Medical Law

Ian Kennedy LLM, LLD
Barrister and Honorary Bencher of the Inner Temple,
Professor of Health Law, Ethics and Policy,
School of Public Policy, University College, London
and President, Centre of Medical Law
and Ethics, King's College, London

Andrew Grubb MA (Cantab), LLD (Lond), FMedSci
of the Inner Temple, Barrister,
Professor of Medical Law
and Head of Department,
Cardiff Law School

Third edition by Andrew Grubb

Butterworths
London, Edinburgh, Dublin
2000

Members of the LexisNexis Group worldwide

United Kingdom	LexisNexis Butterworths Tolley, a Division of Reed Elsevier (UK) Ltd, Halsbury House, 35 Chancery Lane, LONDON, WC2A 1EL, and 4 Hill Street, EDINBURGH EH2 3JZ
Argentina	LexisNexis Argentina, BUENOS AIRES
Australia	LexisNexis Butterworths, CHATSWOOD, New South Wales
Austria	LexisNexis Verlag ARD Orac GmbH & Co KG, VIENNA
Canada	LexisNexis Butterworths, MARKHAM, Ontario
Chile	LexisNexis Chile Ltda, SANTIAGO DE CHILE
Czech Republic	Nakladatelství Orac sro, PRAGUE
France	Editions du Juris-Classeur SA, PARIS
Hong Kong	LexisNexis Butterworths, HONG KONG
Hungary	HVG-Orac, BUDAPEST
India	LexisNexis Butterworths, NEW DELHI
Ireland	Butterworths (Ireland) Ltd, DUBLIN
Italy	Giuffrè Editore, MILAN
Malaysia	Malayan Law Journal Sdn Bhd, KUALA LUMPUR
New Zealand	LexisNexis Butterworths, WELLINGTON
Poland	Wydawnictwo Prawnicze LexisNexis, WARSAW
Singapore	LexisNexis Butterworths, SINGAPORE
South Africa	Butterworths SA, DURBAN
Switzerland	Stämpfli Verlag AG, BERNE
USA	LexisNexis, DAYTON, Ohio

A CIP Catalogue record for this book is available from the British Library.

ISBN 0 406 90325 5

Printed and bound in Great Britain by The Bath Press, Bath

Visit Butterworths LexisNexis *direct* at www.butterworths.com

Preface

hours, collecting and passing the final manuscript and generally keep me together
whilst I felt a loss with the enormity of the task. She has my eternal thanks.

The manuscript was submitted to Butterworths on 1 March 20__ and I have been
able to include some recent legal developments. Other unfortunately will
have to await future edition.

Andrew Grubb
Cardiff Law School

The corpus of medical law is almost unrecognisable from that which we sought
to set out and analyse when this book was first published in 1989. In fact, so
much has changed even since the previous edition, and so many new developments
have occurred, that the length of this edition has grown more than perhaps we
would have wished. The last few years have seen resort to the courts in England
to resolve many issues of medical law. Whilst these were once exclusively
concerned with medical negligence (or clinical negligence in the modern
vernacular), today they encompass family law and public law cases of real legal
significance. The latter, in particular, have assumed an increasing importance
which the Human Rights Act 1998, when it comes into force on 2 October 2000,
can only help to flourish, though with what actual impact is less clear. There is
no avoiding the fact that medical law is today a highly complex and subtle area
of law replete with its own ever increasing volume of case law and legislation.
The latter is not in our context restricted to primary legislation. Indeed, the
plethora of statutory instruments and quasi-legislation such as Directions,
Circulars etc has now come to dominate the regulation of health care delivery.

We have in this edition retained our aim of providing the reader with as full as
possible a collection of materials and analysis of the law in England and Wales.
Devolution has meant, however, that differences between England and Wales
sometimes exist, particularly in the structure and regulation of the NHS. We
have tried to note what differences do exist but our account is predominantly of
the NHS in England. Of course, the common law still flows with its customary
inclusiveness across the Severn. As with previous editions, we make no claims
to provide an account of the law in Scotland. And devolution has only accentuated
the diversity of substantive law that we have in the United Kingdom, as the
recent Adults with Incapacity (Scotland) Act 2000 well illustrates. Our book
remains firmly rooted in English law.

This is the first edition with which one of the authors has not been involved
because of his public service commitments. The book has been that much more
difficult to write and so much less enjoyable to complete as a result. His influence
is ever present and I have tried to continue writing in the composite style –
which belonged wholly to neither of us individually – that we developed as a
result of composing and shaping each sentence together sitting around a table. I
greatly missed the camaraderie and creative process that I uniquely experienced
at those times and look forward to renewed enjoyment of them in the future.

I am grateful to Oxford University Press for allowing me to include material
which previously appeared in the *Medical Law Review*. Also, my thanks go to all
those at Butterworths who worked so hard on the manuscript. Finally, I must
express my thanks to two people. First, my secretary at Cardiff Law School,
Dawn Morgan, who typed the entire manuscript. It remains a mystery to me how
she ever read my handwriting. Thanks Dawn. Secondly, I owe a considerable
debt of gratitude to Jess Gardner, my research assistant, who was generously
funded by Cardiff Law School. She helped me track down material, spent endless

hours 'scissors and pasting' the final manuscript and generally kept me together when I felt all was lost with the enormity of the task. She has my special thanks.

The manuscript was submitted to Butterworths on 1 March 2000 but I have been able to include some more recent developments. Others, unfortunately, will have to await future editions.

Andrew Grubb
Cardiff Law School
1 August 2000

Contents

PART III
MEDICAL LAW IN ACTION: A THE BEGINNING OF LIFE 1137

Chapter 9 Contraception and sterilisation 1139

Chapter 10 Medically assisted reproduction 1211

PART III
MEDICAL LAW IN ACTION: C THE END(ING) OF LIFE 1905

Chapter 16 The end(ing) of life: the competent patient 1907

Acknowledgments

The publishers and authors wish to thank the following for permission to reprint material from the sources indicated. The publishers would also be pleased to hear from those copyright holders from whom permission has been sought but not yet received.

AB Academic Publishers: Grubb 'I, Me Mine: Bodies, Parts and Property' (1998) 3 Med L Int 299; Longley 'Who is Calling the Piper?' (1998) 3 Med L Int 319; Ngwana and Chadwick 'Genetic Diagnostic Information and the Duty of Confidentiality' (1993) 1 Med L Int 73; Savas and Treece 'Fertility Clinics: One Code of Practice' (1998) 3 Med Law Int 243; Daniels, Ericsson and Burn 'The Views of Semen Donors Regarding the Swedish Insemination Act 1984' (1998) 3 Med Law Int 177.

American Psychiatric Association: Roth, Meisel and Lidz 'Tests of Competency to Consent to Treatment' (1977) 134 Am J Psychiatry 279.

American Society of Law and Medicine: Battin 'Voluntary Euthanasia and the Risk of Abuse' (1992) 20 Law, Medicine and Health Care 133; Gostin 'A Moment in Human Development' (1985) 11 American Journal of Law and Medicine 32; Mady 'Surrogate Mothers: The Legal Issues' (1981) American Journal of Law and Medicine 324; Weir 'The Morality of Physician-Assisted Suicide' (1992) 20 Law, Medicine and Health Care 116.

Amsterdam University Press: Griffiths et al *Euthanasia and Law in the Netherlands* (1998).

Barry Rose Law Publishers Ltd: Lee 'Vaccine Damage: adjudicating scientific dispute' in Howells (ed) *Product Liability, Insurance and the Pharmaceutical Industry: An Anglo-American Comparison* (1991).

British Institute of International and Comparative Law: Norrie 'Human Tissue Transplants: Legal Liability in Different Jurisdictions' (1985) ICLQ 442.

Blackstone Press: Wadham and Mountfield *Blackstone's Guide to the Human Rights Act 1998* (1999); Mulcahy and Allsop in Leyland and Woods (eds)

Administrative Law Facing the Future (1997); Bartlett and Sandland *Mental Health Law* – Policy and Practice (2000).

Blackwell Publishers: Allen 'Contracts in the National Health Service Internal Market' (1995) 51 MLR 321; Dworkin 'The Law Relating to Organ Transplantation in England' (1970) 33 MLR 353; Feenan 'Common Law Access to Medical Records' (1996) 59 MLR 101; Hodges 'Development Risks: Unanswered Question' (1998) 61 MLR 560; Hughes 'The Reorganisation of the National Health Service' (1991) 54 MLR 88; Leng 'Death and the Criminal Law' (1982) 45 MLR 206; Lowe and Juss 'Medical Treatment – Pragmatism and the Search for Principle' (1993) 56 MLR 865; Mildred and Howells 'Comment on Development Risks' (1998) 61 MLR 570; Montrose 'Is Negligence an Ethical or a Sociological Concept?' (1958) 21 MLR 259; Pace 'Civil Liability for Pre-Natal Injuries' (1977) 40 MLR 141.

Blackwell (Basil) Ltd: Warnock *A Question of Life* (1985); Report of the Committee of Inquiry into Human Fertilisation and Embryology (Cmnd 9314) (1984).

Blackwell Scientific Publications Ltd: Raymond 'The Employment Rights of the NHS Hospital Doctor' in Dyer (ed) Doctors, Patients and the Law (1992).

British Medical Association: 'Diagnosis of Brain Death' (1976) 2 BMJ 1187; 'Memorandum on the diagnosis of death' (1979) 1 BMJ 332; Gillon 'Editorial' (1988) 296 BMJ 1212; Jochemsen and Keown 'Voluntary Euthanasia Under Control?' (1999) 25 JME 16; Tunkel 'Abortion: How Early, How Late and How Legal?' (1979) BMJ 253; Van Delden 'Slippery Slopes in Flat Countries – a Response' (1999) 25 JME 22; *Withholding and Withdrawing Life-prolonging Medical Treatment: Guidance for decision making* (1999); Boyd (ed) *The New Dictionary of Medical Ethics* (1997); Pallis and Harley *ABC of Brainstem Death* (2nd edn, 1996).

Canada Government Publishing Centre: Canadian Law Reform Commission *Medically Assisted Procreation* (Working Paper 65) (1992); Keyserlinck 'Sanctity of Life or Quality of Life' (1979).

Canada Law Books Inc: Reible v Hughes (1980) 114 DLR (3d) 1; Snell v Farrell (1990) 72 DLR (4th) 289; Stamos v Davies (1985) 21 DLR (4th) 507; ter Neuzen v Korn (1995) 127 DLR (4th) 577; Tremblay v Daigle (1989) 62 DLR (4th) 634; Urbanski v Patel (1978) 84 DLR (3d) 650; Winnipeg Child and Family Services (Northwest Area) v G (DF) (1997) 152 DLR (4th) 193; Yepremian v Scarborough General Hospital (1980) 110 DLR (3d) 513; Zimmer v Ringrose (1981) 124 DLR (3d) 215; B v Children's Aid Society of Metropolitan Toronto; A-G of Canada, Interveners (1995) 122 DLR (4th) 1; Lawson v Laferrière (1991) 78 DLR (4th) 609; McInerney v MacDonald (1992) 93 DLR (4th) 415; Prindham v Nash (1986) 33 DLR (4th) 304;

Ciarlariello v Keller (1993) 100 DLR (4th) 609; R v Bolduc and Bird (1967) 63 DLR (2d) 82; R v Maurantonio (1967) 65 DLR (2d) 674; Norberg v Wynrib (1992) 92 DLR (4th) 449; Re Eve (1981) 115 DLR (3d) 283; Girard v Royal Columbian Hospital (1976) 66 DLR (3d) 676; Hollis v Dow Corning Corp (1995) 129 DLR (4th) 609; Re Superintendent of Family and Child Service and Dawson (1983) 145 DLR (3d) 610.

Carswell Co Ltd: Halushka v University of Saskatchewan (1965) 52 WWR 608; Rodriguez v British Columbia (A-G) (1993) 82 BCLR (2d) 273; League of Life in Manitoba Inc v Morgentaler [1985] 4 WWR 663.

Cass (Frank) & Co Ltd: Brazier 'Revised Consent Forms in the NHS' (1991) 6 Professional Negligence 148; Brazier 'Sterilisation: Down the Slippery Slope?' (1990) 6 Professional Negligence 25; Brazier 'Liability of Ethics Committee and their Members' (1990) Professional Negligence 186; McHale 'Elective Ventilation – Pragmatic Solution or Ethical Minefield' (1995) 2 Professional Negligence 23.

Cavendish (Australia) Pty Ltd: Devereux *Medical Law: Text, Cases and Materials* (1997).

Clarendon Press: Skegg *Law, Ethics and Medicine* (1984); Holm 'Ethical Issues in Pre-implantation Diagnosis' in Harris and Holm (eds) *The Future of Human Reproduction* (1998); Newdick *Who Should We Treat? Law, Patients and Resources in the NHS* (1995).

Croom Helm: Lamb *Death, Brain Death and Ethics* (1985).

DoH Publications: *AIDS/HIV Infected Health Care Workers: Guidance on the Management of Infected Health Care Workers and Patient Notification* (1999); *Ethics Committee Review of Multi-Centre Research: Establishment of Multi-Centre Research Ethics Committees* (1997) HSG (97)23; *A Code of Practice for the Diagnosis of Brain Stem Death* (1998); *Local Research Ethics Committees* HSG (91(5)); *The Protection and Use of Patient Information* (1996).

Dramire Printers Ltd: Bolt 'Dealing with Errors of Clinical Judgment' (1986) 54 Medico-Legal Journal 220.

Family Law: Grubb and Pearl *Blood Testing, AIDS and DNA Profiling* (1990).

General Medical Council: *Protecting and Providing Information* (2000); *Professional Conduct and Discipline: Fitness to Practise* (1987); *Serious Communicable Diseases* (1997).

Hastings Center: Capron 'Anencephalic Donors: Separate the Dead from the Dying' (1987) 17 Hastings Center Report 5; Foley and Hendin 'The Oregon

Report: Don't Ask, Don't Tell' (1999) 29(3) Hastings Center Report 37; Dresser 'Dworkin on Dementia: Elegant Theory, Questionable Policy' (1995) 25 Hastings Centre Report 32; Caplan 'Organ Procurement: It's Not in the Cards' (1984) 14(5) Hastings Center Report 9; Annas 'From Canada with Love: Anencephalic Newborns as Organ Donors' (1987) 17 Hastings Center Report 36.

Jordan & Sons Ltd: Re C (A Minor) [1985] FLR 846; Re C (Detention: Medical Treatment) [1997] 2 FLR 180; Re C (A Minor) (Detention for Medical Treatment) [1997] 2 FLR 180; Re J (Specific Issue Orders: Muslim Upbringing and Circumcision) [1999] 2 FLR 678; Re MW (Adoption: Surrogacy) [1995] 2 FLR 759; Re C (HIV test) [1999] 2 FLR 1004; Re P (Minors) (Wardship: Surrogacy) [1987] 2 FLR 421; Re Q (Parental Order) [1996] 1 FLR 369; Re S (A Minor) (Consent to Medical Treatment) [1994] 2 FLR 1065; Re S (A Minor) (Medical Treatment) [1993] 1 FLR 376; Re S (Medical Treatment: Adult Sterilisation) [1998] 1 FLR 944.

King's College, London, Centre of Medical Law and Ethics: Schlyter *Advance Directives and AIDS* (1992).

King's Fund Publishing and Press Office: New, Solomon, Dingwall, McHale *A Question of Give and Take* (1994).

Kluwer Publishing: Lanham 'Transplants and the Human Tissue Act 1961' (1971) 11 Med Sci Law 16; Skegg' Criminal Liability from the Unauthorised Use of Corpses for Medical Education and Research' (1992) 37 Med Sci Law 51; Skegg 'The Use of Corpses for Medical Education and Research: the Legal Requirements' (1991) 31 Med Sci Law 345; Skegg 'Human Tissue Act 1961' (1976) 16 Med Sci Law 197; Skegg 'Liability for the Unauthorized Removal of Cadeveric Transplant Material' (1974) 14 Med Sci Law 53; Harpwood 'The Health Service Commissioner: The Extended Role in the New NHS' (1996) 3 European Journal of Health Law 207; Jones 'Medical Malpractice in the England and Wales' (1996) European Journal of Health Law 109; Stern 'The Regulation of Assisted Conception in England' (1994) 1 European Journal of Health Law 53; Grubb 'The Persistent Vegetative State: A Duty (Not) To Treat and Conscientious Objection' (1997) 4 European Journal of Health Law 157.

The Law Book Company Ltd: Breen v Williams (1996) 70 ALJR 772; Ellis v Wallsend District Hospital (1989) 17 NSWLR 553; Secretary, Department of Health v JWB and SMB (1992) 66 ALJR 300; Rogers v Whittaker (1992) 67 ALJR 47; Chappel v Hart (1998) 72 ALJR 1344; Fleming *Law of Torts* (9th edn, 1998);

Linacre Centre: Gormally (ed) *Euthanasia, Clinical Practice and the Law* (1994).

Lloyd's of London Press Ltd: North West Lancashire HA v A, D and G [1999] Lloyd's Rep Med 399; Penney v East Kent HA [2000] Lloyd's Rep Med 41; Palmer v Tees HA [1999] Lloyd's Rep Med 375; R v North and East Devon Health Authority, ex p Coughlan [1999] Lloyd's Rep Med 306; Wimpey Construction UK Ltd v Poole [1984] 2 Lloyd's Rep 499; R v Secretary of State for Health, ex p Pfizer Ltd [1999] Lloyd's Rep Med 289; Roylance v General Medical Council [1999] Lloyd's Rep Med 139; Re C (a minor) (medical treatment) [1998] Lloyd's Rep Med 1; Ratcliffe v Plymouth & Torbay HA, Exeter & North Devon HA [1998] Lloyd's Rep Med 162; M v Calderdale & Kirklees HA [1998] Lloyd's Rep Med 157.

McGill Law Journal: Somerville 'Structuring the Issues in Informed Consent' (1981) 25 McGill Law Journal 740; Picard 'The Liability of Hospitals in Common Law Canada' (1981) 26 McGill LJ 997.

Michigan Law Review Association: Dukeminier 'Supplying Organs for Transplantation' (1970) 68 Michigan Law Review 811.

New England Journal of Medicine: Beecher 'Ethics and Clinical Research' (1966) 274 New England Journal of Medicine 1354.

Ontario Law Reform Commission: *Human Artificial Reproduction and Related Matters* (1985).

Oxford University Press, for allowing the inclusion of material which previously appeared in the Medical Law Review. Price 'Assisted Suicide and Refusing Medical Treatment' (1996) 4 Med L Rev 270; Otlowski 'Re Evelyn – Reflections on Australia's First Litigated Surrogacy Case' (1999) 7 Med L Rev 38; Longley 'Complaints After Wilson' (1997) 5 Med L Rev 172; Blake 'Physician-Assisted Suicide' (1997) 5 Med L Rev 294; Freeman 'Does Surrogacy Have Future After Brazier?' (1999) 7 Med L Rev 1; Gunn 'The Meaning of Incapacity (1994) 2 Med L Rev 8; Cica 'Sterilising the Intellectually Disabled' (1993) 1 Med L Rev 186; Matthews 'The Man of Property' (1995) 3 Med L Rev 251; Lewis 'Feeding Anorexic Patients Who Refuse Food' (1999) 7 Med L Rev 21; Wilson 'The Law Commission's Report on Mental Incapacity' (1996) 4 Med L Rev 227; Whitfield 'Common Law Duties to Unborn Children' (1993) 1 Med L Rev 28; Dworkin and Kennedy 'Human Tissue; Rights in the Body and its Parts' (1993) 1 Med L Rev 29; Capron 'A National Commission on Medical Ethics' in Bryne (ed) *Health, Rights and Resources* (1988); Otlowski *Voluntary Euthanasia and the Common Law* (1997); Harris *Clones, Genes and Immortality* (2nd edn, 1998); Montgomery *Health Care Law* (1997); Kennedy and Grubb *Principles of Medical Law* (1998); Grubb 'Problems of Medical Law' in Markesinis and Deakin *Tort Law* (4th edn, 1999).

Penguin Books Ltd: Brazier *Medicine, Patients and the Law* (2nd edn, 1992); Scott *The Body as Property* (1981).

Princeton University Press: Robertson *Children of Choice: Freedom and the New Reproductive Technologies* (1994).

Royal College of Physicians: Barton 'The basis of the licensing authority and its advisers under the Medicines Act 1968 to an individual' and Hodges 'Harmonisation of European Controls over Research' in Goldberg and Dodds-Smith *Pharmaceutical Medicine and the Law* (1991); Barton 'The basis of liability of the licensing authority and its advisers under the Medicines Act 1968 to an individual' in Goldberg and Dodds-Smith (eds) *Pharmaceutical Medicine and the Law* (1991).

Stevens & Son Ltd: AB v Tameside & Glossop HA [1997] 8 Med LR 91; X and Y v Pal [1992] Med LR 195; Blyth v Bloomsbury HA [1993] 4 Med LR 151; Brushett v Cowan [1991] 2 Med LR 271; Bull v Devon AHA [1993] 4 Med LR 117; Roy v Kensington and Chelsea and Westminster FPC [1990] 1 Med LR 328; Hucks v Cole [1993] 4 Med LR 393; R v North Derbyshire HA, ex p Fisher [1997] 8 Med LR 327; Tredget and Tredget v Bexley Health Authority [1994] 5 Med LR 178; Moyes v Lothian Health Board [1990] 1 Med LR 463; Smith v Barking, Havering and Brentwood HA [1994] 5 Med LR 285; Sion v Hampstead HA [1994] 5 Med LR 170; Re A [1992] 3 Med LR 303; Robertson v Nottingham HA [1997] 8 Med LR 1; Malette v Shulman [1991] 2 Med LR 162; Cane 'A Warning About Causation' (1999) 115 LQR 21; Keown 'Restoring Moral and Intellectual Shape of the Law after Bland' (1997) 113 LQR 481; Robertson 'Informed Consent to Medical Treatment' (1981) 97 LQR 102; Mullany 'Liability for Careless Communication of Traumatic Information' (1998) 114 LQR 380; Hoggett 'The Royal Prerogative in Relation to Mentally Disordered' in Freeman (ed) *Medicines, Ethics and the Law* (1988); Williams Textbook of Criminal Law (2nd edn, 1983).

Sweet & Maxwell Ltd: Lennox-Wright [1973] Crim LR 529; Douglas *Law, Fertility and Reproduction* (1991); Fortin 'Is the "Wrongful Life" Action Really Dead?' [1987] JSWL 306; Eekelaar and Dingwell 'Some Legal Issues in Obstetric Practice' [1984] JSWL 258; Dorking 'Compensation and Payments for Vaccine Damage' [1978] JSWL 330; Keown 'Miscarriage: A Medico-Legal Analysis' [1984] Crim LR 608; Hoggett 'The Abortion Act 1967' [1968] Crim LR 247; Price 'Selective Reduction and Feticide: The Parameters of Abortion' [1988] Crim LR 199; Ferguson *Drug Injuries and the Pursuit of Compensation* (1996); Toulon and Phi's *Confidentiality* (1996); Matthews and Foreman (eds) *Jerks on the Office and Duties of Coroners* (11th edn, 1993); Hoggett *Mental Health Law* (4th edn, 1996); Jacob 'Lawyers go to Hospital' [1990] PL 255.

Taylor & Francis Books Ltd: O'Donovan 'What Shall We Tell the Children?' in Lee and Morgan (eds) *Birthrights: Law and Ethics at the Beginnings of Life* (1989).

The Terrence Higgins Trust and the Centre of Medical Law and Ethics, King's College, London: 'The Living Will' (form).

UC Davis Law Review: Capron 'Alternative Birth Technologies: Legal Challenges' (1987) 20 UC Davis LR 697.

US Government Printing Office: President's Commission for the Study of Ethical Problems in Medicine and Biomedical and Behavioral Research *Deciding to Forego Life-Sustaining Treatment: Ethical, Medical and Legal Issues in Treatment Decisions* (1983); President's Commission *Making Health Care Decisions* (1983).

University of California: Rhoden 'The Judge in the Delivery Room' (1986) 74 Cal LR 1951.

University of Toronto: Dickens 'The Control of Living Body Materials' (1977) 27 University of Toronto Law Journal 142.

West Group Publishing: Furrow, Greaney, Johnson, Jost and Schwartz *Health Law* (1995).

Wiley (John): Grubb 'Treatment Decisions: Keeping it in the Family' in Grubb (ed) *Choices and Decisions in Health Care* (1993).

Yale University Press: Veatch *Death, Dying and the Biological Revolution* (revised edn, 1989).

Table of statutes

Page references printed in bold type indicate where the section of an Act is set out in part or in full.

List of cases

1 List of cases

Part I

Introduction

Chapter 1
Introduction

What is medical law?

Medical law is still a comparatively young subject. It has emerged in English law over the last two decades or so as a distinct subject, both as an area of importance in legal practice and as an academic discipline. As with all areas of English law, the central core of medical law is easier to identify than its boundaries. Indeed, as with any emergent academic discipline, disputes over boundaries and content exist. We see it as essentially concerned with the relationship between health care professionals (particularly doctors and to a lesser extent hospitals or other institutions) and patients. It is made up of, borrows from, and reflects, other areas of law, in particular tort, criminal law, public law and family law. In addition, increasingly, arguments derived from property law and equity are being deployed in medical law cases. It is, however, more than the sum of these parts. It is not, in our view, a subject defined merely by reference to a set of factual circumstances. This is, of course, the traditional approach of the pragmatic common law, but it is an approach which is always intellectually unsatisfying. This is not least because it leaves unstated the criteria for deciding whether any particular factual circumstance falls within or outside a given subject area. Thus, typically, the borders of common law subjects routinely overlap and arguments about how to respond to problems at the edges are commonplace.

There are common issues which permeate all the problems which arise in medical law: respect for autonomy, consent, truth-telling, confidentiality, respect for persons, respect for dignity and respect for justice. All of these ethical issues run throughout the field. Until these common themes are recognised and reflected in legal thinking and analysis, a coherent approach to the emerging problems in medical law will be difficult. Thus, we see medical law as having some conceptual unity.

The unifying legal theme is, to us, that of human rights. In our view, therefore, medical law is a subset of human rights law. This is what provides its intellectual coherence. This is not to say that we will not address discrete factual issues such as transplantation or medically assisted reproduction. Rather, we do it after, and in the light of, a close examination of the general principles of, for example, consent, which inform the analysis of particular areas of medical practice. We do not mean by this that medical law is now solely in the domain of the Human Rights Act 1998 and its incorporation of the European Convention on Human Rights. This constitutional Act will, of course, have deep significance for medical law, as it will for so many other areas of law. We consider its application throughout the book, as well as outlining its structure and application to medical law later in this chapter. Rather, we mean that the common law – that glorious concept of English law – is, in its application to medical law, rich with and informed by human rights notions (see I Kennedy *Treat Me Right* (1991) ch 20).

At the outset we should highlight an important distinction between *medical law* and *medical ethics*. On the whole, this book is unashamedly concerned with the former and not the latter. Medical law, as you will come to see on reading further, is a complex subject in itself. The length of this, and other books, on the subject graphically illustrates that. It coexists with the equally intricate and important area of study of medical ethics which is a specialist sub-discipline of moral philosophy.

A Grubb 'Problems of Medical Law' in B S Markesinis and S F Deakin *Tort Law* (4th edn, 1999)

Medical Law and Ethics

Medicine is about life, quality of life, and death. Ethics is about how we as human beings should live together and what obligations we have to each other: what is 'right'. The stock in trade of ethics is founded in the notions of such things as 'personhood', 'human dignity', 'autonomy' and the 'intrinsic value of human life'. Who counts morally and how much do they count if they do? But not all people share the same view about these basic notions. There is also much disagreement about the correct approach to moral reasoning: is its concern with certain moral fundamentals – as in traditional Judaeo-Christian ethics? Or, is it concerned with attributing 'rights' to rational autonomous persons and, if so, what rights do these rights-bearers possess? How do we resolve situations where the rights of individuals come into conflict? Or is it solely concerned with the consequences of an individual's action – in particular, seeking to achieve the greater good of the utilitarian calculus? How can the interests of different individuals be measured and weighed against one another as part of this calculation? Even if the approach is agreed, its application in particular circumstances may not be. All of these are 'big' questions; questions which philosophers have mused over since the time of Aristotle. The body of philosophical literature is enormous. For every argument or claim, there is a different view or counter claim.

Human life is, of course, greatly valued and effectively protected by all civilised societies – secular or religious. But to some people – devout Catholics and certain Protestant fundamentalists – life is more than valuable: it is a gift from God and hence sacred. Such beliefs, when taken to their logical extremes, can have serious implications for the law. Moreover, the nature of the beliefs is such that those who hold them are unwilling to compromise. Those who are pro-life, for example, are unlikely to make any significant concessions on issues such as abortion, embryo experiments, or neonaticide. Termination of pregnancy, to take the abortion example, is unlikely to appeal to them even during the very early stages of the life of the foetus.

It is obvious that medical law and ethics exist in a close relationship. The latter lies at the heart, or if not is very close to the surface, of many of the issues faced by the law. Yet, courts are courts of law, not morals. Their function is to determine and apply the law to the instant case. Often, however, they and others who determine questions of medical law cannot altogether avoid the fact that their decision involves questions of medical ethics. The legal outcome may not always be the same as some would suggest it should be from a philosophical perspective. This may well be because the law, as an instrument of social regulation, has a more limited (more permissive) role to play or, conversely, it may be because it has a more intrusive (or coercive) function: the moral outcome might be otherwise. An example of the former might be the law's defence of a competent woman's right to refuse medical treatment when she is pregnant even if this will have deleterious consequences for her foetus. An example of the latter may be the law relating to euthanasia and assisted-suicide where, for some, such acts could be morally acceptable in certain compelling circumstances. The law, however, may not be able to contemplate for public policy reasons any relaxation of an absolute prohibition against killing or aiding death for 'good reasons'.

Here is not the place to attempt a detailed examination of medical ethics. That is a task for others.

As is suggested, the morality of a particular course of conduct may help to inform us of how the law should respond to the same situation. But it need not. Law and morality may not always march hand in hand. Importantly, not everything that is immoral need or should be illegal. The law may stay its hand and leave the field to moral censure. Defining when the immoral should be transformed into the illegal is an issue that has long challenged scholars. The Hart/Devlin debate will no doubt be familiar. Although not concerned with medical ethics and medical law, that debate has great importance for us. It surfaced in the debates concerning regulation of infertility treatments and embryo research in the mid-1980s. Baroness Warnock (the Chairman of the Government's Committee of Inquiry into such matters) commented on this.

M Warnock *A Question of Life* (1985)

The relation between morality and the law has been a central issue in jurisprudence for very many years. There is a distinction between the way we approached this issue in the two parts of our report, that concerned with the treatment of infertility and that concerned with research. If the question is what measures to remedy infertility should be permitted in this country, the problem may be put in the following form: Why should the law intervene to prevent people using whatever methods are possible to enable them to have children? Why should not everybody be entitled to whatever is currently the best and most efficient treatment for infertility? The issues here are quite closely parallel to the issues raised in the 1960s by the Wolfenden Report on homosexuality between consenting males. Ought the law to intervene to make such conduct criminal or ought it not? The famous view of Lord Devlin (*The Enforcement of Morals*, Oxford, 1959) was that where there is a consensus of opinion against a certain practice among members of the general public (exemplified by the notorious 'man on the Clapham omnibus') then the law must intervene to prevent conduct which is repellent to that public. A shared moral view, Lord Devlin argued, was the cement that bound society together. If such shared views were not reflected in law, if law did not enforce what society held to be morally right and wrong, then society itself would disintegrate. A society is characterised by a shared moral view; without it there would be no society. Therefore to act against such a shared view should be tantamount to treason. The law could no more permit acts contrary to the shared morality than it could permit treason.

The drawback with Devlin's view is that, increasingly, we are compelled to accept that 'common morality' is a myth. There is no agreed set of principles which everyone, or the majority, or any representative person, believes to be absolutely binding, and especially is this so in areas of moral concern, which are radically and genuinely new. We saw that the concept of a 'rule' breaks down, in novel and hitherto unthought-of cases, and the notion that there is a consensus morality in such cases is equally untenable. The question must be recast: in situations where people disagree with each other as to the rights and wrongs of a specific form of behaviour, how do we decide whether or not the law is to intervene?

H L A Hart (*Law, Liberty and Morality*, Oxford, 1963) identified two moral problems, one 'primary' and the other 'critical'. At the first level the question is whether a certain practice (homosexual acts between consenting males, or AID) is morally right or wrong; at the second level the question is whether, if the law intervened on this matter, the infringement of liberty involved would itself be morally right or wrong. If we consider a case that concerned the Inquiry, the case of AID, it is plain that moral opinions about it vary through the whole spectrum, from those who think it absolutely wrong (like members of the Jewish Community, who think that it is 'bringing orphans into the world', and therefore necessarily wrong) through those who are doubtful, because of the possible risk to AID children, to those who regard it as an absolute right that anyone should have access to AID, whether they are married or single, hetero- or homosexual.

Furthermore, any law enacted to render AID a criminal offence, besides going against the moral views of a fair number of the community, would involve, in itself, a disagreeable intrusiveness, for AID is something that can relatively easily be carried out at home, without any medical intervention. For a law to be enforceable, there would need to be a band of snoopers or people ready to pry into the private lives of others, which might well itself constitute a moral wrong.

Similarly, in the controversial matter of surrogate mothers, the Inquiry agreed unanimously that they disapproved of the practice (largely because of possible consequences for the child); but they also agreed that it could not be prevented by law, because of the intrusiveness of any law that would be enforceable. The Inquiry therefore concentrated on how surrogacy for commercial purposes might be checked, leaving on one side the question whether surrogacy was intrinsically morally right or wrong. We might all of us have answered the primary moral question in a way which made surrogacy wrong. This did not pre-empt the answer to the second-order moral question. Should the law be invoked to stop surrogacy? We all agreed that it would be morally wrong to envisage a law which would intrusively curtail human freedom, and which would in addition be impossible to enforce (how could the law tell whether the child whom Abraham claimed as his own was born to Sara, or to a servant girl who happened to be more fertile?). The Inquiry, then, while unanimously answering the first-order question negatively, holding that surrogacy was wrong, nevertheless held that legislation should not be invoked to prevent it. We did however by a majority recommend that the commercial use of surrogacy arrangements, as a way of making money for an agency, could and should be made a criminal offence. For not only was the wrongness of surrogacy compounded by its being exploited for money, but also a law against agencies would not be intrusive into the private lives of those who were actually engaged in setting up a family.

    ... In some cases it was necessary to distinguish the issue of moral right or wrong, as we saw it, from a further, also moral question, whether it would be right to enforce a moral view, even if such a view were agreed. There was, however, a more testing kind of question, infinitely more important, in my opinion. This was the question of research using human embryos ... No-one felt inclined to argue that the decision whether or not to embark on research with the use of human embryos was a matter of personal conscience, as they might in the case of AID, surrogacy, or, for that matter, homosexuality between adults. Everyone agreed that this was a matter on which there must be legislation, and that whether and to what extent embryos should be used must be a decision for the law.

    The reason for this uncertainty, for the distinction, that is, between what might be thought a private matter and one which was *necessarily* public was somewhat obscure. Nor did the Inquiry draw the distinction explicitly or clearly. But the grounds for it are something like this: research is largely publicly funded. Therefore society, from whom ultimately funding comes, is entitled to know, and even to some extent to control, what research methods are used ... There is a strong feeling that certain possible experiments and research should be subject to criminal law and made a criminal offence, wherever undertaken. ...

    All members of the Committee wanted the criminal law to be invoked in this matter.

Having made the briefest of detours, we should now return to our chosen path – mapping out medical law.

What, then, are the constituent parts of medical law? We shall develop in some detail the underlying legal principles and concepts throughout the book. For present, we only offer a brief overview (see further, B S Markesinis and S F Deakin *Tort Law* (4th edn, 1999) pp 238–297).

Much of the law is judge-made, although increasingly statutory regulation has been put in place by Parliament, eg the Human Organ Transplants Act 1989 and the Human Fertilisation and Embryology Act 1990 (see *infra*, chs 15 and 10 respectively). However, given the controversial nature of many of the issues – and their solution not being 'party political' – the courts will remain the most usual forum for the development of medical law. Parliament is an unwilling participant and the courts must respond, when asked, to fill apparent legal gaps even if the judges are not always comfortable doing so (see eg *Airedale NHS Trust v Bland* [1993] AC 789 (HL)). Indeed, through the 'declaratory procedure' the courts have fashioned, since *Re F (Mental Patient: Sterilisation)* [1990] 2 AC 1 (HL), a mechanism by which important medical law issues can be resolved by the courts. And, as a result, the courts have developed a jurisprudence based upon patient rights in the so-called 'treatment decisions' cases (see *infra*, chs 5 and 6).

Until recently, medical law could largely be described by reference to the tort of negligence and the doctor's duty of care to the patient and any criminal prohibition on, or regulation of, his practice. The latter could be located in the common law, for example, murder (eg *R v Cox* (1992) 12 BMLR 38) or gross negligence manslaughter (eg *R v Adomako* [1995] 1 AC 171) or in statutes such as the Abortion Act 1967 or the Anatomy Act 1984. Of course, medical law was not really that simple but was much richer in fact. The last decade or so has, however, seen the law develop such that it would be unrecognisable to lawyers of an earlier era. The inculcation of family and public law principles is particularly noticeable. But, beyond what might be thought of as 'formal law', medical law is regulated by a plethora of quasi-legislative measures emanating from the Government, for example, Health Circulars (HCs).

A Grubb 'Problems of Medical Law' in B S Markesinis and S F Deakin *Tort Law* (4th edn, 1999)

Both negligence and, most recently, the law of battery have played important roles in the legal regulation of the relationship between health care provider and patient. Also, the tort of false imprisonment should not be forgotten since it is particularly important in the context of detention of mentally disordered patients. Such a patient's detention in hospital (or elsewhere) will amount to false imprisonment unless justified under the Mental Health Act 1983 or the common law. The law of negligence imposes a duty of care not to unreasonably injure the patient or, possibly, another when diagnosing, giving advice and undertaking the treatment of a patient. Battery has, arguably, found its most important modern manifestation in medical cases. ... It is this medieval tort that the courts have used to allow them to recognise a patient's so-called 'right of self-determination'. This, in turn, gave the patient a legally enforceable right to decide about medical treatment (including the right to refuse it) however much others might consider it desirable for him. ... It would be short-sighted in any overview of medical law to confine oneself merely to this subset of civil law or, indeed, the law in general.

Whilst the law of tort is a central part of the emergent discipline of medical law, it is only part of the subject. Medical law is much broader and looks to both civil and public law for its principles. It encompasses, for example, family law, criminal law, public law and even principles of personal property law and equity, although the latter remain controversial. Its sources range across statute law (eg, Abortion Act 1967, Human Tissue Act 1961), delegated legislation (eg, the NHS (General Medical Services) Regulations 1992) and case law.

It would also be wrong to see medical *law* as being confined to the discrete and conventional categories of law with which we are familiar. It is more than law as found in statutes or judgments of the courts. Obviously, these form a considerable corpus of the body of medical law but there are other parts that are just as important. There are thus many other regulatory schemes both statutory and non-statutory which pervade the provision of health care in this country.

There is, for instance, disciplinary regulation of the health care professions through, for example, the General Medical Council (for doctors) and the United Kingdom Central Council for Nursing, Midwifery and Health Visiting (for nurses and others). To these we must add the General Dental Council (for dentists) and other bodies that regulate such practitioners as opticians, osteopaths and chiropractors. The list is, in fact, considerable. In performing what is sometimes called their self-regulatory function, these bodies are actually operating within the broad field of public law.

There are other regulatory bodies which police, monitor, and set standards in particular areas of medical practice. Some are statutory, such as the Human Fertilisation and Embryology Authority (HFEA) created in 1990. This regulates most (but not all) forms of assisted conception and research on human embryos. Others are non-statutory. Among them we can mention the Local Research Ethics Committees (LRECs) and Multi-Centre Research Ethics Committees (MRECs), which control research on humans, the United Kingdom Xeno-Transplantation Interim Regulatory Authority (UKXIRA), dealing with trans-genic tissue transplants, the Human Genetic Advisory Commission (HGAC), the Gene Therapy Advisory Committee (GTAC), and Advisory Committee on Genetic Testing (ACGT), which deal with various aspects of genetic developments and technology. The list can easily be made much longer. These bodies – and one must note that there is no overarching national regulatory or advisory body – operate with or without legal 'teeth'; but in each instance they effectively control the area of medical practice within their remit. Their function and performance is very much part of the regulation of medical practice and as such part of medical law.

Beyond these, there are quasi-legislative mechanisms that regulate the delivery of health care to patients and are properly seen as *law* and thus part of medical law. Some examples would include the complaints procedures, which exist for patients who are dissatisfied with the care they have received from a doctor, a hospital or elsewhere in the National Health Service. Equally, there is a plethora of 'dictats' issued by the Department of Health and NHS Executive, which operate, effectively, as law – certainly regulation – within the NHS system. Some of these are actually binding. For instance, Directions issued under the National Health Service Act 1977 and the National Health Service and Community Care Act 1990. Others, such as Health Service Guidance (HSGs), Circulars (HSCs) and Executive Letters (ELs), are merely 'directory'. In practice, however, they act as strong indicators of what should be done or not done at a policy or, indeed, individual level, with internal and external legal consequences if they are not considered and acted upon, only to be departed from on a reasoned and rational basis.

Certainly, it can be confidently predicted that in the future the importance of public law regulation of health care provisions is going to come to the fore. Increasingly, the structural changes to the NHS have brought with them a managerial bureaucracy. Whatever one may think of the merits of this change, it has brought greater transparency to decision-making at both a macro- and micro-provision level. Decisions have more and more fallen within the purview of discretionary decision-making by a public body. The latter is 'grist to the mill' for public law and, as a result, has created opportunities for patients to challenge decision-making within the NHS that was previously unavailable or, at least, not realised by those acting for patients. One particular development calls for mention. The new clinical standards body, the National Institute for Clinical Excellence (NICE) and its remit to produce 'clinical guidelines' will be important. For example, the latter will have a direct impact upon the standard of care expected of a doctor; they will in effect come to be seen as setting the 'bench-mark' of care for individual patients. Departure will require explanation and justification and not mere 'whim', ignorance or prejudice. The standard of care expected will be transparent and a patient will have an opportunity to challenge any departure in advance by judicial review or subsequently in a negligence action if injury results.

(Notice the HGAC and ACGT have now been replaced by the Human Genetics Commission (HGC).)

You will notice here reference to other accountability mechanisms beyond the legal process such as professional regulation, complaints procedures and the Health Service Commissioners. As we shall see (*infra*, ch 3), professional self-regulation has come under close scrutiny as a result of a number of recent health care scandals (see eg O Quick 'Disaster at Bristol: Explanations and Implications of a Tragedy' (1999) 21(4) JSWFL 307).

We shall also return to take a closer look at the influence that public law has, and will increasingly come to have in the future as a result of the Human Rights Act 1998, on medical law. Here, we should note one other potential influence – equity.

A Grubb 'Problems of Medical Law' in B S Markesinis and S F Deakin *Tort Law* (4th edn, 1999)

The doctor-patient relationship is one in which the one partner commands a pre-eminent position partly due to his superior knowledge, and partly as a result of the feeling of 'dependency' that sick people have on their healers. Moreover, it is a relationship of trust and confidence. It has been suggested that, as a result of this, the relationship manifests aspects of a fiduciary nature giving rise to a duty of loyalty to a patient. This duty could create negative obligations, for example, not to create a conflict of interest as well as positive obligations, for example, to provide information to a patient (before and after treatment) including access to medical records. In England, this proposal has not found favour with academics or the courts. Canadian courts, however, have embraced the notion, whilst Australian courts have not. Whilst English law has, for the present, rejected claims that the doctor-patient relationship is fiduciary in nature, the courts have found ways of giving effect, without any discernible conceptual basis, to one of the principal components of a fiduciary duty. This is the duty to give a patient access to his or her medical records. Even more prominent however, would be the doctor's duty to respect a patient's confidences.

We return to the issue of whether the doctor-patient relationship is 'fiduciary' in nature in Chapter 7. (For further discussion see: A Grubb 'The Doctor As Fiduciary' [1994] CLP 311; I Kennedy, 'The Fiduciary Relationship and its Application to Doctors and Patients' in P Birks (ed), *Wrongs and Remedies in the Twenty-First Century* (1996) at p 111; L Hoyano, 'The Flight to the Fiduciary Haven' in P Birks (ed), *Privacy and Loyalty* (1997) at p 169.)

Public law

We should now turn to consider what we referred to earlier, namely the influence of public law upon medical law.

A. JUDICIAL REVIEW

The development of judicial review, by which the courts control and police the legality of government action, is a well-documented phenomenon of the 1970s and 1980s. The public principles of 'vires', 'legality', 'rationality' and 'procedural fairness' have been deployed by the courts to give content and procedural rigour to decision-making within the NHS (see B Schwehr 'Judicial Review and the National Health Service' (1994) Journal of Personal Injury Litigation 192 and C Newdick *Who Shall We Treat?* (1995) ch 4). Here is not the place to engage in a detailed exegisis of these principles of administrative law (on which, see DeSmith, Woolf and Jowell *Judicial Review of Administrative Action* (5th edn, 1995)).

A recurring theme in the case law is the failure of patients to obtain a particular treatment. As a result, they have resorted to the court seeking an order which they hope will result in them being treated. Here, you will see at once that the court may be faced with the question of 'scarce resources' and an attempt effectively to reallocate them through court action (see eg C Newdick 'Resource Allocation in the National Health Service' (1997) 23 American J of Law and Medicine 291). We discuss some of the case law in Chapter 4. Courts, as we shall see, are reluctant to consider such issues, preferring to leave such matters to the political judgment of politicians and Parliament (see eg *R v Central Birmingham HA, ex p Walker* (1987) 3 BMLR 32). However, if the challenge goes instead to the process by which the decision was made, the courts are more ready to entertain a challenge and quash a Health Authority's decision. Hence, health care decisions must be fair, consistent and coherently reached. We can illustrate these latter points by reference to three cases: *R v Cambridge HA, ex p B* (1995) 23 BMLR 1; *R v North Derbyshire HA, ex p Fisher* [1997] 8 Med LR 327; and *West Lancashire HA v A, D and G* [1999] Lloyd's Rep Med 399.

Let us look first at a case which gained national attention.

R v Cambridge Health Authority, ex parte B (a minor) (1995) 23 BMLR 1 (CA)

B was 10 years old. In 1990 she was diagnosed as suffering from non-Hodgkins lymphoma and she underwent chemotherapy. In 1993 she relapsed and developed acute myeloid leukaemia. She underwent a second course of chemotherapy and a course of total body irradiation, a treatment which it is only possible to undergo once. In March 1994 B underwent a bone-marrow transplant from her younger sibling. In January 1995 B suffered a further relapse. The doctors responsible for her previous treatment believed that no further treatment could usefully be administered to B, beyond palliative care, and estimated that she had then some six to eight weeks to live. Her father sought and obtained an opinion more favourable to B's survival. He obtained medical opinion which estimated B's chances of successfully entering into remission from a third course of chemotherapy at 10 to 20% and which gave her a similar chance of success of surviving a second bone-marrow transplant, consequent upon the success of that chemotherapy. He sought to secure funding from the defendant health authority for that treatment to be carried out. The health authority, taking account of clinical judgment, the nature of the treatment requested and its chances of success, declined to fund the treatment. B's father sought judicial review of the health authority's decision. Laws J granted an order of certiorari quashing that decision and ordering the authority to review its decision. The health authority appealed.

Sir Thomas Bingham MR: In the course of his judgment, quashing the decision of the authority, the judge made four criticisms of the manner in which the authority had reached its decision. Before I turn to those, however, it is important that I should state very clearly, as the judge did, that this is a case involving the life of a young patient and that that is a fact which must dominate all consideration of all aspects of the case. Our society is one in which a very high value is put on human life. No decision affecting human life is one that can be regarded with other than the greatest seriousness.

The second general comment which should be made is that the courts are not, contrary to what is sometimes believed, arbiters as to the merits of cases of this kind. Were we to express opinions as to the likelihood of the effectiveness of medical treatment, or as to the merits of medical judgment, then we should be straying far from the sphere which under our constitution is accorded to us. We have one function only, which is to rule upon the lawfulness of decisions. That is a function to which we should strictly confine ourselves.

The four criticisms made by the judge of the authority's decision were these. First, he took the view that Dr Zimmern as the decision maker had wrongly failed to have regard to the wishes of the patient, as expressed on behalf of the patient by her family, and in particular by her father. Our attention was directed to the affidavits that I have mentioned. The point was made that nowhere does one see an express statement that among the factors that led Dr Zimmern to his decision was a consideration of the wishes of the family. In that situation, the judge held that the authority had failed to take a vitally important factor into consideration and that the decision was accordingly flawed.

I feel bound for my part to differ from the judge. It seems to me that the judge's criticism entirely fails to recognise the realities of this situation. When the case was first presented to the authority, it was presented on behalf of the patient, B, as a case calling for the co-operation and funding of the authority. At all times Dr Zimmern was as vividly aware as he could have been of the fact that the family, represented by B's father, were urgently wishing the authority to undertake this treatment; by 'undertake' I mean, of course, provide the funding for it. He was placed under considerable pressure by the family and, in the first instance, perhaps unfortunately, made reference to his policy of not corresponding directly with patients or their relatives about what he called 'extra-contractual referrals', meaning requests for the purchase of medical services outside the health authority.

The inescapable fact is, however, that he was put under perfectly legitimate, but very obvious, pressure by the family to procure this treatment and he was responding to that pressure. It was because he was conscious of that pressure that he obviously found the decision which he had to make such an agonising one and one calling for such careful consideration. To complain that he did not in terms say that he had regard to the wishes of the patient as expressed by the family, is to shut one's eyes to the reality of the situation with which he was confronted. It is also worthy of note, and there is no hint of criticism in this, that the accusation that he did not take the patient's wishes into account was not made in the grounds annexed to Form 86A. It was not, therefore, recognised as an accusation calling for a specific rebuttal.

The second criticism that is made is of the use of the expression 'experimental' to describe this treatment. The judge took the view, and Mr McIntyre on behalf of B urges, that that is not a fair or accurate description given the estimates of success which have been put by reputable practitioners, and given the willingness of Dr Gravett to accept that there was a worthwhile chance of success. The fact, however, is that even the first course of treatment had a chance of success of something between 10 and 20%. It was only if, contrary to the probabilities, that was totally successful, that it would be possible to embark on the second phase of the treatment which itself had a similar chance of success.

The plain fact is that, unlike many courses of medical treatment, this was not one that had a well tried track record of success. It was, on any showing, at the frontier of medical science. That being so, it does not, in my judgment, carry weight to describe this decision as flawed because of the use of this expression.

The third criticism that is made by the judge is of the reference to resources. The learned judge held that Dr Zimmern's evidence about money consisted only of grave and well-rounded generalities. The judge acknowledged that the court should not make orders with consequences for the use of health service funds in ignorance of the knock-on effect on other patients. He went on to say that 'where the question is whether the life of a 10-year-old child might be saved by however slim a chance, the responsible Authority ... must do more than toll the bell of tight resources'. The judge said that '[t]hey must explain the priorities that have led them to decline to fund the treatment', and he found they had not adequately done so here.

I have no doubt that in a perfect world any treatment which a patient, or a patient's family, sought would be provided if doctors were willing to give it, no matter how much it cost, particularly when a life was potentially at stake. It would, however, in my view, be shutting one's eyes to the real world if the court were to proceed on the basis that we do live in such a world. It is common knowledge that health authorities of all kinds are constantly pressed to make ends meet. They cannot pay their nurses as much as they would like; they cannot provide all the treatments they would like; they cannot purchase all the extremely expensive medical equipment they would like; they cannot carry out all the research they would like; they cannot build all the hospitals and specialist units they would like. Difficult and agonising judgments have to be made as to how a limited budget is best allocated to the maximum advantage of the maximum number of patients. That is not a judgment which the court can make. In my judgment, it is not something that a health authority such as this authority can be fairly criticised for not advancing before the court.

Mr McIntyre went so far as to say that if the authority has money in the bank which it has not spent, then they would be acting in plain breach of their statutory duty if they did not procure this treatment. I am bound to say that I regard that submission as manifestly incorrect. Unless the health authority had sufficient money to purchase everything which in the interests of patients it would wish to do, then that situation would never ever be reached. I venture to say that no real evidence is needed to satisfy the court that no health authority is in that position.

I furthermore think, differing, I regret, from the judge, that it would be totally unrealistic to require the authority to come to the court with its accounts and seek to demonstrate that if this treatment were provided for B then there would be a patient, C, who would have to go without treatment. No major authority could run its financial affairs in a way which would permit such a demonstration.

The fourth criticism which the judge made was that the authority had wrongly treated the problem which they faced as one of spending £75,000 when, in the first instance, the treatment only involved the expenditure of £15,000. It was therefore a two-stage process, so it was held and submitted to us, and not a one-stage process, as the authority wrongly thought. Again, I regret that I differ from the judge's view. It is, of course, true that if the first stage were unsuccessful, then £15,000, or even less than £15,000, would be the maximum that the authority would end up spending. It would not, however, be reasonable for the authority to embark on this expenditure on that basis since, quite plainly, they would have to continue if, having expended the £15,000, it proved successful and the call for the second stage of the treatment came. It was, therefore, an inescapable decision whether they should embark on this process at all. Having weighed the matter up and taken advice, particularly bearing in mind the suffering which even embarking on the treatment would inflict, the authority thought that they should not fund the treatment at all. I regret that I find it impossible to fault that process of thinking on their part.

Such is my sympathy with the father and B herself that I have been tempted, although disagreeing with the judge's reasoning, to leave the order which he made in being and invite the authority to reconsider the matter in the light of the judge's conclusions. I have, however, concluded that that would be a cruel deception, since I would be bound to make clear that, in my judgment, the authority could, on a proper review of all the relevant material, reach the same decision that they had already reached and I would feel obliged, expressly, to dissociate myself from the learned judge's opinion that it would be hard to imagine a proper basis upon which this treatment, at least its initial stage, could reasonably be withheld. In my judgment, it would be open to the authority readily to reach that decision since it is, as I think, the decision they have already reached.

While I have, as I hope is clear, every possible sympathy with B, I feel bound to regard this as an attempt, wholly understandable but none the less misguided, to involve the court in a field of activity where it is not fitted to make any decision favourable to the patient.

Stephen Brown P and Simon Brown LJ agreed.

(For a commentary on *ex p B*, see A Parkin 'Allocating Health Care Resources in an Imperfect World' (1995) 58 MLR 867.)

You will notice Lord Bingham's exhortation that the court is not entitled to investigate the merits of the Health Authority's decision but only its legality. Secondly, the judge strongly rejected any argument that the court could make judgments about 'how a limited budget is best allocated to the maximum advantage of the maximum number of patients'. In other words, the court is not concerned with resource allocation *unless* the decision to allocate in the way it was could be characterised as 'irrational' – a burden which is exceptionally difficult for a patient to discharge. Thirdly, you may feel that the trial judge, Laws J was more 'in tune' with the justice of the case when he made the legally important statement that ((1995) 25 BMLR 5 at 17):

where the question is whether the life of a 10-year-old child might be saved ... the responsible authority must in my judgment do more than toll the bell of tight resources. They must explain the priorities that have led them to decline to find the treatment.

The need for consistency, coherence and rationality in planning and providing health care is illustrated by the next case concerned with a failure to fund a new treatment for multiple sclerosis.

R v North Derbyshire HA, ex parte Fisher **[1997] 8 Med LR 327 (QBD)**

Dyson J: In December 1987 the applicant was diagnosed as having the relapsing/remitting form of multiple sclerosis. He has at all material times lived in the area for which the respondent authority is the health authority. The authority cannot itself provide appropriate neurological services to treat the applicant but is able to purchase such services under the internal market established pursuant to sects 3 and 4 of the National Health Service and Community Care Act 1990 from a provider. The relevant provider in the instant case is the Central Sheffield University Hospital's National Health Service Trust, one of whose hospitals is the Royal Hallamshire Hospital at Sheffield. This hospital does provide neurological services from the Trust either by an NHS contract under sect 3(2) of the 1990 Act or by what are called Extra Contractual Referrals or ECRs under sect 3(5) of the Act.

On November 15, 1995, the NHS executive issued an executive letter EL(95)97, ('the Circular') to, amongst others, all health authorities. It asked purchasing authorities and providers to develop and implement local arrangements to manage the entry into the NHS of a new drug for multiple sclerosis called beta-interferon.

In January 1996 the applicant was referred to the Royal Hallamshire Hospital where Dr Petty, a consultant neurologist, assessed him as suitable for beta-interferon therapy. Dr Grunewald, Dr Petty's successor, was of the same view. No funding was made available for the treatment. It will be necessary to examine in some detail what happened between January and November 1996. The applicant seeks judicial review of the respondents' decision, which was communicated to him by the letter from the Trust dated November 18, 1996, to decline to fund the treatment of the applicant with beta-interferon …

The history

On January 4, 1996, the applicant was admitted to the Royal Hallamshire Hospital. Dr Grunewald prescribed beta-interferon for him, but made it clear that he was uncertain as to the position as regards funding for what was a new and expensive drug since it was the first time he had prescribed it. The prescription was sent in the usual way to the hospital's pharmacy for the pharmacist to process and dispense. By reason of its expense the drug was red lined in the hospital's pharmacy records. Drugs are red lined *inter alia* where they are costly. The policy of red lining is a means of ensuring as far as possible that drugs and treatments are prescribed within the total budget available to the Trust.

In view of the fact that beta-interferon had been red lined, the pharmacist blocked the prescription and referred the matter to the Neuro-Sciences Clinical Directorate, with a view to determining whether the funding of the applicant's treatment with beta-interferon could be met within the block contract of funds allocated by the respondents to the Trust.

A decision was taken by the chief executive of the Trust in conjunction with clinical colleagues not to authorise treatment of any North Derbyshire residents with beta-interferon in the light of lack of funding for this drug therapy.

Dr Grunewald was told by the pharmacy that the Trust was unable to fund beta-interferon as there were insufficient funds. He was told that the hospital would need to contact the respondents to negotiate additional funding. This was the first time in his clinical experience that he had been unable to prescribe a drug to a patient because of insufficient funding.

He explained to the applicant that the hospital was unable to treat him with beta-interferon. Understandably the applicant was disappointed. Meanwhile the respondents had been considering what to do about the Circular. Dr McConville (Director of Public Health to the respondents) and others in the Trent region were unconvinced about the effectiveness of beta-interferon. They felt that it had not been sufficiently tested. Nevertheless as early as December 5, 1995 a minute of one of the respondents' meetings records:

> However, the government had now issued guidelines, and health authorities could not refuse to purchase courses of treatment with the drug, but it could only be prescribed by neurological centres.

Despite this, by January 8, 1996, the respondents were writing to the Trust saying that they had adopted a policy

> … that funding will only be considered for patients who are participating in a randomised control trial.

On the same day Mr Dorrell, who was the Secretary of State for Health, delivered the millennium lecture in which he said:

> There should be no clinically effective treatment which a health authority decides as a matter of principle should not be provided: there will always be the exceptional case where treatment is clinically justified. To ban treatment in such circumstances would be inconsistent with the principles on which the NHS is established and I do not believe that they represent acceptable practice.

This was picked up at this meeting of the regional directors of the Trent region, which included the respondent authority in the following way:

> It was noted in the light of Stephen Dorrell's speech, that blanket bans were not acceptable. However, it would be possible to have creative constraints. Performance Managers at Region would be picking up on this issue and it may be difficult to hold the North Derbyshire line if there was no imminent prospect of a trial.

Sometime in February, the NHS executive wrote to the Directors of Public Health in the Trent region including Dr McConville, saying that any new clinical trials that might be undertaken in the UK would take several years to generate results, and that, for the time being therefore, purchasers must make decisions on the basis of knowledge now available. To hold back on the grounds that the evidence did not conclusively indicate a sufficiently large health gain to justify the costs would be at variance with the national and regional guidance that had been issued.

The applicant had enlisted the support of his member of Parliament, Mr Harry Barnes, who had written to Mr Fewtrell, the chief executive of the respondent. On February 19, 1996, Mr Fewtrell replied to Mr Barnes in the following terms:

> There is widespread concern in the medical profession about the way beta-interferon has been introduced in the treatment of multiple sclerosis. The possible benefits appear quite limited, the side effects potentially severe, and until more experience is gained both the risks and benefits of the treatment cannot be readily assessed. The only way the value of this drug can be assessed would be to undertake randomised controlled trials to compare how patients with the treatment fare as against those who do not receive it. Introduction into routine clinical practice without such a trial would mean there would never be any reliable evidence of the benefits of the drug. Specifically there is no evidence that beta-interferon reduces handicap or extends life expectancy amongst sufferers of multiple sclerosis, and it is unfortunate that expectations have been raised as in this case.
>
> It has now been determined nationally (EL(95)97) that the drug may only be prescribed through neurology centres, and in line with this guidance, but against the consensus of medical opinion in North Derbyshire, the Health Authority is discussing the contractual arrangements with local neurology provider units. Priority for use of the limited funds available will be determined by the neurologists at the specialist centres and whether Mr Fisher receives this treatment will be a clinical decision.

In fact however the respondent was not having discussions with the Trust about contractual arrangements to implement the Circular. It continued to hope that beta-interferon treatment could be limited to patients who participated in a trial. They were told in March that a national trial was planned to start within nine to 12 months coordinated from Edinburgh. On March 22 at a meeting of the Directors of Public Health in the Trent region the directors recommended that all districts in Trent support the use of beta-interferon only in the context of the proposed trial. On April 16 the respondents accepted the recommendation of the directors of public health and agreed to identify a sum within the ECR budget for that purpose. Arrangements would be made to inform GPs and consultants of the policy but it was felt that a public statement on the subject would be inappropriate.

The respondents' policy, however, became public knowledge and was featured in the News at Ten on May 11, 1996. The NHS Executive was contacted by the News At Ten for comment. On May 2 the Executive wrote to the respondents saying:

> Our view, as part of the NHSE is, of course, that we expect Health Authorities in Trent to work within the national guidance. The national R&D directorate have had to make it clear through the media that no firm decision has yet been made to fund further trials.

The Executive had, in fact, issued a press release on May 1 which included the following:

> 2. No firm decisions have yet been taken by R&D to launch such a trial. In any event, as the aim of the trial would be to evaluate beta-interferon for a different purpose than that for which the current drug has been licensed [ie the licensed drug aims to reduce the frequency and severity of relapse in relapsing-remitting MS patients], the approach being recommended by Trent DPH's will – if it is followed – have the effect of cutting across the NHS Executive's suggested prescribing policy [in EL(95)97] and effectively denying eligible MS patients the opportunity of receiving treatment now.
>
> 3. Dr Winyard has been in contact with the Region to discuss the position, and agreed the following line, which is being issued to News at Ten:–
>
> The NHS Executive is currently developing a possible national trial with experts, including neurologists, to measure the effects of beta-interferon on disability for people

with Multiple Sclerosis. Any decision on whether such a trial would proceed is some way off. The NHS Executive issued guidance last year to all Health Authorities in the NHS, which it expected them to follow, to help them plan locally for the prescribing of beta-interferon for patients who would appear to benefit from treatment at the present time. There is no question of a blanket ban on treatment with beta-interferon.

Despite this the respondents did nothing to implement the Circular, but continued to see the solution to the beta-interferon issue in a trial. Thus although a meeting of the directors on May 24 was told that the Department of Health was not going back on the original decision laid out in the Circular and that a blanket ban on beta-interferon was not possible, on May 29 Dr McConville wrote:

1 North Derbyshire health has resolved that beta-interferon will only be prescribed in accordance with the Regional and Pharmaceutical offices protocol as part of the controlled randomised control trial.
2 £50k has been allocated for beta-interferon in the 1996/7 Health Investment plan.

In line with this, on May 30 she wrote to the Trust saying that the respondents were willing to purchase beta-interferon as part of the proposed Edinburgh randomised control trial, and that of the £50,000 in the 1996/7 health investment plan for beta-interferon, a maximum of £40,000 may be available within Sheffield.

By June 26 two possible trials were being investigated: one national (the Edinburgh trial) and one within the region. The respondents were still refusing to consider any treatment outside a trial. During the Summer, representations were made on behalf of the applicant to the Prime Minister. On September 3 Mr Major wrote a letter which included the following:

Quite separately, the Department of Health's Technology Assessment Programme had been considering a possible national clinical trial of beta-interferon drugs, specifically to measure the impact of treatment on disability and earlier this year, some health authorities, particularly in the Trent Region, decided to wait for a decision on this trial before finalising their own arrangements for purchasing and prescribing beta-interferon.

However, following further consideration, I understand that the Trent health authorities have recently reviewed their position and are making arrangements for the treatment to be prescribed in appropriate cases. The proposed national trial has been postponed indefinitely.

[He concludes] I hope that this is helpful in explaining the situation and that given the revised position of health authorities in the Trent region, it may now be possible for Kenneth to be treated with beta-interferon.

Whatever may have been the position with other Trent Health Authorities, the respondents were not making arrangements for the treatment to be prescribed in appropriate individual cases. By mid-September the respondents had became aware that any randomised control test was at least 18 months away. They decided to reconsider their trial only policy. At a meeting held on September 17, three options were considered. These were:

(a) Release of £50K in the ECR budget for neurologists specifically for beta-interferon;
(b) Increasing the value of neurological contracts by the amount identified in the ECR budget, and asking neurologists to use it, on the basis of clinical priority, for new drugs and treatments in neurology.
(c) Maintaining our current policy of funding only as part of the proposed national trial.

Dr McConville's memorandum goes on:

The Professional Advisory Team recommended that the Health Authority maintain its current position, option c, until the contents of Dr Winyard's letter are known. Once this is no longer sustainable, they recommend option b.

On September 17 it was decided by the respondent:

... to maintain the Authority's current policy of funding B interferon only as part of a proposed national trial for as long as possible. When this position was no longer sustainable neurologists would be asked to use their discretion, on the basis of clinical priority, for new drugs and treatment in neurology within an overall contract sum.

On October 10 Dr Winyard, who had been the author of the Circular, notified all health authorities that the randomised control trials had been postponed indefinitely. In his letter he stated that:

There was now no further reason for delaying the introduction of local purchasing policies in line with the circular.

This caused the respondents to look at their policy again. On October 29 Mr Fewtrell and Mr Whitney of the Trust met. The substance of the decision taken by Mr Fewtrell, on behalf of the respondents, was recorded in Mr Whitney's letter to the applicant's father dated November 1, 1996, which includes the following:

At the beginning of 1996, they had thought that there was to be a further national clinical trial on beta-interferon; they are now aware that this will not take place in the foreseeable future. However, they do not believe that the use of beta-interferon is cost effective and therefore would not advocate its use particularly within the finite financial resources which they have available to them. On this basis, therefore, they have told me that they will not support the treatment of North Derbyshire residents using beta-interferon for this particular condition, although they accept they cannot ban its use given that the drug has been licensed. In the light of this, I am afraid that I cannot endorse any decision of my own Consultant Neurology colleagues from within this Trust for treating North Derbyshire residents with beta-interferon for this particular condition without additional resources becoming available from North Derbyshire Health Authority. We have been reminded by North Derbyshire Health Authority that they do not wish us to overspend at the end of the current financial year.

On November 14 Mr Whitney, Mr Fewtrell and Dr McConville met the applicant's father and explained the respondents' policy. That explanation was confirmed in Mr Whitney's letter to the applicant's father dated November 18, 1996, in the following terms:

Mr Fewtrell confirmed that the policy of North Derbyshire Health Authority was that they could not support, in cost effective terms, the use of the drug beta-interferon for relapsing multiple sclerosis patients and also they could not identify any new money to give priority to the use of this drug. This was based on the unanimous views of their professional advisers. However, they also made it clear that they could not restrict clinicians, such as Dr Grunewald, prescribing this drug where appropriate based on individual patient need, and within existing contracts. (It is not North Derbyshire's policy to contract for individual drugs.)

A meeting of the respondents held on November 19 records:

The Authority's policy on the use of beta-interferon had been fully explained and a meeting had been held with the individual to discuss the matter. Both Dr McConville and Mr Fewtrell confirmed that as the clinicians had not accorded the patient priority for the use of B-interferon within the existing contract they could not recommend a change of policy.
It was RESOLVED to note the situation.

The respondents' evidence as to whether it did change its policy at this time, and what considerations it took into account, is far from satisfactory. Dr McConville says at paragraph 15 of her affidavit that, following receipt of Dr Winyard's letter of October 10, she gave consideration to whether or not the respondents should change its policy. She continues:

The alternatives that were available to the Authority included a release of the £50,000 allocated in the Authority's budget as part of the Health Investment Programme. This could only be allocated on a 'first come, first served' basis until the money ran out. This would mean that those who may have the greater clinical need or greater potential to benefit who presented to clinics later in the year would be later denied treatment. Accordingly, the authority resolved that it was reasonable for them to maintain their current policy so as to avoid the iniquities of prescribing on a 'first come first served' basis, rather than clinical need or an ability to benefit, a feature of NHS purchasing which Mr Fewtrell has described in his Affidavit.
A change such as I described was potentially very inequitable. Alternatively, the Authority, but for the fact it had no funds available, could have requested 'within the contract' with its providers that neurologists assess all potential recipients, assess their clinical need and ability to benefit and prioritise that need across all North Derbyshire residents with MS. This would have involved the 3 'regional' neurology departments, an increase in the number of clinics and a corresponding increase in the number of staff the costs of which the authority would not have been able to meet within its allocated budget for the year. There was no evidence from the literature that would suggest the need for the Authority to review the clinical and cost effectiveness information upon which the authority's original decision was founded. Indeed the SCHARR report strengthened the evidence against purchasing beta-interferon.

In my judgment it is clear that she is saying that there was no change in policy following the receipt of Dr Winyard's letter. At paragraph 27 of his affidavit Mr Fewtrell says that:

At the meeting of the Board on 19th November 1996 it was reported that the estimated outturn of overspending for the year would be £1,185,000.

Accordingly, there were no additional resources to fund the applicant's treatment. It is suggested by Mr Seys Llewllyn that Mr Fewtrell's affidavit implies that there was a change of policy, but that the respondents had no new funds to make available for beta-interferon treatment; and the question whether any money available to the Trust within the so-called block contract should be applied in providing beta-interferon treatment remained a matter for the Trust.

On instructions, that is what Mr Seys Llewllyn says the policy was. He also told me on instructions that £50,000, which had been described in Dr McConville's memorandum of September 17, 1996, as "in the ECR budget to neurologists specifically for beta-interferon", and the release of which Dr McConville had said in her affidavit was an available alternative, had not been "ring fenced", and did not in fact exist. I shall return to this when I deal with the issues.

I can complete the narrative quite shortly. The contract agreed between the respondents and the Trust for 1997/1998 includes a statement that in relation to beta-interferon the respondents will consider "special cases" as ECRs. I have not been told what "special cases" are. It seems that the respondents have made something of a move away from their original policy of treatment only within a trial, but I do not find it possible to assess the extent of that move.

Dr McConville records in her report dated April 1, 1997, that:

The position reflects an impasse and is probably not sustainable. It is out of line with other North Trent purchasers who appear to have allocated a budget for beta-interferon to the Royal Hallamshire Hospital, leaving clinicians to prioritise which patients receive treatment.

Finally, although this is not in evidence, Mr Seys Llewellyn told me, again on instructions, that it is now agreed in principle between the respondents and the Trust that the 1997/1998 block contract sum for neurological services generally will be increased by £40,000.

I now turn to the issues.

Was the respondents' policy in relation to the beta-interferon treatment up to November 1996 lawful?

What was the policy?

In my view the within-a-trial-only policy was maintained throughout 1996. It is submitted on behalf of the respondents that (1) the policy only operated to deny additional funds to the Trust and not to prevent the Trust from using money earmarked in the block contract sum for neurological services generally, and (2) in any event the policy changed in November 1996.

As regards the scope of the policy, in the real world, without additional funds, there was bound to be a *de facto* ban on beta-interferon treatment. This was well understood by everyone, and explains why the within-a-trial only policy was regarded as a blanket ban: see the press release dated May 1, 1996, and Dr McConville's memoranda of May 29 and July 5.

If in practice the block contract sums would be able, subject to clinical judgment, to fund beta-interferon in appropriate cases, it is difficult to see why the respondents' within-a-trial-only policy generated the reaction that it did from the NHS Executive.

The fact is that the block contract sums had been agreed before the Circular was issued. Beta-interferon is an expensive drug. The respondents would have known, or at least would not have been surprised, that it was the type of drug that would be red lined and would not be dispensed unless additional funding was provided. Thus when Mr Fewtrell wrote in his letter of February 19, 1996:

Priority for use of limited funds available will be determined by the neurologist at the specialist centres and whether Mr Fisher receives this treatment will be a clinical decision ...

he must have known that, unless additional funds were made available, this was simply not true. No doubt that is why he said in his letter that he was:

Discussing the contractual arrangements with local neurology providing units ...

Although the evidence does not disclose that any such discussions took place. The suggestion that beta-interferon treatment may be available within the block contract was impliedly repeated in the letter of November 18, 1996, viz:

They made it clear that they cannot restrict clinicians such as Dr Grunewald prescribing this drug where appropriate based on individual patient need and within existing contracts.

Of course, they could not stop clinicians writing prescriptions, but the respondents knew that, at any rate within the Trust hospitals, those prescriptions would not be dispensed and treatment would not be given unless additional funds were made available. It is pointed out that one of the respondents' residents did in April 1996 receive beta-interferon treatment from a hospital in Manchester. It is suggested that this shows that the respondents' policy did not amount to a blanket ban on beta-interferon treatment. The evidence does not indicate how this patient came to receive the treatment. The respondents were clearly surprised and Dr McConville's note of August 1, 1996 says:

As they made the decision to treat without reference to us I am not convinced that we should pick it up this year.

This single exceptional case concerning a different Trust does not persuade me that it was part of the respondents' policy that beta-interferon treatment should be given in appropriate cases funded by the sums available for neurological services generally within the block contracts.

Did the policy change in November 1996?
I have already referred to the evidence. The affidavit of Dr McConville is quite clear. There was a review of the policy following receipt of Dr Winyard's letter of October 10 and, for the reasons she gives, it was decided not to change the policy. Nor do I read paragraph 27 of Mr Fewtrell's affidavit as saying, in effect, that there was a change of policy. It would have been very surprising if he had said that the policy changed in November, because as the minutes of the meeting dated November 19 record:

Both Dr McConville and Mr Fewtrell confirm that as the clinicians had not accorded the patient priority for the use of beta-interferon within the existing contract they could not recommend a change of policy.

Was the policy lawful?
Its lawfulness must be judged in accordance with *Wednesbury* principles against the background of national policy which was set out fully and firmly in the guidance to be found in the Circular. The respondents had to have regard to that national policy. They were not obliged to follow the policy, but if they decided to depart from it, they had to give clear reasons for so doing, and those reasons would have been susceptible to a *Wednesbury* challenge: see generally *Grandston v SOS for the Environment* (1987) 54 P & CR 86. Moreover, if the respondents failed properly to understand the Circular, then their policy would be as defective as if no regard had been paid to the policy at all. It is accepted on behalf of the respondents that they were under a duty to give serious consideration to each aspect of the Circular. Mr Seys Llewllyn submits that the respondents' policy was an honest and conscientious way of managing the introduction into the NHS of the new drug, and was at least consistent with the Circular.

In my judgment the policy was plainly not in accordance with the Circular. The Circular asked for purchasing authorities and providers:

To develop and implement local arrangements to manage the entry of such drugs into the NHS
… and in particular to initiate a continued prescribing of beta-interferon through hospitals.

One of the key aims was to "target the drug appropriately at patients who were most likely to benefit from treatment". In other words, the Circular was giving guidance as to how most effectively beta-interferon could be introduced into the NHS as a drug to be prescribed to treat patients. The primary aim of a trial is not to prescribe drugs in order to treat patients, but to test their efficacy. I do not consider that the respondents' policy could at any time have fairly been described as a reasonable way of giving effect to the Circular. The respondents, like others, no doubt honestly and conscientiously believed that the efficacy of beta-interferon had not been sufficiently tested. The assumption that underpinned the Circular was that it had been sufficiently tested. A possible outcome of a further trial would be to demonstrate that beta-interferon should cease to be a drug prescribed on the NHS. This merely serves to underline how far away the respondents' policy was from an implementation of the Circular. This is not a case in which a health authority departed from the national policy because there were special factors which it considered exceptionally justified departure. The respondents failed to implement any aspect of national policy, principally because they disagreed with it altogether. They now seek to argue that at least they acted consistently with that policy, although for the reasons that I have given that is plainly not the case. Accordingly, they do not seek to justify their policy as a rational exception to the national policy. That is hardly surprising, since I expect that the situation in which the respondents found themselves when the Circular was issued was not materially different from that faced by most other health authorities. The respondents did not take the Circular into account and decided exceptionally not to follow it. They decided to disregard it altogether throughout 1996, because they were opposed to it. That is something which in my judgment they were not entitled to do.

I conclude therefore that at no time was the policy a proper application of the Circular and that the respondents did not properly take it into consideration.

If I am wrong about that, then the policy became unlawful in about September 1996 when the respondents became aware that any trial had been postponed "indefinitely" (the Prime Minister's letter from September 3); or "for at least 18 months" (Dr McConville's report of September 17). The matter was put beyond doubt by Dr Winyard's letter of October 1 which said that the trial had been postponed "indefinitely" so that, as he said, there was no longer any reason for delaying the introduction of policies in line with the Circular. The respondents' policy had, to use their own word, become well and truly "unsustainable". Once there was no trial in prospect, in truth the respondents had no policy at all in relation to the implementation of the Circular, and yet they continued to maintain this unsustainable position. For the reasons given earlier, reliance on the block contract sum was not a reasonable response to the Circular.

I must now return to the £50,000. On the material before me, £50,000 had been included in the ECR budget to neurologists specifically for beta-interferon: see Dr McConville's memorandum of September 17. As I said earlier, Mr Seys Llewellyn told me on instructions that by November, when the estimated overspend for the year was put at £1,185,000, the £50,000 did not exist, because it had not been "ring fenced". Evidence as to the financial arrangements between the respondents and the Trust is almost non-existent. But what is clear is that Dr McConville swore an affidavit, on May 29, 1997, saying that

> ... an alternative available to the respondents when it considered its policy in late October 1996 was to release the £50,000 allocated in the respondents' budget as part of the health investment programme.

The affidavit of Mr Fewtrell which was sworn on the same day does not expressly deal with the £50,000, but in my view it is not inconsistent with the evidence of Dr McConville.

The fact that, in November 1996 it was estimated that at the end of the financial year the respondents would have over-spent by more than £1,000,000, is consistent with there being available at that time a sum of £50,000 for the ECR budget allocated specifically for beta-interferon.

I am bound to express surprise that the respondents' case on this important aspect of the dispute should have been dealt with in this unsatisfactory way. No explanation has been given as to why, if paragraph 15 of Dr McConville's affidavit was in error, the true position has not been explained in a further affidavit. I am not willing to accept what I have been told on instructions. I shall proceed on the basis of Dr McConville's affidavit, which is entirely consistent with the contemporary documents in relation to the existence of £50,000. The situation was therefore that part or all of the £50,000 could have been released to the Trust, so that the policy embodied in the Circular could have been implemented. That policy was to target beta-interferon appropriately by the exercise of clinical judgment, having regard to local resources. If that step had been taken, it is difficult to see on what basis the respondents could have been criticised, save for the delay in taking it.

Why was this not done? The reason given by Dr McConville is that the money could only be allocated on a first-come-first-served basis, which was unfair, and that the respondents did not have the resources to enable a more equitable assessment of clinical need of patients across the whole North Derbyshire area to be carried out. I regard this as an irrational reason. If correct, it would be a reason for refusing to make any expensive treatment available in almost all circumstances. When deciding whether to prescribe treatment to a patient, a clinician has to have regard to many factors, including the resources available for that treatment and the needs of and likely benefit to that patient, as compared with other patients who are likely to be suitable for that treatment during the financial year.

It is absurd to suppose that, before any patient is prescribed any expensive treatment, a survey must be made of all patients who are, or might be, in need of the same treatment in the area. I do not accept that this was a rational justification for not releasing additional funds.

Indeed, I have considerable doubts as to whether it was the true reason. It is striking that this was not the reason given by Dr McConville at the time. In the letter of November 18, 1996, a different reason was given. It was said that the respondents "could not identify any new money to give priority to the use of this drug". That was simply not true. They could identify new money, namely the £50,000 referred to by Dr McConville, but decided not to release it. It is implicit in the reasoning now advanced by Dr McConville in her affidavit that she accepts that funds were available at the time. Internally the respondents gave yet another reason. The minutes of the meeting of November 19 state that

> ... as the clinicians had not accorded the patient priority for the use of beta-interferon within the existing contract they could not recommend a change of policy.

I regret to say that I regard that as disingenuous. The patient who was being referred to was, of course, the applicant. It has never been suggested that the reason why the applicant had not been accorded priority for the use of beta-interferon was because of an exercise of clinical judgment by the clinicians, and a refusal on their part to make use of the block contract sum for that purpose. I find it most surprising that this excuse, (for that is what it was) was put forward by Dr McConville and Mr Fewtrell in justification of their inability to recommend a change of policy. I therefore reject each of the three reasons variously relied on in justification of the refusal to abandon the policy which had become admittedly unsustainable. None of them could reasonably be relied on.

Mr Seys Llewellyn emphasised two points. First the respondents were under a statutory duty not to overspend: see sect 97(1) of the 1977 Act and the Department of Health Circular HC 91(25). Secondly, clinical decisions must always be taken with due regard to the resources available: see, for example, *R v Cambridge Health Authority* [1995] 1 WLR 898. I unreservedly accept both propositions as correct. But on the facts of this case, they do not assist the respondents. The respondents had funds available, but chose not to allocate them. As for clinical decisions, they were not for the respondents to take, and it is no part of the applicant's case to suggest that they were.

I conclude therefore that the policy was unlawful because it was not a proper application of the guidance, contained in the Circular, and the respondents did not properly take into account the essential requirements of the Circular in adopting and maintaining their policy. In my judgment, the respondents were aware from an early stage that they were not properly applying or taking account of the Circular. They knew that their own policy amounted to a blanket ban on beta-interferon treatment. A blanket ban was the very antithesis of national policy, whose aim was to target the drug appropriately at patients who were most likely to benefit from treatment. They knew from as early as January 12, 1996, that, if there was no imminent prospect of a trial, it might be difficult to "hold the line". Most revealingly of all, the note of the meeting of that date spoke about the possibility of "creative constraints". This is surprising language to find in the context of health care.

What they had in mind at this early stage was using the possibility of a trial as a creative means of avoiding the implementation of national policy. The reason was plainly that the respondents disagreed with that policy. I fear that "creative" is a euphemism for "disingenuous". The prospect of a trial served its purpose as a creative constraint until that prospect disappeared. Thereafter the respondents resorted to other unacceptable and inconsistent excuses in seeking to hold the line, and hang on to their unsustainable position. My conclusion on this issue, based on the reasons that I have given, is sufficient to dispose of this application, subject to questions of relief.

Other arguments

Mr Grace advanced a number of other arguments. These included the submission that since the respondents' policy involved a blanket ban, it amounted to an unlawful fetter of its discretion to make funds available for beta-interferon treatment. He also submitted that the respondents acted unfairly in writing the letter of February 19, 1996, which concealed the true nature of their policy, thereby denying the applicant the opportunity of making representations about the appropriateness of the policy, whether to the respondent, the department, ministers or others. This was and is a high profile case, and pressure might have been brought to bear if the applicant had known the true position.

I also heard arguments that the letter of February 19, 1996, gave rise to a substantive legitimate expectation that the question whether the applicant received beta-interferon treatment would be a clinical decision, made by neurologists at the specialist centre, taking into account the limited funds available; alternatively that the letter gave rise to a procedural legitimate expectation that, before the respondents decided to implement a policy which was materially different from that which was represented by the letter, they would give the applicant the opportunity to make representations as to why such a policy should not be implemented. Having regard to the clear conclusion that I have reached on the main *Wednesbury* unreasonableness point, it is unnecessary for me to lengthen this long judgment still further and deal with these other issues. Accordingly, I do not propose to do so.

Fisher is an important case because it illustrates that Health Circulars may, despite the fact that they are often only guidance, place 'commissioners' of health care under a legal obligation to comply unless there are justifiable grounds for not doing so. The work of the National Institute of Clinical Excellence (NICE) and national service frameworks may be important here (see *infra*, ch 2). Also, *Fisher* shows how judicial review may indirectly result in the patient receiving treatment even though the courts are not strictly entitled to do this. In *Fisher*, Dyson J stated:

I have no reason whatsoever to doubt that if, as I would expect, the respondents fall into line with the other North Trent purchasers and allocate to the Trust a budget for beta-interferon, then the applicant's case will be reconsidered, and that subject to clinical judgment and availability of resources he will receive the treatment.

Once a decision failing to follow a policy or one that is irrational is quashed, there may in practice be only one outcome to the patient – treatment (see also *R v East Lancashire HA, ex p B* [1997] COD 267 (Jowitt J) whether refusal to offer treatment outside HAS policy challengeable on basis of 'irrationality').

You will also notice in *Fisher* reference to the patient's 'legitimate expectation' as a basis for challenging the decision. Dyson J, however, left the point as unnecessary for him to decide. As a legal device in judicial review cases, the notion of 'legitimate expectation' is of growing significance (see, P Craig 'Legitimate Expectations: A Conceptual Analysis' (1992) 108 LQR 79 and 'Substantive Legitimate Expectations in Domestic and Community Law' [1996] CLJ 289). It can, however, be given two meanings, first, a *procedural* right to a fair process and, secondly, a substantive right – to a particular benefit from the public body. In *R v North and East Devon HA, ex p Coughlan* [1999] Lloyd's Rep Med 306 (CA) (discussed *infra*, ch 2) the court enforced a promise to a patient that they could remain 'for life' at a particular nursing home. Lord Woolf MR summarised the court's view:

> 89. We have no hesitation in concluding that the decision to move Miss Coughlan against her will and in breach of the Health Authority's own promise was in the circumstances unfair. It was unfair because it frustrated her legitimate expectation of having a home for life in Mardon House. There was no overriding public interest which justified it. In drawing the balance of conflicting interests the court will not only accept the policy change without demur but will pay the closest attention to the assessment made by the public body itself. Here, however, as we have already indicated, the Health Authority failed to weigh the conflicting interests correctly. Furthermore, we do not know (for reasons we will explain later) the quality of the alternative accommodation and services which will be offered to Miss Coughlan. We cannot prejudge what would be the result if there was on offer accommodation which could be said to be reasonably equivalent to Mardon House and the Health Authority made a properly considered decision in favour of closure in the light of that offer. However, absent such an offer, here there was unfairness amounting to an abuse of power by the Health Authority.

This must be a salutary warning to NHS institutions who *offer* treatment to a patient. Notice, however, the court accepted that 'overriding public interest' could defeat the patient's expectation. Perhaps, the court had in mind a change in a Health Authority's financial position.

Finally, we should look at an important recent decision concerned with the failure to provide gender reassignment surgery to transsexuals. Again, the court considered the policy not to treat to be incoherent and quashed the decision.

North West Lancashire HA v A, D and G [1999] Lloyd's Rep Med 399 (CA)

The [applicants] were transsexuals who wished to undergo gender reassignment treatment including surgery. The [respondent] Health Authority refused to fund such treatment under the NHS. This decision was based upon a policy first formulated in 1995 and modified in 1998 which allocated a low priority for public funding to a number of procedures which the Authority considered to be clinically ineffective in terms of health gain. Under this policy gender reassignment surgery was, amongst other procedures, listed as a procedure for which no treatment service, save for that provided by the Authority's general psychiatric and psychology services, would be commissioned save in the event of overriding clinical need or exceptional circumstances.

The [applicants] sought judicial review of the decision and, on 21 December 1998, Hidden J granted an order quashing the Authority's decisions and its policy upon which the decisions were based.

The Authority appealed against that order. It accepted that transsexualism is an illness within the meaning of section 128 of the NHS Act 1977 but argued that it was nevertheless open to the Authority, indeed necessary, to prioritise treatment under the NHS against the background of limitations upon its resources and the many demands made upon them. The policy itself did not amount to a "blanket" denial of treatment since it allowed for treatment of transsexualism where exceptional circumstances or overriding need were shown. Since none of the [applicants]' circumstances had, in the Authority's view, shown any such grounds it was reasonable to apply the policy to them.

The [applicants] argued that although it was legitimate to devise a policy which prioritised the treatment of illnesses, such a policy would not achieve the purpose declared in section 1 of the NHS Act 1977 if it imposed a "blanket" denial of treatment even in individual cases where there was a clinical need for it; the Authority's policy misunderstood the nature of transsexualism and the effectiveness of available treatment.

Auld LJ: These are appeals by the North West Lancashire Health Authority against the order of Hidden J on 21 December 1998 quashing its decisions refusing to fund gender reassignment surgery for A, D and G and its policy on which it based those decisions.

A, D and G suffer from an illness called "gender identity dysphoria", commonly known as transsexualism. Each was born with male physical characteristics, but psychologically has a female sexual identity. Each has been living as a woman for some years. At the material time A and G had each been diagnosed by a specialist consultant to have a clinical need for surgery substituting female for male characteristics, a procedure known as "gender reassignment surgery". D was awaiting assessment of suitability for such surgery. They all challenge the Authority's refusal to fund their treatment, including surgery, under the National Health Service because of its policy not to do so in the absence of "overriding clinical need" or other exceptional circumstances. They maintain that they are ill and that the Authority's policy, and refusals pursuant to it, to fund treatment for them are irrational. The Authority justifies its policy and refusals on the ground that it has a statutory obligation to care for all within its area and limited financial resources with which to do so, requiring it to give a lower priority to some medical conditions than to others and that transsexualism rightly has a low priority. ...

The Authority's statutory obligations ...
It is important to note the qualifications in [ss 1 and 3 of the NHS Act 1977], as this court observed in *R v North & East Devon Health Authority, ex p Coughlan* 16 July 1999 (unreported) [now reported [1999] Lloyd's Rep Med 306], at page 8 of the transcript. The first is that section 1(1) does not oblige the Secretary of State to provide a comprehensive health service, but "to continue to promote" such a service. The second and third are that section 3 limits his duty of provision of services "to such extent as he considers necessary to meet all reasonable requirements", and, in the case of the facilities referred to in (e), to those "he considers are appropriate as part of the health service". ...

The qualifications in the statutory duties imposed by the 1977 Act to which I have referred make plain that it is for the Authority to judge what services it should provide, and to what extent, to meet all reasonable requirements for them. In *Coughlan* the court said as to the originating and corresponding obligations of the Secretary of State, at page 9 of the transcript:

> 25. When exercising his judgment he has to bear in mind the comprehensive service which he is under a duty to promote as set out in section 1. However, as long as he pays due regard to that duty, the fact that the service will not be comprehensive does not mean that he is necessarily contravening either section 1 or section 3. The truth is that, while he has the duty to continue to promote a comprehensive free health service and he must never, in making a decision under section 3, disregard that duty, a comprehensive health service may never, for human, financial and other resource reasons, be achievable. Recent history has demonstrated that the pace of developments as to what is possible by way of medical treatment, coupled with the ever increasing expectations of the public, mean that the resources of the NHS are and are likely to continue, at least in the foreseeable future, to be insufficient to meet demand.
>
> 26. In exercising his judgment the Secretary of State is entitled to take into account the resources available to him and the demands on those resources. In *R v Secretary of State for Social Services, ex p Hincks* (1980) 1 BMLR 93 the Court of Appeal held that section 3(1) of the Health Act does not impose an absolute duty to provide the specified services. The Secretary of State is entitled to have regard to the resources made available to him under current government economic policy ...

The Authority's policy
In 1995 the Authority adopted a policy allocating a low priority for public funding of procedures it considered to be clinically ineffective in the sense of achieving no or little clinical gain ...

The Authority set out in paragraph 4.1 a number of procedures which it had identified, after consultation, as falling into the lowest 10 per cent in terms of priority for treatment and which it would not provide "except in cases of overriding clinical need". They included, along with gender reassignment, cosmetic plastic surgery, reversal of sterilisation, correction of shortsightedness, all forms of alternative medicine undertaken outside the National Health

Service and homeopathy "except when the effectiveness of the treatment has been scientifically proven and accepted by a substantial and appropriate body of medical opinion". In the case of gender reassignment, it drew a further distinction, in paragraph 4.3 and resolution (iv), between treatment provided by it and outside its area: "Gender reassignment (surgical treatment and/or specialist counselling outside the District) will not be purchased".

In 1998 the Authority revised its 1995 policy "in the light of two further years of corporate experience and healthcare development". The revision expressed an increased emphasis on the "appropriateness" of treatment for public funding in addition to its medical "effectiveness". It provided, under the heading "Appropriate, effective and cost effective health care":

2.1 Interventions on the human body are not always related to ill health, but may be related to a desire to achieve an ideal body image or a bodily function that cannot currently be achieved. This is complicated by the fact that their supporters often describe the desire for intervention in medical terminology, and indeed point out that a lack of complete well-being may itself be a health problem. Nevertheless reasonable health authorities will wish to define the limits of the interventions which they wish to commission, and thus ensure that the resources are used *appropriately*.

Then, in paragraph 2.2, it set out four possible categories of "[h]ealth care interventions". One of them was for procedures which had not been tested by carefully conducted scientific research and where it was uncertain whether the interventions are effective, ineffective or harmful. The Authority, in its evidence to Hidden J, placed gender reassignment surgery in that category. Such procedures, the Policy stipulated, "should be commissioned only with caution, preferably as part of a formal evaluation" to ensure that resources were used "effectively". The paragraph then concluded with this further cautionary restraint:

2.3 The fact that a service is effective and appropriate still does not mean that it represents a good use of NHS resources. It may produce only a small and unimportant improvement in health. It may produce benefits for only a small number of people. Its uncontrolled use may consume resources that could more appropriately be used for other patients. In such circumstances, protocols and service agreements, supported by clinical judgments will ensure that the service is available to patients who can expect to achieve the greatest benefits. They will also ensure that the service does not consume resources excessively relative to competing priorities. Resources will thus be used *cost effectively*.

Paragraph 3, under the heading "Health care that will not be commissioned or which will be commissioned only with restrictions", included gender reassignment along with a number of other procedures including "alternative medicine", surgery for varicose veins, various forms of cosmetic healthcare such as plastic surgery, tattoo removal, face lift and hair transplantation, and reversal of sterilisation. Paragraph 3.11, in setting out the specific restrictions applicable to gender reassignment, in truth almost completely excludes it as a candidate for treatment:

Gender reassignment Persons wishing to adopt the role of the opposite gender ... have access to the general psychiatric and psychological services available within the contract portfolio. However, no such service will be commissioned extra-contractually. The Health Authority will not commission drug treatment or surgery that is intended to give patients the physical characteristics of the opposite gender.

In the event of requests for special consideration, a diagnosis of a gender identity disorder ..., evidence that the person has successfully adapted to the opposite gender role, or clinical advice that the person is suitable for surgery, will not (separately or in combination) be regarded as overriding clinical need or exceptional circumstances. ...

The second paragraph in that passage indicates, somewhat obliquely, the possibility of some exception to the almost complete ban in the first paragraph. And paragraph 5.1, under the heading "Exceptions", underlines how limited the Authority intended it to be:

... the Director of Public Health and Health Policy is authorised to consider exceptions to this policy on the basis of overriding clinical need. Such exceptions will be rare, unpredictable and will usually be based on circumstances that could not have been predicted at the time when the policy was adopted. They cannot therefore be defined. However, except when indicated otherwise above, the following circumstances may contribute to a case for exceptional funding:
i) When there is evidence (including consultant advice) that the problem is the cause of serious mental illness, which can be expected to be substantially improved if the exception is granted. (This must be distinguished from the disappointment and reactive

depression resulting from ineligibility for treatment, which would not be regarded as exceptional). ...

Thus, the only material illustration in the policy of the degree of overriding clinical need that might justify an exception is serious mental illness which the treatment could be expected substantially to improve. ...

General principles

As illustrated in the *Cambridge Health Authority* ([1995 1 WLR 898) and *Coughlan* cases, it is an unhappy but unavoidable feature of state funded health care that regional health authorities [sc] have to establish certain priorities in funding different treatments from their finite resources. It is natural that each authority, in establishing its own priorities, will give greater priority to life-threatening and other grave illnesses than to others obviously less demanding of medical intervention. The precise allocation and weighting of priorities is clearly a matter of judgment for each authority, keeping well in mind its statutory obligations to meet the reasonable requirements of all those within its area for which it is responsible. It makes sense to have a policy for the purpose – indeed, it might well be irrational not to have one – and it makes sense too that, in settling on such a policy, an authority would normally place treatment of transsexualism lower in its scale of priorities than, say, cancer or heart disease or kidney failure. Authorities might reasonably differ as to precisely where in the scale transsexualism should be placed and as to the criteria for determining the appropriateness and need for treatment of it in individual cases.

It is proper for an authority to adopt a general policy for the exercise of such an administrative discretion, to allow for exceptions from it in "exceptional circumstances" and to leave those circumstances undefined; see *In re Findlay* [1985] 1 AC 318, HL, *per* Lord Scarman at 335H–336F. In my view, a policy to place transsexualism low in an order of priorities of illnesses for treatment and to deny its treatment save in exceptional circumstances such as overriding clinical need is not in principle irrational, provided that the policy genuinely recognises the possibility of there being an overriding clinical need and requires each request for treatment to be considered on its individual merits.

However, in establishing priorities – comparing the respective needs of patients suffering from different illnesses and determining the respective strengths of their claims to treatment – it is vital for an authority: 1) accurately to assess the nature and seriousness of each type of illness; 2) to determine the effectiveness of various forms of treatment for it; and 3) to give proper effect to that assessment and that determination in the formulation and individual application of its policy.

Conclusions

As I have said, the Authority has acknowledged in its evidence before Hidden J and in its stance on this appeal that transsexualism is an illness. But its recognition of it in its two Policies is at best oblique and lacks conviction. Indeed, both Policies, read together and as a whole, and Dr Sudell's elaboration of them strongly indicate that the Authority does not really believe it. The inclusion of transsexualism in the 1995 Policy, which was concerned only with medical procedures which the Authority regarded as of "[n]o beneficial health gain or no proven benefit", and bracketing it with cosmetic plastic surgery and the like are testament to that. The same attitude is evident in the 1998 Policy in its introductory references in paragraph 2, under the heading of "Appropriate, effective and cost effective health care", to "interventions on the human body ... not always related to ill health", and again bracketing it with cosmetic surgery and other comparable treatments as "[h]ealth care that will not be commissioned, or ... only with restrictions". If there were any doubt about the Authority's true attitude to the condition, it is removed by paragraphs 42 to 44 of Dr Sudell's affidavit clearly evidencing its scepticism of the notion that transsexualism is an illness worthy of medical attention beyond psychiatric reassurance....

It may be that there is some medical support for such scepticism, despite the apparently overwhelming evidence before Hidden J that transsexualism is an illness which requires treatment. I say nothing about the scope for debate between doctors on the matter. I do not need to do so because the Authority accepts in these proceedings that it is an illness. It follows that its Policies should, but do not, properly reflect that medical judgment and accord the condition a place somewhere in the scale of its priorities for illnesses instead of relegating it to the outer regions of conditions which it plainly does not so regard.

That basic error, one of failure properly to evaluate such a condition as an illness suitable and appropriate for treatment, is not mitigated by the allowance in both Policies for the possibility of an exception in the case of overriding clinical need or other exceptional circumstances. As I have said, such a provision is not objectionable, but it is important that the starting point against which the exceptional circumstances have to be rated is properly evaluated and that each case is considered on its individual merits, see: *per* Bankes LJ in *R v Port of London*

Authority, ex p Kynoch Ltd ([1919] 1 KB 176), at 184; *per* Lord Reid in *British Oxygen Co v Board of Trade* ([1971] AC 610), at 624G–625A; and *per* Lord Scarman *In re Findlay*, at 335H–336F. The Authority's relegation of what was notionally regarded as an illness to something less, in respect of which an applicant for treatment had to demonstrate an overriding clinical need for treatment, confronted each [applicant] with a very high and uncertain threshold.

The 1995 Policy gave no indication of what might amount to an overriding clinical need or other exceptional circumstances; nor did the 1998 Policy, save in paragraph 5.1 in which it emphasised the likely rarity and unpredictability of such circumstances, and instanced as a possibility when "the problem" … was the cause of serious mental illness. Expert assessment that a patient needs the treatment would not do; demonstration of the existence of some other illness was a necessary condition for consideration for treatment. The Authority gave a hint in its consideration of the case of A that epilepsy caused by her untreated transsexualism, if established, might have qualified. But, given the Authority's reluctance to accept gender reassignment as an effective treatment for transsexualism – and it would follow logically any condition caused by it – the provision for an exception in a case of "overriding clinical need" was in practice meaningless, as Mr Blake observed. It was as objectionable as a policy which effectively excluded the exercise by the Authority of a medical judgment in the individual circumstances of each case; cf *R v Secretary of State, ex p Pfizer Ltd* 26 May 1999 (unreported) (now reported, [1999] Lloyd's Rep Med 289), *per* Collins J at page 10 of the transcript of his judgment. Looked at in that light, Dr Sudell's observation in paragraph 31 of his first affidavit that it was "difficult to imagine what an exceptional clinical need for" gender reassignment might be, is understandable.

I accept, of course, that it is a matter for the medical judgment of the Authority, not the court, what, if any, effective medical treatment there might be for transsexualism and any sequelae. …

[I]f a regional health authority [sc] devises a policy not to provide treatment save in cases of overriding clinical need, it makes a nonsense of the policy if, as a matter of its medical judgment, there is no effective treatment for it for which there could be an overriding clinical need. The same applies to any other condition caused by transsexualism such as a mental illness of the seriousness described by Dr Sudell. If:

> the Authority considers the cause of such a condition to be untreatable by hormonal treatment and surgery, it is hard to see how it could regard the condition itself as an overriding need for such treatment.

In my view, the stance of the Authority, coupled with the near uniformity of its reasons for rejecting each of the [applicants'] request for funding was not a genuine application of a policy subject to individually determined exceptions of the sort considered acceptable by Lord Scarman in *Findlay*. It is similar to the over-rigid application of the near "blanket policy" questioned by Judge J in *R v Warwickshire County Council, ex p Collymore* [1995] ELR 217, at 224 – 226.

> which while in theory admitting of exceptions, may not, in reality result in the proper consideration of each individual case on its merits. …

Accordingly, given the Authority's acknowledgment that transsexualism is an illness, its policy, in my view, is flawed in two important respects. First, it does not in truth treat transsexualism as an illness, but as an attitude or state of mind which does not warrant medical treatment. Second, the ostensible provision that it makes for exceptions in individual cases and its manner of considering them amount effectively to the operation of a "blanket policy" against funding treatment for the condition because it does not believe in such treatment.

I was at first attracted to Mr Pannick's alternative submission that, even if the Authority had not properly evaluated the condition of transsexualism, it could, in its allocation of priorities of funding from its finite resources, have lawfully assessed it as not normally worthy of funding and not an exceptional case for treatment in any of the [applicants'] cases. He suggested that even if the Authority were to reformulate its Policy to meet the concerns that I have indicated, there is an inherent unlikelihood of a different result. In such a circumstance, he submitted, the court should not interfere with the decisions. He relied upon Sir Thomas Bingham MR's additional reason in the *Cambridge Authority* case, at 907C–D, for not disturbing its refusal to fund treatment, that it "could, on a proper review of all the relevant material, reach the same decision that it had already reached".

As Mr Pannick also submitted, the fact that each of the [applicants] may have had a clinical need for treatment would not render unlawful the application of a properly formulated policy refusing them treatment if they could not show some additional element in the form of "an overriding clinical need" or otherwise. However, my view is that, as the Authority has not genuinely taken as its starting point in the case of each [applicants] that her condition is or may be an illness worthy and capable of effective treatment, it would be wrong for the court to assume the Authority's task. That must remain a matter for it both as a matter of medical judgment in the setting of priorities, the allocation of funds to those priorities having regard to its finite resources and in its provision for exceptions in individual cases.

For those reasons, I would quash the Authority's 1995 and 1998 Policies insofar as they concern gender reassignment treatment and the decisions the subjects of this appeal based on them, and remit the matter to the Authority for reconsideration of its policy and the decisions on their individual merits. The Authority should reformulate its policy to give proper weight to its acknowledgment that transsexualism is an illness, apply that weighting when setting its level of priority for treatment and make effective provision for exceptions in individual cases from any general policy restricting the funding of treatment for it.

Buxton LJ: A number of propositions are clearly established, mainly by the decision of this court in *R v Cambridge Health Authority, ex p B* [1995] 1 WLR 898. They are:

1. A health authority can legitimately, indeed must, make choices between the various claims on its budget when, as will usually be the case, it does not have sufficient funds to meet all of those claims.

2. In making those decisions the authority can legitimately take into account a wide range of considerations, including the proven success or otherwise of the proposed treatment; the seriousness of the condition that the treatment is intended to relieve; and the cost of that treatment.

3. The court cannot substitute its decision for that of the authority, either in respect of the medical judgments that the authority makes, or in respect of its view of priorities.

I further agree with Mr Pannick's submission that it follows from the foregoing propositions that a health authority can in the course of performing these functions determine that it will provide no treatment at all for a particular condition even if the condition is medically recognised as an illness requiring intervention that is categorised as medical and curative, rather than merely cosmetic or a matter of convenience or lifestyle.

In all of this, the court's only role is to require that such decisions are taken in accordance with equally well-known principles of public law. Those principles include a requirement that the decisions are rationally based upon a proper consideration of the facts. The more important the interest of the citizen that the decision affects, the greater will be the degree of consideration that is required of the decision-maker. A decision that, as is the evidence in this case, seriously affects the citizen's health will require substantial consideration, and be subject to careful scrutiny by the court as to its rationality. That will particularly be the case in respect of decisions of the nature referred to in the previous paragraph of this judgment, which involve the refusing of any, or any significant, treatment in respect of an identified and substantial medical condition.

I am not satisfied that the decisions of the Health Authority in this case met these criteria.
...

I therefore turn to the Health Authority's two statements of policy, of March 1995 and January 1998. Mr Pannick accepted that clinical effectiveness had been the main thrust of the 1995 paper, as demonstrated by the heading, "medical procedures of no proven health gain or no proven benefit". There was no advice given to the Health Authority about any particular procedure included in the briefing paper, save for the general warning that a wide range of procedures then in use could not be demonstrated in research trials to have any clinical effectiveness. However, as the evidence in this application demonstrated, first, there is a strong and respectable body of medical opinion that considers gender reassignment procedures to be effective in suitable and properly selected cases; and second that it is unreal to submit that body of opinion to research trials of the type envisaged in the health authority's paper. I emphasise that the mere fact that a body of medical opinion supports the procedure does not put the health authority under any legal obligation to provide the procedure: the standard here is far removed from the *Bolam* approach in cases of medical negligence. However, where such a body of opinion exists it is in my view not open to a rational health authority simply to determine that a procedure has no proven clinical benefit while giving no indication of why it considers that that is so.

The January 1998 policy specifically superseded that of March 1995, and it is that policy that applies to the cases before us. The January 1998 document was more expansive in its reasoning than its predecessor, but the treatments that it ruled out of consideration were broadly the same. The policy did not confine itself to treatments of no proven benefit, though that was still an important element in its reasoning. The document however continued, at paragraph 2.3:

The fact that a service is effective and appropriate still does not mean that it represents a good use of NHS resources. It may produce only a small and unimportant improvement in health. It may produce benefits for only a small number of people. Its uncontrolled use may consume resources that could more appropriately be used for other patients. In such circumstances, protocols and service agreements, supported by clinical judgments will ensure that the service is available to patients who can expect to achieve the greatest benefits. They will also ensure that the service does not consume resources excessively relative to competing priorities.

There is, however, no indication that those principles, obviously unobjectionable in themselves, were specifically applied to the case of gender reassignment. Insofar as any detailed reference is made to the latter case, the document contents itself with saying that clinical advice that a patient is suitable for surgery will not be regarded as providing an overriding clinical need or exceptional circumstances justifying intervention: which in its context was tantamount to saying that the service will not be provided at all. It is therefore difficult or impossible to escape the conclusion that gender reassignment is included in 1998 policy for the same reasons as obtained in 1995, and with no more explanation or consideration of why that should be so.

In further explanation of its policy the health authority filed the affidavits of Dr Harrison and Dr Sudell. The former addressed the very difficult decisions that have to be made in allocating resources between treatments and procedures that are clearly all of medical benefit, even of medical need, for those who receive them. These are certainly pressing and legitimate considerations for a health authority to take into account; but that general factor does not assist in the present case, because there is no evidence that the Health Authority reached its conclusion on gender reassignment after any review in which gender reassignment was assessed in terms of clinical need and its cost and benefits compared, even in the most outline way, with treatments for other conditions. Nor, indeed, would such a claim on behalf of the Health Authority be consistent with Dr Sudell's explanation of the basis on which the decision in relation to gender reassignment was in fact taken.

Dr Sudell, in paragraphs 42 and 44 of his first affidavit, explained the position as follows:

It is the view of the Health Authority (paragraph 2 of the 1998 policy) that:

"interventions on the human body are not always related to ill health, but may be related to a desire to achieve an ideal body image or a bodily function that cannot currently be achieved" ... . The Health Authority's view is that the comments above apply to gender dysphoria, and therefore that treatment for gender dysphoria is not a condition for which Health Authority funded treatment is appropriate.

This reasoning does not flow naturally from the arrangement of the 1998 policy document. The general statement at the beginning of the paper about surgery to correct body image applies more naturally to the paragraphs dealing with varicose veins and with a wide range of other cosmetic treatments, which the Health Authority will not fund. No reference is made to this consideration in the short passage in which gender reassignment is specifically discussed. Nevertheless, assuming that that was the Health Authority's reason for the 1998 policy, as my Lord points out, Dr Sudell's account only reiterates the conclusion that the health authority is of the opinion that gender reassignment intervention, and in particular surgery, is of no, or no proven, clinical benefit. Dr Sudell himself cites a substantial literature that, on its face, suggests the contrary. Dr Sudell expresses caution about the conclusions of that literature, a view that, as a senior health professional, is clearly open to him. However, there is no indication at all that the Health Authority had the benefit of those views when adopting its policy, or indeed that they gave any consideration to the actual status and value of gender reassignment intervention.

I am therefore driven to the conclusion that the Health Authority has not demonstrated that degree of rational consideration that can reasonably be expected of it before it decides in effect to give no funding at all to a procedure supported by respectable clinicians and psychiatrists, which is said to be necessary in certain cases to relieve extreme mental distress. The decisions therefore cannot stand and must be reconsidered by the Health Authority. ...

I would therefore quash the decisions of the Health Authority and remit them to the Health Authority for further consideration. Such consideration should address the clinical evidence as to the need for and nature of gender reassignment procedures, and to the extent that such procedures continue to be subordinated to other claims on the Authority's resources indicate, at least in broad terms, the reasons for the Authority's choice.

May LJ: As Auld LJ demonstrates, these policies were made upon the premises that transsexualism is not a disease and that surgical treatment for it is of no proven clinical benefit. But it was accepted before Hidden J and before us that transsexualism is an illness....

The first part of the premise upon which the policies proceeded is therefore erroneous. The strong balance of the evidence before the court is that the second part of the premise is also erroneous. But it is neither necessary nor appropriate for the court to determine that debate.

Health authorities have to make hard and often invidious decisions in the allocation of avowedly inadequate resources. But those decisions must proceed from proper assessments of the conditions competing for treatment. The decisions in the present cases did not so proceed, and I agree that they and the policies, so far as they relate to transsexualism, require reconsideration.

The court's decision reaffirms the orthodox view that resource allocation is not properly for the courts. However, the judges make clear that the court does have a role in reviewing non-funding decisions. The case is more than one where the HA devised a flawed policy and then blindly applied it. Perhaps, for the first time, the court made clear that efficacious treatment if it is not to be provided must be justified (see especially per Auld LJ). Such decisions must be properly informed by the relevant evidence. It remains unclear whether having done so, a HA may still not fund such treatment. Buxton LJ thought that it could; Auld LJ left the matter open; and May LJ did not refer to it.

B. THE HUMAN RIGHTS ACT 1998

The most significant public law development for medical law is, however, the Human Rights Act 1998, which is in force in England from 2 October 2000. The Act incorporates most of the provisions in the European Convention on Human Rights into English law. Many of these rights, as we shall see, are relevant for medical lawyers, eg art 2 ('right to life') and art 8 ('right to respect for private and family life'). What impact will art 2 have upon decisions to withdraw or withhold life-sustaining treatment? (see *infra*, ch 17). To what extent may a patient rely upon art 8 to obtain his medical records or prevent disclosure of his medical confidences? (see *infra*, chs 7 and 8). Does art 2 protect an unborn child? (see *infra*, ch 11). These are just a few of the issues which the English courts will undoubtedly have to deal with in the future. We try to deal with the application of the Convention where we consider it relevant in later chapters. Here, we address two sets of issues: (a) incorporation and applicability problems; and (b) an overview of the European Convention.

1. Incorporation and applicability

The 1998 Act incorporates the European Convention by giving certain Convention rights legal effect (see K D Ewing 'The Human Rights Act and Parliamentary Democracy' (1999) 62 MLR 79). In particular, arts 2-12 and 14 of the Convention are incorporated. The two main effects of incorporation are that: (1) all primary and secondary legislation must be 'read and given effect in a way which is compatible with Convention rights' (s 3(1)) (this is a general provision and, on its face, seems to apply to everyone: court, executive, public body and (even it would seem) private citizens); and (2) it will be unlawful for public authorities to act incompatibly with a Convention right unless it is impossible to do so because of legislation (s 6(1) and (2)). This obligation is restricted to 'public authorities', which are not defined in the Act but do include courts and tribunals (s 6(3)).

Individuals may rely upon their Convention rights either by judicial review or other appropriate procedure against a public authority providing they are 'a victim' of the unlawful act (s 7(1)). The *locus standi* is deliberately more narrowly stated than for judicial review under RSC Ord 53 of 'sufficient interest'. Courts are required to interpret (ie 'read up') legislation to be compatible with the Convention and this may entail effectively ignoring the wording of the legislation. By way of remedies, the courts may make any order it considers 'just and appropriate' (s 8(1)) and this may include damages or compensation in certain circumstances (s 8(2) and (3)). The court cannot quash primary legislation which it cannot read under s 3(1) compatibly with the Convention, though it may make a declaration of incompatibility (s 4) (see generally, I Leigh and L Lustgarten 'Making Rights Real: The Courts, Remedies, and the Human Rights Act' [1999] CLJ 509). What is of particular relevance for medical law?

First, courts will be required to interpret legislation in the medical law field consistently with the 1998 Act, eg the Abortion Act 1967, the Human Fertilisation and Embryology Act 1990 and the Data Protection Act 1998. Its obligation under s 3(1) does not depend upon whether a public authority is involved providing that the patient is entitled to bring the action. Likewise, s 3(1) will require bodies such as the Human Fertilisation and Embryology Authority or NHS bodies when applying legislative provisions in relation to patients to do so compatibly with the Convention. It could be argued that the s 3(1) duty is only placed upon courts and tribunals. Even if correct, s 6(1) may place a duty upon these bodies (as public authorities) to act compatibly with the Convention.

Secondly, then, NHS institutions and bodies such as the HFEA will if 'public authorities' have this duty under s 6(1). Are they 'public authorities'? The 1998 Act is silent, though it is intended that a wide definition should be given (for a general discussion, see N Bamforth 'The Application of the Human Rights Act 1998 to Public Authorities and Private Bodies' [1999] CLJ 159). Section 6 contemplates three situations: (1) bodies which are public bodies for all purposes; (2) private bodies that have some function of a public nature; and (3) purely private bodies. It is most likely that NHS institutions and bodies such as the HFEA will fall into category (1) and thus be subject to the s 6(1) duty in whatever they do even, it would seem, if they engage in private activity such as employment relationships (cf *R v East Berkshire HA, ex p Walsh* [1985] QB 152 (CA) – employment decision not amenable to judicial review). Thus, where a Trust or Health Authority decision is taken as in *ex p B*, *Fisher* and *ex p A, D and G* that we saw earlier, s 6(1) will apply and so therefore, will the Convention. Equally, bodies such as the HFEA or the General Medical Council or other regulatory bodies such as Research Ethics Committees must act compatibly with the Convention. There seems little doubt that local research ethics committees or other bodies (such as primary care groups (*a fortiori* Primary Care Trusts) acting on behalf of health authorities will be 'public authorities' for the purposes of the 1998 Act. What, however, of doctors or other health professions? This leads to our next point.

Thirdly, to what extend will individual health professionals have to act consistently with the Convention when making decisions about their patients? It is important to notice that the 1998 Act does not have 'direct horizontal effect' between private individuals. Thus, it could be argued that the private relationship of doctor-patient remains untouched by the Convention. The courts are not likely to see it this way. Two leading commentators on the Act certainly agree: 'Doctors would be public authorities in relation to their NHS functions, but not in relation to their private patients...' (J Wadham and H Mountfield *Blackstone's Guide to the Human Rights Act 1998* (1998) p 37. See also Lord Irving LC at 583 HL Deb 811 (Nov 27 1997)). Of course, if the doctor's decision is really driven by the Trust or Health Authority's policy or overall decision, the patient will have redress against that public body. But, suppose it is not. There are two arguments.

The court could simply see the doctor (or other health professional) as the agent or alter ego of the Trust (or Health Authority) and equate the two (see *Razzel v Snowball* [1954] 3 All ER 429 (CA) – consultant held to be agent of Minister of Health). Despite the fact that conventional wisdom would see the doctor-patient relationship as a private one, this interpretation seems likely. A further possibility is that, were the court to consider the legality of the decision by the doctor, it (the court) would under s 6(1) have a duty to act compatibly with the Convention and thus would apply the law on the basis of the Convention. Effectively, therefore, the doctor would be required to act compatibly with the Convention. Take, for example, an application to the court for a declaration that certain treatment may be withdrawn from an incompetent patient. Assume, also, that this would infringe art 2 ('right to life') of the Convention. The court *must* act compatibly with art 2. It would be pure sophistry to say anything other than the doctor is effectively so bound also – whatever the Act says or, rather, does not say about him being directly bound. Both steps in this argument are controversial. In particular, the first depends upon the view that the Act has 'indirect horizontal' effect between citizens which is not universally accepted (see eg N Bamforth (*op cit*); G Phillipson 'The Human Rights Act, "Horizontal Effect" and the Common Law: a Bang or a Whimper?' (1999) 62 MLR 824; M Hunt 'The Horizontal Effect of the Human Rights Act' [1998] PL 423). The earlier agency argument avoids these difficulties, which only really surfaces in 'pure' private relationships. It more accurately reflects the nature of the National Health Service as a public service.

2. The Convention

Having seen how incorporation is effected by the Human Rights Act 1998, we now turn to consider some of the more important Convention provisions for medical law. Our purpose is not to give a comprehensive account of the Convention as it might apply in each and every situation, but rather to introduce the relevant articles and to provide a framework for working through the application of the relevant provisions.

The relevant articles are arts 2 (right to life), 3 (prohibition of torture), 5 (right to liberty and security), 6 (right to a fair trial), 8 (right to respect for private and family life), 9 (freedom of thought, conscience and religion), 10 (freedom of expression), 12 (right to marry) and 14 (prohibition on discrimination).

We set these provisions out in full.

Article 2

Right to life

1 Everyone's right to life shall be protected by law. No one shall be deprived of his life intentionally save in the execution of a sentence of a court following his conviction of a crime for which this penalty is provided by law.

2 Deprivation of life shall not be regarded as inflicted in contravention of this article when it results from the use of force which is no more than absolutely necessary:

a in defence of any person from unlawful violence;

b in order to effect a lawful arrest or to prevent the escape of a person lawfully detained;

c in action lawfully taken for the purpose of quelling a riot or insurrection.

Article 3

Prohibition of torture

No one shall be subjected to torture or to inhuman or degrading treatment or punishment.

Article 5

Right to liberty and security

1 Everyone has the right to liberty and security of person. No one shall be deprived of his liberty save in the following cases and in accordance with a procedure prescribed by law:

a the lawful detention of a person after conviction by a competent court;

b the lawful arrest or detention of a person for non-compliance with the lawful order of a court or in order to secure the fulfilment of any obligation prescribed by law;

c the lawful arrest or detention of a person effected for the purpose of bringing him before the competent legal authority on reasonable suspicion of having committed an offence or when it is reasonably considered necessary to prevent his committing an offence or fleeing after having done so;

d the detention of a minor by lawful order for the purpose of educational supervision or his lawful detention for the purpose of bringing him before the competent legal authority;

e the lawful detention of persons for the prevention of the spreading of infectious diseases, of persons of unsound mind, alcoholics or drug addicts or vagrants;

f the lawful arrest or detention of a person to prevent his effecting an unauthorised entry into the country or of a person against whom action is being taken with a view to deportation or extradition.

2 Everyone who is arrested shall be informed promptly, in a language which he understands, of the reasons for his arrest and of any charge against him.

3 Everyone arrested or detained in accordance with the provisions of paragraph 1.c of this article shall be brought promptly before a judge or other officer authorised by law to exercise judicial power and shall be entitled to trial within a reasonable time or to release pending trial. Release may be conditioned by guarantees to appear for trial.

4 Everyone who is deprived of his liberty by arrest or detention shall be entitled to take proceedings by which the lawfulness of his detention shall be decided speedily by a court and his release ordered if the detention is not lawful.

5 Everyone who has been the victim of arrest or detention in contravention of the provisions of this article shall have an enforceable right to compensation.

Article 6

Right to a fair trial

1 In the determination of his civil rights and obligations or of any criminal charge against him, everyone is entitled to a fair and public hearing within a reasonable time by an independent and impartial tribunal established by law. Judgment shall be pronounced publicly but the press and public may be excluded from all or part of the trial in the interests of morals, public order or national security in a democratic society, where the interests of juveniles or the protection of the private life of the parties so require, or to the extent strictly necessary in the opinion of the court in special circumstances where publicity would prejudice the interests of justice.

2 Everyone charged with a criminal offence shall be presumed innocent until proved guilty according to law.

3 Everyone charged with a criminal offence has the following minimum rights:

a to be informed promptly, in a language which he understands and in detail, of the nature and cause of the accusation against him;

b to have adequate time and facilities for the preparation of his defence;

c to defend himself in person or through legal assistance of his own choosing or, if he has not sufficient means to pay for legal assistance, to be given it free when the interests of justice so require;

d to examine or have examined witnesses against him and to obtain the attendance and examination of witnesses on his behalf under the same conditions as witnesses against him;

e to have the free assistance of an interpreter if he cannot understand or speak the language used in court.

Article 8

Right to respect for private and family life

1 Everyone has the right to respect for his private and family life, his home and his correspondence.

2 There shall be no interference by a public authority with the exercise of this right except such as is in accordance with the law and is necessary in a democratic society in the interests of national security, public safety or the economic well-being of the country, for the prevention of disorder or crime, for the protection of health or morals, or for the protection of the rights and freedoms of others.

Article 9

Freedom of thought, conscience and religion

1 Everyone has the right to freedom of thought, conscience and religion; this right includes freedom to change his religion or belief and freedom, either alone or in community with others and in public or private, to manifest his religion or belief, in worship, teaching, practice and observance.

2 Freedom to manifest one's religion or beliefs shall be subject only to such limitations as are prescribed by law and are necessary in a democratic society in the interests of public safety, for the protection of public order, health or morals, or for the protection of the rights and freedoms of others.

Article 10

Freedom of expression

1 Everyone has the right to freedom of expression. This right shall include freedom to hold opinions and to receive and impart information and ideas without interference by public authority and regardless of frontiers. This article shall not prevent States from requiring the licensing of broadcasting, television or cinema enterprises.

2 The exercise of these freedoms, since it carries with it duties and responsibilities, may be subject to such formalities, conditions, restrictions or penalties as are prescribed by law and are necessary in a democratic society, in the interests of national security, territorial

integrity or public safety, for the prevention of disorder or crime, for the protection of health or morals, for the protection of the reputation or rights of others for preventing the disclosure of information received in confidence, or for maintaining the authority and impartiality of the judiciary.

Article 12

Right to marry

Men and women of marriageable age have the right to marry and to found a family, according to the national laws governing the exercise of this right.

Article 14

Prohibition of discrimination

The enjoyment of the rights and freedoms set forth in this Convention shall be secured without discrimination on any ground such as sex, race, colour, language, religion, political or other opinion, national or social origin, association with a national minority, property, birth or other status.

There are a number of points we should note. First, there are *three* types of article: (1) those with an absolute prohibition (eg arts 3, 12 and 14); (2) those with an absolute prohibition but subject to specific exceptions (eg arts 2 and 5); and (3) those where the individual's right must be balanced against the rights of others or society's interests (eg arts 8, 9 and 10) (see A McHarg 'Reconciling Human Rights and the Public Interest: Conceptual Problems and Doctrinal Uncertainty in the Jurisprudence of the European Court of Human Rights' (1999) 62 MLR 671).

Secondly, in applying the articles, the courts must interpret the 'right' specified. Thus, the court must determine, for example, whether the 'treatment' of a patient in withdrawing (or not withdrawing) measures is 'inhuman or degrading' or what is the scope of a patient's 'private' or 'family life'. This will be particularly important where the right is stated as an absolute prohibition or only subject to specified factual exceptions but it will be important in other cases too.

Thirdly, the courts will have to consider the extent to which a 'right' imposes a positive obligation upon the State, For example, to provide particular treatments. It will be easier for the court to see 'positive' obligations where the duty is to 'respect' the patient's right (eg art 8) or the right is to be 'protected' (eg art 2), rather than where it is a free-standing negative right such as not being 'deprived of life' (art 2) (see *Osman v UK* (1998) 5 BHRC 293 (ECt HR) and RD O'Sullivan [1998] PL 389). In the context of medical law the courts will often have to consider patient demands for treatment against a background of scarce health care resources, as we saw earlier. Notice the approach and analysis of the Court of Appeal in *North West Lancashire HA v A, D and G* [1999] Lloyd's Rep Med 399.

Auld LJ: Art 8 imposes no positive obligations to provide treatment. The ECHR in *Sheffield and Horsham v UK* (1998) 27 EHRR 163, which concerned post-operative refusal to accord legal status as a woman, said at 191, para 52:

> The Court reiterates that the notion of "respect" is not clear-cut, especially as far as the positive obligations inherent in that concept are concerned: having regard to the diversity of the practices followed and the situation obtaining in the Contracting States, the notion's requirements will vary considerably from case to case. In determining whether or not a positive obligation exists, regard must be had to the fair balance that has to be struck between the general interest of the community and the interests of the individual, the search for which balance is inherent in the whole of the Convention.

Interestingly, the court added at 193, para 58:

> For the Court it continues to be the case that transsexualism raises complex scientific, legal, moral and social issues, in respect of which there is no generally shared approach among the Contracting States.

As Mr Pannick observed, if the respondents have no case under Art 8 of failure to respect their private and family life, they could not, *a fortiori*, establish that they were victims of inhuman or degrading treatment under Art 3 since the same essential issues arise; see *Olsson v Sweden* (1988) 11 EHRR 259, at 292, paras 85–87. And, as he also observed, a breach of the article requires "a particular level" of severity which, of course depends on the circumstances of the case. It is plain, in my view, that Art 3 was not designed for circumstances of this sort of case where the challenge is as to a Health Authority's allocation of finite funds between competing demands. As Hidden J observed, in rejecting similar submissions below:

> The Convention does not give the applicants rights to free healthcare in general or to gender reassignment surgery in particular. Even if the applicants had such a right it would be qualified by the respondent's right to determine healthcare priorities in the light of its limited resources.

Buxton LJ: Article 3 of the ECHR addresses positive conduct by public officials of a high degree of seriousness and opprobrium. It has never been applied to merely policy decisions on the allocation of resources, such as the present case is concerned with. That is clear not only from the terms of Art 3 itself, and the lack of any suggestion in any of the authorities that it could apply in a case even remotely like the present, but also from the explanation of the reach of Art 3 that has been given by the Convention organs. Thus in *Tyrer v United Kingdom* (1978) 2 EHRR 1, a case concerned with corporal punishment, the Strasbourg Court held, at paragraphs [30] and [35] of its judgment that:

> in order for a punishment to be "degrading" and in breach of Art 3 the humiliation or debasement involved must attain a particular level … the Court finds that the applicant was subjected to a punishment in which the element of humiliation attained the level inherent in the notion of "degrading punishment".

More generally, the Strasbourg Commission has on a number of occasions stressed the degree of seriousness of the conduct that Art 3 addresses. For instance, the Commission said in its report in the *East African Asians* case, 14 December 1973, at page 57:

> The Commission recalls its own statement in the First Greek Case that treatment of an individual may be said to be "degrading" in the sense of Article 3 "if it grossly humiliates him before others or drives him to act against his will or conscience" … the word "grossly" indicates that Article 3 is only concerned with degrading treatment which reaches a certain level of severity.

These strong statements clearly demonstrate, if demonstration were needed, that to attempt to bring the present case under Art 3 not only strains language and commonsense, but also and even more seriously trivialises that article in relation to the very important values that it in truth protects.

The situation is less straightforward with regard to Art 8 of the ECHR. There is no doubt that a person's sexual behaviour is an important element in his private life, respect for which is guaranteed by Art 8 of the ECHR. It is, however, less easy to see that a person's sexuality is, in itself, an aspect of his private life, as that concept is understood in the context of Art 8, as opposed to being an evidently important, possibly even overriding, aspect of his personality and personal integrity. That difficult question does not, however, need to be pursued, because it is plain that in this case there has occurred no *interference* with either the applicants' private life or with their sexuality.

The ECHR jurisprudence demonstrates that a state can be guilty of such interference simply by inaction, though the cases in which that has been found do not seem to go beyond an obligation to adopt measures to prevent serious infractions of private or family life by subjects of the state: see *X and Y v Netherlands* 8 EHRR 235 [93] and, more generally, Harris *et al, law of the European Convention on Human Rights* (1995), pages 320–324. Such an interference could hardly be founded on a refusal to fund medical treatment. And in any event this case plainly falls under the reiterated guidance given by the Strasbourg Court in *Cossey v United Kingdom* (1990) 13 EHRR 622 [37] and *Sheffield and Horsham v United Kingdom* (1998) 27 EHRR 163 [52]...

What we see here is a fairly narrow reading of art 8 and art 3 in the medical law context. It suggests rather strongly that 'claim rights' will not easily be accepted by the courts.

Fourthly, in those articles where a balancing exercise is contemplated, how does the court engage in this process? The jurisprudence of the European Court of Human Rights (which English courts must take into account – s 2(1) of the 1998 Act) has developed a three-stage approach: (1) is the infringement in accordance with (or authorised by) law? (2) is it directed towards a legitimate aim specified in the article? and (3) is it 'necessary in a democratic society', ie proportional (and not excessive for) the aims pursued? (see McHaig (*op cit*) pp 683–695).

John Wadham and Helen Mountfield explain this three-stage process:

John Wadham and Helen Mountfield *Blackstone's Guide to the Human Rights Act 1998* (1999)

2.2 THE RULE OF LAW

A core concept in Convention jurisprudence is the rule of law. No matter how desirable the end to be achieved, no interference with a right protected under the Convention is permissible unless the citizen knows the basis for the interference because it is set out in an ascertainable law. In the absence of such detailed authorisation by the law, any interference, however justified, will violate the Convention.

Article 5 of the European Convention, for example, protects the liberty of the person. It is perhaps best described as protecting individuals from 'arbitrary detention'. Under art 5 the state can lawfully detain a person in prison following conviction, for contempt of court, on arrest on a criminal charge, because he or she is mentally ill or in order to deport or to extradite the detained person. But no detention is permitted unless it is 'in accordance with a procedure prescribed by law' – administrative decisions to detain are not sufficient.

There are similar limitations on the right to free expression (art 10) and assembly (art 11). But, again, any such interference must be 'in accordance with the law' or must be 'prescribed by law'. No such interference can be permitted by executive rules alone.

To be 'prescribes by law' or 'in accordance with law' means that there must be an ascertainable legal regime governing the interference in question. The Strasbourg court explained the concept in *Sunday Times v United Kingdom* (1979) 2 EHRR 245 at para. 49:

> Firstly, the law must be adequately accessible: the citizens must be able to have an indication that is adequate in the circumstances of the legal rules applicable to a given case. Secondly, a norm cannot regarded as a 'law' unless it is formulated with sufficient precision to enable the citizen to regulate his conduct.

The common law may be sufficiently clear for this purpose and statute law or regulation is not necessary. In the *Sunday Times* case the Court said that:

> … whilst certainty is highly desirable, it may bring in its train excessive rigidity and the law must be able to keep pace with changing circumstances. Accordingly, many laws are inevitably couched in terms which, to a greater or lesser extent, are vague and whose interpretation and applicable are questions of practice.

It is not acceptable for an interference with a Convention right to occur without any legal regulation (eg, *Halford v United Kingdom* (1997) 24 EHRR 523 regarding office phone tapping), and codes of practice or internal guidance are very unlikely to meet the requirements of certainty. For instance, in *Malone v United Kingdom* (1984) 7 EHRR 14 the applicant's telephone was tapped by the police. At the time when this took place, the only regulation of the practice was an internal code of guidance produced by the police which was not public. The European Court of Human Rights took the view that Mr Malone was not therefore able to assess whether or not his telephone would be listened in to or what the basis in law for the surveillance might be. The common law was inadequate in this case as was clear from the failure of Mr Malone's proceedings in the High Court (*Malone v Metropolitan Police Commissioner* [1979] Ch 344). Accordingly, the interference violated the Convention because it was not prescribed by law. (The Interception of Communications Act 1985 was introduced as a result of this case.)

2.3 LEGITIMATE AIMS

In order to provide a defence to a claim under the Convention any interference by a public authority with a Convention right must be directed towards an identified legitimate aim. In arts 8, 9, 10 and 11 the legitimate aims are set out in the second part of each article. The sorts of aims which are legitimate are the interests of public safety, national security, the protection of health and morals and the economic well-being of the country or the protection of the rights and freedoms of others.

The Convention provides a large number of acceptable reasons for restricting rights and they have a wide scope. It is not difficult for a country facing an allegation of a breach of human rights to find a reason relevant to any case. The Strasbourg authorities have had difficulty in assessing allegations made by applicants that the legitimate aim identified by the respondent was not the 'real' aim of the restriction. For example, in *Campbell v United Kingdom* (1992) 15 EHRR 137 a prisoner complained about the authorities opening his correspondence with his lawyer. He argued that the real reason was to assess the contents. The government claimed that the interference was for the purposes of the prevention of disorder or crime. More than one aim can be identified by a respondent state although only one is necessary to defeat the claim.

2.4 PROPORTIONALITY

The third important concept which the Strasbourg institutions use when assessing whether a Convention right has been improperly violated is that of proportionality: the test of whether the interference is 'necessary in a democratic society'.

Although a few rights in the Convention are absolute, most are not. The Convention approach is to decide whether a particular limitation from a right is justified in the sense of being 'proportionate to the legitimate aim pursued' (*Handyside v United Kingdom* (1976) 1 EHRR 737).

This means that even if a policy which interferes with a Convention right might be aimed at securing a legitimate aim of social policy, for example, the prevention of crime, this will not in itself justify the violation if the means adopted to secure the aim are excessive in the circumstances. The importance of the aim in question and the actual situation which is subject to dispute are important: 'action for the prevention of crime may be directed against homicide or parking offences: the weight of each compared with the right sought to be limited is not the same' (Harris, O'Boyle and Warbrick, op cit, p 297).

As the European Court of Human Rights put it in the case of *Soering v United Kingdom* (1989) 11 EHRR 439 at para 89:

> inherent in the whole of the Convention is a search for the fair balance between the demands of the general interest of the community and the requirements of the protection of the individual's human rights.

The test of whether the measure adopted by the member state is 'necessary in a democratic society' or proportionate to the end to be achieved is different from that traditionally used in English law. It will therefore alter the standard of review of the actions of public authorities in cases where Convention rights are engaged.

Before the commencement of the Human Rights Act 1998, the test for challenging the actions of public authorities by way of judicial review is that they must be unlawful or else 'irrational'. In Lord Diplock's often quoted explanation 'a decision which is so outrageous in its defiance of logic or accepted moral standards that no sensible person who had applied his mind to the question to be decided could have arrived at it'. (*Council of Civil Service Unions v Minister for the Civil Service* [1985] AC 375 at p 410). This is sometimes described as the 'taken leave of his senses' test, and it is very hard to challenge a decision on this basis, although, in later cases where fundamental rights are at stake, the test has been redefined: see the formulation in *R v Ministry of Defence, ex parte Smith* [1996] QB 517.

Where there has been a prima facie violation of a right protected by the Convention, the Strasbourg Court has adopted a more stringent standard in considering whether the state can justify the limitation of that right. Because the Convention starts with a presumption that a right contained in the first part of a Convention article should be respected, it does not require a decision-maker to have 'taken leave of his senses' before the Court can intervene.

Where the Convention allows restrictions on rights it requires them to be justified by a legitimate aim *and* proportional to the need at hand, that is, 'necessary in a democratic society'. The case law interprets this to mean that there must be a 'pressing social need' for the interference. This is a more stringent standard than 'some logical reason': the state's desire to protect a legitimate aim does not allow it to restrict the right of the individual disproportionately – the state cannot use a sledgehammer to crack a nut.

An example of the necessity doctrine is contained in the case of *Dudgeon v United Kingdom* (1981) 4 EHRR 149. The applicant in that case challenged the law which was then in force in Northern Ireland which made buggery between consenting gay men a criminal offence. The Court accepted that the law in question interfered with the exercise of the applicant's right to privacy as set out in art 8(1) and was prescribed by law. The Court went on to consider the other issues that arose from art 8(2), that is, the objectives said to be served by that law, and whether it was a proportional response to them. It stated that 'The Court recognises that one of the purposes of the legislation is to afford safeguards for vulnerable members of society, such as the young, against the consequences of homosexual practices' and accepted that this was a legitimate aim. However, it went on to say, at para 60, that:

> It cannot be maintained in these circumstances that there is a 'pressing social need' to make such acts criminal offences, there being no sufficient justification provided by the risk of harm to vulnerable sections of society requiring protection or by the effects on

the public. On the issue of proportionality, the Court considers that such justifications as there are for retaining the law in force unamended are outweighed by the detrimental effects which the very existence of the legislative provisions in question can have on the life of a person of homosexual orientation like the applicant. Although members of the public who regard homosexuality as immoral may be shocked, offended or disturbed by the commission by others of private homosexual acts, this cannot on its own warrant the application of penal sanctions when it is consenting adults alone who are involved.

The concept of proportionality has been filtering into English law for many years. In English courts, judges have generally come across it in the context of European Community law. For example, in *R v Secretary of State for Employment, ex parte Equal Opportunities Commission* [1995] 1 AC 1 the House of Lords, having identified that a particular social measure (different service periods for full-time and part-time workers in order to qualify for the right to claim employment protection) had an effect on a higher proportion of women than men, analysed the evidence which the government had put forward to support the assertion that this was an 'appropriate and necessary' way of advancing the policy objective it had identified (promoting part-time work opportunities). The House of Lords found insufficient evidence of this. The language used in Convention case law is a little different, but the concept of proportionality – and the Continental legal traditions from which it has derived – are very similar in both Community and Convention law.

English judges have found the idea difficult. There is evidence of this difficulty in questions 4 and 5 of the reference to the European Court of Justice in *R v Secretary of State for Employment, ex parte Seymour-Smith* [1997] ICR 371 at p 381 concerning the time at which justification must be considered, and the evidence required to support a justification defence as a matter of Community law. (The ECJ's decision in *ex parte Seymour-Smith* (case C-167/97) had not been given when this book went to press.) English judges' experience of Community law will probably inform the way they exercise the proportionality balance in cases where Convention arguments arise.

Fifthly, in addition, the European Court has developed a doctrine of the 'margin of appreciation'. This is closely allied to the 'proportionality' test. Under the doctrine, the European Court acknowledges that States have some freedom in implementing public policy, eg public morality. However, this is a doctrine which is part of a pan-European legal order where an international court recognises its limits in setting absolute standards for States. If so, it will be irrelevant when a domestic court applies the Convention (see, Leigh and Lustgarten (*op cit*) at pp 514-517). Of course, the same 'area of discretion' may reflect the domestic constitutional regime between Parliament and the courts where this is appropriate. The point has already been considered by one Law Lord, Lord Hope in *R v DPP, ex p Kebeline* [1999] 4 All ER 801 (HL) at 843–844:

Lord Hope: This brings me to another matter on which there was a consensus between counsel and which, I believe, needs now to be judicially recognised. The doctrine of the 'margin of appreciation' is a familiar part of the jurisprudence of the European Court of Human Rights. The European Court has acknowledged that, by reason of their direct and continuous contact with the vital forces of their countries, the national authorities are in principle better placed to evaluate local needs and conditions than an international court: *Buckley v UK* (1996) 23 EHRR 101 at 129 (paras 74–75). Although this means that, as the European Court explained in *Handyside v UK* (1976) 1 EHRR 737 at 753 (para 48), 'the machinery of protection established by the Convention is subsidiary to the national systems safeguarding human rights', it goes hand in hand with a European supervision. The extent of this supervision will vary according to such factors as the nature of the convention right in issue, the importance of that right for the individual and the nature of the activities involved in the case.

This doctrine is an integral part of the supervisory jurisdiction which is exercised over state conduct by the international court. By conceding a margin of appreciation to each national system, the court has recognised that the convention, as a living system, does not need to be applied uniformly by all states but may vary in its application according to local needs and conditions. This technique is not available to the national courts when they are considering convention issues arising within their own countries. But in the hands of the national courts also the convention should be seen as an expression of fundamental principles rather than as a set of mere rules. The questions which the courts will have to decide in the application of these principles will involve questions of balance between competing interests and issues of proportionality.

In this area difficult choices may have to be made by the executive or the legislature between the rights of the individual and the needs of society. In some circumstances it will be appropriate for the courts to recognise that there is an area of judgment within which the judiciary will defer, on democratic grounds, to the considered opinion of the elected body or person whose act or decision is said to be incompatible with the convention. This point is well made in *Human Rights Law and Practice* (1999) p 74, para 3.21, of which Lord Lester of Herne Hill QC and Mr David Pannick QC are the general editors, where the area in which these choices may arise is conveniently and appropriately described as the 'discretionary area of judgment'. It will be easier for such an area of judgment to be recognised where the convention itself requires a balance to be struck, much less so where the right is stated in terms which are unqualified. It will be easier for it to be recognised where the issues involve questions of social or economic policy, much less so where the rights are of high constitutional importance or are of a kind where the courts are especially well placed to assess the need for protection. But even where the right is stated in terms which are unqualified the courts will need to bear in mind the jurisprudence of the European Court which recognises that due account should be taken of the special nature of terrorist crime and the threat which it poses to a democratic society: *Murray v UK* (1994) 19 EHRR 193 at 222 (para 47).

None of the other Law Lords referred to the matter. Lord Hope's view is, nevertheless, important and illuminates how the courts may proceed.

(In later chapters we will see a number of significant overseas cases analysing human rights documents in medical law cases, eg *B v Children's Aid Society of Metropolitan Toronto* (1995) 122 DLR (4th) 1 (Can Sup Ct); *Rodriguez v A-G of British Columbia* (1993) 82 BCLR (2d) 273 (Can Sup Ct); *Washington v Glucksberg* (1997) 138 2L Ed 2d 277 (US Sup Ct).)

As we have suggested, human rights cases will often involve 'claims' by patients to treatment (see *ex p A, D and G, supra*). The following case from South Africa sheds some light on how courts can approach constitutional provisions where claim 'rights' are asserted but are met by a plea of limited resources.

Soobramoney v Minister of Health, KwaZulu-Natal (1997) 50 BMLR 224 (SA Constitutional Ct)

Chaskalson P:

[1] The appellant, a 41 year old unemployed man, is a diabetic who suffers from ischaemic heart disease and cerebro-vascular disease which caused him to have a stroke during 1996. In 1996 his kidneys also failed. Sadly his condition is irreversible and he is now in the final stages of chronic renal failure. His life could be prolonged by means of regular renal dialysis. He has sought such treatment from the renal unit of the Addington state hospital in Durban. The hospital can, however, only provide dialysis treatment to a limited number of patients. The renal unit has 20 dialysis machines available to it, and some of these machines are in poor condition. Each treatment takes four hours and a further two hours have to be allowed for the cleaning of a machine, before it can be used again for other treatment. Because of the limited facilities that are available for kidney dialysis the hospital has been unable to provide the appellant with the treatment he has requested.

[2] The reasons given by the hospital for this are set out in the respondent's answering affidavit deposed to by Doctor Saraladevi Naicker, a specialist physician and nephrologist in the field of renal medicine who has worked at Addington Hospital for 18 years and who is currently the President of the South African Renal Society. In her affidavit Dr Naicker says that Addington Hospital does not have enough resources to provide dialysis treatment for all patients suffering from chronic renal failure. Additional dialysis machines and more trained nursing staff are required to enable it to do this, but the hospital budget does not make provision for such expenditure. The hospital would like to have its budget increased but it has been told by the provincial health department that funds are not available for this purpose.

[3] Because of the shortage of resources the hospital follows a set policy in regard to the use of the dialysis resources. Only patients who suffer from acute renal failure, which can be treated and remedied by renal dialysis are given automatic access to renal dialysis at the hospital. Those patients who, like the appellant, suffer from chronic renal failure which is irreversible are not admitted automatically to the renal programme. A set of

guidelines has been drawn up and adopted to determine which applicants who have chronic renal failure will be given dialysis treatment. According to the guidelines the primary requirement for admission of such persons to the dialysis programme is that the patient must be eligible for a kidney transplant. A patient who is eligible for a transplant will be provided with dialysis treatment until an organ donor is found and a kidney transplant has been completed.

[4] The guidelines provide that an applicant is not eligible for a transplant unless he or she is "[f]ree of significant vascular or cardiac disease." The medical criteria set out in the guidelines also provide that an applicant must be

> Free of significant disease elsewhere e.g. ischaemic heart disease, cerebro-vascular disease, peripheral vascular disease, chronic liver disease, chronic lung disease.

The appellant suffers from ischaemic heart disease and cerebro-vascular disease and he is therefore not eligible for a kidney transplant.

[5] The appellant has made arrangements to receive dialysis treatment from private hospitals and doctors, but his finances have been depleted and he avers that he is no longer able to afford such treatment....

[7] The appellant based his claim on section 27(3) of the 1996 Constitution which provides:

> No one may be refused emergency medical treatment

and section 11 which stipulates

> Everyone has the right to life.

[8] We live in a society in which there are great disparities in wealth. Millions of people are living in deplorable conditions and in great poverty. There is a high level of unemployment, inadequate social security, and many do not have access to clean water or to adequate health services. These conditions already existed when the Constitution was adopted and a commitment to address them, and to transform our society into one in which there will be human dignity, freedom and equality, lies at the heart of our new constitutional order. For as long as these conditions continue to exist that aspiration will have a hollow ring.

[9] The constitutional commitment to address these conditions is expressed in the preamble which, after giving recognition to the injustices of the past, states:

> We therefore, through our freely elected representatives, adopt this Constitution as the supreme law of the Republic so as to–
>> Heal the divisions of the past and establish a society based on democratic values, social justice and fundamental human rights;
>
> ...
>
> Improve the quality of life of all citizens and free the potential of each person.

This commitment is also reflected in various provisions of the bill of rights and in particular in sections 26 and 27 which deal with housing, health care, food, water and social security.

[10] Sections 26 and 27 contain the following provisions:

> 26. Housing
>
> (1) Everyone has the right to have access to adequate housing.
> (2) The State must take reasonable legislative and other measures, within its available resources, to achieve the progressive realisation of this right.
> (3) ...
>
> 27. Health care, food, water and social security
>
> (1) Everyone has the right to have access to–
>   (a) health care services, including reproductive health care;
>   (b) sufficient food and water; and
>   (c) social security, including, if they are unable to support themselves and their dependants, appropriate social assistance.
> (2) The State must take reasonable legislative and other measures, within its available resources, to achieve the progressive realisation of each of these rights.
> (3) No one may be refused emergency medical treatment.

[11] What is apparent from these provisions is that the obligations imposed on the State by sections 26 and 27 in regard to access to housing, health care, food, water and social security are dependent upon the resources available for such purposes, and that the corresponding rights themselves are limited by reason of the lack of resources. Given this lack of resources and the significant demands on them that have already been referred

to, an unqualified obligation to meet these needs would not presently be capable of being fulfilled. This is the context within which section 27(3) must be construed.

[12] The appellant urges us to hold that patients who suffer from terminal illnesses and require treatment such as renal dialysis to prolong their lives are entitled in terms of section 27(3) to be provided with such treatment by the State, and that the State is required to provide funding and resources necessary for the discharge of this obligation.

[13] The words "emergency medical treatment" may possibly be open to a broad construction which would include ongoing treatment of chronic illnesses for the purpose of prolonging life. But this is not their ordinary meaning, and if this had been the purpose which section 27(3) was intended to serve, one would have expected that to have been expressed in positive and specific terms.

[14] Counsel for the appellant argued that section 27(3) should be construed consistently with the right to life entrenched in section 11 of the Constitution and that everyone requiring life-saving treatment who is unable to pay for such treatment herself or himself is entitled to have the treatment provided at a state hospital without charge.

[15] This Court has dealt with the right to life in the context of capital punishment but it has not yet been called upon to decide upon the parameters of the right to life or its relevance to the positive obligations imposed on the State under various provisions of the bill of rights. In India the Supreme Court has developed a jurisprudence around the right to life so as to impose positive obligations on the State in respect of the basic needs of its inhabitants. Whilst the Indian jurisprudence on this subject contains valuable insights it is important to bear in mind that our Constitution is structured differently to the Indian Constitution. Unlike the Indian Constitution ours deals specifically in the bill of rights with certain positive obligations imposed on the State, and where it does so, it is our duty to apply the obligations as formulated in the Constitution and not to draw inferences that would be inconsistent therewith.

[16] This should be done in accordance with the purposive approach to the interpretation of the Constitution which has been adopted by this Court (see *State v Makwanyane* [1995] 1 LRC 269 at 282-3 (para 9)). Consistently with this approach the rights which are in issue in the present case must not be construed in isolation

> ... but in [their] context, which includes the history and background to the adoption of the Constitution, other provisions of the Constitution itself and, in particular, the provisions of [the bill of rights] of which [they are] part. (See [1995] 1 LRC 269 at 283 (para 10))

[17] The purposive approach will often be one which calls for a generous interpretation to be given to a right to ensure that individuals secure the full protection of the bill of rights, but this is not always the case, and the context may indicate that in order to give effect to the purpose of a particular provision "a narrower or specific meaning" should be given to it (see [1995] 1 LRC 269 at 384 (para 325)) ...

[18] In developing his argument on the right to life counsel for the appellant relied upon a decision of a two-judge bench of the Supreme Court of India in *Paschim Banga Khet Mazdoor Samity and Others v State of West Bengal and Another* (1996 AIR SC 2426 at 2429), where it was said:

> The Constitution envisages the establishment of a welfare State at the federal level as well as at the State level. In a welfare State the primary duty of the Government is to secure the welfare of the people. Providing adequate medical facilities for the people is an essential part of the obligations undertaken by the Government in a welfare State. The Government discharges this obligation by running hospitals and health centres which provide medical care to the person seeking to avail those facilities. Article 21 imposes an obligation on the State to safeguard the right to life of every person. Preservation of human life is thus of paramount importance. The Government hospitals run by the State and the medical officers employed therein are duty bound to extend medical assistance for preserving human life. Failure on the part of a Government hospital to provide timely medical treatment to a person in need of such treatment results in violation of his right to life guaranteed under Article 21.

These comments must be seen in the context of the facts of that case which are materially different to those of the present case. It was a case in which constitutional damages were claimed. The claimant had suffered serious head injuries and brain haemorrhage as a result of having fallen off a train. He was taken to various hospitals and turned away, either because the hospital did not have the necessary facilities for treatment, or on the grounds that it did not have room to accommodate him. As a result he had been obliged to secure the necessary treatment at a private hospital. It appeared from the judgment that the claimant could in fact have been accommodated in more than one of the hospitals which turned him away and that the persons responsible for that decision had been guilty of misconduct. This is precisely the sort of case which would fall within section 27(3). It is one in which emergency treatment was clearly necessary. The occurrence was sudden, the patient had no opportunity of making arrangements in advance for the treatment that was required, and there was urgency in securing the treatment in order to stabilise his condition. The treatment was available but denied.

[19] In our Constitution the right to medical treatment does not have to be inferred from the nature of the State established by the Constitution or from the right to life which it guarantees. It is dealt with directly in section 27. If section 27(3) were to be construed in accordance with the appellant's contention it would make it substantially more difficult for the state to fulfil its primary obligations under sections 27(1) and (2) to provide health care services to "everyone" within its available resources. It would also have the consequence of prioritising the treatment of terminal illnesses over other forms of medical care and would reduce the resources available to the State for purposes such as preventative health care and medical treatment for persons suffering from illnesses or bodily infirmities which are not life threatening. In my view much clearer language than that used in section 27(3) would be required to justify such a conclusion.

[20] Section 27(3) itself is couched in negative terms – it is a right not to be refused emergency treatment. The purpose of the right seems to be to ensure that treatment be given in an emergency, and is not frustrated by reason of bureaucratic requirements or other formalities. A person who suffers a sudden catastrophe which calls for immediate medical attention, such as the injured person in *Paschim Banga Khet Mazdoor Samity v State of West Bengal*, should not be refused ambulance or other emergency services which are available and should not be turned away from a hospital which is able to provide the necessary treatment. What the section requires is that remedial treatment that is necessary and available be given immediately to avert that harm.

[21] The applicant suffers from chronic renal failure. To be kept alive by dialysis he would require such treatment two to three times a week. This is not an emergency which calls for immediate remedial treatment. It is an ongoing state of affairs resulting from a deterioration of the applicant's renal function which is incurable. In my view section 27(3) does not apply to these facts.

[22] The appellant's demand to receive dialysis treatment at a state hospital must be determined in accordance with the provisions of sections 27(1) and (2) and not section 27(3). These sections entitle everyone to have access to health care services provided by the State "within its available resources".

[23] In the Court *a quo* Combrinck J held that "[i]n this case the respondent has conclusively proved that there are no funds available to provide patients such as the applicant with the necessary treatment". This finding was not disputed by the appellant, but it was argued that the State could make additional funds available to the renal clinic and that it was obliged to do so to enable the clinic to provide life saving treatment to the appellant and others suffering from chronic renal failure.

[24] At present the Department of Health in KwaZulu-Natal does not have sufficient funds to cover the cost of the services which are being provided to the public. In 1996–1997 it overspent its budget by R152 million, and in the current year it is anticipated that the overspending will be R700 million unless a serious cutback is made in the services which it provides. The renal unit at the Addington Hospital has to serve the whole of KwaZulu-Natal and also takes patients from parts of the Eastern Cape. There are many more patients suffering from chronic renal failure than there are dialysis machines to treat such patients. This is a nation-wide problem and resources are stretched in all renal clinics throughout the land. Guidelines have therefore been established to assist the persons working in these clinics to make the agonising choices which have to be made in deciding who should receive treatment, and who not. These guidelines were applied in the present case.

[25] By using the available dialysis machines in accordance with the guidelines more patients are benefited than would be the case if they were used to keep alive persons with chronic renal failure, and the outcome of the treatment is also likely to be more beneficial because it is directed to curing patients, and not simply to maintaining them in a chronically ill condition. It has not been suggested that these guidelines are unreasonable or that they were not applied fairly and rationally when the decision was taken by the Addington Hospital that the appellant did not qualify for dialysis.

[26] Ideally the dialysis machines available at the Addington Hospital should handle no more than about 60 patients. At present they are being used to treat 85 patients and the hospital can barely accommodate those who meet its guidelines. The nurse-patient ratio in the renal unit is 1:4.5 instead of the recommended ratio of 1:2.5. According to Dr Naicker, if the hospital were required to treat all persons who, like the appellant, are suffering from chronic renal failure, it would be unable to do so. She says that if the appellant were to be admitted to the programme it would result in other patients who comply with the guidelines being put at risk. Only about 30% of the patients suffering

from chronic renal failure meet the guidelines for admission to the dialysis programme. If everyone in the same condition as the appellant were to be admitted the carefully tailored programme would collapse and no one would benefit from that.

[27] The appellant avers in his affidavits that better use could be made of the dialysis machines at the Addington Hospital by keeping the clinic open for longer hours. He says that some of the nurses "moonlight" at other hospitals after their normal working hours in order to earn extra income, and that if they were given overtime opportunities at the Addington Hospital more people could be treated.

[28] The appellant's case must be seen in the context of the needs which the health services have to meet, for if treatment has to be provided to the appellant it would also have to be provided to all other persons similarly placed. Although the renal clinic could be kept open for longer hours, it would involve additional expense in having to pay the clinic personnel at overtime rates, or in having to employ additional personnel working on a shift basis. It would also put a great strain on the existing dialysis machines which are already showing signs of wear. It is estimated that the cost to the State of treating one chronically ill patient by means of renal dialysis provided twice a week at a state hospital is approximately R60,000 per annum. If all the persons in South Africa who suffer from chronic renal failure were to be provided with dialysis treatment – and many of them, as the appellant does, would require treatment three times a week – the cost of doing so would make substantial inroads into the health budget. And if this principle were to be applied to all patients claiming access to expensive medical treatment or expensive drugs, the health budget would have to be dramatically increased to the prejudice of other needs which the State has to meet.

[29] The provincial administration which is responsible for health services in KwaZulu-Natal has to make decisions about the funding that should be made available for health care and how such funds should be spent. These choices involve difficult decisions to be taken at the political level in fixing the health budget, and at the functional level in deciding upon the priorities to be met. A court will be slow to interfere with rational decisions taken in good faith by the political organs and medical authorities whose responsibility it is to deal with such matters.

[30] Although the problem of scarce resources is particularly acute in South Africa this is not a peculiarly South African problem. It is a problem which hospital administrators and doctors have had to confront in other parts of the world, and in which they have had to take similar decisions. In his judgment in this case Combrinck J refers to decisions of the English courts in which it has been held to be undesirable for a court to make an order as to how scarce medical resources should be applied, and to the danger of making any order that the resources be used for a particular patient, which might have the effect of denying those resources to other patients to whom they might more advantageously be devoted. ...

[31] One cannot but have sympathy for the appellant and his family, who face the cruel dilemma of having to impoverish themselves in order to secure the treatment that the appellant seeks in order to prolong his life. The hard and unpalatable fact is that if the appellant were a wealthy man he would be able to procure such treatment from private sources; he is not and has to look to the State to provide him with the treatment. But the State's resources are limited and the appellant does not meet the criteria for admission to the renal dialysis programme. Unfortunately, this is true not only of the appellant but of many others who need access to renal dialysis units or to other health services. There are also those who need access to housing, food and water, employment opportunities, and social security. These too are aspects of the right to

> ... human life: the right to live as a human being, to be part of a broader community, to share in the experience of humanity (see *State v Makwanyane* [1995] 1 LRC 145 at 384 (para 326) per O'Regan J).

The State has to manage its limited resources in order to address all these claims. There will be times when this requires it to adopt a holistic approach to the larger needs of society rather than to focus on the specific needs of particular individuals within society.

[32] In his concurring judgment in this matter Madala J refers to the possibility of the appellant being treated by Continuing Ambulatory Peritoneal Dialysis (CAPD). This treatment is dealt with fully by Dr Naicker in a supplementary affidavit lodged by her in response to an averment made by the appellant in his replying affidavit that there is treatment, other than renal dialysis, which would be a benefit to him, but had not been offered to him by the Addington Hospital.

[33] Dr Naicker explains that CPAD treatment makes patients vulnerable to infections and leads to patients having to be put on dialysis for two to three months when such infections occur. If an infection occurs frequently or is severe the patient has to be put onto dialysis permanently. A study undertaken at the hospital shows that over 60% of the patients treated at the hospital by CAPD have had to be placed on dialysis permanently. The cost

of the treatment is high – the fluids used in the treatment call for an expenditure of approximately R4000 per month – and there is the additional cost of having to accommodate the patient at the hospital and treat him or her in the surgery. Because of the high cost of the treatment and the demands that it makes on hospital resources including dialysis facilities, the hospital has also set criteria for treating patients by CAPD. Only patients who are candidates for transplant are placed on CAPD and approximately 130 such patients are being treated in this way at the hospital. The appellant is not a candidate for a transplant and accordingly does not meet the criteria for CAPD treatment.

[34] Counsel for the appellant, correctly in my view, appreciated that there was no material difference between the appellant's claim to be placed on dialysis (which is his preferred option) and the alternative of being treated by CAPD. Neither form of treatment is "emergency treatment", neither is accessible to all patients suffering from chronic renal failure and because of the limited resources both are subject to criteria which the appellant does not meet.

[35] I should add that I do not consider it appropriate to comment on the attitude of the private medical sector to CAPD treatment. No evidence was placed before us in that regard and there is nothing on the papers to show that patients treated privately do not receive proper advice in regard to the availability, risks and costs of such treatment.

[36] The State has a constitutional duty to comply with the obligations imposed on it by section 27 of the Constitution. It has not been shown in the present case, however, that the State's failure to provide renal dialysis facilities for all persons suffering from chronic renal failure constitutes a breach of those obligations. In the circumstances the appellant is not entitled to the relief that he seeks in these proceedings and his appeal against the decision of Combrinck J must fail. This is not an appropriate case for an order for costs to be made and the respondent correctly does not seek such an order.

[37] The following order is made. The appeal against the order made by Combrinck J is dismissed. No order is made as to costs.

(Langa D-P, Ackermann, Didcott, Goldstone, Kriegler, Mokgoro, and O'Regan JJ concurred in the judgment of Chaskalson P. Sachs J delivered a concurring judgment)

Sachs J:

[54] Health care rights by their very nature have to be considered not only in a traditional legal context structured around the ideas of human autonomy but in a new analytical framework based on the notion of human interdependence. A healthy life depends upon social interdependence: the quality of air, water, and sanitation which the State maintains for the public good; the quality of one's caring relationships, which are highly correlated to health; as well as the quality of health care and support furnished officially by medical institutions and provided informally by family, friends, and the community. As Minow put it:

> Interdependence is not a social ideal, but an inescapable fact; the scarcity of resources forces it on us. Who gets to use dialysis equipment? Who goes to the front of the line for the kidney transplant? (Harvard Law School Human Rights Program, Cambridge MA 1995, 1 at 3.)

Traditional rights analyses accordingly have to be adapted so as to take account of the special problems created by the need to provide a broad framework of constitutional principles governing the right of access to scarce resources and to adjudicate between competing rights bearers. When rights by their very nature are shared and inter-dependent, striking appropriate balances between the equally valid entitlements of expectations of a multitude of claimants should not be seen as imposing limits on those rights (which would then have to be justified in terms of section 36), but as defining the circumstances in which the rights may most fairly and effectively be enjoyed.

[55] I conclude with some observations on the questions raised relating to section 11 of the Constitution which states that "[e]veryone has the right to life". The present case does not necessitate any attempt to give a definitive answer to all these questions. yet it does point to the need to establish what Dworkin has in his book *Life's Dominion: An Argument about Abortion and Euthanasia* (1993) p 240, called the "relative importance of the natural and human contributions to the sanctity of life". He concludes his study with the eloquent reminder that if people are to

> retain the self consciousness and self respect that is the greatest achievement of our species, they will let neither science nor nature simply take its course, but will struggle to express, in the laws they make as citizens and the choices they make as people, the best understanding they can reach of why human life is sacred, and of the proper place of freedom in its dominion. (See Dworkin p 241.)

[56] "[T]he timing of death – once solely a matter of fate – is now increasingly becoming a matter of human choice." (See *Life sustaining Technologies and the Elderly* (1998)

OTA, Task Force p 41 quoted by Brennan J (dissenting) in *Cruzan v Director, Missouri Department of Health* (1990) 497 US 261 at 302 ...) In the United States, eighty percent of the two million people who die each year, die in hospitals and long term care institutions, and approximately seventy percent of those after a decision to forego life sustaining treatment has been made. The words of Brennan J of the US Supreme Court, writing in a different context, have resonance (at 303):

> Nearly every death involves a decision whether to undertake some medical procedure that could prolong the process of dying. Such decisions are difficult and personal. They must be made on the basis of individual values, informed by medical realities, yet within a framework governed by law. *The role of the courts is confined to defining that framework, delineating the ways in which government may and may not participate in such decisions.* (My emphasis.)

[57] However the right to life may come to be defined in South Africa, there is in reality no meaningful way in which it can constitutionally be extended to encompass the right indefinitely to evade death. As Stevens J put it: dying is part of life, its completion rather than its opposite (see at 343). We can, however, influence the manner in which we come to terms with our mortality. It is precisely here, where scarce artificial life-prolonging resources have to be called upon, that tragic medical choices have to be made.

[58] Courts are not the proper place to resolve the agonising personal and medical problems that underlie these choices. Important though our review functions are, there are areas where institutional incapacity and appropriate constitutional modesty require us to be especially cautious. Our country's legal system simply "cannot replace the more intimate struggle that must be borne by the patient, those caring for the patient, and those who care about the patient". (See *Re Jobes* (1987) 529 A 2d 434 at 451 (NJ SCt) ...) The provisions of the Bill of Rights should furthermore not be interpreted in a way which results in courts feeling themselves unduly pressurised by the fear of gambling with the lives of claimants into ordering hospitals to furnish the most expensive and improbable procedures, thereby diverting scarce medical resources and prejudicing the claims of others ...

[59] The applicant in this case presented his claim in a most dignified manner and showed manifest appreciation for the situation of the many other persons in the same harsh circumstances as himself. If resources were co-extensive with compassion, I have no doubt as to what my decision would have been. Unfortunately, the resources are limited, and I can find no reason to interfere with the allocation undertaken by those better equipped than I to deal with the agonising choices that had to be made.

Madala J concurred.

Of course, *Soobramoney* involved constitutional provisions different from those in the Convention and, outside of emergencies, specifically required the court to consider the availability of resources: s 27 (2) (for a similar case factually, see *Shortland v Northland Health Ltd* [1998] 1 NZLR 433 (NZ CA) and note *Osman, op cit* at para 116). Nevertheless, the approach of the judges of the South African Constitutional Court in seeking to place human rights in the real world may help us to understand how English judges will respond to the interpretative challenge posed by the Convention (see also *North West Lancashire HA v A, D and G* [1999] Lloyd's Rep Med 399 discussed *supra*).

European Convention on Human Rights and Biomedicine

English medical law no longer develops in isolation. Comparative law techniques mean that judges in this country are exposed to the arguments and approaches of overseas courts when formulating English law (see eg *McFarlane v Tayside Health Board* [1999] 4 All ER 961 (HL)). European Union law imposes regulatory regimes for pharmaceuticals and medical devices (see *infra*, ch 13) and has led to the Data Protection Act 1998 (*infra*, ch 7). However, there is not, as yet, a distinctive European medical law. Indeed, uniformity throughout the diverse cultures of Europe is a virtual impossibility on many of the questions that medical law must address. However, increasingly the Council of Europe is moving towards consensus statements of principle. Most prominently is the European Convention on Human Rights and Biomedicine, which was opened for signature in April 1997. The United Kingdom has yet to sign the Convention, although 24 States already have done so.

Undoubtedly, the Convention will become an important international statement of principle and will influence policy making in England. We set out here a number of the provisions dealing with: (1) consent (arts 5 – 9); (2) information (art 10); (3) genetics (arts 11–14); (4) organ and tissue transplantation (arts 19–20); and (5) exploitation of the human body (arts 21–22). As we shall see, these are all important topics covered in this book. We deal with arts 15–18, concerned with research, in Chapter 14 and do not set them out here.

Chapter II: Consent

Article 5. (General rule)

An intervention in the health field may only be carried out after the person concerned has given free and informed consent to it.

This person shall beforehand be given appropriate information as to the purpose and nature of the intervention as well as on its consequences and risks.

The person concerned may freely withdraw consent at any time.

Article 6. (Protection of persons not able to consent)

1. Subject to Articles 17 and 20 below, an intervention may only be carried out on a person who does not have the capacity to consent, for his or her direct benefit.

2. Where, according to law, a minor does not have the capacity to consent to an intervention, the intervention may only be carried out with the authorisation of his or her representative or an authority or a person or a body provided for by law.

The opinion of the minor shall be taken into consideration as an increasingly determining factor in proportion to his or her age and degree of maturity.

3. Where, according to law, an adult does not have the capacity to consent to an intervention because of a mental disability, a disease or for similar reasons, the intervention may only be carried out with the authorisation of his or her representative or an authority or a person or body provided for by law.

The individual concerned shall as far as possible take part in the authorisation procedure.

4. The representative, the authority, the person or the body mentioned in paragraphs 2 and 3 above shall be given, under the same conditions, the information referred to in Article 5.

5. The authorisation referred to in paragraphs 2 and 3 above may be withdrawn at any time in the best interests of the person concerned.

Article 7. (Protection of persons who have mental disorder)

Subject to protective conditions prescribed by law, including supervisory, control and appeal procedures, a person who has a mental disorder of a serious nature may be subjected, without his or her consent, to an intervention aimed at treating his or her mental disorder only where, without such treatment, serious harm is likely to result to his or her health.

Article 8. (Emergency situation)

When because of an emergency situation the appropriate consent cannot be obtained, any medically necessary intervention may be carried out immediately for the benefit of the health of the individual concerned.

Article 9. (Previously expressed wishes)

The previously expressed wishes relating to a medical intervention by a patient who is not, at the time of the intervention, in a state to express his or her wishes shall be taken into account.

Chapter III: Private life and right to information

Article 10. (Private life and right to information)

1. Everyone has the right to respect for private life in relation to information about his or her health.

2. Everyone is entitled to know any information collected about his or her health. However, the wishes of individuals not to be so informed shall be observed.

3. In exceptional cases, restrictions may be placed by law on the exercise of the rights contained in paragraph 2 in the interests of the patient.

Chapter IV: Human genome
Article 11. (Non-discrimination)
   Any form of discrimination against a person on grounds of his or her genetic heritage is prohibited.

Article 12. (Predictive genetic tests)
   Tests which are predictive of genetic diseases or which serve either to identify the subject as a carrier of a gene responsible for a disease or to detect a genetic predisposition or susceptibility to a disease may be performed only for health purposes or for scientific research linked to health purposes, and subject to appropriate genetic counselling.

Article 13. (Interventions on the human genome)
   An intervention seeking to modify the human genome may only be undertaken for preventive, diagnostic or therapeutic purposes and only if its aim is not to introduce any modification in the genome of any descendants.

Article 14. (Non-selection of sex)
   The use of techniques of medically assisted procreation shall not be allowed for the purpose of choosing a future child's sex, except where serious hereditary sex-related disease is to be avoided.

ChapterVI: Organ and tissue removal from living donors for transplantation purposes
Article 19. (General rule)
1. Removal of organs or tissue from a living person for transplantation purposes may be carried out solely for the therapeutic benefit of the recipient and where there is no suitable organ or tissue available from a deceased person and no other alternative therapeutic method of comparable effectiveness.
2. The necessary consent as provided for under Article 5 must have been given expressly and specifically either in written form or before an official body.

Article 20. (Protection of persons not able to consent to organ removal)
1. No organ or tissue removal may be carried out on a person who does not have the capacity to consent under Article 5.
2. Exceptionally and under the protective conditions prescribed by law, the removal of regenerative tissue from a person who does not have the capacity to consent may be authorised provided the following conditions are met:
i.   there is no compatible donor available who has the capacity to consent,
ii.   the recipient is a brother or sister of the donor,
iii.   the donation must have the potential to be life-saving for the recipient,
iv.   the authorisation provided for under paragraphs 2 and 3 of Article 6 has been given specifically and in writing, in accordance with the law and with the approval of the competent body,
v.   the potential donor concerned does not object.

Chapter VII: Prohibition of financial gain and disposal of a part of the human body
Article 21. (Prohibition of financial gain)
The human body and its parts shall not, as such, give rise to financial gain.

Article 22. (Disposal of a removed part of the human body)
When in the course of an intervention any part of a human body is removed, it may be stored and used for a purpose other than that for which it was removed, only if this is done in conformity with appropriate information and consent procedures.

(For a discussion of the Convention see: H D C Roscam Abbing (1998) 5 European Journal of Health Law 377, and see also *Explanatory Report* Council of Europe (January 1997).)

The provisions are largely consistent with English law. However, one point is worth noting here. Article 18(2) prohibiting the creating of human embryos for research is inconsistent with the Human Fertilisation and Embryology Act 1990 (see *infra*, ch 10). No doubt the UK Government will enter a reservation under art 36 before signing or ratifying the Convention.

Making the law

Who should make that law? Given the often controversial nature of many issues in medical law, are the courts the appropriate forum to resolve (and adjudicate upon) questions of morality and public policy in this area? Clearly the answer must be 'sometimes'. But, of course, these questions are also for others. Perhaps the most obvious alternative to the courts is Parliament.

As Lord Bridge pointed out in *Gillick v West Norfolk and Wisbech AHA* [1985] 3 All ER 402 the courts should be cautious about becoming involved in these areas (at 427):

> ... the occasion of a departmental non-statutory publication raising, as in that case, a clearly defined issue of law, unclouded by political, social or moral overtones, will be rare. In cases where any proposition of law implicit in a departmental advisory document is interwoven with questions of social and ethical controversy, the court should, in my opinion, exercise its jurisdiction with the utmost restraint, confine itself to deciding whether the proposition of law is erroneous and avoid either expressing ex cathedra opinions in areas of social and ethical controversy in which it has no claim to speak with authority or proffering answers to hypothetical questions of law which do not strictly arise for decision.

If we look to Parliament, it is unlikely that help will be forthcoming. There are as many votes to be lost as won in trying to resolve such charged issues. The delay in dealing with the Warnock Report bears witness to this. If any legislation were to be forthcoming, it would probably be couched in the most general terms and therefore of only limited value to those who must make particular decisions in particular contexts.

The concerns of the judges were focused in the 1993 case of *Airedale NHS Trust v Bland* [1993] 1 All ER 821. This case will be considered in detail in Chapter 16. It concerned the legality of withdrawing artificial hydration and nutrition from a permanently unconscious patient in a condition known as a 'persistent vegetative state'. For some, the case raised the issue of the legality of euthanasia and all that entailed. While all the judges (nine in all) agreed that it would be lawful to withdraw treatment, two of the judges in the House of Lords expressed concerns about whether these were not more appropriately matters for Parliament to give the courts guidance upon.

Airedale NHS Trust v Bland [1993] 1 All ER 821 (HL)

Lord Browne-Wilkinson: I have no doubt that it is for Parliament, not the courts, to decide the broader issues which this case raises. ...

Where a case raises wholly new moral and social issues, in my judgment it is not for the judges to seek to develop new, all-embracing, principles of law in a way which reflects the individual judges' moral stance when society as a whole is substantially divided on the relevant moral issues. Moreover, it is not legitimate for a judge in reaching a view as to what is for the benefit of the one individual whose life is in issue to take into account the wider practical issues as to allocation of limited financial resources or the impact on third parties of altering the time at which death occurs.

For these reasons, it seems to me imperative that the moral, social and legal issues raised by this case should be considered by Parliament. The judges' function in this area of the law should be to apply the principles which society, through the democratic process, adopts, not to impose their standards on society. If Parliament fails to act, then judge-made law will of necessity through a gradual and uncertain process provide a legal answer to each new question as it arises. But in my judgment that is not the best way to proceed.

Lord Mustill: The formulation of the necessary broad social and moral policy is an enterprise which the courts have neither the means nor in my opinion the right to perform. This can only be achieved by democratic process through the medium of Parliament.

Given the limitations, however, of all the possible institutional methods for responding to the sort of questions we have been considering, is there any better approach? In 1980 in the United States President Carter established the President's Commission for the Study of Ethical Problems in Medicine and Biomedical and Behavioral Research. In the five years of its existence (it was 'defined' by President Reagan in 1985) the Commission produced sixteen reports which have already become classics (and see now, National Bioethics Advisory Commission).

Professor Alexander Capron, who was the Executive Director of the Commission, explains the Commission's functions and evaluates its impact on medical law and ethics in the US. He does so in the context of an examination of the four model approaches which could be adopted, if it were thought that some sort of commission should, in fact, be set up.

A Capron 'A National Commission on Medical Ethics' in P Bryne (ed) *Health, Rights and Resources* (1988)

Types of commissions

Ad hoc panels

My first task, then, is to explain what I have in mind as the four types of commissions on medical ethics. The first is the ad hoc panel. This has been, as I understand it, the approach taken here in the United Kingdom, where commissions such as the Warnock committee on alternative methods of human reproduction have functioned successfully. In the United States, too, ad hoc panels have been used; indeed, the first major forays into this general field were of this sort. For example, the Department of Health, Education, and Welfare (DHEW) during the late 1960s and early 1970s established several ad hoc bodies to examine the implications of transplanted and artificial organs, such as the totally implantable artificial heart. I think it is noteworthy that such bodies returned several times to this same topic and yet their recommendations did not seem to have much impact on the activities of the Department nor on the development of public policy generally. The absence of follow-through is a decided risk of ad hoc groups when the topic is not one that can be disposed of in a single legislative or administrative stroke.

In 1972, a journalist uncovered a research project that had been going on for 40 years among black men in rural Alabama. Several hundred men had been involved in this government-sponsored study of untreated syphilis. The study was begun in 1932 prior to the development of effective therapies for syphilis, but it continued up until the time that it was revealed to the public, which was plainly shocked to discover that scientific curiosity had apparently won out over medical care in the treatment of the victims of this disease in the study group. As a consequence, the DHEW established the Tuskegee syphilis Ad Hoc Advisory Panel made up of distinguished physicians, ethicists, lawyers, and others. Within a few months they issued a report directed both at the particular problems caused by this study and at the larger issue of government regulation of scientific research conducted under government auspices.

It is characteristic of this first type of committee that groups, usually of about a dozen people from medicine, law, economics, ethics, and often a few with prior government service, attempt to reach fairly concrete recommendations and conclusions on a specific subject. Further, such groups are usually staffed by the agency that set them up, which is usually interested in specific fact-finding and recommendations on an immediate problem. Sometimes larger recommendations about the general process may also emerge, as they did from the Tuskegee panel. That body was effective in clarifying most of the facts, though some crucial facts about the degree of intentional deception of the participants were not uncovered. One panel member has now publicly stated that he believes these facts may have been intentionally suppressed and kept from the panel.

Single-subject standing bodies

The broader recommendations of the Tuskegee panel were quickly overshadowed, however, by the creation of another governmental commission in 1974 – the National Commission for the Protection of Human Subjects of Biomedical and Behavioral Research. I will use this group to illustrate the second category in my list – a standing body with authority to study and make recommendations on a narrow field within medical ethics.

The creation of the National Commission had the same provocation as the Tuskagee panel: namely, revelations about human experimentation run amok. In 1972 and 1973 the Congress of the United States took special interest in this subject. In particular, Senator Edward Kennedy, then the Chairman of the Senate Health Subcommittee, held hearings on this topic, during which a number of troubling cases, in addition to the Tuskagee study, were disclosed, particularly research in prisons and mental hospitals and research on human fetuses. As a result, provisions were included in the National Research Act of 1974: namely, that each institution conducting federally-supported research with human subjects was required to create an institutional review board (IRB); and an eleven-member commission drawn from medicine, research, law, ethics, and related fields was to be appointed by the Secretary of Health, Education, and Welfare. As a result, the National Commission for the Protection of Human Subjects was appointed by Secretary Caspar W Weinberger on 3 December 1974, and was lodged within the National Institute of Health, a subdivision of the Department, under the chairmanship of Dr Kenneth Ryan, head of obstetrics and gynaecology at Harvard Medical School.

Most of the topics assigned by the National Research Act to the Commission dealt with experiments on humans; in particular, the Commission was instructed to prepare a report within four months on the subject of fetal experiments, to be followed by other reports on psychosurgery and on various groups of experimental subjects, such as prisoners, children, and persons institutionalised as mentally disabled. (In addition, the Commission was asked to study the social implications of developments in biomedical research, a rather open-ended topic on which the Commission made little headway compared to its thorough treatment of the topics centrally related to experiments on humans.) To draw together its work and provide guidance to IRBs the Commission also prepared a brief summary report – called the 'Belmont Report' after the federal meeting center at which its conclusions were first debated – in which it set forth several basic principles of bioethics on which it had attempted to base its conclusions.

The staff of the National Commission was a mixed group: some career civil servants mostly from DHEW, and some outside experts from academic medicine and ethics. In addition, consultants from a wide variety of fields were commissioned to write advisory papers. The Commission held open monthly meetings which included an opportunity for public testimony. In some ways the National Commission seems similar to what I know of the Comité National Consultatif d'Ethique, although the French group has only one annual open meeting, includes government officials, and is much larger in size, consisting of about 35 people.

Broad-based standing bodies
As the National Commission was completing its statutory mandate in 1978, Senator Kennedy recommended raising it to the level of a Presidential Commission to look at issues in human research across the entire federal government. In the House of Representatives, however, the view arose that any successive commission should have a broader mandate, encompassing issues in medical practice as well as in research on human subjects. Through the agreements reached by Senator Kennedy and Representative Paul Rogers, Chairman of the House Health Subcommittee, a provision was attached to a statute passed in 1978 authorising the creation of the President's Commission.

I will use this group to illustrate my third type of governmental bioethics committee. The mandate of such a group is general in nature, including potentially all topics in bioethics. The President's Commission was required by its statute to conduct studies of a number of topics – including access to health care, informed consent in treatment as well as in research, genetic screening and counselling, and the definition of death – but the topics could be increased at the request of the President. (President Jimmy Carter, through his Science Advisor, Dr Frank Press, did add a topic – human genetic engineering – to the Commission's mandate.) The topics could also be increased at the option of the Commission itself, and this course was also followed when the Commission chose to add the topic of foregoing life sustaining treatment to its list of studies.

What are the salient characteristics of this third type of commission? Like the National Commission, the President's Commission consisted of eleven members from law, ethics and public affairs, under the chairmanship of Morris B Abrams, a New York lawyer and former President of Brandeis University. Unlike the National Commission, the President's Commission was conceived as a permanent body whose members would serve in groups with staggered terms. Since the Commissioners were not named by the President until the summer of 1979 (and were not sworn in until January 1980), the terms served by the first group of Commissioners expired two years later in the summer of 1981. By the conclusion of the Commission's work, eight of the eleven members were appointees of President Ronald Reagan.

Although the Commission was established in a fashion that contemplated a continuing life (as, for example, the limitation of service to two consecutive four-year terms for any Commissioner), the inclusion of a 'sunset clause' meant that the Commission was scheduled to go out of business in December 1982. The purpose of this clause was to allow the legislature to review the group's work and then, by a simple action, to extend its work. Despite the termination date, I still believe that it makes sense to describe such groups as 'standing committees', both because their lives are of indefinite duration (if the termination date is postponed) and because during the three or four years that the President's Commission functioned, it felt free to range quite widely in the field of bioethics. It is true, nonetheless, that the termination date – with the deadlines it imposed for the completion of reports – was an effective, if somewhat oppressive stimulus for Commissioners and staff alike. It might well be that without this goad, some of the intensity that characterised the Commission would have been lacking. The limited time period also made it sensible to bring in staff from outside government, while a truly permanent body might be more heavily staffed by career civil servants. This is not to condemn such a body as a hopeless bureaucracy, but it has been my experience, especially when part of the subject under scrutiny is the performance of the government itself (as it was in our work), that outsiders are more likely to take a fresh look at an issue and are less likely to temper their findings and recommendations out of a need to be gentle with their fellow civil servants.

Like the National Commission, the President's Commission had to 'do ethics in public', because its work was governed by the Federal Advisory Committee Act which requires that such groups hold their meetings in public unless they make a strong case for the need to hold specific private sessions. Despite the prediction of some people that sensitive subjects of the sort being dealt with by the President's Commission could not usefully be discussed in public (lest there be a great deal of posturing and pointless rhetoric on all sides), the requirement that the meetings were open to the public did not prove an impediment to the effective functioning of the Commission. Indeed, the requirement seems to me to have had mostly salutary effects. All those who spoke, especially Commissioners and staff members, were mindful of the need for responsible comments and thoughtful deliberations. Further, the fact that a stenographic record was being made of the proceedings encouraged witnesses to aim for a high degree of accuracy and emphasised the importance of pointed comments rather than rambling dissertations. Finally, the fact that the sessions were public served to underline that the subject matter before the Commission was not esoteric but was a matter of concern and interest to all citizens; and their interest was furthered by the general press coverage of many of the meetings, particularly those at which reports and conclusions were set forth.

Another characteristic of the President's Commission – actually one of the most important – was that the Commission had no power to regulate. Its only real power was that of persuasion. In 1978, philosopher Ruth Macklin told the House Committee holding hearings on the bill that established the President's Commission, that to have any clout, the work of a commission must be 'clear and understandable to a concerned public as well as satisfying to those of us who work professionally in the field of biomedical ethics and health policy'. Therefore, the Commission made its minutes widely available to thousands of people across the country who requested to be on its mailing list, and members of the Commission and its staff testified frequently before Congressional committees holding hearings on topics germane to the Commission's work and held briefings for Congressional members and their staff. One measure of the effectiveness of the Commission was the frequency with which it was asked to present its work to legislative bodies, as well as the number of times its reports received front-page coverage in the newspapers and were featured on the major news and discussion programmes on radio and television.

Because of the need to persuade, there was a strong drive towards consensus, since a divided body would be unlikely to find its conclusions well respected. Although this may not seem remarkable, it should be remembered that in the eyes of many people the field of bioethics is regarded as highly polarised and subject to political polemics. Yet the only major topic that the Commission chose to avoid was abortion, on which its opinions had not been sought and on which it could add little to the already well-developed medical and ethical arguments on both sides. Otherwise, the Commission tackled many difficult issues. Rather than leading to timid reports, however, the search for consensus actually pushed the Commission's reports further and made tem more influential. The Commissioners worked inductively from specific examples to general principles; that is, they moved outwards from a common core of agreement to the point where agreement was no longer possible. This form of deliberation helped to show that the sphere of consensus was quite large.

Action-oriented panels
Let me describe the fourth type of governmental group on medical ethics with which we have had experience in the United States, namely a standing body with direct involvement in binding decisions. As a result of the work of the National Commission, new regulations were issued by what is now known as the Department of Health and Human Services in 1978. Among the provisions of these regulations was the requirement that research involving certain highly sensitive groups be approved at a national level by an Ethics Advisory board (EAB) appointed by the Secretary as well as review and approval by the IRB of the institution at which the research is to be conducted.

The Secretary of the Department of Health, Education, and Welfare, Joseph Califano, established an EAB in 1978. Its first task was to review the acceptability of *in vitro* fertilisation (IVF) because of a protocol submitted by Dr Pierre Soupart of Vanderbilt University. After one year of hearings and commissioned papers, the EAB issued a report in May 1979 recommending that the Secretary permit research on embryos up to two weeks after fertilisation in the laboratory, provided there was to be no implantation of the embryo thereafter. That report has sat on the table for the past eight years without having a definitive response from Secretary Califano or any of his successors, and, ironically, Dr Soupart has since died while waiting for action by the federal government. With the onset of the President's Commission, the EAB was dissolved. Although the President's Commission and EAB had different functions, with no necessary overlap, the EAB did not have the necessary bureaucratic support to continue.

Structure, functions, and accomplishments of the President's Commission

... The work of the President's Commission was carried out by a staff of about 25 people, mostly professionals, with a small support staff. The Commission was housed independently of any government department or agency and was not part of a standing bureaucracy. Most members of the support staff and one senior professional came from careers in government service but all the rest of the staff were outsiders to government. For example, I took leave from the University of Pennsylvania to run the Commission, and other senior staff members, who included a physician, two of the lawyers, two sociologists, an expert in public health, one economist and a succession of philosophers, plus various research assistants, were drawn from academic settings. The Commission met monthly. During the first several years of its work these meetings took the form primarily of hearings at which experts and other interested parties testified on particular topics that were under study by the Commission and were questioned by the Commissioners and senior staff members. Furthermore, the Commission staff themselves were sometimes in the witness chair, to engage in a dialogue with the Commissioners and attempt to convey the results of their studies and to learn from the Commissioners, in general form, the directions that should be taken by the Commission's reports. Although many of the witnesses were invited – and included the consultants who were writing papers for the Commission – time was always allotted for other experts and members of the general public who wished to appear and make statements.

After the initial phase during which background was provided to the Commissioners, the primary work of the staff was to prepare drafts of the Commission's reports. After these had been reviewed by the Commissioners they were rewritten by the staff. Commissioners who had special expertise in an area under study took a more active hand in the process of revision of these reports. In the end, there was unanimity on all the Commission's ten reports except one, on which there was one dissent. In addition to the ten reports there was one report of the Commission's work in commissioning papers and convening a workshop on *Whistleblowing in Biomedical Research*. The reports were released as finished; the work amounted to 16 volumes because the background papers were published as separate appendix volumes for some of the reports.

Rather than review all of these, I will characterise the results in four ways: (1) laying to rest, (2) the crucible, (3) the watchdog, and (4) the small rock (sometimes called the lightning rod or, less charitably, the dumping ground) but I prefer to think of this last role in Homer's terms when, in *The Odyssey*, he says 'a small rock holds back a great wave'.

Laying to rest

The first category is probably best illustrated by the first report the Commission issued in July 1981 on the 'definition' of death. This topic has been a matter of public concern since December 1967 when Dr Christian Barnard performed the first human-to-human heart transplant. In 1968 an ad hoc committee at the Harvard Medical School promulgated criteria for diagnosing death in comatose bodies whose breathing was being artificially maintained. By 1980 when the President's Commission began, many states had laws recognising criteria of the type promulgated by the Harvard Committee and there was general medical agreement although no up-to-date guidelines had been agreed upon.

Given the fact that the subject was already well advanced, it seemed to the Commission that the major impediment to its mandate – to consider the advisability of legislation on the subject – was the very multiplicity of statutory proposals that had been made by groups such as the American Medical Association, the American Bar Association, and the National Conference of Commissioners on Uniform State laws. Most of the legislative 'definitions' had been adopted by states in the early 1970s, but the process had slowed to a trickle, and the few that were legislating tended to write their own bills (with all the confusion and imprecision one would expect) rather than choose among the competing laws. Therefore, the Commission concluded that the best way to avoid simply adding to the multiplicity of proposals was to develop a proposal on which all the major proponents could agree. The result was the Uniform Determination of Death Act (UDDA) which was endorsed by the AMA, and ABA and the NCCUSL, as well as the Commission, when its report *Defining Death* was issued in July 1981. The UDDA has since become law in many states. It recognises that death occurs when there is a total and irreversible cessation of circulatory and respiratory functions, or a total and irreversible cessation of all functions of the brain including the brain stem. Equally important to the provision of a statute was the drafting of a set of medical guidelines by a group of the leading medical experts convened by the Commission. When these guidelines were published in the *Journal of the American Medical Association* they were hailed as a landmark, and today they provide a reliable statement on medical techniques for determining that death has occurred either on cardiopulmonary or neurological grounds.

To summarise, the 'laying to rest' function of a commission seems to be to develop recommendations for action, in this case for legislation and for professional action, and to bring together a broad coalition of people in the field to ensure that the recommendations will be so broadly accepted that the topic will no longer be a matter of division or contention.

The crucible
I refer to the second category as that of the crucible, thinking of it as a place of publicly grinding out conclusions on controversial issues when a consensus is not yet apparent. In the case of the President's Commission, three of its reports probably fall into this category: the one on informed consent, *Making Health Care Decisions*: on 'pulling the plug'; *Deciding to Forego Life-Sustaining Treatment*; and on equitable access to health care, *Securing Access to Health Care*. These are all topics which had been approached by divergent groups in the previous decade. The Commission's role here was threefold. First, it had to identify those elements underlying the apparently disparate views expressed in previous discussions. Second, it had to correct misunderstanding or errors, particularly as those were responsible for the divisions in the public debates; and finally, it had to articulate the implications for public policy and ethical behaviour in a way that would be broadly acceptable. Plainly these objectives involved the Commission in processes of analysis and synthesis; as such it required more original scholarship than the first ('laying to rest') function because there was less existing agreement. These topics did not in the view of the Commission always lead to recommendations for legislation. In some cases the objective of the Commission was to frame the thinking on the subject of public officials, such as judges and legislators, and to attempt to push the academic experts forward so that the Commission's findings and recommendations could become the starting point for future discussions. This would reduce some of the jagged pieces that had prevented public understanding and the advancement of conclusions.

A good example of this second category was the work of the Commission on patient autonomy, and the necessity for and the means for its preservation in the face of patient incompetence contained in the reports on making health-care decisions and on deciding to forego life-sustaining treatment. These conclusions have been widely influential. For example, in the past year a California Appellate court and the Supreme Court in 'landmark opinions' have placed heavy reliance on the report, *Deciding to Forego Life-Sustaining Treatment*. The weight accorded to this report illustrates that those who perform ethical and social analysis need a clear understanding of the realities of the practice they are scrutinising. Such an understanding was provided for the Commission by its members, its staff and expert consultants who all insisted that the realities be well attended to rather than solely being concerned with ethical or philosophical discourse. A great deal of effort was placed on the clarification of facts as they illuminate issues, such as 'active' versus 'passive' euthanasia – something that can become a matter of heated, but nonetheless rather abstract, discussion until it is grounded in understanding of the realities of hospital practices and nursing home procedures, the means of dealing with pain, and the psychology of physicians and nurses.

Watchdog
The third function of the Commission is well illustrated by its work in the areas of federal regulation of human subject research. This is a topic that had been thoroughly studied by our predecessor, the National Commission for the Protection of Human Subjects. The Commission therefore placed particular emphasis on the portion of its mandate to report biennially on the adequacy and uniformity of the federal oversight of research conducted or funded by the government. Although this was perhaps the least exciting topic assigned to the President's Commission, it was very important for several reasons. First, the government's efforts in this area are plainly a matter of great public concern; indeed, the process of governmental commissions and study panels in biomedical ethics was begun because of what was perceived as abuses of human subjects in research. Second, since the National Commission had gone out of existence there was a strong possibility that some of its conclusions and recommendations would simply fall between the cracks of the federal bureaucracy if the President's Commission did not vigilantly monitor the response of federal agencies. Third, the National Commission had primarily studied the work of what is now the Department of Health and Human Services, the largest sponsor of research with human subjects, but the President's Commission had a broader mandate. It was to examine research issues throughout the federal government, and one of the principal recommendations in this area in the first biennial report on research in 1981 was that the government should adopt a single set of regulatory requirements for all federally sponsored human subject research to simplify the burdens placed on researchers and the local IRBs.

A small rock
The final function that a standing ethics group can serve is illustrated, I believe, by the work of the President's Commission on a very controversial topic – namely, genetic engineering. In 1980, shortly after the Commission began its work, leaders of the Catholic, Protestant,

and Jewish congregations in the United States voiced cries of alarm over the prospect that genetic engineering techniques would be soon extended to human beings. Their concerns, which were addressed to President Carter, led his science advisor to request that the President's Commission add the subject of human genetic engineering to its mandate.

In its report, *Splicing Life*, the Commission took a scientific and a philosophical and religious view of the topic. It attempted to place the concerns in historical context and to show that many forms of manipulation of the genetic basis of human disease were no different from conventional, accepted treatment. But treatment that went beyond the somatic cells to alter the human germ line cells raised moral as well as medical concerns. By the time the Commission had completed its work, a number of newspaper reporters had become interested enough in the topic to write thoughtfully about it for their publications and the Commission's conclusions were greeted with general support by editorial writers. In three days of Congressional hearings, when the report was issued in November 1982, the conclusions of the Commission were accepted by a wide variety of scientific and ethical experts and by representatives of the religious groups that had initially provoked the study.

We will see that England has been slow to develop any institutional framework for analysing issues of medical law and ethics of formulating public policy. The Warnock Committee reviewed the areas of infertility treatment and embryo research and the House of Lords' Select Committee on Medical Ethics looked at euthanasia and issues relating to dying (see *infra*, chs 16 and 17) but both were *ad hoc*. The Law Commission engaged on a review of the law relating to medical treatment and incapacitated adults (see *infra* ch 6). The Human Fertilisation and Embryology Authority has a statutory remit within its particular terms of reference to keep issues of ethics and law under review (see *infra* ch 10). Likewise, the non-statutory Human Genetics Commission (and its predecessors) provides advice to ministers on genetics' issues. But still the Government has not sought to create a national commission, unlike many other countries, for example, France and Denmark.

However, in the summer of 1991 the Trustees of the Nuffield Foundation established the Nuffield Council of Bioethics. Its terms of reference are as follows:

1   to identify and define ethical questions raised by recent advances in biological and medical research in order to respond to, and to anticipate public concern;
2   to make arrangements for examining and reporting on such questions with a view to promoting public understanding and discussion; this may lead, where needed, to the formulation of new guidelines by the appropriate regulatory or other body; and
3   in the light of the outcome of its work, to publish reports; and to make representations, as the Council may judge appropriate.

The Council has undertaken a number of studies, through the mechanism of multi-disciplinary working parties, on, for example, the use of *Human Tissue* (1993), *Genetic Screening* (1994), and *Xenotransplantation* (1996). Beyond this, Government policy continues to be formulated on an *ad hoc* basis.

In the result, of course, medical law remains in large part a matter for the judges. In particular, the principles of medical law, to which we refer at the outset of this chapter and which we will consider in detail in the general part of this book, are judge-made. However, before we consider those principles, in the next chapter we consider the structure of the health service in England.

Chapter 2

The provision of medical care

The system for delivering health care within England and Wales is a mixture of public and private provision. However, by far the greater proportion of services is provided through the publicly funded National Health Service. Doctors work in many areas of public service such as the prison medical service and within the medical service of the armed forces. Here, however, we are interested in the provision of medical services within the National Health Service (NHS). Of course, medical services are provided outside the framework of publicly funded medical care, ie private medical care. While the provision of private care is the subject of some statutory regulation particularly as regards licensing, eg Registered Homes Act 1984 (to be replaced by the Care Standards Act 2000) in respect of nursing homes, for the most part the organisation of private health care providers is not specifically regulated and their relationship with their patients is a matter for the general law.

In this chapter we shall concentrate on the NHS, although we return at the end of the chapter to the question of private health care provision and its regulation. Equally, we focus upon the structure of the NHS and how doctors work within it. There are, of course, many other health care practitioners such as nurses, midwives, physiotherapists, pharmacists, dentists and opticians who work within the NHS. The system is complex and, frankly, ever changing to suit the political aspirations and aims of the Government of the day. For our part, we will focus attention on the provision of primary health care through general practitioners and hospital and community health services through NHS Trusts and, increasingly in the future, the new Primary Care Trusts.

Institutional framework of the NHS

The structure of the NHS is set out in a bewilderingly complicated array of primary and secondary legislation, together with other quasi-legislative measures such as statutory directions and health circulars. The principal legislative provisions can be found in the National Health Service Act 1977 (as amended), the National Health Service and Community Care Act 1990, the National Health Service (Primary Care) Act 1997 and the Health Act 1999.

A. HISTORICAL DEVELOPMENT OF THE NHS

Before examining the modern system, it is helpful to see the historical development of the NHS, established in 1948 by the National Health Service Act 1946. Prior to that, the public provision of health care was limited. The 'poor law' institutions were the main source of public provision of hospital services. In addition, these services were also provided by voluntary hospitals, usually established on a charitable basis. The Local Government Act 1929 transferred to local authorities responsibility for the 'poor law' hospital services. The National Insurance Act 1911 sought to provide free GP services to certain groups of workers. Beyond this, until 1948, health care was a matter for private agreement between doctor and patient.

The 1946 Act created the NHS. The political struggle for a comprehensive scheme of primary and hospital care was not an easy one. Professor Chris Ham, a leading expert on the health service, explains:

Christopher Ham *Health Policy in Britain: The Politics and Organisation of the National Health Service* **(3rd edn, 1993)**

Prolonged negotiations accompanied the birth of the Service, and these negotiations at times seemed likely to prevent the birth taking place at all. Certainly, the medical profession ... fought strongly for its own objectives, and was successful in winning many concessions: retention of the independent contractor system for GPs; the option of private practice and access to pay beds in NHS hospitals for hospital consultants; a system of distinction awards for consultants, carrying with it large increases in salary for those receiving awards; a major role in the administration of the Service at all levels; and success in resisting local government control. The concessions made to hospital doctors led Aneurin Bevan to say that he had 'stuffed their mouths with gold' ... In fact, Bevan cleverly divided the medical profession, winning the support of hospital consultants and specialists with generous financial payments, and thereby isolating and reducing the power of GPs, who were nevertheless successful in achieving many of their aims.

Far less successful were the local authorities, who lost control of their hospitals, despite the advocacy by Herbert Morrison in the Labour Cabinet of the local government point of view. The main reason for this, apart from the opposition of the doctors, was the unsuitability of local government areas for the administration of the hospital service. As a result, Bevan – and this was one of his personal contributions to the organisations of the NHS – decided to appropriate both the local authority hospitals and the voluntary hospitals and place them under a single system of administration. Another major personal contribution made by Bevan was to persuade the medical profession that the service should cover all of the population and not just 90 per cent as many doctors wished. Furthermore, the Service was to be funded mainly out of general taxation, with insurance contributions making up only a small part of the total finance.

The NHS introduced a full and comprehensive public service of healthcare provision, free at the point of consumption. The NHS structure distinguished between the provision of primary health care services (by GPs and others) and hospital services (hospital boards) and community health care services (by local authorities). It was not until the National Health Service Re-Organisation Act 1973 that community health care services were taken out of local authority control and, together with other medical services, were put under the control of Health Authorities. Local authorities retained responsibility for community services involving social services provision such as domiciliary support and residential care for the aged and infirm. ('Social' and 'medical' community services had been split between local authority health and social services departments by the Local Authority Social Services Act 1970.)

It was, however, the 1973 Act which created the structural pattern of statutory Health Authorities (then regional (RHAs) and area (AHAs)) which largely persists today. Professor Chris Ham (*supra*) describes the 1973 reorganisation of the NHS:

Within the new structure, Regional Health Authorities (RHAs) took over from Regional Hospital Boards, with somewhat wider responsibilities and slightly modified boundaries. The members of RHAs were appointed by the Secretary of State for Social Services, and their main function was the planning of health services. Beneath RHAs there were ninety Area Health Authorities (AHAs) in England, and their members were appointed partly by RHAs, partly by local authorities, and partly by members of the non-medical and nursing staff. The AHA chairman was appointed by the Secretary of State. Some AHAs contained a university medical school and teaching hospital facilities, and were designated as teaching areas. AHAs had planning and management duties, but one of their most important functions was to develop services jointly with their matching local authorities. Both RHAs and AHAs were supported by multi-disciplinary teams of officers. Alongside each AHA was a Family Practitioner Committee (FPC) which administered the contracts of GPs, dentists, pharmacists and opticians. FPC members were appointed by the AHA, local professionals and local authorities. Finance for health authorities and FPCs was provided by the Department of Health and Social Security. Most areas were themselves split into health districts, each of which was administered by a district management team (DMT), which in practice became the lowest tier of the Service. At district level were located Community Health Councils (CHCs), introduced as part of the reorganised structure to represent the views of the public to health authorities. There were around 200 Community Health Councils in England.

It is pertinent to note that somewhat different arrangements were made in Wales, Scotland and Northern Ireland, which until reorganisation had had similar structures to those existing in England. The Welsh reorganisation bore the closest resemblance to that of England, the main exception being the absence of RHAs in Wales, where the Welsh Office combined the functions of a central government department and a regional authority ...

Figure 1.2   The structure of the NHS, 1974–82

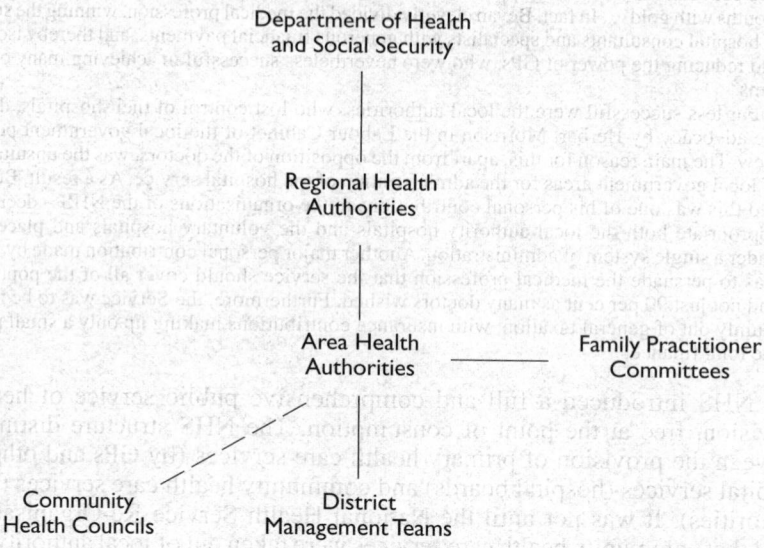

Note: This structure applied only in England. The position in the rest of the United Kingdom is explained in the text.

We see here the beginnings of the modern NHS structure. However, further reform was made as a result of the Royal Commission on the NHS (1979), Cmnd 7615.

Christopher Ham *Health Policy in Britain: The Politics and Organisation of the National Health Service* (3rd edn, 1993)

In its report, the Commission endorsed the view that there was one tier of administration too many, and recommended that there should be only one level of authority beneath the region. A flexible approach to change was advocated, and the Commission pointed out that structural reform was no panacea for all of the administrative problems facing the NHS. Other conclusions in a wide-ranging survey were that Family Practitioner Committees should be abolished, and Community Health Councils should be strengthened.

It fell to the Conservative government which took office in May 1979 to respond to the report ...

In large part, they endorsed the *Patients First* proposals, and in addition announced that Community Health Councils would remain in existence, though their functions would be reviewed. The result was the creation of 192 District Health Authorities (DHAs) in England. The DHAs came into operation on 1 April 1982, and within districts emphasis was placed on the delegation of power to units of management. Detailed management arrangements varied considerably, with some units covering services in districts as a whole, such as psychiatric services, while others were limited to a single large hospital ...

Apart from the reduction in administration, the main change wrought by the reorganisation was the loss in many parts of the country of the principle of coterminosity between health authorities and local authorities. Equally significant was the announcement in November 1981 that Family Practitioner Committees (FPCs) were to be further separated from the mainstream of NHS administration and given the status of employing authorities in their own right. This change was brought into effect by the Health and Social Security Act 1984 and FPCs achieved their independent status on 1 April 1985. In addition, a number of Special Health Authorities were established. Their main responsibility was to run the postgraduate teaching hospitals in London. The structure of the NHS in England after 1982 is shown in Figure 1.3.

In the rest of the United Kingdom different changes were made, reflecting the different administrative structures existing in Scotland, Wales and Northern Ireland. In Wales the main change was the abolition of the district level of management, and the establishment in its place of a system of unit management on a similar basis to that developed in England ...

Figure 1.3 The structure of the NHS, 1982–90

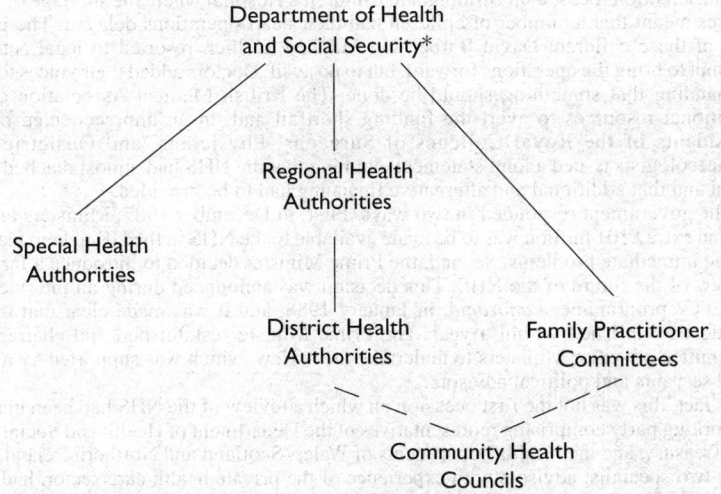

Note: The structure applied only in England. The position in the rest of the United Kingdom is explained in the text.
* The DHSS became the Department of Health in 1988.

Notice two points, First, District Health Authorities (DHAs) were responsible for providing and running hospital and community health services. Secondly, you will notice the emergence of Family Practitioner Committees (FPCs) (later Family Health Service Authorities (FHSAs)), as a statutory health body responsible for making arrangements for the provision of primary care services. Regional Health Authorities oversaw and supervised the activities of both. This bifurcation of 'Health Authority' responsibilities continued until the unification in 1996 of District and Family Health Service Authorities (together with the abolition of Regional Health Authorities) by the Health Authorities Act 1995.

The 1980s were, however, to produce perhaps the most fundamental reform of the NHS structure triggered by the financial crisis that hit the NHS in the late 1980s. In *Management and Competition in the New NHS* (1994) Professor Chris Ham sets the scene for the enactment of the National Health Service and Community Care Act 1990 and the creation of the so-called 'internal market' in the NHS.

Chris Ham *Management and Competition in the NHS* (1995)

Throughout the 1980s expenditure on the NHS continued to grow in real terms but at a slow rate. As the decade wore on there was a widening gap between the money provided by government and the funding needed to meet increasing demands from an ageing population and advances in medical technology. The impact of the funding shortfall became particularly apparent during the course of 1987 and was felt most acutely in the hospital services ... In the autumn of that year, many health authorities had to take urgent action to keep expenditure within cash limits. This included cancelling non-emergency admission, closing beds on a temporary basis, and not filling staff vacancies.

Behind these problems lay a funding system that failed to reward hospitals for treating extra patients. The so-called 'efficiency trap' was caused by the use of global budgets for hospitals that provided a fixed income regardless of the number of patients treated. This meant that hospitals were in practice penalized for productivity improvements because their expenditure increased in line with the number of patients treated but their income remained the same. In this situation, hospitals had little alternative but to reduce workload and cut costs when their budgets ran out.

The financial pressures facing health authorities were compounded by staff shortages. Media attention focused on Birmingham Children's Hospital where the shortage of specialist nurses meant that a number of children had their heart operations delayed. The parents of two of these children, David Barber and Matthew Collier, resorted to legal action in an attempt to bring the operations forward, but to no avail. Doctors added their voices to patients, demanding that something should be done. The British Medical Association called for additional resources to avert the funding shortfall and, in an unprecedented move, the presidents of the Royal Colleges of Surgeons, Physicians, and Obstetricians and Gynaecologists issued a joint statement claiming that the NHS had almost reached breaking point and that additional and alternative financing had to be provided.

The government responded in two ways. First, in December 1987, Ministers announced that an extra £101 million was to be made available to the NHS in the UK to help tackle some of the immediate problems. Second, the Prime Minister decided to introduce a far reaching review of the future of the NHS. This decision was announced during an interview on the BBC TV programme, *Panorama*, in January 1988, and it was made clear that the results would be published within a year. The Prime Minister established and chaired a small committee of senior Ministers to undertake the review, which was supported by a group of civil servants and political advisors.

In fact, this was not the first occasion on which a review of the NHS had been undertaken. A working party comprising representatives of the Department of Health and Social Security, the Treasury, and the Health Departments of Wales, Scotland and Northern Ireland, together with two specialist advisors with experience of the private health care sector, had reported on alternative financing methods in 1982. As the Secretary of State at the time, Norman Fowler, explains in his memoirs, the government decided not to move away from a system in which the NHS was financed largely from taxation, on the basis of the working party's report. This was because other European countries were faced with similar problems to the UK and a centrally run and centrally funded health service like the NHS appeared to be most effective in controlling costs ...

In the absence of any specific proposals to change the basis of health service financing, Ministers pursued a policy of achieving greater efficiency in the NHS and encouraging the growth of private finance and provision alongside the NHS. The result was an expansion in the number of people covered by private health insurance schemes and in the role of private providers. By 1989, 13 per cent of the population in the UK was covered by private insurance. In parallel, the growth of private providers meant that by the end of the 1980s, eight per cent of all acute in-patients were treated privately and 17 per cent of all elective surgery was performed in the private sector. There was an even more rapid expansion of private residential and nursing home provision for elderly people and other vulnerable groups. Taken together, these changes meant that by the end of the decade private and voluntary hospitals and nursing homes supplied an estimated 15 per cent of all UK hospital based treatment and care by value ...

The Ministerial Review
The Ministerial Review, initiated by Margaret Thatcher in 1988, offered an opportunity for alternative methods of financing and provision to be re-examined. The difficulty facing the government in this respect, as Norman Fowler indicates again, was that the NHS performed well when viewed in the international context. Total expenditure on health care, at around six per cent of GDP, was low by comparative standards, and yet for this spending the entire population had access to comprehensive services of a generally high standard. National planning meant that all parts of the country had access to health care, and a well developed system of primary care resulted in many medical problems being dealt with by GPs without the need to refer patients to hospitals. All this was achieved with only a small proportion of the budget being spent on administration ...

While problems clearly existed in relation to waiting lists for some treatments, poor quality of care provided for the so called priority groups, and lack of responsiveness to service users, they did not amount to a decisive case against the NHS. Rather, they indicated the need for a programme of reforms which retained the strengths of the NHS while the weaknesses were tackled. Indeed, for many of those who contributed to the debate, the most urgent requirement was extra money for the NHS to enable the changes that resulted from the *Griffiths Report* to be seen through. According to this school of thought, the key problem confronting the NHS was chronic and long term underfunding; there was nothing wrong with the structure of the NHS that additional resources would not overcome.

From this perspective, the control of health services spending exercised by the Treasury and seen by Norman Fowler as one of the strengths of the NHS, was in fact a major weakness in failing to deliver the volume of resources needed to fund the NHS to an adequate level. At a time when controlling public expenditure was an overriding political priority, it was not surprising that government Ministers were not persuaded by this argument, citing variations in performance across the NHS in support of their argument that existing budgets had to be used more efficiently before extra expenditure on the NHS could be justified ...

In its early stages the Ministerial Review focused on alternative methods for financing. This included looking again at the scope for increasing the role of private insurance and moving from tax funding to a social insurance system on the Western European model. However, this was soon superseded by an analysis of how the delivery of services could be reformed, assuming the continuation of tax funding. It was on this basis that ideas put forward by an American economist, Alain Enthoven, caught the attention of Ministers.

In a report published in 1985, Enthoven argued that an internal market should be developed within the NHS and this idea was elaborated by a number of right-wing think-tanks in their input to the Review ... The contribution of Enthoven's thinking was later acknowledged by Kenneth Clarke who said that he liked Enthoven's idea of the internal market:

> because it tried to inject into a state-owned system some of the qualities of competition, choice, and measurement of quality that you get in well-run, private enterprise ...

It was Clarke who played a major part in the final stages of the Review and who was responsible for presenting the government's proposals following publication of the white paper, *Working for Patients*, in July 1989 . . .

Working for Patients
In the white paper, the government announced that the basic principles on which the NHS was founded would be preserved. Funding would continue to be provided mainly out of taxation and there were no plans to extend charges to patients. Tax relief on private insurance premiums was to [be] made available to those aged over 60, at the Prime Minister's insistence and against the advice of her Chancellor of the Exchequer ... but the significance of this was more symbolic than real. For the vast majority of the population, the NHS would continue to be the provider of health care and the government promised that access to care would be based on need. This was later reiterated by a future Secretary of State, Virginia Bottomley, in a speech to the British Medical Association:

> the government's commitment to the fundamental *principles* of the NHS has not wavered one jot ... During the NHS Review, more radical actions were considered and rejected. They were thrown aside because they were incompatible with the sacrosanct principle of the NHS: that the care and treatment that the service provides should be available to any man, woman or child, on the basis of clinical need, regardless of the ability to pay...

The main changes in *Working for Patients* concerned the delivery of health services. These changes were intended to create the conditions for competition between hospitals and other providers. This was to be achieved through a separation of purchaser and provider roles: the creation of self-governing NHS trusts to run hospitals and other services; the transformation of district health authorities into purchasers of services for local people; the opportunity for larger GP practices to become purchasers of some hospital services for their patients as GP fundholders; and the use of contracts or service agreements to provide links between purchasers and providers.

Fundamental to these proposals was that money would follow patients. This was intended to overcome the efficiency trap facing hospitals and to provide a stronger incentive than global budgets for hospitals to improve their performance. Ministers argued that a system in which providers had to compete for patients and resources would act as a significant stimulus to increase efficiency and to produce a greater responsiveness to patients. The result would be a higher level of uncertainty on the part of providers about the source of their income but it was argued that this was necessary if the NHS was to tackle successfully the problems it faced.

These and other proposals were sketched in broad outline in *Working for Patients*, reflecting the speed with which the white paper had been produced. Subsequently, a series of working papers were published by the Department of Health containing more detail on different aspects of the proposed reforms. Together with the parallel changes to community care planned by the government, the proposals in *Working for Patients* were incorporated in the *NHS and Community Care Bill*. This was published in November 1989 and received the Royal Assent in June 1990, paving the way for the NHS market to come into operation from April 1991.

The debate about *Working for Patients* and the *NHS and Community Care Bill* aroused strong feelings on all sides ... Opposition to the government's proposals was led by the medical profession. The British Medical Association in particular opposed the introduction of market principles into health care. Organizations representing patients shared this concern as did bodies speaking for other professional and staff groups. There was more support for the reforms from managers and health authorities, although the timetable for implementing some of the changes was widely perceived to be unrealistic.

Figure 2 illustrates the organization of the NHS in England as it emerged after 1990. Unlike previous reorganizations, the structure did not change overnight and there was a progressive move away from the old to the new arrangements. Responsibility for overseeing the implementation of the reforms was vested in the NHS management executive working on behalf of Ministers. The management executive continued to be located with the Department of Health but increasingly it took on a separate existence from the policy divisions within the Department.

Figure 2: The structure of the NHS in England after 1990.

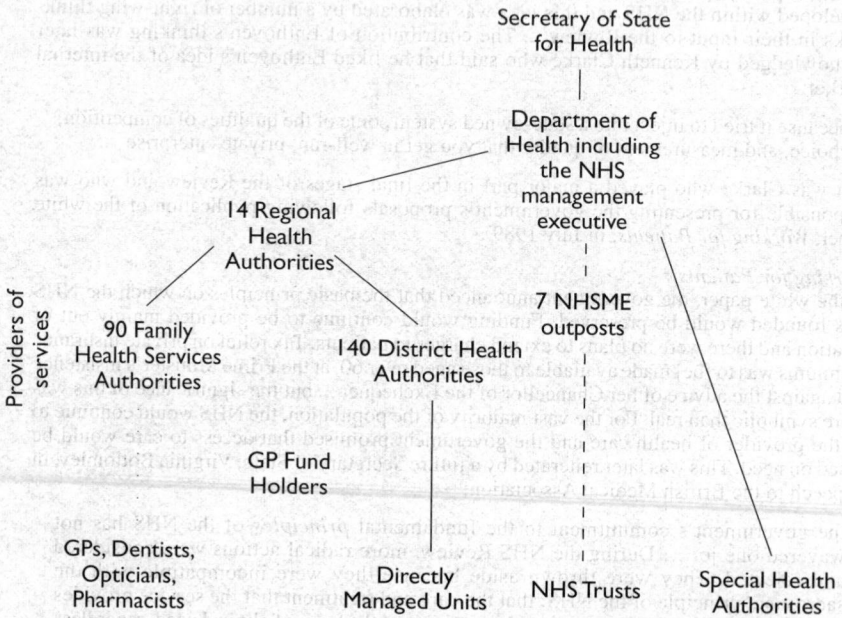

In this role, the Management Executive was used by Ministers to ensure that the reforms were implemented smoothly on the ground. The NHS Chief Executive, Duncan Nichol, assumed a higher profile as implementation gathered momentum, and attracted controversy in 1991 for supporting in public the policies of the government and appearing to criticize the opposition in the process. The NHS management executive worked increasingly with and through regional health authorities and sought to develop its role as the head office of the NHS. This was reinforced by the relocation of the management executive from London to Leeds in 1992.

Importantly, you will notice the separation of the roles of 'providers' of care from that of 'purchasers' of care. Here, is the 'internal market' whereby DHAs and GP fundholders negotiated agreements (usually 'NHS contracts') with providers such as NHS Trusts and directly managed units of DHAs for the provision of services to those for whom they have responsibility. We will see that, in essence, the 'internal market' has been retained by the current Labour Government's NHS reforms though with significant modifications in form and ethos. Importantly, GP fundholding, whereby GPs were funded to purchase hospital and community care for their patients, has been abolished by the Health Act 1999 (s 1). Likewise, the commercial rigours of the market have been substantially diluted to allow for more consultative, inclusive ethos of the 'commissioning' of services by 'primary care groups' ('local health groups' in Wales) made up of GPs, nurses and others responsible for the patients of a particular area. The reforms of the current government have taken the 'sting' out of the internal market. It is, therefore, to the structure of, and services provided by, the modern NHS that we should now turn.

B. THE MODERN NHS

The National Health Service Act 1977 is the principal legislation setting up the National Health Service and imposing statutory duties to provide it (ss 1–5 (Pt I); ss 29, 35, 38 and 41 (Pt II)). The essence of the structure is described by the Department of Health in its *Explanatory Notes* (paras 21-22) to the Health Act 1999.

> 21. Under the 1977 Act, the NHS is essentially split into two different systems. The first is the system which consists primarily in the provision of health care in hospitals. It also covers those services described as "community health services" for example, the services provided by district nurses, midwives or health visitors in clinics or individuals' homes, and the provision of medical services to pupils in state schools. This system is the subject of Part I of the 1977 Act. The responsibility for securing the provision of these services to patients rests with the Secretary of State, although under his powers in section 13 of the 1977 Act he has delegated most of his functions to Health Authorities. Health Authorities enter into arrangements with bodies known as NHS Trusts for the provision by the trusts of hospital and community health services.
> 22. The other main part of the NHS structure is what might be described as "the NHS in the high street". This is dealt with under Part II of the 1977 Act, which governs the arrangements made by Health Authorities for the provision of services by the following professionals: general medical practitioners (GPs), general dental practitioners (GDPs), ophthalmic opticians and ophthalmic practitioners (also known as optometrists), and pharmacists. They provide what are termed general medical services (GMS), general dental services (GDS), general ophthalmic services (GOS) and pharmaceutical services (PhS) respectively. The remainder of Part II contains other provisions relevant to the provision of these high street services, which are often referred to as family health services.

A few general points should be noted. First, NHS services must be provided free of charge unless charging is expressly permitted by legislation (s 1(2)). Examples of this include treatment by GPs following road accidents (hospitals are now covered by the recoupment scheme against compensators in the Road Traffic (NHS Charges) Act 1999), ophthalmic and dental services and, of course, prescription charges (see ss 25, 63, 65, 77–83 and Sch 12 to the National Health Act 1977 for powers to charge). Also overseas visitors may be charged (see National Health Service (Charges to Overseas Visitors) Regulation 1989 (SI 1989 No 306)). Likewise, charges may be made, for example, for accommodation such as private rooms (s 63(1) of the 1977 Act) and NHS Trusts may do so providing it does not significantly affect their other obligations to provide services (National Health Service and Community Care Act 1990, Sch 2, paras 14 and 15 and s 5(9), substituted by Health Act 1999, s 14). Secondly, although the NHS is a public service, it may also make available hospital services and accommodation to private, paying patients (National Health Service Act 1977, s 65 and NHS & CC Act 1990, Sch 2, paras 14 and 15). Again, the power is now restricted so that it cannot be exercised so as to interfere to a 'significant extent' with the Trusts' NHS obligations (1990 Act, s 5(9) inserted by Health Act 1999, s 14).

Let us look first at 'primary care services' provided within the NHS.

1. General medical services (Part II)

(a) Duty to arrange provision

Under the National Health Service Act 1977, Health Authorities have a statutory duty to make arrangements for the provision of primary care services ie general medical services (GP services) (ss 29–34), dental services (ss 35–37), ophthalmic services (ss 38–40) and pharmaceutical services (ss 41–43). Here we are concerned only with the provision relating to services provided by general practitioners.

National Health Service Act 1977

29(1) It is the duty of every Health Authority, in accordance with regulations which shall be made for the purpose, to arrange as respects their area with medical practitioners to provide personal medical services for all persons in the area who wish to take advantage of the arrangements.

(1A) The services so provided are referred to in this Act as "general medical services".

(2) Regulations may provide for the definition of the personal medical services to be provided and for securing that the arrangements will be such that all persons availing themselves of those services will receive adequate personal care and attendance, and the regulations shall include provision—

(a) for the preparation and publication of lists by each Health Authority of a list of medical practitioners who undertake to provide general medical services for persons in the Health Authority's area;

(b) ...

(c) ...

(d) for the issue to patients or their personal representatives by medical practitioners providing those services of such certificates as may be prescribed being certificates reasonably required by them under or for the purposes of any enactment;

(e) for the removal from the list of medical practitioners undertaking to provide general medical services for persons in any area of the name of any one in whose case it has been determined in such manner as may be prescribed that he has never provided, or has ceased to provide, such general medical services for persons in that area.

(f) for the making of arrangements for the temporary provision of general medical services in the area of a Health Authority;

(g) for the circumstances in which a name added to the list by virtue of subsection (6) below may be removed from it.

(3) Regulations under subsection (2) above may provide for the personal medical services there mentioned to include the provision of, and services connected with, any such advice, examination and treatment as are mentioned in paragraph (b) of section 5(1) above.

(4) The remuneration to be paid under the arrangements mentioned in sub-section (1) above to a practitioner who provides general medical services shall not, except in special circumstances, consist wholly or mainly of a fixed salary which has no reference to the number of patients for whom he has undertaken to provide such services.

(5) Regulations shall—

(a) include provision for the making to a medical practitioner providing general medical services of payments in respect of qualifying services provided by a spouse or other relative of his; and

(b) provide that the rates and conditions of payment and the qualifying services in respect of which the payments may be made shall be such as may be determined by the Secretary of State after consultation with such bodies as he may recognise as representing such medical practitioners.

(6) The persons with whom arrangements for the temporary provision of general medical services in an area may be made by virtue of regulations under subsection (2) above include medical practitioners who are not on the list of medical practitioners providing such services in the area, and the power to prepare and publish lists of medical practitioners conferred by paragraph (a) of that subsection accordingly includes power to add the names of medical practitioners with whom such arrangements are made to the list.

(7) Regulations may provide that this Act and any regulations made under it shall apply in relation—

(a) to the making of arrangements for the temporary provision of general medical services; and

(b) to the provision of general medical services in pursuance of any such arrangements,

subject to such modifications as may be specified in the regulations.

(8) ...

(9) ...

We will return shortly to the detail of the services proved by GPs under the National Health Service (General Medical Services) Regulations 1992 (SI 1992 No 635) (as amended). Other regulations govern the other primary care services: National Health Service (General Dental Services) Regulations 1992 (SI 1992 No 661) (as amended) (dental); National Health Service (Pharmaceutical Services) Regulations 1992 (SI 1992, No 662) (as amended) (pharmacy); National Health Service (General Ophthalmic Services) Regulations 1986 (SI 1986 No 975) (as amended) (ophthalmic).

(i) ARRANGEMENTS UNDER PART II OF THE NATIONAL HEALTH SERVICE ACT 1977

What, then, are the arrangements for the provision of 'general medical services' under Pt II of the NHS Act 1977? Each Health Authority is required to prepare and publish a list of general medical practitioners, known as 'the Medical List' who undertake to provide 'general medical services' and additional services such as 'maternity medical services' and 'contraceptive services' in the area for which it is responsible (reg 4 of the National Health Service (General Medical Services) Regulations 1992 (SI 1992 No 635) (as amended) ('the Medical Regulations')). We should notice that the HA may permit a doctor to withdraw his name from any of the lists maintained by the HA on giving three months' notice (reg 6).

The HA must remove a doctor's name from a list where, for example, he is dead, he has ceased to be a registered medical practitioner, he has been convicted of murder or other offences and sentenced to at least six months' imprisonment or he is subject to a direction from the Professional Conduct Committee of the General Medical Council that his name be erased or subject to immediate suspension (reg 7(1)). In addition, the HA must remove the name of any GP from its list who has reached the age of 70 (reg 7(11)).

Another way in which a GP may be removed from the medical list is in the context of disciplinary proceedings for breach of the terms of service in Sch 2 to the Medical Regulations. Where a GP's continued inclusion on a HA's medical list would, in the opinion of the HA 'be prejudicial to the efficiency of the [various] services' provided under the regulations or that the GP has been behaving fraudulently, the HA may refer his case to the statutory NHS Tribunal set up under s 46 (and Sch 9) of the National Health Service Act 1977 (National Health Service (Service Committees and Tribunal) Regulations 1992 (SI 1992 No 664), reg 24. See further, *infra*, ch 3). If the tribunal disqualifies the GP from inclusion in this (or all) HA lists, the HA must remove him from the relevant lists (s 46B (b), NHS Act 1977 inserted by s 40 (1), Health Act 1999).

It is important to notice that the terms of the arrangement between HA and GP are fixed being set out in the Medical Regulations, in particular Sch 2 (the 'terms of service') and Schs 8–13. Whilst there is some flexibility, in the sense that GPs are not required to provide all the primary care services contemplated by the Medical Regulations, for example, maternity and contraceptive services, they are required to provide certain services known as 'personal medical services' (see below). Whatever services they do provide are, however, provided on the terms set out in the Medical Regulations. Breach of the 'terms of service' may give rise to disciplinary proceedings before a Disciplinary Committee of the HA under the National Health Service (Service Committees and Tribunal) Regulations 1992 (SI 1992 No 664) (as amended) (see *infra*, ch 3).

A doctor who wishes to be included on the list of a particular HA must apply to the HA for inclusion (1977 Act, s 30; reg 5(1) of the Medical Regulations). The HA must then refer the application, together with a report containing certain information specified in Pt III of Sch 3 to the Medical Regulations, to the Medical Practices Committee (MPC). The MPC determines applications made under s 30 in accordance with ss 31–34 of the 1977 Act and reg 14 of the Medical Regulations. In particular, reg 15 allows the MPC to specify the conditions under which general medical services may be provided by a GP.

The GP undertakes to abide by 'terms of service' contained in Sch 2 to the Medical Regulations. What is the legal nature of the relationship between a GP and the HA? There are a number of options. First, the relationship is one of contract which, in this situation, would undoubtedly be a contract for services since the GP could never be viewed as an employee of a HA. Secondly, the relationship is one which is *sui generis* defined by statute and lying in the realm of public law. Thirdly, their relationship may be a hybrid, being a creature in part of private law (though not contract) and in part of public law.

Roy v Kensington and Chelsea and Westminster FPC [1990] 1 Med LR 328 (CA); [1992] 1 AC 624 (HL)

On October 25, 1984, the defendant Kensington and Chelsea and Westminster Family Practitioner Committee decided that the plaintiff medical practitioner, Dr Roy, was not devoting a substantial amount of time to his general practice under the National Health Service. The committee reduced his practice allowance by 20 per cent from January 1, 1985. It was not disputed that Dr Roy had been absent from his practice, for reasons of family, sickness or holiday, for lengthy spells over a period of years. During his absence Dr Roy employed a locum who acted as his practice manager when he was not there. There have been no complaints from individual patients of the service that Dr Roy had provided.

Dr Roy claimed that he had a contractual relationship with the committee to provide general medical services to National Health Service patients. He contended that he had fulfilled his obligation by providing a locum during his periods of absence. Other disputes arose between Dr Roy and the committee in respect of, inter alia, payments for ancillary staff. He brought an action against the committee contending inter alia that, by reducing his practice allowance, the committee were in breach of contract.

On an application by the committee to strike out those paragraphs in Dr Roy's statement of claim which claimed to recover the moneys deducted by the committee from his allowance on the ground that they were an abuse of the process of the court, His Honour Judge White held ([1989] 1 Med LR 10), as a preliminary issue, that to allow Dr Roy to proceed would be an abuse of the process of the court because, although there were contractual echoes in the relationship between the doctor and the committee those were deceptive. The rights and duties of the parties were dependent on statute and the duty which the committee discharged was a public law function, an administrative decision, and the court would not substitute its decision for that of the committee. Accordingly, Dr Roy could only proceed on that part of his claim concerned with deductions from his practice allowance by way of an action for judicial review.

Balcombe LJ: In my judgment, the application by a general practitioner in the form prescribed in part II of Schedule 1 to the 1974 Regulations constitutes an offer in writing to perform general medical services in the FPC's locality upon the terms as defined above. When that application is accepted by the FPC and the acceptance is communicated to the applicant (either by letter or by the inclusion of his name in the medical list) a contract between the applicant and the FPC for the performance of services by the applicant is constituted. All the indicia of a contract are present. There is consideration consisting of the promise by the applicant to perform general medical services under the terms of service, in return for the promise by the FPC to pay for those services in accordance with the Statement of Fees and Allowances. The 1974 Regulations also provide for the termination of the relationship: Regulation 5 sets out the circumstances in which the FPC may remove a doctor's name from the medical list, while Regulation 6 enables the doctor to withdraw his name from the list.

Both a general practitioner and a FPC have complete freedom whether and with whom to contract, subject only to the monopoly position of each FPC as the National Health Service employer within its locality, and to the statutory duty of the FPC (under sections 15 and 29 of the 1977 Act) to make arrangements for the provision of general medical services within its locality. The fact that neither the FPC nor the doctor has freedom of contract in relation to the terms of service, which are laid down by the 1977 Act and the 1974 Regulations, is quite immaterial.

If the relationship were not contractual it is difficult to see what else it could be ... I am satisfied that the judge was wrong and that the relationship between Dr Roy and the committee was contractual.

Nourse and Neill LJJ agreed with Balcombe LJ's analysis of the relationship between Dr Roy and the FPC.

Curiously, the Court of Appeal in *Roy* was not referred to the earlier case of *Wadi v Cornwall and Isles of Scilly FPC* [1985] ICR 492 where the Employment Appeal Tribunal held that the relationship was not one of contract. On appeal in *Roy*, the House of Lords was asked to resolve this conflict. Lord Lowry set out the relevant parts of the judgment of the Employment Appeal Tribunal in *Wadi* as follows:

> It is clear from the Act of 1977 and the Regulations of 1974 that the family practitioner committee's designated role in the statutory scheme is merely to administer on behalf of the district health authority the arrangements which it is the duty of the district health authority to make with medical practitioners.

And

> There is in our view little to support Mr Susman's suggestion that the family practitioner committee, still less the medical committee, enters into a contract with the doctor who successfully applies for a vacancy. The family practitioner committee is obliged to cause payments to be made to doctors, but it is a mere conduit pipe for such moneys which the Secretary of State must pay to it and which it must pass on to the doctors. It has no discretion in the amounts or the circumstances of the payments. Nor does the 'light supervision' (to use the industrial tribunal's words) which it exercises over the doctors signify a contract. Still less is there anything to indicate that the medical committee has a contract with the doctor, there being no continuing relationship between them. In summary, our view is that under the statutory arrangements the doctor on the one side and each of the family practitioner committee and the medical committee on the other have rights and obligations conferred by statute rather than by contract. It is not necessary and we think it wrong to seek to import a contract into a scheme of things which is governed by the very detailed statutory arrangements made by neither the family practitioner committee nor the medical committee.

The House of Lords ([1992] 1 AC 624, [1992] 1 All ER 705) chose not to resolve the difference between the Court of Appeal in *Roy* and the Employment Appeal Tribunal in *Wadi*. Instead, the House of Lords decided that Dr Roy's action by writ was properly brought since, whatever the general nature of their relationship in law may be, the statutory framework conferred private rights upon Dr Roy at least as regards payment.

Lord Lowry (with whom the other Law Lords agreed) stated:

> [T]he actual or possible absence of a contract is not decisive against Dr Roy. He has in my opinion a bundle of rights which should be regarded as his individual private law rights against the Committee, arising from the statute and regulations and including the very important private law right to be paid for the work that he has done.

Lord Bridge was content to assume no contract existed and stated:

> I do not think the issue in the appeal turns on whether the doctor provides services pursuant to a contract with the Family Practitioner Committee. I doubt if he does and am content to assume that there is no contract. Nevertheless, the terms which govern the obligations of the doctor on the one hand, as to the services he is to provide, and of the Family Practitioner Committee on the other hand, as to the payments which it is required to make to the doctor, are all prescribed in the relevant legislation and it seems to me that the statutory terms are just as effective as they would be if they were contractual to confer upon the doctor an enforceable right in private law to receive the remuneration to which the terms entitle him. It must follow, in my view, that in any case of dispute the doctor is entitled to claim and recover in an action commenced by writ the amount of remuneration which he is able to prove as being due to him. Whatever remuneration he is entitled to under the Statement is remuneration he has duly earned by the services he has rendered. The circumstances that the quantum of that remuneration, in the case of a particular dispute, is affected by a discretionary decision made by the Committee cannot deny the doctor his private law right of recovery or subject him to the constraints which the necessity to seek judicial review would impose upon that right.

Will it ever be crucial whether or not a GP works under a contract for services? Arguably, as a matter of remedy no procedural problem need necessarily arise. A GP who wishes to dispute some aspect of his relationship with the HA will either have a specific remedy (by, for example, appealing to the Secretary of State) or he could bring an application for judicial review under RSC Ord 53. The latter should be the remedy of first resort (once the statutory remedies have been exhausted) for two reasons: first, challenges to public decisions are appropriately pursued under Ord 53 and secondly, the GP could take advantage of the 'cross-over' provision of Ord 53, r 9(5) which allows the court to regard his action as if it had been begun by writ. This approach would not, however, have assisted Dr Wadi. Judicial review was unavailable since the HA decision not to employ him did not lie within the realm of public law (but quaere any action under the Human Rights Act 1998). Instead, his only right (if any) not to be discriminated against, lay under the Race Relations Act 1976. A precondition to such rights accruing would be that he was seeking 'employment' which, as defined in the Act, requires that had he been successful he would have had a *contract* with the HA. Therefore, the nature of the relationship between the GP and HA is crucial and could not be avoided by the court.

(ii) ARRANGEMENTS UNDER THE NATIONAL HEALTH SERVICE (PRIMARY CARE) ACT 1997

In addition to primary care services provided by GPs under arrangements with Health Authorities pursuant to s 29 of the 1977 Act, the National Health Service (Primary Care) Act 1997 introduced a further set of possible arrangements. The Primary Care Act introduced 'pilot scheme' arrangements (ss 1–20). By virtue of these provisions GPs (and others) may make arrangements with HAs for the provision to patients of primary care services (known as 'personal medical services') outside the traditional framework of the Medical Regulations. The 'pilot scheme' provisions also cover 'dental services' but not other primary care services. The arrangements may be made with a range of health service bodies and employees, including GPs, nurses, NHS Trusts and Primary Care Trusts (1997 Act, s 2).

The two regimes are mutually exclusive in the sense that HAs have no duty under s 29 of the NHS Act 1977 to make arrangements for patients of 'pilot scheme' providers (1990 Act, s 1(5)) and GPs who are such providers may not be on a HA's Medical List and provide services under Pt II of the 1977 Act (1997 Act, s 12). Exceptions exist in respect of the latter, for example, where a doctor is acting as a deputy or outside normal hours for a 'pilot scheme' provider (National Health Service (Pilot Schemes: Pt II Practitioners) Regulations 1998 (SI 1998 No 665)).

It is important to distinguish the HA-Provider arrangement from the delivery (or performance) of services to patients under these arrangements. The arrangement between HA and provider must be on the terms set out in *Directions to Health Authorities Concerning the Implementation of Pilot Schemes (Personal Medical Services)* 1998. As regards the delivery of 'personal medical services', these terms must be adhered to by all GPs who deliver the services and largely mirror the 'Terms of Service' in Sch 2 to the Medical Regulations. Thus, the GP services *delivered* and their relationship to the patient is unchanged. Where a doctor delivers services but is not a party to the 'pilot scheme' arrangements with the HA, the 'pilot scheme' providers remain responsible for compliance by the doctor of the terms of the arrangement (Directions, para 21).

To the extent that the 'provider' is a health service body, the arrangement with the HA will be an 'NHS Contract' under s 4(1) of the National Health Service and Community Care Act 1990 (on which see *infra*). Otherwise, it is likely to be a contract (see, para 22(3) of Directions, *op cit*). This is important since disciplinary matters will not be dealt with under the regime applicable to 'Pt II' GPs but rather through the dispute resolution procedure applicable to NHS Contracts (see *infra*) or through contractual actions and the dispute resolution procedure in Sch 4 to the Directions.

As will be clear, 'pilot scheme' arrangements allow for a 'blurring' of the traditional split between the provision of 'primary care' (NHS 1977 Act, Pt II) and secondary or hospital care (NHS Act 1977, Pt I). Traditional Pt I providers, ie NHS Trusts (alone or in consortia with others), may now become 'providers' of GP services through 'pilot scheme' arrangements, whereby they employ GPs and others on the premises to deliver GP services. (GPs may also be employed by GP practices which are 'pilot schemes' providers.) The Primary Care Act makes it clear that 'pilot scheme' providers must deliver GP services 'equivalent in scope' (Directions, para 3(1)) to those of Pt II GPs (1997 Act, ss 1(1) and (8)) but may also provide hospital and community health services, ie under Pt II of the NHS Act 1977 (NHS Primary Care Act 1997, s 1(3)). Likewise, as we shall see, a blurring will occur when Primary Care Trusts who, in addition to having a commissioning role and are also providers of 'personal medical services' under 'pilot schemes', have been established to provide other services covered by Pt I of the NHS Act 1977 (NHS Act 1977, ss 16A and 18A, inserted by Health Act 1999, ss 2 and 5). Although it is the Government's intention to limit such services, at least in the first instance, to community health services currently provided exclusively by NHS Trusts (see *infra*).

'Pilot Schemes' under the 1997 Act are intended to be temporary, even experimental, arrangements. However, the 1997 Act introduces provisions into the National Health Service Act 1977 to put such arrangements on a permanent basis if they prove successful (1977 Act, see ss 28C–G inserted by Pt II of the 1997 Act).

(b) Provision of Part II services

We now turn to consider some important aspects of the arrangements between GPs and Health Authorities and the services provided. We do so in the context of GPs providing services under Pt II of the National Health Service Act 1977 and the National Health Service (General Medical Services) Regulations 1992 (SI 1992 No 635) (as amended). We do not examine in detail the terms applicable to 'pilot scheme' providers and doctors who perform services under such arrangements. As we noted earlier, these terms are set out in the *Directions to Health Authorities Concerning the Implementation of Pilot Schemes (Personal*

Medical Services) (March 1998) and largely mirror the 1992 Medical Regulations. We will, however, remark on a few matters as we progress.

General practitioners provide 'general medical services' under Pt II of the 1977 Act in accordance with, and on the terms set out in, the Medical Regulations 1992. Paragraph 12(1) of the Terms of Service states that:

> 12(1) Subject to paragraphs 3, 13 and 44, a doctor shall render to his patients all necessary and appropriate personal medical services of the type usually provided by general medical practitioners.

Before we turn to look at what these services are, we should look at a number of the more important conditions upon which all GPs undertake to provide them.

First, we should notice the GP's obligation under para 19(1) of the terms of service which states: 'a doctor shall give treatment personally.' However, this obligation is subject to three important exceptions: treatment by a deputy (or through a deputising service); where it is reasonable to delegate to another, for example a nurse; and where an 'out of hours' arrangement exists.

As regards treatment by a deputy, para 19(2)(a) provides:

> 19(2) Subject to sub-paragraphs (3), (5) and (6), a doctor (in this sub-paragraph referred to as "the patient's doctor") shall be under no obligation to give treatment personally to a patient provided that reasonable steps are taken to ensure the continuity of the patient's treatment, and in those circumstances treatment may be given—
> (a) by another doctor acting as a deputy, whether or not he is a partner or assistant of the patient's doctor; or ...

Paragraph 28(1) requires that:

> 28(1) A doctor shall, before employing any person to assist him in the provision of general medical services, take reasonable care to satisfy himself that the person in question is both suitably qualified and competent to discharge the duties for which he is to be employed.

It is further required that any doctor whom he employs as a deputy has the required qualifications (para 22A) and is not prevented from practising, for example, by virtue of a direction by the NHS Tribunal (para 23).

A GP (or practice) may also make an arrangement with a 'deputising service' who provides GPs (either on a HA list or 'pilot scheme' doctors) with the consent of the HA (para 22). Paragraph 20 of the Terms of Service sets out the liability of the doctor for his deputies.

> 20(1) In relation to his obligations under these terms of service, a doctor is responsible for all acts and omissions of—
> (a) any doctor acting as his deputy;
> (b) any organisation providing deputy doctors as mentioned in paragraph 22 with which he has entered into an arrangement in accordance with that paragraph while acting on his behalf; and
> (c) any person employed by, or acting on behalf of, him or such a deputy or such an organisation,
> except where the act or omission is one for which a deputy is responsible under sub-paragraph (2) or for which the doctor is not responsible, under sub-paragraph (3).
> (2) Where a doctor whose name is included in the medical list of any [HA] is acting as deputy to another doctor whose name is included in the medical list of an [HA], the deputy alone is responsible for—
> (b) his own acts and omissions in relation to the obligations under these terms of service of the doctor for whom he acts as deputy; and
> (b) the acts and omissions of any person employed by him or acting on his behalf.
> (3) Where, in connection with arrangements under a pilot scheme whereby, outside normal hours, pilot doctors and doctors providing general medical services co-operate in such a way that one doctor will cover for another to secure the performance of personal medical services

or, as the case may be, the provision of general medical services for their patients, a pilot doctor acts as a deputy to a doctor whose name is included in the medical list, that doctor is not responsible for the acts or omissions of the pilot doctor.

Hence, by virtue of para 20(2), a GP will not be responsible for any doctor acting as his deputy who is on a HA's Medical List (formerly he had to be on the Medical List of the same HA) (para 20(2)). The deputy remains responsible under his terms of service. A further instance is where a 'pilot scheme' doctor acts for a GP under an 'out of hours' deputising arrangement under para 18A (see *infra*). In such circumstances, the GP will not be responsible for the 'pilots scheme' doctor's acts and omissions (para 20(1) and (3)). However, there is a difference from the previous situation, since the 'pilot scheme' doctor cannot be responsible under any 'terms of service' because he is not subject to them. On the face of it, therefore, no one is responsible in this situation. Where the 'pilot scheme' doctor provides cover other than under an 'out of hours' arrangement, the GP would remain responsible by virtue of para 20(1), since the 'pilot scheme' doctor could not be on the Medical List of a Health Authority (NHS Primary Care Act 1997, s 12(2)). A Pt II GP deputising for a 'pilot scheme' doctor is liable under his 'terms of service' for any act or omission that is a breach of the pilot scheme and would be a breach of his terms of service: National Health Service (Pilot Schemes: Part II Practitioner) Regulations 1998 (SI 1998 No 665), reg 3. The 'pilot scheme' provider also remains responsible for the act and omissions of all doctors (whether deputies or employees) for compliance with the terms of the scheme (*Directions to Health Authorities op cit*, para 21).

As regards delegation by a GP to others, para 19(2)(b) provides that he has no obligation to provide treatment personally:

in the case of treatment which it is clinically reasonable in the circumstances to delegate to someone other than a doctor, by a person whom the doctor has authorised and who he is satisfied is competent to carry out such treatment.

This, of course, unlike the deputising provisions relates to delegation to persons *who are not doctors* which it is reasonable for him to engage (para 28). This provision covers nurses and others working within the GP's practice. The GP remains responsible for their acts and omissions (para 20(1)(c)).

As regards 'out of hours' arrangements, paras 18A–C allow a GP to transfer responsibility for the care of his patients to another doctor with the approval of the Health Authority between 7 pm and 8 am on weekdays, on the weekend after 1 pm on Saturdays and on bank holidays. The GP is thereby absolved from the duty to give treatment personally (para 19(1)), although he may do so (para 18A(5)). This leads to the second important condition GPs agree to.

A GP shall 'normally be available at such times and places as shall have been approved' by the Health Authority and shall 'inform his patients of his availability in such manner as the [Health Authority] may require' (para 29(1)). Thus, the GP's place of practice will be identified and he has an obligation to ensure services are provided on a 24-hour basis (para 18(1)). His personal availability to provide the services will, of course, be less and will be as agreed with the Health Authority. His responsibility under the terms of service will, however, always remain subject to the provisions we have seen in relation to deputies. A GP (or his deputy) must provide the services at one of the places listed in para 13, such as the GP's practice premises or, if it is inappropriate for the patient to attend, he must make a home visit. There are two important exceptions. A GP may arrange with the Health Authority to provide services outside his normal hours at approved premises other than his practice premises, for example, a night clinic (para 29A). This does not, of course, absolve the doctor (or deputy) from making a home visit where that would otherwise be appropriate. Also, as we have seen, a doctor may with the consent of the Health Authority transfer to another doctor(s) responsibility for his patients under an 'out of hours' arrangement pursuant to paras 18A–C.

Thirdly, by para 47 a doctor 'whose name is included in the medical list of an [HA] shall compile in relation to his practice a document ... called a "practice leaflet"'. The information which the practice leaflet should contain is set out in Sch 12 and includes such matters as the personal and professional details of the doctor, times of availability, whether an appointment system is operated and whether he provides special services such as 'maternity medical services' or 'contraceptive services'.

Fourthly, a further duty imposed upon a doctor under the terms of service is to keep adequate records of the illnesses and treatments of his patients (para 36).

Fifthly, notice that a doctor may not demand nor accept payment for the provision of general medical services to, or any other treatment of, patients on his list or who are otherwise his patients under the terms of service (para 38). This general prohibition is subject to a number of exceptions, for example, when attending an examining a patient at a police station (para 38(d)).

Sixthly, another feature of the statutory framework is that there is a limit placed upon the number of persons who may appear on a doctor's list which is generally '3,500 for a doctor carrying on practice otherwise than as an assistant or in a partnership' or '4,500 for a doctor carrying on practice in partnership, subject to a maximum average of 3,500 for each of the partners in the practice' (reg 24(2)).

Seventhly, GPs are required to have a practice-based complaints procedure (para 47A) and have an obligation to co-operate with the Health Authority in the operation of the NHS complaints procedure (see *infra*, ch 3).

Finally, we should notice one omission in the terms of service. There is no requirement for a GP to have insurance or other indemnity cover for medical negligence claims. By contrast, there is an obligation that 'pilot scheme' doctors should be insured (see *Directions to Health Authorities op cit*, para 30). The position as regards Pt II practitioners will be rectified by s 43C of the NHS Act 1977 (inserted by s 9 of the Health Act 1999) which gives the Secretary of State power, by regulation, to require that adequate professional indemnity cover is in place.

(i) GP SERVICES

As part of the reform of the NHS presaged in the Government's White Paper, *Working for Patients*, the terms of service of a GP, previously set out in the National Health Service (General Medical and Pharmaceutical Services) Regulations (SI 1974 No 160) were substantially amended in 1990. In particular the GP's role in health promotions and preventive health care was embodies in the new terms of service. Finally, in 1992 the regulations were consolidated with amendments. They were also divided between 'general medical services' (National Health Service (General Medical Services) Regulations 1992 (SI 1992 No 635): hereafter the 'Medical Regulations'); and 'pharmaceutical services' (National Health Service (Pharmaceutical Services) Regulations 1992 (SI 1992 No 662): hereafter the 'Pharmaceutical Regulations'). A GP's terms of service are now set out in Sch 2 to each of the respective regulations. In essence, the GP is required to provide '*personal medical services*' which are defined in para 12(1) of Sch 2 to the Medical Regulations as follows:

12. (1) Subject to paragraphs 3, 13 and 44, a doctor shall render to his patients all necessary and appropriate personal medical services of the type usually provided by general medical practitioners.

Paragraph 12(2) goes on to state:

12. (2) The services which a doctor is required by sub-paragraph (1) to render shall include the following—
(a)   giving advice, where appropriate, to a patient in connection with the patient's general health, and in particular about the significance of diet, exercise, the use of tobacco, the consumption of alcohol and the misuse of drugs or solvents;
(b)   offering to patients consultations and, where appropriate, physical examinations for the purpose of identifying, or reducing the risk of disease or injury;
(c)   offering to patients, where appropriate, vaccination or immunisation against measles, mumps, rubella, pertussis, poliomyelitis, diphtheria and tetanus;
(d)   arranging for the referral of patients, as appropriate, for the provision of any other services under the National Health Service Act 1977; and
(e)   giving advice, as appropriate, to enable patients to avail themselves of services by a local social services authority.

In the new terms of service additional duties are imposed upon a GP as regards three specific classes of patient: *the newly registered patient, the patient who has not been seen for three years* and *the patient who is 75 or over*.

As regards 'newly registered patients', para 14(1) provides that '... Where a patient has been accepted on a doctor's list ..., the doctor shall, in addition to and without prejudice to his other obligations in respect of that patient under these terms of service, within 28 days ... invite the patient to participate in a consultation ...'. Para 14(2) sets out the detailed obligations of a doctor, during the consultation:

14. (2) Where a patient (or, in the case of a patient who is a child, his parent) agrees to participate in a consultation mentioned in sub-paragraph (1), the doctor shall, in the course of that consultation—
(a) seek details from the patient as to his medical history and, so far as may be relevant to the patient's medical history, as to that of his consanguineous family, in respect of—
      (i)   illnesses, immunisations, allergies, hereditary conditions, medication and tests carried out for breast or cervical cancer;
      (ii) social factors (including employment, housing and family circumstances) which may affect his health;
      (iii) factors of his lifestyle (including diet, exercise, use of tobacco, consumption of alcohol, and misuse of drugs or solvents) which may affect his health; and
      (iv) the current state of his health;
(b) offer to undertake a physical examination of the patient, comprising—
      (i)   the measurement of his height, weight and blood pressure; and
      (ii) the taking of a urine sample and its analysis to identify the presence of albumen and glucose;
(c) record, in the patient's medical records, his findings arising out of the details supplied by, and any examination of, the patient under this sub-paragraph;
(d) assess whether and, if so, in what manner and to what extent he should render personal medical services to the patient;
(e) in so far as it would not, in the opinion of the doctor, be likely to cause serious damage to the physical or mental health of the patient to do so, offer to discuss with the patient (or, where the patient is a child, the parent) the conclusions the doctor has drawn as a result of the consultation as to the state of the patient's health.

(Paragraph 14(4) sets out some exceptions to the duty under para 14(1), for example, where the patient is a child under 5 years of age, or a patient who has had such a consultation within the preceding 12 months with another doctor in the partnership.)

As regards 'patients not seen within 3 years', the Medical Regulations until 1993 required the doctor to offer each patient on his list between the ages of 16 and 75 an opportunity to participate in a consultation with him. In 1993 the terms of service were amended (by SI 1993 No 540) so as to remove this obligation and only to require a consultation if the patient requested it. Paragraph 15(1) now provides that:

15 (1) Subject to sub-paragraph (2), where a patient who—
(a)   has attained the age of 16 years but has not attained the age of 75 years; and
(b)   within the preceding 3 years has attended neither a consultation with, nor a clinic provided
        by, any doctor in the course of his provision of general medical services,
requests a consultation for the purposes of assessing whether he needs personal medical
services, a doctor shall in addition to and without prejudice to any other obligation under
these terms of service, provide such a consultation.

Paragraph 15(4) ensures that the doctor should in the course of the consultation
have the same obligations, as for a new patient, set out in para 14 (2) (*supra*).
As regards 'patients aged 75 and over', para 16(1) provides that:

16 (1) … a doctor shall, in addition to and without prejudice to any other obligations under
these terms of service, in each period of 12 months beginning on 1 April in each year—
(a)   invite each patient on his list who has attained the aged of 75 years to participate in a
        consultation; and
(b)   offer to make a domiciliary visit to each such patient,
for the purpose of assessing whether he needs to render personal medical services to that
patient.

In making the assessment following the consultation under sub-para (1), para
16(5) provides that the doctor shall:

16 (5) … record in the patient's medical records the observations made of any matter which
appears to him to be affecting the patient's general health, including where appropriate the patient's—
(a)   sensory functions;
(b)   mobility;
(c)   mental condition;
(d)   physical condition including continence;
(e)   social environment;
(f)   use of medicines.

Paragraph 16(8) goes on to provide that:

16 (8) Where a patient has participated in a consultation pursuant to sub-paragraph (1),
the doctor shall offer to discuss with him the conclusions he has drawn, as a result of the
consultation, as to the state of the patient's health, unless to do so would, in the opinion
of the doctor, be likely to cause serious harm to the physical or mental health of the
patient.

As a consequence of providing the services already outlined, the regulations
impose on the doctor the duty to prescribe drugs or appliances and to issue certain
certificates in appropriate circumstances. In certain exceptional circumstances a
doctor is even under a duty to *dispense* drugs or appliances.
As regards *prescribing*, para 43 provides:

43 … a doctor shall order any drugs or appliances which are needed for the treatment of any
patient to whom he is providing treatment under these terms of service by issuing to that
patient a prescription form, and such a form shall not be used in any other circumstances.

Under para 44 a doctor is not ordinarily permitted to prescribe, for supply to a
patient under his terms of service, a drug specified in Sch 10 to the Medical
Regulations. This Schedule sets out those drugs or other substances which, in
the view of the Government, should be obtained at the patient's own expense
rather than be a charge on the National Health Service.
Schedule 10 creates the so-called 'black list'. Likewise, Sch 11 creates a restricted
use list of drugs which may only be prescribed in specified circumstances.
The scope of a GP's duty under paras 12 and 43 of his terms of service was
examined in the following case where the Secretary of State sought to restrict a
GP's ability to prescribe the drug Viagra.

R v Secretary of State for Health, ex parte Pfizer Ltd, [1999] Lloyd's Rep Med 289 (QBD)

The manufacturers of a drug, Sildenafil, well known by its trade name, Viagra, applied for judicial review of a circular (No 1998/158) dated 16 September 1998 issued by the Department of Health which gave advice to doctors with a view to restricting the prescribing use of the drug under the NHS.

Viagra is the only drug licensed to be taken orally for the treatment of erectile dysfunction (ED) and is the most desirable medical treatment for that condition because of its effectiveness and relative lack of side effects. In March 1998 Viagra received marketing authorisation in the USA. Similar authorisation within the European Union was expected to follow in the autumn of 1998 and was, in the event, given on 15 September 1998. During the period leading up to these authorisations the Government became concerned at the potential cost implications for the NHS. In January 1998 the National Prescribing Centre in the UK had calculated that the introduction of Viagra in the UK would have a major financial impact upon the NHS unless restrictions were placed on its use. On 22 July 1998 the Standing Medical Advisory Committee (SMAC) were asked by the Government to advise on the introduction of Viagra into NHS use. On about 29 July 1998 SMAC expressed its interim view to be that Viagra should not be routinely prescribed until the committee had finalised its advice on the clinical circumstances in which prescribing would be appropriate. On 16 September 1998 the Department of Health issued a circular in which SMAC's interim guidance was promulgated with a modified form of wording. The circular advised that "as an interim measure SMAC has advised that doctors should not prescribe Sildenafil." It also gave advice to health authorities advising them not to support the prescribing of Sildenafil to patients under the NHS save in exceptional circumstances which were to be cleared in advance.

The effect of this circular was that GP's did not prescribe Viagra. The applicants challenged the lawfulness of the circular both under domestic and European law ...

Collins J: Schedule 10 contains a long list of drugs and substances for which the NHS will not pay. It is largely made up of items such as patent remedies, drugs which are no more effective than cheaper (often generic) alternatives, substances such as sun creams, hair tonics and vitamin supplements and the occasional drug, for example temazepam capsules, which has proved to have been misused and which has no unique positive benefits. Schedule 11 is designed for drugs which, for example, are needed for treatment of particular conditions but which can be used for others where there are cheaper and equally effective alternatives. Alterations to the lists in the two Schedules require an amending statutory instrument.

The Regulations do not indicate the basis upon which drugs or substances should be "black listed" in Schedules 10 or 11. One public announcement of criteria was by the then Secretary of State, Mr Kenneth Clarke in March 1985 (dealing with a precursor to the 1992 Regulations) when he said this:

It follows that the criterion for including drugs in the schedule of medicinal products and other substances not to be available on NHS prescription from 1 April 1985 was that, on expert advice, they had no clinical or therapeutic advantage over other, cheaper, drugs in the categories of antacids, laxatives, analgesics for mild to moderate pain, cough and cold remedies, bitters and tonics, vitamins and benzodiazepine sedatives and tranquillisers. Drugs prescribable only for specific conditions – at present only one, Clobazam for epilepsy – are those which have more than one distinct therapeutic use and which meet this criterion for at least one of those uses but do not meet it for all of them.

In addition, the main schedule includes substances which the Advisory Committee on Borderline Substances has advised are never drugs or medicines in the circumstances of general practice. The independent experts advising us on the contents of the limited list also made a general recommendation, which we accepted. This was that to achieve maximum economy drugs to be retained should wherever possible be specified and prescribed by a non-proprietary name.

There are no cheaper drugs which are equally effective and so those criteria do not apply to Viagra. However, Mr Pannick, QC rightly concedes that the Secretary of State is entitled to include Viagra in Schedule 11 because of resource implications following the likely cost of allowing it to be freely prescribed. On 7 May 1999, the Friday before the Monday on which this application came before me, the Secretary of State issued a circular indicating that he proposed to make regulations on 1 July 1999 to limit the prescription of all treatments for ED on the NHS to men who suffered it as a result of various specified causes or who were receiving treatment (which, of course, would have been other than by Viagra) before 14 September 1998. These proposals were anticipated following a consultation which commenced on 21 January 1999.

I should add that, as the wording of paragraph 44 makes clear, doctors can prescribe Viagra privately, provided that they do not breach paragraphs 40 or 42 …

Mr Pannick, QC has attacked the lawfulness of the circular on the ground that, although couched in the terms of advice, its purpose and effect was to ban or to restrict the prescribing of Viagra to such an extent as to prevent GPs from carrying out their statutory obligations under the terms of service in Schedule 2 of the 1992 Regulations. GPs, submitted Mr Pannick, have a legal and professional duty to exercise their clinical judgment and to give such treatment as they decide to be necessary for a particular patient. If they decide that a particular drug is needed, they can only refuse to prescribe it if it is included in Schedules 10 or 11. Miss Baxendale, QC submits that in exercising his skill and judgment the GP must have regard to advice given by SMAC and by the Secretary of State and, if that advice suggests that a drug which might otherwise seem to be the right treatment should not be prescribed, the GP is entitled, but not bound, to act upon that advice. Furthermore, she submits that the circular clearly states that it contains advice only and does not amount to a direction; accordingly it cannot be held to be unlawful. The Secretary of State is perfectly entitled to take steps to deter GPs from prescribing Viagra having regard to the resource implications for the NHS …

It is clear that, for very understandable and proper reasons, the Secretary of State was concerned that Viagra would prove to have a significantly adverse effect on the resources of the NHS. The press release which accompanied the circular quoted him as stating "doctors are advised not to prescribe Viagra nor health authorities support the provision by NHS Trusts of the drug at NHS expense, until further notice". It was therefore hardly surprising that the press reported the circular as a "ban" on Viagra. Indeed, Mr Moran, the chairman and managing director of the applicants, deposes without contradiction that he understands that the Secretary of State had personally briefed one of the journalists who used the terminology "a ban". Mr Dobson is quoted in the press release in these words:

> Media coverage of this drug to date has created expectations that could prove a serious drain on the funds of the NHS. If this were to happen, other patients could be denied the treatment they need. I cannot allow this to happen.

The advice was initially very effective and its effect was exacerbated because, since Viagra was not "blacklisted" in Schedule 11, it could not be prescribed privately to their patients by NHS GPs: see paragraphs 40 and 42 of Schedule 2 to the 1992 Regulations. The respondent's own evidence shows that between September and December 1998 an average of only 108 NHS prescriptions for Viagra were issued each week across the country. In the light of the feared rush to obtain the drug, that is a clear indication that the advice was largely effective. The "exceptional circumstances" referred to in the circular were never specified, although no doubt the proposals put out to consultation on 21 January 1999 gave from that date some indication of when Viagra should be prescribed.

Some health authorities wrongly interpreted the circular as requiring them to indicate that GPs who prescribed Viagra would be penalised. At best, there was confusion as to the true effect of the circular, so much so that eventually, after much pressure, the Department issued a further circular on 22 February 1999 which reminded health authorities that the circular 1998/158 was "guidance only until such time as substantive proposals, which are currently being consulted upon, are put into effect".

All this, which I have summarised very briefly, enables Mr Pannick to submit that the purpose and effect of the circular was indeed to deter GPs from carrying out their statutory duties under their terms of service. He submitted that paragraph 43 imposed a duty on a GP to prescribe a drug if he was satisfied the patient had a clinical need for it. Paragraph 43 in my judgment does not impose a duty to prescribe a drug. It is dealing with the mechanism to enable a patient to receive a drug if the doctor decides that that drug should be used to treat the patient. The doctor's duty is contained in paragraph 12(1), which really does no more than set out his professional obligations as a doctor and itself reflects the obligations referred to in Regulation 3(1). The doctor must give such treatment as he, exercising the professional judgment to be expected from an average GP, considers necessary and appropriate. Miss Baxendale submits that "appropriate" qualifies "necessary" so that, if a GP considers a particular treatment to be necessary, he must go on to consider whether it is also appropriate. In reaching his final decision, he should have regard to the advice from SMAC and may therefore decide that the treatment is not appropriate. I find this suggested construction impossible. If a GP decides that a particular treatment is necessary, it must inevitably be appropriate. If it were not appropriate, a GP could not rationally decide that it was necessary. "Appropriate" in paragraph 12(1) is included so that GPs will provide services which go beyond those that are needed by their parents. Such services could include, for example, advice on various medical matters or family planning. Some treatment may be considered appropriate but not necessary. No doubt, if a GP in exercising his professional judgment decided that a particular treatment was not appropriate, he would conclude that that treatment was not necessary.

The very fact that the advice in the circular comes from SMAC is likely to make GPs respect it the more and thus to follow it. Mr Pannick has attacked the reasons given for imparting it, castigating them as irrational. I do not think that attack succeeds. I should hesitate long before branding the views on medical matters of eminent practitioners to be irrational. In any event, whether the reasons be good or bad cannot affect the lawfulness of the circular if its purpose and effect is to cause GPs to act contrary to their professional obligations and contrary to their duty as reflected in paragraph 12(1).

In September 1998 the BMA issued its own guidance on the circular. This included the advice that from a legal standpoint GPs could prescribe Viagra since it had not been blacklisted. Miss Baxendale relied on this to make the point that the medical profession could have been in no doubt that the circular was only advisory and could not and did not require GPs not to prescribe Viagra. But the BMA's advice continued that GPs should adhere to SMAC's advice ("as a body representing the medical profession") which was contained in the circular. Thus the BMA's advice does not serve to diminish the effect of the circular and, as it seems to me, the problem with the circular is that the advice was given in a manner which meant that GPs would inevitably regard [it] as overriding their professional judgment. Mr Pannick accepted that advice could be given in strong terms to deter the prescribing of Viagra, but it must make clear that the GPs' clinical judgment is supreme. In essence, the advice should have been reasoned, at least so that GPs knew why they should only prescribe Viagra sparingly. To state in bald terms that Viagra should not be prescribed save in (undefined) exceptional circumstances is tantamount to telling the recipients of the advice to follow it. They cannot know how their professional judgment should be influenced by the advice. In my judgment, the evidence confirms that this was and was intended to be acted upon by GPs independently of whether in their professional judgment a patient needed treatment for ED and so should have the better such treatment available, namely Viagra. Thus I am satisfied that the circular was and is unlawful in terms of domestic law.

You will notice the primacy given by the judge to the GP's duty under para 12 subject to the express exception in para 44 to 'black listed' drugs and substances in Schs 10 and 11. Rather curiously, the judge did not see the duty to prescribe as falling within para 43. His explanation is that it is concerned with 'the mechanism to enable a patient to receive a drug'. That, of course, is the process of prescribing. Supplying or dispensing is a different matter as we shall see shortly. Notwithstanding Collins J's view, para 43 does impose a duty to prescribe, ie provide the authorisation for a pharmacist to dispense a 'needed' drug, namely when it is 'necessary' or 'appropriate' under para 12. Finally, the victory of the applicant drug company was short-lived. Viagra is now a listed drug in Sch 11 which can only be prescribed in certain circumstances (see the National Health Service (General Medical Services) Amendment (No 2) Regulations 1999 (SI 1999 No 1627), amending Sch 11 to the 1992 Regulation).

As regards *certification*, para 37(1) provides:

37. (1) A doctor shall issue free of charge to a patient or his personal representative any medical certificate of a description prescribed in … Schedule 9, which is reasonably required [for the purposes specified in that Schedule], except where, for the condition to which the certificate relates, the patient—
(a) is being attended by another doctor (other than a partner, assistant or other deputy of the first named doctor); or
(b) is not being treated by, or under the supervision of, a doctor.

As regards *dispensing*, the relevant obligations are not set out in the Medical Regulations but are contained in the Pharmaceutical Regulations. Regulation 19 of the Pharmaceutical Regulations provides:

19. A doctor—
(a) *shall provide* to a patient any appliance or drug, not being a Scheduled drug, where such provision is needed for the immediate treatment of that patient before a provision can be otherwise obtained; and
(b) *may provide* to a patient any appliance or drug, not being a Scheduled drug, which he personally administers or applies to that patient [our emphasis].

A 'Scheduled drug' is one listed in Sch 10 or 11 to the Medical Regulations as being a drug which a doctor is not ordinarily permitted to prescribe for supply under his terms of service as we saw above. Notice in relation to regulation 19 only reg 19(a) is mandatory, obviously by reason of the circumstances contemplated therein. Further, reg 20(1) provides for the situations in which a patient either:

> 20.(1)(a) satisfies an [HA] that he would have serious difficulty in obtaining any necessary drugs or appliances from a pharmacy by reason of distance or inadequacy of means of communication; or
> (b) is resident in a controlled locality [ie certain rural areas], at a distance of more than one mile from any pharmacy, and [subject to certain detailed provisions, see paragraph 20(2)]
> he may at any time request in writing the doctor on whose list he is included to provide him with pharmaceutical services.

If, following a request under reg 20(1), the doctor agrees to provide pharmaceutical services to this patient, the HA will then authorise the doctor on his application to do so (reg 20(3)(a)). If, however, the doctor does not agree to provide the services and so does not apply to the HA for permission to provide them, the HA may, nevertheless, require him to do so (reg 20(3)(b)) subject to the doctor demonstrating that he should not be required to provide such services on one of the grounds specified in reg 20(5).

In addition to the services we have seen so far which every GP is *required* to offer there are *four* further services which a GP *may* undertake to the HA to offer to his patients (though this does not entail that he will undertake to provide them to each patient). Paragraph 12(3)(a) of the terms of service contained in Sch 2 to the Medical Regulations provides that:

> 12. (3) A doctor is not required …
> (a) to provide to any person child health surveillance services, contraceptive services, minor surgery services nor, except in an emergency, maternity medical services, unless he has previously undertaken to the [HA] to provide such services to that person.

This paragraph makes it clear, however, that in an emergency a doctor must provide maternity medical services regardless of whether he has previously undertaken to the HA to offer them.

The undertaking referred to in para 12(3)(a) is to the HA since reg 4 of the Medical Regulations requires that the HA 'shall prepare a list, to be called the medical list' (regs 4(1)) and 4(4) goes on to provide:

> 4. (4) In respect of any doctor whose name is included in it, the medical list shall indicate—
> (a) if he is on any of the child health surveillance list, the obstetric list or the minor surgery list;
> (b) if the general medical services he has undertaken to provide include, exclude or are limited to maternity medical services;
> (c) except in the case of a doctor who has requested otherwise, if he has undertaken to provide contraceptive services, and if so—
>   (i) whether he has so undertaken in respect only of patients for whom he or his partners have also undertaken to provide other general medical services, or
>   (ii) whether he has so undertaken without such restriction …

As regards the provision of 'maternity medical services', para 7 of the terms of service provides that a doctor *may* 'undertake to provide maternity services to a woman who has made an arrangement with him in accordance with reg 31(2)'. Regulation 31(2) provides that:

> 31. (2) A woman who, after a doctor has diagnosed that she is pregnant, requires the provision of maternity medical services may arrange for the provision of any or all of the services … with—

(a) any doctor in the obstetric list;
(b) the doctor on whose list she is included; or
(c) any doctor who has accepted her as a temporary resident.

What this means is that where a woman's doctor does not agree to offer maternity medical services, or the woman would prefer to go to a doctor other than her regular GP, she may obtain these services alone from another doctor who is on the obstetric list and who has agreed to make an arrangement with her for their provision.

This is also the case as regards the provision of 'contraceptive services'. Under para 7 of the terms of service a doctor may 'undertake to provide contraceptive services to a woman who has applied to him in accordance with regulation 29'. Regulation 29 provides that:

29. (1) Whether or not she is included in his list for provision of other personal medical services, a woman may apply to a doctor who has undertaken to provide contraceptive services to be accepted by him for the provision of those services.

Where a doctor has made such an undertaking that fact will be indicated on the HA medical list (reg 4(4)).

As regards 'child health surveillance services', which were introduced by the 1990 amendments to the (then) 1974 Regulations, reg 28(1) and (2) of the 1992 Medical Regulations provide that:

28. (1) A parent may, in relation to a child of his who is under the age of 5 years, apply to a doctor—
(a) who is—
   (i) the doctor on whose list the child is included (in this paragraph referred to as 'the child's doctor'),
   (ii) a doctor with whom the child's doctor is in partnership, or
   (iii) a doctor with whom the child's doctor is associated in a group practice; and
(b) whose name is included in any medical list and in the child health surveillance list of the [HA],
for the provision of child health surveillance services in respect of that child for a period ending on the date on which that child attains the age of 5 years.
   (2) A doctor whose name is included in the medical list may, in respect of any person on his list or on the list of a doctor with whom he is in partnership or with whom he is associated in a group practice, undertake to provide child health surveillance services provided that—
(a) his name is also included in the child health surveillance list, and
(b) the person in question is a child who is under the age of 5 years.

As regards 'minor surgery services', which were also introduced in 1990, reg 33(1) and (2) of the Medical Regulations provide that:

33. (1) A person may apply either in writing or in person to a doctor—
(a) who is—
   (i) the doctor in whose list he is included (in this paragraph referred to as 'his own doctor'),
   (ii) a doctor with whom his own doctor is in partnership, or
   (iii) a doctor with whom his own doctor is associated in a group practice; and
(b) whose name is included in the medical list and the minor surgery list of the [HA], for the provision of [minor surgery services] ...
(2) A doctor whose name is included in the medical list may, in respect of any person on his list or on the list of a doctor with whom he is in partnership or with whom he is associated in group practice, undertake to provide minor surgery services, provided that his name is included in the minor surgery list.

You will notice that the opportunity to select, enjoyed by a woman as regards maternity medical services and contraceptive services, does not apply as regards the latter two services.

Further, the relevance of all these provisions is that a doctor may not provide the further optional services to persons who are not his patients unless his name appears on the relevant list maintained by the HA as offering them. Of course, there is nothing to stop a doctor carrying out these services for *his patients* as part of the provision to them of 'personal medical services'. If he does so, however, he will not qualify for payment by the HA specifically associated with the provision of these optional services. This is because he would not be supplying these further services within the terms of the regulations not least because he will not have demonstrated his fitness to do so as called for by the regulations (ie the regulations, as regards these further services, operate *inter alia* as a quality control mechanism).

What then are these four further services a GP may offer?

Maternity medical services are defined in reg 31(1) as:

31. (1) Maternity medical services shall comprise—
(a)   the provision of personal medical services to a woman during the ante-natal period;
(b)   the provision of personal medical services to a woman during labour;
(c)   the provision of personal medical services to a woman and to her baby … during the post-natal period; and
(d)   the provision of a full post-natal examination.

(These services are further particularised in Pt II of Sch 5.)

Contraceptive services are defined in reg 3(1)(c) as follows:

3 (1) (c) (i) the giving of advice to women on contraception;
(ii)   the medical examination of women seeking such advice;
(iii) the contraceptive treatment of such women; and
(iv) the supply to such women of contraceptive substances and appliances.

Child health surveillance services are described in reg 28(3) and Sch 4. Schedule 4 provides in para 1 that:

1. The services … shall comprise—
(a)   the monitoring—
(i)   by the consideration of information concerning the child received by or on behalf of the doctor, and
(ii)   on any occasion when the child is examined or observed by or on behalf of the doctor (whether pursuant to sub-paragraph (b) or otherwise),
of the health, well-being and physical, mental and social development (all of which characteristics are referred to in this Schedule as 'development') of the child while under the age of 5 years with a view to detecting any deviations from normal development;
(b)   the examination of the child by or on behalf of the doctor on so many occasions and at such intervals as shall have been agreed between the FHSA and the health authority in whose district the child resides (in this Schedule called 'the relevant health authority') for the purposes of the provision of child health surveillance services generally in that district.

Paragraphs 2 and 3 go on to specify the record of the child's development which must be compiled and information which must be made available to the relevant health authority.

Minor surgery services are described in reg 33 of the 1992 Medical Regulations and Sch 6 thereto; for example, these services include the excision of warts, the incision of abscesses and the removal of foreign bodies.

(ii) THE DOCTOR-PATIENT RELATIONSHIP

We have seen, in passing, in the previous section how a person may be the patient of different doctors in relation to contraceptive and maternity medical services. Here, we need to consider the mechanisms by which the relationship of GP and patient comes into existence and how, and in what circumstances, that relationship may be terminated.

I. Forming of the relationship

Every person is entitled to have a NHS general practitioner who is their doctor. Section 28F of the National Health Service Act 1977 (inserted by NHS (Primary Care) Act 1997, s 23) provides:

> 28F.—(1) Provision shall be made in regulations for conferring a right on any person to choose the medical practitioner from whom he is to receive primary medical services, subject to—
> (a) the consent of the practitioner concerned; and
> (b) any limit on the number of patients to be accepted by any practitioner.
>   (2) In particular, the regulations—
> (a) shall prescribe the procedure for choosing a practitioner;
> (b) may prescribe a limit on the number of patients to be accepted by a medical practitioner who undertakes to provide general medical services under Part II; and
> (c) shall provide for the distribution among medical practitioners of persons who have indicated a wish to obtain primary medical services but—
>   (i)   have been refused by the medical practitioner of their choice; or
>   (ii) have not chosen a medical practitioner.

'Primary medical services' means 'general medical services' provided under Pt II of the 1977 Act or 'personal medical services' provided pursuant to a 'pilot scheme' (see s 28F(6)).

The mechanism for exercising this 'choice' is set out in the National Health Service (Choice of Medical Practitioner) Regulations 1998 (SI 1998 No 668), which applies to 'primary medical services' as we have seen defined.

Regulation 2 provides as follows:

> 2.—(1) Any person who wishes to receive primary medical services may choose the doctor from whom he is to receive those services (being a doctor who provides general medical services or who is primarily responsible for the performance of personal medical services under a pilot scheme), subject to—
> (a) the consent of that doctor; and
> (b) any limit on the maximum number of persons whose names may be included in the doctor's list of that doctor, imposed by regulation 24 of the GMS Regulations or, as the case may be, directions given under section 28F(3) of the 1977 Act.
>   (2) Subject to paragraph (3), an application for inclusion of a person's name in a doctor's list shall be made by delivering to the doctor a medical card or an application signed (in either case) by the applicant or a person authorised by the applicant to sign on his behalf.

In essence, therefore, the usual mechanism by which the GP-patient relationship is created is through an individual applying by delivery of his medical card or making an application for inclusion on the GP's list of patients. The GP may then accept the individual as a patient. Paragraph 6(1) of the 'terms of service' provides:

> 6 (1) Subject to sub-paragraph (2), a doctor may agree to accept a person on his list if the person is eligible to be accepted by him.

The consequence of this is that the GP, by virtue of his terms of service, undertakes to provide the relevant medical services to his (now) 'patient'. In other words, what is involved is a general request (by the individual) followed by a general undertaking (by the GP) upon acceptance. It is important to notice that the formal establishment of the relationship is not the same thing as saying that the GP owes the patient a duty of care for the purposes of medical negligence. That duty only concretises when the GP is requested to provide, or becomes aware of the need for, the medical service (see *infra* ch 4).

You will recall that a woman may also apply to a GP other than the one on whose list she is included for the provision of 'maternity medical services' providing the doctor is on the HA's obstetric list (reg 31(2)), or for 'contraceptive services', providing he has undertaken the HA to provide them other than to his usual patients (reg 29(1)). In either case, the doctor may agree to provide those services to the woman (paras 7(a) and (c), Sch 2 respectively).

A patient who is already on a GP's list may apply to be included in a different doctor's list (1998 regulations, reg 3(1)). The HA will then remove him from his original doctor's list (1992 regulations, reg 23). Usually, a GP's patients will be resident in his practice area but not always. Temporary residents (ie those who do not intend to reside there for more than three months) may apply, and be accepted, as a patient. Regulation 7 of the 1998 regulations provides:

> 7.—(1) A person requiring treatment who is—
> (a) temporarily residing away from his normal place of residence and is not included in the doctor's list of a doctor who practises in the vicinity of the place where he is temporarily residing, or a pooled list of doctors who practise in that vicinity; or
> (b) moving from place to place and not for the time being resident in any place,
> may apply to any doctor who provides general medical services or is primarily responsible for the performance of personal medical services under a pilot scheme in the area in which he is temporarily resident, to be accepted by him as a temporary resident.
> (2) For the purposes of paragraph (1), a person shall be regarded as temporarily resident in a place if, when he arrives in that place, he intends to stay there for more than 24 hours, but not more than three months.

Children and incompetent adults   What if the individual is a child or incompetent adult? Clearly, if the child is competent, ie able to understand what is involved in making an application to a GP and becoming his patient, the child may make the application themselves (see generally *infra*, ch 5 on competence and children).

What, however, if the child is too young or suffers from disability such that they are not competent? The matter is dealt with in the NHS (Choice of Medical Practitioner) Regulations 1998 (*op cit*). Regulation 2(3)(a) provides:

> 2 (3) An application may be made (otherwise than by the doctor concerned)—
> (a) on behalf of any child—
> (i) by either parent, or in the absence of both parents, the guardian or other adult person who has the care of the child;
> (ii) by a person duly authorised by a local authority to whose care the child has been committed under the provisions of the Children Act 1989; or
> (iii) by a person duly authorised by a voluntary organisation by which the child is being accommodated under the provisions of that Act . . .

Curiously, the 1998 regulations do not define who is a 'child'. The 1992 Medical regulations do and, prior to 1998, these contained the equivalent provisions for children. There, 'child' is defined as one who has not attained the age of 16 (reg 2). Presumably, the 1998 regulations should be read accordingly. Notice the 1998 regulations do not, on their face, restrict the parental (or other) request to cases where the child is incompetent and, probably, consistently with the common law elsewhere, parents may do so even where the child is competent and does not wish the request to be made (see *infra*, ch 6).

In respect of an incompetent adult, reg 2(3)(b) of the 1998 regulations provides as follows:

> 2 (3)(b) An application may be made (otherwise than by the doctor concerned) - on behalf of any adult person who is incapable of making such an application, or authorising such an application to be made on his behalf, by a relative or another adult person who has an interest in the welfare of that person.

A GP's patients   Paragraph 4 of the GP's standard terms of service lists in summary form those individuals who are his patients.

> 4(1) ... a doctor's patients are—
> (a) persons who are recorded by the [HA] as being on his list;

(b) persons whom he has accepted or agreed to accept on his list, whether or not notification of that acceptance has been received by the [HA], and who have not been notified to him by the [HA] as having ceased to be on his list;

(c) for the limited period specified in sub-paragraph (4), persons whom he has refused to accept;

(d) persons who have been assigned to him under regulation 4 of the Choice of Medical Practitioner Regulations;

(e) for the limited period specified in sub-paragraph (5), persons in respect of whom he has been notified that an application has been made for assignment to him in a case to which regulation 4(4) of the Choice of Medical Practitioner Regulations applies;

(f) persons whom he has accepted as temporary residents;

(g) in respect of services under paragraph 8 [ie cervical smears and vaccinations and immunisations], persons to whom he has agreed to provide those services;

(h) persons to whom he may be requested to give treatment which is immediately required owing to an accident or other emergency at any place in his practice area, provided that—

(i) he is not, at time of the request, relieved of liability to give treatment under paragraph 5 [ie is elderly or informed], and

(ii) he is not, at the time of the request, relieved, under paragraph 19(2), of his obligation to give treatment personally [ie by reason of having engaged a deputy], and

(iii) he is available to provide such treatment,

and any persons by whom he is requested, and agrees, to give treatment which is immediately required owing to an accident or other emergency at any place in the locality of any [HA] in whose medical list he is included, provided there is no doctor who, at the time of the request, is under an obligation otherwise than under this head to give treatment to that person, or there is such a doctor but, after being requested to attend, he is unable to attend and give treatment immediately required (or if, in the case of a pilot doctor, more than one such doctor is under an obligation to give treatment, no such doctor practising from the premises to which the request was made is able to attend and give treatment);

(i) persons in relation to whom he is acting as deputy for another doctor under these terms of service;

(j) during the period of an appointment under regulation 25, persons whom he has been appointed to treat temporarily;

(k) in respect of child health surveillance services, contraceptive services, maternity medical services, or minor surgery services persons for whom he has undertaken to provide such services …;

(l) during the hours arranged with the [HA], any person whose own doctor has been relieved of responsibility during those hours under paragraph 18(2) and for whom he has accepted responsibility …; and

(m) any person for whom he has accepted responsibility under an arrangement made under paragraph 18A(2) [ie to provide 'out of hours' services].

(2) Except in a case to which head (h), (i) or (j) of sub-paragraph (1) applies, no person shall be a patient for the purposes of that sub-paragraph if the doctor has been notified by the [HA] that he is no longer responsible for the treatment of that person.

(3) Where a person applies to a doctor for treatment and claims to be on that doctor's list, but fails to produce his medical card on request and the doctor has reasonable doubts about that person's claim, the doctor shall give any necessary treatment and shall be entitled to demand and accept a fee accordingly under paragraph 38(f), subject to the provision for repayment contained in paragraph 39.

(4) Where a doctor—

(a) refuses to accept for inclusion in his list a person who lives in his practice area and who is not included in the list of another doctor practising in that area; or

(b) refuses to accept as a temporary resident a person to whom regulation 7 of the Choice of Medical Practitioner Regulations (temporary residents) applies; or

(c) has requested the removal with immediate effect of a person from his list in accordance with paragraph 9A,

he shall on request give that person any immediately necessary treatment until the expiry of the period of 14 days beginning with the date when that person was refused acceptance (or, as the case may be, with the date when he requested the immediate removal of that person from his list), or until that person has been accepted by or assigned to another doctor, whichever occurs first.

(5) Where the [HA] has notified a doctor that it is applying for the Secretary of State's consent under regulation 4(4) of the Choice of Medical Practitioner Regulations, the doctor shall give the person proposed for assignment any immediately necessary treatment until the [HA] has notified him that—

(a) the Secretary of State has determined whether or not the person is to be assigned to that doctor; and

(b) either the person has been accepted by, or assigned to, another doctor or another doctor has been notified that an application has been made, in a case to which regulation 4(4) of the Choice of Medical Practitioner Regulations applies, to assign that person to him.

As we have seen, and is plain from para 4 of the Terms of Service, the existence of a GP-patient relationship is normally characterised by the twin features of 'request' by the individual and 'undertaking' or 'acceptance' by the doctor. Exceptionally, a patient may be assigned to a GP, ie the GP will have no option but to undertake to provide personal medical services to the individuals. Regulation 4 of the NHS (Choice of Medical Practitioner) Regulations 1998, states:

4.—(1) Where—
    (a) a person whose name is not included in a doctor's list has been refused acceptance by a doctor for inclusion in his doctor's list;
    (b) a person whose name is included in a doctor's list, but who wishes to change doctor, has been refused acceptance by a doctor for inclusion in his doctor's list; or
    (c) a person has applied to a doctor under regulation 7(1) to be accepted by him as a temporary resident and that application has been refused,
he may apply in writing to the Health Authority for assignment to a doctor.
    (2) On receipt of an application for assignment to a doctor, the Health Authority shall—
    (a) subject to paragraph (4), assign the applicant to any doctor with whom the Health Authority has made arrangements for the provision of general medical services, and notify the doctor and the applicant accordingly; or
    (b) require a pilot scheme provider to assign the applicant in accordance with regulation 5 to a doctor who performs personal medical services in connection with a pilot scheme to which the pilot scheme provider is a party.
    (3) In deciding on the doctor to whom a person should be assigned or, as the case may be, the pilot scheme provider who should be required to make such an assignment, the Health Authority shall have regard to—
    (a) the respective distances between the person's residence and the practice premises of the doctors in the part of the Health Authority's area in question;
    (b) whether during the period of six months ending on the date on which the application for assignment is received by the Health Authority the person's name has been removed from the doctor's list or any doctor in that part of the area at the request of that doctor or, as the case may be, a pilot scheme provider;
    (bb) whether the person has been removed from the doctor's list of any doctor in that part of the area at the request of that doctor or, as the case may be, a pilot scheme provider because-
    (i) he has committed an act of violence against the doctor or has behaved in such a way that the doctor has feared for his safety, and
    (ii) the doctor has reported the incident to the police,
    and, if so, which doctor or, as the case may be, which pilot scheme provider, has the most appropriate facilities to deal with such a patient; and
    (c) such other matters as the Health Authority considers to be relevant ...
    (6) A doctor to whom a person is assigned under this regulation or regulation 5 shall not be required to provide child health surveillance services, contraceptive services, maternity medical services or minor surgery services for that person, unless—
    (a) he has accepted him for the provision of such services under the GMS Regulations; or
    (b) he is obliged to provide those services to him in connection with a pilot scheme.

(See also reg 5, in respect of assignment of patient by a 'pilot scheme' provider.)

Regulation 4 (and its predecessor) is the basis for saying that every individual has a right to a GP. However, there is an exception provided for in the regulations where a GP may be exempt from having patients assigned to him. Regulation 4(8) and (9) provides:

4 (8) The Health Authority may exempt from the liability to have persons assigned to him under this regulation any doctor who provides general medical services and who applies to the Health Authority for that purpose.
    (9) In considering an application under paragraph (8) the Health Authority shall have regard to—
    (a) the doctor's age and state of health;

(b) the number of persons whose names are included in his doctor's list; and

(c) where the application relates only to a specified person whose name has previously been removed from his doctor's list, the circumstances of that removal,

and the Health Authority shall notify any such doctor in writing of any decision under this paragraph.

Equally, a GP to whom a patient is assigned has a right to make representations (including an oral hearing) within seven days to the HA seeking to have the decision to assign the patient overturned (1998 regulations, reg 6). The GP remains responsible for the treatment of the assigned individual pending the HA's deliberations (reg 6(1)).

Likewise, under para 4(4), a doctor must provide 'immediate necessary treatment' for up to 14 days (or until assigned to another doctor), even if he refuses to accept the individual as a patient, providing that the individual is not on another doctor's list in the locality.

Paragraph 4(1)(h) is an important provision dealing with accidents and emergencies. In general, the law does not impose an obligation upon a doctor to act as a 'good Samaritan', ie to act as a rescuer in an emergency (see *infra*, ch 4). However, there is an exception in the case of a GP.

Paragraph 4(1)(h) contemplates two types of situation: first, an emergency which arises in the GP's practice area; and secondly, an emergency outside this area but within the area covered by the HA on whose medical list he appears. As regards the latter, he has to agree to provide the emergency medical care once he has been requested to provide it. As regards the former, however, providing the three requirements in (i) to (iii) are satisfied, he has no choice but to render emergency care if requested.

Notice that the GP is only obliged to give treatment that is 'immediately required', ie the emergency care such as applying a tourniquet to stem the blood flow, pending the arrival of the emergency services. Also, this is one of the services for which he may charge when the emergency is a road traffic accident: the fixed fee is £21 (Road Traffic Act 1988, s 158 and 1992 regulations, Sch 2, para 38(d)). One curiosity lies in the wording for the two situations. The first obligation applies to persons '*to* whom he [is] requested to give treatment'. The second, by contrast applies to persons '*by* whom he is requested … to give treatment'. It seems rather strange that the former would apply where a bystander or other said 'doctor, please help', while the latter only applies when the victim of the accident or emergency said 'doctor, I need help'. Surely this difference could not have been intended and no doubt, despite a literal reading of para 4(1)(h), both situations would be covered by *any* request for emergency assistance.

II. Terminating the relationship

The formal relationship between a GP and a patient may be brought to an end when the GP withdraws his undertaking in the manner prescribed in paras 9–11 of the terms of service. Two situations are contemplated: the usual and where the patient is, or threatens to be, violent. As regards the former, paras 9 (patients), 10 (temporary residents) and 11 (maternity medical services) provide for notice to be given by the GP and the HA and his responsibilities will end eight days after it is received or earlier if the patient is accepted by or assigned to another GP.

9 (1) Subject to paragraph 9A, a doctor may have any person removed from his list and shall notify the [HA] in writing that he wishes to have a person removed from his list and, subject to sub-paragraph (2), the removal shall take effect—

(a) on the date on which the person is accepted by or assigned to another doctor, or is accepted for inclusion in a pooled list; or

(b) on the eighth day after the [HA] receives the notice,

whichever is the sooner.

(2) Where, at the date when the removal would take effect under sub-paragraph (1), the doctor is treating the person at intervals of less than 7 days, the doctor shall inform the [HA] in writing of the fact and the removal shall take effect—

(a) on the eighth day after the [HA] receives notification from the doctor that the person no longer needs such treatment; or

(b) on the date on which the person is accepted by or assigned to another.

10. Where a doctor informs the [HA] in writing that he wishes to terminate his responsibility for a temporary resident, his responsibility for that person shall cease in accordance with paragraph 9, as if the temporary resident were a person on his list.

11. (1) A doctor with whom an arrangement has been made for the provision of any or all of the maternity medical services mentioned in regulation 31(1) may agree with the woman concerned to terminate the arrangement, and in default of agreement the doctor may apply to the [HA] for permission to terminate the arrangement.

(2) On an application under paragraph (1), the [HA], after considering any representations made by either party and after consulting the Local Medical Committee, may terminate the arrangement.

(3) Where a doctor ceases to provide any or all of the maternity medical services mentioned in regulation 31(1), he shall inform any woman for whom he has arranged to provide such services that he is ceasing to provide them and that she may make a fresh arrangement to receive those services from another doctor.

Merely by complying with this procedure, a doctor may not necessarily cease to be responsible for the individual. First, until the individual is accepted by (or assigned to) another GP, the formal relationship may come into being once more under para 4(a) if the individual requests treatment which is 'immediately necessary'. Secondly, irrespective of the formal relationship, the doctor may continue to owe any individual who is currently receiving treatment a duty of care until such time as it is reasonable for that treatment to be taken over by another doctor; in other words, whatever the terms of service may say, the doctor may not abandon an individual whom he is treating.

In 1994, the GPs' terms of service were amended (National Health Service (General Medical Services) Amendment Regulations 1994 (SI 1994 No 633)), to deal specifically with 'violent patients'. It was felt that the procedure under para 9 was too slow. Paragraph 9A now provides:

9A(1) Where—

(a) a person on a doctor's list has committed an act of violence against the doctor or has behaved in such a way that the doctor has feared for his safety; and

(b) the doctor has reported the incident to the police,

the doctor may notify the [HA] that he wishes to have that person removed from his list with immediate effect.

(2) Notification under sub-paragraph (1) may be given by any means including telephone or fax, but if not given in writing shall subsequently be confirmed in writing within 7 days (and for this purpose a faxed notification is not a written one).

(3) The time at which the doctor notifies the [HA] shall be the time at which he makes the telephone call or sends or delivers the notification to the [HA].

(4) Where pursuant to this paragraph a doctor has notified the [HA] that he wishes to have a person's name removed from his list with immediate effect, he shall take all reasonable steps to inform the person concerned.

A doctor may give notice by 'any means including telephone or fax' but if not given in writing (including where given by fax) it must be confirmed in writing within seven days (reg 9A(2)). Hence, a patient who uses or threatens violence may be removed from the GP's list with almost immediate effect, at least in the time it takes to telephone or fax the [HA] (regs 9A(3) and 19(6B)). Both the HA must give notice of the removal to the patient (reg 19(6B)) and the doctor must 'take all reasonable steps to inform the person concerned' (reg 9A(4)). Clearly, this latter requirement would not require a doctor to personally inform a violent patient: a telephone call from a member of his staff or a promptly sent letter will suffice. However, the amendments retain the obligation of the GP to provide 'any immediately necessary treatment' for up to 14 days after the doctor has requested the patient's removal or until he has found another doctor (Sch 2, para 4(4)(c)).

The Health Authority has an obligation to 'take all reasonable steps to assign ... the persons to another doctor' by the end of the day the GP gives notification under para 9A (see NHS (Choice of Medical Practitioner) Regulations 1998, reg 4(7)). In doing so, the HA is required to take into account the patient's violent history (1998 regulations, reg 4 (3) (bb) as added by SI 1999, No 3179).

Of course, that GP may rely on para 9A if the patient renews his violent behaviour or simply requests under para 9 to have the patient removed.

The removal of patients by a GP from his list has raised a number of concerns in recent years. There have been reports of patients being removed for financial reasons, because they decline to accept a doctor's advice or because they make a complaint against the GP. In some cases, it has been reported that whole families have been removed from a GP's list. It is generally 'received wisdom' that GPs have an unfettered absolute right to do so under the 1992 regulations. This received wisdom has been called into question in a number of ways. First, the GMC no longer considers that a doctor (including a GP) may not be accountable for terminating the relationship. Since 1998, the GMC's guidance, *Good Medical Practice* (July 1998) has contained the following:

> 21. ... Rarely, there may be circumstances in which you find it necessary to end a professional relationship with a patient. You must be satisfied your decision is fair and does not contravene the guidance in paragraph 13; you must be prepared to justify your decision if called on to do so. In such cases you should usually tell the patient why you have made this decision. You must also take steps to ensure that arrangements are made quickly for the continuing care of the patient. You should hand over records or other information to the patient's new doctor as soon as possible.

Paragraph 13 states:

> 13. The investigations or treatment you provide or arrange must be based on your clinical judgment of the patient's needs and the likely effectiveness of the treatment. You must not allow your views about a patient's lifestyle, culture, beliefs, race, colour, gender, sexuality, age, social status, or perceived economic worth to prejudice the treatment you provide or arrange.

The Health Service Commissioner has addressed the issue in his Annual Report for 1997–98, HC (1997–98) 811 and this was subsequently considered by the House of Commons Select Committee on Public Administration, HC (1998–99) 54.

> 32. ... Under their statutory terms of service, GPs may at any time request the health authority (or board in Scotland) to remove a patient from their list. They are not required to give a reason (The NHS (General Medical Services) Regulations 1992). The British Medical Association believed that there had been an unnecessary raising of anxiety about this. Dr Mac Armstrong, its Secretary, said he did not recognise "the picture that is painted by some who have given this kind of evidence" of "a sense of fear pervading the population that were they to voice their complaints they would immediately find themselves cast out in the street". Unfortunately there are no available figures to show how frequently patients are "cast out in the street". According to the latest published statistics the number of patients transferred at the request of the GP rose from 70,394 in 1993–94 to 82,879 in 1995–96. The vast majority of these transfers are because the patient has moved house, or for similar, administrative reasons. But information is not collected on exactly how many of these transfers occur as the result of a breakdown in the relationship between the GP and the patient. The statistics do, however, separately identify 603 patients in 1993–94, and 986 in 1995–96, who were removed because of an act or threat of violence. Mr Mike Ruane, Chief Executive of Wigan and Bolton Health Authority, told us that "we get around 1,100 requests per annum from GPs. They arrive simply as a request for a list of people to be removed ... It is simply a list". Wigan and Bolton Health Authority was now trying to develop a database which would distinguish the different types of removal.
>
> 33. Both the BMA and the Royal College of General Practitioners have made attempts to identify the scale of the problem. Professor Scott Brown, Vice-Chairman of the RCGP, told

us that the College had funded research within his own faculty in Northern Ireland which had looked at removals over a 10-year period from 1987 to 1996. "Our evidence suggests", he told us, "that removals involve a very small number of patients on a repeat basis and that most of those removed have found other practices to take them on without difficulty". Often hard data, he suggested, does not support what appears in the press. According to the BMA such research as has been done, reveals that the number is very small. A study in Sheffield from 1991 to 1996 showed that an average of 2.4 patients per thousand were removed in each year. Yet there is enough anecdotal evidence given to us to suggest that patients are unfairly removed from GP lists more than just occasionally. Sir Alan Langlands accepted that there was a need for further research on the subject. He indicated, though, that he wanted to proceed in reasonable partnership with the professions, the health authorities and patient groups. **We welcome Sir Alan's commitment to further research on the reasons why doctors remove patients from their lists.**

34. The lack of information makes any effective monitoring of the removals by the health authority impossible. Sir Alan Langlands told us that he thought authorities should be seeking to keep an eye on them. "If there is an unusual pattern and the number is more than the average of three or four a year ...", he told us, "that should trigger some sort of response from the health authority and they should be looking at that, trying to understand the reasons why and trying to uncover whether there is a specific problem with a specific GP". **We agree that health authorities should be doing more to review removals from GP's lists, and recommend that they make inquiries whenever the number of patients removed rises above four a year. Even so, given the statutory terms of service enjoyed by GPs, they may be unable to do very much about it.**

35. There is plenty of evidence, in the cases which have been investigated, to show that some GPs take insufficient care when considering whether to remove a patient from their list. "Some GPs appear to act precipitately to remove a patient from their list", the Ombudsman reported, "rather than taking time to consult colleagues, reflect on alternative courses of action, or discuss the problem with the patient". "They too readily regard the fact", he found, "that a complaint has been made as sufficient evidence that the doctor-patient relationship has broken down, rather than considering the patient's concern and trying to meet it or explain why it is unfounded".

...

37. We accept that doctors do not, in general, act as precipitately in removing their patients as those in some of the cases seen by the Ombudsman. Nor do they remove patients from their lists willingly. Dr Pauline Molony of the Patients Association said that "it goes against the grain" to remove a patient. "You lose a lot of goodwill, not just with the patient but with the patient's family, friends and extended family". But sometimes removal is unavoidable. Dr Molony of the Patients Association told us about the pressure that just ordinarily demanding patients can place on a GP. With violent patients, doctors may themselves be at risk of injury. Professor Scott Brown told us how he had removed one patient (the only one in ten years) because of an act of violence. A recent poll of 100 GPs by the BMA found that forty one per cent had been assaulted in their surgeries or while on-call. In one Berkshire practice all staff are trained in security matters, panic buttons have been installed in every room, and closed-circuit television. Another Midlands GP confessed that his practice removes any patient who they feel may be a threat. One of the last ones they removed had just committed murder. Yet even when patients are difficult and potentially or actually violent, removal is not always much of a solution. When patients are removed from a GP's list they may be returned to it if there is no available alternative. Of the patients removed from a GP's list, SAHC told us, 14 per cent were found to have been removed on more than one occasion, some twice and in extreme cases, 13, 18 and even 23 times. Mr Ruane told us that "there is a small number of patients who, usually because of drug addiction and alcohol addition, personality disorders, are assigned at regular intervals because they are difficult for GPs and the GPs share these people around, so we [the health authority] carry that out". Such "difficult" patients will be a problem for any system, and there is no simple solution to the problems they raise.

38. Should GPs continue to have the right to remove patients from their lists, and should they be able to do so without giving reasons? In his Report the Ombudsman criticised the unwillingness of some GPs to provide an explanation for a patient's removal because "it is only courtesy to do so". Mr Ruane agreed that "there was, and still is to some extent, a culture deeply embedded in both general practitioners and health authority staff who deal with them that there is an absolute right not to give an explanation". The Royal College of General Practitioners issued in June 1997 detailed guidance to its members (printed as an Annex to this Report). It says that a patient who is exacting or highly dependent, or exhibits high levels of anxiety or "demand" about perceived serious symptoms should never be removed, and that complaining or failure to take advice do not normally justify removal. It stresses that the situation should be discussed with the patient before any further steps are taken; and it says that

the doctor should "consider writing to the patient informing him or her of the decision and the reason for removal from the list". Advice was issued by the General Medical Services Committee of the BMA in September 1996 making very similar points.

39. Is such guidance likely to be effective? We took evidence from one general practitioner (Dr Trivedi) who had removed three related households from his list, without explanation, following advice given to the complainant's daughter about breast feeding. The summary of the case given by the Ombudsman is printed below. Dr Trivedi admitted to us that in June 1997 he was still unfamiliar with a document issued by the General Medical Services Committee in September 1996, concerning removal of patients from GPs' lists. "If we had known it, we would have followed it strictly", he told us. Dr Trivedi's example shows how professional guidance can too easily be ignored. Time and time again we have heard evidence during our consideration of the Ombudsman's reports that even where guidance is given it is all too frequently not followed. In any case, one in four doctors do not belong to the BMA and are outside its sphere of influence.

Case No. E.673/97–98
Removal from General Practitioner's list of three households as a result of a complaint; failure by Health Authority to deal with complaint about removal from list.

Matters considered: GP's removal of patients was unreasonable; Health Authority mistaken in believing they could not deal with the complaint.

Complaint against: A GP in the Wigan and Bolton Health Authority area (Dr Trivedi); Wigan and Bolton Health Authority.

Summary of case: On 11 June 1997 Mrs X complained to her GP about advice given to her daughter. The practice attempted to contact the daughter; but she did not wish to speak to the GP concerned. On 13 June, the GP removed three households from his list – Mrs X's, her daughter's, and her son's. On 27 June Mrs X asked the Health Authority's convener to establish an independent review of her complaint. On 9 July the convener replied that he was unable to convene a panel to look at the removal of patients from a GP's list.

Findings: The Ombudsman found that the removal of the daughter from the GP's list was reasonable, but that the consequent removal of Mrs X and her son was not. The Ombudsman concluded that the conveners should have dealt with the complaint through the NHS complaints procedure.

Remedy: The GP apologised and agreed to consider the advice and guidance of his professional bodies about handling problems with patients. The Health Authority apologised and agreed that the convener would handle complaints according to the NHS complaints procedure.

---

40. The professional organisations argued vigorously against the imposition of GPs of any more legally enforceable requirements than apply at present. Dr Armstrong of the BMA said that it would not be acceptable if a reason had to be given in all circumstances. "For example, doctors may be harassed by patients and are in a unique position in relation to the intimacy of the relationship … Is one to insist that as a matter of public record a female doctor should have to write to the health authority stating that Mr X, a pillar of society, has been removed from the list because he persistently attends for an inappropriate consultation and insists on an internal examination?" Even if this correspondence did not come into the public domain, Professor Brown argued, "the practitioner is at risk in that because of personality or other matters the patient may wish to make it public. If he chooses to do so it is up to that patient, but if that bounces back at the general practitioner it will have ramifications for all other relationships including the family". We do not believe that by providing reasons to the health authority for the removal of a patient any of these consequences will flow. If a GP is following the BMA's best practice guidance they will already write to the patient to indicate the reasons for the removal, and therefore a patient, if he or she is so inclined, may already make public the fact that he or she has been removed from a doctor's list. The health authority is unlikely to make public the reasons given by doctors for removal of patients from their lists; and if there was any concern that the fact might become public then it should be possible for the information to be returned in such a way as to provide the authority with the information it requires without revealing unnecessary details about patients' conduct or condition. Dr Trivedi suggested that placing an obligation on a doctor to give reasons for the removal of patients from their lists would be unfair to doctors: "the patients can choose the doctor and leave as and when they

want. They do not have to give any reason why they are leaving; because he is awful or he is good or he is bad or I am moving". No doubt some patients would be only too pleased to give reasons for why they wish to be removed from their doctor's list, but we do not believe that there is any justification for saying that it is unfair to ask doctors, but not patients, to provide reasons. There is in many cases no real choice for a patient but to register with the GP in the area, and de-registration leaves him or her at a serious disadvantage. **We believe that GPs should only be permitted to remove patients from their lists as a last resort, and that their powers to do so should be qualified by amendments to GPs' statutory terms of service. These should ensure:**

— **that information be provided to health authority on the reasons for the removal of any patient not moving out of the area;**
— **that in the event of a breakdown of the doctor-patient relationship, GPs should not be able to remove other members of the patients' family, or other people connected with the patient, unless they are able to show that a similar breakdown has occurred with them as well;**
— **that the health authority agree to removal of any patient from a GP's list;**
— **that an account be provided to the patient of the reasons for the removal; and**
— **that there should be a right of appeal to the health authority or an independent panel by any patient believing himself to have been wrongly removed.**

GPs should be prepared to justify the inconvenience and stigmatisation caused by removal, and health authorities should be prepared to provide better channels of communication between GPs and patients and institute clear and sensible removal mechanisms where conciliation has failed.

You will notice that the Select Committee accepts that legally a GP may remove a patient for any, or no, reason and was not required to provide any explanation to the patient. The criticism of this position led the Committee, in para 40, to propose changes imposing more control over a GP's ability to remove a patient and to prevent removal of family members merely because of their association with a patient whom the GP principally wishes to remove. The Committee also recommended that the GP should be required to give reasons. In its more recent report, the House of Commons Health Committee supported these recommendations (see Report *Procedures Relating to Adverse Clinical Incidents and Outcomes in Medical Care* HC (1998–99) 549-I, para 105).

The Government has accepted that:

New safeguards must be brought in to ensure that patients cannot be penalised for making a legitimate complaint drawing attention to poor practice.

(*Supporting Doctors, Protecting Patients* (Nov 1999), para 2.50.)

Perhaps the crucial question for us is whether the 'received wisdom' represents the law. There are a number of reasons why it may not. The argument would go like this. First, a GP in seeking to remove a patient from his list under para 9 of Sch 2 to the 1992 Regulations is exercising a public law function under the regulations. There seems little doubt about this. What else could be the basis of his action and no action is required of the Health Authority; the removal takes effect by the effluxion of time. Secondly, in doing so, the GP is exercising a discretion which is amenable to judicial review. Thirdly, no such discretion is unfettered and is amenable to challenge on the grounds of illegality, procedural impropriety and irrationality. To this list will have to be added, infringement of a Convention right under the Human Rights Act 1998: we return to this shortly. Fourthly, therefore, attention must turn to the GP's reasons, and the procedure, for removing the patient. Some reasons will be legitimate, others will not be. Alternatively, a decision to invoke para 9 might be irrational in some instances. Removing a patient for exercising their right to complain under the NHS complaints procedure or not to comply with medical advice seems, on the fact of it, to rely upon illegitimate reasons. How can a reliance by a patient upon his rights be sufficient, in itself, to justify removal? The action would, it is suggested, be correctly characterised as irrational (and thus improper) by a court. Such a conclusion can only be supported when the patient's rights under the European Convention are considered, in particular, art 8 – the right to respect for 'private life'. The legitimacy of the aim would find no basis in art 8(2). Likewise, the removal of a patient who is 'costly' or more demanding than other patients seems out of step with a publicly funded National Health Service. Can it really be rationale to remove a patient because they are 'expensive' for a particular GP to treat? If the patient is entitled to the treatment from a GP, it could only be a self-serving motive that would explain the GP's action and thus, by definition, the removal would be illegal. Similarly, removal of a patient's family – even if the patient's removal is reasonable – could only be rational if the circumstances of those family members justified removal rather than merely because they were the patient's family. This is not to say, of course, that a GP may never remove a patient. Clearly, there will be cases where the patient's behaviour, conduct or even attitude, makes a decision to remove them reasonable and lawful. In its guidance in June 1997 (referred to in the Select Committee's Report), the Royal College of General Practitioners offered some guidance on the grounds which could, or could not, justify removal of a patient.

Removal of Patients From GP's List, Royal College of General Practitioners (June 1997)

(A) Guidance on when it is reasonable to remove a patient from a GP's list
The relationship between a doctor and patient should be a therapeutic and beneficial one. However there are a few circumstances where it would normally be considered reasonable to remove a patient although even in these circumstances a GP may decide to retain the patient.

Situations which justify removal
Violence
Where a patient:–
• is physically violent towards a doctor, practice staff or other patients on the practice premises.
• causes physical damage to practice premises or other patient's property.
• gives verbal abuse or makes threats towards the doctor, practice staff or other patients.
• gives racist abuse, orally or physically.
• is violent or uses or condones threatening behaviour to a doctor (or some other member of the primary health care team) who is visiting the patient's home. Such behaviour may involve the patient, a relative, a household member, or pets (such as unchained dogs).

Crime & Deception
Where a patient:–
• fraudulently obtains drugs for non-medical reasons.
• deliberately lies to the doctor or other member of the primary health care team (eg by giving a false name or false medical history) in order to obtain a service or benefit by deception.
• attempts to use the doctor to conceal or aid any criminal activity.
• steals from practice premises.

Distance
• Where a patient has moved out of the designated practice area and has failed to register with another GP.

(B) Guidance on when it is not reasonable to remove patients from a GP's list
Given the current guidelines from the General Medical Council there are a few circumstances where removing a patient is inappropriate.

Situations which never justify removal
• Where there is an exacting or highly dependent patient, condition or disability.
• Where a patient exhibits high levels of anxiety or "demand" about perceived serious symptoms.
• Where preference is displayed by a patient in relation to age, gender, ethnic origin, religion or sexual orientation.
There are a number of other circumstances where it may not be considered reasonable to remove a patient from a GP's list.

Situations which do not normally justify removal

A patient's decision on clinical matters

Where a patient:–
* chooses a home confinement.
* refuses to undertake cervical cytology screening.
* declines immunisation of children.
* does not comply with therapeutic or other health advice.

Critical questioning and/or complaints

Where a patient:–
* persistently questions practice standards or safety (eg sterilisation of instruments, clinical techniques or other practice matters).
* complains via the In-House complaints system.

A final point is that, in any event, given the consequences of the decision to remove for a patient, a court might well require a doctor on the basis of procedural fairness to provide reasons, at least to explain in broad terms why the patient was being removed. The judicial trend is to encourage increased openness in Government and public administration (see *Stefan v The GMC* [1999] Lloyd's Rep Med 90 at 95–96, per Lord Clyde).

2.   Hospital, community health and other services (Part I)

(a) Duty to provide

The main statutory provisions are in the National Health Service Act 1977 (as amended). Sections 1–5 impose a statutory duty upon the Secretary of State for Health to provide, in essence, a National Health Service (apart from primary care services).

National Health Service Act 1977

1(1) It is the Secretary of State's duty to continue the promotion in England and Wales of a comprehensive health service designed to secure improvement—
  (a) in the physical and mental health of the people of those countries, and
  (b) in the prevention, diagnosis and treatment of illness,
  and for that purpose to provide or secure the effective provision of services in accordance with this Act.
  (2) The services so provided shall be free of charge except in so far as the making and recovery of charges is expressly provided for by or under any enactment, whenever passed.
2 Without prejudice to the Secretary of State's powers apart from this section, he has power—
  (a) to provide such services as he considers appropriate for the purpose of discharging any duty imposed on him by this Act; and
  (b) to do any other thing whatsoever which is calculated to facilitate, or is conducive or incidental to, the discharge of such a duty.
  This section is subject to section 3(3) below.
3(1) It is the Secretary of State's duty to provide throughout England and Wales, to such extent as he considers necessary to meet all reasonable requirements—
  (a) hospital accommodation;
  (b) other accommodation for the purpose of any service provided under this Act;
  (c) medical, dental, nursing and ambulance services;
  (d) such other facilities for the care of expectant and nursing mothers and young children as he considers are appropriate as part of the health service;
  (e) such facilities for the prevention of illness, the care of persons suffering from illness and the after-care of persons who have suffered from illness as he considers are appropriate as part of the health service;
  (f) such other services as are required for the diagnosis and treatment of illness.
  (2) …
  (3) Nothing in section 2 above or in this section affects the provisions of Part II of this Act (which relates to arrangements with practitioners for the provision of medical, dental, ophthalmic and pharmaceutical services).
4 The duty imposed on the Secretary of State by section 1 above to provide services for the purposes of the health service includes a duty to provide and maintain establishments (in this Act referred to as "special hospitals") for persons subject to detention under the Mental Health

Act 1983 who in his opinion require treatment under conditions of special security on account of their dangerous, violent or criminal propensities.

5(1) It is the Secretary of State's duty—

(a) to provide for the medical ... inspection at appropriate intervals of pupils in attendance at schools maintained by local education authorities or at grant-maintained schools and for the medical ... treatment of such pupils ...;

(b) to arrange, to such extent as he considers necessary to meet all reasonable requirements in England and Wales, for the giving of advice on contraception, the medical examination of persons seeking advice on contraception, the treatment of such persons and the supply of contraceptive substances and appliances.

(1A) It is also the Secretary of State's duty to provide, to such extent as he considers necessary to meet all reasonable requirements—

(a) for the dental inspection of pupils in attendance at schools maintained by local education authorities or at grant-maintained schools;

(b) for the dental treatment of such pupils; and

(c) for the education of such pupils in dental health.

(1B) ...

(2) The Secretary of State may—

(a) provide invalid carriages for persons appearing to him to be suffering from severe physical defect or disability and, at the request of such a person, may provide for him a vehicle other than an invalid carriage (and the additional provisions set out in Schedule 2 to this Act have effect in relation to this paragraph);

(b) arrange to provide accommodation and treatment outside Great Britain for persons suffering from respiratory tuberculosis;

(c) provide a microbiologies service, which may include the provision of laboratories, for the control of the spread of infectious diseases and carry on such other activities as in his opinion can conveniently be carried on in conjunction with that service;

(d) conduct, or assist by grants or otherwise (without prejudice to the general powers and duties conferred on him under the Ministry of Health Act 1919) any person to conduct research into any matters relating to the causation, prevention, diagnosis or treatment of illness, and into any such other matters connected with any service provided under this Act as he considers appropriate.

(2A) Charges may be made for services or materials supplied by virtue of paragraph (c) of subsection (2) above; and the powers conferred by that paragraph may be exercised both for the purposes of the health service and for other purposes.

(2B) ...

(3) ...

(4) The Public Health Laboratory Service Board continues in being for the purpose of exercising such functions with respect to the powers conferred by paragraph (c) of subsection (2) above as the Secretary of State may determine.

(5) The Board shall continue to be constituted in accordance with Part I of Schedule 3 to this Act, and the additional provisions set out in Part II of that Schedule have effect in relation to the Board.

In fact, as we have seen, the majority of the Secretary of State's functions are delegated to Health Authorities created under s 8 by virtue of the National Health Service (Functions of Health Authorities and Administrative Arrangements) Regulations 1996 (SI 1996 No 708) (as amended) or to Special Health Authorities created under s 11. Examples of the latter include the National Blood Authority established to manufacture blood products (see the National Blood Authority (Establishment and Constitutions) Order 1993 (SI 1993 No 585) and the National Blood Authority Regulation 1993 (SI 1993 No 586) and the United Kingdom Transplant Support Service Authority responsible for maintaining a service for the collection and supply of human organs for transplantation (see the United Kingdom Transplant Support Service Authority (Establishment and Constitution) Order 1991 (SI 1991 No 407) and the United Kingdom Transplant Support Service Authority Regulations 1991 (SI 1991 No 408)).

The Department of Health in its *Explanatory Notes to the Health Act 1999* (*op cit*) helpfully explains the structure:

25. The system provided for under Part I of the 1977 Act is the system under which all of the NHS, apart from family health services, is provided. The core duty to ensure the provision of a

health service is laid upon the Secretary of State (section 1) in extremely broad terms, and is supplemented by the provision of the subsequent sections.

26. Section 2 confers wide-ranging powers for the Secretary of State to provide such services as are appropriate to, and to do any other thing whatsoever which is calculated to facilitate, or is conducive or incidental to, the discharge of any duty imposed on him by the Act. Section 3 sets out those general services which it is the Secretary of State's duty to provide to such extent as he considers necessary to meet all reasonable requirements. Most of the services that may be described as hospital and community health services are included under this section. Section 4 imposes a specific duty on the Secretary of State to provide special hospitals for persons detained under the Mental Health Act 1983 who have dangerous, violent or criminal propensities. The services provided under this section are often referred to as "high security psychiatric services" and are presently managed outside the normal hospital system by Special Health Authorities established under section 11 of the 1977 Act. Further miscellaneous powers and duties are imposed on the Secretary of State by section 5.

27. Part I of the 1977 Act (as amended by the 1995 Act) goes on to provide for the setting up of statutory bodies known as Health Authorities (section 8) and Special Health Authorities (section 11). Health Authorities are established to act for the area set out in their establishment order and together cover all of England and Wales. Special Health Authorities are established for specific functional purposes which the Secretary of State directs them to perform on his behalf (e.g. the National Blood Authority).

28. Although the main functions under Part I of the 1977 Act are conferred on the Secretary of State, the Act provides a mechanism which enables the Secretary of State to devolve to Health Authorities the responsibility for performing these functions, whilst retaining the ability to control how those functions are performed. The Secretary of State may direct a Health Authority or Special Health Authority to exercise his functions on his behalf (section 13). He may also give directions about the exercise of functions by a Health Authority or Special Health Authority (section 17). The Secretary of State has exercised his powers under these sections on many occasions but the principal instrument is the National Health Service (Functions of Health Authorities and Administration Arrangements) Regulations 1996 (S.I. 1996/708). Schedule 1 to those Regulations lists those "specified health service functions" of the Secretary of State that he has delegated to Health Authorities. The Secretary of State has directed Health Authorities to exercise most of his functions under Part I, in particular sections 2, 3, and 5. It is these Regulations by which Health Authorities have their functions in respect of Part I services conferred upon them. There is very little further prescription in primary legislation as to what the Secretary of State must do or how he must do it in relation to the provision of Part I services.

29. Health Authorities and Special Health Authorities are funded under the provisions of section 97 of the 1977 Act, as substituted by paragraph 47 of Schedule 1 to the 1995 Act and amended by section 36 of the Primary Care Act. Health Authorities are paid money in each year under section 97(1) and section 97(3). Section 97(1) concerns the remuneration of persons providing Part II services and is dealt with below. Section 97(3) concerns Part I expenditure and administrative costs. Under section 97(3) a Health Authority is paid money not exceeding the amount allotted to it by the Secretary of State. This amount is allotted towards meeting its "main expenditure" which includes all expenditure attributable to the performance of its Part I functions, all its administrative costs, and certain other expenditure. The money paid in respect of Part I services is therefore cash-limited. To enforce the cash-limits set by the Secretary of State, Health Authorities have various financial duties imposed upon them by section 97A of the 1977 Act (as substituted by paragraph 48 of Schedule 1 to the 1995 Act and amended by paragraph 23 of Schedule 2 to the Primary Care Act).

You will notice here the powers of the Secretary of State to issue directions to health Authorities. Section 16D (inserted by the Health Act 1999, s 12) allows him to direct a Health Authority or Special Health Authority to exercise any functions specified in the direction. The power is very broad indeed provided the function relates to 'the health service'. The direction must be in writing and in some instances by Regulation (see s 18 inserted by the Health Act 1999, s 12). For example, Health Authorities have been directed to establish and operate complaints procedures for GPs (eg the National Health Service (Functions of Health Authorities) (Complaints) Regulations 1996 (SI 1996 No 669)). In addition, the Secretary of State has broad powers to direct Health Authorities, Special Health Authorities and other health service bodies in relation to the exercise of their functions (s 17, inserted by the Health Act 1999, s 12) (see *infra*). Until 1990, those functions which Health Authorities were delegated also entailed a duty to provide services accordingly. However, the National Health Service and Community Care Act 1990 introduced a division between 'purchasing' and 'providing' services under Pt I of the 1977 Act. As a result, NHS Trusts became the main *providers* of services under Pt I with Health Authorities (and GP fundholders) 'purchasing' these services under 'NHS Contracts' (see *infra*). For a time, some Health Authorities retained hospitals as 'directly' managed units but all are now NHS Trusts. As we shall see, the 'commissioning' function (as it is now known) has been taken over by 'primary care groups' ('local health groups' in Wales), which are constituted as committees of the relevant Health Authority and will, in the future, become one of the functions of Primary Care Trusts (PCTs) created under ss 16A–B of and Sch 5A to the National Health Service Act 1977 (as inserted by the Health Act 1999, s 2). Health Authorities may delegate to PCTs such of their functions (subject to some exceptions) as they wish or are required to by the Secretary of State (National Health Service Act 1977, s 17A as inserted by the Health Act 1999, s 12 and see The Primary Care Trusts (Functions) (England) Regulations 2000 (SI 2000 No 695)). It is intended that the responsibility for commissioning the majority of hospital and community health services will eventually be delegated to PCTs (see *Guidance Notes on Health Act 1999 (op cit)*, para 144).

Health Authorities will, thereafter, play an increasingly smaller role in 'commissioning' Pt I services. They will retain responsibility for 'commissioning' some specialist services. Their functions will, therefore, be more focused on strategic planning of healthcare provision at local level. In particular, s 28 of the Health Act 1999 requires Health Authorities to prepare a strategic health improvement plan after local consultation (see generally M Baker *Making Sense of the NHS White Papers* (2nd edn, 1999) pp 45–50 and Part 3). It states:

> 28.—(1) It is the duty of each Health Authority, at such times as the Secretary of State may direct, to prepare a plan which sets out a strategy for improving—
> (a)   the health of the people for whom they are responsible, and
> (b)   the provision of health care to such people.
>   (2) It is the duty of each Health Authority to keep under review any plan prepared by them under this section.

(b) Provision of Part I services

As we have seen, at one time Pt I services were provided directly by health authorities, including until their abolition in 1995 Regional Health Authorities. Since the 1990 Act, Pt I services have been provided by NHS Trusts created under the National Health Service and Community Care Act 1990. These bodies became the 'providers' of services within the 'internal market' of the NHS created by the 1990 Act. Health Authorities and GP fundholders were the 'purchasers' of Pt I services pursuant to 'NHS contracts'. 'Fund-holding' practices were groups of GPs recognised by the Secretary of State pursuant to a procedure under s 14 of the 1990 Act (see National Health Service (Fund-holding Practices) Regulations 1996 (SI 1996 No 706) (as amended)) and given funds ('the allotted sum') otherwise provided to the Health Authority to purchase Pt I services for the practice's patients. Their purchasing powers ranged from purchasing all services to a more limited range, depending upon whether they were a 'standard' or 'community' fund-holding practice (for a detailed discussion see C Newdick *Who Should We Treat?* (1995) pp 212–223). The essence of the system was that 'purchasers' acquired bargaining power in establishing terms for the provision of Pt I services by NHS Trusts (or other providers such as private clinics) who were in competition for the 'business'.

At the time of its inception, the internal market could be described as follows:

THE 'INTERNAL MARKET'

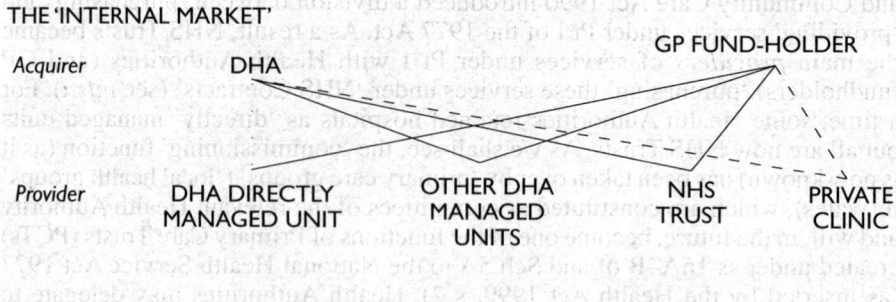

Acquirer   DHA   GP FUND-HOLDER

Provider   DHA DIRECTLY   OTHER DHA   NHS   PRIVATE
           MANAGED UNIT   MANAGED   TRUST   CLINIC
                                 UNITS

[———NHS contract; – – – contract; .... internal accounting procedure]

This diagram introduces two new entities as 'providers', although, in fact, one of them previously existed under a different name. A DHA directly managed unit is a hospital or other service previously provided by a DHA which since 1990 the DHA has continued itself to provide. It is, therefore, both 'acquirer' and 'provider' in these circumstances and financing is a matter of internal accounting within the DHA. The second entity is, however, decidedly novel and is known as the 'NHS Trust'. David Hughes explains the nature, and the place in the system of, the NHS Trust.

The operation of the 'internal market' and the nature of NHS Trusts is discussed by David Hughes in the following extract:

D Hughes 'The Reorganisation of the National Health Service: The Rhetoric and Reality of the Internal Market' (1991) 54 MLR 88

NHSTs represent the Government's attempt to create bodies which possess substantial devolved managerial authority yet remain within the NHS ...

NHSTs are established as bodies corporate having a separate legal status from health authorities and from their own managers and employees (s 5(5)). They will not have Crown immunity, nor will their property be regarded as Crown property (Sched 2, para 18). Each trust will be run by a Board of Directors, and will have certain freedoms not available to DHAs or directly-managed hospitals as well as specific powers and duties. According to DoH guidance, they will be able to acquire and dispose of assets, borrow, retain an operating surplus in normal circumstances, determine their own management structures, decide their own staffing structure and policy, and advertise their services. Although early discussion of 'self-governing hospitals' implied that most NHSTs would develop out of existing hospital units, section 5(1) of the Act provides that a trust may manage 'hospitals or other establishments or facilities', and thus opens up the possibility of a future growth of larger, more comprehensive, provider units. The capital charging scheme will apply to NHSTs as well as to other NHS bodies; however, the originating capital debt of a trust will be divided between an interest-bearing loan and public dividend capital (PDC). The latter carries no fixed repayment obligations but is expected in the long run to yield dividends to the Consolidated Fund at a rate at least equal to the interest that would have been paid. The possibility of deferring payment with respect to PDC for the foreseeable future has been seen by some critics as one of the major financial advantages of NHSTs over directly-managed units.

A NHST will have functions conferred by the Secretary of State under order. While the Act gives little indication of what may be involved, a NHST will have a statutory duty to carry out these functions 'effectively, efficiently and economically' (Sched 2, para 6). The powers vested with [sic] a NHST in furtherance of its functions are specified in more detail. A Trust will be able to enter NHS contracts, to commission research and provide training to charge private patients for accommodation and services, and to generate income under the terms of the Health and Medicines Act 1988 (Sched 2, paras 10, 11, 12, 14, 15). There are also general powers to acquire and dispose of land, to enter contracts with non-NHS bodies necessary or expedient for the discharge of the Trust's functions, to accept gifts and to determine terms of employment of staff (Sched 2, para 16). Additionally, the Health Secretary may confer other powers on Trusts by order made by statutory instrument (s 5(1)).

NHSTs have been among the most controversial of the reforms. Many critics believe that they pave the way for an eventual transfer of units to private ownership, and that the 'playing field' has been decisively tilted to give NHSTs significant financial advantages over directly-managed units. The issue of possible ballots of staff and local electors where a hospital proposed to transfer to NHST status, provided one of the major focal points of opposition in Parliament. Other commentators are concerned that an absence of regulation by health authorities combined with incentives to maximise surpluses may carry a risk of moral hazard, perhaps through encouraging premature discharges or providing misleading information on case-mix. There are also fears that competitive pressures may stimulate the over-provision of sophisticated medical technology along North American lines.

In terms of the intellectual coherence of the reform package, the most significant characteristic of the NHSTs may be the nomenclature that has been chosen. 'NHST' was substituted for the earlier term 'self-governing hospital', in part to open the way for a greater plurality of provider units, but also to combat the charge that such hospitals were 'opting out' of the NHS. Clearly, the major *symbolic* advantage of the term is the connotation of public benefit and the absence of the profit motive. But in what sense may NHSTs be regarded as trusts? Section 90 of the National Health Service Act 1977 provides for a health authority to accept, hold and administer any property on trust for all or any purpose relating to the health service. The 1990 Act enables the Secretary of State to appoint trustees for a NHST, with analogous powers to administer property on behalf of the NHST (s 11). However, this capacity to hold assets on trust hardly resolves the question of overall status. NHSTs are corporations established by statute and run by a Board of Directors appointed by the Health Secretary, which is a separate body from any trustees appointed. Could it be argued that the corporation itself functions as a trust for a beneficiary or beneficiaries?

The trust is a notoriously imprecise and diffuse concept. It is surrounded by a grey area in which, in the absence of any clear determination of status some, though not all of the provisions of trust law – such as a fiduciary duty – may be imposed. Where the specification of a NHST's powers and duties in the Statute leaves gaps, it might be that the title 'trust' would encourage the courts to seek analogies from trust law. However, it seems doubtful, in the case of the NHST, that close parallels will be found. First, although the 1990 Act provides for the transfer of assets to a NHST, it does not specify that these are to be held on trust and, in fact, the newly-established NHST is deemed to have an originating capital debt equal to the assets transferred (s 9). Second, a NHST has uncertain longevity: it may be dissolved if the Secretary of State 'considers it appropriate in the interests of the health service' and its assets transferred to the Secretary or another NHS body, to be used for unspecified purposes (Sched 2, paras 29–30). Third, if the NHST is to be regarded as a public trust, there may be difficulties in establishing charitable status. While it has been assumed that the general purposes of hospitals within the NHS are charitable, it seems unlikely that NHSTs will have this status. A trust is only a charity if it is exclusively for charitable purposes. For example, it must not distribute profits or dividends to individuals. This does not mean that charges cannot be made, but they must be applied for the purposes of the trust. It may be that a NHST's power to charge private patients would cause problems here; certainly, there is the theoretical possibility that an operating surplus might be transferred to the Consolidated Fund and thus removed from the 'trust' (Sched 3, para 6).

Even more importantly, there is the issue of the independence of the NHST. While one may argue that the statute is effectively a charter or deed for the trust, declaring its rights and prescribing its duties, there is nothing to stop these definitions being varied by order. The open-ended nature of the primary legislation means that the NHST is subject to a degree of direct Government control that no ordinary trust or corporation experiences. Thus the Health Secretary may give the NHST such functions as he may specify, and he may determine the membership of NHST boards and the form of proceedings (ss 5(5), 5(7)). NHSTs must achieve the financial objectives set by the Secretary with the consent of the Treasury (s 10(2)). They must comply with the Health Secretary's directions on such matters as officers' qualifications, their appointment and employment, the retention of assets, and (subject to certain caveats) with directions and circulars to health authorities (Sched 2, para 6(2)). With respect to the financing of NHSTs, the Secretary has significant powers to regulate the terms and upper limits of borrowing, and he may direct the transfer of monies judged to be surplus to requirements to the Consolidated Fund (Sched 3, para 1, 3, 6). Finally – as already noted – the Health Secretary may dissolve a NHST and transfer its assets to another body. Against the background of these considerable executive powers, the term 'trust' would seem to be a misnomer. Had the Act used the style 'NHS Corporation' the powers and duties of the body would be the same. Of course, the *symbolic* connotations, in terms of the wider policy debate, might be significantly different.

The arrangements which exist between 'acquirers' and 'providers' differ depending upon who are the parties to the arrangement. Where a 'provider' is outside the NHS, the arrangement will be a contract between a HA or 'fund-holder' and the private 'provider' and like any other commercial contract for the provision of services will be enforceable at law.

Today there are no 'directly managed units'. All former HA facilities are under the control of NHS Trusts and GP fundholders were abolished by s 1 of the Health Act 1999. Today, the 'internal market' would be more appropriately described as follows:

Commissioner   primary care group/Primary Care Trust (PCT)

Provider   NHS Trusts   PCT   Private Clinic

[– – – – contract; ——— NHS Contract]

The new arrangement is simpler. 'Primary Care Groups' ('local health groups' in Wales) have, since 1 April 1999, taken over the 'commissioning role' and are constituted as committees of the relevant Health Authority (see *Direction by the Secretary of State as to the Establishment of Primary Care Groups by Health Authorities* (15 October 1998)).

Sections 16A–B of and Sch 5A to the National Health Service Act 1977 (as inserted by s 2 of the Health Act 1999) allow for the creation of Primary Care Trusts. They are corporate bodies with their own budget for local health care. This allows existing 'primary care groups' to apply to the Secretary of State to become a PCT. PCTs will be able to perform such functions as are specified in their establishment orders (s 16A). PCTs will be able to provide both Pt I services and personal medical and dental services under the National Health Service (Primary Care) Act 1997 (on which see *infra*) (see s 16A(1)). Initially, however, their functions are likely to be limited to 'commissioning-only' Pt I services (level 3 PCT) rather than providing services directly (see *Explanatory Notes to Health Act 1999* (*op cit*) para 55). Although it is intended that they should be allowed to provide 'community health care' services (a level 4 PCT)(for the functions of PCTs see now, The Primary Care Trusts (Functions) (England) Regulations 2000 (SI 2000 No 695)). Each of these arrangements will amount to an 'NHS contract' as Health Authorities and PCTs are 'health service bodies' for the purposes of s 4 of the National Health Service and Community Care Act 1990 (s 4(2)(bb) inserted by Sch 4, para 76 to the Health Act 1999).

David Hughes (*supra*) describes the nature of 'NHS contracts' and identifies some problems which may arise.

Under the present Government, contract has emerged as a key concept in policies designed to establish the primacy of market forces in the provision of public services. The implementation of contractual relations in the NHS is a central plank of the reforms, but this is less straightforward than it seems. One of the most significant features of the 1990 Act is the creation of a new species of contract – here manifested in the form of the *NHS contract* – which may come to have increasing importance in those areas of public provision not amenable to privatisation.

The nature of the contracts to be employed in the re-organised service was one of the most difficult issues in the policy debate that preceded legislation. The outline description in the White Paper and Working Paper 2 has been considerably elaborated in further DoH guidance and discussion papers. Contracts will fall under three major headings. Those between DHAs and private sector providers will take a conventional legal form and be enforceable through the courts in the usual way. This involves very little change from the present situation, although it is expected that the number of such contracts will increase. DHAs and providers within the NHS will, however, stand in quite a different legal relationship, subject to different dispute-resolution mechanisms. The financial arrangements for DHA-managed hospitals will be structured as contracts, but will continue to be enforced through normal management processes. Here, contract seems to be essentially a metaphor, intended to signify a shift in the organisational culture rather than to have a direct practical effect. The 'contracts' to be placed between NHS bodies which have no direct management relationship do not, however, seem to fit either of these forms. These will cover arrangements such as those between a fund-holding GP and a hospital, or between a DHA and a NHST or a directly-managed hospital in another District. The latter, which are to be known as *NHS contracts*, imply a significant departure from the concept of contract in English law and are the subject of section 4 of the 1990 Act.

The classical mode on which English contract law is based defines the contract as a voluntary agreement through which parties make legally binding promises. Each is free to enter other transactions and there is an absence of constraints affecting the operation of ordinary market forces. But *NHS contracts* will fail to meet all these conditions and frequently will meet none of them. First, the introduction of *NHS contracts* will itself be the outcome of central regulation; the product of legislation rather than the market. Public bodies entering such contracts will do so because it is a statutory requirement rather than necessarily because of the inherent economic advantages. Second, the internal market is – on closer inspection – a poor marketplace. Given the inescapable need to provide a range of key services locally and the DoH requirement that the services bought by DHAs reflect general practitioners' existing referral patterns, district general hospitals are likely to continue to be the only realistic contractors for a wide range of services in their local areas. Initially, at least, real choice over contract placement is likely to occur only in those areas of elective surgery where some hospitals have waiting lists and others do not – a rather small proportion of total activity in the health field.

Third, and most significantly, NHS contracts will not be enforceable in the courts in the usual way. In the immediate aftermath of the White Paper the legal status of contracts between NHS bodies was uncertain, but the greater rigour of the Parliamentary drafting process has clearly exposed the inherent difficulties of the *NHS contract* as a legal concept. The 1990 Act defines the *NHS contract* as an 'arrangement under which one health service body (the 'acquirer') arranges for the provision to it by another health service body (the 'provider') of goods and services which it reasonably requires for the purposes of its functions' (s 4(1)). Critically the Act provides that: 'Whether or not an arrangement which constitutes an NHS contract would, apart from this subsection, be a contract in law, it shall not be regarded for any purpose as giving rise to contractual rights or liabilities, but if any dispute arises with respect to such an arrangement, either party may refer the matter to the Secretary of State for determination under the following provisions of this section' (s 4(3)).

As an alternative to litigation or negotiation in the shadow of litigation, the DoH intends to create a special regime of conciliation and arbitration. Use of the courts is ruled out because a system of imposed public sector contracts violates the basic assumptions of contract law, and gives rise to problems – notably the pre-contractual dispute – with which ordinary contract law does not deal. Where parties to a proposed *NHS contract* cannot agree terms, or where collusion, unfair practice or false information is alleged, they will be required to submit to mandatory conciliation by Regional Health Authorities, followed, if necessary, by binding arbitration by the Secretary of State or his appointee. Disputes over alleged breach of contract will also be subject to arbitration. Here the arbitrator will normally be appointed by the parties, but either party retains the right to refer the matter to the Secretary of State for determination. The option of third party enforcement, perhaps through an independent arbitration agency, attracted considerable support in the discussions that followed publication of the White Paper. In the event the Act gives the Health Secretary maximum discretion to deal with disputes that are referred to him: he 'may determine the matter himself or, if he considers it appropriate, appoint a person to consider and determine it in accordance with regulations' (s 4(5)).

These dispute-resolution arrangements are undergirded by a range of reserve powers which appear to go well beyond what a narrow arbitration rule would require. As indicated above, the Health Secretary is empowered to deal not only with disputes over alleged breach (s 4(3)), but also disputes arising out of negotiations regarding a proposed contract (s 4(4)). Since the Secretary may specify terms to be included in a proposed contract and direct that it is proceeded with (s 4(6)), he can effectively impose a contract. With regard to disputes over existing contracts, the Secretary may vary the terms of an arrangement or bring it to an end (s 4(7)). He has power to impose 'directions' (including directions regarding payments) needed to give effect to variation or termination, and these are to be treated as if they were the result of agreement between the parties themselves. This power, of course, significantly exceeds the powers of judges in contract cases. While it is relatively common for judges to imply terms or interpret terms so as to rectify ambiguity or omissions in contracts, the imposition of terms without reference to the original intentions of the parties amounts to a very significant shift from traditional law. It is but one of a very substantial range of powers placed with the Health Secretary by the Act.

Recent DoH guidance suggests that recourse to arbitration may be limited by building 'clear disincentives to non-performance' into the contract itself. Thus a provider which fails to carry out contractual obligations might be required to subcontract the work to another provider at its own expense; or contract prices might be reduced *pro rata* to reflect unsatisfactory performance. However, the use of penalty clauses in a public sector environment is not without difficulties. Monetary penalties simply involve transferring funds between different pockets of the public purse, and are largely ineffective in situations where local monopoly suppliers cannot be allowed to go bankrupt.

NHS contracts will be enforced primarily through an administrative process. They will amount to a system of imposed, public sector contracts which has no obvious precedent in English contract law, and bears little resemblance to the North American system on which it is said to be modelled. As I have argued elsewhere, there may be unexpected and closer parallels with contracts in the planned economies of Eastern Europe. Certainly, problems that have arisen with these contracts – the proliferation of pre-contract disputes, the need to shift the emphasis in remedy from monetary damages to specific performance, and the tendency to blur legal and administrative controls – are also likely to surface in the NHS.

Three points should be noticed. First, three types of 'NHS contract', have developed within the NHS.

Pauline Allen 'Contracts in the National Health Service Internal Market' (1995) 51 MLR 321

There are three types of 'contract' in use in the NHS: block, cost, and volume and cost per case. Block 'contracts' (in their pure form) state that unlimited services must be provided for a fixed sum. The risk is entirely on the provider. Cost and volume 'contracts' amount to a compromise position for each party because, when certain volumes of services are exceeded, further sums must be paid. Cost per case 'contracts' stipulate that the provider is remunerated at an agreed rate in respect of each case treated. The risk is borne by the purchaser. Block 'contracts' which specify an unlimited amount of a certain type of care in return for an annual fee are subject to opportunistic practices by providers to reduce their costs by lowering the quality of care. In order to avoid this occurring, a purchaser would have to incur large *ex post* transaction costs to monitor performance. Furthermore, providers will try to incorporate in their fees an element to protect themselves against the risk (to be borne entirely by them) of having to provide an unlimited amount of care for a fixed price. Risk premia tend to inflate 'contract' prices. Cost per case 'contracts,' on the other hand, stipulate that the provider is remunerated at an agreed rate in respect of each case treated. This can avoid risk premia, but the process of obtaining sufficient costing information (which is an example of *ex ante* transaction costs) is itself costly and time-consuming.

If these transaction costs exceed the costs of the hierarchical administrative system of the NHS which they replace, any advantage in respect of efficiency to be gained from the introduction of the internal market will be vitiated. Williamson's arguments concerning transaction costs and their relevance to the appropriateness of markets and hierarchies indicate that there are circumstances when the use of discretion (which can occur in a vertically integrated hierarchy where contracts are not present) can be more efficient than the use of a market, for which contracts are essential (Williamson, *'Markets and Hierarchies: Analysis and Anti-Trust Implications'* (New York, 1975).) Bartlett (Bartlett, *'Quasi-Markets and Contracts: A Markets and Hierarchies Perspective on NHS Reforms'* (1991) Public Money and Management 11(3), p 53) has argued that the circumstances of the NHS are such that, in accordance with Williamson's criteria, administrative discretion exercised through a vertically integrated hierarchy may be preferable to a market structure. Vincent-Jones (Vincent-Jones, *'The Limits of Contractual Order in Public Sector Transacting'* (1994) 14(3) Legal Studies 364) has also doubted the effectiveness of contractual processes which are part of a quasi-market organisation imposed inappropriately on a particular function or service.

It can be argued that, in the context of the delivery of public services, the contractual approach also creates a structural bias in favour of the delegation of decision-making authority to accountable and effective units. In this way the 'contract' can help the implementation of the 'key measure' of delegating responsibility to local levels. Local knowledge can be used to make explicit and clear choices about services in that area. It is argued in 'Working for

Patients' that such delegation will lead to the NHS being more responsive to the needs of patients. The structure of 'contracting' is not, in itself, automatically conducive to increasing choice for patients because it is the districts and fundholders who are the purchasers, not the patients themselves. However, the Department of Health is exhorting districts to take account of the views of local people (NHS Management Executive, *'Local Voices'* (London: HMSO, 1992), and it can be argued that fundholders are sufficiently close to their patients to be able to enhance their capacity for making choices.

As part of the reform to the 'internal market' it is the Government's intention to stabilise the 'commissioning' process such that agreements will be at least three years long. In addition, we should notice the use of 'extra-contractual' referrals (ECRs), which describe one-off contracts that arise where an individual's care is not covered by existing NHS contracts or where a Trust is reimbursed outside the existing contractual arrangements for services provided (see generally C Newdick *Who Should We Treat?* (*op cit*) pp 186–189). The process was bureaucratic and unsatisfactory. ECRs (technically only in the second sense) are abolished by the Health Act 1999 (Sch 4, para 83(6)). All treatments are now required to be covered by NHS contracts.

Secondly, you will notice the point made by David Hughes that 'NHS contracts' are by virtue of s 4(3) not to be regarded 'as giving rise to contractual rights or liabilities'. Instead, any dispute is to be resolved by a mechanism of conciliation and arbitration by the Secretary of State (s 4(3)). This process includes not only disputes over existing contracts but also in relation to negotiations over the formation of NHS contracts. The dispute resolution mechanism, therefore, goes further than the general law which only deals with the former. The procedure is set out in the National Health Service Contracts (Dispute Resolution) Regulations 1996 (SI 1996 No 623).

Allen (*supra*) discusses the issues of disputes over 'formation' of NHS contracts and their implementation.

(c) Formation of NHS 'contracts'
In the case of the NHS quasi-market, the making of 'contracts' has been imposed on the district by legislation. It is a prerequisite of a legally binding contract that each party entered into the agreement of its own free will. Harden (Harden, *'The Contracting State'* (Buckingham: OUP, 1992)) describes the right not to enter into a contract as an essential aspect of the rule of law because, otherwise, the weak would be exposed to the arbitrary and compulsory imposition of obligations by the strong, who would receive the backing of the state to enforce them. Although it is only the process of contracting which has been imposed on the institutions by the government, not the actual parties with whom agreements must be made, in fact, there may be little choice in many circumstances. It is for this reason that the powers to protect the 'weak' (discussed below) were conferred on the Secretary of State.

There is another way in which the formation of NHS 'contracts' differs significantly from that of the idea type contract. It is axiomatic in classical liberal thought that parties are free to make any bargain they choose. Subject to certain exceptions (notably to protect consumers), parties to contracts are left to come to an agreement which is the result of negotiation. In this way, according to the tenets of neoclassical economics, the wishes of suppliers and demanders are reflected in the contract made and (assuming the prerequisites for the efficient functioning of the market are in existence) the 'invisible hand' of the market will make the optimum allocation of the relevant goods and/or services.

The 1990 Act provides that if the two prospective parties to an NHS 'contract' cannot agree the terms of the 'contract' during their negotiations, because of any reason arising out of their relative bargaining positions, either such party can refer the matter to the Secretary of State for Health 'who may specify terms to be included in the proposed arrangement and may direct that it be proceeded with' (section 4(6)). The NHS Management Executive has issued guidance on resolving disputes (NHS Management Executive, *'NHS Contracts: Guidance on Resolving Disputes'*, EL (91) 11 (London: HMSO, 1991)) which directs potential parties to take their disputes to their regional health authority for informal conciliation before the formal procedure in the 1990 Act is invoked. The guidance also explains that an adjudicator appointed by the Secretary of State would regard an unequal bargaining position as existing if 'either a purchaser threatened to cease securing services, or a provider threatened to cease supplying them, if its terms were not agreed, in circumstances where no alternative practical provider or purchaser was available.' This pre-'contractual' intervention as to the actual terms of the agreement amounts to the imposition of a 'contract' on the parties and, as such, is unprecedented in the arena of legally enforceable contracts.

It is not clear, however, what direct effect the distinctive character of NHS 'contracts' has had and will have on the terms of the 'contracts' actually made or on the capacity of the internal market to deliver the objectives set for it.

The fact that 'contracting' is compulsory could mean that the parties are not as enthusiastic about the process as freely contracting parties would be. This might lead to negotiation and 'contract' drafting not being undertaken in the most effective manner by a workforce in which morale is low and in which the implications of such a large change in culture is not entirely understood or sympathised with. Moreover, existing personnel do not, as yet, possess the skills necessary for negotiating and drafting contracts and, as constraints on resources are great, it is doubtful whether they are in a position to hire these skills on the scale required.

As to the effect of the possibility of the imposition of a 'contract,' it could be that the threat of referral to the Secretary of State induces parties in strong bargaining positions to refrain from 'abusing' those positions and imposing disadvantageous terms on the other party. If this is the case, one could argue that this would have the effect of making the internal market work better than it would otherwise do, because inefficiencies due to any lack of real competition between providers are being vitiated by the fetter on the abuse of monopoly power provided in the 1990 Act.

There is no publicly available evidence that any pre-'contractual' disputes have been referred to the Secretary of State. It is clear, however, that regional health authorities have been acting as informal arbitrators in these circumstances. Many disputes arise out of a difference of opinion as to how fast changes in existing purchasing patterns or prices should be made. For example, one regional health authority issued guidance to all its purchasers that they must give providers one year's notice of any significant changes they wished to make to 'contracts' which were due to be renegotiated. Although this does not amount to the imposition of 'contractual' terms, it is another way in which the internal market is being managed by imposing rules as to the way in which negotiations should be conducted.

Powers of pre-'contractual' dispute resolution have also been used to ensure that contracts are signed at the correct time of year in circumstances where parties were failing to reach agreement in the time specified by the NHS Management Executive. In the case concerned, the disputes officer was of the view that the necessity of the regional health authority intervening was not so much due to real disagreements as to terms but to the inexperience of the parties to the contracting process. The intervention of the region in these circumstances is a way of compensating for the deficiencies in the skills needed for the proper functioning of a market. Presumably, such intervention will become less necessary as staff learn from each contracting round.

(d)   Resolution of contractual disputes

It is an essential attribute of an ordinary commercial contract that it is enforceable by the state at the behest of any of the contracting parties. However, the 1990 Act provides that an NHS 'contract' 'shall not be regarded for any purpose as giving rise to contractual rights or liabilities, but if any dispute arises with respect to such an arrangement, either party may refer the matter to the Secretary of State for determination' (section 4(3)). This is intended to ensure that the resolution of any dispute between the parties is kept out of the courts. The 1990 Act allows the determination of a reference to the Secretary of State to include 'such directions as the Secretary of State ... considers appropriate to resolve the matter in dispute' (section 4(7)). These powers are deemed explicitly to include the possibility of varying the terms of the 'contract' or terminating it (section 4(8)). The latitude given to the Secretary of State by the foregoing is considerably wider than the principles which govern the resolution of real contractual disputes by the courts. A court must interpret what agreement was made by the parties at the time the contract was entered into. It cannot impose on them some other terms.

Despite the wide powers given to the Secretary of State by the 1990 Act, the NHS Management Executive has issued guidelines stating that the principles to be applied in resolving disputes between parties to NHS 'contracts' should recognise the concept of freedom of contract. 'The presumption in determining a dispute is likely to be that the outcome will give effect to the agreement which was originally reached, rather than a new agreement which the parties should have reached.'

Disputes which are referred to the Secretary of State will be subject to the NHS Contracts (Dispute Resolution) Regulations (SI 1991/725 now SI 1996 No 623) in which it is stipulated that the adjudicator appointed by the Secretary of State must give reasons for his decision. Such decisions will be subject to judicial review and, if this were to occur, it would encourage a clear set of principles to emerge as to how such decisions are to be made.

There is no publicly available evidence that any disputes concerning the terms of concluded NHS 'contracts' have been referred to the Secretary of State. However, disputes have been referred to regional health authorities for informal arbitration. As such arbitration is probably not subject to judicial review and it is being encouraged in the place of referral to the Secretary of State, it is possible that no consistent principles concerning the exercise of the power to resolve disputes will emerge.

In summary, the regime governing the resolution of disputes arising out of NHS 'contracts' differs from that which pertains to legally enforceable contracts. It is not clear what principles will be applied when a dispute requires resolution. This makes the task of drafting the 'contracts' difficult because it is not known whether they will be interpreted as ordinary contracts (whether by the Secretary of State, regional health authorities or the court) or whether a wider view will be taken of the arbitrator's powers to alter the original terms. When contracts are subject to the ultimate jurisdiction of the courts, consistent principles of interpretation can develop which can enable those drafting the documents to do so with some certainty as to the implications of the provisions made.

Finally, two points arise out of s 4(3)). First, while NHS contracts are not contracts enforceable by the courts, the courts may, nevertheless, be called upon in certain circumstances to consider (or take account of) their terms. All the potential parties to an NHS contract are public bodies and, as a consequence, are amenable to judicial review if they exceed their statutory powers. As Hughes (*op cit*) points out:

> Since a trust's functions will be defined by the terms of the order by which it is established, any contract placed by it would need to be within the scope of the powers vested in the trust, or it might be subject to a public law action for judicial review seeking to show that the contract is *ultra vires*.

A similar argument could be made in relation to a HA, PCT or (formerly) a GP fundholder.

Another circumstance in which a court may be called upon to take account of the terms of an NHS contract would be in the context of an action in negligence against a 'provider' (or even, possibly, an 'acquirer') of services by an injured patient. A court might have to look to the terms of the NHS contract to determine the scope of any duty owed to the patient. This is a complex issue which we consider in Chapter 4 on medical negligence.

Secondly, the definition of an 'NHS Contract' in s 4(1) may give rise to difficulties. Joe Jacob raises to the points as follows.

J Jacob 'Lawyers Go to Hospital' [1990] PL 255

[S]ection 4(1) of the 1990 Act says that it is an arrangement under which an acquiring health service body arranges for the provision to it 'of goods or services which it reasonably requires for the purposes of its functions'. That is, an arrangement is not an *NHS contract* if the acquirer did not *reasonably* require the goods or services. If the goods or services were not reasonably required, the arrangement cannot be an *NHS contract* and the rest of the section making provision for such *contracts* does not apply. It is not difficult to imagine situations where goods or services may not be reasonably required but nevertheless their acquisition may not be *ultra vires* the corporation. Suppose an NHS body decided to acquire more goods than it reasonably needed for a particular year in order to dispose of a cash surplus (for example, to prevent it committing itself to recurrent expenditure or to guard against projected price rises or to be able to sell them out of a dominant market position). It is perhaps important that these last may be caught by European Community competition rules, and their application may itself depend on whether the arrangement was enforceable as a contract, that is, was not *reasonably required* so as to prevent it becoming an *NHS contract*.

If Jacob is correct, there is, however, a further point to notice. Arguably, the parties will not have an intention to create legal relations (and hence a legally enforceable contract) since they (erroneously) believed that they were creating an NHS contract. The arrangement, as a consequence, would not be subject to the dispute resolution procedure nor amenable to enforcement or interpretation by the courts. This does not seem to have been a situation anticipated by Parliament.

(For discussion of legal issues arising from 'NHS contracts' see: P Allen 'Contracts in the National Health Service Internal Market' (1995) 58 MLR 321; K Barker 'NHS Contracts, Restitution and the Internal Market' (1993) 56 MLR 832 and F Miller 'Competition Law and Anti-Competitive Behaviour Affecting Health Care' (1992) 55 MLR 453.)

3. Community care and NHS provision

We saw earlier the cleaving of social services care which was (and remains) the responsibility of local authorities from community health care and hospital services which became the responsibility of NHS providers. The statutory regime for the former is distinct from the NHS legislation and, like it, is complex (for a full discussion, see L Clements *Community Care and the Law* (1996)). It is important for us to gain an overview of 'social services' care for one significant reason – to determine the extent to which it overlaps, and whether it can legally do so, with NHS services. Jonathan Montgomery provides a useful summary of 'community care' provision.

Jonathon Montgomery *Health Care Law* (1997)

Under the NHS and Community Care Act 1990, local authorities are obliged to prepare and publish plans for community care services in their areas (s 46, see also Chronically Sick and Disabled Persons Act 1970, s 1). These services, sometimes known as social care, comprise a range of services provided by local authorities. (NHS and Community Care Act 1990, s 46(3)) They are the provision of accommodation for adults who cannot look after themselves; (National Assistance Act 1948, s 21) services for adults who are blind, deaf, dumb, or substantially and permanently handicapped by illness, injury, or congenital disability, including the adaptation of homes and provision of meals and special equipment (*ibid*, s 29); and services promoting the welfare of elderly people (Health Services and Public Health Act 1968, s 45) Community care also includes non-residential services for pregnant women and mothers, home help and laundry facilities for households caring for a person who is ill, handicapped, or pregnant. (NHS Act 1977, s 21, Sch 8) With the Secretary of State's approval, local authorities may also provide services for those who are ill, including after-care and preventive care (*ibid*). Finally, community care services cover after-care for those discharged from mental health services (Mental Health Act 1983, s 117).

Under section 47 of the 1990 Act, local authorities must assess the needs of anyone who appears to them possibly to be in need of community care services, and decide whether such services should be provided in the light of that assessment. There is no formal requirement to respond to a request for an assessment, save in respect of those who are blind, deaf, dumb, or substantially and permanently handicapped by illness, injury, or congenital disability. Those clients are entitled to be involved in the assessment process under the Disabled Persons (Services Consultation and Representation) Act 1986. They are also entitled to a written explanation of the assessment and the right to make representations about unsatisfactory aspects of the assessment.

Where a substantial amount of care is already being, or will be, provided (otherwise than for money) for the individual to be assessed special provisions apply. These require the abilities of carers to be taken into account. If the care is being given by someone who is neither employed to do so, nor working for a voluntary organization, then the carer may require a local authority to carry out an assessment of his or her ability to continue to provide the care before deciding what services should be provided.

The provisions of the 1990 Act confer on citizens a right to an assessment, but they do not guarantee them services. However, it may be difficult for local authorities to justify refusing people community care services when an assessment has identified that they are in need of them without acting irrationally. If a local authority does act unreasonably or irrationally, an action for judicial review may be available to challenge the decision. This may be easier if the reasons for an assessment have been revealed under the 1986 Act. Such actions are discussed below. The position of disabled clients, those who are blind, deaf, dumb, or substantially and permanently handicapped by illness, injury, or congenital disability, is stronger. Under section 2 of the Chronically Sick and Disabled Persons Act 1970, local authorities have a duty to provide services that are necessary to meet the client's needs.

One key difference between community care services provided by local authorities and those under the NHS is that the former are not free of charge. Local authorities may recover as much of the cost of providing or securing the services as it is reasonably practical for a client to pay. In the case of residential services, there is a fixed rate, with means testing for those who cannot afford to pay it. The transfer of responsibility for aspects of long-term care and community services from NHS responsibility to that of local authorities has therefore resulted in those services ceasing to meet one of the objectives for the NHS, that health care should be free at the point of delivery.

(For a discussion of the relevance of 'resources' in making assessments under community care legislation see: *R v Gloucestershire CC, ex p Barry* [1997] AC 584 (HL) – Chronically Sick and Disabled Persons Act 1970; *R v Sefton BC, ex p Help the Aged* (1997) 38 BMLR 135 (CA) – National Assistance Act 1948.)

It is this latter point that is vital for us and we shall return to it shortly. However, it is important that s 22 of the National Health Act 1977 (as amended by s 27 of the Health Act 1999) imposes a duty of co-operation between health authorities and other health bodies and local authorities in exercising their respective functions 'in order to secure and advance the health and welfare of the people of England and Wales' (s 22(1)). Thus, there is a statutory duty to work together in providing community care and health services. To this end, there are statutory provisions allowing for the transfer of funds between health bodies and local authorities (NHS Act 1977, ss 28A–28BB, inserted by the Health Act 1999, ss 29–30) and for the 'pooling of resources' (Health Act 1999, s 31). There is also now statutory power allowing flexible arrangements to be made between health bodies and local authorities for 'packaging' of social care and health care by one authority or provider (Health Act 1999, s 31).

The issue can remain, however, of who is responsible for the care of a particular individual whose care has elements of social and health care provision? As Montgomery points out, if provided by the NHS it will be free. If provided by social services departments charges may be made on a means-testing basis. This has been particularly problematic in relation to long-term residential care in nursing homes of the elderly, disabled or infirm. Their care will have 'social care' elements and health care elements such as nursing. Christopher Newdick sets the scene.

Christopher Newdick *Who Should We Treat? Law, Patients and Resources in the NHS* (1995)

The issue arose recently in the case of *White v Chief Adjudication Officer* (1994) (17 BMLR 68 which concerned the long-term care of a group of elderly patients suffering mental illness. They had been cared for in hospital for many years but, in the opinion of a psychiatrist engaged by the health authority, hospital treatment was no longer necessary and they could be placed in a nursing home setting. The question arose as to the right of the residents to income support, so that the dispute was effectively between the Department of Social Security and the Mid Downs District Health Authority as to who was responsible for the cost incurred in providing care and accommodation to the residents. The Court of Appeal reasoned as follows. The nursing home was to be regarded as a 'hospital' within the definition in the National Health Services Act 1977, because it was an 'institution for the reception and treatment of persons suffering from mental illness', namely 'mental disorder within the meaning of the Mental Health Act 1983' (see s 128). On that basis Ralph Gibson LJ said:

> I acknowledge that if the provision of nursing care by professionally trained nurses in an institution is minimal, as for example only rarely expected to be required, such an institution may not be a hospital. In this case, however, the fourteen applicants are mentally ill. They require appropriate nursing for and because of their illness. Forest Lodge [the nursing home] has, and has agreed to maintain, appropriate nurse staffing, including qualified mental nurses. Mr Day, who is in charge, is a mental nurse. All but one of the patients are on medication for their illness. Forest Lodge dispenses drugs on prescription. I would hold that Forest Lodge [is] a hospital (*White v Chief Adjudication Officer* (1994)17 BMLR 68, 80).

Thus, the residents were properly described as 'patients' suffering 'illness'. The nursing home provided care on behalf of the health authority, which was responsible for bearing the costs incurred. Does this decision provide a clear distinction for future cases? Age Concern says that the very use of the word 'illness' is being distorted because decisions to discharge elderly patients are not always based on medical considerations. Rather, the question of an individual's need for care may be determined on managerial and financial grounds. In the result, there are as yet no general rules or standards in use throughout the country. In some areas provision for the elderly may be good, in others it may be appalling, unless funded privately. At this vulnerable time of life, and with the increasing numbers of us who will become dependent, such a haphazard system of responsibility is unacceptable. 'There is an urgent need to clarify the responsibilities of the NHS in providing and/or purchasing continuing care for elderly people. The current position is confused and inequitable. The care available appears to be largely a matter of chance.' (M. Henwood, *'Through a Glass Darkly: Community Care and Elderly People'* (Kings Fund Institute, 1992) 39.)

Curiously, the Department of Health seems until recently to have treated the matter as if it were simply for the patient to decide where he or she wished to stay. It advised that 'no NHS patient should be placed in a private nursing or residential care home against his/her wishes if it means that he/she or a relative will be personally responsible for the home's charges'. (See *Discharge of Patients from Hospital* HC (89) 5 (1989), para 2.) And the minister for health confirmed that 'if the patient in an NHS bed does not feel willing to accept responsibility for private nursing home fees and is not in a condition to return to their home, they should remain under the care of the health authority'. But this is simply to deny the financial pressures under which health authorities operate. In 1995 the Department of Health issued new guidance on *NHS Responsibilities for Meeting Continuing Health Care Needs*, (HSG (95) 8 and LAC (95) 5; (NHSE, 1995)) concerning the obligations of health and social services authorities to provide care to those with long-term needs. The guidance is more forthright. It states that: 'Where patients have been assessed as not requiring NHS continuing inpatient care, they do not have the right to occupy indefinitely an NHS bed ... they do, however, have the right to refuse to be discharged from NHS care into a nursing home or residential care home (*ibid*, para 27).

How is the distinction to be drawn between those who require NHS care and those who do not, and what happens to those who are discharged from hospital against their will? The guidelines specify that the responsibility of the NHS to arrange and fund services includes:

specialist medical and nursing assessment; rehabilitation and recovery; palliative health care; continuing inpatient care under specialist supervision in hospital or in a nursing home; respite health care; specialist health care to support people in nursing homes or residential care homes or the community; community health services to people at home or in residential care homes, primary health care; [and] specialist transport services (*ibid*, para 10).

Responsibility for making these difficult decisions rests with the consultants and nurses responsible for the care of the individuals concerned, on the basis of a multi-disciplinary assessment of need, including where appropriate discussions with staff from social services and housing authorities. This is primarily a matter for clinical discretion which is not effected by the availability of resources, except to this extent. The way in which funds are distributed between health and social services departments may differ from place to place. Some may have invested more heavily in the provision of health services in the community. In such an area discharge from hospital may be more appropriate because adequate health care is available from GPs and health visitors. By contrast, those areas which have less sophisticated facilities in the community may find that adequate care of the type required by the guidelines can only be provided in hospital. This suggests that closer co-operation between health and social services authorities will be required, with respect to both providing care in the present and its purchase for the future.

Those who are discharged from hospital against their wishes will continue to be entitled to receive primary care services from GPs in the same way as before, without the need to pay for them. This is the case whether the care is provided at home, or in a nursing or residential home. Included amongst these services will be specialist nursing advice such as continence and diabetic advice, stoma and catheter care, physiotherapy, speech therapy, and chiropody. However, it would not include meals on wheels or assistance with bathing, dressing, and mobility. They could be provided by the social services authority which may levy a charge for providing them ...

The need to review NHS responsibilities for long-term patients was prompted by the case of the brain-damaged patient who was refused hospital care because his condition had stabilized and nothing more could be achieved for him in hospital. The matter was investigated by the Health Service Ombudsman. The chief executive of the health authority justified the policy on the ground that the authority 'could not meet every health need. Present policy was for shorter inpatient stays with continuing care being provided in the community. The authority did not provide for any long stay beds in hospital or have any contractual arrangements for such beds in private nursing homes.' (*Health Service Commissioner, Second Report for Session*

1993–94. Failure to provide long term NHS care for a brain-damaged patient (HC 197, 1994), para 18)

The Health Service Ombudsman severely criticized the health authority and its policy for failing in its duty to the patient. The Ombudsman considered section 3(1)(e) of the 1977 Act, which imposes on the Secretary of State a duty to provide 'to such extent as he considers necessary to meet all reasonable requirements ... such facilities for ... the after-care of persons who have suffered from illness as he considers appropriate as part of the health service.' He said that the policy of the authority 'was unreasonable and constitutes a failure in the service provided by the authority' (*ibid*, para 22). Arguably, the Court of Appeal would have agreed with the Ombudsman had it been asked to consider the matter. In *White v Chief Adjudication Officer* the Court said that psycho-geriatric patients were 'ill' in the sense that they required constant nursing supervision by skilled nurses. The fact that their condition had stabilized and that they no longer needed treatment in hospital did not prevent them from being patients within the responsibility of the NHS. The two cases are broadly analogous.

The new guidelines on *Continuing Health Care Needs* adopt a similar view. They confirm that decisions about which categories of patient do, or do not, have a right to health care within the NHS are not to be determined by health service managers as a matter of policy. Certainly, managers have their problems, but they do not include making decisions about patient care which are properly the responsibility of clinicians. The guidelines were passed as a response to the Ombudsman's adjudication and the Secretary of State has told the House of Commons' Health Committee that 'Health authorities who follow the new guidelines should not find themselves in a position of being rebuked by the Ombudsman'. (*Priority Setting in the NHS: Purchasing* HC 134-11, Session 1994–95, 162.) This confirmation of the responsibilities of the NHS to elderly patients is reassuring. Any claim to the contrary, intended to reduce their rights to care, has implications which concern the fundamental duty of the Secretary of State under the 1977 Act to provide 'a comprehensive health service'. A decision to restrict that duty would be for Parliament alone.

You will see the reference to the Court of Appeal's decision in *White*. It is not clear whether this decision drew a 'bright line' between social services care and NHS care. On the face of it, it could be argued that the Court of Appeal held that once an element of 'health care' provision was made to a person, their overall 'care' was to be provided under the NHS even if domiciliary or residential care (a classic example of 'social services' care) was also provided. Such a view would have considerable consequences for NHS budgets. Subsequently, the Court of Appeal took a more detailed look at the social care/health care divide.

R v North and East Devon Health Authority, ex parte Coughlan (Pamela), Secretary of State for Health (Intervenor); Royal College of Nursing (Intervenor) [1999] Lloyd's Rep Med 306 (CA)

In 1971 the appellant was involved in a road accident as a result of which she became tetraplegic. She was incontinent, requiring regular catheterisation, and partially paralysed in the respiratory tract, with consequent breathing difficulties. She was subject to the problems of immobility and recurrent headaches.

In 1993 she and other patients were moved with their agreement from Newcourt Hospital to Mardon House, a purpose built facility eventually managed by the local NHS trust. They accepted the move in reliance on an express promise that Mardon House would be their home for as long as they chose, ie a home for life.

In 1992 guidance HSG (92) 50, issued by the NHS Management Executive to District Health Authorities, drew a distinction between "general" nursing care and "specialist" nursing services. The former were to be purchased by social services and the latter by health services. In 1993 the Secretary of State gave approvals and directions under section 21(1) of the National Assistance Act 1948 directing local authorities to make arrangements for the residential accommodation of persons unable through illness to look after themselves. In 1995 guidance was issued by the Secretary of State seeking to delineate further the division of responsibility between the NHS and local authorities.

The Health Authority published policies and eligibility criteria setting out definitions of specialist nursing.

In 1996 the Health Authority reviewed the options for placement and care of the appellant and other patients and concluded they did not meet the eligibility criteria for NHS care. The authority issued a consultation paper on the future of Mardon House, one of the options in which was closure, and contained no alternative provision for the placement of the appellant and others. In April 1998 the Authority chose the closure option, but after an application for judicial review rescinded the decision and conducted further public consultation. Although representations were received from the appellant and other residents the Authority did not disclose to them a report recommending closure.

On 7 October 1998 the Health Authority made a decision to close Mardon House. The appellant applied for judicial review of the decision.

Sedley LJ:

Introduction

1. The critical issue in this appeal is whether nursing care for a chronically ill patient may lawfully be provided by a local authority as a social service (in which case the patient pays according to means) or whether it is required by law to be provided free of charge as part of the National Health Service ("NHS"). If local authority provision is lawful, a number of further important questions arise: as to the propriety of the process by which eligibility for long term health care on the NHS, instead of as a social service, is determined; as to the effect of an assurance given by the Exeter Health Authority, the predecessor of the appellant, the North and East Devon Health Authority ("Health Authority") to the respondent to this appeal (the applicant for judicial review), Miss Coughlan, that she should have a home for life at Mardon House, a NHS facility; and as to the process by which Miss Coughlan has been assigned to local authority care.

2. Normally where a person is assigned to local authority care she will, subject to a means test, be liable to meet the cost of that care. For reasons to which we will come, Miss Coughlan will not in any event be called upon to pay for her care; but, in hearing her claim, which he decided in her favour, Hidden J did not consider that this made the issues and, in particular, the critical issue academic. Now that all issues have been decided in her favour both the Health Authority and (on this appeal) the Secretary of State for Health plainly have a proper interest in challenging the judgment.

3. Miss Coughlan was grievously injured in a road traffic accident in 1971. She is tetraplegic; doubly incontinent, requiring regular catheterisation; partially paralysed in the respiratory tract, with consequent difficulty in breathing; and subject not only to the attendant problems of immobility but to recurrent headaches caused by an associated neurological condition. In 1993 she and seven comparably disabled patients were moved with their agreement from Newcourt Hospital, which it was desired to close, to a purpose-built facility, Mardon House. It is a decision of the Health Authority made on 7 October 1998 to close Mardon House which is the immediate cause of the present litigation …

Nursing care for Miss Coughlan at Mardon House

6. From the time of her accident until the events with which this appeal is concerned, Miss Coughlan's care, which has always included, but has not been confined to, nursing care, was accepted as the responsibility of the NHS acting through the Exeter Health Authority and, more recently, the Health Authority. The Health Authority does not dispute that Miss Coughlan and her fellow long-term patients accepted the move from Newcourt Hospital to Mardon House in 1993 on the basis of a clear promise that Mardon House would be their home for life. Although both Mr James Goudie, QC for the Health Authority and Mr Richard Gordon, QC for Miss Coughlan have based their arguments upon a clear promise to this effect, it will be necessary later in this judgment to look at its precise terms because Mr Gordon contends that when it took the closure decision the Health Authority was presented with a diluted version of the promise.

7. For the first year the John Grooms charity was engaged to run Mardon House, which was leased to the charity and registered as a nursing home under the Registered Homes Act 1984. By the summer of 1994, however, this arrangement had failed and the premises reverted to the local NHS Trust. Section 21(3) of the Registered Homes Act 1984 excludes NHS hospitals from registration as nursing homes. By section 128(1) of the National Health Service Act 1977 ("the Health Act") a "hospital" includes any institution for the reception and treatment of persons suffering from illness, so that Mardon House could no longer be registered as a nursing home, albeit this was the description which most nearly fitted it.

8. Mardon House, although purpose-built for the long-term disabled, had other health service functions as a rehabilitation – "reablement" – unit. For reasons which we do not have to analyse, the Health Authority by 1995 was having to consider whether the reablement service could realistically be kept at Mardon House. This in turn threw up the question whether, if the reablement service were to go, Mardon House could be maintained as a home for younger chronically disabled patients together with some alternative health service use or uses.

NHS Changes: legislation, policy and guidelines

9. Alongside these difficulties of health service provision changes were taking place in health service policy. On 1 April 1993 the National Health Service and Community Care Act

1990 came into force. Among the purposes set out in the long title were "to make further provision about health authorities and other bodies constituted in accordance with the [Health Act], to provide for the establishment of National Health Service Trusts; ... to make further provision concerning the provision of accommodation and other welfare services by local authorities". Mr Gordon's initial charge that this legislation was mistakenly taken by the NHS to permit long-term nursing care to be handed over to local authorities has been defused by Mr Pleming's acceptance, adopted by Mr Goudie, that no material change was introduced by the Act of 1990 and that all the material powers are to be found in the Health Act, the successor to the originating National Health Service Act 1946. It will be necessary to consider in detail the history and significance of those statutory provisions which adjust the relationship between NHS and local authority provision for persons who are ill.

10. The coming into force of the Act of 1990 was accompanied by a guideline document, HSG (92) 50, issued by the NHS Management Executive to District Health Authorities. It is captioned "Local Authority Contracts for Residential and Nursing Home Care: NHS Related Aspects" and begins:

This guidance sets out District Health Authority and Local Authority responsibilities, from April 1993, for funding community health services for residents of residential care and nursing homes who have been placed in those homes by local authorities.

The guidance drew a distinction between "specialist" nursing services, which were to continue to be provided by the NHS, and "general nursing care", which the guidance proposed should be for the local authority to purchase. It said:

Full implementation of the White Paper "Caring for People" will mean that local authorities will have responsibilities for purchasing nursing home care for the great majority of people who need it and who require to be publicly supported. When, after April 1993, a local authority places a person in a nursing home after joint HA/LA assessment, the local authority is responsible for purchasing services to meet the general nursing care needs of that person, including the cost of incontinence services (eg laundry) and those incontinence and nursing supplies which are not available on NHS prescription. Health authorities will be responsible for purchasing, within the resources available and in line with their priorities, physiotherapy, chiropody and speech and language therapy, with the appropriate equipment, and the provision of *specialist* nursing advice, eg continence advice and stoma care, for those people placed in nursing homes by local authorities with the consent of a DHA. Health authorities can opt to purchase these services through directly managed units, NHS trusts, or other providers including the nursing home concerned. Health Authorities continue to have the power to enter into a contractual arrangement with a nursing home where a patient's need is primarily for health care. Such placements must be fully funded by the health authority.

11. In March 1993 the Secretary of State gave approvals and directions under section 21(1) of the National Assistance Act 1948 ("the Care Act") – to which we will come – directing local authorities to make arrangements to provide residential accommodation for persons who were unable through illness to take care of themselves, and to enable such people to obtain nursing attention so long as this did not impinge upon statutory NHS provision.

12. In 1995 further guidance was issued by the Secretary of State for Health, directed both to NHS bodies and to local authorities (HSG (95) 8; LAC (95) 5). It sought to delineate in further detail the appropriate division of responsibility between the NHS and local authorities for those in need of continuing health care. It made clear that access to specialist medical and nursing services should be available and provided at the expense of the NHS for those persons who were no longer eligible for in-patient care. It called on health authorities to develop and publish policies and eligibility criteria for the purchase of continuing health care as from April 1996.

13. The Health Authority published policies and eligibility criteria in conjunction with its twin Devon Health Authority and Devon Social Services. The published document builds upon the distinction made in the 1992 guidelines between specialist and general nursing care, setting out a definition of specialist nursing which Mr Gordon and Mr Havers have submitted is idiosyncratic. It relates specialisation not to qualification but to employment, and it lists as examples of specialist nursing continence care, stoma, diabetic, paediatric, palliative, tissue viability and breast care. It distinguishes these from what it calls core nursing: the work of district nurses, health visitors, practice nurses, community psychiatric nurses, community mental handicap nurses and midwives. Of those areas identified as specialist, none are recognised as such by the United Kingdom Central Council for Nursing. Those listed as non-specialist are arguably all examples of specialist nursing. It is not for us to resolve this difference of approach, but it is relevant to note that the notion of specialist

nursing, introduced by way of policy guidance and not by statute, is, on any view, elusive. As to nursing home care the document says:

> Many people regard care in a Nursing Home as health care, and therefore the purchasing responsibility of the NHS. However, under the NHS and Community Care Act, Social Services were given a new responsibility for purchasing Nursing Home beds. As with the previous arrangement through the Department of Social Security this is subject to a means test. The regulations governing this are laid down nationally. It is anticipated that the majority of placements in Nursing Homes in Devon will continue to be made through Social Services.
>
> Under the terms of the government's guidance it is open to Health Authorities to purchase care from Nursing Homes as NHS Continuing Care (although they do not have to do so if they can meet these responsibilities in other ways ie through contracting for hospital beds). Patients eligible for NHS purchased nursing home care would need to meet the criteria for in-patient care. The care required would be at a higher level than that normally provided by Nursing Homes.
>
> Health and Social Services purchasers are working together to describe more clearly Social Services "normal" expectations of Nursing Homes and how an NHS purchased placement would differ from this.
>
> NHS in-patient care is free at the point of need but Social Services are obliged by law to charge for care; this is decided by Parliament. The questions of charging cannot be taken into account in these eligibility criteria nor in decisions on care for individuals, since these are based on Consultants' clinical judgments.

The policy statement goes on to say:

> The National Health Service Executive recommend that the following services are to be regarded as standard, ie not specialist, in nursing homes: general physical and mental nursing care, artificial feeding, continuous oxygen therapy, wound care, pain control, administration of drugs and medication, catheter care, bladder wash-outs, suction, tracheotomy care, tissue viability.

14. In spite of counsel's best endeavours it has proved impossible to locate the source of the recommendation upon which this passage of the policy is expressly based. Their best guess – that it is HSG (92) 50 – is insufficient because only the broad division between general and specialist nursing care is to be found there. Those instructing Mr Goudie have been able to tell us that from their recollection some recommendations were conveyed in meetings convened by the South West Regional Office of the National Health Service Executive. Mr Pleming has been able to ascertain nothing about these meetings from the departmental end, and neither party has been able to produce a single memorandum or note relating to them. In this situation, which in the experience of the court is unusual, we will take the policy at face value and infer that the allocation of functions is not the work of the Health Authority alone but derives from central NHS guidance …

Grounds of challenge
17. Miss Coughlan's case that the decision to close Mardon House is flawed is put on a number of different grounds by Mr Gordon QC. Any one of those grounds, if established, is sufficient to render the decision unlawful. We shall deal with the points in the following order:
A. Nursing as Health Care and as Social Care (Paras 18–32)
B. Eligibility Criteria (Paras 33–50)
C. The Promise of a Home for Life (Paras 51–90)
D. Human Rights (Paras 91–94)
E. Assessment and Placement (Paras 95–108)
F. Consultation (Paras 109–118)
[We omit from this extract points D-F.]

A.   Nursing as "Health care" and as "Social care"
18. Before Hidden J, the question of the legality of nursing care being provided by a local authority was not the primary issue raised by Mr Gordon on behalf of Miss Coughlan. The decision of the judge has made it the most important issue on this appeal. As to this issue the judge said:

> I accept Mr Gordon's submissions on the question of nursing care that nothing in either NHSCCA or in HSG (95) 8 altered the statutory responsibilities of Health Authorities to provide health services including nursing care. As a result both general and specialist nursing care remain the *sole responsibility* of the Health Authorities. Thus the Respondent Authority was clearly wrong in law in assuming that the law had changed and that it was no longer entitled or empowered to provide or arrange long-term general nursing

care in an NHS setting and/or that there had been a transfer to Social Services Department of such responsibility as a result of "new legislation". Those assumptions were wholly misconceived and led to the Authority taking account of irrelevant matters ... [emphasis added] I conclude that nursing is "health care" and can never be "social care" and that ... HSG (95) 8 did not make any change to any NHS responsibility for health care services including nursing.

19. If the judge's decision is right on this issue, his decision will have significant adverse financial consequences for the Secretary of State and the Health Authority. In addition it will mean that the policy of the Secretary of State as to the provision of nursing care, which has existed for a number of years, has been unlawful. It will, on the other hand, improve the position of those in a similar situation to that of Miss Coughlan. If the judge is right, those who receive nursing care while residing in the community in a nursing or similar home provided by a local authority will be entitled to have that care provided free of charge. This would be the same position as would apply if they were living in their own homes. If the judge is wrong, it means that the nursing services will have to be paid for, unless the financial resources of the person concerned have been nearly exhausted. If these circumstances it is not surprising that a substantial proportion of the argument on this appeal has been devoted to this issue.

20. The answer to this issue depends on the correct interpretation of three sections: sections 1 and 3 of the Health Act and section 21 of Part III of the Care Act. The language of the sections today can be readily traced back to the original legislation which founded the welfare state after the last war. Their legislative history reflects the changes in the manner in which health and care services have been provided since that time. We have, therefore, had the legislative history of the three sections explained to us in depth. (The Health Act is a descendant of the National Health Act 1946. The Care Act has been substantially amended since 1948.) In the end, however, this issue has to be determined by construing the provisions in their current form.

In examining the language of the sections it is desirable to start with the Health Act because, as the Care Act makes clear, the Health Act is the dominant act. This dominance is consistent with the long standing role of local authorities under Part III of the Care Act of only being required to provide assistance for those in need who have no other way of obtaining that assistance. In that sense, assistance under the Care Act is provided as a last resort.

The Health Act
[The judge then set out ss 1 and 3 of the 1977 Act set out *supra*.]
   23. It will be observed that the Secretary of State's section 3 duty is subject to two different qualifications. First of all there is the initial qualification that his obligation is limited to providing the services identified to the extent that he considers that they are *necessary* to meet *all reasonable requirements*. In addition, in the case of the facilities referred to in (d) and (e), there is a qualification in that he has to consider whether they are appropriate to be provided "as part of the health service". We are not concerned here with this second qualification since nursing services would come under section 3(1)(c).
   24. The first qualification placed on the duty contained in section 3 makes it clear that there is scope for the Secretary of State to exercise a degree of judgment as to the circumstances in which he will provide the services, including nursing services referred to in the section. He does not automatically have to meet *all* nursing requirements. In certain circumstances he can exercise his judgment and legitimately decline to provide nursing services. He need not provide nursing services if he does not consider they are reasonably required or necessary to meet a reasonable requirement.
   25. When exercising his judgment he has to bear in mind the comprehensive service which he is under a duty to promote as set out in section 1. However, as long as he pays due regard to that duty, the fact that the service will not be comprehensive does not mean that he is necessarily contravening either section 1 or section 3. The truth is that, while he has the duty to continue to promote a comprehensive free health service and he must never, in making a decision under section 3, disregard that duty, a comprehensive health service may never, for human, financial and other resource reasons, be achievable. Recent history has demonstrated that the pace of developments as to what is possible by way of medical treatment, coupled with the ever increasing expectations of the public, mean that the resources of the NHS are and are likely to continue, at least in the foreseeable future, to be insufficient to meet demand.
   26. In exercising his judgment the Secretary of State is entitled to take into account the resources available to him and the demands on those resources. In *R* v *Secretary of State for Social Services, ex p Hincks* [1980] 1 BMLR 93 the Court of Appeal held that section 3(1) of the Health Act does not impose an absolute duty to provide the specified services. The Secretary of State is entitled to have regard to the resources made available to him under current government economic policy.

The Care Act

27. To ascertain whether local authorities can provide any nursing services as part of their care services pursuant to their Part III responsibilities it is now necessary to turn to the third of the trio of sections, namely section 21 of the Care Act. The section provides:

(1) [Subject to and in accordance with the provisions of this Part of the Act, a local authority may with the approval of the Secretary of State, and to such extent as he may direct shall, make arrangements for providing]—
(a) residential accommodation for persons [aged eighteen or over] who by reason of age, [illness, disability] or any other circumstances are in need of care and attention which is not otherwise available to them; [and
(aa) residential accommodation for expectant and nursing mothers who are in need of care and attention which is not otherwise available to them.]

(2) In [making any such arrangements] a local authority shall have regard to the welfare of all persons for whom accommodation is provided, and in particular to the need for providing accommodation of different descriptions suited to different descriptions of such persons as are mentioned in the last foregoing subsection.

(5) References in this Act to accommodation provided under this Part thereof shall be construed as references to accommodation provided in accordance with this and the five next following sections, and as including references to board and other services, amenities and requisites provided in connection with the accommodation except where in the opinion of the authority managing the premises their provision is unnecessary.

(7) Without prejudice to the generality of the foregoing provisions of this section, a local authority may—

(a) ...

[(b) make arrangements for the provision on the premises in which accommodation is being provided of such other services as appear to the local authority to be required.]

(8) Nothing in this section shall authorise or require a local authority to make any provision authorised or required to be made (whether by that or by any other authority) by or under any enactment not contained in this Part of this Act [or authorised or required to be provided under the National Health Service Act 1977.]

(The passages in square brackets indicate amendments).

The following points should be noted in relation to section 21.

(a) The requirements for approval and directions by the Secretary of State in section 21(1) give the Secretary of State considerable control over both what and how services are provided by local authorities under Part III. (The necessary directions were given in 1993 in an appendix to guidance issued by the Secretary of State on 17 March 1993.)

(b) Under section 21 the primary service provided is accommodation. But the express reference to age, illness and disability as being among the characteristics of the person who is seeking accommodation, which amount to a qualification for the grant of the accommodation, indicate that in many cases there is likely to be a need for nursing services as part of the care provided.

(c) The words in section 21(5), "board and other services" are readily capable of being construed as including nursing services and there appears to be no reason why they should not be so construed. If there were any doubt as to this, it would be removed by the reference in section 26(1B) to "residential accommodation where nursing care is provided".

(d) The nursing services would, however, as section 21(5) requires, have to be "provided in connection with the accommodation".

So far the language of three sections creates no particular difficulty as long as it is subjected to detailed analysis. Section 21(8) remains to be considered. It provides the key to this issue. How are the words "or authorised or required to be provided under" the Health Act to be applied?

28. Each word is of significance. The powers of the local authority are not excluded *by* the existence of a power in the Health Act to provide the service, but they are excluded where the provision is authorised or required to be made *under* the Health Act. The position is different in the case of "any other enactment", where it is sufficient if there is an authority or requirement to be made *by or under* the enactment.

29. The references in section 21 to the Health Act were added by the National Health Service and Community Care Act 1990. The amendment was made in part by section 42 of Part III of that Act. Part III introduced the new arrangements for community care. The same section also added the provision which is now section 26(1B) of the Care Act to which we have already referred. It was clearly contemplated that services which could be provided might include nursing services. Section 21(8) was added to by section 66 and para 5(3) of Schedule 9, entitled

"Minor and Consequential Amendments". The section should not be regarded as preventing a local authority from providing any health services. The subsection's prohibitive effect is limited to those health services which, in fact, have been authorised or required to be provided under the Health Act. Such health services would not therefore include services which the Secretary of State legitimately decided under section 3(1) of the Health Act it was not necessary for the NHS to provide. It would have been remarkable if a minor and consequential amendment of section 21(8) of the Care Act had had the effect, as Mr Goudie contended, of reducing the Secretary of State's important public obligations under the Health Act. The true effect is to emphasise that Care Act provision, which is secondary to Health Act provision, may nevertheless include nursing care which properly falls outside the NHS.

Conclusion

30. The result of the detailed examination of the three sections can be summarised as follows:

(a) The Secretary of State can exclude some nursing services from the services provided by the NHS. Such services can then be provided as a social or care service rather than as a health service.

(b) The nursing services which can be so provided as part of the care services are limited to those which can legitimately be regarded as being provided in connection with accommodation which is being provided to the classes of persons referred to in section 21 of the Care Act who are in need of care and attention; in other words as part of a social services care package.

(c) The fact that the nursing services are to be provided as part of social services care and will have to be paid for by the person concerned, unless that person's resources mean that he or she will be exempt from having to pay for those services, does not prohibit the Secretary of State from deciding not to provide those services. The nursing services are part of the social services and are subject to the same regime for payment as other social services. Mr Gordon submitted that this is unfair. He pointed out that if a person receives comparable nursing care in a hospital or in a community setting, such as his or her home, it is free. The Royal Commission on Long Term Care, in its report, "With Respect to Old Age", (March 1999, Chapter 6, pages 62 *et seq* Cm 4192–1) not surprisingly agrees with this assessment and makes recommendations to improve the situation. However, as long as the nursing care services are capable of being properly classified as part of the social services' responsibilities, then, under the present legislation, that unfairness is part of the statutory scheme.

(d) The fact that some nursing services can be properly regarded as part of social services' care, to be provided by the local authority, does not mean that all nursing services provided to those in the care of the local authority can be treated in this way. The scale and type of nursing required in an individual case may mean that it would not be appropriate to regard all or part of the nursing as being part of "the package of care" which can be provided by a local authority. There can be no precise legal line drawn between those nursing services which are and those which are not capable of being treated as included in such a package of care services.

(e) The distinction between those services which can and cannot be so provided is one of degree which in a borderline case will depend on a careful appraisal of the facts of the individual case. However, as a very general indication as to where the line is to be drawn, it can be said that if the nursing services are (i) merely incidental or ancillary to the provision of the accommodation which a local authority is under a duty to provide to the category of persons to whom section 21 refers and (ii) of a nature which it can be expected that an authority whose primary responsibility is to provide social services can be expected to provide, then they can be provided under section 21. It will be appreciated that the first part of the test is focusing on the overall quantity of the services and the second part on the quality of the services provided.

(f) The fact that care services are provided on a means tested contribution basis does not prevent the Secretary of State declining to provide the nursing part of those services on the NHS. However, he can only decline if he has formed a judgment which is tenable that consistent with his long-term general duty to continue to promote a comprehensive free health service it is not necessary to provide the services. He cannot decline simply because social services will fill the gap.

31. It follows that we do not accept the judge's conclusion that all nursing care must be the sole responsibility of the NHS and has to be provided by the Health Authority. Whether it can be provided by the local authority has to be determined on an assessment of the circumstances of the individual concerned. The Secretary of State accepts that, where the primary need is a health need, then the responsibility is that of the NHS, even when the individual has been placed in a home by a local authority. The difficulty is identifying the cases which are *required* to be placed into that category on their facts in order to comply with

the statutory provisions. Here the needs of Miss Coughlan and her fellow occupants were primarily health needs for which the Health Authority is as a matter of law responsible, for reasons which we will now explain.

B.   *Eligibility criteria*

32. Mr Pleming, on behalf of the Secretary of State, submitted that since the inception of the NHS there has been a broad division between specialist medical services, which are always the NHS's responsibility, and general care services, which can be the responsibility of local authorities. A reflection of this distinction was to be found in section 21(7) of the Care Act prior to its amendment. The section excluded from the services which could be provided by local authorities "specialist services or services of a kind normally provided only on admission to a hospital ..." He also contended that there can be an overlap between the categories of services which can be provided by the NHS and local authorities and that therefore a method needs to exist to determine an individual's eligibility for NHS services for which there would be no charge. The selected method is a combination of guidance by the Secretary of State, to be implemented by health authorities and local authorities, and eligibility criteria drawn up by health authorities in accordance with that guidance. The next issue which has to be determined is whether the guidance and eligibility criteria which have been adopted and applied by the twin Health Authorities and Devon Social Services were flawed. The eligibility criteria could be flawed because they reflected guidance of the Secretary of State, which itself was flawed or they could be flawed because the Health Authorities, in laying down the eligibility criteria, misunderstood, misapplied or failed to follow that guidance.

33. We have already referred to the documents that contained the formal guidance, namely HSG (92) 50 and HSG (95) 8. Those documents could not and, as the judge accepted, did not alter the legal responsibilities of the NHS under the Health Act. They did, however, reflect a change of policy in relation to those who needed long-term care. Although the policy change is not directly relevant to the outcome of this appeal, it probably explains how the legal problems to be resolved by this case arose and some of the confusion on the part of the Health Authority as to its responsibilities.

34. At the request of this court, Mr Pleming, on behalf of the Secretary of State, prepared a helpful note as to how the present policy in relation to long-term care evolved. In general there has been a shift from in-patient hospital care to community provision. This has coincided with advances in the way health and social services treatment and care are provided. Community care can offer improvements in terms of the quality of life it provides over long-term residence in institutions, such as hospitals. We also recognise that, because of that improvement, the scale of health care which is needed may be reduced. However, subject to this, the fact that a patient is being treated in one setting rather than another will not affect their health care needs.

35. In keeping with this change of approach an announcement was made in the House of Commons on 12 July 1989 indicating that the aim of the policy would be to enable people to live as full and independent a life as is possible in the community for so long as they wished to do so. This statement was considered to be in accord with the report by Sir Roy Griffiths in 1988, "Community Care: Agenda for Action". The report accepted the distinction between health and social care and did not alter what should be the responsibility of the NHS for health care. It was, however, intended that local authorities should normally assume responsibility for the care element of public support for people in private and voluntary residential care and nursing homes. A text of the statement was issued under cover of circular HN (89) 18/LASSL (89) 6. Paragraph 25 of the statement confirmed:

> Community care is no longer primarily about providing an alternative to long-stay hospital care. The vast majority of people needing care have never been, nor expect to be in such institutions. The policy aim is to now strike the right balance between home and day care on the one hand, and residential and nursing home care on the other, while reserving hospital care for those whose needs truly cannot be met elsewhere. The changes we propose will for the first time ensure that all public monies are devoted to the primary objective of supporting people at home whenever possible.

36. The policy was developed and implemented by a White Paper, "Caring for People, Community Care in the Next Decade and Beyond" (Cm 849, November 1989) and the National Health Service and Community Care Act 1990 which was brought into force in April 1993. The Act was accompanied by policy guidance "Caring for People: Community Care in the Next Decade and Beyond". Again it was not intended to alter the responsibilities of the NHS. So far as funding was concerned, the change which occurred in April 1993 is that, whereas previously funding for residential nursing home care had been met by central social security funding, after April 1993 this became the direct responsibility of the local authorities. This

was intended to induce a more responsible approach on the part of local authorities as to how the resources were deployed.

37. It is accepted, however, that the NHS continued to be responsible for (a) funding placements for nursing home residents requiring continuing in-patient care and (b) meeting the specialist health care needs of residents of nursing homes for whom the local authority was generally responsible. As we will see, the category (a) responsibility is of significance. It involves the recognition that they will be residents of nursing homes who, while they do not require in-patient care in hospital, do need NHS care in the community.

38. As a result of a report by the Health Service Commissioner in 1994, it was accepted by the then Secretary of State and the Chief Executive of the Health Service that the Health Service had withdrawn too far from its responsibilities in relation to continuing health care. This was followed by the issue of the guidance circular HSG (95) 8/LAC (95) 5 which was intended to address the concerns which had been expressed in the Commissioner's report. This was followed by further guidance on 26 September 1995 provided in Circular HSG (95) 45. The annex to that circular states in para 4.1:

> ... In respect of people being discharged from long stay institutions, the NHS is responsible for negotiating arrangements with local authorities, including any appropriate transfer of resources which assist the local authority meeting the care needs of such people and of their successors who may otherwise have entered the institution ...

It is stated in paragraph 5.1 that Health Authorities are also responsible for the purchase and provision of:

> (ii) specialist or *intensive* medical or nursing support for people in nursing homes ...
> [emphasis added]

39. We have no difficulty with the Secretary of State adopting a policy of treatment in the community where in-patient treatment in a hospital is not required. In determining what health services are to be provided by the NHS, the Secretary of State may take into account what services are and can be lawfully provided by local authorities as care provision. However, the question remains as to whether the correct boundary has been identified between what is the proper responsibility of the NHS and what is the proper responsibility of local authorities.

40. The Secretary of State does not suggest that the NHS need not fund those health services which would not be an appropriate part of the package of care which a local authority can provide under section 21. We recognise that what services can be appropriately treated as responsibilities of a local authority under section 21 may evolve with the changing standards of society. It is always going to be difficult to identify the limits of those services. In the case of the circulars published by the Secretary of State, despite Mr Gordon's submissions on behalf of Miss Coughlan to the contrary, we do not find that they improperly place any responsibilities on local authorities or remove any responsibilities of health authorities. In fact both the judge and Mr Gordon accepted that these circulars had made no change to the responsibilities for health care of the NHS.

41. What Mr Gordon particularly complained of was the distinction which the circulars adopted between general and specialist nursing care. We have already indicated why a dividing line based on this distinction can be described as idiosyncratic. Certainly the expressions should not be regarded as giving anything more than the most general indication of what is and is not health care which the NHS should provide. The distinction between general and special or specialist services does provide a degree of non technical guidance as to the services which, because of their nature or quality, should be regarded in any particular case as being more likely to be the responsibility of the NHS. Where the issue is whether the services should be treated as the responsibility of the NHS, not because of their nature or quality, but because of their quantity or the continuity with which they are provided, the distinction between general and specialist services is of less assistance. The distinction certainly does not provide an exhaustive test. The distinction does not necessarily cater for the situation where the demands for nursing attention are continuous and intense. In that situation the patient may not require in-patient care in a hospital under the new policy, but the nursing care which is necessary may still exceed that which can be properly provided as a part of social services care provision. We read circular HSG (95) 8 as recognising that there can be such cases (see paragraph 21). But the shortcoming of the circular is that it associates such cases only with in-patient treatment and does not make clear whether the in-patient treatment to which it refers has to be in a hospital. What the circulars do not contain are clear statements that the fact that a case does not qualify for in-patient treatment in a hospital does not mean that the person concerned should not be a NHS responsibility. The importance of there being clear statements as to this arise because of the increased emphasis being placed on care in the community. This could result in it being assumed that, because patients who would previously have been treated as in-patients

in hospital no longer qualify for such treatment, they are automatically disqualified from receiving care on the NHS. This is not what is permitted.

42. On this aspect of the case, two things are clear. First, the fact that the resident at a nursing home does not require in-patient treatment in a hospital does not mean that his or her care should not be the responsibility of the NHS. Secondly, as the judge points out, at one time the Health Authority was totally confused as to what the proper division of responsibility between the Health Authority and the local authorities was. Dr Gillian Morgan, the Chief Executive of the Health Authority, in her first affidavit accepts that this was the position. In paragraph 39 of her first affidavit she apologises for the confusion which she and other officers of the authority were under and appear to have caused by their statements. This could be the result of the shortcomings of the circulars.

43. The fact that there is this background of possible confusion makes it important that any eligibility criteria should be drawn up with particular care. They need to identify at least two categories of persons who, although receiving nursing care while in a nursing home, are still entitled to receive the care at the expense of the NHS. First, there are those who, because of the scale of their health needs, should be regarded as wholly the responsibility of a health authority. Secondly, there are those whose nursing services in general can be regarded as being the responsibility of the local authority, but whose additional requirements are the responsibility of the NHS.

44. As to the second of those two categories, in her affidavit Dr Morgan states:

Nursing Homes do not generally divide their charges between accommodation and care. In my view, it would be very difficult if not impossible to distinguish between the elements of nursing care and what otherwise might be called social care – for example help with eating or washing. The difficulty is particularly acute in the context of work carried out by nursing auxiliaries or other carers under the supervision of qualified nurses. This will generally parallel the equivalent arrangements in NHS hospitals where care is delivered by a range of individuals including nursing auxiliaries and others who are not professional nurses. I therefore seriously doubt whether a coherent and consistent division could be maintained between what is a nursing task and what is a carer's task if it were proposed that there should be a different funding regime for the two types of care.

45. We are not in a position to comment on the correctness of this view of Dr Morgan. However if she is correct, then the position can be remedied by the Health Service taking responsibility for the whole cost. Either a proper division needs to be drawn (we are not saying that it has to be exact) or the Health Service has to take the whole responsibility. The local authority cannot meet the costs of services which are not its responsibility because of the terms of section 21(8) of the 1948 Act.

46. Mr Gordon contended that it would be absurd for those who do not meet the Health Authority's eligibility criteria for in-patient care not to be entitled to "general" nursing care services free if they are entitled to "specialist" health care services free. As we have already indicated, there are clearly grounds for saying that for there to be a different regime with regard to payment dependent upon the location where a person is receiving nursing services is unfair, but, that point apart, if a portion of nursing care can still be provided as a service for which the local authority is responsible, then we do not see anything improper in those services being charged for under the local authority regime. Other services for which the NHS is responsible can still be provided on health service terms.

47. It is Criterion 1 of the Eligibility Criteria of the twin Health Authorities and Social Services which is relevant to the issues in this case. It commences by recognising in extremely guarded terms that patients will be eligible for continuing health care "possibly exceptionally in nursing home settings". This follows an introduction which indicates that usually the need for on-site care from doctors (ie not nurses) is a reliable test for eligibility. There are also examples given of "the characteristics which are likely to apply" in cases for which the NHS has a continuing responsibility and they are extreme cases. Core nursing is given the definition which we have already cited. This indicates that nursing is not specialist nursing not because of what nursing services are rendered but because of the title of the nurse, such as district nurses or midwives, who provide the care. This is followed by the statement said to be that of the NHS Executive already quoted.

48. It is for the Health Authority to decide what should be the eligibility criteria in its area in the co-operative framework envisaged by the circulars. In doing so it can take account of conditions in its area. We do not accept the argument that there cannot be variations between the services provided by the NHS in different areas. However the eligibility criteria cannot place a responsibility on the local authority which goes beyond the terms of section 21. This is what these criteria do. Cases where the health care element goes far beyond what the section permits were being placed upon the local authority as a result of the rigorous limits

placed on what services can be considered to be NHS care services. That this is the position is confirmed by the result of the assessment of Miss Coughlan and her fellow occupants. Their disabilities are of a scale which are beyond the scope of local authority services.

49. The relevance of our upholding Miss Coughlan's complaint as to the eligibility criteria is that this could be a factor contributing to the decision to close Mardon House due to lack of support. She argued that, if the proper approach had been adopted as to who qualifies for NHS care, there would not have been this lack of support. Mardon House was an imaginatively conceived NHS facility in part for those who were unfortunate enough to have a similar degree of disability to Miss Coughlan. We agree that the closure decision is called into question by the erroneous view of the Health Authority as to its general legal obligations towards patients such as Miss Coughlan.

In addition, the Court of Appeal also held that the applicant should succeed on the basis of a 'legitimate expectation' of living at Mardon House for life and that the decision infringed her right to respect for her home under art 8 of the European Convention on Human Rights (for a discussion see, Fennell (2000) 8 Med L Rev 145).

The reasoning of the Court of Appeal is detailed and not exactly crystal clear, but you see that, without referring to the earlier decision in *White*, the court seems to have disagreed with its view. 'Nursing care' may be provided by social services and thus subject the patient to charges providing it is not 'health service care'. The Secretary of State may only exclude 'nursing care' from NHS provision to the extent that it is consistent with his duty to promote a comprehensive health service and he cannot do so simply on the basis that social services will fill the gap. What then is 'health care' that falls within NHS provision? Whether it is the latter will depend upon an application of a two-stage test: (i) was the nursing care merely 'incidental or ancillary' to accommodation provided by social services? (a 'quantitative' test); and (ii) was the nursing care of such a nature that it can be expected to be provided by social services? (a 'qualitative' test). This will be no easy test to apply in many instances. The court gives little concrete guidance but indicates that the NHS may remain responsible for nursing care even though the patient no longer requires 'in-patient' treatment in a hospital. The scale of the individual's health needs may mean that they are wholly the responsibility of the NHS or, alternatively, the NHS may be responsible for their specific health needs beyond general nursing services. Importantly, the court points out that in the latter instance the NHS should pay for the whole package if a 'proper division cannot be made, since the local authority cannot meet the costs of services which are not its responsibility' (National Assistance Act 1948, s 21(8)). However, where the division can be made, the court noted the anomaly created by the legislation, namely that in some situations whether nursing care was free may depend on the location of the individual – in hospital, in the community or in a nursing home.

On the facts, the court concluded that the applicant's situation was such that '[her] disabilities are of a scale which are beyond the scope of local authority services'. She was thus entitled to free NHS care.

C. CLINICAL GOVERNANCE AND QUALITY OF SERVICES

Quality assurance mechanisms, risk management systems and modes of accountability for the delivery of services are well recognised elements of good management in business. In delivering healthcare services to the public, no less should be expected from the NHS. Both within the NHS structure, and outside it, a number of features contribute to achieve these goals of good management. For example, as we shall see later, the arrangements for indemnifying NHS Trusts for clinical negligence claims run by the NHS Litigation Authority have within them incentives for such Trusts to have risk management systems in place (see *infra*, ch 4). Accountability is also a key feature of the NHS complaints procedures and the self-regulatory (disciplinary) regimes for health professionals under the auspices of such bodies on the General Medical Council (for doctors) and the United Kingdom Central Council for Nursing, Midwifery and Health Visiting (see *infra*, ch 3). Likewise, standards of training for doctors are supervised and monitored by the Specialist Training Authority, the Joint Committee on Postgraduate Training for General Practice and the medical Royal Colleges. There are, of course, other mechanisms such as clinical audit and the Patient's Charter. The new Labour Government was anxious that quality should be at the heart of the NHS. In three important policy Papers – *The New NHS – Modern … Dependable* (Cm3807) (1997); *A First Class Service* (HSC 1998/113) (1998); and *Quality Care and Clinical Excellence* (1998) – the Government set out its vision for reshaping the NHS and introducing stronger quality assurance mechanisms. The background and proposals are outlines in *A First Class Service.*

A First Class Service HSC 1998/113 (1998)

1.1

High quality care should be a right for every patient in the NHS. The Government wants an NHS that is both modern and dependable. Such a National Health Service should guarantee fair access and high quality to patients wherever they live.

"high quality care should be a right for every patient in the NHS"

1.2

Over the last fifty years the NHS has done a remarkable job. It has banished the fear of becoming ill for millions of our fellow citizens. Every day its staff treat one million people. It is little wonder that the NHS is our country's most popular organisation.

1.3

But no organisation, however great, can afford to stand still. The NHS faces more challenges than ever. They are challenges that are common to other healthcare systems elsewhere in the world, coping with greater and faster medical advances. The challenges posed by a better informed and more demanding public. And the challenges that come from shifts in family structures, changes in working life and an ageing population.

"a series of well publicised lapses in quality have prompted doubts in the minds of patients about the overall standard of care they may receive"

1.4

Today, the public is more likely to question the ability of the NHS to meet these modern challenges. Public confidence has also been undermined by three further factors. By fragmentation in decision making that has prompted accusations of a lottery in care with patients being denied treatment available in neighbouring areas. The sense that the NHS does not match modern expectations of rapid access to high quality services. And a series of well-publicised lapses in quality that have prompted doubts in the minds of patients about the overall standards of care they may receive.

"in a National Health Service there must be a guarantee of excellence for all patients"

1.5

This Government believes that the NHS can meet these challenges and overcome them. But it must be prepared to change and focus on the things that really matter to patients; high quality prompt services wherever they live. At its best the NHS delivers these services and betters anything anywhere in the world. But it is not good enough for such services to be available to some patients while they are unavailable to others. Every patient judges the performance of the whole NHS by the quality of the care he or she receives in their local GP surgery, their local hospital, from their local midwife or health visitor, their local laboratory. In a **National** Health Service there must be a guarantee of excellence for all patients.

1.6

Today's NHS does not fulfil the highest expectations for everyone. For a national public service like the NHS there are unacceptable variations in performance and practice. The inequalities go beyond the provision of medicines and other treatments. There are inequalities in the way that some proven treatments get introduced to the NHS too slowly while other unproven treatments can be introduced too quickly. There are inequalities in waiting times for operations; in the time it takes for patients to receive test results; in the number of people given screening tests. There are inequalities in clinical practice – and in clinical outcomes. In one region, amongst 35 surgeons, rates of mastectomy for breast cancer varied from nil (meaning all women had breast conservation surgery) to 80%. The average was 18%. Similarly, knee replacement is highly effective in removing pain and improving about 90% of cases. Although the number of replacements is increasing, there is still variation even taking into account the different age profiles of local populations with the rate of elective knee replacements ranging from 18–62 per 100,000 population.

1.7
The variations in quality have complex causes but boil down to four main factors. First, the advent of the internal market shattered the national unity of the NHS into hundreds of small competing businesses where there were no incentives to share best practice. Second, even before the internal market, there were no clear national standards of care which all parts of the NHS were expected to achieve. Third, in the history of the NHS there has never been any coherent assessment of which treatments work best for which patients. Fourth, the NHS as a public service has not been sufficiently open and accountable about the quality of the services it offers to the public.

There is concern when it is thought patients are being denied potentially beneficial new treatments. But a wider, if less reported, concern is the number of patients being denied proven treatments because of a delay by health professionals and managers in acting on published evidence. The clot-busting drug streptokinase for heart attack victims and blood-thinning drugs such as heparin, to prevent potentially fatal thrombosis after surgery, all took years to come into routine use despite increasing evidence of their benefits. The time lag between research paper and bedside practice means many patients are being denied effective therapy.

1.8
The variation in care that has resulted is wasteful as well as unfair. The cost to individual patients – let alone the taxpayer – is unacceptable. Patients suffer if resources are not used to best effect, just as they suffer if quality standards very. And such widely differing performance saps the confidence of the public in the very idea of a National Health Service. Taxpayers have the right to expect cash spent wisely. Patients have the right to expect services provided fairly. The Government will ensure there is accountability for both efficiency and quality throughout the NHS.

1.9
The Government has embarked on a ten year programme of modernisation that will see the NHS getting better year by year. Fragmentation in decision-making and two-tier health care are being tackled by abolishing the internal market introduced by the previous government. Quicker access to services will be brought by reducing hospital waiting lists and by the nationwide introduction of the new 24-hour telephone advice service **NHS Direct**. More money is being made available to invest for change. The biggest new hospital building programme in the history of the NHS is now underway to give health service staff the modern facilities they need to deliver modern forms of care.

1.10
This document spells out how the Government's modernisation programme will be taken forward by putting quality at the top of the NHS agenda. The objective is to ensure fair access to effective, prompt high quality care wherever a patient is treated in the NHS. The Government's intention is to ensure clear national standards for services. These will be supported by consistent, evidence-based guidance to raise quality standards in the NHS.

"putting quality at the top of the NHS agenda"

1.11
This will not mean that local variations in need or the different characteristics of different communities will be ignored. Patients experience the NHS as a local service and the needs of the East End of London are different from the needs of East Surrey. Similarly, it must be for the individual clinician to decide what is in the best interest of the individual patient. Each patient is different and treatment must be tailor-made to their specific needs.

"a partnership between the Government and the clinical professions"

1.12
This document describes the Government's approach to matching consistency in quality across the NHS with sensitivity to the needs of the individual patient and local community.

In so doing it moves beyond the NHS models both of the late 1970s and the early 1990s. It rejects the grey uniformity of central control as irreconcilable, both with clinical judgment and with individual patient needs. Equally it dismisses laissez faire local competition as inefficient and incompatible with the drive to ensure that all patients, wherever they live, have access to the same high quality care.

1.13
We propose a new model which marries clinical judgment with clear national standards. It involves a partnership between the Government and the clinical professions. In that partnership, the Government does what only Government can do and the professions do what only they can do.

1.14
The Government's third way involves setting clear national standards but with responsibility for delivery being taken locally and being backed by consistent monitoring arrangements. National yardsticks, drawn up through joint working between the Department of Health and the professions, will guide local decisions by managers and clinicians, not tie their hands. Devolution of responsibility will be matched with accountability for performance – as it has to be in a national public service as important as the NHS (**See Figure 1**).

Figure 1

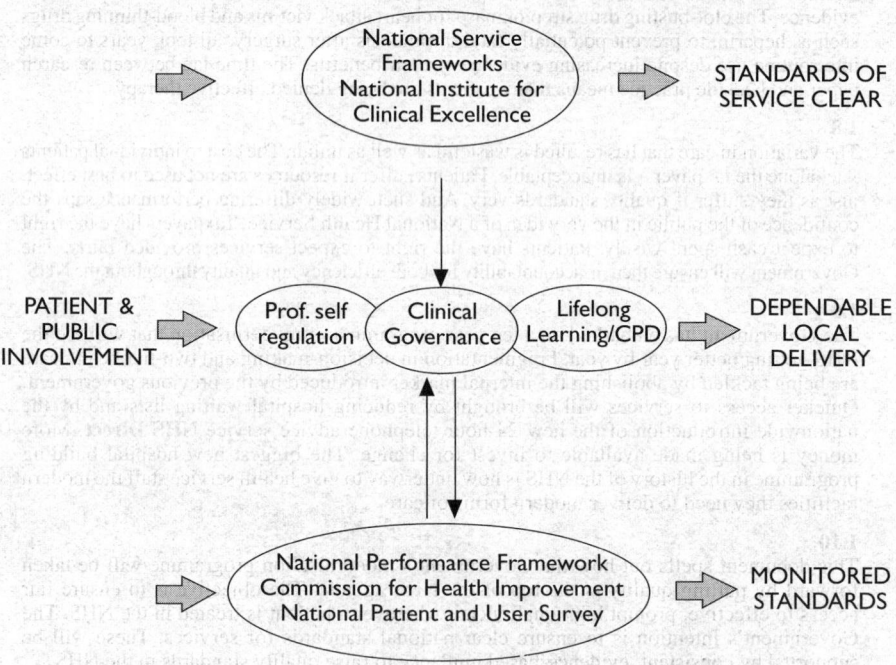

WHAT THE QUALITY FRAMEWORK MEANS FOR PATIENTS

National Service Frameworks
National Institute for Clinical Excellence → STANDARDS OF SERVICE CLEAR

PATIENT & PUBLIC INVOLVEMENT → Prof. self regulation — Clinical Governance — Lifelong Learning/CPD → DEPENDABLE LOCAL DELIVERY

National Performance Framework
Commission for Health Improvement
National Patient and User Survey → MONITORED STANDARDS

"National Standards will be set"

1.15
National standards will be set through National Service Frameworks and through a National Institute for Clinical Excellence (NICE):
the National Service Frameworks will spell out how services can best be organised to cater for patients with particular conditions and the standards that services will have to meet. In all parts of the country the NHS will be required to organise its services to ensure the best quality and the fairest access. The National Service Frameworks, for example, will decide which services are best provided in primary care, in hospitals and in specialist centres: NICE will produce clear guidance for clinicians about which treatments work best for which patients. It will assess new drugs, treatments and devices for their clinical and cost-effectiveness. It

will mean looking, for example, at whether new medicines could replace existing products or reduce the need for complicated surgery.

1.16
Standards will be delivered locally through a new system of clinical governance, extended lifelong learning among staff and modernised professional self-regulation:
clinical governance will be the process by which each part of the NHS quality assures its clinical decisions. Backed by a new statutory duty of quality it will introduce a system of continuous improvement into the operation of the whole NHS. Clinical governance, for example, will provide a means for hospitals to identify and address weaknesses in post operative care lifelong learning will give NHS staff the tools of knowledge to offer the most modern, effective and high quality care to patients. It will provide staff with the opportunity to continuously update their skills and knowledge. Lifelong learning, for example, will allow NHS staff to identify training needs across professions to aid clinical team-working
professional self-regulation provides clinicians with the opportunity to help set standards. A modernised regulatory system will allow the professions to more openly account for how standards are set and enforced. Modern professional self-regulation, for example, will play a fuller part in the early identification of possible lapses in clinical quality.

"standards will be delivered locally"

"standards will be monitored"

1.17
Standards will be monitored through three new mechanisms – a Commission for Health Improvement, a National Framework for Assessing Performance and an annual National Survey of Patient and User Experience of the NHS:
the Commission for Health Improvement will provide an independent means of guaranteeing quality throughout the NHS. Through a rolling programme of reviews of Trusts and the ability to investigate when things are going wrong, the Commission will nip problems in the bud. It will have the power, for example, to intervene at the Government's request, in a hospital where clinical problems have been identified and report to Ministers on remedial action that is needed
the Performance Framework will judge how well each part of the NHS is doing to deliver quality services. The Framework will hold local services to account against objective criteria which measure performance from the patients' point of view. It will, for example, publish information about whether patients have fair access to similar services in all parts of the country
the National Survey of Patient and User Experience will ask those who use the services for their views about clinical quality. Conducted and published annually, the Survey will find out whether local services are meeting patients' needs. The Survey, for example, could trigger the involvement of the Commission for Health Improvement if services in a particular area are consistently failing to deliver patient satisfaction.

"a new emphasis on quality at all levels in the NHS. One that no longer tolerates failure but celebrates success"

1.18
Setting standards, delivering standards, monitoring standards – these are the routes to consistent, prompt, high quality services throughout the NHS. There will be a new emphasis on quality at all levels in the NHS. One that no longer tolerates failure but celebrates success. The approach outlined in this document involves the Government taking responsibility for guaranteeing fair access and high quality throughout the health service. For the first time in the history of the NHS standards will be set for how services should be delivered.

1.19
But the Government cannot deliver high standards by itself. We need the active participation and partnership of clinical professionals and patients throughout the NHS. That is why NICE and the Commission will involve both clinicians and patients. It is why clinical governance arrangements must be developed locally in the NHS. And it is why the Government is setting such store on the views of patients acting as a positive lever for change.

"involving both clinicians and patients"

1.20
The drive to place quality at the heart of the NHS is not about ticking checklists – it is about changing thinking. This document describes how we will do just that. It sets out the Government's approach and, in some places, asks for views about how best our objectives can be achieved. Driving up standards will rely on the commitment and expertise of all those

who work in the health service. The staff of the NHS want a first class service. Patients and the Government want it too. By working in partnership we will deliver first class services to patients wherever they live.

"The drive to place quality at the heart of the NHS is not about ticking checklists – it is about changing thinking"

In essence, therefore, the Government contemplates: (a) effective professional self-regulation; (b) robust systems for monitoring (poor) professional performance; (c) national standards for quality of care through National Service Frameworks and the National Institute for Clinical Excellence (NICE); and (d) policing and monitoring of local quality mechanisms through the Commission for Health Improvement (CHI). (We discuss professional regulation and 'poorly performing' doctors in Chapter 3.) In essence, these new mechanisms collectively make up the arrangements for 'clinical governance', which is defined in *A First Class Service* (*op cit*) (para 3.2) to mean:

> a framework through which NHS organisations are accountable for continuously improving the quality of their services and safeguarding high standards of care by creating an environment in which excellence in clinical care will flourish.

The arrangements for 'clinical governance' apply to all parts of the NHS: to NHS Trusts, Primary Care Trusts and Primary Care Groups.

The Government's description of clinical governance in its document, *A First Class Service* (*op cit*) is as follows:

A First Class Service HSC 1998/113 (1998)

Clinical and corporate governance

3.5 Clinical governance will be part of an overall NHS governance framework. It deliberately echoes the principles of corporate governance. The Chief Executive of each NHS Trust, as accountable officer, will sign an assurance statement on behalf of the Board. A statement to the public on financial risk management and control systems will appear in the 1997/98 Annual Accounts for NHS Trusts and Health Authorities. In future years, this process will be extended to statutory responsibilities in non-financial areas. For the first time in the history of the NHS, there is more than a requirement to meet financial statutory duties.

3.6 Under clinical governance, Chief Executives will be accountable on behalf of NHS Trust Boards, for assuring the quality of NHS Trust services and will provide Boards with regular reports on quality in the same way as they do for finance.

3.7 The principles of clinical governance apply to all those who provide or manage patient care services in the NHS. The principles supporting quality improvement will be the same for large and small organisations. In practice, clinical governance locally will need to take account of the needs, complexity and size of individual NHS organisations. But the emphasis must be on processes that are simple to use and which, above all, produce results. The requirements of clinical governance will be backed by the new statutory duty for quality which will be placed on NHS Trusts and Primary Care Trusts.

3.8 For the first time, the NHS will be required to adopt a structured and coherent approach to clinical quality, placing duties and expectations on local health care organisations as well as individuals. Effective clinical governance will make it clear that quality is everybody's business.

"The principles of clinical governance apply to all those who provide or manage patient care services in the NHS."

3.9 Clinical governance requires partnerships within health care teams, between health professionals (including academic staff) and managers, between individuals and the organisations in which they work and between the NHS, patients and the public.

"effective clinical governance will make it clear that quality is everybody's business"

3.10 Effective involvement of patients and carers is essential to ensuring that everyone is fully engaged in the drive for quality, and that this focuses on what really matters.

The clinical governance framework

3.11 We will introduce a clinical governance framework that:
modernises and strengthens professional self-regulation and builds on the principles of performance review
strengthens existing systems for quality control, based on clinical standards, evidence based practice and learning the lessons of poor performance.
It should include all activity and information that allows an NHS organisation, and those who work within it, to improve the quality of services locally. This will include work to: identify and build on good practice
assess and minimise the risk of untoward events
investigate problems as these arise and ensure lessons are learnt
support health professionals in delivering quality care …

3.12 Key components of the framework will include:
a comprehensive programme of quality improvement activity (such as clinical audit and evidence-based practice) and processes for monitoring clinical care using effective information and clinical record systems. Internal scrutiny within each hospital needs to be supplemented by open and external review. From next year, all hospital doctors will be required to participate in a national audit programme appropriate to their specialty or subspecialty and approved as such by the new Commission for Health Improvement
clear policies aimed at managing risk, including procedures that support professional staff in identifying and tackling poor performance

Main components of clinical governance: NHS Trusts

Clear lines of responsibility and accountability for the overall quality of clinical care through:
the NHS Trust Chief Executive carries ultimate responsibility for assuring the quality of services provided by the Trust
a designated senior clinician responsible for ensuring that systems for clinical governance are in place and monitoring their continued effectiveness
formal arrangements for NHS Trust Boards to discharge their responsibilities for clinical quality, perhaps through a clinical governance committee
regular reports to NHS Trust Boards on the quality of clinical care given the same importance as monthly financial reports
an annual report on clinical governance

A comprehensive programme of quality improvement activities which includes:
full participation by all hospital doctors in audit programmes, including specialty and subspecialty national external audit programmes endorsed by the Commission for Health Improvement
full participation in the current four National Confidential Enquiries
evidence-based practice is supported and applied routinely in everyday practice
ensuring the clinical standards of National Service Frameworks and NICE recommendations are implemented
workforce planning and development (ie recruitment and retention of appropriately trained workforce) is fully integrated within the NHS Trust's service planning
continuing professional development: programmes aimed at meeting the development needs of individual health professionals and the service needs of the organisation are in place and supported locally
appropriate safeguards to govern access to and storage of confidential patient information as recommended in the Caldicott Report on the Review of Patient-Identifiable Information
effective monitoring of clinical care with high quality system for clinical record keeping and the collection of relevant information
processes for assuring the quality of clinical care are in place and integrated with the quality programme for the organisation as a whole

Clear policies aimed at managing risks:
controls assurance which promote self-assessment to identify and manage risks
clinical risk systematically assessed with programmes in place to reduce risk

Procedures for all professional groups to identify and remedy poor performance, for example;
critical incident reporting ensures that adverse events are identified, openly investigated, lessons are learned and promptly applied
complaints procedures, accessible to patients and their families and fair to staff. Lessons are learned and recurrence of similar problems avoided

professional performance procedures which take effect at an early stage before patients are harmed and which help the individual to improve their performance whenever possible, are in place and understood by all staff

staff supported in their duty to report any concerns about colleagues' professional conduct and performance, with clear statements from the Board on what is expected of all staff. Clear procedures for reporting concerns so that early action can be taken to support the individual to remedy the situation

clear lines of responsibility and accountability for the overall quality of clinical care. For Trusts, that will include regular reports to the Board and an annual report on clinical governance.

"successful clinical governance will rely on proper arrangements for accountability, which are seen to be effective by the public"

...

3.14 Clinical governance will provide a systematic framework that can be extended into the clinical community at all levels. Successful clinical governance will rely on proper arrangements for accountability, which are seen to be effective by the public, the wider health service and individual practitioners. Local systems for monitoring quality should be open and fair (whilst respecting the requirement to safeguard patient confidentiality). As a result of participation in national comparative clinical audits, individual hospital doctors will be able to compare their own performance with national averages. Individual doctors will be required to share their results with the medical director of their Trust and the Trust's lead clinician responsible for clinical governance. In turn, doctors from the Commission for Health Improvement will have access to these data when they visit the Trust to review local standards and clinical governance processes.

3.15 Strengthened external audit will help assure patients that services at their local hospital are being monitored and are of a consistently high standard. Doctors with results that fall short of these norms will need to take urgent action to improve their results. Where the outcome has unacceptable mortality or complications, it might be necessary for the clinician to stop performing the procedure. Fellow professionals could provide extra training, supervision and support to correct what had been going wrong. In appropriate circumstances, the **General Medical Council** would be involved.

The Government's strategy has been implemented through the Health Act 1999 and delegated legislation. The detailed provisions can be found in *Clinical Governance: Quality in the new NHS* (HSC 1999/065) (1999) and *Supporting Doctors, Protecting Patients* (November 1999) (for a detailed discussion, see M Baker *Making Sense of the NHS White Papers* (2nd edn, 1999)). For us, there are *three* legal aspects which we should consider.

1. Duty of quality

Section 18 of the Health Act 1999 provides:

18.—(1) It is the duty of each Health Authority, Primary Care Trust and NHS Trust to put and keep in place arrangements for the purpose of monitoring and improving the quality of health care which it provides to individuals.

(2) The reference in subsection (1) to health care which a body there mentioned provides to individuals includes health care which the body provides jointly with another person to individuals.

(3) The Secretary of State may by regulations extend the duty in this section to Special Health Authorities of any particular description.

(4) In this section—

"health care" means services for or in connection with the prevention, diagnosis or treatment of illness,

"illness" has the meaning given by section 128(1) of the 1977 Act.

This 'duty of quality' placed upon HAs, PCTs and NHS Trusts is new. Previously, no statutory duty existed. The only legal duty would be the primary duty of NHS institutions at common law to exercise reasonable care and skill in providing services (see *infra*, ch 4).

The duty is undoubtedly a duty owed to the public at large and subject to the enforcement mechanisms through the Commission for Health Improvement (see *infra*) and the Secretary of State's power to issue directions to these NHS institutions with which they have a duty to comply (see NHS Act 1977, s 17, substituted by the Health Act 1999, s 12) or, in the case of PCTs, directions may be given by a HA (see NHS Act 1977, s 17B, inserted by the Health Act 1999, s 12). Breach of duty under s 18 would not give rise to a civil law action for damages (see *infra*, ch 4).

The effect of s 18 is outlined in the *Explanatory Notes* to the Health Act 1999:

173. Under this section Health Authorities, NHS trusts and Primary Care Trusts will be required to put and keep in place arrangements for monitoring and improving the quality of the health care they provide. A fundamental component of those arrangements will be the implementation of clinical governance arrangements. The concept of "clinical governance" was discussed in the consultation document *A First Class Service* and *Quality Care and Clinical Excellence*, which set out in more detail the Government's plans to improve the quality of NHS healthcare. The main components of clinical governance as described in the consultation documents are:

- clear lines of responsibility and accountability for the overall quality of clinical care;
- a comprehensive programme of quality improvement systems (including clinical audit, supporting and applying evidence-based practice, implementing clinical standards and guidelines, workforce planning and development);
- clear policies aimed at managing risk; and procedures for all professional groups to identify and remedy poor performance.

It is intended that the detail of what is expected of Health Authorities, NHS trusts and Primary Care Trusts in implementing clinical governance will be set out in guidance; The first tranches of clinical governance guidance were published in March 1999 (under HSC 1999/065 in England and WHC (99) 54 in Wales).

2. NICE

In the *New NHS: Modern ... Dependable* (*op cit*), the Government proposed the creation of a new National Institute for Clinical Excellence.

National Institute for clinical Excellence
7.11 A new National Institute for Clinical Excellence will be established to give new coherence and prominence to information about clinical and cost-effectiveness. It will produce and disseminate:

- clinical guidelines based on relevant evidence of clinical and cost-effectiveness
- associated clinical audit methodologies and information on good practice in clinical audit
- in doing so it will bring together work currently undertaken by the many professional organisations in receipt of Department of Health funding for this purpose
- it will work to a programme agreed with and funded from current resources by the Department of Health.

7.12 The National Institute's membership will be drawn from the health professions, the NHS, academics, health economists and patient interests. It will need to have access to an appropriate range of skills, including economic and managerial expertise as well as specialist input on specific issues. The Government will consider developing the role and function of the National Institute as it gathers momentum and experience.

NICE was created as a Special Health Authority under s 11 of the NHS Act 1977 on 26th February 1999 (The National Institute for Clinical Excellence (Establishment and Constitution) Order 1999 (SI 1999 No 220) (as amended by SI 1999 No 2219) and the National Institute for Clinical Excellence Regulations 1999 (SI 1999 No 260) (as amended by SI 1999 No 2218). NICE consists of a chairman, seven appointed members and four officers of the Institute. Its functions are spelt out in art 3 of the Establishment Order (as amended).

The National Institute for Clinical Excellence (Establishment and Constitution) Order 1999 (SI 1999 No 220)

Functions of the Institute
   3. Subject to and in accordance with such directions as the Secretary of State may give, the Institute shall perform such functions in connection with the promotion of clinical excellence and of the effective use of available resources in the health service as the Secretary of State may direct.

In *A First Class Service* (*op cit*), the Government spelt out the content of NICE's functions:

2.8 The work of the
National Institute for Clinical Excellence (NICE) in producing authoritative national guidance is part of the overall approach to achieving consistent clinical standards across the NHS. This approach consists of six stages:
Stage 1: Identification
for **new** health interventions – "scanning the horizon" (that is, identifying at an early stage through available intelligence) for new interventions, including drugs, devices and procedures which are likely to have a significant impact on the NHS
for **existing** interventions – examining current practice to identify unjustified variations in use, or uncertainty about clinical and cost-effectiveness
Stage 2: Evidence collection – undertaking research to assess the clinical and cost-effectiveness of health interventions
Stage 3: Appraisal and guidance – carefully considering the implications for clinical practice of the evidence on clinical and cost-effectiveness and producing guidance for the NHS
Stage 4: Dissemination of the guidance and supporting audit methodologies
Stage 5: Implementation at a local level, through clinical governance and other approaches
Stage 6: Monitoring the impact and keeping advice under review, taking into account the views of patients and their representatives and any relevant new research findings …

Horizon Scanning
The purpose of this work is to identify new interventions and products under development at the earliest possible stage and certainly well before they become available for general use in the NHS. This involves gathering information from a variety of sources, such as published material, contacts with researchers and health care industries and through communication with similar horizon scanning groups abroad, and using expert judgement to assess the potential significance to the NHS …

2.9 NICE will be responsible for appraisal and the production of guidance (**Stage 3**) and its dissemination to the NHS (**Stage 4**). NICE will need to receive feedback on the application of its guidance as this is monitored through clinical audit and through performance assessment (**Stage 6**).

2.10 To fulfil this key role, NICE will need to respond promptly to emerging evidence and may sometimes need to draw attention to gaps in the evidence base. In particular, it will need to be kept aware of:
information emerging from horizon scanning work (**Stage 1**) to be provided by the
Horizon Scanning Centre of the
University of Birmingham in association with the
National Prescribing Centre and the
Drug Information Pharmacists Group
research findings from the NHS R&D programme and other sources (**Stage 2**). In the course of its own work, NICE will identify gaps in evidence and these will be addressed through the NHS R&D programme …

Appraisal and guidance
2.11 There is currently no coherent approach to the appraisal of research evidence and the subsequent production of guidance for clinical practice. Guidance is issued by numerous bodies, at national, regional and local levels, each of which have different ways of appraising the evidence and developing recommendations. The status and implications of the products are not always clear, nor what actions are expected to follow as a result of them. This is confusing for clinicians wanting to know what care they should be expected to give, and for patients wanting to know what care to expect. NICE will reduce duplication of this activity and maximise the use of the academic and professional expertise needed to produce credible guidance. It will provide a single,

national focus for appraisal of significant new and existing interventions, with subsequent guidance. NICE will replace progressively the need for this activity to be duplicated at regional and district levels by such bodies as the regional Development and Evaluation Committees (DECs), the West Midlands Therapeutics Review Advisory Committee (MTRAC) and the **North of England Guidelines Group**.

"there is currently no coherent approach to the appraisal of research evidence and the production of guidance for clinical practice"

2.12 As a body involving professionals, patients and managers, NICE will ensure the production of high quality, evidence-based, guidance to a programme set by the **Department of Health**. This programme will be driven by the information emerging from the horizon scanning work, by the development of National Service Frameworks **(see below)** and other major service priorities.

"NICE will end this confusion by providing a single, national, focus"

2.13 Guidance from NICE will include guidelines for the management of certain diseases or conditions and guidance on the appropriate use of particular interventions. Wherever appropriate, NICE guidance will cover all aspects of the management of a condition – from self care through to primary care, secondary care and more specialist services. It is envisaged that NICE will carry out annually 30–50 appraisals of the most significant new and existing interventions. The various industries which produce drugs and devices involved in these treatments will need to enhance their capacity to produce evidence of clinical and cost-effectiveness. Where evidence of this has not become available at the point that a product comes to market, NICE may recommend that in the first instance the NHS **channels** its use through well controlled research studies, so that patients can be assured of the benefit of treatments used widely throughout the NHS …

2.17 … national guidance will mean that interventions with good evidence of clinical and cost-effectiveness will be actively promoted, so that patients have faster access to treatments known to work. Equally, it will help protect patients from new interventions with inadequate evidence of clinical and cost-effectiveness and ensure that interventions which are effective only in limited circumstances are appropriately used.

2.18 Health professionals need to be able to assess the care they give against established clinical standards. This can be done through clinical audit, which allows them to look at what they are doing against agreed standards and, where necessary, make changes to practice. But health professionals need support in using clinical audit to best effect. Local ownership is vital to the success of implementation and NICE will need to build on and support new and innovative clinical practice at a local level. For that reason, NICE will develop a range of audit methodologies that can be adapted for local use to support the guidance it produces. This will build on the work undertaken by the **National Centre for Clinical Audit (NCCA)**, whose function will be incorporated into NICE.

2.19 Initially, NICE will focus on clinical issues. We recognise there are a range of other interventions, including screening programmes and other public health and health promotion programmes which could come within its orbit in the future.

"local ownership is vital to the success of implementation"

2.20 We propose to bring together under the umbrella of NICE the four established National Confidential Enquiries which look at clinical performance. This will give greater clarity and coherence to the status of their findings. All relevant hospital doctors and other health professionals will be required to participate in the work of the National Confidential Enquiries. Results from their findings will be fed into appropriate NICE guidance and standard setting and will be an important part of ensuring effective clinical governance locally … which is to be independently scrutinised by the Commission for Health Improvement …

Dissemination
2.21 Clear credible guidance and the production of robust audit methodologies are essential. But in themselves, these will not achieve change. Information needs to reach the right people – health professionals, patients, carers and those commissioning services – and be locally owned and acted on in the right way.

"clear, credible guidance"

2.22 NICE will have a key role in co-ordinating the range of current activity in both the active dissemination of information and in responding to specific inquiries. It will provide a single reference point for information on standards and audit methodologies, and will support and complement the new NHS Information Strategy which aims to provide universal desk top access to NICE guidance (on the lines of the PRODIGY computer aided, decision-support system for GPs).

2.23 There is much still to learn on how practice can be changed and this is being actively investigated in the NHS R&D programme (including an emerging Service Delivery and Organisation R&D Programme). NICE will have a developing role in providing information about implementation methodologies to help local clinical teams. There will also be a need to ensure that its clinical guidance is integrated into other appropriate activities, including professional education and training, seminars and workshops, patient education and information, and audit.

"information needs to reach the right people and be acted on in the right way"

2.24 There is already a range of tools available to encourage the implementation of clinical guidance. These include local prescribing policies; formularies and guidelines; audit programmes; and lifelong learning. NICE will provide the focus for such initiatives and for reviewing clinical behaviour and practice. As each NICE guideline is produced, we expect that in each Health Authority area, lead clinicians will be designated to have the responsibility for leading the implementation process.

In 1998, we will publicise a new Information Strategy for the NHS to harness the enormous potential benefits of IT in supporting the drive for quality and efficiency in the NHS. The aim will be to create a powerful alliance between knowledgeable patients advised by knowledgeable professionals as a means of improving health and health care.

Monitoring

2.25 Although NICE will produce clinical guidance against which performance can be assessed, it will not have a direct role in monitoring the uptake of its guidance and audit tools. This will be undertaken through a range of initiatives, in particular through the National Framework for Assessing Performance with its new emphasis on standards and outcomes; through professional self-regulation; and an independent scrutiny of implementation to be provided by the new Commission for Health Improvement through its rolling programme of spot checks on NHS Trusts and Primary Care Trusts. The Commission will also conduct systematic service reviews in which it will follow through the implementation of National Service Frameworks and NICE guidance ... Feedback to NICE will also be provided through the National Survey of Patient and User Experience and its work with a range of other organisations ... However, lessons from this monitoring activity will be reported to NICE to ensure its guidance is sensitive to the needs of the NHS and is responsive to the lessons learned.

Clinical Audit involves systematically looking at the procedures used for diagnosis, care and treatment, examining how associated resources are used and investigating the effect care has on the outcome and quality of life for the patient. Audit is a valuable tool to improve the quality of professional care and, ultimately, patient choice.

2.26 The introduction of clinical governance will mean that variations from expected good practice, as recommended by NICE, will increasingly be challenged locally. We will expect the guidance produced by NICE to be implemented consistently across the NHS. How well this happens in practice, to ensure that unacceptable variations in care for patients are not allowed to persist, will determine whether and how NICE's and the Commission for Health Improvement's powers will be strengthened in the future.

"lead clinicians will be designated to have responsibility for leading the implementation process"

How will NICE work?

2.27 NICE will create a new partnership between the Government, the NHS and clinical professionals. By establishing NICE, the Government will take responsibility for helping to clarify, both for patients and professionals, which treatments work best for which patients and those which do not. For the first time in the history of the NHS the Government, working with clinical bodies, will systematically appraise medical interventions before these are introduced into the NHS. Clear, authoritative, guidance on clinical and cost-effectiveness will be offered to front line clinicians. NICE will offer doctors, nurses and midwives more support than they have had before in making the complex decisions about individual patient care often required in modern health care. That support will enhance the ability of individual clinicians to make such decisions. It will also inform the decisions of those commissioning care.

"we will expect the guidance produced by NICE to be implemented consistently across the NHS"

As will be clear from this, NICE will have a very significant role in setting clinical standards within the NHS. Behind this development is, in part, the Government's desire to eliminate so called 'postcode rationing' where different commissioners (HAs, primary care groups or PCTs) take different views on what treatment should be available to the individuals for whom they have responsibility: such that, in some instances, neighbours on different sides of a street may have different treatments available for the same condition because their respective health authorities have (or have not) commissioned particular services with NHS Trusts. The guidance from NICE – and it is formally no more than that – taken with the National Service Frameworks (initially in mental health and coronary heart disease) will have a significant impact on these anomalies of provision. Increasingly, NICE guidelines will be taken to set the standard and quality of care that a patient is entitled to expect. Thus, while not determinative of the duty of care in negligence, these standards are likely to be seen by the courts as the *expected* level of care, such that departure will require some demonstrable justification relating to the individual patient's particular circumstances. Also, providing care consistent with the guidelines is unlikely to be seen as negligent, even though the courts retain the ability in exceptional cases after *Bolitho v City and Hackney HA* [1998] AC 232, to say that it is (see *infra*, ch 4).

Likewise, failure to provide or commission services recommended by NICE for particular conditions will expose the NHS institutions to challenge by way of judicial review. We saw in Chapter 1 how judicial review has in a number of cases provided a remedy to a patient refused treatment. Largely, as we saw, these successes were built upon procedural errors, failures by Health Authorities to follow their own policies or to do so blindly. The existence of NICE guidance will only enhance the chances of success for refusal to provide treatment where this is inconsistent with its guidance. The guidance will be a relevant – a *very* relevant – consideration in making a decision whether to make available treatment. Of course, there may be *individual* circumstances why this particular patient falls outside the guidance or its recommendation for treatment. Otherwise, the rationality of departing from the guidance may be difficult to sustain before a court. Challenges where the non-provision is founded in a decision as to how to allocate resources have, by and large, been unsuccessful as –

> Difficult and agonising judgments have to be made as to how a limited budget is best allocated to the maximum advantage of the maximum number of patients. That is not a judgment which the court can make.

(*R v Cambridge HA, ex p B* (1995) 23 BMLR 1 at 9, per Sir Thomas Bingham MR.)

This is, and remains, a powerful argument (see *infra*, ch 4). However, the position may change as a result of NICE. First, the guidance is intended to set *national* standards and thus local variations would seem to require strong local reasons to justify a departure. Secondly, and very significantly, in producing guidance NICE is itself enjoined to promote 'the effective use of available resources' (art 3 of the National Institute for Clinical Excellence (Establishment and Constitution) Order 1999 (SI 1999 No 220) (as amended by SI 1999 No 2219, art 2(2))). This aspect of its function was introduced by way of amendment in August 1999. Therefore, the guidelines themselves should take account of the cost-effectiveness of the treatment and, consistent with the NHS body's duty of quality, non-provision of the treatment (or service) would be irrational. That would amount to a 'non-effective' use of available resources.

3. CHI

In *The New NHS – Modern ... Dependable* (*op cit*) the Government set out its plan for the creation of a NHS 'quality watchdog' to be called the Commission for Health Improvement (CHI).

> 7.13 To ensure the drive for excellence is instilled throughout the NHS, the Government will create a new **Commission for Health Improvement**. It will complement the introduction of clinical governance arrangements. Past performance on quality has been variable, and the health service has sometimes been slow to detect and act decisively on serious lapses in quality. As a statutory body, at arm's length from Government, the new Commission will offer an independent guarantee that local systems to monitor, assure and improve clinical quality are in place. It will support local development and 'spot-check' the new arrangements. It will also have the capacity to offer targeted support on request to local organisations facing specific clinical problems.
>
> 7.14 Where local action is not able to resolve serious or persistent problems, the Commission will be able to intervene on the direction of the Secretary of State or by invitation from Primary Care Groups, Health Authorities and NHS Trusts. In these instances, the Commission will both investigate and identify the source of the problem, and work with the organisation on lasting remedies. It will also be able to recommend to the Secretary of State other immediate action. He will have powers to remove NHS Trust Chairs and non-executive directors where there is evidence of systematic failure. The Commission may also undertake an agreed programme of systematic service reviews, following through implementation of the National Service Frameworks and the guidelines developed by the Institute. The Commission will have a membership drawn from the professions, NHS, academic and patient representatives. It will be funded from existing resources.

Section 19 of (and Sch 2 to) the Health Act 1999 create 'a body corporate known as the Commission for Health Improvement'.

CHI came into existence on 1 November 1999. It consists of 14 members, not less than eight of whom must not be health care professionals or be employed by a health service body (see The Commission for Health Improvement (Membership and Procedure) Regulations 1999 (SI 1999 No 2801), reg 2).

The Commission will be accountable to Parliament through the Secretary of State and will produce an annual report and set of accounts (Health Act 1999, Sch 2, paras 12 and 11). In addition, CHI will be subject to the jurisdiction of the Parliamentary Ombudsman (Parliamentary Commissioner Act 1967, Sch 2). The essential functions of CHI are set out in s 20(1) of the Health Act 1999:

> 20.—(1) The Commission has the following functions—
> (a) the function of providing advice or information with respect to arrangements by Primary Care Trusts or NHS trusts for the purpose of monitoring and improving the quality of health care for which they have responsibility,
> (b) the function of conducting reviews of, and making reports on, arrangements by Primary Care Trusts or NHS trusts for the purpose of monitoring and improving the quality of health care for which they have responsibility,
> (c) the function of carrying out investigations into, and making reports on, the management, provision or quality of health care for which Health Authorities, Primary Care Trusts or NHS trusts have responsibility,
> (d) the function of conducting reviews of, and making reports on, the management, provision or quality of, or access to or availability of, particular types of health care for which NHS bodies or service providers have responsibility, and
> (e) such functions as may be prescribed relating to the management, provision or quality of, or access to or availability of, health care for which prescribed NHS bodies or prescribed service providers have responsibility.

Pursuant to s 20 (1)(e) of the 1999 Act, Reg 2 of the Commission for Health Improvement (Functions) Regulations 2000 (SI 2000 No 662) sets out *six* additional functions, as follows:

2. The following functions are prescribed pursuant to section 20(1)(e)—

(a) the function of providing advice or information with respect to the arrangements by Health Authorities, Special Health Authorities or service providers for the purpose of monitoring and improving the quality of health care for which they have responsibility;

(b) the function of providing advice or information with respect to the arrangements by Primary Care Trusts for the purpose of monitoring and improving the quality of health care provided by their relevant service providers;

(c) the function of conducting reviews of, and making reports on, arrangements by Health Authorities to which the duty in section 18 of the Act has been extended, for the purpose of monitoring and improving the quality of health care for which they have responsibility;

(d) the function of conducting reviews of, and making reports on, arrangements by Primary Care Trusts for the purpose of monitoring and improving the quality of health care provided by their relevant service providers;

(e) the function of carrying out investigations into, and making reports on, the management, provisions or quality of health care for which Special Health Authorities have responsibility;

(f) the function of providing advice with respect to the establishment and conduct of health service inquiries.

In addition to performing any functions in relation to NHS care as required by regulations, CHI has *four* core functions (*Explanatory Notes* to the Health Act 1999, *op cit*, para 190).

- providing advice and information on arrangements for the monitoring and improvement of health care provided by NHS trusts and Primary Care Trusts (including "clinical governance" arrangements);
- conducting reviews of the implementation and adequacy of such arrangements;
- investigating, advising and reporting on specific matters relating to the delivery and management of health care provided by NHS bodies;
- conducting national reviews on particular types of health care provided by the NHS . . .

(See also ss 21 and 22 – arrangements with the Audit Commission and Minister respectively.) The Secretary of State may direct the Commission as to the exercise of its functions (s 20(3)) and the Commission has a duty to comply (s 20(4)). Thus, the Secretary of State will have power to shape the operations of the Commission and to focus the areas of investigation or reviews. CHI's jurisdiction covers England and Wales. (As regards the latter, there is an appointed Welsh member and the National Assembly for Wales determines how CHI functions in Wales rather than the Secretary of State.) As we saw, CHI may become involved in the working of an NHS body by invitation of a NHS body or at the direction of the Secretary of State. CHI's remit and powers are wide. It covers all NHS bodies, NHS Trusts, HAs (including primary care groups) and PCTs. As the 'NHS watchdog', CHI will conduct an investigation or review and has extensive powers of entry and to inspect and seize documents. Section 23 provides:

23.—(1) The Secretary of State may by regulations make provision—

(a) conferring a right on persons authorised by the Commission to enter NHS premises at such times, in such cases, for such purposes and on such conditions as may be prescribed in order—

(i) to inspect those premises, or

(ii) to inspect and take copies of prescribed documents held by prescribed persons on those premises,

(b) requiring prescribed persons at such times, at such places, in such cases and for such purposes as may be prescribed to produce prescribed documents or information, or make reports, to the Commission or to persons authorised by the Commission,

(c) requiring prescribed persons at such times, at such places, in such cases and for such purposes as may be prescribed to provide to the Commission, or to persons authorised by the Commission, an explanation of—

(i) any matters which are the subject of the exercise of any functions of the Commission, or

(ii) any documents or information inspected, copied or produced as mentioned in paragraph (a) or (b).

(2) Regulations under this section may not make provision with respect to the disclosure of confidential information which relates to and identifies a living individual unless one or more of the following conditions is satisfied—

(a) the information is disclosed in a form in which the identity of the individual cannot be ascertained,

(b) the individual consents to the information being disclosed,

(c) the individual cannot be traced despite the taking of all reasonable steps,

(d) in a case where the Commission is exercising its functions under section 20(1)(c)—

  (i) it is not practicable to disclose the information in a form in which the identity of the individual cannot be ascertained,

  (ii) the Commission considers that there is a serious risk to the health or safety of patients arising out of the matters which are the subject of the exercise of those functions, and

  (iii) having regard to that risk and the urgency of the exercise of those functions, the Commission considers that the information should be disclosed without the consent of the individual.

(3) Regulations under this section may not make provision with respect to the disclosure of information if that disclosure would be prohibited by or under any other enactment; but where information is held in a form in which the prohibition operates by reason of the fact that the information is capable of identifying an individual, regulations under this section may make provision with respect to the disclosure of the information in a form in which the identity of the individual cannot be ascertained.

(4) Any person who without reasonable excuse—

(a) obstructs a person authorised by the Commission in the exercise of any right conferred by virtue of subsection (1)(a), or

(b) fails to comply with any requirement imposed by virtue of subsection (1)(b) or (c),

is guilty of an offence and liable on summary conviction to a fine not exceeding level 3 on the standard scale.

(5) In this section any reference to documents includes a reference to information held by means of a computer or in any other electronic form; and in the case of information so held, regulations under this section may make provision for it to be made available or produced in a visible and legible form.

(6) In this section—

"confidential information" means information which is held subject to a duty of confidence, and includes information contained in a health record,

"health record" has the meaning given by section 68(2) of the Data Protection Act 1998,

"NHS premises" means premises owned or controlled by a Health Authority, Special Health Authority, Primary Care Trust or NHS trust,

"prescribed" means prescribed by regulations made by the Secretary of State.

You will notice in ss 23(2) and (3) the limitations on the Secretary of State's regulatory power to require disclosure of confidential information, including patient records. (We discuss the 'restrictions on disclosure' of information obtained by CHI when carrying out functions in s 24, *infra* ch 8.)

At the conclusion of an investigation or review, it is not intended that CHI should have any enforcement powers in relation to its recommendations. To the extent that it is necessary, the Secretary of State may effect this through direction under s 17 of the National Health Service Act 1977.

How then will CHI operate? In *A First Class Service* (*op cit*), the range of activities is explained.

4.5 The Commission's role should be seen in the context of proposals for developing clinical governance ... and the more general challenge of strengthening the mechanisms the NHS has at its disposal for improving clinical quality. The Commission will not replace mainstream NHS performance assessment and management, but will complement and reinforce these processes ...

4.7 The Commission will concentrate on clinical issues but will also have the scope to become involved in management issues where these lie behind clinical problems.

"help the NHS identify and tackle serious or persistent clinical problems"

National leadership on clinical governance ...

4.9 The Commission will have a leading role in advice and guidance for the NHS on clinical governance. The Commission will also have the responsibility for endorsing external audit programmes in which all hospital doctors, in the relevant speciality and subspeciality will have to take part.

Reviewing local clinical governance arrangements

4.10 The NHS Executive Regional Offices will lead in overseeing the implementation of local clinical governance arrangements. The Commission will complement and strengthen these mechanisms, by providing a further external and independent check on local arrangements.

4.11 We propose that the Commission should conduct a rolling programme of reviews, visiting every NHS Trust and **Primary Care Trust** provider over a period of around 3–4 years. It will look for evidence that clinical governance arrangements are working, that these are consistent with established standards, and can develop and sustain quality services. Local processes will be assessed on their capacity to support the delivery of quality services. NHS organisations will receive notice of the Commission's visits.

"the Commission should conduct a rolling programme of reviews, visiting every NHS Trust and Primary Care Trust provider over a period of around 3–4 years"

4.12 This rolling programme of reviews will focus on both processes and outcomes. In looking at outcomes, it will take into account strengths and weaknesses which performance management processes and the new Patient Survey may have already identified within specific Trusts. There will be scope to accelerate the place of a particular Trust in the programme if a Regional Office has identified it as needing particular attention. Types of processes the Commission might examine include (for example) complaints handing – ensuring in particular that important lessons from complaints and the Ombudsman's reports are being identified and acted on. A clinical member of the Commission's review teams will have access to individual clinician's external clinical audit results. Recent tragedies demonstrate all too clearly the necessity for supplementing a hospital's internal processes with independent, external, review of clinical quality by the Commission.

"the Commission's reports will not just be about identifying areas for improvement, but will also provide a way of identifying and acknowledging success and good practice and encouraging its dissemination"

4.13 The Commission's findings will be reported to the Trust concerned and shared with the appropriate Health Authority or Regional Office. A summary will be made public. The Commission's reports will not just be about identifying areas for improvement, but will also provide a way of identifying and acknowledging success and good practice, and encouraging its dissemination.

4.14 Regional Offices and Health Authorities will be responsible for ensuring that the recommendations from review visits are acted on, but the Commission may also have a role in following up specific recommendations for action. Follow-up action plans for addressing any identified deficiencies should be agreed between NHS Trusts and Regional Offices (or Primary Care Trusts and Health Authorities), and these plans should be reported to the Commission. An NHS Trust, Health Authority or Regional Office may also wish to invite the Commission to review progress where a need for major development work has been identified; for example, the Commission might agree to accelerate the place of a particular NHS Trust within its next cycle of local reviews.

4.15 The Commission's rolling programme of reviews will cover all NHS Trusts and all Primary Care Trusts. It will not focus explicitly on commissioners of NHS services, though we propose that the Commission should have the power to look at Health Authorities and Primary Care Groups in the course of a review if it considers that their actions are impacting on the issues it is examining. For example, the Commission is likely to take a particular interest in what Health Authorities and Primary Care Groups are doing to encourage the development of clinical governance principles, both in Trusts and in other parts of primary care; and in securing the implementation of National Service Frameworks and NICE standards.

4.16 There will be occasions when the Commission needs to look at those aspects of care delivered in primary care settings in examining whether the whole system of NHS care is working well (for example, for people suffering from heart disease as part of the monitoring of the coronary heart disease National Service Framework). It is right that there should be a strong focus on quality throughout primary care. The principles of clinical governance need to apply in primary as well as secondary care, and all the contractor professionals are expected by their regulatory bodies to deliver the best care they can. We will be working with the relevant professional bodies to explore ways in which other mechanisms – within the framework of the existing national contracts – can in the first instance be used to support quality improvement and the principles of clinical governance in the contractor professions.

"the principles of clinical governance need to apply in primary as well as secondary care"

National Service Frameworks and NICE guidance ...
4.17 Part of each review visit should be devoted to a review of local activity on implementing National Service Frameworks and NICE guidance (for example, by seeking evidence of specific examples where clinical practice has changed). But we also believe that there is merit in reviewing and comparing this work in a more systematic way nationally.

4.18 We propose that the Commission should conduct national "sample" studies of activity to implement National Service Frameworks and associated NICE guidance. The results of these studies should inform the Commission's local review work, as well as wider NHS work to implement the Frameworks ...

Addressing serious or persistent problems ...
4.22 **The new NHS** clearly sets out the measures available to address poor performance in NHS Trusts. Health Authorities can trigger the involvement of the Regional Offices if there are concerns about the failure of NHS Trusts to deliver, and the Regional Offices can also investigate failures to comply with statutory duties. The Commission will supplement not supplant these mechanisms. Most problems will continue to be dealt with by local providers working with Health Authorities and the Regional Offices.

"It will be able to respond quickly and decisively to help identify and address serious problems, providing extra support to managers and clinicians to help put them right"

4.23 The Commission for Health Improvement will provide external help where it is needed. In the past, there has been too much uncertainty about how and when to bring in outside help. The Commission's independence, objectivity and expertise will support its role as an effective "trouble-shooter". It will be able to respond quickly and decisively to help identify and address serious problems, providing extra support to managers and clinicians to help put them right. In doing so, it will need to work very closely with existing sources of expertise (for example, relevant national professional bodies).

Triggering the Commission's involvement
4.24 Strong clinical governance means that problems are far more likely to be identified and addressed at the local level. And strong performance management and the new Patient Survey ... means that there will be a number of "triggers" to sound alarm bells where difficulties continue despite local efforts. Where concerns are raised, service providers, Health Authorities and Regional Offices will have the opportunity to invite support from the Commission to investigate services at a particular Trust.

4.25 Primary Care Groups and Primary Care Trusts will be able to invite the Commission in to look at services provided by their members as contractor professions, but only where other avenues, such as action through contracts, have been shown not to work.

"there will be a number of "triggers" to sound alarm bells where difficulties continue despite local efforts"

4.26 Where the Commission has been invited in to investigate a local problem, follow-up action will be the responsibility of the NHS organisation in question, overseen by the Regional Office or Health Authority. The relevant NHS organisation should share with the Commission its plans for addressing any recommendations for action, and the Commission might be involved in this follow-up action at local request. The Commission is likely to pay particular attention to the implementation of its recommendations when it next visits the organisation as part of its rolling review programme.

4.27 The Commission will work closely with the Regional Offices to ensure that best use is made of its resources and to ensure that help is targeted where most needed. Where the Commission helps to investigate and resolve a problem, a summary of key findings and recommendations will be made public.

"key findings and recommendations should be made public"

Sending in the Commission
4.28 We believe that the Commission must operate in the context of mainstream mechanisms for managing NHS performance and investigating problems. So it will operate to an agreed work programme.

4.29 There may be cases where there is an unacceptable delay in putting serious problems right, or a persistent failure to act. In such cases, the Secretary of State for Health (or Health Authorities for Primary Care Trusts) will be able to ask the Commission to investigate the problem and make recommendations for rapid action. This will usually happen only where there are very serious concerns about the quality of clinical services. NHS organisations will be required to release information that will assist the Commission in its investigation.

4.30 The Commission will not itself be able to impose sanctions on Trusts. Action on its recommendations will usually be followed up through the NHS performance management system. But the Commission may also have a role in follow-up activity, in agreement with a Health Authority or Regional Office. Where there has been serious default in meeting statutory duties, or confidence in the quality of local services has been gravely compromised, the Secretary of State may decide to remove the Trust Board.

4.31 If the Commission discovers or suspects that there are problems with the performance of individual clinicians, it will refer these to the appropriate professional regulatory body (for example, the **General Medical Council**) for it to take action.

"NHS organisations will be required to release information that will assist the Commission in its investigation"

Inquiries
4.32 There is obvious scope for overlap between the Commission's work and the inquiries which NHS organisations or the Secretary of State may sometimes establish into serious service failures. Activity on inquiries is not well co-ordinated and, again, it is often unclear where services can turn for advice.

4.33 We propose that the Commission should, over time, increasingly take on responsibility for overseeing and assisting with external incident inquiries. It should be able to develop the knowledge and expertise to facilitate access to a range of people to serve on inquiry teams, and to help inquiries themselves run more efficiently and effectively.

"overseeing and assisting with external incident inquiries"

Working with other bodies
4.34 The Commission will also need to link with a range of other bodies in the performance of its functions. As well as working closely with NHS bodies, the Audit Commission and the NHS Executive, the Commission will need to develop effective working relationships with organisations such as:
the Health Service Commissioner, whose statutory role is to investigate complaints about NHS services which have not been resolved through the NHS complaints procedure
professional regulatory bodies, such as the GMC, the GDC and UKCC, which are set up under statute to guide and regulate doctors, dentists, nurses and other health care professionals
professional organisations, such as the Royal Colleges, which represent their members and which in some cases set standards for postgraduate education
the Health and Safety Executive, which routinely inspects NHS providers and their health and safety management systems to ensure the health and safety of employees and patients
Social Services organisations and associated regulatory bodies (for example, the Social Services Inspectorate).

"the Commission will need to develop effective working relationships"

(For the detailed functions and workings of CHI, see The Commission for Health Improvement (Functions) Regulations 2000 (SI 2000 No 662).)

Private health care

The provision of health care services within the UK is dominated by public provision under the National Health Service. Private health care has, however, grown considerably, most of it based upon private health care insurance though such organisations as BUPA and PPP, many of whom operate their own hospitals. In addition, of course, private providers may treat NHS patients pursuant to 'NHS contracts'. Conversely, an NHS Trust may have private patients in its 'pay beds'. In this section, we are concerned to examine the regulation of private health care. Of course, professionals such as doctors and nurses are governed by their licensing bodies (eg, the GMC and UKCC) whether they practice in the NHS or in the private sector. However, little else applies. For example, the Commission for Health Improvement's jurisdiction is limited to the NHS. Likewise, the Health Service Commissioner unless the private provider is treating NHS patients. However, private abortion clinics are regulated by the Department of Health through an approval process required under s 1(3) of the Abortion Act 1967 (see *Abortion Act 1967: Compendium of Guidance* (DoH), 1994). The system entails an application process, monitoring and inspection by the DoH. Also, private infertility clinics are regulated by the Human Fertilisation and Embryology Authority (see *infra*, ch 10). Likewise, the Mental Health Act Commission monitors the operation of the Mental Health Act 1983 in independent mental health facilities.

First, we should examine briefly the state of private health care provision in the UK. Secondly, we should examine what regulation exists and, to the extent that it is inadequate, what might be put in place.

A. PRIVATE HEALTH CARE PROVISION

The House of Commons Health Committee in its 5th Report, *The Regulation of Private and Other Independent Health Care* (Session 1998–99, HC 281-1), sets the context.

11. The total value of health services provided by the private and independent sector has been estimated at £14.5 billion for the financial year 1997–98. Table 1 [below] gives some indication of the breadth of the market.

Table 1:

	£ million	£ million
Value of independent sector supply of health care: major markets, UK 1997–98		
Acute sector		2350
Independent medical/surgical hospitals and clinics	1250	
Surgeons', anaesthetists' and physicians' fees	631	
Acute psychiatric and substance dependency treatment	94	
Medical/physical rehabilitation	13	
Screening	34	
Fertility regulation	34	
Private treatment in NHS hospitals	265	
Long term care of elderly and physically disabled and other non acute, no psychiatric care **(annual value at April 1998)**		6917
Private nursing homes	3257	
Voluntary nursing homes	339	
Private residential homes	2085	
Voluntary residential homes	691	
Home Care	545	
Psychiatric rehabilitation & non-acute mental illness Care in private & voluntary psychiatric nursing homes & hospitals		169
Learning disabilities Care in private & voluntary nursing homes & hospitals		77
Pharmaceutical products & medical equipment		3120
General Practice		315
Dentistry		230
Sight tests, spectacles and contact lenses		790
Complementary medicine		570

12. Because the provision of independent health care can be categorised in different ways, there is some variation in published information about the make-up of the sector. The latest published information is contained in the Department's Statistical Bulletin on private hospitals, homes and clinics which is, in turn, drawn from statistics recorded at the date of routine inspection of the premises registered between 1 October 1996 and 31 March 1997. This shows that there were a total of 5,907 establishments with 196,450 beds in England registered under Part II of the Registered Homes Act 1984, which requires the registration of independent nursing homes and mental nursing homes. Within the non-acute sector – mainly nursing homes and mental nursing homes for elderly people – there were 5,559 homes with 185,947 beds. The acute sector comprises two main components:

- The general sector, within which there were 230 hospitals (defined as hospitals with operating theatres) with 9,717 beds having an average occupancy of just over 50%.
- The psychiatric sector of 64 hospitals with some 1,915 beds. The number of beds is estimated because of the difficulty in distinguishing between acute and non-acute mental health provision and between general and mental health provision in multi-speciality hospitals.

13. At mid-1998 the NHS offered about 3,000 private beds, 1,375 of which were in 75 dedicated private patient units (ie occupying entire wards or wings of an NHS Trust hospital). The remainder were pay beds in small numbers, also utilised by NHS patients, whose private patient occupancy has been estimated at only around 10%.

14. The sector is funded mainly by private medical insurance which accounts for about 70% of the market. The remainder comprises direct payment by patients (20%) treatment funded by the NHS (5%) and miscellaneous other groups including patients from overseas (5%). Approximately 11% of the UK population has private medical insurance. The independent hospital sector is dominated by three providers, General Healthcare Group, BUPA Hospitals and Nuffield Hospitals who between them have just over half the total number of beds.

15. It is estimated that 20% of elective surgery in the UK is undertaken within the private sector but this conceals areas where the sector has a more prominent role. The number of patients per year the sector operates on is around 850,000 including almost a third of all hip replacements. Almost half the abortions performed in the UK are carried out in the independent sector. Last year the NHS commissioned some 29,000 elective ordinary admissions and 62,000 day cases from the independent sector. There is evidence to suggest that demand for the independent acute sector is currently fairly static while that for cosmetic surgery and services provided by specialist clinics is growing. The NHS funds very little cosmetic surgery so demands for this market are met almost entirely by the private sector.

16. The NHS makes significant use of the voluntary sector to provide palliative care. Of the 171 hospice units in England, 35 are run by the NHS which manages only 17.5% of all specialist palliative care beds in England.

17. The independent sector provides some 67% of beds for non-acute psychiatric care in independent nursing homes and residential homes. There is a growing demand for beds for mentally ill and mentally infirm people – the figure for the number of beds in 1998, 25,500, represents an increase of 48% compared with 1994. In acute psychiatry, about 55% of the UK's medium and low security beds are provided by the sector. Registered mental nursing homes provide over 80% of beds for the care of brain-injured people. About 30% of occupied independent psychiatric beds are funded by the NHS.

B.   REGULATION

1.   Current

What regulation there is, is largely restricted to Pt II of the Registered Homes Act 1984. The 1984 Act creates a system of registration for 'residential care homes' (administered by the local authority) and 'nursing homes' (administered by the Health Authority). The House of Commons Health Committee examined the present position (*op cit*) (paras 18–23).

18. The current legislation governing the regulation of independent health care in England is Part II of the Registered Homes Act 1984 (the Act), supported by the Nursing Home and Mental Nursing Homes Regulations 1984 (SI 1578). This requires registration of independent acute hospitals, independent psychiatric hospitals, hospices for the provision of specialist palliative care and any premises (unless specifically excluded) where general anaesthetic is administered or where particular procedures are carried out.

19. Nursing homes are defined in the Act in broad categories:

(a) any premises used, or intended to be used, for the reception of, and the provision of nursing for, persons suffering from any sickness, injury or infirmity;

(b) any premises used, or intended to be used, for the reception of pregnant women immediately after childbirth – referred to as a "maternity home";

(c) any premises, not falling within either of the above, which are used, or intended to be used, for the provision of all or any of the following services, namely—

(i)   the carrying out of surgical procedures under anaesthesia;

(ii) the termination of pregnancies;

(iii) endoscopy;

(iv) haemodialysis or peritoneal dialysis;

(v)   treatment by specially controlled techniques.

"Specially controlled techniques" are specified by the Secretary of State by regulation and relate to any technique of medicine or surgery (including cosmetic surgery) which in his view may create a hazard for persons treated or for the staff carrying out the treatment. To date only lasers capable of operating at or above a designated power level have been so designated.

20. A "mental nursing home", for the purposes of regulation, is defined in the Act as: "any premises used, or intended to be used, for the reception of, and the provision of nursing or other medical treatment (including care, habilitation and rehabilitation under medical supervision) for, one or more mentally disordered patients (meaning persons suffering, or appearing to be suffering, from mental disorder), whether exclusively or in common with other persons". In the Act, "mental nursing home" does not include any NHS hospital or any other premises managed by a Government department or provided by a local authority. Mental nursing homes are subject to a subsidiary designation if they wish to accommodate patients detained under the provisions of the Mental Health Act 1983.

21. Under the Act the definition of "nursing home" excludes many facilities. These include premises owned or managed by the NHS, maintained or controlled by a Government department, local authority, or other body instituted by special Act of Parliament or incorporated by Royal Charter; first aid treatment rooms and school sanatoria; premises used wholly or mainly as a private dwelling, by a medical practitioner, for the purpose of consultation with his patients; premises used by a dental practitioner or chiropodist for the purpose of treating his patients; and premises used for the provision of occupational health facilities unless they are used for the provision of treatment by specially-controlled techniques.

22. The Act and regulations place duties on the person registered, and the regulatory authority can lay down few conditions of registration. Most of the duties under the Act are laid on the "person registered" and only if there is a departure from standards of "adequacy" in respect of these can the regulatory authority invoke sanctions. In the event of a person registered failing to comply with statutory or local requirements, health authorities have the power to impose certain conditions, to vary them or to propose refusal or cancellation of registration. Representation and appeal to a Registered Homes Tribunal may be made in these circumstances by the person registered and it is then for the Health Authority to satisfy the Tribunal (whose decision is legally binding) that its proposal is justified. The consequence of this is that the burden of proof lies on the regulatory authority, not the service provider ...

23. The responsibility for both the registration of persons to operate premises and for their subsequent inspection is delegated by the Secretary of State to health authorities who use local management arrangements to carry out these functions. Regulation and inspection units usually comprise a manager (often the senior nurse of the unit) with supporting inspectors and administrative and clerical staff. Specialist inspectors to examine mental health, surgical nursing, the purchasing, storage, administration and disposal of drugs, theatre provision, control of infection, works services and equipment maintenance are employed within the team or contracted to work with it as required. Inspections, which may be unannounced, result in written reports which are required to be made publicly available. Standard practice is that at least one visit should be unannounced but there is no statutory requirement. The Act provides for fees to be paid to health authorities by persons registered both on an annual basis and in relation to initial registration and subsequent major changes. The health authority has powers to investigate complaints in relation to the home concerned provided that it can be shown that the complaint relates to a regulatory matter within the terms of the Act or Regulations...

2. Is this system adequate

The Government acknowledged that there was a need to review the regulatory arrangements and published a Consultation Document, *Regulating Private and Voluntary Healthcare*, in June 1999. The House of Commons Health Committee identified a number of flaws and gaps in the regulation (*op cit*) (paras 34–40).

34. There is almost universal agreement that the current regulatory regime is inadequate to its task (although some health authorities, despite the deficiencies of the Act, have endeavoured to develop effective inspection procedures). As the Secretary of State explained, the existing regulations were drawn up "when there were not very many private acute hospitals and most of those that there were did not do anything very complex". One of the provisions the Act introduced was the facility for dual registration of premises for both residential and nursing care. The scale of non-acute nursing home beds relative to acute (roughly 18:1) has tended to bias inspections towards the non-acute sector. This has increasingly proved a problem. Private acute medicine was regulated under Nursing Homes legislation since, as General Healthcare Group put it, "most surgical work was undertaken in what were, for practical purposes, nursing homes with operating theatres added to them". In written evidence PPP/Columbia told us that, whereas the majority of treatments on which they paid out medical insurance 10 years ago were for relatively minor treatment for varicose veins or hernias, in 1997 four of the 10 treatments most costly to them were coronary artery bypass graft, angioplasty (widening of coronary arteries), hip replacements and knee replacements; treatment for cancer accounted for 15% of their costs.

35. Perhaps the most common criticism of the current regulation we have heard is that it emphasises inspection of facilities but neglects clinical standards. The IHA commented: "there is frequently an undue emphasis on hotel standards such as décor and not sufficient emphasis or expertise into inspecting standards of treatment and care". General Healthcare suggested that the emphasis of inspection was on facilities and service rather than on clinical outcomes. Bromley Health Authority Department of Public Health argued that "present legislation was constraining especially regarding the clinical practice of the medical profession and the hospital's processes whereby they manage medical practice". Joan Morton, Registration Officer for the North Yorkshire Health Authority and representing the National Nursing Home Registration and Inspection Advisory Group, drew attention to the emphasis on "inputs" rather than "outcomes" in the current legislation. In supplementary evidence submitted by the Group, based on a survey of members, which followed up issues arising from oral evidence to us, only 27 out of 51 respondent health authorities claimed that they followed up clinical issues.

36. This last statistic points to another problem with the current regime: the inconsistent way in which health authorities implement the existing regulations, a position stemming from the delegation to health authorities of the regulatory functions under the provisions of the Act. Health authorities vary in the relative priority and thus in the resources – both human and financial – that they devote to this duty. The Department acknowledged that there were "potential difficulties of applying common standards and inspection processes when you have 100 health authorities involved". In oral evidence, Mrs Morton suggested that each registration and inspection unit would know the names of all clinicians working in independent hospitals and registered clinics in the area. The National Nursing Home Registration Inspection and Advisory Group survey of health authorities indicated that in fact only 25 out of 51 held the information or had access to it. More disturbingly, only 33 respondents indicated that they routinely received alert letters issued by NHS Executive regional offices advising health authorities to consult them in respect of individuals whose performance had raised doubts ... According to the Royal College of Nursing (RCN) some inspections might last four to five hours, others to similar facilities might take two days, depending on the inspection unit concerned. Westminster Health Care, who own and operate 91 nursing homes, gave an example of their experience of inconsistent standards of regulation:

In a recent case, we provided extensive evidence that a 30 bed unit could be operated with three at night, a ration of 1:10 which is common throughout the sector but one Health Authority, because [of] their guidelines (which are very old), insisted on four being provided. We have spent considerable time, effort and money in resisting this claim, providing comparative evidence of 12 other identical units and the evidence of a respected Registration Officer from another part of the country. All this was completely ignored ... Inspection reports were satisfactory.

It would appear that national guidelines issued to ensure consistency of inspection are not working. In an attempt to achieve consistency, transparency and targeting of registration the NHS Executive issued fresh guidelines in September 1995 which acknowledged that "Insufficient weight is being given by some registration officers to the series of guidelines published by the National Association of Health Authorities and Trusts".

Gaps in regulation

37. The problems examined above relate to organizations currently subject to regulation. A separate problem is that some medical and clinical activities taking place in the private and independent sector are largely or entirely unregulated. The following table gives an indication of those areas of independent health provision which are not directly regulated:

Table 2: Directly regulated and unregulated health services

Directly regulated	Not directly regulated
Acute Medical/Surgical	
Independent hospitals	Some minor surgery in professional premises (eg minor cosmetic services, GP practices, and dental surgeries) Royal Charter hospitals or hospitals established by special Act of Parliament NHS pay beds and private patient wings within NHS hospitals
Lasers of class 3B or 4	Lasers of class 1, 2 and 3A (when outside independent hospitals)

Directly regulated	Not directly regulated
Termination of pregnancy	Hyperbaric oxygen therapy Free-standing clinical support servicese.g pathology, MRI, CAT scans etc
IVF and other matters regulated by the Human Fertilisation and Embryology Authority	Health screening outside of hospitals Independent consulting practice by healthcare professionals
Mental Health	
Independent mental health homes and hospitals	Therapists and counsellors practising outside of mental health facilities Substance misuse in-patient clinics registered only as residential homes under the Act Substance misuse outpatient facilities Private drug clinics
Nursing	
Nursing homes (including hospices) Dual registered homes Nursing Agencies	Organizations providing domiciliary care Day-care centres Sheltered housing and 'housing with care'
Primary Care and/or community services	
	Private General Practitioners Walk-in primary care services Complementary medicine Retail pharmacy/chemists Private ambulance services Slimming clinics

38. Some of the activities not directly regulated exploit loopholes in the current regulatory framework. For example, private clinics performing minor surgery might be able to evade

regulation by arguing that most of their activity takes place, in the terms of the Act, in "premises used, or intended to be used, wholly or mainly by a medical practitioner for the purpose of consultations with his patients".

39. As has been noted, Section 21 of the Act gives the Secretary of State powers to specify by regulation "any technique of medicine or surgery (including cosmetic surgery) as to which he is satisfied that its use may create a hazard for persons treated by means of it or for the staff of any premises where the technique is used". These powers have to date only been invoked in respect of lasers of class 3B or 4 which have been added to the list of special techniques. There are many other medical techniques which could have been covered. For example, we learned that high-intensity lights were being used for the removal of tattoos or unwanted hair and the treatment of skin blemishes by medically-unqualified beauticians whose sole training was provided by the manufacturers of the equipment. According to Professor Roland Blackwell of University College London, an adviser to Westminster, Kensington and Chelsea Registration and Inspection Unit, these lights posed potential health risks to users and operators equivalent to those of lasers. Poor application of the treatment could, for example, leave those treated with inappropriate scars, or damage the eyesight of those using the equipment. Hyperbaric oxygen therapy, used in a wide variety of procedures ranging from the treatment of decompression sickness to the healing of problem wounds, is another technique not regulated by the Act and not added to it by regulation. There are 15 commercial hyperbaric oxygen treatment chambers in the UK and the potential dangers they might pose was demonstrated by an accident in a chamber attached to a private hospital in Milan in October 1997, when 11 people were killed following the outbreak of fire. Such treatments come to the market with bewildering speed making their regulation a complex task. Any future regulatory regime will need to be able to address the rapid pace of development and change in the independent health sector.

40. The inadequacy of regulation is further highlighted in the area of the provision of information to the consumer. The company P7 Marketing Solutions in a memorandum to us suggested that the majority of private patients were "badly informed" and "obliged to take almost everything on trust". The research they have evaluated indicated that private patients were often ignorant of which consultant would see them, what the qualifications of the consultant were, when they would go to hospital, which hospital they would go to, how long they would stay in hospital and even how much the treatment would cost.

3. A new regulatory structure

Given the emphasis on 'quality' and 'clinical governance' within the NHS, it is, to say the least, curious that nothing analogous exists for the private sector. Also, the oversight of the Health Service Commissioner is absent in the private context. One solution to the relative regulatory void might be to create a regulator for the private sector along the line of Ofsted, Ofgas etc and to extend the jurisdiction of CHI and the HSC. The House of Commons Health Committee in its Report (*op cit*) (paras 90–109) recommended the creation of an independent regulator and that CHI and NICE should have a role to play. (We discuss the Committee's recommendation in respect of the creation of an ombudsman for the private sector in Chapter 3.)

90. It is extremely hard to define what constitutes a medical or surgical procedure presenting a degree of risk requiring regulation by Government. One of the difficulties we have encountered is that medical and surgical technology is fast-changing. Capturing novel techniques within a regulatory framework will be one of the greatest challenges for the Independent Regulator. **We believe that a national moderator will be required to assess whether emerging techniques and technologies pose any risk to patient safety. We recommend that, in addition to those invasive techniques currently subject to regulation, other procedures defined by the moderator should also be regulated. It is important that the list should be kept up to date; in our view the Department's failure to maintain and update the 1984 Act in this regard is unacceptable ... We recommend that the list should be capable of alteration by secondary rather than primary legislation, and that the Moderator reviews the list at least annually.**

91. It then remains to be asked what the target of regulation should be. The evidence we reviewed offered a wide variety of approaches to the preferred regulatory structure. The King's Fund argued that the actual premises where a treatment is carried out are increasingly irrelevant and that regulation should focus instead on clinical activity. The view of HQS, an

organization associated with the King's Fund, was that regulation should be directed not at premises but at organizations. The BMA argued for the primacy of self-regulation within the profession, laying emphasis on the role of MACs. The GMC suggested that individual clinicians ought to be regulated. They told us that their proposals for revalidation for health professionals represented a very significant development in the regulation of health care. The larger providers generally drew attention to organizational audit and requested the inclusion of their services within Government clinical governance initiatives. General Healthcare Group put forward the most comprehensive model of regulation. They told us they believed that "the interests of patients and their safety, would be best served by the introduction of a nationally based system for the accreditation of healthcare *service proprietors*, healthcare *premises*, and healthcare *professionals*". We find this three-pronged approach attractive although we believe that clinical procedures themselves also require regulation. It seems to us that the balance between external regulation by means of an independent regulator and internal quality control is delicate.

92. The form an independent regulator might take occupied much of the evidence we received. Many of the large providers in the independent sector favoured an extension of the jurisdiction of NICE and CHI. The IHA suggested that NICE and CHI should be the "main … location" for regulation of the independent sector. BUPA Hospitals indicated that its "preferred structural option" for regulating independent health care would be so "extend the terms of reference of the Commission for Health Improvement and delegate some responsibility to regional offices and the Royal Colleges". General Healthcare Group concluded their memorandum by suggesting that "the vision of NICE and CHI should embrace the healthcare of the nation as a whole". However, the Secretary of State made clear to us that CHI and NICE would have no specific remit in relation to the regulation of the independent sector. But NICE and CHI will have responsibility for private patients in NHS beds and NHS patients in private settings. The Secretary of State also accepted that the work of these bodies would be in the public domain and thus available to the sector. This last point was expanded in an oral answer from Mr John Hutton MP, Parliamentary Under Secretary of State at the Department:

I can confirm … that the national service frameworks will apply equally to the private sector and to NHS hospitals – they are there for the private sector to use. The new arrangements and guidelines that will come from the National Institute for Clinical Excellence will also be available for use, if the private sector so chooses.

93. Other witnesses shared the Department's reservations of CHI's suitability as a potential regulator. HQS said it did not believe that there was "sufficient evidence to demonstrate that the yet to be established CHI or Commissions for Care Standards are the appropriate bodies" to regulate the sector. They favoured an emphasis on the development of organizational audit, such as that which their organization itself provided, as the most efficient means of improving quality. The RCN pointed out that CHI's functions "do not include registration and issuing licences, and crucially it does not have a statutory enforcement role". Their preferred model was an extension of the Commissions for Care Standards (Care Commissions). They argued that if the Commissions' work extended to the private acute sector it would raise the health component in their activity which, the RCN believed, was in danger of being neglected. They also believed that a single regulator for health and social care would produce savings in overheads.

94. Another advantage of extending the scope of the Care Commissions, in the view of the RCN, was that it would allow the regulatory regime comprehensively to cover those establishments which fell into the grey area between social and health care. The Secretary of State himself told us that "there is a question of where, not the geographical but the functional boundaries are drawn". Ms Sally Tabar of the RCN cited the example of the Horder Centre for Arthritis in East Sussex. This had 24 surgical beds for hip replacements and other orthopaedic surgery and 35 nursing home beds. Because the surgery was often busy some of the nursing home beds were used to nurse post-operative surgical patients. In written evidence the RCN put forward the example of Tadworth Court in Surrey, a children's rehabilitation hospital where children cared for included those recovering from road accidents and those with cerebral palsy. The hospital did not have an operating theatre making it "unclear whether it would be viewed as an acute hospital, or as a nursing home". Other areas where lead responsibility for regulation was unclear included long-term beds in acute hospitals and hospice beds within nursing homes. The NHS Confederation, having surveyed their members, argued that extending the scope of the Care Commissions would be the best means of producing an inspectorate with the necessary mixture of skills to cover the whole range of provision.

95. We find much to commend in the approach of the RCN and NHS Confederation in advocating an enlarged role for the Care Commissions. We have in previous reports argued

in favour of breaking down the boundaries between health and social care wherever possible. We do not, however, believe that the Care Commissions should regulate the independent acute sector. It is our view that the sheer scale of social care provision in the independent sector relative to health care would risk introducing a cultural bias towards a nursing-home oriented inspection system here. We would not, however, wish to jettison what seem to us the considerable advantages of inspectorates drawing on mixed skills and capable of inspecting the mixed social/health care setting. **Accordingly we recommend the creation of an independent regulator for healthcare outside the NHS, responsible to Government, to identify appropriate standards and relevant activity and to provide for its regulation across the country. The wider range of health care services that we recommend to be brought within this remit will require regulation to be operated on a regional basis sharing a common resources centre with each Regional Commission of Care Standards. This common resource centre, we suggest, could be the location of the intellectual property of both the Care Commissions and the Independent Health Regulator. It could negotiate temporary transfers of staff from one regulator to another, giving an extremely flexible inspection regime. It could also co-ordinate training programmes for inspection staff taking account of best practice in both acute and non-acute care. It could provide a common services agency dealing with legal services and general administrative matters. It could operate both regionally and at national board level to ensure consistency of standards.** The following diagram illustrates the model we propose:

Proposed structure for regulation of healthcare outside the NHS

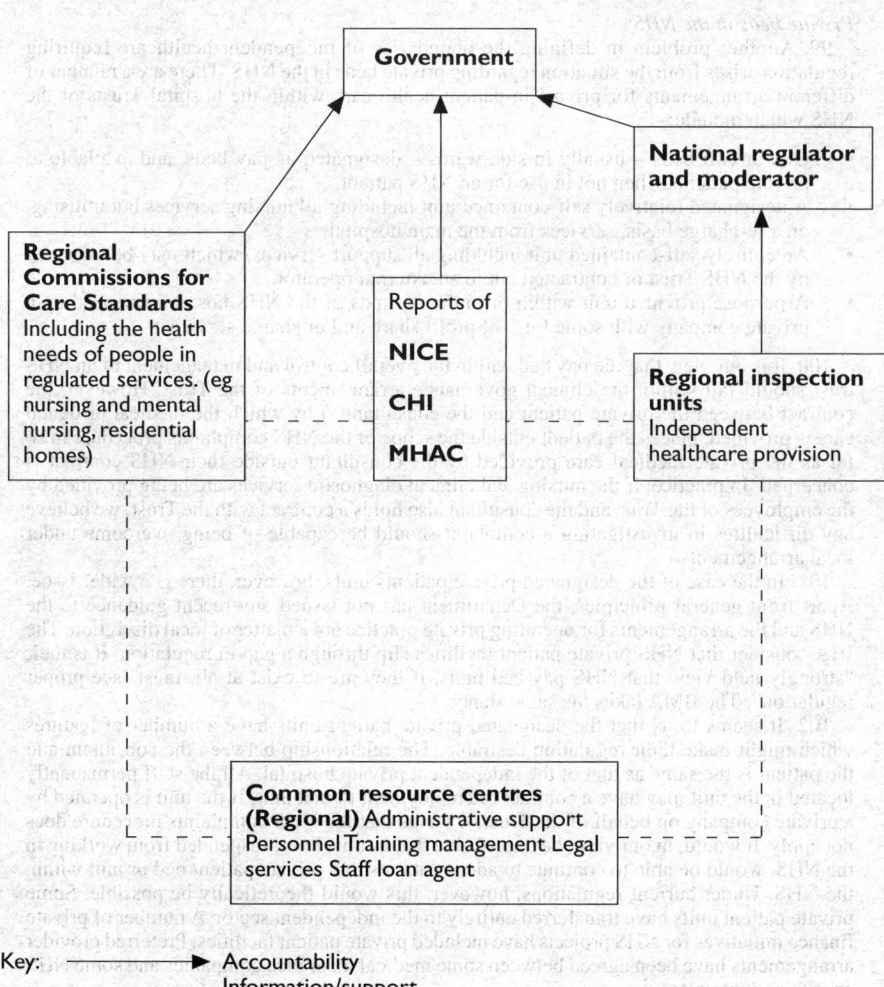

Key: ⟶ Accountability
— — — — — Information/support

96. **We expect all independent acute medical facilities to be brought into inspection so that, for example, there should no longer be exemption for Royal Charter hospitals and those established by Special Act of Parliament.**

97. We believe that such a common resource centre in each region would also be a logical point of interface with NICE and CHI. We accept the Government's argument that these bodies are not regulators but we expect the independent regulator to be influenced by the activity of NICE and CHI so that its judgments are informed by the quality standards applying within the NHS. We also believe that the work of NICE will be compromised if it does not have access to clinical data in the independent sector. To give a simple example, if the independent sector favoured one type of hip replacement on cost grounds and the NHS another, NICE would benefit from having data on failure rates across the sectors. **We recommend that CHI and NICE should inform a common resources centre for an Independent Healthcare Regulator and the Regional Commissions for Care Standards. The Regulator would be expected to draw on the findings of CHI in so far as they are applicable to the individual components under inspection. Independent providers should be obliged on request to submit clinical audit and similar data to CHI and NICE.**

98. We also believe that such a common resources centre would be an ideal point of contact with the MHAC. **We recommend that the Mental Health Act Commission be represented on the national board of the common resource centre for the Independent Healthcare Regulator and Regional Commissions for Care Standards.** We believe that this would enhance the impact of the excellent work which the MHAC is carrying out. The MHAC would have a direct route to the Independent Healthcare Regulator to help it enforce its findings.

Private beds in the NHS

99. Another problem in defining the boundaries of independent healthcare requiring regulation arises from the situation regarding private beds in the NHS. There are a number of different arrangements for private in-patient health care within the hospital Trusts of the NHS which include:–

- One or two beds – usually in side wards – designated as pay beds, and available to private patients when not in use for an NHS patient.
- A designated relatively self-contained unit including all nursing services but utilising, on a re-charge basis, services from the main hospital.
- An entirely self-contained unit including all support services, which may be managed by the NHS Trust or contracted out to an external operator.
- A purpose provided unit within or in the grounds of the NHS hospital financed by a private company with some form of profit share and/or shared services.

100. It is our view that the pay bed within the overall control and management of an NHS trust should fall within the clinical governance arrangements of the Trust. However, the contract between the private patient and the consultant(s) by which the medical or dental care is provided, places the patient outside the scope of the NHS complaints procedure in so far as the private medical care provided by the consultant outside their NHS contract is concerned. In practice, if the nursing and clinical diagnostic services are being provided by the employees of the Trust and the consultant also holds a contract with the Trust, we believe any difficulties in investigating a complaint should be capable of being overcome under local arrangements.

101. In the case of the designated private patients units, however, there is a wider issue. Apart from general principles, the Department has not issued any recent guidance to the NHS and the arrangements for operating private practice are a matter of local discretion. The IHA consider that NHS private patient facilities slip through a gap in regulation. It is their "strongly held view that NHS pay bed units, if they are to exist at all, must face proper regulation". The BMA takes the same stance.

102. It seems to us that the designated private patient units have a number of features which might make their regulation desirable. The relationship between the consultant and the patient is the same as that of the independent private hospital. All the staff permanently located in the unit may have a contract of employment to that unit. If the unit is operated by a private company on behalf of the Trust, it seems that the NHS complaints procedure does not apply. It would, in our view, be improbable that a consultant, suspended from working in the NHS, would be able to continue to admit patients to a private patient bed or unit within the NHS. Under current regulations, however, this would theoretically be possible. Some private patient units have transferred entirely to the independent sector. A number of private finance initiatives for NHS projects have included private patient facilities. Preferred provider arrangements have been agreed between some medical insurance companies and some NHS private patient units.

103. Given these factors, **we consider that all private health care facilities operated within the management of the NHS should be required to function within the clinical procedures and management of the Trust in which they are located. Such an arrangement should require full participation in the Trust schemes of clinical governance and controls assurance. Only consultants with a current service contract or honorary contract with that Trust should be able to admit and treat private patients. This arrangement should include a requirement that any complaint in which the private medical care provided by the consultant outside their NHS contract is an issue which should be dealt with under the full complaints procedure of the NHS including access to the Health Service Ombudsman. This provision should be applicable to any private health care delivered within the terms of the NHS Acts and thus be applicable to the private use of the occasional pay bed as well as the consulting and in-patient private patient units of NHS Trusts.**

104. **Where a private patient unit is operated by a company on behalf of the Trust, we consider that it should fall to be regulated on the same basis as a hospital in the independent sector.**

105. The arrangements set out above, together with the additional and localised services that we propose should be bought into the scope of regulation, make it appropriate that the focus of the operational arm of the independent regulator should relate to the health regions. The following table, drawn up using the predecessor NHS regions which are the most recent comprehensive data, indicate the balance of facilities by region under such arrangements:

Table 3: Independent and NHS designated pay bed units by NHS region

Region	Independent Hospitals/ Clinics	Independent Psychiatric Hospitals	NHS Private Patient Units	Independent Mental National Health	Hospices (Detained patients)	Totals
Anglia & Oxford	29	8	11	14	11	73
North Thames	57	14	21	11	14	117
North West	29	6	8	22	29	94
Northern & Yorkshire	20	8	3	12	21	64
South & West	24	9	8	37	12	90
South Thames	38	15	12	16	25	106
Trent	13	3	5	11	9	41
West Midlands	20	1	7	8	10	46
Totals	230	64	75	131	131	**631**

106. Those figures suggest that each region would have a sufficient number of establishments to inspect to make a regionally-located inspectorate perfectly viable. We do not believe this situation would be very much altered under the new regional structure.

The licensing process

107. The current sanctions available to registration and inspection units have been criticized for their lack of range. Units can cancel the registration of an existing facility, or refuse to register a new one, or issue warnings. The Secretary of State described this choice as being "between a nuclear weapon and a feather duster". We agree with the Secretary of State that a wider range of powers for the regulatory authorities than are presently available would be

appropriate. We think, for example, the regulator should be able to license a home or clinic to carry out certain activities but not others. A possible model might be the Human Fertilisation and Embryology Authority (HFEA), which has powers to grant licences with or without conditions, suspend them or revoke them. In granting licences it requires certain general conditions to be complied with while additional conditions may be added specifically relevant to the centre concerned.

108. We also favour the approach the HFEA takes towards establishing line-management responsibility for the activities of the clinics it deals with. It is the duty of the individual named as the Person Responsible for each centre to ensure that licence conditions are complied with. To assist them, the HFEA is required by law to produce a Code of Practice to guide clinics on how they should carry out their licenced activities. The advantage of this approach, in our view, is that it helps shift the burden of establishing compliance from the regulatory authority to the service provider. **We recommend that the Secretary of State creates a licensing regime for the independent acute sector offering a wide range of powers and sanctions which places the burden of proof of compliance on the provider, not the regulator. We would like the Independent Regulator to issue a detailed code of practice with a view to ensuring that consistent national standards of inspection apply to the independent healthcare sector.**

109. Going beyond formal regulatory structures, we note the view of the RCN that it is important that regulation provides more than a policing function "to include a facilitative, supportive and advisory role too, ie not just identifying what the weaknesses/failures are, but also looking at why they are occurring, and advising on how improvements can be made". One of the criticisms that the Institute of Chartered Secretaries and Administrators made of the current system was that reports "fail to praise good practice or give positive encouragement to staff". It is our view that a good regulatory regime will actively raise standards rather than merely check existing rules are complied with.

In *Regulating Private and Voluntary Healthcare: The Way Forward* (December 1999), the Government proposed a system for regulation through an independent National Care Standards Commission (NCSC) (and, in Wales, an arm of the National Assembly for Wales) replacing that in the Registered Homes Act 1984. The NCSC would set standards for private and voluntary health care services (and 'social care' services, which are not considered here). All independent hospitals and clinics (ie not within the NHS) would be covered, as would nursing homes and premises where certain listed health care services are provided, for example, medical treatment under anaesthesia or sedation, dental treatment under general anaesthesia, obstetric services, abortions, cosmetic surgery and palliative care. Private health care provided within an NHS Trust would not be covered, as this would fall within the remit of the Commission for Health Improvement. The scheme contemplates registration, inspection and monitoring the quality of services provided.

NHS Executive *Regulating Private and Voluntary Healthcare: The Way Forward* (1999)

Regulatory Standards

10. The consultation document raised a number of issues around the standards to be used in inspecting and regulating private and voluntary healthcare establishments. The greater emphasis on standards of care rather than facilities was welcomed. A number of respondents felt it was important that there was linkage between standards to be applied in the NHS and in the private sector. There was a range of views on what new standards should cover and the proposal in the consultation document for further consultation on the standards to be set was generally welcomed as was the proposal for these to be set out in Codes of Practice or secondary legislation rather than in primary legislation in order that they can be kept up to date. **Ministers propose to take the views expressed on the form of standards into account in developing national minimum standards for private and voluntary healthcare.**

11. The consultation document raised a number of specific issues. In particular it asked for views on:
* the arrangements for inspection and how the inspection role might best be carried out;

- a proposal that private and voluntary hospitals should employ only state registered practitioners where such registration exists;
- the links between NHS disciplinary procedures and the private and voluntary sector and the action needed to ensure an appropriate level of exchange of information, particularly in relation to clinical staff who are suspended because of a risk to patients;
- proposals to improve the range of information made available to prospective patients;
- proposals to improve complaints procedures including a requirement for all private and voluntary healthcare establishments to have a clearly laid down complaints procedure as a condition of registration.

12. On the first of these issues the consultation document proposed that, as now, registered healthcare providers should be inspected at least twice a year and be liable to unannounced inspections, that inspection reports should be made publicly available and that inspection teams might be employed either by the regulatory body itself or under contract with other bodies such as the Commission for Health Improvement, Commissions for Care Standards or other bodies. There was a range of views on the frequency of inspections, but a strong view that a mandatory requirement for two inspections per year was unnecessary and likely to overstretch the regulator's resources. A number of respondents suggested that all premises should be inspected once a year and it was suggested that the regulatory body should relate its inspection work to assessed risk. The inspection process could be enhanced if there were proper pre-inspection questionnaires and should concentrate on ensuring that systems were in place to ensure good clinical governance, rather than on inspecting facilities. **Ministers have considered these arguments and decided that all registered premises should be inspected at least once a year with provision as now for unannounced inspections. They would expect the regulatory body to inspect more frequently those establishments where it was concerned about standards of care.**

13. There was little dissent from the proposal that, as now, inspection reports should be made publicly available. There was a strong feeling that the inspection process should concentrate on standards and benchmarks. There was general support for the approach proposed in the consultation document that the regulatory body should be free to draw on expertise from a wide range of other bodies to ensure that appropriately skilled teams of inspectors are established. A number of other points were made by respondents including the importance of training for inspectors, the need to ensure consistency of approach between inspection teams and the need to involve the Mental Health Act Commission in relation to inspections of mental illness hospitals. **Ministers will ensure that the regulatory body can operate flexibly, drawing on a wide range of skills.**

14. There was general support for the proposal that private and voluntary healthcare establishments should ensure that they employ only state-registered staff where state registration exists, and there were concerns about the position of staff groups which do not have state registration or protection of title. There was also general support for the principle of exchanging information about clinicians who may be a risk to patients whether this is identified in the NHS or in the private and voluntary sector. A number of respondents raised concerns about the current alert letters system, which was not seen as adequate and which raised concerns about breach of confidentiality and compromise of the neutral status of suspension within the NHS. **Ministers will take account of the points raised in considering the issue further.** In addition, a number of respondents raised concerns about the slowness of current NHS and professional disciplinary procedures. The Chief Medical Officer's proposals in *Supporting Doctors, Protecting Patients* provide for a comprehensive modernisation of the arrangements for handling poor clinical performance. This would mean a radical overhaul of the current disciplinary procedures to speed them up, and the introduction of a new approach for dealing with performance issues, separate from disciplinary procedures, through a new professional assessment and support service.

15. There was considerable support for the proposal that private and voluntary healthcare providers should ensure that prospective patients have access to a comprehensive range of information about services being provided though concerns were expressed about the need to define more precisely what such information should cover to ensure that it was meaningful to users. **Ministers will ensure that this is taken forward in working up the more detailed regulatory requirements and standards.**

16. Finally, there was general support for the proposal that all private and voluntary healthcare providers should have clear complaints procedures in place, for publication of information on complaints and for an independent investigation mechanism in cases where a complainant was not satisfied with the way in which a private healthcare provider dealt with their complaint. Some respondents were disappointed that the consultation document did not envisage

extending the role of the Health Service Commissioner to cover complaints in the private sector. **Ministers intend to require private and voluntary hospitals and clinics to have complaints procedures as a condition of registration. The Government is considering what would be the most effective arrangements for ensuring the independent investigation of complaints in cases where complainants were dissatisfied with the way in which private or voluntary hospitals or clinics had dealt with their complaints.**

Sanctions

17. The consultation document proposed a more flexible sanctions regime, in particular to allow the regulatory body to require a private or voluntary healthcare provider not to undertake particular forms of treatment until specified conditions such as recruitment of appropriately qualified and trained staff or the provision of access to appropriate support facilities have been fulfilled. It also proposed giving the regulatory body power to close particular wards or other facilities where inspection reports gave cause for concern, without requiring closure of the whole hospital or clinic. Those who commented generally welcomed this approach, though there were a number of comments about the need for proportionality and for a right of appeal. **Ministers will ensure that more flexible sanctions are introduced as part of the overhaul of the existing regulatory arrangements.**

New Regulatory Structure

18. The consultation document sought comments on:
* a proposal to establish a new regulatory body for private and voluntary healthcare separate from the eight Commissions for Care Standards;
* the extent to which hospitals for those with learning disabilities and services particularly in the field of mental illness should be regulated by the Commissions for Care Standards or the new healthcare regulatory body;
* proposals to avoid dual inspection.

19. There was a range of views on the most appropriate regulatory structure for private and voluntary healthcare, though general support for the regulatory body to be independent of the NHS. Of those who expressed a view there was support both for the establishment of a new regulatory body separate from the Commissions for Care Standards and for the Commissions for Care Standards to take on the role of regulating private and voluntary healthcare. Those favouring a separate body considered it important to have a body focused clearly on healthcare issues and able to set national standards. Those who favoured the use of the Commissions for Care Standards raised concerns about the costs of an additional body, the risk of dual regulation for some establishments and the need for seamless regulation.

20. Ministers have considered the issues carefully. **They have decided to establish a single independent regulatory body, the National Care Standards Commission (NCSC), which will have the responsibility for regulating both social care (in place of the planned eight regional Commissions) and private and voluntary healthcare. In order to provide a clear focus on healthcare regulation they expect the NCSC to establish a separate division for this purpose.**

21. As far as regulation of services for those with learning disabilities and those with mental illness is concerned, there was support for the proposal in the consultation document that Commissions for Care Standards should regulate services for those with learning disabilities. There was a range of views on the most appropriate regulatory arrangements for mental illness services, whether they should all be regulated by a single body and if so which, and if not, where the line should be drawn between services which should fall under healthcare regulator and those which should fall under social care regulation. **Ministers' decision to establish a single regulatory body means that the NCSC will be responsible for regulating private mental illness services.**

22. Those who commented generally welcomed the proposal to avoid dual inspection even if some establishments would need to be registered both with a Commission for Care Standards and the new Healthcare Regulatory Body. The decision to have a single regulatory body will avoid the need for establishments to register with two separate bodies.

23. Finally, the proposal that the regulatory regime should be financed by the private and voluntary healthcare sector was generally accepted though concerns were expressed about the need for clarity and transparency of the fee structure. **Ministers have already indicated that they propose to consult further on the last point.**

The Government's proposals will be implemented by the Care Standards Act 2000, introduced into the House of Lords on 2 December 1999.

Chapter 3

Regulation of health professionals, discipline and complaints

Introduction

We saw in the previous chapter the complexity of the structure and organisation of the National Health Service. Within the service and the private sector a myriad of health care professionals can be found: doctors, nurses, dentists, opticians, chiropractors and many others. In this chapter, we are concerned with the regulation of health professionals and the mechanisms for making them accountable to the public for their conduct. For our part, we will concentrate upon doctors. The accountability of the NHS institutions themselves, was dealt with in Chapter 2. Our principal concern is to analyse how regulation and accountability is achieved through *legal* or *quasi-legal* means of disciplinary and complaints procedures. We have already seen in Chapter 1 the role of the courts in judicial review proceedings and we will examine in subsequent chapters civil action, for example, in negligence and battery. We will also see the role played by the criminal law, whether statutory or at common law. Also, we do not engage in a detailed consideration of other mechanisms, for example, managerial ones, which might be of greater interest to political scientists and health policy analysts (for discussions see eg M Moran and B Wood *States, Regulations and the Medical Profession* (1993), D Longley *Public Law and Health Service Accountability* (1993), and D Longley *Health Care Constitutions* (1996) especially ch 5).

Health care professions and regulation

Regulation and accountability of the health professions, particularly doctors, has been a matter of considerable public interest in the recent past. The role of the General Medical Council, its constitution and basis has been challenged. For example, whether it is desirable to continue with a form of self-regulatory body has been questioned. The problems of identifying and dealing with poorly performing doctors has resulted in legal changes to the GMC's powers but has resurfaced as a result of the inquiry into the deaths of neonatal cardiac patients in a Bristol hospital. In the previous chapter we examined the introduction of so-called 'clinical governance' within the NHS by the Health Act 1999 and the creation of the National Institute for Clinical Excellence (NICE) and the Commission for Health Improvement (CHI), which manifest the Government's commitment to improve upon and set appropriate standards of quality of the service provided by the NHS (see The *New NHS: Modern, Dependable* (1997, DoH) Cm 387 and *A First Class Service: Quality in the new NHS* (1998, DoH). Whilst concerned primarily with the National Health *Service*, the mechanisms of 'clinical governance' will also obviously impact on doctors and other health

care professionals and their accountability. What then is meant by 'regulation'?
Writing in the context of doctors, Mike Moran and Bruce Wood (both political
scientists) explain what it entails generally and in relation to doctors.

Michael Moran and Bruce Wood *States, Regulation and the Medical Profession* (1993)

What should medical students be taught in order to qualify as doctors? Who should run
medical education? How should doctors be paid? What controls are needed over the way
they do their job?

Every reader will recognize that these questions are central to the lives of doctors – and to
the lives of their patients. They encapsulate some of the key issues which have to be settled
in the *regulation* of the medical profession. But they are not peculiar to medicine. The needs
of medicine of course demand special arrangements, but there is nothing unique about the
general problems involved in regulating the medical profession, nor about the way those
problems are solved. Doctors provide a service, and regulating the supply of that service
poses issues similar to the regulation of any other good or service supplied in the community.

The issues can be summarized as those concerned *standards, accountability* and *efficiency*.
Any system of regulation has to say something about the standards of technical competence
and ethical probity which will be demanded of practitioners; any system of regulation has to
decide if practitioners will be obliged to give an account of their actions, and if so to whom;
and any system of regulation likewise has to decide how far, if at all, it will be concerned
with the efficiency and effectiveness with which practitioners deliver a service. We will
discover that while these issues are particularly important in the regulation of doctors, they
crop up, not only in medicine, but in regulation as a whole.

*Regulation is the activity by which the rules governing the exchange of goods and services
are made and implemented*. We can see immediately that it is the foundation of social life.
Every kind of market has to be regulated. Making and selling care; supplying banking services;
delivering personal services as varied as hairdressing or burial of the dead: all these take
place within a framework of rules. The study of regulation examines how these rules come
about, how they are implemented and how the institutions responsible for making and
implementing rules come into existence and operate.

The activity of regulation can in turn be broken down into four separate tasks: the control
of market entry and exit, of competitive practices, of market organization and of remuneration.
These tasks have to be carried out regardless of whether the activity in question is the provision
of doctoring or the sale of automobiles.

The *regulation of market entry* is the first task that has to be performed, because the first
questions that have to be answered in regulation are: who can engage in the activity, and what
conditions must they meet in order to have the right to do the job? Rules of market entry vary
from the highly permissive to the exceptionally restrictive: almost anybody can set up as a
window cleaner, whereas to become a banker or a lawyer involves meeting stringent standards
set and enforced by specialized regulatory bodies. One of the central tasks in the study of
regulation is to understand why there exists this spectrum from permissiveness to restrictiveness,
and to discover how far it can be explained by the needs of the activity being regulated.

The second task, the *regulation of competitive practices*, arises because most societies allow
competition in the provision of goods and services, but all place limits on the extent of that
competition. Some limits are set by laws concerned with the overall organization of economic
life: thus laws against fraud and theft, and laws enforcing freely made contracts, are all designed
to restrict the exploitation of the honest by the dishonest. Within this general framework of
regulation, however, almost all goods and services are subject to more particular rules: drugs
may not be marketed by pharmaceutical companies until they have satisfied safety tests; cigarettes
can only be marketed with a health warning, while their advertisement is restricted in some
countries and banned in others; and in some countries particular occupational groups – like
lawyers – are prohibited from competing for business by advertising their services.

The third task is related to the control of competitive practices, but it deserves separate
examination. The *regulation of market structures* is necessary because markets have to be
organized: decisions need to be made about what kinds of institutions will be allowed to
provide goods and services. For instance, most nations have rules governing mergers and
takeovers of private firms; these in effect control the conditions under which the structure of
ownership in markets can be changed. In some cases regulation actually prohibits some
organizations and prescribes others: for example, until recently UK solicitors could not
organize their business in companies enjoying limited liability. In some parts of the insurance
business, for instance, it is only possible to engage in business through partnerships rather
than through companies enjoying limited liability. Some regulations prescribe upper and lower

limits to the size of firms in a market: most banking regulation demands that banks have minimum reserves of capital. In many countries anti-monopoly rules forbid single firms from controlling more than a prescribed percentage of production or sales in a particular market. Market structure regulation also tries to influence the distribution of suppliers. In some instances geographical distribution is regulated: the urban planning system in the UK limits the numbers of particular kinds of shops that can be established in a district; while in the USA most banks are prohibited from operating networks of branches that cross state boundaries.

The fourth and final task that has to be performed is *the regulation of payment*. In any transaction some rules always exist about payment for the good or service being exchanged, even if these rules are only the general framework provided by laws for enforcing contracts and curbing fraud. In many cases there exist more detailed rules governing both scales of charges and actual methods of charging. In professions like law it is common to find fixed scales of charges. In some markets, payment is by collective bargaining between providers and payers; the classic cases lie in labour markets where unions bargain over pay with representatives of employers. At the other extreme – consider the local window cleaner or the haggling that goes on in a used-car showroom – it is the result of an individual deal between the customer and the provider. There are thus great variations in how far payment is regulated: but some decision about the extent and form of regulation has to be made, even if the decision amounts to leaving the customer and supplier free to haggle.

The four tasks outlined here have to be performed in some way in all markets. Their relevance to the medical profession should be clear. In organizing its medical profession each country has to make decisions about the following: how applicants who enter medicine are screened and trained; how far, once in, they will be allowed to compete for business, and what ethical standards will govern their relations with clients; in what institutional settings – hospitals, their own consulting rooms – doctors can practise their profession; and how doctors will be paid? The 'special' problems of regulating doctors are, in other words, only particular instances of the more general problems of regulation.

Of course doctors are not in the marketplace in exactly the same way as window cleaners, bankers or used-car salesmen. On the contrary, one of the distinctive features of medicine as an occupation lies in how far commercial competition is restricted. As we will see in the next section, these controls are often thought to be one of the marks that single out medicine as a *profession*. The controls are the result of particular solutions to the four regulatory tasks identified above. The solutions vary between countries, and have varied over time. There is no single 'model' of regulation – and the pattern in any one country is certainly not the only model. The following illustrations give some indication of the variety.

Entry regulation into the medical profession takes many forms. Acquiring a licence to practise medicine commonly demands acceptance into, and completion of, extended courses in medical education and long periods of practical training but the exact requirements vary from country to country. Most nations – and all those considered in this text – also have their own distinctive rules controlling entry to particular specialisms. In brief, every nation gives an elaborate but different answer to the question: who can become a doctor?

Regulation of competitive practices has been virtually one of the defining features of medicine as a modern profession. As we will see in Chapter 3 there is a long history of efforts to distinguish the doctor from providers of other commercial services. This often took the form of putting limits on competition for patients, and providing 'consumer protection' in the form of ethical codes governing the relations between doctor and patient. All modern health-care systems now have rules restricting, and in some cases prohibiting, advertisements for business by doctors; all regulate the freedom of patients to choose or change doctors; and all have rules governing the personal relations between doctor and patient.

These rules often overlap with *the regulation of market structures*. The practice of medicine has to be organized in some institutions, whether the institution is the 'solo' doctor operating a one-person business or a health service employing all doctors as public servants. The way it should be organized has provided, and continues to provide, some of the most difficult of regulatory issues. For most of this century the preferred solution was to treat the doctor as a species of independent businessman, operating as a 'solo practitioner'. But 'solo practitioners' have always operated alongside other parts of the health-care system, like hospitals. One of the thorniest issues has been the proper division of labour between doctors working inside, and those working outside, hospitals – an issue which, as we shall see, has been settled differently in the three countries examined in this book. More recently, the very idea of the 'solo practitioner' – the doctor operating as a kind of small business – has been challenged by the spread of other ways of organizing the provision of medical services: for instance, by the practice of employing doctors for a salary in profit or non-profit making institutions. The issue of doctors' freedom to operate as independent entrepreneurs does not, however, exhaust the range of problems involved in the regulation of market structures. Among the remainder, one that will recur in these pages is regulation of the geography of markets. It is common for systems to operate some restrictions over where doctors may follow their profession. There is also a continuing debate about how far existing regulations adequately distribute doctors to those areas where they are most needed.

Finally, *payment regulation* is perhaps the most important and controversial task in the regulation of the medical profession. All regulatory systems have to make some decision about what financial relationship, if any, is to exist between the patient and the doctor. The possibilities can be placed on a spectrum. At one end the doctor sets the fee for treatment in the manner of any other private entrepreneur offering a service, and the regulation of payment amounts to no more than the imposition of general rules governing the carrying out of contractual obligations in a market. In the past this was the usual way to regulate payment in many health-care systems; now it is rare. At the other end of the spectrum, no money changes hands at the moment of treatment, and payment is funded by some third party – the government from the public purse, or a health insurance company or fund …

The question of who pays the doctor is, however, not the only important issue in the regulation of remuneration. Just as significant is the way payment is calculated. Again it is helpful to visualize the possibilities along a spectrum. At one end is pure 'payment per service': every possible service that the doctor can perform is costed according to some kind of scale of fees, and the amount paid is simply a result of the sum of services performed for every patient. At the other end of the spectrum is a pure salary system: the doctor is paid a fixed income irrespective of the number of patients seen or the treatments they receive.

Our main focus here will be with regulating the conduct and standards of competence and behaviour of doctors. You will notice, however, the other aspects of regulation particularly in relation to GPs (in Chapter 2) through the 'terms of service' in Sch 2 to the National Health Service (General Medical Services) Regulations 1992 (SI 1992 No 635). As we shall see, it is the role of the regulatory bodies such as the General Medical Council in licensing and disciplining doctors which lies at the heart of regulation of the health professions in the United Kingdom. The State has a legitimate interest in regulating the provision of health care and those who deliver it. This would be the case even if we did not have a National Health Service. Professor Meg Stacey in *Regulating British Medicine: The General Medical Council* (1992) offers the following justification (at p 246):

the particular nature of the doctor-patient relationship, its intimacy and the associated potential for exploitation is one reason; the irremediable and serious nature of mistakes that can be made is another. 'Buyer beware' is little help to the irreparably damaged or dead person – the ultimate risk of falling into the wrong hands in the medical market.

Moran and Wood (*op cit*) illustrate how the State may regulate. They identify *three roles* the State may adopt.

They are: independent self-regulation; state sanctioned self-regulation; and state administered regulation.

Under *independent self-regulation* those concerned with an activity solve the main regulatory tasks independently of the state. This does not necessarily mean that free-market forces are allowed to decide how a good or service is provided. On the contrary, those engaged in a trade or profession may well erect elaborate controls over market entry and competitive practices. In modern society this sort of pure self-regulation is actually quite rare in any important sector of the economy, simply because the modern state is seldom content to leave regulation totally in private hands. Nowadays the best examples of 'pure' models of independent self-regulation are to be found in the fields of leisure, culture and religion. It is common for sporting associations, bodies for the promotion of the arts, and churches, to organize their affairs as purely private associations. Even here, however, independence is on the decline: in recent years in the UK, for instance, the internal conduct of the sport of soccer has increasingly been subject to government control.

This example gives us a hint of how independent self-regulation can turn into *state-sanctioned self-regulation*. The essence of the difference is immediately apparent: in the latter the rules, and the institutions concerned with their formulation and implementation, exist with the consent and support of the state and, in the last analysis, are operated with the support of state sanctions. In recent decades state sanctioning has increasingly displaced pure independent self-regulation. In many cases existing regulatory institutions have been brought under state supervision, while retaining the function of carrying out the detailed tasks of regulation. 'Self-regulation in a statutory framework' is now the standard method of organization in, for example, financial markets in the UK, where a series of 'self-regulatory organizations' control insurance, stock exchanges and allied markets under powers delegated from central government. Likewise many occupations regulate their own arrangements under powers delegated from the state. On the continent of Europe this pattern of self-regulation is especially common. Many regulatory institutions on the continent, especially in the business community, are public law bodies, operated by their own members but endowed with the powers of public agencies.

State-sanctioned self-regulation is widespread for a variety of reasons. In many cases it developed out of older systems of independent self-regulation, when failures in the old arrangements led to reform and state supervision. This is how, for instance, traditional systems of independent self-regulation in the financial markets of the UK and of the USA developed into state-sanctioned self-regulation: in both countries fraud and financial collapse led to demands that government supervise and license the institutions doing the job of regulation. Using the state in this way solves a number of problems simultaneously. Genuinely independent self-regulation often faces serious problems of control, because it is difficult for voluntary associations to wield sanctions against those who break rules. Putting state power behind the system can supply the necessary authority. At the same time, by delegating to private bodies the detailed tasks of regulation states are saved the considerable financial and administrative burden of doing the jobs themselves.

This kind of state licensing poses considerable problems of accountability. By licensing a private body to carry out regulatory functions in its name, the state gives power to that body. The conditions under which that power is granted – the extent to which delegated powers are subject to scrutiny and review, the amount of authority delegated, the powers of punishment devolved – are critical to the functioning of state-sanctioned self-regulation.

State-sanctioned self-regulation in practice 'shades into' the third system identified above, *direct state regulation*. The identifying features of the latter are as follows. Authority to regulate rests on legislation. Regulation may be carried out by a specialized public institution, or by a group of civil servants in a central department of government. The principles of the system are that those who make the rules, and those who implement them, are public servants: they are employees of the state, are subject to rules of public accountability and their actions can be reviewed and challenged in the courts. In principle, direct state regulation ensures public accountability; how far it does so in practice is a matter for investigation of particular cases.

Independent self-regulation, state-sanctioned self-regulation and direct state regulation are three different ways by which the regulatory tasks sketched earlier in this chapter can be carried out.

In the United Kingdom, we adopt 'State-sanctioned self-regulation' though bodies such as the General Medical Council (doctors) (Medical Act 1983); the United Kingdom Central Council of Nursing Midwifery and Health Visiting (nurses, midwives and health visitors) (Nurses, Midwives and Health Visitors Act 1997); the General Dental Council (dentists) (Dentists Act 1984). Other professions which are similarly regulated include pharmacists (Pharmacy Act 1954), opticians (Opticians Act 1989) and nine professions supplementary to medicine, including chiropodists, dieticians, occupational therapists, physiotherapists and radiographers (Professions Supplementary to Medicines Act 1960). Most recently this model has been applied to osteopaths (Osteopaths Act 1993) and chiropractors (Chiropractors Act 1994). The present Government remains committed to this form of self-regulation and has stated:

Health Act 1999, Explanatory Notes (HMSO, 1999)

333 The purpose of professional regulation is to establish a countrywide, professionally set, independent standard of training, conduct and competence for each profession for the protection of the public and the guidance of employers. This is underpinned by personal accountability of practitioners for maintaining safe and effective practice, wherever they are employed and to include effective measures to deal with individuals whose continuing practice presents an unacceptable risk to the public or otherwise renders them unfit to be a registered member of the profession.

(see also *Supporting Doctors, Protecting Patients* (1999), DOH.)

It is worth noting that s 60 of (and Sch 3 to) the Health Act 1999 provides power to modify or repeal any of the regulatory statutes applicable to pharmacists, doctors, dentists, opticians, osteopaths, chiropractors, nurses, midwives and health visitors by Order in Council. The existing regulatory bodies cannot, however, be abolished by such an Order (Sch 3, para 7(1)). However, it is intended to repeal the Nurses, Midwives and Health Visitors Act 1997 so as to replace the current UKCC with a UK-wide regulatory body and to repeal the Professions Supplementary to Medicine Act 1960 and for a new regulatory body to be created by Order in Council to replace the Council for Professions Supplementary to Medicine (s 60(3)). Finally, s 60 allows for the regulation of other professions 'wholly or partly' concerned with 'the physical or mental health of individuals' (s 60(1)(b)). Thus, for example, other complementary medicine practitioners could be regulated providing they constituted a 'profession' and regulation was 'necessary or expedient for the purpose of ... improving the services' provided (s 60(1)(a)). (For a discussion of regulating complementary medicine, see J Stone and J Matthews *Complementary Medicine and the Law* (1996).)

A. DOCTORS

The background to the regulation of doctors and the General Medical Council is discussed by Moran and Wood in *States, Regulations and the Medical Profession* (1993):

UK doctors were organized early. The Royal College of Physicians was chartered in the sixteenth century (in 1518), and the College of Surgeons (later the Royal College) separated from the Company of Barbers in 1745. The less well-off relied on the forerunners of today's general practitioners, who were organized into the Society of Apothecaries ... Each organization constituted a separate self-regulatory body, controlling membership. With medical education and qualifications effectively non-existent, surgeons and physicians in particular were recruited to their organizations more through word of mouth and status than through the display of expertise. Physicians had the highest social status and dominated the supply of medical services, with surgeons in competition.

The collective provision of public health services became essential as the consequences of industrial and urban growth led to water- and sewage-based diseases. Leaders of the public health movement had little time for doctors. Chadwick, the great nineteenth century health-care reformer, spoke of their 'bumbling pretensions' and was critical of the disputes between physicians, surgeons and apothecaries. Many of the latter became parish medical officers under the Poor Law 1834 reforms and, later, District Medical Officers of Health. In a separate development medical directories began to be published in the early 1850s in an attempt by the three branches to clamp down on the thousands of 'doctors' who lacked qualifications (30,000 declared themselves to be doctors in the 1841 Census but only 11,000 appeared in the approved directories).

In terms of taking direct responsibility for services, Parliament restricted its activities to public health and passed a series of acts which initially enabled and later forced local governments to take action. Indirectly it sought to tackle the fragmentation of the medical profession and the inadequacy of medical education and qualifications by establishing a statutory regulatory body under the Medical Act 1858.

Today known as the GMC, or General Medical Council, the new body had the more cumbersome original title General Council of Medical Education and Registration of the United Kingdom. As this suggests, there were two tasks delegated to it – the licensing of individual doctors and the approval of medical schools. Some kind of unity was thus imposed on the fragmented profession, since the registered doctors' list was to include surgeons, physicians, other newer specialists and general practitioners. It still does, with specialist qualifications being determined elsewhere, by the Royal Colleges.

Though statutorily created, the GMC was – and remains – a prime example of state-licensed self-regulation. The 1858 Act – and the several later amending Acts – was a contract between the state and the profession, delegating to the latter responsibility for the standards and quality of those who practise as doctors, a form of contract which UK government has several times utilized to make arrangements with other professions such as law or engineering.

Thus the GMC was initially composed solely of doctors appointed by the main professional societies and academic institutions. Today doctors continue to dominate it, accounting for more than 85 per cent of its members, but many are now elected by the profession at large.

The historical significance of the GMC is twofold. First, unlike some countries where direct regulation by the state prevails, in the UK a tradition of a government–profession contract creating a legal regulatory body and hence legitimizing self-regulation was, and still is, the preferred approach. Certainly the privilege of self-regulation has for many decades been much cherished by the UK medical profession. This formal legitimacy makes the GMC that much more authoritative than would be a non-statutory body. This, in turn, connects to the second aspect of historical significance. State-licensed self-regulation is not the same as independent self-regulation in one important respect. Independent self-regulation would be undertaken by the same body that acts as the doctors' trade union – in the UK, the British Medical Association (BMA). Such a body is clearly partisan, having been established primarily to look after the interests of its members. By divorcing regulation from unionism, the 1858 Act actually strengthened the authority of the profession and the GMC, and gave allopathic medicine enormous prestige and status.

The General Medical Council is today created, and its role primarily defined, by the Medical Act 1983. Diana Kloss describes the GMC's constitution as follows:

Diana Kloss 'The Health Care Professions' in I Kennedy and A Grubb (eds) *Principles of Medical Law* (1998)

This is a body corporate which consists of fifty four elected members, elected by medical practitioners, twenty five appointed members, chosen by certain universities and other bodies, and not more than twenty five members nominated by the Queen. Only nominated members may be, and a majority of the nominated members must be, lay persons without medical qualifications. (Medical Act 1983, s 1 and Part 1 of Sch 1; GMC General Medical Council (Constitution) Order 1979, SI 1979/112, as amended.) Under the Medical Act the Council has power to provide advice for members of the medical profession on standards of professional conduct and medical ethics (Medical Act 1983, s 35).

The GMC controls the education and licensing of doctors in the United Kingdom. As regards its medical education, Diana Kloss (*op cit*) describes its functions:

2.22 The Council, through its Education Committee, controls medical education (Medical Act 1983, s 5). The appointed members still dominate the education committee. The committee must determine the prescribed knowledge and skill required to qualify as a doctor, ensure that instruction given in the universities is sufficient to equip students with that knowledge and skill, determine the standard of proficiency to be expected from candidates in examinations and prescribe patterns of experience in employment in a residential medical capacity in approved hospitals and institutions in order to qualify for full registration. Visitors to medical schools and approved hospitals and institutions, and examination inspectors, may be appointed.

2.23 Before 1978 the GMC had no role in postgraduate medical education, but this was placed under the aegis of the education committee by the Medical Act of that year. However, the content and day-to-day supervision of postgraduate medical education and assessment is left to the universities and the Royal Colleges. Postgraduate education is divided into two stages: basic specialist training for two or three years after full registration and higher specialist training for a further three to five years. Without official accreditation as a specialist, a doctor is highly unlikely to obtain a post as a consultant in the NHS or to be recognised by the private health insurers. However, there is no legal barrier to any doctor with basic medical qualifications setting himself up as a specialist in any field.

2.24 In other states of the European Union specialisation is more common, is undertaken earlier in the doctor's career and is recognised by legal qualifications. Membership of the European Union necessitated the recognition of these qualifications in the Certificate of Specialist Training; however, accreditation by the Royal Colleges maintained its supremacy until it was challenged as being discriminatory by the European Commission, on the ground that it created a two-tier system of UK accredited specialists and those from other member states with the Certificate of Specialist Training whose qualification was regarded as inferior in the UK (*R v Joint Committee on Higher Medical Training, and Specialist Advisory Committee on Rheumatology, ex p Goldstein* [1992] 3 Med LR 278). In January 1991 the GMC began to add the letter T to the medical register against the names of those who were accredited or accorded equivalent status by being appointed a consultant. It did not include the letter T against the names of doctors whose only specialist qualifications were awarded in other member states. The Council maintained an unpublished list of those who had received the Certificate of Specialist training but, as inclusion on this list was not regarded as prima facie evidence of sufficient training to qualify for a consultant post, an entry in the list had little value.

2.25 The Chief Medical Officer, Dr Calman, recommended in his report *Hospital Doctors: Training for the Future* (1993) that each speciality should publish a curriculum and its advice on how that could be provided through a planned, structured training programme, that there should be a new unified training grade to deliver higher specialist training, that progress through the grade and the award of a Certificate of Completion of Specialist Training (CCST) should be based on an assessment of competence and that consultant numbers should be increased well above previous targets. In future, mutual recognition will be afforded to certificates awarded in other member states of the European Union on the same basis as specialist qualifications obtained here. The Government accepted the recommendations in the report, and on 12 January 1996 implementing legislation came into force (European Specialist Medical Qualifications Order 1995, SI 1995/3208).

2.26 Two competent authorities are appointed for the UK in relation to specialist medical qualifications: the GMC and a new body called the Specialist Training Authority of the medical Royal Colleges (STA). The STA issues CCSTs to doctors with the required qualifications and training. The GMC has established and published a register of specialists, including not only those who have been awarded a CCST, but also European doctors with specialist qualifications awarded elsewhere in the EEA whose qualifications are entitled to automatic recognition. From 1 January 1997 it is a condition of appointment as a consultant in the NHS in a speciality other than general practice that the doctor be included in the specialist register. Doctors who are already consultants should apply for inclusion before 1 January 1998. The STA has power to hear appeals against its decisions, and to remove and suspend doctors from the specialist register.

2.27 Control of fitness to practise is in the hands of committees of the Council. The Medical (Professional Performance) Act 1995 has added two new committees to those already established. The Professional Conduct Committee, the Health Committee and the Preliminary Proceedings Committee are charged with the task of establishing whether a medical practitioner has been guilty of serious professional misconduct, or whether his fitness to practise is seriously impaired by reason of his physical or mental condition. (Medical Act 1983, ss 36, 37, 42.) The Assessment Referral Committee and the Committee on Professional Performance were created by the 1995 Act. Their task is to deal with allegations that the standard of professional performance of a doctor has been seriously deficient.

We will return later to consider the disciplinary and performance monitoring functions of the GMC. In addition, the GMC has the power to provide advice to doctors on standards of professional conduct or on medical ethics (Medical Act 1983, s 35). To this end, the GMC produces guidance on such matters as: *Good Medical Practice* (July 1998) (replacing *Professional Conduct and Discipline: Fitness to Practice* ('the Blue Book')); *Confidentiality*; *Protecting and Providing Information* (2000); *Serious Communicable Diseases* (November 1997); and *Seeking Patients' Consent: The Ethical Considerations* (November 1998). This guidance will set the benchmark for the standards expected of a doctor by the GMC.

Who then is a doctor? Curiously, medical practitioners do not ordinarily have doctorates and therefore, the attribution to them of the title 'doctor' is wholly a convention (surgeons, for historical reasons, do not adopt the convention). When we talk of a 'doctor' we are really concerned with a *registered medical practitioner*. By this, we mean a doctor registered with the General Medical Council. Diana Kloss in *Principles of Medical Law* (*op cit*) explains the system of licensing for UK-qualified doctors and for doctors from abroad.

2.10 The medical Register consists of four lists: the principal list, the overseas list, the visiting overseas doctors list and the visiting European practitioners list (Medical Act 1983, s 2). There is also a register of doctors with limited registration. A copy of the printed register which is published annually by the Registrar, is evidence that the persons included are fully registered, and the absence of a person's name from the register is evidence that that person is not registered (Medical Act 1983, s 34).

2.11 Applicants for registration who are qualified to the satisfaction of the Registrar must be issued with a certificate of registration. Any person who holds one or more primary UK qualifications, has passed a qualifying examination and has complied with the regulations laid down by the General Medical Council as to a period of experience is entitled to registration on payment of the appropriate fee (Medical Act 1983, s 3).

2.12 The primary qualifications which entitle an applicant to be entered in the Medical Register are specified in legislation (Medical Act 1983; Medical Qualifications (Amendment) Act 1991). Certain universities, and the Royal Colleges and the Society of Apothecaries, are entitled to hold qualifying examinations with the approval and under the direction of the education committee of the General Medical Council. In addition, a person must satisfy requirements as to experience in employment in a resident medical capacity in one or more approved hospitals or approved institutions, and obtain a certificate to that effect from his examining body, before being entitled to full registration.

2.13 Provisional registration may be sought by those who, having completed the necessary examinations, are undertaking a period of employment in order to obtain the experience necessary for full registration. A person who is provisionally registered is deemed to be registered as a fully registered medical practitioner only so far as it is necessary to enable him to be engaged in employment in a resident medical capacity in one or more hospitals or institutions (Medical Act 1983, s 15).

2.14 The fundamental principle that nationals of member states of the European Union should be free to practise their profession in all other member states has necessitated the mutual recognition of qualifications. In the medical field, two key Directives of 1975 (75/362/EEC; 75/363/EEC) provided that each member state should recognise qualifications obtained in other member states, and also laid down minimum standards which those qualifications must reach, for example, that there must be suitable clinical experience in a hospital under appropriate supervision. At the same time two committees were established by the European Council of Ministers: the Advisory Committee on Medical Training and the Committee of Senior Officials in Public Health. In 1993 a further Council Directive consolidated the Directives of 1975 and subsequent amendments, including a requirement that those entering general practice should have a minimum of two years' specific vocational training. From 1 January 1994 the provisions on training and mutual recognition for doctors have also applied in certain EFTA countries (Austria, Norway, Sweden, Finland and Iceland) which, together with the European Union member states and Leichtenstein, constitute the European Economic Area. Austria, Sweden and Finland became members of the European Union on 1 January 1995.

2.15 A national of a member state of the European Union who is lawfully established in medical practice in a state other than the UK may lawfully render medical services here as a visitor if he makes a written declaration showing the services he intends to provide and produces a certificate showing that he holds recognised medical qualifications in another member state. He may not, other than in an emergency, render medical services except in accordance with his declaration (Medical Act 1983, s 18). If such a person wishes to practise here permanently, he must apply for full registration in the principal list. Although European Directives do not in general permit states to impose a test of linguistic competence on doctors from other European states, doctors seeking employment in the National Health Service may be required by the prospective employer to prove that they can communicate effectively in English.

2.16 Doctors whose qualifications have been obtained outside the European Union are not in such a strong position. Responsibility for establishing the sufficiency of the education received by this group rests with the overseas committee of the GMC. A distinction must be made between recognised foreign qualifications, where the foreign medical school has been recognised by the GMC, and acceptable foreign qualifications which are accepted by the GMC as a sufficient guarantee of the possession of the knowledge and skill required to practise under the supervision of a person who is registered as a fully registered medical practitioner. Many overseas doctors are given only limited registration for a period of up to five years (Medical Act 1983, s 22). Limited registration is obtained by satisfying the Registrar that the applicant has been offered employment in the UK or the Isle of Man, that he holds an acceptable overseas qualification, that he has the necessary knowledge of English, that he is of good character, and that he has the knowledge, skill, and experience required. From 1 January 1996 the GMC has accepted the World Health Organisation's list of primary medical qualifications as acceptable for limited registration. Overseas doctors who undertake postgraduate training in the hospital service and who intend to leave the UK on completion of training are able to enter without a work permit under the Immigration Rules for up to four years. ((1994), HC 395, paras 70, 71). Extension of this period for up to two years may exceptionally be permitted by the Home Office. An alternative to the need to pass the English and clinical tests set by the Professional and Linguistic Assessment Board (PLAB) is that the doctor should be sponsored by a consultant or senior doctor in the NHS who undertakes to supervise and provide training.

2.17 The GMC Annual Report of 1995 concluded that, in future, assessment of all doctors applying for limited registration will be based on objective evidence, either the PLAB tests or, for example, a postgraduate qualification. It is possible for an overseas doctor with only limited registration to apply for full registration. The Review Board for Overseas Qualified Practitioners has power to review decisions of the GMC relating to overseas practitioners under section 29 Medical Act 1983. It was held in *Khan v General Medical Council* ([1994] IRLR 646, CA) that the existence of this right of appeal excluded a right to complain to an industrial tribunal about racial discrimination under the Race Relations Act 1976. The Court of Appeal again considered the powers of the GMC with respect to overseas practitioners in *R v General Medical Council, ex p Virik* ([1996] ICR 433) Dr Virik, who had qualified in Malaysia and India, had obtained limited registration under the Medical Act 1983, s 22, for five years. His application for full registration was refused, and his appeal to the review board was unsuccessful. The GMC's guidance for doctors was limited registration recommended that applicants for full registration should have experience as a registrar or senior house officer and an additional qualification. The same requirements were not specified for holders of UK or European Union qualifications, or those with a recognised overseas qualification. It was held that there was no legal duty to apply a comparative test with UK/European Union doctors. The GMC had a wide discretion, with which the court would only interfere if the decision was manifestly unreasonable. The GMC proposed in 1995 that overseas practitioners should first be granted a training registration which would be similar to limited registration in that they would be required to work under the supervision of a fully qualified medical practitioner.

2.18 Where experience is lacking, an overseas practitioner who has a recognised qualification and good English may be granted provisional registration (Medical Act 1983, s 21). A further possibility is temporary full registration for those who intend to visit the UK for up to a year in order to provide medical services of a specialist nature (Medical Act 1983, s 27). They must possess recognised or acceptable qualifications and special knowledge and skill in a particular branch or branches of medicine. However, the Immigration Rules prohibit such a person with the immigration status of visitor from undertaking paid employment in the UK, that is, the doctor would need a work permit.

2.19 As a result of the publication of the NHS Executive booklet: *Ethnic Minority Staff in the NHS: A Programme of Action* (1993), there has been a review by the Working Group on Specialist Medical Education of the employment and training of overseas doctors entering specialist training. It has recommended that all overseas doctors coming for training, without exception, pass a standard test of English competence before applying to the GMC for registration, and also demonstrate clinical competence to a level comparable with UK doctors.

Being registered as a 'fully registered medical practitioner' has certain consequences for an individual. The most important, perhaps, is that although the legislation does not prevent a person from practising medicine if his name is not on the medical register, he cannot hold himself out as being a registered medical practitioner or profess to be a medically qualified doctor. Section 49 of the Medical Act 1983 provides, *inter alia*:

49. (1) Subject to subsection (2) below, any person who wilfully and falsely pretends to be or takes or uses the name or title of physician, doctor of medicine, licentiate in medicine and surgery, bachelor of medicine, surgeon, general practitioner or apothecary, or any name, title, addition or description implying that he is registered under any provision of this Act, or that he is recognised by law as a physician or surgeon or licentiate in medicine and surgery or a practitioner in medicine or an apothecary, shall be liable on summary conviction to a fine.

On the other hand, being a fully registered medical practitioner confers certain privileges on a doctor. For example, in relation to the recovery of his fees, s 46 of the 1983 Act provides, *inter alia*:

46. (1) Except as provided in subsection (2) below, no person shall be entitled to recover any charge in any court of law for any medical advice or attendance, or for the performance of any operation, or for any medicine which he has both prescribed and supplied unless he proves that he is fully registered.

Is the effect of this section that, for example, a physiotherapist providing medical advice or attendance under a contract could not sue for the fees? On its face, it would seem that the physiotherapists could not recover the fees.

But Jacob and Montgomery in *Encyclopedia of Health Services and Medical Law* (1987) (note to s 46) provide a useful gloss on section 46. They note:

> The section is historic. Subject to the provision in subsection (2) relating to visiting European practitioners it has three parts representing the ancient divisions of medicine. The reference to 'any medical advice or attendance' is to the practice of physicians; that to 'any operation' to the practice of surgeons; and that to 'any medicine which he has both prescribed and supplied' to the practice of apothecaries.

Seen in this light, s 46 only applies to those holding themselves out as registered medical practitioners performing the functions previously associated with the ancient divisions in medicine. Thus, the physiotherapist would be able to recover fees providing there was no representation of being a registered medical practitioner. The section's effect is merely to give the registered medical practitioner a competitive edge in providing services because he alone can describe himself as such and, thereafter, recover any fees.

Similarly, registration allows a doctor to hold certain appointments which he otherwise could not, the most important example being those within the National Health Service. Section 47 of the 1983 Act provides:

47. (1) Subject to subsection (2) below, no person who is not fully registered shall hold any appointment as physician, surgeon or other medical officer –
(a)   in the naval, military or air service,
(b)   in any hospital or other place for the reception of persons suffering from mental disorder, or in any other hospital, infirmary or dispensary not supported wholly by voluntary contributions,
(c)   in any prison, or
(d)   in any other public establishment, body or institution, or to any friendly or other society for providing mutual relief in sickness, infirmity or old age.

More generally, being a fully registered medical practitioner confers on a doctor as a matter of public policy the privilege of doing certain things to other people which would otherwise be prima facie unlawful. (It is no surprise therefore, that the law should wish to hold the doctor to account for what he does in the exercise of this privilege.)

Registered medical practitioners will usually work either within the NHS, as general practitioners or hospital doctors, or in private practice. These are not mutually exclusive. It is often the case that a particular doctor working in a hospital as a consultant will undertake some private work as well as fulfilling his NHS duties.

B. NURSES, MIDWIVES AND HEALTH VISITORS

Nurse, midwives and health visitors are regulated by the United Kingdom Central Council of Nursing, Midwifery and Health Visiting (UKCC). Diana Kloss sets out the functions of the UKCC.

D Kloss in I Kennedy and A Grubb (eds) *Principles of Medical Law* (1998)

2.28 This was established by the Nurses, Midwives and Health Visitors Act 1979, which was consolidated, with subsequent amendments, in the Nurses, Midwives and Health Visitors Act 1997. It consists of such number of members, not greater than sixty, and a multiple of three, as approved by the Secretary of State (Nurses, Midwives and Health Visitors Act 1997, s 1). Two-thirds of the members of the Council are elected and the remaining one-third appointed by the Secretary of State from among persons who are either registered nurses, midwives or health visitors or medical practitioners, or have such qualifications and experience in education or other fields as, in the opinion of the Secretary of State, will be of value to the Council in the performance of its functions. The Secretary of State shall have especially in mind the need to secure a geographical balance, so that each part of the United Kingdom is represented, and the need to ensure that qualifications and experience in the teaching of the relevant disciplines are adequately represented.

2.29 The Council must maintain a register of those qualified in the relevant professions, must determine the training to be undertaken in order to entitle an applicant to be admitted to the register, and also adjudicate on fitness to practise. The Acts establish a national board for each of England, Wales, Scotland and Northern Ireland. The members of the boards are all appointed by the Secretary of State (*ibid*), s 5. The principal function of the national boards is to validate and supervise courses of training and examinations, in accordance with standards laid down by the Council.

2.30 The professional register is divided into fifteen parts. These include first and second level general nurses, first and second level mental illness and mental handicap nurses, paediatric nurses, midwives and health visitors. A person seeking admission to a part of the register must have undergone the training and passed the examinations required by the rules of the Council, must be a person of good character and must pay a fee. Registration is subject to renewal every three years, on payment of a fee.

2.31 The Council is under a duty to make rules regulating the practice of midwives and these rules may, in particular, determine the circumstances in which, and the procedure by means of which, midwives may be suspended from practice, require midwives to give notice of intention to practise to the local supervising authority, the health authority, and require registered midwives to attend courses of instruction in accordance with the rules. The midwifery committee of the UKCC deals with proposals to make, amend or revoke such rules, which must be approved by the Secretary of State in order to come into force.

2.32 A national of any member state of the European Union who applies for registration in the United Kingdom and has professional qualifications designated by statutory instrument as equivalent to UK qualifications must be registered in the relevant part of the register on payment of a fee as long as he satisfies the Council that he is of good character (European Nursing and Midwifery Qualifications Designation Order 1996, SI 1996/3102)). A visiting European Union national who is lawfully practising in another member state as a nurse responsible for general care, or as a midwife, and who holds the appropriate qualifications, may practise in the UK on a temporary basis on making a written declaration to the Council of his intention to practise in the UK and on the production of documents establishing his qualifications in the other state. Registration in a country outside the European Union may be recognised as permitting an individual to the registered in the UK, following individual evaluation of the knowledge and competence of that individual, including proficiency in English (Nurses, Midwives and Health Visitors Act 1997, s 8).

2.33 Fitness to practise is under the control of the Council, which has established a Professional Conduct Committee and a Health Committee. The function of these committees is to determine whether a person on the register has been guilty of professional misconduct, ie 'conduct unworthy of a nurse, midwife or health visitor', (compare the wording with 'serious professional misconduct' in the Medical Act), or whether his fitness to practise has been seriously impaired by reason of his physical or mental condition (Nurses, Midwives and Health Visitors (Professional Conduct) Rules 1993, SI 1993/893).

In 1999 a review of the 1997 Act was published, entitled *The Regulation of Nurses, Midwives and Health Visitors, Report on a Review of the Nurses, Midwives and Health Visitors Act 1997* (J M Consulting Ltd, February 1999). It recommended new legislation, inter alia: to create a single UK-wide regulatory body (the Nursing and Midwifery Council); to require a minimum of one-third lay membership; to simplify the register; to provide additional powers in dealing with misconduct, poor performance and health issues. The government accepted its key recommendations (HSC 1999/030). Section 60 of the Health Act 1999 provides for the repeal of the 1997 Act and for its replacement by Order in Council (ss 60(3) and (2)(b) respectively).

C. SELF-REGULATION

Should self-regulation continue or should the state become directly involved? In its report, *Procedures Related to Adverse Clinical Incidents and Outcomes in Medical Care* (HC 549—I, Session 1999–2000), the House of Commons Health Committee considered this issue.

> 64. Some witnesses, in particular patients and their relatives and carers, felt strongly that the privilege of self-regulation for the medical profession should come to an end. They argued that doctors and nurses were not properly accountable and 'looked after their own'. They believed that lay people were capable of understanding the issues surrounding regulation of the profession and should be partners in the debate. One suggestion was that there should be an independent health regulator, rather as there is for other industries. They also suggested an extension to the role of the Health Service Commissioner. We put these points to the Secretary of State. He disagreed. He felt that self-regulation was the best system and pointed out that any other would, anyway, need medical input on a huge scale. He noted that the medical profession was working hard to improve the extent of regulation, particularly with its proposals for regular re-validation of doctors which are due to be implemented in 2001.
>
> 65. We believe that it is important that there is more lay involvement not only in the membership of the professional bodies and their sub-committees but also within health authorities and trusts at every level. There should be greater partnership between stakeholders within the NHS and clinical governance should provide a mechanism for this. **Whilst recognising the importance of a strong professional input, we recommend that the constitution of the GMC and the UKCC is amended to increase the lay membership to a bare majority and that health authorities and trusts are encouraged to involve local communities in monitoring and maintaining standards.**

As you will see, the (then) Secretary of State favoured continued State-approved self-regulation and the Committee did not demur. Of course, the Order in Council provision of s 60 of the Health Act 1999 will make legislative change to 'beef-up' the regulatory frameworks easier when that is considered necessary. It may also be that the Secretary of State could see no alternative – even if direct state regulation was to exist – to considerable professional involvement in setting educational or other standards.

Not everyone agrees. In a scholarly analysis of the workings of the General Medical Council, Professor Meg Stacey doubts whether the self-regulation model can be sustained.

Margaret Stacey *Regulating British Medicine: The General Medical Council* (1992)

Can self-regulation work?
Professional self-regulation may not be acceptable to the radical right or the radical left, but there is plenty of evidence that the principle is still acceptable to many people. Other occupations continue to follow the model of the GMC or wish they could do so. Social workers, discontented with what they see as the partiality of local authority enquiries, are one such contemporary group.

Smith recognized that there was an underlying question as to whether the self-regulation of doctors is still acceptable ... However, a crucial question is whether his criticisms of the GMC are not *really criticisms of professional self-regulation itself*? Certainly David Bolt *et al* saw that danger, for the bulk of their letter contained the following *credo*:

> Above all we wish to affirm that there is a very substantial majority view among members of the BMA favouring the central principle of professional self regulation, while fully supporting the essential safeguard that such regulation must, in a free society, be undertaken with the benefit of lay opinion and advice such as that which the lay members of the Council provide. We also venture to suggest that this principle would, if seriously challenged, be firmly endorsed by an informed body of public opinion ...

Unreasoned and unsupported arguments of this kind had kept the principle off the agenda of the Merrison committee. Sir Robert Kilpatrick ... put a more reasoned case, including the important point that 'self imposed discipline is much more likely to be accepted by members of the profession than that imposed from outside'. This, however, overlooks the question of just how far 'outside' their everyday lives many members of the profession practising in Britain feel the GMC to be, remote as it still appears, unrepresentative of women, young doctors, non-white doctors as it is. Sir Robert further says that he is sure that no doctor who understands what the principle is all about would wish to lose it and continues 'the GMC will continue to *assert* and uphold the principle' (my emphasis). If the failures of the GMC which Smith pointed to are failures of self-regulation itself then the GMC will not be capable of rising to the challenges which are now facing it.

Stephen Lock ... , in an editorial which followed Richard Smith's articles, called for another enquiry into the role of the GMC 'in both regulation and education', saying, with a bit of exaggeration, that it was almost 20 years since the subject was examined in depth. Lock suggests the profession itself should set up the enquiry, because of the importance of self-regulation, but that it would be better if it was an independent rather than an internal inquiry. He concludes his editorial by pointing out that a GMC which fulfilled its functions properly would be a good deal more expensive, but that doctors should be prepared to pay

both because the benefits will be correspondingly greater (to doctors and to society) and because they need to keep regulation of the profession where it belongs – with the profession.

That call was made in July 1989. There is no indication that the GMC have any intention of proposing an independent enquiry.

My analysis suggests that professionalism as developed in the medical profession may make it impossible to achieve appropriate regulation by the profession. Both the need to maintain unity, in order to self-regulate and the loyalty to the concept of the greater profession, over and above sectional medical interests called forth to sustain that unity tend to restrict and retard what the GMC can do. The felt need to consult and consult again in order to reach consensus decisions greatly slows down the decision-making process. Indeed the procedures may either transform the proposals away from their original intention or hold them up indefinitely, an effective veto. The institutionalization of control in a series of elite groups which have many of their own internal problems to deal with, reduces the sensitivity of their members to what it happening 'out there' and their ability to understand what they hear.

The great advantage of professional self-regulation, when those doing the regulating are sufficiently in touch with the general body of the professionals, is the greater acceptability of self-imposed regulation. Even given the inevitable gap between leaders and led, there it something different about having 'one of us' giving out orders rather than a 'rank outsider' who 'just doesn't understand'. Membership of a self-regulating profession is likely to increase the sense of worth of it members and, given appropriate working conditions, this is likely to enhance the standard of their work. The service ethic, an essential part of medical professionalism, is another major inherent (if sometimes rather latent) advantage.

Professional self-regulation, as we have seen, permeates all aspects of medical regulation, including the law, where medical evidence, unlike evidence from all other professions and occupations, is determinative, not advisory. There is a sense in which the GMC is the standard bearer for medical professionalism, and for that it takes a lot of stick. However, it cannot, as an institution, be held responsible for all the wide array of medical accountability procedures and practices ...

The time has come to look at the entire UK system of regulation of the medical profession as a whole rather than reviewing and reforming its component parts in a piecemeal manner. An independent enquiry should look not only at the GMC, as Lock suggested, or at medical negligence issues, as Havard suggested, but the wider issues of the regulation and accountability of the profession and all the institutions involved. Such an enquiry would look at the component parts, how they are articulated together, including where the GMC fits into that. But above all the enquiry should look at professional self-regulation to establish the balance of advantages and disadvantages it offers. Why has the profession always been so shy, since they are convinced it is so manifestly a good principle, of having self-regulation examined? Dare one whisper that that might be because they know it really is better for the profession than for the public, that its principal purpose is to maintain their power and status?

Given the close-knit interdependence of all health care occupations, it may be that the enquiry should look at regulation and accountability right across the health care professions. Certainly it is unreal that discipline, where blunders may have been made by members of more than one profession, eg nurses and technicians as well as doctors, should be looked at in isolation by each profession in turn as is now the case. The case for dealing with each profession separately depends on the very principle of self-regulation which it would be the first task of the enquiry to examine. This suggests the enquiry should proceed by stages, first examining professional self-regulation. If this should fail, then the subsequent proceedings would follow the course of looking at the regulation of health care professions as a whole. If it were upheld, separate enquiries as to professional regulation for each health care occupation would then be in order.

What kind of regulatory body is needed?

Such an enquiry would need to start by considering what kind of regulatory body is needed. My studies have led me to conclude that an adequate system of regulation should take account of the interests of the practitioners, those they work with and their patients. The criteria by which one might judge whether any medical profession is really well-regulated may be said to include the following:

1. that the profession ensures that only appropriately qualified doctors are admitted to practice;
2. that those continuing in practice are competent;
3. that they work conscientiously;
4. that those allowed to practise do not exploit their patients economically, socially or sexually;
5. that those allowed to practise do not exploit their colleagues or subordinates;
6. that patients or their representatives have ready access to the regulatory body in case of the alleged failure of a practitioner in any of these respects;
7. that patients or their representatives should receive equitable and adequate compensation for any damage resulting from medical accident or misdemeanour;
8. that practitioners are afforded appropriate protection against wrongful actions of patients, employers, colleagues or others.

Would those characteristics be agreed as important by professionals and patients at large? All practitioners would agree that those in practise should be appropriately qualified, competent and work conscientiously also that they should not exploit patients in any way. Practitioners would agree with not exploiting colleagues at least in the sense of not disparaging them. Little attention has been paid in professional codes to the explanation of subordinates. Ready access by patients to regulatory bodies is not something which in the past the profession has been too pleased to offer. It is almost as if, as Smith implies ... , patient and the public are seen as the enemy; however, I imagine that in principal this criterion would be conceded. So far as individual cases are concerned one can expect dispute and challenge about damage and compensation but a professional body, at least theoretically, could surely only be in agreement as to the justice of that criterion. It is unlikely that most patients would recognize that practitioners may need protection against them, but practitioners certainly will.

In thinking about these criteria it is clear that one must distinguish between individual professionals and the profession as a collectivity. This distinction has constantly cropped up in the preceding discussions. It is clearly in the interests of the profession as a collectivity to provide as good a service as modern knowledge, skill and technology can offer; to achieve that may be difficult for any one individual practitioner, for a whole host of reasons. In principle the interests of patients and the profession do not diverge; in practice they often do – from a patient's need for a house call in the early hours of the morning to much more serious issues. Herein lies one of the problems of self-regulation in practice as opposed to in principle.

Does all or part of the regulatory system fulfil these criteria at present? Because the GMC is responsible for ensuring that members of the public can trust any registered medical practitioner whom they consult – which it does by maintaining a register of those fit to practise – it is also responsible for criteria: (1) appropriate qualifications, (2) competence of those in practice, (3) their conscientiousness and (4) no exploitation of patients. The third could be argued to be a matter of wise patient choice, but, given the specialness of medicine, could also reasonably be said to be part of proper professional practice. Given that the GMC has to maintain the register of the competent it could also be said by implication to be responsible for (6), ready access; otherwise, how may it know that its register is reliable? Characteristic (7), compensation, is right outside the GMC's present tasks – it falls to the law. The GMC deals with a small part of (8), protection of practitioners, namely where damage to medical colleagues offends the ethical guidelines, but for the most part the medical trade unions and defence societies and sometimes the law are responsible.

In practice the GMC does not fulfil these tasks at all adequately at present, as we have seen. In addition a number of other authorities – the NHS, other employing authorities – are involved in all except (1), ie ensuring that only appropriately qualified doctors are permitted to practise. The GMC has, furthermore, rested very heavily on the NHS procedures, something for which Jean Robinson has criticized it roundly. The NHS procedures are, of course, no help to patients in private practice who have only the GMC or the law to turn to. Aggrieved patients do not have ready access to the GMC (criterion 6).

A main problem is that professions, including the medical profession, do not think in terms of the kind of regulatory body which I have outlined above. The nature of professionalism as presently understood stands on different premises and ones which I argue are not in the best interests of the profession or its clients. For these reasons … I argue that a new kind of professionalism is needed …

Professional self-reform
[It is] in the interests of medicine itself, as well as of the public that it serves, the profession needs to take a good deal further the self-reforms which it has already initiated in a number of areas, in education, competence, audit, for example. The facet of professionalism in medicine which works well towards good regulation is the service ethic. It is to this that I think both profession and public must look for the future. From this a new professionalism may be developed which will be appropriate for the twenty-first century.

Just as a main advantage of self-regulation is that regulation from peers is likely to be more acceptable than regulation from outside, so there are major advantages for the profession in undertaking its own reform. Medicine as an occupation was a prime leader in establishing the concepts of profession and professionalism. It is now in a good position to lead the way towards the new professionalism which other service occupations could follow.

The new professionalism would realize that the restrictive practices essential to establish the profession in the nineteenth century are now no longer needed. Medicine is well entrenched as the leading healing mode, although practitioners and professional leaders, who receive the flak that flies against their practice and profession, may not feel so secure. Medicine is, however, the individual, practitioner–patient aspect and the collectivity of the profession as a whole. Work has to be done on both counts. Already at the practitioner level a great deal of work has gone on which is laying the foundations for this new professionalism. Medical knowledge, for example, is shared with patients and the public much more freely than it used to be. Many GPs work with or refer their patients to complementary or alternative healers, such as acupuncturists. There are practices where the collegial relationships have been extended to include staff of all kinds. Some hospitals include many non-biomedical healers and counsellors among the services they offer. Numbers of doctors are seeking to establish relationships of greater equality with their patients.

However, the dominant professional ethos, the kind of training many young doctors still receive and the rules and guidance that are offered to practitioners, too frequently still act as a deterrent to such developments. In any case, it is not enough just to change some relationships in this way, although that is important. The collective ethos also has to change so that good developments are no longer shackled.

Tasks towards the new professionalism
The first task in working towards the new professionalism is to ensure that the profession puts the patient and the collectivity of patients not necessarily *first*, but equal to and part of the professional interest. The patients can be, and historically have been, the profession's greatest ally, not only providing work (patients are, after all, the *sine qua non* of the profession) but often providing support in time of trouble. The loyalty that I have seen patients express in the GMC when pleading for their own doctors – including some really rascally ones – to be permitted to continue to practise should reassure practitioners. Those who have had cause for complaint and some other members of the public may be less happy.

To serve the patient well, to put the patient above personal and sectional interests, is already the ideal. In practice, under the old professionalism it has not really worked out that way, as I have shown. In its own interest the profession would be wise to work through all necessary facets to check that it really is providing a good service, both as a collectivity in what it aims to do and so far as the performance standards of its members are concerned. To achieve this the profession will have to listen to what patients say and to understand the way they see things – their conceptual framework …

How quickly can the new professionalism develop?
As professional leaders have already recognized, there is not much time to waste. It will take time, however, to change old ideas, especially ones, such as clinical autonomy and self-regulation, so firmly embedded during initial training and by subsequent repetition. The first step must be to move towards what the profession thinks it already has been doing – seeing that all registered practitioners are reasonably competent. This goal is beginning by some to be seen as more important than blind and unthinking collegial loyalty – as expressed in the ethical guidelines. The importance, for example, of medical audit is recognized by all practitioners who want to see a good job done and who are motivated by the service ethic. Many are not yet convinced and, no doubt, the conviction expressed by some may be mere lip service.

It is understandable that medical practitioners should wish to draw a clear distinction between audit for financial reasons and audit to ensure high standards of practice. It is also understandable that at this stage the profession, only segments of which have hitherto undertaken any systematic reviews of their practice, should insist on audit being closed to any one other than fellow professionals. Those professions which medicine has subordinated understandably wish to undertake their own reviews without medical interference. I would hope, however, that as the new professionalism develops audits would be opened up, not only to other health care workers (for, as I keep saying, so much health care is a joint enterprise with shared responsibility), but also to patients who, after all, in most cases make an active input to their own treatment.

Time must be allowed for the changes at all levels to take place. However, what the profession urgently needs to do is to show that the changes it is proposing are not merely defensive – to change as little as possible and to retain as much power as possible – but that it recognizes that a new kind of professionalism is now needed. If the profession is unable to make such an earnest of intention and to articulate a schedule of the goals to be achieved and how quickly movement can follow, then others are likely to develop the goals and the schedule for the profession. If the profession does not itself set up such a programme it will be because diehards in places of power will not permit it. And here we are back to the problems of self-regulation. However, the GMC, with its statutory responsibilities, its unique understanding of the profession as a whole, is in a position to give such a lead.

Changes needed to create the new professionalism

What the new professionalism will mean is that the profession will have to respond in free and open discussion to the demands of other groups, that proposals will be made and modified, new boundaries drawn and negotiations continued. In some ways this is, of course, what already happens – except for the 'free and open' bit. Negotiations now take place among elites, sometimes reported, sometimes not. Patients' groups are now being included in these negotiations much more than ever before. This is a great advance, but those groups, and particularly their leaders, will have to take care they themselves are not co-opted to the elite system.

Education for the new professionalism

What about the type of education which practitioners should receive? To make way for the new professionalism artificial and inhibiting divisions in medicine will have to be superseded by a more genuine collegiality. Factions within medicine seem to have been deadlocked for too long on the relationship of the various stages of education to each other. The mode of education of young doctors in hospital, modelled essentially on the old professionalism, has been a major factor in undermining that very concept of professionalism. Once junior hospital doctors were granted overtime pay, the old concept of profession received a major dent from within the profession itself.

The damage arose from internal contradictions within medicine whereby the equality of all fully qualified practitioners, strongly upheld, contrasted with the subordinate role of all those in training grades. The carrot, that they would one day achieve full professional status, was not enough for junior hospital doctors in the often alienating conditions of the modern hospital. They took the trade union rather than the professional route to solve their problems. The discomforts of their position again, at the end of 1990, threatened the unity of the profession and the running of the hospital service itself, leading to government intervention ...

The old professionalism failed to solve this problem. A new professionalism would recognize and totally review the conditions of training of young doctors and their relationship to their chiefs as well as to the NHS; indeed, the concept of 'chiefs' itself may well need review. It has to be recognized that the grievances of the junior hospital doctors, while they are exacerbated by the problems facing the NHS as a result of under-funding and reorganization, are in essence created by an old professionalism, deeply imbued with ideas of status and essentially traditional in outlook ('what was good enough for my father ...'; 'I went through it, so can they ...'). More appropriate training conditions would improve service to the patients and reduce the disadvantages which young doctors with responsibility for young children incur. The current conditions of work were devised for an all-male profession where the men undertook no domestic responsibilities. Special conditions for women are not what is needed, but civilized working hours and a less punitive rota or shift system for all junior hospital doctors.

One of the crucial times and places where the values of the old professionalism are instilled into the young practitioner is during the training by chiefs in hospital. A new set of relationships and structures would go along with teaching the more open values of the new professionalism.

Lay involvement in educational control?

Should the control of medical education continue to remain entirely in professional hands? Only the trained have the skills to judge the technical competence of entrants to the profession, but there are other facets where the non-medically qualified have a contribution to make. Educational experts can contribute on topics such as selection of students, examination procedures and teaching methods. Patients and potential patients can comment on the broad outlines of the education medical students receive. For example, a medical training was not needed to observe that, until very recently, doctors were trained in and given experience almost exclusively of hospital medicine while patients most often consulted GPs. That has now been remedied by including general practice as a specialty in the clinical training and the pre-registration year and also by requiring by law vocational training for all intending GPs. Lay advice would have put those advances sooner rather than later: they do not need to be told that most consultations are with GPs and that the quality of their practitioner is of the essence. One cannot always wait for professionalizing ambitions (in this case those of GPs which led to these changes) to catch up with problems patients experience.

So far as the deadlock about putting together all stages of medical education is concerned, it is possible that, had there been a stronger voice from other health care workers and from patients and potential patients, the deadlock might already have been broken. Patients and potential patients have a strong interest in these issues, for the quality of medical care is undoubtedly affected by them and most patients receive a great deal of their treatment from doctors in various stages of training. The problems of junior hospital doctors crucially affect other health care workers also particularly nurses.

Control of entry to the profession has been one of the cornerstones of the old concept of professionalism. Where would it fit into the new? Again following from the criteria of what a well-regulated profession would look like, the already qualified practitioners and the educators would clearly have a major input to make as to what is a properly qualified practitioner. Theirs is the technical knowledge and the practical experience. But, as in the content of the education deemed necessary and the conditions of training, there is a legitimate view from other health care professionals and from patients and potential patients.

How would the new professionalism regulate medicine?

A revised composition for the GMC
A first step would be to propose some crucial changes in the structure and powers of the GMC. Measures to ensure adequate representation of young doctors, women and ethnic minorities would be urgently needed – not simply so that the GMC might appear more representative, but also so that the contribution of all those categories of doctors to the health of the nation, whether in private practice or the NHS, should be fully, fairly and equally taken into account in the Council's deliberations.

The new professionalism would recognize the status of other qualified health care professionals and would accord them adequate places on the Council as of right. The unique contribution they can make by reason of their training and practice experience to the regulation of the profession, both its educational and its disciplinary aspects, would thereby be recognized.

The new professionalism would also wish to seek greatly to increase the proportion of non-medical members on the Council. It would drop the term 'lay', which comes from the out-dated idea of exclusive and esoteric, not to say mystical, knowledge. In their wisdom the new professionals would probably finally decide that all the non-medically qualified taken together should constitute rather more than half of the membership in order to ensure that the service ethic remained to the fore.

A vigorous lead
A new GMC, so constituted, would continue to consult with other medical bodies, as it now does, but would be more vigorous in giving a lead to the profession. It would also restrict more tightly the time and number of these rounds of consultation and would not be afraid to make proposals which might run against the interests of some. It would be more vigorous in its inspection of educational bodies. Legislation would be needed to do these things and, in seeking that, the self-reforming GMC would request stronger powers over all stages of medical education and would propose a specialist register, rather than the voluntary inclusion of special qualifications in the present register.

One body or more?
Thought would have to be given as to whether the functions which the GMC now performs and the enhanced functions I have suggested it should undertake can reasonably be performed by one body. Controlling educational standards and entry qualifications is a large and demanding task and one which is distinct from ensuring that those on the register remain competent to practise. The two functions could be said to overlap at the point of the uptake of continuing medical education. However, to ensure the provisions are there, to indicate what continuing education should be received, when and by whom, is an educational function; to see that practitioners comply with the conditions laid down is a different and disciplinary function. There is no logical reason why the register should not be retained by one authority, the educational standard be set by another and the disciplinary functions as to fitness to

practise in relation to continuing competence, appropriate general behaviour and health be
carried out by a third …

How far, how fast?
Rapid progress to the new professionalism cannot be expected. Changes are likely to come
about in a piecemeal fashion. The grand logical new design is not the British way. The
continual and radical NHS reforms have not encouraged either practitioners or public to be
happy with such wholesale approaches. Progressive elements in the profession – about 20%
are committed to some progressive cause … – will be pushed for change in the direction I
have called 'the new professionalism'. The GMC has already set its face towards important
changes in the area of competence – or performance as they prefer to call it.

Step One: an independent enquiry
Without a sudden conversion to the new professionalism, the existing GMC is before too
long likely to call for a Medical Act to encompass the reforms it will wish to see; these may
include stronger powers to control all stages of medical education, some better ways of
handling competence and possibly the establishment of a separate specialist register. In my
view government would be unwise to accede to such a request without there first having
been an independent, preferably state-sponsored, enquiry into all aspects of the regulation of
the medical profession and of medical accountability. It is to be hoped that government
would find time for such a radical review and the subsequent necessary legislation. Piecemeal
approaches to the question are one reason for the present unsatisfactory state of affairs.
    I have said the profession would itself be wise to call for such an enquiry forthwith and
one which would crucially examine the concept of professional self-regulation. The enquiry
would weigh the advantages and disadvantages of that concept and the way it works and
recommend what principles should in future guide the regulation of the profession.
    In the public interest, as well as in its own interest, medicine needs to remain strong and
united. Nothing I have said about the disadvantages of professional self-regulation should be
taken as suggesting anything other. Any group of workers – and here medicine is no exception
– is right to keep as much control over the working lives of its members as it can. By the
same token no group of workers is entitled to do that at the expense of other workers, customers
or clients.
    Consequently I am looking to the profession for a vigorous lead towards a better mode of
regulation. The GMC is uniquely placed to give such a lead by using its powers to the full,
transforming itself and thus helping in the movement to the new professionalism which is so
urgently needed.

Since Professor Stacey was writing in 1992 a number of changes have occurred,
although the composition of the GMC has remained the same. As we shall see, a
new procedure was introduced in the Medical (Professional Performance) Act
1995 to deal with doctors whose performance is 'seriously deficient' but which
does not amount to 'serious professional misconduct' (see *infra*). The GMC plans
to introduce, with the assistance of the Royal Colleges, a process of continuing
validation to assess the competence of doctors on the GMC's register. Perhaps
most significantly, the GMC has sought to develop ethical standards that are
more sensitive to patients' interests through its publications *Good Medical
Practice* (July 1998) and *Maintaining Good Medical Practice* (July 1998) and
most recently in setting ethical standards for consent and communication in
Seeking Patients' Consent: Ethical Considerations (November 1998).
    These developments represent some moves towards the 'new professionalism'
referred to by Professor Stacey.

Disciplinary and complaint procedures

In this section we consider the disciplinary procedures applicable to doctors
generally and specifically within the NHS and also the complaints procedures
available to NHS patients and to those within the private health care sector.
    It is not always possible to categorise a particular procedure as solely concerned
with either discipline or complaints. For example, the GMC's procedures serve

both functions and, until 1996, likewise the procedure applicable to GPs (and other 'Part II practitioners'). However, others clearly fall into one or other category, for example, the NHS complaints procedure introduced in 1996. This is not at all concerned with disciplinary action against a health professional.

Let us then turn to the General Medical Council and its jurisdiction over doctors. We do not discuss further the disciplinary role of the UKCC in respect of nurses, midwives and health visitors which we referred to earlier (for further discussion, see J Montgomery, *Health Care Law* (1997) at pp 151–160) or of the General Dental Council in relation to dentists.

A. THE GENERAL MEDICAL COUNCIL

We have already seen the licensing and educational roles of the General Medical Council. The GMC has power to take action against a doctor in four situations:

1. where he has been guilty of serious professional misconduct ('misconduct' procedure);
2. where he has been convicted of a criminal offence in Britain;
3. where his professional performance is seriously deficient ('performance' procedure); and
4. where he is seriously ill and it is affecting his ability to practice ('health' procedure).

It may be appropriate to see only the first two situations as concerned with discipline per se. The latter two are intended to be more supportive and remedial but are equally intended to protect the public from doctors who may be a danger to them.

The GMC's procedures may be triggered by a patient complaint. In recent years the GMC has done much to assist patients who wish to complain and now produces a booklet to assist them, entitled, *A Problem With Your Doctor?* (November 1997), which contains a form which may (but need not) be used to make the complaint. Referrals to the GMC may, however, come from any number of sources, for example, the police, other health professionals, other regulatory bodies such as the UKCC, NHS Trusts, Health Authorities or the Health Service Commissioner. (For further discussion of the GMC, see R G Smith *Medical Discipline* (1994) and M Stacey *Regulating British Medicine* (1992).)

Concerns about the conduct or performance of a health professional need to come to the attention of the appropriate body. This may be the employer, Health Authority or regulatory body. In some instances, this may involve a colleague in disclosing confidential information about another colleague. In appropriate circumstances, the 'public interest' defence would justify such a breach of confidence where it is reasonable to consider the professional to be a risk to public health or patient safety (see *Woolgar v Chief Constable of Sussex Police* [1999] 3 All ER 604 (CA), discussed *infra*, ch 8). Likewise, bodies such as the Health Commissioner or Commission for Health Improvement may have material that raises such concerns. Disclosure to the appropriate body, whether regulatory body or employer, may be justified in these instances (see, Health Service Commissioners Act 1993, s 15 and Health Act 1999, s 24(6) respectively, discussed *infra*, ch 8).

For health professionals, however, 'whistleblowing' on a colleague may not be so simple. Certainly, within the NHS the culture has been discouraged. The reasons for the reluctance to 'whistle blow' may be:

> The fear of being labelled a trouble-maker, the fear of appearing disloyal and the fear of victimisation by managers and colleagues are powerful disincentives against speaking up about genuine concerns staff have about criminal activity, failure to comply with a legal duty, miscarriages of justice, danger to health and safety or the environment, and the cover

up of any of these in the workplace (Guidance on Public Interest Disclosure Act 1998, HSC 1999/198).

Some NHS Trusts even imposed so-called confidentiality 'gagging' clauses in health professionals' contracts of employment.

There was also the position taken by the GMC in its guidance offered to doctors. Until 1987, the 'blue book' (*Professional Conduct and Discipline: Fitness to Practise*) came close to equating 'whistleblowing' on a colleague with serious professional misconduct. Even if this was not the GMC's intention, it may have had a 'chilling' effect on the medical profession. The 1983 edition of the 'blue book' stated (at p 15):

> The Council also regards as capable of amounting to serious professional misconduct:
> (i) the depreciation by a doctor of the professional skill, knowledge, qualification or services of another doctor or doctors.

Jean Robinson, who was a lay member of the GMC and a public critic of its operation, comments on this as follows:

Jean Robinson 'Thou shalt not disparage another doctor' (1998) Bull Med Eth 13

> It appeared under the heading 'Advertising, canvassing and related professional offences' and followed a preamble urging doctors to 'refrain from self-advertisement'. The implication was that if a doctor suggested a colleague was not up to scratch, the most likely motive was not to save patients but to drum up trade. In forbidding depreciation the GMC explained it was helping patients, because doctors skilled at self-promotion might not be the best practitioners.
>
> Doctors can get struck off the register only for 'serious professional misconduct', and criticising a colleague clearly rated as such a serious crime it could result in loss of livelihood and reputation. Although in my 14 years on the Council I do not remember any doctor being charged with such an offence, when I spoke at medical schools and conferences I found that students and doctors seemed more aware of that phrase in the Blue Book than any other, and often quoted it when I challenged them for taking no action on incompetent colleagues. No heads had to roll to keep the team in order; the mere existence of the words in the book were enough.

In 1987, the GMC re-worded the 'blue book'. The prohibition on 'depreciation' of colleagues became an injunction against 'disparagement'. Further, it became possible to advise a patient that care by another doctor might be in their best interests. And, importantly, for the first time a duty was imposed upon a doctor to 'whistleblow' to an appropriate body if there was reason to believe he had been guilty of serious professional misconduct or his fitness to practise was called into question.

General Medical Council *Professional Conduct and Discipline: Fitness to Practise* (1987)

> 65. It is improper for a doctor to disparage, whether directly or by implication, the professional skill, knowledge, qualifications or services of any other doctor, irrespective of whether this may result in his own professional advantage, and such disparagement may raise a question of serious professional misconduct.
> 66. It is however entirely proper for a doctor, having carefully considered the advice and treatment offered to a patient by a colleague, in good faith to express a different opinion and to advise and assist the patient to seek an alternative source of medical care. The doctor must however always be able to justify such action as being in the patient's best medical interests.
> 67. Furthermore, a doctor has a duty, where the circumstances so warrant, to inform an appropriate body about a professional colleague whose behaviour may have raised a question of serious professional misconduct, or whose fitness to practise may be seriously impaired

by reason of a physical or mental condition. Similarly, a doctor may also comment on the professional performance of a colleague in respect of whom he acts as a referee.

In 1991, the 'blue book' was further amended. 'Disparagement' was removed and 'comment about professional colleagues' substituted. In addition, the doctor's duty to 'whistleblow' was extended to cases where a doctor's professional performance was 'deficient' – rather reminiscent of the 'performance procedure' introduced by the Medical (Professional Performance) Act 1995 (see *infra*). However, the GMC removed that part which allowed a doctor to advise a patient to seek advice from another.

62. Doctors are frequently called upon to express a view about a colleague's professional practice. This may, for example, happen in the course of a medical audit or peer review procedure, or when a doctor is asked to give a reference about a colleague. It may also occur in a less direct and explicit way when a patient seeks a second opinion, specialist advice or an alternative form of treatment. Honest comment is entirely acceptable in such circumstances, provided that it is carefully considered and can be justified, that it is offered in good faith and that it is intended to promote the best interests of patients.
63. Further, it is any doctors' duty, where the circumstances so warrant, to inform an appropriate person or authority about a colleague whose professional conduct or fitness to practise may be called into question or whose professional performance appears to be in some way deficient. Arrangements exist to deal with such problems, and they must be used in order to ensure that high standards of medical practice are maintained.
64. However, gratuitous and unsustainable comment which, whether directly or by implication, sets out to undermine trust in a professional colleague's knowledge or skills, is unethical.

In 1995 the GMC's replacement publication, *Good Medical Practice* (1995), changed its approach. Paragraph 24 stated:

24.   You must not make any patient doubt a colleague's knowledge or skills by making unnecessary or unsustainable comments about them.

This is repeated in the 1998 edition of *Good Medical Practice* at para 29. At the same time, the duty of the doctor to act so as to protect patients where he believed a colleague created a threat to them was emphasised (paras 18 and 19). In slightly extended form these reappear in the 1998 edition:

23.   You must protect patients when you believe that a doctor's or other colleague's health, conduct or performance is a threat to them.
24.   Before taking action, you should do your best to find out the facts. Then, if necessary, you must follow your employers' procedures or tell an appropriate person from the employing authority, such as the director of public health, medical director, nursing director or chief executive, or an officer of your local medical committee, or a regulatory body. Your comments about colleagues must be honest. If you are not sure what to do, ask an experienced colleague or contact the GMC for advice. The safety of patients must come first at all times.

There remains one curiosity about the GMC's advice, which was highlighted in the House of Commons Health Committee Report on *Procedures Related to Adverse Clinical Incidents and Outcomes* (*op cit*):

45. One anomaly which came to light during our inquiry concerned doctors who worked in the medical defence organisations or who gave expert evidence in court. We discovered that, despite doctors' professional duties, doctors working for the defence organisations do not inform the GMC of any concerns they may have about individual doctors who may be a danger to patients. We asked the Medical Defence Union why this was and whether they felt that when a civil claim was settled on behalf of doctors this should be reported automatically to the GMC. The MDU pointed out that they act as a private organisation, paid for by doctors, and provide advice to doctors where there is a complaint or claim. They felt it would be improper to require doctors in defence organisations to report the doctors who came to them for advice. This would be analogous to defence lawyers reporting a defendant to the police. They suggested that it was more appropriate for other bodies to be obliged to report matters

which may or may not be proved. We asked the Secretary of State about this situation. He agreed to clarify the matter with the GMC. The GMC confirmed to the Secretary of State that all doctors, including those working for medical defence organisations, must report concerns about a colleague's health, conduct or performance if patients may be at risk. They stated that they maintain regular contact with the medical defence organisations and would discuss the position with them.

The GMC's position seems untenable (but notice *Roylance v GMC* [1999] Lloyd's Rep Med 139 (PC), discussed *infra*). It certainly places medico-legal advisers in an impossible position when they are performing functions akin to lawyers providing clients with legal advice.

The GMC's explicit change of stance was matched by the Labour Government's commitment to openness within the NHS 'which encourages staff to feel able to raise concerns about healthcare matters sensibly and responsibly without fear of victimisation' (HSC 1999/198 at p 3). To give legislative effect, *inter alia*, to this, Parliament enacted the Public Interest Disclosure Act 1998, which came into effect on 2 July 1999. The Act introduces a new Pt IVA into the Employment Rights Act 1996.

The Act is not solely concerned with the NHS but provides employees in general with statutory protection when, in certain circumstances, they disclose information in the public interest (ss 43A-H). An employee who is dismissed or subject to victimisation falling short of dismissal can seek compensation from an employment tribunal (Employment Rights Act 1996, ss 47B-49). Further, the Act makes any agreement or contractual term prohibiting 'whistleblowing' void. Section 43J provides:

> 43J.—(1) Any provision in an agreement to which this section applies is void in so far as it purports to preclude the worker from making a protected disclosure.
>
> (2) This section applies to any agreement between a worker and his employer (whether a worker's contract or not), including an agreement to refrain from instituting or continuing any proceedings under this Act or any proceedings for breach of contract.

The legislation is complex (for a detailed analysis see, J Gobert and M Punch, 'Whistle-Blowers, the Public Interest, and the Public Interest Disclosure Act 1998' (2000) 63 MLR 25) . Its application to the NHS may be understood in the following way.

First, the Act applies to all NHS staff, including self-employed NHS professionals such as GPs and to trainees (s 43K).

Secondly, the Act applies to 'qualifying disclosures'. Section 43B provides:

> 43B.—(1) In this Part a "qualifying disclosure" means any disclosure of information which, in the reasonable belief of the worker making the disclosure, tends to show one or more of the following—
> (a) that a criminal offence has been committed, is being committed or is likely to be committed,
> (b) that a person has failed, is failing or is likely to fail to comply with any legal obligation to which he is subject,
> (c) that a miscarriage of justice has occurred, is occurring or is likely to occur,
> (d) that the health or safety of any individual has been, is being or is likely to be endangered,
> (e) that the environment has been, is being or is likely to be damaged, or
> (f) that information tending to show any matter falling within any one of the preceding paragraphs has been, is being or is likely to be deliberately concealed.
>
> (2) For the purposes of subsection (1), it is immaterial whether the relevant failure occurred, occurs or would occur in the United Kingdom or elsewhere, and whether the law applying to it is that of the United Kingdom or of any other country or territory.
>
> (3) A disclosure of information is not a qualifying disclosure if the person making the disclosure commits an offence by making it.
>
> (4) A disclosure of information in respect of which a claim to legal professional privilege (or, in Scotland, to confidentiality as between client and professional legal adviser) could be

maintained in legal proceedings is not a qualifying disclosure if it is made by a person to whom the information had been disclosed in the course of obtaining legal advice.

(5) In this Part "the relevant failure", in relation to a qualifying disclosure, means the matter falling within paragraphs (a) to (f) of subsection (1).

You will notice s 43B(1)(b) and (d), which would cover poorly (or negligently) performing health professionals or professional misconduct by them.

Thirdly, the Act lays down criteria whereby a 'qualifying disclosure' is a 'protected disclosure' such that the individual worker cannot be subject to detriment. For our purposes we can consider three situations: (a) *disclosure to the employer*, ie NHS Trust or Health Authority; (b) *disclosure to regulatory bodies* such as CHI, GMC or Health Commissioner; and (c) *disclosure to others*, such as the police or media. As we shall see, the requirements become progressively more stringent moving from situations (a) to (c).

Disclosure to the employer, broadly understood to include the NHS Trust, Primary Care Trust, Health Authority (if a GP, dentist etc) or the Department of Health, is covered by s 43C. This provides:

43C.—(1) A qualifying disclosure is made in accordance with this section if the worker makes the disclosure in good faith—
(a) to his employer, or
(b) where the worker reasonably believes that the relevant failure relates solely or mainly to—
    (i) the conduct of a person other than his employer or
    (ii) any other matter for which a person other than his employer has legal responsibility, to that other person.
(2) A worker who, in accordance with a procedure whose use by him is authorised by his employer, makes a qualifying disclosure to a person other than his employer, is to be treated for the purposes of this Part as making the qualifying disclosure to his employer.

Section 43C requires that the 'qualifying disclosure' is made in 'good faith'. The 'wrong' may also be disclosed to a third party if it relates to the conduct of that individual and is done in accordance with a procedure authorised by the employer.

Disclosure to a regulatory body will be a 'protected disclosure' if s 43F applies. This permits the Secretary of State to prescribe by Order bodies to whom disclosure may be made.

43F.—(1) A qualifying disclosure is made in accordance with this section if the worker—
(a) makes the disclosure in good faith to a person prescribed by an order made by the Secretary of State for the purposes of this section, and
(b) reasonably believes—
    (i) that the relevant failure falls within any description of matters in respect of which that person is so prescribed, and
    (ii) that the information disclosed, and any allegation contained in it, are substantially true.
(2) An order prescribing persons for the purposes of this section may specify persons or descriptions of persons, and shall specify the descriptions of matters in respect of which each person, or persons of each description, is or are prescribed.

Here, in addition to the requirements for disclosure to an employer, the worker must 'reasonably believe' that the information is 'substantially true'. No doubt the professional regulatory bodies, such as the GMC and UKCC, will be prescribed under this section. In addition, it would seem sensible that the Commission for Health Improvement should also be a prescribed body, given its statutory remit (see *supra*, ch 2).

Finally, disclosure to others under s 43G requires that a number of conditions be satisfied.

43G.—(1) A qualifying disclosure is made in accordance with this section if—
(a) the worker makes the disclosure in good faith,

(b) he reasonably believes that the information disclosed, and any allegation contained in it, are substantially true,

(c) he does not make the disclosure for purposes of personal gain,

(d) any of the conditions in subsection (2) is met, and

(e) in all the circumstances of the case, it is reasonable for him to make the disclosure.

(2) The conditions referred to in subsection (1)(d) are—

(a) that, at the time he makes the disclosure, the worker reasonably believes that he will be subjected to a detriment by his employer if he makes a disclosure to his employer or in accordance with section 43F,

(b) that, in a case where no person is prescribed for the purposes of section 43F in relation to the relevant failure, the worker reasonably believes that it is likely that evidence relating to the relevant failure will be concealed or destroyed if he makes a disclosure to his employer, or

(c) that the worker has previously made a disclosure of substantially the same information—
   (i)   to his employer, or
   (ii) in accordance with section 43F.

(3) In determining for the purposes of subsection (1)(e) whether it is reasonable for the worker to make the disclosure, regard shall be had, in particular, to—

(a) the identity of the person to whom the disclosure is made,

(b) the seriousness of the relevant failure,

(c) whether the relevant failure is continuing or is likely to occur in the future,

(d) whether the disclosure is made in breach of a duty of confidentiality owed by the employer to any other person,

(e) in a case falling within subsection (2)(c)(i) or (ii), any action which the employer or the person to whom the previous disclosure in accordance with section 43F was made has taken or might reasonably be expected to have taken as a result of the previous disclosure, and

(f) in a case falling within subsection (2)(c)(i), whether in making the disclosure to the employer the worker complied with any procedure whose use by him was authorised by the employer.

(4) For the purposes of this section a subsequent disclosure may be regarded as a disclosure of substantially the same information as that disclosed by a previous disclosure as mentioned in subsection (2)(c) even though the subsequent disclosure extends to information about action taken or not taken by any person as a result of the previous disclosure.

You will notice: (1) that the disclosure must not be for financial gain; (2) disclosure to the employer might have resulted in victimisation; (3) there was no prescribed body or there would be a cover-up; and (4) disclosure was reasonable having regard to the matters set out in s 43G(3), such as the identity of the third party, the seriousness of the 'wrong', whether the 'wrong is continuing' etc.

Apart from these situations, however, under s 43H disclosure may be made to others where the 'wrong' is of 'an exceptionally serious nature' and it is reasonable to do so. Section 43H provides:

43H.—(1) A qualifying disclosure is made in accordance with this section if—

(a) the worker makes the disclosure in good faith,

(b) he reasonably believes that the information disclosed, and any allegation contained in it, are substantially true,

(c) he does not make the disclosure for purposes of personal gain,

(d) the relevant failure is of an exceptionally serious nature, and

(e) in all the circumstances of the case, it is reasonable for him to make the disclosure.

(2) In determining for the purposes of subsection (1)(e) whether it is reasonable for the worker to make the disclosure, regard shall be had, in particular, to the identity of the person to whom the disclosure is made.

It should also be noted that an employee may seek legal advice (*quaere* medico-legal advice from a defence organisation?) and this is a 'protected disclosure' (s 43D). To give effect to the 1998 Act within the NHS, the NHS Executive in HSC 1999/198 has required that:

Every NHS Trust and Health Authority should:–

•   Have in place local policies and procedures which comply with the provisions of the Public Interest Disclosure Act 1998. The minimum requirements of local policies should include:–

(i)   the designation of a senior manager or non-Executive Director with specific responsibilities for addressing concerns raised in confidence which need to be handled outside the usual line management chain.

(ii) guidance to help staff who have concerns about malpractice to do so reasonably and responsibly with the right people.

(iii) a clear commitment that staff concerns will be taken seriously, and investigated.

(iv) an unequivocal guarantee that staff who raise concerns responsibly and reasonably will be protected against victimisation.

and should prohibit:–

(v)   confidentiality "gagging" clauses in contracts of employment, and compromise agreements which seek to prevent the disclosure of information in the public interest.

• Ensure that all their staff are aware of local policy and procedures and their own responsibilities for raising genuine concerns in a reasonable and responsible way.

Let us now return to consider the GMC's jurisdiction over doctors.

1.   Misconduct and conviction procedures

The GMC's powers are set out in s 36 of the Medical Act 1983.

36.—(1) where a fully registered person—

(a) is found by the Professional Conduct Committee to have been convicted in the British Islands of a criminal offence, whether while so registered or not; or

(b) is judged by the Professional Conduct Committee to have been guilty of serious professional misconduct, whether while so registered or not;

the Committee may, if they think fit, direct—

(i)   that his name shall be erased from the register;

(ii) that his registration in the register shall be suspended (that is to say, shall not have effect) during such period not exceeding twelve months as may be specified in the direction; or

(iii) that his registration shall be conditional on his compliance, during such period not exceeding three years as may be specified in the direction, with such requirements so specified as the Committee thinks fit to impose for the protection of members of the public or in his interests.

You will notice that the powers to erase, suspend or make conditional a doctor's registration is vested in the Professional Conduct Committee (PCC) of the GMC. The power exists if there is either a finding of 'serious professional misconduct' or where the doctor has been convicted of a criminal offence. Given the nature of the proceedings and that a doctor's ability to practice medicine is at stake, it would seem abundantly clear that the PCC should give reasons for its decision. Also, to assist in determining whether any appeal should be brought. However, the Privy Council left the point open when deciding that the GMC's Health Committee did have a duty to give reasons at common law (*Stefan v The GMC* [1999] Lloyd's Rep Med 90 at 93, per Lord Clyde). There seems little upon which to base such a distinction. The need for reasons as a matter of fairness is just as (if not more) compelling in PCC hearings. A doctor may appeal against such action by the PCC to the Privy Council (Medical Act 1983 s 40). Both the scope of the jurisdiction and the right of appeal should be contrasted with that applicable to nurses etc where only 'misconduct' need be shown (Nurses, Midwives and Health Visitors Act 1997, s 10) and the appeal is to the High Court (*ibid*, s 12). Whilst an appeal to a court is justified given the professional effect on the individual of an adverse PCC decision, there seems little to justify an appeal to the Privy Council rather than the High Court.

However, the misconduct procedure does not begin with the PCC. There is a complex screening procedure involving a professional and lay 'screener' and the Preliminary Proceedings Committee (PCC), which determines whether cases should be referred to the PCC (or Health Committee). The GMC procedure is outlined in its booklet for doctors, *Facing a Complaint* (November 1997):

How we screen cases

When we receive a complaint about a doctor, or find out about a doctor's conviction, we refer the information to a medically-qualified 'screener'. Screeners are GMC members we appoint to decide whether we should take action.

The screener will consider the information carefully, looking at:

* how serious the matter is;
* any other information we may have received about you; and
* the evidence which may be available.

If the screener does not find evidence of serious professional misconduct, they will then consider whether there is evidence to suggest that the standard of your professional performance has been seriously deficient. (You can find details of our performance procedures in our booklet *When Your Professional Performance Is Questioned.*)

If the screener decides that we should not take any action, we refer the papers to a lay (non-medical) member of the Council. If that member agrees with the screener, we will tell both you and the person who sent us the information. The matter will then end there. If the lay member does not agree with the screener, the complaint will proceed to the next stage.

Advice and help

If we want to investigate your conduct, or a conviction, we will write to you. The letter will set out the allegations against you, and ask you to comment. ...

The Preliminary Proceedings Committee

If a screener decides to take action, we refer all the case papers, including the information we have received and your comments in response, to the Preliminary Proceedings Committee (PPC). This is made up of seven members of the GMC – five medical members and two lay members.

The PPC meet in private and consider cases on the basis of the case papers. You will not be called to appear before the PPC except in the most serious cases, which are described below.

The PPC consider all the evidence relating to a case. They can then do any of the following.

* Decide no further action is needed.
* Send you a letter of advice or warning which will end the matter.
* Refer the information for investigation under our health procedures if they believe that you may be unfit to practise medicine because of illness (see our booklet *Helping Doctors Who Are Ill*).
* Refer the case for a public hearing by the Professional Conduct Committee.

If the PPC refer your case to the Professional Conduct Committee or the Health Committee, they may, in rare cases, suspend your registration or apply conditions to it for up to six months. They will do this if they think it is necessary to protect the public, or in your own interest, until the PCC hearing takes place. This order can be renewed for up to three months at a time. If the PPC want to consider making that kind of order, you can attend the meeting and have a legal representative.

The Professional Conduct Committee

If the PPC refer your case for a public hearing, we will prepare one or more charges against you, and the Professional Conduct Committee (PCC) will hear the case.

The PCC usually meet at our offices in London. They follow legal rules of procedure and you may have a legal representative. We will tell you the date and time of the hearing and will expect you to attend. Both you and the people who have complained may be called to give evidence on oath and may be cross-examined. We will also usually call witnesses to attend and be cross-examined, and you may want to do the same.

The panel is usually made up of seven members of the PCC including two lay members. They have to hear the evidence and then consider the following questions.

* Did you behave in the way alleged in the charge?
* If you did, did that behaviour amount to serious professional misconduct?

If the panel find any of the facts proved, you will have an opportunity to present evidence in mitigation (that is, to tell the panel about anything else you want them to take into account) before they decide whether or not you are guilty of serious professional misconduct. They will also consider details of your history and character.

If you have been convicted of a criminal offence, the facts of the case do not have to be proved at the hearing, and the panel do not have to consider whether you have committed serious professional misconduct. The panel will only consider the evidence you give them in mitigation and details of your history and character.

The panel's decision

If they are considering a criminal conviction, or if they find you guilty of serious professional misconduct, the panel will decide on one of the following courses of action.

- To admonish (warn) you and conclude the case. Your registration is not affected by this warning.
- To postpone a decision while they collect more evidence. Your registration is not affected during the postponement.
- To place conditions on your registration for up to three years. During this time the conditions will limit your freedom to practise medicine.
- To suspend your registration for up to a year. During the suspension you will not be able to work as a registered doctor.
- To erase (strike off) your name from the register. This will end your career in medicine unless you can show to us, after a period of time, that you are fit to work as a doctor again.

Conditional registration

The PCC will place conditions on your registration if they believe it will be safe to allow you to continue in some form of medical practice. The conditions might include, for example:

- limiting the specialties you may work in;
- letting you work only if you are supervised;
- preventing you from prescribing controlled drugs; or
- asking you to correct something that is wrong with your conduct or practice.

The PCC will usually hold another hearing before the conditions attached to your registration are due to end. At this hearing they will consider whether to continue the conditions, change them or remove them altogether. If they find you have not met the conditions, you may be suspended or struck off the register.

Suspending your registration

If we suspend your registration, it will be for a set period of up to a year. At the end of that time your registration will automatically restart, unless the PCC decide to hold another hearing to decide on further action.

Being struck off the register

If the PCC decide that your name should be struck off the register, we will not arrange another hearing. After 10 months [now 5 years] you can apply to have your name put back onto the register. The PCC will hear your application in public. You can have a legal representative and witnesses may be called.

Before we let you back onto the register, we have to be satisfied that you are now fit to start working in medicine again without restriction. It is your responsibility to show us that you are fit to do this.

Your right to appeal

The PCC's decision to impose conditions on registration, suspend or strike off a doctor, takes effect about 28 days after it is announced. You will be told the exact date. If the Committee order that you are suspended or struck off, and think you could put others at risk, or that it would be in your own interests to stop medical work at once, they can order your registration to be suspended immediately. You can apply to the High Court (the Court of Session in Scotland) to have that order lifted.

You have 28 days to appeal to the Judicial Committee of the Privy Council against the decision to suspend registration or impose conditions. If the PCC have not ordered that you are suspended immediately, your registration will not be affected until the appeal is settled.

If you appeal against a decision taken at a resumed hearing, and your registration is already suspended or has conditions attached to it, the current period of suspension or conditional registration will remain until the appeal is settled.

You will notice in this description the linkage at an early stage between the misconduct, health and performance procedures (on the latter two see *infra*). As a result, a doctor whose fitness to practise is called into question will be dealt with through the most appropriate procedure within the GMC (for recent changes to the GMC's powers see, The Medical Act 1983 (Amendment) Order 2000 (SI 2000 No 1803)).

(a) 'Serious professional misconduct'

The more difficult part of the GMC's disciplinary powers is that relating to 'serious professional misconduct' in s 36 of the Medical Act 1983. This phrase was first introduced by the Medical Act 1969. Prior to that, the phrase used was 'infamous conduct in a professional respect'. The change in phraseology was not intended, however, to alter the GMC's jurisdiction. Instead, it was intended to explain the jurisdiction in modern terminology, by reference to the way in which 'infamous conduct in a professional respect' had been interpreted by the courts.

Allinson v General Council of Medical Education and Registration [1894] 1 QB 750 (CA)

Lord Esher MR: If it be shown that a medical man, in the pursuit of his profession, has done something with respect to it which would be reasonably regarded as disgraceful or dishonourable by his professional brethren of good repute and competency, then it is open to the General Medical Council to say that he has been guilty of 'infamous conduct in a professional respect'. The question is not merely whether what a medical man has done would be an infamous thing for anybody else to do, but whether it is infamous for a medical man to do it. An act done by a medical man may be infamous though it would not be infamous if done by anybody else, but to bring such an act within s 29 of the Medical Act 1858, it must also be shown to have been infamous 'in a professional respect'. There may be some acts which, though not infamous if done by any other person, yet if done by a medical man in relation to his profession, that is, with regard either to his patients or to his professional brethren, may be fairly considered as 'infamous conduct in a professional respect'. Such acts would, I think, come within s 29.

Lopes and Davey LJJ agreed.

Adopting terminology similar to that of s 36 of the 1983 Act, Scrutton LJ, in *R v General Council of Medical Education and Registration of the United Kingdom* [1930] 1 KB 562 at 569, stated that the GMC's jurisdiction extended to 'serious misconduct judged according to the rules, written or unwritten, governing the profession'. This will usually arise in relation to his conduct whilst acting as a doctor. But, it need not.

Marten v Royal College of Veterinary Surgeons' Disciplinary Committee [1966] 1 QB 1, [1965] 1 All ER 949 (QBD Div Ct)

Marten was a practising veterinary surgeon who owned a farm. During the winter months a number of cattle died on his farm from husk. He was charged before the Disciplinary Committee of the Council of the Royal College of Veterinary Surgeons with, *inter alia*, conduct disgraceful to a man in a professional respect, in that he failed to provide adequate nursing for sick animals in his care and that he allowed conditions to exist on his farm which were likely to bring disgrace on the veterinary profession. He was found guilty and he appealed to the court.

Lord Parker CJ: The second way, however, in which counsel puts the case is this: that conduct, however disgraceful, cannot be conduct disgraceful to a man in a professional respect unless at the time he is actively practising in that profession or acting in pursuit of his profession. To return to the facts of this case, he says that in all these matters the appellant was not acting as a veterinary surgeon, he was acting merely as a farmer, and that what he did in effect had nothing to do with his profession.

Lord Parker CJ then cited Lord Esher MR's judgment in the *Allinson* case and continued:

Counsel for the appellant says that as a matter of law a professional man's conduct cannot be said to be disgraceful to him in a professional respect unless it was done 'in pursuit of his profession', and he would add that 'in pursuit of his profession' meant 'in the course of the practice of the profession'. For my part I see no valid ground for limiting the words in the manner suggested. If, of course, the conduct complained of is equally reprehensible in any one, whether a professional man or not, as for example, conduct constituting some traffic offence, that conduct would not come within the expression. If the conduct, however, though reprehensible in anyone is in the case of the professional man so much more reprehensible as to be defined as disgraceful, it seems to me that it may, depending on the circumstances, amount to conduct disgraceful to him in a professional respect in the sense that it tends to bring disgrace on the profession which he practises. It seems to me, though I do not put this forward in any sense as a definition, that the conception of conduct which is disgraceful to a man in his professional capacity is conduct disgraceful to him as reflecting on his profession, or, in the present case, conduct disgraceful to him as a practising veterinary surgeon. Looked at in that way, which I think is the correct way, there was here abundant evidence on which the Disciplinary Committee could come to the conclusion that the conduct was disgraceful to the appellant in a professional capacity. At any rate, bearing in mind that this court, as has been said many times, is loath to interfere with the findings of a Disciplinary Committee on such a matter as this, I could not myself possibly interfere.

The point arose recently for decision in the Privy Council appeal brought by the Chief Executive of the Bristol Royal Infirmary against the PCC's finding of serious professional misconduct.

Roylance v General Medical Council [1999] Lloyd's Rep Med 139 (PC)

From 1991 until his retirement in 1995 the appellant was Chief Executive Officer of the United Bristol Healthcare NHS Trust. He was also a registered medical practitioner who had been appointed a consultant radiologist in 1964: while Chief Executive he continued under the terms of his contract to carry out one clinical session per week.

The appellant together with two cardiac surgeons appeared before the Professional Conduct Committee of the General Medical Council at a lengthy and highly publicised hearing in 1997 and 1998. All three practitioners were charged with serious professional misconduct relating to cardiac surgery carried out on very young children at Bristol Royal Infirmary between 1990 and 1995. The essence of the case against the appellant was that as the Chief Executive Officer who was also a registered medical practitioner he had failed to take remedial action despite being on notice of the excessive mortality of children undergoing certain types of heart surgery at the Infirmary. The appellant was found guilty of serious professional misconduct and the Committee directed that his name be erased from the Medical Register ...

The appellant appealed to the Judicial Committee of the Privy Council contending that: ...

(3) the subject matter of the allegations against the appellant did not concern the exercise of his professional judgment as a doctor and therefore was not capable of falling within the definition of professional misconduct under section 36 of the Medical Act 1983;

Lord Clyde: The issue here arises on account of the fact that the appellant undoubtedly owed duties to protect patients in his capacity as Chief Executive Officer. But it is not in that capacity that he came before the Professional Conduct Committee. His principal line of defence was that he owed no duty as a doctor. The problem is whether, given the fact of his being a registered medical practitioner in addition to his appointment as Chief Executive Officer, he had any duties in respect of the former capacity in addition to his undoubted duties in respect of the latter.

The appellant's position was set out in its essentials in his letter of explanation of 21 April 1997. His primary submission was there stated to be that during the period in question there had been no exercise by him of his professional judgment as a doctor. In relation to the meeting regarding the proposed operation on the child Loveday he stated that it was beyond his competence to interfere. His position was explored in his evidence and in the course of that he explained that he had a responsibility for patient safety as Chief Executive Officer and not as a doctor. Indeed he could not understand how in exercising the responsibilities of a Chief Executive he could have any additional responsibility in light of his professional knowledge and registration. When asked whether he regarded himself as having any duties as a doctor in relation to paediatric cardiac surgery during the period in question he replied that he had given the matter considerable thought and was obliged to say that the fact that he was a doctor was quite irrelevant. If the appellant's proposition is carried to its full extent he should have challenged the jurisdiction of the Committee to hear the case against him at all. But it is not disputed that the Committee had jurisdiction to try the case. In these circumstances the question may not be about the existence of a duty but about the extent of the duty. But however that may be, in deciding whether the view of his position which the appellant adopted was correct it is necessary to consider the concept of serious professional misconduct.

The expression "serious professional misconduct" is not defined in the legislation and it is inappropriate to attempt any exhaustive definition. It is the successor of the earlier phrase used in the Medical Act 1858 "infamous conduct in a professional respect", but it was not suggested that any real difference of meaning is intended by the change of words. This is not an area in which absolute precision can be looked for. The booklet which the General Medical Council have prepared on Professional Conduct and Discipline: Fitness to Practise, December 1993 indeed recognises the impossibility in changing circumstances and new eventualities of prescribing a complete catalogue of the forms of professional misconduct which may lead to disciplinary action. Counsel for the appellant argued that there must be some certainty in the definition so that it can be known in advance what conduct will and what will not qualify as serious professional misconduct. But while many examples can be given the list cannot be regarded as exhaustive. Moreover the Professional Conduct Committee are well placed in the light of their own experience, whether lay or professional, to decide where precisely the line falls to be drawn in the circumstances of particular cases and their skill and knowledge requires to be respected. However the essential elements of the concept can be identified.

Serious professional misconduct is presented as a distinct matter from a conviction in the British Islands of a criminal offence, which is dealt with as a separate basis for a direction by the Committee in section 36(1) of the Medical Act 1983. Analysis of what is essentially a single concept requires to be undertaken with caution, but it may be useful at least to recognise the elements which the respective words contribute to it. Misconduct is a word of general effect, involving some act or omission which falls short of what would be proper in the circumstances. The standard of propriety may often be found by reference to the rules and standards ordinarily required to be followed by a medical practitioner in the particular circumstances. The misconduct is qualified in two respects. First, it is qualified by the word "professional" which links the misconduct to the profession of medicine. Secondly, the misconduct is qualified by the word "serious". It is not any professional misconduct which will qualify. The professional misconduct must be serious. The whole matter was summarised in the context of serious professional misconduct on the part of a registered dentist by Lord Mackay of Clashfern in *Doughty v General Dental Council* [1988] AC 164 at 173:

> In the light of these considerations in their Lordships' view what is now required is that the General Dental Council should establish conduct connected with his profession in which the dentist concerned has fallen short, by omission or commission, of the standards of conduct expected among dentists and that such falling short as is established should be serious. On an appeal to this Board, the Board has the responsibility of deciding whether the committee were entitled to take the view that the evidence established that there had been a falling short of these standards and also entitled to take the view that such falling short as was established was serious.

In the present case the critical issue is whether, if there was misconduct, the misconduct was "professional misconduct". As counsel for the respondent pointed out it is not simply clinical misconduct which is in issue. Professional misconduct extends further than that. So it is not simply misconduct in the carrying out of medical work which may qualify as professional misconduct. But there must be a link with the profession of medicine. Precisely what that link may be and how it may occur is a matter of circumstances. The closest link is where the practitioner is actually engaged on his practice with a patient. Cases here may occur of a serious failure to meet the necessary standards of practice, such as gross neglect of patients or culpable carelessness in their treatment, or the taking advantage of a professional relationship for personal gratification.

But certain behaviour may constitute professional misconduct even although it does not occur within the actual course of the carrying on of the person's professional practice, such as the abuse of a patient's confidence or the making of some dishonest private financial gain. In *Allinson v General Council of Medical Education and Registration* [1894] 1 QB 750, 761, infamous conduct in a professional respect was held to be established where a doctor by public advertisement had warned the public to avoid other practitioners and recommended them to apply to himself. Lord Esher MR adopted (at pages 760–761) the definition which Lopes LJ propounded in the same case of "at any rate one kind of conduct amounting to 'infamous conduct in a professional respect'". The definition was that such conduct could be established "If it is shewn that a medical man, in the pursuit of his profession, has done something with regard to it which would be reasonably regarded as disgraceful or dishonourable by his professional brethren of good repute and competency". Lord Esher MR then observed, page 761:

> The question is, not merely whether what a medical man has done would be an infamous thing for any one else to do, but whether it is infamous for a medical man to do it ... There may be some acts which, although they would not be infamous in any other person, yet if they are done by a medical man in relation to his profession, that is, with regard either to his patients or to his professional brethren, may be fairly considered "infamous conduct in a professional respect", and such acts would, I think, come within s 29.

But that definition is clearly not, and was not intended to be, exhaustive or comprehensive.

To take the point a stage further, serious professional misconduct may arise where the conduct is quite removed from the practice of medicine, but is of a sufficiently immoral or outrageous or disgraceful character. An example can be found in *A County Council v W (Disclosure)* [1997] 1 FLR 574, where a question arose whether the alleged sexual abuse by a father of his daughter, the father being a medical practitioner, could constitute serious professional misconduct. It was argued that any sexual abuse was too remote from the father's occupation as a doctor since it was outwith any medical treatment of a child. But Cazalet J held (at page 581) that "it seems to me that this doctor can be said, if he has sexually abused his daughter, to have demonstrated conduct disgraceful to him as reflecting on his profession and/or indeed conduct disgraceful to him as a practising doctor". What is important here is not only the fact that disgraceful behaviour remote from the carrying on of a professional practice may constitute serious professional misconduct, but also that the duty of a doctor to himself, if not to his profession, exists outwith the course of his professional practice. One particular concern in such cases of moral turpitude is that the public reputation of the profession may suffer and public confidence in it may be prejudiced.

But moral turpitude is not the only kind of case outwith the conduct of a medical practice which may constitute serious professional misconduct. In *Marten v Royal College of Veterinary Surgeons' Disciplinary Committee* [1966] 1 QB 1 a farmer who was also a veterinary surgeon was found to have failed to give adequate care for animals on his farm. He was not guilty of any moral turpitude, but his conduct was held to constitute conduct disgraceful to him in a professional respect. Lord Parker CJ observed, at page 9:

> But if the conduct, though reprehensible in anyone is in the case of the professional man so much more reprehensible as to be defined as disgraceful, it may, depending on the circumstances, amount to conduct disgraceful of him in a professional respect in the sense that it tends to bring disgrace on the profession which he practises. It seems to me, although I do not put this forward in any sense as a definition, that the conception of conduct which is disgraceful to a man in his professional capacity is conduct disgraceful to him as reflecting on his profession, or, in the present case, conduct disgraceful to him as a practising veterinary surgeon.

Marten was found on account of his work as a farmer to be guilty of conduct disgraceful to him as a practising veterinary surgeon.

In the present case it is not suggested that the appellant's conduct was in the class of moral turpitude or of so outrageous a nature as to bring the profession into disrepute. But that does not mean that the appellant had no duty to have regard to his own capacity as a registered medical practitioner. He was both a registered medical practitioner and Chief Executive of a hospital. In each capacity he had a duty to care for the safety and well being of the patients. As Chief Executive that duty arose out of his holding of that appointment. As a registered medical practitioner he had the general obligation to care for the sick. That duty did not disappear when he took on the appointment but continued to co-exist with it. There was a sufficiently close link with the profession of medicine in the case of the appellant as Chief Executive of a hospital in respect of patients at the hospital. Something of a parallel link can be traced in *Marten* between the profession of veterinary surgery and the care of animals on a farm. Counsel for the appellant sought to argue that any criticism of the appellant derived solely from his holding office as a Chief Executive Officer. But while the failures may as matter of fact be the same, the gravity of the criticism may be increased by him being at the same time a medical practitioner.

Their Lordships would add in relation to the generality of the problem that the philosophy which seeks to divorce the administration from the medical care so as to leave the administrator free from any responsibility for deficiencies in the care of the sick cannot be found. The care, treatment and safety of the patient must be the principal concern of everyone engaged in the hospital service. The medical staff will have the specialist expertise in their various skills. but the idea of a gulf between the medical practitioners and the administration connected by some bridge over which the appellant had passed "from us to them", as appeared in the course of the argument to be a possible aspect of the appellant's case, must be totally unacceptable if the interest of the patient is to remain paramount. The enterprise must be one of co-operative endeavour.

Once it is clear that a duty existed the question remains in the present case what the extent of the duty was in the circumstances. In ordinary circumstances there is no doubt that a medical practitioner who holds the office of Chief Executive Officer of a hospital is perfectly entitled to leave the day to day clinical decisions to the professional staff of the hospital. His duty as a medical practitioner is adequately performed by such a course. But there may occur circumstances in which more may be required of him. In such circumstances his medical skill and knowledge are undoubtedly relevant. Even if he does not have the specialised expertise of the particular area of medicine in which the problem arises, his general knowledge as a doctor will be of service, as for example by enabling him more readily to ask the relevant kinds of question, such as in the present case when was the child last examined and what was the degree of urgency for the operation.

The present has been held to be a case where the professional medical duty required action. The Committee noted the particular circumstances of the history of growing anxiety, of the facts which they found of his knowledge of the concern, especially in the letter of 21 July 1994, of his power to inquire and to intervene. They affirm that as a registered medical practitioner the appellant had a duty to act to protect patients from harm. They held that:

Your own evidence demonstrates that you chose, over a long period, to ignore the concerns which were being brought to your attention, preferring to leave these matters to the consultants concerned. Yet, faced with information suggesting that children were being placed unnecessarily at risk, you took no adequate steps to establish the truth. You knew that your medical director was at the centre of many of these concerns, yet you took no adequate steps to obtain impartial advice from appropriate specialists.

Essentially it was the appellant's own belief that his being a registered practitioner was irrelevant that was the flaw in his defence.

In relation to the particular case of Loveday the Committee pointed out that the appellant had been urged by Professor Angelini and Dr Doyle of the Department of Health not to let the operation go ahead, and that he had decided with Mr Wisheart that an external review was necessary. They continued:

Despite that, without taking appropriate external advice, without making independent inquiries of your own, and without exploring alternatives for safeguarding Joshua Loveday's interests, you took no steps to prevent the operation from proceeding. By your failure to take adequate action, you failed to safeguard Joshua Loveday's proper interests.

In their Lordships' opinion the Committee were entitled in the whole circumstances to find serious professional misconduct established.

Lord Clyde held that the appellant owed a duty to protect patients both as Chief Executive and as a doctor. The former seems correct and would be a judicial reflection of 'clinical governance' and the institutional duty in s 18 of the Health Act 1999. The latter is, however, more problematic. Why did he owe these patients any duty as a doctor? They were not his patients, indeed their care was wholly beyond his competence. Of course, Lord Clyde may not, probably was not, referring to a *legal* duty but rather a professional duty, although the latter characterisation surely begs the question in any event. Lord Clyde's conclusion was that '[t]here was a sufficiently close link with the profession of medicine in the case of the appellant as Chief Executive of a hospital in respect of patients at the hospital'. It might have been different, therefore, if he had been working as an administrator in a non-healthcare context. Or would it? Lord Clyde referred to the veterinary surgeon case of *Marten* and the child abuse case of *W*. Certainly the latter did not involve a healthcare context but a private one. The same could be said of *Marten*, except that it involved caring for animals and he was a vet. Arguably, these cases are correctly decided because the egregious behaviour did cast doubt on the individual's suitability to be a vet and doctor respectively. The conduct was, in the old-fashioned language, 'disgraceful'. Where it is not – and Roylance's was not clearly so – it seems more difficult to forge the professional link with the conduct (see also, *Nwabueze v GMC* (2000) Times, 11 April (PC) – sexual intercourse with a former patient in consulting room of surgery not conduct relating to his professional conduct). Working in a hospital with responsibility for patients may do it. But what of doctors working elsewhere, for example, for medical defence organisations? Arguably not.

What, then, is the modern approach to 'serious professional misconduct'? The leading decision, referred to by Lord Clyde in *Roylance*, is *Doughty v GDC* [1988] AC 164 (PC), concerned with the equivalent words in s 15 of the Dentists Act 1983.

Doughty v General Dental Council [1988] AC 164, [1987] 3 All ER 843 (PC)

Lord Mackay: This is an appeal from a decision of the Professional Conduct Committee of the General Dental Council on 12 March 1987 that the appellant had been guilty of serious professional misconduct in relation to three charges and that his name should be erased from the Dentists Register. The three charges in question were:

That being a registered dentist: (1) Between 10th January and 26th October 1984 you accepted 19 patients, whose names and addresses are shown on List 'A' [which is attached to the charge] for dental treatment as National Health Service patients, and thereafter provided them with dental treatment in the course of which, having obtained radiographs of these patients, you: (a) Failed to retain those radiographs for a reasonable period of time after completion of the treatment; (b) Failed to submit those radiographs to the Dental Estimates Board when required to do so by a letter from the Board dated 27th November, 1984. (2) Between 5th June and 16th November, 1984, you accepted 6 patients, whose names and addresses are shown on List 'B' [which is attached to the charge] for dental treatment as National Health Service patients and thereafter provided them with dental treatment in the course of which you failed to exercise a proper degree of skill and attention. (3) Between 21st August and 5th October, 1984, you accepted 4 patients, whose names and addresses are shown on List 'C' [which is attached to the charge] for dental treatment as National Health Service patients, and thereafter provided them with dental treatment in the course of which you failed satisfactorily to complete the treatment required by the patients ... And that in relation to the facts alleged in each of the above charges you have been guilty of serious professional misconduct.

... The committee announced their decision in the following terms:

In relation to the facts alleged in head 1 of the charge which have been admitted, the Committee finds that you have been guilty of serious professional misconduct. In relation to the facts alleged against you in charge 2 in respect of the five remaining patients and in charge 3 in respect of the three remaining patients, the Committee finds that you have been guilty of serious professional misconduct.

The committee directed that the appellant's name be erased from the Dentists register. ...
[It was argued] by counsel for the appellant ... that in order to prove charges 2 and 3 it was necessary to show that the opinion held by the appellant in relation to the treatment was not honestly held by him and could not honestly be held by a dentist. This submission was founded principally on the observations of Lord Jenkins when giving the judgment of this Board in *Felix v General Dental Council* [1960] 2 All ER 391 at 400, [1960] AC 704 at 721:

With respect to the treatment alleged to have been unnecessary, the evidence (as their Lordships have already observed) showed that, according to the appellant, he honestly believed it to be necessary (or likely to be found necessary) while the dentists who disagreed with him did not claim that the opinion expressed by the appellant was one which no dentist could honestly hold. In this state of the evidence, their Lordships think it would be wrong to impute to the Disciplinary Committee an implied finding to the effect that the appellant did not honestly hold that opinion. An honestly held opinion, even if wrong, in their Lordships' view plainly cannot amount to infamous or disgraceful conduct.

Counsel for the council submitted that the evidence was sufficient to entitle the committee both to hold the facts alleged in charges 2 and 3 proved so far as they had done so and also to hold that those facts constituted serious professional misconduct.

In considering the applicability of Lord Jenkins' observations to the circumstances of the present appeal, it has to be noted that Lord Jenkins was speaking of a case in which dishonesty was very much the issue and in the context of the statutory provision which was the basis of the proceedings in *Felix v General Dental Council*, namely s 25 of the Dentists Act 1957. So far as relevant it was in these terms:

(1) A registered dentist who either before or after registration ... *(b)* has been guilty of any infamous or disgraceful conduct in a professional respect, shall be liable to have his name erased from the register ...

At that time this was the only penalty available in respect of such conduct. The Dentists Act 1983, s 15(1), provided:

For section 25(1) of the [1957] Act (erasure from register for crime or infamous conduct) there shall be substituted – '(1) A registered dentist who (whether before or after registration) ... *(b)* has been guilty of serious professional misconduct, shall be liable to have his name erased from the register, or to have his registration in it suspended, in accordance with section 26(3) of this Act ...'

The suspension referred to is suspension for such period not exceeding 12 months as may be specified in the committee's determination. Counsel for the appellant suggests that this change in language was not intended to effect a change in substance. In *R v General Council of Medical Education and Registration of the UK* [1930] 1 KB 562 at 569, referring to the statutory provision there applicable, namely 'infamous conduct in a professional respect', Scrutton LJ said:

It is a great pity that the word 'infamous' is used to describe the conduct of a medical practitioner who advertises. As in the case of the Bar so in the medical profession advertising is serious misconduct in a professional respect and that is all that is meant by the phrase 'infamous conduct'; it means no more than serious misconduct judged according to the rules written or unwritten governing the profession.

In the General Medical Council's booklet entitled *Professional Conduct and Discipline: Fitness to Practise* (1985) the council stated: 'In proposing the substitution of the expression "serious professional misconduct" for the phrase "infamous conduct in a professional respect" the Council intended that the phrases should have the same significance.'

Their Lordships readily accepted that what was infamous or disgraceful conduct in a professional respect would also constitute serious professional misconduct but they consider that it would not be right to require the council to establish now that the conduct complained of was infamous or disgraceful and therefore not right to apply the criteria which Lord Jenkins derived from the dictionary definitions of these words which he quoted in *Felix v General Dental Council*. Their Lordships consider it relevant, in reaching a conclusion on whether Parliament intended by the change of wording to make a change of substance, to notice that in addition to this change and in close conjunction with it the additional and much less severe penalty of suspension for a period not exceeding 12 months was provided. Further, in terms of s 1(2) of the Dentists Act 1984, which is the statute presently applicable, 'It shall be the general concern of the Council to promote high standards of dental education at all its stages and high standards of professional conduct among dentists ...' In the light of these considerations, in their Lordships' view what is now required is that the council should establish conduct connected with his profession in which the dentist concerned has fallen short, by omission or commission, of the standards of conduct expected among dentists and that such falling short as is established should be serious. On an appeal to this Board, the Board has the responsibility of deciding whether the committee were entitled to take the view that the evidence established that there had been a falling short of these standards and were also entitled to take the view that such falling short as was established was serious.

In the present case the three charges of serious professional misconduct of which the appellant has been found guilty do not impute any dishonesty on his part. It was not suggested that he was carrying out unnecessary treatments for the purpose of enhancing his remuneration. What was suggested was that, judged by proper professional standards in the light of the objective facts about the individual patients that were presented in evidence to the committee, the dental treatments criticised as unnecessary would be treatments that no dentists of reasonable skill exercising reasonable care would carry out. It was for the committee with their expertise in this matter to judge as between the witnesses called by the council and the appellant, who had every opportunity to give his own reasons and explanations for what he did, and to judge whether the allegation was made out subject to the matter already dealt with in relation to charge 3. The point taken by counsel for the appellant at this stage of his submission was pressed primarily in relation to the criticisms of the appellant's treatment as unnecessary. With regard to the other criticisms it appears to their Lordships that the failures admitted in relation to charge 1 and admitted in part and proved to a further extent in relation to charge 2 and proved in relation to charge 3 amounted to professional misconduct. Whether the misconduct was serious depended on a number of factors, for example in relation to charge 1 on the number of patients in respect of whom the failure occurred and the importance of preserving the record for the well being of the patient and as a basis for decision on future treatment of the patient. In relation to charges 2 and 3 the seriousness of the conduct depended on the appreciation of such factors as the number of patients involved, the number of treatments criticised in relation to each patient and particularly in relation to unsatisfactory treatments, and the nature and extent of the failure to complete the treatment properly. On all of these matters the committee were particularly well qualified to reach a view and their Lordships see no reason to disagree with their findings.

Lord Mackay proposes a two-stage test, requiring the PCC to ask itself two questions:

1. Did the doctors' conduct fall short, by act or omission, of the standard of conduct expected among doctors? If yes, then:
2. Was this falling short 'serious'?

The first question relates to a finding of 'professional misconduct' and the second question relates to a finding that it is 'serious'. How does Lord Mackay's approach differ from that adopted by a court in an action for medical negligence? Clearly, there must be cases of negligence which do amount to 'serious professional misconduct'.

The distinction between negligence and serious professional misconduct was, however, emphasised in an earlier decision of the Privy Council not mentioned by Lord Mackay in *Doughty*.

McEniff v General Dental Council [1980] 1 All ER 461, [1980] 1 WLR 328 (PC)

The defendant, a dentist, was found guilty of 'infamous or disgraceful conduct in a professional respect' (s 25 of the Dentists Act 1957) and his name was erased from the register. He had allowed unqualified members of his staff to insert fillings after he had drilled his patients' teeth. He appealed, arguing that the legal assessor had wrongly advised the Disciplinary Committee to the GDC in law. The legal assessor had said:

As far as what constitutes infamous or disgraceful conduct is concerned, to which both advocates have referred, for me the words of Scrutton LJ of *serious* misconduct in a professional respect mean quite plainly that it is for the committee, applying their own knowledge and experience, to decide what is the appropriate standard each practitioner should adhere to, not a special standard greater than is ordinarily to be expected, but the ordinary standard of the profession. I think I have said very little that is in any way new to any member of the committee, but having regard to the submissions made to you I thought I ought at least to say what I have said.

Lord Edmund-Davies: These observations have been criticised as wrong in law in that they failed a distinction between mere negligent conduct and infamous or disgraceful conduct. The submission is that there was a misdirection, in that, although in his opening remarks counsel for the General Dental Council had made passing reference to *Felix v General Dental Council* [1960] AC 704, the legal assessor failed to remind the disciplinary committee of an important passage in the speech of Lord Jenkins, who, in delivering the judgment of this Board in that case, said:

Granted that ... the full derogatory force of the adjectives 'infamous' and 'disgraceful' in s 25 of the Act of 1957 must be qualified by the consideration that what is being judged is the conduct of a dentist in a professional respect, which falls to be judged in relation to the accepted ethical standards of his profession, it appears to their Lordships that these two adjectives nevertheless remain as terms denoting *conduct deserving of the strongest reprobation*, and, indeed, so heinous as to merit, when proved, the extreme professional penalty of striking-off. (Emphasis mine.)

Although the facts in *Felix v General Dental Council* were quite unlike those of the present case, these observations are of compelling significance. For it has respectfully to be said that although prolonged veneration of the oft-quoted words of Lopes LJ has clothed them with an authority approaching that of a statute, they are not particularly illuminating. It is for this reason that their Lordships regard Lord Jenkins' exposition as so valuable that, without going so far as to say that his words should invariably be cited in every disciplinary case, they think that to do so would be a commendable course. But having said that, it has to be added that the committee in the instant case were duly reminded of decisions which have long been approved of by this Board as accurately stating the relevant law. And their Lordships have in mind in this context the following observations of Lord Guest in *Sivarajah v General Medical Council* [[1964] 1 All ER 504]:

The committee are masters both of the law and of the facts. Thus what might amount to a misdirection in law by a judge to a jury at a criminal trial does not necessarily invalidate the committee's decision. The question is whether it can 'fairly be thought to have been of sufficient significance to the result to invalidate the Committee's decision'.

In their Lordships' judgment, it cannot be said that the advice tendered by the legal assessor in this case contained such a defect, and the first ground of criticism must therefore be rejected.

Notice that, in *McEniff*, which was a case concerned with the statute which predated the Dentists Act 1984, the Privy Council expressly approved Lord Jenkins' approach in *Felix* (contrast Lord Mackay in *Doughty*). It may be that Lord Mackay over-emphasised the 'dishonesty' requirement in Lord Jenkins' speech. (See, for example, the view of Lord Parker CJ in *Marten v Royal College of Veterinary Surgeons' Disciplinary Committee* [1965] 1 All ER 949 at 951.) Mr David Bolt, a surgeon (and a frequent chairman of the PCC) offered an explanation in a lecture to the Medico-Legal Society in 1986.

D Bolt 'Dealing with Errors of Clinical Judgment' (1986) 54 Medico-Legal J 220

If you go back to the 1979 Blue Book you will find that it says:

The General Medical Council is not concerned with errors of diagnosis or treatment.

That was a very clear position. However, if you take the 1985 Book, you will find that it is now saying something slightly different. It is saying:

The Council is concerned with errors in diagnosis or treatment and with the kind of matters which give rise to action in the Civil Courts for negligence, only when the doctors' conduct in the case has involved such a disregard of his professional responsibility to patients or such a neglect of his professional duties as to raise a question of serious professional misconduct.

I do not want to labour it too much, but from the same page perhaps I could just read you the little list of the things that the General Medical Council reminds doctors that the public now are entitled to expect from registered medical practitioners. They include 'Conscientious assessment of the history, symptoms and signs of a patient's condition. Sufficiently thorough professional attention, examination and, where necessary, diagnostic investigation. Competent and considerate professional management. Appropriate and prompt action upon evidence suggesting the existence of a condition requiring urgent medical intervention and readiness, where circumstances so warrant, to consult appropriate professional colleagues.'

That, taken altogether, is a fairly strong statement of what the General Medical Council expects of doctors in this context. It is fair, I think, to say that it is a field which is only just developing, because the terms that I have read to you have not been in the Blue Book for more than a short time. The difficulty that we have in looking at cases is that if what you are looking at is an isolated event in the career of an otherwise estimable doctor, it would seem to me very wrong and stupid that the profession should be seeking to take major action on that account. If, on the other hand, what you are looking at seems to you to be just a particular event in, shall we say, a pattern of practice which is casual and unconcerned and careless and generally inferior and shabby, then the Professional Conduct Committee may feel that this merits more substantial action.

In the following case, the PCC took the view that the doctor's negligence on three occasions amounted to serious professional misconduct. On appeal, the Privy Council agreed.

McCandless v General Medical Council (1995) 30 BMLR 53 (PC)

On 16 March 1995 the Professional Conduct Committee of the General Medical Council found the appellant guilty of serious professional misconduct and directed that his name be erased from the Register of Medical Practitioners. The appellant accepted that he had been negligent and that the committee's findings of fact were not open to any material dispute. However, he alleged that the committee, in applying an objective standard, had applied the wrong test as to what constitutes serious professional misconduct. He claimed that serious professional misconduct involves conduct which is morally blameworthy, requiring an examination of why the doctor gave the treatment which he gave. It should exclude honest mistake.

Lord Hoffmann: The chairman of the committee gave the following brief reasons for its finding that he had been guilty of serious professional misconduct:

Dr McCandless, the Committee take a very serious view of the evidence which they have heard about the poor standard of medical care which you provided to all three patients in this case. The care which you provided fell deplorably short of the standard which patients are entitled to expect from their general practitioners.

Mr Mitting submits that these reasons reveal an error of law by the committee. He says that the committee applied the wrong test for what amounts to serious professional misconduct. It thought that it was enough that the treatment given to the three patients fell 'deplorably short' of the standard which would reasonably be expected. Mr Mitting says that poor treatment is not enough. The doctor may nevertheless have been doing his best. He may have been overworked or just not particularly good at the job. But 'serious professional misconduct' means, he said, conduct which is morally blameworthy. This cannot be determined simply by deciding whether the treatment measured up to an objective standard. One has to look at why the doctor gave the treatment which he did. If it fell short of a reasonable standard because he was, for example, too lazy or drunk to examine the patient properly, then he would be guilty of misconduct. But not if he made an honest mistake.

Their Lordships think that some support can be found for Mr Mitting's submission in old cases on the meaning of 'infamous conduct in a professional respect' – the words which were used in nineteenth-century Medical Acts and which continued to be used until replaced by the words 'serious professional misconduct' in the Medical Act 1969. For example, in *Felix v General Dental Council* [1960] 2 All ER 391 at 400, [1960] AC 704 at 721 Lord Jenkins said of a dentist who was alleged to have given unnecessary treatment:

> ... according to the appellant, he honestly believed it to be necessary ... An honestly held opinion, even if wrong, in their Lordships' view plainly cannot amount to infamous or disgraceful conduct.

Since *Felix*'s case, however, much has changed. First, the words 'infamous conduct in a professional respect' were replaced by 'serious professional misconduct'. It is true that the General Medical Council's guide to 'Professional Conduct and Discipline: Fitness to Practise; stated (and continues to state – December 1993, p 7) that the new words were intended to mean the same as the old. On the other hand, it is by no means clear that the council accepted the *Felix* interpretation of what the old words meant. The guide also cites the dictum of Scrutton LJ in *R v General Council of Medical Education and Registration of the United Kingdom* [1930] 1 KB 562 at 569 that: '"infamous conduct" ... means no more than serious misconduct judged according to the rules written or unwritten governing the profession.'

This looks much more like an objective standard. Their Lordships think that the authorities on the old wording do not speak with one voice and that they are of little assistance in the interpretation of the new. Secondly, although there remains the single disciplinary offence now styled 'serious professional misconduct', the possible penalties available to the committee, which used to be confined to the ultimate sanction of erasure, have been extended to include suspension and the imposition of conditions upon practise. This suggests that the offence was intended to include serious cases of negligence. Thirdly, the public has higher expectations of doctors and members of other self-governing professions. Their governing bodies are under a corresponding duty to protect the public against the genially incompetent as well as the deliberate wrongdoers. Fourthly, the meaning of the new wording has been authoritatively stated by this board in *Doughty v General Dental Council* [1987] 3 All ER 843 at 848, [1988] AC 164 at 173 in objective terms:

> ... judged by proper professional standards in the light of the objective facts about the individual patients ... the dental treatments criticised as unnecessary [were] treatments that no dentist of reasonable skill exercising reasonable care would carry out.

This test appears to their Lordships to be, mutatis mutandis, equally applicable to treatment by doctors and in their Lordships' view should make it unnecessary in the future to revisit *Felix*'s case or any of the other earlier authorities.

Once it is accepted that seriously negligent treatment can amount to serious professional misconduct, then it seems to their Lordships that the appeal must fail. The eminent medical practitioners who sat on the committee came to the conclusion that Dr McCandless's treatment of his three patients fell deplorably short of the standard to which patients are entitled to expect from general practitioners. In the circumstances, it is scarcely surprising that they concluded that Dr McCandless was guilty of serious professional misconduct. Their Lordships can see no basis for interfering with that conclusion. Nor can they see any ground for interfering with the committee's decision that the offences merited the penalty of erasure from the register.

Lord Hoffmann's view was that the change in wording that occurred in the Medical Act 1969 was significant and that the increase in the range of penalties that could be imposed less than striking off was also significant. Graphically, he concluded that the GMC had a duty to protect the public against the 'genially incompetent' as well as deliberate wrongdoers. (See also *Hossack v GDC* (1997) 40 BMLR 97 (PC) *infra*.)

(b) Types of conduct amounting to serious professional misconduct

The GMC gives guidance on the type of behaviour and conduct which may amount to 'serious professional misconduct', primarily in its publication *Good Medical Practice* (July 1998). It is important to notice that it is no more than 'guidance'. It explicitly states that it is 'not exhaustive' and cannot cover 'all forms of professional practice or misconduct' which may interest the GMC. The guidance is detailed and duties of a doctor are summarised at the beginning of the booklet.

The duties of a doctor registered with the General Medical Council

Patients must be able to trust doctors with their lives and well-being. To justify that trust, we as a profession have a duty to maintain a good standard of practice and care and to show respect for human life. In particular as a doctor you must:

- make the care of your patient your first concern;
- treat every patient politely and considerately;
- respect patients' dignity and privacy;
- listen to patients and respect their views;
- give patients information in a way they can understand;
- respect the right of patients to be fully involved in decisions about their care;
- keep your professional knowledge and skills up to date;
- recognise the limits of your professional competence;
- be honest and trustworthy;
- respect and protect confidential information;
- make sure that your personal beliefs do not prejudice your patients' care;
- act quickly to protect patients from risk if you have good reason to believe that you or a colleague may not be fit to practise;
- avoid abusing your position as a doctor; and
- work with colleagues in the ways that best serve patients' interests.

In all these matters you must never discriminate unfairly against your patients or colleagues. And you must always be prepared to justify your actions to them.

(For a historical survey of the types of case dealt with by the GMC, see R G Smith *Medical Discipline* (1994) ch 4.)

What role should the Privy Council (on appeal from the PCC) play in setting *legal* limits to the conduct which is capable of being 'serious professional misconduct'? It is clear, that the Privy Council is reluctant to interfere with a finding of 'serious professional misconduct' by the PCC. Only if it can be shown that something has clearly gone wrong at the hearing, whether in the legal principles adopted (or as applied to the facts) or in the procedure itself, will the Privy Council intervene.

The approach of the Privy Council is set out in the following case. As you will see, it was one of those rare instances where the finding of 'serious professional misconduct' was upset.

Hossack v General Dental Council (1997) 40 BMLR 97 (PC)

The Professional Conduct Committee of the General Dental Council determined that the appellant, Robert Julian Hossack, had been guilty of serious professional misconduct and had directed the erasure of his name from the register of dentists. The charge laid against the appellant was that, being a registered dentist, between 29 April 1992 and 29 March 1994 he had accepted three patients for dental treatment as national health service patients in the course of which he had failed to employ a proper degree of skill and attention in providing treatment and, in the case of the first two patients, had failed to carry out the treatments necessary to secure their oral health. It was accepted that, had it not been for the complaint of the third patient, the other two cases would never have come before the Professional Conduct Committee. The committee found the charges proved.

Lord Lloyd: As for the Board's approach in appeals of this type, their Lordships were referred to *Libman v General Medical Council* [1972] 1 All ER 798 at 800, [1972] AC 217 at 221 where it was said that:

… the only circumstances in which an appellate court can reverse a view of the facts taken by the disciplinary committee would be a case where, on examination, it would appear that the committee had misread the evidence to such an extent that they were not entitled to make a finding in the state of the evidence presented before them.

A little later it was said ([1972] 1 All ER 798 at 800, [1972] AC 217 at 221) that it is difficult for an appellant to displace a finding or order of the Committee:

unless it can be shown that something was clearly wrong either (i) in the conduct of the trial or (ii) in the legal principles applied or (iii) unless it can be shown that the findings of the committee were sufficiently out of tune with the evidence to indicate with reasonable certainty that the evidence had been misread.

For the reasons mentioned in *Libman*, and in many subsequent appeals, the Board is always reluctant to take a different view of the evidence than the highly qualified members of a Professional Conduct Committee; but that it will on occasion feel compelled to do so is shown by the recent decision in *Brown v General Dental Council* (30 October 1990), (unreported).

How does the present appeal stand? The expert witness called by Miss Glynn in support of the charge was Mr Martin Kelleher. If he had given evidence in accordance with his report dated 19 December 1995, their Lordships would have dismissed Mr Hossack's appeal without much hesitation. But he did not. His evidence-in-chief was so favourable to the appellant that it was hardly necessary for Mr Williams to cross-examine on the appellant's behalf. Mr Kelleher pointed out that the replacing of the upper canine is regarded as the most complex of all bridge operations, all the more complicated in the present case by reason of the 'outstanding' lower left canine. Me Kelleher commented:

It is difficult to get a good cosmetic result with that particular combination of clinical problems. It is not, in my view, an unusual problem, and if I may be so bold as to say I have probably done something similar myself from time to time and I have had to redo it.

As for the fit, Mr Kelleher considered that the gaps or discrepancies were marginal. From the outside they were imperceptible, and from the inside they could only be seen when photographed in a harsh light from a particular angle. There was no gum disease or tooth decay in way of the bridge. In short, there was no need to replace the bridge, unless Mrs Lawson wanted a replacement for cosmetic reasons. If this were to be done, it would mean making the missing tooth much longer, and bringing it forward to cover the lower tooth where it projected.

So much for Mr Kelleher's evidence. By itself, it could not possibly support a charge of failing to employ a proper degree of skill and attention in the case of Mrs Lawson. But Mr Kelleher was not the only dental practitioner called by Miss Glynn on behalf of the council. She also called Mr Clough. Mr Clough was in a somewhat anomalous position, since he had been a member of the Dental Services Committee in the case of all three patients, and subsequently accepted Mrs Lawson as a patient of his own. It is not clear why he was called. But, in any event, he would be bound to want to defend his decision to replace the bridge. Their Lordships have read his evidence with care. Where it conflicts with that of the consultant, Mr Kelleher, as it did in relation to the alleged deficiencies at the margin, they have no doubt that Mr Kelleher's evidence was to be preferred.

In the absence of any supporting evidence from Mr Kelleher, Miss Glynn argued before their Lordships, as she had before the Professional Conduct Committee, that the appellant should have discussed with Mrs Lawson beforehand the difficulties of making an aesthetically satisfying bridge, and should then have shown her the bridge in a mirror before it was cemented in position. The appellant's evidence was that he did show her the bridge in position before it was cemented, in accordance with his standard practice. But, even if his evidence as to that was not accepted, it would hardly justify a finding of a breach of s 21(1)(a) of Sch 1 [to the Dentists Act 1984].

Finally, there was the allegation that the appellant lost his temper on 2 November. But, as already mentioned, that allegation was not made the subject of any charge. So it obviously had to be excluded altogether from consideration.

Having reviewed the evidence in relation to Mrs Lawson, their Lordships feel bound to conclude that the finding of the Professional Conduct Committee in relation to her was 'out of tune' with the evidence to such an extent that the members of the committee must have misunderstood what Mr Kelleher was saying. Their Lordships repeat that if Mr Kelleher had given evidence in accordance with his report, then they would not have intervened in the finding. But the evidence which he gave at the hearing, both in chief and in cross-examination, was so very different from what he had said in his report, and was so very favourable to the appellant, that the finding of fact by the Professional Conduct Committee in relation to Mrs Lawson cannot stand.

That leaves the question whether the finding of serious professional misconduct can rest on the findings of fact in relation to the other two patients. The answer must surely be no. The finding of serious professional misconduct was explicitly based on the facts found to have been proved in relation to *all* the heads of charge in relation to all three patients. Since in their Lordships' view the Professional Conduct Committee was wrong to find the facts proved in relation to Mrs Lawson, part of the foundation for the overall finding of serious professional conduct has gone. In these circumstances, the overall finding cannot stand.

The Privy Council's reluctance to interfere is even greater if the appeal relates to the sanction imposed. Here, considerable leeway is given to the PCC. In the recent case of *Roylance v GMC* [1999] Lloyd's Rep Med 139 (PC), Lord Clyde stated (at 152):

> ... the appellant submitted that the Committee should not have adopted the most severe method of disposal open to them and that in light not only of the circumstances of the case but of the appellant's own undoubted record of achievement some lesser course would have been just. Their Lordships recognise the force of this submission, but they also note the careful and discriminating view which the Committee expressed in delivering their final determinations in each of the three cases and in the particular case of the appellant they expressly noted the evidence of his contributions to the Health Service over a long period. the decision on disposal is very much a matter for the judgment of the Committee, working through the alternatives presented in rule 31 of the General Medical Council Preliminary Proceedings Committee and Professional Conduct Committee (Procedure) Rules. It has long been recognised that the Board should be very slow to interfere with the discretionary power to impose a sentence of erasure (*McCoan v General Medical Council* [1964] 1 WLR 1107). Their Lordships would not interfere with the disposal unless they were satisfied that the decision was clearly unjust. They have not been persuaded that there was anything improper in the order that the name of the appellant be erased from the Register.

2. Performance procedure

In the light of the GMC's interpretation of its statutory remit in s 36 of the Medical Act 1983 and of the reluctance of the Privy Council to become involved, the question was asked whether the GMC was adequately holding doctors to account so as to further the public interest. Professor Brazier in *Medicine, Patients and the Law* (2nd edn, 1992) observed that 'there is a widespread suspicion that doctors who fail their patients are let off lightly' (at p 13) and called for a re-evaluation of the GMC's procedures. At the heart of the problem was whether the GMC should concern itself only with misconduct which is 'serious' or whether it should cast its net more widely. Some argued that a doctor who is ordinarily competent, but behaves in an incompetent manner in an isolated incident, should not be exposed to a procedure which could result in his being prevented from practising medicine. On the other hand to leave an aggrieved patient only with an action in negligence may not be sufficient to meet his needs or protect the public interest, both in holding the doctor to account and in seeking to ensure that mistakes are not made again.

In 1983, Nigel Spearing MP introduced the Medical Act 1983 (Amendment) Bill to widen the powers of the GMC. It provided:

> **1.** Section 36 of the Medical Act 1983 shall have effect with the addition of the following new subsection—
>
> > (10) Where a fully registered person is judged by the Professional Conduct Committee to have behaved in a manner which cannot be regarded as acceptable professional conduct the Committee may, if they think fit, direct that the registration shall be made conditional in accordance with the foregoing subsection of this section.

The Bill would have removed one barrier which some argue makes it undesirable for the GMC to consider merely negligent conduct, namely that, under the current legislation, the doctor faces (potentially at least) the severe sanction of having his name erased from the register. The argument behind the Bill was that if the GMC had only the lesser sanction available to it, that of making the doctor's registration 'conditional', it could then take jurisdiction over conduct that was itself less serious without the inappropriate threat of erasure being present. The Bill never became law.

The pressure for change remained strong. Professor Margot Stacey in her paper 'Medical Accountability – A Background Paper' in A Grubb (ed) *Challenges in Medical Care* (1992) at p 124 was able to conclude as follows:

The GMC can justly claim that it has changed a great deal in the last 10 years. The mode of dealing with sick doctors is generally agreed to be a great advance on the situation before the 1978 Medical Act. The proportion, as well as the number, of lay members has been increased during the 1980s. A lay person is now involved in initial disciplinary screening; for some time there has even been a lay person on the Finance Committee; there are now two lay members on the disciplinary hearings, not just one as formerly. Furthermore, it was the GMC ... which suggested the introduction of lay persons into the proposed intermediate disciplinary procedures. ...

Council's ethical guidelines (the blue pamphlet) have made it much plainer that bad practice as well as bad behaviour may constitute serious professional misconduct. In the past 10 years more cases involving clinical practice have been passed through to the Professional Conduct Committee, but seem still to be dealt with more leniently than other conduct offences. 'There but for the grace of God ...' tempers judgments.

It has been my belief that really bad practice could always have been construed as serious professional misconduct (and indeed was in gross cases). That more cases were not brought forward was more a matter of will on the part of the members than the powers of the GMC. There is now no doubt about their powers since the judgment about a dentist. Council is in a position to join those who are setting the tone for the profession that self-regulation does include monitoring outcome. Routinely to treat serious clinical errors as serious professional misconduct would constitute a major change in the way professional self-regulation has hitherto been understood, as would setting up any competence procedures under the heading of professional self-regulation.

Notwithstanding these changes, the central question identified by Spearing – what to do about misconduct which was not 'serious' as defined – remained. In 1989 a further GMC Working Party (set up in 1987) issued its report. The terms of reference of the Working Party were to:

examine the issue of the establishment of competence procedures, under its jurisdiction, to help it respond to complaints about standards of care provided by doctors which appear to arise from failure of competence.

Professor Stacey (*supra*) summarised and commented upon the 16 recommendations as follows (at pp 114–116):

This working party reported in May 1989. It made some 16 recommendations in all; in what follows I have grouped them somewhat differently from the way the working party did.

The most innovatory proposal is that there should be new procedures established to deal with doctors alleged to be incompetent, not all within the Council; some should take place at local level. The Council will formulate such proposals and invite the profession to discuss them; the suggested procedures will take account of arrangements for medical audit in the NHS and bear in mind doctors not covered by these procedures.

The working party reiterated the distinction which has in the past been made between 'serious professional misconduct' and incompetence. It rejected the idea that the definition of serious professional misconduct should be widened to include unacceptable or inappropriate conduct of a kind which would not call a doctor's continued registration into question. It also rejected any lowering of the threshold for formal disciplinary proceedings by substituting 'professional misconduct' for 'serious professional misconduct'. Nor did the working party recommend amendment of the 1983 Medical Act along the lines proposed by Nigel Spearing MP to introduce a second, lower tier of 'unacceptable professional conduct'. NHS issues in the category of 'unacceptable conduct' should continue to be dealt with under local NHS disciplinary procedures.

Other recommendations were as follows:

– Initiatives to provide information to patients, both NHS and other, should be taken by local and NHS authorities, Health Councils and consumer and patients' associations. The Council itself should prepare a leaflet about the nature of its own disciplinary jurisdiction and the procedures under which complaints are considered to supplement the individual advice which is already given to complainants.

– No change in the standing instructions whereby NHS patients who complain to the Council are immediately advised by the office to go through NHS procedures in the first instance.

– The GMC should initiate discussions about the improvement of procedures for licensing private clinics, for the appointment of GP locums and for checking the qualifications of doctors employed in the deputising service.

- Lay persons should be involved in the Council's initial screening of disciplinary cases to go forward for committee consideration and matters associated with the formal changes in procedure rules that this would involve.
- Council should convey its view to the Department of Health that lay persons be included in the 'intermediate procedures' proposed for the disciplining of NHS hospital consultants …
- The Department of Health should extend those procedures to junior grades.
- The drafting of charges in conduct cases should be kept under review.

After 18 months of discussion with organisations representing doctors and patients, the NHS and private hospitals, a Consultation Paper, *Proposals for New Performance Procedures* (May 1992), was produced. The GMC adopted the proposals. The proposals were, in essence, enacted in the Medical (Professional Performance) Act 1995. In essence it establishes a 'third fitness to practise procedure to investigate cases where the standard of professional performance of the doctor is "seriously deficient"'.

A new s 36A of the Medical Act 1983 was introduced by the 1995 Act. The 1995 Act came into force on 1 July 1997 (See SI 1996 No 271, SI 1996 No 1631 and SI 1997 No 1315). The Act is not retrospective and hence only applies to a doctor's performance *after* that date.

Professional performance

36A.—(1) Where the standard of professional performance of a fully registered person is found by the Committee on Professional Performance to have been seriously deficient, the Committee shall direct

(a) that his registration in the register shall be suspended (that is to say, shall not have effect) during such period not exceeding twelve months as may be specified in the direction; or

(b) that his registration shall be conditional on his compliance, during such period not exceeding three years as may be specified in the direction, with the requirements so specified.

(2) Where a fully registered person, whose registration is subject to conditions imposed under any provision of this section by the Committee on Professional Performance, is judged by the Committee to have failed to comply with any of the requirements imposed on him as conditions of his registration the Committee may, if they think fit, direct that his registration in the register shall be suspended during such period not exceeding twelve months as may be specified in the direction.

(3) Where the Committee on Professional Performance have given a direction for suspension under any provision of this section the Committee may direct—

(a) that the current period of suspension shall be extended for such further period from the time when it would otherwise expire as may be specified in the direction; or

(b) that the registration of the person whose registration is suspended shall, as from the expiry (or termination under subsection (5)(b) below) of the current period of suspension, be conditional on his compliance, during such period not exceeding three years as may be specified in the direction, with such requirements so specified as the Committee think fit to impose for the protection of members of the public or in his interests;

but, subject to subsection (4) below, the Committee shall not extend any period of suspension under this section for more than twelve months at a time.

(4) The Committee on Professional Performance may make a direction extending a period of suspension indefinitely where—

(a) the period of suspension will, on the date on which the direction takes effect, have lasted for at least two years, and

(b) the direction is made not more than two months before the date on which the period of suspension would otherwise expire.

(5) Where the Committee on Professional Performance have made a direction for indefinite suspension, they—

(a) shall review the suspension when requested to do so by the person whose registration is suspended (but not until two years after the date on which the direction takes effect and not more than once in any period of two years), and

(b) having carried out such a review, may direct that the suspension be terminated.

(6) Where the Committee on Professional Performance have given a direction for conditional registration, the Committee may—

(a) direct that the current period of conditional registration shall be extended for such further period from the time when it would otherwise expire as may be specified in the direction;

(b)   revoke the direction or revoke or vary any of the conditions imposed by the direction; or

(c)   direct that the registration shall be suspended during such period not exceeding twelve months as may be specified in the direction;

but the Committee shall not extend any period of conditional registration under this section for more than three years at a time.

(7) Where the Committee on Professional Performance give a direction under this section for suspension or for conditional registration, or vary the conditions imposed by a direction for conditional registration, the Registrar shall forthwith serve on the person to whom the direction applies a notification of the direction or of the variation and of his right to appeal against the decision in accordance with section 40 below.

(8) In subsection (7) above the references to a direction for suspension and a direction for conditional registration include references to a direction extending a period of suspension or a period of conditional registration.

(9) While a person's registration in the register is suspended by virtue of this section he shall be treated as not being registered in the register notwithstanding that his name still appears in it.

(10) This section applies to a provisionally registered person and to a person registered with limited registration whether or not the circumstances are such that he falls within the meaning in this Act of the expression "fully registered person".

The Act establishes two new committees of the GMC: The Assessment Referral Committee (ARC) and the Committee on Professional Performance (CPP).

The performance procedure is described by the GMC in its booklet, *Performance Procedures: A Guide to the Arrangements* (June 1999).

… the Professional Conduct Committee cannot investigate cases where it appears that the standard of a doctor's professional performance is habitually poor.

The new performance procedures fill that gap. They enable the GMC to investigate cases where it appears that a doctor's general pattern of professional performance is seriously deficient. Where this is proved by the Committee on Professional Performance (CPP) – a GMC committee established under the new arrangements – a doctor's registration will either have conditions attached or it will be suspended.

Seriously deficient performance

Seriously deficient performance is defined by the GMC as a departure from good professional practice – whether or not it is covered by specific GMC guidance – sufficiently serious to call into question the doctor's registration.

A doctor's registration is called into question when there is repeated or persistent failure to comply with the professional standards appropriate to the work being done by the doctor, particularly where this places patients, or members of the public, in jeopardy. This may include repeated or persistent failure to comply with the GMC's guidance in *Good Medical Practice*.

The GMC can use the new procedures where there is *prima facie* evidence of a pattern of seriously deficient professional performance. Doctors are encouraged to cooperate with the procedures. They will not be referred to the CPP unless they refuse, or it is considered that there may be a need to restrict or suspend their registration because the standard of their performance is putting patients at risk.

The new arrangements have been devised to protect patients. They also give doctors the opportunity to update and improve their practice through remedial training. They safeguard doctors against malicious or frivolous complaints. A complaint of seriously deficient performance has to be supported by at least one sworn statement (as with the GMC's conduct and health procedures), unless it originates from the GMC's solicitors, an NHS trust, or a health authority, health board or other public body.

New committees

Two new committees of the GMC have been established – the CPP and the Assessment Referral Committee (ARC).

Some cases will be referred to the CPP which will have the power to impose conditions on, or suspend, a doctor's registration. It has 26 GMC members, including five lay members, although individual cases will be heard by about seven members of the Committee. Hearings will be in private for the next two to three years, but the outcome will be published when a doctor's registration is affected. At the end of this period, the arrangement will be reviewed.

The ARC considers cases where doctors refuse to agree to be assessed. It has power to order an assessment within a fixed period of time. It is composed of 17 GMC members, including four lay members. Each case is heard by about seven members of the Committee, meeting in private.

The procedures
The performance procedures:
* are in the nature of an inquiry, not a trial;
* take account of a doctors' individual circumstances and the environment in which he or she works;
* are thorough and objective.

They have four stages:

Stage 1   **Screening**, to give initial consideration to complaints and what action to take where performance procedures are most appropriate.

Stage 2   **Assessment of performance**, in which the doctor's practice is examined in the context of his or her own environment and circumstances by a team of at least three assessors – two doctors from the relevant specialty and one lay person.

Stage 3   **Remedial training and reassessment**, giving a poorly performing doctor in certain circumstances the opportunity to revise practice and improve performance before undergoing a reassessment.

Stage 4   **Consideration by the Committee on Professional Performance**, where doctors have:
* particularly serious deficiencies identified by an assessment.
* failed to cooperate with the procedures.
* not made sufficient improvements in performance.

The CPP's task is to decide if the standard of a doctor's professional performance is seriously deficient and, if so, whether to put conditions on, or suspend, the doctor's registration. The CPP can also impose similar sanctions where doctors persistently fail to co-operate with assessment …

Stage I: Screening
Complaints about a doctor's performance are dealt with initially in the same way as complaints about serious professional misconduct. They are referred to one of a team of medical members of the GMC appointed as a 'screeners'. The screeners' task is consider individual cases, and decide whether there is evidence of possible serious professional misconduct or serious deficiency of performance, justifying action by the GMC. Each screener can discuss cases as necessary with other screens and, where the screening decision is difficult, the screeners met to discuss the case.

Because the procedures came into force on 1 July 1997, evidence of seriously deficient performance before that date is not evidence which the GMC can taken into account in considering cases.

In many cases where the complaint raises issues about the doctor's performance, the screener may require advice from one or more experts in the specialty concerned before making a decision as to whether the GMC should act. This advice may come from other members of the GMC with expertise in the relevant specialty. In addition, the Royal Colleges or relevant professional associations may be asked to nominate specialists *ad hoc* to advise the screener in individual cases.

The doctor is normally sent a copy of the complaint at an early stage. The screener then directs any further inquiries that may be needed. If the screener considers that no further action is required under the conduct or performance procedures, the case is then referred to a non-medical screener (a lay member of the GMC appointed for this purpose). The case is concluded only with the agreement of the non-medical screener.

Information gained from further inquiries may reveal that the doctor's alleged misconduct or poor performance was apparently caused by serious ill health. If so, the case is passed to the screener for health cases. The flow diagrams in this paper do not show the potential for transfer of cases between the health, conduct and performance jurisdictions of the GMC, because that would make the diagrams extremely complex. However, there are arrangements at various stages for transfer from one procedure (such as performance) to another (such as health) where circumstances so warrant.

In considering whether conduct or performance action is justified, the screener normally first establishes whether any action is already being taken by another body or authority – for example, under NHS disciplinary procedures. If such action is being taken, the screener then has discretion to decide, in the circumstances of each case, whether GMC action should continue, or be postponed until the relevant authority has concluded its procedures.

Where the screener is contemplating instituting the performance procedures, the doctor receives a letter inviting preliminary comments on the complaint, before the screener reaches a final decision. The doctor is then requested to undergo assessment, if the screener decides that this is appropriate and if a lay screener agrees. The complainant is informed of the screeners' decision.

If, having been invited to undergo assessment, the doctor declines to do so, the doctor is referred to the Assessment Referral Committee (ARC).

The ARC has power to direct the doctor to undergo assessment within a fixed period of time, if it regards his or her refusal to be assessed as unjustified. Doctors appearing before the Committee are entitled to legal representation. Similarly, any complainant in the case is entitled to be legally represented.

If a doctor fails to undergo assessment, having been required to do so by the ARC, he or she is then referred to the CPP (see stage IV of the procedures) ...

Stage II: Assessment of Performance

Where the doctor agrees to be assessed, either when initially invited by the screener, or when directed by the ARC, the assessment is conducted by a panel including at least two medically-qualified assessors, drawn from lists of appointed specialists. A lay person is also appointed to the assessment panel in each case. One of the two medically-qualified assessors – the lead assessor – is an experienced assessor from the same general specialty as the doctor being assessed. The other is a peer from the same sub-specialty. In selecting assessors for individual cases, the gender and ethnic background of the doctor are taken into consideration.

At this stage a 'case co-ordinator' takes over the management of each case from the preliminary screener. The case co-ordinators are medically qualified Council members appointed by Council to direct and manage cases referred into the performance procedures.

The assessors are sent information about the case, including a copy of the complaint which led to the doctor being referred for assessment and any preliminary comments received from the doctor. The doctor concerned also has the opportunity to forward evidence to the GMC as to his or her performance, and this is passed on to the assessors.

The content of the assessment varies from specialty to specialty. It includes, for most specialties, a visit to the doctor's place of practice, a review of the doctor's clinical records, observing the doctor in practice, an extended interview with the doctor, exploration of the doctor's clinical reasoning, inquiries of third parties with direct knowledge of the doctor's performance and, where necessary, elements designed to assess the doctor's clinical knowledge, skills and attitudes.

Following the assessment, the assessors submit a report, containing a profile of the doctor's performance, and also offer opinions regarding any measures which might be appropriate to remedy deficiencies in the doctor's performance and to protect the public.

If a doctor refuses to co-operate with the assessment team, the doctor is referred to the CPP (see stage IV of the procedures).

It is open to a doctor who is invited to undergo assessment to decide, either at this stage or at a later stage of the procedures, that he or she would prefer to retire from practice by voluntarily removing his or her name from the Register, as an alternative to continuing along the procedures. If a doctor were to adopt this course, and were subsequently to apply for restoration to the Register, he or she would then have to complete a satisfactory performance assessment ...

Stage III: Remedial Action and Reassessment

The assessors' report is considered by the case co-ordinator, who decides what should happen next in the case. In making their judgments the case co-ordinators follow criteria established by the CPP, and they will report on their decisions regularly to the CPP.

The GMC sends a copy of the report to the doctor. Unless very serious problems have been identified (see below), the doctor is invited to comply with requirements, for example with regard to remedial counselling or training. Those requirements are devised by the case co-ordinator in the light of the findings and opinions expressed in the report. The aim is to proceed in co-operation with the doctor, on the basis of voluntary undertakings, wherever possible and appropriate, rather than resorting to statutory sanctions.

Where the assessment reveals very serious problems which are placing members of the public at risk, the doctor is referred immediately to the CPP.

Details of the remedial action which a doctor might be required to undertake will vary from case to case, depending upon the doctor's specialty and the nature and extent of the problems identified during the assessment.

It is the responsibility of the doctor concerned to seek advice and take steps to undergo any remedial counselling or training recommended, although advice and guidance should in general be available through Regional Postgraduate Deans and Regional Directors of Postgraduate General Practice Education.

After an initial period of remedial action, a reassessment is undertaken.

If it appears that the remedial action has been successful, the case is then concluded.

However, if the initial period of remedial action does not appear to have achieved significant benefit, the doctor is referred to the CPP.

If it appears that it has produced significant benefits, but that further action would be desirable, this is arranged, to be followed by a further reassessment in due course. If the doctor does not wish to pursue further remedial action, or if further training does not produce the required improvement in the doctor's performance, the doctor is referred to the CPP.

Doctors who refuse to take remedial action, or to restrict their practice, when necessary are referred to the CPP (see stage IV of the procedures).

Stage IV: Referral to the Committee on Professional Performance
The CPP meets in private, unless the doctor concerned requests a public hearing. It has powers to impose sanctions on a doctor's registration. The performance screener and case coordinator are able to refer cases to the CPP in the following circumstances:
a. Where the doctor fails to undergo assessment, having agreed to do so at the direction of the screener, or having been directed to do so by the ARC, or
b. Where the case co-ordinator does not accept the opinions expressed by the assessment panel in their report, or
c. Where, on assessment, the doctor's performance is judged to be so poor as to present a serious risk to patients, or
d. Where, having undergone assessment, the doctor refuses to agree to the requirements for further action devised by the case co-ordinator, or
e. Where, having agreed to those requirements, the doctor fails to comply with them, or
f. Where the doctor's performance fails to improve significantly after he or she has taken the recommended remedial action, or
g. Where the doctor in any other way fails to cooperate with the procedures.

The task of the CPP is to determine whether the standard of the doctor's professional performance has been seriously deficient. Where it finds serious deficiency, the CPP has powers to impose conditions on, or to suspend, a doctor's registration.

In all cases where sanctions are imposed, the Committee will resume their consideration of the case after an interval, and may impose further sanctions. In due course, if they have already suspended a doctor's registration for at least two years, they will be able to direct indefinite suspension, and the case will thereafter be resumed only if the doctor requests a review.

The CPP are assisted by one or more independent specialist advisers for each case, so that any necessary expert advice is available to the committee.

The doctor and any complainant in the case have the right to be present and to be legally represented at the Committee.

You will notice the four-stage process envisaged by the procedure: (1) 'screening' by a preliminary screener; (2) 'assessment of performance' by the ARC; (3) 'remedial action and reassessment'; (4) referral to the CPP. Stage 2 will only be reached if the doctor does not agree to be assessed and stage 4 will only be reached if the doctor fails to co-operate with the ARC or the deficiencies are serious enough or, following assessment, improvement or remedial action taken by the doctor is not adequate. The powers of the CPP do not include the power to strike the doctor off the GMC's register and are limited to imposing conditions upon his registration or suspending him (s 36A(1)). Indeed, if the CPP finds a doctor's 'professional performance' to be 'seriously deficient', s 36A(1) imposes a duty upon the CPP either to suspend him for up to 12 months or impose conditions upon registration for a period not exceeding three years. These periods may subsequently be extended by the CPP and there is power to suspend a doctor *indefinitely* (s 36A(4)). A doctor may appeal to the Privy Council within 28 days against a decision of the CPP to suspend him or impose conditions upon his registration (Medical Act 1983, s 40(1)(a)). The appeal is, however, restricted to points of law (Medical Act 1983, s 40(5)).

What precisely is meant by 'seriously deficient' performance? The 1995 Act does not provide a definition. Clearly, however, it was intended to cover conduct or behaviour falling short of 'serious professional misconduct'. In its Consultation Paper in 1992, *Proposals for New Performance Procedures* (*op cit*) the GMC offered some guidance:

> 2.1 The performance procedures are designed for those situations where the doctor's pattern of professional performance appears to be 'seriously deficient' – in other words, so blatantly poor that patients are potentially at risk, and action needs to be taken to resolve the deficiency and/ or to restrict the doctor's freedom to practise.

Later, the GMC states:

> 3.2.1 Nor will the procedures provide a means of investigating every case in which there might be room for criticism of a doctor's professional performance: they will deal only with serious failures to achieve proper professional standards.

The underlying purpose of the new procedure was stated in para 2.3.1:

> 2.3.1 The primary aim of the performance procedures is to protect patients by preventing potential risk from a doctor's poor standard of performance of professional duties.

It is at least clear that the new procedure is not considered by the GMC to be a 'lower tier of professional misconduct', since it is not concerned with 'misconduct' at all (para 3.2.1, *op cit*). Guidance can be found in the GMC's two principal publications concerned with professional standards: *Good Medical Practice* (July 1998) and *Maintaining Good Medical Practice* (July 1998). However, these publications cover the full range of the GMC's jurisdiction including its conduct and ill-health procedures as well. The focus of the jurisdiction seems to be the standard of the doctor's medical practice. Paragraph 2.5.1 of the Consultation Paper (*op cit*) stated:

> 2.5.1 Some reports of the GMC's proposals have called them 'competence procedures', but consideration of a doctor's professional performance goes wider than that. It encompasses all aspects which contribute to a doctor's standard of medical practice, including:
> – standard of professional knowledge
> – standards of professional skills
> – professional attitudes towards patients and colleagues.

And, in *Maintaining Good Medical Practice* (*op cit*), the GMC states that assessment will cover the doctor's 'attitudes', 'knowledge', 'clinical and communication skills' and 'clinical records and audit results' (Annex, p 23 *op cit*). There is some suggestion in the parliamentary debates on the 1995 Act that the doctor's failing must stem from a pattern or series of incidences. Also, the GMC's own literature refers to 'repeatedly failing' to meet professional standards (see *When Your Professional Performance is Questioned* (November 1997) p 3). No doubt this will be the usual situation where 'poor performance' and not misconduct is the issue, but there is no such limitation written into the Act and it is not inherent in the notion of 'seriously deficient' performance.

3. Health procedure

We have already seen mention of the health procedure for doctors whose fitness to practice is impaired by ill-health. The separate procedure to deal with such cases was introduced by the Medical Act 1978. The current statutory provisions are in s 37 of the Medical Act 1983. Section 37(1) sets out the jurisdiction of the Health Committee of the GMC:

> **37.**—(1) Where the fitness to practise of a fully registered person is judged by the Health Committee to be seriously impaired by reason of his physical or mental condition the Committee may, if they think fit, direct—
> (a) that his registration in the register shall be suspended (that is to say, shall not have effect) during such period not exceeding twelve months as may be specified in the direction; or
> (b) that his registration shall be conditional on his compliance, during such period not exceeding three years as may be specified in the direction, with such requirements so specified as the Committee think fit to impose for the protection of members of the public or in his interests.

The powers of the Health Committee are more limited than the PCC. There is no power to erase the doctor's name from the register. The doctor may be suspended (initially for one year but ultimately indefinitely) or conditions placed upon the doctor's registration. The Health Committee has a legal duty under the common law to give reasons, at least brief ones, explaining why the decision was reached (*Stefan v The GMC* [1999] Lloyd's Rep Med 90 (PC) – indefinite suspension). There is a right of appeal to the Privy Council (s 40) but, unlike the right following a finding of 'serious professional misconduct', it is limited to points of law (s 40(5)).

The GMC procedure is somewhat akin to that under the (newer) performance procedure, at least prior to the involvement of the Health Committee. The procedure seeks to encourage consensual compliance with help, advice and medical supervision. It is described in the GMC's guidance, *Helping Doctors Who Are Ill* (Nov 1997):

The health procedures
Most doctors who become ill can deal with the problem themselves, with the support of colleagues where necessary. Our health procedures allow us to deal with cases where patients are at risk because a doctor does not understand how serious their health problem is. The matter we have to deal with nearly always involve mental conditions or addiction. If we use the health procedures in your case, our aim will be to protect patients while you get appropriate medical care and supervision.

The central feature of the health procedures is a medical assessment by experts. If you have a serious health-problem, we aim to encourage you to accept any necessary limitations on your medical work. We also want you to accept a programme of treatment that gives you an insight into your condition, and helps you return to safe medical practice.

Unlike our conduct procedures, which can lead to a public hearing that may be reported in the press, the health procedures are conducted in private at every stage.

How we receive information
Evidence which raises a question about a doctor's state of health comes to us from sources such as concerned colleagues, pharmacists, the police, employers or patients. Occasionally, one of our committees investigating a complaint about a doctor's conduct may refer a case to the health procedures. They will do this if they think that illness may be the underlying cause.

The information we receive usually includes reports from people who have witnessed behaviour which indicates a health problem. It may include reports of local inquiries, which began as a complaint by a patient or information from another member of the medical team. It may be a criminal conviction, such as a drink-driving offence, which brings to light a health problem.

The health screeners
We refer any information of this kind to a 'health screener'. This will be one of our members who is a psychiatrist. The health screener decides whether patients are being put at risk, and considers whether there is enough evidence to suggest that your ability to practise may be seriously impaired by a physical or mental condition.

The health screener will also consider whether the problem has been, or could be, put right by local action. In some cases, colleagues may persuade you to accept treatment and stop work for a time if necessary. There are a number of sources of help available, including procedures managed by local medical committees or within hospitals. Many doctors have benefited from support groups such as the Doctors' and Dentists' Group of Alcoholics Anonymous.

Sometimes the fact that they have been reported to us makes a doctor realise they need help. The health screener may decide not to get involved if they believe that local measures, which are already being taken, will prevent harm to patients and will help you recover.

Medical examination

If the health screener decides on further action, you will be invited to be examined by at least two medical examiners of our choice.

The examiners are not GMC members. They are taken from lists put forward by professional organisations including the royal colleges and the British Medical Association. The examinations will be arranged near your home unless you ask otherwise.

The examiners are likely to be consultant psychiatrists. This is because psychiatric problems, including addiction, are usually the reason a case is referred to the health procedures. We arrange examinations by other specialists, such as a neurologist or physician, where necessary. You have the right to also be examined by examiners of your choice, if you want, but we do not pay for these examinations.

Advice and help

If we tell you we want to investigate your health you should contact your medical defence organisation straight away. The defence societies know our procedures well and are a good source of advice. They can offer you legal support if you need it.

If you are not a member of a defence organisation, you could contact the British Medical Association or another professional organisation to which you belong. They may not be able to provide legal representation but they are a good source of expert advice and support.

Or, you can get your own legal advice, at your own expense. Legal aid is not available to doctors being investigated under our procedures. You cannot claim costs from the other parties involved.

The examiners' reports

The examiners, including any examiners you have chosen, prepare reports answering our questions about your state of health and ability to practise. If they decide you need treatment, they will recommend the kind of medical supervision and support they believe would help you. They may also recommend that you limit your medical work while you receive treatment. Limitations might include, for example:

- avoiding single-handed practice;
- practising only if you are supervised; or
- not practising medicine at all.

The health screener will consider the examiners' reports and send you copies. If the examiners think you are fit for medical work, the health screener will close the case. If they think your ability to practise is seriously impaired by your medical condition, the screener will ask you to accept recommendations for medical supervision and for restrictions on your medical work. If anyone later asks us about your registration, we will tell them about any restrictions on your work that you have agreed to.

Medical supervision

If you agree to medical supervision, the health screener will choose a doctor to supervise you and to arrange necessary treatment. This may be someone who is already treating you, but could be one of the medical examiners or someone else. It will usually be a psychiatrist. Your supervisor will report to the screener from time to time, so that we can monitor your progress towards recovery. If we agree that you can continue to practise medicine while you receive treatment, we will ask your medical supervisor to discuss your progress regularly with anyone who supervises your professional work.

Whether or not the health screener takes further action will depend on your progress. As you return to good health, we will relax the limitations on your medical work. When the screener decides you can practise medicine again without restriction, we will not usually get further reports from your medical supervisor. We will not be involved beyond that point, but we will encourage you to continue to consult your medical supervisor for as long as they think it necessary.

The Health Committee

In most cases, doctors under the health procedures co-operate with what the health screener suggests. There is then no need to refer the case to the Health Committee.

The Committee will become involved in your case only if:

- you do not agree to be medically examined;
- you refuse to accept recommendations for medical supervision or limitations on your medical work;

- you do not keep your agreement to follow the recommendations you have accepted; or
- your state of health deteriorates further.

Occasionally, one of our committees investigating a complaint about a doctor's conduct will refer the case directly to the Health Committee. They will do this if they think illness may be the underlying cause.

The Health Committee meet in private, usually at our offices in London. They follow legal rules of procedure and you may have a legal representative. We may call witnesses to attend and be cross-examined, and you may want to do the same.

There are nine members of the Health Committee. Seven are medical members and two are lay (non-medical) members. All the Health Committee members are GMC members.

At the hearing the Committee receive advice from two specialist medical assessors, selected from lists put forward by professional organisations. One assessor is chosen according to the nature of the condition which is affecting your ability to practise medicine. This assessor is usually a psychiatrist. The other assessor will be selected from the branch of medicine you work in. A legal assessor is present to advise on points of law.

The main evidence at the hearings is the written medical reports. We will send copies of these, with all other papers in the case, to you and the Committee members. The Committee only see the papers that you and your legal advisers have already seen.

You do not have to be present at the hearing, but we advise you to attend.

At the hearing there is an opportunity for you or your representatives to talk to the Committee about the evidence in the papers, or on any other relevant matters. Members of the Committee may ask you, and any witnesses, questions which arise from the papers.

After all the evidence has been heard, the Committee will ask you and your representatives to leave while they consider their decision. They will then tell you their decision. The Committee usually decide on a case on the same day as the hearing.

There are a number of options available. If the Committee want more evidence before they make a decision, they may postpone the hearing for a set period so they can find that evidence. Alternatively, they may adjourn the hearing if you agree to have medical treatment and to limit your professional work.

Under the law, the Committee have to decide whether your ability to practise is seriously impaired by a health problem. If they decide it is, they may:

- suspend your registration for up to 12 months; or
- put conditions on your registration for up to three years. These always include a condition that you must accept medical supervision, and may also include restrictions on your medical work to protect patients and your own health.

The Committee will consider your case again at the end of the period of suspension or when the conditions are due to be reviewed. You will normally be expected to agree to another medical examination before the hearing. The Committee will decide whether there is any risk to patients on the basis of the evidence, including up-to-date reports from your medical supervisor.

If they then decide it is safe to close your case, you will be able to return to medical work, without any restrictions. If they want to keep your case under review, they can impose further conditions, or suspend your registration for up to a year at a time.

In the most serious cases, if the Committee have suspended your registration for two years, they can suspend your registration indefinitely. There would then be no need for further hearings unless you asked for one.

B. NHS DISCIPLINARY PROCEDURES

1. General practitioners

Until 1996, discipline and complaints in relation to GPs were both covered by the procedure set out in the National Health Service (Service Committees and Tribunal) Regulations 1992 (SI 1992 No 664). Under these regulations, as we shall see, Medical Services Committees of Health Authorities inquired into complaints alleging breaches of the 'terms of service' contained in Sch 2 to the National Health Service (General Medical Services) Regulation 1992 (SI 1992 No 635) (as amended) of a practitioner (whether GP, dentist, optician etc) providing services under Pt II of the National Health Service Act 1977 (see discussion in the second edition of this book at pp 589–591). In 1996, as we shall see, a separate complaints procedure was created for the NHS (*infra*). The 1992 Regulations were amended by the National Health Service (Service

Committees and Tribunal) Amendment Regulations 1996 (SI 1996 No 703), creating for the first time a distinct disciplinary procedure for 'Part II' practitioners. Medical Service Committees were abolished and replaced by disciplinary committees of Health Authorities for each of the relevant Part II practitioner groups, ie GPs, dentist, opticians and pharmacists (reg 3). These disciplinary committees, as MSCs before them, investigate breaches of the practitioners' 'terms of service' (reg 4(1)) or where a practitioner is alleged to have been overpaid (reg 4(7)). Provision is made for a practitioner to appeal to the Secretary of State against an adverse finding of a disciplinary committee or subsequent action taken by the Health Authority (reg 9). Appeals are dealt with by the Family Health Services Appeal Authority (see, Family Health Services Appeal Authority (Establishment and Constitution) Order 1995 (SI 1995 No 621) and the Family Health Services Appeal Authority Regulations 1995 (SI 1995 No 622)). The disciplinary system is well described by Jonathan Montgomery.

Jonathan Montgomery *Health Care Law* (1997)

Each health authority is required to have separate committees to deal with the various services: medical, dental, ophthalmic, and pharmaceutical. (SI 1992 No 664, reg 3). There will also be a joint services committee. The procedures of these committees are essentially common and are therefore discussed together. Usually disciplinary committees consist of up to three lay people appointed by the health authority, up to three professionals from a list nominated by the relevant local representative committee, and a legally qualified chairman or woman. However, joint disciplinary committees will comprise two lay people and two members of each of the professions, with a lawyer in the chair (SI 1992 No 664, Sch 2, paras 1, 2 (as amended)).

If a health authority receives information that there may have been a breach of the terms of service, it may decide to take no action (SI 1992 No 664, reg 4(1) (as amended)). If it decides that the matter should go further, it may take one or more of a series of actions. The first is to invoke a disciplinary committee investigation. This is done by referring the matter to another health authority. The second is to inform the NHS Tribunal, which can suspend and disqualify practitioners (NHS Act 1977, ss 46–49E and Sch 9; NHS (Service Committees and Tribunal) Regulations 1992, SI 1992 No 664, reg 3). This happens only rarely. The third is to inform the police or the relevant professional body. If the matter has arisen in the course of a complaint being made against the practitioner, the health authority should await the completion of the complaints procedure. In such circumstances, any referral must be made within twenty-eight days of the resolution of the complaints procedure. In other cases, referral must be within thirteen weeks of the incident (where doctors, opticians, or chemists are concerned). For dentists the period can be extended to up to six months after the completion of treatment (SI 1992 No 664, reg 6 (as amended)).

If a matter is referred to a discipline committee, the health authority must notify the practitioner concerned within two days and send a statement of case to the committee and practitioner within twenty-eight days (*ibid*, Sch 4, para 1 (as amended)). The practitioner then has twenty-eight days to provide a response, which may be extended for a further twenty-eight days at the discretion of the chairman of the discipline committee. A hearing will then be convened by the health authority to whose discipline committee the matter was referred. That hearing will take place in private, and although the practitioner may be assisted by one person, legal representation is not permitted (in that if that person is a barrister or solicitor she or he may not address the committee or question witnesses), (SI 1992 No 664, Sch 4, para 5 (as amended)).

After the hearing, the discipline committee reports to the health authority which referred the case to it. That report will set out the evidence given to it, its findings on relevant questions of fact, the inferences that the committee believes might properly be drawn from those facts as to whether there has been a breach of the terms of service (with reasons for doing so), and its recommendations for action to be taken by the authority (*ibid*, Sch 4, para 7 (as amended). The authority must accept the findings of fact made by the discipline committee, and its inferences as to a breach of the terms of service. It must then consider whether to take further action, having regard to the recommendations of the discipline committee. It is not bound to accept those recommendations, but if it does not accept them it must record its reasons in writing (*ibid*, reg 8(2), as amended). The regulations specify the action available to the authority. Where the authority, after consultation with the local medical committee, believes that the doctor has more patients than she or he is able to give adequate treatment to, it may limit the number of patients the doctor may take on (*ibid*, reg 8(3), as amended). It may also warn the practitioner about compliance with the terms of service, or impose a fine (possibly by deduction from the remuneration to be paid). In the case of dentists, there is also provision to require the practitioner to seek prior approval of some kinds of treatment as specified by the authority (*ibid*, r 8(5), as amended). The authority may also refer the matter to the relevant professional body, so that it may consider disciplinary proceedings (*ibid*, reg 37, as amended).

The Regulations provide for appeal by practitioners to the Secretary of State against the findings of a disciplinary committee or the subsequent decisions of the health authority (*ibid*, reg 9(1), as amended). These appeals are handled by the Family Health Services Appeal Authority. In order to exercise the right of appeal, written notice, including a concise statement of the grounds for appeal, must be sent to the Secretary of State within thirty days of the health authority notifying the practitioner of its decision (*ibid*, reg 9(2), as amended). An appeal may be dismissed without a hearing if the Secretary of State considers that there is no reasonable ground of appeal, or that it is otherwise vexatious or frivolous (*ibid*, reg 10(1), as amended). If not, the other parties will be notified of the particulars of the appeal and given the opportunity to make any comments within twenty-eight days (*ibid*), reg 10(2), as amended). Any such observations will be sent to the appellant, who must make any comments within twenty-one days (*ibid*, reg 10(3), as amended). There will then be an oral hearing unless the appellant does not want one (*ibid*, reg 10(4), (5) as amended). It will take place before a panel of three persons. Two of these must be members of the same profession as the practitioner concerned. The third, who takes the chair, must be a lawyer (*ibid*, reg 10(6), (7), (8) as amended). New evidence of allegations will not be admitted without the agreement of the panel or the Secretary of State (*ibid*, reg 10(11) as amended). The panel will then report to the Secretary of State, who will consider it and decide whether the appeal should be allowed (*ibid*, reg 10(12), as amended). He must provide the parties with a written statement of his reasons (*ibid*, reg 10(14), as amended).

A number of points should be noticed. First, the disciplinary procedures apply only to 'Part II' practitioners. Thus, they have no application to GPs or others who are providing 'personal medical services' etc under pilot schemes by virtue of the National Health Service (Primary Care) Act 1997. Whilst these services will largely be identical to their 'Part II' equivalents (see *supra*, ch 2), the terms upon which the services are provided cannot be enforced via the disciplinary procedure we have just seen. Rather, such action by a Health Authority would have to be contractual in nature or through the dispute resolutions procedure required, for example in the case of GPs, by the *Directions to Health Authorities Concerning the Implementation of Pilot Schemes (Personal Medical Services)* 1998, para 26 and Sch 4. Further, where the GP-providers, are constituted as a 'health service body' under s 4 of the National Health Service and Community Care Act 1990 (see National Health Service (Primary Care) Act 1997, s 16), then any dispute between the Health Authority and provider must be resolved through the dispute resolutions procedure applicable to 'NHS contracts' contained in the National Health Service Contracts (Dispute Resolutions) Regulations 1996 (SI 1996 No 623).

Secondly, you will notice that referral to disciplinary committees is by the Health Authority upon whose list the 'Part II' practitioner is. A patient may raise the issue by way of a complaint which triggers the referral but, unlike the previous system, the patient has no means of triggering the procedure itself. This reflects the fact that it is now exclusively a *disciplinary* procedure by a quasi-employer. The complaints avenue, as we shall see, lies elsewhere.

Finally, you will have seen in the extract reference to the NHS Tribunal. This is an important further disciplinary mechanism applicable to 'Part II' practitioners such as GPs (National Health Service Act 1977, ss 46–49 and Sch 9 (as substituted by Health Act 1999, s 40) and National Health Service (Service Committees and Tribunal) Regulations 1992 (SI 1992 No 664, as amended by SI 1995 No 3091)). The Tribunal is an independent body with a legal chairman, currently Adrian Whitfield QC. The present stature of the Tribunal is reflected in the abolition of the right of appeal to the Secretary of State which existed until 1995 (see the National Health Service (Service Committees and Tribunal) Amendment Regulations 1995 (SI 1995 No 3091), reg 5). Instead, an appeal on a point of law may be brought to the High Court under s 11 of the Tribunals and Inquiries Act 1992 (SI 1992 No 664, reg 26, as amended by SI 1995 No 3091, reg 3(3)).

The NHS Tribunal has jurisdiction in two situations: so-called 'efficiency' and 'fraud' cases – the latter being added by the Health Act 1999.

Where the Tribunal receives representation from a Health Authority that a 'Part II practitioner' (GP etc) may fall within one of the disqualification situations, the Tribunal has a *duty* to inquire (s 46(2)). This may relate to a practitioner already on list or, in the "fraud case", a practitioner who has applied to be included on the Health Authority's relevant list (s 46(2)(a) and (b) respectively). Where the Tribunal receives representations other than from a Health Authority, in the prescribed manner and within any prescribed time limits, the Tribunal has a *discretion* to inquire (ss 46(3) and (4)). Let us now turn to the two grounds for disqualification.

Section 46(6) of the National Health Service Act 1977 states the 'efficiency' case as being where

> the continued inclusion of the person concerned in the list would be prejudicial to the efficiency of the services which those included in the list undertake to provide.

Clearly, GPs who, for example, are incompetent, dangerous or whose personal conduct (drunkenness or abusive behaviour) is seriously called into question could fall within the 'efficiency' ground for disqualification.

The 'fraud' ground was added by the Health Act 1999, s 40. Section 46(7) of the NHS Act 1977 states this as being where the practitioner –

> (a) has (whether on his own or together with another) by an act or omission caused, or risked causing, detriment to any health scheme by securing or trying to secure for himself or another any financial or other benefit, and
> (b) knew that he or (as the case may be) the other was not entitled to the benefit.

'Health Scheme' covers all 'Part II practitioners' and any practitioner providing services under schemes which are prescribed by regulation, such as the prison or defence medical services (s 46(9)).

Section 46(10) elaborates upon 'detriment to a health scheme' as follows:

> Detriment to a health scheme includes detriment to any patient of, or person working in, that scheme or any person liable to pay charges for services provided under that scheme.

Hence, fraud or dishonesty directed against patients *or* the NHS are covered. The practitioner may therefore, for example, be carrying out unnecessary work for which the patient pays, as might arise in the case of a dentist. Or the practitioner may be claiming against the NHS for services that were never provided to patients.

2. Hospital doctors

In essence, disciplinary procedures against doctors (or other health professionals) employed by NHS Trusts are matters for the individual contractual arrangements between the Trust and the doctor. As the House of Commons Health Committee recently commented:

House of Commons Health Committee 'Procedures Relating to Adverse Clinical Incidents and Outcomes in Medical Care' Sixth Report, Vol 1 1998–99

> 50. There is no central NHS disciplinary procedure. Each trust has its own disciplinary procedure, but they are broadly similar based on guidance issued by the NHS. There are two disciplinary processes, one for personal misconduct which is the same for all employees. This

can lead to dismissal in some circumstances. There are also professional procedures in relation to doctors who have been guilty of misconduct for which the punishment falls short of dismissal.

Until the fragmentation of employment relationships following the creation of Trusts, there were some NHS-wide procedures, particularly in relation to allegation of *professional* misconduct or incompetence in HC(90)9. Trusts may well adopt these procedures. The position is explained in the following extract.

B Raymond 'The Employment Rights of the NHS Hospital Doctor' in C Dyer (ed) *Doctors, Patients and the Law* (1992)

The rights provided by the NHS contract

Each health authority has its own standard form of employment contract, but each NHS doctor or dentist has 'written in' to his or her contract certain disciplinary and appeal procedures which provide limited safeguards for practitioners and guidance for health authorities who want to discipline or dismiss doctors in their employment. These may be summarised as:

(a) The disciplinary procedure for cases of *personal conduct* (section 40 of the 'Blue Book').
(b) The procedure for dealing with allegations of *professional conduct* or *professional competence* (Department of Health Circular HC(90)9).
(c) The procedure for appeals to the Secretary of State in all but personal misconduct cases (paragraph 190 of the 'Red Book').

The voluminous labyrinth of national terms and conditions contained in the 'Red' and 'Blue' Books is part and parcel of the hospital doctor's contractual rights and thus section 40 and paragraph 190 will apply to everyone. The position of the HC(90)9 procedure for dealing with allegations of professional misconduct and incompetence – the basis of the Wendy Savage inquiry in 1986 – is slightly less clear. The circular, like its predecessor, HM(61)112, states itself to be *guidance* to health authorities, and in the High Court case brought by Dr Marietta Higgs against the Northern Regional health Authority, the authority argued that the circular was not mandatory and that authorities were free to ignore it if they wished. In that case, the authority had imposed substantial disciplinary sanctions on Dr Higgs following the publication of Lord Justice Butler-Sloss' report on the Cleveland child abuse crisis of 1987, but without having any kind of disciplinary hearing and specifically avoiding using the procedure set out in the circular. In the High Court, the judge upheld this proposition, but Dr Higgs appealed to the Court of Appeal against that decision. In the Court of Appeal, the case was eventually settled on agreed terms and no formal decision was ever made on this point. In the course of argument, however, the Master of the Rolls, Lord Donaldson, expressed the view that the circular obviously represented custom and practice within the Health Service and that large employers within a national public service were therefore bound to observe the procedures laid down by the appropriate Government minister. The net result is that while this issue is tinged with grey, it is sensible to proceed on the basis that every practitioner employed by a health authority can insist that the procedure in the circular is used.

Somewhat less clear is the position of practitioners employed within the NHS trusts. Section 6 of the NHS and Community Care Act 1990 makes it clear that on day one of their existence the trusts take over all the employment duties and liabilities of the health authority, which must therefore include the disciplinary apparatus set out above. On the other hand, it has been stated repeatedly that trusts have the power to determine their own terms and conditions of service for staff and it is therefore open to a trust to introduce different systems by following the appropriate procedures for variation of contracts of employment. The net position for doctors employed by trusts is therefore that they are covered by the mainstream NHS procedures unless their own trust has introduced different procedures, in which case the latter are applicable.

Personal misconduct – section 40
Personal conduct is defined as:

performance or behaviour of practitioners due to factors other than those associated with the exercise of medical or dental skills.

The NHS procedure for dealing with allegations of this nature is set out in section 40 of the 'Blue Book' which comprises the entirety of the system for this category of complaint: there is no right to an HC(90)9 type of inquiry, nor is there any right to a paragraph 190 appeal to the Secretary of State against dismissal.

The section 40 procedure applies to all NHS employees accused of personal misconduct, from hospital porters to consultants, and consists mainly of a procedure for appealing to a committee of the employing authority against disciplinary action (including dismissal) taken at a lower level. The appeal is to a committee of three health authority members, at least one of whom should have a special knowledge of the work of the employee. Where this is not possible, and the appeal is against dismissal, the doctor's representative can ask for the appointment of a specialist assessor who will advise the appeal committee on matters of professional conduct and/or competence. Section 40 then sets out the standard procedure for the appeal hearing, including the usual provisions for the calling and cross-examination of witnesses, final addresses and mitigation.

The significance of section 40 is that since the removal, in March 1990, of the right to a paragraph 190 appeal to the Secretary of State in cases of personal misconduct, this procedure provides health authorities with a 'fast-track' method of dismissing doctors that they wish to be rid of. If your district general manager accuses you of illicit private use of the photocopier, for example, and his recommendation for dismissal is confirmed by the full authority, then only the section 40 appeal committee stands between you and the cold comfort of the industrial tribunal. ... If your contract is held at district level, there is a discretionary right of appeal to the region, but the discretion is theirs, not yours, and they cannot be compelled to hear your appeal at all.

Practitioners would be well advised, therefore, to contact their defence society as soon as any allegation of personal misconduct is raised, even if the subject matter appears to be trivial.

Intermediate procedure

In addition to updating the procedure for inquiries into allegations of professional misconduct and incompetence, Circular HC(90)9 introduced a wholly new procedure for dealing with allegations which were within those categories, but which fell short of the seriousness required for a full-blown inquiry procedure. Faced with such a case (which can include a 'clash of professional views') the Director of Public Health (DPH) of the employing authority may implement the new intermediate procedure.

His first step is to write to the Joint Consultative Committee (JCC) with brief details of the case, asking them to nominate assessors to conduct an investigation, while informing the practitioner at the same time. The assessors (normally two) will come from a different region and at least one will be of the same specialty as the consultant concerned. Once appointed, the assessors receive a written 'statement of the case' from the DPH which is also copied to the doctor concerned. The assessors can then decline to act on the basis that the case is either too serious or too trivial for them or because the case falls within the 'three wise men' procedure of Circular HC(82)13 ... but if they decide to proceed within the intermediate procedure, their next task is to visit the district where the problem has arisen and 'undertake the necessary investigations'.

They then draw up a list of people they would like to see and copy this to the practitioner who may suggest additional names. Anyone who agrees to be interviewed (the assessors have no power of compulsion) will be asked to provide a written statement or to sign an agreed record of the interview. The practitioner will also meet the assessors either alone or in the company of a representative or friend, if he wishes.

Having completed their investigations, the assessors depart to write their report which will comprise a first part containing findings of fact and a second part containing details of which doctors (if any) are at fault and recommendations concerning organisational matters or advice to be given to the consultant. The DPH then receives the report (again copied to the practitioner) and then decides what action to take in accordance with section 40 if appropriate.

It is too early to say how this new procedure will work out in practice and certainly no aspect of its operation has been taken before the courts for review. The welcome aspect of the procedure is the way in which the procedure cannot be implemented behind the practitioner's back, as he must be informed from the very start. What is unwelcome, however, is the apparent inability of the practitioner to have any influence over the choice of assessors. There is nothing to stop the JCC appointing assessors who are either known to favour policies and clinical practices at the opposite end of the spectrum from the practitioner under scrutiny or individuals who are known informal associates of the practitioner's accusers or antagonists in the dispute under review.

Similarly, the inquisitorial method by which evidence is taken in private and in the absence of the practitioner provides abundant opportunity for unfairness, bias and malice. The procedure should provide for the practitioner to be seen twice, once at the outset to respond to the DPH's written statement of case and then again after all the other witnesses have been seen, to respond to any points or allegations which may have been made against him, which the assessors should be bound to disclose. It is a cardinal principle of natural justice, as enforced by the courts, that no information should be used against an individual in these circumstances unless that individual is given the information and an opportunity to rebut or comment. Practitioners who find themselves being made the subject of intermediate procedure should demand that the assessors adopt this method.

The full-blown HC(90)9 – preliminary steps
Where an allegation of professional misconduct or incompetence is too serious to be dealt with via the intermediate procedure – where the practitioner is in jeopardy of serious disciplinary action including (but not confined to) dismissal – the full-blown HC(90)9 procedure must be used. The key figure in the early stages of this system is the health authority chairman, whose first task is to ascertain whether or not there is a *prima facie* case against the doctor concerned. Any preliminary inquiries must be conducted by the DPH who may also invoke the assistance of the authority's legal adviser. At this stage, the chairman is required to inform the practitioner immediately of the nature of the complaint made and that an inquiry, which could lead to dismissal, is under consideration. The practitioner is then given the opportunity to make representations to the chairman.

These 'early warning' provisions are less valuable than they seem. In the Wendy Savage case, which is the best documented example of the system in operation, the first 'complaints' were made over a year before Mrs Savage was notified in accordance with the above provisions. The first she knew that anything was afoot was when she was summoned out of a clinic to see the district medical officer ...

The significance of the Savage case is not just that so much of what is normally conducted behind closed doors was done openly and in the public spotlight, but that it also resulted in her complete exoneration from any suggestion of incompetence. In other words, it was a case that should never have been started at all and having started should have been stopped at the earliest opportunity. Nevertheless, it ran its full course, costing Mrs Savage a 14-month suspension with all the associated personal distress and Tower Hamlets Health Authority £250,000 which could otherwise have been spent on improving patient care. It is nothing less than a tragedy that the new HC(90)9 procedure which replaced the old HM(61)112 should embody none of the lessons which should have been learned as a result of that case. The opening paragraphs of the new procedure are an almost *verbatim* replica of the old procedure and still allow charges to be accumulated without the practitioner's knowledge.

Suspension from duty
The most immediate, humiliating and professionally damaging consequence of an allegation of serious incompetence or misconduct is suspension from duty. Mrs Savage was suspended on 25 April 1985, the day she was notified that the inquiry procedure was under way, and not reinstated until 24 July 1986, after the inquiry had taken place and the report had been produced. By the standards of other doctors in that position, however, she was fortunate: suspensions of three and four years are far from uncommon. The longest is believed to be that of Dr Bridget O'Connell, a consultant paediatrician working in East London who was suspended in December 1982 and remains so at the time of writing.

Despite the devastating impact of suspension, you will search in vain in the HC(90)9 procedure for any discussion of it. The only reference is a sentence which simply states that the inquiry procedure does not 'prejudice the right of the authority to take immediate action (eg suspension from duty) where this is required in cases of a very serious nature' [see now *Lyndon v Yorkshire RHA* (1991) 10 BMLR 49 (CA)].

The unpalatable reality is that employers generally have a very wide freedom to suspend employees from duty and the courts have shown a notable reluctance to intervene. The reason is that the law regards employment as a kind of commercial contract between the employer and employee – the employee provides services and the employer pays money in return. Suspension on full pay therefore is in the blinkered eyes of the law no more than the employer fulfilling his side of the bargain without requiring the employee to put in his or her side of it, rather like a shop giving away goods for nothing. Thus the law regards the suspended doctor not as someone who is undergoing the most professionally damaging experience it is possible to have short of outright dismissal, but as an unusually fortunate individual who is being paid without being required to work. As the law stands at present, therefore, the courts will intervene only if a doctor has been suspended in breach of an established local procedure, as there are none which bind health authorities on a national basis.

Suspension without due cause, or for an unreasonable length of time could constitute constructive dismissal, but where does that leave the practitioner? Once again the industrial tribunal with its inadequate remedies is the only recourse. Sooner or later, the courts are going to have to acknowledge that for highly skilled and dedicated professionals, suspension from duty is not a bonus but a devastating body-blow for which employers should be held fully accountable. For the moment, however, unjustified suspension is a wrong for which English law provides no meaningful or adequate remedy.

HC(90)9 – the inquiry
After hearing from the practitioner, the authority chairman decides whether a *prima facie* case still exists, and if he thinks that it does, he must proceed to the next stage in the inquiry. Note that he is not required to take any expert advice before taking this step and a distinguished

consultant may find himself suspended and subjected to an inquiry on the grounds of incompetence without any expert medical opinion other than that of the Director of Public Health. Even if expert advice is taken, there is nothing to prevent its being obtained from a known opponent or antagonist of the practitioner or someone known for holding opposing clinical views. And even under the new procedure, the health authority chairman can suspend and proceed against any consultant without taking any outside opinion at all.

Once a decision has been made that there is a *prima facie* case, the chairman must proceed to hold a full inquiry unless the facts are undisputed, in which case the section 40 procedure is used. This is also to be used when the facts have been established by an official inquiry or a criminal case. If there is a dispute over whether an official inquiry has dealt with precisely the same issues as in the HC(90)9 allegation, an inquiry panel may be convened to decide whether a full hearing is necessary.

These stipulations about official inquiries are additions introduced by the new procedure and should serve as a warning bell to any practitioners who find themselves involved in such an inquiry. In the Cleveland inquiry, Lord Justice Butler-Sloss was at pains to reassure all concerned that her purpose was not to attribute blame and the normal procedure for warning individuals that they might be subject to criticism in inquiries was not used. Nevertheless, had the health authority decided to use the new procedure against Dr Higgs, they would have been able to attempt to by-pass the HC(90)9 inquiry altogether by invoking this clause. Any doctor involved in an official inquiry, therefore, should regard himself as effectively on trial, regardless of what is said to the contrary.

The inquiry panel specified by HC(90)9 consists of a legally qualified chairman, chosen from a list kept by the Lord Chancellor's Department, together with two side members – a doctor and a lay person in cases of professional misconduct, but two doctors in cases of alleged incompetence, at least one from the same specialty as the doctor accused of incompetence. The circular requires that terms of reference should be drawn up and that these together with copies of correspondence and any written statements made should be provided to the practitioner. He should also be supplied with a list of witnesses to be called for the 'prosecution' together with a note of the main points on which they can give evidence. This again is inadequate. For these proceedings to be conducted fairly, the allegations against the practitioner must be specified in as much detail as possible (there were 55 separate charges in the Savage case) and witnesses should be compelled to provide full statements so that the practitioner knows precisely the case he has to meet.

The proceedings follow the familiar adversarial pattern, save that the circular contains an exhortation to both sides to 'reduce the formality of the proceedings'. In my view, this encouragement should be resisted. Formality of the merely ceremonial or ritualistic kind is of course out of place in a hearing of this nature, but formality in the sense of orderliness of procedure and disciplined attitudes to matters of fact and opinion is essential if the practitioner is to obtain a fair hearing. As far as possible, allegations should be narrowed down, and evidence subjected to sensible but strict tests of relevance and admissibility. When a career is at stake (as it must be in these proceedings) it is not unreasonable for considerable care to be taken to guard against unfairness of any kind and experience shows that a casual, undisciplined approach to these matters is the enemy of justice and fair play.

At the end of the inquiry, the panel produce a two-part report to the authority on the same lines as that described for the intermediate procedure. The panel have no disciplinary powers themselves and the practitioner must be given a chance to make further representations to the authority before sentence is passed. One of the most welcome innovations of the new system is the introduction of a model time scale which envisages a complete HC(90)9 inquiry, from the time of the first decision that a *prima facie* case exists to the final report to the authority, taking no more than 32 weeks. As the Savage inquiry, then one of the fastest on record, took 14 months to make the same progress, there must be a degree of scepticism as to whether this time scale is realistic, but it nevertheless represents a major step forward.

The appeal to the Secretary of State – paragraph 190

A consultant or associate specialist dismissed for any reason other than personal misconduct has an automatic right to appeal to the Secretary of State for Health. This covers, for example, someone made redundant or dismissed after a full HC(90)9 inquiry, or after a section 40 hearing on professional conduct or competence. Notice of appeal must be lodged before the date the dismissal takes effect, but the full statement of case should be provided within four months of the date upon which notice was given, unless an extension is allowed by the Secretary of State. Thus a doctor who received three months' notice of redundancy on 1 January must give notice of appeal before 1 April, and get his statement of case in before 1 May.

On receipt of notice of appeal, the Secretary of State must ask the authority for its written views which must be provided within two months, subject to similar extensions if granted. The Secretary of State must also set up a professional committee to advise him on the case.

This is chaired by the Chief Medical Officer of the Department of Health or his deputy and includes a representative of the Secretary of State and a representative of the practitioner's profession. It is assisted by a qualified solicitor or barrister and may, if it thinks fit, interview the practitioner and representatives of the authority, but is under no obligation to do so. The professional committee usually holds some kind of hearing, but can, if it wishes, conduct the entire procedure on the basis of the written statements and see no one in person.

Having conducted its investigation and deliberations, the committee reports to the Secretary of State, advising termination or continuance of employment or a third course, which is or might be acceptable to both the practitioner and the authority. Within three months of receiving the Committee's report, the Secretary of State must either confirm the termination or direct that the practitioner's employment continue or arrange some other solution acceptable to the practitioner and the authority. Thus the authority has a veto over any solution other than straightforward reinstatement.

First, it should be noted that s 40 of the General Whitely Council Conditions of Service concerned with 'personal misconduct' was replaced by s 42 in 1995 (and for a discussion of the 'personal'/'professional' conduct distinction, see *Chatterjee v City and Hackney Community Services NHS Trust* (1998) 49 BMLR 55). Secondly, the Government has issued a Consultation Paper, *Supporting Doctors, Protecting Patients* (12 November 1999), in which it contemplates a radical overhaul of the NHS disciplinary procedures, including the abolition of the right of appeal to the Secretary of State under para 190 for consultants dismissed for professional misconduct or incompetence. The Consultation Paper also proposes that Health Authorities should have the power to suspend GPs. As we saw, currently that power resides solely in the NHS Tribunal.

The position is far from satisfactory, resulting in confusion (both by professionals and Trusts), delays and manifest procedural unfairness. The House of Commons Health Committee (*supra*) recently had this to say:

> 51. We heard evidence that the disciplinary procedures for doctors in relation to professional matters are expensive, legalistic and complex. This causes problems for managers where a trust wishes to dismiss a doctor for professional reasons and often trusts find another unsatisfactory solution, such as paid leave and ultimately early retirement, or they may leave the matter with a regulatory body. We received evidence that one trust which was concerned about a surgeon's performance had agreed to supply a favourable employer's reference as part of a severance package designed to enable the surgeon to continue to work in another trust, potentially putting subsequent patients at risk. We find this practice absolutely abhorrent and draw attention to the fact that it is not in line with GMC guidelines. Some trusts have developed clauses which allow them to dismiss a doctor for what others might regard as a clinical matter, such as "gross negligence". The MDU felt that the disciplinary procedure as it stands was acceptable, as long as it was properly implemented. However we received evidence that this was not always the case, particularly in relation to the suspension of doctors where we heard that guidelines were not always being met. The Department of Health acknowledges that this is a problem and has established a review of the disciplinary process, including suspensions. This review will be published shortly.

(For further discussion, see V Du-Feu *Employment Law in the NHS* (1995), especially ch 8. See also *Supporting Doctors, Protecting Patients* (1999), DoH paras 2.7–2.15.)

C. COMPLAINTS PROCEDURES

1. Within the NHS

(a) The 'old systems' prior to 1 April 1996

Until April 1996, complaints within the NHS were handled in a number of ways. Complaints against GPs (and other 'Part II' practitioners) were dealt with under the medical service committee (MSC) procedure laid down in the National Health Service (Service Committees and Tribunal) Regulations 1992 (SI 1992 No 664). This, as we have seen, was in reality a disciplinary procedure based upon a failure by the practitioner to comply with his obligations under his 'terms of service' in Sch 2 to the National Health Service (General Medical Services) Regulations 1992 (SI 1992 No 664, as amended).

The process was subject to considerable criticism.

L Mulcahy and J Allsop in Peter Leyland and Terry Woods (eds)
Administrative Law Facing the Future: Old Constraints and New Horizons **(1997)**

From the late 1980s, NHS complaints systems received an increasing amount of attention from policy makers, practitioners and academics' and in the early 1990s criticisms of existing complaint procedures mounted. Interest groups representing consumers, doctors and NHS managers were all concerned about the existing arrangements, including Medical Services Committees. The Council on Tribunals devoted more and more space in its reports to the conduct of these committees and was increasingly outspoken in its comments. Its report for 1988–89 voiced its concerns thus:

> Over the past 12 years or so we have visited service committees on some 120 occasions. That practical experience is, we would claim, of unique value in assessing whether what takes place at service committee hearings can properly be regarded as fair to all those present by comparison with the standards prevailing generally in tribunal systems under our jurisdiction. Based on our observations, we can with confidence assert that very many service committees are well run and dispense justice to complainants and practitioners in an entirely proper fashion within the limits provided by their constitution. But in a significant minority of cases, we are equally confident that there are grounds for concern.

Criticism of the Family Health Service Authorities procedures centred on three main issues. First, the system was said to be biased towards doctors. Secondly, the procedures were thought to be opaque. Lastly, it was said that too much attention was placed on disciplining doctors rather than on resolving disputes. It is significant that while the first two criticisms suggest the need for a move towards more formal protection of the complainant's position, the last reveals a desire for a move away from a formalised legal model.

Bias towards doctors

Inequality of bargaining power
A number of critics suggested there was an inequality of bargaining power between the practitioner and the complainant in the service committee procedure. From their inception, Medical Service Committees represented medical interests to ensure these were protected. They provided a good example of a process which has been called corporatism through which professional interest groups are drawn into government administration to meet the needs of the profession and the state. It has been argued that the profession is more likely to accept that decisions are reasonable if its representatives have taken part in decision making, while government can reach agreement about what is acceptable without public conflict. The fact that doctors were decision makers in Medical Service Committees, albeit in a minority, reflects this. Moreover, lay members were usually appointed by agreement with the Local Medical Committee (LMC). Lastly, professional channels of communication were secured by the fact that the medical members could report back to the LMC and that this has strong links with the GPs' negotiating body, the General Medical Services Committee, a committee of the British Medical Association.

Use of medical networks
Medical influence is also exerted at a less formal level. In a recent study of how GPs respond to complaints, Mulcahy, Allsop and Shirley (see Mulcahy, L, Allsop, J and Shirley, C, '*The Voices of Complainants and GP's in Complaints about Healthcare*' Social Science Research Papers, No 3, London: South Bank University, 1996) found that doctors tend to make extensive use of their medical networks. They are most likely to discuss a complaint with medical colleagues within their own practice, but also commonly contacted their medical defence organisation and LMC secretary for advice, emotional support and help in preparing a formal response. The secretaries are repeat players in the system with an intricate knowledge of the terms of service and a clear understanding of how best to present a defence. Secretaries interviewed for this study estimated that only about 5 per cent of doctors failed to make any contact with them. The secretaries went to some lengths to let doctors know they were there to support and advise them. In two health authorities, information about the LMC secretary was sent out to the GP with a copy of the initial complaint letter. Another health authority

routinely informed the LMC that there was a complaint about a particular doctor and sent out a factsheet to the doctor about what to do and whom to contact. Secretaries provided doctors with help by writing letters for them and by providing various types of support at hearings. This could include anything from help in constructing a defence to actual presentation of their case, despite the fact that representation by paid advocates was not permitted by official guidance. In the words of one LMC secretary: 'I do think I help doctors to make the most of their case ... I always defend them because that's what they're paying me for.'

Mulcahy, Allsop and Shirley also reported that complainants, too, were extremely resourceful in identifying people who could help them to prepare for the service committee. But those who were *most* successful were those who had 'insider knowledge' of the Family Health Service Authority, NHS or other complaints systems. In their study it was noted that the sources that complainants used included a partner who worked in a hospital casualty department and an acquaintance who was a paramedic. But, in contrast to doctors, making contact with 'insiders' was more haphazard. What we cannot tell from these data is how many potential complainants were deterred by a lack of 'insider' support or knowledge.

Closing of ranks and imbalance

Complainants' views of the tribunal process also reveal concerns about bias. What emerged clearly from the research conducted by Mulcahy, Allsop and Shirley (*ibid*) was the complainants' sense of impotence, regardless of the help they received. All the complainants felt that doctors closed ranks to protect one another and that this occurred throughout the medical hierarchy. In the words of one, 'The complaint was a fight with the medical profession. Medics are a very closed shop.' Complainants perceived themselves to be less well supported than the doctor. Many referred to the impression that GPs had a 'professional' or 'experienced' representative to present their case. Despite the impartiality with which the service committee was thought to be conducted, there was a universal feeling amongst complainants that the support of GPs by the medical defence organisations and LMC weighed against complainants who did not have these advantages.

Concern has also been expressed in other quarters about the imbalance in the representation available for hearings. The Council on Tribunals noted that service committees were the only tribunals under its jurisdiction where paid lawyers were barred. This was seen as a problem as doctors were generally more articulate than complainants. Mulcahy, Allsop and Shirley found that while complainants said that they had had no trouble preparing for the hearing, the majority said that it was much more formal than they had anticipated. One complainant said: 'All the questions were abrupt. To me, they were all too miserable, too serious. There were no conversations. It was very formal.' Significantly, it was felt that their misconceptions had had a detrimental effect on their performance on the day. Even a complainant whose complaint was upheld felt on reflection that she had been underprepared. Although she had taken a representative from the Community Health Council to present the case, she was perturbed by having to give her evidence in her own words.

Interestingly, complainants as well as doctors considered the conduct of Medical Service Committees to be fair and well organised. GPs also thought that all the parties to the hearing, including the lay members of the panel, played a full role although there was a recognition that these views might not be shared. In the words of one doctor:

> Yes [it was fair]. I don't think the patient thought it was fair, as she appealed unsuccessfully to the Secretary of State and took legal proceedings. I don't think she understood or cared that it was a hearing about terms of service for the GP.

Opaque procedures

Another criticism of the old Medical Service Committee system was its opacity. If grievance systems are to serve the common good and contribute to the development of a framework of rules understood and acted upon by the relevant communities and known to the public, then Medical Service Committees did not serve their purpose. Hearings were held in private and records of proceedings were not made available to the public. Nor did they appear to have a radiating effect on other doctors. Mulcahy, Allsop and Shirley (*ibid*) found that LMC secretaries reported little feedback to the LMC as a whole, or to rank and file doctors, on the substance and outcome of complaints brought before the Medical Service Committee. In three of the authorities studied, the only information available was an annual report giving overall data on the numbers of complaints but not their substance. In the fourth, a system for discussing anonymous reports from service committees has only just been introduced.

Discipline rather than resolution

Medical Service Committees were not concerned to redress the complainant's grievances but rather to discipline doctors if fault was found. They narrowed the issues at stake to focus on contractual obligations, yet for a dispute to be resolved all the issues of concern to the disputants need to be aired and discussed. The fact that the main purpose of the procedures was disciplinary had three main implications.

First, the procedure could not offer a full range of remedies to the parties. The outcomes of the procedure were disciplinary measures such as financial penalties rather than compensation, apologies or explanations. Mulcahy, Allsop and Shirley's study (*ibid*) reported that all the complainants interviewed, even those whose cases had been successful, thought the *outcome* was unfair; conversely, all the GPs contacted in a parallel study felt that the outcome was fair, even where the complaint against them had been upheld.

Secondly, the procedure encouraged a defensive response to complaints in which positions became entrenched rather than resolution possibilities explored. If complaints about clinical care are taken as an attack on the professional judgement and professional integrity of a clinician, then it is not surprising that strong feelings are aroused. In her study of complaints reaching a Family Health Service Authority service committee, Allsop (Allsop, J, '*Two Sides to Every Story: Complaints' and Doctors' Perspectives about Medical Care in a General Practice Setting*' (1994) Law and Policy, vol 16, No 2, pp 149–84) found that 92 per cent of doctors responded to complaints by denying responsibility. Examples of defensive strategies included claims that: the matter fell outside contractual responsibilities; events were due to the disease process and uncertainty in medical practice; or the failure was due to other people, to external events or to some fault on the part of the complainant or patient. Another reason for defensiveness is the personal cost to doctors if the complaint escalates. This may lead to inquiries by senior colleagues which can threaten reputation, promotion and livelihood. In his study of doctors with problems in the NHS, Donaldson (See Donaldson, L, '*Doctors with Problems in an NHS Workforce*' (1994) 308 British Medical Journal 1277) suggests that certain criticisms are much more likely to be upheld than others through peer review processes. For example, clinical complaints taken to the final stage of the clinical complaints procedure in hospitals were much more likely to be upheld if they concerned communication and behaviour. The author suggests that these were more acceptable and less threatening aspects of professional practice on which to base a peer rebuke (see Bosk, C, '*Forgive and Remember: Managing Medical Failure*', Chicago, 1979).

Ironically, defensive responses tend to exacerbate complaints rather than encourage resolution. One study of GPs showed that if, following a complaint, a GP removed a patient from the practice list, showed lack of sympathy, was hostile or failed to address the issues raised, these then became issues in the dispute. The length of time taken to deal with the complaint, a lack of openness and an unwillingness by those involved to take action when incompetence is revealed, can also induce disillusionment and a determination to pursue the complaint. A breakdown in the relationship between the doctor and patient was a common effect of complaints that went as far as a Medical Service Committee. In their study, Mulcahy, Allsop and Shirley (*supra*) found that, most commonly, this occurred at the instigation of the complainant and was more likely to be prompted by complaints that had reached a Medical Service Committee than by those which had been conciliated.

Despite the propensity for defensiveness, doctors in the same study accepted that complainants' motivations for bringing the complaint were not of the type to endanger the GP's career. Most doctors believed that complainants wanted a social response such as an explanation (26 per cent); an apology (22 per cent); an investigation (21 per cent). Only 17 per cent thought that complainants wanted doctors to be reprimanded, and 2 per cent that they wanted compensation. Paradoxically, their parallel study of complainants revealed that a desire for a doctor to be disciplined was an important motivation for pursuing a complaint, although only a minority wanted a doctor struck off.

The third and final reason why complaints might not be resolved to the satisfaction of the parties was that the issues which could be considered by Medical Service Committees were narrowly defined and did not permit an airing of all the disputant's concerns. The self-employed status of GPs confined investigations to the consideration of whether they had breached their terms of service and, consequently, the processing of complaints had the potential to leave many issues unresolved. For instance, complaints about attitude and behaviour could not be heard, despite the fact that they constituted a significant proportion of allegations made. Yet, Mulcahy, Allsop and Shirley's study (*ibid*) demonstrated that what doctors were prepared to define as a complaint went way beyond the issues which could be considered under the Medical Service Committee procedures. Fourteen per cent of doctors and all complainants mentioned attitude, behaviour and communication problems as being at the crux of the dispute. In summary, the limited research on formal service committee procedures suggests that a mismatch of expectations exists between those making complaints and those responding to them. This reflects the different orders of priority of the disputing parties, which needs to be taken into account if the dispute is to be resolved rather than just managed.

Complaints against hospital doctors, by contrast, were dealt with by governmental circulars which distinguished between complaints which related to clinical judgment and those which did not (HC(88) 37). The latter procedure was less formal and complex than those concerned with clinical judgment. For that, there was a three stage procedure starting with an informal process of conciliation, moving to a more formal stage involving the Regional Medical Officer and ending with an independent professional review by two independent consultants. These procedures were imposed upon Health Authorities and NHS Trusts (Hospital Complaints Procedure Act 1985, ss 1 and 1A respectively). (For a discussion see the Second Edition of this book, pp 591–595 and 600–603 and *Being Heard: The Report of a Review Committee on NHS Complaints Procedures* (May 1994), Annex E.)

Both the non-clinical and clinical procedures were also subject to comment. As regards the former, the Wilson Committee (whose recommendations we shall look at in detail shortly) identified a number of deficiencies.

Wilson Committee *Being Heard – The Report of a Review Committee on NHS Complaints Procedures* (1994)

103 In relation to hospital and community unit procedures, we have received evidence from several trusts describing how they have been able to operate their own systems successfully within existing procedures.

104 There are some reservations about the extent to which the hospital system offers independent investigation staff investigating complaints, even when not responsible for the service complained against, who are employees of the organisation against which the complaint is made and the thoroughness of the investigation depends on their co-operation. Some feel the Chief Executive is likely to be biased.

105 Views are expressed that complainants prefer the formal, if adversarial, family health service procedure over that for hospital complaints. The hospital system is too complicated or adversarial, with patients unsure of who to complain to. Publicity may be poor: an Audit Commission study found 45% of wards visited did not have any posted or written information about the system. Responses from hospitals may not answer questions, but offer alternative descriptions of the patient's experience. There is no visible disciplinary procedure for complaints against managers to be pursued. Investigation of the complaint may be discontinued where the police have decided to pursue a criminal investigation. Oral complaints are not usually recorded.

And, as regards clinical complaints in hospitals, Wilson had the following observations:

106 The majority of criticisms made of the hospital procedure concern the separate procedure for clinical complaints. The procedure pre-dates and does not take account of the recent NHS reforms. The existence of a separate system in itself is confusing and does not encourage access. There is no clear cut distinction between a clinical complaint and a general one about treatment many complaints are a mixture of clinical and non-clinical issues.

107 It can seem to complainants that little or no investigation takes place, and that the process is an exercise in damage limitation. The doctor's own notes may be used as the major evidence with an assumption that the records describe all relevant events adequately despite evidence that they cannot necessarily be relied upon. The complainant has no opportunity to investigate or interrogate. Information may be presented selectively, or even be incorrect. The response may be defensive, evasive, and partial. Too much power may also be seen to lie with the complainant, who may wish to take things as far as possible.

108 Complainants can face a long drawn-out process, particularly before an Independent Professional Review can take place, sometimes "several years". There is a lack of time limits. The procedure does not include any specific mechanism for reference to the General Medical Council or General Dental Council in appropriate cases. Clinical judgement may be made by GPs or by other professions, such as nurses, who are excluded from the procedure.

109 At Stage 1 of the procedure, an initial informal meeting can be intimidating or be viewed by the complainant as a waste of time. There is no compulsion on the individual complained against to be present: while this may be welcomed by the complainant, it can be a cause of anger. If hospitals do not supply the names of those who care for patients, complainants are unable to raise the matter with the professional regulatory bodies. The status of the staff involved may also be important in judging the seriousness of the complaint.

110 Decisions taken at the second stage are discretionary, and it does not include a non-medical element. Its purpose is not always clear, and it can be seen to be slow, secret, and not truly independent. Assessors frequently comment to the Joint Consultants Committee that had Stages 1 and 2 been properly and rapidly addressed, the complaint need have gone no further.

111 At the Independent Professional Review in stage 3, the nature of the procedure makes delays seem inevitable. Complainant may be kept poorly informed about progress. Trusts are increasingly reluctant to release consultants to participate, seeing the procedures as cumbersome, and of doubtful efficiency.

112 The review may not be seen as impartial or truly independent. The second opinions are chosen without reference to the complainant or any other interested party. There is no lay representation, contributing to 'understandable suspicion of "doctors sticking together"' in the words of one doctor. There is also no non-medical input, even where, as in the case of maternity services, a component of care provided may have been from another profession.

113 As Professor Donaldson's study showed, professional peers are more likely to uphold grievances concerning failure in communication than errors of clinical judgement. Neither the complainant, nor the trust, necessarily sees the assessors' report. Meetings may be used as a substitute for a written response. Complainants are often not satisfied with the outcome. AIMS goes so far as not recommending the use of the procedure.

In addition to these mechanisms, there was also the Health Service Commissioners for England and for Wales who came into existence as a result of the National Health Service Reorganisation Act 1973 (subsequently Pt V of the National Health Service Act 1977) but whose jurisdiction is now defined by the Health Service Commissioners Act 1993 (as amended). The HSC was not subject to the same criticisms by Wilson (*op cit*):

114 The Health Service Ombudsman is generally praised very highly for being independent and thorough, although some concern has been expressed about the length of time his investigations take. The normal time limit of twelve months for making complaints is considered restrictive by some. Rare allegations are made that the Ombudsman is biased or that his Office is "paternalistic". Concern is occasionally expressed about a lack of appeal against his judgements.

However, his jurisdiction to deal with patient complaints within the NHS was restricted in two important ways. First, he had no jurisdiction over 'Part II practitioners', ie GPs and others (Health Service Commissioners Act 1993, s 6(1)). Secondly, he could not inquire into 'clinical complaints'. Section 5(1) stated:

5. (1) A Commissioner shall not conduct an investigation in respect of action taken in connection with
(a) the diagnosis of illness, or
(b) the care or treatment of a patient,
which, in the opinion of the Commissioner, was taken solely in consequence of the exercise of clinical judgment, whether formed by the person taking the action or any other person.

Both of these restrictions were criticised despite the fact that the HSC sometimes adopted a liberal approach when considering whether to apply the exclusion of 'clinical judgment' complaints from his jurisdiction (see Select Committee on the Parliamentary Commissioner for Administration 1993–94 *First Report: The Powers, Work and Jurisdiction of the Ombudsman* and Wilson Committee, *op cit*, paras 321–322).

(b) The Wilson Committee and reform

Thus, the climate for change to the NHS complaints system existed. In 1993 the Government established a Committee chaired by Professor Alan Wilson to review the NHS complaints procedures. In May 1994, the Committee published its report, *Being Heard: The Report of a Review Committee on NHS Complaints Procedures*. In the report, the Wilson Committee identified a number of objectives or goals of the parties to complaints, namely patients and the NHS.

Wilson Committee *Being Heard* (*op cit*)

46 The objectives or goals both of patients in making complaints, and of the NHS in responding to them, must be identified in order to consider whether and how NHS complaints procedures might be improved. While following the complaints procedure may not necessarily satisfy the objectives of either party, the objectives are more likely to be met if procedures are designed positively to encourage resolution.

III.2 OBJECTIVES OF COMPLAINANTS

47 Complainants have a variety of objectives in making their grievances known. These objectives need to be at least partially met if the complainant is to be satisfied with the response he or she receives.

48 Who are complainants? Studies show that, compared to the users of the NHS generally, complainants are more likely to be female than male, and under rather than over 45. The reasons for this have not been explored in detail, but it seems likely that younger women are more likely to take a general responsibility for the health of their families (both younger and older relatives), and that a greater sense of entitlement and greater confidence makes younger people more willing to complain. As many as half of those making a complaint may be acting on behalf of someone else, usually a relative.

49 It is rare for a complainant to be motivated by prejudice or malice. There are some complainants who show signs of severe mental disorder, and there are those whose complaints are made out of feelings of grief or guilt. This does not mean that their complaints are unjustified, but it can mean that it may not be possible for action under complaints procedures to satisfy them. The proportion of complaints which follows bereavement is high.

III.2.1 Acknowledgement

50 Complainants want to be taken seriously. They want their views – and the fact that they had reason to complain – to be acknowledged and for the individual or organisation (whether practice, trust, or the NHS generally) they hold responsible to be prepared to take action.

51 People expressing dissatisfaction sometimes do not intend to make "a complaint" although practitioners or staff interpret their comments in this way. Their intention may have been to suggest how things could be improved, and a response which assumes a grievance exists can provoke further concern.

III.2.2 Apology

52 A simple apology can be a very important objective for complainants. If an apology is not provided, or is delayed, the complainant is less likely to be satisfied:

all too often a failure or unwillingness to say "sorry" at an early stage is the reason for complaints proceeding further through the system than is really necessary or appropriate.

53 Apologies can be given without an admission of blame or liability in relation to the substance of the complaint. At the same time, apologies should not be used simply to brush complainants off:

An apology, however gracious, without answers or follow-up action and information, is not going to be sufficient response to the most serious complaints, and can too easily be used as an attempt to get everyone off the hook.

III.2.3. Explanation

54 Complainants usually also want information: an explanation of what happened and why. This explanation must be in language which the patient can understand.

55 If an explanation attempts to deny the complainant's experience of events, it is unlikely to be accepted. Explanations can also degenerate into a form of making excuses.

III.2.4. *Report on action*

56   Complainants often ask for something to be done to prevent the same thing happening again. This is frequently expressed altruistically in terms of others not having the same problems, for example:

> Neither myself or my husband wanted money as no money could ever change the events, however, we did want the hospital to admit they had made a mistake and a reassurance that they had reviewed their procedures to ensure that this did not happen again to anyone else as I would not wish anyone to experience a similar nightmare.

The other side of the coin is that dissatisfied people may not complain if they feel nothing will happen as a result.

57   Many complainants say that getting a commitment to action is their main objective. They are much more likely to be satisfied if information is given about specific measures which have been, or will be, taken.

III.2.5 *Redress and compensation*

58   Complainants can also want action to take place which has a more direct bearing on the care provided to them, or to the patient about whose care they are complaining. This may include redress, such as faster or additional treatment, or financial compensation, particularly in cases such as dentistry where charges may have been incurred.

59   Complainants, even in cases relating to clinical judgement, do not often have financial compensation as a primary goal. It is also apparent that some who take legal action to obtain compensation do so because other goals are not being met.

60   The situation can be different where a charge has been made for a service (eg in relation to dental treatment), other expenditure has been incurred (eg parking charges), or there has been a loss of personal effects.

III.2.6. *Punishment*

61   Complainants do not usually want retribution, but in some cases, they can want steps taken against individual practitioners and members of staff for what they have done, or against managers where they feel mistakes have been covered up. The motive may be a desire to have justice, to help tackle the cause of the complaint or for professionals to be seen to be accountable.

III.2.7. *Voicing the complaint*

62   Finally, a complaint may – at least partially – be an end in itself. This is sometimes overlooked, but the expression of a complaint can provide an outlet for feelings of dissatisfaction, frustration, anger, or grief.

III.3 NHS OBJECTIVES

63   The NHS considers complaints procedures in two ways: firstly, in responding to complainants; and secondly, as the employer or contractor of individual practitioners and staff about whom complaints may be made.

64   From these perspectives, the NHS has several distinct and important objectives: complainant satisfaction; quality enhancement; fairness to practitioners and staff; and avoidance of unnecessary litigation.

III.3.1. *Complainant satisfaction*

65   The NHS needs effective complaints procedures so that complainants can be given a response to their complaints which aims to satisfy them. This may seem obvious, but it has important consequences for how the Service seeks to meet complainants' objectives.

66   Put at its most basic level, the Service has an interest in satisfying complaints to avoid protracted correspondence and unnecessary litigation (see III.3.4 below). While this can encourage standard apologetic responses, these may not meet other objectives of the complainants or of the NHS itself.

67   By providing effective responses to complaints, service providers – both individuals and organisations – can also maintain and enhance their reputation, a factor of increasing importance following the NHS reforms. The damage done to the reputation of providers by not responding adequately to complainants has been demonstrated in other service sectors, as have the positive views generated by good complaints handling. Satisfying a complainant can also enable the relationship between patient and practitioner to be restored.

III.3.2 *Quality enhancement*

68   Complaints can be used positively to improve services. The contribution that complaints can make in this way is now part of the conventional wisdom of quality management within the NHS and elsewhere ... Complaints can help identify or confirm individual or system problems. For example, they can reveal a need for training in communications

skills. Complaints can play a part in purchasers' monitoring of the performance of provider units.

69 The NHS must have complaints procedures which practitioners and staff believe to be fair. This is particularly so as the work undertaken by NHS practitioners and staff involves the care of ill health where outcomes are uncertain. Procedures should allow the views of both sides to be expressed. Otherwise the approach to complaints handling by practitioners and staff may become negative and defensive.

70 We discuss further in Chapter VII the necessary links between complaints and disciplinary procedures, but we simply note here that fairness requires a balance between treating practitioners and staff appropriately and maintaining proper accountability for their actions.

III.3.3 Avoidance of unnecessary litigation

71 Complaints procedures have sometimes been presented as an alternative to, or way of avoiding, civil litigation. This motivation has affected how the procedures themselves have developed and how complaints are handled under them.

72 One effect of this has been a reluctance, particularly by doctors, to provide any statement which might be taken as an admission of liability. Although an apology need not be such an admission, this has sometimes meant apologies have been delayed or denied to complainants. In fact, the policies of the medical defence organisations now encourage apologies to be made.

The Committee identified nine principles upon which a complaints procedure should be based:

161 The principles of any system should embrace the objectives both of complainants and of the NHS ... **We recommend that the following principles should be incorporated into any NHS complaints procedure:**

- responsiveness
- quality enhancement
- cost effectiveness
- accessibility
- impartiality
- simplicity
- speed
- confidentiality
- accountability.

162 In developing these principles we owe a considerable debt to those laid down last year by the Government's Citizen's Charter Complaints Task Force as guidance for public services generally. It could be argued that those listed here might also be applied to any complaints procedures. However, our concern is with the principles that relate most to complaints about NHS services.

VI.2 RESPONSIVENESS

163 In the first place, complaints procedures should be responsive and aim to satisfy complainants. This does not mean that all complainants will be satisfied with the outcome of their complaint, but the procedure should be directed to satisfying their objectives as well as those of the NHS.

VI.3 QUALITY ENHANCEMENT

164 As seen in both private and public sectors ... complaints provide invaluable management information about the quality of services from the perspective of service users and their families and friends. They can help to identify problems and sometimes suggest solutions. The service improvements this can lead to may be to the benefit of all patients and of those involved in providing services for the NHS.

VI.4 COST EFFECTIVENESS

165 Procedures must be cost effective to operate. Although effective in theory, complaints systems which cannot be implemented because resources are not available benefit no one. Where cash limits apply, it is important that investment in complaint handling is not disproportionate to the resources available to improve services. Current information on costs of NHS complaints systems is poor. We have received some helpful information from the Department of health which showed how costly complaint handling for family health services can be and that costs increase substantially the more formally complaints are investigated and considered. It is difficult to measure the costs of missed opportunities for service improvement, but the value of complaints in this respect should not be underestimated.

VI.5 ACCESSIBILITY

166 To satisfy complainants and for management information from complaints to be available, it must be as easy as possible for complainants to make their views known. This should include attempts to reduce potential barriers of class, race, language, and literacy, and to recognise the needs of vulnerable groups such as children, people with mental health problems, and people with learning difficulties. Procedures must be well-published and understandable to all.

VI.6 IMPARTIALITY

167 Once a complaint is made, both complainant and respondent should be able to expect the matter to be considered impartially. This means that procedures should ensure that different points of view are listened to and investigated without prejudice, and that support should be available to both parties involved. As the Institute for Health Services Management observes, "Complainants are more likely to accept outcomes if they feel they have been treated fairly".

VI.7 SIMPLICITY

168 A simple complaints procedure is desirable. It is likely to be more accessible for complainants and easier to use by those operating it. The simplicity of procedures may be constrained by other organisational elements (eg the independent contractor status of GPs within the NHS) or by the complexity of the issues involved (eg in relation to clinical judgement).

VI.8 SPEED

169 Complaints procedures should ensure that complaints receive as fast a response as is possible without jeopardising other principles. This can help to prevent dissatisfaction growing or further complaints arising about delays.

VI.9 CONFIDENTIALITY

170 Complaints systems should encourage people to complain without fear that their current or future care will be compromised. This is of particular relevance to primary care, to priority care services (for people with learning disabilities, mental illness, long-term handicap and so on), and for some patients detained under the Mental Health Act, who may receive long term care from certain staff members or from one particular organisation.

171 The NHS treats patient information as confidential and all those who work within the NHS are bound by a duty of confidence. Confidential information moves only on a need-to-know basis. This must equally apply to exchanges of information taking place within, or as a result of, complaints procedures.

VI.10 ACCOUNTABILITY

172 It is important in relation to complaints that those bodies providing and purchasing services are accountable for what they do, and take responsibility at the most senior levels for the operation of complaints procedures. Chairmen and non-executive members of trusts are therefore to be held ultimately responsible for the operation of their complaints systems.

173 Accountability can also be furthered by openness in publication of complaints statistics by trusts, and health authorities and health boards.

The committee concluded that the current NHS complaints systems were unsatisfactory and made a number of recommendations. Key to these recommendations were: (1) the introduction of a single procedure applicable throughout the NHS; (2) a three-stage procedure involving 'local resolution', 'independent review' and the Health Service Commissioner; and (3) an extension of the HSC's jurisdiction to GPs (and other 'Part II practitioners') so as to cover 'clinical judgment' complaints:

MAXIMUM COMMONALITY

2   We recommend that there should be a common system for complaints by NHS patients so that they can exercise the same rights whichever part of – or provider of services to – the NHS is involved (Para 179).

3   We recommend that NHS practitioners and staff at all levels should make sure that, with the patient's permission, complaints which do not concern matters within their responsibility or involve more than one organisation are quickly passed on so that the complainant will receive a full response (Para 181).

DISCIPLINE

4 We recommend that complaints procedures should be concerned only with resolving complaints, and not with disciplining practitioners or staff (Para 182).

5 We recommend that the Health Departments re-examine existing disciplinary procedures, particularly those for family practitioners, in the light of our other recommendations and our analysis of the shortcomings of existing procedures (Para 183).

6 We recommend that there is an unrestricted flow of information from procedures for handling complaints to management an/or professional bodies, so that they may take any appropriate disciplinary action (Para 186).

PUBLICITY

7 We recommend that every purchaser and provider of NHS services should have simple, readily available written information about how to complain. A short general leaflet on "how to complain about NHS care" should be produced and disseminated. We also recommend that greater publicity should be given to the availability of general information on how to complain from the freephone Health Information Services (Para 187).

8 We recommend that "branding" should be considered as part of the implementation of any new NHS complaints procedures (Para 188).

INFORMAL RESPONSES

9 We recommend that complaints procedures empower NHS staff to give a rapid, often oral, response when a complaint is made about a service within their responsibility, and to initiate appropriate action as a result of the information received (Para 190).

10 We recommend that complaints procedures should encourage those handling complaints, including senior staff, to make early personal contact with complainants (Para 191).

TRAINING

11 We recommend that training in complaints handling should be extended to all NHS practitioners and staff who are, or are likely to be, in contact with patients (Para 192).

12 We recommend that appropriate training is offered jointly to health council staff and others who may be asked to support complainants and respondents (Para 195).

SUPPORT FOR COMPLAINANTS AND RESPONDENTS

13 We recommend that specific resources, including staff, are provided to health councils for their role in supporting complainants, accompanied by guidance from the Health Departments as to the use of these resources and monitoring arrangements (Para 196).

14 We recommend that all NHS practitioners and staff should be made are of the support available when a complaint is made against them (Para 197).

INVESTIGATION

15 We recommend that the degree of investigation carried out within complaints procedures relates to the complainant's required degree of response. Further investigation by management may also be needed into individual, or patterns of, complaints (Para 201).

CONCILIATION

16 We recommend that conciliation is more widely available throughout NHS complaints procedures, and that those attempting conciliation receive appropriate training (Para 203).

TIME LIMITS

17 We recommend that information given out about complaints procedures should encourage people to make complaints known as soon as possible after they become aware of a problem (Para 208).

18 We recommend that the Health Departments examine the desirability of time limits for making complaints in the light of the arguments we have outlined (Para 210).

DEADLINES

19 We recommend that written complaints are acknowledged within two working days (Para 213).

20 We recommend that, if an investigation or conciliation is required, the response to the complainant should normally be made within three weeks of the complaint being received. If this is not possible, the reasons should be explained and a new date given which should be no more than two weeks ahead. Where the complainant is dissatisfied and further action is required by the complaints or chief executive, we recommend that a further two weeks should normally be allowed for this (Para 214).

21 We recommend that all stages of a complaints procedure should normally be completed within three months (Para 215).

CONFIDENTIALITY
22   We recommend that complaints should normally be filed separately from health records (Para 216).

RECORDING AND MONITORING
23   We recommend that a system for the recording and classification of complaints should be developed and implemented on a United Kingdom basis (Para 218).

24   We recommend that non-executive directors should take a key role in monitoring performance on complaints (Para 221).

25   We recommend that all practices and trusts review their complaints handling on at least a quarterly basis, and make an annual published report on these reviews to the relevant health authority or health board, trust board, and main purchaser(s) (Para 222).

26   We recommend that organisations regularly establish what their users think about their handling of complaints (Para 223).

27   We recommend that information derived from complaints is incorporated into quality review mechanisms (Para 224).

28   We recommend that each of the Health Departments publish an annual complaints bulletin on the current quarterly Scottish model (Para 225).

IMPARTIALITY
29   We recommend that all NHS complaints procedures should include at some stage the possibility of complaints being considered by impartial lay people (Para 230).

DESIGNING PROCEDURES
30   We recommend that the broad features of handling and response we describe should be followed. Key aspects should be required by the Health Departments, but detailed implementation and operation should be left to individual organisations (Para 234).

STAGE 1 PROCEDURES
31   We recommend there should be a three-fold approach to complaints in Stage 1: an immediate first-line response; secondly, investigation and/or conciliation; and thirdly, action by an officer of the family health services authority (or equivalent) for family health services or by the Chief Executive for trusts (Para 238).

32   We recommend that there must be well-publicised access for complainants to a named person such as a complaints officer (Para 243).

33   We recommend that special attention should be paid to the needs of vulnerable groups for support and representation in making complaints (Para 244).

34   We recommend that most complaints should receive an appropriate response either immediately or within 48 hours from front-line staff, their immediate managers, or senior clinical staff, or the named person or complaints officer (Para 247).

TRAINING IN COMMUNICATION SKILLS
35   We recommend that NHS practitioners and staff in all disciplines and professions receive thorough training in communications skills and that should this be incorporated at an early stage into training for professional qualification, staff induction courses, and basic training at all levels (Para 250).

36   We recommend that everyone who is likely to receive oral complaints should be trained in active listening skills (Para 251).

ORAL AND WRITTEN COMPLAINTS
37   We recommended that oral and written complaints should receive the same consideration and sensitive treatment (Para 254).

INVESTIGATION AND CONCILIATION
38   We recommend the use of investigation and the offer of conciliation, where an immediate oral response seems inappropriate or where the complainant remains dissatisfied following an earlier response (Para 255).

39   We recommend that the conciliator might be a practitioner or member of staff within the practice or trust, or lay person, specially trained for this role (Para 258).

40   We recommend that, following investigation and/or conciliation, a written response is sent from the senior partner, practice manager, general or clinical managers within the trust, or health authority or health board director (Para 259).

ACTION BY THE COMPLAINTS EXECUTIVE OR CHIEF EXECUTIVE
41   We recommend that in particularly serious cases or where the complainant remains dissatisfied, the complaint should be considered at the most senior level available (Para 261).

42   We recommend that authorities and health boards responsible for family health services – in consultation with local practices and local representative committees – employ "Complaints Executives" (Para 263).

43   We recommend there should be a full range of options at the discretion of the Complaints
     Executive or Chief Executive: conciliation; detailed investigation of the complaint –
     which might include obtaining independent advice or establishing an independent inquiry
     (Para 264).
44   We recommend appropriate professional advice is always sought where complaints
     concern clinical judgement (Para 264).
45   We recommend that whenever a response is sent, the complaint respondent should check
     whether the complainant is satisfied and inform him or her what further action might be
     taken (Para 267).
46   We recommend that the Unit General Manager of directly managed unit should take
     chief executive action where this is required for complaints (Para 269).

COMMUNITY SERVICES
47   We recommend that community service staff should have particular training in responding
     to complaints because they may not have immediate access to advice from more senior
     managers or specialist staff, when they are visiting patients in their own homes
     (Para 271).

NON-NHS PROVIDERS
48   We recommend that purchasers specify complaints requirements in their contracts with
     non-NHS providers (Para 272).

PURCHASERS AND COMPLAINTS ABOUT POLICY DECISIONS
49   We recommend that purchasers should give proper consideration to complainants' views
     on their policies, including deciding whether the original policy decision should be
     changed in the light of the complaint (Para 274).
50   We recommend that, if complaints about purchasing decisions and policy matters cannot
     be resolved locally, complainants should ask the Health Service Ombudsman to
     investigate (Para 275).
51   We recommend that complaints about policy decisions are handled on the same basis as
     those about purchasing (Para 276).

COMPLAINTS INVOLVING MORE THAN ONE ORGANISATION
52   Where a complaint concerns more than one organisation involved in providing or
     purchasing NHS services, we recommend that the organisation receiving the complaint
     should make sure that it receives a full response (Para 277).

COMMUNITY CARE
53   We recommend that the NHS and social services departments liaise closely to develop
     complaints procedures for community care and other areas which embody the principles
     and characteristics we have described. We recommend that the Government should
     consider further integration of NHS and local authority complaints procedures
     (Para 278).

STAGE 2 PROCEDURES
54   We recommend that arrangements are put in place for those complaints which are not
     adequately dealt with under "internal" procedures. These arrangements should take the
     form of screening followed by panel consideration (Para 295).
55   We recommend that whoever operates the Stage 2 procedure must start with *screening*
     each complaint to establish:
     –   firstly, the issues the complainant wishes to be addressed;
     –   secondly, whether these issues could be appropriately considered within Stage 1
         procedures but have not been;
     –   thirdly, what sort of further response is appropriate (including whether the matter
         is more appropriately dealt with under disciplinary procedures) (Para 298).
56   We recommend that the decision to proceed to a Stage 2 panel should rest with the
     screening officer and, in problematic cases, a panel chairman (Para 300).
57   We recommend that panels should normally have three members. If the complaint raises
     issues of professional judgement or requires particular specialist knowledge, two
     additional members might be appointed (Para 301).
58   We recommend that panels should always have a lay majority (including a lay Chairman),
     and vary their members according to the nature of the complaint. If the complaint
     concerns issues relating to clinical judgement, two members should be included from
     the relevant profession acting as independent assessors (other professional reports might
     also be commissioned if necessary). Where the complaint is from a patient detained
     under the Mental Health Act, a commissioner from the Mental Health Act Commission
     (and its equivalents) should normally be co-opted onto the panel. Where the complaint

involves community care, the panel should include representatives from social services. The appointing body should ensure that the list of those available to serve on panels respects equal opportunities principles (Para 302).

59   We recommend that the body appointing panels should be responsible for ensuring that Chairmen and panel members receive adequate training (Para 303).

60   We recommend that the panels should make a report with any appropriate recommendations to be sent to the complainant, and copied to the person(s) against whom the complaint had been made and to the relevant chief executive(s) to judge what management action should follow. If there was an indication that professional codes of practice might have been breached, a copy should also be sent to the relevant regulatory body. We recommend that panels should normally complete their consideration of a complaint within five weeks (Para 305).

ORGANISATIONAL OPTIONS

61   We recommend that the Secretary of State for Health and other UK Health Ministers consider the options for the organisation of the Stage 2 procedures in the light of our recommended principles and features of effective procedures (Para 320).

HEALTH SERVICE OMBUDSMAN

62   We support the recommendations made by the Select Committee on the Parliamentary Commissioner for Administration to extend the Health Service Ombudsman's jurisdiction to GPs and to the operation by family health services authorities of the current service committee procedure. We also suggest that the Government should carefully examine whether the practical difficulties might be overcome which the Select Committee believes prevent the Ombudsman considering complaints about clinical judgement (Para 322).

IMPLEMENTATION

63   We recommend that the introduction of new complaints procedures for family health services should also be accompanied by changes to the national contractual arrangements for family health service practitioners to require practice procedures to be introduced, and co-operation with other aspects of NHS complaints procedures (Para 328).

64   We recommend that purchasers, with guidance from the Health Departments, are made responsible for auditing the complaints procedures operated by those providing services, as part of their contractual monitoring of service quality (Para 331).

65   If general accreditation systems are introduced on a comprehensive basis, we would recommend that complaints procedures should feature in them, and that this should then become the primary means of ensuring complaints procedures are operating effectively (Para 335).

66   We recommend that implementation should be managed through four Implementation Groups within the Management Executives of the four UK countries (Para 340).

67   We recommend that a short annual review of NHS complaints handling in each of the four UK countries should be carried out reporting to the relevant Secretary of State (Para 341).

(c) The 'new system' of complaints

The government accepted the Wilson Committee's recommendations in *Acting on Complaints* in March 1995 (for a critical discussion of Wilson, see J Hanna 'Internal Resolution of NHS Complaints' (1995) 3 Med L Rev 177). On 1 April 1996 the 'new complaints' procedure was introduced into the NHS.

The reforms: (1) replace the existing procedures for GPs (and other 'Part II practitioners') and hospital complaints with a single, uniform procedure; (2) disengage for GPs (and other 'Part II practitioners') complaints from the disciplinary procedures under the National Health Service (Service Committees and Tribunal) Regulations 1995 (SI 1992 No 664) (the National Health Service (Service Committees and Tribunal) Amendment Regulations 1996 (SI 1996 No 703)); (3) extend the jurisdiction of the Health Service Commissioners to complaints against GPs (and other 'Part II practitioners') and to those involving clinical judgment (Health Service Commissioners (Amendment) Act 1996, s 6); and (4) extend the procedure to complaints about purchasing decisions and care and facilities provided in NHS private pay beds. The 'new system' (apart from that relating to the HSC), is effected by a number of directions under s 17 of the

National Health Service Act 1977; *Directions to Health Authorities on Procedures for Dealing with Complaints about Family Health Service Practitioners* (March 1996); *Directions to NHS Trusts and Special Health Authorities on Hospital Complaints Procedures* (March 1996); and *Directions to Health Authorities on Miscellaneous Matters Concerning Complaints* (March 1996).

The directions are binding on Health Authorities and NHS Trusts and, presumably, in due course will apply to Primary Care Trusts created after April 2000. As regards GPs, their 'terms of service' of (and of other 'Part II practitioners') require GPs to have a practice-based complaints procedure and to publicise it. Paragraph 47A of the 'terms of service' in Sch 2 to the National Health Service (General Medical Services) Regulations 1992 (SI 1992 No 635, as amended by SI 1996 No 702, reg 5(7)) provides as follows:

47A (1) Subject to sub-paragraph (2), a doctor shall establish, and operate in accordance with this paragraph, a procedure (in this paragraph and in paragraph 47B referred to as a "practice based complaints procedure") to deal with any complaints made by or on behalf of his patients and former patients.

(2) The practice based complaints procedure to be established by a doctor may be such that it also deals with complaints made in relation to one or more other doctors.

(3) A practice based complaints procedure shall apply to complaints made in relation to any matter reasonably connected with the doctor's provision of general medical services and within the responsibility or control of—
(a)   the doctor;
(b)   any other doctor either employed by him or engaged as his deputy;
(c)   a former partner of the doctor;
(d)   an employee of the doctor other than one falling within paragraph (b),
and in this paragraph and paragraph 47B, references to complaints are to complaints falling within this sub-paragraph.

(4) A complaint may be made on behalf of a patient or former patient with his consent, or—
(a)   where the patient is a child
      (i)   by either parent, or in the absence of both parents, the guardian or other adult person who has care of the child, or
      (ii)   where the child is in the care of an authority to whose care he has been committed under the provisions of the Children Act 1989 or is in the care of a voluntary organisation, by that authority or voluntary organisation, or
(b)   where the patient is incapable of making a complaint, by a relative or other adult person who has an interest in his welfare.

(5) Where a patient has died a complaint may be made by a relative or other adult person who had an interest in his welfare or, where the patient was as described in paragraph (a)(ii) of sub-paragraph (4), by the authority or voluntary organisation.

(6) A practice based complaints procedure shall comply with the following requirements—
(a)   the doctor must specify a person (who need not be connected with the practice and who, in the case of an individual, may be specified by his job title) to be responsible for receiving and investigating all complaints;
(b)   all complaints must be—
      (i)   recorded in writing,
      (ii)   acknowledged, either orally or in writing, within the period of three days (excluding Saturdays, Sundays, Christmas Day, Good Friday and bank holidays) beginning with the day on which the complaint was made or, where that is not possible, as soon as reasonably practicable, and
      (iii) properly investigated;
(c)   within the period of 10 days (excluding Saturdays, Sundays, Christmas Day, Good Friday and bank holidays) beginning with the day on which the complaint was received by the person specified under paragraph (a) or, where that is not possible, as soon as reasonably practicable, the complainant must be given a written summary of the investigation and its conclusions;
(d)   where the investigation of the complaint requires consideration of the patient's medical records, the person specified under paragraph (a) must inform the patient or person acting on his behalf if the investigation will involve disclosure of information contained in those records to a person other than the doctor or a partner, a deputy or an employee of the doctor, and
(e)   the doctor must keep a record of all complaints and copies of all correspondence relating to complaints, but such records must be kept separate from patients' medical records.

(7) A doctor shall inform his patients about the practice based complaints procedure which he operates and the name (or title) of the person specified under paragraph (6)(a).

You will notice the broad scope of the practice-based procedure (para 47A(3)) and the position of who may complain when the patient is a child or otherwise unable to make a complaint, when it may be made by a parent (or other) or a relative (or other adult with an interest in the patient's welfare) respectively (para 47A(4)).

It is part of the prescribed statutory functions of Health Authorities to 'establish and operate in accordance with directions' complaints procedures for GPs (the National Health Service (Functions of Health Authorities) (Complaints) Regulations 1996 (SI 1996 No 669)). General practitioners have a corresponding duty to co-operate with any investigation of a complaint by a Health Authority. Paragraph 47B of Sch 2 (as amended) provides:

47B (1) A doctor shall cooperate with any investigation of a complaint by the Health Authority in accordance with the procedures which it operates in accordance with directions given under section 17 of the Act, whether the investigation follows one under the practice based complaints procedure or not.
(2) The cooperation required by sub-paragraph (1) includes—
(a) answering questions reasonably put to the doctor by the Health Authority;
(b) providing any information relating to the complaint reasonably required by the Health Authority, and
(c) attending any meeting to consider the complaint (if held at a reasonably accessible place and at a reasonable hour, and due notice has been given) if the doctor's presence at the meeting is reasonably required by the Health Authority.

In relation to 'pilot scheme' providers under the National Health Service (Primary Care) Act 1997, these provisions do not apply. Nevertheless, there is an obligation upon Health Authorities to establish and operate similar complaints procedures (see National Health Service (Pilot Schemes: Miscellaneous Provisions and Consequential Amendments) Regulations 1998 (SI 1998 No 646), reg 3). Directions issued to Health Authorities require that they should ensure that any pilot scheme has a complaints procedure which, in the terms specified, is the same as that applicable to 'Part II practitioners' (see *Directions to Health Authorities Concerning the Implementation of Pilot Schemes (Personal Medical Services)* (March 1998), para 25 and Sch 3).

What, then is the new complaints system? It will be helpful to look at the new system as a three-stage process: (a) local resolution; (b) independent review; and (c) the Health Service Commissioner (for discussion, see C Christensen 'Complaints Procedures in the NHS: All Change' (1996) 2 Medical Law International 247 and V Harpwood, 'NHS Complaints' in M Powers and N Harris, *Clinical Negligence* (3rd edn 2000)).

The system is fully and comprehensively explained in the NHS Executive's guidance: *Complaints – Listening … Acting … Improving* (April 1996). In the extracts that follow, those parts of the guidance in italics are mandatory because they are derived from Directions or regulations.

(i) PRELIMINARY MATTERS

NHS Executive *Complaints – Listening … Acting … Improving* (1996)

Formal Procedure
4.1 *Trust/health authority boards/family health services practitioners must establish a complaints procedure and take steps to publicise the arrangements.*
4.2 It will be a requirement for all trusts/health authorities to have a written complaints procedure, that has formally been adopted by the board, for complaints against themselves.

4.3 Family health services practitioners will be required by Regulations to establish and operate practice-based complaints procedures that adhere to national criteria. This applies to all individuals, and public and private companies, who appear on the health authority's list of contractors and practitioners undertaking to provide family health services. ...

Publicity

4.5 *Trusts, health authorities, must ensure that the right to complain, advice about how to use the complaints procedure, and the help available to complainants from staff, community health councils, and other sources, is well publicised to all patients using their services, together with community health councils serving those patients, and to visitors and staff.* (See paragraph 5.14 for family health services practitioners.)

4.6 National publicity material in the form of a poster and leaflet will be made available. In addition, local information will also need to be available to cover

- the arrangements for both Local Resolution and Independent Review of complaints
- how to refer a complaint to the complaints manager or the chief executive
- how to make a request to the convener for an Independent Review panel to be set up
- under what circumstances a complainant may approach a health authority with a complaint about a family health services practitioner
- the role of the community health council in giving individuals advice and support on making complaints
- the way to make a complaint to the Ombudsman.

Who May Complain

4.7 *Trusts*
   Complainants will be existing or former patients using the trust's NHS services and facilities. Complaints may be made on behalf of existing or former patients by anyone who has the patient's consent. If the patient is unable to act, then consent is needed. Where the trust's complaints manager, or convener at the Independent Review stage, does not accept the complainant as a suitable representative of the patient, who is unable to give consent, they may refuse to deal with the complainant and may nominate another person to act on the patient's behalf.

4.8 *Family Health Services Practitioners*
   Complainants will be existing or former patients of a practitioner who has arrangements with a health authority to provide family health services. Complaints may be made on behalf of existing or former patients by anyone who has the patient's consent. It the patient is unable to act, then consent is not needed. Where the health authority's complaints manager, or convener at the Independent Review stage, does not accept the complainant as a suitable representative of the patient, they may either refuse to deal with the complainant, or nominate another person to act on the patient's behalf.

4.9 The complaints procedure will apply to complaints made by or on behalf of patients, for example by their relatives. Trusts, health authorities and family health services practitioners should also, as a matter of good practice, ensure that they deal sensitively and effectively with complaints by visitors, contractors or other users of their facilities.

4.10 The question of whether a complainant is suitable to represent a patient who is unable to give consent depends in particular on the need to respect the confidentiality of the patient, and to any known wishes expressed by the patient that information should not be disclosed to third parties.

Time Limit on Initiating Complaints

4.11.*Trusts, health authorities and family health services practitioners will encourage those who wish to complain to do so as soon as possible after an event. Normally a complaint should be made within six months from the incident that caused the problem, or within six months of the date of discovering the problem, provided that this is within twelve months of the incident. There is discretion to extend this time limit where it would be unreasonable in the circumstances of a particular case for the complaint to have been made earlier and where it is still possible to investigate the facts of the case.*

4.12 The discretion to vary the time limit should be used flexibly and with sensitivity. Wherever possible the complainant's concerns should be addressed constructively, while remaining scrupulously fair to staff. An example of where discretion should be exercised in favour of extending the time limit would be where the complainant has suffered such distress or trauma which prevented him/her from making their complaint at an earlier stage.

4.13 When a complaint is made outside the time limit, it will be for the complaints manager, or appropriate family health services practitioner, to take responsibility for considering an extension of the time limit.

4.14 If the discretionary extension of the time limit is rejected by the complaints manager, then the procedure will be as follows:

- the complainant may complain to the complaints manager about the refusal to exercise discretion to waive the time limits;
- if the refusal is maintained by the complaints manager, the complainant may request the convener to consider setting up a panel for Independent Review of the complaint about refusal to waive the time limit: the normal requirements as to convening decisions will apply – including the time limit for a convening request;
- the convener may then decide
  - to take no further action, or
  - to refer the complaint back for Local Resolution, or
  - to set up a panel to consider the complaint.

If the convener decides to refer the complaint about the time limit back to the trust/ health authority, the complaints manager – or chief executive if it is referred specifically to him/her – should review very carefully the decision not to accept the complaint in the light of the convener's conclusion that further action through Local Resolution is possible.

4.15 If the convener rejects the request, then the complainant may complain to the Ombudsman.

Complaints Manager

4.16 *The trust/health authority must have a designated complaints manager, who is readily accessible to the public. Complainants must be able to refer complaints to the complaints manager. The prime role of the complaints manager is to oversee the complaints procedure. The detailed role and functions of the complaints manager should be decided by the board.*

4.17 It is important to have one person in the organisation who has the overview of the whole complaints system.

The complaints manager may be
- the chief executive,
- a senior manager reporting directly to the chief executive, or
- particularly in large trusts, a senior manager reporting to the chief executive through another director, but with personal access to the chief executive when appropriate.

While it is not essential for the title to be used, it is nevertheless important that the individual with the role of complaints manager is easily identifiable to public and staff alike (see paragraph 4.20 for equivalent role in family health services practices).

4.18 It is for the trust/health authority to decide the exact role of its complaints manager. This role may be either to investigate or advise, or both. He/she needs to have access to all relevant trust/health authority records which are essential for the investigation of any complaint referred to them. He/she should be ready to respond to complaints where the complainant does not wish to raise their concerns with those directly involved with their care, or where front-line staff are unable to deal with the complaint. He/she should always bear in mind the need to consult with those who have been complained against in advance of any response being made to the complainant. The complaints manager needs to be able to provide guidance, help, and sometimes direct support, to other staff who are responding to complaints.

4.19 *Family health services practices must nominate one person to administer the complaints procedure and to identify that person to patients and clients.*

4.20 Family health services practices will decide who is most appropriate to be responsible for its complaints procedure, together with an alternate to act when this person is the subject of the complaint. Complainants may be unhappy at the prospect of having their complaint dealt with by someone who is already involved in their care and who may be the subject of the complaint. If contacted by a complainant, the health authority should be ready to provide assistance to both the complainant and the practitioner to resolve the complaint at practice level, bearing in mind the health authority may become formally involved if the decision is made to proceed to Independent Review (see paragraph 5.15).

Role of Community Health Councils and Patients' Advocates

4.21 Community health council staff have a very important role in assisting complainants at each stage of the process in both the hospital and community services and family health services. Trust and health authority chief executives, as well as family health services practitioners, should ensure advice on how to contact the local community health council for assistance in making a complaint is well publicised, and that community health councils are fully aware of the local arrangements for responding to complaints. The use of patients' advocates and interpreters to assist complainants, either employed directly or through a contract with a local voluntary sector organisation, is also commended. There can be positive advantages to both sides if a patient/complainant is encouraged to access the support of the community health council, or some other appropriate body or individual. The role of interpreting and explaining matters to and on behalf of a complainant may well help with the advancement of the process of Local Resolution.

Appointment of Convener

4.22 *Trusts/health authorities must appoint at least one person to act in the role of convener, who may not be one of its own employees: at least one of the persons appointed must be a non-executive of the trust/health authority.*

4.23 Every trust/health authority must appoint one or more of its non-executives to act as conveners for considering requests by complainants for Independent Review panels to be set up. The discretion to appoint more than one convener to this function is so that the role can be shared, and training of a successor or understudy can be organised more easily. It also provides for the possibility of an alternate convener representing the trust/health authority on the panel, if it is established, relieving the time pressures on the original convener, who may in any case have become involved in a second convening request. The concept of a 'lead' convener or 'convener's office' may be useful. The convener will need staff support. In organising this, the trust/health authority will need to demonstrate impartiality, for example, where the remaining grievance relates in some way to the handling of the complaint during Local Resolution.

4.24 Boards are required to appoint at least one of their non-executive directors as a convenor, who should be fully appraised of guidance and issues relating to the role of the convenor. Conveners may be appointed from any of the non-executives, although chairmen are recommended not to take on this role other than in exceptional circumstances. Trusts/health authorities should be very sensitive to any possible concerns about bias: the appointment to this role of non-executives who are practising or retired clinicians, or recently retired NHS staff, should be exceptional. It is recognised that some trust/health authority boards may wish to appoint additional people on a consultancy basis, specifically to act as conveners, in a similar manner to arrangements that are operated by some boards to help with Mental Health Act reviews of detention. Persons appointed specifically to take on this task may act in the full role of the convener, including serving on the panel. Their terms of appointment by the board should ensure that their role is explicit and that they have appropriate indemnity cover.

4.25 It is suggested that these appointments be for an initial period of at least two years but, where more than one is designated, the appointments might be staggered.

4.26 Conveners will be indemnified for this duty in the same way as for the other duties of non-executive directors.

Complaints and Disciplinary Procedures to be Separated

4.27 *Trusts'/health authorities' complaints procedures must be kept separate from their disciplinary procedures. Family health services practitioners' disciplinary procedures will be separate from the complaints procedure.*

4.28 Policy remains firm on the need for the new complaints procedure to be concerned **only** with resolving complaints and **not** with investigating disciplinary matters. The purpose of the complaints procedure is not to apportion blame amongst staff. It is to investigate complaints with the aim of satisfying complainants (while being scrupulously fair to staff) and to learn any lessons for improvement in service delivery. Inevitably, however, some complaints will throw up information about serious matters which indicate a need for disciplinary investigation.

4.29 In hospital and community/ambulance services, a case for considering disciplinary investigation can be suggested at any point during the complaints procedure, **but** consideration as to whether or not disciplinary action is warranted is a separate matter for management, outside the complaints procedure, and must be subject to a separate process of investigation.

4.30 **Trusts/Health Authorities**
In the case of trusts'/health authorities', papers that have accumulated during the investigation of the complaint may be passed to the appropriate person in the trust/health authority who will be considering the need for a disciplinary or any other form of investigation (see paragraph 4.32 for other relevant forms of investigation). Information gathered in the complaints process can be made available for a disciplinary investigation.

4.31 **Family Health Services Practitioners**
In the case of family health services practitioners there is an important change of procedure. While Service Committee procedures will not be used to investigate complaints made on or after 1 April 1996, formal complaints already under investigation before that date will need to be completed by the appropriate new health authority using the Service Committee procedures. From 1 April 1996, complaints will be investigated using the new procedure and the need for local disciplinary action will only be considered after the handling of a complaint has been concluded. Only if action is necessary to

protect patients, for example such as the need to involve the police, professional registration body, or the NHS Tribunal, would disciplinary investigation interrupt the handling of a family health services complaint. Information gathered in the complaints process by the practitioner as part of Local Resolution, belongs to the practice. This information will be kept separate from the patient's health record. Therefore the health authority has no right of access to it. A practitioner must consent to its release and it cannot be made available automatically for use in disciplinary investigations. However, the Ombudsman has wide-ranging powers which can be used, if necessary, to require the production of information and documents.

Hospital and Community Health Services

4.32 *If any complaint received by a member or employee of a trust/health authority indicates a prima facie need for referral to any of the following*

   i   *an investigation under the disciplinary procedure*
   ii   *one of the professional regulatory bodies*
   iii *an independent inquiry into a serious incident under Section 84 of the National Health Service Act 1977*
   iv   *an investigation of a criminal offence*

the person in receipt of the complaint should at once pass the relevant information to the complaints manager, who will ensure that it is passed on to a suitable person who can make a decision on whether and when to initiate such action: this reference may be made at any point during any stage of the complaints procedure.

Neither the complaints manager nor the convener shall be responsible for deciding whether to initiate any of the action referred to in i–iv above and they should refer such cases to the person designated in the trust/health authority for dealing with such matters. Where it is decided to take action under any of i–iv above before a complaint investigation has been completed, a full report of the investigation thus far should be made available to the complainant.

The complaints procedure will not deal with matters relating to that part of the original complaint which is currently the subject of disciplinary investigation. If action is initiated under i or ii above, the complainant should be advised accordingly so that appropriate action under the complaints procedure can be pursued where there are other matters raised in the complaint which do not relate to disciplinary investigation.

If any action is initiated under iii or iv above, the complaints procedure should be similarly modified until such action is concluded.

When any action under i–iv as set out above has been concluded, that part of the original complaint which has been referred to a different procedure should only recommence through the complaints procedure where there are outstanding matters in the complaint which have not been resolved through that action.

(**Note:** as far as health authorities are concerned, paragraphs 4.32 to 4.36 refer only to complaints about their own services or staff and do not apply to family health services practitioners.)

4.33 When a decision is made to embark upon a disciplinary investigation, the processing of the complaints procedure ceases in respect of all matters that are the subject of the disciplinary proceedings. There may well be other aspects of the original complaint, not covered by the disciplinary inquiry, that should continue to be investigated. It is essential for the person handling the complaint to make clear to the complainant that a disciplinary inquiry is now under way, particularly if the complainant is likely to be asked to take part in this process.

4.34 If there are no outstanding issues from the original complaint to be investigated, in which case the complainant should be advised that no further action will be taken other than that through the disciplinary procedure. The complainant may well ask at this point to be informed of the outcome of the disciplinary inquiry. A judgement will need to be made; on the one hand, in terms of reassuring the complainant, who will be concerned that the matter complained about has been dealt with seriously and satisfactorily; and on the other, the protection of the confidentiality of the member of staff. The guiding principle should be that, when the disciplinary procedure is invoked, the complainant receives the same consideration and level of information as if the matter had been dealt with through the complaints procedure. The complainant should be able to understand what happened, why it happened, and what action has been taken as a consequence to ensure that it does not happen again. The complainant should be informed in general terms of any disciplinary sanction imposed on any staff member.

4.35 It is most important that the complainant is satisfied with the action being taken by the trust/health authority. If a referral for disciplinary investigation has been made during the period of Local Resolution, then this part of the complaints procedure should be rounded off with a formal written explanation of the action taken by the trust/health authority. Where the referral is made later during the Independent Review process, then a similar written explanation needs to be given as part of the completion of this process. Within the context of the complaints procedure, the overall consideration must be that, even if the investigation has been moved into the disciplinary procedure, the complainant is not left dissatisfied, with the feeling that their grievance has only been partially dealt with.

4.36 A similar approach will need to be adopted in a case which has indicated the need for a referral to one of the professional regulatory bodies. A trust/health authority has no control over what then happens and over what period. The complainant should be similarly informed of this decision and, at this point, given as full a response as possible to the complaint, making it clear that any information obtained during the complaints investigation may need to be passed on to the regulatory body. Those parts of the original complaint not included in the reference to the professional regulatory body should continue to be investigated under the complaints procedure.

Possible Claims for Negligence

4.37 *The complaints procedure should cease if the complainant explicitly indicates an intention to take legal action in respect of the complaint.*

4.38 If a complaint reveals a prima facie case of negligence, or if it is thought that there is a likelihood of legal action being taken, the person in receipt of the complaint should inform the persons in the trust/health authority responsible for dealing with risk management and claims management. Even if a complainant's initial communication is via a solicitor's letter, the inference should not necessarily be that the complainant has decided to take formal legal action. A hostile, or defensive, reaction to the complaint is more likely to encourage the complainant to seek information and a remedy through the courts. In the early part of the process it may not be clear whether the complainant simply wants an explanation and apology, with assurances that any failures in service will be rectified for the future, or whether the complainant is in fact seeking information with formal litigation in mind. It may be that an open and sympathetic approach will satisfy the complainant. In a trust, where there is a prima-facie case of clinical negligence, the person dealing with the complaint should seek advice appropriately. This should not prevent a full explanation being given and, if appropriate, an apology offered to the complainant: an apology is not an admission of liability. If formal legal action has been instigated, the complaints procedure should be brought to an end, with the complainant and the complained against being advised appropriately in writing.

4.39 In all prima facie cases of negligence, or where the complainant has indicated the intention to start legal proceedings, the principles of good claims management and risk management should be applied. There should be a full and thorough investigation of the events. In any case where the trust/health authority accepts that there has been negligence, a speedy settlement should be sought.

You will notice a number of matters. First, the time limit of six months for bringing a complaint or within six months of discovering the problem with a 'long-stop' of 12 months from the date of the incident (para 4.11). But there is a discretion to extend the time limit where it would have been 'unreasonable … for the complainant to have made it earlier'. Note this is not the same as saying it is reasonable to allow the extension. The wording is more restrictive than that. Secondly, the complaints procedure must cease, presumably also not begin, where the complainant 'explicitly indicates an intention to take legal action' (for a case upholding the legality of this approach under the previous complaints system, see *R v Canterbury and Thanet DHA, ex p F and W* [1994] 5 Med LR 132 (DC)). The canny complainant would not do this explicitly, even if it was their intention, and the complaints process may unearth relevant material for future negligence litigation.

(ii) LOCAL RESOLUTION

This is at the heart of the new procedures and the guidance emphasises its importance.

NHS Executive *Complaints – Listening ... Acting ... Improving* (1996)

2.4   Ministers have laid great emphasis on resolving complaints as quickly as possible, particularly through an immediate informal response by a front-line member of staff or practitioner, or subsequent investigation and conciliation through staff who are empowered to deal with complaints as they arise, in an open and non-defensive way. Trusts, health authorities and family health services practitioners are urged therefore to concentrate their energies on developing the awareness of front-line staff to the value of satisfying complainants early on, and to establish clear protocols for an open, positive approach to responding to complaints as they arise. For this reason the successful handling of **Local Resolution** should be seen to be the key to the new procedure being successful.

We shall see later that local resolution is not without its problems, particularly in the case of GP complaints. The Government's guidance sets out the system of local resolution:

Trusts and Health Authorities

5.1   *As part of its complaints procedure, the trust/health authority must establish a clear Local Resolution process.* In the case of family health services, Local Resolution is the responsibility of the practitioner.

5.2   The primary objective of Local Resolution is to provide the fullest possible opportunity for investigation and resolution of the complaint, as quickly as is sensible in the circumstances, aiming to satisfy the complainant, while being scrupulously fair to staff. Trusts'/health authorities' complaints procedures must therefore have a well-defined Local Resolution process, which lays emphasis on complaints being dealt with quickly and, where possible, by those on the spot ... The intention of Local Resolution is that it should be open, fair, flexible, and conciliatory. The complainant should be given the opportunity to understand all possible options for pursuing the complaint, and the consequences of following any of these. This explanation should indicate that it might be necessary to look at the patient's health records. The community health council, and indeed any other patient's advocate, in advising and supporting the complainant will be invaluable in this process (see paragraph 4.21). The process should encourage communication on all sides. The aim should be to resolve complaints at this stage, and many should be capable of resolution orally. Local Resolution should not be seen simply as a run-up process to Independent Review: its primary purpose is to provide a comprehensive response that satisfies the complainant. The process of Local Resolution should provide for a range of different options for response to the complainant. Rigid, bureaucratic, and legalistic approaches should be avoided at all stages of the procedure, but particularly during Local Resolution. It is for trusts/health authorities to consider whether there would be advantage in offering access to conciliation (see paragraph 5.16).

Role of Front-Line Staff in Trusts and Health Authorities

5.3   Complaints are most likely to be initiated with front-line staff on the wards, in clinics, at reception desks, or to departmental managers. Management needs to empower front-line staff to deal with complaints on the spot. Local guidance needs to assist front-line staff in distinguishing serious issues which need reference elsewhere, and when to refer complaints for fuller investigation by – or coordinated through – the complaints manager. Steps need to be taken to ensure effective arrangements are in place for dealing with complaints that are received over the telephone. Steps should also be taken to ensure that complainants are made aware of the role of the community health council, and any other patient's advocate available to assist them in pursuing complaints, and how they may be contacted.

5.4   The first responsibility of a recipient of a complaint is to ensure – before doing anything else – that the patient's immediate health care needs are being met. This may require urgent action before any matters relating to the complaint are tackled. Staff should, where possible, deal with the complaint rapidly and in an informal and sensitive manner. Complaints may also be made to clinical staff or even to a member of the trust/health authority board. Whoever within the organisation the complaint is referred to should seek to understand the nature of the complaint and any nuances that are not immediately obvious. Where the recipient is unable to investigate the complaint adequately, or feels unable to give the assurances that the complainant is clearly looking for, then the complaint should be referred on to the complaints manager, either for advice or for handling. Complainants should be encouraged to speak openly and freely about their concerns and should be reassured that whatever they may say will be treated with appropriate confidence and sensitivity.

5.5 Some complainants may prefer to make their initial complaint to someone who has not been involved in their care. In these circumstances they should be counselled to address their complaints to the complaints manager or, if they prefer, to the chief executive. While front-line staff should always encourage complainants to be forthcoming in expressing their concern, apprehension, and anxiety, particularly where they are dissatisfied with the care they have received, this should never be done at the expense of overriding the right of complainants to make their complaint to the complaints manager or the chief executive.

5.6 Front-line staff also need to be empowered to use the information they gain from complaints to improve service quality, particularly oral comments or criticisms which are not actually complaints, where people want something put right or improved, not investigated. Mechanisms for achieving this can be agreed at team level and will be particularly important for sharing information relevant to the work of other teams, for example, those responsible for hotel services.

5.7 When deciding whether or not to pass an oral complaint on to the complaints manager, front-line staff, for example in trusts, will need to take into account the seriousness of the complaint and the possible need for more independent investigation and assessment. While an important role of the complaints manager is to investigate written complaints and to satisfy complainants, this must not preclude the complaints manager from advising front-line and other staff in the resolution of complaints.

Role of the Chief Executive

5.8 The chief executive of the trust/health authority must respond in writing to all written complaints and all oral complaints which are subsequently put in writing and signed by the complainant. In the case of an oral complaint, where the complainant is dissatisfied with the initial response and wants to pursue the matter further, the complaint should be put in writing and signed by the complainant.

5.9 The Citizen's Charter Complaints Task Force defined a complaint as 'an expression of dissatisfaction requiring a response'. In the majority of cases, complaints are made orally. All complaints, whether oral or written, should receive a positive and full response, with the aim of satisfying the complainant that his/her concerns have been heeded, and offering an apology and explanation as appropriate, with reference to any remedial action that is to follow. The chief executive will be responsible for ensuring there is appropriate local policy and procedural guidance available to all staff.

5.10 The Patient's Charter gives patients the right to a written reply from the relevant trust/health authority chief executive in response to a written complaint. The Ombudsman has criticised chief executives of NHS bodies for failure to sign written responses to complainants who have made written complaints, and Ministers have reaffirmed the importance which they attach to performance in this area. The reply might take the form of a full, personally signed, response or a shorter letter covering a fuller report from another member of staff, which the chief executive has reviewed and agreed. Some oral complaints are also sufficiently serious, or difficult to resolve, that they should be recorded in writing by the complaints manager. These complaints ought also receive a written response from the chief executive.

5.11 Consideration should be given to collecting data on oral complaints, even when they are not recorded in writing, so that lessons can be learned which may help with improving service delivery (see paragraph 10.4 on the collection of data on complaints).

5.12 Anyone handling a complaint, and particularly complaints managers handling written complaints, must ensure that any response given to a complainant which refers to matters of clinical judgement is agreed by the clinician concerned and, in the case of medical care, by the consultant responsible for the care of the patient.

5.13 There may be occasions when a communication is critical of a service or the quality of care, but is not intended as a complaint. Chief executives will wish to ensure that their organisations are receptive to comments and suggestions, whether critical or positive, as well as to complaints. Such communications are often a useful form of feedback from patients and their relatives, which can be used to improve quality of service, and also to give encouragement to staff when they are doing well.

Family Health Services Practitioners

5.14 From 1 April 1996 there will be a term of service obligation on family health services practitioners to have in place and to operate practice-based complaints procedures which comply with minimum national criteria:
   • administration of practice-based procedures will be practice-owned and managed entirely by the practice – the health authority will only become involved if the practice procedure does not appear to meet the national criteria

- health authorities will only become involved in an individual complaint if asked to do so by the complainant and/or the practitioner
- one person will be nominated by the practice to be responsible for overseeing the administration of the procedure
- practices must give the procedure publicity
- practices must ensure it is clear how to lodge a complaint and to whom
- an acknowledgement or initial response should normally be made within two working days
- the person nominated to investigate the complaint should make all necessary inquiries such as interviews, if appropriate, of the complainant, general practitioner(s) and practice staff
- an explanation should normally be provided within two weeks (ie ten working days).

It is in everyone's interest that Local Resolution at practice level is successful (see paragraph 1.6). General medical practitioners should keep records to help them bid to their health authority for additional funding under the staff reimbursement scheme to set up and operate new procedures, and health authorities are asked to consider reasonable bids favourably.

Action by the Health Authority

5.15 There are two roles for health authorities in the family health services Local Resolution process. Where, for example, a complainant does not wish for some reason to have a complaint dealt with by the practice, or is having difficulty in getting the complaint dealt with by the practitioner, health authorities will, if both parties agree, act as honest broker between the complainant and the practitioner to resolve the complaint at practice level. Health authorities will also make available lay conciliators as a service to complainants and practices. Arrangements for appointing lay conciliators and, when appropriate, professional advisers to the lay conciliators, is a matter entirely for the health authority. Patients and family health services practitioners need to feel confident in the new complaints system. When a health authority is acting as intermediary between patient and practitioner, providing conciliation or dealing with a request for Independent Review, it will be essential for health authorities to establish clear and constant lines of communication between patients and practitioners. This might be done via a named person in the health authority who can at all times give accurate information about a complaint's progress. Within the health authority, a 'need to know' procedure should be followed: only people who need to be involved in handling a complaint should be aware of its existence. Complaints about treatment provided under family health services arrangements may involve a statutory charge payable by the complainant. Health authorities will need to ensure that conciliators who may become involved fully understand the nature of such charges.

Family Health Services Conciliation

5.16 Conciliation may prove essential if complaints are to be resolved satisfactorily at practice level. Authorities must therefore continue to make conciliators available to practices where a conciliator's assistance is requested, either by the practice or the complainant (see paragraph 5.15). Confidentiality must be strictly observed during the conciliation process. Conciliation is essentially a process of reaching agreement between practitioner and complainant. As a result, conciliators should never be required to report to health authorities on the outcome of conciliations, although they are expected to provide progress reports on their activity from time to time, including informing the health authority when it has ceased. Nor should conciliators provide information which might then be used by the health authority should a complainant prove dissatisfied with Local Resolution and ask for Independent Review.

Completion of Local Resolution

5.17 There is a need to bear in mind that the right of the complainant to request the convener to set up an Independent Review panel is not a right to proceed automatically to Independent Review. The subtlety of this distinction may often be lost on complainants who may well be angry at the time as a result of their dissatisfaction with the outcome of Local Resolution. A clearly documented record of the events of Local Resolution – whether or not a final letter has been sent to the complainant – will assist in reducing the time the convener may have to spend researching the background of the complaint, in the event of an application by the complainant to proceed to Independent Review.

5.18 Trusts and Health Authorities

It may be appropriate for the entire process of Local Resolution to be conducted orally, without any written communication, leaving the complainant completely satisfied with

the outcome. However, where for example
- the person dealing with the complaint suspects the complainant may wish to consider taking the matter further or
- the complainant is satisfied with the oral response but has expressed the wish for a formal response to close the case,

it is recommended that Local Resolution may best be rounded off with a letter to the complainant. Any letter concluding the Local Resolution stage (whether signed by the chief executive because it was a written complaint, or by some other appropriate person) should indicate the right of the complainant to seek an Independent Review of the complaint, or any aspect of the response to it with which the complainant remains dissatisfied and that the complainant has twenty-eight days from the date of that letter to make such a request. This communication should be aimed at satisfying the complainant that the complaint has been fully and fairly investigated, with an appropriately couched apology where things have gone wrong, and what is to be done to prevent a recurrence.

5.19 Family Health Services Practitioners

Guidance to family health services practitioners does not differentiate between the handling of written and oral complaints. In both cases, practices are advised to round off the handling of the complaint by giving a written summary of the investigation and its conclusions to the complainant, also indicating the complainant's right to seek an Independent Review, and that the complainant has twenty-eight calendar days from the date of the letter to make such a request. Local Resolution will end at this point. Practices have been advised to keep detailed records of complaints handling – which they should separate from patients' medical records – both for the purpose of using complaints to improve procedures and services, and in case they are needed to enable the practice to cooperate with later stages of the complaints procedure, including Independent Review.

Performance Targets for Local Resolution

5.20 Recognising the primary purpose of Local Resolution is to satisfy the complainant whenever possible, while being scrupulously fair to staff, the following targets should be used with discretion. Where these targets are not being met, it is very important for the complainant to be informed of the delay and the reasons for it, as well as the likely revised timetable for dealing with the complaint. Similarly, where a complainant withdraws a complaint, it is important that the complained against and, in the case of family health services, the practitioner, are informed immediately.

5.21 Trusts and Health Authorities

Most oral complaints are resolved on the spot or within two working days. Where this is not possible, and for formal written complaints, trusts/health authorities should aim to make either an initial acknowledgement to the complainant within two working days or, if they are able to resolve the complaint fully within this time, to respond in five working days. For written complaints, and oral complaints recorded in writing, acknowledgements should always be in writing. Full investigation and resolution of all types of complaints should be sought within twenty working days, recognising however there is likely to be great variation in the nature of complaints and in the ability of complainants to cope with their part of the process. Given the complexity that arises in some complaints, a clear referencing and dating system is necessary for all communications with patients and family health services practitioners. First class post – or, exceptionally, special delivery mail – should be used in correspondence with complainants and practitioners. All communications should be marked 'Private and Confidential' and/or 'Personal'.

5.22 Family Health Services Practitioners

The aim should be for family health services practitioners to complete the Local Resolution process within ten working days. The possibility however of the health authority being asked to provide support or conciliation (see paragraphs 5.15 and 5.16) will inevitably extend the period of Local Resolution. In these cases it would not be unreasonable for the performance targets to be extended.

(iii) INDEPENDENT REVIEW

What happens if a complainant is dissatisfied with the outcome or process of local resolution – a not atypical event? The answer is that a complainant may within 28 days request that an 'independent review' be set up by the convenor. The government's guidance explains.

NHS Executive *Complaints – Listening ... Acting ... Improving* (1996)

Complainant's Action

6.1 *Complainants who are dissatisfied with the trust/health authority's response, or a practitioner's response, as a result of the Local Resolution process, may refer a request for an Independent Review panel to the convener either orally or in writing. This request should be made within a period of twenty-eight calendar days from the completion of the Local Resolution process. Any request for an Independent Review panel received either orally or in writing by any other member of or employee of the trust/health authority should be passed on to the convener immediately.*

6.2 The twenty-eight calendar days period refers to the period from the date of the letter to the complainant at the conclusion of Local Resolution, including conciliation where it is used (see paragraphs 5.15 and 5.16). A complainant may initially make a request for an Independent Review panel either orally or in writing. The time limit for making the request applies to the initial request and not to the making of the subsequent written statement to the convener (see paragraph 6.4).

Action by the Convener

6.3 The request should be followed up by the appointed convener immediately. The convener should make arrangements so that a complainant's request for an Independent Review panel will be acknowledged.

6.4 *Before deciding whether to convene a panel, the convener must obtain a statement signed by the complainant setting out their remaining grievances and why they are dissatisfied with the outcome of Local Resolution.*

6.5 The convener will want to understand as quickly as possible why the complainant remains dissatisfied. It is important for the convener to obtain the complainant's written statement, in as explicit and detailed a form as possible, before pursuing his/her inquiries. The convener will also need to alert the complained against, including any family health services practitioner who may be involved in the complaint, as soon as possible. The complainant should be encouraged to submit the written statement as quickly as possible when asked to do so by the convener, so that a response to the complainant's request for an Independent Review panel can be made within the twenty-eight days time limit. Experience shows that complainants frequently do not set out clearly what their grievances actually are, or set out clearly why they are dissatisfied with investigations already made. The convener should ensure that complainants are aware of how to seek independent help in drawing up such statements, if they wish, for example, from community health council staff and patients' advocates. Alternatively, the convener, or member of staff, may prepare the statement for the complainant's approval. If, however, the complainant has already clearly set out in writing their remaining grievances, and there is no need to amend this, the convener should not require a new statement to be drawn up. Complainants need to be advised of the various options that are open to the convener for dealing with the complaint at this stage.

6.6 Those who are complained against, including the family health services practitioner, should always be advised in writing of what the complainant has formally stated as his/her grievance. The initial communication to the practitioner advising that there is a request for Independent Review of a complaint involving them might usefully contain details of the secretary or other individual nominated by the local representative committee to help practitioners deal with complaints.

6.7 When dissatisfied with the outcome of Local Resolution, a complainant does not have an automatic right to move to Independent Review (see paragraph 5.17). There may be occasions when the convener feels that Local Resolution has been adequately pursued – in that the complaint has been properly investigated and an appropriate explanation given – and that nothing further can be done, although the complainant remains dissatisfied. The safeguard for the complainant lies in the right to put their case direct to the Ombudsman, should a convener decide not to establish a panel. The Ombudsman will be able to consider whether to recommend:
   • that the initial decision of the convener should be reconsidered
   • that it seems to him more appropriate, to investigate himself.

Role of the Convener

6.8 The role of the non-executive convener is crucial to triggering events under Independent Review ... It is important that he/she distances him/herself from those involved in the complaint. The convener's role is to ensure the complaint is dealt with impartially at the convening stage. It is not his/her function to defend those complained against, or the trust/health authority he/she represents, but rather to ascertain whether all opportunities for satisfying the complainant during Local Resolution have been explored and fully exhausted and what issues, if any, could be referred to a panel. To this end the convener will need to obtain a full picture of the events relating to the complaint. It is not the convener's role to try and resolve the complaint on his/her own.

6.9 Before making the decision on whether to convene a panel, the convener will consult with an independent lay panel chairman from the Welsh Office list. The purpose of this contact is to provide the convener with an external independent view and to aid him/her in assessing the grievance. it is, however, ultimately the convener's decision whether or not to recommend proceeding with the establishment of a panel and to explain why he/she has made this decision (see paragraphs 7.5 and 7.7 – role of the independent lay chairman).

6.10 The convener will decide on the panel's terms of reference. He/she should advise the complainant of any matters which the panel will **not** investigate, for example matters which the trust/health authority has decided should be subject to disciplinary investigation – except for family health services practitioners where disciplinary investigation is not an option at this stage – or matters that have already been dealt with adequately, and those which **will** be dealt with. The convener's statement to the panel outlining terms of reference should not be an interpretation or embellishment of the complainant's written grievance, but set out clearly and concisely what are the issues the panel should investigate. Similarly, the convener must make clear in writing the reasons for deciding against the setting up of a panel. Failure to do so will be criticised by the Ombudsman if the complaint is subsequently referred to him.

6.11 While the convener can decide that a panel be established, it must be set up formally as a committee of the trust/health authority.

Criteria for Establishing a Panel

6.12 *In deciding whether to convene a panel, the convener will consider, in consultation with an independent lay chairman from the Welsh Office list, whether:*
- *the trust/health authority/family health services practitioner can take any further action short of establishing a panel to satisfy the complainant*
- *the trust/health authority/family health services practitioner has already taken all practical action and therefore establishing a panel would add no further value to the process*
- *if either of the circumstances referred to above apply, the convener should not convene a panel. A panel should only be convened if the convener considers that it may be able to resolve the complaint and that nothing short of setting up a panel will do so.*

6.13 The convener will need to take full account of the advice of the independent lay chairman, although ultimately it is for the convener to decide whether or not to direct the establishment of a panel.

6.14 The convener should **not** consider the potential cost of setting up a panel as being a factor in his/her decision to recommend moving to Independent Review.

Clinical Advice to the Convener

6.15 *Where a complaint appears to relate in whole or in part to action taken in consequence of the exercise of clinical judgement, the convener must take appropriate clinical advice in deciding whether to convene a panel.*

6.16 The convener must take appropriate clinical advice in deciding whether to convene a panel when he/she considers a complaint relates wholly, or in part, to action taken in consequence of the exercise of professional clinical judgement – ie any judgement that is made by a member of the clinical professions in the NHS by virtue of their knowledge and skill, which a layman could not make. These will be known as 'clinical complaints'.

6.17 This process will be important in informing the convener about any particular clinical considerations which he/she should take into account, and whether, for instance, there is any further practical action which could still be taken through the Local Resolution process. The key lies in the concept of action taken in consequence of clinical judgement. Clinical judgement can be exercised by any of the recognised clinical professions working within the NHS to provide patient care: doctors, nurses, midwives, health visitors, dentists, pharmacists, optometrists, ophthalmic medical practitioners, clinical psychologists, members of professions supplementary to and allied to medicine, paramedics and ambulance technicians, laboratory and other scientific and technical staff. It is for the convener to decide whether a complaint appears to be a clinical complaint and from whom to seek appropriate clinical advice. Such advice is expected to come at least initially from within the trust/health authority, but not from anyone who is in any way associated with the complaint. It is recognised that advice may sometimes need to be sought from outside the trust/health authority.

6.18 In the case of trust, where clinical advice is needed, conveners are recommended to seek this initially from the medical or nursing director on their board, or the appropriate local professional head. Where the medical or nursing director, or the local professional head, is the subject of the complaint, or where possible conflict of interest arises, or where some other clinical opinion is appropriate, then the advice of an independent professional person should be sought. Such an adviser will be taken from the same list as the list of clinical assessors for panels.

6.19 In the case of family health services, clinical advice to the convener will come from an independent practitioner from the same profession as the practitioner who is being complained about, whose name will come from a list of practitioners, nominated by the relevant local professional representative committee, which is drawn up by the Welsh Office, or in the case of GP fundholders, by the local GP fundholding groups within Wales, or, by agreement, by local medical committees working with local GP fundholding interests.

Decision of the Convener

6.20 Conveners are advised that they should **not** set up an Independent Review panel where
- any legal proceedings have commenced, or there is an explicit indication by the complainant of the intention to make a legal claim, essentially on the same set of circumstances as the complaint, against a trust/health authority/family health services practitioner or one of their employees or
- it is considered the trust/health authority/family health services practitioner has already taken all practicable action and therefore establishing a panel would add no further value to the process: consideration of the cost of instituting an Independent Review is not an appropriate reason for refusing to proceed; or
- it is believed further action as part of Local Resolution is appropriate and practicable:
  - either, referral back by the convener to the trust/health authority chief executive, for further Local Resolution
  - or, an invitation by the convener to the family health services practitioner to reconsider Local Resolution, possibly with conciliation, as preferable to instituting the Independent Review process.
- it is considered there is a prima facie case for a disciplinary investigation (see paragraphs 4.30 and 4.31) so that referral by the convener to the person in the trust/health authority is considered appropriate: the setting up of an Independent Review panel would follow automatically if no disciplinary investigation was pursued.

6.21 *The convener must inform the complainant, and any person alleged in the complaint to have taken any part in the action complained of, in writing of his/her decision as to whether or not a panel should be appointed, setting out clearly the terms of reference if a panel is to be set up, or the reasons for any decision to refuse a panel, and whether or not he/she believes there is further action the trust/health authority/family health services practitioner could take.*

6.22 *Where a panel has been refused, the complainant should be advised of the right to complain to the Ombudsman.*

6.23 *The convener must inform the chief executive of the trust/health authority/family health services practitioner of his/her decision as to whether or not a panel should be set up or whether he/she believes there is further action which the trust/health authority/family health services practitioner should take as part of Local Resolution.*

Response to Complainant

6.24 Both the complainant and the complained about must be informed in writing of the convener's decision as to whether or not an Independent Review panel is to be set up. The convener should send to the trust/health authority chief executive and the family health services practitioner concerned, a copy of his/her communication which explains the decision to the complainant.

6.25 The convener must set out the reasons for any decision to refuse a panel as fully as possible so that the convener's views are clearly available should the complainant decide to exercise the right to refer the complaint on to the Ombudsman. This right should be recorded in the letter from the convener to the complainant. The intention is to ensure that the complainant is fully informed of the reasons for not convening a panel and, if appropriate, why the convener believes there should be a reference back to Local Resolution.

6.26 *If the complainant remains dissatisfied following the reference back to the trust/health authority/family health services practitioner for further action, he/she may refer the complaint once again to the convener to reconsider whether an Independent Review panel should be convened.*

Action by the Trust/Health Authority

6.27 In order to avoid delay, trust/health authority boards are advised to arrange for delegated powers to be given to the chief executive and an alternate executive director to establish a panel formally as soon as the decision of its convener becomes known. The convener will likewise advise the trust/health authority when he/she has decided against establishing a panel. If the recommendation of the convener is that Local Resolution should be reactivated, this should also be expedited by the chief executive.

Performance Targets for Convening

6.28 The convener will arrange for a written acknowledgement of the complainant's request for an Independent Review panel within two working days.

6.29 Convening should not be a re-run of the action taken during Local Resolution. While recognising that assimilation of facts, both written and oral, and the conduct of adequate consultation, all need time if they are to be exercised thoroughly, the period required for a decision to be made as to whether to convene an Independent Review panel should not normally exceed four weeks (ie twenty working days) from the date of the complainant's initial request being received by the convener ...

The independent review process itself involves a panel of three members, including an independent lay chairman, conducting a hearing into the remaining aspects of the complaint referred to the panel. In clinical cases, the panel will be assisted by two medical assessors.

NHS Executive *Complaints – Listening … Acting … Improving* (1996)

Purpose of the Panel

7.1 The purpose of an Independent Review panel is to consider the complaint according to the terms of reference provided by the convener and in the light of the written statement provided to him/her by the complainant. The panel will investigate the facts of the case, taking into account the views of both sides. It will set out its conclusions, with appropriate comments and suggestions, in a written report.

Establishing the Panel

7.2 *Independent Review panels will be composed of three members:*
- *independent lay chairman*
  (from the Welsh Office list)
- *convener*
  (non-executive of the trust/health or appointed person)
- *for trust panels, a representative of the purchaser*
  (either health authority non-executive or, if he/she wishes to be represented, a GP fundholder nominated by the fundholding practice which purchased the service concerned)
  In the case of, health authority panels or special hospital service panels, the third member of the panel will be another independent person from the Welsh Office list.
  Where the convener decides (after consultation with the independent lay chairman and after taking appropriate clinical advice) that the complaint is a clinical complaint, the panel will be advised by at least two independent clinical assessors from a list drawn up by the Welsh Office following advice from the relevant professional bodies.
  The panel is to be established as a committee of the trust/health authority and the assessors are to be appointed by the trust/health authority to advise the panel.

Recruitment & Appointment of Panel Members

7.3 The Welsh Office will be responsible for recruiting panel chairmen and lay panel members, and will organise training. Panel members will be chosen not only for their interest in the subject, but for their impartiality and judgmental skills and, where possible, experience in working in small groups, tasked with producing reports. An outline person specification has been prepared for this role. Recruitment will be in accordance with the equal opportunities policy and the cultural make-up of local communities should be taken into account. People held on the Welsh Office list for the role of panel chairman and third panel members for health authority panels will all be lay people. A prime consideration in their selection will be their independence and ability to act without bias. Practising members of the clinical professions will not be eligible and only exceptionally will recently retired NHS staff or lay non-executives of other trusts/health authorities be chosen. Some health authority boards may wish to recruit additional people on a consultancy basis specifically to act as the third panel member on Trust panels, in a similar manner to appointing additional people to act as conveners. The same principles should apply.

7.4   The Welsh Office will hold a list of independent lay chairman and lay panel members. Trusts and HAs operating locally and co-operatively will be responsible for establishing independent panels and selecting lay chairmen and members. For Trust panels the third panel member will come from the health authority or GP fundholder as representative of the purchaser. Call-off from these lists should be organised in a balanced, independent way, so that no one lay chairman or panel member becomes regularly linked with a particular trust/health authority and geographical bias is avoided.

7.5   It is for trusts/health authorities to issue formal letters covering the appointment of panel members to serve on a specific panel, including indemnity cover, and to ensure that arrangements are made to let panel members have appropriate background and briefing papers, together with the names of the assessors who have been appointed to assist their particular panel. Trusts/health authorities should inform the complainant of the panel members and assessors appointed to conduct the Independent Review.

Role of the Independent Lay Panel Chairman

7.6   The role of the independent lay panel chairman is in two parts ... first, to help the convener by providing independent advice and support during the convening period; second, to chair the panel when established. The convener will consult with an appropriate person chosen from the Welsh Office list of chairmen. The trust/health authority will formally appoint the panel chairman, bearing in mind the need for indemnity cover in respect of the advice given to the convener during the convening period.

7.7   Once the convener's decision has been made to establish an Independent Review panel, and he/she has set out the terms of reference for the panel, responsibility for leading the organisation of the panel's business then falls to its chairman. Arrangements should be established locally within each Health Authority area to ensure that the administration of this function is managed by the Health Authority and relevant Trusts acting co-operatively. It is for the relevant bodies to agree the details of these arrangements; options might include rotating responsibility for the function, establishing a joint secretariat or agreeing that the function should alternate between the HA and Trusts acting corporately.

Functioning of the Panel

7.8   *The function of the panel is to:*
   - *investigate the aspects of the complaint set out in the convener's terms of reference, taking into account the complainant's grievance as recorded in writing to the convener*
   - *make a report setting out its conclusions, with appropriate comments and suggestions.*

The panel will have no executive authority over any action by the trust/health authority, or family health services practitioner, and may not make any suggestion in its report that any person should be subject to disciplinary action or referred to any of the professional regulatory bodies.

7.9   The panel should be proactive in its investigations, always seeking to resolve the complainant's grievance in a conciliatory manner, while at the same time taking a view on the facts it has identified. The panel should be flexible in the way it goes about its business, choosing a method or procedure appropriate to the circumstances of the complaint. It should not allow confrontational situations to arise. Resolution of the complaint may be sought by the full panel, with its assessors, through separate meetings with the complainant and the complained against. It is a matter for the panel to decide whether the complainant and the complained against should be brought together at the same meeting; similarly whether smaller meetings involving, say, any one member of the panel, with or without assessors, are appropriate in the circumstances.

7.10   *The panel will decide how to conduct its proceedings, having regard to guidance issued by the Welsh Office, within the following rules:*
   - *the panel's proceedings must be held in private*
   - *the panel must give both the complainant and any person complained against a reasonable opportunity to express their views on the complaint*
   - *if any of the panel members disagree about how the panel should go about its business, the chairman's decision will be final*
   - *when being interviewed by any members of the panel or the assessors, the complainant and any other person interviewed may be accompanied by a person of their choosing, who may, with the agreement of the panel chairman, speak to the panel members/assessors, except that no person interviewed may be accompanied by a legally qualified person acting as an advocate.*

7.11 The panel will have access to all the records held by the trust/health authority relating to the handling of the complaint; family health service practitioners will be asked to make available their records of the handling of the complaint. If the complaint is a clinical complaint, the panel must have access to the relevant parts of the patient's health record.

7.12 The panel has discretion as to how it should operate. It has a duty to keep responsible records, bearing in mind the possibility of a future investigation by the Ombudsman. Panels should work informally and be flexible in their approach in order to respond appropriately to differing kinds of complaint. The panel chairman will be the final arbiter. The panel process should not be a tribunal process involving formal cross-examination of witnesses: nor should it be confrontational. Panels should not operate in an adversarial, legalistic way. Neither the complainant, nor anybody mentioned in the complaint who is interviewed by the panel, may be legally represented. However, the complainant, and anybody mentioned in the complaint, when being interviewed by the panel, or meeting with individual panel members of the assessors, may be accompanied by a person of their choosing to provide support and advice, but if this adviser is legally qualified he/she may not act as an advocate. A complainant who is accompanied by an adviser may, if desired, be accompanied by a second person, such as a relative, for emotional support. Only with the approval of the panel chairman may those accompanying the complainant, or any other person interviewed, contribute to the panels' proceedings.

Identification of Assessors

7.13 *Where the complaint is wholly or partly related to clinical maters, panels must be advised by at least two independent clinical assessors on relevant matters. The independent clinical assessor's role is to advise and make a report, or reports, to the panel on the clinical aspects of complaints. The assessors should decide, in consultation with the panel, how to exercise their responsibilities, having regard to guidance issued by the Welsh Office and their professional bodies.*

7.14 The role of an assessor is to advise the panel or its individual members. Assessors should not act independently to resolve a complaint. Where a complaint raises issues about more than one medical specialty or health care profession, at least one assessor for each relevant medical specialty or health care profession should be available to advise the panel. In cases where only one discipline is under scrutiny there will be two assessors from the relevant discipline. In some cases it may be appropriate for there to be more than two assessors and it will be for the panel chairman to make this decision.

7.15 The Welsh Office will hold national (England and Wales) lists of assessors for hospital and community health services and an all Wales list of assessors for family health services and GP fundholder complaints, and assessors with experience of exercising clinical judgement in a purchasing context.

7.16 The professional bodies' role in ensuring that lists of appropriate independent assessors, who are acceptable to the profession concerned, are kept up to date, is crucial to ensuring the general standing and efficacy of the assessor system.
   • The Joint Consultants Committee has undertaken to continue this role for hospital medical and dental staff.
   • The Central Committee for Community Dental Services of the British Dental Association will undertake this role for community dentists.
   • Nursing professional bodies will, in close collaboration with trust nurse executive directors, and other senior nurses, ensure that appropriate independent nursing assessors, acceptable to the profession, are identified.
   • Local representative committees will pass on to the Welsh Office names of appropriate assessors in family health services (for GP fundholder see below).
   • Those professional bodies who represent other professions which might be involved will ensure that national lists are available to the Welsh Office.
   • Assessors for GP fundholder complaints will be nominated to the Welsh Office by recognised local fundholding groups working in conjunction with local medical committees.
   • Health authorities will be required to nominate clinicians with experience in exercising clinical judgement in a purchasing context to act as assessors.

Nomination of Assessors

7.17 Trusts/health authorities will need to ascertain the availability of assessors before making formal appointments. Normally assessors for hospital and community health services complaints will be selected from names of those working outside Wales. In the case of family health services panels, assessors should be chosen from a list drawn up by the Welsh Office of assessors nominated by the local representative committees or, in the case of GP fundholders, by recognised local GP fundholding groups working in conjunction with local medical committees. Family health services assessors should not come from within the health authority area of the practice or practitioner against whom the complaint is made. When selecting assessors, it will be important to ensure that they have no connection with any of the parties to the complaint which might call into question their independence or objectivity in respect of the complaint in question. When there is doubt about the choice of an assessor, the appropriate professional body should be contacted.

Appointment of Assessors

7.18 Responsibility for communicating with and ascertaining availability, and formally appointing the chosen assessors will rest with trusts/health authorities, who should issue formal letters covering their appointment to assist a specific panel, including indemnity cover. They will ensure that arrangements are made to let the assessors have appropriate documentation.

Release of Assessors

7.19 The role of the assessor is crucial to the success and impartiality of the new complaints procedure. If the role is to be carried out thoroughly and successfully, then assessors will need to be granted prompt release from their commitments. Trusts and other employers are encouraged to recognise that the system of assessors will only work successfully if there is recognition that release needs to be granted quickly, so that delays in the complaints process can be avoided (see paragraph 7.51).

Role of Assessors

7.20 The role of the assessors is to advise the panel, as and when required, on those aspects of the complaint involving clinical judgements...

7.21 *At least one assessor must be present when the panel, or a member of the panel, interviews either or both of the parties on occasions when matters relating to the exercise of clinical judgement are under consideration.*

7.22 The assessors must have access to all the patient's health records held by the trust/ health authority/family health services practitioner relating to the handling of the complaint. Assessors will need to acquaint themselves of any circumstances where a patient might be denied access to information in the record, or where the patient has expressed the wish for information to be withheld from other parties.

7.23 Assessors may interview/examine complainants, who may if they wish have a person of their choosing present. Assessors should check whether the patient has ever been denied access to all or part of their health record. Where the complainant is not the patient, care must be taken not to disclose information which would breach the patient's-confidence. Care must also be taken not to break third-party confidence. Assessors should not normally explain their findings to either the patient or complainant at this stage, before advising the panel of their views.

7.24 Similarly, assessors may interview any person complained against, who may have a person of their choosing present. Assessors should not normally explain their findings to the complained against before advising the panel of their views.

7.25 There may be occasions when a patient's health record is no longer in the possession of the complained against (including a family health services practitioner against whom the complaint has been made). In these circumstances, every effort should be made by the trust/health authority to provide the complained against with access to it for the purpose of framing a response. In the case of a family health services practitioner, if it is inappropriate to return the health record, then the whole, or relevant part of, the record might reasonably be photocopied or, alternatively, inspected at the health authority's premises.

Assessors' Reports

7.26 It will be open to assessors to provide combined or individual reports. The assessors' reports should **not** be made available to the complainant – or the consultant/clinician complained about – in advance of the reports being made available to panel members. The panel may decide, in consultation with the assessors, to release their reports to the complainant and the complained against, particularly if it is believed this will aid resolution of the complaint. Otherwise assessors' reports will only become accessible to them as part of the panel's final report, initially as a draft (see paragraph 7.30).

7.27 Assessors should take care – since their reports may be made available at a later date to others than just panel members – to ensure their reports contain no information which might cause serious harm to the physical or mental health of the patient or of any individual, or contains information about, or provided by, a third party (other than a health professional involved in the patient" care) who can be identified from the information, unless he/she has consented to its disclosure.

7.28 *The assessors' reports must be attached to the panels' final report when it is issued. If the panel disagrees with the assessors' reports it must state in its report the reasons for doing so.*

7.29 If the panel chairman finds it appropriate, for example, to meet the complainant as a way of rounding off resolution of the complaint, where there are assessors of different disciplines, each should be present if the complaint relates to clinical matters, in order to give a personal explanation to the complainant of any clinical findings.

Panel's Final Report

7.30 The panel may find it helpful to provide the complainant and any people complained against the opportunity to check a draft report – which may not necessarily include the final conclusion of the panel – for factual accuracy within, say, a period of fourteen days, before it is issued formally in its final form. The assessors' reports should be made available in time for their preliminary circulation with the panel's draft report. Those receiving the draft should be reminded that the report is confidential to them and the panel members. The complainant and anyone complained against should be asked to inform the panel if he/she wishes to consult on the content of its draft report with an adviser who has not been previously involved in the complaint, eg the community health council. The responsibility for ensuring the panel finalises its report within the target time limit ultimately rests with the panel chairman.

7.31 *The panel's final report must be sent to:*
 * *the complainant*
 * *the patient, if a different person from the complainant and competent to receive it*
 * *any person named in the complaint*
 * *any person interviewed by the panel*
 * *the clinical assessors*
 * *the trust/health authority chairman and chief executive*
 * *in the case of complaints against family health services practitioners/GP fundholders, the practitioner concerned*
 * *the Welsh Office*
 * *the chairman and chief executive of the independent provider, where the complaint is about services provided by the independent sector*
 * *the health authority chairman and chief executive or GP fundholder who purchased the service concerned.*

 The report will have a restricted circulation. The panel shall not send it to any other person or body. Panel chairmen have the right to withhold any part of the panel's report and all or part of the assessors' reports in order to ensure confidentiality of clinical information.

7.32 The panel's final report should set out the results of its investigations, outlining its conclusions, with any appropriate comments or suggestions. The panel may **not** make any recommendations or suggestions in its report relating to disciplinary matters.

7.33 The complainant may wish to show the report to a representative of the community health council or other appropriate adviser. The chief executive may need to show the report, or sections of the report, to board members. A family health services practitioner may need to show the report, or part of the report, to colleagues in their practice. These, and any similar arrangements, will need to protect the overall confidentiality of the report.

Follow-up Action by Trust/Health Authority Boards

7.34 *Following receipt of the panel's report, the chief executive must write to the complainant informing them of any action the trust/health authority is taking as a result of the panel's deliberations and of the right of the complainant to take their grievance to the Ombudsman if they remain dissatisfied.*

7.35 Trust/health authority boards need to consider what arrangements are necessary for ensuring action is taken on the outcome of Independent Review panel reports, and that subsequent action in individual cases has been taken forward as agreed by the board. Boards are also responsible for ensuring that their decisions are communicated quickly and clearly to the complainant.

Completion of the Complaints Procedure

7.36 It will need to be made very clear to the complainant when the NHS complaints procedure has been completed. The Ombudsman will normally only embark on an investigation when NHS processes have been exhausted.

7.37 **Trusts/Health Authorities/GP Fundholders**

Completion of the complaints procedure for trusts and health authorities – except in cases of complaints involving family health services practitioners (see paragraph 7.42) – is when the chief executive writes to advise the complainant of both the outcome of the consideration by the trust/health authority board of the panel's report and the complainant's right to complain to the Ombudsman if still dissatisfied. It is recognised that it may take a trust/health authority board some time to consider precisely how it will respond to a panel's report, particularly if these are for policy review or changes which require the board to consult with others before making a final decision. Nevertheless, the chief executive should endeavour to communicate to the complainant in writing – within not more than twenty working days from the publication of the panel's report – any matters such as a formal apology; approval of an ex-gratia payment; or an indication of the timescale in which their board has agreed to consider policy issues; plus information about the right of the complainant to complain to the Ombudsman if still dissatisfied. If, following this action, the board takes any further decisions relating to the outcome of the case, then the complainant should be appropriately informed by the chief executive.

7.38 Completion of the complaints procedure for complaints about services purchased by health authorities or GP fundholders from the independent sector, is when the panel's report is sent to the complainant by the health authority chief executive. The chief executive should send the panel's report to the complainant and the independent provider under suitable covering letters as soon as possible after receiving it. The covering letter must advise the complainant of the right to refer their complaint to the Ombudsman if still dissatisfied. If the panel has commented about the possibility or desirability of making changes to the services purchases by a health authority, which are the subject of the complaint, the chief executive should consider, in consultation with the provider as necessary, how those services can be improved and the implications for the health authority's purchasing policy. The chief executive will then wish to follow up the panel's report with a further letter setting out any changes which have been decided on.

7.39 In cases of care purchased by a GP fundholder, the chief executive will also send the panel report to the fundholder. Where suggestions have been made about improvements to a service which has been purchased by a GP fundholder, the chief executive will want to tell the complainant that he is inviting the fundholder to respond personally to the complainant on those matters. Likewise, when the chief executive is writing to the fundholder, he will want to suggest that a response goes from the practice direct to the complainant.

7.40 For services purchased by trusts from the independent sector, the normal trust complaints procedure will apply.

7.41 **Family Health Services Practitioners**
Completion of the complaints procedure is when the panel's report is sent to the complainant by the chief executive. The chief executive should send the panel's report to the complainant and the practitioner under suitable covering letters as soon as possible after receiving it. The covering letter must advise the complainant of the right to complain to the Ombudsman if still dissatisfied. It the panel has commented about the possibility or desirability of making changes to a practitioner's services or organisation, the chief executive will want to tell the complainant that he is inviting the practitioner to respond personally to the complainant on those matters. Likewise, when the chief executive is writing to the practitioner, he will want to suggest that a response goes from the practice direct to the complainant.

Administrative Support, Fees, and Expenses
7.42 The trust/health authority will provide any administrative support which the convener, the chairman, and the panel and its assessors need. All the expenses arising out of the Independent Review process, including any payments and expenses paid to assessors, and expenses and loss of earning allowances paid to panel members, will be met by the trust/health authority establishing the panel.

7.43 Trusts/health authorities will need to agree the level of local administrative support that will be necessary for the convening and Independent Review processes, bearing in mind the fluctuating nature of the demand for this support. The Welsh Office will shortly be arranging to meet each of the 5 Health Authority complaints managers together with the respective Trust complaints managers in each Health Authority area to discuss the detailed arrangements for providing administrative and secretarial support for the Independent Review process.

Panel Members
7.44 Panel members, including conveners, will be eligible to receive travel expenses, and subsistence and loss of earnings allowances.

7.45 Trusts/health authorities should indicate in appointment letters that the particular panel chairman and third panel member will be appropriately indemnified.

Assessors

7.46 Arrangements for payments to independent clinical assessors of all professions while advising a particular panel, together with eligibility for travel expenses and subsistence allowances, will be advised separately.

7.47 Arrangements for funding locum expenses of certain family health services practitioners, and the responsibility for the payment of locum in respect of other assessors, will be advised separately.

7.48 Assessors will be formally appointed by trusts/health authorities to a particular panel and as such will be covered for indemnity while carrying out their role as advisers.

7.49 Where assessors find it more convenient to make their own arrangements for, say, typing their reports, they will need to agree a rate of payment with the trust/health authority in advance.

Performance Targets for Panels

7.50 **Trusts and Health Authorities**

In the case of complaints against trusts or health authorities, the formal appointment of the panel members and assessors should be made within four weeks of the convener's formal letter informing the complainant of the decision that a panel will be set up. While complaints are bound to vary in complexity, a panel should aim to complete its work within twelve weeks of the formal appointment of the panel members and assessors. The chief executive of a trust/health authority should write to the complainants within four weeks of the panel's final report informing them of any action the trust/health authority is taking as a result of the panel's report and of their right to complain to the Ombudsman. Thus the overall target for the Independent Review process is six months from the date when the complainant first request a panel to the date when the chief executive writes following the panel's report.

7.51 **Family Health Services Practitioners**

In the case of family health services complaints, the aim is for panels to complete their work within three months of the date on which the complainant approached the convener with the request for a panel to be set up.

You will notice that the panel is almost acting in a quasi-judicial capacity and yet the convenor, who decided whether to hold the panel hearing, is a member of it. Further, the convenor is usually a non-executive director of the Trust or Health Authority. You will also see the rather tight timescale for the procedure. And, finally, you will notice that the Trust or Health Authority is closely connected in the administration of the panel's functions. These, as we shall see, may be problematic, at least in the perception of complainants.

(iv) HEALTH SERVICE COMMISSIONERS

The Health Service Commissioner sits at the apex of the new NHS complaints procedure. There are separate commissioners for England and Wales. Here, we concentrate on the provisions relating to the former. He becomes involved following completion of the 'independent review' stage. But he might also investigate where a convenor has decided not to hold a panel hearing since the NHS procedures (below him) are then complete.

The work and workload of the Health Service Commissioner's Office for 1997–98 is set out in his Annual Report for that year (HC (1997–98)811) and is summarised in a memorandum he submitted to the House of Commons Select Committee on Public Administration, through which he is accountable to Parliament (Health Service Commissioners Act 1993, Sch 1). (The Welsh Commissioner is accountable to the National Assembly for Wales (Health Service Commissioners Act 1993, Sch 1A).)

Select Committee on Public Administration *Annual Report of the Health Service Ombudsman for 1997–98* HC (1997–98) 811

THE WORK OF THE OFFICE

Workload and investigation time

4. The total number of complaints the Ombudsman received last year increased by 20 per cent on the previous year, to 2,660. But the number of grievances investigated in 1997–98 (270) is lower than in any year since 1988–89. The Annual Report gives as one of the reasons for this the small number of investigations which have been carried forward from the previous year, a by-product of the work in reducing backlogs on which we commented in last year's Report. The other reason is the small number of cases which were accepted for a full investigation. Mr Buckley told us that the proportion of complaints accepted for a formal investigation was very low, at only about 4 per cent of all complaints. The reason for this is that most complaints about administrative handling could be more quickly and effectively dealt with by other means, and many of the clinical complaints related to events which took place before April 1996, and therefore pre-dated the extension of the Ombudsman's jurisdiction to clinical issues. The Deputy Health Service Commissioner, Miss Nisbet, told us that many of the complaints had to be returned to the complainants because they had not exhausted the NHS complaints procedure, and "often had not even started trying. They simply wrote to the Ombudsman because they thought that was a good idea". One thousand complaints were rejected for this reason. A similar number (989) were rejected because there was insufficient evidence of maladministration: as Miss Nisbet said, "for example, somebody has written in distress because their elderly parent died, but they do not say why they thought this was failure of service" …

6. The average time taken to complete investigations was reduced during 1997–98 to 45 weeks. This is "the lowest figure for at least a decade and a considerable improvement on the figure in the mid-1990s" (*ibid*, para 4.16). The table below shows how the average time to complete investigations has changed since 1990. The reduction this year is partly a result of the smaller number of investigations undertaken for the reasons given above. This may not continue, and sustaining the reduction may be a challenge. As the Ombudsman notes in his Business Plan for 1998–99, investigations of complaints about family health service practitioners or the exercise of clinical judgement tend to take longer than nine months, because "their early stages were slower than those of 'traditional' investigations". As they become more common, the Ombudsman's Office may therefore find itself under more pressure to meet its targets. There are also indications that the attempt to resolve as many complaints as possible locally may be only temporary. The Ombudsman's Business Plan says that "from 1998/99 … there will be more scope for HSC to investigate substance, particularly when there is little cause for confidence that further local action will resolve matters. In the last three months of 1997/98, significantly more statements of complaint were issued than in the earlier months, and that trend is expected to continue during 1998/99". This seems to be recognised in the estimate in the 1998–99 Business Plan that the average time taken to complete investigations will go back up to 50 weeks.

Year	90–1	91–2	92–3	93–4	94–5	95–6	96–7	97–8
Grievances investigated	487	442	476	436	508	546	551	270
Average time to complete investigations	58	45.1	45.3	48.6	59.9	66.2	55.9	45

7. Last year we suggested that the Ombudsman should aim to complete all but the most intractable investigations within seven months, rather than the nine months which was his target for 1997; we said that we accepted that this might mean additional resources or new methods of working but believed that the Government should be prepared to allot these if they are required. The Ombudsman responded in his evidence to us that he would "certainly aim to keep to a minimum any delays caused by working practices within my Office". The main difficulty he identified in reducing the time taken for investigations any further was the fact that clinical investigations "inevitably rely heavily on the contributions of external assessors who have many other important demands on their time – including, of course, the care of patients". The Ombudsman's targets for this year appear to reflect this problem: the aim is for 75 per cent of non-clinical investigations completed on or after 1 April 1998 to be completed within 6 months, and for no case of this type to take longer than 9 months; and 75 per cent of clinical investigations which begin on or after 1 April 1998 to be completed within 9 months, and for no case of this type to take longer than 12 months. **It is certainly right for the Ombudsman to use clinical assessors who are practising clinicians, and who therefore are likely to take longer to complete reports. However, we would assume that when choosing clinical assessors, he will choose those who are able to meet reasonably tight deadlines, and will seek to ensure that those deadlines are met. More**

broadly, if there are serious difficulties in achieving further reductions in the time taken to conduct investigations, we would expect the Ombudsman's Office to specify more clearly what those difficulties are. Cases still take far too long to be completed, particularly when many of them have already been through the full gamut of the NHS complaints procedure before reaching the Ombudsman. As we have said before, if the delays can be resolved through additional resources, we believe that the Ombudsman should request, and be given them.

The HSC's jurisdiction and powers are set out in the Health Service Commissioners Act 1993, as amended by the Health Service Commissioners (Amendment) Act 1996, the National Health Service (Primary Care) Act 1997 and the Health Act 1999.

The historical background to the HSC's role is discussed by Vivienne Harpwood in the following extract.

Vivienne Harpwood 'The Health Service Commissioner: The Extended Role in the New NHS' (1996) 3 European Journal of Health Law 207

The powers of the Health Service Commissioner are consolidated in the Health Service Commissioners Act 1993 (Chap 46), but can be traced back to 1973 when the office was established. In theory at present there are three Health Service Commissioners, one for England, one for Wales and one for Scotland, but in practice the Parliamentary Commissioner for Administration, (the Ombudsman), William Reid, who retired in 1996, combines all three posts. In Northern Ireland the position is covered by separate legislation, and there the equivalent post is held by the Commissioner for Complaints who holds the posts of both Health Service Commissioner and Parliamentary Commissioner for Administration. Despite the new culture of health care in the UK, the powers of the Health Service Commissioner have remained substantially the same since for over twenty years. It is therefore not surprising that recommendations were made to expand the role. These have been enacted in the Health Service Commissioners (Amendment) Act 1996. As the Health Service Commissioner is appointed by the Crown, he is independent both of Parliament and the NHS.

Since 1973 individuals have been able to approach the Health Service Commissioner directly with a request to investigate any alleged injustice or hardship caused by (a) a failure in a service provided by a "relevant body" or (b) a failure of such a body to provide a service which it was the function of the body to provide, or (c) maladministration connected with any other action taken by or on behalf of such a body (Health Service Commissioners Act 1993, s 3 (1)). Under the new NHS structure, the Commissioner has also been able to investigate matters arising from arrangements between health service bodies and bodies outside the NHS, such as private clinics which agree to provide services for NHS patients (1993 Act, s 7(2)(b)), and matters concerning NHS contracts, and complaints about purchasing, though some of these powers needed clarifying.

"Relevant bodies" about which complaints could be made under the 1993 Act included Health Authorities, NHS Trusts, Family Health Service Authorities, (now part of Health Authorities), which provide primary care to patients and various other bodies responsible for the provision of NHS care. However, complaints about primary health care practitioners (GPs, opticians, dentists and pharmacists), and about clinical judgment of medical practitioners, were excluded from his jurisdiction at this time.

An addition to the jurisdiction of the Health Service Commissioner came into effect on the first of June 1995 when the Government's Code of Practice on Openness became operational. Members of the public may complain to the Health Service Commissioner about infringements of the Code of Practice after first complaining to the body or person concerned.

Other exclusions on his jurisdiction to investigate include disciplinary and personnel matters (s 7(1)) and commercial or contractual transactions unless arising out of NHS contracts (s 7(2)).

Let us now turn to consider the provision of the Health Service Commissioners Act 1993 (as amended) in detail.

First, what is the jurisdiction and functions of the HSC? Until 1996, the HSC's jurisdiction extended to maladministration by NHS bodies, including Health Authorities, NHS Trusts and Special Health Authorities. He had no jurisdiction to investigate in three areas: (1) where clinical judgment was involved; (2) family health services provision, eg GPs; and (3) provision by independent providers of NHS care. All three of these restrictions were removed by the Health Service Commissioners (Amendment) Act 1996 and the HSC's jurisdiction was further extended to providers of 'personal medical services' (and others) under 'pilot schemes' by the National Health Service (Primary Care) Act 1997 (Sch 2, para 68) and to Primary Care Trusts by the Health Act 1999 (Sch 4, para 85). These provisions are not retrospective and only apply to events on or after 1 April 1996.

Sections 2, 2A, 2B and 3 of the 1993 Act (as amended) provide as follows:

S 2(1) The bodies subject to investigation by the Health Service Commissioner for England are
(a)   Health Authorities whose areas are in England,
(c)   Special Health Authorities to which this section applies exercising functions only or mainly in England,
(d)   National Health Service trusts managing a hospital, or other establishment of facility, in England,
(da) Primary Care Trusts established for areas in England,
(e)   ...
(f)   the Dental Practice Board, and
(g)   the Public Health Laboratory Service Board ...
   (4) References in this Act to a "health service body" are to any of the bodies mentioned above.
   (5) The Special Health Authorities to which this section applies are those—
(a)   established on or before 1st April 1974, or
(b)   established after that date and designated by Order in Council as ones to which this section applies.
   (6) A statutory instrument containing an Order in Council made by virtue of subsection (5)(b) shall be subject to annulment in pursuance of a resolution of either House of Parliament.
S 2A(1) Persons are subject to investigation by the Health Service Commissioner for England if they are persons (whether individuals or bodies) undertaking to provide in England general medical services, general dental services, general ophthalmic services or pharmaceutical services under the National Health Service Act 1977 if they are—
(a)   individuals undertaking to provide in England general medical services or general dental services under Part II of the National Health Service Act 1977;
(b)   persons (whether individuals or bodies) undertaking to provide in England general ophthalmic services or pharmaceutical services under Part II of that Act; or
(c)   individuals performing in England personal medical services or personal dental services in accordance with arrangements made under section 28C of that Act (except as employees of, or otherwise on behalf of, a health service body or an independent provider).
S 2B (1) Persons are subject to investigation by the Health Service Commissioner for England if—
(a)   they are persons (whether individuals or bodies) providing services in England under arrangements with health service bodies or family health service providers, and
(b)   they are not themselves health service bodies or family health service providers ...
   (4) The services provided under arrangements mentioned in subsection (1)(a), ... may be services of any kind.
   (5) In this Act references to an independent provider are to any person providing services as mentioned in subsection (1), (2) or (3).
S 3(1) On a complaint duly made to a Commissioner by or on behalf of a person that he has sustained injustice or hardship in consequence of—
(a)   a failure in a service provided by a health service body,
(b)   a failure of such a body to provide a service which it was a function of the body to provide, or
(c)   maladministration connected with any other action taken by or on behalf of such a body, the Commissioner may, subject to the provisions of this Act, investigate the alleged failure or other action ...
   (1ZA) Any failure or maladministration mentioned in subsection (1) may arise from action of—
(a)   the health service body,
(b)   a person employed by that body,
(c)   a person acting on behalf of that body, or
(d)   a person to whom that body has delegated any functions.

(1A) Where a family health service provider has undertaken to provide any family health services and a complaint is duly made to a Commissioner by or on behalf of a person that he has sustained injustice or hardship in consequence of—

(a) action taken by the family health service provider in connection with the services,

(b) action taken in connection with the services by a person employed by the family health service provider in respect of the services,

(c) action taken in connection with the services by a person acting on behalf of the family health service provider in respect of the services, or

(d) action taken in connection with the services by a person to whom the family health service provider has delegated any functions in respect of the services,

the Commissioner may, subject to the provisions of this Act, investigate the alleged action.

…

(1C) Where an independent provider had made an arrangement with a health service body or a family health service provider to provide a service (of whatever kind) and a complaint is duly made to a Commissioner by or on behalf of a person that he has sustained injustice or hardship in consequence of—

(a) a failure in the service provided by the independent provider,

(b) a failure of the independent provider to provide the service, or

(c) maladministration connected with any other action taken in relation to the service,

the Commissioner may, subject to the provisions of this Act, investigate the alleged failure or other action.

(1D) Any failure or maladministration mentioned in subsection (1C) may arise from action of—

(a) the independent provider,

(b) a person employed by the provider,

(c) a person acting on behalf of the provider, or

(d) a person to whom the provider has delegated any functions.

(2) In determining whether to initiate, continue or discontinue an investigation under this Act, a Commissioner shall act in accordance with his own discretion.

(3) Any question whether a complaint is duly made to a Commissioner shall be determined by him.

(4) Nothing in this Act authorises or requires a Commissioner to question the merits of a decision taken without maladministration by a health service body in the exercise of a discretion vested in that body.

(5) Nothing in this Act authorises or requires a Commissioner to question the merits of a decision taken without maladministration by—

(a) a family health service provider,

(b) a person employed by a family health service provider,

(c) a person acting on behalf of a family health service provider, or

(d) a person to whom a family health service provider has delegated any functions.

(6) Nothing in this Act authorises or requires a Commissioner to question the merits of a decision taken without maladministration by—

(a) an independent provider,

(b) a person employed by an independent provider,

(c) a person acting on behalf of an independent provider, or

(d) a person to whom an independent provider has delegated any functions.

(7) Subsections (4) to (6) do not apply to the merits of a decision to the extent that it was taken in consequence of the exercise of clinical judgment.

(For the relevant provisions applicable to the HSC in Wales see: ss2(2); 2A(2); 2B(2) and 2B(2A); and 3 (1YA).)

You will notice that there can only be an investigation where the complainant alleges he has 'sustained injustice or hardship', (s 3(1)). Likewise, this must arise from a 'failure' in a service or to provide a service or 'maladministration' by the 'health service body' (s 3(1)), GP – whether Part II practitioner or 'pilot-scheme' provider – (s 3(1A)), or 'independent provider' (s 3(1C)). In each case this may arise as a result of action by the provider, an employee of the provider, a person acting on his behalf or someone to whom he has delegated his functions (s 3(1ZA), s 3(1A), s 3(1D) respectively). Notice also that the HSC may not 'question the merits of a decision taken without maladministration' (s 3(4), (5) and (6)). This limitation does not, however, extend to investigations into 'clinical judgments'. Section 3(7) disapplies s 3(4)-(6) in this circumstance. Hence, in this new area of jurisdiction, the HSC's power to investigate is greater than in the case of administrative decisions.

Commenting on this disparity in his powers, Diane Longley states:

Diane Longley 'Complaints After Wilson: Another Case of Too Little Too late?' (1997) 5 Med L Rev 172

Whilst the merits of clinical complaints may be investigated the merits of administrative failures may not. These are restricted to hardship or injustice arising from maladministration. This may make it difficult for the Ombudsman to investigate fully a complaint about purchasing and policy decisions which are often dictated by financial considerations rather than clinical ones. The distinction between administrative and clinical matters in these circumstances is likely to be fine. It is for the Ombudsman to decide whether such a complaint falls within his jurisdiction.

Apart from the extension of jurisdiction to primary care providers, probably the most significant extension was in 'clinical judgment' cases. Vivienne Harpwood examines this new jurisdiction and the historical background.

Vivienne Harpwood 'The Health Service Commissioner: The Extended Role in the New NHS' (1996) 3 European Journal of Health Law 207

In recent years an estimated 25% of cases rejected for investigation by the Commissioner have concerned clinical judgment, *(Select Committee on the Parliamentary Commissioner for Administration, "The Powers, Work and Jurisdiction of the Ombudsman", HC Session 1993–4, para 110)*. Complaints about the clinical judgment of any health care professional were excluded from the jurisdiction of the Health Service Commissioner. "Clinical judgement" was not defined in the Act, and it was left to the Commissioner to decide in each case whether clinical judgment was involved. However, it was generally accepted that wrong diagnosis and treatment could not be the subject of an investigation by the Commissioner.

All too frequently complaints involve allegations both of maladministration and failings in clinical judgement, and such complaints could be dealt with only in part. A recent example from the Health Service Commissioner's Report for April to September 1995 illustrates this point, *(case No E.93/4–95 – Care of an elderly person and unsatisfactory handling of a complaint)*. An elderly woman had fallen at home, and with the help of her son, she sought medical attention at the Accident and Emergency Department of her local hospital. She was discharged from there after her left knee had been x-rayed, despite complaining of pain in her hip and being unable to walk or sit. The following day she was admitted to an elderly care ward and was transferred to another hospital three days later where x-rays revealed fractures to both femurs. She died very soon afterwards. Among other complaints the son maintained that the x-ray taken at the A and E Department should have been obtained by the elderly care unit, and that his mother should have had a bone scan, as it was recorded in her notes that a bone scan was necessary. The son complained to the Trust but the response was extremely slow and the matter was not handled sympathetically. Although the Commissioner was very critical of the dilatory and unsatisfactory response to the complaint, he could not investigate the issues surrounding the bone scan because he considered these to be matters of clinical judgment.

Although excluded from the Commissioner's jurisdiction, clinical complaints have been investigated under the hospital complaints system since 1981, though the Select Committee Report on the Ombudsman in 1993 *(para 110)* condemned this system as "*designed for the convenience of providers of the service rather than of the complainants*". The Wilson Committee in its Report on NHS Complaints (*"Being Heard" HMSO 1994 para 107)*, described the handling of hospital clinical complaints as "*an exercise in damage limitation*". The system did not take into account the recent NHS reforms, and in many cases it was difficult to separate matters of clinical judgment from other aspects of treatment. It was subject to many delays, and was frequently seen as lacking impartiality, as there was no involvement of lay-persons and complainants were not kept abreast of developments in the investigation.

In considering reform of the Complaints system, the Wilson Committee was of the opinion that if a layperson is to be used in the investigation of clinical matters, the Health Service Commissioner would be the obvious candidate for the task, as he already had considerable experience in other dealing with aspects of medical complaints and faced the difficult responsibility of deciding what constituted "clinical judgement". The Select Committee Report in 1993–4, *(1 para 110)*, was ambivalent and contradictory in its views on the use of the

Commissioner to deal with matters of clinical judgement. On the one hand the Report recognised that the Commissioner was *"more than competent to examine such cases"*, and that such a role would introduce greater unity to the Complaints system in the light of the anticipated recommendations of Wilson Committee. On the other hand the Report expressed serious reservations about the enormous increase in work which would undoubtedly be introduced by including clinical complaints in the jurisdiction of the Commissioner. At the time, William Reid himself took the view that such an addition to his workload would require the recruitment of many more staff and would possibly require the separation of the offices of Parliamentary and Health Service Ombudsman. The paragraph dealing with this matter in the 1993–4 Report concluded ambiguously:

> We recommend that clinical judgment remain outside the Health Service Ombudsman's jurisdiction under the existing arrangements, although we believe that the Health Service Commissioner should be seen as the apex of any unified NHS complaints system that may be introduced.

In the event the 1996 Act (section 6) allows the Commissioner to investigate matters of clinical judgment.

Secondly, let us consider how a complaint may be brought.
Who may complain? Section 8(1) and 9(1)–(4) provide as follows:

S 8(1) A complaint under this Act may be made by an individual or a body of persons, whether incorporated or not, other than a public authority.
S 9(1) The following requirements apply in relation to a complaint made to a Commissioner.
  (2) A complaint must be made in writing.
  (3) The complaint shall not be entertained unless it is made—
(a) by the person aggrieved, or
(b) where the person by whom a complaint might have been made has died or is for any reason unable to act for himself, by—
    (i)   his personal representative,
    (ii) a member of his family, or
    (iii) some body or individual suitable to represent him.
  (4) The Commissioner shall not entertain the complaint if it is made more than a year after the day on which the person aggrieved first had notice of the matters alleged in the complaint, unless he considers it reasonable to do so.
  (5), ...
  (6) ...

A 'health service body' (ie Health Authority NHS Trust or PCT) may also refer a complaint to the HSC if received by it from a person who alleges maladministration (s 10).

What are the limitations on investigation? An important limitation here is the time limit of one year in s 9(4). It should be noticed that the HSC has a discretion to extend that period if it is 'reasonable to do so'. Vivienne Harpwood discusses this limitation (*op cit*) at 216–218.

> Complaints which are more than twelve months old are rarely investigated, as it is often difficult to obtain adequate information concerning stale complaints, and it is regarded as unfair on health care professionals that they should be in fear of complaints being made against them after a long period of time has elapsed. As William Reid himself explained:
>
> *This time limit makes sense in protecting professionals from being in permanent jeopardy and also because of the difficulty of getting at the truth when a considerable time period has elapsed.*
>
> (see Reid WK, Appendix to House of Commons Library Research Paper 95/126 December 1995).
>
> There is a clearly a need for some time limit to be placed on the making of a complaint to the Commissioner, but it is difficult to accept that this should differ from that of three years which is placed on claims in civil litigation cases. Apart from obvious evidential problems which also exist in relation to litigation, there is no particular reason for there being a different time limit on complaints to that which applies in civil actions. Many of the potential complainants who are excluded by a one-year time limit could be those who have suffered

the most. Grief or ill-health suffered at the hands of NHS staff may cause temporary inertia or diffidence, and one year may not give such people sufficient time to recover and lodge complaints. From the patient's perspective, the desire to protect staff from the fear of complaints is surely not a good enough reason for imposing a time limit of a single year. The fact that better-informed and well-organised people are able to make their complaints at an early stage does not make sufficient allowance for less aggressive and articulate members of society. It may often be the case, in the words of the poet Yeats that "*The best lack all conviction, the worst are full of passionate intensity*", (Yeats WB, "The Second Coming")

It is important that flexibility be exercised if the complainant is compromised by mental or physical ill-health of bereavement.

Flexibility would also be desirable where the NHS complaints process, at whose apex the HSC sits, has itself exhausted the 12-month period. It should not govern the time schedule we have seen but in practice these are rarely met (see *infra*).

Two further limitations are worth noting. First, the complainant must exhaust the NHS complaints procedure first unless it would not be reasonable to expect that. As we have said, the HSC is now the third stage of that procedure.

S 4(4) Subsection (5) applies where—
(a) action by reference to which a complaint is made under section 3(1), (1A) or (1C) is action by reference to which a complaint can be made under a procedure operated by a health service body, a family health service provider or an independent provider, and
(b) subsection (1), (2) or (3) does not apply as regards the action.
    (5) In such a case a Commissioner shall not conduct an investigation in respect of the action unless he is satisfied that—
(a) the other procedure has been invoked and exhausted, or
(b) in the particular circumstances it is not reasonable to expect that procedure to be invoked or (as the case may be) exhausted.
    (6) Section 1(2) of the Hospital Complaints Procedure Act 1985 (which provides that no right of appeal etc conferred under section 1 of that Act is to preclude an investigation under this Act) shall have effect subject to subsection (5) above.

The exception might arise in the following situation. Vivienne Harpwood (*op cit*) at 225 explains:

The Commissioner himself envisaged such circumstances as arising for example, when there is excessive delay in deciding whether to set up an independent review panel, or where there is evidence of an irretrievable breakdown in the confidence of a complainant in the local procedures, (see "Responsibilities of the Health Service Commissioner", Office of the Health Service Commissioner, Dec 1995).

Secondly, the HSC must not investigate where the complainant has a legal remedy before a court or tribunal, again unless it is not reasonable to expect the complainant to pursue that course.

Section 4(1) provides:

S 4(1) A Commissioner shall not conduct an investigation in respect of action in relation to which the person aggrieved has or had—
(a) a right of appeal, reference or review to or before a tribunal constituted by or under any enactment or by virtue of Her Majesty's prerogative,
or
(b) a remedy by way of proceedings in any court of law,
unless the Commissioner is satisfied that in the particular circumstances it is not reasonable to expect that person to resort or have resorted to it.

Vivienne Harpwood (*op cit*) at 223–234 examines this exclusion:

This is a grey area in which the complainant may suffer injustice by being refused an investigation by the Commissioner on the grounds that the case is one in which litigation would be appropriate. Yet he or she may not be able to obtain legal aid and may be unable to afford the cost of bringing an action in the courts. On the other hand it would be unfair if the Commissioner proceeded with an investigation and upheld a complaint, only to open the way to litigation by having produced all the relevant evidence and made a recommendation in favour of the complainant. However, the Commissioner does not have the power to prevent the commencement of litigation by a complainant, he can merely refuse to investigate a complaint if the circumstances suggest that litigation is appropriate.

Obviously, the legislation seeks to prevent "fishing expeditions" by which would-be litigants seek to establish whether they are likely to win a civil action at public expense by using the good offices of the Commissioner. However, the strict application of this rule may work injustice in individual cases. The same problem has arisen in connection with the system for dealing with hospital complaints, (see Harpwood V, "Medical Negligence Claims and NHS Complaints", Professional Negligence, vol 10, 3, 1994, 73–81). In that context it was been held in *R v Canterbury and Thanet District Health Authority, South East Thames Regional Health Authority Ex Parte F & W, ([1994] 5 Med LR 132)*, that the decision of a Health Authority to abort the investigation into a complaint where litigation was likely was lawful. The case is important because it explores the reasons why the investigation of a complaint is inappropriate where litigation is likely. The reasons given by Stuart Smith LJ included the view that medical staff co-operate in the investigation of complaints, but are less likely to do so if they fear that litigation may be pending, and that in a claim for negligence a far more searching enquiry is likely to be made into the allegations because Courts have the power to subpoena witnesses and to cross examine them on oath. While that is so in the case of the ordinary hospital complaints system which does not involve the Commissioner, the position is rather different if the complaint proceeds to the Commissioner, because he does have significant powers in relation to calling witnesses and obtaining documents, and it would appear that the Commissioner may be in at least as strong a position as a Court to carry out a rigorous investigation and to make appropriate recommendations.

One important distinction between the powers of the Commissioner and those of a Court is that the Commissioner does not have the same power as a Court or Tribunal to award compensation, but can merely recommend the payment of out of pocket expenses. It does appear that in certain cases, such as those discussed above, there are some complainants who fall into a privileged position if the Commissioner decides to investigate their complaints. They are those who are only interested in receiving out of pocket expenses rather then the wider forms of compensation which the courts can award, for pain and suffering, bereavement, nervous shock, future loss of earnings and so on, and who can take their complaint to the Commissioner in the knowledge that they will not be burdened with costs if the complaint proves groundless. They can thus avoid the uncertainty, delay and expense of litigation and are still able to obtain financial recompense for their grievances. This is a discrepancy which it is difficult to reconcile, and it will remain the case that there will be people with genuine grievances who will be unable to obtain redress, either from the Commissioner or through the Courts.

We will return later to the remedies the HSC has at his disposal.

What is the nature of the process of investigation?

S 11(1) Where the Commissioner proposes to conduct an investigation pursuant to a complaint under section 3(1), he shall afford—
(a)   to the health service body concerned, and
(b)   to any other person who is alleged in the complaint to have taken or authorised the action complained of,
an opportunity to comment on any allegations contained in the complaint.
   (1A) Where a Commissioner proposes to conduct an investigation pursuant to a complaint under section 3(1A), he shall afford—
(a)   to the family health service provider, and
(b)   to any person by reference to whose action the complaint is made (if different from the family health service provider),
an opportunity to comment on any allegations contained in the complaint.
   (1B) Where a Commissioner proposes to conduct an investigation pursuant to a complaint under section 3(1C), he shall afford—
(a)   to the independent provider concerned, and
(b)   to any other person who is alleged in the complaint to have taken or authorised the action complained of,
an opportunity to comment on any allegations contained in the complaint.
   (2) An investigation shall be conducted in private.
   (3) In other respects, the procedure for conducting an investigation shall be such as the Commissioner considers appropriate in the circumstances of the case, and in particular—
(a)   he may obtain information from such persons and in such manner, and make such inquiries, as he thinks fit, and

(b)   he may determine whether any person may be represented, by counsel or solicitor or otherwise, in the investigation.

(See also s 12 in respect of evidence and the production of documents.)

What is the outcome of an investigation? The HSC must produce a report to the complainant and the NHS body and, if initiated by an MP, to that MP (s 14). (For the HSC in Wales and his duty to report see, s 14A.) The HSC may also make recommendation to the health body on how to improve their services. He may also recommend that an *ex gratia* payment or apology be made.

Vivienne Harpwood 'The Health Service Commissioner: The Extended Role in the New NHS' (1996) 3 European Journal of Health Law 207

An important aspect of the Commissioner's power is that which enables him to comment upon his findings and to make recommendations if a complaint is upheld. Such recommendations cover a wide range of matters, highlighting the need for health bodies to provide better guidance to medical staff, to review certain practices and to improve complaints-handling mechanisms. The Commissioner may recommend that a particular decision be changed, or that administrative changes be made so that other people do not suffer in future. the Commissioner's decisions are final, unless completely new evidence is produced, when a new investigation may be possible.

7.1   Power to recommend ex gratia payments

While the Commissioner does not have the power to award compensation in the same way as a court of law, an increasingly significant function of the Commissioner is the recommending of ex gratia payments to cover out-of-pocket expenses, where these would provide the best remedy to complainants. The Commissioner's view of this was brought to public attention as long ago as 1988:

> *If I uphold a complaint I generally recommend that the relevant authority grant a remedy. If the remedy I recommend is the introduction or review of administrative procedures this will not be of direct benefit to the complainant. But when they approach me many complainants say that their purpose in doing so is to prevent, if they can, a recurrence of the event which gave rise to their grievance and I believe, therefore, that they achieve some satisfaction from such an outcome. More direct benefit occurs in these cases where I find that a complainant has been caused unnecessary expense due to maladministration by an authority, when I recommend that an ex gratia payment should be made.*

(Introduction to the Annual Report of the Health Service Commissioner for 1987–8, para 6).

A much publicised example of the recommendation of an ex gratia payment attracted considerable media attention in 1994. This concerned a matter of great public debate, relating to the responsibility of Health Authorities for the provision of certain forms of care for infirm people. The complaint related to a man aged fifty five years who had had a stroke in 1989 which had left him with severe brain damage. The hospital in which he had been receiving treatment informed his wife that no more could be done to improve his condition, and the bed was needed for other more acute cases. The man still needed nursing care and was discharged to a medical bed in a private nursing home, at a net cost of £6,000 a year. The complaint to the Commissioner by the patient's wife alleged that an injustice had been suffered because her husband's condition met the criteria which justified treatment paid for by the Health Authority. The issue was essentially one of resources, as the Health Authority claimed that it would be impossible to remain within its budget if it were to provide funding for long term nursing beds in cases such as this. The Commissioner up-held the wife's complaint on the grounds that failure to provide long term care was unreasonable and amounted to a shortcoming in the service provided by the Health Authority. He recommended a payment to her by the Health Authority of a sum to cover the nursing home costs to date. He also recommended that in future the fees for her husband's nursing care should be paid by the Health Authority. He suggested a general review of the policy by which patients were being excluded from NHS care in such cases, (Health Service Commissioner's Second report for 1993–4. Failure to provide long term care for a brain damaged patient (HC 197, 1994).

Another example of the Commissioner's intervention in the controversial area of resource allocation, again concerning the long term nursing care of a stroke patient (Report for the period from April to September 1995, (E264, 94–95)). The wife of the patient in question was awarded the sum of £5,000 to cover out of pocket expenses at the recommendation of the Commissioner.

This type of recommendation which results in the payment of large sums by way of "out of pocket expenses" to the complainant has a special significance because the Commissioner can only investigate matters which cannot be dealt with by litigation. However, there is a very fine line between "out-of-pocket expenses" and compensation for a past financial loss. Bringing a complaint before the Commissioner could become a route to obtaining what is, in reality, compensation. This route is more expeditious and less expensive then pursuing the matter through the Courts.

7.2   Recommendation of an apology

There are many examples in the Commissioner's Reports of emphasis on the need for an apology to be made whenever a grievance is found to be justified. In his 1988 Report, for example, the Commissioner highlighted the importance of the recommendation of an apology to the complainant:

> *This is not, however, the ineffectual outcome that some may suppose. On the one hand it is generally welcomed by the complainant, who sees it as a vindication of his having raised and persisted with his complaint, on the other hand it emphasises to the authority and its staff that they have in fact erred in some way.*

In that year, 1987–8, there were 114 complaints where the Commissioner thought it appropriate that the authority offer an apology, and only eight in which an ex gratia payment was recommended ...

As we have seen, the HSC cannot make an enforceable order requiring the health service body to do anything in the way that a court can. At best, he may make a special report to Parliament if he considers someone has sustained 'injustice or hardship' which has not been, or will not be, remedied (s 14(3)). Thereby, he may 'name and shame' health service bodies – his reports are subject to absolute privilege for the purposes of defamation (s 14(5)) – and as a result have a considerable practicable effect in gaining redress for the patient.

Can the HSC do more if he considers that the complaint has shown that a health care professional is a danger to patients? Can he, for example, inform the employer, the professional disciplinary body such as the GMC or UKCC or the Commission for Health Improvement? Section 15(1) imposes a duty of confidence upon the HSC.

> S 15(1) Information obtained by a Commissioner or his officers in the course of or for the purposes of an investigation shall not be disclosed ...

However, disclosure in the circumstances contemplated would be justified under s 15(1)(e) and (1B) (see *infra*, ch 8). The HSC has a duty to inform the person to whom the information relates (and from whom it was obtained) that he has made the disclosure (s 15(1C) as substituted by s 43(5) of the Health Act 1999).

(d) Criticisms of the 'new' NHS complaints system

The new system has been in operation since 1 April 1996. There have been suggestions that the system is not working as it should. In the course of its inquiry into *Procedures Related to Adverse Clinical Incidents and Outcomes* (HC 549-I, Session 1998–99), the House of Commons Select Committee on Health looked, in some detail, at the NHS complaints procedure and heard evidence critical of its operation:

> 72. According to the evidence we heard, the introduction of a new system had not eliminated criticisms of the complaints procedure, especially in respect of the system's accountability and independence. In particular, patients complained of inconsistencies across the country in the way in which similar matters were dealt with. AVMA called for greater openness and a simplification of the procedures. This corresponded with the Health Service Commissioner's comments on the complexity of the procedures.

73. We also received evidence from the Consumers' Association who carried out a survey in 1997 of patients who had complained. They found that over 40 per cent of respondents were unhappy with the overall way that their complaint had been handled and more than one third did not feel that appropriate action was taken to prevent the problem from happening again. There was also strong feeling that the NHS, and in particular hospital complaints managers and NHS Chief Executives, did not accept responsibility for what happened.

74. The Public Law Project also undertook an independent national evaluation of complainant's views and made their report available to us. They concluded that:

- the initial investigation of the complaint was often poor;
- the convener was not seen as independent;
- the convener and the IRP chair were uncertain of their roles;
- there was a lack of consistency between different areas;
- there was a lack of training for complaint handlers; and
- there was too little external monitoring, and it was therefore unclear how well complaints were reviewed and whether action was taken by GPs or trusts.

75. The Department of Health is currently funding an evaluation of the complaints procedure with an interim report due next year. The aim is to review how the system is working, its strengths and weaknesses, and to recommend improvements. **We welcome this review but recommend that the Department of Health addresses any early indications of problems as quickly as possible.**

Local resolution and the initial investigation

76. Local resolution should allow complaints to be dealt with quickly, flexibly and at the point of complaint. We believe it is a good idea in principle to allow those directly involved to resolve their differences quickly. It also allows an opportunity for conciliation at an early stage. However evidence to us suggested that the initial investigation was not always well conducted. The Health Service Commissioner told us that 40 per cent of complaints addressed to him were sent back because the local procedure had not been exhausted. The Public Law Project's research showed that almost half of the requests for independent review were sent back by the convener for a further attempt at local resolution often because there had been an inadequate investigation of the grievances. This is a strong indication that the initial investigation must be improved.

77. Patients were also dissatisfied with the way their complaint was initially handled. Clearly, patients, their relatives and carers who are unhappy with the service they have received, are entitled to a full and truthful account of the events which occurred. However we were concerned to hear that this was not always given. Witnesses were often dissatisfied with the explanations they received. They felt that these were superficial, biased or did not address all their areas of concern. Patients sometimes felt the version of events presented by NHS staff were more readily believed.

78. Another difficulty with the current system is that there may be several different investigations of the same incident. The Secretary of State commented:

... [a] huge amount of investigatory time is being put in. You could easily have four investigations into one incident – by the local management because there has been a complaint about their outfit, into a complaint from the person concerned or their relative, you could have legal action which would involve investigation and you could have an investigation by the General Medical Council and the UKCC. ... what I would like to see is ... whether it would be possible to have what might be described as a common investigation.

79. **It is clear that the initial investigation of a complaint needs to be much more thorough and should be carried out by well-trained, dedicated staff. We believe that the report from investigations relating to adverse clinical incidents or potential adverse clinical incidents must contain a detailed account of events and be robust enough to be used by other bodies, such as the GMC and UKCC, NHS disciplinary committees, or the courts. It should also contain a recommendation for further action. The implementation of its recommendations should be monitored as part of clinical governance. We recommend that the Department of Health provides a proforma to trusts and health authorities encompassing all the steps which need to be completed as part of the investigation**

80. A key factor in the quality of investigations is the resources available to carry them out. At present each trust and health authority must employ a complaints manager. We heard that these staff were not always adequately trained. There were also concerns that complaints officers were not sufficiently senior. **We recommend that trusts be encouraged to appoint a quality and risk manager with sufficient training, authority and personal skills to**

deal with complaints and bring these issues to Board level where the appropriate action can be taken.

81. We heard other criticisms of local resolution, not just related to the quality of the investigation. Patients felt that there was a defensive attitude from NHS staff. They felt that the responses they had received were inadequate and did not give a full enough explanation. They also considered that no remedial action had been taken to prevent the same thing happening again. In particular witnesses were concerned about the amount of time that the complaints process took. We address this in more detail in paragraphs 100 and 101.

82. Some complaints may be about apparently minor issues, such as staff discourtesy. Others may have serious implications for patient safety and may need to be addressed quickly by a more formal body. **We recommend that the complaints manager in charge of the initial investigation sifts complaints to ensure that those which may contain serious allegations about staff performance and which could endanger future patient care are dealt with speedily and passed to an appropriate authority where necessary. The Department of Health should issue guidance on the types of complaints which would need to be passed on quickly.**

83. Local resolution in principle provides an opportunity for conciliation between complainant and the NHS organisation. Conciliation is one part of this but this method of complaint resolution may be used differently in different areas. It is important that trusts and health authorities do everything in their power to satisfy the complainant, including explaining possible avenues of redress. **We recommend that existing conciliation practices are evaluated to enable good practice to be identified and disseminated.**

The convener

84. A number of bodies, as well as witnesses to us, have expressed concerns about the role of the convener. The Select Committee on Public Administration noted that: "Previous reports of the Health Service Commissioner and this Committee have commented on the poor performance of some conveners and the conduct of IRPs. In his latest Annual Report the Health Service Commissioner has expressed concern at the continuing failure of conveners and IRPs to learn from experience. We took evidence from patient representative bodies and organisations of widespread lack of confidence in these stages of the complaints procedure."

85. Conveners are a vital link in the procedure as they act as gatekeepers to the independent review of complaints following the failure of local resolution. It is crucial that they consider patients' requests for independent review in a fair and impartial way. We found a widespread perception amongst patients, their relatives and carers that conveners were biased because they were members of the trust or health authority board. Witnesses were understandably unhappy if their request was turned down and were inclined to perceive such an outcome as a cover up. The Public Law Project research found similar concerns. Indeed they discovered that 46 per cent of conveners themselves considered it was difficult to maintain independence.

86. Other criticisms of conveners were that they were unclear about their role or carried out their role in an inconsistent way. Some attempted to resolve the complaint themselves, a job which is outside their remit. There was confusion as to whether conveners should deal directly with patients. Furthermore conveners based in a single trust did not necessarily amass a great deal of experience. The Public Law Project's survey showed that trust conveners who had been in post for two years had considered on average only nine requests for independent review.

87. At every stage of the process witnesses were unhappy with the apparent lack of independence; they relied heavily on the Health Service Commissioner and the courts to inject a degree of impartiality which they did not otherwise find. Because the complaints procedure has developed as a "flexible local arrangement" its procedures do not appear to be transparent. The guidance issued by Department of Health is general and there are no suggested good practices. Patients heard of others' complaints being handled differently from their own and could discern no rationale as to why one request for independent review was accepted and another declined. This problem is exacerbated by the perception that the convener is not independent. We put our concerns to the Secretary of State who accepted that criticisms had been voiced, but felt that most people were satisfied with the procedure.

88. **We consider that it is vital that the NHS complaints procedure is made more open and transparent and that the system is seen to be fair and independent. We make recommendations on how this might be done at the independent review stage below. We recommend that the role of convener as it currently stands be abolished. Patients, their relatives and carers who would like an independent review of their complaint should apply directly to the IRP for "leave to appeal". This is similar to those going through the legal process who apply to the court of appeal.**

Independent Review Panels

89. Some witnesses felt strongly that they needed an independent person, such as the Health Service Commissioner, to consider all complaints. We put this to the Health Service Commissioner. He considered it would alter the nature of his work if he were to preside over an inspectorate and noted that any active intervention at an earlier stage would have resource implications and would dilute the work he and his team were already doing. Patients are of course entitled to refer their complaint to the Health Service Commissioner if they are dissatisfied with its outcome, although they must exhaust the local procedures first. We believe that, particularly for serious complaints, it is important that there is an impartial, formal investigation and reconsideration of the complaint if local resolution fails.

90. This role is currently carried out by the IRPs which are established to investigate the complainant's grievances and issue a report setting out conclusions and suggestions for remedying any failings identified. Once an IRP is convened it comprises three members:

- a lay chair (a person nominated by the Secretary of State from a list held by the relevant regional office of the NHS Executive);
- the convener; and
- another lay member (for trust panels this would be a health authority non-executive director; for health authority panels this would be a person nominated by the Secretary of State from the regional office list).

In addition, if the complaint relates to issues concerning clinical judgement, panels must also be advised by two independent clinical assessors.

91. In evidence to us a number of concerns were expressed about the independent review process. Patients were particularly sceptical about the independence of panels. IRPs are established as committees of the trust or health authority and are paid for by the trust or health authority. Although the chair is an independent lay person, patients considered that the convener's membership, and the fact that the panel was usually administered by complaints staff employed by the agency subject to complaint, compromised the panel's independence. They also often perceived the clinical advice provided to be biased. **We recommend that IRPs should consist of a majority of lay members and should not be connected with the trust or health authority which is subject to complaint. We recommend that IRPs should be funded by and accountable to the regional offices of the NHS Executive.**

92. Furthermore, patients considered that the way the panels were conducted was not always transparent. The Public Law Project survey found that in most hearings complainants and staff were seen separately. Although this may avoid an adversarial atmosphere, which can be stressful to both parties, it does not allow patients a chance to question the staff involved or to hear their evidence. This lack of openness meant patients did not feel that NHS staff had explained themselves or had been held to account. In the eyes of patients, relatives and carers already unhappy with their experience, it may encourage the perception that the NHS is covering up and banding together to prevent the truth from coming out. The lack of rigorous central guidance on the workings of independent review means that at the stage where formality and impartiality is most needed, it is almost entirely lacking. Chairs themselves criticised the lack of guidance. **We consider that IRPs should be conducted in a more formal manner, with all parties present, and act as a adjudicatory bodies.**

93. We also heard that chairs and panel members may not receive sufficient training for what is a demanding task. They may also lack experience. The Public Law Project found that chairs on average had been involved in 12 requests for independent review and only three panels in the two years they had been in office. **We recommend that IRPs should be chaired by people with the appropriate background and experience, recruited by the regional office of the NHS Executive. Common standards should apply throughout the country and staff should be properly trained and resourced. Chairs should be fewer in number and operate across the region so that they can build up expertise.**

94. Panels' suggestions or recommendations for action are not required to be implemented. They have no power to call witnesses or evidence and cannot refer cases to the disciplinary process. This is clearly a weakness. **We recommend that panels should have the power to summon witnesses and take evidence. Trusts and health authorities should be required to make a formal response to the panel recommendations. IRPs should refer any major concerns to the Commission for Health Improvement and report annually to the Health Service Commissioner. They should also be able to recommend that disciplinary action may be necessary.**

95. Evidence we received also drew attention to the inconsistencies in the way patients, relatives and carers were dealt with. Some received copies of the full report, others did not. The Consumers' Association research found that, despite the fact that complainants were supposed to receive a written letter from the Chief Executive of the trust or health authority outlining the outcome of the IRP investigation and informing the complainant of action to be taken as a result of the Panel's report, "two of the complainants who had gone through the

IRP process did not receive a copy of the final report. Seven complainants received reports which outlined the IRP's investigations ... only four complainants had an explanation of what went wrong and only two received an apology. Two complainants were not advised that they could ask the Health Service Commissioner to consider their case if they were not satisfied with the outcome of the investigation." **We recommend that the regional offices of the NHS Executive take greater responsibility for independent review, including issuing guidance on good practice. This should include, for example, circulation of the clinical assessors' report to all parties before the panel hearing, that all parties should be present at the hearing, that all parties should receive a copy of the IRP report (including CHCs who should receive an anonymised version), and that patients and relatives should be advised of the role of the Health Service Commissioner.**

96. It is not surprising that many patients, relatives and carers with complaints feel that the Health Service Commissioner is their only hope. If they are not satisfied with the informal, often inadequate, local resolution of their complaint, they are then faced with a review which appears to them to be biased, closed and inconsistent. We consider that our recommendations on independent review will increase the impartiality of the process, perhaps reduce the need for the Health Service Commissioner to become involved and increase patients trust in the system. Some witnesses argued that IRPs should have powers to recommend ex gratia payments to patients, relatives and carers. We discuss ex gratia payments in more detail in paragraph 134.

97. As well as criticisms of each particular stage of the NHS complaints procedure, there were also more general concerns with the process as a whole.

Access to information

98. Throughout the inquiry, patients, their relatives and carers raised several concerns related to their ability to access information. Patients felt they were left in the dark as they struggled to find their way through the complaints maze, often unguided. One particular concern expressed in evidence was access to the clinical assessors' report for those who had taken a case to independent review. The guidance advises that the clinical assessors' report is attached to the IRP's final report, which should then be circulated to the complainant. However this means that complainants do not see the clinical assessors' report until after the hearing. The Health Service Commissioner warned that there may be sound clinical reasons why it would be preferable for the patient not to see the assessors' report, but he noted that these would be exceptional circumstances. **We recommend that the clinical assessors' report is made available to the IRP and the complainant prior to the panel hearing.**

99. Patients, their relatives and carers also reported some difficulties in accessing their medical records, for instance they discovered that their notes had been lost or were incomplete. We were concerned about this because, subject to some provisos, the Access to Health Records Act 1990 enables patients, and in some cases relatives, to obtain a copy of their written notes made from November 1991 onwards. No reason has to be given.

Timescales

100. We heard evidence that the NHS could often not meet the time limits laid out in the guidance on the complaints procedure. For example, in the case of IRPs, there are 10 days to establish the panel and 40 days to draft the report. These deadlines are often not being met. The Consumers' Association found that seven out of 10 initial complaints were not acknowledged within two working days as required by NHS guidelines, and following the investigation, nearly six out of 10 complainants did not get a full reply within the 20 day working deadline. Patients felt it was particularly unfair that their complaints could be rejected on the basis that they fell outside permitted time limits (a particular problem for those who had had poor outcomes to treatment in the long-term, such as patients prescribed benzodiazepines and steroids), but the NHS could miss its own deadlines without apparent sanction.

101. There is a tension between developing a proper and thorough initial investigation and imposing short timescales. As it stands the current timescales are clearly difficult to meet. **We suggest that patients should have as speedy a resolution as possible to their complaint, but we consider that the current time limits for NHS organisations and for patients and relatives should be evaluated and, where appropriate, changed to make them more realistic. We recommend that the NHS regional offices monitor the management of complaints, and emphasise the importance of trusts and health authorities maintaining those deadlines for their overall quality performance.** In addition, as we recommend in paragraph 82, at the initial stage complaints managers should pass serious complaints on to the appropriate body as quickly as possible.

Learning from complaints

102. Complaints provide an opportunity to improve the quality of services provided, but only if lessons are successfully learned. If the NHS learns from experience this will lead to

more cost-effective, as well as better quality, outcomes. We were told that the NHS regional offices were not sufficiently proactive in monitoring complaints. We were concerned that complaints about individual doctors over a period of time did not appear to have been identified. The Department of Health said that it issues guidance, monitors the number of complaints and publishes information and it has also established the *Learning from Experience* panel, which will review how complaints are monitored. In primary care, primary care groups and trusts are required to appoint a senior doctor or nurse to take responsibility at board level for the quality of clinical care and we recognise the work they are undertaking to address clinical standards. However we think more can be done to provide general lessons for management. **We recommend that methods for recording data from complaints, and reporting these, should be clarified as a matter of urgency. We also recommend that GP practices should be required to provide more information to health authorities on how they handle complaints, what the complaints concern, how they are resolved and what action has been taken in response.**

103. One issue that impacts on action taken following a complaint, is that of responsibility for adverse incidents. We discussed in paragraph 23 the advantages of developing a corporate responsibility for dealing with complaints. We believe that, at present, trusts, health authorities and GP practices are not taking their corporate responsibility for complaints sufficiently seriously. The Consumers' Association survey showed that nearly 60 per cent of respondents felt that the NHS, and in particular hospital complaints managers and NHS Chief Executives, did not accept responsibility for what happened. AVMA called for Chief Executives to be professionally accountable for the management of complaints in order to ensure that trusts would be more assiduous in dealing with complaints fully and punctually. Our understanding of the arrangements for clinical governance is that this introduces such an obligation.

Training

104. We have referred several times to the need for proper training of staff. In relation to the complaints procedure we have found that right through the system – from the initial investigation to independent review – staff training has not been given priority nor has it been of sufficient depth, for example it often does not include the opportunity for role play and group work. Concerns were expressed to us that although there was initial funding provided for the training.

Complaints in primary care

105. The NHS complaints procedure is common to hospitals and GP practices. We heard that there is a particular problem with complaints in primary care. The complaints manager is frequently the practice manager and we have been told that some patients are reluctant to complain to their own GP practice for fear it might prejudice their relationship. Patients made it clear that generally they would prefer to complain to someone else. Patients were particularly worried that the GP could remove them, or their family, from the list. At present GPs do not have to give a reason for removing patients from their lists. **The Select Committee on Public Administration recently commented on this issue "we believe that GPs should only be permitted to remove patients from their lists as a last resort, and that an account be provided to the patient of the reasons for the removal". We strongly agree and we hope that having received this recommendation from two select committees the Government will act.**

106. At present patients do have an option to approach the health authority, rather than the practice complaints manager, but we heard that sometimes the health authority acts as little more than a post-box between the complainant and the practice. We recognise that the reason why patients are expected to take their complaint to the practice is that this provides an opportunity for the matter to be sorted out. **However, we believe that there should be an alternative route for complainants through the primary care group, trust or health authority, and recommend that this should be addressed as a matter of urgency.**

You will see a number of criticisms emerge. In particular, you will notice: (1) that the convenor and the independent review panel are not seen as sufficiently independent; (2) that local resolution procedures against GPs are difficult for patients who have to complain to the practice itself; (3) that the IRP process is not sufficiently formal and professional; (4) that the timescale for dealing with complaints is not adhered to; and (5) that IRP's decisions could not be enforced and there was no system of accountability of Health Authorities and GPs in implementing the IRPs recommendations. You may think many of the Select Committee's recommendations would help restore confidence in the complaints system. For the Government's somewhat complacent response see, *Memorandum*

Responding to the Sixth Report of the Health Select Committee (1998-99) Session (Cm 4698, April 2000).

The Health Committee referred to the Public Law Project's (PLP) national evaluation of the complaints procedure through a survey of health bodies and complainants. The committee summarises the PLP's main conclusions in para 74 of its report. The PLP made a number of detailed recommendations for reform of the complaints procedure.

Henrietta Wallace and Linda Mulcahy *Cause for Complaint? An Evaluation of the Effectiveness of the NHS Complaints Procedure* (September 1999)

6.5 Major changes need to be made to the complaints procedure in order to restore public confidence in its independence and effectiveness. Reform is needed to:
* ensure complaints are handled impartially and swiftly at local resolution;
* enhance the independence and powers of the independent review process;
* introduce tighter mechanisms for ensuring that lessons are learned from complaints to improve standards of care across the NHS.

How should local resolution be reformed?
6.6 It is appropriate to have a degree of informality and flexibility in complaints handling at local resolution as it enables health organisations to respond to complaints in whatever way is most likely to satisfy the complainant. However, if health organisations are to be given discretion in how they operate local resolution, then safeguards must be built into the procedure to ensure that they discharge their responsibilities appropriately and fairly. As the seriousness of the allegations in a complaint increase, the need for safeguards becomes all the more important. That there is a second stage to the complaints procedure does not in itself protect complainants against poorly conducted local resolution as it is clear that complainants often choose not to pursue their complaint further, despite remaining dissatisfied. Moreover, at present there is no right to an independent review. Of those who do try to pursue their complaint, only between a fifth and a quarter are referred to the second stage.

The conduct of local resolution
6.7 In PLP's research, participants drew attention to a number of failings in the operation of local resolution which seriously impeded complainants' ability to gain satisfaction. The cause of these failings was attributed primarily to the lack of training or experience among staff in complaints handling and also to the lack of guidance on how to carry out effective local resolution. Poorly conducted local resolution can cause exacerbation of a complaint and lead to unnecessary protraction of the process.

Recommendations:
* **The Department of Health (and its counterparts in the other countries of the UK) should produce national guidance and standards of good practice for the conduct of local resolution. These should include advice on how to carry out a proper investigation and how to write an effective response.**
* **Measures should be introduced which improve the efficiency and speed of local resolution for all complaints and which will allow those which are appropriate for independent review to proceed faster to that stage. For example,**
  - **a time limit to local resolution after which there is an automatic right to independent review;**
  - **complaints to be referred back to local resolution only once;**
  - **poor local resolution itself to be a ground for allowing an independent review.**
6.8 The importance of training for the effective handling of complaints was highlighted in central guidance, yet it is apparent that the training needs of staff who may be in contact with complainants or involved in complaints management have not been adequately addressed.

Recommendations:
* **All new clinical and non-clinical staff who are expected to come into contact with users should be required to undergo training in the complaints procedure and in responding to on-the-spot complaints, as part of their induction programme.**
* **Complaints managers, service managers or other senior members of staff involved in the investigation of complaints should be required to undergo formal training in effective complaints management.**

- **In addition to the training suggested above, continuing staff training should be provided by health organisations, as the need is identified.**
- **Training should place increased emphasis on skills in handling complaints and provide staff with practical advice and tools to carry out effective resolution.**

Local resolution in primary care

6.9 ... at the heart of the problem with local resolution in primary care is the expectation that complainants should take up their grievances directly with the practitioners concerned. In some cases, this is clearly acting as a deterrent to complaining. For complainants' confidence in the procedure to be restored, the procedures for handling complaints about primary care need to be reformed as a *matter of priority*. A means by which a complainant can address their grievances to a person or body who is independent of the practice concerned should be introduced. The function of such an officer would be actively to facilitate local resolution and not to act simply as a post-box for correspondence between the complainant and those complained about. How this process should be established will need to be considered within the context of the current reforms in primary care.

6.10 Proposals which might be explored include:

- chief executives of primary care groups and trusts (and their counterparts in Scotland, Wales and Northern Ireland) to be charged with responsibility for the handling of complaints concerning any practice or practitioner within the group or trust. As with hospital trusts a primary care group/trust might appoint a complaints manager to carry out this function on a daily basis. Users would be advised to direct their complaint to the chief executive or complaints manager rather than to the practitioner concerned. The expectation would be that this person would take responsibility for investigation and for responding to the complainant;
- health authorities to take responsibility for overseeing local resolution of complaints about primary care. Instead of complainants being expected to complain to the practice concerned, complaints would be directed in the first instance to the health authority, which would initiate an appropriate process of investigation and resolution in liaison with the practice concerned. Local resolution would not be by-passed but health authority complaints managers would become much more actively engaged in the process;
- as for the previous option, but with an enhanced role for conciliators in facilitating local resolution, taking into account the recommendations for conciliation proposed below. Conciliation would be offered as the first step in local resolution, rather than as an 'add-on' once initial attempts at resolution had failed, as is often the case at present.

Recommendation:

- **As a matter of priority, the Department of Health should reform local resolution in primary care to enable users to complain to an officer who is independent of the practice concerned and who has responsibility for investigation of the complaint. In planning reform, the proposals suggested above should be considered.**

The role of conciliation

6.11 Although there was wide support among respondents for the concept of conciliation, concerns were expressed about the lack of resources invested in the training of conciliators and also about the lack of guidance about how such conciliation should be conducted. This approach is in marked contrast to the use of conciliation or mediation in other fields where there is intense debate about the advantages of different mediatory models and the level of qualifications required of mediators. If conciliation is to form an important part of local resolution in primary care, it must be both adequately resourced and conducted by trained and professionally qualified conciliators or mediators.

Recommendations:

- **The Department of Health should review current arrangements for conciliation and the appointment and training of conciliators. In particular, training should be run by accredited bodies and it should lead to a formal professional qualification.**
- **Conciliation services should be properly resourced, both in relation to provision of training for conciliators and payment for their services.**
- **Good practice guidance should be developed on the appropriate use and conduct of conciliation. In particular, it should be voluntary for both parties and it should *not* be a requirement for progression to independent review.**

Local resolution and serious complaints

6.12 In PLP's research, respondents were concerned that there were insufficient mechanisms in place to deal appropriately with complaints that raise serious questions about performance, conduct or competence which threaten patient safety. The impartiality of investigations was questioned and, because of the complexity of the complaint, complainants often experienced very protracted local resolution. While the proposals suggested above will help to improve both the quality and speed of local resolution generally, the measures fail to address concerns about independence. They also still rely on complainants having the strength and perseverance to pursue a complaint to independent review. In the public interest, it is important that serious complaints are accorded a higher degree of procedural protection than local resolution currently provides. We propose that such complaints should be identified and directed at an early stage into more formal investigatory and remedial processes, as appropriate, such as independent review, discipline, litigation or to the professional regulatory bodies, such as the General Medical Council. In practice, how would such a process be implemented?

6.13 We propose the following model for discussion:

- as a first step, the classes of complaints which would justify a so-called 'fast-track' approach would need to be defined. The assessment of whether or not a complaint fits the criteria should be as simple as possible if the process is not to become too bureaucratic and cumbersome. It should also allow for health councils and complainants to determine when it was appropriate to request fast-tracking;
- complaints which fit the defined criteria would be referred immediately to an independent screener, based in the regional complaints offices proposed below. Referrals could be made by the health organisation or primary care practitioner concerned, or directly by the complainant or health council. In the case of primary care, complaints referral could also be made by the health authority;
- on the basis of statements provided by both parties, the role of the screener would be to check whether or not the allegations in the complaint indeed met the criteria, and whether there was a case to answer. If both conditions were satisfied the complaint would be referred directly to the most appropriate investigatory and remedial process, such as independent review, discipline or litigation. If not, the complaint would be referred for investigation under local resolution;
- the screening role should be performed by a lay person, who would be required to seek appropriate clinical advice as necessary;

6.14 Those who oppose the introduction of 'fast-tracking' have argued that it might lead to a two-tier complaints procedure with attention being focused on serious complaints to the detriment of others. However, the public interest in seeing that complaints that raise issues of patient safety are speedily and appropriately addressed justifies such an approach, even if a two-tier complaints system is a consequence. Moreover, it could be argued that a two-tier approach is already operating at local resolution, because of the time and resources that are devoted to handling serious complaints, possibly at the expense of others. The early identification and referral of these complaints to other more appropriate investigatory processes would take them out of local resolution and allow trusts, health authorities and primary care practitioners to focus on other grievances which might be satisfactorily resolved at service level. If attempts at local resolution failed for these complaints, complainants could still request an independent review. Thus, no complaints would be excluded from access to the independent review process.

Recommendations:
The Department of Health should:
- **develop a framework for 'fast-tracking' complaints which raise serious questions about performance, conduct or competence which threaten patient safety, taking into consideration the model proposed above;**
- **establish the criteria by which such complaints would be defined, in consultation with the appropriate professional and consumer organisations.**

Monitoring of the operating of local resolution
6.15 It should not be presumed that if a complainant does not proceed beyond local resolution that they are happy with the handling and outcome of their complaint. As was shown in table 2.2 (p13), of those complaints which were completed at local resolution only 29 percent were wholly satisfied with the outcome of the process. More formal procedures for monitoring the conduct of local resolution, and also complainants' satisfaction with the process, should be introduced.

Recommendations:
- **Health organisations should be required to conduct and publish an annual audit of local resolution.**
- **As part of this process they should actively canvass complainants' experiences of the complaints procedure.**
- **As part of its rolling programme of review of clinical governance arrangements in trusts and primary care trusts, the Commission for Health Improvement (and its**

Scottish and Northern Irish counterparts) should undertake to monitor individual trusts' complaints handling performance.

How should convening and independent review be reformed?

6.16 The results of the research suggest that the convening stage of the procedure is one of the most flawed and discredited aspects of the complaints procedure. There is widespread concern about the independence of the convening role, not only among complainants and health councils, but also among conveners themselves. PLP's data also suggest that the way the role is organised is inefficient. The root of these problems lies in having a convener based in every trust and health authority, who is not only usually a non-executive director of the trust or health authority, but also the person who decides whether a complaint concerning that same establishment should be accepted for independent review.

6.17 Concerns were also raised about the impartiality of the independent review process both in terms of how panels are established and conducted. For example, the convener is a member of the panel; in trust cases, the panel is established as a committee of the trust and paid for by the trust; panels are seldom held on neutral premises and are sometimes administered by the same staff who are involved in local resolution.

The case for independent regional complaints centres

6.18 The concerns cited above make a strong case for the establishment of independent regional complaints centres which would be responsible for handling complaints which fail to be resolved at local resolution. Such a proposal is not a novel idea. In submissions to the Wilson review, Action for Victims of Medical Accidents, the Association for Community Health Councils of England and Wales and the British Medical Association all made similar proposals. The UK, furthermore, lags far behind other nations throughout the developed world in establishing complaints procedures which are fully independent of the national health service and also professionally led.

6.19 Under our proposals, the purpose of these centres would be to provide an independent, administratively supported base for all activity relating to convening and independent review. It was *not* to add a further stage to the complaints procedure, but would rationalise existing inefficiencies in the convening and independent review stages of the process.

6.20 The core responsibilities of the regional centres would be to:
- recruit and train chairs, conveners and clinical assessors and to have a role in the training of complaints managers and other senior staff involved in investigation of complaints;
- provide independent administrative support to those undertaking the convening and chairing roles;
- provide a source of independent clinical advice to conveners;
- cover the costs of independent review panels. Local health organisations would be required to pay an annual 'premium' to the regional complaints centre, akin to the risk pooling scheme for sharing clinical negligence costs;
- monitor the implementation of panel recommendations in liaison with the Commission for Health Improvement (to be discussed further in the section on quality enhancement below).

6.21 The main advantage of this arrangement would be not only that it would give stage two greater real and perceived independence but it would also make it more efficient.

Advantages for convening
- Conveners would no longer be part of the organisation complained about, but recruited independently. Most importantly, conveners would be seen to be independent.
- It would no longer be necessary to require conveners to consult a lay chair for an independent opinion. Discretion to consult a lay chair might be retained for complex cases, but in cases where it was obvious that local resolution had not been exhausted the requirement could be removed. This would help to speed up the convening stage and make it more efficient. In cases where a complaint was accepted for independent review, the convener would be expected to *agree* the terms of reference with the lay chair appointed to lead the panel hearing.
- A convener's caseload would no longer be dependent on the number of requests for independent review received by a single trust. The workload would be distributed more evenly between the conveners, thereby ensuring that conveners have a sufficient caseload to sustain their expertise.
- As the regional centres would provide a source of independent clinical advice to conveners, conveners would no longer compromise their impartiality by seeking advice from clinicians within the organisation subject to the complaint.

- The risk that conveners might be influenced in their referral decisions by considerations of the cost of panel hearings would be averted.

Advantages for the independent review process
- The independent review process would be likely to run much more efficiently having a dedicated administrative team responsible for all the arrangements during the review process.
- Chairs would have access to administrative support during the report-writing stage which would help avoid delays at this stage.
- The process would be seen to be more independent, as panel hearings would no longer be established under the aegis of the organisation subject to the complaint nor administered by their staff.
- Where convenient for the parties concerned, the regional centres could provide a neutral location for holding panel hearings.
- The provision of improved support and training for panel members would help boost morale and enhance their skills. This would help to improve performance and the pace of their turnover.

Recommendations:
The Department of Health should:
- **reform the appointment of conveners so that the role is independent of the NHS;**
- **establish independent regional complaints centres which are responsible for handling complaints which fail to be resolved at local resolution, taking into consideration the proposals suggested above.**

The conduct of panel hearings – enhancing accountability and transparency
6.22 A flexible and informal approach to complaints handling may be desirable at local resolution, but is less appropriate at independent review stage. Having failed to achieve satisfaction at local resolution, complainants will expect to see a level of formality in the conduct of stage two of the process which does justice to the seriousness of the grievances being heard. At this stage there is a need for identification of clear standards for the conduct of panels in order to:
- demonstrate to complainants that the process is conducted in a rigorous and fair manner;
- ensure consistency in practice across all panel hearings and that parties are treated equitably;
- improve the transparency of the process;
- instil confidence in the procedure.

Recommendations:
- **The Department of Health should draw up explicit guidance on the rules of procedure for the conduct of panels. This should recommend that:**
  - **proceedings be conducted openly in the presence of both parties unless the complainant desires otherwise. In such situations, alternative arrangements should be agreed with the complainant;**
  - **parties or their representatives be allowed to question each other;**
  - **all information relevant to the investigation, including staff statements and responses at local resolution and also the clinical assessors' reports, be available to parties prior to the start of the panel hearing.**
- **There should also be a contractual requirement for all NHS employees to attend panel hearings if called upon to do so, even if they have moved to another trust or organisation within the NHS. Failure to attend without good reason should become a disciplinary matter.**
- **There should also be a means to require cooperation of those who have left the NHS. Contractually this would be difficult to enforce, but an alternative strategy might be to make failure to cooperate in the investigation of a complaint a ground for a finding of professional misconduct.**

The role of clinical assessors
6.23 While the role of clinical assessors in the independent review process was generally praised, some concerns were raised about their performance and independence. There were also reports of lengthy delays in their appointment to cases due to insufficient numbers.

Recommendations:
- **The Department of Health should review procedures for the appointment of clinical assessors to regional lists. Nominations should be acceptable not only to the profession concerned (as the guidance already suggests), but also to the groups who represent users. To aid lay assessments of the suitability of nominated clinicians,**

information should be supplied by regional offices on why particular clinicians are suitable.
- Improved guidance and training should be offered on the function, duties and responsibilities of clinical assessors.

Recruitment and training of panel members

6.24 Participants in the research expressed concern about the recruitment and training of conveners and other panel members, and the lack of professionalism in the conduct of their duties. Many conveners and chairs themselves reported dissatisfaction with the training they had received for their role, particularly with regard to improving and developing the necessary skills. If the independent review process is to be formalised, as proposed above, the process of recruitment and training of panel members must ensure that they have the necessary skills to perform their duties to a high standard of professionalism.

Recommendations:
- The Department of Health should review procedures for recruiting and training panel members as a matter of priority.
- Panel members should be required to undergo an intensive training programme before undertaking their first case, with particular emphasis on developing skills and good practice in the performance of their duties. This should include training in:
  - quasi-judicial processes and skills;
  - inquisitorial techniques;
  - report writing.
- An on-going programme of regular 'refresher' courses for panel members to update skills and review performance should be provided.
- Other initiatives should be introduced to support conveners and chairs in their work, such as 'mentoring schemes' and regular informal, experience-sharing sessions. Such initiatives should take account of the need to protect the identity of individuals involved in the complaints being discussed.
- In order to recruit and retain panel members of the necessary calibre, the NHS should consider compensating them properly for their time.

Complaints involving more than one health service or sector

6.25 A number of problems were identified in relation to the handling of complaints involving more than one part of the health service or different sectors, such as health and social services. Most particularly, complainants were confused by the different procedures and also frustrated that the grievances raised could not be dealt with under one system.

Recommendations:
- The Department of Health should streamline the processes by which complaints involving more than one part of the health service are heard, both at local resolution and independent review.
- Arrangements for effective handling of cross-sectoral complaints should also be reviewed in discussion with the appropriate agencies.

How can services and performance in the NHS be improved?

6.26 One of the principal aims of the complaints procedure is to ensure that lessons are learned from complaints to improve services not only for complainants but for all potential users. The research revealed, however, that there are only weak mechanisms for ensuring that complaints feed into strategies to improve services, not only within the organisation concerned, but throughout the NHS as a whole. Although the new clinical governance arrangements in the health service will help to address this, there is still a lack of clarity about how complaints will be incorporated into clinical governance processes and also into the work of the Commission for Health Improvement and its counterparts in the other countries of the UK.

Recommendations:
- In addition to the existing reporting requirements, trusts should be required to establish formal procedures by which failings in services identified by complaints are fed routinely into quality strategies, such as audit and risk management. This process would be facilitated if complaints, risk management, clinical audit and other quality initiatives within trusts were fully integrated.
- Trusts should be required to introduce procedures for recording, monitoring and acting on oral complaints.
- Users should also be given opportunities to make comments about the quality of care or services provided, other than through the complaints process.

• In relation to complaints in primary care, health authorities should be given authority to actively monitor complaints handled under practice-based complaints procedures and to establish procedures by which this will be achieved. As part of this process, primary care practitioners should be required under their terms and conditions of service to submit more detailed information to health authorities about complaints, including the nature of the complaints received, how local resolution was approached and the remedial action taken as a consequence.

Quality enhancement following independent review

6.27 Among respondents in the research there was widespread lack of confidence in the independent review process's ability to effectively bring about improvements in services. At the root of their concern was the fact that panel recommendations have no force, nor are there mechanisms in place to monitor whether recommendations have been acted on.

Recommendations:

• The Department of health should require trusts and primary care practitioners to report back fully on action taken to implement a panel's recommendations within a fixed period, say six months following the panel report. Reasons for failure to implement any recommendation should be fully justified.

• These reports should be disseminated to: the complainant, respondent and panel members and, with due regard to confidentiality, to all members of the board of the trust or health authority concerned, the health council, the regional offices, the appropriate purchasers and also the proposed regional complaints centres. Where recommendations have concerned a primary care practitioner, the report should also go to the primary care group or trust.

• The regional complaints centres should be charged with responsibility for monitoring that trusts and primary care practitioners are fulfilling these reporting obligations. They should also be required to collate the information about the improvements in services which have been implemented, and to feed this back to trusts, health authorities and primary care groups across the region, in order that different parts of the health service might learn from each others' experiences. This information should also be published and made publicly available.

• The Commission for Health Improvement, in its review of individual providers, should include inspection of arrangements for addressing quality issues raised by complaints. In liaison with the regional complaints centres, it should also undertake monitoring of trends in panel recommendations to see what national lessons might be learned from complaints that go to independent review panels.

Discipline and complaints

6.28 In some cases, complainants would like disciplinary action to be taken against personnel following a complaint. The motivation is not usually a desire for revenge or recrimination but the need for reassurance that failings in an individual's conduct or performance are addressed so that such events will not happen again. The complaints procedure was not set up to deal with disciplinary issues which are dealt with under separate procedures. While this separation may be appropriate, concerns were raised in the research about the process by which disciplinary matters identified following a complaint were referred into the appropriate disciplinary channels, and also about the visibility of the disciplinary process itself. In particular, in primary care, the very substantial decline in disciplinary cases heard since the introduction of the complaints procedure has raised concerns about the accountability of general practitioners. Some of these concerns might be addressed under the proposals for 'fast-tracking' and improved monitoring recommended above. In addition, further specific areas need attention.

Recommendations:

• At independent review stage, where matters that might require possible disciplinary action are identified, panel reports should be able to recommend explicitly that the need for disciplinary action be considered. (NB we are not recommending that it should become the remit of panels to determine disciplinary action).

• In primary care, there is a need for clarification of the procedure by which complaints may be referred for disciplinary action. In particular, it should not be conditional on a complaint having completed independent review and there should be provision for conveners to suggest referral for disciplinary investigation.

• The disciplinary process itself should be made more transparent and complainants should be fully informed as a matter of course of the outcome of disciplinary action.

- Where alternatives to discipline are recommended, such as a process of retraining and skills' development, complainants should also be informed that this will happen, and of the outcome.

How should complainants be supported and represented?

6.29 For many users of the health service, it is a daunting prospect to make a complaint about one's own care or treatment, or that of a loved one. For those who are particularly vulnerable for reasons, for example, of continuing ill health, mental illness or mental incapacity, or bereavement, access to assistance and support through the process is very important. In some cases the absence of such assistance may result in a justified complaint never being brought against the NHS.

6.30 Health councils currently perform a very valuable role in providing support to complainants and the important role other advice agencies and voluntary sector organisations play must also be recognised. This role was supported by the Wilson Committee and further encouraged in the NHS guidance on the complaints procedure. However, it is not a statutory function of health councils or of other advice agencies to undertake NHS complaints work, and the support they offer varies widely both in quality and quantity across the UK. There is also a lack of clarity for complainants as to what assistance they can expect from health councils.

Recommendations:

The Department of Health should:

- **formally recognise the role of health councils in assisting complainants through the complaints procedure by adding it to their statutory remit;**
- **allocate the necessary resources to support health councils in their work on complaints, including provision of funding for the appointment and central training of a complaints officer for every health council;**
- **develop standards of good practice for advising and supporting complainants;**
- **request the NHS Health Information Service to establish a database of local organisations throughout the UK which provide emotional support, advocacy or other forms of advice and representation for complainants and other users.**

Access to independent medical advice

6.31 In relation to clinical complaints, access to independent clinical advice is particularly important to help complainants understand and clarify the issues involved, yet the availability of such advice is very limited. This imbalance in knowledge places complainants in a vulnerable position, and may result in complaints not being pursued due to lack of awareness or understanding of the failings in care or treatment involved. Conversely, lack of access to early independent clinical advice and information may result in complaints being pursued where there is indeed no case to answer.

Recommendation:

- **The Department of Health should establish a process whereby complainants can receive access to free independent clinical advice in pursuit of a complaint.**

You will notice that there is a similarity in the 'core' recommendations of the Health Committee and PLP. As the Health Committee noted (para 75, *supra*), in November 1998 the Department of Health commissioned its own evaluation of the system which is expected to result in an interim report in 2000. What seems clear is that *two* of the central planks of the Wilson Committees' philosophy for complaints procedures have, in practice, proved untenable and unwanted by complainants (and sometimes health professionals), namely informality (at least at the IRP stage) and a clear distinction between complaints and discipline. In relation to the latter, linkage between the systems albeit that they are separate, now seems desirable.

2.   An alternative model – New Zealand

The Health and Disability Commissioner Act 1994 (NZ) provides an interesting contrast to our own domestic legislation. The Act allows for the appointment of a Health and Disability Commissioner (s 8) and for a Code of Health and Disability Services Consumers' Rights (s 74(1)). The Act provides for a complaints and investigation procedure to the Commissioner and, thereafter to the Complaints

Review Tribunal where a breach of the Code is alleged (ss 31–58). The Code came into force on 1 July 1996. The operation of the legislation is described by Diane Longley.

Diane Longley 'Complaints After Wilson; Another Case of Too Little Too Late? (1997) 5 Med L Rev 172

The remit of the 1994 Act is extensive, covering all health and disability services, whether public or privately provided. It is grounded in the provision of legally enforceable patient rights and its purpose is to facilitate fair, simple, speedy and efficient resolution of complaints relating to the infringement of those rights. The Act refers specifically to rights because this is seen as necessary to redress the imbalance that has traditionally occurred between providers of services and consumers in the health and disability sectors. The rights legislation encompassed in the Act is, as the Commissioner herself has stated, "quite different to comparable legislation anywhere else in the world and is therefore setting new ground" (R Stent (Health and Disability Commissioner), *Gaining an Insight into the Code of Rights* (1996)) and there is a capacity to enjoin health rights with both disciplinary proceedings and other rights tribunals.

The 1994 Act is all encompassing. It defines consumers and providers of health and disability services and the services themselves *inclusively* rather than *exclusively*. In fact, it is difficult to think of any service with some relation to health and disability which does not come within its remit. Not only are those providers whom one would clearly expect to be included covered, but also "alternative medicine" services such as homeopathy, acupuncture, reflexology etc. Also included are health-related services through Housing New Zealand, psychological testing of prisoners by the Justice Department, special schools and rehabilitation, home alteration and accommodation support, amongst others.

The 1994 Act provides for the preparation, content, review and notification of a Code of Patient Rights by the Health and Disability Commissioner (HDC) and the operation of advocacy services independent of the Commission. Although at first sight the Code appears similar to the Patients' Charter, in contrast, the Code creates 10 legally enforceable rights by way of regulation. To ensure that it remains relevant to current situations it may be amended at any time and must be reviewed every three years. Before any such changes may be made there are wide-ranging consultation provisions.

Because the Code is enshrined in regulation it is not as straight-forward as some consumer groups would have preferred and it has consequently been criticised for its rather formal presentation. However, the rights encoded may be presented to consumers in any way providers may choose as long as the latter's duties under the Code are met. Every provider is expected to inform consumers of their rights *and* enable them to be exercised. Where these obligations are not met the onus is on the provider to show that this was reasonable in the circumstances.

It is envisaged that the test of reasonableness will be developed and applied over time as a greater compliance with requirements is expected (ibid at 2.4). This facilitates a necessary degree of flexibility, allowing for the building of standards as well as individuation in the treatment of complaints. This approach of balance grounded on a solid rights base is reflected in the emphasis also given to partnership between consumers and providers in the Code. This states that patients also have a responsibility to communicate as effectively as possible, participate in partnership and learn about their rights so as to empower themselves.

The right to complain is set out in detail in Right 10 of the Code. As is the tradition in New Zealand in approaches made to ombudsmen, there is no provision that a complaint should be written. A consumer may complain in any form appropriate to themselves and may complain to those who provided the service, or any person authorised to receive complaints on behalf of the provider, or any other appropriate person, including an independent advocate provided under the HCC Act, as well as the HDC. This avoids the dilemma that can face patients in Britain in initiating a complaint directly against those who have provided care and may have to provide it in the future.

All complaints are referred in the first instance to the health or disability provider to see if local resolution is possible. Every complaint is expected to be acknowledged within three working days of receipt and the complainant informed of any internal, external or investigating procedures. The consumer must receive all information held by the provider relevant to the complaint. Within 10 working days the provider must either accept the complaint or not or indicate how much additional time is needed to investigate. Monthly updates must be given on any unresolved complaint. There is a requirement that the consumer is informed of the reasons for any of these decisions and told of any action to be taken and any appeal procedures.

Besides the usual rights to respect, freedom from discrimination, dignity, information etc, of particular interest is the right to services of an appropriate standard. Under this heading is included the right of every consumer to have services provided in a manner that minimises the potential harm to, and *optimises the quality of life* of, that consumer; and the right to *co-operation among providers to ensure quality and continuity of services*. It will be interesting to see how these rights are actually interpreted by the HDC as cases arising from breach of the Code begin to bite. There should certainly be no difficulty with multi-agency complaints but there is room for a great deal of discretion in the interpretation of quality of life factors. The health service in New Zealand is as cost containment conscious as the NHS. There, as in the UK, there is no right to particular services and in its initial stages the 1994 Act and the Code were criticised for their procedural focus. However, there appears to be a clear possibility for the HDC in some circumstances to consider more substantive rights and to investigate the merits of purchasing decisions.

The purpose of the advocacy service is "to promote and protect the rights of health and disability service consumers by empowering them through advocacy support" (Health and Disability Commissioner Act 1994, Part III (HDC Act)). Advocacy is seen as the first step in the process of assisting consumers who are unable to resolve their concerns. Advocates may receive complaints from consumers directly, referred by the HDC or by other persons. Their role is to assist consumers to pursue their complaints through formal and informal procedures, including proceedings before health professional bodies. They may also refer unsolved complaints to the HDC and have a duty to report any matter relating to the rights of consumers that in the advocate's opinion should be drawn to the attention of the Commissioner (ibid).

Advocates and the Director of Advocacy act independently of the Minister of Health, health and disability purchasers and providers, and the HDC. But the Director is responsible to the HDC for the efficient, effective and economical management of his/her activities and is charged with the establishment and administration of a nation-wide advocacy service. Under s 28 of the 1994 Act the HDC is authorised to issue guidelines relating to the operation of these independent advocacy services. Advocates are required to assist complainants under an "empowerment model", no judgment or mediation is undertaken in any situation. Consistency of advocacy throughout the New Zealand health service is regarded as fundamental and is achieved through national training, monitoring, guidelines, performance standards and protocols, and information gathering.

In the course of investigation, the HDC may liaise with a number of other bodies, including professional health bodies whose jurisdictions are related to or overlap with that of the Commissioner. If a complaint is made to a professional health body about one of its members, it must be referred to the Commissioner and all action in respect of that complaint suspended until the HDC has investigated it. The HDC also has a discretion to refer a complaint to the Human Rights Commission, the Ombudsman or the Privacy Commissioner if she considers that the matter could be dealt with more properly by them. Where the HDC finds evidence of any significant breach of duty or misconduct, s 48 requires the matter to be referred to the appropriate person or authority including the police or Coroner.

The HDC may call for a mediation conference to resolve a matter by agreement between the parties. Mediation is binding, final and confidential, but it is not he role of the mediator to impose a solution on the parties. Any information, statement or admission disclosed or made during a mediation conference cannot be used as evidence in any court or before any person acting judicially.

The 1994 Act also makes provision for the appointment of a Director of Proceedings (DP) whose role is to assist or represent complainants or others in an action, or to bring an action in his or her own right in respect of a complaint. Like those of the Director of Advocacy, the functions of the Director of Proceedings are exercised independently of the HDC to protect the HDC's investigatory and mediation impartiality. At the conclusion of an investigation the HDC may refer a complaint to the DP for a decision on whether legal proceedings should be brought concerning a breach of the Code. The DP must decide whether to decline to bring an action, bring proceedings before the Complaints Review Tribunal (CRT), or a professional health disciplinary body or, where appropriate, take the matter before the courts. In making the most appropriate decision the DP will take account of the views of the complainant, but also of the wider public interest. The Complaints Review Tribunal hears proceedings brought under the Human Rights Act 1993 and the Privacy Act 1994 as well as the Health and Disability Commissioner Act 1994. Proceedings cannot be brought if the complaint has been resolved by agreement between the parties, for example, in mediation. Proceedings are generally less formal than those of a court but an action before the CRT may result in the award of damages or an order to rectify what has gone wrong, where this directly benefits the individual complainant.

Where the HDC finds that there has been a breach of the Code the report may include recommendations and request that these be implemented within a specified time. Recommendations may include the taking of disciplinary action. If within a reasonable time no appropriate or adequate action has been taken the HDC may make comment and report the matter to the Minister of Health.

As Diane Longley observes, the NZ Code creates ten 'rights' for consumers. She refers to some of them. In full, they are: right to be treated with respect; right to freedom from discrimination, coercion, harassment, and exploitation; right to dignity and independence; right to services of an appropriate standard; right to effective communication; right to be fully informed; right to make an informed choice and give informed consent; right to support; rights in respect of teaching or research; and right to complain.

There is no doubt that these are very extensive indeed. In addition, health providers have a duty to inform consumers of their rights and to enable consumers to exercise their rights (cl 1(3)).

However, as Diane Longley points out, the Code contains two important linked limitations:

Clause 3. Provider compliance—
(1) A provider is not in breach of this Code if the provider has taken reasonable actions in the circumstances to give effect to the rights, and comply with the duties, in this Code.
(2) The onus is on the provider to prove that it took reasonable actions.
(3) For the purposes of this clause, 'the circumstances' means all the relevant circumstances, including the consumer's clinical circumstances and the provider's resource constraints.

Professor Skegg assesses the implications of the New Zealand legislation.

P D G Skegg 'The New Zealand Code of Health and Disability Services Consumers' Rights' (1997) 5 JLM 124

The Act, and the Code for which it provided, have the effect of creating a new form of liability, which takes its place alongside the criminal, tortious, professional disciplinary and other forms of liability to which the provider may already be subject.

At first glimpse the Code appears to promise rather more than it delivers. For all the talk of "rights" of consumers in cl 2, it becomes apparent from cl 3 that providers are not always under an unqualified duty to give effect to these "rights". Their duty is to take "reasonable actions in the circumstances" to give effect to the rights, and comply with the duties, in the Code: cl 3(1). Resource constraints are among the many considerations which will sometimes have a bearing on what conduct is reasonable in the circumstances.

Even when a provider has omitted to take "reasonable actions in the circumstances", there will be no guarantee that the consumer will obtain a remedy. In some cases, the Commissioner may decline to pursue the matter on the ground that it is trivial. Even where the Commissioner completes an investigation and is of the opinion that there has been a breach of the Code, the matter may go no further: the Commissioner is not authorised to institute proceedings against a provider. If proceedings are instituted, and the Complaints Review Tribunal is satisfied both that the Code has been breached and that the consumer has suffered damage in consequence, damages will not always be available.

There will be cases where consumers will obtain statutory remedies which were not available to them previously. However, a focus on the statutory remedies can lead to a distorted understanding of the part the Code will play in the relationship between consumers and providers. In a great many cases consumers will not have the least interest in the statutory remedies – but they will welcome an independent investigation of their complaints, and the explanation and apology that will sometimes follow.

The Code has had the effect of publicising some already established rights, as well as providing some new ones. It will contribute to a raising of consumer expectations, and demands. Even where the Code has simply duplicated rights which had already been conferred on the consumer by other parts of New Zealand law, the complaints procedures provided by the Code and the Act will be of great importance.

It would be easy to exaggerate the importance of the Code, but there is at least as much danger that its importance will be underrated. Along with the accident compensation scheme and the *Health Information Privacy Code*, it is a distinctive and very important element of New Zealand health care law.

For a comparative discussion of complaints procedures, see J Elder, *Who Cares about the Health Victim?* (1998) and YG Nordlund and L Edgren, 'Patient

Complaint Systems in Health Care - A Comparative Study between the Netherlands and Sweden' (1999) 6 European J of Health Law 133.

3. Private practice

All registered medical practitioners and nurses, whether in private practice or within the NHS, are subject to the disciplinary jurisdiction of their professional regulatory bodies, the GMC and UKCC. There is no *imposed* complaints system, except that privately financed infertility clinics are required by the Human Fertilisation and Embryology Authority to have an effective and efficient complaints procedure in place (*Code of Practice* (4th edn, 1998) at paras 12.1–12.7). This does not mean, of course, that a particular private provider does not have its own complaints procedure.

We saw in the previous chapter that in 1999 the House of Commons Health Committee made detailed proposals for the regulation of private and independent health care (5th Report, 1998–99, HC 281-I). The committee examined the issue of complaints in this sector and, as we shall see, recommended that there should be a Ombudsman for the private sector to deal with patient complaints.

House of Commons Health Committee *The Regulation of Private and other Independent Healthcare* (5th Report, 1998–99, HC 281-I)

133. Those wishing to complain about aspects of healthcare in the independent sector currently have only limited options. Provider organizations may deal directly with complaints relating to non-clinical aspects of care (members of the IHA are obliged to have a complaints mechanism in place). Complaints about advertising may be dealt with by the ASA. Dubious commercial practices may eventually cause Trading Standards officers to intervene. Complaints relating to medical insurance can in some cases be dealt with by the insurance ombudsman.

134. Most of the evidence we have reviewed relates not to these matters but to issues arising from clinical care. Miss Perry of the NHS Confederation told us that "there is an expectation on the part of patients that when they go into a private hospital they have the rights to complain that they know exist in the NHS". The arrangements here are influenced by the employment status of clinicians in that, as noted above, independent sector hospitals grant consultants admitting rights but usually take no direct responsibility for the clinical care they administer. Anyone wishing to complain about clinical care has three options all of which are potentially unsatisfactory. They may refer the matter to the health authority for investigation, they may refer a clinician to the GMC or they may pursue legal action.

Health Authority Investigations

135. Health Authorities are empowered to investigate any complaint about the independent sector which can be related to any of the provisions of the Registered Homes Act. We were told by Action for Victims of Medical Accidents (AVMA) that "very few complainants are made aware of this avenue" and that "health authorities vary considerably in terms of how they see their role in responding to complaints". Many health authorities, according to AVMA, would not normally deal with clinical aspects of complaints.

136. We heard first-hand evidence of the lack of clarity surrounding the health authority as an avenue of complaint from Mr Graham Maloney, giving evidence for APROP. Mr Maloney's wife, Christian, was twice given false negative results in tests for breast cancer administered at the Nuffield Hospital Cleveland. Mrs Maloney subsequently died from the disease at the age of 46. Mr Maloney was unhappy not only with the failure to diagnose but also with the care administered by the hospital, to which his wife was admitted when she was dying. Mr Maloney told us he was not informed of the health authority route of complaint but only learned of it in a later conversation with Lord Woolf. The ensuing report from Tees Health Authority was one and a half pages long and, according to Mr Maloney, entirely inadequate. Following the intervention of local Members of Parliament, Tees Health Authority agreed to undertake a second review. It apologised for the inadequacy of the first review. The second review was much longer and more comprehensive. It has subsequently become, in Mr Maloney's words, "the unofficial guideline as to what private patients should expect when a health authority decides to investigate a complaint". Mr Maloney suggested that the only reason the health authority reinvestigated his complaint was because he had removed

from the hospital the relevant drug prescribing chart at the time of his wife's death and had taken professional advice that the drugs administration procedures had been disregarded, a point later confirmed by the health authority investigation. In our view, it should not be necessary for patients with concerns to have to go to these lengths to have their cases reviewed. ...

Litigation

138. The sole function of litigation is to provide compensation in monetary terms for harm that has resulted from negligence. It does not provide the claimant with any explanation as to what went wrong ...

140. In order to minimise the amount of litigation taking place **we think it essential that each provider, as part of their mandatory complaints procedure, offers all complainants an early opportunity for an independent review of their case with a view to achieving an adequate explanation of events.** Any disclosure of information here should not prejudice the person complaining in the event that they choose to proceed to litigation.

Provision of information

141. The Medical Defence Union informed us that "those who represent patients say the single most common reason for initiating medical negligence claims is that they are upset by the doctor's attitude and feel litigation is the only way to get an adequate explanation for what has gone wrong". This seems to us crucial. Many of the witnesses appearing before us told us that they were seeking only information or an apology when they initiated a complaint. With this in mind we think it essential that the complaints procedures for independent hospitals should be far more transparent than is presently the case. A number of measures are required to achieve this. **We recommend that all independent health care providers should be obliged to provide clear and accessible information to their customers on the complaints procedures open to them including external complaint routes such as (at present) via health authorities, or (if our recommendations are accepted) the independent regulator. We believe that the provision of an adequate complaints procedure should be a registration requirement and that the independent inspector should have access to all documentation and records relating to complaints and that these should be taken into account in any decision as to whether to maintain registration.**

142. It has also been brought to our attention that Community Health Councils do not normally have a remit in dealing with complaints relating to treatment within the independent sector. Given the interaction between private and state treatment that characterizes much healthcare today we cannot see that this position remains tenable. A wider role for the Community Health Council would, we believe, be a way of improving the amount of information available to consumers. **We recommend that the remit of Community Health Councils should be extended to include the activity of the independent sector. We believe that any costs accruing from this should be met by the sector itself and come out of the licensing fee.**

Accountability for complaints

143. We think it important that the route for complaint should be clear. At present those complaining are often passed around between clinician, provider and insurer as each tries to shift responsibility to the other. We agree with AVMA when they point out "it may well be that the cause of the complaint rests both with the clinician and the hospital, with neither being prepared to accept responsibility". Moreover, as South East Kent Community Health Council discovered when attempting to follow up complaints against the gynaecologist Mr Rodney Ledward who worked both in the NHS and in the independent sector, medical records remain the property of the consultant not the hospital. We do not believe it is reasonable to place the onus on the consumer to work out who is responsible when something goes wrong in a private hospital or clinic. In almost any other area of consumer activity the consumer associates the product obtained with the organization should not be in a position to stand aside from the consequences of the clinical activities of the clinicians it employs or to whom it grants practising privileges. Accordingly **we recommend that, as a statutory condition, the provider organization should be legally responsible for the investigation of all adverse clinical incidents, including those relating to clinical practice, that take place on its premises and that full medical records should be available at all times to a clinician nominated by the provider as well as to the patient or patient representative. Each provider should be obliged to name and advertise a complaints manager to whom all complaints should be made.**

The case for a Health Commissioner for the independent sector

144. There was widespread support amongst those giving evidence to us for the introduction of a Health Service Commissioner (Ombudsman) for the independent health sector. Currently the Health Service Commissioner only looks at care in the independent sector when it is

purchased by an NHS body. The patient representative groups such as AVMA and APROP, many of the major providers (including PPP/Columbia, BUPA, and Prime Care), the IHA, South East Kent Community Health Council, the BMA and the RCN all advocated a Commissioner for the independent sector. The Consumers' Association went as far as supporting the drawing up of a Private Member's Bill to extend the role of the Health Service Commissioner. Many other organizations and individuals called for an external objective review process without explicitly naming the Commissioner.

145. While there was general agreement on the benefits in principle of a Commissioner for the independent sector there was disagreement on whether the role of the current Health Service Commissioner should be extended or whether a separate Commissioner was required for the independent sector. We wrote to the Health Service Commissioner to establish his views on the merits of extending his remit to cover the independent sector. He felt that such a move would have the advantage of greater simplicity for complainants, in particular those whose treatment was carried out in both the state and independent sectors. A second advantage would be that a single Commissioner would "provide an opportunity to develop and apply common standards in dealing with complaints, particularly in the area of clinical judgment, and to make a contribution to the drive for clinical excellence". However the Commissioner also pointed out to us that such an extension of his powers would require a significant change in the way in which he operated. He felt he would, effectively, become responsible for resolving disputes arising from commercial contracts, which would otherwise be matters for a court; many complainants would be seeking financial compensation which is seldom offered under the NHS complaints procedure; and at present his recommendations are not binding on parties, a situation he felt might not be appropriate in respect of the independent sector. The Commissioner also felt it would not be appropriate for the additional costs he would face to be met from the public purse.

146. **We have considered the argument in favour of extending the role of the Commissioner to cover patients funded privately, but believe it would be preferable for the sector to have a separate Commissioner, with the Health Service Commissioner retaining responsibility for those patients funded by the NHS in the independent sector. We believe it would be more appropriate for such a Commissioner for the independent sector to have powers beyond naming and shaming. We recommend that the findings of such a Commissioner should be transmitted directly to the Independent Regulator who could impose any necessary sanctions. The Commissioner should be accountable to Parliament. We recommend that the costs of a Commissioner for the independent sector should be met in full by the sector.** We believe the funding arrangements would be simpler if such a Commissioner's remit was dedicated to the independent sector. We would not wish our advocacy of a separate Commissioner to create undue barriers in respect of the pooling of information with his or her state sector counterpart. It will clearly be important for both offices to have close working relations to tackle issues relating to patients moving between the NHS and the independent sector.

Mental health complaints

147. We were advised by MIND that there is "a complete lack of complaints procedures in some mental nursing homes" and we received from a patient's relative a detailed description of harm and distress caused, in part, from the absence of an adequate complaints mechanism. The MHAC in its last biennial report expressed concern at the large number of complaints from those detained in the independent sector and at the fact that detained patients felt that their complaints were not taken seriously by some private sector establishments.

148. NHS patients, cared for in the independent sector through a service agreement are able to invoke the NHS complaints procedure, including access to the Health Service Commissioner. These mechanisms are not available to patients self-funded or funded by medical insurers. **We recommend that, in relation to independent mental health services, there should be access to a recognized, nation wide complaints system incorporating an independent review and Ombudsman mechanisms.**

Formal inquiries

A. INQUIRIES BY HEALTH AUTHORITIES

Cicular HM(66)15 contains a further procedure in para 7(iii)(b) which allows for the appointment of an independent person or committee in very serious cases. Paragraph 7(iii)(b) provides:

… [I]n the small number of cases which are so serious that they cannot be dealt with satisfactorily in this way … the investigation should be referred for independent enquiry. Action to refer such cases should be taken by the Board of Governors or the Regional Hospital Board concerned on a reference from the Hospital Management Committee. The general rule should be that an independent lawyer or other competent person from outside the hospital service should conduct the enquiry, or preside over a small committee set up for the purpose, whose membership should be independent of the authority concerned and should include a person or persons competent to advise on any professional or technical matters. The complainant and any other persons who are the subject of the complaint should have an opportunity of being present throughout the hearing, and of cross-examining witnesses, and should be allowed to make their own arrangements to be legally represented if they so wish,

Professor Brazier in *Medicine, Patients and the Law* comments on the HM(66)15 procedure (at pp 205–206).

Where at any stage in an investigation of a complaint further action is found to be necessary, the matter may be referred on to the regional health authority. The authority may appoint one or more of its own members to look into the complaint, or in serious cases may set up an independent inquiry. The inquiry will be conducted by a small committee consisting usually of a legally qualified chairman and two medical practitioners, one from the same specialty as the person whose competence is in issue. All inquiring members will be unconnected with the hospital where the complaint originated. Copies of all documents are circulated to all parties. The complainant and the subjects of the complaint may be legally represented, and cross-examination of witnesses is allowed. Legal aid is not available, and no one can be compelled to attend the inquiry. The committee's findings of fact are then submitted to the staff concerned for further comment. Finally the committee reports its findings and recommendations to the authority.

The inquiry procedure can be effective. … It can also be cumbersome and unfair. And if hospital staff refuse co-operation the procedure may break down altogether. In 1976 Elizabeth Shewin entered hospital for a gall-bladder operation. In the course of the operation she suffered irreversible brain damage. On the advice of their medical defence organization, all ten doctors involved with Miss Shewin refused to give evidence to the inquiry. They finally agreed to appear on condition that the authority met any costs and award that might result if court action were later taken. The inquiry discovered that Miss Shewin's injury resulted from her being given nitrous oxide instead of oxygen because of an improvised and inadequate repair to anaesthetic equipment in the operating theatre. Miss Shewin's relatives sued the authority for negligence and won damages of £262,500. The authority in turn sued the manufacturers of the anaesthetic equipment. The doctors were virtually exonerated.

In a second example, a 26-year-old man, David Woodhouse, entered hospital in 1981 for an appendectomy. He never regained consciousness and ten months later still lay in a coma. Pressure from MPs led the health authority to set up an inquiry. Again, on the advice of their defence organization the doctors refused to testify. The inquiry was abandoned. The authority then asked three independent experts to examine the case. They reported on a series of disasters. For example, the anaesthetist's command of English was poor, he could not spell the names of basic drugs, and neither he nor the duty registrar knew how to use the ventilator. Mr Woodhouse was left without oxygen for twenty minutes. The health authority promised to tighten up procedures. An out-of-court settlement was reached to pay compensation to David Woodhouse and his family.

B. INQUIRIES BY THE SECRETARY OF STATE

The National Health Service Act 1977, s 84(1) provides that: 'The Secretary of State may cause an inquiry to be held in any case where he deems it advisable to do so in connection with any matter arising under this Act or Part I of the National Health Service and Community Care Act 1990.'

Professor Brazier (*op cit*) comments on the s 84 procedure as follows (at pp 206–207):

At such an inquiry all those involved may be compelled to attend and to produce documents, and if the person appointed to hold the inquiry sees fit all evidence may have to be given on oath. The [Secretary of State] rarely uses his coercive power. MPs pressed him to do so in the David Woodhouse case. He refused. Inquiries by the Health Minister are at present limited to cases of national scandal, such as ill-treatment of mental patients or the conditions at Stanley Royde Hospital which led to an outbreak of salmonella food poisoning. Successive [Secretaries of State] have argued that their power to order an inquiry was not intended for use in cases of individual error or even gross incompetence. His powers are to be invoked only to protect the public at large. Yet serious cases of accidents involving individuals may reveal dangers to the public. The [Secretary of State] refused to order an inquiry in the Woodhouse case despite tremendous pressure in Parliament. The authority's own endeavours revealed grave risks to anyone accepting anaesthesia in the area. Was it not in the public interest that this be revealed? Are prospective patients not entitled to know that their health authority may be employing doctors whose knowledge of English and resuscitation procedures may be lamentably and dangerously inadequate?

The recent inquiry set up to look at the events at the Bristol Royal Infirmary was pursuant to s 84 of the 1977 Act.

Part II

Medical law: the general part

Chapter 4

Medical negligence

Introduction

In this chapter we are concerned with the nature of legal actions brought by patients (and others) against doctors and health care institutions for damages to compensate them for injury. The injury may arise out of the treatment provided (so-called iatrogenic injury) or it may be that the patient's illness or disease has not been adequately treated and she is left with permanent harm. As we shall see, the permutations are many. Commonly today, this is referred to as 'clinical negligence'.

Whilst the primary purpose underlying such litigation is compensation, the legal processes may also be seen as mechanisms for holding doctors and others accountable and, in the case of negligence actions, maintaining or improving standards of professional care (for accountability generally see Chapter 3).

In essence, there are three types of action which an injured patient may seek to bring against a doctor or institution: *contract, negligence*, and *products liability*. The latter is dealt with separately in Chapter 13. There is, of course, the possibility of an action in battery where the patient has not given a valid consent to the treatment. We will consider that in Chapter 5, where we also look at the related claims brought in negligence for failure to warn or advise a patient adequately.

Undoubtedly, the negligence action is the principal one by which patients seek compensation for injuries suffered when treated within the NHS. The context of such actions is discussed in the following extract.

Kennedy and A Grubb (eds) *Principles of Medical Law* (1998)

5.02 The frequency and volume of medical negligence actions has increased considerably in recent years. Prior to the 1980s these actions were relatively rare in England; reported cases were few and far between. Since that time a significant upsurge in litigation has occurred and led some to argue that claims for medical negligence are now out of control, just as in the United States of America, and that litigation has reached 'crisis proportions'. (Jones, M 'Medical Negligence' (2nd edn, 1996), Ch 1 and Kennedy, I, 'Confidentiality, Competence and Malpractice' in Byrne, P (ed), *Malpractice in Contemporary Society* (1987)). This trend, it is said, can only have bad consequences for patients because of the transaction and direct costs it imposes upon the limited NHS budget. It is also said that the fear of being sued has, or will, encourage doctors to respond in a defensive and undesirable way and lead them to practise 'defensive medicine' whereby their behaviour towards a patient is modified solely to reduce the risk of legal action. Although it is clear that both the number of claims and their costs are rising, there is no hard evidence of the latter practice. In fact, the introduction of 'risk management' systems – defensive practices of a sort – both in clinical and other services provided within the NHS is more likely to contribute to a higher level of care to patients and others. Awareness of risk and a concern to reduce it will, inevitably, reduce accidents and hence take away the basis for some litigation. It will not, however, contribute to a reduction of claims in some situations, for instance, where a doctor's clinical judgment is at the core of the action. Clinical judgment is notoriously difficult to challenge in court either at the level of showing it was a *mis*judgment or, if it was, that it was a negligent one. However, the development of protocols and, particularly, practice guidelines may have implications by going some way to standardise medical responses and inform doctors (and others) on the available options to treat a particular patient.

5.03 It is also clear that the NHS has taken negligence litigation altogether more seriously in recent years prompted in part by the volume and cost of litigation but also because of the continuing squeeze upon NHS resources and the discipline of the cost-saving regime of the 'internal market'. The introduction of 'NHS Indemnity' in 1990 (Circular HC (89) 34; now updated as HSG(96)48) and the subsequent 'Clinical Negligence Scheme for Trusts' administered by the National Health Service Litigation Authority (The National Health Service Litigation Authority (Establishment and Constitution) Order 1995, SI 1995/2800; The National Health Service Litigation Authority Regulations 1995, SI 1995/2801) introduced on 1 March 1996 (pursuant to the National Health Service and Community Care Act 1990, s 21. See the National Health Service (Clinical Negligence Scheme) Regulations 1996, SI 1996/251, as amended by SI 1997/527) represent attempts at more centralised control to effect a rationalisation of negligence litigation within the NHS. It is also likely that, if introduced, 'conditional fee' agreements and the removal of legal aid for medical negligence actions would 'dampen' the volume of litigation considerably.

Before we turn to consider medical negligence actions in some detail, we should consider first actions in contract brought against doctors both within and outside the NHS.

Contract

In looking at the possibility of a claim for breach of contract by a patient it is important to distinguish between patients treated within the NHS and those treated privately. Actions in contract may be thought to be advantageous to patients, giving rise to more onerous obligations upon the doctor and being actionable *per se*. In reality, these perceived advantages do not exist. As we shall see, by and large, the doctor's legal duty in contract will mirror that in negligence. Also, a claim for more than nominal damages will, in any event, engage all the mechanisms of causation and remoteness associated with negligence actions (see *Chappell v Hart* (1998) 72 ALJR 1344 (HC of A)). But, first we must consider the issue of whether a contract exists between a patient and his doctor or institution.

A. WITHIN THE NHS

The conventional understanding of the doctor/institution-patient-relationship within the NHS is that it is not contractual. However, the orthodoxy has been challenged.

I Kennedy and A Grubb (eds) *Principles of Medical Law* (1998)

(i) *No Contractual Relationship*

5.06 Historically, the legal obligations of a doctor were derived from his status and 'common calling', that is, to exercise the skill and diligence expected of his calling. Whilst delictual in nature, it was recognised that an action in assumpsit and later contract lay against a doctor who treated a patient for payment (*Everard v Hopkins* (1615) 80 ER 1164 and *Slater v Baker and Stapleton* (1767) 95 ER 860). Until the NHS was created in 1948, treatment was either provided privately or on a charitable basis. However, even in the latter instance, when the patient provided no tangible consideration for a contract (*Coggs v Bernard* (1703) 92 ER 107). Within the NHS today it is generally accepted that there is no contractual relationship between a doctor (whether general practitioner or hospital doctor) and the patient (*Pfizer Corp v Ministry of Health* [1965] AC 512 (HL)). Equally, there is no contractual relationship between the patient and the hospital, such as the NHS Trust, where the patient is cared for. Any claim for damages based upon a breach of duty lies only in tort and, in particular, in an action for negligence.

5.07 The basis for the orthodoxy is two-fold. First, medical services within the NHS are provided to the patient pursuant to a statutory obligation. Such compulsion to provide a service is considered to be inconsistent with a contractual arrangement. (*ibid*) Secondly, the patient fails to provide the consideration in return for the doctor (or other's) promise to treat which is necessary if a contract is to exist. This position is not, however, beyond challenge. The statutory context, for example within which a GP functions, is not necessarily inconsistent with a contractual arrangement (see *Roy v Kensington & Chelsea FPC* [1992] 1 All ER 705 (HL)). Also, it could be argued, for example, that in the case of a GP consideration may indirectly be provided by the patient since his inclusion upon the doctor's medical list will result in remuneration being paid by the Health Authority to the doctor. Also, in the case of an NHS Trust, it could be argued again that the patient indirectly provides remuneration in cases where his treatment will generate distinct future (and not past) consideration from the NHS provider whether GP fund-holder or Health Authority. Treatment under an 'extra-contractual' referral most closely fits this description.

5.08 In the Canadian decision of *Pittman Estate v Bain*, ((1994) 112 DLR (4th) 257 (Ont Gen Div)), an Ontario court went even further and held that a contractual relationship existed between the patient and a hospital on the basis that the hospital received funding from the Government funded health insurance scheme. The patient indirectly contributed to this through taxes and health premiums. Further, the hospital obtained a benefit, both financial and in reputation, when patients choose to receive treatment.

5.09 However attractive in principle the arguments may appear, there are two factors which tell against them. And, as we shall see, there is in truth no real reason for an English court to divine a contract between the parties. First, the structure of health care provision within the 'internal market' of the NHS is antithetical to contractual arrangements; for example, the National Health Service and Community Care Act 1990 specifically states that agreements between 'purchasers' and 'providers' are not legally enforceable contracts (s 4(3)). While the 1990 Act does not deal with agreements with patients, the ethos of regulation of the NHS is *ex pactum*. Secondly, the statutory and regulatory context in which health services are provided may led a court to infer that the parties had no intention to create legal relations in the form of a contract. In any event, the argument in *Pittman Estate* is most unlikely to be followed by an English court. It stretches the factual boundaries of what amounts to consideration almost to breaking point: the consideration is probably too remote.

5.10 A contractual claim will not, in most cases, affect the content of the legal rights and obligations of the parties. Even if the courts did determine that a contractual relationship existed, the scope of the duty owed to the patient is unlikely to be any different from that in the tort of negligence. In the end, however, in England a contractual basis for the legal obligations of a doctor or hospital is restricted to treatment which is provided privately. It is important to notice that private treatment is not exclusively provided outside NHS facilities. To the extent that it is provided within the NHS in, for example, 'pay beds' then a contractual basis for the parties legal obligations will apply.

B. PRIVATE TREATMENT

The position is otherwise where the patient is treated privately, whether he pays directly for the treatment or it is paid (directly or indirectly) by an insurance company.

I Kennedy and A Grubb (eds) *Principles of Medical Law* (1998)

5.11 When treatment or other health care is provided privately, a contractual relationship will arise between the doctor and the patient, and usually the clinic or institution and patient. The nature, scope, and terms of these contracts will depend upon the circumstances. Although there are a variety of ways in which contractual relationships may exist for private health care, commonly the patient will make separate arrangements with the doctor (for the treatment and aftercare) and with the clinic for the provision of facilities (such as the operating theatre) and staff (such as nurses). This will be the usual arrangement where the patient consults a doctor privately who then arranges for the patient to be treated at a clinic with which he (the doctor) has an agreement to admit patients. In other situations the arrangement may be directly with the clinic for the provision of the 'services' sought including the doctors who will carry out the procedure. There may, then, be no separate contractual arrangement with the doctor. Examples of this occur in cases of infertility treatment where the patient seeks treatment at an IVF clinic where particular doctors work.

5.12 The terms of these contracts will primarily be a matter for agreement between the parties and then subsequently included expressly in the written contract, if one exists. Terms as to payment, the provision of facilities and staff will be common depending upon the circumstances. The consent form, if any, signed by the patient will form part of the contract (eg *Thake v Maurice* [1986] QB 644 (CA); *Eyre v Measday* [1986] 1 All ER 488). The contract may also specify who is to be the treating doctor and, in such circumstances, it will be a breach of contract if another doctor treats the patient (*Morris v Winsbury-White* [1937] 4 All ER 494). The obligations of the parties will, therefore, be a matter of construing the terms in the contract in each case, subject to the constraints of public policy (eg restricting liability: *Tunkl v Regents of the University of California* (1963) 383 P 2d 441 (Cal Sup Ct)).

Curiously, although the coming into existence of a contract between a doctor and patient is critical, there is little guidance to be found in the law as to when the contract is formed. Given that there must be an offer and acceptance (together with consideration), who is it who offers and who accepts? Is it the patient who offers to pay if the doctor agrees to treat, or the patient who accepts the doctor's offer to treat by agreeing to pay? Picard and Robertson, in *Legal Liability of Doctors and Hospitals in Canada* (3rd edn, 1986) (at pp 1–2), write: 'The offer could be found [in law] in the patient's request for treatment and the acceptance in the doctor's commencement of care. Consideration [is] not a problem unless the patient [is] unable to pay. In such circumstances the law of contract [is] strained somewhat and it was held that the patient's submission to treatment [is] sufficient consideration for the doctor's services' (citing *Coggs v Bernard* (1703) 2 Ld Raym 909 and *Banbury v Bank of Montreal* [1918] AC 626).

What, then, would be the terms of such contracts?

1. Express terms

As regards express terms, as we saw this is entirely a matter of what the parties agree amongst themselves, for example, as to payment or who may carry out a particular procedure. A consent form is an example of an agreement containing express terms (see *Thake v Maurice* [1986] 1 All ER 497 and *Eyre v Measday* [1986] 1 All ER 488).

There are, of course, limits to what the parties may purport to agree through express terms. They cannot, for example, agree to do that which would be regarded as contrary to public policy, for example, selling an organ, nor to waive those obligations implied by law.

2. Implied terms

(a) Reasonable care and skill

In two cases in 1986 involving a sterilisation procedure which failed, the Court of Appeal analysed the legal obligations of the doctor to his patient with whom he had contracted to carry out the procedure. In *Eyre v Measday* [1986] 1 All ER 488, Slade LJ said:

> Applying the *Moorcock* principle, I think there is no doubt that the plaintiff would have been entitled reasonably to assume that the defendant was warranting that the operation would be performed with reasonable care and skill. That, I think, would have been the inevitable inference to be drawn, from an objective standpoint … The contract did, in my opinion, include an implied warranty of *that* nature.

Similarly, in the later case of *Thake v Maurice* [1986] 1 All ER 497 Nourse LJ observed:

The particular concern of this court in *Eyre v Measday* was to decide whether there had been an implied guarantee that the operation would succeed. But the approach of Slade LJ in testing that question objectively is of equal value in a case where it is said that there has been an express guarantee. Valuable too are the observations of Lord Denning MR in *Greaves & Co (Contractors) Ltd v Baynham, Meikle & Partners* [1975] 3 All ER 99 at 103–104, [1975] 1 WLR 1095 at 1100 which I now quote in full:

> Apply this to the employment of a professional man. The law does not usually imply a warranty that he will achieve the desired result, but only a term that he will use reasonable care and skill. The surgeon does not warrant that he will cure the patient. Nor does the solicitor warrant that he will win the case.

Neill LJ in the same case said: 'It is common ground that the defendant contracted to perform a vasectomy operation on Mr Thake and that in the performance of that contract he was subject to the duty implied by law to carry out the operation with reasonable skill and care.'

But notice that Oliver J (as he then was), when talking about the nature of a professional person's obligations, in *Midland Bank Trust Co Ltd v Hett, Stubbs & Kemp* [1979] Ch 384, makes it clear that the implied term that the professional person will use reasonable care and skill is a less than complete description of his obligations.

> **Oliver J:** The classical formulation of the claim in this sort of case as 'damages for negligence and breach of professional duty' tends to be a mesmeric phrase. It concentrates attention on the implied obligation to devote to the client's business that reasonable care and skill to be expected from a normally competent and careful practitioner as if that obligation were not only a compendious, but also an exhaustive, definition of all the duties assumed under the contract created by the retainer and its acceptance. But, of course, it is not. A contract gives rise to a complex of rights and duties of which the duty to exercise reasonable care and skill is but one.
>
> If I employ a carpenter to supply and put up a good quality oak shelf for me, the acceptance by him of that employment involves the assumption of a number of contractual duties. He must supply wood of an adequate quality and it must be oak. He must fix the shelf. And he must carry out the fashioning and fixing with the reasonable care and skill which I am entitled to expect of a skilled craftsman. If he fixes the brackets but fails to supply the shelf or if he supplies and fixes a shelf of unseasoned pine, my complaint against him is not that he has failed to exercise reasonable care and skill in carrying out the work but that he has failed to supply what was contracted for.

Jackson and Powell *Professional Negligence* (4th edn, 1996) comment on Oliver J's views as follows (para 1.10):

> The particular illustration chosen by Oliver J ... must be used with caution, since the obligations of a carpenter to his employer are generally of a different nature to those owed by a professional man to his client. Nevertheless in every contract between a professional man and his client there will be express or implied terms defining the nature of the engagement. Thus if a surveyor is instructed to produce a report on certain property, there is an express or implied obligation to inspect it. If a surgeon agrees with his patient to perform a particular operation, there may be an implied term that he will 'give the necessary supervision thereafter until the discharge of the patient'. If a solicitor is instructed to effect the grant of an option, there are implied terms that he will draw up the option agreement and effect registration. The importance of specific terms such as these is that a professional man will be liable if he breaks them, quite irrespective of the amount of skill and care which he has exercised.

An example of an implied term other than to exercise care and skill arises, for example, in the case of a doctor fitting a prosthesis. In such a case the question arises as to whether the terms implied by law by virtue of the Supply of Goods and Services Act 1982 as to the fitness for the purpose of the goods supplied or that they are of satisfactory quality apply (see generally, Bell (1984) 4 LS 175) and see *infra* ch 14). Similarly, a contract will have implied into it an obligation to keep the patient's medical information confidential (*Furniss v Fitchett* [1958] NZLR 396).

(b) Guarantee of success

It is one thing for the law to expect a contract to be performed properly, it is quite another to demand of the doctor that he guarantee success unless he has expressly agreed to do so. As Nourse LJ stated in *Thake v Maurice (supra)*:

> Lord Denning MR thought [in *Greaves v Baynham, Meikle & Partners*], and I respectfully agree with him, that a professional man is not usually regarded as warranting that he will achieve the desired result. Indeed, it seems that that would not fit well with the universal warranty of reasonable care and skill, which tends to affirm the inexactness of the science which is professed. I do not intend to go beyond the case of a doctor. Of all sciences medicine is one of the least exact. In my view a doctor cannot be objectively regarded as guaranteeing the success of any operation or treatment unless he says as much in clear and unequivocal terms. The defendant did not do that in the present case.

Courts in other jurisdictions have been prepared to find that a doctor has guaranteed a particular result and when he has failed to achieve it, they have allowed the patient to succeed in an action for breach of contract. Two cases involving cosmetic surgery illustrate this. In *Sullivan v O'Connor* (1973) 296 NE 2d 183 (Cal Sup Ct) the plaintiff, a professional entertainer, sued the defendant because of the condition of her nose after he had operated. Justice Kaplan described the plaintiff's condition as follows:

> ... judging from exhibits, the plaintiff's nose had been straight, but long and prominent; the defendant undertook by two operations to reduce its prominence and somewhat to shorten it, thus making it more pleasing in relation to the plaintiff's other features. Actually the plaintiff was obliged to undergo three operations, and her appearance was worsened. Her nose now had a concave line to about the midpoint, at which it became bulbous; viewed frontally, the nose from bridge to midpoint was flattened and broadened, and the two sides of the tip had lost symmetry. This configuration evidently could not be improved by further surgery.

The court allowed the plaintiff to recover for breach of contract. The court went on, however, to warn of the difficulties facing plaintiffs who allege that a doctor guaranteed success:

> It is not hard to see why the courts should be unenthusiastic or skeptical about the contract theory. Considering the uncertainties of medical science and the variations in the physical and psychological conditions of individual patients, doctors can seldom in good faith promise specific results. Therefore it is unlikely that physicians of even average integrity will in fact make such promises. Statements of opinion by the physician with some optimistic coloring are a different thing, and may indeed have therapeutic value. But patients may transform such statements into firm promises in their own minds, especially when they have been disappointed in the event, and testify in that sense to sympathetic juries. If actions for breach of promise can be readily maintained, doctors, so it is said, will be frightened into practising 'defensive medicine'. On the other hand, if these actions were outlawed, leaving only the possibility of suits for malpractice, there is fear that the public might be exposed to the enticements of charlatans, and confidence in the profession might ultimately be shaken.
>
> ... The law has taken the middle of the road position of allowing actions based on alleged contract, but insisting on clear proof. Instructions to the jury may well stress this requirement and point to tests of truth, such as the complexity or difficulty of an operation as bearing on the probability that a given result was promised.

In the Canadian case of *LaFleur v Cornelis* (1979) 28 NBR (2d) 569 (New Brunswick), the defendant, a cosmetic surgeon, performed a procedure to reduce the size of the plaintiff's nose. He failed to inform her that there was a 10% risk of scarring. She, in fact, was scarred. In addition to succeeding in an action in negligence, the plaintiff established a breach of contract.

> **Barry J:** A cosmetic surgeon is in a different position than the ordinary physician. He is selling a special service and he is more akin to a businessman. Therefore, this is not the ordinary malpractice case. Normally a doctor contracts to use the best skill he possesses and he is expected to exercise at least the methods ordinarily employed by similarly trained

professionals. If he does not do so, he may be guilty of negligence in carrying out his contract, as I have found the defendant was in this case.

In the instant case, that was not the kind of a contract which the defendant entered into with the plaintiff. The latter told the defendant what she wanted, namely, a smaller nose. The defendant drew a sketch on his notes to show the changes he would make if the plaintiff paid him a fee of $600.00. There was no misunderstanding whatever. Both parties were *ad idem* as to what each was to do. The plaintiff paid the fee and the defendant failed to carry out his part of the contract. Negligence is not a factor in a straight breach of contract action. There is no law preventing a doctor from contracting to do that which he is paid to do. I appreciate that usually there is no implied warranty of success, in the absence of special circumstances. In this case, the defendant stated to the plaintiff – 'no problem. You will be very happy.' He made an express agreement, which he was not required to, without explaining the risk.

I find that the parties made a contract, and the defendant breached it, leaving the plaintiff with a scarred nose with a minimal deformity.

(See also *Guilmet v Campbell* (1971) 188 NW 2d 601 (Mich Sup Ct): 'specific, clear and express promise' to cure a peptic ulcer: '[O]nce you have an operation it takes care of all of your troubles' (at 606 per Kavanagh J).)

Medical negligence

As we noted earlier, actions for medical negligence are by far the most common legal claims for compensation brought against doctors and hospitals. To maintain such an action, the claimant must establish (a) that a duty of care was owed to him; (b) that the duty was breached; and (c) that he suffered injury (or harm) caused by that breach. There are, of course, the constituent elements of any negligence action. We consider here the particular problems raised for medical lawyers. We first turn our attention to the question of *duty* and, as we shall see, consider not only whether a duty is owed by a doctor or institution to a patient but also what duty, if any, is owed to others such as strangers or those examined for insurance or employment purposes.

A. DUTY OF CARE

1. To patients

(a) Doctors

Margaret Brazier has observed '[a] patient claiming against his doctor ... usually has little difficulty in establishing that the defendant owes him a duty of care' (*Medicine, Patients and the Law* (2nd edn, 1992) at pp 117–118). The precise point at which a duty to take care comes into being may not be easy.

Nevertheless, in general terms the essence of the duty is an undertaking by the doctor towards his patient. As Lord Hewart CJ said in *R v Bateman* (1925) 94 LJKB 791 (CCA) (a case of manslaughter brought against a doctor):

> If a person holds himself out as possessing special skill and knowledge, and he is consulted, as possessing such skill and knowledge, by or on behalf of a patient, he owes a duty to the patient to use due caution in undertaking the treatment. If he accepts the responsibility and undertakes the treatment and the patient submits to his discretion and treatment accordingly, he owes a duty to the patient to use diligence, care, knowledge, skill and caution in administering the treatment. No contractual relation is necessary, nor is it necessary that the service be rendered for reward.

This, of course, assumes something which already exists, namely that the individual has already become the doctor's patient. It may be, however, that

Lord Hewart was using the word 'patient' in the sense (rather obviously) of the person who approaches the doctor and thereafter becomes his patient as a result of the undertaking.

It may seem blindingly obvious who are a doctor's patients. However, the relevant law may not be quite as straightforward. As we shall see, who is a patient analytically turns upon there being an agreement (usually not express) between a doctor and an individual. What is involved in this agreement is a request for medical services by an individual and a consequent undertaking by a doctor to provide these services. Out of this factual request and undertaking, the law forges the legal relationship of doctor and patient. For us the key significance of this legal consequence is that the doctor will, as a matter of law, owe the individual (now, his patient) a duty of care. Given that the law does impose this duty upon a doctor it is, obviously, of critical importance to determine *when* the relationship of doctor and patient is legally created.

While the coincidence of a 'request' by an individual and a resulting 'undertaking' by a doctor adequately captures the normal case, in fact there are situations in which the legal relationship will come into existence without there having been a 'request' on the part of the individual. The doctor, however, must always have given an undertaking of some sort or other to provide medical care on behalf of a young child or where an emergency arises and the individual is unconscious.

(i) GENERAL PRACTITIONERS

In the case of a GP, an individual becomes a patient as a result of the mechanisms created by the National Health Service (Choice of Medical Practitioner) Regulations 1998 (SI 1998 No 668) (whether he is providing 'general medical services', under Pt II of the 1977 Act or 'personal medical services' under a 'pilot scheme' under the 1997 Act) or by virtue of the National Health Service (General Medical Services) Regulations 1992 (SI 1992 No 635) and the *Directions to Health Authorities Concerning Patient Lists (Personal Medical Services)* (1997) and *Directions to Health Authorities Concerning the Implementation of the Pilot Schemes (Personal Medical Services)* (1997) (see *supra*, ch 2).

On one view, the creation of the 'formal' relationship may be thought to create a common law duty of care for the purposes of negligence. Another – and, it is suggested, better – view is that the duty between the GP and the individual only concretises when the GP is requested to provide, or becomes aware of the need for, the medical services. In other words, actual or constructive knowledge is a prerequisite to the existence of the duty (see eg *Goldman v Hargrave* [1967] 1 AC 645 (PC) – landowner's duty to his neighbour for the state of his premises requires knowledge (actual or constructive)). The position might be otherwise where the regulations (or directions) impose a continuing obligation or one that requires the doctor to seek out the patient, eg in relation to patients aged 75 or over who should be offered an annual consultation (see SI 1992 No 635, Sch 2, para 16).

(ii) DOCTORS IN HOSPITALS

Doctors who work within NHS hospitals do not come within the 1992 Regulations or the 'pilot scheme' Directions. Consequently, the creation of the doctor-patient relationship is wholly a matter for the common law, ie the existence or otherwise of an undertaking to take care. The common law position is illustrated by the following case.

Barnett v Chelsea and Kensington Hospital Management Committee [1969] 1 QB 428, [1968] 1 All ER 1068 (QBD)

Nield J: At about 5 am on Jan 1, 1966, three night watchmen drank some tea. Soon afterwards all three men started vomiting. At about 8 am the men walked to the casualty department of the defendants' hospital, which was open. One of them, the deceased, when he was in the room in the hospital, lay on some armless chairs. He appeared ill. Another of the men told the nurse that they had been vomiting after drinking some tea. The nurse telephoned the casualty officer, a doctor, to tell him of the men's complaint. The casualty officer, who was himself unwell, did not see them, but said that they should go home and call in their own doctors. The men went away, and the deceased died some hours later from what was found to be arsenical poisoning. Cases of arsenical poisoning were rare, and, even if the deceased had been examined and admitted to the hospital and treated, there was little or no chance that the only effective antidote would have been administered to him before the time at which he died.

I turn to consider the nature of the duty which the law imposes on persons in the position of the defendants and their servants and agents. The authorities deal in the main with the duties of doctors, surgeons, consultants, nurses and staff when a person is treated either by a doctor at his surgery or the patient's home or when the patient is treated in or at hospital. In *Cassidy v Ministry of Health* [[1951] 2 KB 343], Denning LJ dealt with the duties of hospital authorities and said:

> In my opinion, authorities who run a hospital, be they local authorities, government boards, or any other corporation, are in law under the self-same duty as the humblest doctor. Whenever they accept a patient for treatment, they must use reasonable care and skill to cure him of his ailment. The hospital authorities cannot, of course, do it by themselves. They have no ears to listen through the stethoscope, and no hands to hold the knife. They must do it by the staff which they employ, and, if their staff are negligent in giving the treatment, they are just as liable for that negligence as is anyone else who employs others to do his duties for him. Is there are possible difference in law, I ask, can there be, between hospital authorities who accept a patient for treatment and railway or shipping authorities who accept a passenger for carriage? None whatever. Once they undertake the task, they come under a duty to use care in the doing of it, and that is so whether they do it for reward or not.

> Here the problem is different and no authority bearing directly on it has been cited to me. It is to determine the duty of those who provide and run a casualty department when a person presents himself at that department complaining of illness or injury and before he is treated and received into the hospital wards. This is not a case of a casualty department which closes its doors and says that no patients can be received. The three watchmen entered the defendants' hospital without hindrance, they made complaints to the nurse who received them and she in turn passed those complaints on to the medical casualty officer, and he sent a message through the nurse purporting to advise the three men. Is there, on these facts, shown to be created a relationship between the three watchmen and the hospital staff such as gives rise to a duty of care in the defendants which they owe to the three men?

> … In my judgment, there was here such a close direct relationship between the hospital and the watchmen that there was imposed on the hospital a duty of care which they owed to the watchmen. Thus I have no doubt that Nurse Corbett and Dr Banerjee were under a duty to the deceased …

Here, Nield J found that there was the necessary undertaking on the part of the doctor (Dr Banerjee) such that he had thereafter to behave reasonably. An alternative reading of the case can be that it turns on the hospital's primary duty since Nield J found 'that there was imposed upon the hospital a duty of care which they owed to the watchmen' (see *infra*). In any event, the judge went on to find the doctor in breach of his duty in failing to examine and treat the deceased. His widow, nevertheless, lost her action because she could not show that this breach *caused* his death (see *infra*, p 496-470).

The analysis in *Barnett* is not sophisticated and it does not help us in less obvious contexts. We should try and return to first principles.

When a patient attends a hospital whether as an in-patient or out-patient, at least two distinct legal relationships call for analysis: the relationship between doctor and patient and between the hospital and the patient. (We use the word 'patient' in the context of this second relationship for convenience only. We take the view that a person can only be the patient *stricto sensu* of a doctor, although a hospital may owe him a duty of care under the law of negligence, as we shall see.) Here we are concerned with the relationship between the hospital doctor and the patient.

In the classic (though now dated) work by Lord Nathan, *Medical Negligence* (1957), the underlying explanation of how and why the doctor-patient relationship exists is stated (pp 8 and 10):

> The medical man's duty of care arises . . . quite independently of any contract with his patient. It is based simply upon the fact that the medical man has undertaken the care and treatment of the patient.

Later Nathan continues:

> It is clear then that the duty of care which is imposed upon the medical man arises quite independently of contract. It is a duty in tort which is based upon the relationship between the medical man and the patient, owing its existence to the fact that the medical man has assumed responsibility for the care, treatment or examination of the patient, as the case may be.

This, in our view, properly reflects the position in English law, as far as it goes, as regards the hospital doctor. Of course, it needs some rather more rigorous analysis. At what point can we determine that the doctor has undertaken the care and treatment of the patient? Put another way, when has the doctor 'assumed responsibility' for the patient? It would be difficult to see such an undertaking merely where a patient has been given an appointment as an outpatient. Even the institution itself may not yet have assumed a responsibility, if you like, to bring the individual into its care (see eg *Clunis v Camden and Islington HA* (1997) 40 BMLR 181). More positive steps would be required. The continuing duty would be that of the referring GP.

A patient is admitted to an NHS hospital through a formal procedure of reference by a GP and acceptance by a consultant after consultation with the hospital's manager. The admission is to occupy a bed assigned to the relevant consultant within the hospital. The question immediately arises as to the point at which the doctor-patient relationship is created. You will realise immediately that for the medical lawyer the importance of this is to determine when, if at all, a duty is owed by a doctor to a particular person.

If the principle is that the doctor must have undertaken to care for the person, the question is when, in fact, will that undertaking be judged to have been given in law. It will arise somewhere along the continuum which begins with the patient being at home and ends with the doctor embarking on the first 'laying on of hands'. It is important to remember we are concerned with the *doctor's* undertaking and consequent duty. Others, such as nurses or the hospital itself, may owe a patient their own duty from a different point in time.

Ordinarily, it will be clear in any given case whether a doctor has or has not undertaken to care for someone. At the margins, however, there could be a doubt. For example, it may not always be obvious in a case where the doctor has not yet met (nor is aware of the presence of) the person who has been admitted to the hospital under his care. The patient may meanwhile have been put in the wrong bed or have received inappropriate care such as being given a meal when he should not have been. The duty in this situation may be of the hospital or, perhaps, those who are responsible for allocating the patient to a particular ward.

In determining whether in these situations at the margin there will be an 'undertaking', it may be helpful to bear in mind the following considerations. First, the admitting consultant could be said to have undertaken to make all appropriate arrangements for the individual to be admitted and what follows thereafter. It is unlikely, however, that the doctor will be regarded as having undertaken (absent an express statement to that effect) to be on hand at all times to deal with every eventuality that may arise.

Returning to the general theme of 'undertaking', a patient, in the context of hospital care will be in the care of a team of doctors headed by the consultant. Of course, there will be other teams of professionals not necessarily led by the consultant but our concern here is only with the position of the doctors. Ordinarily each member of the team of doctors will be deemed to have separately undertaken the care of the patient when so assigned by the responsible consultant. However, the consultant as leader of the team remains responsible throughout because his undertaking of the care of the patient continues throughout the care of the patient.

If determining when an undertaking arises is sometimes difficult even *after* admission, it may be equally difficult when the individual is in the hospital but has not yet gone through the formal process of admission. Take, for example, the situation where a person walks into a hospital and suffers an unexpected heart attack requiring immediate care. Here, only in very exceptional circumstances will the admitting doctor be said to have undertaken to care for the person. It does not follow, however, that no duty is owed to the individual. The *hospital* may be judged to have undertaken to care for all those who enter once one of its employees has knowledge that a person needs, or may be in need of, medical attention. In this situation, the hospital could be exposed to primary liability for breach (if established) of its own duty to the individual (*Barnett, supra*).

The last area of difficulty concerning 'undertaking' arises where the doctor is *prima facie* a stranger to a patient who is under the care of another doctor. Take, for example, the situation where a doctor in one team is asked by a nurse to help to care for a patient under the care of another consultant (and he is not part of that consultant's team). The solution to the question whether he becomes that patient's doctor lies in the principle that the law does not require a doctor to act as a good Samaritan towards any person in the absence of an undertaking by the doctor to take care of that person. It is problematic whether the law would deem there to be an undertaking here, but the presence of the doctor and the existence of a need could well lead the law to reach that conclusion.

(iii) CHILDREN

In the case of a child who is too immature to enter into the relationship of doctor and patient, the request for medical services must come from another. In most circumstances, this would be a parent (s 2 of the Children Act 1989). It may, however, be that parental responsibility, as regards medical care, has been acquired by the local authority (under Pts IV and V of the Children Act 1989) to the exclusion of the parents (s 33(3) of the Children Act 1989) or is vested in the court because the child is a ward of court (s 41 of the Supreme Court Act 1981 and RSC Ord 90). In all of these cases the request is made on behalf of another. We are not concerned here with a request by just anyone. The request must be by someone who has the legal authority to act on that other's behalf to bring the relationship of doctor and patient into existence. Of course, that other, ie the child, may well dissent. Assuming (as we are) that the child is incompetent to make decisions on his own by reason of his immaturity, such dissent would have no *legal* force.

To whom does the doctor give his undertaking? The answer must be that the undertaking is given as a matter of fact to the parents or other who acts on behalf of the child. Of course, what flows from this undertaking is the legal duty to care for the child which is owed to the child and no one else. (For the position of GPs and the creation of the 'formal relationship', see The National Health Service (Choice of Medical Practitioner) Regulations 1998, (SI 1998 No 668), reg 2(3).)

The discussion so far has been concerned with the incompetent child; legal orthodoxy would have it that when a child becomes competent (as defined by law) only that child may request medical treatment. No one else can request on the child's behalf and, *ex hypothesi*, no one can request medical services when the child has refused. The Court of Appeal, in the cases of *Re R* [1991] 4 All ER 177 and *Re W* [1992] 4 All ER 627 has suggested that both a court, in the exercise of its inherent jurisdiction, and a parent may request medical services (enter their consent) even in the case of a competent child and even in the face of the child's refusal of those services (for an analysis of this judicial development, see Chapter 6).

(iv) INCOMPETENT ADULTS

The person we are primarily concerned with here is the adult who is unconscious or is otherwise mentally incompetent to request medical treatment. There is of course, covered by reg 2(3)(b) of the National Health Service (Choice of Medical Practitioners) Regulations 1998, *supra*, which as regards a GP provides for the inclusion on his list of a 'person who is incapable of making ... an application' on the application of a 'relative or another adult person who has an interest in the welfare of that person'. This allows for the formal creation of the doctor-patient relationship but no more. As we will see, there is no one who is authorised in law to request medical treatment on behalf of such a person (Chapter 6). Thus, the law must have a mechanism by which treatment which the person needs can lawfully be administered. Until the decision of the House of Lords in *Re F (mental patient: sterilisation)* [1990] 2 AC 1, sub nom *F v West Berkshire Health Authority (Mental Health Act Commission intervening)* [1989] 2 All ER 545 (HL), there had been no authoritative statement by the courts or in legislation recognising the legality of such treatment except in the case of mental disorder (see Mental Health Act 1983, Pt IV). It had been assumed (or argued) that, in appropriate circumstances, such treatment would be lawful (see eg P D G Skegg *Law, Ethics and Medicine* (1988) ch 5 and *Wilson v Pringle* [1986] 2 All ER 440 at 447 per Croom-Johnson LJ).

In *Re F*, the House of Lords acknowledged that the principle of necessity could justify the medical intervention if it was in the patient's 'best interests' (see *supra*, ch 6). Having intervened, the doctor will owe a duty of care. In *Re F*, Lord Goff stated: '... a doctor who has assumed responsibility for the care of a patient may not only be treated as having the patient's consent to act, but may also be under a duty so to act' (at 77). Thus, the doctor's undertaking (without a request from the patient) suffices for the common law. Lord Brandon in the same case more fully stated the position where the patient is unconscious:

> **Lord Brandon:** In many cases, however, it will not only be lawful for doctors, on the ground of necessity, to operate on or give other medical treatment to adult patients disabled from giving their consent; it will also be their common law duty to do so.
>
> In the case of adult patients made unconscious by an accident or otherwise, they will normally be received into the casualty department of a hospital, which thereby undertakes the care of them. It will then be the duty of the doctors at that hospital to use their best endeavours to do, by way of either an operation or other treatment, that which is in the best interests of such patients.

(v) EMERGENCIES

Closely linked to the situation of the incompetent patient, is that of the emergency. Indeed, the House of Lords in *Re F* saw the 'emergency' situation as merely an illustration of the application of the 'principle of necessity'. Of course, it is one thing to say that a doctor *may* treat in an emergency, it is another to say that he *must* treat because he has a duty to do so.

What is important to notice is that even in an emergency the doctor must still have undertaken the care of the individual before any duty in law will arise. Obviously, if the emergency occurs when the individual is already in the care of the doctor, for example, in a hospital, the undertaking will already exist and be deemed to continue. Equally, when a doctor has held himself out as undertaking to treat individuals requiring emergency care, for example, by being on duty in an Accident and Emergency Department of a hospital, he will be deemed to have undertaken to provide emergency care once he is aware of the need for it. No case in England has touched upon this matter but in principle this is the correct approach. Some reliance can be placed upon the only relevant English decision in *Barnett v Chelsea and Kensington HMC* [1968] 1 All ER 1068, which we saw earlier.

Nield J: At about 5 am on Jan 1, 1966, three night watchmen drank some tea. Soon afterwards all three men started vomiting. At about 8 am the men walked to the casualty department of the defendants' hospital, which was open. One of them, the deceased, when he was in the room in the hospital, lay on some armless chairs. He appeared ill. Another of the men told the nurse that they had been vomiting after drinking tea. The nurse telephoned the casualty officer, a doctor, to tell him of the men's complaint. The casualty officer, who was himself unwell, did not see them, but said that they should go home and call in their own doctors. The men went away, and the deceased died some hours later from what was found to be arsenical poisoning. Cases of arsenical poisoning were rare, and, even if the deceased had been examined and admitted to the hospital and treated, there was little or no chance that the only effective antidote would have been administered to him before the time at which he died.

Nield J then asked himself the following question: 'Is there, on these facts, shown to be created a relationship between the three watchmen and the hospital staff such as gives rise to a duty of care in the defendants which they owe to the three men?' The answer he gave was '… I have no doubt that [the nurse] and [the doctor] were under a duty to the deceased …'

This case is, in one sense, an obvious one for us since by giving advice over the telephone the doctor had clearly embarked upon the care of the three watchmen, albeit inadequately. The difficult question is what if the three watchmen had come into the casualty department and the doctor on seeing them declined to treat them despite their apparent need for treatment for no good reason? The position must be that the law would deem there to be an undertaking because of the coincidence of an open Accident and Emergency Department, a doctor on duty and a person apparently in need of emergency care.

The courts would undoubtedly be influenced by the *reliance* of the 'patient' in attending the A&E department on the expectation that emergency care was available. The point is illustrated in the following case, where the 'patient' relied upon the ambulance service to attend but which did not do so for, it was alleged, an unreasonable time, as a result of which she suffered permanent injury.

Kent v Griffiths [2000] Lloyd's Rep Med 109, [2000] 2 All ER 474 (CA)

Lord Woolf MR:

1. The issue on this appeal is whether an ambulance service can owe any duty of care to a member of the public on whose behalf a '999' call is made if, due to carelessness, it fails to arrive within a reasonable time.

The Background

2. The appeal is against a judgment of Mr Justice Turner given on 16 July 1999 by the third defendant, the London Ambulance Service ("LAS"). The judge awarded the claimant

damages amounting to £362,377. He dismissed the claims against the first and second defendants who were the claimant's doctors. The LAS was ordered to pay the claimant's costs of the action, including the costs incurred by the claimant in respect of the claim against the first and second defendants, and to indemnify the claimant in respect of her liability in costs to the first and second defendants. The judge gave the LAS permission to appeal as the case raised a novel point of law. There is no appeal in relation to the decision as to the dismissal of the claim against the first and second defendants. There is a cross-appeal by the claimant as to damages. That cross-claim is to be heard on a later date.

3. The facts relevant to the issue on this appeal can be stated shortly. They are not in dispute. They are set out clearly in the judgment.

4. The claimant is an asthmatic. On 16 February 1991 she suffered an asthma attack. The first defendant attended at her home. At 16.25 the first defendant telephoned the LAS, gave the claimant's name, address and age and indicated that she was suffering from bronchial asthma and asked for an ambulance to take her "immediately please" to casualty where she was expected. The control replied "okay doctor". By 16.38 the ambulance had not arrived so the claimant's husband made a second call. The LAS's response was "Yes. They are well on their way to you … give them another 7 or 8 minutes". At 16.54 the first defendant made a second call as the ambulance had still not arrived. The response was "Well it should be a couple of minutes". The ambulance did not arrive, as the judge found, until 17.05. The claimant arrived at the hospital at 17.17.

5. The record prepared by a member of the ambulance crew indicated that the time of arrival at the claimant's home was not 17.05 but 16.47. The judge found that there had been contemporary falsification of the records by the member of the ambulance crew. He considered that he had not been given any satisfactory explanation for the ambulance taking 34 minutes to travel 6.5 miles from its base to the claimant's home. The judge was satisfied that the crew member had "withheld the true reason, whatever it might have been, why it took so long for the ambulance to reach the claimant's house". The crew member "knew full well just how critical was going to be the record which he made" of the time of arrival. In the absence of any reasonable excuse for the delay, the judge was "driven to conclude that the delay was culpable". The ambulance did not reach the claimant's home within a reasonable time. It could and should have arrived at the claimant's home at least 14 minutes sooner than it did. If it had arrived in a reasonable time, as it should have done, there was a high probability that the respiratory arrest, from which the claimant suffered, would have been averted. The judge also made criticisms as to the information communicated by the LAS to the ambulance crew, which would also amount to carelessness, but he did not base his decision on this additional finding.

6. The doctor gave evidence that if she had been told, when she had first telephoned for the ambulance, that it would be 40 minutes before it arrived she would have probably asked the claimant's husband to drive his wife to the hospital. She would have accompanied them.

7. I should set out the views of this very experienced judge as to the general merits of the claimant's case. He said: "I should have found it offensive to, and inconsistent with, concepts of common humanity if in circumstances such as the present where there had been an unreasonable and unexplained delay in providing the services which LAS were in a position to meet, and had accepted that it would supply an ambulance, the law could not in its turn provide a remedy to the person whose condition was significantly exacerbated in consequence."

8. I have already indicated that the issue on this appeal is whether the claimant was owed a duty of care. Originally in its defence the LAS admitted that it was under a duty to respond. However, after the decision of this Court in the case of *Capital & Counties Plc v Hampshire County Council* [1997] QB 1004 (Stuart-Smith, Potter and Judge LJJ) that a fire brigade was not under a common law duty to answer calls to fires or to take reasonable care to do so, an application was made to withdraw that admission by way of amendment. An application was also made to strike out the allegations against the LAS. This was based on an allegation that the statement of claim disclosed no cause of action in so far as it relied upon the delay in responding to the ambulance call.

9. The application to strike out was dismissed by this Court (Kennedy and Schiemann LJJ and Sir Patrick Russell) [1999] Lloyd's Rep Med 58, [1999] PIQR P192. The Court considered that the *Capital & Counties* case was arguably distinguishable upon the grounds that the duty to fight fires remains throughout a duty owed to the public at large. By contrast once a call to an ambulance service has been accepted, the service is dealing with a named individual upon whom the duty becomes focused. Furthermore, if an ambulance service is called and agrees to attend the patient, those caring for the patient normally abandon any attempt to find an alternative means of transport to the hospital …

The Authorities on Volunteer Rescuers

15. Mr Munby drew our attention to two lines of authorities on volunteers. The first starts with the leading case of *East Suffolk Rivers Catchment Board v Kent* [1941] AC 74 at 84–5, 87, 95, 102 and 104. It deals specifically with the situation where a claim is against a statutory body in relation to the performance of its statutory functions where the statute does not create any duty of care on which the claimant is entitled to rely. As to such a situation Lord Romer made a statement with which Lord Porter agreed. He said (at p 102):

> Where a statutory authority is entrusted with a mere power it cannot be made liable for any damage sustained by a member of the public by reason of a failure to exercise that power. If in the exercise of their discretion they embark upon an execution of the power, the only duty they owe to a member of the public is not thereby to add to the damages that he would have suffered had they done nothing. So long as they exercise their discretion honestly, it is for them to determine the method by which and the time in which and the time during which the power shall be exercised; and they cannot be made liable, except to the extent that I have just mentioned, for any damage that would have been avoided had they exercised their discretion in a more reasonable way.

16. Mr Munby also relies on the *Dorset Yacht* case [1970] AC 1004 and *Capital & Counties* and the other cases that were cited in that case for the proposition I have quoted. However, while the proposition is acceptable, it only applies to this case if the LAS did not owe the usual form of private duty of care to the claimant. I refer to the *usual* form of duty because, as the citation makes clear, even when the responsibility is more limited there is still a residual responsibility.

17. In addition, it is argued that in this case the LAS did "add to the damage [that the claimant] would have suffered if they had done nothing". But for the acceptance of the 999 call the claimant would have been driven to the hospital and would have arrived prior to her "arrest". Furthermore, although I do not regard this as altering the duty that the LAS owed, even if the LAS was not under any private law duty, in this case it would certainly be under a public *duty* to exercise its discretion to provide an ambulance. This is because on the evidence there was no rational reason why would justify the LAS's discretion being exercised in any other manner.

18. The other line of authorities is adequately reflected in the decision of the Canadian courts culminating in the Supreme Court's decision in *"The Ogopogo"* [1971] 2 Lloyd's Rep. 410. They establish that the common law does not require a member of the public to act as would the Good Samaritan. If he does so, however, the law does protect him from being liable in damages except to the extent that his own acts cause damage beyond that which the claimant would have suffered if he had not intervened.

19. While I accept unhesitatingly the good sense of this line of authority I have difficulty in applying it to the present situation. The LAS was under at least a public law duty for the reason I have given already. The provision of ambulances is its statutory function. The LAS and its crews are paid out of public monies to provide their services. It is wholly inappropriate to regard the LAS and its employees as volunteers.

Alexandrou v Oxford

20. In *Alexandrou v Oxford*, the defendant was a Chief Constable who had been sued by Mr Alexandrou after the latter's clothing shop was burgled. The burglar alarm had been activated, but, when the police officers attended, they did not properly inspect the rear of the premises. The judge held that the Chief Constable was liable to Mr Alexandrou because if the inspection had been carried out properly, the theft would have been prevented. The Chief Constable appealed to this Court. This Court allowed the appeal. There were two grounds for the Court doing so. The first ground was that the relationship between Mr Alexandrou and the police was insufficient to create a duty of care. Glidewell LJ stated in the principal judgment of the Court, with which the other members of the Court agreed (at p 334 e–g):

> It is not sufficient for a plaintiff, who seeks to establish that a defendant owed him a duty to take reasonable care to prevent loss being caused to the plaintiff by the activities of another person, simply to prove that if the defendant did not exercise reasonable care it was foreseeable that the plaintiff would suffer the loss. It is necessary for the plaintiff also to show that in the circumstances of the particular case he stands in a special relationship to the defendant, from which the duty of care arose: see per Lord Wilberforce in *McLoughlin v O'Brian* [1982] 2 All ER 298 at 303, [1983] 1 AC 410 at 420: 'That foreseeability does not of itself, and automatically, lead to a duty of care is, I think, clear.'

21. Later Glidewell LJ added (at p 338 g–j):

It is possible to envisage an agreement between an occupier of a property protected by a burglar alarm and the police which would impose a contractual liability on the police. That is not however, the situation in this case. The communication to the police in this case was by a 999 telephone call, followed by a recorded message. If as a result of that communication the police came under a duty of care to the plaintiff, it must follow that they would be under a similar duty to any person who informs them, whether by 999 call or in some other way, that a burglary, or indeed any crime, against himself or his property is being committed or is about to be committed. So in my view if there is a duty of care it is owed to a wider group than those to whom the judge referred. It is owed to all members of the public who give information of a suspected crime against themselves or their property. It follows, therefore, that *on the facts of this case it is my opinion there was no such special relationship* between the plaintiff and the police as was present in the *Dorset Yacht* case."(emphasis added)

22. Having come to the conclusion that the relationship was not "special", in case he was wrong, Glidewell LJ went on to consider whether as a matter of general policy the police should be under such a duty. Here he attached importance to the well-known passage from Lord Keith's speech in *Hill v Chief Constable of West Yorkshire* [1989] AC 53 (at pp 63–64). In that passage of his speech, Lord Keith pointed out that there are some situations where the imposition of a duty of care will result in the exercise of higher standards of care in the carrying out of various activities. However this was not true of police activities. It could result in a "detrimentally defensive frame of mind". In addition Lord Keith considered that police investigations must frequently involve a variety of decisions on matters of policy and discretion as to which particular line of inquiry it was most advantageous to pursue and as to what was the most advantageous way to deploy the available resources. Such decisions were not regarded by the Courts as appropriate to be called into question. Both lines of reasoning of Lord Keith caused Glidewell LJ to express the view that it would not be appropriate for there to be a duty of care.

23. Slade LJ, in giving his additional reasons for allowing the appeal stated (at p 344 c–d):

It is unthinkable that the police should be exposed to potential actions for negligence at the suit of every disappointed or dissatisfied maker of a 999 call. I can see no sufficient grounds for holding that the police owed a duty of care to this plaintiff on or after receipt of the 999 call ... if they would not have owed a duty of care to ordinary members of the public who made a similar call.

24. It is to be noted that, in relation to 999 calls to the police, the law which is laid down in the *Alexandrou* case and the *Hill* case had at least two important strands. The first is that the primary duty which the police are under is to the public at large to prevent crime. The second is that to impose a liability on the police for the benefit of an individual member of the public to prevent a crime could interfere with the performance of that primary duty. Issues will arise when difficult policy decisions have to be made involving conflicts between the interests of different members or sections of the public and those situations should not be made more difficult by possible litigation having to be taken into account.

25. There are however a great variety of situations where the police provide assistance to the public because they decide to do so. In the well known case of *Haynes v Harwood* [1935] 1 KB 146, involving a policeman going to the rescue by stopping a bolting horse, Maugham LJ said (at p 161–2):

In my opinion the police constable was not in any true sense a volunteer. It is true that he was under no positive legal duty to run out into the street and at the risk of his life to stop two galloping horses; and I quite accept that nobody would have thought of reprimanding him if he had done nothing. It is also true that the primary duty of the police is the prevention of crime and the arrest of criminals; but that is only a part of the duties of the police in London. There is a general duty to protect the life and property of the inhabitants; there is a discretionary duty to direct the traffic, to help blind and infirm people to cross the road, and to direct people to cross the road who have lost their way.

26. The obligations of the police are rooted in the common law and not statute: they evolve to meet the current needs of society. I emphasised in my quotation from the judgment of Glidewell LJ that he was careful to refer to the facts of the appeal which the Court was considering. I consider he was right to limit his remarks in this way. The reasoning of the judgments in that case cannot be applied sensibly to the police officer helping pedestrians across the road. If the policeman assumes this task there is no reason of policy or proximity why he should be in any different position from a school teacher who performs this task and, if this is appropriate on the facts, is liable for negligence.

27. Slade LJ used the shorthand of referring to 999 calls. However, it would amount to a misunderstanding of his approach to attach any magic to the fact that the response is to a 999 call. It is the nature of and the circumstances in which the assistance is provided and required which is important. The issue which can be important is whether it is an urgent call made by phone or otherwise for the assistance of the police involving conflicting priorities or difficult decisions as to the best way to protect the public against crime, or whether it is a routine task which involves no policy or resource issues. In the latter situation a duty can readily be inferred. In the former situation it is unlikely it will exist. In between there are a spectrum of different situations which will have to be judged on their facts.

Capital & Counties Plc v Hampshire County Council and Others
28. The decision in the *Alexandrou* case was applied in the *Capital & Counties* case. This was after the Court had examined in detail a large number of authorities and in the course of argument had been referred to further authorities. Stuart-Smith LJ gave the judgment of the Court. It dealt with three different sets of proceedings. In each case, there had been attendance at premises as a result of a 999 call because of a fire. The Court held that the relationship between the owner or occupier of the premises and the fire brigade was not sufficiently proximate so as to impose a duty of care on the fire brigade to protect the property, simply based on the fire brigade's attendance at the site of a fire and involvement in fighting the fire. However, if the fire brigade by their own actions increased the risk of danger they would be liable for negligence in respect of the damage which was caused by the increased risk, unless damage would have occurred in any event …

Was the Judge's Decision Correct? …
40. There are obvious similarities between the facts of this case and the facts in the *Alexandrou* and *Capital & Counties* type of situation. The activities of the fire services are subject to a statutory framework, so are the functions of ambulance services. Section 3(1) of the National Health Service Act 1977 imposes on the Secretary of State a duty to provide, throughout England and Wales, to such extent as he considers necessary to meet all reasonable requirements, "medical, dental, nursing and ambulance services" (Section 1 and 3(1) of the National Health Service Act 1977). This duty is an exhortatory or target duty which does not create a statutory right, the breach of which can give rise to a private law right to damages. As the police and the fire services can be summoned by 999 calls so can the ambulance service, as in this case. However, the tasks which they can be called on to do when summoned can be very different. Mr Munby referred to examples of situations where to distinguish between one emergency service and another would suggest totally different treatment if his argument was not correct. The examples were far from the facts of this case. Here his argument could involve two different services provided under the same section of the same Act being treated very differently. …
42. … I have no reservations about expressing the view that the decision of Turner J was right. The starting point is the fact that even when a statute only establishes a power for a body to act in a particular manner the body can be liable for negligence if there is also a common law duty created on the particular facts of the case. As Lord Browne-Wilkinson states in his significant examination of this subject in *X v Bedfordshire Council* [1995] 2 AC 633 (at p 735 F):

> It is clear that a common law duty of care may arise in the performance of statutory functions. But a broad distinction has to be drawn between (a) cases in which it is alleged that the authority owes a duty of care in the manner in which it exercises a statutory discretion; (b) cases in which a duty of care is alleged to arise from the manner in which the statutory duty has been implemented in practice.

43. In the case of category (b) there is less difficulty in establishing that there is a duty of care, and in this case it is a (b) situation with which we are concerned. In this passage it is duties not powers which are being considered. The distinction between duties and powers is important because, the exercise of a power being discretionary, it is unlikely that there will be any duty of care. This is made clear by Lord Hoffmann in *Stovin v Wise* [1996] AC 923 at P950. But this case is one in which it would have been irrational not to have accepted the request to provide an ambulance and this can alter the situation (see Lord Hoffmann at P951–2).
44. Lord Slynn also deals with this subject in his opinion in *Barrett v Enfield London Borough Council* [1999] 3 WLR 79 at p 95G and 96. He indicates that, if what the authority has done is outside its discretion, the statute is no defence. Lord Slynn cautions against introducing concepts of administrative law into the law of negligence (at p 97 B–C). But reading this comment in its context, it is clear that Lord Slynn is not suggesting that the fact that an authority has acted perversely in a public law sense is to be ignored. On the contrary

he is adopting an approach which I would respectfully endorse of stressing the need to have regard to the facts.

45. Here what was being provided was a health service. In the case of health services under the Act the conventional situation is that there is a duty of care. Why should the position of the ambulance staff be different from that of doctors or nurses? In addition the arguments based on public policy are much weaker in the case of the ambulance service than they are in the case of the police or the fire service. The police and fire services' primary obligation is to the public at large. In protecting a particular victim of crime, the police are performing their more general role of maintaining public order and reducing crime. In the case of fire the fire service will normally be concerned not only to protect a particular property where a fire breaks out but also to prevent fire spreading. In the case of both services, there is therefore a concern to protect the public generally. The emergency services that can be summoned by a 999 call do, in the majority of situations, broadly carry out a similar function. But in reality they can be very different. The ambulance service is part of the Health Service. Its care functions include transporting patients to and from hospital when the use of an ambulance for this purpose is desirable. It is therefore appropriate to regard the LAS as providing services of the category provided by hospitals and not as providing services equivalent to those rendered by the police or the fire service. Situations could arise where there is a conflict between the interests of a particular individual and the public at large. But in the case of the ambulance service in this particular case, the only member of the public who could be adversely affected was the claimant. It was the claimant alone for whom the ambulance had been called.

46. Cases could arise where an ambulance is required to attend a scene of an accident in which a number of people need transporting to hospital. That could be said to be a different situation, but, as the numbers involved would be limited, I would not regard this as necessarily leading to a different result. The result would depend on the facts. I would be resistant to a suggestion that the ambulance service could be regarded as negligent because by an error of judgment a less seriously injured patient was transported to hospital leaving a more seriously injured patient at the scene who, as a result, suffered further injuries. In such a situation, on the facts, it is most unlikely that there would be conduct which could be properly regarded as negligent. The requirement to establish that there has been a lack of care provides the LAS with the necessary protection.

47. An important feature of this case is that there is no question of an ambulance not being available or of a conflict in priorities. Again I recognise that where what is being attacked is the allocation of resources, whether in the provision of sufficient ambulances or sufficient drivers or attendants, different considerations could apply. There then could be issues which are not suited for resolution by the courts. However, once there are available, both in the form of an ambulance and in the form of manpower, the resources to provide an ambulance on which there are no alternative demands, the ambulance service would be acting perversely "in circumstances such as arose in this case", if it did not make those resources available. Having decided to provide an ambulance an explanation is required to justify a failure to attend within reasonable time.

48. Mr Munby does not suggest that the danger to the claimant was not reasonably foreseeable. Nor does he base his case on policy considerations. He focuses on the third strand, proximity, alone. The three strands are often intertwined. In *Caparo* Lord Oliver states (at p 633 B–C) that "what have been treated as three separate requirements are, at least in most cases, in fact merely facets of the same thing, for in some cases the degree of foreseeability is such that it is from that alone that the requisite proximity can be deduced, whilst in others the absence of that essential relationship can most rationally be attributed simply to the Court's view that it would not be fair and reasonable to hold the defendant responsible."

49. So in my judgment here. The fact that it was a person who foreseeably would suffer further injuries by a delay in providing an ambulance, when there was no reason why it should not be provided, is important in establishing the necessary proximity and thus duty of care in this case. In other words, as there were no circumstances which made it unfair or unreasonable or unjust that liability should exist, there is no reason why there should not be liability if the arrival of the ambulance was delayed for no good reason. The acceptance of the call in this case established the duty of care. On the findings of the judge it was delay which caused the further injuries. If wrong information had not been given about the arrival of the ambulance, other means of transport could have been used.

50. The ambulance call having been made, apparently attendance is automatic. This does not prevent acceptance. If having attended there was no reason for the ambulance to go to the hospital there would be no obligation to make an unnecessary journey.

51. The reaction of the judge to the facts of this case accords with the likely reaction of any well-informed member of the public. In such a situation it would be regrettable indeed if

there were not to be a right to compensation. It is clearly a factor which influenced May LJ in another case involving the police, *Costello v The Chief Constable of Northumbria Police* [1999] 1 All ER 550, where the Chief Constable was liable for the negligence of a senior police officer who exposed another police officer to unnecessary risk of injury. May LJ said (at p 564 g):

> I am sure that Astill J was correct to say that the public would be greatly disturbed if the law held that there was no duty of care in this case.

> 52. I would say exactly the same of the facts in this case. As in *Costello* they are out of the ordinary. I would hope that it is unusual in the extreme for an ambulance to be delayed as this ambulance was delayed without the crew being able to put forward any explanation.
> 53. I would dismiss this appeal.
> **Aldous and Laws LJJ agreed.**

The Court of Appeal's decision (which is the subject of appeal to the House of Lords) is based upon the 'acceptance' of the 999 call and the reliance by the patient (and her GP) on the ambulance attending. Lord Woolf MR noted that the decision might have been different if the ambulance service had lacked the resources – whether vehicular or personnel – to send an ambulance. Here, he considered the court might risk being dragged into 'issues which are not suited for resolution by the courts'.

Equally, the court is not saying that there will be a duty of care whenever an ambulance fails to appear. The 999 call must be accepted. Unlike Turner J at first instance, however, the court did not specify that an ambulance must be allocated to the patient ([1999] Lloyd's Rep Med 424 at 453 per Turner J). It would be sufficient that the need for an ambulance was identified and – providing one was available – there was a failure to attend. The 'need' for an ambulance would require that sufficient information was given to recognise the urgency of the situation and the location of the 'patient'. Of course, non-attendance within a 'reasonable' time could still be defended as not negligent if, for example, there were adverse road or weather conditions that prevented prompt attendance. But this would be a question of *breach* rather than the existence of a duty of care (cf Turner J at first instance, *supra* at 453).

Finally, the court rejected the argument that a 'conflict of priorities' at the scene of an accident would prevent a duty of care arising. This type of argument has been very influential in the police, fire service and other emergency service cases. Lord Woolf MR, instead, regarded this (again) as a factor relevant to breach – the need to prove negligence provided the ambulance service 'with the necessary protection'.

However, in general an undertaking will not be held to exist in law merely because of the coincidence of an emergency and a doctor nearby. In general, the law does not impose an obligation upon a doctor to act as a 'good Samaritan', ie to act as a rescuer in an emergency. There is an exception in the case of a GP. Paragraph 4(1)(h) of the terms of service (the National Health Service (General Medical Services) Regulations 1992 (SI 1992 No 635) (as amended), Sch 2) provides as follows:

> 4. (1)(h) ... persons to whom he may be requested to give treatment which is immediately required owing to an accident or other emergency at any place in his practice area, provided that –
> (i)   he is not, at the time of the request, relieved of liability to give treatment under paragraph 5 [ie elderly or infirm], and
> (ii) he is not, at the time of the request, relieved, under paragraph 19(2), of his obligation to give treatment personally [ie by reason of having employed a deputy], and
> (iii) he is available to provide such treatment,
> and any persons by whom he is requested, and agrees, to give treatment which is immediately required owing to an accident or other emergency at any place in the locality of any Health Authority in whose medical list he is included, provided there is no doctor who, at the time

of the request, is under an obligation otherwise than under this head to give treatment to that person, or there is such a doctor but, after being requested to attend, he is unable to attend and give treatment immediately required ...

(Similar provisions exist in relation to 'pilot scheme' doctors: see, *Directions to Health Authorities Concerning the Implementation of Pilot Schemes*) 1997, para 2 (k) and Sch 1, para 13.) Paragraph 4(1)(h) contemplates two types of situation: first, an emergency which arises in the GP's practice area; and secondly, an emergency outside this area but within the area covered by the Health Authority on whose medical list he appears. As regards the latter, he has to agree to provide the emergency medical care once he has been requested to provide it. As regards the former, however, providing the three requirements in (i) to (iii) are satisfied, he has no choice but to render emergency care if requested.

There is one final situation we should consider which may be a further exception to the principle that a doctor need not act as a good Samaritan, ie as a rescuer in an emergency. It is clear that when a call is made in a theatre 'is there a doctor in the house?', a doctor by his mere presence gives no undertaking and can, as a matter of law, ignore the call (see *Re F supra* per Lord Goff at 77–78). However, if the call occurs not in a social setting, but in a professional context the answer is not so clear. Consider the following two examples. First, a hospital doctor leaving for home at the end of his period of duty is confronted by someone who has just entered the hospital and has collapsed. Secondly, a worker carrying out repairs at the offices of a Harley Street physician collapses and is in need of immediate medical attention. Can it be said that the law would deem there to be an undertaking on the part of the doctors in the two cases by virtue of the incident occurring in the context in which the doctor ordinarily acts as a doctor? Arguably, the law would determine that the doctor was not entitled to ignore the call for help in these limited circumstances. In other words, the court would find that the doctor, because what has happened took place in a context where he is practising his profession, is deemed to undertake to render emergency medical care.

The point arose directly in the following Australian case. The New South Wales Court of Appeal (by a majority) adopted this reasoning:

Lowns v Woods (1996) Aust Torts Reports 81-376 (NSWCA)

Cole JA: These two appeals, heard together, are brought by Dr Peter Lowns and Dr Peter Procopis against a judgment of Badgery-Parker J delivered 9 February 1995 in which his Honour held each had been negligent. Regarding Dr Lowns, the trial judge held:

The circumstances were such as to impose upon Dr Lowns a duty of care, the content of which was a duty to attend upon, examine and treat Patrick Woods, and that his refusal to do so constituted a breach of that duty of care for which he may be held liable in damages for negligence ...

The Trial Judge's Findings
1. Patrick Woods was born on 26 August 1976. He suffered a seizure on 29 June 1978 and a second seizure on 13 March 1979. That was the first occasion he was seen by Dr Procopis, a specialist paediatric neurologist. He was again seen by Dr Procopis on 28 March 1979 when phenobarbitone was prescribed. That drug was continued after further consultations on 16 July 1980, 15 July 1981 and until August 1981. Whilst taking the prescribed drug no further seizures occurred. In August 1981 it was decided to endeavour to withdraw the drug but on 31 August 1981 a third seizure occurred resulting in the phenobarbitone being recommenced. That was continued until July 1985 with no further episodes. On 18 July 1985 a further endeavour was recommended at reduction of the medication but on 12 January 1986 a further seizure occurred resulting in the dosage being again increased. In April 1986 the medication was gradually changed from phenobarbitone to carbamazebine.
2. On 20 January 1987 Patrick Woods suffered the seizure the subject of these proceedings ...

The Events of 20 January 1987

Mrs Light, as was her custom, rose and went for a walk on the morning of 20 January 1987. She said she left at 8.00am, insisting that she had looked at her watch and thus was clear on the time of leaving. Her walk took her 20–25 minutes. She was confident of this and, post-incident, had checked that time by repeating her walk in approximately 20 minutes. Thus, she said, she returned at about 8.25am to find Patrick fitting. She immediately called out to her other children and on their attendance first dispatched her eighteen year old son Harry to get an ambulance, and a few minutes later dispatched her fourteen year old daughter, Joanna, to get a doctor. Mrs Light told her daughter, Joanna, to "go and get a doctor". Her daughter immediately changed, took the lift to the ground floor and ran to the doctor's surgery approximately 300 metres away. Joanna estimated she reached the surgery about 5 minutes after her mother's initial request.

The account accepted by the trial judge of what then occurred is as follows:

'I knocked on the door, a man came to the door. I told him, "my mother sent me down here, my brother was having a bad fit, and that we needed a doctor", and could he come up?'

Q. "What did he say?"
A. "He asked me to bring my fitting brother down there. He asked me to bring him down."
Q. "What did you say?"
A. "I said, "he's having a bad fit, we can't bring him down.""
Q. "What did he reply to that?"
A. "To get an ambulance."
Q. "What did you say?"
A. "I said, "we need a doctor. We have already got an ambulance.""
Q. "What did he say to that?"
A. "He said, "no, I won't come.""

There was debate regarding whether the conversation set forth occurred at all, and if it did, whether it occurred with Dr Lowns. It is important to recognise that, at trial, the issue was not whether Dr Lowns should have gone to Patrick Woods; Dr Lowns accepted that, had the request set out in the conversation quoted been made to him, he would, and should, have gone to the child. His case was that the conversation never occurred. The trial judge found that the conversation had occurred with Dr Lowns. That is not challenged on appeal.

Patrick's mother, Mrs Light, said in evidence:

"Joanna came back in and said the doctor wouldn't come" …

Mrs Light knew that Dr Lowns, although refusing to go to the child, had advised the child should be brought to his surgery. Neither ambulance officer apparently knew of this. It was their practice to take patients to doctors other than Dr Lowns.

As I have said Mrs Light instructed her son Harry to go to the ambulance station about 300 metres away and call can ambulance. Harry ran to the ambulance station and within a few minutes of dispatch returned with an ambulance staffed by two officers. Harry travelled back to the unit with the ambulance, passing and waving to his sister Joanna who was hurrying to the doctor, whose premises, so she had been told by Mrs Light, were next to the ambulance station. In fact they were next door but one. Thus when Joanna returned and gave to Mrs Light the message that "the doctor wouldn't come. He said to bring Patrick down to him", Patrick was already in the care of the two ambulance officers.

The importance of these findings of the trial judge is that Mrs Light knew there was an ambulance station within 300 metres and knew there was a doctor within 300 metres. She sent her son Harry first to summons the ambulance, and shortly afterwards sent her daughter Joanna to summons the doctor. She obviously expected both would come to the unit. The trial judge found that, had Dr Lowns gone to the unit, with the assistance of the ambulance officers and members of Patrick's family; valium would have been administered:

I am satisfied on the balance of probabilities that if Dr Lowns had responded to the call to go to treat the plaintiff, he would have been successful in effecting an intravenous injection of valium.

If on the other hand, Dr Lowns had been unable to inject an intravenous injection, the probability is that if Mrs Light had been aware of the possibility of using the rectal route, she would have drawn that to the attention of Dr Lowns, and I am satisfied that on the balance of probabilities that he would have administered valium by that method if unsuccessful intravenously.

His Honour also found that:

> Having injected the medication, he would have directed the ambulance officers to take the patient directly to hospital …

It must be assumed that had Patrick been taken to Dr Lowns' surgery by ambulance the same treatment would there have been given. Subject to the question of timing of the treatment, the trial judge found:

> I find on the balance of probabilities that if Dr Lowns had not breached his duty to treat the plaintiff, the plaintiff's status condition would have been brought to an end before 9.15am and, if a second dose were necessary, before 9.30am. Similarly, I find that if Dr Procopis had given to Mrs Light that advice which he ought to have given, she would have administered rectal valium at such a time as also would have had the effect of bringing the status epilepticus of Patrick Woods to an end by 9.15am., or, should a second dose have been necessary, before 9.30am.

Further his Honour found:

> Acknowledging that there is some chance that the plaintiff may have incurred brain damage prior to 9.15 or 9.30am, I assess the chance of that happening as very low indeed. It follows that I am satisfied as to the plaintiff's case against each defendant that he has established all of the necessary elements thereof, that is to say duty, breach and causation and he is entitled to a verdict against each defendant.

A Critical Question

There is a critical question, on the manner in which Dr Lowns argued his appeal, which was not addressed in specific terms by the trial judge, namely:

> Was Dr Lowns negligent in advising Joanna Woods to bring her brother Patrick to the surgery, if necessary by ambulance which he was informed had been "got", rather than attending on Patrick Woods at his unknown address?

The reason why this issue was not specifically addressed in the evidence at the trial, or in the judgment, becomes clear once the case advanced by Dr Lowns at trial is understood. As I have said, he chose to fight the case against him on a simple issue, namely, whether the conversation with Joanna Woods containing the request occurred. He said it did not. He accepted in cross-examination that if it did occur, he would have gone to Patrick, and should have done so because he could well foresee damage to a fitting child if he did not attend on the child immediately and administer treatment. It was not his case at trial that Mrs Light and the ambulance men should have brought the child to him for treatment. Had it been his case, as Mr Milne QC for the respondents submitted, different and additional questions would have been addressed to Dr Lowns regarding the reasonableness of his not attending on Patrick at his residence rather than at the surgery. …

The Knowledge of Dr Lowns

Dr Lowns denied any knowledge at all of the events because he said there was no conversation between himself and Joanna Woods. However the appeal has been conducted upon an acceptance of the trial judge's findings that it did occur. On that basis the following was the state of his knowledge.

Patrick Woods was not a patient of Dr Lowns. Dr Lowns did not know Patrick Woods' age or anything about him other than that he was the brother of Joanna Woods who would obviously have been about 14 or 15 years of age. He did not know where Patrick Woods was. He knew nothing of his condition apart from being told he was "having a bad fit". He was also told that "we", presumably meaning Patrick Woods' family, could not "bring him down" but was informed that "we have already got an ambulance". He did not know that Patrick Woods was in a unit on the sixth floor of a building, or that there was any difficulty in the ambulance removing him from the unit. Although he did not know where Patrick Woods was situated, he must have assumed that he was in close proximity because his sister had come on foot to the surgery. He had no reason to believe that the ambulance could not bring Patrick Woods to his surgery immediately on the return of Joanna Woods to the place where Patrick Woods was. The trial judge found it would have taken Dr Lowns "a minute or so to collect his bag and perhaps leave a message for the receptionist". Dr Lowns had no reason to think other than that the ambulance could within a time approximate to the time it would take him to go to Patrick Woods, bring Patrick Woods to him.

In those circumstances, whilst denying the conversation occurred, he gave the evidence I have quoted that he would, and should, have gone to Patrick Woods to give him treatment.

Legal Principles

The learned trial judge was correct in his holding:

> In general the common law does not impose a duty to assist a person in peril even where it is foreseeable that the consequence of a failure to assist will be the injury or death of the person imperiled. Something other than the foreseeability of harm is required before the law imposes a duty to intervene. It has been held in other common law jurisdictions that a doctor is under no duty to attend upon a person who is sick, even in an emergency, if that person is one with whom the doctor is not and has never been in a professional relationship of doctor and patient: see Jones, Medical Negligence, Sweet & Maxwell 1991 at p 24, para. 2.21; Kennedy & Grubb, Medical Law, Butterworths, (2nd ed.) 1994 at p 79; *Hurley v Eddingfield* (1901) 59 NE 1058; *Childers v Frye* (1931) 158 SE 744; *Butterworths v Swint* (1938) 188 SE 770; *Findlay v Board of Supervisions of the County of Mohave* (1951) 230 P 2d 526; *Agnew v Parkes* (1959) 343 P 2d 118 at 123; *Hister v Randolf* (1986) 17 P 2d 774. Although there is no Australian authority in which the general proposition has been specifically applied in respect of a medical practitioner, the general principle is clear, and there is certainly no Australian case in which a doctor has been held liable for damages because of a failure to attend upon and treat someone who was not already his patient.

However, a question arises regarding whether the implicit request to Dr Lowns made by Joanna Woods for him to go with her to treat her brother gives rise to such a relationship of proximity as to give rise to a duty of care, and if so what was the content of that duty.

Section 27(2) *Medical Practitioners Act* 1938, applicable at the time, provided that it was "misconduct in a professional respect" for a medical practitioner to:

> "(c) refuse or fail, without reasonable cause, to attend, within a reasonable time after being requested to do so, upon a person for the purpose of rendering professional services in his capacity as a registered medical practitioner in any case where he has reasonable cause to believe that such person is in need of urgent attention by a registered medical practitioner but shall not be guilty under this paragraph of such conduct if he causes another registered medical practitioner to attend as aforesaid."

Dr Lowns, whilst denying the conversation with Joanna, accepted that if it had occurred, as it did, he would have and should have attended upon Patrick at his residence. He did not seek to justify his non-attendance either upon the basis that he had reasonable cause not so to attend because the child was in care of ambulance officers, or upon the basis that the ambulance officers should have brought the child to his surgery. He simply said he was not involved at all.

It was argued that there was no sufficient proximity between Dr Lowns and Patrick Woods to give rise to a duty of care. It was contended there was absent any relevant physical proximity, any circumstantial proximity or any relevant causal proximity in the manner in which those expressions were explained by Deane J in *The Council of the Shire of Sutherland v Hayman* (1985) 157 CLR 424 at 495 and risk of injury in consequence of the omission to attend not being reasonably foreseeable, no duty of care arose.

In my opinion this submission fails. Dr Lowns accepted that injury ("damage") to a fitting child was foreseeable if he, once requested, did not attend to treat the child. There was an obvious physical proximity, for Joanna had come on foot. There also existed an adequate "circumstantial proximity" in the sense that Dr Lowns was a medical practitioner to whom a direct request for assistance was made in circumstances where, on the evidence presented, there was no reasonable impediment or circumstance diminishing his capacity or indicating significant or material inconvenience or difficulty in him responding to the request, in circumstances where he knew, as he must be deemed to have admitted once it is found the conversation occurred, that serious harm could occur to Patrick Woods if he did not respond to the request and provide treatment. Once it is found, as here, that administering valium at the time determined by the trial judge would have brought an end to the status epilepticus before the onset of brain damage causing quadriplegia, causal proximity is also established.

In my opinion the trial judge was correct to find negligence, in this instance, against Dr Lowns.

A number of additional matters were raised on behalf of Dr Lowns:

(1) His Honour should have found Mrs Light left on her walk at 8.00am, not approximately 8.25am. Thus the attack may have occurred for longer than the trial judge found, and on the probabilities brain damage would in any event have occurred by 9.15am when, on his Honour's finding, valium may have been administered by Dr Lowns.

The trial judge accepted as fact the independent, empirical evidence that the ambulance arrived at 9.00am. Thus she found the child fitting at 8.55am. Further, on admission to hospital at about 10.15am Mrs Light gave a history of leaving the child "alone at 8.30am", or alternatively "left unattended for about one and three quarters hours", which could relate back to leaving the child at 8.30am. It followed that either Mrs Light was mistaken as to the duration of her walk which must have been of the order of 55 minutes if she left at 8.00am, or the time when she left, if she walked for only some 20–25 minutes. The trial judge found the latter for reasons which he gave. Those reasons are persuasive. There is no reason for an appellate court to disturb that finding of fact.

(2) Dr Lowns may not have been able to administer valium intravenously. Dr Smeeth and the ambulance officers had difficulty doing so.

First, Dr Lowns gave evidence that would have anticipated being able to give the injection, and second, the trial judge found that had he not been able to do so he would have administered it rectally.

(3) The valium, when administered, may not have stopped the attack of status epilepticus. It is sufficient to say that in the past, Patrick responded to valium. The finding of fact was clearly open to the trial judge.

In my opinion the appeal by Dr Lowns fails …

Mahoney JA dissented on the issue of whether Dr Lowns owed Patrick Woods a duty of care, preferring to see the doctor's obligation as only a moral one.

Mahoney JA:

2.   The Liability of Dr Lowns:

Oversimplified, the position is: (a) the Court must determine whether there is a legal obligation upon a general practitioner to attend a person with whom he has no relationship; (b) before this case, he had no legal obligation to do so; (c) the courts can impose – and on occasion have imposed – a legal obligation where none previously existed; (d) in principle, it should not do so in this case; and (e) the imposition of such an obligation is not required by the way in which the trial was conducted.

(a) The issue in this case:

It is important to emphasise that we are not concerned with obligations in morals or charity, with professional obligations, or with statutory obligations. Dr Lowns is not liable because (if he did) he had a moral or a professional obligation to go to the child in this case.

Assuming the facts to be as found against him, the doctor may have had a moral obligation. Any decent person would help a child in trouble if he could: at least, if special cases be put aside. It may be that charity required that he go.

But moral obligations are not legal obligations. The two must not be confused. A great deal of the time of the legislature is taken up in deciding whether moral obligations should become legal obligations, under what circumstances, and with what qualifications and exceptions. Law, as an instrument of social control, is a blunt instrument. It is often inappropriate to the qualifications and exceptions to which, if made law, a moral obligation should be subject. But the imposition of a legal obligation produces consequences which often make it inappropriate as a means of enforcing moral obligations. We are concerned with whether the moral obligation to which (as I assume) the doctor was subject should be a legal obligation.

Nor are we concerned with professional obligations. As the Court may know, those who, in a learned profession, decide what conduct is to be expected of a member of the profession, would no doubt think that, as a matter of general principle, a general practitioner should answer a call to help a child. But, as every practitioner will know, there are to this many qualifications and exceptions. To take but some examples: the doctor called on may not be (or be simply) a general practitioner. He may not deal with the problem the patient is said to have. He may be otherwise occupied. Any general practitioner will instance patients who call for help needlessly, who seek help at home which could and should be given at the surgery, or whose calls derive from emotional problems rather than actual illness. If professional sanctions are to be imposed, they will ordinarily be imposed in terms which do not impose an absolute obligation and they will be imposed in a way which allows those regulating the profession to assess the circumstances of the case, the qualifications and exceptions to which the general principle is subject, and in the end to do what appears appropriate. That no doubt is why, when failure to attend upon a patient is described as professional misconduct or the like, it is conduct which may, not must, attract professional sanctions: sanctions are applied only when the circumstances require.

I do not doubt that the default here in question is of this kind. Those concerned with the regulation of professional conduct would see the requirement that a doctor attend a sick person as being, first, a qualified requirement, and second, as warranting sanctions only if all the circumstances required them.

I should add that no statutory obligation is here involved. It is accepted that no statutory obligation has been imposed and this part of the child's case was abandoned. The issue is, therefore, whether a legal obligation should now be imposed. ...

(d) In principle, the court should not do so in this case:

I shall not detail at length why this obligation should be imposed. It is sufficient to say that: the obligation to be imposed is not an obligation of the nature proposed by the plaintiffs, viz, an obligation in negligence. The obligation is not, in its nature, one which the courts should impose by judicial decision; the legislature can deal with the matter, it has made some provision in relation to it, and it is best fitted to deal with it; and the effect of imposing an obligation in this case, retrospectively as it must be, would be unjust.

The obligation which the plaintiff contends should be imposed have been pleaded and argued as an obligation in negligence: the plaintiff's claim has been that Dr Lowns breached a duty of care which he owed to them in negligence. The plaintiffs have sought to justify their claim upon the basis, as it has been put, that the doctor was in a position or relationship of proximity to the child and that, because of that relationship, a duty of care in negligence was imposed upon him. The trial judge and the plaintiff in argument, called in aid the "principles of proximity" enunciated by the High Court in *Jaensch v Coffey* (1984) 155 CLR 549; *Sutherland Shire Council v Heyman* (1985) 157 CLR 424; and *Cook v Cook* (1986) 162 CLR 376.

In argument, I asked counsel to address the question whether the obligation sought to be imposed upon the plaintiff was in fact an obligation in negligence or an obligation of a different nature.

The reasoning upon which was based the conclusion that the doctor was subject to a duty of care in negligence was set out clearly and in detail in the learned judge's judgment. Summarised, his Honour concluded that there was the appropriate relationship of proximity and that, as the cases cited showed, if there was proximity there was a duty of care. (I am conscious that I do less than justice to the detail of the judge's judgment). But in the end, it was "the application of the principles laid down in" those cases which led his Honour to the conclusion that "notwithstanding the general principle of the common law that there is no obligation of rescue, circumstances may exist in which a medical practitioner comes under a "duty of care" to go to a person asking for help.

But, with respect, this reasoning mistakes the nature of the question. If a claim is one which is of its nature a claim for damages for the breach of the obligation imposed by the law of negligence, then it is necessary for the plaintiff to show that there was a duty of care, a breach and damages; and to show a duty of care within the tort of negligence, the relation of proximity is necessary or at least relevant. But that is not the present question. If the question be: is this an act or omission to which the tort of negligence extends, that is not to be determined by asking whether (if it be) there is a duty of care. The issue here is not whether the doctor owed a duty of care to go to the child. If he did, his failure to do so, whether deliberate or negligent, was a breach of his legal duty. His default, if there was one, was not one based on the tort of negligence; it was based on a tort or duty of a different kind.

This is not the occasion to analyse the nature of the tort of negligence or the development of that tort. The role of negligence or default in the law of tort or civil wrong is one which may warrant even yet further analysis. I referred to some of these matters in the *San Sebastian* litigation: see (1983) 2 NSWLR 268 at 326 et seq; (1986) 162 CLR 340. In this regard, the law has been concerned, *inter alia*, with two questions. First, it was concerned with the question whether negligence or default was merely part of the various circumstances or situations in which the law would hold one person liable for the loss caused to another. Oversimplified, the law commenced with negligence or default as one of the components of the right to sue persons of particular kinds, eg, agents, persons having the care of the safety of others, and the like. It gradually developed the concept that the defendant might be sued in any case in which his negligence or default had caused damage: cf, eg, *Heaven v Pender* (1883) 11 QBD 503. Cf the differences that existed between eg, Sir John Salmond and P H Winfield and others as to whether there was a tort of negligence and, if there was, whether negligence or default was a necessary element in every tort: see, eg, the Prefaces to Salmond on The Law of Torts (9th ed) and the cases referred to in the text. In due course, of course, the tort of negligence was recognised. Whether, in the light of recent decisions touching absolutely liability, eg, in *Rylands v Fletcher*, and the like, negligence or default may become a necessary element in all torts remains for final determination.

Second, if the tort of negligence being established, it became necessary to formulate the tests for the existence of the essential component of it, the existence of a duty of care. That has proceeded through the *Donoghue v Stevenson* litigation and the cases to which I have referred.

But, in my respectful opinion, none of these matters determines whether there is a duty as such upon a person having goods or skill to provide the benefit of them to another. It does not determine whether, because a person is (in whatever sense the term is used) a doctor, he has such an obligation.

I am conscious that "negligence" has been used in multiple meanings. In, eg, *Fullarton v North Melbourne Electric Tramway and Lighting Co Ltd* (1916) 21 CLR 181 at 189–190, there is an illustration of the early use of the term and the earlier dictionaries provide multiple examples: see, eg, Stroud's Judicial Dictionary (3rd ed) at p 181. But, however the term is used, what remains here is whether there exists, or should be imposed, an obligation of the kind the plaintiffs propose. I do not think that there is such an obligation.

I come now to consider whether, if legislation there is to be, this is legislation which the courts should undertake. I do not presume to detail exhaustively what is the nature of new obligations which the court should properly undertake to impose. The courts may, of course, develop the existing law. This they have done extensively: see *Ballina Shire Council v Ringland*, ubi supra. Whether the *Mabo* decisions are to be seen as merely the reapplication of an existing principle (that occupiers of new lands take them subject to existing proprietary rights) is for others to determine. What is here involved is, in my opinion, the creation of a new civil obligation. It is appropriate to consider whether the nature of the proposed obligation is such that it is appropriate that the courts assume the task of imposing it.

As I have said, the suggested obligation is not one the nature and extent of which is simple nor is it without qualifications and exceptions. As I have said, an experienced general practitioner would immediately suggest the qualifications and exceptions to which any such principle should be subject. The doctor must be a relevant doctor: it is not clear that, eg, an ophthalmologist or a psychiatrist would be obliged to go to a fitting child. There must be qualifications upon when a doctor, a general practitioner, may be expected to go. The time of the night, the doctor's judgment as to the requirements of the stated illness, the appropriateness of treatment at home or in a surgery are some of the matters which would qualify any absolute statement of such an obligation. An experienced doctor may properly conclude that the stated condition was properly accommodated by, eg, ambulance officers or other paramedics or require the hospital rather than him. And there would no doubt be qualifications arising from the nature of the patient and the doctor's previous experience of his complaints.

Matters of this kind indicate that, if an obligation is to be imposed upon a doctor, it cannot be imposed in absolute terms or without qualifications and exceptions. And those qualifications and exceptions will go, not merely to matter which would be, eg, matters of excuse from the application of the general principle, but matters qualifying and limiting the nature and extent of the obligation itself. An obligation of this kind is, in my opinion, not one appropriate to be imposed by judicial fiat.

It is not sufficient to say that the application of qualifications and exceptions, such as exist, can be worked out by the courts over time in the development of the general principle. My purpose in referring to the varied nature of the qualifications and exceptions to which the principle is subject has been to indicate that, if a sanction is to be imposed upon a doctor in such a context, it must be imposed after a consideration and assessment of all of the relevant factors and following the exercise of a careful discretion. This, in my opinion, is not appropriate to the imposition of a general principle of the kind here in question.

The legislature can deal, and has dealt, with this question. It may readily deal with the obligations of medical practitioners and has shown no reluctance to do so. It has indeed dealt with an obligation of this nature: reference was made by counsel to the *Medical Practitioners Act* 1938 s 27. This is not a situation in which the courts must intervene because justice otherwise is not likely to be done.

I have referred to the effect which the imposition of such an obligation will have upon those on whom it is imposed. What is here in question is no small thing. The effect of it may be tested by recalling that in the case of Dr Lowns the application of the principle will require payments by him of the order of more than $3 million.

The effect of the imposition of a new obligation is sometimes minimised by deprecating "flood gates" arguments. That is a traditional response. But, as I have said, the effect of it upon the present defendant and those in his position can be measured. If such an obligation is to be imposed, it should not be imposed retrospectively; it should be imposed to the extent that examination of the consequences of it require and prospectively so that the burden of it may be dealt with.

In saying these things, I am conscious of the great loss which the child has suffered. It is a tragic loss and the burden of it has and will in the future fall upon those of his parents who must deal with him. But the question remains: should that loss be imposed retrospectively upon another? I do not think that that is appropriate for such legislative power as the courts should claim to have.

(e) The present case:

Mr Milne QC, to whose argument I am indebted, has pointed to – as he urged it to be – the way in which the case was conducted at the trial. I shall not pursue all of the matters to which he referred but deal with what are, I think, the main ones. He has submitted, inter alia, that the only – or the only substantial – issue at the trial was: did the doctor refuse to go to the child? The suggestion has been that the other issues were not the subject of argument and that therefore they should not be argued here.

I do not think that the case was so simple. No doubt there was concentration upon the factual issue; the doctor may have expected to win it. But the legal liability of the doctor was in issue. The judge dealt with it in the course of his judgment. It is an issue which remains for determination here.

Mr Milne then emphasised the doctor had himself admitted that he should have gone to the child: if he had been requested, he would, he conceded, have felt obliged to go. But, in my opinion, this does not amount to a concession that he had a legal obligation to go or that there was no issue as to the legal obligation. The doctor may well have been conscious of the moral considerations involved. But such concession as was made was not a concession of legal liability. As I have said, legal liability remained to be determined by the court.

In view of the argument advanced, I shall add a final observation. If it be relevant for a judge of the court to express his opinion upon the matter, I would record that the balance of social utility would lie in favour of the imposition of some form of obligation to attend a person upon call. But that obligation is, for the reasons to which I have referred and otherwise, one which must be subject to qualifications and exceptions. And to have as the sanction for breach of it a simple award of damages would be inappropriate; if a sanction is to be imposed, it must be imposed after consideration of all of the circumstances and only to the extent that, in the particular case, the social considerations requiring the imposition of the obligation warrant. The imposition of the obligation by the creation of a tort sanctioned by damages would, in my opinion, be an inappropriate method of dealing with the problem. ...

Kirby P agreed with Cole JA.

It could be said that the case is not really a 'good Samaritan' case at all, since the defendant did offer help by advising that the child be brought to the surgery. Thus, he did 'assume a responsibility', just as the doctor did in *Barnett*. However, this would be an unduly narrow reading of the majority judgments, which approach the case in a broader perspective. You will notice that, at the end of his judgment, Mahoney JA 'comes clean'. It is not the imposition of a legal duty which troubles him but rather whether the court is the appropriate body to do it. He would leave the matter to the legislature so that it could consider 'all of the circumstances'. Of course, it could be said that in England, at least for GPs, it has done so in the 1992 regulations (and *Directions* for pilot schemes). (For a discussion of *Lowns v Wood*, see D Mendleson (1996) 4 Tort Law Review 242.)

A related, though distinct, point concerns the scope of a doctor's duty if he does render help in an emergency at an accident. Properly understood, this must be a matter of what a 'reasonable doctor' would do (or not do) in the circumstances. It is not a question of whether a duty of care exists but rather a question of whether there has been a breach of duty and, therefore, ultimately a matter of fact for determination in each case. No *a priori* applicable statement of the doctor's obligations can be made. In the particular circumstances, a reasonable doctor might only provide temporary relief, such as stemming the flow of blood. In other circumstances, he might have to go further and provide more treatment for the victim. In *Capital and Counties plc v Hampshire CC* [1997] 2 All ER 865, however, the Court of Appeal has in an *obiter* statement suggested that the doctor's 'only duty as a matter of law is not to make the victim's condition worse.' (per Stuart-Smith LJ at 883. See also, *Powell v Boladz* (1997) 39 BMLR 35 (CA) per Stuart-Smith LJ at 45 and *Phelps v Hillingdon LBC* [1999] 1 All ER 421 (CA) at p 441 per Stuart-Smith LJ. There is no basis for stating this as matter of law and there is no English authority for so limiting the content of the doctor's duty. The Court of Appeal referred to the Canadian decision of *The Ogopogo* [1970] 1 Lloyd's Rep. 257 (Ont CA) and [1971] 2 Lloyd's Rep 410 (Can Sup Ct). This case did not involve a rescue by a professional but rather, the private owner of a boat whose guest fell overboard. The decision of the Ontario Court of Appeal (the point being left open in the Canadian Supreme Court) may be seen as being concerned with the standard of care expected of a rescuer, in effect, no requiring more than not to make the situation worse.

Whilst it is obviously correct that less may be expected in an emergency, perhaps even of professionals, it is not at all clear why professional rescuers such as firemen, police, or doctors are given the benefit of the lower duty. A doctor who allows a road accident victim to die by failing to deal with his injuries does not make the victim's condition 'worse' – even assuming he would not have died with immediate treatment. Yet, there can be no doubt that medical evidence will in many circumstances suggest that the doctor could reasonably have done something to improve, or prevent a deterioration in, the victim's condition. Such a doctor is in breach of his duty to act reasonably in preventing foreseeable injury to the victim and should be liable in negligence.

(b) The institution

We are concerned here principally with the liability of hospitals within the NHS. In practice, of course, this usually means the liability of the relevant NHS Trust. We also have to take account of other institutions: these include the private clinic and, exceptionally, the Secretary of State in the context of the provisions of services which he has not delegated to any other NHS body.

Despite the abolition of much of the machinery of the NHS 'internal market' in the Health Act 1999, there also remains the issue of whether the commissioning 'Primary Care Groups' or Primary Care Trusts may be liable in negligence where there is a failure in the service agreement to make adequate provision for health services.

(i) PRIMARY LIABILITY

The background to the primary liability is discussed in the following extract. (For a fuller discussion, see I Kennedy and A Grubb (eds) *Principles of Medical Law* (1998) paras 8.14–8.33.)

Picard 'The Liability of Hospitals in Common Law Canada' (1981) 26 McGill LJ 997

The earliest hospitals were charitable institutions and protected as such by the courts. They were sustained by endowments and voluntary contributions, which were encouraged in England by the creation of the charitable trust. In order to function hospitals had to purchase supplies of food and equipment, and hire persons to care for the patient and operate the physical plant. Provision was eventually made for some patients to pay for their accommodation. Thus, of necessity, hospitals entered into legal relationships and became accountable under contracts, and by 1907 it was clear that a hospital was liable for the negligence of its employees [*Hillyer v The Governors of St Bartholomew's Hospital* [1909] 2 KB 820]. But it was also held that a hospital could not be liable for the negligence of employees such as nurses or doctors in the execution of their professional duties, as opposed to administrative functions. The rationale for this limitation was that the hospital neither directed nor controlled the exercise of professional judgment.

In the *Hillyer* case the English Court of Appeal concluded that a hospital undertook certain duties toward a patient.

The governors of a public hospital, by their admission of the patient to enjoy in the hospital the gratuitous benefit of its care, do, I think, undertake that the patient whilst there shall be treated only by experts, whether surgeons, physicians or nurses, of whose professional competence the governors have taken reasonable care to assure themselves; and, further, that those experts shall have at their disposal, for the care and treatment of the patient, fit and proper apparatus and appliances.

Thus, approximately seventy-five years ago, a patient had some recourse against a hospital: in contract, depending on the terms thereof, or in tort, if the hospital had breached its duty to select competent staff and to supply proper equipment, or by vicarious liability, subject to the restriction in the *Hillyer* case. ...

The first hospital patients were the cast-offs of society. The middle and upper classes were treated in their own homes by doctors who called on them there and they were cared for by servants and family. It was only the indigent who went to the hospitals, and the hospital and doctor provided their services gratuitously to such patients. A patient injured by either would have had an extremely difficult time pursuing any compensation through legal action. An action in contract might well have failed for lack of intention, uncertainty of terms or lack of consideration. An action in tort might have been brought in trespass to the person but consent could have been implied rather easily. It was the negligence action of the mid-nineteenth century which first brought an opportunity for a patient to demand, in a court of law, that a hospital be held accountable for its actions. But the scope of such an action was quickly restricted by the courts, as outlined earlier. The two main bases for the liability of a hospital, namely a direct duty of care and vicarious liability, were carefully controlled so as to afford hospitals maximum immunity to the suits of patients.

The situation of the modern patient is very different. Today the hospital is the primary institution for health care [in Canada]. It is in the modern hospital that a patient can receive the best health care available because that is where the skill, knowledge and judgment of health-care professionals may be combined with modern medical equipment and technology. Today a patient comes to hospital not seeking charity, but highly skilled medical treatment and he might well have had his name on a waiting-list before being admitted!

... the greatest contract between patients of the earlier hospitals and of the modern hospital lies in the legal relationships formed with the hospital. Any legal relationship the early patient had with a hospital was tenuous and if it gave rise to legal obligations the courts interpreted them restrictively. The modern patient has strong, well-defined legal relationships with his hospital.

... His relationship, in fact, with a hospital is that of being a patient *of the hospital* and it gives rise to certain duties owed to him by the institution. The hospital must not violate his right to be free from unauthorised touching, nor injure him by carrying out its duties in a sub-standard manner. The doctor-patient relationship likewise gives rise to certain duties but it is crucial to any analysis of the patient's position to remember that, while these duties of hospital and doctor may be concomitant, each set of duties is based on a separate and distinct relationship. ...

The earliest duty of care held to be owed by a hospital to a patient was to select competent staff in order that patients would be attended by skilled persons. At first this duty was very narrowly interpreted. A hospital had only to ascertain that its professionals were qualified and competent. This seemed to be the scope of its direct or personal or corporate duty of care. ...

The scope of the direct duty was expanded, first to include the instruction and supervision of personnel employed by the hospital and then to the provision of the systems and organisation to co-ordinate these activities so that the patient received reasonable care. Since a patient is treated in a physical plant with equipment and medical tools, it is not surprising that hospitals were also give a direct duty to provide and maintain proper facilities and equipment.

There is some authority for the existence of other duties but often it is not clear whether the court was basing the hospital's accountability on grounds of direct liability or vicarious liability. These include a duty to establish procedures to prevent patients from harming themselves or being injured by other patients. There are some older cases from which it might be concluded that a hospital has a duty to set up aseptic procedures and to protect patients and even visitors from infection.

Though in theory it is possible for further duties to be created, a review of the cases reveals that the courts have been most cautious when contrasted with their attitude respecting negligence law in general.

In summary, the precedents support these possible direct duties of a hospital to a patient:
(a) to select competent and qualified employees
(b) to instruct and supervise them
(c) to provide proper facilities and equipment
(d) to establish systems necessary to the safe operation of the hospital.
Since the other components of tort law apply, the hospital has to carry out these duties as competently as the reasonable hospital in the circumstances and, even if found sub-standard, would have to be found to have caused the patient's injuries before liability would result. All of the protection of tort law normally available to defendants is available to the hospital.

The quality of the duties owed by a hospital has led to their sometimes being referred to as 'non-delegable'. This has the significant effect of making the employer of an independent contractor strictly liable for any negligence of the contractor in carrying out the duty of care which was the employer's but which he had contracted or delegated to the independent contractor. This is an exception to the general rule that an employer is not liable for the negligence of an independent contractor employed by him.

... Fleming [*The Law of Torts* (5th edn) 1977] discusses the kinds of cases where non-delegable duties have been found and notes that the list is 'long and diverse', extending from dangerous situations, hazardous substances, fire, lateral support for land, maintenance of premises abutting a highway to instances where the duty would normally be to use reasonable care but where the designation of the duty as non-delegable assures that care will be taken (provision of a safe system of work, compliance with statutory safety standards, responsibilities of occupiers of land to certain others and of hospitals to care for their patients).

In establishing that an institution is liable *qua* institution (ie, is in breach of *its* duty), it is important to realise that the *Bolam* test may have no place. Instead, the normal rule of negligence liability should apply, *viz* that the institution will be judged by reference to the norm of practice, that norm being prescriptive rather than descriptive. There would, therefore, be a minimum standard of capability to which the institution will be held. However, in *AB v Tameside & Glossop HA* [1997] 8 Med LR 91 (CA) the Court of Appeal seems to have taken a different view. The case concerned claims by a number of patients (and former patients) for psychiatric injury caused by being informed (they alleged negligently) that a health care worker whom they had been in contact with was HIV positive (for the psychiatric injury aspects of the case, see *supra*, p 402; for the post-treatment duty, see *supra*, p 452). In setting the standard of care, the court rejected the *Bolam* test but it did so only because, in Brooke LJ's words, 'there simply was no adequate well of professional experience on which the court could usefully draw'. Brooke LJ, in finding there had been no negligence merely because the best method of communication had not been used, said the correct approach was as follows:

> **Brooke LJ:** This is not a situation in which it is particularly useful for a court to investigate the previous practices of reasonably competent practitioners when handling a similar situation. With the single exception of the Exeter incident there had been no previous experience in this country, and the evidence showed that the nature of people's irrational concerns, anxieties and ignorance about HIV and AIDS is, and certainly was in April 1991, to a great extent *sui generis*. On the one hand, therefore, the judge was in my judgment wrong to hold that the defendants were negligent because they did not select the best method. On the other hand, I consider that in the particular circumstances of the present case Mr Armitage is confining the freedom of the court too narrowly when he cites the *Bolam* test as providing the solution because there simply was no adequate well of professional experience on which the court could usefully draw in the present case. In such a case the judge has to perform the familiar role of considering the factual evidence carefully, listening to the expert evidence, and forming a view as to whether, in all the circumstances, these public health authorities fell below the standards reasonably to be expected of them when they selected their preferred method of communicating the information to the patients.

The situation was relatively novel, having arisen only once previously in this country. Had the position been otherwise, the Court seems to imply it would have applied the *Bolam* test. Further, where an institution claims to be a centre of excellence it will be held to the standard it claims or professes, by analogy to the specialist doctor (see *Robertson v Nottingham HA* [1997] 8 Med LR 1 at 13 per Brooke LJ and *infra*, p 310).

I. Two strands of liability

Here we are principally concerned with the liability of NHS Trusts (or Primary Care Trusts). We shall deal shortly with the liability, if any, of the Secretary of State. There may, however, be other situations where the issue of primary liability arises: in private clinics or hospitals and GPs' liability for their deputies or locums.

You will see that Ellen Picard (*op cit*) identifies the emergence of two strands of primary liability. The *first*, and probably more conventional, reflects the duty, in effect, to provide a reasonable regime of care, through its staff, facilities and the exercise of supervision. A useful analogy, here, would be with the well-known case of *Wilsons & Clyde Co Ltd v English* [1938] AC 57 and the duty recognised there which an employer owes to an employee in respect of 'the provision of a competent staff, adequate material, and a proper system and effective supervision' (per Lord Wright at 78). For the analogy to work here, 'employer' and 'employee' translate into 'hospital' and 'patient'.

The *second* strand of primary liability is both more conjectural and contentious although it may have a respectable history in judgments of Lord Denning and Morris LJ in the celebrated cases in the 1950s of *Cassidy v Ministry of Health* [1951] 1 All ER 574 and *Roe v Minister of Health* [1954] 2 All ER 131. The choice of which of these strands of liability (if either) is adopted as the law governing institutions' liability will have significant implications as we shall see. The New South Wales Court of Appeal found itself confronted by the need to choose in the following case and, perhaps not surprisingly, the judges differed as to the merits of both approaches.

Ellis v Wallsend District Hospital (1989) 17 NSWLR 553 (NSW CA)

In 1975 the plaintiff, Mrs Marie Ellis, consulted Dr A W Chambers, a neurosurgeon who had treated her on several occasions in the previous years, at his consulting room. Mrs Ellis, who had a background of intractable and very severe neck pain, drug dependence, drug overdoses, and failure of other treatment, was interested in having five-nerve separation microsurgery which Dr Chambers had already mentioned to her. Dr Chambers advised that the only concern that she need have was the risk of slight numbness in her right hand. Mrs Ellis agreed to have the operation. Dr Chambers arranged to have Mrs Ellis admitted to the defendant hospital, Wallsend District Hospital, where he was an 'honorary medical officer'. Under the by-laws and rules Dr Chambers was appointed to the 'honorary medical staff' of the hospital. Honorary medical officers received no payment from the hospital for services performed there. They were allowed to use the operating theatres for their own patients on a roster basis. When the patient was admitted to the hospital on an admission request form the hospital would book the patient in for surgery at a time when the doctor concerned was rostered to use the theatres. The doctor's fee was a matter for the doctor and his patient.

There was evidence that the operation carried a remote risk of paralysis and a more substantial risk of failure to relieve pain. Mrs Ellis gave evidence that if she had been warned of those risks she would not have undergone the operation. On June 18, 1975, Dr Chambers performed a laminectomy and a cervical posterior rhizotomy of the nerve roots at the cervical vertebrae 2 to 6. During the operation there was haemorrhage which was controlled; numerous adhesions surrounding the spinal cord were noted; Dr Chambers did not use magnification available. Six days after the operation Mrs Ellis developed quadriplegia.

Mrs Ellis commenced proceedings against Dr Chambers alleging that Dr Chambers had been negligent in (1) advising her to have the operation; (2) failing to warn her of the risks involved; (3) failing to obtain her consent to the operation; (4) in the performance of the operation. Dr Chambers died in 1986. On June 6, 1988, Mrs Ellis settled her claim against his estate for A$500,000. She then claimed against the hospital on the grounds that (1) the hospital was vicariously liable for Dr Chambers' negligence; (2) that the hospital was in breach of its independent and non-delegable duty to her as its patient to ensure that she received proper medical treatment and was warned of all material risks involved in the surgery. She failed in her claim that the hospital was vicariously liable (Kirby P dissenting). Thus the issue of the primary liability of the hospital became central if she was to recover more than the $500,000 she had recovered from Dr Chambers' insurers.

Samuels JA: There is another possible basis of liability which does not arise out of the hospital's relationship with Dr Chambers, but has its source in its relationship with the patient. Hence I must finally consider whether the hospital, to use the words of Reynolds JA in *Albrighton* [*v Royal Prince Albert Hospital* [1980] 2 NSWLR 542 (NSW CA)] (at 561):

> ... was in breach of a duty which it owed directly to the plaintiff of which it could not divest itself by delegation.

Whether, in other words, the hospital owed the appellant an independent and non-delegable duty. The court in *Albrighton* thought that in that case there was evidence capable of establishing that the hospital did. Reynolds JA (at 561–562) put it thus:

The hospital, by admitting the appellant, could be regarded as undertaking that it would take reasonable care to provide for all her medical needs; and, whatever legal duties were imposed upon those who treated, diagnosed or cared for her needs from time to time, there was an overriding and continuing duty upon the hospital as an organization. It was not a mere custodial institution designed to provide a place where medical personnel could meet and treat persons lodged there, as it might have been regarded in years long since gone by.

That view his Honour regarded as being in conformity with the majority view in *Roe* [v *Minister of Health* [1954] 2 QB 66 (CA)] to which I have already referred. No doubt his Honour had in mind the judgments of Denning and Morris LJJ since Somervell LJ, in a passage which I have earlier set out, viewed the case as one of unvarnished vicarious liability. Certainly, as Blair JA observed in his dissenting judgment in *Yepremian v Scarborough General Hospital* (1980) 110 DLR (3d) 513 at 574, there is 'a clear line linking the views' of Lord Greene in *Gold* [v *Essex CC* [1942] 2 KB 293 (CA)] and those of Denning LJ in *Cassidy* [v *Ministry of Health* [1951] 2 KB 343 (CA)] and of Denning and Morris LJ in *Roe*; and it tends to lead to the proposition stated by Reynolds JA in the first part of the statement which I have just quoted. This line of reasoning is regarded by Professor Fleming, The Law of Torts, 7th edn (1987) at 346, as authorizing a view 'which has gained increasing support' and which tends to render irrelevant the distinction between servants and independent contractors

> ... whenever a hospital offers a complete range of medical treatment to the patient and thereby assumes a non-delegable, personal duty to ensure that he receives careful treatment at the hands of such staff as it provides, including visiting specialists and other independent consultants.

It must be emphasized, however, and is of critical importance in the present case, that in that trilogy of authorities, *Gold, Cassidy* and *Roe*, the judges who were inclined to impose upon the hospital an independent duty to care for those patients whom it received, nonetheless excepted from this prescription the situation of consultants or independent specialists who had not been assigned by the hospital but had undertaken to provide care and treatment by direct arrangement with the patient. In *Gold*, Lord Greene MR (at 302), said, for example:

> So far as consulting physicians and surgeons are concerned, clearly the nature of their work and the relationship in which they stand to the defendants precludes the drawing of an inference that the defendants undertake responsibility for their negligent acts.

But this statement is material to the question of vicarious liability rather than to any restrictions upon breach of the hospital's own independent duty. In *Cassidy*, however, Denning LJ having developed the notion of the hospital's independent liability, added (at 362):

> I think it depends on this: Who employs the doctor or surgeon – is it the patient or the hospital authorities? If the patient himself selects and employs the doctor or surgeon, as in *Hillyer's* case [1909] 2 KB 820, the hospital authorities are of course not liable for his negligence, because he is not employed by them. But where the doctor or surgeon, be he a consultant or not, is employed and paid, not by the patient but by the hospital authorities, I am of opinion that the hospital authorities are liable for his negligence in treating the patient. It does not depend on whether the contract under which he was employed was a contract of service or a contract for services.

In *Roe*, Denning LJ adhered to what he had said in *Cassidy*, but, it may be, took the matter a step further by minimizing the importance of the payment of the doctor (whether consultant or not) by the hospital; and he repeated the same exception. He said (at 82):

> It does not matter whether they are permanent or temporary, resident or visiting, whole-time or part-time. The hospital authorities are responsible for all of them. The reason is because, even if they are not servants, they are agents of the hospital to give the treatment. The only exception is the case of consultants or anaesthetists selected by the patient himself.

I am not wholly confident that Morris LJ in *Roe* did approach the matter as an example of the hospital's independent liability (see at 90–91) but he stressed that the nature of the obligation which a hospital may have assumed:

> ... becomes, as it seems to me, ultimately a question of fact to be decided having regard to the particular circumstances of each particular case ... [at 89].

This observation was taken up by Lord Nathan in *Medical Negligence* (1957) (at 132) where the learned author observes, having discussed the three cases:

> In these circumstances it can be stated with some confidence that the weight of modern authority favours the view that a hospital authority by receiving a patient undertakes a personal obligation or duty towards that patient, for the breach of which it cannot escape liability by saying that it employed competent persons, to discharge the obligation or duty on its behalf; but that the exact extent of the duty is a question of fact in each particular case.

Leaving aside for the moment the recent development in Australia of the doctrine of independent or non-delegable duty, it seems to me that, so far as the responsibility of hospitals to their patients is concerned, the matter has been well stated, if I may say so, by Houlden JA in the second dissenting judgment in *Yepremian*. His Lordship said (at 581):

> First, a general hospital may function as a place where medical care facilities are provided for the use of a physician and his patient. The patient comes to the hospital because his physician has decided that the hospital's facilities are needed for the proper care and treatment of the patient. This use of the hospital is made possible by an arrangement between the hospital and the physician by which the physician is granted hospital privileges. Where a hospital functions as merely the provider of medical care facilities, then, as the trial Judge pointed out, a hospital is not responsible for the negligence of the physician. The present case does not, of course, come with this classification.
>
> Second, a general hospital may function as a place where a person in need of treatment goes to obtain treatment. Here the role of the hospital is that of an institution where medical treatment is made available to those who require it. The present case falls in this second classification. Tony Yepremian was brought to the Scarborough General Hospital because he was in need of treatment. Does a hospital in these circumstances have the duty to provide proper medical care to a patient? In my judgment, it does.

I need only observe that the second of these situations is exactly that which obtained in *Albrighton* and that the first of them is the one which applies in the instant case.

However, before arriving at any final conclusion I must consider whether, and to what extent, the decision of the High Court in *Kondis v State Transport Authority* (1984) 154 CLR 672 compels a particular solution of the problem. This case, if I may respectfully say so, authoritatively determines for this court the nature and scope of non-delegable duties in tort. Mason J, with whom Deane J and Dawson J agreed, notes (at 684 and 686) the criticisms that the notion of a non-delegable duty not only lacks any coherent conceptual foundation, but departs from

> ... the basic principles of liability in negligence by substituting for the duty to take reasonable care a more stringent duty, a duty to ensure that reasonable care is taken.

The justification for this special duty is found in a special relationship between the parties. His Honour said (at 687):

> The element in the relationship between the parties which generates a special responsibility or duty to see that care is taken may be found in one or more of several circumstances. The hospital undertakes the care, supervision and control of patients who are in special need of care. The school authority undertakes like special responsibilities in relation to the children whom it accepts into its care.

He goes on to instance the case of the occupier who invites persons to enter his premises, and that of the landlord who undertakes repairs. And then he continues:

> In these situations a special duty arises because the person on whom it is imposed has undertaken the care, supervision or control of the person or property of another or is so placed in relation to that person or his property as to assume a particular responsibility for his or its safety, in circumstances where the person affected might reasonably expect that due care will be exercised.

I should add that, prior to the reference to the responsibility of hospitals, his Honour had referred to *Gold, Cassidy* and *Roe* as instances of the application of the concept of a personal duty arising in those cases out of the hospital's

> ... undertaking an obligation to treat its patient, an obligation which carries with it a duty to use reasonable care in treatment, so that the hospital was liable, if a person engaged to perform the obligation on its behalf acts without due care [at 686].

The exemplification of the relationships between a hospital and the patients whose care it undertakes, and between the school authority and the children whom it accepts into its care, makes clear that the element which, as Mason J says (at 687):

> … generates a special responsibility or duty to see that care is taken …

involves a particular relationship of dependency, or what Fleming calls (op cit at 362):

> … a special protective relationship.

Hence the special duty arises only in particular circumstances upon which must depend the decision whether or not to assign the relationship they reveal to the special category. *Kondis* is not a direct authority upon the liability of hospitals, but its examples are highly persuasive. Accordingly it may be that once the relationship of hospital and patient is established it follows, as a matter of law, that the hospital owes the patient a non-delegable duty of care. In *Kondis* (at 686) Mason J put the proposition in this way:

> The liability of a hospital arises out of its undertaking an obligation to treat its patient, an obligation which carries with it a duty to use reasonable care in treatment, so that the hospital is liable, if a person engaged to perform the obligation on its behalf acts without due care: *Gold* [1942] 2 KB at 304. Accordingly, the duty is one the performance of which cannot be delegated, not even to a properly qualified doctor or surgeon under a contract for services: *Cassidy* [1951] 2 KB at 364.

It can scarcely be supposed that Mason J was unaware of the limitations upon a hospital's duty of care expressed in *Gold* and *Cassidy*, and in *Roe* as well to which he earlier refers (at 685). It is necessary therefore to read his judgment subject to those statements, so that a hospital is bound to ensure that reasonable care is used in providing the treatment which it undertakes to carry out; but that duty does not extend to treatment which it undertakes to carry out; but that duty does not extend to treatment which is performed by a doctor pursuant to a direct engagement with the patient, and not on behalf of the hospital.

In my opinion therefore while proof of the relationship of hospital and 'patient' will generate a special duty of some kind, closer scrutiny of the facts (cf the analysis proposed by Mason J in *Stevens v Brodribb Sawmilling*) is necessary in order to establish its scope. It is a question of what medical services the hospital has undertaken to supply. In a case such as *Albrighton* where the patient went directly to the hospital for advice and treatment a special duty will arise and may well embrace the provision of the 'complete medical services' which Reynolds JA (at 561) thought it open to conclude that the hospital had undertaken to render, and that duty arose as soon as the plaintiff resorted to the hospital's out-patients' clinic; it did not wait upon admission. In such a case the hospital, by accepting the patient, undertakes to make available all the therapeutic skill and devices which it is reasonably able to deploy. The patients choice is determined by his or her decision to knock at the door of the defendant's hospital, as Lord Greene put it in *Gold* (at 302). If the hospital's response is to open the door and admit the patient to the benefits of the medical and surgical cornucopia within it remains responsible to ensure that whatever treatment or advice the horn disgorges is given with proper care; its duty cannot be divested by delegation.

But the evidence in a particular case may establish that the hospital's undertaking was of a more limited kind. As Morris LJ pointed out in *Roe* (at 89) and (at 91) the nature of the obligation which a hospital has assumed becomes ultimately a question of fact, a proposition which the Court of Appeal adopted in *Albrighton*. In the present case, however, it is quite clear that the appellant did not knock at the hospital's door in the sense contemplated by Lord Greene. It was not the hospital's door but the door of the late Dr Chambers' consulting rooms upon which she knocked, and it was that door which was opened to her and which admitted her to the treatment and advice upon which she thereafter principally relied. I do not think it can be doubted but that it was Dr Chambers and not the hospital to whom the appellant looked for medical care. The hospital, for reasons which I have already discussed and will not repeat, was merely the place in which surgical procedures which he had recommended and which the appellant had agreed to undergo were performed by Dr Chambers. The hospital in the present case was exactly what the hospital was not in *Albrighton*. To reverse Reynolds JA's words in that case (at 562) the hospital here was 'a mere custodial institution designed to provide a place where medical personnel could … treat persons lodged there …'. Of course the appellant stood in a 'special protective relationship' to both the hospital and Dr Chambers, but in respect of different kinds of care. The appellant looked to Dr Chambers for surgical intervention, and to the hospital for nursing care and perhaps the provision of other medical treatment. In rendering that care and treatment the hospital was no doubt under a non-delegable duty which might have been relevant in certain circumstances. But in the event no question arises concerning matters of that sort.

My conclusion does not impose differential duties on a hospital. Following *Kondis* a hospital owes an independent non-delegable duty to ensure that the treatment it undertakes to provide is performed with reasonable care. The question in every case is the nature of that undertaking.
Meacher JA agreed with Samuels JA.

Contrast the approach of the (then) President of the Court of Appeal.

Kirby P: [T]here is now a new and settled basis for the liability of the hospital. It is its direct responsibility pursuant to a non-delegable duty in tort which it owes the patient. The existence of this alternative and additional basis of responsibility in the hospital for the suggested negligence of Dr Chambers may be traced to the judgment of Lord Greene MR in *Gold v Essex County Council*. In *Cassidy*, Lord Denning was later to take pains to acknowledge his error in basing his arguments as counsel in *Gold* upon the grounds of vicarious liability. Lord Greene had not countenanced the error but looked instead to direct liability of the hospital authorities. In *Cassidy*, Lord Denning explained this liability thus (at p 365):

> ... the hospital authorities accepted the plaintiff as a patient for treatment, and it was their duty to treat him with reasonable care ... If those surgeons and nurses did not treat him with proper care and skill, then the hospital authorities must answer for it, for it means that they themselves did not perform their duty to him.

Although Somerville LJ confined his opinion to vicarious liability, Singleton LJ appears to have supported the Denning view that *Gold* established a direct duty on the part of the hospital.

This notion of direct liability soon acquired supporters in Canada. In *Yepremian*, Blair and Houlden JJA, in their dissenting opinions, upheld the plaintiff's claim on the basis of the hospital's primary liability. Blair JA (at 579) gave a social reason for adopting this approach:

> The recognition of a direct duty of hospitals to provide non-negligent medical treatment reflects the reality of the relationship between hospitals and the public in contemporary society. This direct duty arises from profound changes in social structures and public attitudes relating to medical services and the concomitant changes in the function of hospitals in providing them. It is obvious that as a result of these changes the role of hospitals in the delivery of medical services has expanded. The public increasingly relies on hospitals to provide medical treatment and, in particular, on emergency services. Hospitals to a growing extent hold out to the public that they provide such treatment and such services.

Yepremian was appealed to the Supreme Court of Canada: see (1980) 31 OR (2d) 383 (n). However, the case was settled on the payment of a substantial sum to the injured patient (as a report of the approval of the settlement shows). Accordingly the controversy posed by the conflicting opinions in that case has not yet been settled by the Supreme Court: see discussion G H L Fridman 'Hospital Liability for Professional Negligence' (1980) 4 Legal Med Q (Canada) 80 at 88; E Picard, Legal Liability of Doctors and Hospitals in Canada, (2nd edn) (1984) at 322; see also note (1986) 64 Canadian Bar Rev 422 at 423. *Yepremian* was applied in *Van Ginkel v Hollenberg* (1985) 36 Man R 2d 291. The opinion of Blair JA was criticised in J E Magnet 'Corporate Negligence as a Basis for Hospital Liability – A Comment on Yepremian' 6 CCLT 121 at 127.

The theory of the direct non-delegable duty of the hospital has now gained acceptance in England: see *Wilsher v Essex Area Health Authority* [1987] QB 730. Although the case was conducted solely on the basis of the vicarious liability of the health authority, both Sir Nicholas Browne-Wilkinson VC and Glidewell LJ expressed the opinion, obiter, that in some circumstances, an action would lie against the hospital in respect of its own direct and non-delegable duty to the patient in respect of negligent conduct occurring in its operations.

In Australia, this additional basis for the liability of the hospital was accepted in this court in *Albrighton v Royal Prince Alfred Hospital* [1980] 2 NSWLR 542 at 561. Four years later, the High Court of Australia in *Kondis v State Transport Authority* (1984) 154 CLR 672 accepted that, in some relationships, a 'special duty' arises. The relationship of a hospital to patients is one such relationship, as is that of a school authority to children accepted into its care. In the case of the hospital it has a personal non-delegable duty arising out of its (at 686):

> ... undertaking an obligation to treat its patient, an obligation which carries with it a duty to use reasonable care in treatment, so that the hospital is liable, if a person engaged to perform the obligation on its behalf acts without due care. ... Accordingly, the duty is one the performance of which cannot be delegated, not even to a properly qualified doctor or surgeon under a contract for services.

I see no reason to read down these remarks. Nor do I see any justification for superimposing upon them a residual *Hillyer*-type distinction between the liability of the hospital for the negligence of staff surgeons and honorary staff surgeons. Again, I agree with the comment of Professor Giesen [*International Medical Malpractice Law* (1988)] (at 60–61):

> On this basis [direct liability], of course, it makes no difference whether an independent contractor (a specialist, a visiting consultant or a concessionaire) can be brought under the traditional head of 'servant' or not. Even if not, the hospital will still be liable if it has breached its own primary and non-delegable duty of care to the patient.
>
> Courts in Civil Law jurisdictions have arrived at similar results by extending the hospital's primary and non-delegable duty to organize and ensure what can be called a safe hospital system.
>
> Generally speaking, the raison d'etre of direct (corporate) hospital liability is to prevent substandard care in the health care system as a whole. The mere occurrence of a mishap will not necessarily give rise to an inference of substandard care under fault-oriented systems or to a compensable medical injury under no-fault systems. Nevertheless, a patient in a modern and well-staffed hospital is entitled to expect and rely upon the skill, circumspection and experience of hospital physicians and nurses to detect and treat negative occurrences such as sudden and unexpected cardiac arrest during surgery, or a disconnection of life-support equipment … or an infection, before crippling injury results. This goal can only be achieved where reasonable care is taken in securing competent personnel and an organization capable of providing and maintaining a safe hospital system.

It is true that some academic opinion is critical of the development of 'non-delegable duty' in the case of hospitals: see, eg, W P Whippy, 'A Hospital's Personal and Non-delegable Duty to Care for Its Patients – Novel Doctrine or Vicarious Liability Disguised?' (1989) 63 ALJ 182 at 201. However, the doctrine also has its academic supporters: see eg J Bettle, 'Suing Hospitals Direct: Whose Tort was it Anyhow?' (1987) 137 NLJ 573. More to the point, it was adopted by the High Court in *Kondis* in full knowledge (as Mason J indicated (at 686)) of the criticism which had been expressed of the conceptual foundation of the doctrine. It draws strength from the earlier statement of principle by the High Court in *Commonwealth v Introvigne* (1982) 150 CLR 258 – a case concerning the direct liability of the school authority for children in its care.

The authority of the High Court of Australia is binding on this Court. We are not bound by English, Canadian or other opinions to the contrary. As Giesen's text demonstrates, the High Court's principle in *Kondis* is not only in line with developments in other jurisdictions of the common law and civil law. It is supported by reasons of policy and practicality in the modern circumstances of Australian hospitals. It is wrong, in my opinion, to present the respondent hospital as the mere venue for the performance by Dr Chambers of his private surgical procedures. Such a conclusion flies in the face of the consent form, the by-laws and the mutually beneficial arrangement under which Dr Chambers operated at the hospital.

Accordingly, if there was negligence on the part of Dr Chambers, it was negligence for which the hospital was liable. It was so liable either because it was vicariously liable for his negligence as a member of its honorary medical staff, or it was liable directly to the patient which it could not fulfil merely by delegating its operation to a member of the honorary medical staff. As Reynolds JA said in *Albrighton* (at 562), the hospital was not a –

> … mere custodial institution designed to provide a place where medical personnel could meet and treat persons lodged there, as it might have been regarded in years long since gone by.

It was, to the contrary, an integrated institution. And Dr Chambers was part of it.

Both Samuels JA and Kirby P refer to the Ontario case of *Yepremian v Scarborough General Hospital* (1980) 110 DLR (3d) 513. In that case also, the judges differed on the question of primary liability. It may be worthwhile to consider the case more closely.

Yepremian v Scarborough General Hospital (1980) 110 DLR (3d) 513 (Ont CA)

The plaintiff [Tony Yepremian] suffered a cardiac arrest with resultant brain damage at defendant hospital following the commencement of treatment for a diagnosed diabetic condition. The plaintiff had come home from work on a week-end feeling unwell. He was vomiting and had increased frequency of urination and increased frequency of drinking. The family doctor being away, his family took the plaintiff to see G, a physician, who had obtained his degree in medicine a year earlier, and was working in research, but who filled in on some week-ends as a doctor's replacement. G diagnosed tonsillitis, gave a prescription, and said it was unnecessary to take the plaintiff to a hospital. Later that night at home, the plaintiff began to hyperventilate and his family took him to the emergency department of the defendant hospital, where C, a general practitioner with hospital privileges, was on duty. C did not order a urinalysis and made no diagnosis, other than noting plaintiff's hyperventilation on the emergency record. Following two telephone calls to R, the internist on call and an endocrinologist, the plaintiff was admitted to the intensive care unit of the hospital. Eleven hours later, as a result of a nurse's observations, a diagnosis of diabetes was made. The plaintiff was immediately started on insulin. He continued to hyperventilate and remained unconscious or semi-conscious until he suffered the cardiac arrest about 12 hours later.

Arrup JA: Beyond doubt a patient admitted to a hospital expects to receive not only accommodation, food and competent nursing care but also competent medical care. The question still remains: does the hospital undertake to provide that medical care, or does it undertake to select competent doctors who will provide it? ...

The trial Judge has founded liability upon a breach of the hospital's *own* duty – not that of any employed doctor, or of a doctor chosen by it to be on its staff, but an independent duty of its own, which is breached if there is a failure by a specialist on its staff to use reasonable skill and competence in the treatment of a patient in the hospital under his care. I agree that unless there exists in law a 'non-delegable duty of care' owed by the hospital to the patient, the hospital is not liable in this case.

No Court in Canada has ever found before that such a duty exists, and with great respect to the trial Judge, I am not persuaded by his reasons that there is such a duty. I am not dismissing those reasons perfunctorily, nor intending to denigrate them, when I say that he seems to me to be saying, in substance, 'In all the circumstances, the hospital *ought* to be liable.' In my view, if the criterion is to be what is fair and reasonable, it would be fair and reasonable that the highly skilled doctor whose negligence caused the damage should be called upon to pay for it. As the trial Judge did, I must put out of my mind that the plaintiff's chose not to sue him.

I agree with the trial Judge (and have said this earlier in my reasons) that the Yepremians had every right to expect that a large public hospital like Scarborough General would provide whatever was required to treat seriously ill or injured people but I do not think it follows that the public is entitled to add the further expectation: 'and if any doctor on the medical staff makes a negligent mistake, the hospital will pay for it'.

Rather, I think, a member of the public who knows the facts is entitled to expect that the hospital has picked its medical staff with great care, has checked out the credentials of every applicant, has caused the existing staff to make a recommendation in every individual case, makes no appointment for longer than one year at a time, and reviews the performance of its staff at regular intervals.

The minority view was expressed by Blair and Houlden JJA.

Blair JA: It is ... well established that the hospital is liable to a patient directly for failure to provide what, in other areas of tort liability, would be called a 'safe system' ... In some cases, the line is blurred between injury caused by the failure of the hospital to provide proper equipment or organisation and injury caused by the negligence of employees: none the less, the principle of direct liability is well established by the authorities. It is particularly demonstrated by the common law principle, accepted in *Hillyer's* case and elaborated by statute that a hospital is responsible for the proper selection of qualified doctors to serve on its staff ...

[The hospital] contends that its responsibility to the patient is simply to ensure the provision of medical services by properly-qualified doctors without accepting any responsibility to the patient for the manner in which doctors perform those services ...

The recognition of a direct duty of hospitals to provide non-negligent medical treatment reflects the reality of the relationship between hospitals and the public in contemporary society. This direct duty arises from profound changes in social structures and public attitudes relating to medical services and the concomitant changes in the function of hospitals in providing them. It is obvious that as a result of these changes the role of hospitals in the delivery of medical services has expanded. The public increasingly relies on hospitals to provide medical treatment and, in particular, on emergency services. Hospitals to a growing extent hold out to the public that they provide such treatment and such services.

At the outset of my review of the hospital's duty in tort I asked whether the hospital *could* have undertaken a direct duty to provide medical treatment, and whether in the circumstances of this case it *did*. From the foregoing I conclude that the common law does recognise that hospitals *can* in certain circumstances be directly liable to patients for the negligent performance of medical services, as held by Holland J. As Lords Greene, Morris and Nathan have observed, whether and to what extent a hospital assumes a direct duty depends upon the circumstances of the particular case. I am of the opinion that in the circumstances of this case the Hospital *is* liable. It is unnecessary to refer again to the facts which I have quoted from the judgment of Holland J. In the emergency, the Hospital provided, as it held itself out to do, the only means of obtaining medical care for Tony. His life was placed completely in the Hospital's hands. He and his family relied entirely on the Hospital to use its resources of equipment and skilled, but anonymous, personnel to restore his health. With the greatest of respect for those who hold the contrary view, I believe that, in the circumstances of this case, the Hospital's obligation to Tony could not be limited merely to placing a qualified doctor at his disposal. The hospital assumed and would be expected to assume complete responsibility for Tony's treatment.

MacKinnon ACJO and Morden JA agreed with Arrup JA. Houlden JA dissented and agreed with Blair JA.

Kirby P referred in *Ellis* to the case of *Wilsher v Essex Area HA* [1986] 3 All ER 801. Although that case eventually went to the House of Lords, for our purposes it is the judgments of the Court of Appeal which are important.

Wilsher v Essex Area HA [1987] QB 730, [1986] 3 All ER 801 (CA)

The plaintiff was an infant child who was born prematurely suffering from various illnesses, including oxygen deficiency. His prospects of survival were considered to be poor and he was placed in the 24-hour special care baby unit at the hospital where he was born. The unit was staffed by a medical team, consisting of two consultants, a senior registrar, several junior doctors and trained nurses. While the plaintiff was in the unit a junior and inexperienced doctor monitoring the oxygen in the plaintiff's bloodstream mistakenly inserted a catheter into a vein rather than an artery but then asked the senior registrar to check what he had done. The registrar failed to see the mistake and some hours later, when replacing the catheter, did exactly the same thing himself. In both instances the catheter monitor failed to register correctly the amount of oxygen in the plaintiff's blood, with the result that the plaintiff was given excess oxygen. The plaintiff subsequently brought an action against the health authority claiming damages and alleging that the excess oxygen in his bloodstream had caused an incurable condition of the retina resulting in near blindness. At the trial of the action the judge awarded the plaintiff £116,199. In dismissing the appeal, the judge in the Court of Appeal had the following to say on the issue of a health authority's primary duty of care.

Mustill LJ: There is, however, a quite different proposition which might have been advanced, namely that the defendants are directly liable for any adverse consequences of the episode. For example, it might have been said that the defendants owed a duty to ensure that the special baby care unit functioned according to the standard reasonably to be expected of such a unit. This approach would not require any consideration of the extent to which the individual doctors measured up to the standards demanded of them as individuals, but would focus attention on the performance of the unit as a whole. A rather different form of the argument might have been advanced on the following lines. Although the catheter, with its monitor and sampling facility, is a valuable instrument, it will yield misleading and potentially dangerous results if the head is in the wrong place. The defendants therefore owed a duty, if they were to use the catheter on patients entrusted to their care, to ensure that those who were to operate the device knew how to detect when it was wrongly placed, and on their own evidence the junior doctors did not know this. Finally, it might have been said that, if the junior doctors did not have sufficient skill or experience to provide the special care demanded by such a premature baby, the defendants were at fault in appointing them to the posts which they held.

If the nature of the plaintiff's cause of action had been a live issue on this appeal, it would have been necessary to look with care at the developing line of authority on liability for medical negligence. For counsel for the defendants asserted roundly that no health authority ever had been, or in principle ever could be, under any such direct liability as suggested, except perhaps in the case of a person being appointed to a post for which he is not qualified. In the event, however, counsel for the plaintiff explicitly disclaimed on the plaintiff's behalf any intention to put forward a case of direct liability. The trial had been conducted throughout, he made clear, exclusively on the basis of vicarious liability. It is therefore unnecessary to express any opinion of the validity in law of a claim on the alternative basis.

While Mustill LJ thought it was unnecessary to decide the question, as you will see, Sir Nicolas Browne-Wilkinson V-C took the view that the case could not be properly analysed without deciding this point.

Browne-Wilkinson V-C: ... I agree with the comments of Mustill LJ as to the confusion which has been caused in this case both by the pleading and by the argument below which blurred the distinction between the vicarious liability of the health authority for the negligence of its doctors and the direct liability of the health authority for negligently failing to provide skilled treatment of the kind that it was offering to the public. In my judgment, a health authority which so conducts its hospital that it fails to provide doctors of sufficient skill and experience to give the treatment offered at the hospital may be directly liable in negligence to the patient. Although we were told in argument that no case has ever been decided on this ground and that it is not the practice to formulate claims in this way, I can see no reason why, in principle, the health authority should not be so liable if its organisation is at fault: see *McDermid v Nash Dredging and Reclamation Co Ltd* [1986] 2 All ER 676 esp at 684–685, [1986] QB 965 esp at 978–979 (reported since the conclusion of the argument).

Glidewell LJ agreed with the Vice-Chancellor.

Glidewell LJ: I agree with Sir Nicolas Browne-Wilkinson V-C that there seems to be no reason in principle why, in a suitable case different on its facts from this, a hospital management committee [sic] should not be held directly liable in negligence for failing to provide sufficient qualified and competent medical staff.

Perhaps it is surprising that the court was so tentative in accepting the notion of primary or direct liability (and in accepting counsel's assertion that no English cases dealt with the issue) given the background we have already seen. What is important to notice, however, is that the court was not asked to consider, nor did it address, the possibility that the second strand of primary liability represented the law in England ie that the hospital had a non-delegable duty to *ensure* that reasonable care is taken in the provision of health care.

Earlier, we posed the question which, if either, strand of primary liability was recognised in English law. Although the Court of Appeal in *Wilsher* was somewhat tentative there seems little doubt that the first strand of primary liability (ie to provide a safe system etc) is part of English law. It was accepted as such without demur subsequently by the Court of Appeal in *Bull v Devon AHA*.

Bull v Devon AHA [1993] 4 Med LR 117 (CA)

Mrs Bull sued the defendant Health Authority on behalf of herself and her disabled son. He was born at the maternity unit of the Exeter City Hospital for which the defendant and its predecessors were responsible. Mrs Bull claimed that her son was disabled due to asphyxia at birth which was attributable to the negligence of the Health Authority and the staff employed by it. As regards the direct claim against the Health Authority, she alleged that the asphyxia was due to the fact that the delivery of her son was delayed because a doctor was not available to attend her. This, in turn, she alleged, was due to the fact that the hospital had maintained its services on two sites and the system for summoning doctors had broken down.

In the course of holding the Health Authority liable in negligence, the Court of Appeal accepted that the Health Authority owed Mrs Bull and her son a duty of care directly. Slade LJ observed that it was 'indisputable' that the Authority owed a duty of care to Mrs Bull's son. He accepted the plaintiff's submission of the scope of that duty in the following terms (necessarily tailored to the facts of case):

Slade LJ: The duty of a hospital is to provide a woman admitted in labour with a reasonable standard of skilled obstetric and paediatric care, in order to ensure as far as reasonably practicable the safe delivery of the baby or babies and the health of the mother and offspring thereafter.

Applying this to the alleged unsafe system of summoning an obstetrician to look after Mrs Bull, Slade LJ went on to state:

Slade LJ: It is possible to imagine hypothetical contingencies which would have accounted for a failure, without any avoidable fault in the hospital's system or any negligence in its working, to secure for Mrs Bull attendance by any obstetrician qualified to deliver the ...

[plaintiff's son] … In my judgment, however, all the most likely explanations for this failure point strongly either (i) to inefficiency in the system for summoning the assistance of the registrar or consultant, in operation at the hospital in 1970, or (ii) to negligence by some individual or individuals in the working of that system.

Dillon LJ also held the Health Authority liable for breach of its primary duty.

Dillon LJ: In my judgment, the plaintiff has succeeded in proving, by the ordinary civil standards of proof, that the failure to provide for Mrs Bull the prompt attendance she needed was attributable to the negligence of the defendants in implementing an unreliable and essentially unsatisfactory system for calling the registrar.

Mustill LJ cast off his earlier reticence in *Wilsher*. Having examined the evidence relevant to the finding of carelessness against the Health Authority, he concluded that 'the judge had no choice but to decide [that the Authority was in breach of duty]'.

Ten years later, the first strand of primary liability was accepted without question. The courts recognise that 'systems failures' are to be considered as an aspect of the provider's own duty of care to its patients as the case of *Robertson v Nottingham HA* [1997] 8 Med LR 1 (CA) illustrates.

Robertson v Nottingham HA **[1997] 8 Med LR 1 (CA)**

The plaintiff, Jessica Robertson, a minor and a person under disability, suing by her mother and next friend, claimed damages for personal injury caused by alleged negligence of the defendants, Nottingham Health Authority, by their servants or agents prior to and during the birth of the plaintiff on or about July 14, 1983 at the Queen's Medical Centre, Nottingham. Jessica was born with neurological disabilities which resulted in severe spastic quadriplegic cerebral palsy with developmental retardation, visual impairment, epilepsy and microcephaly. It was the plaintiff's case that she suffered from asphyxia in the last period before birth and that she suffered from hypoxic ischaemia encephalopathy (HIE) which in turn caused or substantially contributed to her final condition.

The issue of negligence mainly concerned the interpretation of CTG scans carried out after the plaintiff's mother had been admitted to hospital on July 11, 1983, because her baby was not moving in the usual manner. The first CTG scan, which was taken on July 11, gave no signs to cause concern, but mother was still concerned about continuing reduced foetal activity. The senior house officer, Dr Caroline Robertson, was not happy with the quality of the trace and it was decided to keep mother in overnight and to repeat the scan. On July 12 at 11 10 am a second scan recorded a small but distinct late deceleration lasting some 40 seconds. Trace no 3 commenced at 18 30 on July 12 but contractions were not recorded because the contraction belt had not been fitted. The base line rate was normal and several accelerations were seen in the middle of the tracing.

Trace no 4 started at 13 00 hours on July 13. Dr Robertson examined the trace and discerned three dips. She contacted Dr Pickles (the registrar) who gave instructions for the CTG to be repeated and that a Pinnard's stethoscope was to be used in order to confirm or to discount "dips". Trace no 5 was commenced at 16 00 hours on July 13. Dr Pickles' instructions to listen with the Pinnard's stethoscope were not observed. The midwife recognised decelerations and told Dr Pickles who requested a further scan and "if any loss of contact listen with Pinnards". Trace no 6 was commenced at 21 05 hours. Again the operator was not informed of the need to monitor it with Pinnard's. The trace showed three large decelerations and a raised FHB base line to 160 plus. Trace no 7 started at 13 05. Dr Pickles carried out the scan himself. When the FHB started to drop he listened with a Pinnard's stethoscope. He wrote on the tracing at 23 09 "true deceleration with Pinnards" and similarly at 23 21. At 23 30 Dr Pickles telephoned the consultant who agreed that a caesarean section was appropriate. Mrs Robertson requested an epidural analgesic block. This was inserted some time after midnight. The caesarean section was performed by Dr Pickles and the plaintiff was delivered at 01 18 hours weighing 5 lbs and described as "flat at birth limp and pale". She was resuscitated and given intravenous sodium bicarbonate, but was severely brain damaged …

Brooke LJ: The history of this case revealed two significant types of communications breakdown. The first was concerned with the communication of dependable information, through the use of CTG scans and other means such as a stethoscope, if necessary, about the state of the foetal heart rate to the doctors who were responsible for exercising their clinical judgment in relation to decisions about their patient's future care. The second was concerned with the communication of instructions between the hospital's medical staff and its nursing and midwifery staff.

We will deal with this second set of breakdowns first. Dr Robertson, the senior house officer, told the judge that she had not only passed on orally to the midwives Dr Pickles' instructions on the Wednesday afternoon about the use of a stethoscope for the next scan (T5), but she had also written them down in the medical notes. She said that these notes were kept beside the nursing station and were available to the nursing staff so that the midwives would be able to review them since they had access to both sets of notes, nursing and medical. She believed that the midwives would miss out on relevant information if they did not read the medical notes. Professor Johnson said that he would expect the nurse to follow the note, and he would regard failure to do so as a shooting offence: it was a serious offence not to follow the instructions concerning the Pinnard's stethoscope, and that this was not good practice and not acceptable.

The hospital's doctors repeated these views, in even more marked terms in relation to the later failure to use a Pinnard's stethoscope for T6. Dr Pickles said he regarded it as a serious failure of duty, Professor Johnson "clearly another serious matter" and Professor Symonds regarded it as a failure.

The only member of the nursing or midwifery staff of the hospital to give evidence about these matters was Mrs Morrall. She said that the early staff gave the late staff a "handover" using the nursing cardex but not the doctors' notes. She would not herself look at the medical notes of each patient routinely. She recalled that the day in question had been particularly busy and there had just not been time to look at the medical notes at all. As we have said, she recalled receiving an oral message to do a supervised trace from someone on the early shift. As to the later failure, she accepted that Dr Pickles' instruction at 5pm was directed at any of the medical or nursing staff who were looking after R's mother, but she said that it was not common practice or essential that the midwives should read the medical notes. She believed that Dr Pickles would have also given this instruction orally to the nurses in question, but she just could not remember it having been said. This combination of events led to the midwife who was responsible for the T6 trace immediately after Mrs Morrall went off duty having no knowledge of Dr Pickles' second instruction to use a stethoscope. There was no evidence before the judge as to the systems in place in this hospital for ensuring that there was not a readily avoidable breakdown of communication between the medical staff and the nursing staff, who of course were operating a familiar shift system.

We turn back now to the first set of communications breakdowns. Again, there was unanimity of views among the defendants' senior staff about the duties of nurses or midwives who were responsible for taking CTG scans at that time. Dr Pickles said that with a routine CTG it was right and proper practice for a midwife or nurse to go and check the machine every 15–30 minutes to make sure that the scan was recording properly and that there were no adverse features, and that it would be a breach of proper practice if this was not done. Professor Johnson confirmed that it would be normal and proper practice to check that the machine was recording correctly every 15–30 minutes, and that if there were marked features on the scan that were interpretable by the nursing staff they would call the attention of the medical staff to them. Professor Symonds agreed that it was good practice to go and check the placing of the equipment every 15 minutes and certainly every half an hour, and that if a midwife saw a dip and was not clear about it, she would need to move the transducer or listen herself. So far as T3 was concerned, he admitted surprise that nobody had picked up the fact that the contractions were not properly recorded throughout that scan. Mrs Morrall said that once a midwife was satisfied that the monitor was running all right it could be left, so long as it was checked regularly to make sure that it was running properly. No other evidence was given concerning the instructions in fact given to those who would operate the cardio-tachograph machine or the training they received.

In all this the defendants' witnesses were merely confirming, for the most part, the evidence already given by Professor Steer on behalf of the plaintiff. He considered that in relation to Traces 2–4 the defendants had failed in their duty to improve the quality of the tracing. It is clear from his evidence that, what he had in mind was that if, during the course of a tracing (which usually lasted 75 minutes) a midwife had performed her routine checks, she would (1) have been able to improve the quality of the trace if it had gaps in it where it was making no contact or if the message it was giving was difficult to interpret because the tracing was so poor, or if, as with T3, there was simply no record being made of the contractions at all; and (2) have been able to draw a doctor's attention to clearly interpretable adverse signs midway through a trace, so that a doctor could give any necessary instructions then and there. When Professor Steer said that what he was describing was the standard of care of the majority of obstetricians, his evidence was confirmed to a very considerable extent in this respect by the evidence given to the judge by all the defendants' responsible medical staff.

It is clearly from this analysis of the evidence that there were in these two respects significant breakdowns in the defendants' systems of communication which represented breaches of proper practice. In medical negligence cases the agreed arrangements within the National Health Service between the Department of Health and the professional insurance organisations which were first instituted in Circular HM (54) 32 in 1954 have kept right away from the courts disputes as to whether any negligent breach of duty to a patient arose from negligence by an identifiable member or members of a hospital's professional staff or by a "systems failure". But that a health authority can be liable for a "systems failure" is clear from the recent decision of the Court of Appeal in *Bull v Devon AHA* [1993] 4 Med LR 117.

In that case the trial judge, Tucker J, had held that far too long a time had been allowed to elapse after the birth of a first twin, especially after a vaginal loss of blood, before the second twin was delivered. All three members of the Court of Appeal upheld his decision, ruling that the health authority was negligent in not operating a system whereby, except in unforeseeable contingencies, a responsible doctor would have attended reasonably quickly in relation to such an emergency (see Slade LJ at p 135, left hand column (LHC); Dillon LJ at p 138 (LHC); and Mustill LJ at pp 141 (RHC) – 142 (LHC)).

Although it is customary to say that a health authority is vicariously liable for breach of duty if its responsible servants or agents fail to set up a safe system of operation in relation to what are essentially management as opposed to clinical matters, this formulation may tend to cloud the fact that in any event it has a non-delegable duty to establish a proper system of care just as much as it has a duty to engage competent staff and a duty to provide proper and safe equipment and safe premises (compare *Wilsher v Essex AHA* [1987] QB 730 per Sir Nicolas Browne-Wilkinson at p 778 A–D and Glidewell LJ, agreeing on this point, at p 775 B–C).

A health authority owes its patient a duty to provide her with a reasonable regime of care at its hospital (*Gold v Essex County Council* [1942] 2 KB 293 per Lord Greene MR at pp 302 and 304; and per Goddard LJ at p 309: *Roe v Minister of Health* [1954] 2 QB 66 per Denning LJ at p 72, applying what he said in *Cassidy v Ministry of Health* [1951] 2 KB 343 at pp 359–365, and per Morris LJ at pp 88–89). For examples of analogous cases within a master-servant relationship where an employer was held liable for a systems failure see *McDermid v North Dredging and Reclamation Company Ltd* [1987] AC 906, per Lord Hailsham of St Marylebone at pp 910F–G and 911F–G and per Lord Brandon at pp 918G–H and 919B–D; and *Wilsons & Clyde Coal Co Ltd v English* [1938] AC 57 per Lord Wright at pp 81–84. By a reasonable regime of care we mean a regime of a standard that can reasonably be expected of a hospital of the size and type in question – in the present case a large teaching centre of excellence.

If effective systems had been in place at this hospital for ensuring that so far as reasonably practicable communications breakdowns did not occur in connection with such a significant area of a patient's treatment then the health authority would be vicariously liable for any negligence of those of its servants or agents who did not take proper care to ensure, so far as was reasonably practicable, that the communications systems worked efficiently. If, on the other hand, no effective systems were in place at all – and the evidence is not very complete in this regard – then the authority would be directly liable in negligence for this lacuna.

There is no need, for the purposes of the present case, to go into some of the much wider issues that have been canvassed in Canada (see *Yepremian v Scarborough General Hospital* (1980) 110 DLR (3d) 513) and Australia (see *Ellis v Wallsend District Hospital* [1990] 2 Med LR 103). The only rule that this court has to apply in the present case is that if a patient is injured by reason of a negligent breakdown in the systems for communicating material information to the clinicians responsible for her care, she is not to be denied redress merely because no identifiable person or persons are to blame for deficiencies in setting up and monitoring the effectiveness of the relevant communication systems. She is entitled to say, like the successful plaintiff in *Bull*: "You, the health authority were responsible for my care: you are responsible if there is a breakdown, reasonably attributable to improper practice, in the systems used at your hospital for communicating material information to the clinicians responsible for my care: and I was injured as a result of this negligence." ...

On the facts the court concluded that the negligence had not caused or contributed to the child's brain damage.

A few comments can be made. First, Brooke LJ distinguished between a failure due to a lack of a safe system and one due to a failure to implement effectively or at all that system. The former is an aspect of the institution's *primary* duty whilst the latter is a breach of duty (if at all) by the health care professional for which the institution will be vicariously liable. It is important to note, however, that an institution could be liable itself if it negligently allowed a culture of non-compliance or turned a 'blind eye' to the non-implementation of the system. The latter is also an aspect of the institution's primary duty. Secondly, Brooke LJ (speaking for the Court of Appeal) left open whether English law contemplated liability on the basis of the second strand of primary liability to which we should now turn.

So much, then, for the first strand of primary liability and its acceptance as part of English law. What of the second strand of primary liability – the duty to *ensure* that care is taken in the provision of health services? Is this any part of English law? Properly understood this strand of primary liability amounts to the imposition on a Health Authority of vicarious liability for the negligent acts of anyone working in the institution whether as an employee *or independent contractor*. However attractive Kirby P's analysis in *Ellis* may be that, by analogy, an NHS hospital holds itself out, and thereby undertakes a duty, to ensure that a patient receives reasonable care in the hospital, an English court is unlikely to accept it. Were it to do so it would impose upon a Trust the duty of a guarantor that care be taken, which is a duty rarely imposed upon anyone, as regards the conduct of independent contractors, in English law (see *Tarry v Ashton* (1876) 1 QBD 314; and *Honeywill and Stein Ltd v Larkin Bro Ltd* [1934] 1 KB 191). In other contexts, both the Court of Appeal and House of Lords have set their faces against the expansion of this exceptional group of cases (see *Salsbury v Woodland* [1970] 1 QB 324; *D & F Estates Ltd v Church Comrs for England* [1989] AC 177).

Until recently, no modern case in England considered the more onerous (second) strand of primary liability. In *X (minors) v Bedfordshire CC* [1995] 3 All ER 353, Lord Browne-Wilkinson said the 'negligent acts of [a] servant are capable of constituting a breach of the duty of care (if any) owed directly by the [Health Authority] to the plaintiff' (at 372). It is unclear what to make of this. His reservation about the duty of care – 'if any' – was related to the particular case with which he was concerned, namely an investigation of possible child abuse. On the face of it, his phraseology is that of the second strand: liability because the *employee* is in breach of duty. Yet, his speech is elsewhere more consistent with the first strand (at 392–393) or leaves the issue unresolved (at 372). As we shall see, the first instance case of *M v Calderdale & Kirklees HA* [1998] Lloyd's Rep Med 157 (Huddersfield CC) represents a new departure in favour of the second strand.

Of course, in the context of the NHS the absence of this second strand of primary liability is of little practical significance. Rarely (if ever) will a situation arise where the negligent actor is not an employee of the NHS Trust for whom, as we shall see, the Trust is vicariously liable (but quaere a Primary Care Trust?). It is not impossible however. Illustrations may include agency staff such as nurses working within the hospital who will be independent contractors. Also, a doctor may be 'lent' by one Trust to another. In such circumstances, who would be liable for the doctor's negligence? Arguably, the Trust hospital which 'lent' him would remain his employer and, hence, vicariously Liable (*Mersey Docks and Harbour Board v Coggins and Griffiths (Liverpool) Ltd* [1947] AC 1). Additionally, however, the Trust hospital that has 'borrowed' him could only be liable if this second strand of primary liability is the law (without prejudice to any liability that might incur under the first strands of primary liability) unless, of course, an additional contract of service is entered into between the doctor and the 'borrowing' hospital, which is likely to be the case.

A further situation needs to be considered within the NHS. Increasingly, some services are 'farmed out' to private providers by NHS Trusts, for example, histological testing. What, if any, liability would the NHS Trust have for the negligence of the independent provider. Of course, if there was negligence in the selection or supervision of the independent provider, then liability under the first strand would exist. But what if this was not the case. Could there be liability for a competent but negligent provider? The issue arose in the next case and was answered by the court in the affirmative.

M v Calderdale & Kirklees HA **[1998] Lloyd's Rep Med 157 (Huddersfield CC)**

In February 1992 the plaintiff, M, then aged 17, discovered that she was pregnant. She already had a baby daughter aged six months and did not want another child. She went to her doctor, who referred her to Dr Sykes, senior clinical medical officer for Huddersfield Community Services, who saw the plaintiff at the Princess Royal Community Health Centre on March 2, 1992. Following counselling Dr Sykes arranged for the plaintiff to be treated by the second defendants, the Falladon Private Surgical Hospital. On March 10, 1992, the plaintiff attended at that hospital where a vacuum aspiration of pregnancy was effected by Mr Michael Olabode Fayeye the third defendant.

In May 1992, the plaintiff was found still to be pregnant, confirmed to be some 20 or 22 weeks' duration. She gave birth to a boy on September 22, 1992.

The plaintiff obtained judgments against the third defendant on May 3, 1995, and the second defendant on March 14, 1996. Apparently neither was insured and the second defendants were subject to a winding up order.

On the issue of the liability of the first defendant it was accepted that
(1) the plaintiff was under the care of the first defendant at all material times;
(2) the termination of pregnancy was carried out incompetently;
(3) the first defendant contracted with the second defendants that the second defendants should perform the termination of pregnancy.

It was contended for the plaintiff that
(1) the first defendant had failed in exercising its primary duty under sect 1 of the National Health Service Act of 1977 in that it had failed to provide or secure the effective provision of services as therein set out;
(2) it had been in breach of its duty at common law which was broadly to the same effect, each of those duties being directly owed to the plaintiff;
(3) that they were vicariously liable for the negligence of the second defendants in their selection of the second defendants.

The first defendant's case was that
(1) the court was being asked to create a new category of non-delegable duties and too much reliance was placed on the authorities cited in support of the plaintiff's case;
(2) in relation to the National Health Service Act the first defendant could properly decide whether to provide services itself or secure the provision by an independent contractor chosen reasonably;
(3) the first defendant had no control over the training and monitoring of staff if it chose, as it had done in this case, to secure provision as opposed to providing provision;
(4) there had been no negligence in choosing the second defendants as they were licensed by the appropriate authorities;
(5) the first defendant had exercised a power under the 1977 Act and the question of delegation did not then arise …

Judge Garner: The first defendant's case is that the court is being asked to create a new category of non-delegable duties and too much reliance is placed on the authorities cited in support of the plaintiff's case. The particular medical negligence cases, it is urged, were pre-eminently cases of their time. In relation to the National Health Service Act the first defendant could properly decide whether to provide services itself or secure the provision by an independent contractor chosen reasonably. It was submitted that the first defendant had no control over the training and monitoring of staff if it chose, as it had done in this case, to secure provision as opposed to providing provision. There had been no negligence in choosing the second defendants as they were licensed by the appropriate authorities. What the first defendant had done was to exercise a power under the 1977 Act and the question of delegation did not then arise. The authorities cited by the plaintiff had all to be considered against that background and did not amount to supporting the plaintiff.

In support of their respective cases, Mr Hone and Mr Myerson referred me to a number of authorities and text books and quite properly urged me in different directions. I do not propose to rehearse all their submissions. I have already mentioned some of Mr Myerson's. I prefer to indicate the direction in which the submissions have led me. In the circumstances of this particular case which have to be my perspective I have preferred those of Mr Hone. He placed considerable reliance on *Gold v Essex County Council* [1942] 2 KB p 293, particularly the judgment of Lord Greene, the then Master of the Rolls. I accept that that judgment became the foundation for the assertion made in *Clerk and Lindsell on Tort* in the 17th ed (1995) at paragraph 5.16, and I quote:

> The hospital authority itself is under a duty to its patients which it does not discharge simply by delegating its performance to someone else. No matter whether the delegation be to an employee or an independent contractor and on this basis it makes no difference whether or not a visiting consultant is a servant.

It is clear to me from *Gold* that what must be discovered is the extent of the obligation assumed by the first defendant in relation to this plaintiff. In my view, the first defendant had a duty to bring about for her the effective provision of services either by providing them themselves or causing others to effect this on their behalf. Put another way, the plaintiff could expect an effective termination of her pregnancy from any person or persons in whose hands she was placed by the first defendant because it had the duty to bring that about once she had been accepted by the first defendant into its care. In the circumstances of this case, this plaintiff never questioned what was asked of her by the first defendant, nor was there any element or possibility of choice on her part. She went to her doctor, he referred her to Dr Sykes, she arranged for her to be treated by the second defendants.

Lord Justice Denning in *Cassidy v Minister of Health* [1951] 2 KB 343 has led me in the same direction. I recall Mr Myerson's submissions about the relative position of that learned judge and his solo development of his judgment beyond the central *ratio decidendi* of the case but given the age and authority of that judgment and its lack of challenge I feel bound by it. Not for the first time Lord Justice Denning's words have carried wisdom and relevance prophetically to the present day, particularly these words,

> I take it to be clear law [said Lord Justice Denning] as well as good sense that where a person is himself under a duty to use care he cannot get rid of his responsibility by delegating the performance of it to someone else, no matter whether the delegation be to a servant under a contract of service or to an independent contractor under a contract for services.

I respectfully agree with the views set out in *Street on Torts*, 9th ed (1993) at pages 492 to 494 as drawn to my attention during the hearing that the National Health Service may well owe a non-delegable duty generally. In the particular circumstances of this case I find that they do. I do not accept Mr Myerson's submission based on a consideration of *Rivers v Cutting* [1982] 3 All ER p 69 that the first defendant can satisfy its obligation in this case by asserting that reasonable care was taken in choosing the second defendants. That case related to a power, not a statutory duty. In this case the first defendant has a statutory obligation laid upon it as a matter of principle. Even were it but a matter of fact I am unable to find that the first defendant had taken reasonable care in its dealings with the second defendants in this case. It had no idea whether indemnity insurance was carried or not. It had no available copy of the contract between the parties. It had no up to date information about competence. It seems to me to have relied upon enquiries assumed to be ongoing by others and an apparent absence of complaints. I accept that I cannot find that the second defendants were definitely not insured because the matter was not the subject of direct evidence before me. It seems more than a reasonable assumption that they were not insured, but what I can and do find is that the first defendant was in ignorance about it.

The plaintiff never left the care of the first defendant. She was its patient. She never had an opportunity to divert from the route of treatment arranged on her behalf. In those circumstances she is entitled in my view to remain in the same position as a patient who remains in house relying upon the expectation of an effective provision of services. There will be all the backing of the authority if things go wrong. There is no need to make enquiries about competence; about standards; about insurance because the umbrella of the authority remains above. The patient who remains in-house will have had that provided.

The patient who is sent elsewhere, without having intervened in the choice of destination, will have had that secured. In the event of it being ineffectively provided or secured the patient's rights and remedies must remain the same. If there has been negligence the umbrella of the authority must remain over both that which is provided and that which is secured. If it were different the person who remained in house would be in a more favourable position than the person sent involuntarily elsewhere. That cannot be a proper interpretation of the duty of the first defendant either under the Act or at common law. If the duty of the first defendant were able to be separated off in this way, it could mean that a patient found it necessary to make his or her own enquiries about competence and insurance and other matters possibly in an ambulance en route. That cannot be right.

This does not open floodgates or if I may say so let free unruly horses if the authority in question makes and maintains competent, contractual relationships with others who are properly managed and insured ...

In this case, there would not on the face of it have been a breach of the primary duty to exercise reasonable care in the provision of staff, services or a safe system within the hospital.

There was no suggestion of negligence in selecting the clinic where the termination was performed. By all accounts, the negligence lay in an individual doctor's mistake. It is true that the judge listed a number of failures by the first defendant: not inquiring about the clinic's insurance position, not having a copy of the contract between them and not making up-to-date inquiries about competence. It is extremely difficult to see the relevance of these, except perhaps the final one. In any event, none could be said to have contributed to the plaintiff's injury, ie the 'botched' termination. Whatever inquiries the first defendant would have made, the plaintiff's lot would not have been improved. The doctor would still have made the mistake that led to the failed abortion. If there was any *breach* by the first defendant, it did not *cause* any injury.

Leaving aside the judge's curious and erroneous reliance on s 1 of the National Health Service Act 1977 as giving rise to an action for breach of statutory duty (on which see *infra*, p 329), his decision can, therefore, only be justified on the novel basis he adopted of a non-delegable duty to ensure care is taken. He relied on the 'classic' (or is it 'vintage'?) statements to this effect of Denning LJ (as he then was) in *Cassidy v Ministry of Health* [1951] 2 KB 343 and of Lord Greene MR in *Gold v Essex CC* [1942] 2 KB 293. He could, of course, have also relied upon Denning LJ in *Roe v Minister of Health* [1954] 2 QB 66. It is pretty clear that the motivation in these cases was to obviate the difficulty, that then existed, of relying upon vicarious liability because the staff concerned were not seen to be employees. That, of course, has changed since the 1950s and is probably the main reason why the obiter statements were largely forgotten, at least by the English courts.

It is possible to argue that the approach in those cases could, in some circumstances, result in the imposition of the novel non-delegable duty recognised in the instant case. Even though the judge did not examine the more recent case-law, there is much merit in what he said. The plaintiff never left the care of the first defendant and she ought to be in the same position as if she had been treated 'in house': 'the plaintiff was entitled to expect an effective termination of her pregnancy from any person or persons in whose hands she was placed by the first defendant because it had a duty to bring that about once she had been accepted by the first defendant into its care'.

Of course, the legal difficulties only ensued because the other defendants were uninsured or subject to a winding-up order. Would the judge have been made the same decision if he had, instead, been concerned with contribution proceedings between liquid defendants rather than whether the plaintiff was going to be compensated at all? Legally, it should make no difference; but in reality it does.

The second strand of liability is, also important when deciding the liability of a hospital or clinic outside the NHS. The private clinic or hospital could, of course, be liable under the first strand if the facts show that it negligently failed to set up a 'safe system'. If, however, there is no such negligence (as may well be the case), given that the doctor will ordinarily be an independent contractor using the facilities and staff of the clinic or hospital, the only form of liability the clinic or hospital could face in tort would only impose upon the clinic an implied term to exercise reasonable care; in effect the first strand of primary liability in tort. In tort, there is little doubt that in the usual situation in which the patient selects the doctor who then arranges facilities at a private clinic, the law regards the private clinic as being in precisely the same position as an NHS hospital, ie only the first strand of primary liability applies. It may conceivably be otherwise where the private clinic is judged, by the way in which it holds itself out, to have undertaken to provide a level of service amounting to a guarantee of reasonable care. This could arise where the patient has chosen the clinic on the basis of its reputation in the 'market place'.

II. Liability of the Secretary of State

In addition to the institutions or bodies, which we have just discussed, which may incur primary liability, we must also consider the possible primary liability of the Secretary of State. He may be liable for negligence or, possibly, for breach of statutory duty.

A. Negligence. As regards an action in negligence against the Secretary of State, the courts would have to consider whether, as a matter of law, the Secretary of State owed an individual patient a duty of care. Given that most of the functions which she has not delegated will involve policy decisions at the highest level within the NHS, the patient will face considerable difficulties in bringing a claim. The litigation against the Secretary of State brought by haemophiliacs who claimed to have contracted HIV from infected blood products illustrates this. You will recall that the supply of blood within the NHS is a responsibility retained by the Secretary of State.

Re HIV Haemophiliac Litigation [1996] PNLR 290; (1990) 41 BMLR 171(CA)

The plaintiffs were 962 haemophiliacs and their wives or children who had developed AIDS or would do so as the result of the haemophiliacs being treated under the NHS with blood made out of Factor VIII concentrate imported from the USA which was infected with the HIV virus. They brought an action against, inter alia, the Department of Health, the licensing authority under the Medicines Act 1968, the committee on the safety of medicines ('the central defendants'), all regional and district health authorities in England and Wales, and the central blood laboratories authority. As against the Department of Health the plaintiffs alleged that the department was in breach of its statutory duty under ss 1 and 3(1) of the National Health Service Act 1977 to promote a comprehensive health service in England and Wales designed to secure improvement (a) in the physical and mental health of the people and (b) in the prevention, diagnosis and treatment of illness, and to provide throughout England and Wales facilities for the prevention of illness and the care of persons suffering from illness, and was negligent in failing to ensure that the country was self-sufficient in blood supplies thereby causing haemophiliacs to be treated with infected blood from the USA. The plaintiffs applied for discovery of documents but the department claimed public interest immunity in respect of certain documents on the ground that they related to the formulation of policy by ministers or were briefings for ministers regarding whether a policy of self-sufficiency in blood products should be established, what resources should be allocated to implement such a policy, future planning on the role of the Blood Products Laboratory and whether and how to re-organise the National Blood Transfusion Service. The plaintiffs applied to the court for an order requiring the department to produce the documents in respect of which immunity was claimed. The department contended that production ought not to be ordered because the plaintiffs did not have a good cause of action either for breach of statutory duty or in negligence against the department. Rougier J held that the plaintiffs had no cause of action for breach of statutory duty and no cause of action in negligence for any alleged failure by the department for failure to perform duties imposed by statute but they did have a good cause of action for 'performance related negligence', ie negligence on the part of the department in performing its statutory duties. The judge ordered production of policy documents and exchanges between officials except documents, such as those relating to whether to adopt a policy of self-sufficiency in blood products, which could not be relevant to 'performance' as opposed to 'breach' related negligence. The plaintiffs appealed on the ground that the excluded documents should be made available while the department cross-appealed on the ground that none of the documents in respect of which immunity was sought should be produced.

Ralph Gibson LJ: The main points advanced by Mr Jackson for the plaintiffs were:
(i)   There is no authority to support the proposition that a decision upon the construction of a statute, to the effect that there is no civil remedy available for breach of any duty imposed by it, necessarily means that there can be no claim in negligence in respect of the discharge of carrying out of these duties insofar as any breach of duty consists of a failure to act. Reference was made to *Bux v Slough Metals Ltd* [1973] 1 WLR 1358, 1369–1370; and to *Dorset Yacht Co v Home Office* [1970] AC 1004.

(ii) If, as the judge found, the plaintiffs have sufficiently demonstrated an arguable case on the policy contentions as to proximity, etc, then it was wrong to draw the distinction between 'breach related' and 'performance related' matters as excluding or limiting the duty of care. The distinction between acts and omissions is relevant to the question whether breach of the duty has been shown.

(iii) The distinction between acts and omissions is of significance in cases against public authorities, where the decision within the authority's discretion and policy making function may be impossible to attack as negligent. But the fact that the decision attacked is made as a matter of discretion or policy making does not make the decision immune in law. If it is ultra vires or wholly unreasonable the authority will be liable in negligence if the decision is shown to be negligent by reference to proximity and foreseeability. Reference was made to the *Dorset Yacht* case at pages 1031A–1032A per Lord Reid, 1036F–1037G per Lord Morris, and 1067F–1068C per Lord Diplock; and to *Meade v London Borough of Haringey* [1979] 1 WLR 637 at 647 per Lord Denning MR.

For the Department, Mr Collins did not support the proposition that rejection of the claim for breach of statutory duty must of itself negative any 'coterminous' claim in negligence, but submitted that the same result is achieved by reference to similar aspects of this case by proper application of the requirement that it be just and reasonable to impose the duty of care. The nature of the relationship between the plaintiffs and the Central Defendants, based upon the 1977 Act, is such that it is not just or reasonable to impose a duty of care directly enforceable by any member of the public. His protection should be by an action for negligence, if there is breach of duty, against those who directly provide care and treatment to him; and the remedy for imperfections in the performance of the duties imposed by the 1977 Act should be within Parliament or through the ballot box. All the alleged duties upon which the plaintiffs rely contain the elements of discretion.

Further, as part of the concept of 'just and reasonable' Mr Collins argued that the nature of the discretion, and of the matters relevant to the decision made in discharge of the duties imposed by the 1977 Act, is such that a decision upon alleged negligence in the exercise of those functions should be held to be non-justiciable as unsuitable for judicial decisions: reference was made to *Rowling v Takaro Properties Ltd* [1988] AC 473, 501D–503H. Also it would be against public policy to impose liability in respect of those functions: see *Hill v Chief Constable for West Yorkshire* [1989] AC 53.

For my part, as to those policy contentions I agree with Rougier J that the plaintiffs have made out at least an arguable case. It is obvious that it would be rare for a case on negligence to be proved having regard to the nature of the duties under the 1977 Act, and to the fact that, in the law of negligence, it is difficult to prove a negligent breach of duty when the party charged with negligence is required to exercise discretion and to form judgments upon the allocation of public resources. That, however, is not sufficient, in my judgment, to make it clear for the purposes of these proceedings, that there can in law be no claim in negligence. Nor, on the allegations of fact, can it be said that the plaintiffs have not alleged a case which could be upheld if in law the claim is viable.

I have reached that conclusion on grounds which include the following …

In *Rowling v Takaro Properties* at p 501E the question whether, having regard to all the relevant considerations, it is appropriate that a duty of care should be imposed is a question of

an intensely pragmatic character, well suited for gradual development but requiring most careful analysis …

… in *Murphy's* [*Murphy v Brentwood DC* [1991] 1 AC 398 (HL)] case the claim was for economic loss. These plaintiffs have suffered personal injury. It is possible, in my judgment, that the court, after full consideration, may in this case be driven to hold that in the circumstances of these claims, and notwithstanding the difficulties of proof of negligence for the reasons stated above, yet a duty of care is imposed by the law upon the Central Defendants in the discharge of their functions under the 1977 Act. Those difficulties of proof will, of course, include the matter of exercise of discretion, policy making, allocation of resources and the distinction between failing to confer a benefit as contrasted with the infliction of harm.

Bingham LJ: Mr Andrew Collins QC, for the Department of Health … pointed out, relying on recent authority, that there is no close precedent for such a claim as the present, which differs in nature and scale from the negligence claims with which the courts customarily deal. Furthermore, he argued, the plaintiffs' complaints relate to matters within areas of political and administrative discretion which the courts are incompetent to evaluate (save, where *vires* are in issue, on applications for judicial review). There were, he said, by analogy with *Hill v Chief Constable of West Yorkshire* [1989] AC 53, strong reasons of public policy (or justice and reasonableness) for not holding a minister and a department exercising public functions for the benefit of the community as a whole to owe a duty of care towards individual members of the public.

These are points properly and responsibly argued and they may ultimately prevail, but on the necessarily brief argument which we have heard at this stage I am not at present satisfied that they must do so. Since I agree with the reasons of Ralph Gibson LJ on this point also I shall indicate very briefly the matters which particularly weigh with me:

(1) While there may be no very close precedent for the present claim, there has not perhaps, at least in this country, been any comparable calamity. Of the plaintiffs still living, the great majority have throughout their lives suffered the grave affliction of haemophilia. To this there has now been added the even graver affliction of AIDS, now or in the future. The tragedy was avoidable in the sense that, had different measures been taken in the 1970s and early 1980s, it could, at least in large measure, have been prevented. The law cannot of course redress all ills, however grave, which afflict the human condition and the occurrence of a tragedy, however great, does not compel the conclusion that someone somewhere must be legally answerable. If, however, the plaintiffs can make good their factual allegations against the Department, as one must for present purposes assume in their favour, the law might arguably be thought defective if it did not afford redress.

(2) ...where as here foreseeability by a defendant of severe personal injury to a person such as the plaintiff is shown and the existence of a proximate relationship between plaintiff and defendant is accepted, the plaintiff is well on his way to establishing the existence of a duty of care. He may still fail to do so if it held that imposition of such a duty on the defendant would not in all the circumstances be just and reasonable, but it is by no means clear to me at this preliminary stage that the Department's submissions on that aspect must prevail.

(3) Mr Rupert Jackson QC for the plaintiff's argued that his complaints relate not to any policy decision taken by the Secretary of State but to the Department's failure to implement the policy decision taken, that is, to the implementation not the formulation of policy. I am not persuaded that that contention is wrong, although detailed examination of the facts may well show the line between the two to be blurred.

(4) While the court cannot review the merits of a decision taken by a public authority if it fell within the areas of a discretion conferred by Parliament, it may do so even in a common law action for damages for negligence if satisfied that the decision in question for any of the recognised reasons fell outside the area of such discretion. Whether the plaintiffs can discharge that considerable burden on the facts here I cannot at present determine.

Sir John Megaw agreed.

It could be said that the Court of Appeal is rejecting the too simplistic dichotomy drawn by Stuart-Smith J in *DHSS v Kinnear* (1984) 134 NLJ 886 between the Secretary of State making 'policy' decisions (no liability) and making 'operational' decisions (possible liability). In *Kinnear* Stuart-Smith J held that the decision of the Secretary of State to make the pertussis vaccine available was not amenable to examination in a negligence action despite contradictory views as to its safety. On the other hand, the notice of advice issued by the Secretary of State detailing the circumstances under which the vaccine should be administered could give rise to a cause of action if it was negligently prepared.

Subsequently, the three decisions of the House of Lords in *X (Minors) v Bedfordshire CC* [1995] 3 All ER 353; *Stovin v Wise* [1996] 3 All ER 801 and *Barrett v Enfield LBC* [1999] 3 All ER 193 have explored the potential for private law claims for damages where the defendant is exercising a statutory function, in particular a statutory power. The courts have been concerned about the relationship between the, public law concepts of 'legality', 'fairness' and 'rationality' as bases for challenging the exercise of a statutory *power* and a common law *duty* of care (see P Cane (1996) 112 LQR 13 and J Conbery (1997) 90 MLR 559).

The Court of Appeal had a rare opportunity to consider the issue in the context of the NHS on the following case.

Danns v Dept of Health [1998] PIQR P226 (CA)

Leggatt LJ: The plaintiffs, Roy Allan Danns and his wife Isobel Danns, appeal against the judgment of Wright J given on 18 July 1995 by which he dismissed the plaintiffs' claim and entered judgment for the defendants, the Department of Health.

The claim arises out of an unfortunate sequence of events. The Danns had to children by Mrs Danns' first marriage and two children of their own. By 1981 they had decided that they could manage no more children. That was why, on 12 July 1983, Mr Danns underwent a vasectomy operation. The operation was carried out by a doctor against whom no complain is made. He told both Mr and Mrs Danns that the purpose of the operation, as they well knew, was to render Mr Danns sterile, and that the effect of the operation was irreversible.

The operation was in fact carried out on 11 August 1983. As is customary, sperm samples were taken on two subsequent occasions, both of which were found be negative. A routine letter of 11 December 1983 from the doctor to Mr Danns told him that he could regard himself as sterile and incapable of further parenthood. The result was that neither he nor his wife took any contraceptive precautions. But nevertheless, on 24 March 1991, Mrs Danns gave birth to a son called Jordan, of whom Mr Danns is the father. That had happened because of a process known as late recanalisation of the vas, and the result was that Mr Danns had proved able to pass fertile sperm during intercourse. It is obvious and needs no elaboration what anxiety that caused to the family. In the first instance, no doubt, Mr Danns must have suspected his wife of infidelity, though he has always since stood by her, and now no doubt understands that it was by virtue of rare medical circumstances that he was able, contrary to expectation, to pass fertile sperm to his wife.

The basis of the claim made by the Danns against the Department of Health was a paper published in the British Medical Journal in 1984, referred to as the "Oxford survey", in which the results were given of an analysis of over 14,000 vasectomies. The authors of the paper concluded that after such an operation there remained a 2000 to 1 chance of the vas being joined together months or even years after the operation had been performed, and had been demonstrated, by the giving of samples, to have been initially effective.

The case made by the statement of claim against the Department was that they ought to have known of the risk of pregnancy occurring, notwithstanding the vasectomy in 1984, by virtue of the Oxford paper. Recognising the potentially serious consequences of an unwanted pregnancy, the Department should have by some means communicated the existence of the risk to those such as Mr Danns who could be regarded as at risk of having had a vasectomy that was not wholly effective. It was said that such information could and should have been communicated via the media.

The loss and damage for which the Danns claim was pain and distress, the fact that Mrs Danns had had to give up her job as a machine operator in order to care for Jordan, and the fact that they are put to the expense of bringing up the child.

Included in the defence was reference to two publications. The first, published, in 1979, was the Revised Handbook of Contraceptive Practice in which the Department had said at paragraph, 5.2:

An absolute guarantee that the operation [any sterilisation operation] will be effective can never be given.

That advice was sent to all general practitioners.

The second document referred to was put out by the Family Planning Information Service, which is, indeed, partly funded by the defendants. In a leaflet of July 1980 entitled Male and Female Sterilisation, it was said that it is rare for fertility to return after a sterilisation operation, but occasionally the pathway through the fallopian tubes in the woman or the vas deferens in the man, does reopen and fertility returns. The chance of this happening is approximately 1 in 1,000.

The basis of the plaintiffs' claim originally was a claim that the Department was in breach of statutory duty under section 2 of the Ministry of Health Act 1919, alternatively, in breach of a common law duty of care. In this Court, in circumstances I shall mention, Mr Cartwright, who appears on behalf of the plaintiffs in this Court (as he did in the Court below) has abandoned the claim for breach of statutory duty. In my judgment he was right to do so.

The only section of the Act material for present purposes is section 2. It follows a short title which refers to the exercise of powers by the Ministry of Health which was set up by the Act soon after the first world war. The side-note of section 2 is "General powers and duties of Minister in relation to health". In so far as material it reads as follows:

It shall be the duty of the Minister ... to take all such steps as may be desirable to secure the preparation, effective carrying out and co-ordination of measures conducive to the health of people ... including measures for ... the initiation and direction of research, the collection, preparation, publication, and dissemination of information and statistics relating thereto ...

It is, I believe, common ground that, although the word "duty" is used in course of that section, it in fact represents a duty or power coupled with a discretion. The Judge dismissed the claim on the ground that, by the language of the section, Parliament did not intend to create a private law right of action. He dismissed the claim in negligence because he concluded that, whether to disseminate material of the relevant kind or not was a matter of policy which was exclusively within the discretion of the Department. He also held (although not necessary to his decision) that the plaintiffs had failed to establish a relationship of proximity and that, so far from having fairness, justice and reasonableness on their side, it militated against a claim such as they were making, as public policy would also tend to do. The Judge took the view that the Department had been entitled to leave it to the medical profession how relevant patients should be advised. His conclusion was that the Oxford paper had not resulted in any fundamental change in the thinking of the medical profession, but only a clarification.

The case in this Court has been put before us by Mr Cartwright upon the footing that because, according to him, as many as 50,000 men or more in each year in the early 1980s were receiving a vasectomy and had been doing so for many years before that, there must have been as many as three quarters of a million men who, in the 15 years before 1984, had had such an operation but had received no warning that the effect of the operation might not be final. Allowing for the fact that as many women as men would be affected by the efficacy of the operation, there might have been as many as a million and a half people immediately concerned with the effectiveness of a vasectomy operation.

Mr Cartwright drew our attention to facts which he said, and sought to demonstrate by the evidence, were agreed. First, before 1984 it was generally believed in the medical profession that a failed vasectomy was due to early recanalisation and would be avoided if there was an insistence on use of other contraceptive methods until two negative samples had been provided. That was the general effect of evidence given by witness statements by witnesses for each party. Called on behalf of the plaintiffs was a distinguish Urologist called Mr Owen, and Dr Calman gave evidence for the Department. Another feature of their evidence, as Mr Cartwright submitted, was that after the 1984 paper it was clear that, even after two negative samples, there was a slight chance of returning fertility and patients were warned accordingly. By that is meant that those who became patients after the publication of the 1984 paper were told of the risk to which it drew attention.

It is important then to see how the Judge dealt with that matter. First at page 10B of the transcript of his judgment he said:

… it seems to me that Mr Owen's description of the earlier papers does not really do justice to their contents. The 'One Thousand Vasectomies' paper, which I have already summarised, made it clear that there was experience of re-appearance of motile spermatozoa many months after the operation had taken place; in 1979 Blandy, one of the authors of the earlier paper, wrote in the British Journal of Hospital Medicine that there was not the slightest proof of any statement that if re-union occurred it would be within three months of operation and that this view was that about one per cent of men have spontaneous re-canalisation of the vasa no matter what technique was used to divide them. He added the comment 'no operation can be relied upon to have one hundred per cent certain results'. As I have already observed, the effect of that advice, without any limiting qualifications, appears in the then current edition of the Handbook of Contraceptive Practice.

The Judge added at page 11A of the transcript:

Against this background, although the issue was not before me, and no argument was addressed to me about it, I do not think I would be on safe ground in accepting entirely uncritically the expression of opinion contained in paragraph 9 of Mr Owen's witness statement about the extent to which a general practitioner surgeon, working in 1983, could have been expected to be aware of the possibility of re-canalisation after vasectomy, whenever it happened.

Having made those findings, the Judge towards the end of his judgment, reverted to the topic at page 25C of the transcript saying:

As I have already pointed out, I am satisfied that, by the time that Mr Danns came to undergo his operation in 1983, the medical profession as a whole were perfectly well aware that there was a risk of failure of such an operation and that that risk was not necessarily to be evaluated by reference to any particular period of elapsed time after the operation had been carried out. In my judgment the Department was fully entitled to leave it to the profession to decide what advice or counselling it should give to those coming forward for such an operation. I do not myself accept that the Oxford paper, when it was published in 1984, changed the entire understanding of the profession in relation to the risks of failure of vasectomy as Mr Owen contends. Its importance, in my judgment, lay in the fact that the size of the survey permitted a clearer assessment of the risks of failure to be made.

It seems to me that that was a perfectly fair assessment by the Judge which it was open to him on the evidence to make.

Mr Cartwright has contended that the Department should have faced up to a responsibility of warning patients by taking space in national newspapers. In that way Mr and Mrs Danns would have got to hear of the risk and Mrs Danns could have avoided her unwanted pregnancy by either being sterilised or having her pregnancy terminated at an earlier stage than it was open to her to have done so. The issue in those circumstances, Mr Cartwright submits, is, in essence, whether or not the Department considered the 1984 paper at the time. It is his submission that it escaped the attention of those responsible for dealing with such matters in the Department.

Before the Judge, the case for the Department was that they had considered the matter, albeit informally, and had decided to do nothing. Mr Cartwright accepts that if that was so, as the Judge found, then he would be bound to abandon this appeal because, if a discretion such as is here conferred on the Department is exercised *bona fide*, the exercise of that discretion cannot be challenged. It seems to me that, if the Department failed to exercise its discretion, the appellants would still have to show that, if the Department had exercised its discretion, it would have been bound to decide to disseminate the information, despite the fact that they did not do that when, as the Judge found, they did exercise their discretion. The reasons which they gave for not exercising their discretion are, in my judgment, fatal to the argument that it could only have been exercised in favour of dissemination.

Mr Cartwright submits that the Department should have realised that it was the only organ through which this problem could be addressed. By "problem" he meant, of course, the fact that there were people who had had a vasectomy which they believed to have been totally effective to prevent further fertility, but who might, on the 1,000 or 2,000 to 1 chance of which the publications had spoken, have been in that sense at risk. Mr Cartwright submitted that, if the Department had considered the paper which, according to his submission, they did not, they would have appreciated that there had been a change in clinical practice, that there were a large number of people potentially affected, that it was fair that they should have the benefit of the same warning as was thereafter to be given to those who had the operation, and that many of the problems that beset people in the Danns' position could have been avoided.

He invited our attention to a request that was made by those instructing him for discovery in this matter, which resulted in the assertion by a solicitor who had made appropriate inquiries that the research (referring to the research undertaken by those responsible for the Oxford paper) was not considered at all. How then did the Judge deal with that matter in his judgment? He did so at page 5E of the transcript when he said:

> So far as the Department of Health was concerned, I was told by Dr Kenneth Calman, its current Chief Medical Officer, that his inquiries have revealed that there was no formal consideration of the Oxford survey in the Department in the sense that there were any minuted committee meetings on the subject, nor were any memoranda produced
> …

The Judge went on to refer to the fact that his current deputy, Dr Jeremy Metters, was the coordinator of the revision and update of the Handbook of Contraceptive Practice, which was then in progress, that he was aware of the paper and that there was a team of medical advisers who were also working on the update of the handbook, and the Judge said that they would, in Dr Calman's view, have been aware of the Oxford paper. In particular, the Judge added:

> I accept Dr Calman's evidence about these matters.

He went on to observe that the Department received all issues of the British Medical Journal and the Lancet as they appear, and that about 85 per cent of all registered medical practitioners in the United Kingdom received the British Medical Journal free of charge every week. The Judge concluded (page 6C of the transcript):

> … on the balance of probabilities I am satisfied that all doctors with an interest in reproductive medicine would have become aware, in general terms at least, of the contents of the Oxford survey.

Mr Cartwright invited our attention to considerable passages from the case of *X (minors) v Bedfordshire County Council* [1995] 2 AC 633, and in particular to excerpts from the speech of Lord Browne-Wilkinson. For present purposes it is sufficient to refer to his summary on the subject of statutory discretion at page 738G. I can properly do so without referring to the complicated facts of the conjoined decisions which were the subject of this appeal. His Lordship said (after referring to various authorities):

From these authorities I understand the applicable principles to be as follows. Where Parliament has conferred a statutory discretion on a public authority, it is for that authority, not for the courts, to exercise the discretion: nothing which the authority does within the ambit of the discretion can be actionable at common law. If the decision complained of falls outside the statutory discretion, it *can* (but necessarily will) give rise to common law liability. However, if the factors relevant to the exercise of the discretion include matters of policy, the court cannot adjudicate on such policy matters and therefore cannot reach the conclusion that the decision was outside the ambit of the statutory discretion. Therefore a common law duty of care in relation to the taking of decisions involving policy matters cannot exist.

That is a passage which obviously presents great difficulty for the appellants in this matter. Those difficulties are compounded by the case of *Stovin v Wise* [1996] AC 923 in which the principal speech for the majority was given by Lord Hoffmann who said (at page 953D):

In summary, therefore, I think that the minimum preconditions for basing a duty of care upon the existence of a statutory power, if it can be done at all, are, first, that it would in the circumstances have been irrational not to have exercised the power, so that there was in effect a public law duty to act, and secondly, that there are exceptional grounds for holding that the policy of the statute requires compensation to be paid to persons who suffer loss because the power was not exercised.

It is to be noted that in this context that in course of his cross-examination Mr Owen was asked about a letter from Dr Tacchi who was acting for or advising the Department. That letter (page 119 of the bundle) included a passage which was put specifically to Mr Owen. Counsel said:

'Publications by the Department of Health in the press would in my view only cause distress and distrust amongst the population regarding sterilisation operations which, after all, are in general very effective and well accepted.' That is a perfectly tenable opinion, is it not? It may not be yours but it is a tenable one?

To that Mr Owen replied:

Yes, I would say so.

It seems to me that, whatever explaining Mr Cartwright might attempt of that passage, Mr Owen was indisputably accepting that the point of view expressed in Dr Tacchi's letter which had been put to him was a tenable point of view. From that it follows that it would have been a proper attitude for the Department to have taken so as to found a policy which resulted in the non dissemination of the contents or effect of the Oxford paper.

Mr Cartwright sought to support his submission that the Department was negligent, by looking to the component parts of the tort and contending that there was foreseeability, because it must have been obvious that there could be health consequences from an unexpected pregnancy, as well as proximity on the basis that the reliance of the general public on the Department was also obvious. He sought to reinforce that aspect by inviting attention to the recent case of *Munroe Ltd v London Fire Authority* [1996] 4 All ER 318 in which (at page 329) Rougier J was contrasting the position of the London Fire Authority with a hospital. He said at page 329D:

I consider that against the background of the highly personal element involved in 'adequate medical care', proximity has effectively been imposed upon hospital authorities by the statute. In obedience to that statute, they hold themselves out as being prepared to assume responsibility for the sick and injured. Patients are invited in, whether to the ward or the casualty department, and are entitled to rely upon the hospital assuming responsibility for them.

It seems to me that that kind of proximity is itself to be contrasted in the present context with the position of the Department which is, indisputably, incomparably more remote from the patient than is the casualty department of a hospital.

Mr Cartwright submitted that the overriding public policy consideration is that wrongs should be remedied, and the approach of the Court should be that it takes very potent counter-considerations to override that policy. It seems to me, however, that the policy of the Department was in the circumstances to refrain from causing anxiety on a huge scale to the thousands of people who might have had a vasectomy or who might have been the wife or partner of such a person, merely in the interests of bringing them up to date with the fruits of medical research such as were contained in the Oxford paper.

In my judgment, the Judge was entitled to conclude that consideration, albeit informal, was given to the research paper by the Department. That, Mr Cartwright accepts, is fatal to his appeal. But even if consideration had not been given, still the appellants could not have established that the Department would have been bound to disseminate the results of the latest research. That, as the Judge held, merely permitted a clearer assessment to be made of the risks of failure. There are no grounds for holding that the policy of the Act of 1919 requires compensation to be paid to people like Mr and Mrs Danns who claim to have suffered loss because the power to disseminate information about medical research was not exercised. So far from being irrational not to exercise it in this case, I consider that, upon the evidence, it was sensible in 1984 to refrain from doing so. It follows that I consider that the Judge came to the right conclusion for the right reasons. Nothing since he gave judgment has occurred, save for the reinforcement of it that is now afforded by the cases of *X (Minors) v Bedfordshire County Council* and *Stovin v Wise* to which I have referred. In the light of the Judge's judgment, little that I have said is more than supererogatory.

I would only add this. It is said that Mr and Mrs Danns have had their hopes of obtaining financial support for Jordan raised by advice that they enjoyed some prospects of success on appeal. In face of the Judge's judgment, those prospects were always slight, and they were reduced yet further by the decisions of their Lordships that I have mentioned. But at least they can take consolation from the joy that Jordan must have brought them in the long run.

Roch LJ: There are three reasons why in my opinion the plaintiff's claim against the Ministry was found to fail. First, the Department did not owe the plaintiff a duty at common law to take reasonable care, for the reason that there did not exist as between the plaintiffs and the defendants that degree of the proximity which the law requires. The plaintiffs were not the defendants' neighbours. Although it may be true that the plaintiffs were persons who might foreseeably suffer loss and damage if no warning of the remote possibility of a vasectomy being reversed by natural processes after the two fertility tests have been completed was given, to confine one's attention to that single subject and the Ministry's neighbours to that one class in discharging its functions under section 2 of the Ministry of Health Act 1919, is to ignore the scope and volume of medical research. It further ignores the dissemination of such research to doctors and health authorities by means of the British Medical Journal, the Lancet and Ministry handbooks such as the Handbook of Contraceptive Practice, a copy of which is with our papers.

I agree with the Judge when, at page 24E of his judgment he said:

> Yet further, I would also hold that requirements of fairness, justice and reasonableness do not require the Department to give to the public at large the warnings contended for by the plaintiffs in this action.

The second reason is the Judge's finding at 5E of his judgment that the Ministry did, albeit informally, consider the Oxford survey published in July 1984. That was research of which the appropriate officer of the Department, namely a senior medical officer, would have had notice. If this was so, then the Department did not fail to give consideration to this research. The statute by section 2 requires the Minister, in the exercise or performance of any of his powers and duties, to take all such steps as may be desirable to secure the effective carrying out of measures conducive to the health of the people throughout England and Wales, including measures for the collection, publication and dissemination of information and statistics relating to the prevention and care and cure of diseases, treatment of physical and mental defects, the treatment and care of the blind and the initiation and direction of research. I have paraphrased the wording of the section in a way which I hope is suitable and relevant to this case. There was no evidence that the Department had failed to take such steps as were in their view desirable.

This leads to the third reason why this claim must in my judgment fail. Mr Cartwright accepted that, unless the evidence showed that the giving of the warnings for which he contends was the only way in which the Ministry could reasonably have acted, the chain of causation was broken. In my view, the evidence fell well short of establishing that the publication by the Ministry of such warnings was the only reasonable course for the defendants to pursue.

For those reasons I agree with my Lord that this appeal must fail.

Aldous LJ agreed.

It has long been clear that where the defendant's duty of care is said to arise out of a statutory power a prerequisite to a private law action is that any exercise (or non-exercise) of that power must itself be *ultra vires* (*Home Office v Dorset Yacht Co Ltd* [1970] AC 1004 (HL) and *Anns v Merton LBC* [1978] AC 728 (HL)). The underlying basis is simple: the common law will not allow the recovery of damages for lawful administrative action. It is here that the courts became embroiled in the seemingly helpful, but ultimately, chaotic ordering notions of the 'policy' and 'operational' activities of public bodies (see, *Anns, supra*). The *Bedfordshire* case (and *Rowling v Takaro Properties Ltd* [1988] AC 473 (PC)) showed how this distinction merely masked the real issue: could it be shown that the defendant had acted outside its statutory powers? Further, *Barrett* illustrates that these issues are less relevant where the negligence arises from acts done pursuant to the exercise of the power.

But, in a sense, this only gets the plaintiff to 'first base'. The defendant's action is *ultra vires*, so what? In negligence, the court must still apply the *Caparo* three-stage test. Exercising a power in an *ultra vires* way, *a fortiorii* not exercising it, does not in itself create a 'proximate' relationship or make it 'just, fair and reasonable' to impose a duty of care.

Stovin v Wise and *Barrett* help here. If the claim arises out of the exercise of a statutory power, applying the *ultra vires* doctrine is a prerequisite of liability, but thereafter the ordinary private law concepts of negligence apply (*Stovin, supra*, at 821–822). And, of course, the plaintiff will be faced with all (or none) of the difficulties in establishing 'proximity' etc he would face if the defendant was a private individual or body.

As for the situation where the defendant failed to exercise a statutory power, Lord Hoffmann in *Stovin* left for another day whether it could ever found a negligence action, ie whether anything is left of the *Anns* decision (*supra*, at 828). Assuming it could, Lord Hoffmann made clear that a statutory 'may' can only become a common law 'ought' if two conditions are satisfied (see also *Barrett*). First, there must in effect be a public duty to act. In other words, it must be shown that the defendant's failure to exercise the discretion was irrational. Secondly, there must be exceptional grounds for holding that the policy of the statute requires compensation to be paid. These issues would be reflected in the court's decision on 'proximity' and 'just, fair and reasonableness' (see also *Barrett*). The fact that the defendant has caused injury to the plaintiff by an omission will present difficulties, just as it would against a private defendant.

In *Danns*, the statutory framework imposed a duty upon the defendant but it was a duty coupled with a power as to how to implement it. Hence, the approach in *Stovin v Wise* was applicable. On the facts, the plaintiffs failed to get to 'first base': they could not establish that the Department had gone outside its statutory power. The Court of Appeal held that the judge was correct to conclude that the Department had considered the 'Oxford survey' published in the British Medical Journal in 1984 and its decision not to disseminate the information further was within its statutory discretion under s 2 of the 1919 Act. There is no doubt that this is correct: the evidence showed that the British Medical Journal was received by some 85% of doctors in the UK and there were dangers of causing distress and distrust amongst the public if the Department were to go further and publish the result in the national press. In other words, the Department had not acted illegally (failed to have regard to a relevant matter) nor acted irrationally.

But Leggatt LJ went on to say that even if the Department had not considered whether to disseminate the research, it would have been rational not to distribute it more widely. While this must be so given the Court of Appeal's view about dissemination, this did not mean the Department would have acted *intra vires*. Its failure to consider exercising the discretionary power would itself be unlawful regardless of whether, had it considered it, the Department would or would not then act. It is a fetter of discretion (*British Oxygen Co Ltd v Minister of Technology* [1971] AC 610 (HL)). Of course, in the light of *Stovin v Wise*, this did not help the plaintiffs. Lord Hoffmann, it will be recalled, required that the decision should be *irrational* (ie no reasonable person could have failed to exercise it) and hence create an 'ought' upon which to base the common law *duty*. Additionally, if the Department would not have disseminated the information, their omission to do so (based upon their failure to consider doing so) did not cause the plaintiffs' injury. The plaintiffs would not have satisfied the 'but for' test of factual causation (per Roch LJ).

As if to add insult to injury, the judges went on to consider the plaintiffs action applying the *Caparo* tests. The plaintiffs argued that there was a 'proximate relationship' between the parties because the public placed general reliance upon the Department in performing its statutory functions (on 'general reliance' as an indicator of 'proximity', see *Stovin v Wise, supra,* per Lord Hoffmann at 828–30). There was, of course, no specific or particular reliance – how could there be when the Department had not disseminated the research findings? The court dismissively rejected the plaintiff's argument: the relationship was too 'remote' (per Leggatt LJ) and they were not 'neighbours' (per Roch LJ). The court is surely correct; absent specific reliance by the plaintiffs and knowledge of that by the Department, there was not the necessary 'assumption of responsibility' towards the plaintiffs (see *Henderson v Merrett Syndicates Ltd* [1995] 2 AC 145 (HL) and *Williams v Natural Life Health Foods Ltd* [1998] 2 All ER 577 (HL) per Lord Steyn at 581–584). If it were otherwise, the court would have contradicted its approach to the breach of statutory duty claim that Parliament had not intended to create a cause of action for the benefit of any particular individual.

Roch LJ also agreed with the trial judge that it was not 'fair, just and reasonable' to impose a duty of care. This, it would seem, would be too onerous an obligation for the Department given that the information was already available to doctors in other publications.

Thus, the scope for imposing a duty of care when the Secretary of State (or his delegate) is engaged in the direct exercise of his statutory powers is extremely limited. (The Secretary of State's functions under s 2 of the 1919 Act are now delegated to Health Authorities: see The National Health Service (Functions of Health Authorities and Administrative Arrangements) Regulations 1996 (SI 1996 No 708), reg 3(1) and Sch 1). Likewise, the court has held that a private law action for damages cannot arise out of the 'after care' provision in s 117 of the Mental Health Act 1983. Breach of the statutory duty is remediable only by public law remedies.

Clunis v Camden and Islington HA (1997) 40 BMLR 181 (CA)

From 1987 until 1992 the plaintiff had received psychiatric treatment in several London hospitals. In August 1992 he was detained under s 3 of the Mental Health Act 1983 at Guy's Hospital. The responsible medical officer decided he was fit to be discharged on 24 September 1992. By s 117 of the 1983 Act, the district health authority was under a duty to arrange, in conjunction with the local social services authority, to provide after-care services for the plaintiff, until those authorities were satisfied that he no longer needed the services. The plaintiff having expressed a desire to move to North London and into the defendant health authority's area, a doctor at Guy's contacted the defendant authority and arranged for the plaintiff to be seen at Friern Hospital on 9 October 1992. The plaintiff failed to attend the appointment. Another appointment was made for him to attend on 13 November, but he failed to do so. A further appointment was made, via Haringey social services, for the plaintiff to undergo a mental health assessment visit at his address on 30 November at 3 pm. On that day, the plaintiff left his address, prior to the appointment, and no assessment was made. The plaintiff again failed to attend an appointment on 10 December. On 17 December, the local social services were advised by the police that the plaintiff had been seen 'waving screwdrivers and knives and was talking about devils. The police officer had not exercised his powers of detention under s 136 of the Mental Health Act 1983. Later that same day, the plaintiff killed Jonathan Zito in an unprovoked and sudden attack. On 28 June 1993 the Central Criminal Court accepted the plaintiff's plea of guilty to manslaughter on the grounds of diminished responsibility and ordered his detention under the Mental Health Act 1993, on the grounds that he was suffering from a mental illness, namely schizo-affective disorder. The plaintiff contended that he had suffered injury, loss and damage because the defendant health authority had been negligent and responsible for breaching a duty of care at common law to treat him with reasonable professional care and skill. He claimed that, if he had been assessed prior to 17 December 1992, he would either have been detained or consented to become a patient, and so would not have committed manslaughter and that, as a consequence of the defendant's negligence, he would now be detained for longer than he otherwise would have been. The defendant health authority argued that the claim should be dismissed on two grounds. First, the claim was based on the defendant's own illegal act of manslaughter (ex turpi causa non oritur actio). Secondly, the statutory obligations of the defendant to provide after-care to the plaintiff, following his release from Guy's Hospital, did not give rise to a common law duty of care. ...

Beldam LJ. This is the judgment of the court.

In these proceedings the defendant health authority applies to strike out the claim brought against it by the plaintiff, Christopher Clunis, as disclosing no cause of action. The defendant's application was dismissed by order of Mr R B Mawrey QC, sitting as a deputy judge of the High Court, on 12 December 1996. The defendant now appeals to this court. ...

The next question for the court is the nature and extent of any obligation or duty owed by the defendant health authority to the plaintiff and whether a breach of such duty can give rise to a claim for damages.

The duty to provide after-care which is at the heart of the plaintiff's claim and his submissions arises under s 117 of the Mental Health Act 1983. Section 117 provided:

(1) This section applies to persons who are detained under section 3 above ... and then cease to be detained and leave hospital.

(2) It shall be the duty of the District Health Authority and of the local social services authority to provide, in co-operation with relevant voluntary agencies, after-care services for any person to whom this section applies until such time as the District Health Authority and the local social services authority are satisfied that the person concerned is no longer in need of such services.

(3) In this section "the District Health Authority" means the District Health Authority for the district, and "the local social services authority" means the local social services authority for the area in which the person concerned is resident or to which he is sent on discharge by the hospital in which he was detained.

The Act also provided, by s 124, for the Secretary of State to exercise enforcement powers where an authority is in default:

(1) Where the Secretary of State is of opinion, on complaint or otherwise, that a local social services authority have failed to carry out functions conferred or imposed on the authority by or under this Act or have in carrying out those functions failed to comply with any regulations relating to those functions, he may after such inquiry as he thinks fit make an order declaring the authority to be in default.

(2) Subsections (3) to (5) of section 85 of the National Health Service Act 1977 (which relates to orders declaring, among others, a local social services authority to be in default under that Act) apply in relation to an order under this section as they apply in relation to an order under that section.

Following the analysis of the duties imposed by Parliament on local authorities in *X (minors) v Bedfordshire CC* (1995) 26 BMLR 15, [1995] 2 AC 633, the first question is whether the statutory provisions in this case create duties which give rise to a private law claim for damages if they are not fulfilled or, more particularly, whether a person who has been detained in hospital and who is discharged can claim damages for non-performance of the 'after-care' obligations in s 117(2) of the Act.

Under s 117(2), the authorities named are required to co-operate with voluntary organisations in setting up a system which provides after-care services for patients who have been discharged from hospital after treatment for mental disorder. The services have to be made available to such persons until 'the person concerned is no longer in need of such services'. Undoubtedly, the section is designed to promote the social welfare of a particular class of persons and to ensure that the services required are made available to individual members of the class. However, s 124 provides the Secretary of State with default powers if he is of the opinion, 'on complaint or otherwise', that the functions conferred or imposed under the Act have not been carried out. Thus, the primary method of enforcement of the obligations under s 117 is by complaint to the Secretary of State. No doubt, too, a decision by the district health authority, or the local social services authority, under the section is liable to judicial review at the instance of a patient, see *R v Ealing District Health Authority, ex p F*

(1992) 11 BMLR 59, [1993] 1 WLR 373. The character of the duties created seem to us closely analogous to those described by Lord Browne-Wilkinson in *X (minors) v Bedfordshire CC* (1995) 26 BMLR 15 at 40, [1995] 2 AC 633 at 747 as requiring:

> … exceptionally clear statutory language to show a parliamentary intention that those responsible for carrying out these difficult functions should be liable in damages if, on subsequent investigation with the benefit of hindsight, it was shown that they had reached an erroneous conclusion and therefore failed to discharge their statutory duties.

In our view, the wording of the section is not apposite to create a private law cause of action for failure to carry out the duties under the statute.

Mr Irwin argued that, on discharge from hospital, the patient nevertheless remained a person for whom the district health authority and the local social services authority are responsible, in the sense that they have a duty not only to ensure that the services are available but that the patient receives the benefit of them, and he went on to submit that a duty of care is thereby imposed on the authority which is merely an extension of the care which the plaintiff has been receiving as a patient in hospital. In effect, he submitted, the relationship of doctor and patient which existed between the district health authority and the plaintiff while he was in hospital continued after discharge, so that a common law duty of care was owed by the defendant to continue the plaintiff's treatment. Is it, in the circumstances, just and reasonable to superimpose such a common law duty of care on an authority in relation to the performance of its statutory duties to provide after-care? We do not think so. We find it difficult to suppose that Parliament intended to create such an extensive and wide-ranging liability for breaches of responsibility under s 117 which would, of its nature, apply alike to those engaged as professionals, as well as those in voluntary services, in many disciplines.

After-care services are not defined in the Act. They would normally include social work, support in helping the ex-patient with problems of employment, accommodation or family relationships, the provision of domiciliary services and the use of day centre and residential facilities. No doubt, an assessment of the patient's needs would, in the first instance, be made by the hospital which discharged him. It was for that purpose in this case that the defendant authority sought to arrange appointments with the plaintiff. In that respect, its actions through Dr Sergeant were essentially in the sphere of administrative activities in pursuance of a scheme of social welfare in the community. Bearing in mind the ambit of the obligations under s 117 of the Act and that they affect a wide spectrum of health and social services, including voluntary services, we do not think that Parliament intended so widespread a liability as that asserted by Mr Irwin. The question of whether a common law duty exists in parallel with the authority's statutory obligations is profoundly influenced by the surrounding statutory framework: see per Lord Browne-Wilkinson in *X v Bedfordshire CC* (1995) 26 BMLR 15 at 32, [1995] 2 AC 633 at 739 and per Lord Hoggmann in *Stovin v Wise* [1996] AC 923 at 952–953, [1996] 3 All ER 801 at 828. So, too, in this case, the statutory framework must be a major consideration in deciding whether it is fair and reasonable for the local health authority to be held responsible for errors and omissions of the kind alleged. The duties of care are, it seems to us, different in nature from those owed by a doctor to a patient whom he is treating and for whose lack of care in the course of such treatment the local health authority may be liable.

Nor do we think that Dr Sergeant should be held liable for a failure to arrange for a mental health assessment more speedily. The suggestion that local police had reported that the plaintiff was waving screwdrivers and knives about and talking about devils illustrates to our mind the difficulty of holding her responsible in this case. Under s 136 of the Mental Health Act 1983 a constable finding a person in a public place who appears to be suffering from a mental disorder and to be in immediate need of carer or control may:

> … if he thinks it necessary to do so in the interests of that person or for the protection of other persons, remove that person to a place of safety …

We doubt if even this language, though specifically requiring the constable to act in the interests of a mentally disordered person, creates a duty to take care which gives rise to a claim for damages at the suit of the disordered person.

Moreover, as Lord Browne-Wilkinson pointed out in *X v Bedfordshire CC*, the question whether a doctor owes a duty of care to a patient in certifying that a patient is fit to be detained under the Mental Health Acts was left undecided in *Everett v Griffiths* [1920] 3 KB 163 (*affd* [1921] 1 AC 631) and still remains open for decision in an appropriate case. We have no doubt that it would not be right to hold Dr Sergeant or the defendant health authority liable to the plaintiff in damages for failure to arrange the plaintiff's assessment for the purposes of s 117 more speedily than she did.

For these reasons, we do not think the plaintiff can establish a cause of action arising from a failure by the defendant health authority or Dr Sergeant to carry out their functions under s 117 of the Mental Health Act. Nor do we think that it would be fair or reasonable to hold the defendant responsible for the consequences of the plaintiff's criminal act.

In our view, the defendant's application should have succeeded on both grounds and we would allow the appeal.

The Court of Appeal also held that the plaintiff's action failed because it arose *ex turpi causa* (see *infra*, pp 512-115).

B. Breach of statutory duty. Turning now to breach of statutory duty, the question for consideration is whether the Secretary of State (or his delegate) may be liable in damages for breach of statutory duty. The National Health Service Act 1977, s 3(1) provides:

> 3. (1) It is the Secretary of State's duty to provide throughout England and Wales, to such extent as he considers necessary to meet all reasonable requirements –
> (a) hospital accommodation;
> (b) other accommodation for the purpose of any services provide under this Act;
> (c) medical, dental, nursing and ambulance services;
> (d) such other facilities for the care of expectant and nursing mothers and young children as he considers are appropriate as part of the health service.
> (e) such facilities for the prevention of illness, the care of persons suffering from illness and the after-care of persons who have suffered from illness as he considers are appropriate as part of the health service;
> (f) such other services as are required for the diagnosis and treatment of illness.

(see also ss 1–2 and 4–5 of the 1977 Act.)

In turn, under s 13 of the 1977 Act this duty is delegated to the health authorities created by the legislation: see, The National Health Service (Functions of Health Authorities and Administration Arrangements) Regulations 1996 (SI 1996 No 708 as amended), reg 3 and Sch 1. These functions may be discharged through arrangements with NHS Trusts and other bodies (reg 3(3)). Paragraph 15(1) of Schedule 5 to the Act makes it quite clear that for failure to perform the duty under s 3 it is the delegate and not the Secretary of State who must be sued.

> 15. (1) An authority shall, notwithstanding that it is exercising any function on behalf of the Secretary of State or another authority, be entitled to enforce any rights acquired in the exercise of that function, and be liable in respect of any liabilities incurred (including liabilities in tort) in the exercise of that function, in all respects as if it were acting as a principal.
> Proceedings for the enforcement of such rights and liabilities shall be brought, and brought only, by or, as the case may be, against the authority in question in its own name.

Likewise, in relation to claims based upon the negligent provision of a service, it is the provider, ie Trust, which must be sued: see, National Health Service and Community Care Act 1990, s 8 (NHS Trusts) and National Health Service Act 1977, Sch 5A, para 13 (inserted by the Health Act 1999) (Primary Care Trusts).

Some judges have suggested that an action for breach of statutory duty would lie (*Yepremian v Scarborough General Hospital* (1980) 110 DLR (3d) 513 at 564 per Blair JA; Nathan *Medical Negligence* (1957) p 144 et seq). The issue arose directly, as we have seen, in the *HIV Litigation* case (*supra*).

Re HIV Haemophiliac Litigation (1990) 41 BMLR 171 (CA)

Ralph Gibson LJ: The plaintiffs rely upon section 1 and section 3(1) of the National Health Service Act 1977. ...

[B]y section 13, the Secretary of State may direct certain Health Authorities to exercise on his behalf such of his functions relating to the Health Service as are specified in the direction and (subject to section 14) it then becomes the duty of the body in question to comply with the directions.

The Minister has by statutory instrument delegated many of his functions including that under section 3(1)(e) of the 1977 Act with respect to the provision of facilities for the prevention of illness, the care of persons suffering from illness and the after care of persons who have suffered from illness. It is common ground that the definition of illness under the Act of 1977 includes the condition haemophilia. The Minister has also delegated his function under section 5(2)(d) of the 1977 Act. ...

In *Cutler v Wandsworth Stadium Ltd* [1949] AC 398, Lord Simonds, on the question whether a statute is to be held to provide a cause of action for a breach of duty imposed by it, said at page 407:

> I do not propose to try to formulate any rules by reference to which such a question can infallibly be answered. The only rule which in all circumstances is valid is that the answer must depend on a consideration of the whole Act and the circumstances, including pre-existing law, in which it was enacted. But that there are indications which point with more or less force to the one answer or the other is clear from authorities which ... will have great weight with the House. For instance, if a statutory duty is prescribed but no remedy by way of penalty or otherwise for its breach is imposed, it can be assumed that a right of civil action accrues to the person who is demnified by the breach. For, if it were not so, the statute would be but a pious aspiration.

Under the 1977 Act no remedy by way of penalty or otherwise is prescribed for breach of the duties imposed upon the Secretary of State. Neither side has placed reliance on any aspect of the previously existing law or upon the terms of the statutes which preceded the 1977 Act.

Mr Jackson submitted that because the 1977 Act imposes a duty but provides no remedy for its breach, there is a presumption that Parliament intended that there be such a remedy, and he submitted that no reason is to be found in the provisions of the statute as a whole to justify a different conclusion. He acknowledged that the duties imposed upon the Secretary of State by the Act are of a general nature, and involve the exercise by him of discretion, but Mr Jackson contended that that was no sufficient reason to deny a cause of action for breach of them. Claims for such breach would be rare both because of the difficulty of proving breach of such duties and because the Secretary of State has delegated the performance of most of his functions to Health Authorities. Further, Mr Jackson submitted that paragraph 15 of Schedule 5 supported his argument. That paragraph provides that, upon delegation of a particular function to a Health Authority, it is the Health Authority and not the Secretary of State who is to be used. The proper inference is, it was said, that, with reference to a particular function which has not been delegated, if it is performed negligently, or if it is negligently not performed, the proper defendant is the Department of Health.

Mr Jackson relied upon the decision of Forbes J in *Booth and Co v NEB* [1978] 3 All ER 624 upon the provisions of the Industry Act 1975. A claim for breach of duty imposed by that Act, passed for the benefit of the United Kingdom economy, was held to be arguably good in law. The 1977 Act was passed to protect and to promote the health of the individual citizens of this country and breach of the duties imposed by it should be held to be actionable.

Mr Jackson acknowledged that no duty is imposed by the Act in absolute terms such as are found in statutes such as the Factories Act or in the Road Traffic Acts with reference to insurance. He further acknowledged that, if a claim for negligence is held to be available against the Central Defendants for breach of the common law duty of care in the performance of the functions performed by them under the 1977 Act, it is not possible to think of a claim which could succeed for breach of statutory duty which would fail if put forward as negligence. That concession was, as I understood the argument, not intended to be made if the court should hold the cause of action to be limited as Rougier J held it to be. Mr Jackson argued, however, that the existence of a cause of action in negligence was irrelevant to the process of the court's determination of the intention of Parliament by construction of the statute as a whole.

In answer to these submissions, Mr Collins relied upon the reasons for his decision given by Rougier J. He also relied upon the unreported decision of Wien J in January 1979 in *R v Secretary of State for Social Services and West Midlands R H A, ex p Hincks*, in which at page 29 of the transcript he held that the 1977 Act does not give rise to a right to damages for a breach. The applicants appealed to the Court of Appeal on 18th March 1980 where the decisions and reasons of Wien J were approved. The question of a right of action for damages for breach of statutory duty was not considered in the Court of Appeal. As Mr Jackson submitted the decision of the question by Wien J was obiter.

For my part, I share the judge's view of the apparent nature of the duties imposed by the 1977 Act. They do not clearly demonstrate the intention of Parliament to impose a duty which is to be enforced by individual civil action.

Bingham LJ and Sir John Megaw agreed.

In *Danns v Department of Health* [1998] PIQR P226, the plaintiffs also brought an action for breach of statutory duty against the Secretary of State in respect of his duty under s 2 of the Ministry of Health Act 1919. The claim was unsuccessful (see Commentary (1996) 4 Med L Rev 324 (IK)). At first instance, Wright J rejected this and in the Court of Appeal, the plaintiffs abandoned this part of their action and, in the words of Leggart LJ, they were 'right to do so'. Such an action is in reality simply unarguable. The courts will not interpret Parliament's intention when enacting regulatory frameworks in the social welfare context, of which the NHS is one, as one to create private rights of action for individuals. The general duties – sometimes specific, often coupled with a broad discretion – exist for the benefit of the public at large and operate only in the public law sphere. In the *Bedfordshire* case, Lord Browne-Wilkinson hammered the point home (*supra*, at 364):

> [Y]our Lordships were not referred to any case where it had been held that statutory provisions
> establishing a regulatory system or scheme of social welfare for the benefit of the public at
> large had been held to give rise to a private right of action for damages for breach of statutory
> duty. Although regulatory or welfare legislation affecting a particular area of activity does in
> fact provide protection to those individuals particularly affected by the activity, the legislation
> is not to be treated as being passed for the benefit of those individuals but for the benefit of
> society in general.

In the light of the views expressed by the court in the *HIV Haemophiliac Litigation* case and *Danns* (*supra*), the better view is that the 1977 Act only imposes a duty amenable to control in *public law* through the judicial review procedure under RSC Ord 53.

III. Questions of resource allocation

As is plain from the *HIV Haemophiliac Litigation* case, many decisions involving the provision of health care turn upon the proper allocation of resources. This is so whether the Secretary of State has reserved the responsibility to himself (which is rare in practice) or has delegated his responsibility to the relevant Health Authority and in turn the service is provided by an NHS Trust or Primary Care Trust. The crucial question here is what weight, if any, should the law give to the argument, whether advanced by central Government or by the provider, that the service provided was all that could be done given the available resources? (For further discussion see, I Kennedy and A Grubb (eds) *Principles of Medical Law* (1998), paras 8.54–8.72).

The question of the availability or otherwise of sufficient resources is a troubling one for courts (see the remarks of Lord Donaldson MR in *Re J (a minor) (wardship: medical treatment)* [1992] 4 All ER 614 at 623–634; *R v Cambridge HA, ex p B* [1995] 2 All ER 129 (CA) at 137 per Sir Thomas Bingham MR). While their obligation is to determine the legal standard which defendants must meet, they cannot close their eyes to the fact that these standards must be set in a real world where resources are finite and where there is never enough to go around.

In *R v Cambridge HA, ex p B* [1995] 2 All ER 129 Sir Thomas Bingham MR stated (at 137):

> I have no doubt that in a perfect world any treatment which a patient, or a patient's family,
> sought would be provided if doctors were willing to give it, no matter how much it cost,
> particularly when a life was potentially at stake. It would however, in my view, be shutting
> one's eyes to the real world if the court were to proceed on the basis that we do live in such
> a world. It is common knowledge that health authorities of all kinds are constantly pressed to
> make ends meet. They cannot pay their nurses as much as they would like; they cannot
> provide all the treatments they would like; they cannot purchase all the extremely expensive
> medical equipment they would like; they cannot carry out all the research they would like;
> they cannot build all the hospitals and specialist units they would like. Difficult and agonising
> judgments have to be made as to how a limited budget is best allocated to the maximum
> advantage of the maximum number of patients. That is not a judgment which the court can
> make. In my judgment, it is not something that a health authority such as this authority can
> be fairly criticised for not advancing before the court. ...

If the courts allow themselves to be drawn too far into such questions they will enter territory which traditionally they have regarded the exclusive preserve of Government. If, on the other hand, the courts wash their hands of the question they could face the charge that they were denying compensation to patients and drawing back from their duty to hold the Government accountable when asked to do so.

A. A proposed analysis.   Faced with this dilemma, how should the law respond so that that which is properly for the courts (English-style) is done by the courts, and that which is for Government is left to the Government? The law may develop as follows. It is useful to consider the law and the cases under the headings: (i) inadequate provision of services; (ii) non-provision of services; and (iii) curtailed provision of services.

Inadequate provision – The court could ask whether the complaint before it arises out of inadequacies in the delivery of a system of care which has been created by the provider (NHS Trust or Primary Care Trust), for example, a maternity service with insufficient staff and equipment to meet a level of care which is clearly called for. If, indeed, the complaint does take this form then the court can take refuge in the traditional approach of negligence and avoid the charge of trespassing on foreign territory. The court can ask by reference to expert evidence what can reasonably be expected of a service of the type purportedly created by the provider. This would set the *benchmark* against which to judge the level of service actually provided (of course, setting the benchmark is itself no easy matter). If the level of care did not reach the benchmark, *prima facie* there would be a breach of duty. Then, but not until then, would the question of resources fall for consideration. The provider would then argue that, admittedly, the level of service fell below the legal standard, but the court should modify the legal standard to reflect the available resources in the light of the fact that the provider had done all that it could.

If the court accepts this argument then it is, in effect, agreeing to endorse the decision of the provider. Some would say that this is the only proper course for a court since it cannot consider all the matters which go to balance the books of a provider. However, the better view may be that the courts will say that if an institution offers a service it must reach the 'benchmark' or not provide it at all. If the provider fails in this the court will make it pay for its failings (thereby, of course, further reducing the available resources). While setting the 'benchmark' will often be difficult, the proliferation of protocols and guidelines setting 'clinical standards' may ease a claimant's burden. The work of the National Institute of Clinical Excellence (NICE) under the Health Act 1999 will only further this potential. Likewise, the setting of national policy *may* lead to recognisable basic standards (eg the Citizen's Charter): see *R v North Derbyshire HA, ex p Fisher* [1997] 8 Med LR 327 (Dyson J).

Non-provision – Next, the court may not be faced with a complaint about an existing system but with the *absence of any provision* of service in circumstances where it is said the service should be provided. For example, a Health Authority may choose not to make available kidney-dialysis whereby a patient with renal failure is harmed. This is most likely to be an allegation levied at the health authority or other body responsible for ensuring that the services are provided rather than the Trust who would provide it. In a claim based in negligence the court would have to ask whether the Health Authority had breached its duty to this particular patient by deciding not to provide the service. The court might well distinguish this situation from that of inadequate provision. Here, the choice will be one perhaps exclusively within the legitimate domain of the Health Authority,

It is quite essentially a policy choice and non-justiciable by the courts – at least as its substance. Traditional reasoning in negligence would require the court to ask what a reasonable Health Authority would do in these circumstances. It is difficult to for a court to establish a standard. A court may even be tempted to deny the existence of a duty of care in this situation (see *supra*). In any event, the issues involved in any such decision are so obviously matters of policy and judgment. Thus, a court would almost certainly refuse to contemplate it was a breach of duty on the grounds that the patient's claim was non-justiciable, ie not for *them*.

Curtailed provision – Finally, the complaint before the court may be that a service previously involving a particular amount of resources is now being offered in a curtailed form with a reduced amount of resources. The claim in negligence would be that a patient was harmed not by reason of inadequate provision of care actually delivered, but rather by the absence of that particular care in his case. For example, a Trust may decide to close emergency services for one weekend in four. In such a case, the court may avoid being drawn into the policy of resource allocation by adopting the traditional legal approach of asking the question 'What did the Trust undertake to provide?' and 'Did it do so?' If the Trust undertook only to provide a curtailed service, it would follow that a claim in negligence based upon the lack of provision of that care which would have been available had the service not been curtailed, would fail.

B. The case law. Do the English cases bear out this analysis?

Inadequate provision – A number of cases touch on what we have called the inadequate provision of services where the provider fails to reach the 'benchmark'. The first is inconclusive. In *Wilsher v Essex AHA* [1986] 3 All ER 801, the Vice-Chancellor, Sir Nicolas Browne-Wilkinson, at least raised the question of the extent to which a court should take account of resource allocation. Not surprisingly given the novelty of the argument, he chose to take refuge in the judicial incantation that '[t]hese are questions for Parliament ...' (at 834).

> **Browne-Wilkinson V-C:** Claims against a health authority that it has itself been directly negligent, as opposed to vicariously liable for the negligence of its doctors, will, of course, raise awkward questions. To what extent should the authority be held liable if (eg in the use of junior housemen) it is only adopting a practice hallowed by tradition? Should the authority be liable if it demonstrates that, due to the financial stringency under which it operates, it cannot afford to fill the posts with those possessing the necessary experience? But, in my judgment, the law should not be distorted by making findings of personal fault against individual doctors who are, in truth, not at fault in order to avoid such questions. To do so would be to cloud the real issues which arise. In the modern world with its technological refinements, is it sensible to persist in making compensation for those who suffer from shortcomings in technologically advanced treatment depend on proof of fault, a process which the present case illustrates can consume years in time and huge sums of money in costs? Given limited resources, what balance is to be struck in the allocation of such resources between compensating those whose treatment is not wholly successful and the provision of required treatment for the world at large? These are questions for Parliament, not the courts. But I do not think the courts will do society a favour by distorting the existing law so as to conceal the real social questions which arise.

In *Bull v Devon AHA* [1993] 4 Med LR 117 (CA) (the facts of which we saw above) Mustill LJ was less inclined to judicial abstention. Mustill LJ referred to the hospital's expert evidence that the system operated by the defendant hospital was 'par for the course'.

> **Mustill LJ:** ... it seems to have been assumed by the experts that if this was so, the patient would have nothing to complain about.
> Whatever the apparent appeal of this opinion to practical commonsense, I find its implications to be rather disturbing. Is there not a contradiction in asserting at the same time that the system put the foetus at risk and that it was good enough? ...

The second suggested answer was on these lines: that hospitals such as the Devon and Exeter were in the dilemma of having to supply a maternity service, and yet not disposing of sufficient manpower to provide immediate cover, the more so since the small number of consultants and registrars had to deal with three different sites. They could not be expected to do more than their best, allocating their limited resources as favourably as possible.

Again, I have some reservations about this contention, which are not allayed by the submission that hospital medicine is a public service. So it is, but there are other public services in respect of which it is not necessarily an answer to allegations of unsafety that there were insufficient resources to enable the administrators to do everything which they would like to do. I do not for a moment suggest that public medicine is precisely analogous to other public services, but there is perhaps a danger in assuming that it is completely sui generis, and that it is necessarily a complete answer to say that even if the system in any hospital was unsatisfactory, it was no more unsatisfactory than those in force elsewhere.

It is however unnecessary to go further into these matters, which raise important issues of social policy, which the courts may one day have to address.

I mention the problem only because it underlies the apparent contradiction in the expert evidence, which caused me difficulty in finding the right starting point for a decision on this particular allegation of negligence.

Having considered the observation of Browne-Wilkinson V-C and Mustill LJ, Pill J in *Knight v Home Office* [1990] 3 All ER 237 addressed the same question.

Knight v Home Office [1990] 3 All ER 237, (1989) 4 BMLR 85 (QBD)

The widow of a suicidal prisoner, detained in Brixton Prison hospital wing, alleged that the Home Office was in breach of duty in failing to provide adequate supervision which would probably have prevented him from killing himself. Inter alia she sought to rely on the level of care which would be provided in a specialist psychiatric institution ie that set the benchmark. Pill J disagreed and held that the benchmark was not the optimum level of care provided in a leading specialist hospital and that there had been adequate care on the facts of the case. But he went on to remark as follows.

Pill J: Counsel for the plaintiffs submits that it is not a defence to establish that the standard of care was as good as that in other prisons or that it accorded with government circulars or standing orders in force at the time. While general practice in the prison service is a factor to be taken into account, I accept that the plaintiffs could succeed even if the current practice approved in the prison service had been followed in every respect. As Asquith LJ put it in *Daborn v Bath Tramways Motor Co Ltd* [1946] 2 All ER 333 at 336:

In determining whether a party is negligent, the standard of reasonable care is that which is reasonably to be demanded in the circumstances.

It is for the court to consider what standard of care is appropriate to the particular relationship and in the particular situation. It is not a complete defence for a government department any more than it would be for a private individual or organisation to say that no funds are available for additional safety measures.

I cannot accept what was at one time submitted by counsel for the defendants that the plaintiffs' only remedy would be a political one. To take an extreme example, if the evidence was that no funds were available to provide any medical facilities in a large prison there would be a failure to achieve the standard of care appropriate for prisoners. In a different context, lack of funds would not excuse a public body which operated its vehicles on the public roads without any system of maintenance for the vehicle if an accident occurred because of lack of maintenance. The law would require a higher standard of care towards other road users.

Here, Pill J seems to contemplate a breach of duty not only in the case of a 'below par' service but also where none was provided at all.

By contrast in *Kent v Griffiths* (1998) 47 BMLR 125 (CA), the court was concerned with whether a duty of care was owed by an ambulance service who had received a '999' call (on which see, *supra*, p 283). Accepting there was, Kennedy LJ (in the interlocutory appeal) noted, in a passing comment, that account would have to be taken of the service's 'cash limits' and the 'competing claims on limited resources' when the action proceeded to trial (see also Lord Woolf MR in the second appeal, *supra*, pp 283-289). One may ask the question, 'why'? Particularly when 'benchmarks' exist in this context for 'response times' which are supposed to set the standard for the service regardless of resources.

Non-provision – As for the '*non-provision*' situation, the leading case is the following.

R v Secretary of State for Social Services, ex parte Hincks (1980) 1 BMLR 93 (CA)

Lord Denning MR: Four people living in Staffordshire have come to the court, urging that the health services are insufficient in their area. They desire a declaration of the court saying that the Secretary of State has not fulfilled his duty to provide a comprehensive health service. They are two elderly ladies, an elderly man, and a girl. They have been on a waiting list for surgery in the orthopaedic line for some years. Their complaint is supported by distinguished consultants and surgeons in that area, particularly by Mr John Cozens-Hardy, a Fellow of the Royal College of Surgeons, who was one of the first consultants to the Good Hope Hospital in Sutton Coldfield in Birmingham. As long ago as 1965, his duties were to organise a comprehensive orthopaedic and accident service for the area.

The area is an expanding area, with a large population. The position was that in 1971 plans were made for a section of the Good Hope Hospital to be expanded. Wards were to be opened in replacement of some old huts. That was to be done reasonably quickly. On 25 February 1971 the Department of Health and Social Security approved the reasonable hospital plan in the sum of nearly £2m for what was called 'Phase 3 of the Good Hope Hospital'. Although that plan was approved at that time, a question arose as to it being implemented because costs increased. So much so that by 1973 the estimated cost was just over £3m – but the lowest tender received was £4m. Then, in 1975, the estimated cost was nearly £4 million – but the lowest tender was nearly £7m. So, although the project had been approved for the extensions of the Good Hope Hospital (Phase 3), it could not be done within the cost which had been provided for in the estimate. The tenders were far too high.

This was very distressing for all those concerned with the hospital, as well as the consultants and the patients. Mr Cozens-Hardy speaks of the frustration and the upset which was caused to the medical staff because of these delays and the improbability of the plan going forward.

The matter was put before the Department of Health and Social Security in 1975: and a question was raised in Parliament. On 28 February 1975 the minister, Dr David Owen, wrote to the member of Parliament for the area. After explaining the necessity to cut expenditure, he said:

> It does, however, mean that only those hospitals with the very highest degree of priority will be able to start, and that many desirable hospital building schemes in the country as a whole will have to be postponed. The Good Hope scheme is one of the schemes which will now have to be postponed … I am sorry I cannot give you a more encouraging reply, but in the light of the very difficult economic circumstances we face plans are having to be revised all over the country and many painful decisions are having to be taken.

Then in February 1978 a letter was written to another member of Parliament by Mr Roland Moyle in which he said:

> … it is unfortunately true that there is a national problem of unsatisfactorily long waiting lists for traumatic and orthopaedic surgery because in an increasingly ageing population there are more patients with fractured necks and heads of femur and degenerative joint disease, which can nowadays in many cases best be treated by joint replacements.

As we all know, underlying that statement is the fact that modern surgery is such that many arthritic, rheumatic and other illnesses from which old people suffer can be treated, with very much improved methods. But that means, of course, that hospitals, operating theatres, and the surgeons who treat these people have to be paid for. At the end of the letter, Mr Moyle said:

> Whilst not denying the need for improving and extending facilities in Birmingham the (Regional Health Authority) have had to consider the needs of the other ten areas in the region. Their assessment, in the light of the resources likely to be available for capital developments, is that the Good Hope scheme does not command sufficient regional priority to start within the next ten years.

So in 1978 the scheme was put off for ten years and virtually abandoned – the scheme which had received approval as far back as 1971.

One can imagine, and sympathise with, the feelings of all those concerned in the health service in that area and with the frustration they feel. So, in the last resort, they brought an action to the courts. We are told that these patients received legal aid to bring the proceedings against the department to see if it was really its duty, and to see whether there could be some recourse to the courts.

Mr Blom-Cooper has urged before us all that can be said. He has referred us to the fact that there are no provisions in the statute which limit the expenditure of the Department. Section 3(1) of the National Health Service Act 1977 provides:

It is the Secretary of State's duty to provide throughout England and Wales to such extent as he considers necessary to meet all reasonable requirements – (a) hospital accommodation ... (c) medical, dental, nursing and ambulance services ... (f) such other services as are required for the diagnosis and treatment of illness.

So that is his duty. It is a short point, and an important point that Mr Blom-Cooper raises. He says that that duty must be fulfilled. If the Secretary of State needs money to do it, then he must see that Parliament gives it to him. Alternatively if Parliament does not give it to him, then a provision should be put in the statute to excuse him from his duty. Mr Blom-Cooper says that that duty is plain and imperative, and it ought to be fulfilled by the Secretary of State.

That is an attractive argument, because there is no express limitation on the duty of the Secretary of State in the statute. But, in the course of the argument, many illustrations have been taken showing how necessary it is for a Secretary of State to have regard to forward planning (as it is called), to estimate changes in the population, for instance – or maybe the ageing population. He has to estimate for the future. For instance, when in 1971 the Good Hope Hospital scheme was approved, it was necessarily contemplated that it would be possible within the resources available. Indeed, as the discussion proceeded, it seemed to me inevitable that this provision had to be implied into s 3, 'to such extent as he considers necessary to meet all reasonable requirements such as can be provided within the resources available'. That seems to me to be a very necessary implication to put on that section, in accordance with the general legislative purpose. It cannot be supposed that the Secretary of State has to provide all the latest equipment. As Oliver LJ said in the course of argument, it cannot be supposed that the Secretary of State has to provide all the kidney machines which are asked for, or for all the new developments such as heart transplants in every case where people would benefit from them. It cannot be that the Secretary of State has a duty to provide everything that is asked for in the changed circumstances which have come about. That includes the numerous pills that people take nowadays: it cannot be said that he has to provide all these free for everybody.

I would like to read a few words from the judgment of Wien J, who gave a very comprehensive and good judgment in this matter. He said:

The question remains: has there been a breach of duty? Counsel for the [Secretary of State] submits that s 3 does not impose an absolute duty. I agree. He further submits it does by virtue of the discretion given, include an evaluation of financial resources or the lack of them is at the root of the whole problem in this case. If funds were unlimited, then of course regions and areas could go ahead and provide all sorts of services. But funds are not unlimited. The funds are voted by Parliament, and the health service has to do the best it can with the total allocation of financial resources.

I agree with that approach of the judge in this case. But there is a further aspect which he dealt with. He said, instead of looking at the health service as a whole, could you pinpoint a particular hospital or a particular area like the Good Hope Hospital in Birmingham, and say, 'That does require an extension, and it is a breach of duty for the Secretary of State not to provide for that hospital and that area'? It seems to me – as, indeed, Mr Roland Moyle said in the course of his letter – that you cannot pinpoint any particular hospital or any particular area. The Secretary of State has to do his best having regard to his wide responsibilities. For instance, there are 12 hospitals in this particular area. The service has to be provided over the whole country. Upon that point, the judge said:

I have come to the conclusion that it is impossible to pinpoint any breach of statutory duty on the part of the Secretary of State. If he is entitled to take into account financial resources, as in my judgment he is, then it follows that every thing that can be done within the limit of the financial resources available has been done in the region and in the area. I doubt very much whether under s 3(1) it is permissible to put the spotlight, as it were, upon one particular department of one particular hospital and to say that conditions there are unsatisfactory.

It seems to me that those two paragraphs in the judge's judgment express the position very accurately. It is an interesting point, and it is important from the public point of view because of the grievances which many people feel nowadays about the long waiting list to get into hospital. So be it. The Secretary of State says that he is doing the best he can with the financial resources available to him: and I do not think that he can be faulted in the matter.

I think that the judge was quite right, and I would dismiss the appeal.

Bridge LJ: I agree. The evidence in this case puts a spotlight on the particular difficulties arising from the lack of resources at the Good Hope Hospital in Sutton Coldfield in particular, and more generally in the area of the Birmingham Area Health Authority's districts. But the situations here revealed are not unique. As the evidence shows and as we all know as a matter of common knowledge, the health service currently falls far short of what everyone would regard as the optimum desirable standard. That is very largely a situation which is brought about by lack of resources, lack of suitable equipment, lack of suitably qualified personnel, and above all lack of adequate finance.

The point on which this appeal turns is in the end a very short one which is whether, in performing his duty of considering to what extent it is necessary to meet reasonable requirements by the provisions of accommodation, facilities and services under s 3 of the National Health Service Act 1977, the Secretary of State can in regard to forward planning for the National Health Service, have regard to government economic policy. Mr Blom-Cooper accepts that in relation to current expenditure the Secretary of State can and must have regard to the amount which for any particular year has already been voted by Parliament for the financing of the National Health Service. He accepts that in relation to major projects involving large capital expenditure the Secretary of State and the staff of his department and the regional area health authorities exercising delegated powers and duties under the Secretary of State must all plan forward certainly very much further than one year ahead; but he says nevertheless that, in regard to that forward planning, no regard can be had whatsoever to what government policy may indicate as the likely prospect of future economic stringency limiting the amount of money which is going to be available to the service.

If he is right, then the rather startling conclusion clearly emerges that for the last ten years each successive holder of the office of Secretary of State for Social Services has been in flagrant breach of his duty under the statute and that has gone rather surprisingly unnoticed by Parliament. But, in my judgment, he is not right; and the dilemma in which he finds himself is this. He must either say that, in relation to future planning, the Secretary of State should assume that there will be unlimited resources available for the National Health Service – and, not unnaturally, Mr Blom-Cooper resiles from that extreme and manifestly untenable position – or, alternatively, he must say, as he does say, that the Secretary of State must plan to provide a service within the ambit of some limitation upon the resources which are going to be available to finance the service to be provided.

If there is to be some limitation, I ask myself the question: How is the nature and extent of that limitation to be determined? And the only sensible answer that I find it possible to give to that question is that the limitation must be determined in the light of current government economic policy. I think that is quite clearly an implication which must read into s 3(1) of the National Health Service Act 1977 if it is to be operated realistically. I feel extremely sorry for the particular applicants in this case who have to wait a long time, not being emergency cases, for necessary surgery. They share that misfortune with thousands up and down the country. I only hope that they have not been encouraged to think that these proceedings offered any real prospects that this court could enhance the standards of the National Health Service, because any such encouragement would be based upon manifest illusion.

I too would dismiss this appeal.

Oliver LJ agreed.

The facts of this case demonstrate clearly that when the courts can only avoid being drawn into policy questions in the distribution of resources within the health service by declaring the issue 'non-justiciable', they will have no hesitation in so deciding. (See also, *R v Cambridge HA, ex p B* [1995] 2 All ER 129 (CA) and *R v North Derbyshire HA, ex p Fisher* [1997] 8 Med LR 327 (Dyson J), discussed *supra*, ch 1.)

Curtailed provision – As for the *'curtailed provision'* situation, this has been considered in two cases concerned with cut-backs by a Health Authority in the provision of neonatal intensive care.

R v Central Birmingham HA, ex parte Walker (1987) 3 BMLR 32
(MacPherson J and CA)

MacPherson J: In this case Mr De Mello applies for leave to apply for judicial review of a decision of the Central Birmingham Health Authority, communicated on or about 20 October 1987, that the health authority were satisfied that a baby required an operation but that they were unable to conduct it at this time.

The relief sought is the quashing of that decision and an order that the authority carry out the operation and – I quote from the notice of application – 'provide proper care'. Furthermore, a declaration is sought that the decision not to conduct the operation was unlawful.

The facts of this matter are short and are set out in the affidavit of Mrs Diane Walker. Her baby was born on 9 October 1987. His name is David Barber Walker. He was premature, and he has been cared for in hospital since birth. He is under the care of two consultants. He is not in intensive care, nor is he in an incubator, but he is permanently monitored by hospital equipment and staff in a general ward. He has been treated obviously and, as Mrs Walker unreservedly accepts, with all possible skill. Unfortunately he needs an operation to repair his heart, which has been found to require surgery in order to repair a hole. That is a shorthand, layman's description of the procedure necessary, but I believe that it is all that need be said by way of description of what is required.

On a number of occasions the operation which will have to be performed on this baby has been arranged, or at least forecast to be about to take place, and so far the procedures have been cancelled.

I read now from the affidavit. Paragraph 10 reads:

Apparently the problem is a shortage of specially trained nurses for the intensive care unit that my baby would have to go in after the operation. There are six beds in this unit but currently four trained nurses. There has to be a trained nurse for each bed in use. The four beds are occupied by other babies and, in the period that my baby has been at the hospital, whenever a bed has come free, which has been rare, Mr Giovanni and Mr Sethi have told me that, unfortunately, more urgent cases then [*sic*] my baby's have had to be admitted to the free beds.

Paragraph 11 reads:

Mr Giovanni and Mr Sethi tell me that they are more than willing to carry out my baby's operation but simply cannot do so without the essential after-care available. They have of course said that if my baby's case becomes an 'emergency' then they will have to operate in any event, but there may be no aftercare.

I leave out Mrs Walker's belief as to the question of whether there is at present an emergency and pass to para 12:

I should say at this point that I have absolutely no complaint against Mr Giovanni and Mr Sethi or the other doctors and nurses who are looking after my baby. They have all been wonderful to me and my relatives, and of course my baby. Many have told me privately that they are just as distressed as I am by the whole situation.

Later the affidavit contains this, at para 15:

I ask this Honourable Court to order that the operation take place at once.

The position, then, is that at present the operation has not been done because of a shortage of specially trained nurses and accompanying facilities which do not allow the expansion of the intensive care unit, and this baby's operation has had to be postponed in order that more immediately urgent procedures should be carried out on other babies.

It must be firmly stressed that at present the evidence establishes that there is no danger to the baby. He is being treated and cared for with the fullest possible attention. To move him to another hospital could be risky but to wait will not be – unless of course an emergency develops, in which case, as the doctors have told the applicant, the operation will be done.

I say again that the reason for the postponement is because other more urgent cases have had to be dealt with, and there is a shortage of the human and perhaps also the physical facilities necessary to add this baby at once to the operating list. It need hardly be said that everybody sympathises with all those involved, both mother, baby, doctors and staff. But I have to consider whether this court could conceivably give the relief which is asked, which is in terms to order that the operation be carried out, and to say that the decision to postpone has been reached unlawfully and unreasonably to a point of irrationality.

I say at once that I find it quite impossible to say that there is in the decision made by the health authority, or by the surgeons who act on their behalf, any illegality, nor any procedural defect, nor any such unreasonableness. The fact that the decision is unfortunate, disturbing and in human terms distressing, simply cannot lead to a conclusion that the court should interfere in a case of this kind.

If the suggestion is, as it must be, that additional facilities should be provided, then the argument must be that the Secretary of State has failed, together with the health authority, to provide the necessary facilities, either because of lack of funds or because of the need to balance all the available factors which govern the staffing and running of the National Health Service.

It seems to me that this case is not truly an attack upon the actual decision made (although that is the matter set out in the application itself) and I detect a general criticism of the decisions as to the staffing and financing of the National Health Service and of those who provide its funds and facilities. It has been said before, and I say it again, that this court can no more investigate that on the facts of this case than it could do so in any other case where the balance of available money and its distribution and use are concerned. Those, of course, are questions which are of enormous public interest and concern – but they are questions to be raised, answered and dealt with outside the court.

I am wholly convinced that this decision of the health authority is not justiciable, that is to say that it is not a matter in which the court should intervene. If it were so, then any question of priority or clinical judgment of which case came first could be subject to review where it may depend on the location of available facilities.

I pause to say that there is no possible basis for suggesting that there could be any 'policy' of the health authority to deprive the hospital of staff other than for financial and general reasons which are well-known.

In my judgment the court would do a great disservice to those who have to work in difficult and straitened circumstances if it were to contemplate making an order in this case. No surgeon should be ordered to perform an operation by the court in the circumstances which this case reveals. I deprecate any suggestion that patients should be encouraged to think that the court has a role in a case of this kind.

Mr Demello has to satisfy me that he has no arguable case, upon the facts set out in this application and in the light of the principles which govern judicial review. He has wholly failed so to persuade me. Of course everybody hopes that this matter will be resolved as soon as is humanly possible. But in my judgment I would simply raise false hopes by giving leave. I am convinced that there are no prospects of success in this court in this application – and it must be dismissed.

The Court of Appeal dismissed the applicants' appeal.

Sir John Donaldson MR: This is a renewed application by Mrs Walker for judicial review in the context of facts which are very well known to everybody, namely the inability thus far of the Central Birmingham Health Authority to treat her child, the treatment taking the form of a heart operation.

It is accepted by Mr Bailey, who has appeared for the health authority, that the National Health Service authorities, and indeed the Secretary of State (although no doubt Mr Bailey has no authority to speak on behalf of the Secretary of State), are amenable to judicial review in circumstances in which there is reason to believe that the respondent or potential respondent is in breach of duties laid on him by public law. It is important that that should be known.

But equally, Mr Bailey says – and there is very substantial force in what he says – that in an organisation such as the National Health Service there will always be occasions when patients – with good reason, from their point of view – think that they are not being treated as quickly as they ought to be treated. That stems from the fact that, whatever is the proper level of funding, resources are, and perhaps always will be, finite.

It is not for this court, or indeed any court, to substitute its own judgment for the judgment of those who are responsible for the allocation of resources. This court could only intervene where it was satisfied that there was a prima facie case, not only of failing to allocate resources in the way in which others would think that resources should be allocated, but of a failure to allocate resources to an extent which was *Wednesbury* unreasonable, if one likes to use the lawyers' jargon, or, in simpler words, which involves a breach of a public law duty (see *Associated Provincial Picture Houses Ltd v Wednesbury Corpn* [1947] 2 All ER 680, [1948] 1 KB 223). Even then, of course, the court has to exercise a judicial discretion. It has to take account of all the circumstances of the particular case with which it is concerned.

Taking account of the evidence which has been put before us and all the circumstances, it seems to me that this would be an inappropriate case in which to give leave. If other circumstances arose in this case or another case it might be different, because the jurisdiction does exist. But we have to remember, as I think I have already indicated, that if the court is prepared to grant leave in all or even most cases where patients are, from their points of view, very reasonably disturbed at what is going on, we should ourselves be using up National Health Service resources by requiring the authority to stop doing the work for which they were appointed and to meet the complaints of their patients. It is a very delicate balance. As I have made clear and as Mr Bailey made clear, the jurisdiction does exist. But it has to be used extremely sparingly.

In all the circumstances I would not give leave in this case.

Nicholls LJ and Caulfield J agreed.

Consider the following factually similar case:

R v Central Birmingham HA, ex parte Collier (CA) (6 January 1988)

Stephen Brown LJ: Mr Demello [counsel for the applicant] has sought to distinguish the factual situation in this case by submitting that here, on the evidence of Mr Collier's affidavit, there is an immediate danger to health. I am not sure that I can accept that the affidavit establishes that fact. We have no medical evidence before us, but, even assuming that it does establish that there is immediate danger to health, it seems to me that the legal principles to be applied do not differ from the case of *Re Walker*. This court is in no position to judge the allocation of resources by this particular health authority. Mr Demello recognises that there is no hint of criticism, let alone of complaint, of any action on the part of the surgeon, or any other doctor at the hospital. There is no complaint of bad faith by the health authority. It is not suggested that they are in any way dragging their feet. Mr Demello asserts that, on the basis of what he would say is 'general knowledge', there is a lack of sufficient resources to enable every bed to be in use at the hospital; but there is no suggestion here that the hospital authority has behaved in a way which is deserving of condemnation or criticism. What is suggested is that somehow more resources should be made available to enable the hospital authorities to ensure that the treatment is immediately given.

Of course this is a hearing before a court. This is not the forum in which a court can properly express opinions upon the way in which national resources are allocated or distributed. [There] may be very good reasons why the resources in this case do not allow all the beds in the hospital to be used at this particular time. We have no evidence of that, and indeed, as the master of the Rolls has said [in the *Walker* case], it is not for this court, or any court, to substitute its own judgment for the judgment of those who are responsible for the allocation of resources.

From the legal point of view, in the absence of any evidence which could begin to show that there was a failure to allocate resources in this instance in circumstances which would make it unreasonable in the Wednesbury sense to make those resources available, there can be no arguable case. I am bound to say that, whilst I have for my part every sympathy with the position of Mr Collier and his family and can understand their pressing anxiety in the case of their little boy, it does seem to me unfortunate that this procedure has been adopted. It is wholly misconceived in my view. The courts of this country cannot arrange the lists in the hospital, and, if [there] is [no] evidence that they are not being arranged properly due to some unreasonableness in the Wednesbury sense on the part of the authority, the courts cannot, and should not, be asked to intervene.

Having regard to the very recent decision of *Re Walker* it seems to me unfortunate that the step has been taken of bringing the matter before a court again. It may be that it is hoped that the publicity will assist in bringing pressure to bear upon the hospital; I do not know. This court cannot be concerned with matters of that kind. But simply upon the basis – which is a purely legal basis – that the matter comes before this court I can see no ground upon which the application can be granted.

Neill and Ralph Gibson LJJ agreed.

The language of the judges, at first blush, suggests that the courts do not distinguish the situation of 'curtailed provision' from that of 'non-provision'. A better analysis would be as we have seen, to consider the nature of the Trust's (or other provider's) undertaking as regards the curtailed service. If on the facts the service provided does not comply with the undertaking, the authority will have failed to reach its own 'benchmark'. It could also be liable for a complete failure to comply with its duty as is made clear (albeit in the context of judicial review) by Lord Donaldson MR in *Walker*.

Thus, in both *Walker* and *Collier*, the Health Authorities arguably had not undertaken to provide neonatal intensive care services to all comers. There was, therefore, no failure to reach their own benchmark. it would have been otherwise if they had continued to run the service but with untrained nurses (at times) or cut-price and inadequate facilities by their own standards.

Clearly, in addition, the Trust offering the curtailed service could also face liability if the service was so curtailed as to amount effectively to a non-provision of it. This allows us to notice that, even as regards the non-provision of services although we have said that the courts would regard it as non-justiciable, in an extreme case reference must always be made to the statutory duty imposed on the Secretary of State or his delegates to provide a 'comprehensive health service' (s 1(1) of the National Health Service Act 1977). The complete failure of a Health Authority to provide, for example, any maternity services in an area with an average rate of childbirth could well be justiciable as a breach of this primary duty. However, it remains likely that this breach of duty would only give rise to public law, rather than private law, remedies. Interestingly, as it happens the Health Authority's response to a finding of liability in a case like *Bull* could well be to limit its financial risk by closing down the maternity unit if it could not operate it safely.

IV. The 'internal market' of the NHS
Before leaving the question of institutional liability, we should notice an issue which arises as a consequence of the 'internal market'. Much of the substance of the latter has been 'watered down' by the Health Act 1999 as we saw in Chapter 2. However, the form remains of 'commissioner' and provider. The 'commissioner' may be a primary care group (or local health group in Wales) which will be established as a committee of the relevant Health Authority or a Primary Care Trust established under the 1999 Act. As we have seen, 'NHS contracts' may exist between a 'commissioner' of services and an NHS Trust (as provider). The question arises whether the commissioner may incur primary liability if it agrees to an 'NHS contract' which results in the inadequate provision of services to a particular patient who is harmed. Additionally, could primary liability arise if the commissioner failed properly to monitor either the performance of the contract or the adequacy of the services provided under it, ie failed to meet the reasonable requirements of the community as is its delegated statutory duty under section 3 of the National Health Service Act 1977? In principle, there can be no doubt that such liability could arise if the service provided failed to meet that standard which expert evidence showed was the minimum reasonably necessary. (For a further discussion see, C Newdick, 'Rights to NHS Resources After the 1990 Act' (1993) 1 Med L Rev 53.)

A final issue which arises from the 'internal market' concerns the extent to which an NHS Trust or doctor may argue that the best was done given the available resources under the NHS contract (see K Barker 'NHS Contracting: Shadows in the Law of Tort?' (1995) 3 Med L Rev 161, arguing that the standard of care may be raised as a result of the NHS contract.) In principle, the analysis here would reflect that set out earlier in relation to the NHS more generally albeit that the source of funds (and their limitation) is different. This means that the NHS Trust and the doctor would not be able to avoid liability based upon such arrangement when the care provided fell below the minimum standard. This approach was adopted in an analogous situation by the California Court of Appeal in *Wickline v California*.

Wickline v California (1986) 228 Cal Rptr 661 (Cal CA)

Mrs Wickline, a patient whose care was paid for by Medicaid, was hospitalized for surgery to treat vascular problems in her legs. On July 17, 1977, the date she was to be discharged, her doctors, realizing that she was having a difficult recovery, requested from Medicaid an eight day extension. The Medicaid utilization review nurse, after consulting with a consultant physician, authorized only four days. After four days Mrs Wickline was released. She subsequently suffered from complications that resulted in amputation of her leg. She sued the State, claiming that the complications were the result of the premature discharge, and recovered a jury verdict. The Court of Appeal reversed. Its opinion was based on the following reasoning.

Rowen JA: As to the principal issue before this court, ie, who bears responsibility for allowing a patient to be discharged from the hospital, her treating physicians or the health care payor, each side's medical expert witnesses agreed that, in accordance with the standards of medical practice as it existed in January 1977, it was for the patient's treating physician to decide the course of treatment that was medically necessary to treat the ailment.

The patient who requires treatment and who is harmed when care which should have been provided is not provided should recover for the injuries suffered from all those responsible for the deprivation of such care, including, when appropriate, health care payors. Third party payors of health care services can be held legally accountable when medically inappropriate decisions result from defects in the design or implementation of cost containment mechanisms as, for example, when appeals made on a patient's behalf for medical or hospital care are arbitrarily ignored or unreasonably disregarded or overridden. However, the physician who complies without protest with the limitations imposed by a third party payor, when his medical judgment dictates otherwise, cannot avoid his ultimate responsibility for his patient's care. He cannot point to the health care payor as the liability scapegoat when the consequences of his own determinative medical decisions go sour.

There is little doubt that Dr Polonsky [Mrs Wickline's doctor] was intimidated by the Medi-Cal program but he was not paralyzed by Dr Glassman's [the consultant's] response nor rendered powerless to act appropriately if other action was required under the circumstances. If, in his medical judgment, it was in his patient's best interest that she remain in the acute care hospital setting for an additional four days beyond the extended time period originally authorized by Medi-Cal, Dr Polonsky should have made some effort to keep Wickline there. He himself acknowledged that responsibility to his patient. It was his medical judgment, however, that Wickline could be discharged when she was. All the plaintiff's treating physicians concurred and all the doctors who testified at trial, for either plaintiff or defendant, agreed that Dr Polonsky's medical decision to discharge Wickline met the standard of care applicable at the time. Medi-Cal was not a party to that medical decision and therefore cannot be held to share in the harm resulting if such decision was negligently made.

In addition thereto, while Medi-Cal played a part in the scenario before us in that it was the resource for the funds to pay for the treatment sought, and its input regarding the nature and length of hospital care to be provided was of paramount importance, Medi-Cal did not override the medical judgment of Wickline's treating physicians at the time of her discharge. It was given no opportunity to do so. Therefore, there can be no viable cause of action against it for the consequence of that discharge decision. ...

This court appreciates that what is at issue here is the effect of cost containment programs upon the professional judgment of physicians to prescribe hospital treatment for patients requiring the same. While we recognize, realistically, that cost consciousness has become a permanent feature of the health care system, it is essential that cost limitation programs must not be permitted to corrupt medical judgment. We have concluded, from the facts in issue here, that in this case they did not.

(But see the subsequent case, *Wilson v Blue Cross of Southern California* (1990) 271 Cal Rptr 876, Turner JA *dubitante*.)

(ii) VICARIOUS LIABILITY

Ellen Picard in 'The Liability of Hospitals in Common Law Canada' (1981) 26 McGill LJ 997, 1016–1017, explains the background to vicarious liability in the context of a hospital.

An alternative basis for the liability of a hospital is based on the doctrine of *respondent superior*. It is an older and more settled area of law in regard to hospitals than that of direct, or personal or corporate duty. All of the principles of the law of vicarious liability apply to hospitals, but therein lies the problem. Those principles, set up for masters and servants, shop keepers and clerks, do not fit the hospital and its professional staff. But most courts doggedly try to stretch the old garments to fit the new flesh. The concept that was the material measurement of vicarious liability, the control test, no longer covers modern hospital-doctor relationships. ...

But control of that type is most uncommon today. Indeed almost from the moment the control test went into service its deficiencies were obvious. There is a strong consensus among authorities that it is in respect of its application to professional persons that the control test has broken down. An employer of a professional such as a doctor may know nothing about the practice of medicine. He is not only not in a position to control the doctor but if he attempts to do so will find that the employee has exercised his own form of control over the situation and quit ...

It seems the control test is not providing a credible, reliable measure of when there should be a shift in bearing the loss from the professional who has caused the negligence to the institution responsible for entering into a relationship with him in order to carry out its functions. Put succinctly, the hospital (X) is achieving many of its ends through professionals (Y). In terms of the 'rough justice' sought to be achieved through the concept of vicarious liability, when should X, (a hospital and in law a reasonable person) be held accountable for the negligence of Y (a professional)? Surely the answer is when Y is an integral part of X and is making it possible for X to fulfill its duties and obligations. The theory for determining whether liability should be borne by X has been given a name: the organization test. Fleming has described the organization test as asking whether Y's work was subject to coordinated control as to the *when* and the *where* rather than the *how*.

How has the case law accommodated these views? Picard and Robertson describe the development of the law:

E Picard and G Robertson *Legal Liability of Doctors and Hospitals in Canada* (3rd edn, 1996)

In 1906 an English court [*Evans v Liverpool Corpn* [1906] 1 KB 160] held that a hospital was not vicariously liable for the negligence of a doctor who was an employee because it did not have control over him in his professional activities. Similarly, in a famous English case, *Hillyer v St Bartholomew's Hospital* [[1909] 2 KB 820] the court held that a hospital's responsibilities were to ensure that the persons giving medical care were competent and had proper apparatus and appliances. It would be vicariously liable for negligent acts of professionals while exercising their 'ministerial or administrative duties' but not while they were carrying out professional duties, the reason for the distinction being the perceived absence of control of the employer over those professional activities. It is worth noting that it was also held that in any case at the critical time the nurses were under control of the operator surgeon. This *obiter* comment lives on, seemingly full of potential never realized.

Thus, a hospital was for many years not liable for doctor-employees or for any negligence nurse-employees committed in carrying out their professional duties. Its main responsibility was to select personnel carefully. Eventually, however, in 1942 in *Gold v Essex County Council* [[1942] 2 KB 293], this strange split in responsibility was discarded as being 'unworkable and contrary to common sense'. The negligence involved was that of a radiology technician but the position was held to be the same as that of the nurse. Whatever confusion remained was removed in *Cassidy v Minister of Health* [[1951] 1 All ER 574], where the hospital was held liable for the negligence of a house surgeon employed as part of the permanent staff. The *Hillyer* decision was reviewed and restricted to its facts. Denning LJ said [at 586]:

Relieved thus of *Hillyer's* case, this court is free to consider the question on principle, and this leads inexorably to the result that, when hospital authorities undertake to treat a patient and themselves select and appoint and employ the professional men and women who are to give the treatment, they are responsible for the negligence of those persons in failing to give proper treatment, no matter whether they are doctors, surgeons, nurses, or anyone else. Once hospital authorities are held responsible for the nurses and radiographers, as they have been in *Gold's* case, I can see no possible reason why they should not also be responsible for the house surgeons and resident medical officers on their permanent staff.

Denning LJ pointed out that it is employers who choose and can dismiss employees and this power is the reason that they should be held vicariously liable even where they cannot for various reasons control the employee. Furthermore, the old control test had become somewhat of an anachronism and it was apparent that one of the policy reasons for restricting the liability of hospitals, that of protecting the privately supported or charity hospital, was no longer present as state-supported hospitals became more common. Thus the questions became whether the person's work was an integral part of the hospital organisation and whether the patient employed him. As will be seen, the last question may have come to be paramount. In the last English case in the chain, *Roe v Minister of Health* [[1954] 2 QB6], the English Court of Appeal went a step further by holding that a hospital would be liable for a part-time anaesthetist employed and paid by the hospital as a member of the permanent staff but who also carried on a private practice.

There appears to be no doubt that anyone who is a member of the medical staff of a hospital, whether part-time or full-time, will be judged to be an employee so as to render the Health Authority (whether district or regional) or NHS Trust vicariously liable for their torts. Some uncertainty was initially expressed after the creation of the NHS of the consultant's position. *Razzel v Snowball* [1954] 3 All ER 429, [1954] 1 WLR 1382 is often cited as putting the matter beyond doubt. In that case Denning LJ observed:

> Counsel for the plaintiff pressed us with some observations in the cases concerning consultants. He said that the defendant was a part time consultant, and that a consultant was in a different position from the staff of the hospital. I think that counsel for the defendant gave the correct answer when he said that, whatever may have been the position of a consultant in former times, nowadays, since the National Health Service Act, 1946, the term 'consultant' does not denote a particular relationship between a doctor and a hospital. It is simply a title denoting his place in the hierarchy of the hospital staff. He is a senior member of the staff, and is just as much a member of the staff as the house surgeon is. Whether he is called specialist or consultant makes no difference.

In fact, the case turned on whether a consultant in carrying out treatment was the agent of the Minister, fulfilling the Minister's statutory duty under what was then section 3 of the National Health Service Act 1946. Despite this rather unusual feature, the *dictum* of Denning LJ remains helpful.

Within the NHS the issue of vicarious liability will arise in relation to staff working within a GP's surgery or practice. If the practice nurse or other, for example, is an employee, then the employing GP (and partnership) will be vicariously liable. Likewise in a hospital context, staff may be 'borrowed' from another Trust or may be agency staff. Only if there is a contract of employment will the Trust be vicariously liable – which is likely in the former instance but unlikely in the latter. Otherwise, the Trust's liability will depend upon its primary liability, as we have seen already. (For a discussion of these issues, see *Principles of Medical Law* I Kennedy and A Grubb (eds) (1998) paras 8.03–8.13.)

Outside the NHS, the steady growth of the private sector will inevitably mean that the courts will be faced with issues of *respondent superior*. Are staff working in a private clinic or hospital employed by that institution or, alternatively, are they working as independent contractors? Often nurses will be employed but, depending upon the particular arrangements in place, the doctors may not be. The decision of the New South Wales Court of Appeal in *Ellis v Wallsend DH* (1989) 17 NSWLR 553 is instructive.

Ellis v Wallsend District Hospital (1989) 17 NSWLR 553 (NSWCA)

Samuels JA: I consider first the appellant's submission that the hospital is vicariously liable for Dr Chambers' failure to warn her of the possible dangers and limited benefits of the proposed procedure.

In its conventional formulation the issue is whether Dr Chambers was an employee of the hospital under a contract of service or an independent contractor under a contract for services; in other words whether the relationship between them was one of employer and employee or of principal and independent contractor. Although an employer can be vicariously liable for the wrongs committed by his employees during the course of their employment, it has long been established that the principal of an independent contractor is not, as a general rule, vicariously liable for the wrongs committed by the contractor during the course of the engagement: *Laugher v Pointer* (1826) 5 B & C 547; 108 ER 204; *Quarman v Burnett* (1840) 6 M & W 499; 151 ER 509. Courts have traditionally applied a 'control test' to distinguish servants from independent contractors. An oft-cited formulation of the test is that of Bramwell LJ in *Yewens v Noakes* (1880) 6 QBD 530 at 532–533:

A servant is a person subject to the command of his master as to the manner in which he shall do his work.

Thus, it has been said that an employee, unlike an independent contractor, can be told by his employer not only what work to do, but also how to do it: *Collins v Hertfordshire County Council* [1947] KB 598 at 615 per Hilbery J. Although the quoted formulation of the test suggests the need for actual control over how the work is done, it is now well-established that 'what matters is lawful authority to command so far as there is scope for it': *Zuijs v Wirth Brothers Pty Ltd* (1955) 93 CLR 561 at 571; see also *Humberstone v Northern Timber Mills* (1949) 79 CLR 389 at 404 per Dixon J; *Stevens v Brodribb Sawmilling Co Pty Ltd* (1986) 160 CLR 16 at 24, 29 per Mason J. It is sufficient if this lawful authority to control be 'only in incidental or collateral matters': *Zuijs* (ibid).

Control in the sense discussed, however, is not the only indicium of a master and servant relationship to which a court may or should have regard. The 'modern approach' is to look to factors additional to control. In *Stevens v Brodribb Sawmilling* (at 24) Mason J, with whom Brennan and Deane JJ agreed, placed the control test in its proper context:

> But the existence of control, whilst significant, is not the sole criterion by which to gauge whether a relationship is one of employment. The approach of this Court has been to regard it merely as one of a number of indicia which must be considered in the determination of that question [...] Other relevant matters include, but are not limited to, the mode of remuneration, the provision and maintenance of equipment, the obligation to work, the hours of work and provision of holidays, the deduction of income tax and the delegations of work by the putative employee.

Accordingly, the approach of Australian courts is to look at 'the totality of the relationship between the parties' (at 29), although control remains a significant and therefore relevant indicium of an employer and employee relationship.

This flexible and electric approach to the determination of whether a relationship of employer and employee exists seems inconsistent with the view that an alternative and exclusive manner of ascertaining the existence of the relationship is by the application of the so-called 'organisation test'. This test requires the court to look at the role of a putative employee in the employer's organisation. In *Stevenson Jordan and Harrison Ltd v Macdonald and Evans* [1952] 1 TLR 101 at 111, Denning LJ, a proponent of the test, put it thus:

> One feature which seems to run through the instances is that, under a contract of service, a man is employed as part of the business, and his work is done as an integral part of the business; whereas, under a contract for services, his work, although done for the business, is not integrated into it but is only accessory to it.

See also *Bank voor Handel en Scheepwaart NV v Slatford* [1953] 1 QB 248 at 295 and *Roe v Minister of Health* [1954] 2 QB 66 at 91 per Morris LJ. As a matter of Australian law, the application of the organisation test is, at best, one relevant element in discerning the nature of the relationship between the parties. It is not a conclusive factor. As Mason J said in *Stevens v Brodribb Sawmilling* (at 27–28):

> For my part I am unable to accept that the organisation test could result in an affirmative finding that the contract is one of service when the control test either on its own or with other indicia yields the conclusion that it is a contract for services. Of the two concepts, legal authority to control is the more relevant and the more cogent in determining the nature of the relationship. This comment applies with equal, if not greater, force to the competing view, expressed by Denning LJ in *Bank voor Handel* [1953] 1 QB at 295, that the test is an independent method of determining who is an employee and who is an independent contractor, and in this way seeks to replace the traditional approach of balancing all the incidents of the relationship between the parties.

It is not in dispute that Dr Chambers was an 'honorary medical officer' of the hospital during the relevant period. However, this appellation should not be given an unwarranted significance. The question whether a person is the employee of another is a question of fact: *Zuijs* (at 568–569) and *Albrighton v Royal Prince Alfred Hospital* [1980] 2 NSWLR 542 at 560. (*Davies v Presbyterian Church of Wales* [1986] 1 WLR 323; [1986] 1 All ER 705, in which the House of Lords held that whether a pastor of the Presbyterian Church of Wales is employed under a contract of service is a question of law concerning the true construction of the church's book of rules, is a rather special case and distinguishable.) Accordingly, as the preceding discussion of general principle indicates, one needs to look at all the incidents of the relationship disclosed by the evidence in the instance case, rather than examine in the abstract relationships of the type involved. In *Albrighton*, Reynolds JA (at 559) succinctly states the approach that this court should take in determining whether Dr Chambers, being an honorary medical officer, was a servant of the hospital:

> The submission based on English dicta made to us that honorary medical officers are not servants of a hospital afford no assistance whatever. The problem is to be solved by looking at the evidence in this case to ascertain what it is capable of showing as to the relationship between the hospital and the doctors, however, they may be described. That evidence consists in the account of their activities within the hospital, their use of, and compliance with, hospital forms and routines, and the operation of the by-laws which were admitted in evidence.

... evidence was given by Mr Aitchison, the hospital's accountant between 1966 and 1979, about the practical operation of the by-laws and rules at the hospital during the period in question. This testimony was not generally objected to and is not now disputed.

Mr Aitchison was responsible for all the clerical functions relating to the payment of wages and creditors, for admission processes and for the collection of hospital fees. He testified that honorary medical officers received no payment from the hospital for services performed there. They were allowed to use the hospital's operating theatres for their own patients on a roster basis. In consideration for this right, they were obliged to be on call for emergency admissions and to care for the hospital's public ward patients free of charge. An honorary medical officer would admit patients from his private practice by either telephoning the hospital or giving the patient an admissions request form, as Dr Chambers did in this case, to take to the hospital. The hospital would then book the patient in for surgery at a time which coincided with a period during which the doctor was rostered to use the operating theatres. The doctor's fees in respect of services performed for these patients were regarded by the hospital as a private matter between the doctor and his patient; the hospital made no charge to private or intermediate patients (of which the appellant was one) for services rendered by doctors.

At the cost of some repetition, the evidence discloses the following. Dr Chambers, being an honorary medical officer, was subject to the by-laws and rules of the hospital. Public patients could be assigned to his care: he was obliged to treat them free of charge. But the honorary medical staff made the assignment, reporting their decision to the Board of Directors (rule 78). And the honorary medical staff prepared the 'roster of times during which [they] shall be available for duty' – presumably on call for emergency admissions – forwarding it to the board for consideration (by-law 44). His use of operating theatres for patients he admitted from his private practice was restricted to specified periods; but again this roster was prepared by the honorary medical staff (by-law 44). Visits to his patients in the wards had to be, wherever possible, at times that would not inconvenience the hospital routine. Grievances in respect of treatment of his patients in the hospital had to be reported. He was required, if necessary, to perform medical examinations of hospital personnel and be available for consultation by other members of staff at any time in respect of all cases. If he summarily discharged a patient on any of the grounds included in by-law 83 he had to report the fact to the chief executive officer.

There are other relevant indicia. Dr Chambers was selected and appointed by the board. Appointment was for a fixed three year term and renewable. At the trial it was conceded that his appointment had been successively renewed since the 1950s. The board had power to dismiss him 'after adequate inquiry' and to suspend him until that inquiry took place. He could not absent himself from his duties at the hospital without first obtaining the leave of the board and recommending a replacement. In addition, he was required under the by-laws to give 28 days' notice of his intention to resign.

It follows that the hospital, through the board and, in respect of other than professional matters (an amorphous category to say the least, but see rule 11), through the chief executive officer, possessed a measure of control over the work Dr Chambers did in the hospital. Rules 6 and 11 appear to me to assume, and thus suggest an admission, that the honorary medical officers are employees, although that term is not defined in the rules or by-laws; and although there is no evidence of any written conditions attached to Dr Chambers' original appointment or subsequent renewals (rule 2(b)), or of any acknowledgment under rule 3. But the degree of control revealed by the by-laws and rules was slight. It goes without saying that the hospital could control neither the treatment he prescribed nor the manner in which he performed surgery in its theatres. It is true that members of the honorary medical staff were bound to treat public patients and to be on hand for emergencies, but they themselves distributed the patients and drafted the rosters, and although the board may well have had some implied power of veto or revision it is probable that it was rarely exercised. The authority of the board appears to me to be confined to the formal minimum necessary to be reserved in order to ensure the administrative cohesion and integrity of the organisation in the hospital, but that might be sufficient to satisfy the modified control test enunciated in *Zuijs* (at 571);

and see *Cassidy v Ministry of Health* [1951] 2 KB 343 at 354–355 and Atiyah, *Vicarious Liability in the Law of Torts* (1967) at 46–47.

As I have indicated, the majority judgments in *Stevens v Brodribb Sawmilling* reduce the potency of the control test below the diluted influence conceded to it in *Zuijs*. It is 'a prominent factor', or 'significant', but it is not the sole criterion: cf *Oceanic Crest Shipping Co v Pilbara Harbour Services Pty Ltd* (1986) 160 CLR 626 at 682, where Dawson J held that absence of control was not 'a decisive indication' that no relationship of employer and employee existed. It is merely one of a number of indicia which must be considered in determining whether a relationship is one of employment. 'Other relevant matters' – the list is not exclusive – are set out in the passage from Mason J's judgment in *Stevens v Brodribb Sawmilling* (at 24) which I quoted above.

In the same judgment (at 27) his Honour rejects both the capacity of the organisation test (to which I have previously referred) viewed as one of the relevant indicia, to override a conclusion reached by application of the control test, and its claim to be an independent method of determining the character of the relationship in question. It may be that the organisation test was partially rehabilitated by Wilson J in *Oceanic Crest* (at 646); but probably its apparent endorsement there was an accidental consequence of the special circumstances of the case. Hence *Stevens v Brodribb Sawmilling* authorises and entails consideration of 'the totality of the relationship between the parties' (at 29), a methodology presumably synonymous with 'the traditional approach of balancing all the incidents of the relationship between the parties' (at 28).

With all respect, this prescription seems likely to generate a problem. A balancing exercise assumes conflict, or at least incompatibility, between competing elements. Here I take these to be factors which are compatible with a contract of employment and those which are not. On this view a balance is struck awarding the net advantage of persuasion to one of the contending groups of indicators; and by this means the totality of the relationship is considered and a conclusion reached as to its character.

The problem is that this approach, tending as it does to define the relationship only in terms of its elements, does not provide any external test or requirement by which the materiality of the elements may be assessed. The assertion that a working relationship between A and B will constitute one of employment, provided that it manifests the elements of such a relationship, may be unhelpful unless those elements are certain in number, character, quality and importance, in which case their presence in the prescribed measure will establish the character of the relationship. For example, it was once possible to say that if A enjoyed the right to control B, so far as there was scope for it, in the performance of B's work, the relationship of employer and employee existed between them. When that test was in vogue, it was possible to say that the relationship of employer and employee existed whenever that element of control was present; so that the presence of that element of control manifested the relationship of employer and employee.

However, as Wilson and Dawson JJ observed in *Stevens v Brodribb Sawmilling* (at 35):

The modern approach is, however, to have regard to a variety of criteria.

And then they pose much the same problem as that which I have endeavoured to raise:

The approach is not without its difficulties because not all of the accepted criteria provide a relevant test in all circumstances and none is conclusive. Moreover, the relationship itself remains largely undefined as a legal concept except in terms of the various criteria, the relevance of which may vary according to the circumstances.

Then, their Honours observe that Windeyer J's remarks in *Marshall v Whittaker's Building Supply Co* (1963) 109 CLR 210 at 217 and Denning LJ's formulations of the organisation test really pose 'the ultimate question' in a different way rather than offer a definition capable of providing an answer. But they themselves close this discussion of the concepts involved by stating (at 37) that:

The ultimate question will always be whether a person is acting as the servant of another or on his behalf.

With this proposition may be compared the distinction drawn by Dixon J in *Queensland Stations Pty Ltd v Federal Commissioner of Taxation* (1945) 70 CLR 539 at 552 between a contract of service and 'what in essence is an independent contract', in a passage referred to by Mason J in *Stevens v Brodribb Sawmilling* (at 24) and quoted with approval by Wilson and Dawson JJ in the same case (at 36).

I venture to suggest that, as Wilson and Dawson JJ appear to have concluded in *Stevens v Brodribb Sawmilling*, an accurate formulation of the ultimate question constructively determines the means of answering it. It will at least set the limits of relevance for the indicia to be identified and analysed. It will, so far as this can be done, establish parameters; that is the quantities whose variable values, as they differ from case to case, will favour one answer or another to the ultimate question posed. Such quantities, identical to Mason J's 'indicia', will include the factors which he exemplified and their 'value' will be constituted by their factual content, varying, in the case of mode of remuneration, from fixed salary or wages to amounts determined by reference, for example, to the volume of timber delivered to a mill.

More importantly, the ultimate question will give shape and meaning to the raw facts which examination of the totality of the relationship will reveal. It will constitute the external pattern to which the facts will or will not conform. I would therefore approach the matter by seeking an answer to the question: 'In treating the appellant was Dr Chambers acting as the employee of the hospital (that is to say, on the hospital's behalf) or on his own behalf?'; cf *Oceanic Crest* (at 662) per Brennan J. In seeking the answer I must examine all relevant indicia; that is to say all facts capable of elucidating the question, and thus consider the whole of the relationship between the parties. And in order to point up my external pattern I would reduce my question to more frustian terms by asking whether: 'In treating the appellant was Dr Chambers engaged in his own business or the hospital's ?': cf *Federal Commissioner of Taxation v Barrett* (1973) 129 CLR 395 at 402 per Stephen J.

I must deal with the evidence again, but I can do so this time in a rather more sophisticated way. Dr Chambers at all material times carried on his own business, that is to say, his own specialist medical practice. The performance of surgery was a vital incident of that practice and required the use of facilities which could be obtained only in an hospital which provided operating theatres with their standard fixtures and fittings (I interpolate that Dr Chambers provided other items of the surgeon's kit), together with wards, recovery rooms and trained nursing staff. The list is not exclusive. Without these resources Dr Chambers could not have carried on his practice as a surgeon.

For its parts, the hospital needed senior physicians and surgeons in order to fulfil the objects prescribed by by-law 5, that is, 'to establish and maintain hospital facilities and afford relief to sick persons' in accordance with the provisions of the Public Hospitals Act 1929, section 3 of which defined 'relief' to include treatment of disease or injury and the provision of medical and surgical attention: cf *Razzel v Snowball* [1954] 1 WLR 1382 at 1385; [1954] 3 All ER 429 at 432. Hence Dr Chambers (and other specialist physicians and surgeons) and the hospital entered into an agreement (often renewed) which in 1975 at least represented the standard means of providing a range of surgical services to the community. I have already covered this ground; but at the risk of tedium I repeat its principal incidents. Dr Chambers undertook to treat free of charge those patients who had applied directly to the hospital for relief, in return for operating privileges, nursing care and accommodation in respect of those of his own patients whom he would book into the hospital. By 'his own patients' I mean those who had consulted Dr Chambers directly, or had been referred to him by other doctors, and who had agreed to pay him a fee for his services. They would pay the hospital for nursing and other care for accommodation as private or intermediate patients.

Dr Chambers received no remuneration from the hospital. The hospital through its board and the chief executive officer (save in respect of 'professional matters', that is, matters pertaining to the exercise of medical and surgical art and skill) retained that slight degree of control over the activities of the honorary medical staff (who were generally permitted themselves to manage the discharge of their obligations) necessary, as I said, to maintain administrative efficiency and integrity.

Most of the other indicia mentioned by Mason J do not apply. Considering the totality of the relationship between the parties I conclude that it points convincingly to the conclusion that in treating the appellant Dr Chambers was engaged in his own business and not the hospital's. He was conducting his independent practice as a neuro-surgeon and his relationship with the hospital was not one of employer and employee.

I have so far endeavoured to confine my examination of the relationship between Dr Chambers and the hospital to the manner in which it related to the treatment of the appellant; that is to say, whether he treated her as an employee of the hospital and on its behalf, or whether he treated her on his own account in the furtherance of his independent surgical practice. But I think that I am bound to go further and express a view as to whether there is any basis for the conclusion that he might have fulfilled two roles, being an independent specialist working on his own account in the treatment of those whom I have defined as his own patients, and working as an employee on the hospital's behalf when treating the hospital's patients, that is those who had gone directly to the hospital for relief as the plaintiff did in *Albrighton*. An affirmative answer to this last proposition placing the hospital and Dr Chambers in the relationship of employer and employee would mean that the relationship between them differed without the intervention of any new circumstances save those relating to the manner in which the patient came to the hospital. The degree of control exerted by the hospital over Dr Chambers would be the same whether he was treating a patient of the hospital or one of his own patients as I have defined those terms. The only difference between these two situations would arise from the character of the patient and not from anything in the relationship between Dr Chambers and the hospital. It would be curious, I think, in any case, if while conducting a full-time private practice he combined that undertaking with parallel employment (in the strict sense) by the hospital; and it is no more plausible to postulate that the truth of the situation was that he was an employee of the hospital with a right of private practice such as a member of a university's academic staff might enjoy. It seems to me that, for the reasons which I have already offered, Dr Chambers was never at any time an employee of the hospital, but was at all times an independent specialist who had an agreement with the hospital pursuant to which he provided certain services, and accepted a degree of management, in return for the provision of facilities and resources necessary to enable him to carry on his own practice as a surgeon.

Meagher JA agreed.

Kirby P, however, dissented.

Kirby P: The theory of the liability of hospitals for the acts of persons working within them has changed during the course of the present century. At first, it was held that hospitals were not liable for negligence arising in the course of the exercise of professional skill. The only duty of the hospital towards the patient treated there was to use due care and skill in selecting its medical staff. The relationship of master and servant did not exist between the hospital and the physicians and surgeons who gave their services at the hospital nor between the hospital and the nurses and other attendants assisting in the operation. Because the hospital could not control the way in which those persons performed their tasks, it was not to be held vicariously liable for mistakes which they made. An action brought against the hospital for the damage resulting from negligence alleged to have been caused during an operation was held by the English Court of Appeal to be not maintainable: see *Hillyer v Governors of St Bartholomew's Hospital* [1909] 2 KB 820. The decision called upon an earlier line of United States authority: see discussion S S Bobbe, 'Tort Liability of Hospitals in New York' (1951–52) 37 Cornell LQ 419. It was clearly influenced by 'the gratuitous benefit of its care' which hospitals, at that time, commonly provided to public patients (see ibid at 829).

For several decades, in England and elsewhere, but with waning enthusiasm as time wore on, the holding in *Hillyer* protected hospitals from suits in negligence based on the acts or omissions of professional staff.

The turnaround came in Canada in *Sisters of St Joseph of the Diocese of London in Ontario v Fleming* [1938] SCR 172; [1938] 2 DLR 417: discussed A M Linden, 'Changing Patterns of Hospital Liability in Canada' (1966) 5 Alberta L Rev 212 at 215. Gradually a new doctrine emerged. It reached Australia in *Henson v Board of Management of the Perth Hospital* (1939) 41 WALR 15 and England in *Gold v Essex County Council* [1942] 2 KB 293. It reached South Africa in 1957 in *Esterhuzen v Administrator, Transvaal* 1957 (3) SA 710 (T). Now, almost all common-law countries have rejected the *Hillyer* principle. Ireland did so belatedly: see *O'Donovan v Cork County Council* [1967] IR 173. Despite some early renunciations of hospital immunity (see, eg, *Bing v Thunig* 1653 NYS 2d 3 (1957) (NYCA)), the United States of America was an even more tardy convert; see, eg *Alden v Providence Hospital* 382 F 2d 163 (1967) (DC Circ). The developments are usefully discussed in J D Cunningham, 'The Hospital-Physician Relationship: Hospital Responsibility for Malpractice of Physicians' (1975) 50 Washington L Rev 385.

These changes in the particular context of the relation of professional staff to a hospital parallelled wider changes which were occurring in the law in the definition of the duty of employers to employees generally. The simple 'control' test was no longer considered adequate to determine the relationship of an employer and employee given advances in education, technology, the role of the modern corporation and social changes which necessarily enhance individual autonomy. These changes led to various attempts by the courts to state a new criterion by which the relationship would be defined and by which vicarious liability might be assigned to one body in respect of the acts or omissions of a highly qualified individual performing tasks relevant to its interests. The existence of control over the subordinate (to use a neutral expression) was no longer the principal, still less the sole, criterion accepted by the Australian courts. In place of this test the High Court of Australia suggested the need to look to a number of indicia from which the nature of the relationship and the responsibilities deriving from it would be defined: see *Stevens v Brodribb Sawmilling Co Pty Ltd* (1986) 160 CLR 16 at 24. In England, Lord Denning had earlier suggested a simple test of whether it could be said that the 'subordinate' was working within the 'organisation' of the 'superior'. However, in Australia, although not rejected as irrelevant, the 'organisation test' is not accepted as sufficient or as an independent method for determining that vicarious liability arises: see *Stevens* (at 27).

There are particular reasons why it was necessary for the common law to move away from *Hillyer* in the special context of modern hospitals. One of them, of general application, was explained by Lord Denning (then Denning LJ) in *Cassidy v Ministry of Health* [1951] 2 KB 343 at 359–362:

> If a man goes to a doctor because he is ill, no one doubts that the doctor must exercise reasonable care and skill in his treatment of him: and that is so whether the doctor is paid for his services or not. But if the doctor is unable to treat the man himself and sends him to hospital, are not the hospital authorities then under a duty of care in their treatment of him? I think they are. Clearly, if he is a paying patient, paying them directly for their treatment of him, they must take reasonable care of him; and why should it make any difference if he does not pay them directly, but only indirectly through the rates which he pays to the local authority or through insurance contributions which he makes in order to get the treatment; I see no difference at all. Even if he is so poor that he can pay nothing, and the hospital treats him out of charity, still the hospital authorities are under a duty to take reasonable care of him just as the doctor is who treats him without asking a fee. In my opinion authorities who run a hospital, be they local authorities, government boards, or any other corporation, are in law under the selfsame duty as the humblest doctor; whenever they accept a patient for treatment, they must use reasonable care and skill to cure him of his ailment. The hospital authorities cannot, of course, do it by themselves: they have no ears to listen through the stethoscope, *and no hands to hold the surgeon's knife*. They must do it by the staff which they employ; and if their staff are negligent in giving the treatment, they are just as liable for that negligence as is anyone else who employs others to do his duties for him …
>
> It is no answer to them to say that their staff are professional men and women who do not tolerate any interference by their lay masters in the way they do their work … The reason why the employers are liable in such cases is not because they can control the way in which the work is done – they often have not sufficient knowledge to do so – but because they employ the staff and have chosen them for the task and have in their hands *the ultimate sanction for good conduct, the power of dismissal*. …
>
> [The result then is that] when hospital authorities undertake to treat a patient, and themselves select and appoint and employ the professional men and women who are to give the treatment, then they are responsible for the negligence of those persons in failing to give proper treatment, no matter whether they are doctors, surgeons, nurses, or anyone else. [Emphasis added.]

These remarks concerned the negligence of a junior medical practitioner who was on the staff of the hospital. They are therefore limited, in their terms, to staff professionals actually employed by the hospital. But the reasoning is, in my opinion, applicable to other persons associated with the hospital, over whom the hospital has 'the ultimate sanction for good conduct, the power of dismissal'.

In *Yepremian v Scarborough General Hospital* (1980) 110 DLR (3d) 513 (Ont CA), Blair JA (at 558), in an influential dissenting judgment, traced the

> … oft-told tale of how the Courts in a period of less than 50 years eliminated the anomaly which exempted hospitals from the ordinary rules of liability for negligence of doctors, nurses and other professionals acting within the scope of their employment.

The very nature of hospitals, the growth in the number of publicly funded hospitals, their importance as centres of assistance in times of personal crisis, their emergency wards with a burgeoning accretion of sophisticated equipment all suggested how inapposite was the old 'control' approach to determining the liability of the hospital for the acts of those working 'within it'. But once 'control' was overthrown and attention was paid to a range of considerations governing the relationship of the 'subordinate' to the hospital, the ambit of those for whom the hospital became vicariously liable was pushed ever further.

With copious reference to authority in many common-law countries, Giesen, *International Medical Malpractice Law* (1988) (at 52–54) concludes:

> Hospitals and health care authorities in general are now held liable for negligence of all sorts of staff, including nurses, house pharmacists, laboratory technicians , audiologists, physiotherapists, psychiatrists, radiologists and radiographers, anaesthetists, (house) surgeons, orthopaedic surgeons and neurosurgeons, pathologists, gynaecologists and other specialists, whole-time (or resident) assistant medical officers, part-time medical officers, senior registrars, and consultants.
>
> The same trend prevails in varying degrees in other Commonwealth countries. The same is true of Ireland, South Africa, and, in particular, the United States where, as in England, or in Canada, the immunity of charitable hospitals from negligence liability in

tort for the negligence of their employees has in recent decades almost entirely disappeared. Only vestiges of this doctrine remain, primarily in the form of legislatively imposed restrictions, such as ceilings on the total of recoverable damages or restrictions on those who may bring an action. Absolute immunities, however, are becoming a thing of the past, and increasingly courts are narrowing the areas in which they apply.

This appeal is not the occasion to examine the theoretical bases for vicarious liability. Professor Atiyah has described as many as nine theories to explain why a superior should be liable, in law, for the acts and omissions of a subordinate: PS Atiyah, *Vicarious Liability in Law of Torts* (1967) at 12ff. Once 'control' is abandoned as the test and a range of considerations are taken into account to determine whether vicarious liability arises, it is difficult to see why 'honorary consultants' should, as such, be excluded from the list of those for whom the hospital can be held, in law, to be accountable. The range of specialities and skills already covered in the case of employed staff is clearly established. The hospital has its own reasons for including the 'honorary' amongst its officers. Such persons add to the prestige and community utility of the hospital. They become inseparably connected with the activities of the employed staff. Their activities, in an operation, may be inextricably mixed with those of employed staff. It is in the hospital's financial and professional interest to ensure that its facilities are used to the utmost, including by such 'honoraries'. Upon this basis, I agree with Giesen (op cit at 58) that hospitals should not be allowed to escape responsibility for injury to patients happening on their premises as a result of the activities of health professionals, including honorary surgeons. Other common-law appellate courts have so held: see eg, discussion Cunningham [(1975) 50 Wah L Rev 385] (at 413); the decision of the Illinois Supreme Court in *Darling v Charleston Community Memorial Hospital* 211 NE (2d) 253 (1965); cert denied 386 US 946 (1966). So should we.

Take the present case as an example. The relationship between Dr Chambers and the hospital was defined by the Model By-laws and Rules for Public Hospitals which were admitted into evidence without objection. The relevant provisions are contained in the judgment of Samuels JA. I do not repeat them. It is enough to record that an honorary medical officer (such as Dr Chambers) was appointed to the 'honorary medical staff' of the hospital. He made up, with others in the same category, the 'Honorary Medical Board' of the hospital. That board prepared a roster during which time Dr Chambers was required to be 'available for duty'. He held 'office' for three years from the date of his 'appointment'. He was required to give 28 days' notice of intention to resign. He was not permitted to 'absent himself' from his 'duties' without first obtaining leave of absence from the board and nominating a substitute during such absence. The board retained the ultimate power referred to by Denning LJ in *Cassidy* (at 360) namely, 'the power of dismissal': see by-law 80A. His duty, in association with the hospital, was not confined to public patients. It extended to all patients, including intermediate patients such as Mrs Ellis. It was:

> To render professional services to patients according to their need, give such systematic instruction and training as required by the Board ... and conduct such medical examinations and arrange for such tests ... as are required.

Dr Chambers was required to consult when requested by a colleague. He had the power to discharge summarily any patient refusing to obey a medical direction. Together with other 'officers and employees', he was 'under the control of' the hospital's chief executive officer. The only exception, in the case of 'medical officers (honorary and resident) [was] in respect of professional matters'.

In my opinion, these by-laws, for mutual benefit, tied Dr Chambers inextricably into the organisation of the hospital. True, he could not be directed on how to 'hold the knife' (*Cassidy*). But neither could the other professional staff be so directed. He was integrated into the discipline and direction of the hospital. What he did in his rooms was his affair. But when he came into the hospital, he was part of the hospital. When working on its premises, he was part of its integrated medical team. Nothing could demonstrate this more clearly than the consent form which patients (including Mrs Ellis) were required to sign upon their admission to the hospital. It is set out in full in the judgment of Samuels JA. It includes the statement:

> I understand that an assurance has not been given that the operation will be performed by a particular surgeon.

This showed that, although a patient would have every expectation that her own doctor would perform the operation, once she came into the hospital her relationship with Dr Chambers changes. She was thereafter (as was he) under the discipline, and subject to the requirements, of the hospital. This should not be surprising. More surprising would be the notion, in the necessarily interactive circumstances of a modern hospital conducting advanced microsurgery, that people could be performing health care activities within the hospital but entirely independent of it. This would envisage that in the one operation, if the nursing sister and the honorary surgeon both missed the removal of a swab, though the mistake was common to each and performed in the course of the mutually inter-dependent activity, the hospital would be responsible for one (the nurse) but not for the other (the surgeon). Such artificialities in the law should be avoided. They represent a relic of *Hillyer* thinking. They are especially inappropriate in the facts of the present case, where the integration of Dr Chambers into the activities of the hospital is so clearly shown.

Of course, that the negligent individual should be an employee of the institution is not the only legal requirement for vicarious liability to arise. The negligence must also occur 'in the course of the employment'. This will rarely be a real issue since the professional will be performing duties imposed under their contract of employment in treating or otherwise providing care for the patient. There may be factual difficulties that require resolution where the patient is being treated as a private patient within an NHS institution. The professionals, particularly the nurses, may be caring for the patient on 'NHS time' and thus could be said to be acting 'in the course of their employment' when doing so even if the patient is not strictly an NHS patient.

2.   When engaged by others

There may be a number of situations in which a person may see a doctor in circumstances which do not seem to be those of the normal doctor-patient relationship but rather where the doctor is employed by a third party to give a medical opinion on the individual. Two common examples of this are the physician who examines an employee (or prospective employee) for the employer's purposes and the doctor who is engaged by an insurance company to carry out a medical examination. Others might include the police surgeon called upon to examine the person at a police station prior to detention or to determine his condition to be further detained. The question for us is what has the doctor undertaken to do or what duty, if any, he owes the individual. Obviously, the doctor owes the person a duty to exercise care in performing the specific procedures he uses when examining the person. If he were to injure the person by, for example, negligently taking a blood sample, he would be liable for the harm. The more difficult question concerns whether he has a wider duty. Has he undertaken, and therefore does he owe the individual a duty, to inform the person of his findings to the extent that they may have significance for the individual's health?

The issue first arose in English in *X (minors) v Bedfordshire CC* [1995] 2 AC 633, [1995] 3 All ER 353 (HL) in the context of a psychiatrist and social worker who were asked by a local authority to interview a young child suspected of having been sexually abused. Believing the child to have identified the mother's boyfriend as the abuser, the child was taken into care. The interviewer had made a mistake; the abuser was in fact someone else. The child and the mother brought actions against the local authority, the psychiatrist and the Health Authority which employed her claiming damages in negligence. The House of Lords dismissed all the actions. For our purposes the important issue concerns the claim against the psychiatrist (and her employer) who had interviewed the child. Lord Browne-Wilkinson dealt with the child's action as follows.

Lord Browne-Wilkinson: The claim based on vicarious liability is attractive and simple. The normal duty of a doctor to exercise reasonable skill and care is well established as a common law duty of care. In my judgment, the same duty applies to any other person possessed of special skills, such as a social worker. It is said, rightly, that in general such professional duty of care is owed irrespective of contract and can arise even where the professional assumes to act for the plaintiff pursuant to a contract with a third party: see *Henderson v Merrett Syndicates Ltd* [1994] 3 All ER 506, [1994] 3 WLR 761 and *White v Jones* [1995] 1 All ER 691, [1995] 2 WLR 187. Therefore, it is said, it is nothing to the point that the social workers and psychiatrist only came into contact with the plaintiffs pursuant to contracts or arrangements made between the professionals and the local authority for the purpose of the discharge by the local authority of its statutory duties. Once brought into contact with the plaintiffs, the professionals owed a duty properly to exercise their professional skills in dealing with their 'patients', the plaintiffs. This duty involved the exercise of professional skills in investigating the circumstances of the plaintiffs and (in the *Newham* case) conducting the interview with the child. Moreover, since the professionals could foresee that negligent advice would damage the plaintiffs, they are liable to the plaintiffs for tendering such advice to the local authority.

Like the majority in the Court of Appeal, I cannot accept these arguments. The social workers and the psychiatrists were retained by the local authority to advise the local authority, not the plaintiffs. The subject matter of the advice and activities of the professionals is the child. Moreover, the tendering of any advice will in many cases involve interviewing and, in the case of doctors, examining the child. But the fact that the carrying out of the retainer involves contact with and a relationship with the child cannot alter the extent of the duty owed by the professionals under the retainer from the local authority. The Court of Appeal drew a correct analogy with the doctor instructed by an insurance company to examine an applicant for life insurance. The doctor does not, by examining the applicant, come under any general duty of medical care to the applicant. He is under a duty not to damage the applicant in the course of the examination: but beyond that his duties are owed to the insurance company and not to the applicant.

The position is not the same as in the case of the purchaser of property who is owed a duty of care by a surveyor instructed by the building society which is going to advance the money: see *Smith v Eric S Bush* [1989] 2 All ER 514, [1990] 1 AC 831. In such a case the surveyor is only liable to the purchaser in negligence because he is aware that the purchaser will regulate his (the purchaser's) conduct by completing the purchase in reliance on the survey report. In the child abuse cases, even if the advice tendered by the professionals to the local authority comes to the knowledge of the child or his parents, they will not regulate their conduct in reliance on the report. The effect of the report will be reflected in the way in which the local authority acts.

Nor is the position the same as in *Henderson v Merrett Syndicates Ltd*, where, pursuant to a contract with the members' agents, the managing agents undertook the management of the insurance business of the indirect Names. The managing agents were held to be under a tortious duty of care to the indirect Names, notwithstanding that the managing agents were operating under the terms of a contract with a third party. But the duty of care to the Names in that case arose from, and fell within the ambit of, the terms of the retainer contained in the contract between the managing agents and the members' agents. The Names were not seeking to impose on the managing agents any obligation beyond that which the retainer itself required to be performed. So also in *White v Jones*.

In my judgment in the present cases, the social workers and the psychiatrist did not, by accepting the instructions of the local authority, assume any general professional duty of care to the plaintiff children. The professionals were employed or retained to advise the local authority in relation to the well-being of the plaintiffs but not to advise or treat the plaintiffs.

Sir Thomas Bingham MR in reaching the opposite conclusion relied on the decision in *Everett (pauper) v Griffiths* [1920] 3 KB 163; *affd* [1921] 1 AC 631. In that case a compulsory order for detention of a lunatic had been made under s 16 of the Lunacy Act 1891, a condition precedent to the making of the order being a certificate of incapacity signed by a doctor. The plaintiff, who had been the subject matter of an order under s 16, brought an action against the magistrate who made the order and the doctor who signed the certificate, alleging that the latter had given the certificate negligently. In the Court of Appeal, Atkin LJ expressed the view that the doctor in so certifying owed a duty of care to the plaintiff; Scrutton LJ expressed the contrary view. In the House of Lords, the case against the doctor was dismissed on the grounds that there was no evidence of any negligence. Therefore the question whether the doctor owed a duty of care was not decided. Viscount Haldane (at 657–658) and Viscount Cave (at 680) expressed the tentative view that there was a duty of care, but neither decided the point. I do not consider that this case provides any substantial support for the plaintiffs' case.

Even if, contrary to my view, the social workers and psychiatrist would otherwise have come under a duty of care to the plaintiffs, the same considerations which have led me to the view that there is no direct duty of care owed by the local authorities apply with at least equal force to the question whether it would be just and reasonable to impose such a duty of care on the individual social workers and the psychiatrist.

For these reasons, in my judgment the professionals involved were under no separate duty of care to the plaintiffs for breach of which the local authorities could be vicariously liable.

You will notice that Lord Browne-Wilkinson draws an analogy with the so-called 'insurance doctor'. His assertion that since a doctor is only under a duty 'not to damage the applicant in the course of the examination' is no more than that – an assertion, as there was no English authority to support it. Secondly, Lord Browne-Wilkinson relies on 'public policy' as a second basis for limiting the liability of the interviewers. Earlier in his speech, Lord Browne-Wilkinson identified the arguments telling against a duty of care being imposed on the local authority as follows:

Lord Browne-Wilkinson: Is it, then, just and reasonable to superimpose a common law duty of care on the local authority in relation to the performance of its statutory duties to protect children? In my judgment it is not. Sir Thomas Bingham MR took the view, with which I agree, that the public policy consideration which has first claim on the loyalty of the law is that wrongs should be remedied and that very potent counter-considerations are required to override that policy (see [1994] 4 All ER 602 at 619, [1994] 2 WLR 554 at 572). However, in my judgment there are such considerations in this case.

First, in my judgment a common law duty of care would cut across the whole statutory system set up for the protection of children at risk. As a result of the ministerial directions contained in the HMSO booklet *Working Together* the protection of such children is not the exclusive territory of the local authority's social services. The system is inter-disciplinary, involving the participation of the police, educational bodies, doctors and others. At all stages the system involves joint discussions, joint recommendations and joint decisions. The key organisation is the child protection conference, a multi-disciplinary body which decides whether to place the child on the child protection register. This procedure by way of joint action takes place, not merely because it is good practice, but because it is required by guidance having statutory force binding on the local authority. The guidance is extremely detailed and extensive: the current edition of *Working Together* runs to 126 pages. To introduce into such a system a common law duty of care enforceable against only one of the participant bodies would be manifestly unfair. To impose such liability on all the participant bodies would lead to almost impossible problems of disentangling as between the respective bodies the liability, both primary and by way of contribution, of each for reaching a decision found to be negligent.

Second, the task of the local authority and its servants in dealing with children at risk is extraordinarily delicate. Legislation requires the local authority to have regard not only to the physical well-being of the child but also to the advantages of not disrupting the child's family environment: see eg s 17 of the 1989 Act. In one of the child abuse cases, the local authority is blamed for removing the child precipitately: in the other, for failing to remove the children from their mother. As the *Report of the Inquiry into Child Abuse in Cleveland 1987* (Cm 412) (the Cleveland Report) said (p 244):

It is a delicate and difficult line to tread between taking action too soon and not taking it soon enough. Social services whilst putting the needs of the child first must respect the rights of the parents; they also must work if possible with the parents for the benefit of the children. These parents themselves are often in need of help. Inevitably a degree of conflict develops between those objectives.

Next, if a liability in damages were to be imposed, it might well be that local authorities would adopt a more cautious and defensive approach to their duties. For example, as the Cleveland Report makes clear, on occasions the speedy decision to remove the child is sometimes vital. If the authority is to be made liable in damages for a negligent decision to remove a child (such negligence lying in the failure properly first to investigate the allegations) there would be a substantial temptation to postpone making such a decision until further inquiries have been made in the hope of getting more concrete facts. Not only would the child in fact being abused be prejudiced by such delay: the increased workload inherent in making such investigations would reduce the time available to deal with other cases and other children.

The relationship between the social worker and the child's parents is frequently one of conflict, the parent wishing to retain care of the child, the social worker having to consider whether to remove it. This is fertile ground in which to breed ill feeling and litigation, often hopeless, the cost of which both in terms of money and human resources will be diverted from the performance of the social service for which they were provided. The spectre of vexatious and costly litigation is often urged as a reason for not imposing a legal duty. But the circumstances surrounding cases of child abuse make the risk a very high one which cannot be ignored.

If there were no other remedy for maladministration of the statutory system for the protection of children, it would provide substantial argument for imposing a duty of care. But the statutory complaints procedures contained in s 76 of the [Child Care Act 1980] and the much fuller procedures now available under the [Children Act 1989] provide a means to have grievances investigated, though not to recover compensation. Further, it was submitted (and not controverted) that the local authorities' ombudsman would have power to investigate cases such as these.

Finally, your Lordships' decision in *Caparo v Dickman* lays down that, in deciding whether to develop novel categories of negligence the court should proceed incrementally and by analogy with decided categories. We were not referred to any category of case in which a duty of care has been held to exist which is in any way analogous to the present cases. Here, for the first time, the plaintiffs are seeking to erect a common law duty of care in relation to the administration of a statutory social welfare scheme. Such a scheme is designed to protect weaker members of society (children) from harm done to them by others. The scheme involves the administrators in exercising discretions and powers which could not exist in the private sector and which in many cases bring them into conflict with those who, under the general law, are responsible for the child's welfare. To my mind, the nearest analogies are the cases where a common law duty of care has been sought to be imposed upon the police (in seeking to protect vulnerable members of society from wrongs done to them by others) or statutory regulators of financial dealings who are seeking to protect investors from dishonesty. In neither of those cases has it been thought appropriate to superimpose on the statutory regime a common law duty of care giving rise to a claim in damages for failure to protect the weak against the wrongdoer: see *Hill v Chief Constable of West Yorkshire* and *Yuen Kun-yeu v A-G of Hong Kong* [1987] 2 All ER 705, [1988] AC 175. In the latter case, the Privy Council whilst not deciding the point said that there was much force in the argument that if the regulators had been held liable in that case the principles leading to such liability –

> would surely be equally applicable to a wide range of regulatory agencies, not only in the financial field, but also, for example, to the factory inspectorate and social workers, to name only a few. (See [1987] 2 All ER 705 at 715–716, [1988] AC 175 at 198.)

In my judgment, the courts should proceed with great care before holding liable in negligence those who have been charged by Parliament with the task of protecting society from the wrongdoings of others.

Lords Jauncey, Lane and Ackner agreed with Lord Browne-Wilkinson. Lord Nolan, however, concluded that only the 'public policy' arguments carried weight. He said:

> I respectfully agree with his conclusions and with the whole of his reasoning save that I would, for my part, hold Newham free from vicarious liability for the alleged negligence of the psychiatrist and the social worker towards the child in that case solely on the grounds of public policy (and, in the case of the psychiatrist, the doctrine of witness immunity). Public policy apart, I am unable to accept that the psychiatrist and the social worker were exempt from a general professional duty of care towards the child. I cannot agree that the relationship was analogous to that which arises in the contractual and commercial context of an examination by an insurance company doctor of an applicant for life insurance. I agree with Sir Thomas Bingham MR on this aspect of the matter.

It would, perhaps, have been a curious outcome of the litigation if the Health Authority had been required to carry the burden of the plaintiff's claim, rather than the local authority, when its employee was 'borrowed' in order to assist with the local authority's social services functions.

It is by no means clear that the 'public policy' arguments that were so telling in the *Bedfordshire* case would (or should) have the same impact in the private law contexts of insurance or employment examinations. The most important is, arguably, that of conflict of duty. The courts would be careful to avoid placing the doctor in a position where his (potential) duty to the examinee might conflict with his duty to those who employed him. But even this can be exaggerated, as his duty to exercise reasonable care in examining and advising the examiners would rarely compromise his duty to exercise reasonable care in advising those who engaged him of the examinee's suitability for employment or as an insured. It is worth noting that, in a companion case to the *Bedfordshire* case which reached the House of Lords concerned with the liability of an education authority for its educational psychologists, Lord Browne-Wilkinson saw no difficulty in holding the psychologist to be under a duty of care to the child because '[t]here is no potential conflict of duty between the professional's duties to the [child] and his duty to the educational authority. Nor is there any obvious conflict between the professional being under a duty of care to the [child] and the discharge by the authority of its statutory duties' (at 393). We will return to this issue in the context of the two recent English cases – *Baker v Kaye* (1996) 39 BMLR 12 and *Kapfunde v Abbey National plc* (1998) 46 BMLR 176. For the moment we should return to the issue of 'assumption of responsibility' to the examinee which Lord Browne-Wilkinson denies exists in law. As he noted, Sir Thomas Bingham MR in his dissent in the Court of Appeal disagreed: sub nom *M (a minor) v Newham LBC* [1994] 4 All ER 602 (CA).

M (a minor) v Newham London BC [1994] 4 All ER 602 (CA)

Sir Thomas Bingham MR: Although the mother took the child to see the psychiatrist, she did not herself seek or instigate the consultation and the psychiatrist was plainly engaged to advise the local authority, not the child or the mother on behalf of the child. It was not therefore a normal doctor-patient relationship.

It is on the other hand clear that the relationship between the psychiatrist and the child was very direct and personal. The psychiatrist interviewed the child, it would seem at some length. She would have foreseen that if as a result of her questioning she reached erroneous conclusions and if, basing herself on erroneous conclusions, she gave unsound advice, the child was liable to suffer, whether she remained at home to undergo further abuse (if she had suffered abuse) or by separation from her mother (if she had not suffered abuse or was not likely to continue to do so). She would have recognised the welfare of the child as her paramount concern, not as a matter of legal obligation but of medical duty. Counsel for the health authority and the psychiatrist accepted that the child was the psychiatrist's patient for some purposes, such as confidentiality, but said it was a doctor-patient relationship of a special kind. I agree; but the child was the psychiatrist's patient in the sense that it was for the child alone that the psychiatrist was (as she knew) being invited to exercise her professional skill and judgment. That would ordinarily lead to the conclusion that the psychiatrist owed the child a duty of care, in the absence of reasons why such a conclusion should not follow, and I am not surprised that in the court below the existence of a duty of care was conceded. ...

Since the end of the hearing my attention has been drawn to *Everett (pauper) v Griffiths* [1920] 3 KB 163, a case which was not cited in argument and is not directly in point but which in my view fortifies the conclusions I have reached. A plaintiff acting in person sued two defendants. The first had signed an order under the Lunacy Act 1890 for the plaintiff's reception into an asylum as a pauper lunatic. The second was a medical practitioner on whose certificate the first defendant had relied. The plaintiff alleged a want of care against each and claimed damages. At the trial a special jury could not agree whether the defendants had acted with reasonable care, but Lord Reading CJ entered judgment for the first defendant on the basis that he was immune from suit, as acting in a judicial capacity, and for the medical practitioner on the grounds that the cause of the detention was the first defendant's order and not the medical certificate.

The plaintiff's appeal was unsuccessful, but I think, although much turns in the judgments on the statute in question, that this appeal against the medical practitioner would in principle succeed today. Scrutton LJ, it is true, held that the practitioner incurred no legal liability to the person examined as there was no legal relation between them (see [1920] 3 KB 163 at 195). But Bankes LJ held that there was a duty to exercise reasonable care in making the examination because –

> in a matter of such importance I cannot think that the Legislature could have contemplated any other examination than one conducted with such care as under the circumstances of each case would come up to the standard of what was reasonable. (See [1920] 3 KB 163 at 184.)

It was, however, doubtful in his view whether the practitioner owed a duty to exercise reasonable skill as well as reasonable care. Atkin LJ, in an eloquent dissenting judgment, felt no doubt (at 216):

> Quite apart from general considerations, it appears to me that there was in this case the special relation of doctor and patient between this defendant and the plaintiff, which establishes a duty owed to the plaintiff to take reasonable care in certifying him. I think, moreover, that the duty is not merely a duty to take reasonable care in making inquiries, that is, in ascertaining the necessary data, but includes a duty to exercise reasonable professional skill in forming a conclusion from such data. For what other purpose is a certificate from a medical practitioner required at all?

I find this judgment persuasive.

The plaintiffs failed in his appeal against the first defendant on the ground that he had been honestly satisfied that the plaintiff was a lunatic and a person properly to be detained and that it was therefore immaterial whether or not he had used reasonable care in arriving at his decision. But Atkin LJ dissented on this aspect also, holding that the first defendant also had been bound to take reasonable care to satisfy himself that the plaintiff was a lunatic before signing the order.

The plaintiff appealed to the House of Lords ([1921] 1 AC 631), which unanimously held that the first defendant was immune from liability on the ground favoured by the majority of the Court of Appeal. The House also held, unanimously, that there was no evidence of negligence by the medical practitioner to leave to the jury. The question whether he owed the plaintiff a duty of care was accordingly not argued. Their Lordships were content to assume the existence of a duty without deciding the question, but Viscount Haldane thought it –

> probable that if the matter were argued out [the medical practitioner] would be found to have been under a duty to the [plaintiff] to exercise care ...' (See [1921] 1 AC 631 at 657.)

The Master of the Rolls also reached a contrary conclusion to the House of Lords on the public policy arguments.

Sir Thomas Bingham MR: Imposition of a duty of care on doctors in this context was strongly resisted on grounds of public policy. Stress was laid on the very difficult, delicate and judgmental nature of the doctor's task. The imposition of a duty of care would have adverse practical consequences, causing doctors to act defensively and indecisively and distracting their attention from the task in hand. It would not contribute to the maintenance of high standards. It would undermine the inter-disciplinary co-operation which cases such as the child's demand if some of those involved were liable in negligence and some were not, and if all were liable it would make for complex claims, cross-claims and claims for contribution. It would raise very difficult problems of confidentiality. It would be very unsatisfactory if claims involving children, perhaps very young children, could be prosecuted at any time until the children reached the age of 21. Money is not an appropriate remedy.

I see very considerable force in some of these points but they do not in the end persuade me that it would be just and reasonable on these grounds to deny a right of action to a child foreseeably injured by an act or omission of a doctor in circumstances such as the present if it was an act or omission of which no ordinarily careful and competent member of the medical profession could have been guilty. I give my reasons briefly.

(1) The extreme difficulty and delicacy of the doctor's task in this context, and the highly judgmental nature of it, are very relevant. They present any plaintiff with a formidable task. As always, it will not be enough to show an error or judgment, or to show that other well-qualified members of the profession would have taken a different view. It would have to be shown that the doctor's opinion or conduct fell outside the bounds sanctioned by any responsible body of professional opinion. It can be assumed that few claims would succeed.

(2) A doctor's duty in this as in every other professional situation is to ascertain the facts as best he can, to form the best judgment he can and to give the soundest advice he can, couching his advice in terms appropriate to the judgment he has formed. I do not see why a doctor's performance of this duty in the present context would be inhibited by knowledge that he might be held liable to a child. He might no doubt be anxious to be as sure as possible before expressing any opinion, and would be careful to express no opinion stronger than the facts in his judgment warranted, but both these results are to be encouraged. I do not think he would be deterred from prompt action where the facts appeared to warrant it, since he would be as vulnerable to criticism for failing to advise urgent action when the facts appeared to call for it as for acting precipitately when the facts did not. The doctor's only certain protection would be sound performance of his professional duty, and that is how it should be.

(3) I cannot accept, as a general proposition, that the imposition of a duty of care makes no contribution to the maintenance of high standards. The common belief that the imposition of such a duty may lead to overkill is not easily reconciled with the suggestion that it has no effect.

(4) I am here concerned with the position of the psychiatrist, who was in a special and direct relationship with the child. I consider the position of the social workers below. It by no means follows that if a doctor is subject to a duty the same is true of a policeman, a teacher or a health visitor. Those relationships must be considered when and if they are in issue. The potential complexity of litigation is not of itself a ground for denying relief.

(5) I can well understand that doctors would prefer children and their parents not to see notes and records which they have made of any interview conducted, opinion formed or advice given. But I see no reason to suppose that difficulties would arise different in kind from those with which the courts are familiar, and which they have developed means to overcome and control (see *D v National Society for the Prevention of Cruelty to Children* [1977] 1 All ER 589, [1978] AC 171, *Science Research Council v Nassé, BL Cars Ltd (formerly Leyland Cars) v Vyas* [1979] 3 All ER 673, [1980] AC 1028 and *Re M (a minor) (disclosure of material)* [1990] 2 FLR 36).

(6) Limitation periods have been the subject of much consideration and repeated legislation in recent years. The will of Parliament, reflected in statute, is that minors should be able, on reaching the age of majority, to complain of wrongs done to them before that time. If the courts were to deny children a right of action which they would otherwise grant on the ground that such delayed litigation would be contrary to public policy, they would in my view by substituting their own view of public policy, quite impermissibly, for that of Parliament.

(7) It is not suggested that the child could obtain, or ever could have obtained, any redress of any kind against the psychiatrist save by bringing this action. If she can make good her complaints (a vital condition, which I forbear constantly to repeat), it would require very potent considerations of public policy, which do not in my view exist here, to override the rule of public policy which has first claim on the loyalty of the law: that wrongs should be remedied.

(8) I agree that money is an inadequate remedy for the injury which the child claims to have suffered. So it is for the loss of a leg, or an eye, or a life. But it is usually the best the law can do. If plaintiffs do not want financial recompense they need not claim. It may be assumed that those representing the child regard it as better than nothing. It is not for the courts to refuse the only remedy they can give on the ground that plaintiffs are better without it.

Two English cases directly raise the issue of the duty of care of a doctor examining a person or reaching a decision on his health for the purposes of employment. In the first of these cases (*Baker v Kaye*) the court recognised a duty of care beyond not injuring the person, whilst in the second (*Kapfunde v Abbey National*) the court rejected it.

Baker v Kaye (1996) 39 BMLR 12 (QBD)

As a condition of a contract of employment, the plaintiff was required to obtain a satisfactory medical report from the employing company's doctor, the defendant. During the course of the pre-employment assessment, on 19 February 1991, the defendant took a sample of the plaintiff's blood for assessment. As a result of analysis of the blood, the defendant considered the plaintiff's liver function to be abnormal and requested the plaintiff to give another blood sample, which he did on 21 February. At that time the defendant inquired about the plaintiff's alcohol intake. He consulted a colleague, a consultant gastroenterologist, and concluded that the detected abnormalities were likely to have been produced by excessive consumption of alcohol. Through frequent meetings with the company's seven managers, via regular contact with the company's medical directorate in New York and his lengthy experience with the company, the defendant was aware of the company's requirements and its corporate culture, in particular with regard to employee's consumption of alcohol, which potentially could reflect unfavourably on the company. On receiving the analysis of the second blood sample and, in light of the information solicited from the plaintiff when giving the second blood sample, the defendant decided that he could not recommend the plaintiff to the company for employment which involved high levels of stress, frequent travel and business-related socialising. The plaintiff was informed that he would not be joining the company. The plaintiff alleged that the defendant's assessment was carried out negligently; specifically, that he had failed to weigh him and had not considered obesity of causal significance in considering the results of the blood analysis, and that, as a consequence of that negligence, the plaintiff had suffered financial loss. He had resigned from his previous employment, with immediate effect, on 18 February, although he claimed that the letter of resignation, which he had handed to a director of the company, was to be held by her until he confirmed the satisfactory outcome of the medical assessment to be conducted by the defendant the following day. The plaintiff made no attempt to retrieve the letter. He claimed that he had not done so because statements made to him by the defendant led him to feel confident that he had passed the medical assessment. In April 1991 a consultant physician, to whom the plaintiff had been referred by his own GP, found no evidence of liver disease of any kind.

Robert Owen QC: *The duty of care*

This case raises the question of whether a medical practitioner, retained by a company to carry out pre-employment medical assessments of its prospective employees, owes a duty of care to those whom he assesses in carrying out his assessment and in reporting his conclusion to the company. ...

Mr Bowers, for the plaintiff, contends that the case falls within the well-established category of economic loss caused by negligent misstatement, the *Hedley Byrne & Co Ltd v Heller & Partners Ltd* [1963] 2 All ER 575, [1964] AC 465 category. ...

There is, of course, a fundamental difference between the situation that gave rise to liability in *Hedley Byrne* and the facts of the instant case. In *Hedley Byrne* the advertising agents, who had sought the banker's reference, relied upon it, as the bank knew they would, in placing orders with the company the subject of the reference. In the instant case the plaintiff was dependent upon the medical assessment made by the defendant; but he did not rely upon it in the sense that it did not lead to any action or inaction on his part. His role was entirely passive. It was for the defendant to make a recommendation or non-recommendation, and for NBC to act upon it.

However, that distinction was addressed in *Spring v Guardian Assurance plc* [1994] 3 All ER 129, [1995] 2 AC 296, and resolved by an incremental development of the *Hedley Byrne* principle. The decision is of central importance, not only because it demonstrates that liability may arise where there has not been reliance in the *Hedley Byrne* sense, but also because it is relied upon by the plaintiff as very closely analogous to the instant facts. Mr Spring was dismissed from his position as sales director and office manager by the defendants. He then sought to sell insurance products of another company, but, under the rules of the regulatory body LAUTRO, that company was required to seek, and his former employers to supply, a reference for him. As a result of the unfavourable reference, the company refused to appoint the plaintiff as its representative, and he sued his former employees in negligence and breach of contract. It was held:

> ... that an employer who gave a reference in respect of a former employee owed that employee a duty to take reasonable care in its preparation and would be liable to him in negligence if he failed to do so and the employee thereby suffered economic damage; that the imposition of such a liability was not contrary to public policy on the ground that it might inhibit the giving of full and frank references ... the plaintiff was entitled to succeed on the basis of the principle in *Hedley Byrne & Co Ltd v Heller & Partners Ltd*. (See the headnote of the report [1995] 2 AC 296.)

As in the instant case, Mr Spring did not act in reliance upon the negligent misrepresentation. Like Mr Baker, his role was passive; but that was not fatal to the existence of a duty of care. As Lord Goff of Chieveley said ([1994] 3 All ER 129 at 149, [1995] 2 AC 296 at 319):

> The fact that the inquiry in *Hedley Byrne* itself was directed, in a case concerned with liability in respect of a negligent mis-statement (in fact a reference), to whether the maker of the statement was liable to a recipient of it who had acted in reliance upon it, may have given the impression that this is the only way in which liability can arise under the principle in respect of a misstatement. But, having regard to the breadth of the principle as stated in *Hedley Byrne* itself, I cannot see why this should be so.

Mr Bowers argued that the doctor carrying out a medical assessment on behalf of prospective employers is in the same position as a former employer providing a reference. To test the validity of the analogy that he seeks to draw, it is necessary more closely to consider the basis upon which the House of Lords held that there was liability for a reference given by a former employer. It is clear from the speeches of Lord Goff, Lord Slynn and Lord Woolf that the duty of care had its foundation in the relationship of employer and employee. The contractual situation was complicated by the interrelationship within a group of the four defendants; but it was held by Lord Goff, Lord Slynn and Lord Woolf that it was an implied term of the contract between the plaintiff and the two defendants with whom he was unquestionably in a contractual relationship that: 'they would ensure that reasonable care was taken in the compiling and giving of the reference, and they were in breach of that implied term.' ...

There was, of course, no comparable contractual relationship between Mr Baker and Dr Kaye. I do not consider *Spring* to be as closely analogous as Mr Bowers contends. I certainly do not regard it as determinative of the issue that I have to resolve.

I therefore turn to consider the requirements for a duty of care identified in *Caparo*, namely foreseeability of economic loss, the necessary degree of proximity between the parties, and the proviso that it should be fair, just and reasonable in all the circumstances for a duty to be imposed. But I bear in mind, as did Lord Woolf in *Spring*, that whilst such requirements are of importance '… that importance should not be exaggerated for the reasons which were elegantly explained by Lord Oliver of Aylmerton in *Caparo* …'

First, it is clear that economic loss was a foreseeable consequence of the breach of the duty for which the plaintiff contends.

Secondly, was there sufficiently proximity between the parties to give rise to a duty of care? Before answering that question it is necessary to identify the critical features of their relationship: (i) the defendant was retained by NBC to advise the company as to the plaintiff's suitability for employment; (ii) the plaintiff's employment by NBC was, as the defendant well knew, dependent upon a recommendation by the defendant; (iii) in the course of the medical assessment, the plaintiff provided the defendant with detailed information about his medical history and condition, and supplied samples for analysis; (iv) the information derived from the assessment was regarded by the defendant as confidential to himself and to GE's medical directorate. It was not disclosed to the employing arm of the company; (v) having confirmed the adverse liver function tests by analysis of a second blood sample, the defendant: (a) advised the plaintiff to consult his own medical practitioner; and (b) wrote to his medical practitioner informing her of the results, so as to enable her to take whatever steps were necessary.

In my judgment, there are three features of the relationship which are of particular importance. The first is that, as the defendant well knew, the plaintiff's employment by NBC depended solely upon the assessment. The defendant must have known that to make a non-recommendation could have serious financial consequences for the plaintiff. As he himself said in evidence, 'I don't not recommend people lightly'.

Secondly, in submitting to the assessment the plaintiff agreed to provide detailed information about his state of health to the defendant. He completed the questionnaire, submitted to a physical examination, answered the defendant's questions, and provided samples of blood and urine. It is also noteworthy in this context that the questionnaire authorised disclosure of his medical records to the defendant. There are two points to be made about the information provided by the plaintiff or obtained from the clinical examination or from analysis of the samples provided by him. First, it is clear that the defendant regarded himself as under a duty of confidentiality with regard to such information. Dr Kaye stressed in his evidence to me that he would not disclose it to the company, or rather only to the company's medical directorate, which would itself treat it as confidential. But, secondly, I consider that the plaintiff was entitled to expect that the defendant would exercise due care in the use that he made of such confidential material, and in particular in arriving at conclusions based upon it.

Thirdly, the defendant regarded himself as under a duty to the plaintiff to advise him to seek medical advice if the assessment revealed any indication of a medical condition for which he required medical treatment or advice. The assumption of responsibility for advising the plaintiff to take further advice in the presence of any adverse findings could of itself be said to imply a duty to take reasonable care in carrying out the assessment.

In the course of argument, it was suggested by Mr Seabrook that the obligations to the plaintiff, which were acknowledged by the defendant, and which plainly differentiate the defendant's relationship with the plaintiff from that between the plaintiff and the prospective employer, were ethical as opposed to legal. But legal and ethical duties are obviously not mutually exclusive. To label them as ethical does not assist me in resolving the question of whether a duty of care exists.

The features that I have identified point clearly to a relationship of sufficient proximity to give rise to a duty of care. What is the nature and extent of that duty? In my judgment the defendant was under a duty to the plaintiff to take reasonable care in carrying out the medical assessment, and in making his judgment as to the plaintiff's suitability for employment by NBC by reference to the company's requirements, both general and specific to the post in question.

I turn then to consider the overriding question of whether, in all the circumstances, it is fair, just and reasonable for such a duty to be imposed in relation to the loss contended for by the plaintiff. Mr Seabrook argued that it would not be fair, just and reasonable, so to do because there was a conflict between the discharge of the defendant's duty to the company, his primary duty, and any duty to the plaintiff. In this context Mr Seabrook relied upon a passage from the speech of Lord Browne-Wilkinson in *X (minors) v Bedfordshire CC* (1995) 26 BMLR 15 at 32, [1995] 2 AC 633 at 739 …

Clearly, a conflict between the proper discharge by the defendant of his contractual duties to the company and the putative duty of care to the plaintiff would militate against the imposition of such a duty. Was there such a conflict, actual or potential?

The defendant's duty to the company was to take reasonable care in carrying out the assessment, in eliciting the material information from the plaintiff, in interpreting the test results, and in arriving at a judgment as to whether or not to recommend the plaintiff for employment, bearing in mind the company's requirements, both with regard to the employment position in question and to the company's approach to the consumption of alcohol. The duty to the plaintiff can be couched in identical terms. There could, of course, be a divergence of view between the plaintiff and the company as to what ought to be acceptable to the company in terms of alcohol consumption; but that is not a conflict which would affect the defendant's discharge of his duties to both the company and the plaintiff. It was his duty to judge the plaintiff by reference to the company's requirements; but in so doing he had to exercise reasonable care. I have come to the conclusion that, upon a true analysis of the relationship between the defendant and the company, and between the company and the plaintiff, there is no conflict inconsistent with the imposition of a duty of care. Nor do I consider that there are any other factors that militate against its imposition.

On the facts, the judge held that the defendant had not been careless.

What is perhaps remarkable about the judge's conclusion on duty is not just that he held a duty could be owed in these circumstances but that the plaintiff's claim was for pure economic loss. Such actions are notoriously difficult to bring successfully under English law. Given this, it might be thought a plaintiff's likelihood of success would be *a fortiori* where he suffered personal injury as a result of the failure to diagnose or disclose to him a problem with his health. Of course, it could be argued that the plaintiff had the advantage of falling within the narrow liability recognised in the series of House of Lords' cases beginning with *Hedley Byrne* and ending with *Spring*, even if the judge was not so confident about this.

In *Kapfunde v Abbey National*, however, the Court of Appeal cast considerable doubt upon the decision in *Baker v Kaye*.

Kapfunde v Abbey National plc and Dr D Daniel (1998) 46 BMLR 176 (CA)

The appellant, who had been born in the West Indies, had applied for a permanent post with the respondent firm, where she was employed on a part-time basis. She completed, as required, a confidential medical questionnaire and included information that she had suffered from sickle cell anaemia the previous year. The completed questionnaire was referred by the defendant's occupational health and welfare services to a GP who worked part-time for the respondent, for which she was paid an agreed annual fee. The GP had to consider whether the appellant's medical history indicated that she was likely to have a higher than average level of absence from work. She had so determined and assessed the appellant as unsuitable for permanent employment, with the result that the respondent refused the appellant a permanent post. The appellant, having failed to establish the respondent guilty of racial discrimination, instituted proceedings in 1994 alleging negligence by the GP whom, it was claimed, was a servant of the respondent, pursuant to a contract of service, for whose negligence the respondent was vicariously liable. The negligence alleged was the GP's failure to exercise a proper degree of skill and care in assessing the appellant's suitability for permanent employment. On 12 November 1996, Judge Medawar dismissed the appellant's claim for damages. She appealed against that decision. ...

Kennedy LJ: *Did Dr Daniel owe the appellant a duty of care?*

(a) Constraints applicable to this case

It is, in my judgment, important to stress at the outset when considering whether or not there was duty of care those factors which may be significant when it comes to distinguishing between this and other types of case. I have the following in mind particularly.

1. The lack of any doctor/patient relationship. Dr Daniel never saw the appellant, who, when she submitted her questionnaire probably did not even know of the existence of Dr Daniel. No doubt the appellant expected that the questionnaire which, as Mr Raggatt pointed out, required disclosure of confidential information and made it very clear that frank answers were required, would be seen by someone with occupational health experience, such as a doctor or a nurse. But the evidence showed that, as one would expect, Dr Daniel was not troubled with questionnaires which disclosed nothing of any potential significance. The questionnaire did not authorise Abbey National's Occupational Health and Welfare Service or Dr Daniel to approach the appellant's general practitioner or consultant or authorise access to any medical records. If information from any of those sources was considered to be necessary or desirable such authorisation would had have to be sought.

2. Leaving anti-discrimination law on one side (the appellant's attempt to establish an infringement of such law having failed) the lack of any legal liability upon Abbey National, or any other potential employer, to exercise skill and care in processing applications for employment. As Mr Raggatt accepted at the outset of his submissions, it is still the law that an employer is free to choose who he wishes to employ, and may have quixotic reasons for rejecting apparently worthy candidates.

3. That the claim here is only for economic loss, that is to say the salary and other benefits which the appellant says she would have enjoyed if she had obtained the post for which she applied.

(b)   The appellant's submissions

Mr Raggatt submitted that, despite the three constraints to which I have just referred, Dr Daniel did owe a duty of care to the appellant because: (1) it was reasonably foreseeable that if Dr Daniel negligently over-assessed the risk of the appellant having a higher than average level of absence from work, Abbey National would accept and act upon that assessment, with the result that the appellant would not obtain the permanent post she sought. As a result, she might well suffer some economic loss; (2) in the circumstances, vis-à-vis the appellant, Dr Daniel did assume responsibility in a relationship which was of sufficient proximity to give rise to liability; and (3) it is just, fair and reasonable for this court in these circumstances to impose a legal duty of care.

That legal duty, it is asserted, is no more than a duty to exercise the skill and care to be expected of a reasonably competent occupational health physician carrying out a medical assessment of a job applicant such as this appellant in the circumstances which I have outlined: see *Bolam v Friern Hospital Management Committee* (1957) 1 BMLR 1, [1957] 1 WLR 582.

There was no dispute before us as to the nature of Dr Daniel's duty, if she owed any duty of care at all, and Mr Jarvis QC, for Abbey National, and Mr Seabrook QC, for Dr Daniel, also accepted that if Dr Daniel negligently over-assessed the risk of the appellant having a higher than average level of absence from work, then it was reasonably foreseeable that the appellant might sustain financial loss, so the kernel of the dispute in relation to the existence or non-existence of a duty of care concerns proximity, assumption of responsibility, and the allegation that it is fair and reasonable for such a duty to be imposed.

(c)   Authorities

We were helpfully invited to consider some of the leading authorities dealing with liability for negligent misstatements, starting with the decision of the House of Lords in *Hedley Byrne & Co Ltd v Heller & Partners Ltd* [1963] 2 All ER 575, [1964] AC 465 …

In *Spring v Guardian Assurance plc* [1994] 3 All ER 129, [1995] 2 AC 296 those to whom the plaintiff applied for work in the financial services industry sought a reference from his former employers. The Lautro rules (which then governed the industry) required that such a reference be sought and given. It was given, but it was unfavourable, and was found by the trial judge to constitute a negligent misstatement. In the House of Lords it had to be considered whether a duty of care was owed in contract or in tort, and Lord Goff reached an affirmative conclusion by reference to the principle recognised in *Hedley Byrne*. He said ([1994] 3 All ER 129 at 145, [1995] 2 AC 296 at 318):

> where the plaintiff entrusts the defendant with the conduct of his affairs, in general or in particular, the defendant may be held to have assumed responsibility to the plaintiff, and the plaintiff to have relied on the defendant to exercise due skill and care, in respect of such conduct.

Of course, in the present case the appellant did not entrust Dr Daniel with the conduct of her affairs. Lord Goff held that, because references were an essential common currency of the industry, an employer was under a legal duty to take care when he agreed to provide a reference for a present or past employee, but that approach is not relevant in this case. Lord Woolf recognised that the House was being asked to make a measured extension to the ambit of the law of negligence and pointed to the degree of proximity engendered where there is or has been a contract of employment or services. He also noted that, in an industry where full references are habitually sought and given, it actually benefits an employer asked to give a reference to do as he is asked. As an alternative to liability in tort, Lord Woolf, like Lord Goff and Lord Slynn, was prepared to imply a term in the contract of employment which had existed between the plaintiff and defendant (for simplicity, I assume one defendant and a contract *of* employment) but he concluded his judgment by emphasising that the views which he had expressed were confined to the class of case with which he was dealing. The importance of that qualification is underlined by the fact that, in *Spring*, both Lord Goff and Lord Woolf approved the decision of the New Zealand Court of Appeal in *South Pacific Manufacturing Co Ltd v New Zealand Security Consultants and Investigations Ltd* [1992] 2 NZLR 282, where it was held that an investigator reporting on the causes of a fire to an insurance company owed no duty of care to the insured whose claim was rejected because of the allegedly inaccurate report. Lord Goff found that there had been no assumption of responsibility by the investigator to the insured, and Lord Woolf said that the report of the investigator was made pursuant to their contractual duty to the insurer. Obviously, it can be said that in the present case Dr Daniel is in the position of the investigator.

A decision which at first sight seems to be a great assistance to the appellant is *White v Jones* [1995] 1 All ER 691, [1995] 2 AC 207, in which the defendant's solicitor neglected to comply with a testator's instructions to make a new will including a legacy of £9,000 to each of his two daughters. The testator died and the solicitor was held to have been under a duty of care to the proposed beneficiaries. Lord Goff made a notable reference to the impulse to do practical justice, but, for reasons which will become apparent in dealing with this case, I prefer to concentrate on the speech of Lord Browne-Wilkinson.

He said ([1995] 1 All ER 691 at 716, [1995] 2 AC 207 at 274):

> The law of England does not impose any general duty of care to avoid negligent misstatements or to avoid causing pure economic loss even if economic damage to the plaintiff was foreseeable. However, such a duty of care will arise if there is a special relationship between the parties. Although the categories of case in which such special relationship can be held to exist are not closed, as yet only two categories have been identified, viz (1) where there is a fiduciary relationship and (2) where the defendant has voluntarily answered a question or tenders skilled advice or services in circumstances where he knows or ought to know that an identified plaintiff will rely on his answers or advice.

Obviously, there is no question of a fiduciary relationship in the present case, and, as to the second category, the appellant – as opposed to Abbey National – did not rely on Dr Daniel's advice. The same problem existed in *White v Jones*. As Lord Browne-Wilkinson pointed out, it did not fall within either of the two categories of special relationships so far recognised, but in the opinion of Lord Browne-Wilkinson it was appropriate for the categories of negligence to be incrementally developed so as to provide a remedy in that case. He said ([1995] 1 All ER 691 at 717, [1995] 2 AC 207 at 275):

> In my judgment, this is a case where such development should take place since there is a close analogy with existing categories of special relationship giving rise to a duty of care to prevent economic loss.

It was also found to be fair and reasonable to impose liability on the defendant solicitor in that case, and one of the factors which Lord Browne-Wilkinson considered to be relevant in that context was that there could be no conflict between the solicitor's duty to his client (the testator) and his duty to the intended beneficiary ([1995] 1 All ER 691 at 718, [1995] 2 AC 207 at 276).

Mr Seabrook invited us to regard the decision in *White v Jones* as peculiar to its own facts, a side-alley in the development of the law which is also a dead end. For my part, I am not disposed to look at the decision in quite that way, but it does seem to me that its true significance becomes apparent when one looks at *X (minors) v Bedfordshire CC* (1995) 26 BMLR 15, [1995] 2 AC 633. ...

It seems to me that the position of Dr Daniel is plainly comparable with that of the social workers and doctors in *X (minors) v Bedfordshire CC* (1995) 26 BMLR 15, [1995] 2 AC 633, or with that of a doctor examining for the purposes of life insurance, save that Dr Daniel was making simply an assessment on paper. Furthermore, the way in which Lord Browne-Wilkinson expressed himself in *X (minors) v Bedfordshire CC* makes it absolutely clear that the incremental increase in the categories of negligence made by the decision in *White v Jones*, to which he expressly referred, was a small one, sufficient to cover the facts of that case, but not sufficient to indicate the existence of a duty of care in the sort of circumstances with which we are concerned.

In *Baker v Kaye* (1996) 39 BMLR 12 Mr Robert Owen QC, sitting as a deputy judge, dismissed a claim for damages made against a doctor who had made a pre-employment assessment of the plaintiff which included a physical examination and the taking of blood samples. The deputy judge found that a duty of care was owed, but that there was no breach of that duty. *White v Jones* [1995] 1 All ER 691, [1995] 2 AC 207 does not seem to have been referred to, and in my judgment, although the conclusion was right, it should have also been based upon a finding that there was no duty of care.

(d) Conclusion

In my judgment, there was no special relationship between Dr Daniel and the appellant such as to give rise to a duty of care. I prefer that formulation to saying that there was no sufficient proximity, but it amounts to the same thing. Mr Seabrook submitted that, even if proximity were to be established, it would not be fair, just and reasonable to impose legal liability because of the potential conflict between Dr Daniel's contractual duty to Abbey National and her alleged duty to the appellant. I consider that there is force in that submission, but having regard to the conclusion which I have just expressed, the point is not one which I need explore. ...

On the facts the Judge concluded that Dr Daniel had not been careless.

Millett LJ: I have had the advantage of reading in draft the judgment of Kennedy LJ, with which I am in complete agreement. ...

Spring v Guardian Assurance plc [1994] 3 All ER 129, [1995] 2 AC 296 has encouraged the appellant to argue that Dr Daniel is similarly liable to her if her report was prepared negligently. There is, it is submitted, no rational distinction between an employment reference which is provided to a prospective employer to assist him in deciding whether to employ the subject of the reference and a medical report provided to a prospective employer for the same purpose.

But the reasoning of their Lordships in *Spring v Guardian Assurance plc*, far from supporting the appellant's case, is destructive of it. Their Lordships did not derive the duty of care from the relationship between the maker of a statement and the subject of the statement. They found it in the pre-existing relationship between an employer and his former employee. Three of their Lordships (Lord Goff, Lord Slynn and Lord Woolf) held that it was an implied term of the plaintiff's contract of employment that his employer would take reasonable care in the preparation and giving of a reference; that such a term might be implied despite the absence of any legal obligation to provide a reference; and that it applied even after the plaintiff had left his employment with the employer.

While all four of their Lordships who formed the majority in *Spring* were prepared to find a tortious duty to the same effect, Lord Goff and Lord Lowry considered that this was an application of the principle derived from *Hedley Byrne*, while Lord Slynn and Lord Woolf considered that it represented a measured extension of the principle. Lord Goff explained that the *Hedley Byrne* principle applies whenever the plaintiff entrusts the defendant with the conduct of his affairs, either in general or in a particular respect, so that the defendant may be held to have assumed responsibility to the plaintiff, and the plaintiff to have relied on the defendant to exercise due skill and care, in respect of such conduct.

The decision was firmly based on the pre-existing relationship of employer and employee. It was the existence of this relationship which made it possible for their Lordships to treat the reference as provided, not (or not solely) at the request of the prospective employer, but rather at the request of the former employee and as an incident of his former employment. Lord Goff described the provision of references as a service regularly provided 'by employers *to their employees*' (my emphasis).

The House of Lords revisited this area in *X (minors) v Bedfordshire CC* (1995) 26 BMLR 15, [1995] 2 AC 633, when it held that a psychiatrist owed no duty of care to a child when advising a local authority that the child should be taken into care. ...

The effect of these cases is that the existence of a duty of care on the part of the person who makes a negligent misstatement and the identity of the person to whom the duty is owed depend upon the circumstances in which the statement is made. A duty of care will generally be owed to the person to whom it is made and who relies on it. In the case of a bank reference or medical report, this is normally the person who asks for it or commissions it. A reference by an employer, however, is likely to be regarded as provided to the former employee who is subject of the reference for his use as a passport to future employment rather than as a service to any particular prospective new employer.

This is sufficient to dispose of the appeal. The appellant was required to complete a questionnaire and to provide it to Abbey National. Abbey National was not obliged to consider it with due care, or at all. It was free to employ the appellant, or not to employ her, as it chose, provided that it did not unlawfully discriminate against her on improper grounds. This apart, it could adopt whatever criteria for employment it liked, however capricious, and could apply or disapply its own criteria at will. It was under no duty to the appellant to submit her questionnaire to professional assessment, but it chose to do so. Dr Daniel was instructed by Abbey National to advise it on the appellant's suitability for employment. She was obliged to acquaint herself with Abbey National's criteria for employment and to consider the questionnaire which the appellant had completed with proper professional skill and care in order to give proper advice to Abbey National. But these duties were owed to Abbey National and not to the appellant. There was no pre-existing relationship between Dr Daniel and the appellant from which a duty of care to the appellant could be derived. The only relationship between them was that between the giver of advice and the subject of the advice; and that is not enough. Dr Daniel was in the same position as the social workers and the psychiatrist in *X (minors) v Bedfordshire CC* and the insurance company's doctor to whom Lord Browne-Wilkinson referred in his speech in that case.

In *Baker v Kaye* (1996) 39 BMLR 12 Mr Robert Owen QC held that a doctor retained by an employer to examine a potential employee for his medical suitability for employment owed a duty of care to the potential employee in making his assessment and reporting to the employer. In my judgment this was wrong. In the passage which I have cited from his speech in *X (minors) v Bedfordshire CC*, Lord Browne-Wilkinson made it clear that it made no difference whether or not the doctor physically examined the applicant. Whether he does so or not, financial loss to the applicant employer is clearly foreseeable if a careless error in the doctor's assessment leads to the loss of an opportunity of employment or insurance; but this is not enough. The critical facts are that the applicant is required by the prospective employer or insurer to submit himself to medical examination by a doctor who is instructed by the employer or insurer and not to the applicant, who is a patient only in the sense that he is the subject of the examination and advice. The doctor is taken to assume responsibility for his advice, but only to the employer or insurer who commissioned it and not to the patient who is the subject of the advice.

I agree that the appeal should be dismissed.

Hutchison LJ agreed both judgments.

The Court of Appeal's decision would seem to set English law in stone for the present. The judgments of Kennedy and Millett LJJ are quite emphatic. Two points should be made (for a full discussion, see Commentary (1998) 6 Med L Rev 364 (AG)). First, the defendant and plaintiff were somewhat 'at arms length'. As Kennedy LJ noted, they never met. An assumption of responsibility by the defendant to the plaintiff might be more difficult to find in such circumstances than if the plaintiff had been physically examined. However, Millet LJ did not seem impressed with this distinction and *Baker v Kaye*, where that did occur, was said to be wrongly decided by the court.

Secondly, the case, like *Baker v Kaye*, involved economic loss by the plaintiff. Would the court have been so reluctant if the plaintiff's claim had been for personal injury arising out of misdiagnosis or failure to advise of a physical (or mental) condition from which she was suffering? Perhaps not. Certainly one would expect the court to be more sympathetic to such a claim on the basis that it might be quite reasonable for the examinee to rely on the defendant giving him a 'clean bill of health'. As the following US case illustrates, there is an abundance of US authority to support a duty to advise in these circumstances.

Webb v TD (1997) 95 P 2d 1008 (Mont Sup Ct)

Trieweiler J: The plaintiff, Diana L Webb, filed a complaint in the District Court for the Thirteenth Judicial District in Yellowstone County in which she alleged that she was injured as a result of a negligent orthopedic examination performed by Robert K Snider, MD. Dr Snider had examined her at the request of her employer's workers' compensation insurance carrier. The District Court granted summary judgment to Dr Snider on the basis that he owed claimant no duty because he had no physician-patient relationship with her. Webb appeals from that order and judgment. We reverse the judgment of the District Court ...

FACTUAL BACKGROUND

Diana Webb suffered a work-related injury to her lower back in 1986. From April through August of that year, she received treatment on one occasion from a physical therapist and periodically from a chiropractor for pain relief. The only medical doctor who examined her back was Robert K Snider, MD, an orthopedic surgeon, to whom she was referred by the State Compensation Insurance Fund. She saw Dr Snider on October 7, 1986. He examined her and had her undergo a CAT scan of her back to help determine whether she had herniated an intervertebral disc.

Following Dr Snider's examination and review of the CAT scan film, he wrote her the following letter on October 8, 1986:

Mrs Edward Webb
Box 45
Belfry, MT 59008

Dear Diana:

I have reviewed the CAT scan, and it looks excellent. There is no evidence of a ruptured disc. I think that the problems that you are having are of a back sprain, and I don't feel that any surgical treatment will be necessary.

I indicated to workers' compensation that I feel that you can work, and I gave them an impairment rating of 2 percent applied to the whole person.

If you feel that you cannot return to your original job, then you need to discuss this with workers' compensation.

Sincerely,

Robert K Snider, MD

According to Webb's testimony, because Dr Snider was the only physician who had actually examined her, she relied on his advice and sought no further treatment for her back injury. She eventually returned to an occupation in which she performed heavy labor, severely herniated an intervertebral disc in her lower back, and has significant physical limitations as a result of that additional back injury. ...

DISCUSSION

Does a physician who performs a medical examination of an individual at the request of a third party have a duty of care to the examinee and, if so, what is the scope of that duty?

This is an appeal from an order dismissing Webb's claim by summary judgment. Summary judgment is appropriate when there are no genuine issues of material fact and the moving party is entitled to judgment as a matter of law. See Rule 56(c). MR Civ P Our review of district court orders granting summary judgment is plenary. See *State Farm v Powell* (1995), 274 Mont 92, 95, 906 P 2d 198, 200.

The District Court granted Dr Snider's motion for summary judgment based on its conclusion that he owed no duty to Webb because she was not his patient. The question of whether a legal duty is owed by one person to another, as well as the scope of any such duty, are questions of law. See *Nautilus Ins Co v First Nat'l Ins, In* (1992), 254 Mont 296, 299, 837 P 2d 409, 411.

On appeal, Webb contends that doctors in Montana have a duty to exercise that degree of skill and learning ordinarily exercised by other doctors in the same speciality under like circumstances, and failure to do so is negligence. She cites our decision in *Aasheim v Humberger* (1985), 215 Mont 127, 695 P 2d 824. She contends that she submitted evidence that Dr Snider negligently failed to diagnose her condition and that she suffered further damage as a result of his negligence and, therefore, that the District Court erred by dismissing her claim by summary judgment.

Dr Snider responds that although he has a duty to exercise reasonable care, based on the standards of his profession, when examining, diagnosing, or treating a patient, that duty is based on, and limited to, the doctor-patient relationship. He contends that because he had no doctor-patient relationship with Webb, he owed her no duty as a matter of law. Although Dr Snider concedes that there are no prior decisions to that effect in Montana, he relies on the following decisions from other jurisdictions: *Hafner v Beck* (Ariz App 1995), 185 Ariz. 389, 916 P 2d 1105; *Keene v Wiggins* (Cal Ct App 1977) 69 Cal App 3d 308, 138 Cal Rptr 3; *Peace v Weisman* (Ga App 1988), 186 Ga App 697, 368 SE 2d 319; *Rogers v Horvath* (Mich 1975), 64 Mich App 644, 237 NW 2d 595; *Henkemeyer v Boxall* (Minn Ct App 1991), 465 NW 2d 437; *LoDico v Caputi* (NY App Div 1987) 517 NY S 2d 640; *Promubol v Hackett* (Pa Super 1996), 454 Pa Super 622, 686 A 2d 417; *Tomko v Marks* (Pa App 1992), 412 Pa Super 54, 602 A 2d 890; *Craddock v Gross* (Pa Super 1986), 350 Pa Super 575, 504 A 2d 1300; *Wilson v Winsett* (Tex App 1992), 828 SW 2d 231; *Johnston v Sibley* (Tex Civ App 1977), 558 SW 2d 135. The District Court agreed, and on that basis, granted Dr Snider's motion for summary judgment.

Webb replies that this case is distinguishable from the authorities cited by Dr Snider and relied on by the District Court because in this case Dr Snider undertook to advise Webb regarding her condition, and thereby, assumed a duty to her to exercise reasonable care. She contends that the authorities cited by Dr Snider and relied on by the District Court are inapplicable to the facts in this case because in none of those cases was advice directly provided by the examining physician to the person who had been examined. Webb contends that the more persuasive authorities are the following: *Daly v United States* (9th Cir 1991), 946 F 2d 1467; *Green v Walker* (5th Cir 1990), 910 F 2d 291; *Betesh v United States* (1974), 400 F Supp 238; *Hoover v Williamson* (Md 1964), 236 Md 250, 203 A 2d 861; *Cleghorn v Hess* (Nev 1993), 109 Nev 544, 853 P 2d 1260; *Edwards v Lamb* (NH 1899), 69 NH 599, 45 A 480; *Baer v Regents of*

Univ of California (NM App 1994), 844 P 2d 841; *Ferguson v Wolkin* (NY 1986), 131 Misc 2d 304, 499 NY S 2d 356; *Twitchell v MacKay* (NY App Div 1980), 78 AD 2d 125, 434 NY S 2d 516; *Armstrong v Morgan* (Tex App 1977), 545 SW 2d 45.

We agree that the authorities cited by Dr Snider and relied on by the District Court are not applicable to the facts in this case. All of them involve independent medical examinations at the request of a workers' compensation insurance carrier, state agency, or employer, and all involve allegations that the examination was done negligently, causing some damage to the plaintiff. However, none involved a situation in which the defendant physician was accused of negligently diagnosing a plaintiff's condition and communicating his erroneous conclusions directly to the patient. The closest to a case on point is Promubol where the defendant physician interpreted the plaintiff's x-ray film, sent a report to the plaintiff's insurance company, and sent a copy to the plaintiff. However, critical to that court's decision in favor of the defendant doctor was its conclusion that he had not, in fact, given advice to the plaintiff. That court gave the following explanation for its decision:

> It is clear that the report does not advise appellant. It was neither prepared for appellant nor directed to appellant, and it did not provide recommendations for follow-up. There were no personal notations, whatsoever on the report. Clearly, it represented a gratuitous notification that the information contained therein was being sent to the insurance carrier. Since the exam was reported as normal, sending a copy of the report doubled as notification that appellant Promubol's sought-after insurance increase would likely be granted.

Promubol v Hackett (Pa Super 1996), 454 Pa Super 622, 686 A 2d 417, 420

On the other hand, in *Hoover*, the Maryland Court of Appeals considered a physician's duty under circumstances similar to those in this case. In that case, General Electric Company required annual x-ray examinations of the chests of certain employees due to the effects of silica dust to which they were exposed. One of the employees was the plaintiff, Willard Hoover. The examinations were performed under the direction of the defendant, Dr C Vernon Williamson. The plaintiff alleged that following his annual examination, Dr Williamson advised him that he had "a little infection in the lungs," when, in fact, the examination clearly revealed that he had silicosis. However, his complaint was dismissed based on lack of a physician-patient relationship since Dr Williamson had been retained and paid by his employer. The trial court held that Williamson's duty was to the company and not to Hoover. The Maryland Appellate Court acknowledged that ordinarily recovery for malpractice is limited to situations which involve the relationship of a doctor and patient, but reversed the defendant's dismissal based on the following exception:

> There is, however, a broader, a more fundamental rule of long standing under which a physician may incur a tort obligation which is nonconsensual and independent of contract. This is the general rule that one who assumes to act even though gratuitously, may thereby become subject to the duty of acting carefully, if he acts at all. Restatement, Torts, Sec 325, says the law is that one who gratuitously undertakes to render services which he should recognize as necessary to another's bodily safety, and leads the other in reasonable reliance on the services to refrain from taking other protective steps, or to enter on a dangerous course of conduct, '... is subject to liability to the other for bodily harm resulting from the actor's failure to exercise reasonable care to carry out his undertaking.' See also 2 Harper and James, The Law of Torts, Sect 18.6.

Hoover v Williamson (Md 1964), 236 Md 250, 203 A 2d 861, 863.

That court held that even if the defendant had no duty to the plaintiff to begin with, he assumed a duty when he made affirmative representations to the plaintiff regarding his condition. Hoover is also relied on in *Betesh v United States* (1974), 400 F Supp 238, 245–46, for the principle that a physician performing an independent medical examination can mislead a patient and, therefore, breach a duty to that patient by withholding information, as well as by affirmatively misrepresenting a patient's condition.

Dr Snider contends that if we adopt the plaintiff's theory and allow an exception to the physician-patient requirement in only those situations where a physician makes affirmative representations to the examinee, then in those situations where the examinee does in fact suffer from some physical ailment about which he or she should be notified, ie, the presence of a potentially fatal tumor, then it would be in the physician's best interest not to notify the examinee, and that that would not be in the public's best interest. We agree. Therefore, while we agree with the decision of the Maryland Court of Appeals in Hoover that a physician who performs an independent medical examination has a duty to exercise reasonable care when he or she communicates the results of that examination to the examinee, we conclude that the scope of the duty to the examinee is not limited to those situations in which diagnoses are negligently made and communicated to the person being examined.

Based on the statutory scheme which defines the duty of every person in Montana to exercise ordinary care and skill to avoid injury to others (@ 27-1-701, MCA), we find the decision of the Fifth Circuit Court of Appeals in *Green v Walker*, MD (5th Cir 1990), 910 F 2d 291, persuasive. In Green, the decedent's employer required its employees to undergo an annual physical examination and contracted with the defendant physician to conduct those examinations. The defendant reported that all of Green's test results were normal and that he was employable without restriction. Approximately one year later, he was diagnosed with lung cancer from which he ultimately died. Prior to his death, he brought an action against the examining physician based on his contention that the physician negligently failed to diagnose his condition and that if he had, his chances of survival would have been greater. The district court, however, granted summary judgment in favor of the physician on the basis that no physician-patient relationship existed and, therefore, that the defendant had no duty to Green. The issue on appeal to the Fifth Circuit Court was whether, under Louisiana law, the defendant had a duty to the examinee to perform the examination with due care, and to report his findings, particularly any finding which appeared to pose a threat to the physical or mental health of the examinee. The Fifth Circuit Court held that the defendant had such a duty. That court acknowledged that the traditional principle of law regarding liability for malpractice depends on a physician-patient relationship. See *Green*, 910 F 2d at 296. That court based its decision on Louisiana statutory law, in spite of a decision from Louisiana's Court of Appeals which seemed to require the opposite result. See *Thomas v Kenton* (La App 1982), 425 So 2d 396. It noted that in Louisiana "the Erie obligation is to the [Civil] Code, the 'solemn expression of legislative will.'" Green, 910 F 2d at 294 (quoting *Shelp v National Surety Corp* (5th Cir 1964), cert denied (1964), 379 US 945, 85 S Ct 439, 13 L Ed 2d 543). The statutory provision it relied on provides: "Every act whatever of man that causes damage to another obliges him by whose fault it happened to repair it."

La Civ Code art 2315. That court concluded that Louisiana's Civil Code "permits the articulation of a duty of care that would protect physical examinees, if they are to be deemed other than 'patients,' a position we do not here concede." *Green*, 910 F 2d at 295. It provided the following rationale and conclusion:

> We live in an age in which the drive for an increasingly productive workforce has led employers increasingly to require that employees subject their bodies (and minds) to inspection in order to obtain or maintain employment. See Rothstein, Employee Selection Based on Susceptibility to Occupational Illness, 81 Mich L Rev 1379 (1983) (common procedures include blood tests, urinalysis, pulmonary function tests, and x-rays). In placing oneself in the hands of a person held out to the world as skilled in a medical profession, albeit at the request of one's employer, one justifiably has the reasonable expectation that the expert will warn of "any incidental dangers of which he is cognizant due to his peculiar knowledge of his specialization." *American Mfrs Mut Ins Co v United Gas Corp*, 159 So 2d 592, 595 (La App 1964).
>
> We therefore now hold that when an individual is required, as a condition of future or continued employment, to submit to a medical examination, that examination creates a relationship between the examining physician and the examinee, at least to the extent of the tests conducted. This relationship imposes upon the examining physician a duty to conduct the requested tests and diagnose the results thereof, exercising the level of care consistent with the doctor's professional training and expertise, and to take reasonable steps to make information available timely to the examinee of any findings that pose an imminent danger to the examinee's physical or mental well-being. To impose a duty upon the doctor who performs such tests to do so in accordance with the degree of care expected of his/her profession for the benefit of the employee-examinee, as well as the employer, is fully consistent with the very essence of Civil Code article 2315.

Green 910 F 2d at 295–96 (footnote omitted).

Green has been followed or cited with approval in *Daly v United States* (9th Cir 1991), 946 F 2d 1467; *Cleghorn v Hess* (Nev 1993), 109 Nev 544, 853 P 2d 1260, and *Baer v Regents of Univ of California* (NM App 1994), 118 NM 685, 884 P 2d 841.

Similarly, the Montana Code Annotated provides as follows:

> Except as otherwise provided by law, everyone is responsible not only for the results of his willful acts but also for an injury occasioned to another by his want of ordinary care or skill in the management of his property or person except so far as the latter has willfully or by want of ordinary care brought the injury upon himself.

Section 27-1-701, MCA.

Based on @27-1-701, MCA, we likewise conclude that it is consistent with statutory law in Montana to impose a duty on physicians who perform examinations of an employee, insured, or other person at the request of a third party to exercise the level of care required by the examiner's professional training and experience and to make information regarding the results of that examination available to the examinee if the physician's findings disclose an imminent danger to the examinee's physical or mental well-being.

We do not, by this opinion, conclude that physicians retained by third parties who perform independent medical examinations have the same duty of care that a physician has to his or her own patient. The scope of the duty attendant to an independent medical examination must necessarily be developed on a case-by-case basis. We agree with the observation of the California Court of Appeals in *Keene v Wiggins* (Cal Ct App 1977), 69 Cal App 3d 308, 138 Cal Rptr 3, when it stated that:

> This does not suggest, however, a doctor is required to exercise the same degree of skill toward every person he sees. The duty he owes to each varies with the relationship of the parties, the foreseeability of injury or harm that may be expected to flow from his conduct, and the reliance which the person may reasonably be expected to place on the opinion received. A case-by-case approach is required.

Keene, 138 Cal Rptr at 6.

What we do hold, in this case, is that a health care provider in Montana who is retained by a third party to do an independent medical examination has the following duties:

1. To exercise ordinary care to discover those conditions which pose an imminent danger to the examinee's physical or mental well-being and take reasonable steps to communicate to the examinee the presence of any such condition; and

2. To exercise ordinary care to assure that when he or she advises an examinee about her condition following an independent examination, the advice comports with the standard of care for that health care provider's profession.

For these reasons, we conclude that the District Court erred when it held that the defendant, Robert K Snider, MD, had no duty to the plaintiff, Diana L Webb, to exercise ordinary care under the circumstances alleged in this case. We reverse the order and judgment of the District Court and remand to the District Court for further proceedings consistent with this opinion. **Turnage CJ, Regnier, Nelson and Hunt JJ concurred.**

Two justices, Leaphart and Gray JJ agreed with the decision but only on the basis that the defendant had misrepresented the plaintiff's condition to her.

Leaphart J (specially concurring): I concur in the result reached by the Court, however, I would have only answered the question posed by the appellant Webb. Webb phrased the issue on appeal as follows: "Does a physician who undertakes to advise a patient about her condition following an independent medical examination have an obligation to exercise reasonable care in doing so?"

In responding to the issue framed by Webb, I would hold that an IME doctor who undertakes to advise a patient about her condition following an independent medical examination has an obligation to exercise reasonable care in so advising her.

Unlike the majority, I would not have addressed the broader questions of whether an IME doctor who examines a person must exercise ordinary care to discover mental or physical conditions and to take reasonable steps to communicate the presence of such conditions to the examinee. Those are questions which were not posed by the appellant and are outside the scope of the facts of this appeal. While I do not necessarily disagree with the Court's analysis of those issues, they are issues for another day, another appeal.

In our view, the reluctance of the concurring Justice is unnecessary. Misrepresentation only makes the plaintiff's claim that the doctor assumed a responsibility stronger. It is not, however, crucial.

Having said that, any development in English law would have to be sensitive of the particular contexts in which the duty was sought to be imposed so that policy considerations were, where relevant, taken into account, particularly should the need arise to avoid placing the doctor where his duty to the examinee might conflict with his duty to those who engaged him (for a general discussion, see I Kennedy and A Grubb (eds) *Principles of Medical Law* (1998) paras 5.88–5.104).

3.   Duty to third parties

Are there circumstances in which a doctor may owe a duty of care to someone who is not his patient? A number of situations may be contemplated, for example: a dangerous psychiatric patient causes injury to (or the death of) another; a patient suffering from an infectious disease transmits the disease to another; a patient who is unfit to drive injures another whilst driving; or a patient has a disabling (or worse) genetic condition which may have been inherited by a relative (see I Kennedy and A Grubb (eds) *Principles of Medical Law* (1998) paras 5.47–5.68).

As a preliminary matter, one point should be noted. There is some suggestion in the Court of Appeal that a duty of care may not exist outside the doctor-patient relationship. In *Powell v Boldaz* (1997) 39 BMLR 35 Stuart-Smith LJ came close to stating this when he said that a duty of care to the parents of a boy who died as a result of alleged medical negligence 'depends upon whether [the defendants] are called upon, or undertake, to treat them as patients' (at 45).

Powell v Boldaz (1997) 39 BMLR 35 (CA)

The plaintiffs were the parents of Robert Powell, who died of Addison's disease on 17 April 1990, aged 10. The disease was not diagnosed in time for him to have been treated successfully. Five of the defendants were general practitioners, practising in partnership at a health centre where Robert was a patient. The sixth defendant, West Glamorgan Health Authority, was responsible for the management of Morriston Hospital, Swansea and was vicariously liable for the acts and omissions of the staff thereat, in particular, for Dr Forbes, a consultant paediatrician. On 5 December 1989, one of the defendant GPs visited Robert at home and arranged for his emergency admission to Morriston Hospital, where he was treated as an in-patient of Dr Forbes. A provisional diagnosis of gastroenteritis was made. Despite the fact that subsequent tests caused Dr Forbes to consider the possibility of adrenal insufficiency, a procedure known as ACTH Stimulation, which could determine such an insufficiency, was not carried out and Robert was discharged home on 9 December. The plaintiffs claimed that a clinical summary sheet sent to the GPs (explaining the treatment Robert had received in hospital) indicated his need for an ACTH test; that his parents had been so informed; that he suffered from a hormonal imbalance and that Addison's disease was being considered. The defendant GPs claimed that the sheet contained only an entry under 'Management' which read 'Needs ACHT'. Dr Forbes saw Robert as an out-patient on 18 January 1990, and told Robert's mother that he, Robert, 'looked wonderful' and, by implication, that Addison's disease was no longer considered to be a possibility. Dr Forbes discharged Robert and wrote to his GP. The plaintiffs alleged that the version of his letter produced by the defendants was a forgery. In it, Dr Forbes described Robert's admission to hospital on 9 December as caused by severe gastroenteritis and that on review he seemed 'extremely well'. Robert was seen by one of the defendant GPs on 2 April 1990, complaining of a sore throat and pain in his jaw. The GP detected nothing wrong and Robert returned to school on 3 April. On 5 April he was sent home from school feeling unwell. On 6 April he was seen by one of the defendant GPs. He stayed away from school, and was weak and lethargic. Robert was taken to the GPs' health centre on 11 April, having vomited while eating a meal the previous day. One of the defendant GPs told Robert's parents that he would immediately contact Dr Forbes, but he failed to do so. On 15 April his condition having deteriorated, Robert was taken to his local hospital where Dr Boladz diagnosed glandular fever and arranged for a blood test to be carried out on 17 April. On 16 April, Robert having again vomited, one of the defendant GPs visited him at home, examined Robert, arranged for further blood tests, and told his parents that if Robert's condition deteriorated he would arrange for his admission to hospital. On 17 April Robert's condition worsened further and he collapsed. Another of the defendant GPs visited him at home and was told of her colleague's view that Robert should be hospitalised if his condition worsened. She declined to arrange for his admission and said there was nothing to worry about. Soon thereafter, having contacted Morriston Hospital and been told that Robert's admission required the request of a referring GP, Robert's parents prevailed upon the same GP to refer him. Still of the opinion that such was unnecessary, she eventually agreed to write a letter of reference but declined to order an ambulance for him. His parents drove Robert to hospital, arriving at 7 pm. At 9.45 pm he suffered a cardiac arrest and died. On 30 April 1990 the plaintiffs made a formal complaint to the Family Practitioners Committee about the five defendant GPs. At a hearing before the Medical Services Committee, on 13 December 1990, the complaint against the last of the GPs to visit Robert at home, on the day of his death, was found to be made out, in whole or in part. The complaints against the other four GPs were not upheld. The plaintiffs appealed against these findings to the Secretary of State for Wales. Hearings took place in 1992, but the appeal was not concluded as a result of the plaintiffs withdrawing their appeal. While the appeal process was underway, the Director of Public Prosecutions was approached by counsel for the plaintiffs on the basis that the defendant GPs might have been guilty of forgery and of attempting to pervert the course of justice. A police inquiry ensued over the next two years. In May 1996 the defendants were informed that no prosecution would be brought against any of them. By a writ issued on 13 April 1993, the plaintiffs claimed damages on their own behalf and on behalf of the estate of their son, Robert, pursuant to the Law Reform (Miscellaneous Provisions) Act 1934 and the Fatal Accidents Act 1976, by reason of the negligence of the defendants in causing the death of Robert Powell. The claims originally alleged that the first plaintiff had suffered post-traumatic shock and the second, panic disorder, as a result of witnessing the pain, suffering and subsequent death of their son, Robert. The sixth defendant, the health authority, admitted negligence, primarily on the basis of the failure to diagnose and treat the Addison's disease, and paid the second plaintiff £80,000, plus costs. Subsequently, the plaintiffs alleged that the events after Robert's death, in particular the alleged 'cover-up' operation, gave rise to further causes of action, in causing psychiatric injury to the first plaintiff and exacerbation of the second plaintiff's psychiatric condition. A claim by both for economic loss was also based on post-death events. The plaintiffs had argued, before Butterfield J, five causes of action: (1) negligence involving a breach of duty owed to the plaintiffs; (2) trespass to the person; (3) conspiracy to injure by unlawful means; (4) a breach by the defendant of a fiduciary duty; and (5) the tort of deceit in that there had been an actionable interference of a right which the plaintiff enjoyed. Butterfield J had rejected these submissions and the present appeal was based on the pleaded post-death matters.

Stuart-Smith LJ: I turn then to consider whether the pleaded post-death matters can give rise to an action for negligence. ...

I propose to consider, first, whether a sufficient relationship of proximity existed. It must be appreciated that, prior to 17 April 1990, although the plaintiffs were patients of the defendants in the sense that they were on their register, the only patient who was seeking medical advice and treatment was Robert. It was to him that the defendants owed a duty of care. The discharge of that duty in the case of a young child will often involve giving advice and instruction to the parents so that they can administer the appropriate medication, observe relevant symptoms and seek further medical assistance if need be. In giving such advice, the doctor obviously owes a duty to be careful. But the duty is owed to the child, not to the patients. As Lord Diplock said in *Sidaway v Bethlem Royal Hospital Governors* (1985) 1 BMLR 132 at 147, [1985] AC 871 at 890: 'a doctor's duty of care, whether he be general practitioner or consulting surgeon or physician, is owed to that patient and none other, idiosyncrasies and all.'

After the death, the defendants may owe the plaintiffs a duty of care; but this depends upon whether they are called upon, or undertake, to treat them as patients. There are many situations where a doctor will have close contact with another person, without the relationship of doctor-patient arising so as to involve the duty of care. Two examples are to be found in the speech of Lord Browne-Wilkinson in *X (minors) v Bedfordshire CC* (1995) 26 BMLR 15 at 44–45, [1995] 2 AC 633 at 752–753, one being a psychiatrist examining a child and interviewing a parent for the purposes of discharging the local authority's care responsibilities; the second is the examination of a claimant or plaintiff by a doctor on behalf of an insurance company. In neither of these cases does the doctor undertake to treat the person as a patient and his only duty is not to damage him in the course of the examination.

These are cases where the doctor's obligations are to the local authority or insurance company and there may well be a conflict of interest between them and the person examined. Another example can be found in the case of a doctor who goes to the assistance of a stranger injured in an accident. He does not, as a rule, undertake the patient-doctor relationship so as to make him liable for lack of care, but only a duty not to make the condition of the victim worse (see *Capital and Counties plc v Hampshire CC* [1997] 2 All ER 865 at 883).

I do not think that a doctor who has been treating a patient who has died, who tells relatives what has happened, thereby undertakes the doctor-patient relationship towards the relatives. It is a situation that calls for sensitivity, tact and discretion. But the mere fact that the communicator is a doctor, does not, without more, mean that he undertakes the doctor-patient relationship. It is of course possible that the doctor in such a situation may realise that the shock has been so great that some immediate therapy is needed, but even so, this situation is probably more akin to the doctor giving emergency treatment to an accident victim. Though no doubt it will be a question of fact and degree, in each case, whether doctor-patient relationships came into existence by the doctor undertaking to treat and heal the person as a patient.

If the relatives concerned happen to be on the doctor's register as patients, the position, in my judgment, is no different, though if the doctor perceives that counselling or medicinal treatment is required and it is given by the doctor or is sought by the patient, then the doctor-patient relationship will exist in relation to the advice and treatment given and the duty of care will arise. ...

For these reasons the claims based on breach of the duty of care fail.

Morritt and Schieman LJJ agreed.

It is not entirely clear that Stuart-Smith LJ intended to restrict a doctor's duty of care exclusively to his patients because he acknowledged that a doctor may have a duty of care to, for example, an insurance company on whose behalf he is engaged to examine the individual (on which see *supra*). Perhaps, the best view is that Stuart-Smith LJ meant that a duty to *treat* or *advise*, *qua* doctor, required the relationship of doctor and patient to exist or, more accurately, a relationship where that was the essence of the *undertaking* by the doctor. He referred to the statement of Lord Diplock in *Sidaway v Bethlem Royal Hospital Governors* [1985] AC 871 at 890 that 'a doctor's duty of care … is owed to that patient and none other' which, when read in context, is precisely what Lord Diplock was concerned with. To that extent, his remark is unexceptionable. Of course, if he meant otherwise, then he offers no justification in principle or on the basis of policy for his view and it would be inconsistent with cases such as *Goodwill v BPAS* [1996] 2 All ER 161 (CA) where no such 'blanket' exclusion was contemplated (see *infra*, pp 386-388).

Nevertheless, there are problems facing a third party in establishing that a doctor owes him a duty of care. Often the direct cause of the injury will be the voluntary action of the patient; the claim against the doctor will involve an allegation that he should have acted to avoid that injury by warning the third party or controlling the patient. English law is reluctant to impose liability for omissions or for the voluntary actions of third parties. The alleged duty may involve the doctor in breaching the patient's confidence, which may also be problematic for the law. The risk posed by the patient may be to the general public at large or, at least, to a substantial number of people rather than to the third party specifically. The breadth of potential liability may be a factor which the courts consider tells against a duty of care. Finally, it may be argued that extending liability in a broad way beyond the doctor's patients may create a conflict of interest, impose a disproportionate burden in terms of damages upon the doctor and lead to defensive practices. In short, it would not be 'just, fair and reasonable' to impose a duty of care.

Let us consider some illustrative cases in three situations: (a) dangerous psychiatric patients; (b) transmission of infectious diseases; and (c) inheritable genetic conditions.

(a) Dangerous psychiatric patients

The leading US case is *Tarasoff v Regents of the University of California* (1976) 131 Cal Rptr 14.

Tarasoff v Regents of the University of California (1976) 131 Cal Rptr 14 (Cal Sup Ct)

Tobriner J: On October 27, 1969, Prosenjit Poddar killed Tatiana Tarasoff. Plaintiffs, Tatiana's parents, allege that two months earlier Poddar confided his intention to kill Tatiana to Dr Lawrence Moore, a pscyhologist employed by the Cowell Memorial Hospital at the University of California at Berkeley. They allege that on Moore's request, the campus police briefly detained Poddar, but released him when he appeared rational. They further claim that Dr Harvey Powelson, Moore's superior, then directed that no further action be taken to detain Poddar. No one warned plaintiffs of Tatiana's peril …

Plaintiffs' complaints predicate liability on two grounds: defendants' failure to warn plaintiffs of the impending danger and their failure to bring about Poddar's confinement … Defendants, in turn, assert that they owed no duty of reasonable care to Tatiana … We shall explain that defendant therapists cannot escape liability merely because Tatiana herself was not their patient. When a therapist determines, or pursuant to the standards of his profession should determine, that his patient presents a serious danger of violence to another, he incurs an obligation to use reasonable care to protect the intended victim against such danger. The discharge of this duty may require the therapist to take one or more of various steps, depending upon the nature of the case. Thus it may call for him to warn the intended victim or others likely to apprise the victim of the danger, to notify the police, or to take whatever other steps are reasonably necessary under the circumstances.

In the case at bar, plaintiffs admit that defendant therapists notified the police, but argue on appeal that the therapists failed to exercise reasonable care to protect Tatiana in that they did not confine Poddar and did not warn Tatiana or others likely to apprise her of the danger ...

Plaintiffs can state a cause of action against defendant therapists for negligent failure to protect Tatiana.

The second cause of action can be amended to allege that Tatiana's death proximately resulted from defendants' negligent failure to warn Tatiana or others likely to apprise her of her danger. Plaintiffs contend that as amended, such allegations of negligence and proximate causation, with resulting damages, establish a cause of action. Defendants, however, contend that in the circumstances of the present case they owed no duty of care to Tatiana or her parents and that, in the absence of such duty, they were free to act in careless disregard of Tatiana's life and safety.

In analysing this issue, we bear in mind that legal duties are not discoverable facts of nature, but merely conclusory expressions that, in cases of a particular type, liability should be imposed for damage done. As stated in *Dillon v Legg* 68 Cal 2d 728, 734, 69 Cal Rptr 72, 76, 441 P 2 d 912, 916 (1968): 'The assertion that liability must ... be denied because defendant bears no "duty" to plaintiff "begs the essential questions – whether the plaintiff's interests are entitled to legal protection against the defendant's conduct ... [Duty] is not sacrosanct in itself, but only an expression of the sum total of those considerations of policy which lead the law to say that the particular plaintiff is entitled to protection." (Prosser, Law of Torts [3rd edn 1964] at pp 332–333.)'

In the landmark case of *Rowland v Christian* 69 Cal 2d 108, 70 Cal Rptr 97, 443 P 2d 561 (1968), Justice Peters recognised that liability should be imposed 'for an injury occasioned to another by his want of ordinary care or skill' as expressed in section 1714 of the Civil Code. Thus, Justice Peters, quoting from *Heaven v Pender* (1883) 11 QBD 503 at 509 stated: ' "whenever one person is by circumstances placed in such a position with regard to another ... that if he did not use ordinary care and skill in his own conduct ... he would cause danger of injury to the person or property of the other, a duty arises to use ordinary care and skill to avoid such danger." '

We depart from 'this fundamental principle' only upon the 'balancing of a number of considerations'; major ones 'are the foreseeability of harm to the plaintiff, the degree of certainty that the plaintiff suffered injury, the closeness of the connection between the defendant's conduct and the injury suffered, the moral blame attached to the defendant's conduct, the policy of preventing future harm, the extent of the burden to the defendant and consequences to the community of imposing a duty to exercise care with resulting liability for breach, and the availability, cost and prevalence of insurance for the risk involved'.

The most important of these considerations in establishing duty is foreseeability. As a general principle, a 'defendant owes a duty of care to all persons who are foreseeably endangered by his conduct, with respect to all risks which make the conduct unreasonably dangerous'. (*Rodriguez v Bethlehem Steel Corpn* 12 Cal 3d 382, 399, 115 Cal Rptr 765, 776, 525 P 2d 669, 680 (1974); *Dillon v Legg, supra,* 68 Cal 2d 728, 739, 69 Cal Rptr 72, 441 P 2d 912; *Weirum v RKO General, Inc* 15 Cal 3d 40, 123 Cal Rptr 468, 539 P 2d 36 (1975); see Civ Code, 1714). As we shall explain, however, when the avoidance of foreseeable harm requires a defendant to control the conduct of another person, or to warn of such conduct, the common law has traditionally imposed liability only if the defendant bears some special relationship to the dangerous person or to the potential victim. Since the relationship between a therapist and his patient satisfies this requirement, we need not here decide whether foreseeability alone is sufficient to create a duty to exercise reasonable care to protect a potential victim of another's conduct.

Although, as we have stated above, under the common law, as a general rule, one person owes no duty to control the conduct of another (*Richards v Stanley* 43 Cal 2d 60, 65, 271 P 2d 23 (1954); *Wright v Arcade School Dist* 230 Cal App 2d 272, 277, 40 Cal Rptr 812 (1964); Rest 2d Torts (1965) 315), nor to warn those endangered by such conduct (Rest 2d Torts, *supra,* 314, com c; Prosser, Law of Torts (4th ed 1971) 56, p 341) the courts have carved out an exception to this rule in cases in which the defendant stands in some special relationship to either the person whose conduct needs to be controlled or in a relationship to the foreseeable victim of that conduct (see Rest 2d Torts, *supra* 315–320). Applying this exception to the present case, we note that a relationship of defendant therapists to either Tatiana or Poddar will suffice to establish a duty of care; as explained in section 315 of the Restatement Second of Torts, a duty of care may arise from either '(a) a special relation ... between the actor and the third person which imposes a duty upon the actor to control the third person's conduct, or (b) a special relation ... between the actor and the other which gives to the other a right of protection'.

Although plaintiffs' pleadings assert no special relation between Tatiana and defendant therapists, they establish as between Poddar and defendant therapists the special relation that arises between a patient and his doctor or psychotherapist. Such a relationship may support affirmative duties for the benefit of third persons. Thus, for example, a hospital must exercise reasonable care to control the behaviour of a patient which may endanger other persons. A doctor must also warn a patient if the patient's condition or medication renders certain conduct, such as driving a car, dangerous to others.

Although the Californian decisions that recognise this duty have involved cases in which the defendant stood in a special relationship *both* to the victim and to the person whose conduct created the danger, we do not think that the duty should logically be constricted to such situations. Decisions of other jurisdictions hold that the single relationship of a doctor to his patient is sufficient to support the duty to exercise reasonable care to protect others against dangers emanating from the patient's illness. The courts hold that a doctor is liable to persons infected by his patient if he negligently fails to diagnose a contagious disease (*Hofmann v Blackmon* 241 So 2d 751 (Fla App, 1970)), or, having diagnosed the illness, fails to warn members of the patient's family (*Wojcik v Aluminum Co of America* 18 Misc 2d 740, 183 NYS 2d 351, 357–358 (1959); *Davis v Rodman* 147 Ark 385, 227 SW 612 (1921); *Skillings v Allen* 143 Minn 323, 173 NW 663 (1919); see also *Jones v Stanko*, 118 Ohio St 147, 160 NE 456 (1928)).

Since it involved a dangerous mental patient, the decision in *Merchants National Bank & Trust Co of Fargo v United States* 272 F Supp 409 (DND, 1967) comes closer to the issue. The Veterans Administration arranged for a patient to work on a local farm, but did not inform the farmer of the man's background. The farmer consequently permitted the patient to come and go freely during nonworking hours; the patient borrowed a car, drove to his wife's residence and killed her. Notwithstanding the lack of any 'special relationship' between the Veterans Administration and the wife, the court found the Veterans Administration liable for the wrongful death of the wife.

In their summary of the relevant rulings Fleming and Maximov conclude that the 'case law should dispel any notion that to impose on the therapists a duty to take precautions for the safety of persons threatened by a patient, where due care so requires, is in any way opposed to contemporary ground rules on the duty relationship. On the contrary, there now seems to be sufficient authority to support the conclusion that by entering into a doctor-patient relationship the therapist becomes sufficiently involved to assume some responsibility for the safety, not only of the patient himself, but also of any third person whom the doctor knows to be threatened by the patient.' (Fleming & Maximov, *The Patient or His Victim: The Therapist's Dilemma* (1974) 62 Cal L Rev 1025, 1030.) ...

We recognise the public interest in supporting effective treatment of mental illness and in protecting the rights of patients to privacy (see *Re Liftschutz, supra,* 2 Cal 3d at 432, 85 Cal Rptr 829, 467 P 2d 557), and the consequent public importance of safeguarding the confidential character of psychotherapeutic communication. Against this interest, however, we must weigh the public interest in safety from violent assault. The Legislature has undertaken the difficult task of balancing the countervailing concerns. In Evidence Code section 1014, it established a broad rule of privilege to protect confidential communications between patient and psychotherapist. In Evidence Code section 1024, the Legislature created a specific and limited exception to the psychotherapist-patient privilege: 'There is no privilege ... if the psychotherapist has reasonable cause to believe that the patient is in such mental or emotional condition as to be dangerous to himself or to the person or property of another and that disclosure of the communication is necessary to prevent the threatened danger.'

We realise that the open and confidential character of psychotherapeutic dialogue encourages patients to express threats of violence, few of which are ever executed. Certainly a therapist should not be encouraged routinely to reveal such threats; such disclosures could seriously disrupt the patient's relationship with his therapist and with the persons threatened. To the contrary, the therapist's obligations to his patient require that he not disclose a confidence unless such disclosure is necessary to avert danger to others, and even then that he do so discreetly, and in a fashion that would preserve the privacy of his patient to the fullest extent compatible with the prevention of the threatened danger. (See Fleming & Maximov, *The Patient or His Victim: The Therapist's Dilemma* (1974) 62 Cal L Rev 1025, 1065–1066).

The revelation of a communication under the above circumstances is not a breach of trust or a violation of professional ethics; as stated in the Principles of Medical Ethics of the American Medical Association (1957), section 9: 'A physician may not reveal the confidence entrusted to him in the course of medical attendance ... *unless he is required to do so by law or unless it becomes necessary in order to protect the welfare of the individual or of the community.'* (Emphasis added.) We conclude that the public policy favoring protection of the confidential character of patient-psychotherapist communications must yield to the extent to which disclosure is essential to avert danger to others. The protective privilege ends where the public peril begins.

Our current crowded and computerised society compels the interdependence of its members. In this risk-infected society we can hardly tolerate the further exposure to danger that would result from a concealed knowledge of the therapist that his patient was lethal. If the exercise of reasonable care to protect the threatened victim requires the therapist to warn the endangered party or those who can reasonably be expected to notify him, we see no sufficient societal interest that would protect and justify concealment. The containment of such risks lies in the public interest. For the foregoing reasons, we find that plaintiffs' complaints can be amended to state a cause of action against defendants Moore, Powelson, Gold and Yandell and against the Regents as their employer, for breach of duty to exercise reasonable care to protect Tatiana.

Subsequent cases involving dangerous patients as in *Tarasoff* have interpreted that decision widely so as to impose a duty to warn whenever it is foreseeable that persons will be endangered by the patient (eg *Davis v Lhim* (1983) 335 NW 2d 481 (Mich Sup Ct)). Other courts, on the other hand, have limited the application of *Tarasoff*, requiring not only that a victim be foreseeable, but also that the particular victim be readily identifiable (*Thompson v County of Alameda* (1980) 614 P 2d 728 (Cal Sup Ct), despite a strong dissent by Tobriner J). In a few jurisdictions the courts have refused to apply the *Tarasoff* reasoning at all (*Hasenai v United States* (1982) 541 F Supp 999 (D Md)). (For a discussion of developments since *Tarasoff* see: Franklin and Rabin, *Cases and Materials on Tort Law and Alternatives* (4th edn, 1987) pp 141–151).

Recently, the issue arose in an English case where the plaintiff was the mother of the victim of a psychiatric patient who had sexually abused, murdered and mutilated the body of her four-year-old daughter. In determining whether the plaintiff was owed a duty of care for her claimed psychiatric injury, the Court of Appeal dealt with her action by considering whether a duty of care was owed by the hospital to her daughter.

Palmer v Tees HA [1999] Lloyd's Rep Med 351 (CA)

On 30 June 1994 one Armstrong abducted, sexually assaulted and murdered Rosie Palmer ("Rosie") aged four and thereafter mutilated her body. Armstrong lived in the same street as Rosie. Rosie's mother, Beverley Palmer, brought an action in negligence against the defendants both on her own behalf, claiming post-traumatic stress disorder and pathological grief reaction, and also on behalf of Rosie's estate.

It was alleged that Armstrong had a history of childhood sexual abuse by his mother and neglect by the authorities charged with his protection and care. At the age of 16 he had been diagnosed as very disturbed but nothing had been done by the authorities to address his problems.

It was further alleged that between 1992 and June 1993 Armstrong attempted suicide on five occasions. He had a drink and drugs problem. Between March 1992 and July 1994 Armstrong was under the care of the defendants as a psychiatric patient and was variously diagnosed as suffering from personality disorder or psychopathic personality. He was last admitted to the Hartlepool General Hospital ("the hospital") as an in-patient in June 1993 when it was alleged that he had stated that he had sexual feelings towards children and that a child would be murdered after his discharge. He was discharged from the hospital on 21 June 1993 but remained an out-patient. He was last seen in outpatients on 3 February 1994 with a further appointment to attend on 5 May which he did not keep.

The claimant alleged *inter alia* that the defendants failed to diagnose that there was a real, substantial and foreseeable risk of Armstrong committing serious sexual offences against children and of causing serious bodily injury to any child victims; and that they failed to provide any adequate treatment for Armstrong to reduce the risk of him committing such offences.

The defendants submitted that no duty of care was owed to either Rosie or the claimant and that, even if they did owe a duty, the claimant could not bring herself within the limits of the secondary victim suffering psychiatric injury which was compensatable in law.

On 8 April 1998 Gage J dismissed the claimant's appeal from the decision of Master Hodgson striking out the claim as disclosing no cause of action pursuant to RSC Order 18, rule 19. The learned judge held that there was insufficient proximity between the defendants and Rosie and/or the claimant; and further that it was not fair, just and reasonable to impose a duty of care upon the defendants. Therefore the second and third requirements laid down in *Caparo Industries v Dickman* [1990] 2 AC 605 were not satisfied. He further held that the claimant could not bring herself within the ambit of those who at law could recover damages for psychiatric injury.

Stuart-Smith LJ: 22. Was the judge right to hold that on the facts there was no proximity between the defendants and Rosie or the claimant? Basing himself on the *Dorset Yacht* case and *Hill's* case the judge held that:

> in cases where it is alleged that a defendant by his negligence is responsible for the actions of a third party it must be shown that the victim or injured person was one who came into a special or exceptional or distinctive category of risk from the activities of the third party. It is not sufficient to show that the victim or injured party was one of a wide category of members of the general public.

He held that the potential victim was not identified or identifiable.

23. In the court below Mr Sherman argued that the fact that Rosie and the claimant lived in the same street as Armstrong was sufficient to establish proximity. But he did not rely on this argument before us. Instead he challenged the judge's conclusion stated in the last paragraph. He submitted that in cases of personal injury, it was sufficient that the injury was foreseeable. He relied upon the two passages already cited in paragraphs 16 and 17 above from Lord Oliver's speech in *Caparo* and Lord Steyn's speech in *Marc Rich* approving Saville LJ. But in my opinion the judges, in making those statements, did not have in mind the situation which exists here where there is the interposition of the conscious and voluntary act of a third party.

24. Mr Sherman posed the example of a car mechanic who negligently failed to adjust the brakes of his customer's car, so that it went out of control and killed a psychiatrist's child. Liability would be established because there is sufficient proximity, even though the child was unidentified or unidentifiable, and is merely one of a large class of potential victims. If the psychiatrist negligently failed to diagnose, treat or restrain a psychopathic murderer who killed the mechanic's child why, asks Mr Sherman, should the psychiatrist not be equally liable?

25. The answer to Mr Sherman's question is that a defective machine or mechanical device will behave in a predictable way depending on the laws of physics and mechanics. But a human being will not, save in readily predictable circumstances. Lord Reid said in *Dorset Yacht* at page 1030A:

> These cases show that, where human action forms one of the links between the original wrongdoing of the defendant and the loss suffered by the plaintiff, that action must at least have been something very likely to happen if it is not to be regarded as *novus actus interveniens* breaking the chain of causation. I do not think that a mere foreseeable possibility is or should be sufficient, for then the intervening human action can more properly be regarded as a new cause than as a consequence of the original wrongdoing. But if the intervening action was likely to happen I do not think that it can matter whether that action was innocent or tortious or criminal. Unfortunately, tortious or criminal action by a third party is often, the "very kind of thing" which is likely to happen as a result of the wrongful or careless act of the defendant. And in the present case, on the facts which we must assume at this stage, I think that the taking of a boat by the escaping trainees and their unskilful navigation leading to damage to another vessel were the very kind of thing that these Borstal officers ought to have seen to be likely.

This passage must be read in the context of the facts in that case that the plaintiff was one of a small readily identifiable class of yacht owners whose vessels were moored close by the Borstal boys' camp. The boys had a record of escaping and any escape from the island inevitably required the use of a boat. The plaintiff's boat was readily to hand.

26. Lord Diplock said at pages 1070–1071 in the *Dorset Yacht* case:

> The risk of sustaining damage from the tortious acts of criminals is shared by the public at large. It has never been recognised at common law as giving rise to any cause of action against anyone but the criminal himself. It would seem arbitrary and therefore unjust to single out for the special privilege of being able to recover compensation from

the authorities responsible for the prevention of crime a person whose property was damaged by the tortious act of a criminal merely because the damage to him happened to be caused by a criminal who had escaped from custody before completion of his sentence instead of by one who had been lawfully released or who had been put on probation or given a suspended sentence or who had never been previously apprehended at all. To give rise to a duty on the part of the custodian owed to a member of the public to take reasonable care to prevent a Borstal trainee from escaping from his custody before completion of the trainee's sentence there should be some relationship between the custodian and the person to whom the duty is owed which exposes that person to a particular risk of damage in consequence of that escape which is different in its incidence from the general risk of damage from criminal acts of others which he shares with all members of the public.

What distinguishes a Borstal trainee who has escaped from one who has been duly released from custody is his liability to recapture, and the distinctive added risk which is a reasonably foreseeable consequence of a failure to exercise due care in preventing him from escaping is the likelihood that in order to elude pursuit immediately upon the discovery of his absence the escaping trainee may steal or appropriate and damage property which is situated in the vicinity of the place of detention from which he has escaped.

So long as Parliament is content to leave the general risk of damage from criminal acts to lie where it falls without any remedy except against the criminal himself the courts would be exceeding their limited function in developing the common law to meet changing conditions if they were to recognise a duty of care to prevent criminals escaping from penal custody owed to a wider category of members of the public than those whose property was exposed to an exceptional added risk by the adoption of a custodial system for young offenders which increased the likelihood of their escape unless due care was taken by those responsible for their custody.

I should therefore hold that any duty of a Borstal officer to use reasonable care to prevent a Borstal trainee from escaping from his custody was owed to persons whom he could reasonably foresee had property situated in the vicinity of the place of detention of the detainee which the detainee was likely to steal or to appropriate and damage in the course of eluding immediate pursuit and recapture. Whether or not any person fell within this category would depend upon the facts of the particular case including the previous criminal and escaping record of the individual trainee concerned and the nature of the place from which he escaped.

It should be noted that in this passage Lord Diplock draws a distinction between an escaped prisoner and one who is released. In the present case allegation is one of release or failure to detain.

27. But the critical decision is that of *Hill v Chief Constable of West Yorkshire* [1989] AC 53 which is a case concerned with personal injury. Lord Keith of Kinkel, with whose speech the other members of the House agreed, after citing the passage of Lord Diplock's speech just referred to said:

The *Dorset Yacht* case was concerned with the special characteristics or ingredients beyond reasonable foreseeability of likely harm which may result in civil liability for failure to control another man to prevent his doing harm to a third. The present case falls broadly into the same category. It is plain that vital characteristics which were present in the *Dorset Yacht* case and which led to the imposition of liability are here lacking. Sutcliffe was never in the custody of the police force. Miss Hill was one of a vast number of the female general public who might be at risk from his activities but was at no special distinctive risk in relation to them, unlike the owners of yachts moored off Brownsea Island in relation to the foreseeable conduct of the Borstal boys. It appears from the passage quoted from the speech of Lord Diplock in the *Dorset Yacht* case that in his view no liability would rest upon a prison authority, which carelessly allowed the escape of an habitual criminal, for damage which he subsequently caused, not in the course of attempting to make good his getaway to persons at special risk, but in further pursuance of his general criminal career to the person or property of members of the general public. The same rule must apply as regards failure to recapture the criminal before he had time to resume his career. In the case of an escaped criminal his identity and description are known. In the instance case the identity of the wanted criminal was at the material time unknown and it is not averred that any full or clear description of him was ever available. The alleged negligence of the police consists in a failure to discover his identity. But if there is no general duty of care owed to individual members of the public by the responsibly responsible authorities to prevent the escape of a known criminal or to recapture him, there cannot reasonably be imposed any police force a duty of care similarly owed to identify and apprehend an unknown one. Miss Hill cannot for this purpose be regarded as a person at special risk simply because she was young and female. Where the class of potential victims of a particular habitual criminal is a large one the precise size of it cannot in potential victims of an habitual rapist. The conclusion must be that although there existed reasonable foreseeability of likely harm to such as Miss Hill if Sutcliffe were not identified and apprehended, there is absent from the case any such ingredient or characteristic as led to the liability of the Home Office in the *Dorset Yacht* case. Nor is there present any additional characteristic such as might make up the deficiency. The circumstances of the case are therefore not capable of establishing a duty of care owed towards Miss Hill by the West Yorkshire Police.

While there are, of course, differences between Hill's case and the present, that was a case of the police and not psychiatrists, and the identity of the offender was unknown, the crucial point is that there is no relashionship between the defendant and the victim.

28. Mr Sherman relied on the case of *Holgate v Lancashire Mental Hospital Board* [1937] 4 All ER 19. The facts bear a striking resemblance to those in the present case. L was a defective who had been convicted of serious crimes and sentenced to detention during His Majesty's pleasure. In due course he was transferred to the defendant's institution. He was allowed out on licence without any proper inquiry being made, and the licence was subsequently extended. During the period of his extended licence L visited the plaintiff's house and savagely assaulted her. The action was tried by the jury and the report contains the summing-up of Lewis J. It appears to have been assumed that the defendants owed a duty of care to the plaintiff. The summing up is concerned only with the issue of want of care. It can be said that this decision received some qualified support from Lord Morris in the *Dorset Yacht* case (see pages 1040-1041) and even more qualified support from Lord Reid (page 1031H) but Lord Diplock reserved his opinion as to its correctness. The other two members of the House did not mention it. The case occurred at the time when the essential elements of a duty of care were much less clearly defined than is the position today. In my judgment the case cannot be reconciled with *Hill* on the question of proximity.

29. Mr Sherman referred to a number of American cases. In *Peterson v State of Washington* (1983) 671 Pacific Reports 2nd Series 230, the Supreme Court of Washington held in somewhat similar circumstances that a duty was owed to an unidentified and unidentifiable victim. But the case proceeds on the premise that it is sufficient that there is a special relationship between the defendant and either the third party or the foreseeable victims. In English law it is plainly not sufficient that this relationship exists only between the defendant and third party. Armstrong in this case. That case was followed in the same court in *Taggart v State of Washington* (1992) 822 Pacific Reports 243.

30. But different conclusions were reached in the Supreme Court of California (*Tarasoff v Regents of University of California* (1976) 551 P 2d 334, where the court held that there was a duty to warn an identified victim, but by implication no duty to do so where the victim is unidentifiable (*Thompson v County of Alameda* 614 P 2d 728) and the Federal Court of Appeals 10th Circuit (*Brady v Hopper* 751 F 2d 329). In these cases actions brought by unidentified or unidentifiable victims failed.

31. Mr Moon submitted that in order for there to be proximity there had to be an assumption of responsibility to the victim and there was clearly none in this case. He submitted that except in the conventional case of personal injury such as accidents involving traffic, employers or occupiers' liability, the test of assumption of responsibility is the appropriate one for determining proximity. This test has undoubtedly been used not only in cases of economic loss, but also cases involving physical damage to property and personal injury, including cases of failure to diagnose and treat appropriately a congenital condition (see *X (Minors) v Bedfordshire County Council* [1995] 2 AC 633 at pages 752–753 *per* Lord Browne-Wilkinson referring to a psychiatrist advising a local authority or doctor reporting to insurers; *Capital and Counties plc v Hampshire County Council* [1997] QB 1004 (the Fire Brigade case) 1035–1036; *Phelps v Hillingdon London Borough Council* [1999] 1 WLR 500 at page 514H, an educational psychologist advising a local education authority). But these are all cases where there is a direct contact between the claimant and defendant, but there is no assumption of responsibility or undertaking by the defendant to treat or advise the claimant. I would wish to reserve my opinion as to whether it would be an appropriate test if the victim in such a case as this was identified or identifiable, as for example a child in the household of the abuser.

32. An additional reason why in my judgment in this case it is at least necessary for the victim to be identifiable (though as I have indicated it may not be sufficient) to establish proximity, is that it seems to me that the most effective way of providing protection would be to give warning to the victim, his or her parents or social services so that some protective measure can be made. As Mr Moon pointed out, the ability to restrict and restrain a psychiatric patient is subject to considerable restriction under the Mental Health Act 1983 (see particularly section 3) and is not unlimited in time. Moreover treatment, especially drug treatment of the

patient, depends on his or her co-operation when an out-patient, and is limited when an in-patient. It may be a somewhat novel approach to the question of proximity, but it seems to me to be a relevant consideration to ask what the defendant could have done to avoid the danger, if the suggested precautions ie committal under section 3 of the Mental Health Act or treatment are likely to be of doubtful effectiveness, and the most effective precaution cannot be taken because the defendant does not know who to warn. This consideration suggests to me that the court would be unwise to hold that there is sufficient proximity.

33. For these reasons I would uphold the judge's conclusion that there is no proximity between the defendants and Rosie. The claim in respect of her injury and death must fail and so must the claimant's brought on her own behalf. It is not therefore strictly necessary to consider the second point, namely whether the claimant can bring herself within the ambit of those who can recover damages for psychiatric injury. ...

Pill LJ: Stress has been placed upon the fact that, as in *Dorset Yacht, Hill* and *Osman*, the actions of a third party are interposed between those of the defendant and the impact on the victim. For this purpose, the victim Rosie may be treated as the victim though the further question does arise as to the position of her mother, the plaintiff. Mr Moon fairly includes amongst the facts relevant to proximity the fact that the defendants were aware that Armstrong had said that a child would be murdered after he was discharged from hospital. That being so, Mr Sherman draws attention to the injustice which arises if there is a duty of care to an identified victim (or identified by narrow category as in *Dorset Yacht*) but no duty of care when threats, even very serious ones, are made against an unidentified person or group.

The duty upon the defendant ought not to depend, it is submitted, upon whether a victim is identified. In *Thompson v County of Alameda* 614 P 2d 728, Tobriner J in his dissenting judgment in the Supreme Court of California, put it this way:

If the victim can be identified in advance, a warning to him may discharge that duty: if he cannot be identified, reasonable care may require other action. But the absence of an identifiable victim does not postulate the absence of a duty of reasonable care.

In *Caparo*, Lord Oliver cited Lord Atkin's definition of proximity in *Donoghue v Stevenson* [1932] AC 562, 581:

Such close and direct relations that the act complained of directly affects a person whom the person alleged to be bound to take care would know would be directly affected by his careless act.

Lord Oliver continued:

It must be remembered, however, that Lord Atkin was using his words in the context of loss caused by physical damage where the existence of the nexus between the careless defendant and the injured plaintiff can rarely give rise to any difficulty. To adopt the words of Bingham LJ in the instant case [1989] QB 653, 686:

it is enough that the plaintiff chances to be (out of the whole world) the person with whom the defendant collided or who purchased the offending ginger beer.

In *Caparo*, following the passage from his judgment cited by Lord Oliver, Bingham LJ in the Court of Appeal went on to say that "where careless words causing economic loss are complained of, more is required to establish proximity than the fortuity of suffering damage". It might appear to follow from the statement of Bingham LJ that, where physical damage has been caused, the fortuity of suffering damage is sufficient to establish proximity. The reluctance of the law to expose a defendant in other situations to a liability in "an indeterminate amount for an indeterminate time to an indeterminate class" (Cardozo CJ in *Ultramaris Corporation v Touche* 174 NE 441, 444) may not apply.

Upon authority, however, this is one of the cases of physical damage, described by Lord Oliver as rare, where the existence of the nexus does give rise to difficulty. There is an intervening third party. I see force in the submission that the question whether the identity of a victim is known ought not to determine whether the proximity test is passed. It is forcefully argued that the difference between the threat "I will kill X" and the threat "I will kill the first bald-headed man I meet" ought not to determine whether a duty is placed upon a defendant, though it would obviously go to the extent of the duty and the measures necessary to discharge it. The point does not arise starkly on the present facts because of the passage of time and distance between Armstrong's release and Rosie's murder.

Dorset Yacht and *Hill* are in my judgment binding authority for the proposition that, in circumstances such as the present, the identity of the victim is an important factor in deciding whether the foreseeability test is passed. That being so, I agree with Stuart-Smith LJ that, upon the facts of this case, Rosie does not pass the threshold requirement of the proximity test necessary to establish a duty of care and that the decision to strike out on that ground was correct. The obvious differences between the functions of the police and those of the defendants do not materially affect the decision on that point in the circumstances. I also agree that the decision in *Holgate v Lancashire Mentals Hospitals Board* [1937] 4 All ER 19 cannot be relied upon to establish an arguable case.

Thorpe LJ agreed with Stuart-Smith LJ.

The court went on to hold that, in any event, the plaintiff could not sustain an action for psychiatric injury as she did not fall within the rules established in *McLoughlin v O'Brian* [1983] 1 AC 410 (HL) and *Alcock v Chief Constable of South Yorkshire Police* [1991] 4 All ER 907 (HL) for claims by 'secondary victims'. She had neither witnessed the events involving her daughter nor happened upon their immediate aftermath.

The trial judge, Gage J, had denied liability also on the basis that it would not be 'just, fair and reasonable' to impose a duty of care (see [1998] Lloyd's Rep Med 447). The Court of Appeal accepted that, following the decision of the House of Lords in *Barrett v Enfield LBC* [1999] 3 All ER 193, the court was precluded from doing this at the striking out stage. In *Barrett*, the Law Lords applied the decision of the European Court of Human Rights in *Osman v UK* (1998) 5 BHRC 293 that it was a breach of art 6 of the European Convention to deny an individual a cause of action without exploring the facts: something which is not done on a 'striking out' application. This does not mean that factors relevant to the 'just, fair and reasonableness' limb cannot be taken into account at a trial and we shall return to them shortly. Instead, the Court of Appeal's decision rests firmly on a finding that in law there was no 'proximity' between the hospital and the victim.

Why was there no 'proximity'? The judges relied upon the earlier decisions in *Dorset Yacht* and *Hill*. Both Stuart-Smith and Pill LJJ considered that a special relationship or nexus had to exist between the defendant and the victim. Pill LJ, while not wholly persuaded of the point, concluded that an important aspect of this was whether the victim was known to the defendant. Stuart-Smith LJ, more broadly, also considered that an 'identifiable' victim might satisfy the 'proximity' test. The victim in *Palmer* was neither. It would not be a fair representation of the judgment to see this issue 'was the victim identified or identifiable?' as, itself, a *sufficient* condition for liability. It was, at best, a *necessary* condition only. In particular, Stuart-Smith LJ in his judgment set out a number of other important factors – the inability to warn the victim or authorities to provide protection and the limited powers of control that the defendant had over the patient. It is difficult to see why difficulties over warning an unidentified victim should *a priori* exclude a duty of care. Warning the victim is only one method by which the duty could be discharged. It may not be the only, or best, one. Why not warn the police? This was, of course, what happened in *Tarasoff* itself. As Pill LJ stated, the inability to warn the victim 'would obviously go to the extent of the duty and the measures necessary to discharge it'. Sometimes the argument is put the other way. Because the duty may be discharged by warning, which would be a breach of confidentiality, there should be no duty of care (see eg Gage J, *supra*, at 461). The answer is that, in such cases, any breach is most likely to be lawful as justified in the public interest given the serious risk of harm to another (see *infra*, ch 8). Further, the difficulties of invoking the compulsory powers of detention under the Mental Health Act 1983 may also have been overstated.

In addition, Stuart-Smith LJ specifically referred to a distinction drawn in *Dorset Yacht* between the assailant who is released from detention and causes harm and the one who is simply not caught or detained. To the extent that this suggests that the court might have taken a different view if Armstrong had been detained under the Mental Health Act 1983 and had been negligently released, it might create a false hope for claimants in future cases. The earlier decision in *Holgate v Lancashire Mental Hospitals Board* [1937] 4 All ER 19 was just such a case. Yet, both Stuart-Smith and Pill LJJ considered the case to be wrongly decided. It may be, however, that the time and geographical gap between release and causing harm in that case was significant (contrast *Dorset Yacht* (*supra*) with *Marti v Smith and Home Office* (1981) 131 NLJ 1028). On the facts of *Palmer*, Pill LJ noted as important 'the passage of time and distance between Armstrong's release and Rosie's murder'.

In the result, the court left the law uncertain for the future. There must be more than a sneaking suspicion that the judges would, if the facts were to present themselves, agree with Gage J that liability would arise if 'there existed some distinctive feature or characteristic which demonstrated that [the victim] was at some special risk' ([1998] Lloyd's Rep Med 447 at 461). It remains unclear whether a singled-out victim would be necessary or one of a small group could sue, eg children at school where a known dangerous psychiatric patient or paedophile works. Arguably, there is no distinction that could properly be drawn on the basis of 'proximity' (for a discussion of the US case law, see *Emerich v Philadelphia Center for Human Development Inc* (1998) 720 A 2d 1032 (Pa Sup Ct) – liability to known victim).

Finally, we should look at the issue of 'public policy', which the Court of Appeal did not address because of *Barrett* but Gage J at first instance did ([1998] Lloyd's Rep Med 447):

Gage J: Mr Sherman submits that considerations such as the need to avoid the possibility of doctors practising defensive medicine, in the event of a duty of care being imposed and the burden on health authorities' limited resources if such a duty were to exist are not sufficiently powerful to counter the requirements of justice. He further submits that I should adopt the incremental approach to the issue. The submission was that a finding that a duty of care existed in this case, or arguable existed, would not open the floodgates to other such claims. He submits that the beauty of the incremental approach is that each set of circumstances can be considered on a case by case basis without the danger of the floodgates being opened. The court could limit the duty of care to cases which solely involved death or the most serious injuries.

Attractive as Mr Sherman's arguments are on this issue, having carefully considered them I cannot accept them as correct. While recognizing that the common law should not be frozen in a rigid posture nor be halted by a conservative approach (per Lords Bridge and Scarman in *McLoughlin v O'Brian* [1983] 1 AC 410) in my judgment there are powerful counter arguments. It has to be recognised that one is here dealing with a case where the injuries were caused not directly by the negligence of the defendants but by the activities of a third party.

Mr Moon has pointed to some of the counter considerations. I am not convinced that recognition that health authorities owed a duty of care would lead towards higher standards of medical care, as Mr Sherman submitted. As Lord Keith pointed out in *Hill's* case, on the whole public duty motivates police forces. The same applies to doctors. There is a considerable danger that doctors, to avoid being sued, might lean towards defensive medicine.

To hold that a duty of care existed in such circumstances would considerably widen the category of potential claimants. In my judgment it would be bound to lead to an increase in claims against health authorities and would require them to investigate and deal with such claims. Again, as Lord Keith pointed out in *Hill's* case, the result would be a significant diversion of manpower and attention from health authorities' primary function of caring for patients …

Finally, the plaintiff is not left without any remedy. She is entitled to and has made a claim for compensation from the Criminal Injuries Compensation Board. I realise that obtaining compensation almost certainly comes very low on her list of priorities. I recognise that what she seeks is justice in the form of a judgment against those whom she regards as responsible for this tragic and terrible crime. But it remains the fact that she, as do other victims of crime, has the right to make a claim to the Board.

The judge merely asserted these factors as being relevant. The spectre of the opening of the 'floodgates' and its implications for the defendant's resources is frequently relied upon but is never empirically proven. It is commonly relied upon in actions against the police (eg *Hill*) but it is difficult to see, if relevant in *Palmer*, that it does not also impact upon medical negligence actions in general where it is simply not relied upon by the courts (for a discussion see the different approaches in the Court of Appeal in *M v Newham HA* [1994] 4 All ER 602 (CA)).

(b) Transmission of infectious diseases

Suppose a doctor who failed to diagnose that a patient suffered from an infectious or sexually transmitted disease or otherwise failed to advise the patient of their infection and the patient infected another. Would the doctor owe that other person a duty of care? There do not appear to be any directly relevant English cases. However, the issue has arisen in a number of US decisions (see *Annotation* 3 ALR 5th 370). Clearly, the courts will be concerned to restrict the scope of any potential duty, as we saw in the case of dangerous psychiatric patients. Hence, the likelihood is that only those specifically at risk or even known to the doctor will have any chance of establishing a claim. The nature of this group will depend upon the kind of 'danger' posed by the patient. So, for example, sexually transmitted diseases will affect sexual partners, whilst infectious diseases will affect a broader category of persons close to the patient. The former might be seen in usual circumstances as a small contained group; the latter may not and the courts will, in all probability, restrict the duty (if it exists at all) to close family members (see eg *Gammell v United States* (1984) 727 F 2d 950 (10th Cir) (hepatitis); *Bradshaw v Daniels* (1993) 854 SW 2d 865 (Tenn S Ct) (exposure to ticks causing rocky mountain fever)).

An important contemporary illustration of the legal problems arises in cases where the patient is HIV positive or infected with hepatitis B or C and transmits that to their current (or future) sexual partner. Could the sexual partner sue the doctor for failing to warn him or the patient of the danger?

DiMarco v Lynch Homes – Chester County, Inc (1989) 525 Pa 558 (Sup Ct of Pennsylvania)

Larson J: This appeal presents the issue of whether a physician owes a duty of care to a third party where the physician fails to properly advise a patient who has been exposed to a communicable disease, and the patient, relying upon the advice, spreads the disease to the third party.

On June 18, 1985, Janet Viscichini, a blood technician, went to the Lynch Home in Kimberton, Pennsylvania, to take a blood sample from one of the residents. During the procedure, the patient struck or kicked Ms Viscichini, whose skin was accidentally punctured by the needle which she had used to take blood from the patient. When Ms Viscichini learned that the patient was a carrier of hepatitis and other diseases, she immediately sought treatment from Doctors Giunta and Alwine, appellants herein. The appellants advised her that if she remained symptom free for six weeks, she would not have been infected by the hepatitis virus. Ms Viscichini was not told to refrain from sexual relations for any period of time following her exposure to the disease, but she practiced sexual abstinence until eight weeks after the exposure. As she had remained symptom free during that time, she resumed sexual relations with appellee, Joseph DiMarco, to whom she was not married. In September of 1985, Ms Viscichini was diagnosed as suffering from hepatitis B; in December of 1985, appellee was diagnosed as having the same disease.

Appellee brought an action in the Court of Common Pleas of Philadelphia County against appellants and the Lynch Home. Among appellee's claims is the assertion that it was negligent for the appellants not to have warned Ms Viscichini that having sexual relations within six months of the exposure could cause her sexual partner to contract hepatitis. The trial court granted appellants' preliminary objections and dismissed appellee's complaint with prejudice on the ground that the appellants owed appellee no duty of care because there was no privity between appellee and the appellants. The trial court suggested, however, that a duty may be owed under these facts where the patient and the third party are married.

Appellee filed an appeal to Superior Court, which reversed, holding that the appellants "had a duty to act reasonably in advising [Viscichini] regarding her ability to transmit her communicable disease." *DiMarco v Lynch Homes – Chester County, Inc*, 384 Pa Super 463, 474 n 3, 559 A 2d 530, 535 n 3 (1989). ...

We granted the appellants' petition for allowance of appeal, and we now affirm the decision of the Superior Court. ...

In the instant case, appellee averred in his complaint that he contracted hepatitis after he had intimate relations with a woman who had been exposed to hepatitis eight weeks prior to the sexual relations; that this woman had been told by her doctors, appellants herein, that if she remained symptom free for six weeks, she would not have been infected by the hepatitis virus; that in reliance upon that advice, the woman abstained from sexual relations for eight weeks; and that the advice of the appellants was wrong in that the waiting period should have been twenty-six weeks. ...

When a physician treats a patient who has been exposed to or who has contracted a communicable and/or contagious disease, it is imperative that the physician give his or her patient the proper advice about preventing the spread of the disease. Communicable diseases are so named because they are readily spread from person to person. Physicians are the first line of defense against the spread of communicable diseases, because physicians know what measures must be taken to prevent the infection of others. The patient must be advised to take certain sanitary measures, or to remain quarantined for a period of time, or to practice sexual abstinence or what is commonly referred to as "safe sex."

Such precautions are taken not to protect the health of the patient, whose well-being has already been compromised, rather such precautions are taken to safeguard the health of others. Thus, the duty of a physician in such circumstances extends to those "within the foreseeable orbit of risk of harm." *Doyle v South Pittsburgh Water Co*, 414 Pa 199, 207, 199 A 2d 875, 878 (1964). If a third person is in that class of persons whose health is likely to be threatened by the patient, and if erroneous advice is given to that patient to the ultimate detriment of the third person, the third person has a cause of action against the physician, because the physician should recognize that the services rendered to the patient are necessary for the protection of the third person.

As Superior Court Judge Frank J Montemuro, Jr, writing for the majority, so cogently noted:

[T]his case involves a communicable disease. It hardly needs to be said that the prevention and control of communicable diseases is a momentous task which is of the utmost importance to the health and welfare of our citizens. The Disease Prevention and Control Law of 1955 requires a physician who treats or examines a person suffering from or who is suspected of having a communicable disease to make a prompt report to the local board of health or, if necessary, to the State Health Center of the Department. See 35 PS @ 521.3; 28 Pa Code @ 27.21(a) and (b). We note that 28 Pa Code @27.115 specifically requires physicians to report cases of Hepatitis B. Further, several provisions of the Pennsylvania Code set forth procedures to be followed to prevent the contamination of our blood banks with blood from donors who suffer from or may have been exposed to viral hepatitis. See 28 Pa Code @25.71 and 30.30(7)(i).

384 Pa Super 463, 470, 559 A 2d 530, 533 (1989) (footnote omitted).

Clearly, such measures are mandated by law specifically to protect third persons who will come into contact with those who have been exposed to or who have contracted a communicable disease.

We find, therefore, on the basis of the averments set forth in appellee's complaint, that appellee has stated a cause of action against the appellants. We further hold that the class of persons whose health is likely to be threatened by the patient includes any one who is physically intimate with the patient. Those, like the trial court, who insist that we cannot predict, or foresee, that a patient will engage in sexual activity outside of the marital relationship and that thus, we need not protect those who engage in "casual" sex, are exalting an unheeded morality over reality.

Notice the extent of the duty: it was owed to 'anyone who is physically intimate with the patient'.

Contrast the approach of the minority justices.

Flaherty J: In this case ... the professional service was not performed for the third party, and the doctor did not even know of the existence of the third party. Thus, there was neither privity nor a specific undertaking in favor of the third party and in the absence of privity or specific undertaking, the doctors had no duty of care, and thus no liability, with respect to DiMarco ... the dangers of adopting a negligence concept of duty analyzed in terms of scope of the risk or foreseeability are considerable and are to be avoided. These dangers include not only the imposition of liability in favor of third parties in situations which are beyond the control of the professional rendering the service, but also the prospect of including professionals to narrow their inquires into the client or patient situation, to the detriment of the client or patient, so as to avoid possible liability toward third parties which might come from knowing "too much".

In two footnotes, Flaherty J sets out his objections to extending a professional liability to third parties:

n3 The professional has no control over the client's or patient's disclosures of professional advice, the third parties to whom the advice is disclosed, the nature or circumstances of the communications, the accuracy of what is disclosed, the number of persons to whom disclosures are made, or when disclosures are made. Thus, the professional, under the majority's view, would be subject to an unpredictable number of suits filed by an unpredictable number of persons, some or all of who may be unknown to the professional, at almost any time, claiming that they learned of and relied on the . . .

and then he stated:

n4 The more a professional knows about his client's or patient's situation, the more likely he is to be able to render valuable services, but also the more likely it is that he will learn things which may affect third parties. If liability were imposed for harm which might befall one or more of these third parties, a professional would be forced to analyze each client or patient situation with respect to potential third party risk and to speculate as to the nature, seriousness, likelihood, frequency of risk, the patient's circumstances which might trigger the risk, and the third parties who might be exposed to risk. Obviously, such an undertaking would require much more information from the client or patient, would be very costly and time consuming, and would inevitably result in the sort of narrowing of inquiry referred to above.
      Nix CJ and Zappala J agreed with Flaherty J.

You may think that the approach of the dissenting justices resonates more with English law *unless* an identifiable or identified victim exists. The US courts have, nevertheless, held that the duty could extend to future sexual partners.

Reisner v Regents of the University of California (1995) 31 Cal App 4th 1110 (Cal CA)

Miriam A Vogel AJ: The day after 12-year-old Jennifer Lawson received a transfusion, her doctor discovered the blood was contaminated with HIV antibodies. Although the same doctor continued to treat Jennifer, he never told her or her parents about the tainted blood. Three years later, Jennifer started dating Daniel Reisner and they became intimate. Two years later, the doctor told Jennifer she had AIDS and Jennifer told Daniel. A month later, Jennifer died. Shortly thereafter, Daniel discovered he was HIV positive. Daniel sued Jennifer's doctor and others for negligence ...

Discussion

When the avoidance of foreseeable harm to a third person requires a defendant to control the conduct of a person with whom the defendant has a special relationship (such as physician and patient) or to warn the person of the risks involved in certain conduct, the defendant's duty extends to a third person with whom the defendant does not have a special relationship. (*Tarasoff v Regents of University of California* (1976) 17 Cal 3d 425, 434–436, 131 Cal Rptr 14, 551 P 2d 334.) Dr Fonklesrud and UCLA concede as much but contend this rule does not create a duty where, as here, the third person is both unknown and unidentifiable. We disagree. ...

For several reasons, it is immaterial that, in *Tarasoff*, the therapist knew the identity of his patient's intended victim whereas, in this case, Defendants did not know Daniel or even that he existed.

A.

First, *Tarasoff* dictates the result in our case by holding that the doctor's duty includes the duty to warn "others likely to apprise the victim of the danger ... or to take whatever ... steps are reasonably necessary under the circumstances." (*Tarasoff v Regents of University of California, supra,* 17 Cal 3d at p 431, 131 Cal Rptr 14, 551 P 2d 334.) Daniel does not claim Defendants had to warn *him*, only that they had to warn *Jennifer or her parents,* "others [who were] likely to apprise [him] of the danger" (and, of course, did just that when they learned of it).

B.

Second, there is the case of *Myers v Quesenberry* (1983) 144 Cal App 3d 888, 193 Cal Rptr 733. In *Myers*, two physicians (Quesenberry and Beaumont) were treating a pregnant patient (Hansen) for diabetes.. During an examination at Quesenberry's office, the doctor concluded the fetus had died. When Quesenberry told Hansen to have the dead fetus removed within 18 hours, Hansen became emotionally upset. "The doctors then directed Hansen to drive immediately to [a local hospital] for preliminary laboratory tests. Hansen lost control of her car due to a diabetic attack and struck Myers as he was standing by the side of the road." (*Id.* at pp 890–891, 193 Cal Rptr 733.) Myers sued the doctors. The trial court sustained the doctors' demurrer without leave to amend and the issue on appeal was whether they owed a duty to Myers, with whom they had no relationship, for failing to warn their patient of the foreseeable and dangerous consequences of engaging in the conduct which caused Myers's injuries. (*Id.* at p 890, 193 Cal Rptr 733.)

The Court of Appeal reversed, holding (among other things) that "the fact that Myers was a foreseeable but not a readily identifiable victim of Hansen's driving does not preclude him from stating an action against the doctors for negligently failing to warn her not to drive in an irrational and uncontrolled diabetic condition. *As a practical matter, the doctors here could not have effectively warned Myers of the danger presented by Hansen's driving. ... However, they could easily have warned Hansen not to drive because of her irrational and uncontrolled diabetic condition. Under the facts as alleged here, this probably would not have been a futile act.* Having otherwise complied with her doctors' professional recommendations, Hansen presumably would have continued to follow their advice had they warned her not to drive. ... On these pleadings, we cannot factually presume Hansen would have ignored the doctors' warning. *Thus, under these circumstances where warning the actor is a reasonable step to take in the exercise of the standard of care applicable to physicians ..., liability is not conditioned on potential victims being readily identifiable as well as foreseeable.*" (*Myers v Quesenberry, supra,* 144 Cal App 3d at pp 892–893, 193 Cal Rptr 733, emphasis added.)

Similarly, on the pleadings before us, where warning Jennifer would have been a reasonable step to take in the exercise of the standard of care applicable to physicians, Defendants' liability is not conditional upon Daniel's identity being known or ascertainable, and we cannot factually presume Jennifer or her parents would have ignored Defendants' warning. According to Daniel's complaint, as soon as Jennifer and her parents discovered Jennifer had AIDS, Daniel was immediately notified. As a result, it appears a timely warning to Jennifer probably would have prevented Daniel's injury.

We reject Defendants' efforts to distinguish *Myers* by suggesting there is no "immediate temporal connection" here as there was in *Myers* (where the doctors *told* their patient to *immediately* drive to the hospital) – because Defendants did not *tell* Jennifer to become intimate with Daniel and because at least *three years* "elapsed between the negligent act and [Daniel's] injury." This analysis begs the question. Dr Fonklesrud maintained a physician-patient relationship with Jennifer until she died, which was after Daniel's injury. Just as Dr Fonklesrud knew or reasonably should have known that Jennifer was likely to get AIDS as a result of the contaminated blood, he knew or reasonably should have known that, as she matured, Jennifer was likely to enter an intimate relationship. What happened to Daniel as a result of Defendants' failure to warn Jennifer was just as foreseeable as what happened to Mr Myers – which is why we reject Defendants' euphemistic effort to limit liability on an artificial and immaterial basis.

C.

Third, the facts of this case compel a conclusion designed to encourage the highest standard of care concerning communicable and infectious diseases, and Defendants' arguments to the contrary are red herrings ...

Civil liability for a negligent failure to warn under the circumstances of this case may not hasten the day when AIDS can be cured or prevented but it may, in the meantime, protect one or more persons from unnecessary exposure to this deadly virus.

3.

We summarily reject Defendants' alternative suggestion that a physician ought not to owe *any* duty to a third person because such a duty could adversely affect the doctor's treatment of his patient, to whom his primary duty is owed. As explained above, existing California law already imposes a duty to third persons and the only arguably "new" issue in this case is whether that duty is the same when the third person's identity is unknown to the physician and not readily ascertainable. And, contrary to Defendants' contention, the duty involved in this case – a duty to warn a contagious patient to take steps to protect others – has nothing to do with a physician's decision about how to treat his patient or with a physician's potential liability for the unauthorized disclosure of AIDS test results. (Health & Saf Code, § 199.20

et seq.) Once the physician warns the patient of the risk to others and advises the patient how to prevent the spread of the disease, the physician has fulfilled his duty – and no more (but no less) is required.

4.

We also reject Defendants' suggestion that we ought not to find a duty is owed to Daniel because it would necessarily follow that a duty would be owed to "other persons with whom [Daniel] had sex, and the persons with whom they had sex," and so on ad infinitum. Why? Because "insurance premiums would soar and, quite likely, coverage at any price would not exist long." There are at least two reasons for rejecting this argument.

First, it presumes too much. Arguments premised on opened floodgates and broken dams are not persuasive where, as here, we suspect that only a few drops of water may spill onto a barren desert. To actually recover in this case, Daniel will be required to prove (not merely allege) that a physician and a teaching hospital, knowing they had inadvertently infected a patient with a contagious disease that is almost always deadly, failed to tell her what had happened and failed to warn her about the danger in infecting her loved ones. Daniel will also have to prove causation – not just that Jennifer would have told him about her illness and that he would then have refrained from intimate contact with her but also that he could not have acquired the disease elsewhere. We recognize the sympathetic nature of Daniel's case and the probability that jurors might be inclined to construe the evidence in favor of a young man and against those whose negligence probably sentenced him to death. But the very facts which favor Daniel in this case show how unlikely it is that there are dozens of other Daniels waiting in the wings.

Second, the argument goes too far. We need not decide in this case what the result would be if someone infected by Daniel sued the doctor who failed to warn Jennifer, and the fact that a duty is owed to Daniel does not mean it will be extended without limitation. However, the possibility of such an extension does not offend us, legally or morally. Viewed in the abstract (and *not* with reference to Jennifer or Daniel), we believe that a doctor who knows he is dealing with the 20th Century version of Typhoid Mary ought to have a very strong incentive to tell his patient what she ought to do and not do and how she ought to comport herself in order to prevent the spread of her disease. In any event, the doctor's liability to fourth and fifth persons would by its nature be limited by traditional causation principles. (*Nola M v University of Southern California* (1993) 16 Cal App 4th 421, 427–428, 20 Cal Rptr 2d 97.)

In short, we see no reason to limit duty in this particular case …

Ortega, Acting PJ and Masterson J concurred.

The California Court of Appeal identified positive policy reasons for imposing a *duty to warn the patient* based upon public health concerns. The court saw no conflict in this with the doctor's duties to the patient, including respecting his confidences because no breach was contemplated. Indeed, given the development of drug combinations which may have significant therapeutic benefits to patients who are HIV positive, the duty to warn the patient is in her interest also. Notice the court rejected, rightly, the argument of the defendants that finding for the plaintiff would open up claims by others who were not the sexual partners of the patient. No doubt an English court would express the point in less florid terms than Vogel J, but it would undoubtedly come to the same conclusion, that 'second-' or 'third-hand' actions were simply too remote. It would give rise to a duty owed potentially to the public at large.

There is no English case like *Di Marco* and *Reisner*. The public health policy arguments that featured prominently in the courts' reasoning ought, it is suggested, to point the way for an English court. The only English case that could be relevant does, however, on the face of it not bode well for such claims. The case did not concern the transmission of an infectious disease. Rather, it concerned a claim for damages for the birth of a healthy child following a failed vasectomy. The plaintiff was not the patient of the defendant. Instead, she was a future sexual (and domestic) partner of the patient. She claimed that the defendant's failure to advise her partner (the patient) of the risk of reversal of his vasectomy led him, and her, not to take additional contraceptive precautions to avoid pregnancy. Her claim failed.

Goodwill v British Pregnancy Advisory Service [1996] 2 All ER 161 (CA)

Peter Gibson LJ: Miss Booth put her case on duty of care in this way. A, a doctor, voluntarily agrees to provide a service for B, which includes performing an operation and giving informed advice about the possible consequences of that operation. The purpose of that operation is to render B permanently sterile. It is reasonably foreseeable and accepted that the doctor owes a duty of care to that person's current partner. It is further foreseeable in today's society that the patient may have sexual relations with another partner. It is therefore merely an incremental extension of the law to extend to that partner the duty owed by A to B when A provides the service for B.

In support of that submission Miss Booth referred to the familiar remarks of Lord Morris in *Hedley Byrne & Co Ltd v Heller & Partners Ltd* [1963] 2 All ER 575 at 594, [1964] AC 465 at 502–503:

'My lords, I consider that it follows and that it should now be regarded as settled that if someone possessed of a special skill undertakes, quite irrespective of contract, to apply that skill for the assistance of another person who relies on such skill, a duty of care will arise. The fact that the service is to be given by means of, or by the instrumentality of, words can make no difference. Furthermore, if, in a sphere in which a person is so placed that others could reasonably rely on his judgment or his skill or on his ability to make careful inquiry, a person takes it on himself to give information or advice to, or allows his information or advice to be passed on to, another person who, as he knows or should know, will place reliance on it, then a duty of care will arise.'

In *Henderson v Merrett Syndicates Ltd, Hallam-Eames v Merrett Syndicates Ltd, Hughes v Merrett Syndicates Ltd, Arbuthnott v Feltrim Underwriting Agencies Ltd, Deeny v Gooda Walker Ltd (in liq)* [1994] 3 All ER 506 at 518–519, [1995] 2 AC 145 at 178 Lord Goff referred to that passage and to certain others from the speech of Lord Devlin in *Hedley Byrne* as stating the governing principles.

Miss Booth also relied on *White v Jones* [1995] 1 All ER 691, [1995] 2 AC 207 as providing an example of an analogous situation in which a duty of care has been recognised. In that case a solicitor who was instructed to prepare a will but delayed in carrying out his instructions was held to owe a duty of care to the intended beneficiaries. She submitted that a woman who had a sexual relationship with Mr MacKinlay is in an analogous position to the intended beneficiaries under the will, because just as the solicitor was employed to confer a benefit (in the form of bequests) on a particular class of people (the beneficiaries), so the doctor is employed to confer a benefit (not getting pregnant) on a particular class of people (women who have sexual relationships with Mr MacKinlay). I admire the ingenuity of the suggested analogy, but I have to say that I am wholly unpersuaded that the analogy is real.

It must be recognised that *White v Jones* belonged to an unusual class of cases. A remedy in tort was fashioned to overcome the rank injustice that the only persons who might have a valid claim (the testator and his estate) had suffered no loss and the only persons who had suffered a loss (the disappointed beneficiaries) had no claim. I do not see any comparable injustice in the present case. On the contrary, it might be said that to give a remedy to the plaintiff against the defendants in the circumstances of the present case would not be fair, just or reasonable. The doctor who performs a vasectomy on a man on his instructions cannot realistically be described as employed to confer a benefit on the man's sexual partners in the form of avoiding pregnancy. Still less can he be so described when he is giving advice on tests after the operation. The doctor is concerned only with the man, his patient, and possibly that man's wife or partner if the doctor intends her to receive and she receives advice from the doctor in relation to the vasectomy and the subsequent tests. Whether the avoidance of pregnancy is a benefit or a disadvantage to a sexual partner of the man will depend on her circumstances. If the existence of that partner is known to the doctor and the doctor is aware that she wishes not to become pregnant by the man and the vasectomy is carried out to meet her wish as well as the man's wish, it may be said that the doctor is employed to confer that benefit on her. But that is not this case. In any event, in this case no complaint is made of the vasectomy: it is only the advice following the vasectomy that the doctor gave the man that is the subject of complaint. I cannot accept that the present is a *White v Jones* type of case at all.

Miss Booth also drew our attention to *Thake v Maurice* [1986] 1 All ER 497, [1986] QB 644, which is the case closest to the present one on its facts. That was a successful action in contract and in tort by a husband and wife whom the defendant surgeon had failed to warn of the slight risk that the husband's vasectomy might not leave him permanently sterile. But in that case advice on the husband's vasectomy was given directly to him and his wife, and both signed upon by her without independent inquiry. The defendants could know nothing about the likely course of action of future sexual partners of Mr MacKinlay.

In my judgment on the plaintiff's pleadings the defendants were not in a sufficient or any special relationship with the plaintiff such as gives rise to a duty of care. I cannot see that it can properly be said of the defendants that they voluntarily assumed responsibility to the plaintiff when giving advice to Mr MacKinlay. At that time they had no knowledge of her, she was not an existing sexual partner of Mr MacKinlay but was merely, like any other woman in the world, a potential future sexual partner of his, that is to say a member of an indeterminately large class of females who might have sexual relations with Mr MacKinlay during his lifetime. I find it impossible to believe that the policy of the law is or should be to treat so tenuous a relationship between the adviser and the advisee as giving rise to a duty of care, and there is no analogous situation recognised as giving rise to that duty …

Thorpe LJ: … The reality is that the doctor advised Mr MacKinlay. They are in reality the adviser and the advisee. The plaintiff is no nearer the doctor adviser than one who some three and a half years after the operation commenced a sexual relationship with his patient. Equally, the class to which the plaintiff belongs is in my judgment potentially excessive in size and uncertain in character. Thirdly, the state of knowledge of the adviser militates against the plaintiff. The doctor in the circumstances regards himself as advising the patient, if a married man, the patient's wife. It cannot be said that he knows or ought to know that he also advises any future sexual partners of his patient who chance to receive his advice at second hand. Presented with such a set of facts a doctor is entitled to scorn the suggestion that he owes a duty of care to such a band so uncertain in nature and extent and over such an indefinite future span. Finally, I consider that the plaintiff fails the test of reliance. In reality a woman exploring the development of a sexual relationship with a new partner takes much on trust before experience corroborates or exposes his assurances. Her responsibility is to protect herself against unwanted conception and to take independent advice on whatever facts he presents. Thus I conclude that on an analysis of the pleadings alone the plaintiff's claim discloses no reasonable course of action.

It might be thought curious that the court should analyse the case on the basis that the claim was for economic loss. It was not: the plaintiff had suffered 'personal injury' (see *Walkin v South Manchester HA*) [1995] 4 All ER 132 (CA) and Commentary, (1996) 4 Med L Rev 94 (AG)). Of course, this approach increased the plaintiff's difficulties in establishing a duty of care because of the narrow rules for claiming such loss, especially after *Caparo*. The outcome in the case is, however, explicable. The plaintiff did not rely (see Thorpe LJ) on the defendant's advice. Nor, more importantly at the 'duty' stage rather than for 'causation', would the defendant reasonably expect a future sexual partner to do so. Taking contraceptive measures is, more appropriately, a personal responsibility. The same could, however, be argued for avoiding transmission of sexual diseases such as HIV and, indeed, personal responsibility is an important aspect of the government's public health strategy in this context. Nevertheless, the risk of pregnancy remains a much greater risk than transmission of disease when sexual intercourse takes place. It may well be that we have not yet reached the stage where society *expects* everyone to take personal responsibility especially if the relationship is a long-term one (see Commentary, (1997) 5 Med L Rev 250 (AG)). As we shall see later (*infra*, ch 12), the House of Lords in *McFarlane v Tayside Health Board* [1999] 4 All ER 961 subsequently held that no one (current or future partner of the patient) could bring a claim for the costs of raising a healthy child. This turned upon the nature of the 'wrongful conception' claim rather than the issue of liability to third parties. The importance of *Goodwill* is nevertheless somewhat diminished.

One difference between *Reisner* and *Goodwill* is that, in the former case, the doctor actually created the risk to the plaintiff. He did, you will remember, infect the patient. By contrast, it would be difficult to say that in *Goodwill*, where he failed to advise that nature might reverse the effects of the procedure. The distinction between the defendant who *creates* the risk to the third party and the one who merely allows the risk to continue unabated is often a factually difficult one to draw. It may, however, be one that the court looks to as one which embodies an intuitively felt moral distinction that should be reflected in legal responsibility (see *Hill, supra*). That the defendant created (or increased) the risk of injury to the claimant is important legally, but it is not crucial. If it were, it would make actions based upon the defendant's omission difficult, if not impossible. Also, it is a distinction riddled with practical difficulties of application which would lead the courts to draw lines so fine that the law would run the risk of falling into disrepute.

(c) Genetic conditions

It is increasingly possible for medicine to identify genetic conditions which can be inherited. As a consequence, the diagnosis of a genetic condition in an individual may have health implications for that individual's children or siblings. They too may have inherited the condition. It may be important for them to be aware of this so that they may seek medical advice and, if possible, treatment that may prevent the onset of the inherited condition, slow down its onset or alleviate its symptoms. What, if any, duty of care would a doctor owe the family member of a patient diagnosed with such a genetic condition? To advise that individual of the possibility of their having the genetic condition would, without the consent of the patient, be a breach of confidence. Alternatively, it may be feasible to advise the patient that the issue should be raised with the family member. No English case has yet involved a claim by a family member who has suffered injury as a result of not discovering their genetic condition. The potential for such a claim exists certainly, the identity of claimants may be well within the doctor's knowledge. Other members of the family may even be the doctor's own patients if he is a GP. That a duty of care could arise was accepted by the court in the following American case.

Safer v Pack (1996) 677 A 2d 1188 (NJ Sup Ct, App Div)

Kestin JAD: Donna Safer's claim arises from the patient-physician relationship in the 1950s and 1960s between her father, Robert Batkin, a resident of New Jersey, and Dr George T Pack, also a resident of New Jersey, who practiced medicine and surgery in New York City and treated Mr Batkin there. It is alleged that Dr Pack specialized in the treatment and removal of cancerous tumors and growths.

In November 1956, Mr Batkin was admitted to the hospital with a pre-operative diagnosis of retroperitoneal cancer. A week later, Dr Pack performed a total colectomy and an ileosigmoidectomy for multiple polyposis of the colon with malignant degeneration in one area. The discharge summary noted the finding in a pathology report of the existence of adenocarcinoma developing in an intestinal polyp, and diffuse intestinal polyposis "from one end of the colon to the other." Dr Pack continued to treat Mr Batkin postoperatively.

In October 1961, Mr Batkin was again hospitalized. Dr Pack performed an ileoabdominal perineal resection with an ileostomy. The discharge summary reported pathology findings of "ulcerative adenocarcinoma of colon Grade II with metastases to Levels II and III" and "adenomatous polyps." Dr Pack again continued to treat Mr Batkin postoperatively. He also developed a physician-patient relationship with Mrs Batkin relative to the diagnosis and treatment of a vaginal ulcer.

In December 1963, Mr Batkin was hospitalized once again at Dr Pack's direction. The carcinoma of the colon had metastasized to the liver with secondary jaundice and probable retroperitoneal disease causing pressure on the sciatic nerve plexus. After some treatment, Mr Batkin died on January 3, 1964, at forty-five years of age. Donna was ten years old at the time of her father's death. Her sister was seventeen.

In February 1990, Donna Safer, then thirty-six years of age and newly married, residing in Connecticut, began to experience lower abdominal pain. Examinations and tests revealed a cancerous blockage of the colon and multiple polyposis. In March, Ms Safer underwent a total abdominal colectomy with ileorectal anastamosis. A primary carcinoma in the sigmoid colon was found to extend through the serosa of the bowel and multiple polyps were seen throughout the entire bowel. Because of the detection of additional metastatic adenocarcinoma and carcinoma, plaintiff's left ovary was also removed. Between April 1990 and mid-1991, Ms Safer underwent chemotherapy treatment.

In September 1991, plaintiffs obtained Robert Batkin's medical records, from which they learned that he had suffered from polyposis. Their complaint was filed in March 1992, alleging a violation of duty (professional negligence) on the part of Dr Pack in his failure to warn of the risk to Donna Safer's health.

Plaintiffs contend that multiple polyposis is a hereditary condition that, if undiscovered and untreated, invariably leads to metastatic colorectal cancer. They contend, further, that the hereditary nature of the disease was known at the time Dr Pack was treating Mr Batkin and that the physician was required, by medical standards then prevailing, to warn those at risk so that they might have the benefits of early examination, monitoring, detection and treatment, that would provide opportunity to avoid the most baneful consequences of the condition.

The summary judgment proceeding in the trial court was based upon a scanty record, largely comprised of hospital records. Dr Pack himself had died in 1969; none of his individual records were before the court. The reports of the parties' medical experts and a deposition of plaintiffs' expert were submitted. Ida Batkin, Donna Safer's mother, had also given a deposition in which she testified, among other details, that neither her husband nor Dr Pack had ever told her that Mr Batkin suffered from cancer; and that, throughout the courses of surgery and treatment, Dr Pack advised her that he was treating a "blockage" or an unspecified "infection". On the one or two occasions when Mrs Batkin inquired of Dr Pack whether the "infection" would affect her children, she was told not to worry.

In dismissing, the trial court held that a physician had no "legal duty to warn a child of a patient of a genetic risk[.]" In the absence of any evidence whether Dr Pack had warned Mr Batkin to provide information concerning his disease for the benefit of his children, the motion judge "assumed that Dr Pack did not tell Robert Batkin of the genetic disease."

The motion judge's reasoning proceeded from the following legal premise: "in order for a doctor to have a duty to warn, there must be a patient/physician relationship or circumstances requiring the protection of the public health or the community [at] large." Finding no physician-patient relationship between Dr Pack and his patient's daughter Donna, the court then held genetically transmissible diseases to differ from contagious or infectious diseases or threats of harm in respect of the duty to warn, because "the harm is already present within the non-patient child, as opposed to being introduced, by a patient who was not warned to stay away. The patient is taking no action in which to cause the child harm."

The motion judge relied on *Pate v Threlkel*, 640 So 2d 183 (Fla Dist Ct App 1994), as the only "on point" authority respecting genetically transmissible disease. In holding that a physician owed the patient's child no duty to warn, the Florida Court of Appeals had expressly rejected the general approach of the New Jersey Supreme Court in *Schroeder v Perkel*, 87 NJ 53, 63–65, 432 A 2d 834 (1981), on related questions of foreseeability and duty.

The Florida Supreme Court has since dealt with the issue, reaching a contrary conclusion. Because the case had initially been decided on defendants' motions to dismiss the complaint for failure to state a cause of action, the Supreme Court was required to:

> accept as true the [plaintiffs'] allegations that pursuant to the prevailing standard of care, the health care providers were under a duty to warn [the patient] of the importance of testing her children for [the genetically transmissible]carcinoma.

[Id at 281]

The court held:

> When the prevailing standard of care creates a duty that is obviously for the benefit of certain identified third parties and the physician knows of the existence of those third parties, then the physician's duty runs to those third parties … we hold that privity does not bar Heidi Pate's pursuit of a medical malpractice action. Our holding is likewise in accord with *McCain v Florida Power Corp*, 593 So 2d 500 (Fla 1992) because under the duty alleged in this case, a patient's children fall within the zone of foreseeable risk.
>
> Our holding should not be read to require the physician to warn the patient's children of the disease. In most instances the physician is prohibited from disclosing the patient's medical condition to others except with the patient's permission. See @ 455.241 (2), Fla Stat (1989). Moreover, the patient ordinarily can be expected to pass on the warning. To require the physician to seek out and warn various members of the patient's family would often be difficult or impractical and would place too heavy a burden upon the physician. Thus, we emphasize that in any circumstances in which the physician has a duty to warn of a genetically transferable disease, that duty will be satisfied by warning the patient.

Pate v Threlkel supra 661 So 2d at 282

Because the issue before us arose on a motion for summary judgment, we, too, are obliged to accept plaintiffs' proffer through their medical expert that the prevailing standard of care at the time Dr Pack treated Mr Batkin required the physician to warn of the known genetic threat. The legal standard of care, knowledge and skill is that which is "ordinarily possessed and exercised in similar situations by the average member of the profession practicing in the field." ...

Whether the conduct of a practitioner in established circumstances at a particular time comported with prevailing standards of care is pre-eminently a question to be determined by the finder of fact, not an issue of law to be resolved by the court. *Campo v Tama*, 133 NJ 123, 133, 627 A 2d 135 (1993); *Lopez v Swyer*, 115 NJ Super 237, 251, 279 A 2d 116 (App Div 1971), affd, 62 NJ 267, 300 A 2d 563 (1973). Where, as here, a genuine issue of fact in this regard is presented, the matter is not amenable to resolution on summary judgment. *Brill v Guardian Life Ins Co of America*, 142 NJ 520, 528–30, 536–37, 666 A 2d 146 (1995); *Judson v Peoples Bank & Trust Co of Westfield*, 17 NJ 67, 73–77, 110 A 2d 24 (1954); R 4:46–2.

Whether a legal duty exists is, however, a matter of law ... we see no impediment, legal or otherwise, to recognizing a physician's duty to warn those known to be at risk of avoidable harm from a genetically transmissible condition. In terms of foreseeability especially, there is no essential difference between the type of genetic threat at issue here and the menace of infection, contagion or a threat of physical harm. See generally, eg, *McIntosh v Milano*, 168 NJ Super 466, 483–85, 403 A 2d 500 (Law Div 1979); *Tarasoff v Regents of Univ of Cal*, 17 Cal 3d 425, 551 P 2d 334, 344, 131 Cal Rptr 14 (Cal. 1976); Restatement (Second) of Torts @@ 314, 314A (1965); T A Bateman, Annotation, Liability of Doctor or Other Health Practitioner, 3 ALR 5th 370 (1992). The individual or group at risk is easily identified, and substantial future harm may be averted or minimized by a timely and effective warning.

The motion judge's view of this case as one involving an unavoidable genetic condition gave too little significance to the preferred expert view that early monitoring of those at risk can effectively avert some of the more serious consequences a person with multiple polyposis might otherwise experience. We cannot conclude either, as the trial court did, that Dr Pack breached no duty because avoidable harm to Donna was not foreseeable, i.e., "that Dr Pack's conduct did not create a 'foreseeable zone or risk.'" Such a determination would ignore the presumed state of medical knowledge at the time. It would also tend to undervalue the concepts that inform our case law establishing a cause of action for increased risk of harm, see *Evers v Dollinger*, 95 NJ 399, 412–17, 471 A 2d 405 (1984); see also *Fischer v Canario*, 143 NJ 235, 241–43,670 A 2d 516 (1996); *Scafidi v Seiler*, 119 NJ 93, 108–09, 574 A 2d 398 (1990), as well as the underlying rationale of our rules of law on foreseeability, heretofore held to be specifically applicable in professional negligence cases involving genetic torts. See *Schroeder v Perkel*, supra, 87 NJ at 63–64.

Although an overly broad and general application of the physician's duty to warn might lead to confusion, conflict or unfairness in many types of circumstances, we are confident that the duty to warn of avertible risk from genetic causes, by definition a matter of familial concern, is sufficiently narrow to serve the interests of justice. Further, it is appropriate, for reasons already expressed by our Supreme Court, id at 63–65, that the duty be seen as owed not only to the patient himself but that it also "extends beyond the interests of a patient to members of the immediate family of the patient who may be adversely affected by a breach of that duty." Id At 65; cf *Fosgate v Corona*, 66 NJ 268, 274, 330 A 2d 355 (1974) (patient's daughter-in-law and grandchildren, all members of her household but apparently not, themselves, defendant physician's patients, were entitled to recover for contracting tuberculosis as a result of defendant's malpractice in failing to diagnose the disease in his patient). We need not decide, in the present posture of this case, how, precisely, that duty is to be discharged, especially with respect to young children who may be at risk, except to require that reasonable steps be taken to assure that the information reaches those likely to be affected or is made available for their benefit. We are aware of no direct evidence that has been developed concerning the nature of the communications between physician and patient regarding Mr Batkin's disease: what Dr Pack did or did not disclose; the advice he gave to Mr Batkin, if any, concerning genetic factors and what ought to have been done in respect of those at risk; and the conduct or expressed preferences of Mr Batkin in response thereto. There may be enough from Mrs Batkin's testimony and other evidence for inferences to be drawn, however.

We decline to hold as the Florida Supreme Court did in *Pate v Thelkel*, supra, 661 So 2d at 282, that, in all circumstances, the duty to warn will be satisfied by informing the patient. It may be necessary, at some stage, to resolve a conflict between the physician's broader duty to warn and his fidelity to an expressed preference of the patient that nothing be said to family members about the details of the disease. We cannot know presently, however, whether there is any likelihood that such a conflict may be shown to have existed in this matter or, if it did, what its qualities might have been. As the matter is currently constituted, it is as likely as not that no such conflict will be shown to have existed and that the only evidence on the issue will be Mrs. Batkin's testimony, including that she received no information, despite specific inquiry, that her children were at risk. We note, in addition, the possible existence of some offsetting evidence that Donna was rectally examined as a young child, suggesting that the risk to her had been disclosed.

This case implicates serious and conflicting medical, social and legal policies, many aptly identified in Sonia M. Suter, Whose Genes Are These Anyway? Familial Conflicts Over Access to Genetic Information, 91 Mich L Rev 1854 (1993) and in other sources, including some referred to by the motion judge. Some such policy considerations may need to be addressed in ultimately resolving this case. For example, if evidence is produced that will permit the jury to find that Dr Pack received instructions from his patient not to disclose details of the illness or the fact of genetic risk, the court will be required to determine whether, as a matter of law, there are or ought to be any limits on physician-patient confidentiality, especially after the patient's death where a risk of harm survives the patient, as in the case of genetic consequences. See generally Janet A Kobrin, Confidentiality of Genetic Information, 30 UCLA L Rev 1283 (1983).

Issues of fact remain to be resolved, as well. What was the extent of Donna's risk, for instance? We are led to understand from the experts' reports that the risk of multiple polyposis was significant and that, upon detection, an early full colectomy, i.e. an excision of her entire colon, may well have been the treatment of choice to avoid resultant cancer – including metastasis, the loss of other organs and the rigors of chemotherapy. Full factual development may, however, cast a different light on these issues of fact and others.

Difficult damage issues portend also. Not the least of these will involve distinguishing between the costs of the medical surveillance that would have followed a timely and effective warning, and the costs of medical care attributable to any breach of duty that may be found to have occurred. See *Lanzet v Greenberg*, 126 NJ 168, 188, 594 A 2d 1309 (1991).

Because of the necessarily limited scope of our consideration, we have highlighted only a few of the potentially troublesome issues presented by this case. Such questions are best conceived and considered in the light of a fully developed record rather than in the abstract. ... The order of the trial court dismissing the complaint is reversed.

AM Stein, and Cuff JJ agreed.

Speaking for the court, Kestin J acknowledged the difficulties entailed in the action. The scope of the duty might entail advising the patient, or possibly, the family members directly. Notice the court left open the possibility of the latter, even though it might involve a breach of confidence. *Quaere* whether it would be justified in the public interest? (see *infra* ch8). The important point was that the duty was to take 'reasonable steps ... to assure that the information reaches those likely to be affected or is made available for their benefit'. In the case of young children, the duty to them would be discharged by advising their parents (see eg, in another context *Poynter v Hillingdon HA* (1997) 37 BMLR 192).

4. Psychiatric injury

So far, we have been concerned with physical injury suffered by patients or others. To what extent, if any, could a doctor who negligently carries out medical treatment be liable for psychiatric injury caused to his patients or their relatives? The answer, of course, lies in the rules laid down by the House of Lords in the quartet of cases: *McLoughlin v O'Brian* [1983] 1 AC 410; *Alcock v Chief Constable of South Yorkshire Police* [1992] 1 AC 310; *Page v Smith* [1996] AC 155 and *White v Chief Constable of South Yorkshire Police* [1999] 1 All ER 1. Our concern here is not with psychiatric injury (or indeed distress, shock or anxiety) suffered by a patient consequent upon physical injury. Recovery of damages for the emotional harm follows in such circumstances on normal principles in personal injury claims. Instead, we are concerned with the situation where psychiatric injury alone (and nothing less will suffice) is suffered by the individual. Of course, breach and causation must be established by the claimant, but the real issue of concern to us is whether the law recognises a duty of care to the patient, former patient or relative (see generally I Kennedy and A Grubb (eds), *Principles of Medical Law* paras 5.43–5.46 (patients) and 5.72–5.86 (others)). Here, the distinction between 'primary' and 'secondary' victims is important. A detailed account of the law as most recently stated in *White* can be found elsewhere. For 'primary victims' the law requires no more than foreseeability of injury and resultant psychiatric harm. By contrast, as is well known, for 'secondary victims' (ie those who are themselves not in danger but witness danger to others), the law is more strict, requiring a close relationship with the person in danger and a closeness in time and geography to the incident. The law is summarised, leaving aside the minutiae of the legal issues, in Lord Steyn's speech (for the majority) in *White v Chief Constable of South Yorkshire Police and others* [1999] 1 All ER, 1 (HL):

> **Lord Steyn:** The leading decision of the House of Lords is *Alcock v Chief Constable of the South Yorkshire Police* [1991] 4 All ER 907, [1992] 1 AC 310. …
>
> This decision established that a person who suffers reasonably foreseeable psychiatric illness as a result of another person's death or injury cannot recover damages unless he can satisfy three requirements, viz: (i) that he had a close tie of love and affection with the person killed, injured or imperilled; (ii) that he was close to the incident in time and space; (iii) that he directly perceived the incident rather than, for example, hearing about it from a third person.
>
> Lord Oliver observed that the law was not entirely satisfactory or logically defensible but he thought that considerations of policy made it explicable. …
>
> The decision of the House of Lords in *Page v Smith* [1995] 2 All ER 736, [1996] AC 155 was the next important development in this branch of the law. The plaintiff was directly involved in a motor car accident. He was within the range of potential physical injury. As a result of the accident he suffered from chronic fatigue syndrome. In this context Lord Lloyd of Berwick adopted a distinction between primary and secondary victims: Lord Ackner and Lord Browne-Wilkinson agreed. Lord Lloyd said that a plaintiff who had been within the range of foreseeable injury was a primary victim. Mr Page fulfilled this requirement and could in principle recover compensation for psychiatric loss. In my view it follows that all other victims, who suffer pure psychiatric harm, are secondary victims and must satisfy the control mechanisms laid down in *Alcock's* case.

In *White* the majority limited the 'primary victim' category to those who fell within the 'zone of danger or who reasonably believed they were within it and suffered psychiatric injury'. Consequently, it was held (by the majority) that police officers who had assisted in the aftermath of the Hillsborough disaster could not recover as they were not 'primary victims' because they did not fall within the 'zone of danger', even though some were rescuers. None could fulfil the narrower requirements of liability for 'secondary victims'.

(a) Negligent treatment

In the medical context, a patient could recover as a 'primary victim' if the psychiatric injury arose out of a danger to them or, probably in the obstetric context, a joint danger to the claimant and her child. The point is illustrated by a case which preceded *White*. You will notice in this case that the father of the child also succeeded in his claim. No doubt he would do so even in the light of *White*, but his action would do so solely because he fell within the rules for recovery as a 'secondary victim'. He would no longer be classified as a 'primary victim' as his participation did not expose him to danger.

Tredget and Tredget v Bexley Health Authority [1994] 5 Med LR 178 (City & Mayor's Court)

> **Judge White:** In these proceedings a mother and father of a child who dies within two days of his birth at the defendants' Queen Mary's Hospital at Sidcup in Kent each seek damages

for psychiatric illness and the consequential losses which they subsequently suffered, it being admitted that their son's death was caused by the negligence of the medical staff for whom the defendants are vicariously liable. The parents also claim, pursuant to the provisions of the Fatal Accidents Act 1976, a "bereavement" award of £3,500.00 and funeral expenses of £263.00, but this does not give rise to dispute. What is in dispute, the admission of negligence in the context of the child's death having been made, is the "recoverability" of the damages each parent seeks to compensate for the effect that the death of their child and the circumstances in which it happened had upon them. …

Mrs Tredget, the first plaintiff, who is now thirty-four, has since the age of eleven, been an insulin dependent diabetic. She married the second plaintiff, who is three years younger in the mid-1980s and her daughter, Rebecca, was born to them on August 19, 1987. She was born by Caesarean section at the plaintiffs' local Farnborough hospital, as in her diabetic condition, Mrs Tredget was suffering from polyhydramnios. This pregnancy followed an earlier one in 1984 which miscarried after ten weeks.

She again became pregnant in late 1988, but this was terminated because she then had herpes labalis. The following February she conceived again and it was the birth of this child that has given rise to the proceedings. The pregnancy was normal but having been distressed by the Caesarean section delivery of Rebecca, Mrs Tredget was very anxious to have a vaginal delivery. The obstetrician at Farnborough hospital would not have agreed to this and her GP referred her instead to a Mrs Hanna, the consultant obstetrician and gynaecologist at the defendants' Sidcup hospital, who was prepared to accept her as a patient, understanding her wish to have a normal birth.

During her antenatal care, there were discussions of the risks involved because of her diabetic condition and history, but there is a dispute as to the extent and nature of the warnings that were given. It is accepted that Mrs Hanna warned Mrs Tredget of the possibility of intra-uterine death which was to be countered by inducing labour before term, but the plaintiffs complain in the context of the problems that did develop during delivery, that the risk of her having a larger than normal child and feto-pelvic disproportion resulting in obstruction of labour was never discussed. Had the risks been fully disclosed, Mrs Tredget contends that she would have elected to have a Caesarean section again. This is denied by the defendants whose pleaded case was that the risks of traumatic vaginal delivery were fully explained by Mrs Hanna on every one of the ten antenatal attendances that Mrs Tredget paid to the defendants' hospital.

In the event, the issue as to the nature of the advice and warnings given about the risk of normal delivery remains unresolved, for the matter has sensibly proceeded upon the admission the defendants have made of negligence during the labour.

Mrs Tredget went into hospital on November 5, 1989 at just under thirty-eight weeks, for labour to be induced and, strong contractions having started during the evening of the 7th, she was admitted to the labour ward just before midnight. Up to then, no complications had developed; in particular, no excessive high hydramnios was present but scans had revealed that the baby was larger than average.

Labour progressed normally until 2.00 am when the cervix was noted to be 7 cm dilated, her waters having broken an hour or so earlier. From then on, however, labour slowed and it is now admitted that a decision to perform a Caesarean section, or at least to advise it in very strong terms, should have been taken at about 4.45 am that morning. This is the act of negligence which is established in the proceedings and upon which liability to the plaintiffs has to be founded.

As a consequence of the defendants' medical staff's failure in their management of labour to have the baby delivered by Caesarean section, Mrs Tredget's condition was giving cause for concern by 8.30 am when an attempt was made to stimulate the uterus and the foetal heart having shown deceleration, oxygen was administered. Mrs Hanna saw Mrs Tredget at 9.45 am and observing that there had been no progress since 9.30 am pushed the anterior lip of the cervix over the baby's head to allow it to come down. She gave instructions that the plaintiff was to start pushing at 10.30 am which she did for half an hour without success and a vacuum extraction was then begun. When the baby's head appeared, the umbilical cord was tied around the neck and had to be clamped and cut. The baby's shoulders then became caught within the pelvis and it was necessary for a shoulder bone to be broken to allow the birth process to be completed. When finally delivered at 11.32 am the baby was in a severely asphyxiated condition with no heart beat detectable, but was resuscitated in the labour room behind where Mrs Tredget was lying and then taken to the special care baby unit in another room in the hospital where he was placed in an incubator. His weight at birth was 9lbs 10ounces.

That is the medical history of Mrs Tredget's labour and the delivery which took place just after 11.30 am on November 8 of the baby who was named Callum.

Both mother and father have, in evidence, described their own respective experiences of these events – what they themselves each saw or were aware of – it being their claim that their psychiatric problems that followed, resulted from their involvement in or proximity to the traumas of the birth.

For Mrs Tredget, the birth of Callum with its immediate aftermath was a long, painful and traumatic experience. Recalling the period after 2.00 am when labour had slowed, she said she was not told what was happening – all she knew was that her labour was proceeding. She recalls trying to force the baby down, but by then being too tired and following which, she said there came a time when "all hell was let loose". Up to then her impression was that things had gone forward in a fairly relaxed way but at the point when what her husband described as "pandemonium taking place", she became aware of difficulty in getting the baby out. She has a memory of someone saying "it's out", of two midwives pushing on her abdomen, of someone shouting push and of someone trying to assist the delivery internally. "My feeling", she said "at the time was of fear". It took 4 minutes from the moment the head was out to deliver the rest of the body. By then, Mrs Tredget had been in labour fifteen hours and was physically exhausted.

She did not, because of the state she was in, see the baby when it was delivered, but as she regained her senses she became aware that he was being resuscitated behind her. She had then, she said, a sense that things were wrong and saw that her husband who had been present throughout looked stunned.

Mr Tredget recalled that at this point his legs were shaking and he had to sit down. "I was", he said, "in the state of disbelief. I didn't know what was going on, but I knew there was a problem. I sat down and cried. I was not prepared for it".

He had been with his wife since early the previous evening, coming to the hospital after work. On arrival he had found that there was a mishap over her sugar levels and intervened to give the nurses assistance. The contractions began at 9.00 pm and he remained throughout the night with his wife. He described the atmosphere in the delivery room as being casual until about 10.00 am when he sensed that there were problems and when the delivery was taking place there was what he described as "pandemonium". He played a part in the delivery as he was asked to keep saying to her that she should push while the staff were physically trying to complete the delivery. Although it was four minutes from the time the head emerged until Callum was fully away from his mother; "It seemed", Mr Tredget said, "an eternity". He saw the birth and saw that Callum was more discoloured – black and mauve – than his daughter, at whose birth he had also been when delivered. He saw Callum being resuscitated and taken to the intensive care unit.

At that point, he said, he did not realise how bad his condition was until a doctor came a little later to say, "the good news is that he is alive, but the bad news is that he has a 60/70 percent chance of brain damage".

Mrs Tredget recalls the doctor telling her that Callum had a 60/70 percent chance of survival. "My reaction was", she said, "one of shock. I had no idea the situation was so bad". Later that afternoon, she was brought a photograph one of the nurses had taken of Callum in his incubator as she could not go down to see him that day and had not seen him at birth. It would have been obvious from the photograph which has been produced in Court that he was in a critical condition.

Mrs Tredget was still suffering from the effects of the anaesthesia but was distressed by the tubes visible in the photograph. Although it was put by her bed she could not recall looking at it again. "The events were", she said, "that time more important than the photograph".

The following day both Mr and Mrs Tredget saw Callum in the special care unit. She spent one or two hours with him on her own by his incubator. He was in a bad way and she was distressed as he appeared to be crying. She also felt concern for her husband who was, she observed, not his normal self at all. He recalls crying in disbelief, and their concern not being eased by conflicting reports from the staff as to Callum's chances of survival or of brain damage if he did survive. Callum did, however, during the day appear to improve, but overnight he deteriorated and Mr Tredget was called from home urgently in the early morning of November 10.

On the parents being advised that there was no hope for him, the decision was taken to turn off the life support equipment. Arrangements were made for him to be christened and Mrs Tredget was able to hold him in her arms before he died at 1.00 pm.

I have set out in some detail the history of the management of Mrs Tredget's labour and Callum's death two days after his birth as the sequence of events, and the nature of the parents' experience of them have on the background state of the law been subject to analysis and comment. I will return to them in due course, but for the moment, I merely note how the parents themselves assessed the effect on them at that time of what had happened. Mrs Tredget said,

For me the time between his birth and when he died was very traumatic. There was the uncertainty; neither of us was prepared for what happened. I had shock and disbelief.

Physically, I felt unable to do anything. Mentally there was confusion. I wasn't sure what had happened. We had different explanations. I didn't understand what had happened or why. I subsequently became obsessed with the loss of the baby.

Mr Tredget referred to it as a "nightmare" which started when, as a father, he "saw his son in difficulties during birth". In his statement he said,

I remember being distraught and confused. I was distraught because of what I saw which was chaos and it left me confused. I have never cried so much in my life. To me, Callum was the missing part of my life, albeit a profound statement. It is what I believed then and still do now.

Although until then, the marriage of Callum's parents had been happy, their relationship was immediately affected by his death. It's plain from the evidence that they each suffered psychiatric consequences which have ultimately led or, at least, contributed to the breakdown of their marriage, they having eventually separated in June of last year. I stress that there may well be issues as to the degree to which the misfortunes of the last four years can be attributed to the neonatal death of their child and the effect upon them of it which would become pertinent in a later assessment of quantum, but is not in dispute that they were and, indeed, remain psychiatrically disturbed.

Their relationship deteriorated. Dr Stanford Bourne whose two reports following interviews in May 1992 and May 1993 I have supplemented by his evidence during the hearings, described them as being left blaming themselves, each other and anybody else who might possibly be culpable. The bewildering mixture of anger and guilt, he contends, over this is very pathogenic, tearing their marriage and lives apart.

In fact, another child was conceived in 1991 – a daughter born by elective Caesarean section on January 23, 1992 – but this did not stop the deterioration in their relationship. Indeed, Dr Bourne says that far from producing anticipated relief, a birth of another baby can exacerbate the symptoms that the parents had.

Mr Tredget, who was a garage manager, continued working successfully until 1992, when he had a nervous breakdown and he has been a full time psychiatric patient ever since. As a further complication, he had, before the final breakdown of the marriage, two affairs with other women, one of which was linked to a miscarriage Mrs Tredget had to a further pregnancy. Again, the court at this stage is not concerned with the full implications and assessment for the purposes of quantum of the subsequent history. The tragic fact is, nevertheless, that from being, as Dr Bourne described, a prosperous household with rosy prospects, the parents have become estranged and have now broken up.

Further, it is not in dispute that following the neonatal death of Callum, whatever the legal consequences are, they each suffered psychiatric illness …

Those being the facts, I now turn to the law …

The judge referred to Lord Oliver's two categories in *Alcock* and continued:

… cases in which the injured plaintiff was involved either mediately or immediately as a principal and those in which the plaintiff was no more than a passive or unwilling witness of the injury caused to others. Is the mother who does not actually witness the birth of the damaged child and from whom the child is taken until its death shortly after, a participant; is the father who is present at the birth, who is asked to help by telling his wife to push and who sees the baby taken from her, simply a passive witness; does the law draw a distinction between the role and the duties owed to each parent? Again, in an analysis of the law, can the death of the child as "an event" be separated from the "event" of the birth some 48 hours before or does the lawyer's logic fed by other factual situations in attempting to do so become, as Dr Bourne considered, divorced from reality? …

I simply take the five shorthand tests which the parties in *Sion v Hampstead Health Authority* [1994] 5 Med LR 170 agreed for the purposes of the ruling made by the court had to be applied. Mr Justice Brooke accepted, as a distillation of the law to date, that to succeed in a claim for psychiatric illness caused by shock a plaintiff

… had to prove five things; (1) that he suffered not merely grief, distress and sorrow but a psychiatric illness: (2) that this resulted from shock, i.e. the sudden and direct appreciation by sight or sound of a horrifying event or events, rather than from distress, strain, grief or sorrow or from gradual or retrospective realisation of events; (3) that there was a propinquity in time or space from causative event or its immediate aftermath; (4) the injury was reasonably foreseeable and; (5) that the relationship between the Plaintiff and the Defendant was sufficiently proximate …

Have, therefore, either of the plaintiffs – the mother and father of the child who was directly and fatally affected by the defendants' negligent failure to decide upon a Caesarean section delivery by 4.45 am on November 8, 1989 – succeeded in respect of their own claims in establishing the requirements of liability?

I turn first to proximity of the relationship. They plainly cleared this hurdle without difficulty; being the parents of Callum, they were, as any parents would be, deeply emotionally tied into the birth of their child and the mother, of course, was herself part of the physical process being handled by the defendants.

Secondly, on the evidence, it is plain that they have each suffered more than grief, distress or sorrow following the death of their child. Each has a form of psychiatric illness – pathological grief reaction which, as Dr Bourne explained, is not just a slight exaggeration of the average mourning process, normal grief, – but in each case a serious condition, that of the father being the more severe. This is not now strongly in dispute and in any event, the medical evidence is clear.

What is disputed is that the parents' psychiatric illnesses resulted from shock – the sudden and direct appreciation of sight or sound of a horrifying event – rather than from stress, strain, grief or sorrow from either gradual or retrospective realisation of events, or that the necessary propinquity of time and space from the causative event, if there was one, that the law recognises, or its immediate aftermath has been established.

The defendants' case put simply is that although the parents' suffering may have gone well beyond the consequences of the normal mourning process, it was grief rather than shock which was the causative factor. There was, it is said, no "qualifying event" of the type that has justified "nervous shock" claims in the authorities to date. Although Dr Bourne has referred to the experience of the actual birth for both mother and father as being, in the circumstances "horrific", the anxieties of the time, even making allowance for the "chaos" or "pandemonium" that was experienced, do not amount to a sudden and distinct assault on either's nervous system amounting to "shock" in the accepted understanding of the word. Further allowance is placed on the fact that the death did not take place until two days later and during this time, there would have been a gradual realisation in them of the child's situation. There was no sudden and direct appreciation of the horrifying event. Again, the gradual comprehension came not only from their own perceptions of the birth and what followed, but on information given to them by the medical staff. In other words, not on what they themselves saw or heard, but on what they were told. The mother, it is stressed, did not see the child, or "being in pain, sedated and exhausted", was not fully aware of the true gravity of the situation until she was told later by the doctor of the child's condition. The father at birth did immediately see something was very wrong, but the full realisation only came with time. The cause or negligence, in any event, was several hours before the consequences to the child began to become apparent.

As part of his argument, counsel for the defendants has identified four phases of the child's progression from the negligence to his death nearly two and a half days later, from the negligence to the birth, the period in intensive care up to the morning of his death, the short period after he was taken from the incubator and finally his death, and has submitted that the requirement of an immediacy cannot be satisfied.

Although the birth may have for each contained ingredients which could have given rise to intense emotion and concern, the parents at that moment did not fully comprehend the tragedy; this would only come later and its effect on them has, in any event, been compounded by factors such as guilt, anger and relationship-stresses.

In short, there was no shocking or direct impact sufficient to found a claim the psychiatric illness having been the result of a cumulative process of grief and loss.

Before considering these arguments which I hope I have fairly summarised above, I turn to the remaining pre-condition of liability, namely that of reasonable foreseeability. I find on the evidence that this has been clearly established. Dr Bourne explained that neonatal death is a potent cause of psychiatric disturbance of the kind suffered by these parents: it is bewildering for the parents with a sense of birth and death being wrapped up in one which is more difficult to weather than the death of a child who the parents have had some opportunity to get to know. The risk of disturbance can, he also said, be exacerbated by factors which a death caused by negligence would induce – a horrifying experience at the birth when the circumstances of the death are confused, obscure, difficult to understand or verify, giving cause for feelings of grievance and guilt. Even if the child had lived, Dr Bourne was of the opinion that there would still have been quite serious psychiatric sequelae for the parents.

On the medical evidence, and I only have that of Dr Bourne, I accept that the test of reasonable foreseeability is met but as the authorities show that of itself does not automatically in "nervous shock" cases establish a legal duty of care, and I now return to the disputed issues to which I have referred.

First, was there, as a consequence of the negligence, an "event" as contemplated by the authorities which was horrifying and could have caused shock in either parent in the sense of their having a sudden "appreciation by sight or sound ... which violently agitates the mind"?

On the evidence, the actual birth with its "chaos" or "pandemonium", the difficulties that the mother had of delivery, the sense in the room that something was wrong and the arrival of the child in a distressed condition requiring immediate resuscitation was, for those immediately and directly involved as each of the parents was, frightening and horrifying. I refer in this context to Dr Bourne's appraisal of the effect that there would have been upon them of what was happening.

He concluded

I would have said that the events of delivery – the state of their minds, the pandemonium – it, as it were, 'all blowing up in their faces', would be a very powerful factor in contributing to pathological grief afterwards.

What happened was, of course, happening in full sight of the father with him actually participating at the request of the staff in the efforts to deliver the child by encouraging his wife. Is she to be distinguished because she, in labour, pain, sedated and suffering from exhaustion, was not fully conscious of what was happening about her?

In my judgment this would be quite unrealistic, particularly bearing in mind that although she did not see the child at birth she was, I accept from her own senses – what she heard on seeing her husband's state and no doubt by her instincts – aware that something was wrong. Speaking of the crucial time she said:

I was aware of the difficulty in getting the baby out. I remember someone saying 'it is out'. There were two midwives pushing on my abdomen, someone was shouting 'push' and there was someone internally. My feelings were of fear. It took four minutes for the rest of the body to come out. I did not see the baby when it was delivered. I became aware of the baby being resuscitated behind me and I had a sense that things were wrong. My husband looked absolutely stunned. There was a lot of shouting going on.

Both parents were directly involved in and with the event of the delivery. Of the two broad categories that Lord Oliver identified they were each principals rather than passive witnesses. Further, on the evidence, the event of the delivery was a powerful factor in contributing to the pathological grief each suffered afterwards. There are other contributing or exacerbating factors but that part of the experience was significant in this context, to the point that even had the child lived, psychiatric sequelae could have been expected in any event.

On this approach to the particular circumstances of this case alone, I would say that each of the plaintiffs established liability even though a full appreciation of the gravity of the child's condition only came during his short struggle for life in intensive care during the 48 hours that followed.

In my judgment, however, it is unrealistic to separate out and isolate the delivery as an event, from the other sequence happenings from the onset of labour to Callum's death two days later, as a whole. The problems which beset the difficult and prolonged labour, the traumatic delivery and the short period of his life in intensive care leading to his death were all attributable to the admitted negligent failure by the defendant's medical staff to proceed by way of caesarean section at 4.45 am on November 8. Although lasting for over 48 hours from the onset of labour to the death, this effectively was one event. Of course, it was not in the nature of an immediate catastrophe which lasts only a few seconds – panic in a stadium or a motor accident – but one just as traumatic for those immediately involved as participants as each of the parents were.

The law should be, and in my judgment is, "fluid enough" not simply to recognise one type of traumatic event and to shut its eyes to another such as that upon which this claim is founded, whether or not it is necessary – and in my judgment it is not – to pray in aid the concept of the "aftermath". ...

In *Sion v Hampstead Health Authority* although the relationship of father and son existed, the facts in my judgment can be readily distinguished by the degree of involvement in and the immediacy of the parents to the birth of the child.

There is, of course, underlying the drawing of the line which the courts have sought to do case by case as different circumstances have come before them, the consideration of "policy" – the importance of ensuring that the "flood gates" are not opened or the burden on any tortfeasor unwarrantably increased. In my judgment, if this is a new step in the development of the law, it is not only, as I have indicated, within the principles that have been set out, but has its own in-built limits being founded on the special relationship, with all that follows, of the parent with the child at the unique human moment of birth.

You may also think that the mother's claim, however the judge saw it, was in truth, justified under the 'secondary victim' rules; you will notice his concluding words. It may be, however, that at least part of the psychiatric injury arose from events which also put her in danger (though it may be difficult to say her fear was for herself rather than her child) and thus she could claim the whole of the psychiatric injury as she suffered as a 'primary victim', psychiatric injury which 'materially contributed' to the whole (*Vernon v Bosley* [1997] 1 All ER 577 (CA)).

In any event, in cases of this nature, the *McLoughlin/Alcock* rules will not present any real difficulty to a relative. Where they will, however, is when the relative witnesses the patient suffer or die as a result of medical negligence or where the relatives are called on to identify the patient's body after his death. The leading medical negligence case illustrates this.

Sion v Hampstead HA [1994] 5 Med LR 170 (CA)

Staughton LJ: A young man called Lionel Sion was injured in a motor-cycle accident on September 2, 1988. He was 23 years old at the time. He was taken to the Royal Free Hospital in North London, which is administered by the Hampstead Health Authority. His father, then aged 56 and also called Lionel Sion, went to the hospital to be with him. I shall call the father "Mr Sion". He is the plaintiff in this action. For fourteen days he stayed at his son's bedside, watching him deteriorate in health and fall into a coma. Then on September 16 the son died.

Mr Sion's case is that the staff of the hospital were negligent. In particular, they failed to diagnose substantial and continuing bleeding from the left kidney, which resulted in his son entering a coma on September 5. The allegations of negligence are denied. But as this is a striking-out appeal, we must assume them to be true for present purposes. ...

The circumstances of the son's treatment at the hospital are pleaded at some length. Salient points on which Mr Brennan, for Mr Sion, particularly relies are as follows:

(1) On September 4, two days after he went into hospital, there was a serious deterioration in the son's respiratory condition.

(2) On the next day, there was respiratory arrest and cardiac arrest.

(3) The son thereupon went into a coma and was transferred to the intensive care unit.

(4) On September 16 the son died.

Mr Brennan's submission was that those four events were potentially traumatic events likely to cause shock.

... We are not here considering psychiatric illness caused directly to a plaintiff by negligent treatment, for example by his own psychiatrist. Although the words are not wholly appropriate, these are cases of a primary victim and a secondary victim, the latter being the plaintiff. ...

It is scarcely surprising that the law was agreed by counsel before Brooke J, in the following terms:

> Two propositions are agreed between Counsel. The first is that the term 'nervous shock' is shorthand for psychiatric illness caused by shock. Secondly, that to succeed in a claim for such an injury the plaintiff must prove five things: first, that he suffered not merely grief, distress or sorrow but a psychiatric illness; secondly, that this resulted from shock, i.e. the sudden and direct appreciation by sight or sound of a horrifying event or events, rather than from stress, strain, grief or sorrow or from gradual or retrospective realisation of events; thirdly, that there was propinquity in time or space for the causative event or its immediate aftermath; fourthly, the injury was reasonably foreseeable; and fifthly, that the relationship between the plaintiff and the defendant was sufficiently proximate.

In this court, however, Mr Brennan sought to resile from that agreement; and we readily allowed him to do so. He now submits that Mr Sion does not need to prove sudden shock (or "an external traumatic event", to use the language of Auld J in *Taylor v Somerset Health Authority* [1993] 4 Med LR 34 at page 37), or any shock.

In support of that submission we were referred to a passage in the dissenting judgment of Sir Thomas Bingham MR in *M (A Minor) v London Borough of Newham* [1994] 2 WLR 554 at page 573. However, that was not a case of a claim by a secondary victim. Both the child and her mother were primary victims of the psychiatrist's negligence. ...

No doubt it is true that there is little logic in distinguishing between psychiatric illness caused by sudden shock and any other psychiatric injury. ...

For the present, this court must in my judgment accept the state of the law as declared by the House of Lords, even in a striking-out application. It would not be right for us to impose on the parties the burden of a trial which can only have one conclusion on the present law, against the possibility that this may prove to be a case where the law is changed. In my judgment this application is properly to be determined by the law as it was agreed to be, correctly, before Brooke J. ...

I have to return to the report of Dr Bennett, as providing the general outline of Mr Sion's case but not necessarily containing every detail. As part of the narrative there is this passage:

> During the last three or four days of his son's life he realised that it was almost certain that he would not survive, but he decided to continue to stay in the ICU just in case there was some improvement. By the time his son did actually die on September 16, he was not surprised and felt that in a way he had been preparing himself for this to happen. In retrospect, he cannot be sure whether he knew at exactly what point his son had died, but feels that intuitively he must have been aware of it. He cannot say exactly when the respiration ceased, as by this time this function was carried out entirely by the machine.
>
> He felt uneasy about various points relating to his son's death. In particular he could not see why his son had been fully conscious, alert and lucid for some two and a half days after admission, as he had been told by the Consultant in charge that there was evidence of possibly quite severe brain damage. This was not actually found to be so at the post mortem examination, a fact which I understand emerged clearly at the inquest.
>
> It was only following the inquest which took place several months later, that Mr Sion began to experience real doubts, and to question whether his son's treatment had been competent and satisfactory.

To add to Mr Sion's grief, his wife discovered his suspicion of negligence by the hospital, or may have done, and committed suicide a few days before Christmas 1989.

Under the heading "Sequelae":

> Following his son's death Mr Sion became extremely depressed. He felt that life had virtually lost all its purpose, he was consistently low spirited, with frequent thoughts of suicide. He was understandably very distressed when his wife committed suicide, but in retrospect he feels that his depression was not increased. 'I was so depressed by that time that although I was terribly upset by her death, it just wasn't possible for the depression itself to get any worse.' He felt severe feelings of guilt. These did not arise until after his realisation that there may have been Medical Negligence ... For about three days after he knew his son was dead he 'went numb, I just couldn't think about everything, I felt drained.'

Then under the heading "Summary and Opinion":

> 1 Following his son's tragic death, Mr Sion has experienced a very severe, prolonged, and so far persistent grief reaction, characterised by profound depression, disturbed sleep, impaired appetite and loss of weight, almost constant intrusive memories of all aspects of his son's life, in particular the circumstances of his death and his own, i.e. Mr Sion's experiences at his son's bedside ...
>
> 3 I think it is more probable than not that his prolonged physical proximity to his son throughout the time he was in hospital, with the resultant observation of his deteriorating condition, may well have been a contributory factor to what I would view as an abnormal bereavement reaction...
>
> 5 In view of their nature and timing, I consider his psychiatric symptoms to be a direct result of his son's death, and I think it extremely unlikely that he would have experienced any of these emotional difficulties if his son had survived.

In my opinion there is no trace in that report of "shock" as defined by Lord Ackner, no sudden appreciation by sight or sound of a horrifying event. On the contrary, the report describes a process continuing for some time, from first arrival at the hospital to the appreciation of medical negligence after the inquest. In particular, the son's death when it occurred was not surprising but expected. ...

Peter Gibson LJ: ... Mr Whitfield submitted that the plaintiff's claim could not succeed because the injuries to or the death of a primary victim in themselves or itself do not qualify as the horrifying event causing the shock needed for a valid claim. He said that it was a precondition of a claim that the incident which resulted from a breach of duty should have characteristics of suddenness and violence additional to the injuries or death of the primary victim, and contended that this was demonstrated by the doctrine that a plaintiff may recover if affected by the immediate aftermath of the horrifying event. He relied for those submissions on *Taylor v Somerset Health Authority* [1993] 4 Med LR 34 at page 37 where Auld J accepted an argument on similar lines. I am not persuaded by this argument.

It is of course correct that in most of the decided cases there has been a sudden and violent incident resulting from a breach of duty, but it is the sudden awareness, violently agitating the mind, of what is occurring or has occurred that is the crucial ingredient of shock. In the

McLoughlin case Lord Wilberforce (at pp 417–418) said that the critical question to be decided was whether the wife and mother, who had not been present at the scene of grievous injuries to her family but who in hospital came upon those injuries at an interval of time and space, could recover damages for nervous shock, and he held that she could. I see no reason in logic why a breach of duty causing an incident involving no violence or suddenness, such as where the wrong medicine is negligently given to a hospital patient, could not lead to a claim for damages for nervous shock, for example where the negligence has fatal results and a visiting close relative, wholly unprepared for what has occurred, finds the body and thereby sustains a sudden and unexpected shock to the nervous system.

In *Jaensch v Coffey* (1984) 155 CLR 549 at page 567 Brennan J gave his understanding of "shock":

> … the sudden sensory perception, that is, by seeing hearing or touching, of a person, thing or event, which is so distressing that the perception of the phenomenon affronts or insults the Plaintiff's mind and causes a recognizable psychiatric illness.

That, in my respectful opinion, encompasses the essential elements of "shock" and does not include the additional elements for which Mr Whitfield contended.

But I accept Mr Whitfield's primary submission that the Judge was right to find that on the facts of the present case as appearing from the proposed amended pleadings when read with Dr Bennett's report the plaintiff suffered no sudden and unexpected shock to his nervous system. Instead it is clear that the plaintiff, very understandably, suffered and abnormal grief reaction to his son's death. Staughton LJ has set out the most relevant parts of that report and it is not necessary for me to repeat them. I agree with him that the plaintiff's claim is doomed to fail.

As Peter Gibson LJ makes clear, claims of this sort will not fail simply on the basis that there is no 'unexpected' or 'shocking' event. What is crucial is the *unexpected* or *shocking* nature of the discovery by the relatives. Of course, merely to be *told* of the patient's condition or decline will not do. Likewise, relatives will find it difficult to claim under the so-called 'immediate aftermath' rule in *McLoughlin/Alcock*. Relatives who identify their loved ones in a mortuary following a death caused by medical negligence are unlikely to have the necessary closeness to the 'negligent event' in order to recover as the following case illustrates.

Taylor v Somerset HA (1993) 16 BMLR 63 (QBD)

The plaintiff was a widow who learned of her husband's heart attack at work. The death was the final consequence of the admitted negligence of the health authority in failing to diagnose his serious heart disease. In a state of shock and disbelief she attended the hospital mortuary within an hour after the death to view, at her own request, the body which bore no visible signs of injury, to satisfy her disbelief that he was in fact dead. The sight caused her to suffer nervous shock for which she sought damages from the defendants.

Auld J: The immediate aftermath extension is one which has been introduced as an exception to the general principle established in accident cases that a plaintiff can only recover damages for psychiatric injury when the accident and the primary injury or death caused by it occurred within his sight or hearing. There are two notions implicit in this exception cautiously introduced and cautiously continued by the House of Lords. They are of:
(1) an external, traumatic, event caused by the defendant's breach of duty which immediately causes some person injury or death; and
(2) a perception by the plaintiff of the event as it happens, normally by his presence at the scene, or exposure to the scene and/or to the primary victim so shortly afterwards that the shock of the event as well as of its consequence is brought home to him.

There was no such event here other than the final consequence of Mr Taylor's progressively deteriorating heart condition which the health authority, by its negligence many months before, had failed to arrest. In my judgment, his death at work and the subsequent transference of his body to the hospital where Mrs Taylor was informed of what had happened and where she saw the body do not constitute such an event.

Even if Mr Taylor's fatal heart attack could be considered to be an event to which the 'immediate aftermath' extension applied, the doctor's communication to her of that fact, even within an hour of the death, would not come within the extension. In *McLoughlin v O'Brian* [1982] 2 All ER 298 at 305, [1983] 1 AC 410 at 423 Lord Wilberforce indicated that the law does not compensate for shock brought about by communication by a third party.

Their Lordships in *Alcock* were of the same view, three of them (Lords Keith, Ackner and Oliver [1991] 4 All ER 907 at 915, 918, 932 [1992] 1 AC 310 at 398, 401, 418) expressly doubting the correctness of two first instance decisions in which claims had succeeded based in the main on information received through a third party of a son's death, namely *Hevican v Ruane* [1991] 3 All ER 65, per Mantell J, and *Ravenscroft v Rederiaktiebolaget Transatlantic* [1991] 3 All ER 73 per Ward J. The latter decision has since been reversed by the Court of Appeal ([1992] 2 All ER 470 (note)), in reliance upon their Lordships' views in *Alcock*.

Mrs Taylor also relies on her sight of her husband's body in the hospital mortuary within an hour of his death as coming within the aftermath principle. Mr Lewis submitted that all the events at the hospital, including the visit to the mortuary, should be considered as one. He stressed, as Mrs Taylor's agreed evidence on this point made plain, that part of her reason for agreeing to identify the body at that stage was because she could not believe that what the doctor had told her was true. In *Hevican v Ruane* the claim had been based in part on the plaintiff's sight of his son's body in the mortuary within about three hours after the accident and about two hours after learning of his death, but, as Mantell J made clear ([1991] 3 All ER 65 at 68 and 71), the principal basis of the claim, and of his ruling, was on the communication by others to him of the sad news. It was no doubt for that reason rather than the specific matter of the visit to the mortuary which led their Lordships in *Alcock* to doubt the correctness of the decision. However, in *Alcock*, some of the unsuccessful plaintiffs relied upon their visits to the mortuary some nine hours after the disaster, visits made purely for the purpose of identification. Such visits are well out of time for the immediate aftermath principle to apply, and in Lord Jauncey's expressed view ([1991] 4 All ER 907 at 937, [1992] 1 AC 310 at 424), so was their purpose. This leaves open for argument the question whether a visit to a mortuary within an hour or so after the death for some purpose other than formal identification of the body could come within the aftermath ([1991] 4 All ER 907 at 920–921, [1992] 1 AC 310 at 404–405) suggests by reference to the facts of *McLoughlin v O'Brian* that 'there may be liability where subsequent identification can be regarded as part of the immediate aftermath'. However, *McLoughlin v O'Brian* was a case where the plaintiff saw her injured and distressed husband and children in hospital shortly after their arrival there, and did not depend on any identification of her dead daughter.

Here, the main purpose of Mrs Taylor's visit to the mortuary was to confirm or otherwise the information that she had received from the doctor that her husband was dead. Apart from the obvious shock to her of the sight of his dead body, it bore no marks or signs to her of the sort that would have conjured up for her the circumstances of his fatal attack. In *McLoughlin v O'Brian* an important feature of Mrs McLoughlin's claim was, as Lord Jauncey observed [1991] 4 All ER 907 at 936–937, [1992] 1 AC 310 at 423–434, that the primary victims were still waiting to be attended to when she first saw them in the hospital, and 'were in very much the same condition as they would have been had the mother found them at the scene of the accident'. In my view, the fact that Mrs Taylor's main purpose in viewing her husband's body in the mortuary was to settle her disbelief as to his reported death is not capable of being part of any possible immediate aftermath in the circumstances of this case. It goes to the fact of the death as distinct from the circumstances in which death came about. That distinction, though of doubtful logic, is one upon which I am bound by authority. ...

In my judgment, therefore, Mrs Taylor, even if she had established that there had been an event to which the immediate aftermath extension could be attached, cannot bring her involvement in and about the death of her husband within the third element of constraint expounded by Lord Wilberforce in *McLoughlin v O'Brian* as to the means by which the shock is caused.

As we saw earlier, Auld J's requirement that there be an 'event' was disapproved by the Court of Appeal in *Sion*. His approach to the 'immediate aftermath' remains, however, the law (see *Palmer v Tees HA* [1999] Lloyd's Rep Med 351 (CA); but notice *W v Essex CC* [2000] 2 All ER 237 (HL)).

(b) Breaking bad news

A doctor (or hospital) may be liable to a patient when he carelessly misinforms a patient of his condition (*Allin v City and Hackney HA* [1996] 7 Med LR 167) or provides accurate information but does so in a careless way resulting in psychiatric injury (*AB v Tameside & Glossop HA* [1997] 8 Med LR 91). Thus, the carelessness may arise in respect of the accuracy of the information or in the manner of its disclosure. The duty will also exist in the case of former patients. In either case, the duty arises from the undertaking by the doctor (or hospital) implicit in imparting sensitive information. Liability follows from ordinary negligence principles. In *AB v Tameside & Glossop HA* [1997] 8 Med LR 91, the Court of Appeal accepted the parties' concession of a duty where it was alleged the defendant had carelessly informed current and former patients that a health care worker they may have come into contact with was HIV positive. On the facts, the court held that the defendant had not been negligent (see Commentary, (1997) 5 Med L Rev 338 (IK)). The emerging law is discussed by Nicholas Mullany. He first discusses accurate but carelessly delivered information and then inaccurate information.

Nicholas J Mullany 'Liability For Careless Communication of Traumatic Information' (1998) 114 LQR 380

There is nothing unpalatable about requiring those charged with the onerous and unenviable responsibility of breaking bad news to discharge this obligation in an appropriate manner. To demand accurate and sensitive written or oral dissemination of horrifying information is just and reasonable. *Caparo Industries Plc v Dickman* [1990] 2 AC 605 would not have operated to deny the conceded duty to communicate carefully in *AB*. Such a duty does not impose an intolerable burden on those who bear bad tidings. The fact that certain professionals are trained to perform this task evidences the fact that there is a right way and wrong way to go about it. Bitter pills do not have to be sugarcoated to avoid liability, but insensitive, irresponsible and sensationalist communication of clearly distressing news can and must be avoided. The common law cannot countenance the needless exacerbation of the effect of true traumatic news.

Imposing liability for incompetence of this nature does not diminish the wrong committed by the person responsible for the event announced. To advocate a general duty to communicate carefully is not to ignore the inherent difficulty in breaking bad news, something that should and would be borne in mind by courts in assessing its scope and breach. Such duty does not seriously threaten the timely provision of comprehensive information. Those who fail to disclose information to those who have a right to know it because they fear being sued will be liable for that failure in any event. Social utility is served in that formal training of and the facilities available to police, emergency service workers, doctors, nurses, prison authorities, government agencies and social workers will improve. Specialists will emerge, expert in the delivery of news nobody wants to hear. This will cost, but it is a cost worth paying for a more caring and compassionate society, a goal which not all believe is an inappropriate objective for the law of tort or a threat to its rational reform (*cf.* P S Atiyah, *The Damages Lottery* (1997), pp vii–viii, 2, 56–62).

The duty to communicate carefully should not depend on the presence of a pre-existing professional or other relationship. The mother callously informed by a police officer, a workmate or a stranger that her son has been killed should not be denied recovery for consequent psychiatric injury simply on the basis that there was no relevant bond between them beforehand. If proximity must play a part, it is satisfied by the bond which existed at the time of their meeting for the purpose of the dissemination of the news. Importantly, mental illness was foreseeable. Where there was a pre-existing duty between the parties, as there was in *AB*, the case for the existence of a duty to communicate carefully is particularly strong. It is supported by *Brown v Mount Barker Soldiers' Hospital* [1934] SASR 128, a case sanctioning recovery against conveyers of both true and false bad news which was not referred to by the Court of Appeal. The defendant hospital negligently burned a newborn baby out of sight of the mother. She was told of this true bad news and suffered "shock". Confirming that a duty was owed Piper J said:

Here the defendant in taking charge of Mrs Brown as a patient assumed a care of her involving the need to avoid, so far as reasonably practicable, all things that might prejudice her health or comfort, or increase her need for exertion or care. It would be a breach of duty, actionable if followed by damage, to tell her untruly that her child had been burnt. As the truthfulness of the statement was owing to negligence, the truthfulness was no legal excuse for doing harm by telling her – it was a necessary consequence of the negligence that she had to be told (at p 130).

On what basis can it be said that the duty of a hospital to treat a patient with care and skill does not include a duty to convey objectively distressing news so as to not unnecessarily increase its impact? Careless communication of such news may foreseeably compromise the health of the patient. As *Brown* makes clear, conveying bad news may not involve the positive provision of health care services, but it does carry the obligation not to prejudice mental tranquillity. Preservation of health is paramount.

The suggestion that a general duty of care is somehow indefensible or undesirable as a matter of principle because it will prove notoriously difficult to isolate the precise cause of disorder is baseless. Duty and causation are distinct. The existence of the former can never depend on the ability to prove the latter. The aetiology of psychiatric disorder is a complex subject. It is contested in virtually every suit for damage to the mind: claimants with pre-existing vulnerability to psychiatric injury and evidence of exposure to stressors other than the act the subject of complaint are the norm rather than the exception in modern litigation. Matters of causation will be determined in the "poor communication" cases in the light of detailed expert medical advice as they are in all actions for personal injury. Those claimants who fail to establish the requisite nexus between the manner and method of communicating distressing news (as distinct from the news itself) and proved psychiatric illness will fail. Causation difficulties and the need for proof of recognised disorder will combine to ensure that, far from a general duty leading to an onset of actions, successful suits for careless communication of true bad news will be rare. ...

Liability for careless communication should not turn on whether bad news is accurate. Foreseeability of psychiatric injury is what matters, not whether the news conveyed is true or false. In *Allin* erroneous information was given. A new mother suffered post-traumatic stress disorder when advised, after a very difficult labour and birth, that her baby was dead. Six hours later she learned that it had survived. Following an emergency Caesarean section the baby was in extremely poor condition having lost 80 per cent of her blood. It took 22 minutes to detect a heartbeat. The general consensus of those in the special care baby unit at the hospital managed and controlled by the defendants was that the baby would not survive. After the mother had been returned to the ward from theatre two doctors erroneously, but it seems sensitively, informed her that the baby had died. That negligent misstatement was the main basis of the action, although there was also an allegation that post-trauma counselling had not been provided.

The County Court found that negligence had been proved. As in *AB*, a concession by counsel for the defendants played a part in the determination of the claim: it was not disputed that "the defendants were under a duty of care in respect of statements of this sort made to the mother" (at p 170). Without exploring the threshold duty issue, HH Judge McMullan was moved to express the view that it "would have been an extraordinarily negligent thing to do, to inform a mother that her baby was dead when it was not". The false belief that her baby was dead, even though held for only six hours, was found to have been a substantial causative factor in the onset of the mother's disorder.

The correctness of *Allin* can be tested by reference to the consequence of a denial of duty. It would be offensive if liability could lie under *Hedley Byrne* for economic loss caused by a negligent misstatement but not for psychiatric injury caused by the same wrong. Financial well-being can never be afforded a higher priority than the preservation of physical and mental integrity. Nor does denial of recovery make sense when relief may be had for physical injury caused by negligent misstatement (see *Clayton v Woodman & Son (Builders) Ltd* [1962] 2 QB 533). It is unquestionably right for the common law to insist that those who communicate objectively distressing (indeed, potentially life-shattering) news take all reasonable precautions to ensure that such news is accurate (see *Barnes v Commonwealth* (1937) 37 SR (NSW) 511 at pp 515–516; *Bunyan v Jordan* (1936) 36 SR (NSW) 350, affirmed (1937) 57 CLR 1; *Guay v Sun Publishing Co* [1953] 4 DLR 577 at pp 612–613; Mullany and Handford, *op cit supra* at pp 183–191). How can liability be denied as a matter of principle to the husband told wrongly that he is HIV-antibody positive whose wife divorces him believing he has been unfaithful? What of the woman told wrongly that she has breast or cervical cancer and who, perhaps, endures unnecessary radiation treatment? Psychiatric illness suffered, possibly for years, before these errors are discovered and communicated, is surely compensable. Lord Denning MR's *obiter* opinion that this extension is too "big a step" to endorse should be disregarded (see *D v NSPCC* [1978] AC 171 at pp 188–189) ...

Two further points: what is the position if the bad news is half-true or half-false? If the accuracy of the news is important, how will courts cope with claims where the degree of accuracy is in issue? *Allin* was simple: the baby was either dead or alive. But what if a mother is informed that her child has been very seriously injured in a car accident when the injuries are minor? What if she is told that the injuries are minor when they are in fact life threatening or the child has died (*cf. Petrie v Dowling*)? Are claims based on these mistakes to be determined by reference to duty, breach or causation principles?

The answer to Mullany's last point must be that these matters are relevant only to the issue of breach. Was the doctor careless in determining the accuracy of what he said? In *AB* the information had been volunteered. The court was not concerned with the case where the doctor had failed to inform a patient (or former patient) of the risk of injury arising out of treatment. It may be, as we will see, that as with a duty to disclose medical mistakes, there is a duty to provide *post-treatment* advice about exposure to risks during the procedure, such as HIV infection or Hepatitis B or C (see *infra*, ch 5).

Having considered liability to the patient, what of liability to the patient's relatives for delivering bad news? In *Taylor* the judge referred to the well-known, but nevertheless controversial, rule that a negligent defendant is not liable for psychiatric injury caused where a relative is *told* of their loved one's death or injury by an intermediary (see, *Ravenscroft v Rederiaktiebolaget Transatlantic* [1992] 2 All ER 470n (CA)). What, however, of the intermediary's liability? Could a doctor be liable for negligently communicating 'bad news' to a relative? There is little English case law although *Powell v Boldaz* (1997) 39 BMLR 35 (Commentary, (1998) 6 Med L Rev 112 (IK)) seems against such a claim. We are not here concerned with deliberately misinforming the relative, an unlikely situation one might think, when an action under *Wilkinson v Downton* [1897] 2 QB 57 would arise. The question of liability in negligence is discussed in the following extract.

I Kennedy and A Grubb (eds) *Principles of Medical Law* (1998)

5.84 A final situation which should be considered is where a person is negligently told bad news about a relative and, as a consequence, suffers a shock which causes psychiatric injury. The negligence may lie in the way the information is communicated or in its accuracy. It is clear that an action will not lie against the primary defendant where an intermediary acts as a conduit to tell the plaintiff of injuries that have been inflicted upon the plaintiff's relative. Unlike that situation, however, we are concerned with the liability of the *intermediary* himself. Can a doctor be liable for negligently (see *Wilkinson v Downton* [1897] 2 QB 57 for malicious communication) breaking 'bad news' to the relatives? In principle there is no reason why he should not. (*Jinks v Cardwell* (1987) 39 CCLT 168 (Ont H Ct) (doctor held liable for psychiatric injury caused to a wife when he told her, falsely, that her husband had committed suicide)). The three elements required for a duty of care – 'foreseeability', 'proximity', and the 'fair, just, and reasonable' requirement – seem satisfied. It is readily foreseeable that carelessness might produce an adverse psychiatric reaction. There is a 'close and direct' relationship between the doctor and relative sufficient to create a proximate relationship. Finally, it is not obvious what policy reasons mitigate against imposing liability in this particular context. It should not matter whether the negligence lies in the falsity of the communication or in the method or nature of a (true) communication. As regards the latter situation, there is certainly some analogy with the duty of a doctor to exercise reasonable care when informing his patients post-operatively. (See *AB v Tameside & Glossop HA* [1997] 8 Med LR 91). However, the contrary has been suggested at least where the information is true. (*Mount Isa Mines v Pusey* (1970) 125 CLR 383 (Aust H Ct), per Windeyer J at 407. But note *Guay v Sun Publishing Co* [1953] 4 DLR 577 (Can Sup Ct) (no liability for false story published in newspaper)).

5.85 The decision of the Court of Appeal in *Powell v Boldaz* ((1997) 39 BMLR 35) appears to limit the scope of a doctor's liability in these circumstances. The plaintiffs, a married couple, brought an action claiming damages for psychiatric injury arising out of the death of their son. He suffered from a rare condition known as 'Addison's Disease'. It was accepted that there had been negligence in failing to diagnose and treat his condition and that had he been treated in time he would have survived. Sometime after their son's death, the plaintiffs were told the reason for his death and were shown his medical records. No complaint was made about this. However, they alleged that seven months later they discovered that their son's medical notes had been tampered with by the defendants. They alleged that their general practitioners had conspired to 'cover-up' the cause of their son's death and that their realisation of this caused them each to suffer post-traumatic stress disorder. The judge struck out their actions. The Court of Appeal dismissed the appeal on the basis that no duty of care was owed by the defendants in respect of the post-death allegations. The Court of Appeal held that a duty of care would only arise if the defendants had been called upon or undertook to treat the plaintiffs as patients. While the defendants were the plaintiffs' GPs, the court held that at the relevant time they had not been counselling or treating the plaintiffs. Stuart-Smith LJ said: (ibid, 45).

I do not think that a doctor who has been treating a patient who has died, who tells relatives what has happened, thereby undertakes the doctor-patient relationship towards the relatives. It is a situation that calls for sensitivity, tact and discretion. But the mere fact that the communicator is a doctor, does not, without more, mean that he undertakes the doctor-patient relationship.

Later, he stated that the case law did not establish

some kind of free-standing duty of candour, irrespective of whether the doctor-patient relationship exists in a healing or treating context, breach of which sounds in damages, such damages involving personal injury. This would involve a startling expansion of the law of tort. (ibid., 46)

5.86 Three observations on this decision are worth making. First, the plaintiffs only alleged that their discovery of the 'conspiracy' caused them psychiatric injury and not the communication by the GPs to them of false, inaccurate or insensitively communicated information. Arguably, the plaintiffs' claim would have been stronger if this had been the case. Secondly, the almost mesmeric effect on the Court of Appeal of the label 'doctor-patient relationship' has to be questioned. It is not a necessary condition for a doctor to owe another a duty of care. It is as if the court thought that the plaintiffs were alleging that the defendants had negligently failed to treat them. If they had, the existence of the relationship would have been important, though even then not conclusive, to the action. But this was in fact irrelevant in the case because it was not what they alleged. The real question was whether the defendants owed a duty not to harm the plaintiffs, rather than one not to diagnose or treat them negligently. Thirdly, the Court of Appeal's denial of a duty of care in circumstances such as these was not quite categorical. The court accepted that if the doctor realised that the news he had broken had shocked the recipient such as to call for treatment, he might be liable for not carrying on and treating the individual. Stuart-Smith LJ stated that it would be 'a question of fact and degree in each case whether the doctor-patient relationship came into existence by the doctor undertaking to treat and heal the person as a patient.'

5.87 It is suggested that the reasoning of the Court of Appeal is so open to question that it is extremely unlikely to survive scrutiny in a future case where a doctor negligently *advises* a relative of a patient's death or injuries and thereby causes psychiatric injury.

(c) Fear of injury

Exposure to infectious agents, chemicals or other substances with the potential to harm the individual may result in the fear of developing an injurious condition in the future.

However, for the present, that individual may not be infected or harmed. Instead, the fear causes psychiatric injury. Illustrations may be exposure to asbestos, chemicals such as dioxin or, in the medical context, blood or blood products infected with HIV. In America 'cancer phobia' and 'AIDS phobia' actions have been accepted in some jurisdictions. Some courts require actual infection or injury, others merely require exposure and a reasonable belief in infection. The case law is discussed by the Maryland Court of Appeals in *Faya and Rossi v Almaraz*.

Faya v Almaraz (1993) 620 A 2d 327 (Md CA)

Murphy CJ: These companion cases present the important question whether a surgeon infected with the AIDS virus has a legal duty to inform patients of that condition before operating upon them and, failing that, whether a patient's fear of having contracted the AIDS virus from the infected surgeon constitutes a legally compensable injury where the patient has not shown HIV-positive status...

Dr Rudolf Almaraz, an oncological surgeon specializing in breast cancer with operative privileges at the Johns Hopkins Hospital (Hopkins) in Baltimore, knew himself to be HIV-positive, ie a carrier of the HIV virus, since 1986. On October 7, 1988, Almarez performed a partial mastectomy and axillary dissection on Sonja Faya at Hopkins. He removed an axillary hematoma from Faya the following March. On November 14, 1989, again at Hopkins, Almaraz surgically excised a benign lump from the breast of Perry Mahoney Rossi. The therapeutic outcome of these operations is not in dispute.

On October 27, 1989, Almaraz was first diagnosed as suffering from cytomegalovirus retinitis, the eye infection signalling full-blown AIDS. That diagnosis was confirmed by a second ophthalmologist on November 17, 1989. Thus, as well as knowing his HIV-positive status throughout the period in question, Almaraz knew that he had AIDS prior to the Rossi operation.

Almaraz gave up his practice of medicine on March 1, 1990. He terminated his association with Hopkins in June of that year. He died of AIDS on November 16, 1990. Faya and Rossi learned of their physician's illness for the first time from a local newspaper on or about December 6, 1990, well over a year after Rossi's operation and twenty months after Faya's last contact with Almaraz. Both Faya and Rossi immediately underwent blood tests for the AIDS virus, which came back negative for both. Nevertheless, by December 11 Sonja Faya, Perry Mahoney Rossi, and her husband, Dennis T Rossi (appellants), filed suit against Almaraz's estate, his Maryland professional association business entity, and Hopkins (appellees) for compensatory and punitive damages...

The gist of the complaints was that Almaraz acted wrongfully in operating on the two women without first telling them that he was HIV-positive (and, later, ill from AIDS proper), and that Hopkins was culpable for permitting him to do so. More specifically, appellants alleged that at the time of the consultations and surgeries, Almaraz, knowing of his illness, failed to inform them of any risk of contracting HIV that might result from his performance of the surgical procedures. They alluded to the possibility of a puncture or laceration through the protective garments worn by the surgeon and a consequent commingling of his blood with their blood. They claimed that by undergoing their operations in ignorance of Almaraz's illness, they were exposed to a hazard they would otherwise have avoided by withholding their consent, namely, a risk of AIDS attendant upon invasive surgery...

The representatives of Dr Almaraz asserted that the physician owed no duty to disclose his ailment as part of the doctor-patient exchange leading to informed consent. Hopkins contended, in the main, that it had no duty to investigate and ascertain Almaraz's HIV status; the hospital added that the obligations imposed by the informed consent doctrine did not extend to it in any case. The appellees further averred that the complaints were legally deficient in that appellants failed to allege that the AIDS virus entered their bodies as a result of surgery, and that the claimed injuries were not legally compensable because they rested on fear of a risk that never materialized...

We cannot say as a matter of law that no duty was imposed upon Dr Almaraz to warn the appellants of his infected condition or refrain from operating upon them.

The appellants pleaded that as a result of Dr Almaraz's breach of duty, they were put in fear of having contracted HIV and thereby suffered the derivative consequences of that fear, which were manifested by emotional and mental distress, headaches, sleeplessness, and, in addition, the pain and expense associated with repeated blood tests. We turn now to the question of whether these are legally compensable injuries where the appellants have not alleged in their complaints an actual transmission of the HIV virus into their bodies during the surgical procedures. Instead, appellants allege only that because of Dr Almaraz's HIV positive status, he exposed them to the virus during the surgery. In this regard, the complaints do not allege that subsequent blood tests have revealed that the appellants have, in fact, shown HIV positive status.

Courts have differed on the question of recovery of damages for the feat of AIDS and attendant physical consequences absent an HIV-positive test. In *Burk v Sage Products Inc*, 747 F Supp 285 (ED Pa 1990), the court rejected a paramedic's claim based on fear of contracting AIDS after he suffered a needle-stick from a discarded syringe. The paramedic could not demonstrate that the needle had been used on an AIDS patient, and he himself had tested HIV-negative no fewer than five times during the thirteen months after the incident. The court held first that, in the absence of any allegation that the syringe harbored HIV, the plaintiff had failed to establish an exposure to the AIDS virus sufficient to support a cause of action. Moreover, the court found no compensable injury: "Plaintiff here has alleged no injury which arises out of his exposure to the AIDS virus. Rather, plaintiff's only injuries stem from his *fear* that he has been exposed to the disease." The court deemed such fear to be unfounded, observing that the five negative tests indicated to a high degree of medical certainty that the paramedic would not develop AIDS from his needle-stick.

Other courts have concurred with *Burk* in denying recovery where the plaintiff can demonstrate neither a channel of exposure to the AIDS virus nor demonstrable injury in the form of an HIV-positive test. See *Funeral Services by Gregory, Inc, v Bluefield Community Hospital*, 186 W Va 424, 413 S E 2d 79 (1991)(no recovery for a mortician who had embalmed an AIDS-infected corpse, where he had worn proper protective gear and had not alleged any avenue of exposure); *Hare v State*, 173 A D 2d 523, 570 N Y S 2d 125 (2 Dept 1991)(recovery denied for hospital employee failed to prove that inmate was infected and where plaintiff had tested HIV-negative); *Doe v Doe*, 136 Misc 2d 1015, 519 N Y S 2d 595 (Sup 1987)(recovery denied for "AIDS-phobia" based on husband's alleged homosexual affair, wife having failed to allege that husband was infected with the disease and having failed to allege that she had contracted HIV).

On the other hand, some courts have reasoned differently. In *Johnson v W Va University Hospitals*, 186 W Va 648, 413 S E 2d 889 (1991), the court affirmed a judgment for a police officer attacked in a hospital by an AIDS-infected patient who had first bitten himself on the arm, thereby drawing his own infected blood into his mouth, and then bitten the officer. There, the officer sued the hospital, claiming that it negligently failed to advise him that the patient had AIDS, and that as a result of his exposure to Aids, the officer had suffered from emotional distress. Although regularly tested for the HIV virus after having been bitten by the patient, the tests were negative for the disease. The officer's treating psychologist testified that the officer suffered from post traumatic stress disorder and was unable to sleep. The court noted that, absent physical injury, there would be no recovery for emotional distress. It held, however, that there was evidence of physical injury because of the officer's having been bitten and that his physical injury included sleeplessness, loss of appetite, and other physical manifestations accompanying the emotional distress. The officer's physical injury, the court said, was a factor going to the reasonableness of the officer's fear of contracting AIDS for which he could recover damages for emotional distress, even though he tested HIV-negative. The court emphasized that its decision did not permit recovery of emotional distress damages by anyone who merely comes into contact with an AIDS-infected individual; rather, it said that "recovery of such damages is limited to the situation where the plaintiff is actually exposed to the AIDS virus as a result of a physical injury, and emotional distress, along with physical manifestations of such distress, result therefrom".

In *Carroll v Sisters of St Francis Health Services Inc,* 1992 WL 276717 (Tenn App 1992), certiorari petition filed December 11, 1992, the plaintiff had been pricked by a needle while visiting her sister in the hospital. Even though the plaintiff was unable to show actual exposure to the HIV virus, or that she tested HIV-positive, she sued the hospital for damages which she alleged resulted from fear that she had contracted the disease. In reversing a summary judgment against the plaintiff, the court relied upon *Laxton v Orkin Exterminating Co,* 639 S W 2d 431 (Tenn 1982), in which the Tennessee Supreme Court allowed plaintiffs to recover for fear of harm against an exterminating company which had leaked dangerous chemicals into their drinking supply, even though plaintiffs showed no physical symptoms of illness. *Laxton* specified, however, that "The period of mental anguish ...would be confined to the time between discovery of the ingestion and the negative medical diagnosis or other information that puts to rest the fear of injury." 639 S W 2d at 434.

Explicitly rejecting "the strict rules of actual exposure" required by *Burk* and its progeny, the *Carroll* court read *Laxton* to allow recovery for fear of AIDS even though the plaintiff could show neither actual HIV exposure nor an HIV-positive test. It said:

> We construe *Laxton* to set a standard of 'reasonableness' of the fear... The gravamen of the action in *Laxton* was the effect of defendant's negligence on the plaintiffs' state of mind and the Court found under the peculiar facts of the case that they could reasonably have the fear of acquiring serious medical maladies. The court was quite clear, however, that the period of time considered reasonable for the mental anguish would cease upon information that 'puts to rest the fear of injury.'

Carroll. See also Castro v New York Life Insurance Co, *153 Misc 2d 1, 588 N Y S 2d 695, 697 (Sup 1991) (custodian may recover where stuck by a hypodermic needle discarded in the trash of an insurance company office, insofar as she had "a claim ... tied to a distinct event which would cause a reasonable person to develop a fear of contracting a disease like AIDS").*

[8]In the instant case, we cannot say that appellants' alleged fear of acquiring AIDS was initially unreasonable as a matter of law, even though the averments of the complaints did not identify any actual channel of transmission of the AIDS virus. But *Burk's* requirement that plaintiffs must allege actual transmission would unfairly punish them for lacking the requisite information to do so.

[9]Appellants' *continued* fear of contracting AIDS may, however, be unreasonable after they tested HIV-negative upon learning of Dr Alvaraz's illness, which was well over a year after their last contacts with the physician. As we noted above, there is current credible evidence of a 95% certainty that one will test positive for the AIDS virus, if at all, within six months after exposure to it. Once appellants learned of their HIV-negative status more than a year after their respective surgeries, the possibility of their contracting AIDS from Dr Alvaraz became extremely unlikely and thus, as a matter of law, might be deemed unreasonable. Therefore, appellants may only recover for their fear and its physical manifestations which may have resulted from Almaraz's alleged negligence for the period constituting their reasonable window of anxiety – the period between which they learned of Almaraz's illness and received their HIV-negative results...

In the instant case, appellants allege that their fear and mental and emotional distress are accompanied by headache, sleeplessness, and the physical and financial sting of blood tests for the AIDS virus. *Vance* and its precursors dictate that appellants may recover for these injuries, to the extent that they can objectively demonstrate their existence. Again, however, such damages must be confined to injuries suffered during the appellants' legitimate window of mental anxiety; after this point, for the reasons discussed above, any lingering injuries, as a matter of law, are no longer related to fear that is reasonable.

What would be the position under English law? Importantly, the courts would not require a plaintiff in a situation like *Faya* to satisfy the restrictive *McLoughlin/Alcock* rules applied to so-called 'secondary victims' (see *Alcock v Chief Constable of South Yorkshire* [1992] 1 AC 310 (HL) at 407-408 per Lord Oliver and *McFarlane v EE Caledonia Ltd* [1994] 2 All ER 1 (CA)). Instead, the plaintiff would be a 'primary victim' and would be merely required to establish that injury to her was *reasonably foreseeable*. Indeed, after *Page v Smith* [1995] 2 All ER 736 (HL) it will be sufficient to establish that *any* physical injury was reasonably foreseeable even if psychiatric injury itself was not. Also, it is probably not necessary to establish a 'shocking event' (see *Walker v Northumberland CC* [1995] 1 All ER 737 (Coleman J))- although there would often be one. In any event, even if this was an essential element, the plaintiff would succeed if the *discovery* of the doctor's HIV status (and thus the risk to him) was 'sudden' and 'shocking' (see *Sion v Hampstead HA* [1994] 5 Med LR 170 (CA) per Peter Gibson LJ at 176).

So what of the options offered by the American case law? English law certainly would not require the plaintiff to show actual injury (ie infection with HIV), exposure would suffice (see, *Page v Smith, supra* and *Dulieu v White & Sons* [1901] 2 KB 669 (KB Div)). It is not crucial that the risk of infection is very small because even a remote risk of such serious harm would be considered a reasonably foreseeable risk of injury (see *The Wagon Mound (No 2)* [1967] 1 AC 617 (PC)). After *Page v Smith,* the doctor could be liable to the patient. The doctor's failure to disclose the risk of HIV infection, or his exposing the patient to the risk *per se*, would fall within the approach of the House of Lords in *Page v Smith* as the doctor had exposed the patient to a risk of physical injury, ie HIV infection, even if the patient would remain asymptomatic for some time (see *Cartledge v Jopling & Sons Ltd* [1963] AC 758 – actionable harm does not require proof of 'any symptom or present inconvenience', per Lord Pearce at 778).

But, what if the doctor is not HIV positive? In *Faya*, the court concluded that this was only relevant in determining whether psychiatric injury was reasonably foreseeable. Where the plaintiff's fear is triggered by the doctor's negligence which creates in the mind of the patient a risk of transmission and which would exist if the doctor were HIV positive, for example, by a 'sharps' injury, a patient might succeed on the basis of *Page v Smith*. The foreseeability of physical injury – which, of course, actually occurred – means that the plaintiff does not have to prove that psychiatric injury was reasonably foreseeable. It is difficult to imagine a case where the plaintiff's fear of infection (and the doctor is not infected) does not arise from an injury to the plaintiff. This injury must, of course, have been caused through the negligence of the doctor for the claim for psychiatric injury to have a chance of success. It seems somewhat serendipitous to allow a plaintiff to claim for psychiatric injury arising from the fear of contracting HIV when the defendant's negligence (ie foresight) is likely to relate only to some minor injury. In such a case, the court might well conclude that psychiatric injury itself was not reasonably foreseeable. But, overall this is the effect of the House of Lords' decision in *Page v Smith* (though notice the majority also accepted on the facts that psychiatric injury was reasonably foreseeable: per Lord Ackner at 742; per Lord Browne-Wilkinson at 752; per Lord Lloyd at 767). No doubt if a patient's fear was wholly unreasonable, the court would not entertain the action. The flexibility of such control mechanisms as remoteness would most likely come to the court's aid.

In the litigation concerning *Creutzfeldt-Jakob Disease*, Morland J had to consider claims by children who might have been infected with CJD in human growth hormone used to treat them. The judge considered the application of *Page v Smith.*

The Creutzfeldt-Jakob Disease Litigation, Group B Plaintiffs v Medical Research Council (1997) 41 BMLR 157 (QBD)

All of the plaintiffs in Group B were children, handicapped by dwarfism, who had been selected for treatment by clinicians at growth centres, in a clinical experimental trial. They had been injected, after 1 July 1977, with Hartree HGH, which was capable of infecting them with Creutzfeldt-Jacob Disease (CJD). An unknown number of them might be incubating the disease as a consequence. All of them are aware that they are at risk of developing CJD. On 19 July 1996, Morland J found that to allow new patients, other than those suffering from hypoglycaemia, to receive HGH therapy was a breach of the duty of care owed to them, as it fell below the standard of care and responsibility to be reasonably expected of properly briefed clinicians and experts and that, on the balance of probabilities, cases of CJD among recipients of HGH, whose treatment had begun after 1 July 1997, had been caused by the negligence of the Department of Health. This was a trial of the preliminary issues of: (i) whether the duty was to avoid the risk of psychiatric as well as physical illness; (ii) whether psychiatric injury could, as a matter of law, be held to have been caused by the defendant's negligence; (iii) whether damages for such psychiatric injury were recoverable as a matter of law…

Morland J: It is not disputed that, at the time they were infected with HGH, the defendant's owed a duty of care to the Group B plaintiffs. The Group B plaintiffs were injected with HGH in breach of that duty of care. Mr Irwin made, as his primary submission, that they are primary victims. They were directly owed a duty of care by the defendants, who breached that duty by being responsible for their injection with HGH. The risk of physical injury was foreseeable; that is, the risk of CJD. The psychiatric injury developed as the direct consequence of their becoming aware of that very risk of CJD. The decision of the House of Lords in *Page v Smith* (1995) 28 BMLR 133, [1996] 1 AC 155 applied. It was established that the defendants were in breach of their duty of care to avoid causing personal injury to the Group B plaintiffs. It mattered not whether the injury in fact sustained was physical, psychiatric or both. It was unnecessary to ask whether psychiatric injury was foreseeable. Control mechanisms to limit the number of potential claimants had no place.

Mr Irwin's alternative submission, on the basis that *Page v Smith* was distinguishable or inapplicable because in that case the House of Lords was dealing with a different factual situation – shock induced contemporaneously by direct involvement in a traumatic physical accident – was that on 1 July 1977 it should have been reasonably foreseeable to the defendants that some Group B plaintiffs of ordinary fortitude might develop psychiatric illness after becoming aware of the risk that they might carry a potentially lethal amount of the CJD agent. If the Group B plaintiffs were to be regarded as analogous to secondary victims, control mechanisms were in place and there were no valid public policy reasons why the Group B plaintiffs should not recover.

Mr Irwin submitted that there was no logical or public policy reason why a claimant should not recover for a psychiatric illness caused by becoming aware of the fact that he was at risk of a lethal disease attributable to a physical event negligently occurring years earlier. He submitted that it should matter not whether the news of the risk of the lethal disease induces a sudden shock and consequent psychiatric illness or whether the news is received over a period of time from a variety of sources causing the development of psychiatric illness. A cumulative awareness or a drip-feed of information about the risk of lethal disease are just as foreseeably likely to cause a psychiatric illness as the sudden shock of the initial information.

Mr Irwin further submitted that there were control mechanisms in place which should entitle an individual Group B plaintiff who proves his case to recover and be within any line drawn by public policy. The burden of proof will remain throughout upon the plaintiff. In adversarial litigation, his case and evidence will be subject to careful scrutiny by counsel instructed by the Secretary of State. The individual plaintiff will have to prove that he has suffered a genuine psychiatric illness and that his genuine psychiatric illness was caused by his awareness of the risk of CJD which, in turn, it is not now disputed by the defendants, was caused by the defendants' breach of duty to him in being responsible for commencing HGH injections upon him after 1 July 1977. With regard to the 'floodgates' argument, Mr Irwin submitted that the Group B plaintiffs were a small cohort of people numbering in theoretical terms hundreds but in reality tens. They had special characteristics. They were all children when the defendants breached their duty of care to them and they were adolescents or young adults when they became aware of the risk of CJD. The risk of CJD was not merely the risk of lethal disease but of a disease which would cause the victim ghastly suffering, not capable of treatment or amelioration.

It was fair, just and reasonable for liability to be imposed subject to proof by individual Group B plaintiffs. It is a situation where the court should impose liability. This reflected part of the speech of Lord Bridge in *Caparo Industries plc v Dickman* [1990] 1 All ER 568 at 573-574, [1990] 2 AC 605 at 617-618, who was dealing with a wholly different situation of whether auditors owed a duty of care to investing shareholders and could be liable for economic loss.

Mr Justin Fenwick QC for the defendants submitted that *Page v Smith* was not applicable or was distinguishable. The Group B plaintiffs were not primary victims because their psychiatric injury was not the direct result of a sudden shocking event compressed into a short space of time during which the feared physical injury would have been suffered had it occurred.

He also submitted that the Group B plaintiffs were not secondary victims as that term is used. They were not akin to bystanders of a shocking event negligently caused. There was no proximity of time between the defendants' breach of duty, the negligent injection of Hartree HGH and the later psychiatric illnesses which was consequent upon the awareness of the risk of CJD. There is no case where a plaintiff has succeeded as the result of communication by a third party causing shock.

He submitted that the shock had to be sudden and contemporaneous with an event caused by negligence.

He submitted that to find for the Group B plaintiffs on the trial of the preliminary issues would be a novel step, opening the floodgates, for example, to those exposed to asbestos or radiation. The asbestos worker will inhale or ingest asbestos fibres. Radiation causes physical insult by gamma rays or alpha particles striking cells. There is the potential for many thousands of claims from the victims of asbestos or radiation who could assert, possibly years after, that they learnt that they were at risk from mesothelioma or leukaemia and as a result suffered psychiatric illness. In the present case, although each Group B plaintiff in breach of the defendants' duty of care to him suffered a physical insult when injected with Hartree HGH, there was no proof that any particular injection carried the CJD agent or if it did with sufficient titre to cause CJD.

Mr Fenwick submitted that the line had to be drawn and public policy required that the Group B plaintiffs be excluded from compensation for psychiatric injury. He relied in particular upon the decision of *Metro-North Commuter Railroad v Buckley* (1997) US Lexis 3867, where the Supreme Court held that Buckley, who had been exposed to asbestos on the railroad and had later attended an asbestos awareness course and had, as a result, feared with some cause that he would develop cancer, could not recover emotional distress damages unless and until he manifested the symptoms of a disease. The Supreme Court also held that the 'physical impact' to which *Gottshall* (1994) 114 Sup Ct Reptr 2396 referred does not include a simple physical contact with a substance which might cause a disease at a substantially later time where the substance threatens no harm other than disease related risk.

The Supreme Court gave reasons for this. The 'zone of danger' test involved a threatened physical contact that caused or might have caused immediate traumatic harm. Common law courts have denied recovery for emotional distress to those who are disease-and symptom-free.

In my judgment, American cases are not particularly helpful. The culture of American personal injury litigation is very different from ours and thus public policy considerations. The requirement in England that a plaintiff must prove a genuine psychiatric injury is a powerful control mechanism…:

Mr Fenwick submitted that I should not follow the approach of Harper J in the Supreme Court of Victoria in, I emphasise, a strike-out application, in *APQ v Commonwealth Serum Laboratories Ltd* (2 February 1995, unreported), which has striking factual similarity to the present Group B litigation. The plaintiff was treated with HPG derived from human pituitaries. In course of his judgment, refusing strike-out, Harper J said:

> It is in my opinion beyond argument that the defendants in this case should have foreseen psychiatric harm to a patient treated with HPG upon the patient becoming aware that CJD might follow … In this case, of course, the plaintiff is the primary victim. Her psychiatric illness has resulted from her awareness of the possibility of her own death following an unpleasant disease.

Mr Fenwick has persuaded me that the factual situation in relation to the Group B plaintiffs who suffered psychiatric injury years after receiving the negligent injections of Hartree HGH as the result of becoming aware of the risk of CJD is so far removed from the factual situation in *Page v Smith*, or any factual situation envisaged by their Lordships in their speeches, that *Page v Smith* is not applicable.

In my judgment, Mr Page was truly a primary victim. Mr Smith negligently drove his car into collision with the car driven by Mr Page causing him sudden shock which caused his CFS to become chronic and permanent…

In the case of the Group B plaintiffs, unlike the primary victim envisaged by *Page v Smith*, their psychiatric illnesses result from a fear of the future: will they be struck down by a ghastly untreatable terminal disease which attacks their brains?

The *Page v Smith* primary victim becomes aware of imminent danger and is a participant in the traumatic event. Thus, a sudden shock is produced, resulting in psychiatric illness. By then, all danger of physical, as opposed to psychiatric, injury has passed.

In the *Page v Smith* primary victim situation, the primary victim's awareness of danger and his participation in the traumatic event, his shock and resultant psychiatric illness happen simultaneously or almost contemporaneously.

The Group B plaintiff was specifically owed a duty of care by the defendants, who were responsible for the production of HGH and the supervision of the therapy programme. From 1 July 1977, the defendants were in breach of that duty of care in failing to suspend the programme for new patients. They breached that duty of care by being responsible for a physical impact upon the Group B plaintiffs, their injection with Hartree HGH. Thus far, the Group B plaintiffs can be likened to primary victims.

But the psychiatric injury which they allege was not triggered by that physical event, although the fact of that physical event when they learnt later, that it put them on risk of CJD, was a potent causative factor in the development of the psychiatric injury, although the trigger for the psychiatric injury was their awareness of the risk and the nature of CJD.

I am persuaded that the Group B plaintiffs should not be treated as primary victims. I accept the submissions of Mr Fenwick that, if they were, the ramifications would be incalculable. If they were primary victims so would be those exposed to asbestos or radiation where primary liability may depend not upon common law negligence but on statutory duty or even strict liability, even if they became aware of the risk of physical injury years later and consequently developed psychiatric injury. The potentiality of a huge number of claims in similar situations would arise, making insurance difficult or impossible. It could involve all manner of products and a huge range of potential tortfeasors. It could inhibit the producers, prescribers and suppliers of a product from warning the public of the danger of a product. For example, if a potentially lethal substance had been negligently introduced into a production batch of canned food, it would be disastrous if a supplier or producer were inhibited from warning the public of danger for fear that, among those who had already eaten the canned food, some might bring a claim as a primary victim for psychiatric injury triggered by the warning. Against such a claim the producer could not raise defences either that the psychiatric injury was unforeseeable to a person of normal fortitude or that the law insists upon certain control mechanisms to limit the number of potential claimants.

If the Group B plaintiffs are not to be treated as primary victims, how should the law treat them?

Among the factors to which I have regard is the extent of the defendants' duty of care, the nature of the relationship between the defendants and the Group B plaintiffs, the size of the cohort of potential plaintiffs, the ways in which the plaintiffs might become aware of the risk of CJD, the nature of the suffering in terminal CJD and the defendants' reasonable foreseeability of the effect on HGH recipients if the risk of CJD become a reality.

In my judgment, the relationship between the defendants and the recipients of HGH was, akin to that of doctor and patient, one of close proximity. But they were all children. They themselves did not choose to receive the treatment. They were selected for the treatment by clinicians at growth centres. It was the parents of the children who consented to the treatment. The purpose of the treatment was to improve the child's prospects in adulthood – both physically and, significantly, psychologically – of coping with life. The children were handicapped by dwarfism. They were the objects of a clinical experimental trial, although by 1 July 1977 in reality, because of the increased number of recipients, it was becoming a therapeutic programme.

By 1 July 1977 the defendants were aware of the risk of CJD and, as is now accepted, were negligent in not suspending the programme. When the defendants owed their duty of care to the recipients by being responsible for their injection with HGH, the defendants were not only aware of the risk of CJD, but also that the risk of CJD might not become a reality for years or even decades. The children, their parents and most, if not all, of the clinicians were totally unaware of the risk that in early adulthood or later life they might develop CJD. The extent to which the defendants knew or should have known of the risk and the nature of their negligence is summarised in my judgment of 19 July 1996.

Unlike some of the examples given by Mr Fenwick in his 'floodgates' argument, such as exposure to asbestos, radiation, contaminated blood transfusions, the cohort of potential victims of psychiatric injury is small. It is limited to those whose therapy began after 1 July 1977 and who received Hartree HGH. The total number of children treated between 1959 and 1985 did not reach 2,000. Only a very small number of these could qualify for compensation. They would probably be numbering tens rather than hundreds. The terrible nature of CJD does not need elaboration. Its ghastly and inexorable progress causes great distress and disablement, physically and psychologically, to the victim. It is not susceptible to either treatment or amelioration. Unlike many forms of cancer there is no hope, no chance of prolongation of life and no ability to lead an almost normal form of life during the progress of the disease. Mr Fenwick submitted that it could not be right that the Hartree HGH recipients recover for a psychiatric injury when not only may they never suffer from CJD, but also they may not have been injected with a dose of Hartree HGH with a sufficient titre of the CJD agent capable of triggering CJD. I found this an artificial and unattractive argument. Only on post mortem can a positive CJD diagnosis be made. What is now known is that Hartree HGH was a faulty method of production. On 1 July 1977, although the risk of CJD should have been foreseen and the risk sufficiently serious to require suspension, what was not foreseeable was when the risk might be a reality; indeed, the preponderance of expert opinion was that the awful reality was unlikely to occur.

What knowledge there was as to when the risk might become a reality was obtainable only by extrapolation from the then knowledge about Kuru and laboratory experiments of transmission involving Kuru – or Scrapie-infected tissue to animals and iatrogenic transmission to humans as documented by Duffy and Bernouli.

Such extrapolation was a very inexact guide to any estimation of the time as to when the risk might become an awful reality with the first case of CJD. In the programme the HGH was treated and refined and then injected subcutaneously or intra-muscularly. In Kuru and laboratory and iatrogenic transmission, the HGH was untreated and usually direct to the brain.

In my judgment on 1 July 1977 the defendants, in the state of the then available knowledge, could only have concluded that the risk of CJD becoming a reality could occur within a huge time span, that is within a year or two after injection or within many decades after injection.

Thus, it was reasonably foreseeable that the patient would receive the shocking news that he was at risk of CJD over a very wide time span.

It was reasonably foreseeable that a patient might receive the shocking news towards the end of adolescence, in early adulthood or middle age.

Each CJD death from HGH would increase the fear of other HGH injectees and this should have been foreseen by the defendants. By definition, all the patients were children handicapped by dwarfism.

They had no effective choice but to accept the treatment. The choice was made by their parents on the best motives on the advice of consultant clinicians who believed the treatment safe. When later, maybe several years later, the treatment was stopped, or if their own treatment had already been completed, they learnt that the programme had been suspended because of the risk of CJD. Depending upon the age of the patient, they might learn of the reason for the termination of the programme of their own treatment after their parents or at the same time.

The natural anxiety and distress of their parents – who might regard themselves as being responsible for consenting to a treatment for their child which might be potentially disastrous – however hard the parents tried to disguise it, would be felt by the patient, exacerbating the shock at the news.

Although it may not be reasonably foreseeable that the man of ordinary fortitude would develop psychiatric illness if the information that he was at slight theoretical risk of CJD was given to him by a doctor or counsellor, who would no doubt give the information with optimistic stress, however, in the case of a special therapeutic trial or programme as the HGH programme, it should have been reasonably foreseeable to the defendants by 1 July 1977 that, when news of the potential risk of CJD broke to those who were or had been children when treated, the news would reach Group B plaintiffs not only from considerate and skilled clinicians and counsellors, but also from the media, which foreseeably would tend to highlight or sensationalise the risk of the potential terrible outcome, and from anxious and perhaps angry relations and friends, who would be ignorant of scientific knowledge and likely to use unhelpful language.

In my judgment, the evidence shows that the defendants not only should have reasonably foreseen the risk of psychiatric injury but did in fact do so...

While wholly endorsing what Lord Wilberforce said in *McLoughlin v O'Brian* [1982] 2 All ER 298 at 304, [1983] 1 AC 410 at 422 that persons must be assumed to be possessed of fortitude to enable them to endure the calamities of modern life, and in no way resiling from what I said in my judgment of 19 December 1996, having regard to the special relationship between the Group B plaintiffs and the defendants and the gruesome possibility facing each Hartree HGH recipient, I do not find it surprising that someone of normal fortitude has suffered psychiatric injury and, in my judgment, it should clearly have been reasonably foreseen by the defendants.

I can see no logical reason why foreseeability of, or responsibility for, shock and psychiatric injury should be limited to an area of time contemporaneous or almost contemporaneous with the negligent physical event, ie the injection of Hartree HGH. If the psychiatric injury was reasonably foreseeable, it should be untrammelled by spatial physical or temporal limits (see per Lord Scarman in *McLoughlin v O'Brian* [1982] 2 All ER 298 at 311, [1983] 1 AC 410 at 431).

I do not consider that a delay between the shock of the news of the first cases of CJD and the onset of the psychiatric injury should defeat a plaintiff's claim. A psychiatric injury can be readily induced by an accumulative awareness or drip-feed of information over a prolonged period of time, although the court will scrutinise rigorously a claim so based.

Although I do not consider that in law the Group B plaintiffs are to be treated as primary victims, I am satisfied that when the defendants breached their duty of care to them by being responsible for injecting them with potentially lethal Hartree HGH they should have reasonably foreseen that, if deaths occurred from CJD caused by HGH contaminated with the CJD agent, some of the recipients of that HGH, including some of normal phlegm and ordinary fortitude, might well suffer psychiatric injury o n becoming aware of the risk to them. Therefore, any Group B plaintiff, whether of normal phlegm and ordinary fortitude or having a vulnerable personality, who can prove that his psychiatric illness was caused by his becoming aware of the risk of CJD to him and that he has suffered a genuine psychiatric illness, can recover compensation.

The defendants have urged that I would be taking a novel step, enlarging the type of victim who might recover. If I have taken an incremental step forward, it is a small step. I hope to echo the words of Lord Wright in *Bourhill v Young* [1942] 2 All ER 396 at 405, [1943] AC 92 at 110 that, on the facts of this special situation I have had the good sense to draw the line appropriately.

The defendants as tortfeasors committed a wrong upon the Group B plaintiffs by imperilling their lives from a terrible fatal disease. It was reasonably foreseeable that, if the worst fears were realised and deaths from CJD occurred, Hartree HGH recipients, both those of normal fortitude and those more vulnerable, might suffer psychiatric injury. I cannot see in the facts and circumstances of this litigation why public policy, including social and economic policy considerations, should exclude them from compensation.

You will notice that the judge considered *Page v Smith* and the plaintiffs' reliance on being 'primary victims' as wrong. He did so on the basis that there was no 'shocking event' and public policy ('floodgates') told against liability. His reluctance to characterise the case as one involving 'primary victims' is all the more curious given that he finds for the plaintiffs in the end. In fact, as was suggested earlier, their claims were as 'primary victims' but a 'shocking event' may not be a necessary, though it could be a sufficient, condition for liability. Rather, it is an aspect of the foreseeability of injury caused by actual or apprehended exposure to danger. The plaintiffs were undoubtedly so exposed and, as the judge found, whether infected or not it was reasonably foreseeable they would suffer psychiatric injury.

5. Economic loss

Could a doctor be liable to a patient who suffers economic loss as a result, for example, of a negligently prepared medical report? The Court of Appeal assumed so recently in *Hughes v Lloyds Bank plc* [1998] PIQR P98.

I Kennedy and A Grubb (eds) *Principles of Medical Law* (1998)

5.41 If the doctor is consulted by a patient for a particular purpose which the doctor is aware of, then it is likely that, on the basis of *Hedley Byrne*, a duty of care to exercise reasonable care and skill in preparing the report will be owed by the doctor to the patient. However, where the doctor is unaware that the patient intends to rely upon his advice or, more likely, the patient relies upon it for an unrelated and unexpected purpose, then a duty of care will probably not exist *(Caparo Industries Plc v Dickman* [1990] 2 AC 605 (HL)). The point is illustrated by *Stevens v Bermondsey and Southwark Group HMC* (1963) 107 SJ 478. The plaintiff was advised by a casualty officer at a hospital, following an accident, that there was nothing wrong with him. In fact, the plaintiff had suffered an injury and subsequently developed spondylosis of the spine. However, relying on what he had been told, the plaintiff had already settled his claim against the local authority which was liable for the accident for a small sum of money. He sued the hospital arguing that the doctor's negligent diagnosis had caused him to suffer economic loss since had he been properly advised he would only have settled his claim for more. Paull J held that the defendant was not liable. The hospital doctor had no duty in respect of the plaintiff's financial affairs, only his physical condition. The answer would, as the judge acknowledged, have been different if the doctor had been consulted with a view to providing advice about litigation. The case remains good law in the light of developments since *Hedley Byrne*. The doctor did not know, nor in the circumstances of an A & E department should he have known, that the patient would rely upon his advice in settling his claim. It would have been different if he had known (*McGrath v Keily and Powell* [1965] IR 497 (Ir H Ct)). The doctor had assumed a responsibility to him but only in respect of caring for him *qua* doctor and not as providing the professional services of an expert witness.

5.42 However, a doctor may not only owe a duty of care not to cause his patients financial loss on the basis of a narrow application of the *Hedley Byrne* case. A broader basis of liability was accepted by the House of Lords in *Henderson v Merritt Syndicates Ltd* ([1995] 2 AC 145 (HL)) and *White v Jones* ([1995] 2 AC 207 (HL)) whereby a duty of care may exist where the defendant assumes a responsibility to the plaintiff. The assumption may be express - arising from an undertaking by the defendant – or implied by the law – arising from the conduct of the defendant and surrounding circumstances. Hence, an employer has been held to owe a duty to an ex-employee when he carelessly produced a reference for the employee's new employer thereby causing the employee to lose the job and suffer financial loss (*Spring v Guardian Assurance Plc* [1995] 2 AC 296 (HL)). Likewise, a doctor who was employed by the plaintiff's potential employer to examine him prior to confirming his job owed a duty of care to the plaintiff not carelessly to produce a report resulting in the plaintiff losing the job and suffering financial loss (*Baker v Kaye* [1997] IRLR 219). The plaintiff in this case was not in a conventional doctor-patient relationship with the doctor and, as will be seen, the issue of what duty is owed in such situations is not clear in England. However, if a doctor assumes a responsibility to an examinee in such a case, a fortiori in the case of a patient when he produces a report at the patient's request or otherwise for a particular purpose. *Baker v Kaye* illustrates that a duty of care may arise for negligent advice given by a doctor to a patient who consults him for the purpose of a 'medical reference' which the doctor knows (or ought to know) will be relied upon by the patient or a third party to whom it is to be supplied.

Could he also be liable to a third party to whom a medical report is sent?

5.69 A doctor who is requested by his patient to provide a medical report to a third party, for example, an insurance company or potential employer, may owe a duty of care to that third party to do so carefully so that the third party does not incur economic loss (see eg *Wharton Transport Corp v Bridges* (1980) 606 SW 2d 521 (Tenn Sup Ct). Following *Hedley Byrne v Heller* a doctor, knowing whom the recipient of the report is to be, the purpose for which it will be used, and that the third party will (or is likely to) rely upon it, undertakes (or assumes) a responsibility to the third party sufficient to impose a legal duty to exercise reasonable care and skill in preparing the report. (This should follow from the reasoning in *Spring v Guardian Assurance Plc* [1995] 2 AC 296; [1994] 3 All ER 129 (HL), but notice the reservation by Lord Goff at 147.)

5.70 In the unlikely event that the doctor provides a medical report on the patient without knowing what use it will be put to, or if the report is put to an unexpected use or one which could not reasonably be anticipated by the doctor, it may well be that the all important 'assumption of responsibility' is absent. It will not, however, be necessary for the doctor to know the precise identity of the third party providing he knows the nature of the third party's use, for example, that it is an insurance company.

5.71 The same reasoning would apply if the doctor had no pre-existing relationship with the 'patient' but was specifically engaged directly by the third party to provide the medical report. Here, there would undoubtedly be an undertaking or assumption of responsibility to the third party who requested the report. And, of course, there would almost certainly be a contract between the doctor and third party which would include an implied term which could be the basis for a contractual negligence claim unconstrained by requirements for recovering economic loss in the tort of negligence.

B. BREACH OF DUTY

1. The standard of the reasonable doctor

(a) Generally

Whether the patient's action is for breach of contract or in the tort of negligence, the standard of care is the same. The doctor or other health professional is required by law to exercise the care and skill of a reasonable professional. This, if you like, represents the equivalent of the 'man on the Clapham Omnibus' in the professional context. The standard of the reasonable professional in the medical context is the same, in principle, as it is for other professionals, for example, accountants, lawyers or architects. By holding themselves out as possessing a special skill, doctors and other health professionals are held to the standard of the reasonable person possessing that skill. Negligence is a failure to reach that standard. In the medical context, difficulties have arisen in applying this standard. In particular, the courts have, until recently, seen medical evidence, especially of professional practice, as setting the standard of the reasonable doctor etc. Of course, the latter does not necessarily follow from the acceptance of the former. *Reasonable* practice need not be equated with *accepted* or *common* practice, even less so with expert evidence of what the defendant should have done when there is no relevant professional practice. Yet, the courts have seen the legal standard and proof of breach as inseparable. Together, medical lawyers compositely refer to them as the 'Bolam test', being derived from the summing up of the judge to the jury in the well-known case of that name. In reality, however, the case did not break new ground but was rather stating the law as it had long been accepted.

Bolam v Friern Hospital Management Committee [1957] 2 All ER 118, [1957] 1 WLR 582 (McNair J)

The plaintiff contended that the defendants were vicariously liable for the carelessness of a doctor who administered electro-convulsive therapy to the plaintiff without administering a relaxant drug or without restraining the convulsive movements of the plaintiff by manual control (save for his lower jaw). The plaintiff suffered a fractured hip as a consequence. He brought an action against the defendants in negligence. McNair J directed the jury as follows.

McNair J: I must explain what in law we mean by 'negligence'. In the ordinary case which does not involve any special skill, negligence in law means this: Some failure to do some act which a reasonable man in the circumstances would do, or doing some act which a reasonable man in the circumstances would not do; and if that failure or doing of that act results in injury, then there is a cause of action. How do you test whether this act or failure is negligent? In an ordinary case it is generally said, that you judge that by the action of the man in the street. He is the ordinary man. In one case it has been said that you judge it by the conduct of the man on the top of a Clapham omnibus. He is the ordinary man. But where you get a situation which involves the use of some special skill or competence, then the test whether there has been negligence or not is not the test of the man on the top of a Clapham omnibus, because he has not got this special skill. The test is the standard of the ordinary skilled man exercising and professing to have that special skill. A man need not possess the highest expert skill at the risk of being found negligent. It is well-established law that it is sufficient if he exercises the ordinary skill of an ordinary competent man exercising that particular art. I do not think that I quarrel much with any of the submissions in law which have been put before you by counsel. Counsel for the plaintiff put it in this way, that in the case of a medical man negligence means failure to act in accordance with the standards of reasonably competent medical men at the time. That is a perfectly accurate statement, as long as it is remembered that there may be one or more perfectly proper standards; and if a medical man conforms with one of those proper standards then he is not negligent. Counsel for the plaintiff was also right, in my judgment, in saying that a mere personal belief that a particular technique is best is no defence unless that belief is based on reasonable grounds. That again is unexceptional. But the emphasis which is laid by counsel for the defendants is on this aspect of negligence: he submitted to you that the real question on which you have to make up your mind on each of the three major points to be considered is whether the defendants, in acting in the way in which they did, were acting in accordance with a practice of competent respected professional opinion. Counsel for the defendants submitted that if you are satisfied that they were acting in accordance with a practice of a competent body of professional opinion, then it would be wrong for you to hold that negligence was established. I referred, before I started 'hese observations, to a statement which is contained in a recent Scottish case, *Hunter v Hanley* (1955 SLT 213 at p 217), which dealt with medical matters, where the Lord President (Lord Clyde) said this:

> In the realm of diagnosis and treatment there is ample scope for genuine difference of opinion, and one man clearly is not negligent merely because his conclusion differs from that of other professional men, nor because he has displayed less skill or knowledge that others would have shown. The true test for establishing negligence in diagnosis or treatment on the part of a doctor is whether he has been proved to be guilty of such failure as no doctor of ordinary skill would be guilty of if acting with ordinary care.

If that statement of the true test is qualified by the words 'in all the circumstances', counsel for the plaintiff would not seek to say that that expression of opinion does not accord with English law. It is just a question of expression. I myself would prefer to put it this way: a doctor is not guilty of negligence if he has acted in accordance with a practice accepted as proper by a responsible body of medical men skilled in that particular art. I do not think there is much difference in sense. It is just a different way of expressing the same thought. Putting it the other way round, a doctor is not negligent, if he is acting in accordance with such a practice, merely because there is a body of opinion that takes a contrary view. At the same time, that does not mean that a medical man can obstinately and pig-headedly carry on with some old techniques if it has been proved to be contrary to what is really substantially the whole of informed medical opinion. Otherwise you might get men today saying: 'I don't believe in anaesthetics. I don't believe in antiseptics. I am going to continue to do my surgery in the way it was done in the eighteenth century.' That clearly would be wrong.

The jury returned a verdict for the defendants.

Bolam was accepted and applied by the House of Lords in *Whitehouse v Jordan* [1981] 1 All ER 267, [1981] 1 WLR 246 (treatment) and *Maynard v West Midlands RHA* [1985] 1 All ER 635 (diagnosis).

Whitehouse v Jordan [1981] 1 All ER 267, [1981] 1 WLR 246 (HL)

Lord Edmund-Davies: The principal questions calling for decision are: (a) in what manner did Mr Jordan use the forceps? and (b) was that manner consistent with the degree of skill which a member of his profession is required by law to exercise? Surprising though it is at this late stage in the development of the law of negligence, counsel for Mr Jordan persisted in submitting that his client should be completely exculpated were the answer to question (b), 'Well, at the worst he was guilty of an error of clinical judgment'. My Lords, it is high time that the unacceptability of such an answer be finally exposed. To say that a surgeon committed an error of clinical judgment is wholly ambiguous, for, while some such errors may be completely consistent with the due exercise of professional skill, other acts or omissions in the course of exercising 'clinical judgment' may be so glaringly below proper standards as to make a finding of negligence inevitable. Indeed, I should have regarded this as a truism were it not that, despite the exposure of the 'false antitheses' by Donaldson LJ in his dissenting judgment in the Court of Appeal, counsel for the defendants adhered to it before your Lordships.

But doctors and surgeons fall into no special category, and, to avoid any future disputation of a similar kind, I would have it accepted that the true doctrine was enunciated, and by no means for the first time, by McNair J in *Bolam v Friern Hospital Management Committee* [1957] 2 All ER 118 at 121, [1957] 1 WLR 582 at 586 in the following words, which were applied by the Privy Council in *Chin Keow v Government of Malaysia* [1967] 1 WLR 813:

> ... where you get a situation which involves the use of some special skill or competence, then the test as to whether there has been negligence or not is not the test of the man on the top of a Clapham omnibus because he has not got this special skill. The test is the standard of the ordinary skilled man exercising and professing to have that special skill.

If a surgeon fails to measure up to that standard in *any* respect ('clinical judgment' or otherwise), he has been negligent and should be so adjudged.

As we shall see (*infra*, ch 5), in cases concerned with non-disclosure of information, the House of Lords in *Sidaway v Bethlem Royal Hospital Governors* [1985] AC 871, [1985] 1 All ER 643 was (probably) more circumspect of applying *Bolam* but nevertheless recognised its application elsewhere:

Lord Bridge: Broadly, a doctor's professional functions may be divided into three phases: diagnosis, advice and treatment. In performing his functions of diagnosis and treatment, the standard by which English law measures the doctor's duty of care to his patient is not open to doubt. 'The test is the standard of the ordinary skilled man exercising and professing to have that special skill.' These are the words of McNair J in *Bolam v Friern Hospital Management Committee* [1957] 2 All ER 118 at 121, [1957] 1 WLR 582 at 586, approved by this House in *Whitehouse v Jordan* [1981] 1 All ER 267 at 277, [1981] 1 WLR 246 at 258 per Lord Edmund-Davies and in *Maynard v West Midlands Regional Health Authority* [1985] 1 All ER 635 per Lord Scarman. The test is conveniently referred to as the *Bolam* test. In *Maynard's* case Lord Scarman, with whose speech the other four members of the Appellate Committee agreed, further cited with approval the words of the Lord President (Clyde) in *Hunter v Hanley* 1955 SLT 213 at 217:

> In the realm of diagnosis and treatment there is ample scope for genuine difference of opinion and one man clearly is not negligent merely because his conclusion differs from that of other professional men … The true test for establishing negligence in diagnosis or treatment on the part of a doctor is whether he has been proved to be guilty of such failure as no doctor of ordinary skill would be guilty of if acting with ordinary care…

The language of the *Bolam* test clearly required a different degree of skill from a specialist in his own special field that from a general practitioner. In the field of neuro-surgery it would be necessary to substitute for the Lord President's phrase 'no doctor of ordinary skill', the phrase 'no neuro-surgeon of ordinary skill'. All this is elementary and, in the light of the two recent decisions of this House referred to, firmly established law.

Who then sets the standard? Notice Lord Scarman's comment in *Sidaway*:

> The *Bolam* principle may be formulated as a rule that a doctor is not negligent if he acts in accordance with a practice accepted at the time as proper by a responsible body of medical opinion even though other doctors adopt a different practice. In short, the law imposes the duty of care; but the standard of care is a matter of medical judgment.

We shall return later to consider more fully Lord Scarman's statement. It may seem curious that the law would defer to the medical profession in setting the content of the duty in negligence. As we shall see, the House of Lords in *Bolitho v City and Hackney HA* [1998] AC 232, [1997] 4 All ER 771 has reasserted the court's function as final arbiter of the standard of care expected of the medical profession (*infra*, pp 442–444).

(b) Specialists

You will notice from Lord Bridge's speech in *Sidaway* reference to the 'specialist' doctor. When a doctor holds himself out as being a specialist, the standard of care is that of the reasonable specialist, whether neuro-surgeon, obstetrician or whatever. In *Maynard v West Midlands RHA* [1985] 1 All ER 635, Lord Scarman said (at 638): 'I would only add that a doctor who professes to exercise a special skill must exercise the ordinary skill of his speciality.' Notice the standard is not that of the 'best' or the most experienced specialist. It is of the 'ordinary' or 'competent' specialist (*Defreitas v O'Brien* [1995] 6 Med LR 108 and *O'Donovan v Cork CC* [1967] IR 173 (Ir Sup Ct)). Difficulties may arise over whether the defendant is part of a particular speciality or sub-speciality and new specialities will emerge (see eg *Defreitas v O'Brien* [1995] 6 Med LR 108-spinal surgeons). It will always be a question of what the doctor has held himself out as. If, indeed, he professes to be a 'special' specialist, then he will be judged by the standards to be expected of that sub-discipline or new discipline. He may, as a result, be expected to have greater knowledge and greater skill, requiring more than otherwise would be the case. The point is perhaps, illustrated by the following case.

Wimpey Construction UK Ltd v Poole [1984] 2 Lloyd's Rep 499 (Webster J)

The plaintiffs constructed a quay wall. Cracks occurred in the structure and repairs were effected. The plaintiffs claimed the costs under a professional indemnity insurance policy held with the defendant in respect of 'any omission, error or negligent act in respect of design or specification of work'. The issue which arose was whether the plaintiffs were in breach of their duty.

Webster J: [Counsel] on behalf of Wimpeys sought to put two glosses on the [*Bolam*] test for the purpose of this case. The first is that, as he submits, the test is not 'the standard of the ordinary skilled man exercising and professing to have that special skill' if the client deliberately obtains and pays for someone with specially high skills.

Mr Justice Megarry, as he then was, considered but did not decide the question in the *Duchess of Argyll v Beuselinck* [1972] 2 Lloyd's Rep 172, a claim of negligence against a solicitor. At pp 183-184 he said:

… One question that arose during the argument was that of the standard of care required of a solicitor; and although Counsel did their best to assist me, the question remained obscure. It was common ground that, at any rate in normal cases, an action for negligence by a solicitor is an action in contract: see *Groom v Crocker* [1939] 1 KB 194. At one stage, Mr Arnold asserted that this was of importance only in regard to limitation; but I think that later he accepted that this was too restricted a view. I can see that in actions in tort, the standard of care to be applied will normally be that of the reasonable man: those lacking in care and skill fail to observe the standards of the reasonable man at their peril, and the unusually careful and highly skilled are not held liable for falling below their own high standards if they nevertheless do all that a reasonable man would have done. But to say that in tort the standard of care is uniform does not necessarily carry the point in circumstances where the action is for breach of an implied duty of care in a contract whereby a client retains a solicitor. No doubt the inexperienced solicitor is liable if he fails to attain the standard of a reasonably competent solicitor. But if the client employs a solicitor of high standard and great experience, will an action for negligence fail if it appears that the solicitor did not exercise the care and skill to be expected of him though he did not fall below the standard of a reasonably competent solicitor? If the client engages an expert, and doubtless expects to pay commensurate fees, is he not entitled to expect something more than the standard of reasonably competent? I am speaking not merely of those expert in a particular branch of the law, as contrasted with a general practitioner, but also of those of long experience and great skill as contrasted with those practising in the same field of the law but being of a more ordinary calibre and having less experience. The essence of the contact of retainer, it may be said, is that the client is retaining the particular solicitor or firm in question, and he is therefore entitled to expect from that solicitor or firm a standard of care and skill commensurate with the skill and experience which that solicitor or firm has. The uniform standard of care postulated for the world at large in tort hardly seems appropriate when the duty is not one imposed by the law of tort but arises from a contractual obligation existing between the client and the particular solicitor or firm in question. If, as is usual, the retainer contains no express term as to the solicitor's duty of care, and the matter rests upon an implied term, what is that term in the case of a solicitor of long experience or specialist skill? Is it that he will put at his client's disposal the care and skill of an average solicitor, or the care and skill that he has? I must say that Mr Arnold advanced no contention that it was the latter standard that was to be applied; but I wish to make it clear that I have not overlooked the point, which one day may require further consideration.

According to the research of Counsel that question has not yet received further consideration. Mr Justice Oliver, as he then was, referred to the *Duchess of Argyll's* case in *Midland Bank Trust Co Ltd v Hett, Stubbs and Kemp* [1979] Ch 384 at 403, but without, apparently, modifying the conventional test and for my part, if the question be material, I feel constrained by the clear words of the test as expressed by Mr Justice McNair, and by the approval of that test without qualification by the Privy Council and the House of Lords, to treat it as unqualified. Since the hearing ended I have considered the judgment of Mr Justice Kilner Brown in *Greaves & Co (Contractors) Ltd v Baynham Meikle & Partners* [1975] 1 Lloyd's Rep 31, [1974] 1 WLR 1261 where a similar point was considered. The decision in that case, however, rested on 'special circumstances' (see pp 35 and 1269 C-D) and is not, in my view, inconsistent with the conclusion I have reached.

Likewise, the fact that a doctor has greater skill through his specialism may entail that a 'competent' or 'ordinary' practitioner may undertake a procedure that the less specialised would not (*Defreitas v O'Brien, supra,* and Commentary, (1995) 3 Med L Rev 195 (IK)).

A somewhat similar issue concerns the liability of institutions (see *supra,* p 298). More may be expected at a 'centre of excellence' than at a district general hospital (see *Robertson v Nottingham HA* [1997] 8 Med LR 1 (CA) at 13 per Brooke LJ).

(c) Inexperience

At the other end of the spectrum is the newly qualified or inexperienced doctor. To what level of skill is such a person held? Is his inexperience relevant? There is some authority that it is relevant. In *Junor v McNicol* (1959) Times, 26 March, Viscount Kilmuir LC said that a house officer had a duty to 'display the care and skill of a prudent qualified house [officer], it being remembered that such a position was held by a comparative beginner'. Perhaps not too much should be read into this comment. English law may not look to the rank or employment position of the doctor and, as in the case of a house officer, the inexperience that may necessarily entail.

Perhaps, the appropriate rule of English law can be derived from the case of *Nettleship v Weston* [1971] 2 QB 691, [1971] 3 All ER 581, CA. The case concerned a learner-driver who mounted the kerb in a car and damaged a lamp-post. Her instructor also suffered injuries.

Nettleship v Weston [1971] 2 QB 691 (CA)

Lord Denning MR: Mrs Weston is clearly liable for the damage to the lamp-post. In the civil law if a driver goes off the road on to the pavement and injures a pedestrian, or damages property, he is *prima facie* liable. Likewise if he goes on to the wrong side of the road. It is no answer for him to say: 'I was a learner-driver under instruction. I was doing my best and could not help it.' The civil law permits no such excuse. It requires of him the same standard of care as any other driver. 'It eliminates the personal equation and is independent of the idiosyncrasies of the particular person whose conduct is in question': see *Glasgow Corpn v Muir* [1943] AC 448 *per* Lord Macmillan. The learner-driver may be doing his best, but his incompetent best is not good enough. He must drive in as good a manner as a driver of skill, experience and care, who is sound in wind and limb, who makes no errors of judgment, has good eyesight and hearing, and is free from any infirmity: see *Richley v Faull* [1965] 1 WLR 1454 and *Watson v Thomas S Witney & Co Ltd* [1966] 1 WLR 57.

Salmon LJ: I also agree that a learner-driver is responsible and owes a duty in civil laws towards persons on or near the highway to drive with the same degree of skill and care as that of the reasonably competent and experience driver. The duty in civil law springs from the relationship which the driver, by driving on the highway, has created between himself and persons likely to suffer damage by his bad driving ...

Any driver normally owes exactly the same duty to a passenger in his car as he does to the general public, namely to drive with reasonable care and skill in all the relevant circumstances. As a rule, the driver's personal idiosyncrasy is not a relevant circumstance. In the absence of a special relationship what is reasonable care and skill is measured by the standard of competence usually achieved by the ordinary driver.

Megaw LJ agreed.

The Court of Appeal is saying, in essence, that as a matter of public policy the law must set a standard for the benefit of all below which everyone engaging in risk-creating behaviour may not fall. Thus, a junior doctor would be held to that minimum level of competence necessary for the safety and proper treatment of a patient regardless of his actual level of competence or experience.

The Court of Appeal has settled the question as regards English law in *Wilsher v Essex AHA* [1987] QB 730, [1986] 3 All ER 801. We have already seen the facts of this case set out *supra* at p 308.

Wilsher v Essex AHA [1987] QB 730, [1986] 3 All ER 801 (CA)

Mustill LJ: I now turn to the real content of the standard of care. Three propositions were advanced, the first by junior counsel for the plaintiff. It may, I think, be fairly described as setting a 'team' standard of care, whereby each of the persons who formed the staff of the unit held themselves out as capable of undertaking the specialised procedures which that unit set out to perform.

I acknowledge the force of this submission, so far as it calls for recognition of the position which the person said to be negligent held within this specialised unit. But, in so far as the propositions differs from the last of those referred to below, I must dissent, for it is faced with a dilemma. If he seeks to attribute to each individual member of the team a duty to live up to the standards demanded of the unit as a whole, it cannot be right, for it would expose a student nurse to an action in negligence for a failure to possess the skill and experience of a consultant. If, on the other hand, it seeks to fix a standard for the performance of the unit as a whole, this is simply a reformulation of the direct theory of liability which leading counsel for the plaintiff has explicitly disclaimed.

The second proposition (advanced on behalf of the defendants) directs attention to the personal position of the individual member of the staff about whom the complaint is made. What is expected of him is as much as, but no more than, can reasonably be required of a person having his formal qualifications and practical experience. If correct, this proposition entails that the standard of care which the patient is entitled to demand will vary according to the chance of recruitment and rostering. The patient's right to complain of faulty treatment will be more limited if he has been entrusted to the care of a doctor who is a complete novice in the particular field (unless perhaps he can point to some fault of supervision in a person further up the hierarchy) than if he has been in the hands of a doctor who has already spent months on the same ward, and his prospects of holding the health authority vicariously liable for the consequences of any mistreatment will be correspondingly reduced.

To my mind, this notion of a duty tailored to the actor, rather than to the act which he elects to perform, has no place in the law of tort. Indeed, the defendants did not contend that it could be justified by any reported authority on the general law of tort. Instead, it was suggested that a medical profession is a special case. Public hospital medicine has always been organised so that young doctors and nurses learn on the job. If the hospitals abstained from using inexperienced people, they could not staff their wards and theatres, and the junior staff could never learn. The longer-term interests of patients as a whole are best served by maintaining the present system, even if this may diminish the legal rights of the individual patient, for, after all, medicine is about curing, not litigation.

I acknowledge the appeal of this argument, and recognise that a young hospital doctor who must get onto the wards in order to qualify without necessarily being able to decide what kind of patient he is going to meet is not in the same position as another professional man who has a real choice whether or not to practise in a particular field. Nevertheless, I cannot accept that there be a special rule for doctors in public hospitals; I emphasise *public*, since presumably those employed in private hospitals would be in a different category. Doctors are not the only people who gain their experience, not only from lectures or from watching others perform, but from tackling live clients or customers, and no case was cited to us which suggested that any such variable duty of care was imposed on others in a similar position. To my mind, it would be a false step to subordinate the legitimate expectation of the patient that he will receive from each person concerned with his care a degree of skill appropriate to the task which he undertakes to an understandable wish to minimise the psychological and financial pressures on hard-pressed young doctors.

For my part, I prefer the third of the propositions which have been canvassed. This related to duty of care, not to the individual, but to the post which he occupies. I would differentiate 'post' from 'rank' or 'status'. In a case such as the present, the standard is not just that of the averagely competent and well-informed junior houseman (or whatever the position of the doctor) but of such a person who fills a post in a unit offering a highly specialised service. But, even so, it must be recognised that different posts make different demands. If it is borne in mind that the structure of hospital medicine envisages that the lower ranks will be occupied by those of whom it would be wrong to expect too much, the risk of abuse by litigious patients can be mitigated, if not entirely eliminated.

Glidewell LJ agreed.

Glidewell LJ: In my view, the law requires the trainee or learner to be judged by the same standard as his more experienced colleagues. If it did not, inexperience would frequently be urged as a defence to an action for professional negligence.

If this test appears unduly harsh in relation to the inexperienced, I should add that, in my view, the inexperienced doctor called on to exercise a specialist skill will, as part of that skill, seek the advice and help of his superiors when he does or may need it. If he does seek such help, he will often have satisfied the test, even though he may himself have made a mistake.

Sir Nicolas Browne-Wilkinson V-C dissented.

Browne-Wilkinson V-C: In English law, liability for personal injury requires a finding of personal fault (eg negligence) against someone. In cases of vicarious liability such as this, there must have been personal fault by the employee or agent of the defendant for whom the defendant is held vicariously liable. Therefore, even though no claim is made against the individual doctor, the liability of the defendant health authority is dependent on a finding of personal fault by one or more of the individual doctors. The general standard of care required of a doctor is that he would exercise the skill of a skilled doctor in the treatment which he has taken on himself to offer.

Such being the general standard of care required of a doctor, it is normally no answer for him to say the treatment he gave was of a specialist or technical nature in which he was inexperienced. In such a case, the fault of the doctor lies in embarking on giving treatment which he could not skilfully offer: he should not have undertaken the treatment but should have referred the patient to someone possessing the necessary skills.

But the position of the houseman in his first year after qualifying or of someone (like Dr Wiles in this case) who has just started in a specialist field in order to gain the necessary skill in that field is not capable of such analysis. The houseman has to take up his post in order to gain full professional qualification; anyone else, like Dr Wiles, wishes to obtain specialist skills has to learn those skills by taking a post in a specialist unit. In my judgment, such doctors cannot in fairness be said to be at fault if, at the start of their time, they lack the very skills which they are seeking to acquire.

In my judgment, if the standard of care required of such a doctor is that he should have the skill required of the post he occupies, the young houseman or the doctor seeking to obtain specialist skills in a special unit would be held liable for shortcomings in the treatment without any personal fault on his part at all. Of course, such a doctor would be negligent if he undertook treatment for which he knows he lacks the necessary experience and skill. But one of the chief hazards of inexperience is that one does not always know the risks which exist. In my judgment, so long as the English law rests liability on personal fault, a doctor who has properly accepted a post in a hospital in order to gain necessary experience should only be held liable for acts or omissions which a careful doctor with his qualifications and experience would not have done or omitted. It follows that, in my view, the health authority could not be held vicariously liable (and I stress the word *vicariously*) for the acts of such a learner who has come up to those standards, notwithstanding that the post he held required greater experience than he in fact possessed.

Does the mere reference to the 'post' help? Is not Mustill LJ, with respect, confused by not really talking about a doctor with minimum competence for the task? Arguably Mustill LJ could have decided the case on the basis that the doctor should never have carried out the procedure complained of because he lacked a minimum competence. Certainly, reference to 'post' can lead to confusion. Hence, it has been held that a senior house officer acting as a casualty officer in an A&E department had to be judged by the standard of 'a reasonably competent senior houseman acting as a casualty officer without any reference to the length of experience' (*Djemal v Bexley HA* [1995] 6 Med LR 269 at 271 per Sir Haydn Tudor Evans). Would it not have been better to ask what a reasonably competent doctor performing the task in question would or would not do?

Given the law is as the majority have stated it, how can the law accommodate the needs of public policy that a doctor learns at least part of the job through work experience? The answer must lie in the notion of supervision. If a doctor lacks a minimum competence to carry out a particular procedure but it is proper for him to be present, eg as a learner, then whatever he does must be done under the supervision of the inexperienced doctor. The negligence, if any, will now be that of the experienced doctor for failure adequately to supervise (this is what Glidewell LJ decided in *Wilsher*, as we have seen).

What of the situation, however, where the inexperienced doctor does not realise his own incompetence and so does not seek supervision? You will recall the words of the Vice-Chancellor in *Wilsher* '... one of the chief hazards of inexperience is that one does not always know the risks which exist'. Does *reasonable* supervision contemplate *constant* supervision or something else? If it be the former will the inexperienced doctor *necessarily* be liable? This cannot, in our view, be the law. As a matter of public policy it is recognised that the medical profession, like any other profession, can only acquire some knowledge and skill by taking independent responsibility albeit within the context of overall supervision by the more experienced.

This does leave unanswered the point raised by the Vice-Chancellor: 'the rights of a patient entering hospital will depend on the experience of the doctor who treats him'. This may somewhat overstate the case but certainly there is a problem here. One answer is the Vice-Chancellor's recourse to the primary liability of the hospital. Another answer is to recall the law relating to consent and consider what information the patient ought to be told so as to make any consent valid.

Would a lower standard of care be acceptable if a junior doctor identified himself as such to the patient? In other words, may a patient by agreement lower the standard of care otherwise imposed by law. In *Nettleship v Weston* there was a difference of opinion.

Lord Denning MR: Mrs Weston took her son with her in the car. We do not know his age. He may have been 21 and have known that his mother was learning to drive. He was not injured. But if he had been injured, would he have had a cause of action? I take it to be clear that, if a driver has a passenger in the car, he owes a duty of care to him. But what is the standard of care required of the driver? Is it a lower standard than he or she owes towards a pedestrian on the pavement? I should have thought not. But suppose that the driver has never driven a car before, or has taken too much to drink, or has poor eyesight or hearing; and, furthermore, that the passenger *knows* it and yet accepts a lift from him. Does that make any difference? Dixon J thought it did. In *Insurance Comr v Joyce* [(1948) 77 CLR 39] he said:

If a man accepts a lift from a car-driver whom he *knows* to have lost a limb or an eye or to be deaf, he cannot complain if he does not exhibit the skill and competence of a driver who suffers from no defect... If he knowingly accepts the voluntary services of a driver affected by drink, he cannot complain of improper driving caused by his condition, because it involves no breach of duty.

That view of Dixon J seems to have been followed in South Australia, see *Walker v Turton-Sainsbury*, but in the Supreme Court of Canada Rand J did not agree with it: see *Carr and General Insurance Corpn Ltd v Seymour and Maloney*.

We have all the greatest respect for Sir Owen Dixon, but for once I cannot agree with him. The driver owes a duty of care to every passenger in the car, just as he does to every pedestrian on the road; and he must attain the same standard of care in respect of each.

Megaw LJ agreed on this point. Salmon LJ, however, disagreed.

Salmon LJ:...[T]here may be special facts creating a special relationship which displaces this standard or even negatives any duty, although the onus would certainly be on the driver to establish such facts. With minor reservations I respectfully agree with and adopt the reasoning and conclusions of Sir Owen Dixon in his judgment in *Insurance Comr v Joyce*. I do not however agree that the mere fact that the driver has, to the knowledge of his passenger, lost a limb or an eye or is deaf can affect the duty which he owes the passenger to drive safely. It is well known that many drivers suffering from such disabilities drive with no less skill and competence than the ordinary man. The position, however, is totally different when, to the knowledge of the passenger, the driver is so drunk as to be incapable of driving safely. Quite apart from being negligent, a passenger who accepts a lift in such circumstances clearly cannot expect the driver to drive other than dangerously.

The duty of care springs from relationship. The special relationship which the passenger has created by accepting a lift in the circumstances postulated surely cannot entitle him to expect the driver to discharge a duty of care or skill which ex hypothesi the passenger knows the driver is incapable of discharging. Accordingly in such circumstances, no duty is owed by the driver to the passenger to drive safely ...

In the context of medical treatment the law will probably reflect a court's unwillingness to accept that any agreement by the patient is really *voluntary* rather than reached under the duress of the circumstances. In any event, within a state organised National Health Service, the courts are unlikely to entertain arguments that the standard of care may be lowered by agreement. 'Dumbing down' of the duty is contrary to public policy.

2. Establishing breach

The doctor or other health care professional's duty is to exercise reasonable care. Tort law is familiar with this standard. What is 'reasonable' must be determined taking account of all the circumstances. In determining the reasonableness of a doctor's conduct, as with any other defendant, the law is concerned with the foreseeability of injury, the magnitude of the risk, the cost or practicality of avoiding the risk and the purpose for which the procedure is carried out.

The court is concerned with assessing the reasonableness of the doctor's conduct at the time it occurred rather than with hindsight (*Roe v Minister of Health* [1954] 2 QB 66 (CA)). What may now be foreseeable as a danger or what would now be done may be different but will not lead to a finding of negligence if it was otherwise at the time. This is no more than a statement of general principle in negligence cases.

At one time, the courts drew a 'false antithesis' between an error of judgment and an error amounting to a failure by a doctor to exercise due care and skill. This was conceived by Lord Denning and given a brief moment in the light as Sheila Maclean writes in 'Negligence – A Dagger at the Doctor's Back?' in P Robson and P Watchman (eds) *Justice, Lord Denning and the Constitution* (1981) at p 104:

> In the case of *Roe v Minister of Health* [[1954] 2 QB 66] he said:
>
> > … we should be doing a disservice to the community at large if we were to impose liability on hospitals and doctors for everything that happens to go wrong.
> >
> > …We must insist on due care for the patient at every point, but we must not condemn as negligent that which is only misadventure.
>
> Again in the case of *Hatcher v Black* [(1954) Times, 2 July] he pointed out the risks of holding doctors liable in these circumstances and suggested that to do so would mean that:
>
> > … a doctor examining a patient, or a surgeon operating at a table, instead of getting on with his work, would be forever looking over his shoulder to see if someone was coming up with a dagger – for an action for negligence against a doctor is for him like unto a dagger.
>
> The interests of the community then are seen by Lord Denning not as being the facilitation of compensation in the event of damage as a result of medical intervention, but rather as being that medical practice should be interfered with as little as possible.

Lord Denning returned to his creation in *Whitehouse v Jordan* [1980] 1 All ER 650.

> **Lord Denning MR:** We must say, and say firmly, that, in a professional man, an error of judgment is not negligent. To test it, I would suggest that you ask the average competent and careful practitioner: 'Is this the sort of mistake that you yourself might have made?' If he says: 'Yes, even doing the best I could, it might have happened to me', then it is not negligent. In saying this, I am only reaffirming what I said in *Hatcher v Black* (a case I tried myself), *Roe v Ministry of Health* and *Hucks v Cole* (1968) 112 Sol Jo 483, CA.

Donaldson LJ (as he then was) disagreed:

Donaldson LJ: It is said that the judge lost sight of the fact that the plaintiff had to establish negligence. The basis of this submission was in part that he nowhere referred to 'errors of clinical judgment' and contrasted such errors with negligence. I can understand the omission, because it is a false antithesis. If a doctor fails to exercise the skill which he has or claims to have, he is in breach of his duty of care. He is negligent. But if he exercised that skill to the full, but nevertheless takes what, with hindsight, can be shown to be the wrong course, he is not negligent and is liable to no one, much though he may regret having done so. Both are errors of clinical judgment. The judge was solely concerned with whether or not the defendant's actions were negligent. If they were not, it was irrelevant whether or not they constituted an error of clinical judgment. The question which Bush J [the trial judge] asked himself was whether there had been any failure by the defendant 'to exercise the standard of skill expected from the ordinary competent specialist having regard to the experience and expertise which that specialist holds himself out as possessing', and added the proviso that 'the skill and expertise which we are considering is that applying in 1969-70'. In my judgment, that was not only the correct question, it was the only relevant question.

Lord Fraser delivered the death-blow in the House of Lords ([1981] 1 All ER 267).

Lord Fraser: Referring to medical men, Lord Denning MR said ([1980] 1 All ER 650 at 658): 'If they are to be found liable [*sc* for negligence] whenever they do not effect a cure, or whenever anything untoward happens, it would do a great disservice to the profession itself.' That is undoubtedly correct, but he went on to say this: 'We must say, and say firmly, that, in a professional man, an error of judgment is not negligent.' Having regard to the context, I think that Lord Denning MR must have meant to say that an error of judgment tells us nothing about whether it is negligent or not. The true position is that an error of judgment may, or may not, be negligent; it depends on the nature of the error. If it is one that would not have been made by a reasonably competent professional man professing to have the standard and type of skill that the defendant held himself out as having, and acting with ordinary care, then it is negligent. If, on the other hand, it is an error that a man, acting with ordinary care, might have made, then it is not negligence.

The question is always whether the doctor has exercised reasonable care and skill. Where clinical judgment is entailed it may be more difficult to show that he has not. We shall return to this later. The alleged failure to live up to the standard imposed by law may be founded on a number of factual bases: eg failure to attend or treat the patient, errors in diagnosis, failure to advise the patient at all, or adequately, or in communication to another health professional, and errors in treatment. In truth these are merely factual examples and do not help us address the legal issues (for a full discussion of these (and more) examples, see M Jones *Medical Negligence* (2nd edn, 1996) ch 4).

(a) Common or approved practice

(i) THE '*BOLAM* TEST'

In *Bolam v Friern Hospital Management Committee* [1957] 1 WLR 582, McNair J, in directing the jury in a medical negligence case, gave exceptional prominence to expert evidence of professional practice. He said (at 587):

[A doctor] is not guilty of negligence if he has acted in accordance with a practice accepted as proper by a responsible body of medical men skilled in that particular art ... Putting it the other way around, a man is not negligent, if he is acting in accordance with such a practice, merely because there is a body of opinion who would take a contrary view.

In saying this, McNair J was following the law as it stood. Compliance with *the* practice of the profession would not be negligent. He was referred to the following decision.

Marshall v Lindsey County Council [1935] 1 KB 516 (CA)

Maugham LJ: The practice of the Home in not refusing fresh patients after a single case of puerperal sepsis had occurred, taking, however, the recognised sterilisation precautions, is in accordance with the universal practice of maternity homes and hospitals throughout England. The Ministry of Health is in constant communication with the authorities in charge of maternity homes and hospitals. It has held many inquiries and has issued a number of reports and leaflets in connection with the problem of reducing maternal mortality. It is not suggested that the Ministry has ever proposed the drastic step which the jury appear to favour. In these circumstances I am of opinion that the defendant Council, assuming their responsibility for the acts of the medical officers and nursing staff, have acted in accordance with the recognised practice and are therefore free from liability on the ground of negligence. This is a matter of great importance in relation to the powers of juries. An act cannot, in my opinion, be held to be due to a want of reasonable care if it is in accordance with the general practice of mankind. What is reasonable in a world not wholly composed of wise men and women must depend on what people presumed to be reasonable constantly do. Many illustrations might be given and I will take one from the evidence given in this action. A jury could not, in my opinion, properly hold it to be negligent in a doctor or a midwife to perform his or her duties in a confinement without mask and gloves, even though some experts gave evidence that in their opinion that was a wise precaution. Such an omission may become negligent if, and only if, at some future date it becomes the general custom to take such a precaution among skilled practitioners.

... I do not doubt the general truth ... that a defendant charged with negligence can clear himself if he shows that he has acted in accord with general and approved practice.

Did it enter the mind of the court that the fact that there is unanimity in the profession may not entail the conclusion that this unanimously approved practice is legally appropriate as being *reasonable*? In other words why cannot a judgment of reasonableness be made by anyone other than a doctor?

Maugham LJ referred to the earlier case in the Privy Council of *Vancouver General Hospital v McDaniel* (1934) 152 LT 56. The plaintiff contracted smallpox while being treated in hospital for diphtheria. The Privy Council held that the defendants were not negligent because the expert evidence showed that the hospital's procedures for treating smallpox and preventing other patients catching it were in accordance with the general practice in Canada and the USA. Lord Alness said it was: 'difficult to affirm that negligence on the part of the [defendants] is proved. A defendant charged with negligence can clear his feet if he shows that he has acted in accordance with general and approved practice'. Maugham LJ's *dictum* was approved by the House of Lords in *Whiteford v Hunter* [1950] WN 553 (per Lord Porter).

Subsequently, the House of Lords confirmed that a doctor would not be negligent even where there were 'two schools of thought', providing he acted in accordance with one of them.

Maynard v West Midlands RHA [1985] 1 All ER 635 (HL)

Lord Scarman: My Lords, the question in this appeal is whether a physician and a surgeon, working together in the treatment of their patient, were guilty of an error of professional judgment of such a character as to constitute a breach of their duty of care towards her. The negligence alleged against each, or one or other, of them is that contrary to the strong medical indications which should have led them to diagnose tuberculosis they held back from a firm diagnosis and decided that she should undergo the diagnostic operation, mediastinoscopy. It was an operation which carried certain risks, even when correctly performed, as it is admitted that it was in this case. One of the risks, namely damage to the left laryngeal recurrent nerve, did, as the judge has found and the respondent authority now accepts, unfortunately materialise with resulting paralysis of the left vocal cord. Comyn J, the trial judge, held that the two doctors were negligent. The Court of Appeal (Cumming-Bruce LJ and Sir Stanley Rees, Dunn LJ dissenting) held that they were not. The only issue for the House is whether the two medical men, Dr Ross who was the consultant physician and Mr Stephenson the surgeon, were guilty of an error of judgment amounting to a breach of their duty of care to their patient. Both accept that the refusal to make a firm diagnosis until they had available the findings of the diagnostic operation was one for which they were jointly responsible.

The issue is essentially one of fact; but there remains the possibility, which it will be necessary to examine closely, that the judge, although directing himself correctly as to the law, failed to apply it correctly when he came to draw the inferences on which his conclusion of negligence was based. Should this possibility be established as the true interpretation to be put on his judgment, he would, of course, be guilty of an error of law…

The only … question of law in the appeal is as to the nature of the duty owed by a doctor to his patient…

The present case may be classified as one of clinical judgment. Two distinguished consultants, a physician and a surgeon experienced in the treatment of chest diseases, formed a judgment as to what was, in their opinion, in the best interests of their patient. They recommended that tuberculosis was the most likely diagnosis. But in their opinion, there was an unusual factor, viz swollen glands in the mediastinum unaccompanied by any evidence of lesion in the lungs. Hodgkin's disease, carcinoma, and sarcoidosis were, therefore, possibilities. The danger they thought was Hodgkin's disease; though unlikely, it was, if present, a killer (as treatment was understood in 1970) unless remedial steps were taken in its early stage. They therefore decided on mediastinoscopy, an operative procedure which would provide them with a biopsy from the swollen gland which could be subjected to immediate microscopic examination. It is said that the evidence of tuberculosis was so strong that it was unreasonable and wrong to defer diagnosis and to put their patient to the risks of the operation. The case against them is not mistake or carelessness in performing the operation, which is admitted was properly carried out, but an error of judgment in requiring the operation to be undertaken.

A case which is based on an allegation that a fully considered decision of two consultants in the field of their special skill was negligent clearly presents certain difficulties of proof. It is not enough to show that there is a body of competent professional opinion which considers that theirs was a wrong decision, if there also exists a body of professional opinion, equally competent, which supports the decision as reasonable in the circumstances. It is not enough to show that subsequent events show that the operation need never have been performed, if at the time the decision to operate was taken it was reasonable in the sense that a responsible body of medical opinion would have accepted it as proper. I do not think that the words of the Lord President (Clyde) in *Hunter v Hanley* 1955 SLT 213 at 217 can be bettered:

In the realm of diagnosis and treatment there is ample scope for genuine difference of opinion and one man clearly is not negligent merely because his conclusion differs from that of other professional men… The true test for establishing negligence in diagnosis or treatment on the part of a doctor is whether he has been proved to be guilty of such failure as no doctor of ordinary skill would be guilty of if acting with ordinary care…

… The judge accepted not only the expertise of all the medical witnesses called before him but also their truthfulness and honesty. But he found Dr Hugh-Jones 'an outstanding witness; clear, definite, logical and persuasive'. The judge continued:

I have weighted his evidence against that of the distinguished contrary experts. I do not intend or wish to take away from their distinction by holding that in the particular circumstances of this particular case I prefer his opinions and his evidence to theirs.

My Lords… I have to say that a judge's 'preference' for one body of distinguished professional opinion to another also professionally distinguished is not sufficient to establish negligence in a practitioner whose actions have received the seal of approval of those whose opinions, truthfully expressed, honestly held, were not preferred. If this was the real reason for the judge's finding, he erred in law even though elsewhere in his judgment he stated the law correctly. For in the realm of diagnosis and treatment negligence is not established by preferring one respectable body of professional opinion to another. Failure to exercise the ordinary skill of a doctor (in the appropriate speciality, if he be a specialist) is necessary.

In fact, McNair J in *Bolam* may not have meant that compliance with accepted practice was conclusive. In his summing up he stated (at 587-588):

… it is right to say this, that it is not essential for you to decide which of two practices is the better practice, as long as you accept that what the defendants did was in accordance with a practice accepted by responsible persons; if the result of the evidence is that you are satisfied that his practice is better than the practice spoken of on the other side, then it is really a stronger case.

That final remark seems to leave open the possibility of the court (or jury in *Bolam* itself) having a greater role in setting the standard of care.

Nevertheless, in subsequent cases the *Bolam* test became accepted as stating that professional practice was determinative of the legal standard such as that in *Sidaway v Board of Governors of the Bethlem Royal Hospital* [1985] AC 871, Lord Scarman stated (at 881):

The *Bolam* principle may be formulated as a rule that a doctor is not negligent if he acts in accordance with a practice accepted at the time as proper by a responsible body of medical opinion even though other doctors adopt a different practice. In short, the law imposes the duty of care: but the standard of care is a matter of medical judgment.

This became what might be called that 'conventional' understanding of the *Bolam* test.

(ii) CONVENTIONAL *BOLAM*

Is there not a fundamental problem underlying the approach of McNair J in *Bolam* and which has been followed thereafter? Is not the standard of care a *prescriptive* question rather than merely descriptive? Being prescriptive, is it not unusual for the court to allow a particular group (in this case the medical profession) to prescribe what the law is?

Professor Montrose with characteristic acumen saw the difficulties raised by *Bolam* immediately, as can be seen from the following article.

A Montrose 'Is Negligence an Ethical or a Sociological Concept?' (1958) 21 MLR 259.

Ever since *Blyth v Birmingham Waterworks* [(1856) 11 Exch 781] it has been usual to state the standard for negligence by reference to the 'reasonable man', or the 'prudent and reasonable man', the terms used by Baron Alderson in his judgment. Sometimes mention is made of the 'ordinary' man, the 'man on the Clapham omnibus', but hitherto conduct has not been exonerated from being considered negligent merely because it is of the kind ordinarily done by ordinary people. A motorist is not excused because he shows that he acted in accordance with the common practice of motorists. The question of negligence is one of what *ought* to be done in the circumstances, not what *is* done in similar circumstances by most people or even by all people. In so far as negligence is concerned with what ought to be done, it may be called an ethical concept: in so far as it is concerned with what is done, with practice, it may be said to be a sociological concept.

...[The view of McNair J in *Bolam*] that conformity with practice cannot be negligent stems from a failure to heed the warning of Stallybrass that the 'imagery' of the 'man in the street' may be misleading. McNair J explained the law of negligence to the jury in these terms. 'In the ordinary case which does not involve any special skill negligence in law means this: Some failure to do some act which a reasonable man in the street would not do: and if that failure or the doing of that act results in injury, then there is a cause of action. How do you test whether this failure or cause of action is negligent? In an ordinary case it is generally said that you judge that by the action of the man in the street. He is the ordinary man. In one case it has been said that you judge it by the conduct of the man on the top of a Clapham omnibus. He is the ordinary man.' But the suggested test, though useful as a guide in many cases, is not a universal test: it omits the important qualification stressed by Stallybrass: 'The "man in the street" does not always show the care of a reasonably prudent man in the circumstances.' From the premises of McNair J it does indeed follow that in 'a situation which involves the sue of some special skill or competence', and where there are diverse practices followed by those possessed of that skill, then conformity with one of those practices cannot be negligence. But the qualification which has to be added to the premises has to be added also to the conclusion. It is for the court to say whether the ordinary behaviour of the man in the street, or the ordinary practice of those possessed of 'special skill or competence', is reasonable and prudent.

It is, perhaps, going too far to say the McNair J has entirely omitted the possibility of consideration of a recognised practice as negligence. In the passages already quoted there do occur the epithets 'proper' and 'reasonable', which may refer to objective qualifications and not to subjective beliefs of those following the practice. This attitude appears more clearly in another passage: 'I do not think that I quarrel much with any of the submissions in law which have been put before you by counsel. Counsel for the plaintiff put it this way, that in the case of a medical man negligence means failure to act in accordance with the standards of reasonably competent medical men at the time. That is a perfectly accurate statement, as long as it is remembered that there may be one or more perfectly proper standards; and if a medical man conforms with one of those proper standards then he is not negligent.' Moreover, in his survey on the evidence McNair J referred throughout to the objective reasons for holding that the practice of the defendant was reasonable. He discussed the evidence which had been given of the mortality risk from the use of relaxant drugs, and of the danger of fracture from the use of manual control.

Though it is submitted that the doctrine that mere conformity with practice is legally well established, analysis is required in order that its limits and value may be ascertained. In the first place is it important to distinguish between average practices and average standards, between what the ordinary man does and what the ordinary man thinks ought to be done. His practice is not a necessary determinant of his ethics. *Video meliora proboque, deteriora sequor* applies to peasants and poets. Chorley contends for the view that negligence in motoring cases should be determined by 'that which is regarded as reasonable by motorists generally': this is very different from a statistical average of the conduct of motorists. In the next place, we should consider a distinction suggested by the dictum of Lord Wright in *Lloyds Bank v E B Savory & Co* [[1933] AC 201]. It will be recalled that he considered a banking practice [to be negligent] for failure to provide against a risk. The distinction now to be examined is that between failure to provide against a risk, a fault of omission, and inefficiency in the technique employed to deal with a risk. The failure may be in connection with a known risk, or a risk which ought to have been known. It is true that Lord Wright referred only to risks 'fully known to those experienced in the business of banking', but that limitation arises from the facts of the case. It is surely negligent not to provide against risks which ought to have been known. The fact that it was not appreciated by men experienced in the particular province is, of course, strong evidence that it could not reasonably be expected to have been known and guarded against, but not conclusive evidence. Experts may blind themselves by expertise. The courts should protect the citizen against risks which professional men and others may ignore. A doctor in his enthusiasm for a new cure may not properly appreciate the dangers of his treatment; a trade unionist in his concern for less exhausting labour by his colleagues may not properly appreciate the dangers to others from his easier practice. It is sound ethics and good law for a court, judge or jury to condemn a professional practice which does not provide precautions against risks known to the profession or which the court says ought to have been known. But when the question arises of whether precautions in fact taken are adequate then different considerations may arise. If the practice adopted is one which is designed by those with skill and competence in the particular province to deal with a risk, is it then good law for the court to bring its own judgment to bear on the matter? Frankfurter J, in a case concerned with 'matters of geography and geology and physics and engineering', pointed out that the court had no expertise in these matters. Chorley likewise points out that in motoring cases, where the question is one of precautions to be taken against the well-known risks of collisions, a court does not as such possess expertise in driving, even though 'the learned trial judge is an experienced motorist' [(1938) 2 MLR 69]. Perhaps the attitude of McNair J in *Bolam's* case may be 'explained' as being concerned with the adequacy of precautions designed by those with skill and competence to safeguard against a realised risk. The case for the defence was that free movement of the limbs was the best precaution against injury. It is uniformity with a practice consisting in a technique of precautions against risks which eliminates negligence. We are, however, far from judicial recognition of a distinction between failure to provide against a risk, and adequacy of precautions. The most that can be said is at *Bolam's* case is consistent with the distinction.

Why do you think the courts have adopted the *Bolam* approach? One answer might be in the fact that the court is so often presented with an issue of apparent technical complexity. Finding it difficult to determine what is done and hearing evidence of what *is* done tends to depend upon particular facts of each case, the court has tended to elide the distinct issue of what *ought* to be done with its decision of what *is* done.

Take a simple case. Dr X testifies, supported by his witnesses, that he would never carry out a particular procedure when presented with facts 'P'. The plaintiff, supported by his witnesses, says the procedure should have been carried out when facts 'P' were present. The issue for the court, in essence, is to untangle the reasons offered by the differing medical experts, rather than to be concerned superficially with the description of their practice. The reasons offered may relate to, for example, the consequences of carrying (or not carrying) out the procedure, the risks and benefits associated with it, the quality of information to be gained as against any risk or benefit, the cost in terms of manpower or other expenditure of scarce resources. All of these questions, you will see, are questions of values and not technical medical issues at all. Being questions in value, in all other circumstances they would be properly regarded as for the court.

Another reason for the existing state of the law may be the expressed concern of the courts to avoid what has been called the American disease of malpractice litigation resulting in 'defensive medicine'. In *Whitehouse v Jordan (supra),* Lord Denning MR described 'defensive medicine' thus (at 658):

> Take heed of what has happened in the United States. 'Medical malpractice' cases there are very worrying, especially as they are tried by juries who have sympathy for the patient and none for the doctor, who is insured. The damages are colossal. The doctors insure but the premiums become very high: and these have to be passed on in fees to the patients. Experienced practitioners are known to have refused to treat patients for fear of being accused of negligence. Young men are even deterred from entering the profession because of the risks involved. In the interests of all, we must avoid such consequences in England.

See also Lawton LJ (at 659).

In the *Sidaway* case (*supra*), Lord Scarman offered the following description (at 653):

> The proliferation of medical malpractice in the United States of America has led some courts and some legislatures to curtail or even to reject the operation of the doctrine in an endeavour to restrict the liability of the doctor and so discourage the practice of 'defensive medicine', by which is meant the practice of doctors advising and undertaking the treatment which they think is legally safe even though they may believe that it is not the best for their patient.
>
> The danger of defensive medicine developing in this country clearly exists, though the absence of the lawyer's 'contingency fee' (a percentage of the damages for him as his fee if he wins the case but nothing if he loses) may make it more remote. However that may be, in matters of civil wrong or tort courts are concerned with legal principle; if policy problems emerge, they are best left to the legislature: see *McLoughlin v O'Brien* [1982] 2 All ER 298, [1983] 1 AC 410.

(See also, when *Sidaway* was before the Court of Appeal [1984] 1 All ER 1018, Dunn LJ at 1031; Browne-Wilkinson LJ at 1035.)

What is meant by the notion of 'defensive medicine' is that the state of the law and the consequent fear for litigation cause (or may cause) doctors to carry out procedures which are not called for as a matter of good medical practice but are done to avoid legal liability. Whatever the validity of this as a theory (and you will see that not all judges would give it credence), there is little doubt that it is widely perceived to be a real risk. We shall notice that it may be theoretically incoherent. If the law requires doctors to do only *that which other doctors deem reasonable*, where is the need for defensive medicine? But the notion persists.

Despite the obvious possibility of a different interpretation of *Bolam*, and of limiting its scope of application, it became the common coinage of medical negligence litigation. It was, with one single exception, applied in all medical negligence cases concerned with treatment or diagnosis. It was, as we shall see (*infra*, ch 5), not on the face of it applied in information cases by the House of Lords in *Sidaway* but was subsequently by the Court of Appeal in *Blyth v Bloomsbury HA* [1993] 4 Med LR 151. It was extended to situations where it is difficult to see its relevance. First, where there was no practice but the expert evidence attested to what should have been done (eg *Hughes v Waltham Forest HA* [1991] 2 Med LR 155 (CA)). It is not at all clear why *Bolam* applies to what may be described as 'one-off' decisions by doctors. In *Chapman v Rix* (1960) [1994] 5 Med LR 239, Lord Goddard had said (at 247) that the evidence of two doctors saying that 'they would have acted as [the defendant] did' did not mean the defendant was not negligent. Secondly, the courts applied *Bolam* to determine the scope of a doctor's duty to act in the 'best interests' of an incompetent adult (*Re F (A Mental Patient: Sterilisation*) [1990] 2 AC 1 (HL) and *Airedale NHS Trust v Bland* [1993] AC 789 (HL)). However, by contrast, in evaluating decisions on non-medical matters, *Bolam* has no relevance (see per Lord Mustill at 898 in *Bland*). Likewise, the court must determine questions of fact for itself and thus, rather than apply the *Bolam* test, have to choose between conflicting expert opinion about what happened (see *Loveday v Renton* [1990] 1 Med LR 117 (causation)).

The distinction between pure factual questions and matters of judgment, whether for the profession (under 'conventional *Bolam*') or ultimately the court (following *Bolitho* as we shall see), is illustrated by the Court of Appeal's decision concerned with failures to detect abnormalities in cervical screening.

Penney v East Kent HA [2000] Lloyd's Rep Med 41 (CA)

Lord Woolf MR: 1. This appeal arises out of three actions brought by Sandra Penney, Helen Palmer and Lesley Cannon. The actions were tried in Canterbury before His Honour Judge Peppitt QC sitting as a Deputy High Court Judge. After a hearing lasting two weeks, between 18 – 29 January 1999, the judge gave judgment in favour of the claimants on the issue of liability. With the agreement of the parties, he did not deal with the question of causation. The actions arose out of four cervical smears taken from the three claimants in the years 1989, 1990 and 1992 as part of the national cervical screening programme (CSP). Each of the four smears were reported by the primary screeners as being negative.

2. The consequence of the negative reports was that there was no timely follow up or diagnostic or therapeutic intervention as a result of the screening and each of the subjects went on to develop invasive adenocarcinoma of the cervix. This meant the claimants had to undergo surgery which included a hysterectomy. Prior to the hearing in the court below, Judge Peppitt had declined to transfer the cases to London on the grounds that some of the relevant plaintiffs were very ill, with "time not on their side"...

4. Although the screening programme in its present form began in 1988, screening has a substantially longer history. In the early years there was controversy as to the benefits which CSP was likely to achieve. However, the CSP is now recognised to have been remarkably successful in detecting pre-cancerous changes in squamous cell carcinomas which are known as cervical intra-epithelial neoplasia or "CIN". This is a cancer found in the ectocervix or outer cervix. It was only later that it was appreciated that the screening programme could also be used to identify pre-cancerous changes which can result in adenocarcinoma, endocervical carcinomas. This is possible as a result of the examination of cells taken from the inner cervix. This condition is known as cervical glandular intra-epithelial neoplasia or "CGIN". CGIN is less common and less easy to detect in cervical smears than CIN. However its incidence has for some time been increasing. CGIN is the condition which the claimants allege that screening in their cases should have revealed.

5. If detected at an early stage both these pre-cancerous or cancerous conditions can usually be effectively dealt with by relatively minor surgical treatment. The position can, however, be very different if this does not happen...

9. Before the judge there was an agreed amended general or generic report (the generic report) which provided background information for the purposes of the case. The report had been prepared by Dr Elizabeth Hudson in collaboration with Dr Boon and Dr Hughes, who are the experts called on behalf of the defendants. It was then amended so that it included agreed additions by the claimants' experts, Professor Cotton and Professor Krausz. This report makes the important point that screening should be conducted "so that the best interests of patients are protected" while at the same time attempting to achieve a balance between detecting as many abnormalities as possible without unnecessarily subjecting the individual from whom the smear is taken to unnecessary anxiety.

The Screening
10. The generic report makes it clear that cervical screening does not provide a fault proof test. Even if the manner in which test is taken and interpreted is exemplary, not all cases of cervical pre-cancer or invasive cancer will be detected. This is especially true of adenocarcinoma which is more difficult to detect by cervical smear. As the generic report points out, the abnormality may be high up the endocervical canal out of reach of the usual smear taking instrument. In addition in the case of CGIN the distinction between normal and abnormal results is less well defined. However, reporting needs to be adjusted to take this into consideration.

11. The screening is done by qualified biomedical scientists or qualified cytology screeners. They sit at their microscopes for periods of up to two hours at a time examining methodically the whole of the area of the slide. If screeners consider that a smear is in the normal range (that is negative) or of such poor quality that it should be reported as inadequate and repeated, they report this. If the screener detects or suspects that a smear is abnormal they are required to pass it to a supervisory checker who either confirms the opinion of the primary screener or if it is still considered abnormal, passes it on to a pathologist for examination and report. The report will usually be for a repeat test or referral to a gynaecologist for further investigation.

12. Primary screeners usually screen on average six to eight slides per hour but they should not be subject to pressure to keep to a particular timescale because some slides are more difficult to examine than others. The task of examining the slides can be made more difficult because of the presence of red blood cells or inflammatory cells (white blood cells) which are common contaminants. Cells may also be spread unevenly, and distorted and interpretation is made more difficult when epithelial cells show severe reactive changes.

13. The classification of cells by screeners should be uniform in accordance with the requirement of the CSP. The relevant classes for present purposes are:

Inadequate	Insufficient or poorly visualised cells
Negative	No abnormal cells seen
Borderline changes	Changes of uncertain significance
Mild dyskaryosis	Mild neoplastic squamous changes usually CIN 1.
Glandular neoplasia	Severe glandular cell changes possible adenocarcinoma.

The classification also deals with three more categories of increasingly severe dyskaryosis, namely CIN2 and 3 and invasive squamous carcinoma. The Greek word dyskaryosis refers to an abnormal nucleus.

14. Inadequate smears should result in the test being repeated within three months. Borderline smears should be repeated after three, six or 12 months. The borderline category is used when after examination by the screener, checker and pathologist there is uncertainty whether the cells in a smear are within the normal range. There are "grey areas" between the cells which are clearly normal and cells which are equally clearly abnormal. Borderline is a holding category until the uncertainty is removed as a result of the test being repeated.

15. The generic report makes it clear that even in the best laboratories there will be some false positive and some false negative cervical smear results. A mistake is not necessarily a result of negligence. National standards published in 1996 indicated that primary screeners should detect 85-95% of abnormal smears so that false negative reports do not exceed 5-15%. More recently introduced quality control is intended to reduce false negative reports to 5% or less.

16. The generic report also describes the training of screeners. Screeners, based on their training and experience, have to make a number of judgments, including deciding whether to examine the slides at high magnification. Where a patient who has been tested has developed cervical cancer notwithstanding a negative report, there is a retrospective review. The results of the review vary. There can be no abnormal cells disclosed by the review or there can be a few dispersed dyskaryotic cells which would be unlikely to be detected. In other cases there can be cells which should have been detected by screening but which were wrongly interpreted…

The Law

22. In his judgment, the judge having set out the background facts with admirable clarity, including a detailed account of the task of the cytoscreeners, turned his attention to the law. He began by indicating that both parties agreed that:

"the standard which I have to apply is that of a reasonably competent screener exercising reasonable care at the time when the screening took place. I must ignore any advances in screening practice which have occurred since the relevant events. I must also put out of my mind when considering the extent of the screeners' duty of care the fact that all three [claimants] subsequently developed carcinoma.

Equally importantly I must bear constantly in mind that in cases where an exercise of judgment is called for, the fact that with the benefit of hindsight that judgment was exercised wrongly is not itself proof of negligence."

23. The judge then went on to cite from *Bolam v Friern Hospital Management Committee* [1957] 1 WLR 582, *Maynard v West Midland Regional Health Authority* [1984] 1 WLR 634 and *Bolitho v City and Hackney Health Authority* [1998] AC 232…

26. Both before the judge and before this court counsel were agreed that the approach indicated in the passages which have been cited should be applied to these cases. We agree. The screeners were exercising skill and judgment in determining what report they should make and in that respect the *Bolam* test was generally applicable. Later authorities make clear that this is the appropriate standard to apply. However, as we will explain, the fact that two sets of competent experts genuinely hold differing opinions as to whether or not *at the relevant date*, which is the date of the examination, the screeners could without being negligent have diagnosed the smears as negative does not necessarily provide the solution to the dispute on liability in these cases.

27. …the *Bolam* test has no application where what the judge is required to do is to make findings of fact. This is so, even where those findings of fact are the subject of conflicting expert evidence. Thus in this case there were three questions which the judge had to answer:

> What was to be seen in the slides?
> At the relevant time could a screener exercising reasonable care fail to see what was on the slide?
> Could a reasonably competent screener, aware of what a screener exercising reasonable care would observe on the slide, treat the slide as negative?

28. Thus, logically the starting point for the experts' reasoning was what was on the slides. Except in relation to the slide known as Palmer 2, as to which there was a striking conflict, as a result of a meeting which took place between the experts they were in substantial but by no means total agreement. In so far as they were not in agreement, the judge had the unenviable task of deciding as a matter of fact which of the experts were correct as to what the slides showed. This was a task which required expert evidence. However the evidence having been given, the judge had to make his own finding on the balance of probabilities on this issue of fact in order to proceed to the next step in answering the question of negligence or no negligence. Having come to his own conclusion as to what the slides showed, the judge had, therefore, then to answer the 2nd and 3rd questions in order to decide whether the screener was in breach of duty in giving a negative report. Whether the screener was in breach of duty would depend on the training and the amount of knowledge a screener should have had in order to properly perform his or her task at that time and how easy it was to discern what the judge had found was on the slide. These issues involved both questions of fact and questions of opinion as to the standards of care which the screeners should have exercised. As already indicated, there was virtually no evidence of the actual training provided to the primary screeners. The approach of the experts was to give their opinion, based on their respective interpretations of what was on the slide, on the general question of whether a reasonably competent screener, exercising the appropriate standard of care, could treat the slide as negative.

29. The distinction between issues of fact and issues as to what is or is not an appropriate response to facts when the facts have been ascertained is illustrated by the case of *Loveday v Renton and Welcome Foundation Ltd* [1990] 1 Med LR 117. In summarising his conclusions in that case Lord Justice Stuart-Smith said (at 182):

(1)   The preliminary issue to be determined by the court is, can pertussis vaccine cause permanent brain damage in young children?… The burden of proof rests on the plaintiff and the standard of proof is that of the balance of probability. It must be shown that it is more likely than not that the vaccine can cause permanent brain damage.

(2)   Medical and expert opinion is deeply divided on the issue. The question has to be determined on all the evidence in the case, which is primarily the oral evidence of the witnesses tested in cross examination. The court cannot simply accept the opinion or belief of a witness, however eminent, that such is or is not the case. The basis for the opinion must be examined, tested against other evidence, for consistency and logic and the validity of the reasoning.

(3)   The question is not answered by showing that there is a respectable and responsible body of medical opinion that the vaccine can, albeit rarely, cause permanent brain damage, or that this view may be more widely held than the contrary. The opinion of others not called to give evidence is not admissible to prove the truth of the opinion. The works of learned and qualified authors form part of the general corpus of medical and scientific learning on the subject and can be relied upon and adopted by suitably qualified experts. These experts may have their opinions tested in the light of the literature.

The Appellants' Case

30. The appellants challenge the judge's decision on the central question of the relevant state of knowledge at the time when each of the slides was reported upon. However, it is accepted that the judge asked the right question, that is "How a reasonably competent cytoscreener at the relevant time should have reported her slide?". Mr Faulks submits that

the opinions of the experts called on behalf of the appellants were that abnormalities to be seen on the slides (other than Palmer II, which requires separate treatment) would not have been recognized as such by a reasonably competent cytoscreener at the time. In those circumstances, the classifications of the slides as "negative" could properly have been made by a reasonably competent cytoscreener. It is submitted that these opinions of the appellants' experts were based on a thorough knowledge of the standards of cytoscreeners, the evolution of knowledge, practice in laboratories, examination questions, proficiency tests and all the available literature. They amounted to a good defence upon a proper application of *Bolam* principles. The judge is criticised for holding that *Bolam* did not apply and, in so far as he did, for deciding what were really matters of opinion as if they were questions of fact. He is also criticised for not giving detailed reasons in his judgment for rejecting the appellants' case as to the state of knowledge. It is submitted that at the very least there should be a retrial to permit a judge to come to a reasoned decision on this central issue. At the same time, it is accepted as being highly undesirable that there should be a retrial and Mr Faulks said that the appellants would not wish to put the individual respondents through one. But his instructions did not extend to being able to give any assurance that this would not happen.

31. In addition to what appeared on the slide, Mr Badenoch submitted that the question of what was known at the time of the examination of the slides was a question of fact to which *Bolam* could have no application. This submission we regard as being only partially correct. The state of knowledge may be objectively discernible and therefore be a matter of fact. However, there would be room for differences of opinion as to the extent that screeners at a particular time should be required to be aware of the latest learning on a particular subject. This would be a subject on which respectable opinion could differ as to what is the appropriate standard. Thus, for example, one view might be that the already demanding cytoscreeners' task should not be over-complicated by training them to spot the more subtle and complex changes the relevance of which was not yet fully understood; another view might be that they should be trained to do the best they can to spot and evaluate anything which might be relevant. The evidence did not suggest any divergence of view such as this. Similarly, there might be a difference of opinion as to how much judgment a screener should personally exercise once a potential abnormality was spotted; but again the evidence did not suggest any such divergence of view.

Mrs Penney's Slide

32. The judge's approach to this subject can be illustrated by the slide relating to Mrs Penney dated 31 December 1992. We therefore take her case first. The judge commenced by recording that her slide was by common consent "difficult to interpret though none of the experts argued that the cytoscreener might reasonably have failed to observe what it contained." He then set out the views of the four experts namely the claimants' two experts and Dr Hudson and Dr Boon. Their descriptions of what the slides showed differed in detail. He then set out the fact that a meeting took place on 5 December 1998 when all the disputed smears were reviewed and it was agreed that the slides showed: "Four or five inflamed groups of endocervical cells showing changes in nuclear and cytoplasmic morphology. It was not a normal slide."

33. The judge went on to state that the experts were agreed that at the time they gave evidence (ie not at the time when the screener examined the slide) a reasonably competent cytoscreener would have reported the smear at least as "borderline". At the relevant time that is 1993, a cytopathologist (in other words someone more skilled than a cytoscreener) would at least have reached the conclusion that this smear should have been classified at the time as borderline whereas the other experts took a different view.

On this evidence the judge said:

The issue which I have to decide therefore is whether in the light of what he saw the cytoscreener was negligent in failing to classify the smear as at least borderline. On this issue I prefer the views of Professors Cotton and Krausz. The slide was difficult to interpret even by a Consultant Pathologist. But the abnormality was there to be seen. Whether that abnormality was precancerous or reactive and thus benign it was not for the cytoscreener to decide. His function was to observe and to record. He had neither the knowledge nor the experience to diagnose. In my judgment no competent cytoscreener would have dismissed the possibility that the abnormality on this smear was precancerous. Accordingly if one applies the "absolute confidence" test propounded by Dr Hudson this smear had to be classified at least borderline. Anything less would place the patient in danger.

I have already set out the conflicting views of Doctors Hudson and Boon. In so far as the import of those views is that no cytoscreener could have been expected in 1993 or later to say affirmatively whether the abnormality on the smear was reactive or precancerous I accept them. But that is not the test which both parties agreed that I should apply. I have to consider whether the reasonably competent cytoscreener in 1993 could properly have dismissed the possibility that the abnormality was precancerous. No-one who gave evidence before me sought to suggest how a cytoscreener in 1993 might have been able competently to distinguish between precancerous and reactive changes. Indeed the evidence was to the contrary – that the two are often indistinguishable. In those circumstances I consider that the cytoscreener was wrong to classify this smear as anything less than borderline.

...

35. Pausing there it is important to note that the judge is indicating that his understanding of Drs Hudson and Boon's evidence is that they were saying that a cytoscreener could not in 1993 have been expected to say one way or the other whether the smear was abnormal or not.
36. The judge then went on to say:

I should say at the outset that I find the *Bolam* principle ill-fitting to the facts of Mrs Penney's case. In *Bolam* and the cases which followed the court was concerned with an aspect of professional conduct of which some members of the profession, but not others, disapproved. In other words in those cases the defendants' experts sought to justify as an *acceptable* professional practice what the defendant did or did not do. Here the position is different. All the experts agree that the cytoscreener was wrong. No question of *acceptable* practice was involved. The issue here to which the experts' evidence was directed was whether the cytoscreeners conduct though wrong, was *excusable*. This seems to me to fall outside the *Bolam* principle.

But if I am wrong about this I remain of the view that *Bolam* does not assist the defendants. For I do not consider that the evidence of Drs Hudson and Boon stands up to the logical analysis as that phrase was used by Lord Browne-Wilkinson in *Bolitho* at p 1160 c-d. This is not to disparage the evidence of either. It is rather that in my judgment their opinions cannot stand with 'the absolute confidence' test which Dr Hudson herself propounded with the agreement of the other experts. Here were admitted abnormalities which, to put it most favourably to the cytoscreener, he could not positively have said were not pre-cancerous. Neither Dr Hudson nor Dr Boon suggested that the cytoscreener had the ability to draw any such distinction, still less how they should apply it. It seems to me therefore that having regard to the potentially disastrous consequences of a mistaken classification a reasonably competent cytoscreener should have classified the smear as borderline even though that classification might have caused the patient short-term distress and perhaps the discomfort and embarrassment of a further smear. I cannot believe that any woman would not be prepared to put up with both if the alternative was an undiagnosed potential carcinoma.

It is for these reasons that I have preferred the evidence of Professors Cotton and Krausz to Drs Hudson and Boon in finding as I do that the defendants were negligent and in breach of the duty which they owed to Mrs Penney in failing by their cytoscreener to classify her slide in January 1993 as at least borderline.

In these passages the judge clearly sets out his reasons. In two different passages he sets out the correct standard of care. He also makes it clear by his references to 1993, that contrary to Mr Faulks' submission he appreciates that he has to focus upon that year. He makes findings about what the slide shows. He concluded there was an abnormality which even a consultant pathologist would find difficult to interpret although the abnormality was there to be seen. Because the slide was difficult to interpret in order to protect the patient, in accordance with Dr Hudson's own approach, the slide should have been classified as at least borderline...
38. The judge describes the *Bolam* principle as being "ill fitting to the *facts* of Mrs Penney's case". On an analysis of the judge's reasoning this is an understandable statement for him to make. On the judge's approach, this was not a case where there were two acceptable standards of professional conduct involved. The only comment of the judge which is difficult to understand is his questioning "*whether the cytoscreeners conduct though wrong, was excusable*". However, this does not matter because the judge also, in the alternative, applied the *Bolitho* test. The judge's reasoning was that, if the cytoscreener could not say with a reasonable degree of confidence that the abnormalities were not precancerous, then it was inconsistent with what Dr Hudson and Dr Boon were agreed was the right approach to report her slide as negative.
39. In his submissions, Mr Faulks makes a number of criticisms of the reasoning of the judge. He describes it as simplistic. He submits it amounted to no more than saying that if a slide contains features which *might* be abnormal then a negative classification should not be given. In relation to Mrs Penney's slide, we do not consider this criticism is appropriate. The judge was basing himself on the difficulty of interpreting that particular slide. We do not

regard the reasoning of the judge as inconsistent with the statistics which show that a false negative rate would not be less than 5% to 15%.

40. The judge's reliance on the absolute confidence test is understandable. The phrase 'absolute confidence' was no more than shorthand for the approach which on examination of the transcripts it seems to us all the experts endorsed. To take single passages from the experts' evidence can be misleading, but as an example supportive of the judge's approach reference can be made to the transcript of day 6 at p 79. Dr Hudson was asked "I wonder if you could help the learned judge in terms of the concept of doubt in what is expected of the screener in terms of their response to a relatively difficult smear?".

41. She gave the answer:

Certainly if they have doubt they must pass it on to a checker, and when they are training they have doubts all the time and discuss this with their trainer but once they have passed their exam they are expected to make a certain number of decisions themselves and indeed quite a lot of decisions...

42. The judge also asked:

Is that the test, anything short of absolute confidence within the normal range to pass on? Answer:

Yes, my Lord.

43. What the judge regarded as being an illogical approach on the part of Dr Hudson was explored during her cross examination. For example, (day 6 p 115/116) during her cross examination, she argued that a screener need not refer a particular smear, although earlier she had accepted that in the case of this type of smear a high degree of expertise would be required before it could be confidently stated that the slide was negative.

44. In the case of Dr Boon, he makes it absolutely clear that the cytoscreener should only treat a slide as negative if he or she is satisfied beyond reasonable doubt that this is the position. (Day 7 p 72/73) Dr Hughes, the Authority's other expert, also adopted the same approach as to "the absolute confidence test".

45. The generic report supports the judge's approach to the absolute confidence test. At page 4 it makes the point that "competent cytology screeners should not miss smears with significant numbers of abnormal cells. More subtle abnormalities or small numbers of abnormal cells can inevitably be missed by competent screeners under normal screening conditions."

46. At page 9 it states "The primary screener's job is to make a judgment based on training and experience about the normality or possible abnormality of a smear. The primary screener is encouraged to refer to the checker and pathologist if in any doubt (but population screening by current methodology would not be possible if all cervical smears had to be reported by checkers or pathologists)."...

48. The critical question is whether the judge was entitled to conclude that in the case of Mrs Penney's slide a reasonably competent cytoscreener would have at least been aware that the slide was difficult to interpret. On the judge's findings of fact, this was what the cytoscreener should have concluded. There were abnormalities to be seen on the slide and the reasonably competent cytoscreener could not with confidence have concluded that they were not pre-cancerous. The cytoscreener should then have referred the slide for further examination. Either because of lack of training or because of the way in which the slide was examined, the cytoscreener did not do this.

49. In evidence and in argument before the judge, there was a considerable amount of discussion of the need to have a balance between sensitivity and specificity. There needed to be a balance on the part of the screeners because otherwise there would be an excessive risk of their reaching "false negative" or "false positive" conclusions. However, as the judge made clear, from the point of view of the patient, a false negative could have very adverse consequences. A false positive would have nothing like this disadvantage to the patient. This is because a false negative could have even fatal results for the patient, while as long as the checker or pathologist corrected the mistake made by the screener, a false positive annotation of the slide would have no adverse consequence to the patient. If they repeated the screener's mistake the patient could be caused anxiety, but this is a small price to pay for the protection against the adverse consequences that could result from a slide wrongly being classified as negative. We have no doubt on the evidence that the screening programme should aim by enhanced training of those who operate it to reduce so far as possible the number of false positives and false negatives. On the disputed evidence before the judge however this cannot logically compromise the need for a primary screener to apply the absolute confidence test.

50. Dr Hudson, while adhering to the approach which we have indicated of placing the patient's safety first, did stress that screeners were required to exercise judgment and it was

on the basis of this requirement that the screeners should exercise judgment that she would not criticise the screener who examined Mrs Penney's slide. While this approach may be justified in relation to appropriate smears the judge was entitled to conclude that it could not be justified with regard to the "4 or 5 abnormal groups of endocervical cells" which he found to be present on Mrs Penney's slide. It is correct that the groups were agreed by the experts to be inflamed but this made the screener's task more difficult and to that extent supported the judge's conclusion. Despite the experts' agreement as to what the slide showed Dr Hudson placed less emphasis on what the slide revealed. She considered this to be "slightly atypical endocervical epithelial cells", while Dr Boon based his opinion that it was wholly unreasonable to expect a competent screener to have consistently detected such material on his conclusion that there was no suspicion of glandular neoplasia.

51. The judge did not accept Dr Hudson's and Dr Boon's description of what the slides showed. He was entitled to prefer the evidence of the claimants' experts that there were abnormalities on Mrs Penney's slide which were there to be seen. Applying the agreed absolute confidence test to these abnormalities, the judge was entitled to come to the conclusion which he did. Mrs Penney's case can also provide the answer to Mr Faulks contention that the judge failed to deal adequately with the evidence which was given as to the extent of knowledge of which screeners should have been aware at the relevant time. The judge's approach was to ask himself could a reasonably competent screener pass the slide as negative. Basing himself on his findings as to the abnormalities the slides showed, he considered it was not possible for the reasonably competent screener to do otherwise than take the safe course and did not trust the slide as negative. To come to such a decision it was not necessary to make a detailed analysis of the state of knowledge of screeners in 1993. All the judge had to be satisfied was that the reasonably competent screener should be able to recognise abnormalities which were present, and be unable to conclude with confidence that there was an innocent explanation for their presence...

In addition, the court went on to uphold the judge's findings in relation to the other two claimants that their slides disclosed abnormalities and, applying the test of what a reasonably competent screener would do, these should not have been labelled as 'negative'.

The Court of Appeal then concluded:

67. Before leaving this case, we should stress the following points so that the significance of the decisions of the court in these cases can be properly appreciated:

This judgment only relates to the four slides which were the subject of the claims. It is critical to the findings of the judge and the conclusions of this court that the judge decided that the slides contained obvious abnormalities which meant that their assessment as negative was negligent.

If the abnormalities observable on the slides had been different, the decision of the judge could have been different. This case does not decide that negligence by a cytoscreener can be established by showing that someone who has had a slide labelled negative unfortunately develops cervical cancer. It was not in dispute in this case that cervical cancer can develop even though a relatively recent slide is properly labelled negative. The fact that in the majority of cases this does not happen does not mean that it cannot happen even though a high degree of care is exercised.

The judge was not rejecting the general approach of the Authority's experts and in particular that of Dr Hudson. He was finding that because of the observable abnormalities on the slides the slides should not have been labelled negative in order to comply with the approach (the absolute confidence approach) that those experts supported.

We dismiss the appeal.

The Court of Appeal did not approve the judge's outright rejection of *Bolam* to Mrs Penney's case (set out at para 36 of the Court's judgment). Instead, it dissected the questions that the judge was required to answer into a factual one – what was on the slide? – and a normative one – what should have been done in the light of what was there? The former question was not one where *Bolam* applied: the judge was required to analyse the experts evidence and, if it differed, to choose and determine the factual matter for himself. By contrast, the latter required a standard of care to be applied to the facts on which *Bolam* was relevant. But, as will have been seen, the judge did not blindly follow the expert evidence. He applied the approach of the House of Lords in *Bolitho v City and Hackney HA*

[1998] AC 232. The opinion of the defendants' experts that it was appropriate to classify Mrs Penney's slide as 'negative' was illogical given his factual finding of what the slide disclosed (for further disscution see Commentary (1999) 7 Med L Rev 327 (AG)). Here, we see for the first time a departure from the conventional understanding of *Bolam* to which we now turn.

(iii) THE CHALLENGE TO *BOLAM*

The conventional understanding of *Bolam* was not applied in England in negligence cases not concerned with doctors, eg employee claims (*Cavanagh v Ulster Weaving Co Ltd* [1960] AC 145; *Thompson v Smiths Shiprepairers (North Shields) Ltd* [1984] QB 405) or other professional negligence actions such as those brought against lawyers (*Edward Wong Finance Co Ltd v Johnson Stokes & Masters* [1984] AC 296). While courts often referred to *Bolam* in the latter type of case, they did so either for the proposition that the defendant had to exercise the reasonable care and skill of a professional or for no more than the view that compliance with professional practice was relevant in determining the standard of care but it was not determinative.

It was in this latter sense that courts in other jurisdictions came to understand *Bolam*. For instance in *F v R* (1983) 33 SASR 189 (South Aust Sup Ct), a case involving a failed sterilisation in which the plaintiff alleged she should have been warned of the failure rate, it was said:

> **Bollen J:** Mr Perry's [counsel for the doctor] answer was that the responsible body of medical opinion should prevail over the view of the Court. That would mean that there was no room for the opinion of the Court on vital issues. The Court's function would be limited to ascertaining that there was a responsible body of medical opinion and deciding whether the surgeon had followed it.
>
> Many cases require the calling of expert evidence. These experts frequently express opinions on matters within their field. Sometimes they speak of what is usually done in any activity within that field. Why is the evidence received? It is received to guide or help the court. A court cannot be expected to know the correct procedure for performing a surgical operation. The Court cannot be expected to know why a manufacturer should guard against metal fatigue. A court cannot be expected to know how to mix chemicals. And so on. Expert evidence will assist the Court. But in the end it is the Court which must say whether there was a duty owed and a breach of it. The Court will have been guided and assisted by the expert evidence. It will not produce an answer merely at the dictation of the expert evidence. It will afford great weight to the expert evidence. Sometimes its decision will be the same as it would have been had it accepted dictation. But the Court does not merely follow expert evidence slavishly to a decision. The Court considers and weighs up all admissible evidence which it has received. If the Court did merely follow the path apparently pointed by expert evidence with no critical consideration of it and the other evidence, it would abdicate its duty to decide, on the evidence, whether in law a duty existed and has not been discharged. Acceptance of Mr Perry's first submission could amount to abdication here.
>
> ... I can find nothing in *Bolam v Friern Hospital Management Committee* which justifies any suggestion that evidence of the practice obtaining in the medical profession is automatically decisive of any issue in an action against a surgeon for damages in negligence. Sometimes that evidence will be decisive, sometimes not. It is least likely to be decisive when the allegation is of a failure to warn or to heed complaints of pain ie where no information about the method of procedure or basis of diagnosis is required.
>
> ... I respectfully think that some of the cases in England have concentrated rather too heavily on the practice of the medical profession.

(See also *Albrighton v Royal Prince Alfred Hospital* [1980] 2 NSWLR 542 (NSW CA).)

Some courts acknowledge the 'conventional' understanding of *Bolam* but rejected its application in some medical negligence cases, usually where the doctor was alleged to have failed to provide adequate information to the patient (eg *F v R (supra)* and *Rogers v Whittaker* (1992) 175 CLR 479 (Australia); *Reibl v Hughes*

(1980) 114 DLR (3d) 1 (Canada)). English courts were tempted to follow suit in such cases.

As we shall see the majority of the House of Lords in *Sidaway* ([1985] AC 871) were not wholly content to import the *Bolam* principle into this area of law (*infra* ch 5). In the Court of Appeal in *Sidaway*, Sir John Donaldson MR seemed anxious to point out that *Bolam* had been misunderstood. To him, what doctors do is only to be regarded as lawful provided the law considers what they do to be *right*.

Sidaway v Board of Governors of the Bethlem Royal Hospital [1984] 1 All ER 1018 (CA)

Sir John Donaldson MR: I accept the view expressed by Laskin CJC [in *Reibl v Hughes*] that the definition of the duty of care is not to be handed over to the medical or any other profession. The definition of the duty of care is a matter for the law and the courts. They cannot stand idly by if the profession, by an excess of paternalism, denies its patients a real choice. In a word, the law will not permit the medical profession to play God.

Thus, while I accept the *Bolam* test as the primary test of liability for failing to disclose sufficient information to the patient to enable that patient to exercise his right of choice whether or not to accept the advice proffered by his doctor, I do so subject to an important caveat. This is that the profession, or that section of it which is relied on by the defendant doctor as setting the requisite standard of care, is discharging the duty of disclosure as I have defined it. This, incidentally, accords with the approach of Parliament, which, in s 1(5) of the Congenital Disabilities (Civil Liability) Act 1976, enacted that –

The defendant is not answerable ... if he took reasonable care having *due regard* to the received professional opinion applicable... but this does not mean that he is answerable only because he departed from received opinion.

'Due regard' involves an exercise of judgment, *inter alia*, whether 'received professional opinion' is engaged in the same exercise as the law. This qualification is analogous to that which has been asserted in the context of treating a trade practice as evidencing the proper standard of care in *Cavanagh v Ulster Weaving Co Ltd* [1959] 2 All ER 745, [1960] AC 145 and in *Morris v West Hartlepool Steam Navigation Co Ltd* [1956] 1 All ER 385, [1956] AC 552 and would be equally infrequently relevant ...

I think that, in an appropriate case, a judge would be entitled to reject a unanimous medical view if he were satisfied that it was manifestly wrong and that the doctors must have been misdirecting themselves as to their duty in law.

Another way of expressing my view of the test is to add just one qualifying word (which I have emphasised) to the law as Skinner J summarised it, so that it would read:

The duty is fulfilled if the doctor acts in accordance with a practice *rightly* accepted as proper by a body of skilled and experienced medical men.

But even in circumstances of diagnosis and treatment (rather than disclosure) in which it has been assumed that *Bolam* applied, a number of cases rejected this view. (See also the decision of the Court of Appeal of Manitoba, *Anderson v Chasney* [1949] 4 DLR 71 and cases referred to therein).

Hucks v Cole (1968) [1993] 4 Med LR 393 (CA)

A doctor failed to treat a patient with penicillin and injury resulted when septicaemia occurred. The trial judge held the doctor liable in negligence. His appeal was dismissed by the Court of Appeal.

Sachs LJ: In the present case Dr Cole knew on the 15th October that the septic places from which the plaintiff was suffering had been infected by streptococcus pyogenes; that for this streptococcus in this patient penicillin was bacteriocidal whereas tetracycline, which was being administered, was not; and that penicillin could easily and inexpensively be administered before the onset occurred. It was not administered and the onset occurred: if it had been administered the onset would not have occurred. Thus (unless there was some good cause for not administering it) the onset was due to a lacuna between what could easily have been done and what was in fact done. According to the defence, that lacuna was consistent with and indeed accorded with the reasonable practice of other responsible doctors with obstetric experience.

When the evidence shows that a lacuna in professional practice exists by which risks of grave danger are knowingly taken, then, however small the risks, the Courts must anxiously examine that lacuna – particularly if the risks can be easily and inexpensively avoided. If the Court finds, on an analysis of the reasons given for not taking those precautions that, in the light of current professional knowledge, there is no proper basis for the lacuna, and that it is definitely not reasonable that those risks should have been taken, its function is to state that fact and where necessary to state that it constitutes negligence. In such a case the practice will no doubt thereafter be altered to the benefit of patients.

On such occasions the fact that other practitioners would have done the same thing as the defendant practitioner is a very weighty matter to be put in the scales on his behalf; but it is not, as Mr Webster readily conceded, conclusive. The Court must be vigilant to see whether the reasons given for putting a patient at risk are valid in the light of any well-known advance in medical knowledge, or whether they stem from a residual adherence to out-of-date ideas – a tendency which in the present case may well have affected the view of at any rate one of the defendant's witnesses, who, at a considerable age, seemed not to have any particular respect for laboratory results …

Despite the fact that the risk could have been avoided by adopting a course that was easy, efficient, and inexpensive, and which would have entailed only minimal chances of disadvantages to the patient, the evidence of the four defence experts to the effect that they and other responsible members of the medical profession would have taken the same risk in the same circumstances has naturally caused me to hesitate considerably on two points. Firstly, whether the failure of the defendant to turn over to penicillin treatment during the relevant period was unreasonable. On this, however, I was in the end fully satisfied that in the light of the admissions made by the defendant himself and by his witnesses – quite apart from Dr May's very cogent evidence – that failure to do this was not merely wrong but clearly unreasonable. The reasons given by the four experts do not to my mind stand up to analysis.

It is in this connection perhaps as well at this stage to mention one other point. The fact that great discoveries have been made which by their unremitting use so far eliminate dangers that the modern practitioner is unlikely ever to see the effects of these dangers is no reason for failing to be unremitting in their use even when the risks have become very small. It is not to my mind in point for a practitioner to say, as Dr Cole said (Day 5, page 20) and as Dr June Smith appeared to say (Day 6, page 32) that if he had previously actually seen how dire the effects were of not taking the relevant precaution he would have taken it, but his experience had not up till then led him to see such results. (The potential irrelevance of the rarity of remoteness of the risk, when the maturing of the risk may be disastrous, is incidentally illustrated in *Chin Keow's* case [1967] 1 WLR 813, PC.)

Secondly, as to whether, in the light of such evidence as to what other responsible medical practitioners would have done, it can be said that even if the defendant's error was unreasonable, it was [not] negligence in relation to the position as regards practice at that particular date. On this second point it is to be noted that this is not apparently a case of 'two schools of thought' (see the speech of Lord Goddard in *Chapman v Rix*, on the 21st December, 1960, at page 11): it appears more to be a case of doctors who said in one form or another that they would have acted or might have acted in the same way as the defendant did, for reasons which on examination do not really stand up to analysis.

Dr Cole knowingly took an easily avoidable risk which elementary teaching had instructed him to avoid; and the fact that others say they would have done the same neither ought to nor can in the present case excuse him in an action for negligence however sympathetic one may be to him. Moreover, in so far as the evidence shows the existence of a lacuna of the type to which reference was made earlier in this judgment, that lacuna was, in view of the magnitude of the dangers involved, so unreasonable that as between doctor and patient it cannot be relied upon to excuse the former in an action for negligence.

Lord Denning MR and Diplock LJ agreed that the defendant was in breach of his duty to the plaintiff. (See also *Clarke v Adams* (1950) 94 Sol Jo 599.)

Professor Fleming (the late distinguished torts scholar) recognises the role of the court when he writes in his book *The Law of Torts* (9th edn, 1998), p 121:

English courts adhere to the *Bolam* test whereby physicians acquit themselves by conforming to practices accepted as proper by a responsible section of the profession; in other words, it is not open to judge or jury to find a standard medical practice negligent. By thus deferring to a standard set by the medical profession itself in place of its own usual standard of reasonable care, the law in effect confers a special privilege on the medical profession which it denies to accountants, lawyers and others practising special skills. Its rationale is the layman's ignorance of medical science, coupled with the apprehension of exposing physicians to the vagaries of jury sympathy for victims. This deferential standard is applied in England not only to matters of diagnosis and treatment, but also to information and counselling, and even to non-therapeutic advice such as that relating to abortion and birth-control.

(iv) 'NEW *BOLAM*' EMERGES

Suddenly, in 1993 the Court of Appeal in *Bolitho* ((1992) 13 BMLR 111) reinterpreted *Bolam*, leaving the courts with the final say on whether a doctor had been careless (discussed (1993) 1 Med L Rev 241 (AG)). Subsequently, the Court of Appeal approved the 'new *Bolam*' approach (*Joyce v Merton, Sutton and Wandsworth HA* (1995) 27 BMLR 124; *De Freitas v O'Brien* [1995] 6 Med LR 108) and a series of first instance decisions adopted it (eg *Gascoine v Ian Sheridan & Co (a Firm)* [1994] 5 Med LR 437; *Bowers v Harrow HA* [1995] 6 Med LR 16; *Wiszniewski v Central Manchester HA* [1996] 7 Med LR 248; *Dowdie v Camberwell HA* [1997] 8 Med LR 368. For a discussion of the developing law see (1995) 3 Med L Rev 198 (AG); (1996) 4 Med L Rev 86 (AG) and (1995) 3 Med L Rev 195 (IK)).

Bolitho v City and Hackney HA (1993) 13 BMLR 111 (CA)

The case concerned a claim that a doctor's failure to attend a patient in hospital amounted to a breach of duty and caused asphyxia and consequent brain damage. The defendant admitted a breach of duty. Curiously, a majority of the court (Farquharson and Dillon LJJ) considered *Bolam* to be relevant in determining causation ie whether the doctor probably would have intubated the plaintiff had he attended him. Simon Brown LJ dissented on this point (on which see *infra*). The importance of the case for us here is, assuming *Bolam* to be relevant, the judges' explanation of its relationship to *Hucks v Cole*.

Farquharson LJ: There is, of course, no inconsistency between the decisions in *Hucks v Cole* and *Maynard's* case. It is not enough for a defendant to call a number of doctors to say that what he had done or not done was in accord with accepted clinical practice. It is necessary for the judge to consider that evidence and decide whether that clinical practice puts the patient unnecessarily at risk.

Dillon LJ: In my judgment, the court could only adopt the approach of Sachs LJ and reject medical opinion on the ground that the reasons of one group of doctors do not really stand up to analysis, if the court, fully conscious of its own lack of medical knowledge and clinical experience, was nonetheless clearly satisfied that the views of that group of doctors were *Wednesbury* unreasonable, ie views such as no reasonable body of doctors could have held.

Simon Brown LJ expressed no view on the meaning of *Bolam*. While this is a somewhat radical departure by the Court of Appeal from previous thinking in England, it is fair to say that what the court gives with one hand it takes away with the other. Both judges made it clear that the burden on the plaintiff of demonstrating the unreasonableness of accepted practice is very (perhaps impossibly) onerous. The attraction, however, of the judges' view is that, at least in principle the English Courts could recognise the role they should play (albeit at the margins in cases of treatment and diagnosis) in setting the legal standard of care. This is precisely the residuary role recognised by the leading Commonwealth cases which we have already seen. It was also an approach which appealed to the Irish Supreme Court in reviewing their own line of *Bolam*-type authority in *Dunne v National Maternity Hospital* [1989] IR 91 (Irish Supreme Court).

The other important case was *Joyce v Merton Sutton and Wandsworth HA* [1996] 7 Med LR 1. The Court of Appeal approved the 'new *Bolam*' test and rejected the less interventionist version of *Bolam* as it has been conventionally understood. Roch LJ, for example, stated that the judge's direction to himself that 'a defendant is not guilty of negligence if his acts or omissions were in accordance with accepted clinical practice' – which could have come straight out of McNair J's summing up in *Bolam* – would have been a misdirection if the judge had not added: '[p]rovided that clinical practice stood up to analysis and was not unreasonable in the light of the state of medical knowledge at the time.' And why? According to Roch LJ '[t]he addition is very important because without it, it leaves the decision of negligence or no negligence in the hands of doctors, whereas that question must at the end of the day be one for the courts'.

Hence, the Court of Appeal has approved the signal given in its earlier decision of *Bolitho v City and Hackney HA* (1992) 13 BMLR 111 (CA) and Commentary, (1993) 1 Med L Rev 241 (AG) that the court is required to take a 'hard look' at the professional practice and expert evidence and decide whether it puts 'the patient unnecessarily at risk' (per Farquharson LJ at 119). In *Joyce*, Hobhouse LJ specifically rejected the unfortunate statement by Dillon LJ in *Bolitho* that the court could only find a practice unreasonable in the negligence context if it was '*Wednesbury* unreasonable' in the public law sense, ie one which 'no reasonable body of doctors' could adopt (*supra*, at 132). Along with *Bolam* itself, this has now been shown to be the fallacy it always was.

The stage was set for the House of Lords to make a conclusive shift away from the conventional understanding of *Bolam* when *Bolitho* reached the House of Lords (somewhat belatedly) in 1997 and the Law Lords (Lords Browne-Wilkinson, Slynn, Nolan, Hoffmann and Clyde) did not disappoint in a speech delivered by Lord Browne-Wilkinson with which they all agreed.

(v) *BOLITHO V CITY AND HACKNEY HA*

Bolitho v City and Hackney Health Authority [1997] 4 All ER 771 (HL)

On 16 January 1984 a two-year-old boy, P, who had a past history of hospital treatment for croup, was readmitted to hospital under the care of Dr H and Dr R. On the following day he suffered two short episodes at 12.40pm and 2.00pm during which he turned white and clearly had difficulty breathing. Dr H was called in the first instance and she delegated Dr R to attend in the second instance but neither attended P, who at both times appeared quickly to return to a stable state. At about 2.30pm P suffered total respiratory failure and a cardiac arrest, resulting in severe brain damage. He subsequently died and his mother continued his proceedings for medical negligence as adminstratrix of his estate. The defendant health authority accepted that Dr H had acted in breach of her duty of care to P but contended that the cardiac arrest would not have been avoided if Dr H or some other suitable deputy had attended earlier than 2.30pm. It was common ground that intubation so as to provide an airway would have ensured that respiratory failure did not lead to cardiac arrest and that such intubation would have had to have been carried out before the final episode. The judge found that the views of P's expert witness and Dr D for the defendants, though diametrically opposed, both represented a responsible body of professional opinion espoused by distinguished and truthful experts. He therefore held that Dr H, if she had attended and not intubated, would have come up to a proper level of skill and competence according to the standard represented by Dr D's views and that it had not been proved that the admitted breach of duty by the defendants had caused the injury which occurred to P. The Court of Appeal dismissed an appeal by P's mother and she appealed to the House of Lords.

Lord Browne-Wilkinson: My Lords, this appeal raises two questions relating to liability for medical negligence. The first, which I believe to be more apparent than real, relates to the proof of causation when the negligent act is one of omission. The second concerns the approach to professional negligence laid down in *Bolam v Friern Hospital Management Committee* [1957] 2 All ER 118, [1957] 1 WLR 582...

The Bolam test – should the judge have accepted Dr Dinwiddie's evidence?
As I have said, the judge took a very favourable view of Dr Dinwiddie as an expert. He said:

... I have to say of Dr Dinwiddie also, that he displayed what seemed to me to be a profound knowledge of paediatric respiratory medicine, coupled with impartiality, and there is no doubt, in my view, of the genuineness of his opinion that intubation was not indicated.

However, the judge also expressed these doubts:

> Mr Brennan also advanced a powerful argument – which I have to say, as a layman, appealed to me – to the effect that the views of the defendant's experts simply were not logical or sensible. Given the recent as well as the more remote history of Patrick's illness, culminating in these two episodes, surely it was unreasonable and illogical not to anticipate the recurrence of a life-threatening event and take the step which it was acknowledged would probably have saved Patrick from harm? This was the safe option, whatever was suspected as the cause, or even if the cause was thought to be a mystery. The difficulty of this approach, as in the end I think Mr Brennan acknowledged, was that in effect it invited me to substitute my own views for those of the medical experts.

Mr Brennan renewed that submission both before the Court of Appeal (who unanimously rejected it) and before your Lordships. He submitted that the judge had wrongly treated the *Bolam* test as requiring him to accept the views of one truthful body of expert professional advice, even though he was unpersuaded of its logical force. He submitted that the judge was wrong in law in adopting that approach and that ultimately it was for the court, not for medical opinion, to decide what was the standard of care required of a professional in the circumstances of each particular case.

My Lords, I agree with these submissions to the extent that, in my view, the court is not bound to hold that a defendant doctor escapes liability for negligent treatment or diagnosis just because he leads evidence from a number of medical experts who are genuinely of opinion that the defendant's treatment or diagnosis accorded with sound medical practice. In *Bolam's* case [1957] 2 All ER 118 at 122, [1957] 1 WLR 582 at 587 McNair J stated that the defendant had to have acted in accordance with the practice accepted as proper by a '*responsible* body of medical men' (my emphasis). Later he referred to 'a standard of practice recognised as proper by a competent *reasonable* body of opinion' (see [1957] 2 All ER 118 at 122, [1957] 1 WLR 582 at 588; my emphasis). Again, in the passage which I have cited from *Maynard's* case, Lord Scarman refers to a 'respectable' body of professional opinion. The use of these adjectives - responsible, reasonable and respectable – all show that the court has to be satisfied that the exponents of the body of opinion relied on can demonstrate that such opinion has a logical basis. In particular, in cases involving, as they so often do, the weighing up of risks against benefits, the judge before accepting a body of opinion as being responsible, reasonable or respectable, will need to be satisfied that, in forming their views, the experts have directed their minds to the question of comparative risks and benefits and have reached a defensible conclusion on the matter.

There are decisions which demonstrate that the judge is entitled to approach expert professional opinion on this basis. For example, in *Hucks v Cole* (1968) (1993) 4 Med LR 393, a doctor failed to treat with penicillin a patient who was suffering from septic places on her skin though he knew them to contain organisms capable of leading to puerperal fever. A number of distinguished doctors gave evidence that they would not, in the circumstances, have treated with penicillin. The Court of Appeal found the defendant to have been negligent. Sachs LJ said (at 397):

> When the evidence shows that a lacuna in professional practice exists by which risks of grave danger are knowingly taken, then, however small the risks, the court must anxiously examine that lacuna – particularly if the risks can be easily and inexpensively avoided. If the court finds, on an analysis of the reasons given for not taking those precautions that, in the light of current professional knowledge, there is no proper basis for the lacuna, and that it is definitely not reasonable that those risks should have been taken, its function is to state the fact and where necessary to state that it constitutes negligence.
>
> In such a case the practice will no doubt thereafter be altered to the benefit of patients. On such occasions the fact that other practitioners would have done the same thing as the defendant practitioner is a very weighty matter to be put on the scales on his behalf; but it is not, as Mr Webster readily conceded, conclusive. The court must be vigilant to see whether the reasons given for putting a patient at risk are valid in the light of any well-known advance in medical knowledge, or whether they stem from a residual adherence to out-of-date ideas ...

Again, in *Edward Wong Finance Co Ltd v Johnson Stokes & Masters (a firm)* [1984] AC 296, [1984] 2 WLR 1, the defendant's solicitors had conducted the completion of a mortgage transaction in 'Hong Kong style' rather than in the old-fashioned English style. Completion in Hong Kong style provides for money to be paid over against an undertaking by the solicitors for the borrowers subsequently to hand over the executed documents. This practice opened the gateway through which a dishonest solicitor for the borrower absconded with the loan money without providing the security documents for such loan. The Privy Council held that even though completion in Hong Kong style was almost universally adopted in Hong Kong and was therefore in accordance with a body of professional opinion there, the defendant's solicitors were liable for negligence because there was an obvious risk which could have been guarded against. Thus, the body of professional opinion, though almost universally held, was not reasonable or responsible.

These decisions demonstrate that in cases of diagnosis and treatment there are cases where, despite a body of professional opinion sanctioning the defendant's conduct, the defendant can properly be held liable for negligence (I am not here considering questions of disclosure of risk). In my judgment that is because, in some cases, it cannot be demonstrated to the judge's satisfaction that the body of opinion relied on is reasonable or responsible. In the vast majority of cases the fact that distinguished experts in the field are of a particular opinion will demonstrate the reasonableness of that opinion. In particular, where there are questions of assessment of the relevant risks and benefits of adopting a particular medical practice, a reasonable view necessarily presupposes that the relative risks and benefits have been weighed by the experts in forming their opinions. But if, in a rare case, it can be demonstrated that the professional opinion is not capable of withstanding logical analysis, the judge is entitled to hold that the body of opinion is not reasonable or responsible.

I emphasise that, in my view, it will very seldom be right for a judge to reach the conclusion that views genuinely held by a competent medical expert are unreasonable. The assessment of medical risks and benefits is a matter of clinical judgment which a judge would not normally be able to make without expert evidence. As the quotation from Lord Scarman makes clear, it would be wrong to allow such assessment to deteriorate into seeking to persuade the judge to prefer one or two views both of which are capable of being logically supported. It is only where a judge can be satisfied that the body of expert opinion cannot be logically supported at all that such opinion will not provide the bench mark by reference to which the defendant's conduct falls to be assessed.

I turn to consider whether this is one of those rare cases. Like the Court of Appeal, in my judgment it plainly is not. Although the judge does not in turn say so, it was implicit in his judgment that he accepted that Dr Dinwiddie's view was a reasonable view for a doctor to hold. As I read his judgment, he was quoting counsel's submission when he described the view that intubation was not the right course as being 'unreasonable and illogical'. The appeal of the argument was to the judge 'as a layman' not a conclusion he had reached on all the medical evidence. He refused to 'substitute his own views for those of the medical experts'. I read him as saying that, without expert evidence he would have thought that the risk involved would have called for intubation, but that he could not dismiss Dr Dinwiddie's views to the contrary as being illogical.

Even if this is to put too favourable a meaning on the judge's judgment, when the evidence is looked at it is plainly not a case in which Dr Dinwiddie's views can be dismissed as illogical. According to the accounts of Sister Sallabank and Nurse Newbold, although Patrick had had two severe respiratory crises, he had recovered quickly from both and for the rest presented as a child who was active and running about. Dr Dinwiddie's view was that these symptoms did not show a progressive respiratory collapse and that there was only a small risk of total respiratory failure. Intubation is not a routine, risk-free process. Dr Robertson described it as 'a major undertaking – an invasive procedure with mortality and morbidity attached – it was an assault'. It involves anaesthetising and ventilating the child. A young child does not tolerate a tube easily 'at any rate for a day or two' and the child unless sedated tends to remove it. In those circumstances, it cannot be suggested that it was illogical for Dr Dinwiddie a most distinguished expert to favour running what, in his view, was a small risk of total respiratory collapse rather than to submit Patrick to the invasive procedure of intubation.

Tragic though this case is for Patrick's mother and much as everyone must sympathise with her, I consider that the judge and the Court of Appeal reached the right conclusion on the evidence in this case. I would dismiss the appeal.

Lords Slynn, Nolan, Hoffmann and Clyde agreed.

The issue for the House of Lords was whether the defendant had *caused* the plaintiff's injuries. It was conceded that it was negligent for a doctor not to attend the plaintiff. It was argued by the defendants that even if a doctor had attended he or she would not have intubated the plaintiff and thereby avoided his injury – in other words, there was no 'but for' causation. The House of Lords accepted the trial judge's finding that the doctor would not have intubated the patient had she attended him. However, that was not the only relevant question: causation could also be established by proving that she ought to have intubated, ie her failure would itself have been negligent (on which see below). Expert evidence was given that supported two practices: one which would have intubated the patient and another that would not have. Was this conclusive against the plaintiff on the conventional understanding of *Bolam*? The House of Lords held that it was not: the court could inquire whether the body of professional opinion was 'respectable', 'reasonable' or 'responsible'. Lord Browne-Wilkinson said, having referred to the earlier cases of *Edward Wong (supra)* and *Hucks v Cole (supra)*:

> These decisions demonstrate that in cases of diagnosis and treatment there are cases where, despite a body of professional opinion sanctioning the defendant's conduct, the defendant can properly be held liable for negligence… In my judgment that is because, in some cases, it cannot be demonstrated to the judge's satisfaction that the body of opinion relied upon is reasonable or responsible.

Lord Browne-Wilkinson then went on to explain when such a case would arise. In the vast majority of cases the fact that distinguished experts in the field are of a particular opinion will demonstrate the reasonableness of that opinion. In particular, where there are questions of assessment of the relative risk and benefits of adopting a particular medical practice, a reasonable view necessarily presupposes that the relative risks and benefits have been weighed by the experts in forming their opinions. But if, in a rare case, it can be demonstrated that the professional opinion is not capable of withstanding *logical* analysis, the judge is entitled to hold that the body of opinion is not reasonable or responsible.

His use of the term 'logical' is curious, since many medical decisions will not be based upon logic and deductive reasoning at all but rather upon judgment. What he appears to contemplate is a three-fold review of the expert evidence: (1) have the experts directed their mind to all the relevant matter and facts; (2) have they applied a sensible, coherent and, if appropriate, logical reasoning process to this material to reach a conclusion; (3) is their decision itself defensible as a rational and reasonable one. The first two looked to the decision-making process and the latter to the decision reached itself. On the facts, it was held that neither school of thought was 'illogical' – really they were both defensible in the sense of being properly reached and rational and reasonable in their conclusion.

Lord Browne-Wilkinson acknowledged that it will be a 'rare' or 'exceptional' case where judicial intervention will be justified: 'it will seldom be right for a judge to reach the conclusion that views genuinely held by a competent medical expert are unreasonable.' Nevertheless, the law has been put back on its proper course. Clinical judgments will, in all probability, remain untouched by the court's reviewing hand, as *Bolitho* itself and two subsequent decisions show (*Wiszniewski v Central Manchester HA* [1998] Lloyd's Rep Med 223 (CA) and *Brown v Lewisham and North Southwark HA* [1999] Lloyd's Rep Med 265 (Moore-Bick J)), but medical decisions will be subject to review and that is a very important reaffirmation of the court's role. Experts will have, in future, 'to look to their metal' as the court will require more than sincerely held views; they will require *defensible* views. Any expert who tries to 'lord it' over a judge will find an inquiring mind analysing the basis for his or her conclusion and the process by which it was reached. There is every reason to believe that this will have a salutary effect on expert witnesses and, perhaps, also professional practice thereafter.

Practices based upon habit or uninformed by subsequent medical developments or knowledge may not stand up to this objective scrutiny and rightly so (see, *Dunne v National Maternity Hospital* [1989] IR 91 (Ir Sup Ct)). Practices that expose patients to a risk which the court can objectively determine to be unreasonable will also fall foul of the 'new *Bolam*' test (see *Hucks v Cole, supra*). In some situations, as Gaudron J acknowledged in her concurring judgment in

Rogers v Whittaker (supra), the nature and foreseeability of particular risks or the particular precautionary measures that could (and should) be taken will then be relevant but will 'serve no other useful function' *(ibid)*. Equally, the courts should disengage the *Bolam* test from situations where it really has limited or no application.

Some insight into how the courts may use *Bolitho* can be seen from a similar development in Canadian law. In the following case, the Canadian Supreme Court addressed the same issue: to what extent, if at all, can a defendant who complies with common practice be said to be negligent?

ter Neuzen v Korn (1995) 127 DLR (4th) 577 (Can SC)

The plaintiff was infected with the human immunodeficiency virus (HIV) as a result of artificial insemination by the defendant physician in January 1985. The risk of infection from artificial insemination was not widely known in North America until mid-1985, when the defendant discontinued his program. In January 1985, no test was available in Canada for the detection of HIV in semen or blood. The defendant physician recruited and screened semen donors according to standard practice across Canada at that time. The trial judge directed the jury that it was open to them to find the general practice to be negligent and they did so find. The trial judge also directed the jury that if the contract between the plaintiff and the defendant was primarily for goods, as opposed to services, the *Sale of Goods Act,* RSBC 1979, c 370, would apply and that any common law warranty in a contract for medical services would mirror requirements not to be negligent. The trial judge did not instruct the jury as to the upper limit of non-pecuniary damages. The jury found the defendant negligent and awarded $883,800 in damages, including $460,000 in non-pecuniary damages. The defendant appealed to the British Columbia Court of Appeal, which allowed the appeal and ordered a new trial, holding that this was not a case in which the jury acting judicially could find the common practice of competent Canadian practitioners to be negligent; no common-law warranty and the non-pecuniary damages exceeded the upper limit.

Sopinka J: This appeal raises issues concerning the liability of the respondent physician for conducting an artificial insemination ('AI') procedure which resulted in his patient, the appellant, contracting the Human Immunodeficiency Virus ('HIV') through the infected semen of the donor. Specifically, this court must address whether the respondent physician could be found negligent, notwithstanding conformity with standard medical practice, and whether the trial judge erred in instructing the jury that the prevailing standard of practice could itself be found to be negligent…

ANALYSIS

A. Professional negligence

[30] I agree with the Court of Appeal that there are two aspects to the claim of professional negligence:
(1) breach of duty arising from the failure to be aware of the risk of HIV infection through the use of AI; and
(2) breach of duty with respect to the screening and follow-up of donors.

[31] The alleged departures from the applicable standard of care were:
(1) in respect of the first aspect, failure to discontinue the practice of AI or, in the alternative, to warn the patients of the risk;
(2) in respect of the second aspect, the failure to adequately screen donors so as to eliminate those in a high risk category with relation to the transmission of STDs and to re-interview donors periodically to detect changes in lifestyle. There is also the claim that frozen semen rather than fresh semen should have been used.

[32] In order to properly address the issues relating to professional negligence, it is useful to consider what were the matters which the jury was obliged to decide. In each aspect of the claim the jury was bound to consider whether the evidence established that a standard of practice existed. If the answer was in the affirmative, the next question was whether the defendant conformed to that practice. An affirmative answer to this question would result in a finding of no negligence in favour of the respondent unless the jury was entitled to consider and hold that the standard practice was itself below the required legal standard and that conduct below that standard constituted negligence…

1. *Standard of care and evidence of standard practice*

[33] It is well-settled that physicians have a duty to conduct their practice in accordance with the conduct of a prudent and diligent doctor in the same circumstances. In the case of a specialist, such as a gynaecologist and obstetrician, the doctor's behaviour must be assessed in light of the conduct of other ordinary specialists, who possess a reasonable level of knowledge, competence and skill expected of professionals in Canada, in that field. A specialist, such as the respondent, who holds himself out as possessing a special degree of skill and knowledge, must exercise the degree of skill of an average specialist in his field: see *Wilson v Swanson* (1956) 5 DLR (2d) 113 at pp 124-5, [1956] SCR 804, *Lapointe v Hôpital Le Gardeur* (1992) 90 DLR (4th) 7 at p 13, [1992] 1 SCR 351, 10 CCLT (2d) 101, and *McCormick v Marcotte* (1971), 20 DLR (3d) 345, [1972] SCR 18.

[34] It is also particularly important to emphasize, in the context of this case, that the conduct of physicians must be judged in the light of the knowledge that ought to have been reasonably possessed at the time of the alleged act of negligence. As Denning LJ eloquently stated in *Roe v Ministry of Health,* [1954] 2 All ER 131 (CA) at p 137, '[w]e must not look at the 1947 accident with 1954 spectacles'. That is, courts must not, with the benefit of hindsight, judge too harshly doctors who act in accordance with prevailing standards of professional knowledge. This point was also emphasized by this court in *Lapointe, supra,* at p 14:

> … courts should be careful not to rely upon the perfect vision afforded by hindsight. In order to evaluate a particular exercise of judgment fairly, the doctor's limited ability to foresee future events when determining a course of conduct must be borne in mind. Otherwise, the doctor will not be assessed according to the norms of the average doctor of reasonable ability in the same circumstances, but rather will be held accountable for mistakes that are apparent only after the fact.

No issue is taken with this proposition which was applied both in the trial judge's charge to the jury and by the Court of Appeal.

[35] The Court of Appeal, after a thorough review of the evidence, held that it was not possible for a jury acting judicially to have found that, in 1985, the respondent ought to have known of the risk. This is a power to review a jury verdict which a court of appeal clearly possesses: see *Vancouver-Fraser Park District v Olmstead* (1974), 51 DLR (3d) 416, [1975] 2 SCR 831, 3 NR 326. I agree with this finding and can find no basis upon which it can be questioned. Indeed my review of the evidence leads to the same conclusion. The evidence of standard practice on the first aspect of the case was based entirely on the state of knowledge required of the reasonable practitioner in 1985 and it would have been equally impossible for a jury acting judicially to have found that, given the state of knowledge, the reasonable practitioner ought to either have discontinued AI or warned the patients of the risk. It having been admitted that the respondent continued AI and did not warn his patients, there was no issue concerning his conformity with the standard practice.

[36] The appellant, therefore, can only support a favourable finding on this aspect of the case on the basis that the jury was entitled to find that the standard established by the evidence itself departed from that of a prudent and diligent physician and that the respondent, in failing to conform with a higher standard, was guilty of negligence. This raises the issue as to the correctness of the trial judge's charge to the jury to the effect that the jury was so entitled.

[37] With respect to the second aspect of the claim in professional negligence, the Court of Appeal considered that a verdict for the appellant was open to the jury. It is, however, by no means clear that the evidence establishes a standard practice with respect to the screening and follow-up of donors. This was a matter for the jury to determine. If the jury found that the evidence fell short of establishing the existence of a standard practice, the question arises as to whether the jury could determine the applicable standard without the aid of expert evidence. This is a legal issue upon which the Court of Appeal did not pronounce but which is closely related to the issue raised by the trial judge's instruction referred to above.

[38] It is generally accepted that when a doctor acts in accordance with a recognized and respectable practice of the profession, he or she will not be found to be negligent. This is because courts do not ordinarily have the expertise to tell professionals that they are not behaving appropriately in their field. In a sense, the medical profession as a whole is assumed to have adopted procedures which are in the best interests of patients and are not inherently negligent. As L'Heureux-Dubé J stated in *Lapointe*, in the context of the Quebec *Civil Code* (at p 15):

> Given the number of available methods of treatment from which medical professionals must at times choose, and the distinction between error and fault, *a doctor will not be found liable if the diagnosis and treatment given to a patient correspond to those recognized by medical science at the time, even in the face of competing theories.* As expressed more eloquently by André Nadeau in 'La responsabilité médicale' (1946) 6 R du B 153 at p 155:

[TRANSLATION] The courts do not have jurisdiction to settle scientific disputes or to choose among divergent opinions of physicians on certain subjects. *They may only make a finding of fault where a violation of universally accepted rules of medicine has occurred. The courts should not involve themselves in controversial questions of assessment having to do with diagnosis or the treatment of preference.*

(Emphasis added.)

[39] In *The Law of Torts*, 7th ed (Sydney: Law Book Co, 1987), Professor John G Fleming observed the following with respect to the role of standard practice, at p 109:

Conformity with general practice, on the other hand, usually dispels a charge of negligence. It tends to show what others in the same 'business' considered sufficient, that the defendant could not have learnt how to avoid the accident by the example of others, that most probably no other practical precautions could have been taken, and that the impact of an adverse judgment (especially in cases involving industry or a profession) will be industry-wide and thus assume the function of a 'test case'. *Finally, it underlines the need for caution against passing too cavalierly upon the conduct and decision of experts.*

All the same, even a common practice may itself be condemned as negligent *if fraught with obvious risks.*

(Emphasis added.)

[40] With respect to the medical profession in particular, Professor Fleming noted, at p 110:

Common practice plays a conspicuous role in medical negligence actions. Conscious at once of the layman's ignorance of medical science and apprehensive of the impact of jury bias on a peculiarly vulnerable profession, courts have resorted to the safeguard of insisting that negligence in diagnosis and treatment (including disclosure of risks) cannot ordinarily be established without the aid of expert testimony or in the teeth of conformity with accepted medical practice. *However there is no categorical rule. Thus an accepted practice is open to censure by a jury (nor expert testimony required) at any rate in matters not involving diagnostic or clinical skills, on which an ordinary person may presume to pass judgment sensibly, like omission to inform the patient of risks, failure to remove a sponge, an explosion set off by an admixture of ether vapour and oxygen or injury to a patient's body outside the area of treatment.*

(Emphasis added. Footnotes omitted.)

[41] It is evident from the foregoing passage that while conformity with common practice will generally exonerate physicians of any complaint of negligence, there are certain situations where the standard practice itself may be found to be negligent. However, this will only be where the standard practice is "fraught with obvious risks" such that anyone is capable of finding it negligent, without the necessity of judging matters requiring diagnostic or clinical expertise.

[42] In *Roberge v Bolduc* (1991), 78 DLR (4th) 666, [1991] 1 SCR 374, 39 QAC 81, this court had the opportunity to address this issue in the context of the civil responsibility of a notary under the Quebec *Civil Code*. In that case, it was recognized that there a custom of a profession ignores the *elementary dictates of caution*, it is open to a court to find the professional person negligent. Thus, even if a doctor practises in accordance with common professional practice, he will be liable if that practice is wanting. As L'Heureux-Dubé J stated at pp 710-11:

This brief overview of both doctrine and jurisprudence indicates that courts have discretion to assess liability despite uncontradicted evidence of common professional practice at the relevant time. The standard, in regard to the particular facts of each case, must still be that of a reasonable professional in such circumstances.

It may very well be that professional practice reflects prudent and diligent conduct. One would hope that if a certain practice has developed amongst professionals in regard to a particular professional act, such practice is in accordance with a prudent course of action. The fact that a professional has followed the practice of his or her peers may be strong evidence of reasonable and diligent conduct, *but it is not determinative.* If the practice is not in accordance with the general standards of liability, ie that one must act in a reasonable manner, then the professional who adheres to such a practice can be found liable, depending on the facts of each case.

(Emphasis in original.)

[43] The foregoing principles were also endorsed by this court in *Waldick v Malcolm* (1991), 83 DLR (4th) 114, [1991] 2 SCR 456, 8 CCLT (2d) 1. Thus, it is apparent that conformity with standard practice in a profession does not necessarily insulate a doctor from

negligence where the standard practice itself is negligent. The question that remains is under what circumstances will a professional standard practice be judged negligent? It seems that it is only where the practice does not conform with basic care which is easily understood by the ordinary person who has no particular expertise in the practices of the profession. That is, as Professor Fleming suggests, where the common practice is fraught with danger, a judge or a jury may find that the practice is itself negligent.

[44] As was observed in *Lapointe*, courts should not involve themselves in resolving scientific disputes which require the expertise of the profession. Courts and juries do not have the necessary expertise to assess technical matters relating to the diagnosis or treatment of patients. Where a common and accepted course of conduct is adopted based on the specialized and technical expertise of professionals, it is unsatisfactory for a finder of fact to conclude that such a standard was inherently negligent. On the other hand, matters falling within the ordinary common sense of juries can be judged to be negligent. For example, where there are obvious existing alternatives which any reasonable person would utilize in order to avoid a risk, one could conclude that the failure to adopt such measures is negligent notwithstanding that it is the prevailing practice among practitioners in that area.

[45] Such a case arose in *Anderson v Chasney*, [1949] 4 DLR 71, [1949] 2 WWR 337, 57 Man R 343 (CA); affirmed [1950] 4 DLR 223 (SCC). There, a doctor performed surgery on a child's throat. During the course of the surgery, sponges were used without any tape or strings attached to ensure that none was left in the throat. Nor was a nurse present to count the number of sponges used. One of the sponges was inadvertently left in the throat and after the operation, the child died of suffocation. The surgeon gave evidence that it was not his practice to use sponges with strings, nor to have anyone count the sponges used. This appeared to be standard practice in the hospital, notwithstanding that there were sponges available with strings and nurses could be made available for counting sponges. The Court of Appeal held that the surgeon acted negligently.

[46] The principal reasons, written by McPherson CJM, did not specifically deal with the issue with respect to standard practice. However, McPherson CJM did observe that the fact a sponge was left in a potentially dangerous position is one which 'the ordinary man is competent to consider in arriving at a decision as to whether or not there was negligence' (p 74). By failing to take either of the precautions which were readily available, the majority held that the surgeon was negligent.

[47] In separate concurring reasons, Coyne JA discussed the issue of customary practice among surgeons. He notes that whether or not it is negligent to omit to use sponges with ties or fail to keep count of the sponges is not a matter requiring expert knowledge. Coyne JA observed that general practice is not a complete defence to negligence. I find it useful to quote fairly extensively from his reasons as I believe that they are directly pertinent to the issues in this case. At pp 81-82, he stated:

> Dr Chasney defends on the ground that it has not been his practice, and that it is not the usual practice of operators in the hospital in question and of some operators elsewhere, to take these precautions. But he took a chance in neglecting them. Whether to adopt them or not, he says, is a matter of surgical skill and experience and the general practice of practitioners is conclusive. This, however was not peculiarly a matter of such skill and experience. *His counsel argued that if a general practice of surgeons is followed, negligence cannot be attributed, and that expert evidence is conclusive. But if that were correct the expert witnesses would, in effect, be the jury to try the question of negligence. That question, however, must continue to be one for the petit jury empanelled to try the case, if it is a jury case, and for the Court where it is not.* The experts remain witnesses to give their expert opinions in assistance of the jury or the Court to determine whether there was negligence or not. The opinions of the experts are not conclusive. *But when an operation itself if a complicated and critical one, and acquaintance with anatomy, physiology or other subjects of expert medical knowledge, skill and experience are essential, jury or Court may not be justified in disregarding such opinions and reaching conclusions based on views contrary to those of the experts. That is not the case here. Effective antecedent precautions were not taken and the ordinary every day experience of jurymen or Court is sufficient to enable them to pass upon the question whether such conduct constituted negligence. In my opinion it is clearly so in this case.*

(Emphasis added.)

[48] Coyne JA then adds the following at pp 85-6:

> Whether or not it is negligence to omit to use sponges with ties or to have a count kept is not a matter which requires an expert to decide; it is not special surgical skill that is in question. Such skill is not necessary to answer the question. The point involved is negligence or no negligence. It is not a matter here which requires an expert to decide.

General practice of the defendant and some others does not constitute a complete defence. It is some evidence to be taken into consideration on the question of negligence but it is not conclusive on Court or jury. If it were a defence conclusive on jury or Court, a group of operators by *adopting some practice could legislate themselves out of liability for negligence to the public by adopting or continuing what was an obviously negligent practice, even though a simple precaution, plainly capable of obviating danger which sometimes might result in death, was well known... If a practitioner refuses to take an obvious precaution, he cannot exonerate himself by showing that others also neglect to take it.*

(Emphasis added.)

[49] As well, Coyne JA emphasized that the case involved no difficult or uncertain questions of medical or surgical treatment nor any matters of a scientific or highly technical character. It was simply a matter of whether obvious and simple precautions, easily understood by ordinary individuals, were required to be taken. Coyne JA remarked (at pp 86-7):

Ordinary common sense dictates that when simple methods to avoid danger have been devised, are known, and are available, non-use, with fatal results, cannot be justified by saying that others also have been following the same old, less-careful practice; and that when such methods are readily comprehensible by the ordinary person, by whom, also, the need to use them or not is easily apprehended, it is quite within the competence of Court or jury, quite as much as of experts to deal with the issues; and that the existence of a practice which neglects them, even if the practice were general, cannot protect the defendant surgeon.

(Emphasis added.)

[50] In brief reasons, the Supreme Court of Canada affirmed the reasons of McPherson CJM. The court left open the issue of when it is appropriate for a judge or jury to find a standard medical practice to be unacceptable in terms of taking reasonable care.

[51] I conclude from the foregoing that, as a general rule, where a procedure involves difficult or uncertain questions of medical treatment or complex, scientific or highly technical matters that are beyond the ordinary experience and understanding of a judge or jury, it will not be open to find a standard medical practice negligent. On the other hand, as an exception to the general rule, if a standard practice fails to adopt obvious and reasonable precautions which are readily apparent to the ordinary finder of fact, then it is no excuse for a practitioner to claim that he or she was merely conforming to such a negligent common practice.

[52] The question as to whether the trier of fact can find that a standard practice is itself negligent is a question of law to be determined by the trial judge irrespective of the mode of trial...

Conclusion on professional negligence

[56] After correctly charging the jury with respect to the general standard of care relating to physicians, the trial judge commented on the role of evidence of standard practice as follows:

In deciding what risks should have been known to Dr Korn, evidence of medical experts of custom or general practice is one factor to be considered, but it is not conclusive. *It is open to you as triers of fact to find the custom or general practice negligent.*

(Emphasis added.)

[57] I agree with the following characterization by the Court of Appeal of the issue relating to the standard of care which the jury was called upon to decide in this case (at p 506):

In this case there were difficult, uncertain, highly technical scientific questions requiring information not ordinarily expected of a practising gynaecologist or obstetrician. No jury is capable of deciding on its own what understanding of recent developments the defendant should bring to his practice. As already described, both Dr Stewart and Dr Mascola partially exonerated the defendant ...

Moreover, the evidence established that the state of medical knowledge about AIDS and HIV was highly variable even between highly qualified scientists. There were differences of opinion between public health authorities and practitioners in different medical communities. In our judgment, this was not the kind of case where a judge could properly instruct the jury that it could decide that a practice that conformed to what other practitioners similarly situated were following was negligent. The only proper instruction to be given on at least a part of the case was that the jury should decide whether the defendant conducted himself as a reasonable physician would in similar circumstances. In our judgment, that required the jury to confine itself to prevailing standards of practice.

[58] In light of this characterization, I agree with the conclusion reached by the Court of Appeal that with respect to the first aspect of the case the question of the standard of care was not one which the jury could decide without the aid of expert evidence.

You will see that the approach of the court is broadly similar to that of the House of Lords in *Bolitho*. However, Sopinka J rests the court's inability to hold professional practice as negligent on the sole basis of *technical incompetence*. The only exception is where the risk to the patient is obvious and the necessary precaution to avoid it apparent to a layman. Here, we see shades of *Hucks v Cole* in England.

Commenting on the *Korn* decision, Ellen Picard and Gerald Robertson anticipate that the courts may go further than reviewing 'non technical' matters such as surgical instruments left inside patients as in *Anderson v Chasney*.

Ellen I Picard and Gerald B Robertson *Legal Liability of Doctors and Hospitals in Canada* (1996)

Although it is too early to tell whether this will continue after *Korn*, there are some indications that courts may be willing to take a more expansive view of their power to find negligence in the face of compliance with approved practice. On the one hand this would be ironic, given the Supreme Court's insistence in *Korn* that such compliance is generally *conclusive* evidence of reasonable care. However, by articulating the exception to the general rule in terms of practices which are 'fraught with risk,' the Supreme Court may well have encouraged trial judges to apply that exception beyond the usual non-technical, 'sponge in the body' type of case.

The recent decision in *Tailleur (Tailleur v Grande Prarie General & Auxilary Hospital and Nursing Home District No 14* (1996) 36 Alta LR (3d) 393 (QB)) is an example of this. In that case, a young girl cut her Achilles tendon whilst on a farm, and was treated by an orthopaedic surgeon who applied a full cast just below the knee. Gas gangrene subsequently developed and the patient had to have an emergency above-knee amputation. The doctor was held to have been negligent in failing to use a partial, posterior cast, instead of a full cast, because the former would have allowed for much greater visual inspect for signs of infection. The Court concluded that even if the doctor's choice of a full cast was in accordance with accepted practice, it was still negligent, because it involved obvious risk. Furthermore, according to the Court, this was something which did not involve diagnostic or clinical skill and hence was the type of conduct on 'which an ordinary person may presume to pass judgment sensibly'(ibid at 416).

(For a discussion of *Bolitho*, see H Teff (1998) 18 OJLS 475 and for its application in 'information cases' see, *infra*, ch 5.)

(b) Absence of a practice

One point was raised in *Korn (supra)* which we should address. Sopinka J deals with the situation where there is no 'professional practice' and examines when the court may hold a defendant negligent in such circumstances.

Sopinka J: [55] A related legal issue arises with respect to the second aspect of this case. If the jury finds that the evidence of standard practice does not establish that there did indeed exist a standard practice, can the jury fix the standard without reliance on expert testimony? In my opinion, the answer to this question is the same as the answer previously given. If the alleged act or acts of negligence are such that the jury could reject expert evidence as to standard practice and set the appropriate standard without reliance on expert evidence, then it can do precisely that whether the nature of the issue can be decided on the basis of the ordinary knowledge possessed by the jury or, on the contrary, the matter requires expert evidence because it is beyond the ken of the average juror. Finally, although this is not a matter which arises in this case, I do not foreclose the possibility that exceptionally a jury might find negligence in respect of an issue beyond its ordinary understanding based on expert evidence which it accepts which falls short of establishing a standard practice...

[59] The main contention with respect to this aspect of the claim was that closer questioning and follow-up interviews with donors might have revealed that a donor who infected the appellant was a high risk category relating to the transmission of sexually transmitted diseases. With respect to the foundation in law of this claim the Court of Appeal stated (at pp 507-8):

HIV is one of a number of sexually transmitted diseases. It was the duty of the defendant to take reasonable steps to protect his patients against sexually transmitted diseases. If he failed to do so he would be liable even if the specific disease was one which he did not actually foresee.

As we are not able to know upon what ground the jury's verdict rests, there must be a new trial on the issues raised in the pleadings other than those based upon the defendant's lack of knowledge of the risk of HIV by AI.

[60] I agree that infection with HIV is within the same class of injury as other STDs and that the respondent could be liable for the damage caused notwithstanding that he did not foresee that a failure to take reasonable steps to protect his patients could result in HIV infection. It would be sufficient to found liability if it is established that the respondent ought to have foreseen the class of injury: see *The Queen v Côté* (1974), 51 DLR (3d) 244 at pp 252-3, [1976] 1 SCR 595, 3 NR 341 *sub nom, Kalogeropoulos v Côté*.

[61] The evidence as to standard practice with respect to this aspect of the claim was sketchy and it would be open to the jury to find that there was at the relevant time no standard practice. On the other hand, the jury could also find that the standard practice was not to screen donors or carry out follow-up interviews beyond what the respondent did. In either case, this is an issue that is quite different from that involved in the first aspect of the case. In my opinion, the jury could determine the appropriate standard without reliance on expert evidence. Accordingly, if they decided that no standard practice existed, they can fix the appropriate standard based on their view as to what a prudent and diligent practitioner ought to have done if he or she foresaw or ought to have foreseen that failure to carry out reasonable measures to screen and follow-up donors could result in infection with sexually transmitted diseases other than HIV. As well, if the jury finds that the evidence does establish a standard practice, it is entitled to consider whether that practice is itself consistent with the measures which the hypothetical reasonable prudent practitioner would take in the same circumstances…

His response is somewhat cautious – only when the matter is 'non-technical' can it do so without expert evidence (mirroring the exception to the no-negligence rule). You may feel that this is unduly narrow and is perhaps reflected by the context, namely that he was concerned with a jury trial. Judges may not be so reluctant. It may also confuse *reliance* on expert evidence with *dependence* on professional practice. The former may be helpful even if it is not elevated to the latter. Of course, in *Korn* itself Sopinka J was content that a standard could be set by the court (or jury) in respect of screening and follow up of blood donors (for a discussion of this specific issue see A Grubb and D Pearl *Bloodtesting, AIDS and DNA Profiling* (1990) ch 3). The point has arisen in one English case, where the Court of Appeal did set a standard (absent evidence of a professional practice) where the facts were novel.

AB v Tameside & Glossop HA [1997] 8 Med LR 91 (CA)

Brooke LJ: This is not a situation in which it is particularly useful for a court to investigate the previous practices of reasonably competent practitioners when handling a similar situation. With the single exception of the Exeter incident there has been no previous experience in this country, and the evidence showed that the nature of people's irrational concerns, anxieties and ignorance about HIV and AIDS is, and certainly was in April 1991, to a great extent *sui generis*. On the one hand, therefore, the judge was in my judgment wrong to hold that the defendants were negligent because they did not select the best method. On the other hand, I consider that in the particular circumstances of the present case Mr Armitage is confining the freedom of the court too narrowly when he cites the *Bolam* test as providing the solution because there simply was no adequate well of professional experience on which the court could usefully draw in the present case. In such a case the judge had to perform the familiar role of considering the factual evidence carefully, listening to the expert evidence, and forming a view as to whether, in all the circumstances, these public health authorities fell below the standards reasonably to be expected of them when they selected their preferred method of communicating the information to the patients…

Kennedy and Nourse J delivered concurring judgments.

Like Sopinka J in *Korn*, Brooke LJ looked at all the circumstances in what he described as a *sui generis* situation, and set the appropriate legal standard.

However, unlike Sopinka J, the Court of Appeal did not restrict the kind of care where this would be done. As Brooke LJ made clear at the end of his judgment, the judge must perform the 'familiar role of considering the factual evidence carefully, listening to the expert evidence and form a view' on what should reasonably have been done in the circumstances. In England, therefore, difficulties in determining a standard may make it hard for a claimant to prove breach of duty, but the court is not thereby disentitled from making the inquiry.

One final point to note. The modern trend within the NHS is for clinical guidance, protocols and other formal statements of proper treatment and diagnoses. These may emanate from many 'official' sources, such as government or the Royal Colleges, and their incidence will increased with the work of the National Institute for Clinical Excellence (see *supra*, ch 2). As a consequence, the courts will be presented with thought out and considered standards (note the advice of EAGA in *AB*). Whilst such protocols and guidelines will not necessarily set the legal standard, they will increasingly be seen as providing very good evidence of the standard – subject, as always, to review by the court as *Bolitho* recognises (see eg *Early v Newham HA* [1994] 5 Med LR 214) (for a discussion of clinical guidelines, see: B Hurtwitz *Clinical Guidelines and the Law* (1998) and V Harpwood 'NHS Reform, Audit, Protocols and Standards of Care' (1994) 1 Medical Law International 241).

(c) Departure from approved practice

Is this necessarily a breach of duty?

Hunter v Hanley 1955 SC 200 (Court of Session)

In an action of damages against a doctor, the pursuer, who had suffered injury as a result of the breaking of a hypodermic needle while she was receiving an injection, alleged that the accident had been caused by the fault and negligence of the defender in failing to exercise the standard of care and competence which it was his duty to display in giving the injection. At the trial the presiding Judge directed the jury in the course of his charge that the test to be applied was whether there had been such a departure from the normal and usual practice of general practitioners as could reasonably be described as gross negligence. The jury having returned a verdict for the defender, the pursuer enrolled a motion for a new trial on the ground of misdirection.

The Court of Session (Inner House) ordered a new trial.

Lord President (Clyde): It follows from what I have said that in regard to allegations of deviation from ordinary professional practice – and this is the matter with which the present note is concerned – such a deviation is not necessarily evidence of negligence. Indeed it would be disastrous if this were so, for all inducement to progress in medical science would then be destroyed. Even a substantial deviation from normal practice may be warranted by the particular circumstances. To establish liability by a doctor where deviation from normal practice is alleged, three facts require to be established. First of all it must be proved that there is a usual and normal practice; secondly it must be proved that the defender has not adopted that practice; and thirdly, (and this is of crucial importance) it must be established that the course the doctor adopted is one which no professional man of ordinary skill would have taken if he had been acting with ordinary care. There is clearly a heavy onus on a pursuer to establish these facts, and without all three his case will fail. If this is the test, then it matters nothing how far or how little he deviates from the ordinary practice. For the extent of deviation is not the test. The deviation must be of a kind which satisfies the third of the requirements just stated.

Notice Lord Clyde's third requirement and his use of the word 'established'. It is by no means clear whether Lord Clyde intends it to be for the *court* to determine whether the deviation was justified, or to be a matter on which *doctors'* evidence is conclusive. Note the comment in support of the former view by Sellers LJ in

Landau v Werner (1961) 105 Sol Jo 1008 (CA), that: 'a doctor might not be negligent if he tried a new technique but that if he did he must justify it before the court... Success was the best justification for unusual and unestablished treatment.' Consider in this context the early heart transplant operations: Were they a 'success' even though the patients died, and, if not, was the doctor in breach of his duty to his patient? (See also *Holland v Devitt and Moore Nautical College Ltd* (1960) Times, 4 March, per Streatfield J.)

What, then, is the legal effect of deviating from approved practice?

Clark v MacLennan [1983] 1 All ER 416 (QBD)

The plaintiff, who was about to give birth to her first child, was admitted to a hospital administered by the second defendants, a health authority. The baby was delivered on 11 June 1975. Soon after birth the plaintiff began to suffer from stress incontinence, a not uncommon post-natal condition whereby normal bladder control was lost when the sufferer was subjected to mind physical stress. The plaintiff's disability was particularly acute and after conventional treatment failed to bring about an improvement the first defendant, a gynaecologist, performed an anterior colporrhaphy operation on 10 July 1975. It was normal practice among gynaecologists not to perform such an operation until at least three months after birth so as to ensure its success and to prevent the risk of haemorrhage. The operation was not successful and after it was performed haemorrhage occurred causing the repair to break down. Two further anterior colporrhaphy operations were necessary, and they were carried out on 16 January 1976 and October 1979. Neither was successful with the result that the stress incontinence from which the plaintiff suffered became a permanent disability. She brought an action for damages claiming that the defendants had been negligent in the care and treatment administered to her.

Peter Pain J: Where however there is but one orthodox course of treatment and [the doctor] chooses to depart from that, his position is different. It is not enough for him to say as to his decision simply that it was based on his clinical judgment. One has to inquire whether he took all proper factors into account which he knew or should have known, and whether his departure from the orthodox course can be justified on the basis of these factors.

The burden of proof lies on the plaintiff. To succeed she must show, first, that there was a breach of duty and, second, that her damages flowed from that breach. It is against the second defendants that her attack is principally directed...

On the basis of ... [*McGhee v National Coal Board* [1972] 3 All ER 1008, [1973] 1 WLR 1, HL], counsel for the plaintiff contended that, if the plaintiff could show (1) that there was a general practice not to perform an anterior colporrhaphy until at least three months after birth, (2) that one of the reasons for this practice was to protect the patient from the risk of haemorrhage and a breakdown of the repair, (3) that an operation was performed within four weeks and (4) that haemorrhage occurred and the repair broke down, then the burden of showing that he was not in breach of duty shifted to the defendants.

It must be correct on the basis of *McGhee* to say that the burden shifts so far as damages are concerned. But does the burden shift so far as the duty is concerned? Must the medical practitioner justify his departure from the usual practice?

It is very difficult to draw a distinction between the damage and the duty where the duty arises only because of a need to guard against the damage. In *McGhee's* case it was accepted that there was a breach of duty. In the present case the question of whether there was a breach remains in issue.

It seems to me that it follows from *McGhee* that where there is a situation in which a general duty of care arises and there is a failure to take a precaution, and that very damage occurs against which the precaution is designed to be a protection, then the burden lies on the defendant to show that he was not in breach of duty as well as to show that the damage did not result from his breach of duty.

Applying this, the judge found that the defendants had not discharged this burden and he entered judgment for the plaintiff.

Mustill LJ in the Court of Appeal in *Wilsher v Essex Health Authority* [1986] 3 All ER 801 at 815, cast doubt on the validity of Peter Pain J's analysis.

Mustill LJ: If I may say so, the summary of the evidence contained in the judgment in *Clark v MacLennan* has certainly persuaded me that, as a decision on the facts, the case is unimpeachable. Moreover, although the judge indicated that he proposed to decide the case on burden of proof (at 425), this could be understood as an example of the forensic commonplace that, where one party has, in the course of the trial, hit the ball into the other's court, it is for that other to return it. But the prominence given in the judgment to *McGhee* and the citation from *Clark* in the present case suggest that the judge may have set out to assert a wider proposition, to the effect that in certain kinds of case of which *Clark* and the present action form examples, there is a general burden of proof on the defendant. If this is so, then I must respectfully say that I find nothing in ... general principle to support it.

When the *Wilsher* case reached the House of Lords [1988] 1 All ER 871, it was emphatically affirmed that *McGhee* did not have the effect of shifting the burden of proof (per Lord Bridge at 879, *infra*, pp 470 – 478).

What, however, is Mustill LJ deciding here? Undoubtedly the legal burden of proof does not shift, but is Mustill LJ conceding that the burden of adducing evidence has shifted in that once the plaintiff has established an approved practice and deviation therefrom he *may*, but not necessarily *must*, win unless the defendant brings evidence in reply?

In the end, the effect of deviation from accepted practice is an evidential one. It makes the claimant's case that much stronger but is always subject to the court taking the view that the evidence does not justify a finding that such a departure was unreasonable in the circumstances.

Protocols and clinical guidance may, as we have seen, lead a court to find an accepted or approved practice (see eg *Early v Newham HA* [1994] 5 Med LR 214). Will a departure be negligent? This is, of course, merely a specific instance of the general issue we are considering here. The more general context of professional codes of practice is considered in the following extract.

AM Dugdale and KM Stanton *Professional Negligence* (3rd edn, 1998)

15.23 Codes of practice. Codes of practice applicable to a given professional activity are in substance no more than formalised accepted practice and it is therefore not surprising that conduct which departs from the code may lead to liability. In *Bevan Investments Ltd v Blackhall and Struthers (No 2)* [1973] 2 NZLR 45 at 66 Beattie J summarised the position in relation to engineering codes as follows: 'I am of the view that bearing in mind the function of codes, a design which departs substantially from them is prima facie a faulty design, unless it can be demonstrated that it conforms to accepted engineering practice by rational analysis.' A similar approach towards non-compliance with the codes of accounting and auditing practice was taken by Woolf J in *Lloyd Cheyham & Co Ltd v Littlejohn & Co* (1985) 2 PN 154: 'As to the proper treatment of such statements... While they are not conclusive, so that a departure from their terms necessarily involves a breach of a duty of care, and they are not as the explanatory foreword makes clear, rigid rules, they are very strong evidence as to what is the proper standard which should be adopted and unless there is some justification, a departure from this will be regarded as constituting a breach of duty.' the guidelines relating to valuation issued by the RICS have a similar evidential significance as does the Law Society's Code of Professional Conduct. The operation of the general rule is well illustrated by the decision that the defendant architect in *Voli v Inglewood Shire Council* (1963) 110 CLR 74, HCA as negligent in prescribing floor joists for a stage which were smaller than those required by the Australian Standards Association. This result should be contrasted with that reached in *London Borough of Newham v Taylor Woodrow Anglian Ltd* (1981) 19 BLR 99, a case which concerned the Ronan Point disaster. One of the causes of the failure was the use of a joint which did not conform to the applicable code. However, its use did not establish negligence on the part of the designers, as it was shown that satisfactory calculations had been done as to its likely performance, and that it had been used previously in a large number of buildings and had given no hint of failure.

In the medical context, the courts have held that non-compliance with guidelines was not negligent in particular circumstances where the expert evidence justified departure (eg *Loveday v Renton* [1990] 1 Med LR 117; *Ratty v Haringey HA* [1994] 5 Med LR 413; *Vernon v Bloomsbury HA* [1995] 6 Med LR 297).

(d) Proof and res ipsa loquitur

As we have seen, the *Bolam* test looks to the standards of the medical profession in setting the legal standard of care required of a doctor. It would seem to follow therefore, that to prove his care the plaintiff must adduce medical evidence sufficient to satisfy the burden of proof. Is this always the case? Would, for example, a plaintiff be non-suited if he demonstrated that his doctor had removed the wrong leg, but did not being forward medical evidence to suggest that this was not accepted medical practice? Of course, the answer is 'no'. However, few cases are so obviously comprehensible to the layman. Usually, expert evidence (even if not of professional practice) is beneficial if a plaintiff is to succeed (for the role of experts see *The Ikarian Reefer* [1993] 2 Lloyd's Rep 68 (Cresswell J), especially at 81-82 and *Sharpe v Southend HA* [1997] 8 Med LR 299 (Cresswell J) at 303).

An exception, at least in theory, is *res ipsa loquitur*. Picard and Robertson in *Legal Liability of Doctors and Hospitals in Canada* (3rd edn, 1996), p 305, set the scene:

> There has been judicial recognition in negligence cases of the hardship on plaintiffs who are attempting to prove negligence when they know only that an accident has happened and that they were injured. As the Supreme Court recognized in *Snell v Farrell,* in many instances the details of a medical accident are known only to the defendant. Sometimes the mere fact that an accident happened will itself given rise to a inference of negligence on the part of the defendant because the event is such that it would be unlikely to occur unless there had been negligence. The accident 'speaks of negligence'; hence the term used for this circumstance: *res ipsa loquitur*, 'the thing speaks for itself'.
>
> Variously described as a rule, principle, doctrine and maxim, *res ipsa loquitur* is applied in Canada as part of the law of circumstantial evidence and has been called 'one of the great mysteries of tort law.'
>
> As with much of the law, the essentials of *res ipsa loquitur* are easy to state, but its application is complicated. The doctrine will only apply when:
> 1. there is no evidence as to how or why the accident occurred;
> 2. the accident is such that ordinarily it would not occur without negligence; and
> 3. the defendant is proven to have been in control of or linked to the situation either personally
>   or vicariously.
> The possible effects of the doctrine on the onus of proof vary and are best understood by an analysis of the case-law in point.

In effect there are two reasons why *res ipsa loquitur* will not ordinarily be available to a plaintiff in a medical case. The first turns upon the undoubted uncertainties of medical treatment.

Girard v Royal Columbian Hospital (1976) 66 DLR (3d) 676 (British Columbia Supreme Court)

Andrews J: … [T]he plaintiff underwent an operation at the Royal Columbian Hospital in New Westminster, British Columbia, which is described as being a left femoral popliteal saphenous vein by-pass graft. Shortly after the operation he noticed a weakness in both legs – more on the left than the right. Although there was no further surgical intervention he was in and out of rehabilitative centres for about a year until his condition stabilised to its present one, which consists of a permanent paralysis of the lower limbs accompanied by partial bladder and bowel deficiency and complete impotence. He is ambulatory by using two canes and is constantly uncomfortable from either sitting or standing for an extended period of time and from the loss of some control of both his bladder and bowel…

As to the doctrine of *res ipsa loquitur* which had been relied upon by the plaintiff, he said:

> The human body is not a container filled with a material whose performance can be predictably charted and analysed. It cannot be equated with a box of chewing tobacco or a soft drink. Thus, while permissible inferences may be drawn as to the normal behaviour of these types of commodities the same kind of reasoning does not necessarily apply to a human being. Because of this medical science has not yet reached the stage where the law ought to presume that a patient must come out of an operation as well or better than he went into it. From my interpretation of the medical evidence the kind of injury suffered by the plaintiff could have occurred without negligence on anyone's part. Since I cannot infer there was negligence on the part of the defendant doctors the maxim of *res ipsa loquitur* does not apply.

The second reflects the significant changes in procedure which occurred since the doctrine first developed. Nowadays, it is unlikely that a plaintiff will be at such a disadvantage in terms of knowing what went on that recourse to *res ipsa* will be warranted. The modern developments in the practice of discovery and exchange of evidence coupled with the more careful practice of recording and maintaining medical records has meant that the plaintiff is usually able to know what went on. Mustill LJ makes this point in commenting on the applicability of *res ipsa* in *Bull v Devon AHA* (see also, *Delaney v Southmead HA* (1992) 26 BMLR 111 (CA) per Stuart-Smith LJ).

Bull v Devon AHA **[1993] 4 Med LR 117 (CA)**

Mustill LJ: There still remains on the facts the question whether this interval was so long that negligence should be presumed. For my part, I am not sure that recourse to the maxim *res ipsa loquitur* really advances the matter. In *Bryne v Boadle* (1863) 2 H&C 722 and similar cases, there was an untoward event which the plaintiff put in evidence as constituting the whole of his case. What happened in the warehouse was unknown to the plaintiff, but he was able to say that barrels should not roll out of first storey openings on to passers-by. No further evidence was needed to establish the plaintiff's case, if the defendant chose to call none for himself. Here, the position seems to me different. The plaintiff's advisers were able to put in evidence from the records as part of their case the outlines of what actually happened. They called expert testimony to establish what should have happened, and could point to a disconformity between what the witnesses said should have happened and what actually happened. The defendants themselves also gave some evidence, meagre as it was because of the lapse of time, which added a few more facts about the course of events. I do not see that the present situation calls for recourse to an evidentiary presumption applicable in cases where the defendant does, and the plaintiff does not, have within the grasp the means of knowing how the accident took place. Here, all the facts that are ever going to be known are before the court. The judge held that they pointed to liability, and I agree.

This is not to say that *res ipsa* will never be applied in medical cases, but merely to say that it will be exceptional (eg *Cassidy v Ministry of Health* [1951] 2 KB 343 and *Mahon v Osborne* [1939] 2 KB 14).

The English case law medical cases and the maxim *res ipsa loquitur* was exhaustively examined by the Court of Appeal in the following case.

Ratcliffe v Plymouth & Torbay HA, Exeter & North Devon HA **[1998] Lloyd's Rep Med 162 (CA)**

On September 23, 1989, the appellant plaintiff, John Ratcliffe, 48, underwent a triple arthrodesis of his right ankle at Princess Elizabeth Orthopaedic Hospital, Exeter, following a walking accident two years' earlier. He was given a general anaesthetic and a spinal anaesthetic by Dr Boaden, a consultant anaesthetist. The operation was a success but he suffered a serious neurological defect on the right side from waist downwards. The cause was a mystery but in June 1995 a MRI scan showed a lesion in the spinal cord at T11-T12 level and a more indistinct lesion higher up at T9. The defendants maintained that the spinal injection was administered at L3-L4 level and the neurological weaknesses were consistent with much more extensive damage stretching from T8 to S3.

On the third day of the trial of the plaintiff's action the defendants' expert neurologist and expert neuro-physiologist produced a report on a rare disease Non-Systemic Vasculitis (NSV) which could have been the cause of the neurological defect.

The judge found that Dr Boaden, who impressed the court as a meticulous and conscientious man, administered the spinal injection at L3-L4 with appropriate care; that Mr Ratcliffe's nerve damage had been caused by the injection by some mechanism as to which he was not able to make positive findings; there was a possibility of some kind of asymptomatic weakness in the central nervous system which the stress of the operation had brought to life, and that, accordingly, the plaintiff's claim failed.

On appeal the main argument for the plaintiff was that the judge dismissed the application of the *res ipsa loquitur* doctrine: he should have found that the plaintiff's condition raised an inference of negligence; once the maxim applied the onus was on the defendants to rebut that inference and they could not do so by raising an explanation which only ranked as a possibility…

Brooke LJ: 28. Notwithstanding the judge's clear finding that Dr Boaden had exercised all due care in performing the spinal injection, Mr Burnett nevertheless submitted that the judge ought to have paid more attention to the application of the maxim *res ipsa loquitur* in the way he evaluated the evidence, instead of dismissing it quite briefly towards the start of his judgment. He told us that there is a good deal of inconsistency as between different judges trying medical negligence cases about the way they should handle the operation of the maxim in these cases (if indeed, contrary to the views ascribed to some judges, it applies at all in this type of litigation). In these circumstances he invited us to give some guidance about the appropriate way to approach the maxim in medical negligence litigation. It therefore appears to be necessary to devote a little more attention than usual to this topic.

29. The maxim first appears to have surfaced in reported English cases in *Byrne v Boadle* (1863) 9 LT 450 (where a barrel of flour from a warehouse hit the plaintiff as he was walking by), and its classic exposition appeared four years later in the judgment of Erle CJ in *Scott v The London and St Katherine Docks Company* (1865) 3 H&C 596 at p 667:

> There must be reasonable evidence of negligence. But where the thing is shown to be under the management of the defendant or his servants, and the accident is such as in the ordinary course of things does not happen if those who have the management use proper care, it affords reasonable evidence, in the absence of explanation by the defendants, that the accident arose from want of care.

30. In more modern times, there were two authoritative expositions of the operation of the maxim nearly 30 years ago. In *Henderson v Henry E Jenkins & Sons* [1970] AC 282 Lord Pearson said at p 301:

> In an action for negligence the plaintiff must allege, and has the burden of proving, that the accident was caused by negligence on the part of the defendants. That is the issue throughout the trial, and in giving judgment at the end of the trial the judge has to decide whether he is satisfied on a balance of probabilities that the accident was caused by negligence on the part of the defendants, and if he is not so satisfied the plaintiff's action fails. The formal burden of proof does not shift. But if in the course of the trial there is proved a set of facts which raises a prima facie inference that the accident was caused by negligence on the part of the defendants, the issue will be decided in the plaintiff's favour unless the defendants by their evidence provide some answer which is adequate to displace the prima facie inference. In this situation there is said to be an evidential burden of proof resting on the defendants. I have some doubts whether it is strictly correct to use the expression 'burden of proof' with this meaning, as there is a risk of it being confused with the formal burden of proof, but it is a familiar and convenient usage.

31. In *Lloyde v West Midlands Gas Board* [1971] 1 WLR 749 Megaw LJ said at p 755:

> I doubt whether it is right to describe *res ipsa loquitur* as a 'doctrine'. I think that it is no more than an exotic, although convenient, phrase to describe what is in essence no more than a common sense approach, not limited by technical rules, to the assessment of the effect of evidence in certain circumstances. It means that a plaintiff prima facie establishes negligence where (i) it is not possible for him to prove precisely what was the relevant act or omission which set in train the events leading to the accident; but (ii) on the evidence as it stands at the relevant time it is more likely than not that the effective cause of the accident was some act or omission of the defendant or of someone for whom the defendant is responsible, which act or omission constitutes a failure to take proper care for the plaintiff's safety. I have used the words 'evidence as it stands at the relevant time'. I think that this can most conveniently be taken as being at the close of the plaintiff's case. On the assumption that a submission of no case is then made, would the evidence, as it then stands, enable the plaintiff to succeed because, although the precise cause of the accident cannot be established, the proper inference on the balance of probability is that that cause, whatever it may have been, involved a failure by the defendant to take due care for the plaintiff's safety? If so, *res ipsa loquitur*. If not, the question still falls to be tested by the same criterion, but evidence for the defendant, given thereafter, may rebut the inference. The *res*, which previously spoke for itself, may be silenced, or its voice may, on the whole of the evidence, become too weak or muted.

32. That it is theoretically possible to apply the maxim in medical negligence cases was recognised by this court long ago in *Cassidy v Ministry of Health* [1951] 2 KB 343 (plaintiff's hand rendered useless after a surgical operation on it: inference of negligence not rebutted) and *Roe v Ministry of Health* [1954] 2 QB 66 (plaintiff developed spastic paraplegia following lumbar puncture: inference of negligence rebutted).

33. I see no benefit in returning to the academic discussions of this topic in the 1950s and 1960s, since the operation of the maxim is now well settled by modern authority. Instead, I will consider four medical negligence cases decided by this court in the last 15 years in which the applicability of the maxim was discussed, and the most recent authoritative restatement of the governing principles in an opinion of Lord Griffiths, giving the opinion of five very experienced common law judges in the Judicial Committee of the Privy Council ten years ago.

34. In *Jacobs v Great Yarmouth and Waveney Health Authority* (CA March 29, 1984: [1995] 6 Med LR 192) the trial judge had rejected the plaintiff's case that she had been conscious during an operation, holding that she had mistakenly transposed in her mind the experiences of which she had become aware as she recovered from the anaesthetic after the operation. This court held that the judge was entitled on the evidence to make this positive finding, but Griffiths LJ went on to make some *obiter* observations (with which O'Connor LJ expressly agreed) about her counsel's contention that if this court had been willing to conclude that her recollection was pre-operational then it must follow that negligence had been established against the defendants because of the operation of the doctrine *res ipsa loquitur*.

35. He said at p 198 (LHC) that the doctrine *res ipsa loquitur*:

> … means no more than that, on the facts that the plaintiff is able to prove, although he may not be able to point to a particular negligent act or omission on the part of the defendants, the fair inference to draw is that there has been negligence of some sort on the part of the defendants; but that is an inference to be drawn upon the facts presented by the plaintiff. If there is further evidence presented by the defendant, those facts may be shown in an entirely different light and it may be that at the end of the day it is not possible to draw the inference of negligence.

36. On the facts of the case he said that even if he had been persuaded that this was a pre-operation memory and that the plaintiff had been aware until the moment of the first surgical incision, he would nevertheless not have been able to hold that it was attributable to the negligence of the defendant. The reason for this was that he was satisfied that the defendant had injected a sufficient dose of the anaesthetic drug into the plaintiff's vein, and not outside it, and that the literature shows that in this particular technique there is a risk that even if all proper precautions are taken some patients – admittedly in rare cases – react in an abnormal way to the anaesthetic, and unhappily do remain aware, to a greater or lesser degree, although they are apparently fully anaesthetised. In other words, he was saying that although the plaintiff did set up a case to be answered on the operation of the maxim *res ipsa loquitur*, the defendant on this hypothesis would have answered it by showing that he exercised all proper care, and that it was possible (albeit rare) for this untoward event to occur even when an anaesthetist had exercised all due care.

37. Two members of that court were sitting in the Judicial Committee of the Privy Council four years later in *Ng Chun Pui v Lee Chuen Tat* [1988] RTR 298 when Lord Griffiths, giving the opinion of the Board, quoted at p 301 Erle CJ's dictum in *Scott v London and St Katherine Docks Company* (see para 29 above), and continued:

> So in an appropriate case the plaintiff establishes a prima facie case by relying upon the fact of the accident. If the defendant adduces no evidence there is nothing to rebut the inference of negligence and the plaintiff will have proved his case. But if the defendant does adduce evidence that evidence must be evaluated to see if it is still reasonable to draw the inference of negligence from the mere fact of the accident. Loosely speaking this may be referred to as a burden on the defendant to show he was not negligent, but that only means that faced with a prima facie case of negligence the defendant will be found negligent unless he produces evidence that is capable of rebutting the prima facie case.

38. There are three decisions of this court in medical negligence cases in recent years which show how the court has applied the relevant principles in practice.

39. In *Bull v Devon Area Health Authority* (CA February 2, 1989: [1993] 4 Med LR 117) the evidence showed that there had been a period of 68 minutes between the birth of twins. The second twin was born with serious brain damage, and Slade LJ said at p 131 (LHC) that this was a case where on the evidence the delays in summoning aid in securing the attendance of the registrar or consultant were so substantial as to place upon the defendants the evidential burden of justifying them if it could. In the event they failed to explain the delay satisfactorily and did not discharge the onus. The breach of duty was therefore proved. Mustill LJ, for his part, was not sure that recourse to the maxim *res ipsa loquitur* really advanced the matter, since he did not see that the situation in that case called for recourse to an evidentiary presumption applicable in cases where the defendant does, and the plaintiff does not, have within his grasp the means of knowing how the accident took place. He said at p 142 (LHC):

Here all the facts that are ever going to be known are before the court. The judge held that they pointed to liability, and I agree. It is true that if the defendants had been able to call further evidence, they might have been able to show that what appeared to be an inexcusable delay was in fact to be excused. But they did not do so.

40. Dillon LJ did not refer to the maxim, but he pointed out at p 138 (LHC) that although the onus of proving negligence is on the plaintiff, he does not have to adduce positive evidence to disprove every theoretical explanation, however unlikely, that might be devised to explain what happened in a way which would absolve the defendants of fault.

41. In *Delaney v Southmead Health Authority* (CA June 6, 1992; [1995] 6 Med LR 355) the trial judge had dismissed the plaintiff's complaint that a lesion of the left brachial plexus (which gave her pins and needles in her hand and clawing of two fingers) which followed a surgical operation under general anaesthetic was caused by the negligence of the anaesthetist. Stuart-Smith LJ referred at p 359 (RHC) to an argument by her counsel to the effect that once the judge had accepted or found that the injury had occurred during the operation, and that it was an injury to the brachial plexus (and that there was no narrowing of the thoracic outlet which might have caused the problem), the maxim *res ipsa loquitur* applied. He said:

> For my part, I am doubtful whether it is of much assistance in a case of medical negligence, at any rate when all the evidence in the case has been adduced. But even if [counsel] is right in saying that at that stage the maxim applied, it is always open to a defendant to rebut a case of *res ipsa loquitur* either by giving an explanation of what happened which is inconsistent with negligence (but that is not the limb which the defendants were able to do here) or by showing that the defendants had exercised all reasonable care. In my judgment that is what happened here and that is what the judge accepted.

42. It was a feature of that case that once the alternative explanation had been rejected, nobody really knew what had happened to cause the plaintiff's problems, and counsel had relied on a number of learned articles in support of his contention that proper care could not have been taken on the occasion in question. This court, however, declined to reverse the finding of the judge that proper care had been taken. Stuart-Smith LJ said at p 358 (RHC):

> For my part, I see the force of those submissions and, if the human body was a machine where it is possible to see the internal workings and which operates in accordance with the immutable laws of mechanics and with arithmetical precision, I think that the argument might well be answerable. But in spite of the wonders of modern medical science, even at post-mortem not everything is known about an individual human being. The judge said that it was not possible to explain how the injury had happened. He accepted the evidence of Dr Earl, who he described as a fair witness and who impressed him very much.

43. Dillon LJ at p 360 (RHC) agreed that the judge was not precluded from finding as he did. He said:

> I cannot for my part accept that medical science is such a precise science that there cannot in any particular field be any room for the wholly unexpected result occurring in the human body from the carrying out of a well-recognised procedure.

44. Finally, in *Fallows v Randle* (CA May 7, 1996; [1997] 8 Med LR 160) Stuart-Smith LJ said at p 164 (RHC) that the maxim was not helpful in a case in which a first sterilisation had failed and the plaintiff had had to be re-sterilised six months later. The judge had heard evidence on both sides as to why a Fallope ring was found not to be in the position that it might have been expected to have been in when the second operation was carried out, and when faced with two alternative theories he was entitled to prefer the evidence of the plaintiff's expert, namely that it would not have happened without it being placed in the wrong position, or being dislodged in the course of the operation and not detected, to the somewhat remote theories of the defendants and their expert.

45. In other words, the judge was deciding the case on the evidence, as opposed to applying the maxim in its purest form unbolstered by expert evidence.

46. Counsel for the defendants carried out a study of judgments at first instance in medical negligence cases reported in the Medical Law Reports where the application of the maxim has been considered. The effect of these judgments can be summarised as follows:

(1) Anaesthetic awareness cases

In *Ludlow v Swindon Health Authority* [1989] 1 Med LR 104 Hutchison J said that if the plaintiff were able to establish that she was conscious and experiencing pain during a period when halothane gas should have been administered, then that set of facts would raise an inference of negligence even in the absence of expert evidence that anaesthetic awareness can only occur in the absence of reasonable anaesthetic care.

McKinnon J followed this approach in *Taylor v Worcester & District Health Authority* [1991] 2 Med LR 215.

(2) Untoward consequences of surgery/anaesthesia

In *Bentley v Bristol & Weston Health Authority (No 2)* [1991] 3 Med LR 1, where the plaintiff developed a sciatic nerve palsy following a total hip replacement, Waterhouse J decided in her favour on the evidence but said, *obiter*, at p 16, that if his analysis of the evidence was incorrect, then the maxim was applicable since the defendants had signally failed to rebut the inference of negligence by the evidence of the surgeon, or by other evidence, or by pointing to any tenable explanation of the plaintiff's profound and permanent injury which was consistent with lack of negligence on his part.

In *Moore v Woking District Health Authority* [1992] 3 Med LR 431, where the patient underwent a mastoidectomy and thereafter developed ulnar nerve lesions, Owen J said at p 434 (LHC) that he took the view that a plaintiff who could say that he went into hospital with no impediment to the use of his upper limbs and no obvious risk to them, but came out in effect crippled, had temporarily at least created a situation where there was a prima facie case of negligence. Owen J seems to have been willing to apply the maxim without expert evidence, although the evidence of the plaintiff's expert came close to supporting the maxim. In the event he dismissed the claim on the evidence.

In *Howard v Wessex Regional Health Authority* [1994] 5 Med LR 57, where the plaintiff became permanently tetraplegic following an operation, the plaintiff relied on the maxim at the outset, but at the end of a 3-week trial Morland J said that in view of the way the issues had crystallised, the application of the maxim was inappropriate.

In *Ritchie v Chichester Health Authority* [1994] 5 Med LR 187, where the plaintiff was left with paralysis of the saddle area, incontinence and lack of vaginal sensation, Judge Thompson QC made positive findings of negligence on the evidence and commented at p 205 (RHC) that Stuart-Smith LJ's judgment in *Delaney* seemed to be a confirmation that the maxim does exist in relation to medical negligence cases but that it can be rebutted either by giving a positive explanation, such as some other cause of the damage, or by showing that the defendants had exercised all reasonable care.

(3) Cardiac arrest under general anaesthetic

In *Saunders v Leeds Western Health Authority* (December 6, 1984: [1993] 4 Med LR 355), where the four-year old plaintiff suffered a cardiac arrest during surgery under general anaesthetic, Mann J received evidence from experts that the heart of a fit child does not arrest under anaesthesia if proper care is taken in the anaesthetic and surgical process. The judge found in the plaintiff's favour on the evidence, holding that the only explanation proffered on the defendants' behalf was mistaken, and even if it had been correct, it would have been rejected because it was a chain of occurrence of which only three recorded cases existed in the literature, each of which was in a different field of surgery where the patient was in a different position when the anaesthetic was administered.

In *Glass v Cambridge Health Authority* [1995] 6 Med LR 91, Rix J had received similar expert evidence in the case of an adult. He applied the maxim, holding that the burden of the *prima facie* inference of negligence cast upon the defendants by the doctrine remained unrebutted and undischarged.

47. Most recently of all, in *Widdowson v Newgate Meat Corporation* (CAT November 19, 1997; *The Times* December 4, 1997), a road traffic case in which the defendant had elected to call no evidence, I said of the state of the evidence at the end of the plaintiff's case:

> It appears to me that the suggestions put forward in this passage of cross-examination do not amount to a plausible explanation, consistent with an absence of negligence on the defendant's part, sufficient to rebut a prima facie inference of negligence by the defendant, and a plausible explanation is what the law requires if a defendant is to escape liability in such circumstances (see *Moore v R Fox and Sons* [1956] 1 QB 596 per Evershed MR at p 607 and *Colvilles Ltd v Devine* [1969] 1 WLR 475, per Lord Guest at p 477). In *Clerk & Lindsell on Torts* (17th ed) para 7-180, the editor observes that the defendant cannot hope to redress the balance merely by putting up theoretical possibilities: 'his assertion must have some colour of probability about it'.

48. It is likely to be a very rare medical negligence case in which the defendants take the risk of calling no factual evidence, when such evidence is available to them, of the circumstances surrounding a procedure which led to an unexpected outcome for a patient. If such a case should arise, the judge should not be diverted away from the inference of negligence dictated by the plaintiff's evidence by mere theoretical possibilities of how that outcome might have occurred without negligence: the defendants' hypothesis must have the ring of plausibility about it. It is in this sense that Lord Dunedin's dictum in *Ballard v North British Railway Company* 1923 SC (HL) 43 at p 34 ('if the defenders can show a way in which the

accident may have occurred without negligence, the cogency of the fact of the accident by itself disappears') should be understood.

49. It is now possible to draw some threads out of all this material, by way of explanation of the relevance of the maxim *res ipsa loquitur* to medical negligence cases:

(1) In its purest form the maxim applies where the plaintiff relies on the *res* (the thing itself) to raise the inference of negligence, which is supported by ordinary human experience, with no need for expert evidence.

(2) In principle, the maxim can be applied in that form in simple situations in the medical negligence field (surgeon cuts off right foot instead of left, swab left in operation site; patient wakes up in the course of surgical operation despite general anaesthetic).

(3) In practice, in contested medical negligence cases the evidence of the plaintiff, which establishes the *res*, is likely to be buttressed by expert evidence to the effect that the matter complained of does not ordinarily occur in the absence of negligence.

(4) The position may then be reached at the close of the plaintiff's case that the judge would be entitled to infer negligence on the defendant's part unless the defendant adduces evidence which discharges this inference.

(5) This evidence may be to the effect that there is a plausible explanation of what may have happened which does not connote any negligence on the defendant's part. The explanation must be a plausible one and not a theoretically or remotely possible one, but the defendant certainly does not have to prove that his explanation is more likely to be correct than any other. If the plaintiff has no other evidence of negligence to rely on, his claim will then fail.

(6) Alternatively, the defendant's evidence may satisfy the judge, on the balance of probabilities, that he did exercise proper care. If the untoward outcome is extremely rare, or is impossible to explain in the light of the current state of medical knowledge, the judge will be bound to exercise great care in evaluating the evidence before making such a finding, but if he does so, the prima facie inference of negligence is rebutted and the plaintiff's claim will fail. The reason why the courts are willing to adopt this approach, particularly in very complex cases, is to be found in the judgments of Stuart-Smith and Dillon LJJ in *Delaney* (see para 39 above).

(7) It follows from all this that although in very simple situations the *res* may speak for itself at the end of the lay evidence adduced on behalf of the plaintiff, in practice the inference is then buttressed by expert evidence adduced on his behalf, and if the defendant were to call no evidence, the judge would be deciding the case on inferences he was entitled to draw from the whole of the evidence (including the expert evidence), and not on the application of the maxim in its purest form.

50. In the present case, in which much expert evidence had been given on both sides, Mantell J said:

> The first question to be addressed and one which has occupied most of the hearing is whether it has been shown on a balance of probabilities that the anaesthetist, whoever it was, injected the spinal cord. I put it in that way because although I am far from stating that the maxim *res ipsa loquitur* can never have any application in a medical negligence case I doubt if it helps on the facts of the present. Certainly inferences are there to be drawn from the fact that the plaintiff suffered unexpected neurological damage following the operation but in my judgment that falls short of establishing a prima facie case of negligence... It is not I think necessary for me to refer to authority.

51. The judge went on to find that the plaintiff had not proved that his problems were caused by the Nurick lesion and that it was possible that they were derived from some pre-existing asymptomatic condition which the stress of the operation brought to life. The existence of that remote possibility would not have availed the defendants if the judge was satisfied on the whole of the plaintiff's evidence that he was entitled to infer that the untoward symptoms would not ordinarily have occurred in the absence of negligence by the anaesthetist, and he had received no evidence about what actually happened.

52. In this case, however, the judge made the positive finding that the anaesthetist had performed the spinal injection in the appropriate place with all proper care. In those circumstances any possible inference of negligence falls away, and unless this finding were set aside the plaintiff's case was bound to fail...once the judge was disposed to believe Dr Boaden, and to believe that Dr Clements's note was an accurate contemporary record of what took place, his finding that the injection was inserted in the correct space at the chosen level was really inevitable, and his approach to the applicability of the doctrine *res ipsa loquitur* cannot in my judgment be faulted.

54. For these reasons I would dismiss this appeal...

Hobhouse LJ:... Res ipsa loquitur
Res ipsa loquitur is no more than a convenient Latin phrase used to describe the proof of facts which are sufficient to support an inference that a defendant was negligent and therefore to establish a prima facie case against him...

The burden of proving the negligence of the defendant remains throughout upon the plaintiff. The burden is on the plaintiff at the start of the trial and absent an admission by the defendant is still upon the plaintiff at the conclusion of the trial. At the conclusion of the trial the judge has to decide whether upon all the evidence adduced at the trial he is satisfied upon the balance of probabilities that the defendant was negligent and that his negligence caused the plaintiff's injury. If he is so satisfied he gives judgment for the plaintiff; if not, he gives judgment for the defendant.

Whether or not the plaintiff has at some earlier stage relied upon a prima facie case does not alter this position. The plaintiff may or may not have needed to call evidence to establish a prima facie case. The admitted facts may suffice for that purpose. (*Ng v Lee, sup.*) Conversely, the defendant may have chosen to call no evidence, in which case the court will have to decide whether the evidence adduced by the plaintiff suffices to satisfy the court, in the absence of any evidence to contradict it, that the defendant was negligent and that his negligence caused the plaintiff's injury. In all these situations the task of the judge at the end of the trial is the same. The only difference is that he may be left without direct evidence of what occurred and may have to act upon inferences to be drawn from incomplete evidence. Where the defendant is in a position to adduce evidence as to what occurred but has refrained from doing so, the court will be more willing to draw inferences adverse to the defendant than might otherwise be the case. Where the plaintiff is not in a position himself to give an account himself of what occurred and where the relevant situation was under the control of the defendant and the relevant facts are known to the defendant, the case may come fairly and squarely within the statement of Erle CJ quoted above. But it does so because the facts proved have given rise to an inference that the defendant was negligent. Where there is direct evidence as to what occurred there is no need to rely upon inferences. (*Barkway v South Wales Transport* [1950] 1 All ER 392).

There is no rule that a defendant must be liable for any accident for which he cannot give a complete explanation. Even if there is an inference that, absent some explanation, there probably was negligence, the defendant can always, by showing that he nevertheless took all reasonable care, persuade the court that on the evidence adduced it should not be satisfied that the defendant was in fact negligent. (*Woods v Duncan* [1946] AC 401.)

Medical negligence cases have the potential to give rise to considerations whether the plaintiff has made out a *prima facie* case and whether or not the defendant has provided an adequate answer to displace the inference to be drawn from the plaintiff's *prima facie* case. Further, it is commonplace that the plaintiff will not, himself or herself, have fully known what occurred particularly if the relevant procedure was an operation carried out under anaesthetic. The procedures were under the control of the defendant and what the defendant did or did not do is exclusively within the direct knowledge of the defendant. But in practical terms few if any medical negligence cases are brought to trial without full discovery having been given, particulars having been obtained where necessary of the defendant's pleading, witness statements having been exchanged and experts' reports lodged. Therefore the trial opens not in the vacuum of available evidence and explanation as sometimes occurs in road traffic accident cases but with expert evidence on both sides and defined battle-lines drawn. The aspects of the facts and aetiology which can and cannot be explained with reasonable certainty will have been identified and the rival explanations marshalled. The viable allegations or inferences of negligence will have been identified and the parties and the trial judge will have a reasonable idea of the specific factual issues which are going to have to be investigated and determined at the trial.

To illustrate that from the present case. This case came to trial after all those preparatory procedures had been followed. The plaintiff did not rely solely or even primarily upon the mere appearance of his neurological symptoms after the operation which the defendants had carried out. He relied upon the expert evidence of among others Dr Nurik that the only reasonable explanation of the accident was that the needle injecting the Marcain had been inserted into the plaintiff's spinal cord at T11/12 or T12/L1 and not into the dural sack at L2/3 or L3/4. He had a positive case supported by evidence which unless discredited or contradicted would suffice to enable him to succeed. He also had more general evidence that the neurological symptoms were related to and probably consequential upon the use of a spinal block. Similarly by the start of the trial the plaintiff had abandoned any case that his injuries were caused by contamination of the Marcain. This would have been a possible explanation of damage to the spinal cord but it is not one that he pursued at the trial. So, at the start of the trial the plaintiff was entitled to say that he had a positive case on negligence but that in any event it was a fair inference that the spinal injection was administered in some way which was probably negligent. It was at the same time recognized that the defendants had a positive case to present as well. They contested that the inference was appropriate. They said that they had taken all reasonable care and were ready to call the witnesses to demonstrate it.

They disputed the plaintiff's positive care and presented an alternative thesis which did not involve negligence on their part. All this was simply the state of the issues at the start of the trial.

It was suggested on behalf of the appellants that there is difficulty in deciding in medical negligence cases when an inference of negligence would be justified and whether expert evidence would be necessary. The answer is that it depends upon the facts of the particular case. If the facts of the present case had been that the plaintiff had gone into the operating theatre to have an arthrodesis to his right ankle and had come out of the theatre with his right ankle untouched and an arthrodesis to his left ankle, clearly no expert evidence would be required to support an inference of negligence on the part of the defendants. 'In the ordinary course of things' that does not happen if those conducting the operation have used proper care. But if on the other hand all that one knows is that a baby has been born with some brain defect, more needs to be proved and expert evidence is required to raise an inference of negligence on the part of those in charge of the management of the birth.

The cases of *Cassidy v Ministry of Health* [1951] 2 KB 343 (the plaintiff went into hospital to be cured of two stiff fingers and he came out with four stiff fingers) and *Roe v Ministry of Health* [1954] 2 All ER 131 (routine operations followed by complete paralysis from the waist down) were apparently treated by at least some members of the Court of Appeal as coming into the first category. The vast majority of medical negligence cases will come into the second category and require the plaintiff to adduce some expert evidence before an inference of negligence can be raised.

In practice, save in the most extreme cases of blatant negligence, the plaintiff will have to get his case upon its feet. This is the more so because probably before he commences his action and delivers his pleading he will have seen record of what occurred and obtained some explanation from the defendants. But, even if he has to rely upon some fairly broadly based inference at the outset, by the time he gets to trial he will both be expected to and should be able to make some more specific allegations, supported by expert evidence, as to why he says the defendant was negligent. The essential role of the doctrine of *res ipsa loquitur* is to enable the plaintiff who is not in possession of all the material facts to be able to plead an allegation of negligence in an acceptable form and to force the defendant if the defendant does not make an adequate response. But once the defendant has responded then the question for the court is whether, in the light of that response, that is to say upon all the evidence that has been placed before it at the trial both by the plaintiff and by the defendant, the court is satisfied that the defendant has been negligent and that his negligence caused the plaintiff's injury.

The accepted categories of response that can be made to a case based upon *res ipsa loquitur*, that is to say, upon an inference of negligence, support this analysis. The defendant can displace the inference by showing by reference to a closer examination of the plaintiff's evidence or by reference to evidence adduced by the defendant that the inference that on the balance of probabilities there was negligence is not justified. The plaintiff's case then fails unless a more specific case has been made out. Alternatively the defendant can accept that there is a legitimate basis for the implication but say that in the particular case the defendant in fact exercised reasonable care notwithstanding the outcome and the inability fully to explain how the plaintiff's injury came about.

In my judgment there is no special difficulty involved in medical negligence cases. Each case ultimately depends upon its own facts. In pleading his case the plaintiff will only be expected to particularize his allegations of negligence in a way that is appropriate to the state of his knowledge of what happened at the time of his pleading. What amounts to an acceptable pleaded *prima facie* case of negligence will depend upon the nature of the injuries complained of and the procedures from which they are said to have arisen. By the time the case comes to trial the plaintiff will be able fully to deploy his case by saying that notwithstanding the explanation given by the defendants the appropriate inference still to draw is that the defendants were negligent and by making particularized allegations of negligence against the defendants. At the end of the trial, after all the evidence relied upon by either side has been called and tested, the judge has simply to decide whether as a matter of inference or otherwise he concludes on the balance of probabilities that the defendant was negligent and that that negligence caused the plaintiff's injury. That is the long and short of it.

Medical negligence cases often involve factual questions of complexity and difficulty and require the evaluation of highly technical and conflicting expert evidence but the trial procedure is essentially the same as in other cases. Indeed, the judge will normally have the advantage of expert evidence on both sides and an appropriate level of factual evidence both documentary and oral. Medical negligence cases are unlikely to give rise to the stark problems encountered in road traffic accident cases where there may be a total dearth of evidence or where one or other side may choose, no doubt for tactical reasons, not to present evidence. In my judgment the leading cases already give sufficient guidance to litigators and judges about the proper approach to the drawing of inferences and if I were to say anything further it would be confined to suggesting that the expression *res ipsa loquitur* should be dropped from the litigator's vocabulary and replaced by the phrase a *prima facie* case. *Res ipsa loquitur* is not a principle of law: it does not relate to or raise any presumption. It is merely a guide to help to identify when a *prima facie* case is being made out. Where expert and factual evidence has been called on both sides at a trial its usefulness will normally have long since been exhausted...

The defendants' evidence that they had taken all reasonable care stood uncontradicted. The judge was right to reject the plaintiff's case. Indeed, any other conclusion would have been contrary to the evidence which he had accepted.

The suggestion of the appellant on this appeal was that somehow there remained some residual unanswered inference of negligence which the judge should have used as a basis for finding in favour of the plaintiff. As I have explained earlier, this submission is based upon a misunderstanding of the so-called doctrine of *res ipsa loquitur* and of the correct approach to the drawing of inferences. There was no residual basis. The matter had been fully explored in evidence on both sides and the task of the judge was to make the appropriate findings of fact on the balance of probabilities on that evidence. This is what the judge did and he cannot be faulted. The appeal must be dismissed.

Sir John Vinelott agreed.

C. CAUSATION

It is one thing to show that the defendant doctor owed the plaintiff a duty which was breached and that the plaintiff has been harmed, it is quite another thing to establish that the breach *caused* the harm (see H L A Hart and T Honoré *Causation in the Law* (2nd edn, 1985) But this is what the law requires.

Causation is the legal concept by which the defendant is held responsible for his conduct, which in this context means his negligence. The law only makes a doctor liable if his negligent act or omission resulted in injury to the patient. This seemingly simple concept is in reality both more complex factually and intellectually than it might at first appear. The law requires in general that the doctor's negligent act of omission *made a difference* – what is often called 'but for' causation. There are, as we shall see, exceptions. It is an empirical test: what would have happened if the doctor had not been negligent? Would the patient have been injured (or less injured)? But, the law does not make an individual liable for every outcome that would not have occurred 'but for' his act or omission. To do so would lead to an endless historical chain of responsibility – *reductio ad absurdum*. Equally, what might actually occur to the patient could be quite unexpected or be *more attributable* to another's conduct. The law, as we shall see, draws lines and limits historical connections by notions of 'fairness' 'policy' and 'common sense'. Value judgments may limit responsibility. Here, we are in the realm of legal causation and remoteness.

Although it is somewhat early in a chapter on causation to do so, it is worth looking at a very important judgment, that of Kirby J in the Australian High Court case of *Chappell v Hart* (1998) 72 ALJR 1344. In his judgment he examines, in a reflective and intellectually attractive way, the essence of the legal concept of causation in a medical negligence context. There is no equivalent discussion in the English case law.

The case itself, concerned with a failure to advise of the risks inherent in a medical procedure, is discussed later (*infra*, ch 5). What is of interest to us here is Kirby J's approach and his framework for the law. He was part of the majority (with Gaudron and Gummow JJ) but there is nothing to suggest that the minority (McHugh and Hayne JJ) disagreed. Kirby J begins by identifying that the law is far from easy to understand or apply in this area.

Chappel v Hart (1998) 72 ALJR 1344 (HC of Aust)

Kirby J: 87. Establishing a causal connection between an alleged wrongdoer's conduct or default and the harm complained of is a pre-condition to the legal liability to pay damages...

88. There are no easy solutions to these problems. This is apparent from the many cases concerned with causation in the context of medical negligence coming before final and other courts of appeal in England [(*Hotson v East Berkshire AHA* [1987] AC 750; *Wilsher v Essex AHA* [1988] AC 1074; *Bolitho v City and Hackney HA* [1998] AC 232)], Canada [(*Farrell v Snell* (1990) 72 DLR (4th) 289; *Lawson v Laferrière* (1991) 78 DLR (4th) 609)], the United States of America and Australia [(*CES v Superclinics (Australia) Pty Ltd* (1995) 38 NSWLR 47)]. It is further illustrated by the division of opinions in this case: Gaudron J and Gummow J favouring the dismissal of the appeal; McHugh J and Hayne J being in favour of allowing it. I agree with the remarks of my colleagues that the case is a difficult one involving an unusual chain of events. But, it is not unique. Other cases exist which bear certain similarities [(For example *Sullivan v Micaleff* [1994] Aust Torts Rep 81, 308)]. Whilst avoiding the dangers of endless theoretical argument and acknowledging the disputability of a result depending upon the drawing of lines which fix the outer perimeter of legal liability, this Court must endeavour to give guidance in this case as to the approach to be taken when problems of this kind arise in the future, as surely they will.

Most helpfully, he sets out a number of what he calls 'general legal propositions' relating to causation. We omit those specifically concerned with 'failure to warn' cases (on which see *infra,* ch 5).

Kirby J: 1. *A practical question*: The starting point is to remember the purpose for which causation is being explored. It is a legal purpose for the assignment of liability to one person to pay damages to another. It is not to engage in philosophical or scientific debate, still less casuistry. As Windeyer J explained in *The National Insurance Co of New Zealand Ltd v Espagne* ((1961) 105 CLR 569 at 591))

> Philosophy and science seek the explanation of phenomena and look to relationships and concurrences. Law is not concerned *rerum cognoscere causas*, but with attributing responsibility to persons.

The law allocates responsibility by a process which at once determines the entitlement of the particular plaintiff and sets the standards of conduct that may be expected of other persons in positions analogous to the defendant. The law's concern is entirely practical. 'In the varied web of affairs, the law' said Lord Wright, 'must abstract some consequences as relevant, not perhaps on the grounds of pure logic but simply for practical reasons' (*Liebosch, Dredger v Edison SS (Owners)* [1933] AC 449 at 460). Where a breach of duty and loss are proved, it is natural enough for a court to feel reluctant to send the person harmed (in this case a patient) away empty handed. However, such reluctance must be overcome where legal principle requires it. It must be so not only out of fairness to the defendant but also because, otherwise, a false standard of liability will be fixed which may have undesirable professional and social consequences.

2. *A commonsense approach*: Causation is essentially a question of fact. It is to be resolved as a matter of commonsense. This means that there is usually a large element of intuition in deciding such questions which may be insusceptible to detailed and analytical justification. As Dixon CJ, Fullagar and Kitto JJ remarked in *Fitzgerald v Penn* ((1954) 91 CLR 268 at 277-78)) 'it is all ultimately a matter of common sense' and '[i]n truth the conception in question [ie causation] is not susceptible of reduction to a satisfactory formula'. Similarly, in *Alphacell Ltd v Woodward* ([1972] AC 824 at 847), Lord Salmon observed that causation is 'essentially a practical question of fact which can best be answered by ordinary common sense rather than by abstract metaphysical theory.' Yet, a losing party has a right to know why it has lost and should not have its objections brushed aside with a reference to 'commonsense', at best an uncertain guide involving 'subjective, unexpressed and undefined extra-legal values' (*March v Stramare (E&MH) Pty Ltd* (1991) 171 CLR 506 at 533 per McHugh J (diss). But see now *Bennett v Minister of Community Welfare* (1992) 176 CLR 408 at 428) varying from one decision-maker to another. Nevertheless, despite its obvious defects, the commonsense test has been embraced by this Court as a reminder that a 'robust and pragmatic approach' (*Wilsher v Essex AHA* [1988] AC 1074 at 1090 per Lord Bridge of Harwich) to such questions is the one most congenial to the common law.

3. *The 'but for' consideration*: If, but for the negligent act or omission, the actual damage suffered by a plaintiff would not have occurred, as will often be possible, as a practical matter, to conclude the issue of causation in the plaintiff's favour. Similarly, where the damage would probably have happened anyway, it will often be possible to conclude that the act or omission was not the cause for legal purposes. In this sense, the 'but for' test, so qualified, remains a relevant criterion for determining whether the breach of duty demonstrated is a cause of the plaintiff's damage. However, it is not the exclusive test. Nor is it sufficient on

its own to demonstrate the causal link for legal purposes. It is a mistake to read this Court's cautionary words about the 'but for' test as an expulsion of that notion from consideration where the question of causation is in contest. On the contrary, a sufficient causal connection will, generally speaking, be established if it appears that the plaintiff would not have suffered the damage complained of but for the defendant's breach of duty. The Court has simply added the warning that it is necessary to temper the results thereby produced with 'value judgments' and 'policy considerations'. This qualification has been expressed lest a party, shown to have been in breach of duty, is forever thereafter to be liable for every misfortune that follows in time whatever the breach demonstrated and however irrelevant it may appear to the damage which ensued. As Windeyer J observed in *Faulkner v Keffalinos* ((1971) 45 ALJR 80 at 86):

> But for the first accident, the [plaintiff] might still have been employed by the [defendants], and therefore not where he was when the second accident happened: but lawyers must eschew this kind of 'but for' or sine qua non reasoning about cause and consequence.

In an attempt to assist decision-makers in the task of drawing lines and in the assignment of legal responsibility, various phrases have been proffered by generations of judges to mark out a legally relevant cause (such as 'proximate cause', 'legal cause', 'true cause', 'effective cause', 'substantial cause', 'direct cause', 'foreseeable cause' or 'cause in fact'). These phrases, whilst well-intentioned, beg the question that is to be answered. They also carry dangers of their own. So does the attempt to convert the inquiry, as McHugh J has suggested, from the passive to the active voice as if this will solve the quandary of causation. That quandary remains, however it is expressed in verbal formulation.

4. *The plaintiff's legal onus*: It is elementary to say that it is a pre-condition to recovery of damages for an established breach of a legal duty that the onus is upon the plaintiff to prove that the breach alleged was the cause of the damage shown. It is important to keep separate the questions of liability and the calculation of damages. Where, as in this case, a plaintiff relies on a claim in contract, proof of breach of that contract will entitle the plaintiff to nominal damages at least. For recovery of compensation beyond nominal damages in contract, the plaintiff must prove that the breach was the cause of the damage. This is as true of a claim based on the tort of negligence as of one framed in contract. In this sense, the legal burden of proving causation is, and remains throughout the proceedings, upon the plaintiff. It is not an insubstantial burden. In some medical contexts it has even been described as Herculean. In cases similar to the present, it has been characterised as 'the most formidable obstacle confronting health care consumers' (Milstein, 'Causation in Medical Negligence – Recent Developments' (1997) 6 Australian Health Law Bulletin 21). The reasons include the imprecision of, and uncertainty about, some medical conditions; the progressive nature of others; the complexity of modern medical practice and technology; and the fact that some mistakes, serious enough in themselves, have no untoward results which can properly be attributed to them. In the present case, Dr Chappel argued that he fell into the last stated class of exemption. The recognised difficulties of causation for plaintiffs in medical negligence cases have occasionally given rise to legal devices designed to lighten their burdens. Some of these will be mentioned below.

5. *Displacing apparent causation*: In certain circumstances, the appearance that there is a causal connection between the breach and the damage, arising from the application of the 'but for' test and the proximity of the happening of the damage, has been displaced by a demonstration that:

(a) The happening of the damage was purely coincidental and had no more than a time connection with the breach;

(b) The damage was inevitable and would probably have occurred even without the breach, for example by the natural progression of an undetected, undiagnosed or unrevealed condition, or because the condition presented a life threatening emergency which demanded instant responses without time for the usual warnings and consents;

(c) The event was logically irrelevant to the actual damage which occurred;

(d) The event was the immediate result of unreasonable action on the part of the plaintiff; or

(e) The event was ineffective as a cause of the damage, given that the event which occurred would probably have occurred in the same way even had the breach not happened...

8. *Shifting the evidentiary onus*: One means of alleviating the burden cast by law on a plaintiff to establish a causal relationship between the breach and the damage concerns the evidentiary onus. Australian law has not embraced the theory that the legal onus of proof shifts during a trial. Nevertheless, the realistic appreciation of the imprecision and uncertainty of causation in many cases – including those involving alleged medical negligence – has driven courts in this country, as in England, to accept that the evidentiary onus may shift

during the hearing. Once a plaintiff demonstrates that a breach of duty has occurred which is closely followed by damage, a prima facie causal connection will have been established. It is then for the defendant to show, by evidence and argument, that the patient should *not* recover damages. In *McGhee v National Coal Board* ([1973] 1 WLR 1 at 6; [1972] 3 All ER 1008 at 1012), a Scottish appeal, Lord Wilberforce explained why this was so. Although Lord Wilberforce's statement in *McGhee* has proved controversial in England (*Wilsher v Essex AHA* [1988] AC 1074 at 1087, 1090), it has received support in this Court (eg *March v Stramere (E&MH) Pty* (1991) 171 CLR 506 at 514). Its principle has also been accepted by international experts such as Professor Giesen. I find Lord Wilberforce's exposition compelling ([1973] 1 WLR 1 at 6; [1972] 3 All ER 1008 at 1012):

> [T]he question remains whether a pursuer must necessarily fail it, after he has shown a breach of duty, involving an increase of risk of disease, he cannot positively prove that this increase of risk caused or materially contributed to the disease while his employers cannot prove the contrary. In this intermediate case there is an appearance of logic in the view that the pursuer, on whom the onus lies, should fail – a logic which dictated the judgments below. The question is whether we should be satisfied, in factual situations like the present, with this logical approach. In my opinion, there are further considerations of importance. First, it is a sound principle that where a person has, by breach of a duty of care, created a risk, and injury occurs within that area of that risk, the loss should be borne by him unless he shows that it had some other cause. Secondly, from the evidential point of view, one may ask, why should a man who is able to show that his employer should have taken certain precautions, because without them there is a risk, or an added risk, of injury or disease, and who in fact sustains exactly that injury or disease, have to assume the burden of proving more: namely, that it was the addition of the risk, caused by the breach of duty, which caused or materially contributed to the injury? In many cases … this is impossible to prove, just because honest medical opinion cannot segregate the causes of illness between compound causes. And if one asks which of the parties, the workman or the employers, should suffer from this inherent evidential difficulty, the answer as a matter of policy or justice should be that it is the creator of the risk who, ex hypothesi must be taken to have foreseen the possibility of damage, who should bear its consequences.

9. *Valuing a lost chance*: A further way in which , in some circumstances, the difficulties of causation for a plaintiff are alleviated is by treating the plaintiff's loss as a 'loss of a chance'. In cases in which this approach is permissible, it may allow evaluation of the plaintiff's loss in terms of comparing the chances of suffering harm (given the breach which has occurred) against those that would have existed (if the breach is hypothesised away). In *CES v Superclinics (Aust) Pty Ltd* ((1995) 38 NSWLR 47 at 56-57) I indicated my attraction to this approach as a more rational and just way of calculating damages caused by established medical negligence. It is clearly laid down by the authority of this Court that, in some circumstances, a plaintiff may recover the value of a loss of a chance caused by a wrongdoer's act or omission. The approach also has some judicial support in the context of medical negligence in England, Canada and the United States. A number of commentators favour this approach because of the failure of orthodox reasoning to do justice to some patients' losses and because it invites a more empirical calculation of loss, with the use of statistics which might offer outcomes that are more accurate and fair to all concerned. On the other hand, the weight of judicial opinion in England and Canada and some academic writing appears to be critical of the application of the loss of a chance theory to cases of medical negligence. In part this is because, where medical negligence is alleged, 'destiny …[has] taken its course', arguably making an analysis by reference to chance inappropriate or unnecessary in the view of the critics of this approach (*Lawson v Laferrière* (1991) 78 DLR (4th) 609 at 632-633 per Gonthier J). Alternatively, the loss of a chance calculation has been criticised on the ground that it would discard commonsense, undermine the plaintiff's onus of proving the case and submit the law to the 'paralysis'(*ibid*) of statistical abstractions.

10. *Discounting damages*: If it is established that damage was caused by the breach alleged, it remains to calculate the amount of compensation recoverable. It is then proper to reduce any damages which a defendant should pay for the harm it has caused to a proper proportion actually attributable to its breach. If, independently of the breach on the part of a defendant, the evidence shows that the plaintiff would have suffered loss, the damages may be reduced by reference to the estimate of the chances that this would have occurred. If those chances are less than one percent, this Court has held that they may properly be disregarded as speculative. Dr Chappel argued that, even if he had given the requisite warning to Mrs Hart, and she had postponed the procedure and later undergone an operation by a more experienced surgeon, there was still the same random chance that she would have suffered the complications that occurred; neither more nor less. Mrs Hart argued that the true comparison was between the loss that had in fact occurred to her and the concededly small risk that such loss would have happened at the postulated postponed operation.

She resisted any reduction in her damages, submitting that a chance of injury in a postponed operation was minuscule, ie 'speculative' in the sense described by this Court...

Against that masterly analysis, we now turn to consider the question of *factual causation,* including attempts to relax the conventional approach of the 'but for' test and *legal causation* and *remoteness.*

1. Factual causation

(a) 'but for' test

This is not the place to rehearse in detail the principles of the law of tort concerning factual causation (see HLA Hart and T Honoré, *op cit*, ch v). There are, however, problems particularly relevant in medical law which it is important to notice. They relate *first*, to the need to show that the doctors' or others' conduct *could* cause the plaintiff harm as a medical fact and *secondly*, whether in the particular case the harm *did* arise from the doctors' or others' conduct or was an inevitable consequence of the patient's illness, injury or disease.

The first type of problem is illustrated by the well-known cases relating to the whooping cough vaccine – *Loveday v Renton* [1990] 1 Med LR 117. In *Loveday* the plaintiff alleged that the permanent brain-damage she suffered was caused by the administration of the petussis (whooping cough) vaccine. The court (Stuart-Smith LJ) held that the scientific evidence did not establish a link between brain-damage in young children and the administration of the vaccine. (See also *Kay v Ayrshire and Arran Health Board* [1987] 2 All ER 417 (HL) where the House of Lords relied on the fact that there was no evidence that an overdose of penicillin caused deafness to reach the conclusion that it could not have done so in the case before them.)

The second type of case is the more common giving rise to problems in the case law and is illustrated by the *Barnett* decision. The facts of this case are set out *supra*, p 279. You will recall that the deceased died from arsenic poisoning which was undetected by the hospital he attended because he was not examined.

Barnett v Chelsea and Kensington Hospital Management Committee [1969] 1 QB 428, [1968] 1 All ER 1068 (QBD)

Nield J: It remains to consider whether it is shown that the deceased's death was caused by this negligence or whether, as the defendants have said, the deceased must have died in any event. In his concluding submission counsel for the plaintiff submitted that Dr Banerjee should have examined the deceased and, had he done so, he would have caused tests to be made which would have indicated the treatment required and that, since the defendants were at fault in these respects, therefore the onus of proof passed to the defendants to show that the appropriate treatment would have failed, and authorities were cited to me. I find myself unable to accept this argument and I am of the view that the onus of proof remains on the plaintiff, and I have in mind (without quoting it) the decision quoted by counsel for the defendants in *Bonnington Castings Ltd v Wardlaw* ([1956] AC 613). However, were it otherwise and the onus did pass to the defendants, then I would find that they have discharged it, as I would proceed to show.

There has been put before me a timetable which, I think, is of much importance. The deceased attended at the casualty department at 8.05 or 8.10am. If Dr Banerjee had got up and dressed and come to see the three men and examined them and decided to admit them, the deceased (and Dr Lockett agreed with this) could not have been in bed in a ward before 11am. I accept Dr Goulding's evidence that an intravenous drip would not have been set up before 12 noon. Dr Lockett, dealing with this said 'If [the deceased] had not been treated until after 12 noon the chances of survival were not good.'

Without going into detail into the considerable volume of technical evidence which has been put before me, it seems to me to be the case that when death results from arsenical poisoning it is brought about by two conditions: on the one hand dehydration and on the other disturbance of the enzyme processes. If the principal condition is one of enzyme disturbance – as I am of the view that it was here – then the only method of treatment which is likely to succeed is the use of the specified antidote which is commonly called BAL. Dr Goulding said this is the course of his evidence.

> The only way to deal with this is to use the specific BAL. I see no reasonable prospect of the deceased being given BAL before the time at which he died,

and at a later point in his evidence:

> I feel that even if fluid loss had been discovered death would have been caused by the enzyme disturbance. Death might have occurred later.

I regard that evidence as very moderate, and that it might be a true assessment of the situation to say that there was no chance of BAL being administered before the death of the deceased.

For these reasons, I find that the plaintiff has failed to establish, on the grounds of probability, that the defendants' negligence caused the death of the deceased.

Barnett was a case where the evidence was clear that the breach of duty *did not* cause the deceased's death. *Barnett* is not a typical case. The evidence was all one way. It was *certain* what the outcome would have been for the deceased if there had been no negligence. Also, you should note that the evidence created a straight choice – the negligence was either *the* cause or *not a cause at all*. Often, there will be a number of competing cumulative or alternative causes (we will return to this shortly).

Also, in most cases of medical negligence the evidence of the cause of the plaintiff's harm will be, at best, unclear – either intrinsically so or because of the preparedness of experts so to testify. In such circumstances is it any part of the role of the court to assist the plaintiff to establish causation by, for example, adopting a less stringent definition of causation than is ordinarily employed? The House of Lords had the opportunity to develop the law in this way in *Wilsher v Essex AHA* [1988] 1 All ER 871 but, as you will see, chose not to do so.

Wilsher v Essex AHA [1988] 1 All ER 871, [1988] AC 1074 (HL)

Lord Bridge: My Lords, the infant plaintiff was born nearly three months prematurely on 15 December 1978. He weighed only 1,200g. In the first few weeks of life he suffered from most of the afflictions which beset premature babies. He passed through a series of crises and very nearly died. The greatest danger which faces the very premature baby, on account of the imperfect function of incompletely developed lungs, is death or brain damage from failure of the oxygen supply to the brain. That Martin not only survived but also now retains unimpaired brain function is due both to the remarkable advances of medical science and technology in this field in comparatively recent years and to the treatment he received in the special baby care unit of the Princess Alexandra Hospital, Harlow.

Tragically, however, he succumbed to another well-known hazard of prematurity. He suffers from netrolental fibroplasia (RLF), an incurable condition of the retina which, in his case, has caused total blindness in one eye and severely impaired vision in the other. He sued the Essex Area Health Authority (the authority), who are responsible for the Princess Alexandra Hospital, Harlow, on the ground that his RLF was caused by an excess of oxygen tension in his bloodstream in the early weeks attributable to a want of proper skills and care in the management of his oxygen supply. The action was heard by Peter Pain J and the trial lasted 20 days. In addition to the evidence of the medical and nursing staff at the hospital, the judge heard expert evidence from two paediatricians and two ophthalmologists called for the plaintiff and from three paediatricians and one ophthalmologist called for the authority. All were highly qualified and distinguished experts in their respective fields. In addition, no less than 24 articles from medical journals about RLF covering 129 foolscap pages of print were put in evidence.

The allegations of negligence against the authority related to two quite distinct phases of Martin's treatment. The first concerned the first 38 hours after his birth. In order to monitor the partial pressure of oxygen (PO_2) in the arterial blood of a premature baby, it is standard practice to pass a catheter through the umbilical artery into the aorta. This enables the PO_2 to be measured in two ways. At the tip of the catheter is an electronic sensor connected to a monitor outside the body which, if correctly calibrated, should given an accurate reading of the PO_2. In addition, an aperture in the catheter close to the sensor enables samples of blood to be taken for conventional blood analysis at regular intervals to check and, if necessary, adjust the monitor's calibration. Again it is standard practice to check the location of the sensor by X-ray after the catheter has been inserted. In Martin's case the catheter was inserted by mistake into a vein instead of an artery so that the sensor and the sampling aperture were wrongly located in the heart instead of the aorta. This meant that they would sample a mixture of arterial and venous blood instead of pure arterial blood, which would consequently give a false reading of the level of PO_2 in the arterial blood. The house officer and the registrar who were on duty at the material time and who saw the X-ray which was taken both failed to notice the mistake. The judge held this failure to amount to negligence for which the authority were liable. The plaintiff's case in relation to this first allegation of negligence was that the misplaced catheter gave readings of PO_2 well below the true level of PO_2 in the arterial blood which led to excessive administration of oxygen in an attempt to raise the PO_2 level and that in consequence the true PO_2 level was excessively high for a substantial period until the mislocation of the catheter was realised at 8 o'clock on the morning of 17 December 1978.

A second phase of Martin's treatment alleged to have been negligent was between 20 December 1978 and 23 January 1979. Between these dates it was alleged that there were five distinct periods of differing duration when the medical and nursing staff responsible for Martin's care were in breach of duty in allowing the level of PO_2 in his arterial blood to remain above the accepted level of safety. The judge found that four of these five periods of exposure to an unduly high level of PO_2 were due to the authority's negligence.

In making his finding of negligence in relation to each of the periods of raised PO_2 levels except the first attributable to the misplaced catheter, the judge relied on a principle of law which he thought was laid down by this House in *McGhee v National Coal Board* [1972] 3 All ER 1008, [1973] 1 WLR 1 and which he had stated in his own earlier decision in *Clark v MacLennan* [1983] 1 All ER 416 at 427 in the following terms:

> It seems to me that it follows from *McGhee* that where there is a situation in which a general duty of care arises and there is a failure to take a precaution, and that very damage occurs against which the precaution is designed to be a protection, then the burden lies on the defendant to show that he was not in breach of duty as well as to show that the damage did not result from his breach of duty.

The judge thought that this proposition of law derived support from the decision at first instance of Mustill J in *Thompson v Smiths Shiprepairers (North Shields) Ltd* [1984] 1 All ER 881, [1984] QB 405. He held that the authority failed to prove on a balance of probabilities either that they were not negligent or that their negligence did not cause or materially contribute to Martin's RLF. He therefore held them liable in damages and gave judgment for the plaintiff for £116,119.14.

The Court of Appeal (Sir Nicolas Browne-Wilkinson V-C, Mustill and Glidewell LJJ) affirmed this judgment by a majority, the Vice-Chancellor dissenting (see [1986] 3 All ER 801, [1987] QB 730). It gave leave on terms to the authority to appeal to this House. A number of issues were argued in the Court of Appeal. It unanimously affirmed the finding of negligence against the authority, though by marginally different processes of reasoning, on the ground of the authority's vicarious liability for the registrar's failure to observe from the X-ray that the first catheter inserted into Martin's umbilicus was located in a vein not in an artery. It unanimously reversed the judge's finding of negligence in relation to the later periods when the level of PO_2 in Martin's arterial blood before 8 o'clock on the morning of 17 December 1978 consequent on misplacement of the catheter caused or materially contributed to Martin's RLF.

My Lords, I understand that all your Lordships agree that this appeal has to be allowed and that the inevitable consequence of this is that the outstanding issue of causation must, unless the parties can reach agreement, be retried by another judge. In these circumstances, for obvious reasons, it is undesirable that I should go into the highly complex and technical evidence on which the issue depends any further than is strictly necessary to explain why, in common with all your Lordships, I feel ineluctably driven to the unpalatable conclusion that it is not open to the House to resolve the issue one way or the other, so that a question depending on the consequence of an event occurring in the first two days of Martin's life will not have to be investigated all over again when Martin is nearly ten years old. On the other hand, the appeal raises a question of law as to the proper approach to issues of causation which is of great importance and of particular concern in medical negligence cases. This must be fully considered.

There was in the voluminous expert evidence given at the trial an irreconcilable conflict of opinion as to the cause of Martin's RLF. It was common ground that a sufficiently high level of PO_2 in the arterial blood of a very premature baby, if maintained for a sufficiently long period of time, can have a toxic effect on the immature blood vessels in the retina leading to a condition which may either regress or develop into RLF. It was equally common ground, however, that RLF may occur in premature babies who have survived without any artificial administration of oxygen and that there is evidence to indicate a correlation between RLF and a number of other conditions from which premature babies commonly suffer (eg apnoea, hypercarbia, intraventricular haemorrhage, patent ductus arteriosus, all conditions which afflicted Martin) although no causal mechanisms linking these conditions with the development of RLF have been identified. However, what, if any, part artificial administration of oxygen causing an unduly high level of PO_2 in Martin's arterial blood played in the causation of Martin's RLF was radically in dispute between the experts. There was certainly evidence led in support of the plaintiff's case that high levels of PO_2 in general and, more particularly, the level of PO_2 maintained when the misplaced catheter was giving misleadingly low readings of the level in the arterial blood were probably at least a contributory cause of Martin's RLF. If the judge had directed himself that it was for the plaintiff to discharge the onus of proving causation on a balance of probabilities and had indicated his acceptance of this evidence in preference to the contrary evidence led for the authority, a finding in favour of the plaintiff would have been unassailable. That is why it is conceded by counsel for the authority that the most he can ask for, if his appeal succeeds, is an order for retrial of the causation issue. However, the burden of the relevant expert evidence led for the authority, to summarise it in very general terms, was to the effect that any excessive administration of oxygen which resulted from the misplacement of the catheter did not result in the PO_2 in the arterial blood being raised to a sufficiently high level for a sufficient length of time to have been capable of playing any part in the causation of Martin's RLF. One of the difficulties is that, underlying this conflict of medical opinion, there was not only a substantial difference of view about the aetiology and causation of RLF in general but also a substantial difference as to the inferences which were to be drawn from the primary facts, as ascertained from the clinical notes about Martin's condition and treatment at the medical time and amplified by the oral evidence of Dr Wiles, the senior house officer in charge, as to what the actual levels of PO_2 in Martin's arterial blood were likely to have been during a critical period between 10 pm on 16 December when Martin was first being administered pure oxygen through a ventilator and 8 am the next morning when, after discovery of the mistake about the catheter, the level of oxygen administration was immediately reduced.

Having found the authority negligent in relation to the five periods when the PO_2 level was unduly high, the judge added: 'There is no dispute that this materially increased the risk of RLF.' This statement, it is now accepted, was a misunderstanding of the evidence. Whilst it was common ground that one of the objects of monitoring and controlling the PO_2 level in the arterial blood of a premature baby in 1978 was to avoid or reduce the risk of RLF, it was certainly not accepted by the defence that any of the levels to which Martin was subjected were sufficient in degree or duration to have involved any material increase in that risk. This misunderstanding was one of the factors which led the judge to the conclusion that Martin had established a prima facie case on the issues of causation. He then said:

But it is open to the defendants on the facts of this case to show that they are not liable for this negligence because on the balance of probability this exposure did not cause Martin's RLF.

It was on this premise that the judge examined the issue of causation. In judgment which runs to 68 pages of transcript, only 2 ½ pages are devoted to this issue. The judge repeatedly emphasised that the onus was on the authority, saying at one point:

For the purpose of this action I need go no further than to consider whether the breaches have probably made no substantial contribution to the plaintiff's condition.

And, again, a little later on: 'So I have to consider whether the exposure that occurred probably did no harm.'

After a brief reference to the evidence on one of the plaintiff's witnesses and one of the authority's witnesses whose answers were based on an assumption of fact which he was invited to make, the judge expressed his conclusion in the following passage:

On the basis of this evidence I find that the defendants fail to show that the first and third periods of exposure did not do any damage; *indeed, the probability is that they did*. As to the second, fourth and fifth periods the position is more doubtful. The trouble is the lack of data. The blood gas readings were not sufficiently frequent to enable us to assess whether the excessively high readings were a peak or whether they indicated a longer period; indeed, it is possible that the true figure went higher. The defendants, in my view, have failed to show that these periods did not cause or materially contribute to Martin's RLF. (My emphasis).

Counsel for the plaintiff, seeking to uphold the judgment in Martin's favour, naturally relied heavily on the words I have emphasised in this passage and pointed to the contrast between the judge's view, thereby expressed, of the causative effect of what is now the only relevant period of exposure calling for consideration and his doubts about the effect of three of the four later periods. He urged your Lordships to read this as an indication by the judge that, if he had held the onus to lie on the plaintiff he would have found it discharged on a balance of probabilities. The Court of Appeal did not feel able to accede to a similar submission and I agree with it. As Mustill LJ pointed out ([1986] 3 All ER 801 at 823, [1987] QB 730 at 763), the judge expressed no preference for the plaintiff's experts on this point. Moreover, it is inconceivable that this very careful judge, if he had directed himself that the burden of proof lay on the plaintiff, would not have subjected the complex and conflicting evidence to a thorough scrutiny and analysis before committing himself to an orthodox finding of causation in the plaintiff's favour.

Both parties accepted that the conflict of evidence was of such a nature that it could not properly be resolved by your Lordships simply reading the transcript. Indeed, we were not asked to examine the totality of the voluminous medical evidence. Just as counsel for the authority accepted that it was not open to the House to dismiss the plaintiff's claim, so counsel for the plaintiff accepted that, if he failed in the submission which I have examined and rejected in the foregoing paragraphs, he could not invite the House to make an independent finding in the plaintiff's favour on the simple basis that the expert evidence on a balance of probabilities affirmatively established causation.

The Court of Appeal, although it felt unable to resolve the primary conflict in the expert evidence as to the causation of Martin's RLF, did make a finding that the levels of PO_2 which Martin experienced in consequence of the misplacement of the catheter were of a kind capable of causing RLF. Mustill LJ expressed his anxiety whether 'by making a further finding of an issue where there was a sharp conflict between the expert witnesses, we are not going too far in the effort to avoid a retrial' (see [1986] 3 All ER 801 at 825, [1987] QB 730 at 766). But he concluded that it was 'legitimate, after reading and rereading the evidence', to make this finding based on 'the weight of the expert evidence'. This finding by the Court of Appeal is challenged by counsel for the authority as one which it was not open to it to make. I must return to this later. But assuming, as I do for the present, that the finding was properly made, it carried the plaintiff's case no further than to establish that oxygen administered to Martin as a consequence of the negligent failure to detect the misplacement of the catheter was one of a number of possible causes of Martin's RLF.

Mustill LJ subjected the speeches in *McGhee v National Coal Board* [1972] 3 All ER 1008, [1973] 1 WLR 1 to a careful scrutiny and analysis and concluded that they established a principle of law which he expressed in the following terms ([1986] 3 All ER 801 at 829, [1987] QB 730 at 771-772):

> If it is an established fact that conduct of a particular kind creates a risk that injury will be caused to another or increases an existing risk that injury will ensue, and if the two parties stand in such a relationship that the one party owes a duty not to conduct himself in that way, and if the first party does conduct himself in that way, and if the other party does suffer injury of the kind to which the risk related, then the first party is taken to have caused the injury by his breach of duty, even though the existence and extent of the contribution made by the breach cannot be ascertained.

Applying this principle to the finding that the authority's negligence was one of the possible causes of Martin's RLF, he held that this was sufficient to enable the court to conclude that the negligence was 'taken to have caused the injury'. Glidewell LJ reached the same conclusion by substantially the same process of reasoning. Sir Nicholas Browne-Wilkinson V-C took the opposite view.

The starting point for any consideration of the relevant law of causation is the decision of this House in *Bonnington Castings Ltd v Wardlaw* [1956] 1 All ER 615, [1956] AC 613. This was the case of a pursuer who, in the course of his employment by the defenders, contracted pneumoconiosis over a period of years by the inhalation of invisible particles of silica dust from two sources. One of these (pneumatic hammers) was an 'innocent' source, in the sense that the pursuer could not complain that his exposure to it involved any breach of duty on the part of his employers. The other source (swing grinders), however, arose from a breach of statutory duty by the employer. Delivering the leading speech in the House of Lords, Lord Reid said ([1956] 1 All ER 615 at 617-618, [1956] AC 613 at 619-620):

> The Lord Ordinary and the majority of the First Division have dealt with this case on the footing that there was an onus on the defenders, the appellants, to prove that the dust from the swing grinders did not cause the respondent's disease. This view was based on a passage in the judgment of the Court of Appeal in *Vyner v Waldenberg Bros Ltd* ([1945] 2 All ER 547 at 549, [1946] KB 50 at 55) *per* Scott LJ: 'If there is a definite breach of a safety provision imposed on the occupier of a factory, and a workman is

injured in a way which could result from the breach, the onus of proof shifts on to the employer to show that the breach was not the cause. We think that that principle lies at the very basis of statutory rules of absolute duty.' ... Of course the onus was on the defendants to prove delegation (if that was an answer) and to prove contributory negligence, and it may be that this is what the Court of Appeal had in mind. But the passage which I have cited appears to go beyond that and, in so far as it does so, I am of opinion that it is erroneous. It would seem obvious in principle that a pursuer or plaintiff must prove not only negligence or breach of duty but also that such fault caused, or materially contributed to, his injury, and there is ample authority for that proposition both in Scotland and in England. I can find neither reason nor authority for the rule being different where there is breach of a statutory duty. The fact that Parliament imposes a duty for the protection of employees has been held to entitle an employee to sue if he is injured as a result of a breach of that duty, but it would be going a great deal further to hold that it can be inferred from the enactment of a duty that Parliament intended that any employee suffering injury can sue his employer merely because there was a breach of duty and it is shown to be possible that his injury may have been caused by it. In my judgment, the employee must, in all cases, prove his case by the ordinary standard of proof in civil actions; he must make it appear at least that, on a balance of probabilities, the breach of duty caused, or materially contributed to, his injury.

Lord Tucker said of Scott LJ's dictum in *Vyner v Waldenberg Bros Ltd*:

...I think it is desirable that your Lordships should take this opportunity to state in plain terms that no such onus exists unless the statute or statutory regulation expressly or impliedly so provides, as in several instances it does. No distinction can be drawn between actions for common law negligence and actions for breach of statutory duty in this respect. In both, the plaintiff or pursuer must prove (a) breach of duty, and (b) that such breach caused the injury complained of (see *Wakelin v London & South Western Rly Co* (1886) 12 App Cas 41, and *Caswell v Powell Duffryn Associated Collieries Ltd* [1939] 3 All ER 722, [1940] AC 152). In each case, it will depend on the particular facts proved, and the proper inferences to be drawn therefrom, whether the respondent has sufficiently discharged the onus that lies on him.

(See [1956] 1 All ER 615 at 621, [1956] AC 613 at 624-625.)

Lord Keith said ([1956] 1 All ER 615 at 621, [1956] AC 613 at 625):

The onus is on the respondent [the pursuer] to prove his case, and I see no reason to depart from this elementary principle by invoking certain rules of onus said to be based on a correspondence between the injury suffered and the evil guarded against by some statutory regulation. I think most, if not all, of the cases which professed to lay down or to recognise some such rule could have been decided as they were on simple rules of evidence, and I agree that *Vyner v Waldenberg Bros Ltd* ([1945] 2 All ER 547, [1946] KB 50), in so far as it professed to enunciate a principle of law inverting the onus of proof, cannot be supported.

Viscount Simonds and Lord Somervell agreed.

Their Lordships concluded, however, from the evidence that the inhalation of dust to which the pursuer was exposed by the defender's breach of statutory duty had made a material contribution to his pneumoconiosis which was sufficient to discharge the onus on the pursuer of proving that his damage was caused by the defenders' tort.

A year later the decision in *Nicholson v Atlas Steel Foundry and Engineering Co Ltd* [1957] 1 All ER 776, [1957] 1 WLR 613 followed the decision in *Bonnington Castings Ltd v Wardlaw* and held, in another case of pneumoconiosis, that the employers were liable for the employee's disease arising from the inhalation of dust from two sources, one 'innocent; the other 'guilty', on facts virtually indistinguishable from those in *Bonnington Castings Ltd v Wardlaw.*

In *McGhee v National Coal Board* [1972] 3 All ER 1008, [1973] 1 WLR 1 the pursuer worked in a brick kiln in hot and dusty conditions in which brick dust adhered to his sweaty skin. No breach of duty by his employers, the defenders, was established in respect of his working conditions. However, the employers were held to be at fault in failing to provide adequate washing facilities which resulted in the pursuer having to bicycle home after work with his body still caked in brick dust. The pursuer contracted dermatitis and the evidence that this was caused by the brick dust was accepted. Brick dust adhering to the skin was a recognized cause of industrial dermatitis and the provision of showers to remove it after work was a usual precaution to minimise the risk of the disease. The precise mechanism of causation of the disease, however, was not known and the furthest the doctors called for the pursuer were able to go was to say that the provision of showers would have materially reduced the risk of dermatitis. They were unable to say that it would probably have prevented the disease.

The pursuer failed before the Lord Ordinary and the First Division of the Court of Session on the ground that the had not discharged the burden of proof of causation. He succeeded on appeal to the House of Lords. Much of the academic discussion to which this decision has given rise had focused on the speech of Lord Wilberforce, particularly on two paragraphs. He said ([1972] 3 All ER 1008 at 1012, [1973] 1 WLR 1 at 6):

> But the question remains whether a pursuer must necessarily fail if, after he has shown a breach of duty, involving an increase of risk of disease, he cannot positively prove that this increase of risk caused or materially contributed to the disease while his employers cannot positively prove the contrary. In this intermediate case there is an appearance of logic in the view that the pursuer, on whom the onus lies, should fail – a logic which dictated the judgments below. The question is whether we should be satisfied in factual situations like the present, with the logical approach. In my opinion, there are further considerations of importance. First, it is a sound principle that where a person has, by breach of duty of care, created a risk, and injury occurs within the area of that risk, the loss should be borne by him *unless he shows that it had some other cause.* Secondly, from the evidential point of view, one may ask, why should a man who is able to show that his employer should have taken certain precautions, because without them there is a risk, or an added risk, of injury or disease, and who in fact sustains exactly that injury or disease, have to assume the burden or proving more: namely that it was the addition to the risk, caused by the breach of duty, which caused or materially contributed to the injury? In many cases of which the present is typical, this is impossible to prove, just because honest medical opinion cannot segregate the causes of an illness between compound causes. And if one asks which of the parties, the workman or the employers, should suffer from this inherent evidential difficulty, the answer as a matter of policy or justice should be that it is the creator of the risk who, ex hypothesi, must be taken to have foreseen the possibility of damage, who should bear its consequences. (My emphasis.)

He then referred to *Bonnington Castings Ltd v Wardlaw* and *Nicholson v Atlas Steel Foundry and Engineering Co Ltd* and added ([1972] 3 All ER 1008 at 1013, [1973] 1 WLR 1 at 7):

> The present factual situation has its differences: the default here consisted not in adding a material quantity to the accumulation of injurious particles but by failure to take a step which materially increased the risk that the dust already present would cause injury. And I must say that, at least in the present case, to bridge the evidential gap by inference seems to me something of a fiction, since it was precisely this inference which the medical expert declined to make. But I find in the cases quoted an analogy which suggests the conclusion that, *in the absence of proof that the culpable condition had, in the result, no effect,* the employers should be liable for an injury, squarely within the risk which they created and that they, not the pursuer, should suffer the consequence of the impossibility, foreseeably inherent in the nature of his injury, of segregating the precise consequence of their default. (My emphasis.)

My Lords, it seems to me that both these paragraphs, particularly in the words I have emphasised, amount to saying that, in the circumstances, the burden of proof of causation is reversed and thereby to run counter to the unanimous and emphatic opinions expressed in *Bonnington Castings Ltd v Wardlaw* [1956] 1 All ER 615, [1956] AC 613 to the contrary effect. I find no support in any of the other speeches for the view that the burden of proof is reversed and, in this respect, I think Lord Wilberforce's reasoning must be regarded as expressing a minority opinion.

A distinction is, of course, apparent between the facts of *Bonnington Castings Ltd v Wardlaw*, where the 'innocent' and 'guilty' silica dust particles which together caused the pursuer's lung disease were inhaled concurrently and the facts of *McGhee v National Coal Board* where the 'innocent' and 'guilty' brick dust was present on the pursuer's body for consecutive periods. In the one case the concurrent inhalation of 'innocent' and 'guilty' dust must both have contributed to the cause of the disease. In the other case the consecutive periods when 'innocent' and 'guilty' brick dust was present on the pursuer's body may both have contributed to the cause of the disease or, theoretically at least, one or other may have been the sole cause. But where the layman is told by the doctors that the longer the brick dust remains on the body, the greater the risk of dermatitis, although the doctors cannot identify the process of causation scientifically, there seems to be nothing irrational in drawing the inference, as a matter of common sense, that the consecutive periods when brick dust remained on the body probably contributed cumulatively to the causation of the dermatitis. I believe that a process of inferential reasoning on these general lines underlies the decision of the majority in *McGhee's* case.

In support of their view, I refer to the following passages. Lord Reid said ([1972] 3 All ER 1008 at 1010, [1973] 1 WLR 1 at 3-4):

> The medical witnesses are in substantial agreement. Dermatitis can be caused, and this dermatitis was caused, by repeated minute abrasion of the outer horny layer of the skin followed by some injury to or change in the underlying cells, the precise nature of which has not yet been discovered by medical science. If a man sweats profusely for a considerable time the outer layer of his skin is softened and easily injured. If he is then working in a cloud of abrasive brick dust, as this man was, the particles of dust will adhere to his skin in considerable quantity and exertion will cause them to injure the horny layer and expose to injury or infection the tender cells below. Then in some way not yet understood dermatitis may result. If the skin is not thoroughly washed as soon as the man ceases to work that process can continue at least for some considerable time. This man had to continue exerting himself after work by bicycling home while still caked with sweat and grime, so he would be liable to further injury until he could wash himself thoroughly. Washing is the only practicable method of removing the danger of further injury. The effect of such abrasion of the skin is cumulative in the sense that the longer a subject is exposed to injury the greater the chance of his developing dermatitis: it is for that reason that immediate washing is well recognized as a proper precaution.

He concluded ([1972] 3 All ER 1008 at 1011, [1973] 1 WLR 1 at 4-5):

> The medical evidence is to the effect that the fact that the man had to cycle home caked with grime and sweat added materially to the risk that this disease might develop. It does not and could not explain just why that is so. But experience shows that it is so. Plainly that must be because what happens while the man remains unwashed can have a causative effect, although just how the cause operates is uncertain. I cannot accept the view expressed in the Inner House that once the man left the brick kiln he left behind the causes which made him liable to develop dermatitis. That seems to me quite inconsistent with a proper interpretation of the medical evidence. Nor can I accept the distinction drawn by the Lord Ordinary between materially increasing risk that the disease will occur and making a material contribution to its occurrence There may be some logical ground for such a distinction where our knowledge of all the material factors is complete. But it has often been said that the legal concept of causation is not based on logic or philosophy. It is based on the practical way in which the ordinary man's mind works in the everyday affairs of life. From a broad and practical viewpoint I can see no substantial difference between saying that what the respondents did materially increased the risk of injury to the appellant and saying that what the respondents did made a material contribution in his injury.

Lord Simon said ([1972] 3 All ER 1008 at 1014, [1973] 1 WLR 1 at 8):

> But *Bonnington Castings Ltd v Wardlaw* and *Nicholson v Atlas Steel Foundry & Engineering Co Ltd* establish, in my view, that where an injury is caused by two (or more) factors operating cumulatively, one (or more) of which factors is a breach of duty and one (or more) is not so, in such a way that it is impossible to ascertain the proportion in which the factors were effective in producing the injury or which factor was decisive, the law does not require a pursuer or plaintiff to prove the impossible, but holds that he is entitled to damages for the injury if he proves on a balance of probabilities that the breach or breaches of duty contributed substantially to causing the injury. If such factors do operate cumulatively, it is, in my judgment, immaterial whether they do so concurrently or successively.

Lord Kilbrandon said ([1972] 3 All ER 1008 at 1016, [1973] 1 WLR 1 at 10):

> In the present case, the appellant's body was vulnerable, while he was bicycling home, to the dirt which had been deposited on it during his working hours. It would not have been if he had had a shower. If showers had been provided he would have used them. It is admittedly more probable that disease will be contracted if a shower is not taken. In these circumstances I cannot accept the argument that nevertheless it is not more probable than not that, if the duty to provide a shower had been neglected, he would not have contracted the disease. The appellant has, after all, only to satisfy the court of a probability, not to demonstrate an irrefragable chain of causation, which in a case of dermatitis, in the present state of medical knowledge, he could probably never do.

Lord Salmon said ([1972] 3 All ER 1008 at 1017, [1973] 1 WLR 1 at 11-12):

I, of course, accept that the burden rests on the appellant, to prove, on a balance of probabilities, a causal connection between his injury and the respondents' negligence. It is not necessary, however, to prove that the respondents' negligence was the only cause of injury. A factor, by itself, may not be sufficient to cause injury but if, with other factors, it materially contributes to causing injury, it is clearly a cause of injury. Everything in the present case depends on what constitutes a cause. I venture to repeat what I said in *Alphacell Ltd v Woodward* [1972] 2 All ER 475 at 489-490, [1972] AC 824 at 846: 'The nature of causation has been discussed by many eminent philosophers and also by a number of learned judges in the past. I consider, however, that what or who has caused a certain event to occur is essentially a practical question of fact which can best be answered by ordinary common sense rather than abstract metaphysical theory.' In the circumstances of the present case it seems to me unrealistic and contrary to ordinary common sense to hold that the negligence which materially increased the risk of injury did not materially contribute to causing the injury.

Then, after referring to *Bonnington Castings Ltd v Wardlaw* and *Nicholson v Atlas Steel Foundry and Engineering Co Ltd* he added ([1972] 3 All ER 1008 at 1018, [1973] 1 WLR 1 at 12-13):

I do not find the attempts to distinguish those authorities from the present case at all convincing. In the circumstances of the present case, the possibility of a distinction existing between (a) having materially increased the risk of contracting the disease, and (b) having materially contributed to causing the disease may no doubt be a fruitful source of interesting academic discussions between students of philosophy. Such a distinction is, however, far too unreal to be recognised by the common law.

The conclusion I draw from these passages is that *McGhee v National Coal Board* laid down no new principle of law whatever. On the contrary, it affirmed the principle that the onus of proving causation lies on the pursuer or plaintiff. Adopting a robust and pragmatic approach to the undisputed primary facts of the case, the majority concluded that it was a legitimate inference of fact that the defenders' negligence had materially contributed to the pursuer's injury. The decision, in my opinion, is of no greater significance than that and the attempt to extract from it some esoteric principle which in some way modifies, as a matter of law, the nature of the burden of proof of causation which a plaintiff or pursuer must discharge once he has established a relevant breach of duty is a fruitless one.

In the Court of Appeal in the instant case Sir Nicolas Browne-Wilkinson V-C, being in a minority, expressed his view on causation with understandable caution. But I am quite unable to find any fault with the following passage in his dissenting judgment ([1986] 3 All ER 801 at 834-835, [1987] QB 730 at 779):

To apply the principle in *McGhee v National Coal Board* [1972] 3 All ER 1008, [1973] 1 WLR 1 to the present case would constitute an extension of that principle. In *McGhee* there was no doubt that the pursuer's dermatitis was physically caused by brick dust; the only question was whether the continued presence of such dust on the pursuer's skin after the time when he should have been provided with a shower caused or materially contributed to the dermatitis which he contracted. There was only one possible agent which could have caused the dermatitis, viz brick dust, and there was no doubt that the dermatitis from which he suffered was caused by that brick dust. In the present case the question is different. There are a number of different agents which could have caused the RLF. Excess oxygen was one of them. The defendants failed to take reasonable precautions to prevent one of the possible causative agents (eg excess oxygen) from causing RLF. But no one can tell in this case whether excess oxygen did or did not cause or contribute to the RLF suffered by the plaintiff. The plaintiff's RLF may have been caused by some completely different agent or agents, eg hypercarbia, intraventricular haemorrhage, apnoea or patent ductus arteriosus. In addition to oxygen, each of those conditions has been implicated as a possible cause of RLF. This baby suffered from each of those conditions at various times in the first two months of his life. There is no satisfactory evidence that excess oxygen is more likely than any of those other four candidates to have caused RLF in this baby. To my mind, the occurrence of RLF following a failure to take a necessary precaution to prevent excess oxygen causing RLF provides no evidence and raises no presumption that it was excess oxygen rather than one or more of the four other possible agents which caused or contributed to RLF in this case. The position, to my mind, is wholly different from that in *McGhee*, where there was only one candidate (brick dust) which could have caused the dermatitis, and the failure to take a precaution against brick dust causing dermatitis was followed by dermatitis caused by brick dust. In such a case, I can see the common sense, if not the logic, of holding that, in the absence of any other evidence, the failure to take the precautions caused or contributed to the dermatitis. To the extent that certain members of the House of Lords decided the question on inferences from evidence or presumptions, I do not consider that the present case falls within their reasoning. A failure to take preventative measures against one out of five possible causes is no evidence as to which of those five caused injury.

Since, on this view, the appeal must, in any event, be allowed, it is not strictly necessary to decide whether it was open to the Court of Appeal to resolve one of the conflicts between the experts which the judge left unresolved and to find that the oxygen administered to Martin in consequence of the misleading PO_2 levels derived from the misplaced catheter was capable of having caused or materially contributed to his RLF. I very well understand the anxiety of the majority to avoid the necessity for ordering a retrial if that was at all possible. But, having accepted, as your Lordships and counsel have had to accept, that the primary conflict of opinion between the experts whether excessive oxygen in the first two days of life probably did cause or materially contribute to Martin's RLF cannot be resolved by reading the transcript, I doubt, with all respect, if the Court of Appeal was entitled to try to resolve the secondary conflict whether it could have done so. Where expert witnesses are radically at issue about complex technical questions within their own field and are examined and cross-examined at length about their conflicting theories, I believe that the judge's advantage in seeing them and hearing them is scarcely less important than when he has to resolve some conflict of primary fact between lay witnesses in purely mundane matters. So here, in the absence of relevant findings of fact by the judge, there was really no alternative to a retrial. At all events, the judge who retries the issue of causation should approach it with an entirely open mind uninfluenced by any view of the facts bearing on causation expressed in the Court of Appeal.

To have to order a retrial is a highly unsatisfactory result and one cannot help feeling the profoundest sympathy for Martin and his family that the outcome is once again in doubt and that this litigation may have to drag on. Many may feel that such a result serves only to highlight the shortcomings of a system in which the victim of some grievous misfortune will recover substantial compensation or none at all according to the unpredictable hazards of the forensic process. But, whether we like it or not, the law, which only Parliament can change, requires proof of fault causing damage as the basis of liability in tort. We should do society nothing but disservice if we made the forensic process still more unpredictable and hazardous by distorting the law to accommodate the exigencies of what may seem hard cases.

Leave to appeal was given by the Court of Appeal on terms that the authority should not seek an order for costs in this House or for variation of the orders for costs in the courts below. For the reasons I have indicated I would allow the appeal, set aside the order of the Court of Appeal save as to costs and order retrial of the issue whether the negligence of the authority, as found by the Court of Appeal, caused or materially contributed to the plaintiff's RLF.

Lords Fraser, Lowry, Griffiths and Ackner agreed.

In fact, the *Wilsher* case was settled before re-trial. The House of Lords has adopted a restrictive view of the decision in *McGhee* thereby arguably making the position of the plaintiff in medical negligence cases even more difficult.

Let us first look at the particular issue in *Wilsher*, namely whether it suffices for a claimant to show that the defendant materially increased (or created) the risk of injury even though it cannot positively be demonstrated that he did cause (or contribute to) the injury. The House of Lords held it did not. Lord Bridge explained the earlier decision in *McGhee,* somewhat creatively, as not being an authority for that proposition. Nor was *McGhee* an authority which resulted in the burden of proof shifting to the defendant in such cases. *Wilsher* is, of course, entirely consistent with the conventional approach to factual causation. The approach (allegedly) of the House of Lords in *McGhee* was inconsistent with 'but for' causation and, in the case of Lord Wilberforce, with the traditional view of who bears the legal burden of proof. Lord Bridge, nevertheless, thought *McGhee* was correctly decided – though any observer would have to say, for the wrong reasons – because, taking a 'robust and pragmatic approach' to the facts, the 'negligent' brickdust had contributed to the worker's dermatitis. No such inference could be made in *Wilsher* where there were a number of possible causes of the child's RLF. As Browne-Wilkinson V-C said in his dissent in the Court of Appeal: '[a] failure to take preventative measures against one out of five possible causes is not evidence as to which of those five caused the injury.'

The explanation of *McGhee* is not without its difficulties given that it is a conclusion which the experts were unable to attest to in their evidence – it was the very imponderable of the case. However, if Lord Bridge's approach is given common currency, it may in some cases assist patients faced with evidential uncertainty. Certainly, it will where a judge could take the view 'what else could have caused the injury but the defendant's negligence?' The extent to which it does allow for this will turn upon the court's willingness to 'bridge the evidentiary gap' (for a discussion of *Wilsher*, see Grubb [1988] CLJ 350 and Boon (1988) 51 MLR 508). Subsequently, the Canadian Supreme Court showed the way.

Snell v Farrell (1990) 72 DLR (4th) 289 (Supreme Court of Canada)

The plaintiff lost the sight of an eye following an operation on it performed by the defendant surgeon. The trial judge found that the defendant had acted negligently in continuing the operation after noticing a haemorrhage in the plaintiff's eye. The medical evidence was that the operation was a possible cause of the loss of sight, but the medical witnesses could not say positively that it was the cause. The trial judge held that the burden had shifted to the defendant to disprove causation, that the burden had not been discharged, and accordingly that the defendant was liable.

Sopinka J: Both the trial judge and the Court of Appeal relied on *McGhee,* which (subject to its reinterpretation in the House of Lords in *Wilsher*) purports to depart from traditional principles in the law of torts that the plaintiff must prove on a balance of probabilities that, but for the tortious conduct of the defendant, the plaintiff would not have sustained the injury complained of…

Proof of causation in medical malpractice cases is often difficult for the patient. The physician is usually in a better position to know the cause of the injury than the patient… [T]here is an argument that the burden of proof should be allocated to the defendant. In some jurisdictions, this has occurred to an extent by operation of the principle of *res ipsa loquitur: Cross on Evidence,* 6th edn (1985), at p 138. In Canada, the rule has been generally regarded as a piece of circumstantial evidence which does not shift the burden of proof: see *Interlake Tissue Mills Co v Salmon* [1949] 1 DLR 207, [1948] OR 950 (CA); *Cudney v Clements Motor Sales Ltd* (1969) 5 DLR (3d) 3, [1969] 2 OR 209 (CA); *Kirk v McLaughlin Coal & Supplies Ltd* (1967) 66 DLR (2d) 321, [1968] 1 OR 311 (CA); *Jackson v Millar* (1972) 31 DLR (3d) 263, [1973] 1 OR 399 (CA). As the rule was properly held not to be applicable in this case and no argument was directed to this issue, I will refrain from commenting further upon it…

The question that this court must decide is whether the traditional approach to causation is no longer satisfactory in that plaintiffs in malpractice cases are being deprived of compensation because they cannot prove causation where it in fact exists.

Causation is an expression of the relationship that must be found to exist between the tortious act of the wrongdoer and the injury to the victim in order to justify compensation of the latter out of the pocket of the former. Is the requirement that the plaintiff prove that the defendant's tortious conduct caused or contributed to the plaintiff's injury too onerous? Is some lesser relationship sufficient to justify compensation? I have examined the alternatives arising out of the *McGhee* case. They were that the plaintiff simply prove that the defendant created a risk that the injury which occurred would occur. Or, what amounts to the same thing, that the defendant has the burden of disproving causation. If I were convinced that defendants who have a substantial connection to the injury were escaping liability because plaintiffs cannot prove causation under currently applied principles, I would not hesitate to adopt one of these alternatives. In my opinion, however, properly applied, the principles relating to causation are adequate to the task. Adoption of either of the proposed alternatives would have the effect of compensating plaintiffs where a substantial connection between the injury and the defendant's conduct is absent. Reversing the burden of proof may be justified where two defendants negligently fire in the direction of the plaintiff and then by their tortious conduct destroy the means of proof at his disposal. In such a case it is clear that the injury was not caused by neutral conduct. It is quite a different matter to compensate a plaintiff by reversing the burden of proof for an injury that may very well be due to factors unconnected to the defendant and not the fault of anyone…

I am of the opinion that the dissatisfaction with the traditional approach to causation stems to a large extent from its too rigid application by the courts in many cases. Causation need not de determined by scientific precision. It is, as stated by Lord Salmon in *Alphacell Ltd v Woodward* [1972] 2 All ER 475 (HL), at p 490, '…essentially a practical question of fact which can best be answered by ordinary common sense rather than abstract metaphysical theory'. Furthermore, as I observed earlier, the allocation of the burden of proof is not immutable. Both the burden and the standard of proof are flexible concepts. In *Blatch v Archer* (1774) 1 Cowp 63 at 65, 98 ER 969 at p 970, Lord Mansfield stated: 'It is certainly a maxim that all evidence is to be weighed according to the proof which it was in the power of one side to have produced, and in the power of the other to have contradicted.'

In many malpractice cases, the facts lie particularly within the knowledge of the defendant. In these circumstances, very little affirmative evidence on the part of the plaintiff will justify the drawing of an inference of causation in the absence of evidence to the contrary. This has been expressed in terms of shifting the burden of proof. In *Cummings v City of Vancouver* (1911) 1 WWR 31 at p 34, 16 BCR 494 (CA), Irving JA stated:

> Stephens in his Digest (*Evidence Act*, 1896) says: 'In considering the amount of evidence necessary to shift the burden of proof, the Court has regard to the opportunities of knowledge with respect to the fact to be proved, which may be possessed by the parties respectively.'
>
> *Hollis v Young* (1909) 1 KB 629, illustrates the rule that very little affirmative evidence will be sufficient where the facts lie almost entirely within the knowledge of the other side.

In *Dunlop Holdings Ltd's Application* [1979] RPC 523 (CA) at p 544, Buckley LJ affirmed this principle in the following terms:

> Where the relevant facts are peculiarly within the knowledge of one party, it is perhaps relevant to have in mind the rule as stated in Stephens' Digest, which is cited at page 86 of *Cross on Evidence* [3rd edn]:
>
> > In considering the amount of evidence necessary to shift the burden of proof, the court has regard to the opportunities of knowledge with respect to the facts to be proved which may be possessed by the parties respectively.
> >
> > 'This does not mean,' *Sir Rupert continues,* 'that the peculiar means of knowledge of one of the parties relieves the other of the burden of adducing some evidence with regard to the facts in question, although very slight evidence will often suffice.' *(Emphasis added.)*

See also *Diamond v BC Thoroughbred Breeders' Society* (1965) 52 DLR (2d) 146 at p 158, 52 WWR 385 (BCSC); *Pleet v Canadian Northern Quebec R Co* (1921) 64 DLR 316 at pp 319-20, 50 OLR 223, 26 CRC 227 (CA), and *Guaranty Trust Co of Canada v Mall Medical Group* (1969) 4 DLR (3d) 1 at p 7, [1969] SCR 541.

These references speak of the shifting of the secondary or evidential burden of proof or the burden of adducing evidence. I find it preferable to explain the process without using the term secondary or evidential burden. It is not strictly accurate to speak of the burden shifting to the defendant when what is meant is that evidence adduced by the plaintiff may result in an inference being drawn adverse to the defendant. Whether an inference is or is not drawn is a matter of weighing evidence. The defendant runs the risk of an adverse inference in the absence of evidence to the contrary. This is sometimes referred to as imposing on the defendant a provisional or tactical burden: see Cross , *op cit,* at p 129. In my opinion, this is not a true burden of proof, and use of an additional label to describe what is an ordinary step in the fact-finding process is unwarranted.

The legal or ultimate burden remains with the plaintiff, but in the absence of evidence to the contrary adduced by the defendant, an inference of causation may be drawn, although positive or scientific proof of causation has not been adduced. If some evidence to the contrary is adduced by the defendant, the trial judge is entitled to take account of Lord Mansfield's famous precept. This is, I believe, what Lord Bridge had in mind in *Wilsher* when he referred to a 'robust and pragmatic approach to the ... facts' (p 569).

It is not, therefore, essential that the medical experts provide a firm opinion supporting the plaintiff's theory of causation. Medical experts ordinarily determine causation in terms of certainties whereas a lesser standard is demanded by the law. As pointed out in D W Louisell, *Medical Malpractice*, vol 3 (by Charles Kramer, New York: Matthew Bender, 1977-90), at pp 25-27, the phrase 'in your opinion with a reasonable degree of medical certainty', which is the standard form of question to a medical expert, is often misunderstood. The author explains that:

> Many doctors do not understand the phrase... as they usually deal in 'certainties' that are 100% sure, whereas 'reasonable' certainties which the law requires need only be more probably so, *ie,* 51%...

The issue, then, in this case is whether the trial judge drew an inference that the appellant's negligence caused or contributed to the respondent's injury, or whether, applying the above principles, he would or ought to have drawn such an inference...

The appellant [in this case] was present during the operation and was in a better position to observe what occurred. Furthermore, he was able to interpret from a medical standpoint what he saw. In addition, by continuing the operation which has been found to constitute negligence, he made it impossible for the respondent or anyone else to detect the bleeding which is alleged to have caused the injury. In these circumstances, it was open to the trial judge to draw the inference that the injury was caused by the retro-bulbar bleeding. There was no evidence to rebut this inference. The fact that testing the eye for hardness did not disclose bleeding is insufficient for this purpose. If there was any rebutting evidence, it was weak, and it was open to the trial judge to find causation, applying the principles to which I have referred.

I am confident that had the trial judge not stated that 'I cannot go beyond this since neither doctor did and I should not speculate,' he would have drawn the necessary inference. In stating the above, he failed to appreciate that it is not essential to have a positive medical opinion to support a finding of causation. Furthermore, it is not speculation but the application of common sense to draw such an inference where, as here, the circumstances, other than a positive medical opinion, permit.

The leading Canadian text states that *Snell* has had 'a significant impact on trial level decisions' leading courts to infer causation without the need for 'scientific precision' in the evidence (Picard and Robertson, *Legal Liability of Doctors and Hospitals in Canada* (3rd edn, 1996) p 225). In England, the impact of *Wilsher* has not been so marked (but note the approach of Simon Brown LJ (dissenting) in *Bolitho v City and Hackney HA* (1992) 13 BMLR 111 (CA) but criticised by Lord Browne-Wilkinson on appeal: [1997] 4 All ER 771 at 777).

The discussion of causation in *Wilsher* also draws out a further point. The defendant may not be *the* cause of the patient's injury but he may be a *contributory* cause, ie he may have 'materially contributed' to it (*Bonnington* and *McGhee*). In cases of cumulative causation, whether concurrent or sequential, the doctor will 'materially contribute' to the patient's injury if it would not have occurred without his negligence. It does not matter that it also could not have occurred without another event, providing it is not the case that it would have happened anyway. It is important to notice that 'material contribution' as understood in *Bonnington*, and *Wilsher* applying it, is not established where there are two independent causes (only one of which is the defendant's negligence) and each would have brought about the injury. Causation could only be established in this instance as an exception to the 'but for' test.

Consequently, a summary of the law's general approach to factual causation looks like this (see *Tahir v Haringey HA* [1998] Lloyd's Rep Med 104 (CA)):

1. The burden of proving causation was upon the plaintiff.
2. Causation is a question of past fact, to be decided on a balance of probabilities: see *Mallett v McMonagle* [1970] AC 166.
3. If he proves that the negligence was the sole cause, or a substantial cause, or that it materially contributed to the damage, he will succeed in full: see *Bonnington Castings v Wardlaw* [1956] AC 613 and *McGhee v National Coal Board* [1973] WLR 1.
4. If he fails to cross this threshold then he fails to recover any damages: see *Barnett v Chelsea & Kensington Hospital Management Committee* [1969] 1 QB 428.
    Thus, the plaintiff must establish one of the following:
5. that 'but for' the negligence he would not have suffered *any* injury (plaintiff recovers for all his injuries); or
6. that 'but for' the negligence he would not have suffered *an identifiable part* (X) or *particular aggravation* (Y) of the injuries (plaintiff recovers for X and Y respectively); or

7. that the negligence *materially contributed* to the whole injury (Z) or an identifiable part (X) or particular aggravation (Y) of the injuries (plaintiff recovers for Z, X and Y respectively).

The latter proposition, based upon *Bonnington Castings v Wardlaw* [1956] AC 613, is probably only a refinement of the propositions in 1 and 2, addressing the situation where the defendant's negligence is only one of a number of cumulatively operative factors that effect the injury, rather than being the sole cause.

(b) Departing from the 'but for' test

Exceptionally, a defendant may be held to have caused injury even though it would have happened anyway. The classic illustration of where the courts, taking a commonsense approach, determined causation to be established even where the 'but for' test is not satisfied is in cases of sufficient independent concurrent causes. In *Chappel v Hart, (supra)* Hayne J (in his dissent) gave the standard illustration.

> **Hayne J:** 116. The 'but for' test is, however, neither a comprehensive nor exclusive test of causation. To take but one example where its application is not conclusive, it does not readily resolve the case where two causes are at work and either of them, alone, would have been sufficient to bring about the result. If two separate fires, negligently lit by separate persons, merge to destroy the plaintiff's home, and each fire would have been sufficient in itself to cause the damage, is each of the fire lighters liable? If the 'but for' test were to be applied to each defendant's conduct separately than neither would be liable. And what if neither fire, by itself, would have destroyed the plaintiff's house?

That causation is established here is in part based upon the intuitive reaction that, if one source is not causative, neither is, since both can claim the event would have occurred regardless of their own involvement – the event is 'over-determined'. Attempts to explain the intuitive response have, in the past, led tort scholars to propound an alternative to the 'but for' test, the 'NESS (necessary element in a sufficient set) test' (R Wright 'Causation in Tort Law' (1985) 73, Cal LR 1735, see also T Honoré 'Necessary and Sufficient Conditions in Tort Law' in D G Owen (ed) *Philosophical Foundations of Tort Law* (1995) p 363). The 'NESS test' is as follows:

> a particular condition was a cause of (contributed to) a specific result if and only if it was a necessary element of a set of antecedent actual conditions that was sufficient for the occurrence of the result.

(R Wright 'Causation, Responsibility, Risk, Probability, Naked Statistics and Proof: Pruning the Bramble Bush by Clarifying the Concepts' (1988) 73 Iowa L Rev 1001 at 1019).

Applying this to the 'two fires' example, each is a necessary element of a sufficient set to produce the damage in the actual circumstances: there is a duplication of causes. English law has never articulated the 'NESS test' though it has its academic supporters (see Honoré *(op cit)* and M Staunch 'Causation, Risk and Loss of Chance in Medical Negligence' (1997) 17 OJLS 205). How could the 'NESS test' help in medical negligence cases? 'Not much' is the answer. It will not assist where the evidence establishes that the 'innocent set' injured the patient, for example, the underlying illness and the 'guilty set' had no effect (*Barnet, supra*). Equally, it will have no impact where the evidential uncertainty cannot link the 'guilty set' to the injury (*Wilsher*). In other words, where this is no 'over determination' of causation. Staunch *(op cit)* gives an example where it might be important (at 215, note 35):

... suppose that a patient is suffering from a given disease that if left untreated will injure him. Treatment is available, but to have any effect must be administered simultaneously by Doctor X and Doctor Y. In the event neither X nor Y attend the patient who suffers the injury. On the 'but for' test, both X and Y could claim that their failure to attend made no difference since, had only either one of them attended, the treatment would have failed anyway. The NESS test, however, resolves this problem in to a case of duplicative causation. There are two (overlapping) causal sets simultaneously operating: one contains the illness plus the fact of non-treatment by X, the other the illness plus non-treatment by Y. It then follows, on this test, that X and Y are each a cause of the harm.

The House of Lords has, however, sanctioned a departure from the 'but for' test in the *Bolitho* case. There, the court was faced with the argument that the doctor's negligent failure to attend the patient would have made no difference because the doctor would not have intubated the child and thereby saved him from his injury (from which he subsequently died). Thus, the defendant argued, 'but for' my negligent (non-attendance), the patient would still have suffered his injuries. The House of Lords changed the law.

Bolitho v City and Hackney Health Authority [1997] 4 All ER 771 (HL)

Lord Browne-Wilkinson: Negligence having been established, the question of causation had to be decided: would the cardiac arrest have been avoided if Dr Horn or some other suitable deputy had attended as they should have done. By the end of the trial it was common ground, first, that intubation so as to provide an airway in any event would have ensured that the respiratory failure which occurred did not lead to cardiac arrest and, second, that such intubation would have had to be carried out, if at all, before the final catastrophic episode.

The judge identified the questions he had to answer as follows:

[Mr Owen, for the defendants] submitted, therefore, that (if once it was held that Dr Horn was negligent in failing to attend at either 12.40 or 2 o'clock) the sole issue was whether Patrick would on one or other of these occasions have been intubated. In submitting that on this aspect of the case the issue was what would Dr Horn or another competent doctor sent in her place have done had they attended, Mr Owen was, I think, accepting that the real question was what would Dr Horn or that other doctor have done, *or what should they have done*. As it seems to me, if Dr Horn would have intubated, then the plaintiff succeeds, whether or not that is a course which all reasonably competent practitioners would have followed. If, however, Dr Horn would not have intubated, then the plaintiff can only succeed if such failure was contrary to accepted medical practice (I am not purporting to consider the legal tests in detail, and merely using shorthand at this stage)... Common to both sides is the recognition that I must decide whether Dr Horn would have intubated (or made preparations for intubation) and, *even if she would not, whether such a failure on her part would have been contrary to accepted practice in the profession.* (My emphasis).

As to the first of those issues, Dr Horn's evidence was that, had she come to see Patrick at 2 pm, she would not have arranged for him to be intubated. The judge held that the views of Dr Heaf and Dr Dinwiddie, though diametrically opposed, both represented a responsible body of professional opinion espoused by distinguished and truthful experts. Therefore, he held, Dr Horn, if she had attended and not intubated, would have come up to a proper level of skill and competence, ie the standard represented by Dr Dinwiddie's views. Accordingly, he held that it had not been proved that the admitted breach of duty by the defendants had caused the catastrophe which occurred to Patrick...

Before your Lordships, Mr Brennan QC, for the appellant, submitted, first, that the *Bolam* test has no application in deciding questions of causation and, secondly, that the judge misdirected himself by treating it as being so relevant. This argument, which was raised for the first time by amendment to the notice of appeal in the Court of Appeal, commended itself to Simon Brown LJ and was the basis on which he dissented. I have no doubt that, in the generality of cases, the proposition of law is correct but equally have no doubt that the judge in the circumstances of the present case was not guilty of any self-misdirection.

Where, as in the present case, a breach of duty of care is proved or admitted, the burden still lies on the plaintiff to prove that such breach caused the injury suffered (see *Bonnington Castings Ltd v Wardlaw* [1956] 1 All ER 615, [1956] AC 613 and *Wilsher v Essex Area Health Authority* [1988] 1 All ER 871, [1988] AC 1074. In all cases, the primary question is one of fact: did the wrongful act cause the injury? But in cases where the breach of duty consists of an omission to do an act which ought to be done (eg the failure by a doctor to attend) that factual inquiry is, by definition, in the realms of hypothesis. The question is what would have happened if an event which by definition did not occur, had occurred. In a case of non-attendance by a doctor, there may be cases in which there is doubt as to which doctor would have attended if the duty had been fulfilled. But in this case there was no doubt: if the duty had been carried out it would have either been Dr Horn or Dr Rodger, the only two doctors at St Bartholomew's who had responsibility for Patrick and were on duty. Therefore in the present case, the first relevant question is 'what would Dr Horn or Dr Rodger have done if they had attended?' As to Dr Horn, the judge accepted her evidence that she would not have intubated. By inference, although not expressly, the judge must have accepted that Dr Rodger also would not have intubated: as a senior house officer she would not have intubated without the approval of her senior registrar, Dr Horn.

Therefore the *Bolam* test had no part to play in determining the first question, viz what would have happened? Nor can I see any circumstances in which the *Bolam* could be relevant to such a question.

However, in the present case, the answer to the question 'what would have happened?' is not determinative of the issue of causation. At the trial the defendants accepted that if the professional standard of care required any doctor who attended to intubate Patrick, Patrick's claim must succeed. Dr Horn could not escape liability by proving that she would have failed to take the course which any competent doctor would have adopted. A defendant cannot escape liability by saying that the damage would have occurred in any event because he would have committed some other breach of duty thereafter. I have no doubt that this concession was rightly made by the defendants. But there is some difficulty in analysing why it was correct. I adopt the analysis of Hobhouse LJ in *Joyce v Merton Sutton and Wandsworth Health Authority* (1996) 27 BMLR 124. In commenting on the decision of the Court of Appeal in the present case, he said (at 156):

> Thus, a plaintiff can discharge the burden of proof on causation by satisfying the court *either* that the relevant person would in fact have taken the requisite action (although she would not have been at fault if she had not) *or* that the proper discharge of the relevant person's duty towards the plaintiff required that she take that action. The former alternative calls for no explanation since it is simply the factual proof of the causative effect of the original fault. The latter is slightly more sophisticated: it involves the factual situation that the original fault did not itself cause the injury but that this was because there would have been some further fault on the part of the defendants; the plaintiff proves his case by proving that his injuries would have been avoided if proper care had continued to be taken. In *Bolitho* the plaintiff had to prove that the continuing exercise of proper care would have resulted in his being intubated. (Hobhouse LJ's emphasis.)

> There were, therefore, two questions for the judge to decide on causation: (1) What would Dr Horn have done, or authorised to be done, if she had attended Patrick? and (2) if she would not have intubated, would that have been negligent? The *Bolam* test has no relevance to the first of those questions but is central to the second.

> There can be no doubt that, as the majority of the Court of Appeal held, the judge directed himself correctly in accordance with that approach. The passages from his judgment which I have quoted (and in particular those that I have emphasised) demonstrate this. The dissenting judgment of Simon Brown LJ in the Court of Appeal is based on a misreading of the judge's judgment. He treats the judge as having only asked himself one question, namely the second question. To the extent that Simon Brown LJ noticed the first question – would Dr Horn have intubated? – he said that the judge was wrong to accept Dr Horn's evidence that she would not have intubated. In my judgment, it was for the judge to assess the truth of her evidence on this issue.

> Accordingly, the judge asked himself the right questions and answered them on the right basis…

The House of Lords approved the decision of the Court of Appeal in *Bolitho* and subsequently in *Joyce v Merton Sutton and Wandsworth HA* (1995) 27 BMLR 124 (discussed (1996) 4 Med L Rev 86 (AG)). Where the defendant's negligence consisted of an omission to act (ie a failure of human intervention to prevent harm), the plaintiff may establish causation on one of two bases. By proving, on a balance of probabilities, that:

(i) the defendant would have intervened to prevent the injury; or

(ii) that if she would not have, it would have been negligent not to do so.

The first is, of course, traditional 'but for' causation. The plaintiff failed on this basis. The judge had found, as a fact, that the doctor(s) would not have intubated the plaintiff if they had not been negligent, ie attended the plaintiff. Lord Browne-Wilkinson said that the judges on appeal could not disturb this factual finding and he criticised Simon Brown LJ in the Court of Appeal who had done so. Secondly, the plaintiff failed on the second basis because even applying 'new *Bolam*', the Law Lords held that a reasonable doctor might not intubate given the risks it entailed. It was 'plainly' not an exceptional case. Hence, the defendants' negligence had not caused the plaintiff's injuries from which he subsequently died.

The House of Lords' approach to causation substitutes for the need to establish a causal link between the defendant's negligence and the plaintiff's injuries (basis (i) above), an alternative of establishing a link between a breach of duty which never occurred and the injuries (basis (ii) above).

That *Bolitho* departs from the 'but for' test, is not unique: there are, as we have seen, other illustrations. The 'but for' test is, after all, really an exclusionary rule seeking to identify in general cases where responsibility does *not* lie with a particular person's fault. Intuitively, as a matter of communal common sense, causal links may be forged notwithstanding a failure to establish a 'but for' cause. But to do so, the law must articulate its 'sense of justice' and provide an alternative to the coherent 'but for' test.

Such justifications are difficult enough to articulate where multiple *events* which actually occur seem instinctively to contribute to an injury. In *Bolitho*, the 'event' was hypothetical – the negligence which did not, and never would, occur (failure to intubate). How then did Lord Browne-Wilkinson explain the shift? 'Gut reaction' would be the best description. A sense of not allowing the defendant to 'get away with it'. What Lord Browne-Wilkinson actually said was as follows:

> A defendant cannot escape liability by saying that the damage would have occurred in any event because he would have committed some other breach of duty thereafter.

He recognised that there was 'some difficulty in analysing why it is correct' and there is. He offered no explanation other than to adopt a statement by Hobhouse LJ in the earlier case of *Joyce (supra,* at 156):

> [T]he original fault did not itself cause the injury but this was because there would have been some further fault on the part of the defendants; the plaintiff proves his case by proving that his injuries would have been avoided if proper care had continued to be taken. In *Bolitho* the plaintiff had to prove that the continuing exercise of proper care would have resulted in his being intubated.

The plaintiff can rely upon the defendant's negligence which never occurred, the continuing care that was only hypothetical and link his injuries to the fault that never happened. At least, on the face of it, it must be the hypothetical negligence of the defendant or those for whom he is responsible and not strangers which will be attributed to him. Hence *Bolitho* would not apply where a GP negligently fails to refer a patient to a hospital where it is established further the patient would through the hospital's negligence have not been treated (or treated in time). The GP is not saddled with the hypothetical negligence of the hospital – there is no intuitional imperative here; he is not 'getting away with it' by relying on the hospital's (albeit hypothetical) inadequacies. The problem is the patient is left without a claim since the hospital cannot possibly be liable for a patient it never saw.

Can *Bolitho* be explained on any principled basis? Could it, for example, be justified by adoption of NESS? Was the defendant's fault (in not attending) a necessary element of a set of conditions which are together sufficient to bring about the plaintiff's injury? Where treatment (intubation) should be given – as the *Bolitho* approach contemplates because not to do so would be negligent – the injury only occurs because no one attends the plaintiff and thus fails to do what they should do: together these constitute the sufficient set to bring about the injury. Are both the defendant's fault and the absence of treatment necessary elements of this set? It is doubtful. The negligence (albeit hypothetical) of the defendant is itself sufficient to cause the plaintiff's injuries: the actual negligence of the defendant is not, it would seem, a necessary part of that set or any actually operating set. In any event, this approach – admittedly an exercise in *ex post facto* rationalisation – would also capture the situation where the hypothetical negligence is of a third party for whom the defendant is not responsible.

The better construction of the facts in *Bolitho* may be that the defendant's negligence created a risk of injury to the plaintiff. By not attending, the doctor created a risk that she, or another doctor, might not take the necessary action to prevent the injuries, ie intubation. Seen in this way, *Bolitho* is a case where the defendant merely increased the risk of injury to the plaintiff.

In reality, the doctor's negligence in not attending was an illustration of 'pre-emptive causation' which does not fall within NESS. Staunch (*op cit*, p 210) explains:

> Pre-emptive causation, by contrast, occurs when, through coming about first in time, one causal set 'trumps' another, potential set lurking in the background. The causal potency of the latter is frustrated for, as Wright states, 'a necessary condition for the sufficiency of any set of actual antecedent conditions is that the injury not have occurred already as a result of other actual conditions outside the set' (R Wright 'Causation in Tort Law' (1985) 73 Cal LR 1795). An example offered by Wright of causal pre-emption is where D shoots and kills P as he is about to drink from a cup poisoned by C. Here, the NESS test makes it clear that it is D's act alone which is the cause of P's death (again, compare the unsatisfactory result produced by the 'but for' test, which would exculpate both C and D). C's act, on the other hand, does not satisfy the NESS test: poison does not feature in the list of necessary elements in any operative set of conditions sufficient for P's death; instead it is a necessary part of a potential but, as things turn out, inoperative, causal set...

Likewise, *mutatis mutandis*, the negligence in not intubating does not feature as part of a 'sufficient set' only a 'potential but, as things turn out, inoperative, causal set'.

(c) Loss of a chance

The House of Lords had another opportunity to develop the law in a way more favourable to the plaintiff in *Hotson v East Berkshire AHA* [1987] AC 750, [1987] 2 All ER 909. In that case the plaintiff was unable to establish, on a balance of probabilities, that the defendants' failure to treat him promptly in breach of duty would have alleviated the injuries he suffered from as a result of falling out of a tree. The trial judge, Simon Brown J, found that there had always been a 75% chance that the injuries would have resulted in his disabilities in any event, but that due to the defendants' carelessness, this had become a 100% certainty. Therefore, even though the plaintiff could not show that 'but for' the defendants' carelessness he would be injury-free, he could establish that he had lost a 25% chance of avoiding his eventually permanent injuries. The issue in *Hotson* was whether this could found a claim for damages in the tort of negligence. The trial judge ([1985] 3 All ER 167) and the Court of Appeal ([1987] 1 All ER 210) held that it could.

Hotson v East Berkshire AHA [1987] AC 750, [1987] 2 All ER 909 (HL)

Lord Bridge: My Lords, the respondent plaintiff is now 23 years of age. On 26 April 1977, as a schoolboy of 13, whilst playing in the school lunch hour he climbed a tree to which a rope was attached, lost his hold on the rope and fell some 12 feet to the ground. He sustained an acute traumatic fracture of the left femoral epiphysis. Within hours he was taken to St Luke's Hospital, Maidenhead, for which the appellant health authority (the authority) was responsible. Members of the hospital staff examined him, but failed to diagnose the injury and he was sent home. For five days he was in severe pain. On 1 May 1977 he was taken to the hospital once more and this time X-rays of his hip yielded the correct diagnosis. He was put on immediate traction, treated as an emergency case and transferred to the Heatherwood Hospital where, on the following day, he was operated on by manipulation and reduction of the fracture and pinning of the joint. In the event the plaintiff suffered an avascular necrosis of the epiphysis. The femoral epiphysis is a layer of cartilage separating the bony head from the bony neck of the femur in a growing body. Avascular necrosis results from a failure of the blood supply to the epiphysis and causes deformity in the maturing head of the femur. This in turn involves a greater or lesser degree of disability of the hip joint with a virtual certainty that it will in due course be aggravated by osteoarthritis developing within the joint.

The plaintiff sued the authority, who admitted negligence in failing to diagnose the injury on 26 April 1977. Simon Brown J, in a judgment delivered on 15 March 1985, sub nom *Hotson v Fitzgerald* [1985] 3 All ER 167, [1985] 1 WLR 1036, awarded £150 damages for the pain suffered by the plaintiff from 26 April to 1 May 1977 which he would have been spared by prompt diagnosis and treatment. This element of the damages is not in dispute. The authority denied liability for any other element of damages. The judge expressed his findings of fact as follows ([1985] 3 All ER 167 at 171, [1985] 1 WLR 1036 at 1040-1041):

1. Even had the defendants correctly diagnosed and treated the plaintiff on 26 April there is a high probability, which I assess as a 75% risk, that the plaintiff's injury would have followed the same course as it in fact has, ie he would have developed avascular necrosis of the whole femoral head with all the same adverse consequences as have already ensued and with all the same adverse future prospects. 2. That 75% risk was translated by the defendants' delay in diagnosis denied the plaintiff the 25% chance that, given immediate treatment, avascular necrosis would not have developed. 3. Had avascular necrosis not developed, the plaintiff would have made a very full recovery. 4. The reason why the delay sealed the plaintiff's fate was because it followed the pressure caused by haemarthorisis (the bleeding of ruptured blood vessels into the joint) to compress and thus block the intact but distorted remaining vessels with the result that even had the fall left sufficient vessels to keep the epiphysis alive (which, as finding no 1 makes plain, I think possible but improbable) such vessels would have become occluded and ineffective for this purpose.

On the basis of these findings he held, as a matter of law, that the plaintiff was entitled to damages for the loss of 25% chance that, if the injury had been promptly diagnosed and treated, it would not have resulted in avascular necrosis of the epiphysis and the plaintiff would have made a very nearly full recovery. He proceeded to assess the damages attributable to the consequences of the avascular necrosis at £46,000. Discounting this by 75%, he awarded the plaintiff £11,500 for the lost chance of recovery. The authority's appeal against this element in the award of damages was dismissed by the Court of Appeal (Sir John Donaldson MR, Dillon and Croom-Johnson LJJ)([1987] 1 All ER 210, [1987] 2 WLR 287). The authority now appeal by leave of your Lordships' House...

In analysing the issue of law arising from his findings the judge said ([1985] 3 All ER 167 at 175, [1985] 1 WLR 1036 at 1043-1044):

In the end the problem comes down to one of classification. Is this on true analysis a case where the plaintiff is concerned to establish causative negligence or is it rather a case where the real question is the proper quantum of damage? Clearly the case hovers near the border. Its proper solution in my judgment depends on categorising it correctly between the two. If the issue is one of causation then the defendants succeed since the plaintiff will have failed to prove his claim on the balance of probabilities. He will be lacking an essential ingredient of his cause of action. If, however, the issue is one of quantification then the plaintiff succeeds because it is trite law that the quantum of a recognised head of damage must be evaluated according to the chances of the loss occurring.

He reached the conclusion that the question was one of quantification and thus arrived at his award to the plaintiff of one quarter of the damages appropriate to compensate him for the consequence of the avascular necrosis.

It is here, with respect, that I part company with the judge. The plaintiff's claim was for damages for physical injury and consequential loss alleged to have been caused by the authority's breach of their duty of care. In some cases, perhaps particularly medical negligence cases, causation may be so shrouded in mystery that the court can only measure statistical chances. But that was not so here. On the evidence there was a clear conflict as to what had caused the avascular necrosis. The authority's evidence was that the sole cause was the original traumatic injury to the hip. The plaintiff's evidence, at its highest, was that the delay in treatment was a material contributory cause. This was a conflict, like any other about some relevant past event, which the judge could not avoid resolving on a balance of probabilities. Unless the plaintiff proved on a balance of probabilities that the delayed treatment was at least a material contributory cause of the avascular necrosis he failed on the issue of causation and no question of quantification could arise. But the judge's findings of fact, as stated in the numbered paragraphs (1) and (4) which I have set out earlier in this opinion, are unmistakably to the effect that on a balance of probabilities the injury caused by the plaintiff's fall left insufficient blood vessels intact to keep the epiphysis alive. This amounts to a finding of fact that the fall was the sole cause of the avascular necrosis.

The upshot is that the appeal must be allowed on the narrow ground that the plaintiff failed to establish a cause of action in respect of the avascular necrosis and its consequences. Your Lordships were invited to approach the appeal more broadly and to decide whether, in a claim for damages for personal injury, it can ever be appropriate, where the cause of the injury is unascertainable and all the plaintiff can show is a statistical chance which is less than even that, but for the defendant's breach of duty, he would not have suffered the injury, to award him a proportionate fraction of the full damages appropriate to compensate for the injury as the measure of damages for the lost chance.

There is a superficially attractive analogy between the principle applied in such cases as *Chaplin v Hicks* [1911] 2 KB 786, [1911-13] All ER Rep 224 (award of damages for breach of contract assessed by reference to the lost chance of securing valuable employment if the contract had been performed) and *Kitchen v Royal Air Forces Association* [1958] 2 All ER 241, [1958] 1 WLR 563 (damages for solicitors' negligence assessed by reference to the lost chance of prosecuting a successful civil action) and the principle of awarding damages for the lost chance of avoiding personal injury or, in medical negligence cases, for the lost chance of a better medical result which might have been achieved by prompt diagnosis and correct treatment. I think there are formidable difficulties in the way of accepting the analogy. But I do not see this appeal as a suitable occasion for reaching a settled conclusion as to whether the analogy can ever be applied.

As I have said, there was in this case an inescapable issue of causation first to be resolved. But if the plaintiff had proved on a balance of probabilities that the authority's negligent failure to diagnose and treat his injury promptly had materially contributed to the development of avascular necrosis, I know of no principle of English law which would have entitled the authority to a discount from the full measure of damage to reflect the chance that, even given prompt treatment, avascular necrosis might still have developed. The decisions of this House in *Bonnington Castings Ltd v Wardlow* [1956] 1 All ER 615, [1956] AC 613 and *McGhee v National Coal Board* [1972] 3 All ER 1008, [1973] 1 WLR 1 give no support to such a view.

I would allow the appeal.

As you will see, Lord Bridge allowed the appeal on a 'narrow ground'. Lords Brandon, Mackay, Ackner and Goff agreed with this conclusion.

Lord Bridge left open the issue of whether the plaintiff could have recovered had he established a lost chance of recovery. Lord Mackay in his speech examined this issue in some depth though, again, without reaching any conclusion.

Lord Mackay: I consider that it would be unwise in the present case to lay it down as a rule that a plaintiff could never succeed by proving loss of a chance in a medical negligence case. In *McGhee v National Coal Board* [1972] 3 All ER 1008, [1973] 1 WLR 1 this House held that where it was proved that the failure to provide washing facilities for the pursuer at the end of his shift had materially increased the risk that he would contract dermatitis it was proper to hold that the failure to provide such facilities was a cause to a material extent of his contracting dermatitis and thus entitled him to damages from his employers for their negligent failure measured by his loss resulting from dermatitis. Material increase of the risk of contraction of dermatitis is equivalent to material decrease in the chance of escaping dermatitis. Although no precise figures could be given in that case for the purpose of illustration and comparison with this case one might, for example, say that it was established that of 100 people working under the same conditions as the pursuer and without facilities for washing at the end of their shift 70 contracted dermatitis: of 100 working in the same conditions as the pursuer when washing facilities were provided for them at the end of the shift 30 contracted dermatitis. Assuming nothing more were known about the matter than that, the decision of this House may be taken as holding that in the circumstances of that case it was reasonable to infer that there was a relationship between contraction of dermatitis in these conditions and the absence of washing facilities was likely to have made a material contribution to the causation of the dermatitis. Although neither party in the present appeal placed particular reliance on the decision in *McGhee* since it was recognised that *McGhee* is far removed on its facts from the circumstances of the present appeal your Lordships were also informed that cases are likely soon to come before the House in which the decision in *McGhee* your Lordships cannot affirm the proposition that in no circumstances can evidence of loss of a chance resulting from the breach of a duty of care found a successful claim of damages, although there was no suggestion that the House regarded such a chance as an asset in any sense.

By agreement of the parties we were supplied with a list of American authorities relevant to the question arising in this appeal, although they were not examined in detail. Of the cases referred to, the one that I have found most interesting and instructive is *Herskovits v Group Health Cooperative of Puget Sound* 664 P 2d 474 (1983), a decision of the Supreme Court of Washington en banc. In this case the claim arose in respect of Mr Herskovits's death. He was seen at Group Health Hospital at a time when he was suffering from a tumour but his was not diagnosed on first examination. The medical evidence available suggested that at that stage, assuming the tumour was a stage 1 tumour, the chance of survival for more than five years was 30%. When he was treated later the tumour was a stage 2 tumour and the chance of surviving more than five years was 25%. The defendant moved for summary judgment on the basis that, taking the most favourable view of the evidence that was possible, the case could not succeed. The Superior Court was delivered by Dore J. Early in his judgment he read from the American Law Institute's Restatement of the Law, Second, Torts 2d (1965) vol 2, s 323, which is in these terms:

> One who undertakes, gratuitously or for consideration, to render services to another which he should recognize as necessary for the protection of the other's person or things, is subject to liability to the other for physical harm resulting from his failure to exercise reasonable care to perform his undertaking, if (a) his failure to exercise such care increases the risk of such harm…

After noting that the Supreme Court of Washington had not faced the issue of whether, under this paragraph, proof that the defendant's conduct had increased the risk of death by decreasing the chances of survival was sufficient to take the issue of proximate cause to the jury he said (664 2d 474 at 476):

> Some courts in other jurisdictions have allowed the proximate cause issue to go to the jury on this type of proof … These courts emphasized the fact that defendants' conduct deprived the decedent of a 'significant' chance to survive or recover, rather than requiring proof that with absolute certainty the defendants' conduct caused the physical injury. The underlying reason is that it is not for the wrongdoer, who put the possibility of recovery beyond realization, to say afterward that the result was inevitable… Other jurisdictions have rejected this approach, generally holding that unless the plaintiff is able to show that it was *more likely than not* that the harm was caused by the defendants' negligence, proof of a decreased chance of survival is not enough to take the proximate cause question to the jury… These courts have concluded that the defendant should not be liable where the decedent more than likely would have died anyway. (Dore J's emphasis.)

To the question whether the plaintiff should be allowed, in the case before him, to proceed to a jury he returned an affirmative answer, and gave as the reason (at 477):

> To decide otherwise would be a blanket release from liability for doctors and hospitals any time there was less than a 50 percent chance of survival, regardless of how flagrant the negligence.

In support of this reasoning he referred to *Hamil v Bashline* 481 Pa 256 (1978), a decision of the Pennsylvania Supreme Court, and said:

> The *Hamil* court distinguished the facts of the case from the general tort case in which a plaintiff alleges that a defendant's act or omission set in motion a force which resulted in harm. In the typical tort case, the 'but for' test, requiring proof that damages or death probably would not have occurred 'but for' the negligent conduct of the defendant, is appropriate. In *Hamil* and the instant case, however, the defendant's act or omission failed in a *duty* to protect against harm from *another source*. Thus, as the *Hamil* court noted, the fact finder is put in the position of having to consider not only what *did* occur, but also what *might* have occurred. (Dore J's emphasis).

He goes on to quote from *Hamil's* case 481 Pa 256 at 271:

> Such cases by their very nature elude the degree of certainty one would prefer and upon which the law normally insists before a person may be held liable. Nevertheless, in order than an actor is not completely insulated because of uncertainties as to the consequence of his negligent conduct, Section 323(a) [of the Restatement of the Law, Second, Torts 2d] tacitly acknowledges that difficulty and permits the issue to go to the jury upon a less than normal threshold of proof.

He goes on to refer to another decision, namely *Hicks v US* 368 F 2d 626 at 632 (1966), as containing a succinct statement of the relevant doctrine, which he quotes (664 P 2d 474 at 478):

> Rarely is it possible to demonstrate to an absolute certainty what would have happened in circumstances that the wrongdoer did not allow to come to pass. The law does not in the existing circumstances require the plaintiff to show to a *certainty* that the patient would have lived had she been hospitalized and operated on promptly. (Judge Sobeloff's emphasis).

He refers also to a general observation in the Supreme Court of the United States dealing with a contention similar to that argued before him by the doctors and the hospital. In *Lavender v Kurn* 327 US at 653 (1946) the Supreme Court said:

> It is no answer to say that the jury's verdict involved speculation and conjecture. Whenever facts are in dispute or the evidence is such that fair-minded men may draw different inferences, a measure of speculation and conjecture is required on the part of those whose duty it is to settle the dispute by choosing what seems to them to be the most reasonable inference.

He therefore concluded that the evidence available which showed at maximum a reduction in the 39% chance of five years' survival to a 25% chance of five years' survival was sufficient to allow the case to go to the jury on the basis that the jury would be entitled to infer from that evidence that the delay in treatment was a proximate cause of the decedent's death (see 664 P 2d 474 at 479). He pointed out, however, that causing reduction of the opportunity to recover (also described as a loss of chance) by one's negligence did not necessitate a total recovery against the negligent party for all damages caused by the victim's death. He held that damages should be awarded to the injured party and his family based only on damages caused directly by premature death, such as lost earnings and additional medical expenses and the like.

The approach of Dore J bears some resemblance to the approach taken by some members of this House in *McGhee v National Coal Board* [1972] 3 All ER 1008, [1973] 1 WLR 1 and by Lord Guthrie in *Keynon v Bell* 1953 SC 125. Brachtenbach J dissented. He warned against the danger of using statistics as a basis on which to prove proximate cause and indicated that it was necessary at the minimum to produce evidence connecting the statistics to the facts of the case. He gave an interesting illustration of a town in which there were only two cab companies, one with three blue cabs and the other with one yellow cab. If a person was knocked down by a cab whose colour had not been observed it would be wrong to suggest that there was a 75% chance that the victim was run down by a blue cab and that accordingly it was more probable than not that the cab that ran him down was blue and therefore that the company running the blue cabs would be responsible for negligence in the running down. He pointed out that before any inference that it was a blue cab had been seen in the immediate vicinity at the time of the accident or that a blue cab had been found with a large dent in the very part of the cab which had struck the victim. He concluded that the evidence available was not sufficient to justify the case going to the jury and noted (664 P 2d 474 at 491):

> The apparent harshness of this conclusion cannot be overlooked. The combination of the loss of a loved one to cancer and a doctor's negligence in diagnosis seems to compel a finding of liability. Nonetheless, justice must be dealt with an even hand. To hold a defendant liable without proof that his actions *caused* plaintiff harm would open up untold abuses of the litigation system. (Brachtenbach J's emphasis.)

Pearson J agreed that the appeal should be allowed but did not agree with the reasoning by which that result was supported by Dore J. Pearson J, after examining the authorities and an academic article, stated that he was persuaded that a middle course between the reasoning of Dore and Brachtenbach JJ was correct and concluded 'that the best resolution of the issue before us is to recognise the loss of a less than even chance as an actionable injury' (at 487).

He recognised that this also required that the damage payable be determined by the application of that chance expressed as a percentage to the damages that would be payable on establishing full liability.

I have selected references to the view expressed by the judges who took part in this decision to illustrate the variety of views open in this difficult area of the law. These confirm me in the view that it would not be right in the present case to affirm the general proposition for which counsel for the authority contended. On the other hand, none of the views canvassed in *Herskovits's* case would lead to the plaintiff succeeding in the present case since the judge's findings in fact mean that the sole cause of the plaintiff's avascular necrosis was the injury he sustained in the original fall, and that implies, as I have said, that when he arrived at the authority's hospital for the first time he had no chance of avoiding it. Accordingly, the subsequent negligence of the authority did not cause him the loss of such a chance.

Lord Mackay referred to the relevance of the *McGhee* case to the issue in *Hotson*. One of the reasons for not rejecting outright the plaintiff's argument concerning the recovery of damages for 'loss of a chance' was that the *McGhee* decision in recognising that damages could be recovered, where the plaintiff was able to show that the defendant had 'materially increased the risk' of injuring him, might imply that 'loss of a chance' of avoiding an injury could give rise to compensation in the tort of negligence. But, of course, *Hotson* was decided before *Wilsher* in which the House of Lords, as we have seen, gave *McGhee* a restrictive interpretation.

If *Wilsher* makes plain that a defendant cannot be liable merely if it is proved that he materially increased the *risk* of injuring the plaintiff, neither should he be liable if he merely deprived the plaintiff of a *chance* of recovery. The reasons for this are as follows. First, these are, in reality, two sides of the same coin. Materially to increase the risk of injury to a plaintiff is, at the same time, to decrease the chance of the plaintiff remaining healthy or recovering. We tend to use the language of 'materially increasing the risk' in a *McGhee*- or *Wilsher*-type case where the plaintiff begins healthy and the claim is that the defendant injured him. We tend to use the language of 'loss of a chance' in a *Hotson*-type of case where the plaintiff begins injured and the claim is that the defendant failed to make him better or produce a complete recovery. But these different uses are merely a matter of convenience.

In both situations, therefore, the House of Lords' approach in *Wilsher* is applicable. The 'increased risk' or 'loss of chance' has a merely evidential function from which the court can (though not must) infer that the defendant's negligence (by act or omission) made *the* difference to the plaintiff's condition. Subsequently, in *Tahir v Haringey HA* [1998] Lloyd's Rep Med 104 (CA), Otton LJ interpreted *Hotson* as precluding the recovery of 'damages for the loss of a chance of a complete or better recovery' (at 108).

Secondly, the 'loss of a chance' language is often used in a statistical sense: 1 in 4 recover, 3 in 4 do not. In other words, the statistical evidence is not related to the plaintiff as such but refers to that abstract group of similar individuals familiar to statisticians. Only (as Lord MacKay remarks) if the statistics can be *personalised* to the plaintiff can the inference be made (see T Hill 'A Lost Chance for Compensation in the Tort of Negligence by the House of Lords' (1991) 51 MLR 511 at 516-519). Equally, if the statistics are so overwhelming, the court may feel compelled to take the view that 'how else did the plaintiff get like he is'. This would be the case in *McGhee* itself but not in *Hotson* or *Wilsher* (see Simon Brown LJ's application of *Wilsher* in his dissent in *Bolitho v City and Hackney HA* (1992) 13 BMLR 111 (CA)). Croom-Johnson LJ in the Court of Appeal in *Hotson* puts it as follows (at 223).

Croom-Johnson LJ: In his closing speech, the plaintiff's counsel said:

It is our submission, first of all, that the loss of a chance, even a less than 50% chance, is enough to fund a claim for damages in tort ... damage is proved by proving on the balance of probabilities the loss of a 25% chance.

Put simply that way, the proposition is unsustainable. If it is proved statistically that 25% of the population have a chance of recovery from a certain injury and 75% do not, it does not mean that someone who suffers that injury and who does not recover from it has lost a 25% chance. He may have lost nothing at all. What he has to do is prove that he was one of the 25% and that his loss was caused by the defendant's negligence. To be a figure in a statistic does not by itself give him a cause of action. If the plaintiff succeeds in proving that he was one of the 25% and that the defendant took away that chance, the logical result would be to award him 100% of his damages and not only a quarter, but that might be left for consideration if and when it arises. In this case the plaintiff was only asking for a quarter.

Even the judge at one point in his judgment said ([1985] 3 All ER 167 at 178, [1985] 1 WLR 1036 at 1047):

The defendants' breach of duty here (a) denied the plaintiff the 25% chance of escaping, and thus (b) *may have caused* the very disability which occurred. (My emphasis.)

In the end he decided that the 25/75% split in the chances was something which went to quantification of damages and not to causation.

The role of the 25/75% split as no more than part of the evidentiary material going to proof of liability seems to have been largely lost sight of.

Once the court resolves whether the plaintiff was one of the 75 who do not recover or one of the 25 who do, it then resolves whether the plaintiff has established, on a balance of probabilities, whether the defendant caused the injuries. It is not tenable to talk of lost chances other than at the statistical level. Thus, the 'loss of a chance' argument was a 'red herring' in the *Hotson* case emerging from the unusual finding of fact by the trial judge which confused statistical chances with the actual effects of the defendants' breach of duty on the plaintiff.

It could be said that a discussion of 'loss of a chance' is a resort to labelling rather than analysis. Is not the real question how difficult or easy the courts are prepared to make the plaintiff's task in proving causation? A court could, of course, allow a plaintiff to succeed merely by pointing to statistical probability without more. By demanding more, as in *Hotson*, the plaintiff is forced to fulfil a burden of proof which involves demonstrating precisely that which he cannot, namely particular facts. Lord Mackay's observations in *Hotson* are instructive. Referring to the judgment of Brachtenbach J in the Washington Supreme Court decision of *Herskovits*, Lord Mackay said:

He gave an interesting illustration of a town in which there were only two cab companies, one with three blue cabs and the other with one yellow cab. If a person was knocked down by a cab whose colour had not been observed it would be wrong to suggest that there was a 75% chance that the victim was run down by a blue cab and that accordingly it was more probable than not that the cab that ran him down was blue and therefore that the company running the blue cabs would be responsible for negligence in the running down. He pointed out that before any inference that it was a blue cab would be appropriate further facts would be required as, for example, that a blue cab had been seen in the immediate vicinity at the time of the accident or that a blue cab had been found with a large dent in the very part of the cab which had struck the victim.

Lord Mackay may be right that 'it would be wrong ... therefore that the company ... would be responsible for negligence'. But are the other two propositions wrong in the sentence beginning 'If a person...'? Arguably, Lord Mackay's use of the word 'therefore' indicates that he is moving into a realm of the policy maker. (For a further view see T Hill 'A Lost Chance for Compensation in the Tort of Negligence by the House of Lords' (1991) 54 MLR 511 and J Stapleton 'The Gist of Negligence – II' (1988) 104 LQR 389.)

The Canadian Supreme Court, albeit in an appeal from the Civil Law courts of Quebec, went further than the House of Lords in *Hotson* and specifically rejected an argument based upon recovery for 'loss of a chance'. In effect, they approved the reasoning advanced earlier and the view of Croom-Johnson LJ in *Hotson*.

Lawson v Laferrière (1991) 78 DLR (4th) 609 (Supreme Court of Canada)

In 1971 the defendant physician diagnosed cancer in a patient and removed a lump from her breast, but failed to inform her that the lump was cancerous. Further symptoms appeared, and in 1975 the patient was informed of the earlier diagnosis. She died in 1978 of cancer. An action was commenced by the patient and continued by the plaintiff on the patient's behalf. The trial judge found that the defendant was in breach of a duty to inform the patient, but the medical opinion being divided in 1971 on the proper method of treating breast cancer, the plaintiff's chances of survival would not have been greater if she had been informed. Consequently, he dismissed the action. The majority of the Quebec Court of Appeal held that the defendant's failure to inform the patient of the diagnosis had deprived her of a chance or opportunity of obtaining proper treatment, and that she was entitled to compensation for loss of this chance and for the distress she suffered on hearing of the defendant's failure to inform her of the diagnosis.

On further appeal to the Supreme Court of Canada, held, La Forest J dissenting, allowing the appeal in part, the plaintiff had failed to prove on the balance of probabilities that the defendant had caused the patient's death and, accordingly, the defendant was not, by the civil law of Quebec, liable for the death.

Gonthier J: It is only in exceptional loss of chance cases that a judge is presented with a situation where the damage can only be understood in probabilistic or statistical terms and where it is impossible to evaluate sensibly whether or how the chance would have been realized in that particular case. The purest example of such a lost chance is that of the lottery ticket which is not placed in the draw due to the negligence of the seller of the ticket. The judge had no factual context in which to evaluate the likely result other than the realm of pure statistical chance. Effectively, the pool of factual evidence regarding the various eventualities in the particular case is dry in such cases, and the plaintiff has nothing other than statistics to elaborate the claim in damages. Where the fault of the defendant has already been established and where no other identifiable competing causal factors have been identified, it may be open to the judge to evaluate the damage according to the chance alone. To transform this exceptional case into the theoretical basis for recovery in all loss of chance situations would be necessarily abstract, and, more importantly for the case before us, would give the mistaken impression that the court is more interested in the certainty of statistical chances than in the probable results which those chances represent.

With these considerations in mind, I turn to the role of loss of chance in the medical context.

Loss of chance becomes critically difficult, in France, Belgium and Quebec, as elsewhere, when it is employed as a method of analysis in the complex cases of medical responsibility. In the most difficult cases, such as the one which concerns us, the defendant doctor's fault cannot be easily attached even to any initial actual damage suffered by the plaintiff patient. Accordingly, it is analysis of the lost chance itself which will determine whether the doctor is at all responsible. The lost chance can be analysed in two ways.

In France and Belgium ... it is the chance itself which is considered, usually described as a chance of recovery or survival. The chance must be 'real and serious', and this is said to include chances which are likely or probable... or chances where recovery or improvement is more likely than death or illness... The damages likely are, of course, awarded in relation to the chance itself, and therefore such damages are only partial. According to a recent commentator, loss of a chance analysis is said to be appropriate in cases involving faults of omission. Faults of commission must be analyzed according to a method which connects the fault to the actual death or sickness:... It is acknowledged even by supporters of the full loss of chance analysis in the medical context that by focusing on the lost chance rather than the actual damage which that chance represents the judge is effectively permitted to translate his or her doubts as to the causal link between the fault and the final damage into a reduced award for the patient:...

In Quebec, courts are more inclined to examine the damage which has already occurred, and to consider whether that damage was caused by the doctor's fault or by other identifiable factors. If the fault was causal, then full damages are awarded. Faults of commission are treated in the same manner as faults of omission and, clearly, in more complicated cases both types of fault may be present... The judge attempts, in effect, to determine whether and to what extent the doctor's acts and omissions are responsible for the situation in which the patient now finds himself or herself. A positive result which should have been produced and a negative result which should have been avoided are considered on the same terms, whether they correspond with acts or omissions.

As I have stated earlier, I am inclined to favour an approach which focuses on the actual damage which the doctor can be said to have caused to the patient by his or her fault, and to compensate accordingly. First, as I have said, I can see no basis for treating acts and omissions differently. Accordingly, there is no theoretical imperative directing courts to abandon traditional causal analysis and to adopt instead an essentially artificial loss of chance analysis. Secondly, while I concede that loss of chance analysis is less objectionable when used to evaluate damages in cases where the defendant's responsibility is otherwise clearly established or, perhaps, where no other causal factors can be identified, this type of analysis must be viewed with extreme caution in cases where there are serious doubts as to the defendant's causal role in the face of other identifiable causal factors. Even though our understanding of medical matters is often limited, I am not prepared to conclude that particular medical conditions should be treated for purposes of causation as the equivalent of diffuse elements of pure chance, analogous to the non-specific factors of fate or fortune which influence the outcome of a lottery. Thirdly, as has been pointed out frequently, in the medical context the damage has usually occurred, manifesting itself in sickness or death...the chance is not suspended or crystallised as is the case in the classical loss of chance examples; it has been realized, and the morbid scenario has necessarily played itself out. It can and should be analyzed by means of the generally applicable rules regarding causation.

Overall, then, not only do I question the independent recognition of a lost chance in all but the exceptional classical cases (such as the case of the lottery ticket), but I can certainly see no reason to extend such an artificial form of analysis to the medical context where faults of omission or commission must be considered alongside other identifiable causal factors in determining that which has produced the particular result in the form of sickness or death. As far as possible, the court must consider the question of responsibility with the particular facts of the case in mind, as they relate concretely to the fault, causation and actual damage alleged in the case. While probabilities are unquestionably a part of the assessment of these elements in the finding of responsibility, I am very reluctant to remove the analysis from the concrete to the probabilistic plane.

It is important to recognize that, in cases where the proof indicates that a particular procedure or treatment would probably (though not certainly) have produced a positive result, the patient will usually be able to recover damages under both of the methods described above. If the chance itself is compensated, however, damages will only be measured according to the level of probability. If the actual damage which has been caused is compensated, then the full value of the actual damage will be accorded…

Cases in which the evidence is scarce or seemingly inconclusive present the greatest difficulty. It is perhaps worthwhile to repeat that a judge will be influenced by expert scientific opinions which are expressed in terms of statistical probabilities or test samplings, but he or she is not bound by such evidence. Scientific findings are not identical to legal findings. Recently, in *Snell v Farrell* (1990) 72 DLR (4th) 289 at p 300, [1990] 2 SCR 311, 4 CCLT (2d) 229, this court made clear that '[c]ausation need not be determined by scientific precision' and that '[i]t is not… essential that the medical experts provide a firm opinion supporting the plaintiff's theory of causation' (p 301). Both this court and the Quebec Court of Appeal have frequently stated that proof as to the causal link must be established on the balance of probabilities taking into account *all* the evidence which is before it, factual, statistical and that which the judge is entitled to presume: see, *eg, Shawinigan v Naud* [1929] 4 DLR 57 at pp 59-61, [1929] SCR 341; *Morin v Blais* [1977] 1 SCR 570 at p 580, 10 NR 489; *Laurentide Motels Ltd v Beauport (City)* [1989] 1 SCR 705 at p 808; *J E Construction Inc v General Motors du Canada Ltee* [1985] Que CA 275 at p 278; *Dodds v Schierz* [1986] RJQ 2623 at pp 2635-6, 40 CCLT 167 (CA).

If one takes, for example, a case in which a doctor neglects to employ a recommended procedure which is said to have a 50% chance of complete cure, a judge would not necessarily be bound by expert opinion which declined to conclude that application of the procedure to the patient would have avoided the patient's present worsened condition. The judge might well be justified in finding that the procedure in question would probably have benefited the patient, if other factors particular to that plaintiff support that conclusion. The judge's duty is to assess the damage suffered by a particular patient, not to remain paralyzed by statistical abstraction.

If one moves then to a procedure which is recommended despite a mere 25% chance of success according to expert evidence, it is still not a foregone conclusion that the doctor's fault in not using this procedure must be said to have had no causal role in the patient's death or sickness. If the experts are examined properly, a judge might well find that he or she is justified in concluding that the omission of that procedure did not cause the death or sickness, but that it caused other lesser but clearly negative results (*eg* slightly shorter life, greater pain). The doctor's fault could then be judged causal to the extend of the aggravation of what was otherwise an inevitably terminal or morbid condition.

The plaintiff is aided in establishing his or her case by presumptions (as provided by art 1205 CCLC) and by such factual and statistical evidence as will aid the judge in appreciating what Moisan J described properly as (translation) 'reasonable and prudent behaviour', 'the natural order of things', 'the sequence of cause and effect' and, generally, 'the normal and ordinary course of events'. The judge will want to pay especially close attention to the various causal properties of the doctor's fault as well as the particular character of the damage which has manifested itself. In some cases, where a fault presents clear danger for the health and security of the patient and where such a danger materializes, it may be reasonable for a judge to presume the causal link between the fault and such damage, 'unless there is a demonstration or a strong indication to the contrary': *Morin v Blais* [[1977] 1 SCR 570] at p 580, per Beetz J. If, after all has been considered, the judge is not satisfied that the fault has, on his or her assessment of the balance of probabilities, caused any actual damage to the patient, recovery should be denied. To do otherwise would be to subject doctors to an exceptional regime of civil responsibility.

In conclusion, then, and with all due deference to those who have expressed other opinions, I do not feel that the theory of loss of chance, at least as it is understood in France and

Belgium, should be introduced into the civil law of Quebec in matters of medical responsibility. In the Court of Appeal, Jacques JA states without elaboration that loss of chance is recognized in the common law. I have taken note of the vigorous debate which is taking place in the United States and can find no dominant jurisprudential position favouring loss of chance in that country. In the United Kingdom, the House of Lords has expressed reservations about loss of chance analysis, but has not, as yet, reached a settled conclusion about its possible application: *Hotson v East Berkshire Area Health Authority* [1987] AC 750 (HL). I have also made note of this court's recent decision in *Snell v Farrell, supra*, which I take to endorse traditional principles of causation, properly applied...

In my view, the evidence amply supports the trial judge's finding that the appellant's fault could not be said to have caused Mrs Dupuis' death seven years after the first diagnosis of cancer of the breast. Unfortunately, I must agree with the trial judge that all the evidence clearly confirms the stubborn and virulent nature of this disease.

For an argument that there are identifiable 'loss of chance' cases where the outcome of a particular event/action is not determined because human agency is involved see, H Reece 'Losses of Chances in the Law' (1996) 59 MLR 188. However, that such a 'chance' may exist does not conclude that the law *should* award compensation for its loss. In any event, as Gonthier J points out in *Lawson v Laferrière, (supra)*, when a patient has suffered an injury the law's concern is with compensation for *that injury*. The critical question for the law is whether the patient has established a causal connection between the defendant's negligence and that injury. 'Risk' and 'chance' may be evidentially supportive (or they may not) but that is their role in any claim for the patient's loss (his injury) (see further, *Naxakis v Western General Hospital* [1999] HCA 22 (HC of A), especially per Gaudron J; contrast Callinan and McHugh JJ).

2. Legal causation and remoteness

Medical negligence cases are no different in attracting the traditional analysis adumbrated by the Privy Council in the *Wagon Mound* [1961] AC 388, [1961] 1 All ER 404. Clearly, issues of foreseeability or remoteness (or whatever term of policy is used) *can* arise. An example where the court considered the causal effect of the patient's decision on the defendant's prior negligence is *Emeh v Kensington and Chelsea and Westminster AHA* [1985] QB 1012, [1984] 3 All ER 1044 (CA). The court had to make a policy decision as to whether a woman can properly be expected by the court to undergo an abortion after a failed sterilisation negligently performed rather than bear an 'unwanted child'. (See discussion *infra,* ch 12.)

As we saw earlier, in *Chappell v Hart* (1998) 72 ALJR 1344, the Australian High Court considered in some depth the issue of causation in medical negligence actions. This case concerned a patient who had undergone an operation which resulted in injury to her. She claimed, and it was accepted, that the doctor had negligently failed to warn her of the risk of injury. She contended, and again it was accepted, she would have not consented to the procedure had she known of the risk. However, unlike the usual situation, the evidence was that she would have sought a second opinion and undergone the same procedure sometime later. It was argued that, unlike the usual case, she had failed to establish a causal link between her injury and the defendant's negligent failure to warn (for the usual, see *infra*, ch 5). As you will see, the issue is not one of *factual* causation but of *legal* causation, since it is undoubtedly the case that the patient would not have been injured *at the time* 'but for' the failure to warn.

But, could she recover for injuries when she, herself, accepted she would have undergone the same procedure (and exposed herself to risk) in the future? The Australian High Court divided 3:2 in finding that she could recover. In doing so, they subjected the issue of *legal* causation to careful scrutiny. Here we set out the judgment of Kirby J (with whom Gaudron and Gummow JJ delivered concurring judgments) for the majority and McHugh J (with whom Hayne J delivered a concurring judgment) for the dissent.

Chappell v Hart (1998) 72 ALJR 1344 (HC of A)

Kirby J:

Common ground

91. The issues in the appeal were even further refined before this Court:

1.   Mrs Hart's claim against Dr Chappel was limited to a complaint that he had failed to warn her adequately, or at all, of the dangers involved in the operation: specifically, that there was a danger that her voice could be compromised by the complications which, in fact, occurred. A claim that Dr Chappel had conducted the operation negligently, although initially pleaded, was not supported by evidence and was abandoned at the trial.

2.   Although originally strongly contested, Dr Chappel (for the purpose of the appeal) accepted (as the primary judge had found), that when asking about the risks prior to the operation, Mrs Hart had said to him words to the effect: 'I don't want to wind up like Neville Wran'. This remark was taken to be an allusion to a contemporaneous problem which, following operation, the then Premier of New South Wales (Mr N K Wran) had experienced with his voice which had only been partly restored by a teflon injection to his vocal cords. After the subject operation, Mrs Hart came under the care of Professor B N Benjamin. In treating the damaged laryngeal nerve to allow her improved use of the vocal cords he actually injected teflon. However, this procedure left Mrs Hart's voice weak and affected, much as Mr Wran's voice had been. Dr Chappel fought this appeal on the footing that he had failed properly to respond to his patient's inquiry. To that extent he was in breach of his duty to provide information to his patient which this Court's decision in *Rogers v Whitaker* ((1992) 175 CLR 479) required him to give.

3.   The aetiology of the damage to Mrs Hart's laryngeal nerve was not in doubt. It required the coincidence of three events: (1) the operative tear to the oesophagus; (2) an escape of bacteria from the oesophagus; and (3) consequential impingement of the resulting infection upon the nearby right vocal cord causing paralysis and damage. Each of these preconditions was accepted to be very rare. A tear could occur (according to Professor Benjamin's evidence) once in every 20, 30 or 40 operations. Usually, it resulted in nothing more than the 'escape of a few bubbles of air'. The complication of mediastinitis that occurred in this case was 'very rare indeed'. It had not occurred in the 100 to 150 operations performed by Professor Benjamin. However, it was a recognised possibility. Once a patient asked a question about that possibility, he or she was entitled to have an accurate and candid answer so that the patient could make an informed decision about the surgery. For Mrs Hart, the consequences were important and they were large.

4.   The condition which originally took Mrs Hart to Dr Chappel was 'relentlessly progressive'. Surgery was the 'only relief' for it. Without surgery there would not only be soreness and difficulty in swallowing but the danger that food might become caught in the throat needing emergency attention. It was therefore accepted that, even if Mrs Hart had been warned of the danger of damage to her voice, she would eventually have undergone an operation on her throat. In any such operation the slight risk would exist of the kind that followed Dr Chappel's procedure. Mrs Hart did not dispute this. Dr Chappel conceded that, if the surgery had in fact been postponed and carried out at a different time, '[i]n all likelihood [Mrs Hart] would not have suffered the random chance of injury' to her vocal cord. This represented nothing more than acceptance that such injury was an extremely rare occurrence. It was not even mentioned in some clinical textbooks.

5.   Mrs Hart swore that if she had been told by Dr Chappel of the risks to her voice she would not have gone ahead with the operation by him. She would have sought further advice. She would have wanted the operation performed by the most experienced person available. Professor Benjamin was posited as such a person. The evidence showed that he had performed many more operations of this kind than Dr Chappel had. The primary judge accepted that Mrs Hart was a witness of truth. Her claim must therefore be assessed on the footing that, with the warning that the law required Dr Chappel to give her, she would not have gone ahead with the operation when she did. She would thus not in fact have suffered the damage which ensued.

92. Dr Chappel contended that, in the foregoing facts, Mrs Hart was not entitled to recovery. The random chance of complications could just as easily have struck during an operation at a later time and place and conducted by a different surgeon. In the absence of proof of negligence in the performance of the operation, his accepted failure to warn Mrs Hart had

not caused her damage. Mrs Hart, armed with the decisions below, contended that she had established sufficient facts to demonstrate a causal connection and to retain her damages...

Conclusion: causation was established

94. The application of the foregoing principles to the facts of this case, as now established, presents different puzzles upon which reasonable minds may differ; as indeed they have. The strongest arguments for Dr Chappel, as it seems to me, are those which lay emphasis upon a logical examination of the consequences which would have flowed had he not breached his duty to warn his patient. Dissecting the facts in that way affords a powerful argument which would banish from consideration the events which in fact occurred in the operation which he carried out. All that would have happened, had he given the requisite warning, would have been a change in the timing of the operation and of the identify of the surgeon. For Dr Chappel, these were irrelevant changes as the evidence showed that, whenever the operation was performed and whoever did it, the tripartite chances which had to combine to produce the misfortune which Mrs Hart suffered were extremely rare. There was thus an equivalence of unlikelihood. They were risks inherent in the procedure, not wholly avoidable even by the most skilful and experienced of surgeons. In the view which Dr Chappel urged of the case, Mrs Hart was left with nothing more than the time sequence. To burden a surgeon, in whose actual performance no fault could be found, with civil liability for randomised chance events that followed the surgery would not be reasonable. It would penalise him for chance alone. It would do nothing to establish a superior standard in the performance of the work of surgeons generally.

95. For a time I was attracted to Dr Chappel's arguments. Ultimately, I have concluded against them. The 'commonsense' which guides courts in this area of discourse supports Mrs Hart's recovery. So does the setting of standards which uphold the importance of the legal duty that was breached here. This is the duty which all health care professionals in the position of Dr Chappel must observe: the duty of informing patients about risks, answering their questions candidly and respecting their rights, including (where they so choose) to postpone medical procedures and to go elsewhere for treatment.

96. In *Environment Agency (formerly National Rivers Authority) v Empress Car Co (Abertillery) Ltd* ([1998] 2 WLR 350 at 356-358; [1998] 1 All ER 481 at 487-489), Lord Hoffmann emphasised that commonsense answers to questions of causation will differ according to the purpose for which the question is asked. The answer depends upon the purpose and scope of the rule by which responsibility is being attributed. In *Rogers v Whitaker*, this Court decided that 'a doctor has a duty to warn a patient of a material risk inherent in the proposed treatment' and that:

> a risk is material if, in the circumstances of the particular case, a reasonable person in the patient's position, if warned of the risk, would be likely to attach significance to it or if the medical practitioner is or should reasonably be aware that the particular patient, if warned of the risk, would be likely to attach significance to it. ((1992) 175 CLR 479 at 490).

These standards have fairly been described as onerous. They are. But they are the law. They are established for good reason. When not complied with (as was held to be so in this case) it should occasion no surprise that legal consequences follow. This was an unusual case where the patient was found to have made very clear her concerns. The practicalities are that, had those concerns been met as the law required, the overwhelming likelihood is that the patient would not, in fact, have been injured. So much was eventually conceded. In such circumstances, commonsense reinforces the attribution of legal liability. It is true to say that the inherent risks of injury from rare and random causes arise in every surgical procedure. A patient, duly warned about such risks, must accept them and their consequences. However, she declined to bear the risks about which she questioned the surgeon and received no adequate response. When those risks so quickly eventuated, commonsense suggests that something more than a mere coincidence or irrelevant cause has intervened. This impression is reinforced once it is accepted that Mrs Hart, if warned, would not have undergone the operation when she did.

97. Although no statistical or other evidence was called to demonstrate that recourse to a more experienced surgeon would necessarily have reduced the risk of the kind of injury that occurred (and while some risk was unavoidable), intuition and commonsense suggest that the higher the skill of the surgeon, the less is the risk of any perforation of the oesophagus into the mediastinum. In 100 to 150 operations of this kind, Professor Benjamin had never experienced mediastinitis. Whilst that may indeed be the result of chance and amount to good luck on his part (and on the part of his patients) intuition and commonsense suggest that the greater the skill and more frequent the performance, the less the risk of perforation. And without perforation (already a rare occurrence) the second and third events necessary to produce paralysis of the vocal cords in a patient like Mrs Hart (occurrences even more rare)

would not occur. As Gaudron J points out, the *nature* of the risk would be the same. But the *degree* of risk would be diminished. This was the view taken by the Court of Appeal. It is a view which involved no error.

98. Once Mrs Hart showed the breach and the damage which had immediately eventuated, an evidentiary onus lay upon Dr Chappel to displace the inference of causation which thereupon arose. He failed to do so. Nor, in my view, causation being established, did he prove that Mrs Hart would have been exposed to the same, or substantially the same, possibilities of like injury if she had postponed the procedure and had it done by someone more experienced, as was her right. On the contrary, the evidence demonstrated that the chances of her receiving such injury in any other operation were minuscule. For the reasons stated those chances would probably be even smaller in the hands of a surgeon with the experience and skill of Professor Benjamin.

99. To the complaint that Professor Benjamin (or his equivalent) could not possibly undertake every Dohlman's operation (any more than the most skilful barrister can appear for every client) the answer comes back. This was not an ordinary patient. It was an inquisitive, persistent and anxious one who was found to have asked a particular question to which she received no proper answer. Had a proper answer been given, as the law required, it was found that she would not have undergone the operation at the hands of Dr Chappel when she did. It is virtually certain, then, that she would not have suffered mediastinitis at all. She would not have been injured. She would not have been obliged to bring her case before the courts. She therefore adequately proved causation. Dr Chappel did not displace the inferences to which her evidence gave rise. Nor was it shown that the damages to which she was entitled should be reduced on the footing that they would have occurred in any event.

100. As to the question of loss of a chance, Dr Chappel, by leave, added a ground of appeal to assert that Mrs Hart's damages should have been assessed in those terms. Mrs Hart resisted the amendment but, in any case, said that it mattered not. At trial, the only claim for damages, which she had asserted, was in respect of the physical injury done to her vocal cords and its sequelae. She neither pleaded, nor sought to prove, a case expressed in terms of a loss of a chance. Accordingly, no evidence was tendered as to the value of that chance. The case is therefore not one in which an entirely new perspective should be adopted at such a late stage. One day loss of a chance in this area of discourse will return to this Court. However, this case must be approached on the footing that the loss suffered by Mrs Hart was that claimed: physical injury and its consequence – nothing more.

McHugh J: 22. The question in this appeal is whether a doctor who performed an operation with reasonable care is nevertheless liable for an accidental injury occurring in the course of the operation. The question has to be determined in the context that the doctor, in breach of his duty, failed to warn his patient that such an injury could occur and that the patient, if warned, would have had the operation carried out by 'the most experienced person with a record and a reputation in the field'.

23. Proof of a cause of action in negligence or contract requires the plaintiff to prove that the breach of duty by the defendant caused the particular damage that the plaintiff suffered. In civil cases, causation theory operates on the hypothesis that the defendant has breached a duty owed to the plaintiff and that the plaintiff has suffered injury; but causation theory insists that the plaintiff prove that the injury is relevantly connected to the breach of duty. The existence of the relevant causal connection is determined according to common sense ideas and not according to philosophical or scientific theories of causation. The reason for this distinction was pointed out by Mason CJ in *March v Stramare (E & MH) Pty Ltd* ((1991) 171 CLR 506 at 509):

> In philosophy and science, the concept of causation has been developed in the context of explaining phenomena by reference to the relationship between conditions and occurrences. In law, on the other hand, problems of causation arise in the context of ascertaining or apportioning legal responsibility for a given occurrence.

24. In *March* (ibid) this Court specifically rejected the 'but for' test as the exclusive test of factual causation. Instead the Court preferred the same common sense view of causation which it had expressed in its decision in *Fitzgerald v Penn* ((1954) 91 CLR 268). There, the Court said that the question is to be determined by asking 'whether a particular act or omission … can fairly and properly be considered a cause of the accident' (ibid at 276). As a natural consequence of the rejection of the 'but for' test as the sole determinant of causation, the Court has refused to regard the concept of remoteness of damage as the appropriate mechanism for determining the extent to which policy considerations should limit the consequences of causation-in-fact (*Bennett v Minister of Community Welfare* (1992) 176 CLR 408 at 412-413). Consequently, value judgments and policy as well as our "experience of the 'constant conjunction' or 'regular sequence' of pairs of events in nature" are regarded as central to the common law's conception of causation.

25. The rejection of the 'but for' test as the sole determinant of causation means that the plaintiff in this case cannot succeed merely because she would not have suffered injury but for the defendant's failure to warn her of the risk of injury. However, this failure to warn her of the risk was one of the events that in combination with others led to the perforation of her oesophagus and damage to the right recurrent laryngeal nerve. Without that failure, the injury would not have occurred when it did and, statistically, the chance of it occurring during an operation on another occasion was very small. Moreover, that failure was the very breach of duty which the plaintiff alleges caused her injury. The defendant's failure to warn, therefore, must be regarded as a cause of the plaintiff's injury unless either common sense or legal policy requires the conclusion that, for the purposes of this action, the failure is not to be regarded as a cause of the plaintiff's injury.

26. Underlying the rejection of the 'but for' test as the determinant of legal causation is the instinctive belief that a person should not be liable for every wrongful act or omission which is a necessary condition of the occurrence of the injury that befell the plaintiff. As Macon CJ emphasised in *March* ((1991) 171 CLR 506 at 509), causation for legal purposes is concerned with allocating responsibility for harm or damage that has occurred. So the mere fact that injury would not have occurred but for the defendant's act or omission is often not enough to establish a causal connection for legal purposes. Thus, in *Leask Timber and Hardware Pty Ltd v Thorne* ((1961) 106 CLR 33), members of this Court accepted that the driving of a crane by an uncertified driver was not causally related to the death of the plaintiff's husband, notwithstanding that driving a crane without a certificate was a breach of the law and that the death would not have occurred but for that breach. Windeyer J said (ibid at 46-47):

Possession of a certificate means that the driver has satisfied an inspector that he can drive a crane competently, and is a trustworthy person. If, however, he fails to exercise the competence he has and drives a crane improperly, unskilfully and negligently, it will not avail him or his employer that an inspector had certified that he was capable of doing so properly and skilfully; nor is it material that an inspector thought he was trustworthy if trust in him should prove misplaced. On the other hand, a person might have skill and competence but no certificate. If he drives a crane carefully, skilfully and competently then he is not liable in negligence for the consequences of an accident that occurs without fault on his part. That is how the matter would stand in an action for negligence.

Similarly, in *The Empire Jamaica* ((1955) p 52) Willmer J held that the act of the owners of a ship in sending it to sea with a master who had no certificate, contrary to a local Ordinance, was not a legal cause of a collision occurring on the voyage, notwithstanding that the master was guilty of negligent navigating.

27. Before the defendant will be held responsible for the plaintiff's injury, the plaintiff must prove that the defendant's conduct materially contributed to the plaintiff suffering that injury. In the absence of a statute or undertaking to the contrary, therefore, it would seem logical to hold a person causally liable for a wrongful act or omission only when it increases the risk of injury to another person. If a wrongful act or omission results in an increased risk of injury to the plaintiff and that risk eventuates, the defendant's conduct has materially contributed to the injury that the plaintiff suffers whether or not other factors also contributed to that injury occurring. If, however, the defendant's conduct does not increase the risk of injury to the plaintiff, the defendant cannot be said to have materially contributed to the injury suffered by the plaintiff. That being so, whether the claim is in contract or tort, the fact that the risk eventuated at a particular time or place by reason of the conduct of the defendant does not itself materially contribute to the plaintiff's injury unless the fact of that particular time or place increased the risk of the injury occurring.

28. In principle, therefore, if the act or omission of the defendant has done no more than expose the plaintiff to a class of risk to which the plaintiff would have been exposed irrespective of the defendant's act or omission, the law of torts should not require the defendant to pay damages. Similarly, if the defendant has done no more than expose the plaintiff to a risk for which the defendant has not undertaken responsibility and to which the plaintiff was always exposed, the law of contract should not require the defendant to pay damages for injury arising from that risk even if it follows upon a breach of contract. No principle of the law of contract or tort or of risk allocation requires the defendant to be liable for those risks of an activity or course of conduct that cannot be avoided or reduced by the exercise of reasonable care unless statute, contract or a duty otherwise imposed by law has made the defendant responsible for those risks.

29. For these reasons, in *Carslogie Steamship Co Ltd v Royal Norwegian Government* ([1952] AC 292 at 299), where a vessel was delayed so that damage caused by the defendant's negligence could be repaired, the House of Lords had no difficulty in concluding that further damage to the vessel as the result of a severe storm after it resumed its voyage was not causally connected with that negligence. The House so concluded, notwithstanding that the further

damage probably would not have occurred but for the delay. No doubt the House would have reached a different conclusion if the delay had increased the risk that the vessel might suffer damage from severe storms. Increased risk as the result of breach of duty was the reason that, in *Monarch Steamship Co Ltd v Karlshamns Oljefabriker (A/B)* ([1949] AC 196), the House of Lords held the defendant liable for the cost of transhipment arising from the outbreak of war. The House held that the defendant's breach of duty had resulted in delay which had increased the chance that the cargo would have to be delivered after the outbreak of war.

30. Cases such as *Carslogie* ([1952] AC 292) and *Monarch* ([1949] AC 196) were concerned with damage following negligent acts. But logically the same principles must apply to the wrongful omissions as well as the wrongful acts of the defendant. Thus, if the defendant negligently fails to warn the plaintiff that a particular route is subject to landslides, no causal connection will exist between the failure to warn and subsequent injury from a landslide if every other available route carried the same degree of risk of injury from a landslide. In such a case, the injury suffered is simply an inherent risk in the course of action pursued by the plaintiff. Although the negligence of the defendant has resulted in the plaintiff being in the place where and at the time when the landslide occurred, that negligence is to be regarded as merely one of the set of conditions that combined to produce the injury. Because the negligent failure of the defendant to give a warning did not increase the risk of injury to the plaintiff, the defendant should not incur liability for the plaintiff's injury.

31. On the other hand, if there were alternative routes involving a lesser risk of landslide and the plaintiff would probably have taken one of them, if given a warning, the defendant's failure to warn would be causally connected with the plaintiff's injury. That is because the failure to warn deflected the plaintiff from taking a safer course and increased the chance that he or she would suffer injury. By doing so, the defendant has materially contributed to the occurrence of that injury. The case is *a fortiori* if the plaintiff, on being warned, would have abandoned the journey.

32. Furthermore, a defendant is not causally liable, and therefore legally responsible, for wrongful acts or omissions if those acts or omissions would not have caused the plaintiff to alter his or her course of action. Australian law has adopted a subjective theory of causation in determining whether the failure to warn would have avoided the injury suffered. The inquiry as to what the plaintiff would have done if warned is necessarily hypothetical. But if the evidence suggests that the acts or omissions of the defendant would have made no difference to the plaintiff's course of action, the defendant has not caused the harm which the plaintiff has suffered.

33. Moreover, even when the defendant's wrongful act or omission has exposed the plaintiff to a risk to which the plaintiff would not have been exposed but for that act or omission, the correct conclusion may nevertheless be that no causal connection exists between the negligence and the injury suffered. Thus, in *Central Georgia Railway Co v Price* (32 SE 77 (Ga)(1898)), a railway company was held not liable for injury sustained as the result of a lamp exploding in a hotel where the plaintiff had to stay as the result of the company negligently taking her beyond her destination. The risk of such an event occurring in that hotel on that particular night was so insignificant and therefore so abnormal as to be fairly described as a coincidence, rather than an event causally connected to the defendant's negligence.

34. The foregoing observations lead me to the following conclusions concerning whether a causal connection exists between a defendant's failure to warn of a risk of injury and the subsequent suffering of injury by the plaintiff as a result of the risk eventuating:

(1)   a causal connection will exist between the failure and the injury if it is probable that the plaintiff would have acted on the warning and desisted from pursuing the type of activity or course of conduct involved;

(2)   no causal connection will exist if the plaintiff would have persisted with the same course of action in comparable circumstances even if a warning had been given;

(3)   no causal connection will exist if every alternative means of achieving the plaintiff's goal gave rise to an equal or greater probability of the same risk of injury and the plaintiff would probably have attempted to achieve that goal notwithstanding the warning;

(4)   no causal connection will exist where the plaintiff suffered injury at some other place or some other time unless the change of place or time increased the risk of injury;

(5)   no causal connection will exist if the eventuating of the risk is so statistically improbable as not to be fairly attributable to the defendant's omission;

(6)   the onus of proving that the failure to warn was causally connected with the plaintiff's harm lies on the plaintiff. However, once the plaintiff proves that the defendant breached a duty to warn of a risk and that the risk eventuated and caused harm to the plaintiff, the plaintiff has made out a prima facie case of causal connection. An evidentiary onus then rests on the defendant to point to other evidence suggesting that no causal connection exists. Examples of such evidence are: evidence which indicates that the plaintiff would not have acted on the warning because of lack of choice or personal inclination; evidence that no alternative course of action would have eliminated or reduced the risk of injury.

Once the defendant points to such evidence, the onus lies on the plaintiff to prove that in all the circumstances a causal connection existed between the failure to warn and the injury suffered by the plaintiff.

35. Upon the unusual facts of the present case – they are set out in detail in other judgments – the defendant in my opinion can escape liability only if the proper conclusion is that the plaintiff did not prove that the defendant's failure to warn resulted in her consenting to a procedure that involved a higher risk of injury than would have been the case if the procedure had been carried out by another surgeon...

41. Nothing in the evidence suggested that there was available to the plaintiff the services of a surgeon of such skill that he or she would never perforate the oesophagus while performing this procedure. Nor did the evidence suggest that either Professor Benjamin or any other surgeon was so superior in skill to the defendant that an operation by that person carried with it a statistically significant lesser risk of perforation than an operation by the defendant. Professor Benjamin was no doubt a pre-eminent surgeon in this field and had performed the operation on many more occasions than the defendant. It is also true that risk of perforation will vary depending upon the degree of care taken on a particular occasion. But the evidence did not suggest, let alone prove, that an operation by the defendant carried with it a statistically significant greater risk of perforation than that of any other qualified surgeon. There is not even a suggestion that the defendant had perforated the oesophagus was an inherent risk of the procedure. That is to say, it was an injury that could occur even when reasonable skill and care were exercised. The fact that it happened on this occasion says nothing about whether an operation by the defendant carried with it a statistically significant greater risk of injury.

42. The plaintiff's claim must fail. This follows from her failure to prove that there was open to her an alternative course of action which would have reduced the inherent chance of a perforation and consequent onset of mediastinitis and damage to the recurrent laryngeal nerve. The highest that her case can be put is that the defendant's failure to warn her resulted in her having the procedure at an earlier date and no doubt at a different place with a different surgeon than would have been the case if the defendant had carried out his duty and warned her. On the evidence, the carrying out of the procedure by the defendant on the day and at the place did not increase the risk of injury involved in the procedure. That being so, the defendant's failure to warn did not materially contribute to the plaintiff's injury. Her claim that a causal connection existed between that failure and her injury must be rejected.

43. On the view that I take of the case, it is of no relevance that, if she had been warned, another surgeon would have performed the procedure and that the chance of her suffering damage to the laryngeal nerve in that procedure was very remote. Perforation of the oesophagus with consequential mediastinitis and inflammation resulting in damage to the laryngeal nerve is such a rare event that it is close to a certainty that the plaintiff would have avoided mediastinitis and consequential damage to the laryngeal nerve if another surgeon had performed the procedure. Perforation of the oesophagus can and does occur in carrying out the procedure even though the surgeon exercises reasonable skill and care. When it does occur, it will lead to mediastinitis only if bacteria is present in the oesophagus. According to the evidence of Professor Benjamin, it is 'very rare' for a perforation to be complicated by mediastinitis. Even then, as the learned trial judge found 'the likelihood is that the problems would clear up'. It seems almost certain, therefore, that if the plaintiff had been warned and had had the operation performed by another surgeon she would have avoided damage to the laryngeal nerve.

44. However, it is also close to a certainty that neither mediastinitis nor damage to the laryngeal nerve would have occurred if the defendant had performed the operation on some other day or even at some different hour on that day. He was not as experienced a surgeon as Professor Benjamin but he had performed the operation successfully on previous occasions. If reasonable care is exercised, there is only a remote possibility that damage to a laryngeal nerve resulting from mediastinitis will lead to paralysis of the vocal cords, as happened with the plaintiff, irrespective of which surgeon performs the procedure. Moreover, given the plaintiff's abandonment of any claim that the defendant had *performed* the operation negligently, he must be taken to have exercised reasonable skill and care on this occasion. His performance on this occasion was differentiated from that of others only by the eventuating of a risk that is inherent in the procedure whoever performs it.

45. To hold the defendant liable on the basis that if the plaintiff had been given a warning of the risk of mediastinitis occurring she would have avoided that condition is simply to apply the 'but for' test, a course which *March* rejects. If, as the result of the defendant warning the plaintiff about the risk of perforation, the plaintiff had sought out another surgeon who had operated and accidentally perforated the plaintiff's oesophagus with consequent mediastinitis, only the most faithful adherents to the 'but for' test would argue that the defendant's warning had caused the perforation and mediastinitis. To so argue would seem an affront to common sense. Similarly, with great respect to the learned judges in the courts

below, it seems contrary to common sense to conclude that the defendant's failure to warn caused or materially contributed to him perforating the plaintiff's oesophagus on this occasion. From a common sense point of view, the cause of the perforation and the consequent mediastinitis was the examination of the oesophagus with a rigid endoscope, an examination which carried with it an inherent risk of perforation.

46. The attractiveness of the proposition that the defendant's failure to warn caused or materially contributed to the plaintiff's perforation and mediastinitis derives, I think from the language in which the proposition is expressed. Authorities on writing recognise that using a noun instead of a verb to express action (nominalisation) and omitting an actor from a sentence are fertile sources of imprecise communication. The use of a nominalisation and the omission of an actor can also conceal reasoning errors. The question: 'Did the defendant's failure to warn cause or materially contribute to the perforation of the oesophagus' is more readily answered in the affirmative than the question: 'Did the defendant's failure to warn cause or materially contribute to *him perforating* the defendant's oesophagus?'

47. The first question uses a noun (perforation) instead of the verb (perforate) and expresses no action. Because the perforation follows the failure to warn and the question identifies no action or actor, that question implicitly suggests a connection between the failure to warn and the perforation. But it is merely a temporal or sequential connection between the omission and the injury. When analysed, therefore, the posing of the first question can be of little, if any, assistance in determining whether the defendant by failing to warn of the risk of injury materially contributed to him perforating the oesophagus of the plaintiff.

48. The second question focuses on the defendant and makes his actions central to the inquiry. Its very statement suggests a negative answer. His omission to warn had nothing to do with him perforating the oesophagus on that particular day, except as one of many events that combined to place him in the theatre that day operating on the plaintiff. For the purpose of legal causation theory, his omission to warn was no more causative of the perforation than were his medical qualifications, no more causative of the plaintiff's injury than the lack of a crane driving certificate was causative of the deceased's injury in *Leask Timber* ((1961) 106 CLR 33).

49. It follows that the learned judged of the Supreme Court and the Court of Appeal erred in finding that there was a causal connection between the defendant's failure to warn and the plaintiff's injury.

Our interest in this case lies in the general approach of the judges to legal causation. At one level, the judges' disagreement was a factual one: did the defendant's negligence make the patient's situation any worse – more risky. 'No' according to McHugh J; 'yes' according to Kirby J. At another level, however, the judges may be disagreeing over the central issue in the 'failure to warn' cases. What interest of the patient is the law protecting? Is it to be safe from injury? Or, is it the patient's autonomy, to make an informed decision whether to be exposed to risk? (on this, see *infra*, ch 5). Professor Peter Cane in his comment on *Chappell v Hart* offers the following analysis:

Peter Cane *'A Warning About Causation'* (1999) 115 LQR 21

In *Chappel v Hart* all the Justices were of the opinion that if Dr Chappel had not breached his duty to warn, the combination of factors which led to Mrs Hart's injury would almost certainly not have occurred. However, in the view of the minority, the occurrence of this extremely unlikely combination of circumstances was 'random' (which seems to mean 'beyond the control of the surgeon') and, therefore, a 'coincidence' for which it would not have been fair to hold Dr Chappel liable. Suppose that Mrs Hart had suffered injury as a result of a power surge while Dr Chappel was operating. Since power surges to operating theatres are (one might assume) very rare events, then, on the balance of probabilities, Mrs Hart would not have suffered the hypothetical injury if Dr Chappel had warned her of the risk of injury to her vocal cords. It does not follow, however, that Dr Chappel would have been legally responsible for the hypothetical injury. In the minority's view, there was no significant difference between a power surge and the combination of circumstances which had caused Mrs Hart's injury. They could both be described as coincidental. As far as the majority were concerned, however, what happened to Mrs Hart of precisely the risk which had materialised and caused her injury. The general proposition underlying the majority judgments is that liability for failure to warn will arise if the risk of the injury suffered was one about which the doctor had a duty to warn the patient, but not otherwise. The minority, by contrast, took the view that liability for failure to warn might not arise even if the risk of the injury suffered was one about which the doctor had a duty to warn the patient.

The disagreement between the majority and minority Justices concerned whether there was any good reason why Dr Chappel should be absolved or liability for Mrs Hart's injury even though she would not have suffered it if Dr Chappel had not, by breaching his duty to inform her of the risk inherent in the operation she needed, created the situation in which the injury occurred. On the surface, this was a disagreement about whether or not the combination of circumstances which caused the injury could properly be treated as a coincidence for which it would be unfair to hold Dr Chappel liable. But if we look more carefully, we find that the two sets of Justices also took different views of the facts. It was agreed that surgery of the type performed on Mrs Hart carried a very small risk of injury to her vocal cords no matter when, by whom or how well it was done. What the evidence did not clearly establish was whether, the more skilled and experienced the surgeon, the smaller the risk. Gaudron and Kirby JJ (in the majority) interpreted the evidence as showing that greater skill and experience would reduce the risk, whereas MacHugh and Hayne JJ (in the minority) interpreted it as establishing that the risk was the same no matter how skilled and experienced the surgeon. The importance of this difference of interpretation of the evidence resides in the fact that under Australian law, the question of what the patient would have done if they had been warned is decided subjectively – the inquiry to be made is not what the reasonable patient in the plaintiff's position would have done if warned, but what the plaintiff would have done. The subjective approach gives maximum effect to the 'patient autonomy' justification for the duty to inform. By contrast, an objective approach enables the court to mitigate the consequences of failure to warn for the benefit of doctors. One danger of the subjective approach is well expressed by Kirby J in *Chappel v Hart* (para 93.7): 'Once a disaster has occurred, it would be rare, at least where litigation has commenced, that a patient would not be persuaded, in his or her own mind, that a failure to warn had significant consequences for undertaking the medical procedure at all (where it was elective) or postponing it and getting a more experienced surgeon (as in this case)'. But Kirby J thought that this danger 'should not be over-stated'.

It was accepted that if warned, Mrs Hart would not have had the operation when she did or at the hands of Dr Chappel. It was also assumed that Dr Chappel was not the most experienced surgeon available. If one takes the view of Gaudron and Kirby JJ about the nature of the risk, Mrs Hart's reaction would have been perfectly reasonable, given the importance to her of having a strong voice and the fact that although she needed surgery sooner or later, it was not essential at the time Dr Chappel operated on her. If, by contrast, one takes the view of McHugh and Hayne JJ, her reaction, while perhaps understandable given her special concern about damage to her voice and the fact that the surgery was at that point in time 'elective', would have lacked rational foundation and could not justify holding Dr Chappel liable for the adverse consequences of an operation which he performed without negligence. Because the case was argued and decided in terms which focused on the role of Dr Chappel in the causal chain, this aspect of the disagreement between the majority and the minority did not emerge clearly. All of the Justices simply accepted (either explicitly or implicitly) that so far as the patients' reaction was concerned, the proper approach was a subjective one. So far as Dr Chappel's role in the causal chain was concerned, it seems to me that the majority view is correct. The desirable rule is that a doctor may be held liable for injury about the risk of which fell outside the duty to warn. On this basis, and taking the majority's view of the nature of the risk, the subjective approach worked well enough (although the objective approach would have allowed the majority Justices to reach the same conclusion). However, taking the minority's view of the nature of the risk, the subjective approach produced the wrong answer. Because the case had not been presented in a way which focused on the role of the patient in the causal chain, the minority were forced to take what seems to me to be an unsatisfactory approach to the role of the doctor in order to reach the result they thought correct.

The problem which the minority in *Chappel v Hart* faced is that the subjective test of causation in failure to warn cases gives undue weight to the patient's interest in autonomy and informed decision-making. This is because although the interest protected by the duty to warn is patient autonomy, the practical importance of the duty is that it allows liability to be imposed for physical injury not caused by negligence.

We will return to the test of factual causation as it is deployed in 'failure to warn' cases later (*infra*, ch 5). We will see that the 'subjective' and 'objective' approaches may not be the only options (see *Arndt v Smith* [1997] 2 SCR 539 (Can Sup Ct)).

Legal causation and remoteness rarely presents problems in medical negligence cases. One case where remoteness did arise is *R v Croydon HA* (1997) 40 BMLR 40 (CA).

R v Croydon HA (1997) 40 BMLR 40 (CA)

In October 1988 Mrs R applied for employment with the appellant health authority. As a pre-condition of her employment she was required to undergo a medical examination, including a chest X-ray. Dr Manners, a radiologist, was negligent in his failure to report the presence of a significant abnormality. Had he reported it, Mrs R's general practitioner would have been informed, she would have been referred to a cardiologist, who would have diagnosed primary pulmonary hypertension (PPH). PPH was an untreatable condition where diminished limited life expectancy was exacerbated if the sufferer became pregnant. The appellant accepted that Mrs R would not have become pregnant had she been so diagnosed. However, four months after commencing employment in January 1989, she had become pregnant. She went on maternity leave on 1 October 1989, became ill soon thereafter and PPH was diagnosed. She was delivered of a healthy daughter in November 1989. In January 1990, Mrs R was informed of her reduced life expectancy of three to ten years. In May 1990, following a hysterectomy and cardiac catheterisation, it was obvious that she would not be fit to return to employment which involved dealing with difficult and potentially violent mental patients. Mrs R developed reactive depression and was retired on the grounds of ill health in May 1991. An action for damages against the appellant, based on Dr Manners' negligence, went for trial before Astill J in October 1996. He held: (1) that the pregnancy itself (and not the injury suffered during the pregnancy) was a foreseeable consequence of the failure to diagnose PPH; (2) that the devastating consequences of pregnancy for a woman suffering from PPH were such as should have been at the forefront of the mind of a competent radiologist; (3) that if there had been no breach of duty, Mrs R would have been told of the dangers of pregnancy; (4) that pregnancy and its consequences were the kind of damage from which the appellant must take care to save a plaintiff, so that the present case was no different in principle form 'unwanted birth' cases, arising from failed vasectomy or sterilisation; and (5) that Mrs R was entitled to the reasonable cost of rearing her child. As to the loss of earnings, Astill J found that Mrs R, although she would not have been offered employment by the appellant, would have been found a post which accommodated her disability by her previous employers and that, given that her life expectancy had been revised to 20 years, would have been able to work for a further ten years. With respect to her reactive depression, the judge found that is severity was without doubt greater than the reaction to the news of her PPH would have been in the circumstances which existed in December 1988. The appellant, whilst admitting negligence, contended in this appeal that the plaintiff should not have been awarded damages in respect of: the cost of bringing up her daughter and the expense of pregnancy; loss of earnings and the value of subsidised accommodation; and general damages for reactive depression…

Kennedy LJ: I accept that, subject to questions of remoteness of damage and scope of duty, to which I will turn in a moment, Mrs R may be able to claim, as flowing from the admitted breach of duty, her loss of the opportunity properly to evaluate the arguments for and against pregnancy, but that would hardly be a significant head of damages when, in the result, the hazards of pregnancy are negotiated without disaster, and she gives birth to a healthy and much loved child.

The conclusion which I have just expressed is sufficient to dispose of the appeal in relation to this part of the case, but I turn now to Mr Whitfield's alternative submission, which is that even if in this case conception and pregnancy can be regarded as a form of damage, there is no sufficient connection between that damage and the radiologist's breach of duty to enable a court to say that the damage flowed from the breach. The damage was, as it sometimes said, too remote. The chain of events had too many links. The radiologist reviewing the X-ray of an applicant for employment is not to be compared with a gynaecologist performing a sterilisation operation. The radiologist's duty is to observe and report on abnormalities, but no one expects him to advise as to their aetiology, still less as to what activities, wholly unconnected with employment, the presence of the underlying condition may contra-indicate. We understand that the radiologist never actually saw the plaintiff, and he probably knew very little about her except her age. He would no doubt have accepted that, in so far as he failed to observe an abnormality which could have affected her fitness for work as an employee of the health authority in the immediate future, that was something for which he should be held accountable, but her domestic circumstances were not his affair. In *Smith v Littlewoods Organisation Ltd* [1987] 1 All ER 710, [1987] AC 241, a case about an empty cinema being burnt by vandals, Lord Mackay said ([1987] 1 All ER 710 at 721, [1987] AC 241 at 261):

> what the reasonable man is bound to foresee in a case involving injury or damage by independent human agency, just as in cases where such agency plays no part, is the probable consequence of his own act or omission, but that, in such a case, a clear basis will be required on which to assert that the injury or damage is more than a mere possibility.

In *Doughty v Turner Manufacturing Co Ltd* [1964] 1 All ER 98, [1964] 1 QB 518, a cover was negligently knocked into a hot molten liquid. It was foreseeable that someone might be splashed, but in fact there was an explosion which, it was held, could not reasonably have been foreseen, and for the result of which the defendants were held not to be answerable in law. Mr Whitfield submits that similar considerations arise in this case.

Mr Stewart relied heavily on the recent decision of the House of Lords in *Page v Smith* (1995) 28 BMLR 133, [1996] AC 155, which establishes that, once a defendant owes a duty of care to avoid causing personal injury to a plaintiff, it matters not whether the injury in fact sustained is physical or psychiatric, or both. I accept entirely that a defendant must take his victim as he finds him, but I do not accept that in *Page v Smith* the House of Lords was extending the boundaries of foreseeability in the way that Mr Stewart contends.

As Denning LJ said in a well-known passage in *Roe v Minister of Health* [1954] 2 All ER 131 at 138, [1954] 2 QB 66 at 85:

> Three questions, duty, causation, and remoteness, run continually into one another. It seems to me that they are simply three different ways of looking at one and the same thing which is this: is the consequence fairly to be regarded as within the risk created by the negligence? If so, the negligent person is liable for it: but otherwise not.

That was before the decision in the *Wagon Mound (Overseas Tankship (UK) Ltd) v Morts Dock & Engineering Co Ltd* [1961] 1 All ER 404, [1961] AC 388), but in *Caparo Industries plc v Dickman* [1990] 1 All ER 568 at 573-574, [1990] 2 AC 605 at 617, Lord Bridge adopted a similar approach saying:

> What emerges is that, in addition to the foreseeability of damage, necessary ingredients in any situation giving rise to a duty of care are that there should exist between the party owing the duty and the party to whom it is owed a relationship characterised by the law as one of 'proximity' or 'neighbourhood' and that the situation should be one in which the court considers it fair, just and reasonable that the law should impose a duty of a given scope upon the one party for the benefit of the other.

Mr Whitfield accepts that because of the admissions made in the court below, he cannot argue proximity, but he does invite us to find and I for my part would find, that the plaintiff's domestic life fell outside the scope of the radiologist's duty.

In *South Australia Asset Management Corp v York Montague Ltd* [1996] 3 All ER 365 at 371, [1997] AC 191 at 212, a case concerning an alleged negligent valuation by a surveyor, Lord Hoffmann said;

> The scope of the duty, in the sense of the consequences for which the valuer is responsible, is that which the law regards as best giving effect to the express obligations assumed by the valuer: neither cutting them down so that the lender obtains less than he was reasonably entitled to expect, not extending them so as to impose on the valuer a liability greater than he could reasonably have thought he was undertaking.

The express obligations assumed by the radiologist did not, as it seems to me, extend to the plaintiff's private life. Mr Whitfield in this context invited our attention to three United States decisions, but none of them seemed to me to be of any particular assistance, and I am content to deal with the matter on the basis of those authorities to which I have already referred.

It was agreed before us that if the claim for damages for personal injuries in respect of the pregnancy fails, as in my judgment it does, there can be no award either for the expenses of pregnancy or for the costs of bringing up the child...

Chadwick LJ: It is accepted by the defendant health authority that, in failing to identify and report the presence of a significant abnormality to the main pulmonary artery, the radiologist fell short of the standard of care required of him. It is accepted, also, that, but for his failure to identify and report the abnormality, the plaintiff would not have become pregnant and so would not have given birth to a child in November 1989. In these circumstances, as it seems to me, the entitlement of the plaintiff to damages for the pain and distress suffered in pregnancy and for the expense associated with the birth and up-bringing of her daughter turns on the question whether loss of that nature is within the scope of the duty owed to her by the health authority vicariously as the employer of the radiologist. It is only if that question is answered in the affirmative that it becomes necessary to consider the further question whether any damages can be claimed in respect of the normal expenses and trauma of a planned pregnancy or the costs of bringing up a wanted child.

As Denning LJ observed in the passage of his judgment in *Roe v Minister of Health* [1954] 2 All ER 131 at 138, [1954] 2 QB 66 at 85 to which Kennedy LJ has referred, duty, causation and remoteness are each aspects of the same problem: to what extent should the person found or admitted to have been careless be responsible for the consequences of his carelessness? The consequences must be foreseeable; but they must also be of such a nature that the law regards it as fair, just and reasonable to impose on the person who has been careless liability to compensate the person harmed for the actual harm suffered …

In my view, for the reasons given by Kennedy LJ, a proper examination of the facts in the present case leads to the conclusion that, whatever duty of care was owed to the plaintiff by the health authority, as her prospective employer, the scope and extent of that duty stopped short of responsibility for the consequences of the decision, by the plaintiff and her husband, that she should become pregnant. I think it essential to keep in mind that the relationship between the plaintiff and the health authority was that of prospective employee and employer. There was nothing in the evidence before the trial judge to suggest that the relationship between the plaintiff and her prospective employer had anything to do with whatever plans the plaintiff and her husband may have had for starting a family.

The health authority admitted liability for those medical problems suffered during pregnancy which are attributable to the plaintiff's underlying but undiagnosed condition of primary pulmonary hypertension. It is unnecessary, therefore, to consider what the position would have been if that admission had not been made. It is clear, from the passages set out by Kennedy LJ, that the health authority was not accepting any further liability for the consequences of the pregnancy. I am not persuaded that the admission that was made requires the court to impose a further liability which the health authority has, throughout, put in issue and which is outside the scope of the duty recognised by the law.

Morritt LJ agreed.

You may think that the concession made on behalf of the defendant at first instance that a duty of care was owed would today be inconsistent with the Court of Appeal's decision in *Kapfunde v Abbey National plc* [1999] Lloyd's Rep Med 48 (CA) (see *supra,* pp 361-365). Clearly, the Court of Appeal doubted the validity of the concession. However, the judges found another route to let the defendant 'off the hook' – remoteness. The plaintiff's loss did not fall within the foreseeable risk created by the negligence (see also, *Brown v Lewisham and North Southwark HA* (1999) 48 BMLR 96 (CA)).

The Court of Appeal relied upon a passage in the speech of Lord Hoffmann in *South Australia Asset Management Corpn v York Montagne Ltd* [1996] 3 All ER 365, [1997] AC 191. That case concerned the negligence of a property valuer. However, in the course of his speech Lord Hoffmann, helpfully for us, gave an illustration in the medical context to illustrate the application of the notions of legal causation and remoteness.

Lord Hoffmann: Rules which make the wrongdoer liable for all the consequences of his wrongful conduct are exceptional and need to be justified by some special policy. Normally the law limits liability to those consequences which are attributable to that which made the act wrongful…

A mountaineer about to undertake a difficult climb is concerned about the fitness of his knee. He goes to a doctor who negligently makes a superficial examination and pronounces the knee fit. The climber goes on the expedition, which he would not have undertaken if the doctor had told him the true state of his knee. He suffers an injury which is an entirely foreseeable consequence of mountaineering, but has nothing to do with his knee.

On the Court of Appeal's principle, the doctor is responsible for the injury suffered by the mountaineer because it is damage which would not have occurred if he had been given correct information about his knee. He would not have gone on the expedition and would have suffered no injury. On what I have suggested is the more usual principle, the doctor is not liable. The injury has not been caused by the doctor's bad advice, because it would have occurred even if the advice had been correct…

Your Lordships might, I would suggest, think that there was something wrong with a principle which, in the example which I have given, produced the result that the doctor was liable. What is the reason for this feeling? I think that the Court of Appeal's principle offends common sense because it makes the doctor responsible for consequences which, though in general terms foreseeable, do not appear to have a sufficient causal connection with the subject matter of the duty. The doctor was asked for information on only one of the considerations which might affect the safety of the mountaineer on the expedition. There seems no reason of policy which requires that the negligence of the doctor should require the transfer to him of all the foreseeable risks of the expedition.

It is upon this basis that a doctor ought not to be liable in a failure to warn case where the risk which materialises and results in injury to the patient, was not one which he had a duty to disclose (see *infra*, Chapter 5).

D. DEFENCES

Largely *this* is a matter falling within the general law of torts. We notice here only a few issues which are of interest to the medical lawyer.

We concentrate upon the three defences of *contributory negligence, volenti non fit injuria* and *illegality*. In practical terms, an important defence is that limitation under the Limitation Act 1980. The case law is voluminous and one better dealt with in practitioner works: for discussion, see M Jones *Limitation Periods in Personal Injury Actions* (1995); I Kennedy and A Grubb *Principles of Medical Law* (1998), paras 7.48 – 7.89 and R James 'The Limitation Period in Medical Negligence Claims' (1998) 6 Med L Rev 62.

1. Contributory negligence, volenti and illegality

E Picard and G Robertson *Legal Liability of Doctors and Hospitals in Canada* (3rd edn, 1996)

Patients have certain duties and responsibilities when seeking medical treatment, including a duty to provide information, to follow instructions, and generally to act in their own best interests. In carrying out these duties they are expected to meet the standard of care of a reasonable patient. If they do not, and the breach of this standard is the factual and proximate cause of their injuries, they are contributorily negligent and their compensation will be reduced accordingly. Of course, if the injury is due exclusively to the patient's own negligence, the action will be dismissed...

A simple example of how apportionment legislation works is as follows. Assume a doctor is found to be negligent in treating the patient, but the patient is also found to be contributorily negligent for failing to follow the doctor's instructions. If the judge assesses the patient's damages at $10,000 and apportions liability as 60% to the doctor and 40% to the patient, the result will be that the patient recovers $6,000...

The defence of contributory negligence has been applied in relatively few medical negligence cases in Canada. Theoretically the law and practice in a medical negligence case should be the same as in any other negligence case, and the decision to find contributory negligence has been 'quite frequent' in the ordinary negligence action. One explanation for its rare application in the medical negligence context might be that the seemingly unequal position of the parties, in that the plaintiff patient may have been ill, submissive, or incapable of acting in his or her own best interests, has led the courts to set the standard that patients must meet for their own care at an unreasonably low level. As patients strive for (and achieve) a more equal role in their medical care and in the doctor-patient relationship, it is predictable and just that there will be more patients found to be contributorily negligent, with a consequential reduction in the compensation awarded.

In an older British Columbia case, (*Crossman v Stewart* (1977), 5 CCLT 45 BCSC) a patient was held to be two-thirds to blame for the blindness she suffered, and her doctor (a dermatologist) one-third to blame. She had consulted the dermatologist for a facial skin disorder and he prescribed a drug known as chloroquine or Aralen®, which she took for approximately 6 months under prescription. Because she was a medical receptionist, she was able to obtain the drug from a drug salesman at one-half the price and without a prescription, and for 7 months she took the drug on this basis. At that time, the dermatologist who had been alerted to the possible serious side effects of the drug to vision had all patients whom he had treated with it see an ophthalmologist. Unfortunately, he did not read carefully enough the resulting report on the plaintiff, which would have alerted him to her unorthodox practice. Thereafter for 2 more years the patient obtained the drug from the salesman and when this man retired she went back to the defendant and was prescribed the drug for at least a further eight months. The trial Judge found that at no time was the patient warned of the danger of the prolonged use of the drug, but also that the defendant did not have actual knowledge of her continuous use of it either. The evidence indicated that her eyes would not have been damaged had her consumption been limited to the prescriptions.

The patient's negligence was found to lie in obtaining prescription drugs from an unorthodox source, using them on a prolonged basis, and not consulting her doctor. She had failed to meet the standard expected of a reasonable patient and was the major cause of her own injury. The doctor's negligence was based on his failure to carefully peruse the ophthalmologist's report and to discern from 'corneal changes' noted in that report the probability of recent consumption of the drug. This was obviously a clear case for the application of the contributory negligence rules. In fact, it is even arguable that like the dental patient who nearly bled to death before obtaining medical assistance, (*Murrin v Janes* [1949] 4 DLR 403 (Nfled TD)) this patient was the sole cause of her injury. The standard of care expected of the reasonable patient is tied to the degree of knowledge with respect to medical matters possessed by the lay-person. Just as reasonable people are taken to know that loss of a large volume of blood will seriously endanger health, they also ought to be attributed with the knowledge that obtaining and consuming prescription drugs without medical supervision is risky. However, the fact remains that the patient in this case was given no warning as to the danger of this particular drug and, in fact, after what she would believe was a satisfactory ophthalmological examination, may have had reason to believe that the drug was safe.

In a Quebec case, (*Hôpital Notre-Dame de l'Espérence v Laurent* [1978] 1 SCR 605) the evidence of the doctor and patient was in substantial conflict, but the appellate Courts were not prepared to disturb the trial Judge's holding that the patient was contributorily negligent. The doctor was negligent for failing to diagnose a fracture of the head of the femur, but the patient did not seek further medical treatment for over 3 months and her claim was reduced by one quarter. Unlike the patient in the British Columbia case, who was active in her own treatment, this patient was passive: she failed to seek treatment. The difference in conduct is reflected in the amount by which each patient's compensation was reduced.

Recent medical negligence cases in which the defence of contributory negligence has been applied include a one-fifth reduction because of the patient's failure to use crutches after a bone biopsy (the patient fell and broke her leg), (*Brushett v Cowan* (1990) 69 DLR (4th) 743 (Nfled CA)) a one-half reduction because of the patient's failure to attend a follow up examination after an abortion (the abortion was unsuccessful, and the patient gave birth to twins), (*Fredette v Wiebe* (1986) 29 DLR (4th) 534 (BCSC)) and a 30% reduction for the patient's own carelessness in the misuse of negligently prescribed oral contraceptives, resulting in pregnancy (*Ferguson v Henshaw* [1989] BCJ No 1199 (QL) (SC)).

But, as Picard and Robertson go on to point out, it may not be easy to show that a patient was contributorily negligent.

The defence of contributory negligence has also been pursued without success in some cases. In *Foote v Royal Columbian Hospital*, ((1988) 38 BCLR 222 (SC), att'd (1983), 19 ACWS (2d) 304 (CA)) a doctor was found liable for failing to alert hospital staff to the risk that an epileptic patient whose medication he had changed might have a seizure at any time. During an unsupervised bath, the 15-year-old patient did have a seizure and suffered injuries. The doctor alleged that she should be found contributorily negligent. The trial Judge disagreed, but said that if he had been convinced that the patient had understood instructions not to bathe unsupervised, he would have held her contributorily negligent to the extent of 50%. A man playing touch football broke a lens in his glasses and injured his eye. The optometrist and lens manufacturer whom he sued pleaded contributory negligence, but the trial Judge held that this had not been proven by the defendants. In *Bernier v Sisters of Service (St John's Hospital, Edson)* ([1948] 1 WWR 113 (Alta SC)) the patient was admitted to hospital for an appendectomy. While recovering from the anaesthetic she received second and third degree burns to her feet from hot water bottles placed in her bed. The hospital was found liable for the negligence of the nurses who did not test the temperature of the bottles and placed them without orders. It was argued that the patient was contributorily negligent in failing to call for help, in failing to disclose an earlier bout of frostbite to her feet, and in leaving the hospital early against medical advice. All were rejected by the trial Judge, who was of the opinion that the injury occurred to the patient while she was still anaesthetized and that it was not unreasonable to fail to disclose having frozen her feet upon entering hospital for an appendectomy. Furthermore, her leaving hospital had not aggravated her injuries. All in all this patient had acted as a reasonable patient. It is possible to see, however, that a patient who fails to disclose a material fact to a hospital or doctor might be found contributorily negligent, as might a patient who leaves hospital without notice or against medical advice and as a consequence suffers greater injuries.

One issue which preoccupies some doctors is, what is called in medical journals, 'patient non-compliance'. This is intended to refer to situations in which a patient may not follow the instructions given by his doctor, eg as regards taking a prescribed medicine. Would a court regard this as contributory negligence? Would there be any scope here for the application of the doctrine in American products liability of 'foreseeable misuse' of a product when it is known that patients frequently depart from the instructions in prescriptions?

Consider the following two American cases.

Martineau v Nelson (1976) 247 NW 2d 409 (Sup Ct Minn)

Kelly J: A single issue is dispositive of the appeal: Was the jury's finding of 50% contributory negligence supported by the evidence?

Plaintiff's argue that the issue of contributory negligence was improperly submitted to the jury and that its finding on that issue is not supported by the evidence. This is a case of first impression on the issue of contributory negligence in a sterilisation case. While there have been several reported decisions dealing with actions for malpractice in performing sterilisation operations, including an early Minnesota case sustaining a demurrer to a complaint on a deceit theory, the bulk of the sterilisation cases deal with the burden of proof under theories of negligence and breach of warranty and the problem of provable damages.

Contributory negligence has been recognised as a defence in a number of malpractice cases in other jurisdictions. The defence has been recognised in cases in which the patient has (1) failed to follow the doctor's or nurse's instructions; or (2) refused suggested treatment; or (3) given the doctor false, incomplete, or misleading information concerning symptoms. This court expressly recognised the defence in 1970 in upholding a general verdict for defendant doctor following the submission of his negligence and plaintiff's contributory negligence. In that case, plaintiff had submitted misleading and inaccurate information about her employment status to the doctor and had no telephone, making it difficult for him to contact her regarding the positive result of her Pap smear test. *Ray v Wagner* 286 Minn 354, 176 NW 2d 101 (1970).

Both courts and text writers have emphasised, however, that the availability of a contributory negligence defence in a malpractice case is limited because of the disparity in medical knowledge between the patient and his doctor and because of the patient's right to rely on the doctor's knowledge and skill in the course of medical treatment. Thus, it has been held that it is not contributory negligence to follow the doctor's instructions or to fail to consult another physician when the patient has no reason to believe his pain is caused by the doctor's negligence. It has also been suggested that the patient's neglect of his own health after negligent treatment may be a factor in reducing damages, but should not bar all recovery ...

The relevant issue in this case, which must be considered in light of the record and the authorities just discussed, is whether and to what extent plaintiffs may be charged with acting unreasonably in the face of certain statements and advice of defendant doctors. Confronted with the results of a pathological test showing the removal of a segment of an artery [instead of the intended Fallopian tube], and with equivocation on the part of her doctors as to the success of the operation and the necessity of further procedures, plaintiff wife might have acted unreasonably in failing to at least attempt to persuade her husband to have a vasectomy or, in the absence of vasectomy, in failing to continue a regimen of birth control. The record, however, provides only the barest minimum support for these inferences of negligence. The record does not clearly reveal what plaintiff wife did or did not tell her husband about her conference with the doctors. Furthermore, there is no clear evidence of what birth control methods plaintiff did or did not use after the conference and up to the time the child David was conceived.

The evidence of plaintiff husband's contributory fault is plainly insufficient. The only evidence as to his conduct is that he concluded that his wife could not become pregnant and he elected not to have a vasectomy. There is no evidence that he received any advice directly from the doctors nor any evidence that he acted unreasonably in arriving at his conclusion. Moreover, we think that the law of contributory fault should not compel a 32-year-old husband, who might possibly remarry and later change his mind regarding more children, to undergo sterilisation because of a surgeon's negligence. From our evaluation of the evidence, we have concluded that there must be a new trial for two reasons. First, since we have concluded that plaintiff husband could not have been guilty of any negligence, and since the jury was asked to apportion negligence to husband and wife together, we cannot be certain to what extent the jury relied on erroneous theories as to the husband's negligence in making its apportionment. Second, while there may be some evidence of negligence on the part of plaintiff wife and while the apportionment of such negligence is normally within the province of the jury, we think the 50-50 apportionment in this case is plainly contrary to the weight of the evidence.

We are confronted in this case with the initial failure of the surgeon to properly perform a tubal ligation, coupled with the equivocal statements of the doctors to plaintiff wife regarding the result (ie, both doctors say her tubes are blocked, one encourages vasectomy, the other encourages further procedure if plaintiff would feel uneasy about marital relations), and plaintiffs' reaction in electing not to pursue further procedures. Neither doctor apparently discussed with plaintiff wife the risks of pregnancy notwithstanding the operation or directly informed her that she could become pregnant again. Under these circumstances, plaintiffs cannot be held equally negligent with the surgeon because the subject matter of their negligence is the interpretation of medical matters about which the doctors owed a greater duty to them than plaintiffs owed to themselves. The superior knowledge and skill of the physicians in this case should have been reflected in straightforward, complete, and accurate information and advice to their patient. That patient should not be denied recovery because she could not sift from their equivocation this kind of information and advice.

For the reasons stated above, we have concluded that there must be a new trial against both defendants on the issues of their negligence, of the contributory negligence of plaintiff wife, and of damages.

Schliesman v Fisher (1979) 158 Cal Rptr 527 (Cal CA)

Stephen JA: Robert Fisher, MD and Leonard Lewis, MD (hereinafter appellants) had treated George Schliesman (hereinafter respondent) since 1969 for various medical problems, including diabetes mellitus, arterio-sclerotic heart disease, peripheral vascular disease, gout, hypertension and distal extremity ulcerations. The diabetes was generally controlled with the administration of Orinase in spite of the fact that respondent was approximately 100 pounds overweight and did not adhere to his prescribed diet. The recurrent ulcerations on his feet were treated with antibiotics, hot soaks, and elevation of the affected extremity.

From November 19 to 22 1972, respondent was hospitalised for congestive heart failure. At this time, Dr Fisher discontinued the Orinase, instituted a diabetic diet and recounselled respondent regarding the importance of diet as the preferred means of controlling his diabetes. Dr Fisher's decision to discontinue the Orinase was based upon a recent medical study linking Orinase to increased incidences of heart disease in diabetics. When respondent was seen for follow-up care on December 5, 1972, Dr Fisher felt that the cardiac risks associated with Orinase were sufficiently severe to justify keeping respondent off the medication in spite of elevated blood sugars. Further, Dr Fisher's experience with respondent had been such that he felt the respondent was not responsible enough to be given insulin. Respondent's failure to follow medical advice regarding adherence to his diabetic diet and the need for his discontinuance of beer drinking, together with his tendency to periodically stop taking his medication, led Dr Fisher to believe that respondent was sufficiently unreliable to be prescribed insulin for control of his diabetes, since misuse of that drug could cause rather immediate and life-threatening consequences.

Dr Fisher next saw respondent on December 18, 1972, regarding pain and inflammation of his left foot. The evidence is in conflict as to whether the foot was merely inflamed or had already ulcerated at the time of this examination. The usual antibiotic treatment, hot soaks and elevation were prescribed. Two days later, December 20, 1972, respondent presented at the Santa Monica Emergency Room with a draining ulcer on his left foot. Since the emergency room attending physician could reach neither Dr Fisher nor Dr Lewis by phone, respondent was given a tetanus shot and sent home. When respondent reached Dr Lewis a few hours later, immediate arrangements were made for hospitalisation. Once hospitalised, respondent was treated with a broad-spectrum antibiotic, Erythromycin. Orinase was reinstituted, culture and sensitivity tests were ordered to determine the organism that was causing the infection, and a general surgical consultation requested.

(It was subsequently discovered that the plaintiff's foot was dead. The plaintiff's leg was amputated below the knee.)

Appellants' first contention on appeal is that the trial court erred when it refused to give a preferred instruction for the defence on contributory negligence. For the reasons stated below, we are in agreement with appellants. Here, while the great bulk of testimony was aimed at establishing or refuting that the appellants' care of respondent fell below the applicable standard for medical care, there was still substantial evidence from which the jury could have found that respondent was himself negligent in failing to follow the orders of his physicians regarding diet, weigh reduction and medications and that such negligence proximately contributed to the ultimate loss of his leg.

Robert Uller, MD, testified for appellants. He is a physician who specialises primarily in endocrinology, with approximately 40% or more of his practice dealing with diabetic patients. Dr Uller testified that patients like respondents, who are 'adult-onset diabetics', are generally obese individuals whose pancreas manufactures a relatively normal amount of insulin, but because of the increased body weight, the amount is insufficient for that individual and the individual's blood sugar is correspondingly high. Further, he testified that a reduction in weight is the best treatment for such patients, as it results in a drop in the level of blood sugar, which can then be further controlled by diet. Speaking of respondent specifically, he said: 'In this particular problem the patient is his own worst enemy because you can only tell him what diet to follow, and the big problem here to date with the blood sugars by and large has been obesity. 290 pounds and six-foot-two, 280 pounds in a six-foot-two individual, that's about 100 pounds above ideal body weight for man of, say, large boned structures, six-foot-two individual, so if the individual would follow the diet, you know, the blood sugars would be no problem'. Further, Dr Uller testified that the fact that respondent responded extremely well to insulin therapy while hospitalised was an indication that his diabetes would respond well if he were to follow the recommended diabetic diet. In fact, the hospital records revealed that respondent had to be taken off of insulin after three days because of a suspected insulin reaction. Dr Uller attributed this response to the fact that while hospitalized, respondent was forced to adhere to the diet prescribed by his physicians, which brought his blood sugars close to the normal range. Administering insulin, then, had the effect, of producing an overabundance of insulin in respondent's system. This effect, Dr Uller testified, pointed to the fact that respondent's diabetes would have responded adequately to diet if respondent would have followed his doctors' orders in this regard.

Respondent contends that there is nothing in the record to indicate that there is a direct relationship between the control of diabetes or lack thereof, and the incidence of infection contradicts this assertion. Gerard F Smith, MD, testified of his own experts, however, contradicts this assertion. Gerald F Smith, MD, testified on behalf of respondent. In the course of that testimony he stated: 'Diabetics are more prone to ulcerations, and develop infection because of their high blood sugar. High blood sugar is a media for bacteria to grow. Therefore, if the sugar is out of control and the area to this leg is impaired, we have two factors working: One, we got a good culture media of the existing blood that is there for the bacteria to grow on; Two, we have sugar that is markedly out of control, both of which will cause increased infection.' Also testifying for respondents, Saul Lieb, MD, testified: 'Infection in the presence of diabetes will spread if the treatment of diabetes is not undertaken.'

We note that the foregoing testimony was aimed primarily at the notion that Dr Lewis should not have taken respondent off the Orinase. However, such testimony also provides a foundation from which the jury could have inferred, when coupled with the prior testimony of Dr Uller, that an out-of-control diabetic whose blood sugars are elevated is more likely to get an infection such as the one that invaded respondent's foot and that such an infection will be more difficult to treat and cure as a result of the out-of-control diabetes. That respondent's diabetes could have been controlled by weight reduction and proper diet is a significant fact. While respondent sought to place the blame for his diabetes being out of control on Dr Lewis for discontinuing the Orinase, it was in fact of some significance to be weighed by the jury that respondent could himself have brought his diabetes under control with diet and weight reduction and was, in fact, counselled by his doctors repeatedly to do so. The failure of the trail court to allow an instruction of contributory negligence took this consideration from the jury and denied appellants jury trial on an essential defence.

In England, there does not seem to be a reported case in which a finding of contributory negligence has been made against a patient. There can be no doubt, however, that in principle the Law Reform (Contributory Negligence) Act 1945 could be applied in appropriate circumstances in a medical negligence action or even one for battery (see *Murphy v Culhane* [1977] QB 96 (CA)) or for contractual negligence (see *Forsikringsaktieselskapet Vesta v Butcher* [1988] 2 All ER 43 (CA)).

In the general law of torts, the defence of *volenti non fit injuria*, in effect, means that the plaintiff has agreed to waive the duty owed by the defendant to observe the required standard of care (see generally, *Morris v Murray* [1991] 2 QB 6 (CA)). It need not be an express agreement although the courts are very reluctant to imply such an agreement, particularly since the Law Reform (Contributory Negligence) Act 1945.

You will recall Picard and Robertson's reference to the lack of equality of power between the parties in a doctor-patient relationship in their discussion of contributory negligence. Does not this point apply with even greater force here, so as to suggest that a court would not find a patient had voluntarily waived the doctor's duty save in the most exceptional circumstances? Indeed, do you think a court would find that, as a matter of public policy, a patient should *never* be held to have waived a doctor's duty in the context of medical treatment?

Another defence which could have relevance in a medical negligence action is that of *illegality* or *ex turpi causa non oritur actio*. This defence is founded in public policy and bars an action brought by an individual arising out of illegal or immoral conduct. The following case illustrates its application to the medical content.

Clunis v Camden and Islington HA **(1997) 40 BMLR 181 (CA)**

From 1987 until 1992 the plaintiff had received psychiatric treatment in several London hospitals. In August 1992 he was detained under s 3 of the Mental Health Act 1983 at Guy's Hospital. The responsible medial officer decided he was fit to be discharged on 24 September 1992. By s 117 of the 1983 Act, the district health authority was under a duty to arrange, in conjunction with the local social services authority, to provide after-care services for the plaintiff, until those authorities were satisfied that he no longer needed the services. The plaintiff having expressed a desire to move to North London and into the defendant authority's area, a doctor at Guy's contacted the defendant authority and arranged for the plaintiff to be seen at Friern Hospital on 9 October 1992. The plaintiff failed to attend the appointment. Another appointment was made for him to attend on 13 November, but he failed to do so. A further appointment was made, via Haringey social services, for the plaintiff to undergo a mental health assessment visit at his address on 30 November at 3 pm. On that day, the plaintiff left his address, prior to the appointment, and no assessment was made. The plaintiff again failed to attend an appointment on 10 December. On 17 December, the local social services were advised by the police that the plaintiff had been seen 'waving screwdrivers and knives and was talking about devils'. The police officer had not exercised his powers of detention under s 136 of the Mental Health Act 1983, on the grounds that he was suffering from a mental illness, namely schizo-affective disorder. The plaintiff contended that he had suffered injury, loss and damage because the defendant health authority had been negligent and responsible for breaching a duty of care at common law to treat him with reasonable professional care and skill. He claimed that, if he had been assessed prior to 17 December 1992, he would either have been detained or consented to become a patient, and so would not have committed manslaughter and that, as a consequence of the defendant's negligence, he would now be detained for longer than he otherwise would have been. The defendant health authority argued that the claim should be dismissed on two grounds. First, the claim was based on the defendant's own illegal act of manslaughter (ex turpi causa non oritur actio). Secondly, the statutory obligations of the defendant to provide after-care to the plaintiff, following his release from Guy's Hospital, did not give rise to a common law duty of care. Richard Mawrey QC, sitting as a deputy judge of the High Court, dismissed the defendant's application on 12 December 1996. The defendant now appealed against that decision...

Beldam LJ: *Is the plaintiff's action barred on grounds of public policy?*

Mr Irwin submitted that the rule of policy embraced by the Latin maxim ex turpi causa non oritur actio does not apply to causes of action founded in tort and that the plaintiff's cause of action does not arise from the manslaughter of Mr Zito.

Of this maxim Lord Lindley in *Scott v Brown Doering McNab & Co* [1892] 2 QB 724 at 728, [1891–4] All ER Rep 654 at 657:

> This old and well-known legal maxim is founded in good sense, and expresses a clear and well-recognised legal principle, which is not confined to indictable offences. No Court ought to enforce an illegal contract or allow itself to be made the instrument of enforcing obligations alleged to arise out of a contract or transaction which is illegal, if the illegality is duly brought to the notice of the Court, and if the person invoking the aid of the Court is himself implicated in the illegality. It matters not whether the defendant has pleaded the illegality or whether he has not. If the evidence adduced by the plaintiff proves the illegality the Court ought not to assist him.

The clear and well-recognised legal principle to which Lord Lindley referred has in the ensuing 100 years become blurred by attempts to rationalise its application to different types of claim and to mitigate its consequences where they have appeared to the court to lead to a manifestly unjust result or where the rights of innocent parties may be affected if it is applied.

Comparisons have been made between its application to cases in which contractual rights are pursued, those in which property is claimed and those in which other rights are in issue.

In *Colburn v Patmore* (1834) 1 CR M & R 73 at 83, Lord Lyndhurst LCB said:

> I know of no case in which a person who has committed an act, declared by the law to be criminal, has been permitted to recover compensation against a person who has acted jointly with him in the commission of the crime. It is not necessary to give any opinion upon this point; but I may say, that I entertain little doubt that a person who is declared by the law to be guilty of a crime cannot be allowed to recover damages against another who has participated in its commission.

The argument is even more pertinent if the claim to damages is against someone who has not participated in the crime. The rule stated by Lord Mansfield in *Holman v Johnson* (1775) 1 Cowp 341, [1775-1802] All ER Rep 98 was a rule of public policy that: 'A court will not lend its aid to a man who founds his cause of action on an illegal or immoral act.' The question in that case arose on a claim for goods sold and delivered, but Lord Mansfield did not confine his principle to such cases.

We do not consider that the public policy that the court will not lend its aid to a litigant who relies on his own criminal or immoral act is confined to particular causes of action. Although Mr Irwin asserted that in the present case the plaintiff's cause of action did not depend upon proof that he had been guilty of manslaughter, the claim against the defendant authority is founded on the assertion that the manslaughter of Mr Zito was the kind of act which Dr Sergeant ought reasonably to have foreseen and that breaches of duty by the defendant authority caused the plaintiff to kill Mr Zito. Further, the foundation of the injury, loss and damage alleged is that, having been convicted of manslaughter, the plaintiff will in consequence be detained under the Mental Health Act 1983 for longer than he otherwise would have been. In our view, the plaintiff's claim does arise out of and depend upon proof of his commission of a criminal offence. But whether a claim brought is founded in contract or in tort, public policy only requires the court to deny its assistance to a plaintiff seeking to enforce a cause of action if he was implicated in the illegality and in putting forward his case he seeks to rely upon the illegal acts. As Best CJ said in *Adamson v Jarvis* (1827) 4 Bing 66 at 72-73, 130 ER 693 at 696:

> From the inclination of the Court on this last case, and from the concluding part of Lord *Keynon's* judgment in *Merryweather v Nixan* ((1799) 8 TR 186), and from reason, justice and sound policy, the rule that wrongdoers cannot have redress or contribution against each other is confined to cases where the person seeking redress must be presumed to have known that he was doing an unlawful act.

The restriction of the operation of the policy to cases in which the person seeking redress must be presumed to have known that he was doing an unlawful act was confirmed in the case of *Burrows v Rhodes* [1899] 1 QB 816. In that case the court had to decide whether the plaintiff could recover damages for deceit after he had been duped by the defendants into joining in a military expedition led by one of the defendants into the Transvaal ('the Jameson raid') and who, had he known of the purpose for which he was joining the expedition, would have been guilty of an offence under the Foreign Enlistment Act 1870. The defendants had argued that his action should be dismissed as his case was founded on an illegal act. The court rejected the argument because the plaintiff himself was innocent, had not been convicted and did not have the necessary intention to be involved in the commission of the offence. Kennedy J said (at 828):

> It has, I think long been settled law that if an act is manifestly unlawful, or the doer of it knows it to be unlawful, as constituting either a civil wrong or a criminal offence, he cannot maintain an action for contribution or for indemnity against the liability which results to him therefrom... Where the circumstances constituting the unlawfulness of the act are known to the doer of it, his inability to claim contribution or indemnity appears to me to be clear.

And (at 829-830):

> Certainly there is no right of indemnity where the doer of the act which another has authorized or induced knows it at the time to be a criminal offence. If, in a case in which knowledge is an essential ingredient of the offence, the plaintiff, in his claim for an indemnity, admitted that he was guilty of the offence, his claim would be on the face of it bad. If, in the like case, he was, on the trial of his claim for indemnity, proved to have been convicted of the offence, judgment must be given against him. Nor, in my judgment, can there be any valid claim to indemnity where the doer of the act which constitutes the offence has done it with knowledge of all the circumstances necessary to constitute

the act an offence, but in ignorance that the act done under those circumstances constituted an offence. A man is presumed to know the law. Thirdly, although it is not necessary to decide the point, I am inclined to think that there could be no valid claim to indemnity for being authorized or induced to do an act where the act which is in fact criminal is done in ignorance of the existence of some circumstance which is necessary to make it a crime, or even is done in a belief that such circumstance does not exist, but where it is known that the act is morally a wrong act. In such a case the doer of the act has, it may be said, the mens rea in the sense attributed to that expression by Bramwell B in the well-known case of *R v Prince* (1875) LR 2 CCR 154… But I am unable to accept the defendants' proposition, where the act, though a criminal offence – malum prohibitum – is, upon the state of facts which the doer by the fraudulent misrepresentation of the person against whom he claims indemnity has been induced to believe to be the true state of facts, neither criminal nor immoral.

Later, he said (at 833):

> As I have already pointed out, it can never, in my judgment, be successfully contended that a claim for indemnity can be maintained where the doer of the act knew at the time, or must be presumed to know, of circumstances which make the act either a private wrong or a public crime. Here the gist of the case is that the plaintiff did not know the facts which made his conduct criminal, but, on the contrary, was led by the defendants to believe, and did believe, in the existence of the fact – the sanction of the British Government – which, if it had been given, as he had a right (upon the defendants' representation) to assume it had been given, in the proper way, namely, under the licence of Her Majesty, would have been an answer to any imputation of illegality.

These principles seem to us to be relevant to Mr Irwin's next submission, that not all criminal or illegal acts will prevent the court from entertaining a plaintiff's claim. Pertinently, he said that there are today many summary offences which are not sufficiently serious to warrant the invocation of the maxim; the offence of manslaughter is an offence which varies greatly in its moral blameworthiness, especially if the manslaughter is by reason of diminished responsibility. He urged the court to say that, where the degree of responsibility was diminished by reason of mental disorder, the court should not apply the maxim. He prayed in aid in this regard a test which this court has adopted in other cases between 1986 and 1994, namely whether the result in a particular case would be acceptable to 'the public conscience'.

In *Tinsley v Milligan* [1993] 3 All ER 65, [1994] 1 AC 340 Lord Goff, Lord Keith and Lord Browne-Wilkinson regarded such a test as unsatisfactory. Lord Goff preferred to accept the reason for the rule stated by Ralph Gibson LJ in the Court of Appeal in that case that, in so far as the maxim is directed at deterrence, the force of the deterrent effect is in the existence of the known rule and its stern application. Lord Goff said ([1993] 3 All ER 65 at 80, [1994] 1 AC 340 at 363):

> But, bearing in mind the passage from the judgment of Ralph Gibson LJ which I have just quoted, I have to say that it is by no means self-evident that the public conscience test is preferable to the present strict rules. Certainly, I do not feel able to say that it would be appropriate for your Lordships House, in the face of a long line of unbroken authority stretching back over two hundred years, now by judicial decision to replace the principles established in those authorities by a wholly different discretionary system.

Lord Browne-Wilkinson said ([1993] 3 All ER 65 at 84, [1994] 1 AC 340 at 369):

> My Lords, I agree with the speech of my noble and learned friend, Lord Goff of Chieveley that the consequences of being a party to an illegal transaction cannot depend, as the majority in the Court of Appeal held, on such an imponderable factor as the extent to which the public conscience would be affronted by recognising rights created by legal transactions.

In the present case the plaintiff has been convicted of a serious criminal offence. In such a case, public policy would in our judgment preclude the court from entertaining the plaintiff's claim unless it could be said that he did not know the nature and quality of his act, or that what he was doing was wrong. The offence of murder was reduced to one of manslaughter by reason of the plaintiff's mental disorder but his mental state did not justify a verdict of not guilty by reason of insanity. Consequently, though his responsibility for killing Mr Zito is diminished, he must be taken to have known what he was doing and that it was wrong. A plea of diminished responsibility accepts that the accused's mental responsibility is substantially impaired, but it does not remove liability for his criminal act. We do not consider that in such a case a court can, or should, go behind the conviction and, even if it could, we do not see in the medical report attached to the statement of claim any statement which would justify the court taking the view that this plaintiff had no responsibility for the serious crime to which he pleaded guilty.

The plaintiff in this case, though his responsibility is in law reduced, must, in Best CJ's words, be presumed to have known that he was doing an unlawful act.

The only case cited to us to suggest that the court would entertain a claim to recover damages based on a plaintiff's conviction of a criminal offence, knowingly committed, is *Meah v McCreamer (No 1)* [1985] 1 All ER 367. In that case the plaintiff, who had suffered a head injury in a road accident, was held to be entitled to damages which arose from his subsequent conviction of two offences of rape. Subsequently, in *Meah v McCreamer (No 2)* [1986] 1 All ER 943, he was held not to be entitled to claim as damages sums he had been ordered to pay in compensation to the victims of the rapes. At the first hearing, the judge, Woolf J, recorded that it had not been argued on behalf of the defendant that the plaintiff was not entitled to be compensated for having committed the crimes and was entitled to receive substantial damages in respect of that claim ([1985] 1 All ER 367 at 371). At the second hearing it was argued that it would be contrary to public policy for the plaintiff to be indemnified in respect of the consequences of his crimes ([1986] 1 All ER 943 at 950). Basing himself on the judgment of Lord Denning MR in *Gray v Barr (Prudential Assurance Co Ltd, third party)* [1971] 2 All ER 949 at 956-957, [1971] 2 QB 554 at 568 Woolf J held that public policy –

... would be a further ground for holding that the plaintiff is not entitled to be indemnified for his criminal attacks on the two ladies concerned. (See [1986] 1 All ER 943 at 951).

Whilst any decision of Lord Woolf must be given the greatest weight, we do not consider that, in the absence of argument on the issue of public policy, his decision in *Meah v McCreamer (No 1)* can be regarded as authoritative on this issue.

In *Gray v Barr* a defendant who had shot and killed the plaintiff's husband in circumstances amounting to manslaughter, though acquitted of the criminal offence, was held to be precluded from claiming indemnity under a policy of insurance. Lord Denning MR [1971] 2 All ER 949 at 956, [1971] 2 QB 554 at 568 emphasised that in manslaughter of every kind there must be a guilty mind. He held that, if the defendant's conduct was wilful and culpable, he was not entitled to recover.

In the present case we consider that the defendant has made out its plea that the plaintiff's claim is essentially based on his illegal act of manslaughter; he must be taken to have known what he was doing and that it was wrong, notwithstanding that the degree of his culpability was reduced by reason of mental disorder. The court ought not to allow itself to be made an instrument to enforce obligations alleged to arise out of the plaintiff's own criminal act and we would therefore allow the appeal on this ground.

Obviously, illegality is not a defence which commonly arises in medical law cases.

2. The suicide cases

A group of cases which illustrates attempts to rely upon these (and other) defences in medical negligence actions concerns claims by psychiatric patients for injury caused whilst in hospital. The basic legal position is stated by Professor Michael Jones in *Medical Negligence* (2nd edn, 1996) at para 4-097:

A doctor undoubtedly has a duty to take reasonable steps to protect a psychiatric patient from harming himself, and in an institutional setting a hospital authority may be responsible for injuries inflicted on a patient by himself (*Jinks v Cardwell* (1987) 39 CCLT 168 (Ont HC) or by a fellow patient where the injuries are the result of a failure to provide adequate control and supervision (*Wellesley Hospital v Lawson* (1977) 76 DLR (3d) 688). The duty can include an obligation to make reasonable efforts to prevent suicide attempts. (Jones (1990) 6 PN 107) There will generally be two types of case: (a) where the patient is a known suicide risk; and (b) where it is alleged that the medical staff ought to have realised that he was a suicide risk, but failed to do so.

The cases have concerned injury arising from suicides or attempted suicides. Of course, the plaintiff (or their representatives) will have to show that the defendant was negligent (*Thorne v Northern Group Hospital Management Committee*

(1964) 108 Sol Jo 484 (Edmund-Davies J) and *Hyde v Tameside AHA* (1981) 2 PN 26 (CA) (no negligence); *Selfe v Ilford and District Hospital Management Committee* (1970) 114 Sol Jo 935 (Hinchcliffe J) and *Hay v Grampian Health Board* [1995] 6 Med LR 128 (Lord Johnston) (negligence)).

For us the interesting issues are whether the defendant can successfully raise the defences of contributory negligence, *volenti* and illegality. In addition, can it be said that the patient's act of self-harm was a *novus actus interveniens?* In one medical negligence case – *Hyde v Tameside HA (supra)* – the Court of Appeal adopted a number of devices to deny liability, including public policy and remoteness (especially per Lord Denning MR). The House of Lords has more recently returned to these questions in the context of a prisoner in police custody who commits suicide in *Reeves v Commissioner of Police of the Metropolis.*

Reeves v Comr of Police of the Metropolis [1999] 3 All ER 897 (HL)

The plaintiff sued as administratrix of L, who had committed suicide while in police custody. The police had known that L was a suicide risk because of incidents on earlier occasions when he had been in custody; and because the police surgeon who had examined L on the day in question had considered that he was a suicide risk and that he should be kept under observation, although she had found no evidence of specific mental disturbance. L had hanged himself shortly after the examination, by tying his shirt through the spyhole on the outside of his cell door; he had been able to do that because the flap in the cell door had been left down. The plaintiff claimed damages against the commissioner of police for negligence. The judge found that L was of sound mind at the time of his suicide; that the officers owed L a particular duty to take care to prevent him from committing suicide because they knew he was a suicide risk and that they were negligent in failing to shut the door flap after putting L in the cell. The judge held, however, that the defendant could rely on the defences of volenti non fit injuria and novus actus interveniens, and on the question of contributory negligence assessed L's responsibility in accordance with s 1(1)a of the Law Reform (Contributory Negligence) Act 1945 at 100%. He accordingly dismissed the plaintiff's claim. The plaintiff appealed to the Court of Appeal which, by a majority , allowed the appeal and awarded her damages in the full amount of £8,690. The defendant appealed to the House of Lords.

Lord Hoffmann: The plaintiff in this action is Mrs Sheila Reeves, who had lived with Mr Lynch for some years and had a child by him. She sues the Commissioner of Police of the Metropolis under the Fatal Accidents Act 1976 for negligently causing Mr Lynch's death. The trial judge (Judge White) found that having regard to the fact that the police knew that Mr Lynch was a suicide risk, they owed him a duty to take reasonable care to prevent him from committing suicide while being held in custody. He also found that the police had been negligent and in breach of this duty by failing to shut the wicker hatch after he had been put in the cell. There has been no appeal against these two findings.

The judge found, however, that the breach of duty by the police did not cause Mr Lynch's death. He was of sound mind and his judgment was not impaired. The sole cause of his death was therefore his deliberate act in killing himself. The judge thought that this result could be expressed in Latin either by the maxim volenti non fit injuria (Mr Lynch had consented to the injury he received) or by saying that his suicide was a novus actus interveniens. He also gave the commissioner leave to amend the defence to raise an alternative plea of contributory negligence. On the assumption that the death had been caused partly by the fault of the commissioner and partly by the fault of Mr Lynch, he assessed the responsibility of Mr Lynch in accordance with s 1(1) of the Law Reform (Contributory Negligence) Act 1945 at 100%. The judge was also inclined, without deciding the point, to think that the plaintiff's claim should fail on grounds of public policy in accordance with the maxim ex turpi causa non oritur actio. He held that if the action had succeeded, he would have assessed the damages at £8,690.

Mrs Reeves appealed to the Court of Appeal ([1998] 2 All ER 381, [1999] QB 169). By a majority, the appeal was allowed. Lord Bingham of Cornhill CJ and Buxton LJ said that, as the police did not deny that they owed Mr Lynch a duty to take reasonable care to prevent him from committing suicide or that their breach of duty had enabled him to commit suicide, they could not say that their breach of duty was not a cause of his death. 'So to hold', said Lord Bingham CJ ([1998] 2 All ER 381 at 403-404, [1999] QB 169 at 196) 'would be to deprive the duty of meaningful content.' Morritt LJ dissented, saying that a deliberate act of suicide by a person of sound mind must negative the causal connection between acts which merely created the opportunity and the subsequent death.

On contributory negligence, there was no clear majority view. Buxton LJ, for reasons to which I shall return, thought that the concept really had no application. Lord Bingham CJ said it did, and would have held the commissioner and Mr Lynch responsible in equal shares. Morritt LJ agreed in principle that contributory negligence could apply but said that the judge was right to assess Mr Lynch's responsibility at 100%. In order to have some majority judgment on the point, Lord Bingham CJ, while adhering to the view that Mr Lynch's fault contributed to his death, agreed to assess his share of responsibility at 0%. So the plaintiff recovered the damages in the full amount of £8,690 assessed by the judge.

The commissioner appeals to your Lordships' House. Mr Pannick QC argued two points on his behalf. The first was the question of causation: was the breach of duty by the police a cause of Mr Lynch's death? The way he put the answer was to say that the deliberate act of suicide, while of sound mind, was a novus actus interveniens which negatived the causal connection between the breach of duty and the death. He said at first that he was going to argue the application of the maxim volenti non fit injuria as a separate point. But when it came down to it, he accepted that if the breach of duty was a cause of the death, he could not succeed on volenti non fit injuria. I think that is right. In the present case, volenti non fit injuria can only mean that Mr Lynch voluntarily caused his own death to the exclusion of any causal effect on the part of what was done by the police. So I think it all comes to the same thing: was the breach of duty by the police a cause of the death?

The other point argued by Mr Pannick was contributory negligence. The question of public policy or ex turpi causa non oritur actio, which had not found favour with any member of the Court of Appeal, was not pursued.

On the first question, Mr Pannick relied upon the general principle stated in Hart and Honoré *Causation in the Law* (2nd edn, 1985) p 136: '...*the free, deliberate and informed act or omission of a human being, intended to exploit the situation created by defendant, negatives causal connection.'* (Authors' emphasis). However, as *Hart and Honoré* pp 194–204 also point out there is an exception to this undoubted rule in the case in which the law imposes a duty to guard against loss caused by the free, deliberate and informed act of a human being. It would make nonsense of the existence of such a duty if the law were to hold that the occurrence of the very act which ought to have been prevented negatived causal connection between the breach of duty and the loss. This principle has been recently considered by your Lordships' House in *Empress Car Co (Abertillery) Ltd v National Rivers Authority* [1998] 1 All ER 481, [1998] 2 WLR 350. In that case, examples are given of cases in which liability has been imposed for causing events which were the immediate consequence of the deliberate acts of third parties but which the defendants had a duty to prevent or take responsible care to prevent.

Mr Pannick accepted this principle when the deliberate act was that of a third party. But he said that it was different when it was the act of the plaintiff himself. Deliberately inflicting damage on oneself had to be an act which negatived causal connection with anything which had gone before.

This argument is based upon the sound intuition that there is a difference between protecting people against harm caused to them by third parties and protecting them against harm which they inflict upon themselves. It reflects the individualist philosophy of the common law. People of full age and sound understanding must look after themselves and take responsibility for their actions. This philosophy expresses itself in the fact that duties to safeguard from harm deliberately caused by others are unusual and a duty to protect a person of full understanding from causing harm to himself is very rare indeed. But, once it is admitted that this is the rare case in which such a duty is owed, it seems to me self-contradictory to say that the breach could not have been a cause of the harm because the victim caused it to himself.

Morritt LJ drew a distinction between a prisoner who was of sound mind and one who was not. He said that when a prisoner was of sound mind, 'I find it hard to see how there is any material increase in the risk in any causative sense' (see [1998] 2 All ER 381 at 398, [1999] QB 169 at 190). In *Kirkham v Chief Constable of the Greater Manchester Police* [1990] 3 All ER 246 at 250, [1990] 2 QB 283 at 289–290 Lloyd LJ said much the same. It seems to me, however, they were really saying that the police should not owe a person of sound mind a duty to take reasonable care to prevent him from committing suicide. If he wants to take his life, that is his business. He is a responsible human being and should accept the intended consequences of his acts without blaming anyone else. Volenti non fit injuria. The police might owe a general moral duty not to provide any prisoner with the means of committing suicide, whether he is of sound mind or not. Such a duty might even be enforceable by disciplinary measures. But the police did not owe Mr Lynch, a person of sound mind, a duty of care so as to enable him or his widow to bring an action in damages for its breach.

My Lords, I can understand this argument, although I do not agree with it. It is not, however, the position taken by the commissioner. He accepts that he owed a duty of care to Mr Lynch to take reasonable care to prevent him from committing suicide. Mr Lynch could not rely on a duty owed to some other hypothetical prisoner who was of unsound mind. The commissioner does not seek to withdraw this concession on the ground that Mr Lynch has been found to have been of sound mind. For my part, I think that the commissioner is right not to make this distinction. The difference between being of sound and unsound mind, while appealing to lawyers who like clear-cut rules, seems to me inadequate to deal with the complexities of human psychology in the context of the stresses caused by imprisonment. The duty, as I have said, is a very unusual one, arising from the complete control which the police or prison authorities have over the prisoner, combined with the special danger of people in prison taking their own lives.

Mr Pannick also suggested that the principle of human autonomy might be infringed by holding the commissioner liable. Autonomy means that every individual is sovereign over himself and cannot be denied the right to certain kinds of behaviour, even if intended to cause his own death. On this principle, if Mr Lynch had decided to go on hunger strike, the police would not have been entitled to administer forcible feeding. But autonomy does not mean that he would have been entitled to demand to be given poison, or that the police would not have been entitled to control his environment in non-invasive ways calculated to make suicide more difficult. If this would not infringe the principle of autonomy, it cannot be infringed by the police being under a duty to take such steps. In any case, this argument really goes to the existence of the duty which the commissioner admits rather than to the question of causation.

The decision of the majority of the Court of Appeal is supported by the Commonwealth and United States authority to which we were referred: see in particular *Pallister v Waikato Hospital Board* [1975] 2 NZLR 725, *Funk v Clapp* (1986) 68 DLR (4th) 229 and *Hickey v Zezulka, Hickey v Michigan State University* (1992) 487 NW 2d 106…

On the issues of *novus actus* and *volenti,* Lord Jauncey expressed the following views:

Lord Jauncey: *Novus actus interveniens*
Mr Pannick submitted that the deceased's death was caused not by the negligence of the police officers but by the voluntary act of the deceased while of sound mind. This act broke the chain of causation between the commissioner's breach of duty and the death. He referred to *Kirkham v Chief Constable of the Greater Manchester Police* [1990] 3 All ER 246, [1990] 2 QB 283 and in particular to the following observations of Lloyd LJ ([1990] 3 All ER 246 at 250, [1990] 2 QB 283 at 290):

> So I would be inclined to hold that where a man of sound mind commits suicide, his estate would be unable to maintain an action against the hospital or prison authorities, as the case might be. Volenti non fit injuria would provide them with a complete defence.

Lloyd LJ then pointed out that the plaintiff was not of sound mind. Mr Pannick went on to develop his argument by referring to the fundamental principle of the autonomy of each individual and his or her right of self-determination as expounded in *St George's Healthcare NHS Trust v S, R v Collins, ex p S* [1998] 3 All ER 673 at 685, [1999] Fam 26 at 44. If it is unlawful forcibly to administer food or medicine to a patient against his will because of his right of self-determination it must follow that an adult of sound mind who chooses to take his own life must bear the whole responsibility for his act.

My Lords, I consider that this argument is flawed. In *Clerk and Lindsell on Torts* (17th edn, 1995) p 54, para 2-24 it states:

> … if a particular consequence of the defendant's wrongdoing is attributable to some independent act or event which supersedes the effect of the initial tortious conduct, the defendant's responsibilities may not extend to the consequences of the supervening act or event.

It goes on to state that the novus actus interveniens 'must constitute an event of such impact that it rightly obliterates the wrongdoing of the defendant'. The reference to an independent act superseding the effect of the tortious conduct must, in my view, relate to an act which was outwith the contemplated scope of events to which the duty of care was directed. Where such a duty is specifically directed at the prevention of the occurrence of a certain event I cannot see how it can be said that the occurrence of that event amounts to an independent act breaking the chain of causation from the breach of duty, even although it may be unusual for one person to come under a duty to prevent another person deliberately inflicting harm on himself. It is the very thing at which the duty was directed: see *Stansbie v Troman* [1948] 1 All ER 599 at 600-601, [1948] 2 KB 48 at 51-52 per Tucker LJ. In *Kirkham v Chief Constable of the Greater Manchester Police* [1990] 3 All ER 246 at 254, [1990] 2 QB 283 at 295 Farquharson LJ rejected the defence of volenti non fit injuria as 'inappropriate where the act of the deceased relied on is the very act which the duty cast on the defendant required him to prevent.' These observations are equally apposite to the defence of novus actus interveniens in the present case. In *Pallister v Waikato Hospital Board* [1975] 2 NZLR 725 at 742 Woodhouse J in a dissenting judgment put the matter most succinctly: 'The concept of a novus actus interveniens does not embrace foreseeable acts in respect of which the duty of care has specifically arisen.' It follows that the observations of Lloyd LJ in *Kirkham v Chief Constable of the Greater Manchester Police* [1990] 3 All ER 246 at 250, [1990] 2 QB 283 at 290 cannot apply to a case in which there exists a duty of care on a custodier to prevent a man with known suicidal tendencies from committing suicide.

The individual's right of self-determination is irrelevant here for two reasons. In the first place it is not a defence to a breach of duty but rather an argument against the existence of a duty at all. If an individual can do to his own body what he wills, whether by positive act or neglect then there can be no duty on anyone else to prevent him so doing. In this case, however, it is accepted that the commissioner owed a duty of care to the deceased. In the second place the cases in which the principle has been recognised and to which your Lordships have been referred were cases in which prevention of injury to health or death would have involved an unlawful physical invasion of the individual's rights. In this case performance of the duty of care by closing the flap would have involved no invasion of any rights of the deceased.

Mr Pannick, with his customary fairness, drew the attention of your Lordships to a number of authorities from other common law jurisdictions which he accepted did not support his contention. In the USA the position appears to be that although as a general rule the act of suicide is viewed as an intentional intervening act which relieves the tortfeasor of liability, where a person with known suicidal tendencies is placed in the care of a jailer or other custodian the failure of such person to take reasonable care to prevent the suicide may be a direct and proximate cause of the death: see *Sudderth v White, White v Sudderth, Bowling Green-Warren County Hospital v White, City of Bowling Green v White* (1981) 621 SW 2d 33, *McLaughlin v Sullivan* (1983) 461 A 2d 123 and *Watters v TSR Inc, aka TSR Hobbies Inc* (1990) 904 F 2d 378.

In New Zealand, Richmond J in *Pallister v Waikato Hospital Board* [1975] 2 NZLR 725 at 736 expressed the view that had there been a failure by the hospital board to use reasonable care to guard the deceased against his known suicidal tendencies that failure would have been an effective or substantial cause of his death.

It appears from the decision of the British Columbia Court of Appeal in *Funk v Clapp* (1986) 68 DLR (4th) 229 that in Canada the doctrine of novus actus interveniens does not necessarily break the chain of causation between a jailer's failure in duty of care and the suicide of a prisoner in his charge.

My Lords, I have no doubts that given the admitted breach of duty of care the defence of novus actus interveniens cannot assist the commissioner. The deceased's suicide was the precise event to which the duty was directed and as an actus it was accordingly neither novus nor interveniens.

Volenti non fit injuria

Mr Pannick conceded that if his argument on novus actus interveniens failed so must his argument on volenti non fit injuria. I consider that this concession was rightly made. If the defence were available in circumstances such as the present where a deceased was known to have suicidal tendencies it would effectively negative the effect of any duty of care in respect of such suicide as Farquharson LJ pointed out in *Kirkham v Chief Constable of the Greater Manchester Police* [1990] 3 All ER 246 at 254, [1990] 2 QB 283 at 295 in the passage to which I have already referred.

Lords Mackay and Hope agreed.

However, Lord Hobhouse took a different view:

Lord Hobhouse: The starting point in the present case is the acceptance that the defendant owed Mr Lynch a duty of care. As Lord Bingham CJ put it ([1998] 2 All ER 381 at 403, [1999] QB 169 at 196):

> ... the defendant by his officers at Kentish Town police station owed the deceased a duty to take reasonable care to ensure that he was not afforded an opportunity to take his own life.

(This duty is an application of the more general duty to take reasonable care of a person in one's custody: see *Hague v Deputy Governor of Parkhurst Prison, Weldon v Home Office* [1991] 3 All ER 733, [1992] 1 AC 58.) Lord Bingham CJ emphasised that the duty was a duty to take reasonable care and not to guarantee that a fatality did not occur. He then went on to say in two similar passages ([1998] 2 All ER 381 at 403-404, [1999] QB 169 at 196-197):

Since an act of self-destruction by the deceased was the very risk against which the defendant was bound in law to take reasonable precautions, I cannot see how that act can be regarded as a novus actus. So to hold would be to deprive the duty of meaningful content. This was, after all, the very thing against which the defendant was duty-bound to take precautions. It can make no difference that the deceased was mentally 'normal' (assuming he was), since it is not suggested that the defendant's duty was owed only to the abnormal. The suicide of the deceased cannot in my view be regarded as breaking the chain of causation ... If the defendant owed the deceased a duty of care despite the fact that the deceased was of sound mind, then it again seems to me to empty that duty of meaningful content of any claim based on breach of the duty is inevitably defeated by a defence of volenti.

I would draw attention to three features of these two passages. The first is that Lord Bingham CJ apparently does not accept that any conduct of the suicide would be capable of constituting the sole legal cause of his death. The second is the peculiarity of the present case that the deceased was held by the trial judge to have been of sound mind in contrast with the finding which had been made in *Kirkham v Chief Constable of the Greater Manchester Police* [1990] 3 All ER 246, [1990] 2 QB 283, and had formed the basis of the Court of Appeal's decision in that case. The third is the use of metaphors and Latin tags which I will suggest have outlived their usefulness and now only serve to cause confusion (a view expressed by Lord Sumner as long ago as 1915: see *British Columbia Electric Rly Co Ltd v Loach* [1916] 1 AC 719 at 727-728).

My Lords, in relation to the first feature, let me take two hypothetical situations, neither unduly fanciful. Suppose that the detainee is a political agitator whose primary motivation is to further a political cause. Such persons are liable to see self-destruction, in circumstances which they hope will attract as much publicity and media attention as possible, as an appropriate means of advancing their political cause. Can such a person, having taken advantage of a careless oversight by the police and carried out his purpose, vicariously bring an action against the police and recover damages from them? Or suppose a detainee who and whose family are in serious financial difficulties and who, knowing what the Court of Appeal decided in the present case, says to himself 'the best way for me to help those I love is to commit suicide' and then carries out that purpose by taking advantage of the careless oversight. As Mr Pannick QC said in argument, he might even leave a suicide note for his wife telling her this. In cases such as these it would be surprising if the courts were to say that, notwithstanding the determinative, rational and deliberate choice of the deceased, that choice had not become the only legally relevant cause of the death. It would also in my judgment be contrary to principle. It certainly would be contrary to principle to resort to the fiction of saying that he was guilty of 100% contributory negligence: if the responsibility for his death was his alone, the principled answer is to say that the sole legal cause was his own voluntary choice. Yet, if such a case were hereafter to come before a court, that court, on the basis of the majority decision of the Court of Appeal, would be bound to award the plaintiff damages.

I give these examples to illustrate the need to identify a dividing line unless one is to say that even in such cases the deliberate voluntary choice of the deceased, the quasi-plaintiff, can never break the chain of causation. The view accepted by the majority of the Court of Appeal reduces all such questions to an examination of the scope of the duty of care or remoteness (which in the context of the law of negligence is effectively the same thing: see *Overseas Tankship (UK) Ltd v Morts Dock and Engineering Co Ltd* [1961] 1 All ER 404, [1961] AC 388). The reason why this is contrary to principle is that it is a basic rule of English law that a plaintiff cannot complain of the consequences of *his own* fully voluntary conduct – his own '*free, deliberate and informed*' act: see Hart and Honoré *Causation in the Law* (2nd edn, 1985) p 136 (authors' emphasis). This principle, overlooked by the plaintiff, is to be found in a variety of guises in most branches of the law. In the law of tort it overlaps with other principles and invites recourse to expressions (usually Latin maxims) not all of which have a consistent usage.

One such guise is that a party cannot rely upon his own unlawful or criminal conduct: the so-called ex turpi causa non oritur actio maxim. Until the passing of the Suicide Act 1961, suicide was a crime and accordingly a person who committed that crime could acquire no rights thereby. But it was always open to the interested party to say that the suicide was not criminally responsible because of insanity, usually temporary insanity. The insanity negatived both the criminal character of the conduct and its immorality. This principle is no longer relevant to the present type of case and has not been relied upon by the defendant before us. I agree with the unanimous rejection by the Court of Appeal of this defence. But it is necessary to mention it since the terminology of insanity has properly been used in cases in the past and has, since then, still tended confusingly to colour some of the judicial language. The contrast now is not between sane and insane behaviour but between conduct of the plaintiff which can and cannot be properly described as voluntary.

Suicide is within the range of conduct lawfully open to a person: personal autonomy includes the right to choose conduct which will cause that person's death and the right to refuse to allow others to obstruct that choice: see *Airedale NHS Trust v Bland* [1993] 1 All ER 821, [1993] AC 789 and *St George's Healthcare Trust v S, R v Collins, ex p S* [1998] 3 All ER 673, [1999] Fam 26. Imprisonment does not deprive the prisoner of that autonomy: see *Freeman v Home Office* [1984] 1 All ER 1036, [1984] QB 524. It would also be wrong to treat the principle of illegality or public policy as the answer to the illustrative hypothetical examples which I have given. Our culture has always regarded the willingness to sacrifice one's life for a cause or for the benefit of others as laudable not reprehensible.

In the context of suicide, these points are illustrated by the classic decision of your Lordships' House, *Beresford v Royal Insurance Co Ltd* [1938] 2 All ER 602, [1938] AC 586. There the assured who was sane decided, in circumstances not dissimilar to those postulated by Mr Pannick in argument, that copious life insurance followed by deliberate suicide was the answer to the grave financial problems with which he and his family were faced. The assured's heir was unable to recover under the policies for two primary reasons. '… no system of jurisprudence can with reason include amongst the rights which it enforces rights directly resulting to the person asserting them from the crime of that person' (see [1938] 2 All ER 602 at 605, [1938] AC 586 at 596, quoting Fry LJ in *Cleaver v Mutual Reserve Fund Life Association* [1892] 1 QB 147 at 156, [1891-4] All ER Rep 335 at 340). The other was: 'On ordinary principles of insurance law, an assured cannot by his own deliberate act cause the event upon which the insurance money is payable' (see [1938] 2 All ER 602 at 604, [1938] AC 586 at 595). The causation question is independent of the crime/public policy question and remains notwithstanding the removal of the other.

The legal problem in the present case arises because of the particular findings of fact which the trial judge made about the state of mind of Mr Lynch. Were it not for those findings, the case would have been indistinguishable from the decision in *Kirkham's* case; but, as it was, he rightly considered that he should follow the reasoning of the Court of Appeal in that case and dismiss the claim. Lord Bingham CJ was clearly surprised by the findings which the trial judge had made. I can understand his reaction. It might be thought that any person locked up in a cell was almost certainly being subjected to abnormal stresses which would be liable to cause him to act in an irrational fashion and do things which he would not normally contemplate; he may suffer impulses which he would not normally suffer. He may be in all other respects a normal person. He may not be mentally ill or otherwise suffering from any disturbance of the mind. It is the general experience of those concerned with prison administration and the custody of persons in police stations that the risk of suicide or self-harm exists among those confined whether they be suffering from some frank mental condition or appear to be relatively undisturbed. Your Lordships have been referred to reports and statistics which support this and the risk is clearly recognised in the instructions and recommendations issued by the police authorities and the Home Department. The risk of suicide is a concern of those responsible for holding persons in custody and within their contemplation. But it was the trial judge who heard the evidence, including expert evidence, and made the findings, being fully aware of their significance, and his findings have not been challenged…

Causation
My Lords, causation as discussed in the authorities has been complicated both by conflicting statements about whether causation is a question of fact or of law or, even, 'common sense' and by the use of metaphor and Latin terminology, eg, causa sine qua non, causa causans, novus actus and volenti, which in themselves provide little enlightenment and are not consistently used.

At one level causation is purely a question of fact. It is a question of fact whether event A was a cause of event X. To simplify, it is a factual question whether event X would still have occurred if event A had not. However facts are not that simple. Virtually every event will have a number of antecedent facts which satisfy such a factual test. The ordinary use of language then distinguishes between them, choosing some and discarding others. The presence of oxygen is a necessary cause of combustion yet it is not normally treated as being a cause. This is because it is part of the normal environment and therefore is disregarded when identifying the cause of some abnormal event. (In certain circumstances, oxygen is not or should not be part of the normal environment, eg in tanks used for the sea carriage of petroleum, in which case its presence would be identified as a cause.) The ordinary use of language makes a distinction, independent of any legal cause, between the normal and the abnormal in describing something as a cause.

This use of language is most easily observed in relation to physical events but is also applied to human conduct. Reasonable human responses to situations are not treated as causative; they are a normal consequence of the antecedent event and it is that event which is described as the cause. Thus the reasonable event and it is that event which is described as the cause. Thus the reasonable response of a rescuer to an accident caused by the negligence of another would not without more be described as a cause of an injury suffered by the rescuer. Similarly, to act reasonably on the faith of some misinformation is normally described as a consequence not as a cause. Human conduct, which is not entirely reasonable, for example, where it is itself careless, but is within the range of human conduct that is foreseeable and normally contemplated as not unlikely, may add a further cause of the relevant subsequent event but would not normally mean that an earlier relevant event ceased also to be *a* cause of that later event. Careless conduct may ordinarily be regarded as being within the range of normal human conduct when reckless conduct ordinarily would not.

Any disputed question of causation (factual or legal) will involve a number of factual events or conditions which satisfy the 'but for' test. A process of evaluation and selection has then to take place. It may, for example, be necessary to distinguish between what factually are necessary and sufficient causes. It may be necessary to distinguish between those conditions or events which merely provide the occasion or opportunity for a given consequence and those which in the ordinary use of language would (independently of any imposed legal criterion) be said to have caused the relevant consequence. Thus certain causes will be discarded as insignificant and one cause may be selected as *the* cause. It is at this stage that legal concepts may enter in, either in a way that is analogous to the factual assessment – as for 'proximate' cause in insurance law – or, in a more specifically legal manner, in the attribution of responsibility (bearing in mind that responsibility may not be exclusive). In the law of tort it is the attribution of responsibility to humans that is the relevant legal consideration.

The attribution of human responsibility is often a complex exercise since it involves an examination of the legally relevant features of the consequences in question and the legally relevant features of the conduct complained of (eg *The Empire Jamaica* [1956] 3 All ER 144, [1957] AC 386) in conjunction with or in contrast to other human conduct which may also be factually relevant. Legal criteria (maybe fact sensitive) have to be applied. At this level causation is a question of law. Now is not the time to enter upon an exhaustive examination of the legal criteria. For present purposes two categories are directly relevant.

Before examining these two categories, however, I would stress three points. First, a distinction is drawn between natural and human phenomena. Save in theologically inspired language now long discarded, responsibility is not attached to natural events. The only consideration to which they give rise is remoteness. Secondly, human conduct in contrast can have a double relevance, both to remoteness and to attracting legal and moral responsibility. But, for most purposes in the law, and in particular in the law of tort, all a plaintiff need prove is that the defendant's tort was *a* cause of the loss in respect of which the plaintiff claims. If two or more tortfeasors have each contributed to causing the plaintiff's loss, each of them is severally liable for that loss. Remoteness is, again, the only relevant consideration. Unless the conduct of one tortfeasor has been such as to take the consequence out of the scope of another's tortious duty and render it too remote, the liability of one does not preclude the claim of the plaintiff against each.

Thirdly and most importantly in the present context, there is a radical distinction between the conduct of the plaintiff and the conduct of third parties. To overlook this distinction will inevitably lead to error. At one level where it merely involves some lack of care or breach of duty it reduces but does not negative the plaintiff's right of recovery; this is the position (now) where there is contributory negligence. Failure to mitigate can be similarly analysed (though it can also be analysed pro tanto in terms of remoteness or causation). Where deliberate voluntary conduct of the plaintiff is involved in the knowledge of what the defendant has done, the plaintiff cannot disclaim responsibility for the consequence: he has caused his own loss. His conduct has a different impact to that of a third party.

Remoteness

The first category is the concept of remoteness. In the law of tort, the question is whether the consequence complained of, although factually caused by the defendant's act or omission, was legally too remote. This in turn, in relation to negligence, involves an inquiry into what was reasonably foreseeable by the defendant at the relevant time and what matters came within the scope of the duty of care which the defendant owed to the plaintiff: see *Overseas Tankship (UK) Ltd v Morts Dock and Engineering Co Ltd* [1961] 1 All ER 404, [1961] AC 388 and *Caparo Industries plc v Dickman* [1990] 1 All ER 568, [1990] 2 AC 605. Where other factually causative human conduct is concerned, the application of these tests provides the legal answer. Foreseeable human conduct which falls within the scope of the duty of care is not too remote, even if dishonest or criminal. A clear illustration of this is the well-known case of *Stansbie v Troman* [1948] 1 All ER 599, [1948] 2 KB 48. A decorator was left in charge of the plaintiff's house. He went out to buy some more rolls of wall paper leaving the front door unlocked. As a result a burglar was able to enter and steal the plaintiff's diamond bracelet. The decorator was liable notwithstanding the intervening criminal act of the burglar. The burglar's act was both foreseeable and within the scope of the duty owed by the defendant to the plaintiff. (Of course this does not mean that the burglar was not also legally responsible). The conclusion can be expressed in a number of ways: the defendant's negligence caused the plaintiff's loss; the plaintiff's loss was not too remote; the burglar's act was not a novus actus interveniens. As discussed in *Empress Car Co (Abertillery) Ltd v National Rivers Authority* [1998] 1 All ER 481, [1998] 2 WLR 350, it is necessary to evaluate the subsequent human intervention in conjunction with the essential character of the fault of the defendant.

This principle also extends to conduct of the plaintiff. Was the conduct of the plaintiff foreseeable? Was it within the scope of the duty of care owed by the defendant to the plaintiff? Where the plaintiff is a child, the predictable conduct of the child will not make the child's injury too remote; indeed it is usually the foundation of the defendant's liability to the child: see *Yachuk v Oliver Blais Co Ltd* [1949] 2 All ER 150, [1949] AC 386. Where the defendant's conduct has created a dangerous situation either for the plaintiff or another, the conduct of the plaintiff in response to that danger will not be too remote: see *Scott v Shepherd* (1773) 2 Wm Bl 892, [1558-1774] All ER Rep 295 and *Haynes v Harwood* [1935] 1 KB 146, [1934] All ER Rep 103. Where the defendant has set out to deceive the plaintiff, the success of that deception even though others might not have been deceived does not render the plaintiff's loss too remote; intended consequences are not too remote. Many other examples could be given. Where the conduct of the plaintiff has also been blameworthy, justice is achieved by applying the provisions of the 1945 Act. On the other hand, conduct, whether of the plaintiff or any other person, which is of such a character as to remove the relevant factual consequence from the scope of the relevant duty owed by the defendant to the plaintiff or take it outside the range of what was reasonably foreseeable, will be the same criteria make the consequence too remote for it to be said that it was caused by the relevant act or omission of the defendant.

Thus far, my Lords, these legal principles present no obstacle to the plaintiff in the present case. The suicide of Mr Lynch was foreseeable; it was within the scope of the duty of care owed by the defendant to Mr Lynch. If the plaintiff or some other person had an independent cause of action of their own against the defendant, say for nervous shock, in connection with what occurred that day in Kentish Town police station, the conduct of Mr Lynch would not make the loss suffered by such a person too remote. The Court of Appeal and your Lordships have been right to reject the defence of novus actus. But where, in my judgment, the majority of the Court of Appeal went wrong was to stop there. They rejected wholly any relevance of the second category of legal principle. It would be wrong to be too critical since, as was illustrated by the argument in your Lordships' House, counsel too tended to make the same error.

The responsibility of the plaintiff

The second category of legal principle to which I must refer is that which relates to the responsibility of the plaintiff for that of which he complains. A number of principles are involved. First there is the fundamental principle of human autonomy. Where a natural person is not under any disability, that person has a right to choose his own fate. He is constrained in so far as his choice may affect others, society or the body politic. But, so far as he himself alone is concerned, he is entitled to choose. The choice to commit suicide is such a choice. A corollary of this principle is, subject to the important qualification to which I will refer, the principle that a person may not complain of the consequences of his own choices. This both reflects coherent legal principle and conforms to the accepted use of the word cause: the person's choice becomes, so far as he is concerned, the cause. The autonomy of the individual human confers the right and the responsibility.

To qualify as an autonomous choice, the choice made must be free and unconstrained – ie voluntary, deliberate and informed. If the plaintiff is under a disability, either through lack of mental capacity or lack of excess of age, the plaintiff will lack autonomy and will not have made a free and unconstrained choice. Child plaintiffs come into this category. Both as a matter of causation and the attribution of responsibility, their conduct does not (without more) remove the responsibility of the defendant or transfer the responsibility to the child plaintiff: see *Yachuk v Oliver Blais Co Ltd* [1949] 2 All ER 150, [1949] AC 386. Similarly, plaintiffs suffering from a temporary or a more serious loss of mental capacity (see *Kirkham v Chief Constable of the Greater Manchester Police* [1990] 3 All ER 246, [1990] 2 QB 283, *Pallister v Waikato Hospital Board* [1975] 2 NZLR 725 and *Pigney v Pointers Transport Services Ltd* [1957] 2 All ER 807, [1957] 1 WLR 1121), will not have made the requisite free and unconstrained choice. Where the plaintiff's lack of mental capacity has been caused by the defendant's breach of duty, the entitlement to recover is all the stronger. On the same basis choices made under constraint of circumstances, such as those made by rescuers or persons placed in immediate danger, will not carry with them the consequence that the choice was the sole cause of the subsequent injury to the plaintiff nor will it result in his bearing the sole responsibility for his injury: see *Haynes v Harwood* [1935] 1 KB 146, [1934] All ER Rep 103: cf *Cutler v United Dairies (London) Ltd* [1933] 2 KB 297, [1933] All ER Rep 594. The same applies if the plaintiff's choice was vitiated by misinformation or lack of information. In the context of employment, the question of the reality of the employee's assent and his acceptance of risk has been the subject of many decisions; perhaps the most illuminating discussion for present purposes is to be found in *Imperial Chemical Industries Ltd v Shatwell* [1964] 2 All ER 999 esp at 1008-1009, [1965] AC 656 esp at 680-681 per Lord Hodson where he stresses that the plaintiff's conduct cannot be described as voluntary unless he truly had a free choice. (The case also, like *Stapley v Gypsum Mines Ltd* [1953] 2 All ER 478, [1953] AC 663, illustrates the distinction between lack of care for one's own safety and the true acceptance of risk). These qualifications are fundamental and are the basis of the decisions where a plaintiff has been held entitled still to sue notwithstanding his having made a choice which led to the event of which he complains.

The simplest way in which to express the relevant principles, both the basic principle of the ordinary use of language and as a matter of law it is correct to say that the plaintiff's voluntary choice was *the* cause of his loss. Another partial expression of this principle is the maxim volenti non fit injuria. This maxim, originating from a rather different Roman law context, is a notorious source of confusion: see *Dann v Hamilton* [1939] 1 All ER 59, [1939] 1 KB 509. In intentional torts it means consent by the plaintiff to the act which would otherwise be the tort. In the law of negligence it means the acceptance variously of the risk created by the defendant's negligence or of the risk of the defendant's negligence. In such cases it is probably best confined to cases where it can be said that the plaintiff has expressly or impliedly agreed to exempt the defendant from the duty of care which he would otherwise have owed (*Nettleship v Weston* [1971] 3 All ER 581, [1971] 2 QB 691), a formulation which, it will be appreciated, immediately brings the maxim into potential conflict with s 2 of the Unfair Contract Terms Act 1977. It will also be appreciated that so interpreted the maxim would only have an artificial application to the facts of the present case. The suggestion that Mr Lynch was agreeing to exempt the police authority from anything is both objectionable and wholly unrealistic. (It may be that this consideration understandably coloured counsel's presentation of the defendant's case.)

But, my Lords, if the question raised by Mr Lynch's conduct is seen as a question of causation, these artificialities fall away. If Mr Lynch, knowing that the police officers had put him in a cell with a defective door and had failed to close the hatch, then voluntarily and deliberately, in full possession of his faculties, made the rational choice to commit suicide, principle and language say that it was his choice which was the cause of his subsequent death. He was not, on the judge's findings, acting under any disability or compulsion. He made a free choice: he is responsible for the consequence of that choice.

Conclusion

I would allow the appeal and direct judgment to be entered for the defendant. The argument of the plaintiff and the decision of the majority of the Court of Appeal disclose errors of law. They fail to have adequate regard to the fact that the action is to be decided as if Mr Lynch was the plaintiff. They treat remoteness as the sole criterion of recovery. They do not recognise the principle that a plaintiff who by his own *voluntary* choice deliberately chooses to cause the loss which he seeks to recover from the defendant cannot thereafter say that his choice was not the sole cause of his loss. The decision of the Court of Appeal is also worrying since it fails to provide any dividing line between cases where the plaintiff can recover and those where he cannot and, in view of the findings of fact that were made in the present case, leaves it open for any suicide to recover once some negligence on the part of the prison or police authorities has been shown. I do not consider that this is the law.

On the issue of contributory negligence, the majority held that the defence did apply and damages should be apportioned 50:50. Lord Jauncey most succinctly stated the majority's approach.

Lord Jauncey: *Contributory negligence*
Mr Blake QC for the plaintiff submitted that the act of suicide could not amount to contributory negligence on the part of the deceased inasmuch as it did not amount to fault by him within the meaning of s 4 of the Law Reform (Contributory Negligence) Act 1945. Section 1(1) of that Act provides that where A suffers damage 'as the result partly of his own fault and partly of the fault' of B, the damages recoverable may be reduced 'having regard to the claimant's share in the responsibility of the damage'. Fault is defined in s 4 as meaning 'negligence, breach of statutory duty or other act or omission which gives rise to a liability in tort or

would, apart from this Act, give rise to the defence of contributory negligence'. Mr Blake contended that since an act which was intentional not only as to its performance but also as to its consequences would not have amounted to contributory negligence at common law it followed that the deceased's act of suicide was not 'fault' within the meaning of s 4. He referred to a number of English cases which did not appear to me to bear upon the issue or to advance his argument. In *Pallister v Waikato Hospital Board* [1975] 2 NZLR 725 at 736 Richmond J referred to the possibility of the act of the deceased in jumping from the window amounting to 'fault' within the meaning of the Contributory Negligence Act 1947. Mr Blake also referred to three United States cases, two from the state Court of Appeals and one from a federal Court of Appeals which ruled that a plaintiff's suicide did not amount to contributory negligence. In *Cole v Multnomah County* (1979) Or App 592 P 2d 221 the Court of Appeals of Oregon ruled that acts which a plaintiff's mental illness caused him to commit were the same acts which the defendants had a duty to prevent and therefore could not constitute contributory negligence. In *Alvarado v City of Brownsville* (1993) 865 SW 2d 148 the State Court of Appeals ruled that the Texas Civil Practices and Remedies Code prohibited the use of a plaintiff's suicide as a defence if the suicide was caused in whole or in part by a defendant's breach of duty. In *Myers v County of Lake Indiana* (1994) 30 F 3d 847 the United States Court of Appeals, Seventh Circuit opined that Indiana law would probably not recognise intentional efforts to commit suicide as defences to the tort of negligently failing to prevent suicide attempts. However, this opinion was expressed in the context of a defence which appeared to equiparate contributory negligence to novus actus interveniens and volenti non fit injuria as a complete defence rather than one resulting in reduced quantum of damages. I do not therefore consider that it advances Mr Blake's argument.

On the other hand Mr Pannick referred to three United States cases one from a Federal Court of Appeals and two from state Supreme Courts in which suicide had been treated as amounting to contributory negligence. In *Hickey v Zezulka, Hickey v Michigan State University* (1992) 487 NW 2d 106 the majority of the Supreme Court of Michigan held that the contributory negligence of a prisoner who committed suicide could be taken into account in assessing damages for the jailer's breach of duty. In *Molton v City of Cleveland* (1988) 839 F 2d 240 the United States Court of Appeals, Sixth Circuit refused to disturb the decision of a jury as to the degree of contributory negligence found on the part of a prisoner who committed suicide. In *Champagne v USA* (1994) 513 NW 2d 75 the Supreme Court of North Dakota rejected an argument that the contributory negligence of the victim is never to be considered where suicide is a foreseeable result of a medical provider's failure to take reasonable steps to prevent it, and held that where the patient was responsible for his own care allocation of fault was in order. Although I have referred to the circumstances of each of the six United States cases cited by counsel in relation to contributory negligence the only significant conclusion which I draw from them is that in the United States a deliberate act of suicide by someone in command of his senses does not necessarily bar a plea of contributory negligence in reduction of damages.

My Lords, no United Kingdom authority has been cited in support of Mr Blake's contention so far as the period before 1945 is concerned. This is perhaps not altogether surprising in view of the fact that the effect of contributory negligence at that time was identical to that of the defence of volenti non fit injuria. The authorities from New Zealand and the United States do not suggest that an act intentional both as to performance and consequences can never amount to contributory negligence. If the law is to retain the respect of the public it should where possible walk hand in hand with common sense. There are, of course, occasions where legislation both domestic and European appear to make this impossible but where there is no such legislative inhibition the law should be interpreted and applied so far as possible to produce result which accords with common sense. To take an example, A working beside a tank of boiling liquid which is inadequately guarded negligently allows his hand to come in contact with the liquid and suffers damage; B for a dare plunges his hand into the same liquid to see how long he can stand the heat. It would be bordering on the absurd if A's entitlement to damages were reduced but B could recover in full for his own folly. B's responsibility for the damage which he suffered is undeniable. I see no reason to construe s 4 of the 1945 Act to produce such a result and I agree with Lord Bingham CJ that the word 'fault' in that section is wide enough to cover acts deliberate as to both performance and consequences. An individual of sound mind is no less responsible for such acts than he is for negligent acts and it is his share of responsibility for the damage which reduces the damages recoverable.

In this case the open flap was not a danger to an occupant of the cell acting normally with reasonable regard for his own safety. It only became a danger when it was deliberately used by the deceased as part of the mechanism whereby he strangled himself. The act of the deceased was accordingly a substantial cause of his own demise and any damages recoverable by the plaintiff should be reduced to reflect this.

Were I sitting alone I would have apportioned the blame as to one third to the commissioner and as to two thirds to the deceased. However, I understand that the majority of your Lordships favour a 50/50 division of responsibility and I do not feel inclined to dissent from that view.

The approach of the majority can be applied to psychiatric patients who are a known suicide risk (or who ought to be known to be a risk). As with the police in *Reeves*, the hospital will have undertaken to prevent them injuring themselves and at least because of their psychiatric condition, but probably more broadly. A number of points are worth noting. First, although the Law Lords did reduce the claimant's damages, this may be more difficult to apply where the case concerns a psychiatric patient, who may be of less than sound mind. Lord Hoffmann, for example, stated:

> **Lord Hoffmann:** Buxton LJ ([1998] 2 All ER 381 at 392, [1999] QB 169 at 183) referred to cases in which a defence of contributory negligence failed against child plaintiffs who had injured themselves by taking opportunities to play with dangerous things which the defendant had carelessly given them or left unguarded. He treated these as cases in which the defence failed because the child had done the very thing which it was the defendant's duty to take reasonable care to prevent. In my opinion, however, they have a different explanation. It is because the plaintiffs were children, without full understanding of the dangers they were running, that it would not have been just and equitable to attribute responsibility to them. This may be equally true in the case of a prisoner of unsound mind who commits suicide. In *Kirkham v Chief Constable of the Greater Manchester Police* [1989] 3 All ER 882, where a prisoner suffering from clinical depression committed suicide in his cell, Tudor Evans J decided that no share of responsibility for his death should be attributed to him under the 1945 Act. There appears to have been no appeal against this finding (see [1990] 3 All ER 246, [1990] 2 QB 283).

Lord Hope expressed his agreement with the approach of the Supreme Court of North Dakota:

> **Lord Hope:** In *Champagne v USA* (1994) 513 NW 2d 75, after examining a number of cases about comparative fault in cases of suicide including *Hickey's* case, the Supreme Court of North Dakota rejected the argument that, when a patient's act of suicide is a foreseeable result of a medical provider's failure to treat reasonably to prevent the suicide, it is never appropriate to compare the victim's act of suicide with the medical provider's fault. If the patient was capable of being responsible for his own care, allocation of fault was in order. But a mentally ill patient could only be held to the degree of care permitted by his diminished capacity. The worse the suicidal patient's diminished capacity, the greater the medical provider's responsibility.

Secondly, as regards the defences of *novus actus* and *volenti*, the judges did not draw any distinction between prisoners (and for us patients) who are of sound or unsound mind who commit suicide. The duty to prevent harm 'trumps' the defence.

Thirdly, the judges saw no inconsistency with the duty to prevent suicide and the individual's right of autonomy. We saw Lord Hoffmann and Lord Jauncey's reconciliation above. Lord Hobhouse, in his dissent, disagreed. He saw the 'right' as controlling. The judges were, of course, concerned with a prisoner whom the judge found to be of 'sound mind'. Whilst considering the finding to be surprising, the House of Lords had to accept that. Lord Hobhouse's approach could have no application to a psychiatric patient (whether voluntary or detained) who is undergoing treatment for his mental health. The factual finding would in all likelihood be different from that in *Reeves*.

E. WHO PAYS THE BILL?

Until 1 January 1990 a patient who succeeded in an action in negligence (or battery) or successfully settled such an action looked to the Health Authority or the doctor to meet the bill. It was a matter of no concern to the patient who paid providing one of them did. Obviously, it was a matter of concern to the doctor. A doctor practising in an NHS hospital was contractually obliged to belong to a 'defence organisation' – Medical Defence Union, Medical Protection Society, Medical and Dental Defence Union of Scotland. A general practitioner would customarily also become a member but was not obliged to do so. The functions of such organisations included the provision of legal advice and representation when claims were made against the doctor, and the indemnification of the doctor against any award of damages.

During the 1980s as medical litigation increased so also did the costs of membership of defence organisations (for a discussion of claims see P Hoyte 'Unsound Practice: the Epidemiology of Medical Negligence' (1995) 3 Med L Rev 53 and P Hoyte 'Medical Negligence Litigation, Claims Handling and Risk Management' (1994) 1 Medical Law International 261). Furthermore, one organisation introduced differential rates which reflected the risks of practising in different specialities. Given that within the NHS doctors were largely unable to pass on the cost of these increases to patients, pressure mounted to replace the system. This was notwithstanding the fact that in the hospital sector where most litigation occurs, two-thirds of the cost of a doctor's membership of a defence organisation was borne by the Health Authority.

Health Authorities were equally concerned since they faced an increasing financial burden in meeting the cost of their employees' membership. Additionally, since the Health Authority might itself be liable to contribute to the damages because of its own wrongdoing, it faced a growing charge on its funds as damage claims become more onerous during the 1980s. This was at a time when funds were barely keeping pace with demands placed upon the service.

The basis for arranging the payment of damages was a circular agreed between government and the defence organisations in 1954 (HM(54)32). It sought to distribute the financial burden of litigation between Health Authority and defence organisation, save in so far as one was entirely to blame. The circular contemplated that the Health Authorities and defence organisation should agree the proportion of responsibility which they were prepared to accept without recourse to contribution proceedings. In the absence of such agreement, each would bear 50% of the burden of litigation.

Since the conduct of most litigation was in the hands of the defence organisations, the Health Authorities increasingly realised that they were being held responsible without being able to control the litigation and its financial consequences. Faced with this situation, the Government sought a scheme which would be in their view less expensive since it is they who fund the Health Authorities. On 1 January 1990 the NHS Indemnity Scheme was introduced with the coming into force of circular HC(89)34; 'Claims of Medical Negligence Against NHS Hospitals and Community Doctors and Dentists' subsequently updated by HSG (96) 48 (and 'Arrangements for Clinical Negligence Claims in the NHS' (Oct 1996)).

The Scheme is described and discussed by Professor Michael Jones.

Michael Jones in I Kennedy and A Grubb (eds) *Principles of Medical Law* (1998)

8.74 The arrangement was replaced from 1 January 1990 with the introduction of 'NHS indemnity' under which health authorities assumed responsibility for new and existing claims of medical negligence and no longer require their medical and dental staff to subscribe to a defence organisation. The new scheme was introduced as a result of substantial increases in the subscription rates of the medical defence organisations in the 1980s, and the growing pressure to relate subscription rates to the doctor's speciality, with high risk specialities paying a higher rate. It was considered that this could lead to distortion in pay and recruitment to the medical profession. NHS indemnity covers only health authority responsibilities, namely their vicarious liability for the negligence of staff acting in the course of their employment, and there is no attempt to seek contribution from the employee. This includes consultants and staff provided by external agencies, irrespective of the precise legal relationship between these individuals and the hospital (that is, whether or not they are in law employees of independent contractors).

8.75 Strictly speaking, Health Circular (89)34 did not determine the question whether a health authority was in law vicariously liable for the negligence of, say, agency staff, but simply specified how health authorities were to deal with this in practice. If, for example, an NHS Trust hospital were to take a vicarious liability point in a particular case involving agency staff, the Circular could not change the position in *law*. Health authorities did not, in any event, take this point for agency staff and consultants before 1990. The Circular did not help on this point, since it merely stated that NHS Trusts would be responsible for claims against their medical and dental staff. If visiting consultants and agency staff are not in law employees of the NHS Trust, the Circular could not deem them to be employees. HSG(96)48 and the accompanying documentation updated the guidance given in HC(89)34 and takes the view that in addition to staff acting in the course of their NHS employment, NHS indemnity also covers locums, medical academic staff with honorary contracts, students, researchers conducting clinical trials, charitable volunteers, and people undergoing professional education, training and examinations, 'whenever an NHS body owes a duty of care to the person harmed'.

8.76 Although there were no NHS Trusts constituted when NHS indemnity was introduced, the intention of Health Circular (89)34 was that NHS Trusts should be responsible for claims for negligence against their own medical and dental staff. This was consistent with the objective of giving NHS Trusts financial autonomy and it is the basis upon which the scheme has operated since its inception. From 1 April 1991 NHS Trusts have had to bear their own losses arising out of claims for clinical negligence.

8.77 NHS indemnity does not apply to general practitioners except where the general practitioner has a contract of employment (for example, as a clinical assistant at a hospital or as a public health doctor) with a health authority or NHS Trust and the treatment is being given under that contract. If the health authority or Trust is essentially providing only hotel services and the patient remains in the general practitioner's care, the hospital authority will not be responsible, and the claim will be dealt with by the general practitioner's defence organisation. Where a case involves a claim against both a health authority or NHS Trust and a general practitioner the possibility of a contribution claim exists, but the Circular requests defendants' representatives to seek to reach agreement out of court as to the proportion of their respective liabilities, and to co-operate fully in the formulation of the defence.

However, the changes did not rest there, and in 1995 the Government created the National Health Service Litigation Authority (NHSLA) to administer schemes to cover the liability of Trusts for 'clinical negligence' in England (but not Wales) (see, the NHS Litigation Authority Regulations 1995 (SI 1995 No 2801) and the NHS Litigation Authority (Establishment and Constitutions) Order 1995 (SI 1995 No 2800)). Two schemes were created: the 'Clinical Negligence Scheme for Trusts' (CNST) and the 'Existing Liabilities Scheme' (ELS) (see the NHS (Clinical Negligence Scheme) Regulations 1996 (SI 1996 No 251) (as amended by SI 1997 No 527 and SI 1999 No 1274) and the NHS (Existing Liabilities Scheme) Regulations 1996 (SI 1996 No 686) (as amended by SI 1997 No 526 and SI 1999 No 1275)). In essence, these schemes cover the liabilities of Trusts and others for events on or after 1 April 1995 and before that date respectively. Professor Jones again explains the two schemes.

Michael Jones in I Kennedy and A Grubb (eds) *Principles of Medical Law* (1998)

8.79 The NHS Litigation Authority is a special health authority established in November 1995 with the responsibility for administering schemes set up under section 21 of the NHS and Community Care Act 1990 permitting NHS bodies to pool the costs of injury, loss or damage to property, and liabilities to third parties arising out of their NHS activities (NHS Litigation Authority Document (NHS Executive, 1996)). Its role is to approve or not approve proposals to it by NHS bodies in the conduct of medical negligence claims. The NHS Litigation Authority also has a duty to advise the Department of Health about: novel or contentious claims or claims with major repercussions; claims where the total value, including costs, is more than £1 million; and developments in law and legal practice. It is also responsible for devising and implementing risk management strategies for the NHS. The NHS Litigation Authority administers two principal schemes:

(1) the Clinical Negligence Scheme for Trusts (CNST), covering liabilities for clinical negligence where the adverse event occurred on or after 1 April 1995; (see the NHS (Clinical Negligence Scheme) Regulations 1996, SI 1996) 251, NHS (Clinical Negligence Scheme) (Amendment) Regulations, 1997, SI 1997/527) and

(2) the Existing Liabilities Scheme (ELS) covering incidents of clinical negligence which occurred before that date.

8.80 CNST is funded by contributions from the NHS Trusts who are members of the scheme. (Membership is voluntary). It is not an insurance fund, but a 'pay as you go' scheme which only collects enough money each year in contributions to cover the actual costs which fall into that year, plus a small margin to form a contingency reserve and cover administrative expenses. The object is to permit NHS Trusts to spread the cost of the larger claims, while at the same time leaving the individual Trust responsible for a proportion of the claim. As a result of the significant time gap between an adverse event and settlement of the claim, the expectation is that contributions will be small in the early years, building up in future years. There are discounts of up to a maximum of 5 per cent of the Trust's contribution for putting into place appropriate risk management standards.

8.81 Under the *CNST Membership Rules*, September 1996, there are 'excess' levels which range from £10,000 to £500,000, which are also linked to an 'ultimate threshold' ranging from £100,000 to £1,000,000. For settlements, including costs, which are below the excess there is no financial benefit to the NHS Trust. Where the settlement is above the excess, but below the amount of the ultimate threshold, the Trust must pay the amount of the excess plus 20 per cent of the balance of the settlement. Where the settlement is above the ultimate threshold the Trust pays the amount of the excess plus 20 per cent of the amount between the excess and the ultimate threshold, the remaining amount being paid by the CNST.

8.82 CNST operates on a 'claims paid' basis, which means that it will cover an NHS Trust if the Trust is a member of the scheme continuously at the date of the adverse event which subsequently gives rise to the claim and the date of settlement. There are requirements for Trusts to report claims to CNST, in particular in relation to claims likely to settle for more than £1 million (including costs), claims which have 'significant implications' and claims which may set a precedent or constitute a test case of a 'serial claim'. Although the majority of claims are handled by the Trust's own legal advisers (who are selected and instructed by the Trust), the NHS Litigation Authority has the power to take over the conduct of any claim.

8.83 The Existing Liabilities Scheme (ELS) is funded by the Secretary of State, through the Litigation Authority. Under ELS the health authority or NHS Trust has to bear the first £10,000 of the total cost (damages and costs) of a settlement, 20 per cent of the amount between £10,000 and £500,000, with the remaining cost being met from the existing claims pool administered by the NHS Litigation Authority (FDL (95)96).

A number of further points should be noted. First, both schemes are linked to 'clinical negligence'. This is defined in the National Health Service (Clinical Negligence Scheme) Regulations 1996 (SI 1996 No 251), reg 4 as follows:

4. The Scheme applies to any liability in tort owed by a member to a third party in respect of or consequent upon personal injury or loss arising out of or in connection with any breach of a duty of care owed by that body to any person in connection with the diagnosis of any illness, or the care or treatment of any patient, in consequence of any act or omission to act on the part of a person employed or engaged by a member in connection with any relevant function of that member.

(See also the NHS (Existing Liabilities Scheme) Regulations 1996 (SI 1996 No 686) (as amended) reg 4.)

Thus, the schemes cover clinical negligence claims, whether based upon direct or vicarious liability. What is not clear is whether they would cover claims framed in battery. Would such a claim arise out of a 'breach of a duty of care' owed by the member of the scheme. The answer would appear to be 'no', according to the House of Lords when interpreting the same words in the Limitation Act 1980 so as to exclude actions in battery from the 'personal injury' regime: see *Stubbings v Webb* [1993] AC 498 (HL).

The same point arises in relation to the NHS Indemnity Scheme. There, 'breach of duty of care' is explicitly stated to have 'its legal meaning' (see HSG (96) 48: *Arrangements for Clinical Negligence Claims in the NHS* (October 1996)). It may be this difficulty which has led to actions in negligence being brought by injured patients even through their claims were in essence for battery (see eg *Williamson v East London and City HA* [1998] Lloyd's Rep Med 6).

Secondly, more recently two further schemes have been created, going beyond 'clinical negligence', which are administered by the NHSLA. These cover the liability of Trusts to employees, to the public for the state of their premises and for miscellaneous liability (see the NHS (Liabilities to Third Parties Schemes) Regulation 1999 (SI 1999 No 873) and the NHS (Property Expenses Scheme) Regulations 1999 (SI 1999 No 874). As a consequence, Trusts are also not permitted to carry commercial insurance for any of their non-clinical risks (see HSC 1999/021).

Finally, it should be noted that the schemes do not cover Primary Care Trusts created under the Health Act 1999. No doubt, the schemes will be amended when PCTs come into existence after April 2000.

F. REFORMING THE LAW

1. The context of medical negligence litigation

Litigation between patients and doctors has long been recognised as a less than satisfactory means of regulating the doctor/patient relationship and dealing with patients' unhappiness over treatment. Despite this the system of tort litigation remains the principal process by which patients who are injured are compensated for their injuries, leaving aside the social security system.

The perceived difficulties with the tort system are that it is expensive (the transaction costs are high); there are considerable delays between injury and compensation sometimes in excess of ten years, and such litigation has a disproportionate impact on the NHS. In regard to the latter, awards of damages are often high – perhaps millions of pounds for severe injuries arising out of birth – and the incidence of litigation has increased dramatically in the last 20 years. The system is, therefore, often characterised as not working either from the perspective of claimants or the NHS as a defendant. It can also be said that the litigation process is an adequate mechanism for making doctors and others publicly accountable for the services they provide (see Chapter 3 for other mechanisms). Tort litigation in this context satisfies the aims of neither deterrence or distributive or corrective justice (for discussion of these in the context of 'accident law', including medical negligence, see D Dewes, D Duff and M Trebilcock, *Exploring the Domain of Accident Law* (1996) especially ch 3). Can and should this system be reformed?

The starting point for this inquiry should be the Pearson Report: *Royal Commission of Civil Liability and Compensation for Personal Injury* in 1978 (Cmnd 7054), which made a number of somewhat modest (and some would say disappointing) recommendations about negligence in the context of medical practice.

Criticisms of the present compensation provisions
1325 Criticisms of the present compensation provisions fall into two parts. First, there are those which relate to the difficulty of making claims following negligent treatment. Secondly, there are those concerning the lack of provision for medical accidents.

Proving negligence

1326 The proportion of successful claims for damages in tort is much lower for medical negligence than for all negligence cases. Some payment is made in 30-40 per cent of claims compared with 86 per cent of all personal injury claims.

1327 We received a good deal of evidence about the difficulty of proving negligence. It was said that it was not always possible to obtain the necessary information on which to base a claim. The patient might not know what had happened and he might have difficulty in obtaining the services of a medical expert to assist him. When a doctor was accused of negligence, his colleagues might naturally be reluctant to give evidence. The medical records might not contain all the details of the case, leaving ample scope for different interpretations by witnesses for an against.

1328 One of our number, who attended a Council of Europe colloquy on the civil liability of physicians, held in Lyons in June 1975, reported that most of the doctors and lawyers there agreed that information should be more readily available to the patient's advisers.

1329 In England and Wales, on an order for discovery, the court may direct disclosure of the applicant or his solicitors. The courts have taken the line that, normally, disclosure would be only to a nominated medical adviser of the applicant. In Northern Ireland, the courts have decided that disclosure may be made to the applicant. This is also the position in Scotland.

1330 Any patient may approach the Health Service Commissioners for investigation of his complaint, but the Commissioners are expressly prevented from investigating a claim in respect of which the person aggrieved has or had a remedy in law (unless it would not be reasonable to expect him to resort to it) or in respect of any action taken solely in consequence of the exercise of clinical judgment.

Medical accidents

1331 We have so far discussed the evidence we received about negligence. But there are many more cases where individuals suffer injury which was not due to negligence. We received a good deal of evidence that the position here was unsatisfactory.

1332 The Royal College of Physicians instanced, 'the possible sequelae of coronary arteriograms, kidney biopsies or amniocentesis'. Injury or death might be associated with, 'the development of hypersensitivity to a drug or antibacterial substance that was properly prescribed'. Dr White Franklin pointed out that a patient who stopped breathing under properly administered and controlled anaesthesia might die or recover with faculties grossly impaired.

1333 Some of these patients (or their dependents) would receive social security benefit, but many would receive no cash benefit of any kind.

What should be done?

1334 Our evidence showed that there was considerable dissatisfaction with the present position and some unease about the future.

1335 We considered various ways of compensating medical accidents with or without negligence. We look first at tort, where liability at present is based on negligence, and consider the possibility either of reversing the burden of proof or of imposing strict liability. Then we go on to examine the possibility of a no-fault scheme which would cover medical accidents irrespective of negligence.

Tort compensation

Reversed burden of proof

1336 Some witnesses suggested that, if the burden of proof were reversed, the patient's difficulties in obtaining and presenting his evidence would be largely overcome. It was said that doctors were in a better position to prove absence of negligence than patients were to establish liability. At the Council of Europe colloquy, however, although it was agreed that the patient was at a disadvantage when he sought to establish a claim, serious doubts were expressed on the desirability of making a radical change in the burden of proof. We share these doubts. We think that there might well be a large increase in claims, and although many would be groundless, each one would have to be investigated and answered. The result would almost certainly be an increase in defensive medicine.

Strict liability

1337 We also considered whether strict liability should be introduced. Whilst this would avoid the difficulties of proving or disproving negligence, there would remain the difficulty of proving that the injury was a medical accident, that is to say that it would not have occurred in any event. It would be necessary to define the area to be covered. For example, the foreseeable result of medical treatment such as amputation of a limb in a case of gangrene would not be included. The problems in defining the scope of medical injuries to be included would be the same as those we consider later in connection with the possibility of introducing a no-fault scheme.

1338 Even if it were possible to limit the scope satisfactorily, the imposition of strict liability, as with reversing the burden of proof, might well lead to an increase in defensive medicine.

It would tend to imply rigid standards of professional skill beyond those which the present law requires to be exhibited, and beyond those which (in our view) can fairly be expected. We decided not to recommend that strict liability should be introduced ...

The negligence action

1342 In most of the evidence from the medical profession it was urged that tort should be retained. It was argued that, even if some other system were introduced, the tort action based on negligence should continue alongside. Liability was one of the means whereby doctors could show their sense of responsibility and, therefore, justly claim professional freedom. If tortious liability were abolished, there could be some attempt to control doctors' clinical practice to prevent mistakes for which compensation would have to be paid by some central agency. It was said that this could lead to a bureaucratic restriction of medicine and a brake on progress. It was further argued that the traditions of the profession were not sufficient in themselves to prevent all lapses which, although small in number, might have disastrous effects. Some penalty helped to preserve the patient's opportunity to express disapproval and obtain redress.

1343 We record these views as put to us, although some of us feel that they are unsound and at the least overstated. We also feel bound to ask whether the growth of insurance cover does not mitigate the effect claimed for the value of the tort action. On this point, the Medical Defence Union said that, although they paid the compensation, their investigation into the circumstances brought home to the doctor the part he had played and encouraged a sense of personal responsibility. We add the comment that the cases that come to court must often be those in which the Union advises the doctor to contest the claim because he has a good defence, whereas the much smaller number of cases of gross negligence must usually be settled out of court. The system, therefore, would appear to expose to publicity those doctors whose behaviour is on the face of it the least reprehensible.

1344 Nevertheless, in spite of the doubts we express about the particular arguments put to us by the medical profession for the retention of the tort action, it is clear that there would have to be a good case for exempting any profession from legal liabilities which apply to others, and we do not regard the special circumstances of medical injury as constituting such a case.

1345 We were impressed by the difficulties facing a patient who wishes to establish a case, but we doubt if the confidentiality of medical records adds significantly to the plaintiff's difficulties in view of the powers of the courts to order disclosure.

1346 Although the powers of the Health Service Commissioners are restricted to some extent, we note with interest the possibility of change following a report published in November 1977 by the Select Committee on the Parliamentary Commission for Administration (HC45) about an independent review of hospital complaints in the National Health Service. The Committee considers that there should be a simple straightforward system for handling complaints in every hospital with emphasis on listening carefully to the patient's or relative's concern and dealing with it promptly. When the complainant is not satisfied he should be able to pursue the mater with the district Administrator. For the most serious cases the Secretaries of State should continue to set up inquiries under the relevant Acts. All other cases not resolved by this procedure should be referable to the Health Service Commissioner, including complaints concerning clinical judgment.

1347 We recommend that, subject to our recommendation on volunteers for medical research or clinical trials, the basis of liability in tort for medical injuries should continue to be negligence.

No-fault compensation

1348 Changes made to improve the prospects of getting compensation in the cases of negligence could have no effect on the very much greater number of medical accidents where nobody is at fault.

1349 The employment of new techniques and the development of medical science have increased the ability of the doctor to attempt the treatment of severe diseases and to effect a cure, but at the same time have widened the area in which medical accidents may occur. This trend of greater risks for greater gain is likely to continue.

1350 An operation may have unexpected consequences. Blood products may be used which contain viruses the presence of which could not be foreseen. There are now 3,000 drugs in common use and 10,000 listed drug interactions, both detrimental and beneficial. More will doubtless be discovered.

1351 Many of our witnesses urged us to recommend the introduction of a scheme of no-fault compensation for medical accidents. Dr White Franklin said that negligence should not be the key to any form of monetary compensation. A circuit judge suggested that subsistence level compensation would be appropriate for a medical injury which did not involve negligence. The Royal College of Psychiatrists suggested that over the whole field of personal injury, compensation should not be tied to fault or negligence and should be based on the need of the individual and his family.

1352 Most of our witnesses saw a no-fault scheme as an addition to tort. It was put to us that such a scheme would often overcome the difficulties of proving negligence; and that a special scheme for medical injuries would be justified because of the reliance of the patient on the doctor to preserve his health and perhaps his life.

Overseas experience
1353 No-fault schemes which cover medical accidents have recently been introduced in New Zealand and Sweden. In Volume Three ... we give a detailed description of the provisions; in this chapter we touch only on some relevant features.
1354 New Zealand's accident compensation scheme covers medical, surgical, dental and first aid misadventure. In an appraisal of the first two years' operation of the scheme, Professor Geoffrey Palmer refers to the Accident Compensation Commission's 'restrictive interpretation' of 'medical misadventure' which 'seems concerned to avoid sliding down the slippery slope and compensating illness or death every time medical treatment fails'. This means that in many cases the claimant is left only with recourse to the common law. The view that the Accident Compensation Commission is treading carefully in this difficult area is supported by reported decisions of the Commission.
1355 The Patient Insurance Scheme in Sweden provides no-fault compensation which is based on the rules for the assessment of tort damages. This includes provision for loss of earnings, necessary medical expenses not covered by social insurance, and non-pecuniary loss. The scheme is financed by the Government and by the county councils who are responsible for the hospitals and for public health facilities. Liability is limited to 20 million kronor (about £3 million) for each incident involving injury and there is an overall limitation of 60 million kronor (about £8 ¹/₂ million) for such injuries in the whole country in one year. This is about £1 a head of the population.
1356 Payments under the scheme are relatively modest because they supplement existing social insurance payments which cover virtually all the adult population, including housewives. Social insurance sickness benefit is 90 per cent of earnings with an earnings ceiling of over £10,000 a year. The Patient Insurance Scheme makes up the payments to 100 per cent. Under industrial agreements, benefit for work accidents is made up to 100 per cent and this further reduces the scope for the payments under the Patient Insurance Scheme. Of the compensation paid during the first year only 12½ per cent was for loss of income.
1357 The scheme covers injury or illness which has occurred as a direct consequence of examination, medication, treatment or any other similar procedure, and does not constitute a natural or probable consequence of an act justified from a medical point of view. Mental illness is not covered unless it results from bodily injury. Injuries resulting from risks which are justified in order to avoid a threat to life or of permanent disability or would have occurred regardless of the treatment are also excluded.
1358 The Swedish scheme is administered by the main insurance companies. The amount of compensation is settled in the same way as tort awards. Disputed claims and questions of principle are referred to a panel consisting of a chairman and one member appointed by the government, two members appointed by county councils and two by insurance companies. Specialist medical advice is available. Only 50 cases have been referred to the panel in the first 23 months of the scheme. The advice of the panel has been accepted in every case. There has been no need to use the arbitration machinery under the Swedish Arbitration Act.
1359 The Swedish and New Zealand schemes cater for relatively small populations, so that it is possible to ensure consistency in decisions by dealing with all difficult or borderline cases centrally. Both schemes have been in operation for a short time and claims will take some time to build up. It will be a few years yet before a useful appraisal can be made.

A no-fault scheme for the United Kingdom?
1360 In considering the possibility of a no-fault scheme for this country we looked first at the question of cost. There are two aspects: the overall cost of any scheme; and the machinery for financing it.
1361 It is difficult to be precise about cost. Minor injuries and complications of treatment could reasonably be excluded as in Sweden, where there has to be some incapacity for work for more than 14 days. If there were as many as 10,000 cases a year, and benefits were provided on the same lines as in our suggested work and road schemes, the total additional cost of compensation over the existing form of compensation would be about £6 million a year. Some addition would have to be made for the cost of administration. This could well be substantial. Judging by the Swedish experience there would be at least two claims for every one that was successful.
1362 We think that it would be appropriate to finance any such scheme through the National Health Service. But the question of what to do about medical accidents in private practice would raise difficulties. Although it might be argued that many doctors have both National Health Service and private patients, that private doctors use National Health Service facilities

and that all taxpayers contribute to the National Health Service, nevertheless we think that it is out of the question that a no-fault scheme provided by public funds should cover injuries received in the course of private treatment. There might be other ways of solving the problem. For example, such injuries could be covered by private no-fault insurance, or it might be possible to provide no-fault compensation through a levy on the subscription to medical defence societies. But in view of the decision we come to, as explained below, not to recommend a no-fault scheme because of other even more compelling considerations, we have not worked out in any detail possible ways of meeting this particular difficulty over finance.

1363 Any attempt to devise a no-fault scheme would also run into the problem of whether, and if so, how, treatment given by the 'paramedical' professions should be covered. Most of those in such professions, for example, nurses and physiotherapists, work with or mainly under the direction of doctors or dentists; but there would remain the problem of treatment not given by a medical team, for example chiropody. Outside the National Health Service, there would be the further problem whether other practices, such as osteopathy, should be covered.

Establishing causation

1364 The main difficulty in the way of a no-fault scheme is how to establish causation, since the cause of many injuries cannot be identified. The Medical Research Council said that while future research was likely to establish more causal relationships it would also reveal increasingly complex interactions which would heighten the problems of proving causation in the individual case.

1365 Even with our definition of medical injury we were forced to conclude that in practice there would be difficulty in distinguishing medical accident from the natural progression of a disease or injury, and from a foreseeable side effect of treatment. It is quite normal for a patient not to recover completely for several weeks or months after a major operation; for complications to ensue after operations; and for a patient to find that the drugs prescribed cause serious side effects.

1366 How should words like 'expected' or 'foreseeable' be interpreted? Even rare side effects such as vaccine damage not caused by negligence are often foreseeable in the sense that they are well known to medical science. If such injuries were to be included in a no-fault scheme, where would the line be drawn between them and the accepted risks of treatment? If they were to be excluded, the scheme would do little more than convert the negligence test of tort into a statutory formula, thereby making it easier for the victims of negligence to obtain compensation, but doing nothing for those suffering medical injury from other causes.

1367 In establishing causation, who should take the decision? We envisage that a no-fault scheme would be the responsibility of the DHSS. The use of its adjudication procedure, however, would either place more burdens on the medical manpower available, or would put the onus of making the initial decision on the shoulders of junior officials who have neither the experience nor the training to determine those issues.

1368 To establish causation would involve deciding whether the condition was the result of the treatment and, if so, whether it was a result that might have been expected. This would have to be disentangled from the conditions resulting from the progress of the disease or advancing age or from some other purely fortuitous circumstances.

1369 It is easy to distinguish the completely unexpected result from that which was expected. The grey areas in between pose serious difficulties in knowing where to draw the line.

Conclusions on no-fault compensation

1370 We concluded that we could not recommend the introduction of a no-fault scheme for medical accidents in the United Kingdom. Some of us found this was a difficult decision and thought the arguments were finely balanced. All of us appreciate that circumstances may change, and that our conclusions may have to be reviewed in the future.

1371 We recommend that a no-fault scheme for medical accidents should not be introduced at present; but that the progress of no-fault compensation for medical accidents in New Zealand and Sweden should be studied and assessed, so that the experience can be drawn upon, if, because of changing circumstances, a decision is taken to introduce a no-fault scheme for medical accidents in this country.

'No fault', here, does not mean strict liability (as technically it should) but a system in which compensation is awarded not only without the need to prove fault (though there may be other threshold requirements) but, *more importantly,* without the need to have recourse to litigation to claim compensation.

Ten years on Ham, Dingwall *et al* in their magisterial short paper brought a fresh look to the problems.

C Ham, R Dingwall, P Fenn, D Harris *Medical Negligence: Compensation and Accountability* (1988)

The position today

In the decade that has passed since the Pearson Commission reported, the position in relation to medical negligence has changed significantly. The number of successful claims has risen (see below) and there have been increases in the damages awarded by the courts. These developments have given rise to fears that the UK might be following the example of the USA and may be about to experience a malpractice crisis.

In response, the defence societies have increased their subscription rates substantially. As Table 3 shows, subscription rates rose from £40 in 1978 to £1,080 in 1988. The increase in subscription rates was 71 per cent in 1987 and 87 per cent in 1988. This has created particular difficulties for junior doctors. Although concessionary rates are available to newly qualified doctors (see Table 4) and those on limited incomes, a junior doctor is required to pay the full rate seven years after qualifying. Until the introduction of new arrangements following the 1988 pay award (see below), this meant that subscription rates could amount to the equivalent of a month's salary. As a result of these pressures, the medical profession has reconsidered its position and has called for a review of existing arrangements.

Table 3. Defence Society Subscription Rates 1978-88

Year	Rate £	Annual Increase %
1988	1,080	87
1987	576	71
1986	336	17
1985	288	17
1984	264	35
1983	195	44
1982	135	13
1981	120	26
1980	95	36
1979	70	75
1978	40	-

Table 4. 1988 Defence Society Subscription Rates

	£
Full rate	1,080
Concessionary rates available to members	
Who join within three months of qualification	
1st year	180
2nd year	240
3rd year	396
4th year	492
5th year	600
6th year	744
Non-clinical membership	132
Limited income concessionary rates	
Income ceiling of £6,230	360
Income between £6,231 and £12,460	720

Subscription rates from January 1 1988 for the Medical Protection Society and the Medical Defence Union

At the same time, health authorities have expressed their concern at the impact of increasing awards on cash limited budgets. As well as the cost of awards themselves, health authorities are worried that the threat of legal action will lead to a more defensive medicine. By increasing the use of diagnostic tests and procedures, and by producing greater caution on the part of doctors, it is feared that defensive medicine will add to the pressure on health authority spending, particularly in the acute hospital services.

In parallel with the concern of health authorities and the medical profession, organisations representing patients and their relatives have drawn attention to the shortcomings of the tort system…

First, there is a lengthy and expensive procedure involved in pursuing a claim for damages. This means that cases are often brought only by the rich or those able to obtain legal aid. Cases take a considerable time to work their way through the courts: the average time for settling a claim is four years.

Second, the legal process is by definition adversarial. As such, it may cause doctors and health authorities to close ranks and not offer an adequate explanation to patients and their relatives when things go wrong. In addition, the legal process may itself be distressing in providing a constant reminder of painful or unhappy events.

Third, the emphasis on establishing fault and cause and effect in injury cases turns the tort system into a lottery. Compensation is based not on need but on the ability to prove that somebody was at fault. The rules of the legal process which put the burden of proof on those bringing a claim may create significant difficulties for plaintiffs. As a consequence, similar cases of injury may be compensated quite differently. For example, a child suffering brain damage after contracting encephalitis will receive no compensation, a child suffering brain damage as a result of a vaccine damage will receive £20,000, and a child suffering brain damage following traumatic birth delivery may receive hundreds of thousands of pounds compensation…

Fourth, only a small proportion of people suffering medical injuries are compensated through the tort system. This may mean that the losses incurred as a result of injury are inadequately compensated, although other sources of compensation are available.

Underlying these criticisms is a concern that the arrangements for maintaining high standards of medical practice and holding doctors to account for unacceptable standards of practice are inadequate. Action for the Victims of Medical Accidents (AVMA), established in 1982, has highlighted these issues, and has argued for much greater openness and accountability on the part of the medical profession in dealing with the consequences of accidents. One of the points emphasised by AVMA is that most people who suffer medical injuries are not seeking compensation but want an explanation of what went wrong. An adequate system for dealing with injuries needs to provide for this as well as to offer financial compensation.

Before considering these points more fully, it is worth noting a number of other criticisms levelled at the tort system as it applies to medical injury cases. These are:
- those making a claim may find it difficult to obtain the services of a solicitor with relevant expertise
- there may be difficulty in obtaining the services of doctors willing to act as expert witnesses for patients
- the legal process causes distress and expense to doctors and health authorities as well as to patients
- the availability of legal aid may result in legal action being initiated in inappropriate cases, that is cases where those making a claim have little chance of success…

It is against this background that alternatives to existing arrangements have again come under scrutiny. One widely canvassed option is a no-fault compensation scheme. This has found favour with the British Medical Association (BMA) and the Association of CHCs in England and Wales (ACHCEW). Other possibilities include the introduction of differential premiums for doctors to reflect the risks involved in their work; shifting the cost of providing compensation to the NHS… reforming the tort law to overcome some of the shortcomings identified; providing more support to medical injury cases through the social security system; and extending first party insurance cover.

The view of AVMA is that a change in the existing arrangements is required but it is not clear what that change should be. The view of the Government is that the case for change remains not proven…

To shed more light on this debate, we now consider in more detail the available evidence on the present system and assess whether there is indeed a case for reform…

Before accepting too readily the claim that the UK is experiencing a malpractice crisis, it is important to review the available evidence to establish whether this claim is justified. Ideally, this evidence would include:
- trends in the number of medical accidents occurring expressed as a proportion of patients treated
- trends in the number of medical accidents which result from negligence
- trends in the number of claims made expressed as a proportion of patients treated

- trends in the number of successful claims made expressed as a proportion of patients treated
- trends in damages awarded, including total damages awarded each year, the size of the biggest award and the size of the mean award.

In practice, only some of this information is available. It is not possible to identify either the number of accidents occurring or the number of accidents which result from negligence because this information is not collected routinely. Information is available on claims and damages through the defence societies. The Medical Protection Society (MPS) has published some information on trends in awards (Figures 1 and 2) and has informed us that the number of claims received by the Society increased from around 1,000 in 1983 to over 2,000 in 1987 (personal communication). Similar trends are reported by the Medical Defence Union (MDU): the frequency of claims paid more than doubled between 1984 and 1987, and the average value of damages awarded also doubled in the same period (personal communication). The

Figure 4
Maximum awards paid by the Medical Protection Society for failed sterilisation

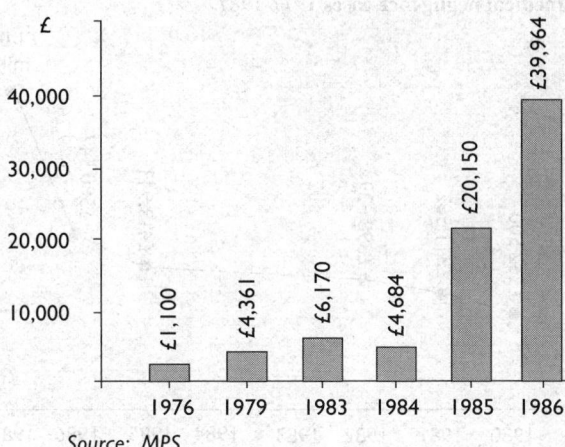

Source: MPS

Figure 6
Average cost of settlements. Percentage increase from January 1976

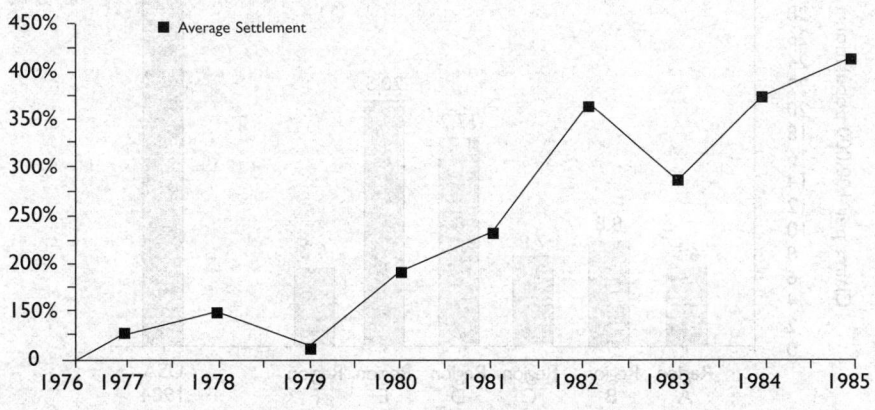

Source: MPS

MDU has published a graph (Figure 3) showing changes in the highest sum awarded in medical negligence cases. More detailed data are not made public because the societies consider that this information is commercially sensitive and might be used by insurance companies seeking to enter the medical insurance market.

Health authorities also collect information on claims and damages but again this has not been fully analysed and published. The DHSS only receives information from health authorities on awards over £100,000 and the Department is currently seeking to improve the quality of this information. The DHSS also collates information on the total payments for losses and compensation made by health authorities. In 1986-7 a total of £9.3 million was paid out by health authorities (Hansard, 24 November, 1987, col 162) but this covers a range of cases including compensation for unfair dismissals and losses due to theft. There is no information held centrally on the proportion of these payments spent on compensation for medical negligence (DHSS, personal communication).

In view of the limited information held by the DHSS, we approached RHA legal advisers for assistance and received detailed replies from six regions. The experience of claims opened in these regions in the most recent available year is shown in Figure 4, together with the US

Figure 3
Highest sum awarded in medical negligence cases 1977-1987

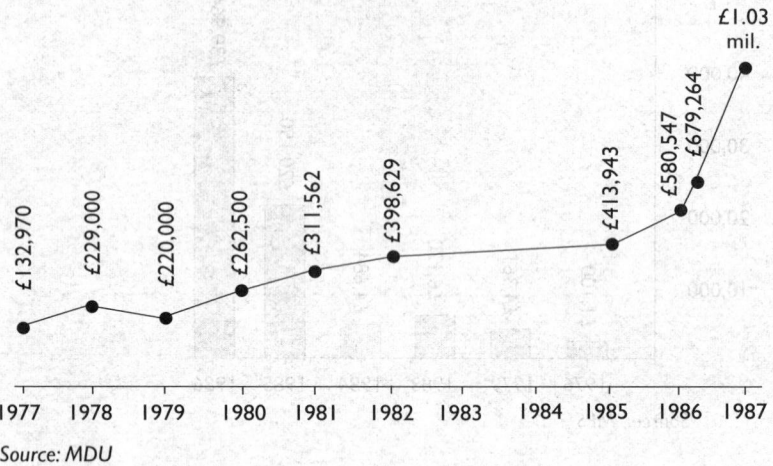

Source: MDU

Figure 4
Annual Claim Rates: Selected English Regions and USA

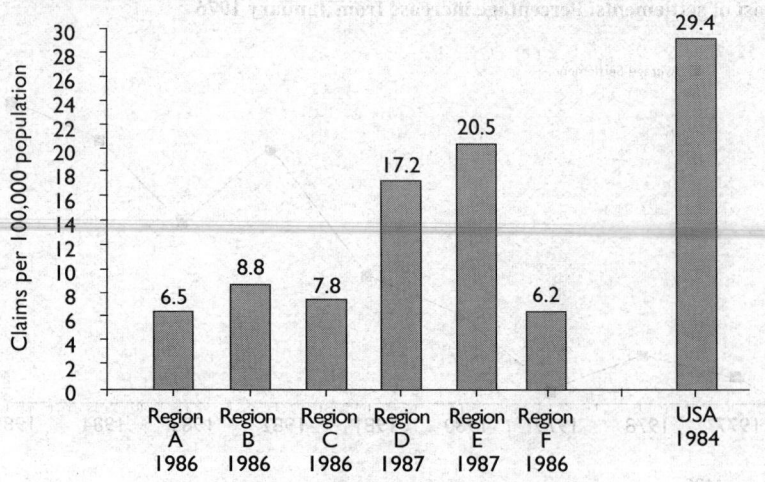

Sources: RHA solicitors and US General Accounting Office

rate for 1984. The variation with the UK is striking: most regions had an annual rate of around 8 claims per 100,000 population between 1986 and 1987, but two adjacent regions had annual rates which were more than double this. Time-series data were readily available for only two of the six regions. Figure 5 shows that Region E has always tended to have a high rate of claiming. As the Figure demonstrates, there is a clear upward trend in the number of claims since 1979/80, but with some indication of a levelling off in 1988.

It is difficult to go beyond these global figures to examine the experience of authorities in managing claims and to identify their specific origins. The most useful published data can be found in a study of 100 cases taken at random from the files of the West Midlands RHA... An audit of these cases found that at the end of three years, 73 actions had been withdrawn, 12 settled out of court and 1 lost in court. Fourteen cases were pending and the authors estimated that nine of these fourteen cases were likely to reach court.

In the context of the Pearson Commission's data, these figures do not suggest that the proportion of claims which are successful is increasing. Indeed the rate at which claims are abandoned would appear to have increased. On the other hand, it would appear that the proportion of claims going to court or likely to go to court is increasing.

Figure 5
Claim Rates for two English Regions 1977-87

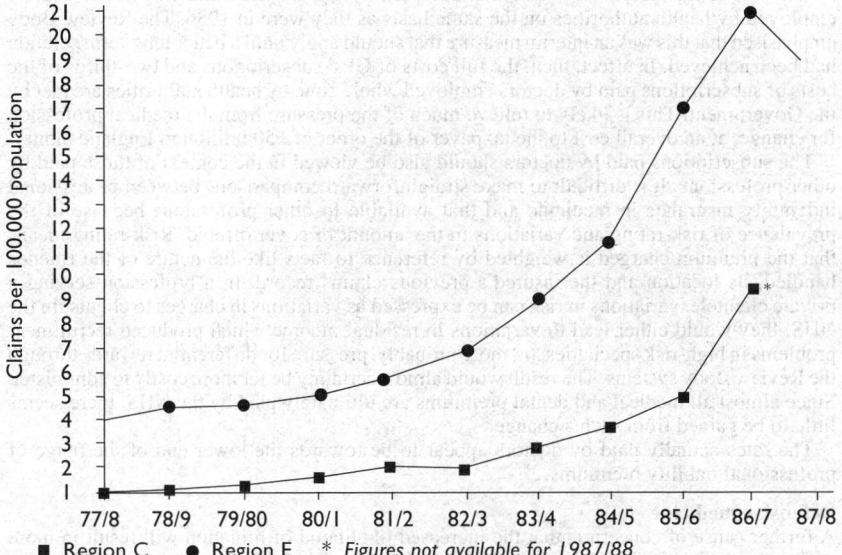

Evidence we have obtained from another health authority confirms that the rate at which claims are abandoned has increased. In this authority, 75 per cent of claims were abandoned in the 1980s compared with around 50 per cent in the 1970s. There is no evidence from this authority that the severity of the claimants' injuries has reduced over time. However, the higher proportion of claims which are abandoned may mean that some claims are being pursued on weaker grounds than they were previously.

The claims experience of this health authority also revealed some interesting patterns in relation to the nature and sources of medical negligence claims. Most claims resulted from temporary injuries, with conditions like iatrogenic infections, fractures caused by mishandling or lack of supervision, and missed diagnosis of fractures being typical. There is some evidence that claim-provoking incidents in hospitals are most likely to occur on the wards rather than in the operating theatre. Moreover, claims arising from events in operating theatres seem more likely to be abandoned. All specialties attract claims, although some attract more claims than others. High risk specialties appear to be obstetrics and gynaecology, anaesthetics, accident and emergency, orthopaedics and neurosurgery.

The evidence from the West Midlands and elsewhere points to a picture in which there is a diversity of claims, many of which arise from relatively minor injuries, with little indication of any systematic variation in the incidence of claim-provoking occurrences. This diversity is reflected in a wide distribution of settlement amounts around a fairly modest average figure. In 1986 prices, the average settlement over the years 1981-86 would appear to be in the region of £15,000 with a standard deviation of £27,000. In addition, health authorities incur legal costs, even where cases are eventually abandoned. Again in 1986 prices, the legal costs of one authority varied between a mean of £210 for abandoned cases, through £1,200 in cases where some payment was made, to £3,000 in cases which were successfully defended in court. Where the authority was required to pay the plaintiff's costs as part of a settlement or award, the mean payment was £2,000.

The impact of subscriptions on the medical profession

As we have noted, a major cause of current concern with compensation arrangements is the impact of increases in defence society subscription rates on the medical profession. In considering this issue, it is worth noting that general practitioners' subscriptions are fully reimbursed by the Government as expenses. As far as hospital doctors are concerned, the increase in defence society subscriptions was taken into account by the Review Body on Doctors' and Dentists' Remuneration in making recommendations on salary levels in 1987.

The Review Body went a stage further in its 1988 report, proposing that two-thirds of the medical rate of subscriptions should be reimbursed as expenses to all whole-time employed practitioners or part-time employed practitioners working wholly for the NHS, with effect from 1 January 1988 (Review Body on Doctors' and Dentists' Remuneration, 1988). The Review Body argued that doctors should continue to bear part of the cost of subscriptions in order to maintain involvement in the handling of claims.

The aim of this proposal, which was accepted by the Government, was to put doctors employed by health authorities on the same basis as they were in 1986. The Review Body emphasised that this was an interim measure that should apply until a better long-term solution had been achieved. In effect, then, the full costs of GPs' subscriptions and two-thirds of the costs of subscriptions paid by doctors employed whole-time by health authorities are met by the Government. This is likely to relieve much of the pressure from the medical profession for change, at an overall cost to the taxpayer of the order of £50 million in England alone.

The subscriptions paid by doctors should also be viewed in the context of those paid by other professions. It is difficult to make straightforward comparisons between professional indemnity insurance in medicine and that available to other professions because of the prevalence of risk-rating and variations in the amount of cover offered. Risk-rating means that the premium charged is weighted by reference to facts like the nature of the Buenos handled, its location and the insured's previous claims record. In a profession serving a private clientele, variations in risk can be expressed as variations in charges to clients. In the NHS, they would either lead to variations in residual income which produced recruitment problems in high-risk specialties, or, more probably, pressure for differential rewards through the Review Body systems. The result would almost certainly be far more costly to administer. Since almost all medical and dental premiums are ultimately paid by the NHS, there seems little to be gained from such a change.

The rates actually paid by doctors appear to be towards the lower end of the range of professional liability premiums…

Defensive medicine

A further cause of concern is that the increased likelihood of litigation will result in more defensive medicine. This claim is made regularly by the BMA and the defence societies. The argument more frequently articulated is that rather than risk legal action doctors will err on the side of caution by requesting additional diagnostic tests which may be clinically unnecessary. Lord Pitt recently summarised this argument:

> If doctors are to face these awards of severe damages they have to make sure of their defence. You are always better off in the witness box if you can say that you have done all the tests that are considered necessary … That means that one is wasting resources. We must therefore face the fact that if we are going to pursue the course that we are now pursuing we shall find an increase in defensive medicine with an alarming waste of resources (*Hansard*, House of Lords, 10 November 1987, cols 1350-51).

In fact, there is little hard evidence that defensive medicine is on the increase. A comprehensive American review of medical malpractice questioned the claim that doctors in the United States were becoming more defensive and noted that if more tests were carried out there could well be benefits for patients … It is also worth reiterating that in the eyes of the law standards of reasonable care in practice are defined by doctors. There is therefore no obligation on doctors to carry out tests and procedures other than those considered reasonable by the profession.

Against this, Harvey and Roberts [(1987) 1 *Lancet* 145] have questioned whether doctors will see this as providing them with sufficient protection. These authors maintain that even where clinical guidelines exist doctors may still judge that tests are needed as a defence against possible litigation. However, Kennedy [*The Unmasking of Medicine* (1983)] argues that what is required is for doctors to be better informed of the legal position and to not feel constrained to practise in a way that is inappropriate. Similarly, Carson [(1982) XCII *Health and Social Service Journal* 1346] has maintained that changes in clinical practice involving reductions in the use of tests need not increase legal liability if the changes are discussed within the profession and receive the support of a reasonable body of doctors. These arguments apply not only to tests but also to other areas of clinical practice, such as obstetrics, where it has been suggested that defensive medicine is also on the increase.

One of the most widely cited examples of defensive practice is the rise in caesarean section rates. This is, however, a phenomenon experienced by many countries with very different patterns of litigation (see Figure 6). The trend seems to be much better explained by other factors. These include changes in the perceived risk/benefit ratio following improvements in anaesthetic technology; changing clinical indications; the preference for conducting further deliveries by repeat caesarean; time management benefits for doctors and patients; and, for a time in the US, greater reimbursement for caesarean sections. Many of these factors are reflected in the rising British rates, independently of any concern over the risk of litigation...

Explanations
Various explanations have been proposed for the growth over the last decade in litigation arising from medical accidents ...[W]e do not think it is plausible simply to attribute the increase in litigation to a direct copying of American experience. Three other types of explanation have been put forward; a real increase in negligence; easier access to legal representation; and a change in the propensity of patients to sue following an adverse outcome.

It is really quite impossible to determine whether rates of medical error have changed in the last ten years. Litigation rates are affected by so many factors that they cannot be treated as a reliable proxy for actual medical behaviour. However, the timing of the increase and the lag between events and claims tend to discount the suggestion that the recent squeeze on the real resources available to the NHS has put excessive pressure on staff and caused higher rates of error. The rates began to rise in relation to incidents occurring in the mid 1970s which predate the most acute stringency in health service resources, although it is not impossible that this is a factor in the recent acceleration of the trend.

A more important observation, though, is that this phenomenon is not unique to the medical profession. Almost without exception, other professions' liability insurers report a similar trend over a similar timescale. In the case of architects, for example, there was one claim for every 7 policies in 1979 and 7 for every 10 in 1987. Claims against veterinary surgeons doubled between 1981 and 1987. The real value of paid and reserved claims against accountants

Figure 6 Caesarean rates for selected countries 1970–84

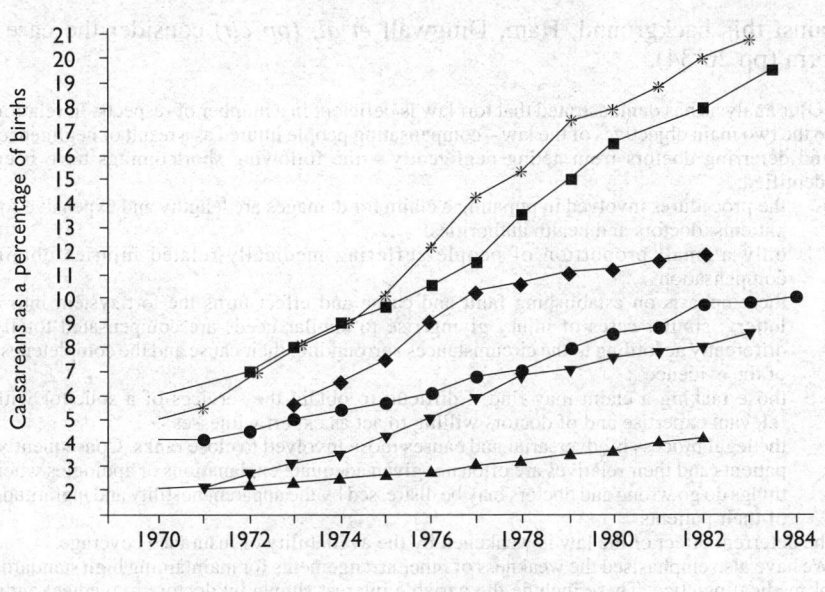

Derived from Macfarlane and Mugford (1986)

increased by 82 per cent between 1979 and 1984. It seems highly improbable that all professions have simultaneously become more prone to error.

There have certainly been important changes in the market for legal services since 1979. A number of medical commentators, as well as insurers for retail pharmacists and veterinary surgeons, have argued that legal aid has become more freely available and that this has encouraged a proliferation of trivial claims. The statistical basis for this latter statement is uncertain. In the case of medicine, it is certainly not substantiated by any of the figures currently available to us.

What is clear is that the capital and income limits for civil legal aid have consistently lagged behind inflation in the last ten years and the proportion of the population eligible for assistance has decreased. It is possible that the changing nature of the market for legal services, especially the growth of specialisation among solicitors, has improved the presentation of applications so that more are likely to be granted. It is also likely that the liberalisation of access to clinical records in recent years has increased the willingness of Legal Aid Committees to support the initial stages of an action because they know that information will be available at a reasonable cost. They can then take a considered decision on whether the action is worth supporting further.

Both of these developments would tend to facilitate more claims from a smaller pool of eligible claimants. This might be experienced by defendants as a growth in 'trivial' claims because many of them will inevitably prove insubstantial once the documents have been studied. Again, though, these developments must be put in the context of the general increase in litigation over the supply of professional services, which is as marked among those serving corporate customers as among those serving individuals. In architecture, the highest risk of litigation arises from work for housing associations. Accountancy cases almost invariably involve company liability.

The most likely explanation, then, relates to claims consciousness, the awareness among victims of the possibility of legal redress and their readiness to pursue this route. The more active marketing of legal services and the efforts of a number of statutory and voluntary bodies like CHCs, Citizens' Advice Bureaux and AVMA may well have had some impact, both in terms of public education and of practical support. If, however, we are dealing here with a particular case of a general phenomenon, more general explanations would be needed.

One possibility is that there may have been a cultural change towards a greater insistence on the right to be compensated for life's misfortunes and an increased distrust of the assumed skill and honour of professionals. Clients may be less ready to accept that adverse outcomes are intrinsic to the uncertainties of professional work and to insist that some dereliction of duty must underlie any failure. In this limited sense, there may be something to be said for the 'Americanisation' thesis.

Against this background, Ham, Dingwall *et al, (op cit)* consider the case for reform (pp 26-34).

[O]ur analysis has demonstrated that tort law is deficient in a number of respects. In relation to the two main objectives of the law – compensating people injured as a result of negligence, and deterring doctors from acting negligently – the following shortcomings have been identified:

- the procedures involved in pursuing a claim for damages are lengthy and expensive for patients, doctors and health authorities
- only a small proportion of people suffering medically-related injuries obtain compensation
- the emphasis on establishing fault and cause and effect turns the tort system into a lottery: similar cases of injury giving rise to similar needs are compensated totally differently according to the circumstances surrounding their cause and the completeness of the evidence
- those making a claim may find it difficult to obtain the services of a solicitor with relevant expertise and of doctors willing to act as expert witnesses
- the legal process is adversarial and causes those involved to close ranks. Consequently, patients and their relatives are often not given adequate explanations or apologies when things do go wrong and doctors may be distressed by the apparent hostility and ingratitude of their patients

the deterrent effect of the law is weakened by the availability of insurance coverage.

We have also emphasised the weakness of other arrangements for maintaining high standards of medical practice. These include the variable interest shown by doctors in medical audit and peer review, and the limitations of complaints and disciplinary procedures as mechanisms for ensuring progressional accountability. Our analysis has demonstrated that the tort system is one element in a package of measures by which the medical profession is held accountable to the public. Any proposals for reform must consider the law's role in ensuring accountability and promoting high standards while recognising its shortcomings as a means of providing compensation.

Against this background, we now consider the range of policy instruments which are, in theory, available to those contemplating reform. Some of these instruments are concerned primarily to deter negligence, while others aim to provide compensation. The instruments may be used singly or in combination. We begin by outlining options for deterring doctors from acting negligently, and then consider methods of providing compensation. In the first part of the chapter, the menu of options is described briefly, and this is followed by more detailed analysis of those options which in our view merit most serious discussion.

Deterrence
There are three main options for deterring doctors from acting negligently. These are legal liability, regulation backed by statute and self-regulation.

Legal Liability
Legal liability for medical accidents can take a number of forms. Doctors can be held strictly liable for all the adverse consequences resulting from medical treatment, or only for the adverse consequences resulting from negligence. Those held liable can be either individual practitioners or groups of individuals acting collectively. Figure 7 sets out the possibilities.

Figure 7 Deference through liability rules

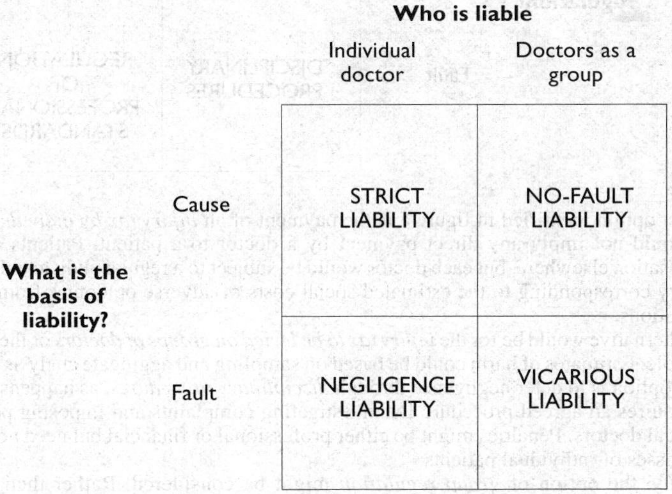

Who is liable

		Individual doctor	Doctors as a group
What is the basis of liability?	Cause	STRICT LIABILITY	NO-FAULT LIABILITY
	Fault	NEGLIGENCE LIABILITY	VICARIOUS LIABILITY

Strict liability exists when individual doctors are held responsible to patients for all the adverse outcomes of medical treatment. *No-fault liability* imposes liability on doctors as a group. The group might be the whole profession or only those doctors involved in the treatment which gave rise to the adverse outcome. *Negligence liability* is the current rule. Under this rule, only those doctors whose standard of care is deemed inadequate by the courts are held liable for the adverse consequences of their actions. The NHS already assumes *vicarious liability* for most of its employees. Under this liability rule the fault of an individual employee renders the employer liable for the adverse consequences resulting form the employee's actions.

All these possibilities can in theory create appropriate incentives for doctors to avoid injuring patients, although in practice the incentives may not operate effectively. Moreover, it is, in principle, possible for patients to contract with individual doctors, hospitals or health authorities in order to agree on a different set of incentives to take care, although again the practical problems of this option may be considerable.

One other possibility should be mentioned, namely that there should be *no liability*. This would shift the entire responsibility to the patient to take his or her own measures to ensure the safety of the care received.

Regulation backed by statute
A second approach to deterrence is to give a regulatory body the power to monitor the adverse consequences of medical intervention. Such a body would receive reports of medical accidents,

which would be required by law, and would determine appropriate action to be taken. This would include the power to levy a fine or injury tax. A body of this kind might develop out of the General Medical Council and would combine its regulatory role with oversight of registration and medical education. If this option were to be pursued, there would be a need to ensure that the regulatory body were genuinely independent and accountable to Parliament. This approach relies on a structure of incentives similar to those generated by the various liability rule options discussed above. Figure 8 illustrates the possibilities.

Figure 8 Deference through regulation

		Who is regulated	
		Individual doctor	Doctors as a group
What is the basis of the regulation?	Cause	INJURY TAX ON INDIVIDUAL	INJURY TAX ON GROUP
	Fault	DISCIPLINARY PROCEDURES	REGULATION OF PROFESSIONAL STANDARDS

The first option identified in figure 8 is the payment of an *injury tax by individual doctors*. This would not imply any direct payment by a doctor to a patient. Patients could seek compensation elsewhere, but each doctor would be subject to a regular audit and the payment of a levy corresponding to the estimated social costs of adverse outcomes from his or her interventions.

An alternative would be for the *injury tax to be levied on groups of doctors* or the profession as a whole. Estimates of harm could be based on sampling and aggregate analysis of injuries. A third option is to deter negligence through *disciplinary procedures*, as happens at present. This requires an agreed procedure for investigating complaints and imposing penalties on individual doctors. Penalties might be either professional or financial but need not be linked to the losses of individual patients.

Finally, the option of *group regulation* might be considered. Rather than having an independent regulatory agency involved with the review of individual doctors, the profession as a whole might be set specific standards of safety and effectiveness and left to develop its own systems of control. The effective sanction here is the risk of losing the privileges of the occupation's protected position in the delivery of health care. The incentive is the concern of colleagues to protect the profession's reputation and maintain public confidence.

Self-regulation
A third approach to deterrence avoids using either the civil or criminal law to impose financial incentives on doctors and instead relies on market-based incentives. Even where no one is held liable, there may be powerful incentives in a market situation for providers to maintain standards, simply as a way of ensuring commercial viability. In the NHS the incentives operate differently, relying more on the concern of the professions and health authorities to protect and improve their reputations. This is again an important element of the present system, although it does not always operate effectively.

Compensation
There are three main options for compensating those injured in medical accidents. These are liability insurance, first-party insurance and social security.

Liability insurance
Any system of legal liability could provide compensation for patients selected by the liability rules as long as those held responsible have the means to pay the damages awarded. Effectively this implies that arrangements must exist for the pooling of liabilities through insurance. Of

course, under a system of group liability, it is possible that some groups will be large enough to bear their own liability losses without insuring. For smaller groups and individuals, third-party liability insurance is a necessary adjunct to civil liability if the latter is to be an effective means of providing compensation.

First-party insurance

If doctors are not held legally responsible for the adverse consequences resulting from medical treatment, either because it is held that no one should be liable, or because only those accidents caused by negligence are compensated, then the burden of loss arising outside the liability system falls directly on the injured patients. Those at risk may therefore choose to insure against the prospective losses, either directly, by means of an income replacement or medical expenses policy with an insurance company, or indirectly, by means of a negotiated sick pay scheme through which employers meet such losses up to a maximum as part of a wages and conditions package. The payments under such schemes are made without necessary reference to the fault or causation of any other party.

Social security

Each of the above insurance options for spreading losses could be made compulsory by a government which was concerned about the possibility of uncompensated losses. Alternatively, government could itself provide social insurance financed out of employee contributions, general taxation, and/or specific levies on goods and services. Entitlement to benefits under such a scheme could be based on the fact of a disability, and not on its cause. In addition, injured patients may be treated and cared for through the further provision of public health care and social services. Effectively, this would be a system of compensation in kind.

Whatever form of compensation is provided, there always remains, in principle, the opportunity for individuals or groups of individuals to contract with each other in order to arrive at an alternative arrangement. For example, patients could agree to waive their rights to compensation through the courts in return for lower cost treatment. Equally, individuals covered by a social insurance fund may be permitted to contract-out in order to obtain preferable cover under a private insurance policy. In practice, however, people may be barred from restricting their coverage beyond a certain point or from completely opting out of compulsory contributions to a common insurance pool because of possible adverse selection problems.

The agenda for reform

Given the range of options available, it is possible to pursue the objectives of compensation and deterrence separately. As an illustration, doctors could be deterred from acting negligently through regulation by an independent agency with the power to levy an injury tax, while compensation could be provided by first-party or social insurance. However, separating the objectives in this way may be inefficient, in that it undervalues the role of the patient in providing information about negligence. This option may also deprive the patient of the satisfaction of securing an improvement in the circumstances which led to his or her injury and it reduces the opportunities available to victims to obtain psychological redress. Although the effectiveness of the tort system in serving these purposes should not be exaggerated, this element of the system may well be significant in some cases in helping to resolve events through the public attribution or exoneration of responsibility for harm.

The medical litigation system in the UK combines negligence liability and disciplinary procedures initiated by complaints with third-party liability insurance for doctors and self-insurance for health authorities. This system gives the individual patient a key role in the process of deterring negligence and obtaining compensation. However, as we have emphasised, the system has a number of shortcomings.

Many of the other options we have identified also have shortcomings. To give some examples, an injury tax levied on individual doctors would be cumbersome and costly to administer; disciplinary procedures may be ineffective as a form of deterrence if they are invoked only in the most serious cases; and self-regulation depends for its effectiveness on a strong commitment by health authorities and doctors to promote high standards through medical audit and quality assurance programmes. This commitment may not always be present.

Market-oriented solutions such as no liability and voluntary first-party insurance place an unreasonable burden on the patient in terms of assessing the quality of the services available. In extreme cases, the patient may be dead before the inadequacy of the care becomes apparent. This may deter others, but it is little consolation to the victim. The marked imbalance in information between patients and doctors is thus a major weakness of market-oriented options.

What then are the policy options which deserve serous consideration in reviewing how the shortcomings of existing arrangements might be overcome? In our view three options merit further analysis. These are:

* the modification of the tort law system and the strengthening of professional accountability

- the introduction of a no-fault compensation scheme, and
- the abandonment of the tort system in favour of providing compensation through social security.

We have selected these options for analysis as they represent different points on the agenda of change facing policy makers. Modifying the existing system and strengthening professional accountability involve incremental reforms, many of which could be introduced at little or no cost. There are obvious attractions in this option to a government committed to tight control of public expenditure. Furthermore, in view of the government's stated position that the case for major reform remains not proven, it may be through a series of minor changes that the best prospects for improvement lie.

No-fault compensation, as we have noted, is an option favoured by a number of organisations active in the field of medical negligence, including the BMA and ACHCEW. There is also relevant overseas experience on which to draw and from which to learn ... If there should be a further increase in the number of legal claims against doctors and in the size of court awards, the feasibility of this option may come under close scrutiny. There is therefore merit in assessing the costs of introducing such a scheme in the UK and the measures that would need to be taken to strengthen professional accountability in the context of no-fault compensation.

Abolishing the tort system in favour of providing compensation through social security – our third option – is a fundamental change which is best viewed as a long-term possibility. Nevertheless, it is an option that deserves analysis, if only to highlight the important part played by social security in supporting those suffering injuries. The issue of income support for disabled people is a major area of analysis in its own right, and in this chapter we are able only to illustrate its potential role in the case of medical negligence.

Changing the existing system

Changes to the existing system fall into three categories. These are increasing access to the courts, transferring negligence liability from individual doctors to health authorities while at the same time strengthening the accountability of doctors, and introducing differential insurance premiums for doctors. We now consider each in turn.

Increasing access to the courts

One set of reforms would seek to increase access to the legal system so that patients could more easily obtain compensation and more cases would result. Specific proposals have recently been put forward by the Citizens Action Compensation Campaign and by the report of the Review Body on Civil Justice to the Lord Chancellor. Both express sympathy for the development of contingency fees in Britain and the Civil Justice Review also discusses at length methods by which legal proceedings could be accelerated.

Our view is that contingency fees and the acceleration of legal proceedings are of limited relevance to medical negligence cases. While it is understandable that both litigants and legal personnel are frustrated by delay in establishing liability and determining compensation, its causes are poorly understood. The pace of litigation towards trial or settlement is determined largely by the plaintiff's solicitor. It may be slowed down in order to establish exactly how serious someone's injuries are so as to calculate what would be an appropriate level of compensation. It may be necessary to wait until a victim can be examined by one of the relatively small number of doctors who are skilled in the preparation of expert evidence for civil cases. If the findings are uncertain or the clinical evaluation is contentious, further time may elapse before other specialists can accommodate the patient. Once a case is prepared, a solicitor may wish to have it presented by a specialist barrister who is fully aware of the complexities of the area. In short, there may be good reasons for delay.

Contingency fees have attracted attention as a possible private alternative to legal aid. In fact, their main virtue is that they substitute the judgment of individual solicitors for the monopoly of the local legal aid committee. The American evidence shows that contingency fees are far from representing a poor person's route to justice. Lawyers will not take on cases unless the certainty of winning and the likely profits are sufficient to justify the risk. Thus, they will take relatively low-value cases arising from road traffic accidents, which are cheap to run and have a highly predictable outcome: they are reluctant to take low-value cases in other areas, including medical malpractice, because the return is insufficient to cover their costs. Moreover, medical malpractice is seen as a particularly risky area, because of the intrinsic uncertainty of causation, so that the lawyer has a strong incentive to reject all but those cases on which his own medical advisers give him strong support. The comparative irrelevance of contingency fees in the British context can be seen from the limited use of speculative actions in Scotland. These are not pure contingency, in that lawyers are only allowed to charge on the basis of the work they have done rather than taking a percentage of the eventual recovery, but they are conditional on the outcome of the case.

A more important consideration is that cases should be handled by solicitors skilled in medical negligence work. Plaintiffs are particularly vulnerable because medical litigation is classically conducted by local law firms with limited knowledge and experience in complex personal injury work. They are opposed by a small group of highly specialised firms with great experience of representing defendants. The real requirement is for a means of identifying and certifying solicitors who are competent to handle such cases on behalf of plaintiffs. AVMA and a number of community health councils have developed panels of solicitors to whom they steer cases and whose effectiveness they attempt to monitor. AVMA has devoted particular effort to the development of a monitoring system in an attempt to improve the effectiveness of their panel members. It would be open to the Law Society to build on these initiatives, as they have done with practitioners in child care and mental health law.

If this change were to be fully effective, it would have to be accompanied by a number of other modifications to the present system. One would be greater publicity for legal services in general, either by encouraging solicitors' own marketing of their services or through the development of schemes like the Law Society's Accident Legal Advice Service (ALAS) initiative which has tried to heighten public awareness of the possibility of claiming for damages. These initiatives might be accompanied by a liberalisation of the rules governing the advertising of legal services to enable members of the public to identify more easily solicitors accredited in medical negligence work and to be better informed about the benefits of approaching a specialist.

It would also be desirable to modify the present rules on fee-splitting, so that generalist, High Street firms had a greater incentive to pass complex cases on to practices with a more appropriate level of skills in return for an introduction fee or a proportion of the eventual profit on a successful case. Some attention would have to be given too to the access barriers represented by the current means testing on civil legal aid. At present, the rewards are too low to encourage specialist firms to develop medical negligence work and the eligibility levels are so restricted as to prevent a considerable section of the population from obtaining redress.

If access to legal aid were made easier, an increase in the rate at which claims are made and pursued would be likely to occur. This might accentuate some of the problems of predicting the financial burden for health authorities. One way of responding would be to pool the risks on a national or regional basis, creating in effect an internal insurance scheme as already happens in some places.

Transferring liability to health authorities and strengthening accountability
A second possible change to the existing system would be to transfer negligence liability from individual doctors to health authorities and [Family Health Service Authorities]. This would put doctors on the same basis as most other NHS staff, with their employer assuming vicarious liability. Such a change would certainly imply a more active role for health authorities and [FHSAs] in promoting high standards of clinical practice and reducing mistakes… Interest in medical audit in the NHS has been uneven, and there are grounds for arguing that a more systematic and rigorous approach is needed.

Health authorities could give a lead by requiring doctors at the appropriate level (firm, department, group practice) to demonstrate that they routinely review the quality of their work. The recent report of the Confidential Enquiry into Perioperative Deaths … recommended that clinicians should assess themselves regularly and that surgeons and anaesthetists should actively audit their results. This recommendation applies with equal force to other branches of medicine.

There is increasing evidence that doctors themselves recognise the importance of audit, both as a form of continuing education and as a means of avoiding mistakes. Thus, several of the royal colleges have taken the initiative recently to encourage doctors systematically to assess their work and to discuss their results with colleagues. Equally, at the local level, a number of enthusiastic individuals have demonstrated what can be achieved when doctors set aside time to gather information about their practice and analyse differences in approach. It should be possible to build on this experience in the future to ensure that audit develops with the support of the profession.

There may also be lessons to learn from developments in the United States in risk management, in particular in encouraging reports of adverse events. Drug reactions, for example, are already monitored by the Yellow Card scheme. Hospitals might introduce similar arrangements for the reporting of surgical or other incidents on a confidential basis, rather in the same way as airline pilots are encouraged to report near misses. One incentive for this might be to impose a collective responsibility on the medical and nursing team for the care of a patient.

Modern health care depends so much on the contribution of a number of specialists in different aspects of any particular case that it is questionable whether the concept of individual liability remains entirely appropriate. If one person makes a mistake which others ignore or cover up, then, at least morally, they would seem to be just as responsible for the adverse outcome. An example might be of a surgeon who commits an error during a common procedure. It is argued by risk managers in the United States that anaesthetists and the theatre nurses should feel an obligation to challenge the surgeon as he makes the mistake and to record their dissent if he persists. If they do not, they should be equally vulnerable at law and to professional sanctions. The medical profession, however, sees this as a receipt for clinical anarchy. Individual liability, it is claimed, is the proper corollary of clinical autonomy...

Differential premiums for doctors
A third way of reforming the existing system, and an alternative to the transfer of negligence liability to health authorities, would be to change the incentive structure facing doctors by introducing differential insurance premiums ... Such risk-rating is common in professional liability insurance and is applied to doctors in the United States. Where professional services are privately provided, there may be some merit in this arrangement. Differential risks can be reflected in differential fees so that there is no direct impact on recruitment to specialties. Doctors can be left with comparable post-premium incomes, or at least, incomes which vary only sufficiently to adjust for the non-pecuniary penalties of a high risk of litigation. Both patients and doctors are given appropriate indications of the hazards associated with different areas of medicine and an incentive either to safe practice or careful selection of doctor.

In the NHS, however, doctors are paid on a uniform scale. Individual effort and initiative are rewarded to an extent by merit awards or list sizes but there are no systematic differences between specialties in terms of the basic income available from NHS practice. In the absence of any variation, it is hard to imagine that recruitment to high-risk specialties would remain unaffected by differential premiums. Moreover, for practitioners working full time for the NHS, the introduction of such premiums would involve little more than an accounting exercise as the government would bear the major share of the cost through its policy of reimbursing two-thirds of the cost of defence society subscriptions.

The one exception to this argument concerns those doctors combining NHS work with private practice. The potential awards to a victim of negligent private treatment are larger than those to NHS patients because private patients would be able to obtain damages based on the assumption of future private care, whereas this might be disputable for NHS patients. It is debatable whether the NHS should in effect cross-subsidise private practice, although whether this happens in practice is difficult to estimate. In global terms, any subsidy is unlikely to be large, and is in any case roughly corrected by the recently announced arrangements which confine reimbursement of the major portion of defence society subscriptions to those doctors working exclusively for the NHS. It is also possible that the risks of private practice are less because of the different case-mix in that sector. Nevertheless, it remains possible that the public payments may be slightly larger than they would be if private medical practice formed a separate pool for insurance purposes.

Moving to no-fault
The term no-fault compensation refers, strictly, to all schemes which abandon the rule than an injured person has to show that someone was negligent in order to obtain redress. However, there is an important distinction between those schemes which still require patients to identify an individual responsible for their condition and those which do not. The former, of which Sweden and New Zealand are examples, share with the negligence system the advantage of being able to make constructive use of the desire of injured patients to obtain redress. Adverse outcomes can be attributed to individual doctors and, at least potentially, used as a basis for promoting high standards. Those schemes which sever the link between victims and the agents of their injuries must find alternative ways of achieving this objective.

The extent to which this is a serious problem depends on the ability of individual doctors to avoid accidents. If it is believed that accidents are better understood as a result of organisational failures, rather than personal mistakes, then the attribution of responsibility to individuals is unnecessary. All that is needed is sufficient information to demonstrate that the patient's injury arose from medical treatment together with a means of referring that information to the appropriate manager or health authorities. Information on claims for compensation might be fed back to those responsible for service delivery at the local level and be used in national reviews to alert all care providers to common problems.

Whether a no-fault scheme is based on proof of individualised caution or not, there is likely to be a need for some form of risk-spreading. Health authorities are large enough to self-insure, although the predictable impact of awards at a time of scarce resources suggests that this may not be the most efficient means of managing their budgets. There may therefore be a case for pooling risks on a regional or national basis, as happens in Sweden. If causation is placed on an individual basis, then doctors would need to continue to obtain some form of insurance and this could be provided by a consortium of the defence societies.

The potential cost of a no-fault scheme varies greatly according to the assumptions that are made about the rate of claiming and the size of awards. At present, there are roughly ten claims relating to hospital treatment per 100,000 population in England each year. Approximately three of these claims are compensated and the average award is around £15,000. The total cost of the system, including both damages payments and legal expenses, is estimated to be £75 million, of which £65 million is attributed to the NHS, either directly or through the cost of subscriptions to the defence societies out of NHS employees' income.

The Swedish scheme generates about 60 claims per 100,000 population from all health care contacts, although, in practice, almost all of these seem to relate to hospital treatment. Fifty per cent of these claims receive compensation, averaging £3,200 at current exchange rates. If we assume that a Swedish-style system were introduced in the UK, at the same rates of claiming and payment, the estimated cost for England alone would be of the order of £50 million per year (see Table 8). This would appear to represent a substantial saving.

Table 8
Estimated costs of a no-fault compensation scheme

A. CURRENT SYSTEM (ENGLAND 1988)	**£ mill**	**B. SWEDISH-STYLE** NO-FAULT SYSTEM	**£ mill**
Estimated health authority cost:	15	Estimated cost if Swedish system replicated:	50
Assumptions:		**Assumptions:**	
Claim rate = 10 per 100,000 population		Claim rate = 60 per 100,000 population	
Abandonment rate = 70%		abandonment rate = 50%	
Average settlement = £15,000		average settlement = £3,200	
Administrative costs = 30%		administrative costs = 15%	
Defence society contribution = 50%			
Estimate defence society costs*:	60	Estimated cost with average settlement £15,000	235
		Estimated cost with average settlement £7,500	117
Assumptions:			
Income generated from doctors practising in England based on a) subscription rates for 1988 as in MPS/MDU annual reports b) breakdown of medical manpower in England as published by DHSS.			
Total	75	*This includes a sum for legal and administrative costs other than those related to negligence cases.	

However, given the more limited nature of the British social security system compared with Sweden, it would also represent a substantial degree of under-compensation. As we noted earlier, the Swedish scheme is designed to top-up other payments in recognition of the pain and suffering involved, and is the sole source of income replacement or service purchase. If a similarly accessible scheme were introduced in England, the lower barriers to access might allow the rate of claims to rise to Swedish levels. If these claims were compensated at current English rates, the overall cost would rise to £235 million per year. On the other hand, one might expect that the average payment per claim would fall, since an increase in the number of claimants is likely to be associated with a reduction in the average severity of claims. In this case, £235 million should be treated as an upper limit. If the average payment per claim were halved, the cost would be around £117 million per year. While this is certainly well above the present cost of tort litigation, it might be thought that the price were justifiable if the shortcomings of the tort system we have identified were overcome.

For this to happen, it would be important to learn from the experience of New Zealand and Sweden. In particular, careful consideration would need to be given to:

- the definition of accidents to be included in the scheme
- the procedures to be used to prevent accidents, to monitor standards of care, and to encourage rehabilitation
- the importance of ensuring equity in the treatment of accident victims and the sick and disabled
- the means by which doctors would be held accountable and patients would receive an explanation of why an accident happened.

In relation to the last of these points, our proposals for reforming the existing system by extending medical audit and strengthening complaints and disciplinary procedures (see above) would have equal relevance under a no-fault scheme.

The issue of equity of treatment for accident victims and the sick and disabled is more complex. As recent developments in New Zealand have demonstrated, the establishment of special schemes for accident compensation can create distinctions which are difficult to defend. It is for this reason that proposals are now under discussion to reduce the benefit available to accident victims in New Zealand. One of the aims of the proposals is to enable the sick and disabled to be eligible for the same benefits as people injured during accidents. In Sweden, this issue is handled through the social security system which provides a generous level of benefits on the basis of need, with accident compensation supplementing these benefits. This suggests that a further radical option for reform is to introduce a general disability income. We now consider this in more detail.

A general disability income

The replacement of tort by social security is both radical and potentially expensive. As such, it is probably best viewed as a long-term possibility. The advantage of a general disability income is that individuals would receive support on the basis of the fact of their injury and its consequences, and would have to establish neither fault nor cause. The payment of benefits periodically rather than as a lump-sum would also remove much of the present uncertainty about whether a sum of money would be adequate to meet future expenses, and would also permit a continuing review of the victim's circumstances.

The principal advantages of social security as a means of providing compensation lie in its relative accessibility and simplicity. As a result, a large number of beneficiaries can be compensated at a low level of administrative expense. However, these advantages are the produce of a generalised, rule-based approach to deciding the appropriate amount of compensation. Benefits may be payable in relation to a schedule of impairments and/or proof of incapacity for work, without specific tailoring of payments to the individual's circumstances, as happens under tort law.

The generosity of the social security system is constrained by the extent to which the payment of benefits affects the recipients' recovery, and, when relevant, their return to work. This is a particular concern when disability benefits are payable to those who are permanently, but partially disabled, and who therefore retain some capacity to work. Designing a set of rules governing the determination of benefits without penalising the decision to return to work for this group of claimants is a task of considerable difficulty....

Two possible solutions are to make awards conditional upon the severity of impairment alone, or to make the assessments irreversible or lump-sum. Either way, this would ensure that subsequent decisions to return to work would not result in a withdrawal of benefit. However, this kind of solution would exaggerate still further the inequities between different types of claimants noted above. The New Zealand approach to this problem has been to limit income replacement to 80 per cent of previous earnings, and to give the Accident Compensation Corporation additional responsibilities for rehabilitation. It is difficult to ascertain the extent to which this has been successful... Clearly, the adoption of a general disability income scheme would not avoid difficult choices between equity and efficiency of the kind which bedevil the tort system.

Moreover, if this option were pursued, a considerable weight would be thrown on the adequacy of other arrangements for monitoring medical standards. Again, this brings into play our proposals... for extending medical audit, and strengthening complaints and disciplinary procedures. As the New Zealand experience has demonstrated, agreement must be reached on how to deter malpractice before radical changes are introduced.

Conclusion

Faced with these options, how should policy makers proceed? In our view there is a good case for reform, because of the considerable shortcomings of the existing arrangements. On the other hand, it is hard to argue strongly for any particular policy option on the basis of present information. Nevertheless, we can broadly summarise the policy choices in relation to both compensation and deterrence.

It is far from clear that the possibilities have been exhausted for improving the tort system as a means of obtaining compensation. As we have noted earlier ... there are a number of ways in which the system could be changed. In summary, the key measures worth pursuing are:

- providing potential claimants with a means of identifying solicitors with appropriate skills in medical negligence cases
- giving greater publicity to legal services through advertising and other means in order to increase public awareness of the general possibilities of claiming for damages
- modifying fee-splitting arrangements among lawyers to create greater incentives for solicitors to pass on cases to specialists
- making access to legal aid easier, and
- developing a system to enable health authorities to pool their risk in order to cope with a larger number of successful claims

While these changes would overcome some of the weaknesses of the present system there would still be a basic inequality between defendants, represented by a small group of experienced and specialised lawyers, and plaintiffs, represented by a dispersed, heterogeneous group of lawyers with infrequent involvement in medical negligence cases. It would also remain difficult to prove fault given the intrinsic uncertainties of human biology and medical technology. In the longer term, then, the inadequacies of the tort system as a method of compensation seem likely to encourage its replacement by a more equitable alternative. If a general disability income is ruled out on grounds of expense, serious consideration could be given to the development of a no-fault scheme.

A no-fault scheme would overcome many of the shortcomings we have identified in the present system: the expense and time involved in pursuing a tort claim; the strong element of lottery; the small proportion of injured patients who receive compensation; and the adversarial nature of the legal process. But ... neither the Swedish nor the New Zealand schemes offer a model which could be imported directly into the United Kingdom. Each has developed under a particular set of institutional conditions which are not reproduced here. Both also illustrate some of the inherent problems of no-fault schemes, such as the question of equity between people disabled as a result of different sorts of mishap and the means by which claims can be mobilised and screened.

The New Zealand experience also demonstrates the greatest weakness of no-fault schemes, namely the reduction in whatever deterrent effect the tort system may exert. The tort system has the unique feature of presenting the victim of negligence with a financial incentive to pursue a claim against the person believed to be responsible. But, given the difficulties of pursuing claims and the intervening effect of insurance, this is inadequate by itself as a method of preventing accidents.

For this reason, consideration needs to be given to a range of other policy options designed to encourage high quality medical care. In the short term, the most promising options worth pursuing are those which aim to strengthen professional accountability. As we have emphasised throughout this Paper, regardless of whether or not a system of no-fault compensation is introduced, a strong case can be made for improving complaints procedures, reforming the procedures used to discipline doctors, and encouraging the extension of medical audit. To summarise the discussion earlier in this chapter, this would involve:

- developing arrangements for medical audit by requiring doctors to demonstrate that they routinely review the quality of their work and by introducing procedures for the reporting of surgical and other incidents on a confidential basis
- extending and simplifying disciplinary procedures against doctors. This applies both to the GMC's procedures and to the procedures followed by health authorities. The aim should be to ensure that adequate arrangements are in place for handling cases where concern about professional conduct and competence arise, not just those involving the most serious consequences
- implementing the recommendations of the Davies Committee on hospital complaints in order to establish independent investigating panels to examine complaints about clinical matters

At the same time, careful consideration should be given to two further changes for implementation in the longer term. These are:

- the introduction of procedures for disciplining doctors based on Sweden's Medical Responsibility Board and involving significant lay participation, and
- the reform of complaints procedures to establish one point of contact whatever the nature of the complaint and to guarantee that those hearing complaints are genuinely independent

If implemented, these measures would help to deter doctors from acting negligently and would assist patients and their relatives to obtain an adequate explanation when things go wrong.

In conclusion, further research would help to clarify the policy choices we have mapped, but even more important is a political commitment to consider carefully ways in which improvements can be brought about to the benefit of all those involved with medical negligence. Above all, what is now required is an informed debate of the issues and the options, a debate which recognises the need both to provide compensation and to promote deterrence.

2.   Procedural and other changes

Since Dingwall *et al* were writing, a number of procedural and other changes have occurred which may affect the 'litigation experience'. First, as we saw earlier, since NHS Indemnity was introduced in 1990, NHS Trusts have been responsible for meeting the awards of damages made against them rather than hospital doctors (and others) themselves. Both this, and the second development we shall see shortly, were intended to reduce the NHS' costs of defending claims by not paying the insurance premiums of doctors and to provide greater institutional control of the litigation by removing from the process the defence organisations (and their lawyers). Secondly, again as we saw earlier, the creation of the Clinical Negligence Scheme for Trusts (CNST) operated by the National Health Service Litigation Authority (NHSLA) has put in place a system of 'mutual insurance', centralised control of litigation and a culture of 'risk management' within NHS Trusts. Thirdly, there has been an increase in the specialisation of lawyers dealing with these cases, particularly for claimants, culminating in the legal aid franchising arrangements with the Legal Aid Board such that only selected firms of solicitors may undertake legal aid work for claimants. In addition, the Law Society has established an accreditation system for specialists in medical negligence. Fourthly, conditional fee arrangements were introduced in 1995 under s 58 of the Courts and Legal Services Act 1990 (see the Conditional Fee Agreements Order 1995 (SI 1995 No 1674) extended by the Conditional Fee Agreements Order 1998 (SI 1998 No 1860)) with the intention of opening up access to the litigation process for those who could not otherwise afford it and were ineligible for legal aid.

By contrast, the volume of litigation has continued to grow and the size of claims is still perceived as increasing (for a study of claims brought against member of the Medical Defence Society in 1989, see P Hoyte 'Unsound Practice: The Epidimiology of Medical Negligence' (1995) 3 Med L Rev 53). Professor Michael Jones describes the situation.

Michael A Jones 'Medical Malpractice in England and Wales – A Postcard from the Edge' (1996) European J of Health Law 109

The first substantial increase in the numbers of claims for medical malpractice was observed in the mid-1980s. The medical defence organisations (the Medical Defence Union and the Medical Protection Society) reported a doubling of the frequency of claims between 1983 and 1987 alone. The Medical Protection Society reported an increase from 1,000 to 2,000 claims per annum in this period. In 1989 the Medical Defence Union paid out £30 million in damages, settlements and costs in the UK, a sum that was more than double the figure for 1985. The increase from the position in the 1970s was remarkable. In 1978 one in 1,000 doctors in Britain had a claim paid. By 1988 this had risen to 13 in 1,000. Data from 1990-91 suggests a claims rate as high as 105 per 1,000 doctors, at an average cost of £27,000, though only about one quarter to one third of claims made will result in a payment to the claimant. Nonetheless, this represents a doubling in the paid claims rate between 1988 and 1990-91.

Since 1990 it would appear that the growth in the numbers of claims has continued, although there are some discrepancies in the figures. From May 31, 1990 Regional Health Authorities and special health authorities were required to make annual returns to the Department of Health about the number and cost of claims for medical negligence in NHS hospitals in England and Wales. Although some returns have been made, unfortunately they are not complete. From 14 Regions the number of cases settled and the total costs (damages plus legal costs) were as follows:

1990-91: 1,618 cases at a cost of £53 million;
1991-92: 1,751 cases at a cost of £51 million;
1992-93: 1,738 cases at a cost of £45 million.

It is not entirely clear how these figures relate to the statement that in 1990 the NHS spent about £45 million on approximately 7,000 malpractice claims, an estimate given in the Department of Health's consultation paper. *Arbitration for Medical Negligence in the National Health Service,1991.* Nor is it apparent how these figures relate to those given by the Deputy Director of Finance and Corporate Information, NHS Executive, speaking at the Institute of Risk Management, in February, 1994, for malpractice costs within the NHS:

    1990-91: £53 million;
    1991-92: £80 million;
    1992-93: £100 million;
    1993-94: £125 million (estimated).

Despite the discrepancies, the overall picture from the figures is one of rising numbers of claims and overall costs (damages plus legal costs).

At the same time as the initial increase in claims was identified in the mid-1980s it was suggested by the defence organisations that there was also a substantial increase in the value of damages awards. Claims made about increases in the level of damages awards are controversial, however. Thus, it has been suggested that the value of awards for non-pecuniary losses (pain and suffering and loss of amenity) has been declining in recent years (see Carling C 'Damages for Pain, Suffering and Loss of Amenity' [1994] JPIL 108). It may be that as lawyers became more sophisticated about the assessment of pecuniary losses which are the consequence of serious disablement, the value of pecuniary awards increased. This tends to suggest that in the past plaintiffs may have been under-compensated. Indeed, empirical evidence produced by the English Law Commission indicates that levels of compensation for personal injury are still too low (see, Law Commission Report No 225, *Personal Injury Compensation: How Much is Enough?* (1994))…

It might have been thought that the continued rise in malpractice claims in the 1990s would have produced an increasing sense of crisis within the NHS. Although there is undoubtedly concern, and doctors do say that they practise defensive medicine, that concern does not appear to have risen to the clamour expressed in the 1980s. In itself the Clinical Negligence Scheme for Trusts will not have a direct effect on doctors' perceptions of the volume of litigation, though the emphasis on clinical risk management may have a laudable long-term effect on the number of medical accidents, or at least reduce the number of patients with a grievance. An injury and a sense of grievance are not the only factors, however, in the potential number of claimants. The overwhelming majority of medical negligence actions are funded by Legal Aid, and with restrictions on eligibility becoming tighter, the ability of injured patients to resort to the legal system is diminished. In practice only the poorest citizens qualify for assistance, whereas 90 to 95 per cent of medical negligence actions are funded by Legal Aid. Success rates for medical negligence actions are substantially lower than for other types of personal injury action. In the 1970s the Pearson Commission estimated that about 85 per cent to 90 per cent of all tort claims were successful, whereas only 30 per cent to 40 per cent of the plaintiffs suing for medical negligence succeeded in recovering some damages. The success rate for medical negligence claims is now put at around 25 per cent.

Notwithstanding the figures available on the frequency of malpractice claims, it is still impossible even to estimate either (i) the number of medical accidents that occur each year, or (ii) the number which result from negligence. It is clear that not all victims of negligence bring a claim for negligence. It would be implausible to suggest, for example, that only the poorest patients are the victims of medical negligence, and yet they represent 90 per cent of claimants. Studies in the USA indicate that the vast majority of victims of medical malpractice do not sue, even in that most litigious of countries. In the absence of any reliable information about how many injuries occur each year as a result of medical negligence it is impossible to say what the appropriate level of litigation should be. It seems likely, however, that there are far more patients who suffer medical injury as a result of negligence who do not sue their doctors, than patients with spurious claims who do. From the patients' perspective it could be argued that the malpractice 'crisis' arises from too few successful claims rather than too much litigation.

(You will notice Professor Jones' reference to US studies that suggest that, even there, most victims of medical negligence do not sue. The reference is to the Report of the Harvard Medical Practice Study to the State of New York – *Patients, Doctors and Lawyers: Medical Injury, Malpractice Litigation and Patient Compensation in New York* (1299) (see summaries in the Second Edition of this book at pp 546-560).)

Concluding on the state of the system in this country, Professor Jones states:

In medical terms a 'crisis' is the turning point of a disease, after which the patient either improves or deteriorates. On this measure there is no medical malpractice crisis in England and Wales. The patient is not about to improve, since the present upward trend of malpractice claims shows no sign of abating. Although paying closer attention to systematic methods of risk management (or mishap prevention) may ultimately have some impact on the number of medical accidents that occur (though this will be difficult to prove given that we do not know how many accidents currently occurring), it is not necessarily the case that this will reduce the number of claims, which appear to be rising from what historically was a very low baseline. The number of accidents occurring is only one factor contributing to the number of claims brought. Given what we know about the large percentage of injured patients who currently do not bring claims, even successful schemes of risk management may only have the effect of reducing the rate of escalation in claims. Improving or restricting access to the legal system may have just as significant an impact on claims rates as efforts to reduce the number of accidents. Lord Woolf is currently undertaking a review of access to the civil justice system, amid a growing recognition of the need for change to enable all individuals with legitimate grounds to have access to law.

On the other hand, it cannot be said that the patient is in terminal decline. The sums spent on medical malpractice litigation have to be put into the context of overall spending on the NHS of over £37 billion a year. Thus, the estimated figure of £125 million for the cost of litigation in 1993-94 represents an expenditure of less than 0.4 per cent on what could be regarded as the NHS 'quality assurance scheme.' (It also compares favourably with the £200 million a year spent by the pharmaceutical industry promoting their products in the UK). Individually, it is true that resorting to the legal system in order to obtain compensation is an extremely expensive and inefficient process, but looked at from a wider perspective it may be that medical malpractice provides a relatively inexpensive incentive scheme for NHS hospitals and doctors to adopt safe practices in the interests of patients. It would seem to be more than mere coincidence that the NHS is only now beginning to take risk management and mishap prevention seriously, as malpractice claim rates are spiralling upwards.

Of course, many of these comments are speculative. Proving a causal connection between litigation and risk reduction is just as difficult as demonstrating a relationship between litigation and defensive practice, given the complexity of the interaction between the legal system and the health care system and the paucity of some of the data. What is certain is that this is an issue that will not disappear. For good or ill the genie is well and truly out of the bottle, and health care providers are simply having to learn to live with the consequences of the growth of medical malpractice litigation.

The National Audit Office estimated that the NHS's potential liabilities in 1997-98 were £1.8bn (*NHS (England) Summarised Accounts* 1997/8, HC 382, para 5.6). As we shall see, the growth in litigation that Professor Jones identifies and the burdens it places upon the NHS have led to calls for its replacement by a 'no fault' system, which we saw referred to by Ham *et al* earlier and which we shall return to later. (For an assessment of a 'litigation crisis' in the UK, see B Markesinis 'Litigation-mania in England, Germany and the USA: Are We So Very Different' [1990] CLJ 233). The difficulties of litigation, however, remain. In his 1996 Report on *Access to Justice*, Lord Woolf singles out medical negligence litigation as being of particular concern.

Woolf *Access to Justice: The Final Report to the Lord Chancellor on the Civil Justice System in England and Wales* (1996)

Medical Negligence

Reasons for looking at medical negligence

1   Why have I singled out medical negligence for the most intensive examination during Stage 2 of my Inquiry? (I am using the term 'medical negligence' in this report to refer to any litigation involving allegations of negligence in the delivery of health care, whether by doctors, nurses or other health professionals.) It may appear a surprising choice, because medical negligence cases have no special procedures or rules of court. They are a sub-species of professional negligence actions, and they also belong to what is

numerically the largest category of cases proceeding to trial, personal injury. Neither of these is singled out for special attention.

2   The answer is that early in the Inquiry it became increasingly obvious that it was in the area of medical negligence that the civil justice system was failing most conspicuously to meet the needs of litigants in a number of respects;

(a)   The disproportion between costs and damages in medical negligence is particularly excessive, especially in lower value cases.

(b)   The delay in resolving claims is more often unacceptable.

(c)   Unmeritorious cases are often pursued, and clear-cut claims defended, for too long.

(d)   The success rate is lower than in other personal injury litigation.

(e)   The suspicion between the parties is more intense and the lack of co-operation frequently greater than in many other areas of litigation.

3   The cost of medical negligence litigation is now so high that smaller claims can rarely be litigated because of any disproportionate cost. It is difficult for patients to pursue a claim of any value unless they are eligible for legal aid. In the Supreme Court Taxing Office survey … 92% of successful parties in medical negligence cases were legally aided. An analysis by the Law Society of a survey by Action for Victims of Medical Accidents (AVMA) of 376 cases conducted by solicitors' firms on its specialist panel indicates that 90% of cases which reached the stage of litigation were legally aided. If these figures are representative of medical negligence litigation generally, then in the vast majority of cases both sides are funded from the public purse. Here the cause for concern is the amount of money spent by NHS trusts and other defendants on legal costs: money which would be much better devoted to compensating victims or, better still, to improving standards of care so that future mistakes are avoided.

4   The new system of case management by the courts which I proposed in my interim report could do much to reduce cost and delay in medical negligence, and to encourage a more co-operative approach, enabling cases to settle on appropriate terms at an earlier stage. In particular:

(a)   Clearer statements of claim and fully pleaded defences should speed up the progress of cases by helping to establish a factual matrix and define the real issues at an earlier stage.

(b)   Claimants' offers will encourage earlier settlements on realistic terms.

(c)   Extended summary judgment may help to weed out weak claims or defences at an earlier stage.

(d)   Improved training and greater specialisation should help judges to identify weak cases, narrow and determine issues and limit the scope of evidence.

(e)   More use of split trials will limit unnecessary work on quantum of damages in cases where liability is in issue (although this should not inhibit early work on quantum in cases where a valuation of the claim is possible).

Greater emphasis on early definition of issues between experts should encourage a more co-operative approach and reduce cost and delay.

5   The difficulty of proving both causation and negligence, which arises more acutely in medical negligence than in other personal injury cases, accounts for much of the excessive cost. The root of the problem, however, lies in the complexity of the law or procedure than in the climate of mutual suspicion and defensiveness which is still all too prevalent in this area of litigation. Patients feel let down when treatment goes wrong, sometimes because of unrealistic expectations as to what could be achieved. Doctors feel they are under attack from aggrieved patients and react defensively. The patients' disappointment is then heightened by what they perceive to be a refusal to acknowledge fault and an attempt to cover up.

6   Case management alone cannot provide the answer to this. A key requirement for achieving the necessary change is designing procedures for handling these cases, both at the pre-litigation stage and by the courts, so that a more co-operative and conciliatory approach to dispute resolution is achieved…

A blueprint for reform

16   A system for resolving disputes about medical treatment must be designed to meet the needs of doctors and other health professionals as well as patients. It should not be designed to suit the interests or convenience of lawyers, except in so far as this is necessary to ensure that the work is done properly.

17   Many people involved in medical negligence litigation have justifiably pointed out to me the importance of establishing at the outset what an injured patient wants. Proceedings often start because the claimant cannot get the information he is seeking, or an explanation or apology, from the doctor or hospital. Historically, solicitors have had no alternative but to advise legal action, which is unlikely to be appropriate in all cases unless the client's main or only objective is to obtain financial compensation.

18   Patients' needs and wishes may not be the same in all cases, and are not always compatible with those of health professionals. An obvious point is that both sides want to win, and for some individuals this may override considerations of speed, economy, or even fairness. Some patients want financial compensation, but they may also want to prevent a repetition of the mistreatment or misdiagnosis which occurred, or to get an apology or explanation for what went wrong. Sometimes, especially in cases where the physical injury was less serious, these non-monetary factors are the most important. Whatever form of redress they are seeking, most patients probably want:

(a)   impartial information and advice, including an independent medical assessment;

(b)   fair compensation for losses suffered;

(c)   a limited financial commitment;

(d)   a speedy resolution of the dispute;

(e)   a fair and independent adjudication; and (sometimes) a day in court.

19   Doctors and other health care professionals agree with patients in wanting a speedy resolution of any disputes, but this is not always compatible with their understandable wish for a fair assessment of their conduct, with a right of comment and hearing. Doctors in particular also want:

(a)   a discreet, private adjudication, which some would prefer to be by a medical rather than a legal tribunal;

(b)   an expert of their own or their solicitor's choice; and

(c)   an economical system, which does not encourage NHS trusts to settle cases over their heads, regardless of liability …

A change of culture

21   The extent of patients' mistrust of doctors and other hospital staff is illustrated by the submission I have received from Action for Victims of Medical Accidents (AVMA). They argue that the real reason for defendants' reluctance to investigate complaints where there is a possibility of legal action is a concern that such an investigation might indeed disclose negligence:

> [The defendants] do not in fact want a relatively simple and cheap way of investigating a complaint which might expose that there has been negligence.

22   If that mistrust is to be removed, the medical profession and the NHS administration must demonstrate their commitment to patients' well being by adopted a constructive approach to claims handling. It must be clearly accepted that injured patients are entitled to redress, and that professional solidarity or individual self-esteem are not sufficient reasons for resisting or obstructing valid claims.

23   Patients and their representatives, for their part, must recognise that some degree of risk is inherent in all medical treatment, and that even the best practitioners do sometimes make mistakes. They should not pursue unrealistic claims, and should make every effort to resolve disputes without recourse to litigation.

24   It is fundamental to my approach to civil litigation in general that legal proceedings should be treated as a last resort, to be used only when other means of resolving a dispute are inappropriate or have failed. When someone has a potential negligence claim against a doctor or hospital, the first essential step is to find out what the patient wants to achieve. If his or her main need is for substantial financial compensation to cover future loss of earnings or the cost of continuing care, then litigation may be (but is not always) the best way to proceed. If the patient is chiefly concerned to get an explanation or apology for what went wrong, or to ensure that procedures are changed so that future accidents can be avoided, then litigation is less likely to be the best course. Recourse to the NHS complaints procedures and, if necessary, the Health Services Ombudsman, may offer a more appropriate means of redress…

28   The best way of dealing with the problem of delay before claims are started would be a policy of more open communication on the part of hospital staff. Effective communication of course, needs to start before things go wrong. All patients who are about to undergo treatment should understand that the outcome of medical treatment can be uncertain, and should be told about the range of possible outcomes in their particular case. Wherever practicable, the advice should be confirmed in writing. Doctors and hospitals should encourage patients to report any unsatisfactory outcome as soon as possible, and to seek an explanation direct from the individual doctor or hospital before going to a solicitor.

29   Every patient who has suffered an adverse outcome is entitled to an explanation, and, where appropriate, an apology. In appropriate cases, there is no reason why an offer of compensation should not be made before any legal claim is notified, provided the patient is encouraged to seek independent advice on the offer. I understand that some hospitals offer to pay for such advice, to ensure that patients are not deterred from seeking it through fear of the cost.

The impact of the Woolf reforms on the litigation process are discussed elsewhere (see M Powers and N Harris (eds) *Clinical Negligence* (3rd edn, 1999)). The essence of the reforms to civil litigation and their impact upon medical negligence litigation was summarised in the Department of Health's written evidence to the House of Commons' Health Committee, *Procedures Relating to Adverse Clinical Incidents and Outcomes in Medical Cases* 6th Report (HC 1998-99), HC 549-II.

> 3. The aim of the reforms is that litigation should be avoided where possible. Where litigation is pursued, it should be more co-operative. It should also be less complex, more predictable and more affordable. The main points of the reforms include:
> – progress of a case will be controlled by the courts and not the parties;
> – proactive judges with increased powers to reduce delay and costs;
> – litigation to be conducted in a way which is proportionate to the amount at issue;
> – a pre-action protocol to encourage openness and co-operation; greater emphasis on Alternative Dispute Resolution, particularly mediation;
> – procedural judges will actively promote early settlement of cases, including the use of alternative dispute resolution, such as mediation, and will have powers to penalise parties who do not genuinely attempt to settle cases promptly;
> – use of experts will be more tightly controlled by the courts, with parties encouraged to sue joint experts and judges able to impose court appointed experts.
> 4. Two aspects of the reforms with immediate relevance for the NHS are the pre-action protocol and the emphasis on mediation as an alternative to litigation. The protocol was developed by a working party of the Clinical Disputes Forum and is an encouraging example of representatives from the NHS, the legal and medical professions and patients groups coming together working together to find less adversarial and more cost effective ways of resolving disputes about medical treatment. The protocol encourages a climate of openness, reflecting the new and developing requirements of clinical governance, and provides general guidance on how this climate might be achieved. The aim is to both ease and speed up the process of exchanging relevant information and increase the prospect of resolving disputes without the need for legal action. Courts will be able to impose sanctions for non-compliance. We recognise the far reaching possibilities of the protocol, and the NHS Executive circulated copies to the NHS in October last year.
> 5. The protocol identifies mediation as a possible alternative to litigation. In future courts will be able, either of their own volition or at the request of the parties, to schedule a break in the timetable specifically to try mediation. Franchised legal aid will also be available for mediation, which is significant recognition of its potential benefit. It is clear that in the current climate there will be considerable impetus behind mediation as an alternative to litigation.

You will notice two of the developments referred to: the pre-action protocols and ADR particularly mediation. The first is intended to 'oil the wheels' of litigation and if possible make going to court unnecessary. The second is intended to be an alternative to court proceedings.

As regards the pre-action protocol for clinical negligence litigation, this was developed by the Clinical Disputes Forum (a multi-disciplinary body comprising key stakeholders in the medico-legal system) and attempts to create a code of best practice for such litigation. The protocol has been given legislative force by virtue of the Civil Procedure Rules 1998 (SI 1998 No 3132) from 26 April 1999. The protocol sets the standard for reasonableness of pre-action conduct, allowing the court to penalise a party in costs or whatever for non-compliance. The CDF considers that the protocol has three aims:

Clinical Disputes Forum 'Pre-action Protocol for the Resolution of Clinical Disputes' (1998) 4 Clinical Risk 139

- encourages a climate of openness when something has gone wrong with a patient's medical treatment or the patient is dissatisfied with that treatment and/or the outcome. This reflects the new requirements for clinical governance within healthcare
- provides *general guidance* on how this more open culture might be achieved when disputes arise

- recommends a *timed sequence of steps* for patients and healthcare providers, and their advisers, to follow when a dispute arises. This should facilitate and speed up exchanging relevant information and to increase the prospects that disputes can be resolved without legal action.

As regards ADR (and mediation), the government initially proposed arbitration (a form of ADR) as a possibility in 1991: see *Arbitration for Medical Negligence in the National Health Service* (DoH 1991). The proposals commanded little support and were heavily criticised (see eg M Jones 'Arbitration for Medical Claims in the NHS' (1992) 8 PN 142) and were never implemented. In 1995, however, the Department of Health established a Mediation Pilot Scheme, which ran between 1995 and 1997. The scheme 'met with a decided lack of enthusiasm by the legal profession' (A Simonowitz 'Mediation in Medical Negligence' (1998) 4 Clinical Risks 63 at 64). The Centre for Dispute Resolution (CEDR), which was involved in the pilot scheme, refers to it in their evidence to the House of Commons' Health Committee (*op cit*) in which they explain ADR (and mediation) and its possible application to medical negligence cases.

House of Commons' Health Committee *'Procedures Relating to Adverse Clinical Incidents and Outcomes in Medical Cases' op cit*

2.1 Our contention is that the mediation process has great benefits to offer to all concerned with clinical negligence disputes, patients, clinicians and NHS executives alike, and that the greater use of mediation in such circumstances should be implemented as soon as possible.

3. DEFINITION AND CONCEPTS

3.1 *ADR* – Alternative Dispute Resolution, a general term covering a range of techniques for resolving disputes, without resorting to litigation or arbitration. The most common of these is mediation.

3.2 *Mediation* – a private, confidential and 'without prejudice' process in which a neutral person assists the parties in reaching an agreed resolution. In particular:

(a) The mediator is not a judge or arbitrator, and cannot impose a solution on the parties.

(b) The confidential forum allows grievances and problems to be aired face-to-face between the people involved.

(c) The process can address both the legal/factual issues, and the more personal ones which inevitably feature in such disputes.

More details of this appear under the paragraph on Benefits (7) below.

4. GROWTH AND DEVELOPMENT OF ADR

4.1 Since CEDR was launched in 1990, the use of ADR in the UK has expanded hugely. Initially progress was slow, and in particular the scepticism of the legal profession limited developments. Latterly, however, growth has been very pronounced, to the point where ADR (and mediation in particular) have become a mainstream feature of the litigation process. In particular:

(a) The new Civil Procedure Rules (CPR) which came into force on 26 April 1999 introduced a power for all judges to stay legal proceedings while the parties attempt to resolve the dispute by mediation or negotiation.

(b) Cases mediated by CEDR have increased to more than one per day. These cover a whole range of areas, including personal injury and clinical negligence.

(c) The result of such activity is the collation of a body of empirical data and evidence which points to profound benefits to be gained from mediation and ADR.

(d) All the top law firms in the UK are members of CEDR and many of their senior staff have undergone detailed training in the use of ADR through CEDR's internationally acclaimed training.

4.2 Conversely, however, the level of use of mediation for clinical negligence disputes still only represent a tiny fraction of those cases in which it could be used.

5. BENEFITS OF MEDIATION IN CLINICAL NEGLIGENCE DISPUTES

5.1 *What do the parties want?*

In our experience, those involved in clinical negligence disputes desire the following by way of process and outcome:

5.2 *Patients*

(a) A process that is speedy, fair, cost-effective, and that will resolve the dispute effectively.

(b) A process that deals not only with the legal issues, but also encompasses their emotional grievances.

(c) A chance to meet with the clinician(s) involved, and not just with their legal and executive personnel.

(d) A chance to 'vent' their grievances, receive explanations, assurances, and even a simple apology.

(e) Compensation at a 'fair' level, if the claim justifies it.

(f) A process that can enable them to retain (if desired) a relationship with the perceived 'negligent' clinician and/or hospital.

5.3 *Clinicians*

(a) A process that is speedy, fair, cost-effective, and that will resolve the dispute effectively.

(b) A process and outcome that allows for vindication of their position, if that is justified, and privacy of resolution to the extent that criticism (justified or not) may attach to them.

(c) A process that can protect or preserve something of the doctor/patient relationship, rather than forcing both into the roles of complainant/defendant.

5.4 *NHS and Hospitals/Trusts*

(a) A process that is speedy, fair, cost-effective, and that will resolve the dispute effectively.

(b) A process which enables a 'fair' sum of compensation to be paid in appropriate circumstances.

(c) A process which mobilises other, broader settlement possibilities (eg apologies, assurances, etc) of a non-monetary nature.

(d) A process in which cost is proportional to the outcomes, and which delivers 'value for money' to the NHS.

(e) A process that enables the hospital/patient relationship to be retained to the extent possible…

7. BENEFITS OF THE MEDIATION PROCESS

In the context of clinical negligence, the main benefits of the mediation process are:

(a) Speed – the average CEDR clinical negligence mediation takes less than one day to conduct. A mediation can be arranged in a matter of days if necessary, a more typical arrangement time is four to six weeks.

(b) Cost-savings – last year alone, the average cost-saving amongst those using CEDR's mediation service was £86,000 per party per case (this represents savings in legal and expert fees alone, excluding all the management time also taken up). Comparable figures are available from CEDR on personal injury cases alone.

If this were multiplied by the number of cases in which medication could/should have been used, the total savings would be vast.

(c) Confidentiality – the confidential nature of the process prevents disclosure of examples, other than anonymously. However, this element is clearly perceived by users as a huge benefit.

(d) Control – Patients, clinicians and hospital trusts alike can retain control of the process and outcome in mediation whereas they have no control over these matters in litigation. In particular, this enhances their dignity, and gives them a chance to 'own' the outcome because they have been responsible for negotiating it. This inevitably leads to greater satisfaction with the outcome.

(e) Breadth of outcomes – While a court is limited simply to awarding compensation (or not), mediation settlements can and usually do incorporate additional 'non-monetary' matters (eg apologies, assurances etc). It is self-evidence that a greater breadth of outcomes creates a greater chance of settlement.

(f) Catharsis – The litigation process tends to stifle the full expression by both patients and clinicians of their emotions regarding the case. This deprives them of a necessary element of catharsis and in turn makes settlement harder to achieve. It also tends to focus all parties on the exact level of compensation to be paid or not, because there is no other focus for their emotional grievances.

By contract, mediation provides a safe, private and entirely frank environment in which these matters can be, and almost always are, properly aired. In CEDR's experience, such an opportunity once taken, almost invariably makes the parties' positions on compensation less entrenched.

The author of this submission, and other CEDR mediators, can all testify to this from their own experience as mediators.

8. NHS EXECUTIVE – ENDORSED MEDIATION PILOT SCHEME

8.1 We also wish to bring to the attention of the Health Committee the existence and experiences of the Mediation Pilot Scheme endorsed by the NHS Executive ('NHSE'). This took place from 1995-97. CEDR was integrally involved in the development and operation of the scheme, providing mediation services for the majority of cases referred under the Scheme, and co-operating in detail with the research conducted into the effectiveness of the Scheme.

8.2 Detailed research was conducted into every case which was mediated, carried out by the University of North London (contact person is Linda Mulcahy). As we understand it, this research was completed last year, although for reasons of which we are not aware, the research has yet to be published.

8.3 Our understanding is that the research broadly reveals the following picture:

  (a) Only a small sample of cases were mediated under the Scheme, and therefore available to be researched.

  (b) However, amongst those whose cases were involved, the perception of both the quality of the process and outcome was extremely high. In other words, the satisfaction of the protagonists was high. This compares powerfully with the litigation process, in which 70 per cent of those who received compensation via that route were dissatisfied with both process and outcome.

  (c) We understand that much of the reason for the low number of cases referred to mediation under the Scheme is attributed to the attitude, scepticism and ignorance of the legal profession. If this is true, it certainly reflects CEDR's wider experience over the last nine years. It is also fair to say, however, that over the last two years such attitudes have softened considerably, as mediation has begun to enter the mainstream of the litigation process.

8.4 We recognise that the material contained in the University or North London research is vital to the debate, and hope that it will be made available to the Health Committee Inquiry.

9. BARRIERS TO GREATER USE OF MEDIATION

9.1 We believe that the case for using mediation in clinical negligence has been demonstrated beyond reasonable challenge, both in CEDR's experience and elsewhere. That said, we also recognise that level of take-up of mediation in clinical negligence cases in the UK has been, and remains, pitifully low.

9.2 There are, in our view, a number of reasons for this:

  (a) Scepticism and ignorance of the legal profession, whilst now waning, has been a major factor. When challenged the law firms on both the plaintiff and defendant sides invariably profess their commitment to its use, and blame the other for its lack of use.

  (b) Absence of a formal sanctioning of the process from those in senior positions within the NHS and/or Hospital Trusts – in our view, many of those handling disputes need to know that any method for dealing with them is formally approved of by their superiors.

  (c) Absence of awareness, by both patients, clinicians and Trusts, of the benefits that mediation can deliver –this results in fewer 'clients' pressing their legal advisors to adopt the mediation route.

  (d) Absence of awareness amongst the same people of the fact that 85 per cent of the cases going to mediation (through CEDR) are successfully resolved on terms acceptable to all concerned, ie that the process is very effective in bringing about resolution.

10. RECOMMENDATIONS

10.1 We would respectfully make the following recommendations to the Health Committee's Inquiry:

  (a) That the research material into the NHSE endorsed Mediation Pilot Scheme be published as soon as possible.

  (b) That the NHSE adopt and publicise a policy statement endorsing and encouraging the use of Mediation in clinical negligence disputes (to be ratified by individual Trusts if necessary).

  (c) That there be a programme of education, training and information on the benefits and effectiveness of mediation, aimed at:

  –   NHS managers and executives (both in risk management and in finance).
  –   Clinicians.
  –   Patients and patient groups.

- Lawyers advising them.
CEDR has already some such programmes for members of:
- ALARM (Association of Litigation and Risk Managers (NHS)).
- AVMA (Action for Victims of Medical Accidents).
- Law firms on Plaintiff and Defendant 'sides'
(d) That an investigation be conducted into why more clinical negligence cases are not going to mediation, and appropriate action taken.
(e) That the views are sought of the Judges dealing with such cases, as to how they intend to exercise their new powers with regard to Mediation (new CPR rule 26(iv)), and what other encouragement should be given (if any) to parties to use mediation.
(f) That law firm instructed by Hospital Trusts demonstrate minimum levels of use and understanding of mediation in clinical negligence cases, as a prerequisite to being instructed.
(g) That in cases where mediation is used there be a detailed audit comparing the financial (and other) implications with those in cases where mediation is not used (unless the University of North London research covers this point adequately).
(h) Now that legal aid has been made available for mediation, that the Health Committee investigate whether the grant of legal aid to pursue a claim for clinical negligence should be made conditional in some way on the use of mediation.
(i) Generally, that all appropriate measures be used to increase the level of use of mediation to resolve cases of clinical negligence.

(See generally, S Burn and L Mulcahy 'The Civil Justice Reform' in M Powers and N Harris *Clinical Negligence* (3rd edn, 1999) ch 7).

Let us now turn to consider the other main contender as an alternative to litigation – a 'no-fault' scheme.

3. 'No fault' scheme

In his evidence to the House of Commons' Select Committee on *Procedures Related to Adverse Clinical Incidents and Outcomes in Medical Care* (1998-9) HC 549-II (at p 233), Frank Dobson, then Secretary of State for Health, remarked that the proper place for lawyers in a hospital 'is on the operating table'. Litigation is seen by some, and certainly by Frank Dobson, as an unsatisfactory process for compensating patients and tantamount to a 'bean feast' for lawyers. Alternatives are then sought and a 'no-fault' scheme, through which compensation could be awarded without recourse to litigation, is the principal option. It avoids the problem of litigation – costs, delay etc as we have seen – and any adverse effects upon professionals of facing court proceedings. We saw at the outset in the Pearson Commission's Report (*op cit*, p 350) the arguments for and against such a scheme in the UK. It did not find favour with the Commission in 1978 and was not endorsed by Ham *et al* in the King's Fund Report (*op cit*) in 1988.

What, then, are the options? And, are they practical for importation to the UK?

(a) A limited scheme

One possibility would be to introduce a limited scheme designed to deal with particular medical injuries. The problem is which injuries? Do any particular stand out as being worthy?

In the US, both Virginia and Florida have created 'no fault' schemes for 'birth-related neurological injury'. In 1988, Virginia enacted the Birth-Related Neurological Injury Compensation Act. The Act applies to:

injury to the brain or spinal cord of an infant caused by the deprivation of oxygen or mechanical injury occurring in the course of labour, delivery or resuscitation in the immediate post-delivery period in a hospital which renders the infant permanently nonambulatory, asphasic, incontinent, and in need of assistance in all phases of daily living. This definition shall apply to live births only.

The scheme is discussed in the following extract.

Barry R Furrow et al *Health Law* vol 1 (1995)

The impact of escalating premiums on the specialty of obstetrics and the severity of obstetric injuries led these states to focus on this narrow category of malpractice claims.

The state of Virginia led the states in implementing a no-fault system for obstetric mishaps. A claim under this Act excludes all other tort remedies, with the exception of a suit 'against a physician or a hospital where there is clear and convincing evidence that such physician or hospital intentionally or wilfully caused or intended to cause a birth-related neurological injury', provided that such suit is filed prior to and in lieu of payment of an award.

Compensation under the statute is for 'net economic loss' only, including medical expenses, rehabilitation expenses, residential and custodial care and service, special equipment or facilities, and related travel, and loss of wages. Compensation for non-economic loss, 'pain and suffering', is disallowed, as are expenses covered by insurance.

The Industrial Commission of Virginia, the state's worker's compensation commission, handles the claims filed. The Commission will decide whether the claimed injury falls within the definition of a birth-related neurological injury, aided by an expert panel of three impartial physicians. This panel will operate according to guidelines developed by the deans of the state's medical schools. A hearing must be held within 120 days of the date of filing. One member of the expert physician panel must be available to testify at this hearing. Each claim filed under this program will also be referred automatically to the state Board of Medicine for evaluation to decide whether the injury resulted from substandard care.

Physicians licensed to practice medicine in Virginia who practice obstetrics or perform obstetrics either full- or part-time, including family physicians, may, but are not required to, participate in the program. Participating physicians must agree in advance with the state Board of Medicine to submit to a review of their obstetric practice in the case of a finding of substandard care. They must also certify to the Commissioner of Health that they will participate in the development of a program to provide maternity care to Medicaid and other low-income patients.

Participating obstetrician-gynaecologists and family physicians will be required to pay $5,000 into the compensation fund annually, while all other physicians in the state will be required to pay $250 per year into the fund. Hospital participation is also voluntary. Participating hospitals will be required to pay $50 per delivery per year into the fund, with an absolute cap of $150,000 per hospital per year. Participating hospitals are also to assist in the development of a state-sponsored maternity care program for low-income women.

It was predicted that the eligibility provisions for brain damage would apply to approximately forty live births in the state each year. In fact, only a handful of claims have qualified each year under the statute, and no claim has been filed. The definition is so narrow that only the most severe injuries are covered, and most of those eligible die as infants. The Virginia reforms hardly pass the test of promoting compensation for serious injury, and must be rated a failure by the standards of any compensation system.

(For further discussion of the Virginia scheme, see D Duff 'Compensation for Neurologically Impaired Infants: Medical No-Fault in Virginia' (1990) 27 Harvard Journal of Legislation 391 and, for the Florida Scheme enacted in 1989, T Tedcastle and M Dewar 'Medical Malpractice: A New Treatment for an Old Illness' (1988) 16 Florida State Univ L Rev 535.)

You will notice a number of features of the legislation. First, a claim under the Act excludes the right to sue for negligence. Secondly, the compensation under the scheme excludes 'non-pecuniary' loss and is limited to 'net economic loss'. Thirdly, the Act does not remove the necessity to establish a causal connection between the claimant's injury and the birth process. Finally, the scheme is funded by a levy imposed upon obstetricians, other doctors and hospitals.

It might be thought that these sorts of cases were ripe to be covered by a 'no fault' scheme in the UK. However, it is far from clear that there would be an overall benefit or gain in doing so. Any such scheme would necessarily have to reduce damages that would otherwise be payable. Yet, care costs etc form the greater part of any such award in any event. Damages for pain and suffering and loss of amenity may be awarded by a court but their removal would not lead to a significant reduction in the claim. Of course, the 'transaction costs' of the scheme may be less than for litigation. However, experts would still be required to establish the causal link that triggers the scheme's operation and to assess the quantum of the claimant's loss. On the other hand, perhaps, less 'lawyering' would be involved. Looking beyond costs, such a scheme would not present a claimant with the problem of establishing negligence but it would require proof of causation. This is often the most difficult factual and legal issue in these 'brain damaged' baby cases. Finally, who would pay for it? Not doctors themselves in the UK, given the current arrangements. It could, however, be a sub-set of the CNST run by the NHS Litigation Authority raised by way of a levy on all Trusts that provide obstetric care. The overall virtue of such a scheme might not, therefore, be all that clear.

(b) 'Medical Injury' scheme

Of course, many of the difficulties with a limited scheme are merely replicated – even accentuated – by a more general scheme covering medical injuries. Here, however, we have a number of overseas illustrations. We have already seen reference to the schemes in New Zealand and Sweden. There is also a scheme operating in Finland. These schemes are described and analysed in the following extract.

Don Dewees, David Duff and Michael Trebilcock *Exploring the Domain of Accident Law: Taking the Facts Seriously* **(1996)**

No-Fault Compensatory Alternatives for Medical Accidents
...Input analysis reviews the structural features of existing and proposed plans in each of five areas (eligibility criteria, benefit levels, claims disposition, financing, and insurance costs); output analysis examines the experience with comprehensive no-fault compensation in New Zealand and Sweden.

Input Analysis

ELIGIBILITY
The first task facing comprehensive no-fault schemes is definition of the compensable event. Unlike fault-based regimes that limit compensation to medical injuries caused by substandard care, comprehensive no-fault expands eligibility to all iatrogenic injuries (injuries attributable to medical care). Thus, as with no-fault workers' compensation plans, the central test would appear to be whether the injury 'arose out of and in the course of' medical treatment. (See P C Williams (1984) 'Abandoning Medical Malpractice' 5 J Legal Med 549 at 583). Nevertheless, as both theoretical analysis and practical experience in New Zealand, Sweden, and Finland made clear, the concept of iatrogenicity is by no means so straightforward.

Theory. To begin, it is not sufficient that the patient's disability be caused by medical intervention; in addition, it must be the *unintended* or *unexpected* result of such treatment. Since many procedures entail adverse consequences as a means of treating patient's underlying condition, no-fault compensation for purely *medical* injuries must exclude these cases in order not to become a general insurance scheme for disability however caused. Thus, for example, temporary disability for a medically obligatory period of convalescence after surgery, or permanent disability associated with a medically necessary removal of a limb or an organ, are properly attributable not to medical cause but to the underlying conditions that made these outcomes medically imperative. In contrast, both temporary disability for a period longer than minimally required after the specific type of surgery performed and permanent disability due to unnecessary removal of a limb or an organ constitute forms of iatrogenic injury. Similarly, commonly encountered side effects that are medically necessary to treat the patient's underlying condition (e.g. routine infections or hair loss with chemotherapy) are properly construed not as medical injuries but as 'unavoidable incidents of the condition which occasioned the therapy.' (Havighurst and Tancredi (1974) 'Medical Adversity Insurance' – 'A No-Fault Approach to Medical Malpractice and Quality' 613 Ins LJ 69). However, adverse results may be iatrogenic when they are more severe than expected or when they represent the random manifestation of a serious low-probability risk inherent in a medically necessary method of treatment.

This test differs from a fault standard in two ways. First, eligibility is measured against a standard of medical possibility rather than customary practice or reasonable care. In other words, as long as the patient's condition can be better treated (whatever the cost), the requisite of medical causation would appear to be satisfied (since the resulting disability is attributable to a medical decision not to employ this alternative procedure). Second, medical necessity is evaluated with the benefit of hindsight, not on the basis of information available prior to the treatment selected. Thus, even if the decision to remove a limb or an organ was correctly indicated on the basis of information obtained by all available diagnostic means (whatever the cost), the resulting disability constitutes iatrogenic injury if subsequent information reveals that this procedure was unnecessary or inappropriate to treat the patient's underlying condition (eg postoperative tissue analysis proves that a tumour was benign).

Iatrogenicity need not involve active medical intervention; it may also occur when a disability is caused or aggravated by a *failure* to prevent or minimise the patient's condition at a stage when it was medically possible to do so. For example, the failure to diagnose and treat preventable blindness from glaucoma or a curable cancer like a lymphoma is properly regarded as a form of medical injury, not a natural progression of the original disease. On the other hand, if diagnosis is medically impossible until the condition is virtually untreatable (or if the patient fails to seek medical attention until corrective measures are no longer possible), the outcome is properly attributed to the underlying condition (or to patient error) rather than to a medical cause. Again, this test differs from a fault standard since eligibility is measured against a standard of medical possibility rather than customary practice or reasonable care. Thus, as long as the patient's condition could have been diagnosed and treated (whatever the cost), the criterion for medical causation is satisfied since the resulting disability is attributable to a medical decision not to employ this method of diagnosis rather than to a natural progression of the disease. Although the definition of medical cause in this context necessarily invokes a standard of medical care, it is mistaken to suggest that this relationship between care and iatrogenicity introduces a notion of fault into an allegedly no-fault patient compensation scheme. The causal question of whether a correct diagnosis *could* have been made is conceptually distinct from the normative question of whether an accurate diagnosis *should* have been made. The standard of care that should actually be employed by a patient compensation scheme (and the criteria for determining a choice of one standard over another) remains a separate question altogether.

A final problem with the concept of medical cause arises because medical science is often probabilistic in nature, and iatrogenicity is typically only one element in a complex causal chain leading to the patient's disability. Unlike victims of automobile accidents or workplace injuries, patients generally submit to medical treatment already experiencing some infirmity. Consequently, if a medical injury occurs, any disability experienced by the victim is frequently attributable both to medical causation and to the patient's underlying condition. For example, if a physician erroneously prescribes a particular drug that is contraindicated for patients with a particular heart condition, the former's error and the latter's heart condition combine to cause the injury. As a result, both the definition and the proof of a compensable event involve difficult issues of probabilistic and proportional causation. Not surprisingly, therefore, many proposals for comprehensive no-fault patient compensation plans specifically limit eligibility to cases in which medical care is both a *probable* cause of the adverse outcome and a *significant* or *material* cause of the resulting disability.

Practice. In establishing actual criteria to govern eligibility for patient compensation, comprehensive no-fault schemes in New Zealand, Sweden, and Finland have had to confront each of the three dilemmas just discussed (intention an expectation, failure to intervene, and difficult issues of probabilistic and proportional causation).

In New Zealand, where the *Accident Compensation Act* refers only to victims of 'medical, surgical, dental, or first aid misadventure,' ([1975] 2 NZ Stat 1409, s 2) these definitional problems have been addressed largely by the courts and the Accident Compensation Corporation (ACC) Appeal Authority. Although the act further stipulates that compensation is not payable for any disability 'caused exclusively by disease, infection, or the ageing process,' (*ibid*, s 2(1)) most questions of eligibility are resolved on a case-by-case basis.

Despite initial reluctance to expand eligibility much beyond traditional fault-based criteria, more recent decisions indicated a growing willingness to grant compensation to the statistically inevitable victims of serious low-probability risks and to patients who experience a medical injury caused by a nonnegligent failure to accurately diagnose their underlying condition. Further, despite legislative language denoting covered and excluded injuries in all-or-nothing terms, the Appeal Authority has invoked notions of probabilistic and proportional causation to determine entitlements under the scheme. On the other hand, neither the ACC nor the New Zealand courts has established a clear test of remoteness to govern compensation for the occurrence of low-probability risks or an explicit specification of the standard of care applicable to cases of non-intervention. Indeed, according to one commentator, recent decisions to compensate victims of misdiagnosis were motivated less by considerations of principle than by the catastrophic nature of the claimants' injuries. (Richard Smith (1982), 'Compensation for Medical Misadventure and Drug Injury in the New Zealand No-Fault Systems: Feeling the Way', 284 Brit Med J 1457, 458).

More recently, however, amendments to the New Zealand scheme have restricted compensation for low-probability risks to adverse consequences that are 'rare' (probability of less than 1%), 'severe' (resulting in death, hospitalisation for more than 2 weeks, or significant disability of more than 4 weeks), and not known by the patient. (Accident Rehabilitation and Compensation Insurance Act 1992, no 13, s 5) In addition, the amendments restore negligence as the standard on which compensation will be based in cases of non-intervention (ibid, s 5 (7)). These amendments represent a reaction to the earlier expansion in eligibility, as well as a response to more general concerns regarding the cost of the compensation scheme as a whole.

Unlike the original New Zealand compensation scheme, patient insurance plans in Sweden and Finland contain detailed provisions describing compensable and excluded injuries. In Sweden, eligibility is accorded to any injury suffered 'in direct connection with health and medical care' (Patient Insurance Conditions of Indemnity, s 1) which:

1. Has arisen in direct consequence of examination, treatment or any similar action, provided that it was not an inevitable consequence of an action which was justified from a medical point of view;
2. Has arisen as direct consequence of a diagnostic incision and which is both of another type and substantially greater than the illness or injury which would have followed if the incision had not been undertaken and the correct diagnosis thus could not have been established;
3. Has arisen or has not been possible to prevent in consequence of the fact that examination results, obtained by means of technical facilities, were incorrect or that observable symptoms of illness were not interpreted, in connection with diagnostic methods, according to commonly accepted practice;
4. Has been caused by an infection due to a contaminative substance probably having been brought to the patient through an action of health or medical care; or
5. Has been caused by an accident [other than a medical injury *per se*] on the premises or within the precincts in which health or medical care is provided or in connection with the transportation of a patient (*ibid*, s 2).

In addition, the Conditions of Indemnity specifically exclude payment for any injury which:

1. Is a consequence of risk-taking, necessary from a medical point of view, to diagnose or treat an injury or illness which, if not treated, threatens life or entails a risk of severe disability;
2. In cases other than those [involving misdiagnosis], has been predominantly caused by an illness or a comparable condition of the patient that has arisen independently of [medical] care;
3. Has been caused by an infection if it is the result of:
   a. An incision or other action in the intestines, the oral cavity, the air passages and other regions that are considered to be unclean from a bacteriological point of view;
   b. An incision in tissue with considerably reduced vitality or comparable degeneration;
   c. Prolonged catheterization or drainage;
   d. Transportation of skin or other plastic surgery with increased risks of infection;
   e. Materials, prostheses or other foreign substances having been applied by an operation, if the infection appears more than one year after the operation;
   f. Reduced resistance to infections due to illness or treatment for illness; or
4. Has been caused by a drug for which the Regulations Relating to the Sale and Prescriptions of Drugs apply and which could not have been avoided by following the directions for the use of the drug (*ibid*, s 3).

In Finland, patient insurance is payable for any injury which:

1. Probably has arisen as a consequence of examination, treatment or any similar action, or neglect of the same;
2. Has been caused by an infection or inflammation which probably has originated in the circumstances connected with examination, treatment, or any similar action; or
3. Has been caused by an accident
   a. Connected with examination, treatment, of any similar action; or
   b. Occurring during ambulance transportation or in connection with fire or other damage to treatment premises or treatment equipment; or
   c. Resulting from a defect in medical care equipment or in a medical care device. (Cited in Diana Brahams (1989), 'The Swedish and Finnish Patient Insurance Systems' in M Martin Halley, Robert J Fowks, F Calvin Bigler, David L Ryan, eds, 'Medical Malpractice Solutions: Systems and Proposals for Injury Compensation')

As in Sweden, compensation is also excluded for any disability that is attributable primarily to the patient's underlying condition, and for the unavoidable effects of medically justifiable treatment and/or medically necessary risk taking (*ibid* at 196, 198). On the other hand, again like the Swedish plan, injuries from diagnostic examinations are compensable only 'if the consequence is unreasonable considering the quality and severity of the illness to be diagnosed and the state of health to the patient as a whole.' (*ibid* at 196-97).

Ignoring for the purposes of this analysis the specific exclusion of drug injuries in the Swedish Conditions, and the category of injuries by accident in both the Swedish and the Finnish plans, one can identify three broad categories of medical injuries compensable under both schemes. First, 'genuine treatment injuries' refer to injuries resulting from 'examination, treatment, or any similar action,' including those injuries listed separately in the Swedish Conditions as injuries from diagnostic intervention. These injuries are compensable provided they are not the inevitable consequences of medically justified treatment and/or medically necessary risk taking. As a result, while both plans embrace a no-fault *ex post facto* test that considers treatment decisions in light of information subsequently brought to light by the procedure itself, each also retains a notion of fault by adopting an exclusion based on medical justification, itself evaluated not according to a standard of medical necessity (optimal care) but in reference to the standard of a senior physician employing actually available facilities. Similarly, except for injuries from diagnostic intervention, random manifestations of statistically inevitable low-probability risks are not compensable if the method of treatment remains justified *ex post facto* from a medical point of view.

The second category of compensable injuries, involving omissions, is entirely fault-based. In Finland, the Conditions of Indemnity refer specifically to 'neglect'; in Sweden, compensable injuries within this category are evaluated according to the traditional tort standard of 'commonly accepted practice' in reference to available technical facilities. As a result, although the Swedish Patient Injury Board actually measures 'commonly accepted practice' against a slightly higher standard of a 'skilled' or 'senior' ('but not a super') specialist, notions of fault rather than medical causation per se govern eligibility for injuries from non-intervention. Finally, infection injuries are governed by a probabilistic assessment as to whether the infection was caused by the patient's own bacteria or whether it was transmitted through surgery. In the former case, the resulting disability is attributed to the patient's original condition and thus excluded from coverage; in the latter case, the infection will be covered as a medically caused injury. For purposes of greater certainty, however, the Swedish plan has also specified a list of designated noncompensable events for infection injuries.

Evaluation. Although accident compensation in New Zealand and patient insurance in Sweden and Finland retain some elements of provider fault to govern entitlement to benefits under each scheme (particularly for the random manifestation of severe low-probability risks and for injuries resulting from non-intervention), each promises to increase significantly the number of injured patients eligible for compensation beyond the 17%-27.6% of all medical injuries compensable under a purely fault-based criterion. Furthermore, despite considerable difficulties in defining the concept of a medical injury and in establishing a causal relationship between medical care and adverse outcomes, appeal decisions in New Zealand and Indemnity Conditions in Sweden and Finland appear to have resolved most of these dilemmas without major controversy.

BENEFITS

To help finance the expansion of eligibility to virtually all medical injuries, comprehensive no-fault schemes typically limit or eliminate benefits for nonpecuniary losses, restrict compensation for income loss to a fixed percentage of pre-disability earnings up to a stated maximum, confine payments to relatively large losses by means of a medical expense or time loss deductible, and preclude double recovery either by compensating only losses not already covered by collateral sources or by establishing a right of subrogation or reimbursement by collateral insurers for benefits paid. Although the Swedish and Finnish insurance policies provide full income replacement for wage loss up to a very high maximum (while New Zealand reimburses income loss at 80% of pre-disability earnings up to a maximum of about US $700 per week), and the New Zealand scheme contains no deductible to exclude small losses (whereas patient insurance plans in Sweden and Finland exclude benefits for injuries not causing death, significant permanent disability or incapacity for more than 2 weeks) each program limits compensation to some extent for nonpecuniary losses and deducts collateral payments from at least some no-fault benefits otherwise payable. As a result, payments should be less variable than under the tort system, and program costs are likely to remain manageable.

DISPOSITION

Comprehensive no-fault patient compensation schemes contain at least four features designed to reduce delays and administrative costs below levels experienced under the existing tort system. Procedurally, comprehensive no-fault circumvents the adversarial character of all liability regimes by separating the process of compensating injured patients from mechanisms for imposing injury costs on health care providers. As a result, other things being equal, claims are likely to be processed more quickly and at lower cost than under the current malpractice system. Similarly, payment of benefits on a periodic basis eliminates the delays and administrative costs involved in calculating compensable losses for lump-sum payment.

Substantively, restrictions on and schedules governing compensation for non-pecuniary losses are likely to reduce the time and cost entailed in determining this difficult-to-measure category of damage. Finally, by predicating eligibility on causation alone, rather than medical cause *and* provider negligence, advocates of comprehensive no-fault patient compensation hope to avoid the delays and administrative costs involved in proving both medical causation and professional negligence. Although several commentators have challenged the view that medical cause would be an easier borderline to administer than medical negligence, recent evidence by the Harvard Medical Practice Study Group suggests that evaluations of medical causation are indeed more easily determined than those of medical negligence. Furthermore, to the extent that the comprehensive no-fault scheme employs specific criteria to address problems of probabilistic and proportionate causation, potential difficulties in application of a strict causation standard are substantially reduced. In fact, the New Zealand scheme avoids many of these borderline problems altogether by paying compensation to all accident victims: to the extent that a significant number of patients seek medical attention on account of injuries incurred in a clearly demonstrable accident (such as an automobile accident), nothing turns on the characterisation of an adverse result as iatrogenic, since entitlement can be established on the basis that the effects of medical treatment were among 'the physical and mental consequences' of the original accident (ACA (*supra*) 52 (1)(a)(i)).

FINANCING
The extent to which comprehensive no-fault patient compensation schemes allocate injury costs to those responsible for medical injuries depends crucially on the manner in which they are financed. First-party schemes – purchases privately by patients themselves or publicly financed through government revenues unrelated to the provision of medical services – impose no direct costs on health care providers. Instead, in the case of private medical maloccurrence insurance, such schemes relegate all incentives for providers to employ efficient care and activity levels to the uncertain mechanisms of the market or professional regulation, or effectively externalise the costs of medical injuries to the broader community on which program costs ultimately fall or (as in Sweden and Finland) through contractual arrangement with a distinct insurance company form which patients claim directly and to which health care providers pay risk-related premiums – internalise program costs to those providers most likely to cause medical injuries. On the other hand, to the extent that comprehensive no-fault schemes reduce compensable benefits by offsetting all payments from collateral sources, injury costs are externalised to these sources and to those upon whom the costs of these collateral insurance plans finally rest.

COST
Unlike automobile injuries, where no-fault insurance is frequently regarded as a potential means of containing auto injury insurance premiums, no-fault patient compensation has generally been dismissed as inordinately expensive. Based on studies indicating that only 17%-27.6% of medical injuries involve provider negligence, and that only 6.25%-8% of negligently injured patients obtain any compensation through the tort system, no-fault patient compensation would be expected to compensate between 45 and 94 times as many injured patients as does the existing tort system. As a result, if a primary reason for considering such a plan is concern over the amount currently expended on malpractice premiums, comprehensive no-fault must immediately appear as a thoroughly unattractive alternative.

Nevertheless, even ignoring philosophical objections that such a plan would not increase costs but merely socialise injury costs that are already privately incurred, there are two reasons why comprehensive no-fault patient compensation schemes need not be as costly as their detractors suggest. First even assuming full (tort level) compensation for all victims of medical injuries, since patients with relatively severe injuries (and large compensable losses) tend to be overrepresented among those who successfully recover through the tort system, program costs should rise at a rate significantly less than the 45- to 94-fold increase in the number of patients compensated relative to the tort system. Moreover, since a substantial fraction of uncompensated injury costs are currently borne by the health care system anyway (and paid for by patients in the form of higher medical insurance premiums), comprehensive no-fault would entail little additional cost for medical expenses but merely reallocate these injury costs within the health care sector. Finally, to the extent that comprehensive no-fault entails lower administrative costs and/or reduces the costs of defensive medicine associated with the current malpractice regime, overall cost increases would be even less.

Second, the ultimate costs of any given comprehensive no-fault scheme depend crucially on the actual benefits paid and on the specific eligibility criteria established by the plan. In particular, since much current malpractice compensation reimburses nonpecuniary losses and losses already covered by collateral sources, comprehensive no-fault schemes that limit compensation for nonpecuniary losses and deduct collateral payments from benefits otherwise available are likely to be considerably more economical than plans that endeavour to compensate injury victims at traditional tort levels. Furthermore, if program costs are still considered to be too high, comprehensive no-fault can be made even more affordable by introducing deductibles or coinsurance arrangements that effectively restrict eligibility to only the most severely injured patients, and which limit compensation to a fixed percentage of confirmed economic losses. On this basis, by imagining a 6-month deductible in a scheme that compensates only net economic losses (after deducting available benefits from collateral sources), the Harvard Study estimates that the total cost of benefits under a comprehensive no-fault patient compensation scheme in the state of New York would have been around $900 million in 1984, which compares favourably to the roughly $1 billion in malpractice premiums paid in the state in 1988. Similarly, although the Swedish scheme pays scheduled benefits for nonpecuniary losses, a 2-week deductible and mandatory collateral source offset (coupled with Sweden's generous social insurance system) should make this plan relatively affordable. In contrast, to the extent that the New Zealand scheme contains no deductible, deducts only collateral public health care benefits, and used to pay limited benefits for nonpecuniary losses, program costs should be significantly higher. Indeed, rising costs were a key reason for the amendments in 1992.

Output Analysis

Empirical analyses of comprehensive no-fault schemes in New Zealand and Sweden are few in number and extremely brief. Nevertheless, scattered statistical and anecdotal evidence together provide a rough picture of the actual performance of each. The following discussion surveys evidence on the frequency of compensation, benefits paid, the disposition of claims, and the experience with insurance costs under each plan.

NEW ZEALAND

Frequency. Despite some initial reluctance to expand eligibility much beyond traditional fault-based criteria (particularly regarding low probability risks and medical omissions), figures indicate that considerably more injured patients are compensated by the accident compensation scheme that obtained benefits through the tort system. While only a handful of injured patients obtained malpractice compensation prior to 1974, 2,035 hospital-based accidents were compensated in 1983 – 91 of these explicitly classified as medical misadventures. On the other hand, anecdotal and statistical evidence suggest that a large number of injured patients may still go uncompensated. According to one expert on the scheme: 'In many cases the patient cannot establish that the treatment is the predominant cause and therefore fails in the claim for compensation.' (Margaret A Vennell (1988), 'The New Zealand Accident Compensation Scheme and Maloccurences' (unpublished) 193). Consistent with this assertion, the British Medical Association reports that only 60% of 'medical misadventure' claims are ultimately granted by the New Zealand Accident Compensation Corporation (British Medical Association, 'Report of No-fault Compensation for Medical Injury working Party (1983)). More recent restrictions on eligibility are likely to reduce the number of victims able to obtain compensation through the accident compensation program.

Benefits. Although separate figures for medical injuries are unavailable, evidence indicates that prior to the 1992 reforms about 20% of all payments under the accident compensation scheme were devoted to nonpecuniary loss. This item and the absence of a deductible to exclude compensation for those experiencing minor and short-term losses were identified by the New Zealand Law Commission as unnecessary payments, partly responsible for recent cost increases experienced by the program, and dispensable under its proposal to expand eligibility to victims of both injury and illness. As already indicated, they were abolished with the 1992 reforms.

Disposition. Reports prior to the 1992 reforms indicate that most claims for 'medical misadventure' were granted with little delay and that administrative costs accounted for less than 10% of total premium dollars collected under the New Zealand scheme – a figure that compares favourably to the 55%-60% figure estimated for the malpractice system. Nevertheless, for at least some injured patients, administrative costs and delays were substantial. Aside from difficulties in determining compensation for nonpecuniary losses (which proved to be one of the most heavily contested areas of the *Accident Compensation Act)*, problems also arose with respect to determinations of medical causation. In one claim reviewed by Richard Smith, (Richard Smith (1982) 'Compensation for Medical

Misadventure and Drug Injury in the New Zealand No-fault System: Feeling the Way' 284 Brit Med J 1457, 1459) the case was still being investigated 5 years after the patient suffered a stroke within 48 hours of receiving an injection of Depo-Provera – a fact, Smith observes, that 'is not a good advertisement for the supposed rapidity of no-fault-systems.' (ibid). Given earlier evidence on the disposition of traditional malpractice claims, it is doubtful that the recent emphasis on provider fault under the 1992 Act will produce any improvement in this regard.

Insurance Costs. Although separate figures on the total costs of medical compensation are unavailable, and cost comparisons are especially difficult where significantly different social systems are involved, the NZ $693 million (NZ $200 per person) cost of the full New Zealand accident compensation scheme in 1987-88 compares favourably to malpractice costs currently experienced in the United States and Canada. Nevertheless, within New Zealand itself, the scheme was sharply criticised for recent cost increases, prompting recommendations for a 2-week deductible and elimination of payments for nonpecuniary losses. This latter proposal was adopted in the 1992 reforms. We are unaware of any attempt to compare the costs of compensation for 'medical misadventure' to the costs of malpractice compensation prior to enactment of the accident compensation scheme.

SWEDEN
Frequency. As with the New Zealand scheme, the Swedish Patient Insurance Plan has achieved a substantial increase in the number of injured patients who obtain compensation – from slightly more than 100 per year before introduction of the scheme to an estimated 4,000 per year in 1986. Nevertheless, also like New Zealand, restrictive eligibility criteria concerning medical omissions and medically justified procedures, and limitations with respect to the requirement of medical causation, contribute to a success rate of only between 55% and 65% of all claims filed.

Benefits. In 1986, the average payment per successful claim under the Swedish Patient Insurance Plan was between about US $4,000 and US $6,000. Although the 2-week deductible likely excludes a large number of small claims, about 27% of claims involved temporary disability of less than 3 months, 36.2% were for temporary disability of more than 3 months, 26.8% involved minor (1%-15%) permanent disability, 8.1% involved moderate (16%-30%) or major (>30%) permanent disability, and about 2% were for death. More significantly, compensation for nonpecuniary losses and mandatory collateral source offset operate in conjunction with Sweden's extensive social and group insurance coverage to ensure that between 60% and 70% of the total compensation paid by the plan relates to pain and suffering, while income loss and medical care each account for only about 15% of total indemnity payments.

Disposition. Most claims under the Swedish plan are resolved quickly and with little expense. Although the British Medical Association reports that processing is very slow in a minority of claims (which may take as long as 2 or 3 years before their final resolution), a 1988 study reported that 58% are resolved within 5 months of filing and 80% within 7 months. This compares quite favourably to the disposition time of US malpractice claims, which take an average of 3 years to be resolved, with roughly 18% taking more than 2 years. With respect to administrative costs, 1983 figures indicate expenses of only 17.5% of total insurance premiums collected – a significant improvement on the 55%-60% estimated for the malpractice regime. Moreover, a more recent review estimates the administrative cost of the Swedish plan at only 14% of total premiums.

Insurance Costs. Reiterating the caution expressed in the New Zealand analysis about meaningful cost comparisons among different social systems, insurance costs under the Swedish plan have been quite economical. In 1983, premiums charged to county councils amounted to roughly US $1.40 per inhabitant, while those levied against private practitioners averaged US $50. Although these rose throughout the 1980s, by 1989 they remained at about only US $2.10 per inhabitant. While these costs have been higher than initially anticipated, they are nowhere near the levels experienced in Canada and the United States.

Summary
Comprehensive no-fault patient compensation ensures that substantially more injured patients will be eligible for benefits than under the current tort system. Furthermore, the no-fault plans in Sweden and New Zealand have had reasonable success in defining the concept of a medical injury and in compensating most injured patients promptly and at relatively low administrative cost. While comprehensive no-fault plans may entail higher overall insurance costs than under the tort system, these costs are not inevitable under such schemes but depend ultimately on the structure of benefits and deductibles that is adopted.

(For further discussion of the New Zealand scheme, see K Oliphant 'Defining "Medical Misadventure": Lessons from New Zealand' (1996) 4 Med L Rev 1.)

Dewees, Duff and Trebilcock identify three normative perspectives of tort law: *deterrence, compensation* and *corrective justice (op cit*, ch 1). How do 'no fault' schemes and the litigation process for medical accidents measure up in optimising these underlying perspectives?

Don Dewees, David Duff and Michael Trebilcock *Exploring the Domain of Accident Law: Taking the Facts Seriously* **(1996)**

Deterrence

. . . With respect to the tort system, from an input perspective quantum rules underdeter medical injuries causing death, and claims initiation rates suggest that only about one in eight negligently injured victims initiates a claim and only one in 16 such victims receives any payment. The ability of many defendants to pass on liability costs to patients and/or health insurers further weakens the deterrent incentives brought to bear on individual physicians. Moreover, many medical injuries appear to be preventable only at the organisational level, although current doctrine in many jurisdictions largely immunises institutional providers of health care from liability.

From an output perspective, empirical evidence suggests that the civil liability system has had a significant impact on medical practice, such as increased record keeping, increased discussion with patients about treatment risks, referrals to other health care professionals, and increased diagnostic testing. However, the effect of these practice changes on the underlying injury rate is much less clear. A recent major study of malpractice litigation in New York State had difficulty identifying a deterrent effect from malpractice litigation, but subsequent and more complex analysis of the data led to the conclusion that malpractice litigation causes a statistically significant but modest reduction in the proportion of injuries caused by negligence. Moreover, whether any marginal gains in injury reduction justify the costs of the tort system is problematic. These costs include not only the costs of legal services, the cost of administering the court system, and the cost of parties' and witnesses' time, but also the cost of defensive medicine engaged in not primarily for its therapeutic qualities but as a liability-reduction strategy. These latter costs have been estimated at between $8.5 billion per year to as high as $40 billion per year in the United States, but these are gross cost estimates ignoring any beneficial impacts from these practical changes. Two areas in which evidence suggests that the civil liability system may have had a positive impact and where the benefits of the practice changes in question probably outweigh the costs are physician discussion of treatment risks and alternatives with patients, and institutional programs of risk management.

Alternative regulatory strategies for injury reduction from medical treatment include individual physician licensure and the related disciplinary processes that regulate both entry and postentry competence of physicians. However, the evidence suggests that criteria for licensing, in particular formal or academic performance, are weakly correlated with future quality of practice and that licensure in itself does not ensure the currency of a practitioner's knowledge in a profession experiencing rapid scientific advances. Mandatory continuing medical education as a condition of licensure and the disciplinary mechanisms of state medical boards also have little effect in promoting competence. Few competence-related delinquencies are reported to a disciplinary authority. Most disciplinary actions relate not to competence but to other aspects of professional ethics such as substance abuse, criminal charges, sexual impropriety, or abetting unlicensed persons to practice medicine. However, recent mandatory reporting obligations by a variety of bodies granting privileges or imposing duties on physicians, a broadening of the range of penal or remedial sanctions available to disciplinary bodies, and an enhancement of nonphysician representation on these bodies has led to some improvements in the efficacy of the disciplinary mechanism as an assurance of physician competence. In addition, the development of quality assurance programs and peer review systems designed to identify inadequate physician practice, with remedial training then targeted to specifically identified practice deficiencies, appear to have some promise. Finally, risk management programs undertaken by institutional health care providers and designed to uncover systemic deficiencies in delivery systems also appear to improve service quality…

Compensation

… As a means of compensating victims of medical injuries, the malpractice system is seriously deficient. Only 17%-25% of injuries are compensable under applicable doctrines, while difficulties of detecting and proving malpractice mean that a most 20% of negligently injured patients even initiate a claim. Further, once within the liability system, compensation is slow, wasteful, and inequitable. The average duration between injury and claim disposition is 3-4 years, and more in cases involving serious injuries. Between 50% and 60% of malpractice premium dollars are consumed in transactions costs, and much of the remainder is devoted to relatively minor injuries and compensation for nonpecuniary losses. Finally, as with automobile accidents, evidence indicates that small losses are typically overcompensated while payments for serious injuries are generally much less than associated economic losses. The income distribution effects are again regressive in that high-income victims recover greater compensation for economic losses, but they do not pay higher implicit premiums.

In contrast, although experience with medical no-fault schemes is limited, evidence suggests that comprehensive programs like those in Sweden and New Zealand can deliver compensation more widely, more quickly, and at much lower cost. While only about 60% of claimants recover under the Swedish and New Zealand plans, the percentage of injured patients obtaining compensation is much higher than under the malpractice regimes that preceded the introduction of these no-fault schemes. Swedish evidence indicates that 80% of no-fault claims are resolved within 7 months of filing. Evidence from both countries indicates that medical no-fault plans can reduce administrative costs to 10%-20% of premiums collected – a significant improvement on the transactions costs incurred under the malpractice system. Although medical no-fault schemes may face some difficulties in distinguishing medical from nonmedical causes, it appears that questions of causation give rise to less ambiguity than questions of negligence. In sum, the evidence suggest that medical no-fault plans are both feasible and vastly superior to the malpractice system as a means of compensating victims of medical injuries...

Corrective Justice
...Doctrinally, the law of medical malpractice is consistent with a corrective justice rationale for liability. Once the relationship between plaintiff and defendant is understood to be primarily contractual rather than tortious, one can view positive duties of care and the applicable standard of customary practice as proxies for the terms to which the parties themselves would likely agree. Nevertheless, difficulties that patients experience in detecting and proving medical malpractice and in settling claims make the liability system deficient as a means of actually achieving corrective justice. At most, only 20% of negligently injured patients initiate malpractice claims, only 40% of these result in some payment, and in cases involving serious injuries these payments are generally much less than economic losses. At the same time, evidence indicates that findings of liability are strongly influenced by compensatory objectives as well as by principles of corrective justice, and that many patients initiate unmeritorious claims in the hope of obtaining some compensation for medical injuries. In turn, physicians often feel that they are unfairly blamed for adverse outcomes that reflect the inherent risks of medical practice rather than substandard practice.

As a result, it is likely that little in the way of corrective justice would be lost by seriously restricting malpractice actions for medical injuries. Furthermore, since the relationship between patients and health care providers is primarily contractual, it should be possible to design an alternative social contract that would better suit the interests of both patients and health care providers. While such a contract could waive current legal rights for some guarantee of no-fault compensation, as in the automobile context we believe that an ideal system should retain a residual role for tort actions in cases of egregious misconduct leading to serious injuries...

Policy Implications
... The current system of malpractice liability is not very successful in achieving the goals considered in this book. As a method of compensating victims of medical injuries, medical malpractice is slow, wasteful, and grossly inadequate. As a vehicle for achieving corrective justice, it is both erratic and deficient. And as a mechanism for promoting accident prevention, its effects are limited and often counterproductive. Overall, too few claims are initiated to substantially achieve any of the goals identified for the liability system.

In contrast, despite some weaknesses in their current operation, both regulatory and no-fault alternatives to the prevention and compensation of medical injuries represent positive directions for future developments in accident policy. Regulatory reforms to enhance the process of peer review, to lessen the burden of proof on and expand the range of sanctions available to professional disciplinary bodies, and to increase non physician representation on these boards promise significant improvements in their effectiveness as a means of identifying and addressing the risks posed by a small minority of truly substandard practitioners. Institutional quality assurance and risk management programs seem far more effective in targeting and eliminating more widespread risks than the uncertain threat of civil liability with its emphasis on individual culpability only for those injuries caused by deviations from customary practice. Finally, a shift from the individual to the institution as the focus of accident prevention can be expected to target organisational practices that are immune to malpractice liability while reducing dramatically the wasteful practice of defensive medicine that stems from individual physicians' risk aversion and fear of personal stigmatisation from a malpractice suit.

On the compensation side, comprehensive no-fault schemes directed primarily at the economic losses of those suffering more severe medical injuries seem both feasible and superior to compensation through malpractice liability. As in the case of no-fault insurance for automobile accidents, several design variables are essential to this scheme. No compensation should be paid for nonpecuniary losses. There should be a high rate of income replacement plus benefits for medical costs and rehabilitation costs. Because a no-fault scheme would greatly increase the number of victims compensated, benefits must be controlled if large premium increases are to be avoided; less than 5% of all patients injured by medical treatment currently recover through the tort system, in contrast to the two-thirds who recover in the case of automobile accidents. The Weiler proposal, similar to that advocated by the American Law Institute study, would address this problem by replacing income losses only after 6 months off work, which focuses the compensation for income loss on the most serious injuries. This is a far longer period than we recommend for motor vehicle accidents. But if a no-fault scheme reduces the transactions and defensive medicine costs of the current system, it would free up resources to satisfy a portion of these additional injury costs. We would support a system that required somewhat higher premiums than the present system to the extent that the increase was offset by a reduction in court costs and defensive medicine costs. We expect that a deductible of 1 or 2 months might achieve this goal, but further research is necessary to determine the appropriate balance.

Finally, risk-rating of premiums would be important to create deterrent incentives. Unlike the New Zealand scheme, where accident costs are largely shifted to the public through general tax revenues, we prefer to internalize these costs to care providers through risk-rated premiums. While individuals practising outside institutional settings would face individual levies, institutional health care providers should be responsible for premiums for medical accidents in institutional settings. In addition to targeting the institution as the focus of accident prevention, this approach would complement proposals for institutional quality assurance and risk management by providing the necessary external stimulus that is otherwise lacking in these forms of self-regulation.

As for corrective justice, there is little role for malpractice liability under the restructured prevention and compensation arrangement outlined here. On the contrary, if the relationship between patient and health care provider is primarily contractual rather than tortious, then both parties would likely be satisfied with an alternative social contract that excludes all malpractice liability in exchange for full compensation for victims of medical injuries. Only in cases of egregious misconduct causing serious and permanent impairment should a tort suit be allowed, and then only if the rule is sufficiently clear that there would be little litigation over the boundaries of the rule itself.

In December 1990, Rosie Barnes (then an MP) introduced the National Health Service (Compensation) Bill as a Private Members Bill. This was intended to create a 'no fault' compensation scheme for injuries suffered during NHS care. The scheme was to be administered by a Medical Injury Compensation Board constituted under the Bill. The scheme was to be funded by moneys from central government. Given the current interest shown both by the Department of Health and the House of Commons' Health Committee (*op cit*) (paras 131-3) in reform in this area, it may be of more than historic interest to look at the terms of the Bill.

National Health Service (Compensation) Bill

Purpose of this Act
1.   The purposes of this Act are:
   (a)   to provide that compensation for injuries suffered due to mishaps during NHS care shall be available without proof of negligence;
   (b)   to secure that NHS patients have the benefit of the same implied terms as to quality and description in respect of goods (including medicines, blood and appliances) as private patients;
   (c)   to seek to ensure that public monies available for caring for and compensating patients injured during NHS care are spent on that; and
   (d)   to minimise mishaps and compensation payments from public funds by enabling other action to be taken so as to maintain standards of care and management within the NHS.

Interpretation

2(1) This section has effect for the interpretation of this Act.

(2) 'The Board' means the Board established under section 3.

(3) 'NHS care' means the provision of treatment, services, goods and facilities to the public under the National Health Service Act 1977 and under Parts I and II of the National Health Service and Community Care Act 1990.

(4) 'Mishap' includes, but is not restricted to, any act or omission which give rise to an action at common law (or for breach of contract or statutory duty) by a patient in respect of NHS care.

(5) A person suffers 'injury', where as a result of a mishap in NHS care and not as a foreseeable and reasonable result of that care or the person's pre-existing condition, he –
  (a) dies;
  (b) requires in-patient hospital treatment for 10 or more days;
  (c) is prevented from engaging in normal activities for 28 or more days;
  (d) suffers significant pain, disability, harm, or distress or significant loss of amenity; or
  (e) suffers a reduction in his life expectancy.

Medical Injury Compensation Board

3(1) There shall a body corporate to be known as the Medical Injury Compensation Board.

(2) The Board shall consist of a Chairman, and not more than 16 other members, appointed by the Secretary of State.

(3) The Chairman shall be a judge of the Supreme Court of England and Wales, and shall be appointed after consultation with the Lord Chancellor.

(4) Of the other members of the Board, who shall be appointed after consultation with such organisations as the Secretary of State considers appropriate –
  (a) 3 shall be medical practitioners;
  (b) 3 shall be practising lawyers;
  (c) 2 shall have experience of management within the NHS;
  (d) 2 shall be health care professionals (other than within (a) above); and
  (e) 6 (and not less than 4) shall be persons other than falling within (a) to (d) above.

(5) In appointing any member who falls within subsection (4)(e) above, the Secretary of State shall have regard to the desirability of appointing persons who have experience in, or knowledge of –
  (a) the provision of health services;
  (b) the provision of legal services;
  (c) consumer affairs;
  (d) social conditions;
  (e) the maintenance of professional standards; or
  (f) counselling or assisting NHS patients who have suffered injury.

(6) The provisions of Schedule 1 shall have effect with respect to the constitution, procedure and powers of the Board and with respect to related matters.

Functions of the Board

4(1) The Board shall establish and maintain a separate medical injury compensation fund.

(2) In exercising its functions, the Board shall have regard to any code of guidance for the time being approved by the Secretary of State under section 8.

(3) On receiving a claim from
  (a) a person who has suffered injury; or
  (b) where that person has died or is a minor or is incapacitated, from his personal representative, or as appropriate guardian, or dependent; or
  (c) in either case, a person acting on his behalf the Board shall investigate the claim.

(4) A claim within subsection (2) is one which is made within 6 months of the claimant becoming aware of the injury and of its relationship with NHS care.

(5) Within 3 months of receiving the claim (or, where that is not practicable, at the earliest practicable opportunity), the Board shall notify the claimant of the results of its investigation.

(6) If the Board considers it appropriate it may offer compensation to the claimant.

(7) An offer of compensation by the Board if not accepted by the claimant shall lapse 2 months after it is received by the claimant, unless the Board agrees to extend it in any particular case.

(8) Where the offer of compensation is accepted any legal claim the claimant might have had in respect of the injury shall pass to the Board.

(9) Having regard to any code of guidance approved by the Secretary of State under section 8, the Board shall also take such other action in respect of a claim as it may consider appropriate.

(10) Schedule 2 sets out further, consequential and ancillary functions of the Board and the value of any legal claim that passes to it...

Relevance of public care provision

6(1) In awarding compensation in respect of any claim relating to NHS care, the Board and the courts shall apply section 2(4) of the Law Reform (Personal Injuries) Act 1948 (which provides that the availability of NHS care shall be ignored when awarding compensation for personal injuries) but with the words 'regard to' substituted for the word 'disregarded'.

(2) Subsection (1) shall not apply in respect of claims brought by the Board or the Secretary of State against suppliers of goods to the NHS or any part of it.

Liability for goods

7(1) A patient supplied with goods in the course of NHS care shall have the benefit of the same implied terms as to description and quality and the same remedies as would apply where the same goods are supplied under a contract of sale within the Sale of Goods Act 1979.

Code of Guidance

8(1) The Secretary of State may, after consulting such persons as he considers appropriate and after making any amendments he considers appropriate, by order –

   (a)　approve any code of guidance prepared by the Board; or

   (b)　approve any modification of the code; or

   (c)　withdraw his approval.

(2) The power to make an order under this section shall be exercisable by statutory instrument subject to annulment in pursuance of a resolution of either House of Parliament.

(For Parliamentary discussion of the Bill, see *Hansard* vol 184 No 47, cols 1223-1289.)

Chapter 5
Consent

Introduction

The ethical principle that each person has a right to self-determination and is entitled to have their autonomy respected finds its expression in law through the notion of consent. As we shall see, any intentional touching of a person without lawful justification or without their consent amounts to the tort of battery and may also constitute a criminal offence. Thus, the law relating to consent – as we will call it – is of the utmost importance in medical law, serving as it does as the means of protection and preserving the right of a patient to decide what is to happen to him. Robins JA in *Malette v Shulman* (1990) 67 DLR (4th) 321 in the Ontario Court of Appeal examined its importance (see *infra* for the facts).

Malette v Shulman (1990) 67 DLR (4th) 321 (Ont CA)

Robins JA: The right of a person to control his or her own body is a concept that has long been recognized at common law. The tort of battery has traditionally protected the interest in bodily security from unwanted physical interference. Basically, any intentional nonconsensual touching which is harmful or offensive to a person's reasonable sense of dignity is actionable. Of course, a person may choose to waive this protection and consent to the intentional invasion of this interest, in which case an action for battery will not be maintainable. No special exceptions are made for medical care, other than in emergency situations, and the general rules governing actions for battery are applicable to the doctor-patient relationship. Thus, as a matter of common law, a medical intervention in which a doctor touches the body of a patient would constitute a battery if the patient did not consent to the intervention. Patients have the decisive role in the medical decision-making process. Their right of self-determination is recognized and protected by the law. As Justice Cardozo proclaimed in his classic statement:

> Every human being of adult years and sound mind has a right to determine what shall be done with his own body; and a surgeon who performs an operation without his patient's consent commits an assault, for which he is liable in damages.

[*Schloendorff v Society of New York Hospital* 211 NY 125 (1914). See also *Videto v Kennedy* (1981) 33 OR (2d) 497, 125 DLR (3d) 127, 17 CCLT 307(CA); Linden, *Canadian Tort Law*, 4th edn (1988) at pp 40–3 and p 59 et seq; Prosser & Keeton, *The Law of Torts*, 5th edn (1984) at pp 39–42; and Fleming, *The Law of Torts*, 7th edn (1987) at pp 23–4.] ...

The right of self-determination ... obviously encompasses the right to refuse medical treatment. A competent adult is generally entitled to reject a specific treatment or all treatment, or to select an alternate form of treatment, even if the decision may entail risks as serious as death and may appear mistaken in the eyes of the medical profession or of the community. Regardless of the doctor's opinion, it is the patient who has the final say on whether to undergo the treatment. The patient is free to decide, for instance, not to be operated on or not to undergo therapy or, by the same token, not to have a blood transfusion. If a doctor were to proceed in the face of a decision to reject the treatment, he would be civilly liable for his unauthorized conduct notwithstanding his justifiable belief that what he did was necessary to preserve the patient's life or health. The doctrine of informed consent is plainly intended to ensure the freedom of individuals to make choices concerning their medical care. For this freedom to be meaningful, people must have the right to make choices that accord with their own values regardless of how unwise or foolish those choices may appear to others: see generally, Prosser & Keeton, *op cit* p 112 et seq; Harper, James & Gray, *The Law of Torts*, 2nd edn (1986), cIII; Linden, *op cit* p 64 et seq; and *Reibl v Hughes* (1980) 114 DLR (3d) 1; [1980] 2 SCR 880; 14 CCLT 1.

In England, the House of Lords has endorsed this understanding of the role and significance of consent in *Sidaway v Governors of Bethlem Royal Hospital* [1985] AC 871, *Re F (a mental patient: sterilisation* [1990] 2 AC 1 and *Airedale NHS Trust v Bland* [1993] 1 All ER 821. In *Re F*, Lord Goff expanded on the views he had expressed earlier concerning the inviolability of every person's body in the absence of their consent.

> **Lord Goff:** I start with the fundamental principle, now long established, that every person's body is inviolate. As to this, I do not wish to depart from what I myself said in the judgment of the Divisional Court in *Collins v Wilcock* [1984] 3 All ER 374, [1984] 1 WLR 1172, and in particular from the statement that the effect of this principle is that everybody is protected not only against injury but against any form of physical molestation (see [1984] 3 All ER 374 at 378, [1984] 1 WLR 1172 at 1177). ...
>
> In the old days it used to be said that, for a touching of another's person to amount to a battery, it had to be a touching 'in anger' (see *Cole v Turner* (1704) Holt KB 108, 90 ER 958 per Holt CJ); and it has recently been said that the touching must be 'hostile' to have that effect (see *Wilson v Pringle* [1986] 2 All ER 440 at 447, [1987] QB 237 at 253). I respectfully doubt whether that is correct. A prank that gets out of hand, an over-friendly slap on the back, surgical treatment by a surgeon who mistakenly thinks that the patient has consented to it, all these things may transcend the bounds of lawfulness, without being characterised as hostile. Indeed, the suggested qualification is difficult to reconcile with the principle that any touching of another's body is, in the absence of lawful excuse, capable of amounting to a battery and a trespass. Furthermore, in the case of medical treatment, we have to bear well in mind the libertarian principle of self-determination which, to adopt the words of Cardozo J (in *Schloendorff v Society of New York Hospital* (1914) 211 NY 125 at 126), recognises that –
>
> > Every human being of adult years and sound mind has a right to determine what shall be done with his own body; and a surgeon who performs an operation without his patient's consent, commits an assault ...
>
> In *Wilson v Pringle* the Court of Appeal considered that treatment or care of such persons may be regarded as lawful, as falling within the exception relating to physical contact which is generally acceptable in the ordinary conduct of everyday life. Again, I am with respect unable to agree. That exception is concerned with the ordinary events of everyday life, jostling in public places and such like, and affects all persons, whether or not they are capable of giving their consent. Medical treatment, even treatment for minor ailments, does not fall within that category of events. The general rule is that consent is necessary to render such treatment lawful. If such treatment administered without consent is not to be unlawful, it has to be justified on some other principle.

After referring to Goff LJ's remark in *Collins v Wilcock*, Brennan J in the Australian High Court case of *Secretary, Department of Health v JWB and SMB* (1992) 66 ALJR 300 at 317–318 (discussed more fully *infra*, chs 6 and 9) emphasised the breadth of the law's protection.

> **Brennan J:** Blackstone declared the right to personal security to be an absolute, or individual, right vested in each person by 'the immutable laws of nature' (Blackstone, ibid, vol 1, pp 124, 129; vol 3, p 119). Blackstone's reason for the rule which forbids any form of molestation, namely, that 'every man's person [is] sacred', points to the value which underlies and informs the law: each person has a unique dignity which the law respects and which it will protect.
>
> Human dignity is a value common to our municipal law and to international instruments relating to human rights (The inherent dignity of *all* members of the human family is commonly proclaimed in the preambles to international instruments relating to human rights: see the United Nations Charter, the International Covenant on Civil and Political Rights (which declares 'the right to ... security of person' Art 9), the Universal Declaration of Human Rights, the International Covenant on Economic, Social and Cultural Rights and the Convention on the Rights of the Child.) The law will protect equally the dignity of the hale and hearty and the dignity of the weak and lame; of the frail baby and of the frail aged; of the intellectually able and of the intellectually disabled. Thus municipal law satisfies the requirement of the first paragraph of the 1971 United Nations Declaration on the Rights of Mentally Retarded Persons which reads:
>
> > The mentally retarded person has, to the maximum degree of feasibility, the same rights as other human beings.

Our law admits of no discrimination against the weak and disadvantaged in their human dignity. Intellectual disability justifies no impairment of human dignity, no invasion of the right to personal integrity. ...

Human dignity requires that the whole personality be respected: the right to physical integrity is a condition of human dignity but the gravity of any invasion of physical integrity depends on its effect not only on the body but also upon the mind and on self-perception.

In *St George's Healthcare NHS Trust v S* [1998] 3 All ER 673 (CA) the Court of Appeal gave its unequivocal support to the law's recognition of a patient's right to decide.

Judge LJ: Even when his or her own life depends on receiving medical treatment, an adult of sound mind is entitled to refuse it. This reflects the autonomy of each individual and the right of self-determination. Lest reiteration may diminish the impact of this principle, it is valuable to recognise the force of the language used when the right of self-determination was most recently considered in the House of Lords in *Airedale NHS Trust v Bland*:

'The first point to make is that it is unlawful, so as to constitute both the tort and crime of battery, to administer medical treatment to an adult, who is conscious and of sound mind, without his consent see *F v West Berkshire Health Authority (Mental Health Act Commission intervening)* [1989] 2 All ER 545, [1990] 2 AC 1. Such a person is completely at liberty to decline to undergo treatment, even if the result of his doing so will be that he will die.' (See [1993] 1 All ER 821 at 860, [1993] AC 789 at 857 per Lord Keith.)

'... it is established that the principle of self-determination requires that respect must be given to the wishes of the patient, so that, if an adult patient of sound mind refuses, however unreasonably, to consent to treatment or care by which his life would or might be prolonged, the doctors responsible for his care must give effect to his wishes, even ... though they do not consider it to be in his best interests to do so ... To this extent, the principle of the sanctity of human life must yield to the principle of self-determination ... and, for present purposes perhaps more important, the doctor's duty to act in the best interests of his patient must likewise be qualified.' (See [1993] 1 All ER 821 at 866, [1993] AC 789 at 864 per Lord Goff of Chieveley.)

'Any treatment given by a doctor to a patient which is invasive (ie involves any interference with the physical integrity of the patient) is unlawful unless done with the consent of the patient: it constitutes the crime of battery and the tort of trespass to the person. Thus, in the case of an adult who is mentally competent, the artificial feeding regime (and the attendant steps necessary to it) constituted to it. A mentally competent patient can at any time put an end to life support systems by refusing his consent to their continuation.' (See [1993] 1 All ER 821 at 881–882, [1993] AC 789 at 882 per Lord Browne-Wilkinson.)

'Any invasion of the body of one person by another is potentially both a crime and a tort ... How is it that, consistently with the proposition just stated, a doctor can with immunity perform on a consenting patient an act which would be a very serious crime if done by someone else? The answer must be that bodily invasions in the course of proper medical treatment stand completely outside the criminal law. The reason why the consent of the patient is so important is not that it furnishes a defence in itself, but because it is usually essential to the propriety of medical treatment. Thus, if the consent is absent, and is not dispensed with in special circumstances by operation of law, the acts of the doctor lose their immunity ... If the patient is capable of making a decision whether to permit treatment and decides not to permit it his choice must be obeyed, even if on any objective view it is contrary to his best interests. A doctor has no right to proceed in the face of objection, even if it is plain to all, including the patient, that adverse consequences and even death will or may ensue.' (See [1993] 1 All ER 821 at 889, [1993] AC 789 at 891 per Lord Mustill.)

The speeches in *Airedale NHS Trust v Bland* did not establish the law, but rather underlined the principle found in a series of authoritative decisions. With the exception of one short passage from the observations of Lord Reid in *S v S, W v Official Solicitor* [1970] 3 All ER 107, [1972] AC 24 no further citation is necessary.

In that case the House of Lords considered whether it was right to order blood tests on two infants to help establish whether or not they were legitimate. Lord Reid examined the legal position and said ([1970] 3 All ER 107 at 111, [1972] AC 24 at 43):

'There is no doubt that a person of full age and capacity cannot be ordered to undergo a blood test against his will ... The real reason is that English law goes to great lengths to protect a person of full age and capacity from interference with his personal liberty. We have too often seen freedom disappear in other countries not only by coups d'état but by gradual erosion; and often it is the first step that counts. So it would be unwise to make even minor concessions.'

The importance of this salutary warning remains undiminished.

(See also Re *T (adult: refusal of treatment)* [1992] 4 All ER 649 (CA).)

As we shall see (*infra*, ch 6), the court applied the principle even where the patient was a pregnant woman and her refusal had a deleterious effect upon her unborn child.

Finally, we should notice that the patient's right would be an aspect of their 'right of privacy' under art 8(1) of the European Convention on Human Rights. Forced treatment against the wishes of a competent patient could also breach their right under art 3 not to be subjected, *inter alia*, to 'inhuman or degrading treatment'.

Issues of consent in the doctor-patient relationship arise in three main contexts: (i) in the crime of battery; (ii) in the tort of battery; and (iii) in the tort of negligence. In reality, consent or lack of it is only an issue in the civil law of torts. Although theoretically, a doctor who ordinarily acts without obtaining a patient's consent may not only be exposed to liability in tort, but also runs the risk of facing a criminal prosecution for the crime of battery, there is little or no chance that this will actually happen in the context of the ordinary practice of medicine in good faith. Obviously there are many circumstances where a doctor can be guilty of a crime involving lack of consent. For example, he may obtain his patient's consent to intercourse by representing it as a legitimate examination (*R v Williams* [1923] 1 KB 340) or he may fraudulently represent that a particular medical procedure is essential and thereby gain financial reward from a private patient by deception. But these are matters which do not concern us here since our concern is with the ordinary practice of medicine in good faith.

The scope of the crime of battery, should it ever arise, is likely to be held by the courts to be the same as the tort of battery, apart from the fact that the doctor's intention will be relevant in determining whether he has the necessary *mens rea* for the crime. (See P D G Skegg *Law, Ethics and Medicine* (1984) at pp 79–80.)

As regards the tort of battery, Professor Fleming in his *Law of Torts* (9th edn, 1998) defines a battery as follows (at p 29):

Of the various forms of trespass to the person the most common is the tort known as battery, which is committed by intentionally bringing about a harmful or offensive contact with another person's body. The action, therefore, serves the dual purpose of affording protection to the individual not only against bodily harm but also against any interference with his person which is offensive to a reasonable sense of honour and dignity. The insult in being touched without consent has been traditionally regarded as sufficient, even though the content is only trivial and not attended with actual physical harm.

There have been relatively few cases in England in which a patient has successfully sued his doctor for battery on the ground that he had not consented to being touched (for a discussion of the cases see G Seabourne 'The Role of the Tort of Battery in Medical Law' (1995) 24 Anglo-Am LR 265 at 275–285). However, there are a few examples: *Hamilton v Birmingham RHB* [1969] 2 BMJ 456 (sterilisation without consent during the performance of a caesarian section); *Michael v Molesworth* [1950] 2 BMJ 171 (operation performed by a different surgeon from the one agreed); *Cull v Royal Surrey County Hospital* [1932] 1 BMJ 1195 (patient consented to an abortion and the doctor carried out a different procedure, a hysterectomy); *Devi v West Midlands RHA* [1981] (CA Transcript 491) (patient consented to an operation to repair a perforation of the uterus, the surgeon performed a sterilisation operation as well). (For a recent example of a dentist held liable in battery for carrying out unnecessary dental work on healthy teeth: see, *Appleton v Garrett* (1995) 34 BMLR 23 (Dyson J), discussed, *infra* pp 661-662.) This does not mean that the tort of battery is unimportant. Its greatest significance lies in the fact that it represents a statement by the law of the importance of an individual patient's right to determine what should or should not be done to his body. Further proof of this is, of course, the fact that, as regards the tort of battery, the plaintiff need not prove that he has suffered harm so as to recover damages. Harm is assumed, since the tort protects the plaintiff from harm which is symbolic as well as that which results in injury. Equally, aggravated damages may be awarded in a battery action (see eg *Appleton v Garrett*, *supra*). It is clear that a battery will be committed by a doctor even if he acts only out of what he sees as the best interests of his patient.

Mohr v Williams (1905) 104 NW 12 (Sup Ct Minn)

Plaintiff consulted defendant, an ear specialist, concerning rouble with her right ear. On examining her, he found a diseased condition of the right ear, and she consented to an operation upon it. When she was unconscious under the anaesthetic, defendant concluded that the condition of the right ear was not serious enough to require an operation; but he found a more serious condition of the left ear, which he decided required an operation. Without reviving the plaintiff to ask her permission, he operated on the left ear. The operation was skillfully performed, and was successful. Plaintiff nevertheless brought an action for battery and succeeded.

Brown J: The last contention of defendant is that the act complained of did not amount to an assault and battery. This is based upon the theory that, as plaintiff's left ear was in fact diseased, in a condition dangerous and threatening to her health, the operation was necessary, and having been skillfully performed at a time when plaintiff has requested a like operation on the other ear, the charge of assault and battery cannot be sustained: that, in view of these conditions, and the claim that there was no negligence on the part of defendant, and an entire absence of any evidence tending to show an evil intent, the court should say, as a matter of law, that no assault and battery was committed, even though she did not consent to the operation. In other words, that the absence of a showing that defendant was actuated by a wrongful intent, or guilty of negligence, relieves the act of defendant from the charge of an unlawful assault and battery.

We are unable to reach that conclusion, though the contention is not without merit. It would seen to follow from what has been said on the other features of the case that the act of defendant amounted at least to a technical assault and battery. If the operation was performed without plaintiff's consent, and the circumstances were not such as to justify its performance without, it was wrongful; and, if it was wrongful, it was unlawful. As remarked in *I Jaggard on Torts*, 437, every person has a right to complete immunity of his person from physical interference of others, except in so far as contact may be necessary under the general doctrine of privilege: and any unlawful or unauthorised touching of the person of another, except it be in the spirit of pleasantry, constitutes an assault and battery. In the case as bar, as we have already seen, the question whether defendant's act in performing the operation upon plaintiff was authorised was a question for the jury to determine. If it was unauthorised, then it was, within what we have said, unlawful. It was a violent assault, not a mere pleasantry: and, even though no negligence is shown, it was wrongful and unlawful.

(For a similar case in Canada, see *Murray v McMurchy* [1949] 2 DLR 442 Supreme Court of British Columbia.) You will also remember Lord Goff's reference in *Re F*: 'surgical treatment by a surgeon who mistakenly thinks that the patient has consented to it … may transcend the bounds of lawfulness.'

The variety of situations in which a battery action may be brought is explored by Allan McCoid in his seminal article.

A McCoid 'A Reappraisal of Liability for Unauthorised Medical Treatment' (1957) 41 Minnesota LR 381

The study of cases involving unauthorised operations or medical treatment indicates the existence of a great diversity of factual situations ranging from a case such as *Schloendorff v Society of New York Hospital* [105 NE 92 (NY, 1914)] in which the doctor operated in direct violation of express prohibitions of the patient and the operation resulted in serious physical injury, to cases such as *Mohr v Williams* [104 NW 12 (1905)] or *Pratt v Davis* [(1906) 79 NE 562], in which the operation was done without the express consent of the patient but probably caused no serious harm to the patient and in point of fact may have conferred some benefit. Between these two extremes lie cases in which there was only a limitation upon a general scope of consent the violation of which did not seriously injure the patient, as in *Tolater v Strain* [(1913) 39 Okla 572] and cases in which there was no express prohibition but substantial harm resulted to the patient from an operation which went beyond the scope of express consent, as in *Wall v Brim* [138 F 2d 478 (5th Circ, 1943)] or *Paulsen v Gundersen* [218 Wis 578, 260 NW 448 (1935)]. Yet the courts tend to group together all of these diverse fact situations under the category of 'assault and battery' and rely upon any one of the early cases as authority for imposing liability upon the doctor which may differ substantially from the nature and scope of liability in a general malpractice action. ...

Traditionally the distinction between an 'assault and battery' and a 'negligent tort' has been drawn on the basis of the existence or nonexistence of 'intent', that state of mind in which the actor acts for the purpose of accomplishing a given consequence or acts with knowledge that such a consequence is substantially certain to occur, although there need be no showing of a hostile or malicious purpose or of an intent to do harm. In all of the cases discussed in this article, the physician knew what he was doing; he knew that he was performing a certain operation or that he was rendering certain treatment affecting the body of the patient. In all but a few of the cases it is to be inferred that he also knew that there was no specific assent to such operation or treatment, and in some of those few the lack of such knowledge was the result of mistake as to the identity of the patient or the identity of a particular portion of the body to be treated, neither of which would constitute a defense. In each of the cases there has been a legal 'harm' in the sense of a physically harmful invasion of the body of the plaintiff-patient or an interference with the patient's personal integrity or right to determine what shall and shall not be done with his body. Following these traditional lines of analysis, one would conclude that except in a very rare case, such as a true emergency, the doctor who acts without the consent of a patient is guilty of an assault and battery.

What appears to distinguish the case of the unauthorized operation from traditional assault and battery cases is the fact that in almost all of the cases, the doctor is acting in relative good faith for the benefit of the patient. It is true that in some cases the results are not in fact beneficial, but the courts have stated repeatedly that doctors are not insurers. The traditional assault and battery, on the other hand, involves a defendant who is acting for the most part out of malice or in a manner which is generally considered as 'anti-social'. And in general the assaulter and batterer is not seeking to confer any benefit upon the plaintiff, even though he may believe, as Dean Prosser has suggested, that he is complimenting the plaintiff by his amatory advances. This leads to the conclusion that there is some basis for separating most of the cases discussed in this paper from the traditional assault and battery. At the same time, there appears to be justification for retaining the 'assault and battery' classification for such situations as occurred in *Bryan v Grace* [(1940) 11 SE 2d 241], *Wellman v Drake* [(1947) 43 SE 2d 57] and *Keen v Coleman* [(1942) 20 SE 2d 175] as well as the 'fraud' cases. Operations, declared to be anti-social in their very nature by statutes making their performance a crime, deserve specialized treatment.

So, the central issue for the medical lawyer here is the legal concept of consent. A legally valid, or real, consent consists of the following elements: (a) it is given by a competent person; (b) it is given voluntarily; (c) it is an adequately informed consent.

For the present it is important to notice the move away from the tort of battery to negligence, reflected in the courts' concern less with the question whether the touching was consented to at all and more with the quality of the information imparted to gain the consent.

Reibl v Hughes (1980) 114 DLR (3d) 1 (Can SC)

Laskin CJ: The tort [of battery] is an intentional one, consisting of an unprivileged and unconsented to invasion of one's bodily security. True enough, it has some advantages for a plaintiff over an action of negligence since it does not require proof of causation and it casts upon the defendant the burden of proving consent to what was done. Again, it does not require the adducing of medical evidence, although it seems to me that if battery is to be available for certain kinds of failure to meet the duty of disclosure there would necessarily have to be some such evidence brought before the Court as an element in determining whether there has been such a failure. ...

The well-known statement of Cardozo J in *Schloendorff v Society of New York Hospital* 211 NY 125 at 129, 105 NE 92 at 93 (1914) that 'every human being of adult years and sound mind has a right to determine what shall be done with his own body; and a surgeon who performs an operation without his patient's consent commits an assault, for which he is liable in damages' cannot be taken beyond the compass of its words to support an action of battery where there has been consent to the very surgical procedure carried out upon a patient but there has been a breach of the duty of disclosure of attendant risks. In my opinion, actions of battery in respect of surgical or other medical treatment should be confined to cases where surgery or treatment has been performed or given to which there has been no consent at all where, emergency situations aside, surgery or treatment has been performed or given beyond that to which there was consent. ...

In situations where the allegation is that attendant risks which should have been disclosed were not communicated to the patient and yet the surgery or other medical treatment carried out was that to which the plaintiff consented (there being no negligence basis of liability for the recommended surgery or treatment to deal with the patient's condition), I do not understand how it can be said that the consent was vitiated by the failure of disclosure so as to make the surgery or other treatment an unprivileged, unconsented to and intentional invasion of the patient's bodily integrity. I can appreciate the temptation to say that the genuineness of consent to medical treatment depends on proper disclosure of the risks which it entails, but in my view, unless there has been misrepresentation or fraud to secure consent to the treatment, a failure to disclose the attendant risks, however serious, should go to negligence rather than to battery. Although such a failure relates to an informed choice of submitting to or refusing recommended and appropriate treatment, it arises as the breach of an anterior duty of due care, comparable in legal obligation to the duty of due care in carrying out the particular treatment to which the patient has consented. It is not a test of the validity of the consent.

You will see from this extract from the leading Canadian case, that the Chief Justice considered that the scope of battery in medical law is restricted (see, further, G Seabourne 'The Role of the Tort of Battery in Medical Law' (1995) 24 Anglo-Am LR 265). Failure of the doctor to provide information will only in exceptional circumstances mean that the patient has not consented to a particular procedure. It is another matter, as we will see, whether an action in negligence may lie for the non-disclosure.

It is clear that the English courts do not favour the action in battery in the context of medical treatment. In *Hills v Potter* [1983] 3 All ER 716 Hirst J said:

I should add that I respectfully agree with Bristow J [in *Chatterton v Gerson*] in deploring reliance on these torts in medical cases of this kind; the proper cause of action, if any, is negligence.

Lord Scarman expressly agreed with these remarks in *Sidaway* (*supra*) when the case reached the House of Lords. Why should this be so? Consider the following remarks of Justice Mosk in the Californian case of *Cobbs v Grant* (1972) 502 P 2d 1:

Mosk J: [M]ost jurisdictions have permitted a doctor in an informed consent action to interpose a defence that the disclosure he omitted to make was not required within his medical community. However, expert opinion as to community standard is not required in a battery count, in which the patient must merely prove failure to give informed consent and a mere touching absent consent. Moreover a doctor could be held liable for punitive damages under a battery count, and if held liable for the intentional tort of battery he might not be covered by his malpractice insurance. Comment, 'Informed Consent in Medical Malpractice', 55 Cal L Rev 1396 (1967). Additionally, in some jurisdictions the patient has a longer statute of limitations if he sues in negligence.

Do any or all of these reasons apply in England?

G Robertson 'Informed Consent to Medical Treatment' (1981) 97 LQR 102

It is submitted that there are two principal reasons for the judicial policy evident in *Chatterton* [*v Gerson* [1981] QB 432] ... against trespass claims in informed consent litigation. First, as can be seen from the decisions in *Fowler v Lanning* [[1959] 1 QB 426] and *Letang v Cooper* [[1965] 1 QB 232] judicial policy appears to be in favour of restricting claims in battery to situations involving deliberate, hostile acts, a situation which most judges would regard as foreign to the doctor-patient relationship. Coupled with this is the stigma and damage to professional reputation which courts repeatedly emphasise are an inevitable by-product of a successful claim against a doctor. These consequences are probably seen as even more serious in an action for battery than in an action for negligence. The second reason stems from the view expressed in the concluding section of this article, namely, that courts in this country will attempt to restrict the scope of the doctrine of informed consent, principally by means of the requirement of causation, the use of expert evidence as to accepted medical practice, and emphasis on the 'best interests of the patient' principle [on which we now have the House of Lords' decision in the *Sidaway* case; *infra*]. Restriction of the doctrine of informed consent in this way would not be possible if it were to be accepted that failure to inform of inherent risks of proposed treatment could ground an action for trespass. As was outlined above, the plaintiff in such an action would not be required to prove, by way of causation, that he would not have consented to the treatment had he been informed of the risks. Similarly, evidence of accepted medical practice has no place in an action for trespass; if failure to disclose a particular risk were to be regarded as vitiating consent, the fact that a reasonable doctor would not have disclosed the risk cannot absolve the defendant from liability for battery. Finally, although the point is not entirely clear, it would seem that a doctor cannot avoid liability for battery simply on the grounds that he was acting in the best interests of his patient. Thus it can be seen that the three principal ways in which the doctrine of informed consent is likely to be restricted would not be available to a court dealing with a case based in trespass.

As we saw, the Crown Indemnity Scheme and the Clinical Negligence Scheme for Trusts whereby NHS institutions pay any damages awarded against doctors in their employment is restricted to claims in negligence (see *supra*, ch 4). It remains uncertain whether a doctor would be covered for a battery claim if he remained a member of a defence organisation (for two cases in which the patients sued in negligence when the essence of their actions was that they had not consented to the procedures: see, *Abbas v Kenney* (1995) 31 BMLR 157 (Gage J) and *Williamson v East London and City HA* (1997) 41 BMLR 85 (Butterfield J)).

A final, and by no means trivial point, concerns the juridical basis of the plea of consent: is it for the plaintiff to prove its absence or for the defendant to prove that the plaintiff consented? In *Freeman v Home Office (No 2)* [1984] QB 524 at 539 McCowan J asserted that it was for the plaintiff to prove lack of consent. There is little or no English case law to determine this issue. In principle, however, consent should be seen as a defence. Given the importance the law places on the bodily integrity of the individual, it is for the defendant to justify the interference. This is the law in other Commonwealth jurisdictions and was convincingly supported by McHugh J in the Australian High Court case of *Secretary, Department of Health v JWB and SMB* (1992) 66 ALJR 300 at 337.

McHugh J: Consent is not necessary, where a surgical procedure or medical treatment must be performed in an emergency and the patient does not have the capacity to consent and no legally authorised representative is available to give consent on his or her behalf.

In England, the onus is on the plaintiff to prove lack of consent (*Freeman v Home Office (No 2)* [1984] QB 524 at 539). That view has the support of some academic writers in Australia (See Balkin and Davis, *Law of Torts*, (1991) pp 38–39; Luntz and Hambly, *Torts: Cases and Commentary* (3rd edn, 1992), pp 680–681; Blay, 'Onus of Proof of Consent in an Action for Trespass to the Person' (1987) 61 *Australian Law Journal 25*), but it is opposed by other academic writers in Australia. (See Fleming, *The Law of Torts* (7th edn, 1987), p 72; Trindade and Cane, *The Law of Torts in Australia*, (1985), pp 39–40.) It is opposed by Canadian authority (*Hambley v Shepley* (1967) 63 DLR (2d) 94 at 95; *Kelly v Hazlett* (1976) 75 DLR (3d) 536 at 556; *Allan v New Mount Sinai Hospital* (1980) 109 DLR (3d) 634). It is also opposed by Australian authority (*Hart v Herron* [1984] Aust Torts Reports 80–201; *Sibley v Milutinovic* [1990] Aust Torts Reports 81–013). Notwithstanding the English view, I think that the onus is on the defendant to prove consent. Consent is a claim of 'leave and licence'. Such a claim be pleaded and proved by the defendant in an action for trespass to land (*Kavanagh v Gudge* (1844) Ad & ER 7 Man & G 316, 135 ER 132; *Wood v Manley* (1839) 11 Ad & El 34, [1835–42] All ER Rep 128; *Plenty v Dillon* (1991) 171 CLR 635 at 647). It must be pleaded in a defamation action when the defendant claims that the plaintiff consented to the publication. (See *Loveday v Sun Newspapers Ltd* (1938) 59 CLR 503 at 525.) The Common Law Procedure Act 1852 (15 & 16 Vict c 76) (Sch B 44) also required any 'defence' of leave and licence to be pleaded and proved. However, those who contend that the plaintiff must negative consent in an action for trespass to the person deny that consent is a matter of leave and licence. They contend that lack of consent is an essential element of the action for trespass to a person. I do not accept that this is so. The essential element of the tort is an intentional or reckless, direct act of the defendant which makes or has the effect of causing contact with the body of the plaintiff. Consent may make the act lawful, but, if there is no evidence on the issue, the tort is made out. The contrary view is inconsistent with a person's right of bodily integrity. Other persons do not have the right to interfere with an individual's body unless he or she proves lack of consent to the interference.

For a discussion of this issue in the context of the crimes of assault and battery see *R v Brown* [1993] 2 All ER 75 HL; contrast Lord Jauncey at 92 and Lord Slynn at 119. Cf Lord Mustill at 103.

Form of consent

A. EXPRESS

Consent is express when the patient explicitly agrees to what is proposed by the doctor. it need not have been set out in any specific form and it need not be in writing: see *Re T (adult: refusal of treatment)* [1992] 4 All ER 649 at 653 per Lord Donaldson MR. Indeed, the vast majority of occasions when patients are touched by doctors take place in a GP's surgery where none of the apparatus of formal consent is present.

Consent forms have, however, long been a part of hospital procedure. The Department of Health (DoH) has published specimen forms in its *A Guide to Consent for Examination or Treatment* (NHS Management Executive, 1990) (HC (90) 22 as amended by HSG (92) 32).

CONSENT FORM   **APPENDIX A(1)**

For medical or dental investigation, treatment or operation

Health Authority .... Patient's Surname ....

Hospital .... Other Names ....

Unit Number .... Date of Birth ....

                                    Sex: (*Please tick*) Male   Female

DOCTORS OR DENTISTS *(This part to be completed by doctor or dentist.)*

                                      (See notes on the reverse.)

Type of operation, investigation or treatment for which written evidence of consent is considered appropriate

I confirm that I have explained the operation, investigation or treatment, and such appropriate options as are available and the type of anaesthetic, if any (general/local/sedation) proposed, to the patient in terms which in my judgment are suited to the understanding of the patient and/or to one of the parents or guardians of the patient.

Signature .... Date ....

Name of doctor or dentist ....

PATIENT/PARENT/GUARDIAN

1.   Please read this form and the notes overleaf very carefully.
2.   If there is anything that you don't understand about the explanation, or if you want more information, you should ask the doctor or dentist.

3.   Please check that all the information on the form is correct. If it is, and you understand the explanation, then sign the form.

I am the patient/parent/guardian (*delete as necessary*).

I agree	■	to what is proposed which has been explained to me by the doctor/dentist named on this form.
	■	to the use of the type of anaesthetic that I have been told about.
I understand	■	that the procedure may not be done by the doctor/dentist who has been treating me so far.
	■	that any procedure in addition to the investigation or treatment described on this form will only be carried out if it is necessary and in my best interests and can be justified for medical reasons.
I have told	■	the doctor or dentist about the procedures listed below I would *not* wish to be carried out without my having the opportunity to consider them first.

Signature   ....

Name   ....

Address   ....

(*if not the patient*)   ....

In addition to this general form, the DoH provides specimen consent forms, *inter alia*, for use in case of sterilisations (Appendix A(2)), for treatment by other health professionals (Appendix A(3)) and as regards treatment of the mentally disordered (Appendix B).

There is no specific form prescribed by law to which the document must conform. It need only record faithfully that which was agreed between the parties and not contemplate that which is unlawful. Indeed, there is no requirement in law that consent be reduced to writing. The written consent form is merely therefore evidence of what was agreed. Notice the words of Bristow J in *Chatterton v Gerson* [1981] 1 All ER 257 at 265:

> I should add that getting the patient to sign a pro forma expressing consent to undergo the operation 'the effect and nature of which have been explained to me', as was done here in each case, should be a valuable reminder to everyone of the need for explanation and consent. But it would be no defence to an action based on trespass to the person if no explanation had in fact been given. The consent would have been expressed in form only, not in reality.

In commenting upon the DoH's form, Margaret Brazier expressed the following views.

M Brazier 'Revised Consent Forms in the NHS' (1991) 6 Professional Negligence 148

> The experienced cynic might well conclude that the new form is longer than its predecessor but how does the extra verbiage actually reinforce patients' rights?
>
> Nothing on the face of the form prevents the doctor scrawling unhelpfully 'D & C' under type of operation and hustling the patient through filling out his part of the form. Note how the doctor certifies that in his judgment the explanation of the proposed treatment is suited to the understanding of the patient. Paternalism enshrined in *Sidaway* [*v Governors of Royal Bethlem Hospital* [1985] AC 871] is given further official blessing. But the Department of Health was not responsible for *Sidaway*. The House of Lords retains that dubious honour. The new form does seek to focus the attention of professional and patient on some of the matters their consultation should cover. At a most banal level more room is made on the form for the explanation of the type of operation, investigation or treatment. The doctor is required to confirm that he has canvassed alternative options available and discussed with the patient the type of anaesthetic. The form prompts the patient to ask questions. In a sense the 'official' form gives the patient express 'permission' to question the doctor. And the patient is offered a specific opportunity to state what additional procedures she would not

wish to be carried out straightaway without an opportunity to consider them first. Those instances where a woman goes into hospital for minor gynaecological surgery and wakes up sterilised 'in her best interests' ought not now to recur.

You will notice that the form states that:

I understand that any procedure in addition to the investigation or treatment described on this form will only be carried out if it is necessary and in my best interests and can be justified for medical reasons.

Two Canadian cases illustrate the questions that can arise from such a clause (for a detailed discussion see, I Kennedy and A Grubb (eds) *Principles of Medical Law* (1998), paras 3.55–3.61).

Brushett v Cowan [1991] 2 Med LR 271 (Newfoundland CA)

Marshall JA: On June 25, 1984 [Miss Brushett] entered hospital to undergo [a] procedure. Prior to the operation she signed a consent which read as follows:

I Brushett Sheila of 198 Pleasant St hereby consent to the submission of myself to the operation or special procedure of Muscle Biopsy Right Distal Thigh the nature and purpose of which have been explained to me by Dr Cowan.

I also consent to such further or alternative measures as may be found to be necessary during the course of the operation or special procedure and to the administration of a general, local or other anaesthetic for any of these purposes.

I further agree that in his discretion Dr Cowan may make use of the assistance of other surgeons, physicians, and hospital staff and may permit them to order or perform all or part of the treatment, special procedure or operative procedure and they shall have the same discretion in my treatment and in the execution of any procedure as Dr Cowan.

After Dr Cowan had excised a portion of the muscle, he went down to the bone and, having observed an area that appeared abnormal he biopsied a portion of it. Miss Brushett was discharged from hospital that same day. No instructions were given to her at that time relating to the use of crutches nor were any provided to her.

Two days later she visited Dr Cowan at his clinic in the hospital for consultation and examination. While arrangements were then made to supply her with crutches, Miss Brushett testified no one advised her to be non-weight bearing. She also maintained she was not made aware that a biopsy had been taken from her bone as well as her muscle and remained unaware of that fact until so advised by a Dr Perkins prior to operating upon her on July 7, 1984, to repair a fracture to her leg. On the other hand, Dr Cowan maintained that during the course of the examination on June 22, 1984, he had advised Miss Brushett of the bone biopsy and instructed her to be non-weight bearing. In support of this contention a letter was produced bearing the same date from the doctor to the Workers Compensation Board relative to Miss Brushett in which he stated:

Today I gave her crutches and advised her to be non-weight bearing.

Miss Brushett testified that she used the crutches intermittently for mobilization, getting in and out of chairs or climbing stairs. She stated that she never used them otherwise inside her home but generally used them outside. However, she was not using them on 6 July 1984, when, in the course of a visit to Old Perlican, she fell and broke her right leg at the site of the bone biopsy. She was subsequently conveyed to the General Hospital in St John's where Dr Perkins operated upon her on 7 July to repair the fracture.

Later Miss Brushett took action against Dr Cowan, the General Hospital and a resident physician at the hospital. Her claim against Dr Cowan was founded in battery arising from the bone biopsy allegedly performed without her knowledge and consent and in negligence primarily related to her post-operative care.

The action against the hospital was discontinued at the commencement of the trial. The claim against the resident physician was dismissed by the trial judge. ... However, the learned trial judge found Dr Cowan liable in battery and in negligence in failing to advise his patient to be non-weight bearing and of the possible effects of normal use of her leg. ...

Citing *Reibl*, the trial judge focused her assessment entirely upon the formal consent signed by Miss Brushett. In so doing, she found para 3 inapplicable and para 2 too vague to permit an interpretation expanding Miss Brushett's consent beyond the muscle biopsy to which she specifically consented in the initial part of the document. As a result she found that the bone biopsy amounted to a battery.

In my respectful opinion the learned trial judge erred in confining her assessment to the formal written consent form. It is noted that Laskin CJC in *Reibl* held that battery should be confined to cases where there has been 'no consent at all' or where medical procedures go 'beyond that to which there was consent'. He did not state that one's inquiry must be limited to the specific formal consent. On the contrary, the statement that battery is predicated upon the absence of any consent 'at all' implies that one must examine all aspects of the situation to determine if the patient had agreed to the medical procedure in respect of which complaint is laid.

Therefore, all relevant circumstances leading up to the surgery should be considered when determining what the patient agreed to when he or she submitted to the procedure. Any written consent will bear obvious weight upon such an assessment. However, inasmuch as many formal consents are signed – as was the one in the case at bar – immediately before the surgery, on the threshold as it were of the operating room, when a patient is experiencing a certain degree of trauma and stress, the circumstances leading up to his or her presence at the hospital are relevant to the patient's intent and the consent form ought to be read in light of them.

In the present case, the circumstances show Miss Brushett to have been referred to Dr Cowan for the purpose of investigating persistent problems associated with an injury which she had sustained. Within a relatively short period of time Miss Brushett had a number of consultations and underwent several investigative procedures at Dr Cowan's instigation, all of which were aimed at determining the cause of her symptoms. Indeed, the biopsy was part of the ongoing investigative process.

It is true that the consent form made specific reference to a muscle biopsy and that the patient must have entered hospital contemplating a part of her muscle was to be excised. However, this was because the bone scan indicated that certain abnormalities detected by it were due to muscle damage. Submission to the surgical procedure was for the purpose of determining the cause of her persistent problem with her right thigh and to achieve this she agreed to undergo a procedure that would enable a portion of her body inside the thigh to be excised for investigation. While the scan caused, at that juncture, both the doctor, Miss Brushett and the written consent to focus upon the muscle in her right thigh, the overriding general purpose and intent must be taken to remain investigatory to determine the cause of the medical problem for which she had first consulted the specialist.

Had the scan signalled potential bone as well as muscle disorders, it is reasonable to assume specific reference would have been made in the consent to bone biopsy and that Miss Brushett would have agreed to it as well. In fact the trial judge, while addressing the doctor's negligence in relation to pre-operative advice, concluded that upon discovery of the discoloured bone and possible malignancy, Miss Brushett as a reasonable patient would have consented to the procedure.

It is, therefore, against the background of these circumstances that the formal consent must be viewed. In doing so the perceived vagueness which the trial judge felt rendered para 2 ineffective becomes clearer. Likewise para 3 acquires a relevance.

Considered from that perspective of the circumstances, the authorization in the second paragraph consenting

> ... to such further or alternate measures as may be found to be necessary during the course of the operation or special procedure ...

may be construed, in my opinion, as consenting to the removal of a necessary sample of the bone adjacent to the muscle in pursuit of the continuing investigative process. The discretion which para 3 records to have been given to the operating surgeon supports this view.

The law has always clearly recognized the individual's right to determine medical treatment upon his or her person: see *Allan v New Mount Sinai Hospital* (1980) 109 DLR (3d) 634, 28 OR (2d) 356; 11 CCLT 299 (HCJ), per Linden J at 642–3. It may not be abridged by considerations of medical convenience. However, this inviolable right must be interpreted in relation to the overall social interest of precluding undue hindrance of the physician legitimately acting within the scope of the consent actually given by adopting too narrow a view of its ambit. The full extent of that consent must be gained by looking at all of the circumstances arising from the relation of doctor and patient, against the background of which the formal consent will be viewed.

In summary, I conclude, with respect, that the trial judge erred in looking exclusively to the signed consent form without regard to all of the factors. Considering all of these circumstances, I am of the opinion that the bone biopsy performed upon Miss Brushett by Dr Cowan did not go beyond the consent given by her to him and, hence, there was no battery.

In the following case the judge also found that the procedure fell within the express consent given.

Pridham v Nash (1986) 33 DLR (4th) 304 (Ontario High Court)

Holland J: This medical malpractice case raises issues of consent to treatment.

Facts

Patricia Pridham is a 39-year-old married woman with four children who works as a driver for Canada Post. The late Dr Nash was an obstetrician and gynaecologist practising in Toronto. Dr Nash delivered three of Mrs. Pridham's children and also performed a tubal ligation and a partial hysterectomy prior to the operation that has given rise to this action.

For about two years before February of 1980, Mrs Pridham had been suffering from periodic pain in the pelvic area. She consulted Dr Nash on 14 February 1980, and told him about her complaints. He then examined her.

Dr Nash's note of the consultation reads as follows:

Feb 14/80 —   Had an operation in Etobicoke General in November 1977 for adhesions.

                      Took out her tube on left side.

                      Still having left sided pain. Has been on antibiotics.

                      Pelvis negative. Pap smear.

                      To have laparoscopy as out patient.

Mrs Pridham testified that after the examination Dr Nash recommended a laparoscopy to find out what was wrong. A laparoscopy is an examination of the abdominal structures within the peritoneum by means of a tubular instrument passed through the abdominal wall. Dr Nash explained there would be a small incision in the area of the navel. A scope would be inserted so that he could look around and he would then let her know what he had found. The procedure was to take place in the hospital under a general aesthetic and a date was fixed for the operation.

Following the consultation Mrs Pridham signed a consent to treatment which was filled out by Dr Nash and reads, in part, as follows:

TO: MOUNT SINAI HOSPITAL, TORONTO, ONTARIO.

1.   I Patricia Pridham consent to the following procedure being performed upon me/upon me
      General Nature of the Treatment: laparoscopy
2.   The anticipated nature and effect of such procedures have been explained to me.
3.   I confirm that I understand the explanations about the nature and effect of the procedures that will be performed upon me.
4.   I consent to all preliminary and related procedures and to the administration of general and other anaesthetics and to additional or alternative procedures as may be necessary or medically advisable during the course of such procedures.
5.   I understand that Mount Sinai Hospital is a teaching hospital and that various medical care personnel may be involved in the procedures.
      '*Patricia Pridham*'

Signature of Patient, Parent or Guardian.

PHYSICIAN'S STATEMENT

On the above date I explained the general nature of the procedure specified above to the person who signed this form and I was witness to that signing.

                                                '*S S Nash*'
                                          Signature of Physician.

Mrs Pridham had undergone a laparoscopic examination before at Etobicoke General Hospital. She said that a similar explanation of the procedure had been given to her at that time. Following that laparoscopic examination there had been a further consultation with her doctor and she had consented to a further operation that had been performed the next day.

On Friday, 29 February 1980, Mrs Pridham was admitted to Mount Sinai Hospital and the operation was performed in the afternoon. Dr Nash's operative report, which is part of the hospital records, reads, in part, as follows:

Surgeon: Dr S Nash.
Anesthetic: General.
Pre-operative Diagnosis: PELVIC PAIN
Post-operative Diagnosis: ADHESION IN PELVIS
Procedure: LAPAROSCOPY AND LYSES OR ADHESIONS

Procedure: Under general anaesthesia, a stab wound was made in the lower end of the umbilicus. The Verres needle was introduced and 8.5(?) litres of (?) carbon dioxide gas was insufflated. The stab wound was increased, and the trocar was pushed through. The laparoscope was put through the sleeve of the trocar.

Evaluation of the pelvis showed no evidence of any uterus. It was difficult to see the ovaries, since they were in the cul-de-sac. There was an adhesive band going from the pelvis to the anterior abdominal wall, and this, I believe, could cause recurrent phases of subacute bowel obstruction.

What was decided was to lyse these two adhesions. A coagulating forceps was then put in, and the two adhesions were lysed using the cutting current. The gas and instruments were removed, and the incision in the umbilicus was closed.

The patient withstood the procedure well, and left the operating room in good condition.

The term lyse used in the report means to cut or divide.

Dr Nash spoke to Mrs Pridham in the recovery room following the procedure and told her that he had found some adhesions, that she would be all right, and that she could go home that day. She said that she just assumed that what was done had to be done and she made no complaint.

After Mrs Pridham returned home she experienced pain in the abdomen. The pain grew in intensity over the week-end and she was admitted, through the emergency department, to Scarborough General Hospital on Monday, 3 March. She came under the care of Dr O'Dwyer, a general surgeon. He diagnosed pelvic peritonitis – inflammation of the peritoneum. He operated and found a perforation of the ileum from which intestinal content leaked readily. There was a surrounding necrotic area (area of dead tissue) which he presumed was the result of cautery. Dr O'Dwyer resected about a three-inch segment of ileum. Mrs Pridham tolerated the operation well and was discharged from the hospital on 21 March.

Mrs Pridham appeared to me to be a hard working, well-motivated person and she was able to get back to work within a reasonable time. She has been left with an unsightly scar on the abdomen and still has some minor complaints.

Issues
The issues raised are as follows:
1. Did Mrs Pridham expressly or by implication consent to the lyseing of the adhesions since it was during this procedure that the damage was caused to the ileum which resulted in peritonitis …

Was there consent, express or implied, to lyse the adhesions?

Counsel for Mrs Pridham submits that although there was consent to an investigative procedure, there was no consent to lyse or cut adhesions during such procedure.

Dr Scott Russell, an obstetrician and gynaecologist, was called as a defence witness. He explained the procedure known as laparoscopy. It is a surgical procedure usually performed under a general anesthetic. A small incision is made in the abdomen and the abdomen is then inflated with carbon dioxide. A trocar is then inserted. A trocar used for such a procedure in 1980 looks like a stainless steel spike about eight inches and one centimetre in diameter. The trocar is covered by a stainless steel sleeve. Once the trocar and sleeve are in place the trocar is withdrawn leaving the sleeve extending through the wall of the abdomen. An optical tube, a laparoscope, is then placed through the sleeve and the surgeon can observe the contents of the abdomen. The laparoscope is about 15 ins long. It is rigid and slightly less than one centimetre in diameter.

Should the surgeon wish to move an internal organ, because it obstructs his view, or wish to cut tissue, or take tissue for biopsy, the surgeon may make a second incision at the public hair-line and, through a trocar, introduce a cutting and coagulating forceps. The forceps may also be introduced through the original incision, using another trocar and sleeve, and this latter procedure was apparently followed in this case.

Laparoscopy is frequently performed and is possibly performed on one in 12 women of child-bearing age in Toronto.

The cutting of adhesions is generally not considered to be serious. Dr Russell said that adhesions can look like cobwebs or can be thicker, like pieces of butchers' cord. Dr Nash apparently thought that Mrs Pridham was well enough following the operation to go home that same afternoon.

The consent form, above-quoted … , reads in part as follows:

4.   I consent to … additional … procedures as may be necessary or medically advisable during the course of such procedures.

If the laparoscopic examination, an investigative procedure, had revealed a major problem requiring surgery then, in my view, the surgeon would not be entitled to rely on the original consent and the general words of the consent, as quoted above, to carry out the major surgery. The surgeon would have been required to consult further with the patient and obtain a further consent to the major operation. However, this case, in my view, is different.

From a practical point of view it would have been foolish for Dr Nash to wait for Mrs Pridham to come out of the anesthetic and then seek her consent to go through the same incision again to cut the two adhesions. The additional curative surgery was of such a minor nature that it falls practically in the same category as taking a sample for biopsy.

It was Dr Russell's opinion that he would consider it part of Dr Nash's mandate to move and clear away obstructions that were in the way and, for this purpose, to introduce a second trocar. Further, in the process of dividing adhesions the doctor would have to cut and coagulate them. Dr Russell testified that if Dr Nash discovered a solitary or simple situation during a laparoscopy it would be reasonable for him to deal with such a situation as a simple curative act undertaken in the process of having the problem discovered. Dr Russel was of the view that Dr Nash properly considered what he did as within his mandate.

In my opinion what happened here came within the wording of the consent and there was, therefore, express consent to this surgery.

(See also *Davis v Barking, Havering and Brentwood HA* [1993] 4 Med LR 85 (McCullough J) and Commentary, (1993) 1 Med L Rev 389 (AG) where an unexpected procedure is performed.)

B. IMPLIED

In *Sidaway v Bethlem Royal Hospital Governors* [1985] 1 All ER 643 at 658 Lord Diplock reminded us that 'consent to battery is a state of mind personal to the victim of the battery …' This being so, if the patient does not explicitly express what is in his mind, a question arises as to whether it is proper to imply from his conduct what his state of mind is. On one view, it is said that the law implies consent from the patient's conduct ie deduces his state of mind. Another view which we think more tenable would describe implied consent as something of a fiction. Without express agreement no one may know what was in the patient's mind but it may be thought appropriate to prevent him complaining after the event that he did not consent. On this view, implied consent properly analysed becomes a form of estoppel whereby a patient, although he may not actually have agreed to some intervention, is estopped from denying that he did so.

The late Professor John Fleming in his authoritative text, *Law of Torts* (9th edn, 1998, p 87) illustrates the kind of situations in which implied consent arises.

J Fleming *Law of Torts* (9th edn, 1998)

Consent may be given expressly, as when a patient authorises a surgeon to perform an operation, but it may just as well be implied: Actions often speak louder than words. Holding up one's bare arm to a doctor at a vaccination point is as clear an assent as if it were expressed in words. A notice warning that unauthorised cars will be wheel-clamped implies consent to that risk. Participants in games or sports involving a likelihood of bodily contact, such as wrestling or boxing, consent to all the risks ordinarily incidental, though not to undue violence or unfair play. Even silence and inaction may in some circumstances be interpreted as an expression of willingness. Failure to resist or protest indicates consent if a reasonable person who is aware of the consequences and capable of protest or resistance would voice his objection. A girl who is silent to an amorous proposal, cannot afterwards capriciously complain of assault.

The best known case in which consent was implied in a medical law context is the following.

O'Brien v Cunard SS Co (1891) 28 NE 266 (Mass Sup Jud Ct)

Knowlton J: ... To sustain the first count, which was for an alleged assault, the plaintiff relied on the fact that the surgeon who was employed by the defendant vaccinated her on ship-board while she was on her passage from Queenstown to Boston. On this branch of the case the question is whether there was any evidence that the surgeon used force upon the plaintiff against her will. In determining whether the act was lawful or unlawful, the surgeon's conduct must be considered in connection with the surrounding circumstances. If the plaintiff's behavior was such as to indicate consent on her part, he was justified in his act, whatever her unexpressed feelings may have been. In determining whether she consented, he could be guided only by her overt acts and the manifestations of her feelings. ... It is undisputed that at Boston there are strict quarantine regulations in regard to the examination of emigrants, to see that they are protected from small-pox by vaccination, and that only those persons who hold a certificate from the medical officer of the steamship, stating that they are so protected, are permitted to land without detention in quarantine, or vaccination by the port physician. It appears that the defendant is accustomed to have its surgeons vaccinate all emigrants who desire it, and who are protected by previous vaccination, and give them a certificate which is accepted at quarantine as evidence of their protection. Notices of the regulations at quarantine, and of the willingness of the ship's medical officer to vaccinate such as needed vaccination, were posted about the ship in various languages, and on the day when the operation was performed the surgeon had a right to presume that she and the other women who were vaccinated understood the importance and purpose of vaccination for those who bore no marks to show that they were protected. By the plaintiff's testimony, which, in this particular is undisputed, it appears that about 200 women passengers were assembled below, and she understood from conversation with them that they were to be vaccinated; that she stood about 15 feet from the surgeon, and saw them form up in a line, and pass in turn before him; that he 'examined their arms, and, passing some of them by, proceeded to vaccinate those that had no mark'; that she did not hear him say anything to any of them; that upon being passed by they each received a card, and went on deck; that when her turn came she showed him her arm; he looked at it, and said there was no mark, and that she should be vaccinated; that she told him she had been vaccinated before, and it left no mark; 'that he then said nothing; that he should vaccinate her again'; that she held up her arm to be vaccinated; that no one touched her' that she did not tell him she did not want to be vaccinated; and that she took the ticket which he gave her, certifying that he had vaccinated her, and used it at quarantine. She was one of a large number of women who were vaccinated on that occasion, without, so far as appears, a word of objection from any of them. They all indicated by their conduct that they desired to avail themselves of the provisions made for their benefit. There was nothing in the conduct of the plaintiff to indicate to the surgeon that she did not wish to obtain a card which would save her from detention at quarantine, and to be vaccinated, if necessary, for that purpose. Viewing his conduct in the light of the surrounding circumstances, it was lawful; and there was no evidence tending to show that it was not. The ruling of the court on this part of the case was correct.

One situation in which it has been said that implied consent justifies intervention is the case of the unconscious patient who is brought in to the emergency department of a hospital. Express consent is impossible, but it is argued the patient would agree to treatment which is in his 'best interests' if he were conscious. The consent may, therefore, be implied (see Skegg 'A Justification For Medical Procedures Performed without Consent' (1974) 90 LQR 512).

Mohr v Williams (1905) 104 NW 12 (Sup Ct Minn)

Brown J: It is not, however, contended by defendant that under ordinary circumstances consent is unnecessary, but that, under the particular circumstances of this case, consent was implied; that it was an emergency case, such as to authorize the operation without express consent or permission. The medical profession has made signal progress in solving the problems of health and disease, and they may justly point with pride to the advancement made in supplementing nature and correcting deformities, and relieving pain and suffering. The physician impliedly contracts that he possesses, and will exercise in the treatment of patients, skill and learning, and that he will exercise reasonable care and exert his best judgment to bring about favorable results. The methods of treatment are committed almost exclusively to his judgment, but we are aware of no rule or principle of law which would extend to him free license respecting surgical operations. Reasonable latitude must, however, be allowed the physician in a particular case; and we would not lay down any rule which would unreasonably interfere with the exercise of his discretion, or prevent him from taking such measures as his judgment dictated for the welfare of the patient in a case of emergency. If a person should be injured to the extent of rendering him unconscious, and his injuries were of such a nature as to require prompt surgical attention, a physician called to attend him would be justified in applying such medical or surgical treatment as might reasonably be necessary for the preservation of his life or limb, and consent on the part of the injured person would be implied.

And again, if, in the course of an operation to which the patient consented, the physician should discover conditions not anticipated before the operation was commenced, and which, if not removed, would endanger the life or health of the patient, he would, though no express consent was obtained or given, be justified in extending the operation to remove and overcome them. But such is not the case at bar. The diseased condition of plaintiff's left ear was not discovered in the course of an operation on the right, which was authorized, but upon an independent examination of that organ, made after the authorized operation was found unnecessary. Nor is the evidence such as to justify the court in holding, as a matter of law, that it was such an affection [sic] as would result immediately in the serious injury of plaintiff, or such an emergency as to justify proceeding without her consent. She had experienced no particular difficulty with that ear, and the questions as to when its diseased condition would become alarming or fatal, and whether there was an immediate necessity for an operation, were, under the evidence, questions of fact for the jury.

While implied consent is one possible justification for the intervention, it is not, we would suggest, the most appropriate. Instead, the doctor's justification for treating an unconscious patient must, if at all, rest in the doctrine of necessity recognised by the House of Lords in *Re F (mental patient: sterilisation)* [1990] 2 AC 1 which we will see in detail later (*infra*, ch 6).

This explanation also applies when the patient's incompetence to consent is permanent, for example, due to intellectual disability. Here, the notion of implying consent when the patient never had, nor will have, capacity to consent is legerdemain. In *Re F* Lord Goff said that to imply consent 'can be regarded as artificial; and in particular, it is difficult to impute consent to those who, by reason of their youth or mental disorder, are unable to give their consent' (at 72). Hence, in *Re F* the legal justification for treating the permanently incompetent was seen as the principle of necessity.

If, as has been argued, the true nature of implied consent is a form of estoppel, what are the criteria which give rise to the estoppel? It could be said that a patient will be estopped from denying that he consented to a procedure in circumstances in which a reasonable person looking at the situation would reach the conclusion that consent had been given in the light of all the circumstances. Of course, the reasonable onlooker would not necessarily possess all the knowledge, nor make all the assumptions, of a doctor. Thus, it is not appropriate to judge whether the patient is consenting from the vantage point of the doctor. Equally, to look at the circumstances from the subjective position of the patient would be unduly harsh and unfair to the medical profession. Thus, a middle position employing the common law stalwart of the 'reasonable person' suggests itself. Much then will depend upon the circumstances and the court's view of what can fairly be said to be the impression left by the patient's conduct. It may be that constructive knowledge of what may happen is a prerequisite as, for example, where prominent notices are displayed (see the discussion of implied consent and breach of confidence, *infra* ch 8 and notice the decision of the Court of Appeal in *Turner v Royal Bank of Scotland* [1999] 2 All ER (Comm) 664 (CA) *infra*, pp 1085-1088).

An example which tests the application of this approach is the oft-cited proposition that any patient admitted to a teaching hospital thereby consents to being touched by students in the course of their training. Let us be clear about this example to avoid misunderstanding. There are two situations in which it may be proposed that the problem of implied consent arise. The first is where a patient agrees to be touched, for example, for the purpose of taking a blood sample and, without her knowledge, it is done by a student. In such a case there is no problem of implied consent. This is not to say there is no legal issue but the issue is whether the express consent given to the procedure is valid given the identity of the person carrying out the procedure (see *infra*). The second situation is where additional, and for the patient, unnecessary procedures are carried out without her knowledge for the purpose of furthering students' training. The paradigm is the vaginal examination of a woman whilst she is under anaesthetic awaiting surgery. This is a case where the legality of the touching turns upon whether consent can be implied. Arguably, without express knowledge that she was in a teaching hospital a reasonable person would not conclude that by consenting to treatment she had thereby impliedly consented to the vaginal examination. Further, even with such knowledge a court should insist that the patient gives express consent particularly bearing in mind the vulnerability of any person who finds herself in a hospital. (For an express recognition of the *ethical* validity of this argument see, *Medical Students in Hospital* (HC (91) 18 (April 1991).)

Perhaps the most controversial recourse to the law of implied consent (or as we would argue, estoppel) has been in the area of HIV testing. It has been argued that testing blood taken from a patient for other purposes with the secret intention of testing for HIV is entirely lawful as merely being an example of implied consent (see the discussion in Keown, 'The Ashes of Aids and the Phoenix of Informed Consent' (1989) 52 MLR 790). As we shall see, the issue is by no means as simple as this. The analysis requires a two-stage approach. The first stage, is a consideration of whether the individual expressly, and with sufficient understanding of what is involved, consents to the taking of the blood for testing for HIV. Secondly, if it is the case that there was no express consent, does the patient's conduct amount to implied consent? Since consideration of the question of implied consent entails examining the question of the 'nature and purpose' of the allegedly express consent, we defer consideration until later (see *infra*, pp 651–670).

The nature of consent

There are three relevant issues which fall to be determined: (1) Did the patient have *capacity* in law? (Was the patient competent to give consent?); (2) Was the person giving consent appropriately *informed* beforehand?; and (3) Was the consent *voluntarily* given?

Each of these issues may be analysed by reference to the nature and extent of the doctor's duty, ie to inform or to ensure voluntariness and competence.

What is the function of the legal requirement of consent? As we saw at the beginning of this chapter, the need for consent derives from the law's respect for the patient's right to decide. Consent, therefore, has a positive and negative property, ie it is as much the exercise of the right to make one's own decision to say 'yes' (consent) or to say 'no' (refuse). It is also a right to change one's mind. Hence, a patient may withdraw their consent to treatment. Obviously, this could be done before the procedure but it may also be done *during* the procedure. The following decision of the Canadian Supreme Court illustrates this.

Ciarlariello v Keller (1993) 100 DLR (4th) 609 (Can SC)

In the course of a medical test, an angiogram, administered after full explanation, the patient became agitated and asked for the test to be stopped. After 10 to 15 minutes the test was resumed and the plaintiff suffered a severe injury of a very rare sort from the resumed test. The trial judge found that, once she had calmed down, the plaintiff "did agree to the final injection and the completion of the angiogram". He held that there was no need for a new explanation of the risks and benefits of the test, and that "whether or not to continue the test is really a matter of medical judgment". He accordingly dismissed the plaintiff's action for damages. An appeal to the Ontario Court of Appeal having been dismissed, the plaintiff appealed to the Supreme Court of Canada.

Cory J: At issue in this appeal is the nature and the extent of the duty of disclosure owed by a doctor to a patient who withdraws the consent given to a medical procedure during the course of that procedure ...

Whether or not there has been a withdrawal of consent will always be a question of fact. The words used by a patient may be ambiguous. Even if they are apparently clear, the circumstances under which they were spoken may render them ambiguous. On some occasions, the doctors conducting the process may reasonably take the words spoken by the patient to be an expression of pain rather than a withdrawal of consent. Obviously, these are questions of fact which will have to be resolved by the trial judge.

For example, in *Mitchell v McDonald* (1987), 40 CCLT 266, 80 AR 16, 53 Alta LR (2d) 46 (QB), the plaintiff was suffering from acute muscular pain in her chest. She consented to receive a cortisone injection directly into the chest muscle. Unfortunately, the injection punctured a lung resulting in its partial collapse. At one point in the procedure, the plaintiff cried out "For God's sake, stop". She argued not unreasonably, that this constituted a withdrawal of consent. However, the trial judge, at p 289, interpreted it as but a cry of pain:

> With respect to the suggestion that the consent might have been withdrawn by her exclamation, "For God's sake, stop," it is beyond dispute that the damage had already been done before her cry. On the evidence, in any event, such a cry could well have been interpreted to mean, "My God, stop hurting me."

While the doctor's interpretation of the patient's cries in *Mitchell v McDonald* may have been reasonable in that case, generally if there is any question as to whether the patient is attempting to withdraw consent, it will be incumbent upon the doctor to ascertain whether the consent has in fact been withdrawn. It should not be forgotten that every patient has a right to bodily integrity. This encompasses the right to determine what medical procedures will be accepted and the extent to which they will be accepted. Everyone has the right to decide what is to be done to one's own body. This includes the right to be free from medical treatment to which the individual does not consent. This concept of individual autonomy is fundamental to the common law and is the basis for the requirement that disclosure be made to a patient. If, during the course of a medical procedure a patient withdraws the consent to that procedure, then the doctors must halt the process. This duty to stop does no more than recognize every individual's basic right to make decisions concerning his or her own body.

This principle has been recognized before. It was very aptly described by Robins JA in *Fleming v Reid (Litigation Guardian)* (1991) 82 DLR (4th) 298 at pp 309-10, 4 OR (3d) 74, 48 OAC 46 (CA), where he stated:

> The right to determine what shall, or shall not, be done with one's own body, and to be free from non-consensual medical treatment, is a right deeply rooted in our own common law. This right underlies the doctrine of informed consent. . . . The fact that serious risks or consequences may result from a refusal of medical treatment does not vitiate the right of medical self-determination. . . . It is the patient, not the doctor, who ultimately must decide if treatment – any treatment – is to be administered.

The same principle was recognized in *Nightingale v Kaplovitch* [1989] OJ No 585 (QL) [summarized 15 ACWS (3d) 42]. In that case the patient was undergoing sigmoidoscopic examination. At one point the examination became extremely painful and the patient screamed "Stop, I can't take this any more" In spite of the patient's cries the doctor continued. The patient made a sudden movement caused by pain and suffered a punctured bowel. RE Holland J of the Ontario High Court stated:

> I conclude on a balance of probabilities that the perforation occurred after Dr [Kapolvitch] had been asked to stop.

> I conclude that the perforation occurred after consent had been withdrawn. This amounted to a battery and liability would generally follow. . . . Quite apart from the question of battery, Dr Kaplovitch was negligent in continuing the procedure when the plaintiff was obviously suffering extreme pain and when he had been asked to stop.

An individual's right to determine what medical procedures will be accepted must include the right to stop a procedure. It is not beyond the realm of possibility that the patient is better able to gauge the level of pain or discomfort that can be accepted or that the patient's premonitions of tragedy or mortality may have a basis in reality. In any event, the patient's right to bodily integrity provides the basis for the withdrawal of a consent to a medical procedure even while it is underway. Thus, if it is found that the consent is effectively withdrawn during the course of the proceeding, then it must be terminated. This must be the result except in those circumstances where the medical evidence suggests that to terminate the process would be either life-threatening or pose immediate and serious problems to the health of the patient.

The issue as to whether or not a consent has been withdrawn during the course of a procedure may require the trial judge to make difficult findings of fact. If sedatives or other medication were administered to the patient, then it must be determined if the patient was so sedated or so affected by the medication that consent to the procedure could not effectively have been withdrawn. The question whether a patient is capable of withdrawing consent will depend on the circumstances of each case. Expert medical evidence will undoubtedly be relevant, but it will not necessarily be determinative of the issue. Indeed, in cases such as this where the patient must be conscious and co-operative in order for the procedure to be performed, it may well be beyond doubt that the patient was capable of withdrawing consent.

In the case at bar, the issue of withdrawal of consent is not an issue. Both the trial judge and the Court of Appeal found that the patient had withdrawn her consent and the respondents have not taken issue with those findings.

Having decided this, Cory J went on to discuss what was a doctor's duty to provide information prior to resuming the procedure.

Cory J: Once a patient withdraws consent to the procedure, the question then becomes under what circumstances a valid consent to the continuation of the process can be given. The appellants contend that before a valid consent to the continuation of the process can be given, the patient must be advised, once again, of all the risks involved in the process. The respondents argue that in the absence of any changes in the circumstances which would result in a greater risk for the patient, no further disclosure need be made.

The argument that the entire disclosure need not be repeated rests on two bases. First, the consent is not referrable to a precise moment in time but, rather, it is a relationship that exists between patient and doctor. That is to say, consent is a process, not an instant in time. As a result, once consent to the procedure has been obtained, then the doctor need not explain and disclose all the risks over again. Rather, all that is necessary is an explanation of any new circumstances which may have arisen which require an explanation.

In this case, the respondents point to six occasions prior to the final injection, when the risks of the procedure were discussed with the patient and an informed consent was given to the process. They note that in *Mitchell v McDonald, supra*, it was held that the patient's past experience with, and informed consent given to cortisone shots meant that the doctor did not need to go over in detail the risks of those shots each time one was administered. However, the presumption that patients have reasonably good memories and have consistently consented to the repetition of a treatment does not necessarily lead to the conclusion that they will also consent when those same patients are in a highly anxious or confused state.

The second argument of the respondents as to why full disclosure need not be repeated addresses the anxiety issue in this way: since the patient is in an emotional state, it would be both pointless and dangerous to increase the patient's fear by outlining all the risks once again. The trial judge gave effect to this submission in these words:

There is no doubt that when a patient is lying on a table and is in the very process of undergoing a surgical procedure, it is not the most desirable point at which to obtain their consent to the continuation of that procedure. Obviously, doctors should avoid obtaining consents under such circumstances. It is difficult, however, to determine beforehand what they should do when such a scenario arises. I have no doubt that whether or not to continue the test is really a matter of medical judgment.

Similarly, the Court of Appeal indicated that once the doctors commenced the angiogram procedure, the issue of informed consent did not arise. In that court's view, the doctors were entitled to exercise their medical judgment and proceed accordingly.

On this issue, I cannot accept the reasoning of the trial judge or the Court of Appeal. Their position constitutes a return to the medical judgment standard which was specifically disapproved in *Reibl v Hughes*, [(1980) 114 DLR (3d) 1]. To give effect to it would permit the doctors to interfere with the bodily integrity of the patients if in their opinion, from a medical point of view, it would be preferable to override the patient's objections and specific refusal to continue the process. Although from the point of view of the medical profession this would undoubtedly be done in the best interest of the patient, none the less, it cannot be accepted.

The appropriate approach is, once again, to focus on what the patient would like to know concerning the continuation of the process once the consent has been withdrawn. Looking at it objectively, a patient would want to know whether there had been any significant change in the risks involved or in the need for the continuation of this process which had become apparent during the course of the procedure. In addition, the patient will want to know if there has been a material change in circumstances which could alter the patient's assessment of the costs or benefits of continuing the procedure. For example, have the circumstances changed in such a way that the procedure is no longer as important to making a diagnosis as it was earlier? Each case, of course, will have to be determined on its own facts. Changes may arise during the course of the procedure which are not at all relevant to the issue of consent. Yet, the critical question will always be whether the patient would want to have the information pertaining to those changes in order to decide whether to continue.

La Forest, Sopinka, McLachlin and Iacobucci JJ agreed.

Notice two points (for commentary, see (1994) 2 Med L Rev 115 (IK)). First, Cory J did not see the right to withdraw consent as absolute where this 'would be either life threatening or pose immediate and serious problems to the health of the patient' (at 619). The basis for this was public policy. It should, however, be seen as a very limited exception to the patient's right to refuse. Also, given that withdrawal of consent will usually only be practicable in minor procedures not carried out under general anaesthetic, circumstances falling within the limitation may be a rarity.

Secondly, the precise formulation of the duty of care may differ between Canada and England but, as we saw, following the decision in *Bolitho v City and Hackney HA* [1997] 4 All ER 771 (HL) the scope of that duty would not be a matter exclusively of professional judgment and evidence (see *supra*, ch 4).

An alternative and more limited view of the true role of consent emerged in the early 1990s in cases concerned with medical treatment and children. In these cases – *Re R (a minor) (wardship: consent to treatment)* [1992] Fam 11 and *Re W (a minor) (medical treatment)* [1992] 4 All ER 627 – the Court of Appeal developed a more restrictive role for consent. In *Re R* Lord Donaldson MR stated:

… Consent by itself creates no obligation to treat. It is merely a key which unlocks a door. Furthermore, whilst in the case of an adult of full capacity there will usually only be one keyholder, namely the patient, in the ordinary family unit where a young child is the patient there will be two keyholders, namely the parents, with a several as well as a joint right to turn the key and unlock the door. If the parents disagree, one consenting and the other refusing, the doctor will be presented with a professional and ethical, but not with a legal, problem because, if he has the consent of one authorised person, treatment will not without more constitute a trespass or a criminal assault.

In *Re W* Lord Donaldson MR returned to the issue.

Lord Donaldson MR: There seems to be some confusion in the minds of some as to the purpose of seeking consent from a patient (whether adult or child) or from someone with authority to give that consent on behalf of the patient. It has two purposes, the one clinical and the other legal. The clinical purpose stems from the fact that in many instances the cooperation of the patient and the patient's faith or at least confidence in the efficiency of the treatment is a major factor contributing to the treatment's success. Failure to obtain such consent will not only deprive the patient and the medical staff of this advantage, but will usually make it much more difficult to administer the treatment. I appreciate that this purpose may not be served if consent is given on behalf of, rather than by the patient. However, in the case of young children knowledge of the fact that the parent had consented may help. The legal purpose is quite different. It is to provide those concerned in the treatment with a defence to a criminal charge of assault or battery or a civil claim for damages for trespass to the person. It does not, however, provide them with any defence to a claim that they negligently advised a particular treatment or negligently carried it out. …

On reflection I regret my use in *Re R* of the keyholder analogy … because keys can lock as well as unlock. I now prefer the analogy of the legal 'flak jacket' which protects from claims by the litigious whether he acquires it from his patient who may be a minor over the age of 16, or a 'Gillick competent' child under that age or from another person having parental responsibilities which include a right to consent to treatment of the minor. Anyone who gives him a flak jacket (ie consent) may take it back, but the doctor only needs one and so long as he continues to have one he has the legal right to proceed.

Of course, as far as it goes Lord Donaldson's analysis is right: consent does provide an answer to a claim in battery. But, as these cases show, at least where children are concerned, Lord Donaldson MR was anxious to assert that competent children do not have an *exclusive* right to determine their own treatment. We will examine this controversial development later (*infra* ch 6). For now it suffices to notice the legal implications of consent given by a child, though not an adult: consent to treatment is effective unless and until the court is involved, refusal of treatment may not be.

Even this statement may need qualification in this somewhat confused area of law. There is, at least, one plausible reading of Lord Fraser's speech in *Gillick v West Norfolk and Wisbech AHA* [1985] 3 All ER 402, (1985) 2 BMLR 11 (HL) which suggests that while a competent child's consent is effective as against any view of the parents as to the child's best interest, it may not be sufficient in that Lord Fraser leaves the final decision whether to treat to the doctor. *Gillick* is, of course, a case concerned with young persons and where young persons are involved the court may be saying that capacity to consent, while being a necessary condition, *may* not be a sufficient one for justifying any doctor's action based on an expression of will. The law may demand that the doctor's action also be in the best interests of the girl as judged by someone other than the young person, ie the doctor. This would, of course, run counter to the thesis contained in the notion of capacity that it is the legal reflection of the ethical principle of respect for autonomy. It may, however, be that Lord Fraser believes this to be the law: (at 412f) 'Nobody doubts, certainly I do not doubt, that in the overwhelming majority of cases the best judges of a child's welfare are his or her parents'; (at 413a) 'The only practical course is, in my opinion, to entrust the doctor with a discretion to act in accordance with his view of what is best in the interests of the girl who is his patient.' Lord Scarman, however, does not subscribe to this view and it is submitted his view is to be preferred.

But, there is another (and better) view of Lord Fraser's speech. Lord Fraser's observations need not be read as undermining the principle that an autonomous person is the best judge of his own interest. An alternative interpretation would be that Lord Fraser is making a far more commonplace point that in any context where a patient seeks medical care from a doctor it is the doctor who has the final word on whether treatment *is* called for. On this reading Lord Fraser's speech does not detract from the thesis developed by him and Lord Scarman concerning the capacity of young persons to decide for themselves once they have sufficient maturity and understanding.

A. CAPACITY OR COMPETENCE TO DECIDE

1. Possible approaches

What is capacity or competence to decide? This question calls for an inquiry into what factors the law regards as important before attaching any significance to any expression of will by the patient. It is a secondary question (which we will consider later) what particular criteria, if any, must be satisfied before the law recognises in the particular case that the abstract notion of capacity has been satisfied. The importance of 'capacity' as a gate-keeper of 'who decides' is clear. A competent patient's decisions call for respect. Hence, a decision to refuse treatment by such a patient is conclusive (but contrast children; *infra*). By contrast, if the patient is incompetent others will make the decision on their behalf in the patient's 'best interests' (see, *infra* ch 6).

Grisso and Applebaum (both psychiatrists) put it well in the context of the mentally ill or disordered.

T Grisso and PS Applebaum *Assessing Competence to Consent to Treatment: A Guide to Physicians and Other Health Officials* **(1998)**

> Competence is a pivotal concept in decision-making about medical treatment. Competent patients' decisions about accepting or rejecting proposed treatment are respected. Incompetent patients' choices, on the other hand, are put to one side, and alternative mechanisms for deciding about their care are sought. Thus, enjoyment of one of the most fundamental rights of a free society – the right to determine what shall be done to one's body – turns on the possession of those characteristics that we view as constituting decision-making competence.

What then are the options? Two seminal works address the issue of capacity/ competence. First, we set out the analysis of the US President's Commission and then that of Loren Roth, Alan Meisel and Charles Lidz.

President's Commission For the Study of Ethical Problems in Medicine and Biomedical and Behavioral Research *Making Health Care Decisions* **(1983)**

> *Identification of incapacity*
> In the light of the presumption that most patients have the capacity to make health care decisions, on what grounds might a person be found to lack such a capacity? Three general criteria have been followed: the outcome of the decision, the status or category of the patient, and the patient's functional ability as a decisionmaker.
> The outcome approach – which the Commission expressly rejects – bases a determination of incapacity primarily on the content of a patient's decision. Under this standard, a patient who makes a health care decision that reflects values not widely held or that rejects conventional wisdom about proper health care is found to be incapacitated.
> Using the status approach, certain categories of patients have traditionally been deemed incapable of making treatment decisions without regard to their actual capabilities. Some of these categories of patients – such as the unconscious – correspond closely with actual incapacity. But other patients who are presumed to be incapacitated on the basis of their status may actually be capable of making particular health care decisions. Many older children, for example, can make at least some health care decisions, mildly or moderately retarded individuals hold understandable preferences about health care, and the same may be true in varying degrees among psychotic persons.
> The third approach to the determination of incapacity focuses on an individual's actual functioning in decisionmaking situations rather than on the individual's status. This approach is particularly germane for children above a certain age (variously described as from seven to mid-teens). For example, rather than considering children under the age of majority incompetent to decide unless they come within one of the exceptions created by the statutory and common law, these patients could be regarded as competent unless shown to lack decisionmaking capacity. Similarly, a senile person may have been declared incompetent by a court and a guardian may have been appointed to manage the person's financial affair, but the functional standard would not foreclose the need to determine whether the senility also negated the individual's capacity to make health care decisions. What is relevant is whether someone is in fact capable of making a particular decision as judged by the consistency between the person's choice and the individual's underlying values and by the extent to which the choice promotes the individual's well-being as he or she sees it.

You will notice their three approaches: *outcome*; *status* and *functional*. A misunderstanding lies in regarding the first 'outcome approach' as being relevant to determining what is capacity. The better view must be that the outcome approach, if it has any significance at all, can only serve as a possible criterion for establishing capacity.

As regards status, we might here be considering categories such as all children, children below a certain age (say 16) or the mentally disordered. As a group, the argument would go, they would be incapable in law of making some (or all) decisions about their life, including medical treatment.

The appropriateness or otherwise of a status approach to capacity can, perhaps, best be judged by reminding ourselves of the very simple question, what are we concerned about here? The answer in short is a patient's expression of will and the question whether that expression of will ought to be respected. The customary answer given is that it ought to be respected in those circumstances where the patient is capable of acting autonomously, ie in exercising self-determination. It is in the words 'autonomy' and 'self-determination' that the key is to be found. These words tell us that the concern of both the law and ethics is with the individual.

It should follow therefore that any notion of capacity should be individual-orientated. It should not consist in mere membership of a group to whom a general classification or status is applied, regardless of the individual's particular circumstances, save where the clearest reasons of public policy demand. Any notion or capacity which did adopt such an approach would, by so doing, undermine the commitment to individual rights which it is the central concern of law and ethics to advance.

The President's Commission's favoured a functional approach and rejected both the outcome and status approaches. The Commission (*op cit*) stated (at pp 171–172):

> The Commission recommends that determinations of incapacity be guided largely by the functional approach, that individuals not in certain basic categories (such as under the age of 14, grossly retarded, or comatose) should be assumed to possess decisionmaking capacity until they demonstrate otherwise, and that incapacity should be found to exist only when people lack the ability to make decisions that promote their well-being in conformity with their own previously expressed values and preferences. The fact that a patient belongs to a category of people who are often unable to make general decisions for their own well-being or that an individual makes a highly idiosyncratic decision should alert health care professionals to the greater possibility of decisional incapacity. But it does not conclusively resolve the matter.

Perhaps the best-known work in this area is that of the American writers Loren Roth, Alan Meisel and Charles Lidz. Their work is extensive and much of it is brought together in *Informed Consent: Legal Theory and Clinical Practice* (1987) by P Appelbaum, C Lidz and A Meisel (see also, Grisso and Applebaum, *Assessing Competence to Consent to Treatment* (1998)). However, the seminal piece is the following.

L H Roth, A Meisel and C W Lidz 'Tests of Competency to Consent to Treatment' (1977) 134 Am J Psychiatry 279

> The concept of competency, like the concept of dangerousness, is social and legal and not merely psychiatric or medical. Law and, at times, psychiatry are concerned with an individual's competency to stand trial, to make a will, and to contract. The test of competency varies from one context to another. In general, to be considered competent an individual must be able to comprehend the nature of the particular conduct in question and to understand its quality and its consequences. For example, in *Dusky v United States* [362 US 405 (1960) (Per curiam)] the court held that to be considered competent to stand trial an individual must have 'sufficient present ability to consult with his lawyer with a reasonable degree of rational understanding – and … a rational as well as a factual understanding of the proceedings against him'. A person may be considered competent for some legal purposes and incompetent for others at the same time. An individual is not judged incompetent merely because he or she is mentally ill.
>
> There is a dearth of legal guidance illuminating the concept of competency to consent to medical treatment. Nevertheless, competency plays an important role in determining the validity of a patient's decision to undergo or forego treatment. The decision of a person who is incompetent does not validly authorise a physician to perform medical treatment. Conversely, a physician who withholds treatment from an incompetent patient who refuses treatment may be held liable to that patient if the physician does not take reasonable steps to obtain some other legally valid authorisation for treatment.
>
> In psychiatry the entire edifice of involuntary treatment is erected on the supposed incompetency of some people voluntarily to seek and consent to needed treatment. In addition, the acceptability of behaviour modification for the patient who is considered dangerous, the resolution of ethical issues in family planning (ie, sterilisation), and the right to refuse psychoactive medications – to cite only a few of the more prominent examples – turn in part on the concept of competency.

As we explain in our companion paper in this issue of the *Journal* [(1977) 134 Am J Psychiatry 285], competency is theoretically one of the independent variables that is determinative in part of the legal validity of a patient's consent to or refusal of treatment. There is therefore a need to specify how competency can be determined. Related questions include the following: Who raises the question of competency? When is this question raised? and Who makes the determination? Answers to these questions are beyond the scope of this paper.

The objective of the present inquiry is to make sense of various tests of competency, to analyse their applicability to patients' decisions to accept or refuse psychiatric treatment, and to illustrate the problems of applying these tests by clinical case examples from the consultation service of the Law and Psychiatry Program of Western Psychiatric Institute and Clinic.

In a brief presentation it is impossible to provide any serious linguistic analysis of a number of words that are frequently used in discussions of competency – words such as 'responsible', 'rational' or 'irrational', 'knowing', 'knowingly', 'understandingly', or 'capable'. These words are often used interchangeably without sufficient explanation or clear behavioural references. Only the rare scholarly article attempts to explain with precision what is meant by such terms; judicial decisions or statutes generally do not.

In evaluating tests for competency several criteria should be considered. A useful test for competency is one that, first, can be reliably applied; second, is mutually acceptable or at least comprehensible to physicians, lawyers, and judges; and third, is set at a level capable of striking an acceptable balance between preserving individual autonomy and providing needed medical care. Reliability is enhanced to the extent that a competency test depends on manifest and objectively ascertainable patient behaviour rather than on inferred and probably unknowable mental status.

Tests for competency
Several tests for competency have been proposed in the literature; others are readily inferable from judicial commentary. Although there is some overlap, they basically fall into five categories: 1) evidencing a choice, 2) 'reasonable' outcome of choice, 3) choice based on 'rational' reasons, 4) ability to understand, and 5) actual understanding.

Evidencing a choice
This test for competency is set at a very low level and is the most respectful of the autonomy of patient decision-making. Under this test the competent patient is one who evidences a preference for or against treatment. This test focuses not on the quality of the patient's decision but on the presence or absence of a decision. This preference may be a yes, a no, or even the desire that the physician make the decision for the patient. Only the patient who does not evidence a preference either verbally or through his or her behaviour is considered incompetent. This test of competency encompasses at a minimum the unconscious patient; in psychiatry it encompasses the mute patient who cannot or will not express opinion.

Even such arch-defenders of individual autonomy as Szasz have agreed that patients who do not formulate and express a preference as to treatment are incompetent. In answer to a question about the right to intervene against a patient's will, Szasz has stated:

> It is quite obvious, and I make this abundantly clear, that I have no objection to medical intervention vis-à-vis persons who are not protesting, ... [for example,] somebody who is lying in bed catatonic and the mother wants to get him to the hospital and the ambulance shows up and he just lies there.

The following case example illustrates the use of the test of evidencing a choice:

> *Case 1.* A 41-year-old depressed woman was interviewed in the admission unit. She rarely answered yes or no to direct questions. Admission was proposed; she said and did nothing, but looked apprehensive. When asked about admission, she did not sign herself into the hospital, protest, or walk away. She was guided to the in-patient ward by her husband and her doctor after being given the opportunity to walk the other way.

This test may be what one court had in mind when, with respect to sterilisation of residents of state schools, it ruled that even legally incompetent and possibly noncomprehending residents may not be sterilised unless they have formed a genuine desire to undergo the procedure.

The guidelines proposed by the US Department of Health, Education and Welfare concerning experimentation with institutionalised mentally ill people also point in this direction by requiring even the legally incompetent person's 'assent to such participation ... when ... he has sufficient mental capacity to understand what is proposed and to express an opinion as to his or her participation'. Although this low test of competency does not fully assure patients' understanding of the nature of what they consent to or what they refuse, it is behavioural in orientation and therefore more reliable in application; it also guards against excessive paternalism.

'Reasonable' outcome of choice

This test of competency entails evaluating the patient's capacity to reach the 'reasonable', the 'right', or the 'responsible' decision. The emphasis in this test is on outcome rather than on the mere fact of a decision or how it has been reached. The patient who fails to make a decision that is roughly congruent with the decision that a 'reasonable' person in like circumstances would make is viewed as incompetent.

This test is probably used more often than might be admitted by both physicians and courts. Judicial decisions to override the desire of patients with certain religious beliefs not to receive blood transfusions may rest in part on the court's view that the patient's decision is not reasonable. When life is at stake and a court believes that the patient's decision is unreasonable, the court may focus on even the smallest ambiguity in the patient's thinking to cast doubt on the patient's competency so that it may issue an order that will preserve life or health. For example, one judge issued an order to allow amputation of the leg of an elderly moribund man even though the man had clearly told his daughter before his condition deteriorated not to permit an amputation.

Mental health laws that allow for involuntary treatment on the basis of 'need for care and treatment' without requiring a formal adjudication of incompetency in effect use an unstated reasonable outcome test in abridging the patient's common-law right not to be treated without giving his or her consent. These laws are premised on the following syllogism: the patient needs treatment; the patient has not obtained treatment on his or her own initiative; therefore, the patient's decision is incorrect, which means that he or she is incompetent, thus justifying the involuntary imposition of treatment.

The benefits and costs of this test are that social goals and individual health are promoted at considerable expense to personal autonomy. The reasonable outcome test is useful in alerting physicians and courts to the fact that the patient's decision-making process may be, but not necessarily is, awry. Ultimately, because the test rests on the congruence between the patient's decision and that of a reasonable person or that of the physician, it is biased in favour of decisions to accept treatment, even when such decisions are made by people who are incapable of weighting the risks and benefits of treatment. In other words, if patients do not decide the 'wrong' way, the issue of competency will probably not arise.

Choice based on 'rational' reasons

Another test is whether the reasons for the patient's decision are 'rational', that is, whether the patient's decision is due to or is a product of mental illness. As in the reasonable outcome test, if the patient decides in favour of treatment the issue of the patient's competency (in this case, whether the decision is the product of mental illness) seldom if ever arises because of the medical profession's bias towards consent to treatment and against refusal of treatment.

In this test the quality of the patient's thinking is what counts. The following case example illustrates the use of the test of rational reasons:

> *Case 2.* A 70-year-old widow who was living alone in a condemned dilapidated house with no heat was brought against her will to the hospital. Her thinking was tangential and fragmented. Although she did not appear to be hallucinating, she seemed delusional. She refused blood tests, saying 'You just want my blood to spread it all over Pittsburgh. No, I'm not giving it.' Her choice was respected. Later in the day, however, when her blood pressure was found to be dangerously elevated (250 over 135 in both arms), blood was withdrawn against her will.

The test of rational reasons, although it has clinical appeal and is probably much in clinical use, poses considerable conceptual problems; as a legal test it is probably defective. The problems include the difficulty of distinguishing rational from irrational reasons and drawing inferences of causation between any irrationality believed present and the valence (yes or no) of the patient's decision. Even if the patient's reasons seem irrational, it is not possible to prove that the patient's actual decisionmaking has been the product of such irrationality. The patient's decision might well be the same even if his or her cognitive processes were less impaired. For example, a delusional patient may refuse ECT not because he or she is delusional but because he or she is afraid of it, which is considered a normal reaction. The emphasis on rational reasons can too easily become a global indictment of the competency of mentally disordered individuals, justifying widespread substitute decision making for this group.

The ability to understand

This test – the ability of the patient to understand the risks, benefits and alternatives to treatment (including no treatment) – is probably the most consistent with the law of informed consent. Decision making need not be rational in either process or outcome; unwise choices are permitted. Nevertheless, at a minimum the patient must manifest sufficient ability to understand information about treatment, even if in fact he or she weights this information differently from the attending physician. What matters in this test is that the patient is able to comprehend the elements that are presumed by law to be a part of treatment decisionmaking. How the patient weights these elements, values them, or puts them together to reach a decision is not important.

The patient's capacity for understanding may be tested by asking the patient a series of questions concerning risks, benefits, and alternatives to treatment. By providing further information or explanation to the patient, the physician may find deficiencies in understanding to be remediable or not. The following case examples illustrate the use of the test of the ability to understand:

Case 3. A 28-year-old woman who was unresponsive to medication was approached for consent to ECT. She initially appeared to be unaware of the examiner. Following an explanation of ECT, she responded to the request to explain its purposes and why it was being recommended in her case with the statement, 'Maul McCartney, nothing to zero', She was shown a consent form for ECT that she signed without reading. Further attempts to educate her were unsuccessful. It was decided not to perform the ECT without seeking court approval.

Case 4. A 44-year-old woman who was diagnosed as having chronic schizophrenia refused amputation of her frostbitten toes. She was nonpsychotic. Although her condition was evaluated psychiatrically as manifesting extreme denial, she understood what was proposed and that there was some risk of infection without surgery. Nevertheless, she declined. She stated, 'You want to take my toes off; I want to keep them.' Her decision was respected. She agreed to return to the hospital if things got worse. A month later she returned, having suffered an auto-amputation of the toes. There was no infection; she was rebandaged and sent home.

Some of the questions raised by this test of competency are, What is to be done if the patient can understand the risks but not the benefits or vice versa? Alternatively, what is the patient views the risks as the benefits? The following case example illustrates this problem:

Case 5. A 49-year-old woman whose understanding of treatment was otherwise intact, when informed that there was a 1 in 3,000 chance of dying from ECT, replied, 'I hope I am the one.'

Furthermore, how potentially sophisticated must understanding be in order that the patient be viewed as competent? There are considerable barriers, conscious and unconscious and intellectual and emotional, to understanding proposed treatment. Presumably the potential understanding required is only that which would be manifested by a reasonable person provided with a similar amount of information. A few attempts to rank degrees of understanding have been made. However, this matter is highly complex and beyond the scope of the present inquiry. Certainly, at least with respect to nonexperimental treatment, the patient's potential understanding does not have to be perfect or near perfect for him or her to be considered competent, although one court seemed to imply this with respect to experimental psycho-surgery. A final problem with this test is that its application depends on unobservable and inferential mental processes rather than on concrete and observable elements of behaviour.

Actual understanding
Rather than focusing on competency as a construct or intervening variable in the decision-making process, the test of actual understanding reduces competency to an epiphenomenon of this process. The competent patient is by definition one who has provided a knowledgeable consent to treatment. Under this test the physician has an obligation to educate the patient and directly ascertain whether he or she has in fact understood. If not, according to this test the patient may not have provided informed consent. Depending on how sophisticated a level of understanding is to be required, this test delineates a potentially high level of competency, one that may be difficult to achieve.

The provisional decision of DHEW to mandate the creation of consent committees to oversee the decisions of experimental subjects implicitly adopts this test, as does the California law requiring the review of patient consent to ECT. Controversial as these requirements may be, they require physicians to make reasonable efforts to ascertain that their patients understand what they are told and encourage active patient participation in treatment selection.

The practical and conceptual limitations of this test are similar to those of the ability-to-understand test. What constitutes adequate understanding is vague, and deficient understanding may be attributable in whole or in part to physician behaviour as well as to the patient's behaviour or character. An advantage that this test has over the ability-to-understand test, assuming the necessary level of understanding can be specified a priori, is its greater reliability. Unlike the ability-to-understand test, in which the patient's comprehension of other material of equivalent complexity (even if this other material is not actually tested), the actual understanding test makes no such assumption. It tests the very issues central to patient decisionmaking about treatment.

Discussion

It has been our experience that competency is presumed as long as the patient modulates his or her behaviour, talks in a comprehensible way, remembers what he or she is told, dresses and acts so as to appear to be in meaningful communication with the environment, and has not been declared legally incompetent. In other words, if patients have their wits about them in a layman's sense it is assumed that they will understand what they are told about treatment, including its risks, benefits, and alternatives. This is the equivalent of saying that the legal presumption is one of competency until found otherwise. The Pandora's box of the question of whether and to what extent the patient is able to understand or has understood what has been disclosed is therefore never opened.

In effect, the test that is actually applied combines elements of all of the tests described above. However, the circumstances in which competency becomes an issue determine which elements of which tests are stressed and which are underplayed. Although in theory competency is an independent variable that determines whether or not the patient's decision to accept or refuse treatment is to be honoured, in practice it seems to be dependent on the interplay of two other variables, the risk/benefit ratio of treatment and the valence of the patient's decision, ie, whether he or she consents to or refuses treatment.

The phrase 'risk/benefit ratio of treatment' issued here in a shorthand way to express the fact that people who determine patient competency make this decision partly on the basis of the risks of the particular treatment being considered and the benefits of that treatment. We do not mean to imply that any formal calculation is made or that any given ratio is determinative of competency. The problems of who decides what is a risk and what is a benefit, the relative weights to be attached to risks and benefits, and who bears the risks and to whom the benefits accrue (eg, the patient, the clinician, society), are beyond the scope of the present inquiry.

Table 1 illustrates the interplay of the valence of the patient's decision and the risk/benefit ratio of treatment. When there is a favourable risk/benefit ratio to the proposed treatment in the opinion of the person determining competency and the patient consents to the treatment, there does not seem to be any reason to stand in the way of administering treatment. To accomplish this, a test employing a low threshold of competency may be applied to find even a marginal patient competent so that his or her decision may be honoured (cell A). This is what happens daily when uncomprehending patients are permitted to sign themselves into the hospital. Similarly when the risk/benefit ratio is favourable and the patient refuses treatment, a test employing a higher threshold of competency may be applied (cell B). Under such a test even a somewhat knowledgeable patient may be found incompetent so that consent may be sought from a substitute decision-maker and treatment administered despite the patient's refusal. An example would be the patient withdrawing from alcohol who, although intermittently resistive, is nevertheless administered sedative medication. In both of these cases, in which the risk/benefit ratio is favourable the bias of physicians, other health professionals, and judges is usually skewed towards providing treatment. Therefore, a test of competency is applied that will permit the treatment to be administered irrespective of the patient's actual or potential understanding.

However, there is a growing reluctance on the part of our society to permit patients to undergo treatments that are extremely risky or for which the benefits are highly speculative. Thus if the risk/benefit ratio is unfavourable or questionable and the patient refuses treatment, a test employing a low threshold of competency may be selected so that the patient will be found competent and his or her refusal honoured (cell C). This is what happens in the area of sterilisation of mentally retarded people, in which, at least from the perspective of the retarded individual, the risk/benefit ratio is questionable. On the other hand, when the risk/benefit ratio is unfavourable or questionable and the patient consents to treatment, a test using a higher threshold of competency may be applied (cell D), preventing even some fairly knowledgeable patients from undergoing treatment. The judicial opinion in the well-known *Kaimowitz* psychosurgery case delineated a high test of competency to be employed in that experimental setting [*Kaimowitz v Michigan Department of Mental Health* 42 USLW 2063 (Mich Cir Ct, (1973))].

Of course, some grossly impaired patients cannot be determined to be competent under any conceivable test, nor can most normally functioning people be found incompetent merely by selective application of a test of competency. However, within limits and when the patient's competency is not absolutely clear-cut, a test of competency that will achieve the desired medical or social end despite the actual condition of the patient may be selected. We do not imply that this is done maliciously either by physicians or by the courts; rather, we believe that it occurs as a consequence of the strong societal bias in favour of treating treatable patients so long as it does not expose them to serious risks.

Conclusions

The search for a single test of competency is a search for a Holy Grail. Unless it is recognised that there is no magical definition of competency to make decisions about treatment, the search for an acceptable test will never end. 'Getting the words just right' is only part of the problem. In practice, judgments of competency go beyond semantics or straightforward applications of legal rules; such judgments reflect social considerations and societal biases as much as they reflect matters of law and medicine.

TABLE 1

Factors in selection of competency tests

Patients' decision	Risk/benefit ratio of treatment	
	Favourable	Unfavourable or questionable
Consent	Low test of competency (cell A)	High test of competency (cell D)
Refusal	High test of competency (cell B)	Low test of competency (cell C)

You will notice here again the running together of the concept of capacity or competence and the criteria for establishing it in any given case.

Here we see a more complex analysis of the possible approaches the law could take to the issue of capacity. Professor Michael Gunn discusses the authors' views in the context of the work of the Law Commission on incapacitated adults. He does so at a time before the Law Commission produced its final report: *Mental Incapacity* (No 231 1995) but in the light of their earlier consultation papers, in particular *Mental Incapacitated Adults and Decision-Making – Medical Treatment* (No 129 1993), to which we will return later. However, in essence, the Law Commission's approach remained the same in its final report.

Michael Gunn 'The Meaning of Incapacity' (1994) 2 Med L Rev 8

In their seminal article on capacity Roth, Meisel, and Lidz (L H Roth, A Meisel and C W Lidz 'Tests of Competency to Conserve to Treatment' (1977) 134 American Journal of Psychiatry 279) recognized the difficulties in formulating a definition of capacity. Indeed they said that the desire to "search for a single test of competency is a search for the Holy Grail (*ibid*, 283). In consequence of this approach some authors have suggested a sliding scale approach to competency (see eg, B Lo, "Assessing Decision-Making Capacity" (1990) 18 Law, Medicine and Health Care). A sliding scale simply misses the point.

Capacity/incapacity are not concepts with clear a priori boundaries. They appear on a continuum which ranges from full capacity at one end to full incapacity at the other end. There are, therefore, degrees of capacity. The challenge is to choose the right level to set as the gateway to decision-making and respect for persons and autonomy. It is not necessary to have a movable definition or a variable standard. It is not necessary to have a simple, single sentence approach since that is likely both to over simplify what is essential to capacity and to create confusion in the minds of those attempting to assess other people's capacity to make decisions. The better approach is to set a definition which does not vary with the medical treatment in question nor does it level vary. It is, though, easier to consent to some medical treatment than other because some treatments are easier to understand or appreciate than others. The definition need not vary in its essential nature from one form of treatment to another. ...

The more important point raised by the article by Roth, Meisel and Lidz is that they identified five possible approaches to capacity, to which we should add a sixth. It must be considered whether the Law Commission has made the best choice of these approaches. The five identified by Roth *et al*. are:

(1) evidencing a choice, (2) 'reasonable' outcome of choice, (3) choice based on 'rational' reasons, (4) ability to understand, and (5) actual understanding (*supra*, at 281).

The sixth approach which must be added to these is the need for the person either to be able to appreciate the treatment and its consequences or that she must actually appreciate the treatment and its consequences.

A. Test 1: Evidencing a Choice ...

This test sets a very low level and "is the most respectful of the autonomy of patient decision making" (*ibid*). All that the patient has to be able to do is to indicate a preference for one treatment rather than another. An indicated choice may merely be a reflex action which if recognised would not be consistent with respect for an individual's autonomy. This is because autonomy would be a hollow concept were a person simply to react rather than choose. This is not to suggest that a choice must not be indicated. It must. But indicating a choice is by itself insufficient.

B. Test 2: Reasonable Outcome ...

The test evaluates whether the patient is able to arrive at a decision which is perceived by others, the treatment providers, as being a reasonable one. As Roth *et al*. point out, this is a test which is probably used more frequently than anyone would care to admit, but it denies capacity to many people who make what may be regarded as strange but not incompetent decisions. For example, had it been accepted in *Re T* that T was actually a Jehovah's Witness taking a decision in the knowledge that it might result in her death, there would have been no doubt about her capacity to make that decision, despite its unreasonableness. If the decision, the outcome, has to be reasonable, as this test demands, a Jehovah's Witness who refuses a blood transfusion (which can be shown to be medically indicated) is necessarily to be found to be incapable of making a decision to refuse that treatment. In addition to being offensive in at least those cases where what appears to be an unreasonable decision is based upon a particular value system or set of beliefs, the danger of this approach is that it may be assumed that a person is competent where she makes a decision with which the treatment provider agrees, but is incompetent where that decision disagrees with that of the treatment provider. In fact, all that such activity may indicate for the allegedly competent patient is rote compliance with the wishes of the treatment provider. It is clear that the Law Commission has rejected this approach (see Consultation Paper No 129 at para 2.14 referring back to Consultation Paper No 119 at para 2.43 and Consultation Paper No 128 at para 3.30). It might be advisable to accept its proposal, made in an earlier Consultation Paper, to adopt a New Zealand approach since "New Zealand law provides that the fact that the client has made or is intending to make any decision that a person exercising ordinary prudence would not have made or would not make is not in itself sufficient for the exercise of [its] jurisdiction by the Court" (Consultation Paper No 128 at para 3.25 quoting from the Protection of Personal and Property Rights Act 1988, s 1(3)).

C. Test 3: Rationality

The third test is one to which courts have alluded but does not appear as central to a definition. Nevertheless it sometimes appears to play a part in the current English test. There are, for example, references in *Re F* to the capacity to make rational decisions or rationally to form a wish not to be treated. In this test it is not the outcome which is being assessed, although that may be used as an indicator which makes it more likely that a person's capacity will be assessed. Instead it is the process by which that decision is made which is to be assessed. If this is thought to be an appropriate test, the first step is to accept the patient's own value base. It may be rejected for example where it is the product of a mental disorder. Ian Kennedy deals with this by arguing that a patient should be regarded as incapable if the beliefs upon which a decision are predicated are the product of a temporary delusion born of some current illness, but not if they are based on beliefs and values which a patient has long held and led his life by, even if they appear to others to be irrational (I Kennedy, in C Dyer, Doctors, Patients and the Law (Blackwell Scientific 1992), at 56–7). Once the value base has been identified, there has to be an assessment of whether the decision is a fairly logical product of it. The test is designed to rule out of competency those people whose decision-making process is seriously affected by mental illness not only when that illness creates a temporary and different value base, but also when it affects the person's reasoning process. A person with an affective disorder may be unable to process information at all so that a decision cannot be regarded as one made as a consequence of a rational process.

The difficulties with this approach are clear. How is a choice to be made between different value bases which are to be accepted and rejected? Even if the ground for rejection is that it should be temporary, why should a person have to evidence long acceptance of a value base for it to be recognised? How can a treatment provider distinguish between what are rational and what are damaging conflicts, eg the treatment provider may not take adequate account of a person's gender, race or culture. Necessarily an assessment of this relies upon the value base of the person carrying out the assessment and so inherently carries with it a potentially dangerous subjective element.

On the other hand, to rely solely on understanding as a proper approach leaves many with a feeling of uneasiness since some people are not thought to be capable of making decisions even if they may understand the information provided. Therefore, some element of rationality appears to creep into all approaches to capacity. This may well be the effect of the Law Commission adopting a "true choice" approach in addition to centring the test of capacity upon understanding.

D. Tests 4 & 5: Ability to Understand and Actual Understanding

The fourth and fifth tests are those most closely aligned to the current state of English law, whether it be the approach created by the courts or that recognised by Parliament in the Mental Health Act Code of Practice. The fourth test demands that the individual have the ability to understand certain information in order to be assessed as being capable of making the treatment decision in question. This approach permits unwise choices, since the weight which the patient places upon the information or how that information is used is not of relevance. This test is to be contrasted with the fifth which is not satisfied by a mere ability to understand but demands actual understanding of the particular treatment and the time of its administration. There is a clear and obvious conceptual difference between the tests. Indeed Stuart-Smith LJ noted the difference in considering Part IV of the Mental Health Act 1983 in *R v Mental Health Act Commission, ex parte X* ((1988) 9 BMLR 77)).

However, there is a difference between being able to identify a theoretical difference and in accepting that that difference has a practical validity. If a person is able to understand treatment and chooses not to, how does that individual then make a choice? Note that the issue cannot be that the person chooses to ignore the information, because that fails to distinguish between the fourth and the fifth test. There is a practical problem. The usual way in which either test can be assessed is by asking the patient to repeat in her own words the information provided. If the information is repeated sufficiently accurately, she will be regarded as understanding the information sufficiently and so be competent to make the decision. If this is the only testing available, how are ability to understand and actual understanding to be differentiated in reality? It would not be an exception to rely on earlier assessments, because these would also rely upon actual understanding and presumptions that the level of understanding persists. If a patient did understand earlier but does not understand now, reliance may be placed upon that earlier decision, rather than on an asserted present ability to understand. Whilst it is accepted that many authors draw a distinction between these two tests, it is difficult to see how the difference translates into practical realities.

E. Test 6: Appreciation

The sixth test sets rather more of a challenge ...

It does not expressly appear in the recommendations of the Law Commission. However, in the discussion of incapacity in Consultation Paper No 128, the Commission states that it prefers an approach "which concentrates upon the person's ability to understand the information relevant to the decision and to appreciate its reasonably foreseeable consequences" (Consultation Paper No 128, at para 3.22). The validity of regarding the sixth test as separate from tests 4 and 5 depends upon understanding not, by definition, including appreciation. It will be seen below that, in fact, it is possible that the one may be included in the definition of the other, as indeed may be the assumption of the Law Commission.

On the assumption that they are different concepts, the need to appreciate the information is an attempt to set the standard of competency higher than mere understanding by pointing out that merely to understand information is insufficient. The decision to be made demands that the patient appreciate the consequences of that decision for herself in order for it to be possible for her to make that decision. It is not sufficient to understand the risks, benefits, consequences, etc. This approach is predicated upon the view that decision-making is not a purely cognitive matter, but has an important emotional content in addition. As S J Anderer has stated (S J Anderer, "A Model for Determining Competency in Guardianship Proceedings" (1990) 14 Mental and Physical Disability Law Reporter 107 at p 111). "Even if the respondent can demonstrate a factual understanding of relevant information, the court may wish to consider evidence that pathological processes are interfering with the respondent's appreciation of risks and benefits or with his or her reasoning process. 'Appreciation' differs from factual understanding in requiring that the individual consider the relevance to his or her own situation of the risks and benefits, and attach an emotional value to those risks and benefits." Margaret Somerville points out (M A Somerville, "Refusal of Medical Treatment in 'Captive' Circumstances" (1985) 63 Canadian Bar Review 59 at 65–8) that this element in capacity would allow a distinction between the Jehovah's Witness refusing blood, who may be regarded as emotionally competent, and the psychiatric patient refusing pharmacotherapy, who would not be, thus the latter may be assessed as incompetent although having no cognitive deficiency. She also notes that this approach deals with a further problem when a person understands all the appropriate information,

> but has some *additional* belief ... which affects his decision concerning treatment, but which is not, in itself, indicative of any disordered cognitive thinking. ... It would be necessary to

postulate the 'additional beliefs' are pertinent to assessing competence, when they cause emotional reactions to the cognitively comprehended information of such a nature and degree that the person can be regarded as emotionally incompetent (*ibid* at 66–7).

Undoubtedly the addition of such a requirement has an inherent appeal since no decision is a purely clinical one removed from emotions and circumstances.

The problems of demanding a "normal" emotional response, include the question whether there is such a normal response. The problem is that it is open to abuse, particularly bearing in mind the dangers of the values of the assessor affecting that assessment. The presence of such an approach might also contravene the acceptance that a competent person is entitled to make objectively silly decisions. One possible solution is that emotional competence would be a factor that could only be taken into account by a court and not a treatment provider when determining competency, so it would be available only in exceptional cases (*ibid* at 67–68).

To introduce such an element into a test would demand a radical rethink of most approaches to the concept of capacity, would present major challenges to explanation and to assessment practices. If understanding may be difficult to assess, how much more so would it be difficult to assess an individual's appreciation.

F.   Tests of Capacity: A Possible Composite Approach

It is possible to argue for an aggregation of the sort of tests considered above. The President's Commission in the United States of American took such an approach, (President's Commission for the Study of Ethical Problems in Medicine and Biomedical and Behavioral Research, 'Making Health Care Decisions' (1983) which was summarised by the Law Commission as

(i) possession of a set of values and goals to provide a stable framework for comparing options, (ii) the ability to communicate and understand information, including linguistic and conceptual skills, plus sufficient life experience to appreciate the meaning of potential alternatives, and (iii) the ability to reason and deliberate about one's choices in a way which enables comparison of the probable impact of alternative outcomes in personal goals and lifestyles. (Consultation Paper No 119, at para 2.41.)

It is suggested, that such an approach sets the standard for capacity to make decisions too high and so does not achieve an appropriate balance between autonomy and paternalism. It is good to know that the Law Commission did not pursue such an approach.

We will return to some of the issues later, in particular the relevance of rationality, outcome etc to an assessment of a patient's capacity to decide. What is plain from what we have seen is that the principled approach to capacity is to look to the *individual* and ask whether they are *able* to understand. Thereby, the law will promote (and permit) individuals to make their own decisions according to their own values and beliefs, ie to make their own autonomous choices. We now turn to consider how the law has developed to this position.

2.   A functional approach – understanding

The threshold notion of 'understanding' as the key to determining capacity to decide should be universal. In other words, it should apply to all persons, whether adult or child. Indeed, it will be in cases of medical treatment of children that the issue of capacity will often arise. In the context of adults, it will not usually do so unless the circumstances call into question the individual's capacity to decide, for example because they suffer from mental disability that may affect their reasoning abilities.

The leading English case which establishes the principled way forward concerned children. In *Gillick v West Norfolk and Wisbech AHA* [1986] AC 112, [1985] 3 All ER 402 Mrs Gillick sought a declaration that a Government circular which contemplated that contraceptive advice and treatment might, in exceptional circumstances, be given to girls under the age of 16 without parental consent was unlawful. *Inter alia*, she asserted that the circular encouraged that which was unlawful because children under 16 were unable in law to give effective consent such that without parental consent the doctor would commit a battery. The Court of Appeal, reversing the decision of Woolf J, agreed with Mrs Gillick's argument.

On appeal, the House of Lords (by a majority) held that a child under the age of 16 could, in law, have the capacity to consent. The judges rejected the 'status' approach based, in this case, upon age and held that liability to understand was the key to capacity or competence to decide.

Gillick v West Norfolk and Wisbech AHA [1986] AC 112, [1985] 3 All ER 402, (1985) 2 BMLR 11 (HL)

Lord Fraser: *1. The legal capacity of a girl under 16 to consent to contraceptive advice, examination and treatment*

There are some indications in statutory provisions to which we were referred that a girl under 16 years of age in England and Wales does not have the capacity to give valid consent to contraceptive advice and treatment. If she does not have the capacity, then any physical examination or touching of her body without her parents' consent would be an assault by the examiner ...

[A] statutory provision which was referred to in this connection is the National Health Service (General Medical and Pharmaceutical Services) Regulations 1974, SI 1974/160, as amended by the National Health Service (General Medical and Pharmaceutical Services) Amendment Regulations 1975, SI 1975/719. The regulations prescribe the mechanism by which the relationship of doctor and patient under the NHS is created. Contraceptive services, along with maternity medical services, are treated as somewhat apart from other medical services in respect that only a doctor who specially offers to provide contraceptive or maternity medical services is obliged to provide them: see the definition of 'medical care' and ; 'treatment' in reg 2(1); see also regs 6(1)(a) and Sch 1, para 13. But nothing turns on this fact. Two points in those regulations have a bearing on the present question although, in my opinion, only an indirect bearing. The first is that by reg 14 any 'woman' may apply to a doctor to be accepted by him for the provision of contraceptive services. The word 'woman' is not defined so as to exclude a girl under 16 or under any other age. but reg 32 provides as follows:

> An application to a doctor for inclusion on his list ... may be made, either – (a) on behalf of any person under 16 years of age, by the mother, or in her absence, the father, or in the absence of both parents the guardian or other adult person who has the care of the child; or (b) on behalf of *any other person who is incapable* of making such an application by a relative or other adult person who has the care of such person ...

The words in para (b) which I have emphasised are said, by counsel for Mrs Gillick, to imply that a person under 16 years of age is incapable of applying to a doctor for services and therefore give some support to the argument on behalf of Mrs Gillick. But I do not regard the implication as a strong one because the provision is merely that an application 'may' be made by the mother or other parent or guardian and it applies to the doctor's list for the provision of all ordinary medical services as well as to his list for the provision of contraceptive services. I do not believe that a person aged 15, who may be living away from home, is incapable of applying on his own behalf for inclusion in the list of a doctor for medical services of an ordinary kind not connected with contraception.

Another provision, in a different branch of medicine, which is said to carry a similar implication is contained in the Mental Health Act 1983, s 131, which provides for informal admission of patients to mental hospitals. It provides by sub-s (2):

> In the case of a minor who has attained the age of 16 years and is capable of expressing his own wishes, any such arrangements as are mentioned in subsection (1) above [for informal admission] may be made, carried out and determined notwithstanding any right of custody or control vested by law in his parent or guardian.

That provision has only a remote bearing on the present question because there is no doubt that a minor under the age of 16 is in the custody of his or her parents. The question is whether such custody necessarily involves the right to veto contraceptive advice or treatment being given to the girl.

Reference was also made to the Education Act 1944, s 48, which dealt with medical inspection and treatment of pupils at state schools. Section 48(3), which imposed on the local education authority a duty to provide for medical and dental inspection of pupils, was repealed and superseded by the National Health Service Reorganisation Act 1973, s 3 and Sch 5. The 1973 Act in turn was replaced by the National Health Service Act 1977, s 5(1)(a). Section 48(4) of the Education Act 1944, which has not been repealed, imposes a duty on the local education authority to arrange for encouraging pupils to take advantage of any medical treatment so provided, but it includes a proviso in the following terms:

Provided that if the parent of any pupil gives to the authority notice that he objects to the pupil availing himself of any of the provisions [for medical treatment etc] so made the pupil shall not be encouraged ... so to do.

I do not regard that provision as throwing light on the present question. It does not prohibit a child under the stipulated age from availing himself of medical treatment or an education authority from providing it for him. If the child, without encouragement from the education authority, 'wishes to avail himself of medical treatment' the section imposes no obstacle in his way. Accordingly, in my opinion, the proviso gives no support to the contention from Mrs Gillick, but on the contrary points in the opposite direction.

The statutory provisions to which I have referred do not differentiate so far as the capacity of a minor under 16 is concerned between contraceptive advice and treatment and other forms of medical advice and treatment. It would, therefore, appear that, if the inference which Mrs Gillick's advisers seek to draw from the provisions is justified, a minor under the age of 16 has no capacity to authorise any kind of medical advice or treatment or examination of his own body. That seems to me to so surprising that I cannot accept it in the absence of clear provisions to that effect. It seems to me verging on the absurd to suggest that a girl or a boy aged 15 could not effectively consent, for example, to have a medical examination of some trivial injury to his body or even to have a broken arm set. Of course the consent of the parents should normally be asked, but they may not be immediately available.

Provided the patient, whether a boy or girl, is capable of understanding what is proposed, and of expressing his or her own wishes, I see no good reason for holding that he or she lacks the capacity to express them validly and effectively and to authorise the medical man to make the examination or give the treatment which he advises. After all, a minor under the age of 16 can, within certain limits, enter into a contact. He or she can also sue and be sued, and can give evidence on oath. Moreover, a girl under 16 can give sufficiently effective consent to sexual intercourse to lead to the legal result that the man involved does not commit the crime of rape: see *R v Howard* [1965] 3 All ER 684 at 685, [1966] 1 WLR 13 at 15, when Lord Parker CJ said:

> ... in the case of a girl under sixteen, the prosecution, in order to prove rape, must prove either that she physically resisted, or if she did not, that her understanding and knowledge were such that she was not in a position to decide whether to consent or resist ... there are many girls under sixteen who know full well what it is all about and can properly consent.

Accordingly, I am not disposed to hold now, for the first time, that a girl aged less than 16 lacks the power to give valid consent to contraceptive advice or treatment, merely on account of her age.

Lord Scarman: The law has ... to be found by a search in the judge-made law for the true principle. The legal difficulty is that in our search we find ourselves in a field of medical practice where parental right and a doctor's duty may point us in different directions. This is not surprising. Three features have emerged in today's society which were not known to our predecessors: (1) contraception as a subject for medical advice and treatment; (2) the increasing independence of young people; and (3) the changed status of women. In time past contraception was rarely a matter for the doctor; but with the development of the contraceptive pill for women it has become part and parcel of everyday medical practice, as is made clear by the department's *Handbook of Contraceptive Practice* (1984 revision) esp para 1.2. Family planning services are now available under statutory powers to all without any express limitations as to age or marital status. Young people, once they have attained the age of 16, are capable of consenting to contraceptive treatment, since it is medical treatment; and, however extensive be parental right in the care and upbringing of children, it cannot prevail so as to nullify the 16-year-old's capacity to consent which is now conferred by statute. Furthermore, women have obtained by the availability of a pill a choice of life-style with a degree of independence and of opportunity undreamed of until this generation and greater, I would add, than any law of equal opportunity could by itself effect.

The law ignores these developments at its peril. The House's task, therefore, as the supreme court in a legal system largely based on rules of law evolved over the years by the judicial process is to search the overfull and cluttered shelves of the law reports for a principle or set of principles recognised by the judges over the years but stripped of the detail which, however appropriate in their day, would, if applied today, lay the judges open to a justified criticism for failing to keep the law abreast of the society in which they live and work.

It is, of course, a judicial commonplace to proclaim the adaptability and flexibility of the judge-made common law. But this is more frequently proclaimed than acted on. The mark of the great judge from Coke through Mansfield to our day has been the capacity and the will to search out principle, to discard the detail appropriate (perhaps) to earlier times and to apply principle in such a way as to satisfy the needs of his own time. If judge-made law is to survive as a living and relevant body of law, we must make the effort, however inadequately, to follow the lead of the great masters of the judicial art.

In this appeal, therefore, there is much in the earlier case law which the House must discard; almost everything I would say but its principle. For example, the horrendous *Agar-Ellis* decisions (see *Re Agar-Ellis, Agar-Ellis v Lascelles* (1878) 10 Ch D 49, (1883) 24 Ch D 317) of the late nineteenth century asserting the power of the father over his child were rightly remaindered to the history books by the Court of Appeal in *Hewer v Bryant* [1969] 3 All ER 578, [1970] 1 QB 357, an important case to which I shall return later. Yet the decisions of earlier generations may well afford clues to the true principle of the law: eg *R v Howes* (1860) 3 E & E 332 at 336, 121 ER 467 at 468, which I also later quote. It is the duty of this House to look at, through and past decisions of earlier generations so that it may identify the principle which lies behind them. Even Lord Eldon (no legal revolutionary) once remarked, when invited to study precedent (the strength of which he never underrated):

> ... all law ought to stand upon principle, and unless decision has removed out of the way all argument and all principle, so as to make it impossible to apply them to the case before you, you must find out what is the principle upon which it must be decided.

(*See Queensberry Leases Case* (1819) 1 Bligh 339 at 486–487, 4 ER 127 at 179, quoted by Lord Campbell *Lives of the Lord Chancellors* (4th edn, 1857) vol 10, ch 213, p 244.)

Approaching the earlier law in this way, one finds plenty of indications as to the principles governing the law's approach to parental right and the child's right to make his or her own decision. Parental rights clearly do exist, and they do not wholly disappear until the age of majority. Parental rights relate to both the person and the property of the child: custody, care and control of the person and guardianship of the property of the child. But the common law has never treated such rights as sovereign or beyond review and control. Nor has our law ever treated the child as other than a person with capacities and rights recognised by law. The principle of the law, as I shall endeavour to show, is that parental rights are derived from parental duty and exist only so long as they are needed for the protection of the person and property of the child. The principle has been subjected to certain age limits set by statute for certain purposes; and in some cases the courts have declared an age of discretion at which a child acquires before the age of majority the right to make his (or her) own decision. But these limitations in no way undermine the principle of the law, and should not be allowed to obscure it.

Let me make good, quite shortly, the proposition of principle.

First, the guardianship legislation. Section 5 of the Guardianship of Infants Act 1886 began the process which is now complete of establishing the equal rights of mother and father. In doing so the legislation, which is currently embodied in s 1 of the Guardianship of Minors Act 1971 [now repealed], took over from the Chancery courts a rule which they had long followed (it was certainly applied by Lord Eldon during his quarter of a century as Lord Chancellor, as Parker LJ in this case (see [1985] 1 All ER 533 at 541, [1985] 2 WLR 413 at 424), quoting Heilbron J, reminds us) that when a court has before it a question as to the care and upbringing of a child it must treat the welfare of the child as the paramount consideration in determining the order to be made. There is here a principle which limits and governs the exercise of parental rights of custody, care and control. It is a principle perfectly consistent with the law's recognition of the parent as the natural guardian of the child; but it is also a warning that parental right must be exercised in accordance with the welfare principle and can be challenged, even overridden, if it be not.

Second, there is the common law's understanding of the nature of parental right. We are not concerned in this appeal to catalogue all that is contained in what Sachs LJ has felicitously described as the 'bundle of rights' which together constitute the rights of custody, care and control (see *Hewer v Bryant* [1969] 3 All ER 578 at 585, [1970] 1 QB 357 at 373). It is abundantly plain that the law recognises that there is a right and a duty of parents to determine whether or not to seek medical advice in respect of their child, and, having received advice, to give or withhold consent to medical treatment. The question in the appeal is as to the extent and duration of the right and the circumstances in which outside the two admitted exceptions to which I have earlier referred it can be overridden by the exercise of medical judgment.

As Parker and Fox LJJ noted in the Court of Appeal, the modern statute law recognises the existence of parental right: eg ss 85 and 86 of the Children Act 1975 and ss 2, 3 and 4 of the Child Care Act 1980 [both Acts now repealed]. It is derived from parental duty. A most illuminating discussion of parental right is to be found in *Blackstone's Commentaries* (1 Bl Com (17th edn, 1830) vol 1, chs 16 and 17). He analyses the duty of the parent as the 'maintenance ... protection, and ... education' of the child (at 446). He declares that the power of parents over their children is derived from their duty and exists 'to enable the parent more effectually to perform his duty, and partly as a recompense for his care and trouble in the faithful discharge of it' (at 452). In ch 17 he discusses the relation of guardian and ward. It is, he points out, a relation 'derived of [the relation of parent and child]: the guardian being only a temporary parent, that is, for so long a time as the ward is an infant, or under age' (at 460). A little later in the same chapter he again emphasises that the power and reciprocal duty of a guardian and ward are the same, pro tempore, as that of a father and child and adds that the guardian, when the ward comes of age (as also the father who becomes guardian 'at common law' if an estate be left to his child), must account to the child for all that he has transacted on his behalf (at 462–463). He then embarks on a discussion of the different ages at which for different purposes a child comes of sufficient age to make his own decision; and he cites examples, viz a boy might at 12 years old take the oath of allegiance; at 14 he might consent to marriage or choose his guardian 'and, if his discretion be actually proved, may make his testament of his personal estate'; at 18 he could be an executor: all these rights and responsibilities being capable of his acquiring before reaching the age of majority at 21 (at 463).

The two chapters provide a valuable insight into the principle and flexibility of the common law. The principle is that parental right or power of control of the person and property of his child exists primarily to enable the parent to discharge his duty of maintenance, protection and education until he reaches such an age as to be able to look after himself and make his own decisions. Blackstone does suggest that there was a further justification for parental right, viz as a recompense for the faithful discharge of parental duty; but the right of the father to the exclusion of the mother and the reward element as one of the reasons for the existence of the right have been swept away by the guardianship of minors legislation to which I have already referred. He also accepts that by statute and by case law varying ages of discretion have been fixed for various purposes. But it is clear that this was done to achieve certainty where it was considered necessary and in no way limits the principle that parental right endures only so long as it is needed for the protection of the child.

Although statue has intervened in respect of a child's capacity to consent to medical treatment from the age of 16 onwards, neither statute nor the case law has ruled on the extent and duration of parental right in respect of children under the age of 16. More specifically, there is no rule yet applied to contraceptive treatment, which has special problems of its own and is a late comer in medical practice. It is open, therefore, to the House to formulate a rule. The Court of Appeal favoured a fixed age limit of 16, basing itself on a view of the statue law which I do not share and on its view of the effect of the older case law which for the reasons already given I cannot accept. It sought to justify the limit by the public interest in the law being certain. Certainty is always an advantage in the law; and in some branches of the law it is a necessity. But it brings with it an inflexibility and a rigidity which in some branches of the law can obstruct justice, impede the law's development and stamp on the law the mark of obsolescence where what is needed is the capacity for development. The law relating to parent and child is concerned with the problems of the growth and maturity of the human personality. If the law should impose on the process of 'growing up' fixed limits where nature knows only a continuous process, the price would be artificiality and a lack of realism in an area where the law must be sensitive to human development and social change. If certainty be thought desirable, it is better that the rigid demarcations necessary to achieve it should be laid down by legislation after a full consideration of all the relevant factors than by the courts, confined as they are by the forensic process to the evidence adduced by the parties and to whatever may properly fall within the judicial notice of judges. Unless and until Parliament should think fit to intervene, the courts should establish a principle flexible enough to enable justice to be achieved by its application to the particular circumstances proved by the evidence placed before them.

The underlying principle of the law was exposed by Blackstone and can be seen to have been acknowledged in the case law. It is that parental right yields to the child's right to make his own decisions when he reaches a sufficient understanding and intelligence to be capable of making up his own mind on the matter requiring decision. Lord Denning MR captured the spirit and principle of the law when he said in *Hewer v Bryant* [1969] 3 All ER 578 at 582, [1970] 1 QB 337 at 369:

I would get rid of the rule in *Re Agar-Ellis* ((1883) 24 Ch D 317) and of the suggested exceptions to it. That case was decided in the year 1883. It reflects the attitude of a Victorian parent towards his children. He expected unquestioning obedience to his commands. If a son disobeyed, his father would cut him off with 1s. If a daughter had an illegitimate child, he would turn her out of the house. His power only ceased when the child became 21. I decline to accept a view so much out of date. The common law can, and should, keep pace with the times. It should declare, in conformity with the recent report on the Age of Majority (Report of the Committee on the Age of Majority (Cmnd 3342) under the chairmanship of Latey J, published in July 1967), that the legal right of a parent to the custody of a child ends at the eighteenth birthday; and even up till then, it is a dwindling right which the courts will hesitate to enforce against the wishes of the child, the older he is. It starts with a right of control and ends with little more than advice.

But his is by no means a solitary voice. It is consistent with the opinion expressed by the House in *J v C* [1969] 1 All ER 788, [1970] AC 668, where their Lordships clearly recognised as out of place the assertion in the *Agar-Ellis* cases (1878) 10 Ch D 49, (1883) 24 Ch D 317 of a father's power bordering on 'patria potestas'. It is consistent with the view of Lord Parker CJ in *R v Howard* [1965] 3 All ER 684 at 685, [1966] 1 WLR 13 at 15, where he ruled that in the case of a prosecution charging rape of a girl under 16 the Crown must *prove* either lack of her consent or that she was not in a position to decide whether to consent or resist and added the comment that 'there are many girls who know full well what it is all about and can properly consent'. And it is consistent with the views of the House in the recent criminal case where a father was accused of kidnapping his own child, *R v D* [1984] 2 All ER 449 [1984] AC 778, a case to which I shall return.

For the reasons which I have endeavoured to develop, the case law of the nineteenth and earlier centuries is no guide to the application of the law in the conditions of today. The *Agar-Ellis* cases (the power of the father) cannot live with the modern statute law. The habeas corpus 'age of discretion' cases are also no guide as to the limits which should be accepted today in marking out the bounds of parental right, of a child's capacity to make his or her own decision and of a doctor's duty to his patient. Nevertheless the 'age of discretion' cases are helpful in that they do reveal the judges as accepting that a minor can in law achieve an age of discretion before coming of full age. The 'age of discretion' cases are cases in which a parent or guardian (usually the father) has applied for habeas corpus to secure the return of his child who has left without his consent. the courts would refuse an order if the child had attained the age of discretion, which came to be regarded as 14 for boys and 16 for girls, and did not wish to return. The principle underlying them was plainly that an order would be refused if the child had sufficient intelligence and understanding to make up his own mind. A passage from the judgment of Cockburn CJ in *R v Howes* (1860) 3 E & E 332 at 336–337, 121 ER 467 at 468–469, which Parker LJ quoted in the Court of Appeal, illustrates their reasoning and shows how a fixed age was used as a working rule to establish an age at which the requisite 'discretion' could be held to be achieved by the child. Cockburn CJ said:

> Now the cases which have been decided on this subject shew that, although a father is entitled to the custody of his children till they attain the age of twenty-one, this Court will not grant a habeas corpus to hand a child which is below that age over to its father, provided that it has attained an age of sufficient discretion to enable it to exercise a wise choice for its own interests. The whole question is, what is the age of discretion? We repudiate utterly, as most dangerous, the notion that any intellectual precocity in an individual female child can hasten the period which appears to have been fixed by statute for the arrival of the age of discretion; for that very precocity, if uncontrolled, might very probably lead to her irreparable injury. The legislature has given us a guide, which we may safely follow, in pointing out sixteen as the age gap up to which the father's right to the custody of his female child is to continue; and short of which such a child has no discretion to consent to leaving him.

The principle is clear; and a fixed age of discretion was accepted by the courts by analogy from the Abduction Acts (the first being the Act 4 & 5 Ph & M c 8 (1557)). While it is unrealistic today to treat a sixteenth century Act as a safe guide in the matter of a girl's discretion, and while no modern judge could dismiss the intelligence of a teenage girl as 'intellectual precocity', we agree with Cockburn CJ as to the principle of the law: the attainment by a child of an age of sufficient discretion to enable him or her to exercise a wise choice in his or her own interests.

The modern law governing parental right and a child's capacity to make his own decisions was considered in *R v D* [1984] 2 All ER 449, [1984] AC 778. The House must, in my view, be understood as having in that case accepted that, save where statute otherwise provides, a minor's capacity to make his or her own decision depends on the minor having sufficient understanding and intelligence to make the decision and is not to be determined by reference to any judicially fixed age limit. The House was faced with a submission that a father, even if he had taken his child away by force or fraud, could not be guilty of a criminal offence of any kind. Lord Brandon, with whom their other Lordships agreed, commented that this might well have been the view of the legislature and the courts in the nineteenth century, but had this to say about parental right and a child's capacity in our time to give or withhold a valid consent ([1984] 2 All ER 449 at 456, [1984] AC 778 at 804–805):

> This is because in those times both the generally accepted conventions of society and the courts by which such conventions were buttressed and enforced, regarded a father

as having absolute and paramount authority, as against all the world, over any children of his who were still under the age or majority (then 21), except for a married daughter. The nature of this view of a father's rights appears clearly from various reported cases, including, as a typical example, *Re Agar-Ellis, Agar-Ellis v Lascelles* (1883) 24 Ch D 317. The common law, however, while generally immutable in its principles, unless different principles are laid down by statute, is not immutable in the way in which it adapts, develops and applies those principles in a radically changing world and against the background of radically changed social conventions and conditions.

Later he said ([1984] 2 All ER 449 at 457, [1984] AC 778 at 806):

I see no good reason why, in relation to the kidnapping of a child, it should not in all cases be the absence of the child's consent which is material, whatever its age may be. In the case of a very young child, it would not have the understanding or the intelligence to give its consent, so that absence of consent would be a necessary inference from its age. In the case of an older child, however, it must, I think, be a question of fact for a jury whether the child concerned has sufficient understanding and intelligence to give its consent; if, but only if, the jury considers that a child has these qualities, it must then go on to consider whether it has been proved that the child did not give its consent. While the matter will always be for the jury alone to decide, I should not expect a jury to find at all frequently that a child under 14 had sufficient understanding and intelligence to give its consent.

In the light of the foregoing I would hold that as a matter of law the parental right to determine whether or not their minor child below the age of 16 will have medical treatment terminates if and when the child achieves a sufficient understanding and intelligence to enable him or her to understand fully what is proposed. It will be a question of fact whether a child seeking advice has sufficient understanding of what is involved to give a consent valid in law. Until the child achieves the capacity to consent, the parental right to make the decision continues save only in exceptional circumstances. Emergency, parental neglect, abandonment of the child or inability to find the parent are examples of exceptional situations justifying the doctor proceeding to treat the child without parental knowledge and consent; but there will arise, no doubt, other exceptional situations in which it will be reasonable for the doctor to proceed without the parent's consent.

Lord Bridge fully agreed with Lords Fraser and Scarman and added nothing further on the issue of consent.

Lord Brandon dealt with the case on the prior question of whether a doctor, by complying with the circular, would act unlawfully by reference to the criminal law or public policy (for which see *infra* ch 9) irrespective of the consent of the child or indeed the parents.

Lord Templeman, however, did address the issue of consent by children and in general agreed with the others. In the context of contraception, however, he took the somewhat idiosyncratic view that contraceptive treatment or advice is special and thus something to which a child could not consent.

In its report, *Mental Incapacity* (No 231 1995), the Law Commission adopted a *functional* test for capacity which it considered largely reflected the common law (*op cit*, para 3.23).

Law Commission *Mental Incapacity* (1995) Report No 231

3.3   In our overview paper we described the variety of tests of capacity which already exist in our law, and we also discussed some medical and psychological tests of capacity (Consultation Paper No 119, paras 2.9–2.42). There are three broad approaches: the "statutes", "outcome" and "functional" approaches. A "status" test excludes all persons under eighteen from voting and used to exclude all married women from legal ownership of property. Under the present law, the status of being a "patient" of the Court of Protection is used in a variety of enactments to trigger other legal consequences. Case-law also suggests that the status of being a "patient" has the extremely significant effect of depriving the patient of all contractual capacity, whether or not as a matter of fact the patient actually had such capacity. The status approach is quite out of tune with the policy aim of enabling and encouraging people to take for themselves any decision which they have capacity to take.

3.4   An assessor of capacity using the "outcome" method focuses on the final content of an individual's decision. Any decision which is inconsistent with conventional values, or with which the assessor disagrees, may be classified as incompetent. This penalises individuality and demands conformity at the expense of personal autonomy. A number of our respondents argued that an "outcome" approach is applied by many doctors; if the outcome of the patient's deliberations is to agree with the doctor's recommendations then he or she is taken to have capacity, while if the outcome is to reject a course which the doctor has advised then capacity is found to be absent.

3.5   We explained in Consultation Paper No 128 that most respondents to our overview paper strongly supported the "functional" approach. This also has the merit of being the approach adopted by most of the established tests in English law. In this approach, the assessor asks whether an individual is able, at the time when a particular decision has to be made, to understand its nature and effects. Importantly, both partial and fluctuating capacity can be recognised. Most people, unless in a coma, are able to make at least some decisions for themselves, and many have levels of capacity which vary from week to week or even from hour to hour.

3.6   In view of the ringing endorsement of the "functional" approach given by respondents to the overview paper, we formulated a provisional "functional" test of capacity and set this out in all three of our 1993 consultation papers. This test focused on inability to understand or, in the alternative, inability to choose. ...

3.13 We took the provisional view in the consultation papers that those who cannot communicate decisions should be included within the scope of the new jurisdiction. We had in mind particularly those who are unconscious. In some rare conditions a conscious patient may be known to retain a level of cognitive functioning but the brain may be completely unable to communicate with the body or with the outside world. In other cases, particularly after a stroke, it may not be possible to say whether or not there is cognitive dysfunction. It can, however, be said that the patient cannot communicate any decision he or she may make. In either case, decisions may have to be made on behalf of such people, and only two respondents expressed the purist view that they should be excluded from our new jurisdiction because they do not suffer from true "mental incapacity". It appears to us appropriate that they should be brought within the scope of our new legislation rather than being left to fend for themselves within the uncertain and inadequate principles of the common law.

The definition of incapacity

3.14 The functional approach means that the new definition of incapacity should emphasise its decision-specific nature. A diagnostic threshold of "mental disability" should be included, except in cases of inability to communicate.

We recommend that legislation should provide that a person is without capacity if at the material time he or she is:
(1)   **unable by reason of mental disability to make a decision on the matter in question, or**
(2)   **unable to communicate a decision on that matter because he or she is unconscious or for any other reason.** (Draft Bill, clause 2(1).)

As you will see, the Law Commission considered that a person would be incapacitated if: (a) he was unable by reason of mental disability to make a decision for himself; or (b) he was unable to communicate his decision for any reason (see cl 2, Draft Mental Incapacity Bill). The latter is important because it identifies a patient who may well be able to (and actually does) understand what is involved but because, for example, he has 'locked-in syndrome' cannot communicate it. Clearly, he too cannot *take* a decision and others must do on his behalf.

As regards the former type of case – where the patient is 'unable ... to make a decision' – the Law Commission offered a further explanation of what this means but, in essence, elaborated and clarified the common law test (see cl 2 of the Draft Mental Incapacity Bill). The Law Commission linked 'understanding' to the criteria for assessing and establishing a patients' capacity, namely the ability to retain the information relevant to making the decision and then actually to make a decision on the basis of that information. What we see here is an approximation to the common law test developed by Thorpe J in *Re C (adult: refusal of medical treatment)* [1994] 1 WLR 290.

(a) Understand what?

It is crucial to determine the level of information that must be understood (or retained) for a person to be competent. The more the information that must be 'processed', the more difficult it may become for a child or mentally disabled adult to be competent.

In *Gillick*, the House of Lords required that the patient to be competent must, in the words of Lord Scarman, 'have sufficient maturity to understand *what is involved*' (our emphasis). Crucially, therefore, we must determine what it is that a patient must be capable of understanding ie what is meant by 'what is involved'? Clearly, 'what is involved' must relate to that information which the law stipulates a patient should be aware of before a valid consent may be given. In large part, it will be the doctor's duty to disclose this information. There may be circumstances in which the patient is aware of 'what is involved' without the need to be told but even here the doctor will have a duty to assess the accuracy of the patient's beliefs.

Put this way, it will be clear that what the patient needs to understand is largely that which the doctor as a matter of law is obliged to inform the patient of. This conclusion does not, however, resolve the problem since, as we shall see, there are two levels of duty imposed upon the doctor by the law. The first, and more fundamental, concerns information that must be disclosed to avoid a claim in battery. What the law requires here is, as we shall see, merely that the doctor inform the patient of the *broad nature and purpose* of the procedure. In *Re C (adult: refusal of medical treatment)* [1994] 1 All ER 819, Thorpe J stated that the patient must understand 'the nature purpose and effect' of the procedure (at 824). In *Re MB (an adult: medical treatment)* (1997) 38 BMLR 175 (CA), Butler-Sloss LJ required that the patient was able to understand 'the information which is material to the decision, especially as to the likely consequences of having or not having the treatment in question' (at 187). This would give to 'what is involved' a very limited content. It is, or course, consistent with Lord Donaldson MR's view that, as we saw above, consent is merely an aspect of the law of battery. However, the better view is that the law of consent goes further and encompasses what we shall see as the more extensive duty (albeit in negligence) to disclose information beyond that minimal level required to avoid a battery claim. Logically, the capacity or ability to understand 'what is involved' must embrace this further information since the basis for requiring disclosure is to allow the patient to make an informed choice and this can only be achieved if the patient is able to understand that further information.

Notice, for example, that in the Age of Legal Capacity (Scotland) Act 1991, s 2(4) requires that the child be capable of understanding the 'nature and *possible consequences* of the procedure or treatment' (our emphasis). This clearly goes beyond the information which a patient must understand in order for the doctor to avoid a claim in battery. (Contrast the Mental Health Act 1983, s 57(2) and 58(3) referring to the 'nature, purpose and *likely effects* of the treatment' (our emphasis). Perhaps the latter wording is more consistent with the individual having a capacity to understand the more limited information necessary for the doctor to avoid a claim in battery.)

The difficulty with *requiring* an ability to understand more than this is the curtailing effect it could have on patients' making decisions for themselves, particularly refusals of treatment where capacity is usually most likely to be at issue. The more a person must be able to understand, the less likely they will have capacity to decide. Thus, while it may seem more logical that a patient should have the ability to understand *all* legally relevant information, to require an ability to understand a more limited set of information would be more empowering. In its *Mental Incapacity* Report (No 231 1995), the Law Commission contented itself with requiring that to be competent the patient should be able to understand or retain the information relevant to the decision, including information about the reasonably foreseeable consequences of deciding one way or another or of failing to make the decision.

(Draft Mental Incapacity Bill, cl 2(2)(a).)

We suggest that this reflects the common law in England. (For a discussion in the context of children, see *infra* pp 643–650.)

(b) Actual understanding versus ability to understand

One final point we should note relates to the concept of capacity.

Does a test which stipulates that the patient 'understands' mean that the doctor must satisfy himself: (a) that the patient *does in fact* understand what is involved; or (b) that the patient is *capable* generally of understanding though, as it may subsequently transpire, he did not understand in the particular case; or (c) that the patient as a *reasonable patient is capable* of understanding or would have understood? Let us assume that (c) can be discounted since it is not concerned with the circumstances of the particular patient which, as we have seen, ought to be the central concern of the law.

While agreeing on the general direction of the law in favour of some notion of 'understanding', in *Gillick* neither Lord Fraser nor Lord Scarman appeared to choose his language with precision or indeed consistency on whether (a) or (b) represents the law. At a number of points in their speeches the judges used language consisted with (a). So, for example, Lord Fraser requires 'that the girl ... *will* understand' the doctor's advice. Similarly, Lord Scarman stated that 'a doctor will have to satisfy himself that she *is* able to appraise' those matters involved in the procedure and its consequences. This is a somewhat equivocal statement by Lord Scarman but on one reading he is saying that the girl must *in fact* understand. The weight of the dicta in *Gillick* is, however, in favour of (b). Consider the following statements:

Lord Fraser stated:

> 'Provided the patient, whether a boy or a girl, is *capable of understanding* what is proposed, and of expressing his or her own wishes, I see no good reason for holding that he or she lacks the capacity to express them validly and effectively and to authorise the medical man to make the examination or give the treatment which he advises' [our emphasis].

Later Lord Scarman said:

> 'It is that parental right yields to the child's right to make his own decisions when he reaches a sufficient understanding and intelligence to be *capable of making* up his own mind on the matter requiring decision' [our emphasis].

and also he said:

> 'It follows that a doctor will have to satisfy himself that she *is able to appraise* these factors before he can safely proceed on the basis that she has at law capacity to consent to contraceptive treatment' [our emphasis].

Notice also that Lord Scarman referred to the Canadian case *Johnston v Wellesley Hospital* (1970) 17 DLR (3d) 139, where Addy J spoke of the child being 'capable' of understanding.

In his judgment in *Re R (a minor) (wardship: consent to treatment)* [1992] Fam 11, [1991] 4 All ER 177, however, Lord Donaldson MR demonstrated how easy it is to use language without the precision which is essential here. In *Re R* the doctor had given evidence that at times R was capable of understanding what was involved in the proposed treatment for her mental illness. Latching onto this, Lord Donaldson MR stated that –

... it is far from certain that [the doctor] was saying that R understood the implications of treatment being withheld, as distinct from understanding what was proposed to be done by way of treatment ... But, even if she was capable on a good day of a sufficient degree of understanding to meet the *Gillick* criteria, her mental disability, to the cure or an alleviation of which the proposed treatment was directed, was such that on other ways she was not only '*Gillick* incompetent' but actually sectionable.

The importance of precision here lies in the following. If the test of understanding is *actual understanding*, ie (a), then whether or not the girl understands *and therefore is competent* to consent (or refuse) may turn on what she is told. Indeed, this seems to have been Lord Donaldson's approach in *Re R* in the quotation above. If the girl is not given certain information she may not understand enough but this would not be the product of any lack of competence but merely that she decided in relative ignorance. It would be an unsatisfactory state of law if doctors could by controlling the information given to a patient thereby grant or deny her competence. Competence or incompetence is a state inherent in the individual patient which cannot depend how much the doctor tells the patient. It must, therefore, be the law that competence is determined by reference to the unvarying conceptual standard of *ability* to understand. Whether, thereafter a patient who is judged competent because she has the capacity or ability to understand, in fact consented, is a distinct question turning upon the reality of the consent based upon legally adequate information.

Unfortunately, the dangers of adopting Lord Donaldson MR's approach are illustrated by *Re L (medical treatment: Gillick competency)* [1998] 2 FLR 810. The case concerned a 14-year-old girl who had suffered extensive and severe burns. Her life was at risk if she did not undergo treatment which might have necessitated a blood transfusion as part of it. She was, however, a practising Jehovah's Witness and refused to consent to the procedure. Her doctor did not explain to her the nature of the 'horrible' death she would endure if she went untreated and gangrene developed. The court was asked to authorise the procedure in her 'best interests'.

In doing so, one basis for Sir Stephen Brown P's decision was that L was incompetent because she did not *actually* understand what was involved in her refusal, namely the manner of her death (on this aspect of the case, see *infra*).

Stephen Brown P asked himself the question whether L *actually* understood what was involved in her decision rather than whether she was *capable* of understanding it. In assessing the patient's ability, the court (or doctor) will often be guided by the patient's actual understanding. How else will an inherent capacity of the individual be judged unless, for example, the patient is unconscious? However, that the patient's state of mind is frequently a yardstick by which to judge the *condition* of their mind, is no reason to confuse the two. The patient's *reasoning power* is the only legally relevant issue at the threshold stage in determining whether the patient is competent to make a decision.

It is only when a patient is unable to decide for themselves that the law should, or needs to, vest decision-making power in another. Usually, of course, the confusion will not matter. Lack of actual understanding may well demonstrate an inability to understand. However, in *Re L* it did matter. L did not understand what was involved in her decision because her doctor had deliberately kept the details from her. The fact that L was ignorant of the detail that the court required her to understand was hardly her fault. Of itself, this did not render her incompetent; rather, it left her uninformed. It cannot be right that a doctor may manipulate a patient's capacity to make a decision by failing to provide relevant information. If relevant to anything, the detail of her death was only of legal interest in determining whether her decision, be it to consent to or refuse the treatment, was *real* and thus valid.

Finally, can we find any guidance in legislation? Not surprisingly, there are few statutes which address this question. The Mental Health Act 1983 in its provisions in ss 57 and 58 (*infra*) clearly endorsed approach (b). Similarly, the relevant provisions of the Children Act 1989 dealing with medical or psychiatric examination or treatment follow this approach (ss 38(6), 43(8) 44(7) and Sch 3, paras 4(4)(a) and 5(5)(a)).

By contrast the Human Organ transplants (Unrelated Persons) Regulations 1989 (SI 1989 No 2480) made pursuant to s 2 of the Human Organ Transplants Act 1989 seem to adopt approach (a), since one of the conditions for approving donations between unrelated persons is that the 'donor *understands* the nature of the medical procedure and risks and consents to the removal of the organ' (reg 2(2)(b)) (our emphasis). Unless it can be argued organ donation between unrelated persons is a special case, it may be that this is merely an example of imprecise drafting.

The most pertinent statutory provision, though only applicable to Scotland, is the Age of Legal Capacity (Scotland) Act 1991. This Act seeks to clarify the law, *inter alia*, in relation to the competence of children to consent to medical treatment in Scotland. Section 2(4) provides:

> 2. (4) A person under the age of 16 years shall have legal capacity to consent on his own behalf to any surgical, medical or dental procedure or treatment where, in the opinion of a qualified medical practitioner attending him, he is *capable* of understanding the nature and possible consequences of the procedure or treatment [our emphasis].

This gives statutory expression to the decision in *Gillick*. For our purposes it is important to notice that Parliament adopted approach (b), ie that the child should be 'capable of understanding' what is involved.

3. Establishing capacity or competence to decide

As has been seen, concern about the establishment of capacity arises out of the two propositions: (1) that a doctor ought to respect his patient's autonomy, but (2) he need only do so when the patient who expresses his will is capable of behaving autonomously. It follows that autonomy is, in effect, a status granted by others, in this case, the doctor. It also follows that in granting the status, it is the doctor's assessment of capacity which is crucial. Thus, capacity is a state of affairs granted by the doctor. In determining capacity, the doctor both as a matter of ethics and law must (ie has a duty to) behave with integrity and satisfy himself that the criteria deemed relevant to determine capacity are present in the particular case. The obverse of this proposition is that if these criteria are present, on any objective assessment, the doctor may not (ie is under a duty not to) impose his own views so as to regard the patient as incapable of understanding and thus, of making his own decisions.

An initial point we should notice is that as Lord Donaldson MR pointed out in *Re T (adult: refusal of treatment)* [1992] 4 All ER 649 at 661 '[e]very adult is presumed to have … capacity [to consent], but it is a presumption which can be rebutted'. (See also *Re MB* (1997) 38 BMLR 175 (CA) per Butler-Sloss LJ at 186.) We shall return shortly to examine the circumstances in which the presumption may be rebutted. Similarly, as a result of section 8 of the Family Law Reform Act 1969 a child aged between 16 and 18 is presumed to be competent in respect of 'surgical, medical or dental treatment'. (discussed *infra*, pp 643–645)

Curiously, Lord Donaldson MR in *Re W (a minor) (medical treatment)* [1992] 4 All ER 627 at 634 stated that s 8 'conclusively presumed' a 16- or 17-year-old to be competent. Section 8 clearly does not do this since it merely puts the child patient in the same position as an adult patient. Hence, as he himself asserted in *Re R*, the presumption is rebuttable. As regards a child under 16 or in circumstances where s 8 is inapplicable, then the child is presumed to be incompetent at common law although this presumption is rebuttable as *Gillick* establishes.

What in law are the criteria for establishing capacity? (See generally MJ Gunn et al 'Decision Making Capacity' (1999) 7 Med L Rev 269.) It is critical to notice here that when we talk of the doctor making a decision as to capacity, there are in fact *two* stages to the process. The first is the reference to the relevant criteria. As will be made clear, these criteria are not for doctors to determine but are a matter for the law. The second stage is the doctor's application of these general criteria. That clearly is a decision for him. In theory it would be subject to review but in practice it is hard to challenge it; hence our insistence upon integrity.

By way of background we should consider the views of the US President's Commission in its 1983 Report, *Making Health Care Decisions*.

President's Commission for the Study of Ethical Problems in Medicine and Biomedical and Behavioural Research: *Making Health Care Decisions* (1983)

Assessments of incapacity

The objective of any assessment of decisional incapacity is to diminish errors of mistakenly preventing competent persons from directing the course of their own treatment or of failing to protect the incapacitated from the harmful effects of their decisions. Health care professionals will probably play a substantial role, if not the entire one, in the initial assessment and the finding may never be reviewed by outside authorities. Nonetheless, since assessment of an individual's capacity is largely a matter of common sense, there is no inherent reason why a health care professional must play this role.

'Decision making incapacity' is not a medical or a psychiatric diagnostic category; it rests on a judgment of the type that an informed layperson might make – that a patient lacks the ability to understand a situation and to make a choice in light of that understanding. Indeed, if a dispute arises or a legal determination of a patient's competence is required, the judge empowered to make the determination will consider the situation not as a medical expert but as a layperson. On the basis of the testimony of health care personnel and others who know the individual well, and possibly from personal observation of the patient, the judge must decide whether the patient is capable of making informed decisions that adequately protect his or her own interests.

Health care professionals are called upon to make these assessments because the question of incapacity to make health care decisions usually arises while a person is under their care. Particularly within institutions such as hospitals, a treating physician often involves colleagues from psychiatry, psychology, and neurology who have ways to accumulate, organise, and analyse information relevant to such assessments. These examinations can yield considerable information about the patient's capabilities. The courses of useful information to be collected include discussions of the situation with relatives and other care-givers, particularly those in close contact with the patient, such as nurses. Ultimately, whether a patient's capabilities are sufficiently limited and the inadequacies sufficiently extensive for the person to be considered incapacitated is a matter for careful judgment in light of the demand of the situation. If the patient improves (or worsens) or if the decision to be made has different consequences, a reassessment of the individual's capacity may be required.

Finally, in any assessment of capacity due care should be paid to the reasons for a particular patient's impaired capacity, not because the reasons play any role in determining whether the patient's judgment is to be honoured but because identification of the causes of incapacity may assist in their remedy or removal. The Commission urges that those responsible for assessing capacity not be content with providing an answer to the question of whether or not a particular patient is incapacitated. Rather, in conjunction with the patient's health care team (of which the assessor may be a member), they should to the extent feasible attempt to remove barriers to decisional capacity.

Earlier, the President's Commission stated (at pp 57–62):

Elements of capacity. In the view of the Commission, any determination of the capacity to decide on a course of treatment must relate to the individual abilities of a patient, the requirements of the task at hand, and the consequences likely to flow from the decision. Decision-making capacity requires, to greater or lesser degree: (1) possession of a set of values and goals; (2) the ability to communicate and to understand information; (3) the ability to reason and to deliberate about one's choices.

The first, a framework for comparing options is needed if the person is to evaluate possible outcomes as good or bad. The framework, and the values that it embodies, must be reasonably stable; that is, the patient must be able to make reasonably consistent choices. Reliance on a patient's decision would be difficult or impossible if the patient's values were so unstable that the patient could not reach or adhere to a choice at least long enough for a course of therapy to be initiated with some prospect of being completed.

The second element includes the ability to give and receive information, as well as the possession of various linguistic and conceptual skills needed for at least a basic understanding of the relevant information. These abilities can be evaluated only as they relate to the task at hand and are not solely cognitive, as they ordinarily include emotive elements. To use them, a person also needs sufficient life experience to appreciate the meaning of potential alternatives; what it would probably be like to undergo various medical procedures, for example, or to live in a new way required by a medical condition or intervention.

Some critics of the doctrine of informed consent have argued that patients simply lack the ability to understand medical information relevant to decisions about their care. Indeed, some empirical studies purport to have demonstrated this by showing that the lay public often does not know the meaning of common medical terms, or by showing that, following an encounter with a physician, patients are unable to report what the physician said about their illness and treatment. Neither type of study establishes the fact that patients cannot understand. The first merely finds that they do not currently know the right definitions of some terms; the second, which usually fails to discover what the physician actually did say, rests its conclusions on an assumption that information was provided that was subsequently not understood. In the Commission's own survey, physicians were asked: 'What percentage of your patients would you say are able to understand most aspects of their treatment and condition if reasonable time and effort are devoted to explanation?' Overall, 48% of physicians reported that 90—100% of their patients could understand and an additional 34% said that 70–89% could understand.

The third element of decision-making capacity – reasoning and deliberation – includes the ability to compare the impact of alternative outcomes on personal goals and life plans. Some ability to employ probabilistic reasoning about uncertain outcomes is usually necessary, as well as the ability to give appropriate weight in a present decision to various future outcomes.

Standards for assessing capacity. The actual measurement of these various abilities is by no means simple. Virtually all conscious adults can perform some tasks but not others. In the context of informed consent, what is critical is a patient's capacity to make a specific medical decision. An assessment of an individual's capacity must consider the nature of the particular decision-making process in light of these developments: Does the patient possess the ability to understand the relevant facts and alternatives? Is the patient weighting the decision within a framework of values and goals? Is the patient able to reason and deliberate about this information? Can the patient give reasons for the decision, in light of the facts, the alternatives, and the impact of the decision on the patient's own goals and values?

To be sure, a patient may possess these abilities but fail to exercise them well; that is, the decision may be the result of a mistaken understanding of the facts or a defective reasoning process. In such instances, the obligation of the professional is not to declare, on the basis of a 'wrong' decision, that the patient lacks decision-making capacity, but rather to work with the patient towards a fuller and more accurate understanding of the facts and a sound reasoning process.

How deficient must a decision-making process be to justify the assessment that a patient lacks the capacity to make a particular decision? Since the assessment must balance possibly competing considerations of well-being and self-determination, the prudent course is to take into account the potential consequences of the patient's decision. When the consequences for well-being are substantial, there is a greater need to be certain that the patient possesses the necessary level of capacity. When little turns on the decision, the level of decision-making capacity required may be appropriately reduced (even though the constituent elements remain the same) and less scrutiny may be required about whether the patient possesses even the reduced level of capacity. Thus a particular patient may be capable of deciding about a relatively inconsequential medication, but not about the amputation of a gangrenous limb.

This formulation has significant implications. First, it denies that simply by expressing a preference about a treatment decision an individual demonstrates the capacity to make that decision. The 'expressed preference' standard does nothing to preclude the presence of a serious defect or mistake in a patient's reasoning process. Consequently, it cannot ensure that the patient's expressed preference accords with the patient's conception of future well-being. Although it gives what appears to be great deference to self-determination, the expressed preference standard may actually fail to promote the values underlying self-administration, which include the achievement of personal values and goals. For these reasons, the Commission rejects the expressed preference standard for decisions that might compromise the patient's well-being.

The Commission also rejects as the standard of capacity any test that looks solely to the content of the patient's decision. Any standard based on 'objectively correct' decisions would allow a health professional (or other third party) to declare that a patient lacks decision-making capacity whenever a decision appears 'wrong', 'irrational', or otherwise incompatible with the evaluator's view of what is best for the patient. Use of such a standard is in sharp conflict with most of the values that support self-determination: it would take the decision away from the patient and place it with another, and it would inadequately reflect the subjective nature of each individual's conception of what's good. Further, its imprecision opens the door to manipulation of health care decision-making through selective application.

Logically, just as a patient's disagreement with a health care professional's recommendation does not prove a lack of decision-making capacity, concurrence with the recommendation would not establish the patient's capacity. Yet, as testimony before the Commission made clear, coherent adults are seldom said to lack capacity (except, perhaps, in the mental health context) when they acquiesce in the course of treatment recommended by their physicians. (Challenges to patients' capacity are rarer still when family members expressly concur in the decision.) This divergence between theory and reality is less significant than it might appear, however, since neither the self-determination nor the well-being of a patient would usually be advanced by insisting upon an inquiry into the patient's decision-making capacity (or lack thereof) when patient, physicians, and family all agree on a course of treatment. Even if the course being adopted might not, in fact, best match the patient's long-term view of his or her own welfare, a declaration of lack of capacity will lead to a substitute making a decision for the patient (which means full self-determination will not occur), yet will rarely result in a different health care decision being made (which means no change in well-being). Substitution of a third party for an acquiescent patient will lead to a different outcome only if the new decision-maker has a strong commitment to promoting previously expressed values of the patient that differ significantly from those that guided the physician. If, as would usually be the case, the substitute would be a family member or other individual who would defer to the physician's recommendation, there would be little reason to initiate an inquiry into capacity. The existing practice thus seems generally satisfactory.

Questions of patient capacity in decision-making typically arise only when a patient chooses a course – often a refusal of treatment – other than the one the health professional finds most reasonable. A practitioner's belief that a decision is not 'reasonable' is the beginning – not the end – of an inquiry into the patient's capacity to decide. If every patient decision that a health professional disagreed with were grounds for a declaration of lack of capacity, self-determination would have little meaning. Even when disagreement occurs, an assessment of the patient's decision-making capacity begins with a presumption of such capacity. Nonetheless, a serious disagreement about a decision with substantial consequences for the patient's welfare may appropriately trigger a more careful evaluation. When that process indicates that the patient understands the situation and is capable of reasoning soundly about it, the patient's choice should be accepted. When it does not, further evaluation may be required, and in some instances a determination of lack of capacity will be appropriate.

Professor Margaret Somerville addresses the particular and troubling issue of rationality.

M Somerville 'Structuring the Issues in Informed Consent' (1981) 26 McGill LJ 740

Does the law require rationality of the patient's decision as a substantive element of a valid consent?

The first consideration is the relationship between understanding and rationality. If the law requires that the patient apparently understand the required disclosure of information in order to give a valid consent, does this mean that the law is seeking to promote rationality of the patient's decision and, further, if his decision is adjudged irrational, may it be ignored or overridden on this basis?

Even if it is accepted that understanding of the required disclosed information is being mandated in order to promote rationality, it must be asked whether this means rationality of the decision-making process or rationality of the decision itself or both. Although understanding may promote rationality in both of these respects, it is usually only the rationality of the decision outcome that is relevant to the law, and understanding may not be an essential condition for this. It is quite possible for a decision to be judged rational by an objective bystander, when the reasons on which it was based were quite irrational. Moreover, the law's requirement of understanding of information by the patient may be seen as promoting autonomy rather than rationality. In this case, to require rationality either of the patient's decision-making process or its outcome would be to contradict directly the value of self-determination which is being promoted by requiring understanding, because self-determination requires recognition of the competent patient's right, for no matter what reason or on what basis, to determine what shall be done to himself.

It is submitted that the preferable approach is to view understanding as promoting autonomy, rather than rationality. Any legal limits to irrationality of a decision-making process or decision outcome should then be set by declaring the person factually or legally incompetent. Thus, the right to autonomy would mean that the competent patient could make irrational decisions concerning himself without the law overriding such decisions. Further, in order to give proper scope to such a rule, it is necessary to recognise that irrationality of the decision-making process or of decision outcomes does not of itself indicate incompetence, although in some circumstances it may be evidence of this.

The issue of irrationality of the patient's decision was considered in *Kelly v Hazlett* [(1976) 75 DLR (3rd) 536]. The defendant surgeon gave evidence that he considered the plaintiff 'irrational', that is, 'irrational from the point of view of not being able to think the way that [he, the doctor] was thinking, which [he] thought was more rational'. The actual irrationality referred to was the patient's decision to undergo the operation only if the cosmetic procedure were included. In the result the Court held that the patient's 'apparent consent' was insufficient to protect the surgeon from liability in negligence on the basis of failure to obtain informed consent. It is not exactly clear how much the irrationality of the patient's decision influenced his holding, but it seems that such irrationality should at least put the physician on notice that the patient's 'decision was not based upon any knowledge or appreciation of the risk', in which case the physician may not rely on the consent as being valid. This case is probably a demonstration of a court looking to the rationality of the patient's decision to indicate both whether the patient had the required understanding of the risks that must be understood in order to give informed consent, and whether the physician had, or ought to have had, knowledge of any lack of understanding on the part of he patient.

In summary, the question of rationality in matters of consent is difficult. To allow (or even more so, require) second-guessing of the patient's decision according to whether that decision is rational may seriously detract from autonomy (which it is the purpose of consent to protect). The more a person's decision deviates from what the person assessing that decision would decide in the same circumstances, and the more serious the consequences of that decision, the more likely it is that the person making the decision will be labelled incompetent and his decision irrational. Rather than judging the rationality of a patient's decision and validating or invalidating consent on that basis, the better solution (which was probably the approach of the Court in *Kelly v Hazlett*) is to adopt understanding by the patient of the information required to be disclosed as the necessary safeguard. Pursuant to such an approach, provided the patient is otherwise judged to be competent, if the physician has no subjective knowledge that the patient lacks understanding and the reasonable physician would have believed that the patient apparently understood the information disclosed, the resulting consent may be relied upon as valid whether or not the patient's decision is considered rational.

In a paternalistic physician-patient relationship, consent was often the *imprimatur* of the doctor's rational decision-making on the patient's behalf. Under a doctrine of informed consent the aim is to enable the patient to make a decision on his own behalf. A remaining question is how far the physician is justified in carrying out a patient's informed, irrational decisions. The physician is far less likely to be acting within legal or ethical limits when implementing such a decision requires a positive intervention on his part, than when it is a situation in which he must desist from violating the patient's physical or mental integrity against his will. More explicitly, a patient's irrational refusal of treatment should be accorded greater respect than his irrational demand for it.

(a) Re C test

English law does not equate assessment of capacity with the right decision, the reasonableness of that decision or the rationality of the reasoning process. The law was developed in the judgment of the Thorpe J in *Re C (adult: refusal of medical treatment)*.

Re C (adult: refusal of medical treatment) [1994] 1 All ER 819 (Fam Div)

Thorpe J: This originating summons was issued on 4 October 1993 by C. It seeks under the court's inherent jurisdiction an injunction restraining Heatherwood Hospital, Ascot from amputating his right leg without his express written consent.

The plaintiff is 68 and of Jamaican origin. He came to England in 1956, his passage being paid by the woman with whom he had lived since 1949. In 1961 she left him, and in 1962 he accosted her at work and after an altercation stabbed her. He was sentenced at the Old Bailey to seven years' imprisonment. While serving that sentence he was diagnosed as mentally ill and transferred from Brixton to Broadmoor. On admission he was diagnosed as suffering from chronic paranoid schizophrenia. He was treated both with drugs and ECT. Over the years he has mellowed and has been accommodated for the past six years on an open ward of the parole house. He is described as neat and tidy, becoming more sociable with staff and other patients in the past two years.

On 6 August 1993 his annual medical revealed no physical problems. However, on 9 September the staff noticed that he had a swollen leg. The Broadmoor surgeon diagnosed gangrene in the foot and he was transferred to Heatherwood Hospital. On 10 September he was seen there by Dr Ghosh, a consultant forensic psychiatrist, and his resident medical officer at Broadmoor. He told her that he had knocked his foot in the shower about three weeks earlier. On the same day he was seen by Mr Rutter, the consultant vascular surgeon at Heatherwood. He found a grossly infected right leg with an necrotic ulcer covering the whole of the dorsum. Mr Rutter considered that he would die imminently if the leg were not amputated below the knee. He assessed the chances of survival with conservative treatment no better than 15%, but C refused to consider amputation. He said that he would rather die with two feet than live with one. Mr Rutter nevertheless booked him in for amputation on 16 September in the hope that consent would be forthcoming when C had had time to adjust to the prospective loss of the limb.

There followed a period of some confusion. At first, Broadmoor thought that the operation could be performed without consent if two consultants agreed that he was not of sound mind to decide. Then Dr Gosh arranged for a solicitor, Miss Scott-Moncrieff, to see him on 14 September. Thereafter she made plain that there would be no consent forthcoming and discussion took place with Mr Leslie, the hospital's solicitor, as to who would initiate court proceedings. In the meantime, Mr Colley was treated with antibiotics and made some improvement.

On 15 September Dr Ghosh applied pressure on C to consent, pressure which reflected her concerns and feelings at the prospect of what she regarded as his imminent and unnecessary death. He did not yield. Since Mr Rutter had made it plain that he was not prepared to amputate without C's unequivocal consent, the operation was abandoned. Thereafter Mr Rutter negotiated more conservative surgery with C. On 22 September he obtained his consent to debridement of the dead tissue under general anaesthetic. C rejected a more localised spinal injection because of the risk of paralysis. The operation was performed on 23 September and was successful. Although the ulcerated area was increased to measure 4 inches by 2.5 inches, the edges of the wound had good blood supply increasing the chance of healing. By 6 October, granulation tissue had reached the level of the surrounding skin and Mr Rutter agreed with C that he would next take skin from his thigh to graft over the wound. So the 85% of imminent death predicted on 10 September had by 6 October been averted.

On 29 September Miss Scott-Moncrieff had requested an undertaking from Mr Leslie that the hospital would not amputate in any future circumstances in recognition of C's repeated refusals. That request was refused on 4 October and on the same day this originating summons was issued. Arrangements were made for it to be heard on 8 October at Heatherwood Hospital. In preparation, Miss Scott-Moncrieff instructed Dr Eastman, who is consultant and senior lecturer in forensic psychiatry at St George's Hospital, and Mr Leslie arranged for Dr Gall, consultant psychiatrist at Heatherwood Hospital, to report.

The evidence on 8 October came from Dr Eastman, Mr Rutter and C. On the second day I heard Dr Gall, Dr Ghosh and legal submissions. Dr Eastman saw C on 6 October and reported comprehensively in writing on 7 October. In his oral evidence he emphasised that schizophrenia is an all-pervasive illness. Features present in C's case include grandiose and persecutory delusions as well as incongruity of affect, a technical term meaning mismatch between the words spoken and the accompanying emotional display. For the patient offered amputation to save life, there are three stages to the decision: (1) to take in and retain treatment information, (2) to believe it and (3) to weigh that information, balancing risks and needs. C had, in Dr Eastman's opinion, achieved the first stage but not the second. Did his disbelief in the imminence of death arise out of his mental illness or other ordinary convictions, or a combination of both? Of course, if to others he showed greater appreciation of the risk of death, that was evidence that he had proceeded further in the progressive stages. It was significant that the persecutory delusions did not include the conviction that his present condition had been caused by agencies at Broadmoor or Heatherwood. For Dr Eastman, the ultimate conclusion should be reached by weighing in the scales the preservation of life against the autonomy of the patient. If the patient's capacity to decide is unimpaired, autonomy weighs heavier, but the further capacity is reduced, the lighter autonomy weighs. Plainly, C's capacity is reduced by his mental illness. But for him the decision as to whether it is sufficiently reduced remains marginal in the absence of any direct link between the persecutory delusions and his present condition.

Mr Rutter had reported in writing on 16 September and 6 October. In contrast to his reports, his evidence was unexpectedly forthright. He said that he had definitely not decided to amputate on 10 September. He had heard later that Dr Ghosh was prepared to authorise the operation, but he was not prepared to accept that. He felt that the only chance for C to regain mobility was to agree to amputation. Accordingly, he took an active decision not operate then or at any future time without C's consent. His assessment was that all C's responses were normal. Even if he deteriorated in future, he would not amputate. Knowing C had made a definitive decision and because he did not regard his mental state as deviating much from the mean, he would respect his wishes and treat him with intravenous antibiotics. He believes in the sanctity of the individual's choice, even if it be wrong. He frequently meets people who do not want amputation and he would not force it on them unless they were so confused or comatose as not to recognise that he was a doctor. For the future, he believes that the condition of the foot will once again threaten C's life. He suffers from peripheral vascular disease with the small vessel variant which is not amenable to bypass surgery. Whilst the wound is healing at present, it is likely that the foot or some other area of his extremities may become necrotic. Infection from the dead tissue would then spread to other organs and cause them to fail. However, there is a possibility that the foot may be maintained in healing to provide a limb contributing to mobility with the aid of a stick or frame. If gangrene returns, it might be in the dry form, resulting in a mummified foot that would still serve as a prop. Only if gangrene returns in the wet form would his life again be threatened. Finally, Mr Rutter established that a below-knee amputation carries with it a 15% mortality risk.

C's oral evidence did not add much to what had been reported by Dr Eastman and Dr Gall. He expressed the grandiose delusions of an international career in medicine during the course of which he had never lost a patient. He affirmed his complete faith in God and, subject to one reservation, in the Bible. He expressed complete confidence in his ability to survive his present trials aided by God, the good doctors and the good nurses. Although he recognised that he would die, death would not be caused by his foot. As he made clear in re-examination, that was his belief, although he could not say that that would not happen. Throughout he expressed his rooted objection to amputation. He did not ascribe the condition of his foot to persecution by authority. As in his interview with Dr Gall, he accepted the possibility of death as a consequence of retaining his limb.

Dr Gall assessed C at interviews on 22 September and 5 October. He reported in writing on 6 October with addendum on 7 October. He heard Dr Eastman's evidence and he agreed with it. He said that the differences between him and Dr Eastman were so fine as not to be worth expressing. Significantly, he also said that he agreed with Mr Rutter's assessment of the extent of C's deviation from the mean, certainly as C now is overall, mentally and physically.

Dr Ghosh has had responsibility for C since May 1992. She has seen him monthly since that date. In addition, she visits his ward weekly. She has developed a relationship within which she has C's trust and confidence. She reported on 15 September and again on 6 October. She disagrees with Dr Eastman and Dr Gall. She considers C incompetent to decide major medical matters because of (1) his grandiose delusion that he was a doctor and (2) his persecutory delusion that whatever treatment is offered is calculated to destroy his body. His capacity to decide is not absent but very seriously reduced. Far from being on the borderline, she regards the case as very clearcut.

Amongst the experts, my very clear conclusion is that the opinion of Dr Eastman and Dr Gall is to be preferred. They did not find any direct link between C's refusal and his persecutory delusions, nor was any to be found in C's oral evidence. Furthermore, it was clear to me that C was quite content to follow medical advice and to co-operate in treatment appropriately as a patient as long as his rejection of amputation was respected.

Unfortunately, Dr Ghosh had never discussed the case with Mr Rutter. When she wrote as she did on 6 October and testified on 11 October, she was unaware of the dramatic aversion of the risk of death over the preceding four weeks. On 11 October she still regarded the limb as dead below the knee and death within a maximum of two years as certain without an amputation. She did not know that amputation carried a significant mortality risk. I have no doubt that this lack of information influenced her appraisal of the critical equation and of C's approach to it.

I was also impressed by the evidence of Mr Rutter, who had obviously considered his professional dilemma profoundly and had made a shrewd appraisal of C's capacity over the weeks in which their relationship had developed.

C himself throughout the hours that he spent in the proceedings seemed ordinarily engaged and concerned. His answers to questions seemed measured and generally sensible. He was not always easy to understand and the grandiose delusions were manifest, but there was no sign of inappropriate emotional expression. His rejection of amputation seemed to result from sincerely held conviction. He had a certain dignity of manner that I respect … submissions divide over the definition of the capacity which enables an individual to refuse treatment. Mr Gordon argues for what he calls the minimal competence test, which he defines as the capacity to understand in broad terms the nature and effect of the proposed treatment. It is common ground that C has the legal capacity to initiate these proceedings without a next friend, within the terms of RSC Ord 80. Mr Gordon contends that the capacity to refuse treatment is no higher and is equally no higher than the capacity to contract. I reject that submission. I think that the question to be decided is whether it has been established that C's capacity is so reduced by his chronic mental illness that he does not sufficiently understand the nature, purpose and effects of the proffered amputation.

I consider helpful Dr Eastman's analysis of the decision-making process into three stages: first, comprehending and retaining treatment information, second, believing it and, third, weighing it in the balance to arrive at choice. The Law Commission has proposed a similar approach in para 2.20 of its consultation paper 129, *Mentally Incapacitated Adults and Decision-Making*. Applying that test to my findings on the evidence, I am completely satisfied that the presumption that C has the right of self-determination has not been displaced. Although his general capacity is impaired by schizophrenia, it has not been established that he does not sufficiently understand the nature, purpose and effects of the treatment he refuses. Indeed, I am satisfied that he has understood and retained the relevant treatment information, that in his own way he believes it, and that in the same fashion he has arrived at a clear choice.

I accept Mr Jackson's submission that C might have the capacity to make a present refusal but lack the capacity to make an anticipatory refusal, but I reject that conclusion because in weighing the consequences of facing a future acute phase without amputation he has the experience of a recent acute attack to guide him.

Thorpe J granted the injunction sought.

You will notice that Thorpe J adopted a three-stage test for establishing a patient's capacity or competence to decide:

1. could the patient *comprehend* and *retain* the necessary information;
2. was he able to *believe* it; and
3. was he able to *weigh* the information, balancing risks and needs, so as to arrive at a choice?

This elaboration can be seen in one of two ways. First, it can be seen as a practical approach to determining whether a patient has the ability to understand, ie satisfy the *Gillick* test. He will not, unless he can comprehend and retain, believe and weigh the relevant information. On this view, Thorpe J has put some 'meat on the bones' of the *Gillick* test. A second interpretation is to see Thorpe J as having gone slightly beyond the *Gillick* test, thereby broadening the category of incompetent patients. Whilst comprehension and belief go to understanding, retaining the information and the capacity to weight it do not, and yet according to Thorpe J, failure to do so will render the patient incompetent in law. There is some force in the second argument. Indeed some judges regard the *Gillick* test as irrelevant outside of cases concerned with the competence of children where their capacity turns upon their developmental stage rather than mental disability or disorder (see *infra*, p 650). In our view, however, the first explanation of Thorpe J's judgment is preferable. In truth, the ability to understand requires all the elements that Thorpe J identifies. For instance, it would be wrong to describe a person as truly understanding the nature of their decision if the long-term implications were retained only transitorily. Likewise, a patient who cannot weigh information in anything like a dispassionate or considered way because their mental disorder ensures they dismiss or disregard certain information, cannot be said, we would suggest, to have the ability to understand what they are purporting to decide.

Subsequently in *Re MB (medical treatment)* (1997) 38 BMLR 175, the Court of Appeal adopted the three-stage test in *Re C*.

Re MB (an adult: medical treatment) (1997) 38 BMLR 175 (CA)

MB, the appellant, aged 23, was admitted to one of the respondent's hospitals on 14 February 1997. She was 40 weeks pregnant and the foetus was in the breech position. She signed a consent form for a caesarian section delivery, but refused to consent to a venepuncture to provide necessary blood samples. She subsequently refused to consent to the insertion of the veneflon, necessary for the anaesthetic to perform the caesarian section delivery. She did agree to anaesthesia by mask, but, following an explanation to her of the risks attendent upon such a procedure, she withdrew her consent to it and to caesarian section delivery. On 18 February she went into labour and agreed to delivery by caesarian section, providing she did not feel the needle involved in the anaesthesia. Later that day, in the operating theatre she refused to consent to anaesthesia by mask and the surgery was cancelled. The defendant health authority then sought and obtained, from Hollis J, a declaration that it would be lawful to perform a caesarian section to deliver the foetus. MB instructed her lawyers to appeal that decision the same evening. On the following day she agreed to the induction of anaesthesia and she was delivered of a healthy male infant by caesarian section on 19 February 1997. The appeal against Hollis J's decision was based on four grounds: (1) that he was wrong to hold that the appellant lacked capacity to consent; (2) that he had failed to make a finding as to what were the appellant's best interests; (3) that the evidence did not establish that the proposed treatment of her was in her best interests and (4) that it was unlawful at common law to use force on a mentally competent patient in order to impose medical treatment upon her.

Here, we only consider the first ground of appeal, namely whether MB was competent to refuse the treatment (for the other issues, see *infra*, ch 6). Speaking for the court, Butler-Sloss LJ approached the issue as follows.

Butler-Sloss LJ: *Conclusions on capacity to decide ...*

(1) Every person is presumed to have the capacity to consent to or to refuse medical treatment unless and until that presumption is rebutted.

(2) A competent woman, who has the capacity to decide, may, for religious reasons, other reasons, for rational or irrational reasons or for no reason at all, choose not to have medical intervention, even though the consequence may be the death or serious handicap of the child she bears, or her own death. In that event the courts do not have the jurisdiction to declare medical intervention lawful and the question of her own best interests, objectively considered, does not arise.

(3) Irrationality is here used to connote a decision which is so outrageous in its defiance of logic, or of accepted moral standards, that no sensible person, who had applied his mind to the question to be decided, could have arrived at it. As Kennedy and Grubb *Medical Law* (2nd edn, 1994) point out, it might be otherwise if a decision is based on a misperception of reality (eg, the blood is poisoned because it is red). Such a misperception will be more readily accepted to be a disorder of the mind. Although it might be thought that irrationality, sits uneasily with competence to decide, panic, indecisiveness and irrationality, in themselves, do not as such amount to incompetence, but they may be symptoms or evidence of incompetence. The graver the consequences of the decision, the commensurately greater the level of competence is required to take the decision: *Re T (adult: refusal of medical treatment)* (1992) 9 BMLR 46, [1993] Fam 95; *Sidaway v Bethlem Royal Hospital Governors* (1985) 1 BMLR 132 at 159, [1985] AC 871 at 904; and *Gillick v West Norfolk and Wisbech Area Health Authority* (1985) 2 BMLR 11 at 19–20, 35, [1986] AC 112 at 169, 186.

(4) A person lacks capacity if some impairment or disturbance of mental functioning renders the person unable to make a decision whether to consent to, or to refuse, treatment. That inability to make a decision will occur when: (a) the patient is unable to comprehend and retain the information which is material to the decision, especially as to the likely consequences of having, or not having, the treatment in question; (b) the patient is unable to use the information and weigh it in the balance as part of the process of arriving at the decision. If, as Thorpe J observed in *Re C*, a compulsive disorder or phobia from which the patient suffers stifles belief in the information presented to her, then the decision may not be a true one. As Lord Cockburn CJ put it in *Banks v Goodfellow* (1870) LR 5 QB 549 at 569: 'One object may be so forced upon the attention of the invalid as to shut out all others that might require consideration.'

(5) The 'temporary factors' mentioned by Lord Donaldson MR in *Re T* (confusion, shock, fatigue, pain or drugs) may completely erode capacity but those concerned must be satisfied that such factors are operating to such a degree that the ability to decide is absent.

(6) Another such influence may be panic induced by fear. Again, careful scrutiny of the evidence is necessary because fear of an operation may be a rational reason for refusal to undergo it. Fear may also, however, paralyse the will and thus destroy the capacity to make a decision.

There are a number of general points to notice here. First, Butler-Sloss LJ did not, in the passage set out above, repeat verbatim the three-stage test of *Re C*. In fact, she omits the middle stage completely – namely, that the patient is able to *believe* the information. It could, therefore, be argued that the law is not as stated in *Re C*. This would, in our view, be a misreading of the Court of Appeal's judgment. The court referred approvingly to the *Re C* test on a number of occasions. Also, the court's own views on the effect of a patient's 'misperception of reality' effectively relies on the middle stage of the *Re C* test to reach a finding of incompetence.

Secondly, the court dispels any basis for equating outcome (reasonable or otherwise) and the rationality of a decision, with incompetence. By 'rationality' is meant that the patient has applied a process of reasoning to the issue and that the conclusion arrived at can be justified by reference to that process. This is an immensely difficult criterion to deploy. Are we not entitled to be irrational? See, for example, decisions about whom we marry, the job we take, the house we buy, the political party we support. Arguably a distinction must be drawn between a decision based upon beliefs or values not commonly held or accepted (eg a Jehovah's Witness's refusal of a blood transfusion) and a decision based upon a misperception of reality (eg that blood is a poison because it is red). In both cases the decisions are based upon premises which most find unintelligible and, therefore, we may be prepared to regard the decisions as irrational. There is, however, an important distinction. The premise of the Jehovah's Witness, for example, is one derived from the individual's value system. Provided the decision is consistent with those values, the decision can only be challenged by refusing to accept (by merely asserting) that the basic premise is wrong. By contrast, in the case of the patient who thinks blood is a poison, the decision can be demonstrated to be based upon a false premise of fact. The individual, unlike the Jehovah's Witness, does not understand what is involved in the treatment (see *Re MB*, *op cit* per Butler-Sloss LJ at 186). The Jehovah's Witness does understand but rejects the treatment for his own reasons based upon his value system. For the sake of completeness, it is of no consequence that the misapprehension that blood is a poison is a result of a temporary delusion, eg in the case of a schizophrenic, or is a long-held view based upon a perverse understanding of the world.

The criterion of rationality more than any other highlights the clash between respect for autonomy and beneficence which is often at the root of decisions about competence. Of course, to talk of beneficence as being in conflict with respect for autonomy is to a certain extent to beg an important question. One of the major drawbacks in appeals to beneficence is that to urge that one should seek to do good does not answer the questions 'What is good?' and 'Who decides?'. Furthermore, on a closer analysis, respect for autonomy may be the most highly prized form of doing good which would mean that the alleged clash between respect for autonomy and beneficence does not materialise. It would also follow that the guiding principle in determining the criteria of competence ought, therefore, to be respect for autonomy.

The courts, in respecting autonomy, must be aware of those circumstances in which the patient's views are the product of a belief or value system or a misperception of reality. Clearly for a court to accept (and to allow the patient to act upon) a decision derived from the latter is not to respect a patient's autonomy but to undermine it. In such a case a court could well take the view that the patient is unable to understand what is involved and is, therefore, incompetent.

Thirdly, the Court of Appeal linked incompetence to 'some impairment or disturbance of mental functioning' (*op cit* at 186). This is important and is reflected in the Law Commission's proposals that a patient's inability to decide must be the result of 'mental disability' (see Draft Mental Incapacity Bill, cl 2(1) and (2)). We put to one side here the patient whose physical disability renders them unable to communicate. The point is that many patients may reject their doctors' advice or see the world in a different way such that the premise (or one of the premises) upon which they reach a decision is different from the doctors' or others. The patient is not thereby rendered incompetent. Rather, this is really the stuff of an individual's ability to make choices for themselves based upon their own values, judgments and reasons (see *infra*).

Fourthly, incapacity may be temporary or permanent and may be due to external factors such as pain, drugs, fatigue and shock (see *Re R (Adult: Refusal of Medical Treatment)* [1993] Fam 95 at 102 per Lord Donaldson MR). As we shall see, there are dangers here of too readily equating the effects of such factors with incompetence, as has occurred in some obstetric cases (see *infra*). The Court of Appeal emphasised the need for the patient's capacity to be 'completely erode[d]'.

Fifthly, the Court of Appeal reiterated the statement of Lord Donaldson MR in *Re T*, *supra* that a patient's capacity must be 'commensurate with the gravity of the decision ... The more serious the decision, the greater the capacity required'. Precisely what this means is unclear. It cannot mean that the courts require greater reasoning powers the more serious the decision. What it can, or course, be understood to require is that the patient should be able to understand more information the more serious the decision and that the courts will give the most careful scrutiny to the process of reaching such decisions, in particular where the patient's life is at stake.

(b) Applying the Re C test

In considering how the *Re C* test has been applied by the courts and how it should be applied, it is useful to consider *four* types of case, always bearing in mind that these are not watertight compartments – there can be overlap – but they are nevertheless helpful, in our view, in developing the analysis: (i) beliefs and value systems; (ii) misperceptions of reality; (iii) compulsive or driven behaviour; and (iv) external factors.

(i) BELIEFS AND VALUE SYSTEMS

It is at the heart of respect for a patient's autonomy that he or she should be permitted to chose whether or not to consent to medical treatment based upon their personal view of their own well-being. In setting the boundary between competence and incompetence the law seeks to give effect to this tenet of a liberal society. However, tensions soon emerge when others (doctors in our context) find the reasons for a patient's choice unfathomable or apparently absurd. To what extent will a patient's religious beliefs affect their capacity to decide? For example, Jehovah's Witnesses may not accept a blood transfusion or the use of blood products according to their faith and some religious groups will refuse all medical intervention.

The point arose directly in *Re T (adult: refusal of treatment)* [1992] 4 All ER 649 (CA) in which an adult woman, apparently a Jehovah's Witness, refused a life-saving blood transfusion. On the facts, the Court of Appeal held that her decision was invalid because it was based solely upon the persuasion, ie undue influence of her mother who was a Jehovah's Witness (see *infra*). Nevertheless, the judges squarely faced up to whether, if she had been a Jehovah's Witness, her decision would have been legally effective. In deciding that it would have been, the court accepted that she would have been competent (ie would have understood what was involved) even though she came to a decision most would find unreasonable and irrational.

Lord Donaldson MR stated that:

> [A patient's] right of choice is not limited to decisions which others might regard as sensible. It exists notwithstanding that the reasons for making the choice are rational, irrational, unknown or even non-existent ...

Later he pointed out:

> That [the patient's] choice is contrary to what is to be expected of the vast majority of adults is only relevant if there are other reasons for doubting his capacity to decide. The nature of his choice or the terms in which it is expressed may then tip the balance.

Similarly, Butler-Sloss LJ stated:

> A man or woman of full age and sound understanding may choose to reject medical advice and medical or surgical treatment whether partially or in its entirely. A decision to refuse medical treatment by a patient capable of making the decision does not have to be sensible, rational or well-considered ...

Subsequently, Lord Donaldson MR in *Re W (a minor) (medical treatment)* [1992] 4 All ER 627 stated that:

> I personally consider that religious or other beliefs which bar any medical treatment or treatment of particular kinds are irrational, but that does not make minors who hold beliefs any the less 'Gillick competent' [*a fortiori* adults]. They may well have sufficient intelligence and understanding fully to appreciate the treatment proposed and the consequences of their refusal to accept that treatment.

You will recall that the Court of Appeal in *Re MB (supra)* confirmed that a religious belief which founds a patient's decision would not lead to a finding of incompetence. There are two explanations of the law's position here.

I Kennedy and A Grubb (eds) *Principles of Medical Law* (1998)

> 3.76 . . . First, the law defers to religiously based decisions made by adults, though not those made on behalf of children, as a matter of social tolerance. Providing the person understands what is entailed in their decision, there is no reason for the law to deprive the individual of decision-making power. It would be an act of unjustified state interference to override decisions made on religious grounds. Secondly, and perhaps of more general importance for medical law, such decisions do not stem from any mental disability or mental malfunctioning on the part of the patient. Apart from situations where the patient is unable to communicate his decision, a necessary condition for depriving an individual of decision-making power, and justifying state intervention in his 'best interests', is that the patient is suffering from a mental malfunctioning having a pathological or psychological etiology. It is the impairment or disturbance in the patient's mental ability to understand which potentially renders him, in law, incompetent.

We should not forget that art 9 of the European Convention on Human Rights protects a person's 'right to freedom of though, conscience and religion'. Enforced treatment contrary to a patient's religious beliefs would undoubtedly infringe art 9 and could not be justified solely by virtue of the argument that it was necessary to protect *that person's* life. (Contrast where the decision is that of parents in relation to their child, *infra*, ch 6.)

It is clear that most of the cases in which the understanding of the patient will be questioned on the grounds that the beliefs giving rise to it are irrational will involve religious beliefs. Jehovah's Witnesses and Christian Scientists are two classic examples. It is possible, however, to postulate decisions being based upon beliefs unrelated to religion. The case of *Re Maida Yetter* provides an illustration.

Re Maida Yetter (1973) 96 D & C 2d 619 (CP Northampton County PA)

> **Williams J:** This matter involves the appointment of a guardian of the person for Maida Yetter, an alleged incompetent, under the Incompetents' Estates Act of February 28, 1956, PL (1955) 1154, as amended, 50 PS $3101, et seq. The petition was filed by Russell C

Stauffer, her brother, a citation issued on May 10, 1973. The citation was served on the alleged incompetent by a deputy sheriff of Lehigh County at Allentown State Hospital, Lehigh County Pa, on May 15, 1973. A hearing was held on May 30, 1973, as specified in the petition. Present at the hearing were petitioner and his counsel, Dr Ellen Bischoff, a psychiatrist on the staff of the hospital; Mrs Marilou Perhac, a caseworker at the hospital assigned to Mrs Yetter's ward; the alleged incompetent and her counsel. Mrs Yetter is married, although she has been separated from, and has had no contact with, her husband since 1947.

From the petition and the testimony it appears that the primary purpose of the appointment of a guardian of the person is to give consent to the performance of diagnostic and corrective surgery.

Mrs Yetter was committed to Allentown State Hospital in June 1971, by the Courts of Northampton County after hearings held pursuant to section 406 of the Mental Health and Mental Retardation Act of October 20, 1966, Sp Sess, PL 96, 50 PS $4406. Her diagnosis at that time was schizophrenia, chronic undifferentiated. It appears that late in 1972, in connection with a routine physical examination, Mrs Yetter was discovered to have a breast discharge indicating the possible presence of carcinoma. The doctors recommended that a surgical biopsy be performed together with any additional corrective surgery that would be indicated by the pathology of the biopsy. When this recommendation was first discussed with Mrs Yetter in December of 1972 by her caseworker, Mrs Perhac, who had weekly counselling sessions with Mrs Yetter for more than a year, Mrs Yetter indicated that she would not give her consent to the surgery. Her stated reasons were that she was afraid because of the death of her aunt which followed such surgery and that it was her own body and she did not desire the operation. The caseworker indicated that at this time Mrs Yetter was lucid, rational and appeared to understand that the possible consequences of her refusal included death.

Mr Stauffer, who indicated that he visits his sister regularly, and Dr Bischoff, whose direct contacts with Mrs Yetter have been since March 1973, testified that in the last three or four months it has been impossible to discuss the proposed surgery with Mrs Yetter in that, in addition to expressing fear of the operation, she has become delusional in her reasons for not consenting to surgery. Her tendency to become delusional concerning this problem, although no others, was confirmed by Mrs Perhac. The present delusional nature of Mrs Yetter's reasoning concerning the problem was demonstrated at the hearing when Mrs Yetter, in response to questions by the court and counsel, indicated that the operation would interfere with her genital system, affecting her ability to have babies, and would prohibit a movie career. Mrs Yetter is 60 years of age and without children.

Dr Bischoff testified that Mrs Yetter is oriented as to time, place and her personal environment, and that her present delusions are consistent with the diagnosis and evaluation of her mental illness upon admission to the hospital in 1971. The doctor indicated that, in her opinion, at the present time Mrs Yetter is unable, by reasons of her mental illness, to arrive at a considered judgment as to whether to undergo surgery.

Mrs Stauffer testified that the aunt referred to by Mrs Yetter, although she underwent a similar operation, died of unrelated causes some 15 years after surgery.

He further indicated that he has been apprised by the physicians of the nature of the proposed procedures and their probable consequences as well as the probable consequences if the procedures are not performed. He indicated that if he is appointed guardian of the person for his sister he would consent to the surgical procedures recommended.

At the hearing Mrs Yetter was alert, interested and obviously meticulous about her personal appearance. She stated that she was afraid of surgery, that the best course of action for her would be to leave her body alone, that surgery might hasten the spread of the disease and do further harm, and she reiterated her fears due to the death of her aunt. On several occasions during the hearing she interjected the statements that she would die if surgery were performed. It is clear that mere commitment to a state hospital for treatment of mental illness does not destroy a person's competency or require the appointment of a guardian of the estate or person. Ryman's case, 139 Pa Superior Ct 212. Mental capacity must be examined on a case by case basis.

In our opinion, the constitutional right of privacy included the right of a mature competent adult to refuse to accept medical recommendations that may prolong one's life and which, to a third person at least, appear to be in his best interests; in short, that the right of privacy includes a right to die with which the State should not interfere where there are no minor or unborn children and no clear and present danger to public health, welfare or morals. If the person was competent while being presented with the decision and in making the decision which she did, the court should not interfere even though the decision might be considered unwise, foolish or ridiculous.

While many philosophical articles have been published relating to this subject there are few appellate court decisions and none in Pennsylvania to our knowledge. The cases are collected in an annotation in 9 ALR 3d 1391. Considering other factors which have influenced the various courts, the present case does not involve a patient who sought medical attention from a hospital and then attempted to restrict the institution and physicians from rendering proper medical care. The State hospital as Mrs Yetter's custodian certainly has acted properly in initiating the present proceeding through the patient's brother and cannot be said to have either overridden the patient's wishes or merely allowed her to die for lack of treatment.

The testimony of the caseworker with respect to her conversations with Mrs Yetter in December 1972, convinces us that at that time her refusal was informed, conscious of the consequences and would not have been superseded by this court. The ordinary person's refusal to accept medical advice based upon fear is commonly known and while the refusal may be irrational and foolish to an outside observer, it cannot be said to be incompetent in order to permit the State to override the decision.

The obvious difficulty in this proceeding is that in recent months Mrs Yetter's steadfast refusal has been accompanied by delusions which create doubt that her decision is the product of competent, reasoned judgment. However, she has been consistent in expressing the fear that she would die if surgery were performed. The delusions do not appear to us to be her primary reason for rejecting surgery. Are we then to force her to submit to medical treatment because some of her present reasons for refusal are delusional and the result of mental illness? Should we now override her original understanding but irrational decision?

There is no indication that Mrs Yetter's condition is critical or that she is in the waning hours of life, although we recognise the advice of medical experts as to the need for early detection and treatment of cancer symptoms. Upon reflection, balancing the risk involved in our refusal to act in favour of compulsory treatment against giving the greatest possible protection to the individual in furtherance of his own desires, we are unwilling now to overrule Mrs Yetter's original irrational but competent decision.

Mrs Yetter's delusion that she had a prospect of becoming a movie star and having babies was judged an irrational delusion which provided strong evidence that she was unable to understand what was being proposed. On the other hand, her aversion to surgery based upon the death of her aunt fifteen years earlier, was not regarded as evidencing an inability to understand though obviously many would regard it as irrational. She had held this view for some time, had lived by it and ordered her life by it. It is of no consequence that others may disagree with it (see also *Re Quackenbush* 383 A 2d 785 (1978) – where a person with a conscientious objection to medical treatment and had shunned treatment for forty years was held competent to refuse life-sustaining surgery).

The Court of Appeal in *Re MB (supra)* pointed out that such views may be some evidence of incompetence because they may lead to the conclusion that the patient is suffering from an impaired or disturbed mental functioning. But it is only some evidence. Much will depend upon the psychiatric evidence, but it is clear that the court will carefully scrutinise this and bizarre behaviour may be consistent with understanding. In *St George's Healthcare NHS Trust v S* (1998) 44 BMLR 160 the Court of Appeal held that a woman was competent to refuse obstetric care and was not suffering from a mental disorder despite the fact that everyone (including the court) could not understand the basis for her behaviour in refusing treatment that was likely to endanger her unborn child. Judge LJ stated as follows:

> The Act cannot be deployed to achieve the detention of an individual against her will merely because her thinking process is unusual, even apparently bizarre and irrational, and contrary to the views of the overwhelming majority of the community at large. The prohibited reasoning is readily identified and easily understood. Here is an intelligent woman. She knows perfectly well that, if she persists with this course against medical advice, she is likely to cause serious harm, and possibly death, to her baby and to herself. No normal mother-to-be could possibly think like that. Although this mother would not dream of taking any positive steps to cause injury to herself or her baby, her refusal is likely to lead to such a result. Her bizarre thinking represents a danger to their safety and health. It therefore follows that she *must* be mentally disordered and detained in hospital in her own interests and those of her baby. The short answer is that she may be perfectly rational and quite outside the ambit of the Act, and will remain so notwithstanding her eccentric thought process.

This final point should, perhaps, be seen in a more general way. The importance lies in applying the second ('ability to believe') and third ('ability to weigh') stages of the *Re C* test. As regards the former, not every patient who disbelieves their doctor's advice fails the second-stage of the test and is incompetent: indeed most will not be incompetent. In *B v Croydon DHA* (1994) 22 BMLR 13 at 20 Thorpe J (at first instance) returning to his earlier creation in *Re C* drew an important distinction between outright disbelief due to mental disorder where the patient is 'impervious to reason, divorced from reality, or incapable of adjustment after reflection' and 'the tendency which most people have when undergoing medical treatment to self assess and then puzzle over the divergence between medical and self-assessment'. Merely to take a different view of the world from a doctor may result in a patient 'disbelieving' him but it should not render the patient incompetent and thus unable to decide, as a matter of law, for themselves. Even a skewed and indefensible view of the world does not have this effect *unless* it has its genesis in what might be termed, mental 'malfunctioning'.

Likewise a patient may have the ability to weigh the information but for reasons particular to him, reach a decision that the doctor (or court) would not. That is the patient's choice and the decision may be based upon the patient's own perception of the world or values providing it is not the product of distorted or deluded perceptions stemming from mental malfunctioning, in particular the very mental disorder for which treatment is needed. The latter occurred in *Tameside and Glossop Acute Services Trust v CH* [1996] 1 FLR 762 (Wall J). Here, the patient refused obstetric intervention which is was considered was necessary to prevent stillbirth. The patient was a paranoid schizophrenic and held a psychotic and deluded belief that her own doctors were malicious and intended to harm the child. The judge authorised her treatment under s 63 of the Mental Health Act 1983 (see, *infra*, ch 6) but concluded that she failed the *Re C* test. Undoubtedly, the patient's lack of belief in her doctors and their advice fell outside the realms of normal scepticism and was based upon a mental disability. As a result, the patient was properly seen as unable to decide for herself.

(ii) MISPERCEPTION OF REALITY

Here the issue is clearer. Someone who is deluded about the world – in our context they do not accept what is happening to them or what treatment may offer for them – is not capable of understanding what is involved.

State of Tennessee v Northern (1978) 563 SW 2d 197 (Tenn Ct App)

Todd J: On January 24, 1978, the Tennessee Department of Human Services filed this suit alleging that Mary C Northern was 72 years old, with no available help from relatives; that Miss Northern resided alone under unsatisfactory conditions as a result of which she had been admitted to and was a patient in Nashville General Hospital; that the patient suffered from gangrene of both feet which required the removal of her feet to save her life; that the patient lacked the capacity to appreciate her condition or to consent to necessary surgery.

Attached to the complaint are identified letters from Drs Amos D Tackett and R Benton Adkins which read as follows:

Mrs Mary Northern is a patient under our care at Nashville General Hospital. She has gangrene of both feet probably secondary to frost bite and then thermal burning of the feet. She has developed infection along with the gangrene of her feet. This is placing her life in danger. Mrs Northern does not understand the severity or consequences of her disease process and does not appear to understand that failure to amputate the feet at this time would probably result in her death. It is our recommendation as the physicians in charge of her case, that she undergo amputation of both feet as soon as possible.

The judge then turned to consider whether Miss Northern had capacity to refuse the treatment.

… Capacity means mental ability to make a rational decision, which includes the ability to perceive, appreciate all relevant facts and to reach a rational judgment upon such facts.

Capacity is not necessarily synonymous with sanity. A blind person may be perfectly capable of observing the shape of small articles by handling them, but not capable of observing the shape of a cloud in the sky.

A person may have 'capacity' as to some matters and may lack 'capacity' as to others. ...

In the present case, this Court has found the patient to be lucid and apparently of sound mind generally. However, on the subjects of death and amputation of her feet, her comprehension is blocked, blinded or dimmed to the extent that she is incapable of recognising facts which would be obvious to a person of normal perception.

For example, in the presence of this Court, the patient looked at her feet and refused to recognise the obvious facts that the flesh was dead, black, shrivelled, rotting and stinking.

The record also discloses that the patient refuses to consider the eventuality of death which is or ought to be obvious in the face of such dire bodily deterioration.

As described by the doctors and observed by this Court, the patient wants to live and keep her dead feet, too, and refuses to consider the impossibility of such a desire. In order to avoid the unpleasant experience of facing death and/or loss of feet, her mind or emotions have resorted to the device of denying the unpleasant reality so that, to the patient, the unpleasant reality does not exist. This is the 'delusion' which renders the patient incapable of making a rational decision as to whether to undergo surgery to save her life or to forego surgery and forfeit her life.

The physicians speak of probabilities of death without amputation as 90% to 95% and the probability of death with surgery at 50-50 (1 in 2). Such probabilities are not facts, but the existence and expression of such opinions are facts which the patient is unwilling or unable to recognise or discuss.

If as repeatedly stated, this patient could and would give evidence of a comprehension of the facts of her condition and could and would express her unequivocal desire in the face of such comprehended facts, then her decision, however unreasonable to others, would be accepted and honoured by the Courts and by her doctors. The difficulty is that she cannot or will not comprehend the facts.

The court was clearly influenced by Miss Northern's refusal to comprehend the facts of her situation. In a concurring judgment, Judge Drowota emphasises this important factor in *Northern*.

Drowota J: In the instant case, the Court found that Miss Northern does not have the capacity to decide whether her feet should or should not be amputated. This finding is not based on any belief by this Court that a competent adult should not be permitted to reject lifesaving treatment. It is *not*, as has been argued to us, based on any idea of this Court that any person who refuses treatment we subjectively think a 'normal' or 'rational' person would choose is 'incompetent' merely because of that refusal. It is based on the Court's finding that Miss Northern is unable or unwilling to comprehend even dimly certain very basic *facts*, without which no one, whether elderly lady, doctor, or judge, would be competent to make such a decision. These facts include the appearance of her feet, which are disfigured, coal black, crusty, cracking, oozing, and rancid. Yet, Miss Northern looks at them and insists that nothing is wrong. Also included was the fact that her doctors are of the opinion that her life is in danger, yet she has expressed no understanding of either the gravity or the consequences of her medical condition. Again, this Court respects Miss Northern's right to disagree with medical condition. Again, this Court respects Miss Northern's right to disagree with medical opinions and advice. Again, if this Court in good faith could find that she perceived as facts that her feet *do* look and smell as they do, and that her doctors *are* telling her that she needs surgery to save her life, we would not interfere with whatever decision she made regardless of how much it conflicted with the substance of her medical advice or with what we ourselves might have chosen. But from our honest evaluation of the facts and evidence of this case, we have been forced to conclude that Miss Northern does not comprehend such basic facts and hence is currently incompetent to decide this particular question. While this finding was made more difficult by Miss Northern's apparent ability to grasp facts not related to the condition of her feet, it is nonetheless correct.

Since Miss Northern was not competent to decide the question of amputation, it fell ... to this Court to do so. Again, the question for me is what would Miss Northern decide if she understood the facts. The presumption with any person must be that he would want surgery that would increase the chance of life from 5–10 to 50% unless some statement made or attitude held while the patient was competent contradicts the presumption. No such contradiction exists in Miss Northern's case. Further, the presumption is strengthened, if anything, by Miss Northern's assertion that she does not want to die. Medically, her feet are dead and lost to her whether or not they are amputated. Psychotic effects are likely if surgery is done, but are quite possible even if Miss Northern survives and loses her feet without surgery. Her prognosis is poor either way, but there is a substantially better chance of life if the surgery is performed. In these circumstances, this Court simply could not find that Miss Northern, if she had a basic understanding of the situation, would not choose the substantially greater chance of life that surgery offers. Our Decision has been made accordingly …

But it is important to distinguish a case such as *Northern*, where the irrationality of the patient's decision affects his understanding, and one in which (albeit rarely) the court takes the view that his understanding remains unimpaired despite the surrounding irrationality.

Lane v Candura (1978) 376 NE 2d 1232 (Mass App Ct)

This case concerns a 77-year-old widow, Mrs Rosaria Candura, of Arlington, who is presently a patient at the Symmes Hospital in Arlington suffering from gangrene in the right foot and lower leg. Her attending physicians recommended in April that the leg be amputated without delay. After some vacillation, she refused to consent to the operation, and she persists in that refusal…

The principal question arising on the record before us, therefore, is whether Mrs Candura has the legally requisite competence of mind and will to make the choice for herself …

A person is presumed to be competent unless shown by the evidence not to be competent … Such evidence is lacking in this case. We recognise that Dr Kelly, one of two psychiatrists who testified, did state that in his opinion Mrs Candura was incompetent to make a rational choice whether to consent to the operation. His opinion appears to have been based upon (1) his inference from her unwillingness to discuss the problem with him that she was unable to face up to the problem or to understand that her refusal constituted a choice; (2) his characterisation of an unwilling[ness], for whatever reason, to consent to life saving treatment … as suicidal; and (3) a possibility, not established by evidence as a reasonable probability, that her mind might be impaired by toxicity caused by the gangrenous condition. His testimony, read closely, and in the context of the questions put to him, indicates that his opinion is not one of incompetency in the legal sense, but rather that her ability to make a rational choice (by which he means the *medically* rational choice) is impaired by the confusions existing in her mind by virtue of her consideration of irrational and emotional factors.

A careful analysis of the evidence in this case, including the superficially conflicting psychiatric testimony, indicates that there is no real conflict as to the underlying facts. Certainly, the evidence presents no issue of credibility. The principal question is whether the facts established by the evidence justify a conclusion of legal incompetence. The panel are unanimous in the opinion that they do not.

The decision of the judge, as well as the opinion of Dr Kelly, predicates the necessity for the appointment of a guardian chiefly on the irrationality (in medical terms) of Mrs Candura's decision to reject the amputation. Until she changed her original decision and withdrew her consent to the amputation, her competence was not questioned. But the irrationality of her decision does not justify a conclusion that Mrs Candura is incompetent in the legal sense. The law protects her right to make her own decision to accept or reject treatment, whether that decision is wise or unwise. …

Similarly, the fact that she has vacillated in her resolve not to submit to the operation does not justify a conclusion that her capacity to make the decision is impaired to the point of legal incompetence. Indeed, her reaction may be readily understandable in the light of her prior surgical experience and the prospect of living the remainder of her life nonambulatory. Senile symptoms, in the abstract, may, of course, justify a finding of incompetence, but the inquiry must be more particular. What is lacking in this case is evidence that Mrs Candura's areas of forgetfulness and confusion cause, or relate in any way to, impairment of her ability to understand that in rejecting the amputation she is, in effect, choosing death over life.

… This case is like *Re Quackenbush*, 156 NJ Super 282, 383 A 2d 785 (Morris County Ct 1978), in which an elderly person, although subject (like Mrs Candura) to fluctuations in mental lucidity and to occasional losses of his train of thought, was held to be competent to reject a proposed operation to amputate gangrenous legs because he was capable of appreciating the nature and consequences of his decision. …

Mrs Candura's decision may be regarded by most as unfortunate, but on the record in this case it is not the uninformed decision of a person incapable of appreciating the nature and consequences of her act. We cannot anticipate whether she will reconsider and will consent to the operation, but we are all of the opinion that the operation may not be forced on her against her will.

The case of *Re C* (*adult: refusal of medical treatment*) (*supra*) itself illustrates the point that a mentally-ill patient may have the capacity to consent or refuse consent even if he suffers from delusions, providing the patient is capable of understanding what is proposed. C was 68 years old and developed gangrene in his right foot. He refused to consent to an amputation of his right leg below the knee. He sought an injunction to restrain his doctors from amputating the leg without his express consent. In granting the injunction, Thorpe J held that C sufficiently understood the 'nature, purpose and effects' of the proposed amputation despite the fact that C was a chronic paranoid schizophrenic and suffered from delusions of grandeur, for example that he had an international medical practice. Thorpe J concluded that C was able to comprehend and retained the relevant information, believe it and weigh the information, balance the risks and needs, and arrive at a choice. He was, therefore, competent to refuse the medical intervention.

There is another circumstance in which a patient may fail to understand what is involved. The patient's illness may be of such a type as to impair understanding of their condition (ie induce a misperception of reality) though in other respects they retain the ability to manage their lives. The paradigms in such cases are the person *suffering from anorexia nervosa* and the person of *fluctuating lucidity* (in particular the manic depressive).

Denial that there is anything wrong their physical conditions is a common aspect of a person with anorexia nervosa. It is tantamount to a statement that they do not need to eat because they have a deluded image of their own body. As we shall see, their compulsive behaviour may render them incompetent applying the third stage of the *Re C* test (*infra*), but they also are not able to believe, just as Mrs Northern was not, that there is anything wrong with them. In *Re KB (adult) (mental patient: medical treatment)* (1994) 19 BMLR 144 the patient refused to eat because she thought she was fat and needed to reduce her weight. The medical evidence was that these 'deranged thought processes' were a product of a mental disorder and rendered the patient incompetent. Ewbank J, in authorising treatment under s 63 of the Mental Health Act 1983, agreed and accepted the evidence that the patient 'does not understand the true situation' (at 145).

The case of a patient with what we have called fluctuating lucidity is also particularly problematical. Between periods of depressive illness or manic moods the patient may experience spells of normality. During such a spell, he may deny that he is ill and refuse the medication which has produced the current spell of normality and is prescribed to prevent the onset of another period of illness, in the mistaken view that he is cured. Once the illness begins to take hold again, the patient becomes unable to understand that he is ill and may have to be restrained so as to be treated. The dilemma for the law is whether to regard the decision to refuse medication while lucid as a valid refusal or whether to regard it as the product of a syndrome the total effect of which is to undermine the patient's capacity to understand what is involved. The latter view allows the patient to be treated before the onset of illness albeit contrary to the apparent will of the patient.

The law is probably otherwise if the patient while lucid does not deny that he suffers swings in mood but simply insists that now that he feels better he will not take the prescribed medication. In our view, in this case the patient is competent in that he is capable of understanding what is involved. Any attempt to save him from himself by averting the onset of another period of illness may only be achieved lawfully (unless he is a child) by treating him under Part IV of the Mental Health Act 1983 which provides for treatment of mental illness or disorder without consent in certain circumstances.

It would, of course, be helpful if the 1983 Act gave us some clear guidance in this sort of case. Not surprisingly, however, the Act speaks in terms of a patient (in order to be competent) being 'capable of understanding the nature, purpose and likely effects of … treatment' (see ss 57(2)(a) and 58(3)(a)). This, of course, leads nowhere in the difficult cases, except that in relation to some treatments for mental illness the Act permits treatment even if the patient is competent and is refusing treatment (s 58).

A case which illustrates the mental conditions we have called fluctuating lucidity is *Re R (a minor) (wardship: consent to treatment)*.

Re R (a minor) (wardship: consent to treatment) [1992] Fam 11, (1991) 7 BMLR 147 (CA)

Lord Donaldson MR: R was born on 15 September 1975 and is therefore 15 years and 10 months old. Her family had been known to the social services for over 12 years and at an earlier stage she had been on the local authority's at-risk register as one who was thought to be a possible victim of emotional abuse. She was a child who gave rise to anxiety because of poor and sometimes violent parental relationships and difficulties generally in establishing boundaries in her life.

Those worries became more acute this year when, on 8 March 1991, she was received into voluntary care after a fight with her father. She claimed she felt it was unsafe to stay in the house with him. She was placed first with emergency foster parents and then at a children's home maintained by the local authority.

While in care she asked not to see her father and showed some ambivalence about her wish to return to live in the care of either parent. Anxiety developed about her mental health. She seemed often flat and expressionless and resistant to being touched by anyone. She appeared to experience visual and auditory hallucinations and sometimes suicidal thoughts. She was accordingly referred to a consultant child psychiatrist, Dr R.

Early in May 1991 her mother went to the children's home and cancelled the voluntary care order under which she had been admitted. R went back home but stayed only a few minutes and then ran off. She was found and returned to the children's home but then ran off again and was found by the police on a bridge over the River Thames threatening suicide. In these circumstances the local authority sought and was granted a five-day place of safety order. R was then placed in a small children's home from which she absconded that night, being found by police the following day at her parents' home.

An interim care order was granted on 24 May and R was persuaded to return to the general children's home to which she had originally been admitted. Her behaviour however was increasingly disturbed. On the same night she had to be the subject of an emergency psychiatric assessment due to her increasingly paranoid and disturbed behaviour.

The psychiatrist who saw her on that occasion was of the opinion that she was ill enough to be the subject of an application under ss 2 and 3 of the Mental Health Act 1983. This view was confirmed by R's subsequent behaviour. She absconded from the children's home and went back to her own house where she ran amok doing serious damage to the building and furniture. She made a most savage attack on her father and also assaulted her mother. Thereafter she calmed down but her behaviour remained highly variable with substantial swings of mood. The downward swings became serious enough for an application to be made on 2 June 1991 for her admission under s 2 of the Mental Health Act 1983. She at once again absconded and attacked her parents, but this time in the presence of an emergency social worker and two psychiatrists.

She was placed in the psychiatric ward of a general hospital and remained there for one week. On 7 June 1991 she was discharged to a more suitable centre for the treatment of someone of her age, namely an adolescent psychiatric unit (the unit) which specialises in disturbance problems in young people of her age.

When the social worker principally concerned with R attended a case review at the unit she was further given a disturbing account of R's progress there. The senior registrar and director of child psychiatry stated that concern was growing over R's mental health to the extent that serious thought was being given to the use of compulsory medication because she was becoming increasingly defiant. Furthermore she was denying her past experience of hallucinations and voices, alleging that she had made it all up. The social worker was advised by the staff of the unit that they had been using sedation from time to time whenever they felt the situation warranted it, but that had always been done with R's consent. When the social worker asked R about this, she replied that she had given her consent because she felt she had no choice, since if she had refused they would have injected her with drugs anyway.

Eventually matters came to a head in events which gave rise to R becoming a ward of court and to the application granted by Waite J. On 28 June 1991 the social worker received a telephone call from a senior consultant at the unit stating that he believed R to be in a psychotic state and that he wanted the permission of the local authority, as the body exercising legal responsibility for R under the care order, to administer anti-psychotic medication to her. The consultant assured the social worker that this was not a decision taken out of the blue, advising her that R was acting extremely paranoid, becoming extremely argumentative, hostile and accusative.

After consulting higher authority within the social services, the social worker telephoned back to the unit giving the local authority's consent to the administration of such medication as the medical authorities of the unit might think necessary.

Later that evening R herself telephoned the social services night duty department. She advised the duty social worker (who happened to be experienced in problems of this kind, being an approved social worker under the Mental Health Act) that the unit were trying to give her drugs. She said she did not need them and she did not want to take them. It was a very long conversation indeed, lasting some three hours. The social worker decided that R sounded lucid and rational and he did not regard her as 'sectionable', ie liable to be made the subject of an application under s 2 and s 3 of the Mental Health Act 1983. Urgent consultation took place within the social services department and as a result a decision was taken that, on reflection, the local authority could not give the necessary permission for R to have the drugs administered to her against her will.

On 3 July 1991 R was again seen by Dr R, the consultant child psychiatrist. R admitted to him that she had been suffering from labile mood swings, fewer suicidal ideas than previously and visual and auditory hallucinations, although not so frequent or persecuting as before. She behaved calmly and was rational.

Dr R reported that:

> I believe that she still requires treatment as an in-patient but that she has improved sufficiently for the Mental Health Act not to be relevant. (She also needs to be involved in later, planned assessment for care proceedings.) She is of sufficient maturity and understanding to comprehend the treatment being recommended and is currently rational. Should she not continue with the [unit] treatment, her more florid psychotic behaviour is likely to return, and she might become a serious suicidal risk. I do not believe that out-patient treatment is adequate for her at this time. I also believe that her family situation is too chaotic for her to be able to return home at this time.

The unit had by then made it clear that it was essential, if R was to remain a patient in its care, that it should have an entirely free hand in regard to the administration of medication to her, whether she was willing or not. Accordingly on 5 July the local authority decided to have recourse to wardship proceedings.

Dr R gave evidence both in the form of report and orally. He explained the nature and functions of the unit. It operated, he said, a very carefully thought out procedure. If an adolescent patient behaved disturbingly, there was first a meeting of the whole community. Then that may have to be followed by exclusion of the adolescent to his or her bedroom and, finally, and only as a last resort, tranquillising medication is administered which is, or often may be, medication of the same nature and effects as drugs prescribed for anti-psychotic purposes. That step was only taken if it was absolutely necessary to enable the staff to cope.

He confirmed that the unit could only continue to accept responsibility for R if their regime was acceptable to whoever had parental responsibility for her. The message from the local authority that they could not give consent to medication administered against her will had the result that, unless that could be changed, the unit would be unable to continue to care for her.

Dr R stated that, if R were to lapse into a fully psychotic state, she would be a serious suicidal risk. She would be potentially very violent and unpredictable in her behaviour and liable to hear persecuting voices. It would be likely, he said, that she would return within some days or weeks to a state of mind in which ss 2 or 3 of the Mental Health Act would have to be invoked. He was asked whether she was familiar with the decision in *Gillick*'s case and said that he was and that he had applied the principles there considered to the circumstances of R's case. He expressed his conclusion in the following answers to questions during his oral examination:

> Q. I think there are two elements we should perhaps look at, and the first of them is whether the proposed treatment is for the benefit and protection of a minor. Could you just comment on that limb for us? *A.* Yes, I think, as I have described, that if [R] were to receive the treatment that has been recommended I think it is highly likely that her condition would improve significantly.
>
> Q. The second matter we must consider is whether, having regard to her development and maturity, she understands the nature and the implications of the treatment proposed.

Can you comment on that? *A*. Yes, I felt that she is mature enough to understand the nature of the proposal. When I saw her on [4 July] she was rational and, I thought, of sufficient understanding to be able to make a decision in her own right.

Q. Have you actually seen for yourself when she has been in a condition displaying mental illness? *A*. No, not a florid state where, or example, at the time she needed to be admitted under a section, but I have seen her when I was extremely concerned about her killing herself and experiencing hallucinations and feeling persecuted, but her behaviour was not as floridly excitable or unpredictable at that time.

Q. When was that that you saw her in that condition, just approximately? *A*. This was the beginning of May.

Q. Would your comments about her understanding and consent be any different when applied to [R] in that condition? *A*. Yes. I also recall that I saw her at the [meeting to assess her suitability for admission to the unit] while she was [in the adult psychiatric ward at the general hospital] when she was behaving very aggressively and, yes, I felt in those circumstances her rationality and capacity to understand recommendations was severely impaired.

Q. When she is in that condition would your assessment of her be one that she is or is not capable of giving an important consent about treatment? *A*. In a florid psychotic stage I think she is unable to give informed consent and therefore I agreed with my colleagues, who decided to section her under the Mental Health Act, even though that is extremely rare in our practice.

Gillick competence

The test of 'Gillick competence', although not decisive in this case is nevertheless of general importance and the evidence of Dr R suggests that it is capable of being misunderstood. The House of Lords in that case was quite clearly considering the staged development of a normal child. For example, at one age it will be quite incapable of deciding whether or not to consent to a dental examination, let alone treatment. At a later stage it will be quite capable of both, but incapable of deciding whether to consent to more serious treatment. But there is no suggestion that the extent of this competence can fluctuate upon a day-to-day or week-to-week basis. What is really being looked at is an assessment of mental and emotional age, as contrasted with chronological age, but even this test needs to be modified in the case of fluctuating mental disability to take account of that misfortune. It should be added that in any event what is involved is not merely an ability to understand the nature of the proposed treatment – in this case compulsory medication – but a full understanding and appreciation of the consequences both of the treatment in terms of intended and possible side effects and equally important, the anticipated consequences of a failure to treat.

On the evidence in the present case it is far from certain that Dr R was saying that R understood the implication of treatment being withheld, as distinct from understanding what was proposed to be done by way of treatment – 'the nature of the proposal' which I take to have been intended as a paraphrase of Lord Scarman's 'to understand fully what is proposed'. But, even if she was capable on a good day of a sufficient degree of understanding to meet the *Gillick* criteria, her mental disability, to the cure or amelioration of which the proposed treatment was directed, was such that on other days she was not only 'Gillick incompetent', but actually sectionable. No child in that situation can be regarded as 'Gillick competent' and the judge was wholly right in so finding in relation to R. ...

'Gillick competence' is a developmental concept and will not be lost or acquired on a day-to-day or week-to-week basis. In the case of mental disability, that disability must also be taken into account, particularly where it is fluctuating in its effect.

Farquharson LJ: Counsel for the Official Solicitor, Mr Munby QC, submitted that the court should determine the application on the *Gillick* principle (see *Gillick v West Norfolk and Wisbech Area Health Authority* [1985] 3 All ER 402, [1986] AC 112). Counsel argued on that authority that the parental right to determine whether a child should have medical treatment terminates if and when the child achieves a sufficient understanding and intelligence to enable him or her to understand fully what is proposed. If the child has the capacity to give a consent valid in law it is not for the court to substitute its own different view. On the other hand, if the child is shown not to have that capacity, then the court has the power and duty to substitute its own decisions if it is different from that of the child.

The learned judge accepted this analysis of the position in law, but came to the conclusion on the evidence available to him that R had not the necessary capacity to make this decision. She was in his judgment a deeply disturbed and unhappy child, who in making her decision had been the victim of her own immaturity. He accordingly granted the application.

The Official Solicitor then brought the present appeal because as counsel informs us it involves important questions of principle. So far as R is concerned however, it seems that the decision of this court will have little impact, as she is likely to be subjected to the medication whether the appeal succeeds or not. If Waite J's decision is upheld, as I think it should be, she will be treated at the unit, otherwise she will receive the medication, at any rate in Dr R's opinion, at an adult hospital.

Mr Munby of course supports the learned judge's statement of the law but complains that there was no evidence upon which he could find that R lacked the capacity to make a decision about her treatment. Counsel relied on the evidence of Dr R about R's state of mind of 3 July which was the most recent account of her condition. Dr R had found on 3 July, just a few days before the judge heard the application, that R was rational and of sufficient understanding to be able to make a decision in her own right. In the face of that evidence counsel submits there was no room for the judge to come to what in effect was the opposite conclusion.

In my judgment, this submission cannot be sustained. It involves assessing the mental state and capacity of the patient at a particular moment in time, isolated from the medical history and background. It is clear from Dr R's evidence and indeed from the evidence of the three-hour telephone conversation that from time to time R had clear intervals when her mental illness was in recession. It is equally clear from Dr R's evidence that this state was neither permanent nor even long term. The prognosis was that if the medication was not given to R she would return to her earlier florid psychotic state. It would be dangerous indeed if the learned judge, or for that matter this court, refused to authorise the medication because on a particular day R passed the *Gillick* test when the likely consequences were so serious. In deciding whether the court's decision is to be substituted for that of the patient it is the task of the court to consider the whole of the medical background of the case as well as the doctor's opinion of the effect of its decision upon the patient's mental state. On the facts of this case, I am clearly of the opinion that the judge's decision was correct.

Staughton LJ agreed that R was incompetent and that, therefore, treatment could be authorised in her best interests.

Although the court undoubtedly arrived at the right result the reasons deployed for doing so are open to criticism. As you will have seen, the court arrived at its decision by concluding that *Gillick* did not apply. This is a somewhat perverse reading of *Gillick* and we return to it later.

The issue in *Re R*, as in all cases, was simply put, if not simply determined, 'Was R able to understand what was involved?' On the evidence, it is arguable that R (like the anorexic) was unable to understand by virtue of her denial that she had suffered a 'past experience of hallucinations and voices' which she claimed she had just made up.

Our conclusion as regards these difficult cases that test the meaning and application of the legal concept of competence is that it is more respectful of patients' autonomy to interpret *incompetence* so as to include the manic depressive and the anorexic (where appropriate) rather than regard them as apparently competent and then do wholesale violence to the law's commitment to the rights of decision-making of the competent.

(iii) COMPULSIVE OR DRIVEN BEHAVIOUR

Some mental disorders may have the effect of rendering an individual incompetent to make a treatment decision because they are unable to weigh at all, or in any satisfactory way, the information relevant to the decision. Illustrations of this include compulsive eating disorders, drug addiction or compulsive phobias or personality disorders. As regards the decision related to their compulsion, these patients would be unable to 'weigh' the information as required by the third stage of the *Re C* test.

Consider first the person suffering from anorexia nervosa (on which, see P Lewis 'Feeding Anorexic Patients Who Refuse Food' (1999) 7 Med L Rev 21). In *Re W (a minor) (medical treatment)* [1992] 4 All ER 627, (1992) 9 BMLR 22 (CA), W, a girl aged 16, was suffering from anorexia nervosa. Her condition was such that it was felt by those caring for her that she should be cared for at a specialist institution and that the doctors should have the option, if they considered it necessary, to force feed her as a last resort. She, however, refused to be moved or treated in this way. The court was asked to decide whether it could authorise her removal and treatment against her stated wishes in the exercise of its inherent jurisdiction. Central to this question, as we shall see later, was whether W was competent to decide about her medical treatment. The trial judge (Thorpe J) held that she was on the basis that '… there is no doubt at all that W is a child of sufficient understanding to make an informed decision'. The Court of Appeal accepted this finding but held, as we shall see, that the court nevertheless could override her competent refusal (*infra*, ch 6). Lord Donaldson MR expressed the view, however, that W could have been considered incompetent. He stated:

> [W]ith all respect I do not think that Thorpe J took sufficiently into account (perhaps because the point did not emerge as clearly before him as it did before us) … that it is a feature of anorexia nervosa that it is capable of destroying the ability to make an informed choice. It creates a compulsion to refuse treatment or only to accept treatment which is likely to be ineffective. This attitude is part and parcel of the disease and the more advanced the illness, the more compelling it may become. Where the wishes of the minor are themselves something which the doctors reasonably consider need to be treated in the minor's own best interests, those wishes clearly have a much reduced significance.

Balcombe LJ also noted that 'it is a feature of anorexia nervosa that it is capable of destroying the ability to make an informed choice', but, unlike Lord Donaldson MR, he did not cast any doubt on Thorpe J's finding that she was competent. Nolan LJ simply accepted Thorpe J's view. In our view, Lord Donaldson MR was correct to doubt W's competence given the effect of anorexia upon a patient's capacity to understand her condition and hence what is involved. Had this been the basis for the court's authorising treatment, the very problematic issue of the court's power to override a competent minor's refusal of treatment would have been avoided.

What Donaldson MR is saying in *Re W* is that the patient has no choice, in effect, because they cannot but refuse the treatment. The effect of the compulsion need not, however, be so great. It may be rather that the patient's mental disorder or disability 'clouds their judgment' such that their decision cannot really be said to be a considered one. The next case illustrates that.

Re C (a minor) (detention for medical treatment) [1997] 2 FLR 180 (Fam Div)

C, aged 16, showed early symptoms of anorexia nervosa at the age of 12. The disease was diagnosed in 1995 when she was admitted to the clinic, a private hospital for the treatment of eating disorders run on boarding-school lines. The local authority funded her treatment, but never sought to take her into care, preferring to cooperate with the family despite the dysfunctional nature of the family situation. After C's discharge from the clinic her health deteriorated rapidly. She was detained in hospital under the Mental Health Act 1983 and later admitted to another hospital. Eventually in November 1996 she was readmitted to the clinic. There her behaviour continued to be disturbed and aggressive and at times suicidal. She absconded four times within a month. At that stage the consultant psychiatrist and the medical director of the clinic both made it clear that they would not readmit C without a court order. In early December 1996 the local authority as plaintiff obtained leave ex parte under s 100 of the Children Act 1989 to invoke the inherent jurisdiction. The matter was confirmed inter partes and an order made giving leave for C to be detained at the clinic for such treatment as was prescribed, with the use of force if necessary. The court gave liberty to apply, fixed the hearing for 17 February 1997 and invited the Official Solicitor to act as amicus curiae. The principal questions raised were (1) whether the court when exercising its inherent parens patriae jurisdiction in relation to a child of 16 has power to direct the detention of the child in a specific institution for the purpose of medical treatment; and (2) whether, in the event of the child consenting to treatment, the deprivation of liberty was an essential part of the treatment or was irrelevant to the treatment process, and whether in the latter case the inherent jurisdiction was being used solely for the deprivation of liberty. C stated that she was content to stay in the clinic voluntarily and receive treatment but she disputed the need for an order.

Here we only consider the issue of C's competence to decide. Wall J concluded she lacked competence in law.

Wall J: *The psychiatric assessments of C: is she competent to consent to or refuse treatment within Re C?*
As I have already made clear, the test which I have to apply if I exercise the inherent jurisdiction is whether or not an order such as that being sought is in C's best interests. It is also common ground that in deciding what is in C's best interests I must have regard to her wishes and feelings, although, plainly, I can override her wishes if what she wants is not in her best interests.

C's capacity to give or refuse consent to treatment is relevant to my decision, but is not determinative of it. Clearly, however, if the evidence is that C has the capacity to give or refuse consent then the weight which should be given to her wishes is increased. C is currently saying that she wishes to remain in the clinic on a voluntary basis and will accept the treatment programme offered. What weight should I give to that expression of intent?

In *Re C (Refusal of Treatment)* [1994] 1 FLR 31, 33E, Thorpe J (as he then was) accepted Dr Eastman's analysis of the decision-making process as comprising three stages, namely (1) comprehending and retaining treatment information, (2) believing it, and (3) weighing it in the balance to arrive at choice. I apply those three tests to C.

On this point, the psychiatric evidence is crucial. Dr D is not a psychiatrist. Apart from the historical psychiatric reports I had up-to-date reports from Dr W, the psychiatrist at the clinic and Dr D2, instructed on behalf of C herself. Dr W was unwilling to give oral evidence on the grounds that he was engaged in an ongoing therapeutic relationship with C and her parents, and Mr Wood did not insist on his presence in court. I did, however, hear oral evidence from Dr D2.

On paper there was no disagreement between the psychiatrists. Both agreed that C failed the third of the *Re C* tests. As Dr D2 put it in her report:

'Regrettably the inherent jurisdiction of the court relates only to in-patient care, the involvement of the court ceasing when C leaves the clinic. Despite this, and despite my considerable misgivings about its use in these circumstances when it has been used as a last-ditch alternative in the absence of care proceedings, I feel that it would be against C's interests at the present time to discontinue the order. Although C appears to be consenting, this is in a very superficial way. She lacks the ability to make a realistic assessment of the short- and long-term consequences of refusal. This is because her desire to minimise events in the past overrides her undoubted intellectual inability to make this evaluation. Consequently her apparent consent is given only to the basics of treatment rather than the whole substance. I believe that it is highly likely that she would cease to co-operate fully in the absence of an order ...'

Dr W agreed. He put the matter this way:

'I am not completely clear as to what is meant by "treatment information" in this situation, but if what is meant is information about the necessary amount of food to maintain weight or similar information then I believe C to be quite capable to taking in, understanding and believing such information. The problem lies in her capacity to use that information, when necessary to balance risks and needs. It is my view that C is easily able to selectively ignore what she knows, or to twist or distort such information so that it suits her immediate purposes without heed for the long-term consequences. I believe that it is likely that these distorting processes happen largely unconsciously and she is not always able to control them. It is a feature of anorexia nervosa and related eating disorders that information is distorted in this way. The immediate gratification involved in being able to override the pangs of hunger, and to feel in control, is such that worries about the effects on the body, and eventually threats to life itself, are ignored.

C had received all the necessary factual information during her first admission to the clinic and her readmission to [the hospital]. However, that she was clearly unable to weigh this information was demonstrated by her immediate and severe loss of weight following discharge.

It is my belief that C is unable to exercise a fully rational capacity to consent to or refuse treatment, as she is unable to access such information when to do so does not suit her immediate aim.'

Dr D2 moved her position slightly in her oral evidence, in that she had become less convinced that the order of the court detaining C in the clinic was having the effect of facilitating treatment. Dr D2 based this, I think, largely on C's abscondence on 13 February 1997. I have to say that insofar as she changed her opinion, that change seemed to me unwarranted. C's abscondence seemed to me to underline the need for an order of detention to facilitate treatment rather than the reverse. In the event, however, Dr D2 did not depart from her recommendation that the court should continue to use its inherent jurisdiction to enforce treatment at the clinic until C was in a fit state to be discharged, and in cross-examination by Mr Munby adhered to her original view that C did not have the capacity to make a realistic assessment of the short- and the long-term consequences of a refusal of treatment. Given Dr D's expanded time-scale, however, Dr D2 recommended that the matter should be kept under review by the court.

I have no hesitation in accepting the psychiatric evidence that C is unable to weigh treatment information, balancing risks and needs, and accordingly is not able to give a valid consent to or refusal of treatment. Whereas C does not wish there to be an order, I accept the evidence of Drs D and W (and the evidence of Dr D2 in her written report) that an order of the court is essential in order to maintain C's treatment at the clinic. I have already made it clear that I consider treatment in the clinic as being in her best interests. Exercising the inherent jurisdiction I plainly have the power to override C's objections to an order being made, if I perceive, as I did, that an order is necessary.

The psychiatric evidence was that C was unable to use the information that she was given about her condition. The effect of her illness was that she minimised past events and selectively ignored or distorted the information. On the basis of this, Wall J concluded that C was not competent to make a decision about the treatment for her mental disorder. In his view, she failed the third stage of the *Re C* three-stage test, namely she was 'unable to weigh treatment information, balancing risks and needs'. There can be no quibble with the actual finding of incompetence in this case in the light of the psychiatric evidence before the court.

We have already alluded to the dangers of necessarily seeing incongruous decisions as ones where the patient was really unable to 'weigh' the information (*supra*). The third stage of the *Re C* test is not an open invitation for a court to make a finding of incompetence simply because the patient's decision is difficult to understand (see *Re MB*, *supra*, at 187).

An example of a 'phobia' which may render a patient unable to make a treatment decision occurred in *Re MB (op cit)* itself (see also *Re L (an adult: non-consensual treatment)* [1997] 1 FCR 609 (Kirkwood J)). There, the patient suffered from 'needle phobia', such that she was quite unable to agree to an injection as a precursor to a caesarean section. In finding her incompetent to make *that* decision, Butler-Sloss LJ speaking for the Court of Appeal said:

We find: (1) MB consented to a caesarian section; (2) what she refused to accept was not the incision by the surgeon's scalpel but only the prick of the anaesthetist's needle. Capacity is commensurate with the gravity of the decision to be taken. (3) She could not bring herself to undergo the caesarian section she desired because, as the evidence established, 'a fear of needles ... has got in the way of proceeding with the operation ... At the moment of panic ... her fear dominated all ... at the actual point she was not capable of making a decision at all ... at that moment the needle or mask dominated her thinking and made her quite unable to consider anything else'.

On that evidence, she was incapable of making a decision at all. She was at that moment suffering an impairment of her mental functioning which disabled her. She was temporarily incompetent. In the emergency, the doctors would be free to administer the anaesthetic if that were in her best interests.

It is important to notice that the Court of Appeal, in stating the principles to be applied which were set out earlier (*supra*, p 624), emphasised that the fear must be extreme, it must 'paralyse the will and thus destroy the capacity to make a decision' (*op cit* at 187).

(For a case concerned with a personality disorder leading to compulsive self-harm, see *B v Croydon HA* (1994) 22 BMLR 13 (CA): 'I find it hard to accept that someone who acknowledges that in refusing food at the critical time she did not appreciate the extent to which she was hazarding her life, was crying inside for help but unable to break out of the routine of punishing herself, could be said to be capable of aiming a true choice as to whether or not to eat' per Hoffmann LJ at 30.)

(iv) EXTERNAL FACTORS

Apart from beliefs that some may find strange or misperceptions of reality, the circumstances in which decisions are made by patients must never be forgotten. Patients are usually under stress and may well be in pain or under the influence of medication. In such circumstances their powers of reasoning may be affected. This is not to argue that these patients are necessarily unable to understand what is involved but merely to suggest that great care must be taken in responding to requests and decisions in each case. As Lord Donaldson MR pointed out in *Re T* (*op cit*):

> Others who would normally have ... capacity may be deprived of it or have it reduced by reason of temporary factors, such as unconsciousness or confusion or other effects of shock, severe fatigue, pain or drugs being used in their treatment.

In *Re MB* (*op cit*) the Court of Appeal entered a cautionary note. Butler-Sloss LJ stated:

> (5) The 'temporary factors' mentioned by Lord Donaldson MR in *Re T* (confusion, shock, fatigue, pain or drugs) may completely erode capacity but those concerned must be satisfied that such factors are operating to such a degree that the ability to decide is absent.

The reason for this is undoubtedly the Court of Appeal's concern over a number of earlier decisions in which pregnant women were held to be incapable of making decisions about their obstetric care whilst in labour. The first of these cases was *Norfolk and Norwich Healthcare (NHS) Trust v W*.

Norfolk and Norwich Healthcare (NHS) Trust v W [1997] 1 FCR 269 (Fam Div)

> The patient arrived at hospital in the last stages of pregnancy. She was fully dilated and ready to deliver her baby but was in a state of arrested labour. However, she denied that she was even pregnant. She had a history of psychiatric treatment and had had three previous pregnancies all terminating by Caesarian section. It was necessary to take action. The consultant obstetrician sought authority to bring the patient's labour to an end by way of forceps delivery and, if necessary, by Caesarian section. If this action was not taken there were two risks to the patient: first that if the foetus was not delivered it would suffocate within the patient which would have life-threatening consequences for the health of the patient; and second that the patient's old Caesarian scars would reopen with a consequent risk to the life of the foetus and the health of the patient. A consultant psychiatrist interviewed the patient. In his opinion she was not suffering from a mental disorder but he was unable to say whether she was capable of comprehending and retaining information about the proposed treatment nor whether she was capable of believing information given to her about the treatment. However, he was of opinion that she was not able to balance the information given to her.

Johnson J held that she was incompetent and that termination of the pregnancy was in her best interest. As regards the former, he stated:

> In reliance upon the opinion of the consultant psychiatrist and taking account of the information I had about the statements made by the patient during the course of the day, I held that although she was not suffering from a mental disorder within the meaning of the statute, she lacked the mental competence to make a decision about the treatment that was proposed because she was incapable of weighing up the considerations that were involved. She was called upon to make that decision at a time of acute emotional stress and physical pain in the ordinary course of labour made even more difficult for her because of her own particular mental history.

In another case, heard the same day, the same judge in *Rochdale Healthcare (NHS) Trust v C* [1997] 1 FCR 274 reached a similar conclusion.

Rochdale Healthcare (NHS) Trust v C [1997] 1 FCR 274 (Fam Div)

The patient was in hospital for the birth of the child. The consultant obstetrician was of opinion that a Caesarian section was necessary. He was of opinion, and told the patient that without the operation both she and the child would die.

The patient would not agree to a Caesarian section as she had had a previous delivery in this way and subsequently suffered backache and pain around the resulting scar. She said she would rather die than have a Caesarian section again.

The operation was required urgently and an application was made to the court less than an hour before it would need to be carried out.

The consultant obstetrician was of opinion that the mental capacity of the patient was not in question and that she seemed to be fully competent. She was capable of comprehending and retaining information about the proposed treatment and of believing such information.

Johnson J: I concluded that he patient was not capable of weighing-up the information that she was given, the third element. The patient was in the throes of labour with all that is involved in terms of pain and emotional stress. I concluded that a patient who could, in those circumstances, speak in terms which seemed to accept the inevitability of her own death, was not a patient who was able properly to weigh-up the considerations that arose so as to make any valid decision, about anything of even the most trivial kind, surely still less one which involved her own life.

You will notice the medical evidence in the latter case and the almost generalised view that painful labour removes a patient's decision-making capacity. In *Re MB* Butler-Sloss LJ rather diplomatically stated:

One may question whether there was evidence before the court which enabled the judge to come to a conclusion contrary to the opinion of the obstetricians that she was competent.

There can be no doubt that the courts have turned their face against making findings of incompetence in situations like the *Rochdale* and *Norfolk and Norwich* cases.

(c) Children

When will a child, ie a person aged under 18, have capacity to consent to medical treatment? This is the central question for us here. We will see that if a child lacks capacity then others with 'parental responsibility' for the child – usually the parents – must make decisions in the child's best interests (*infra*, ch 6). We will also see that, by a curious twist, the courts distinguish between a child's *consent* to treatment and his *refusal* of treatment. Thus, whilst a child's consent (providing he has capacity) will make lawful what would otherwise be a battery, his refusal may be overridden, in certain circumstances, by others such as his parents or the court (*infra*, ch 6). Returning to our central question, it is helpful to look at children who have reached the age of 16 and those below that age.

(i) 16–18 YEAR-OLD CHILDREN

Until 1969, the common law applied to all children. Unfortunately, the law was unclear. Some believed that children could never validly consent to treatment. The law is now to be found in s 8 of the Family Law Reform Act 1969. The background to this legislation is discussed by Lord Donaldson MR in *Re W (a minor) (medical treatment)* [1992] 4 All ER 627 at 634–635:

It is common ground that the Family Law Reform Act 1969 was Parliament's response to the *Report of the Committee on the Age of Majority* (Cmnd 3342 (1967)). The relevant part is contained in paras 474 to 484. These show that the mischief aimed at was twofold. First, cases were occurring in which young people between 16 and 21 (the then age of majority) were living away from home and wished and needed urgent medical treatment which had not yet reached the emergency stage. Doctors were unable to treat them unless and until their parents had been traced and this could cause unnecessary suffering. Second, difficulties were arising concerning—

> operations whose implications bring up the question of a girl's right to privacy about her sexual life. A particularly difficult situation arises in the case of a girl who is sent to hospital in need of a therapeutic abortion, and refuses point blank to enter the hospital unless a guarantee is given that her parents shall not be told about it. (See para 478.)

The committee had recommended that the age of majority be reduced to 18 generally. The report records that all the professional bodies which gave evidence recommended that patients aged between 16 and 18 should be able to give an effective consent to treatment and all but the Medical Protection Society recommended that they should also be able to give an effective refusal (see para 480). The point with which we are concerned was therefore well in the mind of the committee. It did not so recommend. It recommended that—

> *without prejudice to any consent that may otherwise be lawful,* the consent of young persons aged 16 and over to medical or dental treatment shall be as valid as the consent of a person of full age. (My emphasis.)

Section 8 of the Family Law Reform Act 1969 is a follows:

> 8. (1) The consent of a minor who has attained the age of sixteen years to any surgical, medical or dental treatment which, in the absence of consent, would constitute a trespass to his person, shall be as effective as it would be if he were of full age; and where a minor has by virtue of this section given an effective consent to any treatment it shall not be necessary to obtain any consent for it from his parent or guardian.
>
> (2) In this section 'surgical, medical or dental treatment' includes any procedure undertaken for the purposes of diagnosis, and this section applies to any procedure (including, in particular, the administration of an anaesthetic) which is ancillary to any treatment as it applies to that treatment.
>
> (3) Nothing in this shall be construed as making ineffective any consent which would have been effective if this section had not been enacted.

The first and indeed the only occasion upon which this statute has been judicially considered in detail was in *Re W (a minor) (medical treatment) (supra)*. Nolan LJ pointed out that:

> [T]he effect of section 8 is to make it clear that a child of 16 to 17 years of age has the same capacity as an adult to consent to surgical, medical or dental treatment which would otherwise constitute a trespass. The phrase 'surgical, medical or dental treatment' is evidently used in a fairly narrow sense otherwise it would not have been necessary for Parliament to provide, by section 8(2), that the expression includes diagnostic procedures, and ancillary procedures such as the administration of an anaesthetic. The section does not cover, for example, the giving of blood. It does not even include the taking of a blood sample. Separate provision for that is made by section 21 of the Act.

Lord Donaldson MR in *Re W (supra)* also discussed the scope of the section:

> The wording of sub-s (1) shows quite clearly that it is addressed to the legal purpose and legal effect of consent to treatment, namely to prevent such treatment constituting in law a trespass to the person, and that it does so by making the consent of a 16- or 17-year-old as effective as if he were 'of full age' ...
>
> The section extends not only to treatment, but also to diagnostic procedures (see sub-s (2)). It does not, however, extend to the donation of organs or blood since, so far as the donor is concerned, these do not constitute either treatment or diagnosis. I cannot remember to what extent organ donation was common in 1967, but the Latey Committee expressly recommended that only 18-year-olds and older should be authorised by statute to consent to *giving* blood (see paras 485–489). It seems that Parliament accepted this recommendation, although I doubt whether blood donation will create any problem as a 'Gillick competent' minor of any age would be able to give consent under the common law.

Organ transplants are quite different and, as a matter of law, doctors would have to secure the consent of someone with the right to consent on behalf of a donor under the age of 18 or, if they relied upon the consent of the minor himself or herself, be satisfied that the minor was 'Gillick competent' in the context of so serious a procedure which would not benefit the minor. This would be a highly improbable conclusion.

A number of points should be noticed. First, s 8 places the 16–18-year-old in the same position as an adult. Hence, they too are presumed to be competent to make decisions covered by s 8. Secondly, in relation to *other* decisions, 16–18-year-olds are dealt with in the same way as younger children, ie the *Gillick* test of competence applies. Thirdly, s 8(1) applies only to 'surgical, medical or dental treatment'. Thus, organ or blood donation would not be included because it is neither 'treatment' nor 'diagnosis'. Contrast the wording of s 2(4) of the Age of Legal Capacity (Scotland) Act 1991 which, in relation to children under 16, provides that they may consent to 'any surgical, medical or dental *procedure* or treatment' (our emphasis). Arguably, by virtue of the word 'procedure', the limitation would not apply in Scotland. Indeed, this was the intention of the Scottish Law Commission whose Report in 1990 led to the 1991 Act (see *Report on the Legal Capacity and Responsibility of Minors and Pupils* (No 110)).

However, the exclusion from s 8 by Nolan LJ of the taking of a blood sample is wrong. If taken as a 'diagnostic procedure', it is brought within the phrase 'surgical, medical or dental treatment' by virtue of s 8(2). It was wrong of him to consider it excluded because s 21 of the 1969 Act covers the taking of blood samples. That section only does so where it is done for the purposes of paternity testing. Blood taking for any other diagnostic purposes, eg HIV or genetic testing, is not covered by s 21 but by s 8 of the 1969 Act. Fourthly, to the extent that s 8 creates a presumption of competence, as for adults it may be rebutted if the child suffers from a mental disability which affects their understanding. Hence, in *Re C (a minor) (detention for medical treatment)* [1997] 2 FLR 180, which we saw earlier, a 16-year-old girl suffering from anorexia nervosa was held incompetent applying the three-stage *Re C* test. What is more problematic is whether the child's immaturity may be used to rebut their competence once they have reached 16 years of age. Are they subject to the *Gillick* test of competence we saw earlier, albeit that it is presumed to be satisfied under s 8, unlike the situation of a child under 16 where it has to be positively established? The answer should be 'yes'. *Gillick* establishes a legal test of competence which is universal and applies, in principle, to all ages. However, in *Re W* Lord Donaldson MR expressed the view that when s 8 applies 'the test of "*Gillick* competence" is bypassed and has no relevance' (*op cit* at 634). This view is somewhat idiosyncratic and the better view is that expressed by Balcombe and Nolan LJJ that a child aged between 16 and 18 is merely presumed to be competent as if an adult (at 641 and 647 respectively).

(ii) UNDER 16

While s 8 dealt with children who had reached 16, it was not until the decision of the House of Lords in *Gillick v West Norfolk and Wisbech Area Health Authority* [1986] AC 112 that the common law position for children under 16 was resolved. We set out this decision earlier. You will recall that the House of Lords decided that a child under 16 could validly consent to medical treatment if he or she was capable of understanding what was involved. The essence of the decision can be seen in the following extract from the speech of Lord Scarman (with whom Lord bridge agreed).

Lord Scarman: In the light of the foregoing I would hold that as a matter of law the parental right to determine whether or not the minor child below the age of 16 will have medical treatment terminated if and when the child achieves a sufficient understanding and intelligence to enable him or her to understand fully what is proposed. It will be a question of fact whether a child seeking advice has sufficient understanding of what is involved in give a consent valid in law. Until the child achieves the capacity to consent, the parental right to make the decision continues save only in exceptional circumstances. Emergency, parental neglect, abandonment of the child or inability to find the parent are examples of exceptional situations justifying the doctor proceeding to treat the child without parental knowledge and consent; but there will arise, no doubt, other exceptional situations in which it will be reasonable for the doctor to proceed without the parent's consent.

When applying these conclusions to contraceptive advice and treatment it has to be borne in mind that there is much that has to be understood by a girl under the age of 16 if she is to have legal capacity to consent to such treatment. It is not enough that she should understand the nature of the advice which is being given: she must also have a sufficient maturity to understand what is involved. There are moral and family questions, especially her relationship with her parents; long-term problems associated with the emotional impact of pregnancy and its termination; and there are the risks to health of sexual intercourse at her age, risks which contraception may diminish but cannot eliminate. It follows that a doctor will have to satisfy himself that she is able to appraise these factors before he can safely proceed on the basis that she has at law capacity to consent to contraceptive treatment. And it further follows that ordinarily the proper course will be for him, as the guidance lays down, first to seek to persuade the girl to bring her parents into consultation, and, if she refuses, not to prescribe contraceptive treatment unless he is satisfied that her circumstances are such that he ought to proceed without parental knowledge and consent.

Like Woolf J, I find illuminating and helpful the judgment of Addy J of the Ontario High Court in *Johnston v Wellesley Hospital* (1970) 17 DLR (3d) 139, a passage from which he quotes in his judgment in this case ([1984] 1 All ER 365 at 374, [1984] QB 581 at 597). The key passage bears repetition (17 DLR (3d) 139 at 144–145):

> But, regardless of modern trends, I can find nothing in any of the old reported cases, except where infants of tender age or young children were involved, where the Courts have found that a person under 21 years of age was legally incapable of consenting to medical treatment. If a person under 21 years were unable to consent to medical treatment, he would also be incapable of consenting to other types of bodily interference. A proposition purporting to establish that any bodily interference acquiesced in by a youth of 20 years would nevertheless constitute an assault would be absurd. If such were the case, sexual intercourse with a girl under 21 years would constitute rape. Until the minimum age of consent to sexual acts was fixed at 14 years by a statute, the Courts often held that infants were capable of consenting at a considerably earlier age than 14 years. I feel that the law on this point is well expressed in the volume on *Medical Negligence* (1957) by Lord Nathan (p 176): 'It is suggested that the most satisfactory solution of the problem is to rule that an infant who is capable of appreciating fully the nature and consequences of a particular operation or of particular treatment can give an effective consent thereto, and in such cases the consent of the guardian is unnecessary; but that where the infant is without that capacity, any apparent consent by him or her will be a nullity, the sole right to consent being vested in the guardian.'

Lord Templeman in his speech did not dissent from this view in general though he made an exception for contraceptive treatment for young girls.

Lord Templeman: I accept also that a doctor may lawfully carry out some forms of treatment with the consent of an infant patient and against the opposition of a parent based on religious or any other grounds. The effect of the consent of the infant depends on the nature of the treatment and the age and understanding of the infant. For example, a doctor with the consent of an intelligent boy or girl of 15 could in my opinion safely remove tonsils or a troublesome appendix.

Likewise, Lord Fraser agreed that a child under 16 could consent to medical treatment, including contraceptive treatment, if he or she understood what was involved (see his speech, *supra*, pp 606–608).

In practice, therefore, the issue will turn upon the evidence of the child's maturity and development capacity. But what is meant by understanding 'what is involved'? We have already seen that this entails 'the nature, purpose and likely consequences' of undergoing (or not undergoing) the procedure. In *Gillick*, however, Lord Scarman defined 'what is involved' even more extensively, he said:

There are moral and family questions, especially her relationship with her parents; long-term problems associated with the emotional impact of pregnancy and its termination; and there are the risks to health of sexual intercourse at her age ...

As can be seen, Lord Scarman was concerned with contraceptive advice and treatment involving young girls. Perhaps his remarks should be understood to be limited to this context not only in their precise detail but also their reference to wider issues such as 'moral ... questions'. Indeed, in *C v Wren* (1987) 35 DLR (4th) 419, the Alberta Court of Appeal described the obligation as an ethical one but not a legal one in a case concerned with the termination of the pregnancy of a young girl. Kerans JA said:

It is argued before us today that informed consent means consent after consideration of issues like the ethics of an abortion and the ethics of obligation by children to parents. It may be, as Lord Fraser has said in *Gillick v West Norfolk & Wisbech Area Health Authority* [1985] 3 All ER 402, that doctors have an ethical obligation in circumstances like this to discuss issues of that sort with young patients. If so, the doctor would account to the College of Physicians and Surgeons for the performance of that obligation. That is not the issue before us today. Rather, the issue is whether these issues relate to the defence of consent to assault. In our view, they do not.

Kerans JA concluded:

A 16-year-old girl became pregnant by her boyfriend while she was living at home. Several weeks later, she abruptly left home and went elsewhere and has since avoided contact with her parents. She also attended on a physician and surgeon with a view to an abortion and has received approval for it by the statutory committee provided under the *Criminal Code*. The urgency of the matter is that a statutory deadline looms. ...

The ground of appeal is that the learned chambers judge erred in finding that the expectant mother had given informed consent to the proposed surgical procedure.

The law in Alberta is that a surgeon may proceed with a surgical procedure immune from suits for assault if she or he has informed consent from the patient. That test was applied by the learned trial judge, and he found on the evidence before him that this child was capable of giving informed consent and had done so. ...

The law and the development of the law in this respect was analyzed in detail by Lord Scarman in the *Gillick* case. ...

What is the application of the principle [outlined in *Gillick*] in this case? We infer from the circumstances detailed in argument here that this expectant mother and her parents had fully discussed the ethical issues involved and, most regrettably, disagreed. We cannot infer from that disagreement that this expectant mother did not have sufficient intelligence and understanding to make up her own mind. Meanwhile, it is conceded that she is a 'normal intelligent 16-year-old'. We infer that she did have sufficient intelligence and understanding to make up her own mind and did so. At her age and level of understanding, the law is that she is to be permitted to do so.

(See also *Ney v A-G of Canada* (1993) 102 DLR (4th) 136 (BC Sup Ct)). Nevertheless, a number of cases have required a very high level of understanding or appreciation of the consequences of their decisions where children's lives have been at risk: *Re E (a minor)* (1990) 9 BMLR 1 (Ward J); *Re S (a minor) (refusal of medical treatment)* [1994] 2 FLR 1065 (Johnson J) and *Re L (medical treatment: Gillick competency* [1998] 2 FLR 810 (Stephen Brown P).

Re S (a minor) (consent to medical treatment) [1994] 2 FLR 1065 (Fam Div)

The patient, now 15½ years old, had suffered from thalassaemia virtually since birth. She was kept alive by an arduous course of treatment involving monthly blood transfusions in hospital and daily injections, which, since she was 9 years old, she had had to undertake herself. in 1989 she and her mother began to attend meetings of Jehovah's Witnesses. For a time treatment continued, but in May 1994 the patient failed to attend hospital for her blood transfusion. A meeting was held at the hospital between her and her mother and the doctor responsible for her care. Mother and daughter both made it clear that there were to be no more blood transfusions. The local authority issued an application asking the court to exercise its inherent jurisdiction to make an order overriding the patient's expressed wishes. She resisted the application and by her cross-application asked the court to prevent a transfusion being forced on her, on the basis that, in accordance with the beliefs of the Jehovah's Witnesses, further transfusions would have consequences for her in her after-life.

Johnson J: It is now nearly 2 months since S's last transfusion. She looks, to my untutored eye, pale and weak. She gave evidence; I broke off at one point because of my concern about her. Dr J gave evidence meanwhile and S lay at the back of the court with her head on her mother's lap. Her situation is pitiful. S does not wish to die and emotive headlines to that effect would be wholly inappropriate. S's case is simply that she is now of an age when she has the right to decide whether she should have this treatment or not, and she submits no one should override her decision. She has, I believe, not yet been baptised into the church but, none the less, she holds very strongly the beliefs of Jehovah's Witnesses in relation to the giving of blood. As she put it, 'Having someone else's blood is having someone else's soul'.

S told me that for her to submit to further transfusions would have consequences for her in the life hereafter and it is for that reason and not because of any wish to die, so-called, that she resists the local authority's application. Indeed, by her cross-applications, as to the form of which I need make no comment, she asks me to prevent any such transfusion being forced upon her. …

S seemed to me to be not only small, frail and pale of face, but she seemed to me to be less mature than most girls of her age in the way she spoke, responded to questions and generally conducted herself. Of necessity she has had a sheltered upbringing and it seemed to me that she was lacking in the emotional maturity that one would have expected of a girl of her age. Dr S felt that she was not seriously immature in this sense and I defer to Dr S's view, she having had a better opportunity than I have of assessing S's maturity.

I thought too that S had only a very general understanding of some vital matters relating to her treatment and to the consequence for her of that treatment ceasing. That view was shared by Dr S as I shall relate. However, holding her Bible in both her hands as she answered questions, this young woman never wavered in her refusal to have more blood transfusions. She has said on previous occasions that if it was forced upon her it would be like rape and it would be those who had done it who would be the sinners.

In a short report dated 6 June 1994, Dr J said:

> It is clear that in a relatively short number of weeks this girl will die should she not get a blood transfusion. I believe S to have been under considerable pressure in recent years to stop her transfusions. In 1990 we did stop the regular pattern of transfusions in order to show the family that it was not possible for the girl to make her own blood and she got extremely anaemic. They are, therefore, well aware of the dangers of the situation.

In his oral evidence, he elaborated his views. He also explained his familiarity with the problem of teenagers suffering from long-term disability who reject treatment. He explained this by reference to patients suffering from diabetes. He said:

> I find that if I can hold a situation for a year or so, by the age of 17 or so their added maturity leads to a change in attitude …

Dr S had gone at short notice to see S at home. They were alone together for an hour and a half. In her written report, Dr S found that S's cognitive ability was intact and her intelligence in the normal range, but she did not think that she was as bright as her manner might suggest. On closer examination, much of what she said seemed to Dr S to be a repetition of what she had heard or read and seemed not to bear close scrutiny. S had clearly, and I would say very naturally, become fed up with her illness. She told Dr S that at times she cries a lot and prays, 'Please make me better, God, please, I don't want to suffer'. She feels that she has had so much medication she is like a pin-cushion. Clearly, she is missing out on many things in life and even her own physical appearance brings jibes from her peers who call her an 'ironing board'. She said that she's fed up with it all and if it is to go on like this she might as well die, but God might decide to save her.

Dr S says that at one level S knows the basic facts of her medical condition, but she also seemed to genuinely believe a mistake might have been made in the diagnosis. S said:

> They may have got it wrong all these years, and when I stop treatment they'll find it's something else and will treat it. I might not have thalassaemia. Who knows?

Dr S found her surprisingly confused over many details. For example, she was very vague about the need for Deferral and said that if anyone had explained everything to her earlier she would have kept to the treatment more closely.

As to her death, she did not know how that would occur. She hoped she would die in her sleep but, she said, 'You never know, there could be a miracle and God might save me'. As to why God was against her having blood, she seemed uncertain, referring to the risk of HIV, and so on. Strikingly, she spoke to Dr S of 'being free now, free from all these treatments'. Dr S said it was as though she had drawn a line and was going to stick to it.

Dr S found the whole atmosphere in the home puzzling. There seemed to Dr S to be none of the gestures of affection or words of affection that one might have expected whatever one's beliefs. No less than nine times during the interview, S spoke about the possibility of a miracle saving her. Because she was faithful God might decide she should live, maybe she would not die, maybe she did not have thalassaemia.

Doctor S's conclusion was that S does not fully understand the implication of her decision. She doesn't know how death will occur; she certainly, in the view of Dr S, does not believe that a failure to have further transfusions will certainly result in death.

S is very geed up and negative and despondent about her illness, says Dr S. Like Dr J, she finds these feelings are always at their height in adolescence. In her oral evidence, Dr S said that she did not believe that S understood the implication of the decision:

> There were a lot of things that concerned me, the aptness of her replies, some of her phrases. She and her mother were using exactly similar phraseology. S was not able to explain her thoughts except that, "it was said in the Bible". She had no understanding of the manner in which she might die.

The most worrying thing for Dr S was that S seemed to have latched onto the idea that other Jehovah's Witnesses had thalassaemia and survived without transfusion. She said:

> I actually believe that she doesn't believe that she will die. Much of what she said is what I hear from other children who are chronically ill and who are fed up with their treatment. In age terms, this is the peak of such problems.

Cross-examined on S's behalf, Dr S said that she did not consider that she had been tutored to give her answers. She was certainly very determined but she did not agree that S was expressing her own mind. Her feelings about being fed up with treatment makes her susceptible to influence. …

As to her competence to make these decisions, because she is disillusioned with the treatment – one might say, fed up with it – she is susceptible to influence from outside. I do not believe that the mother or any Jehovah's Witnesses have overborne the wish of S in the matter, but I do believe that she has been influenced by them in the sense that she has come to share their faith. She does not understand the full implications of what will happen. It does not seem to me that he capacity is commensurate with the gravity of the decision which she has made. It seems to me that an understanding that she will die is not enough. For her decision to carry weight she should have a greater understanding of the manner of the death and pain and the distress.

Ward J had said in *Re E* (above):

> … I find that he has no realisation of the full implications which lie before him as to the process of dying. He may have some concept of the fact that he will die, but as to the manner of his death and to the extent of his and his family's suffering I find he has not the ability to turn his mind to it nor the will to do so. Who can blame him for that?

In *Re R* (above) Lord Donaldson MR spoke to the same effect.

Is S than '*Gillick*-competent' as to this? In approaching the case beforehand and having the advantage of reading some of the papers over the weekend, I had thought that this was a case of a child who was '*Gillick*-competent'. She is, after all, 15½ years old. But having seen her and heard about her I have no doubt at all but that she is not '*Gillick*-competent'.

'When I was a child, I spoke as a child.' That seemed to me to be how S feels and speaks. There are those who are children and those who are adults and those who are in-between. I do not believe that S is in-between. She is still very much, in my view, a child. Whilst as she gave evidence I was so very strongly impressed by her integrity and her commitment, I believe they were the integrity and commitment of a child and not of somebody who was competent to make the decision that she tells me she has made. She hopes still for a miracle. My conclusion is, therefore, that she is not '*Gillick*-competent'.

Johnson J based his decision to authorise treatment on the power of the court to override a competent child's refusal of treatment where that is in her 'best interests' (see *infra*, ch 6). For good measure, Johnson J found as a fact that S was not '*Gillick*-competent'. He did so on the basis that he considered her to lack emotional maturity and that she was 'still very much … a child'. Competence is, of course, an evidential question which, in the case, was largely based upon the judge's perception of S when giving evidence. It is worth noting, however, that one psychiatric witness doubted whether S was 'seriously immature' for someone of her age. Since she was 15½ years old where does that leave other such teenagers if the judge is correct?

However, S's immaturity and thus her inability to *appreciate* what was involved in her refusal may not have been the real basis for the judge's finding that she as incompetent. Johnson J identified *two* matters which suggested that she did 'not understand the full implications of what will happen'. First, S did not believe that her refusal would lead to her certain death. She hoped for a miracle cure. To the extent that this was seen as undermining her ability to understand it is questionable that it should. Certainly, a denial by a person that they are ill or that their condition is life-threatening can led to a finding of incompetence, as we have seen. But, this is where the denial arises from a mental condition that skews the patient's perception of reality (see *supra*). A finding of incompetence cannot be based upon an individual's different perception (otherwise formed) of their chances of survival. Many terminally-ill people hope for a cure even when their doctors tell them medical science cannot deliver. That 'hope springs eternal' is not a sign of incompetence but a quirk of human nature. S does not seem to have had any underlying mental condition that skewed her sense of reality. All that is left is that she was too immature to 'appreciate' the factors relevant to her decision and is arguably for the court to impose too high a standard.

Secondly, and importantly for us here, Johnson J concluded that 'an understanding that she will die is not enough'. He relied upon the earlier remarks of Ward J in *Re E (a minor)* (1990) 9 BMLR 1 at 6, who said:

> I find that [E] has no realisation of the full implications which lie before him as to the process of dying. He may have some concept of the fact that he will die, but as to the manner of his death and to the extent of his and his family's suffering I find he has not the ability to turn his mind to it nor will he do so.

Johnson J held that for S's 'decision to carry weight she should have a greater understanding of the manner of the death and pain and the distress'. As a standard of competence, the judge is asking a lot of a 15½ year old child. But then, he would be asking a lot of any adult. It is too much to expect of individuals that they come to terms with dying and its processes before they can be said to be competent to make decisions at the end of life.

Commenting on *Re S* and *Re E*, Jane Fortin, in *Children's Rights and the Developing Law* (1998) states (at pp 108–109):

> ... an application of Ward J's views automatically excludes most child patients from being *Gillick* competent in circumstances where the outcome of their refusal to undergo treatment risks their own death. Although few adults could comprehend the process of dying, the pain they would suffer, the fear they would undergo and relatives' distress in watching them die, neither doctors nor the court are entitled to overrule their refusal to undergo treatment for similar reasons. Case law establishes far less stringent requirements when assessing an adult patient's competence to refuse treatment. These requirements are difficult to justify on logical grounds to the teenagers themselves.

The judges' reluctance to allow adolescent children to die, if sound public policy, would be better effected through the courts' protective jurisdiction to override competent refusals rather than by manipulating the legal concept of competence in situations where more is expected of them than would be of adults.

B. INFORMED CONSENT

The aphorism 'informed consent' has entered the language as being synonymous with valid consent. This is, of course, not so and is in fact unhelpful. It gives only a partial view. The requirement that consent be informed is only one, albeit a very important, ingredient of valid consent. Furthermore, the expression informed consent begs all the necessary questions which are the subject of the following section; for example, how informed is informed? It is helpful to consider the law of battery and that of negligence separately.

1. Battery

(a) Nature and purpose

The approach of the English courts was established by Bristow J in the following case in which, for the first time, an English court considered the scope of battery in a medical case.

Chatterton v Gerson [1981] QB 432, [1981] 1 All ER 257 (QBD)

The plaintiff was treated by the defendant, a specialist for chronic pain around the area of an operation scar following a hernia operation. The first treatment was only partially successful. the plaintiff then had a second injection. This also failed to relieve her pain but rendered her right leg completely numb thereby impairing her mobility. The plaintiff alleged that her consent to the treatment was vitiated because she had not been informed of the risk of numbness as a side-effect and that the defendant was, therefore, liable in battery. In dismissing her claim in battery (her claim in negligence was also dismissed) the judge stated the law as follows.

Bristow J: In my judgment what the court has to do in each case is to look at all the circumstances and say, 'Was there a real consent?'. I think justice requires that in order to vitiate the reality of consent there must be a greater failure of communication between doctor and patient than that involved in a breach of duty if the claim is based on negligence. When the claim is based on negligence the plaintiff must prove not only the breach of duty to inform but that had the duty not been broken she would not have chosen to have the operation. Where the claim is based on the trespass to the person, once it is shown that the consent is unreal, then what the plaintiff would have decided if she had been given the information which would have prevented vitiation of the reality of her consent is irrelevant.

In my judgment once the patient is informed in broad terms of the nature of the procedure which is intended, and gives her consent, that consent is real, and the cause of the action on which to base a claim for failure to go into risks and implications is negligence, not trespass. Of course, if information is withheld in bad faith, the consent will be vitiated by fraud. Of course, if by some accident, as in a case in the 1940s in the Salford Hundred Court, where a boy was admitted to hospital for tonsillectomy and due to administrative error was circumcised instead, trespass would be the appropriate cause of action against the doctor, though he was as much the victim of the error as the boy. But in my judgment it would be very much against the interests of justice if actions which are really based on a failure by the doctor to perform his duty adequately to inform were pleaded in trespass.

In *Hills v Potter* [1983] 3 All ER 716, Hirst J approved *Chatterton*, in a case in which the plaintiff alleged non-disclosure of a risk of injury inherent in a medical procedure and claimed that non-disclosure gave rise to an action both in battery and negligence. The judge rejected the battery claim, stating:

As to the claim for assault and battery, the plaintiff's undoubted consent to the operation which was in fact performed negatives any possibility of liability under this head: see *Chatterton v Gerson* [1981] QB 432, [1981] 1 All ER 257. I should add that I respectfully agree with Bristow J in deploring reliance on these torts in medical cases of this kind. The proper cause of action, if any, is negligence.

The leading English case is *Sidaway v Bethlem Royal Hospital Governors* [1984] 1 All ER 1018 (CA); affd [1985] AC 871, [1985] 1 All ER 643 (HL). This case concerned a woman who underwent an operation to relieve pain in her neck and shoulders. The surgeon told her of the possibility of disturbing a nerve root and the consequences of this. However, she alleged that he did not tell her that there was a risk of damaging the spinal cord and the possibly catastrophic consequences if that transpired. In fact, this did occur and the plaintiff sued. She brought her action in negligence, no doubt in light of *Chatterton* and *Hills*. Her action failed, but the Court of Appeal chose to state its view of the scope and application of the tort of battery. In what circumstances, if any, could failure to disclose information give rise to an action in battery?

> **Sir John Donaldson MR:** I am wholly satisfied that as a matter of English law a consent is not vitiated by a failure on the part of the doctor to give the patient sufficient information before the consent is given. It is only if the consent is obtained by fraud or by misrepresentation of the nature of what is to be done that it can be said that an apparent consent is not a true consent. This is the position in the criminal law (*R v Clarence* (1888) 22 QBD 23, 43) and the cause of action based upon trespass to the person is closely analogous. I should add that the contrary was not argued upon this appeal.

> **Dunn LJ:** The first argument was that unless the patient's consent to the operation was a fully informed consent the performance of the operation would constitute a battery on the patient by the surgeon. This is not the law of England. If there is consent to the nature of the act, then there is no trespass to the person. So in *R v Clarence* (1888) 22 QBD 23, a conviction of rape [*sic*] was quashed where the woman did not know that the prisoner was suffering from a venereal disease which he communicated to her. If she had known, she would not have consented to sexual intercourse, even though without knowledge of the probable risk of infection, there was no rape. On the other hand, in *R v Flattery* (1877) 2 QBD 410 where a doctor had had sexual intercourse with a patient under pretence of performing a surgical operation, his conviction of rape was upheld because the patient had only consented to an operation and not the act of sexual intercourse. As Bristow J said in *Chatterton v Gerson* [1981] QB 432, 443: 'once the patient is informed in broad terms of the nature of the procedure which is intended, and gives her consent, that consent is real' so that it affords a defence to a battery.

In dismissing Mrs Sidaway's appeal, the only comment made in the House of Lords on this aspect of the case was by Lord Scarman, who agreed that 'it would be deplorable to base the law in medical cases of this kind on the torts of assault and battery' (at 650).

Finally, in *Freeman v Home Office (No 2)* [1984] 1 All ER 1036, Sir John Donaldson MR reiterated his earlier views in *Sidaway*:

> If there was real consent to the treatment, it mattered not whether the doctor was in breach of his duty to give the patient the appropriate information before that consent was given. Real consent provides a complete defence to a claim based on the tort of trespass to the person. Consent would not be real if procured by fraud or misrepresentation but, subject to this and subject to the patient having been informed in broad terms of the nature of the treatment, consent in fact amounts to consent in law.

You will notice that we refer to the need to know the 'nature *and purpose*' of the touching whereas the courts tend to restrict themselves to the word 'nature'. In our view there is no conflict here. The word 'nature' as used by the judges is intended to connote 'nature' and 'purpose' (see, eg *Re C (adult: refusal of medical treatment)* [1994] 1 All ER 819, where Thorpe J (at 824) stated that the patient must understand 'the nature, purpose and effect' of the treatment).

Since the House of Lords' apparent endorsement in *Sidaway* of the narrow view that consent means only consent sufficient to avoid an action in battery, the argument that battery may also lie where the consent is given in ignorance of relevant material facts seems to have no place in English law. Although the law is unlikely to change, the counter view is both intellectually respectable and, in the light of the interests at stake, may be regarded by some as desirable (see, eg Keng Feng (1987) 7 LS 149). The argument is made by Professor Somerville in the following article.

M A Somerville 'Structuring the Issues in Informed Consent' (1981) 25 McGill Law Journal 740

Battery or negligence?
The proper cause of action when a defective consent is alleged may be either battery or negligence. The difference is significant because:

> It will have important bearing on such matters as the incidence of the onus of proof, causation, the importance of expert medical evidence, the significance of medical

judgment, proof of damage and, most important, of course, the substantive basis upon which liability may be found.

While each of these factors will not be discussed in detail here, it is necessary to be aware of them.

Common law courts in Canada have taken the traditional approach that the consent that is both necessary and sufficient for avoiding a cause of action in battery in medical cases is consent to 'the basic nature and character of the operation or the procedure'. The difficulty in applying this rule is determining which factors form part of the basic nature and character of an act and which do not. Such determinations have been made by judges on a case-by-case basis, with no more definite guidelines than the rule itself. But some judges have tried to formulate a clearer, more objective rule, which would help determine when non-disclosure of information or failure to obtain consent should give rise to a cause of action in battery.

The situation facing the judges can be represented diagrammatically:

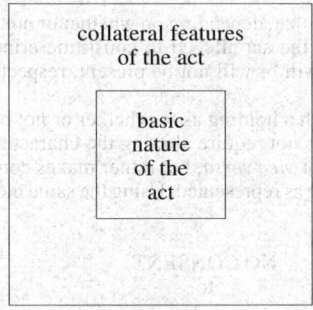

The outer square represents all the consequences or risks to which the patient must consent if liability in tort (battery or negligence) for failure to obtain consent is to be avoided. The inner square represents the factors that make up the basic nature and character of the act of touching. Failure to obtain consent to these factors will give rise to a cause of action in battery. Thus, whether or not battery lies depends on where the inner line is drawn.

That judges will vary in drawing this line, even with respect to the same facts, can be seen by comparing the decision of the majority of the Supreme Court of Canada in *R v Bolduc and Bird* [(1967) 63 DLR (2d) 82] with that of the dissent and that of the Court of Appeal of British Columbia in the same case. Likewise, the judgment of the majority of the Court of Appeal of Ontario in *R v Maurantonio* [(1967) 65 DLR (2d) 674] can be compared with that of the dissent. These are criminal assault (battery) cases, but the rules governing consent in criminal law and in the tort of battery not only have common origins but are directly comparable. Such cases demonstrate that because criminal assault (or battery) will not lie if there is consent as to the basic nature and character of the act, liability will depend on whether or not the feature to which consent has *not* been obtained forms part of the act's basic nature and character. Thus, to the extent that there is discretion involved in determining whether or not a particular feature forms part of the basic nature and character of the act ('basic features'), there is discretion as to the imposition of liability. The two possible alternative analyses of any given fact situation that gives rise to this discretion may be represented as [follows].

Analysis I:

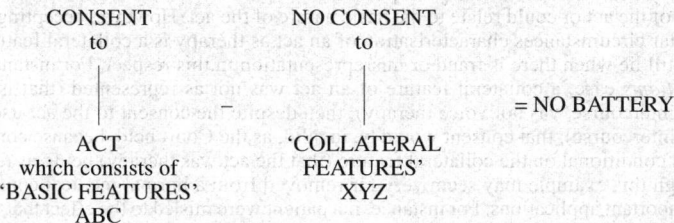

Analysis II:

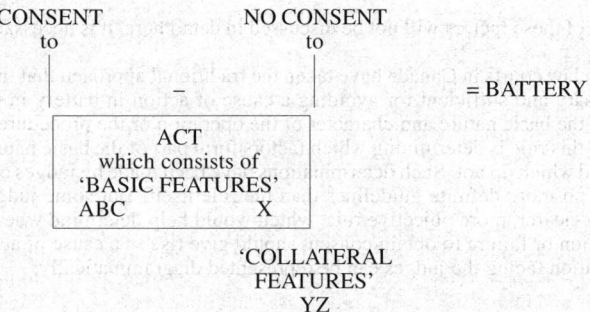

From this diagram it can be seen that, depending on whether or not X is held to be a 'collateral feature' or a 'basic feature' of the act alleged to constitute criminal assault or the tort of battery, the necessary consent will or will not be present, respectively, and liability will be determined accordingly.

There is another way in which a holding as to whether or not battery-avoiding consent is present can be varied. This does not require altering the characterisation of a feature of the act from 'basic' to 'collateral' or *vice versa*, but rather makes consent to the act conditional upon the collateral features being as represented. Using the same model this can be represented as follows:

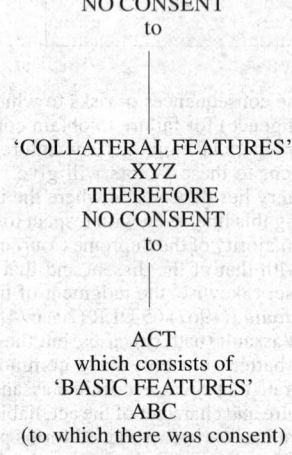

Pursuant to this analysis, it is irrelevant whether X is characterised as a 'basic' or 'collateral' feature, as even if X is a 'collateral' feature, if X is not as represented, the consent will fail to 'flow through' as a valid consent to the act. *R v Williams* ([1923] 1 KB 340), in which the accused, a choir-master, persuaded a young woman that sexual intercourse was therapy for her voice, is probably an example of a court taking such an approach. Depending on the circumstances, whether an act is therapeutic for the patient could be regarded as a 'collateral' feature of the act or could relate to the basic nature of the act. However, accepting that in the particular circumstances characterisation of an act as therapy is a collateral feature, battery could still lie when there is fraud or misrepresentation in this respect. For instance, if, as in the *Williams* case, a collateral feature of an act was not as represented (that is the act of sexual intercourse was not voice therapy), then despite the consent to the act itself (having sexual intercourse), that consent would be invalid, as the Court held, because consent to the act was conditional on the collateral feature (that the act was therapy) being as represented. Although this example may seem very far removed from a normal medical context, it may have important applications. For instance, if a patient were misled to the effect that a particular procedure was therapeutic when in fact it was performed for the purposes of non-therapeutic research, battery-avoiding consent could similarly be vitiated.

How has the law outlined above been applied in the medical relationship? The requirement that there be consent to the basic nature and character of the operation or procedure means that a physician must disclose all inevitable consequences of a proposed procedure in order to obtain battery-avoiding consent. Consequently, all courts faced with the issue have held that there will be a cause of action in battery when a physician does something to which the patient has not consented at all, or which the patient has expressly requested be done or has refused. Battery could also be established where the physician's act was essentially different in nature from that to which the patient consented. For instance, if the patient was told that the purpose of the operation was to relieve pain, but not told that the consequences would include sterility, any consent given would be invalidated and a cause of action in battery would be available.

Some courts have also held that knowledge of certain risks could be so material to understanding of the basic nature and character of an operation that failure to disclose them would vitiate battery-avoiding consent. In other words, it has been held that not only non-disclosure of inevitable results of a procedure can vitiate battery-avoiding consent, but also non-disclosure of risks of which knowledge was 'essential to an informed decision to undergo the operation'. It is with respect to failures to disclose a risk, as compared with an inevitable consequence, that the Supreme Court of Canada has probably restricted the availability of an action in battery.

It is not easy to decide, from a policy point of view, whether or not a cause of action in battery should be allowed for non-disclosure of certain risks. The argument that it should be allowed is that some risks are so serious that they necessarily relate to the basic nature and character of an operation and, therefore, their non-disclosure should give rise to a battery action. The difficulty is that as only some risks have this effect, how is the line to be drawn between those that do and those that do not? The alternative solution, which may be the position adopted by the Supreme Court of Canada in *Reibl v Hughes*, [(1980) 114 DLR (3d) 1] is that any liability for non-disclosure of a risk can only lie in negligence and not in battery.

[A]ctions of battery in respect of surgical or other medical treatment should be confined to cases where surgery or treatment has been performed or given to which there has been no consent at all or where, emergency situations aside, surgery or treatment has been performed or given beyond that to which there was consent … [U]nless there has been misrepresentation or fraud to secure consent to the treatment, a failure to disclose the attendant risks, however serious, should go to negligence rather than to battery. Although such a failure relates to an informed choice of submitting to or refusing recommended and appropriate treatment, it arises as the breach of an anterior duty of due care, comparable in legal obligation to the duty of due care in carrying out the particular treatment to which the patient has consented. It is not a test of the validity of the consent.

That is, non-disclosure of a risk will not give rise to the cause of action in battery except when there has been a 'misrepresentation or fraud to secure consent to … treatment'. But what can constitute misrepresentation within this rule, and why does such misrepresentation allow non-disclosure of a risk to give rise to an action in battery whereas without such misrepresentation it does not?

In exploring these issues it is necessary to determine the basis of the holding of the Supreme Court referred to above. Is it, first, that non-disclosure of a risk does not amount to misrepresentation (although that of an inevitable consequence can); or, second, that information about risks can never relate to the basic nature and character of an operation and thus cannot vitiate battery-avoiding consent; or both propositions; or neither? Presumably, the Court has established the second proposition rather than the first, as it is difficult to draw a distinction between one type of non-disclosure (non-disclosure of inevitable consequences) constituting misrepresentation, and the other (non-disclosure of risks) not doing so. It may be argued that because there is a pre-existing duty to disclose inevitable consequences, but not risks, non-disclosure of inevitable consequences constitutes a misrepresentation, while that of risks does not. But this pre-empts the question to which an answer is sought, that is, just what information is there a duty to disclose so as to avoid an action in battery? Moreover, reliance on a rule that total non-disclosure of a risk does not give rise to a cause of action in battery, because a total non-disclosure cannot constitute misrepresentation, would not exclude a *partial disclosure*. But an approach that recognises partial but not total non-disclosure of risks as misrepresentation would be artificial and could give rise to fortuitous results. Further, the distinction between nonfeasance and misfeasance has no place when there is a pre-existing duty relationship, as there is between physician and patient.

If the Court has not relied on a rule that a non-disclosure is unable to constitute misrepresentation, has it held that the risks of a procedure cannot relate to its basic nature and character? This question can be explored by asking what the situation would be where a significant and serious risk was grossly misrepresented, rather than undisclosed. This could, arguably, give rise to a cause of action in battery within the Court's ruling. However, the fact that misrepresentation of a risk could give rise to a cause of action in battery means, by definition, that the misrepresentation must relate to the basic nature and character of the act. If this is true it shows that the action in battery is not excluded because of the nature of the misrepresentation, that is, because the misrepresentation related to a risk and a risk cannot relate to the basic nature and character of a procedure, but that battery is excluded on some other basis.

If the above analysis is accepted the basis of the Supreme Court's holding is not that total non-disclosure of risks cannot constitute misrepresentation, nor that risks cannot relate to the basic nature and character of a medical procedure. This leaves the question which reveals the key to the basis of the Supreme Court's ruling still unanswered. Why does 'misrepresentation or fraud to secure consent to the treatment' cause non-disclosure of a risk to give rise to a cause of action in battery, where it would not do so if the elements in misrepresentation or fraud were not present?

The true test of whether or not a cause of action in battery will lie for non-disclosure of a risk, provided the risk is serious and sufficiently likely of occurrence to relate to the basic nature and character of the act carried out, depends on the *nature of the physician's conduct with respect to the non-disclosure*. Not only the nature of the undisclosed information is significant, but also the nature of the *failure* to disclose. It is not proposed that, if the physician negligently (ie, unintentionally) fails to disclose or misrepresents a risk, he will be liable in negligence. If he intentionally does either of these things the action will also lie in battery, provided that the risk which is not disclosed or is misrepresented is fundamental enough to relate to the basic nature and character of the procedure. Thus the presence or absence of intention with respect to the non-disclosure of a risk which relates to the basic nature and character of an intervention will determine the cause of action available for failure to obtain consent to that risk. By contrast, when the non-disclosure relates to an inevitable consequence of an intervention, intention or lack of it in relation to the non-disclosure is irrelevant to establishing a cause of action in battery. This is true because the intention necessary to support a cause of action for battery arising from an intentional, non-consensual touching of the kind which occurs is present in carrying out the act which has those inevitable consequences, regardless of the presence or absence of intention with respect to the non-disclosure.

Hence, what is being suggested is that the intention necessary to support an intentional tort will be found in relation to a different element of the tortious act (that is, either the touching or the non-disclosure) depending on whether the failure in obtaining consent relates to failure to inform of risks or of inevitable consequences, but in both cases, the necessary intention may be present.

In relation to determining whether the touching itself was intentional, there is a key concept: the question which must be asked is not simply whether there was consent to a touching, which in most cases there will be, but whether there was consent to touching *of that kind* or *in that manner*. Likewise, it is relevant to ask not only whether there was intention to touch, but whether there was intention to touch *in that manner*. The concept of intention 'to touch in that manner' is broader and more precise than the concept of just touching. It includes the inevitable consequences and purposes of an intervention, as well as the touching itself. Because risks, by definition, may not occur, it is not possible to find the required intention to touch in the manner which results from risks occurring simply by demonstrating their crystallisation. Any proof of intention relates, rather, to the act of non-disclosure of these risks. By contrast, when what occurs is an inevitable consequence of an intervention it can be presumed that this was intended, as in tort a reasonable person is presumed to intend the inevitable consequences of his acts. Consequently, in the latter case, the necessary intention to support intentional touching in that manner and a *prima facie* tort of battery is established by proving the touching, and the only question is whether or not there was sufficient consent.

An objection could be raised here that two different entities are being compared: in one case the question asked is whether or not there is *intentional non-disclosure of information* to which the patient is entitled: that is, is there intentional failure to obtain consent? In the other case the question is whether there is *intentional touching* in a situation where the failure to obtain consent to that touching may have been intentional or unintentional. It is submitted that there is no contradiction between these two approaches. Battery is an intentional tort, which may be established through the intention 'to touch in that manner' or the intentional failure to obtain the necessary consent. It is just that demonstrating the latter is superfluous when it can be shown that there was an intention to touch in a certain manner to which there was no consent.

There is one further problem with the Supreme Court's approach to actions in battery for failure to obtain adequate consent. Some risks are so important that most people would regard them as an essential part of any description of the basic nature and character of a procedure. For instance, the fact that an operation carries a substantial risk of death would cause most persons to characterise that operation as being of a serious nature. Further, can any real distinction be drawn between failure to disclose, for instance, that as a result of an operation a person will certainly be rendered sterile, and failure to disclose that there is a substantial risk of this occurring? It is submitted that the law should not try to draw distinctions that do not accord with generally held views as to what factors constitute the basic nature and character of an act, no matter how conceptually pleasing and easy of application the resulting rule may be.

Thus, with all respect, it is submitted that to the extent that the Supreme Court has limited the availability of an action in battery by stating the law to be that risks do not relate to the basic nature and character of an act and, consequently, their non-disclosure cannot vitiate battery-avoiding consent, the ruling may not be desirable. However, as shown above, the effect of the Supreme Court's ruling on the availability of a battery action will vary, depending on how it is analysed. The analysis suggested accepts the Supreme Court's ruling but minimises its effect of making unavailable a battery action that otherwise would have been available under Canadian common law.

The approach suggested may be summarised as follows: in all cases where lack of consent is alleged, one is arguing either that there was no consent at all to the touching or to touching in that manner. The first question is whether the touching itself and in that manner was intentional. It is highly unlikely that the touching itself will be unintentional, but this is not true of the manner of the touching. The manner of the touching includes two types of consequences: inevitable consequences and risks which eventuate. When the feature of the touching to which it is alleged there was no consent is an inevitable consequence, then there will necessarily have been an *intention* to touch *in that manner*. When, on the other hand, the touching is of that manner because of the crystallisation of a risk, touching *in that manner is unintentional* (unless, possibly, the risk which eventuates was of very high probability, but this case will not be considered here). In the second case, it may initially seem that battery should not lie for non-disclosure of a risk, as the act of which the plaintiff complains – that he was touched in a manner to which he did not consent – was unintentional. However, a second question is relevant: whether the failure to obtain consent was intentional. It is suggested that where it is intentional, and provided the non-disclosure is of a sufficiently serious and probable risk that the risk can be said to form part of the basic nature and character of the intervention, the necessary intention for a cause of action in battery will exist. Such an approach would allow non-disclosure of certain risks because of 'misrepresentation or fraud' to give rise to a cause of action in battery, as the Supreme Court suggests. It would include within the notion of misrepresentation some total non-disclosures; that is, intentional concealment of certain risks would suffice. Thus, only the unintentional non-disclosure of a risk that relates to the basic nature and character of an act would not be actionable in battery. The suggested approach and the correlation of the variables it includes can be demonstrated in the following way:

Non-disclosure:	of inevitable consequence	of 'sufficiently serious and probable' risk
INTENTIONAL	Battery	Battery
UNINTENTIONAL	Battery	Negligence

Defects in consent which do not give rise to a cause of action in battery will be either actionable in negligence (or possibly in contract) or will not be actionable at all. The dividing line between those that are actionable in negligence and those that are not actionable at all is determined by whether or not the physician has breached the standard of care required of him by the law relating to negligence with respect to obtaining the patient's consent …

Finally, it is appropriate here to note that some confusion may be caused because two doctrines 'consent' and 'informed consent' are not distinguished. It is suggested that the word 'consent' be reserved to refer to the substantive entity which must be present to avoid liability in battery and similarly for the term 'informed consent' in relation to negligence. It is proposed that with respect to the substantive content of consent the traditional notion should be retained. This means that consent will be present when there is consent to the basic nature and character of the act. Informed consent is a more extensive concept that also comprehends consent to certain consequences or risks of consequences. But, as further discussion will show, there has not always been consensus as to its requirements. It necessarily includes all elements of the consent doctrine, but the reverse is not true. Thus a physician may have obtained sufficient consent to avoid liability in battery, but not in negligence.

Notwithstanding Professor Somerville's cogent argument, the law in England and Wales undoubtedly reflects a less subtle view of the law (contrast the approach of a majority of the Canadian Supreme Court in *R v Cuerrier* [1998] 2 SCR 371). The distinction is clearly made between information going to the 'nature and purpose' of the proposed procedure and information concerning risks attending it. As regards the latter, action lies, if at all, in the tort of negligence rather than battery. Laskin CJ put it as follows in *Reibl v Hughes* (1980) 114 DLR (3d) 1.

> **Laskin CJ:** In situations where the allegation is that attendant risks which should have been disclosed were not communicated to the patient and yet the surgery or other medical treatment carried out was that to which the plaintiff consented (there being no negligence basis of liability for the recommended surgery or treatment to deal with the patient's condition), I do not understand how it can be said that the consent was vitiated by the failure to disclose so as to make the surgery or other treatment an unprivileged, unconsented to and intentional invasion of the patient's bodily integrity. I can appreciate the temptation to say that the genuineness of consent to medical treatment depends on proper disclosure of the risks which it entails, but my view ... a failure to disclose the attendant risks, however serious, should go to negligence rather than to battery. Although such a failure relates to an informed choice of submitting to or refusing recommended and appropriate treatment, it arises as the breach of an anterior duty of due care, comparable in legal obligation to the duty of care in carrying out the particular treatment to which the patient has consented. It is not a test of the validity of the consent.

For the purposes of the tort of battery, the crucial issue is what facts or information must a patient be aware of in order to be able to understand the 'nature and purpose' of the touching by the doctor so that the patient's consent is valid. Obviously, any analysis of such an indeterminate phrase as this invites judgments of policy which others may not accept. Cases involving fraudulently obtained consent are instructive here since they address the question whether the defendant's fraud denied the plaintiff information crucial to understanding the nature and purpose of the conduct.

The cases fall into three broad categories where the person touched is misled: (i) as to what is being done; (ii) as to who is doing it; and (iii) as to the risks and consequences of the conduct.

(i) WHAT IS BEING DONE?

Two criminal law cases illustrate the extent to which an awareness of what is being done may amount to ignorance of the 'nature and purpose' of the touching and vitiate the consent.

R v Williams [1923] 1 KB 340 (CCA)

> The appellant, who was engaged to give lessons in singing and voice production to a girl of sixteen years of age, had sexual intercourse with her under the pretence that her breathing was not quite right and that he had to perform an operation to enable her to produce her voice properly. The girl submitted to what was done under the belief, wilfully and fraudulently induced by the appellant, that she was being medically and surgically treated by the appellant and not with any intention that he should have sexual intercourse with her. Lord Hewart CJ adopted the statement of the law of the trial judge (Branson J) in dismissing the appeal.
>
> **Lord Hewart CJ:** Branson J stated the law in the course of the summing up in the present case in accurate terms. He said:
>
>> The law has laid it down that where a girl's consent is procured by the means which the girl says this prisoner adopted, that is to say, where she is persuaded that what is being done to her is not the ordinary act of sexual intercourse but is some medical or surgical operation in order to give her relief from some disability from which she is suffering,

then that is rape although the actual thing that was done was done with her consent, because she never consented to the act of sexual intercourse. She was persuaded to consent to what he did because she thought it was not sexual intercourse and because she thought it was a surgical operation.

In the second case, *R v Flattery* (1877) 2 QBD 410, the victim's ignorance was not about the fact that she was having sexual intercourse (the nature of the touching) but its purpose.

R v Flattery (1877) 2 QBD 410 (Court of Crown Cases Reserved)

The prisoner professed to give medical and surgical advice for money. The prosecutrix, a girl of nineteen, consulted him with respect to illness from which she was suffering. He advised that a surgical operation should be performed, and under pretence of performing it, had carnal connection with the prosecutrix. She submitted to what was done, not with any intention that he should have sexual connection with her, but under the belief that he was merely treating her medically and performing a surgical operation, that belief being wilfully and fraudulently induced by the prisoner.

Kelly CB: I think this conviction ought to be affirmed. Counsel for the defendant has ably argued that there was consent on the part of the prosecutrix, and therefore no rape. But, on the case as stated, it is plain that the girl only submitted to the plaintiff's touching her person in consequence of the fraud and false pretences of the prisoner, and that the only thing she consented to was the performance of a surgical operation. Up to the time when she and the prisoner went into the room alone, it is clearly found on the case that the only thing contemplated either by the girl or her mother was the operation which had been advised; sexual connection was never thought of by either of them. And after she was in the room alone with the prisoner, what the case expressly states is that the girl made but feeble resistance, believing that she was being treated medically, and that what was taking place was a surgical operation. In other words, she submitted to a surgical operation and nothing else.

Mellor J: I am of the same opinion … it is said that submission is consent, and that here there was submission. But submission to what? Not to carnal connection. The case is exactly within the words of Wilde, CJ, in *R v Case* [(1850) 1 Den 580]: 'She consented to one thing, he did another materially different, on which she had been prevented by his fraud from exercising her judgment and will.'
Denman and Field JJ and Huddleston B agreed.

Importantly, in *Sidaway* Dunn LJ in the Court of Appeal (see *supra*) approved *Flattery* as a case in which the consent was not valid.

Applying the reasoning in these cases to the context of medical practice may, in many instances, not give rise to difficulties. It will be obvious what is the nature of the procedure, ie what is being done and whether the patient is aware of it. Some cases, however, will remain problematical where it will be difficult to determine precisely what is meant by 'what is being done' for these purposes and hence whether the patient has been adequately informed so as to give a valid consent.

Consider, for example, the fact of *R v Bolduc and Bird* (1967) 63 DLR (2d) 82.

R v Bolduc and Bird (1967) 63 DLR (2d) 82 (Can SC)

[Bolduc, a] physician, about to conduct a vaginal examination and, if necessary, perform a medical procedure in the area to be examined, falsely introduced a lay friend [Bird] of his to the patient as a medical intern and asked if the friend, who, in fact, was present for his own gratification, might observe the examination. The patient consented to the friend's presence and the physician proceeded with the examination during which he touched the patient's private parts and inserted an instrument therein for the purposes of the examination while the friend looked on but at no time touched the patient. Both [Bolduc] and [Bird] were convicted of indecent assault on the patient and their conviction was affirmed by the Court of Appeal.

Hall J: The question for decision is whether on those facts and in the circumstances so described the appellants Bolduc and Bird were guilty of an indecent assault upon the person of the complainant contrary to s 141 of the Criminal Code which reads:

141(1) Every one who indecently assaults a female person is guilty of an indictable offence and is liable to imprisonment for five years and to be whipped.

(2) An accused who is charged with an offence under subsection (1) may be convicted if the evidence establishes that the accused did anything to the female person with her consent that, but for her consent, would have been an indecent assault, if her consent was obtained by false and fraudulent representations as to the nature and quality of the act.

With respect, I do not agree that an indecent assault was committed within the meaning of this section. What Bolduc did was unethical and reprehensible in the extreme and was something no reputable medical practitioner would have countenanced. However, Bolduc's unethical conduct and the fraud practised upon the complainant do not of themselves necessarily imply an infraction of s 141. It is common ground that the examination and treatment, including the insertion of the speculum, were consented to by the complainant. The question is: 'Was her consent obtained by false and fraudulent representations as to the nature and quality of the act?' Bolduc did exactly what the complainant understood he would do and intended that he should do, namely, to examine the vaginal tract and to cauterize the affected parts. Inserting the speculum was necessary for these purposes. There was no fraud on his part as to what he was supposed to do and in what he actually did. The complainant knew that Bird was present and consented to his presence. The fraud that was practised on her was not as to the nature and quality of what was to be done but was as to Bird's identity as a medical intern. His presence as distinct from some overt act by him was not an assault. ...

This case differs from *R v Harms*, 81 CCC 4, [1944] 2 DLR 61, [1944] 1 WWR 12, where the accused was charged with rape following carnal knowledge of an Indian girl, her consent to the intercourse having been obtained by false and fraudulent misrepresentations as to the nature and quality of the act. In that case Harms falsely represented himself to be a medical doctor, and although the complainant in that case knew that he was proposing sexual intercourse, she consented thereto because of his representations that the intercourse was in the nature of a medical treatment necessitated by a condition which he said he had diagnosed. Harms was not a medical man at all. He had no medical qualifications. The Court of Appeal affirmed the conviction by the jury that the Indian girl's consent had been obtained by false and fraudulent representations as to the nature and quality of the act.

The question of fraud vitiating a woman's consent in the case of rape or indecent assault was fully canvassed by Stephen J in *R v Clarence* (1888) 22 QBD 23, and by the High Court of Australia in *Papadimitropoulos v R* (1957) 98 CLR 249, where the court, in concluding a full review of the relevant law and cases decided up to that time, including the *Harms* case, supra, said [at 261]:

> To return to the central point; rape is carnal knowledge of a woman without her consent: carnal knowledge is the physical fact of penetration; it is the consent to that which is in question; such a consent demands a perception as to what is about to take place, as to the identity of the man and the character of what he is doing. But once the consent is comprehending and actual the inducing causes cannot destroy its reality ...

The complainant here knew what Bolduc was proposing to do to her, for this was one in a series of such treatments.

Her consent to the examination and treatment was real and comprehending and it cannot, therefore, be said that her consent was obtained by false or fraudulent representations as to the nature and quality of the act to be done, for that was not the fraud practised on her. The fraud was as to Bird being a medical intern and it was not represented that he would do anything but observe. It was intended that the examination and treatment would be done by Bolduc and this he did without assistance or participation by Bird.

Spence J (dissenting): Let us examine for a moment what was the consent obtained from the complainant. Surely upon the evidence to which I have referred above, it was a consent to the examination of her private parts and the touching of them in the course of treatment in the presence of a doctor, and not a mere medical student or a mere layman who was in some vague fashion considering becoming a medical student.

There was no evidence whatsoever that the complainant knew the accused Bird at all. The name Bird meant nothing to her. She only gave this consent to such a serious invasion of her privacy on the basis that Bird was a doctor intending to commence practice and who desired practical experience in such matters as Bolduc was proposing to engage in. That was the consent which the complainant granted. The indecent assault upon her was not the act to which she consented and therefore I am of the opinion that the two accused were guilty under the provisions of s 141(1).

(For a doctor's duty to inform patients of observers who are unregistered doctors see: HSG (95) 30 applying the guidance in *Medical Students in Hospitals*, HC (91)18.) If it were needed, this case clearly illustrates the inherently uncertain meaning which can be ascribed to 'nature and purpose'. The difference between the judges lies in the degree of specificity ascribed to the term in the particular context. Consider the example of medical research. Blood is taken from the finger of a patient who is otherwise healthy but has a broken leg. He is led to believe or assumes that the taking of the blood is related to the general treatment he is receiving for his leg. In fact, it is to be used for research unrelated to his care. Does his ignorance of the purpose for which the blood is taken mean that he had not validly consented to its being taken? Certainly he understands that blood is being taken. Is this enough or must he also know the reason why? *Flattery* would suggest that he must know the reason why before his consent is real and valid.

Absence of knowledge that a particular 'act' is 'therapeutic' rather than not seems to have been basis for the battery action in the following case.

Appleton v Garrett (1995) 34 BMLR 23 (QBD)

The defendant was a practising dentist in the National Health Service from 1981 to 1988. In 1989 he was struck off the Dental Register as a result of gross overtreatment of patients. The plaintiffs were former patients. Negligence has been admitted by the defendant. The issues before the court were: (i) whether there was liability for trespass to the person; (ii) whether there was an entitlement to aggravated damages; and (iii) the quantification of general damages for pain and suffering and loss of amenity and of damages for the cost of immediate and future treatment.

Dyson J: *Trespass*

It is a necessary but not sufficient condition for the entitlement to recover aggravated damages in this case, that the plaintiffs establish that the defendant's conduct amounted to a trespass to the person, that is assault and battery and not mere negligence: see *Kralj v McGrath* [1986] 1 All ER 54 at 61, approved by the Court of Appeal in *AB v South West Water Services Ltd* [1993] 1 All ER 609 at 625, sub nom *Gibbons v South West Water Services Ltd* [1993] QB 507 at 528.

It is not in dispute that a surgeon who performs an operation without his patient's consent commits an assault for which he is liable in damages ...

The relevant legal principles are not in dispute. Mr Grace QC for the defendant submits that the evidence in this case is insufficient to establish fraud such as would vitiate consent.

The evidence undoubtedly establishes that none of these eight plaintiffs was given any information on which to base a suitably informed consent. None was told why Mr Garrett was of the view that massive restorative treatment was required, often on perfect teeth. Typically, the plaintiff went for a normal routine check-up, and was subjected to the course of treatment without any explanation at all. Only one of the plaintiffs, Mrs Fenton, seems to have questioned the need for the treatment. Her unchallenged evidence was that Mr Garrett retorted in an annoyed and abrupt manner, saying: 'What if I were to question your judgment and capabilities?' I am quite satisfied that the failure to inform in these eight cases was not mere negligence and that Mr Garrett withheld information deliberately and in bad faith. The scale of the unnecessary treatment was so great that it must have been obvious to him that it was indeed unnecessary. The radiographs that he took before he embarked on the treatment showed in many cases that the teeth in these young plaintiffs were free from caries and were in what has been described as 'virgin condition'. Much of the treatment on these teeth was considerable in its scope and extent. For example, several surfaces of virgin teeth were cut heavily and received large fillings, quite often supported by pins. Others received root canal treatment and crowns.

Furthermore, Mr Garrett made many modifications to his dental charts of these patients, typically by adding notations to record fillings to teeth that he had previously marked with a dot. An example appears in an appendix to Professor Elderton's report of 19 October 1993. Professor Elderton said that the dot was a conventional symbol to represent a caries-free tooth. Professor Grieve suggested the dot was probably a symbol simply recording the existence of the tooth. It is significant, however, that the chart in the appendix does not record dots for all the teeth that were undoubtedly present in Mr Hewitt's mouth. I prefer the evidence of Professor Elderton on this point. Mr Garrett did not give evidence. He could have contradicted the evidence of Professor Elderton and explained the significance of the dot. I infer from his failure to do so that he accepts that Professor Elderton is right.

I conclude therefore that Mr Garrett deliberately embarked on large-scale treatment of these plaintiffs which he knew was unnecessary and that he deliberately withheld from them the information that the treatment was unnecessary because he knew that they would not have consented had they known the true position. I think Professor Elderton is probably right when he says that Mr Garrett restricted his treatment almost entirely to the posterior teeth because he knew that the patients would be more likely to question what he was doing if he attacked the anterior teeth. I find, therefore, that none of the plaintiff's consented, at any rate to the treatment of those teeth that required no treatment, and that, at least in relation to those teeth, the tort of trespass to the person has been made out.

While the patients understood that their teeth would be 'treated', it could not be seriously suggested that they were aware of the intrinsic quality of that treatment, ie that it was unnecessary and of no benefit to them. On the contrary, they believed they had unhealthy teeth that needed work. More broadly, they had agreed to therapeutic interventions but got something else.

Contrast with this the Australian case of *R v Mobilio* [1991] 1 VR 339 (Vic App Ct), where a doctor carried out unnecessary vaginal examinations for his own sexual gratification. The court held that the patients had consented since the defendant 'did no act which was essentially different from the act which the women knew he proposed to do' (at 352). He did not carry out a 'therapeutic' procedure *qua* doctor but rather an act of sexual aggression *qua* molester. This case is, we would suggest, wrongly decided and should not be followed. To change the act from a therapeutic to a non-therapeutic procedure is an absolutely crucial shift and one that unquestionably changes the 'nature' of what is being done. (See also J Morgan (1991) 18 MULR 403 for a criticism).

One of the most problematical situations in which this question has arisen involves taking blood for the purposes of testing for the presence of HIV. If a patient has consented to blood being taken in the context of treatment or diagnosis, is this consent sufficient to permit the testing of the blood for the presence of HIV where the context does not suggest that this was called for? Or, is it essential that testing for HIV may only be carried out with the explicit agreement of the patient? Again, the degree of specificity entailed in the words 'nature and purpose' determines these questions. If all that is required is that the patient should agree to the physical touching for consent to be valid, then the subsequent testing for HIV without awareness does not make the touching unlawful. If, on the other hand, 'nature and purpose' is defined in a more general way, it is arguable that an awareness that the blood is to be tested for HIV is necessary before the touching would be lawful. In our view this latter approach more properly reflects the law. The reason is ultimately one of policy. The significance to a patient of being tested for HIV (whatever the result of the test) is so great in terms of possible stigma, discrimination and personal anxiety that the law must insist that the patient must expressly agree to the test. (For a more extended discussion, see our 'Testing for HIV Infection: The Legal Framework' (1989) 86(7) LSG 32 and 86(9) LSG 30 and J Keown 'The Ashes of AIDS and the Phoenix of Informed Consent' (1989) 52 MLR 790.)

(ii) WHO IS DOING IT?

An old American mid-West case illustrates the issue of whether the identity of the person touching can effect the validity of the patient's consent.

De May v Roberts (1881) 9 NW 146 (Sup Ct Mich)

Martson CJ: The declaration in this case in the first count sets forth that the plaintiff was at a time and place named a poor married woman, and being confined in child-bed and a stranger, employed in a professional capacity defendant De May who was a physician; that the defendant visited the plaintiff as such, and against her desire and intending to deceive her wrongfully, etc, introduced and caused to be present at the house and lying-in room of the plaintiff and while she was in the pains of parturition the defendant Scattergood, who intruded upon the privacy of the plaintiff, indecently, wrongfully and unlawfully laid hands upon her and assaulted her, the said Scattergood, which was well known to defendant De May, being a young unmarried man, a stranger to the plaintiff and utterly ignorant of the practice of medicine, while the plaintiff believed that he was an assistant physician, a competent and proper person to be present and to aid her in her extremity. …

The evidence on the part of the plaintiff tended to prove the allegations of the declaration. On the part of the defendants evidence was given tending to prove that Scattergood very reluctantly accompanied Dr De May at the urgent request of the latter; that the night was a dark and stormy one, the roads over which they had to travel in getting to the house of the plaintiff were so bad that a horse could not be ridden or driven over them; that the doctor was sick and very much fatigued from overwork, and therefore asked the defendant Scattergood to accompany and assist him in carrying a lantern, umbrella and certain articles deemed necessary upon such occasions; that upon arriving at the house of the plaintiff the doctor knocked, and when the door was opened by the husband of the plaintiff, De May said to him 'that I had fetched a friend along to help carry my things;' he, plaintiff's husband, said all right, and seemed to be perfectly satisfied. They were bid to enter, treated kindly and no objection whatever made to the presence of defendant Scattergood. That while there Scattergood, at Dr De May's request, took hold of plaintiff's hand and held her during a paroxysm of pain, and that both of the defendants in all respects throughout acted in a proper and becoming manner actuated by a sense of duty and kindness. …

Dr De May therefore took an unprofessional young unmarried man with him, introduced and permitted him to remain in the house of the plaintiff when it was apparent that he could hear at least, if not see all that was said and done, and as the jury must have found, under the instructions given, without either the plaintiff or her husband having any knowledge or reason to believe the true character of such third party. It would be shocking to our sense of right, justice and propriety to doubt even but that for such an act the law would afford an ample remedy. To the plaintiff the occasion was a most sacred one and no one had a right to intrude unless invited or because of some real and pressing necessity which it is not pretended existed in this case. The plaintiff had a legal right to the privacy of her apartment at such a time, and the law secures to her this right by requiring others to observe it, and to abstain from its violation. The fact that at the time, she consented to the presence of Scattergood supposing him to be a physician, does not preclude her from maintaining an action and recovering substantial damages upon afterwards ascertaining his true character. In obtaining admission at such a time and under such circumstances without fully disclosing his true character, both parties were guilty of deceit, and the wrong thus done entitles the injured party to recover the damages afterwards sustained, from shame and mortification upon discovering the true character of the defendants.

Judgment for plaintiff affirmed.

You may think it harsh that a man who went to assist the doctor and comforted the woman during her labour should be held to have committed a battery. But, battery clearly is concerned in part with protecting a person's interest in dignity and undoubtedly the plaintiff's privacy and dignity were invaded. The identity of the defendant, Scattergood was, therefore, crucial in the context of the times since a woman would be affronted if any man other than a doctor assisted her in confinement.

A modern Canadian criminal law case echoes this approach.

R v Maurantonio (1967) 65 DLR (2d) 674 (Ontario CA)

Hartt J: The appellant, Antonio Maurantonio, was convicted by WFB Rogers, Co Ct J, on six counts of indecent assault contrary to s 141 of the Criminal Code, [which we saw earlier in *Bolduc and Bird*] and sentenced to be imprisoned for a period of two years less one day on each count, the sentences to run concurrently. The appeal is from both conviction and sentence.

The convictions arose out of circumstances associated with the attendance of the six female persons upon the appellant at various times while he was allegedly engaged in the practice of medicine for a period of some six months in the City of Toronto.

At the outset of the trial the appellant made the following factual admissions as he is entitled to do pursuant to s 562 of the Criminal Code:

(a) that he was not a medical doctor and did not have any formal education or training and was not entitled to practise medicine;

(b) that he represented to the public and specifically to the complainants that he was a doctor of medicine and licensed to practise medicine; and

(c) that the complainants consented to being treated or examined by the accused only because they believed he was a doctor and that they would not have consented to being examined or treated had they known he was not a doctor.

The evidence called during the course of the trial established the facts covered by these admissions. Clearly, the appellant was not entitled to practise medicine in Ontario or any other jurisdiction and each of the complainants sought his services in the belief that he was a qualified medical practitioner. ...

There is no doubt but that each of the complainants consented to the intimate incidents associated with their own particular examination or treatment and that, but for their consent, the physical activity involved would have clearly constituted an indecent assault. Several grounds of appeal were advanced and disposed of adversely to the appellant during the course of oral argument. The sole point which remains to be determined involves the interpretation of s 141(2), that is, was the consent in each case obtained by 'false and fraudulent representations as to the nature and quality of the act'.

Any consideration of the relationship of fraud to the presence or absence of consent must be prefaced by an appreciation of the distinction between two different kinds of fraud. The general rule is that if deception causes a misunderstanding as to the nature of the act itself there is no legally recognized consent because what happened is not that for which consent was given, whereas consent induced by fraud is as effective as any other consent, if the deceit relates not to the thing done but merely to some collateral matter.

It is urged by counsel for the appellant that the words 'nature and quality of the act' as used in s 141(2) have reference only to the physical touching, that such contact was known to the complainants to be part of the alleged treatment or examination and that each complainant did, in fact, consent to what actually took place. The admitted false representation of the appellant that he was a licensed and duly qualified medical practitioner then becomes only fraud in the inducement and not fraud in the factum. That is, that although the appellant may have fraudulently induced them to submit to the examination or treatment upon the false representation that he was a physician, nevertheless there was no misrepresentation as to the nature and quality of the act to be performed. Therefore, each complainant having consented to the actual physical contact involved, the appellant, despite the admitted fraudulent misrepresentation as to his status, could not be convicted under s 141 of the Criminal Code.

Although superficially appealing, this argument cannot prevail. In my opinion, the words 'nature and quality of the act' as used in s 141(2) should not be so narrowly construed as to include only the physical action but rather must be interpreted to encompass those concomitant circumstances which give meaning to the particular physical activity in question. Here the physical touching was essentially bound up with, and consented to, as part of the medical treatment or examination. It was only to a medical examination or medical treatment, including the reasonable intimate physical contact necessary thereto, that each complainant consented. If that to which they were subjected was not in fact of the nature of a *bona fide* medical examination or treatment then it was something entirely different from that to which they consented. The physical contact in issue here being of an equivocal nature in the circumstances, the question whether or not the complainants received *bona fide* medical attention was dependent upon the intent with which it was carried out and, as such, became a question of fact to be determined on all the evidence by the trial tribunal. On the six counts upon which convictions were registered that issue was found adversely to the appellant by the trial Judge and there is ample evidence to support that finding.

The fraudulent misrepresentation of the appellant that he was a duly qualified and licensed physician was not what induced the complainants to submit to the physical acts entailing the touching of their persons. The false representation which led to consent was that what the appellant was about to do was to conduct a medical examination or administer medical treatment. Since the representation went to the very nature and quality of the act to be performed the consent of each of the complainants, even if given in the full understanding of what physical acts the appellant was about to perform, 'was obtained by false and fraudulent representations as to the nature and quality of the act'. The question is not whether the appellant was a duly qualified and licensed physician but rather an issue of fact as to whether or not the physical touching was a necessary part of a *bona fide* medical examination or treatment, because it was to that and that alone that consent was given. In deciding this issue of fact the trial tribunal would, of course, be entitled to consider the lack of professional qualifications. The weight to be given to this and other relevant facts would depend on the circumstances of a particular case. The authorities, both English and Canadian, dealing with the question of fraud and its relationship to consent are clearly and succinctly reviewed by the High Court of Australia in *Papadimitropoulos v R* (1957) 98 CLR 249, and little would be gained by repeating them here.

In the result, the appeal against the convictions will be dismissed.

Kelly JA agreed.

Laskin JA (dissenting): The sole argument of the Crown to show that consent was obtained 'by false and fraudulent representations as to the nature and quality of the acts' done to the female patients is that these women gave their consent to a medical examination or treatment and this they did not get because of the accused's misrepresentation of his character or qualification. ...

It might just as well be argued that a medically trained person would be guilty of indecent assault if he ministered as did the accused to female patients without being registered as a qualified physician. Crown counsel's admission, previously referred to, makes the question of professional qualification in the present case external to the issue to be decided under s 141(2).

In this state of the matter, it was incumbent on the Crown to prove deceit by the accused as to the 'nature and quality' of the very acts charged against him; whether or not they constituted medical treatment in the abstract would be merely a refined way of challenging professional qualification, and to raise this in the context of s 141(2) would, in my opinion, be begging the question to be decided. the Crown failed completely to show any deceit in this respect.

The plain fact is that the women patients involved in the charges herein against the accused were fully aware of what was being done to them, accepted what was done as medical treatment, and the accused did not delude them into accepting something other than what they expected or sought. I adopt the principle and some of the words of the High Court of Australia in *Papadimitropoulos v R* (1957) 98 CLR 249, when it said (at 261) '... once the consent is comprehending and actual the inducing causes cannot destroy its reality.'

I also find support for my view of the law applicable to this case in the recent judgment of the Supreme Court in *R v Bolduc and Bird* [1967] 3 CCC 294, 2 CRNS 40, present case is *a fortiori*; and I would say of the accused here as was said of the doctor there that [p 295 CCC]: 'There was no fraud on his part as to what he was supposed to do and in what he actually did.'

It follows that the convictions cannot stand, and I would accordingly set them aside and enter verdicts of acquittal.

It could be argued that this case is really a case about 'what's being done' and lack of consent thereto. Certainly, *De May* is a case which turns upon 'who is doing' the touching. But is this true of *Maurantonio*? The explanation of *Maurantonio* which warrants its inclusion alongside *De May* is that the character of what was being done was (for the majority) clearly affected by who was doing it; ie the actor's identity was critical in determining the nature and purpose of the touching. Laskin JA (dissenting), you will notice, was not impressed by the majority's view of the facts.

In our view, the best way to understand these cases is to say that where the identity of the person affects the understanding of *what is being done* then the patient who misapprehends does not validly consent (see *R v Tabassum* (2000) Times, 26 May (CA)). This analysis is borne out by the following decision of the Court of Appeal.

R v Richardson (1998) 43 BMLR 21 (CA)

The appellant was a registered dental practitioner. In 1996 she was suspended from practising. In the month following her suspension, without complaint from them, she treated patients whom she had treated previously. She was charged with assault occasioning actual bodily harm. At her trial, after the judge had ruled that her patients' apparent consent to their treatment was vitiated by her fraud in allowing them to think she continued to be qualified to practise, she changed her plea to guilty. It was accepted that the treatment the patients had been given was of a reasonable standard. She appealed against conviction on the ground that the judge's ruling was incorrect.

Otton LJ: In Smith and Hogan *Criminal Law* (8th edn, 1996) Professor J C Smith QC states at p 420: 'Fraud does not necessarily negative consent. It does so only if it deceives P as to the identity of the person or the nature of the act.'

This statement of principle is derived from *R v Clarence* (1888) 22 QBD 23, [1886–90] All ER Rep133, where the victim consented to sexual intercourse with the accused and although she would not have consented had she been aware of the disease from which D knew he was suffering, this was no assault. Wills J stated ((1888) 22 QBD 23 at 27, [1886–90] All ER Rep 133 at 135): 'That consent obtained by fraud is no consent at all is not true as a general proposition either in fact or in law.'

Stephen J stated ((1888) 22 QBD 23 at 44, [1886–90] All ER Rep 133 at 144):

> ... the only sorts of fraud which so far destroy the effect of a woman's consent as to convert a connection consented to in fact into a rape are frauds as to the nature of the act itself, or as to the identity of the person who does the act.

There is a clear line of authority concerning fraud and the nature of the act. In *R v Williams* [1923] 1 KB 340, [1922] All ER Rep 433, the appellant, a choir master, had sexual intercourse with a girl of 16 years of age under the pretence that her breathing was not quite right and that he had to perform an operation to enable her to produce her voice properly. The girl submitted to what was done under the belief, wilfully and fraudulently induced by the appellant, that she was being medically and surgically treated by the appellant and not with any intention that she should have intercourse with him. The Court of Criminal Appeal held that the appellant was properly convicted of rape. Lord Hewart CJ referred to *R v Case* (1850) 4 Cox CC 220, where a medical practitioner had sexual connection with a girl of 14 years of age upon the pretence that he was treating her medically and the girl made no resistance owing to a bona fide belief that she was being medically treated. It was held that he was properly convicted of an assault and might have been convicted of rape. Lord Hewart CJ also referred with approval to the dicta of Branson J in *R v Williams*:

> The law has laid it down that where a girl's consent is procured by the means which the girl says this prisoner adopted, that is to say, where she is persuaded that what is being done to her is not the ordinary act of sexual intercourse but is some medical or surgical operation in order to give her relief from some disability from which she is suffering, then that is rape although the actual thing that was done was done with her consent, because she never consented to the act of sexual intercourse. She was persuaded to consent to what he did because she thought it was not sexual intercourse and because she thought it was a surgical operation. (See [1923] 1 KB 340 at 347.)

In *R v Harms* (1944) 2 DLR 61 the Supreme Court of Canada considered s 298 of the Canadian Criminal Code, which established that, in order to vitiate consent, the false or fraudulent misrepresentation had to be as to the nature and quality of the act. Harms had falsely represented himself to be a medical doctor. Although the complainant knew that he was proposing sexual intercourse, she consented thereto because of his representations that the intercourse was in the nature of a medical treatment necessitated by a condition which he said he had diagnosed. Harms was not a medical man at all. The court held that a jury was entitled to conclude that the nature and quality of the act as far as the complainant was concerned was therapeutic and not carnal. In other words, the complainant had consented to a therapeutic act, which it was not, and had not consented to a carnal act, which it was. The consent induced by the fraudulent representation was held to have been vitiated.

The later case of *Bolduc and Bird v The Queen* (1967) 63 DLR 82 (2d) was held to be on the other side of the line. The Supreme Court of Canada considered the case of a doctor who falsely represented that his colleague was a medical student and obtained the complainant's consent to the colleague's presence at a vaginal examination. It was held that there was no indecent assault because the fraud was not as to the nature and quality of what was to be done. It was observed that the defendant's conduct was 'unethical and reprehensible, but did not have the effect of vitiating the consent'.

In *Papadimitropoulos v The Queen* (1957) 98 CLR 249 the High Court of Australia considered the case of a complainant who had sexual relations with a man whom she believed to be her husband. Unknown to her no valid marriage ceremony had ever taken place. The complainant had consented to sexual intercourse under the belief, fraudulently induced, that she had contracted a valid marriage to the man whom she believed to be her husband. It was held that these circumstances did not support a conviction for rape. The court stated ((1957) 98 CLR 249 at 261):

> Rape, as a capital felony, was defined with exactness, and although there has been some extension over the centuries in the ambit of the crime, it is quite wrong to bring within its operation forms of evil conduct because they wear some analogy to aspects of the crime and deserved punishment ... the key to such a case as the present lies in remembering that it is the penetration of the woman's body without her consent to such penetration that makes the felony. The capital felony was not directed to fraudulent

conduct inducing her consent. Frauds of that kind must be punished under other heads of the criminal law or not at all: they are not rape ... To return to the central point; rape is carnal knowledge of a woman without her consent: carnal knowledge is the physical fact of penetration; it is the consent to that which is in question; such a consent demands a perception as to what is about to take place, as to the identity of a man and the character of what he is doing. But once the consent is comprehending and actual the inducing causes cannot destroy its reality and leave the man guilty of rape.

And earlier (at 260):

It must be noted that in considering whether an apparent consent is unreal it is the mistake or misapprehension that makes it so. It is not the *fraud* producing the mistake which is material so much as the mistake itself ... tends to distract the attention from the essential inquiry, namely, whether the consent is no consent because it is not directed to the nature and character of the act. The identity of the man and the character of the physical act that is done or proposed seem now clearly to be regarded as forming part of the nature and character of the act to which the woman's consent is directed. That accords with the principles governing mistake vitiating apparent manifestations within other chapters of the law. (My emphasis.)

This result is not altogether surprising, for otherwise every bigamist would be guilty of rape.

The Law Commission in their Consultation Paper No 139 *Consent in the Criminal Law*, having considered fraud and consent generally proposed a lesser offence of obtaining consent by deception and stated (at para 6.27) that:

consent should not in general be *nullified* by deception as to any circumstances other than the nature of the act and the identity of the person doing it, but that deception as to other circumstances should give rise to liability for a lesser offence than that of non-consensual conduct. Where the defendant is aware that the other person is or may be mistaken about the nature of the act or the defendant's identity, we think that the other person's consent should be nullified as if the mistake were induced by fraud ... If a deception as to circumstances in question would give rise to liability *only* for our proposed offence of obtaining consent by deception, as distinct from the more serious offence of acting without any consent at all, liability for taking advantage of a self-induced mistake as to that circumstance could *at most* be for the lesser offence.

It is, thus, unremarkable that neither counsel has been able to cite any authority in which the complainant in a sexual case has been deceived as to the identity of the assailant and her apparent consent has held to have been vitiated by fraud. It is to be noted that s 1(2) of the Sexual Offences Act 1956 provides that a man can be guilty of rape if he induces a married woman to have sexual intercourse with him by impersonating her husband. However, this only covers the type of case where the woman is legally married and for some reason believes that the person with whom she is having sexual relations is her husband when in fact he is not.

Miss Bradley, who argued the case, ably contends that the complainants were deceived neither as to the nature or quality of the act nor as to the identity of the person carrying out the act. The statutory offence was created to punish such conduct as took place here.

Both before the judge and before this court the respondent expressly disavowed reliance upon the nature or quality of the act. Mr Walmsley for the Crown succinctly submitted that the patients were deceived into consenting to treatment by the representation that the defendant was a qualified and practising dentist and not one who had been disqualified. He further submitted that the evidence of the patients was unequivocal: had they known that the defendant had been suspended, they would not have consented to any treatment. If the treatment had been given by a person impersonating a dentist, it would have been an assault. There was no distinction to be drawn between the unqualified dentist and one who is suspended. On this basis, there was a mistake as to the true identity of the defendant.

We are unable to accept that argument. There is no basis for the proposition that the rules which determine the circumstances in which consent is vitiated can be different according to whether the case is one of sexual assault or one where the assault is non-sexual. The common element in both these cases is that they involve an assault, and the question is whether consent has been negatived. It is nowhere suggested that the common law draws such a distinction. The common law is not concerned with the question whether the mistaken consent has been induced by fraud on the part of the accused or has been self-induced. It is the nature of the mistake that is relevant, and not the reason why the mistake has been made. In summary, either there is consent to actions on the part of a person in the mistaken belief that he or they are other than they truly are, in which case it is assault or, short of this, there is no assault.

In essence, the Crown contended that the concept of the 'identity of the person' should be extended to cover the qualifications or attributes of the dentist on the basis that the patients consented to treatment by a qualified dentist and not a suspended one. We must reject that submission. In all the charges brought against the appellant, the complainants were fully aware of the identity of the appellant. To accede to the submission would be to strain or distort the everyday meaning of the word 'identity', the dictionary definition of which is 'the condition of being the same'.

It was suggested in argument that we might be assisted by the civil law of consent, where such expressions as 'real' or 'informed' consent prevail. In this regard, the criminal and the civil law do not run along the same track. The concept of informed consent has no place in the criminal law. It would also be a mistake, in our view, to introduce the concept of a duty to communicate information to a patient about the risk of an activity before consent to an act can be treated as valid. The gravamen of the appellant's conduct in the instant case was that the complainants consented to treatment from her although their consent had been procured by her failure to inform them that she was no longer qualified to practise. This was clearly reprehensible and may well found the basis of a civil claim for damages. But we are quite satisfied that it is not a basis for finding criminal liability in the field of offences against the person.

How did the Court of Appeal approach the issue of the patients' consents? First, the court concluded that the defendant's fraud was only relevant if it vitiated the patients' consents. It was not a free-standing basis for impugning the validity of the consents. This is correct and we will return to it later. Secondly, the Court of Appeal added a second element to the test of whether the patient's consent was real – 'was the patient mistaken about the nature of the act *or the defendant's identity?*' To be fair, this formulation is common currency in criminal law texts (see eg J C Smith and B Hogan *Criminal Law* (8th edn, 1996) p 469) and in the criminal cases concerned with rape (see eg *R v Linekar* [1995] 3 All ER 69 (CA)). Perhaps, it is best seen as a quirk of that area of the criminal law where identity of the actor is, perhaps, most important to the woman. But, analytically, that will not do because in *Richardson* the Court of Appeal concluded that the law of consent was the same in cases of sexual and non-sexual assaults and across both the civil and criminal law. Certainly, as a distinct and separate element of 'understanding', the identity of the actor finds no direct counterpart in the civil (medical law) cases. It is better seen, rather like the so-called 'fraud' or 'bad faith exception', as an aspect of he 'nature' or 'nature and purpose' test. In other words, the identity of the actor may affect the nature of what is being done, for example, as in *Maurantonio* (*supra*) (see, *R v Tabassum* (2000) Times, 26 May (CA) no consent to the 'quality' of the act where the defendant was not medically qualified). If it does not, it is simply irrelevant to the quality of the patient's consent. Thirdly, the patients agreed to therapeutic dental work and that is precisely what they got from a dentist, albeit one who had been suspended by the General Dental Council. The court was correct to hold on the facts that the patients' consents were valid.

A common everyday practice in teaching hospitals offers a troubling example of the relevance to consent of the identity of the person touching. Medical students and trainee (unregistered) doctors routinely, as part of their training, lay hands on patients. Obviously, when the patient knows that the student is a student, and consents to being touched, no problem will ordinarily arise. There are at least two factual situations, however, which do give rise to legal difficulties if the patient is *unaware* that the person is a student.

First, a student may, in fact, examine (ie touch) a patient solely so as to acquire knowledge or experience for himself. The touching plays no part in the care of the patient. In such a circumstance, the consent given by the patient is probably invalid since the identity of the person touching affects the nature of what is being done to the patient, ie training rather than caring.

Secondly, a student may touch a patient as part of the patient's care. Does the lack of awareness by the patient of the identity of the person touching (identity being status here) affect the validity of the patient's consent? You will recall that

Laskin JA in *Maurantonio* thought that if the patient got what he was bargaining for, the identity of the carer was irrelevant. The difficulty, as the majority pointed out, is that the patient may have bargained for a doctor. In our view, the majority's position is correct in principle. It is a nice question as to what conclusion the majority would have reached in the situation posed. It could be said that the difference between a lay person and a doctor is material whereas the difference between a medical student (presumably supervised) and a doctor is not. In our view, unless the patient suffered harm and could establish that the medical student was negligent, an English court would reject any claim by a patient.

Hence, an action in battery would not lie or reverting to the analysis we have adopted: this level of mistake as to identity would not invalidate the consent of the patient. (The need for the explicit consent of the patient to being touched by students as part of their training is recognised in the Government Circular: *Medical Students in Hospitals* (HC (91) 18, April 1991).)

Contrast with the approach we suggest the case of *Perna v Pirozzi* (1983) 457 A 2d 431. In this case, a patient brought an action in battery when she discovered that she had not been operated upon by the doctor whom she had specifically requested when agreeing to the operation.

Perna v Pirozzi (1983) 457 A 2d 431 (NJ Sup Ct)

Pollock J: On the advice of his family physician, Thomas Perna entered St Joseph's Hospital on 8 May 1977 for tests and a urological consultation. Mr Perna consulted Dr Pirozzi, a specialist in urology, who examined Mr Perna and recommended that he undergo surgery for the removal of kidney stones.

Dr Pirozzi was associated with a medical group that also included Drs Del Gaizo and Ciccone. The doctors testified at trial that their medical group customarily shared patients; no doctor had individual patients, and each doctor was familiar with all cases under care of the group. Further, it was not the practice of the group to inform patients which member would operate; the physicians operated as a 'team', and their regular practice was to decide just prior to the operation who was to operate. If, however, a patient requested a specific member of the group as his surgeon, that surgeon would perform the operation. Nothing indicated that Mr Perna was aware of the group's custom of sharing patients or of their methods for assigning surgical duties.

Although Mr Perna had never consulted with Dr Del Gaizo or Dr Ciccone, he had been treated by Dr Pirozzi previously in conjunction with a bladder infection. According to Mr Perna, he specifically requested Dr Pirozzi to perform the operation. None of the defendants directly contradicted Mr Perna's testimony. However, Dr Ciccone testified that he met with Mr Perna on May 16 and, without discussing who would operate, explained that two members of the medical group would be present during the operation. The following day, in the presence of a urological resident, Mr Perna executed a consent form that named Dr Pirozzi as the operating surgeon and authorized him, with the aid of unnamed 'assistants', to perform the surgery …

The operation was performed on 18 May by Dr Del Gaizo assisted by Dr Ciccone. Dr Pirozzi was not present during the operation; in fact, he was not on duty that day. At the time of surgery, Dr Del Gaizo and Dr Ciccone were unaware that only Dr Pirozzi's name appeared on the consent form.

Mr Perna first learned of the identities of the operating surgeons when he was readmitted to the hospital on June 11 because of post-surgical complications…

[The plaintiffs] alleged that there was a failure to obtain Mr Perna's informed consent to the operation performed by Dr Del Gaizo. That is, plaintiffs claimed that Mr Perna's consent to the operation was conditioned upon his belief that Dr Pirozzi would be the surgeon …

… if an operation is properly performed, albeit by a surgeon operating without the consent of the patient, and the patient suffers no injuries except those which foreseeably follow from the operation, then a jury could find that the substitution of surgeons did not cause any compensable injury. Even there, however, a jury could award damages for mental anguish resulting from the belated knowledge that the operation was performed by a doctor to whom the patient had not given consent …

A nonconsensual operation remains a battery even if performed skillfully and to the benefit of the patient. The medical profession itself recognizes that it is unethical to mislead a patient as to the identity of the doctor who performs the operation. American College of Surgeons, Statements on Principles, § IA (June 1981). Participation in such a deception is a recognized cause for discipline by the medical profession. See American College of Surgeons, Bylaws, art VII, § 1(c) (as amended June 1976). By statute, the State Board of Medical Examiners is empowered to prevent the professional certification or future professional practice of a person who '[h]as engaged in the use or employment of dishonesty, fraud, deception, misrepresentation, false promise or false pretence ...' *NJSA* 45: 1–21. Consequently, a statutory, as well as a moral, imperative compels doctors to be honest with their patients.

Few decisions bespeak greater trust and confidence than the decision of a patient to proceed with surgery. Implicit in that decision is a willingness of the patient to put his or her life in the hands of a known and trusted medical doctor. Sometimes circumstances will arise in which, because of an emergency, the limited capacity of the patient, or some other valid reason, the doctor cannot obtain the express consent of the patient to a surrogate surgeon. Other times, doctors who practice in a medical group may explain to a patient that any one of them may perform a medical procedure. In that situation, the patient may accept any or all the members of the group as his surgeon. In still other circumstances, the patient may consent to an operation performed by a resident under the supervision of the attending physician. The point is that a patient has the right to know who will operate and the consent form should reflect the patient's decision. Where a competent patient consents to surgery by a specific surgeon of his choice, the patient has every right to expect that surgeon, not another, to operate.

In our view an English court would be unlikely to adopt the approach in this case for a number of reasons. First, the quality of the touching does not change simply because a different doctor carries out the procedure. Second, and in any event, the standard NHS consent form (which we have already seen) specifically appraises the patient that there is no guarantee that a particular doctor will carry out the procedure. This is not to say that a claim in contract (if one existed) could not be brought where it was an express term of the contract that a particular doctor and no other would carry out the procedure (*Michael v Molesworth* [1950] 2 BMJ 171 (£1 damages awarded)). In our view, a better explanation of *Perna v Pirozzi* is that the patient had only given a *conditional* consent which was not satisfied and therefore there was *no* consent to the procedure (see *Principles of Medical Law* I Kennedy and A Grubb (eds) (1998) at para 3.49). Another example might arise where a patient consents to a blood transfusion but only with blood donated by 'X' and 'Y's' blood is used (see *Ashcraft v King* (1991) 278 Cal Rptr 900).

(iii) RISKS AND CONSEQUENCES

The question here is whether the lack of awareness of risks inherent in a medical procedure or possible consequences of undergoing it, can affect the validity of the patient's consent. As we have seen from cases such as *Chatterton*, *Sidaway* and *Reibl*, the approach of the courts is that knowledge or ignorance of risks or possible consequences are properly to be dealt with by the tort of negligence. Consent for the purposes of the tort of battery is not affected. This modern legal position reflects the view of the law taken in the well-known nineteenth-century cases of *R v Clarence* (1888) 22 QBD 23 and *Hegarty v Shine* (1878) 4 LR Ir 288. In both cases a woman had sexual intercourse with a man as a consequence of which she was infected with a venereal disease. In neither case was her consent held to have been vitiated by her lack of awareness of the risk she ran and the consequences of having intercourse. As we have seen, Professor Somerville argues that some consequences and some risks are so intrinsically a feature of the procedure that the patient must be aware of them in order to understand the 'nature and purpose' of the procedure and therefore give a valid consent for the purposes of an action in battery (see *R v Cuerrier* [1998] 2 SCR 371 (Can Sup Ct) per McLachlin J at para 72: 'Where the person represents that he or she is disease-free, and consent is given on that basis, deception on that matter goes to the very *act* of assault' (our emphasis). See discussion *infra*, 672).

(b) Revisiting the fraud exception

In *Reibl* Laskin CJ stated that a failure to disclose the attendant risks should go to negligence rather than battery 'unless there has been misrepresentation or fraud to secure consent to the treatment ...'. This would suggest, on its face, that where fraud or misrepresentation were involved consent may be vitiated *even* if the patient understood the nature and purpose of the procedure, ie the fraud or misrepresentation went to other things.

The Canadian medical law scholars Ellen Picard and Gerald Robertson analyses Laskin CJ's view in *Reibl*.

E Picard and G Robertson *Legal Liability of Doctors and Hospitals in Canada* (3rd edn, 1996)

One area of great concern springs from the comments of the Supreme Court of Canada on misrepresentation and fraud. Professor Klar has said that the Chief Justice 'was not clear as to what the misrepresentation or fraud must relate or how it will operate' [(1982) 3 SCLR 385]. Professors Gochnauer and Fleming [(1981) 15 UBCL Rev 475] find an internal inconsistency in the Chief Justice's words and asks whether by them he meant to give an illustration of or an exception to the test for battery. Professor Somerville raises a number of concerns about the step taken by the Supreme Court of Canada and says a basic question is: 'Why does "misrepresentation or fraud to secure consent to the treatment" cause non-disclosure of a risk to give rise to a cause of action in battery, where it would not do so if the elements of misrepresentation or fraud were not present?' [(1981) 26 McGill LJ 740]. She suggests an analysis that minimises the Supreme Court ruling and its consequence of making a battery unavailable where it would in the past have been available.

At the bottom of the reservations expressed by a number of commentators is the apparent attempt by the Supreme Court of Canada to separate risk and consent. The criticism is strong. As Professor Somerville has summarised it:

... it is submitted that to the extent that the Supreme Court has limited the availability of an action in battery by stating the law to be that *risks do not relate to the basic nature and character of an act and, consequently, their non-disclosure cannot vitiate battery-avoiding consent*, the ruling may not be desirable [emphasis supplied].

Professors Gochnauer and Fleming say:

The Court's position separating risk and consent is a distortion of our ordinary understanding of the concepts and in a number of cases will defeat our normal, reasonable expectations.

They are critical of the failure of the Supreme Court of Canada to give any policy considerations to justify its position and say:

By cutting us off from our ordinary intuitions in these matters without setting up signposts of policy the decision fails to clarify wholly the applicability of battery and negligence when there has been a breach of the duty to disclose risks of medical treatment.

The parameters of the new battery action have not yet been fully tested by litigation. Although the number of cases where fraud or 'serious' misrepresentation (such as negligent or fraudulent misrepresentation as contrasted with innocent misrepresentation) will be alleged and proven will likely be few, there may be some confusion in the 'grey' areas. For example, in a case where a person is told he will be given an anaesthetic but is not told this will be done by moving a needle into his heart would there be misrepresentation? Would there be misrepresentation if a tonsillectomy was described as a minor, routine and safe procedure when for that patient it was not? What about the prescription of tranquillisers for emotional complaints given without a description of the risks of addiction and misuse? Hopefully future judicial review of battery will provide answers if not an assuagement of the critics.

Communication between the health care professional and the patient is the means by which a valid consent to treatment is given. It is also part of the therapy of good medicine. The absence of good communication is the reason for most lawsuits against health care professionals and hospitals.

In *Chatterton v Gerson* (*op cit*), Bristow J seemed to contemplate 'fraud' or 'bad faith' vitiating consent that would otherwise be valid (see also, *Appleton v Garrett* (1995) 34 BMLR 23 (Dyson J) at 25–26). On the other hand, in *Sidaway* Sir John Donaldson MR (in the Court of Appeal) specifically rejected the view that fraud going to matters other than 'nature and purpose' invalidated consent for the purposes of the tort of battery. In doing so, he approved *R v Clarence*. In our view, Sir John Donaldson MR is correct. The so-called 'fraud exception' is in fact not an exception at all. At all times the issue in a battery case is whether the patient understood the 'nature and purpose' of the procedure. If he misunderstands, in principle the reason for that is irrelevant. If he understands, fraud as to other matters cannot affect this understanding and cannot give rise to an action in battery. It may, of course, (as with a negligence misrepresentation) give rise to liability in the tort of negligence. The Court of Appeal affirmed the view of Sir John Donaldson MR in *R v Richardson* (1998) 43 BMLR 21 (CA), a case we discussed earlier. Otton LJ stated (at 26):

> The common law is not concerned with the question whether the mistaken consent has been induced by fraud on the part of the accused or has been self-induced. It is the nature of the mistake that is relevant, and not the reason why the mistake has been made.

A fortiori, therefore, it will be clear that Laskin CJ's reference to a misrepresentation vitiating consent is not the law in England.

(c) The place of battery in modern medical law

What we have seen is a determined effort by the courts whether in England or elsewhere severely to limit the scope of the tort of battery. The role left for it is virtually vestigial. As a mechanism for compensating injured patients, however, it remains a powerful symbolic and actual deterrent against doctors ignoring the right of autonomy of their patients. It is clear that the courts can manipulate the content of the 'nature and purpose' test in order to expand or contract the scope of battery. This is not really a semantic disagreement however it might appear: it is ultimately a matter of judicial policy.

The judicial process can be seen, albeit in the criminal context, in the Canadian Supreme Court decision of *R v Currier* [1998] 2 SCR 371.

The accused was charged with two counts of aggravated assault pursuant to s 268 of the Criminal Code. Even though he had been explicitly instructed, by a public health nurse, to inform all prospective sexual partners that he was HIV-positive and to use condoms every time he engaged in sexual intercourse, the accused had unprotected sexual relations with the two complainants without informing them he was HIV-positive. Both complainants had consented to unprotected sexual intercourse with the accused, but they testified at trial that if they had known that he was HIV-positive they would never have engaged in unprotected intercourse with him. At the time of trial, neither complainant had tested positive for the virus. The trial judge entered a directed verdict acquitting the accused. The Court of Appeal upheld the acquittals.

The judges all allowed the appeal and ordered a new trial. They did so, however, for differing reasons. Cory, Major, Bastarache and Binnie JJ held that under s 268 fraud extended beyond the 'nature and quality' of the act and included acts where the consent was obtained by the defendant dishonestly exposing the person to a 'significance risk of serious bodily harm'. L'Heureux-Dubé J went further and held that fraud covered any dishonest inducement to consent. For us, the most interesting judgment is that of McLachlin J. Her judgment more closely tracks the common law position and is less dependent upon the specific statutory provision in Canada (s 268 of the Criminal Code) and the intention of the Canadian Parliament when it was amended in 1983. For us, we can see McLachlin J identify the common law post-*Clarence*, and its application of the 'nature and purpose' test and then move on to consider its application it modern society.

R v Currier [1998] 2 SCR 371 (Can Sup Ct)

McLachlin J: *I.   Introduction*
... 25 For more than a century, the law has been settled; fraud does not vitiate consent to assault unless the mistake goes to the nature of the act or the identity of the partner. Fraud as to collateral aspects of a consensual encounter, like the possibility of contracting serious venereal disease, does not vitiate consent. On this appeal the Crown asks us to change this settled law. We are asked to rule that deceiving one's partner about the fact that one has HIV vitiates consent, converting consensual sex into assault.

26 My colleagues L'Heureux-Dubé J and Cory J propose new rules which would criminalize dishonestly obtained sex in a wide variety of circumstances. I sympathize with their goals. The venereal disease of HIV and the AIDS it causes are the cause of terrible suffering and death. The wrong done to a person who is deceived into having unprotected sexual intercourse by a lie about HIV status can be inestimable. However, I respectfully find the approaches they advocate are too broad, falling outside the power of the courts to make incremental changes to the common law. I propose a narrower extension limited to failure to disclose venereal disease . . .

III. The Issues
28 The first issue in this case is whether Parliament, in enacting s 265(3) of the *Criminal Code*, intended to criminalize deceptive sexual conduct. If it did not, a second issue arises: whether the change sought is one the courts may properly make . . .

IV. Analysis

1.   Did Parliament Intend to Change the Law of Fraud for Sexual Assault ...
I turn to what Parliament intended when it adopted a new definition of fraud for assault, including sexual assault, in 1983. Can the intent to radically broaden the crime of assault be inferred from the fact that Parliament omitted the old words "nature and quality of the act"? I think not.

36 First, the phase "nature and quality of the act" did not state the law as it existed even before 1983. The criminal law of assault is an amalgam of the codified provisions of the *Criminal Code* and the uncodified common law. Prior to 1983, the *Code*'s reference to indecent assault described the relevant concept of fraud as "fraud as to the nature and quality of the act". It said nothing about "identity". Yet Canadian courts for over a hundred years accepted that fraud as to identity could negate consent, on the basis of the rule at common law. In 1983 Parliament removed the reference in the *Code* to the other case where the common law recognized fraud vitiating consent to sexual intercourse – fraud as to the nature and quality of the act. The reasonable inference is that Parliament supposed that just as the courts had read "identity" into the criminal law of sexual assault even though the *Code* did not mention it, so the courts would continue to read "nature and quality of the act" into the law even though it was not mentioned. To put it another way, Parliament must be supposed to have expected that the courts would continue to read the *Code* provisions on sexual assault against the background of the common law, unless it used language clearly indicating that it was altering the common law. There is nothing in s 265 of the *Criminal Code* to indicate an intention to remove the common law limitations on fraud for assault. ...

2.   Is it Appropriate for this Court to Change the Law?
42 Parliament has not changed the common law definition of fraud in relation to assault. This leaves the question of whether this Court should do so. ...

58 I have concluded that the broad-based proposals for changing the law put forward by my colleagues go much further than the incremental change to the common law permitted to courts. However, it does not follow that all change to the law of assault is barred. It is open to courts to make incremental changes by extending the common law concepts of nature of the act and identity, provided the ramifications of the changes are not overly complex. Before the appeal can be rejected, it is necessary to consider whether this can be done.

59 It is the proper role of the courts to update the common law from time to time to bring it into harmony with the changing needs and mores of society: *Salituro supra.* This applies to the common law concept of fraud in relation to assault. In *R v Maurantonio*, [1968] 1 OR 145, a majority of the Ontario Court of Appeal held that a man who secured sexual contact by falsely holding himself out to be a doctor had committed a fraud as to the nature and quality of the act. In rejecting a strict interpretation of the phrase "nature and quality of the act" found in the *Criminal Code*, Hartt J (*ad hoc*) stated, at p 153:

> ... the words "nature and quality of the act" ... should not be so narrowly construed as to include only the physical action but rather must be interpreted to encompass those concomitant circumstances which give meaning to the particular physical activity in question. ...

62 In addition to deceit as to venereal disease, the common law recognized deceit as to identity (*R v Dee* (1884), 14 LR Ir 468) and deceit as to whether the act was a medical procedure as opposed to a sexual act, as being capable of vitiating consent to sexual intercourse (*R v Flattery* (1877), 2 QBD 410).

63 *Bennett* and *Sinclair* were disapproved of in *Hegarty v Shine* (1878), 14 Cox CC 145. *Hegarty* involved a civil action for assault and breach of promise of marriage. After having intercourse out of wedlock for a year and becoming pregnant, the plaintiff discovered she and her baby had contracted syphilis from the defendant, who had concealed his condition. The Court of Appeal dismissed the plaintiff's claim on the ground of *ex turpi causa* because they deemed the acts to be immoral and illegal. In particular, the judges held that there was no duty to disclose in such an immoral relation. ...

64 The majority in *Clarence, supra*, noting these comments in *Hegarty*, overruled the cases that had held that deceit as to venereal disease could vitiate consent. Venereal disease, in the majority's view, did not go to the nature of the act. That phrase was confined to whether the act was sexual or non-sexual, as in the "medical act" cases: *Flattery, supra*; *R v Case* (1850), 1 Den 580, 169 ER 381. Stephen J expressed concern that once the law ventured beyond the type of act (ie sexual or non-sexual) and the identity of the perpetrator, no clear line could be drawn between deceptions which should not properly engage the criminal law, and deceptions which could. In essence, the majority's view has stood as law ever since. When Parliament enacted the *Criminal Code* in 1892, the drafters added "quality" of the act to "nature" in describing the type of fraud capable of vitiating consent: *Criminal Code*, SC 1892, c 29, ss 259,266. However, it is unclear what, if anything, that this added to the original common law phrase "nature of the act".

65 Against this background, I return to the conditions for court-made change. The basic precondition of such change is that it is required to bring the law into step with the changing needs of society. This established, the change must meet the condition of being an incremental development of the common law that does not possess unforeseeable and complex ramifications.

66 In the case at bar, I am satisfied that the current state of the law does not reflect the values of Canadian society. It is unrealistic, indeed shocking, to think that consent given to sex on the basis that one's partner is HIV-free stands unaffected by blatant deception on that matter. To put it another way, few would think the law should condone a person who has been asked whether he has HIV, lying about that fact in order to obtain consent. To say that such a person commits fraud vitiating consent, thereby rendering the contact an assault, seems right and logical.

67 Prior to *Clarence*, the common law recognized that deception as to sexually transmitted disease carrying a high risk of infection, constituted fraud vitiating consent to sexual intercourse. Returning the law to this position would represent an incremental change to the law. If it was an increment to reverse the previous common law rule that deceit as to venereal disease could vitiate consent, it is no greater increment to reverse that decision and return to the former state of the law. The change is, moreover, consistent with Parliament's 1983 amendment of the *Criminal Code* to remove the phrase "nature and quality of the act", which suggests that Parliament, while retaining the common law of fraud in relation to consent negativing assault, did not wish to freeze the restrictive mould of *Clarence*.

68 The final and most difficult question is whether the change would introduce complex and unforeseeable changes of the sort better left to Parliament. The first objection under this head is that made by Stephen J. In *Clarence*, that no clear line can be drawn between criminal and non-criminal conduct once the law leaves the certainty of he dual criteria of nature of the act in the sense of whether it was sexual or non-sexual, and the identity of the perpetrator. The argument is made that to go beyond these criteria would be to open the door to convictions

for assault in the case, for example, where a man promises a woman a fur coat in return for sexual intercourse: *Fifteenth Report of the Criminal Law Revision Committee on Sexual Offences* (Cmdn 9213), cited with approval in *R v Linekar* [1995] 3 All ER 69 (CA).

69 This difficulty is a serious one. The courts should not broaden the criminal law to catch conduct that society generally views as non-criminal. If that is to be done, Parliament must do it. Furthermore, the criminal law must be clear. I agree with the fundamental principle affirmed in the English cases that it is imperative that there be a clear line between criminal and non-criminal conduct. Absent this, the criminal law loses its deterrent effect and becomes unjust. For these reasons, I earlier argued against Cory J's imposition of criminal liability for non-disclosure in cases of "significant risk of serious harm", and L'Heureux-Dubé J's approach of finding fraud for every deception inducing consent.

70 The question is whether a narrower increment is feasible that catches only harm of the sort at issue in this appeal and draws the required bright line. In my view, it is. A return to the pre-*Clarence* view of the common law would draw a clear line between criminal conduct and non-criminal conduct. As I have explained, pre-*Clarence*, the law permitted fraud to vitiate consent to contact where there was (a) a deception as to the sexual character of the act; (b) deception as to the identity of the perpetrator; or (c) deception as to the presence of a sexually transmitted disease giving rise to serious risk or probability of infecting the complainant (*Sinclair*, *supra*). This rule is clear and contained. It would catch the conduct here at issue, without permitting people to be convicted of assault for inducements like false promises of marriage or fur coats. The test for deception would be objective, focussing on whether the accused falsely represented to the complainant that he or she was disease-free when he knew or ought to have known that there was a high risk of infecting his partner. The test for inducement would be subjective, in the sense that the judge or jury must be satisfied beyond a reasonable doubt that the fraud actually induced the consent.

71 From a theoretical point of view, the proposed change follows the time-honoured methodology of making changes to the common law on an incremental basis. This, however, is not enough. The addition of a new common law category should reflect some underlying principle that ties it to the logic and policy underlying the existing rule and permits future developments, if any, to proceed on a reasoned, principled basis. If the underlying principle is so broad that it admits of extension into debatable or undesirable areas, then the proposed change should not be made. It was the inability to identify such a principle that seems to have lain behind the decision in *Clarence* to narrow the rule, and the recent decision of the English Court of Appeal in *Linekar* not to extend the rule to deceit as to payment for sexual services.

72 With the greatest of deference to the learned judges in these cases, an explanation may be suggested for why deceit as to venereal disease may vitiate consent while deceit as to other inducements, like promises of marriage or fur coats, does not. Consent to unprotected sexual intercourse is consent to sexual congress with a certain person and to the transmission of bodily fluids from that person. Where the person represents that he or she is disease-free, and consent is given on that basis, deception on that matter goes to the very act of assault. The complainant does not consent to the transmission of diseased fluid into his or her body. This deception in a very real sense goes to the nature of the sexual act, changing it from an act that has certain natural consequences (whether pleasure, pain or pregnancy), to a potential sentence of disease or death. It differs fundamentally from deception as to the consideration that will be given for consent, like marriage, money or a fur coat, in that it relates to the physical act itself. It differs, moreover, in a profoundly serious way that merits the criminal sanction.

73 This suffices to justify the position of the common law pre-*Clarence* that deception as to venereal disease may vitiate consent. The question of whether other categories of fraud could be logically added on the basis that deceit as to them also fundamentally alters the nature of the physical act itself, is better left for another day. It is doubtful that natural consequences, like pregnancy, would qualify, as they are the natural concomitant of the sexual act, and do not fundamentally alter its nature. Similarly, as discussed, promises as to future conduct used to induce consent do not fundamentally change the nature of the physical act. Again, protected sex would not be caught; the common law pre-*Clarence* required that there be a high risk or probability of transmitting the disease: *Sinclair*, *supra*. These observations largely displace the fear of unprincipled overextension that motivated the majority in *Clarence* to exclude deceit as to sexually transmitted disease as a basis on which fraud could vitiate consent.

74 It remains to consider the argument that extending the law, even in this limited fashion, will have unforeseen, complex and undesirable ramifications. Regrettable as it is, it may be that criminalizing deceit as to sexually transmitted disease inducing consent may prevent some people from seeking testing and treatment, out of fear that if they learn about their disease they will be forced to choose between abstaining from unprotected sexual relations

and becoming criminals. On the other hand, it may foster greater disclosure. The message that people must be honest about their communicable disease is an important one. Conduct like that in the case at bar shocks the conscience and should permit of a criminal remedy. In addition, the proposed extension of the law is relatively narrow, catching only deceit as to venereal disease where it is established, beyond a reasonable doubt, that there was a high risk of infection and that the defendant knew or ought to have known that the fraud actually induced consent to unprotected sex. Finally, I note that s 221 of the *Criminal Code* (criminal negligence causing bodily harm) already makes it a crime to engage in unprotected sexual intercourse without disclosing HIV-positive status where the sexual partner contracts HIV as a result: *R v Mercer* (1993), 84 CCC (3d) 41 (Nfld CA). There is no evidence that the application of s 221 has had an adverse effect on testing by extending criminal responsibility to cases where the defendant's partners are unfortunate enough to have been infected. The extension I propose represents only a modest step beyond this offence. Bearing in mind all of these considerations, I am satisfied that this limited change will not have far-reaching, unforeseeable or undesirable ramifications.

75 I conclude that the common law should be changed to permit deceit about sexually transmitted disease that induces consent to be treated as fraud vitiating consent under s 265 of the *Criminal Code*.

Of course, the policy arguments in this context – in particular where an extension of the criminal law is proposed – may have no application in a battery action against a doctor (for a thoughtful discussion, see P Lewis 'The Criminalisation of the Sexual Transmission of HIV in Canada: Implications for the English Position' (1998) 9(1) Dispatches 1–6). Crucial, however, is the nature of the judicial approach – not textual but contextual policy-making. McLachlin J does, after all, seem to 'fit' the facts within the existing rubric of the common law (see para 72). We can conclude by reminding ourselves of Professor Gerald Robertson's explanation of the decline in the tort of battery in the context of medical law.

G Robertson 'Informed Consent to Medical Treatment' (1981) 97 LQR 102

It is submitted that there are two principal reasons for the judicial policy evident in *Chatterton v Gerson* [1981] QB 432 against trespass claims in informed consent litigation. First, as can be seen from the decisions in *Fowler v Lanning* [1959] 1 QB 426 and *Letang v Cooper* [1965] 1 QB 232, judicial policy appears to be in favour of restricting claims in battery to situations involving deliberate, hostile acts, a situation which most judges would regard as foreign to the doctor-patient relationship. Coupled with this is the stigma and damage to professional reputation which courts repeatedly emphasise are an inevitable by-product of a successful claim against a doctor. These consequences are probably seen as even more serious in an action for battery than in an action for negligence. The second reason stems from the view expressed in the concluding section of this article, namely, that courts in this country will attempt to restrict the scope of the doctrine of informed consent, principally by means of the requirement of causation, the use of expert evidence as to accepted medical practice, and emphasis of the 'best interests of the patient' principle. [On which we now have the House of Lords decision in the *Sidaway case*; see *infra*.] Restriction of the doctrine of informed consent in this way would not be possible if it were to be accepted that failure to inform of inherent risks of proposed treatment could ground an action for trespass. As was outlined above, the plaintiff in such an action would not be required to prove, by way of causation, that he would not have consented to the treatment had he been informed of the risks. Similarly, evidence of accepted medical practice has no place in an action for trespass; if failure to disclose a particular risk were to be regarded as vitiating consent, the fact that a reasonable doctor would not have disclosed the risk cannot absolve the defendant from liability for battery. Finally, although the point is not entirely clear, it would seem that a doctor cannot avoid liability for battery simply on the grounds that he was acting in the best interests of his patient. Thus it can be seen that the three principle ways in which the doctrine of informed consent is likely to be restricted would not be available to a court dealing with a case based in trespass.

2. Negligence

A doctor's obligation to provide information in order to obtain a patient's valid consent to treatment is, as we have seen, a somewhat limited one. Indeed, of course, it is not really a question of the doctor's duty, rather of the patient's actual understanding of the 'nature and purpose' of the procedure, however information relevant to that is acquired by the patient. Left at this, the law would be seriously deficient in safeguarding a patient's right to decide whether or not to undergo a particular treatment or procedure. To that end, the law of negligence has been adapted by the courts in the last 20 years to impose a duty to provide infra: mation potentially beyond that sufficient to make the patient's consent valid. This is sometimes referred to as the duty to obtain the patient's *informed consent*. We will not adopt the terminology, as it is unhelpful in understanding the law's approach, though it has become common currency in medical and philosophical circles.

We need to examine a number of issues arising from the application of the law of negligence in this context. Where does the duty to provide information come from? What is the content of that duty? What relevance does medical opinion (or expert evidence) have in setting the legal standard for disclosure of information? Is there any difference in the standard when a doctor is answering questions rather than volunteering information? What is the test of causation in these cases?

Any duty to provide information will usually be owed to the patient. The duty will be discharged by disclosing the information to the patient. However, where consent is sought from a proxy, for example someone with 'parental responsibility' in relation to a child, disclosure to the person who is to make the decision will discharge the duty (see *Thomson v James* (1997) 41 BMLR 144 (CA) and *Poynter v Hillingdon HA* (1997) 37 BMLR 192 (QBD)).

(a) The duty

What, then, is the basis of the legal duty to provide a patient with information?

I Kennedy and A Grubb (eds) *Principles of Medical Law* (1998)

3.102 Any purported consent must also meet the requirements of the tort of negligence. This immediately needs explanation. Negligence is concerned not with the presence or absence of consent, but with the defendant's failure to comply with a legally imposed duty of care. Thus, if the tort of negligence is to have a role, two matters must be established: that a *duty* exists and the *content* of that duty, (the *quantum* of care demanded). Clearly, a duty exists to take care not to harm the patient through careless acts. But what is being considered here are not the doctor's acts. Instead, the concern is with what the doctor must do *prior to* acting, so as to ensure that proper consent has been given for those acts. In particular, the concern is with the knowledge or information which the patient is entitled to be given, (assuming the patient to be competent), before any purported consent is valid. It is important to recognise that, where any complaint arises, what the patient is complaining of is not that a particular procedure was carried out without proper care and skill, (it may have been performed with the utmost skill), but rather, that it was carried out without proper permission.

3.103 Expressed in this way, it is immediately apparent that if the patient is entitled to be informed, the doctor is under a duty to provide the information. To so assert, however, is to place on the doctor a duty of affirmative action. It is trite law that English law regards such a duty as exceptional. While it is one thing to expect people to refrain from careless behaviour, English law, with its aversion to the 'officious intermeddler', will not ordinarily impose a duty to do something on behalf of another. the first step, therefore, is to examine the legal basis for the doctor's duty to inform a patient, so as to obtain valid consent to treatment.

A Duty to Inform

3.104 One well-established ground on which a duty to inform could be based would be to find that, as between the doctor and the patient, there exists a 'special relationship', giving rise to a duty to act. The traditional example is the parent–child and, by extension, the teacher–child relationship. In effect, therefore, the duty is derived from the status of the parties. The common law has not, however, regarded the doctor-patient relationship as falling into the category of special relationship. Its legal origins lay in the law of contract and thus in an assumption that the parties were at arm's length. The notion of vulnerability which underpins the law's recognition of a special relationship, while clearly a central feature of modern medicine, did not colour the earlier development of the law. Thus, a duty to inform cannot be derived from the existence of a special relationship.

3.105   An alternative ground on which English law could base an affirmative duty to inform can be derived from the law of equity. If the relationship between the doctor and patient were fiduciary in nature, a duty to inform could be readily recognised, as an incidence of the more general duty to seek to maximise the interests of the beneficiary. This was the approach adopted by certain courts in the US. Since these courts had previously categorised the doctor–patient relationship as fiduciary, they had little difficulty in carving out and developing a duty to inform. English law, however, has never regarded the doctor–patient relationship as fiduciary. Indeed, when asked to do so, the House of Lords expressly refused. (*Sidaway v Board of Governors of the Bethlem Royal Hospital*) Furthermore, despite some academic support for the idea, (Bartlett, 'Doctors as Fiduciaries' (1997) 5 Med L Rev 193) it is unlikely that there will be a change of mind. Thus, any duty to inform cannot be based on a fiduciary relationship.

3.106   So, where does the duty come from? Curiously, when the English courts very belatedly got round to examining whether a doctor is under a duty to inform a patient, the legal-technical difficulties involved in actually finding some juristic basis for a duty of affirmative action were largely ignored. Instead, the general duty of care owed by a doctor to a patient was interpreted as extending not only to acts but also omissions, in this case the failure properly to inform. As ever, the law of torts displayed the English law's preference for pragmatism over principle. From an analytical point of view, what this appears to mean is that once a doctor's assistance has been sought and the doctor has undertaken to offer treatment, (that is, a doctor–patient relationship has come into existence), this undertaking includes a duty to act affirmatively on the patient's behalf. This, in turn, translates into a duty to inform so as to obtain from a patient a valid consent.

3.107   As regards the existence of the duty, the remaining point to notice is the point at which the duty arises and for how long it continues. Clearly, it arises whenever the doctor proposes a therapeutic intervention. Valid consent must be obtained prior to embarking on therapy, whether it involves touching the patient or prescribing medicines or other such treatment. Moreover, it is a continuing duty. This means that whenever the doctor engages in any new or additional therapeutic intervention, not covered by the previous consent, there arises a fresh duty to obtain consent and, thus, to inform before proceeding. This is rather easier to stipulate than apply, as cases in the US demonstrate. (*Rizzo v Schiller* (1994) 445 SE 2d 153 and *Sinclair by Sinclair v Block* (1993) 663 A 2d 1137) The general law may well be that where the doctor intends to embark on a course of conduct which is sufficiently different from that previously agreed to and as regards which the appropriate legal standard would demand that the patient be informed, a new duty to inform arises.

As you will have noticed, the duty exists prior to treatment commencing but also extends to any *new* treatments or procedures (see eg *Rizzo v Schiller* (1994) 445 SE 2d 153 (Sup Ct Va) and Kennedy (1995) 3 Med L Rev 209 (Commentary)). It would also arise if the patient withdrew consent to a procedure and then agreed to a continuation but the circumstances had changed (see *Ciarlariello v Keller* (1993) 100 DLR (4th) 609 (Can SC), discussed *supra*, p 593). A duty may also arise after treatment has concluded to advise of any mishap etc that has occurred (discussed *infra*).

However, the location of the duty to inform in the tort of negligence is curious and creates difficulties. On the face of it, the duty seems to exist in order to further the patient's ability to decide whether to undergo a particular treatment or procedure. In other words, the rationale for the duty is to require respect for the patient's *autonomy* or *right of self-determination*. The tort of negligence, however, imposes a duty of care in order to protect an individual from exposure to an unreasonable risk of harm (injury or economic loss). It is not concerned directly with respect for the individual's rights. Thus, injury is an essential element of a negligence action as much here as elsewhere. Failure to provide information *only* gives rise to a claim if the injury would have been avoided had it been given to the patient – an application of the 'but for' test of factual causation. Yet, the patient's right to decide – or their autonomy – will have been infringed whether or not injury resulted. The patient would have been denied the liberty to make an informed choice. If the latter were the raison d'être for the duty – and it is not – the patient should have an action for loss of the opportunity to make such a choice. That would be, of course, a 'loss of a chance' claim, which the courts deny these cases are about (see *Chappel v Hart* (1998) 72 ALJR 1344 (HC of A) per Kirby J at paras 93.9 and 100).

(b) The standard

Prior to 1984 a series of decisions at first instance addressed the issue of a doctor's duty in negligence to disclose information to his patient: *O'Malley-Williams v Board of Governors of the National Hospital for Nervous Disease* [1975] 1 BMJ 635 (Bridge J); *Wells v Surrey AHA* (1978) Times, 29 July, (Croom-Johnson J); *Sankey v Kensington and Chelsea and Westminster AHA* (2 April 1982, unreported, Tudor Evans J). These cases, however, left the matter open (for discussion of the early case law, see G Robertson 'Informed Consent to Medical Treatment' (1981) 97 LQR 102).

It was not until the cases of *Chatterton v Gerson* [1981] QB 432 and *Hills v Potter* [1984] 1 WLR 641n (still at first instance) that the English courts had to face the issue head on. Hirst J summarised the position in *Hills v Potter*.

Hills v Potter [1984] 1 WLR 641n

Hirst J: My conclusions are as follows: 1. In my judgment, McNair J in *Bolam v Friern Barnet Hospital Management Committee* [1957] 1 WLR 582 applied the medical standard to advice prior to an operation, as well as to diagnosis and to treatment. This standard is clearly applied without differentiation to all three aspects of the case which McNair J described as 'the three major points': see pp 586–587, 590. The fact that the plaintiff was mentally sick did not affect the legal principle, but might of course affect its application to the facts of the particular case, as McNair J himself said, at p 590.

2. Although the House of Lords in *Maynard v West Regional Health Authority* [1984] 1 WLR 634, did not specifically affirm McNair J in relation to advice as such, the general and unqualified approval given to *Bolam's* case in the House of Lords makes it quite impossible for me to depart from McNair J's decision, especially as it has been applied to advice in the other three first instance cases which I have cited. Indeed I respectfully agree with, and would have thought it right to follow, these first instance cases even without the authoritative guidance contained in *Maynard's* case, which they preceded. I for my part doubt whether the distinction in the medical context between advice on the one hand and diagnosis and treatment on the other is really so clear or so stark as [was] forcefully submitted.

3. ... I hold that the proper standard is the medical standard in accordance with *Bolam v Friern Hospital Management Committee* [1957] 1 WLR 582 and the other first instance cases.

I do not accept [the] argument that by adopting the *Bolam* principle, the court in effect abdicates its power of decision to the doctors. In every case the court must be satisfied that the standard contended for on their behalf accords with that upheld by a substantial body of medical opinion, and that this body of medical opinion is both respectable and responsible, and experienced in this particular field of medicine.

These cases were, however, only first instance decisions. The courts had *three* options in setting the legal standard.

I Kennedy and A Grubb (eds) *Principles of Medical Law* (1998)

3.109 ... The *first* is that the doctor should be under a duty to pass on all that information which the patient being treated wishes to know. This is a subjective test. The underlying philosophy is rights-based. The patient has a right to know as a necessary feature of the overarching right to self-determination. Even as stated, however, this criterion is not free from difficulty. Should it be expressed as what the patient wishes to know or what the patient would wish to know, (if only he knew)? The former is hard enough to satisfy. The latter verges on the impossible.

3.110   A *second* option is that the doctor should pass on that information which any reasonable patient would wish to know before giving consent. The weakness of this approach is clear. It is a compromise. It purports to take account of the patient's right to be informed but does so at the cost of converting the actual patient into a hypothetical reasonable patient. To that extent, the particular circumstances of the patient are in danger of being ignored. At some point, indeed, the purported subjectivity of the test could evaporate into an objective examination of reasonableness.

3.111   A *third* option is that the doctor's duty should be to inform the patient of that which doctors as a profession think it appropriate for the patient to know. Clearly, this test has no element of subjectivity. It reflects a philosophy of paternalism, according to which the doctor is the better judge of what should inform the medical transaction. Not surprisingly, this option has not been free from criticism in an age in which paternalism has fewer defenders. Quite apart from any ethical attack, the option is vulnerable to at least two further criticisms. First, it assumes that information relevant to making a decision about treatment is a matter of technical medical expertise, properly within the purview of medical expertise. Clearly, diagnosis, treatment and prognosis are uniquely matters of medical expertise. How to respond to these; whether to go ahead and accept (ie consent to) treatment, seems to be of a different order. If anything, it would appear to be uniquely within the competence of the patient (the first option set out earlier). Certainly, it would appear hard to describe it as within the *unique* competence of doctors. This is not to say that doctors should have no role in setting the boundaries of the process of gaining consent. If patients expect them to be sensitive to how they communicate what may sometimes be difficult news, doctors are entitled to make judgements as to how to proceed. But this concerns the 'how' of imparting information, which is undoubtedly a matter of medical expertise. It does not relate to 'whether' to inform, which is what is of concern here. It is hard to see how this is a matter for doctors alone. The second criticism which can be raised is that, if the content of the doctor's duty is to pass on that information which other doctors would, it assumes a degree of professional agreement which is unlikely to be demonstrable in practice. Doctors clearly and quite properly may disagree on diagnosis or treatment. There is, however, some structure of learning about these which all (or virtually all) accept and to which all refer, even though they may derive divergent views from it. There is no such body of learning concerning what information a patient should be told which all doctors accept and draw upon. Thus, the idea of a professional standard of disclosure may proceed from a completely false premiss.

What would an appellate court do? In 1985, the scope of the doctor's duty to disclose was finally considered by the House of Lords in the well-known case of *Sidaway*.

Sidaway v Board of Governors of the Bethlem Royal Hospital [1985] AC 871, [1985] 1 All ER 643 (HL)

The plaintiff, who had suffered recurrent pain in her neck, right shoulder and arms, underwent an operation in 1974 which was performed by a senior neuro-surgeon at the first defendant's hospital. The operation, even if performed with proper care and skill, carried an inherent risk, which was put at between one and two per cent, of damage to the spinal column and the nerve roots. The risk of damage to the spinal column was substantially less than to a nerve root but the consequences were much more serious. In consequence of the operation the plaintiff was severely disabled. Her monetary loss was assessed at £67,500.

The plaintiff claimed damages for negligence against the hospital and the executors of the deceased surgeon, the second defendants. She relied solely on the alleged failure of the surgeon to disclose or explain to her the risks inherent in, or special to, the operation which he had advised. Skinner J found that the surgeon did not tell the plaintiff that it was an operation of choice rather than necessity; that whilst he had told her of the possibility of disturbing a nerve root and the consequences, he did not refer to the danger of damage to the spinal cord; that in refraining from informing her of those two factors he was following a practice which in 1974 would have been accepted as proper by a responsible body of skilled and experienced neuro-surgeons; and applying the test formulated in *Bolam v Friern Barnet*

Management Committee [1957] 1 WLR 582 that the standard of care was that of the ordinary skilled man exercising and professing to have that special skill and that a doctor was not negligent if he acted in accordance with the practice accepted at the time as proper by a responsible body of medical opinion, notwithstanding that other doctors adopted different practices, the judge dismissed the plaintiff's claim. The Court of Appeal affirmed Skinner J's decision. On further appeal to the House of Lords, the majority view was given by Lords Bridge, Templeman and Keith.

Lord Bridge: Broadly, a doctor's professional functions may be divided into three phases: diagnosis, advice and treatment. In performing his functions of diagnosis and treatment, the standard by which English law measures the doctor's duty of care to his patient is not open to doubt. 'The test is the standard of the ordinary skilled man exercising and professing to have that special skill.' These are the words of McNair J in *Bolam v Friern Hospital Management Committee* [1957] 1 WLR 582 at 586, approved by this House in *Whitehouse v Jordan* [1981] 1 WLR 246 at 258, *per* Lord Edmund-Davies and in *Maynard v West Midlands Regional Health Authority* [1984] 1 WLR 634 at 638 *per* Lord Scarman. The test is conveniently referred to as the *Bolam* test. In *Maynard's* case, Lord Scarman, with whose speech the other four members of the Appellate Committee agreed, further cited with approval, at 638 the words of Lord President Clyde in *Hunter v Hanley* 1955 SLT 213 at 217:

> In the realm of diagnosis and treatment there is ample scope for genuine difference of opinion and one man clearly is not negligent merely because his conclusion differs from that of other professional men … The true test for establishing negligence in diagnosis or treatment on the part of a doctor is whether he has been proved to be guilty of such failure as no doctor of ordinary skill would be guilty of it acting with ordinary care …

The language of the *Bolam* test clearly requires a different degree of skill from a specialist in his own special field than from a general practitioner. In the field of neuro-surgery it would be necessary to substitute for Lord President Clyde's phrase 'no doctor of ordinary skill', the phrase 'no neuro-surgeon of ordinary skill'. All this is elementary and, in the light of the two recent decisions of this House referred to, firmly established law.

The important question which this appeal raises is whether the law imposes any, and if so what, different criterion as the measure of the medical man's duty of care to his patient when giving advice with respect to a proposed course of treatment. It is clearly right to recognise that a conscious adult patient of sound mind is entitled to decide for himself whether or not he will submit to a particular course of treatment proposed by the doctor, most significantly surgical treatment under general anaesthesia. This entitlement is the foundation of the doctrine of 'informed consent' which has led in certain American jurisdictions to decisions, and in the Supreme Court of Canada, to dicta, on which the appellant relies, which would oust the *Bolam* test and substitute an 'objective' test of a doctor's duty to advise the patient of the advantages and disadvantages of undergoing the treatment proposed and more particularly to advise the patient of the risks involved.

There are, it appears to me, at least theoretically, two extreme positions which could be taken. It could be argued that, if the patient's consent is to be fully informed, the doctor must specifically warn him of *all* risks involved in the treatment offered, unless he has some sound clinical reason not to do so. Logically, this would seem to be the extreme to which a truly objective criterion of the doctor's duty would lead. Yet this position finds no support from any authority, to which we have been referred, in any jurisdiction. It seems to be generally accepted that there is no need to warn of the risks inherent in all surgery under general anaesthesia. This is variously explained on the ground that the patient may be expected to be aware of such risks or that they are relatively remote. If the law is to impose on the medical profession a duty to warn of risks to secure 'informed consent' independently of accepted medical opinion of what is appropriate, neither of these explanations for confining the duty to special as opposed to general surgical risks seems to me wholly convincing.

At the other extreme it could be argued that, once the doctor has decided what treatment is, on balance of advantages and disadvantages, in the patient's best interest, he should not alarm the patient by volunteering a warning of any risk involved, however grave and substantial, unless specifically asked by the patient. I cannot believe that contemporary medical opinion would support this view, which would effectively exclude the patient's right to decide in the very type of case where it is most important that he should be in a position to exercise that right and, perhaps even more significantly, to seek a second opinion as to whether he should submit himself to the significant risk which has been drawn to his attention. I should perhaps add at this point, although the issue does not strictly arise in this appeal, that, when questioned specifically by a patient of apparently sound mind about risks involved in a particular treatment proposed, the doctor's duty must, in my opinion, be to answer both truthfully and as the questioner requires.

The decision mainly relied on to establish a criterion of the doctor's duty to disclose the risks inherent in a proposed treatment which is prescribed by the law and can be applied independently of any medical opinion or practice is that of the District of Columbia Circuit Court of Appeals in *Canterbury v Spence* 464 F 2d 772 (DC, 1972). The judgment of the Court (Wright, Leventhal and Robinson JJ), delivered by Robinson J, expounds the view that an objective criterion of what is a sufficient disclosure of risk is necessary to ensure that the patient is enabled to make an intelligent decision and cannot be left to be determined by the doctors. He said, at 784:

> Respect for the patient's right of self-determination on particular therapy demands a standard set by law for physicians rather than one which physicians may or may not impose upon themselves.

In an attempt to define the objective criterion it is said, at 787, that 'the issue on non-disclosure must be approached from the view point of the reasonableness of the patient's informational needs'. A risk is required to be disclosed 'when a reasonable person, in what the physician knows or should know to be the patient's position, would be likely to attach significance to the risk or cluster of risks in deciding whether or not to forgo the proposed therapy': 464 F 2d 772 at 787. The judgment adds, at 788: 'Whenever non-disclosure of particular risk information is open to debate by reasonable-minded men, the issue is for the finder of facts.'

The court naturally recognises exceptions from the duty laid down in the case of an unconscious patient, an immediate emergency, or a case where the doctor can establish that disclosure would be harmful to the patient.

Expert medical evidence will be needed to indicate the nature and extent of the risks and benefits involved in the treatment (and presumably of any alternative course). But the court affirms, at 792: 'Experts are unnecessary to a showing of the materiality of a risk to a patient's decision on treatment, or to the reasonable, expectable effect of risk disclosure on the decision.' In English law, if this doctrine were adopted, expert medical opinion as to whether a particular risk should or should not have been disclosed would presumably be inadmissible in evidence.

I recognise the logical force of the *Canterbury* doctrine, proceeding from the premise that the patient's right to make his own decision must at all costs be safeguarded against the kind of medical paternalism which assumes that 'doctor knows best'. But, with all respect, I regard the doctrine as quite impractical in application for three principal reasons. First, it gives insufficient weight to the realities of the doctor-patient relationship. A very wide variety of factors must enter into a doctor's clinical judgment not only as to what treatment is appropriate for a particular patient, but also as to how best to communicate to the patient the significant factors necessary to enable the patient to make an informed decision whether to undergo the treatment. The doctor cannot set out to educate the patient to his own standard of medical knowledge of all the relevant factors involved. He may take the view, certainly with some patients, that the very fact of this volunteering, without being asked, information of some remote risk involved in the treatment proposed, even though he describes it as remote, may lead to that risk assuming an undue significance in the patient's calculations. Secondly, it would seem to me quite unrealistic in any medical negligence action to confine the expert medical evidence to an explanation of the primary medical factors involved and to deny the court the benefit of evidence of medical opinion and practice on the particular issue of disclosure which is under consideration. Thirdly, the objective test which *Canterbury* propounds seems to me to be so imprecise as to be almost meaningless. If it is to be left to individual judges to decide for themselves what 'a reasonable person in the patient's position' would consider a risk of sufficient significance that he should be told about it, the outcome of litigation in this field is likely to be quite unpredictable.

I note with interest from a learned article entitled 'Informed Consent to Medical Treatment' by Mr Gerald Robertson, Lecturer in Law, University of Leicester (1981) 97 LQR 102, 108, that only a minority of states in the United States of America have chosen to follow *Canterbury* and that since 1975 'there has been a growing tendency for individual States to enact legislation which severely curtails the operation of the doctrine of informed consent'. I should also add that I find particularly cogent and convincing the reasons given for declining to follow *Canterbury* by the Supreme Court of Virginia in *Bly v Rhoads* 222 SE 2d 783 (1976).

Having rejected the *Canterbury* doctrine as a solution to the problem of safeguarding the patient's right to decide whether he will undergo a particular treatment advised by his doctor, the question remains whether that right is sufficiently safeguarded by the application of the *Bolam* test without qualification to the determination of the question what risks inherent in a proposed treatment should be disclosed. The case against a simple application of the *Bolam* test is cogently stated by Laskin CJC, giving the judgment of the Supreme Court of Canada in *Reibl v Hughes* (1980) 114 DLR (3d) 1 at 13.

To allow expert medical evidence to determine what risks are material and, hence, should be disclosed and, correlatively, what risks are not material is to hand over to the medical profession the entire question of the scope of the duty of disclosure, including the question whether there has been a breach of that duty. Expert medical evidence is, of course, relevant to findings as to the risks that reside in or are a result of recommended surgery or other treatment. It will also have a bearing on their materiality but this is not a question that is to be concluded on the basis of the expert medical evidence alone. The issue under consideration is a different issue from that involved where the question is whether the doctor carried out his professional activities by applicable professional standards. What is under consideration here is the patient's right to know what risks are involved in undergoing or foregoing certain surgery or other treatment.

I fully appreciate the force of this reasoning but can only accept it subject to the important qualification that a decision what degree of disclosure of risks is best calculated to assist a particular patient to make a rational choice as to whether or not to undergo a particular treatment must primarily be a matter of clinical judgment. It would follow from this that the issue whether non-disclosure in a particular case should be condemned as a breach of the doctor's duty of care is an issue to be decided primarily on the basis of expert medical evidence, applying the *Bolam* test. But I do not see that this approach involves the necessity 'to hand over to the medical profession the entire question of the scope of the duty of disclosure, including the question whether there has been a breach of that duty'. Of course, if there is a conflict of evidence as to whether a responsible body of medical opinion approves of non-disclosure in a particular case, the judge will have to resolve that conflict. But even in a case where, as here, no expert witness in the relevant medical field condemns the non-disclosure as being in conflict with accepted and responsible medical practice, I am of opinion that the judge might in certain circumstances come to the conclusion that disclosure of a particular risk was so obviously necessary to an informed choice on the part of the patient that no reasonably prudent medical man would fail to make it. The kind of case I have in mind would be an operation involving a substantial risk of grave adverse consequences, as, for example, the ten per cent risk of a strike from the operation which was the subject of the Canadian case of *Reibl v Hughes* (1980) 114 DLR (3d) 1. In such a case, in the absence of some cogent clinical reason why the patient should not be informed, a doctor, recognising and respecting his patient's right of decision, could hardly fail to appreciate the necessity for an appropriate warning.

In the instant case I can see no reasonable ground on which the judge could properly reject the conclusion to which the unchallenged medical evidence led in the application of the *Bolam* test. The trial judge's assessment of the risk at one to two per cent covered both nerve root and spinal cord damage and covered a spectrum of possible ill effects 'ranging from the mild to the catastrophic'. In so far as it is possible and appropriate to measure such risks in percentage terms – some of the expert medical witnesses called expressed a marked and understandable reluctance to do so – the risk of damage to the spinal cord of such severity as the appellant in fact suffered was, it would appear, certainly less than one per cent. But there is no yardstick either in the judge's findings or in the evidence to measure what fraction of one per cent that risk represented. In these circumstances, the appellant's expert witness's agreement that the non-disclosure complained of accorded with a practice accepted as proper by a responsible body of neuro-surgical opinion afforded the respondents a complete defence to the appellant's claim.

Lord Templeman: In my opinion a simple and general explanation of the nature of the operation should have been sufficient to alert Mrs Sidaway to the fact that a major operation was to be performed and to the possibility that something might go wrong at or near the site of the spinal cord or the site of the nerve root causing serious injury. If, as the judge held, Mr Falconer probably referred expressly to the possibility of damage to a nerve root and to the consequences of such damage, this warning could only have reinforced the possibility of something going wrong in the course of a delicate operation performed in a vital area with resultant damage. In view of the fact that Mr Falconer recommended the operation, Mrs Sidaway must have been told or could have assumed that Mr Falconer considered that the possibilities of damage were sufficiently remote to be ignored. Mrs Sidaway could have asked questions. If she had done so, she could and should have been informed that there was an aggregate risk of between one per cent and two per cent risk of some damage either to the spinal cord or to a nerve root resulting in injury which might vary from irritation to paralysis. But to my mind this further information would only have reinforced the obvious, with the assurance that the maximum risk of damage, slight or serious, did not exceed two per cent. Mr Falconer may reasonably have taken the view that Mrs Sidaway might be confused, frightened or misled by more detailed information which she was unable to evaluate at a time when she was suffering from stress, pain and anxiety. A patient may prefer that the doctor should not thrust too much detail at the patient. We do not know how Mr Falconer explained the operation to Mrs Sidaway and we do not know the reasons for the terms in which he couched his explanation.

On the assumption that Mr Falconer explained that it was necessary to remove bone and free a nerve root from pressure near the spinal cord, it seems to me that the possibility of damage to a nerve root or to the spinal cord was obvious. The operation was skilfully performed but by mishap the remote risk of damage to the spinal cord unfortunately caused the disability from which Mrs Sidaway is now suffering. However much sympathy may be felt for Mrs Sidaway and however much in hindsight the operation may be regretted by her, the question now is whether Mr Falconer was negligent in the explanation which he gave.

In my opinion if a patient knows that a major operation may entail serious consequences, the patient cannot complain of lack of information unless the patient asks in vain for more information or unless there is some danger which by its nature or magnitude or for some other reason requires to be separately taken into account by the patient in order to reach a balanced judgment in deciding whether or not to submit to the operation. To make Mr Falconer liable for damages for negligence, in not expressly drawing Mrs Sidaway's attention to the risk of damage to the spinal cord and its consequences. Mrs Sidaway must show and fails to show that Mr Falconer was not entitled to assume, in the absence of questions from Mrs Sidaway, that his explanation of the nature of the operation was sufficient to alert Mrs Sidaway to the general danger of unavoidable and serious damage inherent in the operation but sufficiently remote to justify the operation. There is no reason to think that Mr Falconer was aware that, as Mrs Sidaway deposed, a specific warning and assessment of the risk of spinal cord damage would have influenced Mrs Sidaway to decline the operation although the general explanation which she was given resulted in her consenting to the operation.

There is no doubt that a doctor ought to draw the attention of a patient to a danger which may be special in kind or magnitude or special to the patient. In *Reibl v Hughes* (1980) 114 DLR (3d) 1, a surgeon advised an operation on the brain to avoid a threatened stroke. The surgeon knew or ought to have known that there was a four per cent chance that the operation might cause death and a ten per cent chance that the operation might precipitate the very stroke which the operation was designed to prevent. The patient ought to have been informed of these specific risks in order to be able to form a balanced judgment in deciding whether or not to submit to the operation.

When a patient complains of lack of information, the court must decide whether the patient has suffered harm from a general danger inherent in the operation or from some special danger. In the case of a general danger the court must decide whether the information afforded to the patient was sufficient to alert the patient to the possibility of serious harm of the kind in fact suffered. If the practice of the medical profession is to make express mention of a particular kind of danger, the court will have no difficulty in coming to the conclusion that the doctor ought to have referred expressly to this danger as a special danger unless the doctor can give reasons to justify the form or absence of warning adopted by him. Where the practice of the medical profession is divided or does not include express mention, it will be for the court to determine whether the harm suffered is an example of a general danger inherent in the nature of the operation and if so whether the explanation afforded to the patient was sufficient to alert the patient to the general dangers of which the harm suffered is an example. If a doctor conscientiously endeavours to explain the arguments for and against a major operation and the possibilities of benefiting and the dangers, the court will be slow to conclude that the doctor has been guilty of a breach of duty owed to the patient merely because the doctor omits some specific item of information. It is for the court to decide, after hearing the doctor's explanation, whether the doctor has in fact been guilty of a breach of duty with regard to information.

A doctor offers a patient diagnosis, advice and treatment. The objectives, sometimes conflicting, sometimes unattainable, of the doctor's services are the prolongation of life, the restoration of the patient to full physical and mental health and the alleviation of pain. Where there are dangers that treatment may produce results, direct or indirect, which are harmful to the patient, those dangers must be weighed by the doctor before he recommends the treatment. The patient is entitled to consider then reject the recommended treatment and for that purpose to understand the doctor's advice and the possibility of harm resulting from the treatment.

I do not subscribe to the theory that the patient is entitled to know everything nor to the theory that the doctor is entitled to decide everything. The relationship between doctor and patient is contractual in origin, the doctor performing services in consideration for fees payable by the patient. The doctor, obedient to the high standards set by the medical profession impliedly contracts to act at all times in the best interests of the patient. No doctor in his senses would impliedly contract at the same time to give to the patient all the information available to the doctor as a result of the doctor's training and experience and as a result of the doctor's diagnosis of the patient. An obligation to give a patient all the information available to the doctor would often be inconsistent with the doctor's contractual obligation to have regard to the patient's best interests. Some information might confuse, other information might alarm a particular patient. Whenever the occasion arises for the doctor to tell the patient the results of the doctor's diagnosis, the possible methods of treatment and the advantages and disadvantages of the recommended treatment, the doctor must decide in the light of his training and experience and in the light of his knowledge of the patient what should be said and how it should be said. At the same time the doctor is not entitled to make the final decision with regard to treatment which may have disadvantages or dangers. Where the patient's health and future are at stake, the patient must make the final decision. The patient is free to decide whether or not to submit to treatment recommended by the doctor and therefore the doctor impliedly contracts to provide information which is adequate to enable the patient to reach a balanced judgment, subject always to the doctor's own obligation to say and do nothing which the doctor is satisfied will be harmful to the patient. When the doctor himself is considering the possibility of a major operation the doctor is able, with his medical training, with his knowledge of the patient's medical history and with his objective position to make a balanced judgment as to whether the operation should be performed or not. If the doctor making a balanced judgment advises the patient to submit to the operation, the patient is entitled to reject that advice for reasons which are rational, or irrational, or for no reason. The duty of the doctor in these circumstances, subject to his overriding duty to have regard to the best interests of the patient, is to provide the patient with information which will enable the patient to make a balanced judgment if the patient chooses to make a balanced judgment. A patient may make an unbalanced judgment because he is deprived of adequate information. A patient may also make an unbalanced judgment if he is provided with too much information and is made aware of possibilities which he is not capable of assessing because of his lack of medical training, his prejudices or his personality. Thus the provision of too much information may prejudice the attainment of the objective or restoring the patient's health. The obligation of the doctor to have regard to the best interests of the patient but at the same time to make available to the patient sufficient information to enable the patient to reach a balanced judgment if he chooses to do so has not altered because those obligations have ceased or may have ceased to be contractual and become a matter of duty of care. In order to make a balanced judgment if he chooses to do so, the patient needs to be aware of the general dangers and of any special dangers in each case without exaggeration or concealment. At the end of the day, the doctor, bearing in mind the best interests of the patient and bearing in mind the patient's right of information which will enable the patient to make a balanced judgment must decide what information should be given to the patient and in what terms that information should be couched. The court will award damages against the doctor if the court is satisfied that the doctor blundered and that the patient was deprived of information which was necessary for the purposes I have outlined. In the present case on the judge's findings I am satisfied that adequate information was made available to Mrs Sidaway and that the appeal should therefore be dismissed.

Lord Keith concurred with Lord Bridge.

By contrast, Lord Diplock, while concurring in the result, differed significantly in his analysis of the doctor's duty to disclose.

Lord Diplock: The merit of the *Bolam* test is that the criterion of the duty of care owed by a doctor to his patient is whether he has acted in accordance with a practice accepted as proper by a body of responsible and skilled medical opinion. There may be a number of different practices which are likely to alter with advances in medical knowledge. Experience shows that, to the great benefit of human kind, they have done so, particularly in the recent past. That is why fatal diseases such as smallpox and tuberculosis have within living memory become virtually extinct in countries where modern medical care is generally available.

In English jurisprudence the doctor's relationship with his patient which gives rise to the normal duty of care to exercise his skill and judgment to improve the patient's health in any particular respect in which the patient has sought his aid, has hitherto been treated as a single comprehensive duty covering all the ways in which a doctor is called upon to exercise his skill and judgment in the improvement of the physical or mental condition of the patient for which his services either as a general practitioner or specialist have been engaged. This general duty is not subject to dissection into a number of component parts to which different criteria of what satisfy the duty of care apply, such as diagnosis, treatment, advice (including warning of any risks of something going wrong however skilfully the treatment advised is carried out). The *Bolam* case itself embraced failure to advise the patient of the risk involved in the electric shock treatment as one of the allegations of negligence against the surgeon as well as negligence in the actual carrying out of treatment in which that risk did result in injury to the patient. The same criteria were applied to both these aspects of the surgeon's duty of care. In modern medicine and surgery such dissection of the various things a doctor has to do in the exercise of his whole duty of care owed to his patient is neither legally meaningful nor medically practicable. Diagnosis itself may involve exploratory surgery, the insertion of drugs by injection (or vaccination) involves intrusion upon the body of the patient and oral treatment by drugs although it involves no physical intrusion by the doctor on the patient's body may in the case of particular patients involve serious and unforeseen risks.

My Lords, no convincing reason has in my view been advanced before your Lordships that would justify treating the *Bolam* test as doing anything less than laying down a principle of English law that is comprehensive and applicable to every aspect of the duty of care owed by a doctor to his patient in the exercise of his healing functions as respects that patient . . .

In matters of diagnosis and the carrying out of treatment the court is not tempted to put itself in the surgeon's shoes; it has to rely on and evaluate expert evidence, remembering that it is no part of its task of evaluation to give effect to any preference it may have for one responsible body of professional opinion over another, provided it is satisfied by the expert evidence that both qualify as responsible bodies of medical opinion. But, when it comes to warning about risks, the kind of training and experience that a judge will have undergone at the Bar makes it natural for him to say (correctly) it is my right to decide whether any particular thing is done to my body, and I want to be fully informed of any risks there may be involved of which I am not already aware from my general knowledge as a highly educated man of experience, so that I may form my own judgment whether to refuse the advised treatment or not.

No doubt, if the patient in fact manifested this attitude by means of questioning, the doctor would tell him whatever it was the patient wanted to know; but we are concerned here with volunteering unsought information about risks of the proposed treatment failing to achieve the result sought or making the patient's physical or mental condition worse rather than better. The only effect that mention of risks can have on the patient's mind, if it has any at all, can be in the direction of deterring the patient from undergoing the treatment which in the expert opinion of the doctor it is in the patient's interest to undergo. To decide what risks the existence of which a patient should be voluntarily warned and the terms in which such warning, if any, should be given, having regard to the effect that the warning may have, is as much an exercise of professional skill and judgment as any other part of the doctor's comprehensive duty of care to the individual patient, and expert medical evidence on this matter should be treated in just the same way. The *Bolam* test should be applied.

Lord Scarman also differed markedly (albeit it in different way) from the majority in his analysis.

Lord Scarman: The *Bolam* principle has been accepted by your Lordships' House as applicable to diagnosis and treatment: see *Whitehouse v Jordan* [1981] 1 All ER 267, [1981] 1 WLR 246 (treatment) and *Maynard v West Midlands Regional Health Authority* [1985] 1 All ER 635 (diagnosis). It is also recognised in Scots law as applicable to diagnosis and treatment; indeed, McNair J in the *Bolam* case cited a Scottish decision to that effect, *Hunter v Hanley* 1955 SLT 213 at 217 per the Lord President (Clyde).

But was the judge correct in treating the 'standard of competent professional opinion' as the criterion in determining whether a doctor is under a duty to warn his patient of the risk, or risks, inherent in the treatment which he recommends? Skinner J and the Court of Appeal have in the instant case held that he was correct. Bristow J adopted the same criterion in *Chatterton v Gerson* [1981] 1 All ER 257, [1981] QB 432. The implications of this view of the law are disturbing. It leaves the determination of a legal duty to the judgment of doctors. Responsible medical judgment may, indeed, provide the law with an acceptable standard in determining whether a doctor in diagnosis or treatment has complied with his duty. But is it right that medical judgment should determine whether there exists a duty to warn of risk and its scope? It would be a strange conclusion if the courts should be led to conclude that our law, which undoubtedly recognises a right in the patient to decide whether he will accept or reject the treatment proposed, should permit the doctors to determine whether and in what circumstances a duty arises requiring the doctor to warn his patient of the risks inherent in the treatment which he proposes.

The right of 'self-determination' – the description applied by some to what is no more and no less than the right of a patient to determine for himself whether he will or will not accept the doctor's advice – is vividly illustrated where the treatment recommended is surgery. A doctor who operates without consent of his patient is, save in cases of emergency or mental disability, guilty of the civil wrong of trespass to the person: he is also guilty of the criminal offence of assault. The existence of the patient's right to make his own decision, which may be seen as a basic human right protected by the common law, is the reason why a doctrine embodying a right of the patient to be informed of the risks of surgical treatment has been developed in some jurisdictions in the USA and has found favour with the Supreme Court of Canada. Known as the 'doctrine of informed consent', it amounts to this: where there is a 'real' or a 'material' risk inherent in the proposed operation (however competently and skilfully performed) the question whether and to what extent a patient should be warned before he gives his consent is to be answered not by reference to medical practice but by accepting as a matter of law that, subject to all proper exceptions (of which the court, not the profession, is the judge), a patient has a right to be informed of the risks inherent in the treatment which is proposed. The profession, it is said, should not be judge in its own cause: or, less emotively but more correctly, the courts should not allow medical opinion as to what is best for the patient to override the patient's right to decide for himself whether he will submit to the treatment offered him. It will be necessary for the House to consider in this appeal what is involved in the doctrine and whether it, or any modification of it, has any place in English law.

The appellant's submissions
The appellant's first submission is that, even if (which she does not accept) the *Bolam* principle determines whether a warning of risk should or should not be given, the facts found establish liability. My Lords, the submission is untenable. It is not possible to hold that the appellant has shown negligence in the *Bolam* sense on the part of Mr Falconer in advising or treating her. His decision not to warn her of the danger of damage to the spinal cord and of its possible consequences was one which the medical witnesses were agreed to be in accordance with a practice accepted as proper by a responsible body of opinion among neuro-surgeons. Further, the medical evidence also emphasised that in reaching a decision whether or not to warn his patient a competent and careful surgeon would attach especial importance to his assessment of the character and emotional condition of his patient, it being accepted that a doctor acting in the best interests of his patient would be concerned lest a warning might frighten the patient into refusing an operation which in his view was the best treatment in the circumstances. Nobody knows what Mr Falconer's assessment of Mrs Sidaway's character, state of mind and emotion was before her operation. There is no evidence to justify an inference that this careful and compassionate man (the history of the case, which I have related, shows that he merited both adjectives) would have failed to consider what was in the best interests of his patient. He could well have concluded that a warning might have deterred her from agreeing to an operation which he believed to be the best treatment for her.

The appellant's second submission is that she has a cause of action which is independent of negligence in the *Bolam* sense. The submission is based on her right to decide for herself whether she should submit to the operation proposed. In effect, she invokes the transatlantic doctrine of informed consent.

The law
The doctrine is new ground in so far as English law is concerned. Apart from the judgment of Bristow J in *Chatterton v Gerson* [1981] 1 All ER 257, [1981] QB 432, I know of only one case prior to the present appeal in which an English court has discussed it. In *Hills v Potter* [1983] 3 All ER 716, [1984] 1 WLR 641n Hirst J followed Skinner J in this case, adding a comment, with which I respectfully agree, that it would be deplorable to base the law in medical cases of this kind on the torts of assault and battery. He did, however, carefully and helpfully devote part of his judgment to a consideration of the transatlantic case which accept a doctrine of informed consent. He was, if I may say so, right to refuse to follow them: he was sitting at first instance and was faced with formidable English authority accepting the *Bolam* test (Skinner J in the present case and Bristow J in respect of advice: and this House in respect of diagnosis and treatment). But the circumstances that this House is now called on to explore new ground is no reason why a rule of informed consent should not be recognised and developed by our courts. The common law is adaptable; it would not otherwise have survived over the centuries of its existence. The concept of negligence itself is a development of the law by the judges over the last hundred years or so. The legal ancestry of the tort of negligence is to be found in the use made by the judges of the action on the case. Damage is the gist of the action. The action on the case was sufficiently flexible to enable the judges to extend it to cover situations where damage was suffered in circumstances which they judged to call for a remedy. It would be irony indeed if a judicial development for which the opportunity was the presence in the law of a flexible remedy should result now in rigidly confining the law's remedy to situations and relationships already ruled on by the judges.

Counsel for the appellant referred to *Nocton v Lord Ashburton* [1914] AC 932, [1914–15] All ER Rep 45 in an attempt to persuade your Lordships that the relationship between a doctor and patient is of a fiduciary character entitling a patient to equitable relief in the event of a breach of fiduciary duty by the doctor. The attempt fails: there is no comparison to be made between the relationship of doctor and patient with that of solicitor and client, trustee and cestui qui trust or the other relationships treated in equity as of a fiduciary character.

Nevertheless, the relationship of doctor and patient is a very special one, the patient putting his health and his life in the doctor's hands. Where *Nocton v Lord Ashburton* does throw light is on the approach of our law to new or special situations and relationships not previously considered by the judges. In that case the House had to consider the field covered by *Derry v Peek* (1889) 14 App Cas 337, [1886–90] All ER Rep 1, the famous case in which the House had held that in an action of deceit it is necessary to prove actual fraud. Viscount Haldane LC had this to say ([1914] AC 932 at 947, [1914–15] All ER Rep 45 at 49):

> My Lords, the discussion of the case by the noble and learned Lords who took part in the decision appears to me to exclude the hypothesis that they considered any other question to be before them than what was the necessary foundation of an ordinary action for deceit. They must indeed be taken to have thought that the facts proved as to the relationship of the parties in *Derry v Peek* were not enough to establish any special duty arising out of that relationship other than the general duty of honesty. But they do not say that where a different sort of relationship ought to be inferred from the circumstances the case is to be concluded by asking whether an action for deceit will lie. I think that the authorities subsequent to the decision of the House of Lords shew a tendency to assume that it was intended to mean more than it did. In reality the judgment covered only a part of the field in which liabilities may arise. There are other obligations besides that of honesty the breach of which may give a right to damages. These obligations depend on principles which the judges have worked out in the fashion that is characteristic of a system where much of the law has always been judge-made and unwritten.

This remains the approach of the judges to new or as yet unconsidered situations.

Unless statute has intervened to restrict the range of judge-made law, the common law enables the judges, when faced with a situation where a right recognised by law is not adequately protected, either to extend existing principles to cover the situation or to apply an existing remedy to redress the injustice. There is here no novelty: but merely the application of the principle ubi jus ibi remedium. If, therefore, the failure to warn a patient of the risks inherent in the operation which is recommended does constitute a failure to respect the patient's right to make his own decision, I can see no reason in principle why, if the risk materialises and injury or damage is caused, the law should not recognise and enforce a right in the patient to compensation by way of damages.

For the reasons already given, the *Bolam* principle does not cover the situation. The facts of this very case expose its limitation. Mr Falconer lacked neither care for his patient's health and well-being nor professional skill in the advice and treatment which he offered. But did he overlook or disregard his patient's right to determine for herself whether or not to have the operation? Did he fail to provide her with the information necessary for her to make a prudent decision? There is, in truth, no evidence to answer these questions. Mrs Sidaway's evidence was not accepted: and Mr Falconer was dead. Assume, however, that he did overlook this aspect of his patient's situation. Since neither his advice nor his treatment could be faulted on the *Bolam* test, his patient may have been deprived of the opportunity to exercise her right of decision in the light of information which she, had she received it, might reasonably have considered to be of importance in making up her mind. On the *Bolam* view of the law, therefore, even if she established that she was so deprived by the lack of a warning, she would have no remedy in negligence unless she could also prove that there was no competent and respected body of medical opinion which was in favour of no warning. Moreover, the tort of trespass to the person would not provide her with a remedy: for Mrs Sidaway did consent to the operation. Her complaint is that her consent resulted from ignorance of a risk, known by the doctor but not made known by him to her, inherent in the operation. Nor would the law of contract offer her a sure way forward. Medical treatment, as in her case, is frequently given today under arrangements outside the control of the law of contract.

One point is clear, however. If failure to warn of risk is actionable in English law, it must be because it is in the circumstances a breach of the doctor's duty of care: in other words, the doctor must be shown to be negligent. English law has not accepted a 'no-fault' basis for the liability of a doctor to compensate a patient for injury arising in the course of medical treatment. If, however, the *Bolam* principle is to be applied to the exclusion of any other test to advice and warning, there will be cases in which a patient who suffers injury through ignorance or a risk known to the doctor has no remedy. Is there any difficulty in holding that the doctor's duty of care is sufficiently extensive to afford a patient in that situation a remedy if as a result she suffers injury or damage? I think not. The root principle of common law negligence is to 'take reasonable care to avoid acts or omissions which you can reasonably foresee would be likely to injure your neighbour': *Donoghue v Stevenson* [1932] AC 562 at 580 *per* Lord Atkin. If it be recognised that a doctor's duty of care extends not only to the health and well-being of his patient but also to a proper respect for his patient's rights, the duty to warn can be seen to be a part of the doctor's duty of care.

It is, I suggest, a sound and reasonable proposition that the doctor should be required to exercise care in respecting the patient's right of decision. He must acknowledge that in very many cases factors other than the purely medical will play a significant part in his patient's decision-making process. The doctor's concern is with health and the relief of pain. These are the medical objectives. But a patient may well have in mind circumstances, objectives, and values which he may reasonably not make known to the doctor but which may lead him to a different decision from that suggested by a purely medical opinion. The doctor's duty can be seen, therefore, to be one which requires him not only to advise as to medical treatment but also to provide his patient with the information needed to enable the patient to consider and balance the medical advantages and risks alongside other relevant matters, such as, for example, his family, business or social responsibilities of which the doctor may be only partially, if at all, informed.

I conclude, therefore, that there is room in our law for a legal duty to warn a patient of the risks inherent in the treatment proposed, and that, if such a duty be held to exist, its proper place is as an aspect of the duty of care owed by the doctor to his patient. I turn, therefore, to consider whether a duty to warn does exist in our law and, if it does, its proper formulation and the conditions and exceptions to which it must be subject.

Some American courts have recognised such a duty. They have seen it as arising from the patient's right to know of material risks, which itself is seen to arise from the patient's right to decide for himself whether or not to submit to the medical treatment proposed. This is the doctrine of informed consent, to which I have already briefly referred.

The landmark case is a decision of the United States Court of Appeals, District of Columbia Circuit, *Canterbury v Spence* 464 F 2d 772 (DC, 1972). This case … has now been approved by the District of Columbia Appeal Court in *Crain v Allison* 443 A 2d 558 (1982) …

It is necessary before discussing the doctrine to bear in mind that it is far from being universally accepted in the United States of America, or indeed elsewhere …

There can be little doubt that policy explains the divergence of view. The proliferation of medical malpractice suits in the USA has led some courts and some legislatures to curtail or even to reject the operation of the doctrine in an endeavour to restrict the liability of the doctor and so discourage the practice of 'defensive medicine' – by which is meant the practice of doctors advising and undertaking the treatment which they think is legally safe even though they may believe that it is not the best for their patient.

The danger of defensive medicine developing in this country clearly exists though absence of the lawyer's 'contingency fee' (a percentage of the damages for him as his fee if he wins the case but nothing if he loses) may make it more remote. However that may be, in matters of civil wrong or tort, courts are concerned with legal principle: if policy problems emerge, they are best left to the legislature: *McLoughlin v O'Brian* [1983] 1 AC 410.

In *Canterbury v Spence* the court enunciated four propositions. (1) The root premise is the concept that every human being of adult years and of sound mind has a right to determine what shall be done with his own body. (2) The consent is the informed exercise of a choice, and that entails an opportunity to evaluate knowledgeably the options available and the risks attendant on each. (3) The doctor must, therefore, disclose all 'material risks'; what risks are 'material' is determined by the 'prudent patient' test, which was formulated by the court (464 F 2d 772 at 787):

[a] risk is … material when a *reasonable person*, in what the physician knows or should know to be the patient's position, would be likely to attach significance to the risk or cluster of risks in deciding whether or not to forgo the proposed therapy. (My emphasis.)

(4) The doctor, however, has what the court called a 'therapeutic privilege'. This exception is that a reasonable medical assessment of the patient would have indicated to the doctor that disclosure would have posed a serious threat of psychological detriment to the patient.

In Canada, in *Reibl v Hughes* (1980) 114 DLR (3d) 1, Laskin CJC expressed broad approval of the doctrine as enunciated in *Canterbury v Spence*, though it would seem that approval of the doctrine was not necessary to a decision in the case. I find no difficulty in accepting the four propositions enunciated in *Canterbury*'s case. But with two notable exceptions they have not yet been considered, so far as I am aware, by an English court. In *Chatterton v Gerson* [1981] 1 All ER 257, [1981] QB 432 Bristow J did consider whether there is any rule in English law comparable with the doctrine of informed consent. He held that a doctor ought to warn of what may happen by misfortune however well the operation may be carried out 'if there is a *real* risk of a misfortune inherent in the procedure' (see [1981] 1 All ER 257 at 266, [1981] QB 432 at 444; my emphasis). He held that whether or not a warning should have been given depended on what a reasonable doctor would have done in the circumstances; and he applied the *Bolam* test to determine the reasonableness of what the doctor did. In *Hills v Potter* [1983] 3 All ER 716, [1984] 1 WLR 641n Hirst J, after discussing the doctrine, also applied the *Bolam* test.

In my judgment the merit of the propositions enunciated in *Canterbury v Spence* 464 F 2d 772 (DC, 1972) is that without excluding medical evidence they set a standard and formulate a test of the doctor's duty the effect of which is that the court determines the scope of the duty and decides whether the doctor has acted in breach of his duty. This result is achieved first by emphasis on the patient's 'right of self-determination' and secondly by the 'prudent patient' test. If the doctor omits to warn where the risk is such that in the court's view a prudent person in the patient's situation would have regarded it as significant, the doctor is liable.

The *Canterbury* propositions do indeed attach great importance to medical evidence, though judgment is for the court. First, medical evidence is needed in determining whether the risk is material, ie one which the doctor should make known to his patient. The two aspects of the risk, namely the degree of likelihood of it occurring and the seriousness of the possible injury if it should occur, can in most, if not all, cases be assessed only with the help of medical evidence. And secondly, medical evidence would be needed to assist the court in determining whether the doctor was justified in his assessment of his patient in withholding the warning.

My Lords, I think the *Canterbury* propositions reflect a legal truth which too much judicial reliance on medical judgment tends to obscure. In a medical negligence case where the issue is as to the advice and information given to the patient as to the treatment proposed, the available options, and the risk, the court is concerned primarily with a patient's right. The doctor's duty arises from his patient's right. If one considers the scope of the doctor's duty by beginning with the right of the patient to make his own decision whether he will or will not undergo the treatment proposed, the right to be informed of significant risk and the doctor's corresponding duty are easy to understand: for the proper implementation of the right requires that the doctor be under a duty to inform his patient of the material risks inherent in the treatment. And it is plainly right that a doctor may avoid liability for failure to warn of a material risk if he can show that he reasonably believed that communication to the patient of the existence of the risk would be detrimental to the health (including, of course, the mental health) of his patient.

Ideally, the court should ask itself whether in the particular circumstances the risk was such that this particular patient would think it significant if he was told it existed. I would think that, as a matter of ethics, this is the test of the doctor's duty. The law, however, operates not in Utopia but in the world as it is: and such an inquiry would prove in practice to be frustrated by the subjectivity of its aim and purpose. The law can, however, do the next best thing, and require the court to answer the question, what would a reasonably prudent patient think significant if in the situation of this patient. The 'prudent patient' cannot, however, always provide the answer for the obvious reason that he is a norm (like the man on the Clapham omnibus), not a real person: and certainly not the patient himself. Hence there is the need that the doctor should have the opportunity of proving that he reasonably believed that disclosure of the risk would be damaging to his patient or contrary to his best interest. This is what the Americans call the doctor's 'therapeutic privilege'. Its true analysis is that it is a defence available to the doctor which, if he invokes it, he must prove. On both the test and the defence medical evidence will, of course, be of great importance.

The 'prudent patient' test calls for medical evidence. The materiality of the risk is a question for the court to decide upon all the evidence. Many factors call for consideration. The two critically important medical factors are the degree of probability of the risk materialising and the seriousness of possible injury, if it does. Medical evidence will be necessary so that the court may assess the degree of probability and the seriousness of possible injury. Another medical factor, upon which expert evidence will also be required, is the character of the risk. In the event of an operation is the risk common to all surgery, eg sepsis, cardiac arrest, and the other risks associated with surgery and the administration of an anaesthetic? Or is it specific to the particular operation under consideration? With the worldwide development and use of surgical treatment in modern times the court may well take the view that a reasonable person in the patient's situation would be unlikely to attach significance to the general risks; but it is not difficult to foresee circumstances particular to a patient in which even the general risks of surgery should be the subject of a warning by his doctor: eg a heart or lung or blood condition. Special risks inherent in a recommended operation procedure are more likely to be material. The risk of partial paralysis, as in this case where the purpose of the operation was not to save life but merely to relieve pain, illustrates the sort of question which may face first the doctor and later the court. Clearly medical evidence will be of the utmost importance in determining whether such a risk is material: but the question for the court is ultimately legal, not medical in character.

If the doctor admits or the court finds that on the prudent patient test he should have disclosed the risk, he has available the defence that he reasonably believed it to be against the best interest of his patient to disclose it. Here also medical evidence, including the evidence of the doctor himself, will be vital. The doctor himself will normally be an essential witness:

and the reasonableness of his assessment may well need the support of independent medical testimony.

My conclusion as to the law is therefore this. To the extent that I have indicated I think that English law must recognise a duty of the doctor to warn his patient of risk inherent in the treatment which he is proposing: and especially so, if the treatment be surgery. The critical limitation is that the duty is confined to material risk. The test of materiality is whether in the circumstances of the particular case the court is satisfied that a reasonable person in the patient's position would be likely to attach significance to the risk. Even if the risk be material, the doctor will not be liable if upon a reasonable assessment of his patient's condition he takes the view that a warning would be detrimental to his patient's health.

Conclusion
Applying these principles to the present case, I ask first: has the appellant shown the risk of damage to the spinal cord to have been a material risk? The risk was slight – less than one per cent – but, if it were to materialise, it could result in severe injury. It was for the appellant, as plaintiff, to establish that the risk was so great that the doctor should have appreciated that it would be considered a significant factor by a prudent patient in the appellant's situation deciding whether or not to have the operation. The medical evidence even of Mr Uttley, the appellant's expert witness, gets nowhere near establishing the materiality of the risk in the sense just outlined. It is, or course, possible that Mr Uttley's evidence was not directed to anything other than negligence in the *Bolam* sense. If so, the appellant, who now relies on the principle of informed consent, must accept the consequences: it was up to her to prove such a case, if she was seeking to establish it. Further, we do not know Mr Falconer's assessment of his patient. It is possible that, had he lived, he could have enlightened the court on much that would have been relevant. After an anxious consideration of the evidence I do not find it possible to say that it has been proved that Mr Falconer failed in his duty when he omitted – as we must assume that he did – to warn his patient of the risk of injury to the spinal cord.

At the end of the day, therefore, the substitution of the *Canterbury*, 464 F 2d 772 (DC, 1972) propositions for the *Bolam* [1957] 1 WLR 582 test of duty and breach of duty does not avail the appellant because the evidence does not enable her to prove that Mr Falconer was in breach of his duty when he omitted the warning. Lack of evidence was always her difficulty; and it remains so, even though, contrary to the submission of the respondents, the law, in my view, recognises a right of a patient of sound understanding to be warned of material risks in the exceptional circumstances to which I have referred. Accordingly, I would dismiss this appeal.

(i) UNDERSTANDING *SIDAWAY*

I. *Bolam* or more?

What is to be made of this 'hotch potch' of speeches is not free from difficulty. Synthesis of the different strands of approach may be impossible and even discerning a majority view is not easy (see I Kennedy *Treat Me Right* (1991) ch 9; M Jones *Medical Negligence* (2nd edn, 1996) para 6–080 et seq and M Brazier (1987) 7 LS 169). Lord Scarman authoritatively restated in *Sidaway* how English law has come to see the decision in *Bolam*. We saw earlier in Chapter 4 how the House of Lords in *Bolitho v City and Hackney HA* [1997] 4 All ER 771 revisited and restated the so-called *Bolam* test or principle somewhat differently. We will return to this later (*infra* p 704). For the present we shall assume the interpretation offered by the judges in *Sidaway*. The *Bolam* principle was formulated as a rule that a doctor is not negligent if he acts in accordance with a practice accepted at the time as proper by a responsible body of medical opinion even though other doctors adopt a different practice. In short, the law imposes the duty of care; but the standard of care is a matter of medical judgment.

With Lord Scarman's statement in mind, the only judge in *Sidaway* to apply the *Bolam* test unequivocally was Lord Diplock. Certainly this was the view of Lord Scarman speaking extra-judicially in a lecture to the Royal Society of Medicine in 1986:

We can ignore Lord Diplock's opinion, as he was in a minority of one; the other three opinions were perhaps truer to the spirit of English law ('Consent, Communication and Responsibility' (1986) 79 J Roy Soc Med 697).

We must therefore turn to the speeches of the other Law Lords. What place does *Bolam* have in the analysis of the law which they severally offer. Certainly Lord Scarman rejected *Bolam* as we saw. We are left, therefore, with Lord Bridge (with whom Lord Keith concurred) and Lord Templeman. Neither judge went so far as to reject *Bolam* explicitly nor did they join Lord Diplock in relying wholly upon it as setting the standard of the duty to disclose.

The key words are those of Lord Bridge:

> ... the issue whether non-disclosure in a particular case should be condemned as a breach of the doctor's duty of care is an issue to be decided primarily on the basis of expert medical evidence, applying the *Bolam* test.

What can Lord Bridge mean by the qualifying adverb 'primarily'? Can it be the same as 'rightly'? Sir John Donaldson MR said in the Court of Appeal in *Sidaway*:

> ... I think that, in an appropriate case, a judge would be entitled to reject a unanimous medical view if he were satisfied that it was manifestly wrong and that the doctors must have been misdirecting themselves as to their duty in law.
>
> Another way of expressing my view of the test is to add just one qualifying word (which I have emphasised) to the law as Skinner J summarised it so that it would read:
>
>> The duty is fulfilled if the doctor acts in accordance with a practice *rightly* accepted as proper by a body of skilled and experienced medical men.

If so, what do either or both of them mean? Without referring explicitly to *Bolam*, Lord Templeman distances himself from the *Bolam* approach when he states that:

> I do not subscribe to the theory that the patient is entitled to know everything *nor* to the theory that the doctor is entitled to decide everything [our emphasis].

And later when he states that:

> At the end of the day, the doctor, bearing in mind the best interests of the patient and bearing in mind the patient's right of information which will enable the patient to make a balanced judgment must decide what information should be given to the patient and in what terms that information should be couched. The court will award damages against the doctor if the court is satisfied that that doctor blundered and that the patient was deprived of information which was necessary for the purposes I have outlined.

Presumably, a doctor 'blunders' when he does not behave 'rightly', ie the rule is a matter of law and not medical practice. If *Bolam simpliciter* does not for the majority in *Sidaway* represent the law of England this must mean that the views of the medical profession are not conclusive on disclosure. (This is not to say they are irrelevant.)

II. Beyond *Bolam*

Let us turn our attention in a little more detail to the speeches of Lord Bridge and Lord Templeman and seek to determine what, beyond *Bolam*, they saw as the doctor's legal standard of disclosure. There are two indications.

A. 'Substantial risk of grave adverse consequence'.

Lord Bridge considered that the court might regard as negligent non-disclosure in accordance with accepted medical practice if in the court's opinion: 'disclosure of a particular risk was so obviously necessary to an informed choice on the part of the patient that no reasonably prudent medical man would fail to make it'. His Lordship gave the example of an operation involving a substantial risk of grave adverse consequences, citing the 10% risk of a stroke in *Reibl v Hughes*. What can 'substantial' mean here? If it is to be regarded in terms of percentage of risks this must carry with it certain difficulties for the law's development. It has at least two drawbacks. The first is that it represents what is really a normative exercise (of what *ought* to be disclosed) as if it were an empirical matter. The danger is that this will suggest that the law's approach is a simplistic and arithmetical one, merely concerned with expert evidence on percentages.

The second objection lies in the danger that reference to percentage risks will merely provoke disagreements among experts as to what is the precise percentage in any particular case. Furthermore, it leaves undecided what percentage is the percentage beyond which a risk is regarded as substantial. Would the law not run the risk of having experts give evidence (hand on heart) that a particular risk has only a 3½% chance of occurring if 4% had become the magic legal limit? A court would have no criteria by which to choose amongst conflicting expert views. The consequence could be that in effect the law would be handed back to the medical profession through experts.

In any event, discussion of the size of risk in isolation overlooks the fact that in matters of risk calculation it is not only whether a risk exists but of what happens if the risk eventuates which are relevant in determining whether a patient is prepared to run that risk. For example, if an operation may bring benefits but carries a high risk of causing a long-term irritating rash, the patient may decide to run that risk whereas he may not decide to run what is represented as a low risk of having a permanent limp as a consequence of the same operation. It is all well and good to refer to 'grave adverse consequences'. The above example tends to suggest that the only judge of what is 'grave' or 'adverse' can be the patient.

B. General and special risks. Lord Templeman's speech is, to say the least, idiosyncratic. He referred neither to the *Bolam* test or the 'reasonable patient' test. Instead, he begins as if the legal canvas is empty and then seeks to paint a new picture. Lord Templeman draws a distinction between risks that are *general* and ones which are *special*. The *former* ordinarily would be known to the patient and no duty to disclose would arise. The latter may call for specific mention by the doctor. Lord Templeman seems to derive this distinction from the Canadian cases. In so doing, however, it is submitted, with respect, he may have read them in a way which others would not. The Canadian cases, particularly *Reibl v Hughes* and *White v Turner* (1981) 120 DLR (3d) 269 (Ont H Ct) are concerned with 'material risks': 'materiality' depending on what a reasonable patient would want to know. The distinction between 'general' and 'special' risks may be relevant to 'materiality' but is not determinative of it. For, ordinarily, a 'general' risk would not be 'material' because the 'reasonable patient' would be presumed to know it. By contrast, a 'special' risk may be 'material' but need not be. Thus, to categorise a risk as 'general' or 'special' is only tangentially relevant to the question of whether the doctor must disclose it.

Even if it be the case that Lord Templeman has reinterpreted Canadian law, the distinction he draws is at least for the time being part of English law for him. It must therefore be asked what are 'general' and 'special' risks in law? One tenable distinction (though as we have seen *prima facie* irrelevant to the issue of 'materiality') could be that a 'general' risk is one that attends all medical procedures, eg risks from anaesthesia in operations. The reasonable patient would, in law, be expected to be aware of these. On this theory the doctor would not be under a specific duty to volunteer information, though he may do if especially questioned (cf Lord Scarman *infra*). A 'special' risk, on the other hand, would be one inherent in the particular procedure either because of the nature of the procedure itself or because of some circumstances particular to the patient. This is the Canadian view. Is it Lord Templeman's? It may be his view. But even if it is, the distinction is unhelpful unless understood in the context of 'materiality' and the 'reasonable patient' which, as we shall see, Lord Templeman appears to reject.

The difficulty is, however, that what Lord Templeman says, suggests it is not his view:

> When a patient complains of lack of information, the court must decide whether the patient has suffered harm from a general danger inherent in the operation or from some special danger.

It is difficult to know how there can be a 'general danger' inherent in the operation as distinct from all operations. Indeed, on the basis of the words used by Lord Templeman the distinction between 'general' and 'special' becomes a distinction without a difference.

The important question then becomes, what is a 'special risk', because whatever else Lord Templeman means he seems to suggest that there may be a duty to disclose such a risk. He defines a special risk as one which may be 'special in kind or magnitude or special to the patient'. Obviously what is 'special to the patient' can *only* be determined by this patient. The reference to 'kind' or 'magnitude' does not seem to take us very far. This is because it is at least arguable that the only judge of what is special here can be the patient himself also. This would mean that Lord Templeman is embracing a legal rule which requires that the doctor must disclose that which the specific patient would need to know, a position expressed nowhere except in Oklahoma (*Scott v Bradford* 606 P 2d 554 (1979)) and, of course, rejected elsewhere in the speech of Lord Templeman himself. This is a legal test going beyond the 'reasonable patient', which again Lord Templeman purports to reject in another part of his speech. The meaning attributed to 'special' is further rendered imprecise by Lord Templeman's reference to *Reibl v Hughes* and the recourse to percentage risks. Reference to percentage risks may be helpful as regards the issue of 'magnitude' but seems to offer no assistance, without more, in determining whether the risk is 'special'.

One conclusion would be that Lord Templeman either embraces a test based upon what the particular patient would wish to know (though he rejects this) or his speech suffers from a degree of internal inconsistency.

Another, less nihilist, interpretation is remarkably conventional and has much to attract it. Starting with the 'reasonable doctor' standard of care Lord Templeman sought to give legal content (or at least guidance) as to how a doctor should approach his duty to provide information and the kinds of risks a reasonable doctor would disclose. It was as if he were saying 'a reasonable driver must balance the risks of driving' but 'drive on the wrong side of the road: well reasonable drivers don't do this' or 'keep their headlights on at night: they do this'. For doctors, then medical opinion whilst relevant, was not conclusive, as in other areas of life, the courts ultimately set the standard. In this, he has much in common with Lord Bridge.

III. The reasonable patient test

The majority in *Sidaway* opted for a duty of disclosure which, while rejecting the *Bolam* test *simpliciter*, leaves the exact nature of the duty somewhat obscure. Lord Scarman declared his commitment to 'the right of his patient to determine for himself whether he will or will not accept the doctor's advice concerning any proposed medical procedure'. This commitment could have led Lord Scarman to opt for either of two positions concerning the legal duty to disclose: the 'reasonable patient' test or the 'particular patient' test. As for the latter, as we have seen Lord Scarman conceded its validity in theory but regarded it as Utopian. It may also be logically impossible to satisfy as a test since it may contemplate an infinite regression of question, answer and subsequent question:

Dr: 'So that is what happens. Is there anything else you need to know?'
Patient: 'I don't know, is there any more I can know?'

Dr: 'Yes, the following happens ... now is there anything else you would like to know?'
Patient: 'I'm not sure, is there anything else you can tell me?'

Lord Scarman therefore opted for the 'reasonable' or 'prudent patient' test as 'the next best thing' to give effect to the patient's right to self-determination. Crucial for the 'reasonable' or 'prudent patient' test in all the jurisdictions in which it has been adopted is the notion of 'materiality', since it is only *material risks* which the doctor must disclose.

How does Lord Scarman define what risks are material? He states 'the test of materiality is whether in the circumstances of the particular case the court is satisfied that a reasonable person in the patient's position would be likely to attach significance to the risk'. As we have seen, Lord Scarman states that this 'is a question for the court to decide upon all the evidence'. Notice that Lord Scarman rejects the distinction between 'general' and 'special' risks as being relevant to 'materiality'. He states:

> With the worldwide development and use of surgical treatment in modern times the court may well take the view that a reasonable person in the patient's situation would be unlikely to attach significance to the general risks; but it is not difficult to foresee circumstances particular to a patient in which even the general risks of surgery should be the subject of a warning by his doctor, eg a heart or lung or blood condition. Special risks inherent in a recommended operational procedure are more likely to be material.

In reaching his view of the law, Lord Scarman draws heavily upon the American decision of *Canterbury v Spence* (1972) 464 F 2d 772 (DC Cir) and the language of rights which is so much more familiar to American courts.

Lord Scarman's approach has clearly not endeared itself to the English courts. There remains an obvious deference to the medical profession. The cultural change that will occur with the Human Rights Act 1998 is likely to have an impact here as elsewhere. An important decision that demonstrates the common law's approach to working out the 'reasonable patient' stand is the landmark decision of the Australian High Court in 1992 in *Rogers v Whittaker*.

Rogers v Whittaker (1992) 67 ALJR 47 (HC of A)

Mason CJ, Brennan, Dawson, Toohey and McHugh JJ: The appellant, Christopher Rogers, is an ophthalmic surgeon. The respondent, Maree Lynette Whitaker, was a patient of the appellant who became almost totally blind after he had conducted surgery upon her right eye. The respondent commenced proceedings against the appellant for negligence in the Supreme Court of New South Wales and obtained judgment in the amount of $808,564.38. After an unsuccessful appeal to the Court of Appeal of New South Wales (1991) 23 NSWLR 600, the appellant now appeals to this Court.

There is no question that the appellant conducted the operation with the required skill and care. The basis upon which the trial judge, Campbell J, found the appellant liable was that he had failed to warn the respondent that, as a result of surgery on her right eye, she might develop a condition known as sympathetic ophthalmia in her left eye. The development of this condition after the operation and the consequent loss of sight in her left eye were particularly devastating for the respondent as she had been almost totally blind in her right eye since a penetrating injury to it at the age of nine. Despite this early misfortune, she had continued to lead a substantially normal life, completing her schooling, entering the workforce, marrying and raising a family. In 1983, nearly forty years after the initial injury to her right eye and in preparation for a return to the paid workforce after a three-year period during which she had looked after her injured son, the respondent decided to have an eye examination. Her general practitioner referred her to Dr Cohen, an ophthalmic surgeon, who prescribed reading glasses and referred her to the appellant for possible surgery on her right eye.

The respondent did not follow up the referral until 22 May 1984 when she was examined by the appellant for the first time. The appellant advised her that an operation on the right eye would not only improve its appearance, by removing scar tissue, but would probably restore significant sight to that eye. At a second consultation approximately three weeks later, the respondent agreed to submit to surgery. The surgical procedure was carried out on

1 August 1984. After the operation, it appeared that there had been no improvement in the right eye but, more importantly, the respondent developed inflammation in the left eye as an element of sympathetic ophthalmia. Evidence at the trial was that this condition occurred once in approximately 14,000 such procedures, although there was also evidence that the chance of occurrence was slightly greater when, as here, there had been an earlier penetrating injury to the eye operated upon. The condition does not always lead to loss of vision but, in this case, the respondent ultimately lost all sight in her left eye. As the sight in her right eye had not been restored in any degree by the surgery, the respondent was thus almost totally blind.

In the proceedings commenced by the respondent, numerous heads of negligence were alleged. Campbell J rejected all save the allegation that the appellant's failure to warn of the risk of sympathetic ophthalmia was negligent and resulted in the respondent's condition. While his Honour was not satisfied that proper medical practice required that the appellant warn the respondent of the risk of sympathetic ophthalmia if she expressed no desire for information, he concluded that a warning was necessary in the light of her desire for such relevant information. The Court of Appeal (Mahoney, Priestley and Handley JJA) dismissed all grounds of the appellant's appeal from the judgment of $808,564.38 on both liability and damages, the Court also dismissed a cross-appeal by the respondent on the question of general damages. The respondent does not pursue the latter issue in this Court but the appellant has appealed on the questions of breach of duty and causation.

Breach of duty
Neither before the Court of Appeal nor before this Court was there any dispute as to the existence of a duty of care on the part of the appellant to the respondent. The law imposes on a medical practitioner a duty to exercise reasonable care and skill in the provision of professional advice and treatment. That duty is a 'single comprehensive duty covering all the ways in which a doctor is called upon to exercise his skill and judgment' [*Sidaway v Governors of Bethlem Royal Hospital* [1985] AC 871 per Lord Diplock at 893]; it extends to the examination, diagnosis and treatment of the patient and the provision of information in an appropriate case. It is of course necessary to give content to the duty in the given case.

The standard of reasonable care and skill required is that of the ordinary skilled person exercising and professing to have that special skill [*Bolam*], in this case the skill of an ophthalmic surgeon specializing in corneal and anterior segment surgery. As we have stated, the failure of the appellant to observe this standard, which the respondent successfully alleged before the primary judge, consisted of the appellant's failure to acquaint the respondent with the danger of sympathetic ophthalmia as a possible result of the surgical procedure to be carried out. The appellant's evidence was that 'sympathetic ophthalmia was not something that came to my mind to mention to her'.

The principal issue in this case related to the scope and content of the appellant's duty of care; did the appellant's failure to advise and warn the respondent of the risks inherent in the operation constitute a breach of this duty? The appellant argues that this issue should be resolved by application of the so-called *Bolam* principle, derived from the direction given by McNair J to the jury in the case of *Bolam v Friern Hospital Management Committee*. ...

Before the primary judge there was evidence from a body of reputable medical practitioners that, in the circumstances of the present case, they would not have warned the respondent of the danger of sympathetic ophthalmia; there was also, however, evidence from similarly reputable medical practitioners that they would have given such a warning. The respondent, for her part, argues that the *Bolam* principle should not be applied if it entails courts deferring to the medical experts in medical negligence cases and that, in any event, the primary judge was correct in the circumstances of this case in not deferring to the views of those medical practitioners who gave evidence that they would not have warned the respondent ...

In *Sidaway*, the House of Lords considered whether the *Bolam* principle should be applied in cases of alleged negligence in providing information and advice relevant to medical treatment. ...

As the speeches in the House of Lords make clear, the action was destined to fail because there was no reliable evidence in support of the plaintiff's central pleading that the surgeon had given no advice or warning. Nevertheless, the majority of the Court (Lord Scarman dissenting) held that the question whether an omission to warn a patient of inherent risks of proposed treatment constituted a breach of a doctor's duty of care was to be determined by applying the *Bolam* principle. However, the members of the majority took different views of the *Bolam* principle. Lord Diplock gave the principle a wide application; he concluded that, as a decision as to which risk the plaintiff should be warned of was as much an exercise of professional skill and judgment as any other part of the doctor's comprehensive duty of care to the individual patient, expert evidence on this matter should be treated in just the same way as expert evidence on appropriate medical treatment. Lord Bridge of Harwich (with whom Lord Keith of Kinkel agreed) accepted that the issue was 'to be decided primarily on the basis of expert medical evidence, applying the *Bolam* test' but concluded that, irrespective of the existence of a responsible body of medical opinion which approved of non-disclosure in a particular case, a trial judge might in certain circumstances come to the conclusion that disclosure of a particular risk was so obviously necessary to an informed choice on the part of the patient that no reasonably prudent medical practitioner would fail to make it. Lord Templeman appeared even less inclined to allow medical opinion to determine this issue. He stated:

[T]he Court must decide whether the information afforded to the patient was sufficient to alert the patient to the possibility of serious harm of the kind in fact suffered.

However, at the same time, his Lordship gave quite substantial scope to a doctor to decide that providing all available information to a patient would be inconsistent with the doctor's obligation to have regard to the patients' best interests. This is the doctor's so-called therapeutic privilege, an opportunity afforded to the doctor to prove that he or she reasonably believed that disclosure of a risk would prove damaging to a patient.

In dissent, Lord Scarman refused to apply the *Bolam* principle to cases involving the provision of advice or information ...

His Lordship referred to American authorities, such as the decision of the United States Court of Appeals, District of Columbia Circuit, in *Canterbury v Spence*, and to the decision of the Supreme Court of Canada in *Reibl v Hughes*, which held that the 'duty to warn' arises from the patient's right to know of material risks, a right which in turn arises from the patient's right to decide for himself or herself whether or not to submit to the medical treatment proposed.

One consequence of the application of the *Bolam* principle to cases involving the provision of advice or information is that, even if a patient asks a direct question about the possible risks or complications, the making of that inquiry would logically be of little or no significance; medical opinion determines whether the risk should or should not be disclosed and the express desire of a particular patient for information or advice does not alter that opinion or the legal significance of that opinion. The fact that the various majority opinions in *Sidaway*, for example, suggest that, over and above the opinion of a respectable body of medical practitioners, the questions of a patient should truthfully be answered (subject to the therapeutic privilege) indicates a shortcoming in the *Bolam* approach. The existence of the shortcoming suggests that an acceptable approach in point of principle should recognize and attach significance to the relevance of a patient's questions. Even if a court were satisfied that a reasonable person in the patients' position would be unlikely to attach significance to a particular risk, the fact that the patient asked questions revealing concern about the risk would make the doctor aware that *this patient* did in fact attach significance to the risk. Subject to the therapeutic privilege, the question would therefore require a truthful answer.

In Australia, it has been accepted that the standard of care to be observed by a person with some special skill or competence is that of the ordinary skilled person exercising and professing to have that special skill. But, that standard is not determined solely or even primarily by reference to the practice followed or supported by a responsible body of opinion in the relevant profession or trade. Even in the sphere of diagnosis and treatment, the heartland of the skilled medical practitioner, the *Bolam* principle has not always been applied. Further, and more importantly, particularly in the field on non-disclosure of risk and the provision of advice and information, the *Bolam* principle has been discarded and, instead, the courts have adopted the principle that, while evidence of acceptable medical practice is a useful guide for the courts, it is for the courts to adjudicate on what is the appropriate standard of care after giving weight to 'the paramount consideration that a person is entitled to make his own decisions about his life'.

In *F v R* [(1983) 33 SASR 189], which was decided by the Full Court of the Supreme Court of South Australia two years before *Sidaway* in the House of Lords, a woman who had become pregnant after an unsuccessful tubal legation brought an action in negligence alleging failure by the medical practitioner to warn her of the failure rate of the procedure. The failure rate was assessed at less than 1 per cent for that particular form of sterilization. The Court refused to apply the *Bolam* principle. King CJ said:

The ultimate question, however, is not whether the defendant's conduct accords with the practices of his profession or some part of it, but whether it conforms to the standard of reasonable care demanded by the law. That is a question for the court and the duty of deciding it cannot be delegated to any profession or group in the community.

King CJ considered that the amount of information or advice which a careful and responsible doctor would disclose depended upon a complex of factors: the nature of the matter to be disclosed; the nature of the treatment; the desire of the patient for information; the temperament and health of the patient; and the general surrounding circumstances. His Honour agreed with the following passage from the judgment of the Supreme Court of Canada in *Reibl v Hughes*:

> To allow expert medical evidence to determine what risks are material and, hence, should be disclosed and, correlatively, what risks are not material is to hand over to the medical profession the entire question of the scope of the duty of disclosure, including the question whether there has been a breach of that duty. Expert medical evidence is, of course, relevant to findings as to the risks that reside in or are a result of recommended surgery or other treatment. It will also have a bearing on their materiality but this is not a question that is to be concluded on the basis of the expert medical evidence alone. The issue under consideration is a different issue from that involved where the question is whether the doctor carried out his professional activities by applicable professional standards. What is under consideration here is the patient's right to know what risks are involved in undergoing or foregoing certain surgery or other treatment.

The approach adopted by King CJ is similar to that subsequently taken by Lord Scarman in *Sidaway* and has been followed in subsequent cases. In our view, it is correct.

Acceptance of this approach does not entail an artificial division or itemization of specific, individual duties, carved out of the overall duty of care. The duty of a medical practitioner to exercise reasonable care and skill in the provision of professional advice and treatment is a single comprehensive duty. However, the factors according to which a court determines whether a medical practitioner is in breach of the requisite standard of care will vary according to whether it is a case involving diagnosis, treatment or the provision of information or advice; the different cases raise varying difficulties which require consideration of different factors. Examination of the nature of a doctor-patient relationship compels this conclusion. There is a fundamental difference between, on the one hand, diagnosis and treatment and, on the other hand, the provision of advice or information to a patient.

In diagnosis and treatment, the patient's contribution is limited to the narration of symptoms and relevant history; the medical practitioner provides diagnosis and treatment according to his or her level of skill. However, except in cases of emergency or necessity, all medical treatment is preceded by the patient's choice to undergo it. In legal terms, the patient's consent to the treatment may be valid once he or she is informed in broad terms of the nature of the procedure which is intended. But the choice is, in reality, meaningless unless it is made on the basis of relevant information and advice. Because the choice to be made calls for a decision by the patient on information known to the medical practitioner but not to the patient, it would be illogical to hold that the amount of information to be provided by the medical practitioner can be determined from the perspective of the practitioner alone or, for that matter, of the medical profession. *Whether* a medical practitioner carries out a particular form of treatment in accordance with the appropriate standard of care is a question in the resolution of which responsible professional opinion will have an influential, often a decisive, role to play; *whether* the patient has been given all the relevant information to choose between undergoing and not undergoing the treatment is a question of a different order. Generally speaking, it is not a question the answer to which depends upon medical standards or practices. Except in those cases where there is a particular danger that the provision of all relevant information will harm an unusually nervous, disturbed or volatile patient, no special medical skill is involved in disclosing the information, including the risks attending the proposed treatment. Rather, the skill is in communicating the relevant information to the patient in terms which are reasonably adequate for that purpose having regard to the patient's apprehended capacity to understand that information.

In this context, nothing is to be gained by reiterating the expressions used in American authorities, such as 'the patient's right of self-determination' or even the oft-used and somewhat amorphous phrase 'informed consent'. The right of self-determination is an expression which is, perhaps, suitable to cases where the issue is whether a person has agreed to the general surgical procedure or treatment, but is of little assistance in the balancing process that is involved in the determination of whether there has been a breach of the duty of disclosure. Likewise, the phrase 'informed consent' is apt to mislead as it suggests a test of the validity of a patient's consent. Moreover, consent is relevant to actions framed in trespass, not in negligence. Anglo-Australian law has rightly taken the view that an allegation that the risks inherent in a medical procedure have not been disclosed to the patient can only found an action in negligence and not in trespass; the consent necessary to negative the offence of battery is satisfied by the patient being advised in broad terms of the nature of the procedure to be performed. In *Reibl v Hughes* the Supreme Court of Canada was cautious in its use of the term 'informed consent'.

We agree that the factors referred to in *F v R* by King CJ must be considered by a medical practitioner in deciding whether to disclose or advise of some risk in a proposed procedure.

The law should recognize that a doctor has a duty to warn a patient of a material risk inherent in the proposed treatment; a risk is material if, in the circumstances of the particular case, a reasonable person in the patient's position, if warned of the risk, would be likely to attach significance to it or if the medical practitioner is or should reasonably be aware that the particular patient, if warned of the risk, would be likely to attach significance to it. This duty is subject to the therapeutic privilege.

The appellant in this case was treating and advising a woman who was almost totally blind in one eye. As with all surgical procedures, the operation recommended by the appellant to the respondent involved various risks, such as retinal detachment and haemorrhage infection, both of which are more common than sympathetic ophthalmia, but sympathetic ophthalmia was the only danger whereby both eyes might be rendered sightless. Experts for both parties described it as a devastating disability, the appellant acknowledging that, except for death under anaesthetic, it was the worst possible outcome for the respondent. According to the findings of the trial judge, the respondent 'incessantly' questioned the appellant as to, amongst other things, possible complications. She was, to the appellant's knowledge, keenly interested in the outcome of the suggested procedure, including the danger of unintended or accidental interference with her 'good', left eye. On the day before the operation, the respondent asked the appellant whether something could be put over her good eye to ensure that nothing happened to it; an entry was made in the hospital notes to the effect that she was apprehensive that the wrong eye would be operated on. She did not, however, ask a specific question as to whether the operation on her right eye could affect her left eye.

The evidence established that there was a body of opinion in the medical profession at the time which considered that an inquiry should only have elicited a reply dealing with sympathetic ophthalmia if specifically directed to the possibility of the left eye being affected by the operation on the right eye. While the opinion that the respondent should have been told of the dangers of sympathetic ophthalmia only if she had been sufficiently learned to ask the precise question seems curious, it is unnecessary for us to examine it further, save to say that it demonstrates vividly the dangers of applying the *Bolam* principle in the area of advice and information. The respondent may not have asked the right question, yet she made clear her great concern that no injury should befall her one good eye. The trial judge was not satisfied that, if the respondent had expressed no desire for information, proper practice required that the respondent be warned of the relevant risk. But it could be argued, within the terms of the relevant principle as we have stated it, that the risk was material, in the sense that a reasonable person in the patient's position would be likely to attach significance to the risk, and thus required a warning. It would be reasonable for a person with one good eye to be concerned about the possibility of injury to it from a procedure which was elective. However, the respondent did not challenge on appeal that particular finding.

For these reasons, we would reject the appellant's argument on the issue of breach of duty. ...

For the foregoing reasons, we would dismiss the appeal.

Gaudron J: There is no difficulty in analysing the duty of care of medical practitioners on the basis of a 'single comprehensive duty' covering diagnosis, treatment and the provision of information and advice, provided that it is stated in terms of sufficient generality. Thus, the general duty may be stated as a duty to exercise reasonable professional skill and judgment. But the difficulty with that approach is that a statement of that kind says practically nothing – certainly, nothing worthwhile – as to the content of the duty. And it fails to take account of the considerable conceptual and practical differences between diagnosis and treatment, on the one hand, and the provision of information and advice, on the other.

The duty involved in diagnosis and treatment is to exercise the ordinary skill of a doctor practising in the area concerned. To ascertain the precise content of this duty in any particular case it is necessary to determine, amongst other issues, what, in the circumstances, constitutes reasonable care and what constitutes ordinary skill in the relevant area of medical practice. These are issues which necessarily direct attention to the practice or practices of medical practitioners. And, of course, the current state of medical knowledge will often be relevant in determining the nature of the risk which is said to attract the precise duty in question, including the foreseeability of that risk.

The matters to which reference has been made indicate that the evidence of medical practitioners is of very considerable significance in cases where negligence is alleged in diagnosis or treatment. However, even in cases of that kind, the nature of particular risks and their foreseeability are not matters exclusively within the province of medical knowledge or expertise. Indeed, and notwithstanding that these questions arise in a medical context, they are often matters of simple commonsense. And, at least in some situations, questions as to the reasonableness of particular precautionary measures are also matters of commonsense. Accordingly, even in the area of diagnosis and treatment there is, in my view, no legal basis for limiting liability in terms of the rule known as 'the *Bolam* test' which is to the effect that a doctor is not guilty of negligence if he or she acts in accordance with a practice accepted as proper by a responsible body of doctors skilled in the relevant field of practice. That is not to deny that, having regard to the onus of proof, 'the *Bolam* test' may be a convenient statement of the approach dictated by the state of the evidence in some cases. As such, it may have some utility as a rule-of-thumb in some jury cases, but it can serve no other useful function.

Diagnosis and treatment are but particular duties which arise in the doctor-patient relationship. That relationship also gives rise to a duty to provide information and advice. That duty takes its precise content, in terms of the nature and detail of the information to be provided, from the needs, concerns and circumstances of the patient. A patient may have special needs or concerns which, if known to the doctor, will indicate that special or additional information is required. In a case of that kind, the information to be provided will depend on the individual patient concerned. In other cases, where, for example, no specific inquiry is made, the duty is to provide the information that would reasonably be required by a person in the position of the patient.

Whether the position is considered from the perspective of the individual patient or from that of the hypothetical prudent patient and unless there is some medical emergency or something special about the circumstances of the patient, there is simply no occasion to consider the practice or practices of medical practitioners in determining what information should be supplied. However, there is some scope for a consideration of those practices where the question is whether, by reason of emergency or the special circumstances of the patient, there is no immediate duty or its content is different from that which would ordinarily be the case.

Leaving aside cases involving an emergency or circumstances which are special to the patient, the duty of disclosure which arises out of the doctor-patient relationship extends, at the very least, to information that is relevant to a decision or course of action which is taken or pursued, entails a risk of the kind that would, in other cases, found a duty to warn. A risk is one of that kind if it is real and foreseeable, but not if it is 'far-fetched or fanciful'. Certainly, the duty to warn extends to risks of that kind involved in the treatment or procedures proposed.

Although on the facts the plaintiff's questioning of her doctor was of central importance, the High Court makes it clear that their judgment is concerned with the doctor's duty to disclose information as a matter of general principle (for discussion see D Chalmers and R Schwartz 'Rogers v Whitaker and Informed Consent in Australia: A Fair Dinkum Duty of Disclosure' (1993) 1 Med L Rev 139). As to the precise nature of the duty it appears clear that the court adopts the 'reasonable patient' test paying due regard to the circumstances of the particular patient. On one reading, the court could be said to have gone further and endorsed, albeit elliptically, the 'particular patient' test rejected by Lord Scarman in *Sidaway*. The joint judgment stated:

> A risk is material if in the circumstances of the particular case, a reasonable person in the patient's position, if warned of the risk, would be likely to attach significance to it *or* if the medical practitioner is or should reasonably be aware that the particular patient, if warned of the risk, would be likely to attach significance to it [our emphasis].

It all depends upon the meaning of 'or'. An alternative interpretation would be that the court is merely stating 'the reasonable patient' test in alternative forms.

As can be seen, the Australian High Court's decision represents another common law jurisdiction's emphatic rejection of *Bolam* and its application in *Sidaway*. The often expressed fears of the courts as to what would follow the adoption of the 'reasonable patient' test would seem to be ill-founded. For example, there is no evidence in Canada that following *Reibl* the floodgates opened and the courts were swamped with cases alleging breaches of a doctor's duty to disclose. Indeed, Professor Robertson, in a careful empirical study of the cases in Canada involving informed consent since *Reibl*, shows that there were only 117 in the following ten years throughout Canada (excluding Quebec), half of them unreported. Moreover, the plaintiff failed in his action in 82% of the cases in which he relied upon a breach of duty to disclose (Robertson 'Informed Consent Ten Years Later: The Impact of *Reibl v Hughes*' (1991) 70 Canadian Bar Review 423). Significantly, in only 13 of the 117 cases (ie about 11%) did the plaintiff rely *solely* upon an alleged failure to disclose information. Thus, although the importance of the legal development in *Reibl* and *Rogers* cannot be overstated its effect on litigation (rather than on the practice of medicine) is minimal (see Robertson 'Informed Consent in Canada: An Empirical Study' (1984) 22 Osgoode Hall LJ 139).

Equally, the concern expressed by the House of Lords in *Sidaway*, particularly by Lord Bridge, that the adoption of the 'reasonable patient' test would mean that the courts could not hear medical evidence and take proper account of medical practice has been shown to be unfounded. Medical evidence remains of relevance, as Lord Scarman pointed out in *Sidaway*. Indeed, it must be determinative of the factual questions of what risks and alternatives exist. Furthermore, it remains of significant persuasive importance when the court comes to decide whether a breach of duty has been established.

Finally, if the 'reasonable patient' test is accompanied by an exception based upon the 'therapeutic privilege' medical evidence again becomes crucial. According to this doctrine, a doctor need not disclose information to a patient, whatever his *prima facie* obligation to do so, if by doing so he may do more harm to the patient than any benefit to be gained from the treatment. English law's continued reliance on the *Bolam* approach avoids the need to establish such an exception since *Bolam* entails that the doctor may exercise appropriate discretion in choosing whether and what to disclose. In keeping with all judicial statements which adopt the 'reasonable patient' test, Lord Scarman in *Sidaway* seeks to make it clear that the law does not make the duty to disclose absolute, but leaves the doctor with some discretion. This is the discretion which has become known as the 'therapeutic privilege'. He states:

> Even if the risk be material, the doctor will not be liable if upon a reasonable assessment of his patient's condition he takes the view that a warning would be detrimental to his patient's health.

Two points must be made. The first is to ask whether in the result the 'reasonable patient' test plus 'therapeutic privilege' is any different from the test advanced in *Sidaway* by Lord Bridge. The answer must be that it is not the same. The difference lies in the fact that under Lord Scarman's (and the North American) view, the doctor has a *prima facie* duty to disclose, and must justify non-disclosure by reference to medical evidence concerning the particular patient's circumstances. Thus, it is for the doctor to advance and prove this justification.

More significantly for a general understanding of *Sidaway*, it is clear from the way Lord Scarman expresses the 'therapeutic privilege' that the doctor may not justify non-disclosure simply by stating that the patient fell into a *class* of patient whom a *responsible body* of medical opinion would not have informed. Lord Scarman appears to reject the relevance of evidence referring to the patient as a member of a particular *class* of patient, and any reliance upon what a responsible body of medical opinion might have done. He states:

> ... it is plainly right that a doctor may avoid liability for failure to warn of a material risk if he can show that he reasonably believed that communication to the patient of the existence of the risk would be detrimental to the health (including, of course, the mental health) of his patient.

The second point which arises concerns the potential implications of adopting the justification of therapeutic privilege. It needs tight control, otherwise, as the President's Commission in America argues in 'Making Health Care Decisions' (*op cit*) (pp 95–96):

> The obvious danger with such an exception is the ease with which it can swallow the rule, thereby legitimating wholesale noncompliance with the general obligation of disclosure.

Accordingly, some courts and commentators hold that the scope of therapeutic privilege should be severely circumscribed, and that, at the least, the privilege should not apply in situations when the potential harm to the patient from full disclosure would result not from the disclosure itself, but from a treatment decision the practitioner fears the patient might make as a result of the information disclosed. More plausible claims of therapeutic privilege might involve certain disclosures to patients previously known to be suicidal or those susceptible to serious physiological effects of stress, and in situations where there is strong reason to believe that a particular disclosure is likely to result in serious self-destructive behaviour that could not be justified in terms of the patients' own long-term values and goals.

Despite all the anecdotes about patients who committed suicide, suffered heart attacks, or plunged into prolonged depression upon being told 'bad news', little documentation exists for claims that informing patients is more dangerous to their health than not informing them, particularly when the informing is done in a sensitive and tactful fashion. On the contrary ... there is much to suggest that the therapeutic privilege has been vastly overused as an excuse for not informing patients of facts they are entitled to know. In light of the values at stake, the burden of justification should fall upon those who allege that the informing process is dangerous to patient health, and information should be withheld on therapeutic grounds only when the harm of its disclosure is both highly probably and seriously disproportionate to the affront to self-determination.

One of the few cases which applies the 'therapeutic privilege' is the following Australian case.

Battersby v Tottman (1985) 37 SASR 524 (SA Sup Ct)

A doctor at a public hospital prescribed a prolonged course of high doses of a particular drug for a patient suffering from mental illness. The doctor was aware that there was a risk of the drug causing serious and permanent eye damage to the patient, but he was of the opinion that the advantages to be derived by the patient from treatment with the drug outweighed the risk of damage to the eyes. The doctor did not warn either the patient or the patient's relatives of the risk of damage to the eyes, or arrange for the patient's eyes to be regularly monitored by an eye specialist, because he was of the opinion that this would have an adverse effect upon the patient. The doctor kept a look out for signs of incipient eye trouble, but the patient nevertheless developed permanent eye damage, and sued the doctor and the hospital for damages for negligence.

There was evidence which the trial Judge (Cox J) accepted that the severe mental illness from which the patient was suffering had responded only to the high doses of the drug in question, that without the prescribed treatment her life was in danger, and that by means of her mental illness the doctor reasonably believed that the patient could not make a rational choice if confronted with the risks to which his treatment exposed her.

The trial judge held on the facts, that it had not been established that the doctor or the hospital had been guilty of any negligence. King CJ (with whom Jacobs J concurred) regarded the facts as justifying the doctor's exercise of the therapeutic privilege.

King CJ: In *F v R* [(1983) 33 SASR, 189, 193] I referred to 'the paramount consideration that a person is entitled to make his own decisions about his life'. The doctor would be in breach of his duty to the patient, in my opinion, if he withheld from a mentally normal and emotionally sound patient information as to a material risk simply because he found that the patient might make an unwise decision, perhaps based upon unreasonable considerations, not to undergo the treatment.

I adhere to what I said in the same case at p 193:

> Even where all other considerations indicate full disclosure of risks, a doctor is justified in withholding information, and in particular refraining from volunteering information, when he judges on reasonable grounds that the patient's health, physical or mental, might be seriously harmed by the information. Justification may also exist for not imparting information when the doctor reasonably judges that a patient's temperament or emotional state is such that he would be unable to make the information a basis for a rational decision.

I think that the appellant's mental and emotional condition as understood by Dr Tottman and as found by the learned trial Judge, placed the doctor in the position of having to make the decision for her for two reasons. First, merely knowledge of the risk to her vision would be sufficient to give rise to a real risk of hysterical blindness. Second, she was quite incapable by reason of her abnormal mental condition of using the information as the basis for calm or rational decision. She was likely to react hysterically and irrationally and to refuse treatment not on rational grounds or as a result of calm deliberation but as a result of distorted mental processes produced by her mental illness. The result of refusal of the treatment, in the belief of the doctor formed on reasonable grounds, was likely to be indeterminate close confinement in a mental institution with a high risk of suicide. I agree with the learned trial Judge that in the circumstances the doctor's decision not to acquaint the patient with the risk to her vision attendant upon the treatment was not negligent.

As if to prove the problematical nature of this concept, Zelling J saw the facts in a different way and dissented.

Zelling J: As the Chief Justice said in *F v R* a doctor may be justified in withholding information where the doctor judges on reasonable grounds that the plaintiff's health, physical or mental, might be seriously harmed by the information. In my opinion, this indicates a balancing test where one has to balance the seriousness of the risk of telling her, against the likelihood of, in this case, serious eye damage, to the plaintiff. My view is, that the balance comes down heavily in favour of telling the patient something as serious as this. After all, as I commented during argument, a doctor could hardly chop off a patient's leg without discussing it with the patient first. I see no reason why a doctor should be able to send a patient blind and be excused by saying 'I thought it was in your best interests for you to be blinded rather than have your treatment hampered'. The matter can easily be tested from the evidence of Dr Cotton, one of the witnesses whom the trial Judge accepted. Dr Cotton said that the most severe side-effect of melleril was not melleri retinopathy but death by cardiac arrest from taking melleril. Surely it could not be put to a court that it was better for the patient to die from cardiac arrest due to the administration of the drug, rather than to tell her of the drug's side-effects and risk a possible suicide. When one deals with effects as serious as the ones I have detailed, and in particular in this case blindness or near blindness or very serious damage which could have led to blindness if persisted in, the patient must be allowed to make her own decision, whether the doctor thinks she is well enough to do so or not, except in the case of a person who is too young to make decisions or is, by reason of mental infirmity, unable to consider and weigh the risks inherent in the treatment. Despite the plaintiff's mental troubles, she was not in that position. The case would have been different if melleril had only been used for a short time, in moderate doses, to stabilize the position.

Battersby deals with only one aspect of the doctrine of therapeutic privilege, *viz* that the doctor may withhold information if his disclosing it to the patient would probably cause actual physical (or mental) harm to the patient (hysterical blindness in this case). There is another situation which gives rise to the privilege which must not be overlooked. As Robinson J put it in *Canterbury v Spence* 464 F 2d 772 (DC, 1972): 'It is recognized that patients occasionally become so ill or emotionally distraught on disclosure as to foreclose a rational decision. … the physician is armed with a privilege to keep the information from the patient …'.

If these two cases both offer valid meanings of 'therapeutic privilege', it is important immediately to reject a third meaning which is sometimes advanced. It may be argued that a doctor may invoke the 'therapeutic privilege' out of a concern for the patient's wider interests as he sees them.

In *Nishi v Hartwell* (1970) 473 P 2d 116 (Haw Sup Ct) it was stated that:

the doctrine [of informed consent] recognizes that the primary duty of a physician is to do what is best for his patient … a physician may withhold disclosure of information regarding any untoward consequences of a treatment where full disclosure will be detrimental to the patient's total care and best interest.

It will be obvious that if this is accepted as being within the scope of the privilege, it would as Robinson J remarked in *Canterbury v Spence* 'devour the disclosure rule itself' (at 789) (and see GMC Guidance, *Seeking Patients' Consent: the Ethical Considerations* (Dec 1998), para 10: relevant information should only be withheld if it would cause 'serious harm' but not merely if the patient would have become upset or decide to refuse treatment).

While the view taken in *Nishi v Hartwell* is clearly bad law, so equally there is a need to avoid responding to such a view by throwing the 'baby out with the bath water' and declaring that where the 'reasonable patient' test is applied there can never be a situation of therapeutic privilege. Such a view has been expressed in the Canadian case of *Meyer Estate v Rogers* (1991) 2 OR (3d) 356 (Ontario High Ct) but must be wrong. It is easy, however, to sympathise with Maloney J in the *Meyers* case since he reached his decision as a reaction against what he saw as the never-ending extension of the doctrine of the 'therapeutic privilege' in the United States.

(ii) The impact of *Bolitho*

English law has not yet adopted the 'reasonable patient' standard. It may do in the future. However, in a most remarkable decision reached shortly after *Sidaway*, the Court of Appeal applied *Bolam* simpliciter.

Gold v Haringey HA [1987] 2 All ER 888, [1988] QB 481 (CA)

In 1979 the plaintiff, who already had two children, became pregnant and agreed with her husband that they would not have any more children. She was referred to a hospital run by the defendant health authority, where the consultant obstetrician suggested sterilisation but made no reference to the alternative of the plaintiff's husband having a vasectomy and gave no warning of the risk of the sterilisation operation failing. The failure rate for sterilisation (20–60 per 10,000) was higher than that for vasectomy (5 per 10,000). The sterilisation operation was performed on the day after the birth of the child but was not a success, with the result that the plaintiff subsequently became pregnant again and gave birth to a fourth child. She brought an action for damages for negligence against the health authority alleging, inter alia, that it had been negligent in not warning her of the risk of failure of the operation and that a statement made to her that the operation would be 'irreversible' amounted to a negligent misrepresentation. The judge held that the operation itself had not been negligently performed but that, having regard to the fact that the contraceptive advice had been given in a non-therapeutic context, the defendants had been negligent in failing to warn the plaintiff of the possibility of failure of the operation. He awarded the plaintiff damaged of £19,000. The defendants appealed.

Lloyd LJ: How then, I ask again, did it come about that the judge found the defendants guilty of negligence, when he accepted that there was a substantial body of responsible medical opinion in 1979 who would not have given any warning? The answer is that he drew a distinction between advice or warning in a therapeutic context and advice or warning in a contraceptive context. In a therapeutic context there was a body of responsible medical opinion which would not have warned of the failure rate. But in a contraceptive context there was no such body of responsible medical opinion. Even if there had been, he would still have found the defendants negligent, since in his view the *Bolam* test does not apply to advice given in a non-therapeutic context. He said:

> I accept that it was the view of the majority of the House of Lords that in the therapeutic context of that case [*Sidaway*] the duty to give advice was subject to the same test as the duty to diagnose and treat, and that this test, known a the *Bolam* test after an earlier case, was that a doctor is not negligent if he acts in accordance with a practice accepted as proper by a responsible body of medical opinion even though other doctors adopt a different practice. This test is different from the one generally applied in actions in respect of negligent advice. I see nothing in the reasons given for adopting the *Bolam* test in the sort of circumstances under consideration in *Sidaway* which compels me to widen the application of this exceptional rule so as to cause it to apply to contraceptive counselling.

So the judge decided against the defendant on two grounds. First, he held that the *Bolam* test did not apply at all in a contraceptive context. Instead he applied his own judgment as to what should have been mentioned in that context. Second, if the *Bolam* test did apply, then he found as a fact that there was no body of responsible medical opinion which would not, in a contraceptive context, have warned of the risk of failure. I have reversed these two grounds, since the first ground raises a question of considerable general importance.

Was the judge right when he held that the *Bolam* test is an exception to the ordinary rule in actions for negligence? If by an 'exceptional rule'; the judge meant that the *Bolam* test is confined to actions against doctors, then I would respectfully disagree. I have already quoted a passage from McNair J's summing up in *Bolam*'s case. In an earlier passage he had said ([1957] 2 All ER 118 at 121, [1957] 1 WLR 582 at 586):

> ... where you get a situation which involves the use of some special skill or competence, then the test whether there has been negligence or not is not the test of the man on top of a Clapham omnibus, because he has not got this special skill. The test is the standard of the ordinary skilled man exercising and professing to have that special skill.

So far as I know that passage has always been treated as being of general application whenever a defendant professes any special skill. It is so treated in *Charlesworth on Negligence* (7th edn, 1983) para 6–17. The *Bolam* test is not confined to a defendant exercising or professing the particular skill of medicine. If there had been any doubt on the question, which I do not think there was, it was removed by the speech of Lord Diplock in the *Sidaway* case [1985] 1 All ER 643 at 657, [1985] AC 871 at 892 where Lord Diplock made it clear that the *Bolam* test is rooted in an ancient rule of common law applicable to all artificers. In *Saif Ali v Sydney Mitchell & Co (a firm)* [1978] 3 All ER 1033 at 1043, [1980] AC 198 at 220 Lord Diplock treated the same test as applicable to barristers, although he did not mention the *Bolam* case by name. The question in that case was whether a barrister is immune from an action in negligence in relation to advice given out of court. It was held that he is not. Lord Diplock said:

> No matter what profession it may be, the common law does not impose on those who practise it any liability for damage resulting from what in the result turned out to have been errors of judgment, unless the error was such as no reasonably well informed and competent member of that profession could have made.

Counsel for the plaintiff did his best to argue that the *Bolam* test is confined to doctors. For the reasons I have given, I cannot accept that augment. I can see no possible ground for distinguishing between doctors and any other profession or calling which requires special skill, knowledge or experience. To be fair to the judge, it was not, I think, on this ground that he regarded the *Bolam* test as exceptional.

In passing, I should mention that the *Bolam* test is often thought of as limiting the duty of care. So in one sense it does. But it also extends the duty of care, as the second of the two passages I have quoted from McNair J's summing up in the *Bolam* case makes clear. The standard is not that of the man on the top of the Clapham omnibus, as in other fields of negligence, but the higher standard of the man skilled in the particular profession or calling.

Why then did the judge think that it would be an extension of the *Bolam* test to apply it in the present case? The reason can only have been that which I have already mentioned, namely the distinction between therapeutic and non-therapeutic advice. Counsel for the plaintiff took us through the *Sidaway* case speech by speech, and paragraph by paragraph, in order to point the distinction. But I remain unconvinced. In the first place the line between therapeutic and non-therapeutic medicine is elusive. A plastic surgeon carrying out a skin graft is presumably engaged in therapeutic surgery; but what if he is carrying out a facelift, or some other cosmetic operation?: Counsel found it hard to say.

In the second place, a distinction between advice given in a therapeutic context and advice given in a non-therapeutic context would be a departure from the principle on which the *Bolam* test is itself grounded. The principle does not depend on the context in which any act is performed, or any advice given. It depends on a man professing skill or competence in a field beyond that possessed by the man on the Clapham omnibus. If the giving of contraceptive advice required no special skill, then I could see an argument that the *Bolam* test should not apply. But that was not, and could not have been, suggested. The fact (if it be the fact) that giving contraceptive advice involves a different sort of skill and competence from carrying out a surgical operation does not mean that the *Bolam* test ceases to be applicable. It is clear from Lord Diplock's speech in *Sidaway* that a doctor's duty of care in relation to diagnoses, treatment and advice, whether the doctor be a specialist or general practitioner, is not to be dissected into its component parts. To dissect a doctor's advice into that given in a therapeutic context and that given in a contraceptive context would be to go against the whole thrust of the decision of the majority of the House of Lords in that case. So I would reject the argument of counsel for the plaintiff under this head, and hold that the judge was not free, as he thought, to form his own view of what warning and information ought to have been given, irrespective of any body of responsible medical opinion to the contrary.

Watkins and Stephen Brown LJJ agreed.

Although the decision in *Gold* offers an unambiguous interpretation of *Sidaway*, it has to be said that it is difficult, at best, to reconcile it with the speeches of *any* of the judges in *Sidaway* apart from that of Lord Diplock. Significantly, Lloyd LJ only referred to (and relied upon) Lord Diplock's speech. Subsequently, in a number of cases, the view taken in *Gold* has been regarded as the authoritative interpretation of *Sidaway: Palmer v Eddie* (18 May 1987, unreported), CA; *Blyth v Bloomsbury HA* [1993] 4 Med LR 151 (CA); *Moyes v Lothian Health Board* [1990] 1 Med LR 463 (Court of Session (Outer House)).

Despite the fact that the House of Lords refused leave to appeal in *Gold*, it should not be assumed that *Gold* has settled the law in England. For example, the Department of Health in its *A Guide to Consent for Examination or Treatment* (HC (90)22), specifically directs the reader's attention to the speeches of Lord Bridge and Lord Templeman (but not of Lord Diplock) in seeking to clarify the duty to disclose established in *Sidaway*. *Gold* does not (and should not) constitute the last word on the meaning of *Sidaway*.

Some judges have interpreted the *Sidaway* decision more creatively than did the Court of Appeal in *Gold*. By synthesising the speeches of Lord Bridge and Lord Templeman (in particular), the courts have concluded that the doctor's duty to volunteer information is not solely a matter for professional practice. In 1994 in *Smith v Tunbridge Wells HA* [1994] 5 Med LR 334 (Morland J) (discussed, (1995) 3 Med L Rev 198 (AG)) the judge held a doctor negligent in failing to disclose the risk of impotence inherent in an operation even though that was accepted as proper practice at the time. The judge took two previously unseen steps here. First, he read *Sidaway* in a far more expansive way than had the court in *Gold*. He referred to all the speeches and sought a common ground. Secondly, he seemed to see *Sidaway* and *Bolam* as representing a single line of authority rather than two.

We saw in Chapter 4 the developments in medical negligence culminating in the House of Lords decision in *Bolitho v City and Hackney HA* [1997] 4 All ER 771. There, the House of Lords interpreted the *Bolam* test consistently with leaving the ultimate judgment on the standard of care to the courts. A 'body of medical opinion' supporting the doctor's conduct must be 'reasonable' and 'responsible': it must be defensible 'logically'. We have already examined the meaning of this new approach but, even if its precise application in the future remains unclear, the court is left with the final say.

Thus, in hindsight, a synthesis of *Bolitho* with *Sidaway* now seems wholly plausible. Lord Bridge (with whom Lord Keith agreed) took a step beyond *Bolam*; where disclosure of the risk was 'so obviously necessary to an informed choice on the part of the patient that no reasonably prudent medical man would fail to [disclose] it' (at 663). There is even common ground here with Lord Templeman who requires the doctor to provide information (particularly about 'special risks') in order to allow the patient to make a 'balanced judgment' (at 666). Lord Diplock also, in applying *Bolam*, refers to the need for the practice to be 'responsible' (at 657). Here, then, we have the 'reasonable' 'responsible' oversight demanded in *Bolitho*. Also, it should not be forgotten that in the Court of Appeal in *Sidaway*, Sir John Donaldson MR spoke of a practice 'rightly' accepted by the medical profession ([1984] 1 All ER 1018 at 1028).

However, the relevance of *Bolitho* – and thus 'new *Bolam*' – to information cases remains uncertain. In *Bolitho*, the House of Lords was only concerned with cases of medical negligence arising out of diagnosis and treatment. Lord Browne-Wilkinson specifically excluded information cases from his 'new *Bolam*' approach (at 779). It is not clear why he did so. Obviously, *Bolitho* was not an information case. It might be argued that his exemption was because he thought that the court had no role in information cases. This would be a perverse explanation. Lord Browne-Wilkinson's exemption is probably better explained as one based more upon caution given that the issue did not arise in *Bolitho* itself. Who could blame him for not wishing to explain the speeches in *Sidaway* if he did not have to.

Subsequently, the Court of Appeal has considered the impact of *Bolitho* upon *Sidaway*.

Pearce v United Bristol Healthcare NHS Trust (1998) 48 BMLR 118 (CA)

The plaintiff was expecting her sixth child. The expected date of delivery was 13 November 1991. The baby had still not arrived on 27 November 1991, when the plaintiff saw the consultant responsible for her care at the respondent hospital, the United Bristol Healthcare Trust. She was very distressed during the consultation, and begged to have an induced labour or a caesarian section. The consultant, however, thought it appropriate to let nature take its course, and for her to have a normal birth without any medical intervention. He explained that it would be very risky to induce the birth, and that it would take longer for her to recover if she had a caesarian section. She accepted this advice. The baby died in utero some time between 2 and 3 December, and the delivery of the stillborn baby was induced on 4 December. The following issues were raised at the trial: (1) Should the consultant have advised the plaintiff that there was an increased risk of stillbirth as a result of the delay in delivery between 13 November and 27 November? (2) If the consultant should have so advised, would his advice have altered the decision made by the plaintiff to have a natural birth? The trial judge dismissed the claim, finding that there had been no negligence on the part of the consultant in not advising the plaintiff of the small risk attached to waiting for a natural labour to begin.

Lord Woolf MR: Mr Richardson submits that, when looking at the question of the advice which a doctor is required to give a patient for whom he is responsible, the courts are not confined, in reviewing the adequacy of that advice, to follow the test laid down in the well-known case of *Bolam v Friern Hospital Management Committee* (1957) 1 BMLR 1, [1957] 1 WLR 582. In other words, the courts are not confined to see whether or not the treatment is in accord with an acceptable body of medical opinion and, in concluding that if it is, there is no liability on the doctor concerned. He submits that the decision of a doctor in relation to the giving of advice can be examined against the background of at least three questions: (1) Is the advice rational having regard to the context and purpose for which it is required? (2) Is the advice responsible in that it alerts the patient to the particular risk of which the patient should know? (3) Is the advice responsive in that it deals with the questions and concerns of the particular patient?

Mr Richardson also submits that if the doctor is not prepared to explain the risks associated with non-intervention to a patient who is concerned, it is his duty to refer the patient to another doctor for a second opinion. Furthermore, he submits that it is only where a patient consents to non-intervention after a proper explanation that that patient can be deprived of his or her entitlement to a second opinion.

So far as the authorities are concerned, in my judgment, Mr Richardson rightly goes to the well-known case of *Sidaway v Bethlem Royal Hospital Governors* (1985) 1 BMLR 132, [1985] AC 871. That case dealt with a situation where the complaint was more conventional – where the risks of operative treatment had not been explained to the patient. Although all the members of the House of Lords were of the view that the plaintiff was not entitled to succeed, the reasons which they gave for this differed. The first speech was given by Lord Scarman. It is a closely reasoned speech, which deals comprehensively with the issues that arise in this situation. The views he expresses are a minority view and do not in this jurisdiction represent the law, although they do reflect the law in the United States and, to some extent, in Canada. They also reflect the developments which have taken place in the law since that decision was given in Australia.

The views of the majority most clearly appear from the speech of Lord Bridge of Harwich, with which Lord Keith of Kinkel agreed. However, Lord Diplock also gave a speech, which adopted the same approach as that of Lord Bridge. That approach involved applying the *Bolam* test to the giving, or failure to give, advice ...

Lord Templeman did not adopt quite the same approach as either Lord Scarman or the majority, but his speech is particularly relied upon by Mr Richardson ...

While recognising that Lord Templeman's approach is not precisely that of the majority, it seems to me that that statement of Lord Templeman does reflect the law and does not involve taking a different view from the majority.

In addition to the *Sidaway* case, Mr Richardson relies on a speech of Lord Browne-Wilkinson in the more recent case of *Bolitho v City and Hackney Health Authority* (1997) 39 BMLR 1 at 10, [1997] 3 WLR 1151 at 1160 ...

In a case where it is being alleged that a plaintiff has been deprived of the opportunity to make a proper decision as to what course he or she should take in relation to treatment, it seems to me to be the law, as indicated in the cases to which I have just referred, that if there is a significant risk which would affect the judgment of a reasonable patient, then in the normal course it is the responsibility of a doctor to inform the patient of that significant risk, if the information is needed so that the patient can determine for him or herself as to what course he or she should adopt.

In *Sidaway* Lord Bridge recognises that position. He refers to a 'significant risk' as being a risk of something in the region of 10%. When one refers to a 'significant risk', it is not possible to talk in precise percentages, but I note, and it may be purely coincidental, that one of the expert doctors who gave evidence before the judge gave the following answer in evidence. I refer to the evidence of Mr Pearson:

> '*A.* If she hadn't asked I wouldn't have mentioned the subject as she was already distressed and the risk is excessively small. I generally practice according to the belief that it is not the doctor's duty to warn of very small risks. If the risk, however, was of the order of 10%, for instance, then of course it would be my duty to warn against such a level of risk.'

Obviously, the doctor, in determining what to tell a patient, has to take into account all the relevant considerations, which include the ability of the patient to comprehend what he has to say to him or her and the state of the patient at the particular time, both from the physical point of view and an emotional point of view. There can often be situations where a course different from the normal has to be employed. However, where there is what can realistically be called a 'significant risk', then, in the ordinary event, as I have already indicated, the patient is entitled to be informed of that risk.

Turning to the facts of this case, the next question is, therefore, 'Was there a significant risk? To what extent was the risk of Jacqueline being a stillborn child increased by delay?' Miss Edwards, on behalf of the respondent, has referred us to the relevant passages in the transcript. They show that, on any basis, the increased risk of the stillbirth of Jacqueline, as a result of additional delay, was very small indeed. The statistical material which was available can be broken down into different classes. Even looked at comprehensively it comes to something like 0.1–0.2%. The doctors called on behalf of the defendants did not regard that risk as significant; nor do I. Indeed, it is right to point out that the operative treatment involved in a caesarian section would inevitably have had some risk.

Miss Edwards also pointed out, rightly, that earlier during the pregnancy the risk of the child being stillborn would have been greater than the figure with which we are concerned after 13 November and 27 November 1991 in this case. Particularly when one bears in mind Mrs Pearce's distressed condition, one cannot criticise Mr Niven's decision not to inform Mrs Pearce of that very, very small additional risk. Mr Niven would know that the baby was not large, which would also mean that the risk would be reduced. This is a case where, in my judgment, it would not be proper for the courts to interfere with the clinical opinion of the expert medical man responsible for treating Mrs Pearce.

Roch and Mummery LJJ agreed.

The approach of the Court of Appeal is highly instructive. There does not now appear to be two lines of authority, ie *Sidaway* and *Bolitho*. Rather, the legal standard in all cases, be they concerned with treatment, diagnosis or disclosure of information, is the same and can be derived from a synthesis of the two House of Lords' decisions. It is as if the more robust approach of the judges to expert evidence and professional practice in *Sidaway* was a precursor of *Bolitho*. At the core of this synthesis is the explicit recognition by the Court of Appeal that it is not for the medical profession to set the standard of disclosure. That, ultimately, is for the court. In reaching this conclusion, Lord Woolf MR relied upon the speeches of the 'majority' in *Sidaway*, namely Lord Bridge (with whom Lord Keith agreed) and Lord Diplock and the speech of Lord Browne-Wilkinson in *Bolitho*. Even the approach of Lord Templeman in *Sidaway* whilst 'not precisely that of the majority', was said to 'reflect the law and does not involve taking a different view from the majority' (per Lord Woolf MR). Welcome though this synthesis is, it must be recognised as 'creative'. A composite view of the speeches in *Sidaway* is problematic as we have seen.

What then does the Court of Appeal make of the standard of disclosure? Here is, perhaps, the most remarkable aspect of the decision. Lord Woolf MR concluded that:

if there is a significant risk which would affect the judgment of a reasonable patient, then in the normal course it is the responsibility of a doctor to inform the patient of that significant risk, if the information is needed so that the patient can determine for him or herself as to what course he or she should adopt.

In one bold step, the Court of Appeal has moved from a synthesis of *Sidaway* and *Bolitho* to a statement of the standard of disclosure remarkably similar to that espoused by the Australian High Court in *Rogers v Whittaker* (1992) 175 CLR 479 (HC of A). There, as we have seen, the High Court spoke of a doctor's duty to disclose all 'material risks' namely any risk which 'a reasonable person in the patient's position, if warned of the risk would be likely to attach significance to it' (at 490). The formulation in *Pearce* is indistinguishable in substance. The High Court appeared to go further and require disclosure of risks which the doctor ought reasonably to know would be significant to the 'particular patient'. Even this difference may evaporate in time and may be implicit in Lord Woolf's overall approach (see *infra*). Interestingly, the Australian High Court thought it was rejecting *Bolam* (see at 487 and 491), while the Court of Appeal applied it, at least in its new-variant form post-*Bolitho*.

Unlike the North American cases, the Court of Appeal has kept to the familiar legal framework of negligence locating the standard in the traditional 'reasonable doctor' test for breach of duty. However, like the Australian High Court before it, the Court of Appeal has nevertheless effectively stated the same standard. In asking the question 'what would a reasonable doctor disclose?', both courts answer 'what a reasonable patient would consider significant'. In the result, there is little, if any, difference. The courts, not the medical profession, retain overall responsibility for setting the standard of disclosure and it is to the needs of the 'reasonable patient' in the setting of the actual patient that the courts will look.

When is a risk 'significant'? In *Pearce* itself, Lord Woolf MR does not provide much guidance. Whether a risk is 'significant' cannot be determined simply in terms of percentages. The doctor will have to:

take into account all the relevant considerations, which include the ability of the patient to comprehend what he has to say to his or her and the state of the patient at the particular time, both from the physical point of view and the emotional point of view ...

It is important to notice that to be 'significant' a risk need not be one, which would have altered the patient's decision to consent to the treatment. A lesser level of importance may suffice. The risk must be one that a 'reasonable patient' would consider *relevant* to, rather than determinative of, his or her decision. Of course, if the patient is also to establish a causal link between the non-disclosure and her injury, the risk must be one which alone or in combination with other risks, would have lead the patient to a different decision (see *Chatterton v Gerson* [1981] QB 432 (Bristow J)). On the facts of *Pearce*, Lord Woolf MR concluded that the 'very, very small additional risk' of stillbirth, somewhere between one and two in 1,000, was not 'significant' particularly bearing in mind the plaintiff's distressed condition. This was not a case where it was proper for the court to interfere with the clinical judgment of the doctor.

In *Pearce*, the courts have moved into uncharted waters. The vigour with which the judges will scrutinise non-disclosure on the basis of the 'new *Bolam*' approach after *Bolitho* is unclear. Certainly, it is arguable that the 'hard look' or 'close scrutiny' of the premises, reasoning process and conclusions of expert evidence has its greatest potential in information cases. Clinical judgments are much less likely to be at the heart of a decision whether to divulge information. Risk/benefit calculations of the kind in play on the facts of *Bolitho* – which the courts are reluctant to disturb – will be less to the fore. More important will be questions of value: respect for the patient's right to choose and decide what is to be done to his or her body. Reasoning based upon 'the need not to trouble the patient', the 'desire to avoid worrying the patient unduly' or 'the fear of refusal' will simply not stand up to analysis because they embody the wrong values.

One thing is clear, doctors must henceforth be on guard; failing to disclose a risk (or alternative) can no longer be met merely by the argument that 'this is what we say'. Courts will perhaps more readily intervene in information cases than in cases of diagnosis and treatment where clinical judgments are more likely to be implicated. In information cases, the courts may want their say more often. Defensive medicine is, as a consequence, likely to lead to greater disclosure. It may be that changes in medical practice, rather than court decisions, will have a greater impact upon the level of disclosure.

In relation to the latter, the General Medical Council has taken a huge step forward in setting professional standards for disclosure of information. In its Guidance, *Seeking Patients' Consent: The Ethical Considerations* (November 1998), the GMC has emphasised the need to provide information and to do so in an intelligible way.

1. Successful relationships between doctors and patients depend on trust. To establish that trust you must respect patients' autonomy – their right to decide whether or not to undergo any medical intervention even where a refusal may result in harm to themselves or in their own death. Patients must be given sufficient information, in a way that they can understand, in order to enable them to exercise their right to make informed decisions about their care. …

3. Effective communication is the key to enabling patients to make informed decisions. You must take appropriate steps to find out what patients want to know and ought to know about their condition and its treatment. Open, helpful dialogue of this kind with patients leads to clarity of objectives and understanding, and strengthens the quality of the doctor/patient relationship. It provides an agreed framework within which the doctor can respond effectively to the individual needs of the patient. Additionally, patients who have been able to make properly informed decisions are more likely to cooperate fully with the agreed management of their conditions.

4. Patients have a right to information about their condition and the treatment options available to them. The amount of information you give each patient will vary, according to factors such as the nature of the condition, the complexity of the treatment, the risks associated with the treatment or procedure, and the patient's own wishes. For example, patients may need more information to make an informed decision about a procedure which carries a high risk of failure or adverse side effects; or about an investigation for a condition which, if present, could have serious implications for the patient's employment, social or personal life.

5. The information which patients want or ought to know, before deciding whether to consent to treatment or an investigation, may include:
   - details of the diagnosis and prognosis, and the likely prognosis if the condition is left untreated;
   - uncertainties about the diagnosis including options for further investigation prior to treatment;
   - options for treatment or management of the condition, including the option not to treat;
   - the purpose of a proposed investigation or treatment; details of the procedures or therapies involved, including subsidiary treatment such as methods of pain relief; how the patient should prepare for the procedure; and details of what the patient might experience during or after the procedure including common and serious side effects;
   - for each option, explanations of the likely benefits and the probabilities of success; and discussion of any serious or frequently occurring risks, and of any lifestyle changes which may be caused by, or necessitated by, the treatment;
   - advice about whether a proposed treatment is experimental; how and when the patient's condition and any side effects will be monitored or re-assessed;
   - the name of the doctor who will have overall responsibility for the treatment and, where appropriate, names of the senior members of his or her team;

- whether doctors in training will be involved, and the extent to which students may be involved in an investigation or treatment;
- a reminder that patients can change their minds about a decision at any time;
- a reminder that patients have a right to seek a second opinion;
- where applicable, details of costs or charges which the patient may have to meet.

6. When providing information you must do your best to find out about patients' individual needs and priorities. For example, patients' beliefs, culture, occupation or other factors may have a bearing on the information they need in order to reach a decision. You should not make assumptions about patients' views, but discuss these matters with them, and ask whether they have any concerns about the treatment or the risks it may involve. You should provide patients with appropriate information, which should include an explanation of any risks to which they may attach particular significance. Ask patients whether they have understood the information and whether they would like more before making a decision.

7. ... if you are the doctor providing treatment or undertaking an investigation, you must give the patient a clear explanation of the scope of consent being sought. This will apply particularly where:
- treatment will be provided in stages with the possibility of later adjustments;
- different doctors (or other health care workers) provide particular elements of an investigation or treatment (for example anaesthesia in surgery);
- a number of different investigations or treatments are involved;
- uncertainty about the diagnosis, or about the appropriate range of options for treatment, may be resolved only in the light of findings once investigation or treatment is underway or during the course of treatment, and when the patient may be unable to participate in decision making. ...

13. Obtaining informed consent cannot be an isolated event. It involves a continuing dialogue between you and your patients which keeps them abreast of changes in their condition and the treatment or investigation you propose. Whenever possible, you should discuss treatment options at a time when the patient is best able to understand and retain the information. To be sure that your patient understands, you should give clear explanations and give the patient time to ask questions. In particular, you should:
- use up to date written material, visual and other aids to explain complex aspects of the investigation, diagnosis or treatment where appropriate and/or practicable;
- make arrangements, wherever possible, to meet particular language and communication needs, for example through translations, independent interpreters, signers, or the patient's representative;
- where appropriate, discuss with patients the possibility of bringing a relative or friend, or making a tape recording of the consultation;
- explain the probabilities of success, or the risk of failure of, or harm associated with, options for treatment, using accurate data;
- ensure that information which patients may find distressing is given to them in a considerate way. Provide patients with information about counselling services and patient support groups, where appropriate;
- allow patients sufficient time to reflect, before and after making a decision, especially where the information is complex or the severity of the risks is great. Where patients have difficulty understanding information, or there is a lot of information to absorb, it may be appropriate to provide it in manageable amounts, with appropriate written or other back-up material, over a period of time, or to repeat it;
- involve nursing or other members of the health care team in discussions with the patient, where appropriate. They may have valuable knowledge of the patient's background or particular concerns, for example in identifying what risks the patient should be told about;
- ensure that, where treatment is not to start until some time after consent has been obtained, the patient is given a clear route for reviewing the decision with the person providing the treatment.

(iii) DISCLOSURE BEYOND RISKS

You will recall that the House of Lords in *Sidaway* spoke of the doctor's duty to disclose only in terms of a duty to disclose risks. None of their Lordships referred to any concomitant duty to advise patients of alternatives to any contemplated treatment, including the alternative not to be treated at all. That this should be an intrinsic element in the duty to disclose is beyond doubt. As a matter of principle if it is intended to empower the patient by informing him, knowledge of alternatives may well be as significant as knowledge of risks. This being so, the courts must regard the types or classes of information that form part of the duty to disclose as a matter of law for them.

The Canadian case of *Haughian v Paine* (1987) 37 DLR (4th) 624 (Sask CA) illustrates that the doctor's duty extends in principle to disclose alternative forms of treatment. There, a failure to advise a patient that a more conservative treatment was available than that advocated by the doctor was held by the Saskatchewan Court of Appeal to be a breach of the doctor's duty to the patient. The Californian case of *Truman v Thomas* (1980) 611 P 2d 902 (Cal Sup Ct) illustrates that, again in principle, the doctor's duty may extend to advising the patient of non-treatment (and its dangers). There, the California Supreme Court found that a failure to advise a female patient of the consequences of refusing a pap smear could constitute a breach of duty by the doctor, when she subsequently died from cancer of the cervix. Likewise, the case of *Pearce v United Bristol Healthcare NHS Trust* (1998) 48 BMLR 118 (CA) (discussed *supra*) concerned a failure to disclose the increased risk of stillbirth if delivery was delayed.

The duty may also extend to disclosure of information about the doctor which exposes the patient to risk during a procedure, for example, that the doctor is HIV positive or infected with hepatitis B or C: see *Faya and Rossi v Almaraz* (1993) 620 A 2d 327 (My CA). In this case the Maryland Court of Appeals held that a surgeon had (arguably) breached his duty of care in not advising two former patients upon whom he had operated that he was HIV positive.

An English court is likely to take a similar view even applying the *Bolam* test and require very compelling reasons indeed to licence non-disclosure. After all, even where the procedure is essential for the patient's health, another doctor could perform it. It is arguable, therefore, that in no circumstances is it reasonable to expose a patient to a risk of HIV infection by transmission from a doctor who is carrying out invasive procedures, for example a surgeon. Indeed, in England professional practice is likely to support a finding of negligence in cases such as *Faya*. At present accepted practice is for an HIV infected doctor to seek appropriate counselling and advice on his continued practice. He must follow that advice which, in the case of a doctor such as a surgeon carrying out invasive or "exposure prone" procedures, is likely to be to cease carrying out such procedures and for him to be reassigned to other work (see, General Medical Council, *Serious Communicable Diseases* (Oct 1997) at paras 24–33 and *Good Medical Practice* (July 1998) at paras 25–27 and *AIDS/HIV – Infected Health Care Workers: Guidance on the Management of Infected Health Care Workers* (March 1999) at paras 4.1–4.13). A court is likely to see a breach of these guidelines as amounting to negligence (see generally B Hutwitz 'Clinical Guidelines: Proliferation and Medicolegal Significance' (1994) 3 Quality in Health Care 37).

It is, perhaps, worth noting that if English law holds that a doctor has a duty to warn a patient of his HIV status, it would be the first time that the risk that had to be disclosed was *not inherent in the procedure* but rather arose because of who was performing it. One strong opponent of requiring disclosure of HIV status by a doctor has said that: 'The doctrine of informed consent was developed to assist patients in making decisions about the benefits and risks of medical treatments, and not to protect them against incompetent or dangerous physicians' (L Gostin 'The HIV-Infected Health Care Professional: Public Policy, Discrimination, and Patient Safety' (1990) 18 Law, Medicine & Health Care 303 at 304). Historically, this may well be correct and there are other mechanisms for dealing with incompetent or dangerous doctors. For example, there are the disciplinary and health procedures of the General Medical Council and, of course, the doctor's employer may also take action (see *supra*, ch 3). However, in principle, the distinction between risks inherent in the procedure and arising because of the operator himself, is one without a legal difference: the patient is in both cases exposed to a risk and the only real question is whether it is careless not to disclose that risk.

Does this mean that an experienced doctor will be required to disclose his inexperience and, thus, the greater likelihood there is of something going wrong? When 'league tables' are available, would this approach require a doctor to disclose his hospital's success rate in a particular procedure or, indeed, his own personal success rate? If not, what is the difference? Perhaps it lies in the specific nature of the risk in *Faya* versus the general risk of 'something going wrong' in the latter cases and patients have no legitimate expectation of the latter. Instead, within the NHS, the issue is whether it is reasonable to allow the inexperienced doctor to carry out the procedure and gain experience and whether there is adequate and proper suspension from someone more experienced (see *Wilsher v Essex AHA* [1986] 3 All ER 801 (CA), *supra* ch 4).

What about conflicts of interest? Must a doctor disclose, for example, that he has a financial interest in the institution where he is advising the patient to go for treatment? The GMC's guidance (*op cit*, para 15) is that he must:

> ... declare any potential conflicts of interest, for example where you or your organisation benefit financially from use of a particular drug or treatment, or treatment at a particular institution.

The issue arose in *Moore v Regents of the University of California* (1990) 51 Cal 3d 120 (Cal Sup Ct).

Moore v Regents of the University of California (1990) 51 Cal 3d 120 (Cal Sup Ct)

The plaintiff John Moore underwent treatment for hairy-cell leukemia at the Medical Center of the University of California at Los Angeles (UCLA Medical Center). The defendants were Dr David Golde, the attending physician; the Regents of the University of California, who own and operate the university; Shirley Quan, a researcher at the University; Genetics Institute; and Sandoz Pharmaceuticals Corporation. The Supreme Court granted review to determine whether Moore had stated a cause of action for breach of the physician's disclosure obligations and for conversion. The Court rejected the conversion cause of action.

II. FACTS

... Moore first visited UCLA Medical Center on October 5, 1976, shortly after he learned that he had hairy-cell leukemia. After hospitalizing Moore and "withdr[awing] extensive amounts of blood, bone marrow aspirate, and other bodily substances," Golde confirmed that diagnosis. At this time all defendants, including Golde, were aware that "certain blood products and blood components were of great value in a number of commercial and scientific efforts" and that access to a patient whose blood contained these substances would provide "competitive, commercial, and scientific advantages."

On October 8, 1976 Golde recommended that Moore's spleen be removed. Golde informed Moore "that he had reason to fear for his life, and that the proposed splenectomy operation . . . . was necessary to slow down the progress of his disease." Based upon Golde's representations, Moore signed a written consent form authorizing the splenectomy.

Before the operation, Golde and Quan "formed the intent and made arrangements to obtain portions of [Moore's] spleen following its removal" and to take them to a separate research unit. Golde gave written instructions to this effect on October 18 and 19, 1976. These research activities "were not intended to have . . . any relation to [Moore's] medical . . . care." However, neither Golde nor Quan informed Moore of their plans to conduct this research or requested his permission. Surgeons at UCLA Medical Center, whom the complaint does not name as defendants, removed Moore's spleen on October 20, 1976.

Moore returned to the UCLA Medical Center several times between November 1976 and September 1983. He did so at Golde's direction and based upon representations "that such visits were necessary and required for his health and well-being, and based upon the trust inherent in and by virtue of the physician-patient relationship. . ." On each of these visits

Golde withdrew additional samples of "blood, blood serum, skin, bone marrow aspirate, and sperm." On each occasion Moore travelled to the UCLA Medical Center from his home in Seattle because he had been told that the procedures were to be performed only there and only under Golde's direction.

"In fact, [however,] throughout the period of time that [Moore] was under [Golde's] care and treatment, . . . the defendants were actively involved in a number of activities which they concealed from [Moore]. . ." Specifically, defendants were conducting research on Moore's cells and planned to "benefit financially and competitively . . .[by exploiting the cells] and [their] exclusive access to [the cells] by virtue of [Golde's] on-going physician-patient relationship. .."

Sometime before August 1979, Golde established a cell line from Moore's T-lymphocytes. On January 30, 1981, the Regents applies for a patent on the cell line, listing Golde and Quan as inventors. "[B]y virtue of an established policy . . . , [the] Regents, Golde, and Quan would share in any royalties or profits . . . arising out of [the] patent." The patent issued on March 20, 1984, naming Golde and Quan as the inventors of the cell line and the Regents as the assignee of the patent. (US Patent No 4,438,032 (Mar 20, 1984).)

The Regent's patent also covers various methods for using the cell line to produce lymphokines. Moore admits in his complaint that "the true clinical potential of each of the lymphokines . . . [is] difficult to predict, [but] . . . competing commercial firms in these relevant fields have published reports in biotechnology industry periodicals predicting a potential market of approximately $3.01 Billion Dollars by the year 1990 for a whole range of [such lymphokines] . . . "

With the Regents' assistance, Golde negotiated agreements for commercial development of the cell line and products to be derived from it. Under an agreement with Genetics Institute, Golde "became a paid consultant" and "acquired the rights to 75,000 shares of common stock." Genetics Institute also agreed to pay Golde and the Regents "at least $330,000 over three years, including a pro-rata share of [Golde's] salary and fringe benefits, in exchange for . . . exclusive access to the materials and research performed" on the cell line and products derived from it. On June 4, 1982, Sandoz "was added to the agreement," and compensation payable to Golde and the Regents was increased by $110,000. "[T]hroughout this period, . . . Quan spent as much as 70 [percent] of her time working for [the] Regents on research" related to the cell line. . .

III. DISCUSSION

A. Breach of Fiduciary Duty and Lack of Informed Consent

Moore repeatedly alleges that Golde failed to disclose the extent of his research and economic interests in Moore's cells before obtaining consent to the medical procedures by which the cells were extracted. These allegations, in our view, state a cause of action against Golde for invading a legally protected interest of his patient. This cause of action can properly be characterized either as the breach of a fiduciary duty to disclose facts material to the patient's consent or, alternatively, as the performance of medical procedures without first having obtained the patient's informed consent.

Our analysis begins with three well-established principles. First, "a person of adult years and in sound mind has the right, in the exercise of control over his own body, to determine whether or not to submit to lawful medical treatment." Second, "the patient's consent to treatment, to be effective, must be an informed consent," Third, in soliciting the patient's consent, a physician has a fiduciary duty to disclose all information material to the patient's decision. . . .

These principles lead to the following conclusions: (1) a physician must disclose personal interests unrelated to the patient's health, whether research or economic, that may affect the physician's professional judgment; and (2) a physician's failure to disclose such interests may give rise to a cause of action for performing medical procedures without informed consent or breach of fiduciary duty.

To be sure, questions about the validity of a patient's consent to a procedure typically arise when the patient alleges that the physician failed to disclose medical risks, as in malpractice cases, and not when the patient alleges that the physician had a personal interest, as in this case. The concept of informed consent, however, is broad enough to encompass the latter. "The scope of the physician's communication to the patient . . . must be measured by the patient's need, and that need is whatever information is material to the decision." (*Cobbs v Grant*, supra, 8 Cal 3d at p 245, 104 Cal Rptr 505, 502 P 2d 1.)

Indeed, the law already recognizes that a reasonable patient would want to know whether a physician has an economic interest that might affect the physician's professional judgment. As the Court of Appeal has said, "[c]ertainly a sick patient deserves to be free of any reasonable suspicion that his doctor's judgment is influenced by a profit motive." (*Magan Medical*

Clinic v Cal State Bd of Medical Examiners (1967) 249 Cal App 2d 124, 132, 57 Cal Rptr 256.) The desire to protect patients from possible conflicts of interest has also motivated legislative enactments. Among these is Business and Professions Code section 654.2. Under that section, a physician may not charge a patient on behalf of, or refer a patient to, any organization in which the physician has a "significant beneficial interest, unless [the physician] first discloses in writing to the patient, that there is such an interest and advises the patient that the patient may choose any organization for the purposes of obtaining the services ordered or requested by [the physician]." (Bus & Prof Code, § 654.2, subd (a). See also Bus & Prof Code, § 654.1 [referrals to clinical laboratories].) Similarly, under Health and Safety Code section 24173, a physician who plans to conduct a medical experiment on a patient must, among other things, inform he patient of "[t]he name of the sponsor or funding source, if any, . . . and the organization, if any, under whose general aegis the experiment is being conducted." (Health & Saf Code, § 24173, Subd (c)(9).)

It is important to note that no law prohibits a physician from conducting research in the same area in which he practices. Progress in medicine often depends upon physicians, such as those practising at the university hospital where Moore received treatment, who conduct research while caring for their patients.

Yet a physician who treats a patient in whom he also has a research interest has potentially conflicting loyalties. This is because medical treatment decisions are made on the basis of proportionality – weighing the *benefits* to the patient against the *risks* to the patient. As another court has said, "the determination as to whether the burdens of treatment are worth enduring for any individual patient depends upon the facts unique in each case," and "the patient's interests and desires are the key ingredients of the decision-making process." (*Barber v Superior Court* (1983) 147 Cal App 3d 1006, 1018–1019, 195 Cal Rptr 484.) A physician who adds his own research interests to this balance may be tempted to order a scientifically useful procedure or test that offers marginal, or no, benefits to the patient. The possibility that an interest extraneous to the patient's health has affected the physician's judgment is something that a reasonable patient would want to know in deciding whether to consent to a proposed course of treatment. It is material to the patient's decision and, thus, a prerequisite to informed consent.

Golde argues that the scientific use of cells that have already been removed cannot possibly affect the patient's medical interests. The argument is correct in one instance but not in another. If a physician has no plans to conduct research on a patient's cells at the time he recommends the medical procedure by which they are taken, then the patient's medical interests have not been impaired. In that instance the argument is correct. On the other hand, a physician who does have a preexisting research interest might, consciously or unconsciously, take that into consideration in recommending the procedure. In that instance the argument is incorrect: the physician's extraneous motivation may affect his judgment and is, thus, material to the patient's consent.

We acknowledge that there is a competing consideration. To require disclosure of research and economic interests may corrupt the patient's own judgment by distracting him from the requirements of his health. But California law does not grant physicians unlimited discretion to decide what to disclose. Instead, "it is the prerogative of the patient, not the physician, to determine for himself the direction in which he believes his interests lie." (*Cobbs v Grant*, supra, 8 Cal 3d at p 242, 104 Cal Rptr 505, 502 P 2d 1.)

Accordingly, we hold that a physician who is seeking a patient's consent for a medical procedure must, in order to satisfy his fiduciary duty and to obtain the patient's informed consent, disclose personal interests unrelated to the patient's health, whether research or economic, that may affect his medical judgment.

The majority of the Californian Supreme Court rests its decision both on the common law duty of care and also because the doctor owes a fiduciary duty to his patient. The latter could be a justification for disclosure but is not accepted in English law (see A Grubb 'The Doctor as Fiduciary' [1994] CLP 311 at 325–329 and P Bartlett 'Doctors as Fiduciaries: Equitable Regulation of the Doctor-Patient Relationship' (1997) 5 Med L Rev 193 at 214–218). However, there is no reason why the obligation cannot be accommodated within the duty of care in negligence if it is relevant to the patient's decision whether to consent to the treatment (cf *Arato v Avendon* (1993) 858 P 2d 598 (Cal Sup Ct) – no duty to disclose medical information that may have affected patient's decision because of the effect on his business interests: see, Grubb (1994) 2 Med L Rev 230 (Commentary)).

(iv) DUTY TO ANSWER QUESTIONS

Thus far we have been concerned with a doctor's duty to *volunteer* information to a patient. To what extent is the analysis different if the patient requests information, ie asks questions. One view might be that the analysis remains unchanged except that the request for information is important, perhaps crucial, in determining what a reasonable doctor would do (see, eg, *Rogers v Whittaker*, *supra*). In England, however, a distinct body of case law has grown up.

Hatcher v Black (1954) Times, 2 July (QBD)

Mrs Hatcher was a lady who occasionally broadcast for the BBC. She went into St Bartholomew's Hospital suffering from a toxic thyroid gland. An operation was advised. She asked if there was any risk to her voice. She was reassured by the doctors. The operation was performed. In the course of it, the nerve was so badly damaged that she could not speak properly. She could not broadcast again. Mrs Hatcher had asked her doctor whether there was any risk to her voice.

Denning LJ: What should the doctor tell his patient? Mr Tuckwell admitted that on the evening before the operation he told the plaintiff that there was no risk to her voice, when he knew that there was some slight risk, but that he did it for her own good because it was of vital importance that she should not worry. In short, he told a lie, but he did it because he thought in the circumstances it was justifiable. If this were a court of morals, that would raise a nice question on which moralists and theologians have differed for centuries. Some hold that it is never permissible to tell a lie even for a just cause: a good end, they say, does not justify a bad means. You must not do a little wrong in order to do a great right. Others, however, hold that it is permissible, if the justification is strong enough, and they point to the stratagems used in war to deceive the enemy. This, however, is not a court of morals but a court of law, and the law leaves this question of morals to the conscience of the doctor himself – though I may perhaps remark that if doctors have too easy a conscience on this matter they may in time lose the confidence of the patient, which is the basis of all good medicine. But so far as the law is concerned, it does not condemn the doctor when he only does that which many a wise and good doctor so placed would do. It only condemns him when he falls short of the accepted standards of a great profession: in short, when he is deserving of censure. Not one of the doctors that have been called before you has suggested that Mr Tuckwell did wrong. All agree that it was a matter for his own judgment. They did not condemn him; nor should we.

This case was, of course, decided in 1954. It might be thought that social attitudes and therefore the law have changed since then. In the *Sidaway* case it was stated (*obiter*) that the doctor has a duty both to answer questions and to do so truthfully.

Lord Bridge: When questioned specifically by a patient of apparently sound mind about risks involved in a particular treatment proposed, the doctor's duty must, in my opinion, be to answer both truthfully and as fully as the questioner requires.

Lords Diplock and Templeman agreed. Notice that Lord Bridge recognises the touchstone of the duty as being to answer 'fully'. What does 'fully' mean? For a long time the leading case was *Smith v Auckland Hospital Board* [1965] NZLR 191.

Smith v Auckland Hospital Board [1965] NZLR 191 (NZCA)

The appellant had entered the respondent board's hospital at Green Lane, Auckland, for an examination, and, if necessary, for surgical treatment for a suspected aortic aneurism. In the course of the proper preliminary investigations he was subjected to a procedure known as aortography, wherein a catheter is inserted into the femoral artery and guided upwards through the arterial passage towards the aorta, into which ultimately an opaque fluid is injected through the catheter, enabling the aorta to be outlined satisfactorily for the proposes of X-ray photography. In the course of this procedure the appellant suffered a surgical mishap through the catheter accidentally dislodging a plaque of atheromatous material from the interior wall of the artery. A condition of clotting supervened, and notwithstanding all due efforts by the surgeons, the appellant's right leg degenerated into a gangrenous condition and ultimately had to be amputated below the knee. Negligence was pleaded in a number of respects, but the jury found for the defence on all issues of negligence alleged in respect of the conduct of the aortogram procedure on the part of the operating radiographer or any members of his team. But it was also alleged that, the risk of the mishap being a reasonably foreseeable one, albeit in only a low percentage of cases, it should have been the subject of a warning to the patient in the circumstances of this case; for the appellant gave evidence, which was uncontradicted, that he had made a specific inquiry as to the risk involved in the procedure, and alleged that the answer given was equivalent to an assurance that there was none. It was contended on his behalf that these facts gave rise to a cause of action in negligence, and an issue was put to the jury accordingly in these terms:

> Was the defendant by its servants or agents negligent so as to involve the plaintiff in the loss of his leg in ... (d), failing to inform the plaintiff adequately of the risks of conducting a femoral aortogram upon him?

to which the jury answered 'Yes'.

Woodhouse J, on an application by the respondent for judgment for the defendant *non obstante veredicto*, upheld the respondent's submissions, and gave judgment for it notwithstanding the jury's finding, holding that there was no evidence on which the jury could find any breach of duty, and alternatively that, even if there had been such evidence, the answer given by the surgeon could not reasonably be found causative of the damage suffered by the appellant. Both these conclusions were attacked in the appeal. Gresson J in the New Zealand Court of Appeal examined what the duty of the doctor was when asked the question 'is there any risk?'

Gresson J: In these circumstances either a refusal to answer at all, which would have carried its own clear implications, or a suggested reference back to Mr Barratt-Boyes, or an honest and reasonably complete and accurate answer was required, and the circumstances did not warrant – as they sometimes may do – *a suppressio veri* ... Here again the distinction lies in the fact that Mr Windsor did not reply to the appellant's question in accordance with what other competent medical men stated was their practice in a similar situation. After all, it was the appellant's prerogative to decide for himself whether he would submit to the proposed procedures, and this placed the doctor under a duty to give a careful and reasonably accurate reply to the appellant's direct inquiry as to the risk involved.

Two comments can be made. First, that Gresson J considers that the duty is, in part, at least, determined by reference to the practice of reasonable doctors and secondly, that this might allow for a range of answers from the *wholly* truthful to the partially truthful to the somewhat deceptive to the '*suppressio veri*'. In the Canadian case of *Hopp v Lepp* (1980) 112 DLR (3d) 67, Laskin CJ found otherwise.

> Apart from situations of this kind, a surgeon need not go into every conceivable detail of a proposed operation so long as he describes its nature, unless the patient asks specific questions not by way of merely general inquiry, and, if so, these questions must be answered, although they invite answers to merely possible risks. If no specific questions are put as to possible risks, the surgeon is under no obligation (although he may do so) to tell the patient that there are possible risks since there are such risks in any operation. It becomes a question of fact of how specific are any questions that are put.

Hopp v Lepp may be reconciled with *Smith* on the basis that in *Smith* the question asked was a '*general*' question and not a '*specific*' one. *Hopp v Lepp* would suggest that where the question is *specific* the doctor has no discretion but to answer and tell the truth. It could be said, therefore, that 'fully' (per Lord Bridge) must mean what Laskin CJ sets out in *Hopp* when the question is *specific*. But can 'fully' be what Gresson J states when the question is a general one? Given that Gresson J contemplates '*suppressio veri*' as a permissible response, it would appear not. It may be, therefore, that Lord Bridge's definition of the doctor's duty, ie that he must answer truthfully and fully (as we have defined it), must be understood as applying to all cases where it is clear to the doctor that the patient is expressly seeking information whether the question be general *or* specific.

How the doctor will respond will depend upon the content of the question. A hard and fast distinction between general and specific questions is consequently unhelpful.

There is some suggestion that a doctor may be justified in withholding information (or perhaps in not telling the truth) when to do so could reasonably be regarded as injurious to his patient's health, applying in effect the doctrine of therapeutic privilege. In *Lee v South West Thames RHA* [1985] 2 All ER 385 (CA) Sir John Donaldson MR said: 'The recent decision of the House of Lords in *Sidaway v Bethlem Royal Hospital Governors* [1985] AC 871, [1985] 1 All ER 643 affirms that a doctor is under a duty to answer his patient's questions as to the treatment proposed ... This duty is subject to the exercise of clinical judgment as to the terms in which the information is given and the extent to which, in the patient's interests, information should be withheld.'

It may be open to question whether leaving the doctor with this discretion is either ethical or should properly be the law. The GMC's guidance states that a doctor must respond 'honestly' to any question and 'answer as fully as the patient wishes' (*Seeking Patients' Consent: the Ethical Considerations* (Nov 1998) at para 9). Does the law follow suit? When the issue of answering questions arose immediately after *Sidaway*, the Court of Appeal took a surprising stance.

Blyth v Bloomsbury HA [1993] 4 Med LR 151 (CA)

Kerr LJ: This is an appeal by the defendant health authority against part of a judgment given by Mr Justice Leonard on 23rd May 1985 after a trial lasting some 10 days. The action had been brought by the plaintiff, Mrs Blyth, against ... the health authority on the ground that negligent advice or information had been given to the plaintiff in December 1989 by a member of staff of University College Hospital ('UCH') in relation to a contraceptive drug called Depo-Provera, which was then injected and had allegedly caused the plaintiff unpleasant side effects after her discharge from the hospital.

The plaintiff, Mrs Blyth, qualified as a nurse in New Zealand. She came here in 1973 and began to take a contraceptive called Minilyn, which caused her considerable problems. It was a combined pill, containing oestrogen and progesterone, and she subsequently gave it up.

She returned to New Zealand in 1975 to nurse her mother, who was unfortunately ill with cancer and died in November of that year. In 1976 she married and returned here; and in 1977 she began to work as a health worker in Hackney. In 1978 she became pregnant, and in May of that year she was referred to UCH for ante-natal care.

In that connection she saw a Miss Aileen Dickins, a consultant at UCH, who gave evidence at this trial. It was then established that she had no, or insufficient immunity to rubella, but fortunately this had no adverse effects on the subsequent history.

However, two consequences followed. First, although it was of course too late to vaccinate her against rubella at that stage of her pregnancy, it was necessary to do so after the birth of her baby in order to protect her and the baby against the risk of infection. Secondly, since the vaccine could itself cause adverse symptoms to a foetus if she were to become pregnant again within three months, it was necessary that she should have some contraceptive protection during this period, since that was certainly her wish.

The general practice at UCH in that regard at that time was to use Depo-Provera for this purpose in many cases unless there were countervailing factors, or the patient did not want it. The judge found that since 1975, when the drug was introduced, it had been administered to about 100 patients a year.

In the result, when Mrs Blyth was admitted to UCH in December 1978 for the birth of her baby, she received (i) a vaccination against rubella and (ii) an injection of the contraceptive Depo-Provera, which was designed to provide her with contraceptive cover for three months. Depo-Provera was a progesterone-only contraceptive and it was therefore thought that it would not have the same adverse consequences for her as the Minilyn which she had used for some years previously.

It is important to bear in mind throughout that there is no complaint in this case about the prescription or administration of the rubella vaccine; nor of the prescription or administration of the Depo-Provera. An allegation to that effect about the latter drug was abandoned at the beginning of the trial.

The remaining complaints of the plaintiff can be summarised as follows: (1) She was insufficiently informed and advised about the possible side effects of Depo-Provera when she was in hospital, and the hospital staff was negligent in that respect. That is the issue raised on this appeal. (2) If she had been informed about the possible side effects more fully than she was, she would not have agreed to have the Depo-Provera injection. This was found by the judge and is not contested. (3) She suffered from manifold side effects, allegedly due to Depo-Provera, for which she claimed damages. All her allegations in that connection were rejected, with the exception of bleeding and menstrual irregularity. The judge held that on the balance of probability these consequences could be attributed to Depo-Provera for some time after her discharge, but that they had certainly disappeared by February 1980, and on one view by July 1979.

An appeal against the award of £3,500 general damages having been abandoned, we are therefore now only concerned with the first of the three issues which I have mentioned …

I must turn to certain parts of the pleadings. The amended statement of claim included the following paragraphs 6 to 9:

6. The Plaintiff agreed to have the said drug after being assured by Dr Burt, a member of the staff of the said hospital:

(a) that the only known side effects of Depo-Provera were occasional spotting and one or two irregular periods;

(b) that all effects contraceptive and otherwise ceased after 3/4 months;

(c) that the drug would not affect breast feeding or pass through to the baby.

7. The said assurances were wrong and inaccurate in the following respects:

(a) that the only known side effects of Depo-Provera included menstrual irregularity, bodyweight changes, mood changes, depression of sexual drive and changes to nails and hair, such side effects lasting for up to a year.

(b) It was known that Depo-Provera would be likely to pass in the milk but it was unknown what effects this would be likely to have on the baby.

8. The Plaintiff would not have agreed to administration of the said drug if she had been told of the possible side effects.

9. As a result of the said drugs the Plaintiff suffered menstrual irregularity, mood changes, loss of sexual drive, eczema, 'galacthorrea' – that is, over-production of milk – 'loss of sleep, loss of weight and hormonal changes including changes in her skin colour and texture, loss of hair, change in hair colour and reduced resistance to infection'.

As will be seen, virtually all of these allegations were rejected by the judge. The only symptoms which he accepted she had after discharge were irregular bleeding and menstruation.

In the particulars of negligence the plaintiff included an allegation that the defendants were negligent by '(iv) failing to answer the Plaintiff's enquiries concerning Depo-Provera accurately and of failing to obtain answers to her questions before attempting to give her the said assurances about the said drug'.

She was asked to supply further and better particulars of that allegation, as to the enquiries she had made, to whom they were addressed and full particulars of the answers that were given and that should have been given, and her reply was as follows:

The Plaintiff informed the Certified Midwife, Sister Nixon, and a Staff Midwife that she was not prepared to have an injection of Depo-Provera until she had discussed the possible consequences of such an injection with a Specialist. The first defendants arranged for Dr Burt to see the Plaintiff. The Plaintiff was able to put various questions to Dr Burt. The relevant questions and answers given by Dr Burt are recorded in the Plaintiff's diary, see under (b) below.

Then it gives the questions and answers as recorded by the plaintiff in her diary, as follows:

1. What is in the drug? A. Progesterone only.

2. Are there any side effects? A. Only occasional spotting.

and then she was asked: 'Does it affect breast feeding? Does it pass in the milk? Does it have an effect on the baby? Are there any known reactions or upsets in anyone at all? All those questions were answered with the word 'No'. 'How long does it take for all effects to wear off: (a) completely, (b) contraceptive, (c) side?', and the answer is: 'All effects completely over within three months.' Then: 'Does it upset periods? (A) Not after three to four months. How does Depo-Provera work in and on the body? (A) Prevention of ovulation.'

There was added: 'The plaintiff should have been told of the known possible side effects of the said drug.'

That alleged record of questions and answers in the plaintiff's diary was rejected by the judge … he said this at p 26D:

For reasons which are inherent in the passages I have cited, it seems to me important to consider whether the plaintiff asked the nursing and medical staff for information and advice about the drug or not. The plaintiff says that she asked the questions which are set out in her diary. The entry is headed 'For Tony' – that is her husband – 'tonight, re DP' – and an abbreviation for 'contraceptive'. In conjunction with the question as to whether the drug would affect breast-feeding the plaintiff has written in brackets '(intend 6/12' – that is six month – 'at least)'. I find an artificial flavour to those two entries, particularly the first, if all of the writing, with minor possible exceptions, was done at the same time as the plaintiff maintains. As I have already indicated, I do not regard it as in any way probable that Dr (Burt) would have answered the question in the form 'Any known reactions, upsets in anyone at all' with a simple negative. Moreover, I do not believe that a person with the plaintiff's professional training would in fact ask such a question. I therefore doubt the accuracy of the plaintiff's evidence as to how precisely the document came to be written. If she had readily been writing the answers, or most of them, down at the time, I think that fact would have been sufficiently unusual to stick in Dr (Burt's) memory, but it does not.

That speaks for itself.

In an earlier part of his judgment he found the following facts about the discussions concerning Depo-Provera between the plaintiff and, first, Sister Nixon, and thereafter Dr Burt. At p 10C the judge said:

Sister Nixon is an experienced midwifery sister. I accept her evidence that she would not have withheld information about the titre reading if she had been asked (that was a reference to the degree of immunity to rubella).

It was she, of course, who administered both injections. She told me that ie was her practice to tell the patient the possible side effects of Depo-Provera. She would have warned of spotting or irregular bleeding which might be light or heavy. If the patient had expressed concern about the injections, it would have been noted in the record and the vaccination would not have been carried out. If the patient requested further advice that would have been recorded and the appropriate arrangements made. The usual practice was to give the vaccine and the Depo-Provera consecutively. As in this case they were administered with an interval of two days the explanation might well be that the plaintiff had been offered the contraceptive injection, for example, by Dr Beatles but was not happy about it initially. Having seen Sister Nixon in the witness box, I am satisfied that she would not have tried to over-persuade the plaintiff into accepting the injection when she did not want it.

He then turns at p 10H to the important discussion about Depo-Provera which the plaintiff had with Dr Burt:

Dr Burt was practising in 1978 under her maiden name of Burt. She had qualified in 1974 and was fully registered in July 1975. She had obtained the Diploma of Child Health in 1977, and in 1981, of course subsequently to the events with which this case is concerned, she obtained her Membership of the Royal College of Obstetricians and Gynaecologists by examination. Membership is the senior qualification by examination given by the college. In 1978 Dr (Burt) was reading for that examination. She had previously held senior house office posts before becoming a senior house officer in obstetrics and gynaecology at University College Hospital on 1st December. It was in the context of this case that she first came across the use of Depo-Provera as a contraceptive, though she had some experience of it in the treatment of cancer. Although she has some memory of a patient who may have been the plaintiff, Dr (Burt) had to accept that she has no memory of events connected with her seeing the plaintiff, apart from what the record contains. This shows that she prescribed the Depo-Provera on 23rd December – that was the Saturday shortly before Christmas. She was then responsible for the obstetric wards and on call for the labour ward and the gynaecological emergencies. Her purpose in seeing the plaintiff was to check her condition prior to discharge. She thinks it was in the course of writing up her notes that she saw that the vaccine had been prescribed and, therefore, appreciated the need for advice that contraceptive action should be taken. The discharge sheet has a section which is headed 'Contraception'. It contains provision for recording whether advice has been requested or offered. That provision has not been used, but the doctor has simply recorded 'Depo-Provera to cover rubella vaccination'. She thought that her suggesting Depo-Provera came about because the sister said that it was often used in these circumstances. She would have referred to the data sheet compendium for the proper dosage and in order to see whether there was any other information which she ought to know. The compendium is a book which contains the manufacturer's information about various drugs. At this time the only relevant comment on side effects relating to a single (injection) was as follows: 'Clinically Depo-Provera is well tolerated. No significant untoward effects have been reported.' However, because of her reading, particularly in preparation for her membership examination, Dr (Burt) was aware that there might be a problem with irregular bleeding. It was her evidence that she would have told the patient of the need for contraception and would have discussed alternative methods. She would have described Depo-Provera as effective, and convenient, and having the appropriate duration of protection, that is to say 90 days. She would have said that it was in common use at the hospital. She would have warned that there might be the problem of irregular bleeding. She would not, she says, have used the word 'spotting' which is attributed to her by the plaintiff. She would have told the plaintiff that the drug was generally acceptable and had no serious or significant side effects. She might have added that progesterone was less associated with side effects than oestrogen and that it would have no adverse effects on the baby. If she had been asked the question postulated by the plaintiff 'Are there any known reactions or upsets in anyone at all?' she would have replied that there might be reactions of which she was not aware, and her answer would have been that she did not know. It was the plaintiff's evidence that she prepared a number of questions before she was seen by the doctor. They were recorded in a diary in which she wrote, at any rate, most of the answers as they were given. Dr (Burt) has no memory of this. The doctor accepted that the delay between the prescribing of the vaccine and the Depo-Provera suggests that there may have been some discussion about the latter. She also accepted that she may have been told that the plaintiff wanted to discuss the drug. She agreed that she would have conveyed the impression to the plaintiff that there were no significant side effects other than bleeding.

The judgment contains no adverse conclusion of any kind concerning Dr Burt, or about her discussion with the plaintiff. Furthermore, none of the medical witnesses criticised her conduct or the information which she gave, as summarised in this account by the judge, other than Professor Huntingford, whose evidence was not accepted as to what was known and required to be disclosed about Depo-Provera in December 1978. On the contrary, the effect of the evidence of all three doctors called by the defendants was to approve the conduct of Dr Burt on the basis of her evidence, which the judge clearly accepted, ie Miss Dickins, Dr Law and an independent highly qualified expert, Dame Josephine Barnes. The judge also clearly accepted the evidence of all these witnesses, and I shall be returning to some short passages in that connection later on.

In effect, therefore, Dr Burt was absolved from any allegation of negligence – indeed, as appears hereafter, not only by the judge but also by counsel for the plaintiff. Nevertheless, somewhat surprisingly in the circumstances, the judge concluded that the defendants had been negligent ... I must refer to some passages in the speeches in the House of Lords in *Sidaway*, on which the judge relied ... there were ... a number of remarks, *obiter* in their context, on the duty to reply to questions. For present purposes I need only refer to two passages. At p 895B Lord Diplock mentioned the natural tendency of many people to want to decide for themselves whether anything should be done to their bodies and whether or not to consent to any treatment which might be advised. In that connection he said:

> No doubt if the plaintiff in fact manifested this attitude by means of questioning, the doctor would tell him whatever it was the patient wanted to know.

Lord Bridge, with whom Lord Keith agreed, said at p 898B:

> I should perhaps add at this point, although the issue does not strictly arise on this appeal, that, when questioned specifically by a patient of apparently sound mind about risks involved in a particular treatment proposed, a doctor's duty must, in my opinion, be to answer both truthfully and as fully as the question requires.

The judge referred to these passages and to another passage in the speech of Lord Bridge before dealing with the questions and answers which appear in the plaintiff's diary, to which I have already referred.

Kerr LJ cited further the judgment of Leonard J, and continued:

(1) It confirms, as I have already mentioned, that the judge absolved Dr Burt from all blame; indeed, he appears to have commended her conduct.

(2) The judge does not find anywhere what enquiries the plaintiff in fact made about Depo-Provera, let alone that she made any specific enquiry. On the contrary, he had already rejected her evidence that she made the specific enquiries recorded in her diary and in the pleading. All that he said in that connection was that it was more probable than not that she asked for some information and advice, and that she had expressed some sort of reservation about Depo-Provera and had made some form of request for reassurances about it. That, so

far as it goes, is of course a finding which the defendants accept, as they must, and it is fully in accordance with the probabilities on the rest of the evidence.

(3) On that assumption, what were the defendants obliged to tell the plaintiff in response, and did they fail in their duty in that regard? In that connection it must be borne in mind that there was no medical evidence on which the judge could properly conclude that the defendants had been negligent by not having given any more information to the plaintiff than what she was told by Dr Burt.

(4) In my view the judge overstated the position on the evidence when he said, at p 28C:

> As Miss Dickins said in evidence, if the patient is making a specific enquiry, it would be right to tell her the whole picture.

The expression 'the full picture' was used by counsel in his cross-examination of Miss Dickins. Her assent to it, at the end of a question occupying nearly eight lines, cannot properly be divorced from the context of her evidence as a whole, and I set out later on the judge's own summary of it.

(5) In the passage which I have read the judge referred to 'such information as is available to the hospital', and to the retrieval of information 'from the files'. What he appears to have had in mind was information, case studies, statistics and other literature which had been collated by Dr Law as part of a piece of research of her own, but which was also available for consultation by others; and he may also have had this in mind when he referred twice to 'the full picture'. ...

For present purposes it is sufficient to take the judge's summary of [the experts'] evidence, though in my view its effect was a good deal stronger and more favourable to the defendants than the summary suggests.

In relation to Miss Dickins, the judge said at p 20:

> Miss Dickins, who was the consultant obstetrician and gynaecologist in charge of the plaintiff from the time of her referral, preceding Daniel's birth, described Depo-Provera as being 'convenient and useful for suitable patients who needed to be without anxiety about becoming pregnant for a period of three months'. Presented with a summary of the answers said to have been by Dr Burt

and I interpolate 'according to Dr Burt's account of the interview (which the judge accepted) and not according to what the plaintiff claims to have been recorded in her diary'

> she was of the opinion that they contained sufficient information for the patient, in the light of the material which was available in 1978. In her view there was no need to mention the other symptoms which were rare, though she thought that it would be necessary to mention them now because of the public discussion. It was common practice to tell the patient about irregular bleeding, but not the minor side effects. However, she added that, if the patient made a specific enquiry, then it would be proper to tell her the full picture.

I have already dealt with the point made again in the last sentence.

Then in relation to Dame Josephine Barnes, the judge said:

> (She) is an obstetrician and gynaecologist of formidable reputation. In addition to her academic and institutional distinctions she is a consultant to the Charing Cross and Elizabeth Garrett-Anderson Hospitals. She regards Depo-Provera as useful in certain applications, including cases in which a woman has been vaccinated against rubella and, therefore, needs to avoid pregnancy for three months. Her evidence was that in 1978 all that was known was that the main side effect of the drug was irregular bleeding. The patient should have been told about it; it was probably unnecessary to warn her of other comparatively trivial side effects of which complaint had been made.

(6) In the light of these comments I conclude that the judge was in error in holding that there was any obligation to pass on to the plaintiff all the information available to the hospital; that is to say in this case the information contained in Dr Law's files. That conclusion could not properly be based upon the evidence. As regards the judge's repeated reference to the need to give a full picture in answer to a specific enquiry, it must be borne in mind, apart from the other matters already mentioned in that regard, that no specific enquiry was found to have been made in this case.

Secondly, I think the judge's conclusions equally cannot properly be based on the remarks of Lord Diplock and Lord Bridge in *Sidaway*. The question of what a plaintiff should be told in answer to a general enquiry cannot be divorced from the *Bolam* test, any more than when no such enquiry is made. In both cases the answer must depend upon the circumstances, the nature of the enquiry, the nature of the information which is available, its reliability, relevance, the condition of the patient, and so forth. Any medical evidence directed to what would be the proper answer in the light of responsible medical opinion and practice – that is to say, the *Bolam* test – must in my view equally be placed in the balance in cases where the patient makes some enquiry, in order to decide whether the response was negligent or not.

In that connection, apart from what was said by Lords Diplock and Bridge, I would also draw attention to the speech of Lord Templeman at p 903D onwards, which suggests to me that the *Bolam* test is all-pervasive in this context. Indeed I am not convinced that the *Bolam* test is irrelevant even in relation to the question of what answers are properly to be given to specific enquiries, or that Lord Diplock or Lord Bridge intended to hold otherwise. It seems to me that there must always be grey areas, with differences of opinion, as to what are the proper answers to be given to any enquiry, even a specific one, in the particular circumstances of any case. However, on the evidence in the present case this point does not arise, since no specific enquiry was found to have been made.

(7) Accordingly, I conclude that the judge erred in finding negligence in relation to what the plaintiff was not told by Dr Burt, whether he relied on the medical evidence or on the *obiter* remarks in *Sidaway*, or both …

Neill LJ: I do not understand that in the decision of the House of Lords in *Sidaway v Board of Governors of the Bethlem Royal Hospital* [1985] AC 871, [1985] 1 All ER 643, in the passages to which my Lord has already drawn attention that Lord Diplock or Lord Bridge were laying down any rule of law to the effect that where questions are asked by a patient, or doubts are expressed, a doctor is under an obligation to put the patient in possession of all the information on the subject which may be available in the files of a consultant, who may have made a special study of the subject. The amount of information to be given must depend upon the circumstances, and as a general proposition it is governed by what is called the *Bolam* test. In 1978 irregular bleeding was the side-effect which was known and recognised. The plaintiff was told about it. In my judgment it was not established, either by means of evidence of some usual system, which broke down in this particular, or by the application of some rule of law, that the plaintiff would, or should, have been put in possession of the material, or the bulk of the material, then in Dr Law's files.

With the utmost respect to the judge, I think he fell into error. Accordingly, I too would allow this appeal.

Balcombe LJ agreed with both judgments.

On one reading of the Court of Appeal's decision it would appear that not much has changed since *Hatcher v Black*, ie that it is still open to the doctor in the exercise of his judgment to decide what information to give even if asked direct questions and that he will be judged by the standards of the profession. There is, however, an alternative and more subtle interpretation of at least the judgment of Neill LJ. While it flies in the face of the conventional view taken of *Blyth*, it merits attention. It is as follows. A close examination of the facts of *Blyth* suggests that the doctor caring for Mrs Blyth did not know the contents of the research in the consultant's (Dr Law's) files. Thus, *Blyth* is not a case of a doctor failing to answer questions of which she knows the answers. Rather, it is a case of whether she should have known the answers (and the court held that she need not have this extra knowledge). Interpreted in this way it is possible to preserve intact the legal force of the views advanced by Lords Diplock, Bridge and Templeman in *Sidaway* by pointing out that *Blyth* is concerned with an entirely different issue.

An additional virtue of this view of *Blyth* is that it prompts a more careful analysis of what may be entailed in their Lordships' view in *Sidaway*. The process of question and answer from a legal point of view involves the following steps, assuming a question is asked.

• *There must be a determination by the doctor of what information the patient is seeking or inquiring about.*

A specific question will clearly identify for the doctor the area to be discussed. A general question will require the doctor to assess what he thinks the patient is interested in. His assessment may lead him to the conclusion that what looks like a general question is, in fact, a request for certain specific information, ie is a specific question.

In determining whether a doctor is in breach of duty by misunderstanding the nature of the patient's request, the law must look to the *Bolam* test since it cannot be doubted that this is a matter, largely, of the exercise of professional skill and judgment.

- *Having reached a view as to what the patient wishes to know, the doctor must give his mind to what he knows in order to answer the question.*

In determining whether a doctor is in breach of duty here, again *Bolam* ought to apply; ie is the doctor's lack of awareness reasonable in the circumstances? (this reflects the alternative view of Neill LJ's judgment in *Blyth* advanced above).

- *Once the doctor has reflected on what he knows, he must decide whether, and if so to what extent, to inform his patient.*

It is at this stage that the legal test for breach of duty need not be the *Bolam* test. Rather it can be as expressed by the judges in *Sidaway*. Indeed, the Australian High Court in *Rogers v Whittaker* (1992) 67 ALJR 47 at 50, went further and stated:

> an acceptable approach in point of principle should be recognized and attach significance to the relevance of a patient's questions. Even if a court were satisfied that a reasonable person in the patient's position would be unlikely to attach significance to a particular risk, the fact that the patient asked questions revealing concern about the risk would make the doctor aware that this patient did in fact attach significance to the risk. Subject to the therapeutic privilege, the question would therefore require a truthful answer.

- *As a variant of the previous situation, the doctor may wish to withhold information because he considers it harmful, ie rely on what we will see is known as the 'therapeutic privilege'.*

Here again evidence from the medical profession must be significant in determining the possible effects on the patient and thus, *Bolam* is again relevant.

Notwithstanding this analysis the courts continue to dilute the duty to answer questions. In *Poynter v Hillingdon HA* (1997) 37 BMLR 192 (QBD), the plaintiff, a baby, underwent heart transplant surgery. His parents were not told of a less than 10% chance of serious complications, namely permanent brain damage, which the child suffered. The parents' claim that they should have been told the risk was dismissed by the judge on the basis that it was in accordance with the (then) prevailing practice. The judge also considered what would have been the position of the parents had they specifically asked about the risks. Having referred to the speeches in *Sidaway* the judge said:

> **Sir Maurice Drake:** If I had to decide the duty owed where a specific question about risks is asked, I would favour the statement to be found in *Clarke and Lindsell on Torts* (17th edn), p 433 that:
>
> > ... in answering express queries about treatment, practitioners are not obliged to give to the patient all the information in their possession. The answers given must ... be judged in the context of good professional practice rather than what the "reasonably prudent patient" might want to know.
>
> But I would consider the duty in the context of what the particular patient wanted to know. That is to say, I would consider it subjectively, not objectively in the context of what a reasonably prudent patient might want to know. ...
>
> Even if, contrary to my findings, these parents had asked directly about the risk of serious permanent brain damage, which I find they did not, it is by no means certain that Dr Radley-Smith, or Professor Yacoub would have been under an unqualified duty to tell them of their assessment of a risk of no more than, and probably less than, 1% – see the

observations of Lord Diplock in the *Sidaway* case and the statement which I think is a correct one to which I have referred in *Clarke and Lindsell on Torts*. Had they been required to exercise their professional skill, in balancing the desire of the parents to have full information against the possibility that the result of giving that information would have been to deter the parents from consenting to the operation, which those experts strongly believed to be in the best interests of Matthew, I think it is arguable that they were entitled to withhold that information. But that issue does not arise for my consideration since I find, on the facts of this particular case, that there was no duty, in view of the questions asked, to disclose that risk.

The judge seems to have adopted an unacceptable version of 'therapeutic privilege' – withholding information to avoid the patient (here the parents) refusing consent to a procedure the doctors consider desirable. This is directly contrary to the GMC's Guidance (*op cit* at para 10) and is, we would suggest, wrong.

Most recently, however, in *Pearce v United Bristol Healthcare NHS Trust* (1998) 48 BMLR 118 (CA), Lord Woolf MR (at 120) accepted as correct the submission that

it is clear that, if a patient asks a doctor about the risk, then the doctor is required to give an honest answer.

The tenor of this statement is more in keeping with emerging concerns within the judiciary to respect patients' rights.

(V) POST-TREATMENT DISCLOSURE

To what extent does a doctor have a legal duty to explain to a patient (or relatives) that something has gone wrong in the patient's treatment?

Robertson 'Fraudulent Concealment and the Duty to Disclose Medical Mistakes' (1987) 25 Alberta LR 215

In recent years a great deal of attention has focused on the duty of a doctor to provide the patient with information prior to performing medical treatment: the concept of 'informed consent'. Very little, however, has been said about a related issue – how much information must a doctor give a patient after the treatment has been performed? In particular, if a mistake is made in the course of treatment (especially surgical treatment), is the doctor under a legal duty to inform the patient of this?

Where a mistake is made in the course of a surgical operation, the doctor's duty to provide reasonable post-operative care requires that proper corrective measures be taken. This will often involve having to inform the patient that something has gone wrong, if this is not already apparent, in order to make the patient aware of the need for further treatment. If the patient is not told, and suffers injury as a result, the doctor is clearly liable. For example, in *Melvin v Graham* [[1973] DRS 659 (Ont HC)] a surgeon who cut into the patient's bladder during a herniotomy was held to have been negligent in not providing proper post-operative care to deal with potential complications arising from his mistake. Similarly, it has been held that failure to inform a patient that a sterilization operation has been unsuccessful [*Cryderman v Ringrose* (1978) 3 WWR 481 (Alta CA)] or that the tip of a hypodermic syringe has broken off during an injection and remains lodged in the patient's body [*Gerber v Pines* (1934) 79 Sol Jo 13 (KB); but see *Daniels v Heskin* [1954] IR 73 (SC) (doctor not negligent in failing to inform patient of presence of broken needle)], renders the doctor liable for any additional injuries suffered as a result of the patient not undergoing corrective treatment. [In *Kueper v McMullin* (1986) 37 CCLT 318 (NBCA), the tip of a dental drill accidentally broke off and lodged in the patients' tooth while the defendant-dentist was performing a root canal. The dentist tried unsuccessfully to remove the drill tip, and decided to seal the tooth. He did not inform the patient of what had happened. The patient's subsequent claim for damages was dismissed. The court held that the dentist ought to have informed the patient of what had happened, and discussed with her the alternative methods of dealing with the problem. However, the court concluded that, even if she had been told, the patient would have consented to having the tooth sealed with the drill tip inside.]

A much more problematic situation arises where the doctor's failure to tell the patient what has happened does not cause any additional physical injury, but merely keeps the patient ignorant of a possible cause of action against the doctor. In many instances a patient who suffers injury during a surgical operation may only discover this (if at all) several years later. In view of the applicable limitation period in Alberta, it becomes especially important to consider whether the law imposes a duty on the doctor to inform the patient of what went wrong in the course of the operation. The recent decision of the English Court of Appeal in *Lee v South West Thames Regional Health Authority* [[1985] 2 All ER 385 (CA)], and the Ontario case of *Stamos v Davies* [(1985) 21 DLR (4th) 507 (Ont HC)] which follows it, suggests that a duty to disclose medical mistakes does exist.

Let us consider in turn the two cases referred to by Robertson at the end of the extract and the further case of *Naylor v Preston AHA* [1987] 2 All ER 353.

Lee v South West Thames RHA [1985] 2 All ER 385 (CA)

Sir John Donaldson MR: It should never be forgotten that we are here concerned with a hospital-patient relationship. The recent decision of the House of Lords in *Sidaway v Bethlem Royal Hospital Governors* [1985] 1 All ER 643, [1985] 2 WLR 480 affirms that a doctor is under a duty to answer his patient's questions as to the treatment proposed. We see no reason why there should not be a similar duty in relation to hospital staff. This duty is subject to the exercise of clinical judgment as to the terms in which the information is given and the extent to which, in the patient's interests, information should be withheld. Why, we ask ourselves, is the position any different if the patient asks what treatment he has in fact had? Let us suppose that a blood transfusion is in contemplation. The patient asks what is involved. He is told that a quantity of blood from a donor will be introduced into his system. He may ask about the risk of AIDS and so forth and will be entitled to straight answers. He consents. Suppose that, by accident, he is given a quantity of air as well as blood and suffers serious ill effects. Is he not entitled to ask what treatment he in fact received, and is the doctor and hospital authority not obliged to tell him, 'in the event you did not only get a blood transfusion. You also got an air transfusion'? Why is the duty different before the treatment from what it is afterwards?

If the duty is the same, then if the patient is refused information to which he is entitled, it must be for consideration whether he could not bring an action for breach of contract claiming specific performance of the duty to inform. In other words, whether the patient could not bring an action for discovery, albeit on a novel basis.

We consider that some thought should be given to what is the duty of disclosure owed by a doctor and a hospital to a patient after treatment, but that is not an issue in this appeal.

Mustill LJ agreed.

Naylor v Preston AHA [1987] 2 All ER 353, [1987] 1 WLR 958 (CA)

Sir John Donaldson MR: I personally think that in professional negligence cases, and in particular in medical negligence cases, there is a duty of candour resting on the professional man. This is recognised by the legal professions in their ethical rules requiring their members to refer the client to other advisers, if it appears that the client has a valid claim for negligence. This also appears to be recognised by the Medical Defence Union, whose view is that 'the patient is entitled to a prompt, sympathetic and above all truthful account of what has occurred' (*Journal of the MDU* (1986) vol 2, no 2, p 2). It was also the view (admittedly *obiter*) of myself and Mustill LJ, as expressed in our judgment in *Lee v South West Thames Regional Health Authority* [1985] 2 All ER 385 at 389–390, [1985] 1 WLR 845 at 850. In this context I was disturbed to be told during the argument of the present appeals that the view was held in some quarters that whilst the duty of candid disclosure, to which we there referred, might give rise to a contractual implied term and so benefit private fee-paying patients, it did not translate into a legal or equitable right for the benefit of national health service patients. This I would entirely repudiate. In my judgment, still admittedly and regretfully *obiter*, it is but one aspect of the general duty of care, arising out of the patient/medical practitioner or hospital authority relationship and gives rise to rights both in contract and in tort.

Professor Robertson (*op cit*) goes on:

It is interesting to note that in *Lee* Sir John Donaldson was repeating what he had said extra-judicially two months earlier, in an address to the Medico-Legal Society [(1985) 53 Medico-Legal J 148]. In that address he admitted that he was simply 'flying a kite' with respect to his views on the duty to disclose medical mistakes. When asked by a member of the audience whether the law does say that doctors must inform their patients if something goes wrong, he replied, 'the law does not say so yet'. Two months later it did.

As was predicted by a leading English barrister [Whitfield (1985) 54 Medico-Legal J 11 at 21], the kite flown by the Master of the Rolls did not stay in the air indefinitely. It landed in Ontario, in the judgment of Mr Justice Kreever in *Stamos v Davies*.

Stamos v Davies (1985) 21 DLR (4th) 507 (Ontario High Ct)

While performing a lung biopsy on the plaintiff, the defendant internist accidentally punctured the plaintiff's spleen. As a result, the spleen had to be removed surgically at a later time. Following the biopsy the defendant did not tell the plaintiff that his spleen had been biopsied and not his lung. The defendant told the plaintiff that he had no result from the biopsy because he had not obtained what he wanted. When asked by the plaintiff what, in fact, he had obtained his reply was simply that he had obtained 'something else' and that there would have to be another biopsy.

Krever J: I hold that, in law, there was a duty on the defendant to inform the plaintiff that he had entered his spleen. The plaintiff asked the defendant what he had obtained at the biopsy. The defendant's failure to be candid with the plaintiff was a breach of duty.

Again, however, the defendant's breach of duty to disclose does not lead to liability. There is no causal connection between the failure to inform the plaintiff about the splenic injury (or, for that matter, the failure to order an ultrasound study or the early discharge from hospital, if I am wrong in my opinion that they did not amount to a breach of duty) and the loss of the spleen. No other conclusion can be drawn from the evidence than that the spleen, in this case, was doomed from the moment it was injured. There is no suggestion in the evidence that anything the plaintiff did at home caused the spleen to rebleed and thus cause its removal. As the defendant's breach of duty to inform the plaintiff of what had happened to his spleen did not cause the damage suffered by the plaintiff, that is, his pain and suffering or the loss of his spleen, the breach of duty was not negligence. The term, negligence, imports the existence of a duty to the plaintiff, a breach of that duty by the defendant and resulting damage to the plaintiff.

Arguably, the legal difficulty identified by Krever J in *Stamos*, ie the inability to show harm *flowing from the breach of duty to disclose post-treatment*, will be common to most cases. No such problem would arise if the duty was an aspect of the fiduciary obligation owed by a doctor to his (ex) patient (See A Grubb 'The Doctor as Fiduciary' [1994] CLP 311 at 335–336) but this is currently not accepted in English law.

The position would be different where the information could help the (ex) patient to avoid future injury. Here, arguably, a duty of care would arise. In *AB v Tameside & Glossop HA* [1997] 8 Med LR 91 (CA), a Health Authority conceded that it had a duty to advise current and past patients that one of its employees health workers who had given obstetric treatment was HIV positive (see Brooke LJ at 93). The case concerned allegedly negligent post-treatment communication, rather than a failure to communicate, which caused psychiatric injury. However, the concession was, rightly in our view, based upon the existence of a 'pre-existing relationship of care' which would not differentiate between negligent communication and non-communication.

The ethical obligation has now been given force by the GMC in its guidance, *Good Medical Practice* (July 1998).

17. If a patient under your care has suffered serious harm, through misadventure or for any other reason, you should act immediately to put matters right, if that is possible. You should explain fully to the patient what has happened and the likely long- and short-term effects. When appropriate you should offer an apology. If the patient is under 16 and lacks the maturity to consent to treatment, you should explain the situation honestly to those with parental responsibility for the child.
18. If a patient under 16 has died you must explain, to the best of your knowledge, the reasons for, and the circumstances of, the death to those with parental responsibility. Similarly, if an adult patient has died, you should provide this information to the patient's partner or next of kin, unless you know that the patient would have objected.

You will notice the ethical duty extends to advising parents of children and, in the case of death, also partners and relatives of patients. There does not, however, appear to be a *legal* duty to advise relatives following the death of a child: *Powell v Boldaz* (1997) 39 BMLR 35 (CA) (discussed *supra*, ch 4). We have already criticised the court's reasoning in reaching this negative conclusion. The reasoning would have no application, of course, where the parents needed the information in order to avoid further injury to their child. They would then be in the same position as the patient who needed to know, as in *AB v Tameside & Glossop HA* (*supra*).

(c) Causation

The plaintiff may establish a breach of duty properly to inform but will only succeed in the action if he can also show that the breach of duty caused him some injury. It would appear that injury here must mean more than a sense of grievance at not being told or of being misinformed. It must mean physical injury or nervous shock as understood in the law of torts (economic loss would be recoverable but would usually arise as a consequence of the physical injury of which complaints had already been made).

(i) FACTUAL CAUSATION

Some would say that the need to prove causation makes much of the heart-searching over the duty to inform irrelevant, since the patient may win the argument over the duty to inform yet lose the action because he cannot show causation. This is because it may be hard for him to say that if he were a 'reasonable person' he would still have refused the treatment concerned even with knowledge of the material (but undisclosed) risks, since evidence may well have been given by doctors that the treatment involved was, all things being equal, medically desirable.

The question is, of course, whether the test of causation is based upon what the 'reasonable patient' would have consented to had he been properly informed or what the 'particular patient' would have consented to if informed. That the test for the duty to inform may be the 'reasonable patient' standard in some jurisdictions and edging towards it in English law, does not necessarily mean that causation should also be governed by a criterion of reasonableness.

The leading reported English case in *Chatterton v Gerson* [1981] QB 432 in which Bristow J adopted (*obiter*) a subjective test of causation:

> When the claim is based on negligence the plaintiff must prove not only the breach of duty to inform but had the duty been broken *she* would not have chosen to have the operation [our emphasis].

He regarded as relevant what the patient *would* have decided. As it happens, however, even in the face of her evidence as to what she felt she would have done, the judge determined that she would have consented because she was 'a lady desperate for pain relief'. This approach is no more than using the 'reasonable patient' test as a yardstick by which to assess the particular patient's evidence. If this is so, it means that the plaintiff faces a considerable difficulty in succeeding in his action even if he can show a breach of duty to inform. He could, of course, show that he was not a reasonable patient, but some type of eccentric. In such a case he would win but it may be hard to satisfy the judge on the facts.

The following case illustrates the English courts' approach.

Smith v Barking, Havering and Brentwood HA [1994] 5 Med LR 285 (QBD)

Hutchinson J: Miss Sharon Smith, whose twenty-eighth birthday fell on the first day of the hearing, claims damages against the Barking, Havering and Brentwood Health Authority in respect of alleged negligent surgical treatment in January 1981. The defendants are sued on the basis that they are responsible for the alleged negligence of Mr Fairburn, the neurosurgeon who carried out an operation on the plaintiff's cervical spinal cord. Mr Fairburn died on 12 October 1984 ...

In March 1970, when she was nine-year-old, the plaintiff was admitted to Oldchurch Hospital in Romford under the care of Mr Fairburn, with complaints of pain in the cervical spine associated with mild quadriparesis and upper motor neurone signs in all limbs, particularly the legs. There was also some hypoaesthesia in the upper limbs. X-rays showed widening of the upper cervical canal. A myelogram was carried out – the report has been lost – and in April an operation was undertaken for what was described as 'drainage of hydromyelia'. There has been some suggestion that this was a wrong diagnosis, but nothing turns on that. There is no doubt about the nature of the problem that was discovered, which I shall briefly describe.

The operation involved an incision above the cervical spine, with exposure of the spines. Portions of bone were then removed to expose the covering of the spinal cord, which was opened to reveal the cord itself. Within the cord a thin-walled cyst was found occupying two-thirds of the transverse diameter of the cord. The cyst had been caused by the access of cerebro-spinal fluid into the vestigial central canal in the spinal cord and its accumulation there. At the operation Mr Fairburn drained the cyst and, discovering a mid-line funnel-shaped opening at the apex of the obex, thought to be responsible for this condition, he took steps to close it.

The operation was successful in the sense that, after an initial and quite long recovery period, the plaintiff's symptoms abated and she was able to live a more or less normal life for some nine years. Over that period she made regular visits of decreasing frequency to the hospital where she was seen by Mr Fairburn, and ultimately, when the plaintiff was eighteen, she was discharged.

By that time she was working as a clerk for an export business and was living an independent life away from home. However, very shortly after her discharge from medical care she began again to experience symptoms. First she noticed tingling in the fingers with some loss of sensation at the ends, and this was followed by weakness in the arms of gradual onset. She had trouble picking things up and came to be unable to distinguish between hot and cold. Ultimately her legs became so weak that it took her a very long time to get up the two flights of stairs to her home, she had difficulty walking, she could only comb her hair if she supported one arm with the other, and she was quite severely disabled.

Of course, once the symptoms began, Miss Smith consulted her doctor and again attended Oldchurch Hospital under the care of Mr Fairburn. The view was taken that she was experiencing a recurrence of the condition which had led to the operation nine years previously. It will be appreciated – and I do not need to go into great detail because it is not a matter of controversy – that the effect of an internal cyst in the spinal cord is that the cord is expanded and becomes compressed against adjacent structures. This leads to interference with the nerve pathways leading from the spinal cord, and they quite quickly sustain irreversible degeneration. The opinion of Dr Turner, the neurologist called on behalf of the defendants, was that had nothing been done the plaintiff's condition would have continued to deteriorate quite rapidly, so that within about three months of 20 January 1981, the date of the operation I am about to describe, she would have been in a wheelchair and within a further six months she would have been tetraplegic. [Counsel for the plaintiff] ultimately accepted that this opinion was correct.

Mr Fairburn considered that a further operation was advisable. What he had hoped to achieve was the location and drainage of the cyst which he believed had re-formed in the hope that this would arrest the progress of the condition, as had happened before. The documents that survive show, however, that Mr Fairburn regarded such an operation as a very difficult one and that he was to some extent reluctant to undertake it. ...

Mr Fairburn carried out the second operation on 20 January 1981, and it was unsuccessful. The plaintiff suffered immediate and permanent tetraplegia. It is unnecessary that I should describe why that came about – nor indeed is it positively known. It is sufficient to say that it is believed to have resulted from some damage to the spinal cord occurring during the second operation ... The plaintiff's claim, and the only matter with which this action is concerned, arises out of Mr Fairburn's failure to warn her of the risks inherent in the operation or to afford her any opportunity to reach an informed decision as to whether to submit to it.

... it was common ground that Mr Fairburn should have given the plaintiff some advice as to the risks involved and the desirability of submitting to the operation and that her evidence that he had not done so must be accepted ...

Given the admitted necessity for such an explanation and the fact, as I find, that there was none, the only significant issue in this case has been whether the plaintiff, had she been given proper advice, would have elected against the operation ...

There was some discussion as to whether the issue of causation would be approached on what was called the objective or the subjective basis – ie, was the question to be resolved by deciding what a reasonable person in the plaintiff's position would have chosen to do or by deciding what the plaintiff herself would have chosen to do. In support of the former approach I was referred to the Canadian authority of *Reibl v Hughes* [1980] 2 SCR 880 and in support of the latter to the decision of Hirst J in *Hills v Potter* [1983] 3 All ER 716, [1984] 1 WLR 641n. Both counsel invited me to accept that in the end the matter must be one for decision on a subjective basis. This must plainly as a matter of principle be right, because the question must be: if this plaintiff had been given the advice that she would have been given, would she have decided to undergo the operation or not?

However, there is a peculiar difficulty involved in this sort of case – not least for the plaintiff herself – in giving, after the adverse outcome of the operation is known, reliable answers as to what she would have decided before the operation had she been given proper advice as to the risks inherent in it. Accordingly, it would, in my judgment, be right in the ordinary case to give particular weight to the objective assessment. If everything points to the fact that a reasonable plaintiff, properly informed, would have assented to the operation, the assertion from the witness box, made after the adverse outcome is known, in a wholly artificial situation and in the knowledge that the outcome of the case depends upon that assertion being maintained, does not carry great weight unless there are extraneous or additional factors to substantiate it. By extraneous or additional factors I mean, and I am not doing more than giving examples, religious or some other firmly held convictions; particular social or domestic considerations justifying a decision not in accordance with what, objectively, seems the right one; assertions in the immediate aftermath of the operation made in a context other than that of a possible claim for damages; in other words, some particular factor which suggests that the plaintiff had grounds for not doing what a reasonable person in her situation might be expected to have done. Of course, the less confidently the judge reaches the conclusions as to what objectively the reasonable patient might be expected to have decided, the more readily will he be persuaded by her subjective evidence.

I should make it clear that nothing I have said is intended to reflect adversely on the plaintiff or to suggest that I have any doubts as to her honesty; but as I listened to her grappling with the different hypothetical questions which were put to her, I felt the greatest sympathy for her and reflected that one would need almost to be a saint to answer such questions objectively – ie, without allowing one's reaction to be influenced by the knowledge of what had, in fact, happened and appreciation of the vital significance of the question. Hence the importance of giving proper weight to an objective assessment of what a reasonable patient could be expected to decide in the light of such proper advice as should have been given. ...

The plaintiff was first asked [when giving evidence] what would have been her reaction had Mr Fairburn told her that if she had the operation there was a chance that it might stop her getting worse coupled with a remote possibility that it would actually produce some improvement, and a risk that if unsuccessful she would be paralysed. She responded, sensibly, that she would have wanted some assurance that the risk of being paralysed was balanced with the risk of not being paralysed: she would have wanted to know the degree of risk. She said that if she had been told that the risk of paralysis was substantial, she would not have had the operation. She was asked, in anticipation of Mr Galbraith's evidence, what her response would have been had she been told that the risk of paralysis was one in four, and she said that she would not have had the operation. She was asked what would have been her response had Mr Fairburn brought together all the material factors. By that counsel meant the hope on the one hand of arresting the progress of the disease for a significant time and on the other hand the risk of making her condition worse or perhaps even causing total paralysis. She said, echoing her earlier answers, that she would have wanted to know what the risk of success was as compared with the risk of failure and that she might have discussed the matter with her parents but would, ultimately, have made up her own mind. She was asked to consider her response to advice to the effect that if she had the operation and it was successful, the condition was in any event likely to recur sooner or later, whereas if she did not have it she would be paralysed within at most two years. She said that she would have wished to wait for a time to see how things worked out. As to this, the evidence shows that if anything was going to be done it was a matter of urgency, because of the speed at which she was deteriorating, and that accordingly she could not sensibly have postponed the decision for more than a week or two. She was asked whether she would have questioned Mr Fairburn and she said that she did not think that she would have done unless invited to do so.

In cross-examination the ground was covered again. [Counsel for the defendant], in a question which attempted to include all the relevant factors on each side, asked her what she would have said, and she responded again that she would have wished to know the risk of paralysis. If she had been told that it was a quarter and that the doctor nevertheless recommended the operation what would she have said, [counsel] asked. She said that if it was a great risk she wouldn't have had the operation.

I have to say that as a means of resolving the all-important question as to what the plaintiff would have decided in January 1981 I found these questions and answers of little assistance. I did, however, derive from her evidence certain material conclusions which are as follows:

(a) The plaintiff was not somebody imbued with any particular views or prejudices on the subject of operations. On the contrary, like most people, she was temperamentally disposed to follow the advice of her doctors – a tendency which would be particularly strong in the case of Mr Fairburn whom she knew and in whom she must have had considerable trust as a result of the long period of their association.

(b) The plaintiff plainly found it, as it seemed to me, extremely difficult to imagine herself back into the situation as it was in January 1981, and I had the impression that in the main, though doing her best, she was not really convinced of her own answers. In truth, I think, she just did not know what she would have done.

(c) There were not, so far as I can discover, any pressing personal or social considerations which would have made her tend to decide one way or the other.

In submitting that I should conclude that the plaintiff would have chosen not to have the operation, [counsel for the plaintiff] invited me to have regard to the circumstances as they were at the time and, in particular, to the following factors. First, he submitted, and I accept, that the plaintiff was a reasonably intelligent young woman capable of independent judgment, shown by the medical records to be cheerful and not depressed and well able to make up her own mind. He submitted, furthermore, that her condition, though grave in fact, might not have appeared so to her. This I cannot accept, because it seems to me inescapable that the degree of disability which she suffered in the period immediately preceding the operation would have been perceived by anyone to be serious. Moreover, part of the advice that she ought to have been given would have involved an explanation about continued and quite rapid deterioration. He invited me to give full weight to the plaintiff's attitude towards operations and desire to be assured that the risk balanced the expected benefits and also to remember how unpleasant she had found the myelogram which had preceded the first operation. Finally, he reminded me that there were no immediate family responsibilities such as a husband or child and no factors connected with her work or economic circumstances which would have impelled her to elect for an operation: although as to that I have already implied that that fact is neutral in the sense that there was nothing of this sort militating in favour of a decision against the operation.

Turning to the appreciation of the operation from the doctors' side, [counsel for the plaintiff] invited me to remember that it was very definitely an elective rather than an essential operation; that it was very rare and that the reason for the risks and benefits were self-evidently difficult to assess and that the doctors recommended it reluctantly. He further submitted that, while it had ultimately been agreed that the proper view was that the plaintiff would have been tetraplegic within nine months, I should not assume that this was the advice she would have necessarily been given at the time. He instanced Mr Galbraith's view that she might have survived a year or even possibly two before reaching that state. He asked me not to confuse the advice with influence and again emphasised that, as Mr Garfield plainly accepted, this was not the sort of decision where the doctor would feel that a plaintiff was necessarily wrong to elect against surgery. He suggested that there is a danger that lawyers tend to weight the choices in a legal as opposed to a human way and argued that the proper approach was to concentrate on the fact that there was a substantial risk up to 25% of total paralysis an that in that situation the plaintiff's approach would have been that she would require to be persuaded of the advisability of the operation, which was by no means an obvious solution. I must, he submitted, give full weight to the plaintiff's own evidence.

Nothing that [counsel for the plaintiff] said in the course of his submissions suggested that there was anything about the plaintiff or her views of reactions which differentiated her from an ordinary reasonable patient. This does not, of course, mean that the response which it is assumed she would have given to a question which she was never asked must be predicted on a purely objective basis, but it does again emphasise the importance to be attached in this difficult field to an objective assessment of what a reasonable patient might be expected to have decided if properly acquainted with all the relevant factors.

It seems to me that in the light of the evidence I have heard from three distinguished neurosurgeons, it is not possible to say with absolute certainty what ought to have been said. Plainly different doctors approach the matter in different ways and further uncertainty is introduced by the possibility that the patient will respond by asking questions to a greater or lesser extent. However, there are some things that I can in the light of their evidence say with confidence. First, there is no doubt that the plaintiff should have had a full and careful explanation of the risks and benefits inherent in the operation. Secondly, I have no doubt that she should have been told in general terms as to the prognosis if she did not have an operation.

Thirdly, as I have already said, I accept Mr Garfield's and Professor Hankinson's view that part of the advice she should have been given should have included a clear indication that the surgeon, weighing all the considerations as best he could, had reached the view that an operation was in her best interests. It may be, as [counsel for the defendant] indicated, that Mr Fairburn was reluctant to carry out the operation because of its difficulties, but he had plainly decided that despite that reluctance it was an operation to be recommended, and it is not to be supposed that he would then have undermined the plaintiff's confidence in his decision and abilities by leaving her with the impression that he did not want to do it.

I consider that what Mr Fairburn ought to have told the plaintiff was something along the following lines. He should have explained to her that the indications were that the condition from which she had previously suffered had recurred and that it was getting worse quickly. He should have explained that if nothing was done she would be totally disabled within quite a short period. If he had been pressed for an estimate, he would, I think, have been talking in terms of less than rather more than a year. If he had been questioned further, he would have indicated that in the course of that deterioration the plaintiff would very soon be in a wheelchair even though not at that stage tetraplegic. He should then have gone on to explain that the operation held out a reasonable chance of arresting the progress of the disease for a significant period – possibly a few years. If questioned, he would have made it clear that this benefit could not be expected to be anything like as great as that achieved by the first operation. Against that reasonable chance of benefit, however, he should have explained that there was a significant risk that her condition would be made worse and that, instead of postponing the onset of total disability, the operation might even markedly accelerate it. He should have made it clear to the plaintiff that, while in his expert view the operation was one which, because it presented a worthwhile chance of significant benefit, she should undergo, the decision was very much for her to take and that in taking it she should bear in mind the risks which he had explained. He should have suggested that she might like to discuss the matter with her parents or her boyfriend and indicated that he would answer any questions that she had so as to assist her to make up her mind.

It seems to me that if, after such a discussion, the plaintiff had quietly considered what to do, the factors which would principally have weighed with her were the following:

(a) First and most important, that if nothing was done she would quite quickly be more or less totally disabled.

(b) Second, that the risk to which the operation exposed her, if it were unsuccessful, was not a risk of something worse than she was going to have to experience anyway but merely of the earlier onset of a condition which she was going to experience anyway.

(c) Third, that while the operation did not hold out any hope of a permanent cure, it would, if successful, result in the postponement of total disability for a significant period.

(d) Finally, and hardly of less significance than the first factor, the plaintiff would inevitably in my view have been much influenced by the reflection that the surgeon in whom she had cause to repose her trust had himself concluded that the chances of success were such as to justify attempting the operation.

Looking at the matter objectively, I cannot escape the conclusion that these factors pointed very strongly towards agreeing to have the operation. Reflection on what she was told would have led a reasonable patient to say to herself: 'Well, it seems I'm going to be paralysed anyway in a very short time. This operation gives me a reasonable chance of avoiding that condition perhaps for a few years. True, there is a real risk he operation will not be successful and I'll then be paralysed even sooner, but the possible benefits clearly considerably outweigh the possible detriment and the chance is one well worth taking.'

In the light of these conclusions I ask myself what the plaintiff would have decided, had she been given advice along the lines I have indicated. For reasons already foreshadowed in this judgment I unhesitatingly conclude that the strong probability is that the plaintiff would have agreed to have the operation. While, of course, there is no certainty about matters of this sort, and the possibility must remain that the plaintiff would have refused, it seems to me in the highest degree unlikely that she would have done so.

One consequence of this blending of the objective to the subjective approach may be that a plaintiff would be more believable when the treatment was not urgently pressing but rather was in a real sense something the patient could take or leave, for example, certain forms of cosmetic surgery.

When an appellate court in England has to determine the test of causation it is unlikely that it will follow the approach adopted in Canada (notice the Court of Appeal's application of the 'subjective' test in *Thomson v James* (1997) 41 BMLR 144 and *O'Keefe v Harvey-Kemble* (1998) 45 BMLR 74). There will be two questions for the court: (i) What is the correct test of causation? and (ii) How is that to be established? What evidentiary burden should be cast upon the claimant? The court may adopt a subjective test of causation but may demand that in seeking to establish that he would not have consented, the plaintiff must meet a standard of evidence which incorporates an element of reasonableness. Given the acceptance of a subjective test (but with an objective ingredient) in England albeit by trial court judges who have not analysed in depth the alternative objective test, it would be useful to look to decisions in Commonwealth jurisdictions where the merits of the two tests have been examined.

There are two significant decisions: the Canadian Supreme Court decision in *Arndt v Smith* [1997] 2 SCR 539 and the New South Wales Court of Appeal decision in *Ellis v Wallsend District Hospital* (1989) 17 NSWLR 553. As we shall see, they reach opposite conclusions on the appropriate rule. The Canadian Supreme court recently considered the respective merits of the 'subjective' and 'objective' tests.

Arndt v Smith [1997] 2 SCR 539 (Can SC)

A sued her physician S for costs associated with rearing her daughter, who was congenitally injured by chickenpox A had contracted during her pregnancy. She contended that had S properly advised her of the risk of injury to her fetus, she would have terminated the pregnancy and avoided the costs she now incurs. S contended that A would not have terminated the pregnancy even if she had been fully advised, and therefore asserted that the loss claimed was not caused by the failure to advise of risk. The trial judge dismissed A's claim. Evaluating her testimony at trial that she would have had an abortion against the fact that she desired a child, that she was sceptical of "mainstream" medical intervention, that an abortion in the second trimester held increased risks and that an abortion would have required the approval of a committee on health grounds, the trial judge concluded that A would not, on a balance of probabilities, have aborted the pregnancy. Also supportive of the trial judge's conclusion was evidence that the risk of serious injury to the fetus was very small and medical advisers would have recommended against an abortion. The Court of Appeal held that the trial judge had applied the wrong test and directed a new trial.

Cory J: [2] The starting point for this question must be *Reibl v Hughes*, [1980] 2 SCR 880, 114 DLR (3d) 1, which set out the basic principles for assessing causation in cases involving allegations of negligence by doctors. *Reibl* involved an action by a patient against a surgeon for failing to warn him of the risk of paralysis associated with the elective surgery performed by that surgeon. One of the defences raised was that even if the surgeon had disclosed all of the risks of the procedure, the plaintiff would nonetheless have gone ahead with the operation. In other words, the physician disputed whether his negligent failure to disclose had, in fact, caused the plaintiff's loss.

[3] The question presented to the Court was how to determine whether the patient would have actually chosen to decline the surgery if he had been properly informed of the risks. In trying to craft the appropriate test, Laskin CJ for a unanimous Court quoted with approval an article from the New York University Law Review, entitled "Informed Consent – A proposed Standard for Medical Disclosure" (1973), 48 NYUL Rev 548. The article distinguished between a subjective test, which asks whether the particular patient would have foregone treatment if properly informed, and an objective test, which asks whether the average prudent person in the patient's position would have foregone treatment if informed of all material risks. The authors preferred the objective test, since the subjective standard suffered from what they deemed to be a "gross defect": "[I]t depends on the plaintiff's testimony as to his state of mind, thereby exposing the physician to the patient's hindsight and bitterness" (p 550).

[4] Laskin CJ shared the authors' concerns about the subjective test, and rejected the pure subjective approach to causation. He explained at p 898 that the plaintiff's testimony as to what he or she would have done, had the doctor given an adequate warning, is of little value:

It could hardly be expected that the patient who is suing would admit that he would have agreed to have the surgery, even knowing all the accompanying risks. His suit would indicate that, having suffered serious disablement because of the surgery, he is convinced that he would not have permitted it if there had been proper disclosure of the risks, balanced by the risks of refusing the surgery. Yet, to apply a subjective test to causation would, correlatively, put a premium on hindsight, even more of a premium than would be put on medical evidence in assessing causation by an objective standard.

In other words, the plaintiff would always testify that the failure to warn was the determining factor in his or her decision to take the harmful course of action. Accordingly the subjective test would necessarily cause the trier of fact to place too much weight on inherently unreliable testimony.

[5] While an objective test would prevent an inappropriate emphasis being placed on the plaintiff's testimony, Laskin CJ thought that a purely objective test also presented problems. At p 898, he discussed his paramount concern with an approach based on the actions of a hypothetical reasonable person:

… a vexing problem raised by the objective standard is whether causation could ever be established if the surgeon has recommended surgery which is warranted by the patient's condition. Can it be said that a reasonable person in the patient's position, to whom proper disclosure of attendant risks has been made, would decide against the surgery, that is, against the surgeon's recommendation that it be undergone? The objective standard of what a reasonable person in the patient's position would do would seem to put a premium on the surgeon's assessment of the relative need for the surgery and on supporting medical evidence of that need. Could it be reasonably refused?

In short, the purely objective standard might result in undue emphasis being placed on the medical evidence, essentially resulting in a test which defers completely to medical wisdom.

[6] To balance the two problems, Laskin CJ opted for a modified objective test for causation, which he set out at length at pp 898–900:

I think it is the safer course on the issue of causation to consider objectively how far the balance in the risks of surgery or no surgery is in favour of undergoing surgery. The failure of proper disclosure pro and con becomes therefore very material. And so too are any special considerations affecting the particular patient. For example, the patient may have asked specific questions which were either brushed aside or were not fully answered or were answered wrongly. In the present case, the anticipation of a full pension would be a special consideration, and, while it would have to be viewed objectively, it emerges from the patient's particular circumstances. So too, other aspects of the objective standard would have to be geared to what the average prudent person, the reasonable person in the patient's particular position, would agree to or not agree to, if all material and special risks of going ahead with the surgery or foregoing it were made known to him. Far from making the patient's own testimony irrelevant, it is essential to his case that he put his own position forward.

The adoption of an objective standard does not mean that the issue of causation is completely in the hands of the surgeon. Merely because medical evidence establishes the reasonableness of a recommended operation does not mean that a reasonable person in the patient's position would necessarily agree to it, if proper disclosure had been made of the risks attendant upon it, balanced by those against it. The patient's particular situation and the degree to which the risks of surgery or no surgery are balanced would reduce the force, on an objective appraisal, of the surgeon's recommendation. Admittedly, if the risk of foregoing the surgery would be considerably graver to a patient than the risks attendant upon it, the objective standard would favour exoneration of the surgeon who has not made the required disclosure. Since liability rests only in negligence, in a failure to disclose material risks, the issue of causation would be in the patient's hands on a subjective test, and would, if his evidence was accepted, result inevitably in liability unless, of course, there was a finding that there was no breach of the duty of disclosure. In my view, therefore, the objective standard is the preferable one on the issue of causation.

In saying that the test is based on the decision that a reasonable person in the patient's position would have made, I should make it clear that the patient's particular concerns must also be reasonably based; otherwise, there would be more subjectivity than would be warranted under an objective test. Thus, for example, fears which are not related to the material risks which should have been but were not disclosed would not be causative factors. However, economic considerations could reasonably go to causation where, for example, the loss of an eye as a result of non-disclosure of a material risk brings about the loss of a job for which good eyesight is required. In short, although account must be taken of a patient's particular position, a position which will vary with the patient, it must be objectively assessed in terms of reasonableness.

These words are as persuasive today as they were when they were written. The test enunciated relies on a combination of objective and subjective factors in order to determine whether the failure to disclose *actually* caused the harm of which the plaintiff complains. It requires that the court consider what the reasonable patient *in the circumstances of the plaintiff* would have done if faced with the same situation. The trier of fact must take into consideration any "particular concerns" of the patient and any "special considerations affecting the particular patient" in determining whether the patient would have refused treatment if given all the information about the possible risks. ...

[9] Some of the criticisms directed at the *Reibl* test may stem from confusion as to what Laskin CJ intended in his adoption of a modified objective test. The uncertainty surrounds the basic premise that the test depends upon the actions of a reasonable person *in the plaintiff's circumstances*. Which aspects of the plaintiff's personal circumstances should be attributed to the reasonable person? There is no doubt that objectively ascertainable circumstances, such as a plaintiff's age, income, marital status, and other factors, should be taken into consideration. However, Laskin CJ did not stop there. He went on and stated that "special considerations" affecting the particular patient should be considered, as should any "specific questions" asked of the physician by the patient. In my view this means that the "reasonable person" who sets the standard for the objective test must be taken to possess the patient's reasonable beliefs, fears, desires and expectations. Further, the patient's expectations and concerns will usually be revealed by the questions posed. Certainly, they will indicate the specific concerns of the particular patient at the time consent was given to a proposed course of treatment. The questions, by revealing the patient's concerns, will provide an indication of the patient's state of mind, which can be relevant in considering and applying the modified objective test.

[10] An example may serve to illustrate this. Imagine a patient considering plastic surgery on his nose. During a pre-operative consultation, the patient asks if the surgery will affect his sense of smell. The physician fails to fairly and adequately explain the attendant risks to this sensory function and does not mention that a certain percentage of patients suffer a permanent loss of a small fraction of their ability to smell. After the surgery, the patient can no longer smell with the same acuity food that is cooking. Under Laskin CJ's test in *Reibl*, the patient's question about the risks to his sense of smell are clearly relevant. The question posed suggests that the patient had a special concern about losing the sense of smell. This is not an unreasonable concern. The loss of a keen sensory perception of smell which is so closely related to the sense of taste is crucial to both those who artistically prepare and those who have a particular appreciation for finely prepared food. This special fear of the loss of a keen sense of smell could be considered by the trier of fact in determining whether the reasonable person with the particular expressed concern of the plaintiff would have consented to the proposed course of treatment if all the risks had been disclosed.

[11] As another example, let us consider a patient who asks his doctor about a proposed procedure, and particularly poses questions as to whether there might be any effect on his hearing, without advising the doctor of his particular passion for the singing of operatic sopranos. If the doctor fails to inform the patient of the possibility that the procedure could limit his ability to hear in the upper ranges, the *Reibl* test would allow the trier of fact to consider the questions posed by the patient in determining whether he would have consented to the proposed treatment if he had been properly informed of all the risks. Again, the questions asked by this patient may act as an indication of his own reasonable fears and concerns, which are appropriate modifiers of the hypothetical reasonable person.

[12] As further evidence that the patient's state of mind is relevant to the *Reibl* test, Laskin CJ goes on at pp 899–900 to caution that the trier of fact may only take into account those particular concerns of the patient which are reasonable.

> [T]he patient's particular concerns must be reasonably based ... Thus, for example, fears which are not related to the material risks which should have been but were not disclosed would not be causative factors.

Clearly, evidence of *reasonable* fears and concerns can be taken into consideration and this is evidence which could go to establishing the plaintiff's subjective state of mind. Therefore, it is apparent that Laskin CJ intended that the reasonable subjective beliefs of the patient should be attributed to the hypothetical reasonable person used to set the objective standard in order to properly reflect the circumstances of the plaintiff.

[13] If the patient's fears and beliefs were not considered when assessing how the "reasonable person in the plaintiff's position" would have responded had all risks of a procedure been disclosed, absurd verdicts could be produced. For example, let us suppose that a plaintiff brought an action based on her doctor's failure to disclose that there was a very significant risk of her giving birth to a disabled child, that the risk was material and the only issue was causation. If the plaintiff's beliefs are not to be considered, the trier of fact could conclude that a reasonable person in the position of the plaintiff would have chosen to terminate the pregnancy and find in favour of the patient even if the plaintiff was

so resolutely and unalterably opposed to abortion that she would never have terminated the pregnancy. The failure to disclose would not have been the actual cause of the harm. Despite this, under the purely objective standard, the plaintiff could recover. This example demonstrates why it is important to include some subjective aspects in the assessment of what the reasonable person in the position of the plaintiff would have done if all the risks had been disclosed.

[14] Laskin CJ carefully noted that purely subjective fears *which are not related to the material risks* should not be taken into account in applying the modified objective test. In other words, fears which are idiosyncratic, which do not relate directly to the material risks of a proposed treatment and which would often be unknown to a physician, cannot be considered. This is what ensures that the objective standard truly is based on the actions of a "reasonable person". It means that a doctor will not be held responsible for damages attributable to a plaintiff's idiosyncrasies. It ensures that a plaintiff would not be able to successfully prove causation simply by demonstrating an irrational fear which, had the physician disclosed all the risks, would have convinced the plaintiff to forego medical treatment. For example, if a doctor failed to tell the patient that one of the risks of a procedure was an allergic reaction which could cause a temporary red rash on the skin, and the patient had an irrational belief that a rash is a highly significant and dangerous sign of evil spirits in the body, the patient could not successfully prove causation by demonstrating that he would not have proceeded with the treatment on the basis of this irrational fear.

[15] *Reibl v Hughes* is a very significant and leading authority. It marks the rejection of the paternalistic approach to determining how much information should be given to patients. It emphasizes the patients' right to know and ensures that patients will have the benefit of a high standard of disclosure. At the same time, its modified objective test for causation ensures that our medical system will have some protection in the face of liability claims from patients influenced by unreasonable fears and beliefs, while still accommodating all the reasonable individual concerns and circumstances of plaintiffs. The test is flexible enough to enable a court to take into account a wide range of the personal circumstances of the plaintiff, and at the same time to recognize that physicians should not be held responsible when the idiosyncratic beliefs of their patients might have prompted unpredictable and unreasonable treatment decisions.

[16] The *Reibl v Hughes* test has had the desired effect of ensuring that patients have all the requisite information to make an informed decision regarding the medical procedure they are contemplating. Members of the medical and legal professions are familiar with its requirements. It strikes a reasonable balance, which cannot be obtained through either a purely objective or a purely subjective approach. A purely subjective test could serve as an incitement for a disappointed patient to bring an action. The plaintiff will invariably state with all the confidence of hindsight and with all the enthusiasm of one contemplating an award of damages that consent would never have been given if the disclosure required by an idiosyncratic belief had been made. This would create an unfairness that cannot be accepted. It would bring inequitable and unnecessary pressure to bear upon the overburdened medical profession. On the other hand, a purely objective test which would set the standard by a reasonable person without the reasonable fears, concerns and circumstances of the particular plaintiff would unduly favour the medical profession.

[17] It has been said that a subjective test, despite its dangers, is the most logical. Yet pure logic cannot achieve the fairness attained by the application of the *Reibl* test. It is said that there is nothing to distinguish between the subjective test and the modified objective test. If that were the case there could be no grounds for complaint from those who favour the subjective test. Yet in my view there is a very real distinction. The modified objective test serves to eliminate from consideration the honestly held but idiosyncratic and unreasonable or irrational beliefs of patients. The *Reibl* test is fair and has recently been approved in the *Dow Corning* case. No useful purpose would be served by changing it. Indeed, to do so may unnecessarily add to the high cost of providing medical care. In short, I see no reason to abandon the modified objective test to causation set down in *Reibl v Hughes*, a test which asks whether a reasonable person in the circumstances of the plaintiff would have consented to the proposed treatment if all the risks had been disclosed.

[18] Turning now to this appeal, it is appropriate to infer from the evidence that a reasonable person in the plaintiff's position would not have decided to terminate her pregnancy in the face of the very small increased risk to the fetus posed by her exposure to the virus which causes chickenpox. Ms Arndt did make a very general inquiry concerning the risks associated with maternal chickenpox. However, it should not be forgotten that the risk was indeed very small. In the absence of a specific and clearly expressed concern, there was nothing to indicate to the doctor that she had a particular concern in this regard. It follows that there was nothing disclosed by Ms Arndt's question which could be used by the trier of fact as an indication of a particular fear regarding the possibility of giving birth

to a disabled child which should be attributed to the hypothetical reasonable person in the patient's situation. Further, factors such as the plaintiff's desire for children and her suspicion of the mainstream medical profession can be taken into consideration when determining what a reasonable person in the plaintiff's position would have done if informed of the risks. It is not necessary to assess the relative importance these beliefs would have in the determination of the question of causation. It is sufficient to observe that all these are factors indicating the state of mind of the plaintiff at the time she would have had to make the decision, and therefore may be properly considered by the trier of fact. I agree with the trial judge that the failure to disclose some of the risks to the fetus associated with maternal chickenpox did not affect the plaintiff's decision to continue the pregnancy to term. It follows that the failure to disclose did not cause the financial losses for which the plaintiff is seeking compensation.

Lamer CJ and LaForest, L'Heureux-Dubé, Gonthier and Major JJ agreed with Cory J.

(Professor Gerald Robertson points out that a significant consequence of adopting the objective test is that in 56% of cases decided in the ten years since *Reibl*, the plaintiff failed to meet the test of causation notwithstanding that there was a breach of duty to inform by the doctor: Robertson, 'Informed Consent 10 Years Later: The Impact of *Reibl v Hughes*' (1991) 70 Canadian Bar Review 423 at 428. For further discussion of the impact of *Reibl* see A Dugdale 'Diverse Reports: Canadian Professional Negligence cases' (1984) 2 PN 108.)

By contrast, McLachlin J in *Arndt* favoured the subjective test.

McLachlin J: [39] Applying the law of negligence, is the proper test what the particular plaintiff before the court would have done had she been fully informed, or what a hypothetical reasonable person would have done?

[40] The fundamental principles of negligence law suggest that the test is what the particular plaintiff before the court would have done. Breach established, the question in a negligence action is whether the breach caused loss to the plaintiff. This is a factual, not a hypothetical, inquiry. In cases of negligence action or misfeasance, the matter is clear. If a plaintiff breaks her leg as a result of being struck by a negligently driven automobile, the question is not whether a reasonable person so struck would have broken her leg; it is whether she, the particular plaintiff at bar, in fact broke her leg. There is no reason in principle why the inquiry should be different where the claim is based on the defendant's failure to act or non-feasance, raising the question of what the plaintiff would have done in a hypothetical state of affairs …

[42] The physician's failure to advise constitutes a failure to take an action required by law. A finding of breach is a finding that the physician should have done something which he or she negligently failed to do. This, like the case of the employee injured as a result of the absence of a helmet required by law, raises the hypothetical question of what the plaintiff would have done had the physician discharged his or her duty. General tort principles suggest that this question is a purely factual inquiry to be answered by reference to all the evidence. This evidence may include evidence from the plaintiff at trial as to what she would have done. But it also includes relevant evidence of her situation, circumstances and mind-set at the time the decision would have been made. The trial judge must look at all the evidence and determine whether the plaintiff would have taken the suggested course on a balance of probabilities. One way of expressing this is to say that the plaintiff's hindsight assertion at trial of what she would have done is tested or evaluated by reference to the evidence as to her circumstances and beliefs at the time the decision would have been made. These circumstances include the medical advice she would have received at the time which might have influenced her decision. In this way, the plaintiff's subjective evidence as to what she would have done is evaluated by reference to the reasonableness of the competing courses of action. As Sopinka J. (dissenting, but not on this ground) put it in *Hollis v Dow Corning Corp*, [1995] 3 SCR 634, at p 689, 129 DLR (4th) 609: "the most reliable approach in determining *what would in fact have occurred* is to test the plaintiff's assertion by reference to objective evidence as to what a reasonable person would have done" (emphasis in original). …

[44] The approach suggested by the fundamental principles of tort law is subjective, in that it requires consideration of what the plaintiff at bar would have done. However, it incorporates elements of objectivity; the plaintiff's subjective belief at trial that she would have followed a certain course stands to be tested by her circumstances and attitudes at the time the decision would have been made as well as the medical advice she would have received at the time. …

[56] This brings us to the arguments against the position that the trial judge's task is to determine what the particular plaintiff at bar would have done had she been properly advised of the risk. The most formidable is the submission that this Court rejected such an approach in *Reibl v Hughes, supra*.

[57] *Reibl v Hughes* concerned a patient who had suffered a stroke and paralysis as a result of an endarterectomy performed to reduce the risk of stroke in the future. His physician had failed to advise him of a risk of stroke or death during or in the aftermath of surgery. He told him only that his risk of having a stroke was greater without the surgery than with it. The patient argued that had he been informed of the risk of stroke consequent on surgery, he would have postponed the surgery for a year and one-half until a lifetime retirement pension from his employment vested. He also asserted that he would have opted for a shorter, normal life rather than a longer life as a cripple. The issue before the Court was how to assess whether the patient would in fact have foregone the surgery had he been properly informed.

[58] The Court, *per* Laskin CJ, began by rejecting the argument that the real wrong was being deprived of the right of choice or consent, giving rise to the tort of battery. Laskin CJ stated at pp 891–92:

> I can appreciate the temptation to say that the genuineness of consent to medical treatment depends on proper disclosure of the risks which it entails, but in my view, *unless there has been misrepresentation or fraud to secure consent to the treatment, a failure to disclose the attendant risks, however serious, should go to negligence rather than to battery*. Although such a failure relates to an informed choice of submitting to or refusing recommended and appropriate treatment, it arises as the breach of an anterior duty of due care, comparable in legal obligation to the duty of due care in carrying out the particular treatment to which the patient has consented. It is not a test of the validity of the consent. [Emphasis added.]

[59] The Court went on to approach the problem on the assumption that a plaintiff suing for negligent non-disclosure will always assert that he or she would have acted differently had he or she been fully informed. Laskin CJ wrote [at p 898]:

> It could hardly be expected that the patient who is suing would admit that he would have agreed to have the surgery, even knowing all the accompanying risks. His suit would indicate that, having suffered serious disablement because of the surgery, he is convinced that he would not have permitted it if there had been proper disclosure of the risks, balanced by the risks of refusing the surgery.

[60] Laskin CJ dismissed a purely subjective approach on the ground that "it depends on the plaintiff's testimony as to his state of mind, thereby exposing the physician to the patient's hindsight and bitterness" (quoting at p 898 from "Informed Consent – A Proposed Standard for Medical Disclosure" (1973), 48 NYUL Rev 548, at p 550). Laskin CJ observed that "the issue of causation would be in the patient's hands on a subjective test, and would, if his evidence was accepted, result inevitably in liability unless, of course, there was a finding that there was no breach of the duty of disclosure". For this reason, Laskin CJ rejected a purely subjective approach based on what the plaintiff at trial asserted he would have done.

[61] At the same time, Laskin CJ was alive to the problems presented by a purely objective approach based on what a hypothetical reasonable person would have done. He noted (at p 898):

> … a vexing problem raised by the objective standard is whether causation could ever be established if the surgeon has recommended surgery which is warranted by the patient's condition. Can it be said that a reasonable person in the patient's position, to whom proper disclosure of attendant risks has been made, would decide against the surgery, that is, against the surgeon's recommendation that it be undergone? The objective standard of what a reasonable person in the patient's position would do would seem to put a premium on the surgeon's assessment of the relative need for the surgery and on supporting medical evidence of that need. Could it be reasonably refused?

[62] Having rejected both a purely subjective and a purely objective approach, Laskin CJ crafted a test that fell between the two, the "modified objective" test. While approaching the issue of what the patient would have done objectively, the judge should take into account "special considerations affecting the particular patient" (p 898). This would, in his view, avoid the problem of leaving the matter of causation entirely in the surgeon's hands: "The patient's particular situation and the degree to which the risks of surgery or no surgery are balanced would reduce the force, on an objective appraisal, of the surgeon's recommendation" (p 899). At the same time, consideration of all factors that might have "reasonably" affected the decision avoids exclusive reliance on the plaintiff's assertion at trial.

[63] While "the patient's particular concerns" at the time should be considered (pp 899–900) (for example, the judge might consider specific questions which the patient may have asked, evincing specific concerns (p 899)), they must be "reasonably based" to avoid excessive subjectivity. Thus "fears which are not related to the [undisclosed] material risks would not be causative factors". Summing up, Laskin CJ stated (at p 900):

> In short, although account must be taken of a patient's particular position, a position which will vary with the patient, it must be objectively assessed in terms of reasonableness.

[64] There is little profit in debating whether the test Laskin CJ had in mind should be labelled objective or subjective. Suffice it to say it contains elements of both the subjective and objective and has been read in different ways. Two assertions can, however, be ventured. First, the Court was concerned to ensure that the plaintiff's particular concerns and circumstances be considered. To hold otherwise would be to virtually place the outcome of the causation inquiry in the hands of the physician. Second, the Court was concerned to ensure that the plaintiff's subjective assertion of what she would have done had she been properly advised be tested "in terms of reasonableness". To hold otherwise would give undue weight to the plaintiff's hindsight assertion that she would have acted in a way that supports her claim for damages. The approach suggested above – that causation is a question of fact for the trial judge to determine on all the evidence including the plaintiff's assertion at trial examined in the light of her circumstances, mind-set and the medical advice she would have received at the time – satisfies both these concerns.

[65] This brings us to the ultimate objection to the proposed test: that it treats the plaintiff unfairly by diminishing her right to choose. As noted earlier, absent extraordinary conduct such as fraud or abuse of power, the inquiry into the damages that flow from failure to advise of medical risks is governed by the law of negligence. The issue is not the plaintiff's right to choose, as it would be for the tort of battery or an action for fraud, but whether as a factual matter the negligent act caused the loss.

[66] Applying the standard appropriate to the law of negligence, the question is whether the proposed test is fair to both plaintiff and defendant. In my view, it is. It avoids the trap of determining the issue of causation either solely by the physician's opinion of what a reasonable person would have done or solely by the plaintiff's unilateral assertion at trial that he or she would have acted differently. Instead, it places the issue in the hands of the trial judge for determination on all the evidence. It takes into account the plaintiff's right of choice, rather than presuming that choice on the basis of a hypothetical reasonable person. And it permits serious consideration of the plaintiff's evidence as to what that choice would have been. As the California Supreme Court stated in *Cobbs v Grant*, 502 P 2d 1 (1972), at pp 11–12, cited by Sopinka J. in *Hollis, supra*, at p 689: "The patient-plaintiff may testify on this subject but the issue extends beyond his credibility." At the same time, it is fair to the physician, who may introduce evidence of what the reasonable patient would have done as it bears on the choice the particular patient at bar would have made.

[67] The proposed test also meets the need, eloquently voiced by Wood JA in the British Columbia Court of Appeal, for a test which accommodates cases where the decision involves a "delicate balancing of overlapping personal, ethical, and medical considerations which can lead to more than one 'reasonable' choice" (p 225 BCLR). The objective test, based on the hypothetical reasonable person, depreciates the plaintiff's personal choice in such situations and deprives her testimony of any weight. the test of what the particular plaintiff at bar would have done, determined in the light of all the circumstances and his or her own values and attitudes, avoids these problems. Nor does the fact that there was more than one reasonable choice present a problem. The question is what choice this plaintiff would have made on all the evidence and on a balance of probabilities.

Sopinka and Iacobucci JJ agreed with McLachlin J's analysis of the law but disagreed with her that the trial judge had applied the test.

The majority in *Arndt v Smith* adopt and endorse the view of the Laskin CJ expressed in *Reibl*. They note that while he rejected the 'pure' subjective approach, Laskin CJ was equally uneasy with a purely objective approach. For this reason, he opted for a 'modified objective' test. Our question here is, what did the majority regard this test as meaning, or putting it in the language suggested earlier, what moderating factors qualify its reliance on the reasonable person. If we can identify them, we can then take a view whether, from the point of legal principle and of fairness, it is a test which an English appellate court should introduce into English law.

The majority, having rehearsed Laskin CJ's analysis, begin by making the crucial but often overlooked point that there is something special in the analysis of causation in cases of breach of the duty to obtain informed consent. The court is being asked to resolve a hypothetical problem, what would the plaintiff have done if properly informed. This has at least two ramifications which are intrinsic in both Laskin CJ's approach and that of the majority. It argues for a cautious approach and it suggests that invoking the traditional approach of the common law to causation as being a matter of evidence is less persuasive than it may appear. There is no evidence in the ordinary sense of an event *X* following a prior event *Y*. This is because *Y*, by definition did not take place, in that the plaintiff was not properly informed.

The hypothetical nature of the issue before the court cannot, therefore, be ignored. It serves to explain the care with which the courts proceed. What, then was the majority's next step? In clarifying what he describes as the 'confusion' surrounding the true meaning of Laskin CJ's 'modified objective' test, Cory J introduces a gloss which at first appears to make the test very close to the subjective test. He reminds us that Laskin CJ's test refers to the actions of the reasonable person in the plaintiff's circumstances. To Cory J this means that the reasonable person 'must be taken to possess the patient's reasonable beliefs, fears, desires and expectations'. He then, however, goes on to assert that such beliefs 'will usually be revealed by the questions posed [by the patient]', citing examples of exchanges between patient and doctor in different contexts. This immediately should raise concerns. It means, in effect, that the plaintiff's case, based, as it must be, on what she would have done, will materially be affected by how questioning and assertive she was. This cannot be the correct approach. The duty to inform is placed by law on the doctor. The law should not introduce, as a measure of compliance, what the plaintiff did or did not do, particularly as some plaintiffs may find the environment sufficiently unnerving that they ask no questions at all. There is no duty on the plaintiff to ask questions, although, of course, it is wise to do so and the more educated and self-confident patient will do so.

Cory J is at pains to highlight that in taking account of the patient's concerns, the test requires that these concerns be 'reasonable'. How significant is this insistence on the reasonableness of the patient's concerns? An initial reaction could well be that any real commitment to an element of subjectivity has been abandoned, by insistence on this qualifying criterion. But, on closer analysis, the picture is less clear.

To justify the demand that the plaintiff's subjective concerns be reasonable, Cory J explains that 'fears which are idiosyncratic, which do not relate directly to the material risks of a proposed treatment and which would often be unknown to the physician, cannot be considered'. This explanation is, of course, somewhat question-begging in that it leaves undefined what 'idiosyncratic' and 'material' (to whom?) may mean and leaves unclear the extent of the doctor's duty to become familiar with the patient's circumstances. But, at the same time, it could be said merely to be insisting that some measure of objective scrutiny of the patient's assertions is appropriate. It denies the plaintiff the right to rely on his true feelings, if no reasonable person would have felt that way and the doctor had no ground for suspecting their existence. But, on the other hand, this may be an inevitable trade-off given the majority's concern, as Cory J puts it, to ensure 'that our medical system will have some protection in the face of liability claims from patients influenced by unreasonable fears and beliefs, while still accommodating all the reasonable individual concerns and circumstances of plaintiffs'. Of course, it can be objected that plaintiffs are not, nor do they have to be, rational or reasonable on many occasions. Why should they be here? Cory J's answer clearly is so that litigation is kept under control.

What conclusion can be drawn from Cory J's analysis? Is it one which should recommend itself to an English appellate court? The answer must be that the initial determinant is whether the underlying policy objectives of allowing in the valid claims of plaintiffs while preventing unwarranted or unmanageable litigation are served. For Cory J they can best be served by beginning with an objective approach, allowing in elements of subjectivity, but subjecting these to a further dose of objectivity. He denies, rightly, that this approach is indistinguishable from the subjective test: 'The modified objective test serves to eliminate from consideration the honestly held but idiosyncratic and unreasonable or irrational beliefs of patients.'

McLachlin J applied the subjective test: what would the plaintiff have done looking at all the evidence? (para 32). McLachlin J explores what is meant by 'the evidence'. It 'may include evidence from the plaintiff at trial as to what she would have done. But it also includes relevant evidence of her situation, circumstances and mind-set at the time the decision would have been made ... [T]he plaintiff's hindsight assertion at trial of what she would have done is tested or evaluated by reference to the evidence as to her circumstances and beliefs at the time'. One interpretation of this approach is that any assertion of the plaintiff is tested simply by whether, in the context, it is believable, or put another way, whether a reasonable person, listening to the plaintiff, would be persuaded.

This may not, however, be what McLachlin J meant. For, she goes on immediately to state that '[i]n this way, the plaintiff's subjective evidence as to what she would have done *is evaluated* by reference to the reasonableness of the competing courses of action' (emphasis added). She cites with approval Sopinka J's observation in *Hollis v Dow Corning Corpn* [1995] 4 SCR 634 that 'the most reliable approach in determining what would in fact have occurred is to test the plaintiff's assertion by reference to objective evidence as to what a reasonable person would have done'.

The role of reasonableness goes to the believability of the plaintiff, not to the standard against which any evidence must be measured. Support for this interpretation is provided by McLachlin J's rebuttal of the dangers of hindsight by stating that 'it is open to a court to disbelieve evidence found [*quaere* believed] to be tainted by hindsight'. This observation is critical. It stresses that it is the believability of the plaintiff's evidence which is to be tested or evaluated rather than its reasonableness. As if to reinforce the point, McLachlin J goes on to echo the comment that concern about the subjective test's excessive reliance on the plaintiff's evidence, may be misplaced. 'Causation is not proved', she states, 'solely by the plaintiff's testimony. The court must make an assessment of credibility which would appear not to be easier nor more difficult than in other contexts. There may also be relevant evidence from third parties to assist the trier of fact'.

Having reached this view, McLachlin J moves to support it on policy grounds. It is the right approach not least because the objective test has proved, since *Reibl*, 'a formidable obstacle to plaintiffs', even if they were able to prove breach of the duty to inform (citing in support Professor Gerald Robertson's well-known paper, 'Informed Consent Ten Years Later: The Impact of *Reibl v Hughes*' (1991) 70 Can Bar Rev 423). She then makes her peace with Laskin CJ and his decision in *Reibl*. First, she asserts that the labels 'subjective' and 'objective' may not be entirely helpful and have themselves been interpreted in different ways. Then she goes on to state that the approach she adopts in fact meets the concerns properly expressed in *Reibl*, that the plaintiff's beliefs be taken account of but at the same time evaluated. Thus, her decision is not really a departure from *Reibl*, if properly understood.

The New South Wales Court of Appeal adopted the approach favoured by McLachlin J in *Arndt v Smith* and in 1989. The approach of the majority in *Arndt v Smith* and *Reibl* was rejected.

Ellis v Wallsend District Hospital (1989) 17 NSWLR 553 (NSWCA)

In 1975 the plaintiff, Mrs Marie Ellis, consulted Dr A W Chambers, a neurosurgeon who had treated her on several occasions in the previous years, at his consulting room. Mrs Ellis, who had a background of intractable and very severe neck pain, drug dependence, drug overdoses, and failure of other treatment, was interested in having five-nerve separation microsurgery which Dr Chambers had already mentioned to her. Dr Chambers advised that the only concern that she need have was the risk of slight numbness in her right hand. Mrs Ellis agreed to have the operation.

There was evidence that the operation carried a remote risk of paralysis and a more substantial risk of failure to relieve pain. Mrs Ellis gave evidence that if she had been warned of those risks she would not have undergone the operation.

On June 18, 1975, Dr Chambers performed a laminectomey and a cervical posterior rhizotomy of the nerve roots at the cervical vertebrae 2 to 6. During the operation there was haemorrhage which was controlled; numerous adhesions surrounding the spinal cord were noted; Dr Chambers did not use magnification available. Six days after the operation Mrs Ellis developed quadriplegia.

In 1981 Mrs Ellis commenced proceedings in the New South Wales court against Dr Chambers alleging that Dr Chambers had been negligent in (1) advising her to have the operation; (2) failing to warn her of the risks involved; (3) failing to obtain her consent to the operation; (4) in the performance of the operation. She also alleged breach of contract and assault.

Dr Chambers died in 1986. On June 6, 1988, Mrs Ellis settled her claim against his estate for A$500,000. She then claimed against the hospital on the grounds that (1) the hospital was vicariously liable for Dr Chambers' negligence; (2) that the hospital was in breach of its independent and nondelegable duty to her as its patient to ensure that she received proper medical treatment and was warned of all material risks involved in the surgery.

The hospital contended that Mrs Ellis was not its patient but that of Dr Chambers.

In dismissing Mrs Ellis's claim, Cole J held inter alia that:
(1)   Dr Chambers negligently failed to warn Mrs Ellis of the risk of developing paraplegia and low prospect of achieving pain relief;
(2)   applying a subjective test, Mrs Ellis had failed to establish a causative link between that negligence and her damage.

Samuels JA: The test by which causation is determined in cases of medical negligence has not yet been established in Australia by any decision of the High Court. In *Gover v State of South Australia* (1985) 39 SASR 543 at 564, Cox J summarized the possible views thus:

> ... if a doctor negligently fails to notify his patient of a particular risk of treatment, and the treatment is given and things do in fact go wrong, will the patient, on suing for damages, have to satisfy the Court that he would not have accepted the treatment had the warning been given? Or is it a matter of what a reasonable man would have done in the patient's situation? Or is there no causation element of this sort at all to be proved before a patient can recover?

On the assumption that there is a burden upon the plaintiff to establish a 'causation element' the contest is between the response to the information which the plaintiff would have made had it been furnished (which has been called the subjective test) and the response which a reasonable person in the plaintiff's situation would have made (which has been called the objective test). As Cox J's review of the authorities indicates, the subjective test has been adopted by single judges in England in *Bolam v Friern Hospital Management Committee* [1957] 1 WLR 582 at 590, [1957] 2 All ER 118, by McNair J, and in *Chatterton v Gerson* [1981] QB 432 at 442 and at 445, by Bristow J. Although *Sidaway* was directed to a different question, that of the nature and extent of any warning which a surgeon should give his patient about the possible risks inherent in the proposed procedure, it contains dicta which tend both to favour and deny the subjective test. For example (at 887 Lord Scarman, summarizing the plaintiff's case, said: '... and that, had she been warned, she would not have consented to the operation.'

... [I]n the judgment in *Smith v Auckland Hospital Board* [1965] NZLR 191 as Cox J pointed out in *Gover* (at 565) a majority of the judges favoured the subjective test.

The objective test has been applied in two cases, one in the United States and one in Canada, which are commonly regarded as conveying the leading exegesis of that view. One is *Canterbury v Spence* 464 F 2d 772 (1972), a decision of the United States Court of Appeals for the District of Columbia, and the other *Reibl v Hughes* (1980) 114 DLR (3d) 1, a decision of the Supreme Court of Canada delivered by Laskin CJC. Both these cases dealt primarily with the doctrine of 'informed consent', but each prefers, to quote from *Canterbury* (at 791):

> ... to resolve the causality issue on an objective basis: in terms of what a prudent person in the patient's position would have decided if suitably informed of all perils bearing significance.

The subjective test was regarded in *Reibl* (in which *Canterbury* was applied) as 'hypothetical and thus unreliable' and, as Laskin CJC observed (at 16) calculated to 'put a premium on hindsight, even more of a premium than would be put on medical evidence in assessing causation by an objective standard'.

I do not myself find these objections to the subjective test persuasive. I respectfully agree with Cox J in *Gover* (at 566) when he said:

> ... At any rate the basic causation principle governing actions in negligence plainly supports, in my opinion, the subjective test. ...

It is, of course, true that a patient's evidence about what he or she would have done if told of certain risks may be coloured by the fact that the risks did in fact eventuate; but it is open to a court to disbelieve evidence found to be tainted by hindsight: Manderson, 'Following Doctors' Order: Informed Consent in Australia' (1988) 62 ALJ 430 at 434. Obviously, in endeavouring to ascertain what the plaintiff's response would have been to adequate information had it been conveyed a the appropriate time, a court will be greatly assisted by evidence of the plaintiff's temperament, the course of any prior treatment for the same or a like condition, the nature of the relationship between patient and doctor including pre-eminently, so far as it can be established, the degree of trust reposed in the doctor by the patient. The extent to which the procedure was elective or imposed by circumstantial exigency and the nature and degree of risk involved will all be matters of considerable importance: see Robertson, 'Informed Consent to Medical Treatment' (1981) 97 LQR 102 at 122.

Despite these practical difficulties I agree with the learned judge that the subjective test is the correct one to apply. It is supported by persuasive authority and is consistent with the principle by which proof of causation is governed in other areas of the law of negligence. To the extent that there may be a choice to be determined upon grounds of policy (there being no decision of any appellate court in Australia upon the point), while there are difficulties inherent in both tests, I would more readily accept the threat of hindsight than adopt medical practice as the determinant. As Manderson (*op cit* at 434) points out the causation question, on the objective view:

> ... resolves itself into a consideration of whether reasonable persons would have refused treatment if they had known the information concealed from them. The answer must be that reasonable persons would have gone ahead with the proposed treatment despite the risks, if it was likely to be beneficial to their health. Yet how is the court to determine whether medical risks are, in short, worth taking, except by asking the opinion of the medical profession?

And the learned author quotes the comment of Laskin CJC in *Reibl* (at 15):

> The objective standard of what a reasonable person in the patient's position would do would seem to put a premium on the surgeon's assessment ...

As I have indicated, Cole J favoured the subjective test but found that, whichever test he applied, he was not satisfied on the balance of probabilities that had the appellant been told that there was a slight risk that the operation might cause paralysis, she would have declined to proceed. This conclusion involved rejection of the following evidence of the appellant:

> Q: Was anything ever suggested to you at that stage as to paralysis or possible paralysis as the outcome? A: Definitely not, if he had mentioned anything, I would have run to Bourke.

It is true that, as his Honour points out, adequate information upon this aspect would have been to the effect that there was a slight risk of paralysis coupled with a recommendation that the operation should be performed. Furthermore, it is plain that the appellant had faith in Dr Chambers with whom she was on friendly and comfortable terms, and her probable response to the warning she should have been given must be considered, as the judge indicated, against the background of intractable and very severe pain, drug dependence, the occasions of drug overdoses and the failure of all other treatment. Moreover, it was correct for the judge to take heed, as he did, of the likelihood that the appellant's account of her hypothetical response must be coloured by the catastrophe which the operation brought in its wake.

It was therefore essential for his Honour to examine with great care the evidence which the appellant gave upon this critical point. This attention was all the more necessary since Dr Chambers' death deprived the court of a witness whose evidence would have been highly relevant to this issue. I do not doubt that his Honour did consider the evidence closely although he does not analyze it at any length in his judgment. As I have said, he mentions the background factors which I have summarized above. He refers to the appellant's evidence that had the risk of paralysis been suggested she 'would have run to Bourke'; and he adds the comment: 'A very real question arises as to whether this evidence should be accepted.' It is evident that his doubt about its credibility arises from what I have called the background factors coupled with the undoubted element that the subjective test necessarily entails the risk of distortion by hindsight. Ultimately, Cole J expressed his material findings thus:

> Applying the subjective test, I am satisfied, on the balance of probabilities, that Mrs Ellis would not have rejected the operation if the slight risk of paralysis had been mentioned. I find that her position was such, all else having been tried and failed, she would have accepted the advice of Dr Chambers in whom she had such faith and on whom she placed such reliance, had he recommended the rhizotomy operation yet coupled it with a warning that there was a slight risk of paralysis.

… Cole J did not explicitly say that he derived assistance from the appellant's demeanour; nor did he offer any other general assessment of her credibility. Certainly, he seems to have accepted everything she said concerning her dealings with Dr Chambers, and no attack was made upon her credit in any particular. Nevertheless, it seems to me inescapable that in arriving at a conclusion as to what the appellant was likely to have done in 1975 if faced with warnings about the possible consequences of a surgical procedure which had been in fact represented to her in an almost entirely favourable light, he must have taken account of how the witness presented herself to him. The question which the learned judge had to decide, which, to me, is a very difficult one, did not only depend upon his view of the appellant's truthfulness, but also upon her capacity, assuming that she was endeavouring to be honest, to restore herself in recollection to the situation in which she stood when the critical decision had to be made. Indeed, it would have been necessary for her to attribute to that decision a significance far greater than any that it could have assumed at the time.

Examining merely the written record, there seems to me much to be said in favour of our view that the circumstances that the appellant hesitated for as long as she did, and sought assurance as often as she did, about a procedure which, so far as she knew, offered only the most minor risk, suggest that her reaction to the true state of affairs would probably have been retreat. Moreover, on the face of it, she appeared to minimize to some extent the gravity of the pain and to diminish its influence upon her decision. But, no doubt, his Honour considered all these matters and was able to do so with the advantage of having seen the appellant in the witness-box. …

There are … cogent reasons for concluding that it is not open to an appellate court to differ from this critical finding.

However, there are powerful considerations in this case which make in the contrary direction. First, his Honour does not appear to have considered the fact that this crucial passage in the appellant's evidence stood unchallenged; certainly, he makes no mention of it. … There was, so far as I can see, no other evidence in contradiction of the appellant's statement. …

Secondly, the judge evidently took the view that the appellant's failure to offer any evidence as to how she would have reacted to information about the low prospect of success put her out of court on this issue. I do not consider that that was a justifiable view. The omission to offer the evidence was of considerable materiality. But it did not follow that a likely hypothetical response could not have been inferred from the appellant's evidence as a whole, taking advantage of the light which that cast upon her character and likely attitudes. I do not think, therefore, that it is correct to say, as the learned judge did, that in the 'absence of any evidence which permits a determination on a subjective basis whether she would have proceeded or not' the plaintiff failed to prove the necessary link. The absence of direct evidence as to how she thought she would have behaved at the time did not preclude consideration of the issue on a subjective basis.

Additionally, the learned judge did not give any attention to the possible subjective response which the appellant might have made had the information conveyed to her contained both a warning about possible paralysis and an accurate assessment of the likely prospects of success.

This is curious, if I may say so, because he found that Dr Chambers' negligence involved failure to warn about both these matters. But he took this course, I would judge, because of the way in which he eliminated from consideration the possible influence of the low rate of statistical success. But, in my respectful opinion, he was not only bound to consider that matter alone from a subjective standpoint, but bound also to consider it from the same standpoint as one of two combined elements in the warning which the appellant should have received.

For these reasons, it is my opinion that the finding that the appellant failed to establish any causative link cannot stand.

Kirby P: I consider that Cole J was correct in applying the 'subjective' test rather than an 'objective' one to the question whether Mrs Ellis would have undergone the operation had she been more fully informed of its risks both of paralysis (remote) and failure to relieve her pain (more substantial). For the reasons given by Samuels JA, I consider that the question to be asked is whether, in the particular circumstances, the risk was such that the particular patient should have been told and, if told, would not have accepted the treatment. It is not whether a hypothetical 'reasonable' patient or even the hybrid 'reasonable patient in the position of the particular patient' would have accepted or rejected the treatment if fully and properly informed of the risks involved in it: cf Cox J in *Gover v South Australia* (1985) 39 SASR 543 at 564; *Smith v Auckland Hospital Board* [1965] NZLR 191; *Bolam v Friern Hospital Management Committee* [1957] 1 WLR 582; [1957] 2 All ER 118; cf *Sykes v Midland Bank Executor and Trustee Co Ltd* [1971] 1 QB 113 at 127, 141 (CA); see also *Sidaway v Bethlem Royal Hospital and Maudsley Hospital Board of Governors* [1985] AC 871 at 894 (HL).

It is true that in Canada and the United States an 'objective' test of 'what a prudent [or reasonable] person in the patient's position would have decided if suitably informed of all perils bearing significance' has been adopted: see *Reibl v Hughes* (1978) 89 DLR (3d) 112 (SCC); *Haughian v Paine* (1987) 37 DLR (4th) 624 (Sask CA); *Schanilec Estate v Harris* (1987) 39 CCLT 279 (BCCA) and *Canterbury v Spence* 464 F 2d 772 at 791 (1972). However, that approach was trenchantly criticized by Lord Diplock in *Sidaway* (ibid at 894). It has also been criticized in Canadian academic literature: see, eg. M A Somerville, 'Structuring the Issues in Informed Consent' (1981) 26 McGill LJ 740. The courts in Canada, whilst remaining loyal to the language of the Supreme Court in *Reibl*, have sought to develop the notion of the hybrid: see eg. *White v Turner* (1981) 120 DLR (3d) 269. We are under no such compulsion to conform to *Reibl*. Deference to respect for the integrity of the patient as an individual, entitled to have command over his or her body, suggests that the common law should uphold the right of the patient to

> … decline operative investigation or treatment however unreasonably or foolish this may appear in the eyes of his [or her] medical advisers … [*Smith v Auckland Hospital Board* at p 210].

The same approach has been adopted in civil law jurisdictions: see discussion. D Giesen, *International Medical Malpractice Law*, Martinus Nijhoff, London, (1988) at 345. It is the one which I would apply.

Although Cole J stated that he would reach the same conclusion whether the 'subjective' or 'objective' test were applied, his correct specification of the 'subjective' test made all the more important the accurate ascertainment of what Ms Ellis, herself, would have done, had she been properly advised of the risks involved in the operation.

It is true that answering the question involves an exercise in retrospective reasoning. The patient cannot, when the mishap leading to damage and litigation has occurred, determine the answer authoritatively by the response in court to the question of what he or she would have done had only full and proper advice been given. However honest the patient may try to be, self-interest and the knowledge of the misfortunes that have followed the treatment will necessarily colour the patient's response to that question. Nonetheless, the answer remains an important ingredient in the decision by the fact finding tribunal as to what it thinks the patient, subjectively and at the time before operation, would have done if properly and fully advised.

Mrs Ellis (in the passages incorporated in Samuels JA's judgment) gave clear evidence on this point. Had she known that paralysis or possible paralysis was an outcome of the operation she would 'definitely not' have had the operation: 'If he had mentioned anything, I would have run to Bourke.' This colloquial expression, poignant in the case of a quadriplegic, envisaging as it does a race to one of the most remote outback towns of Australia, leaves in no doubt what Mrs Ellis was asserting to be (albeit retrospectively) the stance she would have taken at that time.

Other evidence tends to support her assertion. She emerges from the written testimony as a somewhat obsessive person, with strong views, for example, on the taking of tablets. Her step-daughter, according to the evidence, specifically pressed Dr Chambers in her presence to an assurance about the risks of the operation. Once before she had been admitted to hospital in 1971 for an operation but she elected not to have it. Far from assisting the hospital's case, this answer, secured in cross-examination, suggests to my mind that she was the kind of person who would have thought carefully about the risks of the operation as they were explained to her. It is true that she was suffering pain. But according to her, Dr Chambers built the operation up, describing it as 'terrific'. In these circumstances she was certainly entitled, in modern conditions, to be given a more detailed or fanciful risks or those minuscule, freak, unpredictable risks that can sometimes occur. But the bigger the devastation of the possible risk, the greater is the obligation to lay it before the patient so that he or she can make an informed decision.

Cole J found (in terms which are not challenged and appear anyway to be manifestly right) that Dr Chambers did not warn Mrs Ellis that there was a high chance that the operation would not relieve her from pain and that there was a small, but not fanciful, risk of a resultant paralysis. The two risks are obviously inter-related. An operation with a very high success rate and a very low risk of paralysis may, rationally, be accepted much more readily than one where the prospects of success were more circumscribed, though the risk of paralysis was still slight. Dr Chambers undoubtedly thought it in the best interests of Mrs Ellis that she should undergo the operation, but the decision was hers, not his (or the hospital's) to make.

Despite Mrs Ellis' emphatic evidence, Cole J concluded as he did. He had the advantage of seeing Mrs Ellis give her testimony. No doubt this entered into his evaluation of the issue. Mrs Ellis was not cross-examined directly on her statement. Nor was it put to her, specifically, that she would have undergone the operation, contrary to her assertion. The death of Dr Chambers and his consequent absence from the trial did not, in my view, explain or justify the failure of the hospital to challenge Mrs Ellis' direct assertion and to do so in plain terms so that she might meet the challenge ... Mrs Ellis' evidence not being 'inherently incredible' or 'inherently improbable', I am of the opinion that an error had occurred in Cole J's reasoning which is of critical importance. It is one sufficiently serious to require relief from this court. No other explanation is given by Cole J as to why he rejected Mrs Ellis' unchallenged statement. There is no express reference to her demeanour. ... But in the face of emphatic, unchallenged evidence which had support from several objective or unchallenged facts, the conclusion by his Honour to the contrary without adequate or any explanation demands correction.

Meagher JA agreed with Samuels JA.

(ii) LEGAL CAUSATION AND REMOTENESS

Generally speaking, no particular problems arise specific to informed consent involving remoteness of damage (for a general discussion see *supra*, ch 4).

We saw in Chapter 4 the important Australian High Court decision of *Chappel v Hart* (1998) 72 ALJR 1344. This decision raised directly the issue of legal causation in a failure to warn case. You will recall that *Chappel v Hart* concerned a patient who underwent an operation on her oesophagus that entailed an inherent risk that she might suffer damage to her laryngeal nerves and consequent voice loss. In fact, this occurred and it was accepted that it had been negligent of the surgeon not to advise the patient of the risk relying on *Rogers v Whittaker* (1992) 175 CLR 479 (HC of A). For us the important issue is what would the patient have done if she had known of the risk? It was accepted that the operation would inevitably have had to be performed, albeit not when it was. The patient argued that she would have postponed the operation (this was accepted) and sought a second opinion from a more experienced surgeon who would have carried out the procedure. Thereby, the patient would have avoided the injury since the risk was most unlikely to eventuate and, it was argued, would in any event have been reduced because of the surgeon's greater expertise. In a series of very important judgments analysing legal causation and remoteness, a majority of the High Court (Gaudron, Gummow and Kirby JJ) accepted the patient's arguments, whilst two judges (McHugh and Hayne JJ) rejected them. We have already seen these judgments in some detail (see, *supra*, ch 4). We do not repeat those here, instead we set out short passages from the judgment of Gaudron J (in the majority) and Hayne J (dissenting) addressing the essential issue of legal causation in this context.

Chappel v Hart (1998) 72 ALJR 1344 (HC of A)

Gaudron J:

4. The primary contention made on behalf of Dr Chappel is that there was no causal connection between his failure to give adequate warning of the risks involved in the surgery and the damage suffered by Mrs Hart. the contention was made in a context in which it is clear that the surgery was performed with skill and care and the infection which set in and led to the injuries which Mrs Hart sustained was a random event which might occur no matter when or by whom the surgery was performed. It was put that, as surgery was inevitable and carried the risk which, in fact, eventuated, "[t]here was no loss of any 'real and valuable change', nor ... any *substantial prospects* of the risk being diminished or avoided". Alternatively, it was put that the damage sustained by Mrs Hart resulted from the random risk which, in fact, eventuated and her "voluntary willingness to undertake that risk". ...

8. It was not disputed in this Court that Dr Chappel was under a duty to inform Mrs Hart of the possible consequences in the event of the perforation of her oesophagus and subsequent infection, including the possibility of damage to her voice. The duty was called into existence because of the foreseeability of that very risk. The duty was not performed and the risk eventuated. Subject to a further question in the case of a duty to provide information, that is often the beginning and the end of the inquiry whether breach of duty materially caused or contributed to the harm suffered. As Dixon J pointed out in *Betts v Whittingslowe*, albeit in relation to a statutory duty, "breach of duty coupled with an accident of the kind that might thereby be caused is enough to justify an inference, in the absence of any sufficient reason to the contrary, that in fact the accident did occur owing to the act or omission amounting to the breach".

9. Where there is a duty to inform it is, of course, necessary for a plaintiff to give evidence as to what would or would not have happened if the information in question had been provided. If that evidence is to the effect that the injured person would have acted to avoid or minimise the risk of injury, it is to apply sophistry rather than common sense to say that, although the risk of physical injury which came about called the duty of care into existence, breach of that duty did not cause or contribute to that injury, but simply resulted in the loss of an opportunity to pursue a different course of action.

10. The matter can be put another way. If the foreseeable risk to Mrs Hart was the loss of an opportunity to undergo surgery at the hands of a more experienced surgeon, the duty would have been a duty to inform her that there were more experienced surgeons practising in the field. Because the risk was a risk of physical injury, the duty was to inform her of that risk, And that particular duty was imposed because, in point of legal principle, it was sufficient, in the ordinary course of events, to avert the risk of physical injury which called it into existence. And the physical injury having occurred, breach of the duty is treated as materially causing or contributing to that injury unless there is "sufficient reason to the contrary".

11. The ... argument with respect to causation is that there is "sufficient reason to the contrary" to preclude a finding that Dr Chappel's failure to inform Mrs Hart of the risks involved was causally related to the injuries which she sustained. More precisely, it was argued that, even if he had adequately informed her of those risks, it would not have averted the harm suffered. There are two aspects to that argument. The first is that, as surgery was inevitable and the risk which eventuated was inherent in that surgery, Mrs Hart did not, in fact, suffer any damage. The second aspect asserts that the harm resulted from the "random risk" of infection, which, in fact eventuated, and Mrs Hart's "voluntary willingness to undertake that risk".

12. The first aspect of the argument must be rejected. It assumes that the degree of risk – as distinct from the nature of the risk – was the same regardless of the experience of the surgeon concerned. That is a matter to which it will be necessary to return. For the moment, however, it can be put to one side. There is a more fundamental flaw. The argument proceeds on the erroneous footing that the damage sustained by Mrs Hart was simply exposure to risk, not the harm which eventuated. And to say that Mrs Hart would inevitably have been exposed to risk of the harm which she suffered is not to say that she would inevitably have suffered that harm.

13. The second aspect of the argument, which asserts that the harm suffered by Mrs Hart resulted from the "random risk" of infection which eventuated and her "voluntary willingness to undertake that risk", must also be rejected. It may be that, at some stage, Mrs Hart would have voluntarily undertaken whatever risk was involved in the surgery then necessary for her condition. However, it cannot be said that that or any other risk was voluntarily undertaken when Dr Chappel operated but nothing presently turns on that point. The second aspect of the argument must be rejected because it treats the infection which occurred as a supervening event breaking the chain of causation which would otherwise begin with Dr Chappel's failure to inform Mrs Hart of the possible consequences in the event of perforation and subsequent infection. It is contrary to common sense to treat part of the very risk which called the duty

into existence as a supervening event breaking the chain of causation beginning with the breach of that duty.

14. The question whether the infection which set in following perforation of Mrs Hart's oesophagus broke the chain of causation can also be answered by asking what would or would not have happened if Dr Chappel had provided her with adequate information as to the risk involved. If he had, Mrs Hart would not then have undergone surgery and would not then have suffered the injuries which she did or their consequences. Thus, Dr Chappel's "breach was 'still operating', or, continued to be causally significant when [those injuries were sustained]."

15. The arguments advanced on behalf of Dr Chappel with respect to causation cannot succeed.

(Gaudron J went on to refuse to reduce the plaintiff's damages as the risk was 'random' and it had not been established, on the evidence, that the injury would probably have eventuated in any event.)

Hayne J:

115. If the damage of which the plaintiff complains would not have happened without the intervention of the negligent behaviour, it will often be possible to conclude that the negligent behaviour was a cause of that damage. Thus, the plaintiff in *Rogers v Whittaker* ((1992) 175 CLR 479) would not have had surgery on her blind eye if she had been warned of the risk that the operation posed to her good eye. The negligent failure to warn her of that risk was held to be a cause of her damage …

117. The "but for" test is of most use as a negative test. If it is not satisfied, it is unlikely that there is the necessary causal connection. But showing that "but for" the defendant's conduct, the plaintiff would not have suffered damage does not demonstrate the required degree of connection between the defendant's act or omission and the plaintiff's damage. The application of a "but for" test does not identify what might be called the "quality" of the causal connection. No doubt it is with this in mind, that the cases and literature use many different epithets to describe the kind of causation that is necessary – "proximate cause", "legal cause" and so on – as opposed to "causation in fact". (No doubt also, those epithets will sometimes reflect the value judgments or policy considerations mentioned in cases like *March v Stramare (E & M H) Pty Ltd* ((1991) 171 CLR 506.)

118. The importance of examining the nature of the connection between the negligent conduct and the damage can be demonstrated in this way. If the respondent had not been operated on when she was, but had had her operation on another day, the chances are that she would not have suffered the damage to her laryngeal nerve that she did. There may have been no perforation of the oesophagus, there may have been no infection, there may have been no damage to the nerve. The whole tenor of the evidence given at the trial was that if it was the infection that led to paralysis of the laryngeal nerve (and this was the explanation favoured by Professor Benjamin in his written report) infection was such a rare event that it was unlikely (indeed very unlikely) that it would have happened if the operation had been performed on another day. Of course, the respondent did suffer a perforated oesophagus, she did suffer an infection, she did suffer paralysis of the laryngeal nerve. But if she had not attended the hospital on that day, the probabilities are that none of this would have happened. And if the appellant had told her of the risk to her voice, she would not have had the operation when she did. But precisely the same argument would be open if, instead of suffering damage to her voice, as she has, the operating theatre in which her procedure was performed had been struck by lightning, or a runaway truck, and she had been injured. But for the negligent failure to warn she would not have been in harm's way.

119. No doubt the case of the lightning strike or the runaway truck invite consideration of novus actus interveniens and whether, although "the earlier wrongful act or omission may have amounted to an essential condition of the occurrence of the ultimate harm, it was not the true cause or a true cause of that harm" (*Bennett v Minister of Community Welfare* (1992) 176 CLR 408). But that is no more than a particular example of the general proposition that the tort of negligence requires a particular kind of causal relationship between the negligent act or omission of the defendant and the damage suffered by the plaintiff.

120. Being able to say that the damage would not have happened but for the negligent act or omission is not enough. …

121. In my view, the only connection between the failure to warn and the harm the respondent has suffered is that but for the failure to warn she would not have been in harm's way. The appellant's conduct did not affect whether there would be pathogens present in the respondent's oesophagus when the procedure was carried out; his conduct did not affect whether the pathogens that were present would, in all the circumstances, produce the infection

which they did; his conduct did not affect whether that infection would damage the laryngeal nerve as it did. Of course, he manipulated the instrument which perforated the oesophagus but he did so without negligence. …

123. The law of negligence may be seen as directed to several purposes but purposes of compensating the injured and promoting reasonable conduct are prominent among them. In this particular area of negligent advice by a medical practitioner it is important to bear in mind "the paramount consideration that a person is entitled to make his own decisions about his life" (*F v R* (1983) 33 SASR 189).

124. With these purposes in mind, it may be suggested that a sufficient causal relationship is established by showing that the subject-matter of the negligent conduct – a failure to warn of risk to the voice – is the very subject-matter of the damage. But that connection is not enough. If it were enough, it would follow that if the operating theatre had been struck by lightning and the respondent had suffered damage to the laryngeal nerve (because of the resulting power surge affecting the diathermy equipment being used in the operation) the appellant would be liable but that he would not if the power surge caused burns to her body. Similarly, it would mean that the appellant would be liable if the respondent's voice were damaged as a result of an infection stemming from some failure of the hospital to sterilise, properly, instruments or other items used in the procedure.

125. No doubt the fact that what I have called the subject-matter of the negligent conduct and the subject-matter of the damage are the same is important to that intuitive process of analysis that is referred to when it is said that questions of causation are questions of fact to be resolved as a matter of commonsense. But important as this consideration is, it is not determinative.

126. Nor is it enough to say that a purpose of this area of the law is to promote reasonable conduct by medical practitioners and, particularly, the giving of advice necessary to enable people to make their own decisions about their lives. Enlarging the circumstances in which damages will be awarded if there has been a negligent failure by a medical practitioner to advise a patient of risks may well tend to promote the giving of fuller advice. So too may the imposition of a penalty for failing to give proper advice. But the ambit of the liability is not to be decided only according to whether enlarging that ambit will promote careful conduct. The question of causation must still be answered. What is the connection between the negligent act or omission and the damage sustained?

127. The difficulty in the analysis that looks *only* to whether the subject-matter of the negligent conduct (failure to warn of risk to voice) and the damage suffered (damage to the voice) are the same is that it does not pay sufficient heed to the comparison that the law requires between the facts of what happened and the hypothetical facts of what would have happened if there had been no negligent act or omission.

128. It was accepted in this case that, if the respondent had been given proper advice of the risks of the operation, she would, nevertheless, have had the operation which she did. She would have had it at a different time and may have had it performed by a different doctor but she would have had it done. Until she had the operation, she would have continued to suffer the discomforts and dangers that she was suffering when she consulted he appellant – persistent sore throat, difficulty in swallowing, a constant danger of food being caught in her throat. But the hypothetical situation that was to be considered was one in which the respondent had the operation in any event.

129. If she had had the operation at some later time and if she had engaged the appellant to perform it, the risk of her suffering the consequences to her voice that in fact befell her would, for all practical purposes, have been the same. If she had been given proper advice, even if she would have then deferred the operation, that would not have altered the risk that her voice would be affected (any more than it would have affected the risk that the operating theatre would be struck by lightning).

130. If, on being given proper advice, she would have deferred the operation, I would conclude that the respondent did suffer damage and would suffer damage because she did not defer the operation. But the damage she would suffer in those circumstances would not be the damage to her voice – it would be the loss of the period for which she would have deferred the operation and have had her voice and her job, subject nevertheless to the continuing disabilities of her untreated condition. Thus, if, because of the failure to warn, she had the operation (say) two years earlier than she otherwise would have had it and if the damage to her voice thus occurred two years earlier than it *might* have occurred in a later operation, she would have lost two years of employment and attendant enjoyment of life, discounted to take account of the disabilities she would have suffered during that period of two years. But the damage to her voice would not be caused by the failure to warn.

131. The respondent's claim focused upon the damage to her voice. The evidence that was led, and the arguments that were advanced on her behalf, were all directed to showing that the appellant's failure to warn caused the respondent the physical damage which she had

suffered (the damage to the laryngeal nerve with consequent effects on her voice) and the economic consequences that were said to follow from that damage. No evidence was led to suggest that the respondent, if advised of the risks to her voice, would have deferred the operation for any significant period. She said that she would have sought "a second opinion … perhaps several opinions" and no doubt this would have taken time but it was not suggested that she would then have put off the operation for some months let alone years. Thus no factual foundation was laid for a claim based upon delaying the operation.

132. It will be seen that the comparison I have drawn is between the times at which she would have confronted the risk about which she should have been warned. It is not a comparison that involves any prediction of whether that risk would have occurred if the operation had been deferred. That is because the operation has risks even if reasonable care is exercised; those risks cannot be eliminated by the exercise of reasonable care. It was *not* alleged in this case that the appellant performed the procedure negligently. That is, it was *not* alleged that the risk which the respondent faced in undergoing this operation could be eliminated if the surgeon was careful. This is not to deny that professional performance varies: that some surgeons are better than others. But the law is not concerned to do more than enforce standards of *reasonable* care. The respondent could ask no more than that the doctor she engaged to perform this procedure should exercise reasonable care in doing so, and the appellant did just that...

133. There was evidence that if she had been properly advised of the risks to her voice, the respondent would not have had the procedure performed by the appellant, but by another doctor. There was, as I have said, some evidence which suggested that the better the doctor, the less the chance of perforation of the oesophagus. That evidence was, at best, exiguous and stopped far short of identifying any sound basis for assessing what effect the surgeon's skills may have had on the unusual chain of events which happened in this case. Nevertheless, it was submitted that the evidence permitted the conclusion that the appellant's failure to give a proper warning of the risks deprived the respondent of a chance to seek better treatment, or exposed the respondent to a greater risk of injury than she faced in undergoing the procedure at the hands of the appellant. …

146. I agree with McHugh J that there is insufficient evidence in this case to say, on the balance of probabilities, that the appellant's failure to warn exposed the respondent to greater risk of injury. The respondent would have had the operation at some time. The operation has risks even if performed by the most skilled surgeon available. There was very little evidence on the difference between the risk of injury actually faced by the respondent and the risk that she would have faced had the operation been performed by, say, Professor Benjamin.

The complexity of the judgments in *Chappel v Hart* can, perhaps, be said to obscure the simple issue for the court. How did the defendant's negligence make the plaintiff's situation worse apart from the short period during which she would have deferred the operation? The answer lies elsewhere if one analyses these cases as concerned with enhancing the patient's autonomy, ie the right to choose whether *and* when to undergo a medical procedure. The majority's approach is more consistent with the latter, although the judges eschew this as being the essence of the failure to warn cases apart, that is, from Kirby J (see *supra*). On balance, we prefer the argument of the majority based as they are upon a commonsense intuitive reaction to the unusual factual situation in the case. Their arguments are also, we would suggest, more consistent with, what Kirby J called, 'reinforcing the duty to warn' (para 93) (for a less welcoming view, see J Clarke 'Causation in *Chappel v Hart*: Common Sense or Coincidence?' (1999) 6 J of Law and Medicine 335).

One particular problem which we ought to notice, however, is what we can call the problem of the 'unrelated risk'. This involves the following. A patient is advised by his doctor of risk 'X' but not of risk 'Y' and, thereafter, consents to the treatment, ie agrees to run risk 'X'. Let us assume, for these purposes, that the failure to disclose risk 'Y' is a breach of the doctor's duty to his patient. Further, let us assume it can be proved that the patient would not have undergone the procedure had he been informed of risk 'Y'. During the treatment risk 'X' eventuates and the patient is injured. The patient brings an action against the doctor alleging a breach of duty in failing to warn of risk 'Y' relying upon the harm suffered unrelated to risk 'Y' since risk 'Y' has not eventuated.

This issue was considered by the Court of Session (Outer House) in the following case.

Moyes v Lothian Health Board [1990] 1 Med LR 463 (CS(OH))

A patient was advised to undergo angiography. She was informed of the risk of suffering a stroke inherent in such a procedure. She was not, however, informed that the risk was increased given her particular medical condition of hypersensitivity to the contrast medium used in the procedure and the fact that she had a history of migraine. In the event she suffered a stroke. It was not associated with her hypersensitivity but with the standard risk of suffering a stroke about which she had been informed. In her action in negligence, Lord Caplan at one stage assumed that not warning her of the increased risk associated with her hypersensitivity constituted a breach of duty to inform. On this basis he addressed the question whether she could claim where the harm she suffered was unrelated to the breach of duty.

Lord Caplan: The ordinary person who has to consider whether or not to have an operation is not interested in the exact pathological genesis of the various complications which can occur but rather in the nature and extent of the risk. The patient would want to know what chance there was of the operation going wrong and if it did what would happen. If we were to suppose a situation where an operation would give rise to a 1 per cent risk of serious complication in the ordinary case but where there could be four other special factors each adding a further 1 per cent to the risk, a patient to whom all five factors applied might have a 5 per cent risk rather than the 1 per cent risk of the average person. It is perfectly conceivable that a patient might be prepared to accept the risk of one in 100 but not be prepared to face up to a risk of one in 20. If a doctor contrary to established practice failed to warn the patient of the four special risks but did warn the patient of the standard risk and then the patient suffered complications caused physiologically by the standard risk factor rather than by one or other of the four special risk factors I do not think the doctor should escape the consequences of not having warned the patient of the added risks which that patient was exposed to. A patient might well with perfect reason consider that if there were five risk factors rather than one then the chance of one or other of these factors materializing was much greater. The coincidence that the damage which occurred was due to the particular factor in respect of which a warning was given does not alter the fact that the patient was not properly warned of the total risks inherent in the operation and thus could not make an informed decision as to whether or not to go through with it. In the example I give, by going through an operation with five risk factors rather than one the patient was exposed to a degree of risk materially in excess of what the patient had been warned about and was prepared to accept. If he had been given due warning he would have not risked suffering adverse complications from that particular operation and the fact that such complications occurred is causal connection enough to found a claim against the doctor.

While Lord Caplan's judgment is correct as far as it goes, it treats the issue wholly in terms of *factual* causation. Lord Caplan, however, did not recognise that there was also an issue of legal causation or remoteness of damage. It is axiomatic in the law of torts that not every factual cause founds a claim even though harm is produced. The issue which Lord Caplan should have addressed is whether the patient's harm was too remote from the breach of duty. It may well be that Lord Caplan would still have held the doctor liable assuming as he did there was a breach of duty to inform. Other cases may arise, however, where the result of the case may be different depending on whether the question is recognised to be one of factual or legal causation. In other words, if the court chooses to address this issue as a question of remoteness, a claim by a plaintiff may be less likely to succeed. This is because a court may have an intuitive sense that liability should not arise for a harm which is *unrelated* to the doctor's breach of duty to inform and so organise the legal test to achieve this result.

In *Chappel v Hart* (1998) 72 ALJR 1344 (HC of A), Gummow J alluded to the situation of the 'unrelated risk' and adopted this reasoning.

Gummow J: 66. In the present appeal, not only was the damage which Mrs Hart suffered reasonably foreseeable, but the fact that the relevant conjunction of circumstances could occur should have been the subject of any adequate warning and the reason for giving it. It is true that in some cases of a failure to warn by a medical practitioner an application of the "but for" test without qualification could lead to absurd or unjust results. Such would have been the situation if, for example, instead of suffering damage to her laryngeal nerve, Mrs Hart had been injured through the misapplication of anaesthetic. Whilst it would still be open to conclude that, but for Dr Chappel's failure to warn her of the possibility of damage to her voice, she would not have opted for the operation at that time and would not have been injured by the anaesthetic, the law would not conclude that the failure to warn of the risk of injury to the laryngeal nerve caused the injury resulting from the anaesthetic.

(See also Hayne J, *supra*, paras 118–119.)

(d) Waiver

The question here is whether a patient may (expressly or impliedly) absolve a doctor from his duty to inform, assuming the situation to be one in which this duty *prima facie* exists. The answer is probably sometimes but not always. Regrettably it is difficult to be much more precise than this. In its 1983 Report the President's Commission 'Making Health Care Decisions' (1983) addresses the issue (at p 94):

> The modest attention paid to the fourth exception – waiver – in the courts and scholarly literature is regrettable given its interesting relationship to the value of self-determination that underlies the doctrine of informed consent ... self-determination encompasses both the moral right to formal control over a decision and the ideal of active participation in the decisionmaking process. Although these two senses of self-determination often go hand in hand, sometimes they do not, as in the case of a waiver, when a patient asks not to be informed of certain matters and/or delegates decisional authority to another person.
>
>> The impact of the waiver exception is that if a waiver is properly obtained the patient remains the ultimate decisionmaker, but the content of his decision is shifted from the decisional level to the metadecisional level – from the equivalent of 'I want this treatment (or that treatment or no treatment)' to 'I don't want any information about the treatment' [Meisel (1979) Wis L Rev 413 at 459].
>
> The legal requirements for effective waiver in the context of informed consent have never been clearly articulated by the courts. There is substantial reason to believe that the courts would respect waivers of certain information (for example, the disclosure of particular risks) or the delegation of certain decisions to others. Yet it is questionable whether patients should be permitted to waive the professional's obligation to disclose fundamental information about the nature and implications of certain procedures (such as, 'when you wake up, you will learn that your limb had been amputated' or 'that you are irreversibly sterile'). In the absence of explicit legal guidance, health care professionals should be quite circumspect about allowing or disallowing, encouraging or discouraging, a patient's use of waiver.

Obviously the court must be satisfied that there was in truth a waiver in that the doctor was prepared to inform and the patient willingly declined. The suggestion is that there is a public policy limitation as to which the extent a patient may waive a doctor's duty.

In our view, while the patient may waive the right to information as to risks or whatever, it would be against public policy to allow him to waive the right to be informed of the 'nature and purpose' of the proposed procedure. In other words, it could be argued that the law recognises that a patient has a duty to inform himself of what is proposed which he cannot waive.

C. VOLUNTARINESS

The third element of consent is that it be voluntarily and freely given. In *Bowater v Rowley Regis Corpn* [1944] KB 476, Scott LJ stated (at 479):

a man cannot be said to be truly "willing" unless he is in a position to choose freely, and freedom of choice predicates, not only full knowledge of the circumstances on which the exercise of choice is conditional, so that he may be able to choose wisely, but the absence of any feeling of constraint so that nothing shall interfere with the freedom of his will.

In the context of medical law detailed consideration of the issue was given by the US President's Commission in its 1983 Report.

President's Commission *Making Health Care Decisions* (1983)

Voluntariness in decisionmaking
The patient's participation in the decisionmaking process and ultimate decision regarding care must be voluntary. A choice that has been coerced, or that resulted from serious care must be voluntary. A choice that has been coerced, or that resulted from serious manipulation of a person's ability to make an intelligent and informed decision, is not the person's own free choice. This has long been recognised in law: a consent forced by threats or induced by fraud or misrepresentation is legally viewed as no consent at all. From the perspective of ethics, a consent that is substantially involuntary does not provide moral authorisation for treatment because it does not respect the patient's dignity and may not reflect the aims of the patient.

Of course, the facts of disease and the limited capabilities of medicine often constrict the choices available to patient and physician alike. In that sense, the condition of illness itself is sometimes spoken of as 'coercive' or involuntary. But the fact that no available alternative may be desirable in itself, and that the preferred course is, only the least bad among a bad lot, does not render a choice coerced in the sense employed here. No change in human behaviour or institutional structure could remove this limitation. Such constraints are merely facts of life that should not be regarded as making a patient's choice involuntary.

Voluntariness is best regarded as a matter of degree, rather than as a quality that is wholly present or absent in particular cases. Forced treatment – the embodiment of coercive, involuntary action – appears to be rare in the American health care system. Health care professionals do, however, make limited intrusions on voluntary choice through subtle, or even overt, manipulations of patients' wills when they believe that patients would otherwise make incorrect decisions.

Forced treatment. The most overt forms of involuntariness in health care settings involve interventions forced on patients without their consent (and sometimes over their express objection) and those based on coerced consent. Although rare in mainstream American health care, such situations do arise in certain special settings, and therefore require brief discussion. Society currently legitimates certain forced medical interventions to serve important social goals such as promoting the public health (with, for example, compulsory vaccination laws), enforcing the criminal law (removing bullets needed as evidence for criminal prosecutions), or otherwise promoting the well-being of others (sedating uncontrollable inmates of mental institutions on an emergency basis, for example, to protect other inmates or staff).

Although it is typically not viewed as forced treatment, a good deal of routine care in hospitals, nursing homes, and other health care settings is provided (usually by health professionals such as nurses) without explicit and voluntary consent by patients. The expectation on the part of professionals is that patients, once in such a setting, will simply go along with such routine care. However, the Commission's study of treatment refusals found that in a hospital setting it was the routine tests that were most likely to be refused. At least some patients expected that participation was voluntary and refused tests and medications ordered without their knowledge until adequate information was provided about the nature, purpose, and risks of these undertakings. Lack of information in such cases may not only preclude voluntary participation but also raises questions about a patient's rationality, and hence competence.

When a situation offers the patient an opportunity to refuse care, then patient compliance or acquiescence may be viewed as implicit consent. But when the tacit communication accompanying such care is that there is no choice for the patient to make, and compliance is expected and enforced (at least in the absence of vigorous objections), the treatment can be properly termed 'forced'. The following conversation between a nurse and a patient regarding postoperative care, obtained in one of the Commission's observational studies, illustrates forced treatment that follows routinely from another decision (surgery) that was made voluntarily.

Nurse: Did they mention anything about a tube through your nose?
Patient: Yes, I'm gonna have a tube in my nose.

Nurse: You're going to have the tube down for a couple of days or longer. It depends. So you're going to NPO, nothing by mouth, and also you're going to have IV fluid.

Patient: I know. For three or four days they told me that already. I don't like it, though.

Nurse: You don't have any choice.

Patient: Yes, I don't have any choice. I know.

Nurse: Like it or not, you don't have any choice (laughter). After you come back, we'll ask you to do a lot of coughing and deep breathing to exercise your lungs.

Patient: Oh, we'll see how I feel.

Nurse: (Emphasis) No matter how you feel, you have to do that!

The interview ended a few minutes later with the patient still disputing whether he was going to co-operate with the postoperative care.

Coerced treatment. Unlike forced treatment, for which no consent is given, coerced treatment proceeds on the basis of a consent that was not freely given. As used in this sense, a patient's decision is coerced when the person is credibly threatened by another individual, either explicitly or by implication, with unwanted and avoidable consequences unless the patient accedes to the specified course of action. Concern about coercion is accordingly greatest when a disproportion in power or other significant inequality between a patient and another individual lends credibility to the threat of harm and when the perceived interests of the individuals diverge.

The disparity in power between patient and health care professional may be slight or substantial, depending on the nature of the patient's illness, the institutional setting, the personalities of the individuals involved, and several other factors. In nonemergency settings, a patient typically can change practitioners or simply forego treatment, thus avoiding the potential for coercion. Further, although health care professionals do have interests distinct from and sometimes in conflict with those of their patients, strong social and professional norms usually ensure that priority is accorded to patients' welfare. To be sure, coercion can be exercised with benevolent motives if practitioner and patient differ in their assessments of how the patient's welfare is best served. Nonetheless, there is little reason to believe that blatant forms of coercion are a problem in mainstream American health care. When isolated instances of abuse do arise, the law provides suitable remedies.

A patient's family and other concerned persons may often play a useful role in the decisionmaking process. Sometimes, however, they may try to coerce a particular decision, either because of what they perceive to be in the patient's best interests or because of a desire to advance their own interests. In such instances, since the health care professional's first loyalty is to the patient, he or she should attempt to enhance the patient's ability to make a voluntary, uncoerced decision and to overcome any coercive pressures.

Manipulation. Blatant coercion may be of so little concern in professional-patient relationships because, as physicians so often proclaim, it is so easy for health professionals to elicit a desired decision through more subtle means. Indeed, some physicians are critical of the legal requirement for informed consent on the grounds that it must be mere window dressing since 'patients will, if they trust their doctor, accede to almost any request he cares to make'. On some occasions, to be sure, this result can be achieved by rational persuasion, since the professional presumably has good reasons for preferring a recommended course of action. But the tone of such critics suggests they have something else in mind: an ability to package and present the facts in a way that leaves the patient with no real choice. Such conduct, capitalising on disparities in knowledge, position, and influence, is manipulative in character and impairs the voluntariness of the patient's choice.

Manipulation has more and less extreme forms. At one end of the spectrum is behaviour amounting to misrepresentation or fraud. Of particular concern in health care contexts is the withholding or distortion of information in order to affect the patient's beliefs and decisions. The patient might not be told about alternatives to the recommended course of action, for example, or the risks of other negative characteristics of the recommended treatment might be minimised. Such behaviour is justly criticised on two grounds: first, that it interferes with the patient's voluntary choice (and thus negates consent) and, second, that it interferes with the patient's ability to make an informed decision. At the other end of the spectrum are far more subtle instances: a professional's careful choice of words or nuances of tone and emphasis might present the situation in a manner calculated to heighten the appeal of a particular course of action.

It is well known that the way information is presented can powerfully affect the recipient's response to it. The tone of voice and other aspects of the practitioner's manner of presentation can indicate whether a risk of a particular kind with a particular incidence should be considered serious. Information can be emphasised or played down without altering the content. And it can be framed in a way that affects the listener – for example, 'this procedure succeeds most of the time' versus 'this procedure has a 40 per cent failure rate'. Health professionals who are aware of the effects of such minor variations can choose their language with care; if, during discussions, they can adjust their presentation of information accordingly.

Because many patients are often fearful and unequal to their physicians in status, knowledge, and power, they may be particularly susceptible to manipulations of this type. Health care professionals should, therefore, present information in a form that fosters understanding. Patients should be helped to understand the prognosis for their situation and the implications of different courses of treatment. The difficult distinction, both in theory and in practice, is between acceptable forms of informing, discussion, and rational persuasion on the one hand, and objectionable forms of influence or manipulation on the other.

Since voluntariness is one of the foundation stones of … consent, professionals have a high ethical obligation to avoid coercion and manipulation of their patients. The law penalises those who ignore the requirements of consent or who directly coerce it. But it can do little about subtle manipulations without incurring severe disruptions of private relationships by intrusive policing, and so the duty is best thought of primarily in ethical terms.

We now turn to consider the extent to which this analysis is reflected in English law. A case in the last century adopted a view which would undoubtedly be regarded now as out of sympathy with the times.

Latter v Braddell (1881) 50 LJQB 448

The plaintiff's mistress requested a doctor to examine the plaintiff, who was a domestic servant, in order to ascertain whether she was pregnant. The plaintiff objected to the examination, but undressed by the doctor's orders, and submitted to be examined. The doctor examined her, and ascertained that she was not pregnant. He used no violence or threats and did nothing more than was necessary for the examination. The mistress was not present.

The plaintiff sued her master and mistress and the doctor for assault. At the trial the Judge directed a verdict for the master and mistress, and the jury found a verdict for the doctor.

Held (affirming the order of the Common Pleas Division), that there was no evidence against the master and mistress, that the verdict in favour of the doctor was right, and that a rule of a new trial was rightly discharged.

The plaintiff appealed.

Bramwell LJ: I am of opinion that Mr Justice Lindley was right; in fact, I may almost say that he was more than right, for it seems to me that he might have directed a verdict for the defendant, Dr Sutcliffe; but if there was any evidence, his direction to the jury was right, and their finding was right, although it may be a practical hardship. Very likely the plaintiff thought the defendants had a right to have her examined; but the truth is, she submitted to it, and it is impossible to say the jury were wrong in finding that she submitted. She may have submitted under an erroneous notion of law, but it was not through fear of violence. It seems to follow that if the verdict for Dr Sutcliffe was right the other defendants are entitled to a verdict. I think Mr Justice Lindley was right in telling the jury that there was no evidence against Captain and Mrs Braddell. There could only be evidence against them if the plaintiff submitted through fear of violence, and if what was done was done by their order.

Baggallay LJ: I am of the same opinion. The argument for the plaintiff is on the ground of misdirection in withdrawing the case against Captain and Mrs Braddell from the jury, and on the ground that the verdict in favour of Dr Sutcliffe was against the weight of evidence. I think the verdict as to Dr Sutcliffe was right. As to Mrs Braddell I am not satisfied that she did more than tell Dr Sutcliffe to do what might be necessary and proper. Order XXXIX rule 3 would be fatal to the appeal, for no wrong was occasioned, even if there was misdirection.

Brett LJ: I am of opinion that Mr Justice Lindley was right. The doctor could only be liable if he did what he did without the consent or submission of the plaintiff; and Captain and Mrs Braddell could only be liable if they authorised the doctor to do what he did, and he did it, without such consent or submission. I think there was no evidence against Captain and Mrs Braddell. As to the doctor, there might be a case against him, though there was not a case against the other defendants. Then, was there any case for the jury as against Dr Sutcliffe? I think Mr Justice Lindley would have been justified in withdrawing the case from the jury. To make out an assault by Dr Sutcliffe, the plaintiff must shew that he used violence, or that she had reasonable cause to believe that he was threatening violence. I think the law laid down in the judgment of Mr Justice Lindley in the Court below is correct. Even if there was any evidence against Dr Sutcliffe I think there was no misdirection; and if the verdict as to him was right the withdrawal from the jury of the case against Captain and Mrs Braddell was immaterial because, if Dr Sutcliffe did not assault the plaintiff, it does not matter if they authorised him.

The judgment was affirmed.

Should such facts arise today, there can be little doubt that the plaintiff would have succeeded.

In *Re T (adult: refusal of treatment)* [1992] 4 All ER 649 the Court of Appeal sought to establish the legal context in which voluntariness should be placed. The court went beyond the identification of involuntariness with the more usual examples of duress and instead analysed it in terms of the more general legal concept of undue influence. In so doing, the court potentially broadened the scope of the factors which could vitiate a patient's consent or, as in the case itself, a refusal of consent.

Re T (adult: refusal of treatment) [1992] 4 All ER 649, (1992) 9 BMLR 46 (CA)

On July 1 1992, Miss T, an adult then 34 weeks pregnant, was involved in a road traffic accident. On July 4 she was admitted to hospital complaining of chest pains. She was diagnosed as suffering from pleurisy or pneumonia and was prescribed antibiotics and analgesics and given oxygen.

Although brought up by her mother, a fervent Jehovah's Witness, Miss T was not a member of that faith. Her paternal family was opposed to the sect.

On the evening of July 5, when she was in considerable pain, coughing up sputum, on various drugs and suffering contractions in the first stage of labour Miss T said that she did not want a blood transfusion. Shortly before this she had been alone with her mother. Miss T did ask whether there was a substitute treatment and was told that there was.

A decision was made that the delivery should be by caesarean section. A form of refusal of consent to blood transfusions was signed by Miss T. Contrary to what was stated on the form, it was not explained to Miss T that it might be necessary to give a blood transfusion so as to prevent injury to her health, or even to preserve her life, nor was the form read or its contents explained to her.

The caesarean section was performed on July 6, but the baby was stillborn. That night Miss T's condition deteriorated ands he was transferred to intensive care. It appeared that an abscess had developed in Miss T's lungs. Miss T remained in a critical condition throughout July 7.

On July 8 Ward J granted a declaration that in the circumstances which were then prevailing, it would not be unlawful for the hospital to administer a blood transfusion to Miss T despite the absence of her consent because that appeared manifestly to be in her best interests.

Thereupon Miss T received a transfusion of blood or plasma.

Lord Donaldson MR: In essence Ward J found that the physical and mental state of Miss T on the Sunday afternoon and evening were such that although she was undoubtedly under the influence of her mother, she was capable of reaching and did reach a decision as to her own treatment …

A special problem may arise if at the time the decision is made the patient has been subjected to the influence of some third party. This is by no means to say that the patient is not entitled to receive and indeed invite advice and assistance from others in reaching a decision, particularly from members of the family. But the doctors have to consider whether the decision is really that of the patient. It is wholly acceptable that the patient should have been persuaded by others of the merits of such a decision and have decided accordingly. It matters not how strong the persuasion was, so long as it did not overbear the independence of the patient's decision. The real question in each such case is 'Does the patient really mean what he says or is he merely saying it for a quiet life, to satisfy someone else or because the advice and persuasion to which he has been subjected is such that he can no longer think and decide for himself?' In other words 'Is it a decision expressed in form only, not in reality?'

When considering the effect of outside influences, two aspects can be of crucial importance. First, the strength of the will of the patient. One who is very tired, in pain or depressed will be much less able to resist having his will overborne than one who is rested, free from pain and cheerful. Second, the relationship of the 'persuader' to the patient may be of crucial importance. The influence of parents on their children or of one spouse on the other can be, but is by no means necessarily, much stronger than would be the case in other relationships. Persuasion based upon religious beliefs can also be much more compelling and the fact that arguments based upon religious beliefs are being deployed by someone in a very close relationship with the patient will give them added force and should alert the doctors to the possibility – no more – that the patient's capacity or will to decide has been overborne. In other words the patient may not mean what he says.

Butler-Sloss LJ: A most relevant factor in this appeal is the extent and effect of the intervention of the mother who was alone with her daughter immediately before each of the two occasions that Miss T indicated her rejection of a blood transfusion. It is an irresistible inference that before 5 pm the mother had discussed the question of blood transfusions with her daughter because Miss T 'out of the blue' according to the nurse raised the subject. The mother was also alone in the ambulance with her daughter when she was transferred about 11 pm to the labour ward in another part of the hospital shortly before she signed the refusal form. The judge referred to the 'mother's fervent belief in the sin of blood transfusion' and that Miss T had reached her decision under the influence of her mother, but nonetheless found that Miss T's decision was not vitiated by any undue influence. ... both at law and in equity it has long been recognized that an influence may be subtle, insidious, pervasive and where religious beliefs are involved especially powerful. It may also be powerful between close relatives where one may be in a dominant position vis a vis the other. In this case Miss T had been during her childhood subjected to the religious beliefs of her mother and in her weakened medical condition, in pain, and under the influence of the drugs administered to assist her, the pressure from her mother was likely to have a considerably enhanced effect. I find it difficult to reconcile the facts found by the judge with his conclusion that the influence of the mother did not sap her will or destroy her volition. The degree of pressure to turn persuasion or appeals to affection into undue influence may ... be very little. In my view the trial judge, dealing as he was with a most difficult and distressing case under the necessity to give a decision immediately, did not sufficiently take into account the degree of pressure required to constitute undue influence in the case of a patient in the position of Miss T. I agree with the Master of the Rolls that there is abundant evidence that she was subjected to the undue influence of her mother which vitiated her decision.

Staughton LJ: It is, I think, misleading to ask whether [the patient's refusal] was made of the patient's own free will, or even whether it was voluntary. Every decision is made of a person's free will, and is voluntary, unless it is effected by compulsion. Likewise every decision is made as a result of some influence: a patient's decision to consent to an operation will normally be influenced by the surgeon's advice as to what will happen if the operation does not take place. In order for an apparent consent or refusal of consent to be less than a true consent or refusal, there must be such a degree of external influence as to persuade the patient to depart from her own wishes, to an extent that the law regards it as undue. I can suggest no more precise test than that. The cases on undue influence in the law of property and contract are not, in my opinion, applicable in the different context of consent to medical or surgical treatment. The wife who guarantees her husband's debts, or the widower who leaves all his property to his housekeeper, are not in the same situation as a patient faced with the need for medical treatment. There are many different ways of expressing the concept that what a person says may not be binding upon him: a Greek poet wrote 'my tongue has sworn, but no oath binds my mind'.

As is clear, *Re T* was a case in which a patient refused treatment. Perhaps the court adopted the undue influence approach out of its desire that the patient should not die. In fact, of course, most questions involving voluntariness arise in the converse situation, ie when it appears that the patient consented but the patient asserts that the consent was not freely given. In such a case any resort to the argument that the consent was involuntary would be so as to protect the patient from unwanted treatment. It could be argued that here the courts would be more reluctant to make a finding of involuntariness since to do so would be to render a doctor liable in battery. But, now that the test has been developed, it cannot be limited to refusals only. Of course, since everything turns on the facts, a court may simply prefer to believe 'refusals' are unreliable while being less doubting of 'consents'.

An interesting analysis of consent and the law's approach to vitiating factors can be found in the judgment of La Forest J in the Canadian Supreme Court decision of *Norberg v Wynrib* (1992) 92 DLR (4th) 449. The case concerned the sexual exploitation of a drug-dependent patient by her doctor. While all the judges found for the patient, their analyses differed. Sopinka J relied upon the tort of negligence and McLachlin and L'Heureux-Dubé JJ rested their decision on the fiduciary nature of the relationship (for discussion, see A Grubb 'The Doctor as Fiduciary' [1994] CLP 311 at 318–325 and L Hoyano 'The Flight to the Fiduciary Haven' in *Privacy and Loyalty* (ed) P Birks (1997), 169 at 226–239). Our interest lies in the reliance by LaForest, Gonthier and Cory JJ on the tort of battery.

Norberg v Wynrib (1992) 92 DLR (4th) 449 (Can SC)

A physician prescribed a drug to a patient who was addicted to it in exchange for sexual favours. The patient was convicted of an offence in obtaining double prescriptions from more than one physician. The patient brought an action against the physician for battery, negligence and breach of fiduciary duty. The trial judge found a breach of professional duty, but dismissed the action on the grounds that the plaintiff's addiction did not deprive her of the ability to reason and that consequently her consent to the sexual acts was voluntary. The action in negligence failed at trial because there was no evidence that the plaintiff had suffered physical injury as a result of the prescriptions and because the plaintiff's claim was based on her own illegal and immoral acts. An appeal to the British Columbia Court of Appeal was dismissed.

La Forest J: ... The alleged sexual assault in this case falls under the tort of battery. A battery is the intentional infliction of unlawful force on another person. Consent, express or implied, is a defence to battery. Failure to resist or protest is an indication of consent "if a reasonable person who is aware of the consequences and capable of protest or resistance would voice his objection": see John G Fleming, *The Law of Torts*, 7th ed (Sydney: Law Book Co, 1987), at pp 72–3. However, the consent must be genuine; it must not be obtained by force or threat of force or be given under the influence of drugs. Consent may also be vitiated by fraud or deceit as to the nature of the defendant's conduct. The courts below considered these to be the only factors that would vitiate consent.

In my view, this approach to consent in this kind of case is too limited. As RFV Heuston and RA Buckley, eds, *Salmond and Heuston on the Law of Torts*, 19th ed (London: Sweet & Maxwell, 1987), at pp 564–5, put it: "A man cannot be said to be 'willing' unless he is in a position to choose freely; and freedom of choice predicates the absence from his mind of any feeling of constraint interfering with the freedom of his will." A "feeling of constraint" so as to "interfere with the freedom of a person's will" can arise in a number of situations not involving force, threats of force, fraud or incapacity. The concept of consent as it operates in tort law is based on a presumption of individual autonomy and free will. It is presumed that the individual has freedom to consent or not to consent. This presumption, however, is untenable in certain circumstances. A position of relative weakness can, in some circumstances, interfere with the freedom of a person's will. Our notion of consent must, therefore, be modified to appreciate the power relationship between the parties.

An assumption of individual autonomy and free will is not confined to tort law. It is also the underlying premise of contract law. The supposition of contract law is that two parties agree or consent to a particular course of action. However, contract law has evolved in such a way that it recognizes that contracting parties do not always have equality in their bargaining strength. The doctrines of duress, undue influence, and unconscionability have arisen to protect the vulnerable when they are in a relationship of unequal power. For reasons of public policy, the law will not always hold weaker parties to the bargains they make. Professor George B Klippert in his book *Unjust Enrichment* (Toronto: Butterworths, 1983), refers to the doctrines of duress, undue influence, and unconscionability as "justice factors". He lumps these together under the general term "coercion" and states, at p 156, that "[i]n essence the common thread is an illegitimate use of power or unlawful pressure which vitiates a person's freedom of choice". In a situation where a plaintiff is induced to enter into an unconscionable transaction because of an inequitable disparity in bargaining strength, it cannot be said that the plaintiff's act is voluntary: see Klippert, *op cit*, at p 170.

If the "justice factor" of unconscionability is used to address the issue of voluntariness in the law of contract, it seems reasonable that it be examined to address the issue of voluntariness in the law of tort. This provides insight into the issue of consent: for consent to be genuine, it must be voluntary. The factual context of each case must, of course, be evaluated to determine if there has been genuine consent. However, the principles that have been developed in the area of unconscionable transactions to negate the legal effectiveness of certain contracts provide a useful framework for this evaluation.

An unconscionable transaction arises in contract law where there is an overwhelming imbalance in the power relationship between the parties ...

It may be argued that an unconscionable transaction does not, in fact, vitiate consent; the weaker party retains the power to give real consent but the law nevertheless provides relief on the basis of social policy. This may be more in line with Lord Denning's formulation of "inequality of bargaining power" in *Lloyds Bank Ltd v Bundy, supra,* when one takes into account his statement that it is not necessary to establish that the will of the weaker party was "dominated" or "overcome" by the other party. But whichever way one approaches the problem, the result is the same: on grounds of public policy, the legal effectiveness of certain types of contracts will be restricted or negated. In the same way, in certain situations, principles of public policy will negate the legal effectiveness of consent in the context of sexual assault. In particular, in certain circumstances, consent will be considered legally ineffective if it can be shown that there was such a disparity in the relative positions of the parties that the weaker party was not in a position to choose freely. ...

An ability to "dominate and influence" is not restricted to the student-teacher relationship. Professor Coleman outlines a number of situations which she calls "power dependency" relationships: see Phyllis Coleman, "Sex in Power Dependency Relationships: Taking Unfair Advantage of the 'Fair' Sex", 53 Albany L Rev 95. Included in these relationships are parent-child, psychotherapist-patient, physician-patient, clergy-penitent, professor-student, attorney-client, and employer-employee. She asserts that "consent" to a sexual relationship in such relationships is inherently suspect. She notes, at pp 96–7:

> The common element in power dependency relationships is an underlying personal or professional association which creates a significant power imbalance between the parties ... Exploitation occurs when the "powerful" person abuses the position of authority by inducing the "dependent" person into a sexual relationship, thereby causing harm.

While the existence of one of these special relationships is not necessarily determinative of an overwhelming power imbalance, it will, at least in the ordinary case, be required.

It must be noted that in the law of contracts proof of an unconscionable transaction involves a two-step process: (1) proof of inequality in the positions of the parties, and (2) proof of an improvident bargain. Similarly, a two-step process is involved in determining whether or not there has been legally effective consent to a sexual assault. The first step is undoubtedly proof of an inequality between the parties which, as already noted, will ordinarily occur within the context of a special "power dependency" relationship. The second step, I suggest, is proof of exploitation. A consideration of the type of relationship at issue may provide a strong indication of exploitation. Community standards of conduct may also be of some assistance. ...

If the type of sexual relationship at issue is one that is sufficiently divergent from community standards of conduct, this may alert the court to the possibility of exploitation.

Application to this case

The trial judge held that the appellant's implied consent to the sexual activity was voluntary. Dr Wynrib, he stated, exercised neither force nor threats of force and the appellant's capacity to consent was not impaired by her drug use. The Court of Appeal agreed that the appellant voluntarily engaged in the sexual encounters. However, it must be asked if the appellant was truly in a position to make a free choice. It seems clear to me that there was a marked inequality in the respective powers of the parties. The appellant was a young woman with limited education. More important, she was addicted to the heavy use of tranquillizers and pain-killers. On this ground alone it can be said that there was an inequality in the position of the parties arising out of the appellant's need. The appellant's drug dependence diminished her ability to make a real choice. Although she did not wish to engage in sexual activity with Dr Wynrib, her reluctance was overwhelmed by the driving force of her addiction and the unsettling prospect of a painful, unsupervised chemical withdrawal ...

In this case, Dr Wynrib knew that the appellant was vulnerable and driven by her compulsion for drugs. It is likely that he knew or at least strongly suspected that she was dependent upon Fiorinal before she admitted her addiction to him. It was he who ferreted out that she was addicted to drugs ...

The respondent's medical knowledge and knowledge of the appellant's addiction, combined with his authority to prescribe drugs, gave him power over her. It was he who suggested the sex-for-drugs arrangement.

However, it must still be asked if there was exploitation. In my opinion there was. Dr Herbert of the Department of Family Practice, Faculty of Medicine, University of British Columbia, expressed the opinion that "a reasonable practitioner would have taken steps to attempt to help Ms Norberg end her addiction by, for example, suggesting drug counselling, or, at the very least, by discontinuing her prescriptions of Fiorinal". However, Dr Wynrib did not use his medical knowledge and expertise to address the appellant's addiction. Instead, he abused his power over her and exploited the information he obtained concerning her weakness to pursue his own personal interests. It seems to me that a sex-for-drugs arrangement initiated by a doctor with his drug addict patient is a relationship which is divergent from what the community would consider acceptable. ...

To summarize, in my view, the defence of consent cannot succeed in the circumstances of this case. The appellant had a medical problem – an addiction to Fiorinal. Dr Wynrib had knowledge of the problem. As a doctor, he had knowledge of the proper medical treatment, and knew she was motivated by her craving for drugs. Instead of fulfilling his professional responsibility to treat the appellant, he used his power and expertise to his own advantage and to her detriment. In my opinion, the unequal power between the parties and the exploitative nature of the relationship removed the possibility of the appellant's providing meaningful consent to the sexual contact ...

Sopinka J disagreed with this reasoning. He concluded that the patient had consented in fact and that unconscionability was a contractual doctrine that led courts to set aside even consensual agreements.

Sopinka J: In assessing the reality of consent and the existence and impact of any of the factors that tend to negate true consent, it is important to take a contextually sensitive approach. In relation to medical procedures, several courts have emphasized the need to consider all relevant surrounding circumstances in assessing whether there was valid consent: see, for example, *Morrow v Royal Victoria Hospital* (1989), 3 CCLT (2d) 87, 35 QAC 259, 18 ACWS (3d) 1009 (CA); *Brushett v Cowan* (1990), 69 DLR (4th) 743, 3 CCLT (2d) 195, 83 Nfld & PEIR 66 (Nfld CA). Such an approach applies equally in other situations. For example, the commentary to §892B, Consent under Mistake, Misrepresentation or Duress, of the American Law Institute's *Restatement of Law of Torts (2d)* (St Paul, Minn: American Law Institute Publishers, 1965–79) states in relation to duress that "[a]ge, sex, mental capacity, the relation of the parties and antecedent circumstances may be relevant".

In my view, these factors must be applied on a case-by-case basis rather than by establishing categories of individuals or relationships with respect to which apparent consent will never or rarely be consider valid. Certain relationships, especially those in which there is a significant imbalance in power or those involving a high degree of trust and confidence may require the trier of fact to be particularly careful in assessing the reality of consent. However, the question of consent in elation to a battery claim is ultimately a factual one that must be determined on the basis of all the circumstances of a particular case ...

The issue then is whether, having regard to the principles which I have stated, there is any basis to set aside the findings of the courts below that the appellant consented to the sexual activity with the respondent. The appellant submits that having regard to her drug addiction and to the respondent's position of influence as her doctor, there was no genuine consent. I will consider each of these factors in turn.

With respect to the appellant's addiction, the trial judge turned his mind to this factor and concluded that although it clearly inspired her willingness to engage in sexual activity, it did not interfere with her ability to reason or her capacity to consent to the sexual activity which took place. He also noted that she was not under the influence of Fiorinal when sexual activity took place. There was evidence to support all of these findings, and I am unwilling to interfere with the trial judge's conclusion on this ground.

With respect to the doctor-patient relationship, as I have already stated, special relationships between the plaintiff and defendant should alert the trier of fact to the possibility that apparent consent is not genuine; however, the existence of a particular relationship is not determinative of the presence or absence of consent. The beneficiary of a fiduciary relationship can still consent to a transaction with the fiduciary but the court will subject such a consent to special scrutiny. There may well be cases in which a doctor, by virtue of his or her status, exercises such control or authority over a patient that the patient's submission will not be considered genuine consent. However, in my view, that cannot be said about this case. The appellant began and continued to participate in the sexual encounters in order to obtain drugs. She acknowledged that she played on the respondent's loneliness in order to continue obtaining prescriptions. While it is clear that the sexual contact was contrary to the appellant's wishes, in my view it cannot be said that it was without her consent. I therefore do not find any basis on which to set aside the conclusion of the courts below on the issue of consent.

This is sufficient, in my view, to dispose of the battery claim. However, since my colleague La Forest J has relied upon the principles relating to unconscionable transactions in addressing the issue of consent, I feel it necessary to explain why I do not find such an approach helpful or appropriate in this context.

As I have emphasized and as LaForest J also observes, the factual context of each case must be evaluated to determine whether there has been genuine consent. La Forest J then reasons that "[i]f the 'justice factor' of unconscionability is used to address the issue of voluntariness in the law of contract, it seems reasonable that it should be examined to address the issue of voluntariness in the law of tort" [*ante*, p 458]. There is, however, a fundamental difference between these two concepts. In the former, the court may refuse to recognize the validity of a transaction voluntarily entered into by reason of the unfair use of power by the strong against the weak. In the latter, the court is asked to saddle a party with damages for a wrong inflicted on the plaintiff. In the latter case, there is no wrong if there was consent. In the former, the issue is not consent but whether it was fairly obtained. The factor of unconscionability would be more appropriate here if the respondent were seeking to enforce the transaction as opposed to defending himself against an allegation that he committed an intentional tort.

Accordingly, the weight of academic and judicial opinion is that the doctrine of unconscionability operates to set aside transactions even though there may have been consent or agreement to the terms of the bargain. It is not that this doctrine vitiates consent but rather that fairness requires that the transaction be set aside notwithstanding consent. ...

Just as discussing the problem of unconscionability in terms of consent obscures the real basis for relief in these contracts cases, importing the principles of unconscionability into the context of a battery claim has the potential to obscure the real question – whether in all the circumstances, the plaintiff actually consented to the touching which constitutes the alleged battery. ...

I therefore do not find the contractual doctrine of unconscionability of assistance in attempting to answer the factual question of whether the appellant consented to sexual contact with the respondent. Furthermore, in my view, the facts of this case are more accurately reflected by acknowledging that the appellant consented to the sexual contact and by considering the respondent's conduct in light of his professional duty towards the appellant. ...

You may think that the reasoning of Sopinka J is more in line with existing legal doctrine and however well intentioned is the analysis offered by La Forest J, it borrows too much from an unrelated area of law to achieve an end that can be reached by adopting reasoning which is less damaging to the internal fabric of the common law (see eg *Taylor v McGillivray* (1993) 110 DLR (4th) 64 (NB QB) and Commentary (1995) 3 Med L Rev 108 (AG). For a discussion of liability for sexual exploitation by doctors, see T Allen 'Civil Liability for Sexual Exploitation in Professional Relationships' (1996) 59 MLR 56).

A further point concerns the issue of voluntaries in an institutional setting, for example, a prison or psychiatric hospital.

Freeman v Home Office (No 2) [1984] QB 524, [1984] 1 All ER 1036 (CA)

By writ of 15 October 1979 the plaintiff, David Freeman, who at all material times was serving a sentence of life imprisonment at HM Prison, Wakefield, claimed damages for assault and for battery and for trespass to the person by the administration to him of certain drugs, namely Stelazin and/or Modecate and/or Serenace by or under the direction of Dr Cedric Melville Xavier, the servant or agent of the defendants, the Home Office and/or certain prison officers at HM Prison, Wakefield, being also servants or agents of the defendants, between in or about September 1972 and in or about December 1972 against the plaintiff's will and/or without his consent. By paragraph 4 of the statement of claim it was alleged that the plaintiff had not consented to the administration of the drugs or any of them and had 'actively resisted it, but was overcome forcibly by the said medical officer and/or prison officers'.

Stephen Brown LJ: Mr Blom-Cooper submits not only should the judge have inferred the absence of consent by reference to the documentary evidence but, furthermore, that it is impossible within the prison context as between a prisoner and a prison medical officer for free and voluntary consent to exist, at least, he added, in the absence of any written consent form. The prison medical officer is not merely a doctor, he is, submits Mr Blom-Cooper, a prison officer within the meaning of the Prison Rules and accordingly is a person who can influence a prisoner's life and his prospects of release on licence. There must inevitably be an atmosphere of constraint upon an inmate in such circumstances. He cited the well-known passage from the judgment of Scott LJ in *Bowater v Rowley Regis Corpn* [1944] KB 476 at 479:

With regard to the doctrine 'volenti non fit injuria' I would add one reflection of a general kind. That general maxim has to be applied with specially careful regard to the varying facts of human affairs and human nature in any particular case just because it is concerned with the intangible factors of mind and will. For the purpose of the rule, it if be a rule, a man cannot be said to be truly 'willing' unless he is in a position to choose freely, and freedom of choice predicates, not only full knowledge of the circumstances on which the exercise of choice is conditioned, so that he may be able to choose wisely, but the absence from his mind of any feeling of constraint so that nothing shall interfere with the freedom of his will.

He also cited the American case of *Kaimowitz v Michigan Department of Mental Health* 42 USLW 2063 (1973) Cir Ct Wayne Co, Mich the decision of a circuit court in the County of Michigan in 1973 which is the subject of a learned article: *Law, Psychiatry and the Mental Health System* (1974), by Alexander Brooks, p 902. the judgment appears in the course of the article. The case concerned an inmate of a state hospital who had been committed to that institution as a criminal sexual psychopath and had signed what was termed an 'informed consent form' to become an experimental subject for experimental surgery and he later withdrew his consent. The court had to consider the nature of a legally adequate 'informed consent'. Although Mr Blom-Cooper recognised that having regard to recent authority 'informed consent' as such does not apply to the law of this country, he nevertheless placed reliance upon a passage of the judgment which appears at p 914 of the article:

We turn now to the third element of an informed consent, that of voluntariness. It is obvious that the most important thing to a large number of involuntarily detained mental patients incarcerated for an unknown length of time, is freedom.

The Nuremberg Standards require that the experimental subjects be so situated as to exercise free power of choice without the intervention of an element of force, fraud, deceit, duress, overreaching, or other ulterior form of constraint or coercion. it is impossible for an involuntarily detained mental patient to be free of ulterior forms of restraint or coercion when his very release from the institution may depend upon his co-operating with the institutional authorities and giving consent to experimental surgery.

At p 915:

Involuntarily confined mental patients live in an inherently coercive institutional environment. Indirect and subtle psychological coercion has profound effect upon the patient population. Involuntarily confined patients cannot reason as equals with the doctors and administrators over whether they should undergo psycho-surgery. They are not able to voluntarily give informed consent because of the inherent inequality in their position.

Mr Blom-Cooper seeks to apply those considerations and that reasoning to the position of the plaintiff in this present case, and he argues that in fact a valid free and voluntary consent cannot be given by a person such as the plaintiff, who is in prison, to a prison medical officer who is an officer of the prison having a disciplinary role in relation to him. Mr Blom-Cooper also drew the court's attention to the statutory provisions of the Mental Health Act 1983 which relate to detained and voluntary patients. The provisions are to be found in sections 57 and 58 of the Act and relate to the question of consent and impose certain statutory safeguards which have to be fulfilled. He submits that a prisoner like the plaintiff is in a similar situation and accordingly that the court should bear in mind such safeguards in considering whether consent is established.

It was Mr Blom-Cooper's intention to argue additionally that even if contrary to his submission a prisoner can give a legally valid consent to treatment by a prison medical officer, such consent must be 'informed consent'. Having regard to the decision of this court in *Sidaway v Board of Governors of the Bethlem Royal Hospital and the Maudsley Hospital* [1984] QB 493, [1984] 1 All ER 1018, in respect of which judgment was delivered on 23 February 1984, it is not open to him to argue that 'informed consent' is a consideration which can be entertained by the courts of this country. Nevertheless, he submitted to the court that in psychiatric treatment the test of consent should be that which is required by sections 57 and 58 of the Mental Health Act 1983.

Although the circumstances and the facts giving rise to the allegations made in this action afford an opportunity for interesting matters of principle and policy to be raised and considered, nevertheless I find myself in complete agreement with the trial judge that the sole issue raised at the trial, that is to say whether the plaintiff had consented to the administration of the drugs injected into his body, was essentially one of fact. The judge considered with care all the evidence, both oral and documentary, and it is clear from his careful judgment that he took into account the various submissions which Mr Blom-Cooper made as to the nature and effect of the documentary evidence and the setting in which the events occurred. The judge said [1984] 2 WLR 130 at 145C-D:

The right approach, in my judgment, is to say that where, in a prison setting, a doctor has the power to influence a prisoner's situation and prospects a court must be alive to the risk that what may appear, on the face of it, to be real consent is not in fact so. I have borne that in mind throughout the case.

Essentially, however, the matter is one of fact. The judge made the positive finding that the plaintiff consented. He rejected Mr Blom-Cooper's submission that the plaintiff was entitled to judgment because he was incapable in law of giving his consent to the treatment by Dr Xavier in question. In my judgment he was right so to do. There was ample evidence to justify his finding of fact and accordingly the decision to which he came. It is not for this court to consider and decide this appeal upon the basis of an alternative and hypothetical set of facts and circumstances.

I would dismiss this appeal.

Sir John Donaldson MR and Fox LJ agreed.

The significance of *Freeman*'s case is that it goes beyond the more obvious proposition that voluntariness turns on the facts, to state a more challenging hypothesis: that what the President's Commission called the 'institutional setting' may make apparent consent valid. In *Freeman* counsel for the plaintiff's argument was that by virtue of his being in prison, Freeman was *ipso facto* incapable of exercising a free choice. The Court of Appeal rejected this, merely commenting that the 'institutional setting' should put doctors and others on notice that they should be especially careful to satisfy themselves that the consent was freely given.

By contrast, in the well-known case of *Kaimowitz v Michigan Department of Mental Health* (1973) 42 USLW 2063 the Michigan Circuit Court saw the institutional setting as crucial.

Kaimowitz v Michigan Department of Mental Health (1973) 42 USLW 2063 (Mich Cir Ct)

We turn now to the third element of informed consent, that of voluntariness. It is obvious that the most important thing to a large number of involuntarily detained mental patients incarcerated for an unknown length of time, is freedom.

The Nuremberg Standards require that the experimental subjects be so situated as to exercise free power of choice without the intervention of an element of force, fraud, deceit, duress, overreaching, or other *ulterior form of constraint or coercion*. It is impossible for an involuntarily detained mental patient to be free of ulterior forms of restraint or coercion when his very release from the institution may depend upon his co-operating with the institutional authorities and giving consent to experimental surgery.

As pointed out in the testimony in this case, John Doe consented to this psycho-surgery partly because of his effort to show the doctors in the hospital that he was a co-operative patient. Even Dr Yudashkin, in his testimony, pointed out that involuntarily confined patients tend to tell their doctors what the patient thinks these people want to hear.

The inherently coercive atmosphere to which the involuntarily detained mental patient is subjected has bearing upon the voluntariness of his consent.

Involuntarily confined mental patients live in an inherently coercive institutional environment. Indirect and subtle psychological coercion has a profound effect upon the patient population. Involuntarily confined patients cannot reason as equals with the doctors and administrators over whether they should undergo psycho-surgery. They are not able to voluntarily give informed consent because of the inherent inequality in their position.

Footnote: It should be emphasised that once John Doe was released in this case and returned to the community he withdrew all consent to the performance of the proposed experiment. His withdrawal of consent under these circumstances should be compared with his response on January 12, 1973, to questions placed to him by Prof Slovenko, one of the members of the Human Rights Committee. These answers are part of exhibit 22 and were given after extensive publicity about this case, and while John Doe was in Lafayette Clinic waiting the implantation of depth electrodes. The significant questions and answers are as follows:

1. Would you seek psycho-surgery if you were not confined in an institution?
A. Yes, if after testing this showed it would be of help.
2. Do you believe that psycho-surgery is a way to obtain your release from the institution?
A. No, but it would be a step in obtaining my release. It is like any other therapy or program to help persons to function again.
3. Would you seek psycho-surgery if there were other ways to obtain your release?
A. Yes, if psycho-surgery were the only means of helping my physical problem after a period of testing.

You may think that neither *Kaimowitz* or *Freeman* is entirely satisfactory. In *Kaimowitz* the court could be said to have been over-protective. In *Freeman* it could be said that the court dismissed the argument that the 'institutional setting' deprived him of his free will too readily.

D. MISTAKE

1. As to capacity

What if a doctor reaches a view concerning a patient's competence that is objectively unjustified on the evidence and then goes on to act on the purported consent of the patient to treat him? What if any cause of action would lie against the doctor? For example, what if a doctor in good faith, but wrongly, should determine that an elderly confused patient agrees to treatment?

Obviously if there were an action it is important to establish which action, that is negligence or battery, since in the later action a patient would not need to prove, in order to maintain the action, that he had suffered injury as a result of the doctor's conduct. Whichever action can be brought, there is no doubt that any mistake made by the doctor must be reasonable before the law will (if at all) excuse him. An *unreasonable mistake* would seem to give rise *prima facie* to a negligence action and *a fortiori* would not excuse the doctor even if battery was relied upon (*Fletcher v Fletcher* (1859) 1 E & E 420).

Let us therefore assume we are only concerned with *reasonable* mistakes. Deciding which action may be brought is by no means simple: the difficulty lies in whether the mistaken view of the doctor is as to a matter of fact or of opinion; ie that whether a patient is competent or not is a matter exclusively of fact or one of opinion. If it is a mistake of fact, then on first principles an action in battery would lie since mistake is not ordinarily a defence to such an intentional tort (see *John Lewis & Co Ltd v Tims* [1952] AC 676). There are however exceptions where a mistake may be a defence. For example, a policeman making an arrest in the mistaken belief, based on reasonable grounds, that a crime has been committed, would at common law quite apart from statute be excused.

Since the House of Lords' decision in *Re F (mental patient: sterilisation)* [1990] 2 AC 1, the doctor will have a defence based upon necessity if on the facts the treatment was in the incompetent patient's best interests. Of course, *Re F* would not apply in the converse position where the doctor decides in good faith that a patient is *incompetent* when this is not so. *Prima facie* the law in these circumstances would consider the doctor to have committed a battery if he treats the patient in the face of a refusal. In *Re T* Staughton LJ stated:

> Some will say that, when there is doubt whether an apparent refusal of consent is valid in circumstances of urgent necessity, the decision of a doctor acting in good faith ought to be conclusive ... However, I cannot find authority that the decision of a doctor as to the existence or refusal of consent is sufficient protection, if the law subsequently decides otherwise. So the medical profession, in the future as in the past, must bear the responsibility unless it is possible to obtain a decision from the courts.

If, by contrast, in law the mistaken view of the doctor as to the patient's understanding is regarded as relating to a matter of *opinion*, assuming the doctor acts in good faith, then the answer may be different. Will the law excuse the doctor from liability in battery when he has formed a judgment which is mistaken, in that the consensus of informed opinion is otherwise? On grounds of public policy it may be desirable that the law should recognise a legal excuse for the doctor in these circumstances.

That the law should as a matter of policy recognise that a doctor should have a defence of mistake, is illustrated by section 2(4) of the Age of Legal Capacity (Scotland) Act 1991.

> s 2(4) A person under the age of 16 years shall have legal capacity to consent on his own behalf to any surgical, medical or dental procedure or treatment where, *in the opinion of* a qualified medical practitioner attending him, he is capable of understanding the nature and possible consequences of the procedure or treatment (emphasis added).

As is clear this provision was intended by the Scottish Law Commission precisely to cover the case in which a doctor makes a wrong but honest assessment of a child's capacity (see the report on the Legal Capacity and Responsibility of Minors and Pupils (No 110), 1988, paras 3.72–3.77). Indeed, section 2(4) may go even further than we would anticipate the common law to go by excusing even an unreasonable but honest mistake. (Notice the Law Commission in its Report, *Mental Incapacity* (No 231) (March 1995) proposes that only if the mistake is reasonable would the doctor have an excuse: see, Draft Mental Incapacity Bill, cl 4(1).)

2. As to information

Here we are concerned with the situation in which a doctor is mistaken as to the extent (if at all) to which a patient is informed or understands the information. It is important here to differentiate between a doctor's possible liability in battery and in negligence.

As for *battery*, if the patient is not informed about, or does not understand, the 'nature and purpose' of the procedure, on the face of it the doctor should be liable in battery since the touching of the patient is not consented to even though the doctor thinks it is. However, an exception to this may be the circumstances where, as Lord Diplock put it in *Sidaway*, 'the patient is estopped from denying that he possessed the relevant information, because he so acted towards the defendant as to lead the latter reasonably to assume the relevant information was known to him' ([1985] 1 All ER 643 at 658).

As for *negligence*, the position of the doctor is explored by Professor Margaret Somerville.

Margaret Somerville 'Structuring the Issues in Informed Consent' (1981) 26 McGill LJ 740

> Must the patient understand the information given by the physician in order to give consent or informed consent? This question was raised in *Kelly v Hazlett* [(1976) 75 DLR (3d) 536] and was dealt with separately in relation to battery and negligence.
>
> The plaintiff-patient, in that case, had been given 100 mg of pethidine just before she purportedly gave consent. In relation to battery-avoiding consent the judge did not believe
>
> > that it could be suggested otherwise than that the giving of the consent under such circumstances, at the very least, leaves the validity of the consent upon to question ... and that it would be incumbent on the defendant to prove affirmatively that the effect of this sedation probably did not adversely affect the patient's understanding *of the basic nature of the contemplated operation.*
>
> In other words, the surgeon must show
>
> > that the combination of sedation, and ... [the patient's] labile condition, had not blotted the information from her mind, respecting the basic nature and character of the operation when she made her demand. In such circumstances he has shown a sufficient consent to avoid liability on the basis of battery.
>
> But, if the plaintiff
>
> > did not know the basic nature of the operation ... and ... all she was asking for was a result *not a procedure, and she manifested this lack of knowledge to the defendant, then*

*her apparent consent to the operation, notwithstanding her clear desire for the result,
would be ineffective.*

In other words, if the doctor *knows* or if he ought to know that the plaintiff does not understand
the basic nature of the operation, the doctor is, in the absence of other justification, liable in
battery if he performs the operation. Moreover, proof of battery-avoiding consent by the physician
will require proof of the necessary degree of understanding of the information by the patient.

With respect to the patient's understanding of any collateral risks that the physician must
disclose in order to avoid liability in negligence, the defendant surgeon in *Kelly v Hazlett*
admitted that he 'could sense that ... [the plaintiff] was *not understanding* what ... [he] was
attempting to communicate with her by words'. That is, in this particular case, the surgeon
had subjective knowledge of the patient's lack of understanding. The Court held that it is the
doctor's 'duty to be satisfied that ... [the risk] had been brought home to the patient before
he could reasonably regard her apparent consent as being valid.' The consent needed to avoid
liability in negligence, that is the consent required in relation to collateral risks, 'involves
both *awareness* and assent'. However, 'it would be quite unreasonable, and the law does not
call for it, to expect the doctor to see into the mind of the patient to satisfy himself that the
patient not only understands the risks but also puts the degree of emphasis on them which the
doctor considers to be reasonable'.

Although the remarks of the Court in *Kelly v Hazlett* in both the battery and negligence
contexts could be read as requiring actual subjective understanding by the patient of the
disclosed information, it is clear that this is not he case, as the physician may rely on the
patient's consent if he could reasonably have thought at that time that she was aware of the
basic nature and character of the special risks of the operation. Hence the physician may rely
on the patient's consent if it is given pursuant to *apparent subjective understanding* by the
patient of the information disclosed. It is submitted that this is the most satisfactory approach.
A fully subjective standard requiring actual understanding by the patient is too onerous for
physicians and may not be in the best interests of patients, as the patient may not want to
understand the information, or to make the intellectual effort to understand it, or have the
physician bothering him to ensure that he does understand. Thus a physician may rely on the
consent of a patient as a defence to an action in battery if the physician shows that a reasonable
physician in those circumstances would have thought that this patient apparently understood the
basic nature and character of the operation, provided, always, that the particular physician had no
subjective knowledge that this patient did not understand. When a patient sues in negligence for
breach of a physician's duty to inform him and alleges that the breach consists in the physician's
failure to ensure that he, the patient, understood the information, the plaintiff-patient must
prove on the balance of probabilities that a reasonable patient in the same circumstances as
those in which the plaintiff found himself would not have understood the information communicated
to him, or that he did not understand the information, and the physician knew this.

This approach can be examined in view of *Reibl v Hughes*. At the trial level the test of
when the requirement of understanding of information by the patient will be fulfilled was
formulated in different terms with respect to battery and negligence. It was held that 'the law
of battery in effect places on a physician a strict duty to explain to his patient, in language
which the patient can *understand*, the essential nature and quality of the treatment he is to
undergo'. To avoid negligence liability, on the other hand, the doctor must have 'take[n]
sufficient care to convey to the plaintiff and *assure* that the plaintiff *understood* the gravity,
nature and extent of risks specifically attendant on the [procedure']. It is not exactly clear
what standard of care is being required of the physician here in order to avoid negligence
liability for non-disclosure, but it seems to vacillate between one of taking all reasonable
means that a reasonable physician would take to ensure understanding and one of actually
requiring that this result be achieved. In comparison, it is much clearer that actual
understanding by the patient of the information is necessary to obtain battery-avoiding consent.

This approach should be contrasted with that of the majority of the Court of Appeal in the
same case. In discussing whether the patient understood the *purpose* for which the surgery
was being undertaken, a matter which would relate to battery-avoiding consent, it was held
that '[i]f as the patient said, the doctor did his best to tell him about the surgery, and the
patient had some difficulty in understanding it, there was some obligation to have told the
doctor what troubled him'. The approach is acceptable to the extent that it maintains that the
test for validity of the patient's consent, as far as non-understanding of information is
concerned, should be determined in the absence of subjective knowledge on the part of the
physician that the patient does not understand, on the basis of whether the reasonable physician,
taking all the circumstances into account, would have thought the patient understood. But, to
the extent that it establishes only an obligation on the physician to ensure understanding by
the patient if the patient expressly indicates that he does not understand, it should not be
accepted. To make the content of the physician's duty depend on the patient fulfilling some
obligation, such as asking questions,

may overlook the power and status differential in the doctor-patient relationship. From a practical point of view, such a power imbalance both makes the patient less likely to ask questions or to understand what he is told and makes him reluctant to disclose this to the doctor. Further, the patient may not even know enough to ask appropriate questions, or to know he does not understand the answers, or he may be too emotionally upset to realize this.

The proposed test requiring 'apparent understanding' of information by the patient avoids such difficulties, as it would require the physician to assess at least, as a reasonable doctor would, whether the patient apparently understands the information he has been given, and to act accordingly.

More recently Professor Robertson has observed that some Canadian courts have imposed 'a potentially onerous duty' on a doctor.

Robertson, 'Informed Consent Ten Years Later: The Impact of *Reibl v Hughes*' (1991) 70 Canadian Bar Review 424

There is … some indication of courts interpreting *Reibl v Hughes* as requiring physicians to satisfy themselves that the patient understands the information which is given, a potentially onerous duty in light of studies which indicate that many patients understand little of what their doctors tell them and remember even less. For example, in finding a surgeon liable for failing to disclose material risk to a 75-year-old patient, the trial judge in *Kellett v Griesdale* commented that [(BCS Ct) 26 June 1985, unreported]:

It may very well be that the defendant gave a warning but, if so, it did not make a sufficient impression on the plaintiff. The defendant was aware of the problem I mentioned earlier about patients tending to push aside any considerations of risk. That being so, *it was incumbent on him to ensure that the plaintiff clearly understood the risk of significant hearing loss* …

Likewise, in *Schanczl v Singh* [[1988] 2 WWR 465] the Alberta Court of Queen's Bench imposed liability on a physician for failure to disclose material risks, and in so doing emphasized the plaintiff's difficulty in understanding English. The court stated that this difficulty 'placed a special duty on … [the defendant] to be certain that his patient understood the alternatives available to him'.

This latter view has now been approved by the Canadian Supreme Court in *Ciarlariello v Schacter* (1993) 100 DLR (4th) 609 at 622–623 per Cory J (: 'the doctor had the duty to ensure that he was understood'). There is no English case law which addresses this specific point (but notice *Smith v Tunbridge Wells HA* [1994] 5 Med LR 334 at 339 per Morland J). Michael Jones in his book, *Medical Negligence* (2nd edn 1996) at para 6.102 argues as follows:

The doctor does not have to make the patient understand; it is a duty to make a reasonable effort to communicate information to the patient. It is not an answer, however, for the doctor to say that he does not have the time to give seminars in medicine or that the information is too complicated or technical for the patient to understand. The duty must be to give an explanation in terms which are reasonably comprehensible to a layman, although there can be no guarantee that the patient will in fact understand the information. Where it is quite apparent to the doctor that the patient has not understood he may have to make further efforts. The Canadian courts, for example, have taken the view that where the patient has language difficulties the doctor is under a special duty to be sure that the patient has understood.

The scope of the duty in English law was considered by the Court of Appeal in *Lybert v Warrington HA* [1996] 7 Med LR 71. The plaintiff underwent a sterilisation but subsequently gave birth to a healthy child after the procedure reversed itself. She claimed she had not been advised of this risk and that was negligent. The Court of Appeal upheld the trial judge's finding in favour of the plaintiff. In the course of his judgment Otton LJ stated:

In my judgment there was a duty upon those responsible for the conduct of this unit to ensure that there was a proper and effective system for giving a proper warning at some stage during her time as a patient. Ideally this warning should be oral and in writing and could have been given on her admission, or before she agreed to the sterilization, or before her discharge.

There was evidence upon which the judge was entitled to come to the conclusion that a sufficiently clear and comprehensible warning was never given. She denied that she was warned. The plaintiff and her husband had impressed the judge both with their honesty and integrity. He believed her. He accepted that they were genuinely concerned about the risk of conception by reason of their previous history, which included three caesarian sections, the agreement to a hysterectomy and the failure of the conventional sheath method of contraception while waiting for the hysterectomy. Thus, in my view, there was an inherent likelihood that they would have heeded a proper warning. Conversely, there was an inherent unlikelihood that they would have ignored or forgotten such a warning had it been given. There was also an inherent likelihood that, if so advised or warned, they would have agreed to use conventional contraception in the interim period before the hysterectomy. The learned judge (at page 23) said:

> I have come to the firm conclusion on the balance of probabilities, but to a degree going beyond the mere balance, that the plaintiff would not, if she had been properly counselled and warned before or after the operation, have engaged thereafter in unprotected sex.

> Thus I am satisfied that a proper inference could be drawn from the evidence that no reasonable or proper warning was given at any stage to the plaintiff or her husband. I can find no basis for setting aside the finding of fact that such a warning was not given and substituting a finding that it was, or that the warning which the judge found was given was a discharge of the duty of care of the defendants.

The Court of Appeal's decision confirms that a doctor may breach his duty of care to a patient even though he advises or warns the patient, if he does so in an unreasonable way. The law, therefore, requires not only that in a given set of circumstances particular information should be provided to a patient prior to, or as part of, medical treatment but also that the doctor must take *reasonable* steps to ensure that the information is *adequate* in scope, content and presentation to convey the risks of, (or alternatives to), the treatment; is *intelligible* to the particular patient having regard to the circumstances of that patient; and is *understood* by the patient. But, the doctor's legal duty is one of *reasonableness* and no more.

3. As to voluntariness

Where it is alleged that the doctor was mistaken that the patient's consent (or refusal) was freely given, the legal analysis mirrors that which we saw above in relation to mistakes concerning a patient's capacity.

E. LIMITS ON CONSENT

The final question to be addressed in an analysis of the law relating to consent is whether the law places any limits on what a competent person may consent to (see generally, *Principles of Medical Law* (eds) I Kennedy and A Grubb (1998 OUP), paras 3.28–3.33). Lord Griffiths in *Re F*, a case concerned with the sterilisation of a mentally incapacitated adult woman (discussed *infra*, ch 9), states the nature of the inquiry.

Re F (mental patient: sterilisation) [1990] 2 AC 1, (1989) 4 BMLR 1 (HL)

Lord Griffiths: I cannot agree that it is satisfactory to leave this grave decision with all its social implications in the hands of those having the care of the patient with only the expectation that they will have the wisdom to obtain a declaration of lawfulness before the operation is performed. In my view the law ought to be that they must obtain the approval of the court before they sterilise a woman incapable of giving consent and that it is unlawful to sterilise without that consent. I believe that it is open to your Lordships to develop a common law rule to this effect. Although the general rule is that the individual is the master of his own fate the judges through the common law have, in the public interest, imposed certain constraints on the harm that people may consent to being inflicted on their own bodies. Thus although boxing is a legal sport a bare knuckle prize fight in which more grievous injury may be inflicted is unlawful (*R v Coney* (1882) 8 QBD 534), and so is fighting which may result in actual bodily harm: see *A-G's Reference (No 6 of 1980)* [1981] QB 715. So also is it unlawful to consent to the infliction of serious injury on the body in the course of the practice of sexual perversion: *R v Donovan* [1934] 2 KB 498. Suicide was unlawful at common law until Parliament intervened by the Suicide Act 1961.

The common law has, in the public interest, been developed to forbid the infliction of injury on those who are fully capable of consenting to it. The time has now come for a further development to forbid, again in the public interest, the sterilisation of a woman with healthy reproductive organs who, either through mental incompetence or youth, is incapable of giving her fully informed consent unless such an operation has been inquired into and sanctioned by the High Court. Such a common law rule would provide a more effective protection than the exercise of parens patriae jurisdiction which is dependent upon some interested party coming forward to invoke the jurisdiction of the court. The parens patriae jurisdiction is in any event now only available in the case of minors through their being made wards of court. I would myself declare that on grounds of public interest an operation to sterilise a woman incapable of giving consent either on grounds of age or mental incapacity is unlawful if performed without the consent of the High Court. I fully recognise that in so doing I would be making new law. However the need for such a development has been identified in a number of recent cases and in the absence of any Parliamentary response to the problem it is my view that the judges can and should accept responsibility to recognise the need and to adapt the common law to meet it. If such a development did not meet with public approval it would always be open to Parliament to reverse it or to alter it by perhaps substituting for the opinion of the High Court judge the second opinion of another doctor as urged by counsel for the Mental Health Tribunal.

In *A-G's Reference (No 6 of 1980)* [1981] 2 All ER 1057, Lord Lane CJ, speaking for the court, held:

We think that it can be taken as a starting point it is an essential element of an assault that the act is done contrary to the will and without the consent of the victim: and it is doubtless for this reason that the burden lies on the prosecution to negative consent. Ordinarily, then, if the victim consents, the assailant is not guilty.

… The question is: at what point does the public interest require the court to hold otherwise?

… The answer to this question, in our judgment, is that it is not in the public interest that people should try to cause or should cause each other actual bodily harm for no good reason.

However, Lord Lane then went on:

Nothing which we have said is intended to cast doubt on the accepted legality of properly conducted games and sports, lawful chastisement or correction, *reasonable surgical interference*, dangerous exhibitions etc. These apparent exceptions can be justified as involving the exercise of a legal right, in the case of chastisement or correction, or as needed in the public interest, in the other cases [our emphasis].

Presumably, Lord Lane would include *any* medical intervention, surgical or otherwise, which might otherwise constitute a battery.

What then is the explanation for this medical exception to the general rule? In *Airedale NHS Trust v Bland* [1993] 1 All ER 821, Lord Mustill (at 889) offered the following view.

1. *Consent to bodily invasion.* Any invasion of the body of one person by another is potentially both a crime and a tort. At the bottom end of the scale consent is a defence both to a charge of common assault and to a claim in tort. … How is it that, consistently with [this proposition] … a doctor can with immunity perform on a consenting patient an act which would be a very serious crime if done by someone else? The answer must be that bodily invasions in the course of proper medical treatment stand completely outside the criminal law. The reason why the consent of the patient is so important is not that it furnishes a defence in itself, but because it is usually essential to the propriety of medical treatment. Thus, if the consent is absent, and is not dispensed with in special circumstances by operation of law, the acts of the doctor lose their immunity.

Lord Mustill makes the question turn upon whether the touching amounts to 'proper medical treatment'. With respect, of course, this may not take us very far. It still leaves open the central question of what is 'proper' and what constitutes 'medical treatment' (ie who decides).

If these judicial pronouncements do not take us very far, let us turn to the views of Professor Glanville Williams.

G Williams *Textbook of Criminal law* (2nd edn 1983)

... the validity of consent to harm is a grey area in the law. It is sufficiently uncertain to have given rise to the opinion that the judges have a commission to pronounce upon the legality of all forms of surgery; and certainly the pronouncement in *A-G's Reference*, conferring the benediction of the judges on 'reasonable surgical interference', seems to confirm that opinion. In practice, of course, the courts would find in favour of such 'interference', if the question ever arose, almost as a matter of routine.

There have been doubts about sterilisation 'of convenience', ie as a form of birth control. However, medical practice came to accept the operation after counsel advised the BMA that it might be performed without fear of legal repercussions. For some time there was less certainty about castration, which, unlike sterilisation, is a de-sexing operation. It may occasionally be recommended as the only way of obtaining relief from abnormalities in the sexual urge, and in these cases the judges would certainly regard it as lawful. Moreover, the so-called sex-change operation has come to be accepted as lawful. A change from male to pseudo-female sex organs involves castration: the penis and testicles are removed and a pseudo-vagina constructed from the scrotum. Now castration was regarded as a maim at common law, because it was thought to reduce the will to fight. Yet the male-'female' sex-change is performed openly by reputable surgeons. If the issue were raised, the operation could be supported as conducive to the patient's mental health; and Ormrod J [in *Corbett v Corbett* [1971] P 83] accepted its legality on this ground. Again, no one has ever doubted the legality of the operation of prefrontal leucotomy, which, by severing the frontal lobes of the brain, changes the personality of the patient in certain cases of mental illness. Therapy also gives moral support to some cosmetic surgery, but not all. The justification for padding bosoms, chiselling noses, and restoring hymens lost in premarital encounters, is that the patient is pleased and it may be socially or maritally advantageous, rather than that the operation is a psychiatric necessity.

A more serious interference with the body is in taking an organ for transplant, such as a kidney. Nevertheless, no serious legal doubts have been expressed about such operations upon adult donors, where a paired organ is surrendered for the benefit of another.

It may be questioned whether the criminal law has any acceptable place in controlling operations performed by qualified practitioners upon adults of sound mind with their consent ...

In a civil case relating to an operation changing a male to a pseudo-female, Ormrod J said:

There is obviously room for differences of opinion on the ethical aspects of such operations but, if they are undertaken for genuine therapeutic purposes, it is a matter for the decision of the patient and the doctors concerned in his case. the passing of section 1 of the Sexual Offences Act 1967 seems to have removed any legal objections which there might have been to such procedures [*Corbett v Corbett* (otherwise Ashley) [1971] P 83 at 99].

There is no reason why the same view should not be taken for all medical procedures, assuming that the patient has capacity to consent. The law would still play a part in determining legal capacity in the case of the young and the mentally abnormal.

If this is so, the only threat presented by the law in respect of operations on the body is to those who are not medically qualified.

Professor Skegg after discussing the 'medical exception' referred to in the *A-G's Reference* offers the following analysis of the limits of consent.

P D G Skegg *Law, Ethics and Medicine* (1984)

Many touchings which occur in the course of medical practice do not involve 'any hurt or injury calculated to interfere with health or comfort'. In these cases, consent can prevent liability in battery, even if there is 'no good reason' for the touching. Surgery, and some other medical procedures, could be said to involve 'hurt or injury calculated to interfere with health or comfort' in a manner which is 'more than merely transient and trifling'. As has already been suggested, conduct which benefits bodily health should not be regarded as causing bodily harm. But even if it were regarded as causing bodily harm, there could be absolutely no doubt that it was possible to give a legally effective consent to such procedures. There is clearly a good reason for them.

Sometimes medical procedures which were intended to benefit the patient will fail in their object, and will cause what is undoubtedly bodily harm. If an application of force was not intended to cause bodily harm, then the undesired consequence should not render ineffective consent which would otherwise have been effective. In the course of medical practice there is often good reason to attempt to benefit a patient's health, even though there is a risk of harm resulting. Here, too, consent will undoubtedly prevent liability being incurred.

Some medical procedures are not intended to benefit the person on whom they are performed. Indeed, sometimes a procedure is performed on a person in the knowledge that it will certainly be to that person's bodily detriment. This is the case when a kidney is removed from a healthy person, for transplantation into someone who is in need of it. The operation is a major one, and is not without risks. But it is not unreasonably dangerous, and the probable benefit to the recipient far outweighs the probable detriment to the donor. Hence, if called upon to deal with a case in which a kidney had been removed from a consenting adult, for transplantation into someone in need of it, the courts may confidently be expected to take the view that the operation did not amount to the offence of battery. Even though the operation causes serious bodily harm, there is clearly a good reason for it. There is also a good reason for some non-therapeutic medical experimentation, even if it may cause bodily harm.

Where judges regard an activity as socially acceptable they are unlikely to question the reasons for it. In the *A-G's Reference (No 6 of 1980)* the court spoke of the 'accepted legality' of properly conducted games and sports, of dangerous exhibitions, and of 'reasonable surgical interference'. The need for these 'apparent exceptions' only arises where an application of force is intended to cause, or does in fact cause, bodily harm. As the Court of Appeal was prepared to accept that dangerous exhibitions are needed in the public interest, it would be extraordinary if a later court took a restrictive view of the scope of permissible medical interventions. A court is not likely to inquire closely into whether there are good reasons for a particular intervention. There is no danger of a court attempting to decide whether there were good reasons for removing a kidney from a living donor, instead of keeping the patient on dialysis in the hope that a suitable cadaver kidney would become available. And there is now very little danger of a court seeking to manipulate the offence of battery so as to prevent individuals reaching their own decisions about whether to be sterilised, or undergo cosmetic surgery. Opinions vary as to the desirability of such operations in particular circumstances, but it is doubtful whether judges would regard these operations as sufficiently against the public interest to warrant their being regarded as constituting the offence of battery, despite the presence of consent.

Were a patient to consent to having his limbs amputated, for no good reason, his consent would not prevent the amputation from amounting to the offence of battery. But the judges' insistence that there are some applications of force to which consent cannot be given, for the purpose of the offence of battery, should not hinder modern medical practice.

One long-standing limit to consent is to be found in the ancient crime of mayhem (maim). Stephen in his *Digest of the Criminal Law* (1878) defines the crime of maim as follows (p 145):

A maim is bodily harm whereby a man is deprived of the use of any member of his body, or of any sense which he can use in fighting, or by the loss of which he is generally and permanently weakened; but bodily injury is not a maim merely because it is a disfigurement.

Does this affect the practice of medicine? Professor Skegg (*op cit*) argues as follows (pp 43–46):

In practice, the common law offence of maim has long been supplanted by statutory offences. But it has not been expressly abolished, and a judge has made an extrajudicial statement which suggests that there is at least a theoretical possibility of the offence of maim applying to operations in which a kidney is removed from a healthy living donor, for transplantation into a person who is in need of it [R Ormrod 'Medical Ethics' (1968) 2 BMJ 7 at 9]. It is therefore desirable to consider the extent to which the offence of maim would apply to medical procedures, and the related issue of whether consent would be effective to prevent liability.

The [institutional] authorities have long distinguished between acts which permanently disable and weaken a man, rendering him less able in fighting; and acts which simply disfigure. The former are maims, the latter are not. There is no shortage of examples of injuries which fall within one category rather than the other. Over many centuries, it has been agreed that it is a maim to cut off, disable, or weaken an arm or foot. It has also been agreed that it is a maim to deprive a man of an eye, foretooth, or 'those parts, the loss of which in all animals abates their courage' [4 BL Com 205]. However, it has also long been accepted that it is not a maim to cut off an ear or nose, as such injuries are said not to affect a man's capacity for fighting, ...

Most medical procedures do not permanently disable a person and render that person less able in fighting. They therefore fall outside even the potential scope of any offence of maim. This is as true of the removal of a healthy kidney for transplantation as it is of the removal of a diseased appendix. But even if a medical procedure did come within the potential scope of an offence of maim, it would not follow that a doctor would commit an offence of maim in going ahead with it. Just as the infliction of maim was sometimes permitted in self-defence, so a maiming operation would not amount to the offence of maim if there was a good reason for it. Hence, even if castration could still be regarded as coming within the potential scope of maim, it would be justified if performed for a therapeutic purpose.

The offence of maim would very rarely apply to any procedure performed in the course of medical practice, even if consent had not been given. But if something was done which did come within the potential scope of maim – as where a member of the armed forces persuaded a friend to cut off his trigger finger for him, in an attempt to obtain a discharge – consent would normally be irrelevant.

(In *R v Brown* [1993] 2 All ER 75, Lord Mustill (dissenting) stated that the crime of maim was now 'obsolete' (at 106) and, in any event, was no part of English Law since it had been omitted from the crimes of violence in the Offences Against the Person Act 1861. The other Law Lords did not regard the key to the limits of consent to be contained within the four corners of the crime of maim.)

An example of a medical intervention which tests the limits of the law is gender reassignment surgery.

Gender reassignment operations are now available within the National Health Service (see eg *North West Lancashire Health Authority v A, D and G* (1999) 53 BMLR 148 (CA)). Their legality was probable established by the case of *Corbett v Corbett (otherwise Ashley)* [1970] 2 All ER 33. Although this case concerned the validity of a purported marriage between a man and another who had undergone a gender reassignment operation and so the legality of the operation did not specifically arise, Ormrod J clearly did not regard it as unlawful. He said (at p 43):

> There is, obviously, room for differences of opinion on the ethical aspects of such operations but, if they are undertaken for genuine therapeutic purposes, it is a matter for the decision of the patient and the doctors concerned in his case. The passing of the Sexual Offences Act 1967, s 1, seems to have removed any legal objections which there might have been to such procedures.

His reference to the Sexual Offences Act 1967 is, perhaps, a little curious since this legalises sexual intercourse between consenting male adults over the age of 21. Since then, however, public policy, and the legality of the procedure, have never been questioned again (eg *R v Tan* [1983] QB 1053 (CA), *Rees v United Kingdom* [1987] 2 FLR 111 (ECtHR) and *Cossey v United Kingdom* (1990) 13 EHRR 622 (ECtHR)).

In addition to the common law there are examples of statutes which limit consent. One such statute is the Prohibition of Female Circumcision Act 1985.

Prohibition of Female Circumcision Act 1985

1. (1) Subject to section 2 below, it shall be an offence for any person –
   (a) to excise, infibulate or otherwise mutilate the whole or any part of the labia majora or labia minora or clitoris of another person; or
   (b) to aid, abet, counsel or procure the performance by another person of any of those acts on that other person's own body.
2. (1) Subsection (1)(a) of section 1 shall not render unlawful the performance of a surgical operation if that operation –
   (a) is necessary for the physical or mental health of the person on whom it is performed and is performed by a registered medical practitioner; or
   (b) is performed on a person who is in any stage of labour or has just given birth and if so performed for purposes connected with that labour or birth by –

(i)   a registered medical practitioner or a registered midwife; or

(ii) a person undergoing a course of training with a view to becoming a registered medical practitioner or a registered midwife.

(2) In determining for the purposes of this section whether an operation is necessary for the health of a person, no account shall be taken of the effect on that person of any belief on the part of that or any other person that the operation is required as a matter of custom or ritual.

You will notice section 2(1)(a). Does this give the clue as to what separates the permissible from the impermissible, ie touching is permissible when it is intended to benefit the person in a therapeutic context and is done by a doctor? The insistence that the touching must be by a doctor does not mean that Parliament has endorsed the view that anything done by doctors is *ipso facto* 'proper medical treatment'. Rather, Parliament has accepted that the involvement of a doctor is a necessary though not a sufficient condition for legitimising certain kinds of touching.

In *R v Brown* [1993] 2 All ER 75, the House of Lords examined the extent to which an individual could consent to physical interference by another. Regardless of their differences over the law relating to violence, their Lordships agreed that surgical (*semble* medical) treatment is justified in law provided it is consented to or is otherwise justified in law.

In its Consultation Paper, *Consent in the Criminal Law*, No 139 (1995), the Law Commission proposed putting the 'medical exemption' on a statutory basis.

8.50 We therefore provisionally propose that –

(1)   a person should not be guilty of an offence, notwithstanding that he or she causes injury to another, of whatever degree of seriousness, if such injury is caused during the course of proper medical treatment or care administered with the consent of that other person;

(2)   in this context "medical treatment or care" –

(a)   should mean medical treatment or care administered by or under the direction of a duly qualified medical practitioner;

(b)   should include not only surgical and dental treatment or care, but also procedures taken for the purposes of diagnosis, the prevention of disease, the prevention of pregnancy or as ancillary to treatment; and

(c)   without limiting the meaning of the term, should also include the following:

(i)   surgical operations performed for the purposes of rendering a patient sterile;

(ii) surgical operations performed for the purposes of enabling a person to change his or her sex;

(iii) lawful abortions;

(iv) surgical operations performed for cosmetic purposes; and

(v)   any treatment or procedure to facilitate the donation of regenerative tissue, or the donation of non-regenerative tissue not essential for life.

8.51 We also provisionally propose that –

(1)   a person should not be guilty of an offence, notwithstanding that he or she causes injury to another, of whatever degree of seriousness, if such injury is caused during the course of properly approved medical research and with the consent of that other person; and

(2)   in this context the term "properly approved medical research" should mean medical research approved by a local research ethics committee or other body charged with the supervision and approval of medical research falling within its jurisdiction.

(For a critical review of the proposals, see P Alldridge 'Consent to Medical and Surgical Treatment – The Law Commission's Recommendations' (1996) 4 Med L Rev 129.)

Chapter 6

Consent by others

In this chapter we are concerned with two issues. First, we consider the extent to which treatment may be lawfully given to an individual who is incompetent, ie lacks the capacity to consent. In particular, we will consider who (if any) may consent on behalf of that individual, ie parents, spouses and the court. Also, we will consider whether a doctor may lawfully treat an incompetent patient without seeking any consent from another. Secondly, we consider the circumstances, if any, in which treatment may be lawfully given to a competent individual in the face of a refusal of consent by that individual, whether a child or an adult, and, if so, who may validly consent to the treatment or indeed whether consent is required.

Treating without consent: the incompetent

The incompetent include those, whether children or adults, who fail to meet the criteria discussed above – *supra*, ch 5 – in relation to *Gillick v West Norfolk and Wisbech AHA* [1986] AC 112 and *Re C (adult: refusal of medical treatment)* [1994] 1 All ER 819 in that they lack the capacity to consent in law by reason of lack of understanding, those who by reason of mental illness also lack understanding and those who are unconscious. Obviously in these cases, *if the law requires consent* it must look to someone other than the patient, ie the consent of a proxy.

A. PROXIES

1. In respect of children

We consider here three issues: (a) who may act as a proxy; (b) the scope and limits, if any, of a proxy's power; and (c) acting without the proxy's consent.

(a) Who may act as a proxy?

A parent is the most obvious proxy in the case of a child. A parent who has 'parental responsibility' under the Children Act 1989 in respect of a child may consent to medical treatment on behalf of that child (until majority) where the child is incompetent. In *Secretary, Dept of Health and Community Services v JWB and SMB* (1992) 175 CLR 218 (HC of A), McHugh J examined the source of the common law power of parents to consent to medical treatment. He rejected the view expressed in *Gillick* (*op cit*) that the power was derived from the parents' duty to the child stating: 'the law imposes no general duty on parents to provide medical treatment for their children' (at 313). He also rejected the view that it derived from 'a natural right of almost absolute control' over the child as inconsistent with current 'social and judicial recognition of children as persons with independent rights' (at 314). In respect of the latter, he is surely correct. But as regards the former, the *Gillick* line of reasoning is highly persuasive. Nevertheless, McHugh J found another basis for the parental power to consent.

Secretary, Dept of Health and Community Services v JWB and SMB (1992) 175 CLR 218 (HC of A)

McHugh J: It follows that the common law gives this power to parents simply because it perceives them to be the most appropriate repository of such power. Both the interests of the child and the interests of society require that, wherever possible, a child should not be deprived of medical treatment that is for his or her benefit. Consequently, a just and rational legal system must make provision for the care of those who, by reason of infancy, lack the capacity to control and manage their own affairs. This means that the legal system must give a person or persons authority to act on behalf of children in respect of matters in which they are unable to act for themselves. In the case of children (Bromley and Lowe, '*Family Law*', 7th ed (1987), p 254.):

> Apart from a public authority, the most obvious candidates are ore or both of the child's parents and it is in such persons that English law, in keeping with most other societies, has rested such authority and responsibility.

> Although the case for making the parents the repository of such authority is not perhaps as clear cut as is conventionally thought, that case is, nevertheless, supported by strong sociological, psychological and administrative considerations. As Dworkin points out, these grounds include respect for the family as the decision making unit, the appropriateness of giving the power to those who possess a moral duty to protect the child and who are, therefore, likely to have the child's best interests in mind, and the cost and inconvenience of vesting the power in others such as government officials.

Others, such as a local authority, may acquire parental responsibility under Pt IV of the Children Act 1989 and, thus, be empowered to consent. It should be noticed, however, that in such a case the child's parents will retain 'parental responsibility' and hence the power to consent unless the local authority restricts their powers as parents (s 33(3) and (4)).

That the power to consent to medical treatment is an aspect of 'all the rights, duties, powers, responsibilities and authority which by law a parent of a child has in relation to the child' (s 3(1)), ie 'parental responsibility' can be clearly deduced from the *Gillick* decision.

In principle, each parent (or other with parental responsibility) has the ability to consent. In other words, the power is exercisable severally. Section 2(7) of the Children Act 1989 provides:

…each of them may act alone and without the other (or others) in meeting that responsibility…

However, this may be subject to two qualifications. First, there may be duty to consult the other parent in relation to major or long-term decisions which could, of course, include decisions about major or controversial medical procedures (see *Re G (a minor) parental responsibility: education*) [1994] 2 FLR 964 (CA) – duty to consult over change of school. Secondly, in the absence of agreement between the parents, the courts may impose a limitation on the power of one parent to consent, for example, in changing a child's surname (see *Re PC (change of surname)* [1997] 2 FLR 730) and require the approval of the court. So, in *Re J (child's religious upbringing and circumcision)* (1999) 52 BMLR 82 (CA), it was held that ritual circumcision did not fall within the power of one parent to consent to, where there was disagreement between the parents.

The Children Act 1989 introduced a further possible proxy. Section 3(5) provides that:

3 (5) A person who—
(a) does not have parental responsibility for a particular child; but

(b)   has care of the child.
may (subject to the provisions of this Act) do what is reasonable in all the circumstances of
the case for the purpose of safeguarding or promoting the child's welfare.

Teachers and child-minders are the sorts of person contemplated by this provision.
It is clear from the Law Commission's Report which led to s 3(5) that the provision
was intended to extend, in principle, to medical care (see *Report on Guardianship
and Custody* (1988) (Law Commission Report No 172, para 2.16)). However, it is
unlikely that s 3(5) has much relevance as regards medical treatment. This is because
it will rarely (if ever) be 'reasonable…for the purpose of safeguarding or promoting
the child's welfare' for someone temporarily caring for the child to consent to
medical treatment without first consulting the parents. The only circumstance in
which it may be 'reasonable' would be in an emergency. But in an emergency, as
we shall see, a doctor would be entitled to treat the child without consent in any event.

Another possible proxy decision-maker is, of course, the court itself. The court's
jurisdiction may take a variety of forms – in *wardship*, under its *inherent
jurisdiction* or under *s 8* of the Children Act 1989 (for a full discussion, see
N Lowe and G Douglas *Bromley's Family Law* (9th edn, 1998) ch 12 (s 8 orders)
and ch 16 (inherent jurisdiction and wardship)).

Latey J described the wardship jurisdiction in *Re X (a minor) (wardship:
restriction on publication)* [1975] 1 All ER 697 at 700–701 as follows:

> What then are the origin and function of the wardship jurisdiction? In my understanding they
> are these. All subjects owe allegiance to the Crown. The Crown has a duty to protect its
> subjects. This is and always has been especially so towards minors, that is to say now, the
> young under the age of 18. And it is so because children are especially vulnerable. They have
> not formed the defences inside themselves which older people have, and therefore, need
> especial protection. They are also a country's most valuable asset for the future. So the
> Crown as parens patriae delegated its powers and duty of protection to the courts.

In a medical case, Lord Donaldson MR put it as follows in *Re C (a minor)
(wardship: medical treatment) (No 2)* [1989] 2 All ER 791 at 793–794:

> The origin of the wardship jurisdiction is the duty of the Crown to protect its subjects and
> particularly children who are the generation of the future. It is exercised by the courts on behalf
> of the Crown (see Latey J in *Re X (a minor) (wardship: restriction on publication)* [1975] 1 All
> ER 697 at 700–701, [1975] Fam 47 at 52). The machinery for its exercise is an application to
> make the child a ward of court. Thereafter, the court is entitled and bound in appropriate cases
> to make decisions in the interests of the child which override the rights of its parents. Furthermore,
> the court is entitled, and bound in appropriate cases, to make orders affecting third parties
> which the parents could not themselves have made. Obvious examples are orders forbidding
> the publication of information about the ward or the ward's family circumstances.

For a detailed discussion of the origins of the jurisdiction see Lowe and White
Wards of Court (2nd edn, 1986) ch 1. Three points are worth noticing. First, the
wardship jurisdiction is vested in the court under s 41 of the Supreme Court Act
1981 (and RSC Ord 90) and ends when a child ceases to be a minor, ie at 18
(Family Law Reform Act 1969, s 1) or dies (*Re A* [1992] 3 Med LR 303 (Johnson J)).
Secondly, the use of wardship has been severely curtailed by s 100 of the Children
Act 1989. In particular, wardship may not be used when a child is in the care of
a local authority (s 100(2)(c)). Nor may the jurisdiction be invoked by a local
authority even where the child is not in care because the court should not grant
leave to the local authority under s 100(3). Leave could only be granted if no
other court order could be made (s 100(4)(a)) and, as we shall see, the local
authority could apply for a s 8 order under the Children Act 1989, or, it would
seem, ask the court to exercise its inherent jurisdiction outside wardship. Wardship
is still available, however, where the child is not in care, to other interested parties
including a Health Authority (which is not a local authority under the Children

Act 1989; see s 105(1)). Most likely here, also, the court's inherent jurisdiction is the better procedure.

Thirdly, it is important to notice that if the court's wardship jurisdiction is invoked then 'no important step in the life of that child, can be taken without the consent of the Court…(see Heilbron J in *Re D (a minor) (wardship: sterilisation)* [1976] Fam 185). Few, if any, forms of medical treatment could therefore be properly embarked upon where the child is a ward without first seeking the authorisation of the court (see eg *Re G-U (a minor) (wardship)* [1984] FLR 811 (Balcombe J) – abortion).

More common today in medical law cases will be the use of the court's inherent jurisdiction. This jurisdiction which, by contrast with wardship, *may* be invoked by a local authority even in the case of a child in care, was described in *Re W (a minor (refusal of treatment))* [1992] 4 All ER 627 (CA).

> **Lord Donaldson MR:**…Before the coming into force of the Children Act 1989 the appropriate step would have been an application to make W a ward of court. Since that Act came into force, a child who is the subject of a care order, as W was and is, cannot be made a ward of court (see s 100(2)(c) of that Act). Instead the appropriate procedure is for the authority to apply to the court for leave under s 100(3) to make an application for the exercise by the court of the inherent jurisdiction of the High Court.
>
> Since there seems to be some doubt about the matter, it should be made clear that the High Court's jurisdiction in relation to children – the parens patriae jurisdiction – is equally exercisable whether the child is or is not a ward of court (see *Re M and N (minors) (wardship: freedom of publication)* [1990] 1 All ER 205 at 210, [1990] Fam 211 at 223). Indeed the only additional effect of a child being a ward of court stems from its status as such and not from the inherent jurisdiction, eg a ward of court cannot marry or leave the jurisdiction without the consent of the court and no 'important' or 'major' step in a ward's life can be taken without that consent.

> **Balcombe LJ:** [E]ven before the 1989 Act made the distinction [between wardship and the court's inherent jurisdiction] clear for all to see, it had long been recognised that wardship was only machinery and that the court's inherent jurisdiction could be exercised whether or not the child was a ward – see eg *Re L* [1968] 1 All ER 20 at 25, [1968] P 119 at 157. The inherent jurisdiction is the exercise by the High Court of the powers of the Crown as parens patriae and is theoretically without limit – see *Re X (a minor) (wardship: restriction on publication)* [1975] 1 All ER 697 at 706, [1975] Fam 47 at 61.

Unlike wardship, the inherent jurisdiction does not result in the court taking to itself all decisions relating to the life of the child. Instead, the court will only determine certain issues in respect of the child's upbringing, for example medical care, but it is not part of this jurisdiction to seek to superintend any other decision about the child's welfare (for a judicial discussion of wardship and the inherent jurisdiction see, *Re Z (a minor) (freedom of publication)* [1995] 4 All ER 961 (CA) at 967–978 per Ward LJ).

The final jurisdiction of the court in this context is that set out in s 8 of the Children Act 1989, in particular the power to make 'specific issue orders' and 'prohibited steps orders'. These are defined as follows in s 8(1):

> 8. (1) In this Act—
> 'a prohibited steps order' means an order that no step which could be taken by a parent in meeting his parental responsibility for a child, and which is of a kind specified in the order, shall be taken by any person without the consent of the court,…
> 'a specific issue order' means an order giving directions for the purpose of determining a specific question which has arisen, or which may arise, in connection with any aspect of parental responsibility for a child.

Again, these orders may not be made when a child is in the care of a local authority (Children Act 1989, s 9(1)). The inherent jurisdiction will remain the most common means of access to the court in that situation. Further, where a child is *not* in local authority care but the local authority wishes to involve the court in respect of a decision about its medical treatment, the proper procedure would seem to be under s 8 (see, s 100(4) and *Re R (a minor) (blood transfusion)* [1993] 2 FLR 757). Having said that, some judges have permitted the local authority to involve the court's inherent jurisdiction (*Re S (a minor) (medical treatment)* [1993] 1 FLR 376); *Re R (a minor)* [1993] 2 FLR 757 and Family Proceedings Rules 1991, r 4.4(4)). Also, it should be noted that only 'exceptionally' can a s 8 order be made if the child has reached 16 or if the order would otherwise run beyond the child's 16th birthday (s 9(6) and (7)).

(b) The scope and limits of a proxy's power

The central question which we must answer is what is the *scope* of a proxy's power in making decisions and what, if any, *limits* are there?

(i) 'BEST INTERESTS'

It is relatively straightforward to state the scope of a proxy's power in principle. Both Parliament and the courts have repeatedly asserted that the guiding principle is that the proxy must act out of a concern for the child's welfare. The principle is customarily represented by the phrase 'acting in the *best interests* of the child' – the 'best interests' test (but for other views see *infra*).

The current parliamentary statement of the proxy's power is contained in s 1(1) of the Children Act 1989 (though it first appeared in the Guardianship of Infants Act 1925, but see also the earlier Act of 1886). It is on its face addressed to the court.

> s 1 (1) When a court determines any question with respect to—
> (*a*) the upbringing of a child; or
> (*b*) the administration of a child's property or the application of any income arising from it,
> the child's welfare shall be the court's paramount consideration.

The court for its part has insisted that all proxies must adopt the same approach, ie act in the child's best interests (see, *Re J (a minor) (wardship: medical treatment)* (1990) 6 BMLR 25 at 29 per Sir John Donaldson MR but for an assertion to the contrary see *Bromley's Family Law* (*op cit*) at p 326). Hence, in *Gillick* Lord Scarman was able, having referred to the legislation, to state that:

> There is here a principle which limits and governs the exercise of parental rights of custody, care and control. It is a principle perfectly consistent with the law's recognition of the parent as the natural guardian of the child; but it is also a warning that parental right must be exercised in accordance with the welfare principle and can be challenged, even overridden, if it be not.

(See also Lord Hailsham in *Re B (a minor) (wardship: sterilisation)* [1987] 2 All ER 206 at 212.)

At the outset it is fair to state that inherent in the notion of 'best interests' is that the medical intervention must be *therapeutic*, ie intended to benefit the particular individual. The law's equating 'best interests' with therapy causes problems, as we shall see, when dispute exists as to whether a particular intervention (or class of interventions) is indeed therapeutic. Examples exist in the concern over the legality of a proxy's consent to the involvement of a child in non-therapeutic medical research, organ or blood donation and sterilisation. As regards these difficult cases, the courts could choose from three options: (1) absolute prohibition; (2) the adoption of different and less rigorous tests (with safeguards); and (3) prohibit them in all circumstances other than when the court authorises the intervention. We will consider this third option in some detail later. Here we need to notice, in the rare cases in which this has arisen, how the courts have chosen between option (1) and option (2).

S v S, W v Official Solicitor (or W) **[1972] AC 24, [1970] 3 All ER 107 (HL)**

In the two appeals heard together, the court was concerned with the paternity of children born to the parties of marriages. During divorce proceedings, the husbands of the children's mothers denied paternity. In each case the parent who had control of the child consented to a blood test. In each case the House of Lords ordered that a blood test should be taken.

Lord Reid: The Official Solicitor argues on behalf of these children that no blood test of any child ought ever to be ordered unless it can be shown to be in the interest of the child that there should be a test...

I must now examine the present legal position with regard to blood tests. There is no doubt that a person of full age and capacity cannot be ordered to undergo a blood test against his will. In my view, the reason is not that he ought to be required to furnish evidence which may tell against him. By discovery of documents and in other ways the law often does this. The real reason is that English law goes to great lengths to protect a person of full age and capacity from interference with his personal liberty. We have too often seen freedom disappear in other countries not only by coups d'etat but by gradual erosion; and often it is the first step that counts. So it would be unwise to make even minor concessions. It is true that the matter is regarded differently in the United States. We were referred to a number of State enactments authorising the courts to order adults to submit to blood tests. They may feel that this is safe because of their geographical position, size, power or resources or because they have a written Constitution. But here Parliament has clearly endorsed our view by the provision of s 21(1) of the 1969 Act [Family Law Reform Act].

But the position is very different with regard to young children. It is a legal wrong to use constraint on an adult beyond what is authorised by statute or ancient common law powers connected with crime and the like. But it is not and could not be a legal wrong for a parent or person authorised by him to use constraint to his young child provided it is not cruel or excessive. There are differences of opinion as to the age beyond which it is unwise to use constraint, but that cannot apply to infants or young children. So it seems to me to be impossible to deny that a parent can lawfully require that his young child should submit to a blood test. And if the parent can require that, why not the court? There is here no overriding requirement of public policy as there is with an adult.

I shall not refer in detail to the authorities. They were all discussed at some length in argument. But I venture to think that there has been some error in applying to this subject principles and authorities which deal with the custody of children. There the question is simple, though a decision may be very difficult – to whom shall the custody be entrusted? There is no competing question of general public interest, and it has long been well recognised that the paramount question is what is in the best interests of the child. But here there is or may be a conflict between the interests of the child and the general requirements of justice. Justice requires that available evidence should not be suppressed but it may be against the interests of the child to produce it.

The argument, as I understand it, is that a court can only order a blood test of a child in the exercise of the old Chancery jurisdiction acting on behalf of the Sovereign as parens patriae, and that when exercising that jurisdiction a court must act solely in the interests of the child disregarding all more general considerations. I greatly doubt that line of argument. Every court in any litigation must see that the interests of a child are not neglected. I am not at all certain that it is accurate to say that a court orders a blood test. What happens is that by appointing guardians ad litem and by a *Practice Direction* of the Probate Divorce and Admiralty Division of 21st October 1968, the court prevents parents who retain care and control of their children from exercising their right to have blood tests. Then, when an order for a test is sought the true position appears to me to be that the court is being asked to lift it, and if, in defiance of the ban, a parent should have his child's blood tested, he might incur penalties, but, if it is the law that evidence is admissible though obtained by unlawful means, the court could not refuse to receive the result of such a test in evidence. No case has yet occurred in which a court has ordered a blood test to be carried out against the will of the parent who has the care and control of the child, and I am not at all certain that it would be proper to do that or that it will be possible to do that after Part III of the 1969 Act comes into operation.

But even if one accepts the view that in ordering, directing or permitting a blood test the court should go no further than a reasonable parent would go, surely a reasonable parent would have some regard to the general public interest and would not refuse a blood test unless he thought that would clearly be against the interests of the child? I cannot assume that in the present cases the husbands are acting in selfish disregard of these children's interests in asking for blood tests.

Lord MacDermott:...Must the court, before exercising its jurisdiction to order a blood test to be taken of an infant, be satisfied that it is in the best interests of the infant that it should do so?

The duty of the High Court as respects the affairs and welfare of infants falls into two broad categories. There is, first of all, the duty to *protect* the infant, particularly when engaged or involved in litigation. This duty is of a general nature and derives from the Court of Chancery and to some extent also, I believe, from the common law courts which were merged along with the Court of Chancery in the High Court of Justice by the [Supreme Court of Judicature Act 1873]. It recognises that the infant, as one not sui juris may stand in need of aid. He must not be allowed to suffer because of his incapacity. But the aim is to ensure that he gets his rights rather than to place him above the law and make his rights superior to those of others. I shall refer to this duty and the powers of the court relative thereto as the 'protective jurisdiction'. Exercising it the court will be alert to see that the infant is separately represented where his interest so requires, and to change his next friend or guardian *ad litem* if not acting with due diligence and in a proper manner. Other examples of the protective jurisdiction are – the payment into court and investment of moneys recovered by an infant in litigation, the appointment of the Official Solicitor to act on his behalf in matters of special difficulty, and the approval of compromises and settlements entered into on the infant's behalf.

In exercising what I have called the ancillary jurisdiction in relation to infants the court must also observe and, if need be, exercise its protective jurisdiction. For instance, if the court were satisfied that – as might possibly be the case on rare occasions – a blood test would prejudicially affect the health of the infant it would, no doubt, exercise its discretion against ordering the test. And, again, if the court had reason to believe that the application for a blood test was of a fishing nature, designed for some ulterior motive to call in question the legitimacy, otherwise unimpeached, of a child who had enjoyed a legitimate status, it may well be that the court, acting under its protective rather than its ancillary jurisdiction, would be justified in refusing the application. I need not, however, pursue such instances as they do not arise on these appeals. The point to be made is that the protective jurisdiction, if of the nature I have described, would not ordinarily afford ground for refusing a blood test merely because it might, in revealing the truth, prove the infant's illegitimacy in duly constituted paternity proceedings.

This case has importance beyond its particular facts which are now covered, in any event, by ss 20–22 of the Family Law Reform Act 1969 (see *Re F (a minor) (blood tests: parental rights)* [1993] 3 All ER 596 (CA) and *Re H (a minor) (blood tests: parental rights)* [1996] 4 All ER 28 (CA) and *Bromley's Family Law (op cit)* at pp 276–282 for the court's approach to its powers under s 20). It is the only English authority which offers guidance on the legality of medical interventions which are not, on their face, therapeutic. The House of Lords held that such interventions would be lawful providing that they were not 'against the interests' of the child. In other words, the House of Lords changed the test – ie adopted option (2). They justified doing so on the basis that there was a public interest in a child's paternity being known and the intervention involved, at worst, a minimal risk of harm to the child. As we shall see later (in Chapter 14) this analysis has been adopted by those commenting on the law of research, and its application is crucial to the question of the legality of such research.

A difficulty in this view is that it requires some creative reading of the speeches. On its face the case could be said to be limited to ordering (or giving consent to) a blood test in the course of litigation so as to ensure that the court has before it the best evidence to ensure a fair trial. This is expressed particularly by Lords MacDermott and Hodson as being in exercise of the court's 'inherent' or 'ancillary' 'jurisdiction to make interlocutory orders for the purpose of promoting a fair and satisfactory trial' (per Lord MacDermott at 114). Thus, a narrow reading of the case could be that the test of 'not against the interests' is not the law except where it is applied by the *court* in these limited circumstances. If this narrow view were right, it would follow that the test would have no relevance generally for determining the legality of non-therapeutic interventions so as, for example, to permit a parent to volunteer a child for non-therapeutic research.

Of course, the court could make these 'difficult cases' go away by simply fudging the distinction between that which is therapeutic and that which is not. This seems to be an approach which has appealed to some American courts in the context of organ and tissue donation by incompetent children. The American courts do not, however, adopt a uniform approach and are helpfully drawn together in the following case.

Curran v Bosze **(1990) 566 NE 2d 1319 (Illinois Sup Ct)**

Calvo J: Allison and James Curren are 3½-year old twins. Their mother is Nancy Curran. The twins have lived with Ms Curran and their maternal grandmother since their birth on January 27, 1987.

The twins' father is Tamas Bosze. Ms Curran and Mr Bosze have never been married. As a result of an action brought by Ms Curran against Mr Bosze concerning the paternity of the twins, both Mr Bosze and the twins underwent a blood test in November of 1987. The blood test confirmed that Mr Bosze is the father of the twins...

Mr Bosze is the father of three other children: a son, age 23; Jean Pierre Bosze, age 12; and a one-year old daughter. Ms Curran is not the mother of any of these children. Each of these children has a different mother. Jean Pierre and the twins are half-siblings. The twins have met Jean Pierre on two occasions. Each meeting lasted approximately two hours.

Jean Pierre is suffering from acute undifferentiated leukemia (AUL), also known as mixed lineage leukemia. Mixed lineage leukemia is a rare form of leukemia which is difficult to treat. Jean Pierre was initially misdiagnosed as having acute lymphocytic leukemia (ALL) in June 1988, in Colombia, South America. Jean Pierre was brought to American in August 1988, and has been treated by Dr Jong Kwon since that time. Jean Pierre was treated with chemotherapy and went into remission. Jean Pierre experienced a testicular relapse in January 1990, and a bone marrow relapse in mid-June 1990. Dr Kwon has recommended a bone marrow transplant for Jean Pierre.

Mr Bosze asked Ms Curran to consent to a blood test for the twins in order to determine whether the twins were compatible to serve as bone marrow donors for a transplant to Jean Pierre. Mr Bosze asked Ms Curran to consent to the twins' undergoing a bone marrow harvesting procedure if the twins were found to be compatible. After consulting with the twins' pediatrician, family members, parents of bone marrow donors and bone marrow donors, Ms Curran refused to give consent to the twins' undergoing either the blood test or the bone marrow harvesting procedure.

On June 28, 1990, Mr Bosze filed an emergency petition in the circuit of Cook County. The petition informed the court that Jean Pierre 'suffers from leukemia and urgently requires a [bone] marrow transplant from a compatible donor. Without the transplant he will die in a short period of time, thereby creating an emergency involving life and death'. The petition stated that persons usually compatible for serving as donors are parents or siblings of the recipient, and Jean Pierre's father, mother, and older brother had been tested and rejected as compatible donors.

According to the petition, '[t]he only siblings who have potential to be donors and who have not been tested are the children, James and Allison.' The petition stated Ms Curran refused to discuss with Mr Bosze the matter of submitting the twins to a blood test to determine their compatibility as potential bone marrow donors for Jean Pierre. The petition stated the blood test 'is minimally invasive and harmless, and no more difficult than the paternity blood testing which the children have already undergone'. According to the petition, there would be no expense involved to Ms Curran.

In the petition, Mr Bosze requested the court find a medical emergency to exist and order and direct Ms Curran to 'forthwith produce the parties' minor children...at Lutheran General Hospital...for the purpose of compatibility blood testing.' Further, Mr Bosze requested in the petition that 'if the children, or either of them, are compatible as donors, that the Court order and direct that [Ms Curran] produce the children, or whichever one may be compatible, for the purpose of donating bone marrow to their sibling.'...[T]he court ruled on July 18, 1990, that it did not have authority to grant Mr Bosze's petition....

Several courts from sister jurisdictions have addressed the issue whether the consent of a court, parent or guardian, for the removal of a kidney from an incompetent person for transplantation to a sibling, may be legally effective. These cases have been addressed by the parties. While not mandatory authority to this court, these cases are illustrative of the complexities involved when otherwise healthy minors or incompetent persons, who lack the legal capacity to give consent, are asked to undergo an invasive surgical procedure for the benefit of a sibling....

Having considered the well known case of *Strunk v Strunk* (1969) 445 SW 2d 145 (Ky CA) (*infra*), Justice Calvo continued:

In *Hart v Brown* (Super 1972), 29 Conn Supp 368, 289 A 2d 386, the parents of identical twins, age 7 years and 10 months, sought permission to have a kidney from the healthy twin transplanted into the body of the seriously ill twin who was suffering from a kidney disease. The parents brought a declaratory judgment action, as parents and natural guardians of the twins, seeking a declaration that they had the right to consent to the proposed operation. Guardians *ad litem* for each of the twins were appointed. Defendants in the declaratory judgment action were the physicians and the hospital at which the proposed kidney transplantation operation was to take place; the defendants had refused to use their facilities unless the court 'declare[d] that the parents and/or guardians ad litem of the minors have the right to give their consent to the operation upon the minor twins.' *Hart* 29 Conn Supp at 369, 289 A 2d 387.

The court in *Hart* concluded it had the power to determine that the parents have the right to consent to the operation 'using the doctrines of law as stated in the *Strunk* case, in the *Bonner* case, and in the Massachusetts cases.' (*Hart*, 29 Conn Supp at 377, 289 A 2D at 391.) The Massachusetts cases referred to by the *Hart* court were unreported cases where the 'commonwealth of Massachusetts ruled that a court of equity does have the power to permit the natural parents of minor twins to give their consent to a procedure such as is being contemplated by this court.' (*Hart*, 29 Con Supp at 370–71, 289 A 2d at 387.) The *Hart* court stated *Bonner v Moran* (DC Cir 1941), 126 F 2d 121, was 'authority…that nontherapeutic operations can be legally permitted on a minor as long as the parents or other guardians consent to the procedure.' (*Hart*, 29 Conn Supp at 376, 289 A 2d at 390.) In *Bonner*, a 15-year-old minor child's consent to removal of a skin patch for the benefit of his cousin was held legally ineffective.

The court in *Hart* noted it was 'not being asked to act where a person is legally incompetent. The matter, however, does involve two minors who do not have the legal capacity to consent.' (*Hart*, 20 Conn Supp at 370, 289 A 2d at 387.) The *Hart* court referred to the *Strunk* court's decision that a court of equity has the power to permit the natural parent of a 27-year-old mental incompetent to give her consent, using the doctrine of substituted judgment, to a kidney transplantation operation. The court in *Hart* stated:

> The court [in *Strunk*] held that a court of equity does have such power, applying also the 'doctrine of substituted judgment'.
> Therefore, this court is of the opinion that it has the power to act in this matter. (*Hart*, 29 Conn Supp at 371, 289 A 2d at 388.)

The *Hart* court reviewed the medical testimony presented concerning the kidney transplant which 'indicate[d] that scientifically this type of procedure is a "perfect" transplant.' (*Hart*, 20 Conn Supp at 375, 289 A 2d at 389.) The court also noted that a psychiatrist examined the proposed donor and testified the proposed donor 'has a strong identification with her twin sister.' (*Hart*, 29 Conn Supp at 374, 289 A 2d at 389.) Further, the psychiatrist testified 'that if the expected successful results are achieved they would be of immense benefit to the donor in that the donor would be better off in a family that was happy than in a family that was distressed and in that it would be a very great loss to the donor if the donee were to die from her illness.' (*Hart*, 29 Conn Supp at 374–75, 289 A 2d at 389.) The court in *Hart* considered the testimony of the psychiatrist to be 'of limited value only because of the ages of the minors.' *Hart*, 29 Conn Supp at 375, 289 A 2d at 390.

Both guardians *ad litem* gave their consent to the procedure. Both parents gave their consent to the procedure. A clergy person testified that the natural parents were 'making a morally sound decision.' (*Hart*, 29 Conn Supp at 375, 289 A 2d at 390.) The *Hart* court found the testimony of the parents showed they reached their decision to consent 'only after many hours of agonizing consideration.' (*Hart*, 29 Conn Supp at 375, 289 A 2d at 390.) The twin who would serve as the kidney donor 'ha[d] been informed of the operation and insofar as she may be capable of understanding she desires to donate her kidney so that her sister may return to her.' *Hart*, 29 Conn Supp at 375, 289 A 2d at 389.

The *Hart* court stated:

> To prohibit the natural parents and the guardians ad litem of the minor children the right to give their consent under these circumstances, where there is supervision by this court and other persons in examining their judgment, would be most unjust, inequitable and injudicious. Therefore, natural parents of a minor should have the right to give their consent to an isograft kidney transplantation procedure when their motivation and reasoning are favorably reviewed by a community representation which includes a court of equity.
> It is the judgment of this court that [the parents] have the right, under the particular facts and circumstances of this matter, to give their consent to the operations. (*Hart*, 29 Conn Supp at 378, 289 A 2d at 391.)

Although purporting to apply the doctrine of substituted judgment, the *Hart* court did not inquire as to what the 7½-year-old minors would do if the minors were competent. The *Hart* court instead determined that 'the natural parents would be able to substitute their consent for that of their minor children after a close, independent and objective investigation of their motivation and reasoning.' *Hart*, 29 Conn Supp at 375, 289 A 2d at 390.

In *Little v Little* (Tex Civ 1979), 576 W 2d 493, the mother of a 14-year-old mentally incompetent daughter petitioned the court to authorize the mother's consent to the removal of a kidney from her daughter for transplantation into her younger son, who suffered from a kidney disease. The mother had been appointed guardian of her mentally incompetent minor daughter. An attorney *ad litem* was appointed by the court to represent the proposed donor. The attorney *ad litem* argued there was no constitutional or statutory provision empowering the probate court to authorize the removal of an incompetent's kidney for the purpose of benefiting another person.

The mother relied on *Strunk*. The *Little* court discussed the doctrine of substituted judgment as it was applied in *Strunk*. The *Little* court also discussed two cases where the court refused to authorize a transplant, *In Re Guardianship of Pescinski* (1975), 67 Wis 2d 4, 226 NW 2d 180, and *In Re Richardson* (La App 1973), 284 So 2d 185.

It is clear in transplant cases that courts, whether they use the term 'substituted judgment' or not, will consider the benefits to the donor as a basis for permitting an incompetent to donate an organ. Although in *Strunk* the Kentucky Court discussed the substituted judgment doctrine in some detail, the conclusion of the majority there was based on the benefits that the incompetent donor would derive, rather than on the theory that the incompetent would have consented to the transplant if he were competent. We adopt this approach. *Little* 576 SW 2d at 498.

The *Little* court determined that 'the testimony…conclusively establish[ed] the existence of a close relationship between [the proposed donor] and [her brother], a genuine concern by each for the welfare of the other and, at the very least, an awareness by [the proposed donor] of the nature of [her brother's] plight and an awareness of the fact that she is in a position to ameliorate [her brother's] burden.' (*Little*, 576 SW 2d at 498.) Both parents of the incompetent minor consented to the kidney donation; there was no evidence that the incompetent minor had been subjected to family pressure; and there were no medically preferable alternatives to the kidney transplant. The *Little* court also found that the dangers of the operation were minimal and there was evidence the incompetent minor would not suffer psychological harm. The kidney transplant would probably be substantially beneficial to the proposed recipient, and the trial court's decision was made 'only after a full judicial proceeding in which the interests of [the incompetent minor] were championed by an attorney ad litem.' (*Little*, 576 SW 2d at 499.) The *Little* court concluded:

Given the presence of all the factors and circumstances outlined above, and limiting our decision to such facts and circumstances, we conclude that the trial court did not exceed its authority by authorizing the participation of [the incompetent minor] in the kidney transplant as a donor, since there is strong evidence to the effect that she will receive substantial psychological benefits from such participation. Nothing in this opinion is to be construed as being applicable to a situation where the proposed [recipient] is not a parent or sibling of the incompetent. *Little* 576 SW 2d at 500.

In *Pescinski*, the sister and guardian of an adult incompetent 39-year-old man petitioned the court for permission for the incompetent brother to donate a kidney to another sister suffering from a kidney disease. The incompetent, 'classified as a schizophrenic, chronic, catatonic type' (*Pescinski*, 67 Wis 2d at 6, 226 NW 2d at 180) for over 17 years, was a mental patient at a State hospital. A physician testified that the ward had a mental capacity of a 12-year-old child. The guardian *ad litem* for the incompetent person would not consent to the procedure.

In *Pescinski*, the Supreme Court of Wisconsin addressed the issue: 'Does a county court have the power to order an operation to be performed to remove a kidney of an incompetent ward, under guardianship of the person, and transfer it to a sister where the dire need of the transfer is established but where no consent has been given by the incompetent or his guardian *ad litem*, nor has any benefit to the ward been shown?' (*Pescinski*, 67 Wis 2d at 5, 226 NW 2d at 180.) The court answered that it did not.

The *Pescinski* court noted that 'no statutory authority [is] given the county court to authorize a kidney transplant or any other surgical procedure on a living person.' (*Pescinski*, 67 Wis 2d at 7, 226 NW 2d at 181.) The court in *Pescinski* discussed the doctrine of substituted judgment approved by the court in *Strunk*. The *Pescinski* court declined to adopt the doctrine of substituted judgment.

An incompetent particularly should have his own interests protected. Certainly no advantage should be taken of him. In the absence of real consent on his part, and in a situation where no benefit to him as been established, we fail to find any authority for the county court, or this court, to approve this operation. *Pescinski*, 67 Wis 2d at 8–9, 226 NW 2d at 182.

In *In Re Guardianship of Eberhardy* (1981), 102 Wis 2d 539, 307 NW 2d 881, the supreme court of Wisconsin discussed its decision in *Pescinski* and clarified that *Pescinski* 'should not be read as a ruling of want of jurisdiction.' (*Eberhardy*, 102 Wis 2d at 565 n 13, 307 NW 2d at 893 n 13.) On the part of a court to authorize the kidney transplant therein considered, the court in *Eberhardy* stated:

Pescinski represents the exercise of judicial restraint under particular circumstances. Those circumstances included the lack of consent of the guardian *ad litem*, no showing of benefit to the ward, and an absence of legislative guidance. *Pescinski* should not be read as a ruling of want of jurisdiction, and, insofar as it may, we disavow that conclusion. *Eberhardy*, 102 Wis 2d at 565 n 13, 307 NW 2d at 893 n 13.

The Louisiana Court of Appeal in *In Re Richardson* (La App 1973), 284 So 2d 185, declined to adopt the doctrine of substituted judgment announced in *Strunk*. Both parents of a 17-year-old incompetent son with a mental age of three or four years consented to a kidney transplant from the son to his sister. As a procedure vehicle to bring the issue before the court, the father filed suit against the mother to compel her to consent to the kidney transplant. The *Richardson* court distinguished the case before it from the case in *Strunk*:

> We find the facts in [*Strunk*], particularly the conclusion relative to the 'best interest' of the incompetent, are not similar to the facts in the instant case and we also find that both the procedural and the substantive aspects of the majority opinion are not in accord with Louisiana law. *Richardson*, 284 So 2d at 187.

The *Richardson* court stated that the law of its State 'is designed to protect and promote the ultimate best interest of a minor.' (*Richardson* 284, So 2d at 187.) Louisiana law did not provide for the *inter vivos* donations of a minor's property either by the minor or by the minor's tutor (guardian). The *Richardson* court stated:

> Since our law affords this unqualified protection against intrusion [*sic*] into a comparatively mere property right, it is inconceivable to us that it affords less protection to a minor's right to be free in his person from bodily intrusion to the extent of loss of an organ unless such loss be in the best interest of the minor. Of course, that statement and our conclusion are restricted to the facts of the present case. *Richardson*, 284 So 2d at 187.

In the concurring opinion in *Richardson*, it was stated:

> The majority, in my opinion, rightfully assumes that the court is empowered to authorize the transplant of the kidney from the minor, provided certain standards are met, ie, the best interests of the minor. However, I am of the opinion that before the court might exercise its *awesome* authority in such an instance and before it considers the question of the best interests of the child, certain requirements must be met. I am of the opinion that it must be clearly established that the surgical intrusion is urgent, that there are no reasonable alternatives, and that the contingencies are minimal. These requirements of prerequisites are not met in this case. Having so determined, we are not confronted with the question of the best interests of the child. (Emphasis in original.) *Richardson*, 284 So 2d at 188 (Gulotta, J, concurring).

In each of the foregoing cases where consent to the kidney transplant was authorized, regardless whether the authority to consent was to be exercised by the court, a parent or a guardian, the key inquiry was the presence or absence of a benefit to the potential donor. Notwithstanding the language used by the courts in reaching their determination that a transplant may or may not occur, the standard by which the determination was made was whether the transplant would be in the best interest of the child or incompetent person.

The primary benefit to the donor in these cases arises from the relationship existing between the donor and recipient. In *Strunk*, the donor lived in a State institution. The recipient was a brother who served as the donor's only connection with the outside world. In both *Hart* and *Little*, there was evidence that the sibling relationship between the donor and recipient was close. In each of these cases, both parents had given their consent.

We hold that a parent or guardian may give consent on behalf of a minor daughter or son for the child to donate bone marrow to a sibling, only when to do so would be in the minor's best interest.

As sole custodian of the twins, Ms Curran 'may determine the child[ren]'s upbringing, including but not limited to, [the] education, health care and religious training, unless the court, after hearing, finds, upon motion by the noncustodial parent, that the absence of a specific limitation of the custodian's authority would clearly be contrary to the best interests of the child[ren]. Ill Rec Stat 1987, Ch 40, par 608(a)....

The evidence reveals three critical factors which are necessary to a determination that it will be in the best interests of a child to donate bone marrow to a sibling. First, the parent who consents on behalf of the child must be informed of the risks and benefits inherent in the bone marrow harvesting procedure to the child.

Second, there must be emotional support available to the child from the person or persons who take care of the child. The testimony reveals that a child who is to undergo general anesthesia and the bone marrow harvesting procedure needs the emotional support of a person whom the child loves and trusts. A child who is to donate bone marrow is required to go to an unfamiliar place and meet with unfamiliar people. Depending upon the age of the child, he or she may or may not understand what is to happen. The evidence establishes that the presence and emotional support by the child's caretaker is important to ease the fears associated with such an unfamiliar procedure.

Third, there must be an existing, close relationship between the donor and recipient. The evidence clearly shows that there is no physical benefit to a donor child. If there is any benefit to a child who donates bone marrow to a sibling it will be a psychological benefit. According to the evidence, the psychological benefit is not simply one of personal, individual altruism in an abstract theoretical sense, although that may be a factor.

The psychological benefit is grounded firmly in the fact that the donor and recipient are known to each other as family. Only where there is an existing relationship between a healthy child and his or her ill sister or brother may a psychological benefit to the child from donating bone marrow to a sibling realistically be found to exist. The evidence establishes that it is the existing sibling relationship, as well as the potential for a continuing sibling relationship, which forms the context in which it may be determined that it will be in the best interests of the child to undergo a bone marrow harvesting procedure for a sibling.

Both Mr Bosze and Ms Curran are informed of the risks inherent in a bone marrow harvesting procedure performed on a child. Mr Bosze has consulted with Dr Kwon, Jean Pierre's treating physician, Ms Curran has consulted the twins' pediatrician, parents of bone marrow donors, and bone marrow donors. Both Ms Curran and Mr Bosze listened to Drs Johnson, Kwon, Leventhal, Lechtor, Camitta, and Kohrman.

The primary risk to a bone marrow donor is the risk associated with undergoing general anesthesia. The risk of a life-threatening complication occurring from undergoing general anesthesia is 1 in 10,000. As noted by the circuit court, the risks associated with general anesthesia include, but are not limited to, 'brain damage as a result of oxygen deprivation, stroke, cardiac arrest and death.'

The pain following the harvesting procedure is usually easily controlled with post-operative medication. Although there is a risk of infection at the needle puncture site, this is rare.

Ms Curran has refused consent on behalf of the twins to the bone marrow transplant because she does not think it is in their best interests to subject them to the risks and pains involved in undergoing general anesthesia and the harvesting procedure. While Ms Curran is aware that the risks involved in donating bone marrow and undergoing general anesthesia are small, she also is aware that when such risk occurs, it may be life-threatening.

On February 16, 1989, Mr Bosze and Ms Curran agreed in the parentage order that Ms Curran would have sole custody of the twins. Allison and James have lived with Ms Curran and their maternal grandmother since their birth. Mr Bosze and Ms Curran also agreed that Mr Bosze would have visitation rights with the twins. Until the twins reached the age of five years, Mr Bosze would have visitation once a week. Ms Curran was to be present during the visitation.

Between February 16, 1989, and February 14, 1990, Mr Bosze exercised his visitation rights 15 times. On two of these occasions, Jean Pierre was present. Before Mr Bosze ever requested Ms Curran to consent to the twins' donating bone marrow to Jean Pierre, Ms Curran requested that Mr Bosze not tell the twins that Jean Pierre was their half-brother. Ms Curran thought that it would be confusing to the twins to be told that they have two half-brothers and a half-sister, each of whom had a different mother. Mr Bosze honored this request.

It is a fact that the twins and Jean Pierre share the same biological father. There was no evidence produced, however, to indicate that the twins and Jean Pierre are known to each other as family.

Allison and James would need the emotional support of their primary caregiver if they were to donate bone marrow. The evidence establishes that it would not be in a 3½-year-old child's best interests if he or she were required to go to a hospital and undergo all that is involved with the bone marrow harvesting procedure without the constant reassurances and support by a familiar adult known and trusted by the child.

Not only is Ms Curran presently the twins' primary caretaker, the evidence establishes she is, the only caretaker the twins have ever known. Ms Curran has refused to consent to the twins' participation in donating bone marrow to Jean Pierre. It appears that Mr Bosze would be unable to substitute his support for the procedure for that of Ms Curran because his involvement in the lives of Allison and James has, to this point, been a limited one....

This court shares the opinion of the circuit court that Jean Pierre's situation 'evokes sympathy from all who've heard [it].' No matter how small the hope that a bone marrow transplant will cure Jean Pierre, the fact remains that without the transplant, Jean Pierre will almost certainly die. The sympathy felt by this court, the circuit court, and all those who have learned of Jean Pierre's tragic situation cannot, however, obscure the fact that, under the circumstances presented in the case at bar, it neither would be proper under existing law nor in the best interests of the 3½-year-old twins for the twins to participate in the bone marrow harvesting procedure.

The English courts have not had to consider such a case involving a child (but see *Re GWW and CMW* (1997) 21 Fam LR 612 (Aust Fam Ct)). In *Re Y (adult patient) (transplant: bone marrow)* (1996) 35 BMLR 111, the court did, however, consider the issue in respect of an incompetent adult. As we shall see, the courts have required these decisions to be taken in the incompetent's 'best interests' and thus it is instructive for us here.

Re Y (adult patient) (transplant: bone marrow) (1996) 35 BMLR 111 (Fam Div)

Connell J: The plaintiff seeks a declaration under RSC Ord 15, r 16 and pursuant to the inherent jurisdiction of the court. The declaration is to the effect that two preliminary blood tests and a conventional bone marrow harvesting operation under general anaesthetic can lawfully be taken from and performed upon her sister, the defendant, despite the fact that her sister cannot give her consent to such activities. The basis for the application for a declaration is that the blood tests and operation, which the plaintiff asks the court to declare as lawful, are in the best interests of the defendant.

The facts relating to this application may be summarised as follows. The plaintiff is aged 36. She is the eldest of four sisters, she is married and has one daughter, E, aged 6. Both the plaintiff's parents are alive. Her father is aged 68, her mother 62. E is their only grandchild. The plaintiff is suffering from a pre-leukaemic bone marrow disorder myelodispastic syndrome.

In 1984, the plaintiff was diagnosed as suffering from non-Hodgkins lymphoma and since that date she has undergone extensive chemotherapy. In May 1993, she underwent a blood stem cell transplant. This treatment was successful for a while, but there has been recent and increasing deterioration in her condition. Her blood count in particular is deteriorating and the strong likelihood is that her situation will progress to acute myeloid leukaemia over the next three months.

The only realistic prospect of recovery for the plaintiff now is a bone marrow transplant operation from a healthy, compatible donor. Preliminary investigations show that of the plaintiff's three sisters, only the defendant would be a suitable donor.

It seems highly likely that the defendant matches the plaintiff in the relevant respects and this match will be finally confirmed, or otherwise, from information which will become available as a result of two preliminary blood tests in respect of which the declaration is also sought.

The prime purposes of these two preliminary blood tests are: (a) to ensure that the defendant is not afflicted by any viruses such as HIV or Aids and (b) to borrow a pint of the defendant's own blood which would be transposed back to her after collection of the bone marrow.

A search for compatible donors other than the defendant has been carried out as recently as 6 June 1996. Dr A is the consultant haematologist who is responsible for the care of the plaintiff. He told me that there is one possibility from several thousand individuals known to the British Bone Marrow Donor panel but this possibility may well not turn out to be suitable if tests are taken.

The Anthony Nolan Research Centre panel discloses one promising donor but the doctor says experience shows with bone marrow transplants that sibling transplantation produces superior results to those produced by unrelated donor transplantation, no matter how good the matching of the latter. Therefore, from the point of view of the plaintiff, her prospects of significant prolongation of life would clearly be best assisted by a transplant from the defendant and the plaintiff's need as described is urgent.

The defendant is aged 25. She is severely mentally and physically handicapped and has been so since birth. She suffers from hydrocephalus and also underwent an early cardiac arrest which may have damaged her brain further. She lived with her family at home until aged 10, then she went to a residential school until aged 17 and for the last eight years she has lived in a community home.

She is quite incapable of giving her consent to bone marrow donation. Evidence shows that she is of a cheerful disposition but she requires assistance with all her daily tasks save that of feeding. She can speak a very few words and communicates mainly by signs. She suffers from fits, about once every eight weeks, as a result of which she is usually incapacitated for about three days.

When the representative of the Official Solicitor, who is her guardian ad litem in these proceedings, visited her recently, it was apparent that the defendant did not understand what was being said to her. Likewise, she did not understand what was being said when told that her older sister is very unwell. Attempts to talk to her in simple terms by the unit manager at the community home likewise met with no success. The defendant understands her own basic needs but cannot understand the needs of others.

The family of the plaintiff and the defendant is a close family. The defendant's three sisters have been loyal in keeping in touch with her and visiting her occasionally but her most regular visitor and the family member with whom she has the closest relationship is undoubtedly her mother.

It is not possible accurately to describe the relationship between the plaintiff and the defendant as particularly strong, because the plaintiff's ill health has reduced her ability to visit the defendant. However, the plaintiff does keep in touch with the defendant, mainly by cards and presents and by sending to the defendant photographs of E and further, during a recent visit by the family to the defendant, the Official Solicitor's representative did notice that the defendant moved her wheelchair closer to the plaintiff.

As far as the defendant's relationship with her mother is concerned, this is noticeably close and there are overt signs of affection on the defendant's part for her mother. The mother visits the defendant almost weekly and she looked after the defendant at home until that became impossible, largely because of the mother's own ill health. Until that time, the defendant had been the main focus of the family life.

In fact, what happened was that the mother had to enter hospital herself for a hysterectomy; then it was that the defendant, aged ten at the time, was moved into a residential school. The defendant has not returned to live at home since. The family in particular were unable to cope with lifting her but happily, her quality of life in the community home is first-class, given her disabilities.

More recently, the mother has had a coronary by-pass operation in 1992 and at the present time she suffers from angina and gets tired very easily. It is clear that her health is precarious and her condition is significantly exacerbated by her anxieties concerning the health of the plaintiff.

The taking of blood tests and the harvesting of bone marrow from the defendant who is incapable of giving informed consent would amount to assaults upon the defendant and would therefore be illegal unless shown to be in the best interests of the defendant and therefore lawful.

The test to be applied in a case such as this is to ask whether the evidence shows that it is in the best interests of the defendant for such procedures to take place. The fact that such a process would obviously benefit the plaintiff is not relevant unless, as a result of the defendant helping the plaintiff in that way, the best interests of the defendant are served.

The approach is as set out in *F v West Berkshire Health Authority* (*Mental Health Act Commission intervening*) (1989) 4 BMLR 1, sub nom *Re F* (*mental patient: sterilisation*) [1990] 2 AC 1, a non-therapeutic sterilisation case. Thus, the giving of medical treatment to mentally disordered adult patients is, save as to treatment for their mental disorder under the Mental Health Act 1983, governed by common law. The lawfulness of the action depends upon whether the treatment is in the best interests of the patient (see (1989) 4 BMLR 1 esp at 8–9 and 19, 20, [1990] 2 AC esp at 56 and 68, 69 per Lord Brandon and Lord Griffiths).

This case is different from *F's* case because it involves the concept of donation of bone marrow by a donor who is incapable of giving consent where a significant benefit will flow to another person. There was no other person in *Re F* who would have benefited directly as a result of the declaration sought, the benefits of sterilisation attaching solely to the mentally incapacitated subject of the application.

None the less, I am satisfied that the root question remains the same, namely, whether the procedures here envisaged will benefit the defendant and accordingly benefits which may flow to the plaintiff are relevant only insofar as they have a positive effect upon the best interests of the defendant.

As indicated, the defendant's family are a very close, supportive family. They are convinced that the defendant would give her consent to the proposals if she was in a position to do so…

In accordance with *F v West Berkshire Health Authority* (1989) 4 BMLR 1, [1990] 2 AC 1, I must look therefore at the situation of the defendant and ask whether the proposals placed before the court would benefit her and, if yes, whether those benefits outweigh any possible detriment to her.

So far as any benefits to the defendant are concerned, I have previously referred to the fact that this is a closely knit family. For the first ten years of her life, the defendant lived at home where she was looked after by her mother, assisted by her father and her sisters.

In the opinion of Dr B, who is a consultant in the psychiatry of learning disability, who is approved under s 12(2) of the Mental Health Act 1983, who was asked by the Official Solicitor on behalf of the defendant to prepare a report in this case and who gave oral evidence to me, the defendant may very well have some recollection of her early years living in the family home.

The information provided by those who now care for the defendant in the residential home make it apparent that the defendant benefits from the visits which she receives from her family and from her occasional involvement in family events, eg the wedding of one of her sisters, particularly because these visits maintain for her a link with the outside world which is helpful to her and which would otherwise be lost to her.

In addition, the Official Solicitor's representative observed affection between mother and daughter during a recent visit which demonstrated that her mother holds a special place in the defendant's world even if the defendant does not appreciate that this lady is in fact her mother.

If this application is not successful, the chances that the plaintiff will not survive are materially increased. She might be able to receive bone marrow from one of the two unrelated donors but Dr A's evidence to me shows that the recipient's chances of survival for 18 months following transplant from a sibling are at least 40%, whereas those chances after donation from a stranger in the case of the plaintiff's illness are at best 30%. The match from strangers is never quite as good as the match from a sibling.

Further, if the plaintiff survives the first six months post transplant then the prospects for survival semi-indefinitely are good. On the other hand, without any transplant her prospects of survival are very poor and are deteriorating fast. If the plaintiff dies, this is bound to have an adverse affect upon her mother who already suffers from significant ill health. One lay witness took the gloomy view that this event would prove fatal to the mother, but in any event her ability to visit the defendant would be handicapped significantly, not only by a likely deterioration in her health, but also by the need which would then arise for her to look after her only grandchild, E.

In this situation, the defendant would clearly be harmed by the reduction in or loss of contact to her mother. Accordingly, it is to the benefit of the defendant that she should act as donor to her sister, because in this way her positive relationship with her mother is most likely to be prolonged. Further, if the transplant occurs, this is likely to improve the defendant's relationship with her mother who in her heart clearly wishes it to take place and also to improve her relationship with the plaintiff who will be eternally grateful to her.

The disadvantages to the defendant of the harvesting procedure are very small. Expert evidence from two anaesthetists has been placed before me. Both agree that, subject to examination of the defendant by an independent anaesthetist to ensure that she has no, so far undetected, personal aversion to anaesthetic and that there is nothing in her medication or her physical state which makes her an unsuitable subject for a general anaesthetic, the risk in her case of such a process are extremely low, ie less than one per ten thousand and are no greater than those faced by the average patient in hospital. It would be advisable for the responsibility for her clinical management to be shared by two consultant anaesthetists and Dr A told me that this would present no problem.

It is an advantage that the defendant has in fact experienced a general anaesthetic on many occasions in her life including for a hysterectomy, without any apparent adverse effects. She can be accompanied to the operating theatre by a relative who can be present during induction and recovery and any subsequent pain can readily be controlled by at most two doses of intra-muscular morphine.

Of course, none of these problems would fall for consideration if the defendant did not act as donor for the plaintiff and it is relevant to ask the question, why subject the defendant to this process? To this the answer, in my judgment and in the judgment of the Official Solicitor, is because it is to her emotional, psychological and social benefit. This is the expert opinion of Dr B, who is very experienced in these matters and it is the conclusion to which I come on the evidence in this case.

I should perhaps emphasise that this is a rather unusual case and that the family of the plaintiff and the defendant are a particularly close family. It is doubtful that this case would act as a useful precedent in cases where the surgery involved is more intrusive than in this case, where the evidence shows that the bone marrow harvested is speedily regenerated and that a healthy individual can donate as much as two pints with no long term consequences at all. Thus, the bone marrow donated by the defendant will cause her no loss and she will suffer no real long term risk.

Accordingly, subject to any indication as a result of the further tests to be taken and the examination of the defendant by the independent anaesthetist as described, I shall grant the declaration sought.

Connell J justified the procedures applying the 'best interests' test. Although they had *no medical* benefit to the individual, he considered they would be for her 'emotional, psychological and social benefit'. In those American cases which have permitted donation by an incompetent child or adult, it has been the psychological benefit to the donor which has been important.

In each case, a very close personal emotional tie between the donor and donee has been crucial to the court's decision (see *Strunk v Strunk* (1969) 445 SW 2d 145 (Ky CA); *Hart v Brown* (1972) 289 A 2d 386 (Conn Super Ct); *Little v Little* (1979) 576 SW 2d 493 (Tex CA)). Indeed, in *Curran v Bosze* (1990) 566 NE 2d 1319, the only American case referred to by Connell J, one of the main reasons for the Illinois Supreme Court's refusal to allow bone marrow harvesting procedures was, as we saw, that the donor and donee (half brothers) hardly knew one another. Thus, it is the existing and continuing close relationship between the parties which is seen as the primary benefit to the individual in donating (see *Curran v Bosze* (*supra*) at 1343–1344 per Calvo J). The evidence of psychological benefit to Miss Y identified by Connell J was that: (i) the family was a close knit one and Miss Y gained from family visits and being involved in family occasions and these would be affected by the death of her sister; (ii) Miss Y was close to her mother (although she did not appear to know that she was her mother) and her mother's already poor health would be adversely affected by the death of the plaintiff which together with the added burden of caring for her grandson would reduce or eliminate her visits to Miss Y; (iii) her relationship with her mother and sister would be improved as they would both be grateful for what Miss Y would have done. On balance, however, the evidence does not seem to have been particularly strong. Miss Y did not live with her sister; nor does there seem to have been much evidence of a particularly close tie between them (cf *Strunk* (*supra*), where the donor was *dependent* upon his brother who needed the transplant).

Of course, the judge recognised that it was insufficient for him merely to identify a 'benefit' to Miss Y without weighing against this any detriment that she might suffer by undergoing the procedures. However, the risks inherent in the procedures – the general anaesthetic and the removal of two pints of bone marrow – were regarded as 'very small' (one in 10,000 risk of death) and non-existent (as bone marrow is regenerative) respectively. Further, any pain that might arise from the harvesting could be controlled by morphine. And, of course, there could be a detriment by *not* undergoing the procedure. In one American case, for instance, the court relied upon psychiatric evidence that the death of the donor's brother would have an 'extremely traumatic effect upon him' (*Strunk v Strunk* (*supra*), per Osborne J at 147). In *Re Y*, Connell J referred to the 'harm' Miss Y would suffer (directly and indirectly) from the death of her sister although the evidence never elevated this to the level of psychiatric injury.

Given the weaknesses in the evidence which have been suggested above, *Re Y* could be seen as giving a 'green light' to support donations by incompetent adults and children in the future. This would, we think, be a misreading of the case and not Connell J's intention for a number of reasons.

First, the case is probably an unusual one in that it concerned a procedure which does have minimal risks for the donor. Given the need to weigh the benefits of the procedure against the risks of doing it, it is not likely that a court would contemplate donation of non-regenerative tissue such as a kidney. Connell J suggested as much when he remarked that his decision should not be considered 'a useful precedent in cases where the surgery involved is more intrusive'. While the long-term risks of having one kidney are not great, they do exist and the nature of the procedure suggests that it would be difficult to satisfy the 'best interests' test.

Secondly, the courts will undoubtedly look for evidence of a 'close relationship' which will be damaged if the donee-patient dies. It is most unlikely, therefore, that the court would contemplate even a minimally risky procedure if the donor's mental disability or if the child's age prevented them forming such a relationship. Donations by babies and the severely mentally disabled may thus be out of court. Also, the court will look for immediate psychological benefit and would reject as too tenuous evidence of the long-term future benefit of not 'living in a family under the shadow of avoidable, premature death' (J Savulescu 'Substantial Harm but Substantial Benefit' (1996) 312 BMJ 241).

Thirdly, the court might well as a rule-of-thumb look for the 'agreement' (though obviously not the consent) of the donor as a condition to allowing the donation. This would also exclude donations from the very young or severely disabled. Also, it is unthinkable that the 'best interests' test could be satisfied if the donor objected to the donation.

Fourthly, there is no suggestion in Connell J's judgment that purely altruistic benefit will satisfy the 'best interests' test. He restricted himself to situations of 'psychological benefit' (see also *Curran v Bosze* (*supra*) at 1343 per Calvo J: 'the psychological benefit is not simply one of personal, individual altruism in an abstract theoretical sense'). There is no support, therefore, in his judgment for permitting non-therapeutic research upon incompetent adults or children even though this does have strong professional support in exceptional cases of 'minimal risk'.

As *Re Y* shows, the 'best interests' test means 'best interests' of the *patient* and not another. Thus, parents cannot consent to a procedure which is in the interests of a sibling (see *Re Y, supra*) or in their own interests (see *Re Eve* (1986) 31 DLR (4th) 1 (Can SC)). The 'authority to act. . . is conferred on parents – for the benefit of the child and not for the benefit of the parents' (*Secretary, Dept of Health and Community Services, supra*, per McHugh J at 316). So a caesarean section could only be permitted on an incompetent pregnant woman if it was in *her*, rather than her unborn child's interests (see *Re MB* (1997) 38 BMLR 175 (CA) at 188 per Butler-Sloss LJ, discussed *infra*).

(ii) DETERMINING BEST INTERESTS

In *Re F (mental patient: sterilisation)* [1990] 2 AC 1 (HL), the judges, in the context of an incompetent adult had this to say about 'best interests'. Lord Brandon stated at (55):

> The operation or other treatment will be in their best interests if, but only if, it is carried out in order either to save their lives, or to ensure improvement or prevent deterioration in their physical or mental health.

Lord Goff spoke of action taken 'to preserve the life, health or well-being' of the incompetent patient (at 76) (see also Neill and Butler-Sloss LJJ in Court of Appeal at 32 and 42 respectively).

The law is looking for overall 'benefit' to the patient, whether medical, psychological *or social* (for a different view see, *infra*). As regards the latter, notice in particular, Lord Goff's reference in *Re F* to the patient's 'well-being' and Butler-Sloss LJ's remark in *Re MB* (*supra*) that '[b]est interests are not limited to best medical interests' (at 188). In reaching a determination few, if any, situations will inevitably involve one choice: there will be alternatives. At least, there will be the option of non-intervention. It is for the court (or other decision-maker) to weigh up the advantages and disadvantages of each option (or of treatment and non-treatment) in reaching a decision on 'best interests' (see, *Re A (medical treatment: male sterilisation)* [2000] 1 FCR 193 (CA) and *Re S (adult: sterilisation)* (2000) Times, 26 May (CA) discussed *infra*). In determining the 'best interests' of the child, s 1(3) of the Children Act 1989 sets out a number of facts which the 'court shall have regard to'.

1. (3) In the circumstances mentioned in subsection (4), a court shall have regard in particular to—
   (a) the ascertainable wishes and feelings of the child concerned (considered in the light of his age and understanding);
   (b) his physical, emotional and educational needs;
   (c) the likely effect on him of any change in his circumstances;
   (d) his age, sex, background and any characteristics of his which the court considers relevant;
   (e) any harm which he has suffered or is at risk of suffering;
   (f) how capable each of his parents, and any other person in relation to whom the court considers the question to be relevant, is of meeting his needs;
   (g) the range of powers available to the court under this Act in the proceedings in question

It is important to notice that this 'check list', as it is sometimes called, is not exhaustive or comprehensive. Also, all the factors may not be relevant in a particular instance. As you will see, the factors include the 'ascertainable wishes and feelings' of the child, considered 'in the light of his age and understanding'. The wishes will not be determinative and the courts' approach was spelt out by Butler-Sloss LJ in *Re P (minors) (wardship: care and control)* [1992] 2 FCR 681 at 687:

> How far the wishes of children should be a determinative factor…must of course vary on the particular facts of each case. Those views must be considered and may, but not necessarily must, carry more weight as the children grow older.

As we shall see, the court may be prepared to override even a *competent* child's view (*infra*). And the court may authorise the use of force to ensure that treatment in the child's 'best interests' is carried out (see *infra*).

Nevertheless, the wishes of the patient may be important where there are treatment choices, particularly where the patient is an adult. For this reason, in the incompetent adult cases the courts have encouraged consultation with the patient's relatives (see *Re F, supra,* per Lord Goff at 78 and *Re G (persistent vegetative state* [1995] 2 FCR 46 and Commentary (1995) 3 Med L Rev 80 (AG)). In *Re T, supra,* at 51-52 Lord Donaldson MR stated:

> Consultation with the next of kin has a further advantage in that it may reveal information as to the personal circumstances of the patient and as to the choice which the patient might have made, if he or she had been in a position to make it. Neither the personal circumstances of the patient nor a speculative answer to the question 'What would the patient have chosen?' can bind the practitioner in his choice of whether or not to treat or how to treat…but they are factors to be taken into account by him in forming a clinical judgment as to what is in the best interests of the patient. For example, if he learnt that the patient was a Jehovah's Witness, but had had no evidence of a refusal to accept blood transfusions, he would avoid or postpone any blood transfusion so long as possible.

(iii) THE ROLE OF THE COURT

It is important to realise, though it may appear trite to say, that the scope of the proxy's power (or what is in the adult patient's best interests) is a matter for the law. The importance of stating this lies in the fact that as the law sets the scope so it necessarily sets the boundaries of the power and thereby imposes limits. At one level, it could be argued that the boundaries established by the court are essentially, indeed inherently, *ad hoc*. The court merely determines whether in the particular case before it a proxy's decision is, or is not, in the child's best interests. This, of course, atomises the legal approach and prevents the emergence of any general outline of the boundaries of the proxy's power by reference to which proxies in the future may be guided or held to account. We can see the explicit recognition (and rejection) of this approach by Brennan, Deane and McHugh JJ in the Australian High Court case of *Secretary, Department of Health and Community Services v JWB and SMB* (1992) 175 CLR 218.

Secretary, Department of Health and Community Services v JWB and SMB (1992) 175 CLR 218

Brennan J: In ascertaining where the welfare of a child lies, the courts have sought to discover what is in the child's 'best interests'. The 'best interests' approach focuses attention on the child whose interests are in question. By asserting that the *child's* 'best interests' are 'the first and paramount consideration', the law is freed from the degrading doctrines of earlier times which gave priority to parental or, more particularly, paternal rights to which the interests of the child were subordinated. But, that said, the best interests approach does no more than identify the person whose interests are in question: it does not assist in identifying the factors which are relevant to the best interests of the child. The summary rejection by the House of Lords of the criterion offered by *Re Eve* left their Lordships without any guidelines by which to decide *In re B* – or, at least, without guidelines that could be articulated for general application.

That is because the best interests approach offers no hierarchy of values which might guide the exercise of a discretionary power to authorize sterilization, much less any general legal principle which might direct the difficult decisions to be made in this area by parents, guardians, the medical profession and courts. It is arguable that, in a field where the law has not developed, where ethical principles remain controversial and where each case turns on its own facts, the law should not pretend to too great a precision…by transforming a 'complex moral and social question' into a question of fact, the best interests approach leaves the court in the hands of 'experts' who assemble a dossier of fact and opinion on matters which they deem relevant 'without reference to any check-list of *legal requirements*'…the best interests approach is useful only to the extent of ensuring that the first and paramount consideration is the interests of the child, not the interests of others. That approach furnishes no general guidance as to the factors which are relevant to the welfare of the child…

Deane J: That which constitutes the welfare of a child in a particular case falls to be determined by reference to general community standards, but making due allowance for the entitlement of parents, within the limits of what is permissible in accordance with those standards, to entertain divergent views about the moral and secular objectives to be pursued for their children…

McHugh J: What is in the best interests of the child is conventionally seen as being synonymous with the welfare of the child. To say that a medical or surgical procedure is in the best interests of a child, however, is merely to record a result. Before the best interests of the child can be determined, some principle, rule or standard must be applied to the facts and circumstances of the case.

Likewise, in *Re J (a minor) (wardship: medical treatment)* [1990] 3 All ER 930 at 942, Balcombe LJ stated:

I would deprecate any attempt by this court to lay down such an all-embracing test since the circumstances of these tragic cases are so infinitely various. I do not know of any demand by the judges who have to deal with these cases at first instance for this court to assist them by laying down any test beyond that which is already the law: that the interests of the ward are the first and paramount consideration, subject to the gloss on that test which I suggest, that in determining where those interests lie the court adopts the standpoint of the reasonable and responsible parent who has his or her child's best interests at heart.

If, however, it is accepted that a court's role, indeed obligation, is to offer an outline or framework for decision-making it would seem that the court has been slow to undertake this quasi-legislative role. Even when the court begins to undertake this responsibility it is in the nature of the judicial process working from case to case that it will take some time before general criteria begin to emerge. We will in future chapters see how the courts have developed criteria in cases of sterilisation (ch 9) and the treatment of severely handicapped babies (ch 17).

I. Criteria, review and *de novo* decision-making
What, then, is the court doing when the decision of a proxy about the best interests of a child is challenged before the court? In situations when the criteria have to be applied in a particular case, there are a number of possible roles which a court might choose to play (see A Grubb 'Treatment Decisions: Keeping it in the Family' in A Grubb (ed), *Choices and Decisions in Health Care* (1993) pp 48–54). The court could become the proxy decision-maker and impose its own view, *de novo*, of the child's best interests. Alternatively, the court could inquire whether the decision-maker had given his mind to, and taken account of, the relevant criteria set by the law and further, if he had, that he had not applied them capriciously. If the court adopts the former role is it not setting itself up as a kind of 'super-parent' all wise and knowing? Leaving aside the factual issue of why a judge should be a better parent than the parent(s) in question, is there any legal basis for this role? That the courts do it is, of course, a legal basis of a sort in itself. At a deeper level, when the question is 'are they entitled to do it?' it can at least be argued that they have no right to substitute their view for that of the parent. This

is because at the level of political philosophy the law makes the assumption that parents are *prima facie* the decision-makers. It is not a good ground for interfering with the parents' decision to say you disagree with it. Lord Mackay LC can be seen reflecting this in his comment on the Children Bill (later the Children Act 1989) when he said:

> The integrity and independence of the family is the basic building block of a free and democratic society and the need to defend it should be clearly perceivable in the law. [Perceptions of the Children Bill and Beyond (1989) 139 New LJ 505 at 505.]

So what of the other role where the court acts to *review* the parents' decision? This is similar to the court's role in public law when a public body's decision is challenged. The legal basis as well as the attractions of this role are that the court does not usurp the function of the *prima facie* decision-maker. Rather, it stands back from the outcome of the particular decision while ensuring that the process of decision-making is legitimate.

In our view the court's proper role should be to *review* but not usurp. An inevitable consequence of adopting this role is that the courts must establish the criteria by reference to which the *prima facie* decision-maker must be guided. This quasi-legislative function in turn demands that in the sorts of cases we are considering the courts must begin to give substance to such general expressions as 'best interests'. This is precisely what the courts, albeit reluctantly, have moved towards in the cases concerning handicapped babies (see *infra*, ch 17). A similar development can be seen in the cases concerned with sterilising the intellectually disabled (see *infra*, ch 9).

One feature of the development of criteria is that the court will begin to identify factors which the proxy may *not* have regard to, such that if he does his decision cannot stand. One example may be where a proxy bases his decision on his particular religious creed. Regard may, of course, be paid to a religious view of a proxy when the effect on the child is not significant (eg ritual male circumcision). The moment the child's life or limb is at risk the court will have regard to the well-known aphorism of Rutledge J in *Prince v Massachusetts* (1944) 321 US 158 at 170:

> Parents may be free to become martyrs themselves, but it does not follow that they are free in identical circumstances to make martyrs of their children before they have reached the age of full and legal discretion when they can make the choices for themselves.

A classic example is, of course, the refusal of a life-saving blood transfusion for a child of a Jehovah's Witness (see also *Re C (a minor) (medical treatment)* [1998] Lloyd's Rep Med 1 – withdrawal of ventilation from a severely disabled baby contrary to the religious based wishes of the parents). The following case illustrates the approach of the English courts.

Re S (a minor) (medical treatment) [1993] 1 FLR 376 (Fam Div)

> S, aged 4½, had recently been diagnosed as suffering from T-cell leukaemia with a high risk of death. The condition was able to be treated by intensified chemotherapy treatment which had four phases. The transfusion of blood or blood products was an essential supplement. S's parents were dedicated Jehovah's Witnesses and the family records and instructions had always opposed blood transfusions. A case conference had explored the irreconcilable gulf between the consultant's need to include transfusion in the range of treatments available and the parents' conscientious objection to consent to the treatment. The local authority had sought leave to invoke the inherent jurisdiction under s 100 of the Children Act 1989, which had been granted, and for an order permitting a blood transfusion. The following day the parents had issued an application under the Children Act 1989 for a prohibited steps order. The consultant paediatrician had given evidence of the medical need to administer a transfusion in emergency and non-emergency categories. He had been of the opinion that it would have been impossible for him to treat S intensively without the discretion to administer blood.

The consultant had already varied the conventional treatment of S's condition to reflect the convictions of the parents. A senior lecturer in paediatric oncology who had a shared responsibility for major decisions with the consultant in relation to S's treatment had also given evidence on behalf of the local authority. He had stated that either the consultant had the authority to treat S intensively with the discretion to administer blood or there was no medical treatment which held any prospect of cure. The father had been fully supportive of any form of medical or scientific intervention provided it did not breach the veto upon the use of blood. Thorpe J granted the local authority the order it sought.

Thorpe J: The case for the defendants rested on the evidence of the father. He is a young man, but impressive in his emotional control and in the sincerity and simplicity with which he states his convictions. He is fully supportive of any form of medical or scientific intervention providing it does not breach the veto upon the use of blood. There was no impression of the bigot, of the closed mind, or of unreasonable obstinacy. His acceptance of the inevitability of life and death coupled with his faith seemed to make it easy for him to conclude that faith comes first and it is not to be abandoned simply because it leads to awful decisions.

At the end of his evidence, Mr Daniel, on his behalf, sought to argue that regard should be had to the risk factor inherent in the use of blood in the course of medical treatment. He specified the risks as falling into the following categories: mismatch of blood types; samples which had been carelessly stored; samples which had been taken from an HIV positive; samples that were contaminated with hepatitis virus and, finally, samples contaminated with diverse other diseases.

It seems to me that that argument is of little weight beside the argument of conviction advanced by the father, although it is accepted by both doctors that there is a theoretical risk in the use of blood in treatment. It is statistically absolutely tiny, so tiny as to be almost minimal. As the second doctor said, it is impossible to say that any medical treatment is absolutely free of risk. In respect of any medical treatment it is necessary for the practitioner to balance the risks against the advantages, and that exercise in the case of the use of blood invariably results in the conclusion that the advantages enormously outweigh the risks.

Then, Mr Daniel relies upon a statement in an American publication which is at p 27 and following in the second exhibit to his client's affidavit. It is issued by the Counsel of Judges in America and is headed, 'Guides to the Judge in Medical Orders Affecting Children'. The passage relied upon by Mr Daniel appears at p 39. It reads thus:

If there is a choice of procedures, if, for example, a doctor recommends a procedure which had an 80% chance of success but of which the parents disapprove, and the parents have no objection to a procedure which has only a 40% chance of success the doctor must take the medically riskier but parentally unobjectionable course.

Well, in relation to that passage I make the general observation that the proposition that it states is not one which seems to me to apply in child cases in which this court exercises its inherent jurisdiction. In this court, the test must remain the welfare of the child as the paramount consideration. Specifically, in this case, the choice is not between two medical procedures with similar, if differing, prospects of success. Here the stark choice is between one medical procedure with no prospect of success and one medical treatment with a prospect of success which is put at even.

So, as I put to Mr Daniel in argument: are the religious convictions of the parents to deny their child a 50% chance of survival? Are those convictions to deny him that 50% chance and condemn him to inevitable and early death? Mr Daniel realistically saw that this was an extreme case and one in which it is difficult to pursue the argument that the religious convictions of the parents should deny the child the chance of treatment.

Finally, Mr Daniel invites the court to look ahead to the later years of childhood. If this treatment is applied in the face of parental opposition what would be the difficulties and stresses for S in years to come – parented by parents who believe that his life was prolonged by an ungodly act? Well, that consideration seems to me one that has little foundation in reality. The reality seems to me to be that family reaction will recognise that the responsibility for consent was taken from them and, as a judicial act, absolved their conscience of responsibility.

(For other such cases see *Re E (a minor)* (1990) 9 BMLR 1 (Ward J); *Re O (a minor) (medical treatment)* [1993] 4 Med LR 272 (Johnson J); *Re R (a minor)*, [1993] 2 FLR 757 (Booth J)).

You will notice that in *Re S*, and indeed in the other cases, the evidence established that there was only one treatment which carried any hope for the child. This may not always be the case. Indeed, Thorpe J refers to the situation where two therapies are available with differing chances of success but, perhaps, equally with differing risks or side-effects.

What should be the court's approach if the parents elect for the treatment with the lower chance of success but with less severe side-effects? The following American case provides some guidance. It suggests that some cases will arise in which the proxy's decision does not fall outside the permitted bounds (by reason of taking account of inappropriate factors) nor is it capricious but is one with which others may disagree, perhaps vehemently. The New York case of *Re Hofbauer* (1979) 395 NE 2d 1109 (NY CA) provides an example. The case involved the use of laetrile (a natural substance derived from apricot pits) as a treatment for a child's leukaemia.

Re Hofbauer (1979) 395 NE 2d 1109 (NY CA)

Jason J: [I]t is important to stress that a parent, in making the sensitive decision as to how the child should be treated, may rely upon the recommendations and competency of the attending physician if he or she is duly licensed to practise medicine in this State, for '[i]f a physician is licensed by the State, he is recognised by the State as capable of exercising acceptable clinical judgment.' (*Doe v Bolton* 410 US 179 at 199, 93 S Ct 739 at 751, 35 L Ed 2d 201 at 217, reh den 410 US 959, 93 S Ct 1410, 35 L Ed 2d 694.) Obviously, for all practical purposes, the average parent must rely upon the recommendations and competency of the attending physician since the physician is both trained and in the best position to evaluate the medical needs of the child.

Ultimately, however, the most significant factor in determining whether a child is being deprived of adequate medical care, and, thus, a neglected child within the meaning of the statute, is whether the parents have provided an acceptable course of medical treatment for their child in light of all the surrounding circumstances. This inquiry cannot be posed in terms of whether the parent has made a 'right' or a 'wrong' decision, for the present state of the practice of medicine, despite its vast advances, very seldom permits such definitive conclusions. Nor can a court assume the role of surrogate parent and establish as the objective criteria with which to evaluate a parent's decision its own judgment as to the exact method or degree of medical treatment which should be provided, for such standard is fraught with subjectivity. Rather, in our view, the court's inquiry should be whether the parents, once having sought accredited medical assistance and having been made aware of the seriousness of their child's affliction and the possibility of cure if a certain mode of treatment is undertaken, have provided for their child a treatment which is recommended by their physician and which has not been totally rejected by all responsible medical authority.

With these considerations in mind and cognisant that the State has the burden of demonstrating neglect (see *Re C Children* 55 AD 2d 646, 390 NYS 2d 10), we now examine the facts of this case. It is abundantly clear that this is not a case where the parents, for religious reasons, refused necessary medical procedures for their child (eg *Re Sampson* 37 Ad 2d 668, 323 NE 2d 253; affd 29 NY 2d 900, 326 NYS 2d 398; *Re Gregory* S 85 Misc 2d 846, 380 NE 2d 620), nor is this a case where the parents have made an irreversible decision to deprive their child of a certain mode of treatment (*Custody of a Minor* 379 NE 2d 1053 [Mass]). Indeed, this is not a case where the child is receiving no medical treatment, for the record discloses that Joseph's mother and father were concerned and loving parents who sought qualified medical assistance for their child.

Rather, appellants predict their charge of neglect upon the basis that Joseph's parents have selected for their child a mode of treatment which is inadequate and ineffective. Both courts below found, however – and we conclude that these findings are supported by the record – that numerous qualified doctors have been consulted by Dr Schachter and have contributed to the child's care; that the parents have both serious and justifiable concerns about the deleterious effects of radiation treatments and chemotherapy; that there is medical proof that the nutritional treatment being administered Joseph was controlling his condition and that such treatment is not as toxic as is the conventional treatment; and that conventional treatments will be administered to the child if his condition so warrants. In light of these affirmed findings of fact, we are unable to conclude, as a matter of law, that Joseph's parents have not undertaken reasonable efforts to ensure that acceptable medical treatment is being provided their child.

(Cf *Custody of a Minor* (1979) 393 NE 2d 836 (Mass Sup Jud Ct) and *Re Hamilton* (1983) 657 SW 2d 425 (Tenn CA)).

The question in English law is whether a court would stay its hand or feel compelled to take its own view. Our view is that the court should stay its hand both because the parents are *prima facie* entitled to form a judgment within the permissible limits, and because the court has no real basis for claiming to be a better parent.

II. *Re T* and reasonableness

In fact, the approach of the English courts does not precisely mirror the view expressed here. The courts do adopt an *ad hoc* approach to decision-making whilst providing some (if albeit limited) criteria for others who must apply the 'best interests' test. The courts have, however, eschewed overt deference to parents expressly rejecting the argument that only 'unreasonable' parental decisions will be overturned. The leading decision is *Re T (a minor) (wardship: medical treatment)* (1996) 35 BMLR 63.

Re T (a minor) (wardship: medical treatment) (1996) 35 BMLR 63 (CA)

C, who was born on 10 April 1995, suffers from biliary atresia, a life-threatening liver defect. Without a liver transplant, he will not live beyond two-and-a-half years of age. His parents, who are not married, are both health care professionals and experienced in the care of sick young children, and are not willing for the transplant surgery to be carried out. Both parents were currently resident in a Commonwealth country. When C's liver defect was first diagnosed, he underwent a Kasai operation at the age of three-and-a-half weeks, but the outcome was unsuccessful. It is as a consequence of the pain and distress which C was caused by that operation that his parents do not wish him to undergo the transplant surgery, notwithstanding that a consultant paediatrician at one of the hospitals which carries out liver transplants, has assessed C and found him suitable for a transplant and that in the consultant's view, it was in C's best interests for the surgery to be carried out. C's mother sought a second opinion which was also supportive of the transplant surgery for C. it was when C was placed on the urgent transplant list at one of the above hospitals that his mother, against the advice of the consultant paediatrician, took him abroad where there were no facilities for a liver transplant. On 27 August 1996 the local authority in which C had lived was granted leave to commence proceedings under s 100(3) of the Children Act 1989 and the Official Solicitor was appointed guardian ad litem for C. On 17 September 1996 Connell J concluded that the decision of C's mother not to consent to the transplant surgery was not the conduct of a reasonable parent and directed the return of C and his mother to the jurisdiction within 21 days, and that C be presented to a hospital in order that he might undergo the liver transplantation. That decision was the subject of the appeal.

Butler-Sloss LJ: At the substantive hearing of the application of the local authority, Connell J heard evidence from Dr P, Mr R and Dr A, all distinguished consultants in this specialist field. Dr P accepted the opinion of Mr R as to the likely success of the transplant operation. In their reports and in their oral evidence the three doctors were unanimous that the prospects of success were good and that this operation was in the best interests of the child. Dr A and her team were prepared to carry out the operation without the consent of the mother if the court gave consent. The judge felt that the breakdown in the relationship between the mother and the team of Dr A made hospital X unsuitable in the best interests of C. Dr P and his team, while strongly recommending the operation, would wish to respect the decision of the mother and would not be prepared to perform the operation without her consent. Mr R was prepared to carry out the operation but could not answer for his team in the event that the mother did not consent.

The local authority in their originating summons sought the answers to three specific questions: (1) whether it was in the best interests of C to undergo surgery for a liver transplant; (2) for permission to be granted to perform the surgery notwithstanding the refusal of the mother to consent; and (3) for the child to be returned to the jurisdiction for the purpose of such surgery. They were neutral before the judge and the proposed surgery was strongly advocated by C's guardian ad litem…

On the appeal Mr Francis QC, for the mother, informed us that the mother has not changed her mind and that she continued to be supported in her views by the father. He challenged the judge's conclusion that the mother's refusal to consent was unreasonable. He relied heavily upon the opinion of Dr P that he and his team respected the mother's decision and would not seek to go behind it and their view of the enormous importance of the total co-operation of the mother to the operation and the consequential treatment. In most medical situations there was more than one answer. The doctors' view was based upon clinical grounds, but where the welfare of a child required a family decision that decision if reasonable ought to be respected and the inherent jurisdiction of the court ought not to be exercised to overrule it. The more borderline the decision the more weight should be given to the parent's view. He stressed the possibility of further operations and further treatment and the effect upon the mother and upon the child. The choice was to allow the child a short life where he was well and happy for most of the time and would be likely to die peacefully or to cause him to undergo major invasive surgery with a good success rate but all the risks, discomfort and distress for a young child and a lifetime of drugs and the possibility of further invasive surgery and other treatment. The consequence of the decision was to commit the mother to a lifetime of care of the child with the requirement of total commitment to the treatment. The importance of the element of morale was not to be underestimated. The mother would find it very difficult to support the treatment, despite her specialist training and her devotion to the child. Since transplant operations have only been performed for 14 years on children, the statistics were inadequate as a guide for the future. He drew a distinction between extending life and allowing a child to die prematurely. The mother's decision was within that band of reasonable decisions with which the court should not interfere and coerce the mother.

Mr Harris QC, for the local authority, and Mr Murdoch QC, for the Official Solicitor as guardian ad litem of C, strongly supported the decision of the judge that the transplant operation was in the best interests of C. They argued that the judge was entitled to come to the conclusion that the mother's refusal of consent was unreasonable in the light of unanimous medical opinion that this was the accepted treatment and the surgery gave the child a good chance of an extended and a reasonable quality of life. The test was welfare of the child and not the reasonableness of the parent. The view of the parents was only one factor in the welfare test. We were reminded of the enormous strides which continue to be made in medical knowledge and techniques which supported the good prospects of success for the child. There was no reason to suppose that, if the operation was carried out, this mother with her special abilities would not respond to the needs of the child and care for him with devotion and competence. Mr Murdoch stressed that the practical difficulties were not insuperable and should be met if or when they arose...

A line of cases from 1981 has, in my judgment, clearly established the approach of the court to these most difficult and anxious questions...

For the decisions to which I have referred which bind this court it is clear that when an application under the inherent jurisdiction is made to the court the welfare of the child is the paramount consideration. The consent or refusal of consent of the parents is an important consideration to weigh in the balancing exercise to be carried out by the judge. In that context the extent to which the court will have regard to the view of the parent will depend upon the court's assessment of that view. But as Sir Thomas Bingham MR said in *Re Z*, the court decides and in doing so may overrule the decision of a reasonable parent.

Applying those principles to the present appeal, the first argument of Mr Francis that the court should not interfere with the reasonable decision of a parent is not one that we are able to entertain even if we wished to do so. His suggestion that the decision of this mother came within that band of reasonable decisions within which a court would not interfere would import into this jurisdiction the test applied in adoption to the refusal of a parent to consent to adoption. It is wholly inapposite to the welfare test and is incompatible with the decision in *Re Z*.

In my view, however, the judge erred in his approach to the issue before the court. He accepted the unchallenged clinical opinion of the three consultants and assessed the reasonableness of the mother's decision against that medical opinion. Having held that the mother was unreasonable, he accepted that the liver transplant would be likely to prolong the life of C and, in the absence of any reasonable argument to the contrary, he came to the clear conclusion that he should consent to the operation. Since he had already decided that the mother's approach was unreasonable, he did not weigh in the balance reasons against the treatment which might be held by a reasonable parent on much broader grounds than the clinical assessment of the likely success of the proposed treatment. Some of the objections of the mother, such as the difficulties of the operation itself, turned out, from the evidence of Mr R, to be less important than the mother believed. Underlying those less important objections by the mother, was a deep-seated concern of the mother as to the benefits to her son of the major invasive surgery and post-operative treatment, the dangers of failure long term as well as short term, the possibility of the need for further transplants, the likely length of life, and the effect upon her son of all these concerns. The judge did not assess the relevance or the weight of such considerations in his final balancing exercise.

In particular he did not consider at that stage the evidence of Dr P and his strong reservations as to the effect of coercing (as Dr P put it) this mother into playing the crucial and irreplaceable part of the aftermath of major invasive surgery, not just during the post-operative treatment of an 18-month-old baby, but also throughout the childhood of her son. She would inevitably be the primary carer (no one suggested that this baby should be taken into care), and would be expected to care for him for many years through surgery and continuing treatment while she, on her present view, believed that this course was not right for her son. The total commitment of the caring parent, in Dr P's view, was essential to the success of the treatment. Mr Harris suggested to us that Dr P's evidence supporting the mother's approach lacked logic and was woolly. That suggestion is, in my view, to underestimate the experience of a distinguished consultant paediatrician in a specialist and still experimental area of medicine. Moreover, his evidence was supported by the advice given to parents by hospital X in its Fact Sheet 10.

I have well in mind the important principles set out by the House of Lords in *G v G* [1985] 2 All ER 225, [1985] 1 WLR 647 and that this most experienced judge saw the witnesses and in particular the mother. If the decision in this case was a matter of assessing the clinical opinions of the doctors, the judge was clearly right to prefer their views to that of the mother, who could not be as well qualified to give an opinion. But this matter has to be looked at more broadly. The mother certainly told the judge that she recognised her son had only a short time to live if no operation was performed. She was focusing, it seems to me, on the present peaceful life of the child who had the chance to spend the rest of his short life without the pain, stress and upset of intrusive surgery against the future with the operation and treatment taking place. That is an alternative point of view to that to which the judge came and, with some hesitation, I doubt that he was right to deem the mother to be unreasonable in her assessment of the broader perspective of whether this operation should be carried out. But, in any event, the reasonableness of the mother was not the primary issue. This mother and this child are one for the purpose of this unusual case and the decision of the court to consent to the operation jointly affects the mother and son and it also affects the father. The welfare of this child depends upon his mother. The practical considerations of her ability to cope with supporting the child in the face of her belief that this course is not right for him, the requirement to return probably for a long period to this country, either to leave the father behind and lose his support or to require him to give up his present job and seek one in England were not put by the judge into the balance when he made his decision.

Despite the conclusion of the judge which I have set out above, I do not believe that he put into the balance these broader considerations. Consequently, in my view his exercise of discretion was flawed and I am satisfied that his decision cannot stand.

It falls therefore for this court to make the decision whether to consent to the operation and require the return of the child to the jurisdiction. I agree with Mr Murdoch that this court ought not to make a decision on so difficult and delicate an issue mainly on the problems of ordering the return of the child when he is out of the jurisdiction, or in ignorance of whether hospital Z would in fact carry out the operation if the mother continued in her refusal to consent. But they are none the less relevant considerations which, in my judgment, have to be taken into account in the balancing exercise, although they are not determinative. More important than those considerations is, to my mind, the evidence of Dr P and the emphasis he placed throughout his evidence upon the requirements both of the consent of the parents and of a total commitment by the caring parent to the proposed treatment. He foresaw grave difficulties in carrying out the operation and the treatment without that wholehearted support of the mother.

In *Re W (a minor) (medical treatment)* (1992) 9 BMLR 22, [1993] Fam 64, a case about the medical treatment of a girl of 16 suffering from anorexia nervosa, Lord Donaldson MR said (1992) 9 BMLR 22 at 29, [1993] Fam 64 at 76) that there were two purposes to seeking consent, clinical and legal:

> The clinical purpose stems from the fact that in many instances the co-operation of the patient and the patient's faith or at least confidence in the efficiency of the treatment is a major factor contributing to the treatment's success.

That passage applies, in my judgment, with equal force to the need for the confidence in and the commitment to the proposed treatment by the principal carer on the unusual facts of this case. Unlike the intestinal obstruction of the Down's Syndrome baby, which could be cured by a simple operation, C's problems require complicated surgery and many years of special care from the mother.

The reservations of Dr P, to which he held despite concessions he made in his evidence, remain of great significance and importance. His view that the decision of a loving, caring mother should be respected, ought to be given great weight, and is reinforced by the Fact Sheet 10 provided by hospital X. The alternative, of the court giving the consent and passing back the responsibility for the parental care to the mother and expecting her to provide the commitment to the child after the operation is carried out in the face of her opposition, is in itself fraught with danger for the child. She will have to comply with the court order, return to this country, and present the child to one of the hospitals. She will have to arrange to remain in this country for the foreseeable future. Will the father stay in country AB and work or come with her to England, giving up his job and having to seek another job? If he does not come she will have to manage unaided. How will the mother cope? Can her professionalism overcome her view that her son should not be subjected to this distressing procedure? Will she break down? How will the child be affected by the conflict with which the mother may have to cope? What happens if the treatment is partially successful and another transplant is needed? The mother may not wish to consent to further surgery. Is the court to be asked again for consent to the next operation?

The welfare of the child is the paramount consideration and I recognise the 'very strong presumption in favour of a course of action which will prolong life' and the inevitable consequences for the child of not giving consent. But to prolong life, as Lord Donaldson MR recognised in somewhat different circumstances, is not the sole objective of the court and to require it at the expense of other considerations may not be in a child's best interests. I would stress that, on the most unusual facts of this case, with the enormous significance of the close attachment between the mother and baby, the court is not concerned with the reasonableness of the mother's refusal to consent but with the consequences of that refusal and whether it is in the best interests of C for this court, in effect, to direct the mother to take on this total commitment where she does not agree with the course proposed. The effect of the evidence of Dr P, respecting the mother's decision, and the prospect of forcing the devoted mother of this young baby to the consequences of this major invasive surgery, lead me to the conclusion, after much anxious deliberation, that it is not in the best interests of this child to give consent and require him to return to England for the purpose of undergoing liver transplantation. I believe that the best interests of this child require that his future treatment should be left in the hands of his devoted parents. Once the pressure of this litigation is over it may be the parents will reconsider whether they should remain in country AB or should return to this country and attend at hospital Y with a view to a further assessment for the purpose of carrying out the operation. That, however, will be a matter for them and not for this court.

I would allow this appeal and would answer the three questions posed in the originating summons in the negative and would set aside the orders of the judge.

Waite LJ: The cases cited by Butler-Sloss LJ are uncompromising in their assertion that the sole yardstick must be the need to give effect to the demands of paramountcy for the welfare of the child. They establish that there are bound to be occasions when such paramountcy will compel the court, acting as a judicial parent, to substitute the judge's own views as to the claims of child welfare over those of natural parents – even in a case where the views of the latter are supported by qualities of devotion, commitment, love and reason. The judge, after anxious consideration, reached the conclusion that this case provides such an occasion. Was he right to do so?…

In this instance, however, in agreement with Butler-Sloss LJ, I consider that the judge was betrayed into an error of law by his concern with the need to form a judgment about the reasonableness of the mother's approach. An appraisal of parental reasonableness may be appropriate in other areas of family law (in adoption, for example, where it is enjoined by statute) but when it comes to an assessment of the demands of the child patient's welfare, the starting point – and the finishing point too – must always be the judge's own independent assessment of the balance of advantage or disadvantage of the particular medical step under consideration. In striking that balance, the judge will of course take into account as a relevant, often highly relevant, factor the attitude taken by a natural parent, and that may require examination of her or her motives. But the result of such an inquiry must never be allowed to prove determinative. It is a mistake to view the issue as one in which the clinical advice of doctors is placed on one scale and the reasonableness of the parent's view in the other. Had the judge viewed the evidence more broadly from the standpoint of his own perception of the child's welfare when appraised in all its aspects, he would have been bound, in my view, to take significant account of other elements in the case. Those include the parents' ties in country AB, and – crucially – the evidence of Dr P. No one disputes that in the aftermath of the operation the child would remain in the primary care of the mother. Dr P maintained a very clear view that – even assuming that the operation proved wholly successful in surgical terms – the child's subsequent development could be injuriously affected if his day-to-day care depended upon the commitment of a mother who had suffered the turmoil of having her child being compelled against her will to undergo, as a result of a coercive order from the court, a major operation against which her own medical and maternal judgment wholeheartedly rebelled.

All these cases depend on their own facts and render generalisations – tempting though they may be to the legal or social analyst – wholly out of place. It can only be said safely that there is a scale, at one end of which lies the clear case where parental opposition to medical intervention is prompted by scruple or dogma of a kind which is patently irreconcilable with principles of child health and welfare widely accepted by the generality of mankind; and that at the other end lie highly problematic cases where there is genuine scope for a difference of view between parent and judge. In both situations it is the duty of the judge to allow the court's own opinion to prevail in the perceived paramount interests of the child concerned, but in cases at the latter end of the scale, there must be a likelihood (though never, of course, a certainty) that the greater the scope for genuine debate between one view and another the stronger will be the inclination of the court to be influenced by a reflection that in the last analysis the best interests of every child include an expectation that difficult decisions affecting the length and quality of its life will be taken for it by the parent to whom its care has been entrusted by nature.

I too would allow this appeal and substitute the order proposed by Butler-Sloss LJ.

Roch LJ: What principles should apply to a case such as this? The paramount principle is that the court must make the decision which it considers to be in the best interests of the child. In reaching that decision how should the court treat the decisions of parents? I would gratefully adopt the words of Sir Thomas Bingham MR in the case of *Re Z (a minor) (freedom of publication)* [1995] 4 All ER 961 at 986, [1996] 2 WLR 88 at 113 where he said:

> I would for my part accept without reservation that the decision of a devoted and responsible parent should be treated with respect. It should certainly not be disregarded or lightly set aside. But the role of the court is to exercise an independent and objective judgment. If that judgment is in accord with that of the devoted and responsible parent, well and good. If it is not, then it is the duty of the court, after giving due weight to the view of the devoted and responsible parent, to give effect to its own judgment. That is what it is there for. Its judgment may of course be wrong. So may that of the parent. But once the jurisdiction of the court is invoked its clear duty is to reach and express the best judgment it can.

The issue then is what is in the best interests of the child? One factor in determining that issue to be taken into account by the court is the decision of devoted and responsible parents. It is, I would suggest, misleading to ask, once it is accepted that the parents are devoted and responsible, whether their decision is reasonable or unreasonable, because parents who are responsible and devoted will almost certainly reach a decision which falls within the range of decisions which can be classed as reasonable. If the decision falls outside the range of permissible decisions, it is unlikely that the parents are responsible and devoted parents who have sought only to decide in the best interests of their child.

In my judgment the judge misled himself by categorising the parents' decision as being unreasonable. I can see nothing to justify the judge's conclusion that the child's mother is deluding herself that with her care the child miraculously will survive beyond that period of time forecast by the doctors, or that the parents have failed to grasp the improvements in operating technique and subsequent treatment which have taken place in the field of liver transplantation in recent years, particularly in view of Dr P's evidence of the protracted and thorough discussions he has had with the mother.

If the proper stance for parents is that whenever there is a treatment which may prolong the life of their child, then that treatment should be accepted, a decision not to accept that treatment would be unreasonable. But in my opinion that cannot be, and will not be, the answer in every case. Nor are such decisions to be taken solely with medical factors in mind. The presumption in favour of the sustaining of life is not irrebuttable and perhaps has less weight where the issue is whether to prolong or not to prolong life by means of organ transplantation.

The view of the parents in a liver transplant case has two aspects. First, if, as here, the parents are devoted and responsible and have the best interests of their child in mind, then their views are to be taken into account and accorded weight and respect by the court when reaching its decision. Second, the views of the parents have a clinical significance because in the absence of parental belief that a transplant is the right procedure for the child, the prospects of a successful outcome are diminished. This factor explains the stance adopted at hospital Y. It may also explain the passage in Fact Sheet 10, published by the Children's Liver Disease Foundation and given to the mother in this case, in which this sentence appears: 'If the family choose not to proceed with the transplantation once they are acquainted with the facts, this decision is respected.'

I have formed the view that the judge was wrong to categorise the parents' decision as unreasonable and to disregard it in the balancing exercise he had to perform; the judge, therefore, misdirected himself, and we, in this court should exercise the court's inherent jurisdiction.

There are formidable practical difficulties in this case which stand in the way of implementing the order which the judge in fact made. The child's father works abroad. The mother and the child and the father at present are living together. If the mother does not comply with the order, it is not certain whether the courts of the country in which they live will assist in any proceedings to oblige the mother to comply or how long such proceedings would take. The order involves the child and the mother returning to this country, although the financial ability of the family to pay for that is uncertain, particularly if it is necessary for a doctor to accompany the child during the journey. The return of the child to this country must involve both mother and child in distress which will arise from leaving the father and their home, and that must in turn increase the risk that such a journey poses for this child. On arrival in this country it is clear that the operation could not be performed at hospital Y, the hospital that the mother would choose were she disposed to seek a transplant for her child, because that hospital will not perform such an operation without the mother's willing consent. There is another possible centre at which such an operation might be performed, hospital Z. Whereas the surgeon at that centre has indicated that he would be prepared to perform such an operation although the mother was not consenting, it is not clear whether the remainder of the medical team at that centre would be of his view or whether they would take the view set out in Fact Sheet 10.

Then there is the question of treatment following the operation. Are the mother and child to stay in this country? If they are to stay, for how long? If further transplant operations become necessary will the mother give or withhold her consent? What will be the position if at such time the mother and child have returned to country AB?

At present the evidence indicates that this child has a happy and secure life with his parents in country AB. It is true that that life will be a very short life which will end when the child is still a baby, but at a time before the child can become aware of the significance of his condition and its consequences. I do not consider that it is in the child's best interests to disrupt his present life by the court giving its consent to his undergoing a liver transplant operation and ordering the mother to return with him to this country with all the distress and uncertainties that that will inevitably entail for the child in the special circumstances that exist in this case.

I agree that this appeal should be allowed.

We should consider two aspects of *Re T:* first, the court's approach as to its role, and, secondly, its view of the child's best interests.

As regards the first, Connell J held that the mother's refusal of consent was unreasonable. The Court of Appeal concluded that legally this was the wrong question. When exercising its inherent jurisdiction the court had to apply the 'welfare principle' and its familiar manifestation the 'best interests' test. It was no part of this approach for the court to determine the reasonableness or otherwise of the parents' decision. It was for the court to determine the 'best' course in the interests of the child.

There is no doubt that the Court of Appeal had to apply this approach. There is clear authority in the Court of Appeal, relied upon by the judges in *Re T*, that the court must 'exercise an independent and objective judgment' and not accept the decision of a 'devoted and responsible parent' (*Re Z (a minor) (identification: restrictions on publications)* [1996] 2 WLR 88 at 113 per Sir Thomas Bingham MR. However, there is another view of what he, and the mother's counsel, were arguing which was not inconsistent with the case law or s 1 of the Children Act 1989.

It is accepted by the courts that the views of parents are very important factors in reaching a decision about a child's 'best interests' (eg *Re Z, supra* at 88, per Sir Thomas Bingham MR: 'decision treated with respect'; and *Re T,* per Butler-Sloss LJ: 'an important consideration'; per Waite LJ: 'relevant, often highly relevant'; per Roch LJ: 'taken into account and accorded weight and respect').

How can this be reflected in the approach of the court in applying the 'welfare principle' and 'best interests' test? The court has a protective jurisdiction which must prevent abuse by parents and exposing children to harm through ill-conceived or badly motivated decisions taken by the parents. The court is not, however, usually the best decision-maker when matters of judgement or 'close calls' have to be made about a child's welfare. The court has the twin roles of *legislator* and *supervisor*. As legislator, the court must determine the criteria which mark out the 'four corners' of legitimate parental discretion and thereafter, as supervisor, must determine whether those criteria have been applied and, if they have, that the decision is not a manifestly absurd or unreasonable one. If the parents sought to 'martyr' a child on the basis of their religious convictions, the court would be justified in holding the decision not to be in the child's 'best interests' since it is based upon a criterion not directed to the child's interests (as widely accepted) (see eg *Re R (a minor) (Blood Transfusion)* [1993] 2 FLR 757 (Booth J)). Similarly, if the parents declined treatment, for example, correction of a cleft-palate on the basis of the child's future quality of life, the court would conclude that the correct criteria directed to the child's interests have been applied but in an absurd and unreasonable way.

This approach recognises that there may well be a range of decisions which parents may conscientiously reach taking account not only of the medical facts but also judgments about the desirability of the operation and the impact upon the child: in short, the child's 'good' or 'well-being' which are matters they are almost uniquely qualified to determine and assess. Reassuringly, the judges in *Re T* consider these 'broader considerations' as important to a determination of the child's 'best interests'. Thus, the medical evidence of what is in a child's *medical* interests and thus only a partial assessment of the child's interests taken as a whole. The Court of Appeal in *Re T* seems to have embraced this model. 'Reasonableness' thus becomes not the test for the court to apply but rather is at the heart of the 'best interests' test in marginal cases where the parents in making the decision have 'asked themselves the correct questions'.

Thus, although Waite LJ was not prepared to substitute a 'reasonableness' test for the 'best interests' test, deference to parental 'know-how' clearly appealed to him. It is, perhaps, worth noting that the other judges (Butler-Sloss and Roch LJJ) – even though it was not the approach they favoured – concluded that the mother's decision was not unreasonable.

As to the particular case, *Re T* is a most unusual case indeed. The Court of Appeal refused consent to life-sustaining treatment upon a young child which was likely to succeed, giving the child the prospect of many years life. Without it, he would die within 12 to 18 months of, presumably, a rather unpleasant death from liver failure and further, on the evidence, his life after a liver transplant would not have been one racked with pain or distress other than that associated with immuno-suppressive drugs.

The court reached its decision, largely, on the basis of the need for the mother's continuing care after the operation and the court's sense that somehow this would be compromised if the operation was done without her agreement: 'a major operation against which her own medical and maternal judgment wholeheartedly rebelled' (per Waite LJ). Butler-Sloss LJ described the mother and child as 'one' in the circumstances where the mother would be expected to care for C after the operation and for the rest of his life. How this view of her stands with the judges' constant reference to the mother as 'loving', 'devoted' and 'caring' is unclear. The medical evidence suggested that parental support would be essential if the child's recovery was to be optimised and, no doubt in part, justified the view of some doctors that the operation should only be done with the parents' agreement. Where, however, was the evidence that *her* maternal nature would change if the court authorised the operation? Even if it would, does this really turn the child's 'best interests' around? Is the Court of Appeal saying that a parent's lack of devotion and support can neutralise the child's interests in living? Clearly, not always and, as Butler-Sloss LJ herself noted, not where the element of 'continuing devotion' is unnecessary (see *Re B (a minor) (wardship: medical treatment)* [1981] 1 WLR 1421 (CA): 'one-off' operation to remove an intestinal blockage in a Down's Syndrome child's 'best interests' notwithstanding parents' refusal).

As was noted above, the court's willingness to look beyond the medical evidence which unanimously concluded the operation was in C's *medical* interests, is refreshing. The mother had not misdirected herself. She was a health-care worker and, as Roch LJ remarked, she had not failed to grasp the medical realities of C's condition; she was not 'deluding herself that with her care the child miraculously will survive beyond that period of time forecast by the doctors'. The weight the court gave to the 'broader considerations', however, seems somewhat dubious. In addition to the need for a committed parent, the judges relied upon the practical difficulties and inconvenience of bringing the child to England and the problem of enforcing the court's order (per Roch LJ). It does not seem that these should carry much weight when the child's life is at stake and the evidence supports a good prognosis. Perhaps, however, the case is really about an assessment of the child's quality of life with or without the operation. In other words, this was a case where two options were presented where there was 'genuine scope for a difference of view' (per Waite LJ). Certainly, the mother's decision seems to have been based upon an assessment of this: that was the correct issue for the mother to address in considering the 'interests' of C and may be it was (just) a reasonable – or putting it another way, not unreasonable – decision of C's 'best interests'. (For further discussion of *Re T*, see: M Fox and J McHale 'In Whose Best Interests?' (1997) 60 MLR 700.)

Contrast with *Re T* the following case, where the parents' refusal to allow HIV testing was considered not to be in the child's best interests.

Re C (HIV test) [1999] 2 FLR 1004 (CA)

The local authority applied for a specific issue order that a baby born to an HIV positive mother be tested for HIV. The mother was sceptical of the conventional treatment for HIV and AIDS, had refused medication during the pregnancy, and intended to continue breast-feeding until the child was about 2 years old. The judge found that there was a 20% or 25% chance that the baby was infected with HIV; the risk had been increased by the breast-feeding. Both parents were strongly opposed to testing the child for HIV and to any form of medical intervention. The judge stated that the views of the parents looked at widely and generously were important factors in the decision, even, to some extent, irrespective of the validity of the underlying ground for those views, and noted that under the Children Act 1989, s 1(5), any applicant for an order had, in effect, to persuade the court that there were positive grounds for taking the matter out of the hands of those with parental responsibility for the child. A court invited to override parental wishes had to move extremely cautiously. However, he concluded that in the instant case the arguments for overriding the wishes of the parents and for testing the baby were overwhelming. The baby had rights of her own recognised in national and international law, the baby's welfare was paramount, and in the baby's interests the test should take place. The parents applied for permission to appeal, but did not attend court on the date their application was due to be heard, having disappeared from their home, taking the child with them.

Butler-Sloss LJ: The consensus of evidence was firmly in favour of a medical test. There was both written evidence from the first consultant, Dr Gibbs, at Great Ormond Street, oral evidence from Dr Novelli from Great Ormond Street, a letter from a professor or doctor at Edinburgh on behalf of the mother which she was obliged to present to the court, and a consultant, Dr Walters, from Imperial College, who is a co-author with Dr Novelli but gave independent evidence, both from Imperial College. He is also at St Mary's, Paddington. All of them were of the opinion that there was a 25–30% chance that this child would be HIV positive and that it was necessary to test the child. If the child was positive further treatment would be highly desirable. The mother has from the onset of the birth breast-fed the baby. If the baby is HIV positive, such breast-feeding obviously can continue. If the child is negative, then the medical experts were unanimous that the mother ought not to breast-feed.

There was one consultant, a Professor of Pathology from Ontario, who had done a study on HIV and similar matters, and his view was in accord with the parents in doubting the existence of HIV as such, doubting its relation to AIDS, and definitely doubting any need either to test or, in particular, to treat.

The judge in his judgment chose, as was his right, to accept the preponderance of medical evidence, from Great Ormond Street and St Mary's Paddington, supported, as it was, from Edinburgh, and took the view that this was the orthodox but also responsible approach of the medical profession to HIV and AIDS. The judge was only dealing, and it is crucial that this should be clear, with the question of the first test. If the child is positive, it would not be necessary to test again but it may be necessary to treat. The consensus was, from all but Professor de Harven from Ontario, that treatment for a baby under 6 months was important. If the child is negative but the mother continues to breast-feed, it may well be necessary to have further tests. Indeed, because the baby has been breast-fed throughout, the test only applies to up to some 8 weeks before the date of the test. It would be likely that it would be necessary to test again and if the mother continues to breast-feed to continue to test until the end of breast-feeding.

Dr Novelli and Dr Walters' view, as set out by Wilson J at 1014H (above), in a passage which it is necessary to read, said this:

> ...if the baby is not tested for HIV, the professionals who should be advising on her care...are under a grave handicap which can only be to the prejudice of the baby. If, in the absence of a test, the baby develops illness, a doctor treating her who knows of the possibility that she is infected will have to cater for that possibility in the proposed treatment; if, in fact, the baby is uninfected, it is likely that the proposed treatment will be unduly aggressive.

The parents do not accept the evidence of the doctors. They do not accept the decision of the judge, and the mother through counsel comes to us to say that they are good parents with very strongly held views. There is no emergency here. The judge recognised that he could not prevent the breast-feeding because to make such a direction would be ineffective with the mother, and that as responsible parents it is wrong for the court to intervene in decisions which are pre-eminently decisions for parents. The judge is criticised for setting out the parents' strongly held views but not evaluating those views, particularly not evaluating the impact upon the parents of any form of medical regime which would have an enormous impact on them and has already had sufficient impact for them to leave their home. They would find it difficult to abide by any step in the process, and the effect of their enormous upset and distress at having imposed upon them a decision to have their baby tested would inevitably affect the care which they are giving to this child and, indeed, although Mr Horowitz was cautious enough not to say so directly, has shown itself by the fact that they have acted irresponsibly, disappearing with this child, instead of giving the child the normal routine that one would expect for a 5-month old baby. This is the effect of the stress upon them of what they consider to be an unwarranted interference with their rights and responsibilities for their child. Mr Horowitz says that there has to be a space within which parents can reject the current orthodoxy, even though that may be based upon good medical evidence. There is an alternative view. They should be entitled to parental autonomy to make that choice, and that is something with which the courts should not intervene. He says that this is a continuing and developing area of medicine and that the parents ought to be free to make these decisions without the interference of the court. The judge therefore was in error in not evaluating the parents' response. He erred in his exercise of discretion in under-emphasising this parental response and the impact upon the child, and that area in life when parents ought to be left to get on with the care of their own children without authorization intervention. I am paraphrasing the rather better way in which Mr Horowitz actually argued this to us.

Mr Horowitz relied upon a decision of this court in *Re T (Wardship: Medical Treatment)* [1997] 1 FLR 502. I have to say, having been one of the judges in that case, which was a liver transplant case, that it was at the other end of any spectrum that one might be considering. In that decision in my judgment I cited a passage from the Master of the Rolls, Sir Thomas Bingham, in *Re Z (A Minor) (Identification: Restrictions on Publication)* [1997] Fam 1, sub nom *Re Z (A Minor) (Freedom of Publication)* [1996] 1 FLR 191, and I read the passage from the Master of the Rolls (at 32–33 and 217B–C respectively):

> I would for my part accept without reservation that the decision of a devoted and responsible parent should be treated with respect. It should certainly not be disregarded or lightly set aside. But the role of the court is to exercise an independent and objective judgment. If that judgment is in accord with that of the devoted and responsible parent, well and good. If it is not, then it is the duty of the court, after giving due weight to the view of the devoted and responsible parent, to give effect to its own judgment. That is what it is there for. Its judgment may of course be wrong. So may that of the parent. But once the jurisdiction of the court is invoked its clear duty is to reach and express the best judgment it can.

I recite one sentence from my judgment (at 509E):

> As Sir Thomas Bingham MR said in *Re Z*, the court decides and in doing so may overrule the decision of a reasonable parent.

The decision of these parents is not to allow this child to have the first test. The issue is not: Should this baby have treatment? That may or may not arise in the future. The issue is to determine the medical status of the child by a test which is likely to be definitive, in the sense that, if it says the child is positive, everyone knows what the position is, but less definitive if the test is negative at that stage. I have no doubt at all, for my part, that it is right that this child should have the test done. I can see no reason whatever for this court to interfere with the clear and careful decision of Wilson J. In my view, he analysed and weighed in the balance the competing arguments of the parents and the overwhelming medical evidence presented by the council and the Official Solicitor.

The issue before this court is an issue of knowledge. What is the position of this child? In my view, the child is clearly at risk if there is ignorance of the child's medical condition. The degree of intrusion into the child of a medical test is slight. The degree of intrusion into the family of taking the child to the hospital for a medical test would for most people be comparatively slight. The parents have magnified this into a major issue because they do not accept any of the premises upon which the tests will be carried out. But the welfare of the child is paramount. The court has been asked to deal with the case. It cannot shirk its duty. The space sought by Mr Horowitz, which is a space in which parental decisions are final, undoubtedly exists, but it exists subject to s 1(1) of the Children Act. It does not matter whether the parents are responsible or irresponsible. It matters whether the welfare of the child demands that such a course should be taken and, as Evans LJ was asking during this hearing in argument: can it be in the child's best interests for the parents to remain ignorant of their own child's state of health? You only have to ask that question for most people to say no. We are not talking about the rights of parents. We are talking about the rights of the child. Wilson J set out various Articles of the UN Convention on the Rights of the Child 1989. We do not in a sense need that. It is all encapsulated in s 1 of the Children Act, but it does give added strength to this most important of all points, that the parents' views, which are not the views of the majority, cannot stand against the right of the child to be properly cared for in every sense. This child has the right to have sensible and responsible people find out whether she is or is not HIV positive, either as a result of the birth to her mother, or as a result of the breast-feeding. There is a 25% chance, according to the doctors, that she is HIV positive because of the birth. There is an increased danger because of breast-feeding. There is a one in three or one in four chance that she may be HIV positive. What seems to me to be crucial is that someone should find out so that one knows how she should be looked after. The idea that she should have aggressive treatment, because doctors who know about it feel, because they do not know if she is or is not HIV positive, that they must give her additional treatment, when it would not be necessary if she was not HIV positive, seems to me as sad as if they will not give her adequate treatment because the parents did not tell the doctor and the child was in fact seriously ill and was not given adequate treatment. Either way this child has her own rights. Those rights seem to me to be met at this stage by her being tested to see what her state of health is for the question of knowledge. That is as far as it goes. I therefore would refuse the application for permission to appeal.

Evans and Thorpe LJJ agreed.

Perhaps the decision in this case was inevitable: the advantages of knowing the child's HIV status clearly outweighed any disadvantages.

(iv) BEST INTERESTS AND HUMAN RIGHTS

Leaving aside the particular case, at first instance the judge (Wilson J) in *Re C (HIV test)* (*op cit*) raised an important question which will arise under the European Convention on Human Rights.

Re C (HIV test) [1999] 2 FLR 1004 (FD)

Wilson J:...under Art 8 of the European Convention for the Protection of Human Rights and Fundamental Freedoms 1950, the parents and the baby all have a right to respect for their family life; and it will be interesting to see, once the Human Rights Act 1998 is in force, whether that Article will require our inquiry into a child's welfare to be analysed in that way.

Will the Convention have the effect of changing the court's approach? Wilson J refers to art 8. Will art 8 protect the sanctity of parental decision-making? In other circumstances, where the parents' decision to refuse treatment has a religious basis, art 9 protecting the parents' right to freedom of religion may be relied upon to create a 'zone of decision-making' for parents alone. It seems most unlikely that art 8 or 9 would be used by the courts so as to permit decision-making which was not in a child's best interests. Thus, the outcomes of these cases are unlikely to be effected. Any 'zone of decision-making' is likely to be no greater than that granted in *Re T*.

In relation to art 8, it is quite possible that the court *could* concede a right to parents to make decisions about their child's upbringing. Equally, however, it is likely that the right could be justifiably infringed under art 8(2) where its exercise is not in the child's 'best interests', ie for the protection of the child's health or to protect his rights and freedoms.

An instructive illustration of this type of human rights reasoning can be found in the following decision of the Canadian Supreme Court.

B v Children's Aid Society of Metropolitan Toronto; Attorney-General of Canada, Interveners (1995) 122 DLR (4th) 1 (Can SC)

The appellants were the parents of a child who was born prematurely and suffered from many physical ailments. The parents, due to religious beliefs, objected to the use of blood transfusions in treating the child. When the child was about a month old, the attending physicians believed that the child's life was in danger and that a blood transfusion might be necessary. After a hearing on short notice to the appellants, a Provincial Court judge granted the respondent Children's Aid Society (C.A.S.) a 72-hour wardship pursuant to the *Child Welfare Act*, R.S.O. 1980, c 66, the child being found to be a 'child in need of protection' pursuant to s 19(1)(*b*)(ix) of the Act because of the parents' failure to permit medical treatment necessary for the child's health or well-being. At the status review hearing the wardship order was extended for a further 21 days on the basis of the evidence of the attending physicians that the child's condition remained marginal and that they wished to maintain the ability to transfuse in case of an emergency and in addition, because a blood transfusion would be required during surgery which was expected to be performed to confirm a diagnosis of infantile glaucoma. The blood transfusion was administered as part of the exploration and operation for the suspected glaucoma and the temporary wardship order was subsequently terminated. The parents appealed the Provincial Court orders granting and terminating wardship on the grounds, *inter alia*, that s 19(1)(*b*)(ix) of the *Child Welfare Act* and related provisions infringed their rights to choose medical treatment for their child in accordance with the tenets of their faith, in violation of their rights under ss 2(*a*) and 7 of the *Canadian Charter of Rights and Freedoms*. The District Court dismissed their appeal…The parents' appeal to the Ontario Court of Appeal was dismissed…The parents appealed to the Supreme Court of Canada.

La Forest J:

Section 7 of the Charter

[70] Turning now to s 7 of the Charter, the appellants argued that the right to choose medical treatment for their infant is a liberty interest protected under s 7 of the Charter, and that the infringement of that interest in the present case did not conform with the principles of fundamental justice….

Section 7 of the Charter and parental liberty

[71] Although I am of the view that the principles of fundamental justice have been complied with in the present case, I none the less propose to comment on the scope of the protection afforded by the Charter as it relates to the right of parents to choose medical treatment for their infant…

[72] The appellants claim that parents have the right to choose medical treatment for their infant, relying for this contention on s 7 of the Charter, and more precisely on the liberty interest. They assert that the right enures in the family as an entity, basing this argument on statements made by American courts in the definition of liberty under their Constitution. While, as I will indicate, American experience may be useful in defining the scope of the liberty interest protected under our Constitution, I agree that s 7 of the Charter does not afford protection to the integrity of the family unit as such. The Canadian Charter, and s 7 in particular, protects individuals. It is the individual's right to liberty under the Charter with which we are here concerned. The concept of the integrity of the family unit is itself premised, at least in part, on that of parental liberty…

[73] The term 'liberty' has yet to be authoritatively defined in this court, although comments have been made on both ends of the spectrum…

On the one hand, liberty does not mean unconstrained freedom: see *Reference re: Section 94(2) of the Motor Vehicle Act* (1985), 24 DLR (4th) 536, 23 CCC (3d) 289, [1985] 2 SCR 486 (per Wilson J, at pp 555–6); *R v Edwards Books & Art Ltd* (1986) 35 DLR (4th) 1, 30 CCC (3d) 385, [1986] 2 SCR 713 (per Dickson CJC, at pp 3–4). Freedom of the individual to do what he or she wishes must, in any organized society, be subjected to numerous constraints for the common good. The state undoubtedly has the right to impose many types of restraints on individual behaviour, and not all limitations will attract Charter scrutiny. On the other hand, liberty does not mean mere freedom from physical restraint. In a free and democratic society, the individual must be left room for personal autonomy to live his or her own life and to make decisions that are of fundamental personal importance. In *Morgentaler, Smoling and Scott v The Queen* (1988) 44 DLR (4th) 385, 37 CCC (3d) 449, [1988] 1 SCR 30, Wilson J noted that the liberty interest was rooted in the fundamental concepts of human dignity, personal autonomy, privacy and choice in decisions going to the individual's fundamental being. She stated, at pp 486–7:

Thus, an aspect of the respect for human dignity on which the Charter is founded is the right to make fundamental personal decisions without interference from the state. This right is a critical component of the right to liberty. Liberty, as was noted in *Singh*, is a phrase capable of a broad range of meaning. In my view, this right, properly construed, grants the individual a degree of autonomy in making decisions of fundamental personal importance.

... [81] While I was in dissent in that case, I agree with this statement, and, indeed, I later observed in *R v Beare* (1988) 55 DLR (4th) 481 at pp 500–1, 45 CCC (3d) 57, [1988] 2 SCR 387, that I was sympathetic to the view that s 7 of the Charter included a right to privacy. On this point, the American experience can give us valuable guidance as to the proper meaning and limits of liberty. The United States Supreme Court has given a liberal interpretation to the concept of liberty, as it relates to family matters. It has elevated both the notion of the integrity of the family unit and that of parental rights to the status of constitutional values, through its interpretation of the Fifth and Fourteenth Amendments, *Meyer v State of Nebraska*, 262 US 390 (1923), and *Pierce v Society of the Sisters of the Holy Names of Jesus and Mary*, 268 US 510 (1915), are the two landmark cases most often cited. In the former, the Supreme Court invalidated a statute that purported to limit the teaching of foreign languages. Its decision was grounded, in part at least, on a finding that the statute interfered with the right of the parents to control the education of their children. In *Pierce v Society of the Sisters*, the Supreme Court declared unconstitutional a statute that required that children attend public schools...

Despite the lack of unanimity on the formulation of liberty and the role of the courts in reviewing legislation, the dicta on liberty, in so far as family matters are concerned, have been consistently broad. In *Prince v Com of Mass*, 321 US 158 (1944), although the court upheld a statute prohibiting child labour, Rutledge J stated, for the court (at p 166): 'It is cardinal with us that the custody, care and nurture of the child reside first with the parents, whose primary function and freedom include preparation for obligations the state can neither supply nor hinder'...

[83] Where to draw the line between interests and regulatory powers falling within the accepted ambit of state authority will often raise difficulty. But much on either side of the line is clear enough. On that basis, I would have thought it plain that the right to nurture a child, to care for its development, and to make decisions for it in fundamental matters such as medical care, are part of the liberty interest of a parent. As observed by Dickson J in *R v Big M Drug Mart Ltd, supra*, the Charter was not enacted in a vacuum or absent a historical context. The common law has long recognized that parents are in the best position to take care of their children and make all the decisions necessary to ensure their well-being. In *Hepton v Maat* (1957) 10 DLR (2d) 1, [1957] SCR 606, our court stated (at p 2): 'The view of the child's welfare conceives it to lie, first, within the warmth and security of the home provided by his parents.' This recognition was based on the presumption that parents act in the best interest of their child. The court did add, however, that 'when through a failure, with or without parental fault, to furnish that protection, that welfare is threatened, the community, represented by the Sovereign, is, on the broadest social and national grounds, justified in displacing the parents and assuming their duties' (p 2). Although the philosophy underlying state intervention has changed over time, most contemporary statutes dealing with child protection matters, and in particular the Ontario Act, while focusing on the best interest of the child, favour minimal intervention. In recent years, courts have expressed some reluctance to interfere with parental rights, and state intervention has been tolerated only when necessity was demonstrated. This only serves to confirm that the parental interest in bringing up, nurturing and caring for a child, including medical care and moral upbringing, is an individual interest of fundamental importance to our society.

[84] The respondents have argued that the 'parental liberty' asserted by the appellants is an obligation owed to the child which does not fall within the scope of s 7 of the Charter...

[85] While acknowledging that parents bear responsibilities towards their children, it seems to me that they must enjoy correlative rights to exercise them. The contrary view would not recognize the fundamental importance of choice and personal autonomy in our society. As already stated, the common law has always, in the absence of demonstrated neglect or unsuitability, presumed that parents should make all significant choices affecting their children, and has afforded them a general liberty to do as they choose. This liberty interest is not a parental right tantamount to a right of property in children. (Fortunately, we have distanced ourselves from the ancient juridical conception of children as chattels of their parents). The state is now actively involved in a number of areas traditionally conceived of as properly

belonging to the private sphere. None the less, our society is far from having repudiated the privileged role parents exercise in the upbringing of their children. This role translates into a protective sphere of parental decision-making which is rooted in the presumption that parents should make important decisions affecting their children both because parents are more likely to appreciate the best interests of their children and because the state is ill-equipped to make such decisions itself. Moreover, individuals have a deep personal interest as parents in fostering the growth of their own children. This is not to say that the state cannot intervene when it considers it necessary to safeguard the child's autonomy or health. But such intervention must be justified. In other words, parental decision-making must receive the protection of the Charter in order for state interference to be properly monitored by the courts, and be permitted only when it conforms to the values underlying the Charter.

[86] The respondents also argued that the infant's rights were paramount to those of the appellants and, on that basis alone, state intervention was justified. This was the conclusion reached by Whealy DCJ. Children undeniably benefit from the Charter, most notably in its protection of their rights to life and to the security of their person. As children are unable to assert these, our society presumes that parents will exercise their freedom of choice in a manner that does not offend the rights of their children. If one considers the multitude of decisions parents make daily, it is clear that in practice, state interference in order to balance the rights of parents and children will arise only in exceptional cases. In fact, we must accept that parents can, at times, make decisions contrary to their children's wishes – and rights – as long as they do not exceed the threshold dictated by public policy, in its broad conception. For instance, it would be difficult to deny that a parent can dictate to his or her child the place where he or she will live, or which school he or she will attend. However, the state can properly intervene in situations where parental conduct falls below the socially acceptable threshold. But in doing so, the state is limiting the constitutional rights of parents rather than vindicating the constitutional rights of children…

[87] Once it is decided that the parents have a liberty interest, further balancing of parents' and children's rights should be done in the course of determining whether state interference conforms to the principles of fundamental justice, rather than when defining the scope of the liberty interest. Even assuming that the rights of children can qualify the liberty interest of their parents, that interest exists none the less. In the case at bar, the application of the Act deprived the appellants of their right to decide which medical treatment should be administered to their infant. In so doing, the Act has infringed upon the parental 'liberty' protected in s 7 of the Charter…

La Forest J went on to hold that the judicial process was in accordance with the principles of fundamental justice. L'Heureux-Dubé, Gonthier and McLachlin JJ agreed with La Forest J.

Of the remaining five justices, Sopinka J found it unnecessary to consider the scope of s 7 relying on the justification for infringement established by La Forest J. Lamer CJ concluded that 'parental liberty' did not fall within s 7 of the Charter: 'liberty' was restricted to freedom from physical interference. The remaining three justices (Iacobucci, Major and Cory JJ) disagreed with La Forest J's analysis.

Iacobucci and Major JJ: [211] It is important to bear in mind that the impugned provisions of the *Child Welfare Act* are geared to the promotion of the health, safety and personal integrity of the child. To this end, although this appeal raises issues related to the right of parents to rear their children without undue influence by the state, it also touches on the s 7 right of the child to life and security of the person. It is this perspective that we find absent from the reasons of La Forest J. As such, we are concerned by the fact that our colleague's decision creates a situation in which the child's right to life or security of the person is reduced to a limitation on the parents' constitutionally protected ability to deny that child the necessities of life owing to parental liberty and freedom of religion.

1.   *Section 7*

[212] We find that the right to liberty embedded in s 7 does not include a parent's right to deny a child medical treatment that has been adjudged necessary by a medical professional. Although the scope of 'liberty' as understood by s 7 is expansive, it is certainly not all-encompassing…

[213] This is clearly a case where S's right to liberty, security of the person, and potentially even to life is deprived. It is important to note that the abridgment of S's s 7 rights operates independently from the question whether the parents honestly believe that their refusal to consent to the transfusion is in the best interests of the child, since such a refusal shall,

according to the appellants, prevent her from being 'defiled in the eyes of God'. Whether or not her parents' motivations are well-intentioned, the physical effects upon S of the refusal to transfuse blood are equally deleterious.

[214] We note that La Forest J holds that 'liberty' encompasses the right of parents to have input into the education of their child. In fact, 'liberty' may very well permit parents to choose among *equally effective* types of medical treatment for their children, but we do not find it necessary to determine this question in the instant case. We say this because, assuming without deciding that 'liberty' has such a reach, it certainly does not extend to protect the appellants in the case at bar. There is simply no room within s 7 for parents to override the child's right to life and security of the person.

[215] In any event, there is an immense difference between sanctioning some input into a child's education and protecting a parent's right to refuse their children medical treatment that a professional adjudges to be necessary and for which there is no legitimate alternative. The child's right to life must not be so completely subsumed to the parental liberty to make decisions regarding that child: *Re K (R)* (1987) 79 AR 140 at p 147, 4 ACWS (3d) 274 (Prov Ct (Fam Div)). In our view, the best way to ensure this outcome is to view an exercise of parental liberty which seriously endangers the survival of the child is falling outside s 7.

[216] Our colleague's reasons open the door to the possibility that a violation of a guardian's s 7 rights will be found should the state deny a guardian his or her right to refuse a child in his or her charge medical treatment and should that denial fail to conform with fundamental justice. In the case at bar, S's condition, although believed to be serious, was not sufficiently urgent to prevent the Children's Aid Society from seeking a court-ordered wardship, thereby complying with procedural fundamental justice. But what if S were injured in a car accident and required an immediate blood transfusion to save her life? Even if her parents would have been in agreement that the transfusion was necessary and urgently required, their personal convictions would still likely have compelled them to refuse their daughter the treatment. To this end, this exercise of parental liberty can engender the death of an infant.

[217] We find it counter-intuitive that 'parental liberty' would permit a parent to deny a child medical treatment felt to be necessary until some element of procedural fundamental justice is complied with. Although an individual may refuse any medical procedures upon her own person, it is quite another matter to speak for another separate individual, especially when that individual cannot speak for herself and, in S's case, has never spoken for herself. The rights enumerated in the Charter are individual rights to which children are clearly entitled in their relationships with the state and all persons – regardless of their status as strangers, friends, relatives, guardians or parents.

[218] The suggestion that parents have the ability to refuse their children medical procedures such as blood transfusions in situations where such a transfusion is necessary to sustain that child's health is consistent with the view, now long gone, that parents have some sort of 'property interest' in their children. Indeed, in recent years, this court has emphasized that parental duties are to be discharged according to the 'best interests' of the child: *Young v Young* (1993), 108 DLR (4th) 193, [1993] 4 SCR 3, 18 CRR (2d) 41; *P (D) v S (C)* (1993) 108 DLR (4th) 287, [1993] 4 SCR 141, 18 CRR (2d) 1. The nature of the parent-child relationship is thus not to be determined by the personal desires of the parent, yet rather by the 'best interests' of the child, In *Young, supra*, at p 219, L'Heureux-Dubé J (discussing the issue of custody in family law) commented that:

> The proposition…is one of duty and obligation to the child's best interests…One cannot stress enough that it is from the perspective of the child's interests that these powers and responsibilities must be assessed, as the 'rights' of the parent are not a criterion.

[219]The exercise of parental beliefs that grossly invades the 'best interests' of the child is not activity protected by the right to 'liberty' in s 7. To hold otherwise would be to risk undermining the ability of the state to exercise its legitimate *parens patriae* jurisdiction and jeopardize the Charter's goal of protecting the most vulnerable members of society. As society becomes increasingly cognizant of the fact that the family is often a very dangerous place for children, the *parens patriae* jurisdiction assumes greater importance. Although there are times when the family should be shielded from the intrusions of the state, S's situation is one in which the state should be readily able to intervene not only to protect the public interest, but also to preserve the security of infants who cannot yet speak for themselves.

[220] It is clear that a purpose of the Charter is to protect the individual from governmental interference. For this reason, as noted by our colleague La Forest J, many Charter rights have been given broad interpretations. In the instant appeal, concern has been raised that whittling down the ambit of 'parental liberty' could deny parents a constitutional remedy should the state, without due process or substantive merit, arbitrarily decide to remove a child from a home. In our estimation, a more appropriate way of mitigating such a possibility would be to view such a removal as an interference with the child's own liberty or security interest, not

that of the parent. With respect, such an approach obliges the state's *parens patriae* jurisdiction to be fairly exercised, both procedurally and substantively, without necessitating that the 'liberty' interest embedded in s 7 be extended to include parents' endangering the lives of children or denying them required medical treatment.

[221] In sum, since we find the parental decision to withhold medical care to be outside the scope of 'liberty', it does not qualify for Charter protection in the first place.

The approach of Iacobucci and Major JJ (with whom Cory J agreed) is superficially attractive. Under the European Convention, it would strike out the claim of an infringement of art 8, by interpreting art 8(1) as not applying to a parental decision not in the child's 'best interests'. Alternatively, the English court could mirror La Forest J's approach and recognise the infringement under art 8(1) but justifying it as 'necessary in a democratic society' under art 8(2). This would be more consistent with giving human rights precedence subject to justification for interference. In any event, the Convention will not effect the outcome of the existing cases.

The Canadian Supreme Court also considered a claim under s 2(a) of the Charter protecting freedom of conscience. A majority of the Court (La Forest, L'Heureux-Dubé, Sopinka, Gonthier and McLachlin JJ) held that the parents had a right to rear their children according to their religious beliefs, including that of choosing medical and other treatments consistent with those beliefs. However, they concluded that any breach of this right was justified under the Charter to protect the child.

La Forest J: [104] Like the other provisions of the Charter, s 2(*a*) must be given a liberal interpretation with a view to satisfying its purpose: see *Reference re: Section 94(2) of the Motor Vehicle Act, supra.* In *R v Big M Drug Mart Ltd supra*, Dickson J stated, at p 353:

The essence of the concept of freedom of religion is the right to entertain such religious beliefs as a person chooses, the right to declare religious beliefs openly and without fear of hindrance or reprisal, and the right to manifest religious belief by worship and practice or by teaching and dissemination. But the concept means more than that.

[105] In *R v Jones, supra*, I observed that freedom of religion encompassed the right of parents to educate their children according to their religious beliefs. In *P (D) v S (C)* (1993), 108 DLR (4th) 287, [1993] 4 SCR 141, 18 CRR (2d) 1, a case involving a custody dispute in which one of the parents was a Jehovah's Witness, L'Hereux-Dubé stated that custody rights included the right to decide the child's religious education. It seems to me that the right of parents to rear their children according to their religious beliefs, including that of choosing medical and other treatments, is an equally fundamental aspect of freedom of religion…

[108] A more difficult issue is whether the freedom of religion of the appellants is intrinsically limited by the very reasons underlying the state's intervention, namely the protection of the health and well-being of S…

[109] This court has consistently refrained from formulating internal limits to the scope of freedom of religion in cases where the constitutionality of a legislative scheme was raised; it rather opted to balance the competing rights under s 1 of the Charter: see *R v Jones, supra*, and *R v Edwards Books, supra*…

[110] In my view, it appears sounder to leave to the state the burden of justifying the restrictions it has chosen. Any ambiguity or hesitation should be resolved in favour of individual rights. Not only is this consistent with the broad and liberal interpretation of rights favoured by this court, but s 1 is a much more flexible tool with which to balance competing rights than s 2(*a*).

A minority of the Justices (Iacobucci, Major and Cory JJ and Lamer CJ) concluded that the right did not include the imposition upon the child of religious practices which threatened his safety, health or life.

Iacobucci and Major JJ: [223] The parents of S are constitutionally entitled to manifest their beliefs and practise their religion, as is their daughter. That constitutional freedom includes the right to educate and rear their child in the tenets of their faith. In effect, until the child reaches an age where she can make an independent decision on her religion for her and raise her in accordance with that religion.

[224] However, the freedom of religion is not absolute. Although La Forest J considered that limitations on this right are best considered under a s 1 analysis, we are of the view that the right itself must have a definition, and even if a broad and flexible definition is appropriate, there must be an outer boundary. Conduct which lies outside the boundary is not protected by the Charter. That boundary is reached in the circumstances of this case.

[225] We are of the view that the constitutional question should be: to what extent can an infant's right to life and health be subordinated to conduct emanating from a parent's religious convictions? With this perspective as a starting point, we find that the appellants do not benefit from the protection of s 2(*a*) of the Charter since a parent's freedom of religion does not include the imposition upon the child of religious practices which threaten the safety, health or life of the child.

[226] Just as there are limits to the ambit of freedom of expression (*eg* s 2(*b*) does not protect violent acts: *R v Zundel* (1992) 95 DLR (4th) 202 at pp 260–1 and 222–3, 75 CCC (3d) 449, [1992] 2 SCR 731; *R v Keegstra* (1990), 61 CCC (3d) 1 at pp 26 and 98–9, [1990] 3 SCR 697, 1 CR (4th) 129), so are there limits to the scope of s 2(*a*), especially so when this provision is called upon to protect activity that threatens the physical or psychological well-being of others. In other words, although the freedom of belief may be broad, the freedom to act upon those beliefs is considerably narrower, and it is the latter freedom at issue in this case...

[231] The appellants proceed on the assumption that S is of the same religion as they, and hence cannot submit to a blood transfusion. Yet, S has never expressed any agreement with the Jehovah's Witness faith, nor, for the matter, with any religion, assuming any such agreement would be effective. There is thus an impingement upon S's freedom of conscience which arguably includes the right to live long enough to make one's own reasoned choice about the religion one wishes to follow as well as the right not to hold a religious belief. In fact, denying an infant necessary medical care could preclude that child from exercising any of her constitutional rights, as the child, due to parental beliefs, may not live long enough to make choices about the ideas she should like to express, the religion she should like to profess, or the associations she should like to join. 'Freedom of religion' should not encompass activity that so categorically negates the 'freedom of conscience' of another.

The definitional approach of the minority again has much to commend it.

As you will see, the judges also adopted a 'conflict of rights' approach resolving the conflict in favour of the child's right (for a discussion of the case see: Commentary (1996) 4 Med L Rev 117 (IK)).

The interplay between a parent's religious beliefs, 'best interests' and the right to religious freedom arose in *Re J (child's religious upbringing and circumcision)* (1999) 52 BMLR 82 (CA).

Re J (child's religious upbringing and circumcision) (1999) 52 BMLR 82 (CA)

Thorpe LJ: On 23 April 1999 Wall J gave a reserved judgment refusing a father's application for a specific issue order that his five year old son be circumcised. No earlier application raising this issue is known and, accordingly, he gave permission to appeal to enable the father to bring his case to this court.

The judge's factual summary could not be bettered. What follows is all extracted from his judgment at points between pages 3 and 8. I quote:

The father is 27. He is Turkish by birth and upbringing, and retains his Turkish nationality, although he is permanently resident in the United Kingdom and also has a British passport. He is a Muslim, although, as he freely accepts, he does not actively observe many of the tenets of his faith.

The mother is 29. She is English and, apart from a short period around the time of her marriage to the father when she lived with him in Turkey, she has lived throughout her life in England. She is notionally a Christian and a member of the Church of England but, like the father, she is non-practising.

The parents met whilst the mother was on holiday in Turkey in the Summer of 1992. Later that year she returned to Turkey, and she and the father were married in Turkey on 18 November 1992. It was a first marriage for both of them.

The father says that whilst the mother was pregnant with J she gave her agreement that any male child would be circumcised. I accept that evidence.

Following the parents' return to England from Turkey in February 1993, the marriage, despite the birth of J in March 1994, did not endure, and they separated on 29 September 1996 when J was aged two and-a-half.

J is five and attending a local state primary school. He is being brought up in an essentially secular household. The only contact he has with Islam is through his father. The mother has no Muslim friends and no connections with any members of the Muslim community. The father, likewise, does not appear to have Muslim friends or mix in Muslim circles.

Against that factual background, the judge then posed the question: what is J's religion? He answered it thus, adopting a submission made by his Guardian ad litem, the Official Solicitor. I quote:

In English Law, therefore, J would seem to be being brought up as a 'non-practising Christian' in accordance with the convictions of his mother with whom he lives and as a non-practising Muslim when he stays with his father. He therefore has a mixed heritage and an essentially secular lifestyle. He does not have a settled religious faith.

The judge turned to decide, first, a substantial issue as to whether the mother should be required to bring J up as a Muslim; an issue which is no longer live in this court since both parties accept the judge's pragmatic resolution under which the father is free during periods of contact to deal with this aspect in his own way.

The judge's approach to the dispute over circumcision was characteristically thorough. He considered the lawfulness of ritual male circumcision, concluding that it was lawful for two parties jointly exercising parental responsibility to arrange the ritual circumcision of their male child.

The judge then recorded medical attitudes to ritual circumcision, having heard evidence from a consultant paediatrician and having read the GMC and BMA guidelines supplied by the Official Solicitor. He concluded that current mainstream medical opinion requires both parents' consent and, particularly, maternal consent when the father lacks parental responsibility. Additionally, he recorded in the consultant's report that circumcision was not medically indicated for J since he did not suffer from any of the three medical conditions that can make circumcision either necessary or advisable. He also accepted the consultant's advice that:

The procedure is not pain free and there are potential risks both physical and psychological, which may be small but which are nonetheless definite.

The judge's summary of the submissions of the parties is full and in many ways favourable to the father. I need quote only this sentence:

By comparison with what I have to say was the mother's pallid and unconvincing statement of her religious beliefs, the father's passionate plea for J to be given his proper identity as a Muslim and for him to be thereby enabled to identify fully with his father was impressive.

In an important section, the judge considered the likely effects on J of being circumcised. There, he made these significant findings:

In Turkish society, a Muslim male child's peers will all be circumcised: in the circles in which J will grow up, he is likely to be in a small minority and he will not have the reassurance that all his contemporaries have been through – or will go through – the same experience.

The incident I have described also makes it clear to me that the mother, as J's primary carer, would find it extremely difficult to present the question of circumcision to J in a positive light, and unlike ritual circumcision occurring in the context of a Muslim family, where the event would be one of celebration and fulfilment, J's circumcision would be likely to be surrounded by tension and stress, even though the mother was able to agree with the father's counsel in cross-examination that she would, of course, care for J after the operation and would have no difficulty changing dressings.

In my judgment the strained relationship between the parents, and the fact that as a circumcised child J would be unlike most of his peers, increases the risk that J will suffer adverse psychological effects from being circumcised.

Against that background, Mr Justice Wall stated his conclusions, marshalling them by reference to the statutory checklist in s 1(3) of the Children Act 1989. However, he preceded that exercise with this concise passage:

The major benefit is that J will be firmly identified with his father, and confirmed in the eyes of Islam as a Muslim. However his circumcision would not be part of a family celebration, and he would not, thereafter, be brought up in a Muslim family environment.

The disadvantages are that despite the father's passionate defence of the procedure, J may be traumatised by it; he will, moreover, be living in the household of his mother, who disagrees with the procedure, and will find great difficulty in presenting it to J in a positive light.

Finally, in refusing the application, the judge stressed that his conclusion was finely balanced and depended on the facts as he had found them. He summarised the factors which had influenced his conclusion in the following four numbered paragraphs:

(1) Although born a Muslim, it is clear to me that J is going to have an essentially secular upbringing in England. He is not going to mix in Muslim circles, and his main contact with Muslims and the Muslim ethos will be his contact with his father. J is therefore not going to grow up in an environment in which circumcision is a part of family life or in which circumcision is a part of family life; or in which circumcision will be in conformity with the religion practised by his primary carer, or in which his peers have all be circumcised and for him not to be so would render him either unusual or an outsider. To the contrary, circumcision in the circles in which J is likely to move will be the exception rather than the rule.

(2) Circumcision is an effectively irreversible surgical intervention which has no medical basis in J's case. It is likely to be painful and carries with it small but definable physical and psychological risks. For it to be ordered there would accordingly have to be clear benefits to J which would demonstrate that circumcision was in his interests notwithstanding the risks. The principal benefits put forward are J's identification as a Muslim and the strengthening of his bond with his father. The strength of each is substantially weakened, in my judgment, by the facts of J's lifestyle and his likely upbringing. As I have already made clear, he is not going to be brought up as a Muslim child, and the strength of his bond with his father – viewed from his perspective rather than the father's – is unlikely to be weakened if he is not circumcised unless the father chooses to allow the absence of circumcision to work to weaken it.

(3) J is in the middle of a hostile battle between his parents over contact. He is to that extent a vulnerable child. The operation and the period leading up to it are likely to be highly stressful for the mother, who would find it difficult to explain to J why it was being undertaken and would have grave difficulty presenting it to J in a positive light. Furthermore, J is of an age and understanding to feel pain and discomfort without at the same time being fully able to understand why the operation was being carried out.

(4) J's mother, who not only shares parental responsibility for him with his father but cares for him on a day to day basis and is currently the most important person in his life, is opposed to his circumcision, and there is a rational basis for her opposition. It is a strong thing to impose a medically unnecessary surgical intervention on a residential parent who is opposed to it. In my judgment, this should only be done if the evidence shows that J's welfare requires him to be circumcised. For the reasons I have given, I do not think that the evidence overall shows that it is in J's interests to be circumcised…

In presenting his father's appeal, Miss Kushner QC faced an uphill struggle with some fortitude. Her principal complaint was that the judge confused the child's religion with the child's religious upbringing. As a child of a Muslim father, J arrived in this world a Muslim. His family, during the first two years of his life, were practising Muslims to a slight degree and the separation of his parents could not terminate his religion, particularly in the absence of any active step by his mother so to do.

That contention seems to me, at best, to be theoretically correct. For what it is worth, it weighs very light in the scale that the judge had to balance to determine whether the relief sought would advance J's welfare. Some faiths recognise their religion as a birthright derived from either the child's mother or the child's father. Some recognise religion by some ceremony of induction or initiation, but the newborn does not share the perception of his parents or of the religious community to which the parents belong. A child's perception of his or her religion generally depends on involvement in worship and teaching within the family. From this develops the emotional, intellectual, psychological and spiritual sense of belonging to a religious faith. So far, for all practical purposes, the courts have been right to focus upon religious upbringing and it is no surprise to me that there is no reported case focusing on a child's religion, as Miss Kushner defines it.

Miss Kushner also submitted that in a number of respects the judge had underestimated the weight of points that told for her client or over estimated the weight of points that told for the mother. It is unnecessary to particularise. These were all fact dependent issues and none was a point of principle. It is impossible to demonstrate that Wall J erred on any issue of fact or in weighing the discretionary balance.

Miss Kushner further submitted that any considerations against circumcision were either transient or, if not transient, speculative. That submission seems to me to disregard the realities of child development. Fear, pain, despair or a sense of betrayal may all be transient in the temporal sense but still inflict emotional and psychological trauma that will burden a child for life.

Miss Kushner finally accused the judge of setting a general standard that has denied her client success in this application and which would make future applications unlikely to succeed. She rests this submission on a single paragraph, where the judge said:

I repeat that my decision in this case turns on its particular facts. I do not think it can be said that the court would not, in any circumstances, order a child to be circumcised. The example which was put in argument was that of a Jewish mother and an agnostic father with a number of sons, all of whom, by agreement had been circumcised as infants in accordance with Jewish laws; the parents then have another son who is born after they have separated; the mother wishes him to be circumcised like his brothers; the father, for no good reason, refused his agreement. In circumstances such as these, it seems to me that the court would be likely to grant the mother a specific issue order.

It is immediately obvious to me that the paragraph does not begin to justify the charge. It merely emphasises that each case must turn on its particular facts. I would not wish to be taken as laying down any more general guidance than the judge. The only certainty is that social attitudes to male circumcision will remain extremely fluid. The only generalisation I would feel confident to express is that, in those communities where it is the practice to carry out the circumcision of a male child within days of birth, there is much less likelihood of forensic dispute. Many of the issues in the present appeal could not have developed but for the practice of the father's community to defer circumcision to the age of about 7...

For all those reasons I would dismiss this appeal.

Schiemann LJ and Dame Elizabeth Butler-Sloss P agreed.

As you will see, the decision was largely based upon the court's view of the child's 'best interests'.

At first instance, Wall J entertained an argument from the child's father based upon Article 9 of the European Convention.

Re J (Specific Issue Orders: Muslim Upbringing and Circumcision) [1999] 2 FLR 678 (Fam Div)

Wall J: Reliance was placed by counsel for the father on Art 9 of the European Convention, soon to be formally enacted into our domestic law by the implementation of the Human Rights Act 1998. That Article reads:

Freedom of thought, conscience and religion

1. Everyone has the right to freedom of thought, conscience and religion; this right includes freedom to change his religion or belief and freedom, either alone or in a community with others and in public or private, to manifest his religion or belief, in worship, teaching, practice and observance.

2. Freedom to manifest one's religion or beliefs shall be subject only to such limitation as are prescribed by law and are necessary in a democratic society in the interests of public safety, for the protection of public order, health or morals, or for the protection of the rights and freedoms of others.

Reference was also made to Art 24.3 of the United Nations Convention on the Rights of the Child, which although ratified by the Government of the UK in 1991 has not been incorporated into English law. That Article requires all ratifying States to 'take all effective and appropriate measures with a view to abolishing traditional practices prejudicial to the health of children'.

The Human Rights Act 1998 is not yet, of course, in force in the UK. Despite this, it seems to me a useful backdrop against which to examine the application of the welfare principle in s 1 of the Children Act to an application to circumcise a male child.

Section 1 of the Human Rights Act 1998 provides that certain Articles (which include Art 9) are to have effect, and s 3(1) provides that primary legislation must be read and given effect in a way which is compatible with Convention rights. Under s 6, it is unlawful for a public authority (which includes a court) to act in a way which is incompatible with a Convention right.

Under Art 9, the father says that his right to manifest his religion in practice includes the right to arrange for the circumcision of his son in accordance with the tenets of his religion. That seems to me plainly correct. It follows that any limitations on that freedom imposed by a court must be (1) as are prescribed by law; and (2) as are necessary in a democratic society for the protection of the rights and freedoms of others – in this case, the rights and freedoms of both the mother and J himself.

The relevant law in this context must be:

(a) ss 2 and 3 of the Children Act 1989, which give both the mother and the father parental responsibility and the right to act alone and without the other in meeting that responsibility (see s 2(7) of the Act);

(b) s 8 of the Act, which empowers the court to authorise or restrict an exercise of parental responsibility by either parent; and

(c)   the welfare principle contained in s 1 of the Act.

Where, as here, two parents have identical rights under Art 9 of the Convention (and also, for that matter, under Art 8) I see no difficulty in imposing limitations on the right of one parent to manifest his religion if the exercise of that right (a) infringes or conflicts with the rights and freedoms of the other parent or the child, and (b) is found by the court not to be in the best interests of the child.

I therefore see nothing inconsistent with the proper operation of Arts 8 and 9 of the Convention in any decision of the court which, on the particular facts of this case and in the exercise of a judicial discretion, refuses to make a specific issue order permitting J's circumcision, alternatively prohibits the father from causing J to be circumcised.

Equally, given the balance which the court has to strike between the competing rights of the mother, the father, and the child, it does not seem to me that an order prohibiting circumcision in the circumstances of this case could properly be described as discriminatory under Art 14.

On appeal, Thorpe LJ merely stated that the 'judge correctly held that the father's right to manifest his religion had to be balanced against the welfare of the child and the rights of the mother'. It could be said that the 'rights' of the child were also in play, namely under art 8 (and conceivably art 3).

You will notice that Wall J opted to decide the human rights point under art 9(2). In other words, he balanced the competing rights and interests rather as La Forest J did in the Canadian decision rather than assert that the father's art 9(1) right was limited by the 'best interests' of the child.

(v) REASONABLE FORCE AND DETENTION

To what extent is it permissible to use force or restraint to treat a patient? This could be an issue where the patient is incompetent but resisting treatment, or even where the patient is competent but it is a situation where the law may allow treatment notwithstanding, for example, where the patient is a child (see *infra*).

The issue first arose in relation to a patient detained under the Mental Health Act 1983 whom it was sought to treat with her consent under s 63 of the Act (see *infra*). In *Tameside and Glossop Acute Services Trust v CH* [1996] 1 FLR 762, Wall J granted a declaration that it was lawful to treat the patient under s 63 and 'to use restraint to the extent to which it may be reasonably required' to carry out that treatment (see also *Riverside Mental Health NHS Trust v Fox* [1994] 1 FLR 614 (CA)) and *infra*). The judge specifically left open whether such an order could be made at common law. Subsequently, in a number of cases where pregnant women had refused caesarean sections, the courts in declaring them incompetent to decide and that medical intervention was in their best interests, did allow the use of reasonable force (eg *Norfolk and Norwich Healthcare (NHS) Trust v W* [1996] 2 FLR 613 and *Rochdale Healthcare (NHS) Trust v C* [1997] 1 FCR 274).

In the first such case to reach the Court of Appeal – *Re MB* (1997) 38 BMLR 175 – the judges accepted that reasonable force (including restraint) could be used. Butler-Sloss LJ stated (at 188–189):

In a number of first instance decisions the declarations have included that it would be lawful for reasonable force to be used in the course of such treatment. That declaration was granted by Hollis J in the present case and is criticised by Mr Francis. It would, however, follow, in our view, from the decision that a patient is not competent to refuse treatment, that such treatment may have to be given against her continued objection if it is in her best interests that the treatment be given despite those objections. The extent of force or compulsion which may become necessary can only be judged in each individual case and by the health professionals. It may become for them a balance between continuing treatment which is forcibly opposed and deciding not to continue with it. This is a difficult issue which may have to be considered in grater depth on another occasion. In our view, the judge was justified in granting the declaration. All that was involved here was the prick of a needle to enable the first part of the anaesthesia to be given to the patient. In the events which happened, these problems did not arise. MB, on hearing the decision of this court, then signed the consent form on the following morning and co-operated in the initial administration of the anaesthesia. No force was necessary.

Notice the reasoning of the Court of Appeal. The court did not conclude that treatment was in the patient's best interests and thereafter 'tag on' an order that the use of reasonable force would also be justified. Rather, as Butler-Sloss LJ put it, it was 'in her best interests that the treatment be given despite [her] objections'. In other words, the court must take account of the extent of the intervention contemplated and that it will have to be carried out, possibly with resistance from the patient. The greater the level of intervention and the more the patient's co-operation is required, the less likely it will be that *en*forced treatment is in the patient's best interests.

Consider, by way of example, the following case:

Re D (1997) 41 BMLR 81 (Fam Div)

D, aged 49, had spent most of his adult life in and out of psychiatric hospitals, including Broadmoor. He lacked capacity to take decisions with respect to his medical treatment. In addition to a long-standing psychiatric illness, a psychosis, D suffered problems in relation to alcohol and drugs and was in the near end stage of renal failure. He needed dialysis up to four times per week, which would require him voluntarily to keep still, or be restrained. As a result of his mental disability, D was unable to recognise the importance of co-operating in order to receive this treatment. The only alternative to D's co-operation, in the receiving of the treatment, was to give it under a general anaesthetic, but this was both impracticable and dangerous. The doctors responsible for his treatment believed that it might become impossible to treat him, and their employer, a hospital trust, sought a declaration that it would be lawful, being in the best interests of D, not to impose haemodialysis on him, in circumstances in which, in the opinion of those responsible for his treatment, it was not reasonably practicable to do so. D was represented by the Official Solicitor.

Sir Stephen Brown P: It is stated by the consultant nephrologist who deals with this aspect of this patient's condition that he suffers from chronic renal failure at what the consultant describes as 'the near end stage'. It is associated too with a long-standing condition of high blood pressure. The result of that is, from the physical point of view, that D requires dialysis, and he would require that perhaps three or four times a week, and that would mean a period of four hours on the dialysis machine, keeping still, restrained in the physical sense in that way, voluntarily of course in the ordinary way, so that the dialysis treatment can be given.

Unfortunately, because of his mental disability, this patient is unable to recognise the importance of co-operating and to actually co-operate. This dialysis treatment cannot be given without the co-operation of the patient. The doctors have been seeking to persuade him to accept the treatment and to co-operate, but it is becoming impossible to do that. He has recently, on one occasion (on 21 November 1997, I believe) co-operated with a period, but not the full period, of treatment. The fact is that the doctors are very worried about the position and concerned about their own position. The obligation of doctors, of course, is to treat their patients in order to seek to improve their life, and, indeed, to cure where that is possible. In this case the doctors are anxious to do all they can to preserve this man's life, but it is becoming increasingly difficult so to do.

The only extreme step which the consultant nephrologist feels could possibly enable dialysis to be carried out is if this man were placed under a general anaesthetic, but that is not practicable and it is also dangerous, particularly in the case of a man with this patient's difficulties and disabilities. So there is no sure way of ensuring the effectiveness of the dialysis treatment.

The result is, and it is a difficult situation to have to face, that the doctors feel that they must seek the protection of the court in case they are unable to give this treatment. It is, of course, a clinical decision as to whether the treatment can and should be given in particular cases, and because of the difficult situation which does arise in such a situation as this, an application has been made for a declaration in the following terms: that notwithstanding the defendant's inability to consent or refuse medical treatment, it is lawful, as being in the best interests of the patient, for the plaintiff (that is, the hospital authority) not to impose haemodialysis upon him in circumstances in which, in the opinion of the medical practitioners responsible for such treatment, it is not reasonably practicable to do so...

It is a sad and serious situation, but I feel that the hospital trust has had no alternative in the circumstances but to seek a declaration in the terms which I have already indicated, and I propose therefore to grant a declaration in the following terms:

that, notwithstanding the defendant's inability to consent to or refuse medical treatment, it is lawful as being in the best interests of the patient that the plaintiff not to impose haemodialysis upon him in circumstances in which, in the opinion of the medical practitioners responsible for such treatment, it is not reasonably practicable so to do...

It will, of course, be still their purpose to seek to treat this man, and this declaration, as it were, only supports the last resort where in fact they are unable to administer the dialysis treatment because of the condition and the situation which I have described. This is not a question of doctors giving up; this is a question of doctors having to say that, in the circumstances, which unfortunately appear to be likely to continue, then they will be fully justified in not seeking to impose dialysis upon him by other means.

The legal underpinning of the declaration is not entirely clear. Was the judge saying it was not in the patient's best interests to be given the treatment? All things being equal, it must have been in the patient's best interests to dialyse him. Of course, all things were not equal, he was refusing – more importantly resisting – the treatment which made it practically impossible to provide it without the use of force and a general anaesthetic. So, was the judge deciding that it was not in his best interests to dialyse the patient if force and general anaesthetic were necessary? There are two possibilities.

On one view, it could be said that Stephen Brown P concluded that it was not in the patient's best interests to be dialysed simply because it was impracticable. With respect, this is not the correct approach for the law to adopt. In principle it is wrong because it does not necessarily have anything to do with the patient's best interests which is what the legal test is all about. Instead, it is generally more likely to be concerned wit the external circumstances surrounding the provision of the treatment, even if this was not the case in *Re D* itself. It is as if a treatment which is medically indicated but which cannot be given because it is unavailable because of cost or whatever, is not in the best interests of the patient when if it were available, it clearly would be in his best interests to be treated. The better view is that the impracticality of providing a treatment merely means that a doctor cannot be required to provide it. In other words, the law does not make doctors provide treatment when it is impracticable to do so because coercive remedies, such as mandatory injunctions, go against the judicial grain and the law does not act in vain (*Re J (a minor) (child in care: medical treatment)* [1993] Fam 15 (CA)).

A second view of the decision is that the judge decided that the treatment using force was not in the patient's best interests. This would be an altogether more palatable basis for the decision. It is also a more likely explanation given that the 'impracticality' stemmed exclusively from the degree and consistency of the force which would be needed to dialyse a patient three or four times a week for about four hours on each occasion. There is no doubt that the 'burden' of a treatment to a patient are relevant in making a 'best interests' decision. *Re D*, in effect, is no more than an application of this approach where the 'burden' is the use of force and, perhaps, restraint (general anaesthetic being really that). The existing case law, as we have seen, accepts that reasonable force (and restraint) may be used at common law when treatment is otherwise in a patient's best interests. This interpretation of *Re D* does not result in the creation of a new heading of 'impracticality' as a basis for making a best interests decision and is preferable.

So far, the cases have been concerned with the common law principle of necessity in respect of incompetent adults (for a case permitting long-term detention of a mentally disordered patient under the common law providing he is compliant: see *R v Bournewood Community and Mental Health NHS Trust, ex p L* [1998] 3 All ER 289 (HL), discussed *infra*).

The court also has the power to authorise restraint and the use of reasonable force under its *parens patriae* power (and it is likely under s 8 of the Children Act 1989) in relation to children. This has the added importance, that as we shall see, in this kind of case the court may override a *competent* child's wishes. The use of restraint and force may be more commonly required here unless the patient capitulates in the face of parental or court authorisation.

Re C (Detention: Medical Treatment) [1997] 2 FLR 180 (Fam Div)

C, aged 16, showed early symptoms of anorexia nervosa at the age of 12. The disease was diagnosed in 1995 when she was admitted to the clinic, a private hospital for the treatment of eating disorders run on boarding-school lines. The local authority funded her treatment, but never sought to take her into care, preferring to co-operate with the family despite the dysfunctional nature of the family situation. After C's discharge from the clinic her health deteriorated rapidly. She was detained in hospital under the Mental Health Act 1983 and later admitted to another hospital. Eventually in November 1996 she was readmitted to the clinic. There her behaviour continued to be disturbed and aggressive and at times suicidal. She absconded four times within a month. At that stage the consultant psychiatrist and the medical director of the clinic both made it clear that they would not readmit C without a court order. In early December 1996 the local authority as plaintiff obtained leave ex parte under s 100 of the Children Act 1989 to invoke the inherent jurisdiction. The matter was confirmed inter partes and an order made giving leave for C to be detained at the clinic for such treatment as was prescribed, with the use of force if necessary. The court gave liberty to apply, fixing the hearing for 17 February 1997 and invited the Official Solicitor to act as amicus curiae. The principal questions raised were (1) whether the court when exercising its inherent parents patriae jurisdiction in relation to a child of 16 has power to direct the detention of the child in a specific institution for the purpose of medical treatment; and (2) whether, in the event of the child consenting to treatment, the deprivation of liberty was an essential part of the treatment or was irrelevant to the treatment process, and whether in the latter case the inherent jurisdiction was being used solely for the deprivation of liberty. C stated that she was content to stay in the clinic voluntarily and receive treatment but she disputed the need for an order.

Wall J: *The power to exercise the inherent jurisdiction to authorise the detention of C in the clinic for the purposes of medical treatment*
This is the first and critical question. Does the court have the power under the inherent jurisdiction to order the detention of a minor over the age of 16 in a specified institution for the purposes of medical treatment being administered to the minor without her agreement?

The leading case for present purposes seems to me to be the decision of the Court of Appeal in *Re W (A Minor) (Medical Treatment: Court's Jurisdiction)* [1993] Fam 64, sub nom *Re W (A Minor) (Consent to Medical Treatment)* [1993] 1 FLR 1. W was 16 and in the care of a local authority. She was suffering from anorexia nervosa. The local authority wished to transfer her to a unit specialising in the treatment of eating disorders. This was contrary to W's wishes. The local authority accordingly sought leave to invoke the inherent jurisdiction. W resisted the application on the ground that s 8 of the Family Law Reform Act 1969 conferred on her the same right as an adult to refuse medical treatment, with the consequence that the court could not override her refusal. The trial judge held that he had jurisdiction to authorise medical treatment without W's consent and made the order sought by the local authority. The Court of Appeal dismissed W's appeal. As Lord Donaldson of Lymington MR put it at 81C–E and 12C–E respectively:

> There is ample authority for the proposition that the inherent powers of the court under its parens patriae jurisdiction are theoretically limitless and that they certainly extend beyond the powers of a natural parent…There can therefore be no doubt that it has power to override the refusal of a minor, whether over the age of 16 or under that age but '*Gillick*-competent'. It does not do so by ordering the doctors to treat which, even if within the court's powers, would be an abuse of them or by ordering the minor to accept treatment, but by authorising the doctors to treat the minor in accordance with their clinical judgment, subject to any restrictions which the court may impose.

The judgements in *Re W* do not deal specifically with the power to detain the minor in the specialist unit, although the existence of such a power can readily be inferred from the fact that the trial judge (Thorpe J) authorised her removal to and her treatment at the unit. Plainly she could not undergo the treatment if she was not on the unit…

It is therefore clear to me that on the authority of *Re W* I have the power, exercising the inherent jurisdiction of the court, to direct that C remain as an in-patient at the clinic until discharged by Dr D or until further order of the court. That power includes the authorisation of her detention in the clinic for the purposes of treatment. In *Tameside and Glossop Acute Services Trust v CH* [1996] 1 FLR 762 I left open the question whether or not the court has the power at common law, as opposed to under the Mental Health Act, to authorise the use of 'reasonable force' as a necessary incidence of treatment (which, as Mr Wood argues, inevitably also incorporates the notion of detention at the place at which reasonable force might be used). Since that decision, an affirmative answer has been given to it by Johnson J in two cases: see *Norfolk and Norwich Healthcare (NHS) Trust v W* [1996] 2 FLR 613 and *Rochdale Healthcare (NHS) Trust v C* [1997] 1 FCR 274. Since I regard C's presence in the unit and her adherence to its regime as integral parts of her treatment programme, I equally have no doubt that under the inherent jurisdiction I have power not only to direct that she reside in the clinic but also to authorise the use of reasonable force (if necessary) to detain her in the clinic.

I am also satisfied that, were it necessary, I have power to authorise the use of reasonable force to C's person in the administration of the clinic's refeeding treatment programme. I would not, however, contemplate making such an order in this case, since the forcible administration of treatment is antipathetic to the ethos of the clinic and no order in these terms is sought by Dr D.

The judge went on to determine that the patient's detention for treatment was in her best interests (see Commentary (1997) 5 Med L Rev 227 (AG). See also, P de Cruz (1999) 62 MLR 595).

The approach of Wall J was inevitable. As Penney Lewis has put it:

Penney Lewis 'Feeding Anorexic Patients Who Refuse Food' (1999) 7 Med L Rev 21

These holdings follow from the application of *Re W*. Logically, if the court has the power to overrule a competent minor's refusal of medical treatment, such power must include the power to detain that minor for treatment, and to use reasonable force against her if necessary for the detention or the provision of treatment. Otherwise, the competent minor's refusal would effectively be respected, despite it having been overruled by the court.

Re C entailed a very serious and prolonged intervention against the patient. As Wall J recognised, there was no point in authorising the use of force for the treatment since this was antithetical to the nature of the treatment required to be offered.

Whilst the courts have established the principle that 'reasonable force' may be used, the precise limits have not been, inevitably perhaps, given the *ad hoc* nature of the 'best interests' test. Limits, of course, there must be and this is explicit in the notion of '*reasonable* force'. Likewise, art 3 of the European Convention prohibiting 'inhuman or degrading treatment' would undoubtedly set outer limits to *enforced* treatment. However, given that major surgery could be authorised by the court against a child's wishes (see *Re M (medical treatment: consent)* [1999] 2 FLR 1097 (Johnson J) – heart transplant against wishes of competent 15½-year-old), why could this not be done even if the patient resisted given that general anaesthesia is all that would need to be 'forced' upon her? The answer may lie in the fact that her treatment would include a life-time of taking immunosuppressant drugs which would require her compliance. Seen as a whole, without the patient's co-operation the treatment may not be in her 'best interests'.

(vi) AUTHORISE OR ORDER TREATMENT?

What is the precise power which the court exercises? It is sometimes said (somewhat carelessly) that a court *orders* that a specific form of treatment be carried out. It may be better analytically to describe the court's power as one of *authorisation* only. For example, Templeman LJ stated that: '...the local authority must be authorised themselves to authorise and direct the operation to be carried out...(*Re B (a minor) (wardship: medical treatment)* (1981) [1990] 3 All ER 927).

This is because first, courts do not make orders which they cannot supervise and secondly, in the context of medical treatment the last word must, save in the most exceptional circumstances, remain with the doctor. As Margaret Somerville put it in her article, 'Refusal of Medical Treatment in "Captive" Circumstances' (1985) 63 Canadian Bar Review 59 at 89:

Consequently, if the treating physician thought that treatment were contra-indicated, because, for instance, the circumstances had suddenly changed (and there was no negligence involved in holding such an opinion, in that a reasonable and competent physician in the same circumstances could be of the same opinion), the physician would not only have no duty to treat, but would have a duty not to treat, breach of which would constitute medical negligence or malpractice.

The point arose directly in the following case.

Re J (a minor) (child in care: medical treatment) [1993] Fam 15, [1992] 4 All ER 614 (CA)

J a 16-month-old child, was profoundly handicapped, both mentally and physically, as a result of hitting his head in an accidental fall when he was one month old. He was severely microcephalic, his brain not having grown sufficiently following the injury, and he suffered from a severe form of cerebral palsy. He had cortical blindness and severe epilepsy. He was largely fed by a nasogastric tube. Medical opinion was unanimous that J was unlikely to develop much beyond his present level of functioning, that that level might well deteriorate and that his expectation of life, although uncertain, would inevitably be short. He required constant attention day and night. He had been placed with foster parents by the local authority, which shared parental responsibility for him. In December 1991 the consultant paediatrician in charge of J, Dr I, wrote a report in which she expressed the view that 'it would not be medically appropriate to intervene with intensive therapeutic measures such as artificial ventilation if [J] were to suffer a life-threatening event' and that although it 'would be appropriate to offer ordinary resuscitation with suction, physiotherapy and antibiotics [it] would not, however, be appropriate to subject [J] to the more intensive measures that would be required if he was unable to breathe spontaneously'. In a further report Dr I stated that if J was unable to breath spontaneously it would be cruel to subject him to intensive care to prolong his life artificially, that he would be unlikely to survive positive pressure ventilation and that all that such treatment would achieve would be artificially to prolong his vegetative state. Dr N, a consultant paediatrician and paediatric cardiologist with a London teaching hospital who had been consulted by the Official Solicitor, broadly agreed with Dr I. On 30 March 1992 the local authority sought and was granted leave under s 100 of the Children Act 1989 to invoke the inherent jurisdiction of the High Court to determine whether artificial ventilation and/or other life-saving measures should be given to J if he suffered a life-threatening event and sought an order requiring the health authority to continue to provide all available treatment to J including 'intensive resuscitation'. The judge made an interim order and injunction to that effect requiring the health authority to use intensive therapeutic measures including artificial ventilation for so long as they were capable of prolonging his life. The health authority, supported by the Official Solicitor as the guardian ad litem and the local authority, which had changed its view, appealed against the order. J's natural mother sought to uphold the order, relying on a report by Professor B, an expert in child health at another London teaching hospital who did not regard artificial ventilation as being a 'cruel treatment' and took a much more optimistic view than Dr I as to the likelihood of it being possible to wean J from such ventilation if it were ever undertaken. The judge's order was stayed pending the appeal.

Lord Donaldson MR: The fundamental issue in this appeal is whether the court in the exercise of its inherent power to protect the interests of minors should ever require a medical practitioner or health authority acting by a medical practitioner to adopt a course of treatment which in the bona fide clinical judgment of the practitioner concerned is contra-indicated as not being in the best interests of the patient. I have to say that I cannot at present conceive of any circumstances in which this would be other than an abuse of power as directly or indirectly requiring the practitioner to act contrary to the fundamental duty which he owes to his patient. This, subject to obtaining any necessary consent, is to treat the patient in accordance with his own best clinical judgment, notwithstanding that other practitioners who are not called upon to treat the patient may have formed a quite different judgment or that the court, acting on expert evidence, may disagree with him.

It is said that the views which I expressed in my judgments in *Re J (a minor) (wardship: medical treatment)* [1990] 3 All ER 930, [1991] Fam 33 and *Re R (a minor) (wardship: medical treatment)* [1991] 4 All ER 177, [1992] Fam 11 which are relevant to this were obiter and did not receive the express assent of those sitting with me. So be it but, remaining as I am of the view that they were a correct expression of the law, I repeat them as part of the ratio of my decision in this case. From *Re J* [1990] 3 All ER 930 at 934, [1991] Fam 33 at 41:

No one can *dictate* the treatment to be given to the child, neither court, parents nor doctors. There are checks and balances. The doctors can recommend treatment A in preference to treatment B. They can also refuse to adopt treatment C on the grounds that it is medically contra-indicated or for some other reason is a treatment which they could not conscientiously administer. The court or parents for their part can refuse to consent to treatment A or B or both, but cannot insist on treatment C. The inevitable and desirable result is that choice of treatment is in some measure a joint decision of the doctors and the courts or parents. This co-operation is reinforced by another consideration. Doctors nowadays recognise that their function is not a limited technical one of repairing or servicing a body. They are treating people in a real life context. This at once enhances the contribution which the court or parents can make towards reaching the best possible decision in all the circumstances. (My original emphasis.)

From *Re R* [1991] 4 All ER 177 at 184, 187, [1992] Fam 11 at 22, 26:

> It is trite law that in general a doctor is not entitled to treat a patient without the consent of someone who is authorised to give that consent...However consent by itself creates no obligation to treat. It is merely a key which unlocks the door...No doctor can be required to treat a child, whether by the court in the exercise of its wardship jurisdiction, by the parents, by the child or anyone else. The decision whether to treat is dependent upon an exercise of his own professional judgment, subject only to the threshold requirement that, save in exceptional cases usually of emergency, he has the consent of someone who has authority to give that consent.

The order of Waite J was wholly inconsistent with the law as so stated and cannot be justified upon the basis of any authority known to me. Furthermore it was, in my judgment, erroneous on two other substantial grounds, only slightly less fundamental than that to which I have just adverted. The first is its lack of certainty as to what was required of the health authority. The second is that it does not adequately take account of the sad fact of life that health authorities may on occasion find that they have too few resources, either human or material or both, to treat all the patients whom they would like to treat in the way in which they would like to treat them. It is then their duty to make choices.

The court when considering what course to adopt in relation to a particular child has no knowledge of competing claims to a health authority's resources and is in no position to express any view as to how it should elect to deploy them. Although the order is subject to the condition precedent that 'the required drugs and equipment are or could reasonably be made available', it makes no reference to the availability of staff and it has to be borne in mind that artificial ventilation of a young child in an intensive care unit is highly intensive of highly skilled staff. It gives no guidance as to what is meant by the concept of being reasonably available, yet it is not difficult to imagine circumstances in which there could be bona fide differences of opinion as to whether equipment or staff was reasonably available. The health authority is entitled to object and does object to being subject to an order of the court with penal consequences in the event of disobedience when it does not know precisely what is required of it.

Balcombe LJ: So recognising that there are limits to the exercise of this inherent jurisdiction, I agree with Lord Donaldson MR that I can conceive of no situation where it would be a proper exercise of the jurisdiction to make such an order as was made in the present case: that is to order a doctor, whether directly or indirectly, to treat a child in a manner contrary to his or her clinical judgment. I would go further, I find it difficult to conceive of a situation where it would be a proper exercise of the jurisdiction to make an order positively requiring a doctor to adopt a particular course of treatment in relation to a child, unless the doctor himself or herself was asking the court to make such an order. Usually all the court is asked, or needs, to do is to authorise a particular course of treatment where the person or body whose consent is requisite is unable or unwilling to do so.

It will be apparent from what I have already said that I agree with the views expressed by Lord Donaldson MR in *Re J (a minor) (wardship: medical treatment)* [1990] 3 All ER 930 at 934–935, [1991] Fam 33 at 41–42. Since the point has now been taken that in my judgment in that case I did not support that particular passage from Lord Donaldson's MR judgment, I should state that the reason was because I did not find it necessary to do so in the particular circumstances of the case. I did then, and do now, agree with what is there stated as well as with the passages to the like effect in *Re R (a minor) (wardship: medical treatment)* [1991] 4 All ER 177 at 184, 187, [1992] Fam 11 at 22, 26.

Apart from the obvious reasons for this limitation of the exercise of the jurisdiction, there is one other matter which should not be overlooked. The court is not, or certainly should not be, in the habit of making orders unless it is prepared to enforce them. If the court orders a doctor to treat a child in a manner contrary to his or her clinical judgment it would place a conscientious doctor in an impossible position. To perform the court's order could require a doctor to act in a manner which he or she genuinely believed not to be in the patient's best interests; to fail to treat the child as ordered would amount to a contempt of court. Any judge would be most reluctant to punish the doctor for such a contempt, which seems to me to be a very strong indication that such an order should not be made.

I would also stress the absolute undesirability of the court making an order which may have the effect of compelling a doctor or health authority to make available scarce resources (both human and material) to a particular child, without knowing whether or not there are other patients to whom those resources might more advantageously be devoted. Lord Donaldson MR has set out in his reasons the condition of J and his very limited future prospects. The effect of the order of Waite J, had it not been immediately stayed by this court, might have been to require the health authority to put J on a ventilator in an intensive care unit, and thereby possibly to deny the benefit of those limited resources to a child who was much more likely than J to benefit from them. At the very least it would in those circumstances have required the health authority to make a further application to the court to vary or discharge the injunction.

Leggatt LJ agreed.

See also, *Re C (a minor) (medical treatment)* [1998] Lloyd's Rep Med 1 (Stephen Brown P) and Commentary (1998) 6 Med L Rev 99 (IK).)

It may be thought that *Re J* goes too far (see Commentary (1993) 1 Med L Rev 95 (IK)). Perhaps courts should be reluctant to say 'never' (see *R v Portsmouth Hospitals NHS Trust, ex p Glass* (1999) 50 BMLR 269 (CA) per Lord Woolf at 279). For example, a court should *order* treatment if what they are really saying is that the child should not be neglected and left to die. In exceptional circumstances a court would be entitled to take the view that a doctor is under a duty to provide certain treatment notwithstanding the medical opinion to the contrary. This might arise, for example, if the denial of treatment was based upon a moral or religious belief which the court does not accept as being in the child's 'best interests' (see the view of Thomas J in *Auckland AHB v A-G* [1993] 1 NZLR 235 at 252).

(c) Acting without the proxy's consent

Will it ever be lawful for a doctor to treat a child patient without first having obtained the consent of the parents (or others with parental responsibility)? In the generality of situations, it will not be lawful because the parents' consent alone provides the legal justification for treatment. This assumes that the procedure (and hence the consent to it) is in the child's best interests. In *Secretary, Dept of Health and Community Services v JWB and SMB* (1992) 175 CLR 218 (HC of A), McHugh J (at 316) stated:

…because parents are given authority to act for the benefit of the child, their authority is limited to those acts which advance or protect the welfare of the child. This criterion is a matter which must be determined objectively and not be reference to the good faith opinions of the parent. A parent has no authority therefore, to consent to medical treatment unless it can be seen objectively that the treatment is for the welfare of the child. If a parent purports to give consent to treatment which is not for the welfare of the child, the consent is of no effect. A person who acts on such 'consent' is guilty of assaulting the child if the treatment involves any physical interference with the child.

The doctor's duty of care to the child will not usually allow him to treat without consent. In *Re J (a minor) (wardship: medical treatment)* (1990) 6 BMLR 25 at 29 (CA) Lord Donaldson stated:

The doctors owe the child a duty to care for it in accordance with good medical practice recognised as appropriate by a competent body of professional opinion (see *Bolam v Friern Hospital Management Committee* (1957) 1 BMLR 1, [1957] 1 WLR 582). This duty is, however, subject to the qualification that, if time permits, they must obtain the consent of the parents before undertaking serious invasive treatment.

Likewise, in *Re R (a minor) (wardship: medical treatment)* [1991] 4 All ER 177 (CA) Lord Donaldson MR repeated his view:

The decision whether to treat is dependent upon an exercise of [the doctors] professional judgment, subject only to the threshold requirement that, save in exceptional cases usually of emergency, he has the consent of someone who has authority to give that consent.

Where an emergency arises and it is impossible or impracticable to seek parental agreement, the law permits the doctor to give such treatment as is reasonably necessary to avoid serious harm or death to the child. You will recall Lord Donaldson MR's reference to the 'emergency' situation. This, of course, assumes he is unable to seek the permission of a court. In *Gillick v West Norfolk and Wisbech AHA* [1985] 3 All ER 402 Lord Scarman stated (at 424):

> Emergency, parental neglect, abandonment of the child or inability to find the parent are examples of exceptional situations justifying the doctor proceeding to treat the child without parental knowledge and consent; but there will arise, no doubt, other exceptional situations in which it will be reasonable for the doctor to proceed without the parent's consent.

Lord Templeman added (at 432):

> Where the patient is an infant, the medical profession accept that a parent having custody and being responsible for the infant is entitled on behalf of the infant to consent to or reject treatment if the parent considers that the best interests of the infant so require. Where doctor and parent disagree, the court can decide and is not slow to act. I accept that if there is no time to obtain a decision from the court, a doctor may safely carry out treatment in an emergency if the doctor believes the treatment to be vital to the survival or health of an infant and notwithstanding the opposition of a parent or the impossibility of alerting the parent before the treatment is carried out. In such a case the doctor must have the courage of his convictions that the treatment is necessary and urgent in the interests of the patient and the court will, if necessary, approve after the event treatment which the court would have authorised in advance, even if the treatment proves to be unsuccessful.

You will notice his inclusion of the situation where the parents refuse but treatment is vital and there is no time to seek the court's permission. If there is time, it is the court which should resolve the dispute. In cases where the parents refuse to consent to treatment which the doctor considers to be in the child's best interests, the doctor's proper approach should generally be to invoke the court's jurisdiction.

In *R v Portsmouth Hospitals NHS Trust, ex p Glass* (1999) 50 BMLR 269 (CA), the parents of a severely disabled child disagreed with the treatment regime proposed by the doctors. The parents sought judicial review of their decision arguing, *inter alia*, that only the court could override their refusal. Although the court found it unnecessary to express a view, Lord Woolf MR went some way when he stated (at 281–282):

> There can be no doubt that the best course is for a parent of a child to agree on the course which the doctors are proposing to take, having fully consulted the parent and for the parent to fully understand what is involved. That is the course which should always be adopted in a case of this nature. If that is not possible and there is a conflict, and if the conflict is of a grave nature, the matter must then be brought before the court so the court can decide what is in the best interests of the child concerned.

2. In respect of adults

(a) No proxy?

Can anyone consent to medical treatment on behalf of an incompetent adult?

Professor Skegg puts the issue well in his book *Law, Ethics and Medicine,* (1988) at pp 72, 73:

> It is sometimes stated or assumed that, where the patient is incapable of consenting, an effective consent may be given by his spouse, or by some near relative. Unfortunately, those who hold this view do not indicate the grounds on which it is based...
>
> The better view is that there is no general doctrine whereby a spouse or near relative is empowered to give a legally effective consent to medical procedures to be carried out on an adult. Of course, doctors are sometimes justified in proceeding without the consent of the patient. But this is not because the consent of others justifies a doctor in proceeding

without the patient's consent, but because in the circumstances the doctor is justified in
proceeding despite the absence of legally effective consent.

Sometimes the contrary claim is made in America. However, those who make it
have difficulty in pointing to authority to support it under the common law (for
legislative authority, see *infra*, ch 16). They sometimes find refuge in the dictum
in *Canterbury v Spence* (1972) 464 F 2d 772 at 789 of Judge Robinson: 'even in
situations of that character where the patient is unconscious or otherwise incapable
of consenting the physician should, as current law requires, attempt to secure a
relative's consent if possible.' The authority cited to support this proposition is
Bonner v Moran (1941) 126 F 2d 121 at 122–123, but this is a case of an adult
consenting on behalf of a child.

The same mistaken reasoning can be seen in the judgment of Croom-Johnson
LJ in *Wilson v Pringle* [1987] QB 237 (CA), where he assumes that in the case of
an unconscious patient, who is, therefore, unable to consent, the next-of-kin may
validly consent on the patient's behalf. But, like the other judges before him, he
cites no authority for this assumption. It is simply not clear how this assumption
arose. One possibility is that, until 1959, the court had power to appoint a 'committee
of the person' where the patient was unable to make decisions for themselves under
its then *parens patriae* jurisdiction (see *infra*). Often, of course, it would be those
relatives closest to the patient who would be appointed with power to make decisions
on behalf of the patient. It may, therefore, be that it was assumed that the next of
kin had an *inherent* power to make decisions when, of course, it was always court-
given and, as we shall see shortly, no longer exists. A similar situation still pertains
in Scotland today where the Court of Session can appoint a 'tutor dative' to make
all (or specified) treatment decisions on behalf of a patient (see *Law Hospital NHS
Trust v Lord Advocate* (1996) 39 BMLR 166 (Ct Sess (IH)) at 178–181 per Lord
Hope; 187–191 per Lord Cullen; and 194–195 per Lord Clyde).

What are the arguments in favour of vesting proxy power in a patient's relative? We
have already seen the arguments in favour of parents where the patient is a child
eloquently stated by McHugh J in the Australian High Court in *JWB and SMB* (see
supra). The US President's Commission in its 1983 Report, *Deciding to Forego Life-
Sustaining Treatment*, identified five reasons for giving power to the family (at p 128):

**President's Commission *Deciding to Forego Life-Sustaining Treatment:
Ethical, Medical and Legal Issues in Treatment Decisions* (1983)**

(1) The family is generally most concerned about the good of the patient.
(2) The family will also usually be most knowledgeable about the patient's goals, preferences,
     and values.
(3) The family deserves recognition as an important social unit that ought to be treated,
     within limits, as a responsible decision-maker in matters that intimately affect its
     members.
(4) Especially in a society in which many other traditional forms of community have eroded,
     participation in a family is often an important dimension of personal fulfilment.
(5) Since a protected sphere of privacy and autonomy is required for the flourishing of this
     interpersonal union, institutions and the state should be reluctant to intrude, particularly
     regarding matters that are personal and on which there is a wide range of opinion in society.

What are the arguments against this?

**Andrew Grubb 'Treatment Decisions: Keeping it in the Family' in A
Grubb (ed) *Choices and Decisions in Health Care* (1993)**

There are, however, dangers and practical problems in vesting a patient's family with decision-
making power. First, the patient may have no family, or the patient may be estranged from
the family such that they are not interested in his treatment. In this situation, another decision-
making process must be sought. Indeed, in some cases a patient's family may not be the

closest to the patient. This has arisen acutely in the case of gay AIDS patients. Often, here, the patient's closest "family" is the partner and not one of the traditional family unit, from which he is often estranged. While the concept underlying family decision-making remains intact in this situation because "family is whomever the individual is most closely associated with", (A Buchanan and D Brock *'Deciding for Others: The Ethics of Surrogate Decision-Making'* (1989)) the law would need to reflect this and give a broad scope to the traditional meaning of "family" for the concept to function appropriately.

Secondly, there may be disagreement amongst the patient's family as to the care the patient would have wanted. (See *in re Nemser* (1966) 273 NYS 2d 624 (NY Sup Ct) (disagreement between two sons over whether the leg of 80-year-old mother should be amputated).) Disagreement would not necessarily be a problem if the law set a priority of decision-makers within the family but it would, of course, make judicial review more likely.

Thirdly, there is often a feeling that members of a family are abusing their position and acting, not out of the interests of the patient, but out of a concern for their own personal interests. (See Presidents Commission Report (1983) 128–9. These may be financial where, in the case of a dying patient, inheritance is at stake or the cost of care is borne by the family or they may be emotional where the burden of caring for the patient will fall upon the family. The more significant the decision, for example, if it concerns life-sustaining treatment, the greater the fear of abuse because of what is at stake. Undoubtedly this influenced the majority of the US Supreme Court in the *Cruzan* case and led them to accept that the State *could* require "clear and convincing evidence" of the patient's wishes. Chief Justice Rehnquist stated that (*Cruzan v Director, Missouri Department of Health* (1990) 110 S Ct 2841 and (1990) 58 LW 4916 US Sup Ct) at 4920–1):

> The choice between life and death is a deeply personal decision of obvious and overwhelming finality…Not all incompetent patients will have loved ones available to serve as surrogate decision-makers…A state is entitled to guard against potential abuses in such situations.

Fourthly, there is the danger that the family may make a mistake and simply misjudge the patient's wishes. In *Cruzan*, Rehnquist CJ opined that (*ibid* at 4922):

> there is no automatic assurance that the views of close family members will necessarily be the same as the patient's would have been had she been confronted with the prospect of her situation while competent.

For fear of this, the majority in *Cruzan* favoured the status quo (*ibid* at 4921 per Rehnquist CJ):

> An erroneous decision not to terminate results in the maintenance of the status quo; the possibility of subsequent developments such as advancements in medical science, the discovery of new evidence regarding the patient's intent, changes in law, or simply the unexpected death of the patient despite the administration of life-sustaining treatment, at least create the potential that a wrong decision will eventually be corrected or its impact mitigated. An erroneous decision to withdraw life-sustaining treatment, however, is not susceptible of correction.

On occasion, there may be some basis for the fear of abuse or an erroneous decision. But why should the law assume that the risk of either of these must always prevent members of a patient's family reaching decisions? It could be that these dangers have constrained the development of the English common law not to recognise family decision-making in the case of incompetent adults…Before we accept these dangers as sufficient to deprive the family members of their natural role, we should ask two questions. First, given the goal of furthering the patient's autonomy, is there a better way to effectuate the patient's wishes, values and preferences? Almost certainly, there is not. There is no reason to believe that doctors or the court are more likely to know or appreciate a patient's preferences or values. This is, arguably, uniquely something that family (in the widest sense) will appreciate (see eg Brennan J (dissenting) *ibid* at 4932). The danger of an erroneous decision, on this basis, may actually be heightened if others, beyond the family, decide. Of course the danger of abuse will be lessened, but at which cost? The greater risk of error and, in the case of the court, the impracticality and cost of court hearings in every case when a decision about medical care has to be made, is a strong argument in favour of a *presumption* in favour of family decision-making.

The second question that should be asked is whether there is a process by which the dangers (if any) of family decision-making can be eliminated or, at least, minimised? The obvious mechanism is through court involvement resulting in judicial review or scrutiny of treatment decisions. In the United States, "right to die" cases come before the courts if there is any disagreement as to what should be done or whether there are any lingering doubts about the family's motives.

However, the position in England is clear and was unequivocally stated by Lord Donaldson MR in *Re T (adult: refusal of medical treatment)* (1992) 9 BMLR 46 (CA) at 50:

Lord Donaldson MR: There seems to be a view in the medical profession that in such emergency circumstances the next of kin should be asked to consent on behalf of the patient and that, if possible, treatment should be postponed until that consent has been obtained. This is a misconception because the next of kin has no legal right either to consent or to refuse consent.

(See also *Re F (mental patient: sterilisation)* [1990] 2 AC 1 at 13–14 per Lord Donaldson MR.)

One final possibility should be considered. Sometimes, in the case of mentally ill patients, a spouse or relative may be appointed a guardian under s 7 of the Mental Health Act 1983. In *T v T* [1988] Fam 52, Wood J considered whether a guardian could consent to medical treatment. The case concerned a 19-year-old incompetent woman whom it was thought should undergo an abortion and a sterilisation operation in her own best interests.

Wood J:...I pose myself the question – is there anyone who can consent on behalf of this defendant? It is submitted that the answer is 'No'.

This defendant is clearly suffering from a mental disorder within section 1 of the Mental Health Act 1983, and I therefore turn to the possibility of a guardianship application and an order under section 7. The procedure for such an application can be cumberous, and it was not suggested that an application *ex parte* on notice, as in the present case, could properly be made. The effect of a guardianship application is set out in section 8 where the relevant words read:

Where a guardianship application, duly made...is accepted by that authority, the application shall, subject to regulations by the Secretary of State, confer on the authority or person named in the application as guardian, to the exclusion of any other person...(*b*) the power to require the patient to attend at places and times so specified for the purpose of medical treatment, occupation, education or training.

Section 145 of the Mental Health Act 1983, which is the definition section, provides: "medical treatment" includes nursing, and also includes care, habilitation and rehabilitation under medical supervision'.

Section 8 replaces section 34(1) of the Mental Health Act of 1959, where subsection (1) reads, materially:

Where a guardianship application, duly made under the foregoing provisions of this Act and forwarded to the local authority within the period allowed by subsection (2) of this section, is accepted by that authority, the application shall...confer on the authority or person therein named as guardian, to the exclusion of any other person – and here is the important point – all such powers as would be exercisable by them or him in relation to the patient if they or he were the father of the patient and the patient were under the age of 14 years.

The wording of section 8 of the Mental Health Act 1983 will be seen to be much more restricted than the wider powers of the guardian under section 34 of the Act of 1959. One important effect is to remove the guardian's implicit power to consent to treatment on behalf of the patient. In my judgment there is no power to consent to the present operation to be found in section 8 of the Mental Health Act 1983, and indeed, on a construction of the statute as a whole I am satisfied that medical treatment in this context means psychiatric treatment.

If spouses and relatives have no authority to consent, does the court?

It is clear that the court's protective wardship jurisdiction comes to an end when a child reaches majority. Until recently, it was thought that thereafter the court had no power to authorise medical treatment on an incompetent adult, however beneficial or necessary the treatment might be (see *Re B* [1987] 2 All ER 206 at 210 (CA) per Dillon LJ). However, in the Canadian case of *Re Eve*, the Supreme Court 'rediscovered' the Crown's ancient prerogative jurisdiction (originally vested in the Lord Chancellor) over 'lunatics, idiots and others of unsound mind'. La Forest J set out the history of the *parens patriae* jurisdiction.

Re Eve [1986] 2 SCR 388 (Supreme Court of Canada)

La Forest J: The origin of the Crown's *parens patriae* jurisdiction over the mentally incompetent, Sir Henry Theobald tells us, is lost in the mists of antiquity; see H Theobald, *The Law Relating to Lunacy* (1924). *De Prerogatica Regis*, an instrument regarded as a statute that dates from the thirteenth or early fourteenth century, recognised and restricted it, but did not create it. Theobald speculates that 'the most probable theory [of its origin] is that either by general assent or by some statute, now lost, the care of persons of unsound mind was by Edward I taken from the feudal lords, who would naturally take possession of the land of a tenant unable to perform his feudal duties'; see Theobald, *supra*, p 1.

In the 1540s the *parens patriae* jurisdiction was transferred from officials in the royal household to the Court of Wards and Liveries, where it remained until that court was wound up in 1660. Thereafter the Crown exercised its jurisdiction through the Lord Chancellor to whom by letters patent under the Sign Manual it granted the care and custody of the persons and estates of persons of unsound mind so found by inquisition, ie, an examination to determine soundness or unsoundness of mind.

Wardship of children had a quite separate origin as a property right arising out of the feudal system of tenures. The original purpose of the wardship jurisdiction was to protect the rights of the guardian rather than the ward. Until 1660 this jurisdiction was also administered by the Court of Wards and Liveries which had been created for the purpose.

When tenures and the Court of Wards were abolished, the concept of wardship should, in theory, have disappeared. It was kept alive, however, by the Court of Chancery, which justified it as an aspect of its *parens patriae* jurisdiction; see, for example, *Cary v Bertie* (1696) 2 Vern 333 at 342, 23 ER 814 at 818; *Morgan v Dillon* (1724) 9 Mod Rep 135 at 139, 88 ER 361 at 364. In time wardship became substantively and procedurally assimilated to the *parens patriae* jurisdiction, lost its connection with property, and became purely protective in nature. Wardship thus is merely a device by means of which Chancery exercises its *parens patriae* jurisdiction over children. Today the care of children constitutes the bulk of the courts' work involving the exercise of the *parens patriae* jurisdiction.

It follows from what I have said that the wardship cases constitute a solid guide to the exercise of the *parens patriae* power even in the case of adults...But proof of incompetence must, of course, be made.

This marks a difference between wardship and *parens patriae* jurisdiction over adults. In the case of children, Chancery has a custodial jurisdiction as well, and thus has inherent jurisdiction to make them its wards; this is not so of adult mentally incompetent persons (see *Beall v Smith* (1873) 9 Ch App 85 at 92). Since, however, the Chancellor had been vested by letters patent under the Sign Manual with power to exercise the Crown's *parens patriae* jurisdiction for the protection of persons so found by inquisition, this difference between the two procedures has no importance for present purposes.

By the early part of the nineteenth century, the work arising out of the Lord Chancellor's jurisdiction became more than one judge could handle and the Chancery Court was reorganised and the work assigned to several justices including the Master of the Rolls. In 1852 (by 15 & 16 Vict, c 87, s 15 (UK)) the jurisdiction of the Chancellor regarding the 'Custody of the Persons and Estates of Persons found idiot, lunatic or of unsound Mind', was authorised to be exercised by anyone for the time being entrusted by virtue of the Sign Manual.

Since historically the law respecting the mentally incompetent has been almost exclusively focused on their estates, the law on guardianship of their persons is 'pitifully unclear with respect to some basic issues'; see P McLaughlin, *Guardianship of the Person* (Downsview 1979), p 35. Despite this vagueness, however, it seems clear that the *parens patriae* jurisdiction was never limited solely to the management and care of the estate of a mentally retarded or defective person. As early as 1603, Sir Edward Coke in *Beverley's Case* (1603) 4 Co Rep 123 at 126 a, 126 b, 76 ER 1118 at 1124, stated that 'in the case of an idiot or fool natural, for whom there is no expectation, but that he, during his life, will remain without discretion and use of reason, the law has given the custody of *him*, and all that he has, to the King' (emphasis added). Later at the bottom of the page he adds:

2. Although the state says, *custodian terrarum*, yet the King shall have as well the custody of the body, and of their goods and chattels, as of the lands and other hereditaments, and as well those which he has by purchase, as those which he has as heirs by the common law.

At 4 Co Rep p 126 b, 76 ER 1125, he cites Fitzherbert's *Natura brevium* to the same effect. Theobald (*supra*, pp 7–8, 362) appears to be quite right when he tells us that the Crown's prerogative 'has never been limited by definition'. The Crown has an inherent jurisdiction to do what is for the benefit of the incompetent. Its limits (or scope) have not, and cannot, be defined...

It was argued before us, however, that there was no precedent where the Lord Chancellor had exercised the *parens patriae* jurisdiction to order medical procedures of any kind. As to this, I would say that lack of precedent in earlier times is scarcely surprising having regard to the state of medical science at the time. Nonetheless, it seems clear from *Wellesley v Wellesley* [(1828) 2 Bli NS 124, 4 ER 1078], that the situations in which the courts can act where it is necessary to do so for the protection of mental incompetents and children have never been, and indeed cannot, be defined. I have already referred to the remarks of Lord Redesdale. To these may be added those of Lord Manners who, at Bli pp 142–42 and 1085, respectively, expressed the view that 'It is...impossible to say what are the limits of that jurisdiction; every case must depend upon its own circumstances.'

Even if *Eve* is correct that it was part of English common law (and it seems to have been), the important question for the English lawyer is whether it remains part of *English* law after the mental health legislation of the twentieth century? This issue was, of course, not relevant, nor discussed in *Eve*. The legislation does not expressly remove the power of the courts which was delegated to the Lord Chancellor and the judges of the Court of Chancery. Instead, the argument must be that since the legislation vests that part of the *parens patriae* power dealing with the 'property and other affairs' of the incompetent in the Court of Protection, the remaining power over the 'person' has impliedly been taken away. This argument does seem to be in direct conflict with the usual approach of constitutional law to see the prerogative as only taken away expressly or by *necessary* implication. Arguably, that does not seem to have occurred here. Even if the power remains, the last delegation to the judges was revoked in 1960 when the Mental Health Act 1959 became law. A new delegation of the Crown's power to the judges would be necessary today (see discussion in A Grubb and D Pearl 'Sterilisation and the Courts' [1987] CLJ 439 at 458–464).

In *Re B (a minor) (wardship: sterilisation)* [1988] AC 199 the House of Lords left the existence of the *parens patriae* power unresolved because its existence was irrelevant to the case since it concerned a child. The House of Lords finally was required to confront the issue in the case of *Re F (mental patient: sterilisation)* [1990] 2 AC 1, which involved the legality of the proposed sterilisation of a 36-year-old mentally handicapped woman. Lord Brandon expressed the following view:

Lord Brandon: I consider first the parens patriae jurisdiction. This is an ancient prerogative jurisdiction of the Crown going back as far perhaps as the 13th century. Under it the Crown as parens patriae had both the power and the duty to protect the persons and property of those unable to do so for themselves, a category which included both minors (formerly described as infants) and persons of unsound mind (formerly described as lunatics or idiots). While the history of that jurisdiction and the manner of its exercise from its inception until the present day is of the greatest interest, I do not consider that it would serve any useful purpose to recount it here. I say that because it was accepted by the Court of Appeal and not challenged by any of the parties to the appeal before your Lordships, that the present situation with regard to the parens patriae jurisdiction was as follows. First, so much of the parens patriae jurisdiction as related to minors survives now in the form of the wardship jurisdiction of the High Court, Family Division. Secondly, so much of the parens patriae jurisdiction as related to persons of unsound mind no longer exists. It ceased to exist as a result of two events both of which took place on 1 November 1960. The first event was the coming into force of the Mental Health Act 1959, section 1 of which provided:

Subject to the transitional provisions contained in this Act, the Lunacy and Mental Treatment Acts, 1890 to 1930, and the Mental Deficiency Acts, 1913 to 1938, shall cease to have effect, and the following provisions of this Act shall have effect in lieu of those enactments with respect to the reception, care and treatment of mentally disordered patients, the management of their property, and other matters related thereto.

The second event was the revocation by Warrant under the Sign Manual of the last Warrant dated 10 April 1956, by which the jurisdiction of the Crown over the persons and property of those found to be of unsound mind by inquisition had been assigned to the Lord Chancellor and the judges of the High Court, Chancery Division.

The effect of section 1 of the Act of 1959, together with the Warrant of revocation referred to above, was to sweep away the previous statutory and prerogative jurisdiction in lunacy, leaving the law relating to persons of unsound mind to be governed solely, so far as statutory enactments are concerned, by the provisions of that Act. So far as matters not governed by those provisions are concerned, the common law relating to persons of unsound mind continued to apply. It follows that the parens patriae jurisdiction with respect to persons of unsound mind is not now available to be invoked in order to involve the court or a judge in the decision about the sterilisation of F.

The 1959 Act contained a provision which allowed guardians (properly appointed) a wide range of powers extending, it appears, to consent to medical treatment (see *T v T* discussed earlier referring to ss 7–8 of the 1959 Act). As a consequence of this provision it was thought that after 1959 the pre-existing common law power of the court was no longer required. The mechanism for bringing this power into effect was therefore revoked in 1960. Unhappily, the Mental Health (Amendment) Act 1982 abolished the power of guardianship to consent to medical treatment but did not, perhaps by oversight, put anything else back into the law in its place.

It is an interesting point of some constitutional importance whether the *parens patriae* power fell into abeyance when the 1959 Act came into effect, ie the statute was necessarily inconsistent with the continued existence of the prerogative and it could only be re-activated if the statute were amended or repealed. Alternatively, the prerogative was only lost by the courts through the procedural device of the revocation of the warrant under the Sign Manual. In that case there can be no question in constitutional law of the power being lost for ever. As you will have noticed, Lord Brandon (*op cit*) refers to the *combined* effect of the 1959 Act and the revocation of the Royal Warrant. By contrast Lord Goff (at 83) and Lord Griffiths (at 70-71) speak of the loss of jurisdiction due to the latter event only.

Brenda Hoggett 'The Royal Prerogative in Relation to the Mentally Disordered: Resurrection, Resuscitation or Rejection' in M D A Freeman (ed) *Medicine, Ethics and the Law* (1988)

[T]he 1959 Act established the jurisdiction and powers of the Court of Protection to deal with the property and affairs of a patient who was adjudged incapable of managing them for himself. There is clearly some overlap between property and personal affairs, for example where the court may direct the use of the patient's assets to maintain him in a particular home or hospital, or where the court may conduct divorce or other proceedings on his behalf. Generally, however, issues relating to the care and treatment of the patient are dealt with under the quite different compulsory procedures for hospital admission or guardianship.

The provisions of the 1959 (and now the 1983) Act dealing with the jurisdiction and powers of the Court of Protection do appear to be a complete code. They no longer refer to or assume the existence of any royal prerogative. All the previous legislation dealing with it, including the relevant parts of 'The Statute Praerogativa Regis' (for which no date is given) is repealed. There is no provision (akin to section 104 of the Children Act 1975) expressly preserving it. Such a provision might have proved hard to explain. Stripped of centuries of legislation and case law based on *praerogativa regis*, what exactly were the Crown's powers? They would certainly contrast oddly with the general liberal tone of the rest of the Act. Neither is there any provision expressly abrogating the prerogative. Most probably it was felt that it would still exist, but that the legislation had covered all the necessary ground. That being so, the Royal Warrant under which the prerogative was delegated was revoked in 1960.

There are at least two reasons why it might appear in 1959 that the Mental Health Act had made any use of the prerogative, even in relation to the person, unnecessary. First, it did indeed look as though the Act had provided comprehensively for all kinds of decisions to be made on behalf of permanently or seriously disordered patients. The definition of mental disorder may have left some gaps, but long term powers could be exercised over the mentally ill and the severely handicapped. Those powers included long term admission to hospital or reception into guardianship. A guardian enjoyed the same powers over the patient as did the father of a child under 14. This would certainly be adequate to provide consent to medical treatment in most cases. Secondly, however, the legislation was strangely silent on the question of consent to treatment. It was probably assumed that compulsorily admitted patients could be treated without consent, at least if they had been admitted 'for treatment' under the Act. It was probably also assumed that non-protesting patients could be treated without formality. The whole aim of the Act was to keep formalities to a minimum, as these were regarded as both inconvenient and stigmatising, and to allow the professionals to proceed on the basis of their professional judgment wherever possible. However strange this may seem to rights-minded lawyers, we should not underestimate the strength and persuasiveness of the view that this is indeed a preferable approach.

The amendments made in 1982 and then consolidated in the Mental Health Act 1983 represented something of a return to the rights-based lawyers' approach. They restricted the scope of compulsory powers, they increased the protection involved in the procedures, and they dealt expressly with the question of consent to treatment for those compulsorily admitted to hospital. However, at the same time, they reduced the scope of long term procedures in relation to mentally handicapped people, they reduced the powers of guardians, and they did nothing to deal with the question of consent to treatment for the informal incapable patient. Whereas the 1959 Act would have provided some solution to the problems in *Re B* [[1988] AC 199] and *T v T* [[1988] Fam 52], supposing that they had at that stage been perceived, the 1983 Act provided no solution at all.

The Prerogative Dead or Dormant?
It is tempting to argue that, as the 1959 Act appeared to cover all the ground which had been covered by the prerogative, and in a manner which was then thought preferable, the prerogative itself has been abrogated and could not be revived by the modifications in the 1983 Act.

Parliament can no doubt legislate to abolish a prerogative in this way, but did not do so expressly in this case. Alternatively, it may retain the prerogative but regulate how it is to be exercised. The nineteenth and twentieth century legislation referred to earlier regulated the exercise of the prerogative, expanded or clarified the powers available, and conferred analagous powers in relation to wider categories of people. Yet again, Parliament may replace the prerogative with a statutory scheme which supersedes and may therefore curtail or expand it. This would now appear to be the position with respect to the 'property and affairs' of a mentally disordered person. Part VII of the 1983 Act has all the appearance of falling within the principle enunciated by Lord Parmoor in *A-G v De Keyser's Royal Hotel* [[1920] AC 508]:

> The constitutional principle is that when the power of the executive to interfere with the property or liberty of subjects has been placed under Parliamentary control, and directly regulated by statute, the executive no longer derives its authority from the Royal Prerogative of the Crown but from Parliament, and that in exercising such authority the executive is bound to observe the restrictions which Parliament has imposed in favour of the subject.

At first sight, that principle appears equally applicable to the Act's scheme of compulsory powers over the person, for these are undoubtedly thought to deal with the 'liberty of the subject'. There is no longer any suggestion, as there was with the earlier legislation, that they exist alongside an alternative prerogative jurisdiction. When, for example, Parliament carefully prescribed the conditions under which psycho-surgery could be performed, could it seriously be said to have intended to leave open some alternative power to authorise it under the Royal Prerogative?

This line of reasoning seems highly persuasive in relation to particular issues which are dealt with in the Act. Once we turn to matters which quite clearly are *not* dealt with in the Act, we are faced with the problem of deciding whether Parliament intended to limit the executive's powers to what was there or whether it intended to leave open an alternative source of power. The 'Catch 22' is obvious. If the statute gives power to do all that the prerogative allows, then the statute may prevail; but if it does not, then the prerogative still survives. However, the 'Catch 22' is only so alarming if this is looked upon as a matter of civil rights and the 'liberty of the subject'. It could be argued that the prerogative was concerned with people who had been found (after inquisition) not to be ordinary subjects, endowed with the usual legal rights and duties, at all. Such an argument, if accepted, could form some theoretical basis for distinguishing these quasi-parental prerogative powers from others. Although their origin, scope and nature were quite different, they have been likened to the court's inherent powers over children. These were described by Lord Eldon in the well-known case of *Wellesley v Duke of Beaufort* [(1827) 2 Russ 1] as belonging to the Crown as *parens patriae* and 'founded on the obvious necessity that the law should place somewhere the care of individuals who cannot take care of themselves'. The case had nothing to do with the prerogative relating to mental disorder, but clearly the rationale for both could be the same, even if the content and machinery were not.

That being so, the courts might well be tempted to apply similar reasoning to the relationship between statute and prerogative. The cases dealing with the relationship between the statutory powers of local authorities and the prerogative jurisdiction over wards of court have reached the following position. The statutory powers of local authorities do not use the prerogative jurisdiction. Nevertheless, the courts should decline to exercise that jurisdiction in a manner which conflicts with the statutory powers. If, therefore, the local authority objects to the court's intervention in a matter which is within its control, the court should decline to proceed. If, however, the local authority does not object, or actively seeks the court's assistance in the exercise of its powers, or invokes the jurisdiction in order to fill the gaps in its statutory powers, the court may proceed. This reasoning does not permit the court to use the jurisdiction in order to supply any gaps which the statutes have left in the rights of children, parents or relatives. It is entirely possible that a similar position would develop were the prerogative in relation to the mentally disordered to be revived: the jurisdiction might be used to fill the gaps in the statutory powers of the mental health authorities but not to improve the position of the patient or his family under those statutes.

This in itself would give rise to controversy, for the same reasons that the present imbalance in the availability of the wardship jurisdiction has done so. In relation to mentally disordered people, there is perhaps even more reason for concern. The statutory definitions of mental disorder, the procedures to be invoked, and the powers which those procedures allow, have all been quite carefully thought about. The notion that the restrictions could be circumvented, the procedures replaced, and the powers increased because of the revival of an ancient prerogative created for quite different reasons raises serious constitutional issues, quite apart from the more mundane questions which follow.

The absence of a formal proxy presents a legal and practical problem. If treatment is necessary, a decision has to be made to do it. The law must accommodate the need to treat in such circumstances. The House of Lords recognised this in *Re F* [1990] 2 AC 1 and, as we shall see, laid the basis for a justification of treating an incompetent adult in the absence of consent (see *infra*). The practical problem was, in effect, solved by making the doctor a 'quasi-proxy', ie the doctor was the person empowered to carry out treatment. The House of Lords recognised the need to indicate the criteria to be followed by the doctor. In deciding whether to treat, Lord Goff (with whom the other Law Lords concurred on this point) identified the test as follows (at 77): '…the doctor must…act in the best interests of his patient, just as if he had received his patient's consent so to do'.

(b) The test: 'best interests' or substituted judgment

Of course, *Re F* concerned a woman who had never been competent to make decisions about medical treatment. What if an adult (or even, for that matter, a mature child) had previously been competent such that he would have had views about the proposed treatment? We are not concerned here with the situation where the person has, in fact, expressly stated his view with the intention of anticipating the situation in which he is now placed (for this see *infra*, ch 16). Instead, we are concerned with the following issue. To what, if any, extent should the views and values of a patient find expression in the test to be used by the quasi-proxy decision-maker? Concern to reflect the views and values of a patient has led to the development of the so-called 'substituted judgment' test. This test requires that the decision-maker who acts as proxy (who is the substitute decision-maker) should seek to make that judgment which the incompetent patient would have made, by reference to the patient's known views and values.

In its Report of 1988 on 'Sterilisation Decisions: Minors and Mentally Incompetent Adults', the Alberta Institute of Law Research and Reform described the test of substituted judgment as follows:

'Substituted judgment' test
9.35 The 'substituted judgment' test has been employed by some American courts in recent years as an alternative to the best interests test. Under the substituted judgment test the decision is to be the one that would be made by the mentally incompetent person if she were

mentally competent. The test requires the application of the subjective values of the individual insofar as they can be known. To apply it, an attempt must be made to ascertain the mentally incompetent person's actual preference for or against such matters as sterilisation, other means of contraception and parenthood.

9.36 The substituted judgment test was developed in terminal illness cases involving decisions about the use or removal of life support systems. The Supreme Judicial Court of Massachusetts used it as the basis for a sterilisation decision in the case of *Re Moe* [(1982) 432 NE 2d 712]. This court found that the substituted judgment test best protects the mentally *incompetent* person by recognising the dignity, worth and integrity of the person and affording him the same personal rights and choices that are afforded to persons in the mainstream of society.

In his article 'Law and Medical Experimentation' (1987) 13 Monash University Law Rev 189 at 200, Professor Gerald Dworkin comments on the 'substituted judgment' test:

Another concept which is creeping into American case-law in contrast to the traditional 'best interests' approach to proxy consent is that of 'substituted judgment'. The proxy, or court, does not attempt to decide what is in the 'best interests' of the patient, but rather what decision would be made by the individual if he were competent. The court 'dons the mental mantle of the incompetent and substitutes itself as nearly as possible for the individual in the decision-making process [*Superintendent of Belchertown State School v Saikewicz* 370 NE 2d 417 (1977)]. It is one of those strange doctrines which was used in England in the early nineteenth century in connection with the administration of the estates of incompetent persons, [*Re Hinde, Ex p Whitbread* (1816) 2 Mer 99, 35 ER 878] forgotten, and then rediscovered recently by American courts. It has been raised in cases involving incompetent persons to help establish whether, for example, to consent to the withdrawal of life support systems or to certain unusual or controversial types of medical treatment, such as shock therapy or psycho-surgery.

It is a controversial concept, not the least because of the inherent difficulties of attempting to assess what an incompetent patient would have decided were he competent, whether that assessment should be subjective or objective and, if objective, how it can really differ from a 'best interests' approach.

Professor Dworkin rightly questions the relationship between the 'best interests' and 'substituted judgment'. On one view, 'substituted judgment' could be thought to be merely an application of the 'best interests', in that if a person's views are known, and, assuming that a person is the best judge of his own interests, the 'best interests' test would require compliance with his views, ie 'substituted judgment'. The conventional view, however, is that the two tests are different and that the 'best interests' test trumps any concern for the views and values of a patient since 'best interests' contemplates that others must be free to reach a judgment in the light of *their view* of the patient's interests and condition. We have already seen that English law has moved someway towards taking account of a patient's views of their own interests when making 'best interests' determinations (*supra*) and, as we shall see, this has found concrete form in the proposals emanating from the Law Commission on decision-making for incapacitated adults (see, *infra*).

The origins of the 'substituted judgment' test and some of its difficulties are also discussed by Professor John Robertson in his article 'Organ Donations by Incompetents and the Substituted Judgment Doctrine' (1976) 76 Columbia LR 48:

Under the substituted judgment doctrine – at least since the 1918 case of *Re Hinde, ex p Whitbread* [(1816) 2 Mer 99] – courts have authorised gifts from the incompetent's estate to persons to whom the incompetent owes no duty of support. The substituted judgment doctrine requires the court to 'don the mental mantle of the incompetent' and to 'substitute itself as nearly as may be for the incompetent, and to act upon the same motives and considerations as would have moved her'. Motives of charity and altruism, self-interest, and even the desire to minimise estate taxes have all been imputed to an incompetent on this basis. To determine whether the incompetent, if sane, would have made a gift, the courts look to several factors that would move one in the incompetent's situation – the needs of the donee, the relationship to the incompetent, the degree of intimacy both before and during incompetency, the ward's past expressions or manifestations of concern or gift-giving, the present and future requirements of the incompetent himself, the extent of others' dependency upon him, and the size and condition of the estate – 'giving to these and any other pertinent matters such weight as the incompetent, if sane, probably would have given'.

The decisions have had little difficulty squaring the concept with a duty to act in the best interests of the incompetent. The justifications asserted include benefit to the incompetent, his likely ratification of the imputed choice upon recovery, or the satisfaction of intentions and patterns of conduct commenced before the period of incompetency. A notion of respect for persons has been implicit in the doctrine: it is in the incompetent's best interests to be treated as nearly as possible as the person he would be if his incompetence had never occurred. As an early commentator on the doctrine put it:

Acting for the general welfare and advantage of a person does not mean merely supplying his or her physical wants or investing his or her money wisely. It is as much to the general advantage and welfare of a mother, for example, that the health of her children be preserved and that they be cared for in sickness, as it is that she herself be provided with a proper means of support.

…Although the substituted judgment doctrine is recognised in most American and British jurisdictions either in judicial or statutory form, there is wide variation in the facts and circumstances upon which courts find that an incompetent, if competent, would make a gift. The varying results reveal internal tensions which limit the scope of the substituted judgment doctrine in the estate area and its applicability to other situations. The main tension stems from attempting to discern what in fact the incompetent would have done, if competent. The courts invariably focus on the desires and preferences which the incompetent would have had if he never had become incompetent, or if he had, if he recovered and essentially retained his pre-incompetency preference schedule. But there is an alternative approach. The courts could ask what a person in the incompetent's situation would do if he had legal capacity; that is, the courts could act to maximise the present subjective interests of the incompetent.

Professor Robertson justifies the substituted judgment test in the following ways at pp 63–68:

If a person because of age or mental disability cannot select or communicate his preferences, respect for persons requires that the integrity of the person still be maintained. As stated by Rawls [*A Theory of Justice*] maintaining the integrity of the person means that we act toward him 'as we have reason to believe [he] would choose for [himself] if [he] were [capable] of reason and deciding rationally'. It does not provide a license to impute to him preferences he never had or to ignore previous preferences.

Paternalistic decisions are to be guided by the individual's own settled preferences and interests insofar as they are not irrational, or failing a knowledge of these, by the theory of primary goods.

If preferences are unknown, we must act with respect to the preferences a reasonable competent person in the incompetent's situation would have.

There are several reasons for treating incompetents in this way. One is that if the person recovered or became competent, and was informed of our actions, he would be most likely to ratify a decision that attempted to ascertain and do that which from the circumstances it appeared that he would have wanted done. For such an attempt would continue to regard him, even during his incapacity, as an individual with free choice and moral dignity, and not as someone whose preferences no longer mattered. Even if we were mistaken in ascertaining his preferences, the person could still agree that he had been fairly treated, if we had a good reason for thinking he would have made the choices imputed to him.

In addition, if a person were to decide in advance how he would want to be treated if he lost his rational faculties, he would be likely to choose a scheme that, to the extent possible, approximated what he would do if rational. His moral worth is recognised since he is treated as the person he was, that is, as a person with the final ends and beliefs he previously expressed. Moreover, since incompetents are treated as persons in other important respects, consistency requires that, when questions arise concerning their treatment in particular situations, they also be treated as persons with wants and preferences. By failing to treat them as we treat competent persons, in similar situations, ascertaining and respecting their lawful choices, we might undercut respect for the incompetent persons in other situations, and eventually diminish respect for all persons.

In most situations respect for the person of incompetents will result in actions which benefit or act in the best interest of the incompetent. A competent person will ordinarily satisfy his wants and preferences. To the extent that the benefits rule advances the incompetent's previously expressed preferences, or procures him more of the primary goods if his references are unknown, there is a firm basis for ascribing to him choices which yield a net benefit.

If the incompetent's apparent best interests conflict with the choice he would make if competent, respect for persons requires that his imputed choice have priority. Thus, the fact that a Jehovah's Witness is unconscious does not justify transfusing blood to save his life, if he has previously made it clear that under no circumstances would he want a transfusion and he would not be required to accept a transfusion if conscious. Nor should an unconscious person be maintained on an artificial life-support system contrary to previously expressed preference if he would have been permitted to refuse treatment when conscious. By a parity of reasoning, the absence of benefit to the incompetent should not prevent an intervention when a choice in favour of the intervention can be imputed to the incompetent. In short, if respect for persons dictates honoring the wishes of competents even when their objective interests are impaired, a like rule should apply to incompetents.

One objection to this approach might be that it is absurd to treat an incompetent as he would choose to be treated if he were competent, when he is not competent, perhaps never has been, and may never be. The actual situation of the incompetent diverges from how he is treated or regarded under the substituted judgment doctrine. But it is precisely such a divergence that respect for persons requires and which generally confers benefits on the incompetent. Eliminating this divergence would mean that we treat the incompetents in all respects as a non-thinking, non-choosing, irrational being – in short, as a non-person.

A more substantial problem is specifying precisely what it means to 'choose as the incompetent would, if competent'. It could mean what the person would have chosen if he had never become incompetent – if he had remained in possession of his faculties. But what if the incompetency is congenital, or the person is a child? Alternatively, it could mean the choice made by the incompetent if his incompetency were suddenly lifted for a moment, only to have the clouds of unreason later descend. Or it could mean the person's choice if he were permanently to recover competency. This latter interpretation would be appropriate in the situation of children who will develop the faculty of reason or persons temporarily psychotic; but not in that of the retarded, the senile, or the chronically insane. Proper application of the substituted judgment test depends on specifying the precise characteristics of the situation into which competency is projected when the court substitutes its judgment for that of the incompetent.

If respect for persons mans that we accede to a person's choice of ends and means, respect for incompetent persons requires that they be similarly treated. It must be determined what choices a competent person with the characteristics, tastes, preferences, history and prospects of the incompetent would make to maximise his interests or wants – both those he presently has and those he is likely to have in the future. These characteristics might include present incompetency, a period of previous incompetency, and the possibility of future incompetency. His interests or wants will thus vary with the length of the incompetency; his preferences as an incompetent; the identity and preferences established before becoming incompetent; and the likelihood of regaining competency. A competent person with the characteristics of this incompetent cannot very well maximise satisfaction of his preferences if he ignores factors such as present incompetency and future institutionalisation which will determine present and future preferences as an incompetent. To assign the incompetent characteristics as if he had never become incompetent would be to misdescribe him. The divergence between the wants thus assigned him and his actual wants is, in fact, of greater significance that the divergence between his actually being incompetent and the treatment of him as competent for the purposes of the substituted judgment doctrine. The latter divergence merely enable us to respect and honor the wants of the incompetent by treating him like a competent person who would try to maximise his wants. The former distorts what his wants are and thus risks abusing his person by never recognising or satisfying his wants. It acts not to advance his interests, but to advance the interests of a person who superficially resembles the incompetent.

The extent to which the preferences to be maximised depend on recognition of present, past and future incompetency will of course vary with particular situations. A 30-year-old man experiencing a transient psychosis has reasonable prospects of resuming his former social role upon recovery and thus maintaining his prior preferences. To maximise his wants during his incompetency we must take into account the fact that previous preferences will soon be reasserted. The fact of incompetency alters some of his present wants, but it does not allow us to ignore altogether his past preferences.

Suppose, however, that the prognosis for recovery of the 30-year-old man is nil. He faces an indefinite future of incompetency and institutionalisation, in which he will be unable to advance his own interests as an incompetent. The fact of future incompetency has significantly altered his situation and thus his present interest. If he had been an avid mountain-climber while competent and would be likely to continue this sport upon recovery, it would be pertinent to whether a kidney transplant, which would limit such activity, should occur. But the fact that a kidney transplant would interfere with his climbing would not be relevant if he had no chance of climbing again. Choosing for him on the basis of a set of preferences which would exist only if he were competent would thus be inappropriate. Respect for persons only demands that we make the best and most reasonable choice for a person given his wants and preferences in the circumstances he is presently and likely to be in, and not the circumstances in which we, if omnipotent, would like to place him.

A third situation is that of a child or a person with a long history of incompetency who will attain competency in the future. This case resembles the first, in that the incompetent's preferences must take account of future competency, but differs from the first two situations in that no preferences have been established during a prior period of competency. The interests to be maximised include the incompetent's existing tastes and preferences and the tastes or preferences the person is likely to have in the future when competent. Since the latter are unknowable, it would be in his interest to preserve maximum flexibility.

The fourth situation is that of one who has only a brief history of competency or none at all and no expectation of competency in the future. Severely mentally retarded persons and persons who become incurably insane or incur brain damage at an early age, *inter alia*, fall into this category. To respect the dignity and integrity of such a person the task of substituted judgment will be to ascertain his actual interests and preferences, which will be circumscribed by his present and future incompetency.

In each of these situations the wants or interests of a person in the incompetent's situation will include his present wants in the state of incompetency. But how do we ascertain the wants of an incompetent? Should they be granted any validity at all? If the incompetent lacks the capacity to communicate his preferences in the ways that people ordinarily do, it may be more difficult or perhaps impossible to know them. If he somehow communicates preferences, his very incompetency means that his preferences are not necessarily to be honored. But it would be erroneous to conclude that none of the expressed wants of incompetents should be satisfied. Incompetency encompasses several types of mental impairment, including the inability to have certain wants, the possession of bizarre wants, or the inability to choose among or satisfy conflicting preferences. Thus some expressed wants, if they appear irrational and indicative of his incompetency (such as a desire to fly) need not be honored. Expressed wants not in this category, however, should be satisfied. Clearly, they define, in part, his interests, of which respect for persons must take account.

Respect for persons, as argued above, requires that previously expressed preferences, or preferences we think the incompetent has or would have, should also be honored. What if a past preference conflicts with a present preference? The present preference should be honored if so doing will have a favourable or trivial impact on the attainment of other wants, present or future, attributed to the incompetent. Present preferences should not be respected if they will foreclose achieving other expressed wants or wants the incompetent would be presumed to have if competent. Overriding a present want in order to satisfy an imputed want is justified especially if it permits the satisfaction of other present wants. Substituted judgment thus combines subjective and objective elements. The subjective elements are the present tastes and preferences of the incompetent and those which he might have if competent, if he has a reasonable chance of becoming so. The objective aspect is the determination of what a reasonable person with the characteristics and present and future wants of the incompetent would choose to maximise his interests.

Substituted judgment has had its greatest impact on the law in cases having to do with dying, as we shall see in Chapter 17. For present purposes the following decision illustrates the application of the substituted judgment test in the case of an incompetent patient whose religious beliefs suggested that she would have refused treatment had she been competent.

Re Lucille Boyd (1979) 403 A 2d 744 (DC Cir)

Ferren JA: This appeal presents one question: whether – in a nonemergency situation – the court may authorise a hospital to administer psychotropic drugs to a patient adjudicated mentally ill and incompetent, when that patient, before her illness and incompetency, had rejected any use of medication on religious grounds.

...She contends that the court, in deciding whether to force medical treatment on an unwilling incompetent, should apply the 'substituted judgment' rule; ie the court should attempt to ascertain, as nearly as possible, the choice which that individual would make if competent. It follows, according to appellant, that if an individual has clearly expressed a religious objection to medical treatment immediately prior to incompetency, that objection must control the trial court's decision...

As appellant has pointed out, in nonemergency situations a number of courts have adopted the 'substituted judgment' approach. The court, as surrogate for the incompetent, is to determine as best it can what choice that individual, if competent, would make with respect to medical procedures...We believe this approach is sound, whether religious preference or other factors are involved, for it is the only way to pay full respect to the individuality and dignity of a person who has expressed clear, deeply felt, even sacred preferences while competent, but no longer has the capacity to decide. The Supreme Judicial Court of Massachusetts recently developed this rationale in *Superintendent of Belchertown State School v Saikewicz*, 370 NE 2d 417, 428 (1977):

> The 'best interests' of an incompetent person are not necessarily served by imposing on such persons results not mandated as to competent persons similarly situated. It does not advance the interest of the State or the ward to treat the ward as a person of lesser status or dignity than others...Nor do statistical factors indicating that a majority of competent persons similarly situated choose treatment resolve the issue. The significant decisions of life are more complex than statistical determinations. Individual choice is determined not by the vote of the majority but by the complexities of the singular situation viewed from the unique perspective of the person called on to make the decision. To presume that the incompetent person must always be subjected to what many rational and intelligent persons may decline is to downgrade the status of the incompetent person by placing a lesser value on his intrinsic human worth and validity.

Obviously, in attempting to make such a subjective evaluation, in contrast with an objective, 'reasonable person' analysis, the court will be engaging, at best, in approximation; any imputation of a preference to an incompetent person will, to some extent, be fictional. But that inherent limitation does not make the 'substituted judgment' analysis less valid than one which purports to be wholly objective, for *any* analysis presupposes the court's judgment as to what a human being would decide for oneself under the circumstances. There is no reason to believe that the court's use of a hypothetical, reasonable person as the role model for its decision is preferable to an approach which attempts, however imperfectly, to account for the particular qualities of mind and preference known about the individual before the court...

With this said, we should underscore that inevitably the substituted judgment approach, because of its obvious limitations, will result in a synthesis of (1) factors known to be true about the incompetent and (2) other considerations which necessarily suggest themselves when the court cannot be sure about an incompetent's actual wishes. Thus, in trying to decide what choice the individual would make if competent, the court is not precluded from filling the gaps in its knowledge about the incompetent by taking into account what most persons are likely to do in a similar situation. See *Saikewicz, supra*, 370 NE 2d at 430...

We turn now, in greater detail, to how the court should construct the 'substituted judgment' synthesis, particularly as it attempts to account for religious views. With respect to a situation in which an individual's life itself is not at stake, we conclude that (a) when an individual, prior to incompetence, has objected, absolutely, to medical care on religious grounds, (b) the evidence demonstrates a strong adherence to the tenets of that faith, and (c) there is no countervailing evidence of vacillation, the court should conclude that the individual would reject medical treatment...

More specifically, as to the previously-expressed objection itself, several factors are important: whether the objection, if religious, is a recognisable, established one, such as the well-known views of a Jehovah's Witness or Christian Scientist; whether the individual has acted upon these views that demonstrate they have been deeply felt; and whether these views have been long held, perhaps as a matter of family tradition, or if more recently adopted, have been the result of demonstrable experience, such as a religious conversion, which would justify a court's conclusion that the views are unequivocal.

Second, the possibility of detrimental side effects may be especially relevant in a case, such as this, concerning psychotropic drugs. Materials filed with the trial court indicate that such medication may produce side effects which commonly motivate even competent patients to reject their use on nonreligious, as well as religious grounds. See *Rennie v Klein* 462 F Supp 1131 (DNJ, 1978).

Third, the likelihood of cure or improvement with or without treatment is likely to have a bearing on one's decision. It may be, as we stated in [*Re Osborne* (1972) 294 A 2d 372] at 374, that absent a conviction as strong as Mr Osborne's when life is threatened and can only be saved with prompt medical assistance, one's 'instinct for survival' may overtake a lifelong conviction that medical care is wrong. But when life cannot be saved – when death is not far off in any event – a patient may be less likely to accept treatment merely to prolong life,...especially when the treatment is likely to cause severe pain...It follows that where the prospect of imminent death is a marginal or nonexistent factor, as in Mrs Boyd's case, there may be even less incentive for one to compromise religious or other principles to accept medication.

...it does not appear that the court gave sufficient consideration, under the 'substituted judgment' concept, to Mrs Boyd's previously expressed religious views...The court should inquire whether the hospital still seeks authorisation for psychotropic medication. If it does, the court should then take the 'substituted judgment' approach by attempting to determine what course of action Mrs Boyd would choose now. If the court decides that Mrs Boyd would reject psychotropic drugs on religious grounds if presently competent and fully aware of her situation, it must refuse to authorise such treatment unless the government can demonstrate that a particular, 'compelling state interest' would justify overriding Mrs Boyd's putative choice...

Do the English cases recognise the 'substituted judgment' test? In *Re T (adult: refusal of treatment)* [1992] 4 All ER 649, (1992) 9 BMLR 46 the Court of Appeal directly addressed the question of substituted judgment. Lord Donaldson MR remarked that:

> Consultation with the next of kin has a further advantage in that it may reveal information as to the personal circumstances of the patient and as to the choice which the patient might have made, if he or she had been in a position to make it. Neither the personal circumstances of the patient nor the speculative answer to the question 'What would the patient have chosen?' can bind the practitioner in his choice of whether or not to treat or how to treat or justify him in acting contrary to a clearly established anticipatory refusal to accept treatment but they are factors to be taken into account by him in forming a clinical judgment as to what is in the best interests of the patient.

It appears that Lord Donaldson considers 'substituted judgment' merely to be an aspect of the 'best interests' test, ie as a relevant factor in deciding, but not determinative of, what should be done (see also *Airedale NHS Trust v Bland* [1993] AC 789 at 833 per Hoffmann LJ and discussion of the Law Commission's proposals for reform, *infra*). It can be argued that if substituted judgment is taken seriously as a test, the view of the Master of the Rolls must be doubted. Once a patient's views and values have been identified any decision should be based upon them and should, in England, be binding upon the doctor.

Some doubt has been cast upon the place in English law of the substituted judgment test by the speeches in *Airedale NHS Trust v Bland* [1993] 1 All ER 821 of Lords Goff and Mustill:

> **Lord Goff:** I wish however to refer at this stage to the approach in most American courts under which the court seeks, in a case in which the patient is incapacitated from expressing any view on the question whether life-prolonging treatment should be withheld in the relevant circumstances, to determine what decision the patient himself would have made had he been able to do so. This is called the substituted judgment test, and it generally involves a detailed inquiry into the patient's views and preferences: see eg *Re Quinlan* 70 NJ 10 (1976) and *Belchertown State School Superintendent v Saikewicz* 373 Mass 728 (1977). In later cases concerned with PVS patients it has been held that, in the absence of clear and convincing evidence of the patient's wishes, the surrogate decision-maker has to implement as far as possible the decision which the incompetent patient would make if he was competent. However, accepting on this point the submission of Mr Lester, I do not consider that any such test forms part of English law in relation to incompetent adults, on whose behalf nobody has power to give consent to medical treatment. Certainly, in *F v West Berkshire Health Authority* your Lordships' House adopted a straightforward test based on the best interests of the patient; and I myself do not see why the same test should not be applied in the case of PVS patients, where the question is whether life-prolonging treatment should be withheld.

> **Lord Mustill:** [Substituted judgment] involved the appointment of a surrogate to make on behalf of the patient the choice which he believes the patient would now make if able to do so. For this purpose the surrogate builds up a picture of the patient's former character, feelings, convictions and so on from which the putative choice is deduced. This process may perhaps have some justification where the patient is sentient but unable to communicate a choice, but it breaks down totally in a case such as the present. To postulate a patient who is in such condition that he cannot know that there is a choice to be made, or indeed know anything at all, and then ask whether he would have chosen to terminate his life because that condition made it no longer worth living is surely meaningless, as is very clearly shown by the lengths to which the court was driven in *Belchertown State School Superintendent v Saikewicz* 373 Mass 728 (1977). The idea is simply a fiction, which I would not be willing to adopt even if

there were in the case of Anthony Bland any materials upon which a surrogate could act, which as far as I can see there are not.

Is it not the case that their Lordships misunderstand the true nature of substituted judgment? As regards Lord Goff two points are worth noting. First, the premise for his view is the decision in *Re F*. But, of course, as we shall see shortly, substituted judgment was inappropriate in *Re F* as F had never been in a position to form competent views. Secondly, the House of Lords in *Re F* never, therefore, gave any consideration to whether the substituted judgment test could ever be a part of English law. As for Lord Mustill, his distinction between the patient who is sentient and one who is not sentient seems odd. Substituted judgment does not involve the patient deciding, but somebody else 'stepping into the patient's shoes' to decide for the patient. Lord Mustill relies on the unsatisfactory nature of the *Saikewicz* case to demonstrate the inappropriateness of substituted judgment. Saikewicz, however, had never been competent to form a competent view and, therefore, substituted judgment was legally inappropriate in that case. (*Saikewicz* is one of a series of cases in which the Massachusetts Supreme Judicial Court has misunderstood and misapplied the substituted judgment test: *Re Moe* (1982) 432 NE 2d 712 (sterilisation of mentally disabled woman) and *Re Jane Doe* (1992) 583 NE 2d 1263 (a PVS case).)

This last point allows us to reiterate the circumstances in which 'substituted judgment' is inappropriate. It is inappropriate in any case in which the patient has *never* been competent to form views or hold values. Examples include the immature minor and the mentally disabled adult.

The impossibility faced by a court or other proxy in applying the substituted judgment test in these situations was recognised in the Institute of Law Research and Reform of Alberta's Report (*supra*):

> 9.37 The obvious difficulty with the application of the substituted judgment standard relates to persons who have been mentally incompetent from birth and who may therefore never have been able to express their values or desires. It may also be difficult to determine the values and desires of a person who was once competent but has been made incompetent by a supervening injury or disease.

Consequently, in *Re Eve* (*supra*) the Supreme Court of Canada rejected the application of the test to Eve who had been incompetent from birth. The reasoning would also apply in the case of an incompetent child.

> **La Forest J:** Counsel for the respondent strongly contended, however, that the Court should adopt the substituted judgment test recently developed by a number of state courts in the United States. That test, he submitted, is to be preferred to the best interests test because it places a higher value on the individuality of the mentally incompetent person. It affords that person the same right, he contended, as a competent person to choose whether to procreate or not.
>
> There is an obvious logical lapse in this argument…it is obviously fiction to suggest that a decision so made is that of the mental incompetent, however much the court may try to put itself in her place. What the incompetent would do if she or he could make the choice is simply a matter of speculation. The sophistry embodied in the argument favouring substituted judgment has been fully revealed in [*Re Eberhardy's Guardianship*, 307 NW 2d 881 (1981)] at p 893 where in discussing [*Matter of Grady* 426 A 2d 467 (1981)], the court stated:
>
> > The fault we find in the New Jersey case is the *ratio decidendi* of first concluding, correctly we believe, that the right to sterilisation is a personal choice, but then equating a decision made by others with the choice of the person to be sterilised. It clearly is not a personal choice, and no amount of legal legerdemain can make it so.
>
> > …We conclude the question is not choice because it is sophistry to refer to it as such, but rather the question is whether there is a method by which others, acting in behalf of the person's best interests and in the interests, such as they may be, of the state, can exercise the decision. Any governmentally sanctioned (or ordered) procedure to sterilise a person who is

incapable of giving consent must be denominated for what it is, that is, the state's intrusion into the determination of whether or not a person who makes no choice shall be allowed to procreate.

In *Curran v Bosze* (1990) 566 NE 2d 1319 (the facts of which are set out *supra*) the Illinois Supreme Court rejected the application of the 'substituted judgment' test in the case of an incompetent child.

Curran v Bosze (1990) 566 NE 2d 1319 (Illinois Sup Ct)

Calvo J: Mr Bosze and the guardian *ad litem* for Jean Pierre strenuously argue that the doctrine of substituted judgment, recognized by this court in *In Re Estate of Longeway*, 133 Ill 2d 33, 139 Ill Dec 780, 549 NE 2d 292 (1989), and *In Re Estate of Greenspan*, 137 Ill 2d 1, 146 Ill Dec 860, 558 NE 2d 1194 (1990), should be applied in this case to determine whether or not the twins would consent, if they were competent to do so, to the bone marrow donation if they, or either of them, were compatible with Jean Pierre. The doctrine of substituted judgment requires a surrogate decision-maker to 'attempt to establish, with as much accuracy as possible, what decision the patient would make if [the patient] were competent to do so.' (*Longeway*, 133 Ill 2d at 49, 139 Ill Dec 780, 549 NE 2d 292.) Mr Bosze and the guardian *ad litem* for Jean Pierre contend the evidence clearly and convincingly establishes that the twins, if competent, would consent to the bone marrow harvesting procedure.

Ms Curran and the guardian *ad litem* for the twins vigorously object to the application of the doctrine of substituted judgment in this case. It is the position of Ms Curran and the guardian *ad litem* for the twins that it is not possible to establish by clear and convincing evidence whether the 3½-year-old twins, if they were competent – that is, if they were not minors but were adults with the legal capacity to consent – would consent or refuse to consent to the proposed bone marrow harvesting procedure. According to Ms Curran and the guardian *ad litem* for the twins, the decision whether or not to give or withhold consent to the procedure must be determined by the best-interests-of-the-child standard. Ms Curran and the guardian *ad litem* for the twins argue that the evidence reveals it is not in the best interests of the children to require them to submit to the bone marrow harvesting procedure.

This court recognized the doctrine of substituted judgment in *Longeway*. The issue addressed by this court in *Longeway* was whether the guardian of a formerly competent, now incompetent, seriously ill adult patient may exercise a right to refuse artificial nutrition and hydration on behalf of his or her ward and, if so, how this right may be exercised…

In *Longeway*, this court held that a guardian may exercise the right to refuse artificial sustenance on behalf of a ward in accordance with certain guidelines. This court determined that the doctrine of substituted judgment had been implicitly adopted by the General Assembly in the Powers of Attorney for Health Case Law, which states: '[Y]our agent will have authority…to obtain or terminate any type of health care, including withdrawal of food and water…if your agent believes such action would be consistent with your intent and desires.' Ill Rev Stat 1987, ch 1101/2, par. 804–10.

This court recognized two sources of appropriate evidence by which a guardian may be guided in determining whether a formerly competent, now incompetent, patient would choose to refuse artificial nutrition and hydration. The first source requires the surrogate to 'determine if the patient had expressed explicit intent regarding this type of medical treatment prior to becoming incompetent.' (*Longeway*, 133 Ill 2d at 49, 139 Ill Dec 780, 549 NE 2d 292.) If there is no clear evidence of such intent, then the patient's personal value system must guide the surrogate:

> [E]ven if no prior specific statements were made, in the context of the individual's entire prior mental life, including his or her philosophical, religious and moral views, life goals, values about the purpose of life and the way it should be lived, and attitudes towards sickness, medical procedures, suffering and death, that individual's likely treatment/ nontreatment preferences can be discovered. Family members are most familiar with this entire life context. Articulating such knowledge is a formidable task, requiring a literary skill beyond the capacity of many, perhaps most, families. But the family's knowledge exists nevertheless, intuitively felt by them and available as an important decisionmaking tool. [*In re*] *Jobes*, 108 NJ [394] at 415, 529 A 2d [434] at 445 [(1987)] quoting Newman, *Treatment Refusals for the Critically Ill: Proposed Rules for the Family, the Physician and the State*, 3 NYL Sch Hum Rts Ann 45–46 (1985). (*Longeway*, 133 Ill 2d at 49–50, 139 Ill Dec 780, 549 NE 2d 292.)

The guardian is required to prove by clear and convincing evidence whether the incompetent patient, if competent, would choose to terminate artificial nutrition and hydration if the guardian is to be allowed to substitute his or her judgment for the incompetent's judgment. *Longeway*, 133 Ill 2d at 50–51, 139 Ill Dec 780, 549 NE 2d 292.

The best-interests standard, by which a guardian, in the exercise of his or her judgment, determines what is best for the ward, was rejected by this court in *Longeway* as an inappropriate vehicle by which a guardian may be guided in determining whether an incompetent patient, in either an irreversible coma or a persistent vegetative state, should have artificial nutrition and hydration withdrawn. This court rejected the best-interests standard because 'it lets another make a determination of a patient's quality of life, thereby undermining the foundation of self-determination and inviolability of the person upon which the right to refuse medical treatment stands.' (*Longeway*, 133 Ill 2d at 49, 139 Ill Dec 780, 549 NE 2d 292.) By requiring a guardian to proceed under the doctrine of substituted judgment instead of the best-interests standard, the inquiry is necessarily focused on whether the formerly competent, now incompetent, patient had ever manifested an intent as to whether he or she would consent or refuse to consent to artificial nutrition and hydration.

In *Greenspan*, this court addressed the issue of the use of the doctrine of substituted judgment by a guardian of an incompetent person in a chronic vegetative state. The guardian of Mr Greenspan requested leave of court to order the withdrawal of artificial nutrition and hydration as 'Mr Greenspan's surrogate and in order to give effect to what are represented as Mr Greenspan's own wishes.' (*Greenspan*, 137 Ill 2d at 15, 146 Ill Dec 860, 558 NE 2d 1194.)...

In *Greenspan*, this court stated: 'though a guardian's duty is to act in a ward's best interest, such a standard is necessarily general and must be adapted to particular circumstances. One such circumstance is a ward's wish to exercise common law, statutory, or constitutional rights, which may sometimes influence or even override a guardian's own perception of best interests.'...

Mr Bosze argues that the twins, if they had the legal capacity, would have the right to consent or refuse to consent to the proposed bone marrow harvesting procedure. Mr Bosze argues that if the doctrine of substituted judgment is not applied in this case, the twins' right to consent or refuse to consent to medical treatment, which they would have if they were competent, would be violated. Since the twins are without legal capacity to consent or refuse to consent to the proposed bone marrow harvesting procedure, and since the parents do not agree, Mr Bosze argues that both his and Ms Curran's opinions regarding whether the twins should serve as bone marrow donors should be read out of the equation, and the court, applying the doctrine of substituted judgment, should look solely to what the twins would decide to do if they were competent...

Concerning the use of the doctrine of substituted judgment, this court in *Longeway* recognized that '[a] dilemma [exists]...when the patient is an infant or life-long incompetent who never could have made a reasoned judgment about his [or her] quality of life.' (*Longeway*, 133 Ill 2d at 49, 139 Ill Dec 780, 549 NE 2d 292.) Mr Bosze argues that this dilemma was resolved by this court in *Longeway* when it stated that 'although actual, specific express intent would be helpful and compelling, the same is not necessary for the exercise of substituted judgment by a surrogate.' *Longeway*, 133 Ill 2d at 50, 139 Ill Dec 780, 549 NE 2d 292.

Immediately following this statement in *Longeway*, however, this court stated: 'In this case, Mrs Longeway's guardian must substitute her judgment for that of Longeway's, based upon *other* clear and convincing evidence of Longeway's intent.' (Emphasis added.) (*Longeway*, 133 Ill 2d at 50–51, 139 Ill Dec 780, 549 NE 2d 292.) This language addressed the instance where a formerly competent, now incompetent, patient had never 'expressed explicit intent regarding [the] type of medical treatment prior to becoming incompetent.' (*Longeway*, 133 Ill 2d at 49, Ill Dec 780, 549 NE 2d 292.) This language did not address the dilemma of a guardian substituting the judgment of one who never has been able to make 'a reasoned judgment about his [or her] quality of life.' (*Longway*, 133 Ill 2d at 49, 139 Ill Dec 780, 549 NE 2d 292.) In applying the doctrine of substituted judgment, 'the key element in deciding to refuse or withdraw artificial sustenance is determining the patient's intent.' *Longeway*, 133 Ill 2d at 51, 139 Ill Dec 780, 549 NE 2d 292.

Under the doctrine of substituted judgment, a guardian of a formerly competent, now incompetent, person may look to the person's lifehistory, in all of its diverse complexity, to ascertain the intentions and attitudes which the incompetent person once held. There must be clear and convincing evidence that the formerly competent, now incompetent, person had expressed his or her intentions and attitudes with regard to the termination of artificial nutrition and hydration before a guardian may be authorized to exercise, on behalf of the incompetent person, the right to terminate artificial sustenance.

If the doctrine of substituted judgment were to be applied in this case, the guardian of the 3½-year-old twins would have to substitute his or her judgment for that of the twins, based upon clear and convincing evidence of the twins' intent. (*Longeway*, 133 Ill 2d at 50–51, 139 Ill Dec 780, 549 NE 2d 292.) Because each twin is only 3½ years of age, neither has yet had the opportunity to develop 'actual, specific express intent,' or any other form of intent, with regard to serving as a bone marrow donor. We agree with Ms Curran and the guardian *ad litem* for the twins that it is not possible to determine the intent of a 3½-year-old child with regard to consenting to a bone marrow harvesting procedure by examining the child's personal value system. It is not possible to discover the child's 'likely treatment/nontreatment preferences' by examining the child's 'philosophical, religious and moral views, life goals, values about the purpose of life and the way it should be lived, and attitudes towards sickness, medical procedures, suffering and death.' (*Longeway*, 133 Ill 2d at 50, 139 Ill Dec 780, 549 NE 2d 292, quoting *In Re Jobes* (1987) 108 NJ 394, 529 A 2d 434.) The twins have not yet developed the power of self-determination and are not yet capable of making an informed, rational decision based upon all the available information concerning the risks and benefits associated with serving as bone marrow donors. There is no evidence by which a guardian may be guided in ascertaining whether these 3½-year-old children, if they were adults, would or would not consent to a bone marrow harvesting procedure for another child, their half-brother whom they have met only twice.

The doctrine of substituted judgment requires clear and convincing proof of the incompetent person's intent before a court may authorize a surrogate to substitute his or her judgment for that of the incompetent. Any lesser standard would 'undermin[e] the foundation of self-determination and inviolability of the person upon which the right to refuse medical treatment stands.' (*Longeway*, 133 Ill 2d at 49, 139 Ill Dec 780 549 NE 2d 292.) A guardian attempting to prove what a 3½-year-old child would or would not do in a given set of circumstances at a given time in the distant future would have to rely on speculation and conjecture.

Neither justice nor reality is served by ordering a 3½-year-old child to submit to a bone marrow harvesting procedure for the benefit of another by a purported application of the doctrine of substituted judgment. Since it is not possible to discover that which does not exist, specifically, whether the 3½-year-old twins would consent or refuse to consent to the proposed bone marrow harvesting procedure if they were competent, the doctrine of substituted judgment is not relevant and may not be applied in this case.

Curiously, however, in *Re J (a minor) (wardship: medical treatment)* [1990] 3 All ER 930, [1991] Fam 33, which concerned the treatment of a severely handicapped baby, two judges in the Court of Appeal adopted a test which could be thought by some to be that of 'substituted judgment'. Taylor LJ stated that:

I consider that the correct approach is for the court to judge the quality of life the child would have to endure if given the treatment and decide whether in all the circumstances such a life would be so afflicted as to be intolerable to that child. I say 'to that child' because the test should not be whether the life would be intolerable to the decider. The test must be whether the child in question, if capable of exercising sound judgment, would consider the life tolerable. This the approach adopted by McKenzie J in *Re Superintendent of Family and Child Services and Dawson* (1983) 145 DLR (3d) 610 at 620–621 in the passage cited with approval by Lord Donaldson MR. It takes account of the strong instinct to preserve one's life even in circumstances which an outsider, not himself at risk of death, might consider unacceptable. The circumstances to be considered would, in appropriate cases, include the degree of existing disability and any additional suffering or aggravation of the disability which the treatment itself would superimpose. In an accident case, as opposed to one involving disablement from birth, the child's pre-accident quality of life and its perception of what has been lost may also be factors relevant to whether the residual life would be intolerable to that child.

Similarly, Lord Donaldson MR approved the British Columbia case of *Re Superintendent of Family and Child Service and Dawson* (1983) 145 DLR (3d) 610, where McKenzie J stated:

it is not appropriate for an external decision maker to apply his standards of what constitutes a liveable life and exercise the right to impose death if that standard is not met in his estimation. The decision can only be made in the context of the disabled person – and in that context he would not compare his life with that of a person enjoying normal advantages. He would know nothing of a normal person's life having never experienced it.

Commenting, Lord Donaldson MR said:

He was considering the best interests of a severely handicapped child, not of a normal child, and the latter's feelings and interests were irrelevant.

Properly interpreted, as Lord Donaldson MR's remarks make clear, the Court of Appeal in *Re J* was in fact merely asserting that the 'best interest' test requires the decision-maker to seek to take account of the actual circumstances of the patient. Thus, neither Taylor LJ's nor the Master of the Rolls' judgments should be taken as legitimising an application of the 'substituted judgment' test in a case where the patient has never been competent.

3. Court as sole proxy?

The question to be considered here is whether there are circumstances in which the courts have or will reserve to themselves the exclusive right to decide whether a child or adult shall undergo certain treatment. Obviously, if a child is already a ward of court, the court thereafter has exclusive power to make all significant decisions concerning medical treatment, ie those that involve a 'serious step' in the upbringing of the child (*Re D (a minor) (wardship; sterilisation)* [1976] 1 All ER 326 at 335 per Heilbron J). We, however, are concerned with whether in principle a parent or other (as proxy) or doctor (as quasi-proxy) may *not* have the power to consent to medical intervention in certain classes of case. If such cases exist, it means that only the court (if anyone) may give consent. In England and elsewhere this issue has arisen in the context of the controversial cases of sterilising mentally disabled girls and women. In *Re B (a minor) (wardship: sterilisation)* [1988] AC 199, Lord Templeman (at 205–206) expressed the following views:

> **Lord Templeman:** In my opinion sterilisation of a girl under 18 should only be carried out with the leave of a High Court judge. A doctor performing a sterilisation operation with the consent of the parents might still be liable in criminal, civil or professional proceedings. A court exercising the wardship jurisdiction emanating from the Crown is the only authority which is empowered to authorise such a drastic step as sterilisation after a full and informed investigation. The girl will be represented by the Official Solicitor or some other appropriate guardian: the parents will be made parties if they wish to appear and where appropriate the local authority will also appear. Expert evidence will be adduced setting out the reasons for the application, the history, conditions, circumstances and foreseeable future of the girl, the risks and consequences of pregnancy, the risks and consequences of sterilisation, the practicability of alternative precautions against pregnancy and any other relevant information. The judge may order additional evidence to be obtained. In my opinion, a decision should only be made by a High Court judge. In the Family Division a judge is selected for his or her experience, ability and compassion. No one has suggested a more satisfactory tribunal or a more satisfactory method of reaching a decision which vitally concerns an individual but also involves principles of law, ethics and medical practice. Applications for sterilisation will be rare. Sometimes the judge will conclude that a sufficiently overwhelming case has not been established to justify interference with the fundamental right of a girl to bear a child; this was the case in *Re D (a minor) (wardship: sterilisation)* [1976] 1 All ER 326, [1976] Fam 185. But in the present case the judge was satisfied that it would be cruel to expose the girl to an unacceptable risk of pregnancy which could only be obviated by sterilisation in order to prevent child bearing and childbirth in circumstances of uncomprehending fear and pain and risk of physical injury. In such a case the judge was under a duty and had the courage to authorise sterilisation.

It is important to notice that in *Re B* only Lord Templeman took this view. When the issue surfaced again in the case of a mentally disabled adult in *Re F (mental patient: sterilisation)* [1990] 2 AC 1, a majority of the House of Lords did not adopt Lord Templeman's view. It could, of course, be that their view was pre-conditioned by the fact, as we have seen, that the court has no *parens patriae* jurisdiction over adults. However, the better view is that this is irrelevant and that the real issue is simply whether the proxy or quasi-proxy other than the court has the power to decide. Only one of the judges, Lord Griffiths, adopted Lord Templeman's robust view.

> **Lord Griffiths:** I cannot agree that it is satisfactory to leave this grave decision with all its social implications in the hands of those having the care of the patient with only the expectation that they will have the wisdom to obtain a declaration of lawfulness before the operation is

performed. In my view the law ought to be that they must obtain the approval of the court before they sterilise a woman incapable of giving consent and that it is unlawful to sterilise without that consent. I believe that it is open to your Lordships to develop a common law rule to this effect. Although the general rule is that the individual is the master of his own fate the judges through the common law have, in the public interest, imposed certain constraints on the harm that people may consent to being inflicted on their own bodies. Thus although boxing is a legal sport a bare knuckle prize fight in which more grievous injury may be inflicted is unlawful (*R v Coney* (1882) 8 QBD 534), and so is fighting which may result in actual bodily harm: see *A-G's Reference (No 6 of 1980)* [1981] QB 715. So also is it unlawful to consent to the infliction of serious injury on the body in the course of the practice of sexual perversion: *R v Donovan* [1934] 2 KB 498. Suicide was unlawful at common law until Parliament intervened by the Suicide Act 1961.

The common law has, in the public interest, been developed to forbid the infliction of injury on those who are fully capable of consenting to it. The time has now come for a further development to forbid, again in the public interest, the sterilisation of a woman with healthy reproductive organs who, either through mental incompetence or youth, is incapable of giving her fully informed consent unless such an operation has been inquired into and sanctioned by the High Court. Such a common law rule would provide a more effective protection that the exercise of parens patriae jurisdiction which is dependent upon some interested party coming forward to invoke the jurisdiction of the court. The parens patriae jurisdiction is in any event now only available in the case of minors through their being made wards of court. I would myself declare that on grounds of public interest an operation to sterilise a woman incapable of giving consent either on grounds of age or mental incapacity is unlawful if performed without the consent of the High Court. I fully recognise that in so doing I would be making new law. However the need for such a development has been identified in a number of recent cases and in the absence of any Parliamentary response to the problem it is my view that the judges can and should accept responsibility to recognise the need and to adapt the common law to meet it. If such a development did not meet with public approval it would always be open to Parliament to reverse it or to alter it by perhaps substituting for the opinion of the High Court judge the second opinion of another doctor as urged by counsel for the Mental Health [Act Commission].

A number of issues arise:

– Is Lord Griffiths correct that the involvement of the courts in some circumstances is mandatory?
– If the involvement of the courts is not mandatory, is it ever desirable?
– What is the appropriate role of the courts in sterilisation, abortion and other cases?

(a) Is Lord Griffiths correct?

Subsequent to *Re F*, there is no English case that has considered this issue. The Australian High Court addressed the question in some detail.

Secretary, Department of Health v JWB and SMB (1992) 66 ALJR 300 (HC of A)

Mason CJ, Gaudron, Toohey and Dawson JJ: *Can parents, as guardians, consent to sterilisation? Conclusion*
There are, in our opinion, features of a sterilisation procedure or, more accurately, factors involved in a decision to authorise sterilisation of another person which indicate that, in order to ensure the best protection of the interests of a child, such a decision should not come within the ordinary scope of parental power to consent to medical treatment. Court authorisation is necessary and is, in essence, a procedural safeguard. Our reasons for arriving at this conclusion, however, do not correspond precisely with any of the judgments considered. We shall give our reasons. But first it is necessary to make clear that, in speaking of sterilisation in this context, we are not referring to sterilisation which is a by-product of surgery appropriately carried out to treat some malfunction or disease. We hesitate to use the expressions 'therapeutic' and 'non-therapeutic', because of their uncertainty. But it is necessary to make the distinction, however unclear the dividing line may be.

As a starting point, sterilisation requires invasive, irreversible and major surgery. But so do, for example, an appendectomy and some cosmetic surgery, both of which, in our opinion, come within the ordinary scope of parental power to consent to medical treatment. However, other factors exist which have the combined effect of marking out the decision to authorise sterilisation as a special case. Court authorisation is required, first, because of the significant risk of making the wrong decision, either as to a child's present or future capacity to consent or about what are the best interests of a child who cannot consent, and secondly, because the consequences of a wrong decision are particularly grave. The factors which contribute to the significant risk of a wrong decision being made are:

(i)   The complexity of the question of consent. Although there are some cases, of which the facts in *Re X* [[1991] 2 NZLR 365] are an example, in which the parents can give an informed consent to an operation of sterilisation on an intellectually disabled child and in which that operation is clearly for the benefit of the child, there is no unproblematic view of what constitutes informed consent…And, even given a settled psychological or legal rule, its application in many cases is fraught with difficulty. The fact that a child is disabled does not of itself mean that he or she cannot give informed consent or, indeed, make a meaningful refusal. And there is no reason to assume that those attempting to determine the capacity of an intellectually disabled child, including doctors, may not be affected by commonly held misconceptions about the abilities of those with intellectual disabilities…There is no doubt that some sterilisation operations have been performed too readily and that the capacity of a child to give consent (and, later, to care for a child) has been wrongly assessed both here and overseas, historically and at the present time…

(ii) The medical profession very often plays a central role in the decision to sterilise as well as in the procedure itself. Indeed the question has been 'medicalised' to a great degree. (See, for example, *Re a Teenager* (1988) 94 FLR, at 221–222, 223–224; *In re F* [1990] 2 AC, per Lord Goff, at 78; *Re Eve* [1986] 2 SCR, at 399; (1986) 31 DLR (4th), at 7–8, citing from the judgment of the provincial Supreme Court in that case.) Two concerns emerge from this. It is hard to share the view of Cook J in *Re a Teenager* (1988) 94 FLR, at 223 that absolute faith in the integrity of all medical practitioners is warranted. We agree with Nicholson CJ in *Re Jane* (1988) 94 FLR at 26 that, as with all professions, there are those who act with impropriety as well as those who act bona fide within a limited frame of reference. And the situation with which they are concerned is one in which incorrect assessments may be made. (See, for example, *In Re D (A Minor)* [1976] Fam 185; [1976] 1 All ER 326; *Re Jane* (1988) 94 FLR 1; *In Re F* [1990] 2 AC 1.) The second concern is that the decision to sterilise, at least where it is to be carried out for contraceptive purposes, and especially now when technology and expertise make the procedure relatively safe, is not merely a *medical* issue. This is also reflected in the concern raised in several of the cases reviewed, that the consequences of sterilisation are not merely biological but also social and psychological. The requirement of a court authorisation ensures a hearing from those experienced in different ways in the care of those with intellectual disability and from those with experience of the long term social and psychological effects of sterilisation.

(iii) The decision by a parent that an intellectually disabled child be sterilised may involve not only the interests of the child, but also the independent and possibly conflicting (though legitimate) interests of the parents and other family members. (See, for example, *Re Jane* (1988) 94 FLR, at 27, 30; *Re K and Public Trustee* [1985] 3 WWR 204, per Wood J, at 224, at first instance and (1985) 19 DLR (4th) 255, per Anderson JA, at 279, cited with approval by Cook J in *Re a Teenager* (1988) 94 FLR, at 208.) There is no doubt that caring for a seriously handicapped child adds a significant overriding criterion of the child's welfare, the interests of other family members, particularly primary care-givers, are relevant to a court's decision whether to authorise sterilisation. However, court involvement ensures, in the case of conflict, that the child's interests prevail.

The gravity of the consequences of wrongly authorising a sterilisation flows both from the resulting inability to reproduce and from the fact of being acted upon contrary to one's wishes or best interests. The fact of violation is likely to have social and psychological implications concerning the person's sense of identity, social place and self-esteem. As a Court said in *Re Grady* (1981) 85 NJ 235, 426 A 2d at 471–472, a decision to sterilise involves serious questions of a person's 'social and biological identity'. As with anyone, reactions to sterilisation vary among those with intellectual disabilities but it has been said (The Canadian Law Reform Commission Report, *Sterilization*, (1979) p 50, reporting on Sabagh and Egerton, 'Sterilized Mental Defectives Look at Eugenic Sterilization' (1962) 9 *Eugenics Quarterly* 213) that 'sterilised mentally retarded persons tend to perceive sterilisation as a symbol of *reduced* or *degraded* status'. Another study found (Roos, 'Psychological Impact of Sterilization on the Individual' (1975) *Law and Psychology Review* 45 at 54, in the Canadian Report pp 50–51 and see generally pp 49–52) that:

> Essential anxieties commonly associated with mental retardation are likely to be seriously reinforced by coercive sterilisation of those who have had no children. Common sources of these anxieties include low self-esteem, feelings of helplessness, and need to avoid failure, loneliness, concern over bodily integrity and the threat of death.

The far-reaching consequences of a general rule of law allowing guardians to consent to all kinds of medical treatment, as well as the consequences of a wrong decision in any particular case, are also relevant. As Nicholson CJ pointed out in *Re Jane* in the passage quoted earlier ((1988) 94 FLR, at 26), such a rule may be used to justify other procedures such as a clitoridectomy or the removal of a healthy organ for transplant to another child.

For the above reasons, which look to the risks involved in the decision, particularly in relation to the threshold question of competence and in relation to the consequences of a wrong assessment, our conclusion is that the decision to sterilise a minor in circumstances such as the present falls outside the ordinary scope of parental powers…This is not a case where sterilisation is an incidental result of surgery performed to cure a disease or correct some malfunction. Court authorisation in the present case is required. Where profound permanent incapacity is indisputable, where all psychological and social implications have in fact been canvassed by a variety of care-givers and where the child's guardians are, in fact, only considering the interests of the child or where their own interests do not conflict with those of the child, court authorisation will ordinarily reproduce the wishes of the guardian. But it is not possible to formulate a rule which distinguishes these cases. Given the widely varying circumstances, it is impossible to apply a single rule to determine what are, in the respondents' words, the 'clear cases'.

Children with intellectual disabilities are particularly vulnerable, both because of their minority and their disability, and we agree with Nicholson CJ (at 27) that there is less likelihood of (intentional or unintentional) abuse of the rights of children if an application to a court is mandatory, than if the decision in all cases could be made by a guardian alone. In saying this we acknowledge that it is too costly for most parents to fund court proceedings, that delay is likely to cause painful inconvenience and that the strictly adversarial process of the court is very often unsuitable for arriving at this kind of decision. These are clear indications of the need for legislative reform, since a more appropriate process for decision-making can only be introduced in that way. The burden of the cost of proceedings for parents would in the meantime, of course, be alleviated by the application being made by a relevant public body pursuant to s 63C(1) of the *Family Law Act*. (See generally Blackwood, 'Sterilisation of the Intellectually Disabled: The Need for Legislative Reform' (1991) 5 *Australian Journal of Family Law* 138.)

One more thing should be said about the basis upon which we have concluded that sterilisation is a special case with respect to parental powers. As we have indicated, the conclusion relies on a fundamental right to personal inviolability existing in the common law, a right which underscores the principles of assault, both criminal and civil, as well as on the practical exigencies accompanying this kind of decision which have been discussed. Our conclusion does not, however, rely on a finding which underpins many of the judgments discussed; namely, that there exists in the common law a fundamental right to reproduce which is independent of the right to personal inviolability. We leave that question open. It is debatable whether the former is a useful concept, when couched in terms of a basic right, and how fundamental such a right can be said to be. (See Kingdom, 'The Right to Reproduce' in Ockelton (ed), *Medicine, Ethics and Law*, (1986), 55; cf Freeman, 'Sterilising the Mentally Handicapped' in Freeman (ed), *Medicine, Ethics and the Law*, (1988) 55.) For example, there cannot be said to be an absolute right in a man to reproduce (except where a woman consents to bear a child), unless it can be contended that the right to bodily integrity yields to the former right, and that cannot be so. That is to say, if there is an absolute right to reproduce, is there a duty to bear children? But if the so-called right to reproduce comprises a right not to be prevented from being biologically capable of reproducing, that is a right to bodily integrity. The same applies, though in a different way, to a woman's 'right to reproduce'. Again, if the right is, in fact, a right to do with one's person what one chooses, it is saying no more than that there is a right to bodily and personal integrity. Furthermore, it is quite impossible to spell out all the implications which may flow from saying that there is a right to reproduce, expressed in absolute terms and independent from a right to personal inviolability. We think it is important, in terms of this judgment, to make it quite clear that it is inviolability that is protected, no more.

You will notice that the majority of the court emphasised three aspects of decision-making in this area which called for the mandatory involvement of the court: (1) the potential for abuse by the proxy; (2) the danger of the proxy making a wrong decision and (3) the seriousness of the decision in question for the patient. The judges in the minority disagreed although their views differ somewhat *inter se*. We set out here extracts from the judgments of Deane and McHugh JJ.

Deane J: [T]he preferable course will ordinarily be to appoint a guardian of the child for the limited period necessary for the authorisation and performance of the surgery. If, however, circumstances were to arise in which there was no appropriate person prepared to accept appointment as such a temporary guardian, the court could, in my view, itself directly authorise it. (See, eg *Re L (An Infant)* (1968) P 119, per Denning MR, at 157; *K v Minister for Youth and Community Services* [1982] 1 NSWLR at 323; *Rolands v Rolands* (1983) 9 Fam LR, at 330, 322; [1984] FLC, at 79, 203, 79, 204.) More important for present purposes, the jurisdiction extends to granting, at the suit of a parent or interested party, declaratory or other relief in relation to the existence and proper exercise of parental authority. That jurisdiction extends to the making of a declaration that a parent or the parents of an incapable child would or would not, in the particular circumstances of a case, be justified in authorising surgery involving irreversible sterilisation.

In *Re B (A Minor)* [1988] AC, at 205, Lord Templeman expressed the opinion that, in England, 'sterilisation of a girl under 18 should only be carried out with the leave' of a judge of the Family Division of the English High Court. The other members of the House of Lords in that case did not express any opinion on that question but a similar view was expressed by Lord Goff of Chieveley in the case of an operation for the sterilisation of an intellectually disabled adult woman who lacked the capacity to consent (*In Re F (Mental Patient: Sterilisation)* [1990] 2 AC, at 79). There are powerful considerations which support those views, including the grave consequences, both physical and psychological, of irreversible sterilisation and the need to protect the weak and vulnerable from eugenic and utilitarian theories which discount the importance of human integrity and complete personality and which are repugnant to the standards of our community. Those considerations also include the fact that there may well exist a divergence or conflict – sometimes unappreciated – between the interests of the incapable child and the interests of those who are or will be responsible for looking after her or him and for caring for any offspring. In a context where the factors militating against surgery involving sterilisation will not be confined to medical considerations, the courts are likely to be better able than medical practitioners, even acting as members of a multidisciplinary team, to ensure that due regard is paid to, and only to relevant factors in ascertaining what is truly in the interests of the welfare of the child. All these considerations strongly support a conclusion that the effect of the requirement that parental authority be exercised only after due inquiry and adequate consideration is that, in the absence of any applicable statutory procedure or jurisdiction in any other competent tribunal, the parents of an incapable child must obtain a declaratory order from the Family Court (or some other court vested with applicable welfare jurisdiction) before they can validly authorise surgery involving irreversible sterilisation for a purpose other than the conventional medical ones of preserving life and treating or preventing grave physical illness.

On the other hand, one cannot be but conscious of the undeniable fact that a general requirement that the parents of an incapable child maintain proceedings for declaratory relief in the Family Court before authorising such surgery would represent an extraordinarily onerous burden upon them. Proceedings in the superior courts of this country are commonly protracted, (for example, *Re a Teenager* (1988) 94 FLR 181; *Re Jane* (1988) FLR 1; *Re Elizabeth* (1989) 13 Fam LR 47; [1989] FLC 92–023 and *A-G (Qld) v Parents (In Re S)* (1989) 98 FLR 41) and, at least in the many cases where legal aid is not provided, oppressively expensive. (See, eg, *Re Marion* (1990) 14 Fam LR, at 462; [1991] FLC, at 78, 312–78, 313; *Re K and Public Trustee* (1985) 19 DLR (4th), at 278; Professor T W Church, 'A Consumer's Perspective on the Courts', The Second Annual Oration in Judicial Administration, 31 October 1990, pp 6–7.) The delays which are likely to be involved in such litigation are notorious. Inevitably, proceedings about whether surgery involving irreversible sterilisation is in the interests of the welfare of an incapable child will impose a heavy and additional load of anxiety upon the shoulders of caring parents. A consequence of such a general requirement would be that the understandable reluctance of parents to become involved in such legal proceedings would prevent such surgery taking place in at least some cases where it was obviously for the welfare of an incapable child.

What then is the legal resolution of the different considerations favouring and militating against a conclusion that the common law requirement of due inquiry and adequate consideration can only be satisfied by recourse to the Family Court (or to the Supreme Court exercising cross-vested or any residual jurisdiction) in the case of surgery involving the irreversible sterilisation of an incapable child in the Northern Territory? That question arises in this Court as a question of law. The processes of legal reasoning by induction and deduction from legal principle are, however, inadequate to provide an answer to it. The reason why that is so is that, while the question arises in a legal context, the issues which it involves are as much social or moral as they are legal and the answer to it is inevitably affected by personal perceptions of current social conditions, standards and demands. The answer which I would give to it is that the reconciliation of the conflicting considerations requires that a distinction be drawn between those cases where the need for such surgery in the interests of the welfare of the child is, according to general community standards, obvious and those cases where it is not. In a case where such surgery is obviously necessary, a requirement of court approval would impose an unjustifiable burden upon the parents of an incapable child. More important, the requirement would itself be undesirable in that its only significant effect would be to prevent parents, who were not prepared to subject themselves and their families to the expense, inconvenience and anxiety of court proceedings, from authorising surgery which was obviously in the interests of the welfare of the child. In a case where such surgery is not obviously necessary, the need to protect an incapable child from unjustified surgery involving irreversible sterilisation outweighs all other considerations. Notwithstanding the expense, inconvenience and other disadvantages of court proceedings, it appears to me that, in the absence of some special statutory procedure, such proceedings represent the only adequate protection.

McHugh J: In principle, no reason exists for denying to parents the power to consent to the sterilisation of a child in their custody. Public policy does not prevent a person from consenting to an operation which will irreversibly sterilise that person (*Thake v Maurice* [1986] QB 644). Since the parent is the person whom the law entrusts with the power and authority to consent to surgical and medical treatment for the welfare of a child, logically the parent must have the power and authority to consent to any operation or treatment for the welfare of the child which is not contrary to law or public policy.

In the United States, however, courts have consistently held that parents do not possess the authority to consent to the sterilisation of their children (*AL v GRH* 325 NE 2d 501 (Indiana Court of Appeals, (1975)); *Ruby v Massey* (1978) 452 F Supp 361 (United States District Court); *In Re Grady* (1981) 85 NJ 235 426 A 2d 467 (New Jersey Supreme Court); *Matter of Moe* (1982) 432 NE 2d 712 (Massachusetts Supreme Judicial Court)). Moreover, in *Stump v Sparkman* (1978) 435 US 349 at 358–359 the United States Supreme Court appeared to approve the decision of the Indiana Court of Appeals in *AL v GRH* which held that parents had no authority to consent to the sterilisation of their child. The reasons given for rejecting parental consent as sufficient authority for sterilising a child include the history of abuse of sterilising the intellectually disabled – particularly the fear that they will be sterilised for the convenience of the guardians; the destruction of 'an important part of a person's social and biological identity – the ability to reproduce'; and the irreversibility of the procedure. The effect of the blanket rule applied in the United States, however, is that parents cannot consent to an operation which results in the sterilisation of a child even though the procedure is necessary to remove or treat a diseased reproductive organ.

Understandable as the United States approach is, as a matter of principle, a line cannot be drawn between sterilisation procedures and other forms of surgical and medical treatment. It is true, as Holmes said (*The Common Law*, (1881), p 5):

The life of the law has not been logic: it has been experience. The felt necessities of the time, the prevalent moral and political theories, intuitions of public policy, avowed or unconscious, even the prejudices which judges share with their fellow-men, have had a good deal more to do with that syllogism in determining the rules by which men should be governed.

But none of these matters provides any sure ground, in my respectful opinion, for a court to hold that sterilisation procedures should be treated as an exception to the rule that parents can consent to medical treatment and surgical procedures involving their child. If the consensus of the community was that parents ought not to have an unsupervised right to consent to the sterilisation of children, it might be proper to mould common law doctrine to give effect to that consensus, even though the demands of legal principle suggest a contrary course. It might be proper, therefore, to hold that parents cannot give consent to such a procedure without the consent of a court. But as no community consensus on the issue exists, and as the subject of sterilisation 'gives rise to moral and emotional considerations to which many people attach great importance' (*In Re F* [1990] 2 AC, at 56), the proper course for a court is to give effect to established principle instead of laying down a rule which gives effect to what that court thinks is the best social solution to the issue.

In any event, the social utility of requiring the consent of the court in all cases of sterilisation is debatable. Beneficial as such a course may prove to be in some cases, it would require a depressing view of the discharge of the responsibilities of parents and doctors to conclude that the unnecessary sterilisation of children is so widespread that a blanket rule is the only remedy which can protect children from the abuse of their right to bodily integrity. This is especially true in an era when litigation is always expensive and frequently protracted with the result that, in cases where sterilisation is warranted, applications for consent might not be made. Moreover, as Lord Brandon of Oakbrook pointed out in *In Re F* (at 56), if every sterilisation operation required curial consent 'the whole process of medical care for such patients would grind to a halt'. A better remedy for the protection of children than requiring curial consent in all cases of sterilisation is the development of objective standards which the courts can supervise and enforce where necessary. Such standards will promote certainty and consistency in decision making. They will also enable parents to give a valid consent to an operation which will sterilise their child without the cost and trauma associated with litigation.

It follows that, as a matter of principle, a parent has authority to consent to the sterilisation of a child in his or her custody if it will advance or protect the welfare of the child. What is the best interests of the child is conventionally seen as being synonymous with the welfare of the child. To say that a medical or surgical procedure is in the best interests of the child, however, is merely to record a result. Before the best interests of the child can be determined, some principle, rule or standard must be applied to the facts and circumstances of the case (cf Kennedy, 'Patients, Doctors, and Human Rights', Blackburn and Taylor (eds), *Human Rights for the 1990s* (1991), pp 90–91).

Since sterilisation has grave consequences for a person's adult life, it cannot be in the best interests of a child to pre-empt a choice about the procedure which the child would otherwise have as an adult person. If there is any real possibility that, at some future time, the child will acquire the capacity and maturity to choose whether he or she should be sterilised, the carrying out of that procedure cannot be in the best interests of the child unless, of course, protection of the child's health urgently requires that the procedure be carried out during incompetency. Moreover, it must not be assumed that, simply because the child is intellectually disabled, he or she does not have or cannot acquire the capacity to consent to sterilisation. Intellectually disabled persons will frequently have the capacity to make the choice as to whether they should be sterilised (Committee on Rights of Persons with Handicaps (SA), *The Law and Persons with Handicaps*, vol 2: *Intellectual Handicaps*, (1981), p 125). Furthermore, sterilisation involves invasive procedures resulting in the permanent deprivation of a person's right or liberty to reproduce, with the potentiality for psychological harm including the lowering – perhaps the destruction – of self-esteem and, in the case of the intellectually disabled, the reinforcement of anxieties which are commonly the result of intellectual disability. (See Law Reform Commission of Canada, (Working Paper No 24 1979), *Sterilization: Implications for Mentally Retarded and Mentally Ill Persons*, pp 49–52.)

So grave are the certain and potential effects of sterilisation that that procedure can only be for the welfare of the child if the circumstances are so compelling and so likely to endure that they justify the invasive surgery or procedure involved in sterilisation. The circumstances may be compelling if the failure to carry out the procedure is likely to result in the child's physical or mental health being seriously jeopardised or if it is likely to result in the suffering of pain, fear or discomfort of such severity and duration or regularity that it is not reasonable to expect the child to suffer that pain, fear or discomfort. In these cases, the right of the incompetent person to have his or her body protected against invasive procedures resulting in removal or destruction of reproductive organs is outweighed by the necessity for appropriate 'treatment'. The circumstances may also be compelling if the failure to carry out the procedure is likely to result in a real risk that an intellectually disabled child will become pregnant and she does not, and never will, have any real understanding of sexual relationships or pregnancy. In such a case, to speak of a fundamental right of reproduction is meaningless. The human dignity of an intellectually disabled child is not advanced, and indeed is denied, by allowing her (by, what is in point of law, rape) to become pregnant and to give birth in circumstances which she cannot understand and which may result in a frightening ordeal for her not only at the time of birth, but for many months prior thereto.

What constitutes sufficiently compelling circumstances to justify sterilisation will have to be worked out on a case by case basis. But, unless the case falls within one of the above categories or a category analogous thereto, it should be held that the sterilisation of a child is not for his or her welfare. In particular, it is not for the welfare of an intellectually disabled child to sterilise that child merely to avoid pregnancy or to give effect to eugenic policies. Nor is it for the welfare of the child to sterilise her merely because of the hygiene problems associated with menstruation. As the Law Reform Commission of Canada has pointed out, intellectually disabled females who require a great deal of assistance in managing their menstruation are already likely to require assistance with urinary and faecal control, problems which are much more troublesome in terms of personal hygiene (at 34). Moreover, even if the case falls within one of the three categories which I have mentioned or an analogous category, it is not in the best interests of a child to sterilise him or her if the harm can reasonably be avoided by means less drastic than sterilisation.

Furthermore, as I have indicated, sterilisation is one area where the potential for conflict between the parent's interests and the child's interests exists. As Justice Horowitz pointed out in *Matter of Guardianship of Hayes* (1980) Wash 608 p 2d 635 at 640:

> unlike the situation of a normal and necessary medical procedure, in the question of sterilisation the interests of the parent of a retarded person cannot be presumed to be identical to those of the child.

Thus, parents may see sterilisation as relieving them of the worry and distress of the child becoming pregnant or of the burden of caring for a grandchild whom the child would not be able or fully able to care for. If a decision to consent is actuated by interests such as these, a conflict of interest arises. In such a case, the parents have no authority to consent to sterilisation of their child. However, since parents have authority to consent to a sterilisation procedure only in cases where the grounds for the procedure are compelling it is unlikely that, in practice, conflict will arise. If it does, a court of general jurisdiction invested with the parens patriae jurisdiction or the Family Court may give consent in substitution for the parents.

The principles which apply to the sterilisation of children, as I have adumbrated them, fall somewhere between the approach of the Supreme Court of Canada in *Re Eve (E (Mrs) v Eve ('Re Eve')* [1986] 2 SCR 388, 31 DLR (4th) 1) and the approach of the House of Lords in *In Re F*. In *Re Eve*, the Supreme Court held that, in the exercise of the parens patriae jurisdiction, a court should not give consent to a non-therapeutic sterilisation. The distinction between therapeutic and non-therapeutic treatment was strongly criticised by members of the House of Lords in *In Re B (A Minor)* [1988] AC 199 at 203–204, 205. I agree with Professor Kennedy, in the article to which I have earlier referred, where he said (Kennedy, op cit, p 102) that, although 'there are problems at the edges' of the two concepts, '[a]n intervention is therapeutic if treatment (therapy) is intended thereby'. This definition would include the first two categories of justification to which I have referred but exclude the third category. However, for the reasons that I have already given, I think that, where the child has no real understanding of sexual relationships or pregnancy, sterilisation may be justified if no method of contraception is reasonably feasible. In that respect, I would go beyond the approach of the Supreme Court in *Re Eve*. Moreover, it would be inconsistent with the historical development of common law principles to close the categories to which they apply. Consequently, unlike the Supreme Court of Canada, I would hold that sterilisation may also be carried out for purposes which are analogous to the three categories to which I have referred. Such an approach allows the law to develop incrementally, guided by the overarching principle that the circumstances must be so compelling that they justify such an invasive procedure as sterilisation.

In *In Re F*, the House of Lords held that sterilisation of an incompetent child was justified if it was necessary or in the public interest and that it would be in the public interest if the procedure was in the best interests of the child. Their Lordships held that it will be in the best interests of the patient if a doctor has formed the opinion that sterilisation should be carried out provided that that opinion corresponds with a respectable body of medical opinion among those experienced in the field. Their Lordships (Lord Griffith dissenting on this point) held that the involvement of a court was highly desirable as a matter of good practice although it was not necessary as a matter of law. The approach of their Lordships goes well beyond what I consider is the proper view of the common law, even when the decision to sterilise is ultimately made by a court.

A similar view to that of the majority in *JMB* was expressed in the well-known Kentucky case of *Strunk v Strunk*.

Strunk v Strunk (1969) 445 SW 2d 145 (Ky CA)

Osborne J: The facts of the case are as follows: Arthur L Strunk, 54 years of age, and Ava Strunk, 52 years of age, of Williamstown, Kentucky, are the parents of two sons. Tommy Strunk is 28 years of age, married, an employee of the Penn State Railroad and a part-time student at the University of Cincinnati. Tommy is now suffering from chronic glomerulus nephritis, a fatal kidney disease. He is now being kept alive by frequent treatment on an artificial kidney, a procedure which cannot be continued much longer.

Jerry Strunk is 27 years of age, incompetent, and through proper legal proceedings has been committed to the Frankfort State Hospital and School, which is a state institution maintained for the feeble-minded. He has an IQ of approximately 35, which corresponds with the mental age of approximately six years. He is further handicapped by a speech defect, which makes it difficult for him to communicate with persons who are not well acquainted with him. When it was determined that Tommy, in order to survive, would have to have a kidney the doctors considered the possibility of using a kidney from a cadaver if and when one became available or one from a live donor if this could be made available. The entire family, his mother, father and a number of collateral relatives were tested. Because of incompatibility of blood type or tissue none were [sic] medically acceptable as live donors. As a last resort, Jerry was tested and found to be highly acceptable. This immediately presented the legal problem as to what, if anything, could be done by the family, especially the mother and the father to procure a transplant from Jerry to Tommy. The mother as a committee petitioned the county court for authority to proceed with the operation. The court found that the operation was necessary, that under the peculiar circumstances of this case it would not only be beneficial to Tommy but also beneficial to Jerry because Jerry was greatly dependent upon Tommy, emotionally and psychologically, and that his well-being would be jeopardised more severely by the loss of his brother than by the removal of a kidney.

A psychiatrist, in attendance to Jerry, who testified in the case, stated in his opinion the death of Tommy under these circumstances would have 'an extremely traumatic effect upon him' (Jerry).

The Department of Mental Health of this Commonwealth has entered the case as *amicus curiae* and on the basis of its evaluation of the seriousness of the operation as opposed to the traumatic effect upon Jerry as a result of the loss to Tommy, recommended to the court that Jerry be permitted to undergo the surgery. Its recommendations are as follows:

> It is difficult for the mental defective to establish a firm sense of identity with another person and the acquisition of this necessary identity is dependent upon a person whom one can conveniently accept as a model and who at the same time is sufficiently flexible to allow the defective to detach himself with reassurances of continuity. His need to be social is not so much the necessity of a formal and mechanical contact with other human beings as it is the necessity of a close intimacy with other men, the desirability of a real community of feeling, an urgent need for a unity of understanding. Purely mechanical and formal contact with other men does not offer any treatment for the behaviour of a mental defective; only those who are able to communicate intimately are of value to hospital treatment in these cases. And this generally is a member of the family.
>
> In view of this knowledge, we now have particular interest in this case. Jerry Strunk, a mental defective, has emotions and reactions on a scale comparable to that of a normal person. He identifies with his brother Tom; Tom is his model, his tie with his family. Tom's life is vital to the continuity of Jerry's improvement at Frankfort State Hospital and School. The testimony of the hospital representative reflected the importance to Jerry of his visits with his family and the constant inquiries Jerry made about Tom's coming to see him. Jerry is aware he plays a role in the relief of this tension. We the Department of Mental Health must take all possible steps to prevent the occurrence of any guilt feelings Jerry would have if Tom were to die.
>
> The necessity of Tom's life to Jerry's treatment and eventual rehabilitation is clearer in view of the fact that Tom is his only living sibling and at the death of their parents, now in their fifties, Jerry will have no concerned, intimate communication so necessary to his stability and optimal functioning.
>
> The evidence shows that at the present level of medical knowledge, it is quite remote that Tom would be able to survive several cadaver transplants. Tom has a much better chance of survival if the kidney transplant from Jerry takes place.

Upon this appeal we are faced with the fact that all members of the immediate family have recommended the transplant. The Department of Mental Health has likewise made its recommendation. The county court has given its approval. The circuit court has found that it would be to the best interest of the ward of the state that the procedure be carried out. Throughout the legal proceedings, Jerry has been represented by a guardian *ad litem*, who has continually questioned the power of the state to authorise the removal of an organ from the body of an incompetent who is a ward of the state. We are fully cognisant of the fact that the question before us is unique. Insofar as we have been able to learn, no similar set of facts has come before the highest court of any of the states of this nation or the federal courts. The English courts have apparently taken a broad view of the inherent power of the equity courts with regard to incompetents. *Ex p Whitbread* (1816) 2 Mer 99, 35 ER 878, LC holds that courts of equity have the inherent power to make provisions for a needy brother out of the estate of an incompetent. This was first followed in this country in New York, *Re Willoughby, a Lunatic* 11 Paige 257 (NY 1844). The inherent rule in these cases is that the chancellor has the power to deal with the estate of the incompetent in the same manner as the incompetent would if he had his faculties. This rule has been extended to cover not only matters of property but also to cover the personal affairs of the incompetent...

The right to act for the incompetent in all cases has become recognised in this country as the doctrine of substituted judgment and is broad enough not only to cover property but also to cover all matters touching on the well-being of the ward. The doctrine has been recognised in American courts since 1844.

Review of our case law leads us to believe that the power given to a committee under KRS 387.230 would not extend so far as to allow a committee to subject his ward to the serious surgical techniques here under consideration unless the life of his ward be in jeopardy. Nor do we believe the powers delegated to the county court by virtue of the above statutes would reach so far as to permit the procedure which we are dealing with here.

We are of the opinion that a chancery court does have sufficient inherent power to authorise the operation. The circuit court having found that the operative procedures in this instance are to the best interest of Jerry Strunk and this finding having been based upon substantial evidence, we are of the opinion the judgment should be affirmed. We do not deem it significant that this case reached the circuit court by way of appeal as opposed to a direct proceeding in that court.

Notably, also as in the *JMB and SWB* case, a strong dissent was registered in *Strunk*:

Steinfeld J: Apparently because of my indelible recollection of a government which, to the everlasting shame of its citizens, embarked on a programme of genocide and experimentation with human bodies, I have been more troubled in reaching a decision in this case than in any other. My sympathies and emotions are torn between a compassion to aid an ailing young man and a duty to fully protect unfortunate members of society.

The opinion of the majority is predicated upon the authority of an equity court to speak for one who cannot speak for himself. However, it is my opinion that in considering such right in this instance we must first look to the power and authority vested in the committee, the appellee herein. KRS 387.060 and KRS 387.230 do nothing more than give the committee the power to take custody of the incompetent and the possession, care and management of his property. Courts have restricted the activities of the committee to that which is for the best interest of the incompetent: *Harding's Administrator v Harding's Executor* 140 Ky 277, 130 SW 1098 (1910); *Miller v Keown* 176 Ky 117, 195 SW 430 (1912) and 3 ALR 3d 18. The authority and duty have to protect and maintain the ward, to secure that to which he is entitled and preserve that which he has. *Ramsay's Executor v Ramsey* 243 Ky 202, 47 SW 2d 1059 (1932): *Aaronson v State of New York* 34 Misc 2d 827, 229 NYS 2d 550, 557 (1962) and *Young v State* 32 Misc 2d 965, 225 NYS 2d 549 (1962). The wishes of the members of the family or the desires of the guardian to be helpful to the apparent objects of the ward's bounty have not been a criterion. 'A curator or guardian cannot dispose of his ward's property by donation, even though authorised to do so by the court on advice of a family meeting, unless a gift by the guardian is authorised by statute.' 44 CJS Insane Persons para 81, p 191.

Two Kentucky cases decided many years ago reveal judicial policy. In *WT Sistrunk & Co v Navarra's Committee* 268 Ky 753, 105 SW 2d 1039 (1937), this court held that a committee was without right to continue a business which the incompetent had operated prior to his having been declared a person of unsound mind. More analogous is *Baker v Thomas* 272 Ky 605, 114 SW 2d 1113 (1938), in which a man and woman had lived together out of wedlock. Two children were born to them. After the man was adjudged incompetent, his committee, acting for him, together with his paramour, instituted proceedings to adopt the two children. In rejecting the application and refusing to speak for the incompetent the opinion stated:

> The statute does not contemplate that the committee of a lunatic may exercise any other power than to have the possession, care, and management of the lunatic's or incompetent's estate. No authority is given by any statute to which our attention has been called, or that we have been by careful research able to locate, giving the committee of a lunatic or an incompetent authority to petition any court for the adoption of a person as heirs capable of the inheritance of his or her estate.

The same result was reached in *Re Bourgeois* 144 La 501, 80 So 673 (1919), in which the husband of an incompetent wife sought to change the beneficiary of her insurance policy so that her children would receive the proceeds. *Grady v Dashiell* 24 Wash 2d 272, 163 P 2d 922 (1945), stands for the proposition that a loan to the ward's adult insolvent son made at a time when it was thought that the ward was incurably insane constituted an improper depletion of the ward's estate.

The majority opinion is predicated upon the finding of the circuit court that there will be psychological benefits to the ward but points out that the incompetent has the mentality of a six-year-old child. It is common knowledge beyond dispute that the loss of a close relative or a friend to a six-year-old child is not of major impact. Opinions concerning psychological trauma are at best most nebulous. Furthermore, there are no guarantees that the transplant will become a surgical success, it being well known that body rejection of transplanted organs is frequent. The life of the incompetent is not in danger, but the surgical procedure advocated creates some peril.

It is written in *Prince v Massachusetts* 321 US 158, 64 S Ct 438, 88 L Ed 645 (1944), that 'Parents may be free to become martyrs themselves. But it does not follow they are free, in identical circumstances, to make martyrs of their children before they have reached the age of full and legal discretion when they can make that choice for themselves.' The ability to fully understand and consent is a prerequisite to the donation of a part of the human body. Cf *Bonner v Moran* 75 US App DC 156, 126 F 2d 121, 139 ALR 1366 (1941), in which a fifteen-year-old infant's consent to removal of a skin patch for the benefit of another was held legally ineffective.

Unquestionably the attitudes and attempts of the committee and members of the family of the two young men whose critical problems now confront us are commendable, natural and beyond reproach. However, they refer us to nothing indicating that they are privileged to authorise the removal of one of the kidneys of the incompetent for the purpose of donation, and they cite no statutory or other authority vesting such right in the courts. The proof shows that less compatible donors are available and that the kidney of a cadaver could be used, although the odds of operational success are not as great in such case as they would be with the fully compatible donor brother.

I am unwilling to hold that the gates should be open to permit the removal of an organ from an incompetent for transplant, at least until such time as it is conclusively demonstrated that it will be of significant benefit to the incompetent. The evidence here does not rise to that pinnacle. To hold that committees, guardians or courts have such awesome power even in the persuasive case before us, could establish legal precedent, the dire result of which we cannot fathom. Regretfully I must say no.

In the *JMB and SWB* case in Australia, Brennan J perceptively remarked:

> Leaving aside for the moment the possibility of statutory investiture of a specific jurisdiction…the only legal explanation advanced is that a court, in exercising its *parens patriae* jurisdiction, enjoys a wider power than parents or guardians possess in respect of the personal integrity of their children. That proposition, in my respectful view, is erroneous in law and disturbing in its social implications.

In our view, Brennan J's remark is well made. There can be no circumstances in which a court should have exclusive power (short of legislation) to make decisions that proxies should not. As we have seen, in our view the court's function is to legislate legitimate criteria for decision-making and thereafter to review particular decisions of *others*.

(b) Desirable if not mandatory?

Although it may be argued that it would be helpful or desirable if certain types of case were routinely brought before the courts, the court cannot, of course, insist upon this. If it were to try to do so, it would be making involvement of the courts, in effect, mandatory. Regardless of the logic of this, the courts have succumbed to the temptation of getting involved. Thus, in *Re F*, having rejected a mandatory role for the court, Lord Brandon stated that:

> …although involvement of the court is not strictly necessary as a matter of law, it is nevertheless highly desirable as a matter of good practice. In considering that question, it is necessary to have regard to the special features of such an operation. These features are: first, the operation will in most cases be irreversible; secondly, by reason of the general irreversibility of the operation, the almost certain result of it will be to deprive the woman concerned of what is widely, and as I think rightly, regarded as one of the fundamental rights of a woman, namely, the right to bear children; thirdly, the deprivation of that right gives rise to moral and emotional considerations to which many people attach great importance; fourthly, if the question whether the operation is in the best interests of the woman is left to be decided without the involvement of the court there may be a greater risk of it being decided wrongly, or at least of it being thought to have been decided wrongly; fifthly, if there is no involvement of the court, there is a risk of the operation being carried out for improper reasons or with improper motives; and, sixthly; involvement of the court in the decision to operate, if that is the decision reached, should serve to protect the doctor or doctors who perform the operation, and any others who may be concerned in it from subsequent adverse criticisms or claims.
>
> Having regard to all these matters, I am clearly of the opinion that, although in the case of an operation of the kind under discussion involvement of the court is not strictly necessary as a matter of law, it is nevertheless highly desirable as a matter of good practice.
>
> There may be cases of other special operations to which similar considerations would apply. I think it best, however, to leave such other cases to be examined as and when they arise.

Further, Lord Goff expressed a similar view:

Although the parens patriae jurisdiction in the case of adults of unsound mind is no longer vested in the courts in this country, the approach adopted by the courts in the United States and in Australia provides, in my opinion, strong support for the view that, as a matter of practice, the operation of sterilisation should not be performed on an adult person who lacks the capacity to consent to it without first obtaining the opinion of the court that the operation is, in the circumstances, in the best interests of the person concerned, by seeking a declaration that the operation is lawful. (I shall return later in this speech to the appropriateness of the declaratory remedy in cases such as these.) In my opinion, that guidance should be sought in order to obtain an independent, objective and authoritative view of the lawfulness of the procedure in the particular circumstances of the relevant case, after a hearing at which it can be ensured that there is independent representation on behalf of the person upon whom it is proposed to perform the operation. This approach is consistent with the opinion expressed by Lord Templeman in *Re B (A Minor) (Wardship: Sterilisation)* [1988] AC 199, 205–206, that, in the case of a girl who is still a minor, sterilisation should not be performed upon her unless she has first been made a ward of court and the court has, in the exercise of its wardship jurisdiction, given its authority to such a step. He said:

> No one has suggested a more satisfactory tribunal or a more satisfactory method of reaching a decision which vitally concerns an individual but also involves principles of law, ethics and medical practice.

(For *locus standi* to invoke the court's declaratory jurisdiction see, *Re S (hospital order: court's jurisdiction)* [1995] 3 All ER 290 (CA) and Commentary (1995) 3 Med L Rev 294 (AG). For use of the declaratory jurisdiction to resolve questions of criminal law, see *Airedale NHS Trust v Bland* [1993] AC 789 (HL) and J Bridgman 'Declared Innocent?' (1995) 3 Med L Rev 117.)

Despite the logical untenability of this approach, subsequent cases have explored the range of its application. In three cases decided by Sir Stephen Brown, (then) President of the Family Division, his Lordship had to decide whether the approval of the court was desirable when it was proposed to perform an abortion (*Re SG (a patient)* (1990) 6 BMLR 95), a hysterectomy for serious menorrhagia in a severely disabled adult (*F v F* (1991) 7 BMLR 135) and in a girl (*Re E (a minor) (medical treatment)* (1991) 7 BMLR 117).

In all three cases, the judge distinguished *Re F* and did not deem the involvement of the court desirable.

Re E (a minor) (medical treatment) (1991) 7 BMLR 117 (Fam Div)

Sir Stephen Brown P: This is an application to the court, formally made as an interlocutory application in wardship proceedings by the Official Solicitor, who is the guardian ad litem of a mentally handicapped minor called J, who was born on 6 August 1973. J, now 17 years old, sadly, suffers from a severe mental handicap and is unable to make decisions on her own account. Her parents are very concerned for her welfare. They undertake her full-time care, but they are particularly concerned because she suffers from serious menorrhagia, which is excessive menstruation. This has serious effects upon J. I need not enlarge upon them because they are fully set out in a statement which has been submitted to the court by Mr Robinson, a consultant surgeon at Addenbrooke's hospital in Cambridge. He is the consultant gynaecologist who has been responsible for treating J. He has not sworn an affidavit because of a cautionary position recommended to him by the Medical Defence Union, which is concerned about the effects of carrying out medical treatment on mentally handicapped persons. However, there is no doubt that his statement sets out very clearly and fully the medical position so far as J is concerned. She is severely overweight, and an attempt to treat her menstrual conditions by hormones would exacerbate the obesity factor. No effective method of treating her unfortunate physical condition is possible which does not involve surgery. The consultant says in terms that the best treatment and, indeed, the only effective treatment in this case would be to perform a hysterectomy. In this case this would involve sterilising J.

I emphasise at once that it would not be the purpose of such an operation to sterilise J. It would be the inevitable and incidental result, however, of the hysterectomy operation which is recommended by the consultant gynaecologist.

J's parents are quite certain that they should accept the medical advice given to them. They are represented before me, and I am very grateful for the assistance of Mr Lane who appears for them. He makes it quite clear that as parents, so far as it rests within their power, they would consider it appropriate and, indeed, essential that they should responsibly grant their consent for such an operation to be carried out in the interests of the health of their daughter. She has been made the subject of a wardship summons solely in order that the matter can come before the court. I say at once that in the light of the evidence before me and the very careful analysis of her position by the Official Solicitor, who is her guardian ad litem, it is clearly in the interests of J that this operation should be carried out. I have no doubt whatsoever about the fact, and if it is necessary for the court to grant its formal consent to the doctors and her parents for that operation to be carried out, the court will very willingly grant that consent.

However, the issue which has been brought before the court is a somewhat different one. Mr Nicholls, for the Official Solicitor, submits that it is not necessary for the formal consent of the court to be granted in this case in order that the operation in question can be carried out. In a detailed skeleton argument, he has analysed what he submits is the correct legal position. This is a case where the operation is required for therapeutic reasons; it is in order to treat J therapeutically that the operation is said to be required. This is not a case where the objective is sterilisation. This is not a case where the doctors are saying that this young girl should be sterilised because it would be wrong for her to become pregnant. That is not the issue in this case, and I make that very clear. In this case, the submission is made to the court that it ought not to be necessary for a responsible doctor to have to seek the formal consent of the court for the carrying out of an operation which is required in order to treat the patient therapeutically.

It is quite clear that, in recent times, the medical profession has become very anxious about its legal position and possible legal liabilities. It was because of this climate of concern, if I may so describe it, that the Medical Defence Union advised Mr Robinson, the consultant in this case, that he should not swear an affidavit or take any step in this matter unless the court made an order in the wardship proceedings. Mr Nicholls, in an attempt to clarify the legal position of doctors and, indeed of parents placed in a similar position to the parents of J, decided that this matter should be clarified by an application to the court.

The case of *Re F* (1989) 4 BMLR 1, [1990] 2 AC 1, recently decided in the House of Lords, is, of course, the basis of the Medical Defence Union's position in this matter. However, that was a wholly different case on its facts, and it is to be observed that the House of Lords did not rule that the consent of the court was required by law. It stated that, as a matter of good practice, it would be wise for consent to be sought.

It is important that the medical profession should be clear about the position in such cases. I am satisfied, after the careful analysis which Mr Nicholls has presented to the court, that there is a clear distinction to be made between cases where an operation is required for genuine therapeutic reasons and those where the operation is designed to achieve sterilisation. That position was recognised by Lord Bridge in *Re F*, and I believe that it is the correct position in the present case. I think that J's parents are in a position to give a valid consent to the proposed operation. I am not dealing in this instance with the case of an adult; I am dealing with the case of a minor, and it is plainly desirable that in order to relieve the particular symptoms of her distressing condition, J should undergo this particular treatment. Accordingly, in this case, I rule that the consent of the court is not required for this operation to be carried out. It is necessary for therapeutic reasons. In any event, if it were to be considered necessary, I would have no hesitation in granting the court's consent.

This is a case where, after careful deliberation and consideration of all the medical factors, the consultant has come to the conclusion that this treatment is necessary for the relief of the condition from which this unfortunate girl suffers. Accordingly the court will rule and declare that on the facts of this case no formal consent is necessary.

F v F (1991) 7 BMLR 135 (Fam Div)

Sir Stephen Brown P: The court has before it a summons issued by the mother of a 29-year-old mentally handicapped woman. The Official Solicitor appears by counsel as the guardian ad litem of the woman in question.

The situation of the woman, to whom I shall refer by the initial G, is a sad one. She has been seriously disabled from birth. Although she is 29 years of age she has the mental age of a five-year-old. She has no sense of balance and is largely confined to a wheelchair. She lives with her parents, who are husband and wife, and it is her mother who has issued the summons before this court.

Unhappily she has suffered for many years from a distressing condition which in ordinary terms may be described as excessively heavy 'periods'. She is unable to take care of her own menstrual hygiene or basic sanitary care. She dreads having her period and is embarrassed and humiliated by the experience. The general practitioner who has been responsible for her care for many years became increasingly concerned about the effect upon G of this distressing condition. At the instance of her general practitioner she has consulted a consultant gynaecologist, who has also discussed the case with a colleague who is a consultant obstetrician and gynaecologist. The position is that her condition cannot be satisfactorily treated in order to provide relief by hormone treatment. In the opinion of all the doctors the only practicable method of treating this condition is by performing a hysterectomy with ovarian conservation. This would in fact have the incidental effect of sterilising the patient. However, the purpose of such treatment is not to achieve sterilisation; it is in order to treat her therapeutically for a condition which is becoming increasingly distressing and disturbing for this unfortunate young woman.

The mother has issued a summons seeking a declaration that the operation may lawfully be carried out. The Official Solicitor, who appears by counsel, has considered the situation with great care, having regard to the desirability of informing the medical profession of the legal position which arises in a case such as this. In a careful skeleton argument further developed orally by counsel before the court, the Official Solicitor has traced the cases on sterilisation, and submits that in this particular case, and in similar cases, where the purpose of the treatment is essentially therapeutic but which may incidentally result in sterilisation, the approval of the court is not necessary provided that two medical practitioners are satisfied that the operation in question is necessary for therapeutic purposes, and that it is in the best interests of the patient. Further, that there is no practicable less intrusive means of treating the condition from which the patient suffers. The Official Solicitor submits that if these criteria are satisfied then the treatment should be capable of being carried out without specific recourse to the court.

In the present case it is clear from the affidavit evidence of the general practitioner, together with the evidence of the consultant gynaecologist and the consultant obstetrician and gynaecologist, that hysterectomy with ovarian conservation is in the best interests of G, and that there does not exist any practicable less intrusive alternative means of treating her condition. It is clear, therefore, that the purpose of the proposed operation is essentially therapeutic and is not designed to achieve sterilisation.

I have no doubt that in this case if the law were to require the approval of the court for the carrying out of such an operation, that approval should be given, and I would make a declaration to that effect in the terms sought by the summons issued by the plaintiff mother. However, it appears to me that the submission of the Official Solicitor is validly made. That is to say, that in a case where the operation is necessary in order to treat the condition in question, it may be lawfully carried out even though it may have the incidental effect of sterilisation. It is appropriate, however, to indicate that the criteria to which I have already referred should be satisfied in any such case. I take the view that no application for leave to carry on such an operation needs to be made in cases where two medical practitioners are satisfied that the operation is, (1) necessary for therapeutic purposes, (2) is in the best interests of the patient, and (3) that there is no practicable less intrusive means of treating the condition.

I propose, therefore, to make a declaration at the invitation of the Official Solicitor in the following terms: that no application to the court is necessary as a matter of good medical practice for a declaration as to the lawfulness of a proposed therapeutic operation which would have the incidental effect of sterilisation of a woman who cannot consent thereto by reason of mental disability, where the operation is necessary in order to ensure the improvement of the health of the patient, or to prevent deterioration in her health.

In the present circumstances, therefore, the declaration sought by the plaintiff is not necessary, but I have in any event indicated that if I were wrong about that then I would have no hesitation in this case in making a declaration in the terms sought. It is quite clear that this operation should be carried out in order to safeguard the health of this unfortunate young woman.

You will notice that in *F v F* the judge imposed the requirement that the opinions of *two* doctors be sought. The basis for this is unclear unless it reflects the need to establish that a body of medical opinion approves of the procedure and hence that the *Bolam* test is satisfied. The final case involved an abortion rather than a procedure with the consequence of sterilising the young woman or girl.

Re SG (a minor) (1991) 6 BMLR 95 (Fam Div)

Sir Stephen Brown P: The court has before it two summons. Firstly there is an originating summons of 4 December 1990 issued by a young woman, Miss SG, by her father and next friend, Mr RG. The unhappy situation is that Miss SG is a 26 year old severely mentally handicapped woman with a mental age equivalent to a seven or eight year old child. She is looked after at home by her mother and father with assistance and attends an adult training centre for the mentally handicapped. The family is unfortunately further burdened with two other children who suffer from various degrees of mental handicap.

It became apparent recently that Miss SG was pregnant; and she is presently believed to be some 17 weeks pregnant. The general practitioner referred her to a consultant gynaecologist and both he and the general practitioner took the view that it would be in the best interests of Miss SG that her pregnancy should be terminated. It is necessary that any termination should be carried out at a special institution, and provisional arrangements have been made for it to be carried out next week on 11 December. The evidence before me is that if there were any delay beyond 11 December there might very well be complications causing pain, distress and other trauma to the applicant, Miss SG. It is therefore a matter of urgency.

Because of the concern in the medical profession generally arising principally as a result of the recent decision of the House of Lords in the case of *F v West Berkshire Health Authority (Mental Health Act Commission intervening)* (1989) 4 BMLR 1, sub nom, *Re F (mental patient: sterilisation)* [1990] 2 AC 1, the applicant by her father and next friend has felt it desirable to apply to the court for a declaration that it would be lawful in the existing circumstances to terminate the pregnancy of Miss SG despite her inability to give her personal consent to it by reason of her mental incapacity. The applicant appears to take the view that in law it may be necessary in the case of a proposed termination of pregnancy to obtain such a declaration. The medical termination of pregnancy is, however, regulated by the Abortion Act 1967. Section 1(1) provides for two conditions to be fulfilled if a pregnancy is to be terminated:

> Subject to the provisions of this section, a person shall not be guilty of an offence under the law relating to abortion when a pregnancy is terminated by a registered medical practitioner if two registered medical practitioners are of the opinion, formed in good faith – (a) that the continuance of the pregnancy would involve risk to the life of the pregnant woman or of injury to the physical or mental health of the pregnant woman or any existing children of her family, greater than if the pregnancy were terminated; or (b) that there is a substantial risk that if the child were born it would suffer from such physical or mental abnormalities as to be seriously handicapped.

Counsel has indicated to me that both those conditions are capable of being met in this case. Accordingly, the submission is made that that being so and having regard to the strict safeguards of the Abortion Act 1967, this is not a situation which should require a formal declaration from the High Court before the treatment can be carried out. It will be understood by those who have made themselves familiar with this branch of the law that it is a developing branch of the law; and I say that advisedly, because at present the Law Commission is considering the position generally in relation to the medical treatment of such persons and there is an extensive debate about the medical treatment of 'incapable' adults within the medical profession. The Medical Ethics Committee and the Mental Health Committee of the British Medical Association are currently considering their representations to the Law Commission.

In the case of *F v West Berkshire HA*, Lord Brandon, while dealing with a case of sterilisation – a very different type of operation – said in the course of his speech that, provided that the operation or treatment concerned is in the best interests of the patient, it may be lawfully carried out and that the common law would permit that to be done. However, as a matter of good practice, said Lord Brandon, the High Court should be asked to declare the lawfulness of proposed medical treatment which falls within a 'special category'. He indicated that sterilisation would fall within such a special category. The termination of pregnancy, on the other hand, has not been described by the House of Lords as being within a special category. I am told that the Master of the Rolls has indicated that he would be prepared so to describe it, but there is no decision about this particular matter.

The court has been assisted in this case by the Official Solicitor. Mr Nicholls has appeared upon this application and has made submissions, supported by an excellent skeleton argument, as to the position in law of the termination of pregnancy. The Official Solicitor submits that since the termination of pregnancy is already so closely regulated by statute, it is not essential as a matter of practice to seek a declaration from the High Court before carrying out such treatment. He emphasises that this is a very different form of treatment from sterilisation. Abortion, of course, raises emotive and sensitive issues. Having regard no doubt to these sensitivities this application has been made to this court for a declaration. However, the applicant, supported by the views of the Official Solicitor, has also issued a summons seeking alternatively a declaration that such a declaration as is envisaged in the case of a 'special category', is not required by this applicant in this case.

I have no doubt on the facts of this case that, if a declaration such as was considered in the case of *F v West Berkshire HA* is required as a matter of good practice, I should make it, but in the light of the present state of the law I accept the submissions of the Official Solicitor that it is not necessary that the specific approval of the High Court should be a condition precedent to the carrying out of a termination of pregnancy. I consider that the Abortion Act 1967 provides fully adequate safeguards for the doctors who are to undertake this treatment. Accordingly, I am prepared to indicate that in my judgment a formal declaration is not required for this particular treatment. However, it is important that I should also make it clear that the conditions of s 1 of the Abortion Act 1967 must be complied with.

I would add that it has to be borne in mind that in *F v West Berkshire HA* the view of the House of Lords was that such a declaration was desirable in cases falling within a 'special category' as a matter of good practice. No doubt the particular situation arising in cases of the termination of pregnancy will be considered in the Law Commission's current investigation and it may be that further guidelines will be issued by the Medical Ethics Committee of the British Medical Association in addition to recommendations which may be made by the Law Commission. For the time being, however, I express my view that a formal declaration is not required in this case such as was considered to be desirable in the case of *F v West Berkshire HA*. However, I also say that on the facts of this case if such a declaration were to be considered necessary I would be prepared to make it.

The net effect of these decisions, if they survive any future attack in the Court of Appeal, is that the court has resiled from any direct involvement in decision-making in any cases other than those which Stephen Brown P describes as 'non-therapeutic' (see also *Re H (mental patient)* (1992) 9 BMLR 71 (Fam Div) – declaration not necessary or desirable before carrying out a diagnostic procedure). The most obvious example of a non-therapeutic procedure is that of contraceptive sterilisation (see *Re S (Medical Treatment: Adult Sterilisation)* [1998] 1 FLR 944), but you will recall that Lord Brandon asked whether there might not be others in a 'special category'. One example of such case may be the removal of tissue from a healthy incompetent person (see, for example Neill LJ in *Re F* [1990] 2 AC 1 at 33 and Lord Bridge at 52).

The latter issue arose in *Re Y (Mental Patient: Bone Marrow Donations)* [1996] 2 FLR 787, which we saw earlier, and which concerned the legality of bone marrow donation by an incompetent adult to her sister. In the course of his judgment, Connell J stated:

...if on any future occasion there was a need or a wish to perform a bone marrow harvesting procedure on an adult incompetent, it was appropriate for the matter first to be ventilated in court before the procedures took place.

In the case of children, the nature of the decision to balance the interests of one child against another may place the parents in an impossible position: it is this conflict of interest and the dangers of a wrong decision which makes court involvement justified. Further, in both adult and children cases, the evidence of psychological benefit which may justify, on Connell J's approach, the donation is of such a fragile nature that it requires examination and consideration in the more detached environment of a court.

One further class of case where court involvement has been deemed desirable is where it is sought to withdraw artificial hydration and nutrition from a patient in a persistent vegetative state (PVS), the House of Lords in *Airedale NHS Trust v Bland* [1993] AC 789 saw a court declaration of legality as desirable prior to withdrawal. In the Court of Appeal, Sir Thomas Bingham MR (at 815) explained the court's view.

Sir Thomas Bingham MR: At the end of his judgment Sir Stephen Brown P held that in cases of this kind application should be made to the court to obtain its sanction for the course proposed. This was in my respectful view a wise ruling, directed to the protection of patients, the protection of doctors, the reassurance of patients' families and the reassurance of the public. The practice proposed seems to me desirable. It may very well be that with the passage of time a body of experience and practice will build up which will obviate the need for application in every case, but for the time being I am satisfied that the practice which Sir Stephen Brown P described should be followed.

In the House of Lords both Lord Keith (at 859) and Lord Goff (at 874) approved this statement (see also Lord Lowry at 876). (For another possible situation where court involvement is desirable, see *In the Matter of the Welfare of A (A Child)* (1993) FLC 92–402 (Aus Fam Ct) – sex re-assignment on teenager.)

(c) The appropriate role?

If the conclusion is accepted that the courts should not make it mandatory, and cannot make it desirable, that particular cases be brought before them for decision-making, what should be the court's role?

As we have seen, the first role should be to establish the legal criteria which must inform a proxy's decision. Also, the second role should be to review or exercise a supervisory jurisdiction over (within the strict limits which we have seen) the proxy's decision. What needs to be explored further, here, is the nature of the first role mentioned above. It is our view that in addition to setting criteria to govern a proxy's decision, the court has a further role. It must define areas of decision-making which do not fall within any proxy's power to decide. An obvious example of this would be that a proxy may not authorise the killing of the patient (see, *Re J (a minor) (wardship: medical treatment)* [1990] 3 All ER 930 at 936 per Lord Donaldson MR). Another illustration arose in the case of *Re J (child's religious upbringing and circumcision)* (1999) 52 BMLR 82 (CA). The case was concerned with whether to carry out a circumcision on a five-year-old boy. His mother, with whom he lived, was a Christian and was against the procedure being carried out. His father, who was a Muslim, wished it to go ahead. In refusing permission for the procedure, the Court of Appeal held that one parent did not have the power to authorise ritual circumcision against the wishes of the other. Only the court could do this.

Thorpe LJ (with whom Schiemann LJ expressed agreement) stated:

> The only point of principle that this appeal decides is to endorse the judge's conclusion that s 2(7) of the Children Act does not enable a parent to arrange circumcision without the consent of the other. Section 2(7) provides:
>
> > Where more than one person has parental responsibility for a child, each of them may act alone and without the other (or others) in meeting that responsibility; but nothing in this Part shall be taken to effect the operation of any enactment which requires the consent of more than one person in a matter affecting the child.
>
> Mr Nicholls, for the Official Solicitor, submitted and the judge accepted that the operation of circumcision is of considerable consequence and irreversible. It must, therefore, join the exceptional categories where disagreement between holders of parental responsibility must be submitted to the court for determination. He has renewed that submission in this court. No-one has opposed it and I would uphold it.

Butler-Sloss P expressly agreed:

> The Official Solicitor recommended to Wall J that where parents sharing parental responsibility were in disagreement over the circumcision of a male child, that issue should be referred to the court for determination. The judge accepted that submission and I entirely agree with him and with the observations made by Lord Justice Thorpe in his judgment.
>
> There is, in my view, a small group of important decisions made on behalf of a child which, in the absence of agreement of those with parental responsibility, ought not to be carried out or arranged by a one-parent carer although she has parental responsibility under s 2(7) of the Children Act 1989. Such a decision ought not to be made without the specific approval of the court. Sterilisation is one example. The change of a child's surname is another. Some of the examples, including the change of a child's surname, are based upon statute (see s 13(1) of the Children Act).
>
> The issue of circumcision has not, to my knowledge, previously been considered by this court, but in my view it comes within that group. The decision to circumcise a child on grounds other than medical necessity is a very important one; the operation is irreversible,

and should only be carried out where the parents together approve of it or, in the absence of parental agreement, where a court decides that the operation is in the best interests of the child. This requirement for a determination by the court should also apply to a local authority with parental responsibility under a care order.

(See also *In the matter of the Welfare of A (a child)* (1993) FLC 92–402 (Aust Fam Ct) – parents have no authority to consent to sex re-assignment surgery.)

The seriousness and irreversibility of the procedures, together with their controversial nature and the real risk of misjudging the patient's 'best interests', may be the courts' justification for limiting the proxy's decision-making authority.

Perhaps the most distinctive device for indicating the outer limit placed upon a proxy's decision-making lies in the contrast between interventions which are *therapeutic* and those which are *non-therapeutic*. We would argue that, ordinarily, interventions which are non-therapeutic are impermissible in law. This is subject to certain exceptions, for example, in some cases of research (see *infra*, ch 14). The distinction was considered in the House of Lords in *Re B* and robustly rejected. Lord Hailsham remarked:

> I find the distinction…between 'therapeutic' and 'non-therapeutic' purposes of this operation in relation to the facts of the present case above as totally meaningless, and, if meaningful, quite irrelevant to the correct application of the welfare principle.

Lord Bridge put it as follows:

> To say that the court can never authorise sterilisation of a ward as being in her best interests would be patently wrong. To say that it can only do so if the operation is 'therapeutic' as opposed to 'non-therapeutic' is to divert attention from the true issue, which is whether the operation is in the ward's best interest, and remove it to an area of arid semantic debate as to where the line is to be drawn between 'therapeutic' and 'non-therapeutic' treatment.

Lord Oliver remarked:

> Something was sought to be made of the description of the operation for which authority was sought in *Re D* as 'non-therapeutic', using the word 'therapeutic' as connoting the treatment of some malfunction or disease. The description was, no doubt, apt enough in that case, but I do not, for my part, find the distinction between 'therapeutic' and 'non-therapeutic' measures helpful in the context of the instant case, for it seems to me entirely immaterial whether measures undertaken for the protection against future and foreseeable injury are properly described as 'therapeutic'. The primary and paramount question is only whether they are for the welfare and benefit of this particular young woman situate as she is situate in this case.

In these speeches, their Lordships choose to turn their backs on the considered analysis of La Forest J in *Re Eve* (1986) 31 DLR (4th) 1 (Can SC).

The validity of the distinction between therapeutic and non-therapeutic interventions was subsequently accepted by the Australian High Court in the *JWB and SMB* case. As we saw above, the majority of the court, though they thought the line between them was imprecise, nevertheless found it 'necessary to make the distinction'. (See also the judgment of McHugh J, set out *supra*)

To say that the distinction between therapeutic and non-therapeutic exists and should be the basis of legal analysis is not to say that simply by relying on it, all problems are solved. If 'therapy' means that which is intended to produce benefit, the word 'benefit' then becomes the focus of attention. Some would say that it is not significantly different from acting in the 'best interests'. Furthermore, particularly in the context of alleged psychological benefit, benefit is capable of widely differing interpretations, as we saw above when discussing (*Re Y* (*supra*) and the US cases of *Bonner v Moran* (1941) 126 F 2d 121 (USCA DC); *Strunk v Strunk* (1969) 445 SW 2d 145; and *Curran v Bosze* (1990) 566 NE 2d 1319 (Illinois Sup Ct).

In the light of the views expressed by the Canadian Supreme Court and Australian High Court, it could therefore be argued that the House of Lords' rejection of the distinction in *Re B* is out of step. It could be said that the distinction is rejected out of a misunderstanding of its true basis. It is not entirely a descriptive distinction to be applied or not mechanistically to any particular intervention. This is because the distinction is also, in part, normative reflecting prior value judgments as to what types of medical interventions are legitimate and acceptable to society. A differing set of values are at the heart of the different results in *Re B* and *Re Eve*. The misunderstanding of the House of Lords in *Re B* is that they applied the simplistic 'best interests' approach, instead of proceeding in two stages. First, the court must determine in general terms the permissible limits of medical interventions. Secondly, the court must then determine whether the particular doctor did what he did with the intention of producing those permissible ends. The value of the distinction between therapeutic and non-therapeutic interventions is that ordinarily, *ex hypothesi*, the court will regard a therapeutic intervention as legitimate. By contrast the court will need to be persuaded that an intervention which has no therapeutic purpose is legitimate. (See the judgment of Brennan J in the *JWB and SMB* case, in which he emphasises the point that the issue is really a matter of judicial choice applying societal values rather than one of identifying the correct descriptive category into which the particular intervention falls without understanding the underlying basis for the categorisation. See further Chapter 9.)

It may be that the insistence of the Australian High Court on the distinction need not *in fact* produce any different result in any particular case from an application of the 'best interests' test. This is because the 'best interests' test also proceeds from judicial and societal values. The question then has to be put, if the result may be the same why should we be concerned? The answer is that the criterion of 'best interests' contains within it, as Brennan J is anxious to point out, virtually no explicit guidelines as to the values it embraces and thereby allows the court free rein and provides no guidance to proxy decision-makers. By contrast, the distinction between therapeutic and non-therapeutic causes the court to identify the values underlying the notion of treatment and then places a not inconsiderable burden on those who would engage in a non-therapeutic intervention to justify it. Finally, we may speculate that the true reason for the House of Lords' preference for the 'best interests' test allowed a consideration of wider matters. Wanting the freedom to take account of non-medical factors, their Lordships opted for the 'best interests' approach. We have concentrated here on the sterilisation cases because these have been the cases in which the courts have, on the whole, sought to struggle with the question of the role of the court and that of others, for example parents. We will return to these, and other cases, in Chapter 9 when we consider the legality of sterilising incapable women and girls.

B. COMMON LAW JUSTIFICATION

We have been considering so far the role and authority of proxies or the court and the criteria to be applied by them in making decisions. We turn now to consider the situation in which, as regards the law as it stands, no one has authority to decide on behalf of an *incompetent adult* (see, *Re T (adult: refusal of medical treatment* (1992) 9 BMLR 46 (CA) at 50 per Lord Donaldson MR). If treatment is to be carried out, we must find some legal justification. It is a matter of commonsense, though until recently the law had not shown its hand, that it must be lawful to give medical treatment to an incompetent person in appropriate circumstances. Otherwise, the mentally disabled adult patient suffering from severe toothache would have to be left to suffer. Since the common law is 'commonsense under a wig' (per Lord Donaldson MR in *Re F (mental patient: sterilisation)* [1990] 2 AC 1 at 17), the question for the law is not *whether* treatment of the incompetent adult is lawful but *how is it to be justified*. It was not until 1989 that the House of Lords addressed this question of principle.

Re F (mental patient: sterilisation) [1990] 2 AC 1, (1989) 4 BMLR 1 (HL)

A 36-year-old mentally handicapped woman, F, who resided as a voluntary in-patient in a mental hospital and who had the mental age of a small child, had formed a sexual relationship with a male patient. The hospital staff considered that she would be unable to cope with the effects of pregnancy and giving birth, and that, since all other forms of contraception were unsuitable and it was considered undesirable to further curtail F's limited freedom of movement in order to prevent sexual activity, it would be in her best interests to be sterilised. F's mother, who for the same reasons also wished her to be sterilised, issued an originating summons seeking a declaration from the court under RSC, Ord 15, R 16, that such an operation would not amount to an unlawful act by reason only of the absence of F's consent.

The judge granted the declaration sought. On appeal by the Official Solicitor, the Court of Appeal upheld the judge's order. In upholding the grant of the declaration Lord Goff explored the position at common law.

Lord Goff: I turn to consider the question whether, and if so when, medical treatment or care of a mentally disordered person who is, by reason of his incapacity, incapable of giving his consent, can be regarded as lawful. As it is recognised in Cardozo J's statement of principle, and elsewhere (see eg *Sidaway v Board of Governors of the Bethlem Royal Hospital and the Maudsley Hospital* [1985] AC 871, 882, per Lord Scarman), some relaxation of the law is required to accommodate persons of unsound mind. In *Wilson v Pringle* [1987] QB 237, the Court of Appeal considered the treatment or care of such persons may be regarded as lawful, as falling within the exception relating to physical contact which is generally acceptable in the ordinary conduct of everyday life. Again, I am with respect unable to agree. That exception is concerned with the ordinary events of everyday life – jostling in public places and such like – and affects all persons, whether or not they are capable of giving their consent. Medical treatment – even treatment for minor ailments – does not fall within that category of events. The general rule is that consent is necessary to render such treatment lawful. If such treatment administered without consent is not to be unlawful, it has to be justified on some other principle.

Upon what principle can medical treatment be justified when given without consent? We are searching for a principle upon which, in limited circumstances, recognition may be given to a need, in the interests of the patient, that treatment should be given to him in circumstances where he is (temporarily or permanently) disabled from consenting to it. It is this criterion of a need which points to the principle of necessity as providing justification.

That there exists in the common law a principle of necessity which may justify action which would otherwise be unlawful is not in doubt. But historically the principle has been seen to be restricted to two cases of private necessity. The former occurred when a man interfered with another man's property in the public interest – for example (in the days before we could dial 999 for the fire brigade) the destruction of another man's house to prevent the spread of a catastrophic fire, and indeed occurred in the Great Fire of London in 1666. The latter cases occurred when a man interfered with another man's property to save his own person or property from imminent danger – for example when he entered upon his neighbour's land without his consent, in order to prevent the spread of fire onto his own land.

There is, however, a third group of cases, which is also properly described as founded upon the principle of necessity and which is more pertinent to the resolution of the problem in the present case. These cases are concerned with action taken as a matter of necessity to assist another person without his consent. To give a simple example, a man who seizes another and forcibly drags him from the path of an oncoming vehicle, thereby saving him from injury or even death, commits no wrong. But there are many emanations of this principle, to be found scattered through the books. These are concerned not only with the preservation of the life or health of the assisted person, but also with the preservation of his property (sometimes an animal, sometimes an ordinary chattel) and even with certain conduct on his behalf in the administration of his affairs. Where there is a pre-existing relationship between the parties, the intervenor is usually said to act as an agent of necessity on behalf of the principal in whose interests he acts, and his action can often, with not too much artificiality, be referred to the pre-existing relationship between them. Whether the intervenor may be entitled either to reimbursement or to remuneration raises separate questions which are not relevant in the present case.

We are concerned here with action taken to preserve the life, health or well-being of another who is unable to consent to it. Such action is sometimes said to be justified as arising from emergency; in *Prosser and Keeton, Handbook on Torts*, 5th ed. (1984), p 117, the action is said to be privileged by the emergency. Doubtless, in the case of a person of sound mind, there will ordinarily have to be an emergency before such action taken without consent can be lawful for otherwise there would be an opportunity to communicate with the assisted person and to seek his consent. But this is not always so; and indeed the historical origins of the principle of necessity do not point to emergency as such as providing the criterion of lawful intervention without consent. The old Roman doctrine of negotiorum gestio presupposed not so much an emergency as a prolonged absence of the dominus from home as justifying intervention by the gestor to administer his affairs. The most ancient group of cases in the common law, concerned with action taken by the master of a ship in distant parts in the interests of the shipowner, likewise found its origin in the difficulty of communication with the owner over a prolonged period of time – a difficulty overcome today by modern means of communication. In those cases, it was said that there had to be an emergency before the master could act as agent of necessity; though the emergency could well be of some duration. But when a person is rendered incapable of communication either permanently or over a considerable period of time (through illness or accident or mental disorder), it would be an unusual use of language to describe the case as one of 'permanent emergency' – if indeed such a state of affairs can properly be said to exist. In truth, the relevance of an emergency is that it may give rise to a necessity to act in the interests of the assisted person, without first obtaining his consent. Emergency is however not the criterion or even a pre-requisite; it is simply a frequent origin of the necessity which impels intervention. The principle is one of necessity, not of emergency.

We can derive some guidance as to the nature of the principle of necessity from the cases on agency of necessity in mercantile law. When reading those cases, however, we have to bear in mind that it was there considered that (since there was a pre-existing relationship between the parties) there was a duty on the part of the agent to act on his principal's behalf in an emergency. From these cases it appears that the principle of necessity connotes that circumstances have arisen in which there is a necessity for the agent to act on his principle's behalf at a time when it is in practice not possible for him to obtain his principal's instructions so to do. In such cases, it has been said that the agent must act bona fide in the interests of his principal: see *Prager v Blatspiel Stamp & Heacock Ltd* [1924] 1 KB 566, 572 *per* McCardie J. A broader statement of the principle is to be found in the advice of the Privy Council delivered by Sir Montague Smith in *Australasian Steam Navigation Co v Morse* (1872) LR 4 PC 222, 230, in which he said:

> When by the force of circumstances a man has the duty cast upon him of taking some action for another, and under that obligation, adopts the course which, to the judgment of a wise and prudent man, is apparently the best for the interest of the persons for whom he acts in a given emergency, it may properly be said of the course so taken, that it was, in a mercantile sense, necessary to take it.

In a sense, these statements overlap. But from them can be derived the basic requirements, applicable in these cases of necessity, that, to fall within the principle, not only (1) must there be a necessity to act when it is not practicable to communicate with the assisted person, but also (2) the action taken must be such as a reasonable person would in all the circumstances take, acting in the best interests of the assisted person.

On this statement of principle, I wish to observe that officious intervention cannot be justified by the principle of necessity. So intervention cannot be justified when another more appropriate person is available and willing to act; nor can it be justified when it is contrary to the known wishes of the assisted person, to the extent that he is capable of rationally forming such a wish. On the second limb of the principle, the introduction of the standard of a reasonable man should not in the present context be regarded as materially different from that of Sir Montague Smith's 'wise and prudent man', because a reasonable man would, in the time available to him, proceed with wisdom and prudence before taking action in relation to another man's person or property without his consent. I shall have more to say on this point later. Subject to that, I hesitate at present to indulge in any greater refinement of the principle, being well aware of many problems which may arise in its application – problems which it is not necessary, for present purposes, to examine. But as a general rule, if the above criteria are fulfilled, interference with the assisted person's person or property (as the case may be) will not be unlawful. Take the example of a railway accident, in which injured passengers are trapped in the wreckage. It is this principle which may render lawful the actions of other citizens – railway staff, passengers or outsiders – who rush to give aid and comfort to the victims: the surgeon who amputates the limb of an unconscious passenger to free him from the wreckage; the ambulance man who conveys him to hospital; the doctors and nurses who treat him and care for him which renders him incapable of speech or movement. It is by virtue of this principle that the doctor who treats him, the nurse who cares for him, even the relative or friend or neighbour who comes in to look after him, will commit no wrong when he or she touches his body.

The two examples I have given illustrate, in the one case, an emergency, and in the other, a permanent or semi-permanent state of affairs. Another example of the latter kind is that of a mentally disordered person who is disabled from giving consent. I can see no good reason why the principle of necessity should not be applicable in his case as it is in the case of the victim of a stroke. Furthermore, in the case of a mentally disordered person, as in the case of a stroke victim, the permanent state of affairs calls for a wider range of care than may be requisite in an emergency which arises from accidental injury. When the state of affairs is permanent, or semi-permanent, action properly taken to preserve the life, health or well-being of the assisted person may well transcend and may extend to include such humdrum matters as routine medical or dental treatment, even simple care such as dressing and undressing and putting to bed.

The distinction I have drawn between cases of emergency, and cases where the state of affairs is (more or less) permanent, is relevant in another respect. We are here concerned with medical treatment, and I limit myself to cases of that kind. Where, for example, a surgeon performs an operation without his consent on a patient temporarily rendered unconscious in an accident, he should do no more than is reasonably required, in the best interests of the patient, before he recovers consciousness. I can see no practical difficulty arising from this requirement, which derives from the fact that the patient is expected before long to regain consciousness and can then be consulted about longer term measures. The point has however arisen in a more acute form where a surgeon, in the course of an operation, discovers some other condition which, in his opinion, requires operative treatment for which he has not received the patient's consent. In what circumstances should he operate forthwith, and in what circumstances he should postpone the further treatment until he has received the patient's consent, is a difficult matter which has troubled the Canadian Courts (see *Marshall v Curry* [1933] 3 DLR 260, and *Murray v McMurchy* [1949] 2 DLR 442), but which it is not necessary for your Lordships to consider in the present case.

But where the state of affairs is permanent or semi-permanent, as may be so in the case of a mentally disordered person, there is no point in waiting to obtain the patient's consent. The need to care for him is obvious; and the doctor must then act in the best interests of his patient, just as if he had received his patient's consent so to do. Were this not so, much useful treatment and care could, in theory at least, be denied to the unfortunate. It follows that, on this point, I am unable to accept the view expressed by Neill LJ in the Court of Appeal, at 32C–H that the treatment must be shown to have been necessary. Moreover, in such a case, as my noble and learned friend Lord Brandon of Oakbrook has pointed out, a doctor who has assumed responsibility for the care of a patient may not only be treated as having the patient's consent to act, but may also be under a duty so to act. I find myself to be respectfully in agreement with Lord Donaldson of Lymington MR, when he said, at 18D–E:

> I see nothing incongruous in doctors and others who have a caring responsibility being required to act in relation to an adult who is incompetent to exercise a right of choice in exactly the same way as would the court or reasonable parents in relation to a child, making due allowance of course for the fact that the patient is not a child, and I am satisfied that that is what the law does in fact require.

In these circumstances, it is natural to treat the deemed authority and the duty as interrelated. But I feel bound to express my opinion that, in principle, the lawfulness of the doctor's action is, at least in its origin, to be found in the principle of necessity. This can perhaps be seen most clearly in cases where there is no continuing relationship between doctor and patient. The 'doctor in the house' who volunteers to assist a lady in the audience who, overcome by the drama or by the heat of the theatre, has fainted away, is impelled to act by no greater duty than that imposed by his own Hippocratic oath. Furthermore, intervention can be justified in the case of a non-professional, as well as a professional, man or woman who has no pre-existing relationship with the assisted person – as in the case of a stranger who rushes to assist an injured man after an accident. In my opinion, it is the necessity itself which provides the justification for the intervention.

I have said that the doctor has to act in the best interests of the assisted person. In the case of routine treatment of mentally disordered persons, there should be little difficulty in applying this principle. In the case of more serious treatment, I recognise that its application may create problems for the medical profession; however, in making decisions about treatment, the doctor must act in accordance with a responsible and competent body of relevant professional opinion, on the principles set down in *Bolam v Friern Hospital Management Committee* [1957] 1 WLR 582. No doubt, in practice, a decision may involve others besides the doctor. It must surely be good practice to consult relatives and others who are concerned with the care of the patient.

Sometimes, of course, consultation with a specialist or specialists will be required; and in others, especially where the decision involves more than a purely medical opinion, an inter-disciplinary team will in practice participate in the decision. It is very difficult, and would be unwise for a court to do more than to stress that, for those who are involved in these important and sometimes difficult decisions, the overriding consideration is that they should act in the best interests of the person who suffers from the misfortune of being prevented by incapacity from deciding for himself what should be done to his own body, in his own best interests.

Lords Bridge, Brandon and Jauncey concurred with Lord Goff. Lord Griffiths also concurred on this point.

If the legal justification is the principle of necessity, what test did Lord Goff lay down as the means of determining when treatment would be lawful? Lord Goff decided that the test should be the 'best interests' of the patient. You will notice that Lord Goff decided that a doctor would act 'in the best interests' of a patient if 'a responsible and competent body of relevant professional opinion' would support the doctor's conduct, ie the *Bolam* test. What Lord Goff means by this is that a doctor will behave reasonably when he intervenes to treat an incompetent patient if the *Bolam* test is satisfied. It should be added, however, that Lord Goff placed a gloss upon the *Bolam* test by setting the criteria which must inform the view of the 'responsible and competent body' of medical opinion. Lord Goff identified the criteria as being the 'life, health or well-being' of the patient.

Even more clearly Lord Brandon stated that:

> The operation or other treatment will be in their best interests if, but only if, it is carried out in order either to save their lives, or to ensure improvement or prevent deterioration in their physical or mental health.

Before proceeding to examine how this test of 'best interests' is to be applied in particular circumstances of incompetence, it may be worthwhile to inquire whether Lord Goff's decision to found his judgment on the *Bolam* principle is satisfactory. As we saw in Chapter 4, it can be said that the *Bolam* test hands over to doctors power to establish the legal duty a doctor owes to his patient (*Sidaway v Governors of Bethlem Royal Hospital* [1985] 1 All ER 643 at 649 per Lord Scarman). At the heart of the *Bolam* test is the flawed assumption that the court is concerned with the matter of purely medical judgment. Expert opinion of proper professional practice thus resolves the issue of what a reasonable doctor should do. Arguably, when the issue is whether a reasonable doctor *should* have a lawful justification for treating an adult patient who is incapable of consenting, more than a purely medical judgment is called for. Professional opinion is certainly relevant but should not be determinative (see *supra,* ch 4). Arguably, the court should reserve to itself the ultimate role of determining whether intervention is justified and should, therefore, set a legal test which is less deferential to professional practice.

Lord Mustill put it as follows in *Airedale NHS Trust v Bland* [1993] 1 All ER 821 at 898, when examining the weight to be given to the views of doctors in determining when treatment should end.

> **Lord Mustill:**...I venture to feel some reservations about the application of the principle of civil liability in negligence laid down in [*Bolam*] to decisions on 'best interests' in a field dominated by the criminal law. I accept without difficulty that this principle applies to the ascertainment of the medical raw material such as diagnosis, prognosis and appraisal and patient's cognitive functions. Beyond this point, however, it may be said that the decision is ethical, not medical, and there is no reason in logic why on such a decision the opinions of doctors should be decisive.

Lord Goff (with whom the others agreed) applied *Re F* (see, in particular per Lord Browne-Wilkinson at 882-883 relying on *Bolam*).

Curiously, given his acceptance of *Bolam*, Lord Goff in *Re F*, at the same time, seemed to recognise that the court did indeed have a role:

Lord Goff: It was urged before your Lordships by Mr Ouseley, on behalf of the Mental Health Act Commission (the Commission having been given leave to intervene in the proceedings), that a court vested with the responsibility of making a decision in such a case, having first ensured that an independent second opinion has been obtained from an appropriate consultant of the appropriate speciality, should not, if that second opinion supports the proposal that sterilisation should take place, exercise any independent judgment but should simply follow the opinion so expressed. For my part, I do not think that it is possible or desirable for a court so to exercise its jurisdiction. In all proceedings where expert opinions are expressed, those opinions are listened to with great respect; but, in the end, the validity of the opinion has to be weighed and judged by the court. This applies as much in cases where the opinion involves a question of judgment as it does in those where it is expressed on a purely scientific matter. For a court automatically to accept an expert opinion, simply because it is concurred in by another appropriate expert, would be a denial of the function of the court. Furthermore, the proposal of the Commission is impossible to reconcile with the American and Australian authorities which stress the need for a court decision after a hearing which involves separate representation on behalf of the person upon whom it is proposed to perform the operation. Having said this, I do not feel that the Commission need fear that the opinions of the experts will in any way be discounted. On the contrary, they will be heard with the greatest respect; and, as the present case shows, there is a high degree of likelihood that they will be accepted.

In the Court of Appeal, Neill LJ (with whom Butler-Sloss LJ agreed) also recognised what to him were the drawbacks of applying *Bolam* here:

Neill LJ: With respect, I do not consider that this test is sufficiently stringent. A doctor may defeat a claim of negligence if he establishes that he acted in accordance with a practice accepted at the time as proper by a responsible body of medical opinion skilled in the particular form of treatment in question. This is the test laid down in *Bolam v Friern Hospital Management Committee* [1957] 1 WLR 582. But to say that it is not negligent to carry out a particular form of treatment does not mean that that treatment is necessary. I would define necessary in this context as that which the general body of medical opinion in the particular specialty would consider to be in the best interests of the patient in order to maintain the health and to secure the well-being of the patient. One cannot expect unanimity but it should be possible to say of an operation which is necessary in the relevant sense that it would be unreasonable in the opinion of most experts in the field not to make the operation available to the patient. One must consider the alternatives to an operation and the dangers or disadvantages to which the patient may be exposed if no action is taken. The question becomes: what action does the patient's health and welfare require?

You will notice that Neill LJ still looks to professional practice though, for him, the 'general body' of medical opinion must approve of the intervention rather than 'a' body of medical opinion.

Whatever the merits of departure to some extent from the *Bolam* test, Lord Goff's flirtation in *Re F* with this approach was not indulged in by the other members of the House of Lords. The four other Law Lords tested the legality of an intervention solely on the basis of the *Bolam* test (per Lord Bridge at 52; Lord Brandon at 66–67; Lord Griffiths at 69; Lord Jauncey at 83–84. See also, *Re S (hospital patient: court's jurisdiction)* [1995] Fam 26 (Hale J)).

An explanation of this reluctance to go beyond *Bolam* lies in the judges' desire to link the scope of a doctor's duty to his incompetent patient with the scope of the legal justification for *treating* an incompetent patient. Since the former is to be judged on the basis of the *Bolam* test, so must the latter. Lord Brandon put it thus:

In many cases, however, it will not only be lawful for doctors, on the ground of necessity, to operate on or give other medical treatment to adult patients disabled from giving their consent; it will also be their common law duty to do so.

In the case of adult patients made unconscious by an accident or otherwise, they will normally be received into the casualty department of a hospital, which thereby undertakes the care of them. It will then be the duty of the doctors at that hospital to use their best endeavours to do, by way of either an operation or other treatment, that which is in the best interests of such patients.

Reiterating this approach of mirroring the doctor's duty to his patient in the test for judging the legality of the intervention, Lord Bridge stated:

> It would be intolerable for members of the medical, nursing and other professions devoted to the care of the sick that, in caring for those lacking the capacity to consent to treatment they should be put in the dilemma that, if they administer the treatment which they believe to be in the patient's best interests, acting with due skill and care, they run the risk of being held guilty of trespass to the person, but if they withhold that treatment, they may be in breach of a duty of care owed to the patient. If those who undertake responsibility for the care of incompetent or unconscious patients administer curative or prophylactic treatment which they believe to be appropriate to the patient's existing condition of disease, injury or bodily malfunction or susceptibility to such a condition in the future, the lawfulness of that treatment should be judged by one standard, not two. It follows that if the professionals in question have acted with due skill and care, judged by the well known test laid down in *Bolam v Friern Hospital Management Committee* [1957] 1 WLR 582, they should be immune from liability in trespass, just as they are immune from liability in negligence.

There are a number of objections to this view. First, it presumes that there is a pre-existing duty owed by a doctor to the incompetent person. Although usually such a duty will be owed, there are circumstances in which this will not be the case, as Lord Goff pointed out:

> ...I feel bound to express my opinion that, in principle, the lawfulness of the doctor's action is, at least in its origin, to be found in the principle of necessity. This can perhaps be seen most clearly in cases where there is no continuing relationship between doctor and patient. The 'doctor in the house' who volunteers to assist a lady in the audience who, overcome by the drama or by the heat in the theatre, has fainted away, is impelled to act by no greater duty that that imposed by his own Hippocratic oath. Furthermore, intervention can be justified in the case of a non-professional, as well as a professional, man or woman who has no pre-existing relationship with the assisted person – as in the case of a stranger who rushes to assist an injured man after an accident. In my opinion, it is the necessity itself which provides the justification for the intervention.

Thus, to define the scope of the justification for intervention in terms of the pre-existing duty would be to limit the justification too narrowly.

Secondly, whatever the position as regards duty, to express the scope of the justification in terms of *Bolam* effectively makes what is an issue of legal principle become a matter of medical evidence. That is to say that whether conduct is justified must rest on principle not on professional practice.

Thirdly, it could be argued that the judges were unduly blinded by the language of duty. The primary issue should be, first, whether the intervention is legal and, secondly, whether the doctor is in breach of his duty to the patient. So, if the patient were competent a precondition would be the need for the patient's consent. Here, given that the patient is incompetent, his consent cannot be a precondition. It seems, however, that the law has finally turned a corner. The Court of Appeal has now decisively rejected the application of *Bolam* to determine the 'best interests' of an incompetent patient. In *Re S (adult: sterilisation)* (2000) Times, 26 May, the Court of Appeal was concerned with an application to carry out a partial hysterectomy on a mentally incompetent adult woman because of the effects menstruation was said to have upon her. In refusing a declaration that the procedure was in her 'best interests' and lawful, the Court of Appeal rejected the trial judge's reliance upon *Bolam* to determine that either a hysterectomy or the fitting of an IUD would be in her best interests. The judges relied upon the views of Butler-Sloss P in an earlier decision of the court in 2000 in *Re A (medical treatment: male sterilisation)* [2000] 1 FCR 193 (discussed *infra*, ch 9).

Re S (adult: sterilisation) (2000) Times, 26 May (CA)

Butler-Sloss P: the doctor, it seems to me, has two duties. I said in *Re A (medical treatment: male sterilisation)* (1999) 53 BMLR 66 at 72-73]:

Another question which arises from the decision in *F v West Berkshire Health Authority* is the relationship of best interests to the '*Bolam* test'. Doctors charged with the decisions about the future treatment of patients and whether such treatment would, in the cases of those lacking capacity to make their own decisions, be in their best interests, have to act at all times in accordance with a responsible and competent body of relevant professional opinion. That is the professional standard set for those who make such decisions. The doctor, acting to that required standard, has, in my view, a second duty, that is to say, he must act in the best interests of a mentally incapacitated patient. I do not consider that the two duties have been conflated into one requirement. To that extent I disagree with the passage in the Law Commission's Report on Mental Incapacity (Law Com No 231) (1995) p 43, para 3.26 and I prefer the alternative suggestion in footnote 40.

I would suggest that the starting point of any medical decision would be the principles enunciated in the *Bolam* test and that a doctor ought not to make any decision about a patient that does not fall within the broad spectrum of the *Bolam* test. The duty to act in accordance with responsible and competent professional opinion may give the doctor more than one option since there may well be more than one acceptable medical opinion. When the doctor moves on to consider the best interests of the patient he/she has to choose the best option, often from a range of options. As Mr Munby has pointed out, the best interests test ought, logically, to give only one answer.

In these difficult cases where the medical profession seeks a declaration as to lawfulness of the proposed treatment, the judge, not the doctor, has the duty to decide whether such treatment *is* in the best interests of the patient. The judicial decision ought to provide the best answer not a range of alternative answers. There may, of course, be situations where the answer may not be obvious and alternatives may have to be tried. It is still at any one point the best option of that moment which should be chosen.

I recognise that there is distinguished judicial dicta to the contrary in the speech of Lord Browne-Wilkinson in *Airedale NHS Trust v Bland* [1993] AC 789 at page 884. The passage in his speech was not however followed by the other members of the House. Hale J in *Re S (Hospital Patient: Court's jurisdiction)* [1995] Fam 26 at page 32 followed the same approach. She said that, in accordance with the *Bolam* test, it followed that a number of different courses may be lawful in any particular case. That may be so, but I do not read *re F* (above), upon which she relied, as relieving the judge who is deciding the best interests of the patient from making a choice between the available options. I respectfully disagree with Lord Browne-Wilkinson and Hale J. I have had the opportunity to read Thorpe LJ's judgment in draft and I agree with his analysis. As I have set out earlier in this judgment, the principle of best interests as applied by the court extends beyond the considerations set out in *Bolam* (above). The judicial decision will incorporate broader ethical, social, moral and welfare considerations . . .

The question . . . for the judge, was not the proposed treatment within the range of acceptable opinion among competent and responsible practitioners, but was it in the best interests of S? The *Bolam* test was, in my view, irrelevant to the judicial decision, once the judge was satisfied that the range of options was within the range of acceptable opinion among competent and responsible practitioners. If it was not, I would hope a surgeon would not operate, even if a declaration *was* given by the court . . .

Mance LJ agreed.

Thorpe LJ also agreed with the President and added the following important remarks about the relationship of *Bolam* to the 'best interests' test.

Thorpe LJ: 3. The *Bolam* test was of course developed in order to enable courts to determine the boundaries of medical responsibility for treatment that has gone wrong, and usually disastrously wrong. So at first blush it would seem an unlikely import in determining the best interests of an adult too disabled to decide for him or herself. True the decision relates to whether or not the adult should receive medical treatment but that is not treatment already delivered but treatment prospectively available and the medical opinion under judicial review is likely to be forensic rather than from a doctor as part of a treatment package . . .

6. . . . Whilst the decision in *Re F* signposted the inadvertent loss of the parens patriae jurisdiction in relation to incompetent adults, the alternative jurisdiction which it established, the declaratory decree, was to be exercised upon the same basis, namely that relief would be granted if the welfare of the patient required it and equally refused if the welfare of the patient did not.

7. I would therefore accept Mr Munby's submission that in determining the welfare of the patient the *Bolam* test is applied only at the outset to ensure that the treatment proposed is recognised as proper by a responsible body of medical opinion skilled in delivering that particular treatment. That may be a necessary check in an exercise where it would be

impossible to be over scrupulous. But I find it hard to imagine in practice a disputed trial before a judge of the Division in which a responsible party proposed for an incompetent patient a treatment that did not satisfy the *Bolam* test. In practice the dispute will generally required the court to choose between two or more possible treatments both or all of which comfortably pass the *Bolam* test. As most of us know from experience a patient contemplating treatment for a physical condition or illness is often offered a range of alternatives with counter-balancing advantages and disadvantages. One of the most important services provided by a consultant is to explain the available alternatives to the patient, particularly concentrating on those features of advantage and disadvantage most relevant to his needs and circumstances. In a developing relationship of confidence the consultant then guides the patient to make the choice that best suits his circumstances and personality. It is precisely because the patient is prevented by disability from that exchange that the judge must in certain circumstances either exercise the choice between alternative available treatments or perhaps refuse any form of treatment. In deciding what is best for the disabled patient the judge must have regard to the patient's welfare as the paramount consideration. That embraces issues far wider than the medical. Indeed it would be undesirable and probably impossible to set bounds to what is relevant to a welfare determination. In my opinion *Bolam* has no contribution to make to this second and determinative stage of the judicial decision.

8. . . . . It is simply not helpful for either the family or the doctors to be presented with a declaration that two or more possible treatments are lawful on the grounds that both or all satisfied the *Bolam* test. It is the judge's function to declare that treatment which is in the best interests of the patient and, as Mr Munby submits, only one treatment can be best.

The Court of Appeal's decision brings welcome clarity and coherence to this area of the law. The judges make clear that *their* role whether when exercising the court's *parens patriae* jurisdiction or its declaratory jurisdiction in *to decide what is in the patient's best interest. Bolam* does not more than re-assure the court that the alternatives it has to chose between are medically appropriate. But, the decision goes much further. As Butler-Sloss P makes clear, *Bolam* and 'best interests' are also different for the primary decision-making; here the doctor (after *Re F*) but elsewhere others such as parents. The duties of the doctor are two-fold: (1) the duty *of care* – to exercise reasonable care and skill (*Bolam*); and (2) the duty *to care* – by acting in the patient's best interests. Although Thorpe LJ's judgment is, on the whole, concerned with the court's function, there is no doubt that he too agrees with the more explicit remarks of Butler-Sloss P in *Re S* and also in the earlier case of *Re A*, in which he also sat.

(For the use of force and restraint for treatment in the incompetent patient's best interests see *supra* and *R v Bournewood Community and Mental Health NHS Trust, ex p L* (1998) 44 BMLR 1 (HL).)

Having considered the principles on which the justification for intervention may be based it is helpful to refer to the three types of situation in which medical intervention may take place: (1) emergencies; (2) the temporarily incompetent; (3) the permanently incompetent. While the principle remains the same in each of these, the application may vary in the sense that greater intervention may be justified in, for instance, the case of the permanently incompetent than the temporarily incompetent.

1. Emergencies

As Lord Goff stated in *Re F*:

Emergency is however not the criterion or even a pre-requisite; it is simply a frequent origin of the necessity which impels intervention. The principle is one of necessity, not of emergency.

Lord Goff gave examples of the situations in which an emergency would justify medical intervention:

Take the example of a railway accident, in which injured passengers are trapped in the wreckage. It is this principle which may render lawful the actions of other citizens – railway staff, passengers or outsiders – who rush to give aid and comfort to the victims: the surgeon who amputates the limb of an unconscious passenger to free him from the wreckage; the ambulance man who conveys him to hospital; the doctors and nurses who treat him and care for him while he is still unconscious.

In the Court of Appeal in *Re F*, Butler-Sloss LJ explained the emergency situation as follows:

> **Butler-Sloss LJ:** Logically the well known exception of emergency or necessity might be difficult to justify. It is, however, well-established by decisions both in the United States and Canada. In *Pratt v Davis* (1906) 224 Ill 300, 309, Scott CJ said:
>
> > Emergencies arise, and when a surgeon is called it is sometimes found that some action must be taken immediately for the preservation of the life or health of the patient, where it is impracticable to obtain the consent of the ailing or injured one or of anyone authorised to speak for him. In such event, the surgeon may lawfully, and it is his duty to, perform such operation as good surgery demands, without such consent.
>
> Chisholm CJ in *Marshall v Curry* [1933] 3 DLR 260, 275, ruled:
>
> > it is the surgeon's duty to act in order to save life or preserve the health of the patient; and that in the honest execution of that duty he should not be exposed to legal liability.
>
> He found that the removal of the diseased testicle by the surgeon was:
>
> > in the interest of his patient and for the protection of his health and possibly his life. The removal I find was in that sense necessary, and it would be unreasonable to postpone the removal to a later date.
>
> In *Murray v McMurchy* [1949] 2 DLR 442, where the decision went the other way, Macfarlane J said at pp 443–444:
>
> > I think the law is clear that if that [sterilisation operation] were necessary as opposed to being convenient, for the protection of the life or even for the preservation of the health of the patient, the surgeon would be entitled to take the intended procedure.
>
> The Court of Appeal in *Wilson v Pringle* [1987] QB 237 interpreted the category formulated by Robert Goff LJ of 'all physical contact which is generally acceptable in the ordinary conduct of daily life' to include an emergency operation on an unconscious patient. I find it difficult in accepting that interpretation and would prefer to see the emergency cases as a separate category based on the American approach that, in situations where a patient of full mental competence is unable to give consent, an operation necessary for the preservation of life or for the preservation of health of the patient not only can but should be performed. It does not appear to me to be based on implied consent but on public policy that it is in the public interest that unconscious patients requiring emergency treatment should be able to receive it and that doctors giving it should not be liable in tort.

Neill LJ also considered emergencies.

> **Neill LJ:** To the general rule that the patient's consent must be obtained before an operation can be carried out there is one well-recognised exception. Thus, if a patient is unconscious and therefore unable to give or to withhold his consent, emergency medical treatment which may include surgical procedures can be lawfully carried out. Indeed, once the care of the patient has been assumed by, for example, admission into hospital, a failure to give necessary treatment may well be a ground for complaint. The treatment which can be so given, however, is, within broad limits, confined to such treatment as is necessary to meet the emergency and such as needs to be carried out at once and before the patient is likely to be in a position to make a decision for himself…
>
> For my part, I would prefer to explain the emergency cases on the basis that it is in the public interest that an unconscious patient who requires treatment should be able to receive it and that those who give this treatment in an emergency should be free from any threat of an action for trespass to the person.

You will notice that Neill LJ is careful to identify the limits to that which may be justified in an emergency, ie that it is both *necessary* and *cannot be reasonably delayed*.

2. The temporarily incompetent

In a sense, the analysis of this category may be no different from emergencies, namely that a temporarily incompetent may only be treated to the extent that it is both necessary and cannot reasonably be delayed. Lord Goff considered (though left open) this category in *Re F*.

> **Lord Goff:** Where, for example, a surgeon performs an operation without his consent on a patient temporarily rendered unconscious in an accident, he should do no more than is reasonably required, in the best interests of the patient, before he recovers consciousness. I can see no practical difficulty arising from this requirement, which derives from the fact that the patient is expected before long to regain consciousness and can then be consulted about longer term measures. The point has however arisen in a more acute form where a surgeon, in the course of an operation, discovers some other condition which, in his opinion, requires operative treatment for which he has not received the patient's consent. In what circumstances he should operate forthwith, and in which circumstances he should postpone the further treatment until he has received the patient's consent, is a difficult matter which has troubled the Canadian Courts (see *Marshall v Curry* [1933] 3 DLR 260, and *Murray v McMurchy* [1949] 2 DLR 442), but which it is not necessary for your Lordships to consider in the present case.

The Canadian cases referred to by Lord Goff and Butler-Sloss LJ *supra* probably reflect English law. Ellen Picard and Gerald Robertson explain the Canadian law in their textbook *Legal Liability of Doctors and Hospitals in Canada* (3rd edn, 1986) (pp 51–52):

> In *Marshall v Curry* [1933] 3 DLR 260, the doctor discovered a grossly diseased testicle in the course of a hernia repair operation. He removed the testicle, firstly because it was necessary for the hernia repair, and secondly because he judged it potentially gangrenous and therefore a menace to the patient's life and health. Because the patient was under general anaesthetic, the doctor proceeded without consent, and subsequently was sued for battery. Prior to this case it had been held that in emergencies, the doctor became the patient's representative with authority to give his consent on the patient's behalf. Here the court refused to employ this reasoning and instead justified the doctor's action in emergency circumstances on 'the higher ground of duty'. The Chief Justice of Nova Scotia said that 'where a great emergency which could not be anticipated arises' a doctor can act without consent in order to save the life or preserve the health of the patient. The action against the doctor was dismissed.
>
> However, in *Murray v McMurchy* [1949] 2 DLR 442 (BCSC), a doctor who tied a patient's fallopian tubes because he had discovered fibroid tumours in the uterine wall during a Caesarian section, and was concerned about the hazards of a second pregnancy, was held liable. The trial judge found that while it was convenient to carry out the procedure at that time, there was no evidence that the tumours were an immediate danger to the patient's life or health.
>
> Similarly, in *Parmley v Parmley and Yule* [1945] 4 DLR 81 (SCC), in which a patient requested the removal of two teeth and the defendant dentist extracted all of her upper teeth because he found advanced tooth decay and pyorrhoea in the gums, the court held the dentist liable. Again there was no evidence of emergency and thus no basis for proceeding without consent. However, an important *obiter* comment was made in the case:
>
> > There are times under circumstances of emergency when both doctors and dentists must exercise their professional skill and ability without the consent which is required in the ordinary case. Upon such occasions *great latitude may be given to the doctor or dentist* [emphasis supplied].
>
> These cases indicate that Canadian courts differentiate between a procedure that is 'necessary' and one that is 'convenient'. Consent is expendable only where the procedure or treatment is immediately necessary in order to save life or preserve health. Consent is required on all other occasions and it is no answer for the doctor to say that it was more convenient to perform the unauthorised procedure at that time, or that he or she believed that the patient would have wanted it done then.

3.   The permanently incompetent

Here, the very situation considered in *Re F*, the range of interventions justified in law may be greater because the doctor cannot wait and see what the patient may subsequently be prepared to consent to. In *Re F* Lord Goff acknowledged this.

> **Lord Goff:** Take the example of an elderly person who suffers a stroke which renders him incapable of speech or movement. It is by virtue of this principle that the doctor who treats him, the nurse who cares for him, even the relative or friend or neighbour who comes in to look after him, will commit no wrong when he or she touches his body…

Another example…is that of a mentally disordered person who is disabled from giving consent. I can see no good reason why the principle of necessity should not be applicable in his case as it is in the case of the victim of a stroke. Furthermore, in the case of a mentally disordered person, as in the case of a stroke victim, the permanent state of affairs calls for a wider range of care than may be requisite in an emergency which arises from accidental injury. When the state of affairs is permanent, or semi-permanent, action properly taken to preserve the life, health or well-being of the assisted person may well transcend such measures as surgical operation or substantial medical treatment and may extend to include such humdrum matters as routine medical or dental treatment, even simple care such as dressing and undressing and putting to bed…where the state of affairs is permanent or semi-permanent, as may be so in the case of a mentally disordered person, there is no point in waiting to obtain the patient's consent. The need to care for him is obvious; and the doctor must then act in the best interests of his patient, just as if he had received his patient's consent so to do. Were this not so, much useful treatment and care could, in theory at least, be denied to the unfortunate.

Importantly, you may notice an inconsistency between the court's apparent adoption of the *Bolam* test as setting the scope of the justification and what the court says as regards intervention in an emergency and where the patient is only temporarily incompetent. As regards the later situations, *the court* sets limits as to what is permissible. By so doing, the court enumerates the criteria which determine the legality of intervention. In any particular case, medical opinion will determine whether these criteria were in fact met, ie whether it was proper for the doctor to consider that the patient's life was threatened or that the treatment could be delayed. The onus, therefore, is thrust upon the doctor to demonstrate that there was an emergency in the sense defined by the courts. By contrast, as regards the permanently incompetent, arguably Lord Goff relies entirely upon the *Bolam* test (but see *supra.*).

Before we leave this discussion of *Re F*, there is one point of general importance that we should deal with. The analysis so far has proceeded upon the basis of the language used by the court in *Re F*: the language of *necessity*. Arguably, it is possible to understand this area of law by recourse to a more general, but at the same time, more familiar justification, namely that of the *public interest*. The significance of seeing the justification of medical interventions on the incompetent adult as depending on the public interest is that it focuses attention upon the need to balance conflicting interests. These must not be seen as the interests of the individual (private interests) as against the interests of society (public interests). Rather, the conflict or tension must be seen as being between competing *public interests*, ie the public interest in protecting the bodily integrity of a patient as against the public interest in caring for a patient who cannot care for himself. Neill LJ's judgment in *Re F* is significant here.

Neill LJ: For my part, I would prefer to explain the emergency cases on the basis that it is in the public interest that an unconscious patient who requires treatment should be able to receive it and that those who give this treatment in an emergency should be free from any threat of an action for trespass to the person…

The law in this field is concerned to achieve a balance between different rights and duties. The doctor who has undertaken the care of a patient is under a duty to offer such appropriate treatment as is available. The patient has the right to be offered that treatment, though the conscious patient over the age of 16 has the right, certainly in the vast majority of cases, either to accept or to refuse it. Where, however, the patient is unconscious, the right either to accept or to refuse the treatment is valueless. Moreover, except in the case of a child, there is in the ordinary way no one who is able to exercise the right on the patient's behalf. In such circumstances the public interest in my judgment provides the justification for the treatment.

Of course, others may argue for another set of general principles – those of human rights. These do not so readily allow for balancing, although some balancing at some point cannot be avoided. Reliance on human rights alerts us to the danger intrinsic in the process of balancing whereby the balance will be struck in a way which gives inadequate weight to the individual patient's interests.

Balancing of interests is unavoidable in the case of treating the incompetent. If the overarching principle is that of regard for the *public interest*, involving a balancing of competing interests, there is a real danger that *the same balancing process*, used in the context of the incompetent patient, may be prayed in aid also in the case of the *competent patient*. The consequences could be that a competent patient who is refusing treatment could be required to submit to treatment on the grounds that it was in the public interest that the treatment be given. Lord Donaldson MR adopted this approach in *Re T (refusal of treatment)* [1992] 4 All ER 649 (see *infra*).

C. A NEW STATUTORY SCHEME

The current position regarding the decision-making process in respect of incompetent adults is unsatisfactory. As best, the courts have fashioned a quasi-proxy, ie the doctor. But, it is not clear that doctors should be left to make these sorts of decisions, if only because the doctor may genuinely feel torn between his desire to respect the interests of the patient and his desire to intervene and render assistance from a general commitment of going good. Further, if the goal of the law is to seek to ensure, so far as practicable, that a proxy decision conforms to the views and values of the patient, the doctor may not generally be best placed to reach such a determination. Of course, in some cases he may be. However, usually such a decision would be better made by someone close to the patient. To this end, therefore, three options present themselves. First, the law could allow a patient to appoint his chosen health care proxy. This option would require legislative change. Secondly, in default of this, the law could presume those close to the patient to be proxies best able to know the patient's likely choice of health care. As we have seen, this is not directly reflected in the common law. Thirdly, if there is no one else then the law could recognise that the doctor must of necessity act, as he sees fit, in the patient's 'best interests'. As we have seen, what is arguably the 'default position', in fact applies universally under the common law after *Re F*.

So too are there problems with the court's involvement. Whilst the common law has fashioned in *Re F* the so-called 'declaratory procedure' in the incompetent adult cases, the courts lack the power *to decide*: to give or refuse consent to a medical procedure on behalf of the incompetent adult. For many this is undesirable and places the court under the undue handicap (see eg *Airedale NHS Trust v Bland* (1993) 12 BMLR 64 at 122 per Lord Lowry).

In 1989 the Law Commission embarked on a comprehensive review of decision-making and incompetent adults. In 1991 it published a consultation paper (*Mental Incapacitated Adults and Decision-Making: An Overview* Paper No 119) followed by three further, more honed consultation papers in 1993 (*Mentally Incapacitated Adults and Decision-Making: a New Jurisdiction* Paper No 128; *Mentally Incapacitated Adults and Decision-Making: Medical Treatment and Research* Paper No 129; and *Mentally Incapacitated and Other Vulnerable Adults: Public Law Protection* Paper No 130). Finally, in 1995 the Law Commission published its final Report, *Mental Incapacity* (No 231), in which it proposed a comprehensive legislative scheme for decision-making, *inter alia*, in respect of medical treatment and other procedures such as research. The political process, however, led the Lord Chancellor's Department to issue a further consultation document, *Who Decides?* (Cm 3803), in 1997 and its concluded views on reforming the law in 1999, *Making Decisions* (Cm 4465).

The proposals address a number of issues: (i) the nature of incapacity; (ii) the effect of 'anticipatory decisions' of patients; (iii) the creation of a statutory scheme for the appointment of health care proxies; (iv) the role (and limits) of doctors as decision-makers; (v) the role of relatives in decision-making; and (vi) the role of the court. For our purposes, we will consider a number of the issues here. We have already considered the material on 'incapacity' in Chapter 5. We will take account of the recommendations on 'anticipatory decisions' and 'health care proxies' in Chapter 16. At the outset we should notice that the Government, in *Making Decisions* (*supra*), has not accepted a number of key recommendations of the Law Commission, for example, the need for legislation on anticipated refusals of treatment and in respect of so-called 'special procedures' which the Law Commission considered required particular safeguards for patients (paras 12–20).

What then would the Law Commission's scheme look like? (For discussions, see P Wilson 'The Law Commission's Report on Mental Incapacity: Medically Vulnerable Adults or Politically Vulnerable Law?' (1996) 4 Med L Rev 227; J McHale 'Mental Incapacity: Some Proposals for Legislative Reform' (1998) 24 Journal of Medical Ethics 322; and A Grubb '*Who Decides?* Legislating for the Incapacitated Adult' (1998) 5 European Journal of Health Law 231.)

1. The general authority

At the heart of the legislative scheme would be the 'general authority to act reasonably' which, in the context we are concerned with, would allow a doctor or other health care professional to treat a patient who lacked capacity in that patient's best interests. In essence, *Re F* would be given a statutory basis. The Law Commission rejected the idea that relatives or others close to the patient should have decision-making power (but see below their role under 'best interests').

Law Commission Report No 231 *Mental Incapacity* (1995)

4.1 ...In all three of the broad areas we have identified – personal, medical and financial – there is and should remain scope for some informal decision-making without certifications, documentation or judicial determinations. The present law governing such action is far from clear, but a passage in the speech of Lord Goff in *Re F* is a most helpful general statement of the relevant legal principles. In the context of medical treatment, Lord Goff said that 'the principle of necessity' governed treatment without consent where:

> not only (1) must there be a necessity to act when it is not practicable to communicate with the assisted person, but also (2) the action taken must be such as a reasonable person would in all the circumstances take, acting in the best interests of the assisted person. (*Re F (Mental Patient: Sterilisation)* [1990] 2 AC 1, 75).

If this 'principle of necessity' applies, actions which would otherwise amount to civil wrongs will be lawful (*ibid*, 76). A similar common law 'defence of necessity' may be available to defendants in criminal proceedings.

4.2 We suggested in our consultation papers that there was a strong case for clarifying in statute the circumstances in which decisions can be taken for people who lack capacity, but without anyone having to apply for formal authorisation. (Consultation Paper No 128, para 210; Consultation Paper No 129, para 3.40.) We did not envisage this conferring any new power on anyone, but rather as a clarification of the uncertain 'necessity' principle. Respondents gave an enthusiastic welcome to our provisional proposals. There was very broad agreement that a statutory provision would be invaluable in dispelling doubt and confusion and setting firm and appropriate limits to informal action.

4.3 Lord Goff referred to the assisted person being unable to communicate. We have already dealt in Part III with our recommendation for a more strenuous requirement that the person concerned must *lack capacity* to make his or her own decision. Lack of capacity is decision-specific and the authority of another person to act will be limited to those matters where the person lacks capacity. Equally, we have discussed our recommendation for a statutory version of the 'best interests' criterion, together with a new checklist of factors to elucidate it. It remains for us to address that part of the law comprised in Lord Goff's statement that any 'action taken must be such as a reasonable person would in all the circumstances take.'

4.4   In the consultation papers we provisionally proposed a new statutory authority whereby 'carers' and 'treatment providers' might act reasonably to safeguard and promote the welfare and best interests of a person without capacity. Our original formulation provoked some misunderstanding on consultation, with respondents fearing that disagreements and disputes would arise as to the identity of 'the carer' or 'the treatment provider' in possession of the authority. In fact, reasonable action at the informal level can be taken by a variety of different people. On any one day it might be reasonable for the primary carer to dress the person concerned in suitable clothes, for the district nurse to give a regular injection and nursing care, for a worker from a voluntary organisation to take the person out on a trip and for another family member to bring round the evening meal and help the person to eat it. Just as the common law affords each person whose actions fall within the principle of necessity a defence to a suit for trespass, so a statutory 'general authority' should make the qualifying actions of any such person lawful. It is not, therefore, helpful to suggest that any one person can be defined and identified as the holder of the authority. We consider it preferable to refer to actions which are reasonable for the person doing them to do. This underlines the fact that a number of people may have power to act on any one day. It also serves as a reminder that independent restrictions on who should be taking action are not superseded. Such restrictions might be imposed by employment contracts, by professional rules of conduct or by the law of negligence. In the example given, it would not be reasonable for the district nurse to administer treatment which requires prior authorisation from a registered medical practitioner; nor for the voluntary organisation worker to take actions expressly prohibited by the terms and conditions of his or her employment.

We *recommend* that it should be lawful to do anything for the personal welfare or health care of a person who is, or is reasonably believed to be, without capacity in relation to the matter in question if it is in all the circumstances reasonable for it to be done by the person who does it. (Draft Bill, clause 4(1).)

The obligation to act in the best interests of the person without capacity, having regard to the statutory factors, will immediately apply to anyone purporting to exercise this 'general authority'.

4.5   It would be out of step with our aims of policy, and with the views of the vast majority of the respondents to our overview paper, to have any general system of certifying people as 'incapacitated' and then identifying a substitute decision-maker for them, regardless of whether there is any real need for one. In the absence of certifications or authorisations, persons acting informally can only be expected to have reasonable grounds to believe that (1) the other person lacks capacity in relation to the matter in hand and (2) they are acting in the best interests of that person.

The Law Commission considered there should be limitations on the statutory authority.

Restrictions on the general authority

4.29 One benefit of setting out a clear general authority in statute is that the statute can then specify which matters fall outside the scope of that general authority. The general law already provides that certain acts can only be effected by a person acting for himself or herself. Examples would be entering into marriage or casting a vote in a public election. For the avoidance of doubt, our draft Bill lists certain matters which must be done by a person acting for him or herself.

We *recommend* that no person should be able to make decisions about the following matters on behalf of a person without capacity:

(1) consent to marriage, (2) consent to have sexual relations, (3) consent to a divorce petition on the basis of two years separation, (4) agreement to adoption or consent to freeing a child for adoption, (5) voting at an election for any public office or (6) discharging parental responsibilities except in relation to a child's property. (Draft Bill, clause 30.)

In many areas, however, it is at present quite unclear whether action may lawfully be taken on behalf of a person without capacity. If no-one is sure what can lawfully be done, then no-one can be sure what cannot and must not be done. We will now consider a number of actions which should never be lawful simply on the basis of the broad general authority to act reasonably in another's best interests.

(1) Coercion and confinement

4.30 We suggested in our consultation papers that a person without capacity should not be forced to comply with a proposed action to which he or she objects without the authorisation of a judicial body. In the light of concern about restraint techniques which are adopted to prevent disruptive or risk-taking behaviour by disabled people, we also suggested that there should be a general prohibition against the confinement of a person without capacity. In each case, we suggested a proviso where the coercive or confining action was essential to prevent an immediate risk of serious harm to the person concerned or to others. As we explain below, we are now persuaded that no reference to harm to *others* is called for in any new provision, since this contingency is adequately covered in the existing law.

4.31 Our respondents confirmed that a line has to be found between justifiable protection and persuasion of people who have impaired decision-making capacity on the one hand and unjustified restraint or coercion, including mental coercion, on the other. The general law already draws certain lines. Most acts of confinement or coercion will amount to criminal offences and/or civil wrongs. The criminal law allows various defences where the act of coercion or confinement is justified by 'duress of circumstances', self-defence or the prevention of crime. The defence of consent will, however, often be more relevant if the reality is that the coercive or confining action was intended to protect the 'victim' himself or herself. Where, in the cases we are considering, the person against whom the coercive or confining action is directed lacks the capacity to consent, then the law may bite against a well-meaning carer in an unduly harsh way. The uncertain defence on necessity may be all that the carer can hope to rely on. Conversely, however, the uncertain defence of necessity might, in some circumstances, give an unduly broad latitude to those who decide to confine or coerce those under their care. Some of our consultees confidently asserted that locking a door on a demented residential is illegal, but we doubt the accuracy of this claim. Others expressed concern about the lawfulness of 'time out' techniques, which can involve both confinement and coercion, used i some behavioural therapies. Taking into account that *Re F* (*Re F* (*Mental Patient: Sterilisation*) [1990] 2 AC 1) established that a major abdominal operation with irreversible effects was lawful according to the principle of necessity, it is highly likely that in appropriate circumstances acts of confinement or coercion could equally be found lawful if performed 'in the best interests of' the person concerned. In any event, it is clear and hardly surprising that many people with day-to-day care of other people who lack capacity have no idea what actions they may or may not take within the law. Our consultees confirmed that there is a pressing need for this lack of clarity to be resolved.

4.32 We saw some force in the arguments put forward by some of our expert legal respondents, to the effect that any stipulation about confinement and coercion would be redundant, since the proposed general authority is already constrained by the notions of both reasonableness and best interests. We also took careful note of the views of those professional and family carers who argued that enactment of the 'high principle' that confinement and coercion are unlawful would mean many homes and hospitals grinding to a standstill. We reject, however, the suggestion made by a small number of respondents, that no 'objection' by a person without capacity need be given any credence. There is an important distinction between a person passively acquiescing in something and a person who raises positive objections, whether in words or by actions, and therefore has to be subjected to physical force to secure compliance.

4.33 We have concluded that two important messages can be conveyed by a new statutory provision about confinement and coercion. First, the fact that the civil liberties of people without capacity are regularly infringed by coercive and restraining treatment can be challenged by the introduction of a statutory prohibition against such treatment expressed in clear terms. On the other hand, however, the difficult realities of the caring situation can be addressed by a clear statement of the circumstances in which coercive or confining behaviour will in fact be justified. This will provide reassurance to people who can at present only rely on common law defences whose scope and very existence are known only to a select band of legal experts.

We *recommend* that the general authority to provide care to a person without capacity should not authorise the use or threat of force to enforce the doing of anything to which that person objects; nor should it authorise the detention or confinement of that person, whether or not he or she objects. This provision is not to preclude the taking of steps which are necessary to avert a substantial risk of serious harm to the person concerned. (Draft Bill, clause 5.)

We are concerned here with informal acts and decision-making. If the court or a court-appointed manager has taken a decision after due consideration and due process then that decision should of course be capable of being enforced in the usual way.

(2) The superior authority of an attorney or manager

4.34 Informal action is only justifiable where it is not in conflict with a judicial decision, or a decision by a person with formal legal powers. The general authority should not validate an action which conflicts with a decision made by an attorney acting under a valid power of attorney or by a manager appointed by the court. Situations may, however, arise where a person without formal authority seeks to challenge some decision by that attorney or manager, on the basis that it is not in the best interests of the person without capacity. In most circumstances, the formal decision-maker's authority will stand until the court removes it, whether by revoking a power of attorney or varying or discharging an order appointing a manager. Special provision needs to be made for those unusual situations where the decision of the person with formal authority would lead to the death of the person without capacity before the court can issue any determination. In those circumstances, the person without formal authority should be entitled to take minimal steps to maintain the other person's life.

We *recommend* that the general authority should not authorise the doing of anything which is contrary to the directions of, or inconsistent with a decision made by, an attorney or manager acting within the scope of his or her authority. However, this restriction will not apply to actions necessary to prevent the death of, or a serious deterioration in the condition of, the person concerned while an order is being sought from the court. (Draft Bill, clause 6.)

(3)   The superior authority of an advance refusal of treatment
4.35 The topic of 'advance directives' for health care was considered in detail in Consultation Paper No 129 and we discuss our recommendations in Part V below. It should be noted here that, in relation to health care decisions, an effective anticipatory refusal of treatment will restrict the scope of the general authority to treat.

(4)   Independent supervision in health care matters
4.36 There was unanimous agreement from our consultees that certain serious and controversial health care procedures should always be subject to independent supervision. Special provisions, which we will discuss in Part VI below, will therefore restrict the scope of the informal general authority in particular cases.

We will return to these latter recommendations shortly when we consider the Law Commission's proposals on 'special procedures'.

Clauses 4–6 of the Mental Incapacity Bill gave effect to these recommendations.

4. – (1) Subject to the provisions of this Chapter, it shall be lawful to do anything for the personal welfare or health care of a person who is, or is reasonably believed to be, without capacity in relation to the matter in question ('the person concerned') if it is in all the circumstances reasonable for it to be done by the person who does it.
   (2) Where what is done by virtue of this section involves expenditure it shall be lawful—
   (a) for that purpose to pledge the credit of the person concerned; and
   (b) to apply money in the possession of the person concerned for meeting the expenditure;
and if the expenditure is borne for him by another person that person shall be entitled to reimburse himself out of any such money or to be otherwise indemnified by the person concerned.
   (3) Subsection (2) above is without prejudice to any power to spend money for the benefit of the person concerned which is exercisable apart from this section by virtue of having lawful control of money or other property of his.
   (4) Schedule 1 to this Act shall have effect for enabling certain payments which would otherwise be made to a person without capacity to be made instead to a person acting on his behalf or to be otherwise dealt with as provided in that Schedule.

Restrictions on general authority
   5. – (1) Subject to subsection (2) below, section 4 above does not authorise—
   (a) the use or threat of force to enforce the doing of anything to which the person concerned objects; or
   (b) the detention or confinement of that person whether or not he objects.
   (2) This section does not preclude the taking of any steps necessary to avert a substantial risk of serious harm to the person concerned.
   6. – (1) Subject to subsection (2) below, section 4 above does not authorise the doing of anything for the person concerned which is contrary to directions given, or inconsistent with a decision made, within the scope of his authority by the donee of a continuing power of attorney granted by him or by a manager appointed for him by the court.
   (2) This section does not preclude any action necessary to prevent the death of the person concerned or a serious deterioration in his condition while an order as respects the matter in question is sought from the court.

The Government, in *Making Decisions* (Cm 4465) (1999), accepted the need for legislation (paras 1.14–1.23).

You will notice *three* features of this proposal. First, the authority applies where the patient is *or is reasonably believed* to lack capacity. Secondly, the authority to act is not limited to any particular, or any particular class of, individual. Instead, the issue is whether 'in all the circumstances' it is 'reasonable for it to be done by the person who does it'. The nature of the proposed procedure and the circumstances (is it an emergency? is there a more appropriate professional to do this?) will shape the answer to this question and hence the legality of the intervention. Thirdly, the general authority does not allow for the use of force against an objecting patient or for their detention whether or not they object (cl 5(1)). On the face of it, this would seem to be a departure from the common law where both force (*Re MB (Medical Treatment)* [1997] 2 FLR 426 (CA)) and detention (*R v Bournewood Community Mental Health NHS Trust, ex p L* [1998] 3 All ER 289 (HL)) may be lawful in an incapacitated patient's 'best interests'. However, in fact both may be lawful under the general authority where they are 'necessary to avert a substantial risk of serious harm' (cl 5(2)). In practical terms, this 'limitation on the limitation' on the general authority may well suffice to allow action to be taken wherever it is really called for.

2. 'Best interests'

(a) General application

The Law Commission considered that the common law test should apply to all decision-making under its proposed statutory scheme (except in the case of certain procedures – see *infra*).

> 3.25 We explained in our overview paper that two criteria for making substitute decisions for another adult have been developed in the literature in this field: 'best interests' on the one hand and 'substituted judgment' on the other. In Consultation Paper No 128 we argued that the two were not in fact mutually exclusive and we provisionally favoured a 'best interests' criterion which would contain a strong element of 'substituted judgment'. It had been widely accepted by respondents to the overview paper that, where a person has never had capacity, there is no viable alternative to the 'best interests' criterion. We were pleased to find that our arguments in favour of a 'best interests' criterion found favour with almost all our respondents, with the Law Society emphasising that the criterion as defined in the consultation papers was in fact 'an excellent compromise' between the best interests and substituted judgment approaches.
>
> **We *recommend* that anything done for, and any decision made on behalf of, a person without capacity should be done or made in the best interests of that person.** (Draft Bill, clause 3(1).)

> *The meaning of 'best interests'*
> 3.26 Our recommendation that a 'best interests' criterion should apply throughout our scheme cannot be divorced from a recommendation that statute should provide some guidance to every decision-maker about what the criterion requires. No statutory guidance could offer an exhaustive account of what is in a person's best interests, the intention being that the individual person and his or her individual circumstances should always determine the result. In our 1993 consultation papers, however, we suggested that certain principles of general application would always be relevant. At least insofar as substitute health-care decisions are concerned, the principles we suggested probably involve a significant departure from the present state of the law. This, as set out in *Re F*, appears to provide that a doctor who acts in accordance with an accepted body of medical opinion is both (1) not negligent and (2) acting in the best interests of a patient without capacity (*Re F (Mental Patient: Sterilisation)* [1990] 2 AC 1, 78, *per* Lord Goff of Chieveley). This apparent conflation of the criterion for assessing complaints about professional negligence with the criterion for treating persons unable to consent has been the butt of vehement criticism. No medical professional or body responding to Consultation Paper

No 129 argued in favour of retaining such a definition of 'best interests'. Many were extremely anxious to see some clear and principled guidance given as to what 'best interests' might involve. The British Medical Association, for its part, supported our provisional proposals for statutory guidance 'without reservation'.

3.27 It should be made clear beyond any shadow of a doubt that acting in a person's best interests amounts to something more than not treating that person in a negligent manner. Decisions taken on behalf of a person lacking capacity require a careful, focussed consideration of that person *as an individual.* Judgments as to whether a professional has acted negligently, on the other hand, require a careful, focused consideration of how that particular professional acted as compared with the way in which other reasonably competent professionals would have acted. Lord Mustill, who was both a member of the appellate committee of the House of Lords which decided the case of *Airedale NHS Trust v Bland* ([1993] AC 789) and a member of the House of Lords Select Committee on Medical Ethics, said during oral evidence to the latter committee that '[o]ne of the things that is not very good is that the phrase 'best interests' has been put into play without any description of what it means. This, I think, actually increases the difficulties for the doctors rather than helps to solve them. What is at the back of my mind is whether perhaps Parliament could give some more specific definition of…what are the relevant factors…'.

A checklist of factors

3.28 In putting forward a 'best interests' criterion in our 1993 consultation papers, we linked it to a checklist of factors which should be taken into account by a substitute decision-maker. Respondents were very supportive of the factors we provisionally identified and largely confined themselves to suggesting refinement of detail. In Consultation Paper Nos 128 and 130 we provisionally proposed three factors; broadly, the person's past and present wishes and feelings, the need to encourage the person to participate and the principle of least restrictive option. In Consultation Paper No 129 three slightly different factors were suggested; broadly, the person's past and present wishes and feelings, any more conservative treatment option and the factors the person concerned would have considered. In that paper we also included a specific and separate duty to consult a 'nearest relative' in relation to treatment options. In considering the various fields of decision-making together, we have now developed a single checklist which includes all the elements originally identified as important and commended by consultees. We take this opportunity to repeat some of the general comments made in our report on Guardianship and Custody when we recommended a checklist of factors relevant to the welfare of children. First, that a checklist must not unduly burden any decision-maker or encourage unnecessary intervention; secondly, that it must not be applied too rigidly and should leave room for all considerations relevant in a particular case; thirdly, that it should be confined to major points, so that it can adapt to changing views and attitudes. All these considerations are equally applicable to this project and we have borne them in mind in deciding upon the final content of the checklist we now recommend.

We *recommend* that in deciding what is in a person's best interests regard should be had to:—

(1) the ascertainable past and present wishes and feelings of the person concerned, and the factors that person would consider if able to do so;

(2) the need to permit and encourage the person to participate, or to improve his or her ability to participate, as fully as possible in anything done for and any decision affecting him or her;

(3) the views of other people whom it is appropriate and practicable to consult about the person's wishes and feelings and what would be in his or her best interests;

(4) whether the purpose for which any action or decision is required can be as effectively achieved in a manner less restrictive of the person's freedom of action. (Draft Bill, clause 3(2).)

(1) Wishes, feelings and putative factors

3.29 This first element in the checklist establishes the importance of individual views. Realistically, the former views of a person who is without capacity cannot in every case be determinative of the decision which is now to be made. Past wishes and feelings may in any event conflict with feelings the person is still able to express in spite of incapacity. People who cannot make decisions can still experience pleasure and distress. *Present* wishes and feelings must therefore be taken into account, where necessary balanced with past wishes and feelings. One of the failings of a pure 'substituted judgment' model is the unhelpful idea that a person who cannot make a decision should be treated as if his or her capacity were perfect and unimpaired, and as if present emotions need not also be considered.

3.30 We have included reference to the factors the person 'would have considered' if able to do so. Case law in relation to the powers of the Court of Protection to make a 'statutory will' has already stressed the importance of considering such matters, whether or not the person concerned has ever had capacity in relation to the act in question. It was said that a judge is to consider the antipathies and affections of the particular person concerned. (*Re D (J)* [1982] Ch 237.) If that person has never had a capacity and 'the record of her individual preferences and personality is a blank on which nothing has been written' then the court will assume that she would have been 'a normal decent person, acting in accordance with contemporary standards of morality'. (*Re C (A Patient)* [1991] 3 All ER 866, 870.)

3.31 It is worth pointing out that the factors the person concerned 'would consider' might include altruistic sentiments and concern for others. Some organisations representing unpaid family carers disputed the applicability of a 'best interests' criterion to situations where one family member is voluntarily caring for another. They argued that such careers should not be expected to consider the best interests of the cared-for person to the exclusion of the interests of anyone else, or of the family as a whole. A number of other respondents argued that people who know they are losing capacity can be anxious to ensure that their deeply felt unselfish desires not to burden their loved ones are still respected in the future. Although we do not accept the argument that the best interests criterion itself is inapplicable in family care-giving situations, we do stress that the inclusion of a specific reference to the factors the person without capacity would have considered if able to do so addresses these very points.

(2) Maximum participation

3.32 Respondents agreed that even where a person does not have capacity to make an effective decision, he or she may have an important contribution to make to any decision-making process. Those who work with young adults with learning disabilities were particularly anxious that any lack of capacity should be seen as a situation which could and should be altered. In response to comments from such respondents, this factor now includes reference to encouraging the development of decision-making skills.

(3) Consultation

3.33 A small number of respondents to both Consultation Paper No 128 and Consultation Paper No 129 regretted the fact that we had provisionally rejected the grant of decision-making authority as an automatic consequence of a family relationship. We have described how a small number of respondents also challenged the idea that an unpaid family carer should have to act in the best interests of a person lacking capacity, when the carer's life and interests are intimately bound up with the other person's. While the vast majority of respondents agreed with our approach on both these points, we see the force of the argument that family members should be made visible in the new statutory scheme. This is particularly true for the parents of children born with mental disability, those who live with sufferers from psychotic illnesses and the carers of elderly dementia sufferers. Such family members take on onerous and often distressing responsibilities thereby relieving society as a whole of a heavy burden of care. It has recently been reported that '[t]he vast majority of disabled and older people live in private households, and the majority of these are supported and assisted by their family, friends and neighbours'(G Parker and D Lawton, *'Different Types of Care, Different Types of Carer: Evidence from the General Household Survey'* (1994) p 3, citing G Parker, *With Due Care and Attention: A Review of Research on Informal Care* (2nd ed 1990)). Others, however, doubted whether it was right in principle that a person should have to execute a document in order to displace a statutory right granted against his or her will to a little-liked relative. There was quite widespread concern that the person conducting the consultation should be able, or indeed obliged, to use discretion in identifying appropriate consultees in each individual case. As Robert Francis QC put it, consultation 'in a world of divided families' is necessarily a delicate process. The many helpful comments made on consultation have led us to a less formulaic approach which will still achieve what we and most respondents sought to establish. We can still provide for the person concerned naming in advance a person who is to be consulted. It is also appropriate to mention any person who is engaged in caring for that person. So as to ensure maximum flexibility we have also included reference to any person who is interested in the welfare of the person without capacity. If the person has appointed an attorney who is to retain authority once the donor loses capacity then it is likely that the attorney will be an appropriate consultee, even in relation to matters falling outside the scope of the authority granted by the power of attorney. The same considerations apply where the court has appointed a manager. It is inevitable, on this approach, that the consultee must be a person whom it is 'practicable' and 'appropriate' to consult. This is not to give absolute discretion to the decision-maker. If challenged, decision-makers will have to be prepared to explain why a consultation which they declined to carry out was either impracticable or inappropriate . . .

3.35 The process of consultation should be tied to two matters which already concern the prospective decision-maker. First, a relative, carer or person who is closely involved with the person's life as attorney or manager is very likely to have information about the wishes and feelings of the person concerned which might not otherwise filter through to the decision-maker. If the person who now lacks capacity has taken the trouble to nominate someone whom he or she would like to see consulted, then it is even more likely that this nominee has such information. Someone who is in close contact with the person may also have the ability to interpret non-verbal or idiosyncratic signs which give an indication of the person's present wishes and feelings.

3.36 Secondly, a person who is in close contact with the person concerned may have a valid and important view as to what action or decision would be in that person's best interests. Thus, in addition to assisting in ascertaining *information* about the person's wishes the consultee should be invited to express a *view* on the question of 'best interests'.

(4) The least restrictive option
3.37 This factor addresses the 'least restrictive alternative' principle which has been developed over many years by experts in this field and is now widely recognised and accepted.

Clause 3 of the draft Mental Incapacity Bill provides:

3. – (1) Anything done for, and any decision made on behalf of, a person by virtue of this Part of this Act shall be done or made in his best interests.

(2) In deciding what is in a person's best interests regard shall be had to the following—
(a) so far as ascertainable, his past and present wishes and feelings and the factors which he would consider if he were able to do so;
(b) the need to permit and encourage that person to participate, or to improve his ability to participate, as fully as possible in anything done for and any decision affecting him;
(c) if it is practicable and appropriate to consult them, the views as to that person's wishes and feelings and as to what would be in his best interests of—
   (i) any person named by him as someone to be consulted on those matters;
   (ii) anyone (whether his spouse, a relative, friend or other person) engaged in caring for him or interested in his welfare;
   (iii) the donee of any continuing power of attorney granted by him;
   (iv) any manager appointed for him by the court;
(d) whether the purpose for which any action or decision is required can be as effectively achieved in a manner less restrictive of his freedom of action.

(3) In the case of anything done or a decision made by a person other than the court it shall be a sufficient compliance with subsection (1) above if that person reasonably believes that what he does or decides is in the best interests of the person concerned.

The Government accepted the Law Commission's approach but considered that two further matters should be listed in the factors to be considered (*Making Decisions* (Cm 4465) (1999)):

1.12 Following comments received on consultation, the Government proposes to make provision in legislation for the following additional factors to be taken into account in determining best interests:
   • whether there is a reasonable expectation of the person recovering capacity to make the decision in the reasonably foreseeable future
   • the need to be satisfied that the wishes of the person without capacity were not the result of undue influence.

You will notice that the decision may lawfully be taken in the patient's 'best interests' or where it is 'reasonably believe[d]' to be in the patient's best interests (cl 3(3)). Curiously, the Government thought this latter modification to the common law had wrongly not been included by the Law Commission (see *Making Decisions* (*supra* para 1.16)).

In these proposals, you will see the final rejection of the notion of vesting proxy power in a patient's relatives and also of the 'substituted judgment' test that we discussed at length earlier. Yet, we see that relatives and others close to the patient have a role: they must be consulted where it is 'practicable and appropriate' (cl 3(2)(c)) both to ascertain the patient's wishes and feelings (cl 3(2)(a) and (c)) and *for their own views* on where the patient's 'best interests' lie (cl 3(2)(c)).

The proposals will raise difficulties in applying the statutory test. Some are raised in the following extract.

J V McHale 'Mental incapacity: Some Proposals for Legislative Reform' (1998) 24 Journal of Medical Ethics 322

In *Re F* the House of Lords indicated that while no one had the power to consent on behalf of a patient, treatment was to be given on the basis of necessity, where this was in the 'best interests' of an adult who lacks capacity. Best interests was to be referable to the *Bolam* test of the responsible body of professional practice. The Law Commission examined the possible options – a best interests test or a substituted judgment test, in which the decision is made on the basis of the approach the patient would have taken had he/she had capacity. While opting for the former, the best interests approach which it adopted differed from that of *Re F*. Rather than a *Bolam*-based test the report set out a number of criteria which should be considered when assessing a patient's best interests...

The government accepted these in principle but invited views as to their application in practice. Questions raised include: how should the decision maker deal with any differences of opinion which may arise between those consulted, and how far will health professionals be required to make enquiries of interested parties and what are the legal consequences should they fail to do so. Aware, obviously, of the social and cultural dimensions of the complex decision-making process, the government has invited views as to whether the guidance 'should take into account religious/cultural factors in establishing a person's best interests? If so, how could this most effectively be done?' Furthermore, it was asked to what extent relatives and carers can be expected 'to put the interests of the person without capacity entirely before their own, especially if their own welfare or that of another relative or close friend is at stake'? This highlights the fact that while such treatment decisions focus on the best interests of the individual, in practice, in a case such as the proposed sterilisation of a mentally incompetent woman being cared for by an aging parent, it may be difficult to divorce the individual from the setting within which treatment decisions are made.

Ultimately, it may well be that the concession to patient and relative involvement in determining 'best interests' will be of little effect where the medical opinion favours intervention. Only if two genuinely equal treatment options are available is it likely that the patient's wishes or the relatives' views will 'tip the scales' in favour of a particular treatment which the treating doctor himself does not favour.

(b) Departure from 'best interests'

Finally, the Law Commission considered a number of procedures which it thought, perhaps, should be lawful but which could not be taken if the 'best interests' test were applied.

(i) PVS PATIENTS

The first concerned patients in a persistent (permanent) vegetative state (PVS). We discuss the legality of withdrawing care from PVS patients under the common law in Chapter 17. The Law Commission was concerned that its scheme should not affect the legality of withdrawing artificial nutrition and hydration in the circumstances which had been recognised by the House of Lords in *Airedale NHS Trust v Bland* [1993] AC 789.

Law Commission Report No 231 *Mental Incapacity* (1995)

6.18 ...Questions as to whether a particular treatment or procedure should be initiated can be decided by reference to the general authority and the best interests criterion. The particular difficulty arises where, as in the case of Anthony Bland, feeding was being provided on an ongoing basis and the doctors sought to take the positive step of terminating that provision. It may no longer be in the best interests of such a patient to be fed, but it can equally be argued that it is not in his or her best interests for the feeding to stop. The upshot may be that the status quo must continue, even though all involved in the case take the view that this is undesirable...

The criteria for discontinuing artificial sustenance

6.22 Not all of our consultees agreed with Lord Mustill's view that decisions to discontinue artificial nutrition for a patient in PVS cannot be justified by reference to the patient's 'best interests'. We prefer to avoid any semantic argument and confusion by disapplying the general rule where such decisions are concerned, and concentrating instead on the individual factors in the best interests checklist. Some of these are equally applicable to any decision as to whether cessation of feeding and hydration should occur. This is especially true of the first factor, namely the wishes and feelings of the person, and the factors he or she would have taken into account if able to do so. Equally important may be the third factor, namely the views of any of the persons who should be consulted as to the patient's wishes and best interests.

We *recommend* that where the court, an attorney, a manager or an independent medical practitioner decides on discontinuance of artificial sustenance for an unconscious patient with no activity in the cerebral cortex and no prospect of recovery, then regard must be had to the factors in the best interests checklist. (Draft Bill, clause 10(3).)...

The Law Commission (*supra*, para 6.21) also considered that such decisions should not fall within the general authority (see *infra*).

The Law Commission's worries may be wholly unjustified relying as they do on the views of Lord Mustill in *Bland* who did not speak for the majority (see *infra*, ch 17). The correct analysis would be that the continued feeding and/or nutrition could only be justified under the general authority if it was in the patient's 'best interests' and, just as for the common law, if it was not it could not continue. There is, in reality, no need to depart from the 'best interest' test at all.

The same cannot be said of other procedures considered by the Law Commission.

(ii) PROCEDURES NOT FOR THE BENEFIT OF THE PATIENT

The Law Commission considered the legality of 'genetic screening' of incompetent adult patients, their elective ventilation, and non-therapeutic research.

Law Commission Report No 231 *Mental Incapacity* (1995)

6.23 In the course of consultation, our attention was drawn to a number of innovative medical procedures which could be applied to patients unable to give consent to them but would appear to be unlawful under the present law. Some respondents argued that the procedures in question were ethical and reasonable and urged that they should also be rendered lawful. The procedure most often referred to by consultees is known as 'interventional' or 'elective' ventilation. Another is genetic screening.

6.24 The law and ethics relating to elective ventilation were recently comprehensively reviewed in a research report published by the King's Fund Institute. The procedure involves the mechanical ventilation of an unconscious patient whose imminent death is considered inevitable, with the express aim of making effective arrangements for the retrieval and subsequent transplantation of donor organs. It has been carried out at a number of English hospitals over recent years. The researchers' conclusion, with which we agree, is that ventilation in such circumstances is an unlawful battery, since it is not being carried out in the best interests of the potential donor. The researchers were less certain that there was any ethical objection to the procedure, but they pointed out that the research necessary to establish whether any ethical objection is made out cannot be carried out if the procedure is unlawful. They suggested that this 'Catch-22 situation' requires resolution. Our recommendations for a comprehensive scheme whereby decisions could be taken in the best interests of a person without capacity do not assist if it is thought appropriate to make elective ventilation lawful.

6.25 Genetic screening or testing involves the taking of a blood or other body sample from a person in order to investigate the genetic make-up of that person. The ethics of this procedure were also comprehensively reviewed in a recent report, published by the Nuffield Council on Bioethics. (*Genetic Screening: Ethical Issues* (1993).) For the purposes of our own work we take the view that where the purpose of the procedure is to plan a treatment which will help the person concerned, then the general authority and the best interests criterion will apply in the usual way, if the person lacks capacity to consent to the procedure. Sometimes, however, the purpose of the procedure is to provide information to a relative about the genetic structure of the extended family. Some screening programmes also have as their purpose the provision of statistical information to health care professionals. We take the view that the testing of a person without capacity in circumstances where the test is not in the best interests of that person is unlawful under the present law. The expert view of those who recently reported on the ethics of genetic screening is, however, that it is 'a matter for consideration' whether the testing of those with incapacitating conditions should be permitted where 'the benefit of the family could be great and the risk of harm to the individual being tested negligible' (*ibid*). Again, law reform recommendations which are entirely dependent on a notion of 'best interests' will not assist in rendering such procedures lawful.

6.26 We did not invite specific views on either elective ventilation or genetic screening in our consultation papers. While the expert reports referred to above suggest that there is a case for legalising both procedures, none of the comments which have been made to us by respondents allow us to be confident that the case has been made out. We are, however, persuaded that there may come a time when Parliament could be confident that a procedure which was not intended to be in the best interests of a person without capacity to consent to it should nevertheless be rendered lawful. We therefore consider that the Secretary of State should have power to introduce such a change in the law, after consultation and subject to an affirmative resolution by each House of Parliament.

We *recommend* that the Secretary of State may make an order providing for the carrying out of a procedure in relation to a person without capacity to consent if the procedure, although not carried out for the benefit of that person, will not cause him or her significant harm and will be of significant benefit to others. (Draft Bill, clause 10(4).)

If any procedures are designated by the Secretary of State in future, there should (in accordance with the recommendations made elsewhere in this report) still be a clear prohibition against things being done to a person who objects or to a person who has made an applicable advance refusal.

6.27 Before making any order of the type referred to in paragraphs 6.21 or 6.26 above, the Secretary of State should be under a statutory obligation to consult with organisations representing persons with mental disability and with the Official Solicitor. It may well be appropriate to consult more widely. In relation to any new designated procedures, the statutory requirements for approval or consent which we recommended in relation to discontinuance of artificial sustenance should apply. Any order made by the Secretary of State must stipulate whether the procedure requires the prior approval of the court; or alternatively, a certificate from an independent medical practitioner. It seems clear that decisions about elective ventilation would have to be taken in circumstances where it would be quite impractical to require prior court approval on every occasion. If an attorney or manager has authority to consent to the procedure then neither the court nor the second opinion doctor need be involved. As with discontinuance of sustenance, the best interests factors will be relevant and regard should be had to them.

In relation to non-therapeutic research, the Law Commission proposed a scheme for approving these non-beneficial procedures in certain narrowly defined circumstances including the need for the approval of a new statutory body, the Mental Incapacity Research Committee. We consider the Law Commission's proposals in detail in Chapter 14.

We have already seen that the common law cannot accommodate procedures that do not benefit the patient and we will see this in relation to 'elective ventilation' in Chapter 15 and research in Chapter 14. In the result, the Government has decided not to proceed with the Law Commission's proposals (*Making Decisions*, *supra*, para 12) and thus the legality of these procedures will continue to be governed by the common law.

3. Special procedures

As we have seen, at common law the courts have indicated that it is desirable that a declaration be sought before certain procedures are carried out, for example, contraceptive sterilisation, withdrawal of nutrition and feeding from a PVS patient and donation of organs and tissue.

The Law Commission was likewise concerned that some procedures should not fall within the general authority. The Law Commission addressed two issues: (1) what procedures required special provision; and (2) if they did, who should be able to authorise them?

Law Commission Report No 231 *Mental Incapacity* (1995)

Treatments requiring court approval

6.3   Respondents to the consultation paper were unanimous in agreeing that some medical decisions should always require prior judicial approval. A clear consensus emerged in relation to certain treatments. In cases involving such treatments an application will have to be made to the court for specific authorisation unless the court has already considered the matter and made a specific order, or granted a manager authority to take the decision in question. The court need not be involved if the patient has appointed an attorney to take the relevant decision on his or her behalf in the event of incapacity.

   We *recommend* **that the general authority should not authorise certain listed treatments or procedures, which will require authorisation by the court or the consent of an attorney or manager.** (Draft Bill, clause 7(1).)

(1)   Sterilisation

6.4   We suggested in the consultation paper that sterilisation operations could be divided into three sub-sets: those intended to treat a disease of the reproductive organs; those intended for 'menstrual management'; and those intended for contraceptive purposes. None of our respondents suggested that statutory supervision should be applied to those in the first category, which can properly be carried out under the general authority, with access to the court if there is a dispute or difficulty. a number of respondents confirmed, however, that the need for 'menstrual management' can too easily be invoked to avoid the judicial supervision which currently apply to any operation intended to sterilise the patient as a method of contraception. We were greatly assisted by discussions with those in the Official Solicitor's Department who have experience of representing patients in actions involving proposed sterilisations. We are persuaded that there is a valid distinction to be drawn between an operation which is intended to address an existing harmful condition associated with menstruation and one intended to guard against any future distress which might arise from an unintended pregnancy. The phrase 'menstrual management' may obfuscate this crucial distinction instead of emphasising it. We take the view that sterilisation operations designed to relieve the immediate and genuine harmful effects of menstruation can be distinguished from those intended to prevent contraception and need not attract supervision by the court. In view of the concern expressed by respondents, however, we suggest a different form of independent supervision for such cases.

   We *recommend* **that any treatment or procedure intended to reasonably likely to render the person permanently infertile should require court authorisation unless it is to treat a disease of the reproductive organs or relieve existing detrimental effects of menstruation.** (Draft Bill, clause 7(2)(a).)

(2)   Donation of tissue or bone marrow

6.5   Respondents supported our suggestion that an operation to facilitate the donation of non-regenerative tissue or bone marrow by a person without capacity should automatically be referred to the court. The need for any such decision will not stem from any existing distressing condition of the person without capacity, but from the illness of some other person. Organ donation will only rarely, if ever, be in the best interests of a person without capacity, since the procedures and their aftermath often carry considerable risk for the donor. There is, however, authority from another jurisdiction that where a transplant would ensure the survival of a close family member it may be in the best interests of a person without capacity to make such a donation.

We *recommend* **that any treatment or procedure to facilitate the donation of non-regenerative tissue or bone marrow should require court authorisation.** (Draft Bill, clause 7(2)(b).)

6.6   There was support on consultation for our provisional view that the Secretary of State should be able to add to any statutory list of treatments, so that changes in medical science may be taken into account without the need for primary amending legislation.

We *recommend* **that the Secretary of State should have power to prescribe further treatments requiring court authorisation.** (Draft Bill, clause 7(2)(c).)

Treatments requiring a second doctor's certificate

6.7   The BMA, the Royal Colleges and the Department of Health all offer guidance to doctors about seeking a second doctor's opinion as a matter of good clinical practice. Statute imposes a requirement for an independent second medical opinion in relation to certain treatments for mental disorder. (Mental Health Act 1983, ss 57–58.) This means of supervision, much quicker and cheaper than the full procedure of a court hearing, could also usefully be applied to certain complex medical procedures where a patient lacks capacity. One advantage would be that consistency in relation to the treatments for mental disorder specified in section 58 of the Mental Health Act 1983 could be introduced by this means, regardless of whether a patient was 'liable to be detained' or not.

6.8   The treatments suitable for a second opinion category all share the characteristic that they are being proposed by the treating doctor to relieve an existing medical condition of the patient concerned. In this sense, they pose a clearer and more focused question than do the treatments in the court category. The second opinion doctor should be one specially appointed by the Secretary of State to fulfil the role of confirming whether the patient lacks capacity to consent to the procedure, and if so whether it would be in that patient's best interests. As with 'court category' treatments, a decision by a properly authorised attorney or court-appointed manager will displace the need for the statutory second opinion to be obtained. Unlike the treatments in the court category, those in the second opinion category may be accompanied by emergency circumstances. It should therefore be stipulated that action to preserve life or prevent deterioration is permitted, while the second opinion doctor's certificate (or the consent of a person with authority to consent) is being obtained.

We *recommend* **that the general authority should not authorise certain listed treatments or procedures, which should require a certificate from an independent doctor appointed for that purpose by the Secretary of State or the consent of an attorney or manager. The independent doctor should certify that the person concerned is without capacity to consent but that it is in his or her best interests for the treatment or procedure to be carried out. This should not preclude action necessary to prevent the death of the person concerned or a serious deterioration in his or her condition while the certificate or consent is sought.** (Draft Bill, clause 8(1), (2) and (6).)

(1)   Sterilisation

6.9   Although we have concluded that a sterilisation operation designed to relieve a patient of any existing pain and harmful effects connected with menstruation should not require authorisation by the court, many of our respondents expressed concern about operations being labelled 'for menstrual management', with the result that no independent supervision at all is required. A consultant in developmental psychiatry who has made a special study of sterilisation of people with learning disabilities suggested that the level of menstrual distress is often misrepresented, and that further investigation can reveal less drastic means of coping with the problem than a sterilisation operation. There is a clear need for independent supervision in such circumstances.

We *recommend* **that any treatment or procedure intended or reasonably likely to render the person concerned permanently infertile should require a certificate from an independent medical practitioner where it is for relieving the existing detrimental effects of menstruation.** (Draft Bill, clause (8(3)(d).)

(2)   Abortion

6.10 There is already a statutory second opinion procedure designed to protect the interests of the foetus in the Abortion Act 1967. We were extremely concerned to note, however, that a number of our expert respondents expressed the view that abortion operations are still being performed on young women with learning disabilities without a proper investigation of their capacity to consent or of their best interests (and in particular their wishes and feelings). An overwhelming majority of respondents said that abortion in such cases should attract independent supervision. It is clear that what is needed is an additional procedure to protect the interests of any mother who lacks capacity. While some respondents said that court authorisation should be required (and others objected to abortion in principle) it was also repeatedly stressed that delay is particularly undesirable where a pregnancy is to be terminated. Balancing all these factors, we take the view that abortion should be placed in the second opinion category.

We *recommend* that abortion should require a certificate from an independent medical practitioner. (Draft Bill, clause 8(3)(c).)

(3)   Treatments for mental disorder

6.11 Respondents welcomed our provisional proposal that the new statutory scheme should apply when it is proposed to administer medical treatment *for mental disorder* to a patient without capacity to consent to that treatment. The alternative would be to introduce a requirement that in such circumstances the patient should always be detained in accordance with the Mental Health Act 1983 and treated pursuant to the statutory provisions. Respondents did not favour this option, which might radically increase the numbers of people being compulsorily detained and treated. They did, however, favour all patients having the same safeguards where special procedures laid down in relation to particular types of treatment for mental disorder.

6.12 If the new statutory scheme can apply to treatments for mental disorder there would in some cases be an overlap between the Mental Health Act scheme and the new 'incapacity' scheme. We do not believe this will cause any difficulty in practice. There is already an overlap between the Mental Health Act scheme and the common law rules in *Re F*, which our scheme is intended to replace. The Mental Health Act Code of Practice stipulates that '[i]t is the personal responsibility of any doctor proposing to treat a patient to determine whether the patient has capacity to give a valid consent' (Mental Health Act 1983 – Code of Practice (2nd ed 1993) para 15.9). If the patient does not have capacity then the common law as set out in *Re F* may justify treatment in certain circumstances (*ibid*, para 15.9). Where a patient is 'liable to be detained' and the treatment proposed is treatment for his or her mental disorder, statute certainly provides that the treatment may be given without the patient's consent (Mental Health Act 1983, s 63). This does not, however, justify the doctor in disregarding the question of capacity, since the Code of Practice states that consent should nonetheless 'always be sought' (Mental Health Act 1983 – Code of Practice (2nd ed 1993) para 16.16). It also suggests that in practice many treatments will require the patient's acceptance and active co-operation. There will of course be no overlap with our scheme if the patient has capacity but refuses consent to treatment.

6.13 Equally, there will be no overlap if a person who now lacks capacity has made an advance refusal of treatment for mental disorder. If valid and applicable, this would preclude treatment being given pursuant to our new scheme after capacity has been lost. If the person meets the statutory criteria for detention under the 1983 Act, however, then the existence of an advance refusal will not be an end of the matter. The patient can be compulsorily detained and treated in accordance with the terms of the 1983 Act.

6.14 The 1983 Act already makes special provision for two forms of treatment, requiring that an independent second doctor's opinion be obtained if the patient is 'liable to be detained' under the Act. These treatments are (1) electro-convulsive therapy (ECT) and (2) the administration of psychotropic medication for a period exceeding three months. MIND and other respondents welcomed our suggestion that all patients unable to consent to these treatments, whether or not detained under the 1983 Act, should have the same protection. Rather than requiring such patients to be compulsorily detained, our respondents agreed that it would be far preferable for them all to be given the protection of a formal second opinion.

We *recommend* that the treatments for mental disorder described in section 58(1) of the Mental Health Act 1983 should require a certificate from an independent medical practitioner. (Draft Bill, clause 8(3)(a) and (b).)

6.15 In this category too we take it to be important that the Secretary of State should have power to add further treatments or procedures to the list we have proposed.

We *recommend* that the Secretary of State should have power to prescribe that other treatments or procedures should be included in the second opinion category. (Draft Bill, clause 8(3)(e).)

Clauses 7 and 8 of the draft Mental Incapacity Bill gave effect to these recommendations.

7. – (1) Section 4 above does not authorise any treatment or procedure to which this section applies unless—
(a) it has been approved by the court; or
(b) consent to the treatment or procedure has been given within the scope of his authority by the donee of a continuing power of attorney granted by the person concerned or by a manager appointed for him by the court.
  (2) This section applies to—
(a) any treatment or procedure intended or reasonably likely to render the person concerned permanently infertile except where it is for disease of the reproductive organs or for relieving existing detrimental effects of menstruation;
(b) any treatment or procedure to facilitate the donation of non-regenerative tissue or bone marrow;
(c) such other treatments or procedures (including treatments or procedures to facilitate the donation of tissue not within paragraph (b) above) as may be prescribed for the purposes of this section by regulations under subsection (2)(c) above shall be exercisable by statutory instrument subject to annulment in pursuance of a resolution of either House of Parliament.
8. – (1) Section 4 above does not authorise any treatment or procedure to which this section applies unless—
(a) a registered medical practitioner other than the one who will be responsible for carrying it out has certified in writing—
  (i)   that the person concerned is without capacity to consent to the treatment or procedure; and
  (ii) his opinion that it is in the best interests of the person concerned for the treatment or procedure to be carried out; or
(b) consent to the treatment or procedure has been given within the scope of his authority by the donee of a continuing power of attorney granted by the person concerned or by a manager appointed for him by the court.
  (2) The practitioner giving the certificate must be one appointed for the purposes of this section by the Secretary of State.
  (3) This section applies to—
(a) any form of treatment for the time being specified under section 58(1)(a) of the Mental Health Act 1983;
(b) the administration to the person concerned by any means of medicine for mental disorder if three months or more have elapsed since the first occasion when medicine was administered to him by any means for his mental disorder;
(c) abortion;
(d) any treatment or procedure intended or reasonably likely to render the person concerned permanently infertile where it is for relieving existing detrimental effects of menstruation;
(e) such other treatments or procedures as may be prescribed for the purposes of this section by regulations made by the Secretary of State.
  (4) In paragraph (b) of subsection (3) above 'mental disorder' has the same meaning as in the said Act of 1983 and the Secretary of State may by order vary the length of the period mentioned in that paragraph.
  (5) The power to make regulations under subsection (3)(e) or an order under subsection (4) above shall be exercisable by statutory instrument subject to annulment in pursuance of a resolution of either House of Parliament.
  (6) This section does not preclude any action necessary to prevent the death of the person concerned or a serious deterioration in his condition while the necessary certificate or consent is sought.

In *Who Decides?* (*supra*), it seemed that the Government was sympathetic to the recommendations (see, paras 5.6–5.22). However, subsequently it has decided not to legislate on these matters. It is, therefore, quite unclear what shape the law will take in the future (see *Making Decisions* (*supra*), para 12). One view would be that such procedures will now fall within the unfettered 'general authority'. This would be a remarkable change of position from the common law position. It is difficult to see how the court could 'graft on' the court involvement requirement developed at common law when the statute will be silent on the matter. Another view is that these procedures will fall wholly outside the statutory scheme. Thus, their legality and the need for the court involvement will remain a matter for the common law. This is equally remarkable, as it would create parallel legal regimes for decision-making and incompetent patients. It would leave those very problematic procedures to the uncertainty and vagaries of the common law. It seems wholly unjustifiable to exclude them from any future statutory scheme and the Government should think again in order to avoid the chaotic situation that will undoubtedly ensue.

4. Role of the court

We have already touched upon the role of the court. As we have seen, the Law Commission (but not the Government subsequently) considered that the court should alone make certain decisions for incompetent adults. Leaving that to one side, the Law Commission recommended that a single jurisdiction court should come into existence with extensive power to take decisions about the health care of incompetent adults and the power to appoint proxies (managers) to take decisions for that individual (*Mental Incapacity* (*supra*) Pt VIII). The recommendations are detailed and often technical. The Government has, in essence, accepted them in *Making Decisions* (*supra*), ch 3. We set out here the Government's view, which summarises the Law Commission's recommendations.

Lord Chancellor's Department *Making Decisions: The Government's Proposals For Making Decisions on Behalf of Mentally Incapacitated Adults* (1999) (Cm 4465)

STRUCTURE AND ROLE OF THE COURT; COURT APPOINTED MANAGERS

Background

3.2. The Law Commission recommended that, in support of their proposals for a unified system of decision-making to cover financial, personal welfare and healthcare matters, there should be a single court jurisdiction, which would deal with all these issues together. It envisaged the court as being principally the option of last resort in cases of dispute.

3.3. *Who Decides?* supported the recommendation in principle, but identified the potential resource implications and sought views on whether the Court of Protection offered the most appropriate base for this jurisdiction.

3.4. Most respondents favoured a single court jurisdiction for all areas of decision-making. Although there were some concerns about the Court of Protection's perceived lack of accessibility and unsuitability for dealing with emergencies, no realistic alternatives were proposed, and a clear majority of respondents supported the Court of Protection exercising this jurisdiction.

The Government has decided that there will be a new single court jurisdiction, which will deal with all areas of decision-making for adults without capacity.

The new jurisdiction will be based at the Court of Protection, and concerns about accessibility will be met by a regionalised structure (see Chapter 4).

POWERS OF THE COURT

3.5. The Law Commission recommended that decision-making by the court should operate in the context of its key principles:
*   decisions should be taken in the best interests of the person without capacity
*   there should be minimal intervention in his or her affairs unless there is a demonstrable need to do so
*   the option least restrictive of the person's freedom of action should be chosen.

3.6. The court would need to consider the nature and extent of the person's decision-making capacity in reaching a decision.

The Government has decided that the court will be able to make decisions on behalf of a person without capacity, or appoint a manager to make decisions.

The Government intends that the court should have the power to make declarations about capacity.

In exercising its powers, the court will follow two principles that support the aim of making the jurisdiction aimed at limiting intervention to the minimum possible:
*   the decision of the court is preferable to the appointment of a manager
*   *the appointment of a manager should be as limited in scope and duration as possible.*

POWERS OF THE COURT IN HEALTHCARE MATTERS

3.7. The Law Commission recommended that the court's powers in this area should extend to:
- approving or refusing approval to particular forms of healthcare
- appointing a manager to consent, or refuse consent, to particular forms of healthcare
- requiring a person responsible for the healthcare of a patient to allow a different person to take over the healthcare of that patient
- obtaining access to healthcare records.

The Government agrees that the court should have these powers

3.8. The Government believes that certain serious healthcare decisions which can currently be made by a court, such as the withdrawal of artificial nutrition and hydration from a patient in a permanent vegetative state or similar condition, and questions of treatment where the patient has made an advance statement should remain a matter for the court, and should not be able to be delegated to a manager…

3.11. The Law Commission recommended that the powers of the court should extend to obtaining access to healthcare records. A manager may need access to healthcare records in order to exercise their function as proxy decision-maker.

3.12. The Government recognises that a manager who is empowered to take healthcare decisions could require access to healthcare records, and proposes that the court should have the power to authorise a manager to do so.

3.13. The Law Commission also proposed a new power for the court to order admission of people without capacity to hospital for assessment and treatment on similar criteria to those contained in the Mental Health Act 1983.

3.14. Responses did not support such a provision. The Law Commission proposal will therefore not be taken forward.

THE 'NO ORDER' PRINCIPLE

3.15. The Law Commission did not believe that there was a need for a 'no order' principle such as that in the Children Act 1989, where the court may not make an order unless it is satisfied that doing so would be better for the child than not doing so.

3.16. The Government sought views on whether a 'no order' principle was appropriate. The majority of responses supported a 'no order' principle. However, authoritative opposition came from the Senior District Judge and the Official Solicitor. Their view was that the requirement that the court adopt the least restrictive option was sufficient and that the situation was not equivalent to that under the Children Act. Under that Act, the basis for the principle is that those with parental responsibility for the child should be left to exercise it without the intervention of the court unless necessary. However, there is no equivalent to parental responsibility for adults without capacity.

There will not be a 'No Order' principle in relation to court orders made for adults without capacity.

APPOINTING A MANAGER

3.17. *Who Decides?* asked whether the court should be able to appoint a manager; what the scope of the manager's responsibilities should be; and what criteria should be used to decide who should be a manager. The great majority of responses supported the court appointment of managers to deal with welfare, healthcare and property and financial decisions.

3.18. The Government's proposals are an extension of, and replacement for, the current receivership system. The court will be able to appoint a manager to make decisions on matters relating to the personal welfare, healthcare, property or financial affairs of a person without capacity.

Transitional Arrangements

3.19. Appropriate arrangements will be put in place in respect of existing receiverships.

The manager's responsibilities

3.20. The court will be able to appoint a suitable manager and set the scope of his or her responsibilities. The court will be able to appoint different managers for different areas of decision-making if appropriate.

POWERS OF A MANAGER

Decisions that cannot be made by a manager

3.21. As is the case with the general authority to act reasonably, and with CPAs (see paragraphs 1.23 and 2.8., above), a manager will not be able to take certain decisions on behalf of people without capacity. In addition, neither the court nor a manager should have power to make decisions which the person without capacity could not lawfully have made, if that person had retained capacity.

Powers of a manager to refuse consent to healthcare

3.22. *Who Decides?* expressed concern about the provision that would allow a court appointed manager to refuse consent to healthcare and asked the views of respondents on this point. The majority of responses opposed a manager having this power, although there was a substantial minority in favour, including the Law Society and Age Concern.

3.23. The Government takes the view that in most healthcare cases, a one-off decision about treatment will be needed. This could be made by the court without the need to appoint a manager. If a dispute then arose, the matter could be returned to court...

TIME LIMITS AND REVIEW

3.31. The Law Commission proposed that the appointment of a manager should be for the shortest duration that the court deemed necessary, and that a maximum time limit of 5 years for an appointment should be fixed by statute. This would necessitate the automatic review of all cases at least every 5 years.

3.32. *Who Decides?* identified a number of practical drawbacks to this proposal. The majority of longer-term appointments would be likely to concern financial matters. At present, the vast majority of the Court of Protection's patients have no prospect of recovering capacity. A requirement for an appointment to expire, be reviewed and renewed every 5 years would thus involve a substantial waste of resources, which would have serious implications for the workload of the court and would be of consequent additional cost to the patient.

3.33. It could also cause problems if the date of expiry was overlooked and resulted in the manager authorising transactions without authority, or coincided with an important decision which could not be delayed – for example selling property.

3.34. Responses to *Who Decides?* were divided on whether time limited appointments would be useful. The Master of the Court of Protection suggested that, rather than time limit all appointments, the court should have the power to fix a time limit or order a review where appropriate. This review received wide support.

The Government has decided, as a result of the responses, that the court should have the power to fix a time limit or order a periodical review where appropriate in cases where managers are appointed to deal with decisions on financial and welfare issues.

Healthcare managers are likely to be needed for a much shorter duration, and the court should always place a time limit on these appointments. Such appointments will be for a fixed period of no more than 5 years, but they will be renewable by the court.

D. UNDER STATUTE

By way of example, the Mental Health Act 1983 and the National Assistance Act 1948 are briefly discussed here.

1. Mental Health Act 1983

We consider in more detail the Mental Health Act 1983 when we examine its application to the compulsory treatment of *competent* patients. However, it is important to note its application to incompetent patients as the legality of their treatment will be determined by the 1983 Act when it is applicable.

The Mental Health Act 1983, s 63 provides as follows:

Treatment not requiring consent

63. The consent of a patient shall not be required for any medical treatment given to him for the mental disorder from which he is suffering, not being treatment falling within section 57 or 58 above, if the treatment is given by or under the direction of the responsible medical officer.

Notice that treatment is limited to medical treatment 'for the mental disorder from which he is suffering' and is limited to patients 'liable to be detained' under the MHA 1983, ie in essence patients actually detained or on leave (see discussion *infra*). Section 63 provides a defence to a battery in these situations. It does not, however, remove the need for any treatment also to be in the detained patient's best interests' (contrast *B v Croyden HA* (1994) 22 BMLR 13 at 25 per Thorpe J, discussed *infra*.)

Any treatment falling within s 57 may only be given with the consent of the patient and a 'second opinion'. Consequently, it may not be carried out on the incompetent, subject to its not being 'urgent treatment' under s 62. Section 57 applies to 'informal' patients as well as those detained under the Act. The treatments covered by s 57 are psychosurgery and, by regulation, the surgical implantation of hormones to reduce male sexual drive (Mental Health (Hospital, Guardianship and Consent to Treatment) Regulations 1983 (SI 1983 No 893), reg 16): see discussion in *R v Mental Health Act Commission, ex p X* (1988) 9 BMLR 77 (QBD)). Section 58 covers the administration of medicines for longer than three months and, by virtue of the above regulations, electro-convulsive therapy (ECT). As regards these treatments, s 58 does permit them to be administered to the incompetent provided that (by s 58(3)(b)) a second medical opinion confirms that:

> the patient is not capable of understanding the nature, purpose and likely effects of that treatment...but that, having regard to the likelihood of its alleviating or preventing a deterioration of his condition, the treatment should be given.

Further, the Mental Health Act 1983 also includes a provision which represents a statutory example of the principle of necessity. Section 62 provides that:

Urgent treatment
62 (1) Sections 57 and 58 above shall not apply to any treatment—
(a)   which is immediately necessary to save the patient's life; or
(b)   which (not being irreversible) is immediately necessary to prevent a serious deterioration in his condition; or
(c)   which (not being irreversible or hazardous) is immediately necessary to alleviate serious suffering by the patient; or
(d)   which (not being irreversible or hazardous) is immediately necessary and represents the minimum interference necessary to prevent the patient from behaving violently or being a danger to himself or to others.
  (2) Sections 60 and 61(3) above shall not preclude the continuation of any treatment of or treatment under any plan pending compliance with section 57 or 58 above if the responsible medical officer considers that the discontinuance of the treatment or of treatment under the plan would cause serious suffering to the patient.
  (3) For the purposes of this section treatment is irreversible if it has unfavourable irreversible physical or psychological consequences and hazardous if it entails significant physical hazard.

(For a detailed discussion of the 1983 Act see B Hoggett *Mental Health Law* (4th edn), 1996 and L Gostin *Mental Health Services: Law and Practice* (1986) *passim*.)

2. National Assistance Act 1948

Removal to suitable premises of persons in need of care and attention
47 (1) The following provisions of this section shall have effect for the purposes of securing the necessary care and attention for persons who—
(a)   are suffering from grave chronic disease or, being aged, infirm or physically incapacitated, are living in insanitary conditions, and
(b)   are unable to devote to themselves, and are not receiving from other persons, proper care and attention.
  (2) If the medical officer of health certifies in writing to the appropriate authority that he is satisfied after thorough inquiry and consideration that in the interests of any such person as aforesaid residing in the area of the authority, or for preventing injury to the health of, or serious nuisances to, other persons, it is necessary to remove any such person as aforesaid from the premises in which he is residing, the appropriate authority may apply to a court of summary jurisdiction having jurisdiction in the place where the premises are situated for an order under the next following subsection.

(3) On any such application the court may, if satisfied on oral evidence of the allegations in the certificate, and that it is expedient so to do, order the removal of the person to whom the application relates, by such officer of the appropriate authority, as may be specified in the order, to a suitable hospital or other place in, or within convenient distance of, the area of the appropriate authority, and his detention and maintenance therein.

Provided that the court shall not order the removal of a person to any premises, unless either the person managing the premises has been heard in the proceedings or seven clear days' notice has been given to him of the intended application and of the time and place at which it is proposed to be made.

(4) An order under the last foregoing subsection may be made so as to authorise a person's detention for any period not exceeding three months, and the court may from time to time by order extend that period for such further period, not exceeding three months, as the court may determine.

(5) An order under subsection (3) of this section may be varied by an order of the court so as to substitute for the place referred to in that subsection such other suitable place in, or within convenient distance of, the area of the appropriate authority as the court may determine, so however that the proviso to the said subsection (3) shall with the necessary modification apply to any proceedings under this subsection.

(6) At any time after the expiration of six clear weeks from the making of an order under subsection (3) or (4) of this section an application may be made to the court by or on behalf of the person in respect of whom the order was made, and on any such application the court may, if in the circumstances it appears expedient so to do, revoke the order.

(7) No application under this section shall be entertained by the court unless, seven clear days before the making of the application, notice has been given of the intended application and of the time and place at which it is proposed to be made—

(a)   where the application is for an order under subsection (3) or (4) of this section, to the person in respect of whom the application is made or to some other person in charge of him,

(b)   where the application is for the revocation of such an order, to the medical officer of health.

(8) Where in pursuance of an order under this section a person is maintained neither in hospital accommodation provided by the Minister of Health under the National Health Service Act 1977 or by the Secretary of State under the National Health Service (Scotland) Act 1978, nor in premises where accommodation is provided by, or by arrangement with, a local authority under Part III of this Act, the cost of his maintenance shall be borne by the appropriate authority.

(9) Any expenditure incurred under the last foregoing subsection shall be recoverable from the person maintained or from any person who for the purposes of this Act is liable to maintain that person; and any expenditure incurred by virtue of this section in connection with the maintenance of a person in premises where accommodation is provided under Part III of this Act shall be recoverable in like manner as expenditure incurred in providing accommodation under the said Part III.

(10) [*Repealed for England and Wales by the National Health Service Reorganisation Act 1973, s 57, Sched 5.*]

(11) Any person who wilfully disobeys, or obstructs the execution of an order under this section shall be guilty of an offence and liable on summary conviction to a fine not exceeding ten pounds.

(12) For the purposes of this section, the appropriate authorities shall be the councils of districts and London boroughs and the Common Council of the City of London [...], and in Scotland the councils of [regions and islands areas].

(13) The foregoing provisions of this section shall have effect in substitution for any provisions for the like purposes contained in, or having effect under, any public general or local Act passed before the passing of this Act:

Provided that nothing in this subsection shall be construed as affecting any enactment providing for the removal to, or detention in, hospital of persons suffering from notifiable or infectious diseases.

(14) Any notice under this section may be served by post.

The first question is, does s 47 extend to the *incompetent* person? Secondly, does it allow for medical treatment of a person coming within this section?

Brenda Hoggett writes in her *Mental Health Law* (4th edn, 1996) at 94–95:

What does an order allow?
The Acts are by no means clear about what may be done with the person once he has been removed. Section 47(1) of the 1948 Act declares that the purpose of the provisions is to secure 'the necessary care and attention' for the people concerned; and section 47(3) provides

that the court may order their removal to the hospital or home, and their 'detention and maintenance therein'. It seems that the [amending] 1951 Act was expressly passed because a doctor had been unable to persuade a person with a broken leg to go to hospital for treatment. Yet the Acts say nothing about imposing medical treatment, as opposed to care, attention and maintenance, without the patient's consent. In this they are very like the Mental Health Act 1959, which seems to have assumed that getting the patient to hospital was the only problem: what happened once he was there could safely be left to the clinical judgment of the doctors. Nowadays, however, we are very much less inclined to read such powers into statutes which do not expressly contain them…and it would be most unwise to go beyond the limits of what is permitted by these Acts and by the common law.

Treating without consent: the competent

Given the law's concern to protect the individual from unwanted invasion of his body and given the law's recognition that consent in the case of the competent patient is the legal safeguard to protect his interest, it could be argued that treatment of a *competent* patient without consent is only lawful if specifically provided for by statute (and then subject to the overarching provisions of the European Convention of Human Rights and Fundamental Freedoms). That being the case, we should examine the law, particularly the extent to which the *common law* may in fact permit treatment without consent.

A. BY STATUTE

Let us first see what (if any) statutory provisions allow for treatment without consent (compulsory treatment) of the competent. We consider three significant examples of legislative action.

1. Mental Health Act 1983

The Mental Health Act 1983 allows for the compulsory civil detention of individuals suffering from a mental disorder so that they may be treated or assessed for treatment. The detail of the civil 'detention' and 'release' provisions of the 1983 Act are not dealt with here (see, generally, B Hoggett *Mental Health Law* (4th edn, 1996); L Gostin *Mental Health Services – Law and Practice* (1986) and P Bartlett and R Sandlands *Mental Health Law: Policy and Practice* (2000)). Our concern is with the *legality of medical treatment* provided to a detained patient. However, a brief outline of the civil 'detention' provisions of the Act is offered by Dame Brenda Hale in the following extract where she discussed Pt II of the 1983 Act.

Brenda Hoggett *Mental Health Law* (4th edn, 1996)

Most compulsory patients are committed to hospital by means of an application made by the patient's nearest relative or an approved social worker (ASW) and supported by one or two doctors. If accepted by the hospital to which it is addressed, the application is sufficient authority to detain and usually treat the patient against his will. There are three types of application for admission to hospital, colloquially known as 'sections' or even 'orders', and two for care in the community. All are subject to review by an independent mental health review tribunal.

(i) Under section 2, an application for admission for assessment authorises the patient's detention for up to 28 days. Most forms of treatment for his mental disorder may be given without his consent during that time. The application must be supported by recommendations from two doctors, one an approved specialist in mental disorder, to the effect that:

(a) the patient 'is suffering from mental disorder of a nature or degree which warrants the detention of the patient in a hospital for assessment (or for assessment followed by medical treatment) for at least a limited period; and

(b) he ought to be so detained in the interests of his own health or safety or with a view to the protection of other persons.'

(ii) Under section 4, an application for assessment may be made in an emergency with the support of only one medical recommendation. The doctor need not be an approved specialist, although he should, if possible, have previous acquaintance with the patient. The grounds are the same as for a section 2 admission, but both the applicant and the doctor must also state that 'it is of urgent necessity for the patient to be admitted and detained under section 2' and that 'compliance with the provisions…relating to applications under that section would involve undesirable delay.' The application authorises detention for up to 72 hours, but the admission may be converted into an ordinary section 2 admission by the provision of a second medical recommendation within that time. Unless and until that is given, however, there is no statutory power to impose treatment without consent.

(iii) Under section 3, an application for admission for treatment may again be made either by the nearest relative or by a social worker. However, if the nearest relative objects to the admission, the social worker must seek authority from a county court. The patient may be detained in the first instance for up to six months. Then the detention may be renewed, on the advice of the responsible medical officer (RMO), for a second six months and thereafter for a year at a time. Most forms of treatment for the patient's mental disorder may be given without his consent. The initial application must be supported by recommendations from two doctors, one an approved specialist, to the effect that:

(a) the patient 'is suffering from mental illness, severe mental impairment, psychopathic disorder or mental impairment and his mental disorder is of a nature or degree which makes it appropriate for him to receive medical treatment in a hospital; and
(b) in the case of psychopathic disorder or mental impairment, such treatment is likely to alleviate or prevent a deterioration of his condition; and
(c) it is necessary for the health or safety of the patient or for the protection of other persons that he should receive such treatment and it cannot be provided unless he is detained under this section.'

(iv) Under section 7, an application for the reception of a patient aged 16 or over into the guardianship of a local social services authority or private individual may be made in the same way as an application for admission for hospital treatment but to the local authority rather than the hospital. The disorders covered are the same but the 'treatability' test (b) does not apply. Instead of (c), it must be 'necessary in the interests of the welfare of the patient or for the protection of other persons that the patient should be so received.' The guardian can dictate where the patient is to live, how he is to spend his time and who must be allowed to see him, but cannot insist that he accepts treatment for his disorder.

(v) Under section 25A, introduced as from April 1996 by the Mental Health (Patients in the Community) Act 1995, an application, supported by an ASW and one other doctor, can be made by the RMO of a patient aged 16 or over who is detained in hospital for treatment for the patient to be supervised after he leaves hospital. The disorders covered are again the same but the other grounds are:

(b) there would be a substantial risk of serious harm to the health or safety of the patient or the safety of other persons, or of the patient being seriously exploited, if he were not to receive the after-care services [to be provided under s 117]; and
(c) his being subject to after-care under supervision is likely to help to secure that he receives [those services].

The powers and other details are equivalent to those of guardianship but under the control of the health rather than social services.

Part IV of the 1983 Act contains the relevant provisions concerned with consent to treatment.

PART IV

CONSENT TO TREATMENT

56. Patients to whom Part IV applies

(1) This Part of this Act applies to any patient liable to be detained under this Act except—
(a) a patient who is liable to be detained by virtue of an emergency application and in respect of whom the second medical recommendation referred to in section 4(4)(a) above has not been given and received;
(b) a patient who is liable to be detained by virtue of section 5(2) or (4) or 35 above or section 135 or 136 below or by virtue of a direction under section 37(4) above; and

(c) a patient who has been conditionally discharged under section 42(2) above or section 73 or 74 below and has not been recalled to hospital.

(2) Section 57 and, so far as relevant to that section, sections 59, 60 and 62 below, apply also to any patient who is not liable to be detained under this Act.

57. Treatment requiring consent and a second opinion

(1) This section applies to the following forms of medical treatment for mental disorder—

(a) any surgical operation for destroying brain tissue or for destroying the functioning of brain tissue; and

(b) such other forms of treatment as may be specified for the purposes of this section by regulations made by the Secretary of State.

(2) Subject to section 62 below, a patient shall not be given any form of treatment to which this section applies unless he has consented to it and—

(a) a registered medical practitioner appointed for the purposes of this Part of this Act by the Secretary of State (not being the responsible medical officer) and two other persons appointed for the purposes of this paragraph by the Secretary of State (not being registered medical practitioners) have certified in writing that the patient is capable of understanding the nature, purpose and likely effects of the treatment in question and has consented to it; and

(b) the registered medical practitioner referred to in paragraph (a) above has certified in writing that, having regard to the likelihood of the treatment alleviating or preventing a deterioration of the patient's condition the treatment should be given.

(3) Before giving a certificate under subsection (2)(b) above the registered medical practitioner concerned shall consult two other persons who have been professionally concerned with the patient's medical treatment, and of those persons one shall be a nurse and the other shall be neither a nurse or a registered medical practitioner.

(4) Before making any regulations for the purpose of this section the Secretary of State shall consult such bodies as appear to him to be concerned.

58. Treatment requiring consent or a second opinion

(1) This section applies to the following forms of medical treatment for mental disorder—

(a) such forms of treatment as may be specified for the purposes of this section by regulations made by the Secretary of State;

(b) the administration of medicine to a patient by any means (not being a form of treatment specified under paragraph (a) above or section 57 above) at any time during a period for which he is liable to be detained as a patient to whom this Part of this Act applies if three months or more have elapsed since the first occasion in that period when medicine was administered to him by any means for his mental disorder.

(2) The Secretary of State may by order vary the length of the period mentioned in subsection (1)(b) above.

(3) Subject to section 62 below, a patient shall not be given any form of treatment to which this section applies unless—

(a) he has consented to that treatment and either the responsible medical officer or a registered medical practitioner appointed for the purposes of this Part of this Act by the Secretary of State has certified in writing that the patient is capable of understanding its nature, purpose and likely effects and has consented to it; or

(b) a registered medical practitioner appointed as aforesaid (not being the responsible medical officer) has certified in writing that the patient is not capable of understanding the nature, purpose and likely effects of that treatment or has not consented to it but that, having regard to the likelihood of its alleviating or preventing a deterioration of his condition, the treatment should be given.

(4) Before giving a certificate under subsection (3)(b) above the registered medical practitioner concerned shall consult two other persons who have been professionally concerned with the patient's medical treatment, and of those persons one shall be a nurse and the other shall be neither a nurse nor a registered medical practitioner.

(5) Before making any regulations for the purposes of this section the Secretary of State shall consult such bodies as appear to him to be concerned.

59. Plans of treatment

Any consent or certificate under section 57 or 58 above may relate to a plan of treatment under which the patient is to be given (whether within a specified period or otherwise) one or more of the forms of treatment to which that section applies.

60. Withdrawal of consent

(1) Where the consent of a patient to any treatment has been given for the purposes of section 57 or 58 above, the patient may, subject to section 62 below, at any time before the completion of the treatment withdraw his consent, and those sections shall then apply as if the remainder of the treatment were a separate form of treatment.

(2) Without prejudice to the application of subsection (1) above to any treatment given under the plan of treatment to which a patient has consented, a patient who has consented to such a plan may, subject to section 62 below, at any time withdraw his consent to further treatment, or to further treatment of any description, under the plan.

61. Review of treatment

(1) Where a patient is given treatment in accordance with section 57(2) or 58(3)(b) above a report on the treatment and the patient's condition shall be given by the responsible medical officer to the Secretary of State—

(a) on the next occasion on which the responsible medical officer furnishes a report in respect of the patient under section 20(3) above; and

(b) at any other time if so required by the Secretary of State.

(2) In relation to a patient who is subject to a restriction order or restriction direction subsection (1) above shall have effect as if paragraph (a) required the report to be made—

(a) in the case of treatment in the period of six months beginning with the date of the order or direction, at the end of that period;

(b) in the case of treatment at any subsequent time, on the next occasion on which the responsible medical officer makes a report in respect of the patient under section 41(6) or 49(3) above.

(3) The Secretary of State may at any time give notice to the responsible medical officer directing that, subject to section 62 below, a certificate given in respect of a patient under section 57(2) or 58(3)(b) above shall not apply to treatment given to him after a date specified in the notice and sections 57 and 58 above shall then apply to any such treatment as if that certificate had not been given.

62. Urgent treatment

(1) Sections 57 and 58 above shall not apply to any treatment—

(a) which is immediately necessary to save the patient's life; or

(b) which (not being irreversible) is immediately necessary to prevent a serious deterioration of his condition; or

(c) which (not being irreversible or hazardous) is immediately necessary to alleviate serious suffering by the patient; or

(d) which (not being irreversible or hazardous) is immediately necessary and represents the minimum interference necessary to prevent the patient from behaving violently or being a danger to himself or to others.

(2) Sections 60 and 61(3) above shall not preclude the continuation of any treatment or of treatment under any plan pending compliance with section 57 or 58 above if the responsible medical officer considers that the discontinuance of the treatment or of treatment under the plan would cause serious suffering to the patient.

(3) For the purposes of this section treatment is irreversible if it has unfavourable irreversible physical or psychological consequences and hazardous if it entails significant physical hazard.

63. Treatment not requiring consent

The consent of a patient shall not be required for any medical treatment given to him for the mental disorder from which he is suffering, not being treatment falling within section 57 or 58 above, if the treatment is given by or under the direction of the responsible medical officer.

64. Supplementary provisions for Part IV

(1) In this Part of this Act 'the responsible medical officer' means the registered medical practitioner in charge of the treatment of the patient in question and 'hospital' includes a mental nursing home.

(2) Any certificate for the purposes of this Part of this Act shall be in such form as may be prescribed by regulations made by the Secretary of State.

A number of points should be made.

(a) Scope of Part IV

You will notice that Part IV applies to patients 'liable to be detained' under the 1983 Act subject to some exceptions (s 56(1)). The statutory phrase is a term of art. It does not mean 'who could be detained' if the machinery of the 1983 Act was invoked. It means, in essence, 'are detained' under the Act or who are 'on leave' in the community under s 17 of the Act (see *Barker v Barking, Havering and Brentwood Community Healthcare NHS Trust* (1998) 47 BMLR 112 at 120 per Lord Woolf MR). Thus, Pt IV does not in general apply to 'informal patients' within s 131(1) of the Act who are competent and voluntarily being treated or who are incompetent and are being treated under the common law principle of necessity as compliant patients (see *R v Bournewood Community and Mental Health NHS Trust, ex p L* (1998) 44 BMLR 1 (HL) discussed *infra*). However, there is an exception to this in the case of some very serious medical procedures covered by s 57 of the Act: psycho-surgery and the surgical implantation of hormones to reduce male sex drive (see, ss 56(2) and 57 and The Mental Health (Hospital, Guardianship and Consent to Treatment) Regulations 1983 (SI 1983 No 893) (as amended), reg 16(1)). The provisions of Pt IV (in particular ss 57 and 62) apply to these medical procedures even if the individual is an 'informal' patient. Likewise, although Pt IV applies to most 'detained' patients such as those detained for assessment (under s 2) or for treatment (under s 5), it does not apply to all of them, for example, those detained in cases of emergency (under s 4).

(b) Sections 57 and 58

Sections 57 and 58 make special provision for certain treatments. Thus, s 57 *requires* the consent of the patient before the treatments covered (psychosurgery and surgical implantation of hormones to reduce male sex drive) may be carried out. They may not, therefore, be given where the patient is incompetent. The only exception is if the treatment amounts to 'urgent treatment' under s 62. In the case of psychosurgery, this could only be justified under s 62(1)(a) where it was 'immediately necessary to save the patient's life', since it is both an 'irreversible' and 'hazardous' procedure (s 62(3)). In practice, perhaps, this is an unlikely situation to arise.

Section 58 covers two types of procedure: the long-term administration of medicines (ie for longer than three months (s 58(1)(b)) and electro-convulsive therapy (ECT) (the Mental Health (Hospital, Guardianship and Consent to Treatment) Regulations 1983 (SI 1983 No 893) (as amended), reg 16(2)). Section 58(3) permits treatment in these instances either where the patient consents or – importantly for our purposes here – where he has not consented (including, it can be assumed, where he dissents) and a 'second opinion' doctor appointed by the Secretary of State has certified, *inter alia*, that 'having regard to the likelihood of [the treatment] alleviating or preventing a deterioration of his condition, the treatment should be given' (s 58(3)(b)).

(c) Section 63

Apart from the particular medical procedures falling within ss 57 and 58 of the Act, it is s 63 which provides the lawful authority for treatment. Section 63 is set out above. You will notice that s 63 applies providing the treatment is 'given by or under the direction of the responsible medical officer'. The responsible medical officer (RMO) is a doctor, usually a consultant, who has the responsibility for supervising the treatment of a detained patient (s 34(1)). Section 63 removes the need for the patient to consent to the treatment – '[t]he consent of a patient shall not be required'. It applies where the patient *refuses* consent and, as we shall see, implicitly authorises the use of force to effect the treatment. Crucially, however, s 63 only applies to 'medical treatment' given 'for the mental disorder'. There are two points here. First, what is to be given must be 'medical treatment'. Medical treatment is given a wide definition in s 145(1) of the Act:

Medical treatment' includes nursing, and also includes care, habilitation and rehabilitation under medical supervision.

Clearly, this is an 'inclusive' and not 'exclusive' definition. As we shall see, the courts have given the statutory expression a broad meaning so as to include, for example, forced feeding. One problematic area concerns 'restraint' or 'seclusion' of a detained patient. It may be that the patient's 'restraint' is a necessary part of administering the treatment and as such it will be covered by s 63 (see *Tameside and Glossop Acute Services Trust v CH* (1996) 31 BMLR 93, discussed *infra*). Where it is not – and *a fortiori* 'seclusion' – the legal justification must be found elsewhere, for example, implicit statutory authority as a necessary incidence of the detention (see *Pountney v Griffiths* [1976] AC 314 (HL)), express provision under the 1983 Act, at common law in order to prevent injury to others or under s 3 of the Criminal Law Act 1967 (see B Hoggett *Mental Health Law, supra*, pp 140–143).

Secondly, the medical treatment must be *for* the mental disorder. Section 63 does not, therefore, authorise any treatment on the detained patient. There must be a connection between the patient's mental disorder and what is to be done. Section 63 would not, therefore, justify the removal of diseased teeth or a gangrenous limb from a detained patient. Such procedures are governed by the common law and, if competent, the patient's consent would be required (see *Re C (adult: refusal of medical treatment)* [1994] 1 All ER 819).

The leading authority on the meaning of the statutory phrase 'for the mental disorder' is the Court of Appeal's decision in *B v Croydon District HA* (1994) 22 BMLR 13.

B v Croydon District HA (1994) 22 BMLR 13, [1995] Fam 133 (CA)

Ms B was 24. She had a history of being sexually abused as a child. In 1991 she was first admitted to psychiatric hospital. She was diagnosed as suffering from a psychopathic disorder, known as borderline personality disorder, coupled with post-traumatic stress disorder. The symptoms included a compulsion to self-harm. The only known treatment was psychoanalytic psychotherapy. In January 1993, she was compulsorily detained under s 3 of the Mental Health Act 1983. Following detention, she was kept under surveillance and deprived of the means of cutting and hurting herself. However, she virtually stopped eating, and in the course of 1993, her weight fell to dangerously low levels. Although, following a threat of nasogastric feeding, her weight rose temporarily, by the end of May 1994 it was down to 32 kilos and her doctor gave her a life expectancy of two to three months. Once again the hospital proposed forcible feeding by nasogastric tube. On 12 June 1994, following an ex parte hearing before Stuart-White J, an injunction was granted to restrain the Croydon Health Authority from feeding Ms B by tube without her consent. Although Ms B had begun to eat again by the time the matter came to full hearing before Thorpe J at the end of June and the beginning of July, both the parties wanted to know whether tube feeding would have been lawful, in case the situation should arise again. Thorpe J concluded that, whilst at common law Ms B had capacity to refuse nasogastric or intravenous feeding, as a medical treatment for mental disorder, the proposed treatment could be given without consent under s 63 of the Mental Health Act 1983. Section 63 limited the autonomy of a detained patient whose capacity is unimpaired to decisions regarding treatments that are not related to the mental disorder for which he is detained. Ms B appealed and the authority cross-appealed on the finding of capacity.

Hoffmann LJ: The argument before the judge centred on whether tube feeding could be called treatment for the mental disorder from which Ms B was suffering. Before us, however, Mr Gordon QC took a new point. He said that tube feeding fell within s 58 and was therefore altogether excluded from the scope of s 63. I do not think that there is anything in this. The relevant parts of s 58 read as follows:

(1)This section applies to the following forms of medical treatment for mental disorder…(b) the administration of medicine to a patient by any means…at any time during a period for which he is liable to be detained as a patient to whom this Part of this Act applies if three months or more have elapsed since the first occasion in that period when medicine was administered to him by any means for this mental disorder…

Mr Gordon says that food is a medicine. He draws our attention to the fact that some special foods (eg gluten-free rice cookies for coeliacs) may be obtained on prescription. In my view, however, this is not relevant to whether food is a medicine within the meaning of s 58. The section is concerned with medicines administered as treatment for mental disorder. The words 'by any means' in the opening phrase show that one identifies a medicine by its chemical composition and not by whether it is administered to the patient through a tube down his throat or by being put before him on a plate. Even gluten-free rice cookies are not administered for mental disorder and in my judgment ordinary food in liquid form, such as would be used in tube feeding, is not a medicine within the meaning of s 58.

That brings one back to the question of whether tube feeding would have been treatment for the mental disorder from which Ms B was suffering. My initial reaction was that it could not be. Ms B suffers from a psychopathic disorder which, according to the evidence, is incapable of treatment except by psychoanalytical psychotherapy. How can giving her food be treatment for that disorder?

Mr Gordon says that it cannot. It may be a prerequisite of a treatment for mental disorder or it may be treatment for a consequence of the mental disorder, but it is not treatment of the disorder itself. He draws attention to s 3 of the 1983 Act, which specifies the grounds upon which a person suffering from a psychopathic disorder may be detained. It is not enough that the disorder must be 'of a nature or degree which makes it appropriate for him to receive medical treatment in a hospital' (sub-s (2)(a)). The proposed treatment must be 'likely to alleviate or prevent a deterioration of his condition' (sub-s (2)(b)) and it must be 'necessary for the health or safety of the patient or for the protection of other persons that he should receive such treatment' (sub-s (2)(c)). So Mr Gordon says that the patient cannot lawfully be detained unless the proposed treatment will alleviate or prevent deterioration of his condition. No less should be required of the treatment which can be given without his consent under s 63.

This is a powerful submission. But I have come to the conclusion that it is too atomistic. It requires every individual element of the treatment being given to the patient to be directed to his mental condition. But in my view this test applies only to the treatment as a whole. Section 145(1) gives a wide definition to the term 'medical treatment'. It includes 'nursing...care, habilitation and rehabilitation under medical supervision'. So a range of acts ancillary to the core treatment fall within the definition. I accept that by virtue of s 3(2)(b) a patient with a psychopathic disorder cannot be detained unless the proposed treatment, taken as a whole, is 'likely to alleviate or prevent a deterioration of his condition'. In my view, contrary to the submission of Mr Francis, 'condition' in this paragraph means the mental disorder on grounds of which the application for his admission and detention has been made. It follows that if there was no proposed treatment for Ms B's psychopathic disorder, s 63 could not have been invoked to justify feeding her by nasogastric tube. Indeed, it would not be lawful to detain her at all.

It does not however follow that every act which forms part of that treatment within the wide definition in s 145(1) must in itself be likely to alleviate or prevent a deterioration of that disorder. Nursing and care concurrent with the core treatment or as a necessary prerequisite to such treatment or to prevent the patient from causing harm to himself or to alleviate the consequences of the disorder are, in my view, all capable of being ancillary to a treatment calculated to alleviate or prevent a deterioration of the psychopathic disorder. It would seem to me strange if a hospital could, without the patient's consent, give him treatment directed to alleviating a psychopathic disorder showing itself in suicidal tendencies, but not without such consent be able to treat the consequences of a suicide attempt. In my judgment the term 'medical treatment...for the mental disorder' in s 63 includes such ancillary acts.

Mr Francis was, I think, right to draw our attention to s 62 as throwing some light upon the question. Sections 57 and 58 place special restrictions upon the use of particular 'forms of medical treatment for mental disorder': surgical operations for destroying brain tissue or implanting hormones (s 57), electro-convulsive therapy and drugs (s 58). There are special procedures which must be followed before these treatments can be given. But s 62(1) says that in certain specified cases of emergency, these special rules need not be complied with. They include:

> ... any treatment – (a) which is immediately necessary to save the patient's life... or (c) which (not being irreversible or hazardous) is immediately necessary to alleviate serious suffering by the patient; or (d) which (not being irreversible or hazardous) is immediately necessary and represents the minimum interference necessary to prevent the patient from behaving violently or being a danger to himself or to others...

Mr Francis says, in my view rightly, that these emergency cases are not primarily concerned with a direct alleviation or the prevention of a deterioration of the mental disorder. The danger to the patient's life or the likelihood of serious suffering or the patient being a danger to himself or others are more likely to be the results of symptoms of the disorder. Nevertheless, the treatment of such symptoms is assumed by s 62 to be a 'form of medical treatment for mental disorder', since otherwise it would not have come within ss 57 or 58 in the first place.

I therefore agree with Ewbank J in *Re KB (adult) (mental patient: medical treatment)* (1994) 19 BMLR 144 at 146 when he said of the tube-feeding of an anorexic: '...relieving symptoms is just as much a part of treatment as relieving the underlying cause'. To similar effect is the judgment of Stuart-White J, quoted by Sir Stephen Brown P in *F v Riverside Health Trust* (1994) 20 BMLR 1 at 6, sub nom *Riverside Mental Health NHS Trust v Fox* [1994] 1 FLR 614 at 619. The case of *Re C (mental patient: medical treatment)* (1993) 15 BMLR 77, sub nom *Re C (adult: refusal of medical treatment)* [1994] 1 WLR 290, in which a schizophrenic was held entitled to refuse treatment for gangrene, is distinguishable. The gangrene was entirely unconnected with the mental disorder.

Mr Gordon said that if the meaning of 'medical treatment for...mental disorder' was wide enough to include ancillary forms of treatment, s 63 would involve a breach of the Convention for the Protection of Human Rights and Fundamental Freedoms (the European Convention on Human Rights) (Rome, 4 November 1950; TS 71 (1953); Cmd 8969). He referred us to *Herczegfalvy v Austria* (1992) 18 BMLR 48 at 68, (1992) 15 EHRR 437 at 485 in which the court said that a measure constituting an interference with private life and therefore prima facie contrary to art 8(1) (like involuntary tube feeding) can only be justified under art 8(2) if, among the other requirements of that article, its terms are sufficiently precise to enable the individual 'to foresee its consequences for him'. This requirement is necessary to prevent such measures from being a source of arbitrary official power, contrary to the rule of law. In my judgment s 63 amply satisfies this test. There is no conceptual vagueness about the notion of treating the symptoms or consequences of a mental disorder, although naturally there will be borderline cases. But there is no question of an exercise of arbitrary power.

I therefore think that the judge was right and would dismiss the appeal. That makes it unnecessary to consider the cross-appeal against the judge's finding that Ms B had capacity at common law. This is perhaps just as well, because I am bound to say that I have some difficulty with the judge's conclusion...

Neill LJ: I also agree. I am satisfied that the words in s 63 of the Mental Health Act 1983 'any medical treatment given to him for the mental disorder from which he is suffering' include treatment given to alleviate the symptoms of the disorder as well as treatment to remedy its underlying cause.

In the first place it seems to me that it would often be difficult in practice for those treating a patient to draw a clear distinction between procedures or parts of procedures which were designed to treat the disorder itself and those procedures or parts which were designed to treat its symptoms and sequelae. In my view the medical treatment has to be looked at as a whole, and this approach is reinforced by the wide definition of medical treatment in s 145(1) as including 'nursing' and also 'care, habilitation and rehabilitation under medical supervision'.

In the second place I too find support for this construction of 'medical treatment' in s 63 in the provisions relating to urgent treatment in s 62. Section 57, which is concerned primarily with medical treatment which involves surgery on brain tissue, contains detailed provisions for the steps which have to be taken before such treatment can be administered. Similarly, s 58, which is concerned with other specified forms of treatment and with the administration of medicine where the medicine has been administered for a period in excess of three months, contains provisions for the steps to be taken before the treatment is given or continued as the case may be...

It seems to me to be clear that s 62 contemplates treatment which is designed to deal with the symptoms of the disorder rather than the disorder itself. It follows therefore that as s 62 excepts urgent treatment from the regimes imposed by ss 57 and 58 medical treatment in those sections includes treatment of symptoms as well as of causes.

In these circumstances I too would dismiss the appeal. It therefore becomes unnecessary to express any final conclusion about the cross-appeal, though I share the doubts expressed by Hoffmann LJ as to the capacity of Ms B at the relevant time.

Henry LJ agreed.

(See also *Re VS (adult: mental disorder)* (1995) 3 Med L Rev 292 (Douglas Brown J) – artificial feeding and hydration of a person who had attempted suicide within s 63.)

The Court of Appeal confirmed the interpretation of s 63 of the Mental Health Act 1983 adopted in the earlier cases of *Riverside Mental Health NHS Trust v Fox* [1994] 1 FLR 614 (Stuart-White J and CA) and *Re KB (adult) (mental patient: medical treatment)* (1994) 19 BMLR 144 (Ewbank J). Section 63 permits the force-feeding of a patient suffering from anorexia nervosa (*Fox* and *Re KB*) or a borderline personality disorder (*B*) because (i) the patient is suffering from a 'mental disorder' and (ii) the force-feeding is 'treatment…for the mental disorder'. The Court of Appeal accepted that s 63 applied not only to the treatment of the 'mental disorder' itself but also its symptoms such as a refusal to eat. Also, s 145(1) of the 1983 Act defined 'medical treatment' very widely indeed and so as to include 'a range of acts ancillary to the core treatment' (per Hoffmann LJ. See also per Neill LJ). As the Court of Appeal noted, the 'emergency' provisions in s 62 of the 1983 Act clearly contemplate the treatment of symptoms as well as the condition itself as falling within Pt IV of the 1983 Act. As has been noted before, this interpretation of s 63 is undoubtedly the most sensible. To differentiate between the mental disorder and its symptoms would be too artificial and difficult to apply in practice (per Neill LJ). The Court of Appeal noted two potential limitations on the scope of s 63.

First, if the underlying condition was not 'treatable' at all, then s 63 would not apply to treatment of its symptoms. The second limitation envisaged by the Court of Appeal is, perhaps, obvious. The condition to be treated must be 'connected' to the mental disorder. Hence, the court distinguished the case of *Re C (adult: refusal of medical treatment)* [1994] 1 All ER 819 (Thorpe J), where a schizophrenic was held entitled to refuse treatment for gangrene. There, the condition (the gangrene) was not the product of the mental disorder, unlike the condition arising from the refusal to eat in *B*. Only the patient's *decision* to refuse treatment in *Re C* was the product, if at all, of the mental disorder. This makes eminent sense otherwise the Mental Health Act 1983 would permit compulsory treatment of any patient who suffered from a medical condition but whose perception of it was in some way affected by their mental disorder. The Act would, in effect, apply to *all* treatment refusals and not those relating to treatment '*for* the mental disorder' in s 63. The 1983 Act was not intended to have the broader scope which would, if it existed, raise profound civil liberties concerns and almost certainly infringe the European Convention of Human Rights.

As a consequence, a number of situations could arise where a detained patient was in need of medical treatment:
1. where the treatment is given to treat directly the mental disorder, for example, psychotropic medication (within s 63);
2. where the treatment is for a physical condition which is causing or contributing to the mental disorder, for example, a brain tumour producing or contributing to psychological effect (within s 63);
3. where the treatment is given to alleviate the symptoms or consequences of (and which are related to) the mental disorder, for example, force-feeding where the patient's mental disorder leads to a refusal of food and/or water or stomach pumping an attempted suicide (within s 63 after *B v Croydon HA, supra*);
4. where the treatment is for a condition (usually physical) which is unrelated to the mental disorder, for example, renal dialysis (not within s 63: *Re JT (adult: refusal of medical treatment)* [1998] 1 FLR 48 (Wall J).) The mental disorder is only relevant to the patient's competence to make the decision to refuse the treatment: *Re C (adult: refusal of medical treatment)* [1994] 1 All ER 819 (Thorpe J).

A rather curious application of s 63 arose in the following case.

Tameside and Glossop Acute Services Trust v CH (a patient) (1996) 31 BMLR 93 (Fam Div)

The defendant was aged 41. Since 1983 she had suffered from paranoid schizophrenia. In July 1995 she was admitted to the psychiatric unit of the hospital and was detained under s 3 of the Mental Health Act 1983. Following her admission, she was discovered to be pregnant.

CH wanted the baby and wished to care for it. At 31 weeks the foetus was found to be suffering from intra-uterine growth retardation. At 37 weeks the foetus was found to have the abdominal circumference equivalent only to 33 weeks. The doctors took the view that this was caused by a poorly functioning placenta and that if the pregnancy was allowed to continue, the foetus would die in utero. CH maintained the belief that the treatment and advice given by the medical staff were malicious and harmful to her child. She believed that her psychotropic medication was harmful to her child. The consultant obstetrician planned to induce labour and, if necessary, to perform a caesarean section. He considered that the defendant was mentally incompetent to make treatment decisions in relation to the delivery and that she might resist these procedures. He applied for a declaration that it would be lawful to carry out a caesarean section, and that, if necessary, reasonable force and restraint might be used to bring about compliance. Counsel for the Official Solicitor, acting as the patient's guardian ad litem, argued that in the absence of any decided case in which the lawfulness of restraint as an incident of treatment had been specifically considered, and, in view of the civil liberties implications, the matter should, if possible, be decided within the statutory framework of the Mental Health Act 1983, rather than by an extension of common law powers…

Wall J: For s 63 to apply to the defendant on the facts of this case, the 'medical treatment'…has to be 'treatment given to her for the mental disorder' from which she is suffering. This is the point which I must shortly address…

Can it be said that the performance of a caesarean section, and, if required, restraint applied to her to enable it to be carried out, is treatment for the defendant's mental disorder?…

The definition section of the Act, s 145(1) defines 'medical treatment' as including 'nursing, and also includes care, habilitation and rehabilitation under medical supervision'. Sections 57 and 58 refer to specified forms of treatment requiring consent and a second opinion which are not applicable to the instant case, although they emphasise the stringent restrictions surrounding certain forms of treatment imposed by the Act.

In *B v Croydon District Health Authority* (1994) 22 BMLR 13, [1995] Fam 133 the patient suffered from a psychopathic disorder for which the only known treatment was psychoanalytic psychotherapy. One of her symptoms was a compulsion to harm herself. While she was detained under s 3 of the Mental Health Act 1983 she stopped eating. She sought an injunction restraining the health authority from tube feeding her without her consent. On the trial of the issue whether tube feeding without her consent would be lawful, the trial judge held that tube feeding constituted medical treatment for the mental disorder from which she was suffering and that her consent was not required by virtue of s 63. The Court of Appeal upheld his decision…

Is the question of inducing the defendant's labour, or causing her to be delivered of her child by caesarean section, 'entirely unconnected' with her mental disorder? At first blush, it might appear difficult to say that performance of a caesarean section is medical treatment for the defendant's mental disorder.

I am, however, satisfied that, on the facts of this case, so to hold would be 'too atomistic a view', to use Hoffmann LJ's phrase in the passage from *B v Croydon District Health Authority* which I have cited and the reasoning of which I respectfully adopt.

There are several strands in the evidence which, in my judgment, bring the proposed treatment within s 63 of the Act. First, there is the proposition that an ancillary reason for the induction and, if necessary, the birth by caesarean section is to prevent a deterioration in the defendant's mental state. Secondly, there is the clear evidence of Dr M that, in order for the treatment of her schizophrenia to be effective, it is necessary for her to give birth to a live baby. Thirdly, the overall structure of her treatment requires her to receive strong antipsychotic medication. The administration of that treatment has been necessarily interrupted by her pregnancy and cannot be resumed until her child is born. It is not, therefore, I think, stretching language unduly to say that achievement of a successful outcome of her pregnancy is a necessary part of the overall treatment of her mental disorder. Treatment of C's gangrene [in *Re C (supra)*] was not likely to affect his mental condition: the manner in which the delivery of the defendant's child is treated is likely to have a direct effect on her mental state.

I am therefore satisfied that the treatment of the defendant's pregnancy proposed by Dr G is within the broad interpretation of s 63 of the Mental Health Act approved by the Court of Appeal in *B v Croydon District Health Authority*: it follows that, since the defendant's consent to it is not required, Dr G is entitled, should he deem it clinically necessary, to use restraint to the extent to which it may be reasonably required in order to achieve the delivery by the defendant of a healthy baby.

As we shall see, Wall J deals with two other important points relating to s 63 – whether force could be used and the relevance of 'best interests' when s 63 is applied. We shall return to those shortly.

How can an induced labour or caesarean section be 'medical treatment given for [the patient's] mental disorder' under s 63? It seems incredible that anyone should so regard it. On the face of it the decision in *CH* seems quite wrong since this treatment does not fall within situations (1) to (3) we set out above but rather straightforwardly and unequivocally within (4). However, the medical evidence gave some credence to the judge's decision that the case in fact fell within (2). The patient's consultant psychiatrist gave evidence first, that stillbirth (the alternative to the procedures) would lead to a profound deterioration in the patient's mental health; and secondly, that the pregnancy had interrupted the patient's treatment with strong anti-psychotic medication because of the dangers to her foetus. Wall J concluded on the basis of this evidence that the treatment of the patient's pregnancy fell within s 63 because

[i]t is not…I think stretching language unduly to say that achievement of a successful outcome to her pregnancy is a necessary part of the overall treatment of her mental disorder.

Both reasons offered by the judge are questionable. The second is plainly wrong. It is tantamount to saying that any physical condition which impedes the direct treatment of the patient's mental disorder is covered by s 63. Suppose, for the sake of argument, in *Re C (supra)*, the patient's gangrenous leg made it medically inadvisable (or physically impossible) for him to receive his medication for his schizophrenia. It cannot be that the amputation would now fall within s 63. It is no more related to, or a manifestation of, his mental disorder that was actually the fact in the case.

Wall J's first reason is somewhat more difficult to reject *in limine*. However, for a number of reasons his view should be rejected. First, it is inconsistent with the position accepted by the Law Lords in *Re F (mental patient: sterilisation)* [1990] 2 AC 1 (HL). Assuming that F, the woman in the case, had been detained under the 1983 Act, the judges accepted that her sterilisation would not fall within Pt IV of the 1983 Act because it would not be treatment for her mental disorder (see, especially per Lord Brandon at 55 and per Lord Griffiths at 70). Yet on Wall J's view, arguably it would have been. The medical evidence supporting the sterilisation was (as it often is) that pregnancy was not in the woman's health interests because she would suffer psychologically by being pregnant, going through labour and raising the child. Why is the alleviation of this deterioration in her mental health not 'treatment for [her] mental disorder' in the same way that inducing labour or the caesarean section was in *CH*?

Secondly, the most potent argument against Wall J's approach is the sheer breadth of his decision on the scope of s 63. There will be many, apparently unrelated, physical conditions which could be shown to have an impact on a mentally disordered patient's mental health. All of these, once the psychiatric evidence is there, will now fall within s 63 and not require the patient's consent. It was not Parliament's intention to licence the treatment of physical conditions which are not a cause (as in (2) above) or symptoms (as in (3) above) of the mental disorder. The Government saw s 63 in far more limited terms covering 'perfectly routine, sensible treatment' per Lord Elton (*Hansard* (HL) 1982, cols 1064–5). It may be defensible, in limited circumstances, to detain and treat patients compulsorily when they suffer from a mental disorder (see *Wintwerp v The Netherlands* (1979) 2 EHRR 387 (ECtHR)), though this is not wholly without difficulty particularly when it is on the basis of their danger to others (see discussion in T Campbell and C Heginbotham *Mental Illness: Prejudice, Discrimination and the Law* (Dartmouth 1991) chs 4 and 5 and DPT Price, 'Civil Commitment of the Mentally Ill: Compelling Arguments for Reform' (1994) 2 Med L Rev 321). Given the exceptional nature of the power of compulsory detention, non-consensual treatment should be restricted to clear cases of 'treatment for the mental disorder', there are considerable dangers in interpreting s 63 too broadly.

Let us now return to the other two issues raised by Wall J in *Tameside*. Does s 63 justify the use of force to effect the treatment authorised by s 63? We saw earlier (*supra*) that the Court of Appeal, subsequently to *Tameside*, held that reasonable force could be used to carry out treatment in an incompetent patient's best interests under the common law (see *Re MB* (1997) 38 BMLR 175 (CA)). In *Tameside* there was concern that the patient would resist her treatment. The judge held that the doctor was entitled 'to use restraint to the extent to which it may be reasonably required in order to achieve the delivery by the defendant of a healthy baby'. By this it was clearly intended that she could be restrained to allow the administration of an anaesthetic. That the judge contemplated the use of force against the patient may seem draconian. Indeed, it could be argued that s 63 does not permit the use of force. It merely dispenses with the need to obtain the patient's consent and as such only provides a substitute 'flak-jacket'. The better view is, however, that once the law sanctions treatment without consent – a rarity outside of the Mental Health Act – it must also entertain the use of reasonable force to carry out the treatment. Otherwise, the resistance of the patient (whether competent or incompetent) would render nugatory the court's decision and the statutory provision permitting treatment. Indeed, in the earlier case of *Riverside Mental Health NHS Trust v Fox* (*supra*), the judge, without comment from the Court of Appeal, had made just such an order but, for example, detention or punishment would require another legal justification (see *supra*).

Finally, we should consider the question of whether treatment authorised by s 63 must also be in a patient's best interests. In *B v Croydon HA* (1994) 22 BMLR 13, Thorpe J (at first instance) seemed to think this was irrelevant (at 25) when he stated 'it seems disquieting that statute [viz s 63] should legalise what the common law would not'. By contrast, in applying s 63 in *Tameside*, Wall J did ask himself whether the treatment was in the patient's 'best interests'. It is suggested that Wall J was correct to do so.

Certainly s 58 of the 1983 Act when it allows treatment without the patient's consent seems to embody by implication a requirement that the treatment for the mental disorder must be, at the very least, in the patient's 'best interests'. This is entailed in the requirement that the 'second opinion' certifying that 'having regard to the likelihood of [the treatment] alleviating or preventing a deterioration of [the patient's] condition, the treatment *should* be given' (see also s 57(2)(b)). It is true that these words are missing from s 63. However, a doctor always has a duty to act in an incompetent (and, perhaps also a competent) patient's 'best interests' (see *Sidaway v Governors of Bethlem Royal Hospital* [1985] 1 All ER 643 at 666 per Lord Templeman). Section 63 provides a statutory substitute for the patient's consent, it does not purport to, nor does it, replace any duty the doctor owes under the general law to his patient.

(d) Section 62

We have already referred to s 62 which permits 'urgent treatment' even though the requirements of ss 57 or 58 are not satisfied. The scope of this provision is discussed in the following extract.

Peter Bartlett and Ralph Sandland *Mental Health Law – Policy and Practice* (2000)

...the scope of s 62 is limited to treatment which is *immediately* and *minimally* necessary, which has been defined tightly at common law in *Devi v West Midlands AHA* [1980] 7 CL 44 (HC). There is no other limitation on life-saving treatment, but for lesser emergencies the treatment must not be 'irreversible', or 'irreversible and hazardous', as the case may be. These terms are defined in s 62(3). Treatment is classified as 'irreversible' if it has unfavourable, irreversible physical or psychological consequences and 'hazardous' if it entails significant physical hazard. Although all physical treatments potentially carry the risk of unfavourable irreversible consequences, it is unlikely that the emergency administration of drugs or ECT would be so classified by a court, or else s 62 would be otiose. These treatments are hazardous in the sense that they may have unwanted detrimental effects, but the definition of this term is limited to *significant, physical* hazards. Treatments under s 57 are more problematic in theory but in practice it is most unlikely that the treatments covered by that section would be given in an emergency: as we have seen, its application to hormone therapy is in reality nonexistent, and psychosurgery is relatively rarely practised, and never in an emergency situation. In their *Third Biennial Report* the MHAC stated that it was unusual for drugs to be given in an emergency situation, but more common for ECT to be given, usually pending a SOAD visit (MHAC, 1989, para 7.6(j)). That this continues to be the case is borne out by more recent research, which found that the use of s 62 to provide treatment prior to the giving of a second opinion is recorded on 11 per cent of MHAC 2s; of 116 such cases, 112 involved ECT (usually one dose), overwhelmingly for women patients suffering from depressive disorders . . . , and the reason for the treatment was to save the life of the patient or prevent a serious deterioration in his or her condition . . . Around 60 per cent of patients were given ECT within a week of detention under the Act, which seems to indicate that s 62 is often used for informal, competent, refusing patients who are sectioned for this purpose. However, this is not always the case. The MHAC has long reported concern that s 62 has been used to justify the emergency treatment of informal patients or those excluded from the ambit of Part IV by s 56 (1993, para 7.12; 1997, para 5.2.7), but such treatment is unlawful unless covered by the common law.

(e) The relationship between the common law and Part IV

Clearly, once a patient is 'liable to be detained', Pt IV governs *medical treatments for the mental disorder* and the common law cannot be relied upon. Likewise, all *other treatments* must be justified under the common law principle of necessity. As we have seen, this would allow treatment of an incompetent patient in his best interests. But, as we shall see shortly, it would not permit treatment against the wishes of a competent patient.

What, however, of the patient who is not detained under the Act but who is an 'informal' patient under s 131(1) of the 1983 Act? To the extent that the patient is a voluntary patient, he will be competent and his consent will be a necessary requirement to any treatment. The machinery of the 1983 Act must be engaged if he refuses consent and treatment is to be given.

What if the patient is not a voluntary patient because he is not competent to consent to his detention or treatment but he is, nevertheless, compliant? The 1983 Act could be invoked, but must it? There are two issues here. Can the patient lawfully remain in hospital? And, if so, can he be treated under the common law? Both issues arose in the following case.

R v Bournewood Community and Mental Health NHS Trust, ex parte L (Secretary of State for Health and others intervening) [1998] 3 All ER 289 (HL)

L was autistic, profoundly mentally retarded and incapable of consenting to medical treatment. After having been a resident of a hospital run by an NHS Trust for over 30 years, he had been discharged into the community in 1994 and had gone to live with paid carers, Mr and Mrs E. On 22 July 1997 while at a day centre which he attended regularly, L became agitated. His carers could not be contacted and a doctor and a social worker were called. L was sedated and taken by ambulance to the Accident and Emergency Department at the hospital, where he was assessed by a psychiatrist as being in need of in-patient treatment. It was decided that it was unnecessary to detain him under the provisions of the Mental Health Act 1983, as he appeared fully compliant and did not resist admission. He was therefore admitted informally. The doctors and staff responsible for treating L thought that he should be returned to live with Mr and Mrs E as soon as practicable and wrote to them explaining what was proposed. Mr and Mrs E were not however satisfied as to the trust's motives, and L applied, by his next friend: (i) for judicial review of the trust's decision to detain him on 22 July 1997 and its ongoing decision to continue to detain him; (ii) for a writ of habeas corpus ad subjiciendum directed to the trust; and (iii) for damages for false imprisonment and assault. The judge refused the applications and L appealed. The Court of Appeal held that L had been detained by the trust, since those who had control over the premises in which he was had the intention that he should not be permitted to leave those premises and had the ability to prevent him from leaving; that the 1983 Act created a complete regime which excluded the application of the common law doctrine of necessity; and that s 131(1) of the Act, which made provision for the informal treatment of patients who were admitted and treated with consent, did not assist the trust, since L was incapable of giving his consent. They held that L's detention had therefore been unlawful and awarded him nominal damages. The trust appealed.

Lord Goff:

Section 131(1) of the 1983 Act

Central to the argument advanced by Mr Pleming QC on behalf of the Secretary of State was the submission that, under the 1983 Act, persons suffering from mental disorder who are treated for their condition as in-patients in hospital fall into two categories. (1) Those patients who are compulsorily, and formally, admitted into hospital, against their will or regardless of their will, who are detained or liable to be detained in hospital. This category may be called 'compulsory patients'. They may be admitted under s 2 of the 1983 Act ('admission for assessment'); s 3 ('admission for treatment'); s 4 ('admission for assessment in cases of emergency'); or s 5('admission of patients already in hospital'). (2) Those patients who enter hospital as in-patients for treatment either (a) who, having the capacity to consent, do consent ('voluntary patients') or (b) who, though lacking capacity to consent, do not object ('informal patients'). Both are admitted under s 131(1) without the formalities and procedures for admission necessary for detention under the Act. Strictly speaking, therefore, both groups could be described as informal patients, but it is convenient to confine that description to those who are not voluntary patients.

As Mr Pleming stressed, s 131(1) of the 1983 Act is in identical terms to s 5(1) of the Mental Health Act 1959. Furthermore the 1959 Act was enacted following the *Report of the Royal Commission on the Law Relating to Mental Illness and Mental Deficiency* (Cmnd 169 (1954–1957)) (the Percy Commission), which recommended that compulsory detention should only be employed in cases where it was necessary to do so. The Percy Commission's views, and recommendation, on this point are to be found in paras 289, 290 and 291 of their report, which read as follows:

> 289. We consider compulsion and detention quite unnecessary for a large number, probably the great majority, of the patients at present cared for in mental deficiency hospitals, most of whom are childlike and prepared to accept whatever arrangements are made for them. There is no more need to have power to detain these patients in hospital than in their own homes or any other place which they have no wish to leave. We strongly recommend that the principle of treatment without certification should be extended to them. Such a step should help to alter the whole atmosphere of this branch of the mental health services. Many parents of severely sub-normal children at present feel that they lose all their rights as parents when their child is admitted to hospital and automatically becomes subject to compulsory detention there. We have no doubt that the element of coercion also increases the resentment of some feeble-minded psychopaths, and of their parents, when they are placed under 'statutory supervision' or admitted to mental deficiency hospitals after leaving school, and that this makes it even more difficult than it need be to persuade them to regard these services in the same way as other social services and other types of hospital treatment, as services which are provided for their own benefit. Equally important, if the procedures which authorise detention become the exception rather than the rule, the attitude towards compulsion on the part of those administering the services should change. These procedures will no longer be a formality which must be gone through before any patient can be given the care he needs. It will be possible to consider the need for care and the justification for compulsion as two quite separate questions in a way which is not possible at present.
> 290. Admission to hospital without using compulsory powers should also be possible for considerably more mentally ill patients than are at present admitted as voluntary patients…291. We therefore recommend that the law and its administration should be altered, in relation to all forms of mental disorder, by abandoning the assumption that compulsory powers must be used unless the patient can express a positive desire for treatment, and replacing this by the offer of care, without deprivation of liberty, to all who need it and are not unwilling to receive it. All hospitals providing psychiatric treatment should be free to admit patients for any length of time without any legal formality and without power to detain…

Here we find a central recommendation of the Percy Commission and the mischief which it was designed to cure. This recommendation was implemented, in particular, by s 5(1) of the 1959 Act. That the Bill was introduced with that recommendation in mind is confirmed by ministerial statements made in Parliament at the time (see 216 HL Official Report cols 668–669, 4 June 1959).

Following the enactment of the 1959 Act, s 5(1) was duly implemented in the manner foreshadowed by the Percy Commission, a practice which (as is plain from the evidence before the Committee) has been continued under s 131(1) of the 1983 Act, which is in identical terms. It is little wonder therefore that the judgment of the Court of Appeal in the present case, which restricts s 131(1) to voluntary patients, should have caused the grave concern which has been expressed in the evidence, both (1) about the need, following the Court of Appeal's judgment, to invoke the power of compulsory detention in many cases, numbered in their thousands each year, which for nearly 40 years had not been necessary and would, on the view expressed by the Percy Commission, be wholly inappropriate, and (2) about doubts whether some categories of patients would or would not, in consequence of the judgment, require compulsory detention.

In the light of the statutory history, Mr Gordon QC, for Mr L, recognised that s 5(1) of the 1959 Act must have the meaning for which Mr Pleming contended; but he boldly suggested that s 131(1) of the 1983 Act should be given a different meaning and be restricted to voluntary patients. This submission was primarily based upon certain provisions of the Mental Health (Amendment) Act 1982, which were incorporated in the 1983 Act, a consolidating Act. I trust that I will not be thought to fail to do justice to the skill with which Mr Gordon formulated and presented his argument if I say that it is, in my opinion, wholly untenable, bearing in mind not only that s 131(1) of the 1983 Act is in identical terms to s 5(1) of the 1959 Act, but that I have been able to discover no trace, either in the 1982 Act or in the White Paper of November 1981 which preceded it (Reform of Mental Health Legislation (Cmnd 8405)), of any intention to depart from, or modify, the recommendations of the Percy Commission upon which s 5(1) was founded, or to amend s 5(1) itself. On the contrary, it was expressly stated in the White Paper (see the Introduction, para 3) that the 1959 Act had worked well. The main objects of the Bill, as summarised in para 5 of the Introduction, were that the Bill improved safeguards for detained patients, clarified the position of staff looking after them and removed uncertainties in the law. The main improvements, summarised in para 6, had no bearing on the position of informal patients admitted under s 5(1) of the 1959 Act, as was borne out by the succeeding paragraphs of the White Paper and indeed by the 1982 Act itself.

I should briefly refer to s 131(2) of the 1983 Act, which was relied on by the Court of Appeal in support of their construction of s 131(1). Subsection (2) reads:

> In the case of a minor who has attained the age of 16 years and is capable of expressing his own wishes, any such arrangements as are mentioned in subsection (1) above may be made, carried out and determined [even though there are one or more persons who have parental responsibility for him (within the meaning of the Children Act 1989)].

The words which I have placed in square brackets were substituted by the Children Act 1989. The section in its original form was identical to s 5(2) of the 1959 Act, except that the word 'minor' was substituted in 1983 for the word 'infant'. It is plain, in my opinion, that sub-s (2) can have no impact upon the admission of informal patients under sub-s (1) which is concerned with patients who consent as well as those who do not object. It is the former category that sub-s (2) addresses, with special reference to minors.

For these reasons, I am unable, with all respect, to accept the opinion of the Court of Appeal on the crucial question of the meaning of s 131(1). I wish to stress, however, that the statutory history of the subsection, which puts the matter beyond all doubt, appears not to have been drawn to the attention of the Court of Appeal, and that they did not have the benefit, as we have had, of assistance from counsel appearing for the Secretary of State.

Treatment and care for informal patients

I turn briefly to the basis upon which a hospital is entitled to treat, and to care for, patients who are admitted as informal patients under s 131(1) but lack the capacity to consent to such treatment or care. It was plainly the statutory intention that such patients would indeed be cared for, and receive such treatment for their condition as might be prescribed for them in their best interests. Moreover the doctors in charge would, of course, owe a duty of care to such a patient in their care. Such treatment and care can, in my opinion, be justified on the basis of the common law doctrine of necessity, as to which see the decision of your Lordships' House in *F v West Berkshire Health Authority (Mental Health Act Commission intervening)* [1989] 2 All ER 545, [1990] 2 AC 1. It is not therefore necessary to find such justification in the statute itself, which is silent on the subject. It might, I imagine, be possible to discover an implication in the statute providing similar justification; but even assuming that to be right, it is difficult to imagine that any different result would flow from such a statutory implication. For present purposes, therefore, I think it appropriate to base justification for treatment and care of such patients on the common law doctrine.

Lord Goff went on to hold that L had not been 'detained' except when being transferred from one institution to another. He then continued:

Two subsidiary points

There are however two subsidiary points which I wish to mention, one relating to the judgment of the Court of Appeal, and the other of a more general nature.

The first is that the Court of Appeal placed reliance on the decision of this House in the Scottish case of *Black v Forsey* 1988 SC (HL) 28 as providing authority for their conclusion. That case was concerned with the invocation of the common law to supplement the statutory power of compulsory detention to fill a lacuna which had appeared in the Scottish Act. This House held that the common law could not be invoked for that purpose, because the powers of detention conferred upon hospital authorities under the Mental Health (Scotland) Act 1984 were intended to be exhaustive. In my opinion, that decision has no relevance in the present case which is concerned with informal admission under the 1983 Act and bringing a patient to hospital to enable him to have the benefit of such admission if he does not object to it. In this connection, I observe that s 17(2) of the Scottish 1984 Act, which is the equivalent to s 131(1) of the 1983 Act, was not referred to in *Black v Forsey*.

The second point relate to the function of the common law doctrine of necessity in justifying actions which might otherwise be tortious, and so has the effect of providing a defence to actions in tort. The importance of this was, I believe, first revealed in the judgments in *F v West Berkshire Health Authority* [1989] 2 All ER 545, [1990] 2 AC 1. I wish, however, to express my gratitude to counsel for the appellants, Mr John Grace QC and Mr Andrew Grubb, for drawing to our attention three earlier cases in which the doctrine was invoked, viz *R v Coate (Keeper of a Madhouse)* (1772) Lofft 73 esp at 75, 98 ER 539 esp at 540 per Lord Mansfield CJ, *Scott v Wakim* (1862) 3 F & F 328 at 333, 176 ER 147 at 149 per Bramwell B and *Symm v Fraser* (1863) 3 F & F 859 at 883, 176 ER 391 at 401 per Cockburn CJ, all of which provide authority for the proposition that the common law permitted the detention of those who were a danger, or potential danger, to themselves or others, in so far as this was shown to be necessary. I must confess that I was unaware of these authorities though, now that they have been drawn to my attention, I am not surprised that they should exist. The concept of necessity has its role to play in all branches of our law of obligations: in contract (see the cases on agency of necessity); in tort (see *F's* case [1989] 2 All ER 545, [1990] 2 AC 1); in restitution (see the sections on necessity in the standard books on the subject) and in our criminal law. It is therefore a concept of great importance. It is perhaps surprising, however, that the significant role it has to play in the law of torts has come to be recognised at so late a stage in the development of our law.

Lords Lloyd and Hope agreed with Lord Goff.

By contrast, Lords Nolan and Steyn held that L had been detained. Nevertheless, they held that his detention and treatment could be justified at common law.

It is clear from *Bournewood* that Pt IV of the 1983 Act need not be invoked to detain, and thereafter treat, an incompetent patient who is compliant. Although only Lords Nolan and Steyn had directly to address this – Lords Goff, Lloyd and Hope determining that there was no detention – there can be no doubt that all the Law Lords would agree. Lord Goff expressly disassociated himself from the Scottish case of *Black v Forsey* 1988 SC (HL) 28, which could be seen as *requiring* the use of the mental health legislation where it *could* be used. There are difficulties here because the common law is less precise and contains none of the safeguards afforded detained patients under the Act. Lord Steyn was particularly concerned:

Lord Steyn: The general effect of the decision of the House is to leave compliant incapacitated patients without the safeguards enshrined in the 1983 Act. This is an unfortunate result. The Mental Health Act Commission has expressed concern about such informal patients in successive reports. And in a helpful written submission the commission has again voiced those concerns and explained in detail the beneficial effects of the ruling of the Court of Appeal. The common law principle of necessity is a useful concept, but it contains none of the safeguards of the 1983 Act. It places effective and unqualified control in the hands of the hospital psychiatrist and other health care professionals. It is, of course, true that such professionals owe a duty of care to patients and that they will almost invariably act in what they consider to be the best interests of the patient. But neither habeas corpus not judicial review are sufficient safeguards against misjudgments and professional lapses in the case of compliant incapacitated patients. Given that such patients are diagnostically indistinguishable from compulsory patients, their is no reason to withhold the specific and effective protections of the 1983 Act from a large class of vulnerable mentally incapacitated individuals. Their moral right to be treated with dignity requires nothing less. The only comfort is that counsel for the Secretary of State has assured the House that reform of the law is under active consideration.

(For a discussion of *Bournewood*, see P Fennell 'Doctor Knows Best? Therapeutic Detention under Common Law, the Mental Health Act, and the European Convention' (1998) 6 Med L Rev 322; and for proposals for reform of the 1983 Act, see *Reform of the Mental Health Act 1983 – Proposals for Consultation* (Cm 4480), (1999) especially ch 11.)

2. Public Health (Control of Diseases) Act 1984

As its name suggests, this Act is concerned with the control of disease rather than with treatment. It is concerned primarily with the interests of the public who are not ill rather than with any particular person who may be ill. Section 37 provides as follows:

Removal to hospital of person with notifiable disease
37. (1) Where a justice of the peace (acting, if he deems it necessary, *ex parte*) is satisfied, on the application of the local authority, that a person is suffering from a notifiable disease and –
(a) that his circumstances are such that proper precautions to prevent the spread of infection cannot be taken, or that such precautions are not being taken, and
(b) that serious risk of infection is thereby caused to other persons, and
(c) that accommodation for him is available in a suitable hospital vested in the Secretary of State or, pursuant to arrangements made by a Health Authority or Primary Care Trust (whether under an NHS contract or otherwise), in a suitable hospital vested in a NHS Trust, Primary Care Trust or other person.
the justice may, with the consent of the Health Authority in whose district lies the area, or the greater part of the area, of the local authority, order him to be removed to it.
   (2) An order under this section may be addressed to such officer of the local authority as the justice may think expedient, and that officer and any officer of the hospital may do all acts necessary for giving effect to the order.

Similarly, s 58 provides power to detain someone already in hospital and suffering from a notifiable disease, if on leaving the hospital they would not have accommodation in which proper precautions could be taken to prevent the spread of the disease. (Notifiable diseases are cholera, plague, relapsing fever, smallpox and typhus: s 10.)

You will notice that s 37 does not specifically authorise treatment without consent. Arguably, such a power to treat without consent must be expressly given since such a power would override the basic principles of the common law having to do with the inviolability of the person, but notice s 13 of the 1984 Act:

Regulations for control of certain diseases
13. (1) Subject to the provisions of this section, the Secretary of State may, as respects the whole or any part of England and Wales, including coastal waters, make regulations –
(a) with a view to the treatment of persons affected with any epidemic, endemic or infectious disease and for preventing the spread of such diseases.

Again, arguably, these regulations, if they were to provide for compulsory treatment, would be *ultra vires* given that the Act is ambiguous and therefore must be read not to affect fundamental rights (see *R v Hallstrom, ex p W* [1986] QB 1090, (1985) 2 BMLR 73 at 83 per McCullough J).

The Act also makes provision for the *examination* of any person found in [a common lodging-house] with a view to ascertaining whether he is suffering, or has recently suffered, from a notifiable disease (s 40). The section is restricted to granting a power to *examine*; this should not be interpreted as authorising *treatment* without consent. Regulations were promulgated by the

Secretary of State under the Public Health (Control of Diseases) Act 1984 so as to apply s 37 to those suffering from AIDS as if it were a notifiable disease (see now Public Health (Infectious Diseases) Regulations 1988, SI 1988 No 1546).

Does this authorise compulsory treatment of the person suffering from AIDS? This particular provision is curious in at least two respects. First, it refers to those only suffering from AIDS and not to those infected with HIV. *If* a police power under the Public Health Regulations were needed, it is rather odd that it does not extend to the person who potentially poses a greater threat than the actual suffer from AIDS, ie the still healthy HIV-infected person. Secondly, the provision may be a response to hysteria since the threat possessed by AIDS to the public health is of a different order calling for different responses.

For an extended discussion of the issues of policy in England and the USA concerning HIV and AIDS, see I Kennedy and A Grubb 'HIV and AIDS: Discrimination and the Challenge For Human Rights' in A Grubb (ed) *Challenges in Medical Care* (1992); M Brazier and J Harris 'Public Health and Private Lives' (1996) 4 Med L Rev 171 and Sullivan and Field 'AIDS and the Coercive Power of the State' (1988) 23 Harv CR – CLL Rev 139.

3. National Assistance Act 1948, s 47

Removal to suitable premises of persons in need of care and attention
47. (1) The following provisions of this section shall have effect for the purposes of securing the necessary care and attention for persons who –
 (a) are suffering from grave chronic disease or, being aged, infirm or physically incapacitated, are living in insanitary conditions, and
 (b) are unable to devote to themselves, and are not receiving from other persons, proper care and attention.
 (2) If the medical officer of health certifies in writing to the appropriate authority that he is satisfied after thorough inquiry and consideration that in the interests of any such person as aforesaid residing in the area of the authority, or for preventing injury to the health of, or serious nuisance to, other people, it is necessary to remove any such person as aforesaid from the premises in which he is residing, the appropriate authority may apply to a court of summary jurisdiction having jurisdiction in the place where the premises are situated for an order under the next following subsection.
 (3) On any such application the court may, if satisfied on oral evidence of the allegations in the certificate, and that it is expedient so to do, order the removal of the person to whom the application relates, by such officer of the appropriate authority, as may be specified in the order, to a suitable hospital or other place in, or within convenient distance of, the area of the appropriate authority, and his detention and maintenance therein;
 Provided that the court shall not order the removal of a person to any premises, unless either the person managing the premises has been heard in the proceedings or seven clear days' notice has been given to him of the intended application and of the time and place at which it is proposed to be made.
 (4) An order under the last foregoing subsection may be made so as to authorise a person's detention for any period not exceeding three months, and the court may from time to time by order extend that period for such further period, not exceeding three months, as the court may determine.

Again, this statute does not appear to authorise the treatment of a person to whom the section has been applied, without that person's consent (see *supra*).

(For a discussion of the 1948 Act see B Hoggett *Mental Health Law* (4th edn, 1996) pp 92–96.)

B. THE COMMON LAW: ADULTS

1. The general principle

The traditional view must be that if a person is competent he may refuse treatment and it would then be unlawful to attempt to treat him because this would amount to the tort of battery and a crime. It would appear to follow that there is no public policy justifying the treatment of the competent against their wishes. This may, however, be easier to accept where the person is obviously competent and/or his condition is not one which is life-(?limb-) threatening. There is, however, a tendency in all of us, and perhaps more so in doctors, to want to treat even though the person refusing is apparently competent, when it is clear that the person's life is threatened or there is very grave risk to his health. How has the law responded to this? In a few early cases there was a tendency in the courts to avoid attacking head on the principle of the inviolability of the person and instead choosing, by and large, to cast doubt on the competence of the person whose *decision* is in question. This had the purported merit of preserving the principle while acting beneficently towards the individual (see eg, *R v Stone; R v Dobinson* [1977] QB 354 (CA) and *R v Smith* [1979] Crim LR 251 (Griffiths J)). If, however, it constitutes an improper manipulation of the concept of competence it does the law no credit (see *supra*, ch 5).

Courts in the United States have had to consider the legality of treating a competent patient who refuses to consent. As we will see later in Chapter 16, this issue often arises in the context of a dying patient. Here, it is important to identify the general principles, and, in the main, we will consider cases concerned with situations where the patient's life is only at risk because of his refusal of the particular treatment (but he is not otherwise dying), for example, a blood transfusion refused upon religious grounds. These cases, in fact, test the strength of the legal principles because the law is faced with a patient whose life *could* be saved.

Bouvia v Superior Court (1986) 225 Cal Rptr 297 (Cal CA)

Beach JA: Petitioner is a 28-year-old woman. Since birth she has been afflicted with and suffered from severe cerebral palsy. She is quadriplegic. She is now a patient at a public hospital maintained by one of the real parties in interest, the County of Los Angeles. Other parties are physicians, nurses and the medical and support staff employed by the County of Los Angeles. Petitioner's physical handicaps of palsy and quadriplegia have progressed to the point where she is completely bedridden. Except for a few fingers of one hand and some slight head and facial movements, she is immobile. She is physically helpless and wholly unable to care for herself. She is totally dependent upon others for all of her needs. These include feeding, washing, cleaning, toileting, turning, and helping her with elimination and other bodily functions. She cannot stand or sit upright in bed or in a wheelchair. She lies flat in bed and must do so the rest of her life. She suffers also from degenerative and severely crippling arthritis. She is in continual pain. Another tube permanently attached to her chest automatically injects her with periodic doses of morphine which relieves some, but not all of her physical pain and discomfort.

She is intelligent, very mentally competent. She earned a college degree. She was married but her husband has left her. She suffered a miscarriage. She lived with her parents until her father told her that they could no longer care for her. She has stayed intermittently with friends and at public facilities. A search for a permanent place to live where she might receive the constant care which she needs has been unsuccessful. She is without financial means to support herself and, therefore, must accept public assistance for medical and other care.

She has on several occasions expressed the desire to die. In 1983 she sought the right to be cared for in a public hospital in Riverside County while she intentionally 'starved herself to death'. A court in that county denied her assistance to accomplish that goal. She later abandoned an appeal from that ruling. Thereafter, friends took her to several different facilities, both public and private, arriving finally at her present location. Efforts by the staff of real party in interest County of Los Angeles and its social workers to find her an apartment of her own with publicly paid live-in help or regular visiting nurses to care for her, or some other suitable facility have proved fruitless.

Petitioner must be spoon fed in order to eat. Her present medical and dietary staff have determined that she is not consuming a sufficient amount of nutrients. Petitioner stops eating when she feels she cannot orally swallow more, without nausea and vomiting. As she cannot now retain solids, she is fed soft liquid-like food. Because of her previously announced resolve to starve herself, the medical staff feared her weight loss might reach a life-threatening level. Her weight since admission to real parties' facility seems to hover between 65 and 70 pounds. Accordingly, they inserted the subject tube against her will and contrary to her express written instructions.

…a patient has the right to refuse *any* medical treatment, even that which may save or prolong her life. (*Barber v Superior Court* 147 Cal App 3d 1006, 195 Cal Rptr 484 (1983); *Bartling v Superior Court* 163 Cal App 3d 186, 209 Cal Rptr 220 (1984).) In our view the foregoing authorities are dispositive of the case at bench. Nonetheless, the county and its medical staff contend that for reasons unique to this case, Elizabeth Bouvia may not exercise the right available to others. Accordingly, we again briefly discuss the rule in the light of real parties' contentions.

The right to refuse medical treatment is basic and fundamental. It is recognised as a part of the right of privacy protected by both the state and federal constitutions. (Calif Const, art I, para 1; *Griswold v Connecticut* 381 US 479, 484, 85 S Ct 1678, 1681, 14 L Ed 2d 510 (1965); *Bartling v Superior Court, supra,* 163 Cal App 3d 186, 209 Cal Rptr 220.) Its exercise requires no one's approval. It is not merely one vote subject to being overridden by medical opinion.

In *Barber v Superior Court, supra,* 147 Cal App 3d 1006, 195 Cal Rptr 484, we considered this same issue although in a different context. Writing on behalf of this division, Justice Compton thoroughly analysed and reviewed the issue of withdrawal of life-support systems beginning with the seminal case of *Quinlan* 355 A 2d 647, *cert den* 429 US 922, 97 S Ct 319, L Ed 2d 289, (NJ, 1976) and continuing on to the then recent enactment of the California Natural Death Act (Health & Saf Code, ss 7185–7195). His opinion clearly and repeatedly stresses the fundamental underpinning of its conclusion, ie, the patient's right to decide: 147 Cal App 3d at page 1015, 195 Cal Rptr 484. 'In this state a clearly recognised legal right to control one's own medical treatment predated the Natural Death Act. A long line of cases, approved by the Supreme Court in *Cobbs v Grant* 8 Cal 3d 229 [104 Cal Rptr 505, 502 P 2d 1 (1972)]…have held that where a doctor performs treatment in the absence of an informed consent, there is an actionable battery. The obvious corollary to this principle is that *a competent adult patient has the legal right to refuse medical treatment*' (emphasis added); 147 Cal App 3d at page 1019, 195 Cal Rptr 484. '[T]he *patient's interests and desires are the key* ingredients of the decision-making process' (emphasis added); at page 1020, 195 Cal Rptr 484, 'Given the general standards for determining when there is a duty to provide medical treatment of debatable value, the question still remains as to who should make these vital decisions. Clearly, the medical diagnoses and prognoses must be determined by the treating and consulting physicians under the generally accepted standards of medical practice in the community and *whenever possible, the patient himself should then be the ultimate decisionmaker*' (emphasis added); at page 1021, 195 Cal Rptr 484, 'The authorities are in agreement that any surrogate, court appointed or otherwise, ought to be guided in his or her decisions first by his knowledge of *the patient's own desires* and feelings, to the extent that they were expressed before the patient became incompetent.' (Emphasis added.)

Bartling v Superior Court, supra, 163 Cal App 3d 186, 209 Cal Rptr 220, was factually much like the case at bench. Although not totally identical in all respects, the issue there centred on the same question here present: ie, 'May the patient refuse even life continuing treatment?'. Justice Hastings, writing for another division of this court, explained: 'In this case we are called upon to decide whether a competent adult patient, with serious illnesses which are probably incurable but have not been diagnosed as terminal, has the right, over the objection of his physicians and the hospital, to have life-support equipment disconnected despite the fact that withdrawal of such devices will surely hasten his death.' (At p 189, 209 Cal Rptr 220.) '(1) Mr Bartling's illnesses were serious but not terminal, and had not been diagnosed as such; (2) although Mr Bartling was attached to a respirator to facilitate breathing, he was not in a vegetative state and was not comatose ; and (3) Mr Bartling was competent in the legal sense…The court below concluded that as long as there was some potential for restoring Mr Bartling to a "cognitive, sapient life", it would not be appropriate to issue an injunction in this case. We conclude that the trial court was incorrect when it held that the right to have life-support equipment disconnected was limited to comatose, terminally ill patients, or representatives acting on their behalf.' (at p 193, 209 Cal Rptr 220.)

The description of Mr Bartling's condition fits that of Elizabeth Bouvia. The holding of that case applies here and compels real parties to respect her decision even though she is not 'terminally' ill. The trilogy of *Cobbs v Grant, supra,* 8 Cal 3d 229, 104 Cal Rptr 505, 502 P 2d 1, *Barber v Superior Court, supra,* 147 Cal App 3d 1006, 195 Cal Rptr 484, and *Bartling v Superior Court, supra*, 163 Cal App 3d 186, 209 Cal Rptr 220, with their thorough explanation and discussion, are authority enough and in reality provides a complete answer to the position and assertions of real parties' medical personnel.

But if additional persuasion be needed, there is ample. As indicated by the discussion in *Bartling* and *Barber*, substantial and respectable authority throughout the country recognises the right which petitioner seeks to exercise. Indeed, it is neither radical nor startlingly new…

Further recognition that this right is paramount to even medical recommendation, is evidenced by several declarations of public and professional policy which were noted in both the *Barber* and *Bartling* cases.

For example, addressing one part of the problem, California passed the 'Natural Death Act', Health and Safety Code sections 7185 et seq. Although addressed to terminally ill patients, the significance of this legislation is its expression as state policy 'that adult persons have the fundamental right to control the decisions relating to the rendering of their own medical care...' (Health & Saf Code, s 7186.) Section 7188 provides the method whereby an adult person may execute a directive for the withholding or withdrawal of life-sustaining procedures. Recognition of the right of other persons who may not be terminally ill and may wish to give other forms of direction concerning their medical care is expressed in section 7193: 'Nothing in this chapter shall impair or supersede any legal right or legal responsibility which any person may have to effect withholding or withdrawing of life-sustaining procedures in any lawful manner. In such respect the provisions of this chapter are cumulative.'

Moreover, as the *Bartling* decision holds, there is no practical or logical reason to limit the exercise of this right to 'terminal' patients. The right to refuse treatment does not need the sanction or approval by any legislative act, directing how and when it shall be exercised.

In large measure the courts have sought to protect and insulate medical providers from criminal and tort liability. (Eg, *Barber v Superior Court, supra*, 147 Cal App 3d 1006, 195 Cal Rptr 484.) The California Natural Death Act also illustrates this approach. Nonetheless, as indicated it too recognises, even if inferentially, the existence of the right, even in a non-terminal patient, which overrides the concern for protecting the medical profession.

This right is again reflected in the statute concerning execution of a power of attorney for health care (Civ Code, s 2500), which states in pertinent part: 'Notwithstanding this document, you have the right to make medical and other health care decisions for yourself so long as you can give informed consent with respect to the particular decision. In addition, no treatment may be given to you over your objection at the time...'

A recent Presidential Commission for the Study of Ethical Problems in Medicine and Biomedical and Behavioral Research concluded in part: 'The voluntary choice of a competent and informed patient should determine whether or not life-sustaining therapy will be undertaken, just as such choices provide the basis for other decisions about medical treatment. Health care institutions and professionals should try to enhance patients' abilities to make decisions on their own behalf and to promote understanding of the available treatment options...Health care professionals serve patients best by maintaining a presumption in favor of sustaining life, while recognizing that competent, patients are entitled to choose to forego any treatments, including those that sustain life.' (*Deciding to Forego Life-Sustaining Treatment*, at p 3, 5 (US Govt Printing Office 1983) (Report of the President's Commission for the Study of Ethical Problems in Medicine and Biomedical and Behavioral Research.).)...

We do not believe that all of the foregoing case law and statements of policy and statutory recognition are mere lip service to a fictitious right. As noted in *Bartling*, 'We do not doubt the sincerity of '[the hospital and medical personnel's] moral and ethical beliefs, or their sincere belief in the position they have taken in this case. However, if the right of the patient to self-determination as to his own medical treatment is to have any meaning at all, it must be paramount to the interests of the patient's hospital and doctors...The right of a competent adult patient to refuse medical treatment is a constitutionally guaranteed right which must not be abridged.' (Fn omitted, 163 Cal App 3d at p 195, 209 Cal Rptr 220.)

It is indisputable that petitioner is mentally competent. She is not comatose. She is quite intelligent, alert and understands the risks involved...

Here, if force fed, petitioner faces 15 to 20 years of a painful existence, endurable only by the constant administrations of morphine. Her condition is irreversible. There is no cure for her palsy or arthritis. Petitioner would have to be fed, cleaned, turned, bedded, toileted by others for 15 to 20 years! Although alert, bright, sensitive, perhaps even brave and feisty, she must lie immobile, unable to exist except through physical acts of others. Her mind and spirit may be free to take great flights but she herself is imprisoned and must lie physically helpless subject to the ignominy, embarrassment, humiliation and dehumanising aspects created by her helplessness. We do not believe that it is the policy of this State that all and every life must be preserved against the will of the sufferer. It is incongruous, if not monstrous, for medical practitioners to assert their right to preserve a life that someone else must live, or, more accurately, endure, for '15 to 20 years'. We cannot conceive it to be the policy of this State to inflict such an ordeal upon anyone.

It is, therefore, immaterial that the removal of the nasogastric tube will hasten or cause Bouvia's eventual death. Being competent she has the right to live out the remainder of her natural life in dignity and peace. It is precisely the aim and purpose of the many decisions upholding the withdrawal of life-support systems to accord and provide as large a measure of dignity, respect and comfort as possible to every patient for the remainder of his days, whatever their number. This goal is not to hasten death, though its earlier arrival may be an expected and understood likelihood.

Real parties assert that what petitioner really wants is to 'commit suicide' by starvation at their facility. The trial court in its statement of decision said:

> It is fairly clear from the evidence and the court cannot close its eyes to the fact that [petitioner] during her stay in defendant hospital, and for some time prior thereto, has formed an intent to die. She has voiced this desire to a member of the staff of defendant hospital. She claims, however, she does not wish to commit suicide. On the evidence, this is but a semantic distinction. The reasonable inference to be drawn from the evidence is that [petitioner] in defendant facility has purposefully engaged in a selective rejection of medical treatment and nutritional intake to accomplish her objective and accept only treatment which gives her some degree of comfort pending her demise. Stated another way, [petitioner's] refusal of medical treatment and nutritional intake is motivated not by a *bona fide* exercise of her right of privacy but by a desire to terminate her life…Here [petitioner] wishes to pursue her objective to die by the use of public facilities with staff standing by to furnish her medical treatment to which she consents and to refrain from that which she refuses.

Overlooking the fact that a desire to terminate one's life is probably the ultimate exercise of one's right to privacy, we find no substantial evidence to support the court's conclusion. Even if petitioner had the specific intent to commit suicide in 1983, while at Riverside, she did not carry out that plan. Then she apparently had the ability without artificial aids, to consume sufficient nutrients to sustain herself, now she does not. That is to say, the trial court here made the following express finding, 'Plaintiff, when she chooses, can orally ingest food by masticating "finger food" *though additional nutritional intake is required intravenously and by nasogastric tube'* … (emphasis added). As a consequence of her changed condition, it is clear she has now merely resigned herself to accept an earlier death, if necessary, rather than live by feedings forced upon her by means of nasogastric tube. Her decision to allow nature to take its course is not equivalent to an election to commit suicide with real parties aiding and abetting therein. (*Bartling v Superior Court, supra*, 163 Cal App 3d 186, 209 Cal Rptr 220; *Lane v Candura*, (1978) 376 NE 2d 1232.)

Moreover, the trial court seriously erred by basing its decision on the 'motives' behind Elizabeth Bouvia's decision to exercise her rights. If a right exists, it matters not what 'motivates' its exercise. We find nothing in the law to suggest the right to refuse medical treatment may be exercised only if the patient's *motives* meet someone else's approval. It certainly is not illegal or immoral to prefer a natural, albeit sooner, death than a drugged life attached to a mechanical device.

It is not necessary to here define or dwell at length upon what constitutes suicide. Our Supreme Court dealt with the matter in the case of *Re Joseph G* 34 Cal 3d 429, 194 Cal Rptr 163, 667 P 2d 1176 (1983), wherein declaring that the State has an interest in preserving and recognising the sanctity of life, it observed that it is a crime to aid suicide. But it is significant that the instances and the means there discussed all involved affirmative, assertive, proximate, direct conduct such as furnishing a gun, poison, knife, or other instrumentality or usable means by which another could physically and immediately inflict some death producing injury upon himself. Such situations are far different than the mere presence of a doctor during the exercise of his patient's constitutional rights.

This is the teaching of *Bartling* and *Barber*. No criminal or civil liability attaches to honouring a competent, informed patient's refusal of medical service.

We do not purport to establish what will constitute proper medical practice in all other cases or even other aspects of the care to be provided…petitioner. We hold only that her right to refuse medical treatment even of the life-sustaining variety, entitles her to the immediate removal of the nasogastric tube that has been involuntarily inserted into her body. The hospital and medical staff are still free to perform a substantial, if not the greater part of their duty, ie, that of trying to alleviate Bouvia's pain and suffering.

(The decision was approved by the California Supreme Court in *Thor v Supreme Court* (1993) 855 P 2d 375 – recognising right of competent adult prisoner who was a quadriplegic to refuse artificial feeding and medication.)

We can deduce the following from the *Bouvia* decision. First, a competent adult has a legal right to refuse medical intervention even if this will lead to his death. Secondly, such a refusal does not amount to suicide because the patient does not in law cause his own death. Thirdly, the court drew no distinction between withholding or withdrawing artificial hydration and nutrition and other medical interventions. Fourthly, however, the patient's enjoyment of this right may be subject to the law's obligation to consider other interests of society which may conflict with those of the patient. For example, in *Bouvia* the court referred to society's interest in preventing suicide. In certain cases *Bouvia* would suggest that society's interests may prevail over those of the patient.

English law, remarkably, did not face up to the question until the 1990s. In 1992 in *Re T (adult: refusal of medical treatment)* [1992] 4 All ER 649, the Court of Appeal confronted the issue of the right of a competent patient to refuse life-sustaining treatment. As we have seen, the court held that on the facts the patient's refusal of treatment was invalid by virtue of the undue influence of her mother (discussed *supra*, ch 5). Nevertheless, all three judges in the Court of Appeal addressed the central issue. You will recall that the case concerned a young woman in need of a blood transfusion following the stillbirth of her baby. She had been brought up by her mother who was a 'fervent Jehovah's Witness'. T was not a member of that faith. After T became unconscious her father, who was opposed to her holding these beliefs along with her boyfriend, sought a declaration from the court that it would be lawful for the doctors to give a blood transfusion notwithstanding her prior refusal.

Re T (adult: refusal of medical treatment) [1992] 4 All ER 649, (1992) 9 BMLR 46 (CA)

Lord Donaldson MR: An adult patient who like Miss T suffers from no mental incapacity has an absolute right to choose whether to consent to medical treatment, to refuse it or to choose one rather than another of the treatments being offered. The only possible qualification is a case in which the choice may lead to the death of a viable foetus. That is not this case and if and when it arises, the courts will be faced with a novel problem of consideration of legal and ethical complexity. This right of choice is not limited to decisions which others might regard as sensible. It exists notwithstanding that the reasons for making the choice are rational, irrational, unknown or even non-existent (see *Sidaway v Bethlem Royal Hospital Governors* [1985] 1 All ER 643 at 666, [1985] AC 871, at 904–905)…

The law requires that an adult patient who is mentally and physically capable of exercising a choice *must* consent if medical treatment of him is to be lawful, although the consent need not be in writing and may sometimes be inferred from the patient's conduct in the context of the surrounding circumstances. Treating him without his consent or despite a refusal of consent will constitute the civil wrong of trespass to the person and may constitute a crime…

[A refusal of treatment in] this situation gives rise to a conflict between two interests, that of the patient and that of the society in which he lives. The patient's interest consists of his right to self-determination – his right to live his own life how he wishes, even if it will damage his health or lead to his premature death. Society's interest is in upholding the concept that all human life is sacred and that it should be preserved if at all possible. It is well established that the ultimate right of the individual is paramount. But this merely shifts the problem where the conflict occurs and calls for a very careful examination of whether, and if so the way in which, the individual is exercising that right. In case of doubt, that doubt falls to be resolved in favour of the preservation of life, for if the individual is to override the public interest he must do so in clear terms…

Butler-Sloss LJ: A man or woman of full age and sound understanding may choose to reject medical advice and medical or surgical treatment either partially or in its entirety. A decision to refuse medical treatment by a patient capable of making the decision does not have to be sensible, rational or well-considered (see *Sidaway v Bethlem Royal Hospital Governors* [1985] 1 All ER 643 at 666, [1985] AC 871 at 904–905). I agree with the reasoning of the Court of Appeal in Ontario in their decision in *Malette v Shulman* (1990) 72 OR (2d) 417 [2 Med LR 162] (a blood transfusion given to an unconscious card-carrying Jehovah's Witness). Robins JA said (at 432):

At issue here is the freedom of the patient as an individual to exercise her right to refuse treatment and accept the consequences of her own decisions. Competent adults, as I have sought to demonstrate, are generally at liberty to refuse medical treatment even at the risk of death. The right to determine what shall be done with one's own body is a fundamental right in our society. The concepts inherent in this right are the bedrock upon which the principles of self-determination and individual autonomy are based. Free individual choice in matters affecting this right should, in my opinion, be accorded very high priority.

He excluded from consideration the interests of the state in protecting innocent third parties and preventing suicide. I agree with the principles set out above...

It is established that the principle of self-determination requires that respect must be given to the wishes of the patient, so that, if an adult patient of sound mind refuses, however unreasonably, to consent to treatment or care by which his life would or might be prolonged, the doctors responsible for his care must give effect to his wishes, even though they do not consider it to be in his best interests to do so . . . To this extent, the principle of the sanctity of human life must yield to the principle of self-determination . . . and, for present purposes perhaps more important, the doctors duty to act in the best interests of his patient must likewise be qualified. On this basis, it has been held that a patient of sound mind may, if properly informed, require that life support should be discontinued: see *Nancy B v Hôtel-Dieu de Québec* (1992) 86 DLR (4th) 385. Moreover the same principle applies where the patient's refusal to give his consent.

Staughton LJ: An adult whose mental capacity is unimpaired has the right to decide for herself whether she will or will not received medical or surgical treatment, even in circumstances where she is likely or even certain to die in the absence of treatment. Thus far the law is clear.

2.   Balancing competing interests

It is possible to discern in the case of *Re T* two distinct (and perhaps inconsistent) approaches. Lord Donaldson MR initially describes the right of a patient to refuse treatment as an 'absolute' right, albeit possibly subject to an exception when the patient is pregnant. Later in his conclusion he describes the right of the patient as being a '*prima facie*' right, the enjoyment of which is to be balanced against possibly countervailing societal interests. The latter view, that there are interests which need to be balanced against each other, is also reflected in the judgment of Butler-Sloss LJ.

In the subsequent case of *Airedale NHS Trust v Bland* [1993] 1 All ER 821, in one of a number of asides dealing with general principles of medical law, the Law Lords endorsed the right of a patient to refuse life-sustaining treatment:

Lord Keith: It is unlawful, so as to constitute both a tort and the crime of battery, to administer medical treatment to an adult, who is conscious and of sound mind, without his consent: see *F v West Berkshire Health Authority (Mental Health Act Commission intervening)* [1989] 2 All ER 545, [1990] 2 AC 1. Such a person is completely at liberty to decline to undergo treatment, even if the result of his doing so will be that he will die...

Lord Goff: The fundamental principle is the principle of the sanctity of human life – a principle long recognised not only in our society but also in most, if not all, civilised societies throughout the modern world, as is indeed evidenced by its recognition both in art 2 of the European Convention on Human Rights (Convention for the Protection of Human Rights and Fundamental Freedoms (Rome, 4 November 1950; TS 71 (1953); Cmd 8969)) and in art 6 of the International Covenant on Civil and Political Rights (New York, 19 December 1966; TS 6 (1977); Cmnd 6702).

But this principle, fundamental though it is, is not absolute. Indeed there are circumstances in which it is lawful to take another man's life, for example by a lawful act of self-defence, or (in the days when capital punishment was acceptable in our society) by lawful execution. We are not however concerned with cases such as these. We are concerned with circumstances in which it may be lawful to withhold from a patient medical treatment or care by means of which his life may be prolonged. But here too there is no absolute rule that the patient's life must be prolonged by such treatment or care, if available, regardless of the circumstances... it is established that the principle of self-determination requires that respect must be given to the wishes of the patient, so that, if an adult patient of sound mind refuses, however unreasonably, to consent to treatment or care by which his life would or might be prolonged, the doctors responsible for his care must give effect to his wishes, even though they do not consider it to be in his best interests to do so ... To this extent, the principle of the sanctity of human life must yield to the principle of self-determination ... and, for present purposes perhaps more important, the doctor's duty to act in the best interests of his patient must likewise be qualified. On this basis, it has been held that a patient of sound mind may, if properly informed, require that life support should be discontinued: see *Nancy B v Hôtel-Dieu de Québec* (1992) 86 DLR (4th) 385.

Lord Mustill: If the patient is capable of making a decision on whether to permit treatment and decides not to permit it his choice must be obeyed, even if on any objective view it is contrary to his best interests. A doctor has no right to proceed in the face of objection, even if it is plain to all, including the patient, that adverse consequences and even death will or may ensue…

Thus it is that the patient who is undergoing life-maintaining treatment and decides that it would be preferable to die must be allowed to die, provided that all necessary steps have been taken to be sure that this is what he or she really desires.

Lord Browne-Wilkinson (at 881-882)also recognised a competent adult patient's right to refuse medical treatment.

You will recall the two distinct approaches in *Re T*. In *Bland* the judges, on the face of it, adopt an 'absolute' approach espoused by Lord Donaldson MR in *Re T*. However, it could be said that their Lordships do accept that the law involves a balancing exercise. What they do is that, as a matter of principle, they resolve the balance where the conflict is between sanctity of life and self-determination in favour of the latter as we saw explicitly in the speech of Lord Goff (see also Lord Keith at 861).

Subsequent case law in England has enshrined the absolute right of a competent adult to refuse *any* medical treatment. Thus, in *Re MB* (1997) 38 BMLR 175 (CA), speaking for the Court of Appeal, Butler-Sloss LJ stated:

A competent woman, who has the capacity to decide, may, for religious reasons, other reasons, for rational or irrational reasons or for no reason at all, choose not to have medical intervention, even though the consequence may be the death or serious handicap of the child she bears, or her own death. In that event the courts do not have the jurisdiction to declare medical intervention lawful and the question of her own best interests, objectively considered, does not arise.

Likewise, in *St George's Healthcare NHS Trust v S* (1998) 44 BMLR 160 (CA), Judge LJ in the judgment of the court referred to the statements in the *Bland* case and stated:

The speeches in *Airedale NHS Trust v Bland* did not establish the law, but rather underlined the principle found in a series of authoritative decisions. With the exception of one short passage from the observations of Lord Reid in *S v S, W v Official Solicitor* [1970] 3 All ER 107, [1972] AC 24, no further citation is necessary.

In that case the House of Lords considered whether it was right to order blood tests on two infants to help establish whether or not they were legitimate. Lord Reid examined the legal position and said ([1970] 3 All ER 107 at 111, [1972] AC 24 at 43):

There is no doubt that a person of full age and capacity cannot be ordered to undergo a blood test against his will…The real reason is that English law goes to great lengths to protect a person of full age and capacity from interference with his personal liberty. We have too often seen freedom disappear in other countries not only by coups d'état but by gradual erosion; and often it is the first step that counts. So it would be unwise to make even minor concessions.

The importance of this salutary warning remains undiminished.

See also *Re C (adult: refusal of treatment)* [1994] 1 All ER 819 (Thorpe J) – right to refuse surgery for life-threatening condition and *Re JT (adult: refusal of medical treatment)* [1998] 1 FLR 48 (Wall J) – right to refuse renal dialysis with consequent risk to the patient's life. (For a discussion of English law, see J Munby 'Rhetoric and Reality: The Limitations of Patient Self-Determination in Contemporary English Law' (1998) 14 Journal of Contemporary Health Law and Policy 315.)

In our view, the balancing approach whereby a patient's rights are understood as being only *prima facie* rights which must be weighted against the interests of society more properly states English law. The American case law has identified four societal interests (1) the preservation of life; (2) preventing suicide; (3) preserving the integrity of the medical profession; (4) protection of an innocent third party (for a classic exposition see, *Re Claire Conroy* (1985) 486 A 2d 1209 (NJ Sup Ct)). As regards the first, clearly by preferring the patient's right to refuse, the courts in *Re T, Bland, Re MB* and the *St George's Case* reached a conclusion that this societal interest could not outweigh the patient's right. As regards the second, again the court in *Re T* does not consider that any interest that society has in preventing suicide transcends the right of the patient, though it is doubtful whether a patient's conduct in such circumstances amounts to suicide (see, on similar facts, *Fosmire v Nicoleau* (1990) 551 NE 2d 77 (NY CA) held by majority of the court that refusing a blood transfusion is not suicide. Contrast the judgment of Hancock and Simons JJ, concurring).

In *Bland* Lord Goff stated (at 866):

> I wish to add that, in cases of this kind, there is no question of the patient having committed suicide, nor therefore of the doctor having aided or abetted him in doing so. It is simply that the patient has, as he is entitled to do, declined to consent to treatment which might or would have the effect of prolonging his life, and the doctor has, in accordance with his duty, complied with his patient's wishes.

Before we move on to the other societal interests, we should pause and consider Lord Goff's view. There are *two* issues. First, is the patient by refusing treatment committing suicide? Secondly, if yes, is the doctor, by withdrawing or withholding treatment, assisting the patient in committing suicide and thereby guilty of an offence under s 2 of the Suicide Act 1961? We have already seen the issue of suicide raised in the *Bouvia* case. We return to consider the issue in Chapter 16. Does the patient in refusing life-sustaining treatment commit suicide? The arguments are well put by David Price in the following paper. He considers two issues: (1) does the patient intend to die and (2) does the patient cause their death?

David P T Price 'Assisted Suicide and Refusing Medical Treatment: Linguistics, Morals and Legal Contortions' (1996) 4 Med L Rev 270

...the English cases do not discuss in detail the rationale behind the view that such decisions can not amount to an attempt to commit suicide, by contrast with many North American authorities – some of which will be considered below.

The concepts of intention and causal agency are at the heart of evaluations as to the nature of suicide. The *Concise Oxford English Dictionary* and *Webster's Dictionary* define 'suicide' fairly typically as 'the intentional killing of oneself' and 'the act of killing oneself intentionally; in law, the act of self-destruction by a person sound in mind and capable of measuring his moral responsibility,' respectively. These concepts also assume pivotal significance in case law. In *In re Colyer* ((1983) 660 P 2d 738 at 743), the Supreme Court of Washington commented: 'A death which occurs after the removal of life support systems is from natural causes, neither set in motion nor intended by the patient', and consequently is not a suicide. The Massachusetts' Supreme Judicial Court in *Superintendent of Belchertown v Saikewicz* ((1977) 370 NE 2d 417 (Mass)) expressed essentially identical views, as did the Florida Supreme Court in *Satz v Perlmutter* ((1978) 362 S 2d 160 (Fla App)). The reasoning in these cases has been widely followed in the USA. In the UK the search must go back much further in time to find any judicial opinion, but in *Clift v Schwabe* ((1846) 3 CB 437 at 464) Rolfe B stated:

> Every act of self-destruction is, in common language, described by the word suicide, provided it be the intentional act of a party knowing the probable consequences of what he is about. This is, I think, the ordinary meaning of the word.

Does a patient *intend to die* when he or she refuses further medical treatment definitely resulting in death? The courts typically adopt a narrow construction of intention in this context, equating it with desire, yet seemingly then deny the self-evident truth. In *Bouvia v Superior Court*, for instance, a 28-year-old mentally competent quadriplegic woman with cerebral palsy and crippling arthritis, who required others to feed her, refused to allow further food to be administered to her. The trial court said ((1986) 225 Cal Rptr 297 at 305–6 (Cal App)):

> It is fairly clear from the evidence and the court cannot close its eyes to the fact that [petitioner] during her stay in defendant hospital, and for some time prior thereto, had formed an intent to die. She voiced this desire to a member of staff of defendant hospital.

The California Court of Appeal, however, disagreed finding that there was no such intent to die. Similarly, in *McKay v Bergstedt* ((1990) 801 P 2d 617 (Nevada Supreme Court)), involving a 31-year-old quadriplegic patient who wished to be disconnected from the life-sustaining respirator. The Nevada Supreme Court found that Kenneth Bergstedt had no intent to take his own life, and thus did not commit suicide, although he realised that death would be the effect of his decision. Yet, he wished to be removed from the respirator because he feared an agonising death and 'despaired over the prospect of life without the attentive care, companionship and love of his devoted father'. It is arguable though that Elizabeth Bouvia *did* intend to die, even in the sense of wanting to do so – she plainly stated her desire to starve herself to death. Likewise Kenneth Bergstedt, who could not face life without his father. In *Satz v Perlmutter* the Florida Supreme Court even held that the competent (ventilator-dependent) patient had no intention to die despite having attempted on several occasions to disconnect himself from the respirator, but having been physically prevented from so doing by hospital staff ((1978) 362 So 2d 160 (Fla App)).

1. Intention: desire or more?

In some US cases the courts have rationalised their decision that a request for the removal of life-support equipment does not manifest an intention to die by declaring that the patient *really wanted to live*. But, even if it is not specious to argue that an individual does not intend to die despite the adoption of a preference for death over life (surely a person may desire, wish or will a result even though it is only the lesser of two evils?), this reasoning relies on the dubious doctrine of double effect. According to the doctrine, all intended, bad ends are morally wrong, and this includes all bad means chosen to achieve ends. Where a consequence is unintended it is perceived as a side-effect which, if bad, can be justified according to the totality of the circumstances. The doctrine in this context appeals to the distinction between desiring death for its own sake and intending to avoid continued existence in an unacceptable condition, knowing death is the consequence of the decision. Elizabeth Bouvia wished to avoid continued existence in her quadriplegic and unbearable condition; Kenneth Bergstedt found the thought of life without his father and of experiencing an agonising death unbearable etc. However, this distinction would lead to treating almost all rational self-killings as *non*-suicides because it is invariably the case that persons only choose death to avoid some other more undesirable fate, for example, continued existence in unendurable pain or indignity. Indeed, such self-killings are commonly perceived as *paradigmatic* instances of suicide.

Accepting for the moment though that death may not be desired in certain treatment-refusal contexts, can a distinction be drawn between cases where it is the burdens of the treatment itself, rather than any underlying disease or other condition of life, which motivated the decision to bring death about? David Meyers argues that where the patient does not want to die but does not want to live with the burdens of treatment that his illness entails, there is no intention to bring about death by refusing further life-prolonging treatment, ie the discontinuance of the treatment only is intended (D Meyers, '*The Human Body and the Law*' (2nd edn) (Edinburgh University Press 1990) at 280). There will certainly be cases where the treatment refusal is motivated by the desire to avoid a continued life of suffering and other cases where it is only the treatment itself which the individual seeks to avoid. It is admittedly more obvious that the former type of case falls within the compass of 'suicide'. In some instances the treatment refusal will simply be the *means* chosen in pursuance of the intended end – release from suffering. It is less obvious that, say, a Jehovah's Witness's refusal of a necessary life-sustaining blood transfusion constitutes a suicide. The doctrine of double effect does not negate moral responsibility for one's own death where death is chosen as being a *means* to the desired (intended) end, for example, the relief of suffering. It *might* though have this effect if death was a *consequence* of the achievement of an intended goal and not a means of achieving it.

Where the 'treatment' is, as in *Bouvia*, simply further feeding, it is hard to see how the intention of the patient could be limited to the burdens of continued feeding rather than the inevitable ensuing effects. But, even generally, to argue that it is the treatment rather than the existence that is unwanted is spurious. The treatment is *part* of the living. The patient's decision is based on an assessment of quality of life taken as a whole. As Springer J stated in *McKay* ((1990) 801 P 2d 617 (Nevada Supreme Court):

> If we reflect for a moment on the nature and use of this ventilator, it does not take long to see that the machine had become an integral part of Mr Bergstedt's person and was not mere 'treatment'.

This remark could apply equally to patients with kidney failure who require regular dialysis or diabetics who require frequent administrations of insulin, it is not to be solely linked to high-tech, hospital-orientated medicine. Even in the least obvious case involving the Jehovah's Witness, who has no wish to die, it is still the case that the person prefers to die rather than to live having had such a transfusion. The treatment is part of the living yet again. The intention extends to the consequences of the decision even in this case – it cannot possibly be of any import that this is a 'one-off' treatment decision rather than an ongoing treatment process. Robert Martin argues, contrasting the self-killer who desires death from the self-killer who does not, that '...each tolerates it [death] only because, under the circumstances, it is necessary for obtaining the good result'. The distinction advanced by Meyers is untenable. Death is the *means* of avoiding the undesirable aspect of life concerned, even where this is medical treatment alone, so that the doctrine of double effect provides no escape from moral responsibility even in such a case. Death is not simply an unintended side-effect.

2.   Foreseen consequences...

Legal aspects   From a legal perspective, courts invariably go to great lengths to ascertain that patients *do* appreciate that a refusal of treatment *will* culminate in death, in order to determine that they have sufficient capacity to be able to make this decision for themselves. However, although in law a person intends a consequence that it is the actor's purpose or desire to produce, the courts consistently assert that intention is *not synonymous* with desire. It has always been the case in law until very latterly that a person has been taken to have intended a prohibited result despite that result being undesired, where the consequence is either (virtually) certainly the result from the actions or is the means chosen in fulfilment of the objective(s) of the action. It is true that today, strictly, foresight of a (virtually) certain consequence is only *evidence* of intention rather than intention *per se* (see *R v Moloney* [1985] AC 905) and that a jury *can* but not *must* draw an inference of intention in such a case, but (assuming for these purposes that such talk has any coherence to it!) it has been said that it will be hard not to draw an inference where the consequence is, and is foreseen as being, little short of overwhelming (see *R v Nedrick* [1986] 3 All ER 1 (CA)). Even the determined attempt in recent years to give intention an 'ordinary, everyday meaning' has been supplemented by the formulation of judicial guidelines for juries in 'problematic' cases, which have the effect of giving the concept an 'extended' or broad meaning in the criminal law (see N Lacey, '*A Clear Concept of Intention: Elusive or Illusory?*', (1993) 56 MLR 621). Criminal responsibility is, therefore, typically perceived as being equivalent between cases of desired consequences and foreseen virtually certain consequences where no excuse or justification exists for it. As George Fletcher observes, 'Though the doctrine of double effect holds that the undesired side-effect is not intended the tendency of Anglo-American legal theory is to encompass both effects within the ambit of intended killings'. (G Fletcher, '*Rethinking Criminal Law*' (Little Brown 1978) at 257)). By total contrast with the doctrine of double effect, the criminal law (through 'defences' primarily) is only able to weigh the relevance of all the factors and features of the case where the defendant *does* intend the consequences – without intention no analysis of justification is implicated, an acquittal automatically follows.

Intention is, therefore, a more expansive concept than desire in law. It is noteworthy that in *Bland*, in the context of physicians deciding to withhold life-sustaining measures from an *incompetent* person, the House of Lords considered that the physicians involved *did* possess the requisite intention to kill. The view that death, and not just the withholding or withdrawal of food or other treatment, is intended in these treatment refusal cases seems compelling.

B.   Causation

In *Bouvia* the California Court of Appeal stated that 'her decision to let nature take its course is not equivalent to an election to commit suicide with real parties aiding and abetting therein'. It has been remarked that *Bouvia* establishes that such a refusal does not amount to suicide because the patient does not in law cause his own death. In *Re Conroy*, the New Jersey Supreme Court considered that declining life-sustaining medical treatment is not properly viewed as an attempt to commit suicide and remarked that 'refusing medical intervention merely allows the disease to take its natural course; if death were eventually to occur, it would be the result, primarily, of the underlying disease, and not the result of a self-inflicted injury' ((1985) 486 A 2d 1209 at 1224). In Canada, in *Nancy B v Hôtel-Dieu de Quebec* ((1992) 86 DLR (4th) 385 at 394 (Quebec Superior Court)) the Quebec Superior Court also stated that if the plaintiff's death occurred following the removal of respiratory support, it would result from 'nature taking its course'. This perception is one fostered by many moral philosophers and medical practitioners alike. Nonetheless, despite its pervasiveness, to say the patient is not the cause of his own death is spurious apart from in circumstances where treatment cannot offer a cure or the prolongation of life.

The law distinguishes between *factual* and *legal* causation. A cause will not be a factual cause unless the result would not have occurred *but for* the defendant's act or omission. There is no doubt though that the patient's refusal of further treatment here *is* a factual cause of the person's death. In such cases the immediate cause of death is the patient's decision to refuse further life supporting mechanisms. Death would not have occurred *when and as it did* without the implementation of the patient's decision. The underlying disease becomes the *means* of death only. Joseph Fletcher puts it in terms of the natural causes having been 'fatally set in motion' by the patient's decision. Even in cases of terminal illness, medical treatment may still be capable of prolonging life. In fact, in many of the North American cases the patient was not even terminally ill – for instance, in *Bouvia* the patient's life-expectancy was 15–20 years, in *Bergstedt* the patient's condition was non-terminal with artificial life-support and in *Nancy B* it was stated that with respiratory aid she could live for a 'considerable time' (G Fletcher, '*Rethinking Criminal Law*'' (*supra*) at 225). Whilst from a 'scientific perspective' the underlying illness or condition 'causes' death, the law is not so much concerned with the 'pathological story' as the effects of an individual's behaviour on outcomes (see M Benjamin, 'Death, Where is Thy 'Cause'?' (1976) 6 Hastings Center Report 15). There has never been any need in law for a cause to be a *sufficient* or sole (or even dominant) cause of an outcome. Thus, if any doubt exists with respect to causation, this relates to *legal* causation only, ie proximate or imputable cause.

Normally, the role of *legal* causation is to place limits on the otherwise endless causes of events and to allocate responsibility for consequences in a fair and even fashion. The enquiry is primarily designed to screen out consequences which are too remote or accidental flowing from the defendant's acts or omissions, assuming that the cause is 'substantial' (ie significant) – which it clearly would be here. There is rarely, however, any problem stemming from causation where the consequences were intended, which it has been contended above that they are. The individual effectively has sole control over the situation and his or her destiny – it would be surprising if the person did not cause the inevitable results of the decision reached, no matter how understandable or blameless the decision. There is no remoteness or accident implicated in the situations under consideration here. Further, it is an accepted principle of causation that, normally, once a voluntary, informed human act or decision has occurred, there is no need to trace back the causal enquiry beyond it. Although there are undoubted exceptions to this in cases where there has been an *earlier* criminal act and a subsequent act which arguably breaks the chain of causation with the final outcome, it applies *a fortiori* to cases where there is only one act or omission set against the background of underlying conditions or circumstances. Moreover, the later act may not be a *novus actus interveniens* yet still constitute a legal cause of an eventual outcome – although there has rarely been a need to consider this judicially…

If an omission can be a cause of one's own death, could it nevertheless be asserted that suicide is incapable of being committed by an omission? It is submitted that, contrary to the views of Glanville Williams (G Williams '*Textbook of Criminal Law*' (2nd edn) (Stevens 1983) at 613), the fact that the patient is (on one view) merely passive and does nothing positive to cause the death is not to the point. One can seemingly commit suicide by failing to act, by deliberately failing to feed oneself for instance. In the Supreme Court of the United States in *Cruzan v Director, Missouri Health Department*, Scalia J stated that:

> It would not make much sense to say that one may not kill oneself by walking into the sea, but may sit on the beach until submerged by the incoming tide ((1990) 111 L Ed 2d 224 at 249).

He later added:

> Starving oneself to death is no different from putting a gun to one's temple as far as the common law definition of suicide is concerned; the cause of death in both cases is the suicide's conscious decision to 'put an end to his own existence' (*ibid*).

It is indeed difficult to see what justification could be advanced for a distinction to be drawn between acts and omissions here. The individual is clearly terminating his own life deliberately by either means – it is the ends not the means which are the essence of suicide.

Thus, neither lack of intention nor the absence of a causal connection provide a proper basis for the conclusion that the refusal of life-sustaining treatment is not suicide.

If it is suicide, is the doctor 'assisting' it when abiding by the patient's refusal? Again, David Price provides the arguments:

> The consequence of the traditional and preponderant view that the patient's decision to refuse treatment is not a decision to commit suicide, is that the doctor's actions (encouragement as well as assistance) are in all instances outside the control of the criminal law. However, it has been argued here that a patient's decision to refuse life-prolonging treatment does constitute a decision to commit suicide. The issue then arises whether a physician assists such a patient to commit suicide. Is respecting the patient's wishes an 'aiding' (assistance) in law? Arguably in such circumstances the doctor merely allows the patient to exercise his legal right to refuse treatment, as his duty dictates. Beauchamp and Childress describe such non-intervention as 'allowed' rather than 'assisted' suicide on the basis that assistance implies aid in reaching or implementing a decision (T Beauchamp and J Childress, '*Principles of Biomedical Ethics*' (3rd edn) (OUP 1989) at 227). Nonetheless, for example, switching off a ventilator *does*, in the ordinary sense, assist the patient to implement the decision to die. Brody contends, 'In sum, it is rather hard to construe the actions of the staff…as *not* having assisted in the patient's suicide, albeit by passive measures' (H Brody 'Causing, Intending and Assisting Death' (1993) 4 The Journal of Clinical Ethics 112 at 116).

Merely failing to administer (or even withdraw) treatment or nutrition/hydration at the patient's request would undoubtedly be perceived in law as an omission. Can an omission constitute 'aiding'? (Glanville Williams (*supra*) at 579). Currently under English law, an individual may be guilty of aiding an offence by omission where the law imposes a duty to act. Although this occurs rarely, medical practice is one sphere where there would be a *prima facie* duty for which responsibility would attach. However, the actual existence of such a duty, and its content, begs the very question at issue. It arises only where there is a duty to control the other individual's behaviour. In this context, the duty is contingent on the competency or otherwise of the alleged 'suicide'. Where a severely depressed and incompetent patient refused life-prolonging treatment, there would be a duty *not* to respect that patient's wishes, and to continue treatment, if that was in the patient's best interests. In the case of a competent individual refusing life-prolonging treatment, however, there can be no duty to stop the patient from exercising this right, because of the individual's right to self-determination. Where a doctor continued life-prolonging treatment in the face of a refusal of consent to that treatment he would be frustrating the patient's action for battery (an example of such an action is the Canadian case of *Malette v Shulman* (1990) 67 DLR (4th) 321 (Ontario Court of Appeal)). Some omissions to act are therefore not only justified but mandated by law and no physician culpability could attach thereto.

Whatever the argument against Lord Goff's view in *Bland*, as we shall see shortly, it was applied by Thorpe J in *Secretary of State for the Home Department v Robb* (1994) 22 BMLR 43.

As regards the third societal interest, although there are a number of American cases which give some weight to concern for the interests of the medical profession (eg *Brophy v New England Sinai Hospital* (1986) 497 NE 2d 626 (Mass Sup Jud Ct)), it is clear that English law would not consider these interests overreaching. Thus, the first three interests identified in *Bouvia* do not outweigh the right of the competent adult patient to refuse treatment.

The court considered these three societal interests and their effect, if any, in the following case.

Secretary of State for the Home Department v Robb (1994) 22 BMLR 43 (Fam Div)

On 27 August 1994 the respondent prisoner, who had been diagnosed as suffering from a personality disorder, indicated not only by repeated criminal offending, addiction to drugs and ambivalence as to his sexual orientation but also by violent tendencies and ill-sustained personal relationships, went on hunger strike. The respondent was advised of the clinical consequences of his decision and medical experts were agreed that he was of sound mind and understanding. The Home Secretary subsequently sought declarations that the Home Office, prison officials and physicians and nursing staff responsible for the respondent (i) might lawfully observe and abide by the respondent's refusal to receive nutrition and (ii) might lawfully abstain from providing him with hydration and nutrition, whether by artificial means or otherwise, for so long as he retained the capacity to refuse the same.

Thorpe J: The relevant law I take from Miss Davies QC's helpful skeleton argument. The first principle is that every person's body is inviolate and proof against any form of physical molestation. The authority for that is *F v West Berkshire Health Authority* (*Mental Health Act Commission intervening*) (1989) 4 BMLR 1, [1990] 2 AC 1. Secondly, the principle of self-determination requires that respect must be given to the wishes of the patient. So if an adult of sound mind refuses, however unreasonably, to consent to treatment or care by which his life would or might be prolonged, the doctors responsible for his care must give effect to his wishes even though they do not consider it to be in his best interest to do so. The authority for that principle is *Re T (adult: refusal of medical treatment)* (1992) 9 BMLR 46, [1993] Fam 95 and *Airedale NHS Trust v Bland* (1993) 12 BMLR 64, [1993] AC 789.

The next proposition drawn from the same authority of *Airedale NHS Trust* is that a patient who is entitled to consent to treatment which might or would have the effect of prolonging his life and who refuses so to consent, and by reason of the refusal subsequently dies, does not commit suicide. A doctor who, in accordance with his duty, complied with the patient's wishes in such circumstances does not aid or abet a suicide...

Against that background, it seems to me that the definition of the duty of the Home Office in relation to prisoners on hunger strike is relatively straightforward. There is a surprising dearth of authority in this jurisdiction and that dearth has led the plaintiff to seek this declaration and judgment. The only seemingly relevant case is *Leigh v Gladstone* (1909) 26 TLR 139, in which

Lord Alverstone CJ directed the jury that it was the duty of prison officials to preserve the health of prisoners in their custody and that that duty extended to force feeding. For many reasons it seems to me that that authority is of no surviving application and can be consigned to the archives of legal history. It was a case in which a suffragette who had been force fed in prison sought damages against the then Home Secretary. It was decided at a time when there was no question in the mind of government that the Home Secretary had both the power and the duty to force feed hunger-striking prisoners. It was decided at a time when suicide was a criminal act, as was the aiding and abetting of that act. It was a decision taken in the climate of dramatic conflict between the suffragette movement and the government of the day. The point does not seem to have been fully argued and the charge to the jury of Lord Alverstone CJ is of little relevance or weight in modern times in determining the current law.

The only reference to the duty of the Home Secretary in modern authority is the briefest passage in the speech of Lord Keith of Kinkel in *Airedale NHS Trust v Bland* (1993) 12 BMLR 64 at 107, [1993] AC 789 at 859, in which he said:

> ...the principle of the sanctity of life...is not an absolute one. It does not compel a medical practitioner on pain of criminal sanctions to treat a patient, who will die if he does not, contrary to the express wishes of the patient. It does not authorise forcible feeding of prisoners on hunger strike. It does not compel the temporary keeping alive of patients who are terminally ill where to do so would merely prolong their suffering.

There have been much fuller developments in other common law jurisdictions, particularly in the United States, and all counsel have drawn attention to and relied upon a number of decisions, all of which consider the right of the individual to refuse nutrition in differing circumstances. I will refer only to recent decision in the United States that is directly concerned with adult prisoners on hunger strike. The most recent, and for me the most helpful, is the decision of the Supreme Court of California, *Thor v Superior Court* (1993) 5 Cal 4th 725. That authority upheld a decision at first instance that the prison authorities failed in their application for an order authorising force feeding of a quadriplegic prison inmate who had determined to refuse food and medical treatment necessary to maintain his life. The conclusion of the court was the right of self-determination prevailed but the court recognised that the right of self-determination was not absolute and that there were four specific state interests that might countervail. They were specifically (i) preserving life, (ii) preventing suicide, (iii) maintaining the integrity of the medical profession, and (iv) protecting innocent third parties.

The other United States case which is relevant to these arguments is the case of *Re Caulk* (1984) 125 NH 226. There, the Supreme Court of New Hampshire identified a very similar balancing exercise but found that the balance tipped against the right of self-determination. It seems that that decision was not specifically considered in the judgments given in the later case of *Thor*, and I have to say that I find more persuasive the dissenting judgment of Douglas J than the judgment of the majority given by Bachelder J.

These decisions are obviously relevant and helpful in reaching a decision as to how the law stands in this jurisdiction. I consider specifically the four countervailing state interests that were set against the individual's right of self-determination.

The first, namely the interest that the state holds in preserving life, seems to me to be but part and parcel of the balance that must be struck in determining and declaring the right of self-determination. The principle of sanctity of human life in this jurisdiction is seen to yield to the principle of self-determination. It is within that balance that the consideration of the preservation of life is reflected.

The second countervailing state interest, preventing suicide, is recognisable but seems to me to be of no application in cases such as this where the refusal of nutrition and medical treatment in the exercise of the right of self-determination does not constitute an act of suicide.

The third consideration of maintaining the integrity of the medical profession is one that I find hard to recognise as a distinct consideration. Medical ethical decisions can be acutely difficult and it is when they are at their most acute that applications for declaratory relief are made to the High Court. I cannot myself see that this is a distinct consideration that requires to be set against the right of self-determination of the individual.

The fourth consideration of protecting innocent third parties is one that is undoubtedly recognised in this jurisdiction, as is evidenced by the decision of Sir Stephen Brown P in *Re S (adult: refusal of medical treatment)* (1992) 9 BMLR 69, [1993] Fam 123. Also recognised within this jurisdiction is a consideration that was given weight in the decision of *Re Caulk*, namely the need to preserve the internal order, discipline and security within the confines of the jail. But neither of these considerations arise in the present case.

It seems to me that within this jurisdiction there is perhaps a stronger emphasis on the right of the individual's self-determination when balance comes to be struck between that right and any countervailing interests of the state. So this decision is not a borderline one: this is a plain case for declaratory relief. The right of the defendant to determine his future is plain. That right is not diminished by his status as a detained prisoner. The rights of the prisoner, as Mr Lloyd has emphasised in his submissions, are plainly stated in *Leech v Parkhurst Prison Deputy Governor* [1988] 1 All ER 485, [1988] AC 533. Against the specific right of self-determination held by the defendant throughout his sentence there seems to me in this case to be no countervailing state interests to be set in the balance. I have no hesitation in making the declarations in the form ultimately agreed between counsel.

It is important to see how Thorpe J approached the four 'societal interests'. He saw them as being placed in the balance against the individual's right of self-determination. He concluded that this right was not, in the circumstances, outweighed by these interests. Neither, on the facts, was the societal interests in preserving good order, discipline etc in a prison implicated (contrast *Leigh v Gladstone* (1909) 26 TLR 139 and in *Re Caulk* (1984) 125 NH 226 (NH Sup Ct)).

It is important also to notice what Thorpe J actually decided. He granted a declaration at the request of the Home Secretary that it would be lawful *not* to force feed the individual. In other words, he held that there was no *duty* to force feed the prisoner (see also *A-G of British Columbia v Astaforoff* [1983] 6 WWR 322 (Bouck J) and [1984] 4 WWR 385 (BC CA)). Thorpe J left open whether the prison authorities *could* force feed, ie that in sufficiently compelling circumstances within the prison, the interest in prison discipline, order etc could outweigh the prisoner's right (see further commentary (1995) 3 Med L Rev 189, at 190–191 (IK) and *Dept of Immigration v Mok* (1994) 2 Med L Rev 102 (Sup Ct NSW)). That, however, casts no doubt upon the situation between doctor and patient – which Thorpe J conceived to be the case in *Robb* – where the right to refuse is unassailable.

Indeed, any contrary view would in all probability offend art 8 of the European Convention (right to private and family life) and could well, in appropriate circumstances, amount to 'inhuman or degrading treatment' contrary to art 3. The 'right to life' protected under art 2 would, necessarily, fall away if a competent adult refused life-sustaining treatment (see *infra*, ch 16).

It is the fourth societal interest which is problematic. There are two situations to consider here: *first*, where the patient's child has been born and it is suggested that its interests will be compromised by the death of the patient; *secondly*, where the patient is pregnant and the refusal of treatment may (or will) deleteriously affect the unborn child, for example, lead to its death.

(a) The pregnant woman and the foetus

Re T recognises only the fourth category of interest as potentially capable of outweighing the right of the adult patient to decide for herself. Subsequently, the High Court in some haste was called upon to consider this potential exception to the patient's right to refuse treatment.

(i)   *RE S* AND *RE AC*

Re S (adult: refusal of medical treatment) [1992] 4 All ER 671, (1992) 9 BMLR 69 (Fam Div)

Sir Stephen Brown P: This is an application by a health authority for a declaration to authorise the surgeons and staff of a hospital to carry out an emergency Caesarean operation upon a patient, who I shall refer to as 'Mrs S'.

Mrs S is 30 years of age. She is in labour with her third pregnancy. She was admitted to a hospital last Saturday with ruptured membranes and in spontaneous labour. She has continued in labour since. She is already six days overdue beyond the expected date of birth, which was 6 October, and she has now refused, on religious grounds, to submit herself to a Caesarean section operation. She is supported in this by her husband. They are described as 'born-again Christians' and are clearly quite sincere in their beliefs.

I have heard the evidence of P, a Fellow of the Royal College of Surgeons who is in charge of this patient at the hospital. He has given, succinctly and graphically, a description of the condition of this patient. Her situation is desperately serious, as is also the situation of the as yet unborn child. The child is in what is described as a position of 'transverse lie', with the elbow projecting through the cervix and the head being on the right side. There is the gravest risk of a rupture of the uterus if the section is not carried out and the natural labour process is permitted to continue. The evidence of P is that we are concerned with 'minutes rather than hours' and that it is a 'life and death' situation. He has done his best, as have other surgeons and doctors at the hospital, to persuade the mother that the only means of saving her life, and also I emphasise the life of her unborn child, is to carry out a Caesarean section operation. P is emphatic. He says it is absolutely the case that the baby cannot be born alive if a Caesarean operation is not carried out. He has described the medical condition. I am not going to go into it in detail because of the pressure of time.

I have been assisted by Mr Munby QC appearing for the Official Solicitor, as amicus curiae. The Official Solicitor answered the call of the court within minutes and, although this application only came to the notice of the court officials at 1.30pm, it has come on for hearing just before 2 o'clock and now at 2.18pm I propose to make the declaration which is sought. I do so in the knowledge that the fundamental question appears to have been left open by Lord Donaldson MR in *Re T (adult: refusal of medical treatment)* [1992] 4 All ER 649, heard earlier this year in the Court of Appeal, and in the knowledge that there is no English authority which is directly in point. There is, however, some American authority which suggests that if this case were being heard in the American courts the answer would be likely to be in favour of granting a declaration in these circumstances: see *Re AC* (1990) 573 A 2d 1235 at 1240, 1246–1248, 1252.

I do not propose to say more at this stage, except that I wholly accept the evidence of P as to the desperate nature of this situation, and that I grant the declaration as sought.

Can the view of Stephen Brown P be reconciled with the decision in *Re T*? (For discussions of *Re S* see: K Stern 'Court Ordered Caesareans – Whose Interests?' (1993) 56 MLR 238; M Thomson 'After Re S' (1994) 2 Med L Rev 127 and Commentary (1993) 1 Med L Rev 92 (AG).) In so far as the court's declaration was based upon its determination of what it saw as the 'vital interests of the mother', then this is quite inconsistent with *Re T*. A medical procedure refused by a competent adult cannot be lawfully carried out due to concern for that individual's interest. The patient determines his own interests. In so far as the judgment in *Re S* prefers the interests of the unborn child to those of the mother, should these interests prevail?

We approach this question in three stages. First, we look at the arguments advanced in the important US case of *Re AC* (1990) 573 A 2d 1235. Secondly, we examine the policy issues involved in formulating the legal position and we pay particular attention to the thoughtful analyses offered in the Canadian Supreme Court in *Winnipeg Child and Family Services (Northwest Area) v G* (1997) 152 DLR (4th) 193. Finally, we see how the Court of Appeal in England has stepped back from *Re S* and re-asserted the pregnant woman's right to refuse treatment whatever its consequences to the unborn child.

The most significant decision in the United States is the case of *Re AC*. You will recall Stephen Brown P's reference to it in *Re S* to support his decision. As we shall see, this is somewhat problematical, to say the least.

Re AC (1990) 573 A 2d 1235 (DC CA)

Terry JA: We are confronted here with two profoundly difficult and complex issues. First, we must determine who has the right to decide the course of medical treatment for a patient who, although near death, is pregnant with a viable fetus. Second, we must establish how that decision should be made if the patient cannot make it for herself – more specifically, how a court should proceed when faced with a pregnant patient, *in extremis*, who is apparently incapable of making an informed decision regarding medical care for herself and her fetus. We hold that in virtually all cases the question of what is to be done is to be decided by the patient – the pregnant woman – on behalf of herself and the fetus. If the patient is incompetent or otherwise unable to give an informed consent to a proposed course of medical treatment, then her decision must be ascertained through the procedure known as substituted judgment. Because the trial court did not follow that procedure, we vacate its order and remand the case for further proceedings…

This case came before the trial court when George Washington University Hospital petitioned the emergency judge in chambers for declaratory relief as to how it should treat its patient, AC, who was close to death from cancer and was twenty six and one-half weeks pregnant with a viable fetus. After a hearing lasting approximately three hours, which was held at the hospital (though not in AC's room), the court ordered that a caesarean section be performed on AC to deliver the fetus. Counsel for AC immediately sought a stay in this court, which was unanimously denied by a hastily assembled division of three judges. *In Re AC* 533 A 2d 611 (DC 1987). The caesarean was performed, and a baby girl, LMC, was delivered. Tragically, the child died within two and one-half hours, and the mother died two days later.

Counsel for AC now maintain that AC was competent and that she made an informed choice not to have the caesarean performed. Given this view of the facts, they argue that it was error for the trial court to weigh the state's interest in preserving the potential life of a viable fetus against AC's interest in having her decision respected. They argue further that, even if the substituted judgment procedure had been followed, the evidence would necessarily show that AC would not have wanted the caesarean section. Under either analysis, according to these arguments, the trial court erred in subordinating AC's right to bodily integrity in favor of the state's interest in potential life. Counsel for the hospital and for LMC contend, on the other hand, that AC was incompetent to make her own medical decisions and that, under the substituted judgment procedure, the evidence clearly established that AC would have consented to the caesarean. In the alternative, counsel for LMC argues that even if LMC's interest and those of the state were in conflict with AC's wishes, it was proper for the trial court to balance their interests and resolve the conflict in favour of surgical intervention.

We do not accept any of these arguments because the evidence, realistically viewed, does not support them…

[T]he trial court made oral findings of fact. It found, first, that AC would probably die, according to uncontroverted medical testimony, 'within the next twenty-four to forty-eight hours' second, that AC was 'pregnant with a twenty-six and a half week viable fetus who, based upon controverted medical testimony, has approximately a fifty to sixty percent chance to survive if a caesarean section is performed as soon as possible'; third, that because the fetus was viable, 'the state has [an] important and legitimate interest in protecting the potentiality of human life'; and fourth, that there had been some testimony that the operation 'may very well hasten the death of [AC],' but that there had also been testimony that delay would greatly increase the risk to the fetus and that 'the prognosis is not great for the fetus to be delivered post-mortem…' Most significantly, the court found:

> The court is of the view that it does not clearly know what [AC's] present views are with respect to the issue of whether or not the child should live or die. She's presently unconscious. As late as Friday of last week, she wanted the baby to live. As late as yesterday, she did not know for sure.

Having made these findings of fact and conclusions of law, and expressly relying on *In Re Madyun*, 114 Daily Wash L Rptr 2233 (DC Super Ct July 26, 1986), the court ordered that a caesarean section be performed to deliver AC's child…there is only one published decision from an appellate court that deals with the question of when, or even whether, a court may order a caesarean section: *Jefferson v Griffin Spalding County Hospital Authority*, 247 Ga 86, 274 SE 2d 457 (1981).

Jefferson is of limited relevance, if any at all, to the present case. In *Jefferson* there was a competent refusal by the mother to undergo the proposed surgery, but the evidence showed that performance of the caesarean was in the medical interests of both the mother and the fetus. In the instant case, by contrast, the evidence is unclear as to whether AC was competent when she mouthed her apparent refusal of the caesarean ('I don't want it done'), and it was generally assumed that while the surgery would most likely be highly beneficial to the fetus, it would be dangerous for the mother. Thus there was no clear maternal-fetal conflict in this case arising from a competent decision by the mother to forego a procedure for the benefit of the fetus. The procedure may well have been against AC's medical interest, but if she was competent and given the choice, she may well have consented to an operation of significant risk to herself in order to maximize her fetus' chance for survival. From the evidence, however, we simply cannot tell whether she would have consented or not.

Thus our analysis of this case begins with the tenet common to all medical treatment cases: that any person has the right to make an informed choice, if competent to do so, to accept or forego medical treatment. The doctrine of informed consent, based on this principle and rooted in the concept of bodily integrity, is ingrained in our common law. *See Crain v Allison*, 443 A 2d 558, 561–562 (DC 1982); *Canterbury v Spence*, 150 US App DC 263, 271, 464 F 2d 772, 780, *cert denied*, 409 US 1064, 93 S Ct 560, 34 L Ed 2d 518 (1972); *Schloendorff v Society of New York Hospital* 211 NY 125, 127, 105 NE 92, 93 (1914). Under the doctrine of informed consent, a physician must inform the patient 'at a minimum' of the 'nature of the proposed treatment, any alternative treatment procedures, and the nature and degree of risks and benefits inherent in undergoing and in abstaining from the proposed treatment.' *Crain v Allison, supra*, 443 A 2d at 562 (footnote omitted). To protect the right of every person to bodily integrity, courts uniformly hold that a surgeon who performs an operation without the patient's consent may be guilty of a battery, *Canterbury v Spence, supra*, 150 US App DC at 274, 464 F 2d at 783, or that if the surgeon obtains an insufficiently informed consent, he or she may be liable for negligence. *Crain v Allison, supra*, 443, A 2d at 561–562. Furthermore, the right to informed consent 'also encompassed a right to informed refusal.' *In Re Conroy*, 98 NJ 321, 336, 486 A 2d 1209, 1222 (1985) (citation omitted).

In the same vein, courts do not compel one person to permit a significant intrusion upon his or her bodily integrity for the benefit of another person's health. *See, eg Bonner v Moran*, 75 US App DC 156, 157, 126 F 2d 121, 122 (1941) (parental consent required for skin graft from fifteen-year-old for benefit of cousin who had been severely burned); *McFall v Shimp*, 10 Pa D & C 3d 90 (Allegheny County Ct 1978). In *McFall* the court refused to order Shimp to donate bone marrow which was necessary to save the life of his cousin, McFall.

> The common law has consistently held to a rule which provides that one human being is under no legal compulsion to give aid or to take action to save another human being or to rescue…For our law to *compel* defendant to submit to an intrusion of his body would change every concept and principle upon which our society is founded. To do so would defeat the sanctity of the individual, and would impose a rule which would know no limits, and one could not imagine where the line would be drawn.

Id at 91 (emphasis in original). Even though Shimp's refusal would mean death for McFall, the court would not order Shimp to allow his body to be invaded. It has been suggested that fetal cases are different because a woman who 'has chosen to lend her body to bring [a] child into the world' has an enhanced duty to assure the welfare of the fetus, sufficient even to require her to undergo caesarean surgery. Robertson, *Procreative Liberty*, 69 Va L Rev at 456. Surely, however, a fetus cannot have rights in this respect superior to those of a person who has already been born.[8]…

This court and others, while recognizing the right to accept or reject medical treatment, have consistently held that the right is not absolute. *Eg, In Re Boyd, supra*, 403 A 2d at 749–750; *In Re Osborne, supra*, 294 A 2d at 374; *In Re President & Directors of Georgetown College, Inc*, 118 US App D C 80, 331 F 2d 1000, *cert denied*, 377 US 978, 84 S Ct 1883, 12 L Ed 2d 746 (1964); *Rasmussen ex rel Mitchell v Fleming, supra*, 154 Ariz at 216, 741 P 2d at 683; *In Re Conroy, supra*, 98 NJ 337, 486 A 2d at 1223; *cf Hughes v United States*, 429 A 2d 1339 (DC 1981) (upholding as reasonable a minor surgical intrusion to remove bullets from a criminal suspect), *United States v Crowder*, 177 US App DC 165, 543 F 2d 312 (1976) (same), *cert denied*, 429 US 1062, 97 S Ct 788, 50 L Ed 2d 779 (1977). In some cases, especially those involving life-or-death situations or incompetent patients, the courts have recognized four countervailing interests that may involve the state as *parens patriae*: preserving life, preventing suicide, maintaining the ethical integrity of the medical profession, and protecting third parties. *See, eg, In Re Boyd, supra*, 403 A 2d at 748 n 9; *Brophy v New England Sinai Hospital, Inc*, 398 Mas 417, 431–433, 497 NE 2d 626, 634 (1986); *Saikewicz, supra*, 373 Mass at 737, 370 NE 2d at 425; *In Re Farrell, supra*, 108 NJ at 350, 529 A 2d at 410–411. Neither the prevention of suicide nor the integrity of the medical profession has any bearing on this case. Further, the state's interest in preserving life must be truly compelling to justify overriding a competent person's right to refuse medical treatment. *In Re Osborne, supra*, 294 A 2d at 374–375; *Tune v Walter Reed Army Medical Hospital, supra*, 602 F Supp at 1455–1456. This is equally true for incompetent patients, who have just as much right as competent patients to have their decisions made while competent respected, even in a substituted judgment framework. *See In Re Boyd, supra*, 403 A 2d at 750; *John F Kennedy Memorial Hospital, Inc v Bludworth, supra*, 452 So 2d at 923–924; *Saikewicz, supra*, 373 Mass at 739, 370 NE 2d at 427–428; *In Re Conroy, supra*, 98 NJ at 343, 486 A 2d at 1229.

In those rare cases in which a patient's right to decide her own course of treatment has been judicially overridden, courts have usually acted to vindicate the state's interest in protecting third parties, even if in fetal state. *See Jefferson v Griffin Spalding County Hospital Authority, supra* (ordering that caesarean section be performed on a woman in her thirty-ninth week of pregnancy to save both the mother and the fetus); *Raleigh Fitkin-Paul Morgan Memorial Hospital v Anderson*, 42 NJ 421, 201 A 2d 537 (ordering blood transfusions over the objection of a Jehovah's Witness, in her thirty-second week of pregnancy, to save her life and that of the fetus), *cert denied*, 377 US 985, 84 S Ct 1894, 12 L Ed 2d 1032 (1964); *In Re Jamaica Hospital*, 128 Misc 2d 1006, 491 NY S 2d 898 (Sup Ct 1985) (ordering the transfusion of blood to a Jehovah's Witness eighteen weeks pregnant, who objected on religious grounds, and finding that the state's interest in the not-yet-viable fetus outweighed the patient's interests); *Crouse Irving Memorial Hospital, Inc v Paddock*, 127 Misc 2d 101, 485 NYS 2d 443 (Sup Ct 1985) (ordering transfusions as necessary over religious objections to save the mother and a fetus that was to be prematurely delivered); *cf In Re President & Directors of Georgetown College, Inc, supra*, 118 US App DC at 88, 331 F 2d at 1008 (ordering a transfusion, *inter alia*, because of a mother's parental duty to her living minor children). But see *Taft v Taft*, 388 Mass 331, 446 NE 2d 395 (1983) (vacating an order which required a woman in her fourth month of pregnancy to undergo a 'purse-string' operation, on the ground that there were no compelling circumstances to justify overriding her religious objections and her constitutional right of privacy).

What we distill from the cases discussed in this section is that every person has the right, under the common law and the Constitution, to accept or refuse medical treatment. This right of bodily integrity belongs equally to persons who are competent and persons who are not. Further, it matters not what the quality of a patient's life may be; the right of bodily integrity is not extinguished simply because someone is ill, or even at death's door. To protect that right against intrusion by others – family members, doctors, hospitals, or anyone else, however well-intentioned – we hold that a court must determine the patient's wishes by any means available, and must abide by those wishes unless there are truly extraordinary or compelling reasons to override them. *In Re Osborne, supra*. When the patient is incompetent, or when the court is unable to determine competency, the substituted judgment procedure must be followed.

From the record before us, we simply cannot tell whether AC was ever competent, after being sedated, to make an informed decision one way or the other regarding the proposed caesarean section. The trial court never made any finding about AC's competency to decide. Undoubtedly, during most of the proceedings below, AC was incompetent to make a treatment decision; that is, she was unable to give an informed consent based on her assessment of the risks and benefits of the contemplated surgery. The court knew from the evidence that AC was sedated and unconscious, and thus it could reasonably have found her incompetent to render an informed consent; however, it made no such finding. On the other hand, there was no clear evidence that AC was competent to render an informed consent after the trial court's initial order was communicated to her.

We think it is incumbent on any trial judge in a case like this, unless it is impossible to do so, to ascertain whether a patient is competent to make her own medical decisions. Whenever possible, the judge should personally attempt to speak with the patient and doctors. See *In Re Osborne, supra*, 294 A 2d at 374; *In Re President & Directors of Georgetown College, Inc, supra*, 118 US App DC at 87, 331 F 2d at 1007. It is improper to presume that a patient is incompetent. *United States v Charters, supra*, 829 F 2d at 495. We have no reason to believe that, if competent, AC would or would not have refused consent to a caesarean. We hold, however, that without a competent refusal from AC to go forward with the surgery, and without a finding through substituted judgment that AC would not have consented to the surgery, it was error for the trial court to proceed to a balancing analysis, weighing the rights of AC against the interests of the state.

There are two additional arguments against overriding AC's objects to caesarean surgery. First, as the American Public Health Association cogently states in its *amicus curiae* brief:

> Rather than protecting the health of women and children, court-ordered caesareans erode the element of trust that permits a pregnant woman to communicate to her physician – without fear of reprisal – all information relevant to her proper diagnosis and treatment. An even more serious consequence of court-ordered interventions is that it drives women at high risk of complications during pregnancy and childbirth out of the health care system to avoid coerced treatment.

Second, and even more compellingly, any judicial proceeding in a case such as this will ordinarily take place – like the one before us here – under time constraints so pressing that it is difficult or impossible for the mother to communicate adequately with counsel, or for counsel to organize an effective factual and legal presentation in defence of her liberty and privacy interests and bodily integrity. Any intrusion implicating such basic values ought not to be lightly undertaken when the mother not only is precluded from conducting pre-trial discovery (to which she would be entitled as a matter of course in any controversy over even a modest amount of money) but also is in no position to prepare meaningfully for trial. As one commentator has noted:

The procedural shortcomings rampant in these cases are not mere technical deficiencies. They undermine the authority of the decisions themselves, posing serious questions as to whether judges can, in the absence of genuine notice, adequate representation, explicit standards of proof, and right of appeal, realistically frame principled and useful legal responses to the dilemmas with which they are being confronted. Certainly courts dealing with other kinds of medical decision-making conflicts have insisted both upon much more rigorous procedural standards and upon significantly more information.

Gallagher, *Parental Invasions and Interventions: What's Wrong with Fetal Rights*, 10 Harv Women's LJ 9, 49 (1987).

In this case AC's court-appointed attorney was unable even to meet with his client before the hearing. By the time the case was heard, AC's condition did not allow her to be present, nor was it reasonably possible for the judge to hear from her directly. The factual record, moreover, was significantly flawed because AC's mental records were not before the court and because Dr Jeffrey Moscow, the physician who had been treating AC for many years, was not even contacted and hence did not testify. Finally, the time for legal preparation was so minimal that neither the court nor counsel mentioned the doctrine of substituted judgment, which – with benefit of briefs, oral arguments, and above all, time – we now deem critical to the outcome of this case. We cannot be at all certain that the trial judge would have reached the same decision if the testimony of Dr Moscow and the abundant legal scholarship filed in this court had been meaningfully available to him, and if there had been enough time for him to consider and reflect on these matters as a judge optimally should do.

B.   Substituted Judgment

In the previous section we discussed the right of an individual to accept or reject medical treatment. We concluded that if a patient is competent and has made an informed decision regarding the course of her medical treatment, that decision will control in virtually all cases. Sometimes, however, as our analysis presupposes here, a once competent patient will be unable to render an informed decision. In such a case, we hold that the court must make a substituted judgment on behalf of the patient, based on all the evidence. This means that the duty of the court, 'as surrogate for the incompetent, is to determine as best it can what choice that individual, if competent, would make with respect to medical procedures.' *In Re Boyd, supra*, 403 A 2d at 750 (citation omitted).

…[T]o determine the subjective desires of the patient, the court must consider the totality of the evidence, focusing particularly on written or oral directions concerning treatment to family, friends, and health-care professionals. The court should also take into account the patient's past decisions regarding medical treatment, and attempt to ascertain from what is known about the patient's value system, goals, and desires what the patient would decide if competent. See *In Re Conroy, supra*, 98 NJ at 343–44, 486 A 2d at 1229–1230; *In Re Dorone, supra*, 349 Pa Super at 68, 502 A 2d at 1278.

After considering the patient's statements, if any, the previous medical decisions of the patient, and the values held by the patient, the court may still be unsure what course the patient would choose. In such circumstances the court may supplement its knowledge about the patient by determining what most persons would be likely do in a similar situation. *In Re Boyd, supra*, 403 A 2d at 751, citing *Saikewicz, supra*, 373 Mass, at 343, 370 NE 2d at 430; *accord*, 1983 President's Commission Report, *Deciding to Forego Life-Sustaining Treatment* at 135; 1982 President's Commission Report, *Making Health Care Decisions* at 180–181. When the patient is pregnant, however, she may not be concerned exclusively with her own welfare. Thus it is proper for the court, in a case such as this, to weigh (along with all the other factors) the mother's prognosis, the viability of the fetus, the probable result of treatment or non-treatment for both mother and fetus, and the mother's likely interest in avoiding impairment for her child together with her own instincts for survival. *Cf In Re Roe, supra*, 383 Mass at 431, 421 NE 2d at 57…

The [trial] court did not go on, as it should have done, to make a finding as to what AC would have chosen to do if she were competent. Instead, the court undertook to balance the state's and LMC's interests in surgical interventions against AC's perceived interest in not having the caesarean performed…

What a trial court must do in a case such as this is to determine, if possible whether the patient is capable of making an informed decision about the course of her medical treatment. If she is, and if she makes such a decision, her wishes will control in virtually all cases. If the court finds that the patient is incapable of making an informed consent (and thus incompetent), then the court must make a substituted judgment. This means that the court must ascertain as best it can what the patient would do if faced wit the particular treatment question. Again, in virtually all cases the decisions of the patient, albeit discerned through the mechanism of substituted judgment, will control. We do not quite foreclose the possibility that a conflicting state interest may be so compelling that the patient's wishes must yield but we anticipate that such cases will be extremely rare and truly exceptional. This is not such a case.

Having said that, we go no further. We need not decide whether, or in what circumstances, the state's interests can ever prevail over the interests of a pregnant patient. We emphasize, nevertheless, that it would be an extraordinary case indeed in which a court might ever be justified in overriding the patient's wishes and authorizing a major surgical procedure such as a caesarean section. Throughout this opinion we have stressed that the patient's wishes, once they are ascertained, must be followed in 'virtually all cases,' *ante* at 1249, unless there are 'truly extraordinary or compelling reasons to override them,' *ante* at 1247. Indeed, some may doubt that there could ever be a situation extraordinary or compelling enough to justify a massive intrusion into a person's body, such as a caesarean section, against that person's will. Whether such a situation may someday present itself is a question that we need not strive to answer here. We see no need to reach out and decide an issue that is not presented on the record before us; this case is difficult enough as it is. We think it sufficient for now to chart the course for future cases resembling this one, and to express the hope that we shall not be presented with a case in the foreseeable future that requires us to sail off the chart into the unknown[23].

Footnotes to majority opinion

8.   There are also practical consequences to consider. What if AC had refused to comply with a court order that she submit to a caesarean? Under the circumstances, she obviously could not have been held in civil contempt and imprisoned or required to pay a daily fine until compliance. C*f United States v United Mine Workers*, 330 US 258, 304–306, 67 S Ct 677, 701002, 91 L Ed 884 (1947); *DD v MT* 550 A 2d 37, 43 (DC 1988). Enforcement could be accomplished only through physical force or its equivalent. AC would have to be fastened with restraints to the operating table, or perhaps involuntarily rendered unconscious by force injecting her with an anesthetic, and then subjected to unwanted major surgery. Such situations would surely give one pause in a civil society, especially when AC had done no wrong. C*f Rochin v California*, 72 S Ct 205, 208. . .

23.   In particular, we stress that nothing in this opinion should be read as either approving or disapproving the holding *In Re Madyun, supra*. There are substantial factual differences between *Madyun* and the present case. In this case, for instance, the medical interests of the mother and the fetus were in sharp conflict: what was good for one would have been harmful to the other. In *Madyun*, however, there was no real conflict between the interests of mother and fetus; on the contrary, there was strong evidence that the proposed caesarean would be beneficial to both. Moreover, in *Madyun* the pregnancy was at full term, and Mrs Madyun had been in labor for two and a half days; in this case, however, AC was barely two-thirds of the way through her pregnancy and there were no signs of labor. If another *Madyun* type case ever comes before this court, its result may well depend on facts that we cannot now foresee. For that reason (among others), we defer until another day any discussion of whether *Madyun* was rightly or wrongly decided.

Belson JA: I agree with much of the majority opinion, but I disagree with its ultimate ruling that the trial court's order must be set aside, and with the narrow view it takes of the state's interest in preserving life and the unborn child's interest in life.

More specifically, I agree with the guidance the opinion affords trial judges as to how to approach a case like this, first determining the mother's competency to make an informed decision whether to have a caesarean delivery and, if the mother is not competent, then making a substituted judgment for the mother. I also agree that, with respect to surgical procedures, the pregnant woman's wishes, either as stated expressly or as discerned through substituted judgment, should ordinarily be respected and carried out unless there are compelling reasons to override them…

[An] aspect of the majority opinion deserves comment. Having determined that the trial court must be reversed, the majority goes on to opine, in dictum, that this particular case is not one of those 'extremely rare and truly exceptional' cases in which a patient's wishes regarding the proposed medical treatment can be overruled by reason of a compelling state interest (here, the interest in protecting the life of the viable unborn child). This is dictum because, as the majority points out, '[w]e have no reason to believe that, if competent, AC would or would not have refused consent to a caesarean.' Majority opinion at 1247. That being the case, and the actual application of the standard the majority adopts to the facts of this case not being necessary to the majority's determination to reverse, one must regard as dictum the majority's statement that this would not be one of those rare cases in which compelling interest might warrant overriding a mother's decision not to consent.

I think it appropriate, nevertheless, to state my disagreement with the very limited view the majority opinion takes of the circumstances in which the interests of a viable unborn child can afford such compelling reasons. The state's interest in preserving human life and the viable unborn child's interest in survival are entitled, I think to more weight than I find them assigned by the majority when it states that 'in virtually all cases the decision of the patient…will control.' Majority opinion at 1252. I would hold that in those instances, fortunately rare, in which the viable unborn child's interest in living and the state's parallel interest in protecting human life come into conflict with the mother's decision to forgo a procedure such as a caesarean section, a balancing should be struck in which the unborn child's and the state's interests are entitled to substantial weight…

…for the purposes that are, at least, relevant to this case, a viable unborn child is a *person* at common law who has legal rights that are entitled to the protection of the courts. In a case like the one before us, the unborn child is a patient of both the hospital and any treating physician, and the hospital or physician may be liable for the child for the child's prenatal injury or death if caused by their negligence…

Without going into the difficult question of the extent to which an unborn viable child may be entitled to protection under the Fifth, the Fourteenth, or other Amendments to the Constitution, the already recognized rights and interests mentioned above are sufficient to indicate the need for a balancing process in which the rights of the viable unborn child are assigned substantial weight. This view is consistent with the decision of the only appellate court which has heretofore considered this issue…

The balancing test should be applied in instances in which women become pregnant and carry an unborn child to the point of viability. This is not an unreasonable classification because, I submit, a woman who carries a child to viability is in fact a member of a unique category of persons. Her circumstances differ fundamentally from those of other potential patients for medical procedures that will aid another person, for example, a potential donor of bone marrow for transplant. This is so because she has undertaken to bear another human being, and has carried an unborn child to viability. Another unique feature of the situation we address arises from the singular nature of the dependency of the unborn child upon the mother. A woman carrying a viable unborn child is not in the same category as a relative, friend, or stranger called upon to donate bone marrow or an organ for transplant. Rather, the expectant mother has placed herself in a special class of persons who are bringing another person into existence, and upon whom that other person's life is totally dependent. Also, uniquely, the viable unborn child is literally captive within the mother's body. No other potential beneficiary of a surgical procedure on another is in that position.

For all of these reasons, a balancing becomes appropriate in those few cases where the interests we are discussing come into conflict. To so state is in no sense to fail or recognize the extremely strong interest of each individual person, including of course the expectant mother, in her bodily integrity, her privacy, and, where involved, her religious beliefs.

Thus, I cannot agree with the conclusion of the majority opinion that while we 'do not quite foreclose the possibility that a conflicting state interest may be so compelling that the patient's wishes must yield…we anticipate that such cases will be extremely rare and truly exceptional.' Majority opinion at 1252. While it is, fortunately, true that such cases will be rare in the sense that such conflicts between mother and viable unborn child are rare, I cannot agree that in all cases where a viable unborn child is in the picture, it would be extremely rare, within that universe, to require that the mother accede to the vital needs of the viable unborn child.[8]…

Despite the majority's admonition that 'nothing in this opinion should be read as either approving or disapproving the holding in *In Re Madyun*,' 114 Daily Wash L Rptr 2233 (DC Super Ct July 26, 1986), majority opinion at 1252–1253 n 23, I am concerned that the majority's emphasis on the 'extremely rare and truly exceptional' nature of the circumstances in which the unborn child's rights may prevail may move the law toward the extinguishment of the rights of unborn children in cases like *In Re Madyun*. In that case, the trial court was faced with a situation in which an expectant mother refused on religious grounds to consent to a caesarean section even though she was already in labor, and sixty hours had passed since her membrane had ruptured. Although the heavy risk of infection and possible death to the fetus in the absence of a caesarean section were explained to both parents, they refused consent to the caesarean section. Because the child could not be delivered through the birth canal, the child faced a serious and increasing danger of death or brain damage, and the mother's health was endangered as well.

After considering the facts and applicable law, the Superior Court granted the hospital's request for authorization to deliver the baby by the most expedient means – a caesarean section. Counsel appointed to represent the unborn child had also joined the hospital's request. A motions division of this court denied a stay of the trial court's order. Pursuant of the trial court's order, the caesarean section was performed, and a healthy child was born and survives.

I next address the sensitive question of how to balance the competing rights and interests of the viable unborn child and the state against those of the rare expectant mother who elects not to have a caesarean section necessary to save her life or her child. The indisputable view that a woman carrying a viable child has an extremely strong interest in her own life, health, bodily integrity, privacy, and religious beliefs necessarily requires that her election be given correspondingly great weight in the balancing process. In a case, however, where the court in an exercise of a substituted judgment has concluded that the patient would probably opt against a caesarean section, the court should vary the weight to be given this factor in proportion to the confidence the court has in the accuracy of its conclusion. Thus, in a case where the indicia of the incompetent patient's judgment are equivocal, the court should accord this factor correspondingly less weight. The appropriate weight to be given other factors will have to be worked out by the development of law in this area, and cannot be prescribed in a single court opinion. Some considerations obviously merit special attention in the balancing process. One such consideration is any danger to the mother's life or health, physical or mental, including the relatively small but still significant danger that necessarily inheres in any caesarean delivery, and including especially any danger that exceeds that level. The mother's religious beliefs as they relate to the operation would appear to deserve inclusion in the balancing process.

On the other side of the analysis, it is appropriate to look to the relative likelihood of the unborn child's survival. This could range from the situation in *Madyun* where the full-term child's chances for survival were apparently excellent, through a case like the one before us where the unborn child's chances of survival were from fifty to sixty percent, and on to cases where the child's chances for survival are less than even. The child's interest in being born with as little impairment as possible should be considered. This may weigh in favor of a delivery sooner rather than later. The most important factor on this side of the scale, however, is life itself, because the viable unborn child that dies because of the mother's refusal to have a caesarean delivery is deprived, entirely and irrevocably, of the life on which the child was about to embark.

Turning to the specifics of this case...[w]eighed in the balance against ordering the procedure were two considerations that were central to the entire proceeding: the invasive and serious nature of the proposed surgery and the fact that such surgery cannot ordinarily be performed without the consent of the patient. Under the peculiar circumstances of this case, the influence of these factors was diminished by the fact that it was not clear whether AC would have consented to the surgery or not. Before events began to close in on her, AC had agreed to a caesarean at twenty-eight weeks. Thus, she was not averse, in principle, to having that particular type of surgery. What was unresolved was whether she would consent to that surgery at twenty-six and one-half weeks, when the unborn child's chances of survival were somewhat reduced and the chances of impairment to the child somewhat enhanced. It was clear that she had intended all along to carry her unborn child until the point the child could be successfully delivered, and she persevered in that intention even when she knew she would not live long, if at all, after her child was born. Even in the tragically difficult circumstances in which AC found herself at the very time of the court's proceedings, she first appeared in her sedated state to agree to the procedure and then apparently to disagree. Under the circumstances, the court could deem these matters, usually more pertinent to a determination of substituted judgment, to lessen the net weight of the factors that weighed against the performance of the surgery. Also to be considered in the balance was the rather minimal, but nevertheless undisputable, additional risk that caesarean delivery presented for the mother.[15]

Turning to the interest of the unborn child in living and the parallel interest of the state in protecting that life, the evidence indicated that the child had a fifty to sixty percent chance of survival and a less than twenty percent chance of entering life with a serious handicap such as cerebral palsy or mental retardation. The evidence also showed that a delay in delivering the child would have increased the likelihood of a handicap. In view of the record before [the trial judge], and on the basis that there had been no plain error in not applying the sort of substituted judgment analysis that we for the first time mandate in today's ruling, I think it cannot be said that he abused his discretion in the way he struck the balance between the considerations that favored the procedure and those that went against it.

Footnotes to dissenting opinion

8.   To the contrary, it appears that a majority of courts faced with this issue have found that the state's compelling interest in protection of the unborn child should prevail. *See* Noble-Allgire, *Court-Ordered Caesarean Sections*, 10 J Legal Med 211, 236 (1989). I added that in mapping this uncharted area of the law, we can draw lines and a line I would draw would be to preclude the use of physical force to perform an operation. The force of the court order itself as well as the use of the contempt power would, I think, be adequate in most cases. *See id*, at 243.

15.   I note that there was no evidence in this case that the caesarean procedure was likely to shorten AC's life. Although the trial judge alluded in his findings to testimony to that effect, he was apparently referring to argument of counsel rather than testimony. After

the judge's findings were made, the record was reopened to receive information from Dr Hamner who had just spoken to AC. In reporting that she seemed more lucid and had three times answered that she assented to a caesarean delivery, he said he had asked her if she realized that she 'may not survive the surgical procedure.' Because Dr Hamner had already testified that in his opinion AC had less than twenty-four hours to live, and because he presumably was concerned with obtaining the consent of a patient informed of even those risks that were less than probable, this cannot be deemed the statement of an opinion that the surgery would probably shorten AC's life.

In effect, this case appears to have stemmed the tide of decisions in the US authorising caesarean sections and other compulsory treatments against the wishes of a competent mother.

Subsequently, in *Re Baby Doe* (1994) 632 NE 2d 326, the Appellate Court of Illinois refused to balance the interests of an unborn child against the right of a competent pregnant woman to refuse a caesarean section. The court left open, however, whether less invasive procedures, such as blood transfusions, could be authorised by the court against the woman's wishes (*ibid* at 323–323 per DiVito J. See also *Raleigh Fitkin-Paul Morgan Memorial Hospital v Anderson* (1964) 201 A 2d 537 (NJ Sup Ct)). (For a further discussion of court-ordered interventions in the United States see, for example: Gallagher 'Pre-natal Invasions and Interventions: What's Wrong with Fetal Rights' (1987) 10 Harvard Women's LJ 9; Johnsen 'The Creation of Fetal Rights: Conflicts with Women's Constitutional Rights to Liberty, Privacy, and Equal Protection' (1986) 95 Yale LJ 599; Field 'Controlling the Woman to Protect the Fetus' (1989) 17 Law, Medicine and Health Care 114; Robertson and Schulman 'Pregnancy and Prenatal Harm to Offspring: The Case of Mothers with PKU' (1987) 17 Hastings Center Report 23 (Aug/Sept).)

The majority view in *Re AC* reflects the position that the patient's right to refuse treatment is determinative even if she is pregnant. In other words, as a matter of law her right outweighs any conflicting interest of the unborn child. On the other hand, the majority leave open the possibility that if there are 'truly extraordinary or compelling reasons' the patient's right must give way. However, such cases (if they exist) will be rare since the majority contemplate that the patient's refusal will be effective in 'virtually all cases'. Thus, *Re AC* rejects, *exceptional cases apart*, the fourth societal interest advanced in the US cases as potentially outweighing the patient's right.

What, then, if anything, amounts to an exceptional case? In *Re AC*, in footnote 23 to their judgment, the majority refer to the earlier decision in Washington DC of *Re Madyun* (1986) 573 A 2d 1259 appended to the judgment in *Re AC*. What is the difference between the facts of *Re AC* and *Madyun* which justifies the different outcomes? In *Madyun* the intervention carried no risk of harm to the pregnant woman beyond that inherent in the procedure itself. By contrast, in *Re AC* the procedure did carry an additional risk, namely of accelerating AC's death because of her weakened physical condition. Of course, this makes the facts of *Re AC* unusual and the situation in *Madyun* the norm. On this basis, the 'exceptional case' recognised by the majority in *Re AC* based upon *Madyun* (where intervention is justified against the pregnant woman's wishes) is *in fact* the usual case, ie the result in *Madyun* would be more common than that in *Re AC*.

Clearly, this was not contemplated in *Re AC*, since it would produce the result that in most cases the mother's right to refuse would be made to give way to the claims of the unborn child; the exact opposite of what the majority intended.

As you will have noticed, the judge in *Re S* relied upon the 'exceptional case' left open in *Re AC*. If we are right that the DC court misstates what is the exception and what is the norm, then the decision in *Re S* could not be sustained.

(ii) ARGUMENTS AND JUDICIAL POLICY

Having doubted the juridical basis for the decision in *Re S* we must now confront
the question of policy: is it right for a court to engage in a balancing exercise so
as deny a pregnant woman the right to refuse treatment? Certainly there are
circumstances in which the law has given some recognition to the claims of an
unborn child (eg *McKay v Essex Area Health Authority* [1982] 2 All ER 771,
[1982] QB 1166 (CA); *Burton v Islington Health Authority* [1993] QB 204, [1992]
3 All ER 833, (CA); Congenital Disabilities (Civil Liability) Act 1976). This
recognition has not been at the expense of the rights of the pregnant woman to
control her own body (see the general exclusion of a mother as defendant in a
pre-natal injury claim under the 1976 Act *infra*, ch 12). There are, of course,
moral arguments which could suggest that the unborn child, particularly as it
develops, may have a legitimate *moral* claim on the mother so as to limit her
freedom of action. But there is a world of difference between moral claims and
legal claims enforceable by the courts – ie between what one *ought* to do and
what one *must* do and can be made to do by the state. The arguments are well
made in the following seminal paper written by the late Nancy Rhoden.

Nancy Rhoden 'The Judge in the Delivery Room: The Emergency of Court-Ordered Caesareans' (1986) 74 Cal LR 1951

Not surprisingly, very few cases involve performing a medical procedure on one person in
order to save the life of another. This dearth of precedent is partially explained by the highly
factual circumstances such cases require – that an organ or bodily substance of *A*, and only
A, may potentially save *B*, yet *A* refuses to donate it. Additionally, few people in even such
desparate straits as *B* are likely to try to compel donation by *A*, because this goes so strongly
against the grain of American insistence on bodily integrity, autonomy, and nonsubordination.
The general law concerning the duty (or lack of duty) to rescue illustrates this. The following
discussion will first briefly review the principles of Samaritan law and then will examine the
few cases that consider bodily interventions intended to aid a third party.

With limited exceptions, Anglo-American law imposes no duty to come to the assistance
of a person in distress. One exception provides that one who injures or imperils another has
a duty to render aid. Another exception requires that a person who begins a rescue attempt
perform it with reasonable care, and that she not abandon the effort if doing so will leave the
imperiled person in a worse position than before. For our purposes, the most important
exception is that some special relationships between the parties justify imposing a duty to
rescue. Special relationships clearly include those such as innkeeper to guest, common carrier
to passenger, and jailer to prisoner. They also include such fundamental relationships as
parent and child, and it has been suggested that other fundamental relationships, such as
husband and wife, should also be recognized as giving rise to a duty to rescue. These exceptions
mitigate the harshness of the general principle that one may be a 'bad Samaritan', a
controversial principle that many commentators have long criticized as being callous and
indifferent both to moral duties and to human life.

Whatever one's view about the general rule, one feature of the law of rescue is quite
uncontroversial: even when rescue is required, rescues that risk life and limb are, and should
remain, optional. Persons to whom the various exceptions apply have an obligation to take
only rather minimal action, such as warning of danger or calling a doctor or other proper
authorities. The few states that have statutorily created a duty to rescue require only such
assistance as can be rendered without danger to the rescuer. It would, therefore, be an
extraordinary revision of American law to require risky rescues, even by a spouse or parent.

In *McFall v Shimp* [10 Pa D and C 3d 90 (1978)] the court wisely recognized that a
plaintiff's claim to mandatory medical intrusion on another so that the plaintiff's life might
be saved fell under the rubric of Samaritan law. Robert McFall was a victim of aplastic
anemia who sought to force David Shimp, his cousin, to donate bone marrow to him. Although
bone marrow extraction is far less risky than major surgery, it is painful and invasive, requiring
multiple insertions of a curved needle into the iliac bones while the donor is under anesthesia.
Shimp underwent initial tests to determine bone marrow compatibility, and was found to be
the only family member with potentially compatible bone marrow. He then refused to undergo
any further testing. Although the court found the defendant's conduct morally reprehensible,
it refused to order him to complete the testing and, if found compatible, to donate. The court

emphasized that there is no legal duty to rescue others, and stated that to require this Samaritan act 'would change every concept and principle upon which our society is founded.' It continued;

> For a society which respects the rights of *one* individual, to sink its teeth into the jugular vein or neck of one of its members and suck from it sustenance for *another* member, is revolting to our hard-wrought concepts of jurisprudence. Forceable extraction of living body tissue causes revulsion to the judicial mind. Such would raise the spectre of the swastika and the Inquisition, reminiscent of the horrors this portends.

Thus, the court would not order this invasion of Shimp's body even though Shimp's refusal to donate meant death for McFall.

McFall is a sad case, but it was not, as the court's strong and even lurid language indicates, a hard one. The principle of privacy, autonomy, and bodily integrity compel the conclusion that however repugnant the refusal to aid may be, the courts cannot mandate assistance of this nature and magnitude. This conclusion almost certainly would not differ had the case involved a father and child. Mandatory organ donation is a standard scholarly example of a practice that would unquestionably lie beyond the limits of the law. As Angela Holder states, 'In no case is an adult ever ordered to surrender a kidney, bone marrow, or any other part of his body for donation to his child, to another relative, or to anyone else.' Likewise, Donald Regan asks rhetorically, 'Would a court impose criminal liability on anyone, even the child's parent, who did not attempt to save the child at the risk of second-degree burns over one or two per cent of his or her body?' Because risky rescues have never been required, even of parents, we must conclude with Holder and Regan that courts would not compel a parent to donate bone marrow to a dying child.

This conclusion is supported by *In Re George* [630 SW 2d 614 (Mo Ct App 1982)] another sad case in which a thirty-three-year-old adoptee suffering from chronic myelocytic leukemia sought a court order to open his adoption records so that he could locate a compatible bone marrow donor. The judge consulted the man's natural mother, who was tested but found not compatible. The judge then contacted the alleged natural father, whose name was obtained from the adoption records. The man denied paternity and was unwilling to be tested for compatibility. The matter stopped there; the court refused to give the dying man his natural father's name.

Ordering a Caesarean to save the fetus is just as extraordinary as ordering a parent to donate bone marrow to save a child. Even so, courts faced with these cases have not recognized this. This is probably because the Caesarean cases *seem* different. The woman is going to give birth anyway – if she just agrees to a surgical delivery rather than insisting on a vaginal one, the baby will survive unharmed. If she refuses, the harm to the baby will be both immediate and in the same location as the woman (literally). In contrast, the victim who is refused a bone marrow donation will succumb more slowly and, perhaps, out of sight. In addition, it is the doctor, with his or her persuasive professional authority, who seeks Caesarean rather than the individual victim.

These differences may affect the emotional responses of participants and judges. They do not, however, legally distinguish the refusals. In each case, a parent is refusing an invasive and somewhat risky procedure without which his or her child will die or suffer severe harm. John Robertson, a proponent of mandatory Caesareans in certain circumstances, accepts this equivalency, and hence supports compulsory parental 'donations' of blood, bone marrow, and perhaps even organs, depending upon the degree of risk. Robertson's consistency of approach helps to demonstrate the equivalency of the two situations. Once equated, however, the degree to which a court-ordered Caesarean violates fundamental tenets of American law also becomes clear; logical consistency demands that if Caesareans can be required, American law concerning duties to rescue must be radically restructured.

It might be objected that a pregnant woman is a special case because the voluntary act of continuing a pregnancy creates special obligations over and above the duty to rescue imposed upon all parents. A further objection might claim that carrying a fetus to term but refusing a Caesarean may cause the child to be far worse off – profoundly retarded, for example – than if it had never been conceived. If construed as suggesting that the woman fits into an additional exception to the 'bad Samaritan' principle as someone who has begun a rescue, these arguments are still insufficient to create a legal duty to run physical risks for the sake of the fetus. Even if one takes the position that a woman who has carried a pregnancy to term has embarked upon a course of action vis-à-vis the fetus that may be viewed as a rescue and that may arguably allow certain demands to be placed upon her, compulsory surgery goes far beyond demands imposed on other voluntary rescuers. For example, the person who begins to rescue a child trapped in a burning building but then realizes it is far more dangerous than he thought, would not have a duty to continue the rescue despite the change in circumstances. In the Caesarean context the mother's act of nurturing the fetus through pregnancy would not require that she undergo additional risks to ensure its safe passage into the world.

Perhaps, though, this legalistic interpretation does not do justice to the claim that the woman has assumed special obligations. Surely what is meant by the claim is not completely captured by the argument that at the time of delivery multiple exceptions to the 'bad Samaritan' principle may apply. Rather, the real thrust of this objection seems to be that the woman is physically and morally responsible for the life within her, and she ought to do more than the minimum to promote its welfare. The extent of a pregnant woman's moral obligations to her developing fetus merits serious consideration, especially as we learn more about substances that may harm the fetus. Fortunately, most women in our society take these obligations very seriously, even subordinating their desires for such things as alcohol, cigarettes, or caffeine to the interests of the fetus. But in this very private and bodily sphere, the issue of moral obligations, even very compelling ones, must be kept distinct from the issue of coercion of individuals to meet their moral obligations. The law of rescue condones many omissions that are morally reprehensible. For that matter, refusal to undertake risk rescues does not normally even invoke moral opprobrium. Morally, we seem to have a different standard for pregnant women. But this moral standard does not justify an unparalleled level of legal constraint.

Although there are no other cases involving *refusal* to donate a bodily order, in a number of cases parents have sought court permission to authorize an incompetent sibling to donate a kidney to a sibling suffering from renal failure. Some courts have granted this permission. One commentator has suggested, in an extraordinary interpretation of these decisions, 'that there is a rather stringent duty to prevent or remove harm, or both, to a member of one's immediate family, a duty that involves significant risk to oneself and is shared by members of the family who are incompetent to shoulder other types of obligations.' She concludes that cases authorizing donation by incompetents can constitute a legal precedent for compelling parents to undergo invasive medical procedures, including organ donation, for the sake of their children and, of course, for analogous forms of parental compulsion.

Cases authorizing donation from incompetents have not even hinted that the incompetent has a moral or legally enforceable obligation to donate. In fact, there is little doubt that even an incompetent refusal would be sacrosanct. The problem is that could he or she understand the issue, the potential donor might, or might not, wish to donate. Many courts faced with these cases have used the substitute judgment test, which asks what the incompetent would most likely want. When courts have permitted donation, they have stressed the incompetent's probable anguish at the sibling's death. Other courts have rejected the claim that the proper test is whether the incompetent would consent to donate if he could do so, and have simply refused to authorize the transplant on the grounds that it is not in the best interest of the incompetent. Some might argue that in the cases that authorize donation, the imputation of devotion and altruism to the incompetent is somewhat suspect. But even if some courts exaggerate notions of filial devotion to allow donation, the focus of the substituted judgment test on the incompetent's probable desires demonstrates that refusal would also be honored.

The law of donations from the dead also reflects the absence of a legal obligation to donate. The current law is that organs cannot be removed unless either the person had, when alive, indicated his donative intent, or consent from the family is obtained. A person opposed to donation may refuse to donate both for 'good' reasons – religious beliefs, for example – and for 'bad' ones ('if I can't live, I don't want to help someone else to live'). Proposals to revise the law to increase the supply of available organs would merely reverse this presumption; routine removal would be allowed unless this individual had previously indicated opposition, or the family objected when informed of this practice. In other words, such proposals still would not violate the prior choices of the deceased by nonconsensual organ removal. Certainly, by way of comparison, an organ taken from a cadaver can save a life just as an emergency Caesarean can. Yet, respect for individual choice extends even to those decisions that can be exercised only after a person's death. In this way, forcing women to undergo major surgery emerges as an anomalous and inconsistent derogation of individual choice…

Why should law allow these tragedies?

We have seen that legal principles support respecting maternal refusals of surgery. This is an extraordinarily complex and troubling area, however. It surely merits something beyond narrowly legal analysis. A taxonomy of woman's moral obligations to the developing fetus is far beyond this Article's scope. Yet, I suspect that most people would find a woman who refused a Caesarean for a frivolous reason such as abhorring abdominal scars to be acting in an immoral manner. They might wonder what is wrong with judicial intervention to prevent the tragic consequences of her reprehensible conduct. After all, pregnancy *is* unique, and the woman in labor is uniquely able to prevent irreparable harm to a vulnerable being by undergoing a quite routine surgical procedure. In these unusual cases, why should not a court hold that the principles of autonomy, nonsubordination, and bodily integrity exemplified in the law of treatment refusal, rescue, and abortion are weighty, but are not weighty enough to justify the predicted harm?

There are broad societal grounds that favour paying this tragic price for maternal freedom. First, court-ordered Caesareans may start us down that 'slippery slope' toward controlling and coercing pregnant women in the name of fetal well-being. In addition…physicians may be overly alarmist in their predictions, causing judges to order unnecessary surgery. But let us hold both 'slippery slope' fears and medical realities in abeyance a bit longer. Assuming that medical predictions are accurate, and that at least some maternal refusals may evoke justifiable moral condemnation, can we argue, at the level of ethical or legal theory, that upholding maternal refusals is the best general policy?

…I argue that despite the strong impulse to save the baby in an individual case, courts that respond to this temptation behave far more problematically than those that resist. My argument seeks to make explicit what is implicit in the *McFall* holding: that in some cases it is wrong for courts to pursue admittedly better consequences because this pursuit involves such significant invasions of individual rights and autonomy that they compromise the integrity of the court and the humanity of those subject to its rulings. In other words, I suggest that in these cases, courts should not decide on the basis of consequences, but rather upon the primacy of individual rights and upon principles that limit the way in which a person (or state) may legitimately treat another.

My argument inevitably has its limitations. These cases are true dilemmas, pitting certain of our most fundamental intuitions against one another. I do not show that upholding refusals is morally unproblematic – no solution here will be ideal…the problems inherent in elevating consequences above rights are extremely serious, and that courts violate our fundamental ethical intuitions and societal precepts when they intervene to compel one individual to assume risks for the sake of another.

It is virtually a truism to say that the issue of court-ordered Caesareans could arise only within a medical system in which Caesareans had become safe and relatively routine. I suspect that few doctors would even consider seeking a court order if the recalcitrant woman faced unusually high surgical risks – for example, if she had a severe bleeding disorder or a family history of unexplained death or paralysis from anesthesia. Analyzing why surgery should not be imposed if there is a significant risk of serious maternal harm, albeit a lesser risk than the fetus would face in a vaginal delivery, may help show why a proper appreciation of the import of harm suggests that even relatively safe major surgery should not be imposed.

Theories of moral and legal obligation uniformly recognise the fundamental fact that human beings tend to value their own lives above those of others, making it unrealistic to expect them to sacrifice themselves for other persons. Hence, using lethal force in self-defence is lawful, even if the attacker is himself innocent. A person under attack by several others can kill all of them, even though the end result is the death of several persons rather than one. Objectively, this result is worse, but an individual is not expected to take an objective stance when his own life is threatened. Likewise, even in countries where rescue is required, no one is under a legal duty to risk his life in a rescue. This is simply too much to demand of a person, in the light of the ingrained human drive for self-preservation.

Needless to say, persons in the position of making decisions about others must respect the fact that an individual's life is, to him, invaluable. This is another reason why it would be unthinkable for a surgeon unilaterally to decide to distribute one person's organs to five other patients who desperately need just those organs. The almost primal revulsion we feel at a person's or government's sacrificing one person to benefit others applies to lesser bodily invasions as well. As Laurence Tribe states, 'That one person's two good eyes, distributed to two blind neighbours, might yield a net increase in happiness on the theory that one blind person will experience less misery than two, cannot justify a governmental decision to compel the exchange.' Were there a serious risk of the woman's suffering permanent harm from the surgery, requiring it would seem too much like these examples, where our intuitions strongly tell us that such decisions are ethically impermissible.

The intuition that it is impermissible to harm one person to aid another is derived from two closely related principles. The first is that any duty to help must be viewed as less weighty or stringent than a duty not to harm, such that if helping *A* requires harming *B*, it is better that we forego helping *A*. The second principle is that, contrary to the consequentialist's views, it is significant that *A's* injury will occur through natural forces or the malevolent act of a third person, but that the harm to *B*, if you choose to aid *A*, will be of your own doing. It is tragic that persons are harmed, but it is wrong that you harm them. These principles explain why physicians and courts would be so unlikely to impose surgery upon, for example, a woman who would be rendered sterile by it; it would be too clear that the fetus could not be rescued without harming her.

But how does all this apply to the typical Caesarean case, given the general safety of surgical delivery? First, we should note that there is at least a risk, albeit a small one, of lasting physical harm. The mortality rate for Caesareans is very low, approximately 4 in 10,000. For the individual woman, however, there is no way to determine the precise risk of death imposed, because statistics apply to groups, not individuals. Nor can the court foresee the extent to which the risk might be increased by the fact that the surgery will often be done on an emergency basis and will be nonconsensual as well. Thus, the court necessarily imposes some small chance of death or permanent damage upon the woman. More importantly, if our society adopts a general policy of mandating Caesarean delivery when the fetus is imperiled, some women, albeit a very small number, will eventually be sacrificed in order to save some much larger number of babies. Thus, although the chances of sacrifice in any individual case are very small, when we view compulsory Caesareans as a general policy, we see that it imposes the very trade-offs between maternal and fetal health that the Supreme Court disallowed in the abortion cases. Although the Court did not provide an ethical analysis of why trade-offs were impermissible, abortion doctrine reflects the view that a woman should not be used without her consent as a means to enhanced fetal health.

We need not, however, rely on the potential for death or lasting disability to hold that forced Caesarean delivery constitutes a harm. Returning to Nagel's example:

> You have an auto accident one winter night on a lonely road. The other passengers are badly injured, the car is out of commission, and the road is deserted, so you run along it till you find an isolated house. The house turns out to be occupied by an old woman who is looking after her small grandchild. There is no phone, but there is a car in the garage, and you ask desperately to borrow it and explain the situation. She doesn't believe you. Terrified by your desperation, she runs upstairs and locks herself in the bathroom, leaving you alone with the child. You pound ineffectively on the door and search without success for the car keys. Then it occurs to you that she might be persuaded to tell you where they are if you were to twist the child's arm outside the bathroom door. Should you do it?

…someone who objected to a pure deontological [ie, rights-based] ethic could readily feel that twisting the child's arm was justifiable because the wrong was de mimimus and the harm it would prevent severe. But how about breaking his arm? If the distraught driver goes this far, he would not only violate the boy's rights but will also cause him significant, though presumably not permanent, physical harm. It is safe to say that most people, except for thoroughgoing consequentialists, would feel this was going too far, because harming the boy to this degree, even in the pursuit of good consequences, transcends the bounds of moral permissibility. The reason it does, of course, hearkens back to the principle that one should not breach the (stringent) duty not to harm in order to comply with the (weaker) duty to do good.

Performing a Caesarean, I submit, imposes harm that is on the order of breaking the child's arm to benefit the passengers. Neither performing a Caesarean nor breaking an arm is likely to have permanent consequences, but they both involve substantial pain, bodily invasion, and subsequent recovery time. Similarly, the *McFall* court's revulsion at imposing the (lesser) harm of bone marrow extraction can be explained by the unwillingness to treat a human being as a means to another's end, especially when doing so entails physical harm. Just as the *McFall* court implied that its judicial integrity would be compromised by 'sinking its teeth' into one citizen to aid another, courts ordering Caesareans compromise their integrity by plunging knives into unconsenting women.

Of course, the court merely authorizes the surgery, it does not perform it. But this only obscures the violence lurking within the court order, violence that can be highlighted by practical realities. For example what are the limits on force that may be imposed on women…who refuse to return to the hospital? Can the police be sent to get them? Or, if a woman is present but resisting, can the doctors hold her down and forcibly anesthetize her? Concerned physicians inevitably raise these issues; they abhor the thought of doing violence to patients. These issues are much more than mere practical problems in enforcement. Rather, they illustrate how, in a very real sense, the state is assaulting the woman even though her compliance in the face of a court order may often obscure this. The court order muffles the disturbing overtones of violence because the court authorizes but does not act, while the doctor acts but can tell himself that the court has given a superior authorization. But even if, in our variant on Nagel's example, someone else gave the driver permission to break the child's arm, or did the actual breaking at the driver's request, the moral responsibility for the broken arm would still be the driver's. Likewise, when the court authorizes nonconsensual surgery, it becomes responsible for the violence it is approving.

The court that orders surgery may also be responsible for real harm. Suppose that the nonconsensual surgery is performed, and despite all due care by the doctors, the woman dies or suffers irreparable injury. Absent negligence, the physicians would not be legally liable, and of course the court would not be legally liable in any case. But, intuitively, the court seems to bear moral responsibility here, just as the man in Nagel's example would be morally responsible if he twisted the child's arm and it broke. The court seems responsible because it imposed the risk and set in motion the harmful series of events, that is, the nonconsensual surgery. The court is heavily involved when it imposes surgery; it takes on responsibility for rescuing the fetus and must therefore be responsible if the woman is ever harmed seriously or even less substantially.

It might be objected that if the court does not order surgery it sacrifices the fetus and will bear responsibility for this. Initially, a decision not to order surgery may appear this way. But the degree of state responsibility is very different when the court orders surgery and when it does not. Because individuals ordinarily make their own medical choices and assume moral responsibility for them, the woman who refuses surgery despite predictions of harm to her baby may be morally to blame if such a result materalzes. It may be appropriate to say that, morally speaking, if surgery could have prevented the harm, its occurrence is the woman's responsibility. But the state is not ordinarily so involved. Only if the state overrides the woman's choice does it become a sufficiently active participant to acquire moral responsibility for the outcome. Surely the driver in our variant of Nagel's example would not be responsible for the passengers' deaths if he failed to break the child's arm to secure the car. No duty to rescue could encompass inflicting such harm. Similarly, it is unlikely that the state has a duty to rescue when doing so requires imposing major surgery upon an unwilling citizen. Therefore, the state is not responsible for the consequences, however tragic, to the fetus, in the same way that it will be responsible for any harm that befalls a woman whom it coerces to have surgery...

It could be objected that while doctors may recommend surgery in questionable cases, thus giving rise to unnecessary Caesareans, they will not seek to mandate it in any but the most clearcut cases – those where, without surgery, disaster will unquestionably ensue. Indeed, two of the Caesarean cases, *Jefferson* and *Jeffries*, involved women with placenta previa, one of the most clearcut and uncontroversial indications for a Caesarean. The successful vaginal deliveries in those two cases were surprising and unexpected, and these are not the sorts of situations in which critics of obstetrical interventionism would claim that the doctors were excessively alarmed. Nonetheless, these cases illustrate a very crucial point here: that physicians *feel certain* that disaster will ensue does not mean that it will.

Physicians' subjective feelings of certainty will be even less likely to translate into objective certainty in situations in which they are relying on technology with inherent limitations such as EFM [Electronic Fetal Monitoring]. As one expert stressed, when doctors can legitimately feel certain about the ominous import of monitoring tracings, such as when the monitor shows a later terminal heart pattern, there is no time to go to court. If the baby is to be saved at all, immediate action is necessary. At that point, however, surgery might either fail to prevent death or save a severely brain damaged infant. In other words, where there is certainty as to peril, it may sometimes be too late to prevent the damage.

A situation that almost became a court-ordered Caesarean illustrates the danger that unnecessary surgery will on occasion be ordered. An African woman failed to progress in labor satisfactorily, and the internal fetal monitor revealed repetitive late decelerations in the fetal heart rate. No fetal scalp blood sampling was done, even though the woman was between five and six centimeters dilated. The physician advised a Caesarean, but the woman and her husband adamantly refused. They argued that after they returned to Africa, there would be no available facilities for a repeat Caesarean. Consequently, the Caesarean would place the woman at significant risk in future pregnancies. They also noted that doctors recommended a Caesarean for failure to progress during her first pregnancy, but she nonetheless delivered vaginally. In this case a judge was contacted and indicated his willingness to order a Caesarean. Before any order could be issued, however, the woman progressed rapidly to the second stage of labor and delivered an infant with excellent Apgar scores – scores that were not suggestive of fetal distress. Had the labor taken even a little more time, this woman might have been subjected to an unnecessary operation – in her case one that would have greatly increased her future reproductive risks.

Naturally, the above discussion is not meant to suggest that the physician will not be right in a great many cases. Moreover, physicians are surely right when they stress that because the goal of gathering data about such things as fetal heart rate is to *prevent* damage before it can occur, achieving a good outcome despite ominous data does not necessarily mean that the data or the approach taken were wrong – only that doctors discovered the problem in time. Certainly, many or most women would want their doctors to use this conservative and time-honored medical strategy. But there are serious problems with courts' *requiring* a woman to abide by this approach, inasmuch as it does mean that some unnecessary operations will be judicially mandated.

One problem with courts' essentially requiring a maximum approach to obstetrical risks is that whether or not the physician's degree of alarm is warranted, a very prompt judicial decision is almost always required. Hence, judges who hear these cases will typically hear only the doctor's side and will learn little or nothing of the risks of surgical delivery or the ambiguity of many fetal diagnostic procedures. If they attempt to balance the maternal and fetal risks, judges will have no choice but to accept the physician's assessment and, therefore, to implement his or her recommendations. This is analogous to holding a civil commitment proceeding without the potential in-patient present or represented. Unlike a civil commitment proceeding, however, where a short delay is seldom a life-or-death matter, here the time needed to provide the woman even marginally adequate representation may render the proceeding futile (the damage having already been done), moot (the baby having already been born vaginally), or both. Given the very real time constraints, there is no solution to this. Thus, a court that tries to balance risks and benefits will almost inevitably have to base its decision on a one-sided presentation of factors. Courts can avoid this only by limiting their inquiry to an evaluation of competency (if it is in question) and firmly refusing to overturn competent refusals.

Along with one-sided decisionmaking is the threat that nonconsensual Caesareans will lead to other intrusions into pregnant women's lives. The Caesarean cases themselves do not always involve surgery alone. For example, the chief of obstetrics at North Central Bronx Hospital was made guardian ad litem for Mrs Headley and her fetus, with authority to consent to whatever diagnostic and therapeutic procedures were necessary for the fetus's health. The police were sent to locate Mrs Jeffries and bring her forcibly to the hospital. If a high-risk woman cannot refuse a Caesarean, it is hard to see how she can refuse the diagnostic procedures that will determine if a Caesarean is necessary. As doctors define 'high risk' to include more and more women, freedom for any woman to opt out of this country's technologically intensive obstetrics may be threatened.

As we learn more about fetal development and the impact of maternal conduct on the fetus, diagnostic procedures and restrictions on women's conduct could be ordered earlier in pregnancy. Already, some courts have ordered transfusions for pregnant Jehovah's Witnesses, and one court has done so even before the fetus was viable. At least one court has involuntarily committed a schizophrenic woman in the last trimester of pregnancy in order to protect the fetus; another has ordered a pregnant heroin addict to report for drug testing; and yet another has required a pregnant diabetic to take insulin despite her religious beliefs. A criminal prosecution was brought against a California woman for the death of her infant son, who was born with brain damage allegedly resulting from her failure to seek immediate medical attention when she began to hemorrhage from placenta previa, though the action was dismissed. Interventions such as brief involuntary hospitalization, testing, or surveillance to control drinking, drug use, diet, etc, may be viewed by some courts as less intrusive than major surgery – though longer lasting, such interventions are, after all, much less risky. Visions of a 'slippery slope' progression appear very real when one begins with mandatory major surgery.

The potential for far-reaching state control of pregnant women also is suggested by the frightening array of prenatal interventions that some proponents of fetal protection advocate. For example, John Robertson states that pregnant women

> may also be prohibited from using alcohol or other substances harmful to the fetus during pregnancy, or be kept from the workplace because of toxic effects on the fetus. They could be ordered to take drugs, such as insulin for diabetes, medications for fetal deficiencies, or intrauterine blood transfusions for Rh factor. Pregnant anorexic teenagers could be force fed. Parental screening and diagnostic procedures, from amniocentesis to sonography or even fetoscopy could be made mandatory. And, in utero surgery for the fetus to shunt cerebroventricular fluids from the brain to relieve hydrocephalus, or the relieve the urethral obstruction of bilateral hydronephrosis could also be ordered. Indeed, even extra-uterine fetal surgery, if it becomes an established procedure, could be ordered. If the risks to the mother were small and it were a last resort to save the life or prevent severe disability in a viable fetus. [Robertson, 'The Right to Procreate and In Utero Fetal Therapy' 3 J Legal Med (1982).]

Margery Shaw goes even further, approving of breathalyzer tests for pregnant women suspected of alcohol abuse, and seeming to countenance mandatory prenatal diagnosis and even abortion in cases of fetal defects so severe that abortion may be deemed in the fetus's best interest.

The civil liberties implications of all this are staggering, as are the equal protection problems, since pregnant women are the only candidates for this unprecedented state control. A more subtle problem is the potential for prenatal coercion to do fetuses as much harm as good. In the *North Central Bronx* case, Mrs Headley had never returned to the hospital and, despite the risk, had a home birth. Mrs Jeffries went into hiding, and the police search for her was unsuccessful. Women of strong religious beliefs may forego care entirely rather than violate their principle, a course that puts the women and their babies at even greater risk. Pregnant women who take illicit drugs or engage in other types of conduct that may cause fetal harm may avoid prenatal care for fear of involuntary hospitalization or treatment. Thus, ironically, efforts at fetal protection may instead increase fetal peril. Moreover, the coercion necessary to prevent 'maternal flight' – surveillance, reporting requirements (as with child neglect), or sending out the 'obstetrics police' – has mind-boggling implications for individual rights in this country.

A final point is that although coercion to protect a fetus may seem tempting in the individual case when the fetus is imperiled, on a societal scale this is an extraordinarily inefficient way to reduce perinatal mortality and morbidity. In this country, many women are still unable to obtain any, or adequate, prenatal care even though good nutrition and basic care can vastly improve the outcome in many pregnancies. the societal tendency to take all measures possible to rescue an identified individual, while foregoing precautions that could prevent many more deaths (though to unidentifiable persons) is perhaps understandable. But in this area, it is irrational to fail to provide prenatal care to all, thus risking *many* mothers and babies, and at the same time make women with atypical religious or medical beliefs choose between accepting care that violates their most cherished beliefs and foregoing care altogether. How much wiser it would be instead to ensure that caregivers work with these women to provide the best medical care possible within the limitations of their belief systems.

Rhoden's argument that the court should stay its hand seems to us to be extremely persuasive. Furthermore if compulsory intervention upon pregnant women were ever to be legally sanctioned, only Parliament should say so. In *Re F (in utero)* [1988] Fam 122, [1988] 2 All ER 193 the Court of Appeal made this quite clear when it rejected the view that an unborn child could be made a ward of court. The case concerned a 36-year-old woman who suffered from mental disturbance accompanied by drug abuse. Very late in her pregnancy she went missing. The local authority were concerned about the welfare of the unborn child. It sought to make the unborn child a ward of court so that the mother could be found and ordered to reside in a certain place and attend a particular hospital. In deciding that the court did not have jurisdiction to ward an unborn child, the court accepted the earlier cases of *C v S* [1988] QB 135, [1987] 1 All ER 1230 and *Paton v British Pregnancy Advisory Service Trustees* [1979] QB 276, [1978] 2 All ER 987, which had held that an unborn child has no legal existence until it is physically independent of its mother (ie it has been born): on which, see *infra*, ch 11. However, the court also accepted the overwhelming practical problems that might arise if wardship were available because of a possible conflict between mother and unborn child.

Re F (in utero) [1988] Fam 122, [1988] 2 All ER 193 (CA)

May LJ: I have considerable sympathy with the local authority in their position on the facts of the instant case, but I am driven to the conclusion that the judge was right and that the court has no jurisdiction to ward an unborn child. If the courts are to have this jurisdiction in a sensitive situation such as the present, I think that this is a matter for Parliament and not for the courts themselves.

Balcombe LJ: Approaching the question as one of principle, in my judgment there is no jurisdiction to make an unborn child a ward of court. Since an unborn child has, ex hypothesi, no existence independent of its mother, the only purpose of extending the jurisdiction to include a foetus is to enable the mother's actions to be controlled. Indeed, that is the purpose of the present application. In the articles already cited Lowe gives examples of how this might operate in practice [Lowe 'Wardship and Abortion Prevention – Further Observations' (1980) 96 LQR 29 at 30]:

> It would mean, for example, that the mother would be unable to leave the jurisdiction without the court's consent. The court being charged to protect the foetus's welfare would surely have to order the mother to stop smoking, imbibing alcohol and indeed any activity which might be hazardous to the child. Taking it to the extreme were the court to be faced with saving the baby's life or the mother's it would surely have to protect the baby's.

Another possibility is that the court might be asked to order that the baby be delivered by Caesarian section: in this connection see Fortin 'Legal Protection for the Unborn Child' (1988) 51 MLR 54 at 81 and the US cases cited in note 16, in particular *Jefferson v Griffin Spalding County Hospital Authority* (1981) 274 SE 2d 457. Whilst I do not accept that the priorities mentioned in the last sentence of the passage cited above are necessarily correct, it would be intolerable to place a judge in the position of having to make such a decision without any guidance as to the principles upon which his decision should be based. If the law is to be extended in this manner, so as to impose control over the mother of an unborn child where such control may be necessary for the benefit of that child, then under our system of Parliamentary democracy it is for Parliament to decide whether such controls can be imposed and, if so, subject to what limitations or conditions. Thus, under the Mental Health Act 1983, to which we were also referred, there are elaborate provisions to ensure that persons suffering from mental disorder or other similar conditions are not compulsorily admitted to hospital for assessment or treatment without proper safeguards: see ss 2, 3 and 4 of that Act. If Parliament were to think it appropriate that a pregnant woman should be subject to controls for the benefit of her unborn child, then doubtless it will stipulate the circumstances in which such controls may be applied and the safeguards appropriate for the mother's protection. In such a sensitive field, affecting as it does the liberty of the individual, it is not for the judiciary to extend the law.

Staughton LJ: When the wardship jurisdiction of the High Court is exercised, the rights, duties and powers of the natural parents are taken over or superseded by the orders of the court. Until a child is delivered it is not, in my judgment, possible for that to happen. The court cannot care for a child, or order that others should do so, until the child is born; only the mother can. The orders sought by the local authority are not by their nature such as the court can make in caring for the child; they are orders which seek directly to control the life of both mother and child. As was said by the European Commission of Human Rights in *Paton v UK* (1980) 3 EHRR 408 at 415 (para 19): 'The "life" of the foetus is intimately connected with, and cannot be regarded in isolation from, the life of the pregnant woman.'

We were urged by counsel to extend the wardship jurisdiction; but, in my judgment, we are being asked to create a new, perhaps similar, jurisdiction to care for mother and foetus together. I can see that there may be arguments that the court should have such powers. One would hope that they would be needed very rarely, but a need may well exist. I do not think that it is for this court to create that jurisdiction. The exercise of it would, in this case, directly impinge on the liberty of the mother. Where Parliament has granted similar powers, for example in the Mental Health Act 1983, safeguards and limits have been provided; there have to be certificates of qualified doctors who have examined the patient, and such like. No doubt that was done after careful consideration of the topic, and of the circumstances in which a person's liberty should be taken away.

This court is in no position to inquire into the problem of mothers who may neglect or harm their children before birth, or to decide in what circumstances and with what safeguards there should be power to restrict the liberty of the mother in order to prevent that happening. Even if the court were entitled to extend the jurisdiction, as counsel puts it, in that way, it is not a power which the court should exercise.

The Canadian Supreme Court's judgments in the following case examines, at length, the arguments for and against judicial intervention so as to control the conduct of a pregnant woman.

Winnipeg Child and Family Services (Northwest Area) v G (DF) (1997) 152 DLR (4th) 193 (Sup Ct of Canada)

A child welfare agency sought an order requiring that a pregnant woman who was addicted to glue-sniffing be committed to a place of safety and refrain from the use of intoxicants during her pregnancy. The trial judge allowed the agency's application and order that the woman be committed to the custody of the director of the agency and detained in a medical centre until the birth of her child, there to follow a course of treatment dictated by the director. One of the bases for the order was the court's *parens patriae* jurisdiction. The order was stayed two days later and set aside on appeal to the Manitoba Court of Appeal. The agency appealed to the Supreme Court of Canada, seeking a restoration of the detention order.

McLachlin J: II. Issues

[9] This appeal raises two legal issues:

(1) Does tort law, as it exists or may properly be extended by the Court, permit an order detaining a pregnant woman against her will in order to protect her unborn child from conduct that may harm the child?

(2) Alternatively, does the power of a court to make orders for the protection of children (its *parens patriae* jurisdiction), as it exists or may properly be extended by the Court,

permit an order detaining a pregnant woman against her will in order to protect her unborn child from conduct that may harm the child?

[10] The appellant does not request that the order for mandatory treatment be upheld. At the same time, treatment, at least in the minimal sense of abstention from substance abuse, emerged as the only justification for the order for detention. Without mandatory treatment, the order for detention would lack any foundation. Thus the question of whether a judge may order detention of a pregnant woman at the request of the state encompasses the issue of whether a judge may make an order for mandatory treatment.

III. ANALYSIS

A. *Does the Law of Tort Permit an Order for the Detention and Treatment of a Pregnant Woman for the Purpose of Preventing Harm to the Unborn Child?*

1. *Does the Existing Law of Tort Support the Order?*

[11] Before dealing with the cases treating the issue in tort law, I turn to the general proposition that the law of Canada does not recognize the unborn child as a legal or juridical person. Once a child is born, alive and viable, the law may recognize that its existence began before birth for certain limited purposes. But the only right recognized is that of the born person. This is a general proposition, applicable to all aspects of the law, including the law of torts.

[12] By way of preamble, two points may be made. First, we are concerned with the common law, not statute. If Parliament or the legislatures wish to legislate legal rights for unborn children or other protective measures, that is open to them, subject to any limitations imposed by the Constitution of Canada. Further, the fact that particular statutes may touch on the interests of the unborn need not concern us. Second, the issue is not one of biological status, nor indeed spiritual status, but of legal status. As this Court put it in *Tremblay v Daigle*, [1989] 2 SCR 530 at p 553, 62 DLR (4th) 634:

> The task of properly classifying a foetus in law and in science are different pursuits. Ascribing personhood to a foetus in law is a fundamentally normative task. It results in the recognition of rights and duties – a matter which falls outside the concerns of scientific classification. In short, this Court's task is a legal one. Decisions based upon broad social, political, moral and economic choices are more appropriately left to the legislature.

[13] What then is the status of the foetus at common law? In *Tremblay v Daigle*, the father of a foetus sought an injunction to prevent the mother from terminating the pregnancy. He argued that a foetus was a 'human being' entitled to the 'enjoyment of life' under s 1 of the *Charter of Human Rights and Freedoms,* RSQ, c C–12. This court unanimously rejected that contention on the ground that neither the Quebec civil law nor the common law of England and Canada recognize the foetus as a juridical person. While injury to a foetus due to the negligence of third parties is actionable, the right to sue does not arise until the infant is born. See: *Montreal Tramways Co v Léveillé*, [1933] SCR 456, [1933] 4 DLR 337; *Paton v British Pregnancy Advisory Service Trustees*, [1979] QB 276 at p 279, citing Lord Russell of Killowen in *Elliot v Lord Joicey*, [1935] AC 209 (HL) at p 333; *Dehler v Ottawa Civic Hospital* (1979), 101 DLR (3d) 686 (Ont HCJ); affirmed (1980), 117 DLR (3d) 512*n* (Ont CA); *Medhurst v Medhurst* (1984), 9 DLR (4th) 252 (Ont HCJ); and *Diamond v Hirsch*, [1989] MJ No 377 (QL) (QB).

[14] The Court summarized the law at p 569 and concluded that the Quebec *Charter* confers no rights on the unborn child:

> the treatment of a foetus in tort law, property law and family law reveals a similar situation as found under the *Civil Code*, namely, that the foetus has no rights in private law. In the field of tort, it is in fact the Quebec case of *Montreal Tramways, supra*, which is most often relied upon for authority in other jurisdictions in Canada (see, eg, *Duval v Seguin*, [1972] 2 OR 686 (HC); *Steeves v Fitzsimmons* (1975), 66 DLR (3d) 203 (Ont HC). As stated earlier, the *Montreal Tramways* decision does not recognize foetuses as legal persons. In the field of property law, Anglo-Canadian law, like Quebec law, has allowed a foetus to be a beneficiary of a will or a donation but it has only protected a foetus' interests where the foetus has been born alive and viable (see *Earl of Bedford's case* (1587), 7 Co Rep 7b, 77 ER 421; *Thellusson v Woodford* (1805), 11 Ves Jun 112, 32 ER 1030, and *Elliot v Lord Joicey*, [1935] AC 209). In family law, a foetus appears to receive some protection, but, as elsewhere in the law, rights take effect and are perfected by birth (see *K v K* [1933] 3 WWR 351 (Man KB), and *Solowan v Solowan* (1953), 8 WWR 288 (Alta SC)).

[15] The position is clear. Neither the common law nor the civil law of Quebec recognizes the unborn child as a legal person possessing rights. This principle applies generally, whether the case falls under the rubric of family law, succession law or tort. Any right or interest the foetus may have remains inchoate and incomplete until the birth of the child.

[16] It follows that under the law as it presently stands, the foetus on whose behalf the agency purported to act in seeking the order for the respondent's detention was not a legal person and possessed no legal rights. If it was not a legal person and possessed no legal rights at the time of the application, then there was no legal person in whose interests the agency could act or in whose interests a court order could be made.

[17] Putting the matter in terms of tort, there was no right to sue, whether for an injunction or damages, until the child was born alive and viable. The law of tort as it presently stands might permit an action for injury to the foetus to be brought in the child's name *after its birth*. But there is no power in the courts to entertain such an action before the child's birth. The action at issue was commenced and the injunctive relief sought before the child's birth. It follows that under the law as it presently stands, it must fail.

2. *Should the Law of Tort Be Extended to Permit the Order?...*
[19] The changes which the agency asks this Court to make to the law of tort may be summarized as follows:
1.   Overturn the rule that rights accrue to a person only at birth (the 'live-birth' rule);
2.   Recognize a foetal right to sue the mother carrying the foetus;
3.   Recognize a cause of action for lifestyle choices which may adversely affect others;
4.   Recognize an injunctive remedy which deprives a defendant of important liberties, including her involuntary confinement.

[20] The proposed changes to the law of tort are major, affecting the rights and remedies available in many other areas of tort law. They involve moral choices and would create conflicts between fundamental interests and rights. They would have an immediate and drastic impact on the lives of women as well as men who might find themselves incarcerated and treated against their will for conduct alleged to harm others. And, they possess complex ramifications impossible for this Court to fully assess, giving rise to the danger that the proposed order might impede the goal of healthy infants more than it would promote it. In short, these are not the sort of changes which common law courts can or should make. These are the sort of changes which should be left to the legislature.

(a)   Overturning the Rule that Rights Accrue only at Birth
[21] A child may sue in tort for injury caused before birth. However, only when the child is born does it have the legal status to sue and damages are assessed only as of the date of birth: see *Montreal Tramways, supra; Duval v Seguin*, [1972] 2 OR 686, 26 DLR (3d) 418 (HCJ), affirmed (1973) 1 OR (2d) 482, 40 DLR (3d) 666 (CA); *Cherry (Guardian ad litem of) v Borsman*, [1992] 6 WWR 701, 94 DLR (4th) 487 (BCCA).

[22] The rule that a foetus does not have a cause of action for prenatal injuries until 'born alive' also governs in other common law countries such as England and Australia. In England, the *Congenital Disabilities (Civil Liability) Act 1976* (UK) 1976, c 28, s 1, creates the basis of civil liability where a child is born disabled in consequence of tortious action of some person before the child's birth. In Australia, the Supreme Court of Victoria in *Watt v Rama*, [1972] VR 353 (Full Ct), in permitting a claim for a prenatal injury residing from an accident to the mother during pregnancy, explained why the right to sue does not exist before birth as follows (at pp 360–61):

> On the birth the relationship crystallized and out of it arose a duty on the defendant in relation to the child. On the facts which for present purposes must be assumed, the child was born with injuries caused by the act or neglect of the defendant in the driving of his car. But as the child could not in the very nature of things acquire rights correlative to a duty until it became by birth a living person, and as it was not until then that it could sustain injuries as a living person, it was, we think, at that stage that the duty arising out of the relationship was attached to the defendant, and it was at that stage that the defendant was, on the assumption that his act or omission in the driving of the car constituted a failure to take reasonable care, in breach of the duty to take reasonable care to avoid injury to the child. On this view the fact that damage was done to the embryo or foetus before birth, if such was sought to be established, was not an independent element in the plaintiff's cause of action, but merely an evidentiary fact relevant to the issue of causation. [Emphasis added.]

[23] To permit intervention prior to birth in recognition of a duty of care owed to the foetus *in utero* would constitute a major departure from the common law as it has stood for decades. It would reverse the long-standing principle of tort law that remedies for negligent behaviour cannot be pursued until a cause of action is brought by a juridical person.

[24] This change to the law of tort is fraught with complexities and ramifications, the consequences of which cannot be precisely foretold. At which stage would a foetus acquire rights? Could women who choose to terminate a pregnancy face injunctive relief prohibiting termination, relief which this Court rejected in *Tremblay v Daigle, supra*? Alternatively, could they face an action for damages brought on behalf of the foetus for its lost life? If a pregnant woman is killed as a consequence of negligence on the highway, may a family sue not only for her death, but for that of the unborn child? If it is established that a foetus can feel discomfort, can it sue its mother (or perhaps her doctor) and claim damages for the discomfort? If the unborn child is a legal person with legal rights, arguments can be made in favour of all these propositions. Some might endorse such changes attracting an array of consequences that would place the courts at the heart of a web of thorny moral and social issues which are better dealt with by elected legislators than by the courts. Having broken the time-honoured rule that legal rights accrue only upon live birth, the courts would find it difficult to limit application of the new principle to particular cases. By contrast, the legislature, should it choose to introduce a law permitting action to protect unborn children against substance abuse, could limit the law to that precise case.

[25] Two arguments are made in favour of this Court abolishing the rule that no legal rights accrue before live birth. The first is that there is no defensible difference between a born child and an unborn child. This is essentially a biological argument. As noted above, the inquiry before this Court is not a biological one, but a legal one: *Tremblay v Daigle, supra*. The common law has always distinguished between an unborn child and a child after birth. The proposition that biologically there may be little difference between the two is not relevant to this inquiry. For legal purposes there are great differences between the unborn and the born child, differences which raise a host of complexities.

[26] The second argument is that the court should overturn the 'live-birth' rule because the present law does not provide a remedy for situations like the case at bar. This argument suffers from two flaws first, it can be made in every case where a court is asked to make a major and complex change to the law. If there were a remedy, the major change would not be required. The Court rejected this argument in *Watkins v Olafson, supra*, and *Salituro, supra*. Nor can it avail in this case. Second, the argument begs the questions of whether a remedy is required, and if so, what remedy and how finely tailored a remedy is best able to achieve the desired social consequence. It is not every evil which attracts court action; some evils remain for the legislature to correct.

(b) Recognizing a Foetal Right to Sue the Mother Carrying the Foetus

[27] Before birth the mother and unborn child are one in the sense that '[t]he life of the foetus is intimately connected with, and cannot be regarded in isolation from, the life of the pregnant woman': *Paton v United Kingdom* (1980), 3 EHRR 408 (Comm) at p 415, applied in *Re F (in utero), supra*. It is only after birth that the foetus assumes a separate personality. Accordingly, the law has always treated the mother and unborn child as one. To sue a pregnant woman on behalf of her unborn foetus therefore posits the anomaly of one part of a legal and physical entity suing itself.

[28] It is therefore not surprising that no case has been cited to us from any jurisdiction in the world where a pregnant woman has been sued on behalf of her foetus. A few cases have accepted that a child, once born, may bring an action against his/her mother for prenatal injuries: *Dobson (Litigation Guardian of) v Dobson* (1997), 148 DLR (4th) 332 (NBCA); *Lynch v Lynch* (1991), 25 NSWLR 411 (CA) at p 415. But none have accepted the proposition that a foetus might sue the woman carrying it. On the contrary, courts which have considered the notion have rejected it: *Paton, supra*; *Re F (In utero), supra*.

[29] To permit an unborn child to sue its pregnant mother-to-be would introduce a radically new conception into the law; the unborn child and its mother as separate juristic persons in a mutually separable and antagonistic relation. Such a legal conception, moreover, is belied by the reality of the physical situation; for practical purposes, the unborn child and its mother-to-be are bonded in a union separable only by birth. Such a dramatic departure from the traditional legal characterization of the relationship between the unborn child and its future mother is better left to the legislature than effected by the courts.

(c) Recognizing a Cause of Action for Lifestyle Choices Which May Adversely Affect Others

[30] If the problem of permitting an unborn child to sue its future mother could be surmounted, a further difficulty presents itself: could the unborn child sue her for lifestyle choices? The difficulty of this question may be discerned from the cases considering the right of born children to sue their mothers for prenatal injuries. To date, courts and legislatures have confined the right to the child suing its mother for prenatal injuries to injuries due to motor vehicle accidents.

[31] In the only Canadian appellate-level case to consider the issue, *Dobson, supra*, Hoyt CJNB, speaking for the court, stated: "*the narrow issue here concerns pre-natal injuries*

received by a child as a result of a mother's negligent driving of her motor vehicle and not injuries occasioned as a result of a mother's lifestyle choices" (p 336 (emphasis added)). In Australia, the same approach was taken: *Lynch v Lynch, supra.*

[32] In England, the rights of infants to sue their mothers for injuries inflicted before birth is confined by statute to injuries resulting from motor vehicle accidents. The same section of the *Congenital Disabilities (Civil Liability) Act 1976*, that allows children to sue for prenatal injuries specifically excludes the child's own mother as a defendant except in cases where the alleged negligence relates to the operation of a motor vehicle (s 2).

[33] Behind the refusal of the courts and at least one legislature to permit a child to sue its mother for prenatal injuries relating to her lifestyle, lies the fear that such suits would take the courts into the difficult policy issue of the extent to which a mother's lifestyle is actionable. Leaving the special relationship between mother and unborn child aside for the moment, there is little precedent for suing any defendant in tort for damages one has suffered as a consequence of his or her lifestyle. While it is not inconceivable that the courts, proceeding properly in their incremental law-making capacity, may one day recognize such claims, the appellant agency faces the difficulty that on this point too it is asking this Court to break new ground in a controversial area. Once again, the consequences for the law of tort generally might be great. Are children to be permitted to sue their parents for second-hand smoke inhaled around the family dinner table? Could any cohabitant bring such an action? Are children to be permitted to sue their parents for spanking causing psychological trauma or poor grades due to alcoholism or a parent's undue fondness for the office or the golf course? If we permit lifestyle actions, where do we draw the line?

[34] The difficulties multiply when the lifestyle in question is that of a pregnant woman whose liberty is intimately and inescapably bound to her unborn child. One faces, to borrow the words of Hoyt CJNB in *Dobson, supra*, the 'spectre of mothers being sued by their children for various activities or lifestyle choices, such as smoking, drinking and the taking or refusal of medication, during pregnancy that injure the child, with the result that mothers will be unable to control their own bodies and make autonomous choices' (p 336). There is no authority in Canada, England or Australia for the proposition that a mother can be sued for negligent behaviour relating to lifestyle choices made during pregnancy. To recognize a duty of care in such situations would constitute yet another marked extension of the common law which would affect a large segment of society. It follows that the Court must approach the issue with great caution.

[35] Before imposing a duty of care in a new situation, the court must be satisfied: (1) that there is a sufficiently close relationship between the parties to give rise to the duty of care; and (2) that there are no considerations which ought to negative or limit the scope of the duty, the class of persons to whom it is owed or the damages to which a breach of it may give rise: *City of Kamloops v Nielsen* [1984] 2 SCR 2, 10 DLR (4th) 641.

[36] The first criterion is met in the present case. The relationship between a woman and her foetus (assuming for the purposes of argument that they can be treated as separate legal entities) is sufficiently close that in the reasonable contemplation of the woman, carelessness on her part might cause damage to the foetus. The more difficult questions arise within the second branch of the test. A host of policy considerations may be raised against the imposition of tort liability on a pregnant woman for lifestyle choices that may affect her unborn child.

[37] Most obviously, recognizing a duty of care owed by a mother to her child for negligent prenatal behaviour may create a conflict between the pregnant woman as an autonomous decision-maker and her foetus. As the Royal Commission on New Reproductive Technologies in its report *Proceed with Care* (1993), vol 2 (Ottowa: The Commission, 1993) eloquently puts it (at pp 957–58):

> From the woman's perspective…considering the interests of her foetus separately from her own has the potential to create adversary situations with negative consequences for her autonomy and bodily integrity, for her relationship with her partner, and for her relationship with her physician. Judicial intervention is bound to precipitate crisis and conflict, instead of preventing them through support and care. It also ignores the basic components of women's fundamental human rights – the right to bodily integrity, and the right to equality, privacy, and dignity.

The potential for intrusions on a woman's right to make choices concerning herself is considerable. The foetus' complete physical existence is dependent on the body of the woman. As a result, any intervention to further the foetus' interests will necessarily implicate, and possibly conflict with the mother's interests. Similarly, each choice made by the woman in relation to her body will affect the foetus and potentially attract tort liability.

[38] The appellant agency argues that the potential intrusions would be minimal because the duty of care could be defined very narrowly. It submits that the duty of care should be to

refrain from activities involved in a woman's right of self-determination – all her choices, or merely some of them? And if some only, what is the criterion of distinction? Although it may be easy to determine that abusing solvents does not add substantial value to a pregnant woman's well-being and may not be the type of self-determination that deserves protection, other behaviours are not as easily classified. At what point does consumption of alcohol fail to add substantial value to a pregnant woman's well-being? Or cigarette smoking? Or strenuous exercise? No bright lines emerge to distinguish tortious behaviour from non-tortious once the door is opened to suing a pregnant mother for lifestyle choices adversely affecting the foetus. As one writer suggests:

> [A woman} could…be held liable for any behaviour during pregnancy having potentially adverse effects on her fetus, including failing to eat properly, using prescription, nonprescription and illegal drugs, smoking, drinking alcohol, exposing herself to infectious disease or to workplace hazards, engaging in immoderate exercise or sexual intercourse, residing at high altitudes for prolonged periods, or using a general anesthetic or drugs to induce rapid labor during delivery.

(See: D E Johnsen, 'The Creation of Fetal Rights: Conflicts with Women's Constitutional Rights to Liberty, Privacy, and Equal Protection' (1986), 95 Yale LJ 599 at pp 606–7.) . . .

[40] These difficulties would be complicated by the fact that determining what will cause grave and irreparable harm to a foetus – the threshold for injunctive relief – is a difficult endeavour with which medical researchers continually struggle. The difference between confinement and freedom, between damages and non-liability, may depend on a grasp of the latest research and its implications. The pregnant women most likely to be affected by such a 'knowledge' requirement would be those in lower socio-economic groups. Minority women, illiterate women, and women of limited education will be the most likely to fall foul of the law and the new duty it imposes and to suffer the consequences of injunctive relief and potential damage awards.

[41] A further problem arises from the fact that lifestyle 'choices' like alcohol consumption, drug abuse, and poor nutrition may be the products of circumstance and illness rather than free choice capable of effective deterrence by the legal sanction of tort. As J E Hanigsberg writes in 'Power and Procreation: State Interference in Pregnancy' (1991), 23 Ottawa L Rev 35 at p 53:

> [W]omen do not abuse drugs out of a lack of care for their fetuses. Drug abusing pregnant women, like other drug abusers, are addicts. People do not want to be drug addicts. In addition, a product of addiction is the inability to control in-take of the substance being abused…
>
> Treating pregnant substance abusers as fetal abusers ignores the range of conditions that contribute to problems like drug addiction and lack of nutrition, such as limited quality pre-natal care, lack of food for impoverished women, and lack of treatment for substance abusers.

While the law may properly impose responsibility for the consequences of addictive behaviour, like drunkenness, the policy question remains of whether extending a duty of care in tort in this particular situation as the remedy for redressing problems which are caused by addition is a wise option. Given the lack of control pregnant women have over many of these harmful behaviours, it is doubtful whether recognizing a duty of care to refrain from them will significantly affect their choices. As a result, the general deterrent value of the proposed new duty of care is questionable.

[42] Recognizing a duty of care in relation to the lifestyle of the pregnant woman would also increase the level of outside scrutiny that she would be subjected to. Partners, parents, friends, and neighbours are among the potential classes of people who might monitor the pregnant woman's actions to ensure that they remained within the legal parameters. Difficulty in determining what conduct is and is not permissible might be expected to give rise to conflicts between the interested persons and the pregnant woman or even between the interested persons themselves. This raises the possibility of conflict which may exacerbate the pregnant woman's condition (and thus the foetus') rather than improve it.

[43] If it could be predicted with some certainty that all these negative effects of extending tort liability to the lifestyle choices of pregnant woman would in fact diminish the problem of injured infants, the change might nevertheless arguably be justified. But the evidence before this Court fails to establish this. It is far from clear that the proposed tort duty will decrease the incidence of substance-injured children. Indeed, the evidence suggests that such a duty might have negative effects on the health of infants. No clear consensus emerges from the debate on the question of whether ordering women into 'places of safety' and mandating medical treatment provide the best solution or, on the contrary, create additional problems.

[44] Indeed, changing tort law to make a pregnant mother liable for lifestyle-related foetal damage may be counterproductive in at least two ways. First, it may tend to drive the problems underground. Pregnant women suffering from alcohol or substance abuse addictions may not seek prenatal care for fear that their problems would be detected and they would be confined involuntarily and/or ordered to undergo mandatory treatment. As a result, there is a real possibility that those women most in need of proper prenatal care may be the ones who will go without and a judicial intervention designed to improve the health of the foetus and the mother may actually put both at serious health risk. Second, changing the law of tort as advocated by the agency might persuade women who would otherwise choose to continue their pregnancies to undergo an abortion. Women under the control of a substance addiction may be unable to face the prospect of being without their addicting substance and may find terminating the pregnancy a preferable alternative. In the end, orders made to protect a foetus' health could ultimately result in its destruction.

[45] It is not necessary for the purposes of this appeal to decide whether, (assuming the difficulties discussed above involved in treating the pregnant woman and her foetus as separate entitles could be overcome) the policy objections to the proposed extension of tort liability for lifestyle related foetal damage to pregnant women, would negate the *prima facie* duty of care which arises under the test in *City of Kamloops v Nielsen, supra.* It suffices to note that serious policy concerns to such an extension of the law exist. The proposed change to the law of tort has the potential to produce considerable uncertainty and affect many peoples' lives adversely, without any assurance of reducing the problem of damage to unborn children from substance abuse. These considerations, as well as the problems associated with assigning separate legal status to pregnant woman and foetus, militate in favour of leaving it to the legislature to address the proper remedy for the problem.

(d) The Extension of Injunctive Relief in Civil Cases to Detention of the Person

[46] In Canada, tort law permits injunctions to detain goods (the *Mareva* injunction), to restrain activities such as unlawful picketing, and sometimes to mandate certain positive action to prevent the occurrence of serious damage. But the principles of tort law have never been used to justify the forcible detention and mandatory treatment of a person. The order at issue on this appeal can be upheld only by a radical extension of civil remedies into the most sacred sphere of personal liberty – the right of every person to live and move in freedom. There exist only two ways in which the state may lawfully involuntarily confine a person: (1) by the criminal law, whose proper concern is the incarceration of those found guilty of criminal offences against society; and (2) by an order made under a provincial *Mental Health Act* that a person is not competent to manage his or her own affairs. It is open to Parliament and the legislature to enact new grounds for involuntary confinement, subject to compliance with the *Canadian Charter of Rights and Freedoms.* But to suggest that judges at common law should do so is unprecedented. To describe such a change as "major" is to understate the matter; to predict that it would have important ramifications is to state the obvious. This final change is one which, if it is to be made, must be left to Parliament or the legislature.

(e) Conclusion as to Whether the Law of Tort Should Be Extended as Proposed

[47] Taken together, the changes to the law of tort that would be required to support the order for detention at issue are of such magnitude, consequence, and policy difficulty that they exceed the proper incremental law-making powers of the courts. Whether such changes should be made, and if so, how far the law should go in making them, is a task more appropriate to the legislatures than the courts.

[48] I conclude that the order for detention cannot be upheld as an application of tort law.

B.   Does the Power of the Court in Parens Patriae Support an Order for the Detention and Treatment of a Pregnant Woman for the Purpose of Preventing Harm to the Unborn Child?

[49] Alternatively, the appellant seeks to sustain the order for the detention of the respondent by an extension of the court's *parens patriae* jurisdiction to permit protection of unborn children. Courts have the power to step into the shoes of the parent and make orders in the best interests of the child: *E (Mrs) v Eve*, [1986] 2 SCR 388, 31 DLR (4th) 1 *sub nom Eve (Re)*. The agency argues that this power should be extended to orders on behalf of unborn children.

[50] I would reject this submission for reasons similar to those enunciated in connection with the submission that the law of tort should be extended to the unborn. The submission requires a major change to the law of *parens patriae*. The ramifications of the change would be significant and complex. The change involves conflicts of fundamental rights and interests and difficult policy issues. Not surprisingly these difficulties have led all appellate courts that have considered the extension to reject it. I share their view.

[51] The law as it stands is clear: the courts do not have *parens patriae* or wardship jurisdiction over unborn children. This is the law in the European Community, Great Britain

and Canada. In Canada, all courts which have considered the issue, save for the trial judge in this case, appear to have rejected the proposition that the *parens patriae* jurisdiction of the court extends to unborn children…

[52] The English Court of Appeal has taken the same view: *Re F (in utero), supra*…

[55] As the English Court of Appeal's reasons eloquently attest, the same problems encountered in relation to extending tort jurisdiction to the unborn, surface in relation to extending the *parens patriae* jurisdiction of the court. The law sees birth as the necessary condition of legal parenthood. The pregnant woman and her unborn child are one. Finally, to make orders protecting foetuses would radically impinge on the fundamental liberties of the pregnant woman, both as to lifestyle choices and how and as to where she chooses to live and be.

[56] It is argued that the *parens patriae* jurisdiction over children necessarily involves overriding the liberty of parents, and that there is nothing new in this. This argument overlooks the fact that the invasion of liberty involved in making court orders affecting the unborn child, is of a different order than the invasion of liberty involved in court orders relating to born children. The *parens patriae* power over born children permits the courts to override the liberty of the parents to make decisions on behalf of their children where a parental choice may result in harm to a child: *B (R) v Children's Aid Society of Metropolitan Toronto*, [1995] 1 SCR 315, 122 DLR (4th) 1. The only liberty interest affected is the parent's interest in making decisions for *his or her child*. By contrast, extension of the *parens patriae* jurisdiction of the court to unborn children has the potential to affect a much broader range of liberty interests. The court cannot make decisions for the unborn child without inevitably making decisions for the mother herself. The intrusion is therefore far greater than simply limiting the mother's choices concerning her child. Any choice concerning her child inevitably affects her. For example, to sustain the order requested in the case at bar would interfere with the pregnant woman's ability to choose where to live and what medical treatment to undergo. The *parens patriae* jurisdiction has never been used to permit a court to make such decisions for competent women, whether pregnant or not. Such a change would not be an incremental change within *Watkins v Olafson, supra*, but a generic change of major impact and consequence. It would seriously intrude on the rights of women. If anything is to be done, the legislature is in a much better position to weigh the competing interests and arrive at a solution that is principled and minimally intrusive to pregnant women.

[57] I conclude that the law of *parens patriae* does not support the order for the detention of the respondent…

IV. CONCLUSION

[59] I conclude that the common law does not clothe the courts with power to order the detention of a pregnant woman for the purpose of preventing harm to her unborn child. Nor, given the magnitude of the changes and their potential ramifications, would it be appropriate for the courts to extend their power to make such an order. The changes to the law sought on this appeal are best left to the wisdom of the elected legislature. I would dismiss the appeal.

Lamer CJ, La Forest, L'Heureux-Dubé, Gonthier, Cory and Iacobucci JJ agreed.

By contrast, Major J (with whom Sopinka J agreed) dissented.

Major J: I respectfully disagree with the conclusion of McLachlin J that an order detaining a pregnant woman addicted to glue-sniffing for which she has rejected abortion and/or medical treatment and decided to carry her child to term, would require a change to the law which cannot be properly made other than by legislation…

III. ANALYSIS

A.   Introduction

[91] The law of this country is consistent with the grant of a remedy in this case. The *parens patriae* jurisdiction of the superior courts is of undefined and undefinable breadth. This Court's decision in *E (Mrs) v Eve*, [1986] 2 SCR 388, 31 DLR (4th) 1 *sub nom Eve (Re)*, indicates that inherent power resides in the provincial superior courts to act on behalf of those who cannot act to protect themselves. A foetus suffering from its mother's abusive behaviour is particularly within this class and deserves protection.

[92] It has been submitted, however, that a foetus acquires no actionable rights in our law until it is born alive. In my view, the "born alive" rule, as it is known, is a common law evidentiary presumption rooted in rudimentary medical knowledge that has long since been overtaken by modern science and should be set aside for the purpose of this appeal…

In my view, the reliance on this rule was misplaced. The rule is a legal anachronism based on rudimentary medical knowledge and should no longer be followed, at least for the purposes of this appeal.

[103] If a foetus is a "person" for purposes of the *parens patriae* jurisdiction, he or she is in a particularly vulnerable position. A foetus, absent outside assistance, has no means of escape from toxins ingested by its mother. The *parens patriae* jurisdiction exists for the stated purpose of doing what is necessary to protect the interests of those who are unable to protect themselves. Society does not simply sit by and allow a mother to abuse her child after birth. How then should serious abuse be allowed to occur before the child is born?

C.   The "Born Alive" Rule

[104] The "born alive" rule, as its name suggests, requires a foetus to be born alive before any legal rights of personhood can accrue. The Court of Appeal relied on this rule as one resolution to the present case, but no inquiry was made into the genesis or purpose of the rule. Once the genesis of the rule is known, it becomes more apparent that it should not apply in this case.

[105] In a persuasive article on this topic, Clarke D Forsythe has traded the genesis of the "born alive" rules as evidentiary, rather than substantive; a principle necessitated by the primitive medical knowledge and technology of the time: "Homicide of the Unborn Child: The Born Alive Rule and Other Legal Anachronisms" (1987), 21 Val UL Rev 563.

[106] Until the early 19th century medical practitioners could not determine with confidence before quickening (the first physical sensation by the mother of the foetus in the womb) whether a woman was pregnant, or further, whether the child *in utero* was alive. Consequently, the common law adopted the presumption that a child was first endowed with life at quickening…

[107] Limited medical knowledge also could not determine whether a child *in utero* was alive at the time it was subjected to an injury unless the child was also born alive, suffering from that injury…

[108] Forsythe examined the history of the "born alive" rule from its oldest common law origins, considering amount others the writings of Bracton, Coke and Blackstone. He concluded that the rule was always one of evidence, and not of substance…

[109] Present medical technology renders the "born alive" rule outdated and indefensible. We no longer need to cling to an evidentiary presumption to the contrary when technologies like real time ultrasound, foetal heart monitors and foetoscopy can clearly show us that a foetus is alive and has been or will be injured by conduct of another. We can gauge foetal development with much more certainty than the common law presumed. How can the sophisticated micro-surgery that is now being performed on foetuses *in utero* be compatible with the "born alive" rule?

[110] However, there is the temptation to assume that the courts of the past that treated the "born alive" rule as one of substantive law knew as much as it known today about foetal development. Since medical technology has improved to the point of eliminating nearly all of the evidentiary problems from which the "born alive" rule sprang, it no longer makes sense to retain the rule where its application would be perverse…

[113] It is no great step for this Court to hold the "born alive" rule not applicable when considering the *parens patriae* jurisdiction of a provincial superior court. While *R v Sullivan*, [1991] 1 SCR 489, held that the wording of s 206 of the *Criminal Code* adopts the "born alive" rule for purposes of criminal law, this does not bar a reassessment of the rule in the context of this case. Here we are dealing purely with the common law, and no enactment of Parliament prevents a re-evaluation of the premises of this rule…

[115] There are contrary authorities to the position adopted in these reasons. In *Paton v British Pregnancy Advisory Service Trustees*, [1979] QB 276, the court cited the "born alive" rule as a bar to a husband obtaining an injunction preventing his pregnant wife from undergoing an abortion procedure. This same reasoning was applied with respect to Quebec civil law in *Tremblay v Daigle*, [1989] 2 SCR 530, 62 DLR (4th) 634, struck down this country's criminal prohibitions against abortion. Nothing in these reasons purports to interfere with the effect of that decision. However, where a woman has chosen to carry a foetus to term, the situation is different. Having chosen to bring a life into this world, that woman must accept some responsibility for its well-being. In my view, that responsibility entails, at the least, the requirement that the pregnant woman refrain from the abuse of substances that have, on proof to the civil standard, a reasonable probability of causing serious and irreparable damage to the foetus. It is not inconsistent to place restraints upon a woman's abusive behaviour towards her foetus that she has decided to carry to term yet continue to preserve her ability to choose abortion at any time during her pregnancy. It is not a question of a woman making a 'declaration' of her intentions. Rather, the law will presume that she intends to carry the child to term until such time as she indicates a desire to receive, makes arrangements for or obtains an abortion.

[117] *Tremblay v Daigle, supra*, noted that the interests of a foetus are legally protected in a number of circumstances, for example, tort law, child welfare, and inheritance rights: pp 569–70. A child can sue to recover for damage inflicted upon it while a foetus: *Montreal*

Tramways, supra. A gift devised by will to a foetus will not fail if the testator dies before birth. The rationale of attributing rights to the foetus in these situations is linked to protecting the interests of the child upon its birth. In this sense, the rationale of protecting the child/foetus by the exercise of the *parens patriae* jurisdiction is no different, as it depends on the intention of the mother to carry the child to term. As was stated in *Tremblay v Daigle*, at p 563:

> A foetus is treated as a person only where it is necessary to do so in order to protect its interests after it is born.

Protecting the unborn child from having to live its life suffering from severe mental and physical disabilities should meet the test of necessity to "protect its interests after it is born"...

[120] The "born alive" rule should be abandoned, for the purposes of this case, as it is medically out-of-date. It may be that the rule has continuing utility in the context of other cases with their own particular facts. The common law boasts that it is adaptable. If so, there is no need to cling for the sake of clinging to notions rooted in rudimentary medical and scientific knowledge of the past. A foetus should be considered within the class of persons whose interests can be protected through the exercise of the *parens patriae* jurisdiction.

D. Standard for Exercising Jurisdiction

[121] In my opinion, it is a modest expansion on La Forest J's statements in *Eve, supra*, to include a foetus within the class of persons who can be protected by the exercise of the *parens patriae* jurisdiction. However, clearly, the only person by law able to choose between an abortion or carrying to term is the mother. She too has the right to decide her lifestyle whether pregnant or not. The court's ability to intervene must therefore be limited. *It will only be in extreme cases, where the conduct of the mother has a reasonable probability of causing serious irreparable harm to the unborn child, that a court should assume jurisdiction to intervene.*

[122] In the Court of Appeal, Twaddle JA grounded his decision denying jurisdiction in part upon a type of "slippery slope" argument (at p 260 DLR):

> The mother's right to sniff solvents may not seem of much importance, but I do not see how a court can select which conduct harmful to an unborn child should be restrained and which not.

This concern was expressed in a variety of ways at the appeal. Serious substance abuse that has a reasonable probability of causing serious and irreparable harm to the foetus should be restrained. Simply because there may be hard cases on other facts not before the Court does not mean we should ignore what is obvious from the evidence in this case. The damage caused to children by serious substance abuse is well documented. It seems derelict to suggest that we should not restrain this abuse because we can imagine some other cases that may not be as clear.

[123] Taking Twaddle JA's argument to its logical extreme, we would be faced with some strange results. It is interesting speculation to wonder what the result of this appeal might have been, had the state been trying to restrain a pregnant mother from taking thalidomide to deal with her morning sickness.

[124] Opposition to this intervention has been strenuously argued by the respondent and her supporting interveners. Exercise of the *parens patriae* jurisdiction will necessarily involve an overriding of some rights possessed by the mother in order to protect her foetus. It is acknowledged that these are serious impositions, accordingly, the test is set at such a very high threshold. We are not simply denying the mother her "right" to sniff solvents but also possibly her liberty. That is why a remedy of confinement should be the final option. Before a court takes the severe step of ordering confinement, a condition precedent should be that it is certain on a balance of probabilities that no other solution is workable or effective. The least rights-diminishing option should always be sought.

[125] In cases such as this any remedy of confinement must be for purposes of treatment, and not punishment. It follows that the *situs* of the confinement should be a residential treatment facility or hospital which can offer a treatment program. The mother remains free to reject all suggested medical treatment. The confinement serves only to prevent her using toxins strong enough to cause serious and permanent damage to the foetus...

[127] The threshold for state intervention is high. In this case the difficult test is met but each case will have to be decided on its facts. The failure of a pregnant woman to quit smoking or act in some way that is optimum for foetal health would not meet the test for state intervention. The familiar "slippery slope" argument has some points of value, however, it cannot be raised as a principled bar to granting an injunction in this case. The "slippery slope" argument if not carefully assessed can easily become an *in terrorem* argument and lose whatever value it may legitimately possess.

[128] In the present case it is clear that DFG has had ample knowledge of the effects of substance abuse on her foetus. She was sadly aware of giving birth to two permanently handicapped children. DFG had been offered counselling and education of various kinds to no apparent avail.

[129] On the other hand, it is somewhat enlightening that once she was confined, her behaviour improved. She voluntarily remained in the hospital after the order of Schulman J was stayed by the Court of Appeal. To the date of this hearing, she has apparently stayed free of solvents. Her child was born healthy and she is raising him primarily alone, but with the aid of CFS and others.

[130] DFG's case indicates that confinement remedies need not last the entire term of the pregnancy, and would be modified as circumstances change. The treatment necessary will vary with the severity of the abuse and the subsequent conduct of the mother.

[131] It is a fundamental precept of our society and justice system that society *can* restrict an individual's right to autonomy where the exercise of that right causes harm to others. Conversely, it would be unjust *not* to restrict one person's right of autonomy when the exercise of that right causes harm to others. In her dissenting opinion in the final report of the Royal Commission on New Reproductive Technologies, *Proceed with Care* (1993), vol 2, ch 30, Dr Suzanne Rozell Scorsone stated, at p 1131:

> Autonomy is a necessary good, but it is not an absolute. All of us have, as the report says, the right to make our own choices, but rights necessarily entail responsibilities; where our choices may or do harm others, our choices are, in fact, limited, and we are held accountable, whatever our gender. It is the suspension of that accountability with respect to pregnant women which would constitute the setting of a different (and lower) standard of behaviour…

[132] When confinement is determined to be the only solution that will work in the circumstances, this type of imposition on the mother is fairly modest when balanced against the devastating harm substance abuse will potentially inflict on her child. The afflicted children may be sentenced to a permanently lower standard of life. To advocate not confining the mother to prevent this harm seems extreme and shortsighted.

[133] The mother's continuing ability to elect an abortion and end her confinement makes the intrusion of her liberty relatively modest when weighed against the child from birth being seriously and permanently impaired.

F.   Conclusion

[138] I do not believe our system, whether legislative or judicial, has become so paralysed that it will ignore a situation where the imposition required in order to prevent terrible harm is so slight. It may be preferable that the legislature act but its failure to do so is not an excuse for the judiciary to follow the same course of inaction. Failure of the court to act should occur where there is no jurisdiction for the court to proceed. Outdated medical assumptions should not provide any licence to permit the damage to continue. Where the harm is so great and the temporary remedy so slight, the law is compelled to act…

[140] It seems fundamentally unfair and inexplicable for this Court to hold that a foetus, upon live birth, can sue for damages to recompense injuries suffered *in utero*, yet have no ability to obtain a remedy preventing that damage from occurring in the first place. This is the one of the clearest of cases where monetary damages are a singularly insufficient remedy. If our society is to protect the health and well-being of children, there must exist jurisdiction to order a pre-birth remedy preventing a mother from causing serious harm to her foetus. Someone must speak for those who cannot speak for themselves…

[142] I would allow the appeal, and declare that Schulman J was within his jurisdiction under *parens patriae* to order the respondent to refrain from the consumption of intoxicating substances, and to compel the respondent to live at a place of safety until the birth of her child.

Both McLachlin and Major JJ refer to the case of *Dobson v Dobson*. The case concerned a claim by a child against its mother having been born injured as a result of the mother's careless driving. In particular, you will notice Major J's reference to it being 'fundamentally unfair and inexplicable' if such an action could be brought *after* birth but the court could not act so as to prevent the injury pre-natally. Subsequently, the Supreme Court of Canada reversed this decision (Major and Bastarache JJ dissenting) and held that a pregnant woman could never owe her unborn child a duty of care and so be sued for pre-natal injuries: see *Dobson (Litigation Guardian of) v Dobson* (1998) 174 DLR (4th) 1 Can Sup Ct) discussed *infra,* ch 12).

How, then, should we understand the decision in *Winnipeg*? There were two arguments in favour of the order to detain and treat the competent pregnant woman against her wishes. First, that an unborn child could be protected under the court's inherent jurisdiction and, secondly, that the woman's conduct amounted to the tort of negligence. In both instances, the court could prevent the harm to the child by injunctive relief.

All judges in the Supreme Court recognised that the law – as it stood – did not permit such an order. Where they disagreed was whether the court could develop the law or whether, if it was to be changed, this was a matter for the legislature. McLachlin J considered that any change was so major and involved complex social and moral issues that it was better addressed by the legislature, which had a more inclusive mechanism for law making. The dissenting justices disagreed: for them the extension could be achieved in a limited way and by the court. It was 'obvious from the evidence' that there was a 'reasonable probability of causing serious and irreparable harm' to the foetus as a result of the woman's 'serious substance abuse'. 'It seems derelict to suggest that we should not restrain this abuse because we can imagine some other cases that may not be so clear' (per Major J).

For both McLachlin J and Major J the legal status of the unborn child was a crucial question. Only if it was a legal person could it be the subject of the court's *parens patriae* jurisdiction and, also, could an action be brought in negligence in advance of its birth to restrain its mother's harmful behaviour. McLachlin J held that the existing law was that any action or rights that an unborn child might have, accrued at birth. There must, in other words, be a 'live birth' before the court can give effect to the interests of the unborn child. This is also the position in England, for example, in actions for pre-natal injury (*de Martell v Merton and Sutton HA* [1993] QB 204 (CA) and s 1 of the Congenital Disabilities (Civil Liability) Act 1976), for murder and manslaughter (*A-G's Reference (No 3 of 1994)* [1997] 3 All ER 936 (HL) and for the court's inherent jurisdiction (*Re F (in utero)* [1988] 2 All ER 193 (CA)). McLachlin J stated that the court was not merely following a rule simply because it was there. She also rejected the argument that there was little or nothing to differentiate the unborn child from one which had been born. For her, this was a biological argument and one which was 'not relevant to this inquiry'. The law was engaged, instead, upon a legal inquiry. There were good reasons for retaining the 'born alive' rule. Major J disagreed and characterised the rule as an anachronism. It was an evidential rule based upon the historical inability to identify the causes of foetal injury until birth. Given modern medical developments, the rule was 'outdated and indefensible'.

McLachlin J identified a number of policy reasons why the courts should not allow an unborn child to sue its mother in negligence for harm caused by her behaviour.

First, the woman and child were 'one' and to introduce such an action would cast them 'as separate juristic persons in a mutually separable and antagonistic relation'. It would deny the reality that they were 'bonded in a union separable only by birth'. This is not, in itself, a wholly persuasive argument. After all, the issue was whether the juristic status quo should be changed. In relying on the 'reality of the physical situation', there is more to worry over if the reality of an action would be to injunct and thereby control the pregnant woman's behaviour. In England, as we shall see the juristic 'oneness' is tempered by the courts' view that the 'mother and foetus [are] two distinct organisms living symbiotically, not a single organism with two aspects' (*A-G's Reference, supra*, at 943 per Lord Mustill). However, this tells us nothing about the *legal* relationship *inter se* and, in particular, whether the mother may be coerced into certain behaviour for the benefit of the foetus. McLachlin J returned to this when considering the court's *parens patriae* power.

Secondly, McLachlin J considered it inappropriate to recognise an action, which would call into question a woman's lifestyle choices. She noted that in those jurisdictions that allowed a child at birth to bring a claim for pre-natal injury against its mother the cases concerned negligence in driving (*Dobson (Litigation Guardian of) v Dobson* (1997) 148 DLR (4th) 332 (NB CA); *Lynch v Lynch* (1991) 25 NSWLR 411 (NSW CA); Congenital Disabilities (Civil Liability) Act 1976, s 2). There, lifestyle choices did not arise. Behind the refusal to allow claims where the woman's lifestyle causes the injury:

> lies the fear that such suits would take the courts into the difficult policy issue of the extent to which a mother's lifestyle is actionable.

McLachlin J stated that it would be difficult for the courts to draw the line of which lifestyle choices to permit: '[n]o bright lines emerge to distinguish tortious behaviour from [the] non-tortious.' Here, although she did not say so, she may have in mind the problem of setting the standard of reasonable care. How is the court to say when activities such as smoking, drinking, exercise, diet or sexual behaviour go 'beyond the pale'? There may, of course, be some obvious and gross over indulgences, but often the court will be faced with borderline situations and no societal standard to apply. It is not necessary, however, for the court to deny that a duty of care arises in all circumstances just because sometimes the going may get tough in setting the standard of care. It is not enough, of course, to say that some activities such as drug or solvent abuse are obviously 'beyond the pale', have no discernible value to the mother and are activities which the law should seek to deter. As McLachlin J pointed out, they may be the 'products of circumstance and illness rather than free choice capable of effective deterrence by the legal sanction of tort'. Thus, it had not been shown that judicial intervention would, on the whole, decrease the risk of harm to unborn children.

McLachlin J also saw other policy reasons pointing the way against judicial development of the law. Changing the law might tend to drive the problem 'underground'. Women might avoid pre-natal care for fear of being detained and mandatorily treated because of their addition. Also, women might seek to avoid the intervention of the state denying them their addiction, by terminating the pregnancy. Thus, in McLachlin J's words 'order made to protect a foetus' health could ultimately result in its destruction'.

You may not find these reasons individually or cumulatively conclusive against the law's intervention. To be fair to her, neither did McLachlin J. For her, these policy considerations simply required resolution by the legislature not the courts. Subsequently, in *Dobson, supra,* this was precisely the view taken by McLachlin J (and a majority of the Supreme Court) in refusing to recognise an action against a woman for injury caused to her child during pregnancy. This is not to say that the legislature had a free choice. As McLachlin J observed, the legislature would have to comply with the Canadian *Charter of Human Rights and Freedoms* both in setting the substance of the law and the procedure for depriving the woman of her liberty. The Human Rights Act 1998 (s 6(1)) will require an English court to shape the common law consistently with the European Convention, in particular Article 5 (freedom from 'inhuman and degrading treatment') and Article 8 (right to 'private life') and, from the unborn child's perspective, Article 2 (right to 'life'). Of course, there is no question that the current English law, as stated in the *St George's* case (*supra*), is inconsistent with the Convention (see *infra*).

The most important (and convincing) part of McLachlin J's reasoning comes right at the end of her judgment. The conflict between unborn child and mother that McLachlin J was at pains to avoid throughout her judgment is, in this case as in many others, deeper than merely placing a limit upon the mother's choices. She considered it relevant both to the existence of a tort action against the mother and whether the *parens patriae* jurisdiction should be extended to protect unborn children *from her.* The law may, and in the case of children frequently does, limit parental choice where it is perceived not to be in the child's 'best interests'. For example, a court would authorise a blood transfusion in a child's best interests notwithstanding the religious objections of the parents (see *B (R) v Children's Aid Society of Metropolitan Toronto* [1995] 1 SCR 315 (Can Sup Ct) and Commentary, (1996) 4 Med L Rev 117 (IK)). *Winnipeg,* as with the *St George's* case in England, involved physical incarceration and treatment against the woman's wishes. It is the nature and degree of this intrusion into the private domain of the woman, specifically her bodily integrity, that is crucial. As McLachlin J pointed out, to detain the woman and then not to treat her would have been pointless. It makes no sense for the minority Justices to authorise her detention but then to allow her to reject all medical treatment. Detention without treatment, and thus for no purpose, is pointless and would be impossible to justify under human rights legislation. Consequently, it is this degree of interference with the woman's private domain (her body) which makes court involvement inappropriate and contrary to her right to 'liberty' (s 7, Charter) or 'private life' (art 8, Convention). McLachlin J adopted the reasoning of the judges in the Court of Appeal in *Re F (in utero) (supra)*, particularly that of Balcombe LJ (at 200–1), eschewing interference with a woman's fundamental liberties. By contrast, Major J (in his dissent) reminds us that:

It is a fundamental precept of our society and justice system that society can restrict an individual's right to autonomy where the exercise of that right causes harm to others.

This statement of the so-called 'harm principle' is well known (see J Feinberg, *Harm to Others* (1984 OUP)). The important word is, however, *'can* restrict' not *must* restrict. Major J goes on to make what is purely and simply a non-sequitur:

Conversely, it would be unjust not to restrict one person's right of autonomy when the exercise of that right causes harm to others.

Here, of course, he is in error. Not every 'harm' must be prevented. It is important to count the cost of doing so to the rights and interests of the person (and others) in doing so. McLachlin J strikes the better balance for the law. The Court of Appeal in *Re F* and the Canadian Supreme Court had in mind interference by the court, but the same is probably true for the legislature.

(iii) ENGLISH LAW AGAIN

Where, then, does this leave English law? The arguments against intervention by the court (or Parliament) seem powerful. Despite *Re S*, the medical profession rejected forced intervention. In its Guidelines, *A Consideration of the Law and Ethics in Relation to Court-Authorised Obstetric Intervention* (1994) the Royal College of Obstetricians and Gynaecologists stated (at para 5.11):

A doctor must respect the competent women's right to choose or refuse any particular recommended course of action…

The courts were soon to follow in *Re MB.*

Re MB (1997) 38 BMLR 175 (CA)

Butler-Sloss LJ: *The unborn child*
Mr Grace sought to persuade us that, even if MB were competent, the court can and should take into account the interests of the unborn child and balance them against the mother's

interests. Strictly speaking, this delicate and difficult question does not arise as we have found this mother not to have been competent. Nevertheless, and despite by the lack of time, not having had the opportunity to hear full and considered oral argument, we have given careful thought to the written submissions and to the material to which reference has been made. Since decisions of this sort invariably have to be made swiftly, we feel obliged to state our conclusions on this issue also.

In our judgment, the court does not have the jurisdiction to take the interests of the foetus into account in a case such as the present appeal and the judicial exercise of balancing those interests does not arise. The nearest one might get to the view that the unborn child should in these circumstances be considered is to be found in the judgment of Lord Donaldson MR in *Re T (adult: refusal of medical treatment)* (1992) 9 BMLR 46 at 50, [1993] Fam 95 at 102:…

The situation postulated by him arose later in 1992 in *Re S*. The interest of the foetus prevailed. It is a decision the correctness of which we must now call in doubt. That is not to say that the ethical dilemma does not remain. None the less, as has so often been said, this is not a court of morals. In the light of earlier authority, to which we now turn, the position in English law appears clear and contrary to the view expressed by Lord Donaldson and by the President.

Butler-Sloss LJ then referred to *Paton v BPAS* [1979] QB 276; *C v S* [1988] QB 135 and *Re F (in utero)* [1988] Fam 122 and continued:

There are decisions which give some acknowledgement to the effect harmful acts have upon the foetus. *Burton v Islington Health Authority* [1992] 3 All ER 833 at 836, [1993] QB 204 at 223 recognised the common law right of action in respect of in utero damage. The opinion of the House of Lords on murder or manslaughter of a child due to injury inflicted before birth is awaited: *A-G's Reference (No 3 of 1994)* [1996] 2 All ER 10, [1996] QB 581. In some circumstances, an unborn child is deemed to be born when its interests require it: *Villar v Gilbey* [1907] AC 139, [1904–7] All ER Rep 779.

None of the above decisions lends any support to the proposition that the court should take into account the interests of the unborn child at risk from the refusal of a competent mother to consent to medical intervention.

Statute law
We turn briefly to a number of statutes which deal specifically with the foetus. First in time was the Offences Against the Persons Act 1861, which made it an offence to procure an abortion. Then the Infant (Life Preservation) Act 1929, by s 1, provided a criminal offence for the intentional destruction of a child, capable of being born alive, before it has an existence independent of its mother. By the Abortion Act 1967, s 1 (as amended by the Human Fertilisation and Embryology Act 1990), pregnancies up to 24 weeks may be terminated where it is necessary to prevent grave injury to the mental or physical health of the pregnant woman. The Act gives precedence to the health of the mother over the unborn child.

By s 1 of the Congenital Disabilities (Civil Liability) Act 1976, if a child is born disabled as a result of an occurrence set out in s 1(2) the child may have a cause of action in respect of the wrongful act, but not against the mother.

Although it might seem illogical that a child capable of being born alive is protected by the criminal law from intentional destruction, and by the Abortion Act from termination, otherwise than as permitted by the Act, but is not protected from the (irrational) decision of a competent mother not to allow medical intervention to avert the risk of death, this appears to be the present state of the law. Moreover, if the competent mother, by refusing medical intervention, is delivered of a handicapped child, she cannot be sued by that child for her decision not to take steps to protect it at the moment of birth. The Law Commission rejected the proposal that a child should be able to have a claim against his mother for injury sustained before birth (Law Com Report No 60). The statute law does not support Mr Grace's submission.

The European Commission of Human Rights
The question of the rights of the unborn child has been considered in a number of cases in the context of the European Convention of Human Rights. In *Bruggemann and Scheuten v Federal Republic of Germany* [1977] 3 EHRR 244, the Commission considered the relationship between the pregnant woman and the foetus in the context of art 8 of the Convention; the right to respect for private and family life. Two German women challenged the restrictions upon abortion in the criminal law of West Germany. In its opinion, the Commission found that there are limits to the personal sphere:

Pregnancy cannot be said to pertain uniquely to the sphere of private life. Whenever a woman is pregnant, her private life becomes closely connected with the developing foetus.

It did not find it necessary to come to a conclusion whether the foetus has rights within art 2.

The 'right to life' set out in art 2 was considered in *Paton v United Kingdom* [1981] 3 EHRR 408. The husband, having failed to obtain an injunction before Sir George Baker (*Paton v British Pregnancy Advisory Service Trustees* [1978] 2 All ER 987, [1979] QB 276), applied to the European Commission. The husband asserted that the Abortion Act 1967, which authorised the termination of his wife's pregnancy, violated several articles of the convention, principally art 2, the right to life, and art 8. In declaring the application inadmissible, the Commission was satisfied, at para 18 of its decision, that art 2 should not be construed as recognising an absolute right to life for a foetus. Since the termination was at ten weeks; was in accordance with the wishes of the mother, and was carried out in order to avert the risk of injury to her physical or mental health, it did not contravene art 2(1). It stated ([1981] 3 EHRR 408 at 415 (para 19):

> The 'life' of the foetus is intimately connected with, and cannot be regarded in isolation from, the life of the pregnant woman. If Article 2 were held to cover the foetus and its protection under this Article were, in the absence of any express limitation, seen as absolute, an abortion would have to be considered as prohibited even where the continuance of the pregnancy would involve a serious risk to the life of the pregnant woman. This would mean that the 'unborn life' of the foetus would be regarded as being of a higher value than the life of the pregnant woman...
>
> 20. The Commission finds that such an interpretation would be contrary to the object and purpose of the Convention...

The Commission did not come to a conclusion on the broader issue whether art 2 recognises the 'right to life' of a foetus at any later stage before birth. It recognised a wide divergence of opinion in different jurisdictions but it did note that: 'the national law on termination of pregnancy has shown a tendency towards further liberalisation.'

This issue came again before the Commission in *H v Norway* (1990) (Case No C–17004/90, unreported) (a lawful abortion of a 14-week foetus for social reasons) and *Open Door Counselling and Dublin Well Woman v Ireland* (1992) 18 BMLR 1, [1992] 15 EHRR 244 (the suppression of communication of information in Ireland about the availability of abortions in the UK). It held in *H v Norway* that the national laws on abortion differ considerably and in such a delicate area the contracting states must have certain discretion. That discretion was not exceeded in the case before them. The Commission avoided expressing an opinion about the scope of art 2 in relation to the protection of the foetus. The Commission did state, however, in *H v Norway* that it would not exclude that in certain circumstances it does offer such protection, but did not indicate what those circumstances were.

It has not yet become necessary for the European Commission to make a decision about the application of art 2 to the foetus at a stage later than ten weeks. Understandably, it has not expressed an opinion on the issue. We do not consider that this court can gain any assistance on this issue from the opinions of the Commission.

American authorities

The American decisions do not point to a clear conclusion from which this court might derive assistance. They are inconclusive although we detect in the most recent trend in appellate decisions a move towards the approach of the English courts. Sir Stephen Brown P in *Re S* was invited to rely upon an incomplete reference to *Re AC* (1990) 573 A 2d 1235 to support a contrary and incorrect conclusion.

Our conclusions on the interests of the unborn child

On the present state of the English law, the submissions made by Mr Grace that we should consider and weigh in the balance the rights of the unborn child, are untenable. The only support in Lord Donaldson's observation in *Re T* cannot stand, in our view, against the weight of earlier decisions, which are far more persuasive as to the present state of the law and which are applicable by analogy to the present appeal. The law is, in our judgment, clear that a competent woman who has the capacity to decide may, for religious reasons, other reasons, or for no reasons at all, choose not to have medical intervention, even though, as we have already stated, the consequence may be the death or serious handicap of the child she bears or her own death. She may refuse to consent to the anaesthesia injection in the full knowledge that her decision may significantly reduce the chance of her unborn child being born alive. The foetus, up to the moment of birth, does not have any separate interests capable of being taken into account when a court has to consider an application for a declaration in respect of a caesarian section operation. The court does not have the jurisdiction to declare that such medical intervention is lawful to protect the interests of the unborn child even at the point of birth.

We respectfully agree with Balcombe LJ, in *Re F (in utero)*, who also considered the possibility of the court being asked to order delivery of the baby by caesarian section. He said ([1988] 2 All ER 193 at 200–201, [1988] Fam 122 at 144):

> If Parliament were to think it appropriate that a pregnant woman should be subject to controls for the benefit of her unborn child, then doubtless it will stipulate the circumstances in which such controls may be applied and the safeguards appropriate for the mother's protection. In such a sensitive field, affecting as it does the liberty of the individual, it is not for the judiciary to extend the law.

Butler-Sloss LJ (giving the judgment of the Court on behalf of Ward and Saville LJJ) effectively consigned *Re S* to the history books (for discussion, see S Michalowski 'Court-Authorised Caesarean Sections – the End of a Trend?' (1999) 62 MLR 115). The court gave pre-eminence to the absolute right of the pregnant woman to refuse *any* medical treatment. The court left for Parliament, referring to Balcombe LJ's view in *Re F (in utero)*, any change to the law which affected the liberty of the woman. We have here, of course, a position reflected in the Canadian Supreme Court's decision in the *Winnipeg* case. Butler-Sloss LJ also gleaned no assistance from the European Convention and its jurisprudence. Whilst the case law is equivocal at present, generally throughout the world unborn children are not seen as 'legal persons' for the purposes of constitutional provisions (see *infra*, ch 11).

Of course, the court's recognition of the right to refuse treatment was for the *competent* patient and therein lies a potential difficulty. The right is wholly dependent upon a judicial finding of competence. On the facts, the court held the woman was not competent because of her needle phobia (see *supra*, ch 5 and *Re L (patient: non-consensual treatment* (1996) 35 BMLR 44 (Kirwood J)). Likewise, in a number of earlier decisions, Family Division judges have, on the basis of rather limited evidence, concluded that a pregnant woman was not competent and thus treatment could be given in *her* interests (see *Rochdale Healthcare (NHS) Trust v C* [1997] 1 FCR 274 (Johnson J) and *Norfolk and Norwich Healthcare (NHS) Trust v W* (1996) 34 BMLR 16 (Johnson J)). The legal difficulties with these cases has already been discussed (*supra*, ch 5 and Commentary (1997) 5 Med L Rev 317 at 320–324 (IK)).

Finally, as a result, the Court of Appeal's views on the 'right to refuse' were strictly speaking obiter. It was, however, unimaginable that a subsequent court would take a different approach. In the following case, the court went out of its way to re-affirm *Re MB* and find the patient in question to be competent.

St George's Healthcare NHS Trust v S, R v Collins, ex parte S (1998) 44 BMLR 160 (CA)

On 25 April 1996, S, who was about 36 weeks pregnant, was diagnosed as suffering from severe pre-eclampsia, severe oedema and protennuria. She was advised that an early delivery was essential. Although understanding that, without treatment, her baby would die and she herself might die or become severely disabled, S's position was that nature should take its course and she refused any treatment. She was seen by an approved social worker, Louize Collins, and a duty psychiatrist. Ms Collins decided that an application under s 2 of the Mental Health Act 1983 ought to be made. The two doctors who completed the necessary form for S to be admitted for assessment, under s 2, referred to S's need to be detained in the interests of her own health and safety and 'with a view to the protection of other persons'. S was admitted to Springfield Hospital on 25 April, when pre-eclampsia and depression were diagnosed. S recorded, in writing, her 'extreme objection to *any* medical or surgical intervention'. Nevertheless, she was transferred, on the night of 25/26 April, to St George's Hospital for obstetric treatment, where she continued to be detained. She had not been granted leave of absence, from Springfield Hospital under s 17 of the Mental Health Act 1983, nor had she been discharged under s 23 of that Act. S contacted a solicitor at midday on 26 April and was advised that she had a right to refuse treatment. An urgent ex parte application, on behalf of the hospital authority was made to Hogg J, sitting in chambers, at lunchtime of the same day. Counsel informed the judge that it was a 'life and death situation and with minutes to spare' and that S had been in labour for about 24 hours. This was incorrect, S not having yet gone into labour. The judge, who had not been informed that S had instructed solicitors, granted a declaration which, in effect, dispensed with the need for S's consent to medical treatment, noting that S's 'capacity to consent ...*may* be affected by her current mental state'. S was later anaesthetised and delivered of a baby by caesarian section the same evening; a final attempt to secure her consent having been made at 20.35. On 30 April, S was transferred back to Springfield Hospital where a consultant psychiatrist examined her the following day and, on finding no clear evidence of mental illness, decided on 2 May that the s 2 order should be discharged. Although advised to remain as a voluntary patient, S discharged herself immediately.

Judge LJ: *The status of the foetus*
Ignoring those occasions when consent may be implied or dispensed with on the ground of incapacity, each woman is entitled to refuse treatment for herself. It does not follow without any further analysis that this entitles her to put at risk the healthy viable foetus which she is carrying. Concern for the sanctity of human life led Lord Donaldson MR in *Re T (adult: refusal of medical treatment)* (1992) 9 BMLR 46 at 50, [1993] Fam 95 at 102 to express a degree of hesitation against making any such assumption:...(See also *Re S (adult: refusal of medical treatment)* (1992) 9 BMLR 69, [1993] Fam 123, where Sir Stephen Brown P granted a declaration that, notwithstanding her refusal of consent on religious grounds, a caesarian section could be performed on a mother to save her life, and that of her unborn child.) Whatever else it may be, a 36-week foetus is not nothing: if viable, it is not lifeless and it is certainly human. In *A-G's Reference (No 3 of 1994)* [1997] 3 All ER 936, [1998] AC 245 the House of Lords considered the status of the foetus before birth in the context of an allegation of murder arising when a pregnant woman was stabbed and, following premature labour, gave birth to a child who survived for 121 days before dying as a result of the stabbing. The conclusion of the Court of Appeal was that the foetus should be treated as an integral part of the mother in the same way as any other part of her body, such as her foot or her arm. This view was rejected in the House of Lords.

Lord Mustill explained the principle ([1997] 3 All ER 936 at 943, [1998] AC 245 at 255–256):

There was, of course, an intimate bond between the foetus and the mother, created by the total dependence of the foetus on the protective physical environment furnished by the mother, and on the supply by the mother through the physical linkage between them of the nutrients, oxygen and other substances essential to foetal life and development. The emotional bond between the mother and her unborn child was also of a very special kind. But the relationship was one of bond, not of identity. The mother and the foetus were two distinct organisms living symbiotically, not a single organism with two aspects. The mother's leg was part of the mother; the foetus was not...I would, therefore, reject the reasoning which assumes that since (in the eyes of English law) the foetus does not have the attributes which make it a 'person' it must be an adjunct of the mother. Eschewing all religious and political debate, I would say that the foetus is neither. It is a unique organism. To apply to such an organism the principles of a law evolved in relation to autonomous beings is bound to mislead.

Lord Hope of Craighead agreed with Lord Mustill ([1997] 3 All ER 936 at 945, [1998] AC 245 at 267):

It [the Human Fertilisation and Embryology Act 1990] serves to remind us that an embryo is in reality a separate organism from the mother from the moment of its conception. This individuality is retained by it throughout its development until it achieves an independent existence on being born. So the foetus cannot be regarded as an integral part of the mother in the sense indicated by the Court of Appeal, notwithstanding its dependence upon the mother for its survival until birth.

Accordingly, the interests of the foetus cannot be disregarded on the basis that, in refusing treatment which would benefit the foetus, a mother is simply refusing treatment for herself.
    In the present case there was no conflict between the interests of the mother and the foetus: no one was faced with the awful dilemma of deciding on one form of treatment which risked one of their lives in order to save the other. Medically, the procedures to be adopted to preserve the mother and her unborn child did not involve a preference for one rather than the other. The crucial issue can be identified by expressing the problem in different ways. If human life is sacred, why is a mother entitled to refuse to undergo treatment if this would preserve the life of the foetus without damaging her own? In the United States, where such treatment has on occasions been forced on an unwilling mother, this question has been described as 'the unborn child's right to live' and 'the State's compelling interest in preserving the life of the foetus' (*Jefferson v Griffin Spalding County Hospital Authority* (1981) 274 SE

d 457) or 'the potentiality of human life' (*Re Madyun* (1986) 573 A 2d 1259). In *Winnipeg Child and Family Services (Northwest Area) v G* (1997) 3 BHRC 611, a decision which will need further examination, in his dissenting judgment Major J commented (at 645): 'Where the harm is so great and the temporary remedy so slight, the law is compelled to act…Someone must speak for those who cannot speak for themselves.' That said, however, how can a forced invasion of a competent adult's body against her will, even for the most laudable of motives (the preservation of life), be ordered without irremediably damaging the principle of self-determination? When human life is at stake, the pressure to provide an affirmative answer authorising unwanted medical intervention is very powerful. Nevertheless, the autonomy of each individual requires continuing protection, even – perhaps particularly – when the motive for interfering with it is readily understandable, and indeed to many would appear commendable: hence the importance of remembering Lord Reid's warning against making 'even minor concessions'. If it has not already done so, medical science will no doubt one day advance to the stage when a very minor procedure undergone by an adult would save the life of his or her child, or perhaps the life of a child of a complete stranger. The refusal would rightly be described as unreasonable, the benefit to another human life would be beyond value, and the motives of the doctors admirable. If, however, the adult were compelled to agree, or rendered helpless to resist, the principle of autonomy would be extinguished.

In *McFall v Shimp* (1978) 127 Pitts Leg J 14 Flaherty J used more dramatic language when sustaining the entitlement of a defendant to refuse to submit to treatment which would save the life of the plaintiff who suffered from a rare bone marrow disease and desperately required a bone marrow transplant from a compatible donor. It was not therefore a case involving a pregnant woman and her foetus. Nevertheless, he highlighted the potential tensions:

> Our society, contrary to many others, has as its first principle, the respect for the individual, and that society and government exist to protect the individual from being invaded and hurt by another. Many societies adopt a contrary view which has the individual existing to serve the society as a whole. In preserving such a society as we have it is bound to happen that great moral conflicts will arise and will appear harsh in a given instance…Morally this decision rests with the defendant, and in the view of the court, the refusal of the defendant is morally indefensible. For our law to *compel* the defendant to submit to an intrusion of his body would change every concept and principle upon which our society is founded. To do so would defeat the sanctity of the individual…(Flaherty J's emphasis.)

In the particular context of the mother's right to self-determination and the interests of her foetus, this tension was considered in *Re MB* (1997) 38 BMLR 175, [1997] 2 FCR 541. In this most difficult area of the law practical decisions affecting the rights of a mother and her unborn child, and the position of those responsible for their care, frequently require urgent resolution without the luxury or time to analyse the complex ethical problems which invariably arise. Accordingly, with the advantage of detailed skeleton arguments, the relevant statutory provisions and authorities were closely studied.

Giving the judgment of the court, Butler-Sloss LJ said ((1997) 38 BMLR 175 at 186, [1997] 2 FCR 541 at 561):

> A competent woman, who has the capacity to decide, may, for religious reasons, other reasons, for rational or irrational reasons or for no reason at all, choose not to have medical intervention, even though the consequence may be the death or serious handicap of the child she bears, or her own death. She may refuse to consent to the anaesthesia injection in the full knowledge that her decision may significantly reduce the chance of her unborn child being alive. The foetus up to the moment of birth does not have any separate interests capable of being taken into account when a court has to consider an application for a declaration in respect of a caesarian section operation. The law does not have the jurisdiction to declare that such medical intervention is lawful to protect the interests of the unborn child even at the point of birth.

As the mother in *Re MB* was found not to have been competent, strictly speaking this question did not arise for decision and, as Butler-Sloss LJ herself recognised, the observation was obiter.

It was, however, consistent with the reasoning in a line of authorities where a husband had made an unsuccessful application to prevent an abortion being performed on his wife (*Paton v Trustees of BPAS* [1978] 2 All ER 987, [1979] QB 276 and *C v S* (1987) 2 BMLR 143, [1988] QB 135, and with *Re F (in utero)* [1988] 2 All ER 193 at 200, [1988] Fam 122 at 143, where, refusing an application that the foetus of an unstable pregnant woman should be made a ward of court, Balcombe LJ observed:

there is no jurisdiction to make an unborn child a ward of court. Since an unborn child has, ex hypothesi, no existence independent of its mother, the only purpose of extending the jurisdiction to include the foetus is to enable the mother's actions to be controlled.

He went on to consider the possibility that the court might be asked to order delivery of the baby by caesarian section, and commented ([1988] 2 All ER 193 at 200–201, [1988] Fam 122 at 144):

it would be intolerable to place a judge in the position of having to make such a decision without any guidance as to the principles upon which his decision should be based. If the law is to be extended in this manner, so as to impose control over the mother of an unborn child, where such control may be necessary for the benefit of that child, then under our system of parliamentary democracy it is for Parliament to decide whether such controls can be imposed and, if so, subject to what limitations or conditions…If Parliament were to think it appropriate that a pregnant woman should be subject to controls for the benefit of her unborn child, then doubtless it will stipulate the circumstances in which such controls may be applied and the safeguards appropriate for the mother's protection. In such a sensitive field, affecting as it does the liberty of the individual, it is not for the judiciary to extend the law.

None of these authorities appears to have been cited either in *Re T* (probably because they were not strictly relevant) or in *Re S (adult: refusal of medical treatment)*, referred to earlier and, although obiter, the principle encapsulated in the language used by Butler-Sloss LJ in *Re MB* reflected the existing state of the law.

A number of authorities from outside this jurisdiction were cited in the present case, which were not before the court in *Re MB*. However, it is unnecessary to go beyond the decision of the Supreme Court of Canada given on 31 October 1997 in *Winnipeg Child and Family Services (Northwest Area) v G* (1997) 3 BHRC 611…Mr Havers invited us to follow the reasoning in the dissenting judgment delivered by Major J. We decline to do so. Quite apart from the problem that the parens patriae jurisdiction on which the dissenting judgment depended has no more validity in this jurisdiction than it does in Canada, the reasoning of the majority coincides with the approach of this court in *Re MB*, reinforced by the observations of Lord Mustill and Lord Hope in *A-G's Reference (No 3 of 1994)*. In the later part of his speech Lord Mustill said ([1997] 3 All ER 936 at 948, [1998] AC 245 at 261):

It is sufficient to say that it is established beyond doubt for the criminal law, as for the civil law (*Burton v Islington Health Authority, De Martell v Merton and Sutton Health Authority* (1992) 10 BMLR 63, [1993] QB 204) that the child en ventre sa mère does not have a distinct human personality, whose extinguishment gives rise to any penalties or liabilities at common law.

In a final observation relevant to the issues in the present case he added ([1997] 3 All ER 936 at 949, [1998] AC 245 at 262):

The defendant intended to commit and did commit an immediate crime of violence to the mother. He committed no relevant violence to the foetus, which was not a person, either at the time or in the future, and intended no harm to the foetus or to the human person which it would become.

The reasoning which led Lord Hope to conclude that the crime of manslaughter could be committed reinforced this observation. After examining the submission based on the proposition that manslaughter could not be established where the victim of an unlawful violent act was already dead, he continued ([1997] 3 All ER 936 at 957, [1998] AC 245 at 271):

If the person is already dead, his life is over and no further harm can be done. No act which is done to him now or in the future can be dangerous. The mens rea which a person has when doing an unlawful act to a person who is dead is not that which is required for manslaughter. So also a person who is already dead cannot be within the scope of the mens rea which the defendant has when he does an unlawful and dangerous act to someone who is alive.

He then went on to examine the 'different problem' of the foetus. He said (1997) 3 All ER 936 at 957, [1998] AC 245 at 271):

For the foetus, life lies in the future, not the past. It is not sensible to say that it cannot ever be harmed, or that nothing can be done to it which can ever be dangerous. Once it is born it is exposed, like all other living persons, to the risk of injury. It may also carry with it the effects of things done to it before birth which, after birth, may prove to be harmful. It would seem not to be unreasonable therefore, on public policy grounds, to regard the child in this case, when she became a living person, as within the scope of the mens rea which B had when he stabbed her mother before she was born.

At the conclusion of his speech he said ([1997] 3 All ER 936 at 960, [1998] AC 245 at 274):

> The fact that the child whom the mother was carrying at the time was born alive and then died as a result of the stabbing is all that was needed for the offence of manslaughter when the actus reus for that crime was completed by the child's death.

In essence, if the child had not been born alive she could not have been the victim of manslaughter. The language of Lord Hope demonstrates that the concept of being 'born alive', rejected in his dissenting judgment by Major J in *Winnipeg Child and Family Services*, remains undiminished.

In our judgment, while pregnancy increases the personal responsibilities of a woman, it does not diminish her entitlement to decide whether or not to undergo medical treatment. Although human, and protected by the law in a number of different ways set out in the judgment in *Re MB*, an unborn child is not a separate person from its mother. Its need for medical assistance does not prevail over her rights. She is entitled not to be forced to submit to an invasion of her body against her will, whether her own life or that of her unborn child depends on it. Her right is not reduced or diminished merely because her decision to exercise it may appear morally repugnant. The declaration in this case involved the removal of the baby from within the body of her mother under physical compulsion. Unless lawfully justified, this constituted an infringement of the mother's autonomy. Of themselves, the perceived needs of the foetus did not provide the necessary justification.

We do not discuss here the court's decision concerning the use of s 2 of the Mental Health Act 1983 to detain the patient which was held to be unlawful (see Commentary (1998) 6 Med L Rev 356 (AG) and for a discussion of *Attorney-General's Reference (No 3 of 1994)*, Commentary (1995) 3 Med L Rev 302 (AG) and (1998) 6 Med L Rev 256 (AG).).

(b) The parent and child

So far we have been concerned with a competent adult making a decision which affects her unborn child. There is another strand of authority which is concerned with the situation where existing children of the patient's family may be affected by the patient's refusal of life-sustaining treatment. It could be said that since the decision of the patient here will not lead to the death of the child (unlike the situation where the patient is pregnant) *a fortiori* the court should not compel treatment when it is refused. In the first case of its kind in America, however, the court seems to have taken a different view.

Application of the President and Directors of Georgetown College Inc (1964) 331 F 2d 1000 and (on rehearing) 331 F 2d 1010 (USCA DCC)

Skelly Wright J: Attorneys for Georgetown Hospital applied for an emergency writ at 4:00 pm, September 17, 1963, seeking relief from the action of the United States District Court for the District of Columbia denying the hospital's application for permission to administer blood transfusions to an emergency patient. The application recited that 'Mrs Jesse E Jones is presently a patient at Georgetown University Hospital,' 'she is in extremis,' according to the attending physician 'blood transfusions are necessary immediately in order to save her life,' and 'consent to the administration thereof can be obtained neither from the patient nor her husband.' The patient and her husband based their refusal on their religious beliefs as Jehovah's Witnesses. The order sought provided that the attending physicians 'may' administer such transfusions to Mrs Jones as might be 'necessary to save her life.' After the proceedings detailed in Part IV of this opinion, I signed the order at 5:20 pm...

Mrs Jones subsequently appeared in the cause, in this court, as respondent to the application. The treatment proposed by the hospital in its application was not a single transfusion, but a series of transfusions. The hospital doctors sought a court determination before undertaking either this course of action or some alternative. The temporary order issued was more limited than the order proposed in the original application, in that the phrase 'to save her life' was added, thus limiting the transfusions in both time and number. Such a temporary order to preserve the life of the patient was necessary if the cause were not to be mooted by the death of the patient...

Mrs Jones was brought to the hospital by her husband for emergency care, having lost two thirds of her body's blood supply from a ruptured ulcer. She had no personal physician, and relied solely on the hospital staff. She was a total hospital responsibility. It appeared that the patient, age 25, mother of a seven-month-old child, and her husband were both Jehovah's Witnesses, the teachings of which sect, according to their interpretation, prohibited the injection of blood into the body. When death without blood became imminent, the hospital sought the advice of counsel, who applied to the District Court in the name of the hospital for permission to administer blood. Judge Tamm of the District Court denied the application, and counsel immediately applied to me, as a member of the Court of Appeals, for an appropriate writ.

I called the hospital by telephone and spoke with Dr Westura, Chief Medical Resident, who confirmed the representations made by counsel. I thereupon proceeded with counsel to the hospital, where I spoke to Mr Jones, the husband of the patient. He advised me that, on religious grounds, he would not approve a blood transfusion for his wife. He said, however, that if the court ordered the transfusion, the responsibility was not his. I advised Mr Jones to obtain counsel immediately. He thereupon went to the telephone and returned in 10 or 15 minutes to advise that he had taken the matter up with his church and that he had decided that he did not want counsel.

I asked permission of Mr Jones to see his wife. This he readily granted. Prior to going into the patient's room, I again conferred with Dr Westura and several other doctors assigned to the case. All confirmed that the patient would die without blood and that there was a better than 50 percent chance of saving her life with it. Unanimously they strongly recommended it. I then went inside the patient's room. Her appearance confirmed the urgency which had been represented to me. I tried to communicate with her, advising her again as to what the doctors had said. The only audible reply I could hear was 'Against my will.' It was obvious that the woman was not in a mental condition to make a decision. I was reluctant to press her because of the seriousness of her condition and because I felt that to suggest repeatedly the imminence of death without blood might place a strain on her religious convictions. I asked her whether she would oppose the blood transfusion if the court allowed it. She indicated, as best I could make out, that it would not then be her responsibility.

I returned to the doctors' room where some 10 to 12 doctors were congregated, along with the husband and counsel for the hospital. The President of Georgetown University, Father Bunn, appeared and pleaded with Mr Jones to authorize the hospital to save his wife's life with a blood transfusion. Mr Jones replied that the Scriptures say that we should not drink blood, and consequently his religion prohibited transfusions. The doctors explained to Mr Jones that a blood transfusion is totally different from drinking blood in that the blood physically goes into a different part and through a different process in the body. Mr Jones was unmoved. I thereupon signed the order allowing the hospital to administer such transfusions as the doctors should determine were necessary to save her life...

This opinion is being written solely in connection with the emergency order authorizing the blood transfusions 'to save her life'. It should be made clear that no attempt is being made here to determine the merits of the underlying controversy. Actually, the issue on the merits is res nova. Because of the demonstrated imminence of death from loss of blood, signing the order was necessary to maintain the status quo and prevent the issue respecting the rights of the parties in the premises from becoming moot before full consideration was possible. But maintaining the status quo is not the only consideration in determining whether an emergency writ should issue. The likelihood of eventual success on appeal is of primary importance, and thus must be here considered.

Before proceeding with this inquiry, it may be useful to state what this case does not involve. This case does not involve a person who, for religious or other reasons, has refused to seek medical attention. It does not involve a disputed medical judgment or a dangerous or crippling operation. Nor does it involve the delicate question of saving the newborn in preference to the mother. Mrs Jones sought medical attention and placed on the hospital the legal responsibility for her proper care. In its dilemma, not of its own making, the hospital sought judicial direction.

It has been firmly established that the courts can order compulsory medical treatment of children for any serious illness or injury, eg, *People ex rel Wallace v Labrenz*, 411 Ill 618, 104 NE 2d 769, cert denied, 344 US 824, 73 S Ct 24, 97 L Ed 642 (1952); *Morrison v State*, Mo App, 252 SW 2d 97 (1952); *Mitchell v Davis*, Tex Civ App, 205 SW 2d 812 (1947), and that adults, sick or well, can be required to submit to compulsory treatment or prophylaxis, at least for contagious diseases, eg, *Jacobson v Massachusetts*, 197 US 11, 25 S Ct 358, 49 L Ed 643 (1905). And there are no religious exemptions from these orders, eg, *People ex rel Wallace v Labrenz, supra*; cf *Hamilton v Regents*, 293 US 245, 55 S Ct 197, 79 L Ed 343 (1934), rehearing denied, 293 US 633, 55 S Ct 345, 79 L Ed 717 (1935). These principles were restated by the Supreme Court in *Prince v Massachusetts*, 321 US 158, 166–167, 64 S Ct 438, 442, 88 L Ed 645, 652, 653 (1944):

...Acting to guard the general interest in youth's well being, the state as parens patriae may restrict the parents' control...Its authority is not nullified merely because the parent grounds his claim to control the child's course of conduct on religion or conscience. Thus, he cannot claim freedom from compulsory vaccination for the child more than for himself on religious grounds. [*Jacobson v Massachusetts*, 197 US 11, 25 S Ct 358, 49 L Ed 643.] The right to practice religion freely does not include liberty to expose the community or the child to communicable disease or the latter to ill health or death. *People v Pierson*, 176 NY 201, 68 NE 243 [63 LRA 187] [see also *State v Chenoweth*, 163 Ind, 94, 71 NE 197; *Owens v State*, 6 Okl Cr 110, 116 P 345, 36 LRA, NS, 633]...

Of course, there is here no sick child or contagious disease. However, the sick child cases may provide persuasive analogies because Mrs Jones was in extremis and hardly compos mentis at the time in question; she was as little able competently to decide for herself as any child would be. Under the circumstances, it may well be the duty of a court of general jurisdiction, such as the United States District Court for the District of Columbia, to assume the responsibility of guardianship for her, as for a child, at least to the extent of authorizing treatment to save her life. And if, as shown above, a parent has no power to forbid the saving of his child's life, a fortiori the husband of the patient here had no right to order the doctors to treat his wife in a way so that she would die.

The child cases point up another consideration. The patient, 25 years old, was the mother of a seven-month-old child. The state, as parens patriae, will not allow a parent to abandon a child, and so it should not allow this most ultimate of voluntary abandonments. The patient had a responsibility to the community to care for her infant. Thus the people had an interest in preserving the life of this mother.

Apart from the child cases, a second range of factors may be considered. It is suggested that an individual's liberty to control himself and his life extends even to the liberty to end his life. Thus, 'in those states where attempted suicide has been made lawful by statute (or the lack of one), the refusal of necessary medical aid [to one's self], whether equal to or less than attempted suicide, must be conceded to be lawful.' Cawley, Criminal Liability in Faith Healing, 39 Minn L Rev 48, 68 (1954). And, conversely, it would follow that where attempted suicide is illegal by the common law or by statute, a person may not be allowed to refuse necessary medical assistance when death is likely to ensue without it. Only quibbles about the distinction between misfeasance and nonfeasance, or the specific intent necessary to be guilty of attempted suicide, could be raised against this latter conclusion.

If self-homicide is a crime, there is no exception to the law's command for those who believe the crime to be divinely ordained. The Mormon cases in the Supreme Court establish that there is no religious exception to criminal laws, and state obiter the very example that a religiously-inspired suicide attempt would be within the law's authority to prevent. *Reynolds v United States*, 98 US (8 Otto) 145, 166, 25 L Ed 244, 250 (1878); *Late Corporation of the Church of Jesus Christ of Latter-Day Saints v United States (Romney v United States)*, 136 US 1, 49–50, 10 S Ct 792, 34 L Ed 478, 493 (1890). But whether attempted suicide is a crime is in doubt in some jurisdictions, including the District of Columbia.

The Gordian knot of this suicide question may be cut by the simple fact that Mrs Jones did not want to die. Her voluntary presence in the hospital as a patient seeking medical help testified to this. Death, to Mrs Jones, was not a religiously-commanded goal, but an unwanted side effect of a religious scruple. There is no question here of interfering with one whose religious convictions counsel his death, like the Buddhist monks who set themselves afire. Nor are we faced with the question of whether the state should intervene to reweigh the relative values of life and death, after the individual has weighed them for himself and found life wanting. Mrs Jones wanted to live.

A third set of considerations involved the position of the doctors and the hospital. Mrs Jones was their responsibility to treat. The hospital doctors had the choice of administering the proper treatment or letting Mrs Jones die in the hospital bed, thus exposing themselves, and the hospital, to the risk of civil and criminal liability in either case. It is not certain that Mrs Jones had any authority to put the hospital and its doctors to this impossible choice. The normal principle that an adult patient directs her doctors is based on notions of commercial contract which may have less relevance to life-or-death emergencies. It is not clear just where a patient would derive her authority to command her doctor to treat her under limitations which would produce death. The patient's counsel suggests that this authority is part of constitutionally protected liberty. But neither the principle that life and liberty are inalienable rights, nor the principle of liberty of religion, provides an easy answer to the question whether the state can prevent martyrdom. Moreover, Mrs Jones had no wish to be a martyr. And her religion merely prevented her consent to a transfusion. If the law undertook the responsibility of authorizing the transfusion without her consent, no problem would be raised with respect to her religious practice. Thus, the effect of the order was to preserve for Mrs Jones the life she wanted without sacrifice of her religious beliefs.

The final, and compelling, reason for granting the emergency writ was that a life hung in the balance. There was no time for research and reflection. Death could have mooted the cause in a matter of minutes, if action were not taken to preserve the status quo. To refuse to act, only to find later that the law required action, was a risk I was unwilling to accept. I determined to act on the side of life.

[On rehearing before Bazelon, Ch J and Wilbur K Miller, Fahy, Washington, Danaher, Bastian, Burger, Wright, and McGowan, Circuit Judges, en banc, in Chambers. . .

Per Curium. Upon consideration of a pleading styled 'Petition for Rehearing En Banc' in the above-cited matter and an opposition thereto, it is

[Ordered by the court en banc that said petition is denied.]

Burger, Circuit Judge: We can assume first that a hospital, like a doctor, has certain responsibilities and duties towards a person who, by choice or emergency, comes under its care. No affirmative act of the patient is suggested as invading or threatening any right of the hospital. So we must decide whether an 'invasion' of legal right can be spelled out of a relationship between the patient's refusal to accept a standard medical treatment thought necessary to preserve life and the possible consequences to the hospital if, relying on her refusal of consent, it fails to give a transfusion and death or injury follows. The possible economic impact, apart from the moral implications inherent in its responsibilities, perhaps presented an arguable basis for the hospital's claim of protected economic right. It stood in an unenviable 'Good Samaritan' posture when the patient categorically refused to consent to a blood transfusion called for by a medical emergency. The choice between violating the patient's convictions of conscience and accepting her decision was hardly an easy one.

However, since it is not disputed that the patient and her husband volunteered to sign a waiver to relieve the hospital of any liability for the consequences of failure to effect the transfusion, any claim to a protected right in the economic damage sphere would appear unsupported.

Can a legally protected right arise out of some other duty-right of the hospital toward a patient, such as a moral obligation to preserve life at all costs?

For me it is difficult to construct an actionable or legally protected right out of this relationship. The affirmative enforcement of a right growing out of a possible moral duty of the hospital toward a patient does not seem to meet the standards of justiciability especially when the only remedy is judicial compulsion touching the sensitive area of conscience and religious belief...

Mr Justice Brandeis, whose views inspired much of the 'right to be let alone' philosophy, said in *Olmstead v United States*, 277 US 438, 478, 48 S Ct 564, 572, 72 L Ed 944, 956, 66 ALR 376 (1928), (dissenting opinion):

The makers of our Constitution...sought to protect Americans in their beliefs, their thoughts, their emotions and their sensations. They conferred, as against the Government, the right to be let alone – the most comprehensive of rights and the right most valued by civilized man.

Nothing in this utterance suggests that Justice Brandeis thought an individual possessed these rights only as to *sensible* beliefs, *valid* thoughts, *reasonable* emotions, or *well-founded* sensations. I suggest he intended to include a great many foolish, unreasonable and even absurd ideas which do not conform, such as refusing medical treatment even at a great risk.

That judicial power is narrow and limited is a concept deeply embedded in our System. Thus the need for external restraints on the powers of Federal Judges was plainly an important corollary to their constitutionally secured tenure. It was quite as clear in the 1780s as it is today that men are not notorious for exercising self-restraint when they possess both permanent tenure *and* plenary power. Under our System no single Branch of Government has both, and no single Branch of Government could safely be entrusted with both.

Confronted by a unique episode such as this, it seems to me we must inquire where an assumption of jurisdiction over such matters could lead us. Physicians, surgeons and hospitals – and others as well – are often confronted with seemingly irreconcilable demands and conflicting pressures. Philosophers and theologians have pondered these problems and different religious groups have evolved different solutions; the solutions and doctrines of one group are sometimes not acceptable to other groups or sects. Various examples readily come to mind: a crisis in childbirth may require someone to decide whether the life of the mother or the child shall be sacrificed; absent a timely and decisive choice both may die. May the physician or hospital require the courts to decide? A patient may be in a critical condition requiring, in the minds of experts, a certain medical or surgical procedure. If the patient has objections to that treatment based on religious conviction, or if he rejects the medical opinion, are the courts empowered to decide for him?

Some of our greatest jurists have emphasized the need for judicial awareness of the limits on judicial power which is simply an acknowledgement of human fallibility.

Cardozo, in The Nature of the Judicial Process, said:

The judge, even when he is free, is still not wholly free. He is not to innovate at pleasure. He is not a knight-errant, roaming at will in pursuit of his own ideal of beauty or of goodness. He is to draw his inspiration from consecrated principles. He is not to yield to spasmodic sentiment, to vague and unregulated benevolence. He is to exercise a discretion informed by tradition, methodized by analogy, disciplined by system, and subordinated to 'the primordial necessity of order in the social life.' Wide enough in all conscience is the field of discretion that remains.

It is at the periphery of the boundaries of power where the guidelines are less clear that an appealing claim presents difficult choices, but this is precisely the area in which restraint is called for in light of the absolute nature of our powers and the finality which often, as here, attends our acts. But we should heed Cardozo's counsel of restraint and reconcile ourselves to the idea that there are myriads of problems and troubles which judges are powerless to solve; and this is as it should be. Some matters of essentially private concern and others of enormous public concern, are beyond the reach of judges. Cf *Pauling v McNamara*, supra.

I am authorized to state that Wilbur K Miller and Bastian, Circuit Judges, join in the above views.

The *Georgetown* case may be explicable on the basis that the judge regarded Mrs Jones as incompetent and, perhaps, in fact she was. To this extent, the case may not be of the greatest help to us here (see the explanation of the case in *Norwood Hospital v Munoz* (1991) 564 NE 2d 1017 at 1024, footnote 7, per Liacos CJ (Mass Sup Jud Ct) *infra*). If Mrs Jones were competent, however, the case can equally be explained (as indeed it was by the judge himself) as a case in which the court made an emergency order to maintain the 'status quo' pending a full review by the court. Either of these explanations is sufficient to warrant Judge Skelly Wright's decision. In the light of the other explanation, it would be wrong to consider the case as an authority justifying treatment on a competent adult patient simply because of the interests of that patient's existing children.

Subsequent cases in America have made this plain.

Norwood Hospital v Munoz (1991) 564 NE 2d 1017 (Mass Sup Jud Ct)

Liacos CJ: In this case, a competent adult, who is a Jehovah's Witness and a mother of a minor child, appears from a judgment of the Probate and Family Court authorizing Norwood Hospital to administer blood or blood products without her consent.

We state the facts, Yolanda Munoz, a thirty-eight year old woman, lives in Dedham with her husband, Ernesto Munoz, and their minor son, Ernesto, Jr. Ernesto's father, who is over seventy-five years old, also lives in the same household.

Ms Munoz has a history of stomach ulcers. Approximately ten years ago, she underwent surgery for a bleeding ulcer. On April 11, 1989, Ms Munoz vomited blood and collapsed in her home. During the week before she collapsed, Ms Munoz had taken two aspirins every four hours to alleviate a pain in her arm. The aspirin apparently made her ulcer bleed. Ernesto took his wife to the Norwood Hospital emergency room. Physicians at Norwood Hospital gave Ms Munoz medication which stopped the bleeding. Ms Munoz was then admitted to the hospital as an inpatient. During the evening, her hematocrit (the percentage of red blood cells to whole blood) was 17%. A normal hematocrit level for an adult woman is approximately 42%. Ms Munoz was placed under the care of Dr Joseph L Perrotto. It was his medical opinion that the patient had a 50% probability of hemorrhaging again. If Ms Munoz started to bleed, Dr Perrotto believed that she would in all probability die unless she received a blood transfusion. Ms Munoz, however, refused to consent to a blood transfusion in the event of a new hemorrhage.

Ms Munoz and her husband were baptized as Jehovah's Witnesses over sixteen years ago. They are both members of the Jamaica Plain Kingdom Hall of Jehovah's Witnesses. Ms Munoz attends three religious meetings every week. A principal tenet of the Jehovah's Witnesses' religion is a belief, based on interpretations of the Bible, that the act of receiving blood or blood products precludes an individual resurrection and everlasting life after death.

Norwood Hospital has a written policy regarding patients who refuse to consent to the administration of blood or blood products. According to this policy, if the patient arrives at the hospital in need of emergency medical treatment and there is no time to investigate the patient's circumstances or competence to make decisions regarding treatment, the blood transfusion will be performed if necessary to save the patient's life. If the patient, in a non-emergency situation, refuses to consent to a blood transfusion, and the patient is a minor, an incompetent adult, pregnant, or a competent adult with minor children, the hospital's policy is to seek judicial determination of the rights and responsibilities of the parties.

The patient in this case, while no longer in an emergency situation once her ulcer stopped bleeding, has a minor child. The hospital sought a court order; on April 12, the hospital filed a complaint for a declaratory judgment in the Norfolk Division of the Probate and Family Court pursuant to GL c 231A (1988 ed.) The hospital requested that Ms Munoz be required to accept blood transfusions which her attending physician believed to be reasonably necessary to save her life. On that same day, the judge granted a temporary restraining order authorizing the hospital to 'administer transfusions of blood or blood products in the event that [the patient] hemorrhages to the extent that her life is severely threatened by loss of blood in the opinion of her attending physicians.' The court also appointed Mr Jonathan Brant to serve as guidance ad litem for five year old Ernesto, Jr.

On April 13, the judge held a full evidentiary hearing. Dr Perrotto stated in an unchallenged affidavit that, if Ms Munoz were to begin bleeding again, she would have an excellent chance of recovering if she received a blood transfusion. If she started to bleed, however, and did not receive a blood transfusion, she would probably die. In addition, Dr Perrotto stated that there was no alternative course of medical treatment capable of saving the patient's life. Ernesto Munoz and James Joslin, Ms Munoz's brother-in-law, testified at the hearing in favour of allowing Ms Munoz to refuse the blood transfusion. The guardian ad litem's report, which recommended that the hospital's request for a declaratory judgment be denied, was admitted in evidence.

On April 14, the judge granted the declaratory judgment authorizing blood transfusions which were 'reasonably necessary to save [the patient's] life.' The judgment also absolved the hospital and its agents from any civil or criminal liability, except for negligence or malpractice, which might arise from a blood transfusion. On May 11, 1989, the judge issued a detailed opinion explaining his reasons for granting the declaratory judgment. The judge found the patient competent; she understood the nature of her illness, and the potential serious consequences of her decision, including the risk of imminent death if her bleeding resumed and blood transfusions were not administered. While recognizing that a competent adult may usually refuse medical treatment, the judge stated that the hospital could administer the blood transfusions because, if they did not and Ms Munoz subsequently died, Ernesto, Jr, would be 'abandoned'. The judge concluded that the State's interests in protecting the well-being of Ernesto, Jr, outweighed Ms Munoz's right to refuse medical treatment.

In order further to understand the judge's reasoning, we need to discuss his factual finding in more detail. Ernesto works sixteen hours a day Monday through Friday and seven hours on Saturday driving his own commercial truck. Ms Munoz works at a beauty salon from 9 am to 3 pm three days a week. Ernesto, Jr, is enrolled in a day-care center Monday through Friday from 9 am until 4 pm. The judge found that Ms Munoz was the 'principal homemaker and principal caretaker of Ernesto, Jr.' the judge also found that, while Ernesto's father was available to assist in caring for Ernesto, Jr, his assistance would be inadequate because of his advanced age, his inability to speak English, his unemployment, his lack of a driver's license, and because he had not, in the past, played a significant role in caring for his grandson. In addition, the judge found, that while Sonia and James Joslin, Ernesto's sister and brother-in-law, expressed a willingness to help Ernesto take care of the child in the event that Ms Munoz died, the family had not formulated a concrete plan for the care and support of Ernesto, Jr. The judge concluded that Ms Munoz's death 'would be likely to cause an emotional abandonment of Ernesto, Jr, which would more probably than not be detrimental to his best interests.' The judge ruled that '[t]he State, as parens patriae, will now allow a parent to abandon a child, as so it should not allow this most ultimate of voluntary abandonments.'

Ms Munoz argues that the judge erred because she has a right, as a competent adult, to refuse life-saving medical treatment, and the State's interests do not override that right. We agree...

1. *The right to refuse treatment.* This court has recognized the right of a competent individual to refuse medical treatment. We have declared that individuals have a common law right to determine for themselves whether to allow a physical invasion of their bodies. See *Brophy v New England Sinai Hospital, supra* 398 Mass at 430, 497 NE 2d 626; *Harnish v Children's Hosp Medical Center*, 387 Mass. 152, 154, 439 NE 2d 240 (1982); *Saikewicz v Superintendent of Belchertown School* (1977) 373 Mass at 738–739, 370 NE 2d 417. See also GL c 214, s 1B

(statutory right of privacy). We have stated that 'a person has a strong interest in being free from nonconsensual invasion of his bodily integrity.' *Saikewicz, supra* at 729, 370 NE 2d 417. Individuals also have a penumbral constitutional right of privacy to reject medical treatment. See *Roe v Wade*, 410 US 113, 93 S Ct 705, 35 L Ed 2d 147 (1973); *Griswold v Connecticut*, 381 US 479, 85 S Ct 1678, 14 L Ed 2d 510 (1965); *Brophy, supra*; *Saikewicz, supra* 373 Mass at 739, 370 NE 2d 417.

The right to bodily integrity has been developed further through the doctrine of informed consent, which this court recognized in *Harnish v Children's Hosp Medical Center, supra*. Under the doctrine, a physician has the duty to disclose to a competent adult 'sufficient information to enable the patient to make an informed judgment whether to give or withhold consent to a medical or surgical procedure.' *Id* 387 Mass at 154–155, 439 NE 2d 240. It is for the individual to decide whether a particular medical treatment is in the individual's best interests. As a result, '[t]he law protects [a person's] right to make her own decision to accept or reject treatment, whether that decision is wise or unwise.' *Lane v Candura*, 6 Mass App Ct 377, 383, 376 NE 2d 1232 (1978). See *Brophy, supra* 398 Mass at 430–431, 497 NE 2d 626.

There is no doubt, therefore, that Ms Munoz has a right to refuse the blood transfusion. Initially, it is for her to decide, after having been informed by the medical personnel of the risks involved in not accepting the blood transfusion, whether to consent to the medical treatment. The fact that the treatment involves life-saving procedures does not undermine Ms Munoz's rights to bodily integrity and privacy, except to the extent that the right must then be balanced against the State's interests. See *Brophy, supra*; *Saikewicz*, supra; *Matter of Conroy*, 98 NJ 321, 348, 486 A 2d 1209 (1985).

Ms Munoz argues that, in addition to her rights to bodily integrity and privacy, she has a right secured by the free exercise clause of the First Amendment to the United States Constitution to object to administration of blood or blood products because to consent to the blood transfusions would violate one of the principal tenets of her Jehovah's Witnesses faith. Some courts have recognized a free exercise right on the part of Jehovah's Witnesses to refuse blood transfusions. See *In Re Estate of Brooks*, 32 Ill 2d 361, 205 NE 2d 435 (1965); *In Re Brown*, 478 So 2d 1033 (Miss 1985). We do not think it is necessary, however, to decide whether Ms Munoz has a free exercise right to refuse the administration of blood or blood products, since we have already held that she has a common law and constitutional privacy right to refuse a blood transfusion. Also, we need not decide whether a patient's right is strengthened because the objection to the medical treatment is based on religious principles.

2.   *The State's interests.* The right to refuse medical treatment in life-threatening situations is not absolute. *Brophy, supra* 398 Mass at 432, 497 NE 2d 626. *Commissioner of Correction v Myers*, 379 Mass 255, 261–262, 399 NE 2d 452 (1979). We have recognized four countervailing interests: (1) the preservation of life; (2) the prevention of suicide; (3) the maintenance of the ethical integrity of the medical profession; and (4) the protection of innocent third parties. *Brophy, supra*, *Saikewicz, supra* 373 Mass at 741, 370 NE 2d 417…

[The court having rejected the relevance of the first three interests moved on to consider the fourth.]

Protection of third parties. The final, and in this case the most compelling, State interest is the protection of the patient's minor child. The State as parens patriae has an interest in protecting the well-being of children. See *Prince v Massachusetts*, 321 US 158, 166–167, 64 S Ct 438, 442–443, 88 L Ed 645 (1944). The issue is whether a competent adult can be prevented from exercising her right to refuse life-saving medical treatment because of the individual's duties to her child.

The Florida State courts recently have addressed this issue. See *Wons v Public Health Trust of Dade County*, 500 So 2d 679 (Fla Dist Ct App 1987), aff'd, 541 So 2d 96 (Fla 1989). The patient in *Wons* was a thirty-eight year old woman, mother of two minor children, who suffered from dysfunctional uterine bleeding. The patient's physicians informed her that she required treatment in the form of blood transfusions. The patient, however, refused to consent to the transfusion because of her beliefs as a Jehovah's Witness. It was the physicians' medical opinion that, if the patient did not consent to the blood transfusions, she would probably die. The trial judge granted an order authorizing the transfusion, but a Florida District Court of Appeals reversed, holding that the State's interest in protecting the patient's children did not override the patient's right to refuse the medical treatment because the patient's possible death would not result in the abandonment of her two children. *Wons v Public Health Trust of Dade County*, 500 So 2d at 688. As the court pointed out, the testimony showed that the patient came from a tightly knit family, all practising Jehovah's Witnesses, and all of whom supported her decision to refuse the blood transfusion. *Id*. The court also pointed out that the patient's husband and mother were willing to take care of the children in the event that the patient died. *Id*. The court concluded that 'there is no showing of an abandonment of minor children, and, consequently, [the patient's] constitutional right to refuse a blood transfusion is not overridden under the circumstances of this case.' *Id.*

In *Fosmire v Nicoleau*, 75 NY 2d 218, 551 NYS 2d 876, 551 NE 2d 77 (1990), the New York Court of Appeals apparently has held that the State's interest in protecting minor children will never be allowed to override the right of a competent individual to refuse medical treatment. The court explained that 'at common law the patient's right to decide the course of his or her own medical treatment was not conditioned on the patient['s] being without minor children or dependents.' *Id.* At 229–230, 551 NYS 2d 876, 551 NE 2d 77.

We need only state that we agree with the reasoning of the Florida court, and hold that, in the absence of any compelling evidence that the child will be abandoned, the State's interest in protecting the well-being of children does not outweigh the right of a fully competent adult to refuse medical treatment. Our review of the record in this case reveals no such compelling evidence.[7] The evidence shows that Ernesto Munoz supported his wife's decision not to consent to the blood transfusion. There is no evidence in the record that Ernesto was unwilling to take care of the child in the event that Ms Munoz died.[8] We note that the father has the financial resources to take care of the child and to make sure that the child's material needs are satisfied. We also note that Ernesto's sister and brother-in-law supported Ms Munoz's decision, and were willing to assist Ernesto in taking care of the child.

There can also be no doubt that, if Ms Munoz had died, the entire family, including the young child, would have suffered a great loss. However, the State does not have an interest in maintaining a two-parent household in the absence of compelling evidence that the child will be abandoned if he is left under the care of a one-parent household. 'The parens patriae doctrine invoked herein cannot, we think, measure increments of love; it cannot mandate a two-parent, rather than a one-parent, family; it is solely concerned with seeing that minor children are cared for and are not abandoned.' *Wons v Public Health Trust of Dade County*, 500 So 2d at 688. In these circumstances the State's interest in protecting the welfare of the patient's child does not outweigh her right to refuse the blood transfusions.

3.   *Conclusion.* The patient had the right to refuse to consent to the blood transfusion even though she would have in all probability died if she had started to hemorrhage. The State's interests in preserving the patient's life, in maintaining the ethical integrity of the profession, and in protecting the well-being of the patient's child, did not override the patient's right to refuse life-saving medical treatment. Accordingly, the judgment is reversed and a new judgment declaring the rights of the parties, consistent with this opinion, is to be entered in the Probate Court.

Footnotes to extract

7.   The case most often cited in support of proposition that the State's interest in protecting the well-being of the patient's children outweighs the patient's right to refuse life-saving treatment is *Application of the President & Directors of Georgetown College, Inc*, 331 F 2d 1000 (DC Cir), cert denied, 377 US 978, 84 S Ct 1883, 12 LE 2d 746 (1964). In that case, however, unlike the case before us, the patient was not competent to decide for herself whether to consent to the blood transfusion. The court stated that the patient was as 'little able competently to decide for herself as any child would be. Under the circumstances, it may well be the duty of a court…to assume the responsibility of guardianship for her, as for a child, at least to the extent of authorizing treatment to save her life' (footnote omitted). *Id* at 1008.

8.   A commentator's criticism of *Application of the President & Directors of Georgetown College, Inc, supra*, is relevant: '[T]he refusal of [the patient's] husband to authorize the transfusion indicates that he acceded to her wishes even though they might result in leaving the child motherless. It would not seem that one parent should be found guilty of child abandonment in a situation where the other parent has agreed to her leaving and, presumably, to provide for the child alone.' Case Comment. Constitutional Law – Transfusions Ordered for Dying Woman over Religious Objections, 113 U Pa L Rev 290, 294 (1964). See *Matter of Farrell*, 108 NJ 335, 352–353, 529 A 2d 404 (1987) (mother's right to refuse treatment upheld where 'father's capacity to care for [the children] in her absence is unquestioned').

Wilkins, Abrams and Greaney JJ agreed. O'Connor, Nolan and Lynch JJ concurred on the more limited ground that Mrs Munoz's decision to refuse treatment based upon her *religious* beliefs could not be overridden.

Thus, a majority of the Massachusetts' Supreme Judicial Court recognised that a competent patient's refusal of life-sustaining treatment could not be overridden by the interests of any existing children. Of course, on the facts, the Munoz children would not be abandoned because their father and the extended family would take of them. Would the result be the same if this were not so? The court left this open, as had the Florida Supreme Court in *Public Heath Trust of Dade County v Wons* (1989) 541 So 2d 96. By contrast, the New York Court of Appeals in *Fosmire v Nicoleau* (1990) 551 NE 2d 77 (another case concerning a Jehovah's Witness who refused a blood transfusion) did not limit the patient's right to refuse life-sustaining treatment. In that case Wachtler CJ (speaking for the majority of the court) stated that:

> On this appeal the hospital argues that a patient's right to decline lifesaving treatment should be limited to cases where the patient has a terminal or degenerative disease. When the patient is otherwise healthy the State has a stronger interest in preserving life, which should be held to outweigh the patient's choice. The State's interest is even stronger, the hospital contends, when the patient is a parent, and that the appellate Division erred in adopting a 'one-parent rule.' The argument here is that it is always in the child's best interest to have two parents and that the State will intervene to protect the child's welfare...
>
> In the absence of any statute or decision from this court limiting the rights of patients who happen to be parents, the hospital turns to the law of domestic relations, and seeks to equate a parent who declines essential medical care with a parent who intentionally abandons a child. It is argued that since the State, as *parens patriae*, will not allow a parent to abandon a child, it will not permit 'this most ultimate of voluntary abandonments' (*Application of President & Directors of Georgetown Coll*, 331 F 2d 1000, 1008). This argument extends the concept of abandonment far beyond the boundaries recognized in this State, and into areas where it would conflict with other substantial interests.
>
> Although the State will not permit a parent to abandon a child, the State has never gone so far as to intervene in every personal decision a parent makes which may jeopardize the family unit or the parental relationship. The laws of adoption and divorce show that the State recognizes competing interests and, in some instances, accords them priority. Indeed the State's need to punish those who violate its laws has never been held to be subordinate to the needs of the prisoner's family (*see, eg Ferrin v New York State Dept of Correctional Servs*, 71 NY 2d 42, 523 NYS 2d 485, 517 NE 2d 1370). Thus the State's concern with maintaining family unity and parental ties is not an interest which it enforces at the expense of all personal rights or conflicting interests.
>
> The State's interest in promoting the freedom of its citizens generally applies to parents. The State does not prohibit parents from engaging in dangerous activities because there is a risk that their children will be left orphans. There are instances, as the hospital notes, where the State has prohibited the public from engaging in an especially hazardous activity or required that special safety precautions be taken by participants. But we know of no law in this State prohibiting individuals from participating in inherently dangerous activities or requiring them to take special safety precautions simply because they have minor children.

3.   Concluding remarks

Before we leave the law relating to refusals of treatment by competent adult patients we should make a few brief final remarks.

The analysis so far has been concerned with adults who are competent at the time of their refusal of treatment. There are, of course, cases in which the adult, though now incompetent, has previously expressed his refusal of treatment. Such 'anticipatory refusals' may be oral or more formally stated in a written document often called an 'advanced directive' (see, for example, *Malette v Shulman* (1990) 67 DLR (4th) 321; *Re T (adult: refusal of medical treatment)* [1992] 4 All ER 649). We shall consider the law relating to 'anticipatory refusals' in detail later (see *infra*, ch 16). In principle, of course, whether a refusal be anticipatory or contemporaneous should not affect its validity (see *Airedale NHS Trust v Bland* [1993] 1 All ER 821 at 860 per Lord Keith; at 866 per Lord Goff; at 892 per Lord Mustill).

It follows also that once a refusal has clearly been given no appeal to 'necessity' can justify the doctor's intervention notwithstanding the good intentions of the doctor (see eg *Mulloy v Hop Sang* [1935] 1 WWR 714 (Alt CA)).

C. THE COMMON LAW: CHILDREN

To what extent may a competent child refuse medical treatment? To talk of a competent child is to rely upon the watershed decision of the House of Lords in *Gillick v West Norfolk and Wisbech AHA* [1986] AC 112, [1985] 3 All ER 402. In that case, you will recall, the House of Lords recognised that a child was in law competent to make his own decisions providing he has 'a sufficient understanding and intelligence to enable him or her to understand fully what is proposed' (per Lord Scarman [1986] AC 112 at 188). It was widely believed that *Gillick* decided that a competent child could not only consent to medical treatment (which is what the case was actually concerned with) but by necessary logical extension could also refuse treatment regardless of the views of others (for the earliest case to the contrary see: *Re E (a minor)* (1990) 9 BMLR 1 (Ward J) – overriding the refusal of a 15-year-old Jehovah's Witness to a life-saving blood transfusion). The Court of Appeal, led by Lord Donaldson MR, decided to set its face against this view of *Gillick*. In two cases – *Re R (a minor) (wardship: medical treatment)* (1991) 7 BMLR 147, [1992] Fam 11; *Re W (a minor) (medical treatment)* [1992] 4 All ER 627: concerned respectively with a competent child patient under 16 and one who had reached the age of 16 – the Court of Appeal accepted that the *Gillick* decision meant that a competent child could *consent* to treatment and that such consent could not be countermanded at least by the parents (or others with 'parental responsibility'). But the Court of Appeal took the view that the *refusal* of a competent child did not have the same force and could be countermanded by others, whether the parents or the courts.

Re R (a minor) (wardship: medical treatment) [1991] 4 All ER 177, [1992] Fam 11 (CA)

A 15-year old girl who had a history of family problems and who had been on the local authority's at-risk register was received into voluntary care after a fight with her father and was placed in a children's home. While in care her mental health deteriorated and she experienced visual and auditory hallucinations and her behaviour became increasingly disturbed. On one occasion she left the children's home and was found on a bridge threatening to commit suicide, while on another occasions she returned to her parent's home where she ran amok causing serious damage and attacked her father with a hammer. The local authority obtained place of safety and interim care orders and placed her in an adolescent psychiatric unit where she was sedated from time to time with her consent. The unit sought permission from the local authority to administer anti-psychotic drugs to her because she was behaving in a paranoid, argumentative and hostile manner. Although she had clear intervals when her mental illness was in recession the prognosis was that if the medication was not administered she would return to her psychotic state. However, in rational and lucid periods, when she had sufficient understanding to make the decision, she objected to taking the drugs. In those circumstances the local authority refused to authorise the administration of drugs against her will, while the unit was not prepared to continue to care for her unless it had authority to administer appropriate medication to control her. The local authority commenced wardship proceedings and applied for leave for the unit to administer medication, including anti-psychotic drugs, whether or not the ward consented. The questions arose (i) whether the judge had power to override the decision of a ward who was a minor to refuse medication and treatment irrespective of whether the minor was competent to give her consent and (ii) whether the ward had the requisite capacity to accept or refuse such medication or treatment. The judge granted the application, holding that although a wardship judge could not override the decision of a ward who had the requisite capacity on the facts the ward did not have that capacity. The Official Solicitor as guardian ad litem of the ward appealed, contending that if a child had the right to give consent to medical treatment the parents', and a fortiori the wardship court's, right to give or refuse consent was terminated. [In this extract we consider only the issue of the court's powers: for a discussion of competence see *supra*, ch 5, and the scope of the parents' powers see *infra*].

Lord Donaldson MR: This appeal from an order of Waite J on 9 July 1991 involves a consideration of the power of the court to override a refusal by its ward, a 15-year-old girl, to undergo medical treatment involving the taking of medication. So far as is known, such a question has arisen on only one previous occasion, namely in *Re E (a minor)* (1990) 9 BMLR 1, decided by Ward J, a 15-year-old boy who had religious objections, supported by his parents, to being given a life-saving blood transfusion. Possibly in that case, and certainly in this, the judge accepted that the effect of *Gillick v West Norfolk and Wisbech Area Health Authority* [1985] 3 All ER 402, [1986] AC 112 was that, if a child had achieved a sufficient understanding and intelligence to enable him or her to understand fully what was proposed and to be capable of making up his own mind on the matter, the parental right (and the court's right) to give or refuse consent yielded to the child's right to make his own decisions (see [1985] 3 All ER 402 at 422, 424, [1986] AC 112 at 186 and 189 per Lord Scarman) and that this applied as much to a situation in which the child was refusing consent (this case and *Re E*) as to the case in which the child was consenting (the assumed position in *Gillick's* case). However, in *Re E*, as in this case, the judge held that the child had not achieved the required degree of understanding...

The wardship jurisdiction
In considering the wardship jurisdiction of the court, no assistance is to be derived from *Gillick's* case, where this simply was not in issue. Nor, I think, is any assistance to be derived from considering whether it is theoretically limitless if the exercise of such a jurisdiction in a particular way and in particular circumstances would be contrary to established practice. It is, however, clear that the practical jurisdiction of the court is wider than that of parents. The court can, for example, forbid the publication of information about the ward or the ward's family circumstances. It is also clear that this jurisdiction is not derivative from the parents' rights and responsibilities, but derives from, or is, the delegated performance of the duties of the Crown to protect its subjects, and particularly children, who are the generations of the future (see *Re C (a minor) (wardship: medical treatment) (No 2)* [1989] 2 All ER 791 at 793, [1990] Fam 39 at 46).

Whilst it is no doubt true to say, as Lord Upjohn did say in *J v C* [1970] AC 668 at 723, [1969] 1 All ER 788 at 831, that the function of the court is to 'act as the judicial reasonable parent', all that, in context, he was saying was the court should exercise its jurisdiction in the interests of the children, 'reflecting and adopting the changing views, as the years go by, of reasonable men and women, the parents of children, on the proper treatment and methods of bring up children'. This is very far from saying that the wardship jurisdiction is derived from, or in any way limited by, that of the parents. In many cases of wardship, the parents or other guardians will be left to make decisions for the child, subject only to standing instructions to refer reserved matters to the court, eg the taking of a serious step in the upbringing or medical treatment of a child, and to the court's right and, in appropriate cases, duty to override the decision of the parents or other guardians. If it can override such consents, as it undoubtedly, can, I see no reason whatsoever why it would not be able, and in an appropriate case willing, to override decisions by 'Gillick competent' children who are its wards or in respect of whom applications are made for, for example, s 8 orders under the Children Act 1989.

Staughton LJ: I agree with the conclusion of Waite J that, on those facts, the court can authorise medication, consistently with the decision of the House of Lords in *Gillick v West Norfolk and Wisbech Area Health Authority* [1986] AC 112, [1985] 3 All ER 402, even if it has no greater powers than a parent.

The alternative solution to this appeal, which gave rise to the bulk of the argument and perhaps to the appeal itself, depends on two questions of law: (1) Does the parent of a competent minor have power to override the minor's decision, either by granting consent when the minor has refused it or vice versa? (2) Does the court have power to override the decision of a competent minor who is a ward? In both questions, I use the word 'competent' in the *Gillick* sense.

As to the first question, we were referred to the speech of Lord Scarman in *Gillick's* case [1986] AC 112 at 188, [1985] 3 All ER 402 at 423:

...I would hold that as a matter of law the parental right to determine whether or not their minor child below the age of 16 will have medical treatment terminates if and when the child achieves a sufficient understanding and intelligence to enable him or her to understand fully what is proposed.

The hypothetical situation under consideration in *Gillick's* case was where a competent child did consent to medical treatment, but the parent either was not asked or expressly did not consent. The House of Lords decided, as it seems to me, that a doctor could lawfully administer treatment in such a case, although he would naturally take into account that the parent had not been asked or had expressly not consented.

Whether the doctor could lawfully administer treatment when the parent did consent, but the competent child either did not consent or had not been asked – save in the case of emergency – was not a question for decision in *Gillick's* case. As Lord Donaldson MR points out, it may be putting a heavy burden on doctors if, having obtained the consent of the parent of a child under 16, they still have to consider whether the child is competent to give or refuse consent. Nevertheless the passage that I have quoted from Lord Scarman's speech, and particularly the words 'whether or not', suggests that the parent's consent is not sufficient in such a case. This is an important question. But it is not essential to the decision in this case, in my opinion, because I consider (as will shortly appear) that a wardship judge can validly consent to medical treatment even if the ward refuses her consent. In those circumstances, I do not suppose that any opinion of mine as to the effect of consent by a natural parent would be of much assistance in resolving the difference between what appears to have been Lord Scarman's view and that of Lord Donaldson MR; so I express none.

The second question is whether the court has power to override the decision of a competent minor who is a ward. Again it can arise in two forms: the court may be minded to consent when the ward does not (which would be the situation here, if I had found on the evidence that the ward is competent to take the decision); or the court may be minded not to consent when the ward does (as in the *Gillick* hypothetical case). I say at once that in my judgment *Gillick's* case did not touch on this question.

It can be argued that a wardship judge, exercising the authority of the Crown as notional parent, should have no greater powers than a natural parent. I have a good deal of sympathy with that argument, for I accept as a general principle that good reason must be shown before the State exercises any power to control the decisions of a competent person, whether adult or minor, which only concern his well-being.

There is, however, a group of decisions, mainly of Family Division judges, which supports the opposite conclusion. Thus in *BRB v JB* [1968] P 466 at 473, [1968] 2 All ER 1023 at 1025 Lord Denning MR said: '…the child's views are never decisive'. That, of course, was before *Gillick's* case. In *Re P (a minor)* [1986] 1 FLR 272 at 279 Butler-Sloss J said that the child's wishes should not be given 'such paramount importance' as to be conclusive. In *Re G-U (a minor) (wardship)* [1984] FLR 811 at 812 Balcombe J said that an abortion required the leave of the court – although presumably the ward consented, as it had already happened. In *Re B (a minor) (wardship: abortion)* [1991] 2 FLR 426 Hollis J said in an abortion case that the ward's wishes were not decisive. And in *Re E (a minor)* (1990) 9 BMLR 1, which concerned a blood transfusion for a boy of 15, Ward J directly addressed the issue. He said:

> Whether or not he is of sufficient understanding to have given consent or to withhold consent is not the issue for me.

For my part, I do not read the judge as deciding that in wardship there is no power to override the decision of a competent minor. It seems to me that, while accepting that a competent minor can override the parent's choice, he held that the situation was different in wardship. Against that, there is the ruling of Waite J in the present case that the wardship judge could not override the decision of a competent minor.

Faced with such a substantial consensus of opinion among judges who have to deal with this problem from day to day, I conclude that the powers of a wardship judge do indeed include power to consent to medical treatment when the ward has not been asked or has declined. If that means that the wardship judge has wider powers than a natural parent (on the extent of which I have declined to express an opinion), it seems to me to be warranted by the authorities to which I have referred.

Farquharson LJ: Counsel for the Official Solicitor, Mr Munby QC, submitted that the court should determine the application on the *Gillick* principle (see *Gillick v West Norfolk and Wisbech Area Health Authority* [1986] AC 112, [1985] 3 All ER 402). Counsel argued on that authority that the parental right to determine whether a child should have medical treatment terminates if and when the child achieves a sufficient understanding and intelligence to enable him or her to understand fully what is proposed. If the child has the capacity to give a consent valid in law, it is not for the court to substitute its own different view. On the other hand, if the child is shown not to have that capacity, then the court has the power and duty to substitute its own decision if it is different from that of the child…

It is to be emphasised that *Gillick's* case was not a wardship case and was concerned with mentally normal children…The authority of a High Court judge exercising his jurisdiction in wardship is not constrained in this way. The judge's well-established task in deciding any question concerning the upbringing of the ward is to have regard to the welfare of the ward as the first and paramount consideration. In some cases, the decision might well be different if the *Gillick* test were applied. That the two approaches are distinct is vividly illustrated in the dramatic case of *Re E (a minor)* (1990) 9 BMLR 1 by the decision of Ward J.

It is clear in the present appeal that, whether R's capacity to withhold consent to medication was tested on the *Gillick* criteria or whether the court approached the issue on the basis of her welfare being paramount, the result would have been the same.

I would dismiss the appeal.

As we saw earlier (*supra*, ch 5), the Court of Appeal in fact held that R was incompetent to make the relevant medical decision because of her fluctuating mental condition. Thus, at one level the case need tell us nothing since all that was subsequently said about the law relating to competent children was unnecessary. But perhaps such a view could be said to be churlish (for a discussion of *Re R*, see G Douglas 'The Retreat from Gillick' (1992) 55 MLR 569).

Certainly, all three judges accept that *the court* has power to override the refusal of a competent child. As regards any conflict between the views of a competent child and those of the parents only Lord Donaldson MR expressed a concluded view.

Lord Donaldson MR: In the instant appeal Mrs James Munby QC, appearing for the Official Solicitor, submits that (a) if the child has the right to give consent to medical treatment, the parents' right to give or refuse consent is terminated and (b) the court in the exercise of its wardship jurisdiction is only entitled to step into the shoes of the parents and thus itself has no right to give or refuse consent. Whilst it is true that he seeks to modify the effect of this rather startling submission by suggesting that, if the child's consent or refusal of consent is irrational or misguided, the court will readily infer that in the particular context that individual child is not competent to give or withhold consent, it is necessary to look very carefully at the *Gillick* decision to see whether it supports his argument and, if it does, whether it is binding upon this court.

The key passages upon which Mr Munby relies are to be found in the speech of Lord Scarman ([1985] 3 All ER 402 at 423–424, [1986] AC 112 at 188–189):

…as a matter of law the parental right to determine whether or not their minor child below the age of 16 will have medical treatment terminates if and when the child achieves a sufficient understanding and intelligence to enable him or her to understand fully what is proposed. It will be a question of fact whether a child seeking advice has sufficient understanding of what is involved to give a consent valid in law. Until the child achieves the capacity to consent, the parental right to make the decision continues save only in exceptional circumstances. Emergency, parental neglect, abandonment of the child or inability to find the parent are examples of exceptional situations justifying the doctor proceeding to treat the child without parental knowledge and consent; but there will arise, no doubt, other exceptional situations in which it will be reasonable for the doctor to proceed without the parent's consent.

And ([1985] 3 All ER 402 at 421–422, [1986] AC 112 at 186):

The underlying principle of the law was exposed by Blackstone (1 Bl Com (17th edn, 1830) chs 16 and 17) and can be seen to have been acknowledged in the case law. It is that parental right yields to the child's right to make his own decisions when he reaches a sufficient understanding and intelligence to be capable of making up his own mind on the matter requiring decision.

What Mr Munby's argument overlooks is that Lord Scarman was discussing the parents' right '*to determine* whether or not their minor child below the age of 16 will have medical treatment' (my emphasis) and this is the 'parental right' to which he was referring in the latter passage. A right of determination is wider than a right to consent. The parents can only have a right of determination if *either* the child has no right to consent, ie is not a keyholder, *or* the parents hold the master key which could nullify the child's consent. I do not understand Lord Scarman to be saying that, if a child was 'Gillick competent', to adopt the convenient phrase used in argument, the parents ceased to have an independent right of consent as contrasted with ceasing to have a right of determination, ie a veto. In a case in which the 'Gillick competent' child refuses treatment, but the parents consent, that consent *enables* treatment to be undertaken lawfully, but in no way determines that the child shall be so treated. In a case in which the positions are reversed, it is the child's consent which is the enabling factor and again the parents' refusal of consent is not determinative. If Lord Scarman intended to go further than this and to say that in the case of a 'Gillick competent' child, a parent has no right either to consent or to refuse consent, his remarks were obiter, because the only question in issue was Mrs Gillick's alleged right of veto. Furthermore I consider that they would have been wrong.

One glance at the consequences suffices to show that Lord Scarman cannot have been intending to say that the parental right to consent terminates with the achievement by the child of 'Gillick competence'. It is fundamental to the speeches of the majority that the capacity to consent will vary from child to child and according to the treatment under consideration, depending upon the sufficiency of his or her intelligence and understanding of that treatment. If the position in law is that upon achievement of 'Gillick competence' there is a transfer of the right of consent from parents to child and there can never be a concurrent right in both, doctors would be faced with an intolerable dilemma, particularly when the child was nearing the age of 16, if the parents consented, but the child did not. On pain, if they got it wrong, of being sued for trespass to the person or possibly being charged with a criminal assault, they would have to determine as a matter of law in whom the right of consent resided at the particular time in relation to the particular treatment. I do not believe that that is the law.

I referred to a child who is nearing the age of 16, because at that age a new dimension is added by s 8 of the Family Law Reform Act 1969 to which Lord Fraser referred (see [1985] 3 All ER 402 at 407–408, [1986] AC 112 at 167). This is in the following terms:

> (1) The consent of a minor who has attained the age of sixteen years to any surgical, medical or dental treatment which, in the absence of consent, would constitute a trespass to his person, shall be as effective as it would be if he were of full age; and where a minor has by virtue of this section given effective consent to any treatment it shall not be necessary to obtain any consent for it from his parent or guardian...
>
> (3) Nothing in this section shall be construed as making ineffective any consent which would have been effective if this section had not been enacted.

Mr Munby submits, rightly as I think, that consent by a child between the ages of 16 and 18 is no more effective than that of an adult if, due to mental disability, the child is incapable of consenting. That is, however, immaterial for present purposes. What is material is that the section is inconsistent with Mr Munby's argument. If Mr Munby's interpretation of Lord Scarman's speech was correct, where a child over the age of 16 gave effective consent to treatment, not only would it 'not be necessary' to obtain the consent of the parent or guardian, it would be legally impossible because the parent or guardian would have no power to give consent and the section would, or at least should, have so provided. Furthermore sub-s (3) would create problems since, if the section had not been enacted, a parent's consent would undoubtedly have been effective *as a consent*.

Both in this case and in *Re E* the judges treated *Gillick's* case as a deciding that a 'Gillick competent' child has a right to refuse treatment. In this I consider that they were in error. Such a child can consent, but if he or she declines to do so or refuses, consent can be given by someone else who has parental rights or responsibilities. The failure or refusal of the 'Gillick competent' child is a very important factor in the doctor's decision whether or not to treat, but does not prevent the necessary consent being obtained from another competent source.

As you will have seen above, Staughton LJ left this matter open although he seemed to suggest that there would be considerable difficulties with Lord Donaldson's approach.

Three issues remained unresolved by *Re R*. First, does the power to override a competent child's wishes extend to those children who are 16 or over, remembering that R was under 16, such that s 8 of the Family Law Reform Act 1969 does not apply? Secondly, what limits (if any) exist to restrict the court in exercising its power to override the refusal of the child? Thirdly, do parents also have the power to override their child's refusal to consent? These three issues were subsequently addressed by the Court of Appeal in *Re W (a minor) (medical treatment)* [1992] 4 All ER 627.

Re W (a minor) (medical treatment) [1992] 4 All ER 627, (1992) 9 BMLR 22 (CA)

W, a girl aged 16, was suffering from anorexia nervosa which first manifested itself in June 1990. By August 1991 her condition had deteriorated to the point at which for a short time and with her consent she was fed by nasogastric tube and had her arms encased in plaster. On 24 January 1992 Cazalet J granted the local authority leave, under the Children Act 1989, s 100(3), to make an application for the exercise by the court of the inherent jurisdiction of the High Court. The authority applied for (1) leave to move the minor to a named treatment unit or such other establishment as the Official Solicitor might approve, without the minor's consent and (2) leave to give the minor medical treatment without her consent.

Thorpe J held that he had the necessary jurisdiction and authorised the removal of W to and her treatment at a specialist London unit, subject to arrangements first being made for the approval of new foster parents.

On 29 June 1992, W's condition was stable or deteriorating slowly, although there had been some further loss of weight. On 30 June, she had not taken solid food since 21 June, her weight had dropped from 39 kg on 16 June, to 35.1 kg on 30 June with a final weight of 5 stone 7 lb for a girl 5 ft 7 in tall. Medical opinion agreed that should she continue in that way, within a week her capacity to have children in later life would be seriously at risk and a little later her life itself might be in danger.

On 30 June the Court of Appeal made an emergency order enabling her to be taken to and treated at a specialist hospital in London notwithstanding the lack of consent on her part.

Lord Donaldson MR:

Section 8 of the Family Law Reform Act 1969
I turn...to s 8 and to the common law against the background of which the section was enacted. The common law was authoritatively considered and defined in *Gillick v West Norfolk and Wisbech Area Health Authority* [1985] 3 All ER 402, [1986] AC 112 and there is no suggestion that it had altered significantly since 1969. Section 8 is in these terms.

> *Consent by persons over 16 to surgical, medical and dental treatment.* – (1) The consent of a minor who has attained the age of sixteen years to any surgical, medical or dental treatment which in the absence of consent would constitute a trespass to his person shall be as effective as it would be if he were of full age; and where a minor has by virtue of this section given an effective consent to any treatment it shall not be necessary to obtain any consent for it from his parent or guardian.
>
> (2) In this section surgical, medical or dental treatment includes any procedure undertaken for the purposes of diagnosis, and this section applies to any procedure (including in particular the administration of an anaesthetic) which is ancillary to any treatment as it applies to that treatment.
>
> (3) Nothing in this section shall be construed as making ineffective any consent which would have been effective if this section had not been enacted.

In *Re R (a minor) (wardship: medical treatment)* [1991] 4 All ER 177, [1992] Fam 11 this court was concerned with a 15-year-old girl and accordingly the meaning and effect of s 8 was not directly in issue. I did, however, express my views on the construction and effect of the section, which, it now appears, were at variance with the views of academic and other writers (see Bainham 'The judge and the competent minor' (1992) 108 LQR 194 at 198, Thornton 'Multiple keyholders – wardship and consent to medical treatment' (1992) CLJ 34 at 36, Kennedy 'Consent to treatment; the capable person', Gostin 'Consent to treatment; the incapable person' and Dodds-Smith 'Clinical Research' in Dyer (ed) *Doctors, Patients and the Law* (1992) pp 60–61, 156–157 and Brazier *Medicine, Patients and the Law* (2nd edn 1992) p 346). Essentially what all are saying is that a right to consent to medical treatment, whether required under the common law (*Gillick*) or under statute (s 8), must and does carry with it a right not only to refuse consent to treatment, but to refuse the treatment itself. As it is put by the Department of Health *Guidelines for Ethics Committee* (August 1991):

> The giving of consent by a parent or guardian cannot override a refusal of consent by a child who is competent to make that decision.

Since my remarks were unnecessary for the decisions, R not having yet attained the age of 16, I am free to reconsider the matter and to reach an opposite conclusion. Let me therefore start afresh by looking at the common law.

Gillick's case
In *Gillick's* case the central issue was *not* whether a child patient under the age of 16 could refuse medical treatment if the parents or the court consented, but whether the parents could effectively impose a veto on treatment by failing or refusing to consent to treatment to which the child might consent. Mrs Gillick accepted that the court had such a power to veto and contended that the parents had a similar power (see [1985] 3 All ER 402 at 406, 412, 418, [1986] AC 112 at 165, 173, 181 per Lord Fraser of Tullybelton and Lord Scarman). Section 8 only came into the argument because it was contended on behalf of Mrs Gillick that, but for s 8, no minor could ever refuse consent to medical treatment and that s 8 was designed only to lower the age of consent to such treatment from 18 to 16 ([1985] 1 All ER 533 at 539, [1986] AC 112 at 123, 144 per Parker LJ and Fox LJ). The area health authority and Department of Health and Social Security on the other hand contended that under the common law a

minor of sufficient intelligence and understanding could always consent to treatment and that the effect of s 8 was to produce an irrebuttable presumption that a child of 16 or 17 had such intelligence and understanding.

The House of Lords decisively rejected Mrs Gillick's contentions and held that at common law a child of sufficient intelligence and understanding (the 'Gillick competent' child) could consent to treatment, notwithstanding the absence of the parents' consent and even an express prohibition by the parents. Only Lord Scarman's speech is couched in terms which might suggest that the refusal of a child below the age of 16 to accept medical treatment was determinative (see [1985] 3 All ER 402 at 423, [1986] AC 112 at 188–189) because there could never be concurrent rights to consent:

> ...the parental right to determine whether or not their minor child below the age of 16 will have medical treatment terminates if and when the child achieves a sufficient understanding and intelligence to enable him or her to understand fully what is proposed.

If the parental right terminates, it would follow that, apart from the court, the only person competent to consent would be the child and a refusal of consent to treatment would indirectly constitute an effective veto on the treatment itself. I say 'indirectly' because the veto would be imposed by the civil and criminal laws, rather than by the refusal of consent.

In the light of the quite different issue which was before the House in *Gillick's* case, I venture to doubt whether Lord Scarman meant more than that the *exclusive* right of the parents to consent to treatment terminated, but I may well be wrong. Thorpe J having held that 'There is no doubt at all that [W] is a child of sufficient understanding to make an informed decision', I shall assume that, so far as the common law is concerned, Lord Scarman would have decided that neither the local authority nor W's aunt, both of whom had parental responsibilities, could give consent to treatment which would be effective in the face of W's refusal of consent. This is of considerable persuasive authority, but even that is not the issue before this court. That is whether *the court* has such a power. That never arose in *Gillick's* case, the nearest approach to it being the proposition, accepted by all parties, that the court had power to override any minor's consent (*not* refusal) to accept treatment.

The purpose of consent to treatment

There seems to be some confusion in the minds of some as to the purpose of seeking consent from a patient (whether adult or child) or from someone with authority to give that consent on behalf of the patient. It has two purposes, the one clinical and the other legal. The clinical purpose stems from the fact that in many instances the co-operation of the patient and the patient's faith or at least confidence in the efficiency of the treatment is a major factor contributing to the treatment's success. Failure to obtain such consent will not only deprive the patient and the medical staff of this advantage, but will usually make it much more difficult to administer the treatment. I appreciate that this purpose may not be served if consent is given on behalf of, rather than by, the patient. However, in the case of young children knowledge of the fact that the parent has consented may help. The legal purpose is quite different. It is to provide those concerned in the treatment with a defence to a criminal charge of assault or battery or a civil claim for damages for trespass to the person. It does not, however, provide them with any defence to a claim that they negligently advised a particular treatment or negligently carried it out.

Is s 8 ambiguous?

The wording of sub-s (1) shows quite clearly that it is addressed to the legal purpose and legal effect of consent to treatment, namely to prevent such treatment constituting in law a trespass to the person, and that it does so by making the consent of a 16- or 17-year-old as effective as if he were 'of full age'. No question of 'Gillick competence' in common law terms arises. The 16- or 17-year-old is conclusively presumed to be 'Gillick competent' or alternatively, the test of 'Gillick competence' is bypassed and has no relevance. The argument that W, or any other 16- or 17-year-old, can by refusing to consent to treatment veto the treatment notwithstanding that the doctor has the consent of someone who has parental responsibilities, involves the proposition that s 8 has the further effect of depriving such a person of the power to consent. It certainly does not say so. Indeed if this were its intended effect, it is difficult to see why the subsection goes on to say that it is not *necessary* to obtain the parents' consent, rather than providing that such consent, if obtained, should be ineffective. Furthermore, such a construction does not sit easily with sub-s (3), which preserves the common law as it existed immediately before the 1969 Act, which undoubtedly gave parents an effective power of consent for all children up to the age of 21, the then existing age of consent (see *Gillick's* case [1985] 3 All ER 402 at 408, 419, [1986] AC 112 at 167, 182 per Lord Fraser of Tullybelton and Lord Scarman).

The most promising argument in favour of W having an exclusive right to consent to treatment and thus, by refusing consent to attract the protection of the law on trespass to the person lies in concentrating upon the words 'as effective as it would be if he were of full age'. If she were of full age her ability to consent would have two separate effects. First, her consent would be fully effective as such. Second, a failure or refusal to give consent would be fully effect as a veto, but only *because no one else would be in a position to consent*. If it is a possible view that s 8 is intended to put a 16- or 17-year-old in exactly the same position as an adult and there is thus some ambiguity, although I do not think there is, it is a permissible aid to construction to seek to ascertain the mischief at which the section is directed.

The Latey Committee report

It is common ground that the Family Law Reform Act 1969 was Parliament's response to the *Report on the Age of Majority* (Cmnd 3342 (1967)). The relevant part is contained in paras 474–484. These show that the mischief aimed at was twofold. First, cases were occurring in which young people between 16 and 21 (the then age of majority) were living away from home and wished and needed urgent medical treatment which had not yet reached the emergency state. Doctors were unable to treat them unless and until their parents had been traced and this could cause unnecessary suffering. Second, difficulties were arising concerning –

> operations whose implications brings up the question of a girl's right to privacy about her sexual life. A particularly difficult situation arises in the case of a girl who is sent to hospital in need of a therapeutic abortion and refuses point blank to enter the hospital unless a guarantee is given that her parents should not be told about it. (See para 478.)

The Committee had recommended that the age of majority be reduced to 18 generally. The report records that all the professional bodies which gave evidence recommended that patients aged between 16 and 18 should be able to give an effective consent to treatment and all but the Medical Protection Society recommended that they should also be able to give an effective refusal (see para 480). The point with which we are concerned was therefore well in the mind of the Committee. It did not so recommend. It recommended that –

> *without prejudice to any consent that may otherwise be lawful*, the consent of young persons aged 16 and over to medical or dental treatment shall be as valid as the consent of a person of full age. (My emphasis.)

Conclusion on s 8

I am quite unable to accept that Parliament in adopting somewhat more prolix language was intending to achieve a result which differed from that recommended by the Committee.

On reflection I regret my use in *Re R (a minor) (wardship: medical treatment)* [1991] 4 All ER 177 at 184, [1992] Fam 11 at 22 of the keyholder analogy, because keys can lock as well as unlock. I now prefer the analogy of the legal 'flak jacket' which protects the doctor from claims by the litigious whether he acquires it from his patient who may be a minor over the age of 16, or a 'Gillick competent' child under that age, or from another person having parental responsibilities which include a right to consent to treatment of the minor. Anyone who gives him a flak jacket (ie consent) may take it back, but the doctor only needs one and so long as he continues to have one he has the legal right to proceed.

The section extends not only to treatment, but also to diagnostic procedures (see sub-s (2)). It does not, however, extend to the donation of organs or blood since, so far as the donor is concerned, these do not constitute either treatment or diagnosis. I cannot remember to what extent organ donation was common in 1967, but the Latey Committee expressly recommended that only 18-year-olds and older should be authorised by statute to consent to *giving* blood (see paras 485–489). It seems that Parliament accepted this recommendation, although I doubt whether blood donation will create any problem as a 'Gillick competent' minor of any age would be able to give consent under the common law.

Organ transplants are quite different and, as a matter of law, doctors would have to secure the consent of someone with the right to consent on behalf of a donor under the age of 18 or, if they relied upon the consent of the minor himself or herself, be satisfied that the minor was 'Gillick competent' in the context of so serious a procedure which could not benefit the minor. This would be a highly improbable conclusion. But this is only to look at the question as a matter of law. Medical ethics also enter into the question. The doctor has a professional duty to act in the best interests of his patient and to advise accordingly. It is inconceivable that he should proceed in reliance solely upon the consent of an under-age patient, however 'Gillick competent', in the absence of supporting parental consent and equally inconceivable that he should proceed in the absence of the patient's consent. In any event he will need to seek the opinions of other doctors and may be well advised to apply to the court for guidance, as recommended by Lord Templeman in a different context in *Re B (a minor) (wardship: sterilisation)* [1987] 2 All ER 206 at 214–215, [1988] AC 199 at 205–206.

Hair-raising possibilities were canvassed of abortions being carried out by doctors in reliance upon the consent of parents and despite the refusal of consent by 16- or 17-year-olds. Whilst this may be possible as a matter of law, I do not see any likelihood, taking account of medical ethics, unless the abortion was truly in the basic interest of the child. This is not to say that it could not happen. This is clear from the facts of *Re D (a minor) (wardship: sterilisation)* [1976] 1 All ER 326, [1976] Fam 185, where the child concerned had neither the intelligence nor understanding either to consent or refuse. There medical ethics did not prove an obstacle, there being divided medical opinions, but the wardship jurisdiction of the court was invoked by a local authority educational psychologist who had been involved with the case. Despite the passing of the Children Act 1989, the inherent jurisdiction of the court could still be invoked in such a case to prevent an abortion which was contrary to the interests of the minor.

Thus far I have, in the main, been looking at the problem in the context of a conflict between parents and the minor, either the minor consenting and the parents refusing consent or the minor refusing consent and the parents giving it. Although that is not this case, I have done so both because we were told that it would be helpful to all those concerned with the treatment of minors and also perhaps the minors themselves and because it seems to be a logical base from which to proceed to consider the powers of the court and how they should be exercised.

W's case

...I have no doubt that the wishes of a 16- or 17-year-old child or indeed of a younger child who is 'Gillick competent' are of the greatest importance both legally and clinically, but I do doubt whether Thorpe J was right to conclude that W was of sufficient understanding to make an informed decision. I do not say this on the basis that I consider her approach irrational. I personally consider that religious beliefs which bar any medical treatment or treatment of particular kinds are irrational, but that does not make minors who hold those beliefs any the less 'Gillick competent'. They may well have sufficient intelligence and understanding fully to appreciate the treatment proposed and the consequences of their refusal to accept that treatment. What distinguishes W from them, and what with all respect I do not think that Thorpe J took sufficiently into account (perhaps because the point did not emerge as clearly before him as it did before us), is that it is a feature of anorexia nervosa that it is capable of destroying the ability to make an informed choice. It creates a compulsion to refuse treatment or only to accept treatment which is likely to be ineffective. This attitude is part and parcel of the disease and the more advanced the illness, the more compelling it may become. Where the wishes of the minor are themselves something which the doctors reasonably consider need to be treated in the minor's own best interests, those wishes clearly have a much reduced significance.

There is ample authority for the proposition that the inherent powers of the court under its parens patriae jurisdiction are theoretically limitless and that they certainly extend beyond the powers of a natural parent (see eg *Re R (a minor) (wardship: medical treatment)* [1991] 4 All ER 177 at 186, 189, [1992] Fam 11 at 25, 28). There can therefore be no doubt that it has power to override the refusal of a minor, whether over the age of 16 or under that age but 'Gillick competent'. It does not do so by ordering the doctors to treat which, even if within the court's powers, would be an abuse of them, or by ordering the minor to accept treatment, but by authorising the doctors to treat the minor in accordance with their clinical judgment, subject to any restrictions which the court may impose.

The remaining issue is how this power should be exercised in the context of a case in which a minor is refusing treatment or, whilst consenting to one form of treatment, is refusing to consent to another. Mr James Munby QC, appearing as amicus curiae, in his most helpful skeleton argument approached the matter as if 16- and 17-year-olds were in a special category. In a sense, of course, they are because s 8 applies to them. But Mr Munby so treated them because, in his submission, s 8 conferred complete autonomy on such minors, thus enabling them effectively to refuse medical treatment irrespective of how parental responsibilities might be sought to be exercised. That submission I have already rejected. This is not, however, to say that the wishes of 16- and 17-year-olds are to be treated as no different from those of 14- and 15-year-olds. Far from it. Adolescence is a period of progressive transition from childhood to adulthood and as experience of life is acquired and intelligence and understanding grow, so will the scope of the decision-making which should be left to the minor, for it is only by making decisions and experiencing the consequences that decision-making skills will be acquired. As I put it in the course of the argument, and as I sincerely believe, 'good parenting involves giving minors as much rope as they can handle without an unacceptable risk, that they will hang themselves'. As Lord Hailsham of St Marylebone LC put it in *Re B (a minor) (wardship: sterilisation)* [1987] 2 All ER 206 at 212, [1988] AC 199 at 202, the 'first paramount consideration [of the court] is the well-being, welfare or interests [of the minor]' and I regard it as self-evident that this involves giving them the maximum degree of decision-making which is prudent. Prudence does not involve avoiding all risk, but it does involve avoiding taking risks which, if they eventuate, may have irreparable consequences or which are disproportionate to the benefits which could accrue from taking them. I regard this approach as wholly consistent with the philosophy of s 1 of the Children Act 1989, and, in particular, sub-s (3)(*a*). It was submitted that whilst this might be correct, such an approach is inconsistent with ss 38(6), 43(8) and 44(7) of that Act and with paras 4 and 5 of the Sch 3. Here I disagree. These provisions all concern interim or supervision orders and do not impinge upon the jurisdiction of the court to make prohibited steps or specific issue orders under s 8 of the 1989 Act in the context of which the minor has no right of veto, unless it is to be found in s 8 of the 1969 Act.

Thorpe J was faced with having to choose between accepting one or other of two courses of action – leaving W where she was or transferring her to London – each of which was supported by responsible medical opinion. One of these doctors had consulted a Dr D, who was the pre-eminent expert in the treatment of anorexic cases. Initially Dr D was in favour of leaving W where she was, but he changed his mind when he came to give evidence. If ever there was a case for respecting the discretionary decision of the judge who had heard the witnesses, including W, this was it.

In seeking to escape from this conclusion it was submitted in argument that the reasoning of the judgment did not show, or show sufficiently, that Thorpe J had given due weight to W's wishes and that accordingly he had misdirected himself. I regard this criticism as wholly misconceived. Although much of the argument before him and much of his judgment were devoted to the legal rights of a 16-year-old, the only reason for exploring this was that W was resisting a change of regime. W's wishes could therefore never have been out of his mind. Furthermore, in explaining that discretionary decision he said:

The past year has not been a year of successful treatment or progress. There are a number of indications of this lack of success. There are the coercive measures of the gastro-nasal tubes and the plastering of the arms to which I have referred. There is the fact that her therapy was interrupted by fortuitous circumstances. There is the fact that consistent care by her consultant was interrupted by his illness. There is the fact that more recently the unit has promulgated stark rules including a drastic sanction in the event of breach. [W] has breached the rules, the sanction has not been applied, [W] is manifestly in control and the unit is reduced to proposing that they should move away from the psychological coercion to offering reward for good behaviour. That announcement to [W] could, in my judgment, only serve to underline to her the extent to which she is in control. The management options for the immediate future have been considerably constricted by recent developments. Although I have great respect for [W's] consultant and for the dedication of the staff, it seems to me that they have been manoeuvred into a position from which a change is necessary, even if it is a change that carries the risk of interpretation by [W] as 'yet another adult rejection and failure'. Obviously there are pros for the solution urged by her consultant. As well as [W's] views and her vulnerability there is the fact that there is a quasi-family bonding where she is. There is also the consideration that she seems to be flirting with the possibility of committing herself to re-entering mainstream education locally. There is also the proximity of the proposed foster parents and her own siblings.

In this passage Thorpe J was quite clearly not only bearing W's wishes in mind, but looking behind them to see why W wished to remain where she was. Not only would I have refrained from interfering with Thorpe J's decision on the footing that he had properly directed himself and that it was for him to decide, but, because, even on the facts as they then were, I consider that his decision was plainly right.

Balcombe LJ: The first issue before us, as it was before Thorpe J, was whether Parliament had, by s 8 of the Family Law Reform Act 1969, conferred on a minor over the age of 16 years an absolute right to refuse medical treatment, in which case the limitation of the court's inherent jurisdiction exemplified by *A v Liverpool City Council* [[1981] 2 All ER 385, [1982] AC 363] would have operated so as to preclude any intervention by the court.

[Having set out s 8 of the 1969 Act, Balcombe LJ continued:]

It will be readily apparent that the section is silent on the question which arises in the present case, namely whether a minor who has attained the age of 16 years has an absolute right to refuse medical treatment. I am quite unable to see how, on any normal reading of the words of the section, it can be construed to confer such a right. The purpose of the section is clear: it is to enable a 16-year-old to consent to medical treatment which, in the absence of consent by the child or its parents, would constitute a trespass to the person. In other words, for this purpose, and for this purpose only, a minor was to be treated as if it were an adult. That the section did not operate to prevent parental consent remaining effective as well in the case of a child over 16 as in the case of a child under that age, is apparent from the words of sub-s (3).

If there were any ambiguity as to the meaning of the section – and in my judgment there is not – it would be resolved by a glance at the *Report of the Committee on the Age of Majority* (Cmnd 3342 (1967)) (the Latey Report) to see what was the mischief which the section was intended to remedy. Paragraphs 471 to 489 of the Latey Report make it clear that doctors felt difficulty in accepting the consent of someone under 21 (the then age of majority) to medical treatment, even though parental consent might be unobtainable or, for reasons of the minor's privacy, undesirable. The nature of the problem is made apparent in para 479 of the Latey Report:

The legal position is in itself obscure. A cause of action to which a hospital authority or a member of its medical staff (or both) may be liable as the result of the performance of an operation is trespass to the person, and treatment administered without the patient's express or implied consent constitutes an assault which may lead to an action for damages. Until recent years the general rule has been to require the consent of a parent or guardian for an operation or an anaesthetic on a person of under 21, but increasingly at the present time it is becoming customary to accept the consent of minors aged 16 and over. There is no rigid rule of English law which renders a minor incapable of giving his consent to an operation but there seems to be no direct judicial authority establishing that the consent of such a person is valid.

It was not until some 18 years after the publication of the Latey Report that the common law position on this topic was resolved by the decision of the House of Lords in *Gillick v West Norfolk and Wisbech Area Health Authority* [1985] 3 All ER 402, [1986] AC 112.

This interpretation of s 8 was given, obiter, by Lord Donaldson MR in *Re R* [1991] 4 All ER 177 at 185–186, [1992] Fam 11 at 24. His judgment attracted a considerable degree of academic criticism. I have to say that I find this criticism surprising since, as I have already said, the section is in my judgment clear, unambiguous and limited in its scope. One writer went so far as to say that this construction 'flies in the face of the settled interpretation of this provision'. Counsel were unable to suggest any case which may have settled the interpretation of the section other than *Gillick's* case and to that I now turn.

The issue in *Gillick's* case [1985] 3 All ER 402 at 406, [1986] AC 112 at 165 was stated by Lord Fraser of Tullybelton in the following terms:

The central issue in the appeal is whether a doctor can ever, in any circumstances, lawfully give contraceptive advice or treatment to a girl under the age of 16 without her parents' consent.

To the like effect was Lord Scarman (see [1985] 3 All ER 402 at 418, [1986] AC 112 at 181). To that issue the construction of s 8 was at best peripheral.

The section was mentioned by both Parker and Fox LJJ in the Court of Appeal (see [1985] 3 All ER 402 at 418, [1986] AC 112 at 181), but neither attempted to give any definitive construction. In the House of Lords Lord Fraser of Tullybelton mentioned the section, but also did not attempt to define its meaning. Lord Bridge of Harwich, Lord Brandon of Oakbrook and Lord Templeman did not even mention the section. Lord Scarman did, however, mention the section at several points in the course of his speech, and after a consideration of its provisions and other matters said ([1985] 3 All ER 402 at 423, [1986] AC 112 at 188–189):

In the light of the foregoing I would hold that as a matter of law the parental right to determine whether or not their minor child below the age of 16 will have medical treatment terminates if and when the child achieves a sufficient understanding and intelligence to enable him or her to understand fully what is proposed.

I accept that the words 'or not' in this passage suggest that Lord Scarman considered that the right to refuse treatment was co-existent with the right to consent to treatment. I also accept that if a 'Gillick competent' child under 16 has a right to refuse treatment, so too has a child over the age of 16. Nevertheless I share the doubts of the Master of the Rolls whether Lord Scarman was intending to mean that the parents of a 'Gillick competent' child had no right at all to consent to medical treatment of the child as opposed to no exclusive right to such consent. If he did so intend then, in the case of a child over the age of 16, his interpretation of the law was inconsistent with the express words of s 8(3) of the 1969 Act. It is also clear that Lord Scarman was only considering the position of the child vis-à-vis its parents: he was not considering the position of the child vis-à-vis the court whose powers, as I have already said, are wider than the parents'.

I am therefore satisfied that there is no interpretation of s 8 of the 1969 Act – and certainly no 'settled' interpretation – which persuades me that my view of the clear meaning of the section is wrong. I express no view on the question whether a young person, whether over the age of 16 or under that age if 'Gillick competent', should have complete autonomy in the field of medical treatment. That is a matter of social policy with which Parliament can deal by appropriate legislation if it wishes to do so. What I am clear about is that Parliament has not conferred such autonomy on a 16- to 18-year-old child by virtue of s 8 of the 1969 Act, and that the common law as interpreted by the House of Lords in *Gillick's* case does not do so either.

Since Parliament has not conferred complete autonomy on a 16-year-old in the field of medical treatment, there is no overriding limitation to preclude the exercise by the court of its inherent jurisdiction and the matter becomes one for the exercise by the court of its discretion. Nevertheless the discretion is not to be exercised in a moral vacuum. Undoubtedly the philosophy behind s 8 of the 1969 Act, as well as being the decision of the House of Lords in *Gillick's* case is that, as children approach the age of majority, they are increasingly able to take their own decisions concerning their medical treatment. In logic there can be no difference between an ability to consent to treatment and an ability to refuse medical treatment. This philosophy is also reflected by some provisions of the Children Act 1989 which give a child, of sufficient understanding to make an informed decision, the right to refuse 'medical or psychiatric examination or other assessment' or 'psychiatric and medical treatment' in certain defined circumstances – see ss 38(6), 43(8) and 44(7) and paras 4(4)(*a*) and 5(5)(*a*) of sch 3. Accordingly the older the child concerned the greater the weight the court should give to its wishes, certainly in the field of medical treatment. In a sense this is merely one aspect of the application of the test that the welfare of the child is the paramount consideration. It will normally be in the best interests of a child of sufficient age and understanding to make an informed decision that the court should respect its integrity as a human being and not lightly override its decision on such a personal matter as medical treatment, all the more so if that treatment is invasive. In my judgment, therefore, the court exercising the inherent jurisdiction in relation to a 16- or 17-year-old child who is not mentally incompetent will, as a matter of course, ascertain the wishes of the child and will approach its decision with a strong predilection to give effect to the child's wishes. (The case of a mentally incompetent child will present different considerations, although even there the child's wishes, if known, must be a very material factor.) Nevertheless, if the court's powers are to be meaningful, there must come a point at which the court, while not disregarding the child's wishes, can override them in the child's own best interests, objectively considered. Clearly such a point will have come if the child is seeking to refuse treatment in circumstances which will in all probability lead to the death of the child or to severe permanent injury. An example of such a case was *Re E (a minor)* [1992] 2 FCR 219, which came before Ward J. There a 15-year-old Jehovah's Witness, and his parents of the same faith, were refusing to allow doctors to give the boy a blood transfusion without which there was a strong risk (on the medical evidence) that the boy would die. Ward J authorised the blood transfusion. In my judgment he was right to do so. In the course of his judgment he said:

> There is compelling and overwhelming force in the submission of the Official Solicitor that this court, exercising its prerogative of protection, should be very slow to allow an infant to martyr himself.

I agree.

At the end of the first day's hearing before us we were told that W's condition had deteriorated rapidly since the hearing at first instance. Her weight had dropped from 41.7 kg at the beginning of May to 36.75 kg on 28 June. She had for ten days refused all solid food. If this pattern continued she would probably die: if it were not shortly reversed she would be likely to suffer permanent damage to her brain and reproductive organs. In those circumstances, the point had clearly been reached when the court should be prepared, in W's own interests, to overrule her refusal to consent to treatment, and we therefore ordered that she should be treated at the appropriate London unit.

I do not think it would be helpful to try to define the point at which the court should be prepared to disregard the 16- or 17-year-old child's wishes to refuse medical treatment. Every case must depend on its own facts. What I do stress is that the judge should approach the exercise of the discretion with a predilection to give effect to the child's wishes on the basis that prima facie that will be in his or her best interests.

If that is, as I believe to be, the correct approach, then it does not appear to have been adopted by Thorpe J in the present case. That is not said by way of criticism, because the case does not appear primarily to have been argued before him on that basis. It would appear from his judgment that the main argument before him on behalf of W was on the basis of s 8 giving W an absolute right to refuse treatment. Once he had (rightly) rejected that argument, he treated the matter as one for the unfettered exercise of his discretion, in which W's views were merely a relatively unimportant factor, and expressed the view that his real choice was between the conflicting medical views of Dr M, the consultant psychiatrist on whose care W had been for over a year, and Dr G, supported in the event by Dr D, another consultant psychiatrist with specialist experience in the field of anorexia nervosa. However, not merely was there a conflict of medical evidence, but even Dr D, upon whose opinion Thorpe J eventually based his decision, described W as having a 'mild case of anorexia nervosa' and that although he (Dr D) had eventually come round to the view that W should be treated at the specialist London unit, the decision was quite finely balanced. It must be remembered that W was not refusing all medical treatment – she was merely expressing her desire to manipulate the situation, her wish was supported by Dr M and, initially at least, by Dr D. In those circumstances I entertain grave doubts that if Thorpe J had directed himself in the way I have suggested, that W's wishes should be respected unless there were very strong reasons for rejecting them, he would have reached the decision which he did. However, as I have said, by the time the case was before us W's condition had changed so drastically that, whatever may have been the previous position, the court would have been in dereliction of its duty had it not overridden W's wishes and effectively confirmed the order made by Thorpe J that W should be treated at the specialist London unit.

In the course of the arguments before us it was suggested that a construction of s 8 of the 1969 Act which denies a 16- or 17-year-old girl an absolute right to refuse medical treatment, but leaves it open to her parents to consent to such treatment, could in theory lead to a case where a pregnant 16-year-old refuses an abortion, but her parents consent to her pregnancy being terminated. So it could in theory, but I cannot conceive of a case where a doctor, faced with the refusal of a mentally competent 16-year-old to having an abortion, would terminate the pregnancy merely upon the consent of the girl's parents. Leaving aside all questions of medical ethics, it seems to me inevitable that in such highly unlikely circumstances the matter would have to come before the court. I find it equally difficult to conceive a case where the court faced with this problem and applying the approach I have indicated above, would authorise an abortion against the wishes of a mentally competent 16-year-old. The dilemma is therefore more apparent than real.

Nolan LJ: I agree with Lord Donaldson MR that the effect of s 8 is to make it clear that a child of 16 or 17 years of age has the same capacity as an adult to consent to surgical, medical or dental treatment which would otherwise constitute a trespass. The phrase 'surgical, medical or dental treatment' is evidently used in a fairly narrow sense: otherwise it would not have been necessary for Parliament to provide, by s 8(2), that the expression includes diagnostic procedures, and ancillary procedures such as the administration of an anaesthetic. The section does not cover, for example, the giving of blood, it does not even include the taking of a blood sample. Separate provision for that is made by s 21 of the Act. In these circumstances it is impossible to my mind to regard s 8 as supporting the general proposition that in the exercise of its inherent jurisdiction the court should allow the child's decision to determine the matter, whether or not the court thinks that this is in the child's best interests. If the court took this view, it would be abdicating its responsibility.

Nor, to my mind, is the significance of s 8 enhanced by the decision in *Gillick's* case. *Gillick's* case was, of course, concerned with children under the age of 16. There were passing references to s 8 in the printed cases submitted to the House of Lords by the parties, but the section does not appear to have been mentioned in the course of oral argument. Lord Fraser described s 8(1) as having been enacted 'merely for the avoidance of doubt' (see [1985] 3 All ER 402 at 408, [1986] AC 150 at 167).

The general approach adopted by the House of Lords to the weight which should be attached to the views of a child who has sufficient understanding to make an informed decision is clearly of great importance, but it is essential to bear in mind that their Lordships were concerned with the extent of parental rights over the welfare of the child. They were not concerned with the jurisdiction of the court. It is of the essence of that jurisdiction that the court has the power and the responsibility in appropriate cases to override the views of both the child and the parent in determining what is in the child's best interests. Authoritative and instructive as they are, the speeches in *Gillick's* case do not deal with the principles which should govern the exercise of this court's jurisdiction in the present case. In my judgment, those principles are to be found in s 1 of the Children Act 1989. The child's welfare is to be the paramount consideration: see s 1(1). In giving effect to that consideration, the court is to have particular regard to the factors set out in s 1(3). That subsection is expressed to apply only in certain defined circumstances, but it is, I think, common ground that it may be treated as having general application. It requires the court to have regard in particular to: (a) the ascertainable wishes and feelings of the child concerned (considered in the light of his age and understanding); (b) his physical, emotional and educational needs; (c) the likely effect on him of any change in his circumstances; (d) his age, sex, background and any characteristics of his which the court considers relevant; (e) any harm which he has suffered or is at risk of suffering; (f) how capable each of his parents, and any other person in relation to whom the court considers the question to be relevant, is of meeting his needs; and (g) the range of powers available to the court.

In other words, in the circumstances of the present case the wishes and feelings of W considered in the light of her age and understanding, are the first of the factors to which the court must have regard, but the court must have regard also to such of the other factors as may be relevant when discharging its overall responsibility for W's welfare.

I would emphasise that the only aspect of W's welfare with which we are concerned in the present case is her refusal to undergo a particular form of treatment for anorexia. So far in this judgment I have been principally concerned to explain why, as it seems to me, the court has not only the power but the inescapable responsibility of deciding, in that specific context, what is to be done in the interests of her welfare. I am very far from asserting any general rule that the court should prefer its own view as to what is in the best interests of the child to those of the child itself. In considering the welfare of the child, the court must not only recognise but if necessary defend the right of the child, having sufficient understanding to take an informed decision, to make his or her own choice. In most areas of life it would be not only wrong in principle but also futile and counter-productive for the court to adopt any different approach. In the area of medical treatment, however, the court can and sometimes must intervene.

It will, I think, be apparent from what I have said that even in the case of normal medical treatment, I cannot accept that Mr Munby's proposition that the child's decision should determine the matter. The determination must always be that of the court. If one is then to try and specify the grounds upon which it would be right for the court to intervene I do not for my part find it particularly helpful to speak in terms of special or extraordinary cases as distinct from normal cases…One must, I think, start from the general premise that the protection of the child's welfare implies at least the protection of the child's life. I state this only as a general and not as an invariable premise because of the possibility of cases in which the court would not authorise treatment of a distressing nature which offered only a small hope of preserving life. In general terms, however, the present state of the law is that an individual who has reached the age of 18 is free to do with his life what he wishes, but it is the duty of the court to ensure so far as it can that children survive to attain that age.

To take it a stage further, if the child's welfare is threatened by a serious and imminent risk that the child will suffer grave and irreversible mental or physical harm, then once again the court when called upon has a duty to intervene. It makes no difference whether the risk arises from the action or inaction of others, or from the action or inaction of the child. Due weight must be given to the child's wishes, but the court is not bound by them. In the present case, Thorpe J was apparently satisfied on the evidence before him that such a risk existed. In my judgment, he was fully entitled to take this view. By the time the matter came to this court, it was impossible to take any other view. For these reasons, I would dismiss the appeal save to the extent of making the necessary variation of the order of Thorpe J.

We are not directly concerned with cases in which the jurisdiction of the court has not been invoked, and in which accordingly the decision on treatment may depend upon the consent of the child or of the parent. I for my part would think it axiomatic, however, in order to avoid the risk of grave breaches of the law that in any case where time permitted, where major surgical or other procedures (such as an abortion) were proposed, and whereby the parents or those in loco parentis were prepared to give consent but the child (having sufficient understanding to make an informed decision) was not, the jurisdiction of the court should always be invoked. I would say the same of a case in which a child of any age consented to donate an organ; such a case is not, of course, covered by s 8 of the Family Law Reform Act 1969 on any view of the matter.

Undoubtedly, *Re W* is a controversial case (for a discussion, see N Lowe and S Juss 'Medical Treatment – Pragmatism and the Search for Principle' (1993) 56 MLR 865). A number of arguments can be deployed to show that the court made a wrong turn in taking to itself and giving parents decision-making powers over their competent children (see, generally, M Brazier and C Bridge 'Coercion or Caring: Analysing Adolescent Autonomy' (1996) 16 LS 84). Let us first consider the arguments concerning the power of the court. In *Re R* and *Re W* the court was exercising its *parens patriae* power (in wardship or under the inherent jurisdiction of the court). While it is undeniable that the court's jurisdiction is theoretically unlimited, this is only true once it has been determined what falls within the jurisdiction in the first place. For instance, it is clear now that it does not cover adults. It is also arguably the case that it does not cover the competent, whether adult or not. Historically, the jurisdiction was concerned with children and 'idiots, lunatics and others of unsound mind' (*Re Eve* [1986] 2 SCR 388). It is also clear that the jurisdiction was 'founded on the obvious necessity that the law should place somewhere the care of individuals who cannot take care of themselves' (*Wellesley v Duke of Beaufort* (1827) 2 Russ 1 at 20). Competent adults would not have been subject to the *parens patriae* jurisdiction before 1960 when it ceased to exist in respect of adults (see *supra*). Only incompetent adults would have been the proper subjects of the court's jurisdiction. *Mutatis mutandis* the legal position should be the same for children. The courts in *Re R* and *Re W* overlook this and falsely move straight to the position that the court's *parens patriae* power is always limitless in its scope.

Even if this were not the case, the theoretically limitless jurisdiction of the court is subject to practical and policy-based limitations. There is a strong argument that just as courts stay their hand where enforcement would be impossible or where they are asked to review the exercise of a power conferred by statute on, for example, a local authority, so too they should stay their hand where the decision-maker subject to review is a *competent* child. This argument does not turn upon the rather arid point that s 8 of the 1969 Act ousts the court's jurisdiction. Rather it is founded upon the underlying ethos represented by s 8 and the *Gillick* decision. Whether or not s 8 and *Gillick* only relate expressly to consent, they both look to a more fundamental value, namely that of respecting the autonomy of the competent person (whether or not falling within the arbitrarily defined category of 'children'). State paternalism has no place simply on the basis that the 'state knows best'. Some disagree with this. Nigel Lowe and Satvinder Juss, for example, offer the following observation on *Re W*:

Nigel Lowe and Satvinder Juss *'Medical Treatment – Pragmatism and the Search for Principle'* (1993) 56 MLR 865

> To those who question how a child can be held able to give a valid consent yet be unable to exercise a power of veto, we would reply that there *is* a rational distinction to be made between giving consent and withholding it. We must start with the assumption that a doctor will act in the best interests of his patient. Hence, if the doctor believes that a particular treatment is necessary for his patient, it is perfectly rational for the law to facilitate this as easily as possible and hence allow a '*Gillick* competent' child to give a valid consent, and also to protect the child against parents opposed to what is professionally considered to be in its best medical interests. In contrast, it is surely right for the law to be reluctant to allow a *child* of whatever age to be able to veto treatment designed for his or her benefit, particularly if a refusal would lead to the child's death or permanent damage. In other words, the clear and consistent policy of the law is to protect the child against wrong-headed parents and against itself with the final safeguard, as *Re W* unequivocally establishes, of giving the court the last word in cases of dispute.

The basis for this must lie in society's unwillingness to trust teenage children to make decisions about themselves which will seriously and irreparably damage their long-term interests. Hence, the law's acceptance that such children may consent to treatment in the best interests (*Gillick v West Norfolk and Wisbech AHA* [1985] 3 All ER 402 (HL)) but its rejection of their ability to refuse treatment which, seen through the objective eyes of the court, will harm them and will set-back their long term developmental interests (see the elegant argument by J Eekelaar 'The Emergence of Children's Rights' (1986) 6 OJLS 161).

In *Re L (medical treatment: Gillick competency* [1998] 2 FLR 810, Stephen Brown P applied this political philosophy when he said (at 813):

> It is also my view, without any doubt at all, that it would be the appropriate order to make even if I were not justified in coming to the conclusion that she was not so-called '*Gillick* competent'. This is an extreme case and her position is grave indeed. It is vital, as I have already said, that she should receive this treatment.

The case concerned a 14-year-old girl who was a Jehovah's Witness who required a life-saving blood transfusion (see Commentary (1997) 7 Med L Rev 58 (AG) at 59–61 and C Bridge, 'Religious Beliefs and Teenage Refusal of Medical Treatment' (1999) 62 MLR 585).

As regards a conflict between the parents and the child, a majority of the court (Nolan LJ *dubitante*) adopted the approach of Lord Donaldson MR in *Re R* that a child's refusal could be countermanded by the parents. Hence, a child may validly consent to medical treatment and this consent may not be overridden by the parents. In *Re K, W and H (minors) (consent to treatment)* [1993] 1 FCR 240 (Thorpe J) the court considered whether a court order was necessary before children in local authority care could be admitted to and treated at hospitals for disturbed adolescents. Thorpe J concluded that the law was clear (at 246):

> a child with *Gillick* competence can consent to treatment but that if he or she declines to do so, consent can be given by someone else who has parental right or responsibilities.

Hence, in relation to these children the local authority could legally consent to their treatment.

The court's view in *Re W* is open to a number of objections. First, it relies upon a literal interpretation of s 8 of the Family Law Reform Act 1969. While it is true that s 8 only speaks of a child over 16 having capacity to consent to medical treatment, the section could (and perhaps should) be interpreted as encompassing the right to refuse. Despite what the judges say in *Re W*, the Latey Committee (whose report led to s 8) is ambiguous and leaves open the point which the court claims that it concludes. More importantly, the common law, as developed in the *Gillick* case, takes a wholly different view of the law than the gloss placed upon it by Lord Donaldson MR. The House of Lords undoubtedly approached the *Gillick* case from the point of view of seeking to identify what *rights* a young person may have in the context of medical treatment. In particular, the majority of the House were concerned with the right of self-determination. From this starting point no distinction may properly be drawn between *agreeing to* and *refusing* treatment. They are merely two ways of exercising the same right. Thus, if the right to consent exists so does the right to refuse. Lord Donaldson's approach is to reject a rights-based analysis. He idiosyncratically believes that the only role of consent in the common law is not to give effect to a right of self-determination, but rather to serve as a piece of legal armour protecting a doctor who might otherwise be sued in battery. Approached in this way, consent is merely a formal device. It has no substance, least of all the substance of rights. Furthermore, it can readily be detached from any consideration of a refusal. But this is to deny the right to decide which is at the heart of the law of consent as was made clear, *inter alia*, by the House of Lords in *Sidaway v Board of Governors of Bethlem Royal Hospital* [1985] AC 871. After all, making *decisions* includes saying 'no' as well as 'yes' (see *Airedale NHS Trust v Bland* [1993] 1 All ER 821 at 865–866 per Lord Goff).

What these arguments, and indeed the Children Act 1989, demonstrate is that whatever the position when the Family Law Reform Act 1969 was passed, the law now does not recognise parental rights but rather parental duties. The latter exist only for the benefit and welfare of a child who has not yet achieved a level of understanding to be judged competent in a particular matter (see *Gillick* and *F v Wirral Metropolitan Borough Council* [1991] Fam 69, [1991] 2 All ER 648 (CA)). The argument of the judges, therefore, that s 8(3) preserves the parental right to consent is simply misplaced since all it tells us is that we must look to the general law to see who (if anyone) may consent when the child refuses. The overwhelming trend has been to say that no one may do so until *Re R* and *Re W*. Further, it may not be enough for the court to dismiss the 'hair-raising possibilities' (per Lord Donaldson MR) of abortions or sterilisations carried out on competent and unwilling, perhaps even protesting, young women with the consent of the court (or parents) as 'a dilemma...more apparent than real' (per Balcombe LJ). It is surely not appropriate for the court to wash its hands of these real and hard cases by simply asserting that they will not happen. Certainly if *the court* were to authorise such a procedure, some doctor would probably be prepared to carry it out, even if he would not do so merely on the basis of the parents' consent. (In *Re M (medical treatment: consent)* [1999] 2 FLR 1097, the court authorised a heart transplant against the wishes of a 15½-year-old young woman and the judge, Johnson J remarked that her parents could have done so.) It would be hard to imagine a legal development more designed to destroy trust in both the law and the medical profession.

A final point which serves to demonstrate how much of a departure from orthodoxy *Re W* constitutes, involves noticing its impact upon the law of confidentiality. Given that *competent* children are entitled to have their confidences respected, how may a parent consent to treatment if a child refuses and insists on the doctor observing confidentiality by not discussing the case with the parents? The only solution would be if the law recognised some sort of public interest exception, here based upon the best interests of the child. The difficulty with such a view is that it undermines the very nature of competence, ie that a person knows his own best interests and must be free to make his own mistakes (for a discussion see *infra*, ch 8).

Despite these major criticisms of *Re R* and *Re W*, and on the assumption that they currently represent the law, it is necessary to examine how the court views its power to override a child's refusal. In *Re R* little or no guidance was offered as to *when* the court would do so and what weight (if any) it would give to the child's refusal. In *Re W*, on the other hand, the judges did address this issue in the context of the *court's* powers. Presumably, *a fortiori* the court's views would define the scope of the parents' power. Balcombe LJ limited the court's power to cases where the refusal 'will in all probability lead to the death of the child or to severe permanent injury'. Similarly, Nolan LJ contemplated cases where 'the child's welfare is threatened by a serious and imminent risk that the child will suffer grave and irreversible mental or physical harm'. At this point, the court had a 'duty to intervene' (per Nolan LJ). Before that point is reached, however, the court should 'approach its decision with a strong predilection to give effect to the child's wishes' (per Balcombe LJ).

Given this approach, Balcombe LJ thought that the trial judge had wrongly overridden W's refusal since *at that time* her life was not threatened. By the time the case came before the Court of Appeal her condition had deteriorated. Nolan LJ was only prepared to accept Thorpe J's decision on the basis that he had found on the evidence that there was a 'serious and imminent risk' of 'grave and irreversible' harm to her mental or physical health. Subsequent cases have, by and large, involved situations where the child's life was seriously at risk (eg, *Re L (medical treatment: Gillick competency)* [1998] 2 FLR 810; *Re S (a minor) (consent to medical treatment)* [1994] 2 FLR 1065 and *Re M (medical treatment: consent)* [1999] 2 FLR 1097).

As ever, Lord Donaldson MR appeared to give the court a wider power. The limit explicitly stated by the other judges is not readily apparent in his judgment and he entirely accepted the trial judge's decision that W's refusal should be overridden.

The case contemplated in *Re W* is that of the child who refuses and whose refusal is overridden – what of the child who wishes to consent but her parents or the court consider this not to be in her 'best interests'? We know, as regards the parents, that after *Gillick* they have no power to veto treatment by seeking to override the child's consent. In Lord Donaldson's picturesque language the child's consent unlocks the door for the doctor (*Re R*) or gives him a 'flak-jacket' (*Re W*). But, what of the court? Is the court's power similarly limited? Only Staughton LJ gave any consideration to this in *Re R* where he said:

> Then there is the converse case in wardship, where the ward consents but the court is minded either not to consent or positively to forbid treatment. Does the judge in such a case have an overriding power, which the natural parent of a competent child under the age of 16 does not have by reason of the *Gillick* decision? If so, there would again be a problem for doctors, who may have to ask if the child is a ward. But the trend of cases seems to show that, if the treatment would constitute an important step in the child's life, the court does have that power.

Certainly, Staughton LJ's view is consistent with the reasoning in *Re R* and *Re W* if the child is a ward of court for the reason he gave (see also Lord Donaldson MR in *Re W* at 633, asserting that the court's power to override a child's consent was accepted by all parties in the *Gillick* case). If the child is not a ward, however, the answer is more difficult. When the court exercises its inherent jurisdiction or makes an order under s 8 of the Children Act 1989, it could grant an injunction in the former care or a 'prohibited steps' order in the latter case which would have the same effect as if the child were a ward. In practical terms, a court minded to refuse treatment fearing that it could be carried out by a doctor always has this option to prohibit treatment.

In conclusion, on any account the decisions in *Re R* and *Re W* are provocative. They threaten to undermine the landmark decision of the House of Lords in *Gillick* and render teenagers insecure of their rights just at the time when they are being encouraged to take responsibility for themselves. It is our view that these cases do not properly represent an ordered development in the law and should be reconsidered by the House of Lords when the opportunity arises. At this time, thought may be given to the following. There is no doubt that cases such as *Re R* and *Re W* are poignant, difficult and attract enormous popular interest. It is not surprising furthermore that the courts should have arrived at the decision that treatment should be given whatever the patient's wishes in the light of the harm that would otherwise ensue (see also *Re S (a minor) (consent to medical treatment)* [1994] 2 FLR 1065 and *Re L (medical treatment: Gillick competency)* [1998] 2 FLR 810).

In reaching this decision the Court of Appeal has done violence to the development of the law begun by *Gillick*. There was another course open to the court. We saw earlier (*supra*, ch 5) that in each of the cases so far the court has determined that the child was incompetent. Ever since *Gillick* and, indeed, before, there had been speculation about the proper course to take in the following three classes of case. The *first* is the patient with fluctuating lucidity, for example the manic depressive who while lucid denies that he has been ill, refuses medication and plunges headlong back into illness. The *second* is the anorexic who is entirely competent in every regard save that she has an utterly distorted view of her body image and therefore embarks on a pattern of behaviour which might ultimately result in death. The *third* is the person addicted to drugs who may lead a perfectly ordered life provided he satisfies his craving for drugs. All of these three types of person could be regarded in law as incompetent as regards their need for treatment. Their incompetence lies in their inability or refusal to comprehend the true nature of their predicament (see *State of Tennessee v Northern* 563 SW 2d 197 (1978)). Such a view would leave intact the framework of the law of competence and the rights that flow from it without in any way artificially manipulating the concept of competence (see *supra*, ch 5).

The same cannot necessarily be said of cases such as *Re S* (*supra*) and *Re L* (*supra*). There, the court may too hastily have held teenagers to be incompetent. Clearly, the court is striving to act on its 'hunch' that society should not let children make a decision to die. In truth, it comes down to no more than the court (as society's instrument) acknowledging that at some point citizens must be allowed to make their own decisions, even ones which others might perceive as harmful to them. That point is the age of majority, which for us is 18, but could be differently located according to the sense of a particular society or culture. Once that point is reached, the state does not have a compelling interest to prevent rational citizens from reaching (most) decisions. Until that point, however, the protective duty of society permits intervention. If this is the public policy of this country, it might be better for the courts in these other instances, simply to say so rather than to obfuscate matters by distorting the legal concept of competence.

Chapter 7
Medical records

Introduction

A doctor needs to maintain medical records as part of the care of his patient. This is expressly set out in the terms of service of a general practitioner as a duty owned to his Health Authority (see the National Health Service (General Medical Services) Regulations, 1992 (SI 1992 No 635), Sch 2, para 36 and for 'pilot scheme' GPs see, *Directions to Health Authorities Concerning the Implementation of Pilot Schemes (Personal Medical Services)*, Sch 1, para 20). It is undoubtedly also a legal obligation owed to patients in the case both of GPs and hospital doctors.

Records may be either written down or electronically stored, but increasingly the latter. A patient may wish to have *access* to his records in order to discover what is said about him or to verify its accuracy. Also the patient may wish to *control* disclosure of the record to others given the sensitive nature of the information.

Our concern in this and the subsequent chapter is with the legal frameworks governing access to, and control of, patient information. It is important, however, to see the context in which the law operates, in particular the extensive internal regulation of the NHS which is a hallmark of the current system.

As regards access, a *Code of Practice on Openness in the NHS* has operated within the NHS since 1 June 1995. This both seeks to regulate access to information but also recognises the need to respect patient confidences (see discussion in D Longley *Health Care Constitutions* (1996) at pp 148–152). It provides a quasi-legislative basis for patient access not only to their medical records but also to other information held by the NHS, for example, management documentation setting out a Health Authority's, or Trust's policy on allocation of resources. The latter will ultimately fall within the purview of the Freedom of Information legislation which was proposed by the Government in 1999. The former, as we will see, has a legislative basis, most recently in the Data Protection Act 1998.

Concerns over the security and use of patient information within the NHS has led the Government to implement a national strategy and structure. The Department of Health has issued guidance in *The Protection and Use of Patient Information* (March 1996, HS (96) 18) dealing with the use of confidential patient information. Structural concerns, however, led to a review of the use of information culminating in the Caldicott Report in December 1997 (*Report on the Review of Patient-Identifiable Information*). The Caldicott Report was particularly concerned with the use of patient information within the NHS and when provided to outside bodies for purposes other than the direct care of patients, eg audit or management purposes. The Committee noted the need for greater awareness that patients' confidentiality should be respected and called for greater security mechanisms throughout the NHS to limit unauthorised disclosure or use. The Committee identified a number of key principles:

(1) justify the purpose(s) for which the information is required
(2) do not use patient-identifiable information unless it is absolutely necessary
(3) use the minimum necessary patient-identifiable information

(4)   access to patient-identifiable information should be on a strict need-to-know basis
(5)   everyone with access to patient-identifiable information should be aware of their responsibilities
(6)   understand and comply with the law

(See Caldicott Report (*supra*), para 4.2.1.)

The Committee made 16 recommendations to improve the situation and provide a clear framework for the use and storage of patient information, including the appointment of so-called 'Caldicott Guardians' within the NHS institutions to oversee and take responsibility for information systems.

The Caldicott Committee: Report on the review of patient-identifiable information (December 1997)

Summary of Recommendations

Recommendation 1: Every dataflow, current or proposed, should be tested against basic principles of good practice. Continuing flows should be re-tested regularly.

Recommendation 2: A programme of work should be established to reinforce awareness of confidentiality and information security requirements amongst all staff within the NHS.

Recommendation 3: A senior person, preferably a health professional, should be nominated in each health organisation to act as a guardian, responsible for safeguarding the confidentiality of patient information.

Recommendation 4: Clear guidance should be provided for those individuals/bodies responsible for approving uses of patient-identifiable information.

Recommendation 5: Protocols should be developed to protect the exchange of patient-identifiable information between NHS and non-NHS bodies.

Recommendation 6: The identity of those responsible for monitoring the sharing and transfer of information within agreed local protocols should be clearly communicated.

Recommendation 7: An accreditation system which recognises those organisations following good practice with respect to confidentiality should be considered.

Recommendation 8: The NHS number should replace other identifiers wherever practicable, taking account of the consequences of errors and particular requirements for other specific identifiers.

Recommendation 9: Strict protocols should define who is authorised to gain access to patient identity where the NHS number or other coded identifier is used.

Recommendation 10: Where particularly sensitive information is transferred, privacy enhancing technologies (eg encrypting identifiers or "patient identifying information") must be explored.

Recommendation 11: Those involved in developing health information systems should ensure that best practice principles are incorporated during the design stage.

Recommendation 12: Where practicable, the internal structure and administration of databases holding patient-identifiable information should reflect the principles developed in this report.

Recommendation 13: The NHS number should replace the patient's name on Items of Service Claims made by General Practitioners as soon as practically possible.

Recommendation 14: The design of new systems for the transfer of prescription data should incorporate the principles developed in this report.

Recommendation 15: Future negotiations on pay and conditions for General Practitioners should, where possible, avoid systems of payment which require patient identifying details to be transmitted.

Recommendation 16: Consideration should be given to procedures for General Practice claims and payments which do not require patient-identifying information to be transferred, which can then be piloted.

The Government accepted the Caldicott recommendations and 'Caldicott Guardians' came into existence on 31 March 1999 (HSC 1999/012). The national strategy for information management within the NHS calls for increasing dependence upon so-called electronic patient records (EPR) (see *Information for Health, and Information Strategy for the Modern NHS 1995–2005* (September 1998) HSC 1998/168). Ultimately, this is likely to lead to electronically stored and disseminated patient records via an NHS network, together with the development of 'smart card' patient records where the information is stored on a card - something like a credit card - which the patient can carry with them.

The NHS is now taking the issues of security and use of patient records and information altogether more seriously and there is copious guidance on a range of matters (see eg *For the Record, Managing Records in NHS Trusts and Health Authorities* (March 1999) HSC 1999/053 and *Preservation, Retention and Destruction of GP General Medical Services Records Relating to Patients*, HSC 1998/217). These seek to set out and share within the NHS best practice for the management of patient and administrative records within the NHS.

At a national level, the Government has created, from April 1999, the NHS Information Authority as a Special Health Authority under s 11 of the National Health Service Act 1977 (see the National Health Service Information Authority (Establishment and Constitution) Order 1999 (SI 1999 No 695) and the National Health Service Information Authority Regulations 1999 (SI 1999 No 694)). This body is charged with the obligation of implementing the NHS information strategy. In particular, it will co-ordinate the development of national clinical information standards, electronic patient records, a national programme to ensure consistent and effective use of IT and an effective information culture and expertise in the NHS.

We should now turn our attention to the law and the twin issues of *access* to and *control* of medical records.

Access

A. THE COMMON LAW

1. The basis for access

Prior to the passage of the Data Protection Act 1984 and Access to Health Records Act 1990, the question of a patient's right of access to his medical records was by no means easy to resolve. This legislation and, latterly, as we shall see, the Data Protection Act 1998, provide a general right of access to medical records with exceptions. The common law is for all intents and purposes irrelevant after the 1998 Act, since claims for access to *all* medical records fall within its scope. The common law remains, however, a mater of great intellectual interest for medical lawyers and may still have practical application in an exceptional circumstance.

As we shall see, the English common law is stated by the Court of Appeal in *R v Mid Glamorgan FHSA, ex p Martin* [1995] 1 All ER 356 (CA). The diversity of the common law is, however, illustrated by the decisions of the Canadian Supreme Court in *McInerney v MacDonald* (1992) 93 DLR (4th) 415 and of the Australian High Court in *Breen v Williams* (1996) 70 ALJR 772. Taken together, these three decisions exhaustively analyse the bases for a common law claim for access, only to reach quite different solutions.

What, then, are the bases for the claim? First, the patient may seek to assert *ownership* over the medical record and his proprietary right to possession. Secondly, he may claim that it is a term of any *contract* between him and the doctor that he be granted access. Thirdly, he may argue that the relationship between him and the doctor is a *fiduciary relationship*, entailing a right of access. These are the main arguments at common law which a patient could deploy. There are others and, as we shall see, in England the Court of Appeal in *Martin* took a different course.

The Australian High Court considered these bases in the important decision of *Breen v Williams* in 1996. As we shall see, they rejected all of them, together with an argument that the claimant had a 'right to know' based upon their earlier 'informed consent' decision of *Rogers v Whitaker* (1992) 175 CLR 479.

Breen v Williams (1996) 70 ALJR 772 (Aust H Ct)

The appellant, a former patient of the respondent medical practitioner, claimed a legal right of access to records kept by the respondent in respect of his professional treatment of the appellant. The claim was made as one founded, not on principles of discovery or enforcement by resort to applications for curial declaration and injunction, but on alleged rights of common law and in equity. Those rights were said to comprehend a "proprietary right and interest" in the actual information in the respondent's records, an implied term in the contract between appellant and respondent, an innominate right of access to medical records, and a fiduciary duty resting upon the respondent to give the appellant access to her personal medical records. The appellant, having failed in proceedings in the Supreme Court of New South Wales and before the Court of Appeal, further appealed to the High Court.

Gaudron and McHugh JJ: The question in this appeal is whether a patient has a right to inspect and/or obtain copies of his or her medical records that are held by that person's doctor.

In the Supreme Court of New South Wales, Bryson J held that the appellant, Ms Julie Breen, a patient of the respondent, Dr Cholmondeley W Williams, did not have a right to copy or to have access to her medical records. A majority of the Court of Appeal of the Supreme Court (Mahoney and Meagher JJA) agreed with the decision of Bryson J. Kirby P, dissenting, held that a doctor owes a patient a fiduciary duty which entitles the patient to inspect or obtain copies of his or her medical records. Pursuant to the grant of special leave, Ms Breen now appeals to this Court against the order of the Court of Appeal. In our opinion, the appeal should be dismissed...

The right of access
A claim that a patient has a right of access to his or her medical records is a question of great social importance. But absent a contractual term, such a claim has no foundation in the law of Australia. Nevertheless, every possible argument that could be made in support of the claim by Ms Breen was put. Dr Cashman, who appeared for Ms Breen, contended that one or more of five legal principles or doctrines supported or gave to Ms Breen a right of access to records in the possession of Dr Williams that relate to his treatment of her, subject to lawful exceptions.

First, the common law gave her a "proprietary right and interest" in the actual information contained in Dr Williams' records. Second, the common law implied a term in the contract between her and Dr Williams to the effect that she had a right of access to the documents in Dr Williams' file. Third, there was an innominate common law right of access to medical records. Fourth, the common law recognised a patient's "right to know" all necessary information concerning his or her medical treatment including, where requested, access to records containing that information. Fifth, the law imposed on Dr Williams a fiduciary duty, enforceable in a court of equity, to give her access to her medical records.

Did Ms Breen have a proprietary right or interest in the medical records?
Dr Cashman did not submit that Ms Breen owned the actual documents which comprised the medical file. She did not, he said, "seek to divest the doctor of the pieces of paper" comprising the records. The concession that Ms Breen did not own the documents was plainly correct. Professional persons are not ordinarily agents of their clients even though they often have express, implied or ostensible authority to enter into contracts on their clients' behalf. Documents prepared by an agent are ordinarily the property of the principal. But documents prepared by a professional person to assist him or her to do work for a client are the property of the professional person, not the lay client. Speaking of documents which a firm of valuers had prepared in the course of its professional employment MacKinnon LJ said: (*Leicestershire County Council v Michael Faraday & Partners Ltd* [1941] 2 KB 205 at 216, followed in *Chantrey Martin v Martin* [1953] 2 QB 286 at 292–293; *Wentworth v De Montfort* (1988) 15 NSWLR 348 at 352).

If an agent brings into existence certain documents while in the employment of his principal, they are the principal's documents and the principal can claim that the agent should hand them over, but the present case is emphatically not one of principal and agent. It is a case of the relations between a client and a professional man to whom the client resorts for advice. I think it would be entirely wrong to extend to such a relation what may be the legal result of the quite different relation of principal and agent ... [The documents in question] are documents which he has prepared for his own assistance in carrying out his expert work, not documents brought into existence by an agent on behalf of the principal, and, therefore, they cannot be said to be the property of the principal.

The doctor-patient relationship, like that of valuer and client, is not one of agent and principal. Dr Williams' notes were prepared to assist him to fulfil his professional duties. The property in the medical records relating to Ms Breen which he prepared belongs to him; Ms Breen has no proprietary right in respect of those records. The right of ownership of Dr Williams is, statute or contract apart, good against the world and entitles Dr Williams to prevent any person from having access to those records.

Although Dr Cashman conceded that Ms Breen did not own the records, he contended that she had a proprietary right or interest in the documents that entitled her to access them. The premise of this argument was that the records were not owned by anybody. However the idea that an item of personal property that has not been abandoned has no owner is ill-founded. Ownership may be divisible in the sense that one or more of the collection of rights constituting ownership may be detached and vested in a number of persons. Ownership may also be divorced from possession in numerous circumstances. (*Halsbury's Laws of England* (4th ed) Vol 35, par 1128.) But the notion that personal property that has not been abandoned may have no owner is one that is foreign to the common law. Statute or contract apart, medical records, prepared by a doctor, are the property of the doctor. That property right entitles the doctor to refuse other persons access to the records. Dr Cashman's argument based on Ms Breen having a proprietary right or interest in the records must fail.

Was a right of access an implied contractual term?

The doctor-patient relationship is contractual in origin. (*Sidaway v Governors of Bethlem Royal Hospital* [1985] AC 871 at 904.) In general terms, "[a] doctor offers a patient diagnosis, advice and treatment", the objectives of which are the "the prolongation of life, the restoration of the patient to full physical and mental health and the alleviation of pain". (*Ibid* at 903. See also *Rogers v Whitaker* (1992) 175 CLR 479 at 483.) Given the informal nature of the relationship, however, a contract between a doctor and a patient rarely contains many express terms. Because that is so, the courts are obliged to formulate the rights and obligations of the parties to the contract. As Lord Wilberforce has put it, in cases where the parties to a contract have not attempted to spell out all the terms of their contract, the function of the court is "simply ... to establish what the contract is, the parties not having themselves fully stated the terms". (*Liverpool City Council v Irwin* [1977] AC 239 at 254 cited in *Hawkins v Clayton* (1988) 164 CLR 539 at 571.) The Court does so by implying terms in the contract in accordance with established legal principles.

The common law draws a distinction between terms which are implied in fact and terms which are implied by law. Leaving aside terms that are presumed to apply because of the custom of a trade or business, the courts will only imply a term in fact when it is necessary to give efficacy to the contract. A term implied in fact purports to give effect to the presumed intention of the parties to the contract in respect of a matter that they have not mentioned but on which presumably they would have agreed should be part of the contract. A term implied by law on the other hand arises from the nature, type or class of contract in question. Some terms are implied by statutes in contracts of a particular class, for example, money lending and home building contracts. Such terms give effect to social and economic policies which the legislature thinks are necessary to protect or promote the rights of one party to that class of contract. Other terms are implied by the common law because, although originally based on the intentions of parties to specific contracts of particular descriptions, they "became so much a part of the common understanding as to be imported into all transactions of the particular description". (*Byrne v Australian Airlines Ltd* (1995) 69 ALJR 797 at 817.) Many of these terms are implied to prevent "the enjoyment of the rights conferred by the contract [being] rendered nugatory, worthless, or perhaps, ... seriously undermined", the notion of necessity being central to the rationale for such an implication. (*Ibid* at 817 citing *Nullangine Investments Pty Ltd v Western Australian Sub Inc* (1993) 177 CLR 635 at 647–648, 659.) The distinction between terms implied by law and terms implied in fact can tend in practice to "merge imperceptibly into each other".

The argument for Ms Breen started with the premise that, by implication of law, a doctor always contracts with a patient to act in the patient's "best interests". To support this premise, Dr Cashman relied on the following statement of Lord Templeman in *Sidaway v Governors of Bethlem Royal Hospital* ([1985] AC 871 at 904.)

> The doctor, obedient to the high standards set by the medical profession impliedly contracts to act at all times in the best interests of the patient.

From this premise, Dr Cashman argued that, as an incident of the "best interests" term, the doctor must make available medical records concerning a patient when the patient seeks access to them. The leap from the premise to the conclusion is a long one. But we can pass that by.

While the notion of "best interests" is a relevant consideration in some areas of the law, such as the law relating to child welfare, a doctor does not impliedly promise that he or she will always act in the "best interests" of the patient. The primary duty that a doctor owes a patient is the duty "to exercise reasonable care and skill in the provision of professional advice and treatment". (*Rogers* (1992) 175 CLR 479 at 483.) The doctor does not warrant that he or she will act in the patient's best interests or that the treatment will be successful. (See *Greaves v Baynham Meikle* [1975] 1 WLR 1095 at 1100; 3 All ER 99 at 103–104.) If a doctor owed such a duty, he or she would be liable for any act that objectively was not in the best interests of the patient. The doctor would be liable for treatment that went wrong although he or she had acted without negligence. That is not the law of Australia.

There are good reasons why Australian courts do not imply a "best interests" term, as a matter of law, into all doctor-patient contractual relationships. First, "[w]here a term is implied into a contract it will usually embody a contractual promise and therefore create a legal duty". (Carter and Harland '*Contract Law in Australia*' (3rd ed 1996) at p 204.) Such a duty would be inconsistent with the existing contractual and tortious duty to exercise reasonable care and skill in the provision of professional advice and treatment. The existence of a tortious duty of care militates against "the implication of … a general contractual duty of care", (*Hawkins* (1988) 164 CLR 539 at 582–83) particularly where "the incidents of an independent general contractual duty of care would differ from those of an independent tortious duty". (*Ibid* at 583.) Second, the meaning and application of an implied term must be reasonably certain. The notion of "best interests" has been criticised as uncertain in the context of child welfare. (See eg *Secretary, Department of Health and Community Services v JWB and SMB* (*Marion's Case*) (1992) 175 CLR 218 at 270–274.) That criticism is just as pertinent, if not more so, in the context of contract law which places a premium on certainty.

Even if Australian law implied a term in the contract between doctor and patient that the doctor would act in the patient's best interests in the sense that Lord Templeman propounded in *Sidaway*, it would not assist Ms Breen's claim to a right of access to medical records concerning her. Lord Templeman was not asserting that a doctor owed a general duty to act in the best interests of the patient. He used the term in the context of medical advice and treatment. In the paragraph preceding the statement upon which Dr Cashman relies, Lord Templeman had said that "[a] doctor offers a patient diagnosis, advice and treatment". (*Sidaway* (*supra*) at 903.) It was in that context that his Lordship went on to say that the doctor "impliedly contracts to act at all times in the best interests of the patient". (*Ibid* at 904.) The duty was not one applying in respect of all matters arising out of the doctor-patient relationship and subsisting for an indefinite period. Only within the context of "diagnosis, advice and treatment" (*ibid* at 903) was the duty to act in the "best interests" of the patient active. Moreover, "[i]t is difficult to see how a duty to act in the patient's 'best interests' can differ in any substantive way from a doctor's duty to exercise reasonable care in practising the skills of medicine". (Jones, '*Medical Negligence*' (1991) at p 16, fn 9.) In addition, Lord Templeman was not formulating an objective test of "best interests". The whole point of his speech in *Sidaway* was that it was primarily a matter for the doctor to determine what was in the patient's best interests. He said (*Sidaway*, (*supra*) at 905) that

the doctor, bearing in mind the best interests of the patient and bearing in mind the patient's right of information which will enable the patient to make a balanced judgment must decide what information should be given to the patient and in what terms that information should be couched.

For these reasons, the common law did not imply a term in the contract between Dr Williams and Ms Breen that he would always act in her best interests or that she had a right of access to his record of her treatment. So far as advice and treatment were concerned, the only relevant contractual term implied by law was to exercise reasonable care and skill.

Finally, no ground exists for implying a "best interests" term as a matter of fact. The term was not "so obvious that 'it goes without saying'", nor was it "necessary to give business efficacy to the contract". (*Hawkins* (1988) 164 CLR 539 at 571 citing *BP Refinery* (1977) 180 CLR 266 at 283; *The Moorcock* (1889) 14 PD 64 at 68; *Shirlaw v Southern Foundries (1926) Ltd* [1939] 2 KB 206 at 227.)

Accordingly, no implied term of the contract between Ms Breen and Dr Williams entitles her to access to the medical records in his possession.

Is there an innominate common law right of access to medical records?
Dr Cashman relied on the decision of the English Court of Appeal (Nourse, Evans LJJ and Sir Roger Parker) in *R v Mid Glamorgan Family Health Services* ([1995] 1WLR 110; 1 All

ER 356) to assert that there is an "innominate" common law right of access to medical records. The Court of Appeal held in that case that a public health authority had a "duty to administer its property in accordance with its public purposes" (*Mid Glamorgan Family Health Services* [1995] 1 WLR 110 at 116; 1 All ER 356 at 363) and that, as the owner of a patient's medical records, the authority may deny a patient access to his or her records if it is in the best interests of the patient to do so. (*Ibid.*) The Court of Appeal upheld the primary judge's conclusion that an offer to make the records of the plaintiff available to his medical advisers satisfied this duty.

Contrary to the view that we have expressed, Nourse LJ thought that Lord Templeman's speech in *Sidaway* ((*Supra*) at 904) had decided that a doctor had a duty to act at all times in the best interests of the patient and that it was a "general duty". (*Mid Glamorgan Family Health Services* [1995] (*Supra*) at 363.) Nourse LJ went on to say that "[t]hose interests would usually require that a patient's medical records ... should usually, for example, be handed on by one doctor to the next or made available to the patient's legal advisers if they are reasonably required for the purposes of legal proceedings in which he is involved". (*Ibid.*) But, as we have said, we do not think that Lord Templeman intended to lay down so sweeping a duty. In any event, for the reasons that we have given, in Australia no such duty is implied in the contractual relationship between a doctor and patient.

It follows that *Mid Glamorgan Family Health Services* is not an authority that has any persuasive effect in this country.

Does a doctor owe a fiduciary duty to a patient to give the patient access to that person's medical records?

Dr Cashman contends that the doctor-patient relationship is fiduciary in nature and that a doctor who denies a patient reasonable access to medical files concerning that patient is in breach of this fiduciary duty. In our opinion, this submission must be rejected.

Australian courts have consciously refrained from attempting to provide a general test for determining when persons or classes of persons stand in a fiduciary relationship with one another. This is because, as counsel for Dr Williams pointed out, the term "fiduciary relationship" defies definition. In *Hospital Products Ltd v United States Surgical Corporation* ((1984) 156 CLR 41 at 69) Gibbs CJ said:

> I doubt if it is fruitful to attempt to make a general statement of the circumstances in which a fiduciary relationship will be found to exist. Fiduciary relations are of different types, carrying different obligations ... and a test which might seem appropriate to determine whether a fiduciary relationship existed for one purpose might be quite inappropriate for another purpose. For example, the relation of physician and patient, and priest and penitent, may be described as fiduciary when the question is whether there is a presumption of undue influence, but may be less likely to be relevant when an alleged conflict between duty and interest is in question.

As the law stands, the doctor-patient relationship is not an accepted fiduciary relationship in the sense that the relationships of trustee and beneficiary, agent and principal, solicitor and client, employee and employer, director and company and partners are recognised as fiduciary relationships. (*Hospital Products*) (1984) 156 CLR 41 at 97). In *Hospital Products* ((1984) 156 CLR 41 at 97) Mason J pointed out that in all those relationships "the fiduciary acts in a 'representative' character in the exercise of his responsibility". But a doctor is not generally or even primarily a representative of his patient.

However, the categories of fiduciary relationship are not closed. (*Hospital Products*) (1984) 156 CLR 41 at 96) and the courts have identified various circumstances that, if present, point towards, but do not determine, the existence of a fiduciary relationship. These circumstances, which are not exhaustive and may overlap, have included: the existence of a relation of confidence; (*ibid* at 69 citing *Tate v Williamson* (1866) LR 2 Ch App 55 at 61; *Coleman v Myers* [1977] 2 NZLR 225 at 325) inequality of bargaining power; (*Hospital Products* (*supra*) 69–70) an undertaking by one party to perform a task or fulfil a duty in the interests of another party; (*Reading v The King* [1949] 2 KB 232 at 236; *Hospital Products* (*supra*) 96–97) the scope for one party to unilaterally exercise a discretion or power which may affect the rights or interests of another; (*Frame v Smith* (1987) 42 DLR (4th) 81 cited in *LAC Minerals v International Corona Resources* (1989) 61 DLR (4th) 14 at 62–63)and a dependency or vulnerability on the part of one party that causes that party to rely on another. (*Johnson v Buttress* (1936) 56 CLR 113 at 134–135.)

Some aspects of the doctor-patient relationship exhibit characteristics that courts have used to find a fiduciary relationship. For example, from the most mundane consultation with a general practitioner through to the most complicated surgical procedure by a specialist surgeon, a patient is invariably dependent upon the advice and treatment of his or her doctor. Patients also invariably confide intimate personal details about themselves to their doctors.

In some circumstances, the dependency of the patient or the provision of confidential information may make the relationship between a doctor and patient fiduciary in nature. But that does not mean that their relationship would be fiduciary for all purposes. As Mason J pointed out in *Hospital Products*, (1984) 156 CLR 41 at 98), a person may stand in a fiduciary relationship to another for one purpose but not for others.

In *Birtchnell v Equity Trustees, Executors & Agency Co Ltd* ((1929) 42 CLR 384 at 409) Dixon J said that in "considering the operation of [fiduciary principles], it is necessary to [ascertain] the subject matter over which the fiduciary obligations extend". In the present case, if Dr Williams owed a fiduciary duty to Ms Breen, the duties and obligations which arose from their fiduciary relationship could only come from those aspects of the relationship which exhibited the characteristics of trust, confidence and vulnerability that typify the fiduciary relationship. (*Daly v Sydney Stock Exchange Ltd* (1986) 160 CLR 371 at 377.) They could only attach in respect of matters that relate to diagnosis, advice and treatment.

A consideration of the fundamental obligations of a fiduciary shows that Dr Williams owed no fiduciary duty to Ms Breen to give her access to the records that he had created. The law of fiduciary duty rests not so much on morality or conscience as on the acceptance of the implications of the biblical injunction that "[n]o man can serve two masters". Duty and self-interest, like God and Mammon, make inconsistent calls on the faithful. Equity solves the problem in a practical way by insisting that fiduciaries give undivided loyalty to the persons whom they serve. In *Bray v Ford*, ([1896] AC 44 at 51–52) Lord Herschell said:

> It is an inflexible rule of a Court of Equity that a person in a fiduciary position, such as the respondent's, is not, unless otherwise expressly provided, entitled to make a profit; he is not allowed to put himself in a position where his interest and duty conflict. It does not appear to me that this rule is, as has been said, founded upon principles of morality. I regard it rather as based on the consideration that, human nature being what it is, there is danger, in such circumstances, of the person holding a fiduciary position being swayed by interest rather than by duty, and thus prejudicing those whom he was bound to protect. It has, therefore, been deemed expedient to lay down this positive rule.

In the present case, it is impossible to identify any conflict of interest, unauthorised profit or any loss resulting from any breach of duty.

Dr Cashman submitted that Dr Williams had a conflict of interest because in his letter to Ms Breen dated 10 August 1993 he offered to release the records subject to the condition that Ms Breen release him from any legal claims arising out of the treatment. Dr Cashman contended that this condition evidenced Dr Williams' desire to secure "a legal advantage out of the release of the information" which conflicted with his duty to act at all times in the best interests of the patient. Leaving aside the problem of identifying the basis upon which this duty to act at all times in Ms Breen's best interests is grounded, this argument is without substance. If it were correct, it would lead to the anomalous result that no breach of fiduciary relationship would exist if the doctor unconditionally denied a request for reasonable access, but that a breach of fiduciary obligation would exist if the denial was conditional. This is unacceptable. Duty must precede breach. In *Tito v Waddell [No 2]*, ([1977] Ch 106 at 230) Megarry VC pointed out:

> If there is a fiduciary duty, the self-dealing rules about self-dealing apply: but self-dealing does not impose the duty. Equity bases its rules about self-dealing upon some pre-existing fiduciary duty: it is a disregard of this pre-existing duty that subjects the self-dealer to the consequences of the self-dealing rules. I do not think that one can take a person who is subject to no pre-existing fiduciary duty and then say that because he self-deals he is thereupon subjected to a fiduciary duty.

In the present case, there was no breach of fiduciary duty in the conditional denial of access because there was no pre-existing duty on the part of Dr Williams to give access to the records.

It is also impossible to identify any profit that Dr Williams may have derived from the relationship beyond the payment of his authorised professional fees. Nor is the case one where Dr Williams seeks to make or has made a profit from confidential information that he obtained in the course of his relationship with Ms Breen.

The problem of reconciling the alleged fiduciary duty to act in the best interests of Ms Breen with other rights and obligations of Dr Williams and Ms Breen also makes it difficult to see how there could be a fiduciary duty to give access to records relating to her medical treatment. In *Hospital Products*, Mason J explained the relationship of fiduciary obligations and contractual rights and obligations as follows: (*supra* at 97)

> That contractual and fiduciary relationships may co-exist between the same parties has never been doubted. Indeed, the existence of a basic contractual relationship has in many situations provided a foundation for the erection of a fiduciary relationship. In these situations it is the contractual foundation which is all important because it is the contract that regulates the basic rights and liabilities of the parties. The fiduciary relationship, if it is to exist at all, must accommodate itself to the terms of the contract

so that it is consistent with, and conforms to, them. The fiduciary relationship cannot be superimposed upon the contract in such a way as to alter the operation which the contract was intended to have according to its true construction.

The right of access claimed by Ms Breen is not one given by the contract between her and Dr Williams. Nor can it arise from any undertaking, express or implied, by Dr Williams to act as the representative of Ms Breen because no such undertaking was given. Moreover, the contract between the parties gives her no right to or interest in the medical records. They remain the property of Dr Williams. (*Estate of Finkle* (1977) 395 NYS 2d 343 at 344–345.) Furthermore, a fiduciary duty that Dr Williams would *always* act in Ms Breen's best interests, which is the foundation of the claim of a fiduciary obligation to provide access to the records, would conflict with the narrower contractual and tortious duty to exercise reasonable care and skill in the provision of professional advice and treatment that Dr Williams undertook.

In addition, Dr Williams is the owner of the copyright in the records. By federal law, ownership of the copyright gives Dr Williams a number of exclusive proprietary rights including the right to reproduce the records in any material form. He is the beneficial owner of those rights. He does not hold them on trust for Ms Breen. In the absence of an undertaking, express or implied, on the part of Dr Williams to allow her to copy the records, it is difficult to see how Ms Breen could be allowed to copy the records even if she had a right of access to the records.

In our view, there is no basis upon which this Court can hold that Dr Williams owed Ms Breen a fiduciary duty to give her access to the medical records. She seeks to impose fiduciary obligations on a class of relationship which has not traditionally been recognised as fiduciary in nature and which would significantly alter the already existing complex of legal doctrines governing the doctor-patient relationship, particularly in the areas of contract and tort. As Sopinka J remarked in *Norberg v Wynrib*: ((1992) 92 DLR (4th) 449 at 481)

> Fiduciary duties should not be superimposed on these common law duties simply to improve the nature or extent of the remedy.

Dr Cashman relied strongly on the decision of the Supreme Court of Canada in *McInerney v MacDonald* ((1992) 93 DLR (4th) 415) to support his contention that Dr Williams owed Ms Breen a fiduciary duty to give her access to the medical records. In *McInerney*, the Supreme Court held that a doctor owed a fiduciary duty to his or her patient to allow access to medical records, subject to certain conditions. La Forest J, who delivered the judgment of the Court, after holding that the doctor owes a duty to his or her patient "to act with utmost good faith and loyalty", (*ibid* at 423) said: (*ibid* at 424)

> The fiduciary duty to provide access to medical records is ultimately grounded in the nature of the patient's interest in his or her records … [I]nformation about oneself revealed to a doctor acting in a professional capacity remains, in a fundamental sense, one's own. The doctor's position is one of trust and confidence. The information conveyed is held in a fashion somewhat akin to a trust. While the doctor is the owner of the actual record, the information is to be used by the physician for the benefit of the patient. The confiding of the information to the physician for medical purposes gives rise to an expectation that the patient's interest in and control of the information will continue.

Later his Lordship said: (*ibid* at 425)

> The trust-like 'beneficial interest' of the patient in the information indicates that, as a general rule, he or she should have a right of access to the information and that the physician should have a corresponding obligation to provide it. The patient's interest being in the information, it follows that the interest continues when that information is conveyed to another doctor who then becomes subject to the duty to afford the patient access to that information.

However, in this country it is not possible to regard the doctor-patient relationship as one in which the doctor is under a general duty "to act with utmost good faith and loyalty" to the patient. When a medical practitioner undertakes to treat or advise a patient on a medical matter, "[t]he law imposes on a medical practitioner a duty to exercise reasonable care and skill in the provision of professional advice and treatment", (*Rogers* (1992) 175 CLR 479 at 483) not a general duty "to act with the utmost good faith and loyalty".

Secondly, with great respect to La Forest J, it does not help analysis of the legal issues in the present class of case to say that the information "is held in a fashion somewhat akin to a trust" or that there is an expectation that the patient's "control of the information will continue". The information is not property. (*Federal Commissioner of Taxation v United Aircraft Corporation* (1943) 68 CLR 525–535.) Moreover, the only control that a patient has over the information that he or she has given to the doctor is to restrain its improper use. (*W v Egdell* [1990] Ch 359 at 389, 415, 419.) Nor is there any trust of it. Equity does not require the doctor to record, account for or even remember the information. Nor can equity at the suit of the patient prevent the doctor from destroying the records that contain the information. The records are the property of the doctor. He or she may be restrained from using the information in them to make an unauthorised profit or from disclosing that information to unauthorised persons. But otherwise the records are his or hers to save or destroy. The idea that a doctor who shreds the records of treatment of living patients is necessarily in breach of fiduciary duties owed to those patients is untenable.

Furthermore, the judgment of La Forest J does not deal with the fact that the medical records of a patient will often, perhaps usually, contain much more than the information that the patient has given to the doctor. In addition to any observations concerning the patient's condition and notes recording treatment and research, the records may contain comments by the doctor about the personality and conduct of the patient. They may also contain information concerning the patient that the doctor has obtained from other sources. The patient has no rights in relation to or control over any information that has not come from him or her. We can think of no legal principle that would give the patient even a faintly arguable case for access to information in the records that is additional to what the patient has given. If the relationship of doctor and patient was a status-based fiduciary relationship in which the doctor was under a general fiduciary duty in relation to all dealings concerning the patient, the patient might be entitled to access to all the information in his or her medical records. But there is no general fiduciary duty.

La Forest J said that the "fiduciary duty to provide access to medical records is ultimately grounded in the nature of the patient's interest in his or her records". (*McInerney* (1992) 93 DLR (4th) 415 at 424.) However the patient has no legal rights in respect of significant parts of the information contained in medical records. If a patient has a legal right of access to medical records merely because he or she has given personal and confidential information to a doctor, it would seem to follow that journalists, accountants, bank officers and anybody else receiving personal and confidential information always had a fiduciary duty to give access to their records to the person who gave that information.

Thirdly, the Canadian law on fiduciary duties is very different from the law of this country with respect to that subject. One commentator has recently pointed to the "vast differences between Australia and Canada in understanding of the nature of fiduciary obligations". (Parkinson "Fiduciary Law and Access to Medical Records: Breen v Williams" (1995) 17 Sydney Law Review 433 at 439–440.) One significant difference is the tendency of Canadian courts to apply fiduciary principles in an expansive manner so as to supplement tort law and provide a basis for the creation of new forms of civil wrongs. (*Ibid.*) The Canadian cases also reveal a tendency to view fiduciary obligations as both proscriptive and prescriptive. However, Australian courts only recognise proscriptive fiduciary duties. This is not the place to explore the differences between the law of Canada and the law of Australia on this topic. With great respect to the Canadian courts, however, many cases in that jurisdiction pay insufficient regard to the effect that the imposition of fiduciary duties on particular relationships has on the law of negligence, contract, agency, trusts and companies in their application to those relationships. Further, many of the Canadian cases pay insufficient, if any, regard to the fact that the imposition of fiduciary duties often gives rise to proprietary remedies that affect the distribution of assets in bankruptcies and insolvencies.

In this country, fiduciary obligations arise because a person has come under an obligation to act in another's interests. As a result, equity imposes on the fiduciary proscriptive obligations – not to obtain any unauthorised benefit from the relationship and not to be in a position of conflict. If these obligations are breached, the fiduciary must account for any profits and make good any losses arising from the breach. But the law of this country does not otherwise impose positive legal duties on the fiduciary to act in the interests of the person to whom the duty is owed. If there was a general fiduciary duty to act in the best interests of the patient, it would necessarily follow that a doctor has a duty to inform the patient that he or she has breached their contract or has been guilty of negligence in dealings with the patient. That is not the law of this country.

In Australia, therefore, *McInerney* cannot be regarded as a persuasive authority. In this country a court cannot use the law of fiduciary duty to provide relief to Ms Breen which, if granted, would have the effect of imposing a novel, positive obligation on Dr Williams to maintain and furnish medical records to Ms Breen. It follows that Dr Williams does not owe Ms Breen any fiduciary duty to give Ms Breen access to the medical records that relate to his treatment of her.

The "right to know"
Dr Cashman contended that the law in Australia governing the doctor-patient relationship has moved to or is moving towards a recognition of the patient's "right to know" and that this was a reason why the Court should hold that a patient has a right of access to medical records concerning that person. He argued, relying particularly on the decision of this Court

in *Rogers v Whitaker*, (1992) 175 CLR 479.) that this movement is recognisable in the law in five ways: an acceptance of the principle of personal inviolability; a rejection of a paternalistic approach which had been previously accepted; the rejection of the notion that the patient's interests are to be determined by standards exclusively fixed by the medical profession; the imposition of judicially imposed standards; and the acceptance of patient autonomy. Dr Cashman did not contend, however, that this "movement" in the law of itself gave Ms Breen the right of access for which he argued. Rather, he suggested that it advanced the validity of his other arguments.

While recent decisions of Australian courts have rejected the attempt to treat the doctor-patient relationship as basically paternalistic, it would require a quantum leap in legal doctrine to justify the relief for which Dr Cashman contends. *Rogers* took away from the medical profession in this country the right to determine, in proceedings for negligence, what amounts to acceptable medical standards. But the decision also rejected the notion of "the patient's right of self-determination" as providing any real assistance in the "balancing process that is involved in the determination of whether there has been a breach of the duty of disclosure". (*Ibid* at 490.)

Any change in the law must be for Parliament
No doubt there are people in this country who think that a patient should have an unrestricted right of access to medical records that concern that patient. Many others, Ms Breen among them, no doubt think that a patient should have access to such records, subject to limited exceptions. Perhaps only a very small minority of persons in Australia would think that in no circumstances should patients have access to information contained in their medical records. But absent a contractual right, the common law of Australia does not give a patient a right to have access to records, compiled by a medical practitioner, which relate to that patient. Nor, for the reasons that we have given, is it possible for this Court to develop existing principles to create such a right.

Advances in the common law must begin from a baseline of accepted principle and proceed by conventional methods of legal reasoning. Judges have no authority to invent legal doctrine that distorts or does not extend or modify accepted legal rules and principles. Any changes in legal doctrine, brought about by judicial creativity, must "fit" within the body of accepted rules and principles. The judges of Australia cannot, so to speak, "make it up" as they go along. It is a serious constitutional mistake to think that the common law courts have authority to "provide a solvent" (*Tucker v US Department of Commerce* (1992) 958 F 2d 1411 at 1413) for every social, political or economic problem. The role of the common law courts is a far more modest one.

In a democratic society, changes in the law that cannot logically or analogically be related to existing common law rules and principles are the province of the legislature. From time to time it is necessary for the common law courts to re-formulate existing legal rules and principles to take account of changing social conditions. Less frequently, the courts may even reject the continuing operation of an established rule or principle. But such steps can be taken only when it can be seen that the "new" rule or principle that has been created has been derived logically or analogically from other legal principles, rules and institutions.

In the present case, it is not possible, without distorting the basis of accepted legal principles, for this Court to create either an unrestricted right of access to medical records or a right of access, subject to exceptions. If change is to be made, it must be made by the legislature.

Order
The appeal should be dismissed.

Breenan CJ, Dawson and Toohey JJ delivered judgments agreeing. Gummow J also agreed. As regards the 'property' claim, he had this to say:

Gummow J:
Property rights
The appellant also sought to draw support for the right she asserts from a complex of equitable institutions and doctrines dealing with fiduciary duty, confidential information, undue influence, and with unconscientious transactions of the nature considered in such authorities as *Louth v Diprose* ((1992) 175 CLR 621).

To some extent these submissions reflect an imperfect understanding of some basic matters of the law of personal property. Other submissions concern classification as "property" of the information contained in the records in question. As the submissions for the appellant appear to reflect some confusion of thought, it is appropriate, before proceeding further, to draw several basic distinctions.

First, as I understand the submissions, the appellant did not contend before us, and she had not contended before the Court of Appeal, (*Breen v Williams* (1994) 35 NSWLR 522 at 561) that she owned the relevant records "as such". That concession (as the Court of Appeal agreed) (*ibid* at 538, 559–561) was correctly made. The documents in question, including any photographs, are chattels, ownership and the right to exclusive possession of which appear to be enjoyed by the respondent. Access to those records would be an incident of those rights. They would be protected against invasion by the law of tort, in particular by actions for detinue and conversion. Thus, in *Moorhouse v Angus & Robertson (No 1) Pty Ltd*, ([1980] FSR 231 at 239–240) McLelland J held that a cause of action in detinue had been established by an author against his publishers by reason of their failure to comply with his demand for the return of his original manuscript.

Again, in New York, it has been held that the ownership of the medical files of a deceased physician passes to the executor, the property therein having been vested in the physician, not the patients. (*Estate of Finkle* (1977) 395 NYS 2d 343 at 344–345.) Further, a former patient of several hospitals in New York wherein she had been a voluntary patient for treatment for mental illness was held to lack sufficient property interest in medical records relating to her treatment for protection, under the Fourteenth Amendment to the United States Constitution, against deprivation of property without due process of law by reason of refusal of the hospitals to grant her access to the records.(*Gotkin v Miller* (1974) 379 F Supp 859 at 864–868.)

Secondly, the appellant's submissions gave insufficient allowance to the operation in this field of copyright law, a matter of federal statute. The composition by the medical practitioner of the material shown on the records may have involved the authorship by him of what, whilst not of literary quality, were nevertheless literary works for the purposes of copyright law. This would vest in him various exclusive proprietary rights, including that to reproduce the work in a material form. In *Pacific Film Laboratories Pty Ltd v Federal Commissioner of Taxation*, ((1970) 121 CLR 154 at 165–170) Windeyer J referred to the fundamental distinction between copyright as incorporeal property and property in the material thing which is the subject of the copyright, the essence of the former being the power to prevent the making of a reproduction in material form. His Honour referred to authorities, including *In re Dickens* ([1935] Ch 267) This illustrates the distinction. On the proper construction of his will, Charles Dickens bequeathed the manuscript of an unpublished work to his sister-in-law and his residuary estate, including the copyright in the unpublished work, to his children. Ownership of the manuscript would not, of itself, carry with it the right to publish it and to reproduce it.

It is unlikely that the medical practitioner would have made the literary works in pursuance of the terms of his employment by the patient under what was classified as a contract of service, so that the patient was the owner of the copyright (s 35(6)). Ownership of the copyright in any photographs, as artistic works would, pursuant to s 35(5) of the *Copyright Act* 1968 (Cth), vest in the patient only if within the meaning of that provision the patient had made for valuable consideration an agreement for the taking of the photographs and they were taken in pursuance of that agreement.

The copyright of the respondent would not be infringed by anything done for the purposes of a judicial proceeding (s 43(1)). Nor would it be an infringement to act pursuant to a licence or permission (which might be express or implied).

However, the circumstances of the present case, as disclosed in the evidence, do not provide support for the existence of any copyright licence or consent given to the appellant either expressly or by implication. Nor does it appear that such a licence is implied in the contract between medical practitioner and patient as a matter of law in the sense I have described earlier in these reasons.

A further distinction is to be drawn between, on the one hand, property in the physical material on which the records appear, and any literary work which might be represented in the records in question and, on the other hand, a third possible source of juristic rights. This may be sought in the information which might be conveyed to the reader of those records. However, in *Federal Commissioner of Taxation v United Aircraft Corporation*, ((1943) 68 CLR 525 at 534) Latham CJ said:

> Authorities which relate to property in compositions &c, belong to the law of copyright and have no bearing upon the question whether knowledge or information, as such, is property. It is only in a loose metaphorical sense that any knowledge as such can be said to be property.

Those remarks are to be understood in the light of developments, largely since they were made, in equitable jurisdiction. In equity, misuse of confidential information may be restrained. The subject matter is not confined to trade secrets. It extends to information as to the personal affairs and private life of the plaintiff, and in that sense may be protective of privacy. (*Foster v Monntford* (1976) 14 ALR 71; *Stephens v Avery* [1988] Ch 449; *X v Y* [1988] 2 All ER 648.)

That such equitable jurisdiction exists has been accepted on at least two occasions in appeals to this Court. (*Moorgate Tobacco Co Ltd v Phillip Morris Ltd [No 2]* (1984) 156 CLR 414 at 437–438; *Johns v Australian Securities Commission* (1993) 178 CLR 408 at

426–427, 455, 459–460.) Further, the outcome before Mason J in *The Commonwealth v John Fairfax & Sons Ltd* ((1980) 147 CLR 39) illustrates that a claim for copyright infringement and for abuse of confidence made in respect of the one factual matrix may fail as to one and succeed as to the other.

A medical practitioner has been said to be under an obligation in equity not to disclose confidential information concerning a patient which is learned in the course of professional practice, an obligation from which the medical practitioner may be released only with the express or implied consent of the patient. (*W v Egdell* [1990] Ch 359 at 389, 415, 419.) But, in the present case, there is no apprehended breach of an obligation of confidence owed by the respondent to the appellant.

Nor is it acceptable to argue that, because, in some circumstances, the restraint of an apprehended or continued breach of confidence may involve enjoining third parties (as Gaudron J explained in *Johns v Australian Securities Commission*, ((1993) 178 CLR 408 at 460–463) it follows that the plaintiff who asserts an obligation of confidence therefore has proprietary rights in the information in question which in turn found a new species of legal right. In my view there is no substance in what appeared to be the appellant's submission that the existence of an obligation of confidence owed to her by the respondent brought with it a proprietary right which founded her claim to the particular relief she seeks in this litigation.

How, then, would English law approach these questions?

2.   Property

It was conceded in *Breen* that the claimant had no proprietary right over the documents comprising the medical records. On the face of it, this could be the position in England, where a patient's records within the NHS are compiled, in the case of GP records, on Health Authority forms (National Health Service (General Medical Services) Regulations 1992 (SI 1992 No 635), Sch 2, para 36 and *Directions to Health Authorities Concerning the Implementation of Pilot Schemes (Personal Medical Services)*, Sch 1, para 20(1) or, in the case of hospital patients, on forms supplied by the NHS Trust. They are, therefore, the property of the relevant NHS institution.

Nonetheless, in *Breen* three different arguments appear to have been advanced. First, the records were compiled by the doctor as agent and thus were held for the patient as principal. The High Court had no difficulty in rejecting this. The notes were prepared by the doctor for his own use and not as agent. Professional advisers ordinarily are not agents, they held, citing *Leicestershire County Council v Michael Faraday and Partners Ltd* [1941] 2 KB 205. Documents they bring into existence for the purpose of rendering advice belong to them. The notion of agency between doctor and patient is hard to apply in the NHS and the patient will rarely pay for any recorded matter (cf private treatment). Further, the approach seems to work only where the document comes into the hands of the doctor from another and not where it originates with him. It is very difficult to see how title could pass in any documentation from the Health Authority or Trust to the patient if it was initially vested in them. There could be no gift since there would be no delivery to the patient. Also, there would be no contract on which to 'piggy back' the transfer of property. Only if the provider of the document (for example, a consultant providing a report to a GP) intended its title not to vest directly in the recipient or Heath Authority or Trust but in the patient, could the title in the document ever vest in the patient. But this is unlikely in the extreme. In many other professional relationships the cocktail of contract, agency and third party provision of the document, breathes some life into this approach. In the NHS it is effectively moribund where the conventional view will still hold: the Health Authority or Trust retain title to the patient's medical records. Indeed, it is probably the case that even if the doctor were to write the notes on the *patient's paper* that the resulting documents would, in law, belong to the doctor. The resulting documents would be a new thing or *nova species* which, by analogy with the

Roman law of specification (*specificatio*), would belong to the creator who had contributed the work to make the new things: in this context the doctor or more accurately his employer (see B Nicholas *An Introduction to Roman Law* (1962) at 136–138).

Secondly, it was argued that the plaintiff had a right to the information contained in the records, if not to the records themselves. This was rejected as representing a misunderstanding of the law relating to information. It is not property. Rather, equity may prevent disclosure of it to others, thus giving the impression of a property right. But, a protection against disclosure cannot be finessed into a right of access, not least because the doctor's property right is good against all-comers, and as such can serve to deny access. Again, this would be the position of an English court. Thirdly, and somewhat forlornly, it was argued that the records did not in fact belong to anyone. Quite apart from how this could avail the patient, such a proposition does significant damage to the foundations of property law. It was peremptorily dismissed as it would be by an English court.

Thus, the property argument is simply not worth pursuing.

3. Contract

This will, of course, not be relevant with the NHS, since the relationship between doctor (or institutions) and patient is not contractual in nature. If, however, the patient was treated privately a contract would exist. An express term could always provide a patient with a right of access. Perhaps this is likely to be exceptional. Instead, the basis for a right of access will be an implied contractual term. In *Breen* the argument was that there was an implied term in the contract between the patient and her doctor that the doctor should act in her best interests and that this included granting her access to her medical records, not just in the context of the unusual facts of the case, but generally. This was rejected. Terms are implied by law only when necessary for the reasonable or effective operation of a contract: per Deane J in *Hawkins v Clayton* (1988) 164 CLR 539. The implied term argued for did not, the majority held, satisfy this criterion. An additional and somewhat different reason was given by Gaudron and McHugh JJ in their concurring judgment. They rejected the very place in the law of any general duty or the doctor to act in the best interests of the patient. 'While the notion of "best interests" is a relevant consideration in some areas of the law, such as the law relating to child welfare', they stated, 'a doctor does not impliedly promise that he or she will always act in the "best interests" of the patient. The primary duty that a doctor owes a patient is the duty to exercise reasonable care and skill in the provision of professional advice and treatment'. Secondly, a duty to act in a patient's best interests would be inconsistent with the duty in both tort and contract to exercise reasonable care and skill. Thirdly, terms which are to be implied must be reasonably certain as to their meaning. Echoing the High Court's judgment in *Secretary, Department of Health and Community Services v JWB and SMB* (1992) 175 CLR 218, they regarded best interests as far too uncertain in its meaning to be implied into any contract. Finally, they rejected the purported reliance placed by the plaintiff on Lord Templeman's speech in *Sidaway v Governors of Bethlem Royal Hospital* [1985] AC 871 at 904. Put shortly, they stated that Lord Templeman did not mean to say that there was a duty to act in the patient's best interest and if he did, this amounted to no more than saying that the doctor should act with due care and skill.

There is no *general* duty to act in a patient's best interests, can it still be argued that English law would imply such a duty where there is a *contract* between doctor and patient? One of the grounds offered by the High Court for refusing to imply this term is weak. To say that such a term is not 'necessary' for the contract is obviously question begging. If access to information is regarded as a crucial requirement for the proper operation of the doctor-patient relationship, the case for the 'necessity' of implying the term is made out. Instead, English law should not imply the term for the other major reason offered by the High Court: it is potentially inconsistent with the implied duty to act with reasonable care and skill. Further, to imply the term would be to invite claims of breach of contract whenever a doctor's conduct viewed with the benefit of hindsight turned out objectively not to have been in a patient's best interests.

In our view, the *Breen* decision reflects how an English court would approach this issue. We shall return later to the Court of Appeal's decision in *Martin* and its reliance upon Lord Templeman's speech in *Sidaway* to impose a general duty to act in a patient's 'best interests' beyond the law of contract.

4. Fiduciary duty

This formed the basis for Kirby P's dissent when *Breen v Williams* was before the New South Wales Court of Appeal: see (1994) 35 NSWLR 522 and Commentary, (1995) 3 Med L Rev 102 (AG). See also P Parkinson 'Fiduciary Law and Access to Medical Records: *Breen v Williams* (1995) 17 Sydney Law Review 433. It was accepted by a unanimous Supreme Court of Canada in *McInerney v MacDonald* (1992) 93 DLR (4th) 415.

McInerney v MacDonald (1992) 93 DLR (4th) 415 (Can Sup Ct)

La Forest J: The central issue in this case is whether in the absence of legislation a patient is entitled to inspect and obtain copies of his or her medical records upon request.

Facts
The facts are simple. The appellant, Dr Elizabeth McInerney, is a medical doctor who is licensed to practice in New Brunswick. The respondent, Mrs Margaret MacDonald, was her patient. Before her consultations with Dr McInerney, Mrs MacDonald was treated by various physicians over a period of years. On Dr McInerney's advice, Mrs MacDonald ceased taking thyroid pills previously prescribed by other physicians. She then became concerned about her medical care before consulting Dr McInerney, and wrote the latter requesting copies of the contents of her complete medical file. The doctor delivered copies of all notes, memoranda and reports she had prepared herself but refused to produce copies of consultants' reports and records she had received from other physicians, stating that they were the property of those physicians and that it would be unethical for her to release them. She suggested that Mrs MacDonald contact the other physicians for release of their records.

Issues
The appellant raises two issues in this appeal:
1.   Are a patient's medical records prepared by a physician the property of that physician or are they the property of the patient?
2.   If a patient's medical records are the property of the physician who prepares them, does a patient nevertheless have the right to examine and obtain copies of all documents in the physician's medical record, including records that the physician may have received which were prepared by other physicians?

Analysis
...I am prepared to accept that the physician, institution or clinic compiling the medical records owns the physical records. This leaves the remaining issue of whether the patient nevertheless has a right to examine and obtain copies of all documents in the physician's medical records. The majority of the Court of Appeal based the patient's right of access on an implied contractual term. While it may be possible to pursue the contractual route in the civil law system, I do not find it particularly helpful in the common law context. Accordingly, I am not entirely comfortable with the approach taken by the Court of Appeal. However, I do agree that a patient has a vital interest in the information contained in his or her medical records.

Medical records continue to grow in importance as the health care field becomes more and more specialized. As L E Rozovsky and F A Rozovsky put it in The Canadian Law of Patients Records (1984), at pp 73–74:

The twentieth century has seen a vast expansion of the health care services. Rather than relying on one individual, a physician, the patient now looks directly and indirectly to dozens and sometimes hundreds of individuals to provide him with the services he requires. He is cared for not simply by his own physician but by a veritable army of nurses, numerous consulting physicians, technologists and technicians, other allied health personnel and administrative personnel.

While a patient may, in the past, have relied primarily upon one personal physician, the trend now tends to favour referrals to a number of professionals. Each of the pieces of information provided by this 'army' of health care workers joins with the other pieces to form the complete picture. As the number and use of specialists increase, the more difficult it is for the patient to gain access to that picture. If the patient is only entitled to obtain particular information from each health care provider, the number of contacts he or she may be required to make may become enormous. The problem is intensified when one considers the mobility of patients in modern society.

Medical records are also used for an increasing number of purposes. This point is well made by A F Westin, Computers, Health Records and Citizen Rights (1976), at p 27:

> As to medical records, when these were in fact used only by the physician or the hospital, it may have been only curiosity when patients asked to know their contents. But now that medical records are widely shared with health insurance companies, government payers, law enforcement agencies, welfare departments, schools, researchers, credit grantors, and employers, it is often crucial for the patient to know what is being recorded, and to correct inaccuracies that may affect education, career advancement or government benefits.

This then is the general context in which medical records are compiled and the broad purposes they serve in our day. The nature of the information contained in medical records must now be examined.

When a patient approaches a physician for health care, he or she discloses sensitive information concerning personal aspects of his or her life. The patient may also bring into the relationship information relating to work done by other medical professionals. The policy statement of the Canadian Medical Association ... indicates that a physician cannot obtain access to this information without the patient's consent or a court order. Thus, at least in part, medical records include information about the patient revealed by the patient, and information that is acquired and recorded on behalf of the patient. Of primary significance is the fact that the records consist of information that is highly private and personal to the individual. It is information that goes to the personal integrity and autonomy of the patient. As counsel for the respondent put it in oral argument: '[The respondent] wanted access to information on her body, the body of Mrs MacDonald'. In *R v Dyment* [1988] 2 SCR 417, 89 NR 249, 73 Nfld & PEIR 13, 229 APR 13, 45 CCC (3d) 244, at p 429, I noted that such information remains in a fundamental sense one's own, for the individual to communicate or retain as he or she sees fit. Support for this view can be found in *Halls v Mitchell* [1928] SCR 125, at p 136. There Duff J held that professional secrets acquired from a patient by a physician in the course of his or her practice are the patient's secrets and, normally, are under the patient's control. In sum, an individual may decide to make personal information available to others to obtain certain benefits such as medical advice and treatment. Nevertheless, as stated in the Report of the Task Force on Privacy and Computers (1972), at p 14, he or she has a 'basic and continuing interest in what happens to this information, and in controlling access to it'.

A physician begins compiling a medical file when a patient chooses to share intimate details about his or her life in the course of medical consultation. The patient 'entrusts' this personal information to the physician for medical purposes. It is important to keep in mind the nature of the physician-patient relationship within which the information is confided. In *Kenny v Lockwood* [1932] OR 141 (CA), Hodgins JA, stated, at p 155, that the relationship between physician and patient is one in which 'trust and confidence' must be placed in the physician. This statement was referred to with approval by LeBel J in *Henderson v Johnston* [1956] OR 789, who himself characterized the physician-patient relationship as 'fiduciary and confidential', and went on to say, 'It is the same relationship as that which exists in equity between a parent and his child, a man and his wife, an attorney and his client, a confessor and his penitent, and a guardian and his ward' (p 799). Several academic writers have similarly defined the physician-patient relationship as a fiduciary or trust relationship: see for example, E L Picard, Legal Liability of Doctors and Hospitals in Canada (2nd edn 1984), at p 3; A Hopper, The Medical Man's Fiduciary Duty (1973), 7 Law Teacher 73; A J Meagher, P J Marr and R A Meagher, Doctors and Hospitals: Legal Duties (1991), at p 2; M V Ellis, Fiduciary Duties in Canada (1988), at pp 10–11. I agree with this characterization.

In characterizing the physician-patient relationship as 'fiduciary', I would not wish it to be thought that a fixed set of rules and principles apply in all circumstances or to all obligations arising out of the doctor-patient relationship. As I noted in *Canson Enterprises Ltd et al v Boughton & Co* [1991] 3 SCR 534, 131 NR 321, not all fiduciary relationships and not all fiduciary obligations are the same; these are shaped by the demand of the situation. A relationship may properly be described as 'fiduciary' for some purposes, but not for others. That being said, certain duties do arise from the special relationship of trust and confidence between doctor and patient. Among these are the duty of the doctor to act with utmost good faith and loyalty, and to hold information received from or about a patient in confidence. (Picard, supra, at pp 3 and 8; Ellis, supra, at pp 10–11 and 10–12, and Hopper, supra at pp 73–74.) When a patient releases personal information in the context of the doctor-patient relationship, he or she does so with the legitimate expectation that these duties will be respected....

The fiduciary duty to provide access to medical records is ultimately grounded in the nature of the patient's interest in his or her records. As discussed earlier, information about oneself revealed to a doctor acting in a professional capacity remains, in a fundamental sense, one's own. The doctor's position is one of trust and confidence. The information conveyed is held in a fashion somewhat akin to a trust. While the doctor is the owner of the actual record, the information is to be used by the physician for the benefit of the patient. The confiding of the purposes gives rise to an expectation that the patient's interest in and control of the information will continue.

Certain textbooks and case law go further and assert that the patient has a 'proprietary' or 'property' interest in the medical records. For example, Meagher et al supra, write, at p 289:

> In the absence of an agreement, a doctor or hospital owns the records of the patient, but the patient is considered to have a property interest in the medical information contained in the record, with a right of access to it, but not to its possession.

Judicial support for the 'proprietary interest' of the patient can be found in *Re Mitchell and St Michael's Hospital* (1980) 112 DLR (3d) 360 (Ont HC). Although Maloney J there held that he did not have jurisdiction to order the release of hospital records on an originating notice of motion, he had this to say, at 364:

> By virtue of s 11 of the [Public Hospitals Act, RSO 1970, c 378], medical records are 'the property of the hospital and shall be kept in the custody of the administrator', but it seems to me that a patient, or the personal representative of a deceased patient, has something akin to a proprietary interest in the contents of those records and s 11 should in no way operate to prevent appropriate inspection or provision of copies.

A similar sentiment is expressed in the American text by R D Miller, Problems in Hospital Law (4th edn 1983). The author has this to say, at pp 276–277:

> The medical record is an unusual type of property because physically it belongs to the hospital and the hospital must exercise considerable control over access, but the patient and others have an interest in the information in the record. One way of viewing this is that the hospital owns the paper or other material on which the information is recorded, but it is just a custodian of the information. Thus, as stated in *Cannell v Medical and Surgical Clinic*, 21 Ill App 3d 383, 315 NE 2d 278 (1974), the patient and others have a right of access to the information in many circumstances, but they do not have a right to possession of the original records.

I find it unnecessary to reify the patient's interest in his or her medical records and, in particular, I am not inclined to go so far as to say that a doctor is merely a 'custodian' of medical information. The fiduciary duty I have described is sufficient to protect the interest of the patient. The trust-like 'beneficial interest' of the patient in the information indicates that, as a general rule, he or she should have a right of access to the information and that the physician should have a corresponding obligation to provide it. The patient's interest being in the information, it follows that the interest continues when that information is conveyed to another doctor who then becomes subject to the duty to afford the patient access to that information.

There is a further patter that militates in favour of disclosure of patient records. As mentioned earlier, one of the duties arising from the doctor-patient relationship is the duty of the doctor to act with utmost good faith and loyalty. If the patient is denied access to his or her records, it may not be possible for the patient to establish that this duty has been fulfilled. As I see it, it is important that the patient have access to the records for the very purposes for which it is sought to withhold the documents, namely, to ensure the proper functioning of the doctor-patient relationship and to protect the well-being of the patient. If there has been improper conduct in the doctor's dealing with his or her patient, it ought to be revealed. The purpose of keeping the documents secret is to promote the proper functioning of the relationship, not to facilitate improper conduct.

Disclosure is all the more important in our day when individuals are seeking more information about themselves. It serves to reinforce the faith of the individual in his or her treatment. The ability of a doctor to provide effective treatment is closely related to the level of trust in the relationship. A doctor is in a better position to diagnose a medical problem if the patient freely imparts personal information. The duty of confidentiality that arises from the doctor-patient relationship is meant to encourage disclosure of information and communication between doctor and patient. In my view, the trust reposed in the physician by the patient mandates that the flow of information operate both ways. As B Knoppers puts it in Confidentiality and Accessibility of Medical Information: A Comparative Analysis (1982), 12 RDUS 395, at p 431:

> In a relationship often characterized as fiduciary, that is, based on mutual trust and confidence, reciprocity implies an exchange. The personal privacy of the patient which he entrusts to a certain extent to the physician must be met with a corresponding openness and full disclosure.... Personal privacy and access to medical information are not incompatible partners but interchangeable rights.

Robinson J, in *Emmett*, supra, at p 935, note 19, also notes the link between disclosure of medical records and doctor-patient trust: 'The duty of disclosure is a concomitant of the patient's inescapable reliance upon the unadulterated good faith as well as the professional skill of those to whom he has entrusted his treatment.' Rather than undermining the trust inherent in the doctor-patient relationship, access to medical records should enhance it. Indeed, H E Emson observes that the practice of giving patients their own records 'has been said to improve patient understanding, co-operation and compliance'; see The Doctor and the Law: A Practical Guide for the Canadian Physician (2nd edn 1989), at p 214. In this sense, reciprocity of information between the patient and physician is prima facie in the patient's best interests. It strengthens the bond of trust between physician and patient which, in turn, promotes the well-being of the patient.

While patients should, as a general rule, have access to their medical records, this policy need not and, in my mind, should not be pursued blindly. The related duty of confidentiality is not absolute. In *Halls v Mitchell*, supra, at p 136, Duff J stated that, prima facie, the patient has a right to require that professional secrets acquired by the practitioner shall not be divulged. This right is absolute *unless* there is some paramount reason that overrides it. For example, 'there may be cases in which reasons connected with the safety of individuals or the public, physical or moral, would be sufficiently cogent to supersede or qualify the obligations prima facie imposed by the confidential relation'. Similarly, the patient's general right of access to his or her records is not absolute. The patient's interest in his or her records is an equitable interest arising from the physician's fiduciary obligation to disclose the records upon request. As part of the relationship of trust and confidence, the physician must act in the best interest of the patient. If the physician reasonably believes it is not in the patient's best interest to inspect his or her medical records, the physician may consider it necessary to deny access to the information. But the patient is not left at the mercy of this discretion. When called upon, equity will intervene to protect the patient from an improper exercise of the physician's discretion. In other words, the physician has a discretion to deny access, but it is circumscribed. It must be exercised on proper principles and not in an arbitrary fashion. Where a person, in this case a doctor, is under a fiduciary duty to inform another, equity acts in personal to prevent that person from acting in a manner inconsistent with the interests of the person to whom the duty is owed. As stated by Dickson, J (as he then was), in *Guerin v Canada* [1984] 2 SCR 335, 55 NR 161, at p 384:

> ...where by statute, agreement, or perhaps by unilateral understanding, one party has an obligation to act for the benefit of another, and that obligation carries with it a discretionary power, the party thus empowered becomes a fiduciary. Equity will then supervise the relationship by holding him to the fiduciary's strict standard of conduct.

I hasten to add that, just as a relationship may be fiduciary for some purposes and not for others, this characterization of the doctor's obligation as 'fiduciary' and the patient's interest in the records as an 'equitable interest' does not imply a particular remedy. Equity works *in the circumstances* to enforce the duty. This foundation in equity gives the court considerable discretion to refuse access to the records where nondisclosure is appropriate.

In my view, the onus properly lies on the doctor to justify an exception to the general rule of access. Not only is the information in some fundamental sense that of the patient; the doctor has primary access to it. In comparison, the records are unavailable to the patient. To some extent, what the documents contain is a matter of speculation for the patient. Consequently, there is a marked disparity in the ability of each party to prove its case. The burden of proof should fall on the party who is in the best position to obtain the facts.

If a physician objects to the patient's general right of access, he or she must have reasonable grounds for doing so. Although I do not intend to provide an exhaustive analysis of the circumstances in which access to medical records may be denied, some general observations may be useful. I shall make these in a response to a number of arguments that have been advanced by the appellant and in the literature for denying a patient access to medical records. These include: (1) disclosure may facilitate the initiation of unfounded law suits; (2) the medical records may be meaningless; (3) the medical records may be misinterpreted; (4) doctors may respond by keeping less thorough notes; and (5) disclosure of the contents of the records may be harmful to the patient or a third party.

The argument that patients may commence unfounded litigation if they are permitted to examine their medical records is not a sufficient ground for withholding them. The comments of Eberle J in *Strazdins v Orthopaedic & Arthritic Hospital Toronto* (1978) 7 CCLT 117 (Ont HC), at pp 119–120, are helpful in this regard. He states:

>...I believe that it is part of our system of government and of the administration of justice that persons are entitled to start law suits against persons whom they feel have wronged them. The persons who start such actions do so at the risk of costs, the risk of having the action dismissed at some stage if it turns out that it is groundless or even if not groundless turns out to be unsuccessful, and that right of any person to start a law suit does carry with it a correlative obligation on the part of every person in our society; that is, that any one of us may be subject to groundless law suits and it may be that our only weapon to fight them is the penalty in costs … I am not forgetting that if any particular person makes a habit of starting groundless law suits or repetitive lawsuits against a particular person or persons, there are controls which may be exercised to prevent such matters from occurring.

Denial of access may actually *encourage* unfounded law suits. If a law suit is started, a patient can generally obtain access to his or her records under rules of civil procedure relating to discovery of documents. Thus, if a patient strongly wishes to see his or her records, one way of achieving this result is to commence an action *before* ascertaining whether or not there is a valid basis for the action.

The arguments that the records may be meaningless or that they may be misinterpreted do not justify nondisclosure in the ordinary case. If the records are, in fact, meaningless, they will not help the patient but neither will they cause harm. It is always open to the patient to obtain assistance in understanding the file. In the Report of the Commission of Inquiry into the Confidentiality of Health Information (Ontario, 1980) (the 'Krever Report'), vol 2, at p 469, Krever J expressed the opinion that habitual use of jargon or technical terminology is not a sufficiently sound reason for denying a patient access to health records. He did note, however, that a re-evaluation of record keeping methodology may be necessary if a general rule of access is established. If it is possible that the patient will misconstrue the information in the record (for example, misinterpret the relevance of a particular laboratory test), the doctor may wish to advise the patient that the medical record should be explained and interpreted by a competent health-care professional.

The concern that disclosure will lead to a decrease in the completeness, candour and frankness of medical records, can be answered by reference to the obligation of a physician to keep accurate records. A failure to do so may expose the physician to liability for professional misconduct or negligence. It is also easy to exaggerate the importance of this argument. Certainly physicians may become more cautious in what they record, but it cannot be assumed as a natural consequence that this will detrimentally affect the standard of care given to the patient. Generally I doubt that the quality of medical records will be measurably affected by a general rule allowing access to the patient. As Krever J put it in the 'Krever Report', supra, at p 487: 'I say, at once, that I do not believe that any responsible and ethical physician would omit from a medical record any information that, in the interests of proper medical care, belongs in it because of the possibility that the patient may ask to inspect it'.

Nondisclosure may be warranted if there is a real potential for harm either to the patient or to a third party. This is the most persuasive ground for refusing access to medical records. However, even here, the discretion to withhold information would not be exercised readily. Particularly in situations that do not involve the interests of third parties, the court should demand compelling grounds before confirming a decision to deny access. As H Beatty observes in The Consumer's Right of Access to Health Care Records (1986) 3:4 Just Cause 3, at p 3, paternalistic assumptions such as the 'best interests of the patient' may have carried more weight in an area where patients had little education or information with respect to health care and relied upon the trusted family doctor. However, these assumptions 'do not apply today, where consumers typically have brief contacts with many health care providers and institutions, none of which knows the person well enough to determine his or her "best interests"'. Assessing the 'best interests of the patient' is a complex task. Nondisclosure can itself affect the patient's well-being. If access is denied, the patient may speculate as to what is in the records and imagine difficulties greater than those that actually exist. In addition, the physical well-being of the patient must be balanced with the patient's right to self-determination. Both are worthy of protection. In short, patients should have access to their medical records in all but a small number of circumstances. In the ordinary case, these records should be disclosed upon the request of the patient unless there is a significant likelihood of a substantial adverse effect on the physical, mental or emotional health of the patient or harm to a third party.

If a physician refuses a request for access to a patient's medical records, the patient may apply to the court for a remedy. The court will then exercise its superintending jurisdiction and may order access to the records in whole or in part notwithstanding the physician's refusal. Even though the court may ultimately disagree with the physician's view that access should be denied, I have no doubt that in many cases it will be satisfied that the physician acted in good faith in the performance of his or her fiduciary duties. However, if the court is not satisfied that the physician acted in good faith, it should not hesitate to exercise its discretion to grant appropriate relief by way of costs. The general rule of access should not be frustrated by the patient's fear of incurring costs in the pursuit of what is fundamentally his or her right.

Since I have held that the tangible records belong to the physician, the patient is not entitled to the records themselves. Medical records play an important role in helping the physician to remember details about the patient's medical history. The physician must have continued access to the records to provide proper diagnosis and treatment. Such access will be disrupted if the patient is able to remove the records from the premises. Accordingly, the patient is entitled to reasonable access to examine and copy the records, provided the patient pays a legitimate fee for the preparation and reproduction of the information. Access is limited to the information the physician obtained in providing treatment. It does not extend to information arising outside the doctor-patient relationship.

Conclusion

In the absence of regulatory legislation, the patient is entitled, upon request, to inspect and copy all information in the patient's medical file which the physician considered in administering advice or treatment. Considering the equitable base of the patient's entitlement, this general rule of access is subject to the superintending jurisdiction of the court. The onus is on the physician to justify a denial of access. The majority of the Court of Appeal came to essentially the same conclusion, although, as is evident from the above discussion, for different reasons.

In this case, there is no evidence that access to the records would cause harm to the patient or a third party; nor does the appellant offer other compelling reasons for nondisclosure. Accordingly, in my opinion, the lower courts quite properly held that the respondent was entitled to copies of the documentation in her medical chart.

(For discussion, see B Dickens (1994) 73 Canadian Bar Review 234.)

An English court would, however, have to take a significant step in developing the law relating to doctors and patients which would go beyond the mere question of access to records. The court would have to redefine the doctor-patient relationship as being, at least in part, a fiduciary relationship. Though this approach has considerable merit (see *Norberg v Wynrib* (1992) 92 DLR (4th) 449 per McLachlin and L'Heureux-Dubé JJ), it may be that an English court would regard it as too radical a step (see *Sidaway v Governors of Bethlem Royal Hospital* [1984] 1 All ER 1018 (CA) at 1031–1032 per Browne-Wilkinson LJ and [1985] 1 All ER 643 (HL) at 650–651 per Lord Scarman). If the court were able to take this step the Canadian Supreme Court offers two important insights which might serve to reassure the doubters. *First*, La Forest J specifically retains the notion of the 'therapeutic privilege', thereby allowing for the situation in which it would not be in the patient's medical interests to allow access. It will be seen that this is an important feature of the statutory schemes which have been established. *Secondly*, La Forest J examines and demolishes the *in terrorem* arguments advanced by those who would prefer secrecy and thereby exclude the patient's right of access.

Fiduciary duty was, as we have seen, rejected as a basis for access by the Australian High Court in *Breen v Williams*. We have already seen the views of Gaudron and McHugh JJ. Of great interest also is the judgment of Gummow J (*supra* at 805–808) on this point, himself a distinguished equity lawyer.

Gummow J: This is not the case of any improvident transaction between medical practitioner and patient which is the product of unconscientious pressure or influence exerted upon the patient. In *Johnson v Buttress*, (1936) 56 CLR 113 Dixon J said that a physician must justify the receipts of a substantial benefit from the patient, in the same way as must a solicitor in respect of the client and a guardian from the ward. His Honour said (*ibid* at 134) that, where the parties antecedently stood in a relation which gave one an authority or influence over the other from the abuse of which it is proper that there should be protection:

> the party in the position of influence cannot maintain his beneficial title to property of substantial value made over to him by the other as a gift, unless he satisfies the court that he took no advantage of the donor, but that the gift was the independent and well-understood act of a man in a position to exercise a free judgment based on information as full as that of the donee.

What is there said does not directly bear upon the situation with which this appeal is concerned. However, Dixon J went on, in the same passage, to observe that the doctrine which throws upon the recipient the burden of justifying such a transaction rests upon a particular principle. Of that principle, his Honour said: (*ibid* at 134–135)

> It applies whenever one party occupies or assumes towards another a position naturally involving an ascendancy or influence over that other, or a dependence or trust on his part. *One occupying such a position falls under a duty in which fiduciary characteristics may be seen.* It is his duty to use his position of influence in the interest of no one but the man who is governed by his judgment, gives him his dependence and entrusts him with his welfare. (Italics added).

This reasoning was further developed by La Forest J in the following passage from his recent judgment in *Hodgkinson v Simms* ([1994] 3 SCR 377 at 406):

> The concepts of unequal bargaining power and undue influence are also often linked to discussions of the fiduciary principle. Claims based on these causes of action, it is true, will often arise in the context of a professional relationship side by side with claims related to duty of care and fiduciary duty ... Indeed, all three equitable doctrines are designed to protect vulnerable parties in transactions with others. However, whereas undue influence focuses on the sufficiency of consent and unconscionability looks at the reasonableness of a given transaction, *the fiduciary principle monitors the abuse of a loyalty reposed* ... Thus, while the existence of a fiduciary relationship will often give rise to an opportunity for the fiduciary to gain an advantage through undue influence, it is possible for a fiduciary to gain an advantage for him or herself without having to resort to coercion ... Similarly, while the doctrine of unconscionability is triggered by abuse of a pre-existing inequality in bargaining power between the parties, such an inequality is no more a necessary element in a fiduciary relationship than factors such as trust and loyalty are necessary conditions for a claim of unconscionability. (Italics added).

Conformably with the reasoning of Gibbs CJ and Brennan J in *Daly v Sydney Stock Exchange Ltd*, ((1986) 160 CLR 371 at 377, 384–385) the relationship between medical practitioner and patient who seeks skilled and confidential advice and treatment is a fiduciary one. That will be so regardless of whether it is because the relationship between the parties is one which gives the medical practitioner a special opportunity to affect the interests of the patient who is vulnerable to abuse by the fiduciary of his position, or because the medical practitioner undertakes to exercise professional skill for the benefits of the patient, and particular reliance is placed upon the medical practitioner by the patient.

Advice given by the physician to the patient involves specialised knowledge and matters of skill and judgment, which render the advice difficult, if not impossible, of objective and unassisted assessment by the patient. Hence the particular reliance placed upon the physician. In a real sense, especially if invasive procedures upon the person of the patient are involved, the patient has delegated control to the person providing health care. Further, for the patient to obtain the benefit sought from the relationship the patient often must reveal confidential and intimate information of a personal nature to the medical practitioner. Finally, the efforts of the medical practitioner may have a significant impact not merely on the economic but upon the fundamental personal interests of the patient. These considerations, as Professor De Mott has pointed out, serve to emphasise why there is a fiduciary element in the relationship between medical practitioner and patient.

However, to reach that stage of reasoning is not to attain the destination desired by the appellant. First, it is necessary to consider not only whether the relationship between the parties is such as to give rise to fiduciary obligations but also the extent of those obligations in the particular case, "the subject matter over which the fiduciary obligations extend", (*Birtchnell v Equity Trustees, Executors & Agency Co Ltd* (1929) 42 CLR 384 at 409, per Dixon J) so that there may be identified the breach or apprehended breach for which the plaintiff seeks relief from a court of equity. The subject matter here is the provision of medical treatment after, or in the course of, consultation with the patient.

Secondly, the discussion of the principle by Deane J in *Chan v Zacharia* ((1984) 154 CLR 178 at 198–199) identifies the fundamental objection by equity to the pursuit by the fiduciary of personal interest in conflict with the interests of those whom the fiduciary is bound to protect. Likewise, the fiduciary is obliged not to enter upon conflicting engagements to several parties. This is because the fiduciary (for example, a solicitor acting for vendor and purchaser) may be unable to discharge adequately the one obligation without conflicting with the requirement for observance of the other obligation. (*Commonwealth Bank v Smith* (1991) 42 FCR 390 at 391–393; *Haira v Burbery Mortgage Finance & Savings* [1995] 3 NZLR 396 at 404–407.)

As indicated earlier in these reasons, one answer to what otherwise would be breach of duty is the presence of informed consent. Further, a court of equity has inherent jurisdiction or power to authorise, at least in some cases, entry into transactions which otherwise would be in breach of duty. (*In re Drexel Burnham Lambert UK Pension Plan* [1995] 1 WLR 32.)

The fiduciary will be brought into account for any benefit or gain which (1) has been obtained or received in circumstances where a conflict or significant possibility of conflict existed between the fiduciary duty and personal interest in the pursuit or possible receipt of the benefit or gain or (2) was obtained or received by use or by reason of the fiduciary position or opportunity or knowledge resulting from it. (*Chan v Zacharia* (1984) 154 CLR 178 at 199, per Deane J.) Where the breach of duty produces not a gain to the fiduciary but a loss to the party to whom the fiduciary duty was owed, then the judgments of Viscount Haldane LC in *Nocton v Lord Ashburton* ([1914] AC 932 at 956) and of Sir Owen Dixon in *McKenzie v McDonald* ([1927] VLR 134 at 146–148) show that there is an obligation to account for the loss by provision of equitable compensation.

But none of this avails the appellant in the circumstances of the present case. The issue here is not that which would arise, for example, where a medical practitioner had advised the patient to undergo treatment at a particular private hospital in which the medical practitioner had an undisclosed financial interest, or where the medical practitioner prescribed one of a number of equally suitable pharmaceutical drugs for the undisclosed reason that this assisted the practitioner to obtain undisclosed side-benefits from the manufacturer.

In *Moore v Regents of the University of California*, ((1990) 793 P 2d 479 at 484) an appeal was allowed against a decision to allow a demurrer to a cause of action pleaded for breach of fiduciary duty. The plaintiff alleged that his physician, who had treated him for leukaemia, had withdrawn from his body blood, bone marrow and other substances which, unknown to the plaintiff, were of use to the physician and his confederates in establishing a "cell line" in respect of which a patent was obtained. The physician then negotiated agreements for commercial development of the cell line and of products to be derived from it. The court, in deciding that a good cause of action was pleaded, pointed to the conflict between interest and duty involved where the research and commercial interests of the physician might tempt him to order a test or procedure which offered marginal or no benefits to the patient. (*Ibid* at 484.)

In such cases, to adapt the language of La Forest J in *Hodgkinson v Simms*, ([1994] 3 SCR 377 at 406; (1994) 117 DLR (4th) 161 at 174) the fiduciary principle would monitor the abuse of loyalty reposed in the medical practitioner by the patient. The abuse of duty would involve derivation of a benefit or gain by use or by reason of the fiduciary position or of an opportunity or knowledge which resulted from it.

The present is not a case where, unless the respondent accedes to the right asserted against him by the appellant in this proceeding, the respondent will have derived a gain or benefit at the expense of the patient, beyond the agreed fee. Nor will Dr Williams have put himself in a position where his interests conflict with those of the patient. As was pointed out in the Court of Appeal in this case, (*Breen v Williams* (1994) 35 NSWLR 522 at 570, per Meagher JA) to show that a medical practitioner owes fiduciary duties in certain circumstances to the patient is not to demonstrate a right in the patient to inspect and to take copies of the notes and records of the medical practitioner.

In this regard, care is required in translating into fiduciary law in general particular principles developed in the administration of trusts, particularly express trusts constituted by will or settlement. For example, in many such cases of what Lord Browne-Wilkinson has identified as the "traditional trust", (*Target Holdings Ltd v Redferns* [1996] 1 AC 421 at 434) the trustee will stand in a fiduciary relationship to a previously unknown (or unborn) beneficiary. Any element of subjective trust and confidence in the trustee will have been reposed by the testator or settlor, not by the beneficiary. Again, in some species of constructive trust, equity imposes the trust irregardless of any confidence reposed in the trustee.

Where an express trust has been effectively constituted and under its terms the trustee is obliged to manage a trust business, the trustee is required both to observe the terms of the trust and, in doing so, to exercise the same care as an ordinary, prudent person of business would exercise in the conduct of that business were it his or her own. There is a well accepted gloss on, or adjunct to, these requirements in relation to the exercise of powers of investment of a trust fund, pending distribution to those who are or who have become absolutely entitled. (In *Australian Securities Commission v AS Nominees Ltd* (1995) 133 ALR 1 at 12–13.) The Trustee is, of course, a fiduciary. But the above obligations arise from a particular characteristic, not of fiduciary obligations generally, but of the trust. This is the holding of the legal title to property with duties to deal with it for the benefit of charitable purposes or for one or more persons, at least one of whom is not the sole trustee.

Nor do these trustee obligations supply any proper foundations for the imposition upon fiduciaries in general of a quasi-tortious duty to act solely in the best interests of their principals. I agree with the observations of Gaudron and McHugh JJ upon what appears to be a contrary tendency in some of the Canadian decisions. I have expressed earlier in these reasons my view of the use in United States authorities of the phrase "informed consent".

Fiduciary obligations arise (albeit perhaps not exclusively) in various situations where it may be seen that one person is under an obligation to act in the interests of another. Equitable remedies are available where the fiduciary places interest in conflict with duty or derives an unauthorised profit from abuse of duty. It would be to stand established principle on its head to reason that because equity considers the defendant to be a fiduciary, therefore the defendant has a legal obligation to act in the interests of the plaintiff so that failure to fulfil that positive obligation represents a breach of fiduciary duty.

Gummow J's treatment of the fiduciary duty issue is particularly damning of it in this context. For him, unlike the Canadian Supreme Court, it provides protection against abuse through conflict of interest but nothing further. In other words, it imposes 'negative' rather than 'positive' duties (see also *A-G v Blake* [1998] 1 All ER 833 at 843 per Lord Woolf MR: '[Equity] tells the fiduciary what he must not do. It does to tell him what he ought to do').

The merits and de-merits of conceptualising the doctor-patient relationship as one with fiduciary elements has been discussed earlier (see *supra* ch 4). It is a matter, one of the very few, over which the two authors take different views (contrast A Grubb 'The Doctor as Fiduciary' (1994) CLP 311 (in favour) with I Kennedy 'The Fiduciary Relationship and Its Application to Doctors and Patients' in P Birks (ed) *Wrongs and Remedies in the Twenty-First Century* (1996) p 67, where the main battle between us takes place). For the present, at least, it finds no place in English law, although apart from the rather dismissive dicta in *Sidaway* (*supra*), the only judicial authority in the first instance decision in *Martin* (1993) 16 BMLR 81, where Popplewell J rejected *McInerney*, simply stating that it was not in accordance with the decision in *Sidaway* (at 94). The Court of Appeal did not consider the fiduciary argument instead, as we shall shortly see, basing the decision on an altogether different legal foundation.

5.   The 'best interests' of the patient

The Court of Appeal considered whether English law recognised that a patient had a right of access to his medical records in the *Martin* case in 1995. This remains the only relevant English authority.

R v Mid Glamorgan Family Health Services Authority, ex p Martin [1995] 1 All ER 356 (CA)

Between 1966 and 1970 the applicant suffered from psychiatric problems for which he received treatment in hospital. In 1990 the applicant wrote to the respondent health authorities, seeking disclosure of his medical records in order to find out more information about specific incidents which had happened in his past. The records were not on computer and, being made before 1991, were not subject to the Data Protection Act 1984 or to the Access to Health Records Act 1990. On 17 July 1990 the first respondent refused to disclose the medical records, stating that it had no authority to do so. On 5 September the second respondent replied to the applicant, making consideration of such disclosure conditional on an assurance from the applicant that no potential litigation was contemplated by him in respect of his treatment. The applicant refused to give that assurance and stated that he was entitled to see his records as of right. On 2 November the second respondent refused the applicant's request for disclosure on the ground that the responsible consultant psychiatrist was of the view that disclosure of the records to the applicant would be detrimental to him and not in his overall best interests. In 1993 the applicant applied for judicial review of the respondents' decisions. Thereafter the respondents' solicitor wrote to the applicant's legal advisers offering to disclose the records to a medical adviser nominated by the applicant, who would then be in a better position to decide whether and to what extent disclosure could be made to the applicant without causing him harm. The applicant did not accept the offer. The judge refused the application for judicial review, holding that the applicant had no right of access to his medical records at common law. The applicant appealed.

Nourse LJ: The application was heard by Popplewell J on 26 and 27 April 1993, when judgment was reserved until 14 May. In a long and careful judgment the judge dealt with the many points raised on the appellant's behalf. Having referred to the relevant legislation, in particular to the Access to Health Records Act 1990, to guidelines issued by the Department of Health and to authority, including the decisions of the House of Lords in *Sidaway v Bethlem Royal Hospital Governors* [1985] 1 All ER 643, [1985] AC 871 and the Supreme Court of Canada in *McInerney v MacDonald* (1992) 93 DLR (4th) 415, the judge held that the appellant had no right of access to his medical records at common law. He was also of the view that there had been no breach of art 8 of the Convention for the Protection of Human Rights and Fundamental Freedoms (Rome, 4 November 1950; TS 71 (1953); Cmnd 8969), and that in any event that article had no bearing on his decision as to the position at common law.

The judge then considered a secondary and alternative argument which had been advanced on behalf of the respondents. If, contrary to their primary argument, there was some right of access to medical records at common law, it was subject to exceptions in cases, first, where it was necessary to protect an informant and, secondly, where disclosure relied on their solicitor's letter of 24 March 1993 as putting forward a fair and reasonable offer which ought to have been accepted by the appellant.

In regard to this argument, the judge thought that the appellant's position at best must be governed by an exception where there was a risk of injury to his own health or that of others. Having observed that the statutory provisions to which he had referred, including the 1990 Act, contained that sort of exception, he continued:

> Accordingly if I were to take the view (which I do not) that the applicant did have some right of access to his records I would be bound to hold that it was conditional. The respondents have offered sight of the records to an independent person namely the applicant's medical advisers for them to consider whether the information was likely to cause harm to him or anyone else. In those circumstances even if I were to hold that there was such a right of access I would hold that it was subject to that condition. Accordingly in the exercise of my discretion I would not grant the applicant relief because it seems to me that the respondents have offered all that is necessary to comply with what is said to be their duty to the applicant.

Finally, the judge rejected the appellant's arguments based on legitimate expectation, failure to give reasons and a number of subsidiary grounds.

The Access to Health Records Act 1990 which, as the judge observed, came into existence as a result of the decision of the European Court of Human Rights in *Gaskin v UK* (1989) 12 EHRR 36, is expressed by its long title to be an Act 'to establish a right of access to health records by the individuals to whom they relate and other persons'. A prima facie right of access is given by s 3. Section 4 provides for cases where the right may be wholly excluded and s 5 for cases where it may be partially excluded. Section 5(1) provides:

> Access shall not be given under section 3(2) above to any part of a health record – (a) which, in the opinion of the holder of the record, would disclose – (i) information likely to cause serious harm to the physical or mental health of the patient or of any other individual; or (ii) information relating to or provided by an individual, other than the patient, who could be identified from that information; or (b) which was made before the commencement of this Act.

Section 12(2) provided that the Act should come into force on 1 November 1991.

It is thus made clear that the statutory right of access is, in a case such as this, qualified and, further, that it does not apply at all in relation to records made before 1 November 1991. The question which arises in this case is therefore likely to remain a live one for some time to come. But, because it can only be answered in reference to particular facts, I propose to go no further than is necessary for a decision of the present case.

Popplewell J said that the claim was a public law claim and did not depend on any contractual rights. Although both those propositions are correct, a public body, as the owner of medical records, can be in a position no different from that of a private doctor whose relationship with his patient is governed by contract. In other words, a public body, in fulfilment of its duty to administer its property in accordance with its public purposes, is bound to deal with medical records in the same way as a private doctor. In that regard the observations of Lord Templeman in *Sidaway v Bethlem Royal Hospital Governors* [1985] 1 All ER 643 at 665–666, [1985] AC 871 at 904 are pertinent:

> I do not subscribe to the theory that the patient is entitled to know everything or to the theory that the doctor is entitled to decide everything. The relationship between doctor and patient is contractual in origin, the doctor performing services in consideration for fees payable by the patient. The doctor, obedient to the high standards set by the medical profession, impliedly contracts to act at all times in the best interests of the patient. No doctor in his senses would impliedly contract at the same time to give to the patient all the information available to the doctor as a result of the doctor's training and experience and as a result of the doctor's diagnosis of the patient. An obligation to give a patient all the information available to the doctor would often be inconsistent with the doctor's contractual obligation to have regard to the patient's best interests. Some information might confuse, other information might alarm a particular patient. Whenever the occasion arises for the doctor to tell the patient the results of the doctor's diagnosis, the possible methods of treatment, the doctor must decide in the light of his training and experience and in the light of his knowledge of the patient what should be said and how it should be said.

These observations provide a sensible basis for holding that a doctor, likewise a health authority, as the owner of a patient's medical records, may deny the patient access to them if it is in his best interests to do so, for example if their disclosure would be detrimental to his health. In the light of the offer made in the respondent's solicitor's letter of 24 March 1993, that is a complete answer to the appellant's application. I agree with Popplewell J that the respondents have offered all that is necessary to comply with their duty to the appellant. The judge was entitled, in the exercise of his discretion, to refuse the appellant the relief that he sought and I would affirm his decision on that ground. Although the respondents have not taken this point, it might also, as a matter of discretion, have been affirmed on the ground that the appellant did nothing effective to pursue his rights against either of the respondents between 1981 and 1990.

It is inherent in the views above expressed that I do not accept that a health authority, any more than a private doctor, has an absolute right to deal with medical records in any way that it chooses. As Lord Templeman makes clear, the doctor's general duty, likewise the health authority's, is to act at all times in the best interests of the patient. Those interests would usually require that a patient's medical records should not be disclosed to third parties; conversely, that they should usually, for example, be handed on by one doctor to the next or made available to the patient's legal advisers if they are reasonably required for the purposes of legal proceedings in which he is involved. The respondents' position seems to be that no practical difficulty could arise in such circumstances, but that they would act voluntarily and not because they were under a legal duty to do so. If it ever became necessary for the legal position to be tested, it is inconceivable that this extreme position would be vindicated.

On all the other points taken by the appellant I agree with Popplewell J. I would dismiss this appeal.

Evans LJ: Like Nourse LJ, I do not consider that the fact that these are public law proceedings alters the nature of the central issue, which is the extent of the appellant's common law rights and of the respondents' correlative duties to provide access. Like him also, I consider that the essential issue is whether they are entitled to deny access on the ground that their disclosure would be harmful to him.

The statutory right under the 1990 Act is qualified in this way. Section 5(1) reads:

> Access shall not be given ... to any part of a health record – (a) which, in the opinion of the holder of the record, would disclose – (i)information likely to cause serious harm to the physical or mental health of the patient or of any other individual ...

Mr Allen submits that this restriction forms no part of the common law. He relied upon the fundamental right of self-determination which is expressed in art 8(1) of the Convention for the Protection of Human Rights and Fundamental Freedoms (Rome, 4 November 1950; TS 71 (1953); Cmnd 8969), as follows: 'Everyone has the right to respect for his private and family life, his home and his correspondence ...', and which is recognised, as he submits, by common law decisions, including *Sidaway v Bethlem Royal Hospital Governors* [1985] 1 All ER 643, [1985] AC 871 regarding the patient's right to know sufficient of the relevant facts to enable him to make his own decision about medical treatment, and *Re C (adult: refusal of medical treatment)* [1994] 1 All ER 819, [1994] 1 WLR 290 demonstrates, he submits, that the right of self-determination now outweighs the public interest in the sanctity of life.

Therefore, the applicant is entitled to decide for himself whether or not to incur whatever risk of damage to his mental or physical health might accompany the disclosure of the records to him.

Mr Allen's reliance upon art 8 of the convention and on the decision of the European Court of Human Rights in *Gaskin v UK* (1990) 12 EHRR 36 does not involve any contention that the convention forms part of English law or that its provisions are directly enforceable here. Rather, he adopts the approach described in Sir John Laws' lecture to the Administrative Law Bar Association, 'Is the High Court the Guardian of Fundamental Constitutional Rights?' [1993] Public Law 59. The fact that the convention does not form part of English law does not mean that its provisions cannot be referred to and relied upon as persuasive authority as to what the common law is, or should be. Article 8 therefore reflects the right of self-determination which now, he submits, forms part of the common law.

For my part, I am prepared unreservedly to adopt this approach but I hope that it is not unduly insular, or even parochial, to remind oneself at the outset that the object of the inquiry is to establish the relevant rules of the common law. That inquiry in the present case reduces itself to the question whether the common law right of access, if there is one, is qualified in the same way as the statutory right now enacted is qualified by s 5(1)(a).

In my judgment, there is no good reason for doubting either that a right of access does exist or that it is qualified to that extent at least. The record is made for two purposes which are relevant here: first, to provide part of the medical history of the patient, for the benefit of the same doctor or his successors in the future; and secondly, to provide a record of diagnosis and treatment in case of future inquiry or dispute. Those purposes would be frustrated if there was no duty to disclose the records to medical advisers or to the patient himself, or his legal advisers, if they were required in connection with a later claim. Nor can the duty to disclose for medical purposes be limited, in my judgment, to future medical advisers. There could well be a case where the patient called for them in order to be able to give them to a future doctor as yet unidentified, eg in case of accident whilst travelling abroad.

But the present case is not one where the records are required for medical purposes, or in connection with any dispute or projected litigation. Both are expressly disavowed. The applicant wishes to have a greater knowledge of his 'childhood, development and history' (see *Gaskin v UK* (1989) 12 EHRR 36) and he seeks disclosure for this reason alone.

The respondents' solicitor's letter of 24 March 1993 offers to produce the records to a medical adviser who can assess their likely effect upon the mental or physical health of the applicant. It is more than 20 years since he was a patient of any doctor whose records they hold, and so they cannot assess this for themselves. The assessment can only be carried out by a medical adviser with knowledge of his present-day condition. To release the records to the applicant himself, when there are grounds for supposing that they might cause harm to his physical or mental health, would be to risk causing or aggravating the kind of injury which previously they undertook to prevent or cure. These are valid reasons, in my judgment, for holding that any common law right of access is limited to this extent.

Sir Roger Parker agreed.

Where does this leave English law? There are *three* issues to consider: (1) is there a 'right' of access? (2) the basis of the 'right' of access; and (3) the application of 'best interests'.

(a) A right of access?

The Court of Appeal dismissed the patient's appeal in this case. However, in doing so the court rejected Popplewell J's view that a patient does not have a right of access to his medical records (see (1993) 16 BMLR 81 and commentary (1993) 1 Med L Rev 378 (IK)). At least, this seems the most plausible reading of the case. Certainly, Evans LJ (and Sir Roger Parker) asserted a patient's right of access (and the doctor's correlative duty to disclose). Nourse LJ appeared to assume the existence of the right. He did, however, say *ex cathedra* that: '[i]f it ever became necessary for the legal position to be tested, it is inconceivable that this extreme position (ie that there was never a legal duty to disclose) would be vindicated.' He preferred to base his decision on the narrower ground that the patient's right was qualified by the fact that disclosure to him (though not his medical advisors) might be detrimental to his health. Hence, the Health Authorities' offers to disclose the records to the patient's medical advisors were sufficient for their action to be lawful. Of course, ultimately both Evans LJ and

Sir Roger Parker decided the case on the same basis. So, at least in principle, the Court of Appeal has rejected Popplewell J's categorically stated view that at common law a patient could not ever require disclosure to him of his medical records. The Court of Appeal rightly made no mention of the untenable argument advanced by Popplewell J that to grant a right of access to medical records would be inconsistent with the doctor's copyright in the records.

(b) The basis of the 'right'

The medical records at issue in *Martin* were written, hence the access provisions of the Data Protection Act 1984 were inapplicable. Equally the records were made before 1 November 1991 and so the Access to Health Records Act 1990 could not be prayed in aid by the patient. In *Martin* the right was founded in a doctor's duty to act in a patient's 'best interests'. As Nourse LJ put it:

> the doctor's general duty, likewise the health authority's, is to act at all times in the best interests of the patient. Those interests would usually require that a patient's medical records should not be disclosed to third parties: conversely, that they should usually, for example, be handed on by one doctor to the next or made available to the patient's legal advisers if they are reasonably required for the purposes of legal proceedings in which he is involved.

Perhaps the view of Nourse LJ is axiomatic: a patient's 'best interests' do require disclosure to him or others on his behalf in general and, of course, we are very familiar with the language of 'best interests' and a doctor's (though less commonly a Health Authority's) duty to further those interests. But there is a problem here. What happens if a patient wishes to enforce his duty, what is the nature of his cause of action? It should be in contract, on the basis of an implied term, but that would be restricted to private medicine. What if, as in *Martin*, the patient is treated within the NHS? The only basis offered by the judges in *Martin* for such a duty was the speech of Lord Templeman in *Sidaway v Governors of the Bethlem Royal Hospital* [1985] AC 871 (HL). Lord Templeman's speech is widely considered to be the most esoteric of those delivered in the *Sidaway* case and his reliance there on the law of contract is quite out of place when considering an NHS patient. But there is an even greater problem. *Sidaway* was a case in which the plaintiff sued in the tort of negligence claiming that the defendant had failed to disclose an inherent risk of injury to the procedure she had consented to. Even if 'best interests' can be said to be a 'fleshing out' of the doctor's duty of *care* in negligence – and this is doubtful (see A Grubb 'The Doctor as Fiduciary' (1994) CLP 1311), it does not help in cases like *Martin*. The patient could not possibly allege that the defendants were in breach of a duty of care to him. To start with, non-disclosure would (at least at the time) be quite consistent with professional practice. Consequently, applying the *Bolam* test, there would be no breach of duty. More importantly, the patient could not establish any harm recognised by the tort of negligence. Indeed, this would usually form no part of the gist of a claim for access by a patient and in *Martin* itself could not possibly have done so given the view that *disclosure* to him might harm him. Of course, a duty derived from the tort of negligence might explain odd cases where a failure to communicate, say by one doctor with another, resulted in harm to the patient (eg *Coles v Reading and District HMC* (1963) 107 Sol Jo 115 (Sachs J), cf *Chapman v Rix* (1960) Times, 22 December (HL)). And, in fact, both Evans LJ and Sir Roger Parker gave, by way of example, just such a case.

In *Breen v Williams* (*supra*) the judges in the Australian High Court were particularly scathing about the jurisprudential basis of *Martin*. Dawson and Toohey JJ remarked that Nourse LJ 'identified no legal source for a right of access' (at 785). Gaudron and McHugh JJ stated that *Martin* 'is not an authority that has any persuasive effect in [Australia], (at 790). Gummow J stated it did not provide 'any adequate foundation for the existence of the particular common law right' of access (at 804).

There is no doubt that the basis of the duty to act in the patient's best interests is remarkably unclear. You will recall the devastating criticism of it by Gaudron and McHugh JJ in *Breen* earlier (*supra*, p 996). It is inconsistent with the usual tortuous (or contractual) duty to exercise reasonable care and skill. Its scope beyond access to record cases is wholly unclear and uncertain.

Of course, the Court of Appeal in *Martin* did not assert a general duty to act in a patient's 'best interests' although Lord Templeman's speech in *Sidaway* did. Nourse LJ stated (at 363).

> a public body, as the owner of medical records, can be in a position no different from that of a private doctor whose relationship with his patient is governed by contract. In other word, a public body, in fulfilment of its duty to administer its property in accordance with its public purposes, is bound to deal with medical records in the same way as a private doctor.

The patient's 'right' arises from the NHS institution's duty. Sir Roger Parker spoke in similar terms (at 366), though his example of a limitation on use due to the law of confidence is a misconception. It confuses the record (property) with the information (not property) contained within it. By contrast, Evans LJ seemed to start from the patient's right (he referred to art 8 of the European Convention of Human Rights) and then proceeds to impose a correlative duty on the NHS institution.

The approach of the majority (if it should be called that) is curious. It is couched in terms of a 'public duty' and hence, presumably, why the patient was entitled to challenge by way of judicial review under RSC Ord 53. However, the context of the public duty is stated to be that found in the private law relationship of doctor and patient, namely to act in the patient's best interests *à la* Templeman. It is, of course, unusual to say the least, that a property owner should be required to deal with his property for the benefit ('best interests') of another without an explicit contractual undertaking. It is more likely in the context of property vested in a public body who may be required to forego some of the property privileges of the private owner because of its statutory duties (see eg *British Airports Authority v Ashton* [1983] 3 All ER 6 per Mann J at 14 and *R v Somerset County Council, ex p Fewings* [1995] 3 All ER 20). Here, however, the statutory context creates the potential for *greater* limitations rather than, as in *Martin*, reading in a (questionable) ordinary incidents of ownership by private individuals (see generally, J Harris *Property and Justice* (1996)).

In the result, the defendants' duty seems to be, in truth, a private law obligation, masquerading as a public law one.

(c) Applying 'best interests'

There is nothing wrong in principle, or unexpected, in *Martin* in the court recognising that access to medical records cannot be absolute. The (then) legislation on access to manual records (Access to Health Records Act 1990, s 5 (1)(a)) and electronically stored records (Data Protection (Subject Access Modifications) (Health) Order 1987 (SI 1987, No 1903), Art 4(2)(a)) encapsulated exceptions to access where there is a likelihood of serious harm to the physical or mental health of the patient. Access under the Data Protection Act 1998 is similarly limited (see *infra*, p 1023-1024). The issue is whether a generalised exception based upon 'best interests' reflects this fairly stringent exception or goes wider where the risk is not so serious in quantity or quality and even justifies non-disclosure where *harm* to the patient is not the issue.

On the facts of *Martin*, all three judges in the Court of Appeal (as did Popplewell J at first instance) refused the patient access because he had been offered disclosure to his medical adviser. Only he could assess whether disclosure to the patient 'might cause harm to his physical or mental health' (per Evans LJ). Thus, it was not in his 'best interests' that, at least at this stage, he should obtain access to his records.

The facts of *Martin* may well fall short of such an exceptional case. At least, there must be a doubt given the terms of the correspondence between the parties referred to in the judgments. Certainly, the initial concerns of the consultant psychiatrist seem to be as much directed to the 'duty to protect retired colleagues' (see letter of 15 October 1990) as protecting the patient from harm. The former concerns would not justify non-disclosure under the 1984 and 1990 Acts nor would they be consistent with the doctor's duty to act only in the patient's 'best interests'. Remarkably, the reluctance to disclose seems to have been based, in part, on the patient's refusal to give an undertaking that he was not contemplating litigation against his doctor. Not only would the possibility of litigation not justify non-disclosure, it would actually warrant it since, if – which is likely – a claim for 'personal injury' was being contemplated, the patient would have been entitled to pre-action disclosure under s 33 of the Supreme Court Act 1981 and RCS Ord 24, r 7A. On this basis, the patient's error was, at worst, to use the wrong form of words when seeking disclosure. The Court of Appeal in *Martin*, perhaps too readily, accepted that non-disclosure was justified either out of a concern for the patient and most certainly for anyone else.

The application of the law to the facts in *Martin* has been criticised.

Dermot Feenan 'Common Law Access to Medical Records' (1996) 59 MLR 101

The framing of the exception in terms only of detriment to the patient seems insufficient protection of a patient's interests in personal health information. The sufficiency of the exception may be tested by reference to analogous law, comprising persuasive Commonwealth and American dicta and British legislation. In the leading American authority on informed consent, *Canterbury v Spence*, (464 F 2d 772 (1972)) the court held that a doctor is not obliged to disclose where disclosure

> poses *such a threat of detriment* to the patient as to become unfeasible or contraindicated from a medical point of view. It is recognised that patients may become *so emotionally distraught* on disclosure as to *foreclose a rational decision*, or complicate or hinder the treatment, or perhaps even pose psychological damage to the patient. Where that is so, the cases have generally held that the physician is armed with a privilege to keep the information from the patient, and we think it clear that *portents of that type* may justify the physician in action he deems medically warranted. (*Ibid* at 788–9).

Here, harm alone was insufficient. There had to be harm of the type envisaged by the court. Similarly, in the South Australian Supreme Court, King CJ approved his dictum in a previous case to the effect that a doctor is justified in withholding information 'when he judges *on reasonable grounds* that the patient's health, physical or mental, might be *seriously* harmed by the information.' (*Battersby v Tottman* (1985) 37 SASR 524.) Here, the grant court imposes two qualifications on the prospect of harm. First, that there must be reasonable grounds for establishing such a prospect, and, second, that the harm must be serious.

It is easy to understand why these courts require more than simply the doctor's view of potential detriment. There appears to be an implicit acknowledgement by them of the danger of paternalistic bias by the doctor regarding information disclosure. Aside from judicial precedent, mounting empirical evidence undermines doctors' assertions designed to restrict or obstruct information disclosure on the basis that patients would be unable to deal with harmful information. IN 1982 the United States President's Commission for the Study of Ethical Problems in Medicine and Biomedical and Behavioral Research stated: '[d]espite all the anecdotes about patients who committed suicide, suffered heart attacks, or plunged into prolonged depression upon being told "bad news", little documentation exists for claims that informing patients is more dangerous to their health than not informing them, particularly when the informing is done in a sensitive and tactful fashion.' (Presidents Commission for the Study of Ethical Problems in Medical and Biomedical & Behavioral Research 'Making Health Care Decisions' Washington DC: US Govt Printing Office, 1982) Similar findings exist in relation to medical records. It is also acknowledged that unless the exception is carefully circumscribed it may swallow up the primary principle of information disclosure. (*Canterbury, supra.*) Arguably, similar considerations apply to access to medical records.

The exception in *Martin* also falls short of similar policy encapsulated in British freedom of information legislation. In the Access to Health Records Act 1990, which gives a statutory right of access to health records, section 5(1)(a) provides that access shall not be given where in the opinion of the holder of the record ... information is '*likely* to cause *serious harm* to the physical or mental health of the patient ...' (*Martin* (*supra*) per Evans LJ at 119.) This section makes clear the gravity of harm and its likelihood. These criteria reflect the fact that the purpose of the legislation, which was to establish a right of access to health records, was not to be circumscribed too easily. Identical wording, and similar policy consideration, are found in the relevant legislative provisions exempting disclosure made under the Data Protection Act 1984 and in the Access to Medical Reports Act 1988.

It seems that the Court of Appeal in *Martin* simply accepted the opinion of the consultant psychiatrist and, thence, respondents' solicitors, that disclosure would be detrimental to the patient. As the above common law dicta and legislation show, detriment alone ought to be insufficient. Since it is plausible that this issue may arise again before courts in England and Wales – most likely in the judicially unadjudicated context of therapeutic privilege – it seems that it would be appropriate to require that a doctor bears the onus of justifying non-disclosure on the basis that such disclosure would be likely to cause serious harm to the patient and that such harm could not reasonably be prevented through counselling with the patient.

(See further J Davies 'Patients' Rights of Access to their Health Records' (1996) 2 Medical Law International 189.)

6. As a human right

You will notice the reference in the judgments in *Martin* to art 8 of the European Convention of Human Rights. Article 8(1) states that 'Everyone has the right to respect for his private life'. There is no doubt, following the decision of the European Court of Human Rights in *Gaskin v UK* (1990) 12 EHRR 36, that this includes personal information relating to an individual's health. The Court of Appeal in *Martin* did not find it necessary to rely upon art 8 but concluded that the common law was consistent with the applicant's art 8 right. As a result of s 6(1) of the Human Rights Act 1998, any decision by a public body, including an NHS institution, whether to grant a patient access to his medical records would have to accord with art 8 of the Convention. It would also be relevant in interpreting the statutory provisions for access which we shall see later in this chapter (Human Rights Act 1998, s 3(1)). *Gaskin* itself concerned access by a person to his social services files, which contained information provided in confidence. However, access was denied unless the provider of the information had given consent to the disclosure. The ECt HR accepted that art 8(1) applied and had been breached because there was no system for independently reviewing whether access should be granted even in the absence of consent. The court stated as follows (at 50):

Gaskin v United Kingdom (1989) 12 EHRR 36 (ECt HR)

In the Court's opinion, persons in the situation of the applicant have a vital interest, protected by the Convention, in receiving the information necessary to know and to understand their childhood and early development. On the other hand, it must be borne in mind that confidentiality of public records is of importance for receiving objective and reliable information, and that such confidentiality can also be necessary for the protection of third persons. Under the latter aspect, a system like the British one, which makes access to records dependent on the consent of the contributor, can in principle be considered to be compatible with the obligations under Article 8, taking into account the State's margin of appreciation. The Court considers, however, that under such a system the interests of the individual seeking access to records relating to his private and family life must be secured when a contributor to the records either is not available or improperly refuses consent. Such a system is only in conformity with the principle of proportionality if it provides that an independent authority finally decides whether access has to be granted in cases where a contributor fails to answer or withholds consent. No such procedure was available to the applicant in the present case.

Accordingly the procedures followed failed to secure respect for Mr Gaskin's private and family life as required by Article 8 of the Convention. There has therefore been a breach of that provision.

Notice the court concluded that art 8(1) had been breached, as the UK system did not provide 'respect' for the applicant's right. The justificatory provisions of art 8(2) were not relied upon. This may be relevant in the future, for example, in relation to access to the identity of donors by children born as a result of the donation of gametes or embryos (see *infra*, ch 10).

The Court of Appeal in *Martin* may have eschewed the language of 'rights' – with the exception of Evan LJ – preferring to couch the debate in terms of the duty owed to the patient. Nevertheless, because of art 8(1) and its incorporation, the substance of the argument in any future common law case would coalesce around art 8 and, in particular, whether denial of access could be justified under art 8(2). Article 8(2) provides as follows:

8(2) There shall be no interference by a public authority with the exercise of this right except such as is in accordance with the law and is necessary in a democratic society in the interests of national security, public safety or the economic well-being of the country, for the prevention of disorder or crime, for the protection of health or morals, or for the protection of the rights and freedoms of others.

The issues here would, therefore, be whether denial of access was: (1) in accordance with the law; (2) for a legitimate purpose, ie public safety, for the prevention of crime, for the protection of health or morals or for the protection of the rights and freedoms of others; and (3) necessary, in a democratic society, ie proportional 'a pressing social need' to further that legitimate aim (see ch 1, *supra*).

Providing there is the appropriate review mechanism, it seems likely that denial of access in circumstances such as *Martin* would comply with art 8(2), at least to the extent that there was a serious risk of mental or physical injury to the patient or others if disclosure occurred. This was the view of Popplewell J at first instance in *Martin* ((1993) 16 BMLR 81 at 97) and of the Government in enacting the Access to Health Records Act 1990 (s 5(1)(a)) in the wake of *Gaskin*. The risk would, however, have to be real, demonstrable by medical evidence, and the decision to deny access being taken balancing the danger against the patient's 'right of access'.

The latter approach will also apply where the denial of access is based upon concerns for the confidential nature of any information provided by a third party and contained in the patient's records. In *Gaskin*, the ECHR did not decide that such third party interests could never justify an infringement of art 8(1). Rather, the court held that a system of independent review was necessary in such cases. On the substantive issue, it seems unlikely that a third party's interest in confidentiality *alone* could justify a denial of access. It would, of course, be different if disclosure would create a danger to that third party. However, each case must depend upon a balancing exercise and the greater the interference with the third party, the more likely a breach of art 8(1) could be justified. So, for example, where the third party was a professional who provided information upon the patient, denial of access would be impossible to justify under the Convention. By contrast, where the information identified an informant of child abuse perpetrated against the patient or identified the donor of gametes used to produce the child, there would be stronger grounds for a court to see denial of access as 'proportionate' or fulfilling a 'pressing social need' to further a legitimate aim under art 8(2) of the Convention.

B. STATUTORY PROVISIONS

1. In the course of litigation

Parties to litigation are required to give disclosure and inspection of all relevant documentation to the litigation (CPR Rule 31). Since 1970, it has been possible for a patient to obtain disclosure of his medical records where a medical negligence action is likely against the party holding the records. Equally, since that time, it has been possible to obtain medical records, relevant to the action, against a third party (eg, a GP) once the litigation has been commenced against another, for example, a hospital Trust. The provisions relating to pre-action disclosure and 'third party disclosure' are now contained in ss 33 and 34 of the Supreme Court Act 1981. They are discussed in the following extract.

Margaret Brazier *Medicine, Patients and the Law* (2nd edn, 1992)

When considering whether he has a claim in respect of negligence and whom he should sue, the patient and his legal advisers will clearly benefit by gaining access to the patient's notes, reports and X-ray and other test records. Disclosure of records benefits the public interest too. A claim may be seen to be fruitless or a particular individual exonerated. Money and effort will be saved. Before 1970 the patient usually had to go ahead in the dark and ask at the trial for a subpoena ordering the health authority and the doctor to produce their records. Legislation in 1970 introduced a right to pre-trial access to records. [Administration of Justice Act 1970, ss 32–35 (the legislation was based on recommendations of the Winn Committee, Cmnd 3691 (1968).] That original legislation has now been replaced by the Supreme Court Act 1981.

The effect of section 33 of the 1981 Act is this. A patient may apply for a court order requiring the doctor or the authority whom he plans to sue to disclose any records or notes likely to be relevant in forthcoming proceedings. Section 34 goes further. The court may order a person *not* a party to proceedings to produce relevant documents. So if the patient has started proceedings against the doctor but believes that the hospital authority or clinic holds notes of value to his claim, the authority or clinic can be made to hand over the notes. This will help the private patient in a dilemma as to whether he should properly proceed against doctor or hospital. And it may of course lead to the hospital being brought into the proceedings.

Once legislation compelling disclosure of documents was enacted, hospitals and medical defence organizations reluctantly became prepared to hand over documents voluntarily. They feared a spate of fishing expeditions by aggrieved patients. But they preferred to disclose records to the patient's medical adviser alone, and not to the patient or his lawyers. Indeed, they sought to argue that this was the limit of their obligation. The House of Lords disagreed. [*McIvor v Southern Health and Social Services Board*, Northern Ireland [1978] 2 All ER 625.] Under the 1970 statute, they said, the patient himself was entitled to see the documents produced. Pleas that patients would be unduly distressed and fail to understand medical data cut little ice with their Lordships. The 1981 Act is less favourable to patients. A court may limit disclosure to (a) the patient's legal advisers, or (b) the patient's legal and medical advisers, or (c) if the patient has no legal adviser, to his 'medical or other professional adviser'. It is up to the court to decide whether the patient sees the records. But as long as he has retained a lawyer, his lawyer must be permitted to examine the documents. Hospitals and medical protection societies offering voluntary disclosure often still try to keep records even from the patient's lawyers. Lawyers in the medico-legal field advise against accepting such an offer: a lawyer may spot relevant material in support of a claim which even the most experienced medical advisers could miss.

Three important matters on disclosure need a mention. First, the intention to bring proceedings and the likelihood that they will go ahead must be real before the court will order disclosure. The patient must have some solid ground for thinking he has a claim. He cannot use an application for disclosure as a 'fishing expedition' on the off-chance that some evidence of negligence will come to light. [*Dunning v United Liverpool Hospitals' Board of Governors* [1973] 2 All ER 454.] Medical defence organizations used to advise doctors to say nothing and disclose no records without first consulting them. The Medical Defence Union and the Medical Protection Society always refuted allegations that they then attempted to obstruct disclosure of records in all cases. And indeed, if a claim by a patient on its face suggested obvious negligence the defence organization representing the doctor's interests had good reason to co-operate with the patient's lawyers and settle quickly and quietly. Whatever the truth of allegations that the defence organizations sought to prevent disclosure of records, in many cases now their views are marginal. Where the claim arises out of alleged mistreatment in an NHS hospital, NHS indemnity means that the health authority or NHS trust controls defence of the action and *their* lawyers decide whether to disclose records voluntarily or force the patient to seek a court order. Problems with health authorities in the past have tended to relate not to any deliberately obstructive attitude but to difficulties in locating the right records. How far regional health authority legal departments have the resources to cope with claims may determine how efficiently those claims are dealt with. It remains to be seen too how far if at all the enactment of the Access to Health Records Act 1990 will change the atmosphere for disclosure of records. That Act gives patients a qualified right to see their records even where no litigation is contemplated. It would be odd if patients with a legal grievance were offered less generous disclosure. And may it be that a knowledgeable patient, believing he has a grievance, might resort first to the 1990 Act?

Second, will the patient be able to see notes of any inquiry ordered by the Health Authority into his misadventure? The position is complex. If the inquiry was held mainly to provide the basis of information on which legal advice as to the authority's legal liability is based, then the records are protected by legal professional privilege. But if the dominant purpose of the inquiry was otherwise, for example to improve hospital procedures or to provide the basis of disciplinary proceedings against staff, then the patient may be allowed access to the notes of the enquiry. [*Waugh v BRB* [1980] AC 521; and see Diana M Kloss (1984) 289 BMJ 66.] That is the legal position. The Court of Appeal has expressed its disquiet about the effect such claims of legal professional privilege may have on the patient's claim. Claims of privilege can be and are used to frustrate the patient's attempt to find out what happened, what went wrong. In *Lee v South West Thames RHA* [[1985] 2 All ER 385] a little boy, Marlon Lee, suffered a severe scold at home but he should have recovered completely. He was taken to a hospital run by health authority A and then transferred to a burns unit controlled by health authority B. The next day he developed breathing problems, was put on a respirator, and still on the respirator was sent back to A in an ambulance provided by health authority C, the South West Thames RHA. When three days later the boy was taken off the respirator he was found to have suffered severe brain damage, probably due to lack of oxygen. In her attempts to find out what went wrong, the child's mother sought disclosure of records and notes on her son prepared by staff of all three authorities. Health authority A asked South West Thames RHA to obtain a report from the ambulance crew. South West Thames RHA complied and forwarded the report to A. It was this report which the plaintiffs went to court to obtain access to. South West Thames RHA had revealed its existence but refused to hand it over to the family. They claimed it had been prepared in contemplation of litigation and to enable legal advice to be given in connection with that litigation. So it had, but it had been prepared on the request of health authority A to obtain advice as to A's liability to the child. Reluctantly the Court of Appeal held that the privilege attaching to the document was enjoyed by health authority A. South West Thames could not be ordered to disclose the report. Even had they been prepared to do so they could not have handed over the report without A's agreement. The principle was the defendants or potential defendants should be '…free to seek evidence without being obliged to disclose the result of his researches to his opponent'.

So a child was damaged for life in circumstances pointing to negligence on someone's part, and the law was powerless to help his mother find out what exactly caused his brain damage. The Court of Appeal expressed their disquiet and called for reform of the law. Within the doctor/patient relationship Sir John Donaldson MR said there was a duty to answer questions put before treatment was agreed to. [See *Sidaway v Board of Governors of the Bethlem Royal and the Maudsley Hospital* [1985] 2 WLR 480.] Why should the duty to be frank with the patient be different once treatment was completed? And in 1987 [*Naylor v Preston AHA* [1987] 2 All ER 353] he again emphasized the importance he placed on what he termed a duty of candour. How such a duty should be enforced is less clear. In *Lee* the president of the Court of Appeal had suggested that some new remedy based on breach of a duty to inform might evolve. Such a remedy came too late for Marlon Lee. What seems to have happened since though is that judges now recognize that patients have a right to see their records. Access to records is not a concession kindly granted or withheld at the discretion of the health authority. Health authorities or other defendants who drag their feet may ultimately be punished by an order of costs against them.

Third, the court retains the power to refuse to order disclosure where to do so would be injurious to the public interest. [Supreme Court Act 1981, s 35.] This is unlikely to be the case where what is asked for is the plaintiff's own medical notes. An attempt by the Secretary of State for Health to plead public interest immunity to avoid disclosure of records in the actions brought by several haemophiliac patients who had contracted HIV and AIDS from contaminated blood products failed. [*HIV: Haemophiliac Litigation, Guardian*, 28 September 1990, CA]

(See *Supply of Information about Hospital Patients in the Context of Civil Legal Proceedings* (HC (82) 16), explaining the application of the legislation. The current rules of court, replacing RSC Ord 24, are in CPR Rules 31.16 and 31.17

respectively. The restriction to personal injury and death cases is removed by the Civil Procedure (Modification of Enactments) Order 1998 (SI 1998 No 2940).)

It is worth noting that even in litigation, following enactment of the Access to Health Records Act 1990, reliance was often placed upon that Act, with its broader scope, than on the specific pre-action disclosure provisions. (The 1990 Act only applied to manual records created on or after 1 November 1991 and has in large measure been repealed by the Data Protection Act 1998, see *infra*.)

2. The Data Protection Act 1998

Prior to the Data Protection Act 1998, access to medical records (outside litigation) was governed by two Acts – the Data Protection Act 1984 and the Access to Health Records Act 1990. The former covered electronically stored records and the latter manual records created on, or after, 1 November 1991 (for discussion see *Second Edition* of this book at pp 625–632).

The Data Protection Act 1984 is repealed by the Data Protection Act 1998 (DPA 1998), which seeks to give effect to the European Directive on Personal Data 1995 (OJ L281).

All electronic and manual health records are covered by the 1998 Act (s 1(1)). The 1998 Act effectively repeals the Access to Health Records Act 1990, because, unlike the 1984 Act, it also applies to written medical records. While there are transitional provisions which phase in the application of the DPA 1998 to written records until 24 October 2001 (Sch 8), the access provisions apply to written *health* records from 1 March 2000 when the Act came into force (Sch 8, Pt II, para 3(2) and 3(1)(a), exempting access to manual data forming part of an 'accessible record' (which includes a 'health record' (s 68(1)(a) and (2)) from the transitional provisions). The effect is that the 1998 Act governs access to *all* medical records, whether written or electronic, and whenever created since the Act is retrospective.

Here we are concerned with the 'subject information provisions' of the DPA 1998, so far as they apply to health records which replace the 'subject access' provisions of the Data Protection Act 1984 (for a discussion of the remainder of the DPA 1998 as it applies to health information, see *infra* p 1035–1046.)

(a) The right of access

Section 7 of the DPA 1998 confers a right of access upon an individual (the 'data subject') to certain information from a 'data controller', ie the person or persons who control the purposes for which, and the manner in which, the personal data are processed (s 1(1)).

RIGHTS OF DATA SUBJECT AND OTHERS
7. – (1) Subject to the following provisions of this section and to sections 8 and 9, an individual is entitled:–
(a) to be informed by any data controller whether personal data of which that individual is the data subject are being processed by or on behalf of that data controller.
(b) if that is the case, to be given by the data controller a description of-
  (i) the personal data of which that individual is the data subject,
  (ii) the purposes for which they are being or are to be processed, and
  (iii) the recipients or classes of recipients to whom they are or may be disclosed,
(c) to have communicated to him in an intelligible form-
  (i) the information constituting any personal data of which that individual is the data subject, and
  (ii) any information available to the data controller as to the source of those data, and
(d) where the processing by automatic means of personal data of which that individual is the data subject for the purpose of evaluating matters relating to him such as, for example, his performance at work, his creditworthiness, his reliability or his conduct, has constituted or is likely to constitute the sole basis for any decision significantly affecting him, to be informed by the data controller of the logic involved in that decision-taking.

(2) A data controller is not obliged to supply any information under subsection (1) unless he has received–
(a)   a request in writing, and
(b)   except in prescribed cases, such fee (not exceeding the prescribed maximum) as he may require. ...
(8) Subject to subsection (4), a data controller shall comply with a request under this section promptly and in any event before the end of the prescribed period beginning with the relevant day.
(9) If a court is satisfied on the application of – (a) any person who has made a request under the foregoing provisions of this section ,or (b) any other person to whom serious harm to his physical or mental health or condition would be likely to be caused by compliance with any such request in contravention of these provisions, that the data controller in question is about to comply with or has failed to comply with the request in contravention of those provisions, the court may order him not to comply or, as the case may be, to comply with the request.
(10) In this section –
"prescribed" means prescribed by the Secretary of State by regulations;
"the prescribed maximum" means such amount as may be prescribed;
"the prescribed period" means forty days or such other period as may be prescribed;
"the relevant day", in relation to a request under this section, means the day on which the data controller receives the request or, if later, the first day on which the data controller has both the required fee and the information referred to in subsection (3).

(Section 7(9) is as substituted by the Data Protection (Subject Access Modification) (Health) Order 2000 (SI 2000, No 413), art 8(b).)

The data controller is required to supply the information 'promptly' and in any event within 40 days (s 7(8) and (10)). The court may require the data controller to supply the information if he fails to do so (s 7(9)). In order to trigger the data controller's obligation to supply: (1) there must be a request in writing to supply information (s 7(2)(a)); (2) the data controller must receive a fee not exceeding the prescribed maximum (£10 usually) (s 7(2)(b) and The Data Protection (Subject Access) (Fees and Miscellaneous Provisions) Regulations 2000 (SI 2000 No 191) reg 3); and (3) the data controller must be supplied with 'such information as he may reasonably require in order to satisfy himself as to the identity of the person making the request and to locate the information which the person seeks' (s 7(3)).

Subject to exemptions and other limitations (see *infra*), the data controller must supply the following information (ss 7(1) and 8)):
(a) whether personal data of which the individual is the subject is being processed by or on behalf of the data controller;
(b) a description of the data, the purposes for which it is being processed and the recipients (or classes of recipients) to whom it may be disclosed;
(c) if required by the data subject, where possible and which would not involve disproportionate effort, a copy in a permanent and intelligible form of the information held including the source of the data – this may include an explanation of any terms used;
(d) the logic of any process of automated data processing applied to the data.

(b) Exemptions and limitations

Part IV of the DPA 1998 contains certain exemptions from the subject information access provisions. In relation to medical records the following are relevant.

First, s 30(1) allows the Secretary of State to exempt (or modify) the subject information provisions for health information. The Data Protection (Subject Access Modification) (Health) Order 2000, (SI 2000, No 413) (hereafter the 'Health Order') creates an exemption from access under s 7.

Article 5(1) sets out the exemption:

5. – (1) Personal data to which this Order applies are exempt from section 7 in any case to the extent to which the application of that section would be likely to cause serious harm to the physical or mental health or condition of the data subject or any other person.

The Order applies to:

3. – (1) ...personal data consisting of information as to the physical or mental health or condition of the data subject.

However, it does not apply to data exempt under s 38(1) of the Act (art 3(2)), for example, information covered by the Human Fertilisation and Embryology Act 1990 (see, *infra*, p 1027).

Notice the exemption is stated in objective terms – 'likely to cause' the harm contemplated. The latter is restricted to 'serious harm' to the 'physical or mental health' of an individual or to his 'condition'. It is not clear what the latter was intended to cover, or add to the more usual wording of 'physical or mental health'. Also, the likelihood of harm may be to the data subject (the patient) or another individual. Hence, this exclusion applies, for example, where the information would harm the patient himself, eg (*R v Mid Glamorgan FHSA, ex p Martin* [1995] 1 All ER 356) or where another such as a health professional who had been involved in his care would be at risk because the patient was dangerous.

Where the 'data controller' under the 1998 Act is a doctor, the assessment of danger under art 5(1) can be made before disclosure is made. However, what if the record is not in the hands of such an individual? The Health Order requires the 'data controller' in such a situation to consult 'an appropriate health professional' before disclosing and may not rely on the exemption without consulting.

'Appropriate health professional' is defined in art 2 as follows:

2. In this Order –
'the appropriate health professional' means –
(a) the health professional who is currently or was most recently responsible for the clinical care of the data subject in connection with the matters to which the information which is the subject of the request relates; or
(b) where there is more than one such health professional, the health professional who is the most suitable to advise on the matters to which the information which is the subject of the request relates: or
(c) where –
    (i) there is no health professional available falling within sub-paragraph (a) or (b), or
    (ii) the data controller is the Secretary of State and data to which this Order applies are processed in connection with the exercise of the functions conferred on him by or under the Child Support Act 1991 and the Child Support Act 1995 or his functions in relation to social security or war pensions,
a health professional who has the necessary experience and qualifications to advise on the matters to which the information which is the subject of the request relates.

Thus, this usually looks to the patient's current or most recent doctor responsible for his care in relation to the matters covered by the information which is sought under s 7. It would, therefore, be his psychiatrist if his in-patient psychiatric records were sought but his GP if those records were requested.

The obligation to consult is in art 6(1) which provides:

6. – (1) Subject to paragraph (2) and article 7(3), section 7 of the Act is modified so that a data controller who is not a health professional shall not *communicate* information constituting data to which this Order applies in response to a request unless the data controller has first consulted the person who appears to the data controller to be the appropriate health professional on the question whether or not the exemption in article 5(1) applies with respect to the information. (Emphasis added.)

Two exceptions exist in arts 6(2) and 7(3) where consultation is not required.

6.(2) Paragraph (1) shall not apply to the extent that the request relates to information which the data controller is satisfied has previously been seen by the data subject or is already within the knowledge of the data subject.

7.(3) Article 6(1) shall not apply in relation to any request where the data controller has consulted the appropriate health professional prior to receiving the request and obtained in writing from that appropriate health professional an opinion that the exemption in article 5(1) does not apply with respect to all of the information which is the subject of the request.

Interestingly, there does not seem to be a requirement that the health professionals agree that the requisite risk of harm exists. The duty is only to consult. Nevertheless, art 5(2) states:

5.(2) Subject to article 7(1), a data controller who is not a health professional shall not withhold information constituting data to which this Order applies on the ground that the exemption in paragraph (1) applies with respect to the information unless the data controller has first consulted the person who appears to the data controller to be the appropriate health professional on the question whether or not the exemption in paragraph (1) applies with respect to the information. (Emphasis added.)

By way of exception to this, art 7(1) and (2) further provide:

7. – (1) Subject to paragraph (2), article 5(2) shall not apply in relation to any request where the data controller has consulted the appropriate health professional prior to receiving the request and obtained in writing from that appropriate health professional an opinion that the exemption in article 5(1) applies with respect to all of the information which is the subject of the request.
(2) Paragraph (1) does not apply where the opinion either –
(a) was obtained before the period beginning six months before the relevant day (as defined in section 7(10) of the Act) and ending on that relevant day, or
(b) was obtained within that period and it is reasonable in all the circumstances to re-consult the appropriate health professional.

On the face of it, the 'data controller' may conclude that the risk does exist following the consultations even though the 'appropriate health professional' does not. In practice, this is an unlikely state of affairs and might make it difficult for the 'data controller' to establish the exemptions under art 5(1) (which is, as we saw, objectively stated) were the matter to be tested in court. Section 7(9) (as amended by the Health Order), allows a person who might be at risk to ask the court to prohibit disclosure, assuming, of course, he is aware that this may occur. It is, nevertheless, strange to say the least that the Health Order does not require a positive response from the 'appropriate health professional' that the risk under art 5(2) does or does not exist. By contrast, where the 'data controller' has sought the opinion of the 'appropriate health professional' before the request for access under s 7, he may disclose, or rely on the exemption, if he has received the written opinion of that professional that the exemption does not or as the case may be, does apply (arts 7(3) and 7(1) and (2)). It seems obvious that the intention was that the 'appropriate health professional' should determine the application of art 5(2) to the particular situation since the 'data controller' is not qualified to do so. The Health Order does not, however, make this explicitly necessary in every instance.

Secondly, personal data which are processed (including held) only for research, statistical or historical purposes are exempt from the right of access under s 7 providing three conditions are met: (1) the data are not processed to 'support measures or decisions with respect to particular individuals'; (2) the processing is not done in such a way as to cause, or be likely to cause 'substantial damage or substantial distress' to the patient; and (3) the results of the research are made available in a form that does not identify any patient (s 33).

Thirdly, s 38(1) allows the Secretary of State to exempt by Order any personal data whose disclosure is prohibited or restricted by or under any enactment if it is necessary for safeguarding the interests of the data subject or the rights and freedoms of any other individual and the exemption should prevail over the right of access. Under s 35A of the 1984 Act, there was a specific exemption in relation to human embryos held under the Human Fertilisation and Embryology Act 1990 (HFE Act). No such explicit exemption is contained in the 1998 Act. The Data Protection (Miscellaneous Subject Access Exemptions) Order 2000 (SI 2000 No 419) Sch, Part I exempts all information held under the HFE Act from the subject information provisions, leaving that Act to determine the availability of such information.

Fourthly, s 31 exempts certain regulatory activities from the access provisions to the extent that it would be likely to prejudice the proper discharge of their functions. Section 31(2)(a)(iii) covers a statutory body, which protects members of the public against dishonesty, malpractice, or other seriously improper conduct by, or the fitness or incompetence of, persons carrying on any profession. Hence, professional regulatory bodies such as the GMC or UKCC and also the Commission for Health Improvement (see, additionally, s 31(4)(b)) will be exempt from the subject information provisions. Likewise, the Health Service Commissioner is exempt (s 31(4)(a)(iii)).

Finally, there are special provisions in respect of so-called 'third party data'.

7. (4) Where a data controller cannot comply with the request without disclosing information relating to another individual who can be identified from that information, he is not obliged to comply with the request unless –
(a) the other individual has consented to the disclosure of the information to the person making the request, or
(b) it is reasonable in all the circumstances to comply with the request without the consent of the other individual or,
(c) the information is contained in a health record and the other individual is a health professional who has compiled or contributed to the health record or has been involved in the care of the data subject in his capacity as a health professional.

(5) In subsection (4) the reference to information relating to another individual includes a reference to information identifying that individual as the source of the information sought by the request; and that subsection is not be construed as excusing a data controller from communicating so much of the information sought by the request as can be communicated without disclosing the identity of the other individual concerned, whether by the omission of names or other identifying particulars or otherwise.

(6) In determining for the purposes of subsection (4)(b) whether it is reasonable in all the circumstances to comply with the request without the consent of the other individual concerned, regard shall be had, in particular, to –
(a) any duty of confidentiality owed to the other individual,
(b) any steps taken by the data controller with a view to seeking the consent of the other individual,
(c) whether the other individual is capable of giving consent, and
(d) any express refusal of consent by the other individual.

Section 7(4) (as amended by the Health Order) provides that a data controller need not supply information relating to an identifiable third party unless that person has consented or it is reasonable in all the circumstances to do so without consent or the information is in a health record and would identify a health professional who had compiled or contributed to it or been involved in his care (subject to the exemption in Art 5(1) of the Health Order, *supra*). This covers not only information about a third party but also information which identifies the third party as the source of the information (s 7(5)). ('Identified individual' includes someone who could be identified taking account of all the information that is, or is likely to be, in the possession of the data subject: s 8(7)).

Notice that the exemption does not apply to the extent that the information can be provided without identifying the individual (s 7(5)). Also, notice that the absolute prohibition on disclosure without the third party's consent, which appeared in the 1984 Act, has been replaced by a 'reasonableness' requirement. This is in order to take account of the European Court of Human Rights decision in *Gaskin v UK* [1990] 1 FLR 167, which found an absolute prohibition to be a breach of art 8 of the Convention. Section 7(6) expands upon the term 'reasonableness' requiring that, in deciding whether it is 'reasonable in all the circumstances' to comply with a request without the consent of the third party, regard is to be had to: (1) any duty of confidentiality owed to the third party; (2) any steps taken to obtain the third party's consent; (3) whether the third party is capable of consenting; and (4) whether the third party has expressly refused.

(c) Children and incompetent adult patients

(i) MAKING AN APPLICATION

There was uncertainty about the application of the Data Protection Act 1984 to children and incompetent adults (see, *Second Edition*, pp 627–628). The DPA 1998 also creates difficulties. There is no express provision concerned with applications by child patients, unlike the Access to Health Records Act 1990, which specifically dealt with it (ss 3(1)(c) and 4(1) and (2)); nor for applications where the patient is an incompetent adult. Also, the express provision in s 21(9) of the 1984 Act allowing the Secretary of State to make regulations in relation to such applications is not repeated – although it has to be said that the power in the 1984 Act was never exercised.

So what is the position under the DPA 1998? It would seem from the absence of specific provisions in the 1998 Act that the Government considered there was no difficulty (see also, the Data Protection (Subject Access Modification) (Health) Order 2000 (SI 2000 No 413), arts 5(3) and (4), where the possibilities are assumed. Whether there is, depends upon the correct interpretation of s 7 of the 1998 Act.

Interpretation 1: On one view, s 7 only permits the 'data subject' to make a request for the information spelt out in s 7(1). The individual may be an adult or child patient who is competent to make such a request, ie is able to understand the nature and likely consequences of seeking his or her medical records (see by analogy: *Re K* [1988] Ch 310). Section 7(1) seems to envisage that the 'data subject' is the applicant in that it states that 'an individual' is entitled to the statutory information if 'personal data *of which that individual is the data subject*' are being processed (s 7(1)(a), emphasis added).

Interpretation 2: An alternative interpretation would see this provision as merely indicating who must receive the information rather than specifying who may request it. The 'requesting' provision in s 7(2) is couched in general terms and is not directly linked to the 'data subject'. Arguably, this interpretation is self-defeating in the case of incompetent children and adults. If only the 'data subject' is entitled to receive the information, even if a parent or relative can make a valid request under s 7, they cannot receive the patient's medical records in response to it!

The uncertainty is manifest and it is remarkable that these issues were not expressly dealt with in the DPA 1998. It would have been relatively straightforward to have included clear statutory provisions, just as was done in the Access to Health Records Act 1990.

If interpretation 1 is correct, the result would create difficulties where the child was incompetent through age or disability and in respect of an incompetent adult. A parent could not exercise the s 7 right of access. However, that does not mean that disclosure to the parents of a child patient would not be lawful under the 1998 Act where to do so would be in the child's 'best interests'. The doctor would have to ensure that he did so consistently with the Act. This would require that 'parents' were included as potential recipients as part of the 'registrable particulars' lodged with the Commissioner (ss 17, 18 and 16(1)(e)). Further, the doctor would have to comply with the Data Protection Principles in Schs 1 to 3, in particular the First and Second Principles. For the 'processing' (ie disclosure) to be 'fair', he would have to satisfy a condition in Sch 2 and, because the health records comprise 'sensitive personal data' (as defined in s 2), he would in addition have to satisfy a condition in Sch 3 to the Act (s 4(4) and Sch 1, Pt 1, para 1). As regards Sch 2, he could probably rely upon para 4 that the 'processing is necessary to protect the vital interests of the data subject', ie the child, providing always that disclosure *was* 'necessary' for the 'vital interests' (ie those connected with, or essential to, the life) of the child. Likewise, the condition in para 8 of Sch 3 would be satisfied if the disclosure was 'necessary for medical purposes' which it would be if the disclosure was in the child's best interests for its treatment.

As regards incompetent patients, it might be assumed that no difficulty arises if a receiver appointed by the Court of Protection applies on behalf of the patient under s 7 of the 1998 Act. This is probably wrong, since the Court of Protection and receiver's powers are restricted to the 'management of property and affairs' of the patient (Mental Health Act 1983, Pt VII). This is limited to 'business matters, legal transactions and other dealings of a similar kind' and does not include questions relating to the medical treatment of the patient (*Re F, supra*, per Lord Brandon at 59). Nor would it include obtaining access to an incompetent patient's medical records.

As a result, much the same reasoning that applies to the incompetent child would also apply where the patient is an incompetent adult. However, disclosure to relatives is much less likely to be 'necessary', and for the patient's 'vital interests' or for 'medical purposes', because the relatives have no legal power to make medical treatment decisions in respect of the patient. It is the doctor who has that power following *Re F* (*supra*). However, the relatives do generally have a real interest in the welfare of the incompetent patient and it might be that disclosure would fall within the Act, since consultation with relatives about the medical treatment of an incompetent adult is good/best practice (*Re F* (*supra*)). Disclosure is, consequently, an adjunct to the treatment of the patient.

If interpretation 2 is correct, and a request for access can be made by someone other than the 'data subject', parents and relatives would, if sufficiently interested in the patient's treatment, fall within s 7. Since, however, granting access would mean that the doctor would disclose information relating to a third party, ie the child or incompetent adult, he may only comply with the request with the consent of that individual or if 'in all the circumstances' it would be 'reasonable' to do so without that person's consent (s 7(4)). It is, of course, the latter which will be important, since the patient is, by definition, incompetent. Section 7(6) sets out a number of factors to consider in determining what is 'reasonable', including whether the individual is incompetent to consent. Granting access to parents or relatives may be reasonable where it is in the best interests of the patient and is necessary for his or her medical treatment.

(ii) EXEMPTIONS

We are here concerned with the specific exemptions applicable to children and incompetent adults, in addition to the generally applicable ones we saw above. The Access to Health Records Act 1990 contained a number of exemptions from the right of access where this would be contrary to the expectation of the child or incompetent adult patient (see s 5(3)). The 1998 Act does not itself repeat these exemptions. However, the Data Protection (Subject Access Modification) (Health) Order 2000 (SI 2000 No 413) does. Articles 5(3) and (4) provide as follows:

5(3) Where any person falling within paragraph (4) is enabled by or under any enactment or rule of law to make a request on behalf of a data subject and has made such a request, personal data to which this Order applies are exempt from section 7 in any case to the extent to which the application of that section would disclose information –

(a) provided by the data subject in the expectation that it would not be disclosed to the person making the request;

(b) obtained as a result of any examination or investigation to which the data subject consented in the expectation that the information would not be so disclosed; or

(c) which the data subject has expressly indicated should not be so disclosed,

provided that sub-paragraphs (a) and (b) shall not apply where the data subject has expressly indicated that he no longer has the expectation referred to therein.

(4) A person falls within this paragraph if –

(a) ...the data subject is a child, and that person has parental responsibility for that data subject; ...

(c) the data subject is incapable of managing his own affairs and that person has been appointed by a court to manage those affairs.

This prohibits a doctor from disclosing information under s 7 when the data subject (child or incompetent adults) expects that it will not be disclosed to the applicant who, if a child, has 'parental responsibility' for him or, if an incompetent adult, has been appointed by the court to manage his affairs (*quaere* whether the latter is possible?). A number of points should be noticed. First, this may create a conflict between the parents, who have consented to the treatment on behalf of the child, and the doctor, who cannot be required to grant access to the medical records relating to that treatment. Secondly, the 'expectation' must be that the information will not be disclosed to the *particular applicant*. Of course, in some instances the child will disclose on the specific understanding that his parents will not be given access to his health information. It would, however, be too narrow a reading of art 5(3) for it not to include situations where the patient did not expect the information to be disclosed *to anyone*. The more general category should properly be understood to embrace the specific parent(s). Thirdly, art 5(3)(a) and (b) cover, respectively, information *provided* by the patient and information *obtained* by the doctor following an examination or intervention. However, the latter is restricted to cases where the child has 'consented' to the examination or investigation. Thus, it is only applicable where the child was *competent* and consented. If the child is incompetent, reliance must be placed upon art 5(3)(a) – information 'provided' by the child but which would seem inapplicable – or art 5(3)(c), where the child (even though incompetent) has 'expressly indicated' that they do not wish the information disclosed to the parent. This provision would not cover an *unspoken* expectation of non-disclosure of information derived from an examination or investigation.

Fourthly, art 5(3) makes clear that access is not prohibited where the 'expectation' has subsequently been expressly retracted by the patient.

Finally, it is important to notice that s 7 and the exemptions are only concerned with applications for access by parents or others with parental responsibility for a child and those, if any, entitled to act on behalf of an incompetent adult. A court concerned with a child's welfare will, of course, have powers to obtain that child's medical records and it has recently been accepted that a new court exercising jurisdiction over incompetent adults should have a similar power (see *Making Decisions* (CM 4465) 1999 at para 3.11).

(d) Remedies

If a doctor fails to comply with a request under s 7, the data subject (or other person making the request) may make an application to the court for access under s 7(9). The court can order the data controller to comply with the request. The patient may also recover compensation for any 'damage' suffered as a result of the doctor's failure to comply with the request (s 13), which may include financial or psychiatric injury. But, compensation for 'distress' alone is not recoverable under s 13 in this instance. On application by the data subject, s 14 also gives a court power to order the data controller to 'rectify, block, erase or destroy' data which is 'inaccurate' (s 14) (notice the more limited remedies in s 12A for manual data until 23 October 2007).

(e) What remains of the Access to Health Records Act 1990?

The Data Protection Act 1998 repeals in large part the provisions of the Access to Health Records Act 1990: see 1998 Act, Sch 16, Pt I. It removes the right of a patient or, if a child, its parents to obtain access to medical records. The right of access to manual records is now covered by the 1998 Act (see *supra*). The sole remaining basis for access to manual health records by virtue of the 1990 Act is under ss 3(1)(f) and 3(2) by the personal representatives of a dead patient or by a person who may have a claim arising out of his death where this is relevant to an action arising out of the patient's death (s 5(4)).

Access to Health Records Act 1990

> **3.** (1) An application for access to a health record, or to any part of a health record, may be made to the holder of the record by any of the following, namely – …
> (f)   where the patient has died, the patient's personal representative and any person who may have a claim arising out of the patient's death.

The subject access provisions of the Data Protection Act 1998 would not apply to this situation since the Act only covers the medical records of a living person (see definition of 'personal data' in s 1(1)). In any event, it is not at all clear that anyone other than the data subject may apply for access under s 7 of the Act (see *supra*). It is not clear, however, why, where litigation is contemplated or undertaken, the situation is not covered by ss 33 and 34 of the Supreme Court Act 1981 and rr 31.16 and 31.17 of the Civil Procedure Rules 1998: it would appear to be.

Access may be excluded where the deceased did not want it. Section 4(3) provides:

> (4)(3) Where an application is made under subsection (1)(f) of section 3 above, access shall not be given under subsection (2) of that section if the record includes a note, made at the patient's request, that he did not wish access to be given on such an application.

Notice the final words – the deceased must have contemplated a post-mortem application by his relatives and excluded it.

However s 5(3) is broader and would not allow exclusion of access to any part of the record if it was provided in the expectation that it would not be disclosed to the applicant, whether port-mortem or not.

> **5.** (3) Access shall not be given under section 3(2) to any part of a health record which in the opinion of the holder of the record would disclose –
> (a)   information provided by the patient in the expectation that it would not be disclosed to the applicant; or
> (b)   information obtained as a result of any examination or investigation to which the patient consented in the expectation that the information would not be so disclosed.

Access may also be excluded to any part of the record to the extent that the disclosure of the information is, in the opinion of the record holder, likely to cause serious harm to an individual (whether the applicant or someone else) or would reveal information about, or provided by, someone other than the patient unless he or she has consented or where that person is a health professional.

> **5.** (1) Access shall not be given under section 3(2) above to any part of a health record –
> (a) which, in the opinion of the holder of the record, would disclose –
> (i)   information likely to cause serious harm to the physical or mental health of any individual; or

(ii) information relating to or provided by an individual, other than the patient, who could be identified from that information ; or
(b)   which was made before the commencement of this Act.
   (2) Subsection (1)(a)(ii) above shall not apply –
(a)   where the individual concerned has consented to the application ; or
(b)   where that individual is a health professional who has been involved in the care of the patient;
and subsection (1)(b) above shall not apply where and to the extent that, in the opinion of the holder of the record, the giving of access is necessary in order to make intelligible any part of the record to which access is required to be given under section 3(2) above.

As you will see, the right of access is also restricted to records that came into existence on, or after, 1 November 1991, when the Act came into force (s 5(1)(b)), except to the extent that they are necessary to 'make intelligible' any part of a record created after that date (s 5(2)).

3.   Access to Medical Reports Act 1988

This Act came into force on 1 January 1989. The Act established a right of access to *medical reports* prepared by a doctor for employment or insurance purposes. When an employer (or potential employer) or an insurance company seeks a medical report on an individual, it must obtain that individual's consent (s 3(1)). As a condition for granting consent, an individual may require that he be given access to the medical report prior to its supply to the employer or insurance company.
   Section 1 sets out the general principle.

1. It shall be the right of an individual to have access, in accordance with the provisions of this Act, to any medical report relating to the individual which is to be, or has been, supplied by a medical practitioner for employment purposes or insurance purposes.

Section 4 provides that:

4. (1) An individual who gives his consent under section 3 above to the making of an application shall be entitled, when giving his consent, to state that he wishes to have access to the report to be supplied in response to the application before it is so supplied; and if he does so, the applicant shall
(a)   notify the medical practitioner of that fact at the time when the application is made, and
(b)   at the same time notify the individual of the making of the application; and each such notification shall contain a statement of the effect of subsection (2) below.
   (2) Where a medical practitioner is notified by the applicant under subsection (1) above that the individual in question wishes to have access to the report before it is supplied, the practitioner shall not supply the report unless –
(a)   he has given the individual access to it and any requirements of section 5 below have been complied with, or
(b)   the period of 21 days beginning with the date of the making of the application has elapsed without his having received any communication from the individual concerning arrangements for the individual to have access to it.

Even if the individual does not stipulate that he be given access as a condition for granting consent, he may none the less by s 4(3) request access prior to the doctor's supplying it by giving notice to the doctor. If it has already been supplied, the individual is entitled to access for up to six months thereafter (s 6). Access is defined in s 6(3) as meaning inspection of a copy of the medical report or obtaining such a copy.
   An individual's right of access is not absolute. Section 7 of the Act provides for *three* situations where a doctor will be justified in not granting access to the whole or part of the report.

7. (1) A medical practitioner shall not be obliged to give an individual access, in accordance with the provisions of section 4(4) or 6(3) above, to any part of a medical report whose

disclosure would in the opinion of the practitioner be likely to cause serious harm to the physical or mental health of the individual or others or would indicate the intentions of the practitioner in respect of the individual.

(2) A medical practitioner shall not be obliged to give an individual access, in accordance with those provisions, to any part of a medical report whose disclosure would be likely to reveal information about another person, or to reveal the identity of another person who has supplied information to the practitioner about the individual, unless –

(a) that person has consented; or

(b) that person is a health professional who has been involved in the care of the individual and the information relates to or has been provided by the professional in that capacity.

In essence, the three situations are: (1) where in the doctor's opinion, disclosure would be 'likely to cause serious harm to the physical or mental health of the individual or others'; (2) where in the doctor's opinion, it could indicate his intentions in respect of that individual (*semble*: where the doctor intends to suggest further investigations in the light of the examination); (3) where disclosure would be likely to reveal information about another or identify another who had supplied information to the doctor unless that other had consented or had been the individual's doctor.

You will notice the subjective language of the first two exceptions: 'in the opinion of the practitioner' and the objective language of the third exception.

If an individual believes that he has wrongly been refused access he may by virtue of s 8 make an application to the county court alleging failure to comply with the Act. If persuaded the court may order compliance.

Finally, it is important to notice that the provisions of the Act only apply where the doctor making the report is a doctor 'who is or has been responsible for the clinical care of the individual' (s 2(1)). Arguably, the employer or insurance company can quite easily circumvent the provisions of the Act and thereby deny the individual any right of access by stipulating that the individual present himself to a doctor who has not previously treated him. The report that follows will not be prepared by a doctor 'responsible for the clinical care of the individual'; and thus there will be no right of access. It is clear from the legislative history that this was Parliament's intention. The converse situation in which the doctor is someone who is caring for the individual whether GP or hospital doctor is clearly within the Act.

There then remains a third situation: where the doctor is an occupational health physician (OHP) within the employer's organisation. If the OHP has undertaken the clinical care of the employee in the past, the Act will apply. This means that the Act may not be avoided where an employer seeks to obtain a report from an OHP (based on his existing knowledge of the employee) even where the employer chooses to categorise the report as an internal memorandum rather than a medical report.

One final point concerns the relationship between the 1988 Act and the Data Protection Act 1998. Could an examinee obtain access under the latter Act of a 'medical report'? And, would the remedies of rectification etc be available? The answer depends upon the issue of whether a medical *report* is an 'accessible record' under s 68 of the 1998 Act, at least to the extent that the report is not in electronic form. If it is, then the 1998 Act would appear to apply and the s 7 right of access to 'personal data' by the data subject. If the medical report is in written form, however, the 1998 Act will only apply if (1) it consists in 'personal data' (s 1(1)), which it undoubtedly will, providing (2) it is an 'accessible record' within s 68 as a 'health record' as defined in s 68(2). Section 68(2) provides as follows:

(2) in subsection (1)(a) "health record" means any record which –

(a) consists of information relating to the physical or mental health or condition of an individual, and

(b) has been made by or on behalf of a health professional in connection with the care of that individual.

Section 68(2)(b) repeats, in essence, the terms of s 2(1) of the 1988 Act and so excludes situations where the report is prepared by a doctor who has not previously treated the examinee. However, what if the doctor is the examinee's GP? There are two difficulties. First, s 68(2)(b) may be more restrictive even than the 1988 Act. The 1988 Act requires that the doctor preparing the report has or had 'clinical care' of the examinee. Section 68(2)(b) is differently worded. It requires that the *record* has been prepared 'in connection with the care' of the individual. It could be argued that a medical report is not so prepared even if it is prepared by the individual's GP.

Preparation of the report is, in other words, independent of the care of the individual and is, rather, prepared in connection with his employment or insurance application. Interestingly, the Access to Health Records Act 1990 contained the same definition. However, 'care' was defined in s 11 of that Act to include 'examination, investigation, diagnosis and treatment'. On the face of it, a doctor could have had the 'care' of an individual unrelated to any diagnosis or treatment. Otherwise, the including of 'examination' and 'investigation' would have been unnecessary if part of 'diagnosis' or 'treatment'. This definition is not included in the 1998 Act. It is, nevertheless, a strong pointer towards a broader interpretation of s 68(2)(b).

Even if s 68(2)(b) can be given a broader meaning, there is a second difficulty. Is a medical *report*, a health *record*. Neither the 1998 Act, nor the Access to Health Records Act 1990 before it, provides any definition of a 'record'. That the legislature has used two terms might lead one to conclude that something different is intended to be covered by each term. And, of course, this must be correct. Most medical or health *records* are not medical *reports*. The latter are prepared for specific purposes, for example, employment, insurance or litigation purposes, and usually for supply to another such as a prospective employer or insurance company. In other words, they tell someone else about the individual's health. Records, by contrast, seem to be a more permanent store of information, usually for the patient's own benefit now and in the future. It may be, therefore, that a medical report will not be a 'health record'; within s 68(2) of the 1998 Act when it is prepared and supplied to another. Only if it is added to the individual's existing medical file or records will it fall within the 1998 Act. It remains a tenable argument, however, that medical reports which are prepared in a permanent form, ie on paper, are also records covered by the 1998 Act. The 1990 Act is of limited application – in the words of its sponsor 'a finely focused and modest measure' – and the more comprehensive provision of the 1998 Act should now be seen as superseding it in practice.

Control

Turning now from the question of access by a patient, we must consider the extent to which the patient may control information about him contained in his medical records so as to prevent others learning of it without his authority. We should look first to the common law and then statute.

A. THE COMMON LAW

We have seen that arguments based upon ownership of the medical record are futile. Except in the rarest of cases, the ownership of the record will not be vested in the patient. Thus the patient can have no right of control based upon ownership.

The alternative, and much more significant, common law device whereby a patient may control if not the record then the disclosure of the information which it contains, is the law of confidentiality. In essence, a doctor breaches his obligation of confidence to his patient if he discloses medical information without the patient's consent save in exceptional circumstances. We examine the law of confidence in the next chapter.

A further possibility links judicial review with the Human Rights Act 1998. In *R v Mid Glamorgan FHSA, ex p Martin* [1995] 1 All ER 356 the Court of Appeal concluded that medical records within the NHS were the property of the relevant Health Authority or NHS Trust. As such, it had a 'duty to administer its property in accordance with its public purposes' (per Nourse LJ at 363). This duty, which the court concluded required it to act in the patient's best interests, was controllable by judicial review. The conclusion seems to be that it is a 'public duty' vested in a public body. As a result of s 6(1) of the Human Rights Act 1998, it is 'unlawful for a public authority to act in a way which is incompatible with a Convention right'. In deciding whether to disclose a patient's medical records (in pursuance of its public duty), a Health Authority or Trust must comply with the European Convention of Human Rights. Disclosure may be a violation of the patient's right to respect for his private life under art 8 of the Convention. In *Z v Finland* (1997) 25 EHRR 371 the European Court of Human Rights has held that the protection of personal data, especially relating to an individual's health, falls within art 8 and its disclosure must comply with art 8(2). We will return to examine this case in the following chapter, concerned with confidentiality, since it seeks to provide a human rights framework within which to set the legality of breach of confidence (*infra*, ch 8).

B. STATUTE

1. Data Protection Act 1998

The Data Protection Act 1998 (DPA 1998) gives effect to the European Directive on Personal Data (1995 OJ L281) and came into force on 1 March 2000. It repeals and replaces the Data Protection Act 1984. We saw some of its provisions earlier in relation to access to medical records. Here we are concerned with the extent to which the 1998 Act controls the use of patient information.

(a) Scope of the 1998 Act

The DPA 1998 is concerned with regulating the 'processing' of 'personal data' of 'data subjects' (patients) by 'data controllers' (s 1(1)). Within the NHS, health service bodies will be 'data controllers' but individual doctors, especially GPs, may also be such. 'Processing' is given a very wide scope and includes virtually anything that is done with the personal data, such as obtaining, storing and using it in any way including disclosing it.

> **1.** – (1) In this Act, unless the context otherwise requires –
> …"processing", in relation to information or data, means obtaining, recording or holding the information or data or carrying out any operation or set of operations on the information of data, including –
> (a) organisation, adaptation or alteration of the information or data,
> (b) retrieval, consultation or use of the information or data,
> (c) disclosure of the information or data by transmission, dissemination or otherwise making available, or
> (d) alignment, combination, blocking, erasure or destruction of the information or data;

'Personal data' is also given a wide definition in s 1(1) of the DPA 1998.

> "personal data" means data which relate to a living individual who can be identified –
> (a) from those data, or
> (b) from those data and other information which is
> in the possession of, or is likely to come into the possession of, the data controller,

and includes any expression of opinion about the individual and any indication of the intentions of the data controller or any other person in respect of the individual.

It includes expressions of opinion about the individual or statements of intention in relation to that individual. It is, however, restricted in two ways: it must relate to a 'living individual' and it must be information which identifies that individual or which may make the individual identifiable from other data or information in, or likely to come into, the possession of the data controller. Thus, the Act does not apply to information held about dead persons or where the information is adequately anonymised.

The DPA 1998 is broader in its reach than was the 1984 Act such that all health records, whether electronic or written, are covered. The personal data may be information held: (1) electronically or with the intention that it should be; or (2) manually either as part of a 'relevant filing system', ie where the information is structured by reference to individuals or criteria relating to individuals such that specific information relating to an individual is readily accessible or as part of an 'accessible record' (s 1(1)). The latter is defined in s 68(2) of the Act to include a

"health record" namely:
"any record which –
(a)   consists of information relating to the physical or mental health or condition of an individual, and
(b)   has been made by or on behalf of a health professional in connection with the care of that individual."

'Health professional' is given an extensive definition in s 69 of the Act to include doctors, nurses, dentists, opticians, pharmacists and scientific heads of department of NHS bodies.

69. – (1) In this Act "health professional" means any of the following –
(a)   a registered medical practitioner,
(b)   a registered dentist as defined by section 53(1) of the Dentists Act 1984,
(c)   a registered optician as defined by section 36(1) of the Opticians Act 1989,
(d)   a registered pharmaceutical chemist as defined by section 24(1) of the Pharmacy Act 1954 or a registered person as defined by Article 2(2) of the Pharmacy (Northern Ireland) Order 1976,
(e)   a registered nurse, midwife or health visitor,
(f)   a registered osteopath as defined by section 41 of the Osteopaths Act 1993,
(g)   a registered chiropractor as defined by section 43 of the Chiropractors Act 1994,
(h)   any person who is registered as a member of a profession to which the Professions Supplementary to Medicine Act 1960 for the time being extends,
(i)   a clinical psychologist, child psychotherapist or speech therapist,
(j)   a music therapist employed by a health service body, and
(k)   a scientist employed by such a body as head of a department.
    (2) In subsection (1)(a) "registered medical practitioner" includes any person who is provisionally registered under section 15 or 21 of the Medical Act 1983 and is engaged in such employment as is mentioned in subsection (3) of that section.
    (3) In subsection (1) "health service body" means –
(a)   a Health Authority established under section 8 of the National Health Service Act 1977,
(b)   a Special Health Authority established under section 11 of that Act,
(bb)   a Primary Care Trust established under section 16A of that Act,
(c)   a Health Board within the meaning of the National Health Service (Scotland) Act 1978,
(d)   a Special Health Board within the meaning of that Act,
(e)   the managers of a State Hospital provided under section 102 of that Act,
(f)   a National Health Service trust first established under section 5 of the National Health Service and Community Care Act 1990 or section 12A of the National Health Service (Scotland) Act 1978,
(g)   a Health and Social Services Board established under Article 16 of the Health and Personal Social Services (Northern Ireland) Order 1972,
(h)   a special health and social services agency established under the Health and Personal Social Services (Special Agencies) (Northern Ireland) Order 1990, or
(i)   a Health and Social Services trust established under Article 10 of the Health and Personal Social Services (Northern Ireland) Order 1991.

There are, however, transitional provisions which phase in many of the requirements of the Act for manual records before 24 October 2001 (the 'first transitional period') and, to a lesser extent, after 23 October 2001 but before 24 October 2007 (the 'second transitional period'): see Sch 8, Pts II and III respectively. The following discussion assumes the Act is fully in force.

(b) The scheme of the Act

This is not the place for a detailed account of the 1998 Act, which is complex (see I Lloyd *A Guide to the Data Protection Act 1998* (1998)). For present purposes the following is sufficient as an outline of the main provisions. The DPA 1998 creates a registration (or notification) system with a Data Protection Commissioner (and Data Protection Tribunal) and processing personal data unless registered is generally a criminal offence (ss 17(1) and 21(1)) but there are exceptions (s17(2)–(4)). The DPA 1998 establishes eight 'Data Protection Principles' (Schs 1–4) which 'data controllers' must observe. The Act creates a system of enforcement procedures by the Commissioner which are subject to a right of appeal to the tribunal (Pt V) and personal remedies for 'data subjects' including rectification (s 14), preventing the processing of data likely to cause damage or distress (s 10) and compensation for damage when the Act is not complied with (s 13). The Data Protection Commissioner may issue an 'enforcement notice' if the Principles are, or have been, breached (s 40) and failure to comply with such a notice is a criminal offence (s 47).

(c) The Data Protection Principles

The Principles are set out in Sch 1, Pt I to the Act and are elaborated upon in Sch 1, Pt II and Schs 2–4. They are as follows:

> 1. Personal data shall be processed fairly and lawfully and, in particular, shall not be processed unless –
> (a)   at least one of the conditions in Schedule 2 is met, and
> (b)   in the case of sensitive personal data, at least one of the conditions in Schedule 3 is also met.
> 2. Personal data shall be obtained only for one or more specified and lawful purposes, and shall not be further processed in any manner incompatible with that purpose or those purposes.
> 3. Personal data shall be adequate, relevant and not excessive in relation to the purpose or purposes for which they are processed.
> 4. Personal data shall be accurate and, where necessary, kept up to date.
> 5. Personal data processed for any purpose or purposes shall not be kept for longer than is necessary for that purpose or those purposes.
> 6. Personal data shall be processed in accordance with the rights of data subjects under this Act.
> 7. Appropriate technical and organisational measures shall be taken against unauthorised or unlawful processing of personal data and against accidental loss or destruction of, or damage to, personal data.
> 8. Personal data shall not be transferred to a country or territory outside the European Economic Area unless that country or territory ensures an adequate level of protection for the rights and freedoms of data subjects in relation to the processing of personal data.

The concern here is with the 'obtaining', 'storage' and 'use', including 'disclosure' of patient information within the NHS. Each of these activities falls within the statutory term 'processing' (s 1(1)).

First, the information must be 'obtained only for one or more specified and lawful purposes'. The information must not be 'further processed' incompatibly with those purposes (Second Principle). These purposes may be specified in the registration with the Commissioner or in a notice given to the data subject (Sch 1, Pt II, para 5). Generally, this will not cause any difficulties within the NHS, providing the 'registrable particulars' spell out the treatment, management, audit or research purposes etc to which patient information may be put. Section 33, however, exempts the processing of data for 'research' purposes to the extent that these may be different purposes from those when it was obtained.

33 –(1) In this section –
"research purposes" includes statistical or historical purposes;
"the relevant conditions", in relation to any processing of personal data, means the conditions –
- (a)   that the data are not processed to support measures or decisions with respect to particular individuals, and
- (b)   that the data are not processed in such a way that substantial damage or substantial distress is, or is likely to be, caused to any data subject.

(2) For the purposes of the second data protection principle, the further processing of personal data only for research purposes in compliance with the relevant conditions is not to be regarded as incompatible with the purposes for which they were obtained.

(3) Personal data which are processed only for research purposes in compliance with the relevant conditions may, notwithstanding the fifth data protection principle, be kept indefinitely.

(4) Personal data which are processed only for research purposes are exempt from section 7 if –
- (a)   they are processed in compliance with the relevant conditions, and
- (b)   the results of the research or any resulting statistics are not made available in a form which identifies data subjects or any of them.

(5) For the purposes of subsections (2) to (4) personal data are not to be treated as processed otherwise than for research purposes *merely because* the data are disclosed –
- (a)   to any person, for research purposes only,
- (b)   to the data subject or a person acting on his behalf,
- (c)   at the request, or with the consent, of the data subject or a person acting on his behalf, or
- (d)   in circumstances in which the person making the disclosure has reasonable grounds for believing that the disclosure falls within paragraph (a), (b) or (c).

This will be important for epidemiological research using existing patient records. Three conditions must be met: (1) the data are not processed to 'support measures or decisions with respect to particular individuals'; (2) the processing is not done in such a way as to cause, or be likely to cause 'substantial damage or substantial distress to the patient; and (3) the results of the research are made available in a form that does not identify any patient.

Second, the patient information must be processed 'fairly' and 'lawfully' (First Principle). This includes its subsequent use, including disclosure. The requirement that the processing be 'lawful' reads into the 1998 Act, *inter alia*, the common law of confidentiality. Any disclosure in breach of confidence (unless justified at common law) will mean that the information has not been 'processed' (ie disclosed) 'lawfully' within the First Principle (but notice *R v Department of Health, ex p Source Informatics Ltd* (1999) 52 BMLR 65 (CA) – discussing the Data Protection Directive).

Additional provisions in Pt II of Sch 1 deal with compliance with the First Principle. 'Fair' processing requires regard to be had to the method by which the data was obtained including whether there was misrepresentation or deceit (para 1(1), Sch 1).

1. – (1) In determining for the purposes of the first principle whether personal data are processed fairly, regard is to be had to the method by which they are obtained, including in particular whether any person from whom they are obtained is deceived or misled as to the purpose or purposes for which they are to be processed.

Further, processing (including disclosure) will only be 'fair' if, 'so far as practicable', the data controller provided the data subject with certain information (Sch 1, para 2(1)). This includes the purposes for which it is intended to be processed (Sch 1, para 2(3)).

2. – (1) Subject to paragraph 3, for the purposes of the first principle personal data are not to be treated as processed fairly unless –
- (a)   in the case of data obtained from the data subject, the data controller ensures so far as practicable that the data subject has, is provided with, or has made readily available to him, the information specified in sub-paragraph (3), and

(b) in any other case, the data controller ensures so far as practicable that, before the relevant time or as soon as practicable after that time, the data subject has, is provided with, or has made readily available to him, the information specified in sub-paragraph (3).

(2) In sub-paragraph (1)(b) "the relevant time" means –

(a) the time when the data controller first processes the data, or

(b) in a case where at that time disclosure to a third party within a reasonable period is envisaged –

    (i) if the data are in fact disclosed to such a person within that period, the time when the data are first disclosed,

    (ii) if within that period the data controller becomes, or ought to become, aware that the data are unlikely to be disclosed to such a person within that period, the time when the data controller does become, or ought to become, so aware, or

    (iii) in any other case, the end of that period.

(3) The information referred to in sub-paragraph (1) is as follows, namely –

(a) the identity of the data controller,

(b) if he has nominated a representative for the purposes of this Act, the identity of that representative,

(c) the purpose or purposes for which the data are intended to be processed, and

(d) any further information which is necessary, having regard to the specific circumstances in which the data are or are to be processed, to enable processing in respect of the data subject to be fair.

On the face of it, therefore, this would seem to impose an obligation upon the data controller to inform the patient at the time it is first processed (ie obtained) of the purposes for which his medical information may thereafter be processed, including used or disclosed. Disclosure otherwise will breach the First Principle. Notice the exemption for 'research purposes' in s 33 of the Act does not apply to the First Principle. It would not seem to suffice that these purposes have been notified to the Commissioner (contrast para 5 of the Second Principle).

The only exemptions are set out in para 3 of Sch 1, Pt II.

3. – (1) paragraph 2(1)(b) does not apply where either of the primary conditions in sub-paragraph (2), together with such further conditions as may be prescribed by the Secretary of State by order, are met.

(2) The primary conditions referred to in sub-paragraph (1) are –

(a) that the provision of that information would involve a disproportionate effort, or

(b) that the recording of the information to be contained in the data by, or the disclosure of the data by, the data controller is necessary for compliance with any legal obligation to which the data controller is subject, other than an obligation imposed by contract.

Also, as regards processing of information within the NHS, para 4 of Sch 1, Pt II contains an important provision. This deals with situations where the processing is done by means of a 'general identifier', for example, patients' NHS numbers. Such data is 'personal data' within the Act since, although anonymised, the patient is identifiable from other information in the NHS data controller's possession (see s 1(1)). By Order, the Secretary of State may prescribe conditions for the 'lawful and fair' processing of such data.

4. – (1) Personal data which contain a general identifier falling within a description prescribed by the Secretary of State by order are not to be treated as processed fairly and lawfully unless they are processed in compliance with any conditions so prescribed in relation to general identifiers of that description.

(2) In sub-paragraph (1) "a general identifier" means any identifier (such as, for example, a number or code used for identification purposes) which –

(a) relates to an individual, and

(b) forms part of a set of similar identifiers which is of general application.

Third, by way of general exemption, disclosures required by law, by statute or court order or which are made in connection with legal proceedings or seeking legal advice are exempt from the Data Protection Principles except for compliance with Schs 2 and 3 (ss 35 and 27(3) and (4)).

35. – (1) Personal data are exempt from the non-disclosure provisions where the disclosure is required by or under any enactment, by any rule of law or by the order of a court.

(2) Personal data are exempt from the non-disclosure provisions where the disclosure is necessary –

(a) for the purpose of, or in connection with, any legal proceedings (including prospective legal proceedings), or

(b) for the purpose of obtaining legal advice,

or is otherwise necessary for the purposes of establishing, exercising or defending legal rights.

Fourth, s 38(2) empowers the Secretary of State by Order to create further exemptions to the non-disclosure provisions of the Act in certain circumstances.

38. – (2) The Secretary of State may by order exempt from the non-disclosure provisions any disclosures of personal data made in circumstances specified in the order, if he considers the exemption is necessary for the safeguarding of the interests of the data subject or the rights and freedoms of any other individual.

Fifth, in determining whether the information has been processed 'fairly' under the First Principle, regard is to be had as to the method by which it has been obtained, including whether the individual has been deceived or misled as to the purposes for which it will be processed (Sch 1, Pt II, para 1(1)). Thus, whilst a use may be compatible with the purposes notified to the Commissioner (or is covered by s 33 for 'research purposes') and so does not offend the Second Principle, misleading or deceiving the patient about its use may still offend the First Principle.

Sixth, the First Principle requires, as a condition to compliance, that personal data must be processed in accordance with Sch 2 and, if it is 'sensitive personal data', must also be processed in accordance with Sch 3. Health information is 'sensitive personal data', as defined in the Act, to include information about an individual's 'physical or mental health or condition' (s 2(e)).

Schedules 2 and 3 set out a number of conditions for processing. Any use of health information (including disclosure) must satisfy one condition in each of the Schedules.

SCHEDULE 2

CONDITIONS RELEVANT FOR PURPOSES OF THE FIRST PRINCIPLE:
PROCESSING OF ANY PERSONAL DATA

1. The data subject has given his consent to the processing.

2. The processing is necessary –

(a) for the performance of a contract to which the data subject is a party, or

(b) for the taking of steps at the request of the data subject with a view to entering into a contract.

3. The processing is necessary for compliance with any legal obligation to which the data controller is subject, other than an obligation imposed by contract.

4. The processing is necessary in order to protect the vital interests of the data subject.

5. The processing is necessary –

(a) for the administration of justice,

(b) for the exercise of any functions conferred on any person by or under any enactment,

(c) for the exercise of any functions of the Crown, a Minister of the Crown, or a government department, or

(d) for the exercise of any other functions of a public nature exercised in the public interest by any person.

6. – (1) The processing is necessary for the purposes of legitimate interests pursued by the data controller or by the third party or parties to whom the data are disclosed, except where the processing is unwarranted in any particular case by reason of prejudice to the rights and freedoms or legitimate interests of the data subject.

(2) The Secretary of State may by order specify particular circumstances in which this condition is, or is not, to be taken to be satisfied.

In Sch 2 the most relevant are as follows:

1. The data subject has given his consent to the processing.

No explanation is given of this, although it contrasts with the first condition in Sch 3, which requires the 'explicit consent' of the individual. Something less than 'explicit' agreement is clearly contemplated. The Directive referred to 'any freely given specific and informed indication of [the data subject's] wishes' (art 2(h)). The Act does not go so far and seems to contemplate any consent accepted by the common law, including implied consent (see *infra*, ch 8). Implied consent to the use of patient information would exist, for example, where it is to be disclosed within the NHS to other professionals for the individual's treatment. It would also arise where the individual has been given reasonable notice of the purposes for which the information might be used and has not 'opted out' by objecting (see, *Innovations (Mail Order) Ltd v Data Protection Registrar* Case DA/92 31/49/1). Thus, well positioned and prominent notices in a GP surgery or hospital indicating the possible uses of information, for example, for teaching, research or management purposes within the NHS may well satisfy this condition.

3. The processing is necessary for compliance will any legal obligation to which the data controller is subject, other than an obligation imposed by contract.

A NHS Trust (or Primary Care Trust) or GP which was required by a binding Direction from the Secretary of State (or, if relevant, Health Authority) to provide certain patient information would fall within this condition. This would also cover disclosures required by statute, court order, or other legal duty.

4. The processing is necessary in order to protect the vital interests of the data subject.

Notice the disclosure must be 'necessary' and not merely convenient. Also, the disclosure (or use) must relate to the patient's 'vital interests'. This should not be read so narrowly as to be limited to 'life and death' situations. Rather, it should be construed as meaning relevant to his life and health. This condition would justify a doctor disclosing information in an emergency in order to protect the life or health of a patient who needed treatment. For example, where a GP informs a casualty doctor that the patient is on a particular medication, that is relevant to his emergency treatment. The condition may also be satisfied where disclosure to other health professionals is required for the treatment of the patient. Although this would also fall within condition 1 (see above), it also might fall within this condition even where the patient refuses. It could be argued that only the 'processing' (ie the disclosure) must be 'necessary' for the stated purpose. The better view is, however, that disclosure in these circumstances is not 'necessary', since it countermands the patient's wishes. (It would, of course, be 'unlawful' and therefore fall outside the First Principle unless it was a justified breach of confidence). For the avoidance of doubt, the condition can have no application to research involving a patient's medical records, since it will usually not affect his 'vital interests' only others when the outcome of the research is known.

6(1) The processing is necessary for the purposes of legitimate interests pursued by the data controller or by the third party or parties to whom the data are disclosed, except where the processing is unwarranted in any particular case by reason of prejudice to the rights and freedoms or legitimate interests of the data subject.

This condition would *prima facie* allow an NHS body to disclose patient information for its, or the recipient's, legitimate interests. This could include disclosure for the purposes of research, financial accounting, management, audit, preventing fraud within the NHS, for maintaining professional standards or for pursuing appropriate legal action against another or defending action brought against a NHS body. All of these would fall within the 'legitimate interests' of the NHS body or the third party to whom the information is disclosed. It is not clear whether the 'legitimate interest' pursued must be that of both discloser and disclosee. The wording seems to suggest a disjunctive reading. The latter reading would allow disclosure to an individual or authority in order to protect that individual from danger, for example, by the patient (see also Sch 3, para 3, *infra*). In any event, the condition requires that the processing should not be 'unwarranted' by reason of the data subject's rights, freedoms and legitimate interests. This may well prevent disclosure where the disclosure is not 'tailored' in scope and content to the particular interests to be pursued. And, arguably, the disclosure would be 'unwarranted; unless the disclosure was for an 'NHS purpose' rather than some other unconnected purpose of the disclosee such as commercial gain (but contrast *R v Department of Health, ex p Source Informatics* (1999) 52 BMLR 65 (CA) per Simon Brown LJ at 77)

As we saw, a further condition in Sch 3 must be satisfied because health information is 'sensitive personal data'. However, the additional requirement will rarely present a problem in the health context, since the condition in para 8 provides an all-embracing condition for processing for 'medical purposes'.

8(1). The processing is necessary for medical purposes and is undertaken by –
(a) a health professional, or
(b) a person who in the circumstances owes a duty of confidentiality which is equivalent to that which would arise if that person were a health professional.
    (2) In this paragraph 'medical purposes' includes the purposes of preventative medicine, medical diagnosis, medical research, the provision of care and treatment and the management of healthcare services.

The only real limitation is that the use should be 'necessary' but, in practice, this is not likely to be problematic. Paragraph 8(2) brings within the provision every conceivable use by the NHS of patient information, whether for treatment, research or management purposes. In effect, this overcomes the need to establish the first condition in Sch 3, which requires the 'explicit consent' of the data subject to the processing. The remainder of Sch 3 is as follows:

SCHEDULE 3

CONDITIONS RELEVANT FOR PURPOSES OF THE FIRST PRINCIPLE:
PROCESSING OF SENSITIVE PERSONAL DATA
    1. The data subject has given his explicit consent to the processing of the personal data.
    2. – (1) The processing is necessary for the purposes of exercising or performing any right or obligation which is conferred or imposed by law on the data controller in connection with employment.
    (2) The Secretary of State may by order –
(a) exclude the application of sub-paragraph (1) in such cases as may be specified, or
(b) provide that, in such cases as may be specified, the condition in sub-paragraph (1) is not to be regarded as satisfied unless such further conditions as may be specified in the order are also satisfied.
    3. The processing is necessary –
(a) in order to protect the vital interests of the data subject or another person, in a case where –
     (i)   onsent cannot be given by or on behalf of the data subject, or
     (ii) the data controller cannot reasonably be expected to obtain the consent of the data subject, or
(b) in order to protect the vital interests of another person, in a case where consent by or on behalf of the data subject has been unreasonably withheld.
    4. The processing –
(a) is carried out in the course of its legitimate activities by any body or association which –
     (i)   is not established or conducted for profit, and
     (ii) exists for political, philosophical, religious or trade-union purposes,
(b) is carried out with appropriate safeguards for the rights and freedoms of data subjects,
(c) relates only to individuals who either are members of the body or association or have regular contact with it in connection with its purposes, and

(d)   does not involve disclosure of the personal data to a third party without the consent of
      the data subject.
   5. The information contained in the personal data has been made public as a result of steps
deliberately taken by the data subject.
   6. The processing –
(a)   is necessary for the purpose of, or in connection with, any legal proceedings (including
      prospective legal proceedings),
(b)   is necessary for the purpose of obtaining legal advice, or
(c)   is otherwise necessary for the purposes of establishing, exercising or defending legal rights.
   7. – (1) The processing is necessary –
(a)   for the administration of justice,
(b)   for the exercise of any functions conferred on any person by or under an enactment, or
(c)   for the exercise of any functions of the Crown, a Minister of the Crown or a government
      department.
   (2) The Secretary of State may by order –
(a)   exclude the application of sub-paragraph (1) in such cases as may be specified, or
(b)   provide that, in such cases as may be specified, the condition in sub-paragraph (1) is not
      to be regarded as satisfied unless such further conditions as may be specified in the
      order are also satisfied. ...
   9. – (1) The processing –
(a)   is of sensitive personal data consisting of information as to racial or ethnic origin,
(b)   is necessary for the purpose of identifying or keeping under review the existence or
      absence of equality or opportunity or treatment between persons of different racial or
      ethnic origins, with a view to enabling such equality to be promoted or maintained, and
(c)   is carried out with appropriate safeguards for the rights and freedoms of data subjects.
   (2) The Secretary of State may by order specify circumstances in which processing falling
within sub-paragraph (1)(a) and (b) is, or is not, to be taken for the purposes of sub-paragraph
(1)(c) to be carried out with appropriate safeguards for the rights and freedoms of data subjects.
   10. The personal data are processed in circumstances specified in an order made by the
Secretary of State for the purposes of this paragraph.

Two conditions in Sch 3 are worth mentioning.

   3. The processing is necessary –
(a)   in order to protect the vital interests of the data subject or another person, in a case where –
      (i)   consent cannot be given by or on behalf of the data subject, or
      (ii) the data controller cannot reasonably be expected to obtain the consent of the data
            subject, or
(b)   in order to protect the vital interests of another person, in a case where consent by or on
      behalf of the data subject had been unreasonably withheld.

To the extent that the disclosure is to protect the vital interests of the patient, this
will usually be covered by the 'medical purposes' condition in para 8. Where,
however, it is to protect a third party, this paragraph permits disclosure even
where the data subject cannot consent or unreasonably refuses consent or where
it is not reasonable to seek it. No doubt situations concerned with dangerous
psychiatric patients, child (or other sexual) abusers or patients carrying an
infectious disease would fall within this provision. For the disclosure to be
'necessary', the manner of disclosure must be tailored to the aim to be achieved,
hence it must be to the appropriate person or authority. Also, we should notice
para 6 which allows processing where it is necessary in connection with legal
proceedings or seeking legal advice.
   You will notice para 10 of Sch 3 to the DPA which allows the Secretary of
State to specify further conditions for processing 'sensitive personal data' by
Order. The Data Protection (Processing of Sensitive Personal Data) Order 2000
(SI 2000 No 417) sets out a number of such conditions, two of which are of interest
here. Paragraph 2 of its schedule seeks to cover processing , for example, by
disciplinary bodies such as the GMC or UKCC when investigating misconduct
or incompetence or by health service bodies such as Trusts, HAs or the
Commission for Health Improvement when investigating mismanagement or
service failures. Paragraph 9 of the schedule covers processing for 'research

purposes' (as defined in s 33 of the DPA) under certain conditions and goes beyond the conditions in para 8 of Sch 3, we saw above, in that the processing need not be done by a health professional or another who owes a similar duty of confidentiality to the patient.

> 2. The processing –
> (a) is in the substantial public interest;
> (b) is necessary for discharge of any function which is designed for protecting members of the public against –
>> (i) dishonesty, malpractice, or other seriously improper conduct by, or the unfitness or incompetence of, any person or
>> (ii) mismanagement in the administration of, or failures in services provided by, any body or association; or
> (c) must necessarily be carried out without the explicit consent of the data subject being sought so as not to prejudice the discharge of that function. ...
>> 9. The processing –
> (a) is in the substantial public interest;
> (b) is necessary for research purposes (which expression shall have the same meaning as in section 33 of the Act);
> (c) does not support measures or decisions with respect to any particular data subject otherwise than with the explicit consent of that data subject; and
> (d) does not cause, nor is likely to cause, substantial damage or substantial distress to the data subject or any other person.

You will notice that both paras 2 and 9 require that the processing be 'in the *substantial* public interest' (emphasis added). It would seem that more than the 'public interest' being served, on balance, is required. Also, you will not in relation to para 2 that to obtain the explicit consent of the individual must 'prejudice' the investigation or whatever before the condition (as opposed to para 1 of Sch 3, to the DPA 1998) applies.

Finally, the Fifth Data Protection Principle requires that information be kept no longer than is necessary for the purposes for which it is processed. Section 33(3) allows information that is processed only for 'research purposes' as defined to be kept indefinitely.

(d) Remedies

The DPA 1998 creates three remedies, which are principally of interest in the medical context. The first two complement the common law of breach of confidence and negligence. The third is an additional remedy.

First, s 10 entitles a data subject to serve a notice upon the data controller requiring him to cease, or not to begin, processing personal data relating to him.

> 10. – (1) Subject to subsection (2), an individual is entitled at any time by notice in writing to a data controller to require the data controller at the end of such period as is reasonable in the circumstances to cease, or not to begin, processing, or processing for a specified purpose or in a specified manner, any personal data in respect of which he is the data subject, on the ground that, for specified reasons –
> (a) the processing of those data or their processing for that purpose or in that manner is causing or is likely to cause substantial damage or substantial distress to him or to another, and
> (b) that damage or distress is or would be unwarranted.
> (2) Subsection (1) does not apply –
> (a) in a case where any of the conditions in paragraphs 1 to 4 of Schedule 2 is met, or
> (3) The data controller must within twenty-one days of receiving a notice under subsection (1) ("the data subject notice") give the individual who gave it a written notice –
> (a) stating that he has complied or intends to comply with the data subject notice, or
> (b) stating his reasons for regarding the data subject notice as to any extent unjustified and the extent (if any) to which he has complied or intends to comply with it.
> (4) If a court is satisfied, on the application of any person who has given a notice under subsection (1) which appears to the court to be justified (or to be justified to any extent), that the data controller in question has failed to comply with the notice, the court may order him

to take such steps for complying with the notice (or for complying with it to that extent) as the court thinks fit.

(5) The failure by a data subject to exercise the right conferred by subsection (1) or section 11(1) does not affect any other right conferred on him by this Part.

The right does not apply if one of the conditions in paras 1 to 4 of Sch 2 is satisfied (see *supra*). The basis for such a notice must be that the processing (or the manner of its processing) is causing or is likely to cause substantial damage to the data subject or another and that damage or distress is unwarranted (s 10(1)). Within 21 days the data controller must give written notice to the data subject that he has complied or intends to comply or stating why he considers it unjustified (s 10(3)). The data subject may apply to the court which may, to the extent it thinks fit, enforce the notice against the data controller if he fails to comply. Certainly, as regards improper disclosure of patient information, the Act may add little to a common law claim for breach of confidence. It does extend the remedies available where the 'processing' does not entail a breach of confidence, for example, because it is being misused without disclosure.

Second, an individual may seek compensation for damage suffered as a result of the breach of the Act by a data controller (s 13).

13. – (1) An individual who suffers damage by reason of any contravention by a data controller of any of the requirements of this Act is entitled to compensation from the data controller for that damage.

(2) An individual who suffers distress by reason of any contravention by a data controller of any of the requirements of this Act is entitled to compensation from the data controller for that distress if –

(a) the individual also suffers damage by reason of the contravention, or
(b) the contravention relates to the processing of personal data for the special purposes.

(3) In proceedings brought against a person by virtue of this section it is a defence to prove that he had taken such care as in all the circumstances was reasonably required to comply with the requirement concerned.

The claimant may be the data subject or another who suffers damage, for example, as a result of disclosure in breach of the Act. Compensation is limited to damage and any consequential distress by a patient or other (s 13(2)(a)). It is a defence for the data controller to establish that he took reasonable care in all the circumstances to comply with the Act (s 13(3)). Given that the claimant must prove damage (physical, financial or psychiatric) and the data controller has a defence of 'no negligence', the remedy may not add much to the common law.

Third, the court may order the data controller to 'rectify, block, erase or destroy' inaccurate data including an expression of opinion which appears to be based upon inaccurate data (s 14).

14. – (1) If a court is satisfied on the application of a data subject that personal data of which the applicant is the subject are inaccurate, the court may order the data controller to rectify, block, erase or destroy those data and any other personal data in respect of which he is the data controller and which contain an expression of opinion which appears to the court to be based on the inaccurate data.

(2) Subsection (1) applies whether or not the data accurately record information received or obtained by the data controller from the data subject or a third party but where the data accurately record such information, then –

(a) if the requirements mentioned in paragraph 7 of Part II of Schedule 1 have been complied with, the court may, instead of making an order under subsection (1), make an order requiring the data to be supplemented by such statement of the true facts relating to the matters dealt with by the data as the court may approve, and
(b) if all or any of those requirements have not been complied with, the court may, instead of making an order under that subsection, make such order as it thinks fit for securing compliance with those requirements with or without a further order requiring the data to be supplemented by such a statement as is mentioned in paragraph (a).

(3) Where the court –

(a)   makes an order under subsection (1), or
(b)   is satisfied on the application of a data subject that personal data of which he was the data subject and which have been rectified, blocked, erased or destroyed were inaccurate,
it may, where it considers it reasonably practicable, order the data controller to notify third parties to whom the data have been disclosed of the rectification, blocking, erasure or destruction.

(4) If a court is satisfied on the application of a data subject –
(a)   that he has suffered damage by reason of any contravention by a data controller of any of the requirements of this Act in respect of any personal data, in circumstances entitling him to compensation under section 13, and
(b)   that there is a substantial risk of further contravention in respect of those data in such circumstances,
the court may order the rectification, blocking, erasure or destruction of any of those data.

(5) Where the court makes an order under subsection (4) it may, where it considers it reasonably practicable, order the data controller to notify third parties to whom the data have been disclosed of the rectification, blocking, erasure or destruction.

(6) In determining whether it is reasonably practicable to require such notification as is mentioned in subsection (3) or (5) the court shall have regard, in particular, to the number of persons who would have to be notified.

2.   Access to Medical Reports Act 1988

We have already considered the access provisions of the Access to Medical Reports Act 1988. The Act also gives an individual a limited right to control a medical report created for employment or insurance purposes. An employer, or insurance company must obtain an individual's consent prior to seeking a medical report upon the individual (s 3(1)). The Act seems to confer an absolute right upon an individual to refuse his consent to this.

The more usual case will be, however, that the individual does consent to the application for the report if he realistically wants the job, promotion or insurance policy that he seeks. Then, the Act contemplates two situations: *conditional* and *unconditional* consent.

First, the individual (as we saw earlier in this chapter), may consent to the making of the application *on condition* that he is granted access to the report. If access has to be granted under the Act (ie the report or the relevant part of it does not fall within the exemption provisions of s 7) then the medical report cannot be supplied to the employer or insurance company without the individual's consent once the individual has obtained access to the report (s 5(1)). Again, the individual's right to refuse consent seems absolute.

However, instead of refusing consent to the supply of the report the individual is entitled, as a condition of his consent, to request that the doctor 'amend any part of the report which the individual considers to be incorrect or misleading' (s 5(2)). Thereafter, the doctor may only supply the report to the employer or insurance company if (i) he accedes to this request (s 5(2)(a)) or (ii) he attaches to the report a statement by the individual concerning the part of the report to which the doctor has refused to amend (s 5(2)(b)).

Secondly, the individual may give his consent to the making of the application for the report *unconditionally*. As we saw earlier, he may still, prior to its supply, notify the doctor that he wishes to have access to the report (s 4(3)). Supply of the report is then subject to the same restrictions as if the consent has been initially conditional.

If, however, the individuals' unconditional consent remains unchanged, the Act confers upon him no right to control the supply or content of the medical report. In other words, requiring (and obtaining) access to a report is, under the Act, a necessary condition to exercising any control over the supply or content of the report.

Chapter 8

Confidentiality

The obligation of confidence

A. INTRODUCTION

We saw in the previous chapter a number of legal mechanisms by which patients may control access to, and the use of, their confidential information contained in their medical records. In particular, the Data Protection Act 1998 (DPA 1998) provides an important legislative framework, in part designed to protect unjustified access to or use of the records. Over time, it may well be that the 1998 Act is seen as the most important legal mechanism in this area. However, there is one other important control mechanism, namely the law of confidentiality. As we saw, the judge-made common law of confidentiality is imported 'lock, stock and barrel' into the 1998 Act by virtue of the First Data Protection Principle, which requires any processing to be done 'fairly and *lawfully*' (our emphasis) (see DPA 1998, Sch 1, Pt I). Whether seen in this context or more generally as a self-standing legal mechanism by which patients may control access to or use of their medical records, the law of confidentiality remains a most significant and potent control mechanism. It does, of course, uniquely apply where the confidential information is not covered by the 1998 Act because it is not contained in a 'health record' as defined in s 68 of the 1998 Act.

1. The ethical obligation

One of the most fundamental *ethical* obligations owed by a doctor to his patient is to respect the confidences of his patient. That this has long been a central premise in our approach to medicine can be seen from the fact that the Hippocratic Oath states:

> Whatsoever things I see or hear concerning the life of men, in my attendance on the sick or even apart therefrom, which ought not to be noised abroad, I will keep silence thereon, counting such things to be as sacred secrets.

The medical and health professionals have long accepted a professional obligation to respect a patient's medical confidences, although that obligation is not an absolute one. The General Medical Council issues guidance to doctors on their ethical obligations. The most recent guidance provides as follows:

General Medical Council *Confidentiality: Protecting and Providing Information* (2000)

1. Patients have a right to expect that information about them will be held in confidence by their doctors. Confidentiality is central to trust between doctors and patients. Without assurances about confidentiality, patients may be reluctant to give doctors the information they need in order to provide good care. If you are asked to provide information about patients you should:

a. seek patient's consent to disclosure wherever possible, whether or not you judge that patients can be identified from the disclosure.
b. anonymise data where unidentifiable data will serve the purpose.
c. keep disclosure to the minimum necessary.
You must always be prepared to justify your decisions in accordance with this guidance.

Protecting information
2. When you are responsible for information about identifiable patients you must make sure that it is effectively protected against improper disclosure at all times.
3. Many improper disclosures are unintentional. You should not discuss patients where you can be overheard or leave patients' records, either on paper or on screen, where they can be seen by other patients, unauthorised health care staff or the public. Whenever possible you should take steps to ensure that your consultations with patients are private.

The general guidance is then elaborated upon in some detail (see *infra*). Likewise, the United Kingdom Central Council for Nursing, Midwifery and Health Visiting (UKCC), which regulates (and licences) nurses, midwives and health visitors, provides in clause 10 of the *Code of Professional Conduct* (3rd edn, 1992) for a duty of confidentiality on practitioners which is further elaborated upon in its *Guidelines for Professional Practice* (1st edn, 1996).

Breaches of the GMC or UKCC guidelines may expose a practitioner to disciplinary proceedings with the possible consequence, if found guilty of 'serious professional misconduct' (GMC) or 'professional misconduct' (UKCC), of being struck off the relevant professional register (see *supra*, ch 3 for professional regulation generally).

That the professions take confidentiality seriously is probably beyond dispute. But how does the law approach patient confidentiality? Before we turn to consider the common law and statutory provisions in England (and Wales), we should first note the importance of confidentiality as a human right protected by the European Convention on Human Rights, which, of course, is now incorporated into English law by the Human Rights Act 1998 (see *supra*, ch 1).

2. As a human right

Two recent decisions of the European Court of Human Rights illustrate the application of art 8 of the Convention, which provides for 'the right to respect for [an individual's] private and family life' (art 8(1)).

Z v Finland (1997) 25 EHRR 371 (ECtHR)

The applicant, Z, is a Swedish national married to X, whom she had met in Africa. During an investigation of X for a number of sexual offences, it was discovered that he was HIV positive. He was consequently tried on several counts of attempted manslaughter. As it was not clear that he had knowledge of his medical condition at the time of commission of all the sexual assaults, the particular point of contention of the trial was when he might have acquired this knowledge. In attempting to discover this, and because Z had invoked her right under Finnish law not to give evidence, orders were issued obliging the medical advisers treating both X and Z to give evidence. At the same time, the police seized medical records concerning Z and added them to the investigation file.

X was convicted on three counts of attempted manslaughter by the City Court, and on two further counts by the Court of Appeal, which disclosed both the applicant's identity and her medical data in the course of its judgment. Both courts also ruled that the confidentiality of the proceedings should be maintained for a period of 10 years, although all parties had requested a longer period. An attempt by the applicant to have the latter decision quashed or reversed by the Supreme Court was dismissed on procedural grounds.

The applicant complained that there had been violations of her right to respect for private and family life under Article 8, invoking in particular (1) the orders obliging her medical advisers to disclose information about her, (2) the seizure of her medical records and their inclusion in the investigation file, (3) the decisions to limit the confidentiality of the proceedings to a period of 10 years, and (4) the disclosure of her identity and medical data in the Court of Appeal's judgment ...

Judges Gölcüklü, Pettiti, Russo, De Meyer, Pekkanen, Mitsud Bonnici, Makarczyk, Repik:

I. *Alleged violation of Article 8 of the Convention*

60. The applicant alleged that she had been a victim of violations of Article 8 of the Convention, which provides:

1. Everyone has the right to respect for his private and family life, his home and his correspondence.

2. There shall be no interference by a public authority with the exercise of this right except such as is in accordance with the law and is necessary in a democratic society in the interests of national security, public safety or the economic well being of the country, for the prevention of disorder or crime, for the protection of health or morals, or for the protection of the rights and freedoms of others.

61. The Government contested this allegation, whereas the Commission concluded that there had been a violation of this provision …

B. Was there an interference with the applicant's right to respect for her private and family life?

71. It was undisputed that the various measures complained of constituted interferences with the applicant's right to respect for her private and family life as guaranteed by Article 8(1) of the Convention. The Court sees no reason to hold otherwise. It must therefore examine whether they fulfilled the conditions in Article 8(2).

C. Were the interferences justified?

1. "In accordance with the law"

72. The applicant complained that the four contested measures all stemmed from the fact that her medical data had been communicated in the proceedings against X in application of Chapter 17, Article 23(3), of the Code of Judicial Procedure, which provision was in her view couched in "dangerously" broad terms. She submitted that that provision failed to specify the group of persons whose medical information could be used in criminal proceedings. Nor did the relevant law afford a right for the persons concerned to be heard prior to the taking of such measures or a remedy to challenge these. The seizure of medical records and their inclusion in an investigation file did not even require a court order. Thus the legislation could not be said to fulfil the requirements of precision and foreseeability flowing from the expression "in accordance with the law".

73. The Court, however, sharing the views of the Commission and the Government, finds nothing to suggest that the measures did not comply with domestic law or that the effects of the relevant law were not sufficiently foreseeable for the purposes of the quality requirement which is implied by the expression "in accordance with the law" in Article 8(2).

2. Legitimate aim

74. The applicant maintained that the medical data in question had not been of such importance in the trial against X as to suggest that the impugned measures had pursued a legitimate aim for the purposes of Article 8(2).

75. However, the Court is not persuaded by this argument which is essentially based on an *ex post facto* assessment by the applicant of the importance of the evidence concerned for the outcome of the proceedings against X. What matters is whether, at the time when the contested measures were taken, the relevant authorities sought to achieve a legitimate aim.

76. In this respect the Court agrees with the Government and the Commission that, at the material time, the investigative measures in issue were aimed at the "prevention of … crime" and the "protection of the rights and freedoms of others".

77. As regards the 10-year limitation on the confidentiality order, the Court recognises that there is a public interest in ensuring the transparence of court proceedings and thereby the maintenance of the public's confidence in the courts. The limitation in question would, under Finnish law, enable any member of the public to exercise his or her right to have access to the case material after the expiry of the confidentiality order. It could therefore, as suggested by the Government and the Commission, be said to have been aimed at protecting the "rights and freedoms of others".

On the other hand, unlike the Government and the Commission, the Court does not consider that it could be regarded as being aimed at the prevention of crime.

78. As to the publication of the applicant's full name as well as her medical condition following their disclosure in the Court of Appeal's judgment, the Court, unlike the Government and the Commission, has doubts as to whether this could be said to have pursued any of the

legitimate aims enumerated in Article 8(2). However, in view of its findings in paragraph 113 below, the Court does not deem it necessary to decide this issue.

3.   *"Necessary in a democratic society"*

(a)   *Arguments of those appearing before the Court*

(i)   *The applicant and the Commission*

79. The applicant and the Commission were of the view that her right to respect for her private and family life under Article 8 had been interfered with in a manner which could not be said to have been "necessary in a democratic society".

However, their conclusion on this point differed. Whereas the applicant alleged that each measure on its own constituted a violation of Article 8, the Commission found a violation by considering them globally. The Delegate explained that, because of the strong links between the various measures and their consequences for the applicant, an overall assessment provided a better basis for the balancing of interests to be exercised under the necessity test.

There were also certain differences between their respective arguments. They could be summarised in the following way.

80. In the applicant's submission, there was no reasonable relationship of proportionality between any legitimate aim pursued by the measures in question and her interest in maintaining the confidentiality of her identity and her medical condition.

As regards the orders requiring her doctors and psychiatrist to give evidence, she observed that the conviction of X on five, as opposed to three, counts of attempted manslaughter had hardly affected the severity of the sentence and the possibility for the victims of obtaining damages from him. He would in any event have been sentenced for sexual offences in relation to the two remaining counts. In view of the obligation of an HIV carrier under Finnish law to inform his or her doctor of the likely source of the disease, the contested orders were likely to have deterred potential and actual HIV carriers in Finland from undergoing blood tests and from seeking medical assistance.

As to the seizure of the medical records and their inclusion in the investigation file, a substantial part of this material had clearly been irrelevant to the case against X and none of it had contained any information which could have been decisive for determining when X had become aware of his HIV infection. There were certain isolated annotations in the records of statements by Z concerning X, but their importance was only theoretical. The City Court was under no obligation to admit the filing of all of the evidence derived from the seizure.

Against this background, there could be no justification for the decision to make the trial record accessible to the public as early as 10 years later, in the year 2002.

Nor had it been "necessary" for the Court of Appeal to disclose her identity and details of her medical condition in its judgment and to fax this to Finland's largest newspaper, which measure had been particularly damaging to her private and professional life. At the Court of Appeal's hearing, X's lawyer had made it entirely clear that Z did not wish any information about her to be published.

81. Unlike the applicant, the Commission was satisfied that the measures in issue were justified on their merits in so far as the competent national authorities had merely sought to obtain evidence on when X had become aware of his HIV infection. It had regard to the weighty public and private interests in pursuing the investigation of the offences of attempted manslaughter.

On the other hand, the Commission, like the applicant, was of the opinion that the measures in question had not been accompanied by sufficient safeguards for the purposes of Article 8(2).

82. In the first place, the Commission observed that the applicant had been given no prior warning of the first order to senior doctor L to give evidence, nor of the fact that her medical records were to be seized and that copies thereof were to be included in the investigation file. As she had not been properly informed of the various investigatory measures in advance, she had not been able to object to them effectively. Also, in this connection, the applicant pointed out that, not being a party to the proceedings and the court hearings being held *in camera*, she had had no means of appearing before the court to state her views.

It was not clear why it had been necessary to hear all the doctors and what, if any, efforts had been made to limit the questioning in such a way as to minimise the interference complained of.

83. Moreover, there was no indication that the police had exercised their discretion to protect at least some of the information emanating from the applicant's medical records, notably by excluding certain material from the investigation file.

On this point, the applicant also contended that she had not been afforded a remedy to challenge the seizure of the records or their inclusion in the file.

84. Furthermore, whilst it was possible under Finnish law to keep court records confidential for up to 40 years and all the parties to the proceedings had requested 30 years, the City

Court had decided to limit the order to 10 years, which decision had been upheld by the Court of Appeal.

Any possibility which the applicant might have had to ask the Supreme Court to quash the confidentiality order would not have provided her with an adequate safeguard. There was no provision entitling her to be heard by the Court of Appeal and all the parties who had been heard on the matter had unsuccessfully asked for an extension of the order.

85. In addition, the Court of Appeal, by having the reasoning of its judgment published in full, had disclosed the applicant's identity and her HIV infection. She had had no effective means of opposing or challenging this measure.

(ii) The Government

86. The Government contested the conclusions reached by the applicant and the Commission. In the Government's opinion, the various measures complained of were all supported by relevant and sufficient reasons and, having regard to the safeguards which existed, were proportionate to the legitimate aims pursued. They invited the Court to examine each of the measures separately.

87. In the Government's submission, both the taking of evidence from the applicant's doctors and psychiatrist and the production of her medical records at the trial had been vital in securing X's conviction and sentence on two of the five counts of attempted manslaughter. The purpose of these measures had been confined to seeking information on when X had become aware of his HIV infection or had reason to suspect he was carrying the disease.

88. It further maintained that it had been necessary to hear all the doctors because of the nature of the information sought, the seriousness of the offences in question and what was at stake for the accused.

The orders requiring the doctors and the psychiatrist to give evidence had been taken by the City Court and the applicant's objections thereto had been drawn to its attention on 3 March 1993, when senior doctor L had read out her letter to the court.

89. Moreover, the Government argued that since all the records had had a potential relevance to the question as to when X had become aware of or had reason to suspect his HIV infection, it had been reasonable that the material in its entirety be seized and included in the investigation file. Having regard to the variety of symptoms of an HIV infection and the difficulty of judging whether an illness had been HIV related, it had been essential that the competent courts be able to examine all the material. To exclude any of it would have given rise to doubts as to its reliability.

In addition, the Government pointed out that the applicant could have challenged the seizure under section 13 of Chapter 4 of the Coercive Means of Criminal Investigation Act 1987.

90. Bearing in mind the public interest in publicity of court proceedings, the Government considered it reasonable in the circumstances of the case to limit the confidentiality order to 10 years. When heard as a witness, Mrs Z had not expressly requested that her medical data remain confidential and that she should not be identified in the Court of Appeal's judgment.

91. The reference to the applicant as X's wife in the Court of Appeal's judgment had been an indispensable element of its reasoning and conclusion. The fact that the judgment had disclosed her name had been of no significance to her interests. As with the victims of the offences committed by X, it would have been possible to omit mentioning her name, had she expressed any wish to this effect.

92. Finally, in addition to the above safeguards, the Government pointed to the civil and criminal remedies for breach of confidentiality by civil servants which had been available to the applicant under Finnish law and to the possibility of lodging a petition with the Parliamentary Ombudsman or with the Chancellor of Justice.

93. In the light of the foregoing, the Government was of the view that the Finnish authorities had acted within the margin of appreciation left to them in the matters in issue and that, accordingly, none of the contested measures had given rise to a violation of Article 8 of the Convention.

(b) The Court's assessment

94. In determining whether the impugned measures were "necessary in a democratic society", the Court will consider whether, in the light of the case as a whole, the reasons adduced to justify them were relevant and sufficient and whether the measures were proportionate to the legitimate aims pursued.

95. In this connection, the Court will take into account that the protection of personal data, not least medical data, is of fundamental importance to a person's enjoyment of his or her right to respect for private and family life as guaranteed by Article 8 of the Convention. Respecting the confidentiality of health data is a vital principle in the legal systems of all the Contracting Parties to the Convention. It is crucial not only to respect the sense of privacy of a patient but also to preserve his or her confidence in the medical profession and in the health service in general.

Without such protection, those in need of medical assistance may be deterred from revealing such information of a personal and intimate nature as may be necessary in order to receive appropriate treatment and, even from seeking such assistance, thereby endangering their own health and, in the case of transmissible diseases, that of the community. (See Recommendation No. R (89) 14 on 'The ethical issues of HIV infection in the health care and social settings' adopted by the Committee of Ministers of the Council of Europe 24 October 1989.)

The domestic law must therefore afford appropriate safeguards to prevent any such communication or disclosure of personal health data as may be inconsistent with the guarantees in Article 8 of the Convention.

96. The above considerations are especially valid as regards protection of the confidentiality of information about a person's HIV infection. The disclosure of such data may dramatically affect his or her private and family life, as well as social and employment situation, by exposing him or her to opprobrium and the risk of ostracism. For this reason it may also discourage persons from seeking diagnosis or treatment and thus undermine any preventive efforts by the community to contain the pandemic. The interests in protecting the confidentiality of such information will therefore weigh heavily in the balance in determining whether the interference was proportionate to the legitimate aim pursued. Such interference cannot be compatible with Article 8 of the Convention unless it is justified by an overriding requirement in the public interest.

In view of the highly intimate and sensitive nature of information concerning a person's HIV status, any state measures compelling communication or disclosure of such information without the consent of the patient call for the most careful scrutiny on the part of the Court, as do the safeguards designed to secure an effective protection. (See *mutatis mutandis*, *Dudgeon v UK* (A145): (1982) 4 EHRR 149 para 52: And *Johansen v Norway* (1996) 23 EHRR 33.)

97. At the same time, the Court accepts that the interests of a patient and the community as a whole in protecting the confidentiality of medical data may be outweighed by the interest in investigation and prosecution of crime and in the publicity of court proceedings.

98. It must be borne in mind in the context of the investigative measures in issue that it is not for the Court to substitute its views for those of the national authorities as to the relevance of evidence used in the judicial proceedings.

99. As to the issues regarding access by the public to personal data, the Court recognises that a margin of appreciation should be left to the competent national authorities in striking a fair balance between the interest of publicity of court proceedings, on the one hand, and the interests of a party or a third person in maintaining the confidentiality of such data, on the other hand. The scope of this margin will depend on such factors as the nature and seriousness of the interests at stake and the gravity of the interference.

100. It is in the light of the above considerations that the Court will examine the contested interferences with the applicant's right to respect for her private and family life.

Since the various measures were different in character, pursued distinct aims and infringed upon her private and family life to a different extent, the Court will examine the necessity of each measure in turn.

101. Before broaching these issues, the Court observes at the outset that, although the applicant may not have had an opportunity to be heard directly by the competent authorities before they took the measures, they had been made aware of her views and interests in these matters.

All her medical advisers had objected to the various orders to testify and had thus actively sought to protect her interests in maintaining the confidentiality of her medical data. At an early stage, her letter to senior doctor L, urging him not to testify and stating her reasons, had been read out to the City Court.

In the abovementioned letter, it was implicit, to say the least, that she would for the same reasons object also to the communication of her medical data by means of seizure of her medical records and their inclusion in the investigation file, which occurred a few days later. According to the applicant, her lawyer had done all he could to draw the public prosecutor's attention to her objections to her medical data being used in the proceedings.

Moreover, before upholding the 10-year limitation on the confidentiality order, the Court of Appeal had been informed by X's lawyer of the applicant's wish that the period of confidentiality be extended.

In these circumstances, the Court is satisfied that the decision-making process leading to the measures in question was such as to take her views sufficiently into account for the purposes of Article 8 of the Convention. Thus, the procedure followed did not as such give rise to any breach of that Article.

In this connection, the Court takes note of the fact that, according to the Government's submissions to the Court, it would have been possible for the applicant to challenge the seizure before the City Court. Also, as is apparent from the Supreme Court's decision of 1 September 1995, she was able under Finnish law to apply – by way of an extraordinary procedure – for an order quashing the Court of Appeal's judgment in so far as it permitted the information and material about her to be made accessible to the public as from 2002.

(i) The orders requiring the applicant's doctors and psychiatrist to give evidence

102. As regards the orders requiring the applicant's doctors and psychiatrist to give evidence, the Court notes that the measures were taken in the context of Z availing herself of her right under Finnish law not to give evidence against her husband. The object was exclusively to ascertain from her medical advisers when X had become aware of or had reason to suspect his HIV infection. Their evidence had the possibility of being at the material time decisive for the question whether X was guilty of sexual offences only or in addition of the more serious offence of attempted manslaughter in relation to two offences committed prior to 19 March 1992, when the positive results of the HIV test had become available. There can be no doubt that the competent national authorities were entitled to think that very weighty public interests militated in favour of the investigation and prosecution of X for attempted manslaughter in respect of all of the five offences concerned and not just three of them.

103. The Court further notes that, under the relevant Finnish law, the applicant's medical advisers could be ordered to give evidence concerning her without her informed consent only in very limited circumstances, namely in connection with the investigation and the bringing of charges for serious criminal offences for which at least six years' imprisonment was prescribed. Since they had refused to give evidence to the police, the latter had to obtain authorisation from a judicial body – the City Court – to hear them as witnesses. The questioning took place *in camera* before the City Court, which had ordered in advance that its file, including transcripts of witness statements, be kept confidential. All those involved in the proceedings were under a duty to treat the information as confidential. Breach of their duty in this respect could lead to civil and/or criminal liability under Finnish law.

The interference with the applicant's private and family life which the contested orders entailed was thus subjected to important limitations and was accompanied by effective and adequate safeguards against abuse.

In this connection, the Court sees no reason to question the extent to which the applicant's doctors were ordered to give evidence. As indicated above, the expediency of obtaining evidence is primarily a matter for the national authorities and it is not for the Court to substitute its views for theirs in this regard.

104. In view of the above factors, in particular the confidential nature of the proceedings against X, as well as their highly exceptional character, the Court is not persuaded by the applicant's argument that the various orders to give evidence were likely to have deterred potential and actual HIV carriers in Finland from undergoing blood tests and from seeking medical treatment.

105. In the light of the foregoing, the Court finds that the various orders requiring the applicant's medical advisers to give evidence were supported by relevant and sufficient reasons which correspond to an overriding requirement in the interest of the legitimate aims pursued. It is also satisfied that there was a reasonable relationship of proportionality between those measures and aims. Accordingly, there has been no violation of Article 8 on this point.

(ii) Seizure of the applicant's medical records and their inclusion in the investigation file

106. The seizure of the applicant's medical records and their inclusion in the investigation file were complementary to the orders compelling the medical advisers to give evidence. Like the latter measures, the former were taken in the context of the applicant refusing to give evidence against her husband and their object was to ascertain when X had become aware of his HIV infection or had reason to suspect that he was carrying the disease. They were based on the same weighty public interests.

107. Furthermore, they were subject to similar limitations and safeguards against abuse. The substantive conditions on which the material in question could be seized were equally restrictive. More importantly, the material had been submitted in the context of proceedings held *in camera*, and the City Court had decided that the case documents should be treated as confidential, which measure was protected largely by the same rules and remedies as the witness statements.

108. It is true, however, that the seizure, unlike the taking of evidence from the doctors and psychiatrist, had not been authorised by a court but had been ordered by the prosecution.

Nevertheless, under the terms of the relevant provision in Chapter 4, section 2(2), of the Coercive Means of Criminal Investigation Act, a condition for the seizure of the medical records concerned was that the applicant's doctors would be "entitled or obliged to give evidence in the pre-trial investigation about the matter contained in the document[s]". The legal conditions for the seizure were thus essentially the same as those for the orders on the doctors to give evidence.

Furthermore, prior to the seizure of the documents, the City Court had already decided that at least two of the doctors should be heard, whilst it required all the other doctors to give evidence shortly afterwards. The day following the seizure, the City Court, which had power to exclude evidence, decided to include all the material in question in its case file. In addition, as already noted, the applicant had the possibility of challenging the seizure before the City Court.

Therefore, the Court considers that the fact that the seizure was ordered by the prosecution and not by a court cannot of itself give rise to any misgivings under Article 8.

109. As to the applicant's submission that parts of the material had been irrelevant and that some of it had been decisive in the trial against X, the Court reiterates that the expediency of the adducing and admission of evidence by national authorities in domestic proceedings is primarily a matter to be assessed by them and that it is normally not within its province to substitute its views for theirs in this respect. Bearing in mind the arguments advanced by the Government as to the variety of data which could have been relevant for the determination of when X was first aware of or had reason to suspect his HIV infection, the Court sees no reason to doubt the assessment by the national authorities on this point.

110. Therefore, the Court considers that the seizure of the applicant's medical records and their inclusion in the investigation file were supported by relevant and sufficient reasons, the weight of which was such as to override the applicant's interest in the information in question not being communicated. It is satisfied that the measures were proportionate to the legitimate aims pursued and, accordingly, finds no violation of Article 8 on this point either.

(iii) Duration of the order to maintain the medical data confidential

111. As regards the complaint that the medical data in issue would become accessible to the public as from 2002, the Court notes that the 10-year limitation on the confidentiality order did not correspond to the wishes or interests of the litigants in the proceedings, all of whom had requested a longer period of confidentiality.

112. The Court is not persuaded that, by prescribing a period of 10 years, the domestic courts attached sufficient weight to the applicant's interests. It must be remembered that, as a result of the information in issue having been produced in the proceedings without her consent, she had already been subjected to a serious interference with her right to respect for private and family life. The further interference which she would suffer if the medical information were to be made accessible to the public after 10 years is not supported by reasons which could be considered sufficient to override her interest in the data remaining confidential for a long period. The order to make the material so accessible as early as 2002 would, if implemented, amount to a disproportionate interference with her right to respect for her private and family life, in violation of Article 8.

However, the Court will confine itself to the above conclusion, as it is for the State to choose the means to be used in its domestic legal system for discharging its obligations under Article 53 of the Convention.

(iv) Publication of the applicant's identity and health condition in the Court of Appeal's judgment

113. Finally, the Court must examine whether there were sufficient reasons to justify the disclosure of the applicant's identity and HIV infection in the text of the Court of Appeal's judgment made available to the press.

Under the relevant Finnish law, the Court of Appeal had the discretion, firstly, to omit mentioning any names in the judgment permitting the identification of the applicant and, secondly, to keep the full reasoning confidential for a certain period and instead publish an abridged version of the reasoning, the operative part and an indication of the law which it had applied. In fact, it was along these lines that the City Court had published its judgment, without it giving rise to any adverse comment.

Irrespective of whether the applicant had expressly requested the Court of Appeal to omit disclosing her identity and medical condition, that court was informed by X's lawyer about her wishes that the confidentiality order be extended beyond 10 years. It evidently followed from this that she would be opposed to the disclosure of the information in question to the public.

In these circumstances, and having regard to the considerations mentioned in paragraph 112 above, the Court does not find that the impugned publication was supported by any cogent reasons. Accordingly, the publication of the information concerned gave rise to a violation of the applicant's right to respect for her private and family life as guaranteed by Article 8.

Recapitulation

114. The Court thus reaches the conclusions that there has been no violation of Article 8 of the Convention (1) with respect to the orders requiring the applicant's medical advisers to

give evidence or (2) with regard to the seizure of her medical records and their inclusion in the investigation file.

On the other hand, it finds (3) that making the medical data concerned accessible to the public as early as 2002 would, if implemented, give rise to a violation of this Article and (4) that there has been a violation thereof with regard to the publication of the applicant's identity and medical condition in the Court of Appeal's judgment.

In his partial dissent, Judge de Meyer went further, and would have held that it was a violation of art 8 to require the applicant's doctors to give evidence and for her records to be included in the investigative file.

Judge de Meyer: I. The Court accepted that the applicant's right to respect for her private and family life was not infringed by either the orders requiring her doctors and her psychiatrist to give evidence or the seizure of her medical records and their inclusion in the investigation file.

It held that these measures were justified in order to determine when X, her husband, had learnt or had had reason to believe that he was HIV positive for the purpose of establishing whether the offences he was accused of having committed before 19 March 1992 should be classified as attempted manslaughter, like those he had committed after that date, or only as sexual assault.

In my opinion, whatever the requirements of criminal proceedings may be, considerations of that order do not justify disclosing confidential information arising out of the doctor/patient relationship or the documents relating to it.

II. By indicating that the 10-year "limitation on confidentiality" decided on by the Finnish courts in this case was too short, the Court appears to imply that public access to medical data might be permissible after a sufficient length of time has elapsed.

Without prejudice to what might be acceptable with regard to other information in criminal case files, I consider that medical data in such files must remain confidential indefinitely.

The interest in ensuring that court proceedings are public is not sufficient to justify disclosure of confidential data, even after many years have elapsed.

III. In the present judgment the Court once again relies on the national authorities' "margin of appreciation".

I believe that it is high time for the Court to banish that concept from its reasoning. It has already delayed too long in abandoning this hackneyed phrase and recanting the relativism it implies.

It is possible to envisage a margin of appreciation in certain domains. It is, for example, entirely natural for a criminal court to determine sentence – within the range of penalties laid down by the legislature – according to its assessment of the seriousness of the case.

But where human rights are concerned, there is no room for a margin of appreciation which would enable the states to decide what is acceptable and what is not.

On that subject the boundary not to be overstepped must be as clear and precise as possible. It is for the Court, not each state individually, to decide that issue, and the Court's views must apply to everyone within the jurisdiction of each state.

The empty phrases concerning the State's margin of appreciation – repeated in the Court's judgments for too long already – are unnecessary circumlocutions, serving only to indicate abstrusely that the states may do anything the Court does not consider incompatible with human rights.

Such terminology, as wrong in principle as it is pointless in practice, should be abandoned without delay.

As you will see, the crucial area of legal dispute lay in applying art 8(2) to justify the disclosure of the patient's information. That the disclosure was a breach of art 8(1) was readily accepted. The court's deployment of the three-stage test under art 8(2), namely that the disclosure was 'in accordance with the law', was for a 'legitimate aim' and, was 'necessary in a democratic society', illustrates how English law will need to take account of the basis for, and scope of, disclosure in formulating the common law justifications.

The ECtHR returned to the application of art 8 to disclosures of confidential information in *MS v Sweden* (1997) 45 BMLR 133. Of particular interest here is the fact that the court was not concerned with disclosure for the purposes of criminal proceedings but rather with disclosure to a government agency adjudicating upon an individual's social security entitlement. The latter is, perhaps, a more frequent possibility and one of potentially wider application. As we shall see, the court unanimously held that disclosure was justified by art 8(2), given the safeguards imposed by the Swedish law on the receiver of the information.

MS v Sweden (1997) 45 BMLR 133 (ECtHR)

The applicant, MS, was a Swedish citizen. At the age of 14 she was diagnosed as having spondylolisthesis, a condition affecting the spine which can cause chronic back pain. In 1981 she slipped and fell at work, injuring her back. As she was pregnant at the time and had been seeing a doctor at a women's clinic at the hospital, she consulted the same clinic about the injury. Following this incident, she was unable to work for any sustained period of time because of severe back pain and was granted a temporary disability pension and, from 1994, a disability pension. In 1991 she made a claim for compensation under the Industrial Injury Insurance Act (*Lagen om arbetsskadeförsäkring*) 1976 (the Insurance Act) from the Social Insurance office (SIO). During the proceedings, MS discovered that the SIO had requested, and received, from the woman's clinic details from her medical records containing information on treatment she had received in 1981, 1982 and between October 1985 and February 1986. MS had not been consulted about the disclosure. The medical records showed that in 1985 MS had requested an abortion because pregnancy exacerbated her back complaint, but there was no indication that she had alleged that she had injured herself at work. In 1992 the SIO rejected her claim for compensation on the ground that her sick leave had not been caused by an industrial injury. All her domestic appeals were rejected and, in September 1992, she lodged a complaint with the European Commission of Human Rights complaining, inter alia, that the submission of her medical records to the SIO constituted a violation of her right to respect for private and family life as guaranteed by art 8 of the European Convention on Human Rights 1950. In 1995 the Commission declared the application admissible. Before the court the Swedish government disputed that art 8(1) was applicable to the matter complained of by the applicant and maintained that, in any event, there had been no interference with any of her rights guaranteed by that provision. In the alternative it was argued that the measure had been justified under art 8(2) …

Judge Ryssdal (President), Judges Gölcüklü, Palm, Pekkane, Freeland, Mifsud Bonnici, Makarczyk, Gotchev, Jambrek:

A. Article 8(1)

1. Was art 8(1) applicable?

31. In contesting the applicability of art 8(1) the government submitted that, by having initiated the compensation proceedings, the applicant had waived her right to confidentiality with regard to the medical data which the clinic had communicated to the Office (see para 11 above). The measure had constituted a foreseeable application of the relevant Swedish law, from which it clearly followed that the Office was under an obligation to request the information in issue, which the clinic had a corresponding duty to impart (see paras 18–19 above). In this connection, they stressed that the data had not been made public but remained confidential in the Office (see para 16 above).

32. The court observes that, under the relevant Swedish law, the applicant's medical records at the clinic were governed by confidentiality (see para 16 above). Communication of such data by the clinic to the Office would be permissible under the Insurance Act only if the latter authority had made a request and only to the extent that the information was deemed to be material to the application of the Insurance Act (see para 18 above). This assessment was left exclusively to the competent authorities, the applicant having no right to be consulted or informed beforehand (see para 21 above).

It thus appears that the disclosure depended not only on the fact that the applicant had submitted her compensation claim to the Office but also on a number of factors beyond her control. It cannot therefore be inferred from her request that she had waived in an unequivocal manner her right under art 8(1) of the Convention to respect for private life with regard to the medical records at the clinic. Accordingly, the court considers that this provision applies to the matters under consideration.

2. Was there an interference?

33. With reference to the arguments set out in para 31 above, the government disputed that the communication of data in question amounted to an interference with the applicant's right to respect for private life under that article.

34. The applicant and the Commission, stressing that information of a private and sensitive nature had been disclosed without her consent to a certain number of people at the Office, maintained that the measure constituted an interference.

35. The court notes that the medical records in question contained highly personal and sensitive data about the applicant, including information relating to an abortion. Although the records remained confidential, they had been disclosed to another public authority and therefore to a wider circle of public servants (see paras 12–13 above). Moreover, whilst the information had been collected and stored at the clinic in connection with medical treatment, its subsequent communication had served a different purpose, namely to enable the Office to examine her compensation claim. It did not follow from the fact that she had sought treatment at the clinic that she would consent to the data being disclosed to the Office (see para 10 above). Having regard to these considerations, the court finds that the disclosure of the data by the clinic to the Office entailed an interference with the applicant's right to respect for private life guaranteed by art 8(1).

It remains to be determined whether the interference was justified under art 8(2).

B. Article 8(2)

1. 'In accordance with the law'

36. The applicant submitted that the disclosure of her medical records by the clinic had exceeded the Office's request. Whilst the Office had only asked for medical records relating to the time of her back injury allegedly sustained at work on 9 October 1981, the clinic had produced records covering a period up to February 1986 (see para 12 above). The information disclosed did not therefore meet the requirement contained in ch 8, s 7 of the Insurance Act that only data requested should be produced (see para 18 above), and its communication had consequently not been 'in accordance with the law'.

37. However, in the court's view the terms of the above provision suggest that the decisive factor in determining the scope of the imparting authority's duty to provide information is the relevance of the information rather than the precise wording of the request (see para 18 above). The court is satisfied that the interference had a legal basis and was foreseeable; in other words, that it was 'in accordance with the law'.

2. Legitimate aim

38. The object of the disclosure was to enable the Office to determine whether the conditions for granting the applicant compensation for industrial injury had been met. The communication of the data was potentially decisive for the allocation of public funds to deserving claimants. It could thus be regarded as having pursued the aim of protecting the economic well-being of the country. Indeed, this was not disputed before the court.

On the other hand, the court does not consider it necessary to examine the second aim invoked by the government, namely protection of the 'rights ... of others'.

3. 'Necessary in a democratic society'

39. In the applicant's submission, the disclosure of her medical records could not be regarded as having been necessary in a democratic society. She maintained that, while there was no dispute as to the fact that her disability prevented her from working, there was disagreement as to its cause, whether it was spondylolisthesis or the alleged work injury (see paras 9–10 above). Information about her abortion in 1985 had been irrelevant to the issue to be determined by the Office (see paras 12–13 above). In addition, she argued that the duty of confidentiality to which public servants at the Office were subject provided a weaker protection of the applicant's interests than that applying to medical personnel at the clinic. Thus, whilst it was for the patient to show that he or she had suffered damage as a result of disclosure by an ordinary public servant, a doctor had to show that disclosure had not caused damage.

In addition, she maintained that an effective protection of her rights under art 8 required that she should have been notified of the clinic's intention to communicate the data and afforded an opportunity to exercise judicial remedies against that decision before it was implemented (see para 21 above).

40. The government and the Commission were of the view that the disclosure was 'necessary'. Not only had the medical records been relevant to the Office's decision, but the fact that they might be relevant must also have been apparent to her when she made her claim. Even the information concerning the abortion had related to her back problems (see para 13 above). If the Office had been requested to rely exclusively on the applicant's submissions, there would have been a risk of her withholding relevant evidence. Since the data remained confidential while they were in the possession of the Office (see para 16 above), the interference which the disclosure had entailed was of a limited nature.

41. The court reiterates that the protection of personal data, particularly medical data, is of fundamental importance to a person's enjoyment of his or her right to respect for private and family life as guaranteed by art 8 of the Convention. Respecting the confidentiality of health

data is a vital principle in the legal systems of all the contracting parties to the Convention. It is crucial not only to respect the sense of privacy of a patient but also to preserve his or her confidence in the medical profession and in the health services in general. The domestic law must afford appropriate safeguards to prevent any such communication or disclosure of personal health data as may be inconsistent with the guarantees in art 8 of the Convention: see *Z v Finland* (1997) 45 BMLR 107 at 124 (para 95).

Bearing in mind the above considerations and the margin of appreciation enjoyed by the state in this area, the court will examine whether, in the light of the case as a whole, the reasons adduced to justify the interference were relevant and sufficient and whether the measure was proportionate to the legitimate aim pursued: see *Z v Finland* (1997) 45 BMLR 107 at 124 (para 94).

42. Turning to the particular circumstances, the court notes that the applicant's medical data were communicated by one public institution to another in the context of an assessment of whether she satisfied the legal conditions for obtaining a benefit which she herself had requested (see paras 11–14 above). It recognises that, in deciding whether to accept the applicant's compensation claim, the Office had a legitimate need to check information received from her against data in the possession of the clinic. In the absence of objective information from an independent source, it would have been difficult for the Office to determine whether the claim was well founded.

That claim concerned a back injury which she had allegedly suffered in 1981 and all the medical records produced by the clinic to the Office, including those concerning her abortion in 1985 and the treatment thereafter, contained information relevant to the applicant's back problems. As appears from the records of 1985, her back pains constituted the main reason for the termination of pregnancy (see paras 12–13 above). Moreover, the data covered the period in respect of which she claimed compensation under the Insurance Act (see paras 10–11 above). In the court's view, the applicant has not substantiated her allegation that the clinic could not reasonably have considered her post 1981 medical records to be material to the Office's decision.

43. In addition, under the relevant law it is a condition for imparting the data concerned that the Office has made a request and that the information be of importance for its application of the Insurance Act (see para 18 above). Staff of the clinic could incur civil and/or criminal liability had they failed to observe these conditions (see para 22 above). The Office, as the receiver of the information, was under a similar duty to treat the data as confidential, subject to similar rules and safeguards as the clinic (see paras 20 and 22 above).

In the circumstances, the contested measure was therefore subject to important limitations and was accompanied by effective and adequate safeguards against abuse: see *Z v Finland* (1997) 45 BMLR 107 at 126–127 (para 103).

44. Having regard to the foregoing, the court considers that there were relevant and sufficient reasons for the communication of the applicant's medical records by the clinic to the office and that the measure was not disproportionate to the legitimate aim pursued. Accordingly, it concludes that there has been no violation of the applicant's right to respect for private life, as guaranteed by art 8 of the Convention.

Again, we see the ECtHR's unequivocal view that confidential patient information is, in principle, protected from disclosure by art 8(1). The justification under art 8(2) is an interesting one. In *Z v Finland* (*supra*), the court relied upon the familiar ones of 'preventing crime' and 'protecting the rights and freedoms of others'. By contrast, in *MS v Sweden*, the court relied on the need to protect 'the economic well-being of the country', ie to prevent claimants who are 'swinging the lead' or behaving dishonestly from claiming from the public purse. This could have broad application within the administrative regimes in England for sharing information between agencies, for example, social security and inland revenue. The justification, you will notice, does not rest upon the view that the applicant waived her rights by impliedly agreeing to disclosure because she made an application for compensation (see para 35 *supra*). Although the court regards the protecting of personal information (particularly medical information) to be of 'fundamental importance', the court found that the 'state's needs' outweighed her rights *because* the information was protected from further disclosure once received. It should be noted that this requirement will readily be satisfied in England, since a person who knowingly receives confidential information is themselves bound by a duty of confidence (see *A-G v Guardian Newspapers (No 2)*

[1990] 1 AC 109 at 261 per Lord Keith and at 281 per Lord Goff). Interestingly, the court reached its conclusion even though *irrelevant* information relating to an abortion was also disclosed.

3. The common law

Does the common law recognise a legal obligation of confidence? That is the central question which will lead to an examination of when a doctor will owe his patient such a duty, the scope of that duty and when, if ever, the duty may be breached.

(a) The legal basis of the duty

Francis Gurry in *Breach of Confidence* (1985) examines the law relating to breach of confidence (pp 58–60):

> While the jurisdictional basis is fundamental to the breach of confidence action, considerable uncertainty still surrounds it. For this reason, any conclusions drawn about it must necessarily be tentative and devoid of dogmatism. The view offered here is that the courts have relied on principles freely drawn from the fields of contract, equity, and property, and that the liberal use of these principles points to the existence of a *sui generis* action which has, in terms of conventional categories, a composite jurisdictional basis.
>
> The approach adopted by the courts seems to have two dominant characteristics. First, the courts' attitude to jurisdiction has been a *pragmatic* one. What has mattered, it seems, is the existence of *a* jurisdiction on which to act in the case immediately in hand. Considerations of conceptual neatness have been secondary to this pragmatic question:
>
> > The true question is whether, *under the circumstances of this case*, the Court ought to interpose by injunction, upon the ground of breach of faith or of contract.
> >
> > That the Court has exercised jurisdiction in cases of this nature does not, I think, admit of any question. Different grounds have indeed been assigned for the exercise of that jurisdiction … but upon whatever grounds the jurisdiction is founded, the authorities leave no doubt as to the exercise of it [*Morison v Moat* (1851) 9 Hare 241 at 255, 68 ER 492 at 498 per Turner VC].
>
> Secondly, the courts' approach to the question of jurisdiction has been a *flexible* one. This flexibility is nowhere better illustrated than in the relationship between contract and equity. Here the courts have been prepared to introduce an obligation of confidence based on implied contract when the independent jurisdiction in equity has cast doubt on their ability to award damages as well as an injunction [*The Nichrotherm* case [1957] RPC 207]. Similar flexibility is demonstrated within the scope of contract alone, where the courts have supplemented a limited express term of confidence with a broader obligation based on the implied terms of the contract [*Thomas Marshall (Exporters) Ltd v Guinle* [1979] Ch 227].
>
> This flexibility indicates that something more basic than jurisdictional source lies at the foundation of the breach of confidence action. This can be found, it is submitted, in the policy which underlies the circumstances in which relief has been granted – the policy of holding confidences sacrosanct. Thus, the broad notion of a confidence existing between two parties has provided, in the language of the American realists, 'a sort of doctrinal bridge' [*L Fuller 'American Legal Realism'* (1934) 82 University of Pennsylvania L Rev 492-62, 441] between contract, equity, and property. The confidence arises out of both the circumstances in which information has been disclosed and the nature of the information itself. The circumstances of a disclosure may be such that the confider is placing the confidant in a position of trust. If so, either equity or contract will provide a means by which the trust can be honoured. But a disclosure will not betray a confidence if what has been disclosed is common knowledge. It is only when the information is private or 'confidential', when its general publication would reveal something which the confider wishes to keep secret, that the confidence can be regarded as having been reposed by one person in another. Here, the notion of confidence links contract and equity with property, for the courts have recognised that the publication or misuse of confidential information may injure a person either emotionally [*Prince Albert v Strange* (1849) 2 De G & Sm 652, 64 ER 293; (on appeal) 1 Mac & G 25, 41 ER 1171] or materially [*Exchange Telegraph Co v Howard* (1906) 22 TLR 375] even though no *immediate* relationship of trust has been broken. By acknowledging a right of property in information of this kind, the courts have been able to grant relief where the

defendant has acquired the information by reprehensible means. But, it may be said, how can the acquisition of confidential information by reprehensible means, rather than the abuse of a relationship of confidence created by a limited disclosure, involve a breach of a *confidence*? The answer may lie in the combination of two factors. First, the person who has the confidential information and who guards its secret places a trust in the rest of society by demonstrating that he wishes to preserve an element of himself or his business free from general publicity. Secondly, the acquirer, as a member of society, can be said to breach that confidence or trust because of the means which he has used to gain the information. These means force an unwanted communication of the information on the possessor of the information. The act of resorting to such means on the part of the acquirer indicates that he is aware of the other's desire to preserve the confidentiality of the information in respect of which his means have forced a disclosure.

In *A-G v Guardian Newspapers (No 2)* [1990] 1 AC 109, [1988] 3 All ER 545 ('the *Spycatcher* case') at 658, Lord Goff summarised the law:

> I start with the broad general principle ... that a duty of confidence arises when confidential information comes to the knowledge of a person (the confidant) in circumstances where he has notice, or is held to have agreed, that the information is confidential, with the effect that it would be just in all the circumstances that he should be precluded from disclosing the information to others. I have used the word 'notice' advisedly, in order to avoid the ... question of the extent to which actual knowledge is necessary, though I of course understand knowledge to include circumstances where the confidant has deliberately closed his eyes to the obvious. The existence of this broad general principle reflects the fact that there is such a public interest in the maintenance of confidences, that the law will provide remedies for their protection.
>
> I realise that, in the vast majority of cases, in particular those concerned with trade secrets, the duty of confidence will arise from a transaction or relationship between the parties, often a contract, in which event the duty may arise by reason of either an express or an implied term of that contract. It is in such cases as these that the expressions 'confider' and 'confidant' are perhaps most aptly employed. But it is well-settled that a duty of confidence may arise in equity independently of such cases.

The jurisprudential basis of the legal duty is, as you will have seen, not beyond dispute. Often, the duty arises in the commercial context when the dealings between the parties gives rise to a contractual relationship where the duty of confidence may be an express or implied term of that contract. Outside of private treatment, this cannot be the situation in the doctor-patient relationship. There is no contractual relationship between doctor and patient within the NHS (see *supra*, ch 2). A basis in property or tort law is now a most unlikely candidate in English law. Information (confidential or otherwise) is not characterised as 'property' in English law or something over which an individual may exercise property rights (see discussion in *Breen v Williams* (1996) 70 ALJR 772 (Aust H Ct) per Gummow J at 801–803 and *supra*, ch 7). Nor has a claim in tort found favour in English law giving rise to a common law action for damages *per se*. (There may in appropriate circumstances be an action in negligence for breach of a duty of care: see *infra*.) The duty lies instead in equity and the formulation of Lord Goff, and the other Law Lords, in the *Spycatcher* case leaves little doubt that this is the legal foundation of the duty. There are principally two reasons why this may in practice be important: first, the precise circumstances when the duty will be imposed and, secondly, the possible remedies that may lie for breach of confidence, in particular, claims for damages. We will return to both of these points later in the chapter.

Although there had been little doubt that a legal obligation of confidence is owed in law by a doctor to his patient, curiously there was until recently relatively little authority directly on the point (see *Hunter v Mann* [1974] QB 767 at 772 per Boreham J; *Goddard v Nationwide Building Society* [1986] 3 All ER 264 at 271 per Nourse LJ; *A-G v Guardian Newspapers (No 2)* [1988] 3 All ER 545 at 639 per Lord Keith). The cases of *X v Y* [1988] 2 All ER 648 and *W v Egdell*

[1990] 1 All ER 835, (1989) 4 BMLR 96 (CA) put the matter beyond doubt. In both cases the court moved to a consideration of allegations of breach of confidence assuming, without feeling the need to establish, the existence of the duty of confidence in general terms. For example, in *Egdell*, Bingham LJ (as he then was) stated:

> It has never been doubted that the circumstances here were such as to impose on Dr Egdell a duty of confidence owed to W. He could not lawfully sell the contents of his report to a newspaper, as the judge held. Nor could he, without a breach of the law as well as professional etiquette, discuss the case in a learned article or in his memoirs or in gossiping with friends, unless he took appropriate steps to conceal the identity of W. It is not in issue here that a duty of confidence existed. ...
>
> We were referred, as the judge was, to the current advice given by the General Medical Council to the medical profession pursuant to s 35 of the Medical Act 1983. Rule 80 provides:
>
>> It is a doctor's duty, except in the case mentioned below, strictly to observe the rule of professional secrecy by refraining from disclosing voluntarily to any third party information about a patient which he has learnt directly or indirectly in his professional capacity as a registered medical practitioner ...
>
> I do not doubt that this accurately states the general rule as the law now stands, and the contrary was not suggested.

Indeed, the obligation of confidence is not only recognised by the common law. There are specific instances where Parliament has chosen to put the obligation into a statutory form because of the particular circumstances, for example, National Health Service (Venereal Diseases) Regulations 1974 (SI 1974 No 29); Abortion Regulations 1991 (SI 1991 No 499); Health Act 1999, ss 23 and 24 (Commission for Health Improvement); Health Service Commissioners Act 1993, s 15 (investigations by HSC); Human Fertilisation and Embryology Act 1990, s 33. (But notice that the law does not recognise a 'privilege' against disclosure of medical confidences in court proceedings: *Duchess of Kingston's Case* (1776) 20 State T 355 and *Cross on Evidence* (ed Tapper) (7th edn, 1990) at pp 448–449.)

(b) Scope of the duty

Granted the law does recognise a duty of confidence between a doctor and his patient, the next question to be considered is the precise scope of the duty. Gurry, in his book *Breach of Confidence* (1985) (at 148–149), writes:

> A doctor is under legal obligation not to disclose confidential information concerning a patient which he learns in the course of his professional practice:
>
>> [I]n common with other professional men, for instance a priest ... the doctor is under a duty not to disclose [voluntarily], without the consent of his patient, information which he, the doctor, has gained in his professional capacity [*Hunter v Mann* [1974] QB 767 at 772 per Boreham J].
>
> By analogy with the banker's obligation, it would seem that the doctor's duty of non-disclosure applies not only to information acquired directly from the patient, but also to information concerning the patient which the doctor learns from other sources *in his character as the patient's doctor*. Thus, the obligation of secrecy would extend to reports received by a doctor about a patient from medical specialists or from para-medical services.

You will notice that Gurry considers that the obligation would extend to all information received by the doctor 'in his character as the patient's doctor'. Perhaps, this needs further elaboration.

Where the doctor acquires information directly from the patient or by his own examination or observation of the patient, there can be no doubt that the obligation of confidence attaches to this information.

Where the doctor acquires this information from a third party in circumstances in which the third party knows of the doctor-patient relationship, there would seem to be no reason to distinguish this from the usual case already mentioned. It may be asserted, however, that there should be some distinction between the doctor acquiring information from another health care professional as distinct from a lay person. We do not subscribe to this view since, in both situations, the doctor receives the information *qua* professional vis-à-vis the third party (see, eg, *The Protection and Use of Patient Information* (March 1996), DoH, HSG (96) 18 at para 2.4).

Where the doctor acquires the information from a third party in circumstances in which the third party is unaware that he is speaking to the patient's doctor, the answer is not so clear. On one view, since the doctor does not receive the information *qua* professional vis-à-vis the third party, he has no professional obligation of confidence. The better view, perhaps, is that a court would recognise a duty to respect confidentiality since what lies at the root of the doctor-patient relationship is the patient's trust that the doctor will not reveal any *clinical* information to another without permission and this would extend to all such information however received.

All of these situations could be seen as equity imposing an obligation where it would be 'unconscionable' for the doctor to disclose the information. It is true that in *A-G v Guardian Newspapers (No 2)* [1990] 1 AC 109, Lord Goff acknowledged that this could be the basis for the duty of confidence but declined to decide whether it was (at 281). Nevertheless, this is an attractive legal basis and one which might well find favour with a court. Lord Goff did no more than leave the matter open as it was not necessary for him to reach a concluded view in the case. Applying this approach, it would be unconscionable for the doctor to disclose information about his patient which relates to his patient's health (or probably personal information in general) whether or not the provider of the information knew that he was speaking to the patient's doctor (on 'unconscionability' as a basis for the obligation, see *infra*).

(c) The nature of breach of confidence

It may be self-evident that a breach of confidence has occurred in particular circumstances. Usually it will entail *deliberate disclosure* by the doctor of the information. However, the question arises whether disclosure must be deliberate and whether something other than disclosure may amount to a breach of confidence.

As regards the former, the disclosure need not be deliberate. In *A-G v Guardian Newspapers (No 2)* [1990] 1 AC 109, Lord Goff stated that the disclosure may be 'inadvertent, as well as deliberate' (at 281). More recently, in *Swinney v Chief Constable of Northumbria Police* [1996] 3 All ER 449, the Court of Appeal refused to strike out an action for breach of confidence where the police alleged negligently to have disclosed the identity of an informant. Of course, the Court of Appeal only held that the claim was arguable. It may seem surprising that an equitable claim, if that be the basis of the duty of confidence, can arise for inadvertent disclosure; usually equity requires dishonesty or something more than failure to exercise reasonable care (see *Royal Brunei Airlines v Tan* [1995] 2 AC 378, [1995] 3 All ER 97 (PC) – liability for procuring or assisting in a breach of trust or fiduciary duty). The point is unlikely to be crucial in the medical law context.

More pertinent for us is whether a breach of confidence requires *disclosure* of the information. We are not here raising the issue of interlocutory actions for anticipated disclosures; clearly injunctions may be granted in appropriate circumstances for anticipated disclosures of confidential information. Rather we are concerned with whether other 'wrongful' acts or uses of confidential information may give rise to an action. It has been suggested that 'misuse' of information may give rise to an action.

R G Toulson and C M Phipps *Confidentiality* (1996)

3.13... There is no definitive formulation of what constitutes misuse. Misuse will typically take the form of disclosure to another, but it need not do so. An ex-employee may misuse his former employer's customer list without disclosing it to anyone else. Conversely, not every disclosure of information imparted in confidence will amount to misuse. What constitutes misuse must in each case depend on the scope of the duty owed ...

With respect, this confuses in our view the specific action for breach of confidence with a more general action for infringement of privacy (to the extent that such an action forms part of the common law: see *Kaye v Robertson* [1991] FSR 62 (CA)) or an infringement of the Data Protection Act 1998. Nothing short of *disclosure* of the confidential information, it is suggested, will suffice. Other misuses may amount to a legal wrong, but it will not be a breach of confidence.

A final issue concerns anonymised confidential information. Will it be a breach of confidence to disclose information which does not identify the person to whom it relates? This is a point which arises in relation to *personal* confidences including medical confidences but is, of course, not an issue where the disclosure is of commercial confidences usually for financial gain. Is the legal wrong the disclosure or is it the association of the individual with the information of a personal nature which is disclosed to another beyond the confider? In the medical context, this is an important issue. Anonymised patient information is used for research, statistical and management purposes within the NHS. Photographs of patients, presented in a way that they cannot be identified, are often used for teaching purposes and in publications. There has been an assumption that such disclosures are not breaches of confidence providing the patient is not identified or cannot reasonably be identified from the information, ie is not 'identifiable'. The latter is important because it would be as much a breach of confidence to disclose information describing the person to whom the information relates as 'living at 29, Acacia Avenue, Croydon' as it would be if the patient was actually named. If, however, disclosure even of anonymised information is prima facie a breach of confidence, disclosure will have to be justified on the basis, for example, of consent or the public interest.

Surprisingly, the question of anonymity did not directly arise before a court until 1999. However, in *W v Egdell* [1990] Ch 359, Bingham LJ (as he then was) seemed to assume that anonymising the information prevented a breach of confidence. He stated (at 319), speaking of a doctor who had examined a patient:

nor could he without a breach of the law as well as professional etiquette, discuss the case in a learned article or in his memoirs or in gossiping with friends, *unless he took appropriate steps to conceal the identity of [the patient]*. (Our emphasis.)

By contrast, the Department of Health in its guidance, *The Protection and Use of Patient Information* (1996) at para 4.5, took a different view, stating:

... the fact that information has been anonymised does not of itself remove the duty of confidence.

The point arose directly in the following case in 1999.

R v Department of Health, ex parte Source Informatics Ltd **(1999) 49 BMLR 41 (Latham J)**

The applicants were a data collecting company seeking to persuade GPs and pharmacists to allow them to collect data as to the prescribing habits of GPs. They believed this information would be of commercial value to drug companies, and would provide useful data for those interested in monitoring prescribing patterns. The proposal was that, with the consent of the GPs, the pharmacists would, for a fee, and using software provided by the applicants download onto disc the name of the GP and the identity and quantity of the drugs prescribed, but nothing which could identify the patient.

In July 1997 the respondent issued a policy document to health authorities which stated inter alia as follows:

> You may be aware that the Department published guidance – The Protection Use of Patient Information – March 1996. The guidance makes it clear that under common law and Data Protection Act principles, the general rule is that information given in confidence may not be disclosed without the consent of the provider of the information. In this instance, both patients and GPs may be regarded as providers of the data in question.
>
> The letter from the data company to Doctor X suggests that no patient information or diagnostic details would be collected. Anonymisation (with or without aggregation) does not, in our view, remove the duty of confidence towards the patients who are the subject of the data ... Anonymisation of the data (with or without aggregation) would not obviate a breach of confidence.

The applicants sought declaratory relief in relation to the policy document issued by the respondent. Upon the assumption that anonymity could be guaranteed for patients the applicants contended that the policy guidance was wrong in law in asserting that what was proposed would amount to a breach of confidence.

Latham J: In these proceedings the applicants seek certain declaratory relief in relation to a policy document issued in July 1997 by the respondent to health authorities. This followed a request to general practitioners (GPs) from a data collecting company (not the applicants) for their consent to obtain certain information relating to the treatment provided for patients in a form which would ensure the anonymity of those patients. . .

I am asked by the applicants to assume that anonymity can be guaranteed for patients. In these circumstances, it is said, the policy guidance is wrong in law in asserting as it does in the second paragraph, that what is proposed would amount to a breach of confidence ...

Mr Beloff QC, on behalf of the applicants, accepts that when the patient hands in the prescription to the pharmacist for the pharmacist to dispense the relevant drugs, the contents of the prescription are confidential information. The confidence is partly that of the GP, as the prescriber, and partly that of the patient. As far as the patient is concerned, it identifies the fact that he is taking drugs; and the nature of the drugs he is taking could identify his mental or physical condition. He submits, however, that the material supplied to and used by the applicants once abstracted from the prescription, is no longer imprinted with any confidentiality. As far as the GP is concerned, assuming that he has agreed to the applicant's proposal, he will ipso facto have consented to the use of the information. So far as the patient is concerned, the information will have become purely statistical, carrying with it no information of a personal or private nature. It follows that there has been no breach of confidence. In any event, it is submitted, an essential element in any claim for breach of confidence is that the claimant should have suffered detriment; and no detriment could be suffered by the patient so long as anonymity is secured. It is yet further submitted that the process of abstracting the information for the applicants does not involve any misuse by the pharmacist of the information contained in the prescription. The process of sorting the information so as to exclude the name of the patient is not in itself use of the material; when used, that is delivered to the applicants, it no longer contains confidential information. Finally, it is submitted that statistical information of the sort which the applicants wish to obtain is collected routinely within the health service for the benefit of the service, and the patients, and in the interests of medical research. Mr Beloff points to the fact that although the applicants clearly wish to use the material for commercial purposes, there are many research and other disinterested organisations who have written to the respondent indicating that the applicants proposal, if implemented, would provide valuable research material, and could be a useful administrative tool.

Mr Sales, for the respondent, accepts that this court can in its discretion determine the lawfulness or otherwise of the policy guidance. He submits that it is correct as a matter of law. In his submission, the information contained in the prescription can only be used for the purpose for which it was provided, namely dispensing the relevant drugs. Any other use, other than one for which actual or implied consent had been given, will amount to a misuse of the information. As it is accepted that the information is confidential, its misuse ipso facto amounts to a breach of confidence. The misuse consists of the manipulation of the information and its transmission to the applicants for the commercial benefit of the pharmacist. He submits that it is unnecessary, in order to establish a breach of confidence, that the confider suffer any detriment. If he is wrong about that, he submits that the patients would, in fact, suffer detriment by reason of the misuse of the confidential information.

It is a curious fact that this issue has never before been the subject matter of litigation, either in the context of the relationship of a doctor and his patient, or any other similar relationship which carries with it the duty of confidence. I say that it is curious because it is common knowledge that material gleaned from patients records is routinely used, as has been pointed out on behalf of the applicants, for the purposes of medical literature and research, and to obtain relevant statistics. The applicants submit that the absence of controversy is of itself a powerful indication that no one has ever considered that information obtained in a way which secures anonymity can amount to a breach of confidence. It is also surprising that there is little discussion of the matter in the literature. . .

The scope of the action was first enunciated in this form by Megarry J in *Coco v A N Clark (Engineers) Ltd* [1969] RPC 41 at 47 as follows:

> . . . three elements are normally required if, apart from contract, a case of breach of confidence is to succeed. First, the information itself, in the words of Lord Greene MR in the *Saltman* [*Saltman Engineering Co Ltd v Campbell Engineering Co Ltd* (1948) [1963] 3 All ER 413 at 415], must "have the necessary quality of confidence about it." Secondly, that information must have been imparted in circumstances importing an obligation of confidence. Thirdly, there must be an unauthorised use of that information to the detriment of the party communicating it."

As to the latter element, Megarry J expanded on it later ([1969] RPC 41 at 48):

> Thirdly, there must be an unauthorised use of the information to the detriment of the person communicating it. Some of the statements of principle in the cases omit any mention of detriment; others include it. At first sight, it seems that detriment ought to be present if equity is to be induced to intervene; but I can conceive of cases where a plaintiff might have substantial motives for seeking the aid of equity and yet suffer nothing which could fairly be called to detriment to him, as when the confidential information shows him in a favourable light but gravely injures some relation or friend of his whom he wishes to protect. The point does not arise for decision in this case, for detriment to the plaintiff plainly exists. I need therefore say no more than that although for the purpose of this case I have stated the propositions in the stricter form, I wish to keep open the possibility of the true proposition being that in the wider form.

This analysis of the action for the breach of confidence has repeatedly been cited with approval and was adopted by Lord Griffiths in *A-G v Guardian Newspapers (No 2)* [1988] 3 All ER 545 at 649, [1990] 1 AC 109 at 268.

The question at issue in the present case depends upon consideration of the third element. For it is not disputed that the information in the prescription handed to the pharmacist has the necessary quality of confidence about it; nor is it disputed that in receiving that information, the pharmacist is under a duty of confidence in relation to it. The question is whether, in acceding to the applicants' proposal, the pharmacist will be making unauthorised use of that information, and if so the extent which detriment to the patient would have to be shown in order properly to describe what had occurred as a breach of confidence. I put it in that way because I am asked to make a declaration in relation to the wording of the policy guidance, and not in relation to any specific case.

As I have already said, Mr Beloff submits that there has been no unauthorised use of the information. He does so in two separate ways. First he argues that when anonymised, the information loses its confidential character and it is only publication and dissemination of the confidential information which could amount to a breach of confidence. He referred me to the speeches in *A-G v Guardian Newspapers (No 2)*, and in particular the speech of Lord Goff ([1988] 3 All ER 545 at 659, [1990] 1 AC 109 at 281) in which he states that the vice in such a situation is the disclosure of the information. Mr Beloff submits that in no sensible way can anonymised use of the information relating to the drugs in the prescription for statistical purposes be described as disclosure. Alternatively, he submits that the process of anonymisation carried out by the pharmacist is not of itself a use of the information. The information is only used when passed on to the applicants, by which time the information has lost its confidential character. For this submission he relies on the case of *R v Brown* [1996] 1 All ER 545, [1996] 1 AC 543. The defendant in that case, a police officer, was entitled to use the police national computer database in his duties as a police officer, ran checks on two vehicles on behalf of a friend who ran a debt collection agency. On the first occasion the search did not reveal any personal data as defined by the Data Protection Act 1984; on the second occasion, although personal data was revealed, there was no evidence that any subsequent use was made of the information obtained. He was charged with using the data by retrieving information from the computer onto his screen. The House of Lords held that this did not amount to use; there had to be something more than merely the retrieval of the information onto a screen.

Mr Sales makes the straightforward submission that the confidential information is given to the pharmacist only for the purpose of obtaining the drugs; and any use for any other purpose would be unauthorised, unless the pharmacist could point to an express or implied consent to such a use. It is not suggested in the present case that a patient could properly be said to give implied consent to the use of the information for the commercial purposes of the pharmacist and the applicants. In those circumstances the use proposed will clearly be unauthorised. As far as the case of *R v Brown* is concerned, he submits that it is of no assistance to the applicants. In the present case, what is envisaged is not merely the manipulation of the material on the computer, but also its use in the sense that their Lordships considered would amount to an offence under s 5 of Data Protection Act 1984. He submits that there is no need for him to show that there would be any detriment to a patient. It is sufficient that information of an intimate nature has been used for an unauthorised purpose. In any event, he submits, that patient suffers detriment in that material which is conceded to be of commercial value is obtained from him without his having the opportunity to consider whether or not he wishes to exploit that information himself.

In my view, it is impossible to escape the logic of Mr Sales' argument that the proposal involves the unauthorised use by the pharmacist of confidential information. I reject the sophistry of Mr Beloff's submission that the process can be divided into two stages. In my judgment what is proposed will result in a clear breach of confidence unless the patient gives consent, which is not part of the proposal at present …

In one sense this is sufficient to answer the question raised in these proceedings. But I recognise that the thrust of the policy guidance is that pharmacists who agree to take part in the applicants' proposals will expose themselves to the risk of successful actions for breach of confidence. Mr Beloff's argument is of course that if anonymity can be guaranteed, no patient could conceivably suffer detriment, which is a necessary ingredient of such an action. The real question is therefore, what part detriment plays in a cause of action for breach of confidence. This subsumes a further question, which is: what constitutes detriment for the purposes of such an action?

In *A-G v Guardian Newspapers (No 2)* [1988] 3 All ER 545, [1990] 1 AC 109 differing views were expressed by their Lordships …

The clearest statement of principle is that expressed by Lord Griffiths. He considered that the answer to the question was dependant upon whether or not what would otherwise be a breach of confidence, in the sense that it was an unauthorised use of confidential information, had had an effect which justified the grant of relief. The examples given by Lord Keith, and indeed the example given by Lord Griffiths, show that all of their Lordships were aware of the fact that an unauthorised use of confidential information might have subtly and not overtly detrimental consequence. The same concern appears to lie behind the caution expressed by Megarry J in his judgment in *Coco v A N Clark (Engineers) Ltd* [1969] RPC 41.

This suggests that there may, in truth, be little or no difference between the robustly expressed view of Lord Griffiths and the more cautious views of Lord Keith and Lord Goff. It seems to me that all three recognised that there must be some effect on the confider from which the court considers that he is entitled to protection before the court will provide a remedy …

In any given case, it seems to me that it is necessary to identify with some care precisely what it is that the action for breach of confidence is there to protect. In situations such as that with which I am concerned, confidence is essentially imposed because of the personal information which the prescription contains. Professor Wacks, in his monograph *Personal Information: Privacy and the Law* (1989) p 26, defines personal information as follows:

Personal information consists of those facts, communications, or opinions which relate to the individual and which it would be reasonable to expect him to regard as intimate or sensitive and therefore want to withhold or at least to restrict their collection, use or circulation.

Dr Gurry (*Breach of Confidence* (1984)) describes the function of the action in protecting personal confidences as being closely associated with the notion of privacy. He approves (at p 13) the idea that the state of perfect privacy is the state of complete inaccessibility to others, so that a loss of privacy occurs as others obtain information about an individual, pay attention to him or gain access to him. Approaching the problem from this perspective, namely that it is the privacy of the claimant which the action is designed to protect, it is difficult to see how any relevant effect could arise from the use of successfully anonymised information. In that form, the information provides nothing which could link it to the individual's identity; therefore it is no longer personal information, nor is it information which provides any access to the individual whose information is so used.

However, Mr Sales sought to persuade me that sufficient harm could be caused even if anonymity could be guaranteed. Lord Keith is *A-G v Guardian Newspapers* [1988] 3 All ER 545 at 640, [1990] 1 AC 109 at 256 said ...

> Further, as a general rule, it is in the public interest that confidences should be respected, and the encouragement of such respect may in itself constitute a sufficient ground for recognising and enforcing the obligation of confidence even where the confider can point to no specific detriment to himself.

Mr Sales has submitted that this case provides an example of just such a situation. The information is so intimate and personal that its use for anything other than the purpose for which it is divulged constitutes a detriment to the confider and is *ipso facto* justification for restraining any unauthorised use.

This submission merges with two other submissions that he makes on this topic. First he submits that some patients might legitimately feel outraged at the fact that, without their consent, information which they may feel to be peculiarly personal to them can be used for the commercial gain of the pharmacist, and ultimately the applicants. Second, given that the information has commercial value, he submits that they may feel that they have been deprived of the opportunity to exploit that commercial value themselves.

These arguments are difficult to evaluate in the abstract, which is what I am being asked to do in these proceedings. The majority of patients would, I suspect, be unconcerned by the prospect that statistical information obtained from their prescriptions was being used in this way, recognising that, if anonymity is guaranteed, their privacy would not be invaded, and that the commercial value of their prescriptions would individually be infinitesimal. But I recognise that, for some, the sensitivity, as they would see it, of the information may be such that they would feel that any use of the information without their consent, would be unconscionable. In other words it would be a breach of the trust which they were reposing in the pharmacist. Should the law provide them with a remedy even if anonymity can be guaranteed, so that the essential purpose for which confidentiality is imposed on the pharmacist is protected?

I have come to the conclusion that Mr Sales is correct in categorising this type of situation as one in which there is a public interest in ensuring that confidences are kept. It is important that those who require medical assistance should not be inhibited in any way from seeking or obtaining it. As I have indicated, I believe that there may be some patients who will feel very strongly that the pharmacist should not give any information obtained from the prescription without their consent. This will enable them to make a decision as to whether to allow the information to be used.

This touches on one other unsatisfactory aspect of this particular action. So far, I have discussed the case on the basis that anonymity can be guaranteed. However, the applicants have themselves accepted that there is a remote risk that certain information of a rare kind might conceivably enable a patient to be identified. I fully accept that there is no evidence before me which sets out any rational basis for such concerns. Nonetheless, it highlights the fact that systems may not always be perfect. In these circumstances, why should the patient be deprived of the opportunity of making up his own mind as to the risk, such as it may be? This approach also has the merit, it seems to me, of placing the debate in its correct context. Pharmacists provide a service to the community as a whole. It is a matter of real importance that they retain the trust of the public. For them to breach their patients' confidence for their personal gain does not seem to me to be acceptable unless it could be said that the breach of confidence is in itself in the public interest. The applicants in the present case did not seek to persuade me that disclosure of the information would be in the public interest, although I can see that this may well be an alternative solution to the problem of the use by doctors and health authorities of information gleaned from patients. On the other hand I do not consider that the fact that the information has commercial value is likely, of itself to justify the court intervening at the behest of an individual patient. Leaving aside for the moment the difficult question of whether this is an interest which an action for breach of confidence will protect, the value to him of the information will, as I have already said, be infinitesimal. As Rose J said in *X v Y* [1988] 2 All ER 648 at 657: 'There must (as in common ground) be a substantial not trivial, violation of the plaintiffs' rights to justify equitable relief.'

This case was relied on by Mr Sales for the more fundamental proposition that no detriment at all need be shown in order to found the right to relief. In that case a health authority worker disclosed to a member of the press information identifying two general practitioners as suffering from AIDS. The health authority sought, inter alia, an injunction against the reporter and the newspaper which employed him restraining them from making use of that information. The defendants had made contact with the doctors concerned, and were threatening to reveal their identity. They argued at trial that even if, contrary to their main contention, they were not protected by the public interest in disclosing the information, none the less they were entitled to publish the story so long as it ensured the anonymity of the doctors as there would be no detriment to the plaintiffs, that is the health authority in that eventuality. Rose J said, (at 657):

> Counsel for the plaintiffs submitted that detriment is not a separate question but part of the balancing exercise. Further he said there *is* detriment, first, in the breach of contract, second, in the special arrangements which had to be made in order to continue treatment of one of the doctors (as described by the physician), third, in the pursuit of one of the doctors as appears from first defendants notes of conversation and unpublished draft article and in the information that the other doctor was "very suicidal", and, fourth, in the apparent breach of the plaintiffs' duties of medical confidentiality and under the National Health Service (Venereal Diseases) Regulations 1974. In my judgment detriment *in the use of* the information is not a necessary precondition to injunctive relief. (Rose J's emphasis)

He then went on to consider those cases in which injunctions had been granted to restrain those who had obtained confidential commercial information from exploiting it. He noted that in a number of those decisions, no reference to the necessity for detriment in use was made. He continued (at 658):

> But use of the information (as the defendants now seek) in a way which identifies neither the hospital nor the patients does not mean that the plaintiffs have suffered no detriment. Significant damage about which the plaintiffs are entitled to complain has already been done. This is also the answer to the additional submission of counsel for the first defendant that, though there was a breach of confidence in obtaining the information there is, on the evidence, none in publishing it, if the doctors are not identified. In my judgment it is, in the present case, the initial disclosure and its immediate consequences, not subsequent publication, which have found the plaintiffs claim in breach of contract and breach of confidence.

Mr Sales submits that, properly understood, this establishes that once there has been a breach of confidence, there is no need to show detriment in order to obtain a remedy. I do not, however, consider that it supports such a broad proposition as that. It identifies that the breach of confidence in itself might carry with it sufficient detriment to justify the grant of a remedy. With that, I respectfully agree. That is my reason for concluding that in the present case, the breach of confidence by the pharmacist is capable of providing the basis for a successful action.

In coming to this conclusion, I am fully aware of the fact that this would appear to be contrary to the dictum of Bingham LJ in *W v Egdell* (1989) 4 BMLR 96, [1990] ch 359.. In that case a doctor was retained by the plaintiff to support his application for a transfer to a regionally secure unit from a special hospital where he was detained without limit of time. The report was adverse to the plaintiff. He refused to permit the defendant doctor to disclose the report to the medical staff at the hospital. The defendant was so concerned at the danger the patient represented that he took it on himself to disclose the report. The court held that the public interest in the circumstances outweighed the doctor's duty of confidence to the plaintiff. No question arose in the case as to the effect in a breach of confidence case of making the patient's details anonymous. The case itself was concerned with the precise opposite. It does not seem to me that the remark of Bingham LJ formed any part of his reasoning. I do not therefore consider that it precludes me in any way from coming to the conclusion that I have although, obviously, I have considered it with some care.

In refusing to grant the applicant's the declaration they sought, Latham J noted that it was not suggested that the patients had expressly or impliedly consented to the disclosure of the information or that it was justified in the public interest (on which see *infra*).

There are, as you will notice, two threads to the judge's decision: (1) can disclosure of anonymised information be a breach of confidence? and (2) if so, must there be *detriment* to the patients to sustain an action? We have not before considered the second thread but we will consider it here for convenience. As regards anonymity, the judge recognised that he was 'flying in the face' of Bingham LJ's statement in *Egdell*. He does so by asserting that 'the proposal involves the unauthorised use ... of confidential information' and that 'will result in a clear breach of confidence'. It is not entirely clear, however, why he reached this conclusion. Clearly, there was an unauthorised *use* of the information in anonymising it. Certainly, there would appear to be non-compliance with the Data Protection Act 1998 (on which see *supra*, ch 7). First, there would seem to be a breach of the First Data Protection Principle, in that the 'processing' was 'unfair' under Sch 1, Pt I para 1 and Pt II, para 1 when patients were ignorant that this might occur. 'Processing' here means the process of anonymisation itself, since the disclosure of *anonymised* information is not covered by the 1998 Act (see definition of 'personal data' in s 1(1)). The Second Principle would not be breached providing the 'use' was one of the purposes notified to the Commissioner or given to the patients: Sch 1, Pt II, para 5).

Secondly, it is difficult to see how one of the conditions in Sch 2 would be satisfied in the absence of consent (Sch 2, para 1). The only basis being that 'processing is necessary for the purposes of legitimate interests' pursued by the pharmacist or by the pharmaceutical companies (para 6(1)). Perhaps, the facts would fall within this condition but there is a proviso

except where the processing is unwarranted in any particular case by reason of prejudice to the rights and freedoms or legitimate interests of the data subject.

Given Latham J's view that patients would not expect such use and they had an important interest in the use of their data, there might be difficulties of overcoming the proviso.

Thirdly, because the information was 'sensitive personal data', a further condition in Sch 3 would need to be satisfied. Usually, this does not present difficulties in the medical context because of the broadly worded condition in para 8 covering processing necessary for 'medical purposes' (see *supra*, ch 7). The latter phrase is defined to include 'preventative medicine, medical diagnosis, medical research, the provision of care and treatment and the management of healthcare services' (para 8(2)). Only the latter purposes – 'management of healthcare services' – could conceivably have applied on the facts. But, arguably, it does not since the processing was not for 'management' purposes (audit, financial etc) but rather for the 'commercial' purposes of the pharmaceutical companies who wished to track GP prescribing habits. What might save the situation is that para 8(2) only states that 'medical purposes' *includes* the specified purposes. Other purposes might, therefore, possibly be covered. However, it is not easy to see how the 'commercial' interests of pharmaceutical companies can be brought within the underlying statutory phrase 'medical purposes'.

Returning to the important issue – even if an unauthorised *use* took place, why was this a breach of confidence? Perhaps the judge meant the 'misuse' itself (ie the process of anonymisation) was such a breach. If so, as we have suggested earlier, he was wrong. Disclosure is a prerequisite of an action for breach of confidence; and the judge seemed to agree with this referring to Lord Goff's comments to that effect in *Spycatcher* (at 281). He really offered no basis for the disclosure itself amounting to a breach of confidence. Arguably, he was wrong to do so. The analogy may be drawn with an action for libel or slander. In addition to publication (the equivalent of disclosure) to a third party the action requires, *inter alia*, that the plaintiff be identified (or at least be identifiable by others with particular knowledge) (see *Morgan v Odhams Press* [1971] 1 WLR 1239 (HL)). The reason for this is that, without it, the underlying 'wrong' to the claimant will not have occurred – he will not have his reputation diminished. Likewise, it could be argued, the underlying 'wrong' to the patient will not occur unless his personal confidences are available to the public and reflect upon him – ie he does not wish others to know 'x, y and z' *about him*. Not, as the rule Latham J adopts would suggest, that he does not want others to know his information at all – that rationale is more applicable to commercial or other valuable confidences rather than personal ones. The latter really requires embarrassment at the world knowing 'x, y and z' about oneself. If properly anonymised this will not be so.

This way of looking at breach of confidence for personal confidences is closely linked to the second thread of Latham J's judgment, namely whether 'detriment' to the patient must be proved. At his citation of the Law Lords in *Spycatcher* makes clear, they left the matter somewhat uncertain. He concluded that the disclosure could *in itself* be sufficient detriment rather than requiring further additional detriment. In effect, this finesses the 'detriment' issue in medical cases. If it is necessary, it will almost always be present. Others argue, persuasively, that detriment plays no part in actions for breach of *private* confidences. At best, it may be relevant to the remedies a court is likely to make available to the claimant.

R G Toulson and C M Phipps *Confidentiality* (1996)

6.04... In the case of private confidences, the confider may have an interest in the information being kept confidential, regardless of whether disclosure would be positively harmful to him, for reasons which may be perfectly understandable (and which would be understood by any reasonable person in the position of the confidant). If so, for the reasons suggested by Lord Keith in the *Spycatcher* case, that should be sufficient to found a cause of action; and the question whether unauthorised disclosure in such circumstances is considered to involve "detriment" is an exercise in semantics. If on the other hand the confider has no substantial interest in the information being kept confidential, it would follow that the information would not possess the necessary quality of confidence to found an obligation of confidentiality. (*Moorgate Tobacco Co Ltd v Philip Morris Ltd (No 2)* (1984) 156 CLR 414 at 438.)

In the case of public confidences, the interest intended to be protected is the public interest, and it is therefore logical that the jurisdiction should only come into play in circumstances where disclosure would be injurious to the public interest. It is for that reason that cases of public confidence involve what Lord Goff referred to in the *Spycatcher* case as the additional requirement of establishing that the public interest would be harmed by publication. ([1990] 1 AC 109 at 283.) Conversely, it is misleading in such cases to speak of a public interest defence, since the injurious effect of publication on the public interest is an ingredient required to be established in order for the jurisdiction to arise.

The last sentence of the first paragraph does, in our view, shed some light on the approach that should be taken to 'anonymised' information. What is the patient's interest in it if it cannot reflect upon him?

Subsequently, the Court of Appeal reached a different view to Latham J and allowed an appeal by Source Informatics.

R v Department of Health, ex parte Source Informatics (1999) 52 BMLR 65 (CA)

Simon Brown LJ: The points taken by Source on the appeal are, first that the information is confidential to the patient only if it can be identified with him: thus the information downloaded for Source is by definition not confidential; second, that even if (contrary to submission 1) the downloading to Source constitutes anonymisation of confidential information, that itself involves no misuse of the information: it is, indeed, the very antithesis to a breach of confidence. Third, in any event, detriment is required and, as the judge below accepted, here the patient suffers none ...

Mr Sales' response, again put at its shortest, is that Source's first argument is artificial. It is the information as a composite whole which is confidential because it identifies the patient as someone requiring treatment for his condition and that, as no one doubts, the pharmacist could not properly reveal: the patient is entitled to keep his ailments to himself. Source's second argument – that to anonymise confidential information is not to misuse it – Mr Sales confronts head on. He submits that the confidential information is given to the pharmacist by the patient for the sole purpose of obtaining the prescribed drugs; any other use of it (or any part of it) for any other purpose, he argues, is unauthorised and, absent an express or implied consent or a justifying public interest, involves a breach of confidence. As for detriment, Mr Sales submits, first, that on true analysis of the law this is never a specific requirement; alternatively, second, that it is only sometimes so and certainly not in a case like this involving intimate information; alternatively, third, that patients in fact *do* suffer detriment: the confider's feelings are hurt when his confidence is breached. The patient's autonomy, he submits, must be respected ...

Both *W v Egdell* and *X v Y*, it will be noted, concerned (as does the present appeal) the duty of confidence owed in respect of personal information confided in the context of a professional relationship of trust. As Dr Francis Gurry points out in his monograph on *Breach of Confidence* (1984), this is the second of four main classes of information which traditionally have been protected, or whose use has been restricted, by the enforcement of confidences: trade secrets, personal confidences, Government information, and artistic and literary confidences. As Dr Gurry explains, the notion of privacy lies close to the heart of the courts' interest in securing personal confidences. I mention that at this stage because most of the authorities in this field appear to have been decided in respect of other classes of information and, as I shall suggest, that may have some significance ...

To my mind the one clear and consistent theme emerging from all [the] authorities is this: the confidant is placed under a duty of good faith to the confider and the touchstone by which to judge the scope of his duty and whether or not it has been fulfilled or breached is his own conscience, no more and no less. One asks, therefore, on the facts of this case: would a reasonable pharmacist's conscience be troubled by the proposed use to be made of patients' prescriptions? Would he think that by entering Source's scheme he was breaking his customers' confidence, making unconscientious use of the information they provide?

In contending for the answer 'Yes', Mr Sales urges in particular these considerations. The patient's sole purpose in handing over the prescription is so that the pharmacist may dispense the drugs prescribed. That, therefore, is the only use of it that is authorised. By anonymising the information the pharmacist does not cease to be under a duty of confidence with regard to it. Indeed the very act of anonymisation involves "manipulation" of the information and is itself objectionable. The only reason the pharmacist has something to sell is because the patient has handed over his prescription. Even when it is anonymised, it is still not in the public domain. To sell any part of it is to misuse it.

For my part I find these arguments not merely unconvincing but wholly unreal. True it is that even when stripped of anything capable of identifying the patient, the information which the pharmacist proposes to sell to Source is still not in 'the public domain'. But whether or not that matters must surely depend upon the interest at stake. I referred earlier to the different classes of information identified by Dr Gurry as traditionally having attracted the law's protection. If, of course, Government information is involved, then whether or not the information has entered the public domain may well prove decisive – as in *Spycatcher* itself. If trade secrets (which clearly include intellectual property rights) are involved, then the position may be different – consider the final passage quoted above from Dr Gurry and the spring-board principle. What then of a case like the present which involves personal confidences? What interest, one must ask, is the law here concerned to protect?

In my judgment the answer is plain. The concern of the law here is to protect the confider's personal privacy. That and that alone is the right at issue in this case. The patient has no proprietorial claim to the prescription form or to the information it contains. Of course he can bestow or withhold his custom as he pleases – the pharmacist, note, has no such right: he is by law bound to dispense to whoever presents a prescription. But that gives the patient no property in the information and no right to control its use provided only and always that his privacy is not put at risk. I referred earlier to Mr Sales' plea for respect for 'the patient's autonomy'. At first blush the submission is a beguiling one. My difficulty with it, however, is in understanding how the patient's autonomy is comprised by Source's scheme. If, as I conclude, his only legitimate interest is in the protection of his privacy and if that is safeguarded, I fail to see how his will could be thought thwarted or his personal integrity undermined. By the same token that, in a case concerning Government information, 'the principle of confidentiality can have no application to it ... once it has entered ... the public domain' (per Lord Goff), so too in a case involving personal confidences I would hold by analogy that the confidence is not breached where the confider's identity is protected.

This appeal concerns, as all agree, the application of a broad principle of equity. I propose its resolution on a similarly broad basis. I would not distinguish between Source's first and second arguments and nor would I regard the case as turning on the question of detriment. Rather I would stand back from the many detailed arguments addressed to us and hold simply that pharmacists' consciences ought not reasonably to be troubled by cooperation with Source's proposed scheme. The patient's privacy will have been safeguarded, not invaded. The pharmacist's duty of confidence will not have been breached ...

Participation in Source's scheme by doctors and pharmacists would not in my judgment expose them to any serious risk of successful breach of confidence proceedings by a patient (any more than were a prescribing doctor, asked by a manufacturer's representative what medicine he ordinarily prescribes for a given condition, to answer candidly on the basis of his current practice). If the Department continue to view such schemes as operating against the public interest, then they must take further powers in this already heavily regulated area to control or limit their effect. The law of confidence cannot be distorted for the purpose.

I would accordingly allow this appeal and let our judgments stand as the court's declaration in the matter.

Aldous and Schiemann LJJ agreed.

As you will see, the Court of Appeal has returned the law to the more orthodox (and we have argued correct) position that breach of confidence does not extend to disclosure of anonymised personal information. You may, however, consider that the reasoning of Simon Brown LJ is not wholly satisfactory. There is a danger in conceptualising the basis for protecting confidences as an aspect of 'privacy'. Clearly, it is, as we saw earlier, but it is not the same as 'privacy', for example, as protected under art 8 of the European Convention. The main danger lies in misunderstanding the essence of a breach of confidence as going beyond unauthorised disclosure of the information so as to include other unauthorised or improper *uses* of the information. As we have argued, the latter is properly seen as a 'privacy' issue but it is not the issue in breach of confidence actions. Latham J fell into the trap at first instance. Simon Brown LJ does not wholly avoid the trap himself. The law should deal with the misuse of personal information through the protective scheme of the Data Protection Act 1998.

Finally, as we shall see, Simon Brown LJ considered a number of arguments that, had there been a breach of confidence, it was lawful due to implied consent or justified by the public interest. We return to these issues later in this chapter.

(d) Doctors with dual responsibilities

There may be situations where a doctor, through examination or otherwise, obtains information about an individual but does so at the behest of another. For example, he may be engaged by an insurance company or employer to examine the patient for the latter's purposes. Other examples might be police surgeons who take samples, for instance of blood, of a suspect or examine such an individual in order to determine their fitness to be detained in a police station overnight. A further example would be an occupational health physician who may have the general care of an employee or examine an employee for the employer's purposes such as determining his fitness to work or eligibility for retirement on grounds of ill health. We saw earlier, in Chapter 4, similar situations concerned with the scope of the doctor's duty of care in negligence to such individuals. Here we are concerned with the related question of the scope of the doctor's duty of confidence to the individual. In its Guidance, the General Medical Council offers the following advice:

General Medical Council *Confidentiality: Protecting and Providing Information* **(2000)**

Disclosures where doctors have dual responsibilities

33. Situations may arise where doctors have contractual obligations to third parties, such as companies or organisations, as well as obligations to patients. Such situations may occur, for example, when doctors:

a.   Provide occupational health services or medical care for employees of a company or organisation.

b.   Are employed by an organisation such as an insurance company.
c.   Work for an agency assessing claims for benefits.
d.   Provide medical care for patients and are subsequently asked to provide medical reports or information for third parties about them.
e.   Work as police surgeons.
f.   Work in the armed forces.
g.   Work in the prison service.

34. If you are asked to write a report about and/or examine a patient, or to disclose information from existing records to a third party to whom you have contractual obligations you must:
a.   Be satisfied that the patient has been told at the earliest opportunity about the purpose of the examination and/or disclosure, the extent of the information to be disclosed and the fact that relevant information cannot be concealed or withheld. You might wish to show the form to the patient before you complete it to ensure the patient understands the scope of the information requested.
b.   Obtain, or have seen, written consent to the disclosure from the patient or a person properly authorised to act on the patient's behalf. ...
c.   Disclose only information relevant to the request for disclosure: accordingly, you should not usually disclose the whole record. ...
d.   Include only factual information you can substantiate.
e.   . . . In all circumstances you should check whether patients wish to see their report, unless patients have clearly and specifically stated that they do not wish to do so.

35. Disclosures without consent to employers, insurance companies, or any other third party, can be justified only in exceptional circumstances, for example, when they are necessary to protect others from risk of death or serious harm.

The advice contemplates disclosure in two instances: (1) with the consent of the individual; and (2) in the public interest to protect others from risk of death or serious harm.

We will discuss these modifications of the obligation of confidence shortly in this chapter. What, however, is the proper legal analysis? First, it must be determined whether a duty of confidence exists and, if so, its scope. Secondly, it must be decided whether disclosure would be a breach of that duty.

Clearly, the information provided to the doctor would attract a duty of confidentiality to some extent. It has the necessary qualities that we saw identified by Lord Goff in *A-G v Guardian Newspapers (No 2)*, *supra*. The personal information will have the necessary *quality* of confidence and the confidant (the doctor) will have received it in circumstances where he is (or ought to be) aware of this. Thus, it will have been communicated in circumstances importing an obligation of confidence. There can be no doubt that a doctor who disclosed the information to, for example, a newspaper would commit a breach of his duty of confidence owed to the individual. However, that duty would not *exist*, let alone be breached, where he acquired the information from the patient (by communication or examination) in circumstances where the individual knew (or reasonably ought to know) that it would be disclosed to another, for example, the insurance company, employer or police station officer. In other words, the scope of the duty of confidence is limited by the circumstances in which it is confided. Of course, as the GMC Guidance recognises, informing the individual ('patient' in the Guidance) of the reasons for the examination or whatever and that the information will be disclosed to another explicitly creates a *limited* obligation of confidence. It must also be the best practice since the doctor's duty is unambiguous when the individual continues with the examination. Thus, on the basis of our analysis offered above, the second question of whether disclosure would be a breach of confidence does not arise provided disclosure is *limited* to the purposes for which the examination took place. Otherwise, it would have to be justified on the basis of the *subsequent* consent of the individual or the public interest (see eg *Woolgar v Chief Constable of Sussex Police* [1999] 3 All ER 604 (CA) discussed *infra*).

There is no medical case, to our knowledge, which deals with the situation of dual obligations. However, the analysis is, we would suggest, supported by the judgment of Laws J in the following case concerned with the use by police of photographs of a suspected shoplifter obtained during a police investigation. The police supplied the photographs to shopkeepers as part of a scheme to reduce shoplifting.

Hellewell v Chief Constable of Derbyshire [1995] 4 All ER 473 (QBD)

Laws J: There is only one potential cause of action in play here, namely breach of confidence. Although that is not made explicit in the statement of claim, it clearly emerges from the plaintiff's further and better particulars where it is pleaded that 'the use to which the photograph was put was a breach of ... confidence'.

I entertain no doubt that disclosure of a photograph may, in some circumstances, be actionable as a breach of confidence. If a photographer is hired to take a photograph to be used only for certain purposes but uses it for an unauthorised purpose of his own, a claim may lie against him: *Pollard v Photographic Co* (1889) 40 Ch D 345. That case concerned portrait photographs of a lady taken for her private use by a hired photographer who then used one of the pictures for a Christmas card which was put on sale in his shop. North J upheld the plaintiff's claim, both in contract and breach of confidence. If someone with a telephoto lens were to take from a distance and with no authority a picture of another engaged in some private act, his subsequent disclosure of the photograph would, in my judgment, as surely amount to a breach of confidence as if he had found or stolen a letter or diary in which the act was recounted and proceeded to publish it. In such a case, the law would protect what might reasonably be called a right of privacy, although the name accorded to the cause of action would be breach of confidence. It is, of course, elementary that, in all such cases, a defence based on the public interest would be available ...

The chief constable says that no basis is laid in the pleading, either here or in the particulars, for the proposition that the police owed a duty of confidence in relation to the photograph at all. There is no plea of a confidential relationship or of any notice given by the plaintiff that the material contained in the photograph was to be held in confidence. As regards this latter point, it is clear on authority that a duty of confidence may be created simply out of the relationship between the parties with no requirement of any express notice from confider to confidant (see eg *A-G v Guardian Newspapers Ltd* (*No 2*) [1988] 3 All ER 545 at 658, [1990] 1 AC 109 at 281 per Lord Goff). Of course, the idea that a detained suspect might formally notify the police that the photograph just taken of him ... is to be treated by them as confidential information amounts to a Gilbertian scenario only capable of existence in a lawyer's fertile mind. ...

The first question which I must address, therefore, is whether the facts pleaded here are capable of sustaining a cause of action for breach of confidence.

In *Marcel v Comr of Police of the Metropolis* [1992] 1 All ER 72, [1992] Ch 225 the police had seized certain documents in the course of a criminal investigation. Thereafter, a subpoena duces tecum was served on them to produce the documents in civil proceedings. An injunction was sought to prohibit the police from dealing with the documents otherwise than in the course of the criminal investigation. It was granted at first instance but set aside by the Court of Appeal on the basis that it was no abuse of power by the police to obey a subpoena issued by a civil court of competent jurisdiction, and, had such a subpoena been served on the party originally holding the documents, it could not properly have been set aside, save as regards some of the documents, on grounds of legal professional privilege.

The case is far distant from the present on its facts but the following passages are important for the decision I must make. Dillon LJ expressly approved these words from Browne-Wilkinson V-C at first instance ([1992] 1 All ER 72 at 80–81, [1992] Ch 225 at 255–256):

> However, there manifestly must be *some* limitation on the purposes for which seized documents can be used. Search and seizure under statutory powers constitute fundamental infringements of the individual's immunity from interference by the state with his property and privacy – fundamental human rights ... In my judgment, subject to any ... express statutory provision in other Acts, the police are authorised to seize, retain and use documents only for public purposes related to the investigation and prosecution of crime and the return of stolen property to the true owner. (See [1991] 1 All ER 845 at 851–852, [1992] Ch 225 at 234–235; Browne-Wilkinson V-C's emphasis.)

> Nolan LJ also expressed his full sympathy with Browne-Wilkinson V-C's view that strict limits had to be placed on the use to which seized documents could properly be put by the police. He went on ([1992] 1 All ER 72 at 85, [1992] Ch 225 at 261):

The statutory powers given to the police are plainly coupled with a public law duty. The precise extent of the duty is, I think, difficult to define in general terms beyond saying that the powers must be exercised only in the public interest and with due regard to the rights of individuals. In the context of the seizure and retention of documents, I would hold that the public law duty is combined with a private law duty of confidentiality towards the owner of the documents. The private law duty appears to me ... to be of the same character as that which formed the basis of the House of Lords decision in *A-G v Guardian Newspapers Ltd (No 2)* [1988] 3 All ER 545, [1990] 1 AC 109. It arises from the relationship between the parties.

The right of confidentiality was summarised in general terms by Megarry V-C in *Malone v Comr of Police of the Metropolis (No 2)* [1979] 2 All ER 620 at 645, [1979] Ch 344 at 375:

... three elements are normally required if a case of breach of confidence is to succeed: "First the information itself, in the words of Lord Greene MR ... must 'have the necessary quality of confidence about it'. Secondly, that information must have been imparted in circumstances importing an obligation of confidence. Thirdly, there must be an unauthorised use of that information to the detriment of the party communicating it" ...

One may compare the passage from the speech of Lord Goff in *A-G v Guardian Newspapers Ltd (No 2)* [1988] 3 All ER 545 at 658, [1990] 1 AC 109 at 281, to which I have referred but not so far cited:

I start with the broad general principle (which I do not intend in any way to be definitive) that a duty of confidence arises when confidential information comes to the knowledge of a person (the confidant) in circumstances where he has notice, or is held to have agreed, that the information is confidential, with the effect that it would be just in all the circumstances that he should be precluded from disclosing the information to others. ...

In my judgment, having regard to the general principles of the law of confidence and to the approach canvassed in the dicta from *Marcel*'s case which I have cited, where the police take a photograph of a suspect such as that in question here, and do so at the police station in circumstances where at least the suspect's consent is not required, they are not, by law, free to make whatever use they will of the picture so obtained. Such a photograph will, as I have said, convey to anyone looking at it the knowledge that its subject is or has been known to the police. That is not what I may call a public fact. It may be described, prima facie at least, as a piece of confidential information. The circumstances in which the photograph is taken, where the suspect has no choice, save to insist that physical force be not used upon him, impose obligations on the police, breach of which may sound in an action at private law ...

In my judgment, the use which the police may make of a photograph such as this is limited by their obligations to the photograph's subject as follows. They may make reasonable use of it for the purpose of the prevention and detection of crime, the investigation of alleged offences and the apprehension of suspects or persons unlawfully at large. They may do so whether or not the photograph is of any person they seek to arrest or of a suspected accomplice or of anyone else. The key is that they must have these and only these purposes in mind and must, as I have said, make no more than reasonable use of the picture in seeking to accomplish them ...

The better analysis is in terms of the public interest defence, which is always available, where the facts support it, against a confidence claim. The short point, at all events, is that common sense and law alike dictate that the police should be subject to no legal sanctions if they make honest and reasonable use of a suspect's photograph in the fight against crime. I take Megarry V-C to be of the same view in *Malone v Comr of Police of the Metropolis* [1979] 2 All ER 620 at 646, [1979] Ch 344 at 377, which was concerned with telephone tapping. Where the use made of such photographs lies within these bounds, the police will have a public interest defence to any action brought against them for breach of confidence ...

Laws J's analysis was that: (1) a duty of confidence was owed to the photographed suspect; (2) the photographs could be used for the purpose for which they were taken; and (3) they could only be used for other purposes if the latter fell within the 'public interest' defence.

The analysis was followed by the Court of Appeal in *Woolgar v Chief Constable of Sussex Police* [1999] 3 All ER 604. The case concerned the disclosure by the police of an interview given by a nurse to her regulatory body, the United Kingdom Central Council for Nursing, Midwifery and Health Visiting. The Court of Appeal accepted that the disclosure was justified in the public interest (see *infra*). For us, the importance of the case lies in the court's statement of the limited duty of confidentiality. Kennedy LJ stated:

> Undoubtedly when someone is arrested and interviewed by the police what he or she says is confidential. Plainly it may be used in the course of a criminal trial if charges are brought arising out of that investigation, but if it is not so used the person interviewed is entitled to believe that, generally speaking, his or her confidence will be respected.

B. SPECIAL CASES

1. Children

Obviously the responsibility a parent has for a child means that the parent will be anxious to know all about the child's life and what the child is involved in. As it grows to maturity so the child will want to have its own secrets even from its parents. How this process is managed is, of course, the key to successful parenting. Complications arise when a third party, for example a doctor, knows something about a child. The child may not wish the parents to be told. The example most often referred to is that of a young girl who seeks contraceptive advice or treatment but asks the doctor to keep the consultation and any treatment secret. There is a danger, however, that this example is so overladen with moral controversy that if it is used as the paradigm for legal analysis it may distort our approach to the law.

What little case law there is supports the view that a duty of confidentiality is owed by a doctor to a child patient. In *Re C (a minor) (wardships: medical treatment) (No 2)* [1989] 2 All ER 791 (CA) the Court of Appeal considered whether to grant an injunction preventing disclosure of information relating to the treatment of a severely handicapped baby. In granting the injunction, the court, in part, relied upon the health professionals' duty of confidentiality owed to the child.

Lord Donaldson MR stated:

> ... Each one of these carers has in fact been involved with C in a professional capacity and, as such, owed C a duty of confidentiality.
> ... In the absence of a compelling public interest pointing in the other direction, in my judgment the court is entitled and bound to safeguard C's right to confidentiality by reinforcing the former carers' professional obligation and creating an obstacle to third parties' possible attempts to induce them to breach it and to the exploitation of any such breaches ...

Balcombe LJ stated:

> ... the welfare of baby C, and the protection of the confidentiality to which she, as much as any other patient, is entitled concerning her medical treatment, requires that those caring for her be protected from being identified publicly, or from being subjected to solicitation for information about her.

Nicholls LJ stated:

> Those who have previously been involved in her care, as social workers or as medical staff, owe a duty of confidence to her in respect of the information they have acquired about her and her background. Likewise, all the staff at the hospital where baby C is being cared for. Such information could not properly be disclosed by any of these individuals to the media.

Subsequently, in *Re Z (a minor) (freedom of publication)* [1995] 4 All ER 961 (CA), the Court of Appeal referred to *Re C* and Ward LJ stated (at 979):

> Whilst there is no difficulty in recognising that a doctor and medical staff owe their patient a duty to keep confidential all aspects of medical treatment, and that the parent of a child owes the child a similar duty, it is far from clear how far this duty extends. ... Mr Robertson does not now challenge before us the judge's finding, with which I agree, that this child has

the right of confidentiality in respect of her treatment and/or education at the institute. He also rightly concedes that the right to waive confidentiality is a right to be exercised by the parent on the child's behalf ...

Ward LJ went on to recognise that 'waiver' of the duty of confidentiality was an aspect of 'parental responsibility' which had to be exercised by the parents in the child's best interests.

The position seems clear in outcome but the courts have offered little or no analysis of why a child is owed a duty of confidentiality. We propose *three* analyses: (1) a status approach; (2) a capacity approach; and (3) an equitable unconscionability approach. As we shall see, the first and third approaches are most consistent with the views expressed in *Re C* and *Re Z*. The remaining approach – though having much in principle to attract it – would not be.

A principled analysis would proceed as follows. Under what circumstances does a legal duty of confidence arise between a child and a doctor?

(a) A status approach

On one view, when a child is taken to a doctor for treatment by its parent (and thus becomes the doctor's patient), there arises out of that status relationship a duty of confidence. The implication of this view is that *prima facie* the doctor has a duty to observe the child's confidences. Should the doctor choose to tell the parent he will need to demonstrate that his breach of confidence falls within one of the recognised exceptions justifying disclosure of confidential information. But a doctor must usually inform the parents of a young child what he discovers in order to obtain consent to further treatment and so enable the parents to carry out their duty to care for the child. Thus, this view, based as it is upon status, seems out of consonance with the legal and actual reality flowing from the parents' responsibilities to their child. It must be open to doubt, therefore, that the law begins with the premise that the doctor should tell no one and then allows the doctor (or others later if the doctor's decision is called into question) to judge whether in the particular circumstances of the case disclosure to a parent is justified. Such a view leaves much discretion to the doctor. It is, nevertheless, consistent with the Court of Appeal's views in *Re C* and *Re Z* (*supra*). It also would seem to be the view of the General Medical Council in its ethical guidance to doctors.

General Medical Council *Confidentiality: Protecting and Providing Information* (2000)

38. Problems may arise if you consider that a patient is incapable of giving consent to treatment or disclosure because of immaturity, illness or mental incapacity. If such patients ask you not to disclose information to a third party, you should try to persuade them to allow an appropriate person to be involved in the consultation. If they refuse and you are convinced that it is essential, in their medical interests, you may disclose relevant information to an appropriate person or authority. In such cases you must tell the patient before disclosing any information, and, where appropriate, seek and carefully consider the views of an advocate or carer.

You will see that the guidance begins with an obligation of confidence owed to the child (or incompetent adult) and moves to recognise a justification based upon the patient's *medical interests*.

(b) A capacity approach

Another (and analytically preferable) view would have it that the obligation of confidence arises between a child and a doctor when, but only when, the child is competent to form a relationship of confidence, ie to understand what secrecy entails. Analytically, an approach based upon competence is more in keeping with the general law as regards children since generally the courts, and Parliament, have moved away from a status approach towards a concern for a child's capacity (eg Children Act 1989 and *Gillick v West Norfolk and Wisbech AHA* [1986] AC 112).

The implication of this approach is significant. It is that *prima facie* when the child is *incompetent* to form a relationship of confidentiality the doctor is obliged to disclose information which he has learned to the parents. Only if the doctor can provide good reasons can he be justified in not doing so. The balance is struck in favour of disclosure. This is entirely in keeping with the fundamental principle that the law's paramount concern is with the welfare of the child and *prima facie* that welfare is best served by others coming to know what the doctor has learnt. Ordinarily, it will be the parents who need to know so as to care for their child. The parents will themselves come under a legal duty of confidence which the court would require them to perform in the best interests of the child (*Re Z (supra)* per Ward LJ at 979, 980–981 and 983–984). On occasions, it will be others, for example, the social services department when the doctor discovers evidence of parental abuse. The General Medical Council's advice in such circumstances is as follows:

General Medical Council *Confidentiality: Protecting and Providing Information* (2000)

39. If you believe a patient to be a victim of neglect or physical, sexual or emotional abuse and that the patient cannot give or withhold consent to disclosure, you should give information promptly to an appropriate responsible person or statutory agency, where you believe that the disclosure is in the patient's best interests. You should usually inform the patient that you intend to disclose the information before doing so. Such circumstances may arise in relation to children, where concerns about possible abuse need to be shared with other agencies such as social services. Where appropriate you should inform those with parental responsibility about the disclosure. If for any reason you believe that disclosure of information is not in the best interests of an abused or neglected patient, you must still be prepared to justify your decision.

(See also *The Protection and Use of Patient Information* (1996) (DoH) para 4.11.)

Adopting this latter approach, ie of capacity, there are three distinct sets of circumstances which fall to be examined.

(i)   THE CHILD WITH COMPLETE INCAPACITY

Here we consider the child who lacks the capacity to consent to treatment and also lacks the capacity to enter into a confidential relationship. In such a case, the child would ordinarily be very young. By contrast to the status approach, no obligation of confidence will arise between the child and the doctor. Ordinarily, therefore, as we have seen, the doctor will be entitled to disclose to the parent what he has learned so as to advance the care of the child.

To test the validity of this approach we can imagine a situation in which the doctor learns from the child information, unassociated with the reasons for the parent's bringing the child to the doctor. Assume further that it is information which causes the doctor to suspect that the child is at risk of harm. The general law requires that the doctor must act in the child's 'best interests'. The law of confidence reflects this by requiring that in such a case the doctor should tell those who can protect the child from the risk. There cannot be any doubt that the balance, in law, is struck in favour of disclosure. The doctor would need very strong reasons for not disclosing what he has learnt. Does this mean that a doctor has a *duty* to disclose this information to parents (or exceptionally to others)? Or, does it mean that he has a *discretion* to do so? In our view, his obligation to act in the 'best interests' of the child will create a very strong presumption in favour of disclosure. Normally, this would be reflected by the law imposing a duty upon the doctor the breach of which would give rise to a claim in negligence for damages if harm resulted. It does not follow, of course, that it should always be the parents who should be informed. The doctor in acting in the 'best interests' of the child must determine whether the information should more properly be disclosed to others if the child is at risk from a parent (see *Confidentiality: Protecting and Providing Information* (GMC) (2000) *supra*, at para 39 and *The Protection and Use of Patient Information* (DoH) (1996) at para 4.11).

To deduce that no obligation of confidence is owed to a child who lacks capacity to understand the nature of a confidential relationship provokes its own difficulties. What if, for example, a doctor decided to disclose information learned about the child to a newspaper for no good reason? If the doctor's intention was discovered before publication, the newspaper could be enjoined, but on what basis? Arguably, an interested party would have to invoke the court's inherent jurisdiction to act in the 'best interests' of the child (see, eg, *Re C* and *Re Z*, *supra*). What if, however, the newspaper had already published the information. What legal action, if any, could be brought against the doctor? If the status approach were adopted, the doctor would be liable for breach of confidence but we have doubted this approach. In our view a civil action will lie at the suit of the child or the parents if the disclosure causes harm because a negligence action could be brought on behalf of the child. However, if the capacity approach is adopted, where the child lacks capacity to form a confidential relationship, no action for breach of confidence *per se* can arise. This may not be an outcome to which a court would be sympathetic if faced with a child who has suffered injury as a result of a breach of confidence. The 'unconscionability' approach discussed below might overcome this difficulty. Absent any action for the infringement of parental rights, no claim could be brought, of course, by the parents (see *F v Wirral MBC* [1991] Fam 69).

(ii) THE CHILD WITH CAPACITY

Here we consider the child who has the capacity both to consent to treatment and to enter into a confidential relationship. In such a case, an obligation of confidence arises and in principle the law is no different from that applicable to adults. As with adults the obligation is not absolute. A breach of confidence may be justified if, for example, it is made in the public interest. This justification (which we shall consider later) suggests in this context that if a doctor can show that disclosure is in the 'best interests' of his child patient he will act lawfully (*Re C (a minor) (evidence: confidential information)* (1991) 7 BMLR 138, CA) in appropriately compelling circumstances such as cases of physical or sexual abuse.

It is important to state that this should not be interpreted as giving the doctor *carte blanche* to inform others just because he disagrees with his child patient's views and wishes to ignore the prohibition against disclosure. In our view, appropriately compelling circumstances should be limited to cases where the child's life is threatened or the child is exposed to a demonstrable risk of serious harm (see *Re W (a minor) (medical treatment)* [1992] 4 All ER 627).

Some support for the position argued here could be found in the (now repealed) Access to Health Records Act 1990. This recognised that a parent might only claim a right of access to the health records of a child if *either* the child was incompetent to make an application for access and access by the parent was in that child's best interests *or* the child was competent and consented (s 4(2)).

(iii)   THE CHILD WITH INCOMPLETE CAPACITY

Here we refer to the child who has the capacity to enter into a confidential relationship but lacks the capacity to consent to treatment. On the basis that competence to enter into a confidential relationship is the guiding principle in establishing whether there is a duty of confidence, the law in this situation is the same as that set out in (ii) above.

(c) Equity and unconscionability

Some of these difficulties would be avoided if the equitable basis for the duty of confidence was 'unconscionability'. In *Morison v Moat* (1851) 9 Hare 241, Turner V-C stated (at 255):

> the Court fastens the obligation on the conscience of the party, and enforces it against him in the same manner as it enforces against a party to whom a benefit is given the obligation of performing a promise on the faith of which the benefit has been conferred.

In *R v Department of Health, ex p Source Information* (1999) 52 BMLR 65 (CA) (at 76 and 77) Simon Brown LJ gave some support to this basis of the duty when he stated that the touchstone of liability was the confider's 'own conscience' and that the court was concerned to apply 'a broad principle of equity'.

The equitable duty exists because of the *context* in which the information is acquired by the doctor. It has similarities to the 'status approach' we discussed earlier. Equally, it would provide a useful framework in the case of incompetent adult patients and dead patients (see *infra*). The child's capacity to enter a confidential relationship would be *a* factor relevant to the court in determining whether *disclosure* should be prohibited but it would not be determinative. Hence, there might be exceptional circumstances where disclosure would not be unconscionable even though the child was competent (see *supra*). More significantly, even if the child were not competent, an obligation of confidence would usually arise as disclosure would be unconscionable because of the doctor's position vis-à-vis the child as his patient, unless disclosure was in the child's 'best interests'.

2. The incompetent adult

In the case of an adult patient who has always been incompetent, the capacity approach leads to the conclusion that no duty of confidence is owed to the patient since the patient is incompetent to enter into a relationship of confidence. This surprising conclusion could have been avoided, of course, if the status approach or unconscionability approach were adopted: the incompetent adult merely by being a patient would be owed a duty of confidence and could sue through a next friend if any breach occurred. We doubted the status approach on the ground that we thought the balance of law in the case of the incompetent child was in favour of there being a presumption in favour of disclosure so as to serve the incompetent's interests. This conclusion is driven by a concern for situations in which it is desirable for the doctor to disclose information and that the law should be seen to endorse this, eg where the doctor learns that a child may have been abused. Indeed, the law would recognise a duty in negligence to prevent the child from suffering avoidable harm.

You will recall that we accepted that this view is problematic in some situations. If no obligation of confidence is owed by the doctor, absent a legal right to restrain him, what then is to stop the doctor, for example, from disclosing information about his incompetent adult patient to a newspaper? In the case of a child patient, as we have seen, a parent or other may invoke the inherent jurisdiction of the court. But, as regards an incompetent adult, you will recall that the court has no *parens patriae* jurisdiction. Thus a court cannot, *prima facie*, restrain the doctor from disclosing information simply because it is not in the patient's interest to have it disclosed.

There are two solutions to this unsatisfactory state of affairs. First, the court could be given back the *parens patriae* power over adults that it lost in 1960. Secondly, the court could adopt the 'unconscionability' approach and so impress an equitable obligation upon the doctor not to disclose confidential information unless otherwise justified. In many ways, this might be seen as part of a more radical solution which would recognise that the relationship between a doctor and a patient is a fiduciary relationship from which would flow, of course, an obligation not to disclose information when it is not in the patient's interests to do so (see on 'fiduciary relationship').

The GMC's most recent guidance would seem, as it does for incompetent children, to contemplate an (ethical) obligation of confidence owed to the incompetent patient but justify disclosure to others if in the patient's *medical interests*.

General Medical Council *Confidentiality: Protecting and Providing Information* (2000)

38. Problems may arise if you consider that a patient is incapable of giving consent to treatment or disclosure because of immaturity, illness or medical incapacity. If such patients ask you not to disclose information to a third party, you should try to persuade them to allow an appropriate person to be involved in the consultation. If they refuse and you are convinced that it is essential, in their medical interests, you may disclose relevant information to an appropriate person or authority. In such cases you must tell the patient before disclosing any information, and, where appropriate, seek and carefully consider the views of an advocate or carer.

(See also *The Protection and Use of Patient Information* (1996) (DoH) para 4.9: 'decision to pass on information will in practice usually be taken by the health professionals concerned, taking into account the patient's best interests and, as necessary, the views of relatives and carers'.)

3. The dead

What effect does the death of a patient have on the obligation of confidence? The traditional ethical principle is stated by the GMC in its Guidance *Confidentiality: Protecting and Providing Information* (2000) the GMC states as follows:

40. You still have an obligation to keep personal information confidential after a patient dies. The extent to which confidential information may be disclosed after a patient's death will depend on the circumstances. These include the nature of the information, whether that information is already public knowledge or can be anonymised, and the intended use to which the information will be put. You should also consider whether, and if so to what extent, the disclosure of information may cause distress to, or be of benefit to, the patient's partner or family...
42. Particular difficulties may arise when there is a conflict of interest between parties affected by the patient's death. For example, if an insurance company seeks information in order to decide whether to make a payment under a life assurance policy, you should release information in accordance with the requirement of the Access to Health Records Act 1990 or with the authorisation of those lawfully entitled to deal with the person's estate who have been fully informed of the consequences of disclosure. It may also be appropriate to inform those close to the patient.

Is this the legal position? We are not considering here the separate and equally difficult question of whether an action for a breach of confidence which occurred during the life of a patient survives his death (on which see *Morison v Moat* (1851) 9 Hare 241; affirmed (1852) 21 LJ Ch (NS) 248). Instead, we are concerned with an action by a patient's estate for disclosures after the death of the patient. Such a claim could only be brought if the estate had itself suffered a legal wrong. Arguably, the estate can only be legally wronged in this context if it inherits a right of the deceased which is unlawfully interfered with after death. So, for example, the right to sue on a contract passes to the estate. Similarly, where property passes to the estate on death any unlawful dealing with it by others will give the estate a right of action. Thus, the crucial question is whether the right to have confidences observed is a right which passes as a chose in action to the estate. There is no clear answer. It could be argued that since what is at stake is the deceased's feelings and reputation the analogy with the law of defamation is persuasive (ie the cause of action does not survive death). Of course, in relation to defamation, the position is governed by statute. In our view the courts would reflect this policy in the case of breach of medical confidence. The Law Commission in its 1981 Report, *Breach of Confidence* (Cmnd 8388) took the same view as we do.

Law Commission *Breach of Confidence* Report No 110 (1981)

4.107...there is the situation in which a person who has imparted information in confidence to another dies before any breach of confidence has taken place. His personal representatives will have a right of action for any subsequent breach only if the information is of a 'quasi proprietorial' character – such as information relating to 'know-how' – which can be regarded as an asset of the deceased person's estate. The personal representatives of a deceased patient cannot employ the action for breach of confidence to protect the relations or friends of the deceased from distress resulting from the doctor's disclosure of his deceased patient's confidences.

Others take a different view, reflecting the GMC's position:

R G Toulson and C M Phipps *Confidentiality* (1996)

13.17...Equity may impose a duty of confidentiality towards another after the death of the original confider. The question is not one of property (whether a cause of action owned by the deceased has been assigned) but of conscience.
It is open to the courts to regard divulgence by a doctor of information supplied in confidence by a patient who has since died as being unconscionable as well as unprofessional. If so, there is no reason in principle why equity should not regard the doctor as owing a duty of confidence to the deceased's estate, consonant with the maxim that equity will not suffer a wrong to be without a remedy...

Earlier, Toulson and Phipps respond to the Law Commission's view with an example of such an instance (at para 6–04):

...It is doubtful whether that would be a correct statement of law today. If a doctor who treated a celebrity suffering from AIDS during his final illness were subsequently to sell to a newspaper intimate details which had been revealed to him by his former patient in confidence, and in the expectation that the doctor would continue to respect that confidence after the patient's death, it is more probable that a court would regard the obligation of confidence as subsisting after his death; and would grant to the personal representatives (depending on the circumstances) an injunction and/or an account of profits as the only effective means of enforcing the obligation. In such a case it could not be said that the deceased would suffer detriment from the publication, but it would seem contrary to justice that the doctor should make a windfall from his breach of his obligation. Privilege may survive in favour of a deceased's estate (*Bullivant v A-G for Victoria* [1901] AC 196) and it is hard to see why a court should not recognise the survival of an obligation of confidentiality...

In this last example, the information concerns the patient and its disclosure after his death would embarrass or cause distress to others. Suppose, however, that the patient disclosed information *about another* to the doctor which if disclosed, whether during the life or after the death of the patient, would reflect adversely on the other person. Could post-mortem disclosure be restrained to protect the other person from harm, distress or embarrassment? On one view, this is no different from the previous situations. The duty of confidentiality arise between patient and doctor and the issue is, does it survive the former's death? An alternative analysis might see the third party (about whom the information relates) as someone who is also owed a duty of confidence. There are difficulties with this analysis. The third party may not even be aware that the patient disclosed this information about them to the doctor. How could a duty be owed to that person in these circumstances? An alternative view would be that equity can operate upon the 'conscience' of the doctor to protect the third party from disclosure rather as legislation often protects from disclosure information supplied by a patient about another (eg Data Protection Act 1998, s 7(4) and Access to Health Records Act 1990, s 5(1)(a)(ii)). Toulson and Phipps (*op cit*) in their treaties on confidentiality argue for such an action (at para 13–17):

> 13.17...It is possible also that a doctor might owe a duty in conscience towards others. A patient might disclose to his doctor information about X, another member of his family (who might or might not also be his patient), publication of which would be damaging or embarrassing to X, in the understandable belief that there was no risk to X of the doctor making the information public. It would be most unsatisfactory if, on the patient being killed the next day, the doctor became free to make disclosure.
>
> A professional man may owe a duty to persons other than his client, provided that such duty does not conflict with his duty to the client. If the doctor knew that the patient was concerned for X and did not want the information to get out for X's sake, it would be open to a court to hold that publication by the doctor on the patient's death would be unconscionable conduct towards X. *White v Jones*, ([1995] 2 AC 207) although not a case on confidentiality, nevertheless provides an interesting parallel. If under concepts derived from *Nocton v Lord Ashburton* 'best interests' ([1914] AC 932) a solicitor may owe a duty in respect of the economic well being of his client's surviving intended beneficiary, (*White v Jones* [1995] 2 AC 207 at 270–272 and 275–276 per Lord Browne-Wilkinson) so should the doctor's conscience move him to continue to respect his former patient's confidence on behalf of X.

Here, again, we see, reliance on the 'unconscionability' approach of equity as the basis of the duty of confidence.

Modification of the obligation

It is beyond doubt that the legal duty of confidence owed by a doctor to his patient may be subject to exceptions. In *W v Egdell* [1990] 1 All ER 835 the Court of Appeal accepted that the obligation of confidence was not absolute (see Bingham LJ at 848). This is well recognised, as Gurry (*op cit*) points out in his book (at 148–149):

> As is the case with all obligations of confidence, the doctor's duty is not absolute but is subject to the requirement of disclosure under compulsion of law and in the public interest. Furthermore, his obligation can be released with the express or implied consent of the patient.

Gurry identifies three exceptions: (1) consent; (2) compulsion of law; and (3) the public interest. There are few judicial statements of the range of possible exceptions. Most situations will, on analysis, fall within one or more of these justifications. In a New Zealand case, the judge explored in a little more detail the possible exceptions to the duty of confidentiality.

Duncan v Medical Practitioners Disciplinary Committee [1986] 1 NZLR 513 (NZ HCt)

Jeffries J: The foregoing embodies the principle of medical confidence, but it cannot be left there without identifying the existence of qualifications and modifications for I have described, not defined exhaustively the concept. Confidentiality is not breached by private discussions with colleagues in pursuance of treatment, but this may require full disclosure and consent. The confidentiality may be waived by the patient. The doctor may be required by law to disclose. A doctor may be in a group practice where common filing systems are used. Staff who have access to information must be impressed with the requirement of confidence. Limited information to some outside agencies may be made available by a doctor from his files for statistical, accounting, data processing or other legitimate purposes. A doctor may be treating more than one person that requires, or mandates, exchange of information, but here caution and prudence must be carefully observed and consents obtained. As this very case demonstrates a doctor may reveal confidences and secrets if he is required to defend himself, or others, against accusations of wrongful conduct. There may be occasions, they are fortunately rare, when a doctor receives information involving a patient that another's life is immediately endangered and urgent action is required. The doctor must then exercise his professional judgment based upon the circumstances, and if he fairly and reasonably believes such a danger exists then he must act unhesitatingly to prevent injury or loss of life even if there is to be a breach of confidentiality. If his actions later are to be scrutinised as to their correctness, he can be confident any official inquiry will be by people sympathetic about the predicament he faced. However, that qualification cannot be advanced so as to attenuate, or undermine, the immeasurably valuable concept of medical confidence. If it were applied in that way it would be misapplied, in my view, because it would be extravagant with what is essentially a qualification to the principle. Some might say that is line-drawing and if they do then so be it. The line-drawing is not arbitrary but based upon reason and experience, and is the exercise of professional judgment which is part of daily practice for a doctor. The foregoing, either in the description or the qualifications, is not advanced as anything but an outline.

You will notice that, in addition to the conceptual categories above, Jeffries J contemplated disclosure for 'statistical, accounting, data processing or other legitimate purposes' and for the purposes of the doctor defending himself in legal or disciplinary proceedings. We will return to these *factual* situations later. First, we examine the conceptual categories by way of exceptions to the duty of confidence.

A. CONSENT

The General Medical Council's Guidance, *Confidentiality: Protecting and Providing Information* (2000), acknowledges that the patient's consent will justify disclosure (see paras 1 and 13-17 of the Guidance). Likewise, the Department of Health's guidelines, *The Protection and the Use of Patient Information* (1996), states that information may be passed to someone else 'with the patient's consent for particular purpose' (para 2.6).

Although consent is often regarded as an exception to the obligation of confidence, in fact it is not. It is merely a recognition by the patient that the doctor is no longer under an obligation to keep the confidence – it defeats the *existence* of the obligation (see eg Hirst J in *Fraser v Thames Television Ltd* [1983] 2 All ER 101 at 122: 'Counsel for the plaintiffs accepts that...the communication...in the spring or summer of 1974 was legitimate, since it was done with the plaintiff's consent.')

What precisely is meant by 'consent' to disclosure? Clearly this is a legal concept and it means more than 'agreement'. Like consent to treatment, which we considered in Chapter 5, consent must require that the patient: (1) has capacity to decide; (2) has sufficient information to make a decision; (3) is acting voluntarily or not under the undue influence of another. Perhaps it is only the second requirement that calls for specific comment here. How much information is necessary to make a decision? You will recall the limited amount that is necessary for a consent to treatment to be valid: in 'broad terms' the 'nature and purpose' of the procedure. In its Guidance, the GMC provides as follows:

14... When seeking express consent you must make sure that patients are given enough information on which to base their decision, the reasons for the disclosure and the likely consequences of the disclosure. You should also explain how much information will be disclosed and to whom it will be given ....

The ethical standard largely reflects the legal standard which would require a broad understanding of what may be disclosed and for what purposes it might be used. This could include whether the information will identify the patient or be anonymised and whether the recipients will themselves hold the information under a legal obligation of confidence (see para 9, GMC Guidance, *op cit*). They will, of course, whether or not they have a professional obligation if they receive it with actual or constructive knowledge of its confidential character.

Consent to disclose is usually *express* but it may also be *implied*. The legal notion of implied consent is not without its difficulties as we saw when considering consent to treatment (*supra,* ch 5). The precise contours of implied consent are unclear. As we saw, it is arguably a kind of estoppel whereby a patient by virtue of his conduct and the circumstances is denied the ability to say 'I did not consent to this'. Thus, it requires a consideration of all the circumstances such that it can be said that a reasonable person would, looking on, believe the patient was consenting.

Arguably something more than professional practice is needed to establish implied consent, as the following case concerned with disclosure by a bank of its customer's confidential information illustrates.

Turner v Royal Bank of Scotland plc [1999] 2 All ER (Comm) 664 (CA)

Sir Richard Scott V-C: In 1984 Mr Neil Owen Turner opened a business account with the Royal Bank of Scotland (the bank) at the Bank's London Road, Southampton branch. He later opened a personal account at the same branch.

There was nothing at all special in the circumstances in which the accounts were opened; Mr Turner simply signed a bank mandate and gave the bank a specimen of his signature. That was all there was to the opening of the accounts.

Between 19 March 1986 and 24 May 1989 the Bank, on eight separate occasions, responded to so-called status enquiries about Mr Turner. The status enquiries were made by the local branch of the National Westminster Bank.

A status enquiry is an enquiry as to the creditworthiness of the individual. The Bank responded to the National Westminster's status enquiries in terms unfavourable to Mr Turner. In responding in those terms, the Bank made use of information about the state of Mr Turner's accounts...

The Bank...has not contended that Mr Turner expressly authorised it to give references about him. It has accepted that Mr Turner did not know about the general banking practice upon which the Bank relies. But it contends that the existence of the general practice, whether or not known to Mr Turner, binds Mr Turner and that, in opening an account with the Bank, he impliedly authorised the Bank to give information about his creditworthiness to other enquiring banks. The issue on this appeal is whether those contentions are right.

...The modern law as to the duty of confidentiality owed by a banker to its customers starts with the Court of Appeal judgments in *Tournier v National Provincial & Union Bank of England* [1924] 1 KB 461. Bankes LJ, at page 471, said this in reference to the duty of confidentiality:

At the present day I think it may be asserted with confidence that the duty is a legal one arising out of contract, and that the duty is not absolute but qualified. It is not possible to frame any exhaustive definition of the duty. The most that can be done is to classify the qualification, and to indicate its limits.

And then at the bottom of page 472, he said:

In my opinion it is necessary in a case like the present to direct the jury what are the limits, and what are the qualifications of the contractual duty of secrecy implied in the relation of banker and customer. There appears to be no authority on the point. On principle I think that the qualifications can be classified under four heads: (a) Where disclosure is under compulsion by law; (b) where there is a duty to the public to disclose; (c) where the interests of the bank require disclosure; (d) where the disclosure is made by the express or implied consent of the customer.

After giving examples of the first three of these qualifications, Bankes LJ said this, about the fourth:

The familiar instance of the last class is where the customer authorises a reference to his banker.

Scrutton LJ, who dissented on a point not material to this appeal, said at page 480:

The Court will only imply terms which must necessarily have been in the contemplation of the parties in making the contract. Applying this principle to such knowledge of life as a judge is allowed to have, I have no doubt that it is an implied term of a banker's contract with his customer that the banker shall not disclose the account, or transactions relating thereto, of his customers except in certain circumstances.

Then, at the next page, page 481, he said:

I doubt whether it is sufficient excuse for disclosure, in the absence of the customer's consent, that it was in the interests of the customer, where the customer can be consulted in reasonable time and his consent or dissent obtained.

Atkin LJ, at page 484, said:

The facts in this case as to the course of business of this bank do not appear to be in any degree unusual in general banking business. I come to the conclusion that one of the implied terms of the contract is that the bank enter into a qualified obligation with their customer to abstain from disclosing information as to his affairs without his consent.

At page 586 Atkin LJ went on:

I have already stated the obligation as an obligation not to disclose without the customer's consent. It is an implied term, and may, therefore, be varied by express agreement. In any case the consent may be express or implied, and to the extent to which it is given the bank will be justified in acting. A common example of such consent would be where a customer gives a banker's reference. The extent to which he authorises information to be given on such a reference must be a question to be determined on the facts of each case. I do not desire to express any final opinion on the practice of bankers to give one another information as to the affairs of their respective customers, except to say it appears to me that if it is justified it must be upon the basis of an implied consent of the customer.

The principles laid down in these dicta in *Tournier* regarding a bank's obligation of confidentiality to its customer have been confirmed in this Court on a number of occasions. They are not open to doubt (see *Lipkin Gorman v Karpnale Ltd* [1992] 4 All ER 409, [1989] 1 WLR 1340 per May LJ at page 1357G of the latter report).

So there really is only one issue: does the banking practice on which the Bank relies justify imputing to Mr Turner an implied consent to the bank using information that would otherwise be confidential in order to give other banks references about his creditworthiness?

There are a number of factual findings made by the judge to which I should at this point refer. The judge found:

(1) that Mr Turner was unaware of the banking practice under which the Bank gave references in response to status enquiries;

(2) that nothing was said or disclosed to Mr Turner to put him on notice of the existence of this banking practice; and

(3) that the Bank went to considerable lengths to conceal from its customers the fact that it was giving references about their creditworthiness.

The Bank's case is that the general practice of bankers regarding status enquiries is contractually binding on customers whether or not they know about it, or have any reasonable means of finding out about it.

In *Chitty on Contract*, 27th edition Vol I Paragraph 12–014, the circumstances in which usage can become contractually binding are set out:

To be binding the usage must be notorious, certain and reasonable and not contrary to law.

How can the bankers' practice on which the Bank relies be regarded as notorious? It is not to the point that all banks may have known of it. The question is whether it was also notorious among the customers, the ordinary members of the public who open accounts with banks. There is no evidence whatever that in that sense this banking practice was notorious. Mr Turner did not know of it. Ordinary banking customers do not read *Paget* or any other banking text books. There was no evidence of any banking literature, prepared for the purpose of persuading individuals to open accounts with banks, that drew attention to the practice. There was no evidence of any documents put before customers, when opening an account with banks, that drew attention to it. As I have said, the evidence in this case disclosed a policy on the part of the Bank that customers should, if possible, be kept unaware of the practice.

The law holds a person contractually bound by an established usage even if he does not know of it. But it cannot become an established usage unless it is notorious. How can a banking practice be notorious if the existence of the practice is kept from customers?

The proposition that banks can agree among themselves upon a banking practice and put the practice into effect without the knowledge of their customers and then claim that, because the practice is common to all banks, it is binding upon their customers is, in my judgment, unacceptable. There is some authority supporting that reaction.

In *Barclays Bank plc v Bank of England* [1985] 1 All ER 385 Bingham J, as he then was, rejected an argument that because it was the usage of bankers to clear cheques through the clearing house system, the obligation of a presenting banker to present the cheque for collection at the branch of the paying bank where the drawer had his account was discharged by delivery of the cheque to the clearing house (see page 391). He made this comment:

The drawer of a cheque has a clear statutory right under section 45 of the [Bills of Exchange Act 1882] (subject to section 46) to be discharged from liability if the cheque is not duly presented to him or his branch of the paying bank for payment. If it is to be said that the drawer loses that right as the result of a private agreement made between the banks for their own convenience, the very strongest proof of his knowledge and assent would be needed. . .

That comment has, in my judgment, a resonance in the present case. In the present case, the bankers' practice on which the Bank relies seems to me to be no more than a private agreement among banks to respond to status enquiries made by other banks by giving opinions based on the state of their customers' accounts. But their customers are entitled, under the *Tournier* rule, that bankers should treat the state of their accounts as confidential. Customers cannot, in my judgment, be deprived of these rights by bankers establishing among themselves a bankers' practice...

Judge LJ: It is a well established principle of banking law that as part of bank customer relationship, a banker owes a qualified contractual obligation to every customer, not to disclose information about the customer's affairs to a third party, without his consent. The duty is not absolute. In *Tournier v The National Provincial & Union Bank of England* [1924] 1 KB 461, four exceptional circumstances qualifying the duty were identified and their existence has not subsequently been doubted. Neither has the principle of confidentiality.

The present appeal is based on the assertion that the disclosure was made with the express or implied consent of the customer; that is within the fourth qualification in Lord Justice Bankes' judgment in *Tournier*. Express consent presents no problem. If given, the bank's confidentiality obligation is waived for the purpose for which the consent is given. Implied consent too should normally be straightforward. Thus in an example given in *Tournier*, if a customer gives the name of the bank as an institution which may be approached for a reference, he is plainly consenting to the bank's consequent response. The value generally of a reference system of this kind both to customers and to commerce generally is obvious.

However, the consent in the present case depends on a banking practice said to have been current at the time when Mr Turner's account with the Royal Bank of Scotland was opened. Banks and similar institutions would give opinions or references about individual customers to other bankers, without their customer's consent or knowledge.

Assuming, without deciding, that this practice did indeed exist, it undoubtedly suited the banks and may have suited some of their customers, but it will not have suited all their customers, or even a vast majority of them, and many of those it may have suited would probably have preferred either to be told at the time or at least warned that this disclosure might happen, without any further reference to them.

In reality, many customers, including Mr Turner, were ignorant of the practice, and unaware that information which came into the possession of their banks through the banker/customer relationship was being disclosed to others who were not privy to it. On the face of it, such disclosure constituted a breach of the principle of confidentiality.

Properly analysed the operation of this practice, without the knowledge of customers over many years, means that, in truth, the banks unilaterally dispensed with the need for the customer's consent. The purported justification on the basis of the customer's implied consent, implied that is, not for the purpose of giving efficacy to the contract, but on the basis of the practice is itself circular. If the operation of the practice constituted a breach of the principle of confidentiality, its constant representative repetition did not validate it, at any rate, in relation to customers, who like Mr Turner were unaware of and could not be expected to know of it, and from whom it was apparently intended to be concealed. Yet the Royal Bank of Scotland had ample opportunity to inform Mr Turner of the practice and elected not to do so, either at the inception of the bank/customer relationship or before making the disclosures and, if he objected, simply to inform the enquiring bank of that fact. To regard Mr Turner's inactivity when none was sought, or could reasonably be expected of him, as consent, would be entirely unwarranted…

Thorpe LJ agreed.

Applying the approach of the judges, it can reasonably be concluded that implied consent may, as a basic minimum, require that a patient is at least aware of the practice of disclosure, is given an opportunity to object and does not do so. Reasonable effort must be made to bring the potential uses to the attention of patients. An 'opt-out' basis for implied consent would be consistent with the Department of Health's policy of encouraging notification to patients within the NHS by notices, leaflets etc of the uses to which their information may be put (see *The Protection and Use of Patient Information* (1996) (DoH) paras 3.1–3.6). It is also somewhat analogous to the approach of the Data Protection Tribunal in construing the data protection legislation requiring consent to the processing (now Sch 2, para 1 of the Data Protection Act 1998 – see *Linguaphone Institute v Data Protection Registrar*, Case DA/9431/49/1 and *British Gas v Data Protection Registrar* (1998)).

Implied consent in the medical context may be important in determining the use of medical information for research and 'NHS purposes' ie audit, management and teaching. On the analysis we suggest here, it may be difficult to justify such uses on this basis. Reliance upon the 'public interest' justification may be better. We return to this later.

A common example of implied consent as a basis for disclosure is when the patient is in the care of more than one person. In such a case the patient may be assumed to consent to all medical and nursing members of the team being informed so as properly to carry out their respective obligations. The members of the 'team' who receive the information receive it in confidence.

The importance of sharing of information for a patient's medical treatment and care is recognised by the GMC in its Guidance.

General Medical Council *Confidentiality: Protecting and Providing Information* (2000)

7.   Where patients have consented to treatment, express consent to disclosure is not usually needed before relevant information is shared to enable the treatment to be provided. For example, express consent would not be needed for general practitioners to disclose relevant personal information so that a medical secretary can type a referral letter. Similarly, where a patient has agreed to be referred for an X-ray physicians may make relevant information available to a radiologist when requesting an X-ray. Doctors cannot treat patients safely, nor provide the continuity of care without having relevant information about the patient's condition and medical history.

8. You should make sure that patients are aware that personal information about them will be shared within the health care team, unless they object, and of the reasons for this. It is particularly important to check that patients understand what will be disclosed if it is necessary to share personal information with anyone employed by another organisation or agency providing health or social care. You must respect the wishes of any patient who objects to particular information being shared with others providing care, except where this would put others at risk of death or serious harm.

9. You must make sure that anyone to whom you disclose personal information understands that it is given to them in confidence, which they must respect. Anyone receiving personal information in order to provide care is bound by a legal duty of confidence, whether or not they have contractual or professional obligations to protect confidentiality.

10. Circumstances may arise where a patient cannot be informed about the sharing of information, for example, because of a medical emergency. In these cases you should pass relevant information promptly to those providing the patients' care.

(See also *The Protection and Use of Patient Information* (1996) (DoH) para 2.6: 'the recipient needs the information because he or she is or may be concerned with the patient's care and treatment'. Though, curiously, this seems to be justified under a 'need to know' basis, which is distinct from consent to disclosure.)

The GMC Guidance not only reflects good practice, it would undoubtedly be supported by a court as reflecting English law. Notice, however, *three* limitations: (1) the patient must be aware that sharing may occur; (2) implied consent will not apply where the patient has objected; and (3) only information relevant to treating or caring for the patient should be disclosed. A further limitation must be added: that the patient is competent. As Lord Goff remarked in *Re F (mental patient: sterilisation)* [1990] 2 AC 1 at 72, implied consent is 'artificial' and 'difficult to impute' where the patient is incompetent. Disclosure, whether to health professionals, relatives or others, must in this instance be justified on a different principle (see *infra*).

It is a continually vexing question whether information should be imparted to those members of the team who do not belong to a profession with a strictly enforced professional code and who may not preserve records under the same circumstances of confidentiality and yet may have a legitimate interest. Interestingly, the GMC in its Guidance (*op cit*, para 9) does contemplate sharing information in this context without explicit consent but notes that the 'receiver' must be made to understand that the information is held in confidence regardless of their professional obligations.

Likewise, the Department of Health Guidelines, require the patient's express knowledge and acknowledges he may veto the disclosure.

The Protection and Use of Patient Information Department of Health (1996)

4.14 In all areas of health and social care the various agencies involved, including the NHS, should be aiming to deliver a 'seamless' service. In some instances particular agencies have a statutory obligation to assist each other or to work together. Essential patient information must therefore be able to pass between the NHS, local authority social services and other services (such as housing, education, voluntary or independent bodies) where those agencies are contributing to or planning a programme of care, or where one may need to be initiated. The patient needs to be aware that some information sharing will be necessary and this can usually be discussed with him or her as part of the care planning process.

4.15 If the patient raises any objections, the possible consequences for a coordinated care programme should be explained and assurances given that other agencies would receive only information which they really need to know. However, as at paragraph 4.4, the patient's ultimate decision should be respected unless there are overriding considerations to the contrary: for example, in some cases involving a history of violence, or where an elderly frail person shows signs of non-accidental injury, it may be justified to pass information to another agency without his or her agreement (see paragraph 5.6).

It may be that the practical needs involved in the management of a patient would lead to a court to say that a doctor has a discretion to disclose to all those professionals who also 'need to know' so as properly to serve the medical needs of the patient. Such a discretion must necessarily be exercised with caution and information should only be disclosed to others who are made aware of the confidential nature of the information and that they will have a *legal* duty to respect that confidence (on which, see *The Protection and Use of Patient Information* (1996) (DoH) para 4.1).

One final issue concerning consent. You will recall that in *Duncan v Medical Practitioners' Disciplinary Committee* [1986] 1 NZLR 513, Jeffries J contemplated the lawful disclosure of confidential information by a doctor 'if he is required to defend himself, or others, against accusations of wrongful conduct'. What is the legal justification for this? Could it be implied consent by the patient? The argument would be at its strongest where the patient initiates the proceedings against his own doctor. In such circumstances, it could be argued that the patient implied consents to relevant medical records being disclosed by the doctor, for example to his lawyers, for the purposes of defending himself (see *Hay v University of Alberta Hospital* (1990) 69 DLR (4th) 755 (Alta QB)). Where, however, the action is not brought by a patient or is not brought against the doctor, the argument is at its weakest and the better view would be that the patient's consent to disclosure would be required or an order of the court under r 31 of the Civil Procedure Rules 1998 should be sought (for a statutory provision dealing with such disclosure in respect of assisted reproduction, see, s 33(6)(f) of the Human Fertilisation and Embryology Act 1990).

B. PUBLIC INTEREST

An important exception to the duty of confidentiality is where the public interest in disclosure is engaged and outweighs the public interest in protecting the confidence. The exception took form, perhaps first, in the context of disclosing wrongdoing or iniquitous behaviour by an individual.

Lion Laboratories Ltd v Evans [1984] 2 All ER 417 (CA)

Griffiths LJ: The first question to be determined is whether there exists a defence of public interest to actions for breach of confidentiality and copyright, and, if so, whether it is limited to situations in which there has been serious wrongdoing by the plaintiffs, the so-called 'iniquity' rule.

I am quite satisfied that the defence of public interest is now well established in actions for breach of confidence and, although there is less authority on the point, that it also extends to breach of copyright: see by way of example *Fraser v Evans* [1969] 1 All ER 8, [1969] 1 QB 349; *Hubbard v Vosper* [1972] 1 All ER 1023, [1972] 2 QB 84; *Woodward v Hutchins* [1977] 2 All ER 751, [1977] 1 WLR 760 and *British Steel Corpn v Granada Television Ltd* [1981] 1 All ER 417, [1981] AC 1096.

I can see no sensible reason why this defence should be limited to cases in which there has been wrongdoing on the part of the plaintiffs. I believe that the so-called iniquity rule evolved because in most cases where the facts justified a publication in breach of confidence the plaintiff had behaved so disgracefully or criminally that it was judged in the public interest that his behaviour should be exposed. No doubt it is in such circumstances that the defence will usually arise, but it is not difficult to think of instances where, although there has been no wrongdoing on the part of the plaintiff, it may be vital in the public interest to publish a part of his confidential information.

To the extent that there was any doubt about the existence of the 'public interest' justification, those doubts were laid to rest by the House of Lords in *A-G v Guardian Newspapers (No 2)* [1990] 1 AC 109, [1988] 3 All ER 545.

A-G v Guardian Newspapers (No 2) [1988] 3 All ER 545

Lord Griffiths: The courts have, however, always refused to uphold the right to confidence when to do so would be to cover up wrongdoing. In *Gartside v Outram* (1856) 26 LJ Ch 113 it was said that there could be no confidence in iniquity. This approach has been developed in the modern authorities to include cases in which it is in the public interest that the confidential information should be disclosed: see *Initial Services Ltd v Putterill* [1967] 3 All ER 145, [1968] 1 QB 396; *Beloff v Pressdram Ltd* [1973] 1 All ER 241 and *Lion Laboratories Ltd v Evans* [1984] 2 All ER 417, [1985] QB 526. This involves the judge in balancing the public interest in upholding the right to confidence, which is based on the moral principles of loyalty and fair dealing, against some other public interest that will be served by the publication of the confidential material.

Lord Goff: The third limiting principle is of far greater importance. It is that, although the basis of the law's protection of confidence is that there is a public interest that confidences should be preserved and protected by the law, nevertheless that public interest may be outweighed by some other countervailing public interest which favours disclosure. This limitation may apply, as the judge pointed out, to all types of confidential information. It is this limiting principle which may require a court to carry out a balancing operation, weighing the public interest in maintaining confidence against a countervailing public interest favouring disclosure.

Embraced within this limiting principle is, of course, the so-called defence of iniquity. In origin, this principle was narrowly stated, on the basis that a man cannot be made the 'confidant of a crime or a fraud' (see *Gartside v Outram* (1856) 26 LJ Ch 113 at 114 per Page Wood V-C). But it is now clear that the principle extends to matters of which disclosure is required in the public interest (see *Beloff v Pressdram Ltd* [1973] 1 All ER 241 at 260 per Ungoed-Thomas J and *Lion Laboratories Ltd v Evans* [1984] 2 All ER 417 at 432–433, [1985] 1 QB 526 at 550 per Griffiths LJ).

Clearly, this is potentially a very widely drawn modification to the obligation of confidence. If interpreted too widely, it might swallow up the obligation. What guidance do the cases give to the doctor as to when it is in the public interest to disclose confidential information? Lord Wilberforce was anxious to make clear that: 'there is a wide difference between what is interesting to the public and what it is in the public interest to make known' (*British Steel Corpn v Granada Television Ltd* [1981] 1 All ER 417 at 455).

The extent to which concern for the public interest may serve as a justification for breach of medical confidences is considered in the following case.

X v Y [1988] 2 All ER 648, (1987) 3 BMLR 1 (QBD)

In February 1987 one or more employees of the plaintiffs, a health authority, supplied the first defendant, a reporter on a national newspaper owned and published by the second defendants, with information obtained from hospital records which identified two doctors who were carrying on general practice despite having contracted the disease AIDS. The second defendants made one or more payments of £100 for the information. On 28 February the plaintiffs obtained an order restraining the defendants from 'publishing…or making any use whatsoever of any confidential information' which was the property of the plaintiffs and contained in their hospital records. On 15 March the second defendants published an article written by the first defendant, under the headline 'Scandal of Docs with AIDS', which implied that there were doctors in Britain who were continuing to practise despite having contracted AIDS and that the Department of Health and Social Security wished to suppress that fact. The defendants intended to publish a further article identifying the doctors. The plaintiffs sought (i) an injunction restraining the defendants from publishing the identity of the two doctors, (ii) disclosure by the defendants of their sources…The question arose whether the second defendants were justified in the public interest in publishing and using the information disclosed to the first defendant.

Rose J: Under the National Health Service (Venereal Diseases) Regulations 1974 the plaintiffs and their servants have a statutory duty to take all necessary steps to secure that any information capable of identifying patients examined or treated for AIDS shall not be disclosed except to a medical practitioner, or a person under his direction, in connection with and for the purpose of treatment, or prevention of the spread, of the disease. Confidentiality is of paramount importance to such patients, including doctors. The plaintiffs take care to ensure it. Their servants are contractually bound to respect it. If it is breached, or if the patients have grounds for believing that it may be or has been breached they will be reluctant to come forward for and to continue with treatment and, in particular, counselling. If the actual or apprehended breach is to the press that reluctance is likely to be very great. If treatment is not provided or continued the individual will be deprived of its benefit and the public are likely to suffer from an increase in the rate of spread of the disease. The preservation of confidentiality is therefore in the public interest…Is publication of this confidential information justified in the public interest? …

On the one hand there are the public interests in having a free press and an informed public debate; on the other, it is in the public interest that actual or potential AIDS sufferers should be able to resort to hospitals without fear of this being revealed, that those owing duties of confidence in their employment should be loyal and should not disclose confidential matters and that, prima facie, no one should be allowed to use information extracted in breach of confidence from hospital records even if disclosure of the particular information may not give rise to immediately apparent harm.

I keep in the forefront of my mind the very important public interest in freedom of the press. And I accept that there is some public interest in knowing that which the defendants seek to publish (in whichever version). But in my judgment those public interests are substantially outweighed when measured against the public interests in relation to loyalty and confidentiality both generally and with particular reference to AIDS patients' hospital records. There has been no misconduct by the plaintiffs. The records of hospital patients, particularly those suffering from this appalling condition should, in my judgment, be as confidential as the courts can properly keep them in order that the plaintiffs may 'be free from suspicion that they are harbouring disloyal employees'. The plaintiffs have 'suffered a grievous wrong in which the defendants became involved…with active participation'. The deprivation of the public of the information sought to be published will be of minimal significance if the injunction is granted; for, without it, all the evidence before me shows that a wide-ranging public debate about AIDS generally an about its effect on doctors is taking place among doctors of widely differing views, within and without the BMA, in medical journals and in many newspapers, including the Observer, the Sunday Times and the Daily Express. Indeed, the sterility of the defendants' argument is demonstrated by the edition of the second defendants' own newspaper dated 22 March 1987. It is there expressly stated, purportedly quoting a Mr Milligan, that three general practitioners two of whom are practising (impliedly in Britain) have AIDS. Paraphrasing Templeman LJ in the *Schering* case, the facts, in the most limited version now sought to be published, have already been made available and may again be made available if they are known otherwise than through the medium of the informer. The risk of identification is only one factor in assessing whether to permit the use of confidential information. In my judgment to allow publication in the recently suggested restricted form, would be to enable both defendants to procure breaches of confidence and then to make their own selection for publication. This would make a mockery of the law's protection of confidentiality when no justifying public interest has been shown. These are the considerations which guide me, whether my task is properly described as a balancing exercise, or an exercise in judicial judgment, or both.

No one has suggested that damages would be an adequate remedy in this case.

It follows that the answer to the first question is No. The plaintiffs are entitled to a permanent injunction in the form of para 1(i) of the interlocutory order made by Ian Kennedy J.

You will notice that Rose J rightly characterises the law's concern with the protection of confidences as being a public interest. Some have characterised the right to confidence as a private interest. The danger of doing so is that private interests tend to give way to the public interest when they are weighed against each other. Interests are far more fairly balanced when public interest is set against public interest and private interest against private interest.

It will be helpful at this point to identify the types of situation in which the 'public interest' may be prayed in aid to justify disclosures of confidential information. We can usefully consider these under the following headings: (1) danger (risk) to the health or safety of others; (2) prevention or detection of crime; and (3) teaching, research and management purposes.

1. Danger to the health or safety of others

This situation arose in the leading English case concerned with the 'public interest' exception in the medical context.

W v Egdell [1990] 1 All ER 835, (1989) 4 BMLR 96 (CA)

W was detained as a patient in a secure hospital without limit of time as a potential threat to public safety after he shot and killed five people and wounded two others. Ten years after he had been first detained he applied to a mental health review tribunal to be discharged or transferred to a regional secure unit with a view to his eventual discharge. His responsible medical officer, who had diagnosed him as suffering from schizophrenia which could be treated by drugs, supported the application but it was opposed by the Secretary of State. His solicitors instructed a consultant psychiatrist, E, to examine W and report on his mental condition with a view to using the report to support W's application to the tribunal. In his report E strongly opposed W's transfer and recommended that further tests and treatment of W would be advisable, and drew attention to W's long-standing interest in firearms and explosives. E sent the report to W's solicitors in the belief that it would be placed before the tribunal, but, in view of the contents of the report, W through his solicitors withdrew his application. When E learnt that the application had been withdrawn and that neither the tribunal nor the hospital charged with W's clinical management had received a copy of his report he contacted the medical director of the hospital, who, having discussed W's case with E, agreed that the hospital should receive a copy of the report in the interests of W's further treatment. At E's prompting the hospital sent a copy of his report to the Secretary of State, who, in turn, forwarded the report to the tribunal when referring W's case to them for consideration.

When W discovered that the report had been disclosed he issued a writ against E and the recipients of the report seeking (i) an injunction to restrain them from using or disclosing the report, (ii) delivery up of all copies of the report and (iii) damages for breach of the duty of confidence. Scott J held that the duty of confidentiality owed by E to W as his patient was subordinate to E's public duty to disclose the results of his examination to the authorities responsible for W because such disclosure was necessary to ensure that the authorities were fully informed about W's mental condition when making decisions concerning his future. The judge accordingly dismissed W's claim against E and the recipients of the report. W appealed against the dismissal of his action against E, contending that the public interest in the duty of confidentiality owed by E to W should override any public interest considerations in disclosing the report to the authorities responsible for W.

Stephen Brown P: In the course of his judgment Scott J said ([1989] 1 All ER 1089 at 1101–1102, [1989] 2 WLR at 709–710):

The basis of W's case is that his interview with Dr Egdell on 23 July 1987 and the report written by Dr Egdell on the basis of that interview is, or ought to have been, protected from disclosure by the duty of confidence resting on Dr Egdell as W's doctor. It is claimed that Dr Egdell was in breach of his duty of confidence in telling Dr Hunter about the report, in sending a copy of the report to Dr Hunter and in urging the despatch of a copy to the Home Office…It is convenient for me first to ask myself what duty of confidence a court of equity ought to regard as imposed on Dr Egdell by the circumstances in which he obtained information from and about W and prepared his report. It is in my judgment plain, and the contrary has not been suggested, that the circumstances did impose on Dr Egdell a duty of confidence. If, for instance Dr Egdell had sold the contents of his report to a newspaper, I do not think any court of equity would hesitate for a moment before concluding that his conduct had been a breach of his duty of confidence. The question in the present case is not whether Dr Egdell was under a duty of confidence; he plainly was. The question is as to the breadth of that duty. Did the duty extend so as to bar disclosure of the report to the medical director of the hospital? Did it bar disclosure to the Home Office? In the *Spycatcher* case [*A-G v Guardian Newspapers Ltd (No 2)*] [1988] 3 All ER 545 at 658–659, [1988] 3 WLR 776 at 805, 807 in the House of Lords Lord Goff, after accepting 'the broad general principle…that a duty of confidence arises when confidential information comes to the knowledge of a person (the confidant) in circumstances where he has notice, or is held to have agreed, that the information is confidential, with the effect that it would be just in all the circumstances that he should be precluded from disclosing the information to others', formulated three limiting principles. He said: 'The third limiting principle is of far greater importance. It is that, although the basis of the law's protection of confidence is that, there is a public interest that confidences should be preserved and protected by the law, nevertheless that public interest may be outweighed by some other countervailing public interest which favours disclosure. This limitation may apply, as the learned judge pointed out, to all types of confidential information. It is this limiting principle which may require a court to carry out a balancing operation weighing the public interest in maintaining confidence against a countervailing public interest favouring disclosure'. In *X v Y* [1988] 2 All ER 648 at 653, a case which concerned doctors who were believed to be continuing to practise despite having contracted AIDS, Rose J said: 'In the long run, preservation of confidentiality is the only way of securing public health; otherwise doctors will be discredited as a source of education, for future individual patients "will not come forward if doctors are going to squeal on them". Consequently, confidentiality is vital to secure public as well as private health, for unless those infected come forward they cannot be counselled and self-treatment does not provide the best care...' The question in a particular case whether a duty of confidentiality extends to bar particular disclosures that the confidant has made or wants to make requires the court to balance the interest to be served by non-disclosure against the interest served by disclosure. Rose J struck that balance. It came down, he held, in favour of non-disclosure. In the *Spycatcher* case that balance too was struck. In that case the balance did not come down in favour of non-disclosure. I must endeavour to strike the balance in the present case.

Counsel for W agreed that the judge was required to carry out a balancing exercise. He said that it is a question of degree.

As a starting point Scott J turned to 'Advice on Standards of Professional Conduct and of Medical Ethics' contained in the General Medical Council's 'Blue Book' on professional conduct and discipline. The judge said ([1989] 1 All ER 1089 at 1103, [1989] 2 WLR 689 at 711–712):

These rules do not provide a definitive answer to the question raised in the present case as to the breadth of the duty of confidence owed by Dr Egdell. They seem to me valuable, however, in showing the approach of the General Medical Council to the breadth of the doctor/patient duty of confidence.

These rules do not themselves have statutory authority. Nevertheless, the General Medical Council in exercising its disciplinary jurisdiction does so in pursuance of the provisions of the Medical Act 1983. Under the heading 'Professional Confidence', rr [80] to 82 provide as follows:

80. It is a doctor's duty, except in the cases mentioned below, strictly to observe the rule of professional secrecy by refraining from disclosing voluntarily to any third party information about a patient which he has learnt directly or indirectly in his professional capacity as a registered medical practitioner.

81. The circumstances where exceptions to the rule may be permitted are as follows...
   (b) Confidential information may be shared with other registered medical practitioners who participate in or assume responsibility for clinical management of the patient. To the extent that the doctor deems it necessary for the performance of their particular duties, confidential information may also be shared with other persons (nurses and other health care professionals) who are assisting and collaborating with the doctor in his professional relationship with the patient. It is the doctor's responsibility to ensure that such individuals appreciate that the information is being imparted in strict professional confidence...
   (g) Rarely, disclosure may be justified on the ground that it is in the public interest which, in certain circumstances such as, for example, investigation by the police of a grave or very serious crime, might override the doctor's duty to maintain his patient's confidence...
   82. Whatever the circumstances, a doctor must always be prepared to justify his action if he has disclosed confidential information. If a doctor is in doubt whether any of the exceptions mentioned above would justify him in disclosing information in a particular situation he will be wise to seek advice from a medical defence society or professional association...

The judge said that paras (b) and (g) of r 81 seemed to him to be particularly relevant. He then rehearsed the circumstances of the disclosure by Dr Egdell of his report and asked the question ([1989] 1 All ER 1089 at 1104, [1989] 2 WLR 689 at 713):

Did these circumstances impose on Dr Egdell a duty not to disclose his opinions and his report to Dr Hunter, the medical director at the hospital? In my judgment they did not. Dr Egdell was expressing opinions which were relevant to the nature of the treatment and care to be accorded to W at the hospital. Dr Egdell was, in effect, recommending a change from the approach to treatment and care that Dr Ghosh was following. He was expressing reservations about Dr Ghosh's diagnosis. The case seems to me to fall squarely within para (b) of r 81. But I would base my conclusion on broader considerations than that. I decline to overlook the background to Dr Egdell's examination of W. True it is that Dr Egdell was engaged by W. He was the doctor of W's choice. Nonetheless, in my opinion, the duty he owed to W was not his only duty. W was not an ordinary member of the public. He was, consequent on the killings he had perpetrated, held in a secure hospital subject to a regime whereby decisions concerning his future were to be taken by public authorities, the Home Secretary or the tribunal. W's own interests would not be the only nor the main criterion in the taking of those decisions. The safety of the public would be the main criterion. In my view, a doctor called on, as Dr Egdell was, to examine a patient such as W owes a duty not only to his patient but also a duty to the public. His duty to the public would require him, in my opinion, to place before the proper authorities the result of his examination if, in his opinion, the public interest so required. This would be so, in my opinion, whether or not the patient instructed him not to do so.

The judge then referred to the submission of counsel for W that the dominant public interest in the case was the public interest in patients being able to make full and frank disclosure to their doctors, and in particular to their psychiatrist, without fear that the doctor would disclose the information to others. The judge said ([1989] 1 All ER 1089 at 1104–1105, [1989] 2 WLR 689 at 713–714):

> I accept the general importance in the public interest that this should be so. It justifies the General Medical Council's r 80...In truth, as it seems to me, the interest to be served by the duty of confidence for which counsel for W contends is the private interest of W and not any broader public interest. If I set the private interest of W in the balance against the public interest served by disclosure of the report to Dr Hunter and the Home Office, I find the weight of the public interest prevails...In my judgment, therefore, the circumstances of this case did not impose on Dr Egdell an obligation of conscience, an equitable obligation, to refrain from disclosing his report to Dr Hunter, or to refrain from encouraging its disclosure to the Home Office.

In this court counsel for W acknowledges that, in addition to the duty of confidence admittedly owed by Dr Egdell to W, it was necessary for the judge to consider the public interest in the disclosure by Dr Egdell of his report to the authorities. There are two competing public interest considerations. However, he submitted that the dominant public interest was the duty of confidence owed by Dr Egdell to W. The burden of proving that that duty was overridden by public interest considerations in disclosing his opinion to the public authorities rested fairly and squarely on Dr Egdell. He contended that, where the public interest relied on to justify a breach of confidence is alleged to be the reduction or elimination of a risk to public safety, it must be shown (a) that such a risk is real, immediate and serious, (b) that it will be substantially reduced by disclosure, (c) that the disclosure is no greater than is reasonably necessary to minimise the risk and (d) that the consequent damage to the public interest protected by the duty of confidentiality is outweighed by the public interest in minimising the risk. He relied on the decision of Rose J in *X v Y* [1988] 2 All ER 648. He also cited a passage from the judgment of Boreham J in *Hunter v Mann* [1974] 2 All ER 414 at 417–418, [1974] QB 767 at 772:

> The second proposition is this: that in common with other professional men, for instance a priest and there are of course others, the doctor is under a duty not to disclose, without the consent of his patient, information which he, the doctor, has gained in his professional capacity, save, says counsel for the appellant, in very exceptional circumstances. He quoted the example of the murderer still manic, who would be a menace to society. But, says counsel, save in exceptional circumstances, the general rule applies. He adds that the law will enforce that duty.

He referred to the American case of *Tarasoff v Regents of the University of California* (1976) 17 Cal 3d 358 as an example of extreme circumstances and submitted that only in the most extreme circumstances could a doctor be relieved from observing the strict duty of confidence imposed on him by reason of his relationship with his patient. In this instance, said counsel for W, there was no immediate prospect of W being released or of being detained other than under secure conditions and furthermore any change in his circumstances would be conditional on further expert analysis and recommendation.

The two interests which had to be balanced in this case were both public interests. The judge was wrong to refer to W's 'private' interest. The judge was also in error, said counsel for W, in saying: 'The case seems to me to fall squarely within para (*b*) of r 81' (of the General Medical Council's rules). Dr Egdell did not have any clinical responsibility for W and accordingly that particular rule could not be relied on by Dr Egdell in the present circumstances...

Counsel for Dr Egdell argued that Dr Egdell is acknowledged to be a responsible and experienced consultant psychiatrist having particular knowledge of the procedures relating to the management and treatment of restricted patients detained in secure conditions under the provisions of the Mental Health Act 1983. His evidence on matters of fact was not challenged. It must be accepted that he was genuinely seriously concerned by the revelation of what seemed to him to be entirely new facts relating to W's long-standing interest in guns and explosives. It is not challenged he said, that he acted in good faith in disclosing his report to Dr Hunter and in urging its disclosure to the Home Secretary. He plainly believed that he was acting in the public interest.

The balance of public interest clearly lay in the restricted disclosure of vital information to the director of the hospital and to the Secretary of State who had the onerous duty of safeguarding public safety.

In this case the number and nature of the killings by W must inevitably give rise to the gravest concern for the safety of the public. The authorities responsible for W's treatment and management must be entitled to the fullest relevant information concerning his condition. It is clear that Dr Egdell did have highly relevant information about W's condition which reflected on his dangerousness. In my judgment the position came within the terms of r 81(*g*) of the General Medical Council's rules. Furthermore, Dr Egdell amply justified his action within the terms of r 82. The suppression of the material contained in his report would have deprived both the hospital and the Secretary of State of vital information, directly relevant to questions of public safety. Although it may be said that Dr Egdell's action in disclosing his report to Dr Hunter fell within the letter of r 81(*b*), the judge in fact based his conclusion on what he termed 'broader considerations', that is to say the safety of the public. I agree with him.

In so far as the judge referred to the 'private interest' of W, I do not consider that the passage in his judgment (see [1989] 1 All ER 1089 at 1105, [1989] 2 WLR 689 at 714) accurately stated the position. There are two competing public interests and it is clear that by his reference to *X v Y* [1989] 2 All ER 648 the judge was fully seised of this point. Of course W has a private interest but the duty of confidence owed to him is based on the broader ground of public interest described by Rose J in *X v Y*.

Accordingly I agree with the judge's decision to dismiss W's claim. Dr Egdell was clearly justified in taking the course that he did.

Bingham LJ: The breadth of [a duty of confidence] in any case is...dependent on circumstances. Where a prison doctor examines a remand prisoner to determine his fitness to plead or a proposer for life insurance is examined by a doctor nominated by the insurance company or a personal injury plaintiff attends on the defendant's medical adviser or a prospective bidder instructs accountants to investigate (with its consent) the books of a target company, the professional man's duty of confidence towards the subject of his examination plainly does not bar disclosure of his findings to the party at whose instance he was appointed to make his examination. Here, however, Dr Egdell was engaged by W, not by the tribunal or the hospital authorities. He assumed at first that his report would be communicated to the tribunal and thus become known to the authorities but he must, I think, have appreciated that W and his legal advisers could decide not to adduce his report in evidence before the tribunal.

The decided cases very clearly establish (1) that the law recognises an important public interest in maintaining professional duties of confidence but (2) that the law treats such duties not as absolute but as liable to be overridden where there is held to be a stronger public interest in disclosure. Thus the public interest in the administration of justice may require a clergyman, a banker, a medical man, a journalist or an accountant to breach his professional duty of confidence (*A-G v Mulholland* [1963] 1 All ER 767 at 771, [1963] 2 QB 477 at 489–490, *Chantrey Martin & Co v Martin* [1953] 2 All ER 691, [1953] 2 QB 286). In *Parry-Jones v Law Society* [1968] 1 All ER 177, [1969] 1 Ch 1 a solicitor's duty of confidence towards his clients was held to be overridden by his duty to comply with the law of the land, which required him to produce documents for inspection under the Solicitors' Accounts Rules. A doctor's duty of confidence to his patient may be overridden by clear statutory language (as in *Hunter v Mann* [1974] 2 All ER 414, [1974] QB 767). A banker owes his customer an undoubted duty of confidence, but he may become subject to a duty to the public to disclose, as where danger to the state or public duty supersede the duty of agent to principal (*Tournier v National Provincial and Union Bank of England* [1924] 1 KB 461 at 473, 486, [1923] All ER Rep 550 at 554, 561). An employee may justify breach of a duty of confidence towards his employer otherwise binding on him when there is a public interest in the subject matter of his disclosure (*Initial Services Ltd v Putterill* [1967] 3 All ER 145, [1968] 1 QB 396, *Lion Laboratories v Evans* [1984] 2 All ER 417, [1985] QB 526). These qualifications of the duty of confidence arise not because that duty is not accorded legal recognition but for the reason clearly given by Lord Goff in his speech in (*A-G v Guardian Newspapers Ltd (No 2)* [1988] 3 All ER 545 at 659, [1988] 3 WLR 776 at 807, *the Spycatcher* case), quoted by Scott J ([1989] 1 All ER 1089 at 1102, [1989] 2 WLR 689 at 710):

> The third limiting principle is of far greater importance. It is that, although the basis of the law's protection of confidence is that there is a public interest that confidences should be preserved and protected by the law, nevertheless that public interest may be outweighed by some other countervailing public interest which favours disclosure. This limitation may apply, as the judge pointed out, to all types of confidential information. It is this limiting principle which may require a court to carry out a balancing operation, weighing the public interest in maintaining confidence against a countervailing public interest favouring disclosure.

These principles were not in issue between the parties to this appeal. Counsel for W accepted that W's right to confidence was qualified and not absolute. But it is important to insist on the public interest in preserving W's right to confidence because the judge in his judgment concluded that while W had a strong private interest in barring disclosure of Dr Egdell's report he could not rest his case on any broader public interest (see [1989] 1 All ER 1089 1104–1105, [1989] 2 WLR 689 at 713–714). Here, as I think, the judge fell into error. W of course had a strong personal interest in regaining his freedom and no doubt regarded Dr Egdell's report as an obstacle to that end. So he had a personal interest in restricting the report's circulation. But these private considerations should not be allowed to obscure the public interest in maintaining professional confidences. The fact that Dr Egdell as an independent psychiatrist examined and reported on W as a restricted mental patient under s 76 of the Mental Health Act 1983 does not deprive W of his ordinary right to confidence, underpinned, as such rights are, by the public interest. But it does mean that the balancing operation of which Lord Goff spoke falls to be carried out in circumstances of unusual difficulty and importance…

…[T]he judge regarded r 81(*b*) as accurately stating the law and held that Dr Egdell's disclosure in the present case fell squarely within it. I have some reservations about this conclusion. It is true that the disclosure here may be said to fall within the letter of the first sentence of para (*b*). But I think the paragraph is directed towards the familiar situation in which consultants or other specialised experts report to the doctor with clinical responsibility for treating or advising the patient, and the second sentence shows that he doctor whose duty is in question is regarded as having a continuing professional relationship with the patient. I rather doubt if the draftsman of para (*b*) had in mind a consultant psychiatrist consulted on a single occasion –

> for the purpose of advising whether an application to a Mental Health Review Tribunal should be made by or in respect of a patient who is liable to be detained or subject to guardianship under Part II of this Act or of furnishing information as to the condition of a patient for the purposes of such an application…' (See s 76(1) of the Mental Health Act 1983).

Nor do I think that Dr Egdell, in making disclosure, was primarily motivated by the ordinary concern of any doctor that a patient should receive the most efficacious treatment. Had that been his primary object, I think he would, consistently with the spirit of para (*d*), have tried to reason with W to obtain his consent to disclosure in W's own interest. I need not, however, reach a final view. The judge preferred to rest his conclusion on a broader ground, which was in effect the exception set out in r 81 (*g*) of the General Medical Council advice, and I think that if the disclosure cannot be justified under that exception it would be unsafe to justify it under any other.

Rule 81 (*g*) provides:

> Rarely, disclosure may be justified on the ground that it is in the public interest which, in certain circumstances such as, for example, investigation by the police of a grave or very serious crime, might override the doctor's duty to maintain his patient's confidence.

It was this exception which, as I understand, the judge upheld and applied when he held, in what is perhaps the crucial passage in this judgment ([1989] 1 All ER 1989 at 1104, [1989] 2 WLR 689 at 713):

> In my view, a doctor called on, as Dr Egdell was, to examine a patient such as W owes a duty not only to his patient but also a duty to the public. His duty to the public would require him, in my opinion, to place before the proper authorities the result of his examination if, in his opinion, the public interest so required. This would be so, in my opinion, whether or not the patient instructed him not to do so.

Counsel for W criticised this passage as wrongly leaving the question whether disclosure was justified or not to the subjective decision of the doctor. He made the same criticism of a passage where Scott J said ([1989] 1 All ER 1089 at 1105, [1989] 2 WLR 689 at 714):

> If a patient in the position of W commissions an independent psychiatrist's report, the duty of confidence that undoubtedly lies on the doctor who makes the report does not, in my judgment, bar the doctor from disclosing the report to the hospital that is charged with the care of the patient if the doctor judges the report to be relevant to the care and treatment of the patient, nor from disclosing the report to the Home Secretary if the doctor judges the report to be relevant to the exercise of the Home Secretary's discretionary powers in relation to that patient.

In my opinion these criticisms are just. Where, as here, the relationship between doctor and patient is contractual, the question is whether the doctor's disclosure is or is not a breach of contract. The answer to that question must turn not on what the doctor thinks but on what the court rules. But it does not follow that the doctor's conclusion is irrelevant. In making its ruling the court will give such weight to the considered judgment of a professional man as seems in all the circumstances to be appropriate.

The parties were agreed, as I think rightly, that the crucial question in the present case was how, on the special facts of the case, the balance should be struck between the public interest in maintaining professional confidences and the public interest in protecting the public against possible violence. Counsel for W submitted that on the facts here the public interest in maintaining confidences was shown to be clearly preponderant. In support of that submission he drew our attention to a number of features of the case, of which the most weighty were perhaps these.

(1) Section 76 of the Mental Health Act 1983 shows a clear parliamentary intention that a restricted patient should be free to seek advice and evidence for the specified purposes from a medical source outside the prison and secure hospital system. Section 129 ensures that the independent doctor may make a full examination and see all relevant documents. The examination may be in private, so that the authorities do not learn what passes between doctor and patient.

(2) The proper functioning of s 76 requires that a patient should feel free to bare his soul and open his mind without reserve to the independent doctor he has retained. This he will not do, if a doctor is free, on forming an adverse opinion, to communicate it to those empowered to prevent the patient's release from hospital.

(3) Although the present situation is not one in which W can assert legal professional privilege, and although tribunal proceedings are not strictly adversarial, the considerations which have given rise to legal professional privilege underpin the public interest in preserving confidence in a situation such as the present. A party to a forthcoming application to a tribunal should be free to unburden himself to an adviser he has retained without fearing that any material damaging to his application will find its way without his consent into the hands of a party with interests adverse to his.

(4) Preservation of confidence would be conducive to the public safety; patients would be candid, so that problems such as those highlighted by Dr Egdell would become known, and steps could be taken to explore and if necessary treat the problems without disclosing the report.

(5) It is contrary to the public interest that patients such as W should enjoy rights less extensive than those enjoyed by other members of the public, a result of his judgment which the judge expressly accepted (see [1989] 1 All ER 1089 at 1105, [1989] 2 WLR 689 at 714).

Of these considerations, I accept (1) as a powerful consideration in W's favour. A restricted patient who believes himself unnecessarily confined has, of all members of society, perhaps the greatest need for a professional adviser who is truly independent and reliably discreet. (2) also I, in some measure, accept, subject to the comment that if the patient is unforthcoming the doctor is bound to be guarded in his opinion. If the patient wishes to enlist the doctor's wholehearted support for his application, he has little choice but to be (or at least convince an expert interviewer that he is being) frank. I see great force in (3). Only the most compelling circumstances could justify a doctor in acting in a way which would injure the immediate interests of his patient, as the patient perceived them, without obtaining his consent. Point (4), if I correctly understand it, did not impress me. Counsel's submissions appeared to suggest that the problems highlighted by Dr Egdell could be explored and if necessary treated without the hospital authorities being told what the problems were thought to be. I do not think this would be very satisfactory. As to (5), I agree that restricted patients should not enjoy rights of confidence less valuable than those enjoyed by other patients save in so far as any breach of confidence can be justified under the stringent terms of r 81 (*g*).

Counsel for Dr Egdell justified his client's disclosure of his report by relying on the risk to the safety of the public if the report were not disclosed. The steps of his argument, briefly summarised, were these.

(1) As a result of his examination Dr Egdell believed that W had a long-standing and abnormal interest in dangerous explosives dating from well before his period of acute illness.

(2) Dr Egdell believed that this interest had been overlooked or insufficiently appreciated by those with clinical responsibility for W.

(3) Dr Egdell believed that this interest could throw additional light on W's interest, also long-standing and in this instance well documented, in guns and shooting.

(4) Dr Egdell believed that exploration of W's interest in explosives and further exploration of W's interest in guns and shooting might lead to a different and more sinister diagnosis of W's mental condition.

(5) Dr Egdell believed that these explorations could best be conducted in the secure hospital where W was.

(6) Dr Egdell believed that W might possibly be a future danger to members of the public if his interest in firearms and explosives continued after his discharge.

(7) Dr Egdell believed that these matters should be brought to the attention of those responsible for W's care and treatment and for making decisions concerning his transfer and release.

Dr Egdell's good faith was not in issue. Nor were his professional standing and competence. His opinions summaries in (1), (2), (3) and (4) (although not accepted) were not criticised as ill-founded or irrational. Dr Egdell deferred to the greater knowledge of another medical expert relied on by W concerning the regime in a regional secure unit but did not (as I understood) modify his view that the explorations he favoured should take place before transfer.

Counsel for W contended that Dr Egdell's belief summarised in (6) did not in all the circumstances justify disclosure of the report. There was, he said, no question of W's release, whether absolutely or conditionally, in the foreseeable future. The Home Office had made plain that it would not sanction transfer to a regional secure unit for about 18 months. Even if he were transferred he would remain a patient of the special hospital for the first 6 months and the high staff ratio in such units would ensure a very high level of security thereafter. Much further testing would in any event be done before W was again at large. Disclosure of the report would do nothing to protect the public.

I do not find these points persuasive. When Dr Egdell made his decision to disclose, one tribunal had already recommended W's transfer to a regional secure unit and the hospital authorities had urged that course. The Home Office had resisted transfer in a qualified manner but on a basis of inadequate information. It appeared to be only a matter of time, and probably not a very long time, before W was transferred. The regional secure unit was to act as a staging post on W's journey back into the community. While W would no doubt be further tested, such tests would not be focused on the source of Dr Egdell's concern, which he quite rightly considered to have received inadequate attention up to then. Dr Egdell had to act when he did or not at all.

There is one consideration which in my judgment, as in that of the judge, weighs the balance of public interest decisively in favour of disclosure. It may be shortly put. Where a man has committed multiple killings under the disability of serious mental illness, decisions which may lead directly or indirectly to his release from hospital should not be made unless a responsible authority is properly able to make an informed judgment that the risk of repetition is so small as to be acceptable. A consultant psychiatrist who becomes aware, even in the course of a confidential relationship, of information which leads him, in the exercise of what the court considers a sound professional judgment, to fear that such decisions may be made on the basis of inadequate information and with a real risk of consequent danger to the public is entitled to take such steps as are reasonable in all the circumstances to communicate the grounds of his concern to the responsible authorities. I have no doubt that the judge's decision in favour of Dr Egdell was right on the facts of this case.

Counsel for W argued that even if Dr Egdell was entitled to make some disclosure he should have disclosed only the crucial paragraph of his report and his opinion. I do not agree. An opinion, even from an eminent source, cannot be evaluated unless its factual premise is known, and a detailed 10-page report cannot be reliably assessed by perusing a brief extract.

No reference was made in argument before us (or, so far as I know, before the judge) to the European Convention on Human Rights (Convention for the Protection of Human Rights and Fundamental Freedoms (Rome, 4 November 1950; TS 71 (1953); Cmd 8969)), but I believe this decision to be in accordance with it. I would accept that art 8(1) of the convention may protect an individual against the disclosure of information protected by the duty of professional secrecy. But art 8(2) envisages that circumstances may arise in which a public authority may legitimately interfere with the exercise of that right in accordance with the law and where necessary in a democratic society in the interests of public safety or the prevention of crime. Here there was no interference by a public authority. Dr Egdell did, as

I conclude, act in accordance with the law. And his conduct was in my judgment necessary in the interests of public safety and the prevention of crime.

I would dismiss the appeal. Having reached that conclusion I do not think it necessary to consider whether, had W succeeded, he could have recovered damages in contract for shock and distress.

Sir John May agreed.

Given the court's acceptance of the fact that confidence may be breached in the public interest, are there any factors which limit the extent to which information may be disclosed? *Egdell* suggests that there may be several.

First, as Bingham LJ makes clear the disclosure may be made only to those whom it is necessary to tell so as to protect the public interest.

> **Bingham LJ:** He could not lawfully sell the contents of his report to a newspaper, as the judge held. Nor could he, without a breach of the law as well as professional etiquette, discuss the case in a learned article or in his memoirs or in gossiping with friends, unless he took appropriate steps to conceal the identity of W.

Of course, it may be necessary in a particular circumstance to disclose the confidence more widely in order, for example, to protect the public from a danger. An analogy which may assist here is the law of defamation and the defence of qualified privilege (see, for example, *Blackshaw v Lord* [1983] 2 All ER 311 per Stephenson LJ). That publication may need to be limited in its scope to be justified was recognised by the Law Lords in *A-G v Guardian Newspapers (No 2), supra.*

> **Lord Griffiths:**...Even if the balance comes down in favour of publication, it does not follow that publication should be to the world through the media. In certain circumstances the public interest may be better served by a limited form of publication perhaps to the police or some other authority who can follow up a suspicion that wrongdoing may lurk beneath the cloak of confidence. Those authorities will be under a duty not to abuse the confidential information and to use it only for the purpose of their inquiry. If it turns out that the suspicions are without foundation, the confidence can then still be protected: see *Francome v Mirror Group Newspapers Ltd* [1984] 2 All ER 408, [1984] 1 WLR 892. On the other hand, the circumstances may be such that the balance will come down in favour of allowing publication by the media: see *Lion Laboratories Ltd v Evans* [1984] 2 All ER 417, [1985] QB 526. Judges are used to carrying out this type of balancing exercise and I doubt if it is wise to try to formulate rules to guide the use of this discretion that will have to be exercised in widely differing and as yet unforeseen circumstances...

> **Lord Goff:**...It does not however follow that the public interest will in such cases require disclosure to the media, or to the public by the media. There are cases in which a more limited disclosure is all that is required (see *Francome v Mirror Group Newspapers Ltd* [1984] 2 All ER 408, [1984] 1 WLR 892)...

The 'need to know' limitation is also emphasised by the GMC in its most recent guidance on confidentiality.

General Medical Council *Confidentiality: Protecting and Providing Information* (2000)

> 36. Disclosure of personal information without consent may be justified where a failure to do so may expose the patient or others to a risk of death or serious harm. Where third parties are exposed to a risk so serious that it outweighs the patient's privacy interest, you should seek consent to disclosure where practicable. If it is not practicable, you should disclose information promptly to the appropriate person or authority. You should generally inform the patient before disclosing the information.

Secondly, to justify disclosure the risk must be 'real' rather than fanciful (see Bingham LJ at 853).

Thirdly, the risk in *Egdell* was to physical safety of members of the public (per Stephen Brown P at 846 and Bingham LJ at 853). It can be argued that the court only contemplated disclosure where there is a risk involving the *danger of physical harm*, given the emphasis placed on this aspect of the case by all the judges. As we shall see, this is probably not a limitation in all situations.

There is a further point in *Egdell* which does not appear to have been acknowledged by the court. It is not clear whether Dr Egdell in his examination of W discovered new facts about W's propensity to be a danger or whether he merely disagreed with other doctors' interpretation of the same facts. If the former is the case, then clearly there is fresh evidence, which on the court's view of public interest, Dr Egdell was justified in bringing to the attention of the proper authorities. If, however, the latter is the case, the decision becomes more problematic. All we have is a difference of opinion among experts, one of whom claims that his opinion is right where the consequences of holding that view will undoubtedly lead to the continued detention of W. Arguably, the fact that the evidence was merely a difference of opinion should have been a relevant factor in determining whether the public interest justified disclosure. Of course, if the medical evidence is the *only* evidence in the case relevant to the patient's dangerous conduct the argument against disclosure has less force since *ex hypothesi* this medical opinion is adding something new (*R v Crozier* (1990) 8 BMLR 128 (CA)). At the very least the doctor would be entitled to press that further medical opinion be obtained and, perhaps, as a last resort if he judges the situation to be sufficiently serious to disclose his views to the proper authorities.

Egdell concerned a dangerous psychiatric patient who created a risk to the safety of the public. Other situations may involve risks created by patients, including patients who cannot drive safely (as in *Duncan v Medical Practitioners Disciplinary Ctte* [1986] 1 NZLR 513) and parents who are abusing their children. Bearing in mind the 'need to know' requirements, disclosure to the appropriate agency, for example, social services or the police will be relevant in determining whether the disclosure is justified, together, of course, with other factors such as the perceived danger of the individual. The Department of Health in its Guidance, *The Protection and Use of Patient Information* (1996), at para 5.7 outlines the correct approach:

5.7. Each case must be considered on its merits, the main criterion being whether the release of information to protect the public should prevail over the duty of confidence to the patient. The possible therapeutic consequences for the patient must be considered whatever the outcome. Decisions will sometimes be finely balanced and may concern matters on which NHS staff find it difficult to make a judgment. Therefore it may be necessary to seek legal or other specialist advice or to await or seek a court order.

A further situation where a patient may create a danger to another is where the patient is infected with a communicable disease and there is a risk of transmission, for example, to a sexual partner or member of the patient's family. The general approach we have discussed here applies in this situation also.

Special difficulties as regards confidentiality have always attended infectious diseases, in particular those that are sexually transmitted. The information is particularly sensitive given its potential for stigmatising those infected. HIV infection and AIDS are at the same time merely another example of this and *sui generis*, given the extraordinary potential for discrimination against those infected. It is not surprising, therefore, that HIV infection (in particular) and sexually transmitted diseases (in general) have attracted considerable concern in the context of confidentiality.

We have already seen the National Health Service (Venereal Diseases) Regulations 1974 (SI 1974 No 29) which represent the long-standing recognition by Parliament of the need to safeguard confidence in this sensitive area. Building on this general approach, the GMC issued specific guidance concerning HIV infection in August 1988 (amended in June 1993). What is clear from the guidance is the recognition by the GMC of the need to balance the importance of observing confidence in this situation against a legitimate concern for the interests of others who may be affected by the person infected with HIV. The GMC's Guidance has now been extended and covers 'serious communicable diseases' so as to include such infections as Hepatitis B and C: see *Duties of a Doctor: Serious Communicable Diseases* (1997). As regards disclosure to a patient's sexual partners or relatives of information about his medical condition, the GMC's Guidance provides as follows:

General Medical Council *Serious Communicable Diseases* (1997)

Giving information to close contacts

22. You may disclose information about a patient, whether living or dead, in order to protect a person from risk of death or serious harm. For example, you may disclose information to a known sexual contact of a patient with HIV where you have reason to think that the patient has not informed that person, and cannot be persuaded to do so. In such circumstances you should tell the patient before you make the disclosure, and you must be prepared to justify a decision to disclose information.

23. You must not disclose information to others, for example relatives, who have not been, or are not, at risk of infection.

And, in relation to disclosure to other health professionals such as his general practitioner it provides as follows (paras 18–19):

Informing other health care professionals

18. If you diagnose a patient as having a serious communicable disease, you should explain to the patient:
    - The nature of the disease and its medical, social and occupational implications, as appropriate.
    - Ways of protecting others from infection.
    - The importance of giving the professionals who will be providing care information which they need to know about the patient's disease or condition. In particular you must make sure the patient understands that general practitioners cannot provide adequate clinical management and care without knowledge of their patient's conditions.

19. If patients still refuse to allow other health care workers to be informed, you must respect the patients' wishes except where you judge that failure to disclose the information would put a health care worker or other patient at serious risk of death or serious harm. Such situations may arise, for example, when dealing with violent patients with severe mental illness or disability. If you are in doubt about whether disclosure is appropriate, you should seek advice from an experienced colleague. You should inform patients before disclosing information. Such occasions are likely to arise rarely and you must be prepared to justify a decision to disclose information against a patient's wishes.

The GMC's guidance reflects, in our view, the law limiting, as it does, the justification for disclosure to where there is demonstrable danger to the sexual partner or other health professional (see further, A Grubb and D Pearl *Bloodtesting, AIDS and DNA Profiling* (1990) ch 2). It is not self-evident why the justification for disclosure to other health professionals is considered as a 'serious risk' of death or serious harm (para 19), whilst *any* risk of these outcomes will suffice for a sexual partner (para 22). The magnitude of the risk is, we would suggest, always a factor when engaging in the balancing process of whether the public interest justifies disclosure in breach of confidence.

The infected person, as in *X v Y* (*supra*), may also be a doctor who has treated patients who may as a result have been at risk of exposure. The patient, though a doctor, is just as entitled to have his confidences respected as anyone else. However, it may be necessary to contact his patients (or other health professionals) for them to determine whether they have been infected through contact with him. The Department of Health has issued guidance on the management of such cases: *AIDS/HIV Infected Health Care Workers* (1999). It seeks to encourage responsible behaviour by health professionals who believe they may have been infected including seeking advice from a specialist occupational health physician.

Department of Health *AIDS/HIV Infected Health Care Workers: Guidance on the Management of Infected Health Care Workers and Patient Notification* (1999)

6. THE ROLE AND RESPONSIBILITIES OF THE OCCUPATIONAL HEALTH SERVICE AND HIV PHYSICIANS

6.1 All matters arising from and relating to the employment of HIV infected health care workers should be coordinated through a specialist occupational health physician.

6.2 The HIV physician providing the necessary regular care to an infected worker should liaise with the occupational health physician and preferably they should jointly manage the case.

6.3 Occupational health services which do not employ a specialist occupational physician should refer individuals to such a physician in another unit. The Association of National Health Service Occupational Physicians (ANHOPS) [see Annex D] has issued guidance to its members and has given a list of specialist occupational physicians who can be contacted by those working in occupational medicine in the field. The close involvement of occupational health departments in developing local procedures for managing HIV infected health care workers is strongly recommended.

6.4 It is recommended that all health authorities, boards and trusts should identify a suitable specialist occupational health physician who should also be available for consultation by general medical and dental practitioners and their employees, and should liaise with local private health care providers and offer them such a service if they wish.

6.5 If such arrangements do not exist, the Faculty of Occupational Medicine or ANHOPS [see Annex D] will also put independent contractors and other non NHS staff in touch with a specialist occupational health physician. Alternatively, the physician looking after the worker may contact the UKAP for advice.

6.6 Whilst the occupational health physician has responsibility for occupational medical management and assessment, where a physician is not immediately available, some infected health care workers may initially seek advice from an occupational health nurse. The nurse should make every effort to arrange for the health care worker to see the occupational health physician as soon as possible. If necessary the occupational health nurse should seek confidential advice directly from the UKAP. As for any other referral to the UKAP, identification of the worker should be avoided.

6.7 Patient safety and public confidence are paramount and dependent on the HIV infected, or potentially infected, health care worker observing their duty of self-declaration to an occupational physician. It is extremely important that HIV infected health care workers receive the same rights of confidentiality as any patient seeking or receiving medical care. Occupational health practitioners, who work within strict guidelines with respect to confidentiality, have a key role in this process, since they are able to act as an advocate for the health care worker and adviser to the employing authority. They should adopt a proactive role in helping health care workers to assess if they have been at risk of HIV infection [see 4.6] and encourage them to be tested for HIV if appropriate [see 4.5].

6.8 Occupational health notes are held separately from other hospital notes and can be accessed only by occupational health practitioners, who are obliged ethically and professionally not to release notes or information without the consent of the individual. Conversely, occupational health practitioners do not have access to hospital notes. There are occasions when an employer may need to be advised that a change in duties should take place, but HIV status itself normally would not be disclosed without the health care worker's consent. However it may be necessary in the public interest for

the employer to have access to confidential information where patients are or may
have been at risk.

6.9   Occupational physicians are well placed to act as advocates for the worker on issues
of retraining and redeployment, or, if indicated, medical retirement. Occupational
health departments could develop local policies for the management of infected health
care workers' future employment.

As you will have noticed, the guidance reflects the law as we have stated it,
namely that the doctor owes a duty of confidentiality to the infected health
care worker but disclosure may be necessary in the public interest to protect
others. The guidance elaborates on this:

10.   CONFIDENTIALITY CONCERNING THE INFECTED HEALTH CARE WORKER

10.1 There is a general duty to preserve the confidentiality of medical information and
records. Breach of the duty is very damaging for the individuals concerned, and it
undermines the confidence of the public and of health care workers in the assurances
about confidentiality which are given to those who come forward for examination or
treatment. In dealing with the media, and in preparing press releases where necessary,
it should be stressed that individuals who have been examined or treated in confidence
are entitled to have their confidence respected.

10.2 Every effort should be made to avoid disclosure of the infected worker's identity, or
information which would allow deductive disclosure. This should include the use of a
media injunction as necessary to prevent publication or other disclosure of a worker's
identity [see 11.45]. The use of personal identifiers in correspondence and requests
for laboratory tests should be avoided and care taken to ensure that the number of
people who know the worker's identity is kept to a minimum [see 8.4]. Any
unauthorised disclosure about the HIV status of an employee or patient constitutes a
breach of confidence and may lead to disciplinary action or legal proceedings.
Employers should make this known to staff, to deter open speculation about the identity
of an infected health care worker.

10.3 The duty of confidentiality, however, is not absolute. Legally, the identity of infected
individuals may be disclosed with their consent, or without consent in exceptional
circumstances where it is considered necessary for the purpose of treatment, or
prevention of spread of infection. Any such disclosure may need to be justified.

10.4 In balancing duty to the infected health care worker and the wider duty to the public,
complex ethical issues may arise. As in other areas of medical practice, a health care
worker disclosing information about another health care worker may be required to
justify their decision to do this. The need for disclosure must be carefully weighed
and where there is any doubt the health care worker considering such disclosure may
wish to seek advice from his or her professional body.

10.5 The fact that the infected worker has died, or has already been identified publicly,
does not mean that duties of confidentiality are at an end.

The health care worker's personal responsibility for the safety of his patients is
reflected in the GMC's guidance.

General Medical Council *Serious Communicable Diseases* (1997)

Responsibilities of doctors who have been exposed to a serious communicable disease

29.   If you have any reason to believe that you have been exposed to a serious communicable
disease you must seek and follow professional advice without delay on whether you
should undergo testing and, if so, which tests are appropriate. Further guidance on
your responsibilities if your health may put patients at risk is included in our booklet
Good Medical Practice.

30.   If you acquire a serious communicable disease you must promptly seek and follow
advice from a suitably qualified colleague – such as a consultant in occupational
health, infectious diseases or public health on:

- Whether, and in what ways, you should modify your professional practice.
- Whether you should inform your current employer, your previous employers or
any prospective employer, about your condition.

31.   You must not rely on your own assessment of the risks you pose to patients.

32.   If you have a serious communicable disease and continue in professional practice you
must have appropriate medical supervision.

33. If you apply for a new post, you must complete health questionnaires honestly and fully.

(See also, GMC *Good Medical Practice* (1998) paras 23–27.)

The treating doctor's professional obligations to respect confidence are also set out.

Treating colleagues with serious communicable diseases

34. If you are treating a doctor or other health care worker with a serious communicable disease you must provide the confidentiality and support to which every patient is entitled.
35. If you know, or have good reason to believe, that a medical colleague or health care worker who has, or may have, a serious communicable disease, is practising, or has practised, in a way which places patients at risk, you must inform an appropriate person in the health care worker's employing authority, for example an occupational health physician, or where appropriate, the relevant regulatory body. Such cases are likely to arise very rarely. Wherever possible you should inform the health care worker concerned before passing information to an employer or regulatory body.

You will notice reference in para 35 of the GMC's guidance to disclosure to the 'relevant regulatory body', eg GMC (doctors), UKCC (nurses) and GDC (dentists). This leads us into one final situation which we should notice, namely where a doctor (or nurse) becomes aware that another doctor (or nurse) is performing poorly or otherwise creating a danger to patients. An infected health care worker is one illustration of this but there are many others, for example, incompetence or ill health. We saw in Chapter 3 how the NHS has moved from its anti-'whistleblowing' policy to a more open and accountable culture. We also saw that legislation in the shape of the Public Interest Disclosure Act 1998 has provided statutory protection to employees and other workers', including health care workers, who disclose wrongdoing etc within the employment context (see, generally, HSC 1999/198). There may be confidentiality issues in these cases but not necessarily doctor-patient confidences although there may be if the doctor (or nurse) is also a patient. What is the position if he is, and another health professional considers it necessary to disclose that he is a danger, incompetent or whatever? There is no doubt that the public interest may justify disclosure to the health professional's employer and, in appropriate circumstances, to the relevant regulatory body. Usually, of course, disclosure to the employing Trust will be the best course, but this may not prove effective or the problem is so serious that referral to a regulatory body such as the GMC is appropriate (see GMC *Good Medical Practice* (1998) at paras 23–24 and GMC *Maintaining Good Medical Practice* (1998) pp 14–15).

Would such disclosures in breach of confidence be justified in the public interest? All will depend upon the 'balancing exercise' of weighing one public interest against another. There are, however, legislative precedents to support it: Health Act 1999, s 24(6)(g) and (h) (CHI) and Health Service Commissioners Act 1993, s 15(1)(e) (Health Service Commissioner). The following case illustrates the approach a court is likely to take. It did not concern disclosure by a doctor to the regulatory body but rather disclosure by the police of a confidential interview. Nevertheless, the Court of Appeal's application of the 'public interest' justification is illuminating.

Woolgar v Chief Constable of the Sussex Police **[1999] 3 All ER 604 (CA)**

W, a registered nurse and the matron of a nursing home, was arrested and interviewed by the police following the death of a patient in her care. Although the police concluded the investigation without bringing any charges, the matter was referred to the United Kingdom Central Council for Nursing, Midwifery and Health Visiting (the UKCC), the regulatory body for the nursing profession, whose normal practice was to ask the police to release any relevant information. The police practice was to seek authority to disclose from those who had given statements, but W refused to give such consent. The police nevertheless indicated that they would listen to the tape of the interview in order to decide whether it should be disclosed to the UKCC. W sought an injunction to restrain the police from disclosing the contents of the interview, but the application was dismissed. She appealed, contending that, in order to safeguard the free flow of information to the police, it was essential that those who gave information should have confidence that it would not be used outside criminal proceedings ...

Kennedy LJ: (1) This is an appeal from a decision of Astill J, who on 3 September 1998 dismissed the appellant's application for an order that the chief constable be restrained from disclosing to the United Kingdom Central Council for Nursing, Midwifery and Health Visiting (the UKCC) the contents of an interview between the appellant and the police which took place at Worthing police station on 6 December 1997.

(2) Background facts
The background facts are simple and not contentious. The appellant is a registered nurse, and in 1997 she was matron of a nursing home at Worthing. After the death on 23 November 1997 of a patient in her care allegations were made which led to her being arrested and interviewed by the police on 6 December 1997. The officer concerned was Det Sgt Julie Buchan, and it is clear from her affidavit that the allegation with which she was particularly concerned was one of over-administration of diamorphine, but she was also aware of other allegations which were matters of concern to the Registration and Inspection Unit (the RIU) of the West Sussex Health Authority.

At the conclusion of her investigation Det Sgt Buchan notified the appellant, and also the owner of the nursing home and the RIU, that the evidence did not meet the evidential test required for criminal charges, and the matter was then referred by the RIU to the UKCC which is the regulatory body for nursing, midwifery and health visiting. It is a disciplinary body, with power to remove nurses from the register if that is necessary to protect patients. The allegations which the UKCC had to investigate were more wide-ranging than those which had been considered by the police. Other patients were involved, and in addition to allegations of misuse of drugs there were allegations of other forms of maltreatment. The UKCC began to investigate in April 1998, and on 24 June 1998 the appellant was officially informed of what was afoot ...

(6) The issue
Undoubtedly when someone is arrested and interviewed by the police what he or she says is confidential. Plainly it may be used in the course of a criminal trial if charges are brought arising out of that investigation, but if it is not so used the person interviewed is entitled to believe that, generally speaking, his or her confidence will be respected. If authority be required for that proposition, it can be found in *Taylor v Serious Fraud Office* [1998] 4 All ER 801, [1998] 3 WLR 1040 but, as all of the authorities cited to us indicate, there are exceptional circumstances which justify the disclosure by the police, otherwise than in the course of a criminal trial, of what has been said by a suspect during the course of an interview, in circumstances where the suspect, or former suspect, does not consent to such disclosure. The question which arises in this case is whether, if the regulatory body of the profession to which the suspect belongs is investigating serious allegations and makes a formal request to the police for disclosure of what was said in interview, the public interest in the proper working of the regulatory body is or may be such as to justify disclosure of the material sought. If the answer to that question is in the affirmative how, as a matter of procedure, should contentious issues in relation to disclosure be resolved?

(7) Authorities
Mr Wadsworth QC, for the appellant, submits that it is right to start from the position that, as Millett LJ said in the Court of Appeal in *Taylor v Serious Fraud Office* [1997] 4 All ER 887 at 904:

> Members of the public who volunteer information to the police are entitled to expect that it will be used only for the purpose of the investigation and subsequent criminal proceedings. Their expectations should be respected...

The first of the English authorities we were invited to consider is *Beloff v Pressdram Ltd* [1973] 1 All ER 241, and Mr Wadsworth submits that it should now be read in the light of later authorities. It concerned a breach of copyright, and Ungoed-Thomas J when dealing with the submission that public interest might justify disclosure, cited (at 260) from Lord Denning MR's judgment in *Initial Services Ltd v Putterill* [1967] 3 All ER 145 at 148, [1968] 1 QB 396 at 405, where Lord Denning MR said that the exception which justified disclosure –

should extend to crimes, frauds and misdeeds, both those actually committed as well as those in contemplation, provided always – and this is essential – that the disclosure is justified in the public interest.

Ungoed-Thomas J then looked at later cases and continued ([1973] 1 All ER 241 at 260):

> The defence of public interest clearly covers and, in the authorities does not extend beyond, disclosure, which as Lord Denning MR emphasised must be disclosure justified in the public interest, of matters carried out or contemplated, in breach of the country's security, or in breach of law, including statutory duty, fraud, or otherwise destructive of the country or its people, including matters medically dangerous to the public; and doubtless other misdeeds of similar gravity.

Here again the respondents invite our attention to 'matters medically dangerous to the public'.

In *A-G v Guardian Newspapers Ltd (No 2)* [1988] 3 All ER 545, [1990] 1 AC 109 (the 'Spycatcher' case) the claim was for an injunction to restrain future publication of information derived from a former member of the security services. Lord Griffiths said ([1988] 3 All ER 545 at 649–650, [1990] 1 AC 109 at 268–269):

> The courts have…always refused to uphold the right to confidence when to do so would be to cover up wrongdoing. In *Gartside v Outram* (1856) 26 LJ Ch 113 it was said that there could be no confidence in iniquity. This approach has been developed in the modern authorities to include cases in which it is in the public interest that the confidential information should be disclosed: see *Initial Services Ltd v Putterill* [1967] 3 All ER 145, [1968] 1 QB 396, *Beloff v Pressdram Ltd* [1973] 1 All ER 241 and *Lion Laboratories Ltd v Evans* [1984] 2 All ER 417, [1985] QB 526. This involves the judge in balancing the public interest in upholding the right to confidence, which is based on the moral principles of loyalty and fair dealing, against some other public interest that will be served by the publication of the confidential material. Even if the balance comes down in favour of publication, it does not follow that publication should be to the world through the media. In certain circumstances the public interest may be better served by a limited form of publication perhaps to the police or some other authority who can follow up a suspicion that wrongdoing may lurk beneath the cloak of confidence. Those authorities will be under a duty not to abuse the confidential information and to use it only for the purpose of their inquiry. If it turns out that the suspicions are without foundation, the confidence can then still be protected …

Lord Goff said ([1988] 3 All ER 545 at 659, [1990] 1 AC 109 at 282):

> …although the basis of the law's protection of confidence is that there is a public interest that confidences should be preserved and protected by the law, nevertheless that public interest may be outweighed by some other countervailing public interest which favours disclosure. This limitation may apply…to all types of confidential information. It is this limiting principle which may require a court to carry out a balancing operation, weighing the public interest in maintaining confidence against a countervailing public interest favouring disclosure.

In both speeches there is recognised the possibility of countervailing public interests, and of the need to balance one against the other.

In *Re a company's application* [1989] 2 All ER 248, [1989] Ch 477 Scott J considered an application by a company to restrain an ex-employee from disclosing confidential information or documents to the Financial Intermediaries Managers and Brokers Regulatory Authority (FIMBRA). The judge said ([1989] 2 All ER 248 at 251, [1989] Ch 477 at 481):

> If this were a case in which there were any question or threat of general disclosure by the defendant of confidential information concerning the way in which the plaintiff carries on its business or concerning any details of the affairs of any of its clients, there could be no answer to the claim for an injunction; but it is not general disclosure that the defendant has in mind. He has in mind only disclosure to FIMBRA, the regulatory authority, and, in relation to a particular case that he has identified in his affidavit, the Inland Revenue. I ask myself whether an employee of a company carrying on the business of giving financial advice and of financial management to the members of the public under the regulatory umbrella provided by FIMBRA owes a duty of confidentiality that extends to barring disclosure of information to FIMBRA.

The judge recognised the possibility that the defendant was activated by malice, and continued ([1989] 2 All ER 248 at 251, [1989] Ch 477 at 482):

But, if that is so, then I ask myself what harm will be done. FIMBRA may decided that the allegations are not worth investigating. In that case, no harm will have been done. Or FIMBRA may decide that an investigation is necessary. In that case, if the allegations turn out to be baseless, nothing will follow the investigation. And, if harm is caused by the investigation itself, it is harm which is implicit in the regulatory role of FIMBRA. It may be that what is put before FIMBRA includes some confidential information. But that information would, as it seems to me, be information which FIMBRA could at any time obtain by the spot checks that it is entitled to carry out.

The judge expressly declined to carry out any investigation into the allegations, saying ([1989] 2 All ER 248 at 252, [1989] Ch 477 at 483):

> ...it is for FIMBRA, on receiving whatever information the defendant puts before it, to decide whether there is a matter for investigation. If there is not, then I cannot see that any harm has been done to the plaintiff. If there is, then it is right for FIMBRA rather than the court to investigate.

Obviously the respondents place considerable reliance upon the decision in *Re a company's application*, but Mr Wadsworth submits that it is a very different type of case. There was no element of public interest immunity, only a conflict between the rights of the employer and the rights of the regulator. Mr Wadsworth submits that if the UKCC want the information held by the chief constable and the appellant withholds consent the UKCC should issue a witness summons, not at the investigatory stage, but when the matter goes before the conduct committee, if it reaches that stage. That is the moment at which the matter could be properly tested. That, he submits, is the course envisaged by this court in *Marcel v Comr of Police of the Metropolis* [1992] 1 All ER 72, [1992] Ch 225 where the issue was whether the police were entitled to disclose seized documents to a third party for use in civil litigation. Voluntary disclosure was not approved. Dillon LJ ([1992] 1 All ER 72 at 81, [1992] Ch 225 at 256) cited with approval what had been said by Browne-Wilkinson V-C at first instance ([1991] 1 All ER 845 at 852, [1992] Ch 225 at 235), namely:

> In my judgment, subject to any express statutory provision in other Acts, the police are authorised to seize, retain and use documents only for public purposes relating to the investigation and prosecution of crime and the return of stolen property to the true owner...if communication to others is necessary for the purpose of the police investigation and prosecution, it is authorised. It may also be (though I do not decide) that there are other public authorities to which the documents can properly be disclosed for example to City and other regulatory authorities or to the security services...

In *R v Chief Constable of the North Wales Police, ex p AB* [1998] 3 All ER 310, [1999] QB 396 convicted paedophiles sought declarations that the decision of the police to inform a caravan site owner of their conviction was unlawful. They failed. In the Divisional Court Lord Bingham CJ said ([1997] 4 All ER 691 at 698, [1999] QB 396 at 409–410):

> When, in the course of performing its public duties, a public body (such as a police force) comes into possession of information relating to a member of the public, being information not generally available and potentially damaging to that member of the public if disclosed, the body ought not to disclose such information save for the purpose of and to the extent necessary for performance of its public duty or enabling some other public body to perform its public duty.

After referring to two authorities, Lord Bingham CJ continued ([1997] 4 All ER 691 at 699, [1999] QB 396 at 410):

> It seems to me to follow that if the police, having obtained information about an individual which it would be damaging to that individual to disclose, and which should not be disclosed without some public justification, consider in the exercise of a careful and bona fide judgment that it is desirable or necessary in the public interest to make disclosure, whether for the purpose of preventing crime or alerting members of the public to an apprehended danger, it is proper for them to make such limited disclosure as is judged necessary to achieve that purpose.

It is worth noting in passing that there is no suggestion that it is necessary for the police to seek court approval for making a disclosure. Buxton J said ([1997] 4 All ER 691 at 703, [1999] QB 396 at 415):

> ...information acquired by the police in their capacity as such, and when performing the public law duties that Lord Bingham CJ has set out, cannot be protected against disclosure in the proper performance of those public duties by any private law

obligation of confidence. That is not because the use and publication of confidential information will not be enjoined when such use is necessary in the public interest, though that is undoubtedly the case. Rather, because of their overriding obligation to enforce the law and prevent crime the police in my view do not have the power or vires to acquire information on terms that preclude their using that information in a case where their public duty demands such use.

The Court of Appeal upheld the decision of the Divisional Court. Lord Woolf MR giving the judgment of the court, said ([1998] 3 All ER 310 at 321, [1999] QB 396 at 429):

The issue here is not the same as it would be in private law. The fact that the convictions of the applicants had been in the public domain, did not mean that the police as a public authority were free to publish information about their previous offending absent any public interest in this being done. As Lord Bingham CJ stated, before this happens it must at least be a situation where in all the circumstances it is desirable to make disclosure. Both under the convention and as a matter of English administrative law, the police are entitled to use information when they reasonably conclude this is what is required (after taking into account the interests of the applicant), in order to protect the public and in particular children.

Another recent example to which we were referred is *Bunn v BBC* [1998] 3 All ER 552. A plaintiff who had faced trial for conspiracy to defraud tried to stop the defendants from including in a broadcast and in a book admissions he had made when interviewed by the police which had been referred to in open court. He failed because the material was already in the public domain, but Lightman J (at 557) recognised that:

There is a substantial public interest in an accused person being able to make full disclosure in a statement to the police without fear of that statement being used for extraneous purposes ...

Finally there is the decision of the House of Lords in *Taylor v Serious Fraud Office* [1998] 4 All ER 801, [1998] 3 WLR 1040. I have already cited from the judgment of Millett LJ in the Court of Appeal. The case was concerned with whether those involved in investigating fraud, including witnesses, could be sued for defamation. In the House of Lords it was held that material disclosed by the prosecution to a defendant in criminal proceedings was subject to an implied undertaking that such material would not be used for any purpose other than the defence in the instant case. The House of Lords also held that witnesses, potential witnesses, and those who take part in a criminal investigation with a view to a prosecution or possible prosecution, are immune from suit. Lord Hoffman said ([1998] 4 All ER 801 at 813, [1998] 3 WLR 1040 at 1052): 'The policy of the immunity is to enable people to speak freely without fear of being sued, whether successfully or not'.

(8) The UKCC procedure

In the course of his submissions Lord Lester took us through the statutory powers and duties of the UKCC as set out in the Nurses, Midwives and Health Visitors Act 1997, which includes the duty to maintain a register of qualified nurses (s 7) and to determine circumstances in which a person may be removed from the register (s 10(1)(a)). Paragraph 1(b) of Sch 2 gives power to require witnesses to attend for the purposes of proceedings under s 10 before the council or a committee, and the proceedings are further governed by the Nurses, Midwives and Health Visitors (Professional Conduct) Rules 1993 Approval Order 1993, SI 1993/893. A practitioner may be removed from the register if she has been guilty of misconduct (r 2(1)(a)), the question of misconduct having been investigated and referred to the conduct committee where misconduct has been proved to that committee's satisfaction (r (2)(2)). Before the matter reaches the conduct committee it is considered by a preliminary proceedings committee (the PPC) which also considers any written response which the practitioner may offer to the allegations, and it is only if the PPC so decides that disciplinary proceedings are formally commenced (rr 7, 8 and 9). The point to be noted is that this is a staged procedure, and the stage in the procedure with which this case is concerned is the initial investigatory stage.

(9) Conclusion

Essentially Mr Wadsworth's submission was and is that when the appellant answered questions when interviewed by the police she did so in the reasonable belief that what she said would go no further unless it was used by the police for the purposes of criminal proceedings. The caution administered to her so indicated, and in order to safeguard the free flow of information to the police it is essential that those who give information should be able to have confidence that what they say will not be used for some collateral purpose.

However, in my judgment, where a regulatory body such as the UKCC, operating in the field of public health and safety, seeks access to confidential material in the possession of the police, being material which the police are reasonably persuaded is of some relevance to the subject matter of an inquiry being conducted by the regulatory body, then a countervailing public interest is shown to exist which, as in this case, entitles the police to release the material to the regulatory body on the basis that save in so far as it may be used by the regulatory body for the purposes of its own inquiry, the confidentiality which already attaches to the material will be maintained. As Mr Horan said in para 14 of his skeleton argument:

> A properly and efficiently regulated nursing profession is necessary in the interest of the medical welfare of the country, to keep the public safe, and to protect the rights and freedoms of those vulnerable individuals in need of nursing care. A necessary part of such regulation is the ensuring of the free flow of the best available information to those charged by statute with the responsibility to regulate.

Putting the matter in convention terms Lord Lester submitted, and I would accept, that disclosure is 'necessary in a democratic society in the interests of...public safety or...for the protection of health or morals, or for the protection of the rights and freedoms of others'.

Even if there is no request from the regulatory body, it seems to me that if the police come into possession of confidential information which, in their reasonable view, in the interests of public health or safety, should be considered by a professional or regulatory body, then the police are free to pass that information to the relevant regulatory body for its consideration.

Obviously in each case a balance has to be struck between competing public interests, and at least arguably in some cases the reasonableness of the police view may be open to challenge. If they refuse to disclose, the regulatory body can, if aware of the existence of the information, make an appropriate application to the court. In order to safeguard the interests of the individual, it is, in my judgment, desirable that where the police are minded to disclose, they should, as in this case, inform the person affected of what they propose to do in such time as to enable that person, if so advised, to seek assistance from the court. In some cases that may not be practicable or desirable, but in most cases that seems to me to be the course that should be followed. In any event, in my judgment, the primary decision as to disclosure should be made by the police who have the custody of the relevant material, and not by the court.

I would therefore dismiss this appeal.

Otton and Waller LJJ agreed.

The case concerned a nurse who was potentially a risk to the safety of patients. Not all cases of poorly performing health professionals or misconduct by them will involve such dangers. What if the doctor or nurse was suspected of dishonesty or fraud directed against patients on the NHS? You will have noticed the reference by the Court of Appeal to *Re a Company's Application* [1989] Ch 477. This concerned disclosure of confidential documents to a regulatory body that was not concerned with the physical safety of individuals but rather regulation in the financial sector. The GMC, UKCC and GDC all concern themselves with fraud or dishonesty by the professionals they respectively regulate. There is no reason in principle to exclude such situations from the 'public interest' justification. Promoting honesty and integrity in the context of a public service is in the public interest (see *MS v Sweden* (1997) 45 BMLR 133 (ECtHR) applying art 8(2) of the ECHR). Whether disclosure is justified will, in part, depend upon the seriousness of the allegation. Of course, if conduct appears to fall within the regulatory bodies' remit, it is likely to be of a serious nature in any event.

It is important to notice that here we are concerned with a doctor's *discretion* to disclose confidential information. There is another question: is he ever under a duty to do so, such that a failure to inform another about the patient's dangerousness could give rise to an action in negligence for damages? We discussed this earlier, in Chapter 4 (*supra*).

2. Prevention or detection of crime

Guidance from both the General Medical Council and the Department of Health contemplates disclosure to prevent or detect serious crime as being capable of falling within the public interest justification.

General Medical Council *Confidentiality: Protecting and Providing Information* (2000)

37. ... for example:...
c. Where a disclosure may assist in the prevention or detection of a serious crime. Serious crimes, in this context, will put someone at risk of death or serious harm, and will usually be crimes against the person, such as abuse of children.

Likewise, the DoH in its guidance refers to disclosure for 'the prevention of serious crime' and provides:

DoH *The Protection and Use of Patient Information* (1996)

Tackling serious crime
5.8. Passing on information to help tackle serious crime ... may be justified if the following conditions are satisfied:
i. without disclosure, the task of preventing, detecting or prosecuting the crime would be seriously prejudiced or delayed;
ii. information is limited to what is strictly relevant to a specific investigation;
iii. there are satisfactory undertakings that the information will not be passed on or used for any purpose other than the present investigation.
5.9. Requests for information relating to a number of patients in order to identify one or more is likely to be justified only if there is a very strong public interest.

On the face of it, both sets of guidance see this as a practical application of the 'danger to others' sub-set of public interest. The GMC directly refers back to a patient who creates a 'risk of death or serious harm' (*supra*, para 37 referring to para 36). Likewise, the DoH's guidance links this situation to 'danger to the general public'. Clearly, of course, many instances where patient information is relevant to 'serious crime' will be to the detection of crimes of physical or sexual violence (see eg *R v Crown Court at Cardiff, ex p Kellam* (1993) 16 BMLR 76 and *R v Singleton* [1995] 1 Cr App Rep 431 (both murder)). Usually, if the suspect is still at large, there will be a continuing risk to the public. This may also be argued if there is a possibility of the suspect being released from custody if the information is not provided, though the case is not so strong (but note *Egdell, supra*). However, this may not always be so. The suspect may not be a likely (or even possible) re-offender or the offence may not involve danger to the physical safety of others. In such cases, is the 'public interest' justification applicable? It is suggested that it is – for two reasons. First, there is a general public interest in facilitating the due processes of the criminal justice system. In principle, any offence may justify disclosure. However, the less serious it is, the less likely the public interest in maintaining patient confidentiality will be outweighed. It is for this reason that the DoH, in its guidance, refers to 'serious crime' and by way of illustration in Annex D (*op cit*) lists 'serious arrestable offences' defined in the Police and Criminal Evidence Act 1984, s 116. Secondly, in any event, to restrict the 'public interest' justification to dangers to the *physical* safety of others is too limiting. Other serious consequences to the public, such as fraud and dishonesty, should fall in principle within the justification (see eg *Price Waterhouse v BBCI Holdings (Luxembourg) SA* [1992] BCLC 583 (Millet J)). Whether disclosure is, in fact, justified will depend again on balancing the public interest in favour and against it.

3.   Teaching, research and clinical audit

Access to patient information may be essential for the conduct of medical research, teaching of health professionals and to maintain standards by clinical audit. To what extent does the law permit disclosure of confidential information for these purposes? This is not an easy question to answer but it must lie, if at all, either in the realm of *consent* or in the justification for breach of confidence because of the *public interest*.

In *Duncan v Medical Practitioners' Disciplinary Committee* [1986] 1 NZLR 513, a case we saw earlier, Jeffries J stated:

> Limited information to some outside agencies may be made available by a doctor from his files for *statistical, accounting, data processing or other legitimate purposes.* (Our emphasis.)

Jeffries J refers to disclosure for some purposes which might compendiously be described as 'NHS management' purposes. We shall return to this shortly. He does not directly refer to research and it might be important to gain access to patient records either in itself for research purposes, eg epidemiological research, or as part of a larger research project. On disclosure for research purposes, there is precious little authority. However, in one nineteenth-century Scottish case the legality of disclosure for these purposes was acknowledged. In *AB v CD* (1851) 14 D 177, Lord Fullerton stated (at 179–180):

> **Lord Fullerton:** the question here is…whether the relation between [a medical] adviser and the person who consults him, is or is not one which may imply an obligation to secrecy, forming a proper ground of action if it be violated. It appears to me that it is, and that the present case, as stated on the record, is one to which the principle may apply. The obligation may not be absolute. It may and must yield to the demands of justice, if disclosure is demanded in a competent Court. It may be modified, perhaps, in the case alluded to in the argument of the disclosure being conducive to the ends of science, though even there concealment of individuals is usual.

In its guidance, the General Medical Council acknowledges the proprietary of disclosure for research, education and clinical audit in some circumstances.

General Medical Council *Confidentiality: Protecting and Providing Information* (2000)

> *Consent where the disclosure is unlikely to have personal consequences for patients*
> 15. Disclosure of information about patients for purposes such as epidemiology, public health safety, or the administration of health services, or for use in education or training, clinical or medical audit, or research is unlikely to have personal consequences for the patient. In these circumstances you should still obtain patients' express consent to the use of identifiable data or arrange for members of the health care team to anonymise records.
> 16. However, where information is needed for the purposes of the kind set out in paragraph 15, and you are satisfied that it is not practicable either to obtain express consent to disclosure, nor for a member of the health care team to anonymise the records, data may be disclosed without express consent. Usually such disclosures will be made to allow a person outside the health care team to anonymise the records. Only where it is essential for the purpose may identifiable records by disclosed. In all such cases you must be satisfied that patients have been told, or have had access to written material informing them:
>
> a.   That their records may be disclosed to persons outside the team which provided their care.
> b.   Of the purpose and extent of the disclosure, for example, to produce anonymised data for use in education, administration, research or audit.
> c.   That the person given access to records will be subject to a duty of confidentiality.
> d.   That they have a right to object to such a process, and that their objection will be respected, except where the disclosure is essential to protect the patient, or someone else, from risk of death or serious harm.

17. Where you have control of personal information about patients, you must not allow anyone access to them for the purposes of the kind set out in paragraph 15, unless the person has been properly trained and authorised by the health authority, NHS trust or comparable body and is subject to a duty of confidentiality in their employment or because of their registration with a statutory regulatory body ...

Clinical audit and education
22. Anonymised data will usually be sufficient for clinical audit and for education. When anonymising records you should follow the guidance on obtaining consent in paragraphs 15-17 above. You should not disclose non-anonymised data for clinical audit or education without the patient's consent ...

Medical research
31. Where research projects depend on using identifiable information or samples, and it is not practicable to contact patients to seek their consent, this fact should be drawn to the attention of a research ethics committee so that it can consider whether the likely benefits of the research outweigh the loss of confidentiality. Disclosures may otherwise be improper, even if the recipients of the information are registered medical practitioners. The decision of a research ethics committee would be taken into account by a court if a claim for breach of confidentiality were made, but the court's judgement would be based on its own assessment of whether the public interest was served. More detailed guidance is issued by the medical royal colleges and other bodoes.

Publication of case-histories and photographs
32. You must obtain express consent from patients before publishing personal information about them as individuals in media to which the public has access, for example in journals or text books, whether or not you believe the patient can be identified. Express consent must therefore be sought to the publication of, for example, case-histories about, or photographs of, patients. Where you wish to publish information about a patient who has died, you should take into account the guidance in paragraphs 40-41 before deciding whether or not to do so.

You will notice three guiding themes here: (1) anonymise the data if possible; (2) normally obtain the express (and informed) consent of the patient; (3) disclosure may be justified without such consent in some circumstances. It is important to notice that the GMC does not seem to contemplate use for teaching or clinical audit without *express* consent if the information is not anonymised (para 22; but contrast para 16). By contrast, for research disclosure is contemplated in exceptional circumstances without consent but with the agreement of the appropriate Research Ethics Committee (para 31). As we have seen, it has recently been decided that it is not a breach of confidence to disclose anonymised patient information: see *R v Department of Health, ex p Source Informatics Ltd* (1999) 52 BMLR 65(CA) (*supra*). Of course, anonymisation if possible, and consistent with the proposed usage, would still be best practice and may be relevant in setting the limits of justified disclosure on the basis of consent or the public interest.

Clearly, there is no legal difficulty with disclosure if the patient specifically consents to it. Subject, that is, to the issues of competence, understanding and voluntariness. But, can a patient's consent be implied in certain circumstances? We have previously examined the notion of *implied* consent (see *supra*, ch 6 (treatment), *supra*, (confidentiality)). In our view, it has nothing to do with consent at all, which is subjective, being a state of mind of the patient. Rather, it is objective, being akin to estoppel whereby the patient because of his conduct and the circumstances is prevented from asserting that he did not in fact consent. For this reason it cannot be invoked in the case of incompetent adult or child patients and it can have no application where the patient has actually refused his consent. Equally, we have seen that a professional practice of which the individual is unaware cannot give rise to a defence of implied consent: see *Turner v Royal Bank of Scotland* [1999] 2 All ER (Comm) 664 (CA), discussed *supra*. The key question is 'can it reasonably be inferred that, in the circumstances they find themselves and with the knowledge they had, the patient must have agreed to the use of his confidential information for the particular purpose?'

It might be claimed that patients within the NHS must realise that their information could be used for teaching, research or clinical audit. But why? In *ex p Source Informatics* (1999) 49 BMLR 41, Latham J touched on this (at 48-9):

> **Latham J:**...Nor is it suggested that the patient can be said to have given implied consent. This may be the position where doctors and the Health Service itself use anonymous material for the purposes of research, medical advancement or the proper administration of the Service. That is not, however, a matter on which I have heard sufficient evidence or argument to enable me to come to any conclusion; nor is it necessary for me to do so for the purposes of these proceedings.

(Notice the tentative view of Simon Brown LJ in the Court of Appeal: (1999) 52 BMLR 65 at 81, preferring implied consent to the public interest justification.)

Notice Latham J's view on implied consent relates to *anonymised* information only but really that is a 'red herring' here. The answer to the crucial question – what would it be reasonable for a patient to believe would happen to his confidential information? – is probably not significantly affected by its anonymisation. Would a patient contemplate any of this? We seriously doubt it. Indeed, the NHS' own *Patients Charter* (1995) states:

> You have the *right* to choose whether or not you want to take part in medical research or medical student training.

While this seems to contemplate direct personal involvement in research or teaching, it is capable of a broader construction so as to cover research on a patient's records. In any event, its existence is highly destructive of the reasonableness of inferring implied agreement to indirect involvement of the latter sort. Patients do not read and construe such documents as if they were parliamentary draftsmen, rather they do as lay people making reasonable assumptions and reaching reasonable interpretations. A reasonable interpretation is that consent to *involvement* in research or teaching is the patient's right.

It may, however, be reasonable to imply agreement to the use of information held in confidence if a patient has had notice of the potential use and not refused his consent. Having been given a reasonable opportunity to 'opt out', the patient could reasonably be said to be estopped from denying his agreement. There will be difficult factual problems encountered in determining whether the patient had actual notice of the use or reasonable attempts were made to bring it to the patient's attention. It is the advice of the Department of Health that such written notices should be developed and in its guidance, *The Protection and Use of Patient Information* (1996), it is stated:

> 3.1. **All NHS bodies must have an active policy for informing patients of the kind of purposes for which information about them is collected and the categories of people or organisations to which information may need to be passed.** Where other bodies are providing services for or in conjunction with the NHS, those concerned must be aware of each others' information policies.
>
> 3.2. Subject to some important common elements (see paragraph 3.6), the precise arrangements for informing patients are for local decision, taking account of views expressed by community health councils, local patient groups, staff, and agencies with which the NHS body is in close contact. However, those concerned should bear in mind that:
>
> i.   as a general rule, patients should be told how information would be used before they are asked to provide it and must have the opportunity to discuss any aspects that are special to their treatment or circumstances;

ii.   advice must be presented in a convenient form and be available both for general
       purposes and before a particular programme of care or treatment begins.
3.3. Methods of providing advice include:
•   leaflets enclosed with patients' appointment letters or provided when prescriptions
     are dispensed;
•   GP practice leaflets and/or notification on initial registration with a GP;
•   routinely providing patients with necessary information as a part of care planning;
     identifying someone to provide further information if patients want it.
3.4. There must be arrangements for people whose first language is not English or who
have restricted vision or reading skills.
3.5. Notices in waiting areas, newsletters, and other publicity materials can help to reinforce
the general approach, but are insufficient on their own.

In Annex A, a model notice is provided which states, *inter alia*:

...We *may use* some of this information for other reasons: for example, to help us protect
the health of the public generally and to see that the NHS runs efficiently, plans for the
future, trains its staff, pays its bills and can account for its actions. Information may also
be needed to help educate tomorrow's clinical staff and to carry out medical and other
health research for the benefit of everyone...

Arguably, such notices would, if a patient had not 'opted out', justify the
implication of their consent. It may even be that prominent notices in patient
areas in hospitals and GP surgeries would suffice (contrast, DoH Guidance
(*supra*) at para 3.5).

Where, however, this approach does not assist is in the use of information
collected without any notice, perhaps many years ago where the use presently
contemplated was never brought to the patient's attention. A typical, though
not unique, instance of this would be in the area of epidemiological research
on patient records, whether anonymised or not. Contacting patients to obtain
their consent now will often be impractical and costly and may even be
impossible. So what other justification might be prayed in aid here? Could the
'public interest' justification apply?

As regards research, the Government's guidance to Research Ethics
Committees states:

DoH *Local Research Ethics Committees* (HSG (91(5))

3.11. Researchers should be asked to confirm that personal health information will be
kept confidential, that data will be secured against unauthorised access and that no individual
will be identifiable from published results, without his or her explicit consent. All data
from which an individual is identifiable should be destroyed when no longer required for
the purposes of the original research. If, exceptionally, the researcher wishes to retain
confidential information beyond the completion of the research, the LREC, the relevant
NHS body and the research subject must first be made aware of the reasons for retaining
the information and the circumstances in which this might be disclosed. The subject's
consent to these arrangements must be recorded.
3.12. Epidemiological research through studies of medical records can be extremely
valuable. Patients are however entitled to regard their medical records as confidential to
the NHS and should in principle be asked if they consent to their own records being released
to research workers. However, there will be occasions when a researcher would find it
difficult or impossible to obtain such consent from every individual and the LREC will
need to be satisfied that the value of such a project outweighs, in the public interest, the
principle that individual consent should be obtained. Where a patient has previously
indicated that he or she would *not* want their records released then this request should be
respected.
3.13. The LREC will need to be assured that this kind of research will be conducted in
accordance with current codes of practice and data protection legislation. Wherever possible
consent should also be sought from the health professional responsible for the relevant
aspect of the subject's care. Once information has been obtained from the records no
approach should be made to the patient concerned without the agreement of the health
professional currently responsible for their care.

3.14. Certain enquiries and surveys, involving only access to patient records, such as the national morbidity surveys and post-marketing surveillance of drugs, which are in the public interest, do not need prior approval of an LREC. Appendix A gives a list of these.

Clearly these guidelines begin from a premise requiring the research subjects' consent to disclosure. They do, however, address the issue of the public interest where consent may be 'difficult or impossible to obtain'. Arguably, this single example of the public interest in research outweighing the public interest in confidence is limited to the conduct of epidemiological research or other research involving patient records where consent and anonymisation are impossible or impractical. That conducting research, including in respect of patient records, is in the public interest in principle is illustrated by s 2 of the Ministry of Health Act 1919, which places a duty upon the Secretary of State to take: 'all such steps as may be desirable for … the initiation and direction of research.' (See also s 5(2)(d) of the National Health Service Act 1977: power to 'conduct, or assist by grants or otherwise … any person to conduct research…')

This, of course, does not determine whether any *particular* research using patient information is justified – that will require a balance to be struck taking account of the value of the project, the possibility of anonymisation and the practicality and possibility of seeking patient agreement. Public interest would seem also to be the basis of the General Medical Council's advice (*supra*, para 31). It may also underlie the Government's guidance, *The Protection and Use of Patient Information* (1996), which states:

4.20. Advice to patients about the use of personal information must emphasise:
   i. the importance of teaching and research to the maintenance and improvement of care within the NHS, inter-agency care and public health generally;
   ii. that such information, anonymised or aggregated wherever possible, may sometimes be used for teaching and research (and that universities or other bodies carrying out approved research are required to treat it in confidence and must not use it for other purposes);
   iii. that any research proposals involving access to patient records require clearance by the relevant Local Research Ethics Committee, which must be satisfied in particular that:
      a. arrangements to safeguard confidentiality are satisfactory;
      b. any additional conditions relating to the use of information that the LREC thinks are necessary can be met;
      c. any application to use *identifiable* patient information is fully justified: for example, because this is essential to a study of major importance to public health. If not, approval to proceed would not be given;
   iv. that their specific consent will be sought to any activity relating to teaching or research that would involve them personally;
   v. that any published research findings will not identify them without their specific agreement.

Such use is justified by the Department of Health on a 'need to know' basis, which is juxtaposed to disclosure with the patient's consent (*op cit*, para 2.6). It can only be, we would suggest, a manifestation of the 'public interest' justification. In *Source Informatics* (*supra*), Latham J (at 52) offered the latter as legal justification: 'The applicants . . . did not seek to persuade me that disclosure of the information would be in the public interest, although I can see that this may well be an alternative solution to the problem of the use by doctors and health authorities of information gleaned from patients.' However in the Court of Appeal, Simon Brown LJ (at 81) seems to have preferred the 'implied consent' explanation for using patient records for research (and management) purposes rather than the public interest justification. His view was only tentative, being irrelevant to the case itself and, for the reasons we have given, the public interest justification is preferable.

4. Management and NHS administrative purposes

As regards management, the BMA in its book *Rights and Responsibilities of Doctors* (1992) offers the following observation in para 3.8:

> With the development of an 'internal market' in the NHS concerns have arisen about safeguarding the confidentiality of patient data which might appear on bills for extra-contractual referrals, etc. The Department of Health booklet *NHS Review Information Systems: Action for Managers* stated that 'very strict, tightly controlled administrative and computer security arrangements will be necessary to safeguard confidentiality and to deal with subject access requests'. This emphasis on such a breach of confidentiality as a very serious matter has been reinforced in NHS management executive letter EL(91)49.
>
> All grades of NHS staff, including clerical officers who might handle confidential bills relating to individual patients, are reminded in this letter that breach of confidence is a disciplinary offence, and arrangements for handling data containing patients' details must be agreed with an appropriate senior medical officer. Despite these guidelines pressure is mounting for a coding system on NHS bills and contracts which would ensure complete confidentiality.

The difficulty with the view expressed by the BMA is that it proceeds from a misunderstanding of what confidentiality is about. A patient confides in his doctor. He does not confide in the staff in general, eg accountants, managers and office staff (or, indeed, other doctors not concerned with his care). To purport to justify disclosure to these on the grounds that they will keep the patient's secret misses the point. The patient may not want (or expect) them to know in the first place. This is what confidentiality is about.

Of course, a patient's information has always been available to lots of eyes. But this has been regarded as something that is wrong and to be avoided though almost a fact of life. It is another thing to institutionalise the practice and thereby legitimise it. No one can doubt the need of management in the current NHS to have access to patients' information. Equally, no one can doubt that routinising such access may drive a 'coach and horses' through confidentiality. Can administrative use be justified on the basis of implied consent or the public interest? The General Medical Council in its Guidance (*op cit*) promotes disclosure in anonymised form (para 23) but contemplates, as for teaching etc, disclosure of identifiable information where that is necessary (para 16).

General Medical Council *Confidentiality: Protecting and Providing Information* (2000)

Administration and financial audit

23. You should record financial or other administrative data separately from clinical information, and provide it in anonymised form, wherever that is possible.

24. Decisions about the disclosure of clinical records for administrative or financial audit purposes, for example where health authority staff seek access to patients' records as part of the arrangements for verifying NHS payment, are unlikely to bring your registration into question, provided that, before allowing access to patient's records, you follow the guidance in paragraphs 15-17. Only the relevant part of the record should be made available for scrutiny.

The basis for disclosure under para 16 may well be implied consent. Some legal commentators have also justified disclosure on the basis of implied consent.

R G Toulson and C M Phipps *Confidentiality* (1996)

3.11 General practitioners and hospitals have to maintain records. Increasingly they are computerised. The storing of information, whether manually or on computer, to which as a matter of practical reality others may have access involves actual or potential loss of secrecy. Moreover information may be stored not merely for medical but for management purposes, eg in the case of a private hospital patient so that the accounting department bills the patient correctly. The legal justification may be put in alternative ways. Since no medical practice or hospital could operate properly or efficiently without maintaining medical records, it may be said that the patient impliedly consents to it. Alternatively it may be said that the keeping of records is in part for the purpose of the patient's present or future treatment and in part for the protection of the doctor's or hospital's proper interests, and therefore does not in itself infringe upon any duty of confidentiality to the patient. Infringement will occur if records are leaked for other purposes, for example, by disclosure to the press (as in *X v Y* [1988] 2 All ER 648).

You will notice that two purposes are contemplated here – the *interests of the NHS* and the *private interest of the doctor*. The latter is, perhaps, more difficult to entertain than the former. We have already discussed the issue of consent when considering disclosure for the purposes of research, teaching or clinical audit. What we said there has equal application here. In reality, the legal justification lies elsewhere.

There is, in our view, an arguable public interest in maintaining and monitoring the efficient use of public funds within the NHS. Indeed, there is statutory backing for financial auditors to access patient information (National Health Service Act 1977 s 98). The public interest is also reflected in the European Court of Human Rights' reliance on art 8(2) of the Convention in *MS v Sweden* (1997) 45 BMLR 133 (*supra*), namely that disclosure to monitor proper use of public funds was necessary for 'the economic well-being of the country'. In *ex p Source Informatics* (1999) *supra*, as we saw earlier, Latham J, at first instance, inclined to the view that the use of patient information by doctors and others within the health service for administrative purposes might be justified either on the basis of implied consent or as being in the public interest. Simon Brown LJ, however, in the Court of Appeal preferred 'implied consent' without rejecting the alternative of the public interest. In our view, the public interest approach is preferable.

In the end, we are again concerned with the balancing exercise of *when* the public interest justifies disclosure and controls over the dissemination of information within (and sometimes outside) the NHS (see *supra*).

5. Genetics

One further illustration of the public interest justification is worth considering given its contemporary importance in health care. To what extent may a doctor disclose genetic information obtained from examining or testing a patient to other members of that patient's family? The importance of this question lies in the fact that, almost uniquely, genetic (medical) information about one person may be very relevant to the health of a family member because of their common genetic heritage.

The following extract explains the situation.

British Medical Association *Human Genetics: Choice and Responsibility* (1998)

The general principles of confidentiality apply equally to genetic information as to other medical records. With the results of genetic testing, however, there is the added dimension that genetic testing of one individual has relevance for other family members. This can present health professionals with a conflict between their duty to maintain patient confidentiality and their duty to protect others from avoidable harm and suffering. Some geneticists have argued that in genetics the true patient is the family rather than the individual and, as they share a common genetic inheritance, the duty of confidentiality to the individual is less clear . . . , the concept of a purely personal decision is challenged by genetics where information obtained has relevance for other people with whom the individual has close family ties and to whom he or she has certain moral duties and responsibilities. The level of confidentiality required for genetic information has been interpreted differently throughout Europe, with some countries wanting to strengthen confidentiality in this area, others suggesting grounds to weaken it and still others suggesting that the usual norms of medical practice should apply. The BMA believes that, as with other areas of health care, the doctor's duty of confidentiality to the individual patient is of fundamental importance and should only be breached when there is a legal requirement or an overriding public interest...however, individuals should be encouraged to consider the implications of their decisions for other people.

There are two main ways in which genetic information about one individual affects another. First, testing for a dominant disorder inevitably reveals information about the genetics status of certain other people. Take, for example, the case of a woman whose maternal grandfather has Huntington's disease. Her mother has not begun to show symptoms of the disorder and has declined pre-symptomatic testing. If the daughter has the test, and it proves positive, the daughter knows that her mother also carries the defective gene. In this case, the daughter's decision to know her own genetic status gives her information about her mother which her mother herself lacks. In the majority of cases sensible discussion can lead to a mutually satisfactory decision about whether the test should go ahead and how much or how little information should be revealed to whom. Genetic counsellors and other health professionals can help to facilitate this discussion, assuming, as in most cases, that both parties are willing to try to reach agreement in this way. If they are not willing to discuss the issue or if agreement cannot be reached, careful thought will need to be given to how the situation will be handled. In most cases, however, a health professional should not refuse to provide testing solely on the grounds that it will reveal information about a relative which that relative does not wish to know.

Once the information is generated the issue is more a question of how the confidentiality of the mother can be protected, given that every time the patient's status is disclosed, the status of her mother can be inferred. The daughter may be unwilling to share information about her own genetic status with other people, including her mother, despite being informed of the relevance of the information for other family members. This will result in the anomalous position of the daughter having information about her mother which her mother does not have. If the mother knows that the test is being carried out and wants to know the result she should seek testing herself, accompanied by appropriate counselling and support. In the very rare cases where, despite discussion and counselling, the daughter decides to have the test without informing her mother, the question arises of whether the health professionals concerned should, or perhaps even have a duty to, inform the mother of the result...

Another way in which genetic information may be relevant to others is if an individual discovers from testing that other family members may be at risk of developing or passing on a serious genetic disorder. Take, for example, the mother of a son with Duchenne muscular dystrophy who has tested positive for carrier status and whose sister was known to be planning children. Information about the woman's carrier status would be an important factor for her sister to consider in making reproductive decisions. Many cases have been reported in which parents have expressed their anger at being denied the opportunity to make informed decisions because information about their at-risk status was not shared with them. In addition to information affecting reproductive decisions, genetic information would also be of great relevance to relatives where those known to be at risk could seek pre-symptomatic testing or early diagnosis leading to action to delay or prevent the onset of the condition. The fact that information would be useful, relevant, or interesting to a relative, however, does not justify the disclosure of that information without the individual's consent. Such disclosure would only be justified in very limited circumstances . . .

How, then, should we approach disclosure to others? Can it be justified in the public interest? The BMA thinks it can, in exceptional circumstances, where the patient cannot be persuaded to agree (*ibid* pp 70–72).

The difficulty of confidentiality in relation to genetics is highlighted by the conflicting conclusions reached by the House of Commons Science and Technology Committee and the Nuffield Council on Bioethics, both of which have produced reports on genetics. The former gave precedence to the duty of confidentiality stating that 'if counselling cannot persuade someone to consent to sharing information with their relatives the individual's decision to withhold information should be paramount'. (House of Commons Science and Technology Committee 'Human Genetics: The Science and Its Consequences' (HMSO, 1995) para 228). This conclusion was reached on the grounds that failure to guarantee confidentiality would discourage people from participating in research or seeking information which could be beneficial to their own health. The Nuffield Council on Bioethics, however, concluded that in some cases warning others of potential serious harm was more important, stating 'in exceptional circumstances, health professionals might be justified in disclosing genetic information to other family members, despite an individual's desire for confidentiality'. (Nuffield Council on Bioethics, 'Genetic Screening: Ethical Issues' (1993)). Both reports emphasised the importance of trying to persuade the individual to disclose the information voluntarily. This point is also emphasised in…the Genetic Interest Group's report *Confidentiality and Medical Genetics*. (Genetic Interest Group, 'Confidentiality and Medical Genetics' (1998)).

From an ethical perspective an individual can be seen to have a moral obligation to share relevant information with people with whom he or she has close family links. The fact that the individual is perceived to have moral obligations, however, does not mean that health professionals, or anyone else, can compel that person to fulfil them. The extent to which a refusal to share information can be justified on moral grounds will depend to a large extent upon the individual factors of the case such as the closeness of the relationship, the degree of certainty, the level of risk or benefit to others, whether the other people are aware of their genetic risk, and the individual's reasons for the refusal.

The BMA, whilst emphasising a doctor's duty of medical confidentiality, has always argued that this duty is not absolute. It is recognised, both in law and ethics, that in some limited circumstances there may be an overriding public interest in disclosing confidential medical information to an appropriate person or body. Any doctor who decides to disclose information to a third party, without consent, must be prepared to justify his or her actions to the General Medical Council (GMC), which regulates the medical profession. The GMC's guidelines on confidentiality state that disclosure of information, without consent, 'may be necessary in the public interest where a failure to disclose information may expose the patient, or others, to risk of death or serious harm'. (General Medical Council 'Confidentiality: Guidance from the General Medical Council para 18.) The Association believes that, as a general rule, genetic information should not be disclosed without the consent of the individual concerned. People seeking testing should be informed of the implications for other family members before they consent to testing and should be strongly encouraged to share the information with those affected. Experience has shown that the vast majority of individuals are happy to share genetic information with their relatives. If, however, after counselling and persuasion, the individual refuses to share the information, this refusal should be respected unless the limited criteria set out by the GMC are met. In such circumstances there may be grounds for breaching confidentiality. The type of factors which should be considered in reaching this judgement are:

- the severity of the disorder;
- the level of predictability of the information provided by testing;
- what, if any, action the relatives could take to protect themselves or to make informed reproductive decisions, if they were told of the risk;
- the level of harm or benefit of giving and withholding the information; and
- the reason given for refusing to share the information.

In resolving these very difficult dilemmas health professionals may find it helpful to discuss the circumstances within the health care team or, on an anonymous basis, with other colleagues. In some exceptional cases disclosure of information, without consent, will be justified. At this stage, before any contact with the relatives has been made, the doctor should inform the patient of his or her intention to pass the information to family members and explain the reasons why this is considered to be justified. Wherever possible information should be passed to relatives in a way that does not identify the patient. This might be done by simply informing the individual that information has been obtained from 'a relative' without naming the person or the relationship.

Reliance here is being placed upon the 'public interest' justification and, in particular, the 'harm' or 'injury to others' aspect we have seen earlier. You will notice the factors set out in the extract which must be taken into account in determining whether breach of confidence is justified.

We agree with this general approach. The approach of the law is further explored in the following extract.

C Ngwana and R Chadwick 'Genetic Diagnostic Information and the Duty of Confidentiality: Ethics and the Law' (1993) 1 Med Law Int 73

PUBLIC INTEREST AND DISCLOSURE TO THIRD PARTIES

Genetic Relations as Third Parties
English courts have yet to determine as a direct issue whether it would be in the public interest to disclose the counsellee's confidence to genetically related third parties so as to prevent or ameliorate the effects of genetic disease. However to the extent that, . . . it is firmly established that the obligation of confidence is relative, the more pertinent question is determining the contours of the public interest exception in genetic disease. A starting point is a closer appreciation of analogous cases where courts have countenanced the doctor's decision to override the duty of confidence in the interest of a third party.

...To what extent then does the public interest exception...translate to disclosure of genetic confidence to genetically related third parties so as to prevent or ameliorate the harmful effects of the disease? An initial point to note here, as some commentators have observed, is that courts have enunciated the public interest exception in wide and vague terms. (Grubb, A and Pearl D A (1990) '*Bloodtesting, Aids and DNA Profiling*' Family Law, Bristol, 43). It is apparent from decided cases that the public interest exception can be invoked to protect an open rather than closed category of interests of which the physical and mental health of an identified individual or class of subjects is but one. (*A-G v Guardian Newspapers (No 2)* [1988] 3 All ER 545). What is crucial is the establishment of tangible anticipated harm to a third party. In principle, therefore, the interest in preventing the deleterious effects of genetic disease in a genetically related third party prima facie falls within the public interest exception. Indeed, it is in similar vein that it has been suggested that where the patient is carrying HIV or suffering from AIDS, the public interest exception would justify disclosure of confidence so as to protect an unwitting third party from the risk of contracting the infection and developing the serious and/or fatal disease through sexual intercourse. However, notwithstanding the vague and inconclusive nature of the manner in which courts have articulated the public interest exception, it is possible to derive some criteria from the decided cases.

Circumstances justifying disclosure must be compelling
The onus is on the confidant to justify excepting the duty of confidence. In this connection, courts have emphasised that the circumstances justifying disclosure must be *exceptional* or *compelling* otherwise the duty of confidence would cease to have any real meaning at all. This parallels the ethical point made earlier that on a utilitarian calculation confidentiality is not as vulnerable as it might appear because it is not an easy matter to find sufficient utility from a breach of confidence to outweigh the harm done to an individual confider *and* damage to the respect for confidentiality generally that may result as a side effect. Hence in the Egdell case, Bingham LJ had this to say about the circumstances justifying disclosure:

> ...only the most *compelling* circumstances could justify a doctor in acting in a way which could injure the immediate interests of his patient as the patient perceives them without his consent [1990] 1 All ER 835 at 851j; (1989) 4 BMLR 96 at 115.

Disclosure of confidence in the face of an express or implied objection by the confider is likely to injure the interest of the confider, such that in the medical context, unless the exception to disclose is invoked sparingly, patients as a class would cease to have confidence in the medical profession with the inevitable counterproductive results to public health in general. It would seem to follow, therefore, that the mere fact that a third party is at risk from a genetic disease would not necessarily be sufficient by itself to justify disclosure of confidence in the public interest. It is thus important to attempt to identify criteria, other than the mere fact of risk of genetic disease, that the courts are likely to treat as constituting compelling circumstances justifying disclosure.

Probability and magnitude of harm to be averted or ameliorated
The degree of harm that would come to the third party unless confidence is disclosed is a most important factor when determining whether disclosure was justifiable in the public interest. The more probable and the more serious the magnitude of harm in question, then the more likely that courts will hold the disclosure to be in the public interest.

Courts have not systematically employed a risk model to evaluate the probability and magnitude of harm before coming to a conclusion whether disclosure was or is in the public interest. However, it is apparent from analogous cases that judges appeal implicitly if not explicitly to such considerations...

In the light of the above, the question whether it is justified in the public interest to disclose confidence to a genetically related third party will depend primarily on the peculiarities of the genetic disease in question. Genetic disease neither exhibits homogeneity nor certainties in terms of probability and magnitude of risk to third parties. There are about 5,000 known genetic diseases whose mode of inheritance is not always predictable and which manifest with varying severity. (Nichols, E K (1988) *'Human Gene Therapy'* Chapter 1 Harvard University Press; Cambridge, Mass, London.) It is conventional to classify genetic diseases into three main groups: unifactorial, multifactorial and chromosomal disorders, depending on the nature of the defect. (Ibid.) In unifactorial disorders, only a single gene is defective. They follow a Mendelian inheritance making it possible to predict the probability of the disorder being transmitted to descendants. (Examples of unifactorial diseases: Huntington's disease, Myotonic dystrophy, cystic fibrosis, sickle cell anaemia, Duchenne muscular dystrophy, haemophilia.) In multifactorial disorders, the defect is of several rather than a single gene. The mode of inheritance in descendants is unpredictable. (Prime examples are neutral tube defects as spina bifida and anencephaly.) In chromosomal disorders, there is an abnormal alteration in the structure and number of chromosomes. The mode of inheritance, as with multifactorial disorders, is unpredictable. (A prime example is Down's Syndrome.) Thus far, it is apparent that short of conducting an investigation on the third party genetically related to the confidant, the prior determination of risk insofar as establishing probability as a relevant factor in the determination of the question whether disclosure is in the public interest, is more feasible in unifactorial rather than multifactorial and chromosomal disorders where the mode of inheritance is unpredictable.

It is also more important to bear in mind that even with unifactorial disorders, there is no necessary homogeneity in terms of probability of risk in descendants. Much will depend on whether the disorder is a dominant one, where there would a 1:2 chance of manifesting in offspring, or a recessive, where the probability would be 1:4; or a sex- or X- linked one, where manifestation of the disease and carrier status will depend on gender of offspring.

Further, as Beauchamp and Childress (Beauchamp, T L and Childress, J F (1989) *'Principles of Biomedical Ethics'* 3rd Edn, OUP, New York) have noted, even if it is possible to ascertain on a numerical scale the statistical probability and the magnitude of the risk, there still remains the problem of deciding objectively which risks are not acceptable to run. The problem of establishing objective criteria for determining risk acceptability is not peculiar to genetic medicine. It has received attention in other areas of medicine. As Rowe has observed, whilst risk identification and estimation are relatively capable of objectification, evaluating risk acceptability allows a very wide margin of subjective appreciation. Much will depend on the value system of the party doing the evaluation. Generally speaking, the medical profession and the lay do not always evaluate risks from the same stand-point. In medical research for example, there is evidence suggesting that the desire to advance medical knowledge and secure a therapeutic breakthrough, may influence the researcher in running a risk that the research subject regards as unacceptable. In genetic medicine it is possible that the desire to reduce the burden of genetic disease on society or prevent suffering, may influence geneticists to treat as unacceptable, risks that the lay are otherwise prepared to run.

From the above observations it will be apparent that consensus may be difficult to attain in that there are likely to be appreciable differences of opinion on what kind of genetic diseases would be in the public interest to disclose. In so far as ascertaining the legal standards, however, much will depend on the prevailing custom of the geneticist. Courts do not require mathematical accuracy in the exercise of clinical discretion. *(Re J (a minor) (Wardship: Medical treatment)* [1990] 3 All ER 930 at 945f per Taylor LJ.) The crucial consideration is whether a particular practice has the confidence of the profession or a section of it. This follows from the *Bolam* standard where a doctor is regarded as competent by the courts if he exercises his skill in a manner which a responsible doctor in a comparable position would have done. (*Bolam v Friern Hospital Management Committee* [1957] 2 All ER 118, (1957) 1 BMLR 1, [1957] 1 WLR 582.) This is so notwithstanding that there may be diametrically opposed schools of thought in relation to a given clinical activity. (Ibid; *Whitehouse v Jordon* [1981] 1 All ER 267, 1 BMLR 14, [1981] 1 WLR 246.) Although courts have reiterated the point that ultimately it is for the law rather than the medical profession to set the requisite standard, decided cases demonstrate not only consistent but also a remarkable judicial deference towards standards set by the profession. (*Whitehouse v Jordan* supra; *Sidaway v Bethlem Royal Hospital Governors* [1985] 1 All ER 643, (1985) 1 BMLR 132.)

The extent to which disclosure is necessary to avert or ameliorate harm
The rationale for disclosing otherwise confidential information is to enable the third party to avoid or ameliorate harm…

In genetic disease, however, the benefits of disclosure of confidence are not always axiomatic. This is primarily due to the fact that for the great majority of genetic disease, other than palliative measures, there is no curative or prophylactic therapy which the third party at risk can take. Diseases such as adenomatous polyposis coli, a precursor to malignancy, which can be cured if detected and treated early, represent the exception rather than the rule. (Harper, P S and Clarke, A (1990) *'Should we treat children for 'adult' genetic diseases?'* Lancet, 1205–6.) What then would be the rationale for disclosure where curative therapy was not available?

Even where curative therapy is unavailable it is possible to argue that the third party can at least take palliative measures to minimise the deleterious effects of the disease. However, this argument does not deal adequately with the fact that there may be cases where even the palliative measures do very little to influence the course of the disease. (Ibid.) In such cases the only real benefit of disclosure might be in providing the third party with an opportunity to prevent harm by exercising informed reproductive decision-making. The question arises as to whether it is ever justifiable to break a confidence on this ground alone. This question is considered below in the section dealing with the spouse/partner.

The third party must exist as an identifiable individual or belong to an existing class of subjects
Courts have implicitly developed the public interest exception to protect from harm existing people identifiable as individuals or by reason of class…

It is worth noting, however, that few of the documents on genetic disease and confidentiality *explicitly* mention the harm to future offspring as a reason for breach of confidence. In as much as under English civil law the unborn child has no independent legal status, it is submitted, the public interest exception does not obtain to prevent harm to future people since legally they cannot be harmed. (*Paton v Trustees of BPAS* [1978] 2 All ER 987; *C v S* [1987] 1 All ER 1230, (1987) 2 BMLR 143; *Re F (in utero)* [1988] 2 All ER 193.) Ethically, however, we take the view that it is possible to speak of harm to as yet unborn people regardless of whether they are in an embryonic or foetal state. The RCP report, *Ethical Issues in Clinical Genetics* (1991) (Royal College of Physicians (1991) 'Ethical Issues in Clinical Genetics: A Report of a Working Group of the Royal College of Physicians Committees on Ethical Issues in Medicine and Clinical Genetics' prepared by Janet Radcliffe Richards and Martin Bobrow Royal College of Physicians; London. See para 4.9) may be implying this when it goes on to suggest a move from a *right* to make reproductive choices in the light of full information to a *duty* to do so. On the other hand, what they have in mind may be the economic and social costs of caring for sufferers from genetic disease.

We take the view, as we have argued elsewhere (Chadwick, R F and Ngwena, C G (1992) *'The development of a normative standard in counselling for genetic disease: ethics and law'* Journal of Social Welfare and Family Law No 4, 276) that suffering is a bad thing whenever and wherever it occurs, and it is good to try to prevent it. Effort put into this activity, however, inevitably has costs elsewhere, and it is uncertain whether preventing such future possible harm could outweigh the certain harm of breach of confidence now. This again would require some assessment of the seriousness of the future harm and the probability of its occurrence. It is worthy of note at this point that the BMA has expressed the view that 'any breach of confidentiality without consent would have to be justified on the basis of the severity of the disorder and implications for other family members'. (British Medical Association (1992) *'Our Genetic future: The Science and Ethics of Genetic Technology,* p 201; OUP, Oxford.) Whether 'other family members' here can be taken to include the unborn is not clear. Apparently that possibility is not ruled out.

SPOUSE/PARTNER AS THIRD PARTY
Thus far a genetic relationship has been assumed between the confider and the third party. It is important to consider the position of the confider's spouse or reproductive/procreative partner as third party and whether the public interest exception obtains. At one level, the spouse or partner is in a different position from the genetically related party. Genetic disease is vertically rather than horizontally transmitted. Thus the spouse or partner's sexual and reproductive relationship with the confidant does not put him/her at a direct risk in terms of contracting disease unlike the position with infections, for example. What then would be the possible justification for invoking the public interest exception?

It might be argued that the spouse or partner has a right to informed reproductive decision-making. There is a view that individuals have the right to make reproductive decisions in the light of as much information as possible. (Royal College of Physicians (1991) (*supra*) para 4.7) If this is the case then to deny a person information that might be pertinent to his or her decision is a harm, in so far as it violates a right. The denial undermines their capacity to make an informed choice. It is not clear, however, why we should think that there is such a right, and further why, even if it is accepted as a good we ought to pursue, choice in this area should be given higher priority than choice over the use of personal information. As suggested above, it might be argued that in this conflict situation the burden of proof should be on the one who would break a confidence, and it is not clear that harm to choice *itself* is sufficiently serious to warrant disclosure. Moreover, unless the confidant is under a tortious duty of care to provide such information, the law would not recognise a right to reproductive decision-making. (*Sidaway v Bethlem Royal Hospital Governors* [1985] 1 All ER 643, (1985) 1 BMLR 132.) Something more then needs to be added to constitute a harm of sufficient magnitude.

The costs of rearing a handicapped child

A harm that might be considered relevant by the law is the cost (financial, emotional and physical) of rearing a handicapped child. Someone who is aware of relevant genetic information can take steps to avoid those costs, and can therefore reasonably claim to be harmed if he or she takes decisions in ignorance and then incurs the costs.

This kind of cost is played down in reports such as that of the RCP, in favour of a stress on reproductive choice. This may be because it is considered to come dangerously close to talking about social costs of genetic disease with their eugenic connotations. The *Purchaser's Guide to Genetic Services* however is quite explicit about this. (Royal College of Physicians (1991) '*Purchasers' Guide to Genetic Services in the NHS: A Report of a Working Group of the Clinical Genetics Committee of the Royal College of Physicians,*' London.) It is moreover harm that has been taken seriously by the courts in wrongful birth cases, (*Emeh v Kensington an Chelsea and Westminster Area Health Authority* [1984] 3 All ER 1044; *Udale v Bloomsbury Area Health Authority* [1983] 2 All ER 522; *Thake v Maurice* [1984] 2 All ER 513) despite the fact that they have been loathe to recognise claims for wrongful life. (*McKay v Essex Area Health Authority* [1982] 2 All ER 771.)

Again a balancing exercise is required, if it is thought that any of these harms is sufficiently serious that steps should then be taken to avert them. However, what also has to be considered is whether a breach of confidentiality is the only way of going about this. Wachbroit has argued that if issues of reproductive choice are important, then it is open to the couple making the reproductive decision to have genetic testing. While this may be true in theory, the argument depends not only on awareness of the issues but also on the availability of resources, which are likely to be in short supply.

Non-paternity

There is, however, another ethical consideration. Some of the information that becomes available to a genetics counsellor will have been positively confided by the client. Other information, however, will become known to the counsellor as a result of some screening procedure. This may include discovery of non-paternity. It might be argued that the harm to a spouse who is kept ignorant of such facts is the harm of deception. It may be difficult to find enough weight in the harm of deception *itself* to outweigh the harm of breach of confidence unless it has further consequences. Whether or not it does will in part depend on the relationship between the confidant and the spouse – is he or she also a client of the confidant? If so then the deception may damage their relationship. Also, a man who falsely supposes himself to be the father of a child with a particular genetic status may take unwarranted decisions about his reproductive future. This raises the question discussed above. What has to be borne in mind is that to reveal information about non-paternity might lead to harm to the confider, not only of the breach of confidentiality itself, but also harm (in some cases violence) within the relationship. These harms have to be weighed against each other...

CONCLUSION

From an ethical point of view it has been argued that confidentiality cannot be an absolute duty. Whether it is based on autonomy or utility a balancing exercise has to be carried out. It has been suggested, however, that there is a presumption in favour of confidentiality, and that the burden of proof is on the would-be disclosure. Considerations in favour of disclosure have to be sufficiently great to outweigh not only the harm to individual confiders but also the danger of weakening respect for confidentiality generally, with the attendant consequences for the professional-client relationship. In these respects ethics and law appear to be in agreement. It has been argued that the recent trend towards undermining the presumption in favour of confidentiality has not been well supported by compelling reasons. When the balancing exercise counts in favour of disclosure, all things considered, it is then what the confidant ought to do, and thus can be described as his or her duty. This is where a difference between ethics and law emerges…[R]ather than merely countenance unquestioningly the prevailing custom(s) in genetic medicine, as is the judicial trend in other areas of medicine, it would be desirable for the circumstances justifying disclosure to be clearly articulated, if the occasion arose to lay down the legal standard. But since judicial intervention depends on the initiative of individual parties, such an occasion might never arise. Moreover, the law tends to lay down standards retrospectively rather than prospectively. For these reasons it would be desirable in the meantime to promulgate a code of ethics following an inquiry into the attendant ethical and legal considerations so as to give clear and consistent guidance to clinicians in genetic medicine…

(For discussion of whether a *duty* to disclose exists in law see, *supra*, ch 4 and for further discussion in an international context, see L Skene 'Patients' Rights or Family Responsibilities?' (1998) 6 Med L Rev 1.)

C. STATUTORY

We have already made mention of a number of statutory provisions that create a legal duty of confidentiality. Often, these provisions are backed by criminal sanctions for breach unless disclosure falls within one of the stated exceptions. In what follows, we examine six instances: the Abortion Regulations 1991; the Public Health (Control of Disease) Act 1984; the National Health Service (Venereal Diseases) Regulations 1974; the Police and Criminal Evidence Act 1984; the Health Act 1999 ss 22–24; and finally, the Health Service Commissioners' Act 1993, s 15.

The Abortion Regulations 1991 (SI 1991 No 499)

5.   A notice given or any information furnished to a Chief Medical Officer in pursuance of these Regulations shall not be disclosed except that disclosure may be made –
(a)   for the purposes of carrying out their duties.
   (i)   to an officer of the Department of Health authorised by the Chief Medical Officer of that Department, or to an officer of the [National Assembly of Wales] authorised by the Chief Medical Officer of that Office, as the case may be, or
   (ii)   to the Registrar General or a member of his staff authorised by him: or
(b)   for the purposes of carrying out his duties in relation to offences under the Act or the law relating to abortion, to the Director of Public Prosecutions or a member of his staff authorised by him; or
(c)   for the purposes of investigating whether an offence has been committed under the Act or the law relating to abortion, to a police officer not below the rank of superintendent or a person authorised by him; or
(d)   pursuant to a court order, for the purposes of criminal proceedings which have begun; or
(e)   for the purposes of bona fide scientific research; or
(f)   to the practitioner who terminated the pregnancy; or
(g)   to a practitioner, with the consent in writing of the woman whose pregnancy was terminated; or
(h)   when requested by the President of the General Medical Council for the purpose of investigating whether there has been serious professional misconduct by a registered medical practitioner, to the President of the General Medical Council or a member of its staff authorised by him.

The regulation only applies to the notice of termination and the information contained in it.

Wilful disclosure in breach of reg 5 is a summary offence (Abortion Act 1967, s 2(3)). Notice the breadth of the exceptions to the duty of confidentiality in addition to consent by the patient to include purposes related to the performance and enforcement of the abortion law, other criminal proceedings, pursuant to court order, scientific research and for disciplinary proceedings against a doctor. In essence, reg 5 sets out many of the instances that could fall within the 'public interest' exception at common law (see *supra*). But notice, as regards professional disciplinary proceedings, that there is no mention of the United Kingdom Central Council for Nursing, Midwifery and Health Visiting (UKCC). It would appear, therefore, that disclosure to the UKCC, unlike to the GMC, would be an offence. Likewise, there could not be disclosure for the purposes of investigating a complaint. Of course, in both cases disclosure could not even be done with the written consent of the patient or patients, which only licenses disclosure to 'a practitioner' (reg 5(g)). Although these limitations do not seem to have caused any practical difficulties, experience in relation to other statutes, eg the Human Fertilisation and Embryology Act 1990 and Health Service Commissioners Act 1993, where disclosure is stated in very limited terms, suggests that there may be difficulties in the future.

Public Health (Control of Disease) Act 1984

Notifiable diseases
10. In this Act, 'notifiable disease' means any of the following diseases –
(a) cholera;
(b) plague;
(c) relapsing fever;
(d) smallpox; and
(e) typhus.

Cases of notifiable disease and food poisoning to be reported
11. (1) If a registered medical practitioner becomes aware, or suspects, that a patient whom he is attending within the district of a local authority is suffering from a notifiable disease or from food poisoning, he shall, unless he believes, and has reasonable grounds for believing, that some other registered medical practitioner has complied with this subsection with respect to the patient, forthwith send to the proper officer of the local authority for that district a certificate stating –
(a) the name, age and sex of the patient and the address of the premises where the patient is,
(b) the disease or, as the case may be, particulars of the poisoning from which the patient is, or is suspected to be, suffering and the date, or approximate date, of its onset, and
(c) if the premises are a hospital, the day on which the patient was admitted, the address of the premises from which he came there and whether or not, in the opinion of the person giving the certificate, the disease or poisoning from which the patient is, or is suspected to be, suffering was contracted in the hospital…
    (4) A person who fails to comply with an obligation imposed on him by subsection (1) above shall be liable on summary conviction to a fine not exceeding level 1 on the standard scale.

These provisions are supplemented by the Public Health (Infectious Diseases) Regulations 1988 (SI 1988 No 1546), which refer to a wide range of further infectious conditions which must be reported by doctors.

National Health Service (Venereal Diseases) Regulations 1974 (SI 1974 No 29)

2. Every [Health Authority] shall take all necessary steps to secure that any information capable of identifying an individual obtained by officers of the Authority with respect to persons examined or treated for any sexually transmitted disease shall not be disclosed except –
(a) for the purpose of communicating that information to a medical practitioner, or to a person employed under the direction of a medical practitioner in connection with the treatment of persons suffering from such disease or the prevention of the spread thereof, and
(b) for the purpose of such treatment or prevention.

This regulation was introduced so as to give statutory emphasis to the obligation of confidence in this area of medical practice (see discussion in A Grubb and D Pearl *Bloodtesting, AIDS and DNA Profiling* (1990) pp 55–56). The reasons are obvious: thus, the circumstances under which disclosure can be made are carefully circumscribed. Curiously, the regulations have not been amended to apply to NHS trusts (but see NHS Trust (Venereal Disease) Directions 1991). Although it is often said that reg 2 creates a duty of confidentiality, strictly speaking it does not. Rather, it imposes a statutory duty upon a Health Authority *to enforce* a duty of confidentiality that arises by virtue of the common law (or statute) between the patient and doctor or Health Authority. It could be argued that the wording of the provision is such as to allow a patient's GP to be informed by those working in a Genito-Urinary Clinic without the consent of, and even in the face of the refusal of, the patient. This has particular significance in the context of HIV infection where some have argued for the right of the GP to be informed of a patient's HIV status, allegedly in the interests of the patient so as to ensure any future care is medically optimal but, in the case of some doctors at least, in their own perceived interests.

A careful reading of the words of the regulation suggests that it is only information relating to treatment for venereal disease *and* only when the GP himself is also treating the disease that the exception comes into play. In essence it is merely an example of sharing information in the context of team care.

Even if this is wrong, a further point can be made. The notion of *treatment* entails the need for the patient's consent which itself entails agreement to share information about his condition. Arguably reg 2(b) can have no application in the absence of the patient's agreement to the transfer of the information to his GP.

A small, but important, point to notice is that the obligation of confidence under the regulations applies to any disease which is 'sexually transmitted'. If this is so, a patient who is HIV positive may need to look to the common law for protection of his confidence if he became infected by some other means as, for example, if he is a haemophiliac or has otherwise become HIV positive as a result of an infected blood donation. Alternatively, a 'sexually transmitted disease' within the regulations could be said to be one usually transmitted through sexual contact but which may be transmitted by other means. Blood, for example, may be infected with syphilis and transfused into someone who then develops the disease. The disease remains a 'sexually transmitted disease'. On this analysis HIV infection would be within the regulations regardless of the means of infection. (See *X v Y* [1988] 2 All ER 648, in which Rose J assumes the latter to be the case.)

Police and Criminal Evidence Act 1984

Special provisions as to access

9. (1) A constable may obtain access to excluded material…for the purposes of a criminal investigation by making an application under Schedule 1 below and in accordance with that Schedule [ie, to a circuit judge]…

Meaning of 'excluded material'

11. (1) Subject to the following provisions of this section, in this Act 'excluded material' means –
(a) personal records which a person has acquired or created in the course of any trade, business, profession or other occupation or for the purposes of any paid or unpaid office and which he holds in confidence;
(b) human tissue or tissue fluid which has been taken for the purposes of diagnosis or medical treatment and which a person holds in confidence…

(2) A person holds material other than journalistic material in confidence for the purposes of this section if he holds it subject –
(a) to an express or implied undertaking to hold it in confidence or
(b) to a restriction on disclosure or an obligation of secrecy contained in any enactment, including an enactment contained in an Act passed after this Act.

Meaning of 'personal records'
12. In this Part of this Act 'personal records' means documentary and other records concerning an individual (whether living or dead) who can be identified from them, and relating –
(a) to his physical or mental health;
(b) to spiritual counselling or assistance given or to be given to him;
(c) to counselling or assistance given or to be given to him, for the purposes of his personal welfare, by any voluntary organisation or by any individual who–
    (i) by reason of his office or occupation has responsibilities for his personal welfare; or
    (ii) by reason of an order of a court, has responsibilities for his supervision.

These provisions apply to medical records of an identified individual whether alive or dead and, human tissue or tissue fluid taken for the purposes of diagnostic or medical treatment. The courts have given a broad ambit to the scope of s 12. In *R v Cardiff Crown Court, ex p Kellam* (1993) 16 BMLR 76 (DC), it was held that 'records…relating…to…physical or mental health' included records of a patient's movements and absences from a psychiatric hospital. As a result, they were 'excluded material', which could not be obtained under Sch 1 to PACE for the purposes of a murder investigation (see Commentary (1994) 2 Med L Rev 370 (AG)). Likewise, in *R v Singleton* [1995] 1 Cr App Rep 431 (CA), the cast of a patient's teeth was held to be 'excluded material' being 'other records' relating to the patient's physical health (s 12(a)).

The provisions of PACE seek to protect the confidentiality of certain sensitive material from being accessed by the police without an order of a circuit judge. Two further points should be noticed: first, some material may not be obtained under PACE because of the limitations in Sch 1 to the Act, in particular that, prior to the Act, a search warrant could have been issued to a police constable to search for the material (see Sch 1, para 3). Thus, for example, Sch 1 does not allow for access to material relevant to a murder investigation because no such warrant could have been issued before the Act (see *ex p Kellam, supra*). Secondly, PACE only deals with *access* by the police. It does not prevent a doctor or other health professional disclosing medical records or other excluded material providing this would be a justified breach of confidence, for example, as being in the public interest. The following case illustrates this second point.

R v Singleton [1995] 1 Cr App Rep 431 (CA)

The appellant was charged with murder. After his arrest he was asked by the police to provide a sample of tooth marks because the victim had marks on her chin which were thought to have been made by a human bite. He refused, but his dentist voluntarily gave his dental records to the police. The appellant sought at his trial to have the dental evidence excluded on the ground that it was excluded material within the terms of section 11 of the Police and Criminal Evidence Act 1984 and as such could only be disclosed to the police by means of an application to a circuit judge under section 9 and paragraph 3 of Schedule 1 to the 1984 Act. The judge ruled that the evidence was admissible and the appellant was convicted.

Farquharson LJ: …it is pointed out, if the prosecution had made an application under Schedule 1 the learned circuit judge would have been bound to refuse it. Once again, that proposition is not contested by the Crown.

The prosecution case is that the provisions of the 1984 Act are, in the present circumstances, irrelevant. It is argued by counsel that the Act would only be invoked where production of the material is refused by a person holding it or in possession of it. Section

9 of the Act, he points out, provides that a constable *may* obtain access to the excluded material by invoking the procedures of the section, but not that he has to do so. In this case the appellant's dentist produced the records on request and volunteered delivery of the model. If the police can obtain the evidence by the co-operation of the person holding it, Mr Seabrook argues, they are entitled to do so...

Plainly the object of the Act is to protect disclosure of such confidential personal records. It seems equally clear that the person to be protected from disclosure is not the suspect in any particular case, but the person who has acquired or created the personal record. Accordingly, if that person voluntarily discloses the record he does not seek or require the protection given by the Act to that class of record. It is for the person identified in section 11(1) to decide whether he wishes to make this disclosure, bearing in mind the degree of confidence reposed in him. If he decided that it is his duty to retain the record the Act provides the procedure the police must follow to obtain access to it. It would then be open to the person who is the holder of the document to make representations to the circuit judge that an order should not be made under Schedule 1. That seems to us to be a sensible and practical way of interpreting the provision. It highlights the fact that the issue, if it arises, is to be resolved as between the police and the holder of the record. The suspect's consent is not required and his refusal does not affect the decision of the holder. In any criminal inquiries it would be foolish to put the suspect on notice that the police were attempting to obtain access to this kind of material, see *Leicester Crown Court, ex p Director of Public Prosecutions* (1987) 86 Cr App R 254 [1987] 1 WLR 1371.

For the reasons already explained in this judgment, if the appellant's dentist had refused to disclose the records (which of course includes the cast), the police would not have been successful on an application for access under section 9. This of course illustrates the seriousness with which Parliament regarded the protection of this material; see for example another case helpfully cited by Mr Moses, *Cardiff Crown Court, ex p Kellam, The Times,* May 3, 1993, but that does not, in our judgment, affect the option to disclose voluntarily which is open to the holder of the record.

In concluding that this is a practical interpretation of the Act, the Court has in mind the difficulties with which the police would otherwise be faced when seeking access to prohibited material. In every case whether the person holding the material is prepared to give access to it or not, the police would have to make an application to a circuit judge. We do not believe that Parliament could have had such a cumbersome process in mind. If Parliament intended the application under section 9 to be the exclusive method of obtaining access to this type of material, it could easily have said so. It would, after all, be placing a restriction on the powers of the police to obtain this type of evidence to such an extent that one would have expected it to have been expressly dealt with in the text of the Act. This particular area of medical records is, of course, of great value to police officers investigating serious crime, as time and again it is by recourse to the dental records or casts possessed by the dentists that the identity of persons who have been killed is established...In our judgment no...ambiguity is disclosed by subsection (1) of section 9 and for the reasons that we have already given, it would not inhibit the prosecution from tendering the evidence which they obtained in the way that I have described.

For those various reasons this appeal is dismissed...

Whilst the thrust of the Court of Appeal's approach seems correct, the statement that PACE was designed to protect the holder of the record is not. Clearly, the purpose of the procedure under Sch 1 of obtaining access to 'excluded material', including medical records etc, is to protect *the patient* whose confidence is being breached. Nevertheless, that underlying protection is not removed *if* disclosure is, in any event, justified at common law in the public interest.

1. Health Act 1999

We saw in Chapter 2 that the Health Act 1999 creates a body known as the Commission for Health Improvement (CHI) (see ss 19 and 20 and Sch 2). To the extent that CHI is the 'NHS policeman', s 23 of the 1999 Act allows the Secretary of State to make regulations authorising CHI to enter and inspect NHS premises and take copies of documents including patient records. Sections 23 and 24 of the 1999 Act create an elaborate scheme, backed by criminal sanctions, of the circumstances in which CHI may obtain access to confidential information about patients and in which it may be disclosed by CHI to others (see, The

Commission for Health Improvement (Functions) Regulations, (SI 2000 No 662) regs 17-20).

Section 23(2) of the Health Act 1999 limits the circumstances in which the information may be obtained to four situations.

> **23.** (2) Regulations under this section may not make provision with respect to the disclosure of confidential information which relates to and identifies a living individual unless one or more of the following conditions is satisfied –
> (a) the information is disclosed in a form in which the identity of the individual cannot be ascertained,
> (b) the individual consents to the information being disclosed,
> (c) the individual cannot be traced despite the taking of all reasonable steps,
> (d) in a case where the Commission is exercising its functions under section 20(1)(c)–
>   (i)   it is not practicable to disclose the information in a form in which the identity of the individual cannot be ascertained,
>   (ii) the Commission considers that there is a serious risk to the health or safety of patients arising out of the matters which are the subject of the exercise of those functions, and
>   (iii) having regard to that risk and the urgency of the exercise of those functions, the Commission considers that the information should be disclosed without the consent of the individual.

Further, s 23(3) does not allow regulations permitting CHI to obtain access to information that is prohibited under a statutory provision, eg s 33 of the Human Fertilisation and Embryology Act 1990, unless the prohibition would not apply if the patient was not identified and it can be accessed by CHI in that form.

Section 23(6) defines 'confidential information' as information held subject to a duty of confidentiality and includes 'health records' as defined in s 68(2) of the Data Protection Act 1998 (see *supra*). Notice that s 23(2) only applies to confidential information relating to a 'living individual' and thus does not cover the records of a 'dead person', though, as we saw, a legal duty may survive the death of the patient, (*supra*).

The reference in s 23(2) to CHI exercising its functions under s 20(1)(c) is to its investigatory powers in respect of the management, provision or quality of health care. Section 20(1)(c) provides:

> **20.** (1) The Commission has the following functions– ...
> (c) the function of carrying out investigations into, and making reports on, the management, provision or quality of health care for which Health Authorities, Primary Care Trusts or NHS trusts have responsibility.

In this situation, the limitations of s 23(2)(a)–(c) are disregarded, in effect in the public interest because of the serious risk to the health or safety of patients.

Information acquired by CHI is statutorily protected and may only be disclosed with 'lawful authority' which is closely defined in the Act. It is a criminal offence otherwise to 'knowingly or recklessly' disclose confidential information obtained under s 23(2) (s 24(1)) or other information obtained in confidence by CHI, provided that in the latter instance the information alone, or taken together with other information held by CHI, would identify the patient (s 24(2) and (7)). In both cases the disclosure must be during the lifetime of the patient. However, it is not an offence to disclose information when the patient is not identified in the information itself or cannot be so identified from other information disclosed by CHI (s 24(8)). It is also a defence to disclose information which has previously been disclosed lawfully under s 24 (s 24(4)(b)) or when the individual reasonably believes it has been (s 24(5)(b)).

The crucial defence to disclosure is, however, disclosure with 'lawful authority' (s 24(6)) or where the individual reasonably believes that it would be (s 24(5)(a)).

Section 24(6) provides as follows:

24. (6) For the purposes of this section a disclosure of information is to be regarded as made with lawful authority if, and only if, it is made –

(a) with the consent of the individual to whom the information relates,
(b) for the purpose of facilitating the exercise of any functions of the Commission,
(c) for the purpose of facilitating the conduct of any investigation under the Health Service Commissioners Act 1993,
(d) in accordance with any enactment or order of a court,
(e) in connection with the investigation of a serious arrestable offence,
(f) for the purposes of criminal proceedings in any part of the United Kingdom,
(g) in a case where the information appears to the Commission to reveal –
   (i) that the performance of a health professional in his capacity as such has or may have fallen substantially below that which is expected,
   (ii) that a health professional has or may have been guilty of serious professional misconduct, or
   (iii) that the fitness of a health professional to practise as such is or may be seriously impaired by reason of his physical or mental condition,
  and the person to whom the information is disclosed is a person to whom the Commission considers that it should be disclosed in order for appropriate action to be taken, or
(h) in a case where –
   (i) the information reveals that a person is likely to constitute a threat to the health or safety of individuals, and
   (ii) the person to whom it is disclosed is a person to whom the Commission considers that the information should be disclosed in the interests of the health and safety of individuals.

These provisions largely mirror in statutory form the 'public interest' justification for disclosure at common law (leaving aside the consent provision in s 24(6)(a)). In particular, s 24(6)(g) provides for disclosure to an appropriate person information which is relevant to disciplinary action against a health professional. Usually, this would allow for disclosure to the regulatory body, the GMC in the case of a doctor (see the specific wording of s 24(6)(g)(ii) *supra*) but it might include disclosure to others, such as the Chief Executive of the Trust for action to be taken. Section 24(6)(g)(ii) would not, however, allow this disclosure to the registration bodies of other health professions where the statutory powers are concluded in a different language, eg 'misconduct' in the case of nurses (s 7(c) of The Nurses, Midwives and Health Visitors Act 1997) unless, of course, the particular misconduct is elevated to the level of 'serious' even though this is not a necessary condition for the registration body to take action. Section 24(6)(g)(i) seems to be written in the language of the new performance procedures operated by the GMC for doctors for 'seriously deficient performance' (see Medical (Professional Performance) Act 1995, and *supra* ch 3). By contrast s 24(6)(g)(iii) encompasses more generally the health procedures of bodies such as the GMC, the UKCC and the GDC (see, Medical Act 1983, s 37, Nurses, Midwives and Health Visitors (Professional Conduct) Rules 1993 Approval Order 1993 (SI 1993 No 893) and Dentists Act 1984, s 28 respectively).

Section 24(6)(h) contemplates the situation where an individual (whether a health professional or patient) is likely to be a danger to others. The provision requires that there is *likely* (not *possible*) danger and permits the CHI to disclose information to an appropriate person to avert the danger. Who that is will depend upon the circumstances and may include the doctor's employer (where the patient is in danger) or the police or other responsible agency (such as social services) where a patient is the danger.

2. Health Service Commissioner Act 1993

We saw in Chapter 3 the role of the so-called 'Health Service Ombudsmen' (*supra*). Section 15 of the 1993 Act (as amended by s 11 of the Health Service Commissioner (Amendment) Act 1996 and s 43 of the Health Act 1999) provides as follows:

15. (1) Information obtained by a Commissioner or his officers in the course of or for the purposes of an investigation shall not be disclosed except –

(a) for the purposes of the investigation and any report to be made in respect of it,

(b) for the purposes of any proceedings for –

   (i)   an offence under the Official Secrets Acts 1911 to 1989 alleged to have been committed in respect of information obtained by virtue of this Act by a Commissioner or any of his officers, or

   (ii) an offence of perjury alleged to have been committed in the course of the investigation,

(c) for the purposes of an inquiry with a view to the taking of such proceedings as are mentioned in paragraph (b),...

(d) for the purposes of any proceedings under section 13 (offences of obstruction and contempt), or

(e) where the information is to the effect that any person is likely to constitute a threat to the health or safety of patients as permitted by subsection (1B).

   (1A) ...

   (1B) In a case within subsection (1)(e) the Commissioner may disclose the information to any persons to whom he thinks it should be disclosed in the interests of the health and safety of patients.

   (1C) If a Commissioner discloses information as permitted by subsection (1B) he shall –

   (a) where he knows the identity of the person mentioned in subsection (1)(e), inform that person that he has disclosed the information and of the identity of any person to whom he has disclosed it, and

   (b) inform the person from whom the information was obtained that he has disclosed it.

   (2) Neither a Commissioner nor his officers nor his advisers shall be called on to give evidence in any proceedings, other than proceedings mentioned in subsection (1), of matters coming to his or their knowledge in the course of an investigation under this Act.

   (3) The reference in subsection (2) to a Commissioner's advisers is a reference to persons from whom the Commissioner obtains advice under paragraph 13 of Schedule 1 or paragraph 6(6) of Schedule 1A.

The present legislation is far more permissive than was the case under the original 1993 Act or, indeed, in its amended form after the 1996 Act. Originally, only the most unusual circumstances were covered, eg breach of the Official Secrets Act. Otherwise, information obtained by the Commissioner could not be disclosed. However, the current legislation is broader, allowing disclosure, *inter alia*, of patient information where 'any person is likely to constitute a threat to the health or safety of patients'. This would allow disclosure to the appropriate regulatory authorities, enforcement agencies such as the police or social services, CHI or, indeed, the doctor's employer. Section 15(1C) ensures that the person to whom the information relates and the source are informed that disclosure has taken place and to whom.

In addition, there are a number of other statutory modifications where a duty to disclose will displace the obligation of confidence: National Health Service (Notification of Births and Deaths) Regulations 1982 (SI 1982 No 286); Misuse of Drugs (Notification of, and Supply to Addicts) Regulations 1973 (SI 1973 No 799); see further, *Rights and Responsibilities of Doctors* (1992) ch 3. We discuss earlier the provisions of the Data Protection Act 1998 and its relevance to breach of confidence (*supra*, ch 7).

Remedies

It goes without saying that a patient may obtain an injunction if he acts in time to restrain an unlawful breach of confidence. But, can he seek damages after the event for the fact of disclosure and any distress, harm or loss it may have caused him? (For a discussion, see Capper (1994) 14 LS 313.) By analogy with the cases related to commercial confidence, it seems clear that the patient may recover any foreseeable economic loss arising from the breach, for example, if he loses his job (*Seager v Copydex Ltd* [1967] 1 WLR 923), (for a general discussion of remedies available for breach of confidence, see Toulson and Phipps, *Confidentiality* (1996) ch 10). As regards physical harm, the patient may be able to establish a claim in negligence.

Furniss v Fitchett [1958] NZLR 396 (NZ HCt)

The defendant doctor, at the invitation of the plaintiff's husband, wrote the following letter, which he then gave to the husband. The plaintiff (and, indeed, the husband) were patients of the defendant.

Mrs Phyllis C L Furniss   21.5.56
32 Mornington Road
The above has been attending me for some time and during this period I have observed several things:
(1) Deluded that her husband is doping her.
(2) Accuses her husband of cruelty and even occasional violence.
(3) Considers her husband to be insane and states that it is a family failing.
On the basis of the above I consider she exhibits symptoms of paranoia and should be given treatment for same if possible. An examination by a Psychiatrist would be needed to fully diagnose her case and its requirements.
Yours faithfully
A J Fitchett

The husband later used the letter in separation proceedings brought by the plaintiff. This was the first that she knew of its existence. She sued the defendant for breach of confidence.

Barrowclough CJ: The relationship between the plaintiff and the defendant was that of doctor and patient. The doctor knew – he admitted that he knew – that the disclosure to his patient of his opinion as to her mental condition would be harmful to her. He was careful not to tell her directly what that opinion was. Nevertheless, he wrote out and gave to Mrs Furniss's husband a certificate, expressing that opinion. If he ought reasonably to have had in contemplation that Mrs Furniss might be injured physically, though not financially, as the result of his giving that certificate – and that on the evidence is beyond dispute – then it seems clear that he should have regarded her as 'his neighbour' in Lord Atkin's phrase. If she was his neighbour in that sense, he was under a duty to take care to avoid an act which he could reasonably foresee would be likely to injure her – again physically though not financially...

On the facts, it is clear that if Mrs Furniss were to be confronted by this certificate, it was likely to do her harm. The certificate was handed to Mr Furniss, who was then living with his wife. Their relations were extremely strained. She regarded him as mentally unsound and as intent on doping or poisoning her. She had not hesitated to make these accusations against him, and it was because of her accusations that he had been brought to the distraught condition in which he found himself when he begged the doctor to give him a certificate. In these circumstances, it seems to me not only likely, but extremely likely, that when the husband was charged by his wife with mental instability, he would be goaded into a 'tu quoque' retort, and that he would disclose to her either the certificate or at all events its contents. That he apparently did not disclose it, and that the certificate remained hidden from Mrs Furniss for a whole year, speaks volumes for the husband's restraint. It is also to be noted that, in giving the certificate to Mr Furniss, the doctor placed no restrictions on its use. It was not even marked 'confidential'. On that evidence I can only conclude that Dr Fitchett ought reasonably to have foreseen that the contents of his certificate were likely to come to his patient's knowledge, and he knew that if they did, they would be likely to injure her in her health.

I do not hold that the doctor ought to have foreseen the precise manner in which the contents of his certificate did in fact come to Mrs Furniss's knowledge; though, I think, that, in the circumstances disclosed by the evidence, he ought to have foreseen that the certificate could be expected to be used in some legal proceedings, in which his patient would be concerned and thus come to her knowledge. It is sufficient to say that, in my view, on the evidence in the special circumstances of this case, Dr Fitchett should have foreseen that his patient would be likely to be injured as the result of his action in giving her husband such a certificate as he did give, and in giving it to him without placing any restriction on its use. In these circumstances, I am of opinion that, on the principle of *Donoghue v Stevenson* [1932] AC 562, there arose a duty of care on his part. I have not forgotten that the certificate was true and accurate, but I see no reason for limiting the duty to one of care in seeing that it is accurate. The duty must extend also to the exercise of care in deciding whether it should be put in circulation in such a way that it is likely to cause harm to another.

The plaintiff's action was for nervous shock. There is no doubt that the special nature of the doctor-patient relationship is such that it would allow the courts to award damages for psychiatric injury for negligent disclosure of confidential information. What, however, if the action is for breach of confidence itself?

One possibility is that damages may be awarded in lieu of an injunction under s 50 of the Supreme Court Act 1981, where an injunction could be granted for breach of the equitable obligation of confidence (*Saltman Engineering Co Ltd v Campbell Engineering Co Ltd* (1948) 65 RPC 203 (CA) and *A-G v Guardian Newspapers (No 2)* [1990] 1 AC 109 per Lord Goff at 286). Damages would cover both past and future losses (see Law Commission *Report on Breach of Confidence* (1981) Cmnd 8388 at para 4.73). The difficulty arises, however, if no injunction can be granted because, for example, the breach of confidence has already occurred. The patient's harm will usually be distress or injured feelings because personal information is known by others. In their book, *Confidentiality* (1996), Toulson and Phipps argue that damages may be recovered in this kind of situation and may include non-pecuniary loss of this sort.

R G Toulson and C M Phipps *Confidentiality* (1996)

10–10 ...It is suggested that, quite apart from Lord Cairns' Act, compensation in equity (also known as equitable damages) may be awarded generally for breach of an equitable duty of confidence, just as for breach of duty by a fiduciary; and that the same compensation principles underlie compensation or damages in equity as underlie damages at common law. (*Royal Bank of Brunei v Tan*) [1995] 2 AC 378.) If this is correct, damages are available for breach of duty of confidence, whether in contract or in equity...

10–11 Other unresolved questions are whether damages may be awarded for mental stress or injury to feelings caused by breach of confidence, and whether exemplary or punitive damages may be awarded.

Damages cannot ordinarily be recovered for injury to reputation or feelings (*Addis v Gramophone Co Ltd* [1909] AC 488) but there are exceptions. Defamation has always been an exception, because injury to reputation is the essence of the wrong. The courts have also made an exception in cases of contract where the subject matter of the contract is the provision of pleasure (*Jarvis v Swan Tours Ltd* [1973] QB 233) or protection from distress, (*Heywood v Wellers* [1976] QB 446) as distinct from other contracts where mental distress is a foreseeable consequence of breach. (*Bliss v South East Thames Regional Health Authority* [1987] ICR 700 at 718; *Hayes v Dodd* [1990] 2 All ER 815 at 826; *Watts v Morrow* [1991] 1 WLR 1421 at 1439.)

10–13 ...The problem is most likely to arise where confidential information of a personal nature is leaked to, or otherwise obtained by, the press in breach of a duty of confidence, in circumstances where the plaintiff may suffer considerable upset, but no monetary loss, and an account of profits may be an impracticable remedy. The questions which arise are, firstly, whether such a plaintiff is entitled to compensation for the non-pecuniary harm caused to him; and secondly, whether he is entitled to claim exemplary damages on the basis that the conduct was calculated to generate a profit exceeding the amount of any compensatory damages (which, if the answer to the first question is negative, would *ex hypothesi* be nil). Professor Cornish has commented: ('*Intellectual Property Patents, Copyright, trade Marks and Allied Rights*' (2nd ed, (1989)) para 8–042):

> There remains the question as yet unexplored in the case-law, whether damages for injury to feelings are available for breach of confidence, as they are for defamation and copyright infringement. All that can usefully be said is this. Breach of confidence is slowly becoming one of the ways in which the law accords protection to privacy and those aspects of personal reputation that are associated with it. Infringement of copyright and defamation fulfil the same function in ways that are differently limited. But since both allow damages for injured feelings, it would seem quixotic to bar this form of monetary compensation from the third field, for the sake of yet another historical point.

> It may be argued that, in a case where a duty of confidentiality exists to protect personal privacy, its object is to protect the feelings of the confider, and therefore it would be in accordance with principle to allow damages for injury to feelings caused by breach of that duty. But whether the courts will adopt that approach remains to be seen. If they do, the case for exemplary damages would be weakened, because the plaintiff would be entitled to compensation for the non-pecuniary injury caused to him as well as to an account.

What little case law there is may, however, suggest that the law is otherwise.

The law was examined by Scott J in *W v Egdell* [1989] 1 All ER 1089 (not discussed on appeal: [1990] 1 All ER 835). W's action, it will be recalled, was based upon a contractual obligation of confidence though, as we shall see, the judge did not regard this as necessarily significant.

W v Egdell [1989] 1 All ER 1089 (QBD)

Scott J: I think [it] open to question whether shock and distress caused by the unauthorised disclosure of confidential information can, in any event, properly be reflected in an award of damages.

In *Bliss v South East Thames Regional Health Authority* [1987] ICR 700 at 717–718 Dillon LJ said:

> the general rule laid down by the House of Lords in *Addis v Gramophone Co Ltd* ([1909] AC 488, [1908–10] All ER Rep 1) is that where damages fall to be assessed for breach of contract rather than in tort it is not permissible to award general damages for frustration, mental distress, injured feelings or annoyance occasioned by the breach. Modern thinking tends to be that the amount of damages recoverable for a wrong should be the same whether the cause of action is laid in contract or in tort. But in the *Addis* case Lord Loreburn regarded the rule that damages for injured feelings cannot be recovered in contract for wrongful dismissal as too inveterate to be altered, and Lord James of Hereford supported his concurrence in the speech of Lord Loreburn by reference to his own experience at the Bar. There are exceptions now recognised where the contract which has been broken was itself a contract to provide peace of mind or freedom from distress: see *Jarvis v Swans Tours Ltd* ([1973] 1 All ER 71, [1973] QB 233) and *Heywood v Wellers* ([1976] 1 All ER 300, [1976] QB 446). Those decisions, do not however cover this present case. In *Cox v Philips Industries Ltd* [1976] 3 All ER 161, [1976] 1 WLR 638 Lawson J took the view that damages for distress, vexation and frustration, including consequent ill-health, could be recovered for breach of contract of employment if it could be said to have been in the contemplation of the parties that the breach would cause such distress etc. For my part, I do not think that that general approach is open to this court unless and until the House of Lords has reconsidered its decision in the *Addis* case.

This Court of Appeal authority seems to me to preclude W from recovering damages (save nominal damages) to the extent that his claim is based on breach of an implied contractual term. I do not see any reason, on this point, why equity should not follow the law.

Accordingly, in my judgment, W would not, even if I had found Dr Egdell to be liable, have been entitled to damages. He would have had to be content with a declaration and an injunction.

By contrast, the Law Commission in its Report No 110, entitled *Breach of Confidence* (Cmnd 838, 1981) recommended that damages for mental stress caused by a breach of confidence should be available (see paras 6.5 and 6.114), but the recommendation has not been enacted into law.

Part III

Medical law in action

A: The beginning of life

Chapter 9

Contraception and sterilisation

In this chapter we examine the legality of the use of contraception and sterilisation procedures. Our particular concerns are with children, in the case of contraception, and with the intellectually disabled, in the case of sterilisation. We are not here concerned with liability issues and damages claims for failed sterilisations or contraceptive measures whether in negligence, contract or as an aspect of products liability. These can be found elsewhere in the book (*infra*, ch 12 and 14 respectively). What is important for us to examine here are the distinct legal issues which arise in relation to contraception and from the body of case law and practice that has evolved in England (and Scotland) in relation to surgical sterilisation of incompetent women and children for contraceptive purposes or for, what is sometimes called, the purposes of menstrual management.

Non-surgical methods

The forms of contraception considered here are the condom, the intra-uterine device (IUD), long-acting injectable contraceptives (Depo-provera), and the female contraceptive pill (the pill). Apart from the condom, these require the involvement of doctors to prescribe or fit them. A threshold question is whether these amount to medical treatment.

Lord Scarman, in *Gillick v West Norfolk and Wisbech AHA* [1985] 3 All ER 402 at 418, said:

> ... as is clear in the light of s 5 of the National Health Service Act 1977 (re-enacting earlier legislation) and s 41 of the National Health Service (Scotland) Act 1978, contraceptive medical treatment is recognised as a legitimate and beneficial treatment in cases in which it is medically indicated. ...

Section 5(1)(b) of the National Health Service Act 1977 imposes a duty upon the Secretary of State:

> to arrange, to such extent as he considers necessary to meet all reasonable requirements in England and Wales, for the giving of advice on contraception, the medical examination of persons seeking advice on contraception, the treatment of such persons and the supply of contraceptive substances and appliances.

Lord Fraser, in *Gillick, op cit* at 407, pointed out:

> These, and other, provisions show that Parliament regarded 'advice' and 'treatment' on contraception and the supply of appliances for contraception as essentially medical matters. So they are, but they may also raise moral and social questions on which many people feel deeply, and in that respect they differ from ordinary medical advice and treatment.

A. CONTRACEPTION AND CHILDREN

Non-surgical forms of contraception in the context of the young are typically identified with prescribing contraceptive pills for a girl. This is the medical example we analyse here.

The law identifies three areas of difficulty. They are: first, problems of *consent*; secondly, problems of *confidentiality*; and thirdly, problems of *public policy* and the criminal law. We have already examined in detail the circumstances under which a child may give consent to medical treatment (*supra*, ch 5). Of course, the leading case of *Gillick* specifically concerns the legal capacity of a child to give consent to contraceptive advice and treatment. As we saw, the House of Lords, by a majority, found that providing the child has sufficient maturity and understanding of what is involved, her consent is legally valid.

Further, we have also examined the law relating to confidence and how it applies to children (*supra*, ch 8). The only question which remains, therefore, is the extent to which, if at all, public policy or the criminal law constrains doctors from providing contraceptive treatment to children who have the capacity to consent.

Gillick v West Norfolk & Wisbech AHA [1986] AC 112, [1985] 3 All ER 402 (HL)

The Department of Heath and Social Security, in the exercise of its statutory functions, issued a circular to area health authorities containing, inter alia, advice to the effect that a doctor consulted at a family planning clinic by a girl under 16 would not be acting unlawfully if he prescribed contraceptives for the girl, so long as in doing so he was acting in good faith to protect her against the harmful effects of sexual intercourse. The circular further stated that, although a doctor should proceed on the assumption that advice and treatment on contraception should not be given to a girl under 16 without parental consent and that he should try to persuade the girl to involve her parents in the matter, nevertheless the principle of confidentiality between doctor and patient applied to a girl under 16 seeking contraception and therefore in exceptional cases the doctor could prescribe contraceptives without consulting the girl's parents or obtaining their consent if in the doctor's clinical judgment it was desirable to prescribe contraceptives. The plaintiff, who had five daughters under the age of 16, sought an assurance from her local area health authority that her daughters would not be given advice and treatment on contraception without the plaintiff's prior knowledge and consent while they were under 16. When the authority refused to give such an assurance the plaintiff brought an action against the authority and the department seeking (i) as against both defendants a declaration that the advice contained in the circular was unlawful, because it amounted to advice to doctors to commit the offence of causing or encouraging unlawful sexual intercourse with a girl under 16, contrary to s 28(1) of the Sexual Offences Act 1956, or the offence of being an accessory to unlawful sexual intercourse with a girl under 16, contrary to s 6(1) of that Act, and (ii) as against the area health authority a declaration that a doctor or other professional person employed by it in its family planning service could not give advice and treatment on contraception to any child of the plaintiff below the age of 16 without the plaintiff's consent, because to do so would be unlawful as being inconsistent with the plaintiff's parental rights. The plaintiff conceded that, in order to be entitled to the first declaration sought, she was required to show that a doctor who followed the advice contained in the circular would necessarily be committing a criminal offence or acting unlawfully.

Lord Fraser: Three strands of argument are raised by the appeal. These are (1) whether a girl under the age of 16 has the legal capacity to give valid consent to contraceptive advice and treatment including medical examination; (2) whether giving such advice and treatment to a girl under 16 without her parents' consent infringes the parents' rights; and (3) whether a doctor who gives such advice or treatment to a girl under 16 without her parents' consent incurs criminal liability. I shall consider these strands in order.

[Having considered the first two strands of argument, Lorder Fraser continued:]

3. Is a doctor who gives contraceptive advice or treatment to a girl under 16 without her parents' consent likely to incur criminal liability?

The submission was made to Woolf J on behalf of Mrs Gillick that a doctor who provided contraceptive advice and treatment to a girl under 16 without her parents' authority would be committing an office under s 28 of the Sexual Offences Act 1956 by aiding and abetting the commission of unlawful sexual intercourse. When the case reached the court of Appeal counsel on both sides conceded that whether a doctor who followed the guidelines would be committing an offence or not would depend on the circumstances. It would depend on the doctor's intentions; this appeal is concerned with doctors who honestly intend to act in the best interests of the girl, and I think it is unlikely that a doctor who gives contraceptive advice or treatment with that intention would commit an offence under s 28. It must be remembered that a girl under 16 who has sexual intercourse does not thereby commit an offence herself, although her partner does: see the Sexual Offences Act 1956, ss 5 and 6. In any event, even if the doctor would be committing an offence, the fact that he had acted with the parents' consent would not exculpate him as Woolf J pointed out ([1984] QB 581 at 595, [1984] 1 All ER 365 at 373). Accordingly, I regard this contention as irrelevant to the question that we have to answer in this appeal. Parker LJ in the Court of Appeal dealt at some length with the provisions of criminal law intended to protect girls under the age of 16 from being seduced, and perhaps also to protect them from their own weakness. Parker LJ expressed his conclusion on this part of the case as follows ([1985] 2 WLR 413 at 435, [1985] 1 All ER 533 at 550):

> It appears to me that it is wholly incongruous, when the act of intercourse is criminal, when permitting it to take place on one's premises is criminal and when, if the girl were under 13, failing to report an act of intercourse to the police would up to 1967 have been criminal, that either the department or the area health authority should provide facilities which would enable girls under 16 the more readily to commit such acts. It seems to me equally incongruous to assert that doctors have the right to accept the young, down, apparently, to any age, as patients, and to provide them with contraceptive advice and treatment without reference to their parents and even against their known wishes.

My Lords, the first of those two sentences is directed to the question, which is not in issue in this appeal, of whether contraceptive facilities should be available at all under the NHS for girls under 16. I have already explained my reasons for thinking that the legislation does not limit the duty of providing such facilities to women of 16 or more. The second sentence, which does bear directly on the question in the appeal, does not appear to me to follow necessarily from the first and with respect I cannot agree with it. If the doctor complies with the first of the conditions which I have specified, that is to say if he satisfies himself that the girl can understand his advice, there will be no question of his giving contraceptive advice to very young girls.

For those reasons I do not consider that the guidance interferes with the parents' rights.

Lord Scarman also rejected Mrs Gillick's argument based on the criminal law. Like Lord Fraser he adopted the views of Woolf J at first instance.

Woolf J: So far as the offence against section 6 of the Sexual Offences Act 1956 is concerned, I accept that a doctor who is misguided enough to provide a girl who is under the age of 16, or a man, with advice and assistance with regard to contraceptive measures with the intention thereby of encouraging them to have sexual intercourse, is an accessory before the fact to an offence contrary to section 6. I stress the words 'with the intention thereby of encouraging them to have sexual intercourse'. However, this I assume, will not usually be the attitude of a doctor.

There will certainly be some cases, and I hope the majority of cases, where the doctor decides to give the advice and prescribe contraceptives despite the fact he was firmly against unlawful sexual intercourse taking place but felt, nevertheless, that he had to prescribe the contraceptives because, whether or not he did so, intercourse would in fact take place, and the provision of contraceptives would, in his view, be in the best interests of the girl in protecting her from an unwanted pregnancy and the risk of a sexually transmitted disease. It is as to whether or not in such a situation the doctor is to be treated as being an accessory, that I have found the greatest difficulty in applying the law.

The judge then referred to the well-known cases of *National Coal Board v Gamble* [1959] 1 QB 11 and *DPP for Northern Ireland v Lynch* [1975] AC 653 and continued:

> ... three matters have to be borne in mind. First of all, contraceptives do not in themselves directly assist in the commission of the crime of unlawful sexual intercourse. The analogy of providing the motor car for a burglary or providing poison to the murderer, relied on in argument, are not true comparisons. While if the man wears a sheath, there may be said to be a physical difference as to the quality of intercourse, the distinction that I am seeking to draw is clearer where the woman takes the pill or is fitted with an internal device, when the unlawful act will not be affected in any way. The only effect of the provision of the means of contraception is that in some cases it is likely to increase the likelihood of a crime being

committed by reducing the inhibitions of the persons concerned to having sexual intercourse because of their fear of conception or the contraction of disease. I therefore see a distinction between the assistance or aiding ... and the act of the doctor in prescribing contraceptives. I would regard the pill prescribed to the women as not so much 'the instrument for a crime or anything essential to its commission' but a palliative against the consequences of the crime.

The second factor that has to be borne in mind is that the girl herself commits no offence under section 6 since the section is designed to protect her from herself: see *R v Tyrell* [1894] 1 QB 710. This creates problems with regard to relying upon any encouragement by the doctor as making him the accessory to the offence where the girl alone attends the clinic. The well-known case, *R v Bourne* (1952) 36 Cr App Rep 125, has to be distinguished because there, the woman can be said to have committed the offence although she was not criminally responsible because of duress. The doctor, if he is to be an accessory where the woman alone consults him, will only be an accessory if it can be shown that he acted through the innocent agency of the woman, the situation dealt with in *R v Cooper* (1833) 5 C & P 535.

The final point that has to be borne in mind, is that there will be situations where long-term contraceptive measures are taken to protect girls who, sadly, will strike up promiscuous relationships whatever the supervision of those who are responsible for their well-being, the sort of situation that Butler-Sloss J had to deal with in *Re P (a minor)* (1982) 80 LGR 301. In such a situation the doctor will prescribe the measures to be taken purely as a safeguard against the risk that at some time in the future, the girl will form a casual relationship with a man when sexual intercourse will take place. In order to be an accessory, you normally have to know the material circumstances. In such a situation the doctor would know no more than that there was a risk of sexual intercourse taking place at an unidentified place with an unidentified man on an unidentified date – hardly the state of knowledge which is normally associated with an accessory before that fact.

Under this limb of the argument, the conclusion which I have therefore come to is, that while a doctor could, in following the guidance, so encourage unlawful sexual intercourse as to render this conduct criminal, in the majority of situations the probabilities are that a doctor will be able to follow the advice without rendering himself liable to criminal proceedings. Before leaving this limb of the argument, I should make it absolutely clear that the absence of consent of the parents makes no difference to the criminal responsibility of the doctor. If his conduct would be criminal without the parents' consent, it would be equally criminal with their consent.

Lord Bridge agreed on the impact of the criminal law on the outcome of the case. By contrast, Lord Brandon in his vigorous dissent saw the case *wholly* in terms of criminal law and the public policy underlying it. Questions of consent for him were irrelevant.

Lord Brandon: In my opinion the formulation of the question whether such activities can be lawfully carried on without the prior knowledge and consent of the parents of any girl of the age concerned ... involves the rolling up in one composite question of two separate and distinct points of law. The first point of law is whether the three activities to which I have referred [giving advice, examining and prescribing] can be carried on lawfully in any circumstances whatever. If, on the one hand, the right answer to the first point of law is No, then no second point of law arises for decision. If, on the other hand, the answer to the first question is Yes, then a second point of law arises, namely whether the three activities referred to can only be lawfully carried on with the prior knowledge and consent of the parents of the girl concerned.

The first point of law appears to me to be one of public policy, the answer to which is to be gathered from an examination of the statutory provisions which Parliament has enacted from time to time in relation to men having sexual intercourse with girls either under the age of 13 or between the ages of 13 and 16.

It is, I think, sufficient to begin with the Criminal Law Amendment Act 1885 and then to go on to the Sexual Offences Act 1956, by which the former Act was repealed and largely replaced.

Part 1 of the 1885 Act, which contained ss 2 to 12, had the cross-heading 'Protection of Women and Girls'. Sections 4 and 5 provided, so far as material:

4. Any person who unlawfully and carnally knows any girl under the age of thirteen years shall be guilty of felony, and being convicted thereof shall be liable at the discretion of the court to be kept in penal servitude for life, or for any term not less than five years, or to be imprisoned for any term not exceeding two years, with or without hard labour ...

5. Any person who – (1) Unlawfully and carnally knows or attempts to have unlawfully carnal knowledge of any girl being of or above the age of thirteen years and under the

age of sixteen years … shall be guilty of misdemeanour, and being convicted thereof shall be liable at the discretion of the court to be imprisoned for any term not exceeding two years, with or without hard labour …

In *R v Tyrell* [1894] 1 QB 710, [1891–4] All ER Rep 1215 it was held by the Court for Crown Cases Reserved that it was not a criminal offence for a girl between the ages of 13 and 16 to aid and abet a man in committing, or to incite him to commit the misdemeanour of having carnal knowledge of her contrary to s 5 of the Criminal Law Amendment Act 1885 set out above. The ground of this decision was that the 1885 Act had been passed for the purpose of protecting women and girls against themselves: see the judgment of Lord Coleridge CJ [1894] 1 QB 710 at 712, [1891–4] All ER Rep 1215 at 1215–1216.

The Sexual Offences Act 1956 represents the latest pronouncement of Parliament on these matters. Sections 5 and 6 provide, so far as material:

5. It is a felony for a man to have unlawful sexual intercourse with a girl under the age of thirteen.

6. (1) It is an offence … for a man to have unlawful sexual intercourse with a girl under the age of sixteen …

Further, by s 37 and Sch 2, the maximum punishment for an offence under s 5 is imprisonment for life, and that for an offence under s 6 imprisonment for two years. Since the passing of the 1956 Act the distinction between felonies and misdemeanours has been abolished. For the purposes of this case, however, nothing turns on this change of terminology.

My Lords, the inescapable inference from the statutory provision of the 1885 and 1956 Acts to which I have referred is that Parliament has for the past century regarded, and still regards today, sexual intercourse between a man and a girl under 16 as a serious criminal offence so far as the man has such intercourse is concerned. So far as the girl is concerned, she does not commit any criminal offence, even if she aids, abets or incites the having of such intercourse. The reason for this, as explained earlier, is that the relevant statutory provisions have been enacted by Parliament for the purpose of protecting the girl from herself. The having of such intercourse is, however, unlawful, and the circumstances that the man is guilty of such a criminal offence, while the girl is not, cannot alter that situation.

On the footing that the having of sexual intercourse by a man with a girl under 16 is an unlawful act, it follows necessarily that for any person to promote, encourage or facilitate the commission of such as act may itself be a criminal offence, and must, in any event, be contrary to public policy. Nor can it make any difference that the person who promotes, encourages or facilitates the commission of such an act is a parent or a doctor or a social worker.

The question then arises whether the three activities to which I referred earlier should properly be regarded as, directly or indirectly, promoting, encouraging or facilitating the having, contrary to public policy, of sexual intercourse between a man and a girl under 16. In my opinion there can be only one answer to this question, namely that to give such a girl advice about contraception, to examine her with a view to her using one or more forms of protection and finally to prescribe contraceptive treatment for her, necessarily involves promoting, encouraging or facilitating the having of sexual intercourse, contrary to public policy, by that girl with a man.

The inhibitions against the having of sexual intercourse between a man and a girl under 16 are primarily twofold. So far as the man is concerned there is the inhibition of the criminal law as contained in ss 5 and 6 of the 1956 Act. So far as both are concerned there is the inhibition arising from the risk of an unwanted pregnancy. To give the girl contraceptive treatment, following appropriate advice and examination, is to remove largely the second of these two inhibitions. Such removal must involve promoting, encouraging or facilitating the having of sexual intercourse between the girl and the man.

It has been argued that some girls under 16 will have intercourse with a man whether contraceptive treatment is made available to them or not, and that the provision of such treatment does not, therefore, promote, encourage or facilitate the having of such intercourse. In my opinion this argument should be rejected for two quite separate reasons. The first reason is that the mere fact that a girl under 16 seeks contraceptive advice and treatment, whether of her own accord or at the suggestion of others, itself indicates that she, and probably also the man with whom she is having, or contemplating having, sexual intercourse, are conscious of the inhibition arising from the risk of an unwanted pregnancy. They are conscious of it and are more likely to indulge their desire if it can be removed. The second reason is that, if all a girl under 16 needs to do in order to obtain contraceptive treatment is to threaten that she will go ahead with, or continue, unlawful sexual intercourse with a man unless she is given such treatment, a situation tantamount to blackmail will arise which no legal system ought to tolerate. The only answer which the law should give to such a threat is, 'Wait till you are 16'.

The DHSS has contended that s 5(1) of the National Health Service Act 1977 imposes on it a statutory duty to carry out, in relation to girls under 16 as well as to older girls or women, the three activities to which I referred earlier. That provision reads:

> It is the Secretary of State's duty ... (b) to arrange, to such extent as he considers necessary to meet all reasonable requirements in England and Wales, for the giving of advice on contraception, the medical examination of persons seeking advice on contraception, the treatment of such persons and the supply of contraceptive substances and appliances.

This provision does not define the 'persons' who are the subject matter of it, nor is there any definition of that expression anywhere else in the Act. In these circumstances it seems to me that a court, in interpreting the provision, must do so in a way which conforms with considerations of public policy rather than in a way which conflicts with them. For the reasons which I have given earlier, I am of the opinion that, in the case of girls under 16, the giving of advice about contraception, medical examination with a view to the use of one or other form of contraception, and the prescribing of contraceptive treatment are all contrary to public policy. It follows that I would interpret the expression 'persons' in s 5(1)(b) above as not including girls under 16. Alternatively, I would say that the expression 'all reasonable requirements', which occurs earlier in the provisions, cannot be interpreted as including the requirements of a girl under 16 which, if satisfied, will promote, encourage or facilitate unlawful acts of sexual intercourse between a man and her.

My Lords, reference was made in the course of the argument before you to a decision of Butler-Sloss J in *Re P (a minor)* (1982) 80 LGR 301. In that case the judge, in wardship proceedings, ordered that a girl of 15, who had been pregnant for the second time and was in the care of a local authority, should be fitted with a contraceptive appliance because it appeared that it was impossible for the local authority, in whose care she was, to control her sexual conduct. It was contended that this decision was authority for the proposition that, in wardship proceedings at any rate, an order could lawfully be made for the supply and fitting of a contraceptive appliance to a girl under 16.

I do not know what arguments were or were not addressed to Butler-Sloss J in that case, and it is, in any event, unnecessary for your Lordships to decide in these proceedings the limits of the powers of a court exercising wardship jurisdiction. As at present advised, however, I am of opinion, with great respect to Butler-Sloss J, that the order which she made was not one which she could lawfully make.

My Lords, great play was made in the argument before you of the disastrous consequences for a girl under 16 of becoming pregnant as a result of her willingly having unlawful sexual intercourse with a man. I am fully conscious of these considerations, but I do not consider that, if the views which I have so far expressed are right in law, those considerations can alter the position.

It is sometimes said that the age of consent for girls is presently 16. This is, however, an inaccurate way of putting the matter, since, if a man has sexual intercourse with a girl under 16 without her consent, the crime which he thereby commits is that of rape. The right way to put the matter is that 16 is the age of a girl below which a man cannot lawfully have sexual intercourse with her. It was open to Parliament in 1956, when the Sexual Offences Act of that year was passed, and it has remained open to Parliament throughout the 29 years which have since elapsed, to pass legislation providing for some lower age than 16, if it thought fit to do so. Parliament has not thought fit to do so, and I do not consider that it would be right for your Lordships' House, by holding that girls under 16 can lawfully be provided with contraceptive facilities, to undermine or circumvent the criminal law which Parliament has enacted. The criminal law and the civil law should, as it seems to me, march had in hand on all issues, including that raised in this case, and to allow inconsistency or contradiction between them would, in my view, serve only to discredit the rule of law as a whole.

Since I am of opinion that the first question which I posed earlier, namely whether the provision of contraceptive facilities to girls under 16 was lawful in any circumstances at all, should be answered in the negative, the second question which I posed, relating to the need for prior parental knowledge and consent, does not arise. This is because, on the view which I take of the law, making contraception available to girls under 16 is unlawful, whether their parents know of and consent to it or not.

Lord Templeman in his dissenting speech similarly concentrated on public policy. For him, however, public policy was relevant not in determining the ambit of the criminal law, but, in the context of medical care, whether a child could consent to *contraceptive* as distinct from other forms of medical treatment.

Lord Templeman: I accept also that a doctor may lawfully carry out some forms of treatment with the consent of an infant patient and against the opposition of a parent based on religious or any other grounds. The effect of the consent of the infant depends on the nature of the treatment and the age and understanding of the infant. For example, a doctor with the consent of an intelligent boy or girl of 15 could in my opinion safely remove tonsils or a troublesome appendix. But any decision on my part of a girl to practise sex and contraception requires not only knowledge of the facts of life and of the dangers of pregnancy and disease but also an understanding of the emotional and other consequences to her family, her male partner and to herself. I doubt whether a girl under the age of 16 is capable of a balanced judgment to embark on frequent, regular or casual sexual intercourse fortified by the illusion that medical science can protect her in mind and body and ignoring the danger of leaping from childhood to adulthood without the difficult formative transitional experiences of adolescence. There are many things which a girl under 16 needs to practise but sex is not one of them. Parliament could declare this view to be out of date. But in my opinion the statutory provisions discussed in the speech of my noble and learned friend Lord Fraser and the provisions of s 6 of the Sexual Offences Act 1956 indicate that as the law now stands an unmarried girl under 16 is not competent to decide to practice sex and contraception …

In the present case it is submitted that a doctor may lawfully make a decision on behalf of the girl and in so doing may overrule or ignore the parent who has custody of the girl. It is submitted that a doctor may at the request of a girl under 16 provide contraceptive facilities against the known or assumed wishes of the parent and on terms that the parent shall be kept in ignorance of the treatment. The justification is advanced that, if the girl's request is not met, the girl may persist in sexual intercourse and run the risk of pregnancy. It is not in the interests of a girl under 16 to become pregnant and therefore the doctor may, in her interests, confidentially provide contraceptive facilities unless the doctor can persuade the girl to abstain from sexual intercourse or can persuade her to ensure that precautions are taken by the male participant. The doctor is not bound to provide contraceptive facilities but, it is said, is entitled to do so in the best interests of the girl. The girl must be assured that the doctor will be pledged to secrecy otherwise the girl may not seek advice or treatment but will run all the risks of disease and pregnancy involved in sexual activities without adequate knowledge or mature consideration and preparation. The Department of Health and Social Security (DHSS) memorandum instructs a doctor to seek to persuade the girl to involve the parent but concludes that 'the decision whether or not to prescribe contraception must be for the clinical judgment of a doctor'.

There are several objections to this approach. The first objection is that a doctor, acting without the views of the parent, cannot form a 'clinical' or any other reliable judgment that the best interests of the girl require the provision of contraceptive facilities. The doctor at the family planning clinic only know that which the girl chooses to tell him. The family doctor may know some of the circumstances of some of the families who form his registered patients but his information may be incomplete or misleading. The doctor who provides contraceptive facilities without the knowledge of the parent deprives the parent of the opportunity to protect the girl from sexual intercourse by persuading and helping her to avoid sexual intercourse or by the exercise of parental power which may prevent sexual intercourse. The parent might be able to bring pressure on a male participant to desist from the commission of the offence of sexual intercourse with a girl under 16. The parent might be able and willing to exercise parental power by removing the family or the girl to a different neighbourhood and environment and away from the danger of sexual intercourse.

The second objection is that a parent will sooner or later find out the truth, probably sooner, and may do so in circumstances which bring about a complete rupture of good relations between members of the family and between the family and the doctor. It is inevitable that, when the parent discovers that the girl is practising sexual intercourse, the girl will in self-justification and in an attempt to reassure the parent reveal that she is relying on contraceptive facilities provided by the doctor in order to avoid pregnancy. The girl and the doctor will be the losers by this revelation.

The third and main objection advanced on behalf of the respondent parent, Mrs Gillick, in this appeal, is that the secret provision of contraceptive facilities for a girl under 16 will, it is said, encourage participation by the girl in sexual intercourse and this practice offends basic principles of morality and religion which ought not to be sabotaged in stealth by kind permission of the National Health Service. The interests of a girl under 16 require her to be protected against sexual intercourse. Such a girl is not sufficiently mature to be allowed to decide to flout the accepted rules of society. The pornographic press and the lascivious film may falsely pretend that sexual intercourse is a form of entertainment available to females on request and to males on demand but the regular, frequent or casual practice of sexual intercourse by a girl or a boy under the age of 16 cannot be beneficial to anybody and may cause harm to character and personality. Before a girl under 16 is supplied with contraceptive facilities, the parent who knows most about the girl and ought to have the most influence with the girl is entitled to exercise parental rights of control, supervision, guidance and advice in order that the girl may, if possible, avoid sexual intercourse until she is older. Contraception should only be considered if and when the combined efforts of parent and doctor fail to prevent the girl from participating in sexual intercourse and there remains only the possibility of protecting the girl against pregnancy resulting from sexual intercourse.

These arguments have provoked great controversy which is not legal in character. Some doctors approve and some doctors disapprove of the idea that a doctor may decide to provide contraception for a girl under 16 without the knowledge of the parents. Some parents agree and some parents disagree with the proposition that the decision must depend on the judgment of the doctor. Those who favour doctor power assert that the failure to provide confidential contraceptive treatment will lead to an increase in pregnancies amongst girls under 16. As a general proposition, this assertion is not supported by evidence in this case, is not susceptible to proof and in my opinion is of doubtful validity. Availability of confidential contraceptive treatment may increase the demand for such treatment. Contraceptive treatment for females usually requires daily discipline in order to be effective and girls under 16 frequently lack that discipline. The total number of pregnancies amongst girls of under 16 may, therefore, be increased and not decreased by the availability of contraceptive treatment. But there is no doubt that an individual girl who is denied the opportunity of confidential contraceptive treatment may invite or succumb to sexual intercourse and thereby become pregnant. Those who favour parental power assert that the availability of confidential contraceptive treatment will increase sexual activity by girls under 16. This argument is also not supported by evidence in the present case and is not susceptible to proof. But it is clear that contraception removes or gives an illusion of removing the possibility of pregnancy and therefore removes restraint on sexual intercourse. Some girls would come under pressure if contraceptive facilities were known to be available and some girls under 16 are susceptible to male domination.

Parliament could decide whether it is better to have more contraception with the possibility of fewer pregnancies and less disease or whether it is better to have less contraception with the possibility of reduced sexual activity by girls under 16. Parliament could ensure that the doctor prevailed over the parent by reducing the age of consent or by expressly authorising a doctor to provide contraceptive facilities for any girl without informing the parent, provided the doctor considered that his actions were for the benefit of the girl. Parliament could, on the other hand, ensure that the parent prevailed over the doctor by forbidding contraceptive treatment for a girl under 16 save by or on the recommendation of the girl's general medical practitioner and with the consent of the parent who has registered the girl as a patient of that general practitioner. Some girls, it is said, might pretend to be over 16 but a doctor in doubt could always require confirmation from the girl's registered medical practitioner.

In sum, therefore, the House of Lords in *Gillick* has decided that a doctor need not fear the criminal law in the form of the crime of aiding and abetting an offence under s 6 of the Sexual Offences Act 1956 if he gives contraceptive advice or treatment to a young girl under the age of 16. This is clear from the judgment of Woolf J adopted by both Lords Fraser and Scarman (with whom Lord Bridge concurred).

Lord Brandon's dissenting speech is not, as you will have seen, exclusively concerned with the niceties of the criminal law but with larger questions of social policy. Lord Templeman is also concerned with the wider question of the relationship between the criminal law and public policy. Both Lord Brandon and Lord Templeman interpret social policy as requiring that contraception be treated separately by the law and not be made available to young persons.

The majority, however, saw public policy as pointing in the opposite direction.

Lord Fraser: Once the rule of the parents' absolute authority over minor children is abandoned, the solution to the problem in this appeal can no longer be found by referring to rigid parental rights at any particular age. The solution depends on a judgment of what is best for the welfare of the particular child. Nobody doubts, certainly I do not doubt, that in the overwhelming majority of cases the best judges of a child's welfare are his or her parents. Nor do I doubt that any important medical treatment of a child under 16 would normally only be carried out with the parents' approval. That is why it would and should be 'most unusual' for a doctor to advise a child without the knowledge and consent of the parents on contraceptive matters. But, as I have already pointed out, Mrs Gillick has to go further if she is to obtain the first declaration that she seeks. She has to justify the absolute right of veto in a patent. But there may be circumstances in which a doctor is a better judge of the medical advice and treatment which will conduce to a girl's welfare than her parents. It is notorious that children of both sexes are often reluctant to confide in their parents about sexual matters, and the DHSS guidance under consideration shows that to abandon the principle of confidentiality for contraceptive advice to girls under 16 might cause some of them not to seek professional advice at all, with the consequence of exposing them to 'the immediate risks of pregnancy and of sexually-transmitted diseases'. No doubt the risk could be avoided if the patient were to abstain from sexual intercourse, and one of the doctor's responsibilities will be to decide whether a particular patient can reasonably be expected to act on advice and abstain. We were told that in a significant number of cases such abstinence could not reasonably be expected. An example is *Re P (a minor)* (1981) 80 LGR 301, in which Butler-Sloss J ordered that a girl aged 15 who had been pregnant for the second time and who was in the care of a local authority should be fitted with a contraceptive appliance because, as the judge is reported to have said (at 312):

> I assume that it is impossible for this local authority to monitor her sexual activities, and, therefore, contraception appears to be the only alternative.

There may well be other cases where the doctor feels that because the girl is under the influence of her sexual partner or for some other reason there is no realistic prospect of her abstaining from intercourse. If that is right it points strongly to the desirability of the doctor being entitled in some cases, in the girl's best interests, to give her contraceptive advice and treatment if necessary without the consent or even the knowledge of her parents. The only practicable course is, in my opinion, to entrust the doctor with a discretion to act in accordance with his view of what is best in the interests of the girl who is his patient. He should, of course, always seek to persuade her to tell her parents that she is seeking contraceptive advice, and the nature of the advice that she receives. At least he should seek to persuade her to agree to the doctor's informing the parents. But there may well be cases, and I think there will be some cases, where the girl refuses either to tell the parents herself or to permit the doctor to do so and in such cases the doctor will, in my opinion, be justified in proceeding without the parents' consent or even knowledge provided he is satisfied on the following matters: (1) that the girl (although under 16 years of age) will understand his advice; (2) that he cannot persuade her to inform her parents or to allow him to inform the parents that she is seeking contraceptive advice; (3) that she is very likely to begin or to continue having sexual intercourse with or without contraceptive treatment; (4) that unless she receives contraceptive advice or treatment her physical or mental health or both are likely to suffer; (5) that her best interests require him to give her contraceptive advice, treatment or both without the parental consent.

That result ought not to be regarded as a licence for doctors to disregard the wishes of parents on this matter whenever they find it convenient to do so. Any doctor who behaves in such a way would, in my opinion, be failing to discharge his professional responsibilities, and I would expect him to be disciplined by his own professional body accordingly. The medical profession have in modern times come to be entrusted with very wide discretionary powers going beyond the strict limits of clinical judgment and, in my opinion, there is nothing strange about entrusting them with this further responsibility which they alone are in a position to discharge satisfactorily.

As is clear, speaking for the majority Lord Fraser sees public policy as concerned to protect young girls from the harmful consequences of engaging in sexual intercourse without contraception. Furthermore, Lord Fraser sees the true purpose of the criminal law as being to protect young girls since they are under the Sexual Offences Act 1956 'victims' of others' crimes. Why victimise them further by denying them contraception is a question implicit in both his speech and that of Lord Bridge. This is not to say that Lord Fraser contemplated that contraception should be made available to young girls without any legal constraint beyond the consent of the child. Conscious of the gravity of such decisions he is anxious to establish guiding criteria which condition the circumstances under which doctors may prescribe contraception. In effect, what Lord Fraser is doing is vesting in the doctor the authority to determine what it is in the girl's 'best interests' while defining in general terms the criteria which must inform the doctor's decision.

Lord Fraser's approach may be distinguished from that of Lord Scarman. For Lord Fraser the young girl's consent is a necessary but not sufficient condition for treating her. There must be a further enquiry conducted by the doctor as to whether it would be in her 'best interests' to treat her. This inquiry invites the doctor to go beyond concern for 'medical' or even 'health interests' to consider the wider social and moral factors. Lord Scarman, on the other hand, appears to regard consent alone as the key, always assuming, as we must, that the doctor is prepared on medical grounds to treat the patient. He does not invite the doctor to engage in any inquiry about wider interests. He does, however, insist that in determining whether the child *is* consenting the doctor must consider a range of factors far greater than those normally associated with the issue of capacity (see *supra*, ch 3). This is clearly Lord Scarman's attempt to recognise the special nature of contraceptive treatment by setting a higher threshold for capacity while at the same time ensuring that young girls are not completely denied access to treatment.

Lord Bridge pithily addresses the issue of public policy in agreeing with Lord Fraser and Scarman as follows:

> **Lord Bridge:** On the issue of public policy, it seems to me that the policy consideration underlying the criminal sanction imposed by statute on men who have intercourse with girls under 16 is the protection of young girls from the untoward consequences of intercourse. Foremost among these must surely be the risk of pregnancy leading either to abortion or the birth of a child to an immature and irresponsible mother. In circumstances where it is apparent that the criminal sanction will not, or is unlikely to, afford the necessary protection it cannot, in my opinion, be contrary to public policy to prescribe contraception as the only effective means of avoiding a wholly undesirable pregnancy.

We should permit Professor Sir John Smith to have the last word. In his commentary ([1986] Crim LR 114) on *Gillick*, he proposes an alternative mechanism within the criminal law in order to give effect to the public policy conclusions reached by the majority.

> The case decides no more than that such conduct [ie, contraceptive treatment] is sometimes lawful and it leaves open the possibility that the doctor will on other occasions by acting unlawfully and even criminally by aiding and abetting the offence under the Sexual Offences Act 1956, s 6. It is with this aspect of the case that this commentary is concerned.
>
> Lord Brandon's dissenting speech is based mainly on his interpretation of the relevant principles of the criminal law. He drew from the Criminal Law Amendment Act 1885 and the Sexual Offences Act 1956 (which replaced it) the 'inescapable inference' that Parliament has for the past century regarded, and still regards, sexual intercourse by a man with a girl under 16 as a serious criminal offence by the man though not by the girl, even though she may have incited, aided, abetted, counselled and procured the man to do the act. Such intercourse is 'unlawful' and 'it follows necessarily that for any person to promote, encourage or facilitate the commission of any such act may itself be a criminal offence and must, in any event, be contrary to public policy'. The commission of the act is, of course, a criminal offence, so anyone who promotes, encourages or facilitates it would seem to be, prima facie, guilty of the crime as a secondary party. Lord Brandon's caution in saying that it *may be* a criminal offence is probably due to his regard for the fact that it would be necessary to prove *mens rea* in the case of any alleged abettor. In his Lordship's opinion the giving of contraceptive advice to the girl *necessarily* involves promoting, encouraging or facilitating the having of sexual intercourse by the girl with the man. For both parties, contraceptive advice to the girl largely removes the inhibition of the risk of an unwanted pregnancy and thus *necessarily* promotes, encourages or facilitates the sexual intercourse. Since these consequences, in Lord Brandon's opinion, necessarily follow, such advice is always unlawful – and this is so whether the parent concurs in it or not. If the reasoning is correct, the doctor giving the advice might find it hard to raise any doubt whether he was aware of consequences which would necessarily follow from his advice; and so would appear to be liable as a secondary party when these consequences did follow.

Lord Brandon was dissenting, but one of the majority, Lord Bridge, acknowledged the 'logical cogency' of this reasoning and it is indeed difficult to see any flaw in it. Yet the decision of the majority is that, sometimes at least, the doctor may prescribe contraception to the girl under 16 without committing an offence. According to Lord Fraser, he acts lawfully if he is satisfied:

> (1) that the girl (although under 16 years of age) will understand his advice; (2) that he cannot persuade her to inform her parents or to allow him to inform the parents that she is seeking contraceptive advice; (3) that she is very likely to begin or to continue having sexual intercourse with or without contraceptive treatment; (4) that unless she receives contraceptive advice or treatment her physical or mental health or both are likely to suffer; (5) that her best interests require him to give her contraceptive advice, treatment or both without the parental consent.

The question now to be considered is how such considerations exclude the application of the doctrine of secondary liability. None of their Lordships gave detailed consideration to this question, Lord Scarman and Lord Bridge being content to adopt the relevant passage of the judgment of Woolf J, [1984] QB 581, 593–595. In the light of this and the other observations of the House, why is the doctor who gives advice in accordance with the conditions stated not guilty of aiding and abetting?

1. Is it because he lacks the necessary intent? There is considerable support for this view in the judgment and speeches but it deserves closer examination. Woolf J recognised that a doctor who provided contraceptive advice to the girl or to the man 'with the intention thereby of encouraging them to have sexual intercourse' would be guilty of an offence; so he was of the opinion that the innocent doctor has no such intent. Unfortunately, as in other contexts, the meaning of 'intention' is obscure. Woolf J recognised that, where a person has such an intention, an 'unimpeachable motive' is not an answer, following Devlin J in *National Coal Board v Gamble* [1959] 1 QB 11, 20 and Lord Simon's consideration of that judgment in *DPP for Northern Ireland v Lynch* [1975] AC 653, 698–699. Where all the conditions specified by Lord Fraser are satisfied, the doctor may well be aware that the provision of contraception will make it more likely that the girl will begin or continue having sexual intercourse – indeed, accepting Lord Brandon's realistic approach, he can hardly fail to be aware of it. If he knows that this will be the result, does he not intend it? Of course, it is not the result he desires, but Devlin J, in the passage cited by Woolf J expressly rules out any necessity to prove that the aider and abettor desires the proscribed result – 'If one man deliberately sells to another a gun to be used for murdering a third, he may be indifferent whether the third man lives or dies and interested only in the cash profit to be made out of the sale, but he can still be an aider and abettor'. It is true that Devlin J also said, 'I would agree that proof that the article was knowingly supplied is not conclusive evidence of intent to aid', citing *Fretwell* (1862) 9 Cox CC 152 and *Steane* [1947] KB 997. These, however, were both cases which depended on the fact that the court required desire to produce a result in order to constitute the particular intent; and in *A-G v Able* [1984] 1 All ER 277, 287 (the 'Exit' case) Woolf J himself held that *Fretwell* was inconsistent with *National Coal Board v Gamble* and was to be 'confined to its own facts'. What is this further mental element called 'intent to aid' of which the defendant's knowledge, that the act he is doing will aid, is evidence, but not conclusive evidence? Hard thought by many students has produced nothing but the desire to aid – and that has been expressly ruled out. There is only one proper way to deal with a proposition to which no meaning can be given and that is to ignore it. It follows then, that a person who *knows that his acts will* aid or encourage an act by another *intends* to aid or encourage that act. If that is right, the doctor who is aware of the obvious fact that his advice will encourage the commission of the crime intends to encourage it and cannot be exempted from liability on the ground that he lacks the intent ordinarily required for an aider and abettor.

2. Having quoted *Gamble's* and *Lynch's* cases, Woolf J took account of three matters. (i) Contraception does not directly assist sexual intercourse, as the provision of a motor car may assist a burglary, or poison a murderer. (ii) The girl commits no offence so the doctor can be accessory to the man's offence only through the innocent agency of the girl. (iii) In some cases the doctor will know no more than that there is a risk of sexual intercourse taking place 'at an unidentified place with an unidentified man on an unidentified date'. With respect, however, it is by no means clear that the presence of any or all of these considerations will negative the principles of secondary liability. Consider the matter in the context of burglary. Suppose (i) D sends a message to E: 'If you must commit burglary (I hope you won't) I will be prepared to swear that you were elsewhere at the relevant time'; (ii) he sends this message by a nine year old child; and (iii) he has no idea where and when the contemplated burglary might take place. The encouragement is indirect, it is given through an innocent agent, and the time, place and victim are all unascertained. But if E is

encouraged to commit a burglary (whether or not he would have committed that burglary without that encouragement) D would surely be liable to conviction as a secondary party.

3. Is the doctor not liable because the unlawful sexual intercourse will (or probably will) take place anyway, whether he prescribes contraceptives or not? Again it is submitted that in principle this is not an answer to the charge. In *A-G v Able* [1984] 1 All ER 277 Woolf J had to consider whether the publishers of a booklet containing advice on how to commit suicide were guilty of aiding and abetting suicide. He held that there had to be a connection between the suicide and the supply of the booklet to make the supplier responsible but added: 'This does not mean that the suicide or attempted suicide would not have occurred but for the booklet'; [1984] 1 All ER 287. A charge of procuring requires proof of causation but 'the same close causal connection is not required when what is being done is the provision of assistance'. Cf *Calhaem* [1985] 2 All ER 266. One out of 20 spectators at an unlawful prize-fight who shouts encouragement to the contestants is clearly guilty of aiding and abetting, although it is perfectly clear that the fight would have begun and continued in exactly the same way if he had not been there. The doctor's case is no different in principle.

4. Is the answer that the doctor is not liable because the man may well not know that the girl has been supplied with contraceptive advice and so will not be encouraged thereby? Again, it is submitted that the answer is in the negative – at least if the commission of the offence has in fact been facilitated. If assistance is in fact given, it should not be necessary to prove that the principal offender knew it had been given. If P's butler, D, leaves P's door unlocked with the intention and effect of facilitating the entry of a burglar, E, it is submitted that D is guilty of aiding and abetting the burglary even though the assistance was given without the burglar's knowledge or consent. To take a closer analogy, D would surely be guilty of aiding and abetting an offence under section 6 if he gave a 15 year old girl an aphrodisiac or other drug with the intention and effect of causing her more readily to submit to sexual intercourse with E, even if E was quite unaware of D's conduct.

A concealed defence of necessity
The conclusion is that a doctor who satisfies all the conditions for accessory liability will not be liable to conviction in the limited circumstances by the majority of the House of Lords. Lord Scarman, like Lord Fraser (above), suggested specific restrictions on the doctor's right to prescribe:

> He may prescribe only if she has the capacity to consent or if exceptional circumstances exist which justify him in exercising his clinical judgment without parental consent. The adjective 'clinical' emphasises that it must be a medical judgment based on what he honestly believes to be necessary for the physical, mental and emotional health of his patient. The bona fide exercise by a doctor of his clinical judgment must be a complete negation of the guilty mind which is an essential ingredient of the criminal offence of aiding and abetting the commission of unlawful sexual intercourse.

Where the conditions specified by Lords Fraser and Scarman are satisfied, it is clear that the doctor does not commit an offence. Yet he may be well aware that the provision of contraception will encourage both the girl and the man to have intercourse and that what is likely will become more likely. Their Lordships make no condition that he should not be so aware.

The assistance or encouragement given to the man may be exactly the same whether these conditions exist or not. So, if the doctor may be sometimes liable and sometimes not, the difference depends on his motive in prescribing contraception. Yet it is recognised that 'an unimpeachable motive' is generally no answer. The answer to this conundrum, it is suggested, is that we have here encountered a concealed defence of necessity. The doctor is acting lawfully if he is doing what he honestly believes to be necessary. All the normal conditions for liability as an aider and abettor may be satisfied; yet the doctor is to be excused. The commission of the offence may be, as Lord Brandon asserts it is, promoted, encouraged or facilitated; but the evil of the encouragement, etc, of the offence is outweighed by the good which flows from the provision of the advice.

The second dissenting judge, Lord Templeman, also seems, in effect, to have recognised a defence of necessity but of a more limited nature than that propounded by Lords Fraser and Scarman. The additional condition is that the parents must concur in giving the contraceptive advice.

> Section 6 of the Sexual Offences Act 1956 does not, however, in my view, prevent parent and doctor from deciding that contraceptive facilities shall be made available to an unmarried girl under the age of 16 whose sexual activities are recognised to be uncontrolled and uncontrollable. Section 6 is designed to protect the girl from sexual intercourse. But if the girl cannot be deterred then contraceptive facilities may be

provided, not for the purpose of aiding and abetting an offence under s 6 but for the purpose of avoiding the consequences, principally pregnancy, which the girl may suffer from illegal sexual intercourse where sexual intercourse cannot be prevented.

The American Model Penal Code propounds a general defence of necessity:

Conduct which the actor believes to be necessary to avoid a harm or evil to himself or to another is justifiable, provided that:

(a) the harm or evil sought to be avoided by such conduct is greater than that sought to be prevented by the law defining the offence charged.

Our law clearly does not recognise any such general defence but the courts, while reluctant to admit it, do from time to time allow the application of something very like it in exceptional circumstances. The most obvious example is *Bourne* [1939] 1 KB 687 where it was held that it was a defence to the statutory felony of procuring an abortion to show that the act was done in good faith for the purpose only of preserving the life of the mother although there was no provision for any such defence in any statute.

It is submitted that it would be better to recognise that the same has been done in the present case than to attempt to justify the result by straining the accepted principles of secondary liability, with possibly harmful results in later cases.

(See also Glanville Williams 'The Gillick Saga Parts I and II' (1985) 135 NLJ 1156 and 1179; I Kennedy *Treat Me Right* (1991), ch 5 and A Grubb and D Pearl 'English Law and Issues Relating to Medicine, Health and the Family in E K Banakas *UK Law in the 1980s* (1988) pp 144–158.)

B. CONTRACEPTION AND THE MENTALLY ILL OR DISABLED

The other apparently special case apart from children involves contraceptive treatment for the mentally ill and disabled. In our view, this only raises the issue of capacity to consent and is not, as a matter of law, special in any other way. It may be otherwise, of course, if, for example, the pill or long-acting injectable contraception were actually being given for reasons of managing personal hygiene rather than contraception. This would raise questions as to the propriety of the action and whether it amounted to treatment. It cannot be treatment, of course, if it is done for the interests of others.

As the Panel of Persons appointed by the Licensing Authority to Hear the Application for a Product Licence to Market the Drug Depo-Provera as a long-term contraceptive stated in their Report (1983, paras 5.4, 5.6):

There was considerable discussion before us on the issue of consent. We believe that the use of a drug that is long acting and with common and often unpleasant side effects is only acceptable if informed consent is obtained from the recipient. Some potential recipients would, of course, be able to understand and weigh the issues involved and give valid consent to treatment. A number of witnesses told us that these would include some of the mentally ill and mentally handicapped in institutional care, and the socially disadvantaged or socially maladapted in the community, provided that proper counselling was given to them. We believe, however, that for a number of reasons it will be difficult for many potential recipients to give informed consent. This is due to such factors as the lack of time available for explanation and counselling by medical and nursing staff, the lack of training and skills in such counselling among doctors not specialising in family planning, patients not being given information on which to make a decision, the inability of patients to understand and weigh the issues, whether through lack of intelligence, general inadequacy, mental handicap, psychiatric illness or through language difficulties, or because they are unable or unwilling to question or challenge the doctor's guidance.

It would only be in very exceptional circumstances that patients who were unable to give real consent would be given the drug. The type of situation that we have in mind is that mentioned by Dr Rona McClean in her written evidence, where the patient is mentally handicapped to such a degree that she cannot give consent to any type of medical treatment. In such circumstances the doctor concerned should apply the same criteria to treatment with Depo-Provera as would be applied when considering any form of medical treatment.

Surgical methods

A. WITH CONSENT

1. Legality

Can an individual give a valid consent to a surgical operation for sterilisation?

Bravery v Bravery **[1954] 1 WLR 1169 (CA)**

Denning LJ: An ordinary surgical operation, which is done for the sake of a man's health, with his consent, is, of course, perfectly lawful because there is just cause for it. But when there is no just cause or excuse for an operation, it is unlawful, even though the man consents to it.
... Likewise with a sterilisation operation. When it is done with a man's consent for a just cause, it is quite lawful; as, for instance, when it is done to prevent the transmission of an hereditary disease. But when it is done without just cause or excuse, it is unlawful, even though the man consents to it. Take a case where a sterilisation operation is done so as to enable a man to have the pleasure of sexual intercourse, without shouldering the responsibilities attaching to it. The operation then is plainly injurious to the public interest. It is degrading to the man himself. It is injurious to his wife and to any woman whom he may marry, to say nothing of the way it opens to licentiousness; and, unlike contraceptives, it allows no room for a change of mind on either side.

This view, however, probably did not represent the law even in 1954 as Hodson LJ indicated in *Bravery* itself.

Hodson LJ: In our view these observations are wholly inapplicable to operations for sterilisation as such, and we are not prepared to hold in the present case that such operations must be regarded as injurious to the public interest.
In the circumstances of the present case and for the reasons we have given, we are unable to accept the conclusion of Denning LJ at the end of his judgment.
Sir Raymond Evershed MR agreed with Hodson LJ.

Today, there can be no doubt that such operations are lawful and cannot be said to be contrary to public policy since sterilisation for contraceptive purposes is recognised as 'just cause'. If confirmation be needed, Parliament has provided for vasectomy operations to be carried out within the NHS, see the NHS Act 1977, s 5(1)(b):

It is the Secretary of State's duty ...
(b) to arrange, to such extent as he considers necessary to meet all reasonable requirements in England and Wales, for the giving of advice on contraception, the medical examination of persons seeking advice on contraception, the treatment of such persons and the supply of contraceptive substances and appliances.

Other jurisdictions have reached a similar view, eg Canada (*Cataford v Moreau* (1978) 114 DLR (3d) 585), and New Zealand where s 61A of the Crimes Act 1961 provides that:

61A. Further provisions relating to surgical operations – (1) Every one is protected from criminal responsibility for performing with reasonable care and skill any surgical operation upon any person if the operation is performed with the consent of that person, or of any person lawfully entitled to consent on his behalf to the operation, and for a lawful purpose.
(2) Without limiting the term 'lawful purpose' in subsection (1) of this section, a surgical operation that is performed for the purpose of rendering the patient sterile is performed for a lawful purpose.

2. Involvement of others

Are there circumstances in which the law requires not only the consent of the person to be sterilised, but also of some other person, such as a spouse or, in the case of a child, a parent?

(a) Spouse

At one time, it was common for consent forms to require the 'agreement' of a spouse to a sterilisation operation. The general consent form recommended by the Medical Protection Society for all surgical procedures, including sterilisations, until 1988 contained the following clause:

I, husband/wife,* of the above-named patient, hereby confirm my consent to the above.†

Date .... Signature of spouse ....

* Delete whichever inapplicable.

† It is recommended that if the patient be married and the procedure likely to affect sexual or reproductive functions, the signature of the spouse should also, when reasonably possible, be obtained.

(The MPS's current suggested consent form does not require a doctor to obtain a spouse's consent.) Arguably, the pre-1988 clause was aimed more at maintaining good domestic relations rather than meeting any legal requirement. If it were a valid legal limitation on a spouse's capacity to be sterilised, it would mean uniquely that in this area of medical treatment an adult competent person would not have the right to self-determination nor be entitled to confidentiality. Furthermore, it would suggest that a spouse who opposed the sterilisation could apply for an injunction if it were thought that the procedure would be carried out without his consent. If a person may not obtain an injunction to prevent a spouse from having an abortion (*Paton v British Pregnancy Advisory Service* [1979] QB 276, [1978] 2 All ER 987), it must be the case that *a fortiori* no action could lie to prevent sterilisation. Thus, it cannot be the case that a requirement of spousal consent has any force in law. It is, of course, another matter whether a sterilisation carried out without the knowledge or consent of a spouse could serve as evidence of 'irretrievable breakdown' for the purpose of divorce. On the other hand, there would seem to be no legal remedy available to a person whom a doctor refuses to sterilise unless the spouse consents; short, perhaps of complaining to the General Medical Council.

Support for the proposition that this analysis reflects the common law can be found in the Oklahoma case of *Murray v Vandevander* (1974) 552 P 2d 302, which unlike the well-known case of *Planned Parenthood of Missouri v Danforth* 428 US 52 (1976) and its progeny does not rely on constitutional law arguments.

Murray v Vandevander (1974) 522 P 2d 302 (Oklahoma CA)

Box J: The question presented on appeal is whether a husband can recover from a physician and hospital for damage to a marital relationship resulting from an operation on the wife, consented to by her. It is the opinion of this court that such recovery was rightfully denied by the trial court.

… The natural right of a married woman to her health is not qualified by requiring that she have the consent of her husband in order to receive surgical care from a physician …

We have found no authority and plaintiff has cited none which hold that the husband has a right to a childbearing wife as an incident to their marriage. We are neither prepared to create a right in a husband to have a fertile wife nor to allow recovery for damage to such a right. We find that the right of a person who is capable of competent consent to control his own body is paramount.

There is no allegation in the petition that plaintiff's wife of diminished capacity or otherwise incapable of consent. There was no necessity for the physician in the instant case to obtain the consent of the plaintiff. No duty was breached by performance of the operation without consent of the husband of the patient.

The current consent form recommended by the Department of Health in its *A Guide to Consent for Examination or Treatment* (HC (90) 22 as amended by HSG (92) 32) is set out in Appendix A(2) as follows:

CONSENT FORM   **APPENDIX A(2)**

For sterilisation or vasectomy

Health authority .... Patient's Surname..................................

Hospital .... Other Names ....

Unit Number .... Date of Birth ....

Sex: (please tick) Male Female

DOCTORS *(This part to be completed by doctor. See notes on the reverse)*
Type of operation: Sterilisation or Vasectomy

Complete this part of the form
I confirm that I have explained the procedure and any anaesthetic (general/local) required,
to the patient in terms which in my judgment are suited to his/her understanding.

Signature .... Date ....

Name of doctor ....

PATIENT
1.   Please read this form very carefully.
2.   If there is anything that you don't understand about the explanation, or if you want
     more information, you should ask the doctor.
3.   Please check that all the information on the form is correct. If it is, and you
     understand the explanation, then sign the form.

I am the patient

I agree	■	to have this operation, which has been explained to me by the doctor named on this form.
	■	to have the type of anaesthetic that I have been told about.
I understand	■	that the operation may not be done by the doctor who has been treating me.
	■	that the aim of the operation is to stop me having any children and it might not be possible to reverse the effects of the operation.
	■	that sterilisation/vasectomy can sometimes fail, and that there is a very small chance that I may become fertile again after some time.
	■	that any procedure in addition to the investigation or treatment described on this form will only be carried out if it is necessary and in my best interests and can be justified for medical reasons.
I have told	■	the doctor about the procedures listed below I would <u>not</u> wish to be carried out straightaway without my having the opportunity to consider them first.

....

....

For vasectomy

| I understand | ■ | that I may remain fertile or become fertile again after some time. |
| | ■ | that I will have to use some other contraceptive method until 2 tests in a row show that I am not producing sperm, if I do not want to father any children. |

Signature   ....

You will notice that there is no longer any clause concerning spousal agreement.

(b) Parent

In the case of sterilisation the same considerations apply concerning the role of parents and doctors and the capacity of children to consent as were discussed in our analysis of *Gillick* in Chapter 5 and its particular application to contraception earlier in this chapter.

B. WITHOUT CONSENT

We are concerned here with issues of substantive law: the circumstances in which it may be lawful to sterilise an incompetent person. This inquiry does not require us to distinguish between adults and children. We have already seen that the inherent jurisdiction of the court to authorise medical treatment extends to children but not to adults. As a consequence, a court may not authorise the sterilisation of an adult incompetent. But, as the House of Lords made clear in *Re F (mental patient: sterilisation)* [1990] 2 AC 1, any case in which sterilisation is proposed should be brought before the court and a declaration of its legality sought (see *supra*, ch 6).

As regards the *principles* to be applied in determining the legality of the sterilisation, it is largely irrelevant whether the incompetent person is an adult or a child. We propose first to set out the judgments in the leading cases in England and Canada. They represent two polar points on a spectrum of approaches to sterilising the intellectually disabled. Thereafter, we shall rely upon a subsequent decision of the Australian High Court to explore and comment critically upon the English and Canadian approaches.

1. Canada: 'best interests' and therapy/non-therapy

Re Eve [1986] 2 SCR 388: (1981) 115 DLR (3d) 283 (Sup Ct Can)

La Forest J:

Background
When Eve was a child, she lived with her mother and attended various local schools. When she became twenty-one, her mother sent her to a school for retarded adults in another community. There she stayed with relatives during the week, returning to her mother's home on weekends. At this school, Eve struck up a close friendship with a male student: in fact, they talked of marriage. He too is retarded, though somewhat less so than Eve. However, the situation was identified by the school authorities who talked to the male student and brought the matter to an end.

The situation naturally troubled Mrs E. Eve was usually under her supervision or that of someone else, but this was not always the case. She was attracted and attractive to men and Mrs E feared she might quite possibly and innocently become pregnant. Mrs E was concerned about the emotional effect that a pregnancy and subsequent birth might have on her daughter. Eve, she felt, could not adequately cope with the duties of a mother and the responsibility would fall on Mrs E. This would understandably cause her great difficulty; she is a widow and was then approaching sixty. That is why she decided Eve should be sterilised. Eve's condition is more fully described by McQuaid J as follows:

> The evidence established that Eve is 24 years of age, and suffers from what is described as extreme expressive aphasia. She is unquestionably at least mildly to moderately retarded. She has some learning skills, but only to a limited level. She is described as being capable of being attracted to, as well as attractive to, the opposite sex. While she might be able to carry out the mechanical duties of a mother, under supervision, she is incapable of being a mother in any other sense. Apart from being able to recognise the fact of a family unit, as consisting of a father, a mother, and children residing in the same home, she would have no concept of the idea of marriage, or indeed, the consequential relationship between, intercourse, pregnancy, and birth.

Expressive aphasia was described as a condition in which the patient is unable to communicate outwardly thoughts or concepts which she might have perceived. Particularly in the case of a person suffering from any degree of retardation, the result is that even an expert such as a psychiatrist is unable to determine with any degree of certainty if, in fact, those thoughts or concepts have actually been perceived, or whether understanding of them does exist. Little appears to be known of the cause of this condition, and even less of its remedy. In the case of Eve, this condition has been diagnosed as extreme.

From the evidence, he further concluded:

[t]hat Eve is not capable of informed consent, that her moderate retardation is generally stable, that her condition is probably non-inheritable, that she is incapable of effective alternative means of contraception, that the psychological or emotional effect of the proposed operation would probably be minimal, and that the probable incidence of pregnancy is impossible to predict.

General considerations

Before entering into a consideration of the specific issues before this Court, it may be useful to restate the general issue briefly. The Court is asked to consent, on behalf of Eve, to sterilisation since she, though an adult, it unable to do so herself. Sterilisation by means of a tubal ligation is usually irreversible. And hysterectomy, the operation authorised by the Appeal Division, is not only irreversible; it is major surgery. Eve's sterilisation is not being sought to treat any medical condition. Its purposes are admittedly non-therapeutic. One such purpose is to deprive Eve of the capacity to become pregnant so as to save her from the possible trauma of giving birth and from the resultant obligations of a parent, a task the evidence indicates she is not capable of fulfilling. As to this, it should be noted that there is no evidence that giving birth would be more difficult for Eve than for any other woman. A second purpose of the sterilisation is to relieve Mrs E of anxiety about the possibility of Eve's becoming pregnant and of having to care for any child Eve might bear.

The *parens patriae* jurisdiction is, as I have said, founded on necessity, namely that need to act for the protection of those who cannot care for themselves. The courts have frequently stated that it is to be exercised in the 'best interest' of the protected person, or again, for his or her 'benefit' or 'welfare'.

The situations under which it can be exercised are legion; the jurisdiction cannot be defined in that sense. As Lord MacDermott put it in *J v C* [1970] AC 668, at 703, the authorities are not consistent and there are many twists and turns, but they have inexorably 'moved towards a broader discretion, under the impact of changing social conditions and the weight of opinion ...'. In other words, the categories under which the jurisdiction can be exercised are never closed. Thus I agree with Latey J in *Re X* ([1975] 1 All ER 697), at 699, that the jurisdiction is of a very broad nature, and that it can be invoked in such matters as custody, protection of property, health problems, religious upbringing and protection against harmful associations. This list, as he notes, is not exhaustive.

What is more, as the passage from *Chambers* cited by Latey J underlines, a court may act not only on the ground that injury to person or property has occurred, but also on the ground that such injury is apprehended. I might add that the jurisdiction is a carefully guarded one. The courts will not readily assume that it has been removed by legislation where a necessity arises to protect a person who cannot protect himself.

I have no doubt that the jurisdiction may be used to authorise the performance of a surgical operation that is necessary to the health of a person, as indeed it already has been in Great Britain and this country. And by health, I mean mental as well as physical health. In the United States, the courts have used the *parens patriae* jurisdiction on behalf of a mentally incompetent to authorise chemotherapy and amputation, and I have little doubt that in a proper case our courts should do the same. Many of these instances are related in *Strunk v Strunk* 445 SW 2d 145 (Ky 1969), where the court went to the length of permitting a kidney transplant between brothers. Whether the courts in this country should go that far, or as in *Quinlan*, permit the removal of life-sustaining equipment, I leave to later disposition.

Though the scope or sphere of operation of the *parens patriae* jurisdiction may be unlimited, it by no means follows that the discretion to exercise it is unlimited. It must be exercised in accordance with its underlying principle. Simply put, the discretion is to do what is necessary for the protection of the person for whose benefit it is exercised; se the passages from the reasons of Sir John Pennycuick in *Re X* at 706–07, and Heilbron J in *Re D* [(*a minor*) (*wardship: sterilisation*) [1976] 1 All ER 326] at 332, cited earlier. The discretion is to be exercised for the benefit of that person, not for that of others. It is a discretion, too, that must at all times be exercised with great caution, a caution that must be redoubled as the seriousness of the matter increases. This is particularly so in cases where a court might be tempted to act because failure to do so would risk imposing an obviously heavy burden on some other individual.

There are other reasons for approaching an application for sterilisation of a mentally incompetent person with the utmost caution. To begin with, the decision involves values in an area where our social history clouds our vision and encourages many to perceive the mentally handicapped as somewhat less than human. This attitude has been aided and abetted by now discredited eugenic theories whose influence was felt in this country as well as the United States. Two provinces, Alberta and British Columbia, once had statutes providing for the sterilisation of mental defectives; *The Sexual Sterilization Act* RSA 1970, c 341, repealed by SA 1972, c 87; *Sexual Sterilization Act,* RSBC 1960, c 353, s 5(1), repealed by SBC 1973, c 79.

Moreover, the implications of sterilisation are always serious. As we have been reminded, it removes from a person the great privilege of giving birth, and is for practical purposes irreversible. If achieved by means of a hysterectomy, the procedure approved by the Appeal Division, it is not only irreversible; it is major surgery. Here, it is well to recall Lord Eldon's admonition in *Wellesley's* case, [*Wellesley v Duke of Beaufort*] *supra*, at 2 Russ p 18, 38 ER p 242, that 'it has always been the principle of this Court, not to risk the incurring of damage to children which it cannot repair, but rather to prevent the damage being done'. Though this comment was addressed to children, who were the subject matter of the application, it aptly describes the attitude that should always be present in exercising a right on behalf of a person who is unable to do so.

Another factor merits attention. Unlike most surgical procedures, sterilisation is not one that is ordinarily performed for the purpose of medical treatment. The Law Reform Commission of Canada tells us this in *Sterilisation*, Working Paper 24 (1979), a publication to which I shall frequently refer as providing a convenient summary of much of the work in the field. It says at p 3:

Sterilisation as a medical procedure is distinct, because except in rare cases, if the operation is not performed, the *physical* health of the person involved is not in danger, necessity or emergency not normally being factors in the decision to undertake the procedure. In addition to its being elective it is for all intents and purposes irreversible.

As well, there is considerable evidence that non-consensual sterilisation has a significant negative psychological impact on the mentally handicapped; see *Sterilisation, supra*, at pp 49–52. The Commission has this to say at p 50:

It has been found that, like anyone else, the mentally handicapped have individually varying reactions to sterilisation. Sex and parenthood hold the same significance for them as for other people and their misconceptions and misunderstandings are also similar. Rosen maintains that the removal of an individual's procreative powers is a matter of major importance and that no amount of *reforming zeal* can remove the significance of sterilisation and its effect on the individual psyche.

In a study by Sabagh and Edgerton, it was found that sterilised mentally retarded persons tend to perceive sterilisation as a symbol of *reduced* or *degraded* status. Their attempts to *pass for normal* were hindered by negative self perceptions and resulted in withdrawal and isolation rather than striving to conform …

The psychological impact of sterilisation is likely to be particularly damaging in cases where it is a result of coercion and when the mentally handicapped have had no children.

In the present case, there is no evidence to indicate that failure to perform the operation would have any detrimental effect on Eve's physical or mental health. The purposes of the operation, as far as Eve's welfare is concerned, are to protect her from possible trauma in giving birth and from the assumed difficulties she would have in fulfilling her duties as a parent. As well, one must assume from the fact that hysterectomy was ordered, that the operation was intended to relieve her of the hygienic tasks associated with menstruation. Another purpose is to relieve Mrs E of the anxiety that Eve might become pregnant, and give birth to a child, the responsibility for whom would probably fall on Mrs E.

I shall dispose of the latter purpose first. One may sympathise with Mrs E. To use Heilbron J's phrase, it is easy to understand the natural feelings of a parent's heart. But the *parens patriae* jurisdiction cannot be used for her benefit. Its exercise is confined to doing what is necessary for the benefit and protection of persons under disability like Eve. And a court, as I previously mentioned, must exercise great caution to avoid being misled by this all too human mixture of emotions and motives. So we are left to consider whether the purposes underlying the operation are necessarily for Eve's benefit and protection.

The justifications advanced are the ones commonly proposed in support of non-therapeutic sterilisation (see *Sterilisation, passim*). Many are demonstrably weak. The Commission dismisses the argument about the trauma of birth by observing at p 60:

For this argument to be held valid would require that it could be demonstrated that the stress of delivery was greater in the case of mentally handicapped persons than it is for others. Considering the generally known wide range of post-partum response would likely render this a difficult cause to prove.

The argument relating to fitness as a parent involves many value-loaded questions. Studies conclude that mentally incompetent parents show as much fondness and concern for their children as other people; see *Sterilisation, supra*, p 33 et seq, 63–64. Many, it is true may have difficulty in coping, particularly with the financial burdens involved. But this issue does not relate to the benefit of the incompetent; it is a social problem, and one, moreover, that is not limited to incompetents. Above all it is not an issue that comes within the limited powers of the courts, under the *parens patriae* jurisdiction, to do what is necessary for the benefit of persons who are unable to care for themselves. Indeed, there are human rights considerations that should make a court extremely hesitant about attempting to solve a social problem like this by this means. It is worth noting that in dealing with such issues, provincial sterilisation boards have revealed serious differences in their attitudes as between men and women, the poor and the rich, and people of different ethnic backgrounds; see *Sterilisation, supra*, at p 44.

As far as the hygienic problems are concerned, the following view of the Law Reform Commission (at p 34) is obviously sound:

... if a person requires a great deal of assistance in managing their own menstruation, they are also likely to require assistance with urinary and faecal control, problems which are much more troublesome in terms of personal hygiene.

Apart from this, the drastic measure of subjecting a person to a hysterectomy for this purpose is clearly excessive.

The grave intrusion on a person's rights and the certain physical damage that ensues from non-therapeutic sterilisation without consent, when compared to the highly questionable advantages that can result from it, have persuaded me that it can never safely be determined that such a procedure is for the benefit of that person. Accordingly, the procedure should never be authorised for non-therapeutic purposes under the *parens patriae* jurisdiction.

To begin with, it is difficult to imagine a case in which non-therapeutic sterilisation could possibly be of benefit to the person on behalf of whom a court purports to act, let alone one in which that procedure is necessary in his or her best interest. And how are we to weigh the best interests of a person in this troublesome area, keeping in mind that an error is irreversible? Unlike other cases involving the use of the *parens patriae* jurisdiction, an error cannot be corrected by the subsequent exercise of judicial discretion. That being so, one need only recall Lord Eldon's remark, *supra*, that 'it has always been the principle of this Court, not to risk damage to children which it cannot repair' to conclude that non-therapeutic sterilisation may not be authorised in the exercise of the *parens patriae* jurisdiction. McQuaid J was, therefore, right in concluding that he had no authority or jurisdiction to grant the application.

Nature or the advances of science may, at least in a measure, free Eve of the incapacity from which she suffers. Such a possibility should give the courts pause in extending their power to care for individuals to such irreversible action as we are called upon to take here. The irreversible and serious intrusion on the base rights of the individual is simply too great to allow a court to act on the basis of possible advantages which, from the standpoint of the individual, are highly debatable. Judges are generally ill-informed about many of the factors relevant to a wise decision in this difficult area. They generally know little of mental illness, of techniques of contraception or their efficiency. And, however well presented a case may be, it can only partially inform. If sterilisation of the mentally incompetent is to be adopted as desirable for general social purposes, the legislature is the appropriate body to do so. It is in a position to inform itself and it is attuned to the feelings of the public in making policy in this sensitive area. The actions of the legislature will then, of course, be subject to the scrutiny of the courts under the *Canadian Charter of Rights and Freedoms* and otherwise.

Many of the factors I have referred to as showing that the best interests test is simply not a sufficiently precise or workable tool to permit the *parens patriae* power to be used in situations like the present are referred to in *Re Eberhardy's guardianship*, [307 NW 2d 881 (1981)]. Speaking for the court in that case, Heffernan J had this to say, at p 894:

Under the present state of the law, the only guideline available to circuit courts faced with this problem appears to be the 'best interests' of the person to be sterilised. This is a test that has been used for a number of years in this jurisdiction and elsewhere in the determination of the custody of children and their placement – in some circumstances placement in a controlled environment ...

No one who has dealt with this standard has expressed complete satisfaction with it. It is not an objective test, and it is not intended to be. The substantial workability of the test rests upon the informed fact-finding and the wise exercise of discretion by trial courts engendered by long experience with the standard. Importantly, however, most determinations made in the best interests of a child or of an incompetent person are not irreversible; and although a wrong decision may be damaging indeed, there is an opportunity for a certain amount of empiricism in the correction of errors of discretion. Errors of judgment or revisions of decisions by courts and social workers can, in part at least, be rectified when new facts or second thoughts prevail. And, of course, alleged errors of discretion in exercising the 'best interest' standard are subject to appellate review. Sterilisation as it is now understood by medical science is, however, substantially irreversible.

Heffernan J also alluded to the limited capacity of judges to deal adequately with a problem that has such general social overtones in the following passage, at p 895:

What these facts demonstrate is that courts, even by taking judicial notice of medical treatises, know very little of the techniques or efficacy of contraceptive methods or of thwarting the ability to procreate by methods short of sterilisation. While courts are always dependent upon the opinion of expert witnesses, it would appear that the exercise of judicial discretion unguided by well thought-out policy determination reflecting the interests of society, as well as of the person to be sterilised, are hazardous indeed. Moreover, all seriously mentally retarded persons may not *ipso facto* be incapable of giving birth without serious trauma, and some may be good parents. Also, there has been a discernible and laudable tendency to 'mainstream' the developmentally disabled and retarded. A properly thought-out public policy on sterilisation or alternative contraceptive methods could well facilitate the entry of these persons into a more nearly normal relationship with society. But again this is a problem that ought to be addressed by the legislature on the basis of fact-finding and the opinions of experts.

The foregoing, of course, leaves out of consideration therapeutic sterilisation and where the line is to be drawn between therapeutic and non-therapeutic sterilisation. On this issue, I simply repeat that the utmost caution must be exercised commensurate with the seriousness of the procedure. Marginal justifications must be weighed against what is in every case a grave intrusion on the physical and mental integrity of the person.

It will be apparent that my views closely conform to those expressed by Heilbron J in *Re D, supra*. She was speaking of an infant, but her remarks are equally applicable to an adult. The importance of maintaining the physical integrity of a human being ranks high in our scale of values, particularly as it affects the privilege of giving life. I cannot agree that a court can deprive a woman of that privilege for purely social or other non-therapeutic purposes without her consent. The fact that others may suffer inconvenience or hardship from failure to do so cannot be taken into account. The Crown's *parens patriae* jurisdiction exists for the benefit of those who cannot help themselves, not to relieve those who may have the burden of caring for them.

I should perhaps add, as Heilbron J does, that sterilisation may, on occasion, be necessary as an adjunct to treatment of a serious malady, but I would underline that this, of course, does not allow for subterfuge or for treatment of some marginal medical problem. Heilbron J was referring, as I am, to cases where such treatment is necessary in dealing with a serious condition. The recent British Columbia case of *Re K*, [(1985) 19 DLR (4th) 255], is at best dangerously close to the limits of the permissible.

… However, [counsel] also argued that there is what he called a fundamental right to free procreative choice. Not only, he asserted, is there a fundamental right to bear children; there is as well a fundamental right to choose not to have children and to implement that choice by means of contraception. Starting from the American courts' approach to the due process clause in the United States Constitution, he appears to base this argument on s 7 of the *Charter*. But assuming for the moment that liberty as used in s 7 protects rights of this kind (a matter I refrain from entering into), counsel's contention seems to me to go beyond the kind of protection s 7 was intended to afford. All s 7 does is to give a remedy to protect individuals against laws or other state action that deprive them of liberty. It has no application here.

Another *Charter*-related argument must be considered. In response to the appellant's argument that a court-ordered sterilisation of a mentally incompetent person, by depriving that person of the right to procreate, would constitute an infringement of that person's rights to liberty and security of the person under s 7 of the *Canadian Charter of Rights and Freedoms*, counsel for the respondent countered by relying on that person's right to equality under s 15(1) of the *Charter*, saying 'that the most appropriate method of ensuring the mentally incompetent their right to equal protection under s 15(1) is to provide the mentally incompetent with a means to obtain non-therapeutic sterilisations, which adequately protects their interests through appropriate judicial safeguards'. A somewhat more explicit argument along the same lines was made by counsel for the Public Trustee of Manitoba. His position was stated as follows:

> It is submitted that in the case of a mentally incompetent adult, denial of the right to have his or her case presented by a guardian *ad litem* to a Court possessing jurisdiction to give or refuse substituted consent to a non-therapeutic procedure such as sterilisation, would be tantamount to a denial to that person of equal protection and equal benefit of the law. Such a denial would constitute discrimination on the basis of mental disability, which discrimination is prohibited by Section 15 of *The Canadian Charter of Rights and Freedoms*.

> Section 15 of the *Charter* was not in force when these proceedings commenced but, this aside, these arguments appear flawed. They raise in different form an issue already dealt with ie, that the decision made by a court on an application to consent to the sterilisation of an incompetent is somehow that of the incompetent. More troubling is that the issue is, of course, not raised by the incompetent, but by a third party.

> The court undoubtedly has the right and duty to protect those who are unable to take care of themselves, and in doing so it has a wide discretion to do what it considers to be in their best interests. But this function must not, in my view, be transformed so as to create a duty obliging the court, at the behest of a third party, to make a choice between the two alleged constitutional rights – the right to procreate or not to procreate – simply because the individual is unable to make that choice. All the more so since, in the case of non-therapeutic sterilisation as we saw, the choice is one the courts cannot safely exercise.

> *Other issues*
> In light of the conclusions I have reached, it is unnecessary for me to deal with the *Charter* issues raised by the appellant and some of the interveners. It is equally unnecessary to comment at length on some of the subsidiary issues such as the burden of proof required to warrant an order of sterilisation and the precautions that judges should, in the interests of justice, take in dealing with applications for such orders. These do not arise because of the view I have taken of the approach the courts should adopt in dealing with applications for non-therapeutic sterilisation. Since these issues may arise in cases involving applications for sterilisation for therapeutic purposes, however, I will venture a few words about them. Since, barring emergency situations, a surgical procedure without consent ordinarily constitutes battery, it will be obvious that the onus of proving the need for the procedure is on those who seek to have it performed. And that burden, though a civil one, must be commensurate with the seriousness of the measure proposed. In conducting these procedures, it is obvious that a court must proceed with extreme caution; otherwise as MacDonald J noted, it would open the way for abuse of the mentally incompetent. In particular, in any such proceedings, it is essential that the mental incompetent have independent representation.

Even though Eve was not a minor, but an incompetent adult, the Supreme Court held that it had jurisdiction akin to wardship derived from the Crown's *parens patriae* prerogative power. We have already seen that this is not so in England (see *supra*, ch 6).

You will have noticed the reference to the earlier of the Court of Appeal of British Columbia in *Re K and Public Trustee* (1985) 19 DLR (4th) 255 in La Forest J's judgment. The Supreme Court regarded this case as illustrating the difference between a therapeutic sterilisation and the non-therapeutic sterilisation in *Re Eve*.

> More germane for the present purposes is the recent case of *Re K and Public Trustee* (1985) 19 DLR (4th) 255, where the Court of Appeal of British Columbia ordered that a hysterectomy be performed on a seriously retarded child on the ground that the operation was therapeutic. The most serious factor considered by the court was the child's alleged aversion to blood, which it was feared would seriously affect her when her menstrual period began. It should be observed, and the fact was underscored by the judges in that case, that *Re K and Public Trustee* raised a quite different issue from that in the present case. As Anderson JA put it at p 275: 'I say now, as forcefully as I can, this case cannot and must not be regarded as a precedent to be followed in cases involving sterilisation of mentally disabled persons for contraceptive purposes'.

Re K was followed by a Saskatchewan Court in *Re H (EM)* (1995) 130 Sask R 281, where the court authorised endometrial ablation (destruction of the lining of the uterus) where a young, mentally disabled girl suffered great distress and physical discomfort when menstruating. The court, however, applied *Re Eve* in refusing to authorise tubal ligation as this, unlike the other procedure, was non-therapeutic.

2. England: 'best interests' without more

Re B (A Minor) (Wardship: Sterilisation) [1988] AC 199, [1987] 2 All ER 206 (HL)

A local authority had the care of a mentally handicapped and epileptic 17-year-old girl who had a mental age of five or six. Expert advice was that she had no understanding of the connection between sexual intercourse and pregnancy and birth, and would not be able to cope with birth nor care for a child of her own. She was not capable of consenting to marriage. She was, however, exhibiting the normal sexual drive and inclinations for someone of her physical age. There was expert evidence that it was vital that she should not be permitted to become pregnant and that certain contraceptive drugs would react with drugs administered to control her mental instability and epilepsy. There was further evidence that it would be difficult, if not impossible, to place her on a course of oral contraceptive pills. The local authority, which had no wish to institutionalise her, applied to the court for her to be made a ward of court and for leave to be given for her to undergo a sterilisation operation. The application was supported by the minor's mother. The Official Solicitor, acting as the minor's guardian *ad litem*, did not support the application. The judge granted the application, and an appeal by the Official Solicitor was dismissed by the Court of Appeal. The Official Solicitor appealed to the House of Lords.

Lord Hailsham of St Marylebone LC: There is no doubt that, in the exercise of its wardship jurisdiction, the first and paramount consideration is the well-being, welfare or interests (each expression occasionally used, but each, for this purpose, synonymous) of the human being concerned, that is the ward herself or himself. In this case I believe it to be the only consideration involved. In particular there is no issue of public policy other than application of the above principle which can conceivably be taken into account, least of all (since the opposite appears to have been considered in some quarters) any question of eugenics. The ward has never conceived and is not pregnant. No question therefore arises as to the morality or legality of an abortion.

The ward in the present case is of the mental age of five or six. She speaks only in sentences limited to one or two words. Although her condition is controlled by a drug, she is epileptic. She does not understand and cannot learn the causal connection between intercourse and pregnancy and the birth of children. She would be incapable of giving a valid consent to contracting a marriage. She would not understand, or be capable of easily supporting, the inconveniences and pains of pregnancy. As she menstruates irregularly, pregnancy would be difficult to detect or diagnose in time to terminate it easily. Were she to carry a child to full term she would not understand what was happening to her, she would be likely to panic, and would probably have to be delivered by Caesarean section, but, owing to her emotional state, and the fact that she has a high pain threshold she would be quite likely to pick at the operational wound and tear it open. In any event, she would be 'terrified, distressed and extremely violent' during normal labour. She has no maternal instincts and is not likely to develop any. She does not desire children, and, if she bore a child, would be unable to care for it.

In these circumstances her mother, and the local authority under whose care she is by virtue of a care order, advised by the social worker who knows her, a gynaecologist, and a paediatrician, consider it vital that she should not become pregnant, and in any case she would not be able to give informed consent to any act of sexual intercourse and would thus be a danger to others. Notwithstanding this, she has all the physical sexual drive and inclinations of a physically mature young woman of 17, which is in fact what she is. In addition, she has already shown that she is vulnerable to sexual approaches, she has already once been found in a compromising situation in a bathroom, and there is significant danger of pregnancy resulting from casual sexual intercourse. To incarcerate her or reduce such liberty as she is able to enjoy would be gravely detrimental to the amenity and quality of her life, and the only alternative to sterilisation seriously canvassed before the court is an oral contraceptive to be taken daily for the rest of her life whilst fertile, which has only a 40% chance of establishing an acceptable regime, and has serious potential side effects. In addition, according to the evidence, it would not be possible in the light of her swings of mood and considerable physical strength to ensure the administration of the necessary daily dose. As her social worker put it, 'if she [the ward] is ... in one of her moods ... there is no way' she would try to give her a pill.

In these circumstances, Bush J and the Court of Appeal both decided that the only viable option was sterilisation by occlusion of the Fallopian tubes (not hysterectomy). Apart from its probably irreversible nature, the detrimental effects are likely to be minimal. For my part, I do not myself see how either Bush J or the Court of Appeal could sensibly have come to any other possible conclusion applying as they did as their first and paramount consideration the correct criterion of the welfare of the ward.

The ward becomes of age (18) on 20 May next. There seems some doubt whether some residual *parens patriae* jurisdiction remains in the High Court after majority (cf Hoggett *Mental Health Law* (2nd edn, 1984) p 203 and 8 Halsbury's Laws (4th edn) para 901, note 6). I do not take this into account. It is clearly to the interest of the ward that this matter be decided now and without further delay. We should be no wiser in 12 months' time than we are now and it would be doubtful then what legal courses would be open in the circumstances.

We were invited to consider the decision of Heilbron J in *D (a minor) (wardship: sterilisation)* [1976] 1 All ER 326, [1976] Fam 185 at 193, when the judge rightly referred to the irreversible nature of such an operation and the deprivation, which it involves, of a basic human right, namely the right of a woman to reproduce. But this right is only such when reproduction is the result of informed choice of which this ward is incapable. I have no doubt whatsoever that that case was correctly decided, but I venture to suggest that no one would be more astonished than that wise, experienced and quite learned judge herself if we were to apply these proper considerations to the extreme and quite different facts of the present case.

We were also properly referred to the Canadian case of *Re Eve* (1986) 31 DLR (4th) 1. But whilst I find La Forest J's history of the *parens patriae* jurisdiction of the Crown (at 14-21) extremely helpful, I find, with great respect, his conclusion (at 32) that the procedure of sterilisation 'should *never* be authorised for non-therapeutic purposes' (my emphasis) totally unconvincing and in startling contradiction to the welfare principle which should be the first and paramount consideration in wardship cases. Moreover, for the purposes of the present appeal I find the distinction he purports to draw between 'therapeutic' and 'non-therapeutic' purposes of this operation in relation to the facts of the present case above as totally meaningless, and, if meaningful, quite irrelevant to the correct application of the welfare principle. To talk of the 'basic right' to reproduce of an individual who is not capable of knowing the casual connection between intercourse and childbirth, the nature of pregnancy, what is involved in delivery, unable to form maternal instincts or to care for a child appears to me wholly to part company with reality.

In the event, I am quite sure that the courts below had jurisdiction, and applied the right criterion for the right reasons, after careful consideration of all the evidential material before them.

Lord Bridge: It is unfortunate that so much of the public comment on the decision should have been based on erroneous or, at best, incomplete appreciation of the facts and on mistaken assumptions as to the grounds on which the decision proceeded. I can only join with others of your Lordships in emphasising that this case has nothing whatever to do with eugenic theory or with any attempt to lighten the burden which must fall on those who have the care of the ward. It is concerned, and concerned only, with the question of what will promote the welfare and serve the best interests of the ward.

There is no reason to doubt that the Canadian decision in *Re Eve* was correct on its own facts. La Forest J, delivering the judgment of the Supreme Court, emphasised (at 9) that 'there is no evidence that giving birth would be more difficult for Eve than for any other woman'. The supposed conflict between the views of the Supreme Court in Canada and of the Court of Appeal in England arises from the passage where it is said (31 DLR (4th) 1 at 32):

> The grave intrusion on a person's rights and the certain physical damage that ensues from non-therapeutic sterilisation without consent, when compared to the highly questionable advantages that can result from it, have persuaded me that it can never safely be determined that such a procedure is for the benefit of that person. Accordingly, the procedure should never be authorised for non-therapeutic purposes under the *parens patriae* jurisdiction.

This sweeping generalisation seems to me, with respect, to be entirely unhelpful. To say that the court can never authorise sterilisation of a ward as being in her best interests would be patiently wrong. To say that it can only do so if the operation is 'therapeutic' as opposed to 'non-therapeutic' is to divert attention from the true issue, which is whether the operation is in the ward's best interests, and remove it to an area of arid semantic debate as to where the line is to be drawn between 'therapeutic' and 'non-therapeutic' treatment.

In *Re D (a minor) (wardship: sterilisation)* [1976] 1 All ER 326 at 332, [1976] Fam 185 at 193 Heilbron J correctly described the right of a woman to reproduce as a basic human right. The Supreme Court of Canada in *Re Eve* (1986) 31 DLR (4th) 1 at 5 refer, equally aptly, to 'the great privilege of giving birth'. The sad fact in the instant case is that the mental and physical handicaps under which the ward suffers effectively render her incapable of exercising that right or enjoying that privilege. It is clear beyond argument that for her pregnancy would be an unmitigated disaster. The only question is how she may best be protected against it. The evidence proved overwhelmingly that the right answer is by a simple operation for occlusion of the Fallopian tubes and that, quite apart from the question whether the court would have power to authorise such an operation after her eighteenth birthday, the operation should now be performed without further delay. I find it difficult to understand how anybody examining the facts humanely, compassionately and objectively could reach any other conclusion.

Lord Oliver: My Lords, none of us is likely to forget that we live in a century which, as a matter of relatively recent history, has witnessed experiments carried out in the name of eugenics or for the purpose of population control, so that the very word 'sterilisation' has come to carry emotive overtones. It is important at the very outset, therefore, to emphasise as strongly as it is possible to do so, that this appeal has nothing whatever to do with eugenics. It is concerned with one primary consideration and one alone, namely the welfare and best interest of this young woman, an interest which is conditioned by the imperative necessity of ensuring, for her own safety and welfare, that she does not become pregnant. …

What prompted the application to the court was the consciousness on the part of her mother and officers of the council responsible for her care that she was beginning to show recognisable signs of sexual awareness and sexual drive exemplified by provocative approaches to male members of the staff and other residents and by touching herself in the genital area. There was thus brought to their attention the obvious risk of pregnancy and the desirability of taking urgent and effective contraceptive measures. Although at present she is subject to effective supervision, her degree of incapacity is not such that it would be thought right that she should, effectively, be institutionalised all her life. The current approach to persons of her degree of incapacity is to allow them as much freedom as is consistent with their own safety and that of other people and although the likelihood is that she will, for the foreseeable future, continue to live at the residential institution, she visits her mother and her siblings at weekends and will, inevitably, be much less susceptible to supervision when she goes to an adult training centre. At the same time the risks involved in her becoming pregnant are formidable. The evidence of Dr Berney is that there is no prospect of her being capable of forming a long-term adult relationship such as marriage, which is within the capacity of some less mentally handicapped persons. She has displayed no maternal feelings and indeed has an antipathy to small children. Such skills as she has been able to develop are limited to those necessary for caring for herself at the simplest level and there is no prospect of her being capable of raising or caring for a child of her own. If she did give birth to a child it would be essential that it be taken from her for fostering or adoption although her attitude towards children is such that this would not cause her distress. So far as her awareness of her sexuality is concerned, she has, as has already been mentioned, been taught to manage for herself the necessary hygienic mechanics of menstruation, but it has not been possible to teach her about sexuality in any abstract form. She understands the link between pregnancy and a baby but is unaware of sexual intercourse and its relationship to pregnancy. It is not feasible to discuss contraception with her and even if there should come a time when she becomes capable of understanding the need for contraception, there is no likelihood of her being able to develop the capacity to weigh up the merits of different types of contraception or to make an informed choice in the matter. Should she become pregnant, it would be desirable that the pregnancy should be terminated, but because of her obesity and the irregularity of her periods there is an obvious danger that her condition might not be noticed until it was too late for an abortion to take place safely. On the other hand, the risks if she were permitted to go to full term are serious, for although it is Dr Berney's opinion that she would tolerate the condition of pregnancy without undue distress, the process of delivery would be likely to be traumatic and would cause her to panic. Normal delivery would be likely to require heavy sedation, which would be injurious to the child, so that it might be more appropriate to deliver her by Caesarean section. If this course were adopted, however, past experience of her reaction to injuries suggests that it would be very difficult to prevent her from repeatedly opening up the wound and thus preventing the healing of the post-operative scar. It was against this background and in the light of the increasing freedom which must be allowed her as she grows older and the consequent difficulty of maintaining effective supervision that those having the care of the minor concluded that it was essential in her interests that effective contraceptive measures be taken. Almost all drugs appear to have a bad effect on her and the view was formed, in which her mother concurred, that the only appropriate course offering complete protection was for her to undergo sterilisation by occluding the Fallopian tubes, a relatively minor operation carrying a very small degree of risk to the patient, a very high degree of protection and minimal side effects. There is, however, no possibility that the minor, even if of full age, would herself have the mental capacity to consent to such an operation. Hence the application to the court.

The necessity for the course proposed has been exhaustively considered by the Official Solicitor on the minor's behalf and there have been obtained two very careful and detailed reports from Dr Berney who is a consultant in child and adolescent psychiatry, and Mr Barron, a consultant of obstetrics and gynaecology to the Newcastle Health Authority. Both agree on the absolute necessity of taking effective contraceptive measures and the report of Mr Barron, in particular, contains a detailed consideration of the various options. It is unnecessary for present purposes to dilate on the numerous possible courses which have been considered. Her limited intelligence effectively rules out mechanical methods while at the same time the way in which certain contraceptive drugs are likely to react with anti-convulsant drugs administered for her epileptic condition severely limits the available choices. In the end it emerges as common ground that the only alternative to sterilisation which even merits consideration is the administration daily in pill form of the drug progesterone supplemented for the present, at any rate, by the danazol which she is presently taking. This involves a number of disadvantages and uncertainties. In the first place, it involves a regular and uninterrupted course which must be pursued over the whole of the minor's reproductive life of some 30 years or so. Secondly, it involves a *daily* dosage, a matter which has given great concern to those having the care of the minor. Miss Ford, the social worker most closely connected with her, was of the opinion that if the minor was in one of her violent moods there was no possible way in which the pill could be administered. Thirdly, the side effects of the drug over a long term are not yet known. Possibilities canvassed in the course of the evidence of Dr Lowry, the consultant paediatrician at Sunderland District General Hospital, were weight-gain, nausea, headaches and depression. But fourthly, and perhaps even more importantly, the effectiveness of this course is entirely speculative. The matter can perhaps best be summed up on the answer given by Mr Barron when he was asked in examination-in-chief for an assessment of the prospect of achieving a satisfactory contraceptive regime by way of pill. He said:

> It would be very speculative because you have a problem here of a girl who is obese, who is still quite young, who has all kinds of problems like, for example, taking anti-convulsant therapy for epilepsy, which affect the manner of working certainly of oestrogens, all of which make her a particularly difficult person in whom to perform a normal judgment. Therefore, I think that we might find a successful modus vivendi, but it is difficult to be certain. I think it is perhaps – if you want a kind of guess, I would say that we have a 30 to 40% chance of getting some formulation that would be successful. But of course it would have to be taken for a very long time.

In answer to a further question he surmised that an experimental period of 12 to 18 months might be required.

Here then is the dilemma. The vulnerability of this young woman, her need for protection, and the potentially frightening consequences of her becoming pregnant are not in doubt. Of the two possible courses, the one proposed is safe, but irreversible, the other speculative, possibly damaging and requiring discipline over a period of many years from one of the most limited intellectual capacity. Equally it is not in doubt that this young woman is not capable and never will be capable herself of consenting to undergo a sterilisation operation. Can the court and should the court, in the exercise of its wardship jurisdiction, give on her behalf that consent which she is incapable of giving and which, objectively considered, it is clearly in her interests to give?

My Lords, I have thought it right to set out in some detail the background of fact in which this appeal has come before your Lordships' House because it is, in my judgment, essential to appreciate, in considering the welfare of this young woman which it is the duty of the court to protect, the degree of her vulnerability, the urgency of the need for protective measures and the impossibility of her ever being able at this age or any later age either to consent to any form of operative treatment or to exercise for herself the right of making any informed decision in matters which, in the case of a person less heavily handicapped, would rightly be thought to be matters purely of personal and subjective choice.

My Lords, the arguments advanced against the adoption of the expedient of a sterilisation operation are based almost entirely (and, indeed, understandably so) on its irreversible nature. It was observed by Dillon LJ in the Court of Appeal that the jurisdiction in wardship proceedings to authorise such an operation is one which should be exercised only in the last resort and with that I respectfully agree. What is submitted is that, in concluding as it did that the instant case was one in which, as the last resort, that jurisdiction ought to be exercised, the Court of Appeal was in error and had not given sufficient weight to the alternative course of experimentation with the progesterone pill. That submission has been reinforced before your Lordships by a further submission not made in either court below that there lies in the court an inherent jurisdiction in the case of a mentally handicapped subject of any age to sanction, as *parens patriae*, an operation such as that proposed whenever it should be considered necessary. Thus, it is argued, some of the urgency is taken out of the case, for further application can be mounted at any time should alternative methods of contraception prove ineffective. My Lords, speaking for myself, I should be reluctant to express any view regarding the correctness of this submission without very much fuller argument than it has been possible for counsel in the time available to present to your Lordships. But in fact I do not consider that in the instant case the point is of more than of academic interest for I am, for my part, prepared to assume for present purposes that the *parens patriae* jurisdiction continues into full age. Making that assumption, I remain wholly unpersuaded that the Court of Appeal failed to give full weight to the alternative proposed or that it erred in any way in the conclusion to which it came. It was faced, as your Lordships are faced, with the necessity of deciding here and now what is the right course in the best interests of the ward. The danger to which she is exposed and the speculative nature of the alternative proposed are such that, on any footing, the risk is not one which should properly be taken by the court. For my part I have not been left in any doubt that Bush J and the Court of Appeal rightly concluded that there was no practicable alternative to sterilisation and that the authority sought by the council should be given without further delay.

Your Lordships attention has, quite properly, been directed to the decision of Heilbron J in *Re D (a minor) (wardship: sterilisation)* [1976] 1 All ER 326, [1976] Fam 185, a case very different from the instant case, where the evidence indicated that the ward was of an intellectual capacity to marry and would in the future be able to make her own choice. In those circumstances Heilbron J declined to sanction an operation which involved depriving her of her right to reproduce. That, if I may say so respectfully, was plainly a right decision. But the right to reproduce is of value only if accompanied by the ability to make a choice and in the instant case there is no question of the minor ever being able to make such a choice or indeed to appreciate the need to make one. All the evidence indicates that she will never desire a child and that reproduction would in fact be positively harmful to her. Something was sought to be made of the description of the operation for which authority was sought in *Re D* as 'non-therapeutic', using the word 'therapeutic' as connoting the treatment of some malfunction or disease. The description was, no doubt, apt enough in that case, but I do not, for my part, find the distinction between 'therapeutic' and 'non-therapeutic' measures helpful in the context of the instant case, for it seems to me entirely immaterial whether measures undertaken for the protection against future and foreseeable injury are properly described as 'therapeutic'. The primary and paramount question is only whether they are for the welfare and benefit of this particular young woman situate as she is situate in this case.

Your Lordships have also been referred to *Re Eve* (1986) 31 DLR (4th) 1, a decision of the Supreme Court of Canada which contains an extremely instructive judgment of La Forest J in which he considered the extent of the *parens patriae* jurisdiction over mentally handicapped persons. His conclusion was that sterilisation should never be authorised for non-therapeutic purposes under the *parens patriae* jurisdiction. If in that conclusion the expression 'non-therapeutic' was intended to exclude measures taken for the necessary protection from future harm of the person over whom the jurisdiction is exercisable, then I respectfully dissent from it for it seems to me to contradict what is the sole and paramount criterion for the exercise of the jurisdiction, viz the welfare and benefit of the ward. La Forest J observed (at 32-33):

If sterilisation of the mentally incompetent is to be adopted as desirable for general social purposes, the legislature is the appropriate body to do so.

With that I respectfully agree but I desire to emphasise once again that this case is not about sterilisation for social purposes; it is not about eugenics, it is not about the convenience of those whose task it is to care for the ward or the anxieties of her family; and it involves no general principle of public policy. It is about what is in the best interests of this unfortunate young woman and how best she can be given the protection which is essential to her future well-being so that she may lead as full a life as her intellectual capacity allows. That is and must be the paramount consideration as was rightly appreciated by Bush J and by the Court of Appeal. They came to what, in my judgment, was the only possible conclusion in the interests of the minor. I would accordingly dismiss the appeal.

(*Re B* is discussed in M D A Freeman 'Sterilising the Mentally Handicapped' in M D A Freeman (ed) *Medicine, Ethics and the Law* (1988) p 55; A Grubb and D Pearl 'Sterilisation and the Courts' [1987] CLJ 439.)

The test which the English court adopts is the same as that in *Eve*, namely that of 'best interests'. Of course, they reach diametrically opposed conclusions in applying the test. We must, therefore, consider the fundamental issue: what is the meaning of 'best interests' here? There are, in fact, two distinct ways of determining 'best interests'. The *first*, and narrower, approach may be that ordinarily adopted by the English family law which tends to invite a court to form a judgment based upon the particular case before it. This approach tends to eschew regard for any general principle governing all children or incompetent adults. Furthermore, and this may be a jurisprudential flaw, it tends to treat normative issues as if they were issues of fact. Facts do not suggest what *ought* to be done; it is the values and policies by reference to which these facts are evaluated which perform this function. The *second*, and wider approach, neglected (or rejected) by the English courts, is that which would import into 'best interests' issues related to human rights – in this case the rights of the child. This was the approach, as we saw earlier, adopted by the Canadian Supreme Court in *Re Eve*, curiously without reliance upon the Canadian Charter of Rights and Freedoms.

Given the approach adopted by the House of Lords in *Re B*, there is, of course, a most significant issue which is left untouched by the Law Lords. Should not the court articulate guidelines both for itself and others who have to determine whether a sterilisation operation is in an incompetent individual's best interests? We know from *Re B* that a sterilisation performed for eugenic reasons does not fall within the 'best interests' test, but this is all we know. In the next case the House of Lords had an opportunity to take the development of the law further.

Re F (a mental patient: sterilisation) [1990] 2 AC 1, [1989] 2 All ER 545 (HL)

Lord Brandon: My Lords, this appeal concerns the proposed sterilisation of an adult woman, F, who is disabled by mental incapacity from consenting to the operation. ...

The material facts relating to F, which are not in dispute, are these. She was born on 13 January 1953, so that she is now 36. She suffers from serious mental disability, probably as a consequence of an acute infection of the respiratory tract which she had when she was about nine months old. She has been a voluntary in-patient at Borocourt Hospital (a mental hospital under the control of the health authority) since 1967, when she was 14. Her mental disability takes the form of an arrested or incomplete development of the mind. She has the verbal capacity of a child of two and the general mental capacity of a child of four to five. She is unable to express her views in words but can indicate what she likes or dislikes, for example people, foods, clothes and matters of routine. She experiences emotions such as enjoyment, sadness and fear, but is prone to express them differently from others. She is liable to become aggressive. Her mother is her only relative and visits her regularly. There is a strong bond of affection between them. As a result of the treatment which F has received during her time in hospital she has made significant progress. She has become less aggressive and is allowed considerable freedom of movement about the hospital grounds, which are large. There is, however, no prospect of any development in her mental capacity.

The question of F being sterilised has arisen because of a relationship which she has formed with a male patient at the same hospital, P. This relationship is of a sexual nature and probably involves sexual intercourse or something close to it, about twice a month. The relationship is entirely voluntary on F's part and it is likely that she obtains pleasure from it. There is no reason to believe that F has other than the ordinary fertility of a woman of her age. Because of her mental disability, however, she could not cope at all with pregnancy, labour or delivery, the meaning of which she would not understand. Nor could she care for a baby if she ever had one. In those circumstances it would, from a psychiatric point of view, be disastrous for her to conceive a child. There is a serious objection to each of the ordinary methods of contraception. So far as varieties of the pill are concerned she would not be able to use them effectively and there is a risk of their causing damage to her physical health. So far as an intrauterine device is concerned, there would be danger of infection arising, the symptoms of which she would not be able to describe so that remedial measures could not be taken in time.

In the light of the facts set out above Scott Baker J concluded that it would be in the best interests of F to have an operation for sterilisation by ligation of her Fallopian tubes. The Court of Appeal unanimously affirmed that conclusion, and no challenge to its correctness was made on behalf of any party at the hearing of the appeal before your Lordships …

In my opinion … a doctor can lawfully operate on, or given other treatment to, adult patients who are incapable, for one reason or another, of consenting to his doing so, provided that the operation or other treatment concerned is in the best interests of such patients. The operation or other treatment will be in their best interests if, but only if, it is carried out in order either to save their lives or to ensure improvement or prevent deterioration in their physical or mental health …

There is one further matter with which I think that it is necessary to deal. That is the standard which the court should apply in deciding whether a proposed operation is or is not in the best interests of the patient. With regard to this Scott Baker J said:

> I do not think they [the doctors] are liable in battery where they are acting in good faith and reasonably in the best interests of their patients. I doubt whether the test is very different from that for negligence.

This was a reference to the test laid down in *Bolam v Friern Hospital Management Committee* [1957] 2 All ER 118, [1957] 1 WLR 582, namely that a doctor will not be negligent if he establishes that he acted in accordance with a practice accepted at the time by a responsible body of medical opinion skilled in the particular form of treatment in question.

All three members of the Court of Appeal considered that the *Bolam* test was insufficiently stringent for deciding whether an operation or other medical treatment was in a patient's best interests. Lord Donaldson MR said:

> Just as the law and the courts rightly pay great, but not decisive, regard to accepted professional wisdom in relation to the duty of care in the law of medical negligence (the *Bolam* test), so they equally would have regard to such wisdom in relation to decisions whether or not and how to treat incompetent patients in the context of the law of trespass to the person. However, both the medical profession and the courts have to keep the special status of such a patient in the forefront of their minds. The ability of the ordinary adult patient to exercise a free choice in deciding whether to accept or to refuse medical treatment and to choose between treatments is not to be dismissed as desirable but inessential. It is a crucial factor in relation to all medical treatment. If it is necessarily absent, whether temporarily in a emergency situation or permanently in a case of mental disability, other things being equal there must be greater caution in deciding whether to treat and, if so, how to treat, although I do not agree that this extends to limiting doctors to treatment on the necessity for which are 'no two views' (per Wood J in *T v T* [1988] 1 All ER 613 at 621, [1988] Fam 52 at 62]. There will always or usually be a minority view and this approach, if strictly applied, would often rule out all treatment. On the other hand, the existence of a significant minority view would constitute a serious contra-indication.

Neill LJ said:

> I have therefore come to the conclusion that, if the operation is necessary and the proper safeguards are observed, the performance of a serious operation, including an operation of sterilisation, on a person who by reason of a lack of mental capacity is unable to give his or her consent is not a trespass to the person or otherwise unlawful. It therefore becomes necessary to consider what is meant by 'a necessary operation'. In seeking to define the circumstances in which an operation can properly be carried out Scott Baker J said: 'I do not think they are liable in battery where they are acting in good faith and reasonably in the best interests of their patients. I doubt whether the test is very different from that for negligence'. With respect, I do not consider that this test is sufficiently stringent. A doctor may defeat a claim in negligence if he establishes that he acted in accordance with a practice accepted at the time as proper by a responsible body of medical opinion skilled in the particular form of treatment in question. This is the test laid down in *Bolam v Friern Hospital Management Committee*. But to say that it is not negligent to carry out a particular form of treatment does not mean that that treatment is necessary. I would define necessary in this context as that which the general body of medical opinion in the particular speciality would consider to be in the best interests of the patient in order to maintain the health and to secure the well-being of the patient. One cannot expect unanimity but it should be possible to say of an operation which is necessary in the relevant sense that it would be unreasonable in the opinion of most experts in the field not to make the operation available to the patient. One must consider the alternatives to an operation and the dangers of disadvantages to which the patient may be exposed if no action is taken. The question becomes: what action does the patient's health and welfare require?

Butler-Sloss LJ agreed with Neill LJ.

With respect to the Court of Appeal, I do not agree that the *Bolam* test is inapplicable to cases of performing operations on, or giving other treatment to, adults incompetent to give consent. In order that the performance of such operations on, and the giving of such other treatment to, such adults should be lawful, they must be in their best interests. If doctors were to be required, in deciding whether an operation or other treatment was in the best interests of adults incompetent to give consent, to apply some test more stringent than the *Bolam* test, the result would be that such adults would, in some circumstances at least, be deprived of the benefit of medical treatment which adults competent to give consent would enjoy. In my opinion it would be wrong for the law, in its concern to protect such adults, to produce such a result.

Lord Griffiths: My Lords, the argument in this appeal has ranged far and wide in search of a measure to protect those who cannot protect themselves from the insult of an unnecessary sterilisation. Every judge who has considered the problem has recognised that there should be some control mechanism imposed on those who have the care of infants or mentally incompetent women of child bearing age to prevent or at least inhibit them from sterilising the women without approval of the High Court. I am, I should make it clear, speaking now and hereafter of an operation for sterilisation which is proposed not for the treatment of diseased organs but an operation on a woman with healthy reproductive organs in order to avoid the risk of pregnancy. The reasons for the anxiety about sterilisation which it is proposed should be carried out for other than purely medical reasons, such as the removal of the ovaries to prevent the spread of cancer, are readily understandable and are shared throughout the common law world ...

In the United States and Australia the solution has been to declare that, in the case of a woman who either because of infancy or mental incompetence cannot give her consent, the operation may not be performed without the consent of the court [see now, *Dept of Health and Community Services v JWB* (1992) 66 ALJR 300 (Aust High Ct)]. In Canada the Supreme Court has taken an even more extreme stance and declared that sterilisation is unlawful unless performed for therapeutic reasons, which I understand to be as a life-saving measure or for the prevention of the spread of disease: see *Re Eve* (1986) 31 DLR (4th) 1. This extreme position was rejected by this House in *Re B (a minor) (wardship: sterilisation)* [1987] 2 All ER 206, [1988] AC 199, which recognised that an operation might be in the best interests of a woman even though carried out in order to protect her from the trauma of pregnancy which she could not understand and with which she could not cope. Nevertheless Lord Templeman stressed that such an operation should not be undertaken without the approval of a High Court judge of the Family Division. In this country *Re D (a minor) (wardship: sterilisation)* [1976] Fam 185 stands as a stark warning of the danger of leaving the decision to sterilise in the hands of those having the immediate care of the woman, even when they genuinely believe that they are acting in her best interests.

I have had the advantage of reading the speeches of my noble and learned friends Lord Brandon and Lord Goff and there is much therein with which I agree. I agree that those charged with the care of the mentally incompetent are protected from any criminal or tortuous action based on lack of consent. Whether one arrives at this conclusion by applying a principle of 'necessity' as do Lord Brandon and Lord Goff or by saying that it is in the public interest as did Neill LJ in the Court of Appeal, appear to me to be inextricably interrelated conceptual justifications for the humane development of the common law. Why is it necessary that the mentally incompetent should be given treatment to which they lack the capacity to consent? The answer must surely be because it is in the public interest that it should be so.

In a civilised society the mentally incompetent must be provided with medical and nursing care and those who look after them must do their best for them. Stated in legal terms the doctor who undertakes responsibility for the treatment of a mental patient who is incapable of giving consent to treatment must give the treatment that he considers to be in the best interests of his patient, and the standard of care required of the doctor will be that laid down in *Bolam v Friern Hospital Management Committee* [1957] 2 All ER 118, [1957] 1 WLR 582. The doctor will however be subject to the specific statutory constraints on treatment for mental disorder provided by Pt IV of the Mental Health Act 1983. Certain radical treatments such as surgical destruction of brain tissue cannot be performed without the consent of the patient and if the patient is incapable of giving consent the operation cannot be performed, however necessary it may be considered by the doctors. Other less radical treatment can only be given with the consent of the patient or, if the patient will not or cannot consent, on the authority of a second medical opinion. There are however no statutory provisions that deal with sterilisation ...

I cannot agree that it is satisfactory to leave this grave decision with all its social implications in the hands of those having the care of the patient with only the expectation that they will have the wisdom to obtain a declaration of lawfulness before the operation is performed. In my view the law ought to be that they must obtain the approval of the court before they sterilise a woman incapable of giving consent and that it is unlawful to sterilise without that consent. I believe that it is open to your Lordships to develop a common law rule to this effect. Although the general rule is that the individual is the master of his own fate the judges through the common law have, in the public interest, imposed certain constraints on the harm that people may consent to being inflicted on their own bodies. Thus, although boxing is a legal sport, a bare knuckle prize fight in which more grievous injury may be inflicted is unlawful (see *R v Coney* (1882) 8 QBD 534), and so is fighting which may result in actual bodily harm (see *Re A-G's Reference (No 6 of 1980)* [1981] 2 All ER 1057, [1981] QB 715). So also is it unlawful to consent to the infliction of serious injury on the body in the course of the practice of sexual perversion (see *R v Donovan* [1934] 2 KB 498, [1934] All ER Rep 207). Suicide was unlawful at common law until Parliament intervened by the Suicide Act 1961.

The common law has, in the public interest, been developed to forbid the infliction of injury on those who are fully capable of consenting to it. The time has now come for a further development to forbid, again in the public interest, the sterilisation of a woman with healthy reproductive organs who, either through mental incompetence or youth, is incapable of giving her fully informed consent unless such an operation has been inquired into and sanctioned by the High Court. Such a common law rule would provide a more effective protection than the exercise of parens patriae jurisdiction which is dependent on some interested party coming forward to invoke the jurisdiction of the court. The parens patriae jurisdiction is in any event now only available in the case of minors through their being made wards of court. I would myself declare that on grounds of public interest an operation to sterilise a woman incapable of giving consent on grounds of either age or mental incapacity is unlawful if performed without the consent of the High Court. I fully recognise that in so doing, I would be making new law. However, the need for such a development has been identified in a number of recent cases and in the absence of any parliamentary response to the problem it is my view that the judges can and should accept responsibility to recognise the need and to adapt the common law to meet it. If such a development did not meet with public approval it would always be open to Parliament to reverse it or to alter it by perhaps substituting for the opinion of the High Court judge the second opinion of another doctor as urged by counsel for the Mental Health Act Commission.

As I know that your Lordships consider that it is not open to you to follow the course I would take I must content myself by accepting, but as second best, the procedure by way of declaration proposed by Lord Brandon and agree to the dismissal of this appeal.

Lord Goff: We are searching for a principle on which, in limited circumstances, recognition may be given to a need, in the interests of the patient, that treatment should be given to him in circumstances where he is (temporarily or permanently) disabled from consenting to it. It is this criterion of a need which points to the principle of necessity as providing justification.

That there exists in the common law a principle of necessity which may justify action which would otherwise be unlawful is not in doubt ...

We are concerned here with action taken to preserve the life, health or well-being of another who is unable to consent to it. Such action is sometimes said to be justified as arising from an emergency; in Prosser and Keeton *Torts* (5th edn, 1984) p 117 the action is said to be privileged by the emergency. Doubtless, in the case of a person of sound mind, there will ordinarily have to be an emergency before such action taken without consent can be lawful; for otherwise there would be an opportunity to communicate with the assisted person and to seek his consent. But this is not always so; and indeed the historical origins of the principle of necessity do not point to emergency as such as providing the criterion of lawful intervention without consent ... when a person is rendered incapable of communication either permanently or over a considerable period of time (through illness or accident or mental disorder), it would be an unusual use of language to describe the case as one of 'permanent emergency', if indeed such a state of affairs can properly be said to exist. In truth, the relevance of an emergency is that it may give rise to a necessity to act in the interests of the assisted person without first obtaining his consent. Emergency is however not the criterion or even a prerequisite; it is simply a frequent origin of the necessity which impels intervention. The principle is one of necessity, not of emergency ... the [legal] principle, [is that] not only (1) must there be a necessity to act when it is not practicable to communicate with the assisted person, but also (2) the action taken must be such as a reasonable person would in all the circumstances take, acting in the best interests of the assisted person.

Take the example of an elderly person who suffers a stroke which renders him incapable of speech or movement. It is by virtue of this principle that the doctor who treats him, the nurse who cares for him, even the relative or friend or neighbour who comes in to look after him will commit no wrong when he or she touches his body.

[This is an example of] a permanent or semi-permanent state of affairs. Another example of the latter kind is that of a mentally disordered person who is disabled from giving consent. I can see no good reason why the principle of necessity should not be applicable in his case as it is in the case of the victim of a stroke. Furthermore, in the case of a mentally disordered person, as in the case of a stroke victim, the permanent state of affairs calls for a wider range of care than may be requisite in an emergency which arises from accidental injury. When the state of affairs is permanent, or semi-permanent, action properly taken to preserve the life, health or well-being of the assisted person may well transcend such measures as surgical operation or substantial medical treatment and may extend to include such humdrum matters as routine medical or dental treatment, even simple care such as dressing and undressing and putting to bed ...

I have said that the doctor has to act in the best interests of the assisted person. In the case of routine treatment of mentally disordered persons, there should be little difficulty in applying this principle. In the case of more serious treatment, I recognise that its application may create problems for the medical profession; however, in making decisions about treatment, the doctor must act in accordance with a responsible and competent body of relevant professional opinion, on the principles set down in *Bolam v Friern Hospital Management Committee* [1957] 2 All ER 118, [1957] 1 WLR 582. No doubt, in practice, a decision may involve others besides the doctor. It must surely be good practice to consult relatives and others who are concerned with the care of the patient. Sometimes, of course, consultation with a specialist or specialists will be required; and in others, especially where the decision involves more than a purely medical opinion, an inter-disciplinary team will in practice participate in the decision. It is very difficult, and would be unwise, for a court to do more than to stress that, for those who are involved in these important and sometimes difficult decisions, the overriding consideration is that they should act in the best interests of the person who suffers from the misfortune of being prevented by incapacity from deciding for himself what should be done to his own body in his own best interests.

In the present case, your Lordships have to consider whether the foregoing principles apply in the case of a proposed operation of sterilisation on an adult woman of unsound mind, or whether sterilisation is (perhaps with one or two other cases) to be placed in a separate category to which special principles apply. Again, counsel for the Official Solicitor assisted your Lordships by deploying the argument that, in the absence of any parens patriae jurisdiction, sterilisation of an adult woman of unsound mind, who by reason of her mental incapacity is unable to consent, can never be lawful. He founded his submission on a right of reproductive autonomy or right to control one's own reproduction, which necessarily involves the right not to be sterilised involuntarily, on the fact that sterilisation involves irreversible interference with the patient's most important organs, on the fact that it involves interference with organs which are functioning normally, on the fact that sterilisation is a topic on which medical views are often not unanimous and on the undesirability, in the case of a mentally disordered patient, of imposing a 'rational' solution on an incompetent patient. Having considered these submissions with care, I am of the opinion that neither singly nor as a whole do they justify the conclusion for which counsel for the Official Solicitor contended. Even so, while accepting that the principles which I have stated are applicable in the case of sterilisation, the matters relied on by counsel provide powerful support for the conclusion that the application of those principles in such a case calls for special case.

It was urged before your Lordships by counsel for the Mental Health Act Commission (the Commission having been given leave to intervene in the proceedings) that a court vested with the responsibility of making a decision in such a case, having first ensured that an independent second opinion has been obtained from an appropriate consultant of the appropriate specialty, should not, if that second opinion supports the proposal that sterilisation should take place, exercise any independent judgment but should simply follow the opinion so expressed. For my part, I do not think that it is possible or desirable for a court so to exercise its jurisdiction. In all proceedings where expert opinions are expressed, those opinions are listened to with great respect; but in the end, the validity of the opinion has to be weighed and judged by the court. This applies as much in cases where the opinion involves a question of judgment as it does in those where it is expressed on a purely scientific matter. For a court automatically to accept an expert opinion, simply because it is concurred in by another appropriate expert, would be a denial of the function of the court ... I do not feel that the Commission need fear that the opinions of the experts will in any way be discounted. On the contrary, they will be heard with the greatest respect; and, as the present case shows, there is a high degree of likelihood that they will be accepted.

Lord Bridge and Lord Jauncey agreed with the speeches of Lord Brandon and Lord Goff.

When comparing the approaches of the House of Lords and the Supreme Court of Canada two particular strands of analysis warrant careful attention. These are: the distinction between 'therapeutic' and 'non-therapeutic' interventions and the 'best interests' criterion. Unlike the court in *Eve*, the House of Lords in *Re B* flatly rejects the distinction between 'therapeutic' and 'non-therapeutic' interventions as unhelpful and meaningless. In *Re F* the House of Lords simply ignores the point. Instead, the Law Lords rely wholly on the criterion of 'best interests'. Again, however, unlike the Canadian Supreme Court they give barely any substantive content to it. And, what content they do supply cannot be said to offer precise guidance in what is a controversial area of medical decision-making. Lord Brandon, you will recall, speaks of an intervention as being in a patient's 'best interest' if carried out 'in order either to save [the individual's life], or to ensure improvement or prevent deterioration in [his] physical or mental health'. Lord Goff talks of action taken by a doctor 'to preserve the life, health or well-being of another'. It could be thought that Lord Goff's reference to 'well-being' offers the decision-maker a virtual carte blanche. Somewhat revealing is the comment of Lord Keith (himself not a party to the decisions in *Re B* and *Re F*) in *Airedale NHS Trust v Bland* [1993] 1 All ER 821 at 860 that:

In *In Re F (mental patient: sterilisation)* [1990] 2 AC 1 this House held that it would be lawful to sterilise a female mental patient who was incapable of giving consent to the procedure. The ground of the decision was that sterilisation would be in the patient's best interests because her life would be fuller and more agreeable if she were sterilised than if she were not.

The approach to 'best interests' epitomised by Lord Goff's language is in stark contrast to that employed in *Re Eve* where La Forest J recognised that what is at stake is a consideration of fundamental human rights. Concern for human rights is a far cry from someone making a judgment about an incompetent person's 'well-being'. The difference between the courts is even more sharply drawn when it is realised that the House of Lords in *Re F* held that it will be doctors who determine the patient's 'best interests', ie her 'well-being'. This is because the Law Lords in *Re F* import into their decision the *Bolam* test. *Bolam*, of course, embodies a test used to establish breach of duty in a negligence action. It is questionable whether the *Bolam* test has any place in determining what is clearly not a matter of medical fact such as diagnosis, prognosis or treatment (*Airedale NHS Trust v Bland* [1993] 1 All ER 821 at 895 per Lord Mustill). It is beyond doubt that what is involved are questions of value and social policy which are not the unique domain of doctors. The more one moves from an obvious therapeutic (ie medically indicated) sterilisation towards a sterilisation carried out for social management, the less weight need be given to the views of doctors. As we saw, even Lord Goff at the end of the speech in *Re F* appeared to doubt the wisdom of relying on *Bolam*. (*Re F* is discussed in I Kennedy *Treat Me Right* (1991) ch 20; J Shaw (1990) 53 MLR 91; A Grubb and D Pearl [1989] CLJ 380; D Morgan [1990] JSWL 204.) In *Re A (medical treatment: male sterilisation)* (2000) 53 BMLR 66 (CA) (also cited as *R-B (a patient) v Official Solicitor* [2000] Lloyd's Rep Med 87), Dame Elizabeth Butler-Sloss P (at 72–73) made clear that *Bolam* and the 'best interests' test were not linked but were 'two duties' which had not been conflated into one requirement. In any event, the President went on to point out that once an application was before the court for its approval of a sterilisation procedure, the court had to make a decision in the patient's best interests alone (see also, *Re S (adult patient: sterilisation)* (2000) Times, 26 May (CA) – court must determine the patient's 'best interests' not apply *Bolam* test; for a discussion of *Bolam* and its relationship to 'best interests', see *supra* ch 6).

3. Australia: 'best interests' analysed

In *Re Eve* the Canadian Supreme Court addressed society's values and reached a conclusion on what social policy called for. The House of Lords, by contrast, it could be said, did not make explicit the values which they considered and the weight they ascribed to them. Subsequently, the High Court of Australia undertook an altogether more systematic review of the issues involved in sterilising incompetent patients in *Secretary, Department of Health and Community Services v JWB and SMB* (1992) 175 CLR 218; (1992) 66 ALJR 300. As you will see, the majority of the court adopted as a means of analysing the law the distinction between 'therapeutic' and 'non-therapeutic' procedures, while recognising the inherent uncertainty in these terms. For the majority, only therapeutic sterilisation could be lawfully carried out on the basis of parental consent alone. But, unlike the Canadian Supreme Court in *Re Eve*, the majority held that some sterilisations albeit non-therapeutic in nature could be carried out with the court's permission. For the majority, only if the sterilisation was 'a by-product of surgery appropriately carried out to treat some malfunction or disease' would it be therapeutic. For these judges, therefore, all procedures performed or carried out for the benefit of an intellectually disabled girl but solely intended to result in sterilisation required the approval of the court. The court would not, however, approve a sterilisation where the intention was eugenic or entirely for the convenience of others, such as those caring for her. Therefore, a sterilisation performed solely for contraceptive purposes could be lawful if it were demonstrated to be necessary for the girl's general welfare. The court recognised the need to develop guidelines so as to give content to the criterion of 'best interests' in the context.

Deane J, in essence, agreed with the majority that a sterilisation for purely contraceptive purposes could be lawful with the court's approval. McHugh J in large part also accepted the legality of such procedures where 'the child has no real understanding of sexual relationships or pregnancy … if no [other] method of contraception is reasonably feasible'. But, in any event, as we shall see, for him these procedures could be consented to by the parents.

Brennan J, however, considered that all non-therapeutic procedures intended to sterilise the girl were unlawful. Hence, for him, purely contraceptive sterilisations would never be lawful. His view of what amounted to a non-therapeutic sterilisation was, however, somewhat narrower than that of the majority of the court. Like Deane J, he considered that where the procedure was carried out to avoid demonstrable future physical or mental harm to the girl, the procedure could be lawful and could be consented to by the parents. Hence, the Canadian case of *Re K and Public Trustee* (1985) 19 DLR (4th) 255 (BCCA) (where the girl has a 'phobic aversion' to blood) and the New Zealand case of *Re X* [1991] 2 NZLR 365 (where menstruation would have had disastrous psychological consequences) were cases in which the performance of a hysterectomy was justified on therapeutic grounds.

Department of Health and Community Services (NT) v JWB and SMB (1992) 175 CLR 218; (1992) 66 ALJR 300 (High Court of Australia)

Mason CJ, Dawson, Toohey and Gaudron JJ: Marion, the pseudonym of the teenager who is the subject of this appeal, is now 14 years old. She suffers from mental retardation ('mental retardation' is the language of the application to the Family Court. Throughout this judgment different expressions are used to reflect the terminology of argument and of decisions under consideration. Current usage prefers the term 'intellectual disability'), severe deafness and epilepsy, has an ataxic gait and 'behavioural problems'. She cannot care for herself. Her parents, who were married in 1976 and who, with their children, are residents of the Northern Territory, applied to the Family Court of Australia for an order authorising performance of a hysterectomy and an ovariectomy (referred to in the application as ovarienectomy) on Marion; alternatively, a declaration that it is lawful for them to consent to the performance of those procedures. A hysterectomy is proposed for the purpose of preventing pregnancy and menstruation with its psychological and behavioural consequences; an ovariectomy is proposed in order to stabilise hormonal fluxes with the aim of helping to eliminate consequential stress and behavioural responses. While the term 'sterilisation' is used throughout this judgment, it must be understood that what the Court is concerned with are the two procedures proposed for Marion. The term is used as a shorthand for these procedures in the particular circumstances unless the context indicates that sterilisation in a different sense or in different circumstances is intended.

The issue specifically before the court was procedural: who, if anyone, could authorise the proposed sterilisation? The court necessarily, however, had also to address the question of the legality of the sterilisation itself.

In arguing that there are kinds of intervention which are excluded from the scope of parental power, the Commonwealth submitted that the power does not extend to, for example, the right to have a child's foot cut off so that he or she could earn money begging, and it is clear that a parent has no right to take the life of a child. But these examples may be met with the proposition that such things are forbidden because it is inconceivable that they are in the best interests of the child. Even if, theoretically, begging could constitute a financially rewarding occupation, there is a presumption that other interests of the child must prevail. Thus, the overriding criterion of the child's best interests is itself a limit on parental power. None of the parties argued, however, that sterilisation could never be said to be in the best interests of a child with the result that it could never be authorised. On the contrary, the question whether parental power is limited only arises because the procedure may be authorised. But, the question whether it is in the best interests of the child and, thus, should be authorised is not susceptible of easy answer as in the case of an amputation on other than medical grounds. And the circumstances in which it arises may result from or involve an imperfect understanding of the issues or an incorrect assessment of the situation. (See, for example, *In Re D (A minor)* [1976] 2 WLR 279 at 288; [1976] 1 All ER 326 at 334; *Re Jane* (1988) 94 FLR 1 at 26, 27. See also *In Re F* [1990] 2 AC 1, per Lord Griffiths, at 69 and per Lord Goff, at 79.)

It is useful, at this point, to look at how sterilisation has been treated in this regard in relevant cases. That is to say whether, and on what bases, sterilisation has been treated as a special case, outside the ordinary scope of parental power to consent to medical treatment.

Australia
There are four relevant Australian decisions concerning sterilisation, apart from the Family Court's decision in the present case. They are: *Re a Teenager* (1988) 94 FLR 181; *Re Jane*; *Re Elizabeth* (1989) 13 Fam LR 47; [1989] FLC 92-023; and *Attorney-General (Qld) v Parents ('In Re s')* (1989) 98 FLR 41. All were first instance decisions, all involved minors, and the result of each decision was to permit the sterilisation of the girl or young woman involved. With respect to the question of mandatory court involvement, however, authority is evenly divided. *Re a Teenager* and *In Re S* held that it was unnecessary for parents, as guardians, to seek approval from a court to authorise sterilisation; further, that parental consent was sufficient. *Re Jane* and *Re Elizabeth* held that a court's consent was required.

In *Re a Teenager* an application was made by an intellectually disabled 14 year old girl, through her next friend, to restrain her parents from permitting a planned hysterectomy on her to proceed. She was assessed as having the mental ability of a child of about two and a half years. A member of staff of a government centre, on hearing about the operation, contacted a solicitor. The solicitor, acting bona fide, informed the doctor who intended to carry out the operation that the procedure was unlawful without a court order. In dismissing the application, Cook J held that it is within the scope of the powers of parents to authorise the sterilisation of their child. He said (*Re a Teenager* (1988) 94 FLR, at 220–221):

So far as the *Family Law Act* is concerned, prima facie thoughtful, caring and loving parents, acting in concert, aided by appropriate medical advice, have a right and indeed a duty to make decisions as to medical treatment including major operations in respect of the children of their marriage, whether such children are normal or are mentally handicapped. There must be some clear and obvious factors, over and above those usually attendant on such operative treatment, before any form of interference by the Court at the behest of the child or any other person, is justified.

Sterilisation in itself, in his Honour's opinion, involved no such 'clear and obvious factors'.

His Honour's conclusion appears to have been based on the principle that in the 'intimate environment' of family life 'parents are given a unique opportunity to become aware of the special needs' (at 196) of their child and that, as against this experience and proximity, a court has no special expertise. Moreover, taking such a decision 'out of the hands of thoughtful, caring and loving parents' (at 197) would risk the denial of the protection granted families by s 43(b) of the *Family Law Act* which provides that the Court shall have regard to 'the need to give the widest possible protection and assistance to the family as the natural and fundamental group unit of society, particularly while it is responsible for the care and education of dependent children'.

In *Re Jane*, the Acting Public Advocate of Victoria applied to the Family Court to be appointed the next friend of Jane and, on Jane's behalf, sought an injunction restraining her parents from permitting a hysterectomy to be performed on her without the approval of the Family Court. The Human Rights Commission intervened. Jane was 17 years old and was assessed to have the mental ability of a child of two. The purpose of the proposed operation was to prevent menstruation and the risk of pregnancy. In deciding that only a court, as distinct from the guardians of a child, can give lawful consent to a hysterectomy, Nicholson CJ appears to have considered the fundamental, independent rights of a child involved in a sterilisation decision to be at too great a risk without the safeguard of a court's participation. His conclusion also rested on the characterisation of the sterilisation as 'non-therapeutic' (*Re Jane* (1988) 94 FLR, at 30–31). The Chief Justice identified two rights recognised by the common law and which might be said to be affected by such a decision: the fundamental principle that every person's body is 'inviolate' (at 8) and the right, or liberty, to reproduce or to choose not to do so (at 9–11). It was argued before his honour that if the Family Court has the power to consent to this kind of operation under its parens patriae jurisdiction, then parents have such power also because in the exercise of its parens patriae jurisdiction the Court simply stands in the place of the parents. Nicholson CJ relied on the judgment of Sachs LJ in *Hewer v Bryant* [1969] 3 WLR 425 at 433; [1969] 3 All ER 578 at 584–585 to conclude that the powers of the Crown as the historic parens patriae were more extensive than those of a parent. He then went on to consider the consequences of the Court's consent being held to be unnecessary (*Re Jane* (1988) 94 FLR, at 26):

> The consequences of a finding that the court's consent is unnecessary are far reaching both for parents and for children. For example, such a principle might be used to justify parental consent to the surgical removal of a girl's clitoris for religious or quasi cultural reasons, or the sterilisation of a perfectly healthy girl for misguided, albeit sincere, reasons. Other possibilities might include parental consent to the donation of healthy organs such as a kidney from one sibling to another.

And his Honour did not accept that unqualified trust in the medical profession expressed by Cook J in *Re a Teenager* (1988) 94 FLR, at 223, saying (*Re Jane* (1988) 94 FLR, at 260):

> Like all professions, the medical profession has members who are not prepared to live up to its professional standards of ethics … Further, it is also possible that members of that profession may form sincere but misguided views about the appropriate steps to be taken.

In defining the circumstances in which a court's consent is required for an operative procedure to be performed on a minor or an intellectually retarded person, Nicholson CJ employed, though somewhat tentatively, the distinction between 'therapeutic' and 'non-therapeutic' operations (at 30–31), where the term 'therapeutic' means treatment of some malfunction or disease. This criterion was used as a test in the Canadian case of *E(Mrs) v Eve* ('*Re Eve*') [1986] 2 SCR 388; (1986) 31 DLR (4th) 1, but was criticised in *In Re B (A Minor)* [1988] AC 199 at 203–204, 205, 211–212 by the House of Lords as a test for determining the scope of the parens patriae jurisdiction. In the end Nicholson CJ found both the distinction between therapeutic and non-therapeutic treatment and the idea of a basic human right to be determinative. He concluded that consent to a medical procedure which involves 'interference with a basic human right such as a person's right to procreate' and which has as 'the principal or a major aim' a non-therapeutic purpose was outside the scope of parental power (*Re Jane* (1989) 94 FLR, at 31).

Ross-Jones J in *Re Elizabeth* agreed with Nicholson CJ, and for the same reasons, that the approval of the Family Court is required. His Honour also relied on the judgment of Lord Donaldson MR in the Court of Appeal's decision in *In Re F* saying (*Re Elizabeth* (1989) 13 Fam LR, at 62; [1989] FLC, at 77,376) that a sterilisation operation is 'irreversible and is of an emotive, sensitive and potentially controversial character'. But his Honour found it unnecessary to examine these factors any further or explain why they should mean that court involvement was necessary.

In *In Re S*, Simpson J relied on the conclusion of the House of Lords in *In Re F*, that there is no necessity for the consent of a court to be obtained for medical procedures to be performed on an adult person under a feasibility, to come to the same conclusion with respect to a minor.

In the case now before the Court Nicholson CJ adhered to the conclusion he had reached in *Re Jane*, saying (*Re Marion* (1990) 14 Fam LR, at 558; [1991] FLC, at 78,301):

I think it can be said of sterilisation that it does stand in the category of procedures that require the authorisation of a court for all the reasons contained in the various passages from the speeches of the House of Lords in *Re B* and *Re F*, which I have cited, to which further support is given by the American and Canadian authorities.

He drew further support from the *Human Rights and Equal Opportunity Commission Act*. It is necessary to turn now to some of the decisions upon which Nicholson CJ relied and later to the *Family Law Act*.

New Zealand

In *Re X* [1991] 2 NZLR 365 Hillyer J, in the exercise of the parens patriae jurisdiction, made an order consenting to a child of 15 years, with a mental age of three months, undergoing a hysterectomy operation to prevent menstruation, which, according to the evidence, would have had extremely harmful consequences for the child who, by virtue of the relevant New Zealand legislation, had authority to consent to such an operation. Hillyer J considered that doctors undertaking an operation which would result in sterilisation were obliged to satisfy themselves that the parental consent was an informed one and that the operation would be in the best interests of the child. His Honour held that, although this would in many cases call for an exercise of the court's jurisdiction, there would be obvious cases in which the existence of a consensus of opinion would make it unnecessary to approach the courts and for the parents to incur the expense, inconvenience and anxiety which such an approach would entail.

England

In *In Re B*, a case concerning the sterilisation of a 17 year old girl assessed to have the understanding of a normal six year old, the House of Lords endorsed ([1988] AC, per Lord Bridge of Harwich, at 205; see also Lord Templeman, at 206 and Lord Oliver of Aylmerton, at 211) the reasoning of Heilbron J in *In Re D*, a case decided some 12 years earlier. In the earlier case Heilbron J said ([1976] 2 WLR, at 286; [1976] 1 All ER, 332):

> The type of operation proposed is one which involves the deprivation of a basic human right, namely, the right of a woman to reproduce, and, therefore, it would be, if performed on a woman for non-therapeutic reasons and without her consent, a violation of such right.

Much of the discussion by the House of Lords in *In Re B* about this 'basic human right' was, however, in the context of the main question before the Court – whether or not sterilisation of a mentally disabled person could be authorised by the Court in *any* circumstances – and was in response to the issues raised by the decision of the Canadian Supreme Court in *Re Eve* that such a procedure 'should never be authorised for non-therapeutic purposes under the parens patriae jurisdiction', ([1986] 2 SCR, at 431; (1986) 31 DLR (4th), at 32. See *In Re B* [1988] AC, at 203–204, 204–205). The House of Lords found that the basic human right to reproduce did not preclude a sterilisation of a minor in appropriate circumstances but only Lord Templeman commented on the issue of mandatory court authorisation. He concluded ([1988] AC at 205) that consent to sterilisation of a minor was outside the scope of parental power and 'should only be carried out with the leave of a High Court judge'. Again, since the major issue before the House of Lords was the question whether *any* person or body could consent to sterilisation on behalf of a disabled minor, his Lordship did not elaborate his view that court authorisation is necessary. He said (at 206) that '[n]o-one has suggested a more satisfactory ... method [than proceedings before a judicial tribunal] of reaching a decision which vitally concerns an individual but also involves principles of law, ethics and medical practice', and he referred again to 'the fundamental right of a girl to bear a child'.

Between publication of the judgments in *Re Elizabeth* and *In Re S* in Australia, the judgment of the House of Lords in *In Re F* was delivered. The House of Lords there held that a court's consent to the sterilisation of a 36 year old woman was unnecessary ([1990] 2 AC, per Lord Bridge, at 51–52; per Lord Brandon of Oakbrook, at 56; per Lord Goff, at 79; per Lord Jauncey of Tullichettle, at 83–84), and that the procedure was lawful if it was in the best interests of the woman (per Lord Bridge, at 51–52; per Lord Brandon, at 83–84). However, as Nicholson CJ said in the present case (*Re Marion* (1990) 14 Fam LR, at 437; [1991] FLC, at 78,291), the decision of the House of Lords is consistent with the proposition that, in the case of a minor, a court's consent is required. Furthermore, the House of Lords' decision was influenced by the particular jurisdictional framework involved. A lacuna in jurisdiction resulted from the revocation by Royal Warrant in 1960 of the parens patriae jurisdiction of the High Court with respect to adults with mental disability. Therefore, in the circumstances, the Court had no jurisdiction to authorise sterilisation. Even so, Lord Griffiths held (*In Re F* [1990] 2 AC, at 70–71) that it should, on the grounds of 'public interest', be the law that the consent of the High Court is necessary. Furthermore, each of their Lordships urged the wisdom of making an application to the Court (per Lord Bridge, at 51; per Lord Brandon (with whom Lord Jauncey agreed), at 57; per Lord Goff, at 79), though such an application was not mandatory. In this regard Lord Brandon elaborated the special features of the procedure which make it 'highly desirable' that the Court be involved (at 56):

> These features are: first, the operation will in most cases be irreversible; secondly, by reason of the general irreversibility of the operation, the almost certain result of it will be to deprive the woman concerned of what is widely, and as I think rightly, regarded as one of the fundamental rights of a woman, namely, the right to bear children; thirdly, the deprivation of that right gives to moral and emotional considerations to which many people attach great importance; fourthly, if the question whether the operation is in the best interests of a woman is left to be decided without the involvement of the court, there may be a greater risk of it being decided wrongly, or at least of it being thought to have been decided wrongly; fifthly, if there is no involvement of the court, there is a risk of the operation being carried out for improper reasons or with improper motives; and, sixthly, involvement of the court in the decision to operate, if that is the decision reached, should serve to protect the doctor or doctors who perform the operation, and any others who may be concerned in it, from subsequent adverse criticisms or claims.

United States

The constitutional bases mentioned at times in the United States cases differ from our own, as does the social and legal history of that country, particularly with regard to the widespread acceptance in North America during the early part of this century of the theory of eugenics. (See the statement of Holmes J in *Buck v Bell* (1927) 274 US 200 at 207, that '[t]hree generations of imbeciles are enough'; Law Reform Commission of Canada (Working Paper No 24, 1979), *Sterilization: Implications for Mentally Retarded and Mentally Ill Persons*, (hereafter 'the Canadian Report'), pp 24–29; see also Goldhar, 'The Sterilization of Women with an Intellectual Disability' (1991) 10 *University of Tasmania Law Review* 157.) Nevertheless, much of what is said in those cases derives from and discusses common law principles; given the number of cases concerning sterilisation in those jurisdictions, some reference to them is warranted.

The case of *AL v GRH* (1975) 325 NE 2d 501 is directly in point. AL filed a complaint seeking a declaration of her right under the common law attributes of the parent-child relationship to have her son, GRH, sterilised. The boy, aged 15, had suffered brain damage as the result of a car accident during his childhood. The Court of Appeals of Indiana said (at 502):

> [T]he facts do not bring the case within the framework of those decisions holding … that the parents may consent on behalf of the child to medical services necessary for the child …
>
>   [T]he common law does not invest parents with such power over their children even though they sincerely believe the child's adulthood would benefit therefrom.

In *Stump v Sparkman* (1978) 435 US 349 the Supreme Court of the United States held that a judge who had authorised, after an ex parte hearing, a sterilisation of a minor on the application of the minor's mother, had jurisdiction to do so under an Indiana statute conferring general jurisdiction on the Court. There, a 'somewhat retarded' 15 year old girl was sterilised, having been told she was to have her appendix removed. Two years later, when she was married and unable to become pregnant, she was told that she had been sterilised. The Supreme Court referred without disapproval to the opinion of the court below with respect to parental powers of consent, which was in accordance with the decision in *AL v GRH* just mentioned (at 358–359).

One of the leading United States cases in this context is that of *In Re Grady* (1981) NJ 426 A 2d 467 in which the Supreme Court of New Jersey held that the Court could, within its parens patriae jurisdiction, decide whether to authorise sterilisation of a legally incompetent person and that the decision should, ultimately, be made by a court, not by the guardian of the person concerned. The Court began with the idea of a fundamental right to procreate. It said (at 471–472).

> Sterilisation may be said to destroy an important part of a person's social and biological identity – the ability to reproduce. It affects not only the health and welfare of the individual but the well-being of all society. Any legal discussion of sterilisation must begin with an acknowledgement that the right to procreate is 'fundamental to the very existence and survival of the race' (*Skinner v Oklahoma* (1942) 316 US 535 at 541) … This right is 'a basic liberty' of which the individual is 'forever deprived' through unwanted sterilisation.

The Court then examined the constitutional right of privacy which involved the right to choose among procreation, sterilisation and other methods of contraception. This was based on United States constitutional provisions but, as Nicholson CJ said in the present case (*Re*

Marion (1990) 14 Fam LR, at 443; [1991] FLC, at 78,296), that basic right has been held to be allied with, or to have been derived from, the common law principle of bodily inviolability as well as from written constitutional guarantees.

According to the Supreme Court of New Jersey, the right to procreate and the right to privacy could only be protected adequately if the decision to sterilise was the subject of independent, judicial decision-making (*In Re Grady* (1981) NJ 426 A 2d at 475):

> We need not determine here the full range of persons who may assert such a right on behalf of the incompetent. The parents are unquestionably eligible to do so. The question of who besides the parents has standing to represent the purported interests of the incompetent can await future determination. Nevertheless, we believe that an appropriate court must make the final determination whether consent to sterilisation should be given on behalf of an incompetent individual. It must be the court's judgment, and not just the parents' good faith decision, that substitutes for the incompetent's consent.

Thus, the two fundamental rights involved in the decision to sterilise required, in the Court's opinion, reference to the court to ensure sufficient protection against their abuse. That is to say, the nature of the rights themselves distinguished this decision from others made by parents in the ordinary course of caring for their children.

Other United States cases which have held that the court's consent is required on the basis that the operation interferes with the fundamental right to procreate include *Ruby v Massey* (1978) 452 F Supp 361, *Master of Guardianship of Hayes* (1980) Wash 608 P 2d 635 and *Matter of Moe* (1982) Mass 432 NE 2d 712.

Summary of earlier decisions

In summary, Australian authority prior to the present case is evenly divided on the question whether court authorisation is a mandatory requirement. The New Zealand decision in *Re X* depended on legislation which enabled parents of an intellectually handicapped child to consent to an operation resulting in sterilisation. Neither of the English cases is directly in point, but in *In Re B* Lord Tempoleman expressed the opinion that court authorisation was required. *In Re F* concerned an adult, not a minor. It held that court authorisation was not required though this was in the context of the court having no jurisdiction to order a sterilisation. In *Re Eve* the Canadian Supreme Court held that non-therapeutic sterilisation can never safely be said to be in the best interests of a person and so can never be authorised by a court under the parens patriae jurisdiction. There is, on the other hand, strong United States authority to the effect that sterilisation for contraceptive purposes is outside the scope of parental power but comes within the scope of the court's parens patriae jurisdiction.

In the cases reviewed, the bases which emerge for isolating the decision to sterilise a child as a special case requiring authorisation from a source other than the child's parents appear to be: first, the concept of a fundamental right to procreate; secondly, in some cases, a similarly fundamental right to bodily inviolability or its equivalent; thirdly, the gravity of the procedure and its ethical, social and personal consequences, though these consequences are not examined in any detail.

Can parents, as guardians, consent to sterilisation? Conclusion

There are, in our opinion, features of a sterilisation procedure or, more accurately, factors involved in a decision to authorise sterilisation of another person which indicate that, in order to ensure the best protection of the interests of a child, such a decision should not come within the ordinary scope of parental power to consent to medical treatment. Court authorisation is necessary and is, in essence, a procedural safeguard. Our reasons for arriving at this conclusion, however, do not correspond precisely with any of the judgments considered. We shall, therefore, give our reasons. But first it is necessary to make clear that, in speaking of sterilisation in this context, we are not referring to sterilisation which is a by-product of surgery appropriately carried out to treat some malfunction or disease. We hesitate to use the expressions 'therapeutic' and 'non-therapeutic', because of their uncertainty. But it is necessary to make the distinction, however unclear the dividing line may be.

As a starting point, sterilisation requires invasive, irreversible and major surgery. But so do, for example, an appendectomy and some cosmetic surgery, both of which, in our opinion, come within the ordinary scope of a parent to consent to. However, other factors exist which have the combined effect of marking out the decision to authorise sterilisation as a special case. Court authorisation is required, first, because of the significant risk of making the wrong decision, either as to a child's present or future capacity to consent or about what are the best interests of a child who cannot consent, and secondly, because the consequences of a wrong decision are particularly grave.

(i)   The complexity of the question of consent. Although there are some cases, of which the facts in *Re X* are an example, in which the parents can give an informed consent to an operation of sterilisation on an intellectually disabled child and in which that operation is clearly for the benefit of the child, there is no unproblematic view of what constitutes informed consent ... And, even given a settled psychological or legal rule, its application in many cases is fraught with difficulty. The fact that a child is disabled does not of itself mean that he or she cannot give informed consent or, indeed, make a meaningful refusal. And there is no reason to assume that those attempting to determine the capacity of an intellectually disabled child, including doctors, may not be affected by commonly held misconceptions about the abilities of those with intellectual disabilities ... the Canadian Report, pp 50, 60–70; and note the striking results of unconscious race, class and gender bias on decisions to sterilise which are recorded at pp 42–44. There is no doubt that some sterilisation operations have been performed too readily and that the capacity of a child to give consent (and, later, to care for a child) has been wrongly assessed both here and overseas, historically and at the present time. (Strahan (ed) *On the Record: A Report on the 1990 STAR conference on sterilisation* (Vic), pp 6–7; the Canadian Report, pp 36–49; Goldhar, op cit, at p 157 (reference to recent government reports). See also *In Re D and Stump v Sparkman*. In the latter case there was court involvement but the application for sterilisation was heard ex parte.)

(ii) The medical profession very often plays a central role in the decision to sterilise as well as in the procedure itself. Indeed the question has been 'medicalised' to a great degree. (See, for example, *Re a Teenager* (1988) 94 FLR, at 221–222, 223–224; *In Re F* [1990] 2 AC, per Lord Goff, at 78; *Re Eve* [1986] 2 SCR, at 399; (1986) 31 DLR (4th), at 7–8, citing from the judgment of the provincial Supreme Court in that case.) Two concerns emerge from this. It is hard to share the view of Cook J in *Re a Teenager* (1988) 94 FLR, at 223 that absolute faith in the integrity of all medical practitioners is warranted. We agree with Nicholson CJ in *Re Jane* (1988) 94 FLR, at 26 that, as with all professions, there are those who act with impropriety as well as those who act bona fide but within a limited frame of reference. And the situation with which they are concerned is one in which incorrect assessment may be made. (See, for example, *In Re D (A Minor)* [1976] 2 WLR 279; [1976] 1 All ER 326; *Re Jane* (1988) 94 FLR 1; *In Re F* [1990] 2 AC 1.) The second concern is that the decision to sterilise, at least where it is to be carried out for contraceptive purposes, and especially now when technology and expertise make the procedure relatively safe, is not merely a *medical* issue. This is also reflected in the concern raised in several of the cases reviewed, that the consequences of sterilisation are not merely biological but also social and psychological. The requirement of a court authorisation ensures a hearing from those experienced in different ways in the care of those with intellectual disability and from those with experience of the long term social and psychological effects of sterilisation.

(iii) The decision by a parent that an intellectually disabled child be sterilised may involve not only the interests of the child, but also the independent and possibly conflicting (though legitimate) interests of the parents and other family members. (See, for example, *Re Jane* (1988) 94 FLR, at 27, 30; *Re K and Public Trustee* [1985] 3 WWR 204, per Wood J, at 224, at first instance and (1985) 19 DLR (4th) 255, per Anderson JA, at 279, cited with approval by Cook J in *Re a Teenager* (1988) 94 FLR, at 208.) There is no doubt that caring for a seriously handicapped child adds a significant burden to the ordinarily demanding task of caring for children. (See Yura, 'Family Subsystem Functions and Disabled Children: Some Conceptual Issues' in Ferrari and Sussman (eds), 'Childhood Disability and Family Systems' (1987) 11 *Marriage and Family Review*, 1/2, 135; Kazak, 'Professional Helpers and Families with Disabled Children: A Social Network Perspective' in Ferrari and Sussman (eds), op cit, 177.) Subject to the overriding criterion of the child's welfare, the interests of other family members, particularly primary care-givers, are relevant to a court's decision whether to authorise sterilisation. However, court involvement ensures, in the case of conflict, that the child's interests prevail.

The gravity of the consequences of wrongly authorising a sterilisation flows both from the resulting inability to reproduce and from the fact of being acted upon contrary to one's wishes or best interests. The fact of violation is likely to have social and psychological implications concerning the person's sense of identity, social place and self-esteem. As the Court said in *In Re Grady* (1981) NJ 426 A 2d at 471–472, a decision to sterilise involves serious questions of a person's 'social and biological identity'. As with anyone, reactions to sterilisation vary among those with intellectual disabilities but it has been said (The Canadian Report, p 50, reporting on Sabagh and Edgerton, 'Sterilized Mental Defectives Look at Eugenic Sterilisation' (1962) 9 *Eugenics Quarterly* 213), that 'sterilised mentally retarded persons tend to perceive sterilisation as a symbol of *reduced* or *degraded* status'. Another study found (Roos, 'Psychological Impact of Sterilization on the Individual' (1975) 1 *Law and Psychology Review* 45 at 54, in the Canadian Report, pp 50–51 and see generally pp 49–52) that:

Existential anxieties commonly associated with mental retardation are likely to be seriously reinforced by coercive sterilisation of those who have had no children. Common sources of these anxieties include low self-esteem, feelings of helplessness, and need to avoid failure, loneliness, concern over body integrity and the threat of death.

The far-reaching consequences of a general rule of law allowing guardian to consent to all kinds of medical treatment, as well as the consequences of a wrong decision in any particular case, are also relevant. As Nicholson CJ pointed out in *Re Jane* in the passage quoted earlier ((1988) 94 FLR, at 26), such a rule may be used to justify other procedures such as a clitoridectomy or the removal of a healthy organ for transplant to another child.

For the above reasons, which look to the risks involved in the decision, particularly in relation to the threshold question of competence and in relation to the consequences of a wrong assessment, our conclusion is that the decision to sterilise a minor in circumstances such as the present falls outside the ordinary scope of the powers, rights and duties of a guardian under s 63E(1) of the *Family Law Act*. This is not a case where sterilisation is an incidental result of surgery performed to cure a disease or correct some malfunction. Court authorisation in the present case is required. Where profound permanent incapacity is indisputable, where all psychological and social implications have in fact been canvassed by a variety of care-givers and where the child's guardians are, in fact, only considering the interests of the child or where their own interests do not conflict with those of the child, court authorisation will ordinarily reproduce the wishes of the guardian. But it is not possible to formulate a rule which distinguishes these cases. Given the widely varying circumstances, it is impossible to apply a single rule to determine what are, in the respondents' words, the 'clear cases'.

Children with intellectual disabilities are particularly vulnerable, both because of their minority and their disability, and we agree with Nicholson CJ (at 27) that there is less likelihood of (intentional or unintentional) abuse of the rights of children if an application to a court is mandatory, than if the decision in all cases could be made by a guardian alone. In saying this we acknowledge that it is too costly for most parents to fund court proceedings, that delay is likely to cause painful inconvenience and that the strictly adversarial process of the court is very often unsuitable for arriving at this kind of decision. These are clear indications of the need for legislative reform, since a more appropriate process for decision-making can only be introduced in that way. The burden of the cost of proceedings for parents would in the meantime, of course, be alleviated by the application being made by a relevant public body pursuant to s 63C(1) of the *Family Law Act*. (See generally Blackwood, 'Sterilisation of the Intellectually Disabled: The Need for Legislative Reform' (1991) 5 *Australian Journal of Family Law* 138.)

One more thing should be said about the basis upon which we have concluded that sterilisation is a special case with respect to parental powers. As we have indicated, the conclusion relies on a fundamental right to personal inviolability existing in the common law, a right which underscores the principles of assault, both criminal and civil, as well as on the practical exigencies accompanying this kind of decision which have been discussed. Our conclusion does not, however, rely on a finding which underpins many of the judgments discussed; namely, that there exists in the common law a fundamental right to reproduce which is independent of the right to personal inviolability. We leave that question open. It is debatable whether the former is a useful concept, when couched in terms of a basic right, and how fundamental such a right can be said to be. (See Kingdom, 'The Right to Reproduce' in Ockelton (ed), *Medicine, Ethics and Law* (1986), 55; cf Freeman, 'Sterilising the Mentally Handicapped' in Freeman (ed), *Medicine, Ethics and the Law* (1988), 55.) For example, there cannot be said to be an absolute right in a man to reproduce (except where a woman consents to bear a child), unless it can be contended that the right to bodily integrity yields to the former right, and that cannot be so. That is to say, if there is an absolute right to reproduce, is there a duty to bear children? But if the so-called right to reproduce comprises a right not to be prevented from being biologically capable of reproducing, that is a right to bodily integrity. The same applies, though in a different way, to a woman's 'right to reproduce'. Again, if the right is, in fact, a right to do with one's person what one chooses, it is saying no more than that there is a right to bodily and personal integrity. Furthermore, it is quite impossible to spell out all the implications which may flow from saying that there is a right to reproduce, expressed in absolute terms and independent from a right to personal inviolability. We think it is important, in the terms of this judgment, to make it quite clear that it is inviolability that is protected, not more.

Brennan J:

The social and legal context

The question raised by this case starkly demonstrates the quandry of the law when it is invoked to settle an issue which is a subject of ethical controversy and there are no applicable or analogous cases of binding authority. Although the issues in this case relate to the law's protection of the physical integrity of a person suffering from an intellectual disability, there is no clear community consensus on these issues which the courts or the legislature can translate into law. Nevertheless, concrete and poignant cases – Marion's among them – arise for decision. In such a case, a court must try to identify the basic principles of our legal system and to decide the issues in conformity with those principles.

The appeal to this Court does not require the ultimate merits of the application to be decided, but the questions of authority and jurisdiction raised by the amended stated case cannot be answered except by reference to the principles which define and govern the law's protection of physical integrity. The questions of authority and jurisdiction are adjectival and it is not possible to answer them without determining the substantive law which the respective repositories of authority and jurisdiction are to apply. To determine the repository of a power to grant a valid authority for sterilisation without reference to the governing principles is simply to leave the repository to decide for or against sterilisation according to an unguided discretion. Conversely, to ascertain the governing principles without determining the repository of the power is to state a rule without providing for its application.

The questions in the amended stated case are directed to ascertaining the repository of a power to grant a valid authority for the removal of Marion's organs without her consent but those questions do not in terms refer to the scope of the power. The questions, though stated with specific reference to Marion, were posed before the facts have been ascertained and the only fact which can therefore be assumed is Marion's incapacity to consent or to refuse consent to surgery. If the questions be understood as inquiring whether a parent, a guardian or a court has power validly to authorise the sterilisation of any child who is intellectually incapable of giving or refusing consent to his or her sterilisation, the answer is that there is no such broad power: neither parents nor other guardians nor courts have power to authorise sterilisation simply because a child is intellectually disabled …

I turn to examine the circumstances in which a repository of a power to authorise sterilisation can be justified in exercising it. An obvious justification exists when the proposed treatment is therapeutic.

Therapeutic medical treatment

It is necessary to define what is meant by therapeutic medical treatment. I would define treatment (including surgery) as therapeutic when it is administered for the chief purpose of preventing, removing or ameliorating a cosmetic deformity, a pathological condition or a psychiatric disorder, provided the treatment is appropriate for and proportionate to the purpose for which it is administered. 'Non-therapeutic' medical treatment is descriptive of treatment which is inappropriate or disproportionate having regard to the cosmetic deformity, pathological condition or psychiatric disorder for which the treatment is administered and of treatment which is administered chiefly for other purposes.

The distinction between therapeutic and non-therapeutic medical treatment was adopted by the Supreme Court of Canada in *Re Eve (E(Mrs) v Eve (Re Eve)* [1986] 2 SCR 388; (1986) 31 DLR (4th) 1) as the criterion for distinguishing permissible from impermissible sterilisation of an intellectually disabled child, though the definitions which I have attempted were implied rather than expressed in the judgment of the Court delivered by La Forest J. Notwithstanding the unanimous judgment of that Court, in *In Re B (A Minor)* [1988] AC 199 at 204, Lord Hailsham of St Marylebone LC dismissed the distinction in relation to the facts in that case as 'totally meaningless, and, if meaningful, quite irrelevant to the correct application of the welfare principle' which his Lordship stated in these terms (at 202; see, to the same effect, the speech of Lord Oliver of Aylmerton, at 211):

> in the exercise of its wardship jurisdiction the first and paramount consideration is the well being, welfare, or interests (each expression occasionally used, but each, for this purpose, synonymous) of the human being concerned, that is the ward herself or himself.

Similarly, Lord Bridge of Harwich (at 205) thought that the drawing of a distinction between therapeutic and non-therapeutic operations would 'divert attention from the true issue, which is whether the operation is in the ward's best interest'.

The welfare principle is, in England and elsewhere, statutorily binding on courts exercising jurisdiction over the guardianship and custody of infants. The effect of a statute which declares the welfare of an infant to be 'the first and paramount consideration' was explained by Dixon J in *Storie v Storie* (1945) 80 CLR 597 at 611–612:

> The word 'first' as well as the word 'paramount' shows that other considerations are not entirely excluded and are only subordinated. The provision proceeds, however, to deny superiority to the claim of one parent over the other 'from any other point of view' scil other than the welfare of the child. Section 145, which comes from the earlier

Guardianship of Infants Act 1886 s 5, gives the court power to make such order as it thinks fit 'having regard to the welfare of the infant and to the conduct of the parents and to the wishes as well of the mother as of the father'.

In administering these provisions the courts do not assume the functions of a children's welfare board seeking to discover, independently of parental and family relationship, the most eligible custodian, locality and environment for the upbringing of the infant: cf per Lord Clyde and Lord Sands, *Hume v Hume* 1926 SC 1008 at 1014 and 1015 respectively.

The traditional view is still followed in the courts that prima facie it is for the welfare of a child that it should enjoy the affection and care of parents and be brought up under their guidance and influence.

In ascertaining where the welfare of a child lies, the courts have sought to discover what is in the child's 'best interests'. The 'best interests' approach focuses attention on the child whose interests are in question. By asserting that the *child's* 'best interests' are 'the first and paramount consideration', the law is freed from the degrading doctrines of earlier times which gave priority to parental or, more particularly, paternal rights to which the interests of the child were subordinated. (As in *In Re Agar-Ellis. Agar-Ellis v Lascelles* (1878) 10 Ch D 49.) But, that said, the best interests approach does no more than identify the person whose interests are in question: it does not assist in identifying the factors which are relevant to the best interests of the child. (As Grubb and Pearl point out in 'Sterilization and the Courts' (1987) 46 *Cambridge Law Journal* 439 at 442.) The summary rejection by the House of Lords of the criterion offered by *Re Eve* left their Lordships without any guidelines by which to decide *In Re B* – or, at least, without guidelines that could be articulated for general application.

That is because the best interests approach offers no hierarchy of values which might guide the exercise of a discretionary power to authorise sterilisation, much less any general legal principle which might direct the difficult decisions to be made in this area by parents, guardians, the medical profession and courts. It is arguable that, in a field where the law has not developed, where ethical principles remain controversial and where each case turns on its own facts, the law should not pretend to too great a precision. Better, it might be said, that authority and power conferred on a suitable repository – whether it be parents or guardians, doctors or the court – decide these difficult questions according to the repository's view as to the best interests of the child in the particular circumstances of the case. In that way, it can be said, the blunt instrument of legal power will be sharpened according to the exigencies of the occasion. The absence of a community consensus on ethical principles may be thought to support this approach. But it must be remembered that, in the absence of legal rules or a hierarchy of values, the best interests approach depends upon the value system of the decision-maker. Absent any rule or guideline, that approach simply creates an unexaminable discretion in the repository of the power. Who could then say that the repository of the power is right or wrong in deciding where the best interests of an intellectually disabled child might lie when there is no clear ethical consensus adopted by the community? An authorisation to sterilise might be reviewable by a tribunal, but what guidance would the best interests approach give the tribunal? The problem was identified by Professor Ian Kennedy (in his paper 'Patients, Doctors and Human Rights', in Blackburn and Taylor (eds), *Human Rights for the 1990s* (1991), pp 90–91).

> To decide any case by reference to the formula of the best interests of the child must be suspect. To decide *Re B* this way is profoundly to be regretted. The best interests formula may be beloved of family lawyers but a moment's reflection will indicate that although it is said to be a test, indeed *the* legal test for deciding matters relating to children, it is not really a test at all. Instead, it is a somewhat crude conclusion of social policy. It allows lawyers and courts to persuade themselves and others that theirs is a principled approach to law. Meanwhile, they engage in what to others is clearly a form of '*ad hocery*'. The best interests approach of family law allows the courts to atomise the law, to claim that each case depends on its own facts. The court can then respond intuitively to each case while seeking to legitimate its conclusion by asserting that it is derived from the general principle contained in the best interests formula. In fact, of course, there is no general principle other than the empty rhetoric of best interests; or rather, there is some principle (or principles) but the court is not telling. Obviously the court must be following *some* principles, otherwise a toss of the coin could decide cases. But these principles, which serve as pointers to what amounts to the best interests, are not articulated by the court. Only the conclusion is set out. The opportunity for reasoned analysis and scrutiny is lost.

Of course the variable circumstances of each case require evaluation and judicial evaluations of circumstances vary, but the power to authorise sterilisation is so awesome, its exercise is so open to abuse, and the consequences of its exercise are generally so irreversible, that guidelines if not rules should be prescribed to govern it. The courts must attempt the task in the course of, and as a necessary incident in, the exercise of their jurisdiction. That is not to say that the courts should arrogate to themselves the power to authorise sterilisations of intellectually disabled children, but it is to say that it has become the duty of the courts – and, in the present case, specifically the duty of this Court – to define the scope of the power to authorise sterilisations of intellectually disabled children and the conditions of exercise of the power, and to determine the repository of the power. The power cannot be left in a state so amorphous that it can be exercised according to the idiosyncratic views of the repository as to the 'best interests' of the child. That approach provides an insubstantial protection of the human dignity of children; it wraps no cloak of protective principle around the intellectually disabled child. And yet, as Professor Kennedy points out, that is the very purpose of involving the legal process – a purpose which the best interests approach defeats so that 'the law fails the woman-about-to-be-sterilised' (Kennedy, ibid, at p 91).

The anxious goodwill of the repository of the power – whether parents, guardians or courts – can generally be assumed, but there are too many factors which tend to distort a dispassionate and accurate assessment of the true interests of the child. There are some powerful if unarticulated influences affecting, albeit in good faith, the presentation of information on which a decision as to the best interests of the child is to be made and the making of that decision. I mention some of those influences: the interests of those who bear the burden of caring for the child, the interests of those who will be involved in the sterilisation if it proceeds, the scarcity of public resources, the widespread tendency to dismiss intellectually disabled people as not deserving of full human dignity (especially if their powers of communication are defective) and common misconceptions (see the factors referred to by Professor F J Bates, 'Sterilising the Apparently Incapable: Further Thoughts and Developments' (1987) 12 *Australian Child and Family Welfare* 4 at 5) (for example that there is a substantial risk that any intellectually disabled female will bear defective children). Again, Professor Kennedy points out that, by transforming a 'complex moral and social question' into a question of fact, the best interests approach leaves the court in the hands of 'experts' who assemble a dossier of fact and opinion on matters which they deem relevant 'without reference to any check-list of *legal requirements*' (Kennedy, op cit, at pp 91–92). It is not possible for the law to neutralise those influences, but it is possible for the law to define the issues with sufficient objectivity to minimise the prospect that those influences will undermine the law's protection of the human dignity of the intellectually disabled child.

If the pragmatism of the best interests approach were to be embraced for want of principle to govern the exercise of the power, the choice of the repository of power would be extremely difficult. On the one hand, parents and guardians, who bear the immediate responsibility for a child's welfare and frequently bear the burden of her care, would have a strong claim to be the repository of the power. On the other, the courts, whose judges are removed from the burdens of and pressures upon parents and guardians and the would bear no personal responsibility for any decision they might make, could offer some check upon abuses of the power. A third choice would be to require the concurrence both of parents or guardians and of the court as a condition of the exercise of the power. If no principle other than the best interests approach is to govern the exercise of the power, it would be necessary to adopt the third choice to secure for the child the protection which neither of the first two choices could offer, making provision for a special procedure (as was proposed in *In Re F (Mental Patient: Sterilization)* [1990] 2 AC 1 at 65; and cf *In Re Grady* (1981) NJ 426 A 2d 467 at 481–483; *Matter of Guardianship of Hayes* (1980) Wash 608 P 2d 635 at 639–641, 643) in an attempt to safeguard the interests of the child. That would be a cumbersome and costly expedient which, if the approach in *Re Eve* is followed, need not be adopted.

With the greatest respect for the views expressed by their Lordships in *Re B*, I find the decision of their Lordships in *Re Eve* more conductive to the maintenance of the human dignity of the intellectually disabled and more in accord with legal principle. The test of therapeutic medical treatment recognises the importance of personal integrity and of the maintenance and enhancement of natural attributes to the welfare of the child. By comparison, the best interests approach is useful only to the extent of ensuring that the first and paramount consideration is the interests of the child, not the interests of others. That approach furnishes no general guidance as to the factors which are relevant to the welfare of the child.

Of course, factual difficulties are unavoidable in deciding whether medical treatment is therapeutic or non-therapeutic but, in principle, the distinction is clear and, in particular, the purpose of therapeutic medical treatment can be clearly distinguished from other purposes. Therapeutic medical treatment is calculated to enhance or maintain as far as practicable the physical or mental attributes which the patient naturally possesses; it is not calculated to impair or destroy those attributes and the capacities they afford. Thus, there is a rationale which justifies the administration of therapeutic medical treatment without the patient's consent when the patient is incapable of consenting or refusing consent. It needs no argument to show that a malignant tumour of the uterus justifies the performance of an hysterectomy or that multiple cysts on an ovary may dictate its surgical removal. However, where menstruation produces or is likely to produce a psychiatric disorder of such severity as to require its suppression – as occurred in *Re X* [1991] 2 NZLR 365 – consideration must be given to the different treatments reasonably available and appropriate to suppress menstruation and to their medical advantages and disadvantages in order to ensure that the least invasive of the treatments is selected. Proportionality and purpose are the legal factors which determine the therapeutic nature of medical treatment. Proportionality is determined as a question of medical fact. Purpose is ascertained by reference to all the circumstances but especially to the physical or mental condition which the treatment is appropriate to affect.

The propriety of authorising sterilisation for therapeutic purposes is not reasonably open to doubt. Therapeutic medical treatment falls clearly within the exception of 'medical treatment ... reasonably needed' in s 187(c) of the [Northern Territory Criminal] Code. When the purpose of a proposed sterilisation is therapeutic, the invasion of the child's physical integrity, the disquieting of her mind and any change in her self-perception are justified by the need to maintain to the maximum extent or to enhance the child's natural physical and mental attributes. The invasion of the child's personal integrity is then the means of maintaining or enhancing the attributes and functions which, so far as they may, contribute to her human dignity. The propriety of authorising sterilisation for non-therapeutic purposes is more problematic.

Non-therapeutic sterilisation
If sterilisation is contemplated to secure a non-therapeutic purpose, the invasion of the child's personal integrity can be justified only if it can be shown that the non-therapeutic purpose possesses some higher value than the preservation of her physical integrity. Clearly, sterilisation could not be justified in order to secure some base purposes – for example, to prevent the birth of a child who would disappoint the testamentary expectations of a residuary beneficiary. Another base purpose which would now be commonly recognised as such, though it was given a higher value in earlier days (see per Homes J in *Buck v Bell* (1927) 274 US 200 at 207) before the uncivilised practices of Nazism revealed its hideous implications, is the purpose of eugenic selection. Economic arguments can be mounted in support of a policy of preventing the birth of defective children and those arguments can be supported by a desire to alleviate the emotional and physical burden of caring for them but, even in a case where an intellectual disability is transmissible, the involuntary sterilisation of a girl is too high a price to pay to avoid the risk. A law which sacrifices the human dignity of individuals in order to avoid reasonable calls by the disabled upon public resources and to avoid the need for compassionate assistance to the disabled inverts the civilised priority of values and depletes the humanity of society. Financial security and comfort, though legitimate objectives in themselves, are not to be preferred over the equal protection by the law of the human rights of every member of the community. The sterilisation of a human being simply in order to prevent him or her from becoming a parent is an extreme denial of that person's human rights.

However, between therapeutic purposes on the one hand and manifestly base purposes on the other, a variety of different purposes may appear which many would regard as of significant value in assessing the 'best interests' of an intellectually disabled child. The purposes which fall into this category can be gathered under the broad description of 'preventative': to prevent the risk of a pregnancy which the child could not properly understand and the concomitant risk of parenthood with responsibilities beyond the capacity of the child to discharge. These risks are an understandable source of anxiety to parents, guardians and others who have a genuine concern for the welfare of an intellectually disabled child. These are risks which create an understandable anxiety in many parents, guardians and others who have a genuine concern for the welfare of a normal child. In the case of a normal female child, it would be wholly unacceptable to permit sterilisation in order to prevent pregnancy or parenthood, though those events might be thought to be tragedies in particular circumstances by reasonable persons concerned with the welfare of the child. Depending on the circumstances, the use – or, a fortiori, the exploitation – of the sexual attributes of a female child may entail tragic consequences, yet the risk of even the likelihood of tragic consequences affords no justification for her sterilisation. What difference does it make that the risk is occasioned by an intellectual disability? The answer to this question depends on the view taken of the proposition earlier set out in the Declaration on the Rights of Mentally Retarded Persons: they are entitled to the *same* rights as other humans to the maximum degree of feasibility. To accord in full measure the human dignity that is the due of every intellectually disabled girl, her right to retain her capacity to bear a child cannot be made contingent on her imposing no further burdens, causing no more anxiety or creating no further demands. If the law were to adopt a policy of permitting sterilisation in order to avoid the imposition of burdens, the causing of anxiety and the creating of demands, the human rights which foster and protect human dignity in the powerless would lie in the gift of those who are empowered and the law would fail in its function of protecting the weak.

Where it is desirable to avoid the risk of pregnancy, the risk may be avoidable by means which involve no invasion of the girl's personal integrity. Those who are charged with responsibility for the care and control of an intellectually disabled girl (by which I mean a female child who is sexually mature) – whether parents, guardians or the staff of institutions – have a duty to ensure that the girl is not sexually exploited or abused. If her disability inclines her to sexual promiscuity, they have a duty to restrain her from exposing herself to exploitation. It is unacceptable that an authority be given for the girl's sterilisation in order to lighten the burden of that duty, much less to allow for its neglect. In any event, though pregnancy be a possibility, sterilisation, once performed, is a certainty. If a non-therapeutic sterilisation could be justified at all, it could be justified only by the need to avoid a tragedy that is imminent and certain. Such a situation bespeaks a failure of care, and sterilisation is not the remedy for the failure. Nor should it be forgotten that pregnancy and motherhood may have a significance for some intellectually disabled girls quite different from the significance attributed by other people. Though others may see her pregnancy and motherhood as a tragedy, she, in her world, may find in those events an enrichment of her life.

Because non-therapeutic purposes are, by definition, related to social values or values other than the maintenance and enhancement of the natural attributes and functions of the intellectually disabled female child, I am unable to postulate a case where it would be justifiable to authorise her sterilisation. I am conscious that courts which have adopted the best interests approach have been accustomed to balance the risks of what may appear to be likely social tragedies against the physical invasion, incapacitation and mental and emotional impact of sterilisation. In my respectful opinion, a balancing exercise is impossible to perform. On one side is the immediate and serious invasion of physical integrity with the resulting grave impairment of human dignity. On the other, there is a risk of what is adjudged to be a future tragedy involving dependence on others, inability to cope, social incompetence or some other matter apparently diminishing the quality of the child's life. The values on either side of the balance are not comparable. If there is to be a rule – as, in my view, there must be – the rule must give priority to the right to physical integrity and the human dignity it protects, even though such a rule imposes burdens on parents, guardians and those having the care of the intellectually disabled child who are entitled to the active support of the State which must bear the ultimate burden.

Such a rule, it may be said, is too idealistic and is out of touch with contemporary community standards. There is much force in that criticism but this is an area of the law in which it is necessary to guard against the tyranny which majority opinion may impose on a weak and voiceless minority. The history of intellectually disabled people contains a surfeit of examples of degrading treatment administered under laws which reflected the standards of the time – standards which were a reproach to the civilisation then enjoyed. If equality under the law, human rights and the protection of minorities are more than the incantations of legal rhetoric, it is in this area of the law that they have real work to do.

I would hold that the power to authorise sterilisation of an intellectually disabled child extends to therapeutic sterilisations but no further ... the power to authorise non-therapeutic sterilisation of an intellectually disabled child is a novel power which some courts have, by their own decision, assumed to themselves. (In the United States, judicial opinion as to the existence of the power has fluctuated: see the cases collected in *In Re Grady* (1981) NJ 426 A 2d at 480.) It is not only the assumption of a novel power which is significant but the assertion that it is assumed in exercise of the wardship or parens patriae jurisdiction. If that be so, the power is exercisable over the objection of parents or guardians and simply on the footing that the court deems its exercise to be in the 'best interests' of the child. Of course the parents or guardians will be heard on any application to the court, but the idiosyncratic views of the judge are given, by this theory, overwhelming effect.

In the United States, the assumption by courts of a power to authorise sterilisation of intellectually disabled people has been accompanied by judicial prescription of protective procedures and criteria for determining whether sterilisation is in the patient's best interests: see *In Re Grady* (at 481–483) and *Matter of Guardianship of Hayes* (1980) Wash 608 P 2d at 639–643. Though the desirability of protective procedures and criteria is manifest, their prescription gave the Courts' decisions a legislative character in the eyes of Rosselini J who, speaking for the minority in *Matter of Guardianship of Hayes*, expressed his concern that the courts do not become 'an imperial judiciary' (at 646). I share his concern. The hypothesis that a court is empowered to authorise the non-therapeutic sterilisation of intellectually disabled children is asserted in order to satisfy what the court perceives to be a lacuna in the powers which ought to be available to satisfy the exigencies of the situation of some disabled children. But the court is an instrument of State power, and the powers of the State to authorise interference with the personal integrity of any of its subjects otherwise than for therapeutic purposes is not self-evident. If such a power can be exercised to secure what the court may deem to be the welfare of an intellectually disabled child, may not a like power be exercised to secure what the court may deem to be the welfare of any child? It is a power which would be exercised not by an anxious and anguishing parent or guardian who can be called to account, but by a judge to whom the case is assigned in a court's list and who, having exercised his or her discretion, is discharged from all responsibility for the consequences. The case of *Stump v Sparkman* (1978) 435 US 349, which left the sterilised woman and her husband without remedy, despite a demonstrably erroneous exercise of judicial power to authorise her sterilisation, is a distressing reminder that courts, for all their independence and wisdom, are not appropriate repositories of so awesome a power.

Moreover, the assumption of a power to authorise non-therapeutic sterilisations without legislative authority is tantamount to the assumption of a power to disperse from compliance with the criminal laws which otherwise protect personal integrity. Justification by court order for what is otherwise an offence is neither an orthodox doctrine of the common law nor consistent with the proper function of a court. Though some statutes create offences exempting instances in which a court is satisfied that particular circumstances exist, the proposition that a court can assume a power to dispense from the criminal laws which protect personal dignity when the judge believes the dispensation is for the welfare of a child is truly judicial imperialism. If that proposition were valid, the laws which presently bear on organ and tissue donations, medical experimentation, abortion or other surgical procedures could be overridden if an application were made to a judge vested with the parens patriae jurisdiction who took the view that the application of the law in the particular circumstances of the case would not be in the child's best interests. It is one thing for a court to exercise the power possessed by parents and guardians to authorise surgical procedures on a child and for the criminal law to accept that authorisation, as it accepts an authorisation by the parents or guardians, to be the equivalent of consent to what would otherwise be an unlawful application of force. It is another thing for a court to exercise an exclusively curial power to authorise a surgical procedure and to require that authorisation to be treated both as an effective consent and as conclusively determining the lawfulness of the procedure. In the former case, the criminal law is simply construed to take account of the parental power which has always been recognised; in the latter case, protection which the criminal law has been fashioned to provide is undone by the exercise of a novel power, created by declaration of the instrument of government claiming to exercise it.

Deane J: Irreversible sterilisation involves the destruction of a natural human attribute and the removal of an integral part of complete human personality. Its eventual psychological consequences will commonly be unforeseeable. They may include emotional devastation, destruction of self-esteem and perceived deprivation of an essential element and purpose of life itself. Nonetheless, circumstances can arise in which surgery involving irreversible sterilisation is, according to general community standards, clearly conducive to the welfare of an incapable child. The most obvious example of such circumstances is where such surgery is necessary to preserve the life of the child: eg, excision or other treatment to avert death by reason of cancer of the ovaries or testicles. Where that is so, it is, as a matter of general principle, within the authority of parents to authorise the surgery in the same way as it is within the authority of parents of an incapable child to authorise the amputation of an incurably gangrenous limb. Similarly, the parents of an incapable child have authority to authorise surgery involving irreversible sterilisation in a case where such surgery is, according to competent medical advice, necessary for the conventional purpose of treating or preventing grave physical illness. In such cases, the common law requirement of due inquiry and adequate consideration is satisfied by competent medical advice, including or supplemented by appropriate multi-specialist and inter-disciplinary input (eg, psychological or vocational).

In the present case, the reasons for the suggested surgery are not purely medical. In some judgments in the decided cases, and in argument in the present case, the phrases 'therapeutic surgery' and 'non-therapeutic surgery' have been used to distinguish between surgery for the traditional medical purpose of preserving life or directly treating or preventing physical illness and surgery for other or wider purposes, such as the enhancement or preservation of the quality of life. The use of those phrases in a context such as the present must, however, be accompanied by two important caveats. The first is that the borderline between 'therapeutic' and 'non-therapeutic' surgery is far from precise and, particularly where psychiatric illness is involved, may be all but meaningless. In particular, surgery involving the sterilisation of a young intellectually disabled female to avoid the special and aggravated problems of menstruation would not appear to me to be for conventional medical purposes but is often described as being for 'therapeutic purposes'. (See, eg, *Re E (A Minor) (Medical Treatment)* [1991] 2 FLR 585 at 586; *Re GF (A Patient)* [1991] FCR 786 at 787–788.) the second is that the common law does not, as a matter of principle, draw a general distinction between 'therapeutic' and 'non-therapeutic' surgery for the purposes of parental authority. (See, eg, per Lord Hailsham of St Marylebone LC, *In Re B (A Minor)* [1988] AC, at 203–204.) ...

... [T]here are circumstances in which it is plain that, according to the general standards of our society, surgery involving sterilisation of an incapable child for reasons other than the conventional medical ones of preventing death or treating or preventing physical illness is or is not clearly in the interests of the welfare of the child. The New Zealand case of *Re X* [1991] 2 NZLR 365 provides a convenient example of circumstances in which such surgery is plainly in the interests of the welfare of an incapable child.

The judgment in *Re X* was delivered on X's 15th birthday. She was a profoundly multi-handicapped girl with the intellectual capacity (other than as regards gross motor skills such as walking) of a three to eight-month-old infant. She could not speak, was not toilet-trained despite intensive efforts by both her family and the staff of the special school which she attended, had no 'control whatever over her bodily functions' (at 367) was, and would obviously remain, quite incapable of understanding human relations, sex or human procreation. This lack of understanding and her inability to express herself meant that the only indications that she gave when sustaining pain were non-specific reactions which included fits of irritability capable of lasting for an entire day and involved threatening conduct and violence towards others and a degree of self-mutilation.

The onset of menstruation was imminent and the overall evidence, both lay and medical, led inevitably to the conclusion that the child's reaction to menstrual pain would be uncomprehending irritability involving likely violence and some self-mutilation. X's parents, who were unusually knowledgeable about retarded children and heroically devoted to X and her interests, were convinced that she could not cope either with menstrual periods or with the associated hygienic problems. The trial judge, Hillyer J, summarised (at 368) their approach, with which he agreed, as follows:

> X's parents believe there is very little point in her having monthly periods for the next 30 years. She has a very strong heart and is likely to live that long. She will never be able to have children, and that function in her life is quite unnecessary. They believe X goes through enough pain and agony without having to deal with monthly periods as well. She has had to have operations to cure club feet and to straighten her back. She came through these well, and in hospital was given pain relief mainly by suppositories because of the difficulty in getting her to swallow anything, let alone giving her injections. The mother says X is hopeless with medicines. She will not let other people touch her or put anything in her mouth except food.

In circumstances where there was no prospect of any significant improvement in X's condition as she grew older it was obvious – as Hillyer J found (at 367) – that it was 'absolutely vital' that 'she should not become pregnant' since she 'most certainly could not cope with motherhood, pregnancy or labour' and the 'only way she could become pregnant would be by being raped, because she is unable under any circumstances to consent'. The application by X's parents for an order consenting to a hysterectomy operation upon X was supported by medical evidence that the surgery was desirable and that there was no less drastic treatment which would, in the circumstances, be appropriate. Hillyer J held that the High Court of New Zealand had jurisdiction to make such an order under its residual parens patriae jurisdiction (see, generally, per Cooke J, *Pallin v Department of Social Welfare* [1983] NZLR 266 at 272), and that, in the circumstances of the case, such an order should be made. His Honour made clear ([1991] 2 NZLR, at 369) that he saw the purpose of the operation as not sterilisation but the prevention of menstruation. That being so, the importance of his Honour's conclusion that it was 'absolutely vital' that X should never become pregnant was that it turned what would, in the case of a normal child, have probably been a decisive countervailing consideration into a supporting factor.

As I have indicated, the reason for my referring at length to the facts of *Re X* is that the case provides an example of circumstances in which it is quite clear that surgery involving irreversible sterilisation for other than conventional medical purposes in necessary for the welfare of an incapable child. Once it is recognised that parental authority to authorise medical treatment extends, in some circumstances, to the authorisation of surgery involving irreversible sterilisation (eg for the treatment of serious illness), there is no basis in legal principle for excluding from the scope of that parental authority circumstances such as those involved in *Re X*. Certainly it cannot be said that such surgery for the treatment of a serious illness, in a case where it involves the sterilisation of a mentally normal child, is more obviously for the overall welfare of the child than surgery involving irreversible sterilisation in a case such as *Re X* where there are, from the point of view of the child's interests and welfare, compelling physical and social reasons for such surgery and where there is no significant countervailing detriment. It is true that there is a passage in the judgment of La Forest J in *Re Eve* (see (1986) 31 DLR (4th) at 32) which, if read in isolation, suggests that the Supreme Court of

Canada accepted the proposition that it can never be safely concluded that 'non-therapeutic sterilisation' is for the benefit of a person incapable of consenting to it. *Re Eve* was, however, a case involving the suggested sterilisation for contraceptive purposes of an intellectually disabled woman of whom it was said (at 9) that 'there is no evidence that giving birth would be more difficult for Eve than for any other woman'. The circumstances of the case were simply not comparable to a case such as *Re X* and it seems to me to be quite clear that the references to 'non-therapeutic sterilisation' in the judgment of La Forest J should not be understood as intended to cover a case where what is involved is surgery upon a profoundly mentally disabled girl to prevent extraordinary difficulty, discomfort and pain which would accompany menstruation. (See, in particular, La Forest J's comments (ibid, at 22) about *Re K and Public Trustee* (1985) 19 DLR (4th) 255; and see, also, the use of the phrases 'therapeutic reasons' and 'therapeutic purposes' in *Re E (A Minor) (Medical Treatment)* [1991] 2 FLR, at 586 and *Re GF (A Patient)* [1991] FCR, at 787.) Be that as it may, I respectfully agree with Lord Bridge of Harwich (*In Re B (A Minor)* [1988] AC, at 205) that:

> To say that the court can never authorise sterilisation of a ward as being in her best interests would be patently wrong. To say that it can only do so if the operation is 'therapeutic' as opposed to 'non-therapeutic' is to divert attention from the true issue, which is whether the operation is in the ward's best interests, and remove it to an area of arid semantic debate as to where the line is to be drawn between 'therapeutic' and 'non-therapeutic' treatment.

Nor can such a confinement of the authority of parents be justified by reason of the gravity of irreversible sterilisation since, as has also been seen, it is plainly within the authority of parents to authorise surgery involving irreversible sterilisation in at least some circumstances. Indeed, the consequences of surgery involving irreversible sterilisation are immeasurably less grave in a case, such as *Re X*, where it is meaningless to speak of the fundamental right to procreate than they are in the case of such surgery upon an intellectually normal child for conventional medical purposes.

On the other hand, the requirement that parental authority to authorise surgery be exercised for the purpose, and only for the purpose, of advancing the welfare of the child necessarily excludes from the scope of that authority some categories of case involving the surgical sterilisation of an incapable child for other than conventional medical purposes. The most obvious example of such a category of case is surgery for so-called 'eugenic' purposes. Whatever may have been the approach accepted in other times and in other places, surgery upon a retarded person cannot, within the limits imposed by general community standards in this country, be justified by eugenic or 'public welfare' reasons such as those advanced by Holmes J in *Buck v Bell* (1927) 274 US 200 at 207. Nor can such surgery upon a mentally retarded child be justified as necessary for the welfare of the child *merely* because it will make easier the task of those responsible for the child's protection and care. That is not, of course, to deny that the easing of the burden of protecting and caring for an incapable child may, in most cases, be also at least indirectly in the interests of the welfare of the child.

Between the extreme categories of cases, where surgery involving irreversible sterilisation plainly can and plainly cannot be justified as necessary for the welfare of an incapable child are other cases in which there may be room for legitimate differences of opinion about what promotes the welfare of an incapable child in the circumstances of a particular case. Within that area, the welfare principle embodied in the common law propositions stated earlier operates at two levels to define the extent of parental authority. If the circumstances of a particular case are such that surgery involving irreversible sterilisation can reasonably be seen, according to general community standards, as being necessary for the welfare of the particular child, it will lie within the scope of parental authority to authorise it. That parental authority is, however, confined to the authorisation of what the parents, after due inquiry and adequate consideration, consider to be in the interests of the welfare of the child.

In what has been written above, I have already identified the two principal categories of case in which surgery involving irreversible sterilisation of an incapable child is, according to general community standards, obviously necessary for the welfare of the child. The first is where such surgery is immediately necessary for conventional medical purposes, that is to say, the preservation of life or the treatment or prevention of grave physical illness.

The second category is that of which *Re X* constitutes an example. (See, also, *Re E (A Minor) (Medical Treatment)* [1991] 2 FLR 585; *Re GF (A Patient)* [1991] FCR 786.) A case will fall into this category if, but only if, it involves surgery upon a girl and the following conditions are all clearly and convincingly satisfied. (See the discussion of standard of proof in *Re K and Public Trustee* (1985) 19 DLR (4th), at 268–272; and the implicit approval of the 'clear and convincing' standard in *Re Jane* (1988) 94 FLR, at 20–21.) First the child is so profoundly intellectually disabled that she is not and never will be capable of being a party to a mature human relationship involving informed sexual intercourse, of responsible procreation or of caring for an infant. Second, the surgery must be necessary to avoid grave and unusual problems and suffering which are or would be involved in menstruation which has either commenced or which is virtually certain to commence in the near future. These problems could arise from inability to comprehend or cope with pain; a phobic aversion to blood; a complete inability to cope with problems of hygiene with psychiatric or psychological consequences; or any of a variety of other possible complications. The problems or suffering which would result from menstruation must be such that it is plain that, according to general community standards, it would be quite unfair for the child and ultimate adult to be required to bear the additional burden of them. Third, the surgery must be a treatment of last resort in the sense that no alternative and less drastic treatment would be appropriate and effective. I would expect that the second and third requirements could not be satisfied in many cases until menstruation had actually commenced. Fourth, there must be competent medical advice from a multidisciplinary team, acting on the basis of appropriate paediatric, social and domestic reports, that the above conditions are all satisfied. When parents have received such multidisciplinary advice, they will have discharged the obligation of due inquiry and adequate consideration and will be justified in authorising the particular surgery.

The question arises whether there are any other categories of case in which surgery involving irreversible sterilisation of an incapable child can be said to be obviously necessary for the welfare of the child. On balance, it seems to me that there are not. Like Hillyer J in *Re X* [1991] 2 NZLR, at 369–370, Anderson JA in *Re K and Public Trustee* (1985) 19 DLR (4th), at 274–275 and Brown P in *Re E (A Minor) (Medical Treatment)* [1991] 2 FLR, at 586, I would draw a distinction between the category of case (see above) in which the primary purpose of the surgery is to prevent pain and extraordinary behavioural and personal problems which are, in the circumstances of a particular case, involved in menstruation and the case where the purpose of the operation is sterilisation for contraceptive purposes. Notwithstanding the views expressed by the Supreme Court of Canada in *Re Eve* (1986) 31 DLR (4th), esp at 32, it appears to me that there may well be circumstances in which surgery involving sterilisation of a profoundly intellectually disabled child for contraceptive purposes may, in the circumstances of a particular case, be necessary for the welfare of the child. I am not, however, persuaded that sterilisation for contraceptive purposes could ever be said to be so obviously necessary for the welfare of an incapable child that parents would be justified in dispensing with the impartial and independent advice of a court or other statutory tribunal which has the capacity to deliver an authoritative and binding opinion on the question.

The judges of the Family Court have, in earlier cases and in the present case, made evident their appreciation of the multiplicity of factors which may be relevant to the question whether parents would be justified in authorising surgery involving irreversible sterilisation in the circumstances of a particular case. A list of a number of those factors is set out near the end of the thoughtful and helpful judgment of Hillyer J in *Re X* [1991] 2 NZLR, at 376–378. His Honour, in my view correctly, places at the forefront of those factors the need to identify the child's level of functioning and development and to consider whether there is any real likelihood of a significant increase in the child's capabilities in the future. The importance of those two aspects cannot be over-emphasised. In dealing with them, a court must be vigilant against the danger of making false and adverse assumptions about the ability of an intellectually disabled person to become a party to a mature human relationship involving informed sexual relations, to engage in responsible procreation and to care for an infant. A court must also be vigilant against the danger of discounting the possibility of significant future improvement in the capabilities of an intellectually disabled person with regard to those matters. Indeed, unless the case is one in which there is no real likelihood that the child in question will ever be able to make a responsible decision for herself or himself about surgery involving irreversible sterilisation, it is difficult to envisage circumstances in which a court would be justified in pre-empting that decision in a case where such surgery was not at that time necessary for compelling medical or quasi-medical (eg the near certainty of trauma or psychological damage) reasons.

The material before the Court in the present case does not establish that the case falls within either of the categories of case (conventional medical reasons or the *Re X* type of case) in which it can be said that surgery involving sterilisation of an incapable girl is obviously justified in the interests of the child's welfare. On the other hand, the material before the Court does not seem to me to preclude the possibility that the present case does fall within the second of those categories.

McHugh J: [A] parent has authority to consent to the sterilisation of a child in his or her custody if it will advance or protect the welfare of the child. What is in the best interests of the child is conventionally seen as being synonymous with the welfare of the child. To say that a medical or surgical procedure is in the best interests of a child, however, is merely to record a result. Before the best interests of the child can be determined, some principle, rule or standard must be applied to the facts and circumstances of the case (cf Kennedy, 'Patients, Doctors, and Human Rights', Blackburn and Taylor (eds), *Human Rights for the 1990s* (1991), pp 90–91).

Since sterilisation has grave consequences for a person's adult life, it cannot be in the best interests of a child to pre-empt a choice about that procedure which the child would otherwise have as an adult person. If there is any real possibility that, at some future time, the child will acquire the capacity and maturity to choose whether he or she should be sterilised, the carrying out of that procedure cannot be in the best interests of the child unless, of course, protection of the child's health urgently requires that the procedure be carried out during incompetency. However, it must not be assumed that, simply because the child is intellectually disabled, he or she does not have or cannot acquire the capacity to consent to sterilisation. Intellectually disabled persons will frequently have the capacity to make the choice as to whether they should be sterilised (Committee on Rights of Persons with Handicaps (SA), *The Law and Persons with Handicaps*, vol 2: *Intellectual Handicaps* (1981), p 125). Furthermore, sterilisation involves invasive procedures resulting in the permanent deprivation of a person's right or liberty to reproduce, with the potentiality for psychological harm including the lowering – perhaps the destruction – of self-esteem and, in the case of the intellectually disabled, the reinforcement of anxieties which are commonly the result of intellectual disability. (See Law Reform Commission of Canada (Working Paper No 24 1979), *Sterilization: Implications for Mentally Retarded and Mentally Ill Persons*, pp 49–52.)

So grave are the certain and potential effects of sterilisation that that procedure can only be for the welfare of the child if the circumstances are so compelling and so likely to endure that they justify the invasive surgery or procedure involved in sterilisation. The circumstances may be compelling if the failure to carry out the procedure is likely to result in the child's physical or mental health being seriously jeopardised or if it is likely to result in the suffering of pain, fear or discomfort of such severity and duration or regularity that it is not reasonable to expect the child to suffer that pain, fear or discomfort. In these cases, the right of the incompetent person to have his or her body protected against invasive procedures resulting in removal or destruction of reproductive organs is outweighed by the necessity for appropriate 'treatment'. The circumstances may also be compelling if the failure to carry out the procedure is likely to result in a real risk that an intellectually disabled child will become pregnant and she does not, and never will, have any real understanding of sexual relationships or pregnancy. In such a case, to speak of a fundamental right of reproduction is meaningless. The human dignity of an intellectually disabled child is not advanced, and indeed is denied, by allowing her (by, what is in point of law, rape) to become pregnant and to give birth in circumstances which she cannot understand and which may result in a frightening ordeal for her not only at the time of birth, but for many months prior thereto.

What constitutes sufficiently compelling circumstances to justify sterilisation will have to be worked out on a case by case basis. But, unless the case falls within one of the above categories or a category analogous thereto, it should be held that the sterilisation of a child is not for his or her welfare. In particular, it is not for the welfare of an intellectually disabled child to sterilise that child merely to avoid pregnancy or to give effect to eugenic policies. Nor is it for the welfare of the child to sterilise her merely because of the hygiene problems associated with menstruation. At the Law Reform Commission of Canada has pointed out, intellectually disabled females who require a great deal of assistance in managing their menstruation are already likely to require assistance with urinary and faecal control, problems which are much more troublesome in terms of personal hygiene (at 34). Moreover, even if the case falls within one of the three categories which I have mentioned or an analogous category, it is not in the best interests of a child to sterilise him or her if the harm can reasonably be avoided by means less drastic than sterilisation.

Furthermore, as I have indicated, sterilisation is one area where the potential for conflict between the parent's interests and the child's interest exists. As Justice Horowitz pointed out in *Matter of Guardianship of Hayes* (1980) Wash 608 P 2d 635 at 640:

> unlike the situation of a normal and necessary medical procedure, in the question of sterilisation the interests of the parent of a retarded person cannot be presumed to be identical to those of the child.

Thus, parents may see sterilisation as relieving them of the worry and distress of the child becoming pregnant or of the burden of caring for a grandchild whom the child would not be able or fully able to care for. If a decision to consent is actuated by interests such as these, a conflict of interest arises. In such a case, the parents have no authority to consent to the sterilisation of their child. However, since parents have authority to consent to a sterilisation procedure only in cases where the grounds for the procedure are compelling it is unlikely that, in practice, conflict will arise. If it does, a court of general jurisdiction invested with the parens patriae jurisdiction or the Family Court may give consent in substitution for the parents.

The principles which apply to the sterilisation of children, as I have adumbrated them, fall somewhere between the approach of the Supreme Court of Canada in *Re Eve (E(Mrs) v Eve ('Re Eve')* [1986] 2 SCR 388; 31 DLR (4th) 1) and the approach of the House of Lords in *In Re F. In Re Eve*, the Supreme Court held that, in the exercise of the parens patriae jurisdiction, a court should not give consent to a non-therapeutic sterilisation. The distinction between therapeutic and non-therapeutic treatment was strongly criticised by members of the House of Lords in *In Re B (A Minor)* [1988] AC 199 at 203–294, 205. I agree with Professor Kennedy, in the article to which I have earlier referred, where he said (Kennedy, op cit, p 102) that, although 'there are problems at the edges' of the two concepts, '[a]n intervention is therapeutic if treatment (therapy) is intended thereby'. This definition would include the first two categories of justification to which I have referred but exclude the third category. However, for the reasons that I have already given, I think that, where the child has no real understanding of sexual relationships or pregnancy, sterilisation may be justified if no method of contraception is reasonably feasible. In that respect, I would go beyond the approach of the Supreme Court in *Re Eve*. Moreover, it would be inconsistent with the historical development of common law principles to close the categories to which they apply. Consequently, unlike the Supreme Court of Canada, I would hold that sterilisation may also be carried out for the purposes which are analogous to the three categories to which I have referred. Such an approach allows the law to develop incrementally, guided by the overarching principle that the circumstances must be so compelling that they justify such an invasive procedure as sterilisation.

In *In Re F*, the House of Lords held that sterilisation of an incompetent child was justified if it was necessary or in the public interest and that it would be in the public interest if the procedure was in the best interests of the child. Their Lordships held that it will be in the best interests of the patient if a doctor has formed the opinion that sterilisation should be carried out provided that that opinion corresponds with a respectable body of medical opinion among those experienced in the field. Their Lordships (Lord Griffith dissenting on this point) held that the involvement of a court was highly desirable as a matter of good practice although it was not necessary as a matter of law. The approach of their Lordships goes well beyond what I consider is the proper view of the common law, even when the decision to sterilise is ultimately made by a court.

In effect, the approach of their Lordships transfers the issue to the medical profession for determination. As Professor Kennedy points out (at pp 89–90, 91, 98), once the doctors approve the procedure, the court gives its consent to the procedure on the basis of what the doctors and social workers 'regard as important or significant'. In substance, as Professor Kennedy asserts (at p 90):

> The courts will be presented with a fait accompli. Those who wish to challenge it will have what amounts to a near impossible task. They will have to persuade the court to reject, wholly or in part, the evidence of the 'experts', evidence that is often unanimous and which has all the trappings of expertise. It will be too late to argue that the answers may be wrong because the questions were wrong.

Whatever may be the position in England, the approach of their Lordships is not consistent with the common law of Australia.

(Subsequently, the Family Court authorised Marion's sterilisation as being in her interests: *Re Marion (No 2)* [1994] FLC 92–448 (Fam Ct Aust). For further Australian case law, see: *P v P* (1994) 120 ALR 545 (Aust H Ct) and Commentary (1995) 3 Med L Rev 97(IK); *L and GM v MM* [1994] FLC 668 (Fam Ct Aust) discussed *infra*, p 1193.)

The decision of the Australian High Court is instructive for two reasons. *First*, whatever the merits of the position adopted by the majority or by the other judges, at least the court shows its hand. The majority state expressly what factors and values they regard as important, as do the judges in the minority. If it does nothing else this provides the basis for an informed debate on what is clearly an issue which, it may be thought, has been resolved for the present in the UK but which may attract Parliamentary attention in the future. *Secondly*, the variety of judgments and the significant differences in the analysis adopted illustrate how complex and troubling is the question of sterilising incompetent patients. This also prompts the inquiry whether a court is the proper arbiter of the issue or whether it should be a matter for Parliament.

The Australian High Court's decision is a most significant one. It is particularly of interest because of the judges' use of language – that of human rights. It is, of course, an approach rejected by the House of Lords in *Re B* and one which does not surface in *Re F*. In the light of the Human Rights Act 1998, it is crucial to see how 'rights talk' may cause the English courts to re-evaluate *Re F* and (what we will see to be) its progeny. In particular, art 8's protection of an individual's 'right to privacy' may be engaged when their 'personal integrity' is violated and art 12, conferring the right to 'found a family', may be implicated. It is even conceivable that the prohibition on 'inhuman or degrading treatment' in art 3 will be prayed in aid. The extent to which these rights may be negated and how the courts will accommodate the perceived need to protect incapable girls and women from harm will be at the heart of the human rights argument. No doubt English courts will be reluctant to change their position given their perception of the latter. The Australian High Court's approach is discussed in the following paper by Natasha Cica.

Natasha Cica 'Sterilising the Intellectually Disabled' (1993) 1 Med L Rev 186

… [The] extensive theoretical and practical weaknesses of the 'best interests' test lead to its wholesale rejection by Brennan J in *Department of Health v JWB and SMB*. He argued that application of the 'best interests' test requires the decision-maker to balance 'the risks of what may appear to be likely social tragedies' against 'the physical invasion, incapacitation and mental and emotional impact of sterilisation' ((1992) 66 ALJR 300 at 322). In his opinion such a balancing exercise is impossible to perform, because the values on either side of the balance cannot be compared. Brennan J stated that priority must always be given to the intellectually disabled person's 'right to physical integrity and the human dignity it protects', regardless of the burdens this places upon carers and ultimately the State. (*Ibid*.) He argued that any legal rule which does not ensure the protection of the human dignity of the intellectually disabled should be rejected. He saw the 'best interests' text as such a rule. He claimed it 'provides an insubstantial protection of the human dignity of children; it wraps no cloak of protective principle around the intellectually disabled child' (*ibid*, at 320). For Brennan J the only protective principle which was adequate was that enunciated by La Forest J in *Re Eve*: that it is never lawful to authorise the performance of a non-therapeutic sterilisation upon an intellectually disabled person (*ibid*, at 320 and 323). For Brennan J this blanket prohibition was necessary to safeguard the human rights of a particularly weak and powerless group of people (*ibid*, at 322).

The human right in question was said to be the right to 'integrity of the person'. Brennan J traced common law recognition of this right to Blackstone's declaration that every person has the absolute right to personal security, 'every man's [*sic*] person being sacred, and no other having a right to meddle with it, in any the slightest manner'. (*Ibid*, at 317.) Protection of the right to personal integrity is the underlying rationale of the crime and tort of battery: (*ibid*, at 317 per Brennan J and at 312 per Mason CJ, Dawson, Toohey and Gaudron JJ)

> The fundamental principle, plain and incontestable, is that every person's body is inviolate, it has long been established that any touching of another person, however slight, may amount to a battery … The breadth of the principle reflects the fundamental nature of the interest so protected. (*Collins v Wilcox* [1984] 3 All ER 374 at 378 per Robert Goff LJ.)

Brennan J stated that the value underlying and informing the common law is therefore that 'each person has a unique dignity which the law respects and which it will protect' ((1992) 66 ALJR 300 at 317). Not only was this an important principle at common law, it had been recognised in numerous international human rights instruments (*ibid*, at 318). Both the common law and international law were said to admit of no discrimination against the weak and disadvantaged, including the intellectually disabled, in protection of their human dignity (*ibid*). Involuntary sterilisation was said to involve a substantial invasion of a person's physical integrity, affecting not only her body but also her mind and self-perception. Respect for the human dignity of the intellectually disabled child therefore demanded that sterilisation only be permitted if there was 'justification of a compelling kind' ((1992) 66 ALJR 300 at 319–19). For Brennan J such justification only existed if the procedure was therapeutic in nature.

The language of human rights was also used by Mason CJ, Dawson, Toohey and Gaudron JJ. They expressed concern at the particular vulnerability of intellectually disabled children and at the likelihood of (intentional or unintentional) abuse of their rights (*ibid*, at 312). Like Brennan J, they stated the need to protect 'a fundamental right to personal inviolability existing in the common law' (*ibid*). They wished to make it clear that their conclusions were not based upon recognition of a fundamental common law right to *reproduce*. Although they left open the question of whether such a right exists, they expressed doubts as to the usefulness of a notion of a basic, absolute right to reproduce which is independent of the right to personal inviolability. They stated that if the so-called right to reproduce comprises either a right not to be prevented from being biologically capable of reproducing, or a right to do with one's person what one chooses, that right is simply an aspect of the right to bodily and personal integrity.

Despite their recognition of the important human rights dimension of this issue, Mason CJ, Dawson, Toohey and Gaudron JJ did not reject the 'best interests' test. It was their opinion that the right to personal inviolability would be adequately protected by the requirement of mandatory court involvement. They admitted that the phrase 'best interests' is imprecise. They emphasised, however, that the requirement that sterilisation only be performed as 'a step of last resort' would narrowly confine the scope of lawful non-therapeutic sterilisations ((1992) 66 ALJR 300 at 315. Recall that the House of Lords in *Re B* similarly stated that sterilisation must be viewed as 'a step of last resort'.) These judges also emphasised that non-therapeutic sterilisation would only be in the 'best interests' of an intellectually disabled child if sterilisation was 'necessary to enable her to lead a life in keeping with her needs and capacities' (*ibid*). They did not specify exactly which needs and capacities, nor exactly whose perception of a life 'in keeping' with those needs and capacities was to guide the judge in each case. Indeed they stated that it was impossible to formulate a rule to identify cases in which sterilisation would be in the 'best interests' of an intellectually disabled child (*Ibid*). They were nonetheless confident that

> within the range of expertise available to them, judges will develop guidelines to give further content to the phrase 'best interests of the child' in responding to the situations with which they will have to deal. (*Ibid.*)

The remaining two High Court judges also adopted the 'best interests' test. Deane J stated that sterilisation of an intellectually disabled child will only be lawful if it is necessary for the welfare of that child (*ibid*, at 335 and 330). He claimed that 'there may well be circumstances' in which sterilisation of a profoundly intellectually disabled child for contraceptive purposes may be considered to be necessary for that child's welfare (*ibid*, at 335). He neither specified those circumstances nor gave any guidance as to how the decision-maker (the court) should determine whether those circumstances existed. By comparison, McHugh J did attempt to provide criteria to guide the decision-maker (the parent(s)). He also stated that parents may only authorise sterilisation if it will advance or protect the welfare of the child. He acknowledged that to say something is in a child's welfare or her 'best interests' is 'merely to record a result' (*ibid*, at 341). He argued that this problem must be overcome by the development of objective standards, to promote certainty and consistency in decision-making (*ibid*). McHugh J suggested an overarching principle: that sterilisation should only be authorised in circumstances 'so compelling and so likely to endure' that sterilisation may be justified (*ibid*, at 342). He also articulated a number of criteria to guide parental decision-making. He also clearly described the type of case in which non-therapeutic sterilisation would be justified. This was his third category of permissible sterilisations: cases where failure to perform the procedure 'is likely to result in a real risk that an intellectually disabled child will become pregnant' and where 'she does not, and never will, have any real understanding of sexual relationships or pregnancy' (*ibid*, at 342).

With respect, it is difficult to share the confidence of these six members of the High Court that their versions of the 'best interests' test guarantee that unjustifiable non-therapeutic sterilisations will not be performed upon intellectually disabled people. Admittedly the approaches of McHugh J and of Mason CJ, Dawson, Toohey and Gaudron JJ represented an improvement upon those of the House of Lords in *Re B* and *Re F*, insofar as the Australian judges acknowledged that the words 'best interests' mean nothing without principles or criteria to guide their application. Despite this, none of the six advocates of the 'best interests' test produced adequate criteria. Mason CJ, Dawson, Toohey and Gaudron JJ left the task of developing detailed guidelines to be worked out in the future by judges on a case-by-case basis. Deane J provided no guidance. McHugh J did outline a more principled scheme to guide parental decision-making; but unfortunately his principles displayed an inadequate commitment to human rights. Given that Mason CJ, Dawson, Toohey and Gaudron JJ (and of course Brennan J) characterised the sterilisation issue as one involving human rights, this shortcoming should not be overlooked. The problem lies in McHugh J's statement that non-therapeutic sterilisation of an intellectually disabled child will be permissible if there is a real risk of pregnancy and she does not and never will have *any real understanding* of sexual relationships and pregnancy. This comes dangerously close to asserting that a person only has human rights, or that her human rights only deserve respect, insofar as she has a 'real understanding' of those rights (see also *Re B* [1988] AC 199 at 203 per Lord Hailsham). This in turn suggests an approach in which human rights give way to 'practicalities', In *Re W* ([1993] 1 FLR 381). Hollis J stated that '[n]o-one in this case has suggested any practical reason why such an operation – that is, sterilisation – would be to W's detriment'. Yet surely the role of human rights is to ensure that the weak are protected at all times, regardless of whether or not it is 'practical' to do so. And surely the weak are *most* in need of protection when it is most inconvenient and impractical to assert their human rights. Brennan J countered the argument that a human rights-based approach to sterilisation is too 'idealistic' and 'out of touch with contemporary community standards' as follows:

> There is much force in that criticism but this is an area of the law in which it is necessary to guard against the tyranny which majority opinion may impose on a weak and voiceless minority. The history of intellectually disabled people contains a surfeit of examples of degrading treatment administered under laws which reflected the standards of the time – standards which were a reproach to the civilisation then enjoyed. If equality under the law, human rights and the protection of minorities are more than the incantations of legal rhetoric, it is in this area of the law that they have real work to do ((1992) 66 ALJR 300 at 322–3) ...

The subsequent Australian Family Court case of *L and GM v MM* (1994) FLC 92–449 is of particular interest since the judge, in dismissing the application to perform a hysterectomy upon a 17-year-old physically and intellectually disabled girl, shows how a court may (and we would say should) approach the issue of risk of pregnancy and the dangers of sexual abuse. As we shall see later, English courts have just begun to grapple with this.

L and GM v MM; *The Director-General, Department of Family Services and Aboriginal and Islander Affairs* (1994) FLC 92 (Aust Fam Ct)

This was an application by parents for authorisation to consent to the performance of an abdominal hysterectomy upon their 17-year-old physically disabled and intellectually handicapped child, Sarah.

Sarah lived in a disabled persons' ward in a country hospital and was dependent on health care providers for her daily needs. She was unable to communicate and could not walk without the assistance of at least one other person. She could not operate her wheelchair. Her condition would not improve and might be expected to deteriorate. She began to menstruate in 1991. It was possible that at some time in the future she might be accommodated outside the hospital system.

The parents argued that hysterectomy was necessary to assist in maintaining hygiene, to control Sarah's epilepsy and to prevent pregnancy. They placed strong reliance on their wishes and the 'weight' to which those wishes were entitled.

Warnick J:

... The evidence in particular

Much of the evidence was common ground, though, as just noted, difference of opinion did exist in some significant areas. Where I have made findings of fact it is either because those facts were common ground or I have preferred one view to another, without necessarily, in every instance, discussing the reasons for that preference.

The contentions and evidence as to the benefits and detriments of the operation for Sarah can be categorised and discussed as follows.

Hygiene

Menstrual blood is a sterile solution. Given Sarah's double incontinence, the addition for a period of days every four or five weeks of menstrual discharge is of no significance to the risks of infection of Sarah.

There is evidence that on a couple of recorded occasions Sarah has removed the additional padding with which she is provided during menstruation and discarded this on the floor. It was suggested that some other occasions of such conduct may not have been recorded. On the evidence, I am satisfied that such is the degree of supervision of Sarah and others in the ward where she currently resides or to be expected of Sarah in other residences, if she moves into residential accommodation, that no real risk of infection to Sarah or others arises from this occasional conduct by her.

Further, I am not satisfied that all means of potentially controlling this intermittent conduct by Sarah have been explored. She has never been observed to remove the padding at school, where she spends a great amount of her time. Ms C, an occupational therapist, suggests that much can be done by the choice of clothing to prevent Sarah having access to the passing.

I am satisfied that any improvement to Sarah's hygiene arising from the proposed procedure would be of the most minor nature.

Proposed move to residential accommodation

Any views that Sarah's menstruation would have to be controlled or stopped or that she would need to be self-sufficient with regard to her hygiene during menstruation, before she could move to residential accommodation, have been entirely dispelled by the evidence of Ms T.

Risk of sexual abuse

Sarah's condition is such that she could not provide knowing consent to sexual contact. Ms C's researches have disclosed that most of the research into pregnancy in, and sexual abuse of, intellectually disabled persons has been in respect of groups other than persons in need of high support and supervision. It is difficult to gauge the magnitude of risk, but there is evidence from Ms T to suggest that such risk is minor. Ms C refers to a consideration, which it does not require expertise to recognise, that is, the proposition that sexual abuse would, if it occurred, be more likely to be perpetrated by a carer than a non-carer and may be more likely by carers, if there was a knowledge that Sarah could not conceive. Speculation as to the workings of an abuser's mind may be an especially hazardous business, but it does seem reasonable to observe that there is certainly no correlation between sterilisation and removal of the *risk* of abuse, as distinct from *one potential consequence*.

Pregnancy

It is considered that Sarah could not possibly understand the connection between intercourse and pregnancy, would almost certainly have no understanding of the biological changes in her arising from pregnancy and would probably not understand the process of birth and even a connection between her pregnancy and any child born.

Pregnancy does carry with it the possibility of difficulties controlling epileptic seizures, which possibilities are later discussed.

During consideration of this matter, I became concerned to know what the medical response would likely be, if Sarah fell pregnant. I informed the parties of this concern. Some further evidence has been placed before me as a result, but it really provides no further information about the likely medical response to such a development.

The parents say that they do not believe in abortion and would not make an application to the court. Dr Py has provided a report about the methods and consequences of termination of pregnancy. He has also declared his personal position to be that he does not perform termination. He says:

A pregnancy would be a traumatic event in Sarah's life, but termination of pregnancy would be an added assault on her body and psyche which I would never support.

Dr Py is the practitioner who would perform the sterilisation operation, if authorised. The view of Dr Py that pregnancy would be a traumatic event for Sarah, does not accord with the medical evidence of her incapacity to understand her surroundings and her own body.

All concerned in this matter evidence horror at the prospect of a pregnancy for Sarah. It is the understandable and anticipated reaction from any humane and sensitive person. When analysed however, much of the horror seems likely to arise from the contemplation of the prospect of any male abusing a person in Sarah's circumstances, or perhaps more specifically, from the contemplation of pregnancy, as the evidence of such abuse. The point has already been noted, that sterilisation will not prevent abuse and may arguably increase the risk thereof.

Removal of risk of uterine and cervical pathology

It is thought that, given Sarah's inability to communicate, there is a risk that if pathological conditions did arise in her uterus or cervix, she might be unable to inform her carers of symptoms. There was no evidence directed to the risks of pathological conditions developing, if the operation is not carried out, nor to the magnitude of advantage to a patient, in obtaining treatment, represented by an ability to recognise and communicate symptoms, particularly in Sarah's circumstances where she is attended to regularly by trained personnel. The matter was referred to almost in passing, and in the circumstances, I consider that the advantages for Sarah's health, arising from this consideration, are minor and difficult of measurement, depending as they do on a number of hypothetical situations becoming reality.

I maintain this view, notwithstanding a reference by Dr A to Sarah's inability to communicate problems to her carers, as a significant factor. Dr A also regarded parental concern about pregnancy to be a significant factor, though he himself did not regard the possibility of pregnancy as important a consideration as questions of hygiene. Dr A's opinion is discussed in more detail later.

Epileptic seizures during menstruation
Some suggestions were made that Sarah experienced increased incidence of epileptic seizures during menstruation. Overall however, the evidence does not support a conclusion to this effect, and Dr P opined that the proposed procedure was not likely to decrease the incidence of epileptic fits.

Sarah's emotional state and pain about and during menstruation
Carers have observed Sarah's behaviour to change at these times. She seemed to become depressed, tearful and agitated. Insofar as these mood changes are not the result of pain experienced (and it is not known whether they are or not), they will not be improved by the removal of the uterus, as it is (unless caused by pain) the consequence of ovarian function, that such moods are experienced.

There are at least two causes of pain at this time. The removal of the uterus may diminish the pain but could not be considered likely to remove all pain, if in fact it is being experienced.

While it is not known if Sarah experiences pain, the hospital records note that on some occasions at and about the time of Sarah's menstruation, she has been given pain relievers and the behaviour or mood which was assumed to be due to pain, has improved.

On the evidence there is room for further consideration and exploration of the use of analgesics at the time of Sarah's menstruation.

The position of Sarah's carers
I might be said (without any reflection on Sarah's carers, but merely in recognition of the limits of humankind) that the easier Sarah is to care for, the better care she is likely to receive. There is, however, no evidence that this would be so, and indeed, there is evidence that menstruation adds an insignificant burden for those involved in her care. She already attends school, participates in the family link program and is not prevented by menstruation and the difficulties associated therewith from entering residential accommodation. There is no evidence then, that her quality of life will be improved by way of expansion of the activities in which she might be involved, or by decreasing the burden on carers, upon the cessation of menstruation.

The parents' view
The parents bring their application, at least in part, in reliance upon views of responsible professions. They are obviously particularly concerned by the prospect of Sarah falling pregnant. Their views are readily understandable and deserving of respect. The parents see Sarah about four times a year.

Whether the view of the parents is entitled to special weight in the court's deliberations is discussed later.

Risks of operation
These were primarily referred to in the evidence of Dr Py, the Director of Medical Services at the hospital. They involve the risk of infection and of damage to other bodily parts during the operative procedure. I did not take it from Dr Py's evidence that the risks were other than what might be described as usual risks of any operative procedure, though they could not be described as of no significance.

Alternative procedures to prevent menstruation
In some cases, suppressant drugs can be used to prevent menstruation. The use of such drugs is not an alternative for Sarah because it would interfere with the effectiveness of the anti-convulsants prescribed for her ...

Summary of benefits/detriments

Benefits:
　(i) A minor or insignificant, if any, improvement in hygiene.
　(ii) A risk of pregnancy avoided. However with regard to this risk I consider there are good safeguards against the possibility of pregnancy. Pregnancy is not, of itself, to be considered necessarily harmful to Sarah, save for the possible interference with the operation of the anti-convulsant drugs.
　(iii) Possible relief of some pain, but this benefit must be seen in light of the consideration that it is not known if Sarah suffers pain. It is unlikely that all pain would be removed and alternative means of pain relief may be successful.

(iv) Removal of the concern that the treatment of uterine or cervical pathology may be impeded by Sarah's inability to communicate. This series of sequential 'possibilities' does not amount to a significant concern.

(v) The parents' wishes would be met.

Detriments:

(i) Risks of operation.

(ii) Long-term effects of removal of the uterus *may* be harmful ...

Conclusion

The proposed procedure will not with any certainty (subject to the removal of the risk of pregnancy) increase Sarah's capacity to enjoy life or meet a presently unmet need.

Expected improvement to hygiene, and lessening of the risks of infection are, in Sarah's circumstances of such a high degree of support and dependence anyway, minimal. Even then, in respect of pad removal, improvements in prevention can still be explored. The possibility that a uterine or cervical infection or disease might occur, and then escape detection because of Sarah's inability to communicate, was not convincingly explored and, I infer from the passing reference to it, has such a degree of remoteness, that the drastic step of sterilisation would not be justified to remove that possibility.

Sterilisation is unnecessary to enable Sarah to move to residential-style accommodation. It will not demonstrably improve the attitude towards Sarah of her carers.

Sterilisation will not improve Sarah's health. It may, but by no means certainly, decrease pain she may experience at times of menstruation, but alternative means of pain relief may also be successful.

Whether the parents' wishes are met or not, is not an event which will, of itself, impact on Sarah.

There are risks attached to the operation itself, though these are small. It is possible that removal of the uterus will produce harmful effects in the long term. Sterilisation may increase the risk of sexual abuse.

I am of the clear opinion that upon the factors considered thus far, sterilisation is not in Sarah's best interests.

I return to the factor which seems the primary consideration motivating this application, and which is, in my view, the most significant consideration, ie the removal of the risks of pregnancy. I make the following observation:

(i) It is probable, *but not certain*, that Sarah can become pregnant.

(ii) She could only become pregnant as a result of advantage being taken of her, that is, abuse.

(iii) There are substantial safeguards against the possibility of abuse.

(iv) The effect of pregnancy upon Sarah cannot be gauged with confidence, but she will not have any understanding of the condition.

(v) I do not know what the medical response to a pregnancy for Sarah would be. Termination remains, at least, a possibility.

(vi) If Sarah became pregnant and if the pregnancy was not terminated, there is a possibility of difficulty in managing Sarah's epilepsy.

(vii) There is a possibility (not previously discussed), of harm to the foetus, either from Sarah's medication or as a result of her seizures.

(viii) Sterilisation does not have to be done at this time, but can remain an option if circumstances change.

Thus pregnancy itself is a number of steps removed from probability. Possible consequences (other than the termination itself) are further distanced by the prospect of termination. Harm to Sarah arising from pregnancy is more removed again and harm to the foetus is yet more distant.

In strict logic, the prospect of harm to the foetus, in Sarah's circumstances, is probably not a matter bearing upon her best interests, and the issue should therefore be disregarded. If, compassionately, regard can be had to such matters, the prospect is so remote as not to be a significant consideration.

To make a decision in this case, in favour of sterilisation, would be virtually equivalent to establishing a policy that all females, with profound disabilities resembling those afflicting Sarah, should be sterilised. There is nothing substantial about the risk, nor clearly detrimental to Sarah about pregnancy, which justifies the interference with personal inviolability, unless it be that where there is any risk (as there must always be) sterilisation should occur.

I cannot think that such an approach is consistent with human dignity, the fundamental nature of the right to personal inviolability, and the responsibility of the capable for the incapable.

When the position is so put the 'negative premise' that the 'right to reproduce' is of no 'value' to Sarah does not 'counter-balance' the positive duty to ensure the protection of the fundamental right to personal inviolability. If from the procedure there were real benefits to capacity to enjoy life or to quality of life, then the fact that the right to reproduce was valueless would take on significance in the equation.

In *Re B (A Minor) (Wardship): Sterilisation* [1988] AC 199 Lord Oliver said (at 211):

... the right to reproduce is of value only if accompanied by the ability to make a choice.

In the same case Lord Hailsham (at p 204) said:

To talk of the 'basic right' to reproduce of an individual who is not capable of knowing the cause or connection between intercourse and childbirth, the nature of pregnancy, what is involved in delivery, unable to form material instincts or to care for a child appears to me wholly to part company with reality ...

It is to be noted that their Lordships were speaking of the 'right to reproduce' by which their Lordships might not have meant the same thing as 'the right to personal inviolability'.

If all their Lordships meant was that the capacity to reproduce was of no practical advantage to the incompetent person, I would not take exception. However, I would not, with respect, accept, if it was intended, that the degree of entitlement of an individual to a basic human right, such as the right to personal inviolability, varied according to the individual's level of understanding and appreciation of that right. This is distinct from the question of the readiness with which the right might be interfered with, if the capacity to enjoy or exercise it or an element of it, was missing, and positive benefits were clearly to be gained by the interference.

I note that Nicholson CJ, in *In re Jane* (supra) took a similar view of the attachment of rights to individuals, when considering the judgment of the Court of Appeal of British Columbia in *Re K and Public Trustee* [1985] 4 WWR 724. The Chief Justice said (at p 77, 257):

... It seems to me, with respect, that the child's rights were not removed by her lack of appreciation of them, although this factor was properly a matter for the Court to consider in determining whether the procedure was for the welfare of the child. ...

... I repeat that, in my view, it is important in addressing the prospect of a pregnancy, the thought of which immediately evokes a variety of emotions ranging from anger at the hypothetical abuser, to revulsion at the baseness of which we are capable, to separate the consequence from the cause. Much of the emotion is responsive to the contemplation of the abuse. The risk of that is not removed by sterilisation.

I am not satisfied, on the balance of probabilities, but to a firm degree on clear and convincing proof, that sterilisation is in Sarah's best interests. It follows that I intend to declare that the proposed procedure is not in Sarah's best interests ...

(For a discussion of the case, see Commentary (1995) 3 Med L Rev 94 (IK).)

4. England: the cases post *Re F*

In the meantime, given that the English courts must follow the law as established by the House of Lords, this will involve (as we have seen) the application of a less than precise criterion of 'best interests'. The consequences of this approach can already be seen from a series of first instance cases. Professor Margaret Brazier discusses two early decisions: *Re M (A Minor) (Wardship: Sterilisation)* [1988] 2 FLR 497 (Bush J) (tubal ligation) and *Re P (A Minor) (Wardship: Sterilisation)* [1989] 1 FLR 182 (Eastham J) (tubal ligation).

Margaret Brazier 'Sterilisation: Down the Slippery Slope?' (1990) 6 Professional Negligence 25

The judgments in *Re M* and *Re P* [requiring the authorisation of a judge] cast doubt on how effective the judicial safeguard has turned out to be. M was another seventeen-year-old girl with a mental age of five or six. Like Jeannette [in *Re B*], she appeared to have no maternal feelings. Two features of her case are pertinent. First, the gynaecologist who was intending to carry out the operation testified, and the judge placed great emphasis on his testimony, that with the improvements in tubal surgery there was a 50 to 75 per cent chance of successfully reversing sterilisation should M's condition ever improve. Second, there was said to be a 50 per cent chance any child born to M might suffer from some degree of mental retardation. Bush J stated very firmly that eugenic considerations were in themselves irrelevant but then did appear to take into account evidence that if M should become pregnant an abortion on the ground of foetal handicap might be recommended. And he was clearly influenced in his decision to authorise sterilisation by the evidence advanced of the operation's reversibility.

Perhaps, apart from a slight inference that eugenics banned from the front door is being let in at the back, the decision in *Re M* is little different from *Re B*. But *Re M* laid the foundation for the next and truly disturbing judgment of Eastham J in *Re P*. P was a seventeen-year-old of normal and attractive appearance who was said to have a mental age of six. In contrast to Jeannette, her communication skills were good, at least at the level of the average six-year-old. Her intellectual development would, it was thought, not improve although her social skills were advancing with care and training. She appeared to be vulnerable to seduction and seemed to have some maternal feelings. Her mother feared that if she became pregnant and understood what was happening she would refuse to agree to an abortion. Taking her child away from her at birth would be traumatic. It would be a disaster for her to have a child.

Eastham J authorised the sterilisation of P. He found that she might eventually attain the level of understanding needed for capacity to marry. He agreed that, as at present P regarded sexual intercourse as painful, there was no current risk of pregnancy. She was quite clearly a young woman with greater understanding of human relationships and maternity than B. The 'right' to reproduce, to bear a child and give birth appeared to be something P might well value. So what persuaded Eastham J to authorise an operation said just two years earlier to be a measure of 'last resort'? Three factors stand out as crucial to his decision: (1) he agreed with arguments advanced that P was vulnerable to exploitation by unscrupulous males; (2) he was concerned by evidence that if P gave birth and her child was taken from her that event would be traumatic and damaging for her; (3) and most importantly, the judge was impressed by the evidence of Professor Robert Winston that reversal of female sterilisation carried out by clips on the Fallopian tubes now has a 95 per cent success rate. On the basis of this evidence, his Lordship concluded that in 1989 sterilisation should no longer be regarded as the 'last resort' The House of Lords in *Re B* in 1987 had perceived female sterilisation as irreversible:

> The situation today is that the operation is not irreversible, although it is still current ethical practice to tell patients that it is an irreversible operation as part of the information to be given to them when they are giving consent for the operation to be carried out, although if such a patient changes her mind, no doubt it would be explained to her that the more serious reversal operation could be contemplated.

The judgment in *Re P* must cast doubt on the validity of criteria applied to the question of sterilising mentally handicapped girls. It is no doubt the case that Professor Winston, a world-renowned expert in tubal surgery, achieves a 95 per cent rate in sterilisation reversals. However, 50 to 75 per cent would be considered a good success rate by most competent gynaecologists. Can the possibility, even probability, of successful reversal justify no longer treating sterilisation as the 'last resort' but rather as a convenient method of contraception? Resources for non-urgent gynaecological surgery are scarce. Waiting lists in many districts are long. How easy would it be for M or P to find a surgeon willing to reverse their sterilisation if their mental conditions improved? They are never likely to be of high or even average intelligence. It is doubtful whether a gynaecologist would be willing to reverse the sterilisation of even a relatively mildly mentally impaired woman. And as Eastham J acknowledged, reversal is more complex and serious surgery than the original sterilisation operation. He is in effect saying to P that because there is available the technology to reverse her sterilisation, the initial decision to sterilise may be taken more lightly, albeit the actual chances of her obtaining a reversal operation are minimal and that the operation, if undertaken, would be attended by greater risk and discomfort to her than the original surgery.

What of the other reasons for sterilising P? Clearly she is vulnerable to seduction and must be protected from exploitation, particularly as her current perception of sexual intercourse is of something unpleasant and painful. Sterilisation will do nothing to safeguard her from unscrupulous men. It protects her only against one possible consequence of seduction, pregnancy. She remains exposed to venereal disease, trauma, and perversion. And indeed, in the knowledge that she cannot now conceive, her carers may understandably be less stringent in their efforts to protect P from unwanted or damaging sexual experience. Pregnancy, the judge found, would be a disaster for P. No doubt that is true. But of itself that finding is manifestly insufficient to justify non-consensual sterilisation. Pregnancy is a disaster for all too many women. Yet no one suggests that all women likely to be incapable of coping with childbirth and/or child care should be forcibly sterilised. P was to be sterilised because she is labelled as 'mentally handicapped'. That label appeared to enable the judge to address the question of whether sterilisation was in P's best interests with only a cursory analysis of the girl's competence or potential competence to decide for herself or whether to agree to sterilisation.

The incompetence of the several young women now sterilised by order of the court in England has tended to be assumed rather than explained; much is made of the girl's mental age. P, like Jeannette, was said to have a mental age of six. Such a statement conjures up an image of a little girl whose chronological age and mental age coincide and the idea of allowing a child who is actually six to decide whether or not to be sterilised seems ludicrous. However, P is in reality a girl of 17 who understands to some extent the workings of her body and copes with its needs. Her social skills are good and, unlike Jeannette, she communicates with others quite well. Presumably, it is her reasoning capacity which is to be equated with a six-year-old's. What does a patient have to understand to be competent to give a valid consent to medical treatment? For a competent patient's consent to be valid, he must have been informed in broad terms of the nature and purpose of the treatment proposed. His consent will not be vitiated by a failure to explain the risks, implications and side effects of treatment. It must therefore follow that to be competent to give a valid consent, the patient need only be able to understand in broad terms the nature and purpose of treatment. In the context of sterilisation that means that she should understand that she will be put to sleep while a doctor operates on her tummy to ensure that she is never able to have babies. Most six-year-olds who have learned something of how babies are born would comprehend that information. And P, of course, adds to the reasoning capacity of the child of six the appearance of puberty and an understanding of menstruation.

The judge expressly conceded that with further development and training P might attain the necessary capacity to marry. Her mother testified that she was naturally concerned that if P became pregnant she would refuse an abortion. Neither of those factors suggest that P's handicap was such that she would *never* be capable of making a choice for herself of whether or not to bear a child, or that she could not comprehend pregnancy and birth. Childbirth for P might well be an unwise choice, but if she had or may have developed the ability to make a choice at all then the decision on her interests should have remained hers and hers alone.

It was suggested at one stage at the hearing in *Re P* that, as it is now clear that adult women may be lawfully sterilised where a woman herself is and always will be incapable of giving her own consent to sterilisation, the decision on whether or not to sterilise P should be delayed. Those caring for P should 'wait and see' how she developed. The judge felt delay was unnecessary, a finding heavily influenced by his fallacious emphasis on the potential reversibility of sterilisation. *Re P* has, however, disturbing implications for the practice of sterilising adult handicapped women. The House of Lords held in *F v West Berkshire Health Authority* that the court had no jurisdiction to give or withhold consent to sterilisation of a woman over 18. Such surgery was, however, lawful where the woman is incapable of giving consent herself, and the operation is in the existing circumstances in her best interests, and is carried out in conformity with good medical practice. Good medical practice is to be judged by the *Bolam* test and not by any more stringent measure. While as a matter of law application to a court to authorise sterilisation was not required, their Lordships laid down a procedure whereby an application might be made for a declaration that the proposed operation was not unlawful. Lord Goff commented at the end of his judgment:

> If, however, it became the invariable practice of the medical profession not to sterilise an adult woman who is incapacitated from giving her consent unless a declaration that the proposed course of action is lawful is first sought from the court, I can see little, if any, practical difference between seeking the court's approval under the *parens patriae* jurisdiction and seeking a declaration as to the lawfulness of the operation.

Adult women, like girls under 18, thus enjoy *de facto* if not *de jure*, the safeguard of judicial protection from over-hasty or ill-considered sterilisation. But what is that safeguard worth? The *Bolam* test defines the question of whether sterilisation of the woman is 'good practice'. The *Bolam* test lays down that a practitioner is not negligent if he conforms with a responsible body of medical opinion even though another equally responsible body of opinion dissents. Confronted by evidence from gynaecologist A that he and gynaecologists B–L now regard sterilisation as a reversible operation, a sort of surgical Depo-Provera, must a judge ignore gynaecologists M–Z who doubt the success or even the relevance of reversibility?

A declaration that a proposed sterilisation is not unlawful is a valuable safeguard but a safeguard for the doctor not the patient. A surgeon sterilising a young woman having first obtained a declaration that the operation is not unlawful eliminates the risk that she might later sue him from negligence. For the woman, if the *Bolam* test and the *Bolam* test alone establishes the lawfulness of surgery, then judicial intervention does little more than protect her from the complete maverick whom none of his colleagues would back in his decision to sterilise her. Of course, judicial intervention *ought* to serve one other function too, to ascertain that the woman is in face incapable of consenting to or refusing treatment on her own behalf. The judgments in *Re M* and *Re P* do not inspire confidence in the judiciary's readiness to develop and apply clear guidelines defining competence.

Again and again in the judgments on sterilisation lipservice is paid to the serious import of a decision to sterilise a woman. Reference is made to 'a right to reproduce' or to 'reproductive autonomy'. How is it then that a decision of such import may appear to be taken, as in *Re P*, without proper analysis of what should be the *primary* question, is the woman capable of consenting to, or refusing, sterilisation herself? For what may be in her best interests cannot be relevant unless and until it is established that she is and will continue to be incapable of understanding what is entailed in sterilisation, that she is incapable of determining her own interests. The likelihood that she may make an unwise choice cannot justify depriving her of choice. Perhaps the reality is that doctors and judges do not, maybe cannot, assess the woman's interests alone divorced from the circumstances of her life. Sterilising P may be justifiable in her mother's interests, relieving her of anxiety and enabling her to give P more freedom and a better quality of care. The burden on those charged with the institutional care of handicapped girls may be eased by sterilising those girls, and certainly community care becomes a more viable option where there is no risk of pregnancy. Ensuring P does not have a baby who may either be cared for inadequately by his mother or condemned to a series of foster homes is certainly in the baby's interest. Yet in *Re B* an assurance was given that non-consensual sterilisation was lawful only in the girl herself's interests and as a measure of last resort. Experience must cause us to wonder whether, in the event, the Canadian supreme Court was right in proclaiming in *Re Eve* that non-therapeutic involuntary sterilisation should never be lawful. In England we have slithered down the slippery slope at a frightening speed.

(See the further cases of *Re W (Mental patient) (Sterilisation)* [1993] 1 FLR 381 (Hollis J) (tubal ligation); *Re HG (Specific Issue Order: Sterilisation)* [1993] 1 FLR 587 (Peter Singer QC) (tubal ligation); *Re E (A Minor) (Mental Treatment)* [1991] 2 FLR 585 (Stephen Brown P) (hysterectomy); *Re GF (A Patient)* [1992] 1 FLR 293 (Stephen Brown P) (hysterectomy).)

Interestingly, the Official Solicitor, once the House of Lords had handed down its decision in *Re F*, sought extra-judicially to do the very thing which the House of Lords had been reluctant to do, ie make explicit the factors relevant to deciding whether an incompetent person should be sterilised: see [1989] 2 FLR 447, [1990] 2 FLR 530 and [1993] 2 FLR 222. The Official Solicitor chose to do this in what he described as a 'Practice Note'. The most recent Practice Note, [1996] 2 FLR 111, in addition to providing procedural guidance, sets out in para 10 the following:

10. The Official Solicitor anticipates that the court will particularly require evidence clearly establishing the following:

Mental capacity
(1) That the patient is incapable of making her own decision about sterilisation and is unlikely to develop sufficiently to make an informed judgment about sterilisation in the foreseeable future, having regard to the most up-to-date medical knowledge in this field. In this connection it must be borne in mind that –
(i)   the fact that a person is legally incompetent for some purposes does not mean that she necessarily lacks the capacity to make a decision about sterilisation; and
(ii) in the case of a minor her youth and potential for development may make it difficult or impossible to make the relevant finding of incapacity.

Risk of pregnancy
(2) That there is a need for contraception because the patient is fertile and is sexually active or is likely to engage in sexual activity in the foreseeable future. (*Re W (Mental Patient: Sterilisation)* [1993] 1 FLR 381.)

Potential psychological damage
(3) That the patient is likely if she becomes pregnant or gives birth to experience substantial trauma or psychological damage greater than that resulting from the sterilisation itself.

Alternative methods of contraception
(4) That there is no appropriate reversible method of contraception available having regard to the most up-to-date medical knowledge in this field.

This Note has no legal force and the court is free to disregard it (see *J v C* (1990) 5 BMLR 100 (Thorpe J) and *L v L's Curator ad Litem* 1997 SLT 167, (1996) 32 BMLR 87 (Lord MacLean)).

It does, however, provide important guidance on the nature of any application that will attract the Official Solicitor's support in court. The latter is not essential but highly desirable, since the court will take great notice of the Official Solicitor's stance in relation to a particular application.

In the two recent cases of *Re LC Medical Treatment: Sterilisation* [1997] 2 FLR 258 (Thorpe J) and *Re S (Medical Treatment; Adult Sterilisation* [1998]] 1 FLR 944 (Johnson J), Family Division judges have refused to permit the sterilisation of incapable adult women. In doing so, the courts in England have, for the first time, required proof that there is a *real risk* of pregnancy with deleterious consequences. These decisions halt an unbroken line of decisions, dating back to *Re B* in 1987, when the outcome has been different.

Re S (Medical Treatment: Adult Sterilisation) [1998] 1 FLR 944 (Fam Div)

Johnson J: S is 22. She is a charming and attractive young woman and to all outward appearances entirely normal. However her mental and emotional state is such that she is quite unable to look after herself. She has virtually no ability to communicate except by making some very basic noises. She requires help in dressing and looking after her own basic physical needs. She could not be left to walk alone along a street. She has no understanding of sexuality. In sum, she is vulnerable. In particular, in the world as unhappily it is, she is vulnerable to sexual exploitation.

So it is that her parents decided, and I emphasise after much thought, that it would be best for S if she were to be sterilised. In these proceedings, brought nominally in the name of S herself, her mother asks the court to declare that it would be lawful for the necessary medical procedures to be performed.

S's parents have devoted themselves to her upbringing. They are caring, responsible parents, committed to the care of their child. There is no hint of any selfish motivation in the present application; their thought is only to do what is best for S. So far nothing untoward has happened to S but the anxiety is that at some unguarded moment in the future, some man will be able to contrive a situation in which S is subjected to sexual intercourse and may become pregnant. S has no appreciation of what is involved in the sexual act, in pregnancy or in childbirth. There could never be any question of S being able to keep a child were it born to her, even with the most enormous support. This case is all about future risk. There is no question here of any infringement of S's right to reproduce. ...

Clearly sensible steps must be taken to prevent S being exposed to risk of sexual assault because that would be very serious for her. For a sexual assault to result in pregnancy would of course be even more serious, the probability being that the pregnancy would have to be terminated. The purpose of the proposed sterilisation is to achieve complete elimination of the risk of pregnancy. An alternative method of avoiding a pregnancy is contraception and in S's case the only practical method would be long-term administration of the contraceptive pill. She does not have the ability to adhere to the necessary regime so there would be an ongoing commitment for perhaps 25 years for someone to ensure that the pill was taken daily.

Briefly stated, the issue before the court is whether the risk of pregnancy is such as to require sterilisation, with the consequent imposition on S of the necessary invasive procedures which carry with them a risk of fatality, largely because of the general anaesthesia involved, put by doctors at 4 in 50,000.

Some might have supposed that such a decision should be made for S by her parents, whose devotion to her I have already described. After all, the European Convention on Human Rights seeks to protect family life. In *Re KD (A Minor) (Ward: Termination of Access)* [1988] AC 806, sub nom *Re KD (A Minor) (Access: Principles)* [1988] 2 FLR 139 the House of Lords, and I think particularly of the speeches of Lord Templeman and Lord Oliver, emphasised in compelling terms the right of a minor child to be brought up in the child's own family and, one supposes, such an upbringing would include the entitlement of the child for decisions about medical treatment to be made within the family. One remembers too the powerful statements of Lord Mackay of Clashfern at the time of the passing of the Children Act 1989 to the effect that the State, whether in the guise of the local authority or the court, should not interfere in family life unless there are compelling reasons to do so.

However this concept has no application to the decision which I have to make. Sterilisation raises different issues. This is not simply because it is a topic on which opinion and emotions are strongly divided. It is because sterilisation, at least in a case such as this, is proposed not to cure any medical malaise but for less tangible, the opponents would say social, reasons.
....

I have ventured into the background to the legal position governing applications such as this because it may seem unfair that the law should not give effect to the wishes of caring, informed and responsible parents. ...

The judge referred to *Re B* and then continued:

A similar situation came before Hollis J in *Re W (Mental Patient) (Sterilisation)* [1993] 1 FLR 381. The young woman was 20 and similarly vulnerable. She was to live in the community as much as was possible and there would be occasions for her to be involved socially with young people of both sexes in similar situations. Again the choice of protection lay between contraception and sterilisation. There was no suggestion there on the part of the Official Solicitor that there was 'any practical reason why such an operation – that is sterilisation – would be to W's detriment'. In granting the declaration sought, Hollis J said:

> Here there is clearly a responsible body of medical opinion skilled in the particular field of diagnosis and treatment in favour of sterilisation, notwithstanding the fact there is only a small risk of W becoming pregnant at the present time. From what I know about this case, I agree ... that sterilisation would, in all the circumstances, clearly be in W's interests.

In *Re LC (Medical Treatment: Sterilisation)* [1997] 2 FLR 258 Thorpe J was concerned with a young woman of 21 who, at the time of the hearing, was in a residential home where the level of care and supervision was said to be exceptionally high. In rejecting the application Thorpe J said:

> What is to be decided today is not whether sterilisation is a better protective procedure than 20 or 25 years of prescribed (oral contraceptive), but whether the standard of care and supervision are sufficient to protect L against the only physical experience foreseeably likely to lead to conception, which is of course an invasive sexual assault ... In the end, I decide the issue ... upon the basis that the evidence that has been called has established that the present level of care and supervision at X House is of such an exceptionally high quality that it would not be in L's best interest to impose upon her a surgical procedure which is not without risks nor without painful consequences. I simply cannot in conscience conclude that it would be in her best interest to subject her to that as long as she is receiving the very specialist dedicated care that she is ... Leave could not be justified upon the basis of some vague and unsubstantiated fear that L in future would be exposed to risks from which she is presently protected.

Counsel appearing before me on behalf of the Official Solicitor told me that the decision of Hollis J in *Re W* had not been cited to Thorpe J in *Re LC*. None the less, whilst at first blush there may seem to be no distinction between the two decisions, there is in fact a very important difference. In *Re W* the young woman was likely to be in unsupervised situations with young men and indeed Hollis J referred to the evidence of an occasion when a boy had taken W by the hand and tried to take her out of the place where the disco was being held. In *Re LC* on the other hand, the young woman was the subject of such care and supervision that a risk of sexual activity was extremely unlikely. In the one case there was a foreseeable risk, in the other there was not.

It is ironic that if a young woman is being cared for and supervised by caring and responsible parents, then the wish of the parents is to be overridden; whereas a similar decision will be upheld if made by parents who are careless and irresponsible.

The detriment that is advanced by the Official Solicitor relates only to the medical procedures involved in sterilisation. The procedures are carried out under general anaesthetic which of course carries a risk of fatal or other injury. Overnight stay in hospital is not usually necessary although it might be helpful in S's case. The patient suffers significant pain for a few hours after the operation. In *Re B* (above) the House of Lords seemed to attach lesser importance to these effects than appears from later cases. Lord Hailsham of St Marylebone said:

> Apart from its probably irreversible nature, the detrimental effects are likely to be minimal.

Lord Bridge of Harwich said:

> The evidence proves overwhelmingly that the right answer is by a simple operation.

Lord Oliver of Aylmerton spoke of sterilisation as:

> A relatively minor operation carrying a very small degree of risk to the patient, a very high degree of protection.

The risk

The concern of S's mother is that someone might assault her. That might become more likely if S's parents became too old or infirm to protect her and of course there is, sadly, the ever-present risk nowadays that a care worker might take advantage of his position.

There are three situations in which S is away from her parents' supervision. Every weekday S is taken to the A Training Centre where she stays from 9 am to 4 pm. She is taken there and returned by a local authority minibus. The staff there are alert to ensure that S is always closely supervised.

Every Wednesday night S attends the Gateway Club. There are usually about 75 people there who have problems similar to S and there are between 10 and 12 supervising helpers. Mrs G, from the club, told me that she could recall no more than four occasions in her 20 years' experience when there had been any inappropriate touching and that had always been in public and of the most simple nature. She told me that S does not make advances to others but is receptive to a kindly gesture or a touch.

Every year arrangements are made for S to be away from home for 4 weeks in a respite home run by Mrs W. The staff is all female and there are three staff to ten residents. Four of the residents are usually male. Mrs W told me that S has to have a high degree of supervision for her own personal safety, for example in relation to the dangers of road traffic. She certainly cannot be allowed out of the building unaccompanied. S loves you to hold her hand and be attentive to her – this is with boys as well as girls. Mrs W had seen her at a disco go up to a boy and ask him to hold her hand and stroke it. Mrs W demonstrated. S seems to get a nice feeling from this.

The factual conclusion to which I feel driven, a word I choose deliberately, by this evidence is that the circumstances of S both now and in the foreseeable future are really indistinguishable from those in *Re LC*. So far there has been no identifiable occasion when S has been at risk, as was the case in each of the cases to which I have referred in which the relief sought was granted. I would wish to have upheld the decision of the parents which many observers would have described as being entirely reasonable. None the less, it is particularly important in this field of law that there should be consistency, identifiable consistency, in the decisions that are made. In the absence of any risk that can be called identifiable rather than speculative, it seems to me to follow that I should refuse the mother's applications. …

The healthy scepticism of Johnson J and of Thorpe J in the earlier case of *Re LC* is welcome (see discussion in Commentary (1998) 6 Med L Rev 354 (AG)). There remains a danger that the courts may, in cases where there is an 'identifiable risk' of pregnancy, still seek to avoid such a risk and its consequences almost at all costs (see, eg, *Re X (Adult Sterilisation)* [1998] 2 FLR 1124 (Holman J)). This would be unfortunate and *Re S* does not support it. Sterilisation will not be in the woman's 'best interests' just because there is a risk of pregnancy: the risk of harm must be considered, both in maintaining the status quo and in having the procedure, and other alternatives must be considered (see Practice Note, *supra*, para 10, *Re S (adult patient: sterilisation)* (2000) Times, 26 May (CA) and *L and GM v MM*, *supra* 1193). As *Re S* illustrates, the views of the woman's parents (or other carers) will not be determinative (see also *Re S* (2000), *supra*). The court has the final say and, as we shall now see, the court must be involved if contraceptive sterilisation is contemplated.

Of course, as you will have noticed, all the cases we have considered so far have involved *female* patients. Could it ever be in the best interests of an incompetent *male* patient that he be sterilised? In such an instance, the patient would not, of course, endure the burdens of pregnancy, labour etc. How, therefore, could his best interests be served by undergoing a surgical procedure? Could it neverthless be for his general 'well-being' on the basis that it might free him from constraints in his care that would otherwise be thought necessary? It might be thought that such procedures could only be for the benefit of others, for example, potential sexual partners who would often themselves have an intellectual disability or his carers who could be freed of the most onerous obligation of supervising him for fear of such consequences. The issue arose for the first time in England in the following case.

Re A (Medical Treatment: Male Sterilisation) (2000) 53 BMLR 66 (CA)

A, who was now 28 years old, had Down's syndrome and had been assessed as being on the borderline between significant and severe impairment of intelligence. He lived with his 63-year-old mother who provided him with a high degree of care and supervision. However, the mother's health was not good and her major concern was that, when A moved into local authority care, he might have a sexual relationship resulting in the birth of a child and he would be unable to understand the consequences, and she disapproved very strongly of a man walking away from responsibility. Accordingly, the mother, acting as A's next friend, applied to the High Court for a declaration that a vasectomy operation was in A's best interests and could lawfully be performed on him despite his inability to consent to it. The Official Solicitor opposed the application. The judge found that whilst A was sexually aware and active, he had no understanding of the link between sexual intercourse and pregnancy. He held that, while in the care of his mother A was unlikely to enter into any casual sexual relationship with a woman, but were a pregnancy to occur the effect on A would be minimal, and concluded that a vasectomy operation was not essential to A's future well-being. On appeal to the Court of Appeal, the mother argued that sterilisation ought to be seen as a form of contraception; that the decision should be taken now and not later; and that the main consideration was the quality of life which it was possible for A to enjoy.

Dame Elizabeth Butler-Sloss P: It is clear . . . that, whether the application was concerned with an adult or with a child, the decision of the court was made in the best interests of that person and that principle was applied to the individual facts of each case.

An application on behalf of a man for sterilisation is not the equivalent of an application in respect of a woman. It is not a matter of equality of the sexes but a balancing exercise on a case by case basis. There are obvious biological differences and sexual intercourse for a woman carries the risk of pregnancy which patently it does not for a man. Indeed there is no direct consequence for a man of sexual intercourse other than the possibility of sexually transmitted diseases. There may be psychological consequences for him in pregnancy or in the birth of his child. He may be required to take responsibility for the child after birth and may, in certain circumstances attract disapproval and criticism. In the case of a man who is mentally incapacitated, neither the fact of the birth of a child nor disapproval of his conduct is likely to impinge on him to a significant degree other than in exceptional circumstances. His freedom of movement might in certain instances be restricted and consequently his quality of life might be diminished. It is possible that there may be other disadvantages to the person concerned which might lead a court to decide to approve the operation. It may be necessary to evaluate the nature and degree of risk attached to approval of or refusal to approve the operation to sterilise. But the task in each case is to balance all the relevant factors and to decide what are the best interests of the person unable to make his own decision.

In the present appeal it is necessary to focus upon the best interests of A himself. It is clear from the evidence of his mother that, as long as she cares for him, he will continue to be subjected to the present regime of close supervision. The refusal to approve the operation will inevitably upset A's mother but her care of him will not be diminished nor will he be aware that she is upset. If sterilisation did take place, it would not save A from the possibility of exploitation nor help him cope with the emotional implications of any closer relationship that he might form. It is also clear from the evidence of those who care for him in the day centre that the level of supervision does not depend upon his fertility. His mother has raised her concerns with them over inappropriate behaviour with women attending the day centre. The supervisors stop inappropriate behaviour because it is conducted in a public place and, it would appear, will continue to do so whether or not he has the operation. From my understanding of the evidence, Dr Campbell's assessment of the present supervision of A is incorrect and that the operation will not free him to enjoy a more relaxed regime. When in due course he goes into local authority care, the degree of freedom might be affected by the fear that he might form a sexual relationship with another resident. It would however, in my view, be likely that the woman concerned would be the object of protection rather than A. If his quality of life were, however, to be diminished, that would be a reason to seek at that time a hearing before a High Court judge to grant a declaration that sterilisation would then be in A's best interests.

I would dismiss the appeal.

You will notice that the court did not say 'never', only 'hardly ever' but not on these facts. Thorpe LJ added:

Thorpe LJ: I share [the view of Dr Campbell] that A's fertility is of no advantage to him but of real disadvantage. In our society vasectomy has become the preferred method of contraception for many males who wish to separate their sexual and procreative functions. The obligation of society is to minimise the consequence of disability by vouchsafing for the disabled wherever possible the rights and freedoms vouchsafed to the majority who have been spared disability. If there are opportunities of replacing with reality the fantasies that stimulate A's isolated masturbatory sexual activity then they should be grasped. Of course it might be said that Dr Campbell's assumption that sexual intercourse with a female partner would be likely to prove enjoyable for A might be said to be optimistic. Any balanced appraisal must recognise the possibility of painful experiences such as the ending of the relationship in circumstances which A might not comprehend or which might cause him distress. That said my conclusion is that Dr Campbell's expert evidence provided a foundation upon which other evidence might have been laid in the construction of a successful outcome.

However supportive evidence from A's carers was either not established or not called. When cross-examined by Mr Francis QC, A's mother effectively conceded that there would be no relaxation in the level of supervision were a vasectomy performed. As she explained, that was a consequence of her basic distaste for sex outside marriage. As well as the control which she was able to exert within her own house, she would not accept a placement at a home or day centre that adopted a permissive attitude to sexual intercourse between disabled people in their care.

The claimant called no evidence from A's other carers and the evidence as to the practice of the day centre and the respite home came from attendances taken by the Official Solicitor's representative. Those attendances clearly demonstrate that their present practice is to prevent sexual intercourse between disabled people in their care by watchful supervision. Therefore in my judgment the crucial missing piece in the construction of the evidential jigsaw was evidence from A's mother and/or from A's alternative carers that, whether nor not in reliance on Dr Campbell's expert evidence, supervision post vasectomy would be at a reduced level and opportunities for A to develop sexual experience and intimacy with a woman countenanced. Clearly the onus is on the claimant to establish that the vasectomy would be in his best interests. In my opinion the construction of the positive case was incomplete . . .

In conclusion although I agree that this appeal must be dismissed I would like to emphasise that its failure does not preclude a fresh application in the future on fresh evidence . . .

The court left open whether the consequences to others could be taken into account (see per Butler-Sloss P at 73 and Thorpe LJ at 75 (see discussion *supra*, ch 6).

You might feel that the 'positive case', as Thorpe LJ calls it, might not be too difficult to establish were it not, as in *Re A*, for a restrictive attitude of his personal and professional carers. Indeed, it was argued in *Re A* that there was the potential here, at least for males with moderate learning disability, for the 'floodgates' to open. Thorpe LJ's specific response (at 77) was that each application would need to be considered on its merits as to that individual's 'best interests'. Whilst, of course, this is obviously true, the point argued is nevertheless worth noticing.

5. The involvement of the court

We saw earlier (*supra*, ch 6) that the courts have taken to themselves the role of policing and regulating decision-making in relation to some medical treatments or procedures. It was in the contraceptive sterilisation cases of *Re B* and *Re F* that this first emerged.

The judges have distinguished *therapeutic* from *non-therapeutic* interventions. The latter *should* be brought before the court while the former need not. Notice that the courts cannot, and do not, require their involvement as a matter of law but rather consider it desirable as a matter of good practice. Contraceptive sterilisations fall into the latter category (*Re F*), while procedures intended to treat a physical condition such as a diseased uterus but which also result in sterilisation of the patient, do not (per Lord Griffiths in *Re F*). Likewise, in *Re E (a minor) (medical treatment)* (1991) 7 BMLR 117 (Stephen Brown P) and *F v F* (1991) 7 BMLR 135 (Stephen Brown P) the court has held that a hysterectomy performed to alienate the effects of menstruation which will have demonstrable consequences for the health of the girl or woman, do not have to be brought before the court, since they are 'therapeutic' in nature. It suffices that, as a matter of good practice, the procedure is supported by two doctors as being necessary for therapeutic purposes and in the best interests of the patient.

In its Report (No 231), *Mental Incapacity* (1985), the Law Commission approved, in essence, of this approach. Although, in doing so, it arguably has gone further than would the common law in requiring court approval.

Law Commission *Mental Incapacity* Report No 231 (1995)

6.4   We suggested in the consultation paper that sterilisation operations could be divided into three sub-sets: those intended to treat a disease of the reproductive organs; those intended for "menstrual management"; and those intended for contraceptive purposes. (Consultation Paper No 129, paras 6.4–6.8.) None of our respondents suggested that statutory supervision should be applied to those in the first category, which can properly be carried out under the general authority, with access to the court if there is a dispute or difficulty. A number of respondents confirmed, however, that the need for "menstrual management" can too easily be invoked to avoid the judicial supervision which should currently apply to any operation intended to sterilise the patient as a method of contraception. (The court's involvement is not necessary if an operation will only have the incidental effect of sterilising the patient, *Re GF (Medical Treatment)* [1992] 1 FLR 293.) We were greatly assisted by discussions with those in the Official Solicitor's Department who have experience of representing patients in actions involving proposed sterilisations. We are persuaded that there is a valid distinction to be drawn between an operation which is intended to address an existing harmful condition associated with menstruation and one intended to guard against any future distress which might arise from an unintended pregnancy. The phrase "menstrual management" may obfuscate this crucial distinction instead of emphasing it. We take the view that sterilisation operations designed to relieve the immediate and genuine harmful effects of menstruation can be distinguished from those intended to prevent conception and need not attract supervision by the court. In view of the concern expressed by respondents, however, we suggest a different form of independent supervision for such cases.

We recommend that any treatment or procedure intended or reasonably likely to render the person permanently infertile should require court authorisation unless it is to treat a disease of the reproductive organs or relieve existing detrimental effects of menstruation. (Draft Bill, clause 7(2)(a).).

6.9   Although we have concluded that a sterilisation operation designed to relieve a patient of any existing pain and harmful effects connected with menstruation should not require authorisation by the court, many of our respondents expressed concern about operations being labelled "for menstrual management", with the result that no independent supervision at all is required. A consultant in developmental psychiatry who has made a special study of sterilisation of people with learning disabilities suggested that the level of menstrual distress is often misrepresented, and that further investigation can reveal less drastic means of coping with the problem than a sterilisation operation. There is a clear need for independent supervision in such circumstances.

We recommend that any treatment or procedure intended or reasonably likely to render the person permanently infertile should require a certificate from an independent medical practitioner where it is for relieving the existing detrimental effects of menstruation. (Draft Bill, clause 8(3)(d).)

In *Who Decides?* (1997 Cm 3803) the LCD makes one sensible point that seems to have been overlooked by the Law Commission. It deals with a category of case which should be excluded from the need for court approval because it is wholly therapeutic in nature.

The Lord Chancellor's Department '*Who Decides?* (1997) Cm 3803

… The Government notes that treatment of diseases other than those affecting the reproductive organs, such as chemotherapy for cancer, may be likely to render a person permanently infertile …

As we saw earlier (*supra* ch 6), the Government has decided not to take forward the Law Commission's recommendations, *inter alia*, in relation to contraceptive sterilisations (*Making Decisions* (1999), Cm 4465, para 12).

6.   Starting again

What is required given the limitations of judicial law-making and the controversial subject matter, is a thoroughgoing review of the whole subject: the medical and psychiatric realities, the social implications, the ethical concerns and the appropriate legal framework. The following example of such a review can be found in the work of the Institute of Law Research and Reform, in Alberta, Canada: *Competence and Human Reproduction* (Report No 52, February 1989).

Factors for Judge to Consider

(1) The Factors

Before making an order authorizing a sterilization the judge would be required to consider the factors enumerated in a statutory list – factors of the sort that a person who is competent would ordinarily weigh in coming to a personal decision. All of the factors would be weighed from the perspective of their impact on the best interests of the person for whom sterilization is being considered, and not from the perspective of their impact on the interests of others.

The factors are simply listed in this section and will be discussed in paragraphs (2) to (4) below.

(a) Elective Sterilization

For an elective sterilization, the foremost factor would be:

* the wishes and concerns expressed by the person for whom sterilization is being sought, to the extent they can be ascertained.

(These wishes and concerns would be ascertained and introduced in evidence after steps have been taken to inform the person of the factors affecting the decision, and to assist the person, to the full extent her intellectual capacity allows, to participate in making a decision.)

There would be fifteen other specific factors:

* the age of the person.
* the likelihood that the person will become competent to consent to the proposed sterilization,
* the physical capacity of the person to reproduce,
* the likelihood that the person will engage in sexual activity,
* the risks to the physical health of the person if the sterilization is or is not performed,
* the risks to the mental health of the person if the sterilization is or is not performed,
* the availability and medical advisability of alternative means of medical treatment or contraception,
* the previous experience, if any, of the persons with alternative means of medical treatment or contraception,
* the likelihood that any child of the person would be born with a physical or mental disability and the likely effect of that disability on the ability of the person to cope,
* the ability of the person to care for a child at the time of the application and any likely changes in that ability,
* the likelihood that a child of the person could be cared for by some other person,
* the likely effect of foregoing the proposed sterilization on the life of the person as it limits or otherwise affects the ability of those who care for the person to provide required care (it is the consequential effect on the person for whom sterilization is being considered that would be weighed in considering this factor),
* the likely effect of the proposed sterilization on the opportunities the person will have for satisfying human interaction,
* the religious beliefs, cultural and other values of the person, and
* the wishes, concerns, religious beliefs, cultural and other values of the family or other person providing personal care insofar as they affect the interests of the person.

(We emphasize that the decision must be made in the best interests of the person whose sterilization is in issue. The views of family members or other personal caregivers are relevant only to the extent that they affect the best interests of the person. We have kept the category narrow because we think that a real and substantial connection with the person ought to be shown before the views of any other person are taken into consideration.)

To these would be added as a residual factor:

* any other matter that the judge considers relevant.

(b) Hysterectomy for Menstrual Management

For a hysterectomy for menstrual management, the following would be added to the above list of factors:

* the availability and medical advisability of alternative means of menstrual management, and
* the previous experience, if any, of the person with alternative means of menstrual management

As well, the proposed legislation would permit the judge to make the order authorizing the performance of a hysterectomy only where no less drastic alternative method of menstrual management is reasonably available.

(c) In General

In a situation where evidence on a factor is not available or not readily available, the judge would be able to make an order in the absence of evidence only if he is satisfied that evidence cannot reasonably be obtained.

As one respondent observed, the requirement that the factors *must* be considered is a strength of our proposal in that it goes a long way toward ensuring that a decision would be based on the fullest possible information and consideration.

(2) Factors Raising Risk of Confusion with Interests of Others

The choice of the 'best interests' test confirms our guiding principle that a sterilization should be authorized only where it would be for the benefit of the person to be sterilized. Benefit to others – be it the family, caregivers, a future spouse, or a child who may be conceived and born – is not a consideration.

In consultation, a number of respondents expressed the concern that some of the factors listed in the proposed legislation would permit the interests of others to be brought in through the back door. They pointed to factors such as:

* the ability of the person to care for a child at the time of the application and any likely changes in that ability,
* the likelihood that any child of the person would be born with a physical or mental disability and the likely effect of that disability on the ability of the person to cope,
* the likelihood that a child of the person could be cared for by some other person,
* the likely effect of foregoing the proposed sterilization on the ability of those who care for the person to provide required care, and
* the wishes, concerns, religious beliefs, cultural and other values of the family or other person providing personal care insofar as they affect the interests of the person.

We hasten to dispel any such misapprehension. Under our proposal, these factors are to be considered only insofar as they have an impact on the best interests of the person for whom sterilization is sought. We emphatically do not intend that the consideration of these factors should derogate from our overriding principle of benefit to the person herself. They are *not* to be considered from the point of view of the interests or welfare of any other person.

At the same time, we think it would be a mistake to pretend that persons who are not competent to make sterilization decisions live in a social vacuum when in fact they depend on a network of family, friends and others to assist them in living as normal a life as possible. As we see it, the nature and extent to which a person can count on others is relevant to the determination of her present and likely future circumstances and this, in turn, is relevant to the consideration of her best interests.

Admittedly, the distinction between the interests of others insofar as they affect the interests of the person whose sterilization is sought and the interests of others in their own right carries with it the risk of misapplication. However, we think the risk is minimized, if not eliminated, by the choice of a superior court judge as decision maker and by the provision of a broad range of substantive and procedural safeguards for the judge to observe. We have revised the proposed legislation in an effort to make it irrefutably clear that these factors are to be considered only insofar as they relate to and impact on the best interests of the person for whom sterilization is sought.

Finally, in our tentative recommendations, the last factor set out above was phrased to include the wishes, concerns, religious beliefs and other values of the family 'or other interested person' insofar as they affect the interests of the person. The definition we propose for an 'interested person' would be an adult who, because of his relationship to the person in respect of whom an order is sought, is concerned for the welfare of the person. The judge would have the authority to decide whether a person is or is not an interested person for a purpose named in the legislation.

Some respondents felt that the definition of 'interested person' would require consideration of the wishes, concerns, religious beliefs and other values of primary caregivers including medical professionals and persons who are employed in an institution where the person is resident. We do not think a judge would interpret the words this widely. However, we do agree that the definition of 'an interested person' is overly broad for this section. In our final proposal we have substituted the words 'or other person providing personal care' for the words 'an interested person' in this factor. Where the judge considers the views of an individual who is not a family member to be relevant, he would be obliged to consider them under the residual factor in any event.

(3) Other Factors Attracting Specific Comment

(a) Wishes of the Person for Whom Sterilization is Sought

As already stated, the factor to receive the foremost attention of the judge would be:

* the wishes and concerns expressed by the person for whom sterilization is being sought. These would be ascertained after the person has been informed of the factors affecting the decision and assisted, to the full extent of her intellectual capacity, to participate in making a sterilization decision.

Embodied in this factor is the recognition that a person who is not competent to consent may nevertheless indicate preferences or wishes that should be considered. A minor would be able to do so more and more expressly as she approaches adulthood when the presumption of competence would apply.

Some respondents felt that the objection to sterilization by a normally developing minor should be decisive of the issue. While we are of the view that a case in which the decision of the judge would prevail over the wishes of a normally developing minor would be highly unusual, we have stopped short of this position for two reasons. First, a minor is, by our definition, a person who is not competent to make a decision about an elective sterilization or a hysterectomy for menstrual management. Second, it should not be overlooked that sterilization for optional medical treatment and for the protection of mental health comes within the statutory regime. Bearing these points in mind, we think it best to entrust the decision to the judge after hearing all the facts of an individual case.

(b)   Religious Beliefs, Cultural and Other Values
In Report for Discussion No 6, we listed the religious beliefs and other values of the person for whom sterilization is being sought along with the wishes and concerns of the person. In the final proposals we have added *cultural* values to this factor in response to a suggestion received during consultation. *Cultural* values have also been added to the parallel factor which now requires the judge to consider the wishes, concerns, religious beliefs, *cultural* and other values of the family or other person providing personal care to the person for whom sterilization is sought.

(c)   Likelihood of Future Competence
Another factor the judge would be required to consider is:
•   the likelihood that the person will become competent to consent to the proposed sterilization.
The discussion of the wishes and concerns of the person to be sterilized underscores the significance of the likelihood of future competence as a factor in the case of a normally developing minor. The latter factor is also significant for a person whose lack of competence stems from a mental disability that is transient in nature and unlikely to persist for the whole of the person's reproductive life.

One respondent submitted that if there is evidence of past competence and evidence making it reasonable to conclude that the person may be competent again in the future, such evidence should be conclusive and no non-therapeutic sterilization decision ought to follow. We take the point, but can imagine a case in which the likelihood of return to competence is remote and the reasons for sterilization lie at the medical treatment end of the spectrum of sterilization purposes under the new regime. Again, we think it preferable to trust to the discretion of the judge who is in a position to weigh this evidence along with all the other circumstances in an individual case.

(d)   Age
Discussion on the issue of the likelihood of future competence has prompted us to add as a specific factor:
•   the age of the person.
One reason for specifying age is that its inclusion in the list helps to draw attention to the fact that maturation can be expected of minors for whom sterilization is being considered. Another reason for enumerating age is that reproductive choices tend to vary with age. For example, in the general population persons nearing the end of their reproductive years are more likely to choose sterilization than persons in younger age groups. Recognizing such tendencies would facilitate normalcy in decision making on behalf of persons who are not competent to consent personally.

(e)   Physical Capacity to Reproduce
A further factor the judge would be required to consider is:
•   the physical capacity of the person to reproduce.
In the Report for discussion, we tentatively recommended that a presumption of fertility should be raised if the medical evidence indicates normal development of sexual organs and the evidence does not otherwise raise doubts about fertility. We made our recommendation because fertility is difficult to prove. Nevertheless, it would obviously be pointless and wrong to perform a sterilization on a person who is physically unable to reproduce.

Some respondents observed that the presumption has the effect of placing the onus on the person under a disability to prove there is some existing physical dysfunction that has rendered her sterile. They suggested that the more appropriate and reasonable evidentiary requirement would be to place the onus on the applicant to prove that the person is capable of reproduction. This point was made by respondents who are opposed in principle to sterilization for birth control or menstrual management. The onus they suggest would be virtually impossible to meet in cases where no prior offspring have been conceived.

We are satisfied that the proposed presumption reflects the more reasonable likelihood of normal reproductive functioning.

(f) Alternative Means of Birth Control or Menstrual Management
Two further factors the judge would be required to consider are:
- the availability and medical advisability of alternative means of medical treatment or contraception, or of menstrual management, and
- the previous experience, if any, of the person with alternative means of medical treatment or contraception, or of menstrual management.

The tentative recommendations in the Report for Discussion referred only to the 'availability and medical advisability' of alternatives. The factor referring to 'the previous experience, if any, of the person' has been added for both elective sterilization and hysterectomy for menstrual management as a result of a suggestion made in consultation on our tentative recommendations. Although information about previous experience is likely to form part of the foundation for an expert opinion on medical advisability, we agree that it would be helpful to specify it for consideration by the judge.

(4) Factors Attracting Little or No Comment
Most of the remaining factors received little or no specific comment one way or the other. We have omitted from our final proposals one factor that was included in our tentative recommendations. It is the likelihood that the person might in the future be able to marry. We are not persuaded that flagging this factor would be misconceived. Because we are living in an era when reproduction decisions are being made independently of marriage, marriage is not of direct relevance to the sterilization issue. The reference to the likelihood of marriage in the future could unduly arouse the traditional view that having children is fundamental to marriage and unacceptable outside of marriage, thereby tipping the balance against the weight of other factors in an individual case. That is to say, it could lead to the undue approval of sterilization in cases where marriage is unlikely and the undue refusal of sterilization where marriage is a possibility.

Where there is a chance that a future spouse would be able to provide help with the care of a child, our proposals cover the possibility in the factor relating to any other care that might be available for a child if born.

(g) Method of Sterilization
The choice of surgical operation or other medical procedure to be used for sterilization would, in most instances, be a matter for medical decision. Our proposals do, however, contain two provisions relating to the method of sterilization. In the case of an *elective sterilization*, the proposed legislation would prohibit the sterilization from being performed by hysterectomy unless the judge, by order, expressly authorizes it on the basis of persuasive medical evidence. In the case of a *hysterectomy for menstrual management*, the proposed legislation would permit the judge to make an order authorizing the performance of a hysterectomy only where no less drastic alternative method of menstrual management is reasonably available.

In both cases, our proposals reflect the principle that the least injurious or least intrusive means of accomplishing the intended purpose should be used.

At present, the law in England and Wales is a matter for the courts. In its Report on *Mental Incapacity* (No 231) in 1995, the Law Commission did not seek to make any recommendations for specific changes to the substantive law as it applied to sterilisation of incompetent adults. It was content that the proposed scheme with 'best interests' at its heart should apply. Its recommendations, as we have seen, were restricted to procedural questions of the need for court approval or other safeguards taking such decisions out of the 'general authority' of doctors and the Government has decided that these will not find a place in any future legislation (on which see *supra* ch 6).

Chapter 10

Medically assisted reproduction

Introduction

Medicine has made extraordinary advances in responding to the desire of women (and their partners) to have a child. These advances, as it may be imagined, have not been free from moral and legal difficulties. In this chapter we explore how the law has responded to these developments. The medical background to the problem of infertility is well described by the Canadian Law Reform Commission.

Canadian Law Reform Commission *Medically Assisted Procreation* (Working Paper 65) (1992)

Infertility
Infertility is the involuntary, significant reduction of reproduction capacity. In North America, the generally recognized threshold of infertility is an inability to become pregnant after one year of unprotected intercourse. The World Health Organization's standard is two years.

Although Canadian studies of infertility prevalence are scarce, it has been reported that 15 percent of couples seek medical advice for infertility. In the United States the prevalence of infertility has not changed significantly from 13.3 percent in 1965 to about 13.9 percent in 1982, excluding surgically induced sterility.

Some of the factors influencing the prevalence of infertility are: (1) trends toward childbearing later in life; (2) environmental factors, such as infection from sexually transmitted diseases, and occupational exposure; (3) medical treatments such as those used for high blood pressure, stomach ulcer and cancer, as well as non-therapeutic drugs such as narcotics, alcohol and tobacco.

A. Evaluation of the Infertile Couple
The infertile couple seeking medical help undergoes a series of procedures to determine the nature and severity of the problem. First a medical history is taken and, if necessary, counselling about timing effective intercourse is given.

The woman is tested to detect hormonal dysfunction. There may be a biopsy of the uterine lining, and a hysterosalpingogram, which is an X-ray that reveals blockages of the fallopian tubes. Laparoscopy, which is the introduction of an endoscope into the abdomen, may be used to inspect the outer surfaces of the uterus, fallopian tubes and surrounding structures for any abnormalities. These procedures are often painful, include slight risks of infection, and may result in the puncture of the uterus, although this last is rare. Medical precautions, such as the administration of antibiotics, are therefore taken to minimize risks.

The man must undergo a semen analysis to evaluate the number and quality of sperm. If the semen is abnormal, blood tests may be performed to detect hormonal abnormalities. A post-coital test may also be used to determine if there is incompatibility between the semen and female reproductive factors. This test requires the couple to have sexual intercourse timed to coincide with ovulation; within a few hours, post-coital tests of cervical mucus are performed.

B. Causes of and Treatments for Infertility
Infertility may be traced to one partner, both partners, or to biochemical or immunological incompatibility between partners. Most female infertility is due to: ovulation disorders, usually because of hormonal abnormality; tubal blockage as a result of infection and other

disease processes; endometriosis; and other causes, including abnormalities of the vagina or cervix, and mucous incompatibilities with sperm.

Treatments for female infertility include hormone or drug therapy, surgery, and medically assisted procreation technologies such as IVF and GIFT.

Infertility due to an ovulation disorder is treated with ovulatory stimulants, which are very successful if infertility is due only to an ovulation disorder. Other medical treatments include drugs to treat endometriosis, infection, and immune incompatibilities. For fallopian tube blockage, surgery may be used. When other infertility treatments are unsuccessful, artificially assisted procreation may be employed, but as a last resort.

Male infertility typically results from decreased numbers or an absence of sperm in the semen, abnormal motility and structural abnormalities, all of which prevent normal fertilization of the egg. Precise causes of male infertility are often undetectable, but varicocele (varicose veins of the testes) or infection may play a role. The absence of sperm (azoospermia) may be caused by impaired production of sperm or blockage of passageways. Although greatly reduced numbers of sperm (oligospermia) reduce fertility, there is still controversy as to the number of sperm necessary for normal reproductive functioning.

When sperm counts fall below five million, fertility is significantly reduced. Therefore, couples unwilling to wait the several years often necessary to achieve 'natural' pregnancy may seek treatment for male factor infertility. These treatments include hormonal therapy and such laboratory techniques as the 'swim up' procedure that aim to improve the concentration of normal sperm available for fertilization. However, the success of these procedures in conjunction with the use of artificial insemination is less than 20 percent.

In theory, one might expect that IVF could be useful in the treatment of male factor infertility. Once the egg is placed directly in a container with the partner's sperm, the normal sperm, even if there are relatively few, should be able to fertilize the egg. This would provide the couple with a child genetically related to both parents. But the ability of the sperm to fertilize the egg appears to be only half as successful as in cases of IVF with non-male factors. Nevertheless, there are reports that find IVF for male factor infertility as successful as IVF for other reasons. In any event, artificial insemination by donor (AID) is considered a leading remedy for both the infertile and sterile male because it is less costly, less invasive, and statistically much more successful than IVF.

The various developments in treating the infertile include, principally, artificial insemination using donated sperm (AI); *in vitro* fertilisation techniques (IVF) including ICSI (Intra Cytoplasmic Sperm Injection), and surrogacy. While AI and surrogacy have been with us for a long time and may, in some cases, be accomplished without any medical involvement, IVF was developed in the 1970s and requires medical intervention. Of course, AI and surrogacy will usually be carried out under medical supervision. More recently, developments in cloning techniques, the use of ovarian tissue and stem-cell research have promised much by way of therapeutic potential. At the same time, legal, ethical and social concerns about these developments have taxed public policy makers. We will return to examine the issues later in this chapter.

Medically assisted reproduction sometimes involves treating infertile couples using their own genetic material. In other cases, the treatment will involve the use of donated material, whether sperm, eggs or even embryos. It was the development of IVF procedures which raised concerns about the practices of medically assisted reproduction and led to a call for regulation. In response, the government set up a Committee of Inquiry into Human Fertilisation and Embryology chaired by Baroness Warnock (as she became) which reported in 1984 (Cmnd 9314). The 'Warnock Committee', as it became known, identified the range of concerns which arose from the rapid developments in medically assisted reproduction.

Report of the Committee of Inquiry into Human Fertilisation and Embryology (Cmnd 9314) (1984)

2.1 In the past, there was considerable public ignorance of the causes and extent of infertility, as well as ignorance of possible remedies. At one time, if a couple were childless, there was very little they could do about it. Generally the cause of infertility was thought to be something in the woman which made her childless; only occasionally was it thought that there might be something wrong with the man. Even today, there is very little factual information about the prevalence of infertility. A commonly quoted figure is that one couple in ten is childless, but accurate statistics are not available, nor is it known what proportion of this figure relates to couples who choose not to have children. In certain religious and cultural traditions, infertility was, and still is, considered sufficient grounds for divorce. In our own society childless couples used to be advised to adopt a child. Now, as a result of improved contraception, the wider availability of legal abortion and changed attitudes towards the single mother, far fewer babies are placed for adoption.

2.2 Childlessness can be a source of stress even to those who have deliberately chosen it. Family and friends often expect a couple to start a family, and express their expectations, either openly or by implication. The family is a valued institution within our present society: within it the human infant receives nurture and protection during its prolonged period of dependence. It is also the place where social behaviour is learnt and where the child develops its own identity and feeling of self-value. Parents likewise feel their identity in society enhanced and confirmed by their role in the family unit. For those who long for children, the realisation that they are unable to found a family can be shattering. It can disrupt their picture of the whole of their future lives. They may feel that they will be unable to fulfil their own and other people's expectations. They may feel themselves excluded from a whole range of human activity and particularly the activities of their child-rearing contemporaries. In addition to social pressures to have children there is, for many, a powerful urge to perpetuate their genes through a new generation. This desire cannot be assuaged by adoption.

2.3 Arguments have been put to us both for and against the treatment of infertility. First, we have encountered the view that in an over-populated world it is wrong to take active steps to create more human beings who will consume finite resources. However strongly a couple may wish to have children, such a wish is ultimately selfish. It has been said that if they cannot have children without intervention, they should not be helped to do so. Secondly, there is a body of opinion which holds that it is wrong to interfere with nature, or with what is perceived to be the will of God. Thirdly, it has been argued that the desire to have children is no more than a wish; it cannot be said to constitute a need. Other people have genuine needs which must be satisfied if they are to survive. Thus services designed to meet these needs must have priority for scarce resources.

2.4 In answer to the first point, it is never easy to counter an argument based on the situation of the world as a whole with an argument relying on the desires of individuals. We saw it as our function to concentrate on individuals rather than on the world at large. Questions about the distribution of resources within the world as a whole lie far outside our terms of reference. In any event, the number of children born as a result of techniques to assist in the treatment of infertility will always be insignificant in comparison with the naturally increasing world population. On the second point, the argument that to offer treatment to the infertile is contrary to nature fails to convince in view of the ambiguity of the concepts 'natural' and 'unnatural'. We took the view that actions taken with the intention of overcoming infertility can, as a rule, be regarded as acceptable substitutes for natural fertilisation. Thirdly, the argument that the desire to have children is only a wish, not a need, and therefore should not be satisfied at the expense of other more urgent demands on resources can be answered in several ways. There are many other treatments not designed to satisfy absolute needs (in the sense that the patient would die without them) which are readily available within the NHS. Medicine is no longer exclusively concerned with the preservation of life, but with remedying the malfunctions of the human body. On this analysis, an inability to have children is a malfunction and should be considered in exactly the same way as any other. Furthermore infertility may be the result of some disorder which in itself needs treatment for the benefit of the patient's health. Infertility is not something mysterious, nor a cause of shame, nor necessarily something that has to be endured without attempted cure. In addition, the psychological distress that may be caused by infertility in those who want children may precipitate a mental disorder warranting treatment. It is, in our view, better to treat the primary cause of such distress than to alleviate the symptoms. In summary, we conclude that infertility is a condition meriting treatment.

In the light of its analysis, the committee recommended statutory regulation of medically assisted reproduction. In the immediate aftermath of the Warnock Report, the Medical Research Council and the Royal College of Obstetricians and Gynaecologists set up the Voluntary (later Interim) Licensing Authority. This body served to provide a self-regulatory mechanism for licensing infertility treatment and research on human embryos and gametes. It ceased to exist on

1 August 1991 when the Act establishing the Human Fertilisation and Embryology Authority came into force. It is the framework of the Human Fertilisation and Embryology Act 1990 which resulted from the recommendations of the Warnock Committee that we are concerned with here. However, by way of introduction, before we turn to a detailed account of the 1990 Act, it will be helpful to consider one or two preliminary matters.

First, the complexities of the issues to be considered are well illustrated by the following table set out in Professor Bernard Dickens's article, 'Reproduction Law and Medical Consent' (1985) 35 Toronto Law Journal 255 at 280:

Table of reproductive options

Sperm	Ovum	Uterus	Means of conception	Intended child custody	Explanation
H	W	W	natural	H and W	normal conception
H	W	W	AI	H and W	AI by husband
H	W	W	IVF	H and W	IVF
D	W	W	AI/IVF	H and W	conception by sperm donor
H	D	W	IVF or IV + F and ET	H and W	conception by ovum donor
H	D1	D1	AI	H and W	'SM' and SPA by W
H	W	D	any and ET	H and W	SM and SPA by W
H	D1	D2	any and ET	H and W	ovum donation, SM and SPA by W
D	W	D	any and ET	H and W	SM of W's ovum and adoption
D	D	W	any and ET	H and W	W bears (unrelated) child and SPA by H
D	D1	D1	any	H and W	adoption
D	D1	D2	any and ET	H and W	adoption
F	M	M	any	F and M	child of the union
F	D1	D1	any	F	father has child
D	M	M	any	M	mother has child
F	D1	D2	any and ET	F	father has true surrogate child
D	M	D	any and ET	M	mother has true surrogate child
D	D1	D2	any and ET	D2	true surrogate has child
D	D1	D1	any	third party	adoption
D	D1	D2	any and ET	third party	adoption
H	W	W	posthumous AI/IVF	W	widow has child
H	W	D	posthumous IVF/IV + F and ET	W	widow has true surrogate child
H	W	D	posthumous IVF and ET	H	widower has true surrogate child

H	= husband (legal or common law)	F = single father
W	= wife (legal or common law)	M = single genetic mother
D	= donor of sperm, ovum, or uterine service	SPA = step-parent adoption
AI	= artificial insemination	IVF = *in vitro* fertilisation
ET	= embryo transplantation	IV + F = *in vivo* fertilisation (by AI) and flushing
'SM'	= so-called surrogate motherhood	any = natural conception, AI, IVF, or IV + F
SM	= surrogate motherhood	

A slightly different scheme is offered by Professor Alexander Capron in 'Alternative Birth Technologies: Legal Challenges' (1987) 20 UC Davis Law Review:

Review possibilities

No	Name of Method	Genetic Source	Fertilization	Gesta-tion	Social Parent
1	Traditional Reproduction	X_M & Y_M	Natural	M	M & M
2	Artificial Insemination, Husband	X_M & Y_M	AI	M	M & M
3	Test Tube Baby	X_M & Y_M	IVF	M	M & M
4	Artificial Insemination, Donor	X_M & Y_D	AI	M	M & M
5A	Donated Egg	X_D & Y_M	IVF	M	M & M
5B	Transferred Egg	X_D & Y_M	AI with embryo flushing	M	M & M
6	Surrogate Motherhood	X_D & Y_M	AI	D	M & M
7A	Test Tube Baby in Rented Womb	X_M & Y_M	IVF	D	M & M
7B	Transfer to Rented Womb	X_M & Y_M	Natural or AI w/embryo flushing	D	M & M
8	Post-natal Adoption	X_D & Y_D	Natural, AI, or IVF	D	M & M
9	Substitute Father	X_M & Y_D	IVF	M	M & M
10	Brave New World	X_1 & Y_2	IVF or Natural/AI/ w/embryo flushing	3	4 & 5

Abbreviations: X = female, Y = male, AI = artificial insemination, IVF = *in vitro* fertilization, D = donor, M = member or married couple

To these can be added a further permutation where cloning is contemplated.

Secondly, as we saw earlier, the Warnock Committee recommended legislation as the mechanism for regulation. We should pause to consider other ways in which society may respond to the issues raised by medically assisted reproduction. It should be noticed that, in general, particular aspects of medical practice are rarely regulated by statute in England. The 1990 Act is a significant exception to this, perhaps reflecting the fine balance between assisting the infertile and the fears of what could flow from the technologies as they are developed.

In an important report, the Ontario Law Reform Commission examined in detail the arguments for and against regulation and the options for regulation if appropriate.

Ontario Law Reform Commission *Human Artificial Reproduction and Related Matters* (1985) (2 vols)

In this chapter, the Commission has set forth the extent to which the common law, existing statutory and regulatory provisions, and professional rules of conduct may bear on the use and consequences of the new reproductive technologies in Ontario. At the outset, we cautioned that the 'law' in this area is, in a sense, astigmatic – in the main, ignoring or inadvertently applying to the various legal issues arising from the growth of artificial conception services. While the relatively recent advent of these services goes some distance to explain the present state of affairs, the novelty of at least some of the procedures is rapidly diminishing. As a consequence, hitherto reasonable explanations for the dearth of law in the area of artificial conception are beginning to wear thin.

The Commission is quite aware ... that the fact that legislation does not speak directly to a certain matter is not, in itself, a damning criticism necessitating immediate remedial action. Silence may well reflect continuing, deep-seated controversy, so that there may be a justifiable wish to permit the law to develop without legislative fetters. Even inadvertent solutions may be equitable responses – a manifestation of the capacity of the legal regime, created to deal with one set of circumstances, to grow and flourish in a new milieu.

On the other hand, the Commission is acutely conscious of the pervasive notion in many circles that the dictates of medical science, when followed to their logical extremes, will lead inexorably to horrors hitherto characterised as fantasy or science fiction. The spectre of cloning, wholly 'test tube' babies, genetic engineering and manipulation – these and other fears frequently feed the view that the only proper response of the law in this area is prohibition and criminalisation.

While, like others, we are seriously concerned about the nature and implications of certain types of medical and other related research and experimentation, we do not subscribe to his rather cataclysmic, certainly pessimistic view. The automatic invocation of 'logical extremes' and 'worst case scenarios' is not, of course, unique to the present context. But, as a precept for action, these arguments must be viewed with extreme caution; they ought not to animate the proper reaction of the law to all developments in the field of medicine. Keeping pace with new and beneficial scientific advances does not thereby make the law an accomplice with regard to those facets of science unacceptable to the community. The law need not meekly trim its sails to accommodate such unwanted developments. Law and law reform comprehend more than merely wholesale endorsement or outright prohibition; as a manifestation of the perceived needs and wishes of the community, they can also, for example, limit or actively facilitate, encourage, or discourage certain kinds of activity to one degree or another. The Commission's reaction to, and perception of, the present law and its adequacy, insofar as it relates to the new reproductive technologies, largely mirrors this more flexible approach to what we believe to be the proper role of the law in this area.

Some issues are of such fundamental importance to parents, children, and third parties that they no longer ought to be left to the uncertainties and vicissitudes of evolutionary legal development. Perhaps the most obvious example concerns the status of an artificially conceived child. Leaving aside the contentious issue of surrogate motherhood, should the law expressly acknowledge the social reality of a child conceived with the use of donor gametes, so that the social parents are recognised in law as the only parents? Or should the gamete donor, the biological parent, who is almost invariably, but not always, anonymous, be treated in law as a parent, with all the rights and responsibilities attendant upon such a role? Should the rules respecting birth registration further acknowledge the social realities and reflect the intentions and expectations of all the parties? Is society well served by legislation that basically ignores artificial conception in this context and even, occasionally, encourages subterfuge and prompts individuals to evade strictures of the law, for example, by registering children to suit their own predilections?

In relation to these technologies, the vision of the present law is uncomfortably out of focus; indeed, it simply has been overtaken by events. To a significant degree, the existing legal regime cannot escape the confines of the natural reproduction mould. And the search for doctrine that is even remotely relevant to the many serious, complex questions raised in the context of artificial conception involves arduous and generally fruitless legal circumnavigation around frequently foreign principles. It is this uncertainty in the legal implications of various activities – particularly, but not exclusively, in relation to status, parentage, and surrogate motherhood – that pervades the law and practice relating to the use of the new reproductive technologies. A broad cross-section of society, from lawyers to doctors, social workers, ethicists, and others, has decried the absence of clear legal rules to guide the actions of all persons participating, or wishing to participate, in artificial conception programmes. Accordingly, we believe that the law must be re-examined and refashioned. It must reflect the benefits of the new technologies and the reasonable hopes of infertile men and women, while at the same time guarding against those excesses perceived to be injurious to the fabric of society. ... we are constrained to caution against any wholesale abandonment of the view that the law may, and should, act as a progressive, normative guide, not simply a reflection of present community standards. When we consider state intervention in the case of the new reproductive technologies, we may view the issue, at lest in part, as a privacy matter. And when the law deals with matters of personal privacy, it frequently swings its pendulum in favour of individual interests. This issue of personal privacy is critical to our study, and any wish on the part of a segment of society to constrict or limit the ability of individuals to choose whatever method they wish to bring a child into a family, and to regularise their relationship with that child, must be balanced against the human costs attending such intervention. The law may reflect the community's level of tolerance; but it may also stretch or fashion it in the interests of a worthy goal.

For the purpose of our conceptual analysis in this chapter, we shall differentiate between two fundamental approaches to reform, representing the two extreme points on what is clearly a continuum. One basic approach we shall term the 'private ordering' approach, where the legal regime is designed to give effect to the intentions of the parties. The other basic approach we shall call the 'state regulation' approach, where the free choice of the parties does not determine what they may do or the consequences of their actions, but where the state actively intervenes to set mandatory normative standards of conduct. With the latter approach, there are certain ancillary matters that must be addressed. For example, how should the state attempt to persuade people to comply with the rules of behaviour to which adherence is deemed essential?

It bears mentioning here that the so-called private ordering model – exemplified, for example, in the case of one's choice to conceive children by natural reproduction – does not necessarily eschew legislative initiatives. Statutory provisions may indeed be required to give effect to, or preclude interference with, the wishes of individuals. This type of legislation differs from that contemplated by the state intervention approach in its essentially facultative animus: it does not, in effect, tell people what to do or not to do, but serves to facilitate their activities where necessary.

We also wish to note that the two basic approaches set forth in this chapter represent conceptual paradigms of how the law might deal with reproductive choices and their consequences. Accordingly, they each provide a theoretical model against which we may measure the kind of legal regime that ought to govern our conduct. However, a consideration of these general approaches is but one stage in the development of our proposals for reform: it is necessary to determine whether this macroscopic approach to law reform — where all aspects of the subject matter are governed by the same broad conceptual approach – is appropriate in the context of artificial conception. Indeed, it may become clear that the special characteristics of the various artificial reproduction technologies, or certain facets of these technologies, must be dealt with differently. In other words, the legal regime governing such matters need not necessarily be uniform and all-embracing; rather, a more flexible approach, sensitive to the requirements of different aspects of the problem in different ways, may be desirable. Such a hybrid approach may, then, marry aspects of the private ordering and state regulation approaches, and then leave room for common law evolution and for the development of normative guidelines outside the Legislature ...

... the Commission came to the conclusion that the law must take special cognisance of the new artificial conception technologies. In the present chapter, we have examined two main conceptual approaches to law reform in this area, the state regulation approach and the private ordering approach.

When attempting to assess which of the two approaches ought to be adopted in the case of artificial reproduction – or indeed, whether some hybrid approach is preferable – the models of natural reproduction and adoption immediately spring to mind. More specifically, we inevitably come face to face with a general, fundamental question: should the law treat artificial reproduction differently than the manner in which it treats natural reproduction, at least insofar as the decision to conceive a child is concerned? If the private ordering approach is eschewed in favour of the state regulation approach in the case of artificial reproduction, on what basis is such a determination to be made? ...

... while no one can legitimately assume to speak for all segments of the community on so controversial a topic as artificial reproduction, the Commission can attempt to give serious consideration to the conflicting views presented to us directly or gleaned from the increasingly voluminous literature. Our proposals for reform, then, are based on our perception of prevailing community standards, however amorphous they may appear to be, and our view of what members of the community appear to want or be willing to tolerate. Without slavishly and uncritically adopting such standards, they do serve to indicate how members of society believe we ought to be governed. We cannot simply ignore prevailing views, in a sense placing ourselves above the community, enlightening it concerning the 'best' ordering of society. In the area of human conception, whether natural or artificial, it would be presumptuous to take such licence.

Having regard to the considerations just described, we have come to the conclusion that the law must impose a degree of intervention in the case of artificial conception that is neither desirable nor possible in the case of natural reproduction. The wishes of the parties – particularly, the desire of the prospective social parents to have a child – are, in fact, only one of many considerations that should affect the determination of the nature of the new legal regime. Given the implications of artificial conception for persons other than the prospective parents, we strongly believe that 'private ordering' cannot be the sole governing factor. In our view, there are sound philosophical and practical reasons for embracing, at least in some areas, an approach that does not give free rein to the wishes of the parties ...

Having concluded that, under certain circumstances, the state ought to intervene in respect of artificial conception in the interest of broader societal values, several subsidiary, but no less critical, questions arise. For example, to what extent and in respect of what activities, if any, should such intervention take the form of either outright prohibition or regulation? If regulation is desirable in respect of any or all of the activities in question, how should the guiding norms be set, and who should set and apply them?

(a) Prohibition or regulation?

We turn first to consider the two forms by which limits may be placed on an individual's private activities, namely, prohibition and regulation. It should first be made clear that the law need not necessarily adopt only one of these two interventionist means. While clearly a wholesale prohibition respecting the use of artificial conception services would leave nothing to regulate, it is entirely reasonable to envisage a legal regime in which some aspects of the new technologies are prohibited, some are strictly controlled, and some are the subject of minimal regulation.

For example, one might wish to prohibit minors from donating ova for use in IVF programmes because extraction of ova may involve surgical intrusion and because a woman's complement of ova is finite. One might believe it essential to prohibit all forms of what may be termed 'genetic engineering', but countenance research at approved or licensed research centres that have ethical review committees to oversee such activities. Or some latitude might be tolerated in respect of payment of semen donors of their reasonable expenses.

The list of possible permutations and combinations involving prohibition and regulation could easily be expanded. But the essential point is that our perception of the different facets of the subject matter should not be static or rigid; we must be open to the suggestion that a hybrid regime, in which a spectrum of responses, from total prohibition to slight regulation, may be both desirable and possible.

The determination of where specific activities ought to be placed on this spectrum – and not left to the unfettered discretion of individuals – is influenced by several more or less obvious factors. As we indicated in the Introduction to this chapter, matters of logic almost inevitably mix with basic human fears and emotions to produce in each of us a sense of what we may be willing or able to tolerate. The spectre of cloning or experimental genetic manipulation may well be anathema to almost everyone in the community, so that a doctrinaire stance – outright prohibition – may be palatable. But, in other areas, consensus may be difficult, even impossible, to achieve. For example, there has been a continuing debate concerning whether adopted children ought to be entitled to have access to information respecting their natural parents, a debate that arises as well in the context of artificial conception where 'anonymous' donor gametes are used. Rational reasons favouring disclosure vie with concerns respecting the possible emotional reactions of the various parties. And so, insofar as adoption law in Ontario is concerned, we have moved slowly away from an extreme posture of secrecy to a regulated access regime.

Aside from assessing the necessity for, or desirability of, either prohibition or some type of regulation based on the particular attributes of each activity, it must be borne in mind that complete prohibition or strict regulation, however justifiable in the abstract, may produce evasion, especially by the desperate or more affluent who may seek to obtain services in more accommodating jurisdictions. And such violation of the law may well be seen as legitimate in the eyes of the majority or a substantial minority of the population.

But the danger of evasion as such is not the only problem respecting strict punitive measures directed at certain activities. For example, given the relative simplicity of the artificial insemination procedure, its prohibition or strict control may encourage laypersons to perform the insemination on themselves and others, without medical supervision. In other words, this type of artificial reproduction may be driven underground, away from physicians who have the requisite skills and knowledge to prevent or remedy any medical complications that may arise in the recipient or child.

In the case of surrogate motherhood, it is clear that key medical, legal, and other services are available – and have been delivered, to our knowledge, on at least one occasion – outside Ontario to Ontario residents, largely because of the perceived, and correct, view that surrogate motherhood agreements are not enforceable in this Province. Again, attempted suppression does not necessarily result in the elimination of the activity, but may create more perils than anticipated. Indeed, one of the dangers of any prohibition of artificial conceptions is that it may prejudicially affect children conceived in this fashion. We have already seen that the present law deals only inadvertently with such critical issues as the legal status of an artificially conceived child.

There are, then, important human and other costs of prohibition that must be weighed in the balance before seeking to render a particular practice illegal, even though it may be deemed not to be worthy of any active protection. As in the case of our choice between the state regulation and private ordering as a general approach to law reform in this area, these factors have led us to the conclusion that a hybrid regime is both necessary and desirable. Such a regime most adequately reflects the complexity of the subject and the differing norms that, we believe, ought to govern different aspects of each of the new technologies.

(b) The instruments of regulation

Assuming the adoption of a regulatory approach, at least for some purposes, a second set of issues concerns the particular instruments of regulation. Who should set the requisite standards, how should they be set, and who should apply them? Again there are several alternative approaches to the resolution of these questions.

The establishment of norms governing conduct may be left to the Legislature, by means of legislation, to the courts, through the development of common law principles, to governmental or other tribunals, to professional bodies, such as the College of Physicians and Surgeons of Ontario, or to a combination of such institutions. In some cases, a statute or regulation may set a standard to be applied by the medical profession itself. In other cases, legislation may be monitored and interpreted by an administrative body or by the courts. Again, there is no universal rule; the particular combination selected in respect of the establishment and application of normative guides depends on several factors, including the type of the particular activity in question and the nature and extent of the control sought.

Regulation need not, of course, take the form of formal, written norms emanating from some body specifically charged with developing applicable guidelines, for example, the Legislature or even the College of Physicians and Surgeons of Ontario (by means of rules of professional conduct). Regulation of conduct may take place incrementally, through the medium of the courts. The courts, utilising existing common law or developing new rules, may either interpret or add glosses on legislation or written guidelines from some other source, or may deal with controversial issues in respect of which there is no universal social policy or consensus and, hence, no 'legislated' philosophy.

Courts may, for example, exercise a valuable role in determining such issues as the standard of care that is to be applied by practitioners of artificial conception, and whether institutions such as clinics and hospitals, through their infertility units, bear responsibility for their practitioners' negligence. The advantage of leaving such matters to judicial development is that such development will occur within a generalised jurisprudence, and not be, without justification, distinctive or anomalous to artificial conception.

Further, regarding the establishment of the requisite standard of care, court decisions in some cases may reflect developments in the state of the reproductive art as they occur, unfettered by a legislated or regulated framework that may become based upon outmoded techniques or discredited practices. This may be particularly important, since artificial conception technologies are still evolving and many variations in clinical practice exist, the relative advantages of which have yet to be determined by properly conducted studies. A legislated scheme that embodies any particular practice may give undue preference to a procedure that proves to be no better than others and possibly worse, and may inhibit development of superior alternatives. Courts may well compel the raising of standards by finding that the existing practice – for example, on screening gamete donors for adverse genetic traits or venereal infection – does not satisfy legal requirements respecting the standard of care.

It has been observed that '[t]he most ethically and politically controversial aspect of IVF is the status of the embryo'. A legislated solution to this controversy would be of far-reaching effect, and would have implications for many areas of the law. A judicial approach would define the fact situations in which a particular judicial decision is to apply, and the purposes for which a given solution is designed. Judicial explanation, which itself may undergo several reinterpretations, may be preferable to the structured and traditional language of legislation to say within what limits a particular resolution is to operate.

However, a difficulty with entrusting matters to the courts is that, in some cases, they may adhere to precedents that are not related to advances in artificial conception technologies. Judgments may continue to embody public policy perceptions conditioned by the supposition that conception results only from sexual intercourse, or, perhaps at some future time, that artificial conception results only from artificial insemination or IVF, or a particular mode of artificial conception. The early disposition to equate AID with adultery shows how judicial attitudes, while perhaps understandable in one era, may become and remain part of the problem in another era, which legislation may be required to resolve. Courts may take strict and limiting views, for instance, regarding the inheritance rights of a child not genealogically related to a testator, such as the parent of a husband whose wife had the child by AID, when the testator made a bequest to the husband and the 'heirs of his body'.

There is, however, a dynamic interaction between legislation and judicial attitudes, since courts tend to note the thrust of legislative initiatives, and often take leads from them. If legislation were enacted specifically to accommodate all or certain types of artificial conception, for instance, it might be unlikely that the courts would regard agreements made in furtherance of such particular conceptions as void as against public policy. Courts may, of course, decline to admit a new kind of claim, on the ground that the matter raises a significant issue of public policy that should be tackled by the Legislature before a solution is incorporated into the law by the courts; and they may similarly feel that private arrangements regarding sensitive areas, such as surrogate motherhood agreements, should be approved by an Act of the Legislature rather than by a court. Once generally accommodating legislation has been passed, however, the courts may find such legislation to be an expression of public acceptance or tolerance in which they may find inspiration and direction.

It is never certain, on the other hand, that courts will follow the lead of legislation, or interpret, apply, or extend its provisions in a collaborative way. Judges may hesitate to go further than recent legislation, reasoning that, had the Legislature intended its scheme to embrace an additional step, it would have so provided, and that its failure so to provide is evidence of a contrary intention. For avoidance of doubt, legislation may have to be drafted comprehensively in order to address foreseeable areas of possible application. Oversights and issues beyond anticipation may then have to be left to the courts, but the legislative design may, in principle, aim to be all-embracing, as a self-contained and definitive code.

Alternatively, it may not be necessary to resolve every detail in order to achieve legislation that is sufficiently comprehensive to address a given issue. Depending on the particular issue, minimal legislation may be enacted, fashioning the critical skeleton of a new policy, but leaving the developed form to be supplied by an emerging jurisprudence. Legislation also may properly be structured in order to anticipate and accommodate further developments in related case law, without seeking to affect its direction. If the case law fails to develop, or follows an unsatisfactory direction the Legislature always retains its residual power to supplement or supersede judgments.

In the same way that certain matters may be left to be resolved by the courts, other matters may best be resolved according to medical professional ethics, bearing in mind that the practice of medicine may include artificial conception and, accordingly, that such a practice may be undertaken only by doctors or persons under their supervision or direction.

We have seen that the Legislature has granted the College of Physicians and Surgeons of Ontario wide powers of self-government. Among other things, the College may regulate the practice of medicine and establish standards of knowledge, skill, qualification, and practice among members. In addition, the College may set ethical standards for doctors.

Having regard to the fact that the statutory mandate of the College is exercised 'in order that the public interest may be served and protected', it is not surprising that persons who are authorised to practise medicine by the College are subject to compulsory discipline for professional misconduct. 'Professional misconduct' is defined in regulations made under the *Health Disciplines Act*, primarily in collaboration with the provincial Ministry of Health. The list of activities constituting professional misconduct tends to be specific, but a residual category exists for 'conduct or an act relevant to the practice of medicine that, having regard to all the circumstances, would reasonably be regarded by members as disgraceful, dishonourable or unprofessional'.

The College of Physicians and Surgeons of Ontario conscientiously consults with those whom it regulates and with the wider community beyond, in the process of formulating its ethical position on various matters, and it is open to public and media comment and ministerial influence. It may strike committees to address particular issues and may involve non-professionals in its deliberations and recommendations. Accordingly, it may reflect an ethical consensus with considerable credibility, although it may be expected that the opinions of the professionals it regulates, who are also strongly represented on the governing council, will be heard with special clarity.

The College periodically updates its principles of ethical practice, and contributes to public education and discussion concerning such principles. It attempts to respond to past events and to anticipate future possibilities, so that practitioners generally are offered guidance when they contemplate innovative practices. Further, unlike courts of law, the College will accommodate requests from doctors for *ad hoc* ethical rulings based upon hypotheses and anticipated scenarios. Its familiarity with the realities of practice and its access to scientific and technical data may afford its judgments a conviction that more abstract theorising may lack.

Contributions to the debate of the ethics of professional practice may come through initiatives of many organisations other than the provincial College. The views of responsible bodies, such as the Medical Research Council, may be of significance regarding, for example, research concerning the use of gametes and embryos. Moreover, the reports of governmental agencies or professional bodies in Canada and around the world can be expected to be seriously considered. Professional ethical principles may, therefore, be informed by a variety of national and international considerations that may influence perceptions of what provincial ethical practice requires. Inasmuch as the ethical assessments of the College of Physicians and Surgeons of Ontario may draw from the same body of knowledge that would be relevant to the design of statutes or regulations, such assessments may serve equally to control conduct within the medical profession, and may even enjoy the greater confidence and sympathetic compliance of individual physicians.

Accordingly, it is possible to leave some matters unaddressed by statute, to be determined by authorised practitioners acting under professional guidance. Practitioners are accountable both through the courts, for the injuries they wrongfully cause to individuals they have a legal duty to protect, and through their professional disciplinary councils, for breach of ethical rules, professional misconduct, or falling below the established standards of their profession. Further, while legislation may be introduced to govern such activities as research, it may be equally appropriate, and perhaps preferable, to confine sensitive research, such as research on embryos, to special centres that maintain credible ethical screening of research proposals through institutional review boards, and that undertake departmental and other monitoring of clinical and research practices.

An advantage of this approach to the control of individual practice is that it would utilise existing personnel, institutions, and established mechanisms, whereas new regulatory legislation might require a policing and enforcement service that might be less than comprehensive, costly, and poorly received among professionals conscious of their responsibilities. By the same token, some may argue that professionals are generally too socially conservative, health professionals in particular having been suspected of undue paternalism in pursuing patients' perceived interests rather than patients' expressed wishes. These and other advantages and disadvantages that attach to the control of artificial conception through medical and related professional guidelines must be balanced against the advantages and disadvantages of seeking control through express legislation.

In light of the Commission's philosophy and previous conclusions respecting the appropriate approach to law reform in the case of the new reproductive technologies and respecting the nature of the limits that should be placed on an individual's private actions, it should come as no surprise that, in the present context, we once again eschew a dogmatic approach that would require uniform treatment to be provided in all cases. We believe that some matters – clearly those that involve outright prohibition of certain activities – necessitate statutory control. Other matters, setting out procedural details or licensure requirements, may be left to the regulations. And yet further matters, involving essentially medical judgment or involving ethical issues relating to the conduct of physicians, may be determined by the medical profession, either formally or informally. In all, or most, of these cases, recourse may well be had to the courts to interpret legislation or relevant codes of ethics or professional conduct.

The first legislation in the world to regulate assisted reproduction was the Infertility (Medical Procedures) Act 1984 in Victoria, Australia (since replaced by the Infertility Treatment Act 1995 (Vic)). Subsequently a number of jurisdictions have legislated, including South Australia (Reproductive Technology Act 1988) and Western Australia (Human Reproductive Technology Act 1991). As we saw, the Government in the UK has regulated through the Human Fertilisation and Embryology Act 1990 (hereafter the 1990 Act). The regulatory framework took effect on 1 August 1991 and, apart from surrogacy, seeks to establish a comprehensive legislative framework. In Europe, legislation also exists in a number of countries, for example, France, Germany, Austria, Norway, Sweden, Denmark and Spain (for a comparative overview see, D Evans (ed), *Conceiving the Embryo: Ethics, Law and Practice in Human Embryology* (1996) and D Evans (ed), *Creating the Child: The Ethics, Law and Practice of Assisted Procreation* (1996) generally).

Assisted reproduction technology

Our main concern here is with the regulation of treatments for infertility but we also consider the regulation of research on embryos. The infertility treatments regulated by the 1990 Act are those that involve the use of donated genetic material (whether sperm, eggs or embryos) or those which involve the creation of an embryo outside the human body. In addition, the 1990 Act regulates the storage of all reproductive material. What is not directly regulated by the 1990 Act is the practice of surrogacy. Only in so far as a surrogate birth is achieved through the use, in part or whole, of donated genetic material or using IVF techniques is the framework of the 1990 Act applicable. Otherwise, the practice of surrogacy is regulated, again in part, by the Surrogacy Arrangements Act 1985 (which we will consider later in this chapter).

At the heart of the 1990 Act is the establishment of an authority charged generally with the implementation of the statute. This is the Human Fertilisation and Embryology Authority (HFEA) (s 5). The membership of HFEA is prescribed in Sch 1 to the 1990 Act. It consists of a chairman and deputy chairman and such other members as the Secretary of State appoints. In appointing such members the Secretary of State must ensure that there is a majority of members who are neither doctors nor research scientists. Similarly, the chairman and deputy chairman must not be drawn from these professional groups.

The principle functions of the HFEA are as follows:

(i) to license treatment services, the storage of gametes and embryos and research on embryos (s 11);
(ii) to monitor and inspect premises and activities carried out under statutory licence (s 9);
(iii) to submit an annual report to the Secretary of State on its activities (s 7); and
(iv) to maintain a code of practice as guidance for the proper conduct of activities carried out under a licence (s 25).

By s 8 of the 1990 Act, the HFEA has the following additional 'general' functions:

8. General functions of the Authority

The Authority shall –
(a) keep under review information about embryos and any subsequent development of embryos and about the provision of treatment services and activities governed by this Act, and advise the Secretary of State, if he asks it to do so, about those matters,
(b) publicise the services provided to the public by the Authority or provided in pursuance of licences,
(c) provide, to such extent as it considers appropriate, advice and information for persons to whom licences apply or who are receiving treatment services or providing gametes or embryos for use for the purposes of activities governed by this Act, or may wish to do so, and
(d) perform such other functions as may be specified in regulations.

A. LICENSING

The 1990 Act divides activities involving human gametes and embryos into three categories. First, there are those activities, for example, cloning (but perhaps not all instances of it, see *infra*), which are illegal (ie criminal) and cannot be licensed. Secondly, there are those activities which are illegal (ie criminal) unless carried out pursuant to a licence granted by the HFEA, for example, the creation of an embryo *ex utero* or the storage of gametes or embryos. Thirdly, there are those activities which are not covered by the Act and so are lawful even without a licence, for example, the treatment of a couple using the sperm of the male partner (ie artificial insemination by the husband or Gamete Intra-Fallopian Transfer (GIFT)):

1. The general scheme

The basic framework for regulation can be found in ss 1–4 of the Human Fertilisation and Embryology Act 1990:

Principal terms used

1. Meaning of 'embryo', 'gamete' and associated expressions

(1) In this Act, except where otherwise stated –
(a) embryo means a live human embryo where fertilisation is complete, and
(b) references to an embryo include an egg in the process of fertilisation, and, for this purpose, fertilisation is not complete until the appearance of a two cell zygote.
(2) This Act, so far as it governs bringing about the creation of an embryo, applies only to bringing about the creation of an embryo outside the human body; and in this Act –
(a) references to embryos the creation of which was brought about *in vitro* (in their application to those where fertilisation is complete) are to those where fertilisation began outside the human body whether or not it was completed there, and
(b) references to embryos taken from a woman do not include embryos whose creation was brought about *in vitro*.
(3) This Act, so far as it governs the keeping or use of an embryo, applies only to keeping or using an embryo outside the human body.

(4) References in this Act to gametes, eggs or sperms, except where otherwise stated, are to live human gametes, eggs or sperms but references below in this Act to gametes or eggs do not include eggs in the process of fertilisation.

2. Other terms

(1) In this Act –

'the Authority' means the Human Fertilisation and Embryology Authority established under section 5 of this Act, ...

'Licence' means a licence under Schedule 2 to this Act and, ...

'treatment services' means medical, surgical or obstetric services provided to the public or a section of the public for the purpose of assisting women to carry children.

(2) References in this Act to keeping, in relation to embryos or gametes, include keeping while preserved, whether preserved by cryopreservation or in any other way; and embryos or gametes so kept are referred to in this Act as 'stored' (and 'store' and 'storage' are to be interpreted accordingly).

(3) For the purposes of this Act, a woman is not to be treated as carrying a child until the embryo has become implanted.

Activities governed by the Act

3. Prohibitions in connection with embryos

(1) No person shall –

(a) bring about the creation of an embryo, or

(b) keep or use an embryo,

except in pursuance of a licence.

(2) No person shall place in a woman –

(a) a live embryo other than a human embryo, or

(b) any live gametes other than human gametes.

(3) A licence cannot authorise –

(a) keeping or using an embryo after the appearance of the primitive streak,

(b) placing an embryo in any animal,

(c) keeping or using an embryo in any circumstances in which regulations prohibit its keeping or use, or

(d) replacing a nucleus of a cell of an embryo with a nucleus taken from a cell of any person, embryo or subsequent development of an embryo.

(4) For the purposes of subsection (3)(a) above, the primitive streak is to be taken to have appeared in an embryo not later than the end of the period of 14 days beginning with the day when the gametes are mixed, not counting any time during which the embryo is stored.

Prohibition in connection with germ cells

3A. – (1) No person shall, for the purpose of providing fertility services for any woman, use female germ cells taken or derived from an embryo or a foetus or use embryos created by using such cells.

(2) In this section –

'female germ cells' means cells of the female germ line and includes such cells at any stage of maturity and accordingly includes eggs; and

'fertility services' means medical, surgical or obstetric services provided for the purpose of assisting women to carry children.

4. Prohibitions in connection with gametes

(1) No person shall –

(a) store any gametes, or

(b) in the course of providing treatment services for any woman, use the sperm of any man unless the services are being provided for the woman and the man together or use the eggs of any other woman, or

(c) mix gametes with the live gametes of any animals,

except in pursuance of a licence.

(2) A licence cannot authorise storing or using gametes in any circumstances in which regulations prohibit their storage or use.

(3) No person shall place sperm and eggs in a woman in any circumstances specified in regulations except in pursuance of a licence.

(4) Regulations made by virtue of subsection (3) above may provide that, in relation to licences only to place sperm and eggs in a woman in such circumstances, sections 12 to 22 of this Act shall have effect with such modifications as may be specified in the regulations.

(5) Activities regulated by this section or section 3 of this Act are referred to in this Act as 'activities governed by this Act'.

A number of points should be noted arising from these sections establishing the basic framework.

First, the Act wholly regulates the creation, use and storage of human embryos *ex utero*, whether for treatment or research purposes. By contrast, the Act only partially regulates dealing with human gametes. Storage of sperm or eggs does require a licence. And, given that a licence is required for the storage of 'gametes' (s 4(1)(a)), a single licence will cover both 'eggs' and 'sperm'. However, the use of human gametes is only regulated in the case of use for treatment if donated gametes are involved and, in the case of research, if the gametes are to be mixed with gametes of an animal. In general, therefore, other use of gametes for research (not involving storage) is unregulated. (For exceptions to the need for a storage licence for gametes to be used for certain purposes such as teaching and research see, The Human Fertilisation and Embryology (Special Exemptions) Regulations 1991 (SI No 1588 1991).) Similarly, infertility procedures involving the patients' own gametes and not involving the creation of embryos are also unregulated. The best known example of this is the procedure known as GIFT. At the time the legislation was passing through Parliament a move was made to include GIFT within the regulatory framework. In the event this failed but, as you will see, s 4(3) and (4) permit the making of regulations which could bring procedures such as GIFT within the Act: there are none at present. Curiously, the HFEA takes the view that some parts of the regulatory provisions apply to *unlicensed* treatments such as GIFT carried out at licensed centres. In its *Code of Practice* (4th edn, 1998) the HFEA states that the licence conditions that require the 'welfare of any child' born or already existing be considered by a doctor prior to giving treatment also applies to unlicensed procedures, for example, GIFT (*supra*, para 3.13). It is not clear what the legal basis for this is. It may well be good practice to consider the welfare of the child, perhaps even an aspect of the doctor's common law duty, but it cannot be required by the 1990 Act. Only those activities which would be unlawful without a licence need authorisation from, and can be authorised by, the HFEA.

Secondly, the 1990 Act was amended in 1994 (by s 156 of the Criminal Justice and Public Order Act 1994) to introduce s 3A. Section 3A came into force on 10 April 1995 (see The Criminal Justice and Public Order Act 1994 (Commencement No 6) Order 1995 (SI 1995 No 721)). The new section makes it a criminal offence, punishable by a maximum penalty of ten years' imprisonment, to use foetal eggs or embryos derived therefrom in medically assisted reproduction. In order to ensure that immature foetal eggs are covered, s 3A uses the statutory phrase 'female germ cells' which is defined in s 3A(2) to cover immature as well as mature eggs. What s 3A does not prohibit, on its face, is *research* using foetal eggs. (Research on any resulting embryos is regulated by the 1990 Act: s 3 and Sch 2 in particular.) Of course, a great deal of research on foetal eggs would probably be directed towards their use in infertility treatment. Since the latter is now prohibited, effectively this kind of research will not be undertaken.

It is recognised that there is a shortage of eggs for donation to infertile women particularly from ethnic groups. Harvesting the eggs from aborted foetuses would, at a stroke, overcome any general shortage. (Other rich sources could be transplantation of ovarian tissue from live donors and from cadavers.) Section 3A is, in fact, a pre-emptive strike by those opposed to use of foetal eggs. It is not feasible yet to use them in clinical practice, though it might not be long before the techniques are developed.

Curiously, s 3A was enacted at a time when the Human Fertilisation and Embryology Authority was conducting a public consultation process on the use of eggs obtained from foetuses, live donors and cadavers for research and treatment. Parliamentary intervention through s 3A somewhat shortcircuited this process, at least in part. Although, ultimately, the Authority took a view consistent with s 3A (see Report on *Donated Ovarian Tissue in Embryo Research and Assisted Conception* (July 1994) at para 20).

We will return to the issue of the use of ovarian tissue later in this chapter (*infra*). You will, however, notice one feature of s 3A: it is intended to cover both mature and immature eggs and does so by utilising the phrase 'female germ cells' which is defined to include both (s 3A(2)). The reason for this is that it is not clear whether the 1990 Act would otherwise cover immature eggs (or sperm). The argument is that the statutory term 'gamete(s)' includes only mature eggs or sperm. Unfortunately, the 1990 Act does not provide any guidance in s 1 where 'gametes, eggs or sperm' are merely stated to refer to 'live human gametes, eggs or sperm' (s 1(4)). This question is crucial when considering the application of the 1990 Act to the storage of ovarian and testicular tissue. As we shall see, the HFEA has adopted a narrow interpretation of 'gamete(s)' so as to exclude 'immature' eggs or sperm from the scope of the 1990 Act (see *infra*).

Thirdly, the Act permits research on human embryos providing HFEA has licensed the research project. However, s 3(3)(a) and (4), when read together, limit the power to grant a licence for such research to embryos which have not developed a primitive streak. Section 3(4) irrebuttably presumes that this takes place 'not later than the end of the period of 14 days beginning with the day when the gametes are mixed, not counting any time during which the embryo is stored'. (For a discussion of the arguments surrounding the use of human embryos for research, see *First Edition* of this book at pp 660–682.)

Fourthly, it is important to notice the statutory definition given to the word 'embryo' by s 1(1) given that any activity which results in the creation of an embryo *ex utero* triggers the need for the activity to be licensed. The wording of s 1(1) is curious. It contemplates an embryo being the product of the 'complete' fertilisation of an egg by a sperm. Further, in order to bring within the Act research at an early stage of fertilisation, s 1(1)(b) broadens that definition so as to include 'an egg in the *process* of fertilisation'. So far so good. However, s 1(1)(b) goes on to state that 'fertilisation is not complete until the appearance of a two cell zygote'. The definition of 'embryo' now contradicts itself. An embryo is both 'complete' in the process of fertilisation and not 'complete' until that process is over. Parliament's intention is clear; the wording of the Act is, however, unfortunate. As we shall see, the definition of 'embryo' is crucial to the question of whether some 'cloning' techniques may be licenced by the HFEA or, by contrast, are largely left unregulated by the Act (see *infra*).

Fifthly, artificial insemination which does not involve donated gametes is outside the Act. This is clear from the wording of s 4(1)(b). As can be seen from s 4(1)(b), the Act is concerned, on the whole, with the provision of 'treatment services'. The Act makes it clear that it is only concerned with infertility treatments provided 'to the public or a section of the public', arguably, by the appropriate medical personnel (s 2(1)). Thus, do-it-yourself artificial insemination, even using sperm donated by someone else, does not fall within the Act (unless the sperm has been stored).

Finally, we should notice the definition of 'store' or 'storage' in s 2(2) of the Act. This provision defines the relevant terms widely. Of course, the most obvious form of storage is cryopreservation (ie freezing). But under the Act, any form of 'keeping while preserved' gametes or embryo amounts to storage. The definition is, however, limited in this respect. It would not cover the 'keeping' of gametes or embryos in the laboratory or clinic while fresh before use *unless* preservative measures have been taken. Mere 'keeping' is not storage although what mounts to 'preservation' is not entirely clear. Does it, for example, cover 'dry shippers' used to allow transfer of sperm for home insemination? (See *Code of Practice*, *supra*, para 7.16). Arguably, it includes anything which prevents deterioration in the condition of the gametes or embryos - whether this involves chemical or cooling agents or, in some cases, maintaining the ambient temperature. If so, and this would seem to be a proper interpretation of the Act, the patient (who is not licensed) may be unable to take them without themselves having a storage licence (see s 14(1)(b), 1990 Act)! That is unless receipt of the sperm is seen as supply 'in the course of providing treatment services' to the patient (*ibid*) which it might be even though self-insemination is contemplated.

2. Licensed activities

(a) The scheme

The HFEA has statutory power to grant licences for the following activities: infertility treatment, research and storage. While storage licences may be combined with licences for treatment or research, licences may not be granted combining research and treatment. The detail of the licensing procedure is set out in ss 9, 10 and 16–22 of the 1990 Act and The Human Fertilisation and Embryology Authority (Licence Committee and Appeals) Regulations 1991 (SI 1999 No 1889) (and see HFEA, *Manual for Centres* (March 1996)). The essence of the scheme is described in the HFEA's *Second Annual Report* in 1993:

Once an application has been received, the process is as follows:
  i.   a site visit by a team of inspectors;
  ii.   consideration of the application and inspection report by a licence committee;
  iii. notification of the outcome to the applicant.
If the applicant is not content with the decision, representations may be made to the committee before the decision takes effect. This may be followed by an appeal to the full Authority and finally, on a point of law, an applicant may appeal to the High Court.

One of the most important aspects of the whole inspection and licensing process is to promote and sustain good practice and, in doing so, to ensure a consistent approach. At the beginning, the Authority established a number of procedures to ensure that these objectives are met and regularly reviewed. ...

After an inspection, a report is submitted to a licence committee. The committee's decision to issue or refuse a licence takes account of the recommendations of the inspection teams.

... Licence Committees
Licence committees consist of five members of the Authority, with a quorum of three. ...

In considering licence applications and the standards to be met, licence committees must be guided by the Act and the Code of Practice. Where new or major issues arise, such as home insemination, licence committees have taken policy advice from the Authority. Guidance has then been given as an addition to the Code of Practice which, following consultation, has been revised accordingly.

To ensure that the Authority maintained a consistent approach to licensing, a strategy was developed for assessing and monitoring standards in centres based on the following:

(i) As well as the standard conditions attached to all licences, additional conditions are attached to licences on occasions where the inspection team or the licence committee discovers a breach (or breaches) of the Act or of the Code of Practice. Centres may be given a certain amount of time to comply with conditions of licence or, alternatively, compliance may be assessed at the next full inspection. Licence conditions have been used, when appropriate, as a means of applying pressure on centres to conform quickly in areas where there have been observed deficiencies in their practice. In this first year, it has been only those centres where this approach was not thought to be sufficient to achieve the required result which have been refused treatment licences. Monitoring of conditions is also carried out by the inspector coordinators who act as the point of contact between the Authority and the centre.

(ii) Licences are issued for a specific period of time with twelve months being the standard duration. A number of fifteen month licences were issued in the first year in order to spread the expiry dates more evenly throughout the year. Centres which have particularly stringent (or numerous) conditions attached to their licence have normally been given short-term licences so that the concerns of a licence committee can be reassessed at further inspections.

The licence committee judges what is a reasonable length of time within which the centre should be expected to meet the conditions before a decision is made on the duration of the licence.

The following table shows the length of time for which treatment licences were issued in the first year of licensing.

Length of licence issued (months)

	Three	Six	Twelve	Fifteen
No. of Centres	4	3	81	19

(iii) Licence committees may ask that a letter be sent to a centre which includes specific recommendations. Generally a recommendation is practical advice, based on the Authority's experience of good practice.

The Authority has reviewed all of the conditions and recommendations attached to licences issued in the first year. Not only has this demonstrated a good degree of consistency in the decision-making process, but it has also led to standardisation in the wording of some of the more common conditions and recommendations.

(iv) Centres are commended for particularly high standards of practice and their procedures and methods may be used by the Authority to help other centres obtain equally high standards. Communication between centres is encouraged ...

... Licences Issued and Refused
The Authority currently licenses 107 treatment centres of which 65 are for IVF and 37 for donor insemination only. A total of 32 research and 8 storage only licences have been issued. Lists of currently licensed centres and research projects are set out at Annexes 3 and 4. Five licence applications have been refused, including 2 research applications.

Where treatment licences have been refused the reasons for the refusal have been given to the applicants. Generally these have been cases where the centres failed in significant ways to meet the standards required by the Act and Code of Practice, and where it appeared to the licence committee that the centre would be unable to meet the required standard within a reasonable period of time.

Licence conditions have related to aspects of the Code of Practice. However, given the emphasis placed on certain issues in the Act and the Code of Practice, it is not surprising that many of the conditions relate to counselling, confidentiality and security, the welfare of the child and information for patients. These are all new statutory obligations which some centres are considering for the first time. It is reasonable therefore for the Authority to recognise that in some centres it may take a little time to develop adequate procedures ...

... Appeals
Appeals against licence committee decisions may be made to the full Authority. If the appellant is unhappy with the outcome of an appeal and believes there are grounds, on a point of law, a further appeal may be lodged with the High Court. The Authority has, so far, heard one appeal against a licence committee's decision to refuse a treatment licence application. This was an application for an IVF licence in a centre which offered GIFT as a treatment and the centre wished to use IVF as a diagnostic means of establishing the likelihood of fertilisation in vivo. The Authority took the view that the quality of embryology support needed to make this procedure worthwhile in these circumstances was as great as that demanded in an IVF treatment centre and that it should therefore only be used in centres which had the expertise to offer IVF treatment. In this particular case the centre was unable to meet that standard and the resulting appeal did not succeed. The principle that emerged from this has subsequently been included in the Authority's revised Code of Practice.

Breaches of the Code of Practice
Licence committees have also considered cases where centres are in breach of Code of Practice guidelines. Most notably there have been some cases where centres have transferred to a woman four embryos during a single treatment cycle. The limit stated in the Code of Practice is three. In each case the centres concerned had done this on only a single occasion which was shortly after the Code of Practice took effect on 1 August 1991. Each of the centres concerned provided the licence committee with a report of how the breach had occurred. They also gave assurances that this was the only occasion on which four embryos had been transferred, and that their policies were to limit the number to three in all cases. Having seen the centres' reports, the licence committees asked the Chief Executive to write to the centres concerned informing them of the seriousness with which the Authority viewed the breach and warning them of the possible consequences of any further breach of this limit. This might include suspension or revocation of licences ...

. . . Review Procedures

While much of the licensing procedure is set out in statute, the corresponding administrative arrangements are entirely at the discretion of the Authority. The Authority is aware that it is important to ensure that the right information is available to centres, to inspectors and to licence committees.

The Licensing and Fees Committee has therefore examined the inspection and licensing procedures in the light of experience from the first year. The views of centres and of inspectors have been taken into account in this review process.

The Authority's first year of licensing has been very successful. In order to maintain consistency, licence conditions will, in future, be standardised as far as possible to show how they relate to particular parts of the Code of Practice. Information gained from experience of licensing will continue to be used to develop and improve the licensing process.

The manual for centres is being updated to take account of recent amendments to the Code of Practice, and to other procedures and guidance.

The Inspection Process

For some centres the inspection process was an entirely new experience and was somewhat daunting. Over the last year inspections lasted between two hours and a full day depending on the size of the centre, the applications made and the services offered. The aim has been to ensure that the centre is adhering to the Act and the Code of Practice, that the staff are properly qualified and that the facilities are of an appropriately high standard.

During the inspection the team meets the 'Person Responsible', whose duty it is to ensure that the centre complies with the requirements of the Act and the Code of Practice. The team also meets the medical and scientific staff, nurses, counsellors and staff in charge of recordkeeping. Each is questioned about the procedures at the clinic and about their particular role. In addition questions are asked and investigations made in the following areas:

Staff
The inspectors ensure that all staff have appropriate qualifications and experience.

Facilities
The visiting team inspects the facilities used during treatment and research. Particular consideration is given to ensuring that the facilities and laboratory conditions are of a sufficiently high standard and that attention has been given to overall security as well as to monitoring clinical, counselling and laboratory practice.

Assessing Clients
Centres are required, by law, to take account of the welfare of any child who may be born or affected by the treatment. Questions are asked about what medical and social investigations are performed before treatment begins and the criteria used in deciding whether to treat and which treatment is most appropriate.

Donors
Centres using donated eggs, sperm or embryos are asked about their procedures for the recruitment and counselling of donors and the screening performed before donated material is used. The team also ensures that there are suitable procedures for limiting the number of children born from a single donor.

Information and Consent
Centres are required, by law, to provide information to those considering treatment. Any written information given to patients before, during or after treatment is assessed by the inspection team to ensure that it is accurate, comprehensive and easily understood. In particular, it should not be misleading, any success rates quoted should be accurate for that particular centre and all charges should be clearly set out with no hidden costs. The consent forms are also reviewed.

Counselling
All centres are required, by law, to offer counselling to those considering or undergoing treatment and to potential donors. On inspection visits consideration is given to when, where and how the offer of counselling is made.

Handling, Use, Storage and Disposal of Gametes and Embryos
By speaking to staff and inspecting the facilities, a judgment is made on the standard of service offered and the centre's adherence to the guidelines on good practice set out in the Code of Practice.

Records
Particular attention is given to the precautions taken for the security of patient and donor records and the system of record-keeping.

Research
In those centres undertaking licensed research, the inspection team meets the chairman or a member of the local research ethics committee and the staff involved in the research. The reasons for undertaking the research, its aims, the justification for the use of human embryos and the ethics committee's deliberations are all discussed.

Other
Centres are required to have a formal complaints procedure and questions about the number, nature and outcome of any complaints are asked during the inspection visit. Enquiries are also made about any other issues which may be of interest to the HFEA.

A number of points to notice arising from this account by the HFEA. First, the HFEA is currently moving to a three-year licensing cycle (see 7th *Annual Report* (1998) (HFEA) p 1). Secondly, the most recent figures show that 72 clinics are licensed for IVF and DI, one for IVF only, 31 for DI only, eight for storage of sperm only and two had only research licences: a total of 114 clinics. A total of 24 research projects are licenced (see, 7th *Annual Report* (*supra*) pp 1 and 22).

(b) Licences and conditions

As we have seen, the regulatory framework is a creature of statute. The Act is complex. Here is not the place to engage in a detailed exegesis of all the statutory provisions. Instead, we will set out for completeness the essential provisions governing the terms under which licences will be granted in Sch 2 and ss 12–15. Then, we will take up and examine a number of important issues concerning access to treatment, consent to use and control of genetic material, access to and control of information and the status of children born after infertility treatment.

Schedule 2 to the 1990 Act lays out the HFEA's powers concerning the granting and scope of licences under the Act (see also s 11).

SCHEDULE 2

ACTIVITIES FOR WHICH LICENCES MAY BE GRANTED

Licences for treatment
1. – (1) A licence under this paragraph may authorise any of the following in the course of providing treatment services –
(a) bringing about the creation of embryos *in vitro*,
(b) keeping embryos,
(c) using gametes,
(d) practices designed to secure that embryos are in a suitable condition to be placed in a woman or to determine whether embryos are suitable for that purpose,
(e) placing any embryo in a woman,
(f) mixing sperm with the egg of a hamster, or other animal specified in directions, for the purpose of testing the fertility or normality of the sperm, but only where anything which forms is destroyed when the test is completed and, in any event, not later than the two cell stage, and
(g) such other practices as may be specified in, or determined in accordance with, regulations.
(2) Subject to the provisions of this Act, a licence under this paragraph may be granted subject to such conditions as may be specified in the licence and may authorise the performance of any of the activities referred to in sub-paragraph (1) above in such manner as may be so specified.
(3) A licence under this paragraph cannot authorise any activity unless it appears to the Authority to be necessary or desirable for the purpose of providing treatment services.
(4) A licence under this paragraph cannot authorise altering the genetic structure of any cell while it forms part of an embryo.
(5) A licence under this paragraph shall be granted for such period not exceeding five years as may be specified in the licence.

Licences for storage
2. – (1) A licence under this paragraph or paragraph 1 or 3 of this Schedule may authorise the storage of gametes or embryos or both.

(2) Subject to the provisions of this Act, a licence authorising such storage may be granted subject to such conditions as may be specified in the licence and may authorise storage in such manner as may be so specified.

(3) A licence under this paragraph shall be granted for such period not exceeding five years as may be specified in the licence.

Licences for research

3. – (1) A licence under this paragraph may authorise any of the following –

(a)   bringing about the creation of embryos *in vitro*, and

(b)   keeping or using embryos,

for the purposes of a project of research specified in the licence.

(2) A licence under this paragraph cannot authorise any activity unless it appears to the Authority to be necessary or desirable for the purpose of –

(a)   promoting advances in the treatment of infertility,

(b)   increasing knowledge about the causes of congenital disease,

(c)   increasing knowledge about the causes of miscarriages,

(d)   developing more effective techniques of contraception, or

(e)   developing methods for detecting the presence of gene or chromosome abnormalities in embryos before implantation,

or for such other purposes as may be specified in regulations.

(3) Purposes may only be so specified with a view to the authorisation of projects of research which increase knowledge about the creation and development of embryos, or about disease, or enable such knowledge to be applied.

(4) A licence under this paragraph cannot authorise altering the genetic structure of any cell while it forms part of an embryo, except in such circumstances (if any) as may be specified in or determined in pursuance of regulations.

(5) A licence under this paragraph may authorise mixing sperm with the egg of a hamster, or other animal specified in directions, for the purpose of developing more effective techniques for determining the fertility or normality of sperm, but only where anything which forms is destroyed when the research is complete and, in any event, not later than the two cell stage.

(6) No licence under this paragraph shall be granted unless the Authority is satisfied that any proposed use of embryos is necessary for the purposes of the research.

(7) Subject to the provisions of this Act, a licence under this paragraph may be granted subject to such conditions as may be specified in the licence.

(8) A licence under this paragraph may authorise the performance of any of the activities referred to in sub-paragraph (1) or (5) above in such manner as may be so specified.

(9) A licence under this paragraph shall be granted for such period not exceeding three years as may be specified in the licence.

General

4. – (1) A licence under this Schedule can only authorise activities to be carried out on premises specified in the licence and under the supervision of an individual designated in the licence.

(2) A licence cannot –

(a)   authorise activities falling within both paragraph 1 and paragraph 3 above,

(b)   apply to more than one project of research,

(c)   authorise activities to be carried on under the supervision of more than one individual, or

(d)   apply to premises in different places.

Three general points need to be made briefly. First, a licence (of whatever kind) is granted to an individual known as the 'person responsible' (see ss 16 and 17) or, if someone else, the 'nominal licensee'. There must always be, however, a 'person responsible' and this individual remains responsible for complying with the terms and conditions of the licence. A 'nominal licensee' may be a manager or other administrative employee of a clinic but the 'person responsible' will always be a Clinician or, where appropriate, a scientist. Secondly, treatment licences authorise particular classes of treatments to be carried out under the control of the 'person responsible' at the designated premises (similarly in the case of a storage licence). By contrast, licences for research are granted for a specific project of research for one or more of the purposes set out in para 3 of Sch 2. Thirdly, licences for all activities are subject to a maximum time-limit: five years in the case of licences for treatment and storage and three years for research.

As you will notice from the terms of Sch 2, licences are subject to conditions. The Act spells out a number of standard conditions for all licences (s 12) and for the particular activities contemplated by the Act (s 13 (treatment); s 14 (storage); s 15 (research)).

Licence conditions

12. General conditions

The following shall be conditions of every licence granted under this Act –

(a) that the activities authorised by the licence shall be carried on only on the premises to which the licence relates and under the supervision of the person responsible,

(b) that any member or employee of the Authority, on production, if so required, of a document identifying the person as such, shall at all reasonable times be permitted to enter those premises and inspect them (which includes inspecting any equipment or records and observing any activity),

(c) that the provisions of Schedule 3 to this Act shall be complied with,

(d) that proper records shall be maintained in such form as the Authority may specify in directions,

(e) that no money or other benefit shall be given or received in respect of any supply of gametes or embryos unless authorised by directions,

(f) that, where gametes or embryos are supplied to a person to whom another licence applies, that person shall also be provided with such information as the Authority may specify in directions, and

(g) that the Authority shall be provided, in such form and at such intervals as it may specify in directions, with such copies of or extracts from the records, or such other information, as the directions may specify.

13. Conditions of licences for treatment

(1) The following shall be conditions of every licence under paragraph 1 of Schedule 2 to this Act.

(2) Such information shall be recorded as the Authority may specify in directions about the following –

(a) the persons for whom services are provided in pursuance of the licence,

(b) the services provided for them,

(c) the persons whose gametes are kept or used for the purposes of services provided in pursuance of the licence or whose gametes have been used in bringing about the creation of embryos so kept or used,

(d) any child appearing to the person responsible to have been born as a result of treatment in pursuance of the licence,

(e) any mixing of egg and sperm and any taking of an embryo from a woman or other acquisition of an embryo, and

(f) such other matters as the Authority may specify in directions.

(3) The records maintained in pursuance of the licence shall include any information recorded in pursuance of subsection (2) above and any consent of a person whose consent is required under Schedule 3 to this Act.

(4) No information shall be removed from any records maintained in pursuance of the licence before the expiry of such period as may be specified in directions for records of the class in question.

(5) A woman shall not be provided with treatment services unless account has been taken of the welfare of any child who may be born as a result of the treatment (including the need of that child for a father), and of any other child who may be affected by the birth.

(6) A woman shall not be provided with any treatment services involving –

(a) the use of any gametes of any person, if that person's consent is required under paragraph 5 of Schedule 3 to this Act for the use in question,

(b) the use of any embryo the creation of which was brought about *in vitro*, or

(c) the use of any embryo taken from a woman, if the consent of the woman from whom it was taken is required under paragraph 7 of that Schedule for the use in question,

unless the woman being treated and, where she is being treated together with a man, the man have been given a suitable opportunity to receive proper counselling about the implications of taking the proposed steps, and have been provided with such relevant information as is proper.

(7) Suitable procedures shall be maintained –

(a) for determining the persons providing gametes or from whom embryos are taken for use in pursuance of the licence, and

(b) for the purpose of securing that consideration is given to the use of practices not requiring the authority of a licence as well as those requiring such authority.

14. Conditions of storage licences

(1) The following shall be conditions of every licence authorising the storage of gametes or embryos –

(a) that gametes of a person or an embryo taken from a woman shall be placed in storage only if received from that person or woman or acquired from a person to whom a licence applies and that an embryo the creation of which has been brought about *in vitro* otherwise than in pursuance of that licence shall be placed in storage only if acquired from a person to whom a licence applies,

(b) that gametes or embryos which are or have been stored shall not be supplied to a person otherwise than in the course of providing treatment services unless that person is a person to whom a licence applies,

(c) that no gametes or embryos shall be kept in storage for longer than the statutory storage period and, if stored at the end of the period, shall be allowed to perish, and

(d) that such information as the Authority may specify in directions as to the persons whose consent is required under Schedule 3 to this Act, the terms of their consent and the circumstances of the storage and as to such other matters as the Authority may specify in directions shall be included in the records maintained in pursuance of the licence.

(2) No information shall be removed from any record maintained in pursuance of such a licence before the expiry of such period as may be specified in directions for records of the class in question.

(3) The statutory storage period in respect of gametes is such period not exceeding ten years as the licence may specify.

(4) The statutory storage period in respect of embryos is such period not exceeding five years as the licence may specify.

(5) Regulations may provide that subsection (3) or (4) above shall have effect as if for ten years or, as the case may be, five years there were substituted –

(a) such shorter period, or

(b) in such circumstances as may be specified in the regulations, such longer period, as may be specified in the regulations.

15. Conditions of research licences

(1) The following shall be conditions of every licence under paragraph 3 of Schedule 2 to this Act.

(2) The records maintained in pursuance of the licence shall include such information as the Authority may specify in directions about such matters as the Authority may so specify.

(3) No information shall be removed from any records maintained in pursuance of the licence before the expiry of such period as may be specified in directions for records of the class in question.

(4) No embryo appropriated for the purposes of any project of research shall be kept or used otherwise than for the purposes of such a project.

Of course, the HFEA can, and does, impose further conditions in particular cases where circumstances make it appropriate. As we saw in its Annual Report for 1993, the HFEA often imposes conditions relating to matters in the *Code of Practice* maintained pursuant to the statutory duty in s 25 of the Act. These conditions may be standard (see *Manual for Centres* (*supra*) pp 15–18) or specifically tailored for the particular centre or research project.

Breach of a condition in a licence may lead HFEA to revoke a licence. We will return to consider particular aspects of the *Code of Practice* later, and here we should note that breach of its provisions *may* also lead to revocation or variation of a licence. Section 25(6) provides:

25. (6) A failure on the part of any person to observe any provision of the code shall not of itself render the person liable to any proceedings, but –

(a) a licence committee shall, in considering whether there has been any failure to comply with any condition of a licence and, in particular, conditions requiring anything to be 'proper' or 'suitable', take account of any relevant provision of the code, and

(b) a licence committee may, in considering, where it has power to do so, whether or not to vary or revoke a licence, take into account any observations of or failure to observe the provisions of the code.

(c) Particular techniques

Over time, a number of new techniques have been developed, or are anticipated, which involve the use of embryos or, possibly, gametes in treatment or research: pre-implantation genetic diagnosis (PGD); storage and use of ovarian and testicular tissue; cloning and stem-cell research. Each of these poses questions for the HFEA in regulating IVF techniques or the storage of gametes under the 1990 Act. Of course, many new techniques will emerge in the future. These, however, are arguably the most significant new ones for the present. How, if at all, are these dealt with under the current legislation and how should they be?

(i) PRE-IMPLANTATION GENETIC DIAGNOSIS (PGD)

What is PGD? The HFEA and Advisory Committee on Genetic Testing (ACGT) explain the background in their joint consultation document:

HFEA/ACGT Consultation Document *Pre-Implantation Genetic Diagnosis* (1999)

The history of PGD

10. PGD has now been practised for several years and has developed because of the availability of *in vitro* fertilisation and new genetic testing techniques. In passing the Human Fertilisation and Embryology Act 1990 (HF&E Act), Parliament made the decision that embryo research should be permitted. The possibility of developing methods for detecting the presence of gene or chromosome abnormalities in embryos before implantation was recognised at that time. The provision was enacted against the background of a clinical trial which had just been undertaken to establish the technique of pre-implantation genetic diagnosis in the case of a life threatening sex-linked disorder. The HFEA has accepted the position implicit in the legislation and has licensed PGD for certain severe or life-threatening disorders at a limited number of clinics. Following a public consultation in 1993 the HFEA rejected the use of PGD for sex selection for social reasons (HFEA Public Consultation on Sex Selection – January 1993).

Current Use of PGD

11. Four centres in the UK are currently licensed to carry out PGD and one centre for the embryo biopsy part of the procedure only. The technique was first successfully used in 1990 to produce two sets of twin girls where families were at high risk of passing on a serious X-linked disorder. The first autosomal recessive disorder where PGD resulted in the birth of an unaffected child was cystic fibrosis. Sexing an embryo to avoid X-linked disorders and testing for age related aneuploidy (an abnormal number of chromosomes) are the most common reasons for preimplantation diagnosis world-wide. Testing for cystic fibrosis remains the most common use of PGD for a single gene defect.

12. PGD has been used to detect a number of other inherited disorders. These include autosomal recessive disorders, where the specific gene defect is identified, such as Tay Sachs disease and Rh D blood typing. X-linked disorders where PGD, by sex determination, has been used include conditions such as Duchenne's muscular dystrophy and Lesch Nyhan syndrome. With some X-linked disorders, eg Duchenne's muscular dystrophy, the specific defect can now be identified in a proportion of families, which means that male embryos free of the disorder can now be implanted along with female embryos. PGD has also been used to test for two autosomal dominant conditions; the gene predisposing to polyposis coli. As new tests become available this list will continue to grow.

13. A further reason for requesting PGD is where one partner is at high risk of transmitting a chromosome anomaly, such as a translocation. Such couples have often experienced repeated miscarriages and periods of infertility and are already receiving assisted conception treatment. For such patients, PGD may be a way to achieve a successful pregnancy where they would otherwise have difficulty. In some instances, PGD may also help individuals at risk of having a child with severe developmental problems because of a chromosomal imbalance.

As you will see, PGD is a technique whereby embryos are selected so as to exclude those which would result in the child inheriting a genetic condition. The technique may result in the identification of that *specific* genetic condition or, if not and the condition is an x-linked disorder, to select out male (xy) embryos which might be affected.

As a technique, PGD involves the creation and use of embryos. As a consequence, it must be licensed by the HFEA for it to be lawful. You will notice the reference in the HFEA/ACGT consultation document to the fact that, since 1993, the HFEA has only licensed the procedure for *medical* reasons, in particular, to prevent inheritance of certain severe or life-threatening conditions. The HFEA has decided, following a consultation process in 1993, not to allow the selection of embryos purely for *social* reasons (see HFEA *Public Consultation on Sex Selection* (January 1993)). Reflecting these two situations, some jurisdictions have enacted specific legislation. For example, the Victorian legislation, the Infertility Treatment Act 1995 – provides as follows:

Infertility Treatment Act 1995 (Victoria)

50. Ban on sex selection
(1) If a person is carrying out artificial insemination or a treatment procedure, that person must not –
(a) use a gamete, zygote or embryo; or
(b) perform the procedure in a particular manner –
with the purpose or a purpose of producing or attempting to produce a child of a particular sex.
Penalty: 240 penalty units or 2 years imprisonment or both.
(2) Sub-section (1) does not apply if it is necessary for the child to be of a particular sex so as to avoid the risk of transmission of a genetic abnormality or a disease to the child.

Let us first consider PGD for *medical* reasons.

There is no doubt that Parliament envisaged PGD when the 1990 Act was enacted. Schedule 2 contemplates research licences being granted for the purpose of 'developing methods for detecting the presence of gene or chromosome abnormalities in embryos before implantation' (para 3(2)(e)). Further, treatment licences may authorise 'practices designed to ensure that embryos are in a suitable condition to be placed in a woman or to determine whether embryos are suitable for that purpose' (para 1(1)(d)).

PGD might be seen as an alternative to pre-natal diagnosis (PND), where an adverse test result would give the woman the opportunity for a termination of the pregnancy. PGD avoids the need for a termination, leading, it is said, merely to the discarding of affected (or particular sex) embryos. The link between PGD and PND is made by the HFEA/ACGT in its consultation paper such that the availability of PGD could reflect the availability of a termination on the grounds of foetal abnormality under s 1(1)(d) of the Abortion Act 1967 (see *infra*, ch 11).

HFEA/ACGT Consultation Document *Pre-Implantation Genetic Diagnosis* (1999)

Options for families at risk of passing on a serious genetic disorder: PND and PGD compared
24. As has been mentioned, prenatal diagnosis (PND) is an option currently available to people at risk of passing on a serious genetic disorder to their children. Methods of PND include amniocentesis, chorionic villus sampling (CVS) as well as fetal blood and tissue sampling. These methods can be used to provide tissue for chromosome or DNA analysis and also for the detection of metabolic errors in the fetus. Amniocentesis and CVS carry a small risk of miscarriage. Amniocentesis takes place relatively late in pregnancy so that where a termination is being considered this may not be possible until 18 weeks or later.

25. While PND may involve making decisions about the termination of an existing pregnancy, PGD will involve the disposal of affected embryos at their earliest stages of development. PGD therefore provides an opportunity to begin a pregnancy knowing that only unaffected embryos have been transferred. For this reason, some people may find PGD more acceptable and less traumatic. The Human Fertilisation and Embryology Act 1990 allows research on embryos up to 14 days following fertilisation. This was based on the Warnock Committee's argument that this was the earliest possible point for development of a central nervous system. For this reason PGD is likely to be more acceptable to some people than PND. However, it is acknowledged that some do not accept this distinction as they view the status of an embryo as being no different from that of the fetus.

26. Because embryos in PGD are tested at their earliest stages of development some may fear it will be too easy to test and discard them where no serious disorder exists. Currently, access to PGD is confined to individuals having a known family history of a serious genetic disorder. Furthermore, PGD cannot be considered an easy option because of the need to undergo IVF. It is therefore not a treatment that will be undertaken lightly or offer any guarantee of success. These factors appear to offer substantial practical barriers to the casual use of PGD.

27. There is already substantial professional experience and development of services with respect to the use of PND. Both PND and PGD raise the same general issues in relation to the seriousness of inherited conditions. In addition, both provide possible solutions to families who have to make difficult choices where there is a risk that their children may be affected …

Access to PGD
29. As previously mentioned, PGD is currently used by individuals at risk of having a child with a serious genetic disorder or of transmitting a chromosomal anomaly. However, there are others who may want access to PGD in the future. One potential group will be IVF patients without a known genetic risk who may wish to have the viability of their embryos assessed through a process of screening for chromosomal anomalies. It is known that embryos with chromosomal abnormalities are much less likely to implant and develop, as well as being a frequent cause of miscarriage.

30. To take the possibilities one step further, the wider public may wish to have access to PGD so that embryos could be tested for a number of common disorders in circumstances where the individuals concerned are not themselves at an increased risk of passing on a genetic disorder. However, it should be stressed that there are significant problems with this approach. First of all, there is difficulty in testing individual cells for a variety of genetic conditions, and secondly, performing extra tests may have little impact on the overall risk of any genetic disorder occurring in a given pregnancy. However, the general aim would be to ensure, as far as possible, that a healthy child is born. **In due course what restrictions should there be on access to PGD?**

"Seriousness" of disorder
31. Compiling a list of disorders where the use of PGD might be acceptable would necessitate defining exactly what was considered serious enough for inclusion. As knowledge about the genetic basis of certain disorders increases, the list would have to be constantly reviewed. Furthermore, individual judgments on seriousness will vary depending on personal and family circumstances and on the nature and severity of the condition and the likelihood of transmission.

32. If a couple already have an affected child or have had one or more terminations because of a genetic disorder in the fetus, they may feel less able to cope with the demands of another affected child or a further termination. In addition, they have experience of members of their family suffering or dying from a particular disorder.

33. Furthermore, many disorders vary in the severity with which they present. Cystic fibrosis can contribute to death within a few days of birth, but some individuals may survive into their thirties and beyond. In addition, medical advances in the treatment of some genetic conditions may result in the relief of symptoms and an increased life expectancy. For example, the outlook for those with adult polycystic kidney disease has improved dramatically with dialysis and kidney transplantation. The outcome for those affected by cystic fibrosis may improve in the future with gene therapy.

34. If the HFEA does not provide a list of conditions for which PGD is permitted the decision on testing will be for the clinical team to consider with the patient. At present where the suitability of PGD is being considered, centres are understood to be applying

the criteria for termination of pregnancy for fetal abnormality published by the Royal College of Obstetricians and Gynaecologists (RCOG) (Annex C). This limits the use of PND to cases where there is a precise diagnosis and a "substantial risk" of "serious handicap".

35. The HFEA and the ACGT concluded that the approach to PGD should mirror that adopted for PND and that general guidance rather than a list of specific conditions should be provided to guide clinicians on their approach to considering the use of PGD with individual patients. **Should the seriousness of a genetic condition be a matter of clinical judgment based on general guidance? If so, what aspects might such general guidance cover?**

Of course, the symmetry between s 1(1)(d) of the Abortion Act 1967 and the availability of PGD is, on the face of it, attractive. It could even be argued that Parliament may well have had this in mind when passing the 1990 Act, always remembering, as we shall see in the next chapter, that they also took the opportunity during the passage of the Bill to amend and 'tidy up' the Abortion Act 1967. Others disagree in the appropriateness of the symmetry.

Søren Holm 'Ethical Issues in Pre-implantation Diagnosis' in J Harris and S Holm (eds) *The Future of Human Reproduction* (1998)

Pre-implantation and Pre-natal Diagnosis: Similarities and Differences
The similarities in the ethical analysis of pre-implantation and pre-natal diagnosis are obvious. The main aim of the techniques is similar (both are primarily aimed at finding and removing embryos and fetuses with undesired characteristics), and the medical setting where the techniques are performed is also similar.

If the ethical analysis is primarily based on a conception of the moral status of the embryo and fetus which does not entail any major changes in this status in the time span from conception to birth, then pre-implantation and pre-natal diagnosis are morally on a par. If the embryo attains full moral status at conception then it is wrong to destroy it at any point thereafter, and if it does not attain full moral status before it is born (or even later) then it is not wrong to destroy it at any time during pregnancy ...

There are differences between pre-natal and pre-implantation diagnosis, even if neither fetuses nor zygotes have moral status. It may be psychologically easier to ask for an eight-cell zygote to be destroyed than to ask for an abortion (and it does not affect the mother's health in the same way), and this could lead to pre-implantation diagnosis being used for conditions, or by people in situations, where pre-natal diagnosis and abortion would never be contemplated. Another difference lies in the position of the zygote relative to the position of the fetus. When pre-implantation diagnosis is performed the zygote is in the laboratory in a Petri dish, whereas pre-natal diagnosis is performed on a fetus inside a woman's body. Arguments relying on a woman's right to control her body therefore support a right to have the embryo/fetus destroyed only in one of those situations and not in the other. This has implications for a range of consent issues surrounding pre-implantation diagnosis ...

Pre-implantation diagnosis is not cheap in itself, and in cases where it is sought by fertile couples who would not normally have IVF treatment the quite substantial price of IVF should be added on top. If the use of the technique becomes widespread it will therefore represent a serious drain on health care resources. There will undoubtedly be savings in not having to care for the handicapped persons who were destroyed while they were still embryos, but these savings will mainly fall outside the health care sector and cannot be directly converted to health care funding. Pre-implantation diagnosis will therefore have to compete in the normal priority setting process. If we compare the technique with other similar techniques this would mean that pre-implantation diagnosis and IVF would first be offered to couples with known risk of genetic disease; the next group to get it (if funds are available) would be couples already being offered publicly funded IVF procedures; and it is probably unlikely that couples wanting pre-implantation diagnosis just in order to choose a child of a specific kind would ever be funded by the public health care system ...

Restriction of Pre-implantation Diagnosis to Serious or Severe Conditions?
In the public debate and in legislative proposals it is often suggested that pre-natal and pre-implantation diagnosis should be restricted to looking for serious or severe conditions. Some have operationalized this idea and suggested the creation of a positive list of conditions for which pre-implantation diagnosis will be available and a negative list of conditions for which it will be prohibited. The underlying idea is probably an extension of the requirement

in many European abortion laws that late abortions on eugenic grounds are only allowable if the fetus suffers from a serious or severe condition. The English Abortion Act of 1967, for instance, allows late abortions if there is: 'a substantial risk that, if the child were born, it would suffer from such physical or mental abnormalities as to be severely handicapped' (J K Mason, and R A McCall Smith '*Law and Medical Ethics*' 3rd edn (Edinburgh: Butterworths, 1991) 104.) There are at least two problems with this suggestion for a restriction on pre-implantation diagnosis.

First of all it is questionable whether the state has any right to impose restrictions on pre-implantation diagnosis if such a restriction is not based on an argument giving the zygote moral status. This problem will be dealt with more extensively in the next sections of the chapter.

Secondly, it is very difficult to produce a non-arbitrary dividing line between severe conditions and non-severe conditions. It is reasonable to assume that the notion of severity which is at play here is a global notion of severity which is closely linked to the notion of disability, and which should perhaps ultimately be cashed in terms of an ability to have a good life. The exact understanding of severity is, however, not important for the present argument as long as it is agreed that severity cannot be reduced to mere medical/physical severity in this context.

Despite the political correctness lobby and its attempts to force the view upon us that there are no disabled people but only differently abled people, there can be little doubt that some conditions are actually disabling in any realistically conceivable human society. It is disabling to be blind and deaf at the same time, and no amount of re-description can change that. Conditions which are universally disabling in this sense (ie disabling in any realistically conceivable human society) are clearly paradigmatic exemplars of severe conditions. The same could be said of a condition like Lesch-Nyhan syndrome which leads to mental retardation and compulsive self-mutilation (children with this condition may bite off their fingers or toes, or gouge out their own eyes). An individual with Lesch-Nyhan syndrome has a degree of suffering which clearly places this condition in the category of severe conditions.

There are, however, many conditions where the situation is not nearly as clear. Many conditions are not universally disabling but only disabling in specific circumstances. Severe myopia (near-sightedness) is only marginally disabling in our society, whereas it was a severe disability before the invention of glasses. If changes in the disabling effects of a given condition were only of this historical kind, it would not pose any serious problem to an attempt to find a dividing line between the severe and the non-severe conditions. It would mean that specific conditions would move relative to the dividing line, but at any one point in time a condition would either be severe or non-severe.

A more serious problem is that severity varies not only historically but according to the precise social context of each affected person. Even if we assume that the physical and psychological manifestations of a given condition are constant, there will be many conditions where the impact on the person with the condition will vary quite markedly. The degree to which for instance a severe case of club foot will affect a person will depend on both the kind of family he or she is born into – whether physical or more sedate pursuits are the centre of family life – and the kind of other abilities which the person has. The severity in the global sense of a severe case of club foot is thus not determined by the medical severity of the condition. Two persons with the same medical severity might end up being widely separated on the global severity scale. This indicates that a dividing line operating on the level of specific conditions is at risk of misclassifying individuals. The conceptual basis of the categorization therefore seems to force us towards a case-by-case classification, and away from a classification of a number of cases falling under the same condition label.

It is furthermore unclear whose assessment of severity should count. There will undoubtedly be differences between the general population, politicians, physicians, persons with the condition, and prospective parents in this assessment, both for specific conditions and for the cut-off point. This uncertainty opens the field for pressure groups wanting to have a specific condition classified in a specific way. It is probably most likely that the pressure will be in the direction of labelling more and more conditions as severe, because that would be the only way to get access to pre-implantation diagnosis for these conditions. Because of the conceptual ambiguity underlying the original classification of conditions and the original placing of a dividing line it will be difficult to offer principled arguments against a re-classification. It is therefore foreseeable that 'severity creep' will take place over time, and that more and more conditions will be labelled as severe.

Despite these difficulties of definition, the HFEA/ACGT consultation document, as we saw, opts for the PND analogy. They suggest the approach of the Royal

College of Obstetricians and Gynaecologists in its report, *Termination of Pregnancy for Fetal Abnormality* (January 1996):

> 3.3.2   The World Health Organisation has defined disability as follows:
>
> *... any restriction or lack (resulting from an impairment) of ability to perform an activity in the manner or within the range considered normal for a human being.*
>
> In interpreting the definition, the WHO considers that:
>
> 3. Assisted performance. Includes the need for a helping hand (ie: the individual can perform the activity or sustain the behaviour, whether augmented by aids or not, only with some assistance from another person.)
>
> 4. Dependent performance. Includes complete dependence on the presence of another person (ie: the individual can perform the activity or sustain the behaviour, but only when someone is with him most of the time).
>
> 3.3.3   A person is only likely to be regarded as seriously handicapped if they need the support described in the WHO Points 3 or 4. However, an opinion that a particular fetal abnormality would be associated with serious handicap should be based on a careful consideration of the following factors, not all of which will be relevant in every case.
>
> These are:
> –   the probability of effective treatment, either *in utero* or after birth;
> –   the probable degree of self-awareness and of ability to communicate with others;
> –   the suffering that would be experienced;
> –   the extent to which actions essential for health that normal individuals perform unaided would have to be provided by others;
>
> Judgments should be cautious, recognising that it is not possible to give an authoritative view of the meaning of 'seriously handicapped' as this has not been interpreted by the courts.

As with PND (see *infra*, ch 11), there are problems in applying the test of 'substantial risk' of 'serious handicap' to, for example, late on-set disorders such as Huntington's disease and to pre-dispositional testing for genetic conditions (see HFEA/ACGT Consultation document (*supra*) paras 39–47).

Let us now turn to consider the use of PGD for *social* purposes, including selection to achieve the birth of a child of a particular sex or to obtain children with particular characteristics such as hair or eye colour. At present, as we have seen, the HFEA will not permit this. Should it?

S Holm 'Ethical Issues in Pre-implantation Diagnosis' in J Harris and S Holm (eds) *The Future of Human Reproduction* (1998)

A recurrent feature of the ethical debates about pre-natal diagnosis and about gene therapy is the suspicion that these techniques may be used to promote the selection or creation of children with certain characteristics which the parents just happen to want. The same suspicion can obviously be raised about the use of pre-implantation diagnosis. Such choices could be about the sex of the child or about other characteristics such as height, colour of the hair or eyes, or intelligence (not all of these choices are technically possible at the moment, and it may never become possible to test for intelligence). Sometimes such choices are described in the public debate as 'frivolous choices'. Would it be appropriate for the state to try to restrain such choices, either through direct prohibition, or by leaving them out of the range of services funded by the public health care system?

The focus here will mainly be on arguments supporting a general or partial prohibition of pre-implantation diagnosis. The issues concerning restriction of public funding are extremely interesting, but would require an in-depth analysis of justice in health care resource allocation. I have therefore decided to leave the funding issues out of this chapter.

There can be no doubt that examples can be created, and real life situations do occur, where a prohibition against selection according to a certain criterion goes against some persons' deeply felt desires, and causes them harm. This is clearly so in the case of sex selection where for instance British hereditary peers may have a strong desire to select for male offspring (with the ethical blessing of Mary Warnock), or perhaps more importantly women in certain ethnic groups may need male children to maintain their marriages and social status. Are such cases sufficient to vitiate any attempt of state intervention?

If we look at the question of direct prohibition it seems that the state would have to show that allowing people to exercise these kinds of choices would harm other people or other societal interests. Whether such harm could plausibly be argued to exist depends to a very great extent on (1) what kinds of states of affairs we allow to count as harms, and (2) what kind of connection we require between the action of making a specific reproductive choice and the harmful state of affairs.

Harm in the Family

Very direct harm can be imagined within family units if parents want to select against characteristics which already existing children have. Statements like 'it is not because we don't like black hair and brown eyes, it is just that we would also like to have a blond, blue-eyed child' are unlikely to do much toward alleviating any feeling of psychological rejection the already existing child with black hair and brown eyes might feel. But if people only select characteristics for their first child this problem could be alleviated.

We can also envisage scenarios where parents will want to select embryos with a specific condition which is normally seen as a handicap or disability. There is anecdotal evidence that some American deaf couples have used pre-natal diagnosis to detect and abort non-deaf fetuses, so that they could be certain to have a deaf child which could be fully integrated in the deaf culture. Pre-implantation diagnosis could be used for the same purpose. Intuitively most would probably feel that this is a perverse use of the technique and that the child who is born deaf has been harmed in some way. There are, however, arguments purporting to show that this is not the case. These arguments proceed from the observations that (1) if a woman conceives a child this month, the child will be different from the child she could have conceived next month, because they will come from the union of different gametes and be genetically different, and more generally (2) any change in reproduction which entails a change in the timing or manner of conception leads to the production of different children (children with different identities). In the case of the deaf child we may believe that we are comparing the welfare of the child growing up deaf with the welfare of the same child growing up hearing and deciding which would be the better life for the child, but this is not true. What we are doing is comparing two different children, the child growing up deaf and another child growing up hearing. The life of the deaf child is the only life this child can have, and what we have to decide is not whether there are better lives, but whether the life of this child is so bad that it would be better not to have it. This is an unlikely proposition in most cases, so the argument that it would be better for the child not to be born than to be born disadvantaged is in most circumstances false. What we have to decide is whether parents are allowed to choose to bring into the world a child with an impairment, when they could have produced another and 'better' child, or whether they are only allowed to bring 'the best possible' child into the world. If we decide that they are only allowed to bring 'the best possible child' into the world, this will clearly have implications which reach far beyond questions about pre-implantation diagnosis.

Societal Harm

Harm outside the family context is also possible but it will probably be of a much more indirect nature, not mediated through the direct effects of the choice made, but through its symbolic meaning. To choose a specific characteristic must necessarily imply a preference for that specific characteristic when compared to other members of the same set of mutually exclusive options (eg the members of the set of eye colours). To deliberately choose brown eyes must imply a preference for brown eyes over other possible colours. It is arguable that to prefer something is to value it more highly than the other possible options, and this assumption actually plays a major role in rational choice theory when the implicit value structure of an individual is determined from his explicit choices and preferences. This entails that by choosing a specific characteristic I signal that it is more valuable to me than the other possible options.

Let us imagine that a person with the less favoured characteristic (characteristic A) claims that he or she feels devalued by the choice made, and that he or she is thereby harmed. What defence could the person choosing have against such a claim? One possibility would be to say something like 'my choice and my values are specific to my situation and it is not intended to entail a general evaluation of all persons with characteristic A'. That defence would, however, be implausible if an analysis of the aggregate of all the choices made in similar situations showed that there was a general tendency to choose against characteristic A. Such a general bias would indicate that the values of the chooser were less situation specific than he or she would have us believe, and would furthermore indicate the existence of an underlying social value structure biased against characteristic A.

Persons with A could in that case plausibly claim that allowing people to choose against A legitimizes and reinforces the underlying social bias against A. What is wrong is thus not the individual acts of choice but their combined effect. In this way the problem resembles the well-known 'problem of the commons' in social co-operation where individual actions which are rational and acceptable lead to an unacceptable combined result. It may not be wrong for any individual couple to select for characteristic A, but it becomes wrong when taken together with all the other choices made by other couples.

If this line of argument is accepted it can support a prohibition of specific forms of pre-implantation diagnosis, but not a general prohibition of the whole technique.

(For further discussion, see J Harris *Clones, Genes and Immortality* (1998) ch 1; H Draper and R Chadwick 'Beware! Pre-implantation Genetic Diagnosis May Solve Some Old Problems But It Also Raises New Ones' (1999) 25 J Med Ethics 114; and Health Council of the Netherlands *IVF-Related Research* (1998) ch 2.)

(ii) STORAGE AND USE OF OVARIAN AND TESTICULAR TISSUE

I. Children

The Human Fertilisation and Embryology Act 1990 states that gametes may only be stored pursuant to a licence (s 4(1)(a)). A particular difficulty arises with this in the case of young children who, for example, undergo treatment that may result in them becoming infertile. It is now possible to remove and store ovarian tissue (in the case of girls) and testicular tissue (in the case of boys) with the intention of harvesting eggs or sperm subsequently in order to allow the patient when grown up the opportunity to have a genetically related child. What if the child is not competent to consent to the removal and/or storage of the tissue? While the tissue may be removed with the consent of those with parental responsibility, if in the child's best interests, such proxy consent does not allow 'gametes' to be stored under the 1990 Act. Under Sch 3 to the Act, 'effective consent' (ie appropriate consent in writing) is required from the gamete-provider, namely the child herself or himself. Yet they may be insufficiently mature to have the capacity to consent under the *Gillick* test (see *supra*, ch 5). On the face of it, this is an insurmountable hurdle to a sensible, beneficial practice. One solution would be to amend the 1990 Act so as to permit, at least, storage when removal is in the child's best interests, as it surely would be, if it left open the possibility of giving the child an opportunity to procreate in the future. In her review for the Government, Professor Sheila McLean proposes such a change in the law, albeit not specifically in the context of children but incompetent patients generally.

Sheila A M McLean *Review of the Common Law Provisions Relating to the Removal of Gametes and of the Consent Provisions in the Human Fertilisation and Embryology Act 1990* (1998)

2.6   However, there is one set of circumstances in which it might be thought that the written consent requirement could be waived. If it has been possible to ascertain that the 'best interests' exception to the general requirements of the common law can be invoked to permit the removal of gametes then it clearly could be the case that lawfully obtained gametes would still need to be stored before use. If the interests which render the removal lawful are to be vindicated, then it would be anomalous not to permit such storage. *Thus, it may be necessary specifically to amend the legislation to provide that the Human Fertilisation and Embryology Authority has the discretion to waive the consent requirements in schedule 3 to the 1990 Act for storage only in such cases. This will be only until that person is deemed competent to reach an independent decision within the terms of schedule 3 to further storage and/or use.*

However, such an amendment may be unnecessary in the case of children. The licensing scheme only applies to the storage of 'gametes'. Could it be said that the reproductive material in ovarian tissue or the testicular tissue of young boys does not amount to 'gametes'? What else could they be? The 1990 Act does not contain a definition. However, the HFEA has defined 'gamete' as:

> a reproductive cell, such as an ovum or a spermatozoon, which has a haploid set of chromosomes and which is able to take part in fertilisation with another of the opposite sex to form a zygote.

When applied to the testicular tissue of young boys and to ovarian tissue of young girls, this definition excludes the immature 'sperm' or 'eggs' which are often present. Hence, their storage would not fall within the provisions of the 1990 Act and would not require the patient's (unobtainable) written consent. As regards testicular tissue, the HFEA has issued the following guidance:

HFEA Guidance *Storage and Use of Testicular Tissue* (1998)

3. Using this definition in conjunction with the six grades of puberty described by Professor Tanner, the storage of testicular tissue from boys who have reached Tanner Grade 2 or beyond would require a licence from the HFEA. In addition consent to storage would be required as explained below.

4. Substituted consent is not possible under the 1990 Act. Thus consent to storage cannot be given on behalf of any child who has reached Tanner stage 2 and whose testicular tissue is to be stored by a person with parental responsibility. However, a child under the age of 16 can give an effective consent in accordance with the 1990 Act's requirements if he is "Gillick" competent. It is for the treating doctor to assess whether or not a child has that competence.

5. If a boy is pre-pubertal (pre Tanner Grade 2) then his testicular tissue can be stored on unlicensed premises. However, if such material were subsequently to be developed *in vitro* in some way so as to create "gametes" within the definition above, the storage or use of that material would require a licence. At that stage an effective consent would also have to be given in accordance with the 1990 Act.

6. **NB** The common law on consent applies to the *removal* of testicular tissue from any male. In the case of a pre-pubescent child who is not "Gillick" competent it would be for the person with parental responsibility to consent to such a procedure where this is in the child's best interests.

The position is slightly more complex for ovarian tissue but applies even to adult women.

HFEA Guidance *Storage and Use of Ovarian Tissue* (1998)

4. For much of the menstrual cycle, ovarian tissue will not contain gametes according to the above definition. Any gamete or gametes that are present will be localised in certain parts of the ovary. Clinicians will need to consider on a case by case basis whether ovarian tissue contains any gametes either by reference to the stage of the woman's cycle or by appropriate testing or assessment of the tissue itself.

5. Where a licence is needed for the tissue's storage because a gamete or gametes are present, the provisions of the 1990 Act requiring effective consent to the storage have to be complied with. Effective consent under the 1990 Act can only be provided by the individual whose gametes are to be stored. If, therefore, it is necessary to obtain consent from a female under the age of 16 for storage for subsequent use for a purpose requiring a licence, this can only be provided if she is competent in law to consent, ie if she is capable of understanding the implications of the proposed course of action. Neither parents nor anyone else can provide effective consent under the 1990 Act.

6. It will be apparent from the above that a licence is not required if tissue does not contain gametes according to the definition in paragraph 2 above. However, if immature gametes are taken from the tissue and matured *in vitro*, the provisions of the 1990 Act will apply. This includes the requirement for effective consent to be obtained when gametes according to the above definition are created and where any storage and subsequent use of the gametes in licensable treatment or licensable research is contemplated.

7. **NB** The common law on consent applies to the *removal* of ovarian tissue from any female. Section 8 of the Family Law Reform Act 1969 provides that anyone who has attained the age of 16 years and is of sound mind may give a legally valid consent to surgical or medical treatment or procedures. Some children, though under the age of 16, are perfectly able to understand the implications of medical decisions that affect them and are legally capable of giving or refusing consent to treatment. Their consent should always be sought. For those children who cannot understand it would be for the person with parental responsibility to consent to the medical procedure of removal where this is in the child's best interests.

Is the HFEA correct to construe the statutory term 'gamete' to mean, in effect, 'mature gamete'? As we shall see, the same issue arises in relation to foetal eggs taken and stored. In relation to the latter, Aurora Plomer and Norma Martin-Clement offer the following:

Aurora Plomer and Norma Martin-Clement, 'The Limits of Beneficence: Egg Donation Under the Human Fertilisation and Embryology Act 1990' (1995) 15 LS 434

As the HFEA report notes, the Act as originally drafted appears to control only the use of *mature* eggs or 'gametes' (HFEA Report on Donated Ovarian Tissue in Embryo Research and Assisted Conception (London, July 1994) para 20). But foetal eggs are not 'gametes'. Foetal tissue may contain primary oocytes or even primordial germ cells. Primordial germ cells appear in human embryos in the third week of development. They divide into oogonia by the fifth week. By the end of the twelfth week oogonia differentiate into primary oocytes which at birth contain the same number of chromosomes as other body tissue. The number of chromosomes of primary oocytes remains the same until sexual maturity where the number is reduced by half and then only in sequence. The end-product of each process of myotic division is a gamete. When a female gamete is combined with a male gamete it gives rise to a zygote (definition of 'gamete' in Oxford Dictionary). Under Schedule 3 a licence is required and the donor's consent must be obtained only for the storage or use of gametes (HFE Act 1990, sch 3 para 2(1), 2(2), 5(1), (2), 6(1), (3) and para 8). In the absence of a statutory definition, the dictionary definition applies and the word 'gamete' must be construed as referring to reproductive cells which give rise to a zygote when combined. If so, the storage and use of foetal eggs would not be controlled by the Act.

When a word in an Act is ambiguous, the courts may now consult Parliamentary debates as an aid to statutory construction (*Pepper v Hart* [1992] 3 WLR 1032). But there was no detailed discussion of the scope of the term 'gametes' in the Parliamentary debates or in the report of the Warnock Committee, on the basis of which the Act was drafted. Warnock simply stated in a footnote that 'gamete' is the collective term for both sperm and eggs, while the Lord Chancellor, introducing the Bill's Second reading to the House of Lords referred, in parenthesis, to 'gametes' as the collective noun for human sperm and eggs (513 HL Official Report (5th series) col 1004). The courts would therefore find no clear guidelines in the Parliamentary materials to determine whether Parliament's intention was to leave the use of immature reproductive cells unregulated. It is however improbable that Parliament intended to regulate or control only the use of mature reproductive cells/eggs since an embryo created with donated eggs will be genetically linked to the donor whether the egg was mature or immature at the time of extraction.

One statutory provision may be of assistance in construing the term 'gamete'? Section 3A of the 1990 Act was enacted in 1994 in order to prohibit the use of foetal 'eggs' in IVF treatment. However, Parliament did not use the term 'egg' but rather chose that of 'female germ cell', which s 3A(2) defines to mean: 'cells of the female germ line and includes such cells at any stage of maturity and accordingly includes eggs.'

Hence, in 1994 at least, Parliament was aware that foetal germ cells might not be, in fact, eggs and so chose the phrase 'female germ cell' and defined it, in effect, to include mature *and immature* 'eggs'. This would support the HFEA's definition of 'gamete' in the broader context. Nevertheless, the point remains that in 1990 Parliament did not seem to draw any distinction between mature and immature eggs and sperm. The later enactment of s 3A cannot affect the interpretation of the whole Act and Parliament's earlier (it could be argued) intention to regulate eggs and sperm, however mature.

II. Donation of ovarian tissue

The 1990 Act allows gametes to be donated for treatment or research. It is recognised that there is a shortage of both donated sperm and eggs for use in treatment. Ovarian tissue is rich in immature eggs. The tissue could be derived from adult women, children, cadavers or dead foetuses. If such tissue were available and the eggs harvested or the tissue grafted into the patient, there might be benefits to that woman in seeking to establish a pregnancy. Equally, the availability of eggs in order to create embryos for research could be increased if these sources were permissible.

How, if at all, does the 1990 Act apply to these situations? As we have seen, the storage and donation of gametes for treatment is regulated by the 1990 Act (s 4(1)). Likewise, the creation of embryos, whether for treatment or research, falls within the 1990 Act and can only be done pursuant to a licence (s 3(1)). We have already seen that the HFEA defines 'gamete' so as to exclude immature eggs or sperm. Thus, the storage and donation of ovarian tissue taken from a live person is not regulated by the Act unless the immature eggs are extracted, matured and then used to create embryos or donated for treatment. In the case of cadavers and dead foetuses, the difficulties are multiplied. The removal and use of tissue taken from a dead person is governed by the Human Tissue Act 1961 (see *infra*, ch 15). Is the use of ovarian tissue also covered by the 1990 Act? If it is, the consent requirements in Sch 3 would have to be complied with. These are, of course, more stringent than the requirements of the Human Tissue Act 1961(see *infra*, ch 15). The answer turns upon a construction of the 1990 Act. We must always bear in mind that the Act does not (apart from s 3A) apply to immature eggs (see *supra*). The question is, therefore, only concerned with the use or donation of *matured* eggs originally taken from a dead person or foetus. It seems that the creation of embryos whatever the origins of their constituent gametes (and necessarily these will be 'mature') is covered by the Act (s 3 prohibiting the creation, storage and use of embryos). Thus, the consent requirements of Sch 3 must be satisfied, ie the 'donor' must have given written explicit consent to the creation of embryos, their storage and use in treatment or research (compare especially s 1(2) of the Human Tissue Act 1961). This could, of course, occur if the source is a dead adult (or competent child). It is impossible, however, if the source is an aborted foetus. What if the eggs are donated but not used to create an embryo, for example, for GIFT? Section 4(1) of the 1990 Act prohibits the use of eggs for treatment without a licence from the HFEA where the procedure involves the 'use [of] the eggs of *any other woman* (s 4(1)(b)) (our emphasis). Here, there is arguably a difference between the situation where the source is a dead 'woman' and where it is a dead foetus – the latter does not seem to fall within the statutory licensing scheme and would, as a consequence, be unregulated and so uncontrolled. Using the eggs of a dead woman would, however, always fall within the Act. This loophole in the regulatory scheme is, nevertheless, by the way since the amendment of the 1990 Act in 1994, introducing s 3A of the Act, which *prohibits* the use of fetal 'germ cells' (immature and mature eggs) taken from a foetus (or embryo) for the treatment of others. In Victoria, the legislation bans use in treatment or research. Section 42 of the Infertility Treatment Act 1995 states:

42. Ban on procedures involving oocytes derived from a foetus
A person must not use oocytes derived from a foetus in a treatment procedure or research.

By contrast, s 3A does not prohibit their use for research but, of course, the use of *gametes* in general for research is not regulated and, as we have seen, the creation and use of embryos for research will require a licence from the HFEA even for eggs taken from a dead foetus (but see *infra* for further difficulties over consent).

Some have taken the view that donation of eggs from cadavers is only covered by the Human Tissue Act 1961 and have called for the law to change (see Plomer and Martin-Clement 'The Limits of Beneficience: Egg Donation Under the Human Fertilisation and Embryology Act 1990' (1995) 15 LS 434 at 448–454). Our view is, as has been seen, otherwise.

In 1994, the HFEA produced a report, following a public consultation process, *Donated Ovarian Tissue in Embryo Research and Assisted Conception.* In the report, the HFEA stated its position on the use of ovarian tissue taken from live donors, cadavers and fetuses.

HFEA *Donated Ovarian Tissue in Embryo Research and Assisted Conception* (July 1994)

The Authority's position

Infertility Treatment
4. In the case of infertility treatment, the Authority believes that different considerations apply to the use of ovarian tissue from the three sources discussed: live donors, cadavers and fetuses. Balancing benefits against risk of harm, the HFEA has concluded that in treatment it would be acceptable to use ovarian tissue only from live donors. Whilst the Authority has no objection in principle to the use in infertility treatment of cadaveric ovarian tissue from adult women, it will not currently approve its use. The authority does not consider the use of fetal ovarian tissue in treatment to be acceptable.

Embryo research
5. In the case of embryo research, the Authority has concluded that, again balancing benefits against the risk of harm, the use of ovarian tissue from all three sources to produce embryos is acceptable. This would be subject to existing controls and provided that informed written consent specifically for the purpose had been obtained from the live donor, the woman who has died or the woman undergoing abortion. The process would require all relevant information and counselling to be available to the woman before she could give consent.

General considerations
6. It is in the nature of human beings to intervene to try to shape their world. Medical treatment is by definition interventionist and has been developed through research and practice to overcome problems which afflict and distress men and women. Few would argue against interfering in the natural order for the purpose of healing, but some people have reservations about intervention in order to relieve infertility. However, infertility can often be alleviated. Society through Parliament has permitted the possibility of producing embryos outside the body and the use of donated eggs and sperm for fertility treatment and embryo research. All are subject to specific controls. The use of fetal tissue is already permitted in research or in treatment under the Polkinghorne guidelines adopted by the Department of Health (Polkinghorne report – 'Review of the Guidance on the Research Use of Fetuses and Fetal Material' 1989 Cm 762 HMSO).
7. The Polkinghorne guidelines say that consent to use fetal tissue obtained from a woman undergoing an abortion should be general and that the woman should not know the use to which the fetal tissue may be put, or if it is used at all. The guidelines also say that the woman's decision to allow the fetal tissue to be used should be separated from her decision to undergo abortion, and they recommend that a third party should be interposed between the person wishing to use the tissue and the woman. These guidelines need to be reconciled with the requirement of the Human Fertilisation and Embryology Act 1990 (HFE Act) for informed specific consent from the woman providing eggs if fetal ovarian tissue is to be used in embryo research.
8. There is no question of the Authority issuing licences for any treatment procedures until they have been adequately proved through licensed research. The Authority must also be satisfied that they are necessary or desirable for the purpose of treatment. There is no question of the Authority issuing licences for research projects unless it is satisfied that the research is necessary or desirable and that the use of human embryos is essential.
9. The HFE Act sets out the conditions which must apply before licensed research or fertility treatment is undertaken. Information about the implications of the procedure to be undertaken must be given, and counselling must be offered before consent to use or store eggs or sperm is obtained. Before accepting a particular woman for treatment, clinics are required to take into consideration the welfare of any child who may be produced and the welfare of any

other child who may be affected. These procedures are subject to close monitoring by the Authority.

10. In addition to taking account of the requirements of the HFE Act, the Authority bases its considerations on the principles underlying the HFEA Code of Practice:

 – the respect which is due to human life at all stages in its development;
 – the right of people who are or may be infertile to the proper consideration of their request for treatment;
 – a concern for the welfare of children, which cannot always be adequately protected by concern for the interests of the adults involved; and
 – a recognition of the benefits, both to individuals and to society, which can flow from the responsible pursuit of medical and scientific knowledge.

The supply of eggs

11. The deep distress felt by people who are unable to have children in the normal way is widely acknowledged. In some cases this could be alleviated but for the fact that there is a shortage of donated eggs. The Authority therefore believes that it is acceptable to seek to increase the supply of eggs for infertility treatment.

12. Eggs are used to produce embryos for research for the purposes permitted in the HFE Act. These are promoting advances in the treatment of infertility; increasing knowledge about the causes of congenital disease and miscarriages; developing more effective contraception techniques; detecting genetic or chromosomal abnormalities in embryos. The availability of eggs from all three sources mentioned earlier could therefore enable embryo research to increase understanding of the causes of infertility and of birth abnormalities. Techniques to improve the treatment of infertility may be developed through this research which could reduce the need for egg donation in the future. The Authority therefore considers that it is acceptable to seek to increase the supply of eggs for embryo research.

13. The ways sought to increase the supply of eggs should comply with HFEA directions, minimise risk to the donor and, in the case of infertility treatment, minimise risk to the recipient and to the potential child.

Embryo Research

14. The Authority considers that the moral difficulties presented by using tissue from any of the proposed sources for embryo research permitted by licence under the HFE Act are not new. Donation of eggs and sperm for the purpose of embryo research is already permitted under the HFE Act.

Live donors and cadavers

15. The special status accorded to the embryo in the HFE Act requires informed specific written consent by the person providing eggs to their use to produce embryos. This can be obtained from live donors. Written decisions made before death or donor cards would be needed in the case of post mortem donation. There is no provision for proxy consent to the use of eggs and embryos in the HFE Act, and the Authority does not consider that next-of-kin should be able to give consent on behalf of a woman who has died or to override her consent. However, the Authority believes that it should be possible to develop a system for written informed consent by the woman before death which did not impinge on the existing donor card system for organ donation.

Minors

16. The Authority is satisfied that at present 18 is the age at which it can be confident that the full implications of donating ovarian tissue for the purpose of embryo research can be understood. This is the age limit set in the Code of Practice for live donors. However, the Authority recognises the concept of a child's maturity and understanding in relation to consent and intends to explore this further in the context of the use of ovarian tissue, including issues relating to post mortem donation.

Fetuses

17. In the case of fetal tissue the woman undergoing an abortion is recognised in the Polkinghorne guidelines as having a special position with regard to the fetus so that her explicit consent should be obtained to the use of the fetus or fetal tissue for research (see Polkinghorne report, Chapter 6). The use of eggs was not considered separately in the Polkinghorne report but consent to their use in embryo research could be obtained by an additional consent option.

Infertility Treatment

Live donors

18. The Authority has concluded that it would be acceptable to use ovarian tissue in infertility treatment from adult live donors provided informed specific written consent has been given.

This can be carried out in accordance with the current provisions of the HFE Act and Code of Practice, which sets an age limit of 18. The Authority is satisfied that it is possible to control the number of offspring from one donor. Only a limited amount of ovarian tissue would be available from a single donor. Control would be in line with the Authority's policy on gamete donors set out in its Code of Practice, ie the limit of 10 offspring.

Cadavers

19. In the case of the use of ovarian tissue in infertility treatment from females under 18 who have died, the same concerns about obtaining specific informed consent from minors mentioned in paragraph 16 lead the Authority to the view that tissue from this source should not currently be used. In the case of an adult woman who has died, there is no objection in principle. This is provided that the woman has given informed consent specifically to donate her tissue for the treatment of others, for example, by means of a special donor card or a will. However, more can and should be done to find out about the psychological consequences for the recipient couple and particularly for the prospective child. The Authority will then reconsider licensing treatment using ovarian tissue from women or girls who have died.

Fetuses

20. The use of fetal ovarian tissue raises difficult social, medical, scientific and legal concerns. No arguments emerging from the consultation have convinced the Authority that these can be put aside. The Authority considers that the issue of the possible psychological consequences for the offspring is most difficult. There is widespread and fundamental objection to using fetal tissue in this way. Accordingly, it would be particularly difficult for a child to come to terms with being produced from a fetus because of prevailing social attitudes. The HFEA, therefore, does not consider the use of tissue from this source to be acceptable in infertility treatment. Other developments are taking place involving ovarian tissue from adults which look likely to reduce the need to consider the use of fetal ovarian tissue in infertility treatment.

It is not entirely clear what view the HFEA has taken on the application of the 1990 Act. Clearly, its views on the use of foetal eggs for treatment have now been enshrined in s 3A of the 1990 Act, as we saw earlier. It would, however, limit the use of ovarian tissue for treatment to that taken from live donors. Because of the perceived difficulties of obtaining 'specific informed consent' from the woman before her death and possible psychological effect on any child born, it would exclude donation from cadavers (for a legislative provision prohibiting the use of gametes taken from a dead man or woman, see Infertility Treatment Act 1995 (Vic), s 43). As we have seen, the HFEA would seem to have power to do so.

As regards research, the HFEA accepts the use of eggs to create embryos for research. There are *two* difficulties here. First, where the source is a dead foetus there is a clash of 'consent cultures'. Research on foetal material is, as the HFEA notes, governed by the Code of Practice developed by the Polkinghorne Committee (*Review of the Guidance on the Research Use of Fetuses and Fetal Material*, Cm 762 (1989), see *infra*, chs 14 and 15). The guidelines recommend that the mother of the aborted foetus should consent to its use for research and that her consent should be *general* and not specific and be separated from the decision to have the abortion. The woman should not be able to specify particular research uses for the material. These are 'at odds' with the consent requirements of Sch 3 to the 1990 Act (see HFEA Report, *supra*, para 7).

Secondly, the HFEA requires the consent of the *woman* (paras 5 and 17). The 1990 Act requires the consent of the gamete-providers to the creation and use of an embryo for research (Sch 3, para 6(1) and (3)). It is not immediately apparent why the *woman* is the gamete-provider. It is not *her* eggs that are being used, but those of the foetus. The foetus is genetically unique and its 'germ cells' are different from those of the woman. Unless the foetus and mother are regarded in law as one, it is the foetus which is the gamete-provider. But herein lies the difficulty, *its* 'effective consent' under Sch 3 to the 1990 Act is impossible to obtain. The law does not see the pregnant woman and her foetus as legally one (see *Attorney-General's Reference (No 3 of 1994)* [1997] 3 All ER 936 (HL) per Lords Mustill and Hope). Thus, whatever the common sense of the HFEA's position, it would seem that the creation and use of embryos using eggs taken from aborted foetuses cannot be done without amendment of the 1990 Act.

(For discussions of the use of foetal and cadaveric tissue, see Plomer and Martin-Clement (*op cit*) and C Erin 'Some Comments on the Ethics of Consent to the Use of Ovarian Tissue from Aborted Fetuses and Dead Women' in J Harris and S Holm (eds) *The Future of Human Reproduction* (1998) ch 9.)

(iii)   CLONING

In February 1997 it was announced that a sheep known as 'Dolly' had been produced by fusing nuclear DNA extracted from the mammary cell of an adult sheep and an egg cell from which the nuclear DNA had been removed ((1997) 385 Nature 753). 'Dolly' was the first cloned mammal and brought closer the possibility of cloning humans. In fact, 'Dolly' was not a perfect clone – ie a exact genetic double – since the mitochondrial DNA of the enucleated egg remained. However, this represents only about 20 genes in 'Dolly', whilst the nucleus of the donated genetic material contained some 70,000 genes.

What precisely is cloning?

Pat Walsh and Andrew Grubb 'I Want to Be Alone' (1997) 7 Dispatches 1

... In essence, cloning in humans would involve replacing the genetic material in the nucleus of *A*'s cell ("the clone") with the distinct genetic material taken from *B*'s cell ("the cloned"). As a consequence, the resulting cell of *A*, would develop by division with the same genetic make-up as *B*, the person from whom the nuclear genetic material was taken. How the "product" might be allowed to develop thereafter would depend upon whether the reason for the cloning was purely experimental or intended to create a live human clone.

There seem to be three methods by which this "transplantation" of genetic material may be achieved. First, there is "*embryo nucleus replacement*" where the nucleus from *B*'s cell is placed into *A*'s cell (which is part of an embryo); *A*'s cell has had its own nuclear genetic material removed and discarded. Second, and by way of variation of the first method, there is "*cell nucleus substitution*" where the nucleus of an egg of *A*'s is removed and replaced with the nucleus of a cell taken from *B*. The final method, "*cell fusion*", involves removing the genetic material from an egg cell of *A*'s and fusing it with a cell taken from *B* which retains its nucleus.

Each of these methods is distinguished by the source of the receiving cell of *A* (the clone). In addition, the cell of *B* (the cloned), which contains the sought after genetic material, may be different: it may (1) be a part of an embryo; (2) be a cell derived from an embryo, or (3) be a fully formed cell of a fetus or person ...

Why might cloning of humans be contemplated?

Two categories of case can be identified where cloning might be contemplated. The first involves producing a live born person whose genome is the same as the cloned source. This might be called *reproductive cloning*. Secondly, another type of cloning involves the production of cells or tissue which does not result in the creation of a cloned person. The cells or tissue may be important for the treatment of the 'source' of the cells. This might be called *therapeutic cloning*. It may be important to keep the distinction between these two categories in mind. Whilst both employ cloning techniques, there may be significant differences morally and for public policy makers in setting the limits to what may be done.

I. The current law

Is cloning lawful, prohibited or regulated? The Warnock Committee considered the possibility of developing cloning techniques, in particular, the nuclear transfer technique that led to the birth of 'Dolly' (see *Report of the Committee of Inquiry into Human Fertilisation and Embryology* (Cmnd 9314), 1984 at paras 12.11 and 12.14). The Government indicated that such techniques would be prohibited, and be criminal offences, under what became the 1990 Act (see *Human Fertilisation and Embryology: A Framework For Legislation* (Cm 259) (1987) at para 38). In the result, Parliament enacted s 3(3)(d) of the Human Fertilisation and Embryology Act 1990.

> **3.** (3) A licence cannot authorise – ...
> (d) replacing a nucleus of a cell of an embryo with a nucleus taken from a cell of any person, embryo or subsequent development of an embryo.

This, however, is only a partial ban, and does not cover nuclear transfer techniques. If not banned, is the technique subject to the regulatory framework of the 1990 Act? The answer depends upon whether an 'embryo' is created and used.

Pat Walsh and Andrew Grubb 'I Want to be Alone' (1997) 7 Dispatches 1

Prohibition on Cloning When Parliament passed the Act, it sought to prohibit cloning *absolutely*. Speaking on the second reading of the Bill in the House of Lords, Lord Ennals said, *inter alia*, of cloning that "everyone in your Lordships' House and all scientists involved are in agreement that this kind of research should be banned and that such ban should be enforced with stiff penalties." The prohibition was intended to prevent both cloning research and the possibility of creating a cloned person. The relevant provision in the Act is section 3(3)(d) which provides that: "A licence cannot authorise ... replacing a nucleus of a cell of an embryo with a nucleus taken from a cell of any person, embryo or subsequent development of an embryo." Of course, this provision, in fact, prohibits *only* "embryo nucleus replacement" carried out for any purpose and this was Parliament's intention (*Hansard HL* Vol 513, col 1013 per Lord Mackay of Clashfern). The fact of the matter is that Parliament did not contemplate cloning being achieved by any other method: hence the prohibition was narrowly drawn. But, since "cell nucleus substitution" and "cell fusion" do not involve the replacement of the nucleus of a cell of *an embryo*, the prohibition in s 3(3)(d) of the Act simply does not apply.

Does this mean that these latter methods are permitted under the Act?

The answers are not straightforward because the Act is unclear. The crucial questions are: (1) does the particular method of cloning involve the "use" or "creation" of an embryo? – if so a licence will be required from the Authority; and (2) are there any further provisions of the Act preventing genetic manipulation of embryos or cells which fetter the Authority's licensing powers? As regards both of these, of course, the application of the Act to cloning is an *unintended* effect because Parliament thought it had prohibited it by express provision in section 3(3)(d).

Cell Nucleus Substitution So, does the source of the genetic material "transplanted" involve the "use" of an embryo? "Cell nucleus substitution" involves the "use" of a cell from *B* that is to provide the nucleus, and therefore genetic material, for the clone, *A*. The Act, however, only requires a licence before *an embryo* is *used* (s 3(1)(b)). So that, where the source cell is part of, or was taken from, an embryo "cell nucleus substitution" could only be done either for research or other purposes, if the Authority permitted it.

Nevertheless, the Act may not allow the Authority always to licence this method of cloning even if it wanted to. The Act places limits upon tinkering with the genetic material of the cell of an embryo as part of a research project or for treatment, ie implantation with a view to creating a cloned double. As regards the former, paragraph 3(4) of Schedule 2 of the Act states that a research licence "cannot authorise altering the genetic structure of any cell *whilst it forms part of an embryo*, except in such circumstances (if any) as may be specified in or determined in pursuance of regulations" (emphasis added). Similarly as regards the latter, paragraph 1(4) of Schedule 2 states that a treatment licence "cannot authorise altering the genetic structure of any cell *while it forms part of an embryo*." (emphasis added). Consequently where "cell nucleus substitution" involves the taking of the nucleus of a cell whilst *part of an embryo*, the Authority cannot licence it, if treatment is contemplated, and if research is contemplated, can only licence it to the extent permitted by regulations – which do not currently exist. These provisions would, however, have no impact where the source cell (*B*) had already been separated from an embryo – which may be easy and usual. Here, the Authority *could* licence the use of the embryo to be used as the source of the nucleus. We will discuss below whether it should.

By contrast, where the source of the nucleus (*B*) is not an embryo but a fetus or person then the Act's provisions which regulate the *use of an embryo* obviously do not apply. Is this variation of "cell nucleus substitution", therefore, wholly unregulated? The answer requires us to look not at the regulation of the source of the genetic material, but rather of the "product" of the cloning exercise and depends upon whether the recipient cell (*A*) is allowed to develop by dividing and thereby to become an embryo. If it is, then the Act requires this activity to be licenced as it involves the creation *ex utero* of an embryo (s 3(1)(a)).

Whether or not division takes place is a matter of fact. Whether, if it does, it results in an embryo may seem rather obvious – what else is it? But, in fact, because of the definition of embryo contained in the Act it is not clear. Section 1(1) of the Act provides an artificial definition of "embryo" for the purposes of the Act as follows: "(a) embryo means a live human *where fertilisation is completed*, and (b) references to an embryo *include an egg in the process of fertilisation*, and, for this purpose, fertilisation is not complete until the appearance of a two cell zygote." (emphasis added). Thus, to qualify as such under the Act an embryo must have, at least, two cells and it must result from fertilisation. The definition does not contemplate a dividing cell which has not been fertilised but rather has been produced by "*cell* nucleus substitution". This is most unfortunate since we are left in the position of having an entity which looks like an embryo, behaves like an embryo but is not, under the Act, an embryo. Indeed, it is not clear what it is. Embryologists would regard it as such and, no doubt, so would have Parliament if they had thought about it – but they did not since they thought they were absolutely prohibiting cloning – and the result is that this 'dividing cell' is not an embryo within the Act. Thus "cell nucleus substitution" where the source cell (*B*) comes from a person or fetus is not regulated by the Act and therefore, remarkably, can be carried out without a licence.

Cell Fusion This rather perplexing outcome for "cell nucleus substitution" due to the narrow definition of "embryo" in the Act also affects the regulation of cloning by "cell fusion". Here the analysis is almost identical. If the fusion occurs using a source cell (*B*) taken from an embryo, the *use of that embryo* requires a licence. If the fusion occurs using a source cell (*B*) taken from a fetus or person, two questions arise. First, have you thereby immediately *created* an embryo by fusion? If so, this in itself requires a licence (s 3(1)(a)). Secondly, even if you have not immediately created an embryo, if division occurs have you, therefore, *created* an embryo *ex utero*? The latter question is identical to that raised above for "cell nucleus substitution".

So, is the fused entity *itself* an "embryo" under the Act? The answer is probably not. The creation of the fused entity is not, and what develops from it cannot be described as, an embryo under the Act. The conjoined cells (*A* and *B*) may look like a constructed embryo and have the necessary "two cells" required under the Act – at least if the receiving cell (*A*) stripped of its nucleus can still count as a cell. But, more importantly, the entity produced by fusion is not the result of "fertilisation" which is a stated pre-condition to an "embryo" under the Act. Thus, "cell fusion" is only regulated to the extent that a cell (*B*) from an embryo is used as a source of genetic material. Where, therefore, the source cell is a fetus or person, again the activity is wholly unregulated and does not require a licence from the Authority.

The upshot of this analysis of the 1990 Act's application to cloning is that it lacks clarity and consistency. Quite unexpectedly, the 1990 Act partly prohibits, partly regulates and partly leaves untouched cloning of humans.

This analysis is not shared by everyone. Its implications are, of course, startling: the 'Dolly' technique is lawful and unregulated. The matter was considered by the House of Commons Select Committee on Science and Technology in the immediate aftermath of the birth of 'Dolly'. The Committee took evidence from the HFEA and the Department of Health. In its report (*The Cloning of Animals From Adult Cells*, HC 373, 2 vols, Session 1996–1997), the Committee noted that both the HFEA and the Department had been advised that the product of the 'nuclear transfer' was an 'embryo' and thus fell within the 1990 Act and thus could only be lawfully created pursuant to a licence from the HFEA (see para 26). Not satisfied that this was sufficiently clear, the Select Committee recommended that the 1990 Act should be amended to make sure the technique fell within the legislative scheme (para 29). The HFEA in its Report on Cloning (with the Human Genetics Advisory Commission) maintained that the law is clear but, as we shall see shortly, recommended that consideration be given to a legislative ban on reproductive cloning (see *Cloning Issues in Reproduction, Science and Medicine* (HFEA/HGAC, December 1998) para 3.4 and 9.2). In its response to the report, the Government remained content that the 1990 Act was adequate to control cloning but would keep the matter under review (Government Response to the Report by HGAC and HFEA on *Cloning Issues in Reproduction, Science and Medicine* (Cm 4387) June 1999, para 1–4).

An illustration of an explicit legislative ban on cloning is found in the Infertility Treatment Act 1995 (Vic). Section 47 states: 'A person must not carry out or attempt to carry out cloning.' However, as the definition of 'clone' in s 3(1) of the Act shows that it is important in order to achieve a comprehensive ban on cloning, that close attention must be given to the wording of the legislation. 'Clone' is defined as: 'to form, outside the human body, a human embryo that is genetically identical to another human embryo or person.'

Leaving aside the difficulty of defining 'embryo', the definition of 'clone' would not cover the product of the nuclear substitution technique. It is not 'genetically identical' to its source cell because, as we noted earlier, the mitochondrial DNA of the enucleated egg forms part of it and is not part of the source.

Is cloning licensable?   The answer depends upon the definition of the legislative term 'embryo'. Accepting the HFEA's interpretation of 'embryo' means that cloning may be carried out pursuant to a treatment or research licence. However, as regards the former, the HFEA has indicated that it will not licence 'reproductive cloning' (see Report on Cloning (*supra*) at para 3.8) and has, since 1994, prohibited the creation of clones by embryo splitting for treatment purposes (at para 3.9).

II. Changing the law

Should 'reproductive' or 'therapeutic' cloning be permitted in the UK?

Reproductive cloning   Reproductive cloning was considered and rejected in the report of the HGAC/HFEA on cloning that we referred to earlier, which was published in December 1998. The report followed a public consultation earlier in 1998 (*Cloning Issues in Reproduction Science and Medicine – A Consultation Document* (HGAC/HFEA, Jan 1998)).

HFEA/HGAC *Cloning Issues in Reproduction, Science and Medicine* (1998)

4.2 The consultation document set out a number of scenarios where cloning technology could be applied to make a "copy" of another human being, envisaging single or multiple "copies" of a living or a dead fetus, baby, child or adult. These included parents who might wish to "replace" an aborted fetus, dead baby or child killed in an accident, produce a sibling to be a compatible tissue or organ donor for a child dying from, say, leukaemia or kidney failure; or an individual attempting to "cheat death" by using cloning technology. Mention was also made of the possibility of selecting characteristics in offspring or to assist human reproduction in the case of infertile couples or lesbian couples. Views were sought on the acceptability of cloning in all, or any, of these circumstances.

4.3 The response to the consultation was conclusive. There was very little support for reproductive cloning, though there were a few who saw benefit in certain circumstances, mainly in connection with infertility treatment. 80% of the respondents thought it was an ethically unacceptable procedure, an opinion that was endorsed within each of the different groupings of those responding …

4.4 Safety is itself an ethical issue. Nuclear replacement in animals is at present very inefficient. Few of the reconstructed embryos develop, some develop abnormally, some die at or soon after birth. In humans, the wastage of human eggs and the high risks of miscarriage and congenital malformation alone would exclude any realistic prospect of reproductive cloning. However, since issues of efficiency and safety may eventually be resolved, it is necessary to analyse further the reasons why human reproductive cloning is so widely judged to be ethically unacceptable.

4.5 A central ethical issue is the widely accepted moral principle that human beings may never be treated merely as means to an end, but only as an end. Many of the suggested reasons for which reproductive cloning might be employed have a strongly instrumental character to them, for they contemplate bringing human beings into existence for reasons outside the persons themselves. Examples would be the 'replacement' of a lost relative or the making available of compatible tissue for transplantation into another. It would be morally demeaning and psychologically damaging for someone to learn that the primary reason for their existence lay not in their own value, but in their utility for another purpose, as the substitute for someone else or for the benefit of someone else. Moreover, in the case of attempted 'replacement', the action would be based on the fallacious equation of a person with their genome ...

4.6 These particular ethical arguments would not apply to the possible use of cloning as an extreme measure to relieve infertility in a case where nuclear replacement seems the only way to produce an embryo for implantation which incorporated genetic material derived from one of the intending parents. In these latter circumstances there would be good reason to suppose that the person brought into being would be highly valued for his or her own sake. However, other ethical considerations would also be relevant. The relief of the pain of infertility is, in general, a good end, but it is not an absolute end to be achieved without regard to the ethical acceptability of the means employed for that achievement. The wish for genetic offspring is a natural human aspiration, but this has to be held in balance with other desirable aspects of human well being and it cannot be given an overriding priority above all other considerations. While the desire for children, and feelings of solidarity with kin are the source of much human good, too exclusive an emphasis on genetic connection can lead to distortions.

4.7 The use of reproductive cloning to relieve infertility would involve risks likely to be ethically unacceptable for human use in the foreseeable future (see paragraph 4.4 above). There are further ethical difficulties about the source of the genetic material which could be used in nuclear replacement to relieve infertility. If the nucleus was derived from one of the parents, this would generate an unbalanced genetic relationship of an entirely unprecedented kind within the family. A child cloned in this way would have a unique set of family relations, as he or she would inherit their *complete* genetic make up from one of their "parents" and have no genetic connection with the other. This complete genetic identity between the child and one parent would constitute a novel situation of which there is no previous experience and there must be uncertainties and doubts about the effects this would have on the family and the child. For these psychological and social reasons, there must be serious ethical doubts about the propriety of bringing about such a set of relationships. All these considerations give rise to serious ethical concerns about reproductive cloning as a means to relieve infertility. There is a difference from donor insemination where an entirely new individual is conceived as a result of the fertilisation of a gamete produced from one parent with a donor gamete, so there is a partial connection with one parent and none with the other.

4.8 In relation to using reproductive cloning as a means to relieve infertility it is also necessary to consider the wider question of public policy. Decisions about what may be done involve not only the couple themselves and their medical advisors but also society as a whole. For any type of infertility treatment to function satisfactorily there has to be a degree of social acceptance of the measures being taken. It is quite clear that human reproductive cloning is unacceptable to a substantial majority of the population. A total ban on its use for any purpose is the obvious and straightforward way of recognising this. The results of the consultation fully support Government policy in this respect.

Others take a more liberal view, arguing that 'procreative autonomy' or 'procreative liberty', absent compelling arguments against, should not rule out reproductive cloning altogether (see eg J Harris ' "Goodbye Dolly?" – The Ethics of Human Cloning' (1997) 23 J of Med Ethics 353).

A scholarly and full analysis is offered by Professor John Robertson in the following extract.

John A Robertson 'Liberty, Identity, and Human Cloning' (1998) 76 Texas LR 1371

III. The Demand for Human Cloning and Procreative Freedom

A proper assessment of cloning requires that it be viewed in light of the realities of how it might be used once it is shown to be safe and effective. The most likely uses would be as extensions of current reproductive and genetic-selection technologies. Several plausible uses can be articulated; ones quite different than the horrific scenarios originally imagined. The question then becomes: Do these uses fall within main-stream understandings of why procreative freedom warrants special respect as one of our fundamental liberties? Investigation of this question will set the stage for examining what the possible harms of cloning are and, thus, what public policy toward human cloning should be. ...

B.   *Human Cloning and Procreative Liberty*

The question to be asked about each likely use of cloning is whether it is an exercise of procreative liberty that deserves the special protection ordinarily accorded to procreative choice. To answer this question, we must consider the meaning and scope of procreative liberty and then ask whether different types of cloning fit within that meaning. Here cloning of embryos and existing children may initially have different status than cloning oneself or third parties …

In some cases the family needs sought through cloning can be satisfied by cloning embryos or children. In others, somatic cell transfer from adults will be necessary. Threats to individuality, autonomy, and lineage can arise with any form of cloning, although some harms, such as confusion about family lineage and autonomy may be more likely with adult cloning of somatic cells than with the cloning of embryos. The discussion assumes that all forms of cloning are equally effective although important differences in the ability to clone successfully may exist among them.

1. The Meaning and Scope of Procreative Liberty. – Procreative liberty is the freedom to decide whether or not to have offspring. It is a deeply accepted moral value and pervades many of our social practices. Its importance stems from the impact which having or not having offspring has in our lives. This is evident in the case of a choice to avoid reproduction. Because reproduction imposes enormous physical burdens upon the woman, as well as social, psychological, and emotional burdens on both men and women, it is widely thought that people should not have to bear those burdens unless they voluntarily choose to do so.

But the desire to reproduce is also important. It connects people with nature and the next generation, gives them a sense of immortality, and enables them to rear and parent children. Depriving persons of the ability or opportunity to reproduce is a major burden and should not occur without their consent.

Reproductive freedom – the freedom to decide whether or not to have offspring – is generally thought to be an important instance of personal liberty, indeed, given its great impact on a person, a fundamental personal liberty. Of course, both the liberty to avoid and the liberty to engage in reproduction are contested in certain instances, as controversies over abortion and population limits illustrate. In recent years the emergence of assisted reproduction, noncoital means of conception, and prebirth genetic selection has also raised controversies about the limits of procreative freedom. Questions about cloning and procreative liberty are situated in those controversies.

The question of whether cloning is part of procreative liberty is a serious one only if noncoital, assisted reproduction and genetic selection are themselves part of that liberty. A strong argument exists that the moral right to reproduce does include the right to use noncoital or assisted means of reproduction. Infertile couples have the same interests in reproducing as coitally fertile couples and the same abilities to rear children. Coital infertility should no more bar them from reproducing with technical assistance than visual blindness should bar a person from reading with Braille or with the aid of a reader. It thus follows that married couples (and arguably single persons as well) have a moral right to use noncoital assisted reproductive techniques, such as in vitro fertilization (IVF) and artificial insemination with a spouse or partner's sperm, to beget biologically related offspring for rearing. It should also follow – although this is more controversial – that the infertile couple would have the right to use gamete donors, gestational surrogates, and even embryo donors if necessary. Although third-party collaborative reproduction procedures do not replicate exactly the genes, gestation, and rearing unity that ordinarily arises in coital reproduction, they come very close and should be treated accordingly. Each of these procedures, with varying degrees of closeness, enables the couple to have or rear children biologically related to at least one of them.

Some right to engage in genetic selection would also seem to follow from the right to decide whether or not to procreate. People make decisions to reproduce or not because of the package of experiences that they think reproduction or its absence would bring. In many cases, they would not reproduce if it would lead to a packet of experiences X, but they would if it would produce packet Y. Since the makeup of the packet will determine whether or not they reproduce, a right to make reproductive decisions based on that packet should follow. Some right to choose characteristics, either by negative exclusion or positive selection, should follow as well, for the decision to reproduce may often depend upon whether the child will have the characteristics of concern.

From this brief account, one sees that procreative liberty is clearly accepted in many respects but contested in others, particularly with regard to the use of donors and surrogates and choosing and selecting offspring characteristics. Many contested areas involve technological innovations that have not yet been fully assimilated. Although the scope of procreative liberty has not yet been clearly defined, a process or methodology for addressing these issues has now been identified. It involves looking closely at a new practice, say IVF or gamete donation or surrogacy, and investigating its connection with the interests and understandings that make coital reproduction a valued activity. Such an inquiry leads to the conclusion that most new reproductive techniques should be presumptively viewed as part of procreative liberty because they enable an infertile couple to rear offspring who are related by genes or gestation to one or both of the rearing pair. The same is true of many forms of genetic selection, at least negative selection.

If most current forms of assisted reproduction and genetic selection fall within prevailing notions of procreative freedom, then a strong argument exists that some forms of cloning share certain aspects of procreative liberty as well, for cloning shares many features with assisted reproduction and genetic selection. For example, the most likely uses of cloning would enable a married couple, usually infertile, to have healthy, biologically related children for rearing. Or it would allow them to obtain a source of tissue for transplant to enable an existing child to live.

Cloning, however, is also different in important respects. Unlike the various forms of assisted reproduction, cloning is concerned not merely with producing a child, but rather with producing a child with a *particular* set of genes. Many prebirth genetic-selection techniques are now in wide use, but they operate negatively by excluding undesirable genetic characteristics, rather than positively as cloning does. Moreover, none of them are able to select the entire nuclear genome of a child as cloning does.

Furthermore, cloning is not the final or even the most threatening form of genetic selection. Eventually, scientists will develop techniques of gene alteration by insertion or deletion of genes. The motivating purpose will be to cure disease at the genetic level. Once developed, however, those techniques might also be used to enhance the genetic makeup of offspring or even to diminish them prior to birth. The prospect of more extensive genetic manipulation of offspring is hardly a reason to allow human cloning. If anything, it creates even greater pressure to come to terms with cloning now so that we may deal more effectively with genetic enhancement and diminishment once they are developed ...

2. Constituting Procreative Liberty. – ... cloning is directly involved with procreative liberty in situations in which the couple initiating the cloning intends to rear the resulting child. This protected interest is perhaps clearest when they are splitting embryos or using DNA from their own embryos or children, but it also exists when one of the rearing partner's DNA is used. Using the DNA of another person is less directly reproductive, but still maintains a gestational connection between the cloned child and its rearing parents, as now occurs in embryo donation.

In considering the relation between cloning and procreative liberty, we see once again how blurred the meanings of reproduction, family, parenting, and children become as we move away from sexual reproduction involving a couple's egg and sperm. Blurred meanings, however, can be clarified. The test must be how closely the marginal or deviant case is connected with the core. Applying this test elucidates several plausible cases involving a couple who seek to clone the DNA of embryos, their existing children, themselves, or consenting third parties, each of which is sufficiently connected with the core so as to fall within the scope of procreative liberty. In all of these instances the couple will be seeking a child whom they will gestate and rear. Unless all selection is to be removed from reproduction, the couple's interest in selecting the genes of their children deserves the same protection accorded other reproductive choices.

It is not necessary to be convinced by all aspects of this argument to grant its effect. A strong presumption in favor of individual choice is essential in procreative matters because they are so intimate and personal, and so fraught with meaning for our lives and those around us, that only the individuals and couples directly involved can decide whether to go forward. One need not personally accept all the ways of achieving reproductive goals to still recognize that choice must be presumptively left to the individuals directly involved. Some instances in which children would be cloned so closely resemble distinctively reproductive methods that individual freedom to clone and rear in those cases should also be respected.

The root of the problem is the uncertain meaning assigned to genes in determining whether reproduction has occurred. Always relevant, sometimes genes are determinative and sometimes they are not. Genes may be a necessary condition, but they are never sufficient for determining whether the distinctively procreative is at stake. In making intent to rear (and gestate) so significant, reproduction is defined in terms of *some* biologic connection plus rearing. We do no great violence to prevailing understandings of procreative choice when we recognize DNA cloning to produce children whom we will rear as a legitimate form of family or procreative choice. Whether we wish to allow families to be formed in this way will then depend upon whether cloning imposes such significant harm on others that this valid method of family formation should be restricted ...

Having established that 'procreative liberty' is engaged in choosing to reproduce through cloning, Professor Robertson moves on to analyse what harms may arise from the practice. We set out this discussion at some length because it is here that the 'battle ground' over reproductive cloning is really located and will be if English Law is challenged under arts 8 or 12 of the European Convention in the future (see *supra*, ch 1) and his discussion is particularly rich.

IV   The Harms of Human Cloning

The initial response to the idea of cloning humans has been overwhelmingly negative, with many persons, politicians, religious bodies, and advisory commissions calling for its prohibition. Some find it repugnant because it denies the essence of being human or threatens the individuality and uniqueness of resulting children. Others stress threats to autonomy caused by rigid parental expectations or the risks of physically unsafe experimentation. Still others believe that cloning will confuse traditional notions of kinship and lineage, which are so key to our sense of self and our place in the world. Finally, there are fears of the slippery slope: permitting cloning in even limited cases might inevitably lead to abusive scenarios or make it impossible to stop the onslaught of genetic manipulation and engineering of offspring that future technologies could make possible.

Many of these objections to human cloning were made in the abstract or with the fantasy scenarios of instant replication of all-determining genes in mind. Even when popular images of cloning are put to rest, grave concerns about the welfare of resulting children persist. Having examined more realistic situations in which cloning, if shown to be safe and effective in humans, is likely to be used and cloning's connection with prevailing conceptions of procreative freedom, it is time to analyze claims of harm to see whether they constitute a sufficient basis for banning or severely restricting human cloning.

The following section will consider the main objections to human cloning in light of its likely use in family formation. The question to be addressed is whether the feared harm is sufficient in itself or in conjunction with other harms to justify prohibition or severe restrictions of human cloning. Views as to the sufficiency of the alleged harms are, of course, intimately connected with assessments of whether cloning is so closely involved with reproductive choice that it should be protected from governmental intervention except in cases of compelling harm.

If protected uses of cloning are not involved, then most of the fears raised about cloning will suffice to justify a ban or other regulation. Government may generally restrict liberty if it has a rational basis for action, and the concerns raised about cloning are rational concerns that may properly inform public policy as long as they do not infringe on fundamental liberties. Of course, whether those social or community concerns are worth pursuing at the price of nonfundamental liberty interests will remain a contested issue of public policy. But if the most likely uses of cloning will enable couples to form families in ways that are reasonably viewed as exercises of procreative liberty, then concerns regarding the harms of cloning will have to reach a higher level than mere rationality to justify overriding individual choice.

A.   *The Problem of Wrongful Life*

Most of the harms said to flow from human cloning focus on the welfare of children who are given the same DNA as another individual. Whether the feared harm is physical safety, individuality, autonomy, instrumentalization, or threats to lineage, all are claims that the child who results is intrinsically or irrevocably harmed by the experience and, thus, that the best policy would be to prevent cloning from occurring to prevent the harm that the resulting child would experience.

Such claims have wide appeal, but they raise a central conceptual problem that calls into question whether preventing harm to offspring ever justifies preventing their birth altogether. The problem arises because, but for the technique in question, the cloned person would not exist. Banning the technique may prevent a child from being born into the circumstances of concern, but it does so, not by assuring that it is born in different circumstances, but by preventing it from being born at all.

Preventing existence as a way to prevent harm to the person who would exist makes sense for that person only if it reasonably appears that once born, the child's existence would be so full of pain and suffering that its interests would be best served by nonexistence. But it is rare that the techniques at issue – whether cloning or other genetic manipulations – would cause harm or suffering to such an extent. The strongest case would be a child born with Tay Sachs disease, who after six months or so of normal development, begins a progression toward inevitable death at about two years. Other genetic defects, such as sickle cell anaemia, cystic fibrosis, or Down's Syndrome, do not have such devastating effects that a child born with those conditions would be better off, from its own perspective, never living at all. None of the assisted reproductive techniques, including those using donors and surrogates, lead to a child whose life would be invariably full of such great suffering that it too never should be born. Nor is being born with the DNA of another likely to have such devastating effects on the child that it is better off, once it exists, in not continuing life.

There have been two main responses by those who reject the implications of this position (Tort law in the United States has almost universally rejected claims of wrongful life based on the birth of a child who could not have existed but with the condition of concern. See eg *Smith v Cote*, 513 A 2d 341, 351–355 (NH 1986)). One is to deny its premises; the other is to grant it but find reasons other than concern about offspring welfare for calling the birth wrongful. The first strategy – denying the argument's premises and conclusion – is commonly asserted in bioethical writing, but there is usually little argument or analysis, and when there is, it usually misses or confuses key steps in the argument (see eg, Cynthia B Cohen "Give Me Child or I Shall Die!: New Reproductive Technologies and Harm To Children" Hastings Center Report Mar–Apr (1996), at 19).

An exception to the lack of analytic rigor are the views of philosophers Derek Parfit and Dan Brock, who would replace an individual or person-based notion of harm, on which my argument rests, with a class-based notion (Derek Parfit, *Reasons and Persons* 396–401, 487–90 (1984); D W Brock 9 Bioethics 269, 271-75 (1995)). Yet even they acknowledge that the notion of harm to a class, rather than to an individual, can be sustained only if the number of the members of the class is kept constant – for example, when a member of the class of all children born, who has a defect such as cloning, can be replaced with another child without that defect. If that condition cannot be met, they admit that they have not shown that the person-regarding concept of harm fails. But the couple seeking to have the cloned child ordinarily cannot have another healthy child, or they would not have resorted to cloning in the first place.

A different strategy is to accept the argument but assert that the child's birth was harmful for reasons other than the welfare of the child per se. Here the response comes close to asserting that the offense that others feel because less than normal children are born is a sufficient ground for preventing couples from producing such children. But an argument based on offense still seems to rest either on the assumption that the child would have been better off never being born at all, or that the parents are acting without regard for the child's welfare.

Proponents of the wrongful life theory may also think that the parents could have easily had another "non-defective" child. But this too overlooks the interests of the child who is now born, albeit with the defect or condition in question. From the now existing child's perspective – the perspective of *this* particular child – it is not harmed by existence, because it has no alternative to existing with the defect or condition of concern, and it finds its current existence, being the only one available to it, very fine indeed. Moreover, the argument assumes that the parents who intentionally bring a disabled child into the world have no concern for that child. If they are prepared to rear and love it regardless of its condition, it is wrong to say that its birth denigrates respect for life or persons.

An added problem is that proponents of this response seem unaware of the implications of their position. If their claim that parents act wrongfully when they knowingly allow children to be born in some less than ideal or normal condition, then parents in many situations would be acting wrongfully. The underlying principle on which their claim rests would condemn women who, after prenatal diagnosis, test positive for Down's syndrome, cystic fibrosis, or Tay Sachs and then refuse to abort, or who refuse testing after getting pregnant when they know that there is a one-in-four risk of having a child with severe genetic disease, or who refuse carrier screening in the first place. These decisions are much more likely to cause the birth of children with special problems or conditions than assisted reproduction or cloning. Surely offense alone that one would knowingly bring a disabled or handicapped child into the world is not a sufficient basis for prohibiting couples from making that choice, at least when they plan to rear the child themselves and have the resources to do so.

Despite these difficulties, proponents of the view that birth can be prevented because the child can only be born harmed seem genuinely concerned about the welfare of children. They see the physical and psychological difficulties that they think cloned or genetically selected or engineered children will have, and they blame the parents for knowingly bringing this situation about. Indeed, they perceive the opposite position as seriously confused and insensitive to the plight of children. In their eyes, that view would always excuse as harmless *any* parental prebirth manipulation because the parents could always claim that *this* child would not even have been born but for the very act claimed to have harmed it. The problem is that their position leads them to prevent the birth – to deny existence – to the very people they claim to respect. If the children whose welfare is at issue are to exist at all, it can only be in the condition which proponents of this argument say justifies preventing their birth.

The debate between these positions is likely to continue, for each side thinks that the other is causing harm to children, although they see it occurring in different ways. In such a conflicted situation the best solution is to move the discussion to a different level or to ask a different question in the hope of identifying areas of agreement. One area of agreement might lie in defining the likely effects of giving particular DNA to individuals. If we can agree that on closer analysis the effects of cloning are much less serious or ominous than originally considered, then there may be no need to resolve the wrongful life issue, for there will be no serious claim that the resulting lives are wrongful, or indeed, that they are greatly diminished or inferior to non-cloned lives (which are not available to them). In making this inquiry, we should compare the effects of cloning to the effects that we tolerate in other reproductive and genetic selection decisions. Only if cloning presents substantial risks of untoward effects over current practices do we need to confront the differences in the approaches outlined here.

Another ground for agreement may lie in recalling why a decision about whether the child is harmed when it has no other way to be born matters. As a legal or policy matter, that issue is important because harm to the child by virtue of its own birth would constitute the substantial harm to others necessary to justify infringements of procreative liberty. But if procreative liberty is not involved, then lesser degrees of harm will suffice to support restrictions on liberty. If the effects on children of greatest concern occur in situations in which the initiator or clone source will not rear, then those uses might not fall within the zone of procreative liberty and therefore do not deserve special respect. If so, concerns about the child's welfare, even if not technically involving harm to the child, may legitimately be taken into account.

A third area of potential agreement lies in evolving understandings of proper parenting and reproductive behavior. Whatever one's views about wrongful life, people might find some consensus based on their assessment of whether cloning is necessary, in light of accessible alternatives, for a couple to have and rear healthy, biologically-related children in a committed family setting. A couple who, due to infertility or other needs, chooses to have and rear a cloned child would be manifesting the character that is ordinarily expected in parents committed to their child's well-being. We might properly question their character if they fail to show plausible reasons for choosing to clone or if they fail to show proper regard for the well-being of the resulting child. Here we could distinguish couples who are interested in having a healthy, genetically-related child whom they will rear, from couples who are interested in changing or altering genes to serve an agenda that seems divorced from the child's well-being once it exists. Ultimately, the questions here will concern norms and understandings of good parenting and reasonable parent-child relations.

The fact that the family and child will face a novel psychological situation does not necessarily mean that parents act wrongfully or violate prevailing conceptions of good parenting in choosing this route to form a family. As with procreative liberty, we construct and constitute the normative underpinnings of parental and child-rearing relations as we confront them in novel situations such as cloning.

B.   Potential Harms from Human Cloning

I examine seven harms alleged to follow from human cloning and consider whether they are sufficient to justify prohibition of a couple's use of cloning techniques to form a family.

1. Violation of Human Dignity and Identity. – The initial reaction to human cloning, particularly in Europe, was that it was a violation of human dignity and identity. In the United States, Professor George Annas expressed one aspect of this view when he told the United States Senate that it was unacceptably inhuman to create a clone because a person's essential humanness requires being born from the combination of two separate sets of chromosomes, not one set, as would occur in cloning. Yet whether an individual has one or two genetic parents is but one particular view of what constitutes our humanity, and has no greater, indeed, arguably a lesser, claim to define humanity than rationality, consciousness, language, or some other factor. In any event, persons created through nuclear transfer cloning do have two genetic parents – the same genetic parents as the clone source.

In Europe, the emphasis on human dignity, without further efforts to specify its content, has been effective at the national and regional political levels (Council of Europe: Draft Additional Protocol to the Convention on Human Rights and Biomedicine on the Prohibition of Cloning Human Beings with Explanatory Report and Parliamentary Assembly Opinion', Sept 22 1997, 36 ILM 1415, 1419). But appeals to human dignity, without further specification of the content of that dignity, so that it can be evaluated and compared to other conceptions and practices, will hardly do as a compelling justification for overriding procreative liberty. (For an incisive critique of the European reliance on dignity, see John Harris, *"Goodbye Dolly?" The Ethics of Human Cloning*, 23 J Med Ethics 353, 354–355 (1997), claiming that appeals to human dignity do not provide sufficient justification for outlawing human cloning.) As the following discussion shows, a more specific content can be given to "human dignity" by focusing on issues of safety, individuality, autonomy, objectification, and kinship, and asking whether those risks are sufficient to justify a ban on human cloning undertaken for family or reproductive purposes.

2. Physical Safety. – Issues about physical safety arise with any new medical procedure. The danger that physicians who have an interest in developing and using innovative procedures will mislead patients about the prospect of success is always present. In some cases patients may demand procedures when the risks and likelihood of success are unknown. A variety of formal and informal regulatory procedures, from institutional review board assessments of research to clinical practice standards, exist to assure the safety and efficacy of new procedures.

The risk of premature use leading to physically damaged children exists with human cloning as it does with other medical and reproductive procedures. The risk is greatest when the procedure is new and not yet established. With cloning, the risks are: that eggs and DNA will be donated, embryos created, and then placed in the uterus without a realistic chance of success; that implantation will occur, but a high rate of miscarriage will result; and that resulting children will be deformed, will prematurely age, or will have a higher rate of cancer or other disease. On the other hand, cloning will assure that chromosomal aneuploidies or other defects, which are always a risk with coital reproduction, will not occur, for it is unlikely that DNA with such anomalies will have been cloned.

Considerable animal and laboratory research will be necessary to establish human cloning as a safe and effective procedure. The NBAC cited the need for more research establishing the physical safety of cloning as a reason for enacting a federal criminal ban, even though there was little risk that anyone would begin cloning before safety and efficacy had first been established in animals. Although reasonable people might differ in their willingness to accept risks to have a biologically-related family, few couples and doctors would be willing to use cloning techniques to form families if there were a significant risk of physical damage to offspring, or even high rates of miscarriage. With Food and Drug Administration or other regulatory control to assure safety of the technique, concerns about physical safety will rarely provide a sound basis for prohibiting cloning by couples seeking to have biologically-related children for rearing.

3. Cloning and Threats to Individuality. – Much opposition to human cloning has been based on concerns about a diminished sense of uniqueness and individuality in persons who are created with the DNA of other persons. Dr Ian Wilmut, in supporting his claim that human cloning would be repugnant, pointed to a denial of individuality, as did President Clinton in calling for Congress to ban human cloning for five years. Their underlying theory is that a unique genome is essential to individuality and that if one has the same DNA as another, she will inevitably be viewed as a copy of the person from whom the DNA came. This will produce such a reduced sense of individuality that it is in the childs' best interests not to be born at all.

Oddly, proponents of this view do not view identical twins as lacking individuality even though they have the same genome (including mitochondrial DNA). In fact, some twins have a sense of unity or nonseparateness that does not resolve itself into separate identities until later in childhood. Usually, however, we think of identical twins as having a special closeness and intimacy that other siblings do not share. Rather than suffer from a loss of individuality, identical twins created by cloning, even if born years apart, may have a special closeness that outweighs the risk of being confused with, or judged by, or expected to conform to the earlier twins' phenotype.

Couples who choose the DNA of another embryo or person for their child will face issues of their child's identity and individuality. If they use cloning as a legitimate way to solve a problem of family formation, they will be interested in having their child profit from the chosen genes while also experiencing its own individuality. One can choose a particular genome for one's child without regarding the child as a mere copy or replica of the DNA source. One can grant genes importance without granting them total importance, for nurture and environment also matter significantly in creating personal identity.

The DNA source and the resulting child may have the same nuclear DNA, but they are clearly separate persons who are born at different times and who occupy separate bodies. Their uterine, early childhood, and overall rearing environment and experiences will be different, and they ordinarily will not have the same mitochondrial DNA. While sharing many features, identical twins born at the same time are clearly separate persons. Identical twins born at different times are likely to be even more different. Thus using the DNA of another to make a child will not result in a mere copy or replica of the DNA source, must less make its life so full of suffering or reduced individuality that its life is not worth living.

A more sophisticated criticism based on individuality asserts not that the clone and the clone source are not physically separate or legally different persons, but rather that they will not be viewed or will not view themselves as truly separate. Because they have X's DNA, the danger is that their rearing parents, they themselves, and perhaps others will treat or perceive them as being X.

But several conditions would have to coalesce to create this effect. First, the rearing parents would have to know the clone source's phenotype and believe that its genotype will control the child's personal identity, despite the temporal and environmental differences that will occur in the child's rearing. Second, the concern about individuality would be magnified if other people also knew that the child is the clone of another person. But most people will have no idea or information about the origin of a person's DNA. Even if they did, they may still regard the later born child as an individual in his own right. Finally, and most importantly, the child would have to be informed of its status as a clone and believe that genes are all or largely determinative of who an individual is, while also ignoring the importance of being born and reared at a later time and in a different environment.

It is highly unlikely that all these conditions would manifest themselves in the most likely cloning scenarios. Take the case where parents, either through embryo splitting, nuclear transfer from embryos, or cloning of an existing child, produce a child with the same DNA as an existing or previously existing child. Because parents of identical twins view them as separate, and indeed often go to some trouble to treat them as different, no reason exists why they would not do so with later born identical twins, even though they have an earlier child with whom the later born twin may be compared. If they want the best possible life for their child, one would expect them to do everything possible to give the child its own sense of individuality and avoid viewing her merely as a copy of the existing child.

Consider also situations in which cloning is sought as a substitute for embryo or gamete donation. In the case of embryo donation, the DNA of a third party is chosen because that DNA has some special characteristic or meaning. The couple hopes that the clone will have at least some of the characteristics of the clone source, for example, her looks, intelligence, health, or merely her family connection. But it does not follow that they will view the child as identical to that source or that the child will be loved only to the extent that she emulates or resembles that source. They too will know that genes, while important, are not all-determinative of identity or personality. They will also know that rearing the child in a different setting at a later time is also likely to make her different from the DNA source. Although there will be some physical similarity, it is hard to think that parents interested in having a healthy child will not rear her as an individual in her own right.

Consider also cases in which a couple agrees to use the DNA of one of them in lieu of gamete donation from a stranger to produce the child whom they will gestate and rear. The rearing parent and child may share many physical characteristics, but it will be very difficult to view an infant and child as identical to its much older genetic twin who is also functioning as its rearing father. Even the rearing father will be hard-pressed to view the child as identical to himself, even though he might view it as part of or derived from himself, or have a very special parental relationship because of the genetic similarity.

In sum, the claim that human cloning necessarily violates a person's individuality because one does not have a unique genome is not convincing given the widespread existence of twins and the intent of a couple to gestate and rear the resulting child. Similarity in genotype does not mean that there will be similarity in phenotype, particularly when the rearing occurs in a different environment at a later time. If cloning occurs as part of a couple's efforts to have and rear offspring, we can expect that the rearing parents will attempt to inculcate difference rather than similarity and make strenuous efforts to ensure the child's sense that she is a special individual. To be sure, issues about the child's individuality are important matters to be addressed in the consent and counselling process of a couple contemplating the use of cloning to form a family. They do not, however, constitute the tangible harm needed to justify infringements on procreative rights to use cloning for the purpose of family formation.

4. Cloning as a Violation of Autonomy. – Many fears about human cloning involve the freedom or autonomy of the resulting child. A major limitation of freedom would occur if the resulting clone were the property, subject, or slave of the clone source or initiator of the cloning. But the decision to use another's DNA in bringing a child into the world gives neither the clone source nor the initiator of the cloning absolute or despotic power over that child. Any child born as a result of cloning would legally be a person with all the moral and legal rights of persons, and would no more be the property or subject of the person who commissions or carries out the cloning than any other child. Murder, assault, child abuse, and other laws protective of children would apply to all children, whether they are the product of cloning or coital conception. The power to determine whether another person will be born, and even what genes she carries, does not give one any additional power over that person once she does exist.

A second sense in which cloning might be thought to violate the resulting child's autonomy rests on a crude form of genetic determinism. It assumes that in picking one set of genes for the person, one is depriving her of the autonomy that she would have had if she possessed a different set of genes. This view assumes that genes control a person's actions and that in selecting genes, one is controlling or determining who or what the person is. It also overlooks the key fact that at a certain point, if given different genes, the resulting child would be a different person.

The position as stated claims too much. If it is true that the clone source's genes determine who the clone is and leave him no freedom to be otherwise, then no person has autonomy because we are all controlled by our genes. Of course, a prior phenotypic expression of one's genome is not available to constrain us in advance as it may be in the case of cloning, but the phenotype of the parents is close enough to impose similar constraints. Yet none of us think that we are totally determined by our parental genes, and we often engage in actions, particularly in adolescence, to distinguish ourselves from them. There is good reason to think that a child given the DNA of a sibling, a parent, or a third party would not also engage in that separation or would lack the ability to do so, particularly if the parents were interested in having the child develop its own sense of identity.

A third sense in which cloning could affect autonomy is through parental expectations based on the chosen genome. The fear is that because the genes chosen have special meaning for the parents, the couple will demand or expect the child to emulate or copy the life of the gene source. They will guide or mold the child to fit those expectations, thus depriving it of the ability to make its own choices. Given the power of parental influence, the child might come to view herself as having no freedom to act other than as she thinks her DNA source would have acted. Yet this fear also founders on the more likely possibility that parents, while hoping that their child will follow certain paths and even guiding or encouraging them to do so, will in the end have to accept the cloned child as a separate individual with his or her own preferences and path in life.

The concern about excessive parental expectations shares features with a fourth sense in which the resulting child may lack autonomy – denial of an "open future" because of phenotypic knowledge of the clone source. The philosopher Hans Jonas has articulated this point:

> The simple and unprecedented fact is that the clone knows (or believes to know) altogether too much about himself and is known (or is believed to be known) altogether too well to others. Both facts are paralyzing for the spontaneity of becoming himself. ... It is the known donor archetype that will dictate all expectations, predictions, hopes and fears, goal settings, comparisons, standards of success and failure, of fulfillment and disappointment, for all "in the know" – clone and witnesses alike; and this putative knowledge must stifle in the *pre-charted subject* all immediacy of the groping quest and eventual finding "himself" with which a toiling life surprises itself for good and for ill. (Hans Jonas 'Biological Engineering – A Preview' in *Philosophical Essays: From Ancient Creed To Technological Man* at 161.)

Jonas notes further that this effect is independent of the actual effects of genotype on a person's life. According to Jonas, genotype "is made his fate by the very assumptions in cloning him, which by their imposition on all concerned become a force themselves." (Ibid.) Jonas concludes that the clone is "antecedently robbed of the *freedom* which only under the protection of ignorance can thrive; and to rob a human-to-be of that freedom deliberately is an inexpiable crime that must not be committed even one." (Ibid.)

Jonas's eloquently stated concerns do not, of course, apply to every case involving human cloning. (Indeed, they were addressed to the situation of improving the quality or performance of the human race generally, and not to the procreative uses of cloning described above). They would not, for example, apply to cloning embryos or children who have not lived very long, for little will be known about them. Nor would they apply to a third party DNA source about whom little is known. Finally, this effect requires that the resulting child be informed of the origin of its DNA. Denial of an open future would not be a great danger if the child does not learn that he is cloned, does not know details of the clone source's life, or does not think that he is bound to copy or emulate that model.

Jonas's concerns, however, are theoretically applicable in the many cases in which parents are likely to have some information about the clone source's phenotype and have chosen its DNA for the value or meaning that phenotype carries for them. The danger exists, but it exists in noncloning situations as well. Based on what we know now about parental wishes in having and rearing offspring, the separate moral and legal status that children have, and how cloning is most likely to be used, parents will have a great interest in the well-being and autonomy of their child. Rearing a child with the DNA of another will present special challenges, but there is no basis for thinking that well-meaning parents cannot master them and allow the child the necessary room and freedom to become herself, regardless of what is known about the clone source.

No doubt parents interested in their child's well-being will strive to avoid constricting the child's future with overly rigid expectations. Indeed, no couple should embark upon cloning without considering the dangers of overly identifying the child with the clone source. No reputable program should provide cloning services without counselling couples about those dangers and screening out those couples who do not appear able to deal with the psychological challenges presented, as many assisted reproduction programs now do with couples seeking gamete donation or surrogacy. A major rearing task of parents will be to support the child's development toward being her own person, independent of the clone source's characteristics.

One may thus recognize the challenge of assuring the child an open future without concluding that all cloning will inevitably lead to perceptions of the child as a "clone" or copy of the clone source without the freedom to develop her own identity. In such circumstances, the chance that cloning will so harm the child's autonomy or sense of identity that it is preferable for her not to have been born at all is highly unlikely. Threats to autonomy thus do not constitute a compelling ground for denying couples the right to use cloning to form families.

5. Objectification and Instrumentalization. – A commonly asserted danger of human cloning is that it will lead to children being treated as means to parental ends and not as ends in themselves, thus violating the Kantian maxim to treat people as ends and not merely as means. Such a risk would be great if, as in *Brave New World* (Aldous Huxley *Brave New World* 10–12 (Time Inc Books 1963)), cloning were used to produce a worker class or many copies of a particular genome to serve societal or individual utilitarian goals without regard for the welfare of the resulting individual. But such scenarios do not recognize that cloning requires gestation and rearing of a child, much less that cloning may be part of a married couple's efforts to have and rear children.

The danger of objectification and instrumentalization might still exist, although to a lesser extent, with married couples who gestate and rear the children whose DNA they have chosen. After all, they are choosing to give the child a particular genome for a reason. Even if they do not view genes as all-determinative, they are expecting something because of the genome chosen for the child. The danger is that they will view the child primarily as a means to fulfil the goals that motivate the choice of that genome, thus rendering the child's life full of expectations and consequent suffering that make it preferable that it not be born at all.

In evaluating this claim, however, we cannot ignore the reasons that ordinarily motivate persons to have children. These reasons may range from continuing one's genetic line to connecting with nature after death, making provisions for a caretaker in one's old age, saving the marriage or relationship, demonstrating virility, obeying God's commandments, or simply experiencing the joy and pleasure of children. Many of these motives or purposes may continue to exist once the child is born, and indeed, may exist simultaneously with love for the child herself. Ordinarily, the existence of ulterior or mixed motives for wanting children does not cast doubt on the ethical acceptability of reproduction, for they do not prevent parents from loving children for themselves or respecting them as persons in their own right.

Similarly, parents may choose to have a child with a particular genome because they want the child to be tied to a certain lineage, to be healthy, to have certain other genetic attributes, to be like another child or person, to avoid the use of unknown tissue or embryo donors, or to be a source of organs or tissue. While some parents could end up viewing the child as a mere means to other agendas and ignore the child's own needs, it is more realistic to think that they will love and respect resulting children for themselves, even as the children serve these other goals, for they will have embarked on intrusive medical procedures, gestation, and childrearing in order to have the child.

As we have seen in other contexts, the child's genes could matter enormously for the parents without also causing the parents to deny or negate the child's own uniqueness, freedom, or worth as a person. This is clear when parents choose to have a later-born twin of an existing child or use the DNA of a third party or one of the spouses in lieu of gamete or embryo donation. It is also true when the motivating reason for cloning is to produce organs or tissue for transplant in an existing child. In the latter case, the child's own good and status as an end in herself can coexist with the parents' desire to help an existing child.

An instructive parallel to the use of cloning to obtain tissue or organs for transplant for an existing child arose in the Ayala case. The Ayala's eighteen-year-old daughter Anissa suffered from leukemia. Although in remission, there was a chance that the disease would recur and that eventually a bone marrow transplant would be necessary. Because neither her siblings nor her parents were a suitable match, her parents decided to have another child so that it might serve as a donor if necessary. After Mr Ayala underwent a reversal of a previous vasectomy, the couple conceived coitally and gave birth to a child who turned out to be an excellent tissue match for Anissa when the need for a bone marrow donation arose. Although a few ethicists raised concerns about conceiving a child to be a donor for another, it was clear that the Ayalas loved the new child as much as their other children and would continue to love her, whether or not she was able to save their older daughter's life.

If the Ayalas acted ethically because they were prepared to love the child whose conception was motivated by another child's potential need for bone marrow, then using an existing child's DNA in order to have another child as a source of organs or tissue should also be acceptable. Indeed, the ability to replicate existing DNA eliminates the risk that the resulting child will not be a proper match, thus lessening the chance that the child will be aborted in utero or rejected after birth because it is not an ideal donor. If the need for donation arises, the rights of the child with the chosen DNA still have to be respected. Its organs or tissue cannot be used without its consent, or if incompetent to consent, without a showing that the benefits it receives from the donation outweigh the harms (*Strunk v Strunk*, 445 SW 2d 145, 148–49 (Ky 1969)).

The example of cloning to obtain tissue or organs for an existing child shows that the threat of objectification or instrumentalization is not significantly greater with cloning that it is with coital reproduction. In either case, usually only couples seriously interested in rearing the resulting child would have a child for an ulterior purpose in addition to the interests of that child herself. In either case the genes matter, but the child matters as well. The fact that the child was also desired to serve as a source of tissue or organ does not negate the love that parents will have for that child.

The question of objectification is somewhat different if cell biology advances to the point that tissue or organs for transplant can be obtained from embryonic stem cells or early abortions. In that case cloning another to obtain tissue or organs for transplant need only produce cloned embryos or fetuses, and not live-born children, thus avoiding the problem of instrumentalizing a child created in part to serve as an organ source. In addition, a wider range of transplants becomes possible because obtaining organs from a living donor is limited to donations that do not unduly harm it (eg, blood, bone marrow, and possibly kidney).

Creating cloning embryos and fetuses to obtain tissue, while avoiding the problem of harm to resulting children, must confront the equally divisive issue of whether it is ethically acceptable to create and destroy embryos, or to conceive and abort fetuses, in order to obtain tissue and organs for transplant. Previous debates over the use of fetal tissue transplants to treat Parkinson's disease and the creation of embryos solely for research purposes demonstrate the ethical issues that thereby arise. An important distinction in those debates was whether a person believed that embryos or fetuses had rights in themselves as persons or subjects with independent moral status, or whether persons found such practices offensive even if they did not believe that embryos or fetuses had independent moral status. Persons who hold the latter view are best viewed as opposing those practices for symbolic, as opposed to rights-based reasons, because they acknowledge that embryos and fetuses do not independently have rights not to be discarded or aborted. If so, the issue will be resolved by a policy judgment about whether the transplant benefits of such sources outweigh the symbolic harm to respect for life that such practices would entail. In either case, however, the debate is not directly relevant to the ethical issues that arise from creating children by nuclear transfer cloning, but it concerns the different problem of creating and then destroying prenatal life in order to serve the health interests of others.

In sum, there is no reasonable basis for thinking that choosing particular DNA for a child is more likely to instrumentalize or objectify that child than choosing to have children born for any of the myriad reasons that drive persons in coital reproduction. Surely the risk that children with chosen DNA will have a life full of suffering because of the reasons motivating the choice of DNA does not appear great. That risk is not sufficient to prevent couples from cloning another when that choice is a reasonable way for the couple to achieve their goals of having and rearing biologically-related offspring.

6. Kinship, Lineage, and Family Relations. – A major source of concern with human cloning is the confusion that it could create in family lineage and kinship (see National Bioethics Advisory Comm'n, *Cloning Human Beings: Reports and Recommendations of the National Bioethics Advisory Commission*, 104 (1997) USA at P 70 (describing several examples in which cloning potentially could threaten family stability – hereinafter NBAC Cloning Report)). As with other objections to cloning, the argument takes the following form: (1) some forms of cloning could give rise to problems in identifying the lineage and kinship of resulting children; (2) these problems make the child's life much less happy than it would otherwise be; (3) therefore, all cloning should be prohibited.

The following discussion will focus on the kinship effects of the transfer of nuclear material and not on the effects arising from an egg donor's contribution to the enterprise, even though human cloning will raise family and kinship issues for the egg source as well. Because some of a person's DNA is in the mitochondria found in the egg's cytoplasm, a woman providing the egg into which the source DNA is transferred will also be contributing bits of DNA to the resulting child. This fact creates the novel possibility of separating the female *genetic* contribution in reproduction into two parts – nuclear DNA and mitochondrial DNA in the egg into which the nucleus of the source cell is placed. In sexual reproduction the same female provides both sources of female DNA. Nuclear transfer cloning permits DNA derived from the female to be provided by different women, or by the same woman at different points in time. Cloning thus further partializes biologic motherhood by presenting the novel possibility of a third biologic mother, in addition to the separate gestational and genetic mothers that IVF technology now makes possible.

An important issue in coming to terms with human cloning will be how to regard the contribution of an egg donor who neither gestates nor provides nuclear DNA. Is her effort in providing eggs sufficient to give her a kinship role? If effort alone does not qualify her as kin, does the contribution of cytoplasm and mitochondrial DNA give her a biologic or genetic status that deserves treatment like other biological contributors to a child's birth? We do not know the answer because the question has never previously arisen. It would certainly be plausible to continue the cultural emphasis on nuclear DNA and ignore the role that the donor of enucleated eggs provides, viewing her as more kin than nanny or wetnurse but less than the person who provides the nuclear DNA. The question of what meanings to construct for this relationship is another example of how human cloning and other forms of genetic selection require us to define reproductive meanings in the very process of using the technologies.

a. Cloning one's child. – The kinship problem is not salient in all cloning situations. A couple's use of their embryo's or an existing child's DNA to have another child raises no issue of kinship between rearing parents and child, for the child is clearly their genetic child. If the wife provides the egg into which the child's DNA is inserted, she will be the provider of both kinds of DNA, while also serving as gestational mother. If she does not provide the egg, she is nevertheless the major source of DNA (albeit at an earlier point in time) and will gestate. In that situation, role or lineage confusion from the existence of an egg source is unlikely.

The only relational oddity is that the child will have an older sibling with an identical nuclear genome. But this does not confuse kinship as such, although it does raise the novel question of the relation between an earlier and later born identical twin because the earlier born twin is the DNA source for the later. Unlike most twins, they will not share the same uterine or rearing environment. Indeed, given the differences in time and environment, they may consider themselves more as non-twin siblings than twins. The problems of individuality, autonomy, and objectification that cloning an existing child presents are not usefully understood as problems of kinship, for the kinship relationship between the two twins individually and between each of them and their rearing parents is not in question.

b. Cloning an unrelated third party. – The lineage problem is more relevant when another person's DNA is used in lieu of an anonymous embryo donation. In this case the couple will gestate and rear a child with whom they have no genetic tie. The party who consents to be cloned will have a later born identical twin with whom it has no rearing or social relation. The genetic parents of the clone source will also have no assigned rearing or social relation with the clone of their genetic offspring. While this situation is a deviation from the kinship relations that exist in coitally-created families, it does preserve a rearing relation with the woman who gestated and with her marriage or life partner.

The resulting kinship relations are similar but not identical to the splits among genetic, gestational, and social parentage that occur in certain kinds of assisted reproduction. Some forms of assistance (sperm and egg donation and gestational surrogacy) involve a genetic connection with at least one of the rearing partners – a connection that is missing here. With cloning, however, as with embryo donation, there is still a gestational relation. Embryo donation, to the extent it is now practiced, is socially and ethically accepted because of the gestational relationship and the recipient's commitment to rear. A similar situation exists with the cloning of a third party in lieu of embryo donation. In both cases the gestating mother and her partner will rear a child with whom they have no genetic connection.

Because it is unlikely in this scenario that the woman gestating and rearing the cloned embryo will provide the eggs that receive the nuclear transfer, a donor egg cycle will have to be initiated in another woman to provide the needed eggs. If donor eggs are used, the lineage becomes slightly more complicated because another woman will be providing the egg that receives the transfer of nuclear DNA. The resulting child will then have two different genetic mothers, as well as a gestating mother (who also will rear). A genetic purist might find this significant, but it is reasonable to expect that for the foreseeable future most people will view nuclear DNA rather than mitochondrial DNA as the primary carrier of kinship relations. In either case, however, as in embryo donation, the gestational and rearing relationship will be more significant.

An important kinship aspect of using the DNA of an individual unrelated to the couple is that the genetic parents of the clone source will be the resulting child's genetic parents. Without having done anything, they will have new genetic progeny – a later born identical twin of their offspring. Just as an embryo donor's parents will have no say in the genetic replication of their child, they may have no say over whether their child chooses to be cloned. This is likely to be true even though embryo donation results in genetic grandchildren, while cloning of their child leads to genetic reproduction. If they are aware of the cloning, they probably will have no rearing role with the resulting child. Nor will the child in many cases have any knowledge of or relation with either his elder identical twin or his genetic parents, just as the children of gamete or embryo donation seldom have social relations with genetic kin.

The concerns about kinship and lineage raised by cloning third-party DNA thus affect the parent-and-child rearing relation less than they affect the relation between the child and the DNA source, and the child and the DNA source's genetic parents. Its difference from embryo donation is again not substantial. Embryo donation also assumes that genetic parents will have no relation with genetic offspring. In that case, however, the genetic parents (the donors of the embryos) have consented to the possibility of genetic offspring. In cloning, it will often be the case that only the first born identical twin and not the genetic parents must give consent. If the genetic parents acquire no rearing rights or duties from their genetic relation alone, one can question whether the creation of additional genetic progeny without more is a significant burden that requires their consent.

  c. Rearing a clone of self. – A major challenge to understandings of kinship arises if the DNA of one of the rearing partners is used to create the child whom they gestate and rear. Given that twenty percent of a couple's infertility is due to male factors, and that thirty thousand to forty thousand children are born each year through the use of donor sperm, some demand for this form of cloning is likely.

  The kinship problem is that the social parent is genetically a sibling of the child – indeed, is an older identical twin – thus changing the traditional generational relation between parent and child. The danger of kinship confusion occurs on several levels. The rearing parent could forget that this child is a person in his own right and view him as merely an earlier version of himself. Such overidentification or attachment could make the child's efforts to detach from the parent more difficult. Alternatively, the parent could project fantasies on the child of what the parent wishes he had done when younger, again confusing the psychological boundaries between the two. The problem in the latter case, however, is less a problem of kinship or lineage than of the effects of the social parent's identification and expectations on the child's welfare. If those problems are successfully negotiated, then no problem of kinship as such arises.

  The situation involving self-cloning and rearing also affects the kinship relations between the clone source's own parents and the resulting child. The decision to clone and rear oneself means that one's parents have new genetic progeny through no effort, or even decision, of their own. Socially, the clone source will be rearing his own clone, thus putting his parents in the position of social grandparents when they are also genetic parents. In fact, they may not have consented to have another genetic child or even know of its existence. Whether or not they have consented to the cloning, the intention of the offspring who is cloned to rear the resulting child should define kinship relations, with the clone source and his spouse recognized as rearing parents. Although the clone source's parents may experience a strong emotional attachment to the new child, they have not undertaken to have and rear an additional child, and they should not be assigned rearing rights or duties beyond those of grandparents. (This result should follow even if they have consented to the cloning of their offspring. Grandparents are not, however, without rights in situations where rearing relations have already existed. See eg *Moore v City of East Cleaveland* 431 US 494, 504–06 (1977).) This result seems fair because their adult child's decision to clone and rear fits more closely with the next generation's project of having children.

  In situations in which the husband rather than the wife is the source of the child's nuclear DNA, several different relations are possible between the wife and the child. In the most appealing case, she will also provide the eggs which are enucleated to receive the husband's DNA, and then gestate the child. This procedure will require egg retrieval and probably stimulation of the ovaries as well. In this scenario, the child's nuclear genetic mother and gestational mother are different, even though the wife will have provided small bits of mitochondrial DNA and the egg into which the transferred nuclear DNA is inserted. If she gestates without providing the egg or nuclear DNA, the child will have the same gestating and rearing mother, and a different major and minor genetic mother. If the couple uses a gestational surrogate as well, then a fourth female aspect of motherhood will be realized.

  Does this further fragmentation of motherhood into two genetic parts adversely affect the child or kinship relations among the various parties? It will depend on the social and psychological importance of the mitochondrial DNA in the enucleated egg that makes a resulting child possible and the relation between clones and clone sources. At the present time no cultural meanings attend those relationships because they have not previously existed. In terms of effort alone, the role of the egg donor should be significant. Yet she contributes so little mitochondrial DNA relative to the nuclear DNA that her genetic role may well be marginalized. If only to simplify matters, she should not be regarded as socially significant kin at all.

  In the end, it is hard to see that kinship confusion for any of the parties is so great that it is likely to clash with reasonable judgments about forming families through nuclear transfer cloning. True, a couple will be rearing a smaller physical version of one of them, and a danger exists that pathological projections or identifications will occur. With advance counselling and a desire for the child's well-being, however, the novelty of the situation may be successfully managed. After all, the couple's goal is a normal family rearing situation, which they typically cannot achieve coitally. The danger to kinship relations from rearing one's clone is not so great that bans on self-cloning or other forms of cloning are justified.

  d. Cloning and rearing one's parent. – Cloning raises more serious problems of family and kinship confusion when the DNA source is one's parent. Using the DNA of a cousin, uncle, or aunt should raise no kinship problems in and of itself. Using the DNA of a sibling should also pose no major problems. In that case, one of the rearing partners will be rearing a younger, identical twin of an existing sibling. The practice of older siblings raising younger ones is not unknown in our culture and should be manageable even when those relations result from cloning.

The situation, however, is more problematic if a couple uses the DNA of one of their parents to create the embryo, which the wife gestates and which the husband and wife then rear. In that case, one would be carrying and then rearing a genetic replica of one's mother or father, or one's spouse's mother or father. A split between the gestating woman and the egg source only complicates what will, in any event, be a highly complicated matter.

Here, through cloning the resulting child would be the genetic parent of the person who is serving as its rearing parent. The danger is that the traditional lines between social and genetic parent and child might be blurred or confused, even beyond that which arises with self-cloning, leading to psychological and social complications for all the parties. Without more experience, one cannot tell how problematic such a situation would be. Given the great differences in age and development between genetic child and parent, special or severe developmental problems may not arise. If the couple has a good reason for using this source of DNA and has been fully counselled about the risks of psychological projection or conflict, then perhaps the risks are not appreciably greater than in rearing one's own clone or other situations of donors and surrogates.

On the other hand, the situation is sufficiently novel that a couple requesting it may be hard-pressed to convince doctors and other gatekeepers to the validity of their choice. Although not necessarily leading to a situation of such psychological suffering that the life of either child or parent becomes wrongful, insistence on cloning one's parent indeed seems distant from the usual parental or family project. Precisely because it is so problematic and strange, requests for it are likely to be rare. A key question will be whether a couple requesting parental cloning is plausibly exercising procreative liberty. If they are not, the risk of confusing kinship and family relations would be a sufficiently rational basis for banning this form of cloning. In any event, the risks of cloning one's parent would not justify a ban on the use of other familial sources of DNA, much less on all cloning.

e. Summary of kinship issues. – In sum, concerns about kinship and lineage provide no compelling basis for overriding a married couple's or an individual's wishes to use different forms of cloning to form a family. Kinship issues are only marginally relevant when the DNA of one's embryo or existing children is used. They are more relevant when the DNA of a third party is used, but that situation is similar to the kinship problems that arise with embryo donation. Cloning oneself or one's parent poses the greatest problems. In either case, the expected psychological harm or conflict would not amount to a wrongful life for the resulting child, but the question of whether either is so deviant from ordinary reproductive arrangements as to be perceived as beyond the pale of procreative liberty remains to be seen. Determining whether an exercise of procreative liberty is involved is another example of the constitutive value choices required by human cloning and other genetic selection techniques.

7. Eugenics. – Another feared harm of human cloning is that it will lead to wide-scale positive or negative eugenics, in which reproduction – whether by cloning or other methods – will occur only if social approved genes are used (NBAC Cloning Report (*supra*) at 74–75 (pointing out that determining which human traits and characteristics are to be favoured requires an assumption that is based on selective superiority, which has been linked to racist thinking)). As a ground for banning human cloning, the argument assumes a slippery slope between any use of human cloning and large-scale eugenics. To forestall an inevitable slide to eugenics, it concludes that a ban on all or most human cloning is justified.

a. Public eugenics. – The deepest fears generated by cloning are that it will lead to government-imposed or -conducted reproduction involving genetic selection and engineering, akin to the heavily regimented system portrayed in Huxley's *Brave New World* (between 1907 and 1963, more than 60,000 persons were sterilized under state involuntary sterilization laws) or in Margaret Atwood's *The Handmaid's Tale* (*supra*). Given our current democratic system, it seems highly implausible that the government could require people to clone as a way of improving the gene pool or assuring the most fit offspring. Nor does it seem likely that the government will identify desirable genomes, hire women to gestate the clones, and then rear them. (Margaret Atwood, *The Handmaid's Tale* (1986) (depicting a future dystopia in which society enslaves women as institutionalized surrogates.)) Nor would the government be likely to produce children through extrauterine, mechanical gestation if that became possible. Even if such practices did not violate anyone's rights, they are well outside our understandings of the role of government. The possibility of public eugenic policies in the future is too tenuous and speculative a basis to justify limiting or infringing personal choice in matters central to the family now.

Other government policies could encourage or cause widespread eugenics, but they are not directly related to human cloning. The government, for example, could require that people know their genomes or the genome of their embryos or fetuses, so that they could make appropriate planning decisions. It could even require that they avoid prenatal actions that harm offspring who could be born without the harm. The goals of such policies exist independently of cloning and might be sought regardless of whether human cloning ever becomes a common practice. The possibility of somatic cell nuclear transfer cloning does raise public awareness about genes, but it is unlikely in itself to increase mandatory government programs for genetic selection of offspring. As with slippery slope arguments generally, even if the feared state of affairs at the bottom of the slope is the unmitigated horror it is alleged to be, it is that sheer speculation that such eugenic policies would inevitably result from a step in that direction now through cloning.

Nor is human cloning to form or maintain families likely to lead to a government-imposed negative eugenics program, in which persons with certain characteristics or traits are prohibited from reproducing. Both cloning and genetic restraints on reproduction involve aspects of genetic selection of offspring characteristics. But the goal of restricting the incidence of certain genes is a far cry from the use of cloning to choose the genome of children. Given past abuses with compulsory sterilization, the absence of a strong need for such programs, and the lack of any group lobbying for a negative eugenics program, the adoption of such policies is highly unlikely. In addition, the intrusion on reproductive rights and bodily integrity makes such policies constitutionally dubious. (In *Re Moe* 432 NE 2d 712, 719–20 (Mass 1982); In *re Grady* 426 A 2d 467, 473–75 (NJ 1981); In *re Guardianship of Hayes*, 608 P 2d 635, 639–41 (Wash 1980). In *Re Guardianship of Hayes*, 307 NW 2d 881, 891–94 (Wis 1981) (all recognizing that an incompetent individual could only be sterilized for therapeutic contraceptive purposes, not eugenic ones, and then only if it were clearly shown to be in the incompetent's best interest – that is, she would choose the procedure herself if she were competent to do so.) It is highly implausible to think that cloning for the family-related reasons discussed above would lead directly to publicly-imposed negative eugenics.

b. Private eugenics. – The concern about eugenics may actually reflect fears about the growing spread of private eugenics. The ability to choose the genome of children through embryonic or somatic cell nuclear transfer may legitimate and therefore encourage increased use of all forms of genetic selection. As commercial firms enter the field and choice replaces chance, the fear is that parents will increasingly try to engineer offspring traits and characteristics, thus creating a regime of private eugenics.

But this fear is not a sufficient basis for restricting cloning or other genetic selection techniques. It is arbitrary to hold cloning responsible for such a future state. Indeed, people have been very interested in their children's genes before cloning appeared likely, though they have been largely limited to techniques of selection and exclusion, rather than positive engineering. Current practices of screening most pregnancies for genetic anomalies and projects for mapping and sequencing the entire human genome play a much greater role in creating the growing genetic consciousness that pervades society. The willingness to use cloning in forming families will reflect the increasing geneticization of society. It is implausible, however, to think that the relatively small number of cases in which embryo splitting or nuclear transfer cloning would be used to form families would greatly affect the willingness to use other forms of genetic selection.

Increased emphasis on the genes of offspring is likely regardless of whether human cloning is available to couples seeking to have and rear biologically related offspring. Other selection techniques will grow in power and specificity, regardless of the fate of human cloning. The fear that a regime of private eugenics will soon dominate human reproduction is too general and speculative a fear to justify stopping family-centered uses of human cloning.

(For other discussions of 'harms', see: Williamson (1999) 25 J of Med Ethics 96; McCarthy (1999) 25 J of Med Ethics 98; Burley and Harris (1999) 25 J of Med Ethics 108; Holm (1998) 7 Camb Q Health Care Ethics 160 and Harris (1997) 7 Camb Q Health Care Ethics 163.)

Therapeutic cloning In their report (*supra*), the HGAC and HFEA explain the developments that might involve cloning techniques to create cells, tissue or even organs that could have therapeutic benefits for an individual. The report also considers the extent to which research to such ends could be licensed under the 1990 Act.

HGAC and HFEA *Cloning Issues in Reproduction, Science and Medicine* (1998)

5.3 The most likely objective of a research project involving the use of CNR [cell nuclear replacement] would be to create a cultured cell line for the purposes of cell or tissue therapy. People who have tissues or organs damaged by injury or disease (eg skin, heart muscle, nervous tissue) could provide their own somatic nuclei and, by using these to replace nuclei in their own or donated eggs, individual stem cells (not embryos) could be produced in culture. These cells could then be induced (by exposure to appropriate growth factors) to form whichever type of cell or tissue was required for therapeutic purposes with no risk of tissue rejection and no need for treatment of the patient with immunosuppressive drugs.

5.4 For some processes somatic non-cloned cultured cells can be used for some kinds of tissue repair. They have a disadvantage, however, in that, depending on the age of the individual, they may have a limited life span. Other approaches to the treatment of degenerative disease and the repair of tissue damage, avoiding the risk of tissue rejection, may have been perfected before any success has been achieved with the types of embryo research outlined in paragraph 5.3 above. It may prove possible to treat tissues in such a way as to abolish their antigenicity, or custom-made "humanised" transgenic animals may provide tissues that can be successfully transplanted to any recipient, without the need for permanent treatment with immunosuppressive drugs. However, these possibilities are again speculative, and unlikely to be available for clinical testing for a decade or two. it would therefore seem unwise to rule out absolutely any lines of research no involving reproductive cloning that might prove of therapeutic value.

5.5 Some research has already been licensed by the HFEA into the possible generation *in vitro* of stem cell lines from human embryos for the purposes of analysing the factors that affect the development of embryos fertilised and grown *in vitro* and assessing their developmental potential. There is a recent report from the USA of the successful derivation from human embryos (fertilised *in vitro* and donated for research) of cell lines resembling stem cells in many respects ('Embryonic Stem Cell Lines derived from Human Blastocysts" Science, 282, 1145–1147: 1998). It therefore seems likely that applications for research projects involving CNR in human oocytes may be received by the HFEA within the next few years. Any such project would require a source of oocytes donated for research which at present are not widely available. However, *in vitro* techniques for maturing very immature oocytes from human ovaries are being devised, and these could possibly provide a source of enucleated oocytes adequate for research use (within the confines of its remit HFEA will be looking at stem cell technology).

5.6 The eventual clinical use of such procedures would be to provide immunologically compatible tissues for the treatment of degenerative diseases of, for example, the heart, liver, kidneys and cerebral tissue, or repair damage to skin or bone. The potential value of such techniques to human medicine is enormous. However, restrictions have been placed on the Authority in Schedule 2 of the HFE Act on the circumstances in which a licence may be issued.

5.7 Schedule 2 of the 1990 Act states that the HFEA cannot authorise a research project "unless it appears to the Authority to be necessary or desirable for one the following purposes:
(a)   promoting advances in the treatment of infertility;
(b)   increasing knowledge about the causes of congenital disease;
(c)   increasing knowledge about the causes of miscarriage;
(d)   developing more effective techniques of contraception;
(e)   developing methods for detecting the presence of gene or chromosome abnormalities in embryos before implantation.
or for such other purposes as may be specified in regulations."

5.8 The 1990 Act further requires that such licences can only be granted if the HFEA is satisfied that any proposed use of embryos is necessary for the purposes of the research.

5.9 Since therapeutic approaches to disease or tissue damage are not at present included in the purposes for which research can be licensed under the HFE Act (see paragraph 5.7), the making of new regulations would be required to extend the scope of the Act to include these purposes.

5.10 One potential future application of CNR would be for the avoidance of mitochondrial diseases. These life threatening and debilitating diseases are caused by defects in the mitochondria, which are small organelles located in the cytoplasm of each cell. Defective mitochondria are transmitted from the mother, in her egg cells, to all her offspring. It has been suggested that a woman suffering from such a disease could have a healthy child if the nuclear material from one of her eggs was transferred before fertilisation into a donor egg from which the nuclear material had been removed. Nuclear replacement between eggs has been successful in animals. It is not followed by the high incidence of embryonic mortality and abnormal development that characterises nuclear replacement procedures using somatic nuclei that require genetic reprogramming (as with Dolly). Nuclear replacement from one egg to another is not cloning, since after fertilisation the embryo is not identical to the mother, nor to any other embryo. Similarly, because the use of CNR for the avoidance of mitochondrial disease is not at present included in the purposes for which research can be licensed under the HFE Act (see paragraph 5.7), the making of new regulations would be required to extend the scope of the Act to include this purpose.

5.11 A significant number of respondents expressed fears and reservations about the possible commercialisation of therapeutic uses of CNR techniques. Similar anxieties arise in connection with any major advance in medical intervention. There is an understandable desire on the part of the public that curative procedures should not simply be exploited as sources of financial gain for their developers, but that there should be respect for the public good and corresponding access to these techniques for those who would benefit from them. A balance has to be struck between affording a reasonable recompense to those who have exercised initiative (and undertaken the risk involved in major and costly development programmes) and ensuring that the needs of the sick are properly met. The system of patenting is intended to provide a degree of such safeguard, for it requires that knowledge relevant to the new invention is available in the public domain, whilst granting the discoverer a limited period of protected benefit. There does not seem to be any reason why developments in the field of nuclear replacement therapy should differ significantly from other kinds of medical advances in this respect.

5.12 It has been questioned whether the 14 day limit for human embryo research could be breached by serial nuclear transfer. The HFEA and the HGAC take the view that this is not the case. Whether the nucleus to be replaced in an enucleated oocyte is taken from an adult or from another embryo, the clock is put back to the beginning, embryonic development starts over again, and the primitive streak stage specified in the Act would still not be reached within the 14 day time limit.

In the result, this led to the following recommendation:

9.3 When the 1990 HFE Act was passed, the beneficial therapeutic consequences that could potentially result from human embryo research were not envisaged. We therefore *recommend* that the Secretary of State should consider specifying in regulations two further purposes to be added to the list in paragraph 3(2) of Schedule 2 (as described in paragraph 5.7 of this report) being:
• *developing methods of therapy for mitochondrial diseases*
• *developing methods of therapy for diseased or damaged tissues or organs.*

It is perhaps worth noting that Sch 2, para 3(3) states that regulations may only specify research purposes, *inter alia,* 'which increase knowledge … about disease, or enable such knowledge to be applied'. This wording would not seem to permit regulations authorising research for therapy for *damaged* tissues or organs, as opposed to *diseased* tissues or organs. Legislation would be required for this.

One final point of interest arises out of the report's reference to the creation of 'stem cell lines' (see para 5.5). Scientifically and medically, this will be an exciting and important development. The following describes the science and its possible issues.

Julian Savulescu 'Should We Clone human beings? Cloning as a Source of Tissue for Transplantation' (1999) 25 J Med Ethics 87

Stem cells are cells which are early in developmental lineage and have the ability to differentiate into several different mature cell types. Totipotent stem cells are very immature stem cells with the potential to develop into any of the mature cell types in the adult (liver, lung, skin, blood, etc). Multipotential stem cells are more mature stem cells with the potential to develop into different mature forms of a particular cell lineage, for example, bone marrow stem cells can form either white or red blood cells, but they cannot form liver cells.
    Multipotential stem cells can be used as
a.   a vector for gene therapy.
b.   cells for transplantation, especially in bone marrow.
Attempts have been made to use embryonic stem cells from other animals as vectors for gene therapy and as universal transplantation cells in humans. Problems include limited

differentiation and rejection. Somatic cells are differentiated cells of the body, and not sex cells which give rise to sperm and eggs. Cloning of somatic cells from a person who is intended as the recipient of cell therapy would provide a source of multipotential stem cells that are not rejected. These could also be vectors for gene therapy. A gene could be inserted into a somatic cell from the patient, followed by selection, nuclear transfer and the culture of the appropriate clonal population of cells in vitro. These cells could then be returned to the patient as a source of new tissue (for example bone marrow in the case of leukaemia) or as tissue without genetic abnormality (in the case of inherited genetic disease). The major experimental issues which would need to be addressed are developing clonal stability during cell amplification and ensuring differentiation into the cell type needed. It should be noted that this procedure does not necessarily involve the production of a multicellular embryo, nor its implantation in vivo or artificially. (Indeed, cross-species cloning – fusing human cells with cow eggs – produces embryos which will not develop into fetuses, let alone viable offspring.)

A related procedure would produce totipotent stem cells which could differentiate into multipotent cells of a particular line or function, or even into a specific tissue. This is much closer to reproductive cloning. Embryonic stem cells from mice have been directed to differentiate into vascular endothelium, myocardial and skeletal tissue, haemopoietic precursors and neurons. However, it is not known whether the differentiation of human totipotent stem cells can be controlled in vitro. Unlike the previous application, the production of organs could involve reproductive cloning (the production of a totipotent cell which forms a blastomere), but then differentiates into a tissue after some days. Initially, however, all early embryonic cells are identical. Producing totipotent stem cells in this way is equivalent to the creation of an early embryo.

As we saw, the HFEA can only licence such research if it is 'necessary or desirable' and is for one of the stated purposes (Sch 2, para 3(2)). The HGAC/HFEA report illustrates that this *new* development may require amending legislation to permit some research (for an argument in favour of the research, see Savulescu 'Should we Clone Human Beings? Cloning as a Source of Tissue for Transplantation' (1999) 25 J of Med Ethics 87). Once the stem cells have been removed from the embryo (whether or not cloned), it is difficult to see how the HFEA would have any ability to regulate what was done with the *cells*. Its powers are limited to licensing research on *embryos*.

The Act may also need amendment here if regulation is considered desirable, as it surely must be (see generally, Symposium 'Human Primordial Stem Cells' (1999) 29(2) Hastings Centre Report 30–42 and Nuffield Council on Bioethics, *Stem Cell Therapy: The Ethical Issues* (1999)).

(d) Treatment ethics committees

One matter which is not dealt with in the regulatory framework is that of ethics committees. Many of the decisions taken by clinicians in this context raise more than clinical matters but rather ethical and social considerations. Who should have access to infertility treatments? Should it be available to single women or gay couples? Should post-menopausal women or patients who are HIV positive be treated? To assist in making such decisions, the Interim Licensing Authority (the HFE's predecessor) required clinics to have ethics committees. Guideline 13(a) of the ILA's *Guidelines for Both Clinical and Research Applications of Human In Vitro Fertilisation* (6th Report, ILA, 1991 Annex 1) stated:

> . . . each centre must have access to an ethical committee, and no procedure should be undertaken without the knowledge and consent of the ethical committee.

Detailed guidelines were provided by the ILA on the role, membership and working of such committees (Annex 2). As you will have seen, the 1990 Act does not contain the requirement that a licensed centre should have an ethics committee. It could have so easily been made a standard condition in every licence under s 12 of the 1990 Act. The HFEA has also not made it a requirement either through additional conditions or in the *Code of Practice* (4th edn, 1998) in respect of *treatment*. As regards embryo research, the *Code of Practice* states (at para 10.7): 'Centres should refer each research project to a properly constituted ethics committee for approval before applying for a research licence'.

Thus, embryo research is dealt with in the same way as other research on human subjects (see *infra*, ch 14). Nevertheless, many clinics do have ethics committees who assist in making decisions which are ethically and socially difficult or controversial. In a survey of clinics, Savas and Treece obtained data on the frequency and work of ethics committees.

Diane Savas and Stephen Treece 'Fertility Clinics: One Code of Practice' (1998) 3 Medical Law International 243

SURVEY AND RESULTS
The survey was conducted by means of a questionnaire sent to all licensed Fertility clinics actively involved in treatment in the UK. The questionnaire was a mixture of "open", "closed", and "weighted" questions and respondents were assured of anonymity, (it was felt that anonymity would allow far more openness in the answers provided by respondent clinics). Questionnaires were sent to all 107 clinics listed in the HFEA's Patients Guide to DI and IVF Clinics. 57 clinics replied, representing a 53% response rate. Of these 57, two were returned unanswered with notes stating that one clinic had closed and the other amalgamated with an existing clinic. The remaining 55 responses represented a 51% viable response rate and comprised the final survey sample. Two clinics waived their right to anonymity, (in respect of the authors only), in order to request a copy of the findings of the survey. They also included for the authors' information, copies of their patient questionnaire, and one also included a copy of the questionnaire sent out to patients' general practitioners.

Of the respondents, five treated NHS referrals exclusively, seventeen were private clinics, and the remaining twenty nine had a mix of both private and NHS clients.

If it is to be accepted that assisted conception services should be regulated in a way naturally occurring pregnancies are not, an obvious starting point in any investigation into decision making in this area has to be the approach adopted by clinics when dealing with the dilemma of to whom they are prepared to offer their services, and conversely, which prospective parent(s) they would refuse to help. This process forces providers of fertility services into making decisions as to who will make the 'better' parents by implication. Such decisions will inevitably involve economic, religious and moral as well as clinical considerations and as such can generally be considered under the head of 'ethics'.

The first question asked whether a clinic had its own ethics committee. Thirty-six, (65%), respondents reported that they had a committee responsible to their particular clinic or department, although one respondent reported that although they possessed such a committee, it had never been consulted. Nineteen, (35%), respondents reported that they had no ethics committee, although of these, nine had access to an alternative body, often a Local Research Ethics Committee, (LREC). The remaining ten, (18%), respondents reported that they made ethical decisions based on the views of the treatment team.

The solving of ethical dilemmas is fraught with difficulty. Those charged with that responsibility must often choose whether their role is to reflect the perceived views of the majority of society or alternatively, perhaps, to break new ground and provide a lead to the public at large. This is particularly pertinent in the field of assisted conception which is so often operating at the frontiers of research. It was therefore considered important to obtain information not only in respect of the proportion of clinics with ethics committees, but also to examine the composition of those committees. The responses illustrated that thirteen ethics committees comprised a majority of lay members, and twelve had a majority of medical personnel, (including nurses and midwives). There was an equal number of medical and lay members in two clinics. In nine cases, it was either impossible to enumerate the professional backgrounds of members, or the respondents did not answer the question.

One of the most striking features in respect of the composition of the ethics committees was the overwhelming majority of members with middle class, professional backgrounds. In only six instances, did the possibility exist that these members *may* have had working class backgrounds. The largest single professional group mentioned, perhaps not unexpectedly, was that of doctors from varying disciplines. Doctors were mentioned 85 times and made up 34% of the total number of members mentioned by the respondents. 'Lay' members, again as defined by the respondents, were mentioned 52 times and were the second largest group, followed by nurses [35], lawyers, [24], clergymen, [18], social workers, [10], school teachers [8], and counsellors, [8]. Other professions categorised as 'lay' by respondents, included four pharmacists and two radiographers.

In their research, the authors went on to ask how certain ethical decisions – such as access to treatment by patients other than married couples and 'welfare of the child' issues – would be made. Having done so, the authors comment on the evidence they had elicited about ethics committees as follows:

OBSERVATIONS

... Firstly, it is submitted that they provide an interesting yet worrying profile of the composition of ethics committees. Those clinics who responded to the survey appear to be receiving ethical advice from an overwhelmingly middle class, professional perspective. In addition, doctors appear to be represented to a greater degree than any other profession, and when nurses and other medically related disciplines are aggregated together, they total 49% of committee members mentioned. The size of this group of medically oriented professionals could expose committees to the charge, perhaps unfairly in the majority of cases, that ethical decisions are being taken with too close an eye on clinical and research led grounds, rather than with reference to the Code of Practice requirements. Of course doctors and nurses are not a homogenous group. Nurses and midwives have their own professional obligations to fulfil in accordance with guidelines issued by their regulatory body. (The United Kingdom Central Council for Nursing and Midwifery.) There can be little doubt however, that for both structural and clinical reasons, Doctors will hold the balance of power in any debate as to the merits or otherwise of a decision to treat or not to treat. The very fact that the term 'treatment' is used in relation to the provision of fertility services ensures this. That is not to say doctors are incapable of making difficult decisions on ethical rather than clinical grounds, far from it. However, the decision will perhaps inevitably be to a greater or lesser extent, from a medical perspective, (even when taking into account the differing 'specialities' of those Doctors), rather than that of the 'man on the Clapham Omnibus.' There can be little doubt that the presence of Doctors on ethical committees is a necessity. The fact that treatment in this field is often highly technical and research led requires their expertise in advising others as to the feasibility or risks involved in certain procedures. The question must be however, should the medical profession be represented to quite the extent it appears to be? As Juli[e] Stone comments,

> Are doctors uniquely competent to decide who will be fit parents? Indeed, apart from the question of medical suitability for a particular treatment, we should ask whether this is a medical decision at all or whether it is rather a moral, social and political question. (Stone J (1990), Infertility Treatment: a selective right to reproduce? in *Ethics and Law in Health Care and Research*, ed Byrne P.)

Given the number of high profile assisted pregnancies in which the decision has been criticised on ethical grounds by the media, there would appear to be an argument that all fertility clinics should refer ethical matters to a dedicated ethics team. Currently, many clinics claiming to have such a committee appear to have been heavily influenced by the guidelines issued by the NHS Management Executive relating to the composition and objectives of Local Research Ethics Committees (NHS Management Executive letter (HSG (91) 5) paras 2.4, 2.6, 2.7) (our italics). The guidelines state that members of an LREC should include hospital medical staff, nursing staff, general practitioners and at least two or more lay persons. Perhaps somewhat unrealistically, the guidelines also state that professional members are not, "... in any way the representatives of those groups. They are appointed in their own right, to participate in the work of the LREC as individuals of sound judgement and relevant experience." (Ibid., para 2.6).

It is not advocated that ethics committees considering difficult questions in either the field of research or treatment should blindly follow the views of 'society' as interpreted by the popular press, both tabloid and broadsheet. Such views may be ill judged, and based on ignorance. However, in order to obtain a broad spectrum of opinion and the opportunity to make reference to the current social, political and moral nexus, it is suggested that any ethics team should have a lay membership of at least fifty per cent of the total. Members should also be more representative of the general public in respect of social and economic background. This is a difficult area in which the provision of an arena in which varied opinions can be heard, should be the aim. The results of this survey would indicate that at present, ethics committees are generally the preserve of an academic and social elite ...

CONCLUSION

... If it is appropriate for ethics committees to oversee research proposals, there is no reason that a similar ethics committee should not be appointed by fertility clinics to monitor and advise on problem cases which arise during treatment of patients, yet there is no requirement for the formation of such committees in the Code of Practice. Until this is the case, the provision of fertility treatment will continue to generate controversy ...

B. ACCESS TO TREATMENT

The 1990 Act does not specifically address the entitlement of a person to gain access to treatment services. The issue was recognised as important by the Warnock Committee (*supra*). The conclusions arrived at may be regarded as conventionally satisfactory but somewhat under-argued.

Report of the Committee of Inquiry into Human Fertilisation and Embryology (1984) (CM 9314)

2.5 It is sometimes suggested that infertility treatment should be available only to married couples, in the interests of any child that may be born as a result. While we are vitally aware of the need to protect these interests, we are not prepared to recommend that access to treatment should be based exclusively on the legal status of marriage.

2.6 In discussing treatment for infertility, this report takes the term *couple* to mean a heterosexual couple living together in a stable relationship, whether married or not. We use the words *husband* and *wife* to denote a relationship, not a legal status (except where the context makes differentiation necessary, for example in relation to legitimacy).

2.7 In the evidence, concern was expressed that infertility treatment may be provided for couples without due regard for the interests of any child that may be born as a result. For example the couple may have a previous conviction for child abuse. It has been argued that the greater the degree of intervention in the creation of a child, the more responsibility must be taken for that child. However, the evidence also drew attention to the absence of any restrictions of procreation by fertile couples, whatever their circumstances. Indeed, some of the evidence referred to the fact that Articles 8 and 12 of the European Convention on Human Rights guarantee a respect for family life and the right to found a family. It has been argued that these provisions create a right to take full advantage of the techniques which are available to alleviate infertility.

2.8 There are other considerations which many believe should be taken into account. For example, a woman may seek treatment when she has herself, at an earlier stage, been sterilised at her own request. Perhaps because of a new marriage, she now very much wants children. The question may be raised whether, if she has children, albeit from another marriage, she should be eligible for infertility treatment. Again, a woman who has had a child may subsequently become infertile. Opinions may be divided about whether she should be eligible for treatment.

2.9 Furthermore, the various techniques for assisted reproduction offer not only a remedy for infertility, but also offer the fertile single woman or lesbian couple the chance of parenthood without the direct involvement of a male partner. To judge from the evidence, many believe that the interests of the child dictate that it should be born into a home where there is a loving, stable, heterosexual relationship and that, therefore, the *deliberate* creation of a child for a woman who is not a partner in such a relationship is morally wrong. On the other side some expressed the view that a single woman or lesbian couple have a right under the European Convention to have children even though those children may have no legal father. It is further argued that it is already accepted that a single person, whether man or woman, can in certain circumstances provide a suitable environment for a child, since the existence of single adoptive parents is specifically provided for in the Children Act 1975 [now repealed].

2.10 In the same way that a single woman may believe she has a right to motherhood, so a single man may feel he has a right to fatherhood. Though the feminist position is perhaps more frequently publicised, we were told of a group of single, mainly homosexual, men who were campaigning for the right to bring up a child. Their primary aim at present is to obtain in practice equal rights in the adoption field, but they are also well aware of the potential of surrogacy for providing a single man with a child that is genetically his. There have been cases in other countries of surrogacy in such circumstances. It can be argued that as a matter of sex equality if single women are not totally barred from parenthood, then neither should single men be so barred.

2.11 We have considered these arguments, but, nevertheless, we believe that as a general rule it is better for children to be born into a two-parent family, with both father and mother, although we recognise that it is impossible to predict with any certainty how lasting such a relationship will be.

2.12 We have considered very carefully whether there are circumstances where it is inappropriate for treatment which is solely for the alleviation of infertility to be provided. In general we hold that everyone should be entitled to seek expert advice and appropriate investigation. This will usually involve referral to a consultant. However, at the present time services for the treatment of infertility are in short supply, both for initial referral and investigation and for the more specialised treatments considered in this report. In this situation of scarcity some individuals will have a more compelling case for treatment than others. In the circumstances medical practitioners will, clearly, use their clinical judgment as to the priority of the individual case bearing in mind such considerations as the patient's age, the duration of infertility and the likelihood that treatment will be successful. So far this is not contentious. However, notwithstanding our view that every patient is entitled to advice and investigation of his or her infertility, we can foresee occasions where the consultant may, after discussion with professional health and social work colleagues, consider that there are valid reasons why infertility treatment would not be in the best interests of the patient, the child that may be born following treatment, or the patient's immediate family.

2.13 This question of eligibility for treatment is a very difficult one, and we believe that hard and fast rules are not applicable to its solution. We recognise that this will place a heavy burden of responsibility on the individual consultant who must make social judgments that go beyond the purely medical, in the types of case we have discussed. We considered whether it was possible for us to set out the wider social criteria that consultants, together with their professional colleagues, should use in deciding whether infertility treatment should be provided for a particular patient. We decided it was not possible to draw up comprehensive criteria that would be sensitive to the circumstances of every case. We recognise however that individual practitioners are on occasions going to decline to treat a particular patient and **we recommend that in cases where consultants decline to provide treatment they should always give the patient a full explanation of the reasons.** This would at lease ensure that patients were not kept in ignorance of the reason for refusal, and would be able to exercise their right to seek a second opinion.

During the course of the legislation passing through Parliament, an attempt was made to restrict access to infertility treatment to married couples or, at least, to heterosexual couples in a stable relationship. The Bill was not amended to take account of this. However, s 13(5) was introduced so as to provide some limits upon access to treatment. It provides:

13 (5) A woman shall not be provided with treatment services unless account has been taken of the welfare of any child who may be born as a result of the treatment (including the need of that child for a father), and of any other child who may be affected by the birth.

The important principle of the welfare of the child which runs through legislation concerned with children is, therefore, made part of the doctor's obligation in determining whether to make infertility treatment available to any given person(s). It is, of course, the requirement that the doctor should take account of 'the need of [the] child for a father' and 'of any other child who may be affected by the birth' that is significant. In these words, Parliament has required that the clinical judgment of the doctor must be exercised having regard to others and not just in the 'best interests' of his patient. In this respect, the 1990 Act departs from what would be the normal understanding of a doctor's duty to his patient.

We are concerned with what are, in fact, two distinct but related issues: first, the general question of the suitability of *anyone* to be a parent; and secondly, the suitability of an applicant who is not married. These two issues, together with the possibility of a judicial remedy for denying access to treatment, are discussed by Professor Gillian Douglas.

Gillian Douglas *Law, Fertility and Reproduction* (1991)

Fitness to parent
This arises in two ways. First, suppose a couple present for treatment, but the doctor considers them as unsuitable to act as parents because of their life-style or previous history. Those with a record of child abuse, or drug-taking, might fall into this category. The doctor could argue that it is preferable to deny them treatment rather than have to take emergency measures to protect any resulting child from harm at their hands. A refusal to treat by a private clinic could not be legally challengeable unless it infringed the Sex Discrimination Act 1975 or the Race Relations Act 1976. But it is hard to see how the first could be prayed in aid, and it will be very difficult to prove racial discrimination in order to rely upon the second.

It is also debatable whether a refusal in the NHS could be challenged on other grounds, although an action for judicial review was brought in *R v Ethical Committee of St Mary's Hospital (Manchester), ex p H* ([1988] 1 FLR 512). There, the applicant had been turned down as a suitable foster or adoptive parent, because she had a criminal record involving prostitution offences, and a 'poor understanding' of fostering. She accordingly sought IVF treatment, but was removed from the waiting list after the hospital became aware of her background. At St Mary's, the criteria for offering treatment were that couples

> must, in the ordinary course of events, satisfy the general criteria established by adoption societies in assessing suitability for adoption ... [and there] must be no medical, psychiatric or psychosexual problems which would indicate an increased probability of a couple not being able to provide satisfactory parenting to the offspring or endanger the mother's life or health if she became pregnant. ...

She sought judicial review of the refusal to treat her, but failed on the basis that she had been given an opportunity to make representations against the refusal, so that there was no procedural unfairness. Schiemann J was prepared to accept, *obiter*, that a blanket policy to refuse treatment to 'anyone who was a Jew or coloured' might be illegal. But here, the hospital's criteria were apparently regarded as acceptable. ...

Centres offering IVF treatment were required by the ILA guidelines to have an ethical committee to scrutinise their treatment and research programmes, and their objectives included the protection of the interests of patients and of any children resulting from the use of assisted reproduction. No guidance was given on how this was to be done. It is therefore unsurprising that the St Mary's Hospital committee might have had regard to the adoption criteria, which were the only semi-official tests of fitness to parent available. Under section 13(5) of the 1990 Act, treatment licences must contain a condition that

> A woman shall not be provided with treatment services unless account has been taken of the welfare of any child who may be born as a result of the treatment (including the need of that child for a father), and of any other child who may be affected by the birth.

Under section 25(2) the code of practice must also contain guidance on this for those providing treatment services [*Code of Practice* (1993) paras 3.12–3.30]. Such a provision is undesirable. The concept of welfare is hard enough to apply in cases concerning children who are in existence, let alone those who are only a twinkle in the doctor's eye. It is also open to many different assessments, depending on the values of the person making the judgment.

This becomes particularly important in relation to the second type of situation which raises the question of fitness to parent. This is where a woman (or, perhaps less likely, a man) does not have, or seek a partner of the opposite sex, but wants a child. Here, the question is whether children should always ideally be brought up in a household containing a mother and a father. The matter was considered by the Warnock Committee, whose view was that 'as a general rule it is better for children to be born into a two-parent family, with both father and mother' although they did not make a recommendation to limit treatment to members of a couple.

Attempts during the passage of the Act through Parliament to limit treatment to the married, or at least to members of a heterosexual cohabiting couple, were unsuccessful, but section 13(5) does require consideration to be given to the child's need for a father – presumably meaning a man who will fulfil the *social* role of father. This requirement was put in as an amendment expressly to prevent the creation of one-parent families through assisted reproduction (and implicitly to prevent lesbian woman from receiving treatment). Yet there is no evidence for the supposition that the children of such families suffer *because* they are cared for by only one parent, homosexual or otherwise. Children from one-parent families might experience poverty, or the emotional trauma of their parents' relationship breaking up, but children who are born after assisted reproduction are arguably less likely to experience such problems, since their birth was planned when the parent was already settled into her life-style.

In addition to the welfare test operating as a means of excluding those regarded as unfit to parent from the benefits of treatment, it has been suggested that section 38, which provides that a person who has a conscientious objection to participating in any activity governed by the Act is under no duty to do so, will be relied upon by those who oppose not only the principle of donation, or creation of embryos in vitro, but also, for example, by those who do not wish to treat lesbians. Such an approach would mirror that found in relation to abortion, where doctors may help or hinder women seeking terminations, depending upon their own views of the 'rightness' of the woman's case. ...

Although there were almost 60 clinics (both NHS and private) offering insemination in 1990, only about six were prepared to treat single or lesbian women. The requirement in section 13 is likely to deter any more clinics from offering treatment to these women, and may force them to resort to unlicensed treatment.

Gillian Douglas talks of how hard it is to apply the concept of welfare concerning children 'who are only a twinkle in the doctor's eye'. Arguably, we can go further and suggest that s 13(5) is, in fact, incoherent. If there is an option to bring about the birth of a child, it can never (or almost never) be in its welfare or interests not to be born. Existence for the child is preferable to non-existence. Thus, the reference in s 13(5) to the child's 'welfare' cannot have its ordinary family law meaning. Instead, s 13(5) must be directing us elsewhere and this can only be to the suitability of the proposed parent(s). Given that those who become parents by conventional means do not need to pass any suitability test, the dangers of prejudice and discrimination are obvious. For example, if suitability to be a parent means the ability to meet the needs of the child, it is arguable that the more affluent the applicant for treatment, the more likely a child's *material* needs would be met. Assuming that the capacity to meet the child's spiritual needs does not vary according to social class and status, it would follow that treatment should primarily be offered to the affluent (as those who can afford to pay for this treatment often are). Only by arguing that s 13(5) imports some element of equality of opportunity could this approach, distasteful as it is, be rebutted.

HFEA's *Code of Practice* (4th edn, 1998) accepts 'the right of people who are or may be infertile to the proper consideration of their request for treatment' (p 5). This, on its face, seems to endorse (or come close to endorsing) the principle of equality of access. It seeks to give substance to the basic principle in the detailed provisions of the *Code of Practice* dealing with access to treatment.

HFEA, *Code of Practice* (4th edn, 1998)

Factors to be Considered

3.15 Centres should take all reasonable steps to ascertain who would be legally responsible for any child born as a result of the procedure and who it is intended will be bringing up the child. When clients come from abroad, centres should not assume that the law of that country relating to the parentage of a child born as a result of donated gametes is the same as that of the United Kingdom.

3.16 People seeking treatment are entitled to a fair and unprejudiced assessment of their situation and needs, which should be conducted with the skill and sensitivity appropriate to the delicacy of the case and the wishes and feelings of those involved.

3.17 Where people seek licensed treatment, centres should bear in mind the following factors:
a.   their commitment to having and bringing up a child or children;
b.   their ability to provide a stable and supportive environment for any child produced as a result of treatment;
c.   their medical histories and the medical histories of their families;
d.   their health and consequent future ability to look after or provide for a child's needs;
e.   their ages and likely future ability to look after or provide for a child's needs;
f.   their ability to meet the needs of any child or children who may be born as a result of treatment, including the implications of any possible multiple births;
g.   any risk of harm to the child or children who may be born, including the risk of inherited disorders or transmissible diseases, problems during pregnancy and of neglect or abuse; and
h.   the effect of a new baby or babies upon any existing child of the family.

3.18 Where people seek treatment using donated gametes, centres should also take the following factors into account:
a.   a child's potential need to know about their origins and whether or not the prospective parents are prepared for the questions which may arise while the child is growing up;
b.   the possible attitudes of other members of the family towards the child, and towards their status in the family;
c.   the implications for the welfare of the child if the donor is personally known within the child's family and social circle; and
d.   any possibility known to the centre of a dispute about the legal fatherhood of the child (see paragraphs 5.6 to 5.8, below).

3.19 Further factors will require consideration in the following cases:
a.   where the child will have no legal father. Centres are required to have regard to the child's need for a father and should pay particular attention to the prospective mother's

ability to meet the child's needs throughout their childhood. Where appropriate, centres should consider particularly whether there is anyone else within the prospective mother's family and social circle willing and able to share the responsibility for meeting those needs, and for bringing up, maintaining and caring for the child. ...

Enquiries to be Made

3.23 Centres should take a medical and social history from each prospective parent. They should be seen together and separately. This should include all the information relevant to paragraphs 3.12 to 3.19 above.

3.24 Centres should seek to satisfy themselves that the GP of each prospective parent knows of no reason why either of them might not be suitable for the treatment to be offered. This would include anything which might adversely affect the welfare of any resulting child.

3.25 Centres should obtain the client's consent before approaching the GP. However, failure to give consent should be taken into account in considering whether or not to offer treatment.

3.26 If any of these particulars or inquiries give cause for concern, eg, evidence that prospective parents have had children removed from their care, or evidence of a previous relevant conviction, the centre should make such further inquiries of any relevant individual, authority or agency as it can.

3.27 Centres should obtain the client's consent before approaching any individual, authority or agency for information. However, failure to give consent should be taken into account in deciding whether or not to offer treatment.

Multidisciplinary Assessment

3.28 The views of all those at the centre who have been involved with the prospective parents should be taken into account when deciding whether or not to offer treatment. Prospective parents should be given a fair opportunity to state their views before any decision is made and to meet any objections raised to providing them with treatment.

3.29 If a member of the team has a cause for concern as a result of information given to them in confidence, they should obtain the consent of the person concerned before discussing it with the rest of the team. If a member of the team receives information which is of such gravity that confidentiality *cannot* be maintained, they should use their own discretion, based on good professional practice, in deciding in what circumstances it should be discussed with the rest of the team.

3.30 The decision to provide treatment should be taken in the light of all the available information. Treatment may be refused on clinical grounds. Treatment should also be refused if the centre believes that it would not be in the interests of any resulting child, or any child already existing, to provide treatment, or is unable to obtain sufficient information or advice to reach a proper conclusion.

3.31 If treatment is refused for any reason, the centre should explain to the woman and, where appropriate, her husband or partner, the reasons for this and the factors, if any, which might persuade the centre to reverse its decision. It should also explain the options which remain open and tell clients where they can obtain counselling.

3.32 Centres should record in detail the information which has been taken into account when considering the welfare of the child or children. The record should reflect the views of all those who were consulted in reaching the decision, including those of potential parents.

On its face the *Code of Practice* does not exclude anyone *in limine* from treatment, leaving the decision to turn upon the suitability of the particular applicant(s). Whether this is a satisfactory means of ensuring equality is, at best, debatable. it may be that judicial review, as cases such as *Harriot* (referred to by Gillian Douglas, *supra*), will operate to provide guidance and ensure that patent discrimination of whatever kind does not occur. In particular, the courts are likely to achieve this by requiring (as does the *Code of Practice*) that reasons for refusal of access be given by the responsible clinician.

Harriott was, of course, a case where the applicant's challenge was to the procedural fairness of the decision to refuse her access to fertility treatment. In the following case, the challenge went to the substance of the decision.

R v Sheffield Health Authority, ex parte Seale (1994) 25 BMLR 1 (QBD)

The applicant sought in vitro fertilisation treatment, from the respondent health authority, in order to become pregnant. She was refused on the grounds that, being 37, she was outside the age range within which the authority provided treatment. The upper age limit of 35 had been imposed in order to ration treatment, within a limited budget, to women upon whom it was likely to have the greatest benefit. The applicant asserts that the restriction is illegal, being contrary to s 3 of the National Health Service Act 1977, under which the Secretary of State is under a duty to provide medical services to meet all reasonable requirements. The applicant further asserts that the decision is irrational, not being founded on any sustainable clinical approach, and in failing to take account of individual circumstances.

Auld J: Mr Straker challenges the decision made in this case, based on the criteria set out in the letter of 22 April 1994, under three heads. The first is illegality. As I understand his submission, it is that as the Secretary of State has given no directions or imposed no limitations on the provision of in vitro fertilisation, and it is not for the district health authority, once it has committed itself to providing such a service, to restrict that provision if in the case of any patient there is a chance, a reasonable probability, a possibility – I do not quite know where the line is to be drawn – of the treatment being effective. As I understand Mr Straker's argument, it is that if any such qualification beyond efficacy is to be introduced, that is for the Secretary of State, and she has not done it here.

In my view, it is not possible to erect out of the absence of a direction by the Secretary of State, or of the imposition by her of a limitation on the provision of such a service, a denial to the regional or district health authority of itself determining the circumstances in which such a service can be provided. It is not arguable, in my view, that it is bound, simply because it has undertaken to provide such a service, to provide it on demand to any individual patient for whom it may work, regardless of financial and other constraints upon the authority. Accordingly, I reject as unarguable any submission based on illegality here. In my view it is clear that if the Secretary of State has not limited or given directions as to the way in which such a service, once undertaken, should be provided; the authority providing it is entitled to form a view as to those circumstances and when they justify provision and when they do not.

The second argument of Mr Straker is that the decision here is irrational, that is, absurd. That is what he has to show as arguable to succeed on this application for leave. He says it is irrational because it is not founded on any sustainable, clinical approach. The basis of that argument appears to be that there is more than one view of the appropriate 'cut-off' age for such treatment. In short, he submits, and refers me to the views of other doctors, that 35 years old is too low an age. It is possible to achieve success certainly up to the age of 42. I cannot, nor could the court when deciding the matter as a substantive issue, if it came to that, form a view as to the rightness or wrongness of competing medical views on the effective cut-off date for the utility of such treatment. The decision letter does not say that the treatment cannot be effective after the age of 35, but merely that it is 'generally less effective in women aged over 35 years'.

If that is so, can Mr Staker challenge the decision as irrational on the basis that it is absurd to apply the age of 35 years as a blanket cut-off point, taking no account of individual circumstances? His submission is that every case should be considered individually. Clinically speaking, there is no doubt good sense in such a submission. And a clinical decision on a case by case basis is clearly desirable and, in cases of critical illness, a necessary approach. However, it is reasonable, or it is at least not *Wednesbury* unreasonable (see *Associated Provincial Picture Houses Ltd v Wednesbury Corp* [1947] 2 All ER 680), of an authority to look at the matter in the context of the financial resources available to it to provide this and the many other services for which it is responsible under the National Health Service legislation. I cannot say that it is absurd for this authority, acting on advice that the efficacy of this treatment decreases with age and that it is generally less effective after the age of 35, to take that as an appropriate criterion when balancing the need for such a provision against its ability to provide it and all the other services imposed upon it under the legislation.

The third matter upon which Mr Straker relied as part of his argument based on irrationality was a reference to a particular condition from which this applicant suffers for which pregnancy is said to be a cure. However, that matter does not appear to have loomed large, or at all, in the circumstances giving rise to the decision of 22 April. Nor does it appear to have been particularly prominent as a reason for special treatment in this case in the correspondence that followed that decision.

Under the heading of 'Irrationality' Mr Straker relies upon the fact that privately paying patients can secure such treatment until the age of 42. It seems to me that that argument does not meet the central problem here of an authority coping with a finite budget and a myriad of services which it is bound to provide under it. I am, therefore, of the view that there is no arguable case that this decision was irrational, applying the high test that that word imports under the *Wednesbury* decision.

Lastly, Mr Straker submits that there was a procedural impropriety here. I confess I find it difficult to see any procedural hook on which Mr Straker could base his application. It seems to me, to whatever extent there was a procedural element upon which he relied, it falls to be considered under the heading of 'Irrationality'. I certainly can see no procedural basis upon which he can challenge this decision.

Accordingly, despite the very well organised and highly persuasive arguments of Mr Straker, I feel bound to refuse this application.

In *Seale*, the applicant could not even persuade the judge that she had an arguable case that would justify granting leave to bring an application for judicial review. First, it was argued that it was illegal to have a policy which limited access to IVF – which might be successful – in the absence of a direction from the Secretary of State. This is a patently untenable argument which would have profound implications within the health service since it would require limitless resourcing. Auld J would, as we saw, have none of it.

Of course, as a statement of general principle Auld J's view is correct. However, it does not mean that an authority will always act lawfully by limiting provision of its services. It must do so rationally and this was the second line of attack made by the applicant. She argued that the age of 35 was irrational. It was too low an age to set as a cut-off point. Looking as it *de novo*, one could conclude that there was some substance in this argument. Many woman now conceive their first child in their mid to late thirties. It is well recognised that fertility decreases with age, but 35 is really no age at all. But this is to do precisely what the court in a judicial review case cannot do. The court may only look to see if the decision is rational and not whether it is right. Lord Diplock in *Council of Civil Service v Minister for the Civil Service* [1985] AC 374 at 410 explained 'irrationality' as follows:

> It applies to a decision which is so outrageous in its defiance of logic or of accepted moral standards that no sensible person who had applied his mind to the question to be decided could have arrived at it.

In *Seale*, the cut-off age in the authority's policy was based on the view that IVF treatment was 'generally less effective in women aged over 35 years'. In itself, this would not rebuff an argument that 35 was an irrational age, since it would remain an arbitrary cut-off point. Why not 34 or 36 years of age? Age has a progressive effect on fertility – though less markedly so if donated eggs are used. Indeed, it is not until later in the average woman's life (perhaps in her early 40s) that a sharp drop in fertility can be identified at any particular age. A recent survey of the records of IVF treatments carried out in Britain between 1991 and 1994 identified success rates for women aged 25 of 16%; aged 30 of 17% and aged 35 of 14%. However by the age of 40 the success rate has dropped to 7% and by 45 it is 2% (see A Templeton, J K Morris and W Parslow 'Factors that Affect Outcome in *In-Vitro* Fertilisation Treatment' (1996) 348 The Lancet 1402). It might be, therefore, that a policy of limiting IVF to those under 35 would be irrational if *likely success* was the *sole* criterion for the policy. In *Seale*, of course it was not because the authority was seeking to allocate its resources most effectively. Hence, Auld J concluded that it was not 'absurd' for the authority 'to take [35] as an appropriate criterion when balancing the need for such provision against its ability to provide it and all the other services imposed upon it under the legislation'.

The best argument for the applicant seems to have been that she should have been considered an exceptional case outside the policy. It is a well-known principle of administrative law that while a public body may lawfully adopt a policy, it must not fetter its discretion by blindly applying that policy (*British Oxygen Co Ltd v Ministry of Technology* [1971] AC 610 (HL)). In short, the body must retain a willingness to consider each case on its merits, particularly if the individual claims to be an exceptional case (*ibid*, at 625 per Lord Reid). It is not entirely clear from the judgment of Auld J, but it does seem that this was part of Mrs Seale's complaint. It seems she suffered from a medical condition for which pregnancy is a cure. On the face of it, Auld J chose to dismiss this aspect of her case as being one which did not seem to have featured in the authority's decision against her. But surely this is her best point? The authority should have considered this. A policy to exclude from IVF treatment all those over 35 – even if lawful – must be applied flexibly. If the authority did not consider whether she was an exceptional case, in effect, on medical grounds, it unlawfully fettered its discretion and the correct remedy would be to quash the decision and require the authority to consider her claim again. At least, there seems to have been an arguable case justifying the grant of leave under RSC Ord 53 (see *supra*, ch 1 discussing judicial review).

Finally, it is important to notice what *Seale* was not about. It was not a case where the court was concerned to consider denial of access to IVF treatment other than on the basis of financial constraints. The decision has no implications for claims by single women, gay or lesbian couples or others who are excluded from IVF (or other techniques for assisting reproduction).

What, if any, impact will the Human Rights Act 1998 have? Articles 8, 12 and 14 of the European Convention on Human Rights may be relevant.

ARTICLE 8. RIGHT TO RESPECT FOR PRIVATE AND FAMILY LIFE

1. Everyone has the right to respect for his private and family life, his home and his correspondence.

2. There shall be no interference by a public authority with the exercise of this right except such as is in accordance with the law and is necessary in a democratic society in the interests of national security, public safety or the economic well-being of the country, for the prevention of disorder or crime, for the protection of health or morals, or for the protection of the rights and freedoms of others.

ARTICLE 12: RIGHT TO MARRY

Men and women of marriageable age have the right to marry and to found a family, according to the national laws governing the exercise of this right.

ARTICLE 14: PROHIBITION ON DISCRIMINATION

The enjoyment of the rights and freedoms set forth in this Convention shall be secured without discrimination on any ground such as sex, race, colour, language, religion, political or other opinion, national or social origin, association with a national minority, property, birth or other status.

As a preliminary point, we must notice that the Convention may not apply. Clearly, it will if the decision to exclude a particular individual from treatment is part of a Health Authority's commissioning policy as in *Seale* as it will be a decision of a public authority (s 6). Equally, it may well apply to any decision taken within the NHS as the doctor will be seen as 'part of' or the 'alter ego' of the public authority be it an NHS Trust or Health Authority (see *supra*, ch 1). Outside the NHS, however, if the treatment is sought privately the argument is more difficult and depends upon the 'indirect horizontal effect', if any, of the Human Rights Act 1998 (see *supra*, ch 1).

Putting this 'applicability' point to one side, would art 8, 12 or 14 be infringed if an individual was denied access to infertility treatment on the basis of their sexual orientation or age?

First, consider the 'right to marry and to found a family' in art 12. The right to have a family (ie at least one child) is applicable only to married couples. It might assist when the exclusion from treatment is aged based but would not be applicable to other relationships (see eg *Rees v UK* (1986) 9 EHRR 56 (ECtHR)). Secondly, art 14 is not a general 'equal treatment' or 'equality' provision but rather only requires that other Convention rights be applied equally without discrimination. Usually, it will be the substantive right that will lead to a successful challenge under the Convention rather than through reliance on art 14 (for a case holding that a restriction of IVF treatment to married couples discriminated unlawfully against a single woman on the grounds of marital status, see *Pearce v South Australian Health Commission* (1996) 66 SASR 486 (SA Sup Ct (FC))). Thirdly, it is, therefore, to art 8 that we should turn our attention.

It has long been argued in other jurisdictions that a 'right to procreate' is part of more general 'liberty' or 'privacy' rights (see eg J Robertson *Children of Choice: Freedom and the New Reproductive Technologies* (1994) pp 22–42 and discussion of 'cloning' *supra*). While the matter has not been addressed by the European Court of Human Rights or, of course, an English court, nevertheless it is clearly arguable that conceiving, bearing and rearing a child is an aspect of an individual's 'private and family life' (see B Hale *From the Test Tube to the Coffin* (1996) p 8). Attention must focus, therefore, on whether the infringement would be justified under art 8(2). What would be the 'legitimate interest'? Reliance would probably be placed on the phrase 'protection of the rights and freedoms of others'. A decision to exclude from access on the basis of the 'welfare of the child' (relying on s 13(5) of the 1990 Act) could fall within the latter phrase if 'others' were construed to include future 'others'. However, a blanket ban would be difficult to sustain as a 'proportional' response to this legitimate aim under art 8(2). Individual consideration would be essential in order to decide whether *in the particular case* denial of access to treatment was justified. Further, exclusion on the basis of a preconceived view about the life-style of unmarried couples or individuals or because of their sexual orientation might be defended under the head of 'protection of morals' in art 8(2). This if, of course, the most objectionable basis for denying access. It seems to be out of step with the HFEA's *Code of Practice* and would be, it is suggested, be undefendable under art 8(2) if it were to be relied upon. However, returning to the likely basis for denial of access, namely 'protection of others' (ie the welfare of the child), the evidence of psychological harm of being brought up in a single parent family or by a homosexual couple is examined and its relevance tested in the following extract.

Jonathan Glover *The Glover Report on Reproductive Technologies to the European Commission: Fertility and the Family* (1989)

Some people think that reproductive technology should only be available in the 'standard' case of the infertile couple. Others disagree. A doctor who wants to stick to helping the infertile couple should of course be free to follow his or her conscience. But what should we say about a doctor or clinic deciding to give help in the non-standard cases? Are they doing good by helping satisfy the need for children in women who would previously have been denied them? Or are they doing something to which there are ethical objections?

The non-standard cases are not all the same, and it may be consistent to take one view of the widow and a different one of the lesbian couple. We will here briefly take the case of the lesbian couple as an example. This is an interesting case for its possible impact on how the family is to evolve.

Semen donors may not want their biological children to grow up with two lesbian parents. But this is not a central issue, as no doubt some donors could be found. (Apart from sympathetic heterosexuals, some male homosexuals might see donation as a contribution to defeating prejudice.) The interesting ethical issues start when this problem is overcome.

What is the case *against* helping? In these non-standard cases we would not be overcoming a medical problem, but would be circumventing biological limits to parenthood. The normal state for a child is to have one parent of each sex. It is surely right to be very cautious about tampering with something so fundamental, involving the possible risk of psychological damage. For instance, there is the question of how the child will think of sexuality and procreation. And growing up in a lesbian family might frustrate a boy's need for a male role model, or a girl's need to develop an intuitive understanding of the other sex. (The same points could be made in reverse about children being brought up only by men.) If the lesbian couple becomes a common alternative nucleus for a family, any psychological losses will become accordingly widespread.

What is the case *for* helping? Homosexuals have suffered, and still suffer, from an appalling degree of prejudice and discrimination. This has often made homosexuality a sad condition, and the extension of the idea of the family to include a version with lesbian parents is a large move towards greater equality.

It could be said that there cannot be equality *in procreation* between heterosexuals and homosexuals. Just as the heterosexual woman who does not want children must always take this possibility into account (for instance by using contraception), so must the lesbian who wants children accept that she cannot have them with her female partner.

One reply to this is: just as heterosexuals use contraception, why should not lesbians use reproductive technology? Such a reply is in one way an over-simplification. There is a difference between using contraception to control one's own reproductive capacities and using reproductive technology. The latter helps homosexuals by introducing heterosexuality into the relationship in a depersonalized form, via the semen donor. There are complications about the status of the donor in a lesbian family. It would be possible to admit of lesbians having children through adoption, while wishing to draw the line at tampering with the idea that reproduction requires people of both sexes.

Yet it is surely right to be predisposed in favour of anything that removes some of the barriers against homosexuals having a fulfilled family life. Lesbians who want to have children are not different in their needs from heterosexual women. Like many other women, lesbians may care about what adoption does not provide: having a child genetically theirs and to whom they give birth. They may care as much about having *their* children as an infertile wife, and their lives may be as much enriched by such children as anyone else's.

. . . Some thoughts on policy

Removal of discrimination against homosexuals in such a fundamental matter would be a great gain. But obviously there are strong grounds for unease about reproductive help where the family circumstances may impose a serious handicap on the child. The anxieties are based partly on the child's own interests, and partly on the social impact of the spread of such families. Everything depends on how well founded these anxieties are. People differ over the hypothesis that children born through AID to one of a lesbian couple are likely to be at a disadvantage. Some think that, in the light of what we know of human nature, the hypothesis is very plausible, while others think there is no such presumption in favour of it.

The fullest study we have been able to find is suggestive, but not conclusive (Golombok, Spencer and Rutter: *Journal of Child Psychology and Psychiatry*, 1983).

Thirty-seven children aged between five and seventeen, being brought up in twenty-seven lesbian households, were compared with thirty-eight children in twenty-seven single-parent families, being brought up by a heterosexual mother. Psychosexual and psychiatric appraisals were based on interviews with the children, on interviews with the mothers, and on questionnaires given to the mothers and to teachers. The two groups did not differ in gender identity: all the children said they were glad to be the sex they were. (But gender identity is usually established at an early age, and in some cases *could* have been established before the lesbian partnership was set up.) The two groups did not differ in sex-role behaviour. And there were no signs of differences in sexual orientation between the two groups. (This was based on the reported patterns of friendship in pre-pubertal children, and also on reports of romantic friendships in the small number who were past the age of puberty.)

These negative findings suggest that anxieties about the effects of being brought up in a lesbian family may be unfounded. But they cannot completely exclude the hypothesis of disadvantage.

Because the control group were in single-parent families, conclusions depend on the evidence that children brought up by single parents are not themselves different in these respects. To test the disadvantage hypothesis, it would be more satisfactory to have a direct comparison with children brought up by heterosexual couples. And the great majority of the lesbians in the study had previously had heterosexual relationships. (Of those who had not, one had an adopted child, and the other had one adopted child and one child by AID.) It *may* be misleading to extrapolate from that group to all those seeking reproductive help, if the majority of the latter group have not had heterosexual relationships. Also, as the authors of this study themselves stress, the question of sexual orientation cannot fully be settled without a follow-up study when the children are older.

If children were worse off having two female social parents, this would have to be set against the elimination of discrimination against homosexuals. But the claimed disadvantage, while not finally refuted by the evidence, is certainly not supported by it. And, if there is any disadvantage, it is hardly like to be so bad that it would be better if the children had not been born. So the objection is at most one about 'moderately severe' disadvantage.

We expect that, until the disadvantage hypothesis is overwhelmingly supported or refuted empirically, those who have to decide about helping will divide in their views, as we do. It seems right to doctors and others to follow their consciences, some giving help and some refusing it. (However, in some countries, such as Germany, professional guidelines forbid non-standard use of AID.) The result of those who believe in giving help doing so can be expected to be some growth in the numbers of such families.

This is likely to go further as feminist or lesbian groups start themselves to provide the help denied by more traditional clinics. In the United States, feminist health centres have started to do this; in 1982, the Oakland Feminist Women's Health Center set up the first feminist sperm bank (Francie Hornstein: 'Children by Donor Insemination: A New Choice For Lesbians', in Rita Arditti *et al: Test-Tube Women*, London, 1984). It is likely that self-help arrangements, supplemented by women's clinics where necessary, will spread in Europe.

The other possible basis for opposing reproductive help to lesbians is its impact on society. There are two parts to this case. One is linked to the hypothesis that the children are disadvantaged, and is based on the view that larger numbers of disadvantaged people may affect society for the worse. The other part of the case is the need to protect the institution of the family.

We take the view that the restriction of liberty involved in any legal ban on reproductive help to lesbian couples could only be justified by grounds for believing that harm would be done by that help. Because the view that the children would be worse off than others is itself speculative, losses to others as a result of their disadvantages are even more speculative.

It could be argued that future people would suffer psychological losses through the dilution of the traditional concept of the family. But, because this is again such a speculative claim, we think this case is insufficient to justify a legal ban. And we are sceptical about using the law in an attempt to freeze our changing family structure. One of the costs of widespread adultery is its weakening of that structure, but to criminalize it would seem a heavy-handed response. And that seems equally true of the more speculative weakening resulting from helping lesbians to be mothers.

While the members of this committee are divided about the desirability of providing help, we are agreed that it should not be legally prevented. Those of us who are inclined to think it wrong to help do not wish to criminalize the behaviour of those who take a different view. The case that the children are disadvantaged is too weak to support that.

Rather little is known with certainty of the effects of lesbian parenthood. On the one hand, this is an argument for caution. But, on the other hand, it can be an argument for letting the future shape of the family evolve experimentally. No doubt people should be discouraged from taking high risks of major family disasters. And it goes without saying that new forms of family life must only be tried voluntarily. But, subject to these qualifications, we prefer a society predisposed in favour of 'experiments in living' to one in which they are stifled.

We may find that *not* all happy families are alike.

There is evidence that many clinics will not treat a single woman or a lesbian or gap couple (see D Savas and S Treece 'Fertility Clinics: One Code of Practice?' (1998) 3 Medical Law International 243 at 250). Their position may not survive a challenge under art 8 unless in the particular case the evidence of harm is clear.

A final comment on the Human Rights Act 1998. In *R v North West Lancashire HA ex p A, D and G* [1999] Lloyd's Rep Med 399 (CA) (see *supra* ch 1), Auld LJ made two remarks about Article 8 and the Human Rights Act 1998. First, he observed that in the context of the provision of treatment, art 8 may not take the common law any further. He may well be right in this. Secondly, he asserted that art 8 imposed no positive obligation to provide treatment. This is not strictly true, in that the European Court has countenanced negative *and* positive obligations under art 8, albeit that the court will be more circumspect in imposing the latter (see eg *Stjerna v Finland* (1995) 24 EHRR 195). In any event, as in *ex p A* itself, once the treatment is provided to some, it must be provided to all consistently with arts 8 and 14. There must be a legitimate basis for not doing so and the infringement must be proportional to that aim. As Dame Brenda Hale has put it in her Hamlyn Lectures, *From the Test Tube to the Coffin* (1996) at 8–9:

> The State cannot have a duty to supply a service on demand. Would-be parents may, however, be entitled to expect fair treatment from those who allocate what the State does supply or who regulate what others will supply either voluntarily or for reward.

C. CONSCIENTIOUS OBJECTION

Like the Abortion Act 1967, the 1990 Act contains a 'conscientious objection' provision designed to permit individuals to opt out of participating in any of the activities covered by the Act, Section 38 provides as follows:

> **38.** (1) No person who has a conscientious objection to participating in any activity governed by this Act shall be under a duty, however arising, to do so.
>
> (2) In any legal proceedings the burden of conscientious objection shall rest on the person claiming to rely on it.

This provision is closely modelled upon that which appears in s 4 of the Abortion Act 1967 (discussed *infra*, ch 11). Unlike s 4 of the Abortion Act 1967, however, s 38 does not contain an exception to the right to object where action is necessary to save the patient's life or to prevent grave permanent injury (see Abortion Act 1967, s 4(2)). This omission from the 1990 Act probably reflects the fact that such a situation is very unlikely to arise in the context of infertility treatment (*a fortiori* research on embryos) and hence is unnecessary.

Under s 38 the objection must, of course, be a matter of conscience and the burden is on the individual to establish it (s 38(2)). But a matter of conscience is widely understood to cover, for example, religious, moral or other principled beliefs which lead the individual to conclude that the activity is wrong. Section 38 allows a doctor, nurse or other individual to refuse to 'participate' in a licensed activity to which they have such a conscientious objection.

There may be difficulties in some cases of determining when an individual is being asked to 'participate' (see, *Janaway v Salford HA* [1989] AC 537, discussed *infra*, ch 11). However, there is no doubt that a doctor or nurse who objected to IVF treatment because it involved the creation of an embryo outside the body could not be required to 'participate' in infertility treatment using IVF. Similarly, a research scientist or laboratory technician could not be required to work in a research project involving human embryos if he objected to this.

The right of 'conscientious objection' applies to *any* activity governed by the 1990 Act. It follows that an individual may object to some but not all the activities, for example, to IVF treatment but not artificial insemination. A difficult question is whether the individual must object to participating in a whole class of activity, as in the examples so far, or whether he may also object (a) to participating in particular instances or (b) parts of a licensed activity. Two examples will illustrate the point.

Could, for example, a doctor refuse to treat a lesbian woman by artificial insemination because he 'objected' to her life-style and sexual orientation even though he has no objection to artificial insemination in principle? In our view, he could not (contrast, G Douglas, *supra*). There are two reasons. First, it could be argued that the doctor's objection is not conscientious as usually understood since it appears to be the product of prejudice rather than principle. Secondly, and more importantly, his objection is not to participating in *an activity* governed by the 1990 Act but rather to treating *this patient*.

By way of further example, could an individual object to participating in part of a licensed activity? Would an individual's objection to being involved in embryo biopsy (to detect a genetic defect) or to allowing a surplus embryo to perish after successful IVF treatment, fall within s 38 even if that individual had no objection to IVF in principle? The answer is not clear from the statute. But, again it could be argued that s 38 only permits an individual to have a conscientious objection to a class of activity licensed under the Act, ie IVF treatment, artificial insemination, storage or research and so on. Beyond this, the Act does not allow the individual to pick and choose which parts of licensed activities that he is prepared to be involved in (contrast, Mrs Virginia Bottomley, *Hansard* (Standing Committee B) 15 May 1990, col 203).

D. CONSENT TO USE AND CONTROL OF GENETIC MATERIAL

As we saw in Chapter 5, consent is a (if not *the*) central legal issue in determining the legality of medical treatment. It is no less so in the case of medically assisted reproduction. Here, however, the 1990 Act has given further prominence to the consent of those involved in the medical procedures. Consent is relevant in two distinct ways. *First*, there is the need for those who are donating genetic material and those being treated for infertility to consent to the medical procedure. As we shall see, the need for, and content of the consents is a matter of common law supplemented by the statute (and *Code of Practice*). *Secondly*, consent is relevant (as a result of the statute) to the future use or storage of an individual's genetic material. Schedule 3 to the 1990 Act requires that a donor of genetic material should give written consent to its future use. Similarly, the Act requires that those who wish their genetic material to be stored should consent to that storage. We shall return to consider the relevant provisions relating to use and storage shortly. For the present, however, it can be seen that the consent of the provider of the genetic material will often determine the fate of that material subject to certain limitations imposed by the statute.

When the 1990 Act came into force on 1 August 1991, there already existed in storage quantities of sperm and embryos, since infertility treatment had been part of medical practice for some years. This caused a number of problems because to continue to store or to use the genetic material required compliance with the detailed consent and information provisions of the Act. Many (if not most) of the donors were untraceable and, therefore, their consents to storage or future use under the Act could not be obtained. In order to obviate the need to destroy the sperm or embryos, the Human Fertilisation and Embryology Act 1990 (Commencement No 3 and Transitional Provisions) Order 1991 (SI 1991 No 1400) permitted their storage (without consent) until such time as consent might be obtained for use in the future. Of course, contacting some donors has proved impossible and hence the stored material may not be used. Once the statutory maximum storage period has expired it will have to be destroyed.

1. Consent to the procedure

A donor of genetic material (for example, of eggs) or a patient undergoing infertility treatment must consent to the medical interventions involved. This is no more than to state the position at common law. In the *Code of Practice* (4th edn, 1998) Annex D, HFEA sets out two standard consent forms for use by patients receiving infertility treatment. Only one point of particular interest is worth noting. The forms, which are examples only, contain a section for the husband or male partner of the patient to complete whereby he agrees to the treatment. The purpose of this is not, as the form itself makes clear, because the partner's consent is necessary 'to make the treatment lawful'. Rather, it is designed to avoid any evidential difficulty that might arise when establishing the parentage of any child born after treatment (see *infra*, discussion of ss 27 and 28 of the 1990 Act).

The 1990 Act acknowledges the common law position and provides in s 13(6) in the case of those receiving treatment services as follows:

13. (6) A woman shall not be provided with any treatment services involving –
  (a) the use of any gametes of any person, if that person's consent is required under paragraph 5 of Schedule 3 to this Act for use in question.
  (b) the use of any embryo the creation of which was brought about *in vitro*, or
  (c) the use of any embryo taken from a woman, if the consent of the woman from whom it was taken is required under paragraph 7 of that Schedule for the use in question,

unless the woman being treated and, where she is being treated together with a man, the man have been given a suitable opportunity to receive proper counselling about the implications of taking the proposed steps, and have been provided with such relevant information as is proper.

There are two requirements before consent can be given, therefore: an *opportunity for counselling* and the *provision of relevant information*. Similarly, donors and those storing genetic material must also be given the opportunity of counselling and be provided with relevant information prior to donation or storage (see Sch 3, para 3). It is important to notice that the obligations are different as regards counselling and information: namely *a duty to give the opportunity* of counselling but *a duty to provide* information.

HFEA's *Code of Practice* (4th edn, 1998) seeks to provide guidance as to the meaning of the statutory provisions. As regards counselling, the *Code of Practice* provides as follows:

General

6.1 People seeking licensed treatment (ie, *in vitro* fertilisation or treatment using donated gametes) or consenting to the use or storage of embryos, or to the donation or storage of gametes, **must** be given 'a suitable opportunity to receive proper counselling about the implications of taking the proposed steps', before they consent.

6.2 Counselling should be clearly distinguished from:

    a.   the information which is to be given to everyone, in accordance with the guidance in Part 4 [see below];

    b.   the normal relationship between the clinician and the person offering donation or seeking storage or treatment, which includes giving professional advice; and

    c.   the process of assessing people in order to decide whether to accept them as a client or donor, or to accept their gametes and embryos for storage, in accordance with the guidance given in Part 3.

6.3 No-one is obliged to accept counselling. However, it is generally recognised as beneficial.

6.4 Three distinct types of counselling should be made available in appropriate cases:

    a.   *implications counselling:* this aims to enable the person concerned to understand the implications of the proposed course of action for themselves, for their family, and for any children born as a result. It may include genetic counselling;

    b.   *support counselling*: this aims to give emotional support at times of particular stress, eg when there is a failure to achieve a pregnancy.

    c.   *therapeutic counselling*: this aims to help people to cope with the consequences of infertility and treatment, and to help them to resolve the problems which these may cause. It includes helping people to adjust their expectations and to accept their situation.

Centres **must** make implications counselling available to everyone. They should also provide support or therapeutic counselling in appropriate cases or refer people to sources of more specialist counselling outside the centre.

6.5 Centres should present the offer of counselling as part of normal routine, without implying either that the person concerned is in any way deficient or abnormal, or that there is any pressure to accept. Centres should allow them sufficient time to consider the offer.

6.6 Centres should allow sufficient time for counselling to be conducted sensitively, in an atmosphere which is conducive to discussion. The length and content of counselling, and the pace at which it is conducted, should be determined by the needs of the individual concerned.

6.7 Centres should offer people the opportunity to be counselled by someone other than the clinician responsible for their treatment, donation or storage. Such counselling should be independent of the clinical decision-making process.

6.8 Centres should offer people the opportunity to be counselled individually and with their partner if they have one. Group counselling sessions may also be offered, but it is not acceptable for a centre to offer only group sessions.

6.9 People should be able to seek counselling at any stage of their investigation or treatment. However, counselling should normally be made available after the person seeking treatment or providing the gametes or embryos has received the oral and written explanations described in paragraph 4.4 and 4.5 [see below]. Discussion may then focus on the meaning and consequences of the decision, rather than on its practical aspects.

Implications Counselling

6.10 Counsellors should invite potential clients or providers of gametes and embryos to consider the following issues:

a. the social responsibilities which centres and providers of genetic material bear to ensure the best possible outcome for all concerned, including the child;

b. the implications of the procedure for themselves, their family and social circle, and for any resulting children;

c. their feelings about the use and possible disposal of any embryos derived from their gametes;

d. the possibility that these implications and feelings may change over time, as personal circumstances change;

e. the advantages and disadvantages of openness about the procedures envisaged, and how they might be explained to relatives and friends.

6.11 Counsellors should invite *clients* to consider in particular:

a. the client's attitude to his or her own, or partner's infertility;

b. the possibility that treatment will fail.

6.12 Where treatment using donated gametes or embryos is contemplated, clients should also be invited to consider:

a. their feelings about not being the genetic parents of the child;

b. their perceptions of the needs of the child throughout his or her childhood and adolescence.

6.13 If a woman is already undergoing infertility treatment when the question of treatment with donated gametes or embryos derived from them arises, counselling about the implications of receiving donated material should be offered separately from counselling about the other implications of treatment. Treatment with donated material should not proceed unless the woman and, where appropriate, her partner have been given a suitable opportunity to receive counselling about it.

6.14 If a woman is undergoing infertility treatment and the possibility of her or her partner becoming a donor also arises, counselling about the implications of donation should be undertaken separately from counselling about the implications of treatment in the first instance. If the possibility of donation arises at a later stage in the treatment, donation should not proceed unless the woman and, where appropriate, her partner have been given a suitable opportunity to receive counselling about it.

6.15 Counselling about the implications of donation may be combined with counselling about the other implications of treatment at a later stage, if this is advisable in the light of the initial counselling sessions and the client's or potential donor's wishes.

6.16 Counsellors should invite potential *donors* of gametes and embryos to consider in particular:

a. their reasons for wanting to become a donor.

b. their attitudes to any resulting children, and their willingness to forego knowledge of and responsibility for such children in the future;

c. the possibility of their own childlessness;

d. their perception of the needs of any children born as a result of their donation;

e. their attitudes to the prospective legal parents of their genetic offspring;

f. their attitudes to allowing embryos which have been produced from their gametes to be used for research.

6.17 If person seeking to donate or store genetic material is married or has a long-term partner, the centre should counsel them together if they so wish. If a partner wishes to be counselled separately about the implications of donation or storage, centres should take all practicable steps to offer counselling at the centre, or to assist him or her in contacting an external counselling organisation.

Genetic Counselling

6.18 Centres should have arrangements in place to make genetic counselling available for patients and donors. Centres should ensure that when patients and donors are referred for genetic counselling the confidentiality provisions of the HFE Act are taken into account.

Later Counselling

6.19 Centres should take all practicable steps to provide further opportunities for counselling about the implications of treatment, donation or storage after consent has been given, and throughout the period in which the person is providing gametes, or receiving treatment, if this is requested. If someone who has previously been a donor or client returns to the centre asking for further counselling, the centre should take all practicable steps to help them obtain it.

Support Counselling

6.20 Centres should also take all practicable steps to offer support to people who are not suitable for treatment, whose treatment has failed, prospective donors who are found to be unsuitable and people who have previously unsuspected defects, to help them come to terms with their situation.

6.21 These steps should include, wherever practicable, reasonable assistance in contacting or establishing a support group.

6.22 Centres should ensure that, as part of their training, all staff are prepared to offer appropriate emotional support at all stages of their investigation, counselling and treatment to clients who are suffering distress.

Therapeutic Counselling
6.23 Procedures should be in place to identify people who suffer particular distress and to offer them, as far as is practicable, therapeutic counselling, with the aim of helping them to come to terms with their situation.
6.24 If a client experiences mental ill-health or a severe psychological problem which may or may not be related to infertility, for which it would be more appropriate to seek help and advice outside the centre, the centre should take all practicable steps to help him or her to obtain it.

Records
6.25 A record should be kept of all counselling offered and whether or not the offer is accepted.
6.26 All information obtained in the course of counselling should be kept confidential, subject to paragraph 3.29, above.

As regards the duty to give information, the *Code of Practice* provides as follows:

General Obligation
4.1 Before anyone is given licensed treatment (ie, *in vitro* fertilisation or treatment using donated gametes) or consents to the use or storage of embryos, or to the donation or storage of gametes, they **must** be given 'such relevant information as is proper'. This should be distinguished from the requirement to offer counselling, which clients and donors need not accept.
4.2 Clients and donors should be given oral explanations supported by relevant written material. They should be encouraged to ask for further information and their questions should be answered in a straightforward, comprehensive and open way.
4.3 Centres should devise a system to ensure that:
    a.   the right information is given;
    b.   the person who is to give the information is clearly identified, and has been given sufficient training and guidance to enable them to do so; and
    c.   a record is kept of the information given.

Information to be Given to Clients
4.4 Information should be given to people seeking treatment on the following points:
    a.   the limitations and possible outcomes of the treatment proposed, and variations of effectiveness over time. This should include the centre's own live birth rate per treatment cycle and the national live birth rate per treatment cycle;
    b.   the possible side effects and risks of the treatment to the woman and any resulting child. This should include:
        (i)   the possible side effects of ovarian stimulation (where relevant) for the women, including the risks associated with ovarian hyperstimulation syndrome (OHSS)
        (ii)   the risks to the women and fetus associated with multiple pregnancy and the possible practical, financial and emotional impact of a multiple birth on the family unit;
    c.   the genetic and other screening that donors at the centre undergo. This should include the sensitivity of the tests that are carried out and the likelihood that a screened donor will be a carrier;
    d.   the availability of genetic testing, especially if the donors that are used at the centre are not screened for cystic fibrosis;
    e.   the possible disruption of the client's domestic life which treatment will cause, and the length of time he or she will have to wait for treatment;
    f.   the techniques involved, including (where relevant) the possible deterioration of gametes or embryos associated with storage, and the possible pain and discomfort;
    g.   the availability of embryo freezing facilities, including the likelihood of success of embryo freezing, thawing, transfer and implications of storage;
    h.   any other infertility treatments which are available, including those for which a licence is not necessary;
    i.   that counselling is available;
    j.   the cost to the client of the treatment proposed and of any alternative treatments;
    k.   the importance of telling the treatment centre about any resulting birth;
    l.   who will be the child's parent or parents under the Act. Clients who are nationals or residents of other countries, or who have been treated with gametes obtained from a foreign donor should understand that the law in other countries may be different from that of the United Kingdom ...;
    m.   the child's right to seek information about his or her origins on reaching 18 or on contemplating earlier marriage;

n.   the information which centres must collect and register with the HFEA and the extent to which that information may be disclosed to people born as a result of the donation;

o.   a child's potential need to know about their origins;

p.   the centre's statutory duty to take account of the welfare of any resulting or affected child; and

q.   (where relevant) the advantages and disadvantages of continued treatment after a certain number of attempts.

Information to be Given to People Providing Gametes and Embryos

4.5 Information should be given to people consenting to the use or storage of embryos, or to the donation or storage of gametes, on the following points:

a.   the procedures involved in collecting gametes, the degree of pain and discomfort and any risks to that person, eg, from the use of superovulatory drugs;

b.   the screening which will be carried out, and the practical implications of having an HIV antibody test, even if it proves negative;

c.   the genetic testing that will be carried out, its scope and limitations and the implications of the result for the donor and their family;

d.   the purposes for which their gametes might be used;

e.   whether or not they will be regarded under the Act as the parents of any child born as a result;

f.   that the Act generally permits donors to preserve their anonymity;

g.   the information which centres must collect and register with HFEA and the extent to which that information may be disclosed to people born as a result of the donation;

h.   that they are free to withdraw or vary the terms of their consent at any time, unless the gametes or embryos have already been used;

i.   the possibility that a child born disabled as a result of a donor's failure to disclose defects, about which they knew or ought reasonably to have known, may be able to sue the donor for damages;

j.   in the case of egg donation, that the woman will not incur any financial or other penalty if she withdraws her consent after preparation for egg recovery has begun;

k.   that donated gametes and embryos created from them will not normally be used for treatment once the number of children believed to have been born from them has reached 10, or any lower figure specified by the donor; and

l.   that counselling is available.

It is undoubtedly the case that the level of detail required to be disclosed under the *Code of Practice* goes beyond that which the common law would otherwise require (see *supra*, ch 5). What would the consequence be if a doctor failed to comply with the Code? You will have noticed that s 25(6) begins, 'A failure on the part of any person to observe any provision of the code shall not of itself render the person liable to any proceedings …' A literal meaning may suggest that the Code is not intended to set any standard for the purposes of civil liability in negligence (though it may be relevant in proceedings concerning revocation of a licence). On the other hand, a good argument could be made that the Code establishes what a reasonable doctor should do, ie the *Bolam* test, such that failure to comply with the Code would constitute a breach of duty. The prominence the Code has in this area of treatment suggests that the latter view will prevail.

2.   Control of gametes and embryos

We are concerned with the issue of the extent to which the providers of gametes and embryos may exercise legal control over their genetic material. For example, who may decide the fate of spare embryos stored after infertility treatment is completed or abandoned? Do the gamete-providers have any proprietary claims over their genetic material?

The 1990 Act seeks, in essence, to vest control of gametes and embryos in the providers of the genetic material. It does so through an elaborate scheme of consents. Schedule 3 to the Act requires that a gamete-provider must, at the time that the gametes are procured, indicate in a written consent what use(s) those gametes may be put to. The gametes (or any resulting embryos) may only be used in accordance with the consents or, as we shall see, in accordance with those consents as subsequently varied under the Human Fertilisation and Embryology Act 1990 (s 12(c) and Sch 3). Schedule 3 provides as follows:

CONSENTS TO USE OF GAMETES OR EMBRYOS

Consent
1. A consent under this Schedule must be given in writing and, in this Schedule, 'effective consent' means a consent under this Schedule which has not been withdrawn.
2. – (1) A consent to the use of any embryo must specify one or more of the following purposes –
(a) use in providing treatment services to the person giving consent, or that person and another specified person together,
(b) use in providing treatment services to persons not including the person giving consent, or
(c) use for the purposes of any project of research,
and may specify conditions subject to which the embryo may be so used.
    (2) A consent to the storage of any gametes or any embryos must –
(a) specify the maximum period of storage (if less than the statutory storage period), and
(b) state what is to be done with the gametes or embryo if the person who gave the consent dies or is unable because of incapacity to vary the terms of the consent or to revoke it,
and may specify conditions subject to which the gametes or embryo may remain in storage.
    (3) A consent under this Schedule must provide for such other matters as the Authority may specify in directions.
    (4) A consent under this Schedule may apply –
(a) to the use or storage of a particular embryo, or
(b) in the case of a person providing gametes, to the use or storage of any embryo whose creation may be brought about using those gametes,
and in the paragraph (b) case the terms of the consent may be varied, or the consent may be withdrawn, in accordance with this Schedule either generally or in relation to a particular embryo or particular embryos.

Procedure for giving consent
3. – (1) Before a person gives consent under this Schedule –
(a) he must be given a suitable opportunity to receive proper counselling about the implications of taking the proposed steps, and
(b) he must be provided with such relevant information as is proper.
    (2) Before a person gives consent under this Schedule he must be informed of the effect of paragraph 4 below.

Variation and withdrawal of consent
4. – (1) The terms of any consent under this Schedule may from time to time be varied, and the consent may be withdrawn, by notice given by the person who gave the consent to the person keeping the gametes or embryo to which the consent is relevant.
    (2) The terms of any consent to the use of any embryo cannot be varied, and such consent cannot be withdrawn, once the embryo has been used –
(a) in providing treatment services, or
(b) for the purposes of any project of research.

Use of gametes for treatment of others
5. – (1) A person's gametes must not be used for the purposes of treatment services unless there is an effective consent by that person to their being so used and they are used in accordance with the terms of the consent.
    (2) A person's gametes must not be received for use for those purposes unless there is an effective consent by that person to their being so used.
    (3) This paragraph does not apply to the use of a person's gametes for the purpose of that person, or that person and another together, receiving treatment services.

In vitro fertilisation and subsequent use of embryo
6. – (1) A person's gametes must not be used to bring about the creation of any embryo *in vitro* unless there is an effective consent by that person to any embryo the creation of which may be brought about with the use of those gametes being used for one or more of the purposes mentioned in paragraph 2(1) above.
    (2) An embryo the creation of which was brought about *in vitro* must not be received by any person unless there is an effective consent by each person whose gametes were used to

bring about the creation of the embryo to the use for one or more of the purposes mentioned in paragraph 2(1) above of the embryo.

(3) An embryo the creation of which was brought about *in vitro* must not be used for any purpose unless there is an effective consent by each person whose gametes were used to bring about the creation of the embryo to the use for that purpose of the embryo and the embryo is used in accordance with those consents.

(4) Any consent required by this paragraph is in addition to any consent that may be required by paragraph 5 above.

Embryos obtained by lavage, etc.
7. – (1) An embryo taken from a woman must not be used for any purpose unless there is an effective consent by her to the use of the embryo for that purpose and it is used in accordance with the consent.

(2) An embryo taken from a woman must not be received by any person for use for any purpose unless there is an effective consent by her to the use of the embryo for that purpose.

(3) This paragraph does not apply to the use, for the purpose of providing a woman with treatment services, of an embryo taken from her.

Storage of gametes and embryos
8. – (1) A person's gametes must not be kept in storage unless there is an effective consent by that person to their storage and they are stored in accordance with the consent.

(2) An embryo the creation of which was brought about *in vitro* must not be kept in storage unless there is an effective consent, by each person whose gametes were used to bring about the creation of the embryo, to the storage of the embryo and the embryo is stored in accordance with those consents.

(3) An embryo taken from a woman must not be kept in storage unless there is an effective consent by her to its storage and it is stored in accordance with the consent.

(a) The consents

Schedule 3 makes clear that it is the gamete-provider who must specify the purpose to which the gametes may be put, ie, whether they may be used for treatment (and, if so, for whose treatment) (paras 5(1) and 6(2) and (3)); may be stored (para 8(1) and (3)) or used to create embryos (para 6(1)). In the last of these, the gametes providers must *both* consent to the future use for that use to be lawful, ie, for treatment, (and if so, whose treatment) and/or for research and/or storage of the embryos (paras 2(1), 6(3) and 8(2)). However, it is perfectly lawful for a gamete-provider, or providers in the case of embryos, to consent *only* to storage without giving any consent to use. Of course, subsequent consent to any particular use must be given before anything may be done with these gametes or embryos.

In addition, a consent to storage of gametes and embryos must address *three* specific issues (para 2(2)); the maximum period of storage (if less than the statutory maximum); what is to be done if the gamete-provider(s) dies; and what is to happen if the gamete-provider(s) becomes incapable of varying or revoking consent. The consent forms HFEA (00) 6 and (00) 7 provide respectively for the use and storage of sperm and embryos and for eggs and embryos.

In essence, therefore, the statutory scheme confers a power of veto upon each (of the) gamete-provider(s) over what use the gametes (or embryos created using their gametes) may be put to. This power of veto must be seen in the light of certain statutory limits. *First*, s 14(1)(b) makes it a condition of every storage licence:

(b) that gametes or embryos which are or have been stored shall not be supplied to a person otherwise than in the course of providing treatment services unless that person is a person to whom a licence applies.

Thus, the gamete-provider(s) may not indicate transfer to someone other than a person who is being provided with licensed treatment or is another licence-holder.

Secondly, the Act sets a maximum storage period for gametes and embryos and requires that at the end of the period if stored they 'shall be allowed to perish' (s 14(1)(c)) regardless of the wishes of the gamete-providers. The maximum storage period in respect of gametes is ten years (s 14(3)) and in respect of embryos is five years (s 14(4)). Section 14(5) permits these periods to be varied by regulation. This has occurred both for gametes and embryos. The Human Fertilisation and Embryology (Statutory Storage Period) Regulations 1991 (SI 1991 No 1540) extend the storage period for gametes where in the terms of regulation 2(2):

> ... the gametes were provided by a person –
> (a)   whose fertility since providing them has or is likely to become, in the written opinion of a registered medical practitioner, significantly impaired,
> (b)   who was aged under 45 on the date on which the gametes were provided, and
> (c)   who does not consent to the gametes' being used for the purpose of providing treatment services to persons other than that person, or that person and another together, and never has so consented while the gametes were ones to which this regulation applied.

The regulations extend the period from ten years by the difference between the patient's current age and the age of 45 (ie the storage period for a 30-year-old would be $(45 - 30) + 10 = 25$ years). The justification for this extended period is to permit, for example, patients undergoing radiotherapy for cancer to store gametes for an extended period.

It is important to notice what the 1991 regulations actually say. First, they apply to 'gametes'. At the time, the intention was to deal with the storage of sperm. However, it is now possible to store eggs and since the statutory term 'gametes' includes 'eggs', in principle the regulations apply to the latter also. Secondly, and more significantly, the regulations do not create a general extension of the statutory storage period for gametes. The individual's medical condition must, in the opinion of a doctor, be such that his (or her) fertility 'has or is likely to become ... significantly impaired' *and* that this condition has or will occur '*since* providing [the gametes]'. Thus, as we suggested in our illustrations, it applies where a treatment (such as a vasectomy), disease or illness *since* the gametes were first stored affects the individual's fertility in the specified manner. It does not apply, therefore, to the ordinary situation where the gametes are in storage for infertility treatment. However, since female fertility will necessarily become 'significantly impaired' in time through natural processes, arguably and rather paradoxically, the *healthy* female patient who stores her eggs for future use is covered by the longer storage period.

The very specific situation contemplated by the 1991 regulations for stored gametes is to be contrasted with the regulations applicable to stored embryos. The Human Fertilisation and Embryology Authority reported in July 1995 that the maximum period of five years for the storage of embryos should be increased (*Statutory Storage Period for Embryos: Report by the Human Fertilisation and Embryology Authority to the Health Ministers of the United Kingdom* (DOH July 1995)). The Authority reported that there was 'no evidence of lack of safety for patients or their potential children in the use of frozen embryos in treatment' and that experts had assured them that there was 'no reason to believe that viable embryos stored in proper conditions would suffer harm from longer, even indefinite, storage' (at para 24). The Authority was disposed to the view that storage should be a matter to be decided in each instance upon the twin principles of the welfare of the child and the informed consent of the gamete-providers but that this was not consistent with the terms of the 1990 Act (ie ss 14(3)–(5)) and so rejected it (at para 44). The Authority also rejected two specific options: first, of setting the time limit by reference to a 'natural time limit' based upon a woman's childbearing years (say 50 or 55) as 'virtually impossible to define adequately' (at para 47(a)); and secondly, of a fixed time limit of 10 or 15 years as too inflexible and not catering for a 'few very exceptional cases, such as young cancer patients' (at para 47(2)). Instead, the Authority proposed a modest, but flexible, extension of that time limits (at para 45). It proposed that while the 'normal storage period' should remain at five years, regulations should permit the storage period to be extended by a further five years at the end of the 'normal storage period' for medical or social reasons compatible with the welfare of the child with the specific renewed consent of the gamete-providers. For the Authority, ten years would allow couples more control over their lives without creating unmanageable numbers of embryos in storage (at para 45). There should be a presumption against storage beyond ten years which could be rebutted in special cases such as cancer patients or where the woman had, or might, cease to produce her own eggs (at para 46). In addition the Authority proposed that there should be a continuing review procedure which 'would serve as an important, regular reminder to clinics and couples storing embryos of the special status of embryos, and of the need to address the issue of what to do with them' (at para 46).

In the result, Parliament approved the Human Fertilisation and Embryology (Statutory Storage Period for Embryos) Regulations 1996 (SI 1996 No 375). Regulation 2 provides as follows:

Extension of statutory storage period in respect of embryos
2. – (1) In the circumstances specified in paragraph (2) below, section 14(4) of the Act (statutory storage period in respect of embryos) shall have effect as if for five years there were substituted the appropriate period specified in the Schedule to these Regulations.
　　(2) Those circumstances are that –
(a)　each of the relevant persons has confirmed in writing that that person has no objection to any embryo which is created using gametes provided by that person being stored for a period in excess of five years for use in the provision of treatment services;
(b)　the woman being treated is aged under 50 on the relevant date and the treatment in question would not result in her being a surrogate mother within the meaning of section 1(2) of the Surrogacy Arrangements Act 1985(b); and
(c)　in the written opinion of two registered medical practitioners, one of the relevant persons, or, where she is not one of those persons, the woman being treated, has or is likely to become prematurely and completely infertile.
　　(3) In the circumstances mentioned in paragraph (4) below, section 14(4) of the Act shall have effect as if for five years there were substituted –
(a)　if the woman being treated is aged 45 or under on the relevant date, ten years; or
(b)　if she is aged 46 or over, the appropriate period specified in the Schedule to these Regulations.
　　(4) Those circumstances are –
(a)　the circumstances specified in paragraph (2)(a) and (b) above; and
(b)　that in the written opinion of a registered medical practitioner one of the relevant persons or, where she is not one of those persons, the woman being treated –
　　(i)　has, or is likely to develop, significantly impaired fertility, or
　　(ii)　has a gene or genes such that a child born with that gene or those genes may suffer from such physical or mental abnormalities as to be seriously disabled.

Regulation 1 provides the following definitions of the terms contained in reg 2.

　　(2) In these Regulations – ...
'the relevant date' is either 1st August 1991 or the date on which the embryo in question is first placed in storage, whichever is the later;
'the relevant persons' means the two persons whose gametes are used to bring about the creation of an embryo; and
'the woman being treated' means the woman in whom, at the relevant date, it is intended that such an embryo may be placed, whether or not she is one of the relevant persons.

By and large, the regulations give effect to the Authority's recommendations and proposals to extend the statutory storage period where there is a genuine need to do so although they differ in some respects. The regulations are relatively short but majestically opaque to interpret. The regulations set out a number of conditions that must be satisfied for extended storage.

'*No objection' by the gamete-providers* The regulations only permit an extension of the five year storage period with the written agreement of the gamete-providers. It appears that this agreement may be given *either* at the time of storage *or* before the five year period expires. Notice that the agreement of one or both of the *treated* couple will only be required if they have provided the gametes that produced the embryos. If donated gametes have been used it will be the *donor(s)* whose agreement must be given.

Further, because the regulations require the gamete-providers to have 'confirmed' in writing that they do not object to the extended storage, it is clear that an existing or original (written) consent to store for longer than five years will not satisfy the regulations. A written reaffirmation is required (see form HFEA (96)8).

The regulations do not require the gamete-providers' 'consent' but rather that he or she 'has confirmed in writing that [he or she] has *no objection*' to storage beyond five years 'for use in the provision of treatment services'. The regulations seem to have been deliberately couched in this negative language so as to differentiate the 'agreement' requirements under them from the (positive) consent provisions of Sch 3 to the 1990 Act. This is important because it emphasises that the regulations merely allow for an extension of the storage period; the *use* of the embryos thereafter is governed by the 1990 Act and, in particular, the consent provisions of Sch 3 (see *infra*).

The 'woman being treated' The regulations make clear that there must be a 'woman being treated' at 'the relevant date' (ie the time the embryos are first stored (or on 1 August 1991 if they were stored prior to that date) (regs 2(2) and 1(2)). And the regulations define her as 'the woman in whom [on that date] it is intended that [the stored embryo(s)] may be placed' (reg 1(2)). Thus, the regulations will not apply unless on the 'relevant date' the embryos were (or are) appropriated for the treatment of a *particular* woman. It is not enough, therefore, that the gamete-providers have consented (under Sch 3) in general terms for their use in treatment services and confirmed they have 'no objection' to such use in the extended storage period (under reg 2(2)), the embryo(s) must *in fact* be assigned to a particular woman for her treatment by the clinic: always, of course, consistently with the Sch 3 consents of the gamete-providers. It does not necessarily follow, however, that the embryos must thereafter be used for *her* treatment (see discussion *infra*).

Also, the 'woman being treated' must be under 50 on the 'relevant date' (reg 2(2)(a)). Since the regulations never extend the storage period beyond the 55th birthday of the 'woman being treated' (see *infra*), the ordinary five-year storage period will allow for storage *at least* until the woman is aged 55 if at the time the embryos are first stored she is already over 50.

Further, the regulations are only intended to cover situations where an infertile couple are seeking to have a child using IVF technology *for themselves*. Hence the regulations specifically exclude the situation where the 'woman being treated' will be acting as a surrogate mother if a pregnancy is established (reg 2(2)(b)). Hence, a couple could not have 'their' embryos stored for longer than five years so as to establish a second surrogate pregnancy to produce a genetically related child to their first born. Whilst the Government is content that couples should be able to plan their family using IVF technology over the extended timescale allowed by the regulations, this is only so if the birth mother is to be the social mother. There is no justification for this limitation other than a gut reaction against surrogacy. Given the more relaxed recent parliamentary attitude to surrogacy, evidenced in s 30 of the 1990 Act, this exclusion looks rather odd. Here, again, however the drafting of the regulation creates a loop-hole because it only does not apply where the surrogacy is contemplated *at the time of storage* (or 1 August 1991 if later). Just as it seems a *subsequent* intention to donate fits the wording of the regulation (see *infra*), so will an intention to donate to a surrogate. This was not Parliament's intention.

Grounds for (and period of) extended storage The regulations contemplate *three* factual circumstances pertaining to either the 'woman being treated' or the gamete-providers which justify extended storage. First, if (in the written opinion of one doctor) one of the gamete-providers or woman being treated 'has, or is likely to develop, *significant impaired fertility*' (reg 2(4)(b)(i)) or secondly 'has a gene or genes such that *a child* with that gene or those genes *may suffer from such physical or mental abnormalities as to be seriously disabled*' (reg 2(4)(b)(ii)), then the storage period is extended to ten years or until the woman being treated is 55 whichever is shorter (reg 2(3)). The Government views the former of these grounds as the most common in practice if the five-year period is to be extended in any given case (see *First Standing Committee on Delegated Legislation: Draft Fertilisation and Embryology (Statutory Storage Period for Embryos) Regulations 1996 Hansard* (30 April 1996) at col 22 (per Mr Horam MP Parliamentary Under-Secretary of State for Health)). The first ground will be widely used since it covers the usual case of an infertile couple who are undergoing treatment and plan to have another (genetically related) child in the future, possibly more than five years after the embryos were initially stored. The second, perhaps less common, covers the situation where a couple undergo IVF treatment using donated embryos to avoid transmitting a serious genetic condition (carried by them) to their children and wish to have more (genetically related) children in the future again, possibly beyond the initial five year period. Thirdly, if (in the written opinion of two doctors) one of the gamete-providers or the woman being treated 'has or is likely to become *prematurely and completely infertile*' (reg 292)(c)), then the statutory storage period may be extended until the woman being treated is 55 (reg 2(1) and Sch). This ground for extension, potentially allowing storage for up to 39 years (where the woman being treated is 16), is intended to be 'exceptional'. The example given by the Government was of a woman being treated by radiotherapy for cancer and the regulations allow for the 'embryos to be transferred to her womb after waiting for a period of several years to ensure that the risk of cancer recurring will remain low' (per Mr Horam MP, at col 23).

The extension of the storage period is, unlike the proposals of the Authority, a 'one-off'. There is no required review process over the period of storage to determine whether the embryos should remain in storage in the future nor staged extension of the storage period although this is stated to be best practice by the Authority (see *Guidance For Centres on the Changes to the Statutory Storage Period for Embryos* (HFEA, April 1996) at paras 16–17). Also, in extreme cases of 'complete infertility' a longer period of storage than that recommended by the Authority is envisaged, ie until the treated woman reaches the age of 55 which, again unlike the Authority's recommendations, looks very much like the 'natural time limit' the Authority rejected as inflexible and impossible to define.

Use of embryos during extended storage period A cursory reading of the regulations might lead one to think that embryos stored pursuant to the regulations must be used in treatment services and possibly even restricted to the treatment of the particular woman for whom they were intended at the 'relevant date' ie when the first stored (or 1 August 1991 if stored earlier). Certainly, the spirit underlying the regulations is to allow infertile couples to store 'their' embryos for longer than the five-year period for *their* treatment and the grounds for extending the storage period reflect this. However, they most probably do not have this effect. The regulations are concerned only with the circumstances in which the *storage period* for embryos may be extended. Although there is some reference to their use in treatment services in the regulations, this is only relevant in establishing the basis for extending the storage period. Thus, there must be a 'woman being treated' (for whose treatment the embryo(s) are intended) at the 'relevant time', the 'agreements' of the gamete-providers and the grounds for extension, but once the storage period has been extended, the use of the embryos thereafter is governed by the 1990 Act. In particular, the consent provisions of Sch 3 apply just as much during the extended storage period allowed by the regulations as otherwise (see, HFEA *Guidance For Centres* (*supra*) at para 11 and consent forms HFEA (96)6 and (96)7). The embryos may then be used only in accordance with the gamete-providers 'effective consents' (Sch 3, para 6). Consequently, either of the gamete-providers could vary their statutory consent *to use* under Sch 3 (Sch 3, para 4(1)) during the 'extended period' so as to frustrate the purpose underlying the extension, for example, by revoking consent to the use of the embryo(s) for treatment purposes or for use by the particular 'woman being treated'. Equally, the embryo(s) could subsequently be used for the treatment of another woman or, as we saw earlier, as part of a surrogate arrangement, or even for research providing this was consistent with the existing (or varied) consents of the gamete-providers under Sch 3 to the 1990 Act and even though the latter use is not contemplated by the regulations.

Turning now to a *third* issue relating to the gamete-providers' consents, you will have noticed that Sch 3, paras 2(1) and 2(2) permit gamete-providers to specify conditions subject to which an embryo may be used or gametes or embryos may be stored. It is not clear whether conditions may be laid down by a gamete donor as to the use of gametes themselves. No mention is made of this in para 2 of Sch 3. However, since any condition will qualify his (or her) consent to use and they may only be used in accordance with the donor's consent (para 5(1)), perhaps the point is academic.

Are there limits to conditions which may be specified? For example, could a gamete-provider validly stipulate that his gametes may not be used for the treatment of individuals from a particular ethnic or religious group? The Act does not provide an answer to this question. We must look, therefore, to the general law. There is little doubt that a court would regard as invalid a condition which discriminated for no good reason against certain members of society (see, by analogy *Re Dominion Students' Hall Trust* [1947] Ch 183 (gift for the benefit of students of European origin only); and *Re Lysaght* [1966] Ch 191 (gift for the creation of medical studentships excluding students of the Jewish or Roman Catholic faiths)).

The question then arises whether such a condition if found to be unlawful would invalidate the 'effective consent' of the gamete-provider *in toto* or could the invalid condition be severed if that were possible? English law offers two analogies. The first – the charitable trust analogy – would suggest that if the consent could be valid with the condition excised, then it should be regarded as valid so as to serve the public interest in having gametes and embryos available. This, of course, could not happen if to excise the condition would leave a gap in the gamete-provider's consent which the statute did not permit, for example, as to what is to happen on the death of the gamete-provider. The second – the testamentary analogy – would suggest that the consent would only be valid if what remained once the condition was excised still gave effect to the gamete-provider's underlying intention. In our view, the former analogy should be followed by a court. The testamentary approach would be more likely to lead to failure of donations given that the abhorrent condition is likely to be central to the donor's intention. It is, in our view, more appropriate for the law to further the availability of gametes for treatment (subject to public policy constraints). This will be best achieved by applying a 'blue pencil' approach to void conditions.

Fourthly, we should notice s 12(e), which provides:

(e) that no money or other benefit shall be given or received in respect of any supply of
     gametes or embryos unless authorised by directions.

The directions made by the HFEA (Ref D 1998/1) provide that individual donors
of gametes may be paid up to a maximum of £15 for each donation plus any
reasonable expenses incurred (para 3). Other benefits may also be given to the
donor but are limited to 'treatment services and sterilisation' (para 4). Licence-
holders who supply other licence-holders with gametes or embryos may only be
paid reimbursement of reasonable expenses which may include all the supplier's
costs and not just out-of-pocket expenses (paras 7 and 8). The Directions also
prohibit licensed clinics accepting donors whom they know to have received
money or benefits not permitted by the Directions from third parties (para 5). It
is a summary offence under s 41(8) of the 1990 Act if the condition in s 12(e) is
not complied with. The effect of these provisions is to prohibit trade in human
gametes and embryos (see also Human Organ Transplants Act 1989, s 1(3)
discussed *infra*, ch 15). The Directions do, however, continue to permit 'paid'
sperm donation and what is sometimes called 'compensated egg sharing' whereby
an infertility patient donates some of her eggs in return for IVF treatment which
is free or offered at a reduced rate, for example, paying only for the drugs used.
This is despite the fact that the HFEA wishes to move towards 'altruistic' donation
but has not done so because of the perceived effect this would have on the supply
of gametes for donations, particularly sperm (see Chairman's letter to clinics
December 1998 and also *Consultation on the Implementation of Withdrawal of
Payments to Donors* (February 1998) (HFEA)).

The *final* matter to notice in relation to consents is that of variation and
withdrawal. Paragraph 4 of Sch 3 provides:

Variation and withdrawal of consent
4. – (1) The terms of any consent under this Schedule may from time to time be varied, and
the consent may be withdrawn, by notice given by the persons who gave the consent to the
person keeping the gametes or embryos to which the consent is relevant.
     (2) The terms of any consent to the use of any embryo cannot be varied, and such consent
cannot be withdrawn, once the embryo has been used –
(a)   in providing treatment services, or
(b)   for the purposes of any project of research.

You will recall that, by para 1, consent by a gamete-provider must be in writing
for it to be an 'effective consent'. Paragraph 4 refers to 'notice' – it does not
specify that this must be in writing. However, the definition of 'notice' in s 46
implies that 'notice' should be in writing and this would be consistent with the
need for the gamete-providers' intentions as to the use of their gametes (or
embryos) to be certain and provided in recorded form to the HFEA. Paragraph 4(2)
limits the gamete-providers' capacity to vary or withdraw their consents. If an
embryo has not been used it follows that consent to its use can be withdrawn.
Patently being in storage with a view to use for treatment does not fall within the
exclusion 'has been used … in providing treatment services' (para 4(2)(a)). More
than an intention, even an appropriation for a particular use is required. Thus,
para 4(2) seeks to avoid the problems created by disputes over the fate of frozen
embryos which may arise when the gamete-providers disagree, for example, in
the case of marital breakdown (see discussion of *Davis v Davis* (1992) 842 SW
2d 588, *infra*).

Once consent to storage is validly withdrawn by at least one gamete-provider,
para 8 of Sch 3 (see above) applies such that any gametes or embryos may no
longer be lawfully stored. They must, thereafter, either be used in accordance

with any remaining consents to their use or, if no such consent exists, the gametes and embryos must be 'allowed to perish'. Although the Act does not spell out this latter consequence, it is the only conclusion that the statute allows. The procedure for disposal should be 'sensitively devised' because of the special status of the human embryo (see *Code of Practice* (1998) paras 7.24–7.26).

(b) Posthumous use of gametes and embryos

We have already seen the requirement in Sch 3, para 2 of the 1990 Act that any consent to storage of gametes or embryos requires that the gamete-providers state 'what is to be done with the gametes or embryos if the person who gave the consent dies'. Likewise, the gametes or embryos could only be used for treatment or research after the death of a gamete-provider in accordance with their existing consents (para 2(1) and para 5(1) and (3)). Thus, the 1990 Act permits posthumous use of sperm or embryos by a widow providing that her husband or partner has given written consent prior to his death. English law gives prominence to the procreative liberty of the gamete-providers even following the death of one of them (for a full discussion of the issues, see J Robertson 'Posthumous Reproduction' (1994) 69 Indian LJ 1027). Some jurisdictions take a different view, making it a criminal offence to use gametes or embryos of the dead, for example s 43 of the Infertility Treatment Act 1995 (Vict) provides as follows:

> **43. *Ban on procedures involving gametes of people known to be dead***
> A person must not –
> (a)   inseminate a woman with sperm from a man known to be dead; or
> (b)   transfer to a woman a gamete from a person known to be dead; or
> (c)   transfer to a woman a zygote or an embryo formed from a gamete from a person known to be dead; or
> (d)   form a zygote with sperm from a man known to be dead; or
> (e)   form a zygote, if the woman who produced the oocyte used to form the zygote is known to be dead.

The issue of posthumous use of sperm arose in the Diane Blood case in 1997.

R v Human Fertilisation and Embryology Authority, ex parte Blood [1997] 2 All ER 687 (CA)

The applicant and her husband were married in 1991. Towards the end of 1994 they decided to try and start a family, but before the applicant could conceive, her husband contracted meningitis and lapsed into a coma. The applicant asked for samples of his sperm to be collected by electro-ejaculation for use by her at a later date in treatment for artificial insemination. The husband died shortly afterwards. The samples of sperm were entrusted to the Infertility Research Trust for storage. The applicant wished to use the samples to have her husband's child, but the Human Fertilisation and Embryology Authority refused either to give the necessary consent to treatment in the United Kingdom under the provisions of the Human Fertilisation and Embryology Act 1990 on the grounds that to do so would be contrary to the provisions of s 4(1) of and Sch 3 to the 1990 Act requiring the written consent of a donor to the taking of his sperm, or to exercise its discretion to authorise export of the sperm for treatment abroad. The applicant sought judicial review of the authority's decision, but the judge refused her application on the ground that the 1990 Act, which permitted no discretion on the part of the authority, expressly required the written consent of the donor to the use and storage of his gametes, unless a couple were undergoing 'treatment together' within the terms of that Act. The applicant appealed, contending (i) that treatment in the United Kingdom could lawfully take place because, on its proper construction, the statutory exception in s 4(1)(b) of the 1990 Act permitting treatment without written consent for a couple together applied in the applicant's case, and (ii) that the authority's refusal to exercise its power to authorise export of the sperm for treatment abroad was an infringement of the applicant's right to obtain medical services in another member state of the European Community.

Lord Woolf MR:
(1) Storage and use in this country
Having referred to the statutory provisions and general directions which are relevant, it is now possible to resolve the 'construction issues'. These are as to what are the requirements of the 1990 Act as to storage and treatment and whether they have been complied with in the case of Mr Blood's sperm. Here Community law plays no part.

The parties have provided extra statutory material intended to help on the issues as to the construction of the 1990 Act. However, it is not necessary to refer to that material to resolve the issues which we have to decide.

Turning therefore to the provisions of s 4(1), the first comment that can be made is that it makes a different provision for the *storage* of gametes from that made for the *use* of the male gamete, ie sperm.

As to storage, s 4(1) makes it clear that it must always be pursuant to a licence. That means that storage can only take place lawfully in accordance with the requirements of the licence which for the present purposes are those contained in Sch 3. This means that there must be a consent in writing (paras 1 and 8), which complies with paras 2(2) and 3, before the storage can lawfully take place.

The position as to storage
Sperm can be used fresh or after it has been preserved. Its life, if not preserved is extremely limited, a matter of a few hours. If it is preserved, then it is being stored for the purposes of the 1990 Act and, therefore, is subject to the requirements of a licence. This is made clear by the definition of keeping or preserving sperm contained in s 2(2). The Act, therefore, takes the preservation process as the beginning of storage. This is understandable since preservation involves the processing of gametes and Parliament has required that this should be done subject to the control of the licensing process. The result is that in the ordinary way, no preservation can take place unless the required written consents exist. This would also apply in the case of the preservation of sperm intended for export unless a particular direction was obtained prior to preservation which permitted the storage to take place notwithstanding that there were not the requisite consents.

It follows that Mr Blood's sperm should not, in fact, have been preserved and stored. Technically therefore, an offence was committed by the licence holder as a result of the storage under s 41(2)(b) of the 1990 Act by the licensee. There is, however, no question of any prosecution being brought in the circumstances of this case and no possible criticism can be made of the fact that storage has taken place because Professor Cook of the IRT was acting throughout in close consultation with the authority in a perfectly bona fide manner, in an unexplored legal situation where humanity dictated that the sperm was taken and preserved first, and the legal argument followed. From now on, however, the position will be different as these proceedings will clarify the legal position. Because this judgment makes it clear that the sperm of Mr Blood has been preserved and stored when it should not have been, this case raises issues as to the lawfulness of the use and export of sperm which should never arise again.

Treatment
The question of the lawfulness of the storage is quite separate from the lawfulness of the taking of the sperm from Mr Blood as he lay unconscious. The 1990 Act does not deal with this and the propriety of the treatment involved in taking the sperm in this case is governed by common law principles relating to the patient's consent to the electro-ejaculation which have not been argued before us. It is therefore, not necessary to make any comment about this. But the authority made it clear that though they did not make an issue of this point, they should not be taken as accepting that proper consent was given to that procedure.

The fact is that whether or not it was proper to do so, treatment was being provided to Mr Blood even though he was unconscious when the sperm was obtained. The next question is, therefore, as to whether the obtaining of the sperm amounted to treatment services, which were being provided for Mr and Mrs Blood together in the sense that s 4(1)(b) refers to the provision of services 'for the woman and man together'.

If Mr Blood had survived and the sperm had been immediately used as part of a course of treatment for himself and his wife while he was still alive, then the exception to the requirement of a licence for this treatment under s 4(1)(b) would apply. Furthermore, as it would not be necessary for the treatment to be 'in pursuance of a licence' there would be no statutory requirements for the consent of Mr Blood to its use because the treatment would be outside the statutory control. In this situation, the fact that Mr Blood was unconscious would only be relevant to questions of the legality of the consent given on his behalf under the common law. As already indicated, treatment of a patient who is unaware of what is happening is not in itself a contravention of the 1990 Act. The important question is whether this position is altered as a result of Mr Blood dying before the sperm was used for the treatment of Mrs Blood. It is the time of treatment which is critical under s 4(1)(b).

In answering this question, it is to be borne in mind that s 4(1)(b) creates a criminal offence. In addition, s 4(1)(b) can interfere with Mrs Blood's ability to have a child by her former husband. Both these considerations suggest that a narrow interpretation should be given to its provisions. Lord Lester prays in aid s 28(6) as indicating that the 1990 Act contemplates the use of a person's sperm after his death. Section 28(6) provides that when –

the sperm of a man, or any embryo the creation of which was brought about with his sperm, was used after his death, he is not to be treated as the father of the child.

While this subsection clearly presupposes that there will be the use of the sperm posthumously, this provision does not provide any assistance either way as to the ambit of the exception to the general prohibition against use of sperm contained in s 4(1)(b). Section 28(6)(b) would apply to cases where it was not necessary to rely on the exception to s 4(1)(b) because the man providing the sperm had given the necessary consent required by Sch 3 …

The 1990 Act clearly regards the situation where the donor of the gametes dies before their use as being one which requires special safeguards. Thus, under para 2(2)(b) of Sch 3, a consent must state what is to happen to gametes if the donor dies. There are also the different provisions in the Act as to paternity where the father dies contained in s 28(6). This, together with the obvious difficulty in regarding a person who is dead as being treated together with someone else, means it is really not possible to regard treatment as being together for the purposes of s 4(1)(b), once the man who has provided the sperm has died. And, in any event, the exception to the need for written consent in the case of gametes for 'treatment together' only applies where the sperm is used at once and so does not need to be preserved. The keeping of sperm requires written consent under s 4(1)(a) and the terms of the licence.

This means that in this case, because of the effect of the section, Mrs Blood is not entitled to rely on the exception to s 4(1)(b) or to para 5 of Sch 3. Accordingly, the authority and Sir Stephen Brown P are correct so far as treatment in the United Kingdom is concerned. The absence of the necessary written consent means that both the treatment of Mrs Blood and the storage of Mr Blood's sperm would be prohibited by the 1990 Act. The authority has no discretion to authorise treatment in the United Kingdom …

Having established the facts so far as use in this country is concerned, all the courts and the authority can do is give effect to the clear language of the 1990 Act. Our decision means that, unless fresh sperm are being used, there will always be a need for a written consent which complies with the schedule. It seems, therefore, that in the future, those who are responsible for treating a man and woman together should take the precaution of having the necessary consent not only to storage but also to enable that treatment to continue if the man should have the misfortune to die before the sperm is used.

(2) The law which applies to the export of sperm

It has already been pointed out that s 24(4) of the 1990 Act gives a discretion to the authority as to when and subject to what conditions to permit any person to whom a licence applies to export sperm in any particular case. The authority has made general directions on this subject but those directions do not prevent the authority making a specific direction permitting export in any particular case.

It is a particular direction which Mrs Blood seeks. Mr Pannick, on behalf of the authority, accepts that under arts 59 and 60 of the EC Treaty, Mrs Blood as a citizen of the Community has a right, which is directly enforceable by her (and therefore part of English law) to receive medical treatment in another member state. It is submitted on behalf of Mrs Blood that the authority's prohibition of the export of her late husband's sperm is an infringement of the freedom to provide (and receive) cross-border services in other member states. Those articles are not relevant to receiving treatments in a non-member state such as the United States.

There cannot be any question of the 1990 Act itself infringing those articles. Because of the width of the discretion given to the authority, the authority is in a position by granting consent to avoid any issue of any possible infringement of arts 59 and 60 arising. The possibility of infringing Mrs Blood's rights under those article arises when the authority refuses consent for export as it has done in this case or imposes conditions on the consent which it gives. Her rights would be infringed if the authority misdirects itself as to the effect of those articles or comes to a decision which contravenes them.

Mr Pannick submits that there is no possible infringement here because Mrs Blood is entitled to receive what treatment she likes in Belgium or elsewhere. He contends that all that is being refused is the export of the gametes and that cannot amount to infringement of her rights under arts 59 and 60 of the Treaty.

Mr Pannick's approach does not make sufficient allowance for the reality of the situation. It is to this which regard has to be had when considering the entitlement to the provision of services under art 59. The refusal to permit exports prevents Mrs Blood having the only treatment she wants …

First, the court or decision-taker must consider whether the challenged actions or decisions are an infringement of the relevant cross-border rights of the affected Community citizen, and then whether they are justified by the legitimate requirements of the state whose actions or decisions are challenged.

The first question of infringement must be approached on a practical (functional) basis …

In the case where a wife wishes to receive artificial insemination services using sperm of her late husband, it is artificial to treat the refusal of permission to export the sperm as not withholding the provision of fertilisation treatment in another member state. From a functional point of view, the ability to provide those services is not only substantially impeded but made impossible.

However, the fact that there is interference with the freedom to provide services does not mean that art 59 is infringed. It means no more than the second stage has been reached and the interference has to be justified in accordance with the well-established principles if it is not to contravene art 59. Those principles are correctly summarised by Lord Lester in the case of an administrative decision as being that the decision must be non-discriminatory, it must be justified by some imperative requirement in the general interest, it must be suitable for securing the attainments of the objects which it pursues and it must not go beyond what is necessary to attain that objective. One justification which is recognised by the authorities which is relied on by Mr Pannick is that the member state is going no further than is necessary to prevent persons from evading the application of national legislation (see *R v Immigration Appeal Tribunal, ex p Secretary of State for the Home Dept* Case C-370/90, [1992] ECR I-4265 at 4286, 4295 (paras 14, 24)).

Furthermore, the provision of services in relation to artificial insemination raise difficult ethical and moral considerations which member states can appropriately feel it is necessary to protect by imposing regulations to prevent abuse and undesirable practices occurring.

Accordingly, Parliament was acting well within its powers in passing the 1990 Act, with its requirement for informed written consent from the donor before gametes were stored. And the authority were rightly faithful to and acting consistently with the clear intention of Parliament in giving the 1991 directions imposing a general restriction on export. But arts 59 and 60 give Mrs Blood the right to seek a particular direction permitting export in her case, under ss 23 and 24 of the 1990 Act.

Article 59 cannot, therefore, be relied on as preventing the authority from imposing any restriction on the export of sperm, where a particular direction is sought, and in each case it is a question of degree whether the restriction is justified by the considerations to which reference has already been made. This, in the first instance, is a question for the authority. The courts will only intervene in one of two situations. First, where the authority does not comply with the usual administrative law standards which are enforced by judicial review, including directing themselves correctly as to the law. Secondly, where the authority's decision wrongly evaluates the considerations Lord Lester identified to an extent which goes beyond the margin of appreciation Community law allows in the case of administrative decisions of this sort.

Finally, as to the law on export, it is important to stress that unless the question of export is raised with the authority before the sperm is obtained from the donor and the authority, for reasons it is difficult to imagine, dispenses with the requirement for consent before storage, storage will be unlawful without that consent and so, in practice, it will only be sperm stored with consent which will be capable of being the subject of export.

(3) The authority's decision in this case

… Parliament did not place any express restriction on the authority's discretion. Parliament by the 1990 Act had left issues of public policy as to export to be determined by the authority. It is the authority's decision that, therefore, has to be capable of being justified in relation to art 59. In coming to its decision, the authority was required to take into account that to refuse permission to export would impede the treatment of Mrs Blood in Belgium and to ask whether, in the circumstances, this was justified. The material which was placed before the authority in order to assist them to perform this task is known. Unfortunately, it makes no mention of this requirement.

Turning next to consider the reasons given by the authority bearing this in mind, the position appears to be as follows. (1) The first reason given by the authority is a correct statement that in this case there has not been compliance with the 1990 Act in relation to storage or use in the United Kingdom. This is the starting point for the subsequent reasoning which is the essence for the explanation why the authority was not prepared to exercise its undoubted discretion to permit export in Mrs Blood's favour. It was a permissible and proper starting point: in giving a particular direction, the authority is using delegated powers, which should be used to serve and promote the objects of the legislation, which clearly attach great importance to consent, the quality of that consent, and the certainty of it. The authority must balance that against Mrs Blood's cross-border rights as a Community citizen. (2) The second reason, by referring to the fact that Mrs Blood has no prior connection with any country to which she wishes to export the sperm, ignores the fact that she has the right to receive treatment in Belgium and that Parliament has placed no restriction on the authority's discretion to permit this. It, therefore, tends to confirm that the authority was unaware of the extent of those cross-border rights. (3) The third reason given by the authority, is based on the desirability of the consent being in clear and formal terms. This is unexceptional. However, it does not acknowledge that the evidence that Mrs Blood puts forward that her husband would have given his consent in writing if he had had the opportunity to do so is compelling. (4) The fourth reason given by the authority that Mr Blood had not considered or given his consent to the export of his sperm is a consideration to which the authority was entitled to have regard.

Parliament has delegated to the authority the responsibility for making decisions in this difficult and delicate area, and the court should be slow to interfere with its decisions. However, the reasons given by the authority, while not deeply flawed, confirm that the authority did not take into account two important considerations. The first being the effect of art 59 of the Treaty. The second being that there should be, after this judgment has been given, no further cases where sperm is preserved without consent. The authority is not to be criticised for this because, in relation to the law, it was dependant upon the guidance it received. However, the fact remains that having not received the appropriate guidance, the authority did not take into account two matters which Mrs Blood is entitled to have taken into account.

From the argument before us and those reasons, it is reasonably clear that it was a concern of the authority that if they gave Mrs Blood consent to export, this would create an undesirable precedent which could result in the flouting of the 1990 Act. While as already indicated this can, in the appropriate case, be a legitimate reason for impeding the provision of services in another member state it is a consideration which can not have any application here. The fact that storage cannot lawfully take place without written consent, from a practical point of view means that there should be no fresh cases. No licensee can lawfully do what was done here, namely preserve sperm in this country without written consent. If the authority had appreciated this, it could well have influenced its decision and, in particular, overcome its reluctance to identify Mr Blood's wishes on the basis of Mrs Blood's evidence and the material which she can produce to support that evidence. It would be understandable for the authority not to wish to engage on an inquiry of this nature where there can be other cases where the evidence is not so credible since it could lead to invidious comparisons. However, the position is different if this case will not create an undesirable precedent.

If the authority had taken into account that Mrs Blood was entitled to receive treatment in Belgium unless there is some good reason why she should not be allowed to receive that treatment, the authority may well have taken the view that as the 1990 Act did not prohibit this, they should give their consent. The authority could well conclude that as this is a problem which will not reoccur there is not any good reason for them not to give their consent. If treated in Belgium, Mrs Blood is proposing to use a clinic which in general terms adopts the same standards as this country. The one difference being that they do not insist upon the formal requirements as to written consent which are required in this country. The need for formal requirements is not obvious in this situation.

Apart from the effect of Community law, the authority's view of the law was correct. It is not possible to say even taking into account Community law that the authority are bound to come to a decision in Mrs Blood's favour. What can be said is that the legal position having received further clarification, the case for their doing so is much stronger than it was when they last considered the matter. The second decision cannot stand because it is by no means clear that the authority would have come to the same decision if it had taken into account these two additional considerations. The appeal must, therefore, be allowed. As to what relief should be granted in the light of this judgment can be determined after we have had the opportunity of hearing submissions of counsel.

In this case, there is no need to make a reference to the Court of Justice for the European Communities. The principles to be applied are clear. Any difficulty relates to their application.

If the authority is to reconsider their decision it will have to direct itself correctly as to the law, that is the law including Community law. This will involve starting from the premise that to refuse to allow the export of the sperm is contrary to art 59 of the Treaty unless there are appropriate reasons to justify this. The onus is, therefore, on the authority to provide reasons which meet the standards set by Community law. In deciding whether it can be justified, the authority are entitled to take into account the public interest. The authority will also have to take into account the nature of the present case; again a matter of which it was not aware when it came to its recent decision.

It is unnecessary to consider whether the present reasons would have passed the scrutiny to which they could be subject under Community law since the underlying decision is flawed. It will, however, be apparent from what has been stated that this is unlikely.

It is regrettable if the agonising situation of Mrs Blood will be prolonged by this judgment. Unfortunately, her case raises problems for which there are no clear precedents and in relation to which the law is only clarified by the passage through the courts. This is bound to be a slow process even where the courts have done their best to ensure expedition.

The Court of Appeal upheld the judge's view of the application of the 1990 Act to the domestic use (and storage) of the sperm. However, the court allowed the appeal on the narrow ground that the HFEA had not lawfully exercised its discretion under ss 23 and 24 to allow export. The court did so for two reasons: first, the HFEA had failed to take account of (or have sufficient regard to) in the exercise of its discretion, the applicant's treaty right to obtain medical services (including infertility treatment) in another member state; and secondly, because the HFEA had wrongly been concerned that to allow this applicant to export sperm (without the requirements of the 1990 Act being satisfied) would create an undesirable precedent for future cases. In allowing the appeal, the court acknowledged that the HFEA was not bound to allow Mrs Blood to export her dead husband's sperm, however, in the light of the court's approach to the EU right 'the case for their [sic] doing so is much stronger than it was when they [sic] last considered the matter' (per Lord Woolf MR). In re-exercising its discretion, however, the HFEA was left with a clear picture of the judges' views. Lord Woolf MR had said that 'the evidence that Mrs Blood puts forward that her husband would have given his consent in writing if he had had the opportunity to do so is *compelling*' (emphasis added).

Blood appears to be a superficially simple case. However, it is deceptively so (for discussion, see D Morgan and R Lee 'In the Name of the Father? Ex parte Blood: Dealing with Novelty and Anomaly' (1997) 60 MLR 84). There are three issues we should consider: (1) the use of sperm posthumously within the UK: (2) its export to an EU country; and (3) the legality of taking sperm from an unconscious or dead patient for posthumous use.

(i) POSTHUMOUS USE IN UK

It is clear that the storage of sperm and, subject to one exception, its use for treatment is *only* lawful if done in accordance with the written consent ('effective consent' under Sch 3, para 1) of the sperm provider (Sch 3, paras 8(1) and 5(1)). Consequently, on the face of it the husband's sperm could not be stored or used for his widow's treatment since it was accepted he had not provided a written consent complying with the requirements of Sch 3 to the 1990 Act.

As regards the *use* of the sperm, there is an exception in Sch 3 to the need for written consent. (There was, however, as the Court of Appeal acknowledged, simply no argument that the Act allowed the *storage* of his sperm; it was illegal without his written consent.) Written consent is not required 'to the use of a person's gametes for the purpose of that person, or that person and another together, receiving treatment services (para 5(3)). Was the husband's sperm being used for '[him] and [his widow] together, receiving treatment services'? The Court of appeal agreed with Stephen Brown P that the insemination of Mrs Blood would not fall within these words. It seems almost ridiculous to regard a widow and her dead husband as being treated *together* and it is the use, not the taking, of the sperm which must be done 'together'. The court's conclusion just has to be correct. In fact, there is, as a matter of statutory construction, a conclusive argument against the applicant. Paragraph 5(3) of Sch 3 to the 1990 Act requires two 'persons' to be treated together and the deceased husband is not, in law, a 'person' *at the time of its use*, which is the crucial time when applying the 1990 Act.

We will return later to the meaning within the 1990 Act of 'treatment together', since it is important, not only in defining when insemination with sperm is a licensed activity but also, in determining a child's parentage under s 28 of the Act.

In *Blood*, the couple had not begun undergoing treatment prior to his falling into a state of unconsciousness. What would have been the position in *Blood* if the treatment had commenced before the husband's lapse into unconsciousness but was completed after his death? Certainly if a man whilst alive withdrew from the 'joint enterprise' of establishing a pregnancy, he and his (former) partner would not be receiving treatment 'together'. His sperm could only be used with his written consent (Sch 3, para 5(1)). Is death the equivalent of 'withdrawal'? Of course, as regards the storage and use of the sperm, the man's written instructions will exist because this is one of the matters which must be addressed by a gamete-provider as part of his written consent given *prior to storage* (Sch 3, para 2(2)(b)). An absence of indication on storage or use posthumously would be so fundamental to the consent (and the provisions of Sch 3, para 2(2)) that it ought to vitiate his consent to storage *ab initio*. Thus, no problem will arise in respect of its use whether or not his widow is being treated 'together' with him (either para 5(1) or (3) will be satisfied). Equally, he cannot in law be the father of the child (s 28(6)(a)). However, in one respect the scope of the statutory phrase is very important. If the widow is not being treated 'together' with her dead husband, what would previously have been unlicensed treatment (s 4(1)(b)) could after death only be done in pursuance of a licence. The better view, it is suggested, is that they are no longer being treated 'together' – there are not two 'persons' involved – and it is appropriate that the licensing conditions (and regulatory mechanisms) of the Act should apply where a posthumous child is to be conceived using a *dead* man's sperm. The Court of Appeal seems to have accepted this but not realised that the matter is dealt with fully in the 1990 Act (Sch 3, para 2(2)).

Equally, if the couple are being 'treated together' and the sperm is stored (with his written consent of course) and the man falls into a coma in which he lingers for sometime, the 1990 Act deals with the matter. The better view is that the couple are no longer being 'treated together' *at the time of use*: his total incapacity must be inconsistent with any other view. Schedule 3, para 2(2) requires that, in consenting to storage, the man state, what is 'to be done with the gametes' if he 'is unable because of incapacity to vary the terms of the consent or to revoke it'. Here, again, the man's wishes will be known – there will be, or not as the case may be, the sought after 'written consent' – and his wishes must be adhered to by those dealing with his sperm.

The only circumstance where the 1990 Act leaves a gap is rather farcical. Suppose the couple were being treated using the man's fresh sperm, ie storage was not contemplated and thus the consent process for that was not utilised and he then died, for example at the clinic, before the insemination (with the fresh sperm) could be carried out. (Exactly the same situation would arise if the man fell into a coma and was still alive when the insemination was to take place.) The sperm could not be stored and neither could it be used to complete the insemination: both would require the man's written consent which he would not have given. In order to avoid this situation, it will be necessary as a precaution to obtain the written consent of the man to posthumous storage and use even where the actual intention is to use his sperm immediately.

(ii) EXPORT TO EU COUNTRY

The applicant would have had an uphill task to persuade the court that the HFEA's directions on the export of gametes (1991/98) were *ultra vires* given that they, in terms, reflected the provisions of the 1990 Act in the material respect of requiring the gamete-provider's written consent. There is no suggestion in the Court of Appeal's judgment that the HFEA were not entitled lawfully to make the directions.

A plausible argument might have been that the HFEA had fettered its discretion to make an exception to the directions in the applicant's case. It would, for example, have been unlawful for the HFEA simply to state that the directions contained a rule without considering whether it should apply to the circumstances. However, the HFEA did not do that; just prior to the court proceedings and again subsequently the HFEA thought about whether to treat Mrs Blood as an exceptional case and make a specific direction under s 24(4) permitting export of the sperm (see 'Widow Barred from Going Abroad to have Husband's Baby' Times, 22 November 1996).

At first instance, Stephen Brown P could not fault the HFEA's behaviour procedurally. It was entirely reasonable for the HFEA not to make an exception in this case. It was, after all, an attempt to avoid the provisions of the 1990 Act. Perhaps it would have been different if the applicant had a *real connection* with the country to which export was sought. For example, if the applicant had been a Belgian national who, on marrying a UK citizen, had moved to the UK and now after his death wished to return to Belgium to live. But, that was not this case. The Court of Appeal disagreed: the HFEA had acted ultra vires on *Wednesbury* principles.

First, the court determined that art 59 of the Treaty of Rome created a directly enforceable right to receive medical treatment in another EU country (see *Society for the Protection of Unborn Children Ireland Ltd v Grogan* Case C-159/90 (1991) 9 BMLR 100 (EC)). This right was, prima facie, infringed where Mrs Blood was not permitted to export her dead husband's sperm so as to obtain infertility treatment in Belgium. The court rejected the, rather too cute, argument that she was not being prevented from receiving treatment merely because she could not export the sperm. The court thought, rightly, that this did not 'make sufficient allowance for the reality of the situation' because 'the ability to provide those services is not only substantially impeded but made impossible' (per Lord Woolf MR). The court held that an infringement of Mrs Blood's right could be justified by the legitimate requirements of the state: ie, the decision must be: (1) non-discriminatory; (2) justified by an imperative requirement in the public interest; (3) suitable for attaining the objects pursued; and (4) a proportionate response. In the view of the Court of Appeal, the HFEA, in its decision on 21 November, had failed to take account of Mrs Blood's EU right and the need for its infringement to be justified. The onus was upon the HFEA to provide reasons justifying the infringement of Mrs Blood's right. It had, in administrative law language, failed to take any (or sufficient) account of a relevant consideration.

Secondly, the HFEA was, in the view of the Court of Appeal, wrong to take into account the argument that to allow this applicant to export would create a precedent for future cases 'flouting the Act' because this was a unique case. Since the storage of sperm was illegal without the written consent of the man, the question of export in these circumstances would not arise in the future. The sperm would never be taken in the first place because it could not be stored (see below the argument about the legality of the 'taking'). By and large this is true, however, the HFEA can dispense with the need for consent to storage (as well as to use) if the sperm is to be exported. Section 24(4) of the 1990 Act allows the HFEA to make a specific direction in which it can provide for 'such modifications' of ss 12–14 of the Act 'as may be specified in the direction' including, of course, the consent provisions of Sch 3. Necessarily, the HFEA would have to be consulted prior to the taking of the sperm for export and, as Lord Woolf MR stated, the reasons for this would be 'difficult to imagine'. That, of course, had not happened in this case. Why, therefore, was the storage of Mr Blood's sperm lawful *in this case* pending reconsideration by the HFEA's of its decision? The Court of Appeal never addressed this issue. It seems that it was unlawful and, despite the court's decision, remained unlawful and a criminal offence under s 41(2)(b) of the 1990 Act which carries a maximum term of imprisonment of two years!

(For a discussion of the EU issues, see T Hervey, 'Buy Baby: The European Union and Regulation of Human Reproduction' (1998) 18 OJLS 207.)

(iii) THE LEGALITY OF TAKING SPERM

The most curious aspect of the case is that no question was asked about the legality of the taking of the sperm from the applicant's husband. The Court of Appeal merely reported that it was not argued before them, they made no comment upon it and the HFEA reserved its position on the matter.

Mr Blood was unconscious when the two samples were taken. He was, in law, incompetent for all purposes. The legality of the takings was not governed by the 1990 Act but rather by the common law. In the *Blood* case, there is no doubt that the removal of sperm from the applicant's comatose husband was illegal. It constituted a battery: a deliberate touching without consent or other lawful justification. What treatments or procedures may legally be performed upon an incompetent adult are governed by the House of Lords' decision in *Re F (Mental Patient: Sterilisation)* [1990] 2 AC 1 (HL) (see *supra* ch 6). Removal of the sperm could not be justified under the 'principle of necessity' as being in *his* 'best interests'. On the conventional view of an individual's interests, there can be no 'benefit' to him in having a posthumous child. His wife wholly derives the benefit and the 'taking' is in *her* interests alone. A contrary argument can be put that an individual may possess 'interests' which transcend his incapacity or even death: so-called 'critical' or 'persisting' interests (see generally, A Grubb 'The Persistent Vegetative State: A Duty (Not) To Treat and Conscientious Objection' (1997) 4 European Journal of Health Law 39 at 52–55). Included amongst these could be an individual's endeavour to found a family with his partner. Such a view would require a radical change in English law as it currently stands. It may be that in future English law will have to adapt to take account of a married couple's 'right to found a family' under art 12 of the European Convention of Human Rights, which the courts will have to apply when reaching 'best interests' decisions (see Human Rights Act 1998, s 6(1) and (3)(a)). (It is unclear whether an unmarried couple fall within art 12.) While this right may not be an absolute one, particularly when it is sought to impose positive obligations, a total deprivation of the practical ability to procreate because of the conventional legal construction of 'best interests' would seem to be an infringement of art 12 providing, that is, that the right survives the death of one partner. Even then, the surviving person's right to 'private life' under art 8 will be engaged and, in itself, would require a realignment within the 'best interests' test.

Having said that, in some instances the removal of sperm (and tissue) from an unconscious man could be in the individual's best interests even applying a conventional approach. For example, if he was only temporarily unconscious and undergoing treatment which would render him infertile, eg radiation or chemotherapy treatment. Removing sperm in order to preserve for him an opportunity to have children in the future when he regains consciousness, would be in *his* interests. Of course, in the usual situation, the man's consent could be obtained in advance, and that would be the legal justification for the taking. More likely is the situation where the individual is a child and is incompetent. Those who can consent to the removal on his behalf, such as his parents, could do so in his 'best interests' prior to the treatment. The problem here is that the sperm could not lawfully be stored under the Human Fertilisation and Embryology Act 1990 without the child's written consent (Sch 3, para 8(1) and see discussion *supra* in relation to testicular tissue) – the same would apply in the case of the temporarily incompetent adult but he may have provided written consent to storage prior to becoming incompetent. The 1990 Act, unlike the common law, does not allow for proxy consent. It must be the individual whose gametes are to be stored who gives consent: an incompetent child obviously could not. Subject, that is, to this: the child may be pre-pubertal and physically immature such that his testicular tissue does not contain 'sperm' covered by the 1990 Act but merely has the potential in the future to produce sperm (see *supra*). This tissue could be stored outside the licensing scheme of the 1990 Act and hence the child's consent would not be necessary under Sch 3 (see HFEA *Seventh Annual Report* (1998) at 26–27). However, if there were sperm in the tissue, the 'taking' would be lawful but it would be pointless, since the sperm could not be preserved. Only legislative amendment can overcome this disparity between the common law and the Act. It could do so by allowing for proxy consent to storage (but not use) or by allowing storage (but not use) where it is in a child's best interests until such time as the child became competent to give, or not as the case may be, written consent to storage (and use thereafter) under the 1990 Act (see S McLean *Review of the Common Law Provisions Relating to the Removal of Gametes and of the Consent Provisions in the Human Fertilisation and Embryology Act 1990* (July 1998) para 2.6, discussed *infra*).

What, however, would have been the position if the male partner were dead when the removal of the sperm was contemplated? The common law approach of 'best interests' would be irrelevant because the individual was dead. How would a court decide whether posthumous removal was lawful? One approach would be to recognise that under the common law the removal was lawful unless prohibited by some positive law.

The Human Tissue Act 1961 seems to contemplate removal at common law when in s 1(8) it states: '[n]othing in this section shall be construed as rendering unlawful any dealing with, or with any part of, the body of a deceased person which is lawful apart from this Act.' The legality at common law of removing organs for transplantation has been the subject of close scrutiny by academic medical lawyers (see P D G Skegg (1974) 14 Medicine, Science and the Law 53; I Kennedy (1976) 16 Medicine, Science and the Law 49 and P D G Skegg (1977) 17 Medicine, Science and the Law 123 and *infra* ch 15). The courts have never considered this question. As regards criminal liability, a number of possible offences have been mooted, for example, preventing a lawful burial or disposal, infringement of the Human Tissue Act 1961 or indecent interference with a dead body. It seems, however, most unlikely that any criminal liability would arise where sperm is removed by a doctor. Of course, if the death involves the coroner, then his consent must be sought for any dealing to be lawful. Likewise, there would be no basis for a civil claim by the relatives, not least because the interference with the body would be with the consent of the deceased's next of kin but, in any event, no such action would lie (see Commentary (1996) 4 Med L Rev 216 (AG)).

The alternative approach is to consider whether the removal would be lawful under the Human Tissue Act 1961. On the face of it, the 1961 Act could apply (contrast S McLean (*supra*) at para 3.11). First, the Act applies to donation of 'any part' of the 'body'. Sperm and its associated tissue would seem to fall easily within this statutory phrase. (But *quaere* sperm alone?) Secondly, the

Act permits removal where the 'part' is to be used, *inter alia*, for 'therapeutic purposes'. Assisting the deceased's widow to conceive and bear a child, again, comfortably comes within this requirement of the Act. Thereafter, the 'person lawfully in possession of the body' (most probably the hospital), may authorise the removal of the 'part' either because of the deceased's prior request (s 1(1)) or because he had not objected to it prior to his death and his surviving spouse (or relatives) does not object (s 1(2)). The requirements of s 1(1) and (2) have been simplified but this is the essence of them (see for full discussion, *infra* ch 15). There is, nevertheless, one impediment to bringing this type of situation within the 1961 Act. Section 1(3) of the Human Tissue Act states that an authorisation under the Act makes lawful 'the removal and *use*' of the body part (emphasis added). There is here a conflict with the Human Fertilisation and Embryology Act 1990. The *use* of the sperm is controlled by the latter legislation. So, for example, treatment of the widow would require the deceased's written consent since this would not be 'treatment together' (s 4(1)(b) as interpreted in *Blood* (*supra*). It would be a perverse interpretation of the 1961 Act to understand it as authorising 'removal' but not 'use' of such 'parts' of the body to which it applies. Section 1(3) of the 1961 Act is explicit: it authorises both. Parliament clearly intended the 1990 Act to regulate the 'use' of sperm (and ova). The only possible reconciliation of the two Acts is, therefore, to construe the 1961 Act as not applying to the removal of sperm (or indeed ova). Thus, it is the common law alone which determines the legality of 'removal', and the 1990 Act alone which regulates the 'use' of gametes.

(iv) REFORMING THE LAW

Following the *Blood* decision, the Government set up a review of the law. In July 1998 Professor Sheila McLean produced her report. As regarding the 'written consent' requirement of the 1990 Act, she concluded that it should remain.

Sheila A M McLean *Review of the Common Law Provisions Relating to the Removal of Gametes and of the Consent Provisions in the Human Fertilisation and Embryology Act 1990* (1998) (DoH)

2.3   The range and complexity of the decisions which a potential donor must address in the provision of consent to storage and use of gametes are potentially very strong reasons why the process of obtaining a consent is given such close attention in the Act. The requirement that consent be in writing is one additional measure which adds weight both to the process of obtaining consent and to its ultimate validity. Even some of those who responded to the Consultation Document who felt that the requirement for written consent was not always justified noted the clarity and lack of ambiguity which written consent could provide.

2.4   One other reason for maintaining the current requirement (which was supported by 60% of those who responded to the specific question (57 out of 95)) related to the functioning of the Human Fertilisation and Embryology Authority (HFEA) itself. These functions include most importantly the regulation of clinics and enforcement of good practice which are underpinned by inspection, collection of statistical information and audit. Without the documentation provided by written evidence of consent, these functions could be weakened.

2.5   For others, the inherent nature of genetic material provided the rationale for written consent to be required for storage and use. A general view of many respondents was that the clarity provided by a formally recorded, and carefully worded, consent was important in such a sensitive area. What is clear is that there are a number of reasons, some procedural and some ethical, why gametes and those who donate them are treated differently by the law ...

2.7   In addition, a general point arises in respect of those who, by reason, for example, of physical disability, are unable to sign a document. In accordance with the general rules of the law, written consent could be substituted by witnessed verbal agreement in such cases. There is no obvious reason to believe that this would not also apply to the terms of the Human Fertilisation and Embryology Act, as it would in other circumstances, but *if there is doubt* the relevant section should be clarified to make this specific.

The review also considered whether the common law should be changed so that gametes could be removed from unconscious patients without their explicit consent. Professor McLean recommended no change in the law (para 1.13). However, she noted that in exceptional circumstances removal of gametes from an unconscious person could be in his 'best interests':

> **1.9** ... where the individual is thought likely to recover, and the treatment will result in sterility on recovery, it is likely that it could be held to be in that person's best interests to be able, after treatment, to have the ability to choose whether or not to parent.

As regards this situation, Professor McLean recommended that the 1990 Act be amended to do away with the requirements of written consent to storage.

> **2.6** However, there is one set of circumstances in which it might be thought that the written consent requirement could be waived. If it has been possible to ascertain that the 'best interests' exception to the general requirements of the common law can be invoked to permit the removal of gametes then it clearly could be the case that lawfully obtained gametes would still need to be stored before use. If the interests which render the removal lawful are to be vindicated, then it would be anomalous not to permit such storage.
> *Thus, it may be necessary specifically to amend the legislation to provide that the Human Fertilisation and Embryology Authority has the discretion to waive the consent requirements in schedule 3 of the 1990 Act for storage only in such cases. This will be only until that person is deemed competent to reach an independent decision within the terms of schedule 3 to further storage and/or use.*

(For a discussion of questions of the status of any child born posthumously and of inheritance rights, see *infra*).

(c) Remedies

As we have seen, the 1990 Act determines what must happen to gametes or embryos in any given circumstance. Either the gamete providers' consents must be acted upon or, where statutory provisions dictate an outcome, they must be 'allowed to perish'. But what happens if the licence-holder fails to comply with the consents or fails to allow the gametes or embryos to perish? Obviously, the HFEA could review the relevant licence given that this would amount to a breach of a condition of the licence. This would not, of course, necessarily assist the providers of the gametes. Would they have any remedy in law? On its face, the 1990 Act does not provide a remedy. However, there may be four possible avenues of redress.

(i) JUDICIAL REVIEW

The gamete providers might seek a remedy, whether a declaration or, perhaps, an order of *mandamus*, by way of an application for judicial review under RSC Ord 53, against the licence-holder. The crucial question in such a case would be: is the licence-holder exercising a *public* function? The courts have given a broad meaning to this (see *R v Take-Over and Mergers Panel, ex p Datafin* [1987] QB 815 (CA)). It is possible that the courts would conclude that a licence-holder was exercising a public function. However, it is unlikely. The licence-holder is, in reality, operating or carrying out a *private* activity, heavily regulated by statute but nevertheless no different in principle from any provider of services whether doctor or company. The fact that the licence-holder may be a public employee within the health service is irrelevant if the functions he is performing are *private* in nature (*R v East Berkshire HA, ex p Walsh* [1985] QB 152 (CA)).

(ii) CONTRACT

Where infertility treatment (or storage) is provided outside the NHS, there will be a contract between the licence-holder and the relevant parties. Of course, express provision may be made in the contract which, providing it is not inconsistent with the 1990 Act, would give the contracting parties a remedy for breach of contract if the licence-holder did not act in relation to the gametes or embryos as required. This, however, would be unusual. More likely is that the terms of Sch 3 (ie the relevant consents of the parties) could be said to be implied into the contract such that a claim for breach of contract could be brought against the licence-holder. The terms are clear; the parties will have known of their existence and will appreciate that they are intended to apply to regulate the relationship between them. On this basis, remedies would include injunction or specific performance as well as damages (perhaps even for any distress caused given the personal nature of the contract: *Bliss v South East Thames RHA* [1987] ICR 700 (CA) and *Hayes v James & Charles Dodd* [1990] 2 All ER 815 (CA)).

Even if the treatment or storage occurs within the NHS, payment may be made by the patients. Hence, the above argument would also apply in that context.

(iii) BREACH OF STATUTORY DUTY

Section 17 of the 1990 Act imposes a statutory duty upon the licence-holder, *viz* that 'the conditions of the licence are complied with'. Failure to comply with the provisions of Sch 3 or the duty to allow the embryos or gametes to perish under s 14(1)(c) would constitute a breach of that duty. Would such a breach give rise to a private right of action? The Act is silent on whether civil liability should arise for breach of the Act (but note s 25(6) as regards breach of the *Code of Practice*, *supra*). In our view, the 1990 Act is so emphatic in its commitment to the wishes of gamete-providers that a court might well take the view that a private right of action should arise. The provisions of Sch 3 clearly contemplate gamete-providers as the beneficiaries of the obligations imposed upon licence-holders. The argument gains force from the fact that otherwise an aggrieved party might not have a remedy in law for breach of the terms of the Act.

(iv) THE 'PROPERTY' CLAIM

Could any gamete-provider alleging non-compliance with the Act by the licence-holder claim that the non-compliance interferes with a property right he has in the gametes or embryos? A 'property' claim was considered in the following case.

Davis v Davis (1992) 842 SW 2d 588 (Tenn Sup Ct)

Daughtrey J: This appeal presents a question of first impression, involving the disposition of the cryogenically-preserved product of *in vitro* fertilization (IVF), commonly referred to in the popular press and the legal journals as 'frozen embryos.' The case began as a divorce action, filed by the appellee, Junior Lewis Davis, against his then wife, appellant Mary Sue Davis. The parties were able to agree upon all terms of dissolution, except one: who was to have 'custody' of the seven 'frozen embryos' stored in a Knoxville fertility clinic that had attempted to assist the Davises in achieving a much-wanted pregnancy during a happier period in their relationship.

... Introduction
Mary Sue Davis originally asked for control of the 'frozen embryos' with the intent to have them transferred to her own uterus, in a post-divorce effort to become pregnant. Junior Davis objected, saying that he preferred to leave the embryos in their frozen state until he decided whether or not he wanted to become a parent outside the bounds of marriage.

Based on its determination, that the embryos were 'human beings' from the moment of fertilization, the trial court awarded 'custody' to Mary Sue Davis and directed that she 'be permitted the opportunity to bring these children to term through implantation.' The Court of Appeals reversed, finding that Junior Davis has a 'constitutionally protected right not to beget a child where no pregnancy has taken place' and holding that 'there is no compelling state interest to justify ordering implantation against the will of either party.' The Court of Appeals further held that 'the parties share an interest in the seven fertilized ova' and remanded the case to the trial court for entry of an order vesting them with 'joint control ... and equal voice over their disposition.'

Mary Sue Davis then sought review in this Court, contesting the validity of the constitutional basis for the Court of Appeals decision. We granted review, not because we disagree with the basic legal analysis utilized by the intermediate court, but because of the obvious importance of the case in terms of the development of law regarding the new reproductive technologies, and because the decision of the Court of Appeals does not give adequate guidance to the trial court in the event the parties cannot agree.

We note, in this latter regard, that their positions have already shifted: both have remarried and Mary Sue Davis (now Mary Sue Stowe) has moved out of the state. She no longer wishes to utilize the 'frozen embryos' herself, but wants authority to donate them to a childless couple. Junior Davis is adamantly opposed to such donation and would prefer to see the 'frozen embryos' discarded. The result is, once again, an impasse, but the parties' current legal position does have an effect on the probable outcome of the case, as discussed below.

At the outset, it is important to note the absence of two critical factors that might otherwise influence or control the result of this litigation: when the Davises signed up for the IVF program at the Knoxville clinic, they did not execute a written agreement specifying what disposition should be made of any unused embryos that might result from the cryopreservation process. Moreover, there was at that time no Tennessee statute governing such disposition nor has one been enacted in the meantime ...

... [We] have no statutory authority or common law precedents to guide us, we do have the benefit of extensive comment and analysis in the legal journals. In those articles, medical-legal scholars and ethicists have proposed various models for the disposition of 'frozen embryos' when unanticipated contingencies arise, such as divorce, death of one or both of the parties, financial reversals, or simple disenchantment with the IVF process. Those models range from a rule requiring, at one extreme, that all embryos be used by the gamete-providers or donated for uterine transfer, and, at the other extreme, that any unused embryos be automatically discarded. Other formulations would vest control in the female gamete-provider – in every case, because of her greater physical and emotional contribution to the IVF process, or perhaps only in the event that she wishes to use them herself. There are also two 'implied contract' models: one would infer from enrolment in an IVF program that the IVF clinic has authority to decide in the event of an impasse whether to donate, discard, or use the 'frozen embryos' for research; the other would infer from the parties' participation in the creation of the embryos that they had made an irrevocable commitment to reproduction and would require transfer either to the female provider or to a donee. There are also the so-called 'equity models': one would avoid the conflict altogether by dividing the 'frozen embryos' equally between the parties, to do with as they wish; the other would award veto power to the party wishing to avoid parenthood, whether it be the female or the male progenitor.

Each of these possible models has the virtue of ease of application. Adoption of any of them would establish a bright-line test that would dispose of disputes like the one we have before us in a clear and predictable manner. As appealing as that possibility might seem, we conclude that given the relevant principles of constitutional law, the existing public policy of Tennessee with regard to unborn life, the current state of scientific knowledge giving rise to the emerging reproductive technologies, and the ethical considerations that have developed in response to that scientific knowledge, there can be no easy answer to the question we now face. We conclude, instead, that we must weigh the interest of each party to the dispute, in terms of the facts and analysis set out below, in order to resolve that dispute in a fair and responsible manner ...

... The 'Person' vs 'Property' Dichotomy

One of the fundamental issues the inquiry poses is whether the preembryos in this case should be considered 'persons' or 'property' in the contemplation of the law. The Court of Appeals held, correctly, that they cannot be considered 'persons' under Tennessee law:

> The policy of the state on the subject matter before us may be gleaned from the state's treatment of fetuses in the womb. ... The state's Wrongful Death Statute, Tenn. Code Ann. S 20-5-106 does not allow a wrongful death for a viable fetus that is not first born alive. Without live birth, the Supreme Court has said, a fetus is not a 'person' within the meaning of the statute. *See eg, Hamby v McDaniel*, 559 SW 2d 774 (Tenn 1977); *Durrett v Owens*, 212 Tenn 615, 371 SW 2d 433 (1963); *Shousha v Matthews Drivurself Service*, 210 Tenn, 384, 358 SW 2d 471 (1962); *Hogan v McDaniel*, 204 Tenn 235, 319 SW 2d 221 (1958). Other enactments by the legislature demonstrate even more explicitly that viable fetuses in the womb are not entitled to the same protection as 'persons'. Tenn Code Ann S 39-15-201 incorporates the trimester approach to abortion outlined in *Roe v Wade*, 410 US 113 [93 S Ct 705, 35 L Ed 2d 147] (1973). A woman and her doctor may decide on abortion within the first three months of pregnancy but after three months, and before viability, abortion may occur at a properly regulated facility. Moreover, after viability, abortion may be chosen to save the life of the mother. This statutory scheme indicates that as embryos develop, they are accorded more respect than mere human cells because of their burgeoning potential for life. But, even after viability, they are not given legal status equivalent to that of a person already born. This concept is echoed in Tennessee's murder and assault statutes, which provide that an attack or homicide of a viable fetus may be a crime but abortion is not. *See* Tenn. Code Ann. SS 39-13-107 and 39-13-210.

Junior Lewis Davis v Mary Sue Davis, Tennessee Court of Appeals at Knoxville, No. 190, slip op at 5–6, 1990 WL 130807 (Sept. 13, 1990).

Nor do embryos enjoy protection as 'persons' under federal law ...

Left undisturbed, the trial court's ruling would have afforded preembryos the legal status of 'persons' and vested them with legally cognizable interests separate from those of their progenitors. Such a decision would doubtless have had the effect of outlawing IVF programs in the state of Tennessee. But in setting aside the trial court's judgment, the Court of Appeals, at least by implication, may have swung too far in the opposite direction.

The intermediate court, without explicitly holding that the preembryos in this case were 'property', nevertheless awarded 'joint custody' of them to Mary Sue Davis and Junior Davis, citing TCA SS 68-30-101 and 30-15-208, and *York v Jones*, 717 F Supp 421 (ED Va 1989), for the proposition that 'the parties share an interest in the seven fertilized ova.' The intermediate court did not otherwise define this interest ...

The intermediate court's reliance on *York v Jones*, is troublesome. That case involved a dispute between a married couple undergoing IVF procedures at the Hones Institute for Reproductive Medicine in Virginia. When the Yorks decided to move to California, they asked the Institute to transfer the one remaining 'frozen embryo' that they had produced to a fertility clinic in San Diego for later implantation. The Institute refused and the Yorks sued. The federal court assumed without deciding that the subject matter of the dispute was 'property'. The *York* court held that the 'cryopreservation agreement' between the Yorks and the Institute created a bailment relationship, obligating the Institute to return the subject of the bailment to the Yorks once the purpose of the bailment had terminated. 717 F Supp at 424–425.

In this case, by citing to *York v Jones* but failing to define precisely the 'interest' that Mary Sue Davis and Junior Davis have in the preembryos, the Court of Appeals has left the implication that it is in the nature of a property interest. For purposes of clarity in future cases, we conclude that this point must be further addressed.

To our way of thinking, the most helpful discussion on this point is found not in the minuscule number of legal opinions that have involved 'frozen embryos,' but in the ethical standards set by The American Fertility Society, as follows:

> Three major ethical positions have been articulated in the debate over preembryo status. At one extreme is the view of the preembryo as a human subject after fertilization, which requires that it be accorded the rights of a person. This position entails an obligation to provide an opportunity for implantation to occur and tends to ban any action before transfer that might harm the preembryo or that is not immediately therapeutic, such as freezing and some preembryo research.
>
> At the opposite extreme is the view that the preembryo has a status no different from any other human tissue. With the consent of those who have decision-making authority over the preembryo, no limits should be imposed on actions taken with preembryos.

A third view – one that is most widely held – takes an intermediate position between the other two. It holds that the preembryo deserves respect greater than that accorded to human tissue but not the respect accorded to actual persons. The preembryo is due greater respect than other human tissue because of its potential to become a person and because of its symbolic meaning for many people. Yet, it should not be treated as a person, because it has not yet developed the features of personhood, is not yet established as developmentally individual, and may never realize its biological potential.

Report of the Ethics Committee of The American Fertility Society, *supra*, at 34S–35S.

Although the report alludes to the role of 'special respect' in the context of research on preembryos not intended for transfer, it is clear that the Ethics Committee's principal concern was with the treatment accorded the transferred embryo. Thus, the Ethics Committee concludes that 'special respect is necessary to protect the welfare of potential offspring ... [and] creates obligations not to hurt or injure the offspring who might be born after transfer [by research or intervention with a preembryo].' *Id* at 35S.

In its report, the Ethics Committee then calls upon those in charge of IVF programs to establish policies in keeping with the 'special respect' due preembryos and suggests:

> Within the limits set by institutional policies, decision-making authority regarding preembryos should reside with the persons who have provided the gametes. ... As a matter of law, it is reasonable to assume that the gamete-providers have primary decision-making authority regarding preembryos in the absence of specific legislation on the subject. A person's liberty to procreate or to avoid procreation is directly involved in most decisions involving preembryos.

Id at 36S.

We conclude that preembryos are not, strictly speaking, either 'persons' or 'property,' but occupy an interim category that entitles them to special respect because of their potential for human life. It follows that any interest that Mary Sue Davis and Junior Davis have in the preembryos in this case is not a true property interest. However, they do have an interest in the nature of ownership, to the extent that they have decision-making authority concerning disposition of the preembryos, within the scope of policy set by law.

... The Enforceability of Contract

Establishing the locus of the decision-making authority in this context is crucial to deciding whether the parties could have made a valid contingency agreement prior to undergoing the IVF procedures and whether such an agreement would now be enforceable on the question of disposition. Under the trial court's analysis, obviously, an agreement of this kind would be unenforceable in the event of a later disagreement, because the trial court would have to make an ad hoc 'best interest of the child' determination in every case. In its opinion, the Court of Appeals did not address the question of the enforceability of prior agreements, undoubtedly because that issue was not directly raised on appeal. Despite our reluctance to treat a question not strictly necessary to the result in the case, we conclude that discussion is warranted in order to provide the necessary guidance to all those involved with IVF procedures in Tennessee in the future – the health care professionals who administer IVF programs and the scientists who engage in infertility research, as well as prospective parents seeking to achieve pregnancy by means of IVF, their physicians, and their counsellors.

We believe, as a starting point, that an agreement regarding disposition of any untransferred preembryos in the event of contingencies (such as the death of one or more of the parties, divorce, financial reversals, or abandonment of the program) should be presumed valid and should be enforced as between the progenitors. This conclusion is in keeping with the proposition that the progenitors, having provided the gametic material giving rise to the preembryos, retain decision-making authority as to their disposition.

At the same time, we recognize that life is not static, and that human emotions run particularly high when a married couple is attempting to overcome infertility problems. It follows that the parties' initial 'informed consent' to IVF procedures will often not be truly informed because of the near impossibility of anticipating, emotionally and psychologically, all the turns that events may take as the IVF process unfolds. Providing that the initial agreements may later be modified *by agreement* will, we think, protect the parties against some of the risks they face in this regard. But, in the absence of such agreed modification, we conclude that their prior agreements should be considered binding.

It might be argued in this case that the parties had an implied contract to reproduce using *in vitro* fertilization, that Mary Sue Davis relied on that agreement in undergoing IVF procedures, and that the court should enforce an implied contract against Junior Davis, allowing Mary Sue to dispose of the preembryos in a manner calculated to result in reproduction. The problem with such an analysis is that there is no indication in the record that disposition in the event of contingencies other than Mary Sue Davis's pregnancy was ever considered by the parties, or that Junior Davis intended to pursue reproduction outside the confines of a continuing marital relationship with Mary Sue. We therefore decline to decide this case on the basis of implied contract or the reliance doctrine.

We are therefore left with this situation: there was initially no agreement between the parties concerning disposition of the preembryos under the circumstances of this case; there has been no agreement since; and there is no formula in the Court of Appeals opinion for determining the outcome if the parties cannot reach an agreement in the future.

In granting joint custody to the parties, the Court of Appeals must have anticipated that, in the absence of agreement, the preembryos would continue to be stored, as they now are, in the Knoxville fertility clinic. One problem with maintaining the status quo is that the viability of the preembryos cannot be guaranteed indefinitely. Experts in cryopreservation who testified in this case estimated the maximum length of preembryonic viability at two years. Thus, the true effect of the intermediate court's opinion is to confer on Junior Davis the inherent power to veto any transfer of the preembryos in this case and thus to insure their eventual discard or self-destruction.

As noted [above], the recognition of such a veto power, as long as it applies equally to both parties, is theoretically one of the routes available to resolution of the dispute in this case. Moreover, because of the current state of law regarding the right of procreation, such a rule would probably be upheld as constitutional. Nevertheless, for the reasons set out [below] we conclude that it is not the best route to take, under all the circumstances.

... *The Right of Procreational Autonomy*

Although an understanding of the legal status of preembryos is necessary in order to determine the enforceability of agreements about their disposition, asking whether or not they constitute 'property' is not an altogether helpful question. As the appellee points out in his brief, '[as] two or eight cell tiny lumps of complex protein, the embryos have no [intrinsic] value to either party.' Their value lies in the 'potential to become, after implantation, growth and birth *children*.' Thus, the essential dispute here is not where or how or how long to store the preembryos, but whether the parties will become parents. The Court of Appeals held in effect that they will become parents if they both agree to become parents. The Court did not say what will happen if they fail to agree. We conclude that the answer to this dilemma turns on the parties' exercise of their constitutional right to privacy ... the right of procreational autonomy is composed of two rights of equal significance – the right to procreate and the right to avoid procreation. ...

The equivalence of and inherent tension between these two interests are nowhere more evident than in the context of *in vitro* fertilization. None of the concerns about a woman's bodily integrity that have previously precluded men from controlling abortion decisions is applicable here. We are not unmindful of the fact that the trauma (including both emotional stress and physical discomfort) to which women are subjected in the IVF process is more severe than is the impact of the procedure on men. In this sense, it is fair to say that women contribute more to the IVF process than men. Their experience, however, must be viewed in light of the joys of parenthood that is desired or the relative anguish of a lifetime of unwanted parenthood. As they stand on the brink of potential parenthood, Mary Sue Davis and Junior Lewis Davis must be seen as entirely equivalent gamete-providers.

It is further evident that, however far the protection of procreational autonomy extends, the existence of the right itself dictates that decisional authority rests in the gamete-providers alone, at least to the extent that their decisions have an impact upon their individual reproductive status. As discussed ... above, no other person or entity has an interest sufficient to permit interference with the gamete-providers' decision to continue or terminate the IVF process, because no one else bears the consequences of these decisions in the way that the gamete-providers do.

Further, at least with respect to Tennessee's public policy and its constitutional right of privacy, the state's interest in potential human life is insufficient to justify an infringement on the gamete-providers' procreational autonomy. ...

... [T]he state's interest in the potential life embodied by these four to eight-cell preembryos (which may or may not be able to achieve implantation in a uterine wall and which, if implanted, may or may not begin to develop into fetuses, subject to possible miscarriage) is at best slight. When weighed against the interests of the individuals and the burdens inherent in parenthood, the state's interest in the potential life of these preembryos is not sufficient to justify any infringement upon the freedom of these individuals to make their own decisions as to whether to allow a process to continue that may result in such a dramatic change in their lives as becoming parents.

The unique nature of this case requires us to note that the interests of these parties in parenthood are different in scope than the parental interest considered in other cases. Previously, courts have dealt with the child-bearing and child-rearing aspects of parenthood. Abortion cases have dealt with gestational parenthood. In this case, the Court must deal with the question of genetic parenthood. We conclude, moreover, that an interest in avoiding genetic parenthood can be significant enough to trigger the protection afforded to all other aspects of parenthood. The technological fact that someone unknown to these parties could gestate these preembryos does not alter the fact that these parties, the gamete-providers, would become parents in that event, at least in the genetic sense. The profound impact this would have on them supports their right to solo decisional authority as to whether the process of attempting to gestate these preembryos should continue. This brings us directly to the question of how to resolve the dispute that arises when one party wishes to continue the IVF process and the other does not.

... Balancing the Parties' Interests

Resolving disputes over conflicting interests of constitutional import is a task familiar to the courts. One way of resolving these disputes is to consider the positions of the parties, the significance of their interests, and the relative burdens that will be imposed by differing resolutions. In this case, the issue centres on the two aspects of procreational autonomy – the right to procreate and the right to avoid procreation. We start by considering the burdens imposed on the parties by solutions that would have the effect of disallowing the exercise of individual procreational autonomy with respect to these particular preembryos.

Beginning with the burden imposed on Junior Davis, we note that the consequences are obvious. Any disposition which results in the gestation of the preembryos would impose unwanted parenthood on him, with all of its possible financial and psychological consequences. The impact that this unwanted parenthood would have on Junior Davis can only be understood by considering his particular circumstances, as revealed in the record.

Junior Davis testified that he was the fifth youngest of six children. When he was five years old, his parents divorced, his mother had a nervous break-down, and he and three of his brothers went to live at a home for boys run by the Lutheran Church. Another brother was taken in by an aunt, and his sister stayed with their mother. From that day forward, he had monthly visits with his mother but saw his father only three more times before he died in 1976. Junior Davis testified that, as a boy, he had severe problems caused by separation from his parents. He said that it was especially hard to leave his mother after each monthly visit. He clearly feels that he has suffered because of his lack of opportunity to establish a relationship with his parents and particularly because of the absence of his father.

In light of his boyhood experiences, Junior Davis is vehemently opposed to fathering a child that would not live with both parents. Regardless of whether he or Mary Sue had custody, he feels that the child's bond with the non-custodial parent would not be satisfactory. He testified very clearly that his concern was for the psychological obstacles a child in such a situation would face, as well as the burdens it would impose on him. Likewise, he is opposed to donation because the recipient couple might divorce, leaving the child (which he definitely would consider his own) in a single-parent setting.

Balanced against Junior Davis's interest in avoiding parenthood is Mary Sue Davis's interest in donating the preembryos to another couple for implantation. Refusal to permit donation of the preembryos would impose on her the burden of knowing that the lengthy IVF procedures she underwent were futile, and that the preembryos to which she contributed genetic material would never become children. While this is not an insubstantial emotional burden, we can only conclude that Mary Sue Davis's interest in donation is not as significant as the interest of Junior Davis has in avoiding parenthood. If she were allowed to donate these preembryos, he would face a lifetime of either wondering about his parental status or knowing about his paternal status but having no control over it. He testified quite clearly that if these preembryos were brought to term he would fight for custody of his child or children. Donation, if a child came of it, would rob him twice – his procreational autonomy would be defeated and his relationship with his offspring would be prohibited.

The case would be closer if Mary Sue Davis were seeking to use the preembryos herself, but only if she could not achieve parenthood by any other reasonable means. We recognize the trauma that Mary Sue has already experienced and the additional discomfort to which she would be subjected if she opts to attempt IVF again. Still, she would have a reasonable opportunity, through IVF, to try once again to achieve parenthood in all its aspects – genetic, gestational, bearing and rearing.

Further, we note that if Mary Sue Davis were unable to undergo another round of IVF, or opted not to try, she could still achieve the child-rearing aspects of parenthood through adoption. The fact that she and Junior Davis pursued adoption indicates that, at least at one time, she was willing to forego genetic parenthood and would have been satisfied by the child-rearing aspects of parenthood alone.

... Conclusion

In summary, we hold that disputes involving the disposition of preembryos produced by *in vitro* fertilization should be resolved, first, by looking to the preferences of the progenitors.

If their wishes cannot be ascertained, or if there is dispute, then their prior agreement concerning disposition should be carried out. If no prior agreement exists, then the relative interests of the parties in using or not using the preembryos must be weighed. Ordinarily, the party wishing to avoid procreation should prevail, assuming that the other party has a reasonable possibility of achieving parenthood by means other than use of the preembryos in question. If no other reasonable alternatives exist, then the argument in favor of using the preembryos to achieve pregnancy should be considered. However, if the party seeking control of the preembryos intends merely to donate them to another couple, the objecting party obviously has the greater interest and should prevail.

But the rule does not contemplate the creation of an automatic veto, and in affirming the judgment of the Court of Appeals, we would not wish to be interpreted as so holding.

For the reasons set out above, the judgment of the Court of Appeals is affirmed, in the appellee's favor. This ruling means that the Knoxville Fertility Clinic is free to follow its normal procedure in dealing with unused preembryos, as long as that procedure is not in conflict with this opinion.

Reid CJ and Drowota, O'Brien and Anderson JJ concurred.

We are not concerned here with the detailed analysis of the Tennessee court in determining what should be done with any particular frozen embryo (see also *Kass v Kass* (1998) 91 NY 2d 554 (NY CA) – enforcing parties' agreement as to disposition of frozen embryos. For discussion see, J Robertson 'In the Beginning: the Legal Status of Early Embryos' (1990) 76 Virginia LR 437 and J Robertson 'Prior Agreements for Disposition of Frozen Embryos' (1990) 51 Ohio St LJ 407). Rather, we are concerned to notice what the court called the 'person v property dichotomy'. Having decided that an embryo is not a 'person', the court also decided that the embryo is not 'property' either. It occupies, therefore, some special category *sui generis* (see our discussion of the 'dead body' *infra*, ch 18). The court, however, concluded that gamete providers have dispositional control over embryos produced from their gametes. This conclusion echoes the position under the 1990 Act (although in England, unlike Tennessee, each gamete-provider has, as we have seen, a power of veto over what may be done).

Davis v Davis, therefore, provides no support for the gamete providers' claim to exercise a 'property' right over their embryos in the case of non-compliance with the 1990 Act (for a 'property' approach, see A Grubb 'The Legal Status of the Frozen Human Embryo' in A Grubb (ed) *Challenges in Medical Care* (1992) pp 69–90). It may be otherwise as regards sperm or eggs in that it could be argued that they are property in the same way as it could be said that blood and other body tissue is property once separated from the individual (see *infra*, ch 15). The California case of *Hecht v Superior Court* (1993) 20 Cal Rptr 2d 275 (Cal CA) accepted this view holding that sperm could be bequeathed in a will (see B Steinbock 'Sperm as Property' in Harris and Holm (eds) *The Future of Human Reproduction* (1998) 150–161). Whatever is right, whether as regards embryos or sperm, the framework established by the 1990 Act makes such inquiries pointless. This is because wherever the 'property' approach may lead us, it cannot take us further than the 1990 Act already allows.

There are, however, two examples where a court could be drawn into determining whether the 'property' claim exists. The first is where a gamete-provider requests that the gametes or embryo be transferred to another licence-holder and the licence-holder who currently has the gametes or embryos refuses (eg *York v Jones* (1989) 717 F Supp 421 (ED Va)). In such a case, (assuming the gamete-providers withdraw their consent to storage) the court could avoid the need to be drawn into a property analysis by deciding that the appropriate remedy lay in an action for breach of statutory duty.

The second is where the gametes or embryos are lost, damaged or destroyed. Of course, even here a claim might be brought in negligence for any psychiatric damage caused to the gamete-providers by the loss (see eg *Del Zio v Columbia Presbyterian Medical Centre* (SDNY, 12 April 1976) see *First Edition*, pp 656–660). Could they, however, also succeed in a claim for conversion? Here, the Act will not provide a way out. Given that there is no reasoned solution of what is essentially a question of metaphysical proportions it would be idle to predict the outcome of such a case should these very limited circumstances, which are the only ones that pose the problem, arise.

E. ACCESS TO AND CONTROL OF INFORMATION

Section 31 of the 1990 Act imposes upon the HFEA a statutory obligation to keep a register of information which relates to the following information specified in s 31(2):

> (a) the provision of treatment services for any identifiable individual, or
> (b) the keeping or use of the gametes of any identifiable individual or of an embryo taken from any identifiable woman.
> or if it shows that any identifiable individual was, or may have been, born in consequence of treatment services.

In essence, this information consists of that relating to patients receiving infertility treatment, gamete donors and any children born as a consequence (hereafter 'the statutory information'). The Act requires licence-holders to collect this information and provide it to HFEA (see ss 12–15). Two issues arise: (a) who, if anyone, may gain access to this statutory information? and (b) beyond these circumstances when may the statutory information be disclosed by the HFEA or a licence-holder?

1. Access

(a) Information held by HFEA

First, let us consider access to the statutory information held by HFEA. There are a limited number of situations contemplated by the 1990 Act.

(i) SECTION 31(3)–(5)

The following provisions of s 31 require that the authority give access to certain statutory information in the case of a person who has reached the age of 18.

> **31.** (3) A person who has attained the age of eighteen ('the applicant') may by notice to the Authority require the Authority to comply with a request under subsection (4) below, and the Authority shall do so if –
> (a) the information contained in a register shows that the applicant was, or may have been, born in consequence of treatment services, and
> (b) the applicant has been given a suitable opportunity to receive proper counselling about the implications of compliance with the request.
> (4) The applicant may request the Authority to give the applicant notice stating whether or not the information contained in the register shows that a person other than a parent of the applicant would or might, but for sections 27 to 29 of this Act, be a parent of the applicant and, if it does show that –
> (a) giving the applicant so much of that information as relates to the person concerned as the Authority is required by regulations to give (but no other information), or
> (b) stating whether or not that information shows that, but for sections 27 to 29 of this Act, the applicant, and a person specified in the request as a person whom the applicant proposes to marry, would or might be related.
> (5) Regulations cannot require the Authority to give any information as to the identity of a person whose gametes have been used or from whom an embryo has been taken if a person to whom a licence applied was provided with the information at a time when the Authority could not have been required to give information of the kind in question.

The applicant is entitled to be informed by the HFEA that he was or might be born as a result of donated gametes or an embryo. He (or she) may also discover whether a named individual whom they propose to marry are genetically related. Presumably, although this is not spelt out in the Act, the important information is whether they fall within the prohibited relationships but for the provisions of the 1990 Act. There may be considerable practical difficulties and inaccuracies in identifying precise relationships.

In addition to the information which an 18-year-old may gain access to, there is a special category of information which may be made available to someone between the ages of 16 and 18 where the person is concerned that someone whom he or she proposed to marry may be genetically related to them (s 31(6)–(7)):

> **31.** (6) A person who has not attained the age of eighteen ("the minor") may by notice to the Authority specifying another person ("the intended spouse") as a person whom the minor proposes to marry require the Authority to comply with a request under subsection (7) below, and the Authority shall do so if –
> (a)   the information contained in the register shows that the minor was, or may have been, born in consequence of treatment services, and
> (b)   the minor has been given a suitable opportunity to receive proper counselling about the implications of compliance with the request.
>   (7) The minor may request the Authority to give the minor notice stating whether or not the information contained in the register shows that, but for sections 27 to 29 of this Act, the minor and the intended spouse would or might be related.

The most significant issue concerns access to information relating to the *genetic origins* of the child. Only that information permitted by regulations must, in deed may, be disclosed (s 31(4)(a)). The effect of s 31(5) is to ensure that, at any given time, a donor of gametes (or embryos) will know what information may subsequently (ie 18 years later) be divulged to any child. The donor looks to the terms of the regulations in force at the time of the donation. The regulations cannot retrospectively affect what HFEA has to disclose as to genetic identity, although this is not so for *other information*. The Act would require amendment to achieve this. To illustrate this point, imagine two children are born on a certain day, one as a result of sperm donated at a time when the regulations specified that identifying information could be disclosed while the other child was conceived using sperm donated under a different regime of regulations which did not permit such disclosure. The effect would be that, although they would both become 18 on the same day, what they may learn about their genetic background would be significantly different. Currently, there are no regulations and hence any children conceived using donated material will not be able to obtain *any* identifying information about their genetic background. A contrast, therefore, has been made between children who are adopted – who at 18 have a legal right to discover their natural parents (see Adoption Act 1976, s 51) – and children born through medically assisted reproduction. The Warnock Committee recommended that certain 'basic information', though not identifying information, should be made available.

Report of the Committee of Inquiry into Human Fertilisation and Embryology (Cm 9314) (1984)

> **4.19** It is the practice of some clinics in the USA to provide detailed descriptions of donors, and to permit couples to exercise choice as to the donor they would prefer. In the evidence there was some support for the use of such descriptions. It is argued that they would provide information and reassurance for the parents and, at a later date, for the child. They might also be of benefit to the donor, as an indication that he is valued for his own sake. A detailed description also offers some choice to the woman who is to have the child, and lack of such choice can be said to diminish the importance of the woman's right to choose the father of her child.
> **4.20** The contrary view, also expressed in the evidence, is that detailed donor profiles would introduce the donor as a person in his own right. It is also argued that the use of profiles devalues the child who may seem to be wanted only if certain specifications are met, and this may become a source of disappointment to the parents if their expectations are unfulfilled.
> **4.21** As a matter of principle we do not wish to encourage the possibility of prospective parents seeking donors with specific characteristics by the use of whose semen they hope to

give birth to a particular type of child. We do not therefore want detailed descriptions of donors to be used as a basis for choice, but we believe that the couple should be given sufficient relevant information for their reassurance. This should include some basic facts about the donor, such as his ethnic group and his genetic health. A small minority of the Inquiry, while supporting the principle set out above, and without compromising the principle of anonymity, consider that a gradual move towards making more detailed descriptions of the donor available to prospective parents, if requested, could be beneficial to the practice of AID, provided this was accompanied by appropriate counselling. **We recommend that on reaching the age of eighteen the child should have access to the basic information about the donor's ethnic origin and genetic health and that legislation be enacted to provide the right of access to this.** This legislation should not be retrospective.

The current legislation, as you will have noticed, does not allow for the disclosure of *any* information about the donor.

The arguments for and against semen donors remaining anonymous are made by Jonathan Glover in the following extract from his Report to the European Commission on Reproductive Technologies (pp 35–38).

Glover Report *Fertility and the Family* (1989)

Most semen donors express a preference for anonymity. This is partly to avoid paternity suits. (In most countries, the legal position is unclear.) But it is also to avoid unwanted later contact with their 'offspring'.

Swedish law has given the child the right to know the identity of the semen donor, on reaching maturity at the age of eighteen. Paternity suits are eliminated by assigning paternity to the married woman's husband, who gives his irrevocable written consent. The donor remains anonymous as far as the social parents are concerned. The law equates AID with adoption, so the donor has a social recognised position, though one without rights. Is this alternative model preferable to anonymity?

Let us look first at the family in which the child will grow up. Social parenthood often out-ranks biological parenthood. Being a social father is much more important in life than being a semen donor. And the emotional bond with the social father is usually far more important to children than the genetic links with the donor.

The social parents may want their family to be a closed unit, as much like other families as possible, unencumbered by ambiguous half-relationships with donors. A social father may feel rejected if he sees the donor as a rival.

Parents often prefer anonymous donors who will disappear afterwards. But some opponents of anonymity favour the Swedish model, where the potential identification of the donor would only take place eighteen years after the child's birth. This seems to give plenty of time for the development of family bonds which will survive. And parents themselves sometimes prefer a known or related donor. This can be because they think they have some idea of the likely genetic characteristics of the child. And, in the case of related donors, they may value the extra genetic link with the child this gives, as well as their more intimate knowledge of the kind of person the donor is. It is possible to have a known or related donor whose identity is kept from the child; but this involves the drawbacks of family secrets. The desire for a genetic or other link may lead some social parents to prefer a system without anonymity.

What about the position of donors? As in the Swedish system, the donor can be given complete legal protection, so that the child has no rights against the donor other than knowledge of his identity.

The effect of abolishing anonymity in Sweden seems to have been an initial decline in numbers of donors. This may suggest that many donors prefer to be anonymous, quite apart from fear of paternity suits. But this must be linked to two other effects of the new law. There was a decline in demand: couples felt less comfortable at the thought that the child might eventually wish to contact the donor. And physicians in some AID centres refused to continue offering AID under the new law. In the centres still continuing with AID, the numbers of donors have returned to normal, although they are now more often older and more often married …

Policies on anonymity represent a social choice about the meaning of donation. Do we accept and recognise the donor's contribution as an act of altruism, perhaps as part of a system in which a husband donates with the full agreement of his wife? Or do we prefer the anonymous student as a source, treating the contribution as an embarrassment, to be accepted but swept under the carpet? There may be more dignity for the donor in a system of openness rather than anonymity. In the case of donors, there seems something to be said for eliminating anonymity, but against this must be set what appears to be their own widespread preference for retaining it.

What about the children? The child's concern with his or her origin was the main motive for the Swedish policy.

Some adopted children find they come to care very much who their biological parents are, and may go to great lengths to find out. Our sense of who we are is bound up with the story we tell about ourselves. A life where the biological parents are unknown is like a novel with the first chapter missing. Also there are the marked similarities between children and their biological parents. The child may wonder who is the person, perhaps among those passed in the street, who has that degree of closeness.

On the other hand, for young children who know who the semen donor was, there may be problems about their identity. They may see neither person as being unambiguously their father. This suggests that it may not be in the children's best interest to be told who the donor is at an early age, but is not a point against a system of the Swedish type, setting the right to know at the age of eighteen. And, since the legal right to know need not be exercised, no child loses anything by it. Since some people care so much about their origins, seeing them as an important part of their identity, the interests of the children count strongly in favour of the right to know.

What relative weight should be given to the different interests of the various people involved? This is the kind of problem where no absolute general rule is likely to give best results in all cases. So much depends on the individual case: who the particular people are, their relationships and what they care about. As a committee we unsurprisingly found ourselves differing in the weight we gave to the different interests.

Some of us felt that it can be very hard on the parents to have the donor intrude on the family. But most of us were inclined to think that, by the time the child is eighteen, the family should usually be strong enough to weather this.

Some of us were inclined to see knowledge of one's origins as so central to identity as to be a right. We all accept that ignorance of it can be a severe psychological disadvantage, and we give this great weight in thinking about policy. But the claim that this knowledge is an absolute right suggests, for instance, that it should always outweigh any degree of unwillingness by donors to discard the protection of anonymity. Is this plausible?

In a system without anonymity, donors need not themselves be hugely disadvantaged. As in Sweden, their legal position can be protected. There may be some disadvantages in later contact by their offspring. But no-one need become a donor if they think this possibility is a terrible one. Perhaps the interests of the children count for more than the possible disadvantages to the donors.

But the case for anonymity does not here simply rest on a direct appeal to the interests of the donors. The fear is that, through putting off potential donors, abolition of anonymity will damage the whole programme. The losers will be infertile couples who will no longer be able to have this help in having children because potential donors have voted with their feet.

The extreme views are, on the one hand, that knowledge of the donor is an inviolable right, and, on the other hand, that anonymity should always be guaranteed. Perhaps a reasonable middle course can be found.

We suggest that the child's interests create a strong *presumption* in favour of openness, but with protection for the various parties involved. As in the Swedish model, the social parents should be protected from intrusion when the 'child' still *is* a child, and the donor should be protected from paternity claims. But, although we favour openness, this is a presumption rather than an absolute right. There is a case for adopting a Swedish-type law for an experimental period, and seeing what happens to donor recruitment. If it slumps disastrously, public appeals could be tried to counteract the effects of the new system. If none of this worked, there would then be case for abandoning the experiment.

To put the point briefly: it can be better for a child to be born without the right to know the biological father than for that child not to be born at all. But, if the donor programmes can be kept up, best of all might be to be born with the right to know.

Less positive in her support for disclosure of identity information is Professor Katherine O'Donovan, when she considers the issue in the context of the adoption experience (see also S Maclean and M Maclean 'Keeping Secrets in Assisted Reproduction' (1996) 8 Child & Family LQ 243).

Katherine O'Donovan 'What Shall We Tell the Children? Reflections on Children's Perspectives and the Reproduction Revolution' in Robert Lee and Derek Morgan (eds) *Birthrights: Law and Ethics at the Beginnings of Life* (1989)

THE BACKGROUND

... *Anonymity* has been part of the legal institution of adoption since its inception in England and Wales in 1926 (The Adoption of Children Act 1926). It was believed that biological and adoptive parents' interests were best served by this policy. A special register was created to record and make traceable the connection between the entry in the birth register and the entry in the adoption register. This was maintained by the Registrar General. However, access to this special register was unobtainable except by special permission of a court. Approval for inspection was rarely granted. This meant that adopted persons , who did not know the names of genitors, could not obtain copies of their original birth certificates. Adoption practice has generally involved the giving of a new name to the child (ibid. s 11 (7). It has always been possible for an adopted person to obtain the original birth certificate, provided the birth name is known).

Anonymity was reinforced by the Adoption Act of 1949 which permitted adopters to conceal their identity from the biological parents during court proceedings. The theory of 'matching' the child's physical appearance to that of the adopters also enabled concealment. The adoption itself could be hidden, from the child and from the world. Social policy in adoption, until fairly recently, was to mimic so far as possible the arrival of a newborn child into a biological family. The notes of registration in the Adoption Act 1950 state: 'the substitution ... of the original birth certificate is considered desirable where that certificate revealed the fact of illegitimacy or where it is desired to conceal the origin of the child' (Adoption Act 1950).

Artificial insemination by a donor is almost as common a way of becoming a parent today as adoption. It is estimated that 2.5 per cent of live births in the United Kingdom are through AID, and that 250,000 people in the United States were conceived through this process. Donors of sperm are guaranteed anonymity where the medical profession is involved. This policy is justified by the confidentiality of medical treatment, the doctor/ patient relationship. It is also said to be necessary to protect donors, and to ensure that donation continues. Medical practice has been to advise AID parents to keep the matter secret. A leaflet from the Royal College of Gynaecologists (1979) advises that 'unless you decide to tell the child there is no reason for him (or her) ever to know that he (or she) was conceived by AID. Whether or not you do so is entirely up to you (Snowden and Mitchell *'Artificial Family'* p 84). This goes further than anonymity; for it introduces secrecy.

Secrecy is a darker concept than anonymity. It is possible for a child to know that its genetic and social parentage have been separated, even though the genitors remain anonymous. But where parentage is a secret, the child may not know anything.

The first indication that the policy of secrecy on adoption might not be entirely sound came with the Hurst Report in 1954. There it was stated: 'A number of witnesses in England thought that the adopted person has a right to this information [about origins] and expressed the view that it is not in the interests of adopted children to be permanently precluded from satisfying their natural curiosity.' (Report of the Departmental Committee on the Adoption of Children (the Hurst Report), Cmnd 9248 (London: HMSO, 1954) p 53.) The committee recommended that the adoption application should include a pledge to tell the child of the adoption. This was not implemented in the subsequent Adoption Act 1958. The Home Office did produce an explanatory memorandum for all adopters. This stressed that children should be told of adoption but added: 'You may prefer not to tell him anything; but that would be unwise, because he would be likely to find out himself sooner or later and if you had not told him, the discovery might be a shock' (Appendix of Home Office Letter (HO58/59, March 1959)). The evidence from life histories of adopted persons is that discovery is more than a shock; it can undermine a lifetime's security.

The opinion was growing that not only was it good adoption practice to tell children of their status, but also that they should be given some information about their birth parents. The adoption law in Scotland, from its inception in 1930, had permitted adoptees, on reaching the age of 17, to apply for their original birth certificates direct from the Registrar General. John Triseliotis had done research on Scottish adoptees applying for birth records and was forceful in recommending to the Houghton Committee, set up in 1969, that England and Wales should follow Scottish practice. The reason was grounded on the concept of identity. (See J Triseliotis, *In Search of Origins* (London: Routledge & Kegan Paul, 1973).)

The first Working Paper published by the Houghton Committee in 1970 still emphasized concealment:

anonymity serves as a protection both for the child and the adoptive parents on the one hand and the natural parents on the other – for the adoptive home against interference from the natural parents or the fear of this; for the natural parents against any temptation to watch the child's progress or in any other way to feel the links still in existence. (Adoption of Children: Working Paper of the Department Committee on the Adoption of Children (the Houghton Report)(London: HMSO, 1970) p 231.)

And although greater openness with the child about adoption was advocated, the committee still felt that this 'does not, however, necessarily entail a knowledge of the actual names of the natural parents and other identifying information' (ibid. p 234).

Secrecy in family life is a strong subject in fiction and autobiographies. Philosophical reflections thereon suggest that family secrets, whilst forming part of the fabric and history of the group, may have a deleterious effect. Sissela Bok argues that deceit over an important matter, such as parentage, is a form of control and even assault. The secret excludes the child whom it concerns, evoking a sense of being an outsider (S Bok '*Secrets*' (New York: Vintage, 1984) ch 3). There is both an attraction to, and a repulsion from, the secret. The telling may be experienced by the child as an aggressive attack on the centre of her life. Instead of clearing up the dark hints, the sense of exclusion, the feeling of not belonging, the revelation may create greater mysteries.

Underlying this are issues of interaction and power within the family unit.

> Secrets and myths may ... be started by an individual member of the family. Like everything else that happens in families, they do not remain the property of the individual, as the responses of other family members set in motion processes of interaction, which strengthen or weaken the effects of secrets and myths (L Pincus and C Dare '*Secrets in the Family*' (London: Faber & Faber, 1978) p 16).

The prevailing secrecy may set up doubts and insecurities. The awareness of a family secret may place the child of donation in a similar position to the child of adoption in the past. 'Silence and secrecy are a shelter for power'; feelings of powerlessness and guilt may follow.

The outcome of the Houghton Committee's 1972 report was the Children Act 1975. Section 26 provides that, on reaching the age of 18, adopted people have the right to receive a copy of their original birth certificate. Because of the promise of anonymity to parents, those adopted before 12 November 1975 receive mandatory counselling, as part of an official effort to ensure that genitors are not suddenly confronted by genes (Children Act 1975).

The manner of discussion of access to birth certificates in Parliament reveals a number of assumptions surrounding the institution of adoption. On one hand were those who feared for the security of the biological mother confronted by the child placed for adoption. These feelings were expressed in terms of 'her guilty secret', her embarrassment and shame of her past, her rejection by family and neighbours (Official Report, House of Commons, Hansard, Vol 893 (20 June 1975) on the Children Bill). This discourse reveals much about the status of women, notions of female chastity, and the stigma of bearing an illegitimate child. On the other hand there were those who spoke of 'a basic human right that every child should know his origins', (ibid.) of being 'physically whole', (ibid.) of the adopted child who 'wishes to know who and what he is' (ibid.).

The idea underlying section 26 has been summed up by Triseliotis in the words, 'no person should be cut off from his origins'. But the notion of origins and its accompanying phrase 'identity' have not been subjected to critical scrutiny.

Rather they have been greeted with acclaim by writers on this area of social policy and law.

Identity in discussions of adoption policy serves as a concept concerned with psychology. Researchers have linked 'genealogical and personal information to the development of a positive sense of identity and of a whole self'. Triseliotis, who influenced the passing of section 26, writes of 'a psychological need', in 'the formation of a positive concept of self' for 'personal history material'. Such information is 'a fundamental right' in 'the quest for roots, origins and reunions', where adoptees are 'seeking to "complete" themselves'. (J Triseliotis, 'Obtaining birth certificates', in P Bean (ed), *Adoption: Essays in Social Policy, Law and Sociology* (London, 1984)). The question which is neither asked nor answered is whether the identity crisis suffered by adoptees is socially and discursively constructed.

Other writers have criticized this model of identity as pathological. Haimes and Timms argue that there is a distinction between ego identity and social identity.

> The rhetoric of the pathological model used concepts such as the 'identity crisis' to describe the effect of a bad adoptive experience on the individual's ego identity, that private 'internal' sense of self. We argue that adoption can be better understood in terms of the individual's *social* identity: adoption is, after all, a social arrangement rather than a natural process happening to the individual. (Haimes and Timms, '*Adoption*' p 98).

The concept of social identity is explained as 'the presentation of self in everyday life' and the appraisal and judgment of others. Adopted persons are aware of themselves as different but are, according to this view, attempting to account for themselves in their 'search for origins'.

A social identity open to questioning does not imply, as a damaged ego identity might, a degree of psychological disturbance, but rather that extra care is required by the social act or interaction, and often that extra work is needed to ensure the individual is taken as a serious, competent but non-threatening member of society (ibid.).

This idea of identity seems to be an 'image of ourselves projected to other people' (J Glover, (1984)). But identity has other senses, such as that of oneself as a particular kind of person. The two models of identity, ego and social, erected by writers on adoption, are underpinned by visions of normality and difference. This is a vision of family structure in which there is a 'natural' family, which is assumed. Triseliotis, and Haimes and Timms are committed to a discourse which does not question the concept of identity as a response to socially produced situations. Yet, as Derek Morgan argues, 'appeals to the "natural order" of the family and claims of its necessary retention can be seen, from the perspective of social history, as an attempt to legitimate and reinforce a specific form of structure and specific relationships of authority and dependence' (D Morgan, 'Making Motherhood male: Surrogacy and the moral economy of women' Journal of Law and Society, vol 12 (1985), p 219). The 'search for identity' as the quest of adopted children for their genetic parents has been termed, does not exist in a vacuum. It is produced by legal and social structures which attach value to concepts of identity linked to genitors. The case histories of those whose searches have ended in finding a parent do not necessarily suggest that such quests should be encouraged (P Toynbee, 'Lost Children' (1985)).

THE EXPERIENCE OF ADOPTED CHILDREN

The literature on adoption and identity used case-studies to bring out what are perceived as crucial issues. These are knowledge of genetic origins as important for psychological health and openness by genetic and social parents. Yet a recent popular account of nine case histories, revealingly entitled *Lost Children*, shows that the quest and subsequent discoveries may be disastrous for the searcher. This account does not question the desire to trace genetic parents which is perceived as 'natural'; the adopted child is said to have 'some fate, some identity, some natural identity which drives him on to seek out his own origins' (ibid.). Adopted children are described as growing up with a desperate longing to discover more about themselves and their roots; even where the adoption has been successful and happy, many feel incomplete without some knowledge of their blood origins (ibid.).

It is an open question as to whether this description is accurate. But what is revealing is a language suffused with the notion that we are our genes; that blood matters. In this account secrecy is explained as having been necessary originally to overcome the stigma of illegitimacy, but now to be in the interest of the adopters: 'giving them the emotional security of knowing that the natural mother has gone for ever, and they are entirely free to simulate natural parenting as best they can'. However, a 'sense of alien, different, foreign, unknown blood and genes may not ever be totally obliterated from the relationship between new parents and child'. (Ibid.)

The concept of stigma is introduced by writers on adoption to account for perceived differences on the part of others between the adoptive family and the 'natural' family. Erving Goffman has argued that those who are perceived as different are stigmatized as a form of 'management of spoiled identity'.

The attitude we normals have towards a person with a stigma and the actions we take in regard to him, are well known, since these responses are what benevolent social action is designed to soften and ameliorate ... We construct a stigma theory, and ideology to ... account for the danger he represents. (E Goffman *'Stigma: Notes on the Management of Spoiled Identity'* (New York: Prentice-Hall, 1963) p 45.)

Adoptive parents, it seems, are stigmatized because 'by admitting that their child is adopted, they are telling the world of the shame of their own infertility' (P Toynbee, *'Lost Children'* p 22). Adoptive children are stigmatized as 'unknown blood, unknown genes' the 'cuckoo in their nest' (ibid. p 24). The 'spoiled identity' of both arises, in part, from an inability on the part of normals to place the adoptive family.

In most literature on child care the concept of placement is used to convey a sense of a new family for a child whose initial placement with biological parents has broken down. But there is another sense of placement, to do with 'social identity – their ability to place themselves in their own and in the life-histories of others'. Section 26 is said to be important in this process 'not simply because it confers access to information but also because it allows for the public requesting of an account'.

Uneasiness about adoption among normals and adoptees is reflected in stigma and marginal status. Adopted children are seen as having an 'achieved' role, as having to prove themselves and who they are; whereas the biological child has an ascribed role. One adoptee reflected: '[Y]ou know, I wasn't a blood relation – and blood counts in families – they never accepted me.' (Haimes and Timms '*Adoption*' p 67.)

The hidden agenda of section 26 is that adopted children have an unrequited desire to know their genitors, and that this is a natural and understandable need which can be met by legislation. Although I have argued that writings on this need should be subjected to critical scrutiny, nevertheless we must take seriously the question whether other children brought up by a genetically unrelated parent also have this desire and require legislation to meet it.

Before we leap into extending section 26 of the Children Act 1975 to cover all children with 'unknown genes' perhaps we should investigate further the research data on adopted children. It has been said that all adopted children experience the need to contact their genitors. But does the empirical evidence support this assertion? Closer inspection reveals that there was an initial flood of applications on the coming into force of section 26 but that this has diminished to a trickle. Furthermore, application for one's original birth certificate does not necessarily mean a desire to trace, or to contact genitors. Of the first 500 applicants to the General Register Office, only 46 gave locating a natural parent or relative as their prime reason, but 140 overall declared an intention to trace.

This data does not suggest an overwhelming urge on the part of adoptees to seek out genitors. The literature is insufficiently critical of the idea of a 'search for identity'. There are two questions to be asked: first, to what extent is the perceived psychological need culturally produced? Second, might this need not be a displacement of other personal problems, or part of the adolescent crisis experienced by most persons?

It is true that in Polly Toynbee's popular account of the experience of adoptees the subjects wished to contact their genitors. Some were obsessed with this desire. However, this was a self-selecting group. Of the eight searchers, one found a mother who was a hopeless derelict, another was obsessed with a mother who refused to have anything to do with him, and a third discovered her mother to be Ruth Ellis, the last woman to be hanged in England.

That these searchers experienced a desire to fill a gap in their lives cannot be denied. But the majority were not adopted as babies. Furthermore their quest appears to have arisen because they shared a popular view expressed by Toynbee that 'every human civilization has held family and blood kinship in high esteem' (supra). The literature on the search for origins continually emphasizes the blood tie. If this has any meaning then it ought to apply also to children of donation. Yet the unspoken text that the search for genitors is natural, that infertile adults are to be stigmatized, might be sufficient argument for secrecy on the part of social parents.

BLOOD TIES MATTER

The notion of blood relationships suffuses the work on adoption and identity. But is it blood that is under discussion? Most subjects of case studies were interested in their mothers, rather than in their fathers. Does this mean that the nine months *in utero* create a perceived bond? If that is so, then children born through sperm, egg, or embryo donation may have identity problems. But children produced through surrogacy and womb-leasing arrangements may have similar experiences to adoptees. However, it seems that genes, inherited appearance, traits, intelligence, are emphasized by some subjects. As Oliver O'Donovan reflects: 'From now on there is no knowing what a parent is.'

Modern social policy theory has been to de-emphasize the blood tie. Too many tragedies, such as that of Maria Colwell, have arisen from claims by parents based on biological relationships (O O'Donovan '*Begotten or Made?*' (1984)). Feminist theorists have persistently attacked John Bowlby's depiction of mother love as based on genetic bonds. Carers have been shown to form relationships with small children on a day-to-day basis and not on blood. This resurrection of blood as of great significance in parent/child relationships seems a retrograde step.

In what sense might the blood tie matter? Elsewhere I have identified three aspects: materials, medical, and the cultural notion of identity. In the case of adoption there can be no material interest, as the adoption order severs the legal tie with the biological parents, and therefore adoptees cannot look to them for inheritance or financial support. Donation, however, does not sever the legal tie between genitor and child. So far as medical interest is concerned we do know that a genetic family history of certain diseases may be important knowledge to any person. When founding a family future parents will be greatly helped by knowledge of genetic diseases such as haemophilia or Huntington's chorea. No legislative effort has been made in ascertaining and recording such information for adoptees, although this is a feasible task. Nor has the medical profession shown any concern despite advances in scientific work or genetic diseases. The *Warnock Report* has proposed that this be done for children born through egg and sperm donation. (Report of the Committee of Inquiry into Human Fertilisation and Embryology (Warnock Report) Cmnd 9314 (London, HMSO, 1984)). It is however the confused concept of identity that has been the focus of law makers, social workers and the published work on adoption.

IMPLICATIONS FOR THE CHILDREN OF DONATION

What does this mean for the children of donation? Are they in an analogous position to the children of adoption, or can significant distinctions be drawn? At present it seems that donation is surrounded by the secrecy, anonymity, and stigma, so familiar from the adoption story. As secrecy has been an important aspect of the adoption experience it is likely to be so also the donation experience. Why does secrecy surround donation? Medical ethics require confidentiality in the relationship between doctor and patient. In the case of donation the duty has been interpreted by the Royal College of Gynaecologists as owed both to the donor and to future parents. Concern to protect the privacy of donors was the reason given by physicians in the United States for their failure to keep records of donations.

There is also reason to suspect that donors would not participate in donation if anonymity were not guaranteed. A study of sixty-seven donors in Melbourne showed that half would not participate if their names were available to parents. It seems however that fear of legal complications was one source of desire for anonymity and some donors held softer attitudes towards the children produced. Recent experience in Sweden, where anonymity is no longer promised to donors, supports the hypothesis that donations will be significantly reduced by the legislative creation of rights to know the donor's identity.

Male infertility, the major reason for attempts at conception through artificial insemination by a donor, is a source of shame. Studies show that feelings of masculinity have been damaged by the discovery of infertility. AID parents do not tell. Yet many of those interviewed by Snowden and Mitchell were tormented by the secrecy they had initially so eagerly sought (Snowden and Mitchell '*Artificial family*' Ch 5). The shame men feel because of infertility seems to be related to cultural attitudes, to meanings given to masculinity. A misfortune leads again to stigma.

Marginal status and a failure of placement are also said to be a common feature of adoption and donation. Although the children may suffer a marginal identity because of 'their ignorance about certain key people and events in their lives' (Haimes and Timms (supra) p 50), the parents are marginalized by their failure to conceive. Section 26 is said to be important to the children of adoption, not just in opening the way to secret information, but also by permitting the adoptee to request a public account of the adoption. The idea of an account or public explanation arises from the institution of adoption as legally constituted and sanctioned. Its intrusion makes the state accountable for the transfer of parental rights. Views are influenced by legal structures, and adoption is subjected to the full rigours of legal control. Private adoptions, and private contracts for transfer of parental rights are unenforceable, and illegal (Adoption Act 1976, s 11; Children Act 1975, s 85(2); Guardianship Act 1973, s 1(2)). If the state takes control of donation, as it proposes to do, then a similar accountability will be expected by the children of donation.

The experience of adoption is highly relevant in discussions of the new reproductive technology. What was seen in parliamentary discussions of section 26 as an issue of children's rights versus parents' rights, has become an issue of moral responsibility in terms of power and choice. It is true that power and choice are lacking for all children. The old taunt thrown by child at parent, 'I didn't ask to be born', is indicative of the powerlessness of all, not just the adopted. It is evident that adoptive children do not choose their adoptive parents, in most cases; but neither do they choose their birth parents. Is there some sense in which the fusion of egg and sperm of biological parents is seen as outside their control, whereas the decision to adopt, sanctioned by law, is an exercise of power and choice? But choice is now exercised in the decision to become biological parents. It is odd that adoptive parents or parents by donation should be perceived as more powerful than biological parents. In adoption the process of application, interview, vetting, trial period and supervision before the adoption is granted emphasizes the powerlessness and marginal status of the infertile. State control of the new technology of conception is likely to increase the feelings of powerlessness of parents by donation, who are already subjected to the power of the medical profession.

Secrecy removes power and choice from the adopted. This is made clear in personal histories. It is highly likely to be true also of the children of donation. But secrecy arises from the stigmatizing of infertility and illegitimacy. It serves to preserve certain perceived standards of morality and normality. Perhaps it is these that must change.

It has been suggested that there is an uneasiness about adoption in society as a whole and that it is this which gives rise to stigma (Haimes and Timms (supra) p 81). But the stigma attaches also to infertility. And recent debates suggest great unease in relation to new modes of conception. Therefore, a likely outcome is that the children will be stigmatized. Given this hypothesis, it is hardly surprising that social parents are reticent and secretive.

The general advice given by social workers to AID parents is to tell. Thus Haimes and Timms:

> whether the children have a right to know their genetic origins, possibly at the expense of the adults involved, is a debate that was thoroughly rehearsed prior to the introduction of Section 26. It would seem that Section 26 is the answer. It is difficult to argue a special case for AID. (Ibid.)

We know very little about what AID children feel. There is pressure in the United States and elsewhere for information to be released. In Sweden this has led to legislation. Given the prevailing secrecy and confidentiality of treatment, how many of the 250,000 people alive in the United States estimated to have been conceived after AID know of their status? The corresponding estimate for the United Kingdom is 50,000. Writers have put forward the hypothesis that

> children and adults are likely to suspect something, not just through family interaction but also through basic genetic knowledge. Other temporal and social, as well as physical cues work to confirm their suspicion, but given the lack of publicity of AID until recently, they are far more likely to suspect adoption or even adultery, rather than the truth. (Ibid.)

The prevailing secrecy may set up doubts and insecurities. The awareness of a family secret may place the child of donation in a similar position to the child of adoption in the past. At first glance there seem to be distinctions to be drawn, but on closer inspection these seem less obvious. Is it likely that in future we shall regard telling the children of donation in the same light as we now regard telling the children of adoption? Or are the distinctions sufficiently great to put donation in a different light? In order to probe this, two aspects demand further thought. The first is the reasons why genetic parentage is of interest to children. The second is social attitudes to donation.

In its exclusive concentration on psychological needs the literature on 'the search for origins' overlooks the practical reasons why their genetic parentage is of interest to children. A major practical interest is medical and genetic history. It is not too far-fetched to suggest that a reason why more adopted women than men go in search of their origins is that women's particular closeness to family medical history raises these issues in an immediate way. There is also evidence to show that it is at the stage of the life cycle when considering founding a family of one's own that interest is highest. Thus Philip Whitehead, an adopted child, stated in the parliamentary debate on section 26 that the adopted child

> wishes to know who and what he is. This is true as he approaches marriage … It is at such moments that a person wishes to know all the relevant facts and data about his past. (Official Report, House of Commons, Hansard, vol 893, col 1901 (20 June 1975) on the Children Bill.)

Furthermore, as Yoxen points out, the risks of genetic diseases, and of consanguineous marriage, do exist. Medical advances have enabled the identification of particular genes. Where these carry genetic disease parents should be informed. These are arguments for 'quality control' of donors (Yoxen, *'Unnatural Selection?'* p 29), but they are also directed at openness about genetic origins. This makes it all the more curious that the medical profession should encourage secrecy …

ATTITUDES TO DONATION

The *Feversham Committee Report* of 1960 on artificial insemination by donor took the view that 'the role of donor is of such a kind that it is liable to appeal to the abnormal and the unbalanced' (Report of the Departmental Committee on Human Artificial Insemination, Cmnd 1105 (London: HMSO, 1960)). And the medical establishment's view is that anonymity of donors must be retained, for those who do not object to being identified are seen as psychologically suspect (Haimes and Timms 'Adoption' p 97). From the donor's point of view there are several good reasons for wanting guaranteed anonymity. These have arisen in part from legal structures which are slow to adapt to donation. Thus while the AID child was illegitimate at law, the genetic father had , in theory, the duties to the child of an illegitimate father, that is, of financial support. The child could have claimed against the donor's estate on his death (Under the Inheritance (Provision for Family and Dependents) Act 1975). Hence the recent change to remove all liabilities from the donor (Family Law Reform Act 1987, s 27).

Cultural attitudes raise other issues. There is no evidence that donors are stigmatized, but they do seem to share the general public unease about displaced children. The French example is of some interest here. The state controls a nationally co-ordinated network of AID centres. Donors are unpaid and are encouraged to see their donation as a gift to meet the needs of infertile couples. Only married donors are accepted and the gift is represented as being from the 'donor couple' to the 'recipient couple'. It is the cultural significance attached to the act which is of interest. The organizers intend to create 'a new social understanding' (Yoxen (supra) p 29) of AID, as a social duty, a charity to others, something to be valued by those involved. Desirable thought it may be to give a positive social meaning to donation, the French example also represents 'a pervasive system of moral control' (ibid. p 30) over AID.

No doubt cultural attitudes elsewhere could change. But would this cultural change lie in the direction of saying that egg and sperm donation are analogous to blood donation? The consequences of such a view might be that genetic parentage would not be considered important and the notion of a search for origins bizarre. Or would the cultural change lie in the direction of genetic parents identifying themselves without difficulty to their genetic offspring? The latter direction seems unlikely. Relationships are the result of social interaction, and not of blood. But if openness is a social goal then the cultural meaning of parenthood must change to give full recognition to those who care for children and are psychological parents. At the same time the stigmatizing of adoptive and other 'different' children must cease …

CONCLUSION

The trouble with the concept of the need to know one's origins in the context of parentage is that it is an imprecise concept which is socially constructed. The imprecision of the concept has already been discussed and it has been suggested that it be broken down further into psychological, medical, and legal aspects. The assertion that the notion of need is socially constructed does not represent a denial that it may be experienced in a profound sense by adopted and other persons. But it does arise partially from the cultural significance attached to the blood tie. By this is meant that 'the psychological need to feel whole' through identification of genetic parents arises from the value placed on such blood relationship. This value is made up of self-interest, pride, love. But it also is reflected in and reflects the legal structures surrounding parent and child relationships.

In most cases genetic parentage and social parentage are united. Legal rights and duties of parents are designed to cover that situation. But where genetic and social parentage are separated, or where both genetic and social fathers are missing or unknown, law and social attitudes stigmatize those children conceived in a different pattern from the majority. Removing the stigma might ensure that some of the secrecy and tension surrounding these matters is dispelled.

O'Donovan refers to the effect removing donor anonymity would have on the supply of semen for donation – there is, it is said, a risk it will dry up. This is an important point and if a correct empirical assertion, one that could not lightly be disregarded by policy makers. You will have noticed in the earlier piece by Jonathan Glover reference to the law in Sweden – the Swedish Insemination Act 1984 – which since 1984 has given children born as a result of donor insemination the right to seek out the identity of the donor on reaching maturity. Other countries have followed suit, for example, Victoria, Australia (Infertility Treatment Act 1995, ss 79–80) and in New Zealand where, without legislation, it has become culturally expected that such information will be available and, it has been reported, that most clinics will not accept donors unless they agree to allow their identity to be available (see K Daniels 'The Semen Providers' in Daniels and Haimes (eds) *Donor Insemination – International Social Science Perspectives* (1998) p 77).

The Swedish system has been the subject of much empirical study (see eg K Daniels 'The Swedish Insemination Act and its Impact' (1994) 34 New Zealand J of Obstetrics and Gynaecology 437 and K Daniels and O Lagos 'The Swedish Insemination Act and the Availability of Donors' (1994) 10 Human Reproduction 1871). In a recent project Daniels and colleagues carried out a study of the attitudes of male donors at a donor insemination clinic in Malmo, Sweden. In the course of reporting their study, the authors discuss the background to the Swedish law.

K R Daniels, H L Ericsson and I P Burn 'The Views of Semen Donors Regarding the Swedish Insemination Act 1984' (1998) 3 Med Law Int 117

Traditionally, semen donors have been completely anonymous, the doctor or clinic often destroying information about the donor upon the birth of the child so that there is no possibility of the donor and the recipient couple, or the offspring coming into contact with each other. Couples have also traditionally been counselled not to inform the offspring about his or her DI conception. A number of the reasons for both these forms of secrecy have been suggested.

First, secrecy has been necessary to protect the offspring from social and psychological trauma, resulting from the stigma associated with DI, and from the frustration of not being able to contact the donor if they are told about his existence. Second, secrecy has been necessary to protect the couple, and particularly the infertile husband, from the stigma of infertility. Couples may also fear that offspring, if told about their DI conception, will reject the father. Third, secrecy has been necessary to protect the donor from legal liability for the offspring, and from the possible disruption to the donors own family if the offspring were to seek to contact him. Fourth, secrecy has been seen as a way of protecting the members of the medical profession who provide this service. Some aspects of DI, notably sperm banking, are quite profitable particularly in the USA, and the removal of secrecy from DI may reduce this profitability. Also, some medical professionals prefer secrecy as they fear adverse public reaction to their being identified as providers of a service which is seen by many as being less than respectable. Finally, secrecy about DI is seen to protect the ideal of 'family', and the importance of the rights of families to privacy in these matters.

There are, however, many problems associated with this secrecy and the resulting complete separation that it entails between the donor, and the recipient couple or the offspring. First, it denies the offspring the right to information about their genetic background. This is important both psychosocially and medically. Psychosocially, research in adoption has indicated the importance for offspring of having the ability to have access to information about their genetic parents even if the majority of offspring choose not to exercise the right. There can be seen to be important parallels between adoption and DI in this regard. There are also medical benefits associated with offspring being able to contact the donor in that, potentially, the donor could be the best person to provide, for example, a bone marrow transplant for the offspring. Second, secrecy can have a negative impact on family relations in that keeping the secret can be a psychological burden on the couple. It may also force the parents to lie to or at least deceive the offspring, and this is likely to have an impact on the level of trust between the family members. Even if parents do not tell their offspring, the latter may find out, by accident, about their conception. The consequences of this may be quite devastating. Third, secrecy may reinforce the negative attitudes to DI held by many in the community, and increase the stigma of infertility. Greater openness about both infertility and DI could lead to greater awareness of these issues, and potentially to a reduction in the associated stigma, and to an increase in public sympathy for the suffering of the infertile. Fourth, secrecy frustrates the desires of donors for more access to information about the offspring. Finally, secrecy creates an environment in which it is difficult for health and welfare professionals to obtain information about infertility issues and to train to respond to the needs of the infertile. Consequently, the level of service they are able to provide is compromised.

The question of how to regulate DI in Sweden was first considered by a Government Commission in the late 1940s and early 1950s. However, the report of this Commission was not acted upon at the time. In 1981, partly in response to the lack of regulation in the area, an Insemination Committee (IC) was formed by the Swedish parliament. Lack of regulation had led to the situation, such as that in 1983, when the court ruled, in a divorce proceeding, that a husband did not have to pay support for a DI offspring conceived by his former wife, on the grounds that the child was not biologically his.

The brief of the IC was not, however, just to make recommendations in regard to issues of the paternity of the DI offspring, but also to consider IVF, the rights of the unborn, situations in which pregnant women drink heavily, and foetal diagnosis. However, in regard to DI, it recommended that a man who has consented to his wife or partner receiving DI should become the legal father of, and be responsible for, any resulting offspring from the moment that the insemination takes place. Of greater importance, in relation to this research, are the recommendations made by the IC in regard to the offspring's rights to know about their DI conception and their rights of access to information about the donor. The IC recommended that parents should be open with the child about its DI origins and should seek to tell the child of this at the earliest possible opportunity. It also recommended that doctors should try to make prospective parents aware of the importance of being open with the child in this matter. These recommendations gained the support of the Swedish parliament, were passed into law, and came into effect in 1985.

The question of whether DI offspring should have access to the identity of the donor was heavily debated at the time the IC was considering this issue. The authorities and organisations consulted were roughly equally divided for and against anonymity, although nearly all the medical authorities consulted were in favour of anonymity. Those who favoured anonymity argued that its removal would lead to a decrease in the number of donors, and consequently couples seeking DI would be forced either to undertake it outside of the protection of the state system or to go abroad to be treated. Arguments were also made regarding the effect that a restriction on the import of semen from abroad without the approval of the National Board of Health and Welfare would have on the supply of donors. It was argued that this provision would restrict the availability of semen for people from minority ethnic groups, for whom there was a shortage of donors from within Sweden, despite the fact that the legislation specifically allowed for the import of semen in such situations. It was also argued that telling offspring about their DI conception might cause them to suffer considerable psychic conflict as a result of having 'two fathers'. This argument is used by the French Sperm Bank Federation, CECOS, as justification for its policy of anonymity. Similarly, it has been argued that making information available to offspring which will allow them to contact the donor, enables a potentially conflictual situation to arise. Consequently, the legislation in question is not taking the rights of the donor seriously enough.

Arguments opposing anonymity were primarily concerned with the rights of offspring to information about their genetic background. Other arguments were also made concerning the potentially negative consequences of offspring learning about the nature of their conception other than by being told directly by their parents. Offspring may feel that since their parents have deceived them about something as basic as their conception then they can no longer trust them in a variety of other matters. In response to this, those in favour of anonymity noted that in Sweden approximately 10% of all children are offspring not of their mothers husband, as indicated by their birth records, but of someone else. Those opposed to anonymity did not consider this necessarily to be a desirable state of affairs and consequently did not consider it to be a good reason for anonymity in relation to DI. It was also noted that, in order to protect the donor, legislation required that information could only be divulged to the offspring upon reaching maturity and not to the parents, or any third party.

As discussed earlier DI, and other infertility treatments involving gamete donation, are unique in that they exist at the interface of welfare, medical and legal areas of concern. The reluctance of some doctors to co-operate with the new legislation can be seen partially as a rejection by them of welfare and legal approaches to this issue, and partially as a reluctance by them to cede control of this area to professionals operating out of different frameworks.

The study sheds some light on the impact of removing donor anonymity on the supply of semen. The researchers gave questionnaires to 52 current and past semen donors (who had reached the maximum number of permitted resulting pregnancies). Forty-three questionnaires were returned, giving a response rate of 83%. The results were as follows (*op cit* at pp 119–123):

RESULTS

Demographic Characteristics
Table 1 shows that the 43 respondents in the study were between 21 and 53 years of age, and that 63% of them were married or living in permanent relationships. Previous donors were on average 2 years older than current donors. Sixty-seven per cent of donors had contributed to non-DI conceptions, and 30% intended to have children, or more children, while 35% did not. Donors were spread across a range of occupations; 53% being in professional/managerial/technical positions and 12% being students. Fifty-eight per cent of the respondents stated that they had no religion and 37% indicated some form of Christian belief.

TABLE 1
Demographics

Age		
Mean	37.4	
Range	21–53	
Median	37	
Occupation	No	%
Professional/managerial/technical/admin.	23	53
Service and sales	10	23
Student	5	12
Other, eg production, clerk	3	7
Unemployed	2	5
Marital status		
Married	15	35
Live together	12	28

Single in steady relationship	7	16
Single	5	12
Engaged	3	7
Previously married/lived tog.	17	40

Contributed to Non-DI conceptions?

Yes	29	67
No	14	33

Do you intend to have children or further children?	N	%
Yes	13	30
No	15	35
Unsure/No Answer	15	35
Religion		
None	25	58
Protestant	12	28
Roman Catholic	4	9
Nominal only	2	5
Other	2	5

The Swedish Law on Artificial Insemination
Donors were asked an open ended question about their attitude towards the Swedish law on artificial insemination which, as stated previously, gives donor offspring the right to know the identity of their biological father upon maturity. Thirty-three per cent of donors approved of the law and an additional 21% believed that everyone had the right to know their father, or that all who asked about their biological father should be told. This brings the total of donors who agreed with the law's position on identification to 54%, as compared to the 14% who disagreed with the law or thought that it was wrong. The remaining 12% had some doubts or concerns. Further comments in relation to this issue came from a small percentage of donors (5%) who believed that the law helped to *create the need* to know the biological parent, and a similar percentage who believed that only non-identifying information should be made available. Twenty-three per cent of donors gave responses which were not directly relevant to the question and 9% did not answer. Others answered this question in more than one way.

Donors were specifically asked whether they should have the right to remain anonymous. Forty-four per cent thought that they should, 30% disagreed and 26% were unsure. When asked to comment upon this the donors responded giving the reasons outlined in Table 2. These responses show a variety of opinions about the positive and negative aspects of anonymity and openness for donors, recipient couples and offspring.

Donors were also asked about their understanding of the changes to the law. They were asked if they thought that the husband or partner of the woman who received their donation was the legal father of the resulting child. Ninety-three per cent correctly answered 'yes', 1 donor (2%) answered 'no', and 2 donors (5%) were unsure. Donors were also asked what was their understanding of their legal rights and responsibilities to the child. Forty-nine per cent responded correctly that they had no rights and responsibilities and 12% noted, again correctly, that the child could learn their identity and meet them upon maturity. Thirty per cent were unsure of their rights or responsibilities.

Future contact with Offspring
When asked how they would feel if traced by their offspring 46% of donors said that they would be happy to meet them, or that their feelings would be positive ones of curiosity or surprise. Sixteen per cent of donors said that they were unsure about how they would feel about meeting their offspring, and 7% said they would not be happy to do so. One donor gave no answer.

TABLE 2

Donor comments on their right to anonymity

	No	%
No Comment	15	35
Everyone should have the right to know their biological father	6	14
Anonymity benefits the donor	5	12
Child already has a mother and father	3	7
If child learns of their DI conception they should have the right to know their father	2	5
It could be disturbing for the child to find out about DI or about their biological father	2	5
No need for anonymity	2	5
Should depend on each case and be up to the donor	2	5

*More than one response possible

The remaining 19% of donors mentioned only the types of feelings, or the concerns they thought they might have, upon meeting their offspring. These, however, were not the only donors to make comments of this nature. A list of the wide range of feelings and concerns that donors thought they would experience is presented in Table 3.

Donors were also asked what they thought about the secrecy surrounding DI. Twenty-one per cent responded that the situation was 'OK as it is', 12% were more obviously approving of secrecy in commenting that it was appropriate, or that it served to avoid embarrassment or liability for children. Nine per cent made comments about specific types of secrecy in DI, and five per cent thought that it would be better if there were less secrecy. Fifty-three per cent of respondents did not answer this question.

Donors were informed that it is now the practice of adoption agencies that children should be told of their adoption. Donors were asked if they thought that this also applied to DI. Twenty-eight per cent of the donors thought, that it did, 40% disagreed and 35% were unsure. In commenting on this; 26% of donors said that they thought it was up to the parents; 12% said that disclosure may disrupt the child or the family's life; 9% said that the offspring should be told only if they suspect or need to know, and 7% each said that every child had a right to know their father, that there were issues of medical information or consanguinity, and that DI and adoption are different.

TABLE 3

Donors feelings about being traced by their offspring

	No	%
Happy to meet them/positive/curious/surprised	24	56
Unhappy/don't want to meet them	3	7
Unsure	7	16
Mentioned that they had no fatherly feelings or that offspring already had fathers	5	12
Depends on what child is like	3	7
Mixed feelings, strong feelings: bewilderment, stress, pride	3	7
Feel nothing/would take it well and be calm	2	5
Would want to know how parents felt about it	1	2
Worried and responsible if things had not gone well for child	1	2

'I already think ahead to what I would say at that very important moment'	1	2
Honesty is better than lies	1	2
Wouldn't mind, but wife does not like the possibility	1	2
No answer	1	2

*More than one response was possible

Commenting on their results, the authors make the following observations (at pp 127–132)

The demographics and responses of the donors in this study lend support to the conclusion that donors now come from a variety of backgrounds (Table 1), tend to be older (median age, 37), have contributed to non-DI conceptions (67%) and have had contact with people who are infertile (19%), or are donating out of a desire to help infertile couples (53%).

It is also of note, in assessing the characteristics and attitudes of donors in this study, that while a considerable number of them (44%) thought that they should have the right to remain anonymous, that this figure is considerably lower than the percentages of donors answering similar questions to this effect in studies in other countries (Rowland R (1984), Lansac (1993) and Neilson A F, Pederson B and Lauritsen J G (1995) 'Psychological aspects of donor insemination. Attitudes and opinions of Danish and Swedish donor insemination patients to psychosocial information being supplied to offspring and relatives' Acta Obstetrica Et Gynecologica Scandanavia 74 45–50). The percentage of donors answering similar questions in this way ranged from 100% in Belgium to 63% in the UK. While these differences may partly be due to differences in the ways in which the questions were asked, they do seem to indicate that the Swedish donors are less concerned with anonymity than donors in other studies. A possible explanation for this is that the Swedish legislation has created an environment for semen donation which is not so attractive to donors for whom anonymity is important.

There is a discrepancy between the 54% of donors who said that they supported the law and the 30% of donors who said that they did not think donors should have a right to anonymity. Part of this discrepancy may be due to the fact that anonymity is not a simple concept. Experts arguing for either secrecy or openness in regard to anonymity are often talking about different things. Joyce, in trying to alleviate some of the misunderstanding in these arguments, outlined four degrees of openness in DI families:

(1) The fact of DI may be shared with chosen members of the family or close friends, (2) the fact of DI may be shared with the child, (3) the fact of DI may be shared with society in general, and (4) the identity of the donor may be made known to the DI child, and perhaps, to the family (Joyce D N (1984) 'The implications of greater openness concerning AID', in 'AID and After: papers from BAAF, BASW and a Scottish Working Party, London').

The type of anonymity that was probably in the mind of the donors when they answered the questions in this study is the fourth option about the child, and possibly the family gaining access to the donor's identity (although the law only allows the offspring to gain access to information about the donor). This point is backed up by the publicity given to this type of anonymity during the passage of the Law on Artificial Insemination prior to it coming into force in 1985. Out study indicated that 30% of the donors were unsure of their rights or responsibilities under the 1984 legislation. This may mean that they are thinking of different definitions of anonymity than the type of anonymity which is denied by the Swedish law. If all the donors were clear in their understanding of the situation then there may have been less of a discrepancy between those who supported the law and those who did not think donors had a right to anonymity. An example of donors making a distinction between different types of anonymity is noted in an Australian study by Rowland (Rowland R (1984) *supra*). Donors in this study drew a distinction between a situation where the names of donors would be available to offspring by mutual consent, and a situation where their names would be handed out automatically to parents. Rowland also noted that the way questions about anonymity issued were worded could effect the answers that donors gave. Donors in this current study may consequently have responded positively to the question about rights, without connecting this to their earlier response about the law.

Another reason for the discrepancy may be that donors consider that few offspring will seek to trace donors, few couples will tell their offspring about their DI conception. In other words, in Joyce's terms, they may believe that the fourth degree of openness will not occur because the second degree of openness has not. Donors may have associated the idea that they are unlikely to be contacted by offspring with their having a right to anonymity. While this association may not be particularly logical, in issues as complex as this where feelings and assumptions about such things as genetic linkage are difficult to articulate, it is easy for thinking to become confused. If donors are making such an association between the likelihood of their being contacted and their right to anonymity, this would perhaps explain some of the discrepancy between their being in favour of the law which makes their identification possible, while also believing that they have a right to anonymity.

Further, it is interesting to note the difference between the 41% of current donors and 19% of previous donors who did not think that they had a right to anonymity. It would be instructive to undertake research on the opinions of donors about anonymity over a longer time period than was possible with this study. Such research could ascertain whether the increase in donors who do not regard anonymity as a right continues as time passes, and donors become more accustomed to the operation of the legislation.

The passage of the 1984 legislation has probably led to many infertile couples who did not wish to either tell their offspring about their DI conception, or did not wish their offspring to have access to information about the donor, either to inseminate themselves, or possibly receive insemination illegally from a sympathetic doctor, or to go to another country to receive DI. In one Danish clinic Swedish couples made up 39% of the couples who received DI between 1983 and 1992 (Neilson A F et al (1995) supra), while in a Finnish clinic couples from Sweden made up an estimated 50% of those receiving DI. This latter course of action is perfectly legal and Swedish citizens are respected in this matter.

There are, however, policy implications for such actions, in that couples undertaking DI informally within Sweden, or those going to other countries for treatment, may not receive the level of counselling assessment that those using the Swedish system are required to undergo. Further, these couples will probably not be subject to the same degree of rigour in the screening of donors and semen as is possible in the state system. Consequently, in making DI available only to couples under the condition of donor identifiability, the legislation may have increased the psychosocial and medical risks involved in DI for those who seek to avoid its measures and consequently may have increased both the number of families who are not properly prepared for the difficulties of having a DI offspring, and the number of children born with otherwise avoidable hereditary medical conditions.

Swedish welfare services will, however, have to resolve the issue of the extent of their involvement in helping interested DI offspring find the relevant donor, and consider the ways in which they will respond to any potential conflicts between the donor and the offspring. The first offspring eligible to seek information will come forward in approximately 2004 as the legislation effectively places the age of 'maturity' at 18. Prior to this, there will be other issues to deal with in relation to training staff to counsel and work with families who are having difficulties in telling their offspring about the DI conception, or where the offspring has learnt about their conception accidentally. They may also have to respond to the needs of offspring who were conceived outside of the state system, who now know about their DI conception, and who also know that their parents, chose to forego a system which would have allowed them relatively straightforward access to information about the donor if they so desired it. It is difficult to know how various offspring will respond to these situations. The little information from adult offspring that there is, is of an anecdotal nature and tends to infer that the way in which offspring are told or come to hear about their conception, and the way in which they have been brought up, impacts on the way in which they respond to being conceived by DI, and the attitude they have towards the donor; if they can find him ...

CONCLUSION

A slight majority of donors in this study were in favour of the Swedish law and its provisions about anonymity, and only a small minority were opposed to it. However, a much larger minority of donors were of the opinion that donors should have a right to be anonymous. This discrepancy is perhaps explicable in terms of the wide variety of meanings that are attached to 'anonymity', the way the two questions were worded, and by the fact that nearly a third were unsure of their rights and responsibilities with regard to DI offspring. The majority of donors who commented on the secrecy surrounding DI in Sweden were satisfied with the situation as it was, although there was a sizeable minority who thought there should be more secrecy.

Donors in Sweden were less concerned with the right to anonymity than donors in many other countries around the world. This would seem to indicate that the Swedish legislation is attracting men with different types of attitudes to anonymity than are donating in other parts of the world. The legislation has not resulted in an ongoing decrease in the number of men who are willing to donate semen, and there is, in fact, evidence that there has instead been an increase in the number of men donating.

The 1984 legislation has, however, encountered considerable opposition from the medical professional, and there is evidence that initial decreases in the number of donors in Sweden after the law was changed may, partially, have been due to doctors refusing to recruit donors under the new legislation. There is also evidence that many infertile couples rather than use DI under the Swedish legislation, have chosen to undertake this procedure in neighbouring countries, thereby circumventing the possibility that offspring will be able to access identifying information about the donor upon maturity and subsequently contact him. The implications of this development for these DI families and for welfare services in Sweden may be considerable in years to come.

There may well be some lessons here for us about the change of profile of donors if anonymity is removed, the question of whether couples undergoing infertility treatment will welcome such a change in the law, the importance of a positive professional response in any new legislative climate and, finally, the issue of 'openness' between parents and children about the latter's origins (see also Rumball and Adair 'Telling the Story: Parents' Scripts for Donor Offspring' (1994) 14 Human Reproduction 1329 – 30% of respondents in a New Zealand survey had given their children such information).

Any regulations made under the 1990 Act (s 45) would have to be formulated consistently with the European Convention of Human Rights. There are probably *three* possibilities: (1) no access to donor identity (no change in the law); (2) access to donor identity with the donor's consent; and (3) access to donor identity regardless of the donor's wishes. At least for the present, options (2) and (3) could not be retrospective (s 31(5)).

How would the European Convention apply? The most relevant provision is art 8, which provides as follows:

Article 8

Right to respect for private and family life

1. Everyone has the right to respect for his private and family life, his home and his correspondence.

2. There shall be no interference by a public authority with the exercise of this right except such as is in accordance with the law and is necessary in a democratic society in the interests of national security, public safety or the economic well-being of the country, for the prevention of disorder or crime, for the protection of health or morals, or for the protection of the rights and freedoms of others.

Could a child born as a result of donated gametes or an embryo argue that a prohibition on obtaining the identity of a donor infringed their right to 'private and family life'? There is no clear jurisprudence upon this in the European Court. However, an individual's 'personal identity' is a matter protected by art 8 (see eg *B v France* (1992) 16 EHRR 1 (ECtHR) and *Burghartz v Switzerland* (1994) 18 EHRR 101 (ECtHR)). It is dangerous to 'lift' phrases out of judgments of the European Court of Human Rights and translate them into contexts unrelated to the facts of that particular case. Nevertheless, the court has observed that '[r]espect for private life must also comprise to a certain degree the right to establish and develop relationships with other human beings' (*Dudgeon v UK* (1981) 4 EHRR 149 at para 29). *A fortiori*, a relationship with a genetic parent. Likewise, the opportunity for, and the establishment of, a relationship with a genetic parent may be an aspect of the right to 'family life' (*Anderson v Sweden*) (1992) 14 EHRR 615, para 72). In *U v W (A-G intervening)* (1997) 38 BMLR 54, Wilson J had this to say in relation to the application of art 8 (at 73):

Wilson J: The argument is that the exclusion of the respondent from non-genetic paternity is an infringement of the right of the boys to respect for their family life.

In *Marckx v Belgium* (1979) 2 EHRR 330 at 342 (para 31) the European Court of Human Rights said:

The object of the Article is "essentially" that of protecting the individual against arbitrary interference by the public authorities. Nevertheless, it does not merely compel the State to abstain from such interference: in addition to the primarily negative undertaking, there may be positive obligations inherent in an effective "respect" for family life. This means, amongst other things, that when the State determines in its domestic legal system the regime applicable to certain family ties such as those between an unmarried mother and her child, it must act in a matter calculated to allow those concerned to lead a normal family life.

There is no doubt that the Court of Human Rights has given a wide construction to the notion of the family in art 8. It covers the relationship between the genetic father and this child, even where he is not married to the mother and ceased to cohabit with her prior to the birth: *Keegan v Ireland* (1994) 18 EHRR 342. It also covers some non-genetic relationships, obviously including the child's relationship with his adoptive father or stepfather ... Nevertheless, [counsel for the applicant] has failed to persuade me ...There is no genetic link and there has never been any de facto relationship between the respondent and the boys ...

He saw a 'genetic link' or a 'de facto relationship' as a necessary trigger to the application of art 8. Thus, there is every reason to believe that a restriction on access to identifying information about a donor would amount to an infringement of art 8(1). The crucial issue, we would suggest, is whether a total prohibition, or a limited prohibition allowing access only with the donor's consent, can be justified under art 8(2). Such a restriction must be: (1) in accordance with the law; (2) for a legitimate purpose set out in art 8(2); and (3) 'proportionate' (see *supra*, ch 1). There is no difficulty with the first requirement in this context. As regards the legitimate purpose, it could be argued that the rights of the donor himself to his 'private and family life' are at stake and thus the restriction would fall within the phrase 'for the protection of the rights and freedoms of others' in art 8(2).

On the face of it, this looks correct. However, the donor's rights would not be infringed if he agreed to his identity being disclosed. Thus, a legislative scheme – such as option (2) above – whereby the donor must consent to disclosure could not be incompatible with the Convention. His rights would be respected and so would the child's under art 8, providing only donors who consented to disclosure were allowed to donate. Consent at the time of donation would be the crucial requirement which would be irrevocable after the treatment had taken place. To disallow a change of heart by the donor subsequent to donation, would be a justified restriction on the donor's right under art 8 given the child's right, providing the original consent was freely given and the donor was fully counselled about the implications for him of donating. A scheme which allowed a donor to 'opt out' of disclosure but still donate would arguably be contrary to art 14 by unjustifiably discriminating against some children in their art 8 right on the ground of their 'social origin' or 'other status'.

If, however, the legislative scheme contemplated disclosure even without the donor's consent (option (3)), it would be much harder to justify under art 8(2). It would override a donor's rights when they could be respected, at least in a prospective scheme, by requiring donor consent at the time of donation. Retrospective disclosure of a donor's identity, when donation has taken place *in an expectation of anonymity*, seems doomed to fall foul of the Convention unless the donor's consent *at the time of disclosure* is sought and obtained. In this instance, the donor's right to his 'private and family life' is particularly strong.

What, then, about maintaining the status quo *prohibiting* access to the donor's identity in any circumstances? What justification under art 8(2) could be made? Clearly, the rights of the donor again come into play. Here, probably, such a blanket ban would not be a proportionate response because of the possibility of a 'donor consent' scheme. It could also be argued that the 'rights of others' could include those of infertile couples either under art 8 itself, or 'to found a family' under art 12. Article 12 may not necessarily apply (the right being a single right to marry *and* found a family). Whether reliant on art 8 or 12, the argument would have to be premised on the fact that to remove the blanket ban would affect the supply of donor sperm and thereby deprive others of the opportunity to found a family. Even if empirically demonstrable, and that may be difficult, it is doubtful whether the rights of unidentified 'others' in society such as infertile couples in general could properly justify overriding the rights of particular children to 'know their genetic origins'.

In the result, the most likely Convention-compliant regulations would be ones that allowed access to a donor's identity with his consent given either at the time of donation (in the case of prospective legislation) or at the proposed time of disclosure (if retrospective effect as with adoption were contemplated).

Recent legislation in Victoria – the Infertility Treatment Act 1995 – has permitted a child (on reaching 18) to obtain access to information about a donor, including identifying information. Sections 79–80 provide as follows:

79. Application by person born as a result of a donor treatment procedure or descendant for information about donor

(1) A person who is or may have been born as the result of a donor treatment procedure or who is the descendant of such a person may, on attaining the age of 18 years, apply to the Authority for information required to be recorded in the central register about a donor whose gametes were used in the procedure or whose gametes were used to form a zygote or embryo used in the procedure, being either or both of the following –
(a)   information about the donor (other than information from which the donor will or may be identified);
(b) information which will or may identify the donor.
(2) An application under this section must –
(a)   be in writing; and
(b)   be in the prescribed form and accompanied by the prescribed fee.

80. Authority to give information about donor to person born as the result of a procedure

(1) On receiving an application for information under section 79(1)(a) the Authority must give, in writing, any such information recorded in the central register to the applicant, if the Authority is satisfied that the applicant has been offered counselling about the potential consequences of the disclosure of that information from a counsellor who has been approved under Part 8 to give counselling to persons applying for information under section 79.
(2) On receiving an application for information under section 79(1)(b), the Authority must –
(a)   give, in writing, any such information recorded in the central register to the applicant if it is satisfied that the applicant has received counselling about the potential consequences of the disclosure of the information from a counsellor who has been approved under Part 8 to give counselling to persons applying for information under section 79; and
(b)   prior to the giving of the information make reasonable efforts –
(i)   to advise the donor that the information is about to be given; and
(ii)   to advise the donor that he or she may need counselling and provide the donor with the names of counsellors approved under Part 8 to give counselling to persons in respect of whom applications have been made under section 79.

The legislation, in general, requires that the child should undergo counselling and imposes a duty on the Infertility Treatment Authority to advise the donor that the information is to be given. The donor's consent to disclosure is not, however, required. The provision is only prospective. Where the donation preceded the commencement of the Act, the donor's identity may only be given with his consent (s 184(4) and (5)). In essence, the Victorian scheme follows the one we suggest would be most likely to be compliant with the European Convention. Retrospective disclosure is only permitted with the donor's consent. Whilst consent is not formally required for prospective cases, all donors know the situation and presumably would not continue to donate if they did not agree to disclosure of their identity in the future. Undoubtedly, explicit consent at the time of donation would be preferable.

Two final points: first, you will see that the right in s 79 of the Victorian Act also applies to a 'descendant' of a child born by assisted reproductive techniques. No provision is made for this in the UK in the 1990 Act. It may be just as important for the child of someone born by AI or IVF techniques to know the identity of the donor as it is for the actual person so born. In many instances this will not matter;

the individual who was born may already have discovered the information and can pass it on. Alternatively, he may be willing to do so in order to satisfy the curiosity of his own child. But this will not always be so where, for example, that individual is already dead or is unwilling to make an application or his child is unwilling to approach his parent to make an application. Arguably, whatever 'right to know' the person born has should also be seen as a right of each of his descendants, at least direct descendants, who have just as strong an interest in knowing who their grandparents, great-grandparents etc were. Here, of course, the interests of the donor may be less significant as time will have passed and he (or she) may even be dead.

Secondly, the Victorian legislation also vests a 'right' in the donor to obtain information about the child including its identity providing in the latter instance the child (if over 18) or the parents consent to disclosure (ss 76 and 77). The Act also allows parents to obtain information about the donor prior to, and following, treatment including identifying information if he consents (ss 71–72 and 74–75). There are also provisions allowing donors to obtain information about the use of his gametes and the treated couple, including their identity with their agreement (ss 72–73) which we discuss below.

(ii) SECTION 32

The Registrar General may request information from the HFEA in fulfilling his statutory functions:

Information to be provided to Registrar General
32. (1) This section applies where a claim is made before the Registrar General that a man is or is not the father of a child and it is necessary or desirable for the purpose of any function of the Registrar General to determine whether the claim is or may be well-founded.
(2) The authority shall comply with any request made by the Registrar General by notice to the Authority to disclose whether any information on the register kept in pursuance of section 31 of this Act tends to show that the man may be the father of the child by virtue of section 28 of this Act and, if it does, disclose that information.

(iii) SECTION 34

A court may require the HFEA to disclose information (excluding that relating to any donor) where a dispute over parentage arises:

Disclosure in interests of justice
34. (1) Where in any proceedings before a court the question of whether a person is or is not the parent of a child by virtue of sections 27 to 29 of this Act falls to be determined, the court may on the application of any party to the proceedings make an order requiring the Authority –
(a) to disclose whether or not any information relevant to that question is contained in the register kept in pursuance of section 31 of this Act, and
(c) if it is, to disclose so much of it as is specified in the order, but such an order may not require the Authority to disclose any information falling within section 31(2)(b) of this Act.
(2) The court must not make an order under subsection (1) above unless it is satisfied that the interest of justice requires it to do so, taking into account –
(a) any representations made by any individual who may be affected by the disclosure, and
(c) the welfare of the child, if under 18 years old, and of any other person under that age who may be affected by the disclosure.
(3) If the proceedings before the court are civil proceedings, it –
(a) may direct that the whole or any part of the proceedings on the application for an order under subsection (2) above shall be heard in camera, and
(c) if it makes such an order, may then or later direct that the whole or any part of any later stage of the proceedings shall be heard in camera.
(4) An application for a direction under subsection (3) above shall be heard in camera unless the court otherwise directs.

(iv) SECTION 35

A court may require the HFEA to disclose the identity of a donor when a child wishes to bring a claim for injury caused before the birth under s 1 of the Congenital Disabilities (Civil Liability) Act 1976. The section seems to contemplate the situation where, for example, the proposed action will be against the donor for *his* negligence and, of course, the donor's identity is necessary to begin the action.

> **Disclosure in interests of justice: congenital disabilities, etc.**
> 35. (1) Where for the purposes of instituting proceedings under section 1 of the Congenital Disabilities (Civil Liability) Act 1976 (civil liability to child born disabled) it is necessary to identify a person who would or might be the parent of a child but for sections 27 to 29 of this Act, the court may, on the application of the child, make an order requiring the Authority to disclose any information contained in the register kept in pursuance of section 31 of this Act identifying that person …
> (3) Subsections (2) to (4) of Section 34 of this Act apply for the purposes of this section as they apply for the purposes of that.

(v) DATA PROTECTION ACT 1998

We have already discussed the application of the Data Protection Act 1998 (see *supra*, ch 7). It applies to the computerised records of HFEA, s 35A of the Data Protection Act 1984 prevented access by a child to information concerning their origins unless that information may be obtained under s 31 of the 1990 Act. The 1998 Act does not contain a similar exemption. However, the Data Protection (Miscellaneous Subject Access Exemptions) Order 2000 , (SI 2000 No 419) made under s 38(1) of the 1998 Act, excludes access to all information covered by s 31(2) of the 1990 Act. Unlike the previous exemptions, therefore, it covers not only access to information about any child born, but also information about treatment services for identifiable individuals and about donors of gametes or embryos.

(b) Information held by the licence-holder

The licence-holder would, in principle, have to comply with a request for access under the Data Protection Act 1998 (if he is a health professional). We discussed these statutory provisions in Chapter 7.

As regards the DPA 1998, we have already seen the limitation imposed in The Data Protection (Miscellaneous Subject Access Exemptions) Order 2000, (SI 2000 No 419). The Access to Health Records Act 1990 curiously imposed no such limitation. As we saw in Chapter 7, the Access to Health Records Act 1990 has a very limited application after the enactment of the Data Protection Act 1998. Only access by the personal representatives of a deceased is now contemplated (s 3(1)(f)) and the manual records must be relevant to a claim relating to that person's death (s 5(4)). This could conceivably apply where a child (or parent) dies during treatment and a claim is made. To that extent, the Access to Health Records (Control of Access) Regulations 1993 (SI 1993 No 746) closes the gap by providing, in reg 2:

> 2. Access shall not be given under section 3(2) of the [Access to Health Records] Act to any part of a health record which would disclose information showing that an identifiable individual was, or may have been, born in consequence of treatment services within the meaning of the Human Fertilisation and Embryology Act 1990.

2. Disclosure of information

Section 33 of the 1990 Act imposes a strict secrecy requirement for statutory information held by the HFEA of a licence-holder. As regards the HFEA, s 33(1) and (2) provide:

33. (1) No person who is or has been a member or employee of the Authority shall disclose any information mentioned in subsection (2) below which he holds or has held as such a member or employee.

    (2) The information referred to in subsection (1) above is –

(a) any information contained or required to be contained in the register kept in pursuance of section 31 of this Act, and

(c) any other information obtained by any member or employee of the Authority on terms or in circumstances requiring it to be held in confidence.

As regards a licence-holder, s 33(5) provides:

33. (5) No person who is or has been a person to whom a licence applies and no person to whom directions have been given shall disclose any information falling within section 31(2) of this Act which he holds or has held as such a person.

The strict limits (and limited exceptions) of the 1990 Act as originally drafted proved problematic and led to the passage of the Human Fertilisation and Embryology (Disclosure of Information) Act 1992 which amended s 33 considerably so as to permit a greater degree of disclosure by licence-holders.

(a) By HFEA

As regards statutory information, disclosure by HFEA is permitted in the following circumstances:

33. (3) Subsection (1) above [ie the non-disclosure rule] does not apply to any disclosure of information mentioned in subsection (2)(a) above made –

(a) to a person as a member or employee of the Authority,

(b) to a person to whom a licence applies for the purposes of his functions as such,

(c) so that no individual to whom the information relates can be identified,

(d) in pursuance of an order of a court under section 34 or 35 of this Act,

(e) to the Registrar General in pursuance of a request under section 32 of this Act, or

(f) in accordance with section 31 of this Act.

Section 33(7) also permits HFEA to disclose information to patients or donors which relates exclusively to themselves. It provides:

33. (7) [section 33(1) and (5)] does not apply to the disclosure to any individual of information which –

(a) falls within section 31(2) of this Act by virtue of paragraph (a) or (b) of that subsection, and

(b) relates only to that individual or, in the case of an individual treated together with another, only to that individual and that other.

Would it be lawful for the HFEA to disclose information held on its register for the purposes of research, for example, follow-up studies? Clearly, if the information were anonymised this would be exempt from non-disclosure by virtue of s 33(3)(c). However, this may not be practicable given the nature of any given research. It would seem that this information cannot be disclosed even to members of the Authority or licence-holders (or others named on the licence) who wish to carry out the research. In the former case it would not be given to the member 'as a member … of the Authority' (s 33(3)(a)) but rather *qua* researcher. As regards the latter, disclosure would not be for the "purposes of his functions" as a licence-holder. Again, it would be in the capacity as researcher. To allow what may be highly desirable research, it seems that the 1990 Act will require amendment. The same argument, precisely, is applicable to disclosure by a licence-holder to others under s 33(6) (see s 33(6)(a) and (b)).

As regards confidential information held by HFEA which is not 'statutory information', the Act in s 33(2)(b) imposes a statutory obligation of confidence. Section 33(4) permits disclosure in the following circumstances.

33. (4) Subsection (1) [ie the non-disclosure rule] above does not apply to any disclosure of information mentioned in subsection (2)(b) above –

(a)   made to a person as a member or employee of the Authority,

(b)   made with the consent of the person or persons whose confidence would otherwise be protected, or

(c)   which has been lawfully made available to the public before the disclosure is made.

(b) By the licence-holder

It must always be remembered that the general law relating to confidentiality applies to the licence-holder. What s 33 is concerned with is the statutory information held by the licence-holder and its provisions may go further than the general law in limiting disclosure. It is also a criminal offence to breach the provisions of s 33 (see s 41(8)).

Section 33(6), (6A), (6B), (6C), (6D), (6E), (6F), (6G), (7) and (9) set out the *only* circumstances in which disclosure of statutory information is permitted.

33. (6) Subsection (5) [ie the non-disclosure rule] above does not apply to any disclosure of information made –

(a)   to a person as a member or employee of the Authority,

(b)   to a person to whom a licence applies for the purposes of his functions as such,

(c)   so far as it identifies a person who, but for sections 27 to 29 of this Act, would or might be a parent of a person who instituted proceedings under section 1A of the Congenital Disabilities (Civil Liability) Act 1976, but only for the purpose of defending such proceedings, or instituting connected proceedings for compensation against that parent,

(d)   so that no individual to whom the information relates can be identified,

(e)   in pursuance of directions given by virtue of section 24(5) or (6) of this Act.

(f)   necessarily –
   (i) for any purpose preliminary to proceedings, or
   (ii) for the purposes of, or in connection with, any proceedings,

(g)   for the purpose of establishing, in any proceedings relating to an application for an order under subsection (1) of section 30 of this Act, whether the condition specified in paragraph (a) or (b) of that subsection is met, or –

(h)   under section 3 of the Access to Health Records Act 1990 (right of access to health records).

(6A) Paragraph (f) of subsection (6) above, so far as relating to disclosure for the purpose of, or in connection with, any proceedings, does not apply –

(a)   to disclosure of information enabling a person to be identified as a person whose gametes were used, in accordance with consent given under paragraph 5 of Schedule 3 to this Act, for the purposes of treatment services in consequence of which an identifiable individual was, or may have been, born, or

(b)   to disclosure, in circumstances in which subsection (1) of section 34 of this Act applies, of information relevant to the determination of the question mentioned in that subsection.

(6B) In the case of information relating to the provision of treatment services for any identifiable individual –

(a)   where one individual is identifiable, subsection (5) above does not apply to disclosure with the consent of that individual;

(b)   where both a woman and a man treated together with her are identifiable, subsection (5) above does not apply –
   (i) to disclosure with the consent of them both, or
   (ii) if disclosure is made for the purpose of disclosing information about the provision of treatment services for one of them, to disclosure with the consent of that individual.

(6C) For the purposes of subsection (6B) above, consent must be to disclosure to a specific person, except where disclosure is to a person who needs to know –

(a)   in connection with the provision of treatment services, or any other description of medical, surgical or obstetric services, for the individual giving the consent,

(b)   in connection with the carrying out of an audit of clinical practice, or

(c)   in connection with the auditing of accounts.

(6D) For the purposes of subsection (6B) above, consent to disclosure given at the request shall be disregarded unless, before it is given, the person requesting it takes reasonable steps to explain to the individual from whom it is requested the implications of compliance with the request.

(6E) In the case of information which relates to the provision of treatment services for any identifiable individual, subsection (5) above does not apply to disclosure in an emergency, that is to say, to disclosure made –

(a) by a person who is satisfied that it is necessary to make the disclosure to avert an imminent danger to the health of an individual with whose consent the information could be disclosed under subsection (6B) above, and

(b) in circumstances where it is not reasonably practicable to obtain that individual's consent.

(6F) In the case of information which shows that any identifiable individual was, or may have been, born in consequence of treatment services, subsection (5) above does not apply to any disclosure which is necessarily incidental to disclosure under subsection (6B) or (6E) above.

(6G) Regulations may provide for additional exceptions from subsection (5) above, but no exception may be made under this subsection –

(a) for disclosure of a kind mentioned in paragraph (a) or (b) of subsection (6A) above, or

(b) for disclosure, in circumstances in which section 32 of this Act applies, of information having the tendency mentioned in subsection (2) of that section.

(7) This section does not apply to the disclosure to any individual of information which –

(a) falls within section 31(2) of this Act by virtue of paragraph (a) or (b) of that subsection, and

(b) relates only to that individual or, in the case of an individual treated together with another, only to that individual and that other . . .

(9) In subsection (6)(f) above, references to proceedings include any formal procedure for dealing with a complaint.

Until the amendments to s 33 in 1992, the range of disclosure was limited to the circumstances set out in s 33(6)(a) to (e) and 33(7). As regards these, only that in s 33(6)(c) calls for comment. It permits disclosure of the identity of a donor by a licence-holder who is sued by a disabled child for negligence arising from the infertility treatment in order to defend himself (see *infra*, ch 12 for a discussion of these actions and s 1A of the Congenital Disabilities (Civil Liability) Act 1976).

As regards the amended provisions, there are five important areas to consider:

(i) LEGAL PROCEEDINGS

The Act permits disclosure where it is *necessary* for the purpose of, or in connection with, 'proceedings' or as a preliminary to such proceedings (s 33(6)(f)). This provision is, on its face, both wide and general in its application. It is important to notice, however, that disclosure must be *objectively* necessary. It would not suffice, in itself, for the doctor to believe that disclosure was necessary or otherwise to act in good faith since these subjective terms are conspicuous by their absence from s 33(6)(f). The provision applies to 'any proceedings' and this term is not defined other than to state that it includes 'any formal procedure for dealing with a complaint' (s 33(9)). Clearly, however, it would include: any legal proceedings brought against a licensed doctor; disciplinary action brought against a general practitioner (where, perhaps, she is licensed to provide artificial insemination) under the National Health Service (Service Committee and Tribunal) Regulations 1992 (SI 1992 No 664); and a complaint against an NHS doctor under the NHS complaints procedure (see *supra*, ch 3). Given the generality of the wording of s 33(6)(f), disclosure might also be permitted in, or as a preliminary to, legal proceedings to which the doctor is not a party. Subject to this disclosure would still have to be required by law or otherwise not be a breach of confidence by the doctor. Importantly, under this new provision disclosure is restricted to information which relates to *the patient or any children born*: information that identifies a donor is not permitted at least where a child has subsequently been born (s 33(6A)(a)). The latter information may be important where the medical negligence claim is based upon inadequate screening of the donor(s) or testing of the donated material. Here what passed between the doctor and the donor may well be important to the doctor's defence and yet he cannot disclose any identifying information to his legal advisers. Only the court has power to order disclosure of information which identifies a donor (eg s 35) and then only for the purpose of instituting proceedings against the donor. Presumably, such proceedings would be under the Congenital Disabilities (Civil Liability) Act 1976, brought by a disabled child who alleges that the donor negligently failed to disclose his medical or genetic history which subsequently affected the child. Is it really necessary to protect a donor's identity and related information at all costs? Surely, at the very least, the court should have power to order disclosure here also?

(ii) CONSENT OF PATIENT

Disclosure of information relating to a patient's infertility treatment is now permitted with the consent of the patient or both parents if they are being treated together (s 33(6B)–(6D)). Where it is necessarily incidental to disclosure of this information, it is also permissible to disclose information relating to the birth of any child as a result of treatment services (s 33(6F)). A patient's consent will not be valid unless reasonable steps have been taken to explain to the patient the implications of disclosure (s 33(6D)). Where disclosure is to be to another concerned with the medical care of the patient or for audit or accounting purposes, the consent to disclosure may be general; but where it is to others the patient must consent to disclosure to a *specific person* (see model consent form, *Code of Practice* (4th edn, 1998)(HFEA) Annex A). This amendment overcomes one of the major perceived problems with the 1990 Act as originally drafted. It obviates the need to use the circumlocutory procedure advised by the Authority whereby the patient would be given a sealed envelope to deliver to the patient's general practitioner (see *Code of Practice* (1991) at para 3.6).

It is not unknown for patients undergoing treatment to wish to know about, or contact, donors. Likewise, sometimes donors wish to know what has happened to their gametes. The 1990 Act makes no special provision for these situations. The Victoria Infertility Treatment Act 1995 in Australia does have specific provisions allowing patients to obtain non-identifying information and, with consent, identify information about a donor prior to treatment (ss 71 and 72) and after a child is born (ss 74 and 75). Also, the donor may find out what has happened to his gametes (or embryos) (s 73) and may obtain non-identifying information about the patients (s 72). What is the position in English law? Of course, there is no prohibition on a licence-holder disclosing non-identifying information to a donor or to patients about the others. The donor's general background is commonly revealed to patients in order to match them up as much as possible. However, information *identifying* the donor cannot be disclosed to the patients in order for them to contact the donor, even with the donor's consent. The 1990 Act is clear and narrowly drawn and, it should be noted, contains a specific exemption from the non-disclosure rule for disclosure *to* the patients or donor of information about *themselves* (s 33(7)). Could the licence-holder, however, disclose to the donor information identifying the patients and, thereby allow the donor to contact the patients if he wishes? Section 33(6B) contains a more broadly worded provision allowing disclosure of patient information with their consent, as we have seen. However, there is, even here, a difficulty. Section 33(6B) requires that the patient(s) consent to disclosure to a 'specific person' unless it is for one of the specified purposes, ie treatment, clinical audit or financial audit (s 33(6C)). Clearly, this situation does not fall within any of these. Normally, the patient(s) will consent to disclosure to 'Dr X' or 'Dr Y' as the 'specific person'. Here, that is impossible, since the donor's name cannot be revealed. Would it suffice to say 'I consent to disclosure to the donor(s) of the gametes/embryos'? Arguably, this is a 'specific' person, albeit that it is not a 'named' person. The Act does not require that it be the latter. If it did, it could have said so. Since s 33(6B) was enacted to allow patients, having been counselled, to permit controlled disclosure of information about themselves, we would suggest tht the disclosure to the donor is within the Act in these circumstances. Of course, this will not help the patients if the donor does not wish to have contact with them. That, however, is and remains his right under the legislation and, of course, it is explicitly in the Victoria statute.

(iii) EMERGENCIES

The Act permits disclosure of information relating to treatment services given to a patient in an emergency where the doctor is '*satisfied that it is necessary* to avert an imminent danger to the health' of the patient and 'it is not reasonably practicable to obtain that patient's consent' (s 33(6E), emphasis added). Although, as in the provision relating to legal proceedings (discussed above), disclosure must be necessary, this provision is more subjectively worded and so may be more easily satisfied. It should however be noted that the doctor must be satisfied that the danger to the patient is *imminent*; foreseeable danger will not of itself suffice. In other words, the danger must be faced there and then before it can properly be said to be 'imminent'. It should also be noted that the patient's consent must be sought if that is reasonably practicable. Again, it is permissible to disclose information relating to the birth of any child as a result of treatment services providing this is necessarily incidental to the disclosure of the patient information (s 33(6F)).

(iv) DECLARATION OF PARENTAGE

Disclosure is permitted for the purpose of establishing the genetic parenthood of a child who is the subject of an application for a parental order in a surrogacy case under s 30 of the 1990 Act (s 33(6)(g)).

(v) BY REGULATIONS

Disclosure of 'statutory information' is permitted in such circumstances as may be specified in Regulations promulgated by the Secretary of State (s 33(6G)). The Act therefore now avoids the problem faced until its amendment in 1992, namely that unforeseen problem situations required primary legislation to make disclosure lawful.

F. STATUS OF CHILDREN

You will recall that early in this chapter we set out tables devised by Professors Dickens and Capron demonstrating the potential complexities of the relationship between donors of gametes and offspring. For the law the question is quite simple. In the case of any child who, in law, is the mother and who, in law, is the father?

At common law, parenthood was almost certainly defined by genetic make-up. In other words, where sperm was donated, the donor was the legal father of the child albeit that presumptively if the child were born within a marriage the husband would be rebuttably deemed the father. As regards egg or embryo donation, the common law's unfamiliarity with these practices (which separate the gestational from the genetic) would probably have led it to prefer the claims of the gestational mother. The inconsistency between the two positions could, however, have persuaded a court to opt for the genetic determination of parenthood both as regards the mother and father (see eg *Johnson v Calvert* (1993) 851 P 2d 776 (Cal Sup Ct) but notice *In re the Marriage of Buzzanca* (1998) 61 Cal App 4th 1410 (Cal CA) – commissioning couple in a surrogacy arrangement were parents of child born following embryo donation from third parties even though genetically unrelated to the child).

As regards sperm donation, Parliament acted in s 27 of the Family Law Reform Act 1987 to reverse the common law rule and make the husband of a patient who was artificially inseminated the father of any child unless it was proved that he did not consent to the procedure.

In the 1990 Act, Parliament acted to resolve questions of parenthood (whether it be mother or father) whenever a child was born as a consequence of infertility treatment.

1. The mother

Sections 27 and 29 of the 1990 Act provide as follows:

Meaning of 'mother'
27. (1) The woman who is carrying or has carried a child as a result of the placing in her of an embryo or of sperm and eggs, and no other woman, is to be treated as the mother of the child.

(2) Subsection (1) above does not apply to any child to the extent that the child is treated by virtue of adoption as not being the child of any person other than the adopter or adopters.

(3) Subsection (1) above applies whether the woman was in the United Kingdom or elsewhere at the time of the placing in her of the embryo or the sperm and eggs.

Effect of sections 27 and 28
29. (1) Where by virtue of section 27 or 28 of this Act a person is to be treated as the mother or father of a child, that person is to be treated in law as the mother or, as the case may be, father of the child for all purposes.

(2) Where by virtue of section 27 or 28 of this Act a person is not to be treated as the mother or father of a child, that person is to be treated in law as not being the mother or, as the case may be, father of the child for any purpose.

(3) Where subsection (1) or (2) above has effect, references to any relationship between two people in any enactment, deed or other instrument or document (whenever passed or made) are to be read accordingly.

These provisions make clear that the gestational woman (and no one else) is, in law, the mother of any child born as a result of IVF procedures or, for example, GIFT. A potential omission would arise where egg donation occurs but does not involve IVF or GIFT, ie where the egg is directly implanted in the woman for natural fertilisation. This is not a procedure currently used. Here, however, the common law would apply.

2. The father

Section 28 of the 1990 Act provides as follows:

Meaning of 'father'
28. (1) This section applies in the case of a child who is being or has been carried by a woman as the result of the placing in her of an embryo or of sperm and eggs or her artificial insemination.

(2) If –
(a) at the time of the placing in her of the embryo or the sperm and eggs or of her insemination, the woman was a party to a marriage, and
(b) the creation of the embryo carried by her was not brought about with the sperm of the other party to the marriage,

then, subject to subsection (5) below, the other party to the marriage shall be treated as the father of the child unless it is shown that he did not consent to the placing in her of the embryo or the sperm and eggs or to her insemination (as the case may be).

(3) If no man is treated, by virtue of subsection (2) above, as the father of the child but –

(a) the embryo or the sperm and eggs were placed in the woman, or she was artificially inseminated, in the course of treatment services provided for her and a man together by a person to whom a licence applies, and

(b) the creation of the embryo carried by her was not brought about with the sperm of that man,

then, subject to subsection (5) below, that man shall be treated as the father of the child.

(4) Where a person is treated as the father of the child by virtue of subsection (2) or (3) above, no other person is to be treated as the father of the child.

(5) Subsections (2) and (3) above do not apply –

(a) in relation to England and Wales and Northern Ireland, to any child who, by virtue of the rules of common law, is treated as the legitimate child of the parties to a marriage,

(b) in relation to Scotland, to any child who, by virtue of an enactment or other rule of law, is treated as the child of the parties to a marriage, or

(c) to any child to the extent that the child is treated by virtue of adoption as not being the child of any person other than the adopter or adopters.

(6) Where –

(a) the sperm of a man who had given such consent as is required by paragraph 5 of Schedule 3 to this Act was used for a purpose for which such consent was required, or

(b) the sperm of a man, or any embryo the creation of which was brought about with his sperm, was used after his death,

he is not to be treated as the father of the child.

(7) The references in subsection (2) above to the parties to a marriage at the time there referred to –

(a) are to the parties to a marriage subsisting at that time, unless a judicial separation was then in force, but

(b) include the parties to a void marriage if either or both of them reasonably believed at that time that the marriage was valid; and for the purposes of this subsection it shall be presumed, unless the contrary is shown, that one of them reasonably believed at the time that the marriage was valid.

(8) This section applies whether the woman was in the United Kingdom or elsewhere at the time of the placing in her of the embryo or the sperm and eggs or her artificial insemination.

(9) In subsection (7)(a) above, 'judicial separation' includes a legal separation obtained in a country outside the British Islands and recognised in the United Kingdom.

The effect of this provision, in essence, is fivefold. First, if the woman who is being treated (and gives birth) is married, her husband is, as always, presumed to be the father of the child because of the presumption of legitimacy (s 28(5)(a)). Of course, a husband may seek to rebut this presumption through, for example, DNA profiling. If successful, he will still be deemed in law to be the father under s 28(2) unless he proves that he did not consent to the infertility treatment. As we saw earlier, the HFEA's *Code of Practice* includes, in the relevant standard consent form, a requirement that the husband acknowledge his consent to the infertility procedure. Although, of course, this is only evidence of his consent, it will be difficult to show that it does not truly represent his state of mind.

Secondly, if the woman is not married and she receives 'treatment services provided for her and a man *together*' (s 28(3), our emphasis) her partner is deemed to be the father even though donated sperm or an embryo is used. Where his own sperm is used the section does not apply (s 28(3)(b)) but it is, of course, unnecessary since he remains the father under the common law. Unlike the case of the husband, it would appear that the unmarried partner cannot displace his deemed parenthood under s 28(3) even if he is subsequently able to show that he did not really consent to what was done. Perhaps to avoid any arguments, again the relevant consent form in the *Code of Practice* should be used to record his consent. At the very least this will put him on notice if he continues to agree to be treated together with the woman.

Section 28(3) was intended to cover the unmarried couple who live in what is sometimes called a *de facto* or common law marriage. The Act seeks to put them in the same position as the married couple. The statutory phrase, that the 'treatment services' should be 'provided for her and a man together', is not, however, defined in the Act. Could it be construed to go further and include, for example, the case of an unmarried woman who brings along to the infertility clinic a male friend for support? In one sense, they are being treated 'together'. However, it would be absurd to regard the male friend as the child's father. On the other hand, if he is not the father, the child will be legally fatherless if donated sperm is used in accordance with the provisions of the Act (s 28(6)(a) below) and the court might be tempted to strive to avoid such a conclusion.

Another view is, however, that s 28(3) should be given a more narrow and limited interpretation. Parliament was probably only contemplating treatment by unmarried 'couples' in situations closely analogous to that of married couples (see, Hansard, HL vol 517, cols 210–11). Thus, s 28(3) only applies when the couple are seeking treatment with a view to having a child to bring up together. On this basis, the male friend who accompanies the woman to the clinic would not be the father of the child under s 28(3).

This interpretation of s 28(3) is bolstered by the wording of s 4(1) of the Act which is very similar to that of s 28(3). As we saw earlier, s 4(1)(a) seeks to bring within the regulatory framework infertility treatment using donor sperm but not treatment where the sperm of the male partner being treated is used. Hence, a licence is required where sperm is used 'in the course of providing treatment services for any woman, us[ing] the sperm of any man *unless the services are being provided for the woman and the man together*' (s 4(1)(b), our emphasis). These words closely mirror those in s 28(3). Suppose a woman brought a friend who was to act as the sperm provider to the clinic with her. The Act's regulatory provisions would only apply if the treatment services were not being provided for them 'together' since *his sperm* is being used. Can this situation really be distinguished from the situation where an anonymous sperm donor is used? We would suggest not. Where artificial insemination is carried out, the regulatory framework should apply unless the couple are seeking a child which is genetically theirs and intended to be brought up as their child. This is, of course, the interpretation offered above of the same words in s 28(3).

The courts have considered the statutory phrase 'treatment together' on four occasions: *Re Q (Parental Order)* 1 FLR 369 (Johnson J); *Re B (Parentage)* [1996] 2 FLR 15 (Bracewell J); *R v HFEA, ex p Blood* [1997] 2 All ER 687 (CA) and *U v W (A-G intervening)* (1997) 38 BMLR 54 (Wilson J). The cases are considered in the most recent decision of Wilson J.

U v W (A-G intervening) (1997) 38 BMLR 54 (Fam Div)

From November 1990, for a period of three and half years, the applicant, Miss U, and the respondent, W, had been virtually living together. Following their attempt for U to become pregnant, they undertook tests in August 1991, when it was discovered that W's sperm was defective, being of poor mobility. In May 1993 they underwent in vitro fertilisation treatment, involving sub-zonal insemination, in Nottingham. In April 1994 they travelled to Rome to consult Dr A, who had pioneered a treatment involving implanting the embryo in the uterus using a laser. They agreed to this treatment and, on 29 May 1994, U returned to Rome, followed by W on 4 June. Prior to this, both had taken medication specified by Dr A. The £3,750 cost of the treatment was wholly paid by U. On 5 June it was understood by all parties that, while every effort would be made to use W's sperm, recourse to donor sperm would be a last resort. On 6 June Dr A informed U and W that he had fertilised 12 of U's ova, but only one by W's sperm. Overnight, it was decided that U would receive the donor embryos as well as W's. On 7 June they signed a statement agreeing to treatment involving donor gametes and whereby U agreed to undertake to acknowledge maternity, W paternity, of any resulting children. W returned to England. Subsequently, Dr A told U that W's embryo had died and she agreed to be implanted with six donor embryos, three of which would be lasered on to her uterus. This treatment having been carried out, U returned to England on 9 June where she was met at Heathrow Airport by W. A row ensued and the relationship terminated. Three embryos had successfully implanted, although one was subsequently removed. Twin boys were born on 8 February 1995, since when W had had no contact with them. Genetic tests have confirmed U's maternity of the twins and excluded W's paternity.

Wilson J: *C. The Scheme of the Act*
… Section 28 provides for paternity. It applies in the case of a child who is being or has been carried by a woman as the result of the placing in her of an embryo or of sperm and eggs or her artificial insemination: s 28(1).

Subsection (2) provides for non-genetic paternity in the case of some married men. …

Thus, apart from any question of consent, s 28(2) does not apply to the respondent because he was not married to the applicant.

Then follows s 28(3), which is central to these proceedings … It is important to note the contrast in the provision for non-genetic paternity between that of the married man under s 28(2) and that of the unmarried man under s 28(3). The former is treated in law as the father unless it is shown that he did not consent to the placement within his wife. The latter is treated in law as the father only if it is shown that the placement within the woman occurred in the course of treatment services provided for her and him together by a person to whom a licence applies.

The enactment of s 28(2) did not altogether represent new law: it was an enlargement of the provision for the paternity of a married man following artificial insemination by a donor set out in s 27 of the Family Law Reform Act 1987. By contrast, s 28(3) represented entirely new law; and in section D below I will consider its genesis.

Subsection (4) provides that, where a person is treated as the father of the child by virtue of s 28(2) or (3), no other person is to be treated as the father of the child. So the sperm donor is excluded from paternity whenever non-genetic paternity arises. But s 28(6)(a) provides for exclusion of the sperm donor from paternity in certain circumstances, even when non-genetic paternity does not arise: the circumstances are, broadly, that the donor should have given a written and informed consent to the use of his sperm pursuant to Sch 3 to the Act. In that the anonymous donor of the sperm used by Dr A did not give such a consent (or, to be pedantic, there is no evidence that he did), he would technically be the father of the boys in the event that this application was dismissed.

Mr Vaughan QC, on behalf of the applicant, places considerable reliance on s 28(8), which provides:

> This section applies whether the woman was in the United Kingdom or elsewhere at the time of the placing in her of the embryo or the sperm and eggs or her artificial insemination.

There is no problem about the application of s 28(8) to s 28(2): the location of the treatment is made as irrelevant to the non-genetic paternity of the husband as to the non-genetic maternity of the carrying woman under s 27(3). But it is impossible to apply s 28(8) to s 28(3) because the latter requires treatment under licence and such will not be granted for treatment overseas. Section 28(8) would have been better drafted if, at the beginning, it had referred to 'Subsection (2) above' rather than 'This section'.

D. Treatment … together
The applicant has to establish that the embryos were placed in her in the course of treatment services provided for her and the respondent together. The respondent concedes that, in so far as, in the course of their relationship, treatment services were provided with a view to the use of his own sperm in the fertilisation of the applicant's eggs, the services were provided for them together. Thus, he concedes that the services provided by Nurture in May 1993 were provided for them together. It must follow, I think, that, in so far as Dr A was providing services with a view to the use of the respondent's own sperm, the services were provided for them together. But the respondent stresses that the issue is whether the embryos were placed in the applicant in the course of such treatment. The embryos placed in the applicant were not embryos fertilised with the respondent's sperm. The objective of using his sperm had been abandoned by the time when the embryos were placed in her. The treatment which Dr A was providing at the relevant time was treatment with the use of donated sperm and such treatment, says the respondent, was being provided for the applicant alone.

The respondent's contention raises a conundrum about what the unmarried man must have said and/or intended and/or done before it can be concluded that treatment services not involving the use of his own sperm were provided for the woman and him together. The conundrum vexed Johnson J in *Re Q (a minor) (parental order)*, [1996] 1 FLR 369. He needed to look at s 28(3) only in passing, so as to note its patent inapplicability to the facts of his case. But he said (at 371):

It seems plain to me that the subsection envisages a situation in which the man involved himself received medical treatment, although as presently advised I am not sure what treatment is envisaged since the subsection refers to a man whose sperm was not used in the procedure.

He added (at 372):

I need further instruction as to who might be a man *treated* together with the carrying woman but who is not the sperm donor.

The notion of the provision or receipt of treatment services for or by a woman and a man together is found in other parts of the Act, specifically in s 4(1)(b) and para 5(3) of Sch 3, both of which Bracewell J addressed in *Re B (minors) (parentage)* [1996] 2 FLR 15, a decision upon which the applicant relies. But the facts did not give rise to the same conundrum: for there it was the woman's boyfriend himself who had, under medical supervision, donated the sperm with which, five months later, after the breakdown of their relationship, she was inseminated. The judge concluded that the man's gametes had been used (ie presumably at the time of the insemination) for the purpose of their receiving treatment services together.

In *R v Human Fertilisation and Embryology Authority, ex p Blood* (1997) 35 BMLR 1, [1997] 2 WLR 806 (a decision pending delivery of which this judgment has been delayed) the Court of Appeal approved the analysis of *Re B (minors) (parentage)* by Sir Stephen Brown P in the court below ((1997) 35 BMLR 1 at 8) namely that the man –

was a willing, consenting party to the treatment which they had commenced together when the sperm sample was taken and that he had not subsequently withdrawn his deemed consent.

Notwithstanding the factual differences, I must note the robust construction of the words 'treatment ... together' adopted in *Re B (minors) (parentage)* and now approved, albeit by reference to its 'special facts', by the Court of Appeal. In *ex p Blood* itself the man (a husband) had died and so, by contrast, posthumous use of sperm taken from him while in a coma was inevitably held not to be capable of constituting 'treatment ... together'.

The applicant stresses the width of the statutory definition of 'treatment services' set out at the beginning of section C above and contends that it makes no distinction between the use in treatment of the man's or a donor's sperm. But the distinction is so fundamental that, in my judgment, it must be addressed in considering whether the services were provided for the woman and the man together. The code of practice highlights the distinction. Paragraphs 5.2 and 5.3, which address the need for the woman to consent to treatment, provide:

No licensed treatment should be given to any woman without her written consent to *that particular treatment*. The written consent should explain the nature of the treatment and the steps which are to be taken ... If it is possible that the question of treatment with donated gametes or embryos derived from them may arise, the centre should raise the matter with the client or clients beforehand. The centre should allow clients sufficient time to reflect before asking for consent to *treatment with donated material*. (My emphases.)

And paragraph 6.13 provides:

If a woman is already undergoing infertility treatment when the question of treatment with donated gametes or embryos derived from them arises, counselling about the implications of receiving donated material should be offered separately from counselling about the other implications of treatment ...

I have no doubt that there is a mental element inherent in the notion of 'treatment ... together' and that, if the respondent had believed at all material times that the treatment which was being provided was treatment in which his sperm alone was to be used, Dr A's treatment of the applicant with donor sperm would not have amounted to services provided for them together.

That hypothesis, however, does not fit the facts of this case. On 5 June it was understood by the respondent, as well as by the applicant, that, albeit as a last resort, recourse would be had to donor sperm. On 6 June it was understood by the respondent, as well as by the applicant, that, unless embryos fertilised by donor sperm were placed along with that fertilised by his sperm, the treatment stood a negligible chance of success. By that point, the respondent thus knew that, if the treatment was to proceed, donor sperm, as well as his sperm, was to be used. It is important to notice the respondent's reaction to that knowledge. There occurred no ostensible change in his role, no lesser degree of his participation in the dialogue. On the contrary, in his own words, as amended, 'we needed time to consider'. It was not just the applicant who needed the time: together they needed the time and together they used it in the discussions later that day.

On the following day, the respondent went, as usual, to the clinic together with the applicant. As usual, he participated in the discussion with Mrs B. And, together with the applicant, he signed the declaration. That he chose to add his signature to hers on a form which, as he knew, purported to permit the use of donor sperm is, in my view, a clear indication that the treatment with such sperm was 'treatment ... together'. That he was then obliged to leave the clinic, prior to the placement of the embryos in the applicant, is irrelevant.

The relevance of the long history of admitted 'treatment ... together ' with a view to the use of his own sperm is, in my view, that it became more incumbent on the respondent to make clear any disassociation on his part from the move into treatment which included donor sperm. But from what he said or did, neither the applicant nor those at the clinic could have inferred such disassociation; still less was it expressed. Even the respondent agrees that in Rome he never indicated to the applicant that he wanted nothing to do with any treatment with donor sperm or that he would not want to commit himself to a child so conceived. In truth, the respondent associated himself with the new treatment.

The test in s 28(3)(a) is not whether the man consented either to be deemed in law to be the father of the prospective child or to become legally responsible for him: it is whether the relevant treatment services were provided for the woman and him together. It stretches the requisite mental element in the man too far to require either form of such consent. In my view, what has to be demonstrated is that, in the provision of treatment services with donor sperm, the doctor was responding to a request for that form of treatment made by the woman and the man as a couple, notwithstanding the absence in the man of any physical role in such treatment.

I conclude that Dr A placed the embryos in the applicant in the course of treatment services provided for her and the respondent together ...

In this case, Wilson J gave some helpful guidance on the scope of s 28(3).

First, Wilson J accepted that there was a mental element inherent in the notion of 'treatment together'. Hence, it would have been fatal to an application of s 28(3) if the male partner had thought that the woman was going to be treated using *his* sperm, rather than a donor's. On the facts, Wilson J concluded that the man knew full well that donor sperm was to be used to create the embryos to be implanted in the woman.

Secondly, Wilson J considered it was important that the man had bee involved throughout the woman's treatment in Rome and had signed a declaration with her acknowledging the use of donor sperm and the couple's parentage of any resulting child. Indeed, the judge considered that the man's course of conduct showed that he associated himself with the treatment of the woman using embryos created with donor sperm.

Thirdly, Wilson J held that it was not necessary for the man to have consented to become in law the child's father or to be legally responsible for him. That was not a requirement of s 28(3). Instead Wilson J said:

> In my view what has to be demonstrated is that, in the provision of treatment services with donor sperm, the doctor was responding to *a request for that form of treatment made by the woman and the man as a couple*, notwithstanding the absence in the man of any physical role in such treatment. (Emphasis added.)

In stating this, Wilson J has knocked on the head, hopefully once and for all, the absurd suggestion by Johnson J in *Re Q (Parental Order) (supra)* that the statutory phrase could only be satisfied if the man was 'receiv[ing] medical treatment' himself by which he meant a 'laying on of hands' by a doctor. In this narrow sense of 'treatment', since the couple are conceiving using donor sperm rather than the man's, it would have been an impossible requirement to meet. Johnson J's view was wrong given that s 28(3) is only concerned, on its face, with situations where donor sperm is used (see Commentary (1996) 4 Med L Rev 207 at 208–210 (AG)). Wilson J would have none of that as his concluding words quoted above show.

Wilson J's approach is probably only a reformulation of that offered by Bracewell J in *Re P (supra)*, namely, that the couple are engaged on a 'joint enterprise' which envisages 'providing medical services to a couple to help the woman conceive' (*supra* at 20–21). Importantly and correctly, Wilson J requires that the 'joint enterprise' is, of course, to involve the use of donor sperm. While he did not consider that the man must consent to be the child's legal father in order the 'treatment' to be 'together', the man's agreement to the course of treatment is relevant. Indeed, as long as the man is aware of what is taking place, it is difficult to see how the couple could not be said to be receiving 'treatment together'. The point is, of course, in both *Re P* and the instant case, the couple were trying to have a baby for themselves. They were attempting to start a family together. Thus, the consent must go to the 'treatment' and its purpose, ie starting a family 'together'. As we said above, the man next door who comes along to the clinic to provide his neighbour with sperm is not caught by s 28(3). He consents to the use of his sperm but he is not engaged in a 'joint enterprise' of starting a family. He is, for all intents and purposes, a donor; he is just not an anonymous one. As such, the licensing requirements of the 1990 Act apply (s 4(1)(b)) and he is not the father by virtue of s 28(3). Indeed, he is expressly not the father by virtue of s 28(6)(a) because the sperm will have to be used in accordance with his consent under Sch 3 to the 1990 Act.

The general approach of Bracewell and Wilson JJ commends itself as a matter of common sense in interpreting the statutory phrase. There will always be difficult factual situations which will perplex the courts but the thrust of the courts' approach is now clear: are the couple trying to have a child together (involving donated sperm) as part of the treatment for the infertility that prevents them starting (or increasing) their family.

Fourthly, in all circumstances the Act ensures, in s 28(6)(a), that the donor of sperm used in accordance with the Act is not, in law, the father of the child. Unlike the position at common law, therefore, being a sperm donor carries no risk of being exposed to the responsibilities of a father. Thus, the public policy of facilitating sperm donation is furthered.

What, however, is the position if the donor's sperm is used not in accordance with his consent? For example, suppose he has agreed to its use only for research but it is mistakenly used for treatment services. Section 28(6)(a) does not apply. Nevertheless, he may still not be the father of any children. If the woman being treated is married and s 28(2) applies or she is unmarried and s 28(3) applies, her partner is the legal father, then the donor will not be the child's father (s 28(4)). Consequently, the donor will only remain the father in the unlikely event that his sperm is misused *and* either the woman's husband establishes that he did not consent to her treatment or the woman is unmarried and is treated alone. These possibilities are, of course, extremely unlikely in practice.

Fifthly, the position if an infertile couple do not resort to licensed treatment should be noted, ie if 'DIY' insemination is used. The provisions in s 28(2) – where the woman is married – apply to *all* cases of artificial insemination including those not carried out pursuant to a licence under the Act (the presumption of legitimacy will also apply). Consequently, her husband, and not the donor is, as we have seen, the father of the child. However, s 28(3) – which applies where the woman is not married – does not apply to 'DIY' insemination since it is restricted to situations where she, together with a man, receives *treatment services* under the Act, ie at a licensed clinic. Therefore, cases of 'DIY' insemination, where the woman is unmarried, continue to be governed by the common law. The donor remains legally the father of any child born.

Finally, there are a number of circumstances in which the provisions of the Act serve to bring about the result that a child will not have a father in law.

Where the woman has received treatment using donated gametes or embryos in circumstances where, under the Act, her male partner is not the father of the child, the child will be fatherless. An example would be where a husband was able to show that he had not consented to her treatment under s 28(2)(b) or if she was treated alone. The final situation in which a child will be fatherless arises because of s 28(6)(b), where 'the sperm of a man, or any embryo the creation of which was brought about with his sperm, was used after his death'. Hence, although the Act does not prohibit posthumous use of stored sperm or embryos, the Act ensures that any child born will not, for example, have a claim on the estate of the dead man (see, *supra*). The position might have been otherwise at common law: *In the Estate of K* (1996) 5 Tas R 365 (Slicer J) – children born through IVF following posthumous implantation were children of the deceased father for inheritance purposes (see Commentary (1997) 5 Med L Rev 121 (AG) and, more generally, R Atherton 'En Ventre Sa Frigidaire: Posthumous Children in the Succession Context' (1999) 19 LS 139). In the Government's review following the *Blood* case, Professor Sheila McLean recommended that consideration should be given to amending s 28(6) of the Act so as to restore the child's legal relationship to its deceased father but that there should be no change in respect of inheritance (*Review of the Common Law Provision Relating to the Removal of Gametes and of the Consent Provisions in the Human Fertilisation and Embryology Act 1990* (July 1998), paras 3.4 and 3.7 respectively).

Surrogacy

A. INTRODUCTION

In this section we examine the law as it pertains to surrogate motherhood, a modern practice which as Peter Singer and Deane Wells in *New Ways of Making Babies: The Reproduction Revolution* (1984) (pp 107–108) point out, has historical precedents:

> ... there is nothing new about the basic idea of surrogate motherhood. It is even in the Bible. The sixteenth chapter of Genesis tells the following story about Abraham and his wife Sarah (who have, at this stage, not yet been given the new names they received from God after he makes his covenant with Abraham, and hence are referred to by their original names of Abram and Sarai):
>
>> Abram's wife Sarai had born him no children. Now she had an Egyptian slave-girl whose name was Hagar, and she said to Abram, 'You see that the Lord has not allowed me to bear a child. Take my slave-girl; perhaps I shall found a family through her.' Abram agreed to what his wife said, so Sarai, Abram's wife, brought her slave-girl, Hagar the Egyptian, and gave her to her husband Abram as a wife ... He lay with Hagar and she conceived ...

The Warnock Committee in its 1984 Report (*Report of the Committee of Inquiry into Human Fertilisation and Embryology* (1984) (Cmnd 9314)) offered an answer to the question 'What is surrogacy?'

> **8.1** Surrogacy is the practice whereby one woman carries a child for another with the intention that the child should be handed over after birth. The use of artificial insemination and the recent development of *in vitro* fertilisation have eliminated the necessity for sexual intercourse in order to establish a surrogate pregnancy. Surrogacy can take a number of forms. The commissioning mother may be the genetic mother, in that she provides the egg, or she may make no contribution to the establishment of the pregnancy. The genetic father may be the husband of the commissioning mother, or of the carrying mother; or he may be an anonymous donor. There are thus many possible combinations of persons who are relevant to the child's conception, birth and early environment. Of these various forms perhaps the most likely are

surrogacy involving artificial insemination, where the carrying mother is the genetic mother inseminated with semen from the male partner of the commissioning couple, and surrogacy using *in vitro* fertilisation where both egg and semen come from the commissioning couple, and the resultant embryo is transferred to and implants in the carrying mother.

8.2 There are certain circumstances in which surrogacy would be an option for the alleviation of infertility. Examples are where a woman has a severe pelvic disease which cannot be remedied surgically, or has no uterus. The practice might also be used to help women who have suffered repeated miscarriages. There are also perhaps circumstances where the genetic mother, although not infertile, could benefit from the pregnancy being carried by another woman. An example is where the genetic mother is fit to care for a child after it is born, but suffers from a condition making the pregnancy medically undesirable.

8.3 If surrogacy takes place it generally involves some payment to the carrying mother. Payment may vary between reimbursement of expenses, and a substantial fee. There may, however, be some instances where no money is involved, for example, where one sister carries the pregnancy for another.

You will see here the possible ways in which surrogacy may arise including 'full' or 'gestational' surrogacy involving embryo donation and 'partial' surrogacy utilising only the sperm of the commissioning father. The former, but not the latter, necessarily requires medical intervention.

B. THE ISSUES

The modern practice of surrogacy is thought to raise the following problems. The Warnock Committee (*supra*) summarised the arguments as follows:

> **8.10** There are strongly held objections to the concept of surrogacy, and it seems from the evidence submitted to us that the weight of public opinion is against the practice. The objections turn essentially on the view that to introduce a third party into the process of procreation which should be confined to the loving partnership between two people, is an attack on the value of the marital relationship ... Further, the intrusion is worse than in the case of AID, since the contribution of the carrying mother is greater, more intimate and personal, than the contribution of a semen donor. It is also that it is inconsistent with human dignity that a woman should use her uterus for financial profit and treat it as an incubator for someone else's child. The objection is not diminished, indeed it is strengthened, where the woman entered an agreement to conceive a child, with the sole purpose of handing the child over to the commissioning couple after birth.
>
> **8.11** Again, it is argued that the relationship between mother and child is itself distorted by surrogacy. For in such an arrangement a woman deliberately allows herself to become pregnant with the intention of giving up the child to which she will give birth, and this is the wrong way to approach pregnancy. It is also potentially damaging to the child, whose bonds with the carrying mother, regardless of genetic connections, are held to be strong, and whose welfare must be considered to be of paramount importance. Further, it is felt that a surrogacy agreement is degrading to the child who is to be the outcome of it, since, for all practical purposes, the child will have been bought for money.
>
> **8.12** It is also argued that since there are some risks attached to pregnancy, no woman ought to be asked to undertake pregnancy for another, in order to earn money. Nor, it is argued, should a woman be forced by legal sanctions to part with a child, to which she has recently given birth, against her will.

The arguments are more fully considered in the report of the Government's 1998 Review chaired by Professor Margaret Brazier, *Surrogacy: Review for Health Ministers of Current Arrangements for Payments and Regulation* (1998) (Cm 4068).

> 4.2 ... the Warnock Committee unanimously condemned surrogacy for convenience and the majority regarded surrogacy as intrinsically objectionable in almost every case. The Report thus sought to use the law to discourage surrogacy by outlawing any third party assistance in the creation of surrogacy arrangements.
>
> 4.3 The Warnock Report referred to the following arguments against surrogacy: (i) it constituted an attack on the value of the marital relationship by the intrusion of a third party into the process of procreation, in a more personal and intimate way than would be the case with gamete or embryo donation (ii) the use of a woman's uterus for financial profit, as an

incubator for someone else's child, was inconsistent with human dignity; (iii) surrogacy distorted the relationship between mother and child, and might be psychologically damaging to the child, or degrading to the child, when it was treated as a commodity in a financial transaction; and (iv) since pregnancy carries risk, no woman should be asked to undertake it for another, in order to earn money.

4.4 The Report then briefly rehearsed some arguments in support of surrogacy: (i) those who regarded it as an intrusion into the marriage relationship need not seek the treatment for themselves, but should not try to prevent others from doing so: (ii) surrrogacy need not be seen as a degrading use of a woman's body or as commodifying the child, but rather as "a deliberate and thoughtful act of generosity on the part of one woman to another" (paragraph 8.12); (iii) psychological risks to the child (such as separation from the birth mother) were hard to calculate, and in any case some of these risks were already accepted in the case of adoption; and (iv) women had a right to enter into surrogate relationships if they wished, and there was no reason to suppose that they did so lightly, or that payment compromised the voluntary nature of a woman's agreement to enter into a surrogacy arrangement.

4.5 In the course of our review many of the arguments debated in the Warnock Report were raised again with us. The emphasis of debate has nonetheless changed somewhat. Opposition to surrogacy on the grounds of the intrusion of a third party into the marriage relationship was voiced to us, but only by a very small minority of respondents. Couples whose faith or philosophy requires acceptance of the exclusivity of that marriage relationship perhaps now accept that while their private morality excludes surrogacy for themselves such private choices should not dictate public policy. Indeed across a wide spectrum of opinion, we judge that the existence of surrogacy is now accepted, and that the crucial issue is how far the state should intervene to protect the interests of the parties.

4.6 In 1998, the principal concerns relating to surrogacy appear to be these: (i) does existing law and practice adequately safeguard the welfare of the child? (ii) does, and indeed should, existing law and practice protect the interests of the surrogate, her family and the commissioning couple? While there is unanimous agreement that the law must protect children, there was lively debate about how far if at all the state should intervene to limit the choices of the adult parties to surrogacy; and (iii) is payment to the surrogate for her services acceptable? Do payments contravene ethical values and may payments add to the risks of surrogacy?

4.7 At the time of the Warnock Report, very strong concerns were voiced about the prospect of surrogacy for convenience. A scenario where wealthy career women simply wished to avoid the inconvenience of pregnancy and "employed" others to bear children for them was envisaged. We have seen no evidence of such practices. When a woman has no uterus, or suffers from a condition rendering pregnancy dangerous to her health, it is readily seen that these are compelling medical reasons to consider resort to surrogacy. Surrogacy is a last resort. We have, however, been made aware that where a couple has undergone a number of failed IVF cycles surrogacy may be considered even though pregnancy is not absolutely impossible for the commissioning woman. At what point surrogacy becomes an acceptable alternative to other infertility treatment is now a live issue.

Social and Psychological Issues

Surrogacy and the welfare of the child
4.8 Families created by surrogacy differ from the traditional family in two important ways. (1) The gestational mother and the social mother are not the same. Although this is also true of adoption, surrogacy differs from adoption in that the pregnancy was created with the deliberate intention of the surrogate mother handing over the child to the commissioning couple. (2) In the case of partial surrogacy, the child is genetically unrelated to the commissioning mother, and where a donated embryo is used, the child is genetically unrelated to both commissioning parents.

4.9 No systematic information exists about the long-term psychological consequences for children born as a result of a surrogacy arrangement. To the extent that the experiences of adopted children are relevant to children conceived by surrogacy, it is important to note that adopted children do tend to show a greater incidence of emotional and behavioural problems in comparison with their non-adopted counterparts. Not all adopted children experience difficulties, however. It seems that psychological problems are most likely to occur in adoptive families where the quality of parenting is poor, and where the parents do not communicate openly about the adoption to the child. It is also of relevance that the younger children are at the time of the adoption, the less they are at risk.

4.10 There is a growing body of research on the psychological development of children conceived by assisted reproduction suggesting that the quality of parenting in such families is good and that the children themselves are functioning well, whether or not donated gametes had been used in the child's conception. In so far as surrogacy sometimes involves the use of

IVF, and children born as a result of a surrogacy arrangement often lack a genetic link with their commissioning mother and occasionally with their commissioning father as well, these findings can be extrapolated to families created through surrogacy. However, only pre-adolescent children conceived by assisted reproduction have been studies as yet, and their psychological well-being in adolescence and beyond remains unknown. It is at adolescence that issues of identity become salient for children and it is also at adolescence that difficulties in parent-child relationships are most likely to occur.

4.11 It was inevitable that our review was conducted in the absence of empirical data on what happens to children born as a result of a surrogacy arrangement, and we have had to rely instead on knowledge about children in adoptive and assisted reproduction families. Although this body of research indicates that we should not necessarily expect children born as a result of a surrogacy arrangement to be at risk for psychological problems, children born through surrogacy differ from adopted and assisted reproduction children in ways that may be detrimental to their emotional well-being as they grow up. It is not known, for example, how a child will feel about having been created for the purpose of being given away to other parents or, if the surrogate mother remains in contact with the family, what the impact of two mothers will be on his or her social, emotional and identity development through childhood and into adult life, particularly in families where the surrogate mother is also the genetic mother of the child.

4.12 Evidence that we have obtained in the course of this review indicates that it is not unusual for the surrogate mother to remain in contact with the commissioning couple and the child, a situation akin to open adoption whereby the biological mother remains in contact with the adoptive family. Although greater openness is generally believed to be of benefit to adopted children, the direct involvement of the biological mother in the adoptive family remains controversial, with some critics arguing that this could interfere with the security of the child's relationship with the adoptive parents. It is difficult to extrapolate from the experience of open adoption to surrogacy, as children involved in open adoption arrangements had often developed a close relationship with their biological mother before making the transition to an adoptive family.

4.13 Although it might be expected that contact with their surrogate mother would be a positive experience for children in that they could develop a clear understanding of their origins, it remains possible that the involvement of the surrogate mother may be distressing for children and undermine the relationship between the commissioning parents and the child. This may be particularly so where one or both commissioning parents lack a genetic link with the child.

4.14 A further distinction between many children born as a result of a surrogacy arrangement and children who are adopted or born as a consequence of some other form of assisted reproduction is the payment to the surrogate mother. The effect on a child, especially an older child, of learning that the woman who bore him or her was paid to do so is difficult to predict. Particularly in cases where children have a hostile or distant relationship with the commissioning couple, the knowledge that they had been brought into the world as a result of a commercial arrangement may not only have a damaging effect on family relationships but may also interfere with the child's development of a secure sense of identity and positive self-esteem. Furthermore, children who discover that their surrogate mother has had other children as part of a surrogacy arrangement may find this information particularly difficult to accept.

4.15 We are very much aware that the child born in consequence of a particular surrogacy arrangement is often not the only child at risk of psychological harm. It appears that those involved in surrogacy practice strongly recommend that the surrogate should have her own children. We are concerned (as were many of our respondents actively engaged in child welfare) about the impact on the emotional security of these children of seeing their mother give up a sibling, especially for payment, and in some instances on more than one occasion. Awareness of a potential effect on the surrogate's own children is demonstrated by advice from COTS (COTS Booklet 1997: Surrogates Information) that:

> We believe it is unfair on your own children for them to actually see the baby you will be giving up, as this makes it all too real for them and could cause problems later. If you intend to continue the friendship ... wait until your own children have settled down before you all meet again. If this is unavoidable do ensure that you are not holding the baby but the couple are when your children visit.

4.16 We find ourselves lacking direct evidence of the impact of surrogacy on the psychological welfare of children born as a result of surrogacy and the surrogate's own children. We judge, nonetheless, that there is clear potential risk to the welfare of such children. Research to identify and quantify that risk is needed urgently. The paramount importance of the welfare of the child is such that we believe that in making judgments about the regulation of surrogacy, the state must act on the precautionary principle. Society has a duty to minimise any such potential risk.

Surrogacy and the interests of adults
4.17 Just as information is lacking on the outcomes of surrogacy for children, relatively little is known about the consequences for the adults involved in a surrogacy arrangement. Although studies of mothers who give up their babies for adoption have shown that this can be an extremely upsetting experience that remains with them throughout their lives, it is possible that relinquishing a child in the context of a surrogacy arrangement may be less traumatic. A study by Eric Blyth of a small volunteer sample of surrogate mothers recruited through COTS suggests that parting with the child can be difficult but that distress can be accompanied by feelings of satisfaction and happiness for the commissioning couple (Eric Blyth "'Not a Primrose Path': commissioning parents' experiences of surrogacy arrangements in Britain" Journal of Reproductive and Infant Psychology Vol 13 pp 189–198 (1995)). The long-term effects of being a surrogate mother, and whether there are differences in outcome between surrogate mothers who are genetically related to the child and those who are not, remain unknown.
4.18 In the course of our Review, we did receive accounts of women who suffered distress as a result of entering into a surrogacy arrangement. They felt pressured at times to make decisions they regretted and considered that on occasion they were treated in a demeaning way by the commissioning couple. We know of at least two instances where such distress caused the surrogate to decide to keep the child.
4.19 It may be argued that adults who choose to be surrogates must, like everyone else, sometimes make hard choices. Risk of emotional or psychological harm is a factor for the surrogate to weigh when agreeing to enter into an arrangement. We are concerned, however, that women may be entering into surrogacy arrangements without full awareness of the physical and psychological risks. Payments may operate as an inducement to enter into surrogacy for women suffering financial hardship. There is evidence that the majority of surrogates are significantly poorer than commissioning couples and have relatively low educational attainments. A number are unemployed, unsupported by a partner and responsible for children of their own. "Professional" surrogacy may appear to be an attractive option for women in these circumstances. Some women clearly regret taking up that option. We regard it as proper that society seeks to implement measures to ensure that nobody enters into a surrogacy arrangement unaware of its possible risks or motivated principally by financial need.
4.20 The impact on the commissioning couple of having a child through surrogacy is also unknown. Parents of children conceived by assisted reproduction appear to be well-adjusted and have stable marriages, at least in the early years of the child's life. In the case of surrogacy, however, a third party is directly involved until the child is born and may remain in touch with the family as the child grows up. It is possible that the involvement of a third party may have a negative effect on the couple's relationship, and on the woman's security in her mothering role, particularly in families where the surrogate mother and the commissioning father are the genetic parents of the child. The only available information on this issue comes from Eric Blyth's study which indicates that difficulties can sometimes arise in the relationship between the surrogate mother and the commissioning couple (ibid, pp 185–196).
4.21 It was strongly argued before us that only the welfare of the child could justify intervention to limit private choices. We concluded that the especial vulnerability of adults in the uncharted waters of surrogacy does justify some degree of state intervention primarily to ensure that all involved do so freely and on the basis of full and accurate information. We are also aware that in raising a family the welfare of adults cannot entirely be divorced from the welfare of their offspring. Psychological harm suffered by the parents may adversely affect children. For example, the effects on a surrogate of giving up the child may have negative consequences for her own existing children. Or a commissioning mother made insecure by continuing contact with the surrogate may find it more difficult to parent the child.

The ethical debate
4.22 Since the publication of the Warnock Report there has been continuing controversy and debate both regarding the arguments used in the Report and the practical conclusions of the majority. In order for us to make our recommendations within our Terms of Reference we have had to revisit the debate as a whole, even although our remit is much narrower than that given to the Warnock Committee of Enquiry. In addressing the ethics of surrogacy, we consider, first, whether the principal argument given by Warnock, that surrogacy is an unwarranted use of a person as a mere means to an end, is decisive. We then discuss some of the other arguments for and against surrogacy, referred to in the Report but not used when it reached its conclusions: the risks to the child, including psychological trauma and commodification; the limits of procreative rights; and the moral character of the surrogacy relationship.

Exploitation

4.23 Is a surrogacy arrangement potentially exploitative of the surrogate mother, and positively so when financial interests are involved? The Warnock argument is that treating another person as a means to another's ends is "always liable to moral objection". This may be so, but what makes the moral objection valid? The original 18th century version of the moral principle, formulated by the philosopher Immanual Kant, was that we should treat all persons (including ourselves) as ends in themselves, never as *mere* means. To be treated as ends in themselves people must be able to exercise moral agency, to make a free and informed choice to carry out acts that serve the ends of others. Payment for their services does not make people into a mere means: on the contrary lack of payment (as in slavery or breadline wages) may be much more exploitative.

4.24 Even where there is risk in an occupation (eg working as a soldier, or in the police or fire service) payment does not of itself necessarily constitute exploitation. There is unlikely to be exploitation providing that people choosing to undertake such jobs do so with full knowledge and understanding of such risks, and that the payments made to them are not of a nature or at a level to induce them to take such risks against their better judgment.

4.25 The issue of exploitation of the surrogate therefore resolves into the fundamental question of her capacity to foresee the risks entailed. Payment increases the risk of exploitation if it constitutes an inducement to participate in an activity whose degree of risk the surrogate cannot, in the nature of things, fully understand or predict. In our judgment, surrogacy does carry some unpredictable risks which become fully evident only after an agreement has been entered into, perhaps even some time after the baby has been handed over to the commissioning parents. Some women may be particularly vulnerable to these risks, because of their social, economic or personal situation. This is one of our reasons for rejecting the concept of surrogacy as a paid occupation. Even if our Terms of Reference allowed us to recommend the full commercialisation of surrogacy, we would not do so, because it would imply a normalisation of what we believe to be a difficult personal choice, with an unknown degree of psychological risk.

4.26 The degree of risk should not be exaggerated. Evidence we have received from surrogate mothers in response to our questionnaire suggests that many women have found being a surrogate an emotionally rewarding experience, with no obvious ill effects on them or their families. Others, however, describe much less happy experiences. Although there is not strong enough evidence to warrant attempts to ban surrogacy because of its effect on surrogate mothers, there is sufficient cause for concern to make regulation essential.

Welfare of the child

4.27 A second reason for restricting, or at least regulating, surrogacy is the moral imperative to make the welfare of the child our prime concern. As we have noted, we are handicapped by a lack of empirical evidence about the effects of surrogacy on the children born as the result of surrogate arrangements (or of its effect on any other children of the surrogate). Given that the risks are hard to quantify, should we give any weight to this consideration? Some writers have argued that society would have to be quite certain of substantial risks to the child before any disbenefit of being conceived in this unusual manner outweighed the benefit of life itself. After all, they argue, surely we can be confident that most disadvantaged children will still prefer life to non-existence (see Harris J *The Valve of Life* Routledge, 1985, at p 147).

4.28 This argument appears to us to rest on a confusion between possible and actual persons. Unless we have a belief in the pre-existence of the soul, there is no person who suffers from not being alive. A decision not to proceed with a conception because of particular circumstances – or the prevention of achieving conception because of restrictive legislation or lack of adequate resources for infertility treatment – certainly causes unhappiness and a sense of loss to the would-be *parents*. But there is no child who suffers this loss or to whom we or the parents have moral obligations.

4.29 Therefore, we do not have to show certainty of major harm to potential children before we are justified, either through personal decision or legislative restriction, in avoiding conceptions on grounds of risk to the welfare of the child. It is sufficient to show that, if such lives are brought into being, they could be significantly compromised physically or emotionally. By not bringing them into being we do no harm to a child, since none exists. This is not to say that people should aim for perfection in their progeny, or that the state should institute draconian measures to narrow people's procreative choices. Rather, it justifies controlling, at least to some degree, this emotionally complex way of creating a family.

4.30 In practice, welfare considerations of this kind do not lead to major incursions into procreative liberty, but to the creation of institutions which provide guidance to people with difficult procreative choices (examples of this are the provision of genetic counselling services and the HFEA guidelines within which certain fertility services are provided). In respect of surrogacy, we regard there being sufficient concern about its effects on children to justify regulation, which includes measures aimed at ensuring the best protection of the child's welfare.

Procreative liberty

4.31 However, a further objection to any restriction of this kind on procreative choice must now be considered. It has been argued (Harris J correspondence submitted as evidence to the review team) that the whole structure of regulation of infertility treatment recommended by Warnock and enacted in the Human Fertilisation and Embryology Act 1990 is an infringement of human rights, and constitutes discriminatory treatment of infertile people, since they are subject to restrictions not imposed upon those who can conceive by natural means. This argument gains considerable power from the much clearer evidence of likely physical or psychological damage to children in some natural conceptions (eg women infected with the AIDS virus; drug abusers; men who are known to be potential child abusers) than any of the possible risks to children from assisted parenthood. It is outside our remit to consider the wider question of regulation of infertility treatment as a whole. However, the argument has obvious relevance to the narrower question of whether there should be any regulation of surrogacy.

4.32 We accept that people have a *prima facie* right to procreative or reproductive autonomy, and we are certainly opposed to any notion of a state-controlled licensing system (There are those, however, who do argue that all parents should be licensed by the state. See Lafollette H "Licensing Parents", (1980) Philosophy and Public Affairs 1979–80, 182–197) which prevents people from making their own procreative choices, through, for example, limits on numbers of children or enforced contraception or sterilisation. We agree that a consequence of this may be that some children are put in grave hazard by the circumstances of their conception and birth. However, we do not regard procreative autonomy as an absolute right, especially since it can come into conflict with the rights of others. Procreation is not just a matter of individual freedom. It entails bringing about the life of another human, whose welfare and autonomy deserve the highest attention from the state, because of the total dependency of children on others.

4.33 In view of this, we believe that when regulation is practicable and when it does not entail major state intrusion into the lives or bodily integrity of individuals, it may be ethically justifiable. We therefore accept the appropriateness of the "welfare of the child" provision of the Human Fertilisation and Embryology Act, and believe that the principle it embodies can quite fairly be extended to surrogacy arrangements (as is presently the case in the HFEA guidelines) without an undue incursion on the rights of commissioning parents to privacy. Moreover, as we have argued earlier, the rights of the surrogate and of her children are also to be taken into account, and these must be balanced against the claims of infertile people to procreative liberty.

The gift relationship

4.34 A further ethical dimension in the surrogacy debate concerns the notion of "commodification" of childbearing entailed in surrogacy as a financial transaction. It was argued by a number of the respondents to our questionnaire that surrogacy need not be equated with "baby-selling", because any fee paid to the surrogate can be regarded as payment for the pregnancy, *ie* payment for her services, not the baby. We find it difficult to see how this distinction can be maintained, especially because any fully commercial transaction of this kind should be subject to the normal laws of contract. It is unimaginable that a commissioning couple should enter into a contract that required simply that the surrogate become pregnant and give birth. The contract would have to contain a requirement that in return for the fee the child was handed over to those contracting the pregnancy, with penalties for failure to fulfil this aspect of the agreement.

4.35 It is possible to imagine a new legislative framework, which permitted payment of a fee to the surrogate, whilst maintaining her right to retain the child, but any such legislation would rationally have to contain provision for the contracting couple to obtain redress in the event that the child was not handed over. These legal considerations lead us to the conclusion that any financial arrangement that involves remuneration rather than simply expenses has to be regarded as a form of child purchase.

4.36 We fully accept that women who offer themselves as surrogates often do so at considerable inconvenience, discomfort and risk to themselves. We have certainly no wish to encourage the exploitation of such women by creating an environment in which they are involved in such arrangements without realising that there is no financial recompense for their time and effort. But the answer to this is to make quite explicit the social values on which this activity is based. We believe that the core value here, on which many social arrangements in the United Kingdom are based, including blood and live organ donation, is the "gift relationship".

4.37 It appears that, as a society, we believe that the use of our procreative capacities to assist others should also be a gift, not a commercial transaction ... Certainly the "cost" of the gift to the woman who undergoes pregnancy and birth in order to help an infertile couple is much greater than any other form of donation, except perhaps live kidney donation. It may be that few women will be willing to undertake such a commitment, except for a relative or close friend. But, whatever the practical consequences on the frequency of surrogacy arrangements, we have made our recommendations on the assumption that bearing a child for others should be seen within the context of a fully informed and free act of giving, and that neither the child nor the surrogate should be regarded as the subjects of a commercial transaction.

C. POSSIBLE RESPONSES

1. The Warnock Committee

The Warnock Committee's view was as follows (*supra*):

8.17 The question of surrogacy presented us with some of the most difficult problems we encountered. The evidence submitted to us contained a range of strongly held views and this was reflected in our own views. The moral and social objections to surrogacy have weighed heavily with us. In the first place we are all agreed that surrogacy for convenience alone, that is, where a woman is physically capable of bearing a child but does not wish to undergo pregnancy, is totally ethically unacceptable. Even in compelling medical circumstances the danger of exploitation of one human being by another appears to the majority of us far to outweigh the potential benefits, in almost every case. That people should treat others as a means to their own ends, however desirable the consequences, must always be liable to moral objection. Such treatment of one person by another becomes positively exploitative when financial interests are involved. It is therefore with the commercial exploitation of surrogacy that we have been primarily, but by no means exclusively, concerned.

8.18 We have considered whether the criminal law should have any part to play in the control of surrogacy and have concluded that it should. We recognise that there is a serious risk of commercial exploitation of surrogacy and that this would be difficult to prevent without the assistance of the criminal law. We have considered whether a limited, non-profit making surrogacy service, subject to licensing and inspection, could have any useful part to play but the majority agreed that the existence of such a service would in itself encourage the growth of surrogacy. **We recommend that legislation be introduced to render criminal the creation or the operation in the United Kingdom of agencies whose purposes include the recruitment of women for surrogate pregnancy or making arrangements for individuals or couples who wish to utilise the services of a carrying mother; such legislation should be wide enough to include both profit and non-profit making organisations. We further recommend that the legislation be sufficiently wide to render criminally liable the actions of professionals and others who knowingly assist in the establishment of a surrogate pregnancy.**

8.19 We do not envisage that this legislation would render private persons entering into surrogacy arrangements liable to criminal prosecution, as we are anxious to avoid children being born to mothers subject to the taint of criminality. We nonetheless recognise that there will continue to be privately arranged surrogacy agreements. While we consider that most, if not all, surrogacy arrangements would be legally unenforceable in any of their terms, we feel that the positions should be put beyond any possible doubt in law. **We recommend that it be provided by statute that all surrogacy agreements are illegal contracts and therefore unenforceable in the courts.**

8.20 We are conscious that surrogacy like egg and embryo donation may raise the question as to whether the genetic or the carrying mother is the true mother. Our recommendations in 6.8 and 7.6 cover cases where eggs or embryos have been donated. There remains however the possible case where the egg or embryo has not been donated but has been provided by the commissioning mother or parents with the intention that they should bring up the resultant child. If our recommendation in 8.18 is accepted, such cases are unlikely to occur because of the probability that the practitioner administering the treatment would be committing an offence. However, for the avoidance of doubt, we consider that the legislation proposed in 6.8 and 7.6 [ie making the gestational mother the legal mother] should be sufficiently widely drawn to cover any such case. If experience shows that this gives rise to an injustice for children who live with their genetic mother rather than the mother who bore them then in our view the remedy is to make the adoption laws more flexible so as to enable the genetic mother to adopt.

In the introduction to her book *A Question of Life*, Baroness Warnock writes (at p xii):

Similarly, in the controversial matter of surrogate mothers, the Inquiry agreed unanimously that they disapproved of the practice (largely because of possible consequences for the child); but they also agreed that it could not be prevented by law, because of the intrusiveness of any law that would be enforceable. The Inquiry therefore concentrated on how surrogacy for commercial purposes might be checked, leaving on one side the question whether surrogacy was intrinsically morally right or wrong. We might all of us have answered the primary moral question in a way which made surrogacy wrong. This did not pre-empt the answer to the second-order moral question, Should the law be invoked to stop surrogacy? We all agreed that it would be morally wrong to envisage a law which would intrusively curtail human freedom, and which would in addition be impossible to enforce (how could the law tell whether the child whom Abraham claimed as his own was born to Sarah, or to a servant girl who happened to be more fertile?) The Inquiry then, while unanimously answering the first-order question negatively, holding that surrogacy was wrong, nevertheless held that legislation should not be invoked to prevent it. We did however by a majority recommend that the commercial use of surrogacy arrangements, as a way of making money for an agency, could and should be made a criminal offence. For not only was the wrongness of surrogacy compounded by its being exploited for money, but also a law against agencies would not be intrusive into the private lives of those who were actually engaged in setting up a family.

We find helpful the distinction that Baroness Warnock draws between what is morally permissible and the extent to which the law should respond to the immoral. (We are puzzled by the apparent misunderstanding of the Committee's conclusions which, as we have seen, would outlaw *all* agencies whether profit-making or not.)

2. The options

Several possible responses of the law are set out by Shelley Roberts in her paper 'Warnock and Surrogate Motherhood: Sentiment or Argument?' in P Byrne (ed) *Rights and Wrongs in Medicine* (1986) at pp 104–109:

A. Total prohibition
How, then *ought* the issue of surrogacy to be settled? If we are convinced by the argument that no one should be permitted deliberately to avoid her maternal responsibilities, either for love or money, then the obvious solution is to attempt to devise a method of preventing all surrogacy transactions.

This, of course, raises tremendous practical difficulties. First, it is quite possible that couples may be sufficiently determined to have children by surrogacy that they will opt for the practice regardless of whether or not it is prohibited. Secondly, if the law were to make all surrogacy criminally unlawful, it could find itself hindered in the detection and regulation of possible harms and abuses that might result from 'underground' surrogacy. In addition, secrecy in and outside the family about the nature of a child's provenance could well undermine the stability of the families concerned, and consequently, of society.

Finally, the enforcement of laws against surrogacy, given the intimate nature of the arrangements, would be both difficult and possibly counter-productive. What sanctions could be imposed on transgressors? Fines would be unlikely to deter those intent upon paying huge sums of money for a child. If we imprison his parents for conceiving him, it will be the child who will suffer most. Similarly, his position will be jeopardised if we insist he stays with a mother who does not want him, or publicly declare him illegitimate, or refuse to allow the only family that claims him as theirs to have legal recognition as his parents. Thus, it seems that the most obvious response to the problems of surrogate motherhood may be impractical.

B. Licensing and regulation
If indeed it would not be plausible to seek to outlaw surrogacy, then thought must be given to practical methods by which surrogacy could be regulated. How could the most detrimental features of the practice be avoided? One method might be to regulate surrogate transactions by imposing a licensing scheme for agencies, requiring various forms of mandatory screening and counselling for participants.

There are serious problems with this approach. The most obvious is that government interference in, or control of, surrogacy would imply a legitimisation of the practice and perhaps act to encourage participants. If surrogacy clinics were established and licensed, it seems likely that the publicity would increase the popularity of surrogacy as a means of overcoming childlessness. If, however, it is accepted that there are serious problems inherent in surrogacy *per se*, then it is arguable that government ought to discourage rather than encourage the practice. The most serious objections to surrogacy will not be removed even if the process as a whole is subject to close scrutiny, and it would seem wrong to spend sums of public money on the licensing of an activity that has been judged to be contrary to public policy. Thus, it appears that the only legitimate form of regulation would be one which sought to eliminate aspects of surrogacy found to be particularly problematical.

C. Prohibition of commercial surrogacy

1. The role of intermediaries
The solution adopted by the Warnock committee and incorporated into the government's bill is to curtail surrogacy by imposing restrictions on the participation of intermediaries. No person or organisation is to initiate, take part in negotiations or compile information for use in surrogacy arrangements if such is done 'on a commercial basis' (that is, in return for payment to the intermediary).

The prohibition of commercial agencies would certainly limit the growth in the number of surrogate transactions. It would also specifically overcome the sort of abuse seen in the 'stud farms' previously described. One suspects, however, that the measure is designed more to cover up what the public finds distasteful about surrogacy (profit-hungry agencies) than to counteract any ill effects the practice may have upon its participants and on society at large. The more sensational possibilities for exploitation aside, there seems little difference, as regards most of surrogacy's problems, between a commercial agency and a volunteer agency, between a transaction mediated by an agency and one conducted privately.

One of the distinctly counterproductive features of the move to curtail intermediaries recommended by the Warnock committee and found in the bill is the effective exclusion of professionals such as doctors and solicitors from surrogacy arrangements. If no person is permitted, in exchange for payment, to compile information in respect of a surrogate arrangement, then couples and prospective surrogates would not, for example, be able to consult their physicians for genetic testing. If no one may take part in the negotiations, then solicitors would not be allowed to assist in facilitating the legal adoption of children born to surrogates.

A prohibition on professional assistance adds to, rather than detracts from, the difficulties associated with surrogacy. It prevents couples from seeking advice that may either lead them to decide against surrogacy or help them to proceed in the way least prejudicial to the interests of all concerned, especially the child. Without in any way encouraging surrogacy, the availability of professional assistance could point towards an informal screening process and allow the resulting child to be properly incorporated into the family that will be caring for him.

On both sides of the Atlantic, professional bodies have already begun to prohibit their members from any form of active recruiting of surrogates. This might be the most sensible way in which to regulate the participation of doctors, solicitors, psychologists and others in the surrogacy process and would be preferable to excluding them completely.

2. The role of surrogates
Both the Warnock committee and the drafters of the Government's bill recognised that one of the principal problems involved in surrogacy was its commercial aspect. It is suggested, however, that they approached the problem in the wrong way. Instead of seeking to prohibit payment to those assisting in surrogacy arrangements, they should have concentrated on the prohibition of payment to surrogates themselves. Although this solution would not resolve all the fundamental objections to surrogacy, it may be the practical alternative best suited to the protection of those concerned and of society in general.

The result of such a prohibition would probably be to limit the participants in surrogacy arrangements to friends or relatives of the couple seeking a child. Few women would voluntarily bear a child for a stranger. If there were to be an additional ban on advertising, as proposed in section 3 of the bill, then strangers could not ordinarily become involved.

Such a limitation of surrogacy to voluntary arrangements may resolve beneficially a number of the problems associated with surrogacy. First, volunteers would be much less likely to be victims of financial coercion. Equally, they would be unlikely to exploit the couples involved. It is of course arguable that the emotional pressure exerted by a relative or friend could be considerable. However, emotional pressure to perform voluntarily a lawful act is not the sort of duress that is sufficiently severe as to involve sanctions of law.

Secondly, if we refer back to the criteria for organ donations, voluntary womb-leasing ought to fit within the 'approved' category, in that it is the sort of disposition that was thought to be permissible if offered as a donation, but probably contrary to public policy if done in exchange for money. Paid surrogacy, of course, would have been against public policy, according to this test.

A third issue was the disruption of the marriage of the commissioning couple by the surrogate. There is no doubt that the presence of a friend or relative as a 'third party' to the marriage may present a considerable amount of tension. Morally, however, it may be less problematical than a similar intrusion by a stranger. If ties of blood or affection bind the commissioning parents and surrogate, they suggest that the second woman already has a link with the marriage. If anyone could be deemed appropriate as a substitute for the wife, then perhaps it is someone closely related or connected to her and to the family.

The final and perhaps most serious difficulty with surrogacy was the effect of the process upon the children concerned and upon our notions of childhood. At an individual level, the insistence that surrogate transactions be unpaid might well reduce the likelihood of the agreement dissolving into a dispute detrimental to the child. The involvement of friends would result in an arrangement where participants would be inclined to understand and care about each other's interests in the process. An additional benefit is a sort of built-in screening mechanism. A woman who is acting out of love rather than money and who deals directly with the commissioning father is much more likely to ask herself whether or not he is a suitable parent and similarly to consider the prospective mother.

It has been argued, of course, that it is not fair to ask a woman to go through the hardship of a surrogate pregnancy without compensating her for the pain, inconvenience and time. Surely, the better question is whether it is fair to *ask* a woman to undergo a pregnancy for someone else *at all*, and the answer is clearly 'no'. Only if a friend, out of love or compassion, *offers* herself in such a way can the offer be tolerated as a gift of self. The surest way to limit surrogacy to the cases most likely to proceed smoothly is to require an exceptional altruism in the surrogate mother.

However, by allowing even voluntary surrogacy, it is hard to avoid the allegations that surrogacy is equivalent to constructive abandonment and entails the use of a child as the means to an end. The elimination of paid surrogacy would, of course, improve the situation somewhat. The absence of a formal contract and exchange of 'goods' for money would eliminate some of the factors leading to a child-as-product mentality. Although problems could arise either as the result of over-solicitous interference from a surrogate who was a close relative or friend, or confusion for the child as to which woman was his real mother, children might still find it easier to comprehend the idea of 'auntie helping mummy' than of a business transaction between strangers. And it is arguable that a woman who knows the family well into which her child will be adopted, or is herself a member of that family, is committing a less reprehensible act than one who gives her infant to strangers. Nevertheless, the basic philosophical objections remain and nothing short of total prohibition, dismissed as impractical, could remove them. The continuing existence of such problems must serve as a reminder that the scheme proposed here is simply a way in which some forms of surrogacy may be tolerated and not an endorsement of a process which remains fundamentally at odds with public policy.

Given the complexities of the issues arising and the nature of the interests involved, it is inevitable that the law will be involved in some shape or form and to some or other extent. The question then becomes what form that law should take.

One option could be to leave matters to *ad hoc* resolution by the courts as they arise. Alternatively some regulatory scheme could be devised which aims to deal comprehensively with the subject. The latter approach appears to have considerable support. This does not, of course, determine the content of the legal regulation. Professor Alexander Capron, however, adopts an interesting stance urging a minimalist approach through legislation, thereafter relying on traditional family law to achieve the necessary regulation.

A Capron 'Alternative Birth Technologies: Legal Challenges' (1987) 20 UC Davis LR 697

Is legislation desirable?
Should we remedy this problem by legislating a framework for surrogate contracts? On the one hand, to do so may well increase the frequency of such arrangements – not a salutary development in my view. On the other hand, the primary interest in protection of the offspring is not well-served by the absence of a statutorily established system. What ought such a statute encompass? At a minimum, I would suggest the following.

First, careful medical screening should be performed for all participants in 'surrogacy' to prevent avoidable illness. Granted, this does not exist for ordinary reproduction – but, then, surrogacy is not ordinary. The result may well be achieved through the threat of sanctions on the professionals (physicians, social workers, lawyers, etc) who superintend the arrangements; their failure to screen could be a basis for liability. The risk of eugenic controls being exercised by the state places this aspect of a statute into a difficult balancing act, but the interest in protecting the child is strong enough to compel a hard effort to find a solution that stops short of state control of reproduction.

Second, surrogacy should be regarded as a form of prenatal adoption of the child of one parent by the other parent and provisions for state supervision, including confidential record-keeping, should parallel those applicable to postnatal adoption. The harder question is whether standards of 'fitness' ought to be applied to the couples; it may be enough to achieve this indirectly through medical supervision. There may, of course, be some issues that cannot be well resolved by the law but must be left to the development of social norms. For example, should the procedure be limited to infertile couples and those with medical reason (genetic or gestational risks) for not reproducing themselves? Rather than trying to develop clear rules on what qualifies as sufficient 'infertility' or 'medical contraindication,' it may be sufficient to leave the question to physicians and potential surrogates: 'Is this couple's problem serious enough to warrant surrogacy?'

Third, and perhaps most important, the parties to the contract should each be bound by their normal parental obligations of care and support, regardless of the breach or alleged breach of contract by the party. The Malahoff case indicates the potential for abandonment of the child if the parties are free to regard the situation as one of a contract for delivery of a product.

All of these suggestions made thus far aim to protect the interest of the child, which I view as the primary aim of public policy in this field. Other provisions in a statute would expand on this goal, while also attempting to promote additional values.

Fourth, the law should provide that the child is the legal child of the surrogate mother. This was the position of the Warnock Committee in England in 1984. Such a legal rule would do three things. First, it would reinforce the child's interest in having a legally responsible mother at birth. Second, it would place the surrogate in the same position as other women who decide to allow a child to be adopted, which includes having the right to change her mind within a specified time period. Third, it would also discourage surrogacy by exposing the biological father to the risk that he might end up with a financial obligation to the child but without any guarantee of other parental rights (which would lodge instead with the surrogate's husband).

The rule I suggest regarding maternity raises the more difficult issues of the presumption of paternity. Under the law in the thirty or so states with AID statutes, a child born after AID is presumed to be the legal offspring of her husband if he has consented to the insemination. Applying that rule to surrogacy would make the child the legal offspring of the surrogate's husband if he consents, or would open the physician (and others) to suit if the husband 'non-consented' and later became dissatisfied with the situation. A Michigan decision declining to allow the paternity act to be used to declare prenatally the paternal status of a contracting father was revised on appeal, [*Sykowski v Appleyard* (1985) 362 NW 211] while a Kentucky court declined to allow a 'mere affidavit' to rebut the presumption of the paternity of the surrogate's husband [*Re Baby Girl* No 83 AD (Jefferson Circ Ct, March 8, 1983)].

A fifth control that a statute might exercise would be to regulate the amount of payment made. Obviously, such agreements are notoriously difficult to supervise. The major risk that a person runs in going outside the terms permitted in the regulation is the same risk as already exists – namely, holding an unenforceable contract – and that has not deterred hundreds of people so far. Moreover, besides difficulties of enforcement, the question arises, which way should the regulation tend – to hold down payments to the level of actual out-of-pocket expenses (including life and health insurance premiums), which would lead to surrogacy only by true altruists, or to push the price up to a level commensurate with the values of the service and the time and effort involved? The latter would doubtless lead to a flood of eager surrogates, but without at least some control, more cases are likely to arise like the one now being litigated in San Diego, in which a Mexican woman is trying to retain custody of the child she bore under a surrogate contract for $1500.

Suppose that the legal regulations adopted are seen as disadvantaging surrogacy compared to AID. Is this unfair discrimination because it treats couples differently based on male versus female infertility? I do not believe that the claimed objection based on 'procreative freedom' is persuasive, for several reasons. First, there is a substantial difference between the role of the 'donor' in AID (merely contributing the germinal material, which is obtained in a risk-free procedure) and the 'donor' in a surrogate contract (who not only contributes the germinal material but carries the child for nine months and gives birth to it). These differences – in time, in risk, in attachment, and in effects on fetal development – implicate the values of well-being and of exploitation set forth earlier. Second, the legal rule in question – that a child born to a woman is legally hers until she gives the child up for adoption – is facially neutral between the situations of AID and surrogacy. In both instances, it vests parental rights and obligations in the woman who is inseminated and her husband. Third, the analogy between AID and surrogate motherhood is inexact; the correct analogue to AID is egg donation … In that case, the 'adoptive mother', who gestates the donated egg (fertilised by the sperm of her husband or another donor) would be the legal mother.

The development of alternative birth technologies is seemingly pushing back the limits of human biology, and in the process sorely testing the limits of human law. The *Baby M* case in New Jersey reminds us of these limits, since it involves at its core the interest of a child who is not a party to the contract. My sense is that, in the absence of a statute that clearly establishes the rules I have recommended in this essay, the *Baby M* court should rule on grounds of the child's 'best interests' in a custodial sense, not on the basis of the contract. Moreover, in so ruling there must be no presumption that wealth or social class is determinative. As the California Supreme Court recently ruled, in a custody dispute over an out-of-wedlock child whose father was seeking custody based on the greater financial means and better home environment he and his new wife could offer compared with the child's working (and still unwed) mother, 'the purpose of child support awards is to ensure that the [parent] otherwise best fit for custody receives adequate funds,' and not to use the poorer parent's position as a ground for denying custody. [*Burchard v Garay* (1986) 724 P 2d 486.] At the heart of best interests – or 'beyond' it – is stability and continuity for the child. In the *Baby M* case, that consideration could lead custody to be awarded to Dr Stern and his wife (who have had primary custody of most of the child's first year), even if the physician who performed the insemination were now to announce that he had used semen from a man other than Dr Stern.

Given the controversial nature of the issues raised by surrogate arrangements, it is, therefore, perhaps no surprise that legislation in countries around the world had adopted different policy options. Australia, for example, has been in the vanguard in legislating to regulate the provision of infertility services and, in particular, surrogacy arrangements. The following extract summarises the developments.

Margaret Otlowski *'Re Evelyn* – Reflections on Australia's first Litigated Surrogacy Case' (1999) 7 Med L Rev 38

As in other countries, there has been considerable debate in Australia about the ethics of surrogacy, particularly arrangements of a commercial nature. During the 1980s, at the Commonwealth level, and in all but one of the Australian States and Territories, law reform commission bodies and agencies addressed the issue of surrogacy and whether surrogacy arrangements should be permitted. With the exception of the Tasmanian Chalmers' Committee Report, the reports resulting from these inquiries made recommendations against permitting surrogacy, and legislation was subsequently introduced in Victoria, South Australia, Queensland, Tasmania and the Australian Capital Territory (Victoria: Infertility Treatment Act 1995; South Australia: Family Relationships Act 1975; Queensland: Surrogate Parent Act 1988; Tasmania: Surrogacy Contracts Act 1993; Australian Capital Territory: Substitute Parent Agreement Act 1994). However, despite calls for uniformity between States and Territories on the issue, the legislation enacted is by no means uniform and three jurisdictions (New South Wales, Western Australia and the Northern Territory) have not, as yet, introduced surrogacy legislation.

The main focus of the existing legislation is to outlaw the commercial aspects of surrogacy arrangements. With the exception of South Australia, the legislative prohibition extends to the immediate contracting parties who commit an offence under the Act if they enter into a commercial surrogacy arrangement. Under each of the Acts, all surrogacy agreements, whether of a commercial nature or not, are void and unenforceable which effectively puts into statutory form the conclusion that had been reached by the courts in overseas jurisdictions. Queensland is the only jurisdiction which criminalises non-commercial or altruistic arrangements. In the other jurisdictions, whilst the object of the legislation is clearly to discourage surrogacy arrangements, parties entering into non-commercial arrangements are not penalised.

Legal regulation of surrogacy arrangements can, as we have seen, take a number of forms: (i) *total prohibition* (usually linked with criminal sanctions); (ii) *non-regulation* (leaving it to the parties and the 'market' to set permissible limits); and (iii) *partial regulation* (usually preventing third party involvement and advertising; but sometimes limited to commercial arrangements). Few jurisdictions have opted for total prohibition but Queensland's Surrogate

Parenthood Act 1988 is an example in the common law world (see also German Law of 13 December 1990, s 1(1)7). Equally, the regulation of surrogacy arrangements is rarely left entirely to the parties and the market place. Even in America where the market is more likely to be allowed to regulate, certainly the *making* (if not also the *performance*) of surrogacy arrangements, the law always regulates the *outcome* of such arrangements ie it is the law which determines the issues of parentage and the upbringing of any children born (see eg *In the Matter of Baby M* (1988) 537 A 2d 1227 (NJ Sup Ct)).

By way of example, we can see the approach in the Tasmanian Surrogacy Contracts Act 1993 (SCA 1993), referred to by Otlowski (*supra*).The SCA 1993 adopts a model of partial regulation. The SCA 1993 applies to 'surrogate contracts' and this term is very widely defined to include gratuitous agreements as well as contracts *stricto sensu* (s 3). It is also defined to include surrogacy contracts made not only before the surrogate becomes pregnant but also where she is already pregnant (s 3). The effect of the SCA 1993 may be summarised as follows.

First, under the Act all surrogate contracts are 'void and unenforceable' (s 7).

Secondly, it is illegal to 'publish, or cause to be published, an advertisement, notice or other document' offering to be a surrogate, seeking a surrogate or offering to be an intermediary (s 6).

Thirdly, the SCA 1993 seeks to prohibit third parties becoming involved in surrogate contracts. It is illegal to introduce prospective parties to a surrogate contract (s 4(1)); to induce another to enter into a surrogate contract (s 4(2)); to arrange or negotiate a surrogate contract or agree to do so (s 4(3)); and to make or receive payment or reward (defined to include non-monetary benefits (s 3) in relation to a surrogate contract (s 4(4)). The comprehensive provisions of s 4 of the Act prohibit all forms of third party participation in the making of the arrangement.

Fourthly, under the SCA 1993, the parties will commit a criminal offence if they 'make or receive, or agree to make or receive, a payment or reward' (s 4(4)).

It is not entirely clear, but the wording of s 4(2) may be such that third parties are also liable if they 'induce' another to enter into a surrogacy contract. Usually, one side of the surrogacy contract will 'induce' the other side to enter into the contract. If this is the correct interpretation of the SCA 1993, then it will be very difficult in Tasmania lawfully to make surrogacy contracts.

Finally, we should notice the provisions of the SCA 1993 which make it illegal to provide 'technical or professional services in relation to achieving' a pregnancy for a surrogate (s 5). Clearly, therefore, a so-called 'IVF surrogacy' involving donated gametes or embryos is illegal in Tasmania. A doctor would commit a criminal offence were he to help the couple (or is it the surrogate) *achieve* a pregnancy. Of course, it is important to notice what the Act does prohibit – providing services for '*achieving* a pregnancy'. Thus, a doctor may provide medical care to the surrogate once the pregnancy is achieved.

(For a detailed discussion of Australia, see A Stuhmcke 'Surrogate Motherhood: The Legal Position in Australia' (1994) 2 J of Law and Medicine 116.)

3. The response in England

In England, in response to the highly publicised birth of 'Baby Cotton' to a surrogate mother in January 1985 (see *Re C (a minor)* [1985] FLR 846), Parliament enacted the Surrogacy Arrangements Act 1985. We shall discuss this in detail later. It takes a middle ground. While not prohibiting surrogacy, it seeks to discourage it as a practice by, for example, making it illegal to facilitate *commercial* surrogacy arrangements and by prohibiting advertising for surrogates or offering to be a surrogate.

The Report of the *Surrogacy Review* (Cm 4068 1998) (*supra*) summarised the current state of English law:

> 2.24 In the event, the Surrogacy Arrangements Act 1985 and the Human Fertilisation and Embryology Act 1990 (the "1990 Act") embodied in full neither the recommendations of the majority nor the minority in Warnock, and in our judgment the legislative framework which evolved to deal with surrogacy rested on no coherent basis of policy. The 1985 Act, enacted swiftly after publicity surrounding the Baby Cotton case, outlawed commercial surrogacy agencies only.
> 2.25 In a subsequent White Paper *Human Fertilisation and Embryology: A Framework for Legislation* (Cm 259) the Government rejected both the majority proposals to outlaw *any* third party participation in surrogacy arrangements and the minority proposal to license non-profit making surrogacy agencies and to bring surrogacy arrangements within the jurisdiction of what was to become the HFEA.
> 2.26 The White Paper did propose that the statutory licensing authority review surrogacy from time to time and report to Parliament; and that regulations under the proposed legislation should permit the Secretary of State to lay regulations to extend the authority's powers to include power to license non-profitmaking surrogacy agencies. In the event, these proposals did not find their way into what became the 1990 Act and so no express obligations were placed on the HFEA.

The discouragement did not, however, work and the practice continued. The *Surrogacy Review* (*ibid*) explains:

> 3.5 A number of developments over the ensuing years meant that surrogacy did not largely disappear as might have been anticipated: (1) the courts showed themselves (not unsurprisingly) to be more concerned to secure the future of a particular child, than to maintain strict rules on expenses; (2) late in the day section 30 was inserted in the Human Fertilisation and Embryology Act 1990 providing an alternative to adoption for some commissioning couples; (3) professional opinion on the ethics of doctors becoming involved in surrogacy changed significantly; and (4) at least two voluntary organisations came into existence with the objective of assisting commissioning couples to find surrogates and to help the parties set up and follow through surrogacy arrangements.

You will notice reference to the shift in professional opinion about surrogacy and medical involvement. The Report of the *Surrogacy Review* describes the shift in opinion:

> 3.21 In 1984, it appeared that opinion within the medical profession veered against professional involvement in surrogacy and that had the majority proposals in Warnock been implemented, professionals might well have had grounds to fear that any such involvement might be unlawful. By 1990, it was clear that the bar on any third party involvement in surrogacy arrangements would not be implemented, and the BMA had altered its stance significantly from opposition to surrogacy to acceptance that professional involvement in surrogacy might, in appropriate circumstances, be ethical.
> 3.22 In its 1996 publication *Changing Conceptions of Motherhood* the BMA reviewed the practice of surrogacy in Britain. In its guidelines to health professionals endorsing surrogacy as an acceptable option of last resort, the BMA sets out guidance designed to safeguard the welfare of any child to be born and to minimise risks to surrogate mothers. By 1996, it was also clear that a number of clinics licensed by the Human Fertilisation and Embryology Authority (HFEA) had begun to offer full surrogacy services, and, much less frequently, medically supervised insemination.
> 3.23 It is necessary to be clear as to just what level of medical professional involvement in surrogacy is now practised and endorsed by the BMA. Care of the surrogate once there is an established pregnancy was of course never condemned. Indeed it would be unethical not to provide such care. In recent years however doctors have been asked both to provide advice on surrogacy and to provide treatment services. Generally such treatment services, if they involve IVF or use of stored sperm, must be provided in a licensed clinic. There are, however, accounts of general practitioners assisting in insemination with fresh sperm.
> 3.24 Where treatment services to establish pregnancy in the surrogate are provided in a licensed clinic, the clinic is subject to the Code of Practice promulgated by the HFEA and approved by the Secretary of State for Health. The HFEA in its Code stresses that surrogacy should be considered only where it is "physically impossible or highly undesirable for medical reasons" for the commissioning mother to carry the child (Human Fertilisation and

Embryology Authority: Code of Practice (4th edition – July 1998) at paragraph 3.20). Where the intending mother has no uterus, or has suffered from habitual miscarriage, or suffers from a medical condition rendering pregnancy a grave risk to her life or permanent health, such criteria would appear to be met. Evidence has been given to us suggesting that, additionally, surrogacy might be contemplated where the intending mother had undergone a series of failed IVF cycles. Establishing a pregnancy in a healthy and provenly fertile surrogate might be perceived as preferable to continued attempts at IVF. Whether such cases constitute use of surrogacy as "a last resort" where pregnancy is impossible may be open to question.
3.25 The Code lays down procedures in relation to the welfare of the child. Clinics offering treatment services in relation to surrogacy stress (in evidence to us) that over and above what the Code of Practice demands, every effort is made to secure the welfare of the child to be born, and to ensure that all parties to the arrangement understand the implications of what they are agreeing to do.
3.26 The change in attitude within the medical profession has had two significant results. "Medical endorsement" of surrogacy adds to its respectability. Couples who wish to utilise full surrogacy where they are the genetic parents of the child can obtain assistance in establishing a pregnancy *via* IVF at a licensed clinic. Couples who seek partial surrogacy but with the reassurance of medical supervision can also do so. In both cases that ability to seek professional involvement is likely to be dependent on ability to pay. There have been to our knowledge at least two instances of health authorities being asked to pay for surrogacy services, but generally such services are confined to the private sector.
3.27 What medical practitioners do *not* involve themselves in, however, is the process by which commissioning couples find a surrogate. Doctors may often now be willing to advise generally on surrogacy arrangements and assist in establishing a pregnancy. They do not (and might well fall foul of the 1985 Act if they did) assist couples to establish a surrogacy arrangement. A couple seeking medical assistance to establish a pregnancy must either have found their own prospective surrogate independently, or have obtained assistance from one of the non profit-making organisations set up to support commissioning couples and surrogates, such as COTS and SPC (see paragraphs 3.30 and 3.31 below). We understand that some clinics will refer patients contemplating surrogacy to such organisations.

(For a survey of the involvement of licensed clinics in surrogate pregnancies, see A Balen and C Hayden 'British Fertility Survey of all Licensed Clinics that perform surrogacy in the UK' (1998) 1 Human Fertility 6 (29 of 113 licensed clinics perform surrogacy).)

We will discuss later in this section the *Surrogacy Review's* proposals for reform of the law. As we shall see, the report rejects any suggestion that surrogacy arrangements should be outlawed and, instead, proposes a regulatory framework which seeks to prevent effectively the commercialisation of surrogacy and protect the welfare of children (paras 4.38–4.51).

Before we do that, however, we should examine the current law in England and Wales.

D. ENGLISH LAW

1. The validity of the agreement

The typical terms of a surrogacy contract can be seen in the New Jersey case of *In the Matter of Baby M* (1988) 537 A 2d 1227(*infra*). The contract referred to, and set out below, is that used by the Infertility Center of New York (ICNY), the senior executive of which is the attorney, Noel Keane, regarded as the leading exponent of surrogacy arrangements in the United States.

SURROGATE PARENTING AGREEMENT

THIS AGREEMENT is made this   day of , 19   by and between MARY BETH WHITEHEAD, a married woman (herein referred to as 'Surrogate'), RICHARD WHITEHEAD, her husband (herein referred to as 'Husband'), and WILLIAM STERN (herein referred to as 'Natural Father').

Recitals

THIS AGREEMENT is made with reference to the following facts:

(1) WILLIAM STERN, Natural Father, is an individual over the age of eighteen (18) years who is desirous of entering into this Agreement.

(2) The sole purpose of this Agreement is to enable WILLIAM STERN and his infertile wife to have a child which is biologically related to WILLIAM STERN.

(3) MARY BETH WHITEHEAD, Surrogate, and RICHARD WHITEHEAD, her husband, are over he age of eighteen (18) years and desirous of entering into this Agreement in consideration of the following:

NOW THEREFORE, in consideration of the mutual promises contained herein and the intentions of being legally bound hereby, the parties agree as follows:

1. MARY BETH WHITEHEAD, Surrogate, represents that she is capable of conceiving children. MARY BETH WHITEHEAD understands and agrees that in the best interest of the child, she will not form or attempt to form a parent-child relationship with any child or children she may conceive, carry to term and give birth to pursuant to the provisions of this Agreement, and shall freely surrender custody to WILLIAM STERN, Natural Father, immediately upon birth of the child; and terminate all parental rights to said child pursuant to this Agreement.

2. MARY BETH WHITEHEAD, Surrogate, and RICHARD WHITEHEAD, her husband, have been married since 12/2/73, and RICHARD WHITEHEAD is in agreement with the purposes, intents and provisions of this Agreement and acknowledges that his wife, MARY BETH WHITEHEAD, Surrogate, shall be artificially inseminated pursuant to the provisions of this Agreement. RICHARD WHITEHEAD agrees that in the best interest of the child, he will not form or attempt to form a parent-child relationship with any child or children MARY BETH WHITEHEAD, Surrogate, may conceive by artificial insemination as described herein, and agrees freely and readily to surrender immediate custody of the child to WILLIAM STERN, Natural Father; and terminate his parental rights;

RICHARD WHITEHEAD further acknowledges he will do all acts necessary to rebut the presumption of paternity of any offspring conceived and born pursuant to aforementioned agreement as provided by law, including blood testing and/or HLA testing.

3. WILLIAM STERN, Natural Father, does hereby enter into this written contractual Agreement with MARY BETH WHITEHEAD, Surrogate, where MARY BETH WHITEHEAD shall be artificially inseminated with the semen of WILLIAM STERN by a physician. MARY BETH WHITEHEAD, Surrogate, upon becoming pregnant, acknowledges that she will carry said embryo/fetus(s) until delivery. MARY BETH WHITEHEAD, Surrogate and RICHARD WHITEHEAD, her husband, agree that they will cooperate with any background investigation into the Surrogate's medical, family and personal history and warrant the information to be accurate to the best of their knowledge. MARY BETH WHITEHEAD, Surrogate and RICHARD WHITEHEAD, her husband, agree to surrender custody of the child to WILLIAM STERN, Natural Father, immediately upon birth, acknowledging that it is the intent of this Agreement in the best interests of the child to do so; as well as institute and cooperate in proceedings to terminate their respective parental rights to said child, and sign any and all necessary affidavits, documents, and the like, in order to further the intent and purposes of this Agreement. It is understood by MARY BETH WHITEHEAD, and RICHARD WHITEHEAD, that the child to be conceived is being done so for the sole purpose of giving said child to WILLIAM STERN, its natural and biological father. MARY BETH WHITEHEAD and RICHARD WHITEHEAD agree to sign all necessary affidavits prior to and after the birth of the child and voluntarily participate in any paternity proceedings necessary to have WILLIAM STERN'S name entered on said child's birth certificate as the natural or biological father.

4. That the consideration for this Agreement, which is compensation for services and expenses, and in no way is to be construed as a fee for termination of parental rights or a payment in exchange for a consent to surrender the child for adoption, in addition to other provisions contained herein, shall be as follows:

(A) $10,000 shall be paid to MARY BETH WHITEHEAD, Surrogate, upon surrender of custody to WILLIAM STERN, the natural and biological father of the child born pursuant to the provisions of this Agreement for surrogate services and expenses in carrying out her obligations under this Agreement;

(B) The consideration to be paid to MARY BETH WHITEHEAD, Surrogate, shall be deposited with the Infertility Center of New York (hereinafter ICNY), by the representative of WILLIAM STERN, at the time of the signing of this Agreement, and held in escrow until completion of the duties and obligations of MARY BETH WHITEHEAD, Surrogate, (see Exhibit 'A' for a copy of the Escrow Agreement), as herein described.

(C) WILLIAM STERN, Natural Father, shall pay the expenses incurred by MARY BETH WHITEHEAD, Surrogate, pursuant to her pregnancy, more specifically defined as follows:

(1) All medical, hospitalization, and pharmaceutical, laboratory and therapy expenses incurred as a result of MARY BETH WHITEHEAD'S pregnancy, not covered or allowed by her

present health and major medical insurance, including all extraordinary medical expenses and all reasonable expenses for treatment of any emotional or mental conditions or problems related to said pregnancy, but in no case shall any such expenses be paid or reimbursed after a period of six (6) months have elapsed since the date of the termination of the pregnancy, and this Agreement specifically excludes any expenses for lost wages or other non-itemized incidentals (see Exhibit 'B') related to said pregnancy.

(2) WILLIAM STERN, Natural Father, shall not be responsible for any latent medical expenses occurring six (6) weeks subsequent to the birth of the child, unless the medical problem or abnormality incident thereto was known and treated by a physician prior to the expiration of said six (6) week period and in written notice of the same sent to ICNY, as representative of WILLIAM STERN by certified mail, return receipt requested, advising of this treatment.

(3) WILLIAM STERN, Natural Father, shall be responsible for the total costs of all paternity testing. Such paternity testing may, at the option of WILLIAM STERN, Natural Father, be required prior to release of the surrogate fee from escrow. In the event WILLIAM STERN, Natural Father, is conclusively determined not to be the biological father of the child as a result of an HLA test, this Agreement will be deemed breached and MARY BETH WHITEHEAD, Surrogate, shall not be entitled to any fee. WILLIAM STERN, Natural father, shall be entitled to reimbursement of all medical and related expenses from MARY BETH WHITEHEAD, Surrogate, and RICHARD WHITEHEAD, her husband.

(4) MARY BETH WHITEHEAD'S reasonable travel expenses incurred at the request of WILLIAM STERN pursuant to this Agreement.

5. MARY BETH WHITEHEAD, Surrogate, and RICHARD WHITEHEAD, her husband, understand and agree to assume all risks, including the risk of death, which are incidental to conception, pregnancy, childbirth, including but not limited to, postpartum complications. A copy of said possible risks and/or complications is attached hereto and made a part hereof (see Exhibit 'C').

6. MARY BETH WHITEHEAD, Surrogate, and RICHARD WHITEHEAD, her husband, hereby agree to undergo psychiatric evaluation by JOAN EINWOHNER, a psychiatrist as designated by WILLIAM STERN or an agent thereof. WILLIAM STERN shall pay for the cost of said psychiatric evaluation. MARY BETH WHITEHEAD and RICHARD WHITEHEAD shall sign, prior to their evaluations, a medical release permitting dissemination of the report prepared as a result of said psychiatric evaluations to ICNY or WILLIAM STERN and his wife.

7. MARY BETH WHITEHEAD, Surrogate, and RICHARD WHITEHEAD, her husband, hereby agree that it is the exclusive and sole right of WILLIAM STERN, Natural Father, to name said child.

8. 'Child' as referred to in this Agreement shall include all children born simultaneously pursuant to the inseminations contemplated herein.

9. In the event of the death of WILLIAM STERN, prior or subsequent to the birth of said child, it is hereby understood and agreed by MARY BETH WHITEHEAD, Surrogate, and RICHARD WHITEHEAD, her husband, that the child will be placed in the custody of WILLIAM STERN'S wife.

10. In the event that the child is miscarried prior to the fifth (5th) month of pregnancy, no compensation, as enumerated in paragraph 4(A), shall be paid to MARY BETH WHITEHEAD, Surrogate. However, the expenses enumerated in paragraph 4(C) shall be paid or reimbursed to MARY BETH WHITEHEAD, Surrogate. In the event the child is miscarried, dies or is stillborn subsequent to the fourth (4th) month of pregnancy and said child does not survive, the Surrogate shall receive $1,000.00 in lieu of the compensation enumerated in paragraph 4(A). In the event of a miscarriage or stillbirth as described above, this Agreement shall terminate and neither MARY BETH WHITEHEAD, Surrogate, nor WILLIAM STERN, Natural Father, shall be under any further obligation under this Agreement.

11. MARY BETH WHITEHEAD, Surrogate, and WILLIAM STERN, Natural father, shall have undergone complete physical and genetic evaluation, under the direction and supervision of a licensed physician, to determine whether the physical health and well-being of each is satisfactory. Said physical examination shall include testing for venereal diseases, specifically including but not limited to, syphilis, herpes and gonorrhea. Said venereal diseases testing shall be done prior to, but not limited to, each series of inseminations.

12. In the event that pregnancy has not occurred within a reasonable time, in the opinion of WILLIAM STERN, Natural Father, this Agreement shall terminate by written notice to MARY BETH WHITEHEAD, Surrogate, at the residence provided to the ICNY by the Surrogate, from ICNY, as representative of WILLIAM STERN, Natural Father.

13. MARY BETH WHITEHEAD, Surrogate, agrees that she will not abort the child once conceived except, if in the professional medical opinion of the inseminating physician,

such action is necessary for the physical health of MARY BETH WHITEHEAD or the child has been determined by said physician to be physiologically abnormal. MARY BETH WHITEHEAD further agrees, upon the request of said physician to undergo amniocentesis (see Exhibit 'D') or similar tests to detect genetic and congenital defects. In the event said test reveals that the fetus is genetically or congenitally abnormal, MARY BETH WHITEHEAD, Surrogate, agrees to abort the fetus upon demand of WILLIAM STERN, Natural Father, in which event, the fee paid to the Surrogate will be in accordance to Paragraph 10. If MARY BETH WHITEHEAD refuses to abort the fetus upon demand of WILLIAM STERN, his obligations as stated in this Agreement shall cease forthwith, except as to obligations of paternity imposed by statute.

14. Despite the provisions of Paragraph 13, WILLIAM STERN, Natural Father, recognizes that some genetic and congenital abnormalities may not be detected by amniocentesis or other tests, and therefore, if proven to be the biological father of the child, assumes the legal responsibility for any child who may possess genetic or congenital abnormalities. (See Exhibits 'E' and 'F'.)

15. MARY BETH WHITEHEAD, Surrogate, further agrees to adhere to all medical instructions given to her by the inseminating physician as well as her independent obstetrician. MARY BETH WHITEHEAD also agrees not to smoke cigarettes, drink alcoholic beverages, use illegal drugs, or take non-prescription medication or prescribed medications without written consent from her physician. MARY BETH WHITEHEAD agrees to follow a prenatal medical examination schedule to consist of no fewer visits than: one visit per month during the first seven (7) months of pregnancy, two visits (each to occur at two-week intervals) during the eighth and ninth month of pregnancy.

16. MARY BETH WHITEHEAD, Surrogate, agrees to cause RICHARD WHITEHEAD, her husband, to execute a refusal of consent form as annexed hereto as Exhibit 'G'.

17. Each party acknowledges that he or she fully understands this Agreement and its legal effect, and that they are signing the name freely and voluntarily and that neither party has any reason to believe that the other(s) did not freely and voluntarily execute said Agreement.

18. In the event any of the provisions of this Agreement are deemed to be invalid or unenforceable, the same shall be deemed severable from the remainder of this Agreement and shall not cause the invalidity or unenforceability of the remainder of this Agreement. If such provision shall be deemed invalid due to its scope or breadth, then said provision shall be deemed valid to the extent of the scope or breadth permitted by law.

19. The original of this Agreement, upon execution, shall be retained by the Infertility Center of New York, with photocopies being distributed to MARY BETH WHITEHEAD, Surrogate and WILLIAM STERN, Natural Father, having the same legal effect as the original.

WILLIAM STERN   DATE
Natural Father

STATE OF:
COUNTY OF

On the day of   , 19   , before me personally came WILLIAM STERN, known to me, and to me known, to be the individual described in the foregoing instrument and he acknowledged to me that he executed the same as his free and voluntary act.

NOTARY PUBLIC

A central question in English law is to what extent is such a contract enforceable? There are two principal ways in which the parties might seek to enforce the contract. First, the parties might wish to enforce one of the terms during the course of the surrogate's pregnancy, for example, that the surrogate mother undergo certain medical tests or refrains from particular conduct which might be harmful to the unborn child. Secondly, the parties might wish to enforce the terms of the contract requiring the surrogate mother to hand over the baby to the commissioning couple after its birth. We shall return to the latter issue shortly. It was the one that arose in the *Baby M* case. The problems that would be faced if the law were to permit enforcement of the detailed terms of surrogate arrangements are discussed in the following extracts.

C Sappideen 'The Surrogate Mother – A Growing Problem' (1983) University of New South Wales Law Review 79

...[I]f those contracts were enforceable, difficult problems would arise on breach of contract. Independently of the issue of public policy, a court of equity will not specifically enforce contracts for personal services. Two reasons may be given for this rule; the first is that contracts which require constant supervision will not be enforced and secondly, that a court will not order performance of contracts requiring special confidence and trust. A court of law can, however, enforce the contract by awarding damages for breach of contract. Examples will be given to illustrate inherent difficulties.

(a) Breach by the surrogate

The surrogate may breach the contract (depending on its terms) in a variety of ways, for example smoking, drinking during pregnancy, terminating the pregnancy by abortion, or refusal to hand over custody of the baby. Taking the first examples, smoking and drinking during pregnancy – would this breach allow the couple to treat the contract as at an end? Should the contract provide that the breach of any of its terms renders the contract voidable by the innocent party? Would a fraudulent misrepresentation that the surrogate did not smoke or drink allow the innocent party to rescind? If the innocent party reaffirmed the contract and sued for damages, what would be the damages? For example, how could damage be measured and proved if all that could be shown was that the surrogate had had one cigarette, or one drink? If the surrogate terminated the pregnancy what damages could be recovered by the couple? Presumably all that could be obtained here would be damages for emotional distress suffered as flowing naturally from the breach.

(b) Breach by the couple

Depending on the terms of the contract, breaches could include failure to pay, failure to take custody of the child, or failure to provide health insurance or to adopt the child. If the couple refused to take custody of the child, would the surrogate be able to recover the cost of upkeep for the child until aged eighteen, or would the surrogate be obliged to mitigate her loss by placing the child for adoption?

Specific questions which arise from contracts such as these are addressed in Theresa Mady's article. Although some of the discussion concerns uniquely American law, the analysis (and suggested approach) remains of great interest. In this article the following abbreviations are adopted: S = surrogate mother; H = commissioning male; W = commissioning female.

T Mady 'Surrogate Mothers: The Legal Issues' (1981) American Journal of Law and Medicine 324

Given that the surrogate mother arrangement is legal, parties still must determine what terms they can include that will be judicially enforced in a written contract. Although the parties' written agreement may be persuasive to a court in establishing their intent, courts are not bound to enforce provisions which are contrary to public policy. Clearly, public policy concerns permeate the surrogate mother arrangement, especially where the interests of an unborn child are at stake. In addition, attempts to contract to specifically enforce personal services are not necessarily binding, for parties cannot divest a court of law of its power to grant relief.

1. Rights and liabilities of S

The rights and liabilities of the surrogate mother stem from two basic promises that she makes to H and W. First, S promises to be inseminated with H's semen and carry the child to term. This includes the assurance that she will seek the necessary medical attention to maintain and ensure the health and safety of the fetus. Second, S promises to surrender to H and W all rights in the child. If S is married, this second promise may become complicated if her husband wishes to retain custody of the child.

The law presumes that a child born to a married woman is the child of the woman and her husband. Since this presumption is rebuttable, S and her husband should state explicitly that they will make no claim to the child; without this statement the intention of the parties may be undercut. Such a provision would help eliminate emotional strain and probably litigation, and would avoid harming the child by involving it in custody proceedings.

If S breaches by not adhering to one or both of these promises, courts will have difficulty devising appropriate remedies. The proper remedy will depend on the type of breach. Three major possibilities for breach arise: S may wish to abort the child, S may negligently cause harm to the fetus, or S may refuse to give up the child after birth.

If *S* desires to abort for any reason, within certain constitutional limits, it is unclear whether she can be legally prevented from so doing. The United States Supreme Court has held that the right to decide to abort is one of constitutional dimension which cannot be limited by the exercise of state law unless pursuant to a compelling state interest. The Court has also held that a woman may decide to abort irrespective of her husband's consent. If a husband cannot veto his wife's decision to abort, it is unclear whether *H* and *W*, who are merely in a contractual relationship with *S*, can impose their will. However, some constitutional rights can be waived prior to their exercise. It is unclear whether all constitutional rights can be irrevocably waived. It has never been decided which category encompasses the right to choose to abort. If *S* cannot irrevocably waive her right to choose to have an abortion, she will retain this right. If *S* aborts the fetus, however, she breaches by destroying the essence of the contract. Classical contract remedies do not allow recovery for the emotional upset which *H* and *W* would inevitably suffer. Restitution for expenses already paid may be the only viable recourse. Although a tort action for infliction of emotional distress might more appropriately compensate *H* and *W*, few jurisdictions have accepted this cause of action. In addition, wrongful death actions may not presently extend to abortion of a fetus.

The second type of breach can occur if *S* negligently causes harm to the fetus, abrogating the promise to provide proper care during pregnancy. In this event, *H* and *W* have two possible avenues of recovery: an action for breach of the terms of the contract, or a tort action based on negligence. Both actions would require *H* and *W* to prove essentially the same elements, although the likelihood of equitable relief rather than damages increases when predicated on the contract action. In either case, *H* and *W* would have to demonstrate that the contract imposed a duty on *S*, whether explicit or implied, to maintain an adequate level of care during pregnancy. If the contract makes explicit the level of care *S* will undertake, including the activities she must forego, then the extent of her duty will be clear. In the absence of specific terms in the contract, the standard of necessary medical attention that *S* must observe would be the same that a reasonable pregnant woman in the circumstances would receive. The range of activities undertaken by reasonable women during pregnancy is expansive, and proving that any given activity falls outside this range would be difficult. Since this duty is not easily defined in the abstract, parties would be well advised to include an explicit statement in the contract, in order to eliminate ambiguities and needless legal complications.

After establishing a duty and breach of that duty, *H* and *W* must prove that the breach proximately caused or will cause the alleged specific injury in order to succeed under either a tort or contract theory. Proof of proximate cause, however, may be difficult because tracing the origin of a congenital defect in a particular child back to a particular source may be impossible. For example, alcohol or caffeine consumption may cause birth defects, but demonstrating that any specific birth defect resulted from such consumption is difficult. Thus, any suit for breach of that duty to provide adequate care will have to overcome this serious obstacle.

Once *H* and *W* establish the elements of a cause of action, two forms of relief are available. In most legal actions, courts assess the inquiry to the plaintiff and direct the defendant to pay the plaintiff money damages. When payment of money damages is inadequate, because either the harm is not clearly quantifiable, or the underlying basis of the suit depends upon something that money cannot replace or compensate the plaintiff, courts are willing to prescribe equitable relief: to enjoin the defendant from doing an act or to do an act. Injunction, however, is considered an extraordinary remedy and will not ensue absent a showing that the legal remedy is inadequate.

Obtaining either equitable or legal relief will be difficult, since the real purpose of the promise to receive proper care is to protect the welfare of the unborn child. Retrospective legal relief, obtained after a child is born deformed, for instance, clearly is inadequate since money damages will not cure the deformity. Perhaps *H* and *W* can include a liquidated damages clause in the contract, which would provide a specific measure of damages in the event of a specific breach. Yet, courts often strike down liquidated damages as penalties. Thus the damage remedy contains inherent weaknesses that make resort to it unsatisfactory. Given the uncertainties of the equitable remedy, however, the damage remedy may be the only viable means of enforcing this agreement. If *S*'s negligence results in a miscarriage, money damages will be the only possible remedy. Damages are as difficult to determine as if *S* had aborted the fetus, leaving restitution for expenses paid as the only quantifiable measure. Of course, if *H* and *W* are unable to prove negligence on the part of *S*, they would be obligated to pay for the services rendered up to this point. The clearer the contract is concerning the measure of damages, the more likely courts will be to award them.

In the event that *H* and *W* discover, during the term of *S*'s pregnancy, that she has been remiss in obtaining the appropriate level of medical attention, they can request a court to order her compliance. Showing the inadequacy of the legal remedy should not be difficult. Certainly the health and well-being of a child is so unique that a court, if possible, will employ its equity powers to further that end. The problem with injunctions, however, lies in administering orders that direct a woman to receive medical care or to refrain from a certain diet. Courts historically have been reluctant to enjoin parties where the resultant order demands close personal supervision or personal services. Thus, even though the remedy at law would be inadequate, courts may require that alternative, due to the problems inherent in administering equitable orders.

In sum neither remedy for breach of this promise seems satisfactory. Although injunctive relief is more desirable, it may be judicially unacceptable. In that event only the damage remedy would remain. Damages, however, would be difficult to quantify. In addition, the difficulty in proving proximate cause increases when H and W must demonstrate that a particular activity caused a particular defect. This additional burden will not exist in the case of prospective relief, for H and W will only have to show either that it was prohibited in the terms of the contract, or that it may cause birth defects and that a reasonably prudent pregnant woman would not take the risk. In light of these burdens on H and W, the possibility exists that this promise to obtain adequate medical care, although important to the purpose of the contract, may be wholly unenforceable.

The third way that S can breach the contract is by refusing to give up the child after birth. Monetary damages for H and W in this event do not suffice since the whole purpose of the agreement was to provide them with what they could not otherwise obtain, a child of their own. Since in many cases they are willing to pay money to obtain that child, giving them money as damages would be wholly inadequate. In addition there is no ethically acceptable standard by which a jury can measure the worth of the child. Specific performance, that is, forcing S to surrender the child to H and W, is an equally tenuous alternative. Courts have manifested an extreme reluctance to intervene in domestic relationships. Although S is not a part of the family consisting of H and W, and therefore S, H and W do not comprise a domestic relationship, it seems unlikely that a court would force a woman to give up a child she carried merely on the basis of a contract. Therefore H and W would have to obtain relief in a custody suit where a court would determine the best interests of the child. If the custody suit did not prove favorable for H and W, there would be little recourse. Restitution for expenses incurred by H and W provides the only clear-cut compensable contractual damage.

2. Rights and liabilities of H and W

As consideration for the promise of S, H and W promise to pay to S the financial costs of pregnancy and medical care, and to accept the child after birth. Sometimes they also agree to pay S an additional fee for her services. Since H and W have a keen interest in providing good care during pregnancy, presumably they will pay these expenses. However, if H and W breach their promises to pay the costs of pregnancy or to pay the fee to S, recovery would be fairly straightforward, since these expenses either will be delineated in the contract, or easily ascertained by assessing the costs of medical care. If H and W refuse to accept the child after birth, problems will occur in determining the appropriate remedy, similar to those that occur when S refuses to give up the child. Specific performance is unlikely since a court would not force H and W to accept an unwanted child, thereby jeopardizing the child's best interests.

In this instance, S could sue for child support payments. Just as an unwed mother may sue the father of the child for support, S should be able to sue H in the event that he refuses custody. Since S reasonably relied on H and W's promise, she should not have to incur the expenses of bringing up a child that she believed would not be in her custody after its birth. On the other hand, if S wishes to retain custody of the child, she should not be coerced into putting up the child for adoption, despite the rationale of mitigating damages or because she cannot afford to provide adequately for the child. In either case, the father, H should be estopped from denying responsibility. It should be noted, however, that in the typical artificial insemination case a donor of semen usually does not incur liability for child support unless the donor was the donee's husband. However, regarding the surrogate mother arrangement, H not only recognizes that he is the genetic father but also contracts to accept the child and become the father in all respects. The same policy considerations, therefore, which demand insulating the donor from liability in artificial insemination cases do not apply in the surrogate mother cases. In order to make resolution of this issue easier, the contract should include a provision for payment of child support in the event that this sort of breach occurs.

If neither family wants to retain custody of the child, S is free to offer the child for adoption. Perhaps H and W must bear the costs of adoption, but this amount is likely to be small, given the high demand for adoptable babies. The likelihood that either S or H and W will refuse to accept the child increases if the child is born with a deformity or a handicap. Screening procedures should minimize this possibility, and exclude those couples not willing to accept a deformed or handicapped child. Attempting to eliminate these couples at the outset decreases the likelihood of such a problem subsequently arising. In the event, however, that the child is unadoptable, the legal responsibility for care of the child should rest with H and W.

(For a full discussion of the arguments concerning the enforcement of surrogate arrangements, see M Field *Surrogate Motherhood: The Legal and Human Issues*

(1988), arguing that the surrogate mother should have a right to renounce the contract up to the time of the birth of the child.)

So, what is the position in English law: is a surrogate contract valid, unenforceable or void on grounds of public policy?

(a) The criminal law

Is the agreement unlawful *in limine* as constituting a crime? There are at least three possibilities. First, the parties' agreement may constitute a conspiracy to corrupt public morals or outrage public decency. No English case has addressed this question. Arguably, the fact that a number of surrogacy arrangements have been widely publicised and been the object of litigation without prompting any intervention by the DPP is, at least, *prima facie* evidence that the agreement would not amount to a criminal conspiracy in England. Further, it has sometimes been urged that the fulfilment of a surrogacy arrangement amounts to the crime of 'baby selling'. However, it seems clear that no such crime is known to the common law. 'Baby selling' (the handing over of a child for money) is merely treated at common law as conduct *contra bonos mores*. It is a separate question whether the agreement should be so regarded. We would suggest that it should not.

Secondly, an offence may be committed under s 57 of the Adoption Act 1976 if the commissioning couple intend to adopt the child once born:

> 57. (1) Subject to the provisions of this section, it shall not be lawful to make or give to any person any payment or reward for or in consideration of –
> (a) the adoption by that person of a child;
> (b) the grant by that person of any agreement or consent required in connection with the adoption of a child;
> (c) the handing over of a child by that person with a view to the adoption of the child; or
> (d) the making by that person of any arrangements for the adoption of a child.

The forerunner of this section, s 50 of the Adoption Act 1958, was interpreted in the following case.

Re an Adoption Application (Surrogacy) [1987] Fam 81, [1987] 2 All ER 826 (Fam Div)

Latey J: Mr and Mrs A apply to adopt a little child, now aged 2 years and 4 months. The child's mother (whom I shall call 'the mother') is Mrs B. The child was conceived as a result of a surrogacy arrangement, as it is described, between Mr and Mrs A and Mrs B and her husband, Mr B. As a result of that arrangement, Mr A and Mrs B had sexual intercourse on a few occasions and in due course the child was conceived. It was in no sense a love affair. It was physical congress with the sole purpose of procreating a child. As soon as there was conception intercourse ceased.

What led up to this arrangement was this: Mr and Mrs A are a devoted couple. To complete and fulfil their union they dearly wanted a child. For medical reasons Mrs A was and is unable to have a baby. They did everything they could with medical help and advice, including surgery, to overcome this but to no avail. They then tried to adopt a child both in this country and abroad, again to no avail. As to this country, the principal reason given was their ages. This is surprising. At that time Mr A was barely 40, and Mrs A in her mid-30s, well within the normal age of parenthood, I would have thought. Another and subsidiary reason may have been that it was their second marriage, each having been divorced. But there is no doubt that their marriage is solid and stable, especially now that they have the baby, or toddler as it now is.

Then they heard a radio programme, and Mrs A saw a television programme, about surrogacy. They saw it as their last chance.

In the meanwhile, Mr and Mrs B had two children of their own. They decided at that time to have no more (though recently they have had a third child). Mrs B is one who enjoys pregnancy despite sickness and backache. She too heard, saw and read about surrogacy. She was deeply and genuinely moved about the plight of childless couples. There is no question about her sincerity about this. After much thought she decided to embark on this path. She discussed it with her husband, who was not, at first, enthusiastic but acquiesced and later supported her.

She put an advertisement in a magazine. Mr and Mrs A saw it and answered it. They met and the arrangement was made. Finance entered into it and this aspect of it is at the heart of whether an adoption order can be made in this case and, if it can be, whether it should be made. This is because of the terms of certain statutory enactments which I will come to shortly.

The mother, Mrs B, was in full-time employment. She and her husband's joint income enabled them and their children to live in comfort. If she became pregnant it would mean giving up her job and earnings. It would mean incurring other expenses. She had responses from other couples – one couple in particular who offered a very large sum of money. This was not what she wanted.

She agreed with Mr and Mrs A to act as a surrogate because as she says:

I wanted to help a childless couple. My own children are very precious to me and I sympathised greatly with any couple who were unable to have children of their own, so much so that I was willing to have another pregnancy in order to give someone else that joy.

She wanted a couple with whom she could be friendly, empathise, have a rapport. She and Mr an Mrs A found each other and she declined the others, including the couple offering the very large sum.

The two couples agreed a global sum of £10,000. The mother says:

The money represented only my loss of earnings, expenses in connection with the pregnancy, and emotional and physical factors. I emphasise that I did not go into the arrangements for commercial reasons, nor did I accept the money to hand [the child] over. I would have done that in any event. In fact, overall, I was marginally worse off. This does not bother me since my motive was not financial.

In his report the child's guardian ad litem says:

The mother does *not* appear to have been primarily motivated in entering into the arrangements by financial considerations. She appears to have felt strongly that through a surrogacy arrangement she could offer an important service to a childless couple and to have regarded the money mainly as the equivalent of compensation for loss of earnings while pregnant ... Her interest in surrogacy the mother attributes to a particular pleasure she has in having babies and a great sympathy for women who are unable to experience the joy of having and caring for a baby. The public discussions and debates she heard about this subject struck a special chord for her, thus her initiative in advertising herself.

I have heard the mother speak about this in her evidence. I am left in no doubt that it is the plain, unvarnished truth.

Mr and Mrs A paid £1,000 when she was some months pregnant, and £4,000 shortly after the baby was born. The balance of £5,000 was due some months later, but the mother refused to accept it. This was because she and a professional writer as co-author wrote a book: 'Surrogate Mother. One Woman's Story', from which she made money. That book has been put in as part of the material in this case. It was written pseudonymously and with care to conceal the identity of the child and those connected with the child. I have tried to do the same in this judgment. In the interest of the child nothing must be published which might point to the child's identity with serious consequences to the child later in life, if it were publicly known. Mr and Mrs A's close circle know the facts. They accept and love the child. Mr and Mrs A are very intelligent people who adore the child. They have already worked out what and when they are going to tell the child, and done so admirably, as it seems to me. But for any public publicity to happen about this child as it grows up would certainly damage its emotional development and might be disastrous.

If the word 'commercial' has any bearing on what has to be decided in this case and if it connoted a profit or financial reward element there was nothing commercial in what happened. There was no written contract or agreement; no lawyers were consulted until after the baby was born. The arrangement was one of trust which was fully honoured on both sides.

The rest of the history can be told briefly. The child was born in hospital with Mrs A present at the birth and Mr A joining them almost immediately. Two days later the mother and child went to Mr and Mrs A's home. The four of them spent a week together. The mother went back to her own home. Mr and Mrs A and the child have been together since. The child thrived. The three of them have been and are supremely happy. The mother and Mr and Mrs A have kept in contact. The mother and Mr B have a third child. They are closer than they ever have been.

The first question, therefore, is whether in the present case there has been 'any payment or reward' within the meaning of section 50 of the Adoption Act 1958 – 'for adoption', to put it conveniently albeit imprecisely. This is a question of fact to be decided on the evidence. Mr and Mrs A and Mrs B have all given evidence. All are transparently honest. They did not make notes. They did not take legal advice. Not surprisingly, their recollection of the precise sequence of events and what was discussed and when is not clear. What does come out strongly is that what was wanted was a baby and that Mr and Mrs A should have it from birth to care for and bring up. And that it was upon this that they were all concentrating. It was only after the payments had been made and the baby was born that any of them began to turn their minds in any real sense to adoption and the legalities.

In my judgment there was no payment or reward within the meaning of section 50(1) of the Adoption Act 1958.

It may be that in his desire to arrive at a conclusion which he thought served the best interests of all the parties, Latey J was somewhat relaxed in his application of s 50 to the facts. He seems to have concluded that the payment was not made with a view to adoption and also that by its nature it lacked the quality of 'payment or reward'. Contrast the view of the New Jersey Supreme Court on hearing the appeal in the case of *In the Matter of Baby M* (1988) 537 A 2d 1227 (discussed at first instance by Capron, *supra*).

In the Matter of Baby M (1988) 537 A 2d 1227 (NJ Sup Ct)

Wilentz CJ: Our law prohibits paying or accepting money in connection with any placement of a child for adoption … Excepted are fees of an approved agency (which must be a non-profit entity) and certain expenses in connection with childbirth.

Considerable care was taken in this case to structure the surrogacy arrangement so as not to violate this prohibition. The arrangement was structured as follows: the adopting parent, Mrs Stern, was not a party to the surrogacy contract; the money paid to Mrs Whitehead was stated to be for her services – not for the adoption; the sole purpose of the contract was stated as being that 'of giving a child to William Stern, its natural and biological father', the money was purported to be 'compensation for services and expenses and in no way … a fee for termination of parental rights or a payment in exchange for consent to surrender a child for adoption'; the fee to the Infertility Center ($7,500) was stated to be for legal representation, advice, administrative work, and other 'services'. Nevertheless, it seems clear that the money was paid and accepted in connection with an adoption.

The Infertility Center's major role was first as a 'finder' of the surrogate mother whose child was to be adopted, and second as the arranger of all proceedings that led to the adoption. Its role as adoption finder is demonstrated by the provision requiring Mr Stern to pay another $7,500 if he uses Mary Beth Whitehead again as a surrogate, and by ICNY's agreement to 'coordinate arrangements for the adoption of the child by the wife'. The surrogacy agreement requires Mrs Whitehead to surrender Baby M for the purposes of adoption. The agreement notes that Mr *and* Mrs Stern wanted to have a child, and provides that the child be 'placed' with Mrs Stern in the event Mr Stern dies before the child is born. The payment of the $10,000 occurs only on surrender of custody of the child and 'completion of the duties and obligations' of Mrs Whitehead, including termination of her parental rights to facilitate adoption by Mrs Stern. As for the contention that the Sterns are paying only for services and not for an adoption, we need note only that they would pay nothing in the event the child died before the fourth month of pregnancy, and only $1,000 if the child were stillborn, even though the 'services' had been fully rendered. Additionally, one of Mrs Whitehead's estimated costs, to be assumed by Mr Stern, was an 'Adoption Fee', presumably for Mrs Whitehead's incidental costs in connection with the adoption.

Mr Stern knew he was paying for the adoption of a child; Mrs Whitehead knew she was accepting money so that a child might be adopted; the Infertility Center knew that it was being paid for assisting in the adoption of a child. The actions of all three worked to frustrate the goals of the statute. It strains credulity to claim that these arrangements, touted by those in the surrogacy business as an attractive alternative to the usual route leading to an adoption, really amount to something other than a private placement adoption for money.

Arguably, the New Jersey court's approach is more persuasive than that of Latey J in *Re An Adoption Application*.

It should be noted that s 57(3) of the Adoption Act 1976 provides: 'This section does not apply … to any payment or reward authorised by the court to which an application for an adoption order in respect of a child is made.' In *Re An Adoption Application*, Latey J held that 'authorised by the court' in s 50(3) of the 1958 Act (s 57(3)'s forerunner) covered not only authorisation in advance of making a payment but could also cover retrospective authorisation after it had been made. Latey J (at p 36) acknowledged that otherwise:

> ... It would mean, for example, that any payment, however modest and however innocently made, would bar an adoption and do so however much the welfare of the child cried aloud for adoption with all the security and legal rights and status it carried with it: and that, be it said, within the framework of legislation whose first concern is promoting the welfare of the children concerned.
>
> I do not believe that Parliament ever intended to produce such a result (not, anticipating, has it done so in my judgment). The result it intended to produce is wise and humane. It produced a balance by setting its face against trafficking in children, on the one hand, but recognising that there may be transactions which are venial and should not prohibit adoption, on the other hand.

In applying s 50(3) and making the adoption order in favour of the commissioning parents, the judge said:

> It follows that in each case the court has a discretion whether or not to authorise any payment or reward which has already been made or may be contemplated in the future. In exercising that discretion the court would no doubt balance all the circumstances of the case with the welfare of the child as first consideration against what [Counsel for the guardian *ad litem*] well described as the degree of taint of the transaction for which authorisation is asked.

It is at best arguable whether 'authorisation' was intended to include subsequent ratification by a court. If Latey J is right, he should, perhaps, have made clear the grounds for doing so. But, if he had done so, they would in fact probably have been contrary to the spirit of the adoption legislation. Nevertheless in the next case, the judge followed Latey J's view about retrospective authorisation and made an adoption order against the wishes of the surrogate mother.

Re MW (Adoption: Surrogacy) [1995] 2 FLR 759 (Fam Div)

> The applicants for adoption, who were husband and wife, had entered into a surrogacy agreement with the child's mother whereby she was to carry the child following impregnation by AID by the husband. The agreement, set out in a document drafted by the applicants' solicitor and amended by the mother's solicitor, provided that the mother was to receive £7500 and that she endorsed and supported the adoption process. The applicants cared for the child from the time of his birth in January 1992. However, after the birth conflict arose between the mother and the applicants as to contact. The mother launched a publicity campaign in the press and on television, publishing photographs of the baby and causing the applicants considerable distress. An application by her for a residence order was abandoned but she continued to press for contact and opposed the application for adoption.

> **Judge Callman:** In this case I am dealing with applications by Mr W an Mrs W (which are adoption applications) in respect of M who was born on 31 January 1992. He was the result of an arrangement entered into between Ms A (I will call her hereafter 'the mother') and the applicants (whom I will call hereafter 'the applicants'). So far as Mr W is concerned, I will describe him hereafter as 'the father' and I will describe Mrs W hereinafter, for technical reasons, as 'the stepmother' ...

> Then I have to consider questions which are much more complex. When it comes to the question of illegal payments the court has to look at s 57 of the Adoption Act 1976, and that makes it quite plain that there is a prohibition where any person has made or given to any person a payment or award for or in consideration of adoption by that person of a child. The leading case on this is *Re Adoption Application (Payment for Adoption)* [1987] Fam 81, sub nom *Re Adoption Application AA212/86 (Adoption Payment)* [1987] 2 FLR 291, in which Latey J, at pp 86 and 296 respectively, effectively said that on the face of that case there had been no payment or award within the meaning of this section since adoption had been contemplated after the payment of the money and the birth of the child, that there had been nothing commercial or financial regarding the agreement. Then he said that even if the payment did fall within the prohibited ambit the court would exercise its discretion to authorise a payment retrospectively. I have come to the conclusion when looking at the whole of these facts that there is a distinction between the facts in the case of Latey J and

this case because the very document which is headed 'Memorandum of Understanding under the Surrogacy Act' endorses and supports an adoption process undertaken by the applicants. I have no doubt at all that adoption was plainly in the minds of the parties at the beginning, and to that extent there is a breach of s 57 in my judgment in respect, certainly, of the first three payments, and I have considerable doubts about the last payment. I think the last payment was extracted really as an addition to the initial payments under circumstances that I am not quite certain about yet. I think I must really find that these payments were made in breach of s 57.

That leads me to the question of whether I should exercise my discretion in this case, and I have decided that I have power under s 57(3) to authorise the making of these payments retroactively, or on the authority of Latey J and the case I have cited and also in the case of *Re C* [1993] 1 FLR 87. So I hereby retroactively authorise the payments under s 57(3) of the Adoption Act 1976 ...

Unlike Latey J, the judge concluded that the payments had been in contemplation of an adoption and were, therefore, unlawful. He also concluded, again unlike Latey J, that it was a 'payment', seemingly distinguishing Latey J's approach in the earlier case that there was 'nothing commercial or financial regarding the agreement' (per Judge Callman at 764).

(See also, on payment and 'parental orders' under s 30 of the Human Fertilisation and Embryology Act 1990, *Re Q (Parental Order)* [1996] 1 FLR 369 (Johnson J), *supra*.)

Finally, there is the Surrogacy Arrangements Act 1985. We shall return to consider its terms in detail shortly. For the present it is sufficient to note that it creates a number of criminal offences for those involved in *commercial* surrogate arrangements. But it specifically excludes the surrogate mother or commissioning couple from liability under the Act (see s2(2), discussed *infra*).

(b) The civil law

In the New Jersey case of *In the Matter of Baby M* (1988) 537 A 2d 1227 the New Jersey Supreme Court examined the validity of a surrogacy contract.

In the Matter of Baby M (1988) 537 A 2d 1227 (NJ Sup Ct)

Wilentz CJ: In this matter the Court is asked to determine the validity of a contract that purports to provide a new way of bringing children into a family. For a fee of $10,000, a woman agrees to be artificially inseminated with the semen of another woman's husband; she is to conceive a child, carry it to term, and after its birth surrender it to the natural father and his wife. The intent of the contract is that the child's natural mother will thereafter be forever separated from her child. The wife is to adopt the child, and she and the natural father are to be regarded as its parents for all purposes. The contract providing for this is called a 'surrogacy contract', the natural mother inappropriately called the 'surrogate mother'.

... In February 1985, William Stern and Mary Beth Whitehead entered into a surrogacy contract. It recited that Stern's wife, Elizabeth, was infertile, that they wanted a child, and that Mrs Whitehead was willing to provide that child as the mother with Mr Stern as the father.

The contract provided that through artificial insemination using Mr Stern's sperm, Mrs Whitehead would become pregnant, carry the child to term, bear it, deliver it to the Sterns, and thereafter to whatever was necessary to terminate her maternal rights so that Mrs Stern could thereafter adopt the child. Mrs Whitehead's husband, Richard, was also a party to the contract; Mrs Stern was not. Mr Whitehead promised to do all acts necessary to rebut the presumption of paternity under the Parentage Act. NJSA 9:17–43a(1),–44a. Although Mrs Stern was not a party to the surrogacy agreement, the contract gave her sole custody of the child in the event of Mr Stern's death. Mrs Stern's status as a nonparty to the surrogate parenting agreement presumably was to avoid the application of the baby-selling statute to this arrangement. NJSA 9:3–54.

Mr Stern, on his part, agreed to attempt the artificial insemination and to pay Mrs Whitehead $10,000 after the child's birth, on its delivery to him. In a separate contract, Mr Stern agreed to pay $7,500 to the Infertility Center of New York ('ICNY'). The Center's advertising campaigns solicit surrogate mothers and encourage infertile couples to consider surrogacy. ICNY arranged for the surrogacy contract by bringing the parties together, explaining the process to them, furnishing the contractual form, and providing legal counsel.

... After several artificial inseminations over a period of months, Mrs Whitehead became pregnant. The pregnancy was uneventful and on March 28, 1986, Baby M was born.

[The court then examined the legislation of New Jersey in relation to (1) the prohibition of adoption for money; (2) the termination of parental rights; and (3) the surrender of custody and consent to adopt. The court concluded that the surrogacy agreement was in direct conflict with the legislation and hence was invalid and unenforceable. The court then went on to consider public policy considerations.]

... The contract's basic premise, that the natural parents can decide in advance of birth which is to have custody of the child, bears no relationship to the settled law that the child's best interests shall determine custody. ...

The surrogacy contract guarantees permanent separation of the child from one of its natural parents. Our policy, however, has long been that to the extent possible, children should remain with and be brought up by both of their natural parents. ... This is not simply some theoretical ideal that in practice has no meaning. The impact of failure to follow that policy is nowhere better shown than in the results of this surrogacy contract. A child, instead of starting off its life with as much peace and security as possible, finds itself immediately in a tug-of-war between contending mother and father.

The surrogacy contract violates the policy of this State that the rights of natural parents are equal concerning their child, the father's right no greater than the mother's. ... The whole purpose and effect of the surrogacy contract was to give the father the exclusive right to the child by destroying the rights of the mother.

The policies expressed in our comprehensive laws governing consent to the surrender of a child ... stand in stark contrast to the surrogacy contract and what it implies. Here there is no counselling, independent or otherwise, of the natural mother, no evaluation, no warning.

The only legal advice Mary Beth Whitehead received regarding the surrogacy contract was provided in connection with the contract that she previously entered into with another couple. Mrs Whitehead's lawyer was referred to her by the Infertility Center, with which he had an agreement to act as counsel for surrogate candidates. His services consisted of spending one hour going through the contract with the Whiteheads, section by section, and answering their questions. Mrs Whitehead received no further legal advice prior to signing the contract with the Sterns.

Mrs Whitehead was examined and psychologically evaluated, but if it was for her benefit, the record does not disclose the fact. The Sterns regarded the evaluation as important, particularly in connection with the question of whether she would change her mind. Yet they never asked to see it, and were content with the assumption that the Infertility Center had made an evaluation and had concluded that there was no danger that the surrogate mother would change her mind. From Mrs Whitehead's point of view, all that she learned from the evaluation was that 'she had passed.' It is apparent that the profit motive got the better of the Infertility Center. Although the evaluation was made, it was not put to any use, and understandably so, for the psychologist warned that Mrs Whitehead demonstrated certain traits that might make surrender of the child difficult and that there should be further inquiry into this issue in connection with her surrogacy. To inquire further, however, might have jeopardised the Infertility Center's fee. The record indicates that neither Mrs Whitehead nor the Sterns were ever told of this fact, a fact that might have ended their surrogacy arrangement.

Under the contract, the natural mother is irrevocably committed before she knows the strength of her bond with her child. She never makes a totally voluntary, informed decision, for quite clearly any decision prior to the baby's birth is, in the most important sense, uninformed, and any decision after that, compelled by a pre-existing contractual commitment, the threat of a lawsuit, and the inducement of a $10,000 payment, is less than totally voluntary. Her interests are of little concern to those who controlled this transaction.

Although the interest of the natural father and adoptive mother is certainly the predominant interest, realistically the *only* interest served, even they are left with less than what public policy requires. They know little about the natural mother, her genetic makeup, and her psychological and medical history. Moreover, not even a superficial attempt is made to determine their awareness of their responsibilities as parents.

Worst of all, however, is the contract's total disregard of the best interests of the child. There is not the slightest suggestion that an inquiry will be made at any time to determine the fitness of the Sterns as custodial parents, of Mrs Stern as an adoptive parent, their superiority to Mrs Whitehead, or the effect on the child of not living with her natural mother.

This is the sale of a child, or, at the very least, the sale of a mother's right to her child, the only mitigating factor being that one of the purchasers is the father. Almost every evil that prompted the prohibition on the payment of money in connection with adoptions exists here.

The differences between an adoption and a surrogacy contract should be noted, since it is asserted that the use of money in connection with surrogacy does not pose the risks found where money buys an adoption. Katz 'Surrogate Motherhood and the Baby-Selling Laws', 20 *Colum JL & Soc Probs* 1 (1986).

First, and perhaps most important, all parties concede that it is unlikely that surrogacy will survive without money. Despite the alleged selfless motivation of surrogate mothers, if there is no payment, there will be no surrogates, or very few. That conclusion contrasts with adoption; for obvious reasons, there remains a steady supply, albeit insufficient, despite the prohibitions against payment. The adoption itself, relieving the natural mother of the financial burden of supporting an infant, is in some sense the equivalent of payment.

Second, the use of money in adoptions does not *produce* the problem – conception occurs, and usually the birth itself, before illicit funds are offered. With surrogacy, the 'problem', if one views it as such, consisting of the purchase of a woman's procreative capacity, at the risk of her life, is caused by and originates with the offer of money.

Third, with the law prohibiting the use of money in connection with adoptions, the built-in financial pressure of the unwanted pregnancy and the consequent support obligation do not lead the mother to the highest paying, ill-suited, adoptive parents. She is just as well-off surrendering the child to an approved agency. In surrogacy, the highest bidders will presumably become the adoptive parents regardless of suitability, so long as payment of money is permitted.

Fourth, the mother's consent to surrender her child in adoptions is revocable, even after surrender of the child, unless it be to an approved agency, where by regulation there are protections against an ill-advised surrender. In surrogacy, consent occurs so early that no amount of advice would satisfy the potential mother's need, yet the consent is irrevocable.

The main difference, that the unwanted pregnancy is unintended while the situation of the surrogate mother is voluntary and intended, is really not significant. Initially, it produces stronger reactions of sympathy for the mother whose pregnancy was unwanted than for the surrogate mother, who 'went into this with her eyes wide open'. On reflection, however, it appears that the essential evil is the same, taking advantage of a woman's circumstances (the unwanted pregnancy or the need for money) in order to take away her child, the difference being one of degree.

In the scheme, contemplated by the surrogacy contract in this case, a middleman, propelled by profit, promotes the sale. Whatever idealism may have motivated any of the participants, the profit motive predominates, and ultimately governs the transaction. The demand for children is great and the supply small. The availability of contraception, abortion, and the greater willingness of single mothers to bring up their children has led to a shortage of babies offered for adoption ... The situation is ripe for the entry of the middleman who will bring some equilibrium into the market by increasing the supply through the use of money.

Intimated, but disputed, is the assertion that surrogacy will be used for the benefit of the rich at the expense of the poor. See eg Radin 'Market Inalienability', 100 *Harv L Rev* 1849, 1930 (1987). In response it is noted that the Sterns are not rich and the Whiteheads not poor. Nevertheless, it is clear to us that it is unlikely that surrogate mothers will be as proportionately numerous among those women in the top twenty per cent income bracket as among those in the bottom twenty per cent. *Ibid*. Put differently, we doubt that infertile couples in the low-income bracket will find upper-income surrogates.

In any event, even in this case one would not pretend that disparate wealth does not play a part simply because the contrast is not the dramatic 'rich versus poor'. At the time of the trial, the Whiteheads' net assets were probably negative – Mrs Whitehead's own sister was foreclosing on a second mortgage. Their income derived from Mr Whitehead's labors. Mrs Whitehead is a homemaker, having previously held part-time jobs. The Sterns are both professionals, she a medical doctor, he a biochemist. Their combined income when both were working was about $89,500 a year and their assets sufficient to pay for the surrogacy contract arrangements.

The point is made that Mrs Whitehead *agreed* to the surrogacy arrangement, supposedly fully understanding the consequences. Putting aside the issue of how compelling her need for money may have been, and how significant her understanding of the consequences, we suggest that her consent is irrelevant. There are, in a civilized society, some things that money cannot buy. In America, we decided long ago that merely because conduct purchased by money was 'voluntary' did not mean that it was good or beyond regulation and prohibition. *West Coast Hotel Co v Parrish*, 33 US 379, 57 SCt 578, 81 L Ed 703 (1937).

Employers can no longer buy labor at the lowest price they can bargain for, even though that labor is 'voluntary', 29 USC §206 (1982), or buy women's labor for less money than paid to men for the same job, 29 USC § 206(d), or purchase the agreement of children to perform oppressive labor, 29 USC § 212, or purchase the agreement of workers to subject themselves to unsafe or unhealthful working conditions, 29 USC §§ 651 to 678. (Occupational Safety and Health Act of 1970.) There are, in short, values that society deems more important than granting to wealth whatever it can buy, be it labor, love or life. Whether this principle recommends prohibition of surrogacy, which presumably sometimes results in great satisfaction to all of the parties, is not for us to say. We note here only that, under existing law, the fact that Mrs Whitehead 'agreed' to the arrangement is not dispositive.

The long-term effects of surrogacy contracts are not known, but feared – the impact on the child who learns her life was bought, that she is the offspring of someone who gave birth to her only to obtain money; the impact on the natural mother as the full weight of her isolation is felt along with the full reality of the sale of her body and her child; the impact on the natural father and adoptive mother once they realize the consequences of their conduct. Literature in related areas suggests these are substantial considerations, although, given the newness of surrogacy, there is little information.

The surrogacy contract is based on principles that are directly contrary to the objectives of our laws. It guarantees the separation of a child from its mother; it looks to adoption regardless of suitability; it totally ignores the child; it takes the child from the mother regardless of her wishes and her maternal fitness; and it does all of this, it accomplishes all of its goals, through the use of money.

Beyond that is the potential degradation of some women that may result from this arrangement. In many cases, of course, surrogacy may bring satisfaction, not only to the infertile couple, but to the surrogate mother herself. The fact, however, that many women may not perceive surrogacy negatively but rather see it as an opportunity does not diminish its potential for devastation to other women.

In sum, the harmful consequences of this surrogacy arrangement appear to us all too palpable. In New Jersey the surrogate mother's agreement to sell her child is void. Its irrevocability infects the entire contract, as does the money that purports to buy it.

In England, is the agreement void on grounds of public policy or, if not, unenforceable? In two cases (*A v C* [1985] FLR 445 and 543 and *Re P (Minors) (Wardship: Surrogacy)* [1987] 2 FLR 421) the court offered its view on the validity of surrogacy agreements. In *Re P*, Sir John Arnold P said:

> … One possible view about that matter is that there is, or may in certain circumstances be, an element concerning the surrogacy agreement which is repellent to proper ideas about the procreation of children, so as to make any such agreement one which should be rejected by law as being contrary to public policy. It is not necessary in this case, for the reasons which I have indicated, to come to any conclusion upon that point. The existence of the agreement is relevant to this extent, that plainly one of the factors which has to be taken into account in determining where the welfare of the children lies, is the factor of the character of the rival custodians who were put forward for consideration and it might be that the willingness of those persons to enter into a surrogacy agreement would reflect upon their moral outlook so adversely as to disqualify them a potential custodians at all, but I do not think that that factor enters into the present case.

In *A v C*, at first instance, ([1985] FLR 445), Comyn J stated:

> … The agreement between the parties I hold as being against public policy. None of them can rely upon it in any way or enforce the agreement in any way. I need only give one of many grounds for saying this, namely that this was a purported contract for the sale and purchase of a child.

In the Court of Appeal ([1985] FLR 543), Ormrod LJ described the arrangement as 'most extraordinary and irresponsible, bizarre and unnatural' and 'a sordid commercial bargain'. He concluded that the arrangement was a 'wholly artificial situation from the very beginning which should never have happened and which no responsible adult should ever have allowed to happen'. Cumming-Bruce LJ described the arrangement in similar terms, '… a kind of baby-farming operation of a wholly distasteful and lamentable kind'; and 'a guilty bargain which should never have been made'; and a 'lamentable commercial transaction'. Stamp LJ confined his judgment to one sentence but could not resist describing the arrangement as 'this ugly little drama'.

In these cases the courts were not specifically considering the validity of the surrogacy agreements and the remarks were, therefore, no more than judicial comment. How would a court approach this issue if it had to face it squarely? It is likely that the court would in such a situation have endorsed the view of Comyn J at first instance in *A v C* that 'the agreement ... I hold as being against public policy. None of them can rely upon it in any way or enforce the agreement in any way.' Comyn J gives as 'one of the many grounds for saying this ... that this was a purported contract for the sale and purchase of a child'. As we said earlier, the Government in its 1987 White Paper indicated that legislation should put beyond the fact that surrogate arrangements were unenforceable in the English courts (see para 65). Subsequently, the Human Fertilisation and Embryology Act 1990 inserted a new s 1A into the Surrogacy Arrangements Act 1985 to give effect to this:

1A. No surrogacy arrangement is enforceable by or against any of the persons making it.

The section applies to 'surrogate arrangements' as defined in the 1985 Act. We shall see shortly that the Act defines 'surrogate arrangements' widely but that it does not include agreements reached *after* the child is conceived and which are intended to result in the child being handed over by the surrogate mother. Such arrangements would remain governed by the common law.

2. Regulation of surrogate arrangements

English law only partially regulates surrogate arrangements. While it does not prohibit them, it does not seek to encourage them either. Unlike the regulatory framework created for medically assisted reproduction, surrogate arrangements are left largely alone by the law. (For proposals for reform, see *supra*.) As we have already seen, they are, of course, unenforceable in the courts. However, there is regulation in two ways.

A surrogate pregnancy using the genetic material of the commissioning couple will often require the involvement of medical personnel. The use of IVF or AI techniques to achieve the pregnancy will be licensed activities under the Human Fertilisation and Embryology Act 1990. As such, the HFEA may regulate the *use* of the techniques to achieve a surrogate pregnancy. HFEA's *Code of Practice* (4th edn, 1998) provides, in para 3.20 as follows:

3.20 The application of assisted conception techniques to initiate a surrogate pregnancy should only be considered where it is physically impossible or highly undesirable for medical reasons for the commissioning mother to carry the child.

It follows from para 3.20 that a licence-holder may be subject to sanction through variation or withdrawal of his licence if he assists in a surrogate pregnancy which is sought by the commissioning couple merely as a convenient (rather than a medically desirable) way of having a child.

Further, the Surrogacy Arrangements Act 1985 prohibits, through criminal sanction, certain activities carried out 'on a commercial basis'. The Surrogacy Arrangements Act 1985, ss 1-2 provide:

Meaning of 'surrogate mother', 'surrogacy arrangement' and other terms
1. (1) The following provisions shall have effect for the interpretation of this Act.
(2) 'Surrogate mother' means a woman who carries a child in pursuance of an arrangement –
(a) made before she began to carry the child, and

(b)   made with a view to any child carried in pursuance of it being handed over to, and parental responsibility being met (so far as practicable) by, another person or other persons.

(3) An arrangement is a surrogacy arrangement if, were a woman to whom the arrangement relates to carry a child in pursuance of it, she would be a surrogate mother.

(4) In determining whether an arrangement is made with such a view as is mentioned in subsection (2) above regard may be had to the circumstances as a whole (and, in particular, where there is a promise or understanding that any payment will or may be made to the woman or for her benefit in respect of the carrying of any child in pursuance of the arrangement, to that promise or understanding).

(5) An arrangement may be regarded as made with such a view though subject to conditions relating to the handing over of any child.

(6) A woman who carries a child is to be treated for the purposes of subsection (2)(a) above as beginning to carry it at the time of the insemination or of the placing in her of an embryo, of an egg in the process of fertilisation or of sperm and eggs, as the case may be, that results in her carrying the child.

(7) 'Body of persons' means a body of persons corporate or unincorporate.

(8) 'Payment' means payment in money or money's worth.

(9) This Act applies to arrangements whether or not they are lawful.

Negotiating surrogacy arrangements on a commercial basis, etc.

2. (1) No person shall on a commercial basis do any of the following acts in the United Kingdom, that is –

(a)   initiate or take part in any negotiations with a view to the making of a surrogacy arrangement,

(b)   offer or agree to negotiate the making of a surrogacy arrangement, or

(c)   compile any information with a view to its use in making, or negotiating the making of, surrogacy arrangements;

and no person shall in the United Kingdom knowingly cause another to do any of those acts on a commercial basis.

(2) A person who contravenes subsection (1) above is guilty of an offence; but it is not a contravention of that subsection –

(a)   for a woman, with a view to becoming a surrogate mother herself, to do any act mentioned in that subsection or to cause such an act to be done, or

(b)   for any person, with a view to a surrogate mother carrying a child for him, to do such an act or to cause such an act to be done.

(3) For the purposes of this section, a person does an act on a commercial basis (subject to subsection (4) below) if –

(a)   any payment is at any time received by himself or another in respect of it, or

(b)   he does it with a view to any payment being received by himself or another in respect of making, or negotiating or facilitating the making of, any surrogacy arrangement.

In this subsection 'payment' does not include payment to or for the benefit of a surrogate mother or prospective surrogate mother.

(4) In proceedings against a person for an offence under subsection (1) above, he is not to be treated as doing an act on a commercial basis by reason of any payment received by another in respect of the act if it is proved that –

(a)   in a case where payment was received before he did the act, he did not do the act knowing or having reasonable cause to suspect that any payment had been received in respect of the act; and

(b)   in any other case, he did not do the act with a view to any payment being received in respect of it.

In essence these provisions seek to outlaw commercial surrogacy agencies. A number of points arise.

First, the terms of s 2(1) are widely drafted so as to include any activity leading up to, and concluding with, a surrogate arrangement. Also, s 1 defines the terms 'surrogate mother' and 'surrogate arrangement' broadly, although as noted earlier, the Act would not cover an arrangement reached *after* conception (s 1(2)(a) and 1(6)). Contrast the Surrogacy Contracts Act 1993 (Tas), s 3). Importantly, however, the legislation does not cover non-profit making agencies which the Warnock Committee had recommended should also be outlawed (see para 8.18, *supra*). The Act appears, therefore, to endorse the view that it is only the *exploitive* nature of commercial agencies which merits prohibition. The 1985 Act, therefore, stands in stark contrast to legislation in other countries which prohibits even non-profit making agencies (see, for example Surrogacy Contracts Act 1993 (Tas), s 4).

Secondly, the Act does not prohibit the *making* of surrogate arrangements whether or not payment is made to the surrogate. Section 2(2) of the Act specifically excludes the surrogate mother and the commissioning couple from the provisions of the legislation and any payment to the surrogate mother is ignored in determining whether the arrangement was made 'on a commercial basis' (s 2(3)). Again, there is a contrast to be made here with legislation in other countries where (exceptionally) surrogacy itself is illegal (Surrogate Parenthood Act 1988, (Qd) ss 2 and 3), or surrogacy for reward is illegal (Infertility Treatment Act 1995 (Vic), s 59) (see discussion of Tasmanian Surrogacy Contracts Act 1993, *supra*). Indeed, the position under the 1985 Act stands in stark contrast to the provisions in England dealing with organ donation in the Human Organ Transplants Act 1989. That Act prohibits, and makes criminal, the giving or receiving of money in return for the donation of an organ for transplantation (see *infra* ch 15). The difference must be based, if anything, on the avoidance of tainting any child born to a surrogate by the criminal conduct of the surrogate or commissioning parents (see Warnock Report, para 8.19). This danger is, of course, not present in situations covered by the Human Organ Transplants Act 1989.

Finally, the 1985 Act does not prevent medically assisted surrogacy arrangements unless the doctors engage in any of the activities (such as initiating or negotiating the arrangement) prohibited by s 2(1) (see discussion *supra*). Merely to provide medical assistance by, for example, providing IVF treatment does not fall within the Act's provisions even where the treatment is provided privately (and so the doctor is paid) or where the parties to the surrogacy arrangement have *themselves* negotiated a payment to the surrogate. The British Medical Association in its *Changing Conceptions of Motherhood: The Practice of Surrogacy in Britain* (1996) has issued guidelines for practitioners (see especially pp 59–62). In particular, the BMA states, reflecting the HFEA's *Code of Practice (supra)*, that '[s]urrogacy is an acceptable option of last resort where it is impossible or highly undesirable for medical reasons for the intended mother to carry a child herself' (p 59). The BMA opposes surrogacy for social reasons or convenience (p 2).

The BMA's guidances seek to reflect the doctors' responsibilities to the parties to the surrogate arrangement and any resulting child depending upon the degree of professional involvement in the arrangement. We set the guidances out in full as they represent a useful practical approach to medical involvement in surrogate arrangements.

British Medical Association *Changing Conceptions of Motherhood: The Practice of Surrogacy in Britain* (1996)

1. Surrogacy is an acceptable option of last resort in cases where it is impossible or highly undesirable for medical reasons for the intended mother to carry a child herself. In all cases the interests of the potential child must be paramount and the risks to the surrogate mother must be kept to a minimum.
2. Health professionals consulted about a surrogacy arrangement should inform themselves about the legal position before offering advice. In particular, health professionals should be aware of the non-enforceability of surrogacy arrangements and the legal position with regard to parentage of the child.
3. In surrogacy arrangements the level of the health professionals' ethical responsibilities will vary depending on the degree of involvement in the arrangement. The BMA has divided these into three broad categories: (i) health professionals consulted about an established pregnancy; (ii) those consulted by women considering self-insemination; and (iii) those professional teams providing assisted conception techniques for the establishment of a pregnancy involving a surrogacy arrangement. Health professionals have responsibilities to all their patients. However, where health professionals are providing treatment services to assist people to have children they have additional responsibilities to the potential child.
4. Once a surrogate pregnancy has been established, the practitioner's ethical obligations to the surrogate mother and child are no different from those owed to any other pregnant woman

except that additional support may be required. The duty of the health care team is to provide the appropriate level of support and guidance both during and after the pregnancy.

5.   Practitioners approached by people considering self-insemination should encourage those concerned to consider the issues and implications very carefully and should ensure that they are aware of how to obtain accurate information about the medical, psychological, emotional and legal issues involved with surrogacy.

6.   Before agreeing to provide licensed treatment services aimed at establishing a surrogate pregnancy, for example through in vitro fertilisation or donor insemination, the health care team must take all reasonable steps to ensure that the medical, emotional and legal issues have been carefully considered and must, in all cases, take account of the welfare of the child who may be born as a result of the treatment. Such treatment services may only be provided in clinics licensed by the Human Fertilisation & Embryology Authority (HFEA) and in compliance with the HFEA's Code of Practice. Before proceeding with treatment, health professionals should also satisfy themselves that the intended parents have tried all other reasonable treatment options.

7.   Some health professionals who are not providing treatment services or advising on surrogacy may nonetheless be aware that a woman is, or a couple are, considering surrogacy. In such cases, the practitioner should seek to persuade them to share relevant information which might be important to the overall assessment of the interests of the potential child. It is particularly important to divulge information, such as a history of child abuse or neglect, to the medical team providing the treatment services. If such information highlights an *exceptional* risk to the parties involved, the person should be informed that the practitioner might, in a rare and particularly serious case, consider disclosing such details without his or her consent. In such cases the person should first be advised of this intention and be given the opportunity to divulge the relevant information voluntarily, or to challenge the disclosure.

8.   Health professionals providing treatment services or advice about surrogacy, should actively encourage those considering this option to seek counselling and testing for infectious diseases.

9.   Health professionals providing advice or treatment services should also emphasise the importance of discussing with all parties, in advance, the decisions which may need to be made before, during and after the pregnancy. These include decisions about the number of embryos to be replaced in surrogacy using IVF, the level of prenatal testing, the preferred method of delivery and decisions about care in the immediate postpartum period. Ideally these decisions should be reached by mutual agreement but in all cases of dispute, the surrogate mother, in conjunction with the health professionals, should make the final decision.

10.   There should be mutual trust and openness between the health professionals and their patients as much as between the individual parties to the arrangement.

11.   It is important that care and treatment are provided non-judgmentally.

12.   The surrogate mother should usually have successfully borne at least one child prior to the surrogacy arrangement and preferably will have completed her own family and have a partner, family or friends to provide support throughout and after the pregnancy. In some cases, particular attention may be necessary where family support is to be given to the surrogate mother and the intended mother from the same family.

13.   In view of the potential risks to the surrogate mother's health, the intended parents should be advised of the importance of ensuring that proper insurance cover has been arranged for the surrogate mother.

14.   All of the health professionals involved should understand clearly who has overall management of the pregnancy.

15.   After birth, the surrogate mother, her family and the intended parents are likely to need additional support and advice. These needs should be recognised by the health team. Midwives and health visitors have a particularly important role to play at this stage.

16.   Health professionals providing treatment services aimed at establishing a surrogate pregnancy should ensure, before proceeding, that consideration has been given to the long-term medical and psychological needs of those participating in the arrangement.

17.   Openness and truth-telling between parents and children is generally to be encouraged.

18.   Health professionals with a conscientious objection to surrogacy are not obliged to participate in the arrangement but have an ethical duty to refer the patient to another practitioner who would be prepared to consider offering help and advice.

In addition to the provisions concerned with commercial agencies, the 1985 Act goes further in prohibiting advertising by, or for, a surrogate mother. Section 3 provides:

Advertisements about surrogacy

3. (1) This section applies to any advertisement containing an indication (however expressed) –

(a)   that any person is or may be willing to enter into a surrogacy arrangement or to negotiate or facilitate the making of a surrogacy arrangement, or

(b) that any person is looking for a woman willing to become a surrogate mother or for persons wanting a woman to carry a child as a surrogate.

(2) Where a newspaper or periodical containing an advertisement to which this section applies is published in the United Kingdom, the proprietor, editor or publisher of the newspaper or periodical is guilty of an offence.

(3) Where an advertisement to which this section applies is conveyed by means of a telecommunication system so as to be seen or heard (or both) in the United Kingdom, any person who in the United Kingdom causes it to be so conveyed knowing it to contain such an indication as is mentioned in subsection (1) above is guilty of an offence.

(4) A person who publishes or causes to be published in the United Kingdom an advertisement to which this section applies (not being an advertisement contained in a newspaper or periodical or conveyed by means of a telecommunication system) is guilty of an offence.

(5) A person who distributes or causes to be distributed in the United Kingdom an advertisement to which this section applies (not being an advertisement contained in a newspaper or periodical published outside the United Kingdom or an advertisement conveyed by means of a telecommunication system) knowing it to contain such an indication as is mentioned in subsection (1) above is guilty of an offence.

(6) In this section 'telecommunication system' has the same meaning as in the Telecommunications Act 1984.

This section has two effects. First, it makes it a criminal offence to publish an advertisement seeking a surrogate mother or offering to act as a surrogate mother in a newspaper or periodical (s 3(2)). The offence is committed by the proprietor, editor or publisher. An offence is also committed by the 'conveyor' of an advertisement through radio or television (s 3(3)) or otherwise, for example, where a shopkeeper places a notice in his window (s 3(5)).

Secondly, s 3 *may* also cover advertising by a potential surrogate mother or a commissioning couple. (You will recall that this occurred in *Re An Adoption Application* before the 1985 Act was passed.) Section 3 (unlike s 2) does not specifically exempt them from liability. They may, therefore, be accessories to the crimes of others committed under s 3. Also, the wording of s 3(3), 3(4) and 3(5) are sufficiently wide to cover their acts. It could well be said that they 'cause' an advertisement to be conveyed or to be published or to be distributed by *placing* the advertisement with the publisher. (Since these phrases do not appear in s 3(2) dealing with publication in a newspaper, the only liability in such a case would be as an accessory.)

3. Parentage and parental responsibility for the child

Here we are primarily concerned with the question of with whom the child born as a consequence of a surrogacy arrangement should live. Of course, the purpose of a surrogate arrangement is that the child should be handed over to the commissioning couple and live with them. If all the parties are in agreement, as we shall see, this is the most likely outcome. Sometimes, however, there may be disagreement: the surrogate mother may wish to keep the child or, though less likely, none of the parties may want the child where, for example, it is born disabled. In the language of the Children Act 1989 we are concerned here with who will have 'parental responsibility' for the child.

(a) Who are the child's parents?

We have already seen (*supra*) how ss 27 to 29 of the Human Fertilisation and Embryology Act 1990 allocate parenthood when medically assisted reproduction occurs. Those provisions are equally applicable to surrogate pregnancies when IVF or AI is used.

(i) THE MOTHER

As a consequence, the surrogate mother will, in law, be the mother of any child born whether or not she is genetically related to the child. The woman of the commissioning couple will not be the mother even if her eggs were used during an IVF procedure. (For an unusual case holding that a commissioning woman was the mother of a child born to a surrogate following donation of an embryo from a third party, see *In re the Marriage of Buzzanca* (1998) 61 Cal App 4th 1410 (Cal CA).)

(ii) THE FATHER: WHERE THE SURROGATE IS MARRIED

In all cases the surrogate mother's husband will be the father of the child unless he can prove he did not consent to the procedure. Again, the man of the commissioning couple will not be the father of the child even if his sperm is used for AI or IVF (s 28(4)).

The legal position is examined by Kristina Stern in the following extract.

Kristina Stern 'The Regulation of Assisted Conception in England' (1994) 1 European J of Health Law 53

If a child born to a married surrogate mother was conceived by sexual intercourse, the presumption of legitimacy applies and can only be rebutted by medical evidence showing that the surrogate's husband was not in fact the child's genetic father (see the US case *Baby M* (1988) 537 A 2d 1227 (NJ CA)). But where birth follows some form of assisted conception and the woman is married at the time when conception takes place, or when an embryo's sperm or eggs are placed in her, the HFEA deems her husband to be the child's legal father and he cannot absolve himself from legal paternity, and parental responsibility (under s 2(1) of the Children Act 1989 parental responsibility is allocated to both the father and the mother where they were married to each other at the time of the child's birth. One way around the legal formalities might be for the legal parents to arrange for some or all of their parental responsibilities to be met by the commissioning parents, as provided under section 2(9) of the Children Act 1989), by proving that he is not the child's genetic father. The only situation in which he is not deemed to be the child's legal father is where it can be shown that he did not consent to his wife's fertility treatment (s 28(2)). Provided he can also rebut the presumption of legitimacy which stems from the fact that the child is conceived within a marriage, this appears to offer a means by which a surrogate mother's husband can avoid parental responsibility ... unless a parental order is made in favour of the gamete donor (under section 30 when it comes into effect) this would mean that the child is, as a matter of law, without a father. English courts will be understandably reluctant to allow such an outcome in the absence of strong evidence that he is actually *opposed to* the surrogacy (para 5.7 of the Code of Practice recommends that centres obtain written evidence of his consent) ...

(iii) THE FATHER: WHERE THE SURROGATE IS UNMARRIED

What, however, if the surrogate is unmarried? At common law, if the commissioning father's sperm is used he will be the father of the child. Hence, if the child is born after 'DIY' insemination or sexual intercourse, he will be the father since the 1990 Act does not affect the position. He will not, however, have parental responsibility' for the child as he and the child's mother are not married at the time of birth. He will only have 'parental responsibility' if he acquires it under the Children Act 1989 (s 2(2)). (For proposals to reform the law conferring 'parental responsibility' automatically on unmarried fathers who are registered as such after birth see, Lord Chancellor's Department *Consultation on Procedures for the Determination of Paternity and on the Law on Parental Responsibility for Unmarried Fathers* (March 1998).)

However, if a doctor is involved the question arises whether s 28 alters the position. It may do so, as we saw earlier, if the surrogate and the commissioning male are receiving licensed treatment. This will depend upon whether the woman is being treated using the sperm of a man who is being treated *together* with her (s 4(1)). Clearly, we are concerned with the situation where the commissioning male's sperm is being used. But, can it be said that he and the surrogate are being treated *together*? It was argued above that to be treated *together* a couple must be seeking treatment with a view to bringing up the child together. Clearly, this is not the case with a surrogacy arrangement. Consequently, the provision of treatment must be licensed. The commissioning male's consent to the use of his sperm is required under Sch 3 to the 1990 Act and, by virtue of s 28(6)(a), when it is used in accordance with his consent he ceases in law to be the father. He is in effect considered to be, and dealt with under the Act, as a sperm donor. The common law position is, thus, reversed. Section 28(3) does not rescue the situation by deeming him to be the father because (a) he is not being treated *together* with the surrogate and (b) his sperm is being used. Both are requirements for s 28(3) to apply (see *supra*). It should be noted also that if the surrogate has a partner he also cannot be the child's father unless s 28(3) applies to him. It does not as he too is not being treated together with the surrogate since there is no intention for them to bring up the child together.

As we saw earlier, however, the courts may not require such a broad intention for 'treatment together' (see *supra*). It will suffice, it could be argued, that the parties consent or agree to the procedure with the intention of establishing a pregnancy. If so, the treatment will not be licensed treatment under the 1990 Act, and the commissioning male will be the father at common law on the basis of his genetic connection to the child. Kristina Stern (*supra* at pp 70–71) explains this complex situation.

Kristina Stern The Regulation of Assisted Conception in England (1994) 1 European J of Health Law 53

It is difficult to predict how English courts will construe 'treated together' in the context of surrogacy arrangements. One factor which is likely to influence their decision is that, unless the commissioning father and the surrogate mother are regarded as being 'treated together', the child who is born to an unmarried surrogate mother following licensed fertility treatment is legally fatherless. In cases of ambiguity it is likely that English courts will interpret the HFEA so as to ensure that the child has two legal parents. Taking this into account, it may be that courts will construe 'treated together' broadly so as to cover the situation where a female fertility patient is accompanied by a man with whom she shares the common pursuit of achieving pregnancy and, ultimately, the birth of a child. It is likely, after all, that the surrogate mother and the commissioning father will present to the fertility clinic together, and there is nothing in either the HFEA or the Code of Practice to suggest that 'treated together' necessarily involves that the man and woman are cohabiting, or even intending to raise the child together. On the other hand the section was clearly *intended* to cover couples who seek to raise a child *together*, and it may well be found not to apply in the context of a surrogacy arrangement.

Similarly, if an unmarried surrogate mother is implanted with embryos created using the gametes of both of the commissioning parents ("gestational" or "complete" surrogacy) the child's parentage depends upon whether the surrogate mother and the commissioning father are regarded as having been treated together. In this factual context it may be more difficult to so construe their relationship since clearly the commissioning (and genetic) mother must also have been 'treated' together with her partner when the embryos were created *in vitro* or collected by lavage. But if English courts take account of the fact that the consequence of considering them *not to be treated together* is that the child will be legally fatherless, they may be prepared to interpret 'treated together' so as to cover this situation ...

The difficulty with this interpretation is that the HFEA's regulatory powers will be more limited as we discussed earlier (see *supra*). Kristina Stern in a footnote (fn 94) acknowledges the difficulties:

A broad interpretation of treated together could have ramifications for the scope of the Authority's regulatory authority. This is because a licence is required for artificial insemination in every case where a woman is treated using the sperm of a man unless that woman and that man are being treated together (s 4(1)(b)). If 'treated together' is interpreted to apply to any man with whom she presents at a clinic, such treatment would not require a licence. This was clearly not the intention of Parliament.

A further complication arises where the unmarried surrogate is inseminated with the sperm not of the commissioning male, but of a third party donor. (The same issue arises if donated embryos are used.) Clearly, this will be licensed treatment by virtue of s 4(1)(b) of the 1990 Act even if they are being 'treated together', since it will not involve the use of *his* sperm. Clearly, also, the donor cannot be the father by virtue of s 28(6)(a) if used in accordance with his consent. Then who is? No one, unless the commissioning male is being 'treated together' with the surrogate, then s 28(3) will make him the father.

In *Re Q (Parental Order)* [1996] 1 FLR 369, the issue arose, albeit it relation to an application of s 30 of the 1990 Act.

Re Q (Parental Order) [1996] 1 FLR 369 (Fam Div)

An unmarried woman, acting as a surrogate mother for a married couple, carried and gave birth to a child created from the egg of the wife fertilised by sperm donated at a clinic under a licensed arrangement rather than the sperm of the husband. The question arose as to who was to be treated as the father for the purpose of giving consent to the making of a parental order under s 30 of the Human Fertilisation and Embryology Act 1990, which required, under s 30(5), that 'The court must be satisfied that both the father of the child (including a person who is the father by virtue of section 28 of this Act), where he is not the husband, and the woman who carried the child have freely, and with full understanding of what is involved, agreed unconditionally to the making of the order' ...

Johnson J: The question is who is the father in the circumstances of the present case. These were that the child was carried by an unmarried woman who had placed in her an egg of the wife fertilised by the sperm of a donor who was not the husband.

In general the legal father of the child is the man whose sperm led to its creation, but s 28(6) provides two exceptions. One is where a man's sperm is used after his death. The other is where the man is a donor for the purpose of licensed treatment (see Sch 3). In both these cases the donor of the sperm will not be treated as the father of the child ...

Two other situations are envisaged by the Act ...

In the present case s 28(2) has no relevance because the carrying woman was not married. The sperm was donated at a clinic under a licensed arrangement so that the donor is not the father, this being one of the exceptions under s 28(6).

The question therefore becomes whether, applying s 28(3) to the circumstances of this case, the applicant husband was a man *for whom treatment services were provided* by a licence holder, *together with the carrying woman* ...

As a matter of ordinary language when a woman receives medical treatment and both she and a man together visit a doctor and it is understood that he is to pay the doctor's fee, then of course on one interpretation one might say that medical treatment was being 'provided' for him as well as for her because of his undertaking to pay for it. Surely that is not what Parliament intended by s 28(3). It seems plain to me that the subsection envisages a situation in which the man involved himself received medical treatment, although as presently advised I am not sure what treatment is envisaged since the subsection refers to a man whose sperm was not used in the procedure ...

In the case of a carrying mother who is married, *her* husband is to be treated as the father of the child unless it is shown that he did not consent to the carrying mother (his wife) taking part in the process. Unless (and until) that consent is shown *not* to have been given, the consent of the husband of the carrying mother to the making of the order must be obtained. This is the effect of s 28(2).

However, if there is no one treated as father under s 28 either because the carrying mother was unmarried or she was married and *her* husband did not consent to the process – then one turns to s 28(3). Under that subsection the man whose sperm was donated is specifically excluded, and this latter exclusion applies even if the donor was not the subject of one of the exceptions to s 28(6). The applicant husband is excluded because on the facts of this case he was not 'treated' with the carrying woman. I need further instruction as to who might be a man *treated* together with the carrying woman but who is not the sperm donor.

In one commentary on the section I have read that 'commonly this will mean the male cohabitant of the treated woman'. I respectfully disagree, because it does not seem to follow that simply because a man is living with the treated woman he was being provided with treatment services ...

We have already remarked (*supra*) on Johnson J's approach and the need, in effect for actual treatment to be provided to the man for s 28(3) to apply. The resolution of this situation is, in our view, the same as where the commissioning male's sperm is used and it highlights the difficulties with the 'consent to the procedure' approach of the courts. This makes little or no sense when the male makes no genetic contribution to the child.

(b) Allocating parental responsibility

Of course, to be in law the parents of the child at birth is not necessarily to determine with whom the child should live thereafter. (Contrast *Johnson v Calvert* (1993) 851 P 2d 776 (Cal Sup Ct) where the California Supreme Court equated 'parenthood' with who should have custody of a child born to a surrogate mother using the commissioning couple's embryo.) The English courts are required to act on the basis that 'the child's welfare [is] the court's paramount consideration' (Children Act 1989, s 1(1)). It may be that a child's 'best interests' dictate that 'parental responsibility' should be allocated elsewhere, for example, in the commissioning couple. It is to this issue that we now turn.

(i) WHERE THE PARTIES ARE AGREED

Where both the surrogate mother (and her husband or partner) and the commissioning couple are agreed that the child be handed over to be brought up by the commissioning couple, there are a number of legal mechanisms through which this may be achieved. First, the couple may seek to *adopt* the child; secondly, the couple may seek a 'parental order' under s 30 of the Human Fertilisation and Embryology Act 1990; and thirdly, the couple may invoke the court's *inherent jurisdiction* (probably through wardship in this type of case).

As regards adoption, the procedure and technicalities are discussed by Gillian Douglas in *Law, Fertility and Reproduction* (1991), pp 161–162:

> Where the surrogate mother is unmarried, or the pregnancy was achieved after sexual intercourse, or her husband did not consent to the artificial fertilisation procedure, so that the commissioning father is the putative father, he ranks as a relative of the child under section 72(1) of the Adoption Act 1976 and an adoption order could be made provided the child is at least 19 weeks old and at all times during the preceding 13 weeks has lived with the commissioning parents. A joint adoption order can only be made in favour of a married couple under section 14, so that cohabiting commissioning parents could not both be made legal parents. A single applicant can adopt a child under section 15, so that where the surrogacy had been undertaken for a single man, for example, that would not of itself prevent the order being made.
>
> Where the surrogate is married and the child resulted from artificial fertilisation techniques, with her husband's consent, the commissioning father would not be the legal father, but a stranger to the child in law. The child would accordingly have to have lived with the commissioning parents for at least 12 months, [s 13(1) and (2) Adoption Act 1976] but the situation is complicated by section 11(1) of the Adoption Act, which prohibits the placement of a child for adoption other than by a relative, unless arranged by an adoption agency or authorised by an order of the High Court. Contravention of the section is a criminal offence, but it has been held that private placements can be sanctioned after the event by the High Court. Where a child has not been placed by an adoption agency, the applicant for adoption must notify the local authority, and they must report to the court on the suitability of the applicant and whether there has been a contravention of section 11. In all adoption applications, a reporting officer must be appointed to ensure proper parental agreement to the making of the order (including investigating the circumstances relevant to the agreement), and where the child's welfare seems to require it, a guardian *ad litem* must be appointed to safeguard

the child's interests. It is likely that a guardian would be appointed when a surrogacy arrangement is revealed during an adoption application.

As Gillian Douglas points out, the effect of ss 27–29 of the Human Fertilisation and Embryology Act 1990 makes the adoption procedure a cumbersome one. It seems unlikely that adoption will be the preferred procedure where there is agreement, unless some technical reason stands in the way of making a 'parental order' under s 30 of the 1990 Act.

A second procedure is available under s 30 of the Human Fertilisation and Embryology Act 1990 which came into force on 1 November 1994:

Parental orders in favour of gamete donors

30. (1) The court may make an order providing for a child to be treated in law as the child of the parties to a marriage (referred to in this section as "the husband" and "the wife") if –
(a)   the child has been carried by a woman other than the wife as the result of the placing in her of an embryo or sperm and eggs or her artificial insemination,
(b)   the gametes of the husband or the wife, or both, were used to bring about the creation of the embryo, and
(c)   the conditions in subsection (2) to (7) below are satisfied.

(2) The husband and the wife must apply for the order within six months of the birth of the child or, in the case of a child born before the coming into force of this Act, within six months of such coming into force.

(3) At the time of the application and of the making of the order –
(a)   the child's home must be with the husband and the wife, and
(b)   the husband or the wife, or both of them, must be domiciled in a part of the United Kingdom or in the Channel Islands or the Isle of Man.

(4) At the time of the making of the order both the husband and the wife must have attained the age of eighteen.

(5) The court must be satisfied that both the father of the child (including a person who is the father by virtue of section 28 of this Act), where he is not the husband, and the woman who carried the child have freely, and with full understanding of what is involved, agreed unconditionally to the making of the order.

(6) Subsection (5) above does not require the agreement of a person who cannot be found or is incapable of giving agreement and the agreement of the woman who carried the child is ineffective for the purposes of that subsection if given by her less than six weeks after the child's birth.

(7) The court must be satisfied that no money or other benefit (other than for expenses reasonably incurred) has been given or received by the husband or the wife for or in consideration of –
(a)   the making of the order,
(b)   any agreement required by subsection (5) above,
(c)   the handing over of the child to the husband and the wife, or
(d)   the making of any arrangements with a view to the making of the order,
unless authorised by the court. ...

(11) Subsection (1)(a) above applies whether the woman was in the United Kingdom or elsewhere at the time of the placing in her of the embryo or the sperm and eggs or her artificial insemination.

Section 30 is, in many respects, a remarkable provision since it accepts, and gives legal effect, to surrogate arrangements. Given the general Parliamentary distaste for such things as expressed in the Surrogacy Arrangements Act 1985, the existence of s 30 might seem surprising. Of course, the 1985 Act's primary target is commercial surrogate brokers and not the parties (whether surrogate or commissioning couple) themselves and s 30 does not run counter to this legislative statement of public policy. Nevertheless, it must be remembered that the 1990 Act also amended the 1985 Act by introducing a new s 1A which expressly declares, even though there could have been little doubt under the common law, that surrogate arrangements are *legally unenforceable*. Again, perhaps, it can be said that s 30 does not run counter to this statement of policy either or, more particularly, the 1994 regulations do not since the child's welfare or 'best interests' will 'trump' any agreement to the contrary (cf *Johnson v Calvert* (1993) 19 Cal

Rptr 2d 494 (Cal Sup Ct) and Commentary (1994) 2 Med L Rev 239 at 243–244 (AG) – parentage and upbringing of a child born following a 'gestational' surrogacy arrangement determined by intention of parties to the arrangement). In the end, however, s 30 might be seen as a softening of approach by Parliament in its attitude to surrogate arrangements (see E Blyth 'Section 30 – The Acceptable Face of Surrogacy?' (1993) 4 JSWFL 248). In truth, of course, it was the product of a backbencher's intervention to legislate for a particular difficulty faced by his constituents (see *Hansard* (1990) vol 170, cols 944–5 (Michael Jopling MP) and *Re W (Minors) (Surrogacy)* [1991] 1 FLR 385 – twins born to a surrogate following IVF using the commissioning couple's embryos).

It must not be assumed that s 30 will apply to all surrogate arrangements. It will not. The 1990 Act lays down *six* conditions to the making of a s 30 order and cumulatively these considerably limit its application.

(i) **the child must be genetically related to at least one of the commissioning couple** (s 30(1)(b));

Hence, s 30 applies both to 'gestational' surrogacy arrangements where the embryo of the commissioning couple is transferred to the surrogate and to 'traditional' surrogacy arrangements where only the sperm of the male partner of the commissioning couple is used to artificially inseminate the surrogate.

(ii) **the surrogate mother (and her husband or partner) must consent to the 'parental order' (unless they cannot be found or are incapable of giving consent)** (ss 30(5) and (6)) **and these consents cannot be given earlier than six weeks after the birth** (s 30(6));

In effect, therefore, the surrogate mother *or* her partner hold a veto over the making of a 'parental order'. There is no provision equivalent to s 16 of the Adoption Act 1976 which permits the court to dispense with the consent of the birth mother where it has been 'unreasonably withheld' (see eg *Re MW (Adoption: Surrogacy)* [1995] 2 FLR 759 – overriding mother's refusal to an adoption order). Section 30 is very specific about the nature of the parties' consents which must be given 'freely' and 'with full understanding of what is involved'. The 'cooling off' period of six weeks following the birth may help a court to be satisfied that the parties to the arrangement (and particularly the surrogate mother) have thought out what is proposed. Nevertheless, it is likely that the court would require direct evidence from the parties in order to be satisfied that this requirement is fulfilled.

(iii) **the commissioning couple must be at least 18 and married** (ss 30(4) and (1));

Obviously, therefore, an unmarried couple will not be able to obtain a 'parental order' under s 30 and will need to seek an adoption order or other order vesting parental responsibility in them. Also, a single man who enters into a surrogacy arrangement in order to have a child for himself falls outside s 30.

(iv) **the application must be made within six months of the birth of the child or for births before the 1990 Act came into force within six months of that** (s 30(2));

This condition, equivalent to a limitation period for seeking an order under s 30, does on its face create a difficulty. When did the 1990 Act come into force? Some sections came into effect on 1 November 1990 when it received the Royal Assent. If this interpretation were accepted *no* birth before 1 November 1990 could be dealt with under s 30 since the s 30 procedure did not come into effect until 1 November 1994. In fact all births more than six months before 1 November 1994 would fall outside the s 30 procedure. Only births since the 1994 regulations came into force (ie since 1 November 1994) could be dealt with under s 30. Such an interpretation would run counter to the intention of Parliament. Further, this literal interpretation would be 'absurd' and under *Pepper v Hart* [1993] 1 All ER 42 (HL), no doubt, a court looking at Hansard could easily divine Parliament's intention to have been to allow applications to be made under s 30 for *any birth arising before s 30 came into force* and *made within six months of that date.*

(v) **No money or other benefit other than reasonable expenses must have been given or received by the commissioning couple unless authorised by the court** (s 30(7));

This condition limits any payment or the equivalent to the surrogate or by the commissioning couple but does allow *reasonable* expenses to be paid. However, other payments in money or kind may be made with the authorisation of the court. Like s 57 of the Adoption Act 1976, which prohibits any 'payment or reward' being made or given in contemplation of adoption unless authorised by the court, s 30(7) of the 1990 Act is likely to be interpreted to permit both prospective and retrospective authorisation by the court (see *Re Adoption Application (Payment for Adoption)* [1987] Fam 81 (Latey J)).

Nevertheless, s 30 is almost certainly narrower than s 57 of the Adoption Act in what it permits without court authorisation even though the latter has been (perhaps erroneously) interpreted only to prohibit 'commercial' dealings, ie those involving a profit or financial reward element (see per Latey J at 84). Section 30 only permits, without court authorisation, 'expenses reasonably incurred'. Thus, any element of payment is outlawed by s 30, even in the absence of 'commercial' dealings or of one of the parties acting for reward. Section 30 only permits reimbursement of actual expended moneys, eg medical costs or maternity clothes. It would not, for instance, allow payment in lieu of salary if the surrogate gave up work to carry the child (contrast G Douglas, *supra*, at p 159). Of course, once the court is asked to authorise a payment (which is not an expense), it is likely to be guided by its view of whether the 'parental order' is in the child's best interests and condone any reasonable or modest payment whether or not it is an expense (see Latey J's approach to s 57(3) of the Adoption Act 1976 in *Re Adoption Application (Payment for Adoption)* (*supra*) at 87–88). Indeed, even an extortionate payment may be condoned if the court takes the view that making the 'parental order' is in the child's best interests.

(vi) **the child must be living with the commissioning couple (who must be domiciled in the UK) at the time of the application and the court makes an order** (s 30(3)).

This requirement may, in practice, create some problems since it will only be satisfied if the surrogate mother has handed over the child to the commissioning couple after birth at least by the time the application under s 30 is made. Even if she is about to hand over the child, the court may, in the six week period before a s 30 application can be made, take a different view on residence.

It is clear that an order under s 30 will, for all intents and purposes, have the same effect as an adoption order in favour of the commissioning couple. The Parental Orders (Human Fertilisation and Embryology) Regulations 1994 (SI 1994 No 2767) amend and thereby apply certain provisions of the Adoption Act 1976 to 'parental order' cases under s 30 of the 1990 Act.

The amendments effected by Sch 1 to the regulations are detailed and reference should be made to the Department of Health's *Guidance Notes* (August 1994) on the regulations. The main (and most important) features are as follows.

First, the proceedings for a court deciding whether to make a 'parental order' under s 30 are likely to be in private (s 64 of the 1976 Act as amended) and provision is made for the appointment of a guardian *ad litem* to represent the child's interests.

Second, the court is required in making a decision whether or not to make a 'parental order' to have regard as the first consideration to 'the need to safeguard and promote the welfare of the child throughout his childhood' (s 6 of the 1976 Act as amended). Section 30 made no mention of this requirement though the same requirement in s 1 of the Children Act 1989 would have applied to s 30 proceedings anyway. Also, s 6 of the 1976 Act requires the court to have regard to the 'wishes and feelings of the child'. Here, the draftsman may have gone too far in borrowing the provisions of the 1976 Act given that an application for a 'parental order' must be made within six months of the child's birth!

Third, the effect of a s 30 order is to extinguish the 'parental responsibility' of the surrogate mother and of her husband or partner (if any) (s 12 of the 1976 Act as amended). At the same time, the child is to be treated for all purposes as if he (or she) is the child of the marriage of the applicants for the 'parental order' and not the child of anyone else (s 39 of the 1976 Act as amended). There are a number of exceptions, for example, relating to marriage, incest, nationality or titles (ss 47 and 44 of the 1976 Act as amended). Nevertheless, in general the effects of ss 27–29 of the 1990 Act on parentage are reversed. The common intention of the parties to the surrogate arrangement is given effect to and the genetic parentage of the applicants is restored in law. To this extent, s 30 replicates the effect of the decision of the Californian Supreme Court in *Johnson v Calvert* (1993) 851 P 2d 776 (Cal Sup Ct). However, there is an important distinction: there the intention of the parties was used as a 'tie breaker' when a dispute arose over the child's upbringing between the surrogate and the commissioning couple. Under s 30 the common intention of the parties must subsist at the time the court adjudicates: there must be no dispute or the court has no power to make a s 30 order. And further, under s 30 the original (and subsisting) intention of the parties will not be effected by the court unless to do so is in the child's best interests (see *Johnson v Calvert*, per Kennard J dissenting).

Fourth, the Registrar General is required to maintain a distinct 'Parental Order Register' to record the effects of 'parental orders' made by the court (s 50 of the 1976 Act as amended). Significantly, however, a person who is the subject of a 'parental order' will be allowed to obtain details of their birth once they have attained the age of 18 (s 51 of the 1976 Act as amended). This is a departure from the original draft regulations published in 1993 which did not apply the 'right to know' provision in the adoption legislation to individuals subject to a 'parental order'. (See the (draft) Parental Orders for Gamete Donor Regulations 1993.) Such individuals are now unique amongst children born following medically assisted reproduction. All other children are denied access to details of 'third parties' involved in the process (s 31(3) and (4) of the 1990 Act).

The analogy with adoption is, arguably, inappropriate. In adoption cases the 'child' may discover who is her *genetic* mother (and possibly father). In 'parental order' cases, the surrogate mother will only be the *genetic* mother in the situation where the female of the commissioning couple has made no genetic contribution, ie the surrogate was artificially inseminated with the sperm of the male of the commissioning couple (a 'traditional' surrogacy arrangement). Here, the adoption analogy – and the 'child's' right to know her *genetic* origins enshrined in the Adoption Act – may be apt. But if the surrogate makes no genetic contribution because the embryo of the commissioning couple has been implanted in the surrogate (a 'gestational' surrogacy arrangement), to discover *her* identity is not to seek the identity of a *genetic* parent. The genetic parent(s) will be well known to the child as her social parents for the last 18 years or more. (Notice that s 31(3) and (4) of the 1990 Act do not have any practical application to 'parental order' cases since they only allow a child to obtain information (as permitted by regulations) about anyone who would be her parent(s) but for ss 27–29 of the 1990 Act: in context this means 'the commissioning couple' or any third party donor but does not include the surrogate herself.)

In addition, a child under 18 who is subject to a 'parental order' may discover whether a proposed spouse is within the prohibited degrees of relationship for marriage (s 51(2) of the 1976 Act as amended). For this purpose, both the commissioning couple and the surrogate and her partner (if any) will be the child's parents (s 47(1) of the 1976 Act as amended). Hence, for example, the child could not marry the son or daughter of the surrogate who would for this purpose be considered in law the brother or sister of the child.

(For a discussion of the *Surrogacy Review's* proposals for reforming 'parental orders' see, *infra*.)

How, then, will a court acting in the child's 'best interests' determine with whom a child should live? As we have seen, the determination of who should bring up the child is not a matter for the parties to agree amongst themselves. As Sir John Arnold P put it in *Re P (minors) (wardship: surrogacy)* [1987] 2 FLR 421:

> ... [T]he court's duty is to decide the case, taking into account as the first and paramount consideration, the welfare of the child or children concerned and if that consideration leads the court to override any agreement that there may be in the matter, then that court is fully entitled to do.

Even though the parties are agreed that the commissioning parents should bring up the child, the court may choose to disregard the terms of the agreement and place the child with another.

The following case concerned what was said to be the first commercial surrogacy agreement in England. It illustrates that even where all the parties to the agreement are content with who should have custody, the court in the exercise of its wardship jurisdiction must make the ultimate decision, based on its perception of the child's 'best interests'. The case also illustrates the judiciary's uneasiness with the publication of the names of the parties involved – in this case at least the surrogate mother was already well-known – and as we shall see, the judge made an order restraining the press from discovering or publishing the names of the parties.

Re C (A Minor) [1985] FLR 846 (Fam Div)

Latey J: The baby's father is Mr A, as I will describe him. He and his wife, Mrs A, are in their 30s and have been married for several years. Mr A is fertile. Mrs A has a congenital defect which prevents her from ever having children. Both dearly wanted a baby. In their home country adoption is slow and a child is usually aged 4 to 5 at adoption. They wanted a baby to bring up from birth. They made inquiries.

In 1983 the father contacted an agency in America and entered into a contract whereby he paid a sum of money and the agency undertook to find a surrogate mother to bear his child. She also would be paid. In England there is a similar agency. A surrogate mother was found.

In 1984 the father came to England, by arrangement, for the sole purpose of providing seminal fluid for insemination of the surrogate mother. It was so arranged that he provided his semen to a qualified nurse and it was introduced into the mother. The father and the mother did not meet and have not met. The insemination was successful, resulting in conception.

The agreement was that the baby on birth was to be handed over to the father and his wife, Mr and Mrs A, to be theirs to care for and bring up.

The father and his wife came to this country in anticipation of the birth and on Friday, 4 January, the baby was born. On the same day the local authority, the London Borough of Barnet, obtained a place of safety order. The baby remained at the hospital, cared for by the nurses.

On Tuesday, 8 January 1986 the father issued a wardship summons. On the same evening there was a hearing before me, when the father was represented by counsel and solicitors, and the London Borough of Barnet was represented by counsel and its legal department. The father and his wife were present.

At that time the social services department had already carried out a good deal of its inquiries, but still had some to complete. It was a fairly lengthy hearing and I made interim orders and directions.

The social services department thought that they could conclude their inquiries by Friday last and I directed that the matter be restored for hearing on that day. They did complete their inquiries and the matter was heard on Friday last.

The inquiries which were deposed to in evidence, were very full and covered every relevant matter. They established that the father, Mr A, is the natural father of the baby; that the natural mother has voluntarily relinquished all parental rights in the child; and that she in fact left the baby in hospital some hours after birth and has not seen her since. The evidence deals in the fullest details with Mr and Mrs A and their health, living and family circumstances and their suitability as parents, about which I will say a little more in a moment.

In the result, the local authority supports to the full the application that the baby be given into the care and upbringing of Mr and Mrs A.

First and foremost, and at the heart of the prerogative jurisdiction in wardship, is what is best for the child or children concerned. That and nothing else. Plainly, the methods used to produce a child as this baby has been, and the commercial aspects of it, raise difficult and delicate problems of ethics, morality and social desirability. These problems are under active consideration elsewhere.

Are they relevant in arriving at a decision on what now and, so far as one can tell, in the future is best for this child? If they are relevant, it is incumbent on the court to do its best to evaluate and balance them.

In my judgment, however, they are not relevant. The baby is here. All that matters is what is best for her now that she is here and not how she arrived. If it be said (though it has not been said during these hearings) that because the father and his wife entered into these arrangements it is some indication of their unsuitability as parents, I should reject any such suggestion. If what they did was wrong (and I am not saying that it was), they did it in total innocence.

It follows that the moral, ethical and social considerations are for others and not for this court in its wardship jurisdiction.

So, what is best for this baby? Her natural mother does not ask for her. Should she go into Mr and Mrs A's care and be brought up by them? Or should some other arrangement be made for her, such as long-term fostering with or without adoption as an end?

The factors can be briefly stated. Mr A is the baby's father and he wants her, as does his wife. The baby's mother does not want her. Mr and Mrs A are a couple in their 30s. They are devoted to each other. They are both professional people, highly qualified. They have a very nice home in the country and another in a town. Materially they can give the baby a very good upbringing. But, far more importantly, they are both excellently equipped to meet the baby's emotional needs. They are most warm, caring, sensible people, as well as highly intelligent. When the time comes to answer the child's questions, they will be able to do so with professional advice if they feel they need it. Looking at this child's well-being, physical and emotional, who better to have her care? No one.

Accordingly, the orders which I made on Friday evening are that the wardship will continue until further notice; the care and control of the baby is committed to Mr and Mrs A until further order; on their undertaking to return the child to the jurisdiction if the court should so order (an unlikely contingency in this case) there is leave for them to take her to live outside the jurisdiction. There are further orders that RSC Ord 63, r 4 shall not apply, and that no one may search for, inspect or take a copy of any of the documents filed in these proceedings without leave of the court; and an order to similar effect regarding the documents in the possession of the social services department, again without leave of the court.

I also approved arrangements for the immediate handover of the baby to Mr and Mrs A. These were worked out with the object, amongst others, of avoiding the identification of Mr and Mrs A. …

Finally, I issued a specific order that there must be no disclosure or publicity which *might* (and I stress that word) lead to the identification of Mr and Mrs A. The reasons for this are or should be self-evident. Is this baby to grow into childhood, adolescence and adulthood with the finger pointed at her as 'This is the girl who …' It is unthinkable that it should be so. Were it otherwise the injury to her mental and emotional health might be grave indeed. The wardship continues and with it that specific order. Any breach of it would be a very serious contempt.

It is inconceivable that leave ever will be given to publish the identities of Mr and Mrs A. That being so, it would be kind and compassionate to discontinue any inquiries which may be on foot and leave this couple to bring up their child in peace and quietness of mind.

(ii) WHERE THE PARTIES ARE NOT AGREED

Difficulties may arise, where the surrogate mother refuses to surrender the custody of the child to the commissioning couple, as in the following cases: *A v C* (custody to surrogate); *Baby M* (custody to commissioning parents); *Re P (Minors)* (custody to surrogate). Here, of course, the s 30 procedure is not available because the surrogate mother is refusing to consent. While adoption is possible if the court takes the view that she is unreasonably withholding her consent, these types of dispute are most likely to be raised under the court's inherent jurisdiction.

This situation looks the most difficult to resolve since there is a 'tug of war' between the parties to the agreement for the child. A judicial determination of what are the child's best interests will not necessarily result in any particular party to the agreement obtaining parental responsibility. The attitude of Comyn J and the Court of Appeal in *A v C* – which can only be described as open antagonism towards the commissioning father – might not be so likely now.

The American case of *Baby M,* the facts of which we have already seen, illustrates how the court can perceive the child's best interests as lying with the commissioning parents and not with the surrogate who is the natural mother of the child (see also *Re MW (Adoption: Surrogacy)* [1995] 2 FLR 759 – making adoption order in favour of commissioning couple despite refusal of surrogate).

In the Matter of Baby M (1988) 537 A 2d 1227 (NJ Sup Ct)

Wilentz CJ: Having decided that the surrogacy contract is illegal and unenforceable, we now must decide the custody question without regard to the provisions of the surrogacy contract that would give Mr Stern sole and permanent custody. (That does not mean the existence of the contract and the circumstances under which it was entered may not be considered to the extent deemed relevant to the child's best interests.) With the surrogacy contract disposed of, the legal framework becomes a dispute between two couples over the custody of a child produced by the artificial insemination of one couple's wife by the other's husband. ... The applicable rule given these circumstances is clear: the child's best interests determine custody.

We note again that the trial court's reasons for determining what were the child's best interests were somewhat different from ours. It concluded that the surrogacy contract was valid, but that it could not grant specific performance unless to do so was in the child's best interests. The approach was that of a Chancery judge, unwilling to give extraordinary remedies unless they well served the most important interests, in this case, the interests of the child. While substantively indistinguishable from our approach to the question of best interests, the purpose of the inquiry was not the usual purpose of determining custody, but of determining a contractual remedy.

... The question of custody in this case, as in practically all cases, assumes the fitness of both parents, and no serious contention is made in this case that either is unfit. The issue here is which life would be better for Baby M, one with primary custody in the Whiteheads or one with primary custody in the Sterns.

The circumstances of this custody dispute are unusual and they have provoked some unusual contentions. The Whiteheads claim that even if the child's best interests would be served by our awarding custody to the Sterns, we should not do so, since that will encourage surrogacy contracts – contracts claimed by the Whiteheads, and we agree, to be violative of important legislatively-stated public policies. Their position is that in order that surrogacy contracts be deterred, custody should remain in the surrogate mother unless she is unfit, regardless of the best interests of the child. We disagree. Our declaration that this surrogacy contract is unenforceable and illegal is sufficient to deter similar agreements. We need not sacrifice the child's best interests in order to make that point sharper ... Some of Mrs Whitehead's alleged character failings, as testified to by experts and concurred in by the trial court, were demonstrated by her actions brought on by the custody crisis. For instance, in order to demonstrate her impulsiveness, those experts stressed the Whiteheads' flight to Florida with Baby M; to show her willingness to use her children for her own aims, they noted the telephone threats to kill Baby M and to accuse Mrs Stern of sexual abuse of her daughter; in order to show Mrs Whitehead's manipulativeness, they pointed to her threat to kill herself; and in order to show her unsettled family life, they noted the innumerable moves from one hotel or motel to another in Florida. Furthermore, the argument continues, one of the most important factors, whether mentioned or not, in favour of custody in the Sterns is their continuing custody during the litigation, now having lasted for one-and-a-half years. The Whiteheads' conclusion is that had the trial court not given initial custody to the Sterns during the litigations, Mrs Whitehead not only would have demonstrated her perfectly acceptable personality – the general tenor of the opinion of experts was that her personality problems surfaced primarily in crises – but would also have been able to prove better her parental skills along with an even stronger bond than may now exist between her and Baby M. Had she not been limited to custody for four months, she could have proved all of these things much more persuasively through almost two years of custody.

The argument has considerable force. It is of course possible that the trial court was wrong in its initial award of custody. It is also possible that such error, if that is what it was, may have affected the outcome. We disagree with the premise, however, that in determining custody a court should decide what the child's best interests *would be* if some hypothetical state of facts had existed. Rather, we must look to what those best interests *are today* even if some of the facts may have resulted in part from legal error. The child's interests come first ... The custody decision must be based on all circumstances, on everything that *actually* has occurred, on everything that is relevant to the child's best interests. Those circumstances include the trip to Florida, the telephone calls and threats, the substantial period of successful custody with the Sterns, and all other relevant circumstances. ...

There were eleven experts who testified concerning the child's best interests, either directly or in connection with matters related to that issue. Our reading of the record persuades us that the trial court's decision awarding custody to the Sterns (technically to Mr Stern) should be affirmed ...

Our custody conclusion is based on strongly persuasive testimony contrasting both the family life of the Whiteheads and the Sterns and the personalities and characters of the individuals. The stability of the Whitehead family life was doubtful at the time of the trial. Their finances were in serious trouble (foreclosure by Mrs Whitehead's sister on a second mortgage was in process). Mr Whitehead's employment, though relatively steady, was always at risk because of his alcoholism, a condition that he seems not to have been able to confront effectively. Mrs Whitehead had not worked for quite some time, her last two employments having been part-time. One of the Whiteheads' positive attributes was their ability to bring up two children, and apparently well, even in so vulnerable a household. Yet substantial question was raised even about that aspect of their home life. The expert testimony contained criticism of Mrs Whitehead's handling of her son's educational difficulties. Certain of the experts noted that Mrs Whitehead perceived herself as omnipotent and omniscient concerning her children. She knew what they were thinking, what they wanted, and she spoke for them. As to Melissa, Mrs Whitehead expressed the view that she alone knew what that child's cries and sounds meant. Her inconsistent stories about various things engendered grave doubts about her ability to explain honestly and sensitively to Baby M – and at the right time – the nature of her origin. Although faith in professional counseling is not a *sine qua non* of parenting, several experts believed that Mrs Whitehead's contempt for professional help, especially professional psychological help, coincided with her feelings of omnipotence in a way that could be devastating to a child who most likely will need such help. In short, while love and affection there would be, Baby M's life with the Whiteheads promised to be too closely controlled by Mrs Whitehead. The prospects for wholesome, independent psychological growth and development would be at serious risk.

The Sterns have no other children, but all indications are that their household and their personalities promise a much more likely foundation for Melissa to grow and thrive. There *is* a track record of sorts – during the one-and-a-half years of custody Baby M has done very well, and the relationship between both Mr and Mrs Stern and the baby has become very strong. The household is stable, and likely to remain so. Their finances are more than adequate, their circle of friends supportive, and their marriage happy. Most important, they are loving, giving, nurturing, and openminded people. They have demonstrated the wish and ability to nurture and protect Melissa, yet at the same time to encourage her independence. Their lack of experience is more than made up for by a willingness to learn and to listen, a willingness that is enhanced by their professional training, especially Mrs Stern's experience as a pediatrician. They are honest; they can recognize error, deal with it, and learn from it. They will try to determine rationally the best way to cope with problems in their relationship with Melissa. When the time comes to tell her about her origins, they will probably have found a means of doing so that accords with the best interests of Baby M. All in all, Melissa's future appears solid, happy, and promising with them.

Based on all of this we have concluded, independent of the trial court's identical conclusion, that Melissa's best interests call for custody in the Sterns ...

It seems to us that given her predicament, Mrs Whitehead was rather harshly judged – both by the trial court and by some of the experts. She was guilty of a breach of contract, and indeed, she did break a very important promise, but we think it is expecting something well beyond normal human capabilities to suggest that this mother should have parted with her newly born infant without a struggle. Other than survival, what stronger force is there? We do not know of, and cannot conceive of, any other case where a perfectly fit mother was expected to surrender her newly born infant, perhaps forever, and was then told she was a bad mother because she did not. We know of no authority suggesting that the moral quality of her act in those circumstances should be judged by referring to a contract made before she became pregnant. We do not countenance, and would never countenance, violating a court order as Mrs Whitehead did, even a court order that is wrong; but her resistance to an order that she surrender her infant, possibly forever, merits a measure of understanding. We do not find it so clear that her efforts to keep her infant, when measured against the Sterns' efforts to take her away, make one, rather than the other, the wrongdoer. The Sterns suffered, but so did she. And if we go beyond suffering to an evaluation of the human stakes involved in the struggle, how much weight should be given to her nine months of pregnancy, the labour of childbirth, the risk to her life, compared to the payment of money, the anticipation of a child and the donation of sperm?

There has emerged a portrait of Mrs Whitehead, exposing her children to the media, engaging in negotiations to sell a book, granting interviews that seemed helpful to her, whether hurtful to Baby M or not, which suggests a selfish, grasping woman ready to sacrifice the interests of Baby M and her other children for fame and wealth. That portrait is a half-truth, for while it may accurately reflect what ultimately occurred, its implication, that this is what Mary Beth Whitehead wanted, is totally inaccurate, at least insofar as the record before us is concerned. There is not one word in that record to support a claim that had she been allowed to continue her possession of her newly born infant, Mrs Whitehead would have ever been heard of again; not one word in the record suggests that her change of mind and her subsequent fight for her child was motivated by anything other than love – whatever complex underlying psychological motivations may have existed.

We have a further concern regarding the trial court's emphasis on the Sterns' interest in Melissa's education as compared to the Whiteheads'. That this difference is a legitimate factor to be considered we have no doubt. But it should not be overlooked that a best-interest test is designed to create not a new member of the intelligentsia but rather a well-integrated person who might reasonably be expected to be happy with life. 'Best interests' does not contain within it any idealized lifestyle; the question boils down to a judgment, consisting of many factors, about the likely future happiness of a human being, *Fantony v Fantony* 21 *NJ* at 536, 122 *A* 2d 593. Stability, love, family happiness, tolerance, and, ultimately support of independence – all rank much higher in predicting future happiness than the likelihood of a college education. We do not mean to suggest that the trial court would disagree. We simply want to dispel any possible misunderstanding on the issue.

Even allowing for these differences, the facts, the experts' opinions, and the trial court's analysis of both argue strongly in favor of custody of the Sterns. Mary Beth Whitehead's family life, into which Baby M would be placed, was anything but secure – the quality Melissa needs most. And today it may be even less so. Furthermore, the evidence and expert opinion based on it reveal personality characteristics, mentioned above, that might threaten the child's best development. The Sterns promise a secure home, with an understanding relationship that allows nurturing and independent growth to develop together.

The court award custody to Mr and Mrs Stern.

The result reached in the *Baby M* case will not always be the court's solution. All will depend upon the court's view of the child's 'best interests'.

Re P (Minors) (Wardship: Surrogacy) [1987] 2 FLR 421 (Fam Div)

A woman offered her services as a surrogate mother to a married professional man who donated sperm by artificial insemination and agreed to pay a lump sum to adopt the child. During the pregnancy she began to have misgivings about giving up the child and when she had given birth to twins in October 1986 her disinclination hardened increasingly. After a period of indecision, and despite her concern and regret about disappointing the father and his wife, she decided to keep the children. She and the father independently approached the local authority who applied to the court to make the children wards of court and to deal with the matter. By the date of the hearing the twins had been cared for by their mother for 5 months.

Sir John Arnold P: What then are the factors the court should take into account? I have already mentioned on the side of Mrs P the matters which weigh heavily in the balance are the fact of her maternity, that she bore the children and carried them for the term of their gestation and that ever since she has conferred upon them the maternal care which they have enjoyed and has done so successfully. The key social worker in the case who has given evidence testifies to the satisfactory nature of the care which Mrs P has conferred upon the children and this assessment is specifically accepted by Mr B as being an accurate one. I start, therefore, from the position that these babies have bonded with their mother in a state of domestic care by her of a satisfactory nature and I now turn to the factors which are said to outweigh those advantages, so as to guide the court upon the proper exercise of the balancing function to the conclusion that the children ought to be taken away from Mrs P, and passed over, under suitable arrangements, to Mr and Mrs B. They are principally as follows. It is said, and said quite correctly, that the shape of the B family is the better shape of a family in which these children might be brought up, because it contains a father as well as a mother and that is undoubtedly true. Next, it is said that the material circumstances of the B family are such that they exhibit a far larger degree of affluence than can be demonstrated by Mrs P. That, also, is undoubtedly true.

Then it is said that the intellectual quality of the environment of the Bs' home and the stimulus which would be afforded to these babies, if they were to grow up in that home, would be greater than the corresponding features in the home of Mrs P. That is not a matter which has been extensively investigated, but I suspect that that is probably true. Certainly, the combined effect of the lack of affluence on the part of Mrs P and some lack of resilience to the disadvantages which that implies has been testified in the correspondence to the extent that I find Mrs P saying that shortage of resources leads to her sitting at home with little E and overeating, because she has no ability from a financial point of view to undertake anything more resourceful than that. Then it is said that the religious comfort and support which the Bs derive from their Church is greater than anything of that sort available to Mrs P. How far that is true, I simply do not know. I do know that the Bs are practising Christians and do derive advantages from that circumstance, but nobody asked Mrs P about that and I am not disposed to assume that she lacks that sort of comfort and support in the absence of any investigation by way of cross-examination to lay the foundations for such a conclusion. Then it is said, and there is something in this, that the problems which might arise from the circumstance that these children who are, of course, congenitally derived from the semen of Mr B and bear traces of Mr B's Asiatic origin would be more easily understood and discussed and reconciled in the household of Mr and Mrs B, a household with an Asiatic ethnic background, than they would be if they arose in relation to these children while they were situated in the home of Mrs P, which is in an English village and which has no non-English connections. Obviously that is expressed contingently as a factor, although there is no means by which the court can measure the likelihood or otherwise of the contingency which has regard to racial discrimination. The situation in which Mrs P lives is not, as it seems to me, likely to breed that sort of intolerance. She lives in a smallish country community, large in terms of a village but small in terms of a town, where there is very little penetration by any immigrant citizens, which does not seem to me to be a community in which racial discrimination is very likely, but it is a factor which contingently at least may have some importance.

Those are the particular matters which are put forward as counterweights to the advantages to which Mrs P can point, and additionally there is the matter to which I have already referred, that it is said that in the letter of mid-November 1986, Mrs P was, herself, recognising that the balance of advantage, which the court is required to consider for the reason I have indicated, operated in favour of the solution of placing the children with the Bs and taking them away from Mrs P, but I do not think that that last factor is of substantial importance. At the time when that letter was written there was, as independent evidence testifies, a prevalent state of things in which Mrs P was suffering from post-natal depression, or at least post-natal stress, so that her expressions of opinion were not likely to have been very reliable at that time. Secondly, any such opinion was expressed at a stage when the children were 1 month old and might not be valid in the circumstances such as now prevail. They are 5 months old and have consistently been looked after by their mother during that 5 months' period and, thirdly, the court is not only not bound, although it might be influenced, by such an expression of opinion, but is required in the due exercise of the jurisdiction to come to its own conclusion upon that topic.

As regards the other factors, they are, in the aggregate, weighty, but I do not think, having given my very best effort to the evaluation of the case dispassionately on both sides, that they ought to be taken to outweigh the advantages to these children of preserving the link with the mother to whom they are bonded and who has, as is amply testified, exercised over them a satisfactory level of maternal care, and accordingly it is, I think, the duty of the court to award the care and control of these babies to their mother.

One final point requires notice. Although *A v C* began as a dispute about custody of a child, eventually the commissioning father's claim was for access (what today would be a 'contact order' under the Children Act 1989) alone. This the Court of Appeal rejected. Ormrod LJ said (at 458):

I can see absolutely no advantage to this child in continuing to be in contact with the father, except possibility a financial advantage to which I attach no significance whatever, in this case. If the father is to continue to turn up in the mother's house or to keep meeting her somewhere to take over the child, or to meet some member of her family to take over the child and return the child, the whole of this sordid story will be revived weekly or monthly as the case may be. The mother's position will be handicapped, and the handicapping of her position handicaps the child.

Cumming-Bruce LJ said (at 460–461):

In my view, the effect of the access ordered by the judge must, inevitably, be to introduce such a disruptive factor into the mother's emotional life that it is bound to have an adverse effect upon the boy. The boy's interest in this case is identified with the mother's interest, and the boy must be given a mother free from the threat of repeated confrontation with a man with whom she has never had any sort of relationship at all, save one of sordid pecuniary advantage. In my view, any advantage that the father could confer on the child is wholly outbalanced and obviously outbalanced by the disadvantage to the child of being brought up by the mother, who is subject to such a dangerous and persistent reminder of an episode in her life which, though she will never forget it, must be kept as completely in the background as possible.

It is interesting to note that in the *Baby M* case where, by contrast, custody was awarded to the commissioning parents, the Supreme Court of New Jersey remitted the issue of access by the surrogate mother, Mary Beth Whitehead, to the trial court. The court observed:

We have decided that Mrs Whitehead is entitled to visitation at some point, and that question is not open to the trial court on this remand. The trial court will determine what kind of visitation shall be granted to her, with or without conditions, and when and under what circumstances it should commence. ...

While probably unlikely, we do not deem it unthinkable that, the major issues having been resolved, the parties' undoubted love for this child might result in a good faith attempt to work out the visitation themselves, in the best interests of their child.

It seems most unlikely that a court would make a 'contact order' in favour of a surrogate mother if it were minded to grant the commissioning parents parental responsibility.

(iii)   WHERE NONE OF THE PARTIES WANTS THE CHILD

Difficulties are also posed where the parties are agreed that, because it has transpired that the child has been born disabled, neither party should be obliged to have custody. This problem is not resolved merely by saying 'parental responsibility' is inalienable, even though this is true (Children Act 1989 s 2(9)). This begs the question who the parents should be? The court will determine who should have parental responsibility and a 'residence order' on the 'best interests' approach. In doing so, the court will clearly have regard to the fact that the child is unwanted by the parties to the agreement. It may well be in such a case that the child's best interests lie elsewhere than living with any of the parties to the agreement. Adoption or long-term fostering to third parties may be the most likely outcome in this sort of case.

E. REFORMING THE LAW

In 1997, the Government set up a review of surrogacy arrangements in the UK chaired by Professor Margaret Brazier. In October 1998, the review team reported: *Surrogacy – Review for Health Ministers of Current Arrangements for Payments and Regulation* (CM 4068). The Review's terms of reference were as follows:
– to consider whether payments, including expenses, to surrogate mothers should continue to be allowed, and if so on what basis;
– to examine whether there is a case for the regulation of surrogacy arrangements through a recognised body or bodies; and if so to advise on the scope and operation of such arrangements;

– in the light of the above to advise whether changes are needed to the Surrogacy Arrangements Act 1985 and/or s 30 of the Human Fertilisation and Embryology Act 1990.

In the result, the Review made a number of recommendations:

Payments

1. Payments to surrogate mothers should cover only genuine expenses associated with the pregnancy (paragraph 5.24).

2. Additional payments should be prohibited in order to prevent surrogacy arrangements being entered into for financial benefit (paragraph 5.24).

3. The basis on which expenses will be met should be established before any attempt is made to create a surrogacy pregnancy, with a requirement for documentary evidence of expenses incurred in association with the surrogacy arrangement to be produced by the surrogate mother (paragraph 5.24).

4. Legislation should define expenses in broad terms of principle and empower Ministers to issue directions on what constitutes reasonable expenses and the methods by which expenses shall be proven (paragraph 7.11).

Regulation

5. Agencies involved in surrogacy arrangements should be required to be registered by the UK Health Departments and to operate in accordance with the Code of Practice required under the terms of the proposed new Surrogacy Act (paragraph 6.23).

6. The Department of Health, in consultation with the other UK Health Departments, should draw up a Code of Practice after discussion with relevant bodies and individuals. The Code should be binding on registered agencies. The Code should also operate as an *advisory* Code to provide guidance in relation to all surrogacy arrangements whether made through a registered agency or privately (paragraph 6.23).

7. As an interim measure (prior to the necessary legislation) the UK Health Departments should draw up and promulgate a voluntary code and invite relevant bodies to seek voluntary registration. The Code should also be drawn to the attention of professional bodies and of the Human Fertilisation and Embryology Authority, so that they could consider incorporating advice on relevant aspects of it into the guidance they issue to practitioners and clinics (paragraph 6.24).

8. In addition to the Code, the Health Departments should also consider establishing requirements for full record keeping and reporting of specified statistics; and clear guidelines on how research will be facilitated into the outcomes of the arrangements (paragraph 6.26).

Legislation

9. Consideration should be given to the repeal of both the Surrogacy Arrangements Act 1985 and section 30 of the Human Fertilisation and Embryology Act 1990, and their replacement by a new Surrogacy Act. The Surrogacy Act would seek to address in the one statute the main legal principles governing surrogacy arrangements in the United Kingdom, to offer a surrogacy 'code' and include (paragraphs 7.2 and 7.3):

(i) the continuation of the current provisions of Section 1A of the 1985 Act relating to the non-enforceability of surrogacy contracts;

(ii) the continuation of current provisions prohibiting commercial agencies from assisting in the creation of surrogacy arrangements and related provisions prohibiting advertisements in relation to surrogacy arrangements;

(iii) new statutory provisions defining and limiting lawful payments to surrogate mothers;

(iv) provision for the promulgation by the UK Departments of Health of a Code of Practice governing surrogacy arrangements generally;

(v) provision for the registration of non profit-making surrogacy agencies by the Departments of Health and that such agencies should be required to comply with the Departments' Code of Practice on surrogacy arrangements;

(vi) provision to prohibit the operation of unregistered agencies;

(vii) new provisions for the grant of a parental order to commissioning couples (a revised section 30 order). The revised order should provide that applicants for a parental order should establish compliance with the Surrogacy Act and the Code of Practice; and that they have complied with the statutory limitations on payments. The revised order should *not* authorise the judge to approve otherwise impermissible payments.

10. Parental orders should only be obtained in the High Court; Judges should be able to order DNA tests; and Guardians *ad litem* should be able to check criminal records (paragraph 7.24).

11. In order for a parental order to be granted, the commissioning couple should be habitually resident in the United Kingdom, the Channel Islands or the Isle of Man for a period of 12 months immediately preceding the application for a parental order (paragraph 7.24).

As you will see, the Review recommended the enactment of a new Surrogacy Act to give effect to its main recommendations and to bring together the current statutory provisions concerned with surrogate arrangements.

These recommendations are critically examined by Professor Michael Freeman in the following extract.

Michael Freeman 'Does Surrogacy Have a Future After Brazier?' (1999) 7 Med L Rev 1

Brazier recommendations relate to three matters: *payments to surrogates*; the *regulation of surrogacy;* and, *new legislation* to replace the 1985 Act and s 30 of the 1990 Act, tightening up the provisions of these Acts and providing for a new Code of Practice.

A. Payments to Surrogates

It was concern about the "level" (Brazier report para 3.1) of payments being made to surrogate mothers that was a major factor in the initiation of the review. Of course, information was (and is) sketchy but accounts from COTS and elsewhere suggest payments of "£15,000 or more" (para 3.4) are being made by commissioning couples to surrogates. Payments reported to Guardians Ad Litem "ranged from nothing to £12,000, averaging £3,800 where payments were made" (para 1.31) (and, therefore, though the report does not say so, less than this). In fact in cases known to Guardians Ad Litem (GALs) – those where applications for parental orders were made – in only 3 per cent of cases was payment more than £10,000 (para 5.6 and Annex C). The cynic might comment that if there was concern about the "level" of payments it ought to have been because the remuneration appears to be so "low" That those who are not applying for parental orders are the "big spenders", as the report suggests (para 5.7), can only be speculation. It is equally possible that they are ignorant of the law – a possibility which the report countenances in another context (para 6.33). The review found a majority of respondents (56%) were against payments (para 6.33). This excluded COTS members who generally favoured payments. A large majority (83 per cent) believed surrogates should not be "out of pocket as a result of their pregnancy". There was less consensus in relation to loss of earnings: 75 per cent thought payments should reimburse loss of actual earnings (para 5.9), but only 31 per cent that potential earnings should be compensated. In fact, over one in six respondents wanted to prohibit payments of any kind.

Brazier recommends that payments to surrogate mothers should cover only genuine expenses associated with the pregnancy (para 5.24) – a list of permissible expenses is provided (para 5.25) – and actual loss of earnings (the difference between the surrogate mother's usual earnings and state benefits) (para 5.26). A number of reasons are given to support this conclusion. First, children are not commodities to be bought and sold. Of course, this is right, but Brazier is too readily dismissive of the distinction between payment for the purchase of a child and payment for a potentially risky, time-consuming and uncomfortable service. The Report also overlooks the point made by Laura Purdy ('*Reproducing Persons*') (Cornell University Press 1996), ch 11) that paying a woman to bear a child forces us to recognise the process as socially useful and children as socially valuable creatures whose upbringing and welfare are critically important. Secondly, it is in line with emerging policy in relation to egg and sperm donors, as well as with the law on blood and live organ donation (paras 5.12–5.13). This inevitably treats the law and policy in these areas as unproblematic, which they clearly are not. But it was outside the remit of the review to question beyond surrogacy, and it is equally outside the scope of this paper to do so. Thirdly, women should not be influenced to become surrogate mothers by the lure of financial benefit. The review found (unsurprisingly) that many surrogates are "primarily motivated by payment" (para 5.14). The spectre of surrogacy as a profession is also noted (para 5.17). The fears here may well be exaggerated and regulation could police this. Fourthly, though conceded to be speculative, the report believes it is "not necessarily in children's best interests to learn that their surrogate mother benefitted financially from their birth or from giving them away to the commissioning couple" (para 5.19). Clearly, children born of surrogacy arrangements have the right to be told this, but done properly and at the right time, is there any reason to believe that they will be harmed by information that money passed hands? The Report implies that the right time to tell a child of his/her origins is when that child is a teenager (para 5.21). This surely cannot be the right advice and makes one suspicious of the rest of the psychology embedded in the report.

The Report fails to appreciate that withdrawing remuneration from surrogates will only derive potential surrogates away from regulated surrogacy into an invisible and socially uncontrolled world where the regulators will be more like pimps than adoption agencies. There is every reason to control surrogacy and to guard against perceived problems, but most women will expect to be rewarded. Brazier agrees and believes that surrogacy will rarely be undertaken by strangers once its recommendations are implemented. This prognosis is misplaced: surrogacy will continue; it will probably grow as infertility increases; it will go underground and the fees will become larger. We cannot stop women exercising their autonomy, nor can we persuade them that being paid aggravates their exploitation, when common sense tells them the reverse.

B. Regulation

Brazier proposes that surrogacy should be regulated. This was also the view of the minority in the Warnock Report and it is supported by Singer and Wells (*The Reproduction Revolution* (Oxford University Press 1984) at 118–19) and others (eg Ontario Law Reform Commission '*Human Artificial Reproduction and Related Matters*' (1985)). Brazier rests its case for regulation on protection. Regulation, it says, "might reduce the more obvious hazards to the child and the others involved (including any children of the surrogate mother)" (para 6.3). The view that regulation is undesirable because its effect would be to aggravate the current situation – in effect the view of Warnock (para 6.5) – is dismissed: "the risks of not having a regulatory framework are greater than any entailed by introducing one" (para 6.5). Like the minority in Warnock, Brazier would not outlaw surrogacy arrangements made outside the regulated service. Those not using this might find it more difficult to secure a parental order under the new section 30 of the Human Fertilisation and Embryology Act 1990, but that, it is envisaged, would be the only sanction. It is my view that if surrogacy is to be regulated, as I agree it should, then all surrogacy arrangements should be thus controlled. The institution of adoption is a ready-made model: private placements, save within the context of the family, are banned and no adoption order can be made without first being vetted (Adoption Act 1976, s 11(1), (3) and *Gatehouse v Robinson* [1986] 1 WLR 18).

Brazier investigates three options for regulatory bodies. It rejects conferring regulatory powers on infertility clinics or the Human Fertilisation and Embryology Authority: it is not right to perceive surrogacy arrangements as "merely another treatment for infertile people" (para 6.13). Brazier is right to reject this option. Clinics and the HFEA have medical and scientific expertise and this is rarely required in the context of surrogacy. Other skills are, and these are more likely to be found in adoption-like agencies. It also rejected a new licensing authority on the ground that a "complex and expensive regulatory arrangement" (para 6.22) would be "an excessive reaction to current concerns about the practice of surrogacy". It favours instead a "much simpler option": "all agencies involved in surrogacy arrangements would be required to be registered by the UK Health Departments and to operate in accordance with a statutory Code of Practice" (para 6.23).

This modest proposal would not require the establishment of any new Authority. Brazier does not make out a strong case for this method of regulation. Given how few surrogacy arrangements and surrogacy births there are, the logic of decentralisation is weak. Even within the control of a Code of Practice, there are bound to be differences of interpretation and whether surrogacy is approved may depend on geography. One subject of such concern, should not authority speak with one voice? The case for a single licensing authority (Singer and Wells called it a "State Surrogacy Board") is a strong one.

C. Reforming the Law

Brazier recommends a new Surrogacy Act. This would address in one statute "the main legal principles" governing surrogacy arrangements and offer a surrogacy "code" (para 7.2). ...

The new Surrogacy Act would both consolidate and reform the law. ...

The new Surrogacy Act would define and limit lawful payments to surrogate mothers allowing, as we have seen, only prescribed expenses and actual loss of earnings. It would also provide for the promulgation of a Code of Practice as a "model of good practice". Although the details of this are to be left for the Department of Health to settle after a consultation process, the Report offers a detailed blueprint in Chapter 8. This addresses a number of matters.

Commendably, the first concern is the welfare of the child. The Report does not adopt a consistent line on this. In the discussion of the Code of Practice, as in the Executive Summary, the welfare of the child must be "the paramount concern of all parties to the arrangement, the courts and all other agencies involved" (para 18). Elsewhere in the Report, we are told that the welfare of the child "must be accorded the highest priority" (paras 4.46 and 4.50). These are different standards. The paramountcy principle allows no space for other considerations. The child's welfare is more than just the "top item": it "rules upon or determines the course to be followed" (per MacDermott in *J v C* [1970] AC 668, 710). But according a child's welfare – in effect, of course, a child yet to be born – the highest priority, it becomes the "first consideration" but not the only one. It is weighted, though by how much is an unanswerable question. A reading of the Report as a whole suggests that it must intend to accord the child's welfare only the "highest priority" (to use language found in other statutes "the first consideration") because the interests of other parties, in particular the vulnerability of the surrogate, are constantly stressed ...

The Report does address eligibility, albeit briefly, and not in these terms. It argues that there should be a minimum and a maximum age for commissioning parents. It does not address criteria: the thorny question of surrogacy for post-menopausal women is thus not addressed. If the ethical arguments for not permitting post-menopausal women to receive egg donations are weak, and recent essays suggest they are, *a fortiori* the case for limiting surrogacy to younger couples is unconvincing. It is not clear what the Report has in mind. In 1994 the High Court upheld the decision of a Health Authority not to provide publicly-funded fertility treatment for a woman aged 37 on the grounds only of her age (*R v Sheffield HA, ex parte Seale* (1995) 25 BMLR 1). Is surrogacy to be similarly limited and, if so, on what grounds (the rationing of a scarce resource, surrogates?). Is it envisaged that the maximum age will apply to both men and women? Older women have a better claim to consider parenthood since in the natural order of things they will live longer than their male counterparts. On minimum age, the Report says little but implies that the age at which one can apply for a parental order, currently 18, should be raised (para 8.4). It is anyway lower than the minimum age at which an adoption order can be applied for. But whether the age specified is 18 or 21 (and it surely would be wrong to stipulate a higher age, say 25 or 30) is of no consequence: it is inconceivable that people not at least in their twenties would contemplate surrogacy. I have my doubts as to the necessity to specify an age at all.

On surrogates, the Report also indicates criteria: a minimum age (21); a maximum age (no age is mentioned); having had a child and having one still living with her; a minimum period of two years between any pregnancies; a maximum number of surrogate births (one, "save where a commissioning couple seek a sibling for a previous child where the surrogate was the genetic mother"). The surrogate is to be provided with comprehensive information about the risks of surrogacy, and to have access to independent counselling and legal advice. The Report also recommends "a period of reflection between any initial approach to act as a surrogate and any attempt to establish a pregnancy" (para 8.6). The importance of "free, informed consent" in altruistic arrangements is also stressed. The Report says nothing about the marital status of the surrogate but accordingly overlooks questions which relate to her husband's status, where she is married.

The Report sees the relationship between the surrogate and the commissioning parents as being based on a "memorandum of understanding" (para 8.12) (which, though non-contractual, would define and clarify the expectations of the parties) (para 8.14). This should record arrangements to secure the future welfare of the child, and include agreements about contact between the surrogate and the child (para 8.13). (I note not between the child and the surrogate) and/or what the child is to be told about his or her origins. Of course, this suggests that the Report sees contact and identity questions as matters for negotiation between the commissioning parents and the surrogate, rather than as matters of public policy upon which the state has the right to dictate a clear line. On the conduct of pregnancy (matters such as smoking and ante-natal care), the Report is ambivalent. Are these matters of negotiation too? The Report says that they are matters to be addressed, but by whom, the regulatory body or the parties to a particular surrogacy arrangement? If regulation is to fulfil its role, then the screening out of unsuitable surrogates, which clearly includes smokers, must be part of its remit.

D. The Revised Parental Order

The Report makes a number of recommendations to reform the parental order scheme, currently in section 30 of the Human Fertilisation and Embryology Act 1990. First, it recommends that commissioning parents should only be eligible to apply for an order if they can establish that they have complied with the statutory limitations on payments: (para 7.13) otherwise impermissive payments should not be amenable to retrospective judicial authorisation, as is the case at present (s 30(7)). However, commissioning parents in breach would remain eligible to adopt the child. The adoption judge would thus retain the power, as now, to give retrospective authorisation to payments (para 7.13). Adoption as a fall back position is far from satisfactory, but with Brazier I have to agree that some solution must be found so that children are not left in an unsatisfactory limbo position. The concept of a residence order only partially assists: the commissioning parents could acquire parental responsibility in this way but would share it with the surrogate (see Children Act 1989 s 12) (and her husband if the child is produced by means of assisted procreation with his consent) (HFEA Act 1990 s 28(2)). Since this is hardly satisfactory – it is potentially productive of disputes – adoption, however undesirable, would seem the only solution.

Brazier formulates one curious exception to the rule that surrogacy is to go through a registered agency if a parental order is to be sought and made. Where neither the couple nor the surrogate were aware of the requirement that agencies be registered, "their lack of knowledge would not preclude the grant of a parental order" (para 7.23) where all other conditions were met. What looks like misplaced indulgence (why should ignorance of the law excuse in this context?) is compounded when, in the next sentence, it is suggested that a judge "might well be disinclined to exercise his or her discretion to grant a parental order" if it were established that the commissioning couple knew their surrogate "was only 16" and no attempt had been made to provide her with advice or counselling. Those using unregistered agencies should therefore be careful to ensure 16-year-old surrogates are counselled or they use 17 or 18-year-olds or, perhaps, there is some other lesson that I have not grasped! To push the realm of fantasy further, what of a *Gillick*-competent 15-year-old surrogate? (see *Gillick* [1986] AC 112). If she is artificially inseminated, it is difficult to see what offence is committed. If she receives counselling (after falsely representing her age), would Brazier countenance a parental order?

Secondly, Brazier recommends that parental orders should be obtained only in the High Court to ensure "the effective 'approval' of a surrogacy arrangement is given by judges of the highest experience" (para 7.24). I doubt whether this is really necessary or that, should surrogacy continue legitimately, this view will prevail in ten years time.

Thirdly, it is recommended that judges should be empowered to require DNA tests to establish the genetic relationship of the child to at least one of the commissioning couple. As Brazier says, where this is not so, the parties have entered into a pre-natal adoption agreement and the general laws relating to adoption should apply.

Fourthly, Brazier recommends that guardians ad litem should have power to check criminal records to ascertain whether the commissioning couple has any criminal convictions likely to endanger the welfare of the child.

Fifthly, it is recommended that the requirement in the present section 30 that at least one of the applicants be domiciled in a part of the United Kingdom (or in the Channel Islands or the Isle of Man) be replaced by a provision that both should be habitually resident for a period of 12 months immediately preceding the application. As Brazier notes, domicile is a concept of "tortuous complexity" and "habitual residence", though far from simple, is more straightforward.

The proposals for DNA tests (where necessary and it will only happen in the exceptional case), for criminal checks (presumably to establish whether either of the couple is a 'Schedule 1 offender') and for a change in personal connecting factor (though it will affect English domiciliaries who live abroad) should cause no problems.

However, if section 30 is to be revitalised (and it was, after all, a late and rushed amendment in 1990), other changes should be considered. First, if parental responsibility is to be extended to a wider category of unmarried fathers, is it necessary (or desirable) to confine applications for a parental order to couples who are husbands and wives? The government proposals on parental responsibility were made late in Brazier's deliberations. The Report is aware of the problems extensions may cause but throughout assumes that surrogacy arrangements are made with commissioning couples and, although it does not specifically say so, implies that they are persons who are married to each other. Would it be a step too far at this stage to allow those living together as husband and wife to apply for a parental order? If this continues not to be allowed, the unmarried couple is forced into the artificial position of one adopting and the other (or both) seeking a residence order (see *Re AB (Adoption: Joint Residence)* [1996] 1 FLR 27).

Secondly, the provision in s 30(2) which limits applications to the period of six months from the birth of the child seems unduly restrictive and could be relaxed or the limitation period dispensed with totally.

Thirdly, the provision in s 30(4) that at the time of the making of the order (note not the birth of the child) the husband and wife must have attained the age of 18 seems, as indicated above, unnecessary. But, if an age is to be specified, then, in accordance with Brazier's proposals, it will presumably need to be raised, though, it will be remembered, the Report does not indicate to what.

Fourthly, the court must be satisfied that the surrogate and the legal father of the child "have freely, and with full understanding of what is involved, agreed unconditionally to the making of the order". Where the surrogate is married, the legal father will usually be the husband (unless he can prove that he did not consent to the procedure). But if he did, why should his agreement to a parental order be required? Where the surrogate is unmarried, the commissioning man will be the legal father if his sperm was used for donor insemination or in vitro fertilisation. If there is medical intervention, whether he is the legal father will hinge on whether the surrogate and commissioning man are being treated "together". If they are not being treated "together", and this must be the better view, neither he nor any other man is the child's legal father. It may be too much to expect from surrogacy reform that Parliament will look again at these legal parentage rules, but they are complex, confusing and ill-understood.

Fifthly, agreement cannot be dispensed with, though it is not required where the person concerned cannot be found or is incapable of giving agreement. This "ground" is modelled on adoption law, but adoption law makes provision for dispensing with agreement if it is unreasonably withheld, and on a number of other grounds. Consideration should be given to extending the model of adoption law to embrace these other grounds. If a surrogate freely hands over a child and subsequently refuses to agree to the making of a parental order, the opportunity to test her change of heart through the unreasonableness provision should be open. Why should she be treated any differently from any other mother who hands over her child and then changes her mind?

Sixthly, the statutory provision is currently filled out by the Parental Orders (Human Fertilisation and Embryology) Regulations 1994, which applies many of the provisions of the Adoption Act 1976 to section 30 applications and orders. Thus, for example, applications are heard in private, a guardian *ad litem* is appointed for the child, and the court has a duty to safeguard and promote the welfare of the child. The child's welfare is the first consideration (as in adoption). However, the welfare checklist in section 1(3) of the Children Act, which explains the paramountcy test, is, we are advised, to be considered (para 3.18). These are matters which ought to be in primary legislation rather than in regulations or guidance, and, if there is to be a new Surrogacy Act, there is the opportunity for a rethink and a reformulation.

Seventhly, Brazier investigates the GAL's role only in relation to criminal searches. The Report overlooks the fact that children cannot be parties to section 30 proceedings. One result of this is that in this "extraordinarily complicated and sensitive area" (see J E Timms *'Children's Representation: A Practitioner's Guide'* (Sweet and Maxwell) 1995, at 305), guardians are not able to instruct solicitors for the children whose interests they represent. The guardian is thus acting without the benefit of legal advice for the child. Section 30 was designed to satisfy the needs of adults, and here it clearly shows. As Cretney and Masson observe: "Despite the appointment of a guardian *ad litem* it appears that there is an expectation that all applicants who meet the basic qualifications for a parental order will obtain one" (*Principles of Family Law* (6th edn) (Sweet and Maxwell) 1997, at 947). Not surprisingly the Department of Health guidance envisages that it will be exceptional for a guardian to recommend that an order should not be made, a view which was confirmed by evidence given to the Brazier inquiry by guardians (para 3.19).

Chapter 11

Abortion

There are a few, if any, more contentious areas of medical practice than termination of pregnancy or abortion. The practice has been prohibited or regulated since 1803. The struggle by the medical profession in the nineteenth century for supremacy over 'irregulars' and other 'quacks', is well documented (eg Irvine Loudon 'Medical Practitioners 1750-1850 and the Period of Medical Reform in Britain' in A Wear (ed) *Medicine in Society* (1992) at p 219) and has its reflection in the practices of gynaecology and obstetrics including abortion (see J Keown *Abortion, Doctors and the Law* (1988) chs 2 and 3). From Lord Ellenborough's Act of 1903 (the precursor of the current criminal prohibition on abortion) to the case of *Bourne* in 1938 and finally the Abortion Act 1967, we have witnessed the 'medicalisation' of a crime. Absolute prohibition leading to partial acceptance within the medical community then the law and ultimately Parliamentary regulation (see A Grubb 'Abortion Law in England: The Medicalisation of a Crime' (1990) 18 Law, Medicine and Health Care 146). Despite the liberalising provisions of the Abortion Act 1967 and its general acceptance, there remains serious opposition to the availability of abortions that it contemplates, based on religious or moral objections about the value of human life. For some, abortion is murder. The political struggles that are played out in America in the courts and elsewhere have never been part of the English landscape. Opposition remains, nevertheless, and the many attempts to amend the legislation pay witness to this, all – except for the overhaul in 1990 – have failed. Challenges under the Human Rights Act 1998 to the scope of the 1967 Act are no doubt not far away.

In this chapter we provide an analysis of the *law* and regulation of abortion. We do not seek to engage in the debate about the morality of abortion, about which there is a wealth of specialist literature: see Mary Anne Warren *Moral Status* (1998) ch 9 and Joel Feinberg (ed) *The Problem of Abortion* (1985); seminal pieces include: J J Thomson 'A Defence of Abortion: A Reply to Judith Thomson' (1973) 2 Philosophy and Public Affairs 117; P Foot 'The Problem of Abortion and the Doctrine of the Double Effect' (1967) 5 Oxford Review; R Dworkin, *Life's Dominion* (1993).

Historical background

Professor Bernard Dickens sets the scene.

Bernard Dickens *Abortion and the Law* (1966)

The position at common law
... [B]ecause the offence was of ecclesiastical cognisance ... the writings of authorities on English criminal law have few references to abortion. The protection the Common Law afforded to human life certainly extended to the unborn child but whether abortion (ie after quickening) amounted to homicide or a lesser offence is not clear beyond doubt from the authorities, and possibly altered at different periods. Bracton, writing in the early part of the

thirteenth century said that abortion after animation was homicide. Furthermore, George Crabbe alleges this to have been the position long before; 'If, in Bracton's time, anyone struck a pregnant woman so as to cause abortion, it was homicide, after the foetus was formed. This appears to have been the law in the time of the Saxons.'

An epitome of Bracton, written near the end of the thirteenth century by Fleta is more explicit. His chapter 'De Homocidio' asserts 'He, too, in strictness is a homicide who has pressed upon a pregnant woman or has given her poison or has struck her in order to procure an abortion or to prevent conception, if the foetus was already formed and quickened, and similarly he who has given or accepted poison with the intention of preventing procreation or conception. A woman also commits homicide if, by a potion or the like, she destroys a quickened child in her womb.'

Later authorities, however, do not follow this view, and Coke while quoting Bracton an mentioning Fleta, nevertheless denies homicide. 'If a woman be quick with childe (sic), and by a Potion or otherwise Killeth it in her wombe; or if a man beat her whereby the child (sic) dieth in her body, and she is delivered of a dead childe, this is a great misprision, and no murder; but if the childe be borne alive, and dieth in her body, and she is delivered of a dead childe, this is a great misprision, and no murder; but if the childe be borne alive, and dieth of the Potion, battery or other cause, this is murder; for in law it is accounted a reasonable creature, in *rerum natura*, when it is born alive.'

Coke then demonstrates that a man is accessory to murder who counsels a pregnant woman to kill the child when it is born and continues, 'and yet at the time of the commandment, or counsel, no murder could be committed of the childe in *utero matris*.'

The consequence of this 'great misprision' is not described, but Hawkins wrote in 1716 that the procuring of the abortion of a quick child amounts to a Common Law misdemeanour and is murder if the child is born alive but dies in consequence of its premature birth, or of the means employed.

Blackstone, in his *Commentaries on the Laws of England* (1765) suggests that manslaughter was a possible interpretation of Bracton's characterisation of abortion. He wrote 'Life … begins in contemplation of law as soon as an infant is able to stir in the mother's womb. For if a woman is quick with child, and by a potion or otherwise, killeth it in her womb; or if any one beat her, whereby the child dieth in her body, and she is delivered of a dead child; this, though not murder, was by the antient (sic) law homicide or manslaughter (Bracton). But Sir Edward Coke doth not look upon this offence in quite so atrocious a light, but merely as a heinous misdemenor.'

That Blackstone should translate as 'a heinous misdemenor' what Coke earlier called 'a great misprision' may suggest the contemporary evaluation of the crime of abortion, as the law of misprision was well known to Blackstone. In his *Commentaries* he wrote 'Misprisions … are, in the acceptance of our law, generally understood to be all such high offences as are under the degree of capital, but nearly bordering thereon.' His rejection of this word to describe Coke's view suggests that while the antient law regarded abortion as homicide or manslaughter, the contemporary view was that it was not a capital offence, nor even close thereto. After classifying misprisions into negative and positive, the latter consisting in the commission of something which ought not to be done, he continued 'Misprisions, which are merely positive, are generally denominated contempts, or high misdemeanors' and are usually punishable with fines and imprisonment.

Blackstone does not adopt the modern division of crimes into felonies and misdemeanours, but draws the distinction 'A crime or misdemeanour, is an act committed, or omitted, in violation of a public law, either forbidding or commanding it. The general definition comprehends both crimes and misdemeanors; which, properly speaking, are mere synonymous terms; though, in common usage, the word "crimes" is made to denote such offences as are of a deeper and more atrocious dye; while smaller faults, and omissions of less consequence, are comprised under the gentler name of "misdemeanors" only.'

The *Commentaries on the Laws of England* were written by Blackstone for the lay public, and one may suppose that they were intended to be read according to the common usage, by which misdemeanours were 'smaller fruits, and omissions of consequence.'

Nevertheless, even accepting that in Coke's period (1552-1634) abortion was an offence bordering on the capital, it would probably not have been prosecuted in the Common Law courts, as the ecclesiastical courts retained a criminal jurisdiction, and abortion was generally regarded as their province. However, the Reformation in the mid-sixteenth century challenged this jurisdiction, and in 1641, during the political turmoil immediately before the Civil War, Parliament abolished the senior ecclesiastical courts, the Court of High Commission and the Court of Delegates and these took into abolition with them the whole system of ecclesiastical courts. In these new circumstances, the Common Law had an impetus to develop its own principles, but at the Restoration in 1661 the ordinary ecclesiastical courts were re-established, and much of their old criminal jurisdiction revived, in theory. However, in fact, this was becoming increasingly diminished by the growing practice of making ecclesiastical offences statutory felonies, which took them into the Common Law courts. Moreover even where offences were not so removed from the ecclesiastical courts, the Common Law was generating its own concurrent growth, and it was not until 1803 that procuring abortion was made a statutory felony.

Blackstone in 1765 treated it as a Common Law misdemeanour, and support for this is provided in Chitty's *Criminal Law* (1816) which provides precedents from an indictment both under the 1803 Act and under the Common Law, where drawing on a case of 1802 EF is charged in the third count of the indictment with 'unlawfully ... giving and administering to AE, ... pregnant with child divers other ... dangerous pills ... with a wicked intent to cause and procure the said AE to miscarry ... However, references to the procuring of abortion as a crime at Common Law before it became a statutory offence in 1803 are not numerous, and are fairly late in date.

Statutory provisions

It appears that before 1803 the crime of abortion was Common Law misdemeanour capable of commission by the pregnant woman herself and by other persons on her, but in either case only provided that the stage of 'quickening' had been reached. There are scanty records of the crime, because it was mainly regarded as a matter for the ecclesiastical courts and even where prosecuted in the Common Law courts it would be a rare case, as most abortion is committed before the stage of quickening has been reached (a widely accepted time being fourteen weeks after conception).

Lord Ellenborough's Act, receiving the Royal assent on June 24th 1803, for the first time placed the offence of criminal abortion on a statutory basis. Explaining that 'certain ... heinous Offences, committed with Intent to destroy the Lives of his Majesty's Subjects by Poison, or with Intent to procure the miscarriage of Women ... have been of late also frequently committed; but no adequate Means have been hitherto provided for the Prevention and Punishment of such Offences', it provides in section 1 'That if any Person or Persons ... shall wilfully, maliciously, and unlawfully administer to, or cause to be administered to or taken by any of his Majesty's Subjects, any deadly Poison, or other noxious and destructive Substance or Things, with Intent ... thereby to cause and procure the Miscarriage of any Women then being quick with child ... then and in every such case the Person or Persons so offending, their Counsellors, Aiders, and Abettors, knowing of and privy to such Offence, shall be and are hereby declared to be Felons, and shall suffer Death.'

Although this section created a capital offence, introducing a more severe penalty than was available for the Common Law misdemeanour, it did not substantially alter the legal definition. Indeed it may have been more restricted, as it dealt only with the abortion of women quick with child, procured by use of 'poison, or other noxious and destructive substance or thing'. By the *ejusdem generis* rule of construction, 'thing' may have excluded instruments of manipulations or exercises.

There was no specific reference to a woman procuring her own abortion, but the words of the section probably included such a case, and the statute was directed to the punishment of such an offence, which was consistent with the position at Common Law. Nevertheless the infrequent prosecution of offenders prevented the matter from being clarified beyond doubt, and it may have been that where a woman procured her own abortion by another, she would be charged as an aider and abettor to that other's offence, or still be liable for the Common Law misdemeanour.

The great innovation of the 1803 Act was in section 2; abortion before quickening became a crime for the first time, and was a felony, although not punished as severely as abortion after quickening. The practical significance of this provision was widespread, as nearly all woman who procure their own abortion do so in the early months of pregnancy, before quickening.

Section 2 provides 'And whereas it may sometimes happen that Poison or some other noxious and destructive Substance or Thing may be given, or other means used, with Intent to procure Miscarriage or Abortion where the Women may not be quick with Child at the Time, or it may not be proved that the Women was quick with Child, be it therefore further enacted, that if any Person or Persons ... shall wilfully and maliciously administer to, or cause to be administered to, or taken by any Woman, any Medicines, Drug, or other Substance or Thing whatsoever, or shall use or employ, or cause or procure to be used or employed, any Instrument or other Means whatsoever, with Intent thereby to cause or procure the Miscarriage of any Woman not being, or not being proved to be, quick with Child at the time of administering such Things or using such Means', that this shall be felonious, and punishable with fine, imprisonment, whipping or transportation for up to fourteen years.

This section is of interest for two main reasons. First, it adopts the ecclesiastical distinction between the *embryo formatus* and the *embryo informatus*, capital punishment being reserved only for the abortion of the former. Second, this is the only occasion upon which a statute has actually used the word 'abortion'. Other references here and in future statutes, are to 'miscarriage', and one may conclude from the fact that this section is the only one to contain the word, and also the first to deal with the termination of pregnancy before quickening, that the legislature assumed that termination before quickening was probably called 'abortion', and termination after quickening was described as 'procuring a miscarriage'. This linguistic distinction does not appear in Lord Landsdowne's Act of 1828.

This Act, repealing the 1803 Act, preserved the ecclesiastical distinction, and provided in section 8 'That if any Person, with Intent to procure the Miscarriage of any Women then being quick with Child, unlawfully and maliciously shall administer to her, or cause to be taken by her, any Poison or other noxious Thing, or shall use any Instrument or other Means whatever with the like Intent, every such Offender, and every Person counselling, aiding or abetting such Offender, shall be guilty of Felony.' The punishment was imprisonment, transportation or whipping.

The 1828 Act is more explicit than the 1803 Act on the question of whether an unaided women procuring, or attempting to procure her own abortion, is covered by the Act, but the same presumption of inclusion may be made, although the uncertainty must be recognised. No authority has suggested her exclusion, and apart from introducing slightly more lenient punishments for abortion before quickening, the 1828 Act made little change to the statutory position. In any event a woman could be indicted as an accessory before the fact to an abortion committed upon herself, and to an operation performed upon her with like intent before quickening.

The words 'any woman not being, or not being proved to be, then quick with Child' in the Act of 1803 and 1828, probably relate to the method of determining the state of pregnancy, ie to see if the embryo was *formatus* or *informatus*. The same method was adopted where a woman liable to sentence of death for any offence pleaded her pregnancy as a reason why sentence should not be passed upon her in accordance with law. A Jury of Matrons was sworn in, composed of twelve married women then present in court, and these examined the woman to see if she was 'quick with Child'. Medical aid could be sought to ensure a true Jury of Matrons was to be empanelled the doors of the court were locked, to prevent them from leaving. Their reluctance may have been justified in that it may not have been clear at the time just what they were deciding.

If a woman has quickened, the position and the consequences are clear; but if she has been found not to be quick with child, this may be because her pregnancy is not sufficiently advanced, or because she is not pregnant. This latter condition could have affected the position.

In *R v Scudder* [(1828) 1 Mood CC 216], a case under section 2 of the 1803 Act, but equally applicable to section 13 of the 1828 Act, which used identical words, ie 'any woman not being, or not being proved to be, quick with child', it was held a complete answer to an indictment for abortion before quickening, to show that the woman was not pregnant. This judgment was, however, at variance with *R v Phillips* [(1811) 3 Camp 76], where Lawrence J said 'It is immaterial whether … or not it (savin) was capable of procuring abortion, or even whether the woman was actually with child; if the prisoner believed at the time that it would procure abortion, and administered it with that intent, and case is within the Statute.' This judgment is consistent with the words of the Acts of 1803 and 1828, but interprets simply a division between women who have quickened and those who have not, without distinguishing whether the latter are pregnant or not. This lack of distinction assimilates the *embryo informatus* to the absence of any embryo at all, which is inconsistent with the theological conditioning of the law.

The Offences Against the Person Act, 1837 did not adopt the distinction between women quick or not quick with child, and therefore the case of *R v Wycherley* [(1838) 8 C & P 262] can reveal an issue of exclusively academic interest. In this case, where a surgeon was aiding a Jury of Matrons after a verdict of guilty of murder Guerney B distinguished for him ' "With quick Child" is when the child has quickened.' Applying this definition to the Acts of 1803 and 1828, it could be said that the capital offence was committed in the case of a pregnant woman, the less serious offence relating to a woman who was not pregnant. In terms of medical knowledge the critical distinction is between pregnancy and non-pregnancy, and this legal division might therefore have been rational. 'Quickening' is merely a change in the position of the uterus, and is not evidence of animate life coming to the foetus, which might justify the greater protection provided by the greater punishment.

The Offences Against the Person Act, 1837 not only abandoned the distinction between the *embryo formatus* and the *embryo informatus* in applying its sanction, but did not distinguish a pregnant woman from one who was not. It provided in section 6 'That whosoever, with Intent to procure the Miscarriage of any Woman, shall unlawfully administer to her or cause to be taken by her any Poison or other noxious Thing, or shall unlawfully use any Instrument or other Means whatsoever with the like Intent, shall be guilty of Felony.' The punishment was transportation or imprisonment, this being one of Lord John Russell's reform measures abolishing the death sentence.

There was still no express reference to a woman who procured her own abortion, but there was no doubt that the Act was intended and understood to include her within its ambit. An early draft to the section had distinguished the position of such a woman from that of another person charged with procuring her abortion, in whose case there was a requirement of proof of pregnancy. Lord Lyndhurst's criticisms of this requirement prevailed to omit this from the final draft.

One may consider the use of the word 'unlawfully' at this stage in the development of the law relating to abortion. The 1803 Act used the expression 'wilfully, maliciously, and unlawfully' to characterise acts of abortion performed after quickening, and 'wilfully and maliciously' for both cases. Neither of these Acts suggests when abortion could be lawful, and the 1837 Act is equally silent (as indeed is the current statute, passed in 1861). However, although one may dismiss the use of the formulae in early statutes as being part of the prolix style of draftsmanship then favoured, in 1837 the word may have had some distinctive purpose, however elusive. The Criminal Law Commissioners, commenting in 1846 that other countries' codes have this proviso, suggested the expediency of adding to the then existing law 'Provided that no act specified in the last preceding Article shall be punishable when such as is done in good faith with the intention of saving the life of the mother whose miscarriage is intended to be procured.' This proviso was later incorporated into the Infant Life (Preservation) Act, 1929 as a defence in child destruction prosecutions, but regarding abortion, no guidance was given on the meaning of the word 'unlawfully' until nearly a century after this recommended proviso, in the leading case of *R v Bourne* in 1938.

For further discussion of the common law, see: J Keown *Abortion, Doctors and the Law* (1988) Ch 1; A Grubb 'Abortion Law in England: The Medicalisation of a Crime' (1990) 18 Law, Medicine and Health Care 146.

The present law

A. THE CRIME

The law relating to abortion is part of the criminal law. It operates by creating a crime ('procuring a miscarriage') to which the Abortion Act 1967 creates a defence in certain specified circumstances. There are also other lesser crimes that make it unlawful to fail to comply with the reporting, certification and confidentiality provisions set out in the Abortion Regulations 1991 (SI 1991 No 499)(see *infra*). The importance of this in that the processes of criminal justice may have a significant inpact upon the regulations of abortions since the crime of legality is ultimately a matter for the criminal law and its requirement of proof beyond a reasonable doubt of the crime and the existence of prosecutional discretion vested in the Crown Prosecution Service and the DPP.

The following statutory provisions create the criminal offences relating to abortion.

Offences against the Person Act 1861

58. – Every woman, being with child, who, with intent to procure her own miscarriage, shall unlawfully administer to herself any poison or other noxious thing, or shall unlawfully use any instrument or other means whatsoever with the like intent and whosoever, with intent to procure the miscarriage of any woman, whether she be or not with child, shall unlawfully administer to her or cause to be taken by her any poison or other noxious thing, or shall unlawfully use any instrument or other means whatsoever with the like intent, shall be guilty of an offence, and being convicted thereof shall be liable to imprisonment.

59. – Whosoever shall unlawfully supply or procure any poison or other noxious thing, or any instrument or thing whatsoever, knowing that the same is intended to be unlawfully used or employed with intent to procure the miscarriage of any women, whether she be or not be with child, shall be guilty of an offence, and being convicted thereof shall be liable to imprisonment for a term not exceeding five years.

It is important to establish at the outset the parameters of the law of abortion. it must always be remembered that here the law provides a special regulatory scheme beyond that pertaining to medical treatment and procedures in general. It does so, as we saw, out of a concern for the dangers to maternal health but also, importantly, because the killing of human life is entailed.

To an extent the issue can be crystallised in the question: when does 'conception' end and 'abortion' begin? More accurately, for the lawyer, the issue is: when can it be established that a doctor's conduct amounts to a prohibited act of 'intending to procure a miscarriage'? Medicinal substances or devices which act solely to *prevent fertilisation* pose no difficulties. They are contraceptive in nature, no 'miscarriage' is involved and the law of abortion is not implicated. Not all so-called 'contraceptives' operate, however, in the way that the 'pill' or condoms do. Some operate to prevent implantation of a fertilised egg.

One form of contraception poses special legal problems for the law of abortion. It is that form known as post-coital birth control. (See I Kennedy *Treat Me Right* (1991) ch 3.) Is a doctor who prescribes post-coital birth control, sometimes known as the 'morning after' pill, guilty of an offence under s 58 unless he complies with the terms of the 1967 Act? The central question is when, as a matter of law, can a person be said to act 'with intent to procure a miscarriage'? In turn this requires us to understand the meaning of the word 'miscarriage' in ss 58 and 59. Needless to say, there is no definition offered in English law either in statute or in case law.

One view advanced is that a 'miscarriage' is procured whenever a fertilised egg is destroyed or expelled from the body whether or not it had been implanted in the uterus. If this view were correct, it would mean that any intervention after conception done with the intention of 'procuring a miscarriage' as so defined, would amount to an offence under the Offences Against the Person Act 1861. It may be interesting, however, to notice the authority and arguments on which this view is based.

John Keown 'Miscarriage: A Medico-Legal Analysis' [1984] Criminal Law Review 608

Judicial authority

In addition to the guidance afforded by the actual wording of the abortion provisions, the construction of 'miscarriage' has arisen in several reported cases. These cases, drawn from India, Victoria and the United States, are of persuasive value on account of the similarity between section 58 and the statutory provisions with which they deal. They point unanimously to an unrestricted construction of 'miscarriage'.

The leading Indian case on the question is *Ademma* [[1886] ILR IX Mad 369], decided by the Court of Appeal at Madras. The defendant was charged under section 312 of the Indian Penal Code 1860 with procuring her own miscarriage. The evidence showed that she had only been pregnant for about a month and that all that came away was a mass of blood. The Sessions Judge ruled that she had not been 'with child' within the meaning of the section. He observed: 'There was nothing which could be called even a rudimentary foetus or child' [*ibid* 370]. Accordingly, Ademma was acquitted. The Court of Appeal, however, consisting of Muttusami Ayyar and Brandt JJ, ordered a re-trial, holding that the offence could be committed from conception onward:

> The term 'miscarriage' is not defined in the Penal Code. In its popular sense it is synonymous with abortion, and consists in the expulsion of the embryo or foetus, ie the immature product of conception. The stage to which pregnancy has advanced and the form which the ovum or embryo may have assumed are immaterial [*ibid* 370].

The court continued:

> Section 312 requires proof that the woman is 'with child', but it is enough if the fact of pregnancy and the intended expulsion of the immature contents of the uterus are established. The words 'with child' mean pregnant, and it is not necessary to show that 'quickening', ie perception by the mother of the movements of the foetus, has taken place, or that the embryo has assumed a foetal form [*ibid*].

Although the defendant had been pregnant for one month and implantation had, therefore, already occurred somewhere, the broad basis of the court's decision affords sound authority for the legal irrelevance of implantation.

The meaning of 'miscarriage' was also considered by an Australian court in *Trim* [[1943] VLR 109]. There, the defendant was charged with the murder of one Edna Freeman. The Crown alleged that death had resulted from the defendant's use of a syringe with intent to procure Freeman's miscarriage, and secured a conviction for manslaughter. Trim appealed, contending *inter alia* that the judge had been guilty of a misdirection by ruling that the use of the syringe with intent to evacuate the uterus was an offence under section 62 of the Crimes Act 1928 (the section corresponding to section 58) even if the foetus was believed to be dead. By a majority, the Full Court of the Supreme Court of Victoria dismissed the appeal. Martin J delivered the majority judgment. He observed that, as section 62 did not require proof of pregnancy, 'one, and perhaps the chief, evil which the Legislature wished to prevent was the possibility of harm being done to the women' [*ibid* at 115]. In construing 'miscarriage' broadly enough to prohibit the attempt to expel even a dead foetus, he remarked; 'In popular use the word "abortion" frequently is used as synonymous with "miscarriage", and the presence of the heading, "Attempts to procure abortion", to sections 62 and 63 suggests that the Legislature intended the "miscarriage" in those sections to cover "abortion"' [*ibid*]. He continued: 'In *Webster's Dictionary* appears the following comprehensive definition of "Abortion": "Act of giving premature birth; specifically, the expulsion of the human fetus prematurely, particularly at any time before it is viable, or capable of sustaining life; miscarriage" [*ibid*]. Martin J then adverted to the restricted definition of 'miscarriage' as abortion between the 'quickening' of the foetus – around the fourth month of pregnancy – and the point of its viability. However, he concluded that just as the word 'birth' in section 64 of the Crimes Act had been broadly interpreted to include even stillbirth, 'The word "miscarriage" should be given no restricted meaning in sections 61 and 62, as one reason for all three sections is the safeguarding of the health of a woman who is or may be with child' [*ibid* at 116]. In support of this unrestricted construction, Martin J cited the sixth edition of *Taylor's Principles and Practice of Medical Jurisprudence* [6th edn, 1910, (ed F Smith), Vol II, page 142], which declared in relation to section 58:

the statute only uses the word 'miscarriage', including in that term comprehensively the emptying of a pregnant uterus at any time of conception, ignoring altogether the technical terms abortion, miscarriage, premature confinement, which are merely convenient descriptive words for medical men.

By using such a popular term, it added, the law 'intends, thereby, to mean the contents of a gravid uterus, whether such contents be well or ill-formed, living or dead, moles or any other result of conception ...' [*ibid* at 178]. Martin J did not regard this definition as authoritative in relation to section 62, but conceded:

it does convey the sense in which that word is there used, as, by reason of the heading in the material section, and the apparent purpose of the legislation, I consider it is wide enough to include abortion which, in the same work (vol II, p 141) is defined as 'an untimely emptying of a uterus which contains the products of a conception' [*supra* at 116].

A further source of judicial authority supporting an unrestricted interpretation of 'miscarriage' takes the form of a long and substantial line of case law from the United States, which establishes that 'miscarriage' and 'abortion' are legally synonymous and refer to the expulsion of the products of conception at any period of pregnancy. As early as 1850, the Supreme Court of Pennsylvania stated: 'Miscarriage, both in law and philology, means the bringing forth the foetus before it is perfectly formed and capable of living ... The word abortion is synonymous and equivalent to miscarriage, in its primary meaning' [*Mills v Commonwealth* (1850) 13 Pa (1 Harris) 630 at 632]. The court's statement of the law has been consistently supported by the courts of other states. [See, eg, *Wells v New Mutual Life Insurance Co of Boston, Mass* 43 A 126 (SC Penn) (1899); *People v Rankin* 74 P 2d 71 (1937) (SC Calif); *Hall v People* 201 P 2d 382 (1948) (SC Col); *Scott v State* 117 A 2d 831 (1955) (SC Del).]

Victor Tunkel in 'Modern Anti-Pregnancy Techniques and the Criminal Law' [1974] Criminal Law Review 461 seeks to provide a further basis for this position by reference to a sentence in Professor Williams's *Sanctity of Life and the Criminal Law*, published in 1958 (at p 141).

At present both English law and the law of the great majority of the United States regard any interference with the pregnancy, however early it may take place, as criminal, unless for therapeutic reasons. The foetus is a human life to be protected by the criminal law from the moment when the ovum is fertilised.

Relying on this, Tunkel argues (at p 465):

> ... [T]he use of the word 'miscarriage' has always been understood to include any fatal interference with the fertilised ovum: ... To hold otherwise would, in effect, give a sort of free-for-all moratorium of a week or more after intercourse during which every sort of abortionist could ply his craft with impunity. The law may permit the douching of the vagina soon after intercourse, but that seems the limit of allowable post-coital prevention.

These arguments do not appear to be relevant to the discussion concerning the difference between pre-implantation and implantation. They appear to be more concerned with the difference between 'conception' and 'quickening', particularly in the light of the fact that the nineteenth-century authorities were unaware of the detail of the physiological processes involved between conception and birth, save in the most general terms. Furthermore, it should be added that Professor Williams, when he gave his mind to this particular point, in his *Textbook of Criminal Law* (2nd edn, 1983) p 294, wrote as follows:

> Where exactly is the line drawn between contraception and abortion?
> Formerly it was thought that the vital point of time was fertilisation, the fusion of spermatozoon and ovum, but it is now realised (although the point has not come before the courts) that this position is not maintainable, and that conception for legal purposes must be dated at earliest from implantation.
> The legislation is unspecific. The abortion section does not expressly refer to conception; it speaks merely of a 'miscarriage'. There is, therefore, nothing to prevent the courts interpreting the word 'miscarriage' in a way that takes account of customary and approved birth control practices.

As Professor Williams goes on to point out, to hold the view advanced by Keown *et al* carries the further consequence that the fitting of an intra-uterine device (IUD), sometimes known as the 'coil' would also be governed by the Abortion Act and could be unlawful. It cannot be doubted that a doctor who fits an IUD does so with knowledge that intercourse may take place and, in those circumstances, his intention will be to prevent the implantation of a fertilised egg in the uterus. (There is also evidence that an IUD when fitted may prevent fertilisation, but clearly if done with this intention such a practice could never be unlawful under the 1861 Act. It is, however, questionable whether the two intentions could be separable.)

Surely Professor Williams is correct in writing (*op cit*, pp 294-295) that:

> ... [N]o one who uses or fits IUDs supposes that they are illegal or are governed by the Abortion Act. The only way to uphold the legality of present medical practice, to make IUDs contraceptives and not abortifacients, is to say that for legal purposes conception is not complete until implantation.

He goes on to reach the same view concerning post-coital birth control by use of the 'morning after' pill when he concludes that 'the legal argument (concerning IUDs and "morning after" pills) is that the word "miscarriage" in s 58 means the miscarriage of an implanted blastocyst'.

The issue arose, albeit tangentially, in *R v Price* [1969] 1 QB 541, where the defendant, a doctor was charged under s 58 of the 1861 Act having fitted an IUD to a pregnant woman which caused her to abort. The defendant's conviction was quashed because of a misdirection by the judge on an evidential matter. However, the defence was that he did not believe the woman was pregnant when he fitted the coil. In the Court of Appeal, Sachs LJ (at 544) regarded the crucial question to be 'did the appellant at the time ... know or believe that the patient was pregnant and, accordingly, introduce the instrument with intent to procure a miscarriage ...?' By 'pregnant' it is reasonably clear that Sachs LJ had in mind a woman's condition 'post-implantation'.

The view reflected in Professor Williams's conclusion and in *R v Price* was the one accepted by the (then) Attorney-General, Sir Michael Havers QC in a written answer to the House of Commons in May 1983 (42 Parl Deb HC 238 at 239).

> The sole question for resolution therefore is whether the prevention of implantation constitutes the procuring of a miscarriage within the meaning of sections 58 to 59 of the Offences against the Person Act 1861. The principles relating to interpretation of statutes require that the words of a statute be given the meaning which they bore at the time the statute was passed. Further, since the words were used in a general statute, they are *prima facie* presumed to be used in their popular, ordinary or natural sense.
>
> In this context it is important to bear in mind that a failure to implant is something which may occur in the manner described above or quite spontaneously. Indeed in a significant proportion of cases the fertilised ovum is lost either prior to implantation or at the next menstruation. It is clear that, used in its ordinary sense, the word 'miscarriage' is not apt to describe a failure to implant – whether spontaneous or not. Likewise, the phrase 'procure a miscarriage' cannot be construed to include the prevention of implantation. Whatever the state of medical knowledge in the 19th century, the ordinary use of the word 'miscarriage' related to interference at a stage of pre-natal development later than implantation.
>
> In the light of the above I have come to the conclusion that this form of post-coital treatment does not constitute a criminal offence within either section 58 or 59 of the Offences Against the Person Act 1861.

The issue directly arose in *R v Dingra* in 1991. Unfortunately, the case is unreported. The newspaper report (*Daily Telegraph*, 25 January 1991) indicates that the defendant fitted an IUD to a woman 11 days after intercourse had taken place. The judge directed an acquittal on a charge under s 58 on the basis that the woman could not have been pregnant, which he equated with implantation. Leaving aside the fact that this might not be justifiable medically in such a woman, the judge's view is entirely consistent with that expressed by the Attorney General. The defendant's acquittal would be justified on the basis that it would not be possible to establish that he *intended* to procure a miscarriage if he believed implantation had not occurred. That it had not is, of course, irrelevant under s 58, which covers a woman 'whether she be *or not with* child'.

Besides removing doubts about the legality of fitting IUDs, the view of expressed by the Attorney-General of the 'morning after' pill and in *Dingra* in relation to IUDs also can be said to conform with a common-sense understanding of the word 'miscarriage'. To 'miscarry' clearly entails that something has been 'carried'. It would be unusual to say that a woman is carrying anything when all that has transpired is that an egg has been fertilised and is travelling through her body. By contrast, it would accord with common sense and be quite natural to describe her as carrying something once a fertilised egg is implanted in her uterus.

Indeed, the Human Fertilisation and Embryology Act 1990 takes such a view in s 2(3) that '[F]or the purposes of the Act, a woman is not to be treated as carrying a child until the embryo has become implanted'. While this provision does not strictly apply to the 1967 Act – 'the Act' referred to is the 1990 Act – it does clearly demonstrate Parliament's view, at least in 1990, and, it is suggested, is highly persuasive when interpreting the scope of the 1861 Act (cf approach of Brooke J in *Rance v Mid-Downs HA* [1991] 1 All ER 801 at 818 interpreting the Infant Life (Preservation) Act 1929).

It follows, therefore, on this interpretation that the 'morning after' pill may be prescribed up to the point at which medical evidence establishes that implantation is likely to occur, which seems to be anywhere between five and ten days after intercourse has taken place.

An example of this common-sense view being adopted by legislation can be found in the 1977 amendment to the Crimes Act 1961 of New Zealand. Section 182A provides:

182A. For the purposes of sections 183 to 187 of this Act the term 'miscarriage' means –
(a)   The destruction or death of an embryo or fetus after implantation; or
(b)   The premature expulsion or removal of an embryo or fetus after implantation, otherwise than for the purpose of inducing the birth of a fetus believed to be viable or removing a fetus that has died.

B. THE LAWFUL ABORTION: THE ABORTION ACT 1967

1. Introduction

At common law there was thought to be no defence to conduct amounting to a crime under ss 58 and 59. Then, in 1938, Mr Bourne, a well-known surgeon, challenged this view.

R v Bourne [1939] 1 KB 687, [1938] 3 All ER 615 (Central Criminal Court)

Macnaghten J: The evidence called on behalf of the Crown proved that on June 14, 1938, the defendant performed an operation on the girl in question at St Mary's Hospital, and thereby procured her miscarriage. The following facts were also proved: On April 27, 1938, the girl, who was then under the age of fifteen, had been raped with great violence in circumstances which would have been most terrifying to any woman, let alone a child of fourteen, by a man who was in due course convicted of the crime. In consequence of the rape the girl became pregnant. Her case was brought to the attention of the defendant, who, after examination of the girl, performed the operation with the consent of her parents.

The defence put forward was that, in the circumstances of the case, the operation was not unlawful. The defendant was called as a witness on his own behalf and stated that, after he had made careful examination of the girl and had informed himself of all the relevant facts of the case, he had come to the conclusion that it was his duty to perform the operation. He had satisfied himself that the girl was in fact pregnant in consequence of the rape committed on her. He had also satisfied himself that she had not been infected with venereal disease; if he had found that she was so infected, he would not have performed the operation, since in that case there would have been a risk that the operation would cause a spread of the disease. Nor would he have performed the operation if he had found that the girl was either feeble-minded or had what he called a 'prostitute mind', since in such cases pregnancy and child-birth would not be likely to affect a girl injuriously. He satisfied himself that she was a normal girl in every respect, though she was somewhat more mature than most girls of her age. In his opinion the continuance of the pregnancy would probably cause serious injury to the girl, injury so serious as to justify the removal of the pregnancy at a time when the operation could be performed without any risk to the girl and under favourable conditions.

The evidence of the defendant was supported and confirmed by Lord Horder, and also by Dr JR Rees, a specialist in medical psychology. Dr Rees expressed the view that, if the girl gave birth to a child, the consequence was likely to be that she would become a mental wreck ...

The charge against Mr Bourne is made under s 58 of the Offences Against the Person Act 1861, that he unlawfully procured the miscarriage of the girl who was the first witness in the case. It is a very grave crime, and judging by the cases that come before the Court it is a crime by no means uncommon. This is the second case at the present session of this Court where a charge has been preferred of an offence against this section, and I only mention the other case to show you how different the case now before you is from the type of case which usually comes before a criminal court. In that other case a woman without any medical skill or medical qualifications did what is alleged against Mr Bourne here; she unlawfully used an instrument for the purpose of procuring the miscarriage of a pregnant girl; she did it for money; *21 5s* was her fee; a pound was paid on making the appointment, and she came from a distance to a place in London to perform the operation. She used her instrument, and, within an interval of time measured not by minutes but by seconds, the victim of her malpractice was dead on the floor. That is the class of case which usually comes before the Court.

The case here is very different. A man of the highest skill, openly, in one of our great hospitals, performs the operation. Whether it was legal or illegal you will have to determine, but he performs the operation as an act of charity, without fee or reward, and unquestionably believing that he was doing the right thing, and that he ought, in the performance of his duty as a member of a profession devoted to the alleviation of human suffering, to do it. That is the case that you have to try to-day....

Nine years ago Parliament passed an Act called the Infant Life (Preservation) Act 1929 (19 & 20 Geo 5, c 34). Sect 1, of that Act provides that 'any person who, with intent to destroy the life of a child capable of being born alive, by any wilful act causes a child to die before it has an existence independent of its mother, shall be guilty of felony, to wit, of child destruction, and shall be liable on conviction thereof on indictment to penal servitude for life: Provided that no person shall be found guilty of an offence under this section unless it is proved that the act which caused the death of the child was not done in good faith for the purposes only of preserving the life of the mother.' It is true, as Mr Oliver has said, that [the 1929 Act] provides for the case where a child is killed by a wilful act at the time when it is being delivered in the ordinary course of nature; but in my view the proviso that it is necessary for the Crown to prove that the act was not done in good faith for the purpose only of preserving the life of the mother is in accordance with what has always been the common law of England with regard to the killing of an unborn child. No such proviso is in fact set out in s 58 of the Offences Against the Person Act 1861; but the words of that section are that any person who 'unlawfully' uses an instrument with intent to procure miscarriage shall be guilty of felony. In my opinion the word 'unlawfully' is not, in that section, a meaningless word. I think it imports the meaning expressed by the proviso in s 1, sub-s 1, of the Infant Life (Preservation) Act 1929, and that s 58 of the Offences Against the Person Act 1861, must be read as if the words making it an offence to use an instrument with intent to procure a miscarriage were qualified by a similar proviso.

In this case, therefore, my direction to you in law is this – that the burden rests on the Crown to satisfy you beyond reasonable doubt that the defendant did not procure the miscarriage of the girl in good faith for the purpose only of preserving her life. If the Crown fails to satisfy you of that, the defendant is entitled by the law of this land to a verdict of acquittal. If, on the other hand, you are satisfied that what the defendant did was not done by him in good faith for the purpose only of preserving the life of the girl, it is your duty to find him guilty. It is said, and I think said rightly, that this is a case of great importance to the public and, more especially, to the medical profession; but you will observe that it has nothing to do with the ordinary case of procuring abortion to which I have already referred. In those cases the operation is performed by a person of no skill, with no medical qualifications, and there is no pretence that it is done for the preservation of the mother's life. Cases of that sort are in no way affected by the consideration of the question which is put before you to-day.

What then is the meaning to be given to the words 'for the purpose of preserving the life of the mother'? There has been much discussion in this case as to the difference between danger to life and danger to health. It may be that you are more fortunate than I am, but I confess that I have found it difficult to understand what the discussion really meant, since life depends upon health, and it may be that health is so gravely impaired that death results. A question was asked by the learned Attorney-General in the course of his cross-examination of Mr Bourne. 'I suggest to you, Mr Bourne', said the Attorney-General, 'that there is a perfectly clear line – there may be border-line cases – there is a clear line distinction between danger to health and danger to life.' The answer of Mr Bourne was: 'I cannot agree without qualifying it; I cannot say just yes or no. I can say there is a large group whose health may be damaged, but whose life almost certainly will not be sacrificed. There is another group at the other end whose life will be definitely in very great danger.' And then he adds: 'There is a large body of material between those two extremes in which it is not really possible to say how far life will be in danger, but we find, of course, that the health is depressed to such an extent that life is shortened, such as in cardiac cases, so that you may say that their life is in danger, because death might occur within measurable distance of the time of their labour.' If that view commends itself to you, you will not accept the suggestion that there is a clear line of distinction between danger to health and danger to life. Mr Oliver wanted you to give what he called a wide and liberal meaning to the words 'for the purpose of preserving the life of the mother'. I should prefer the word 'reasonable' to the words 'wide and liberal'. I think you should take a reasonable view of those words.

It is not contended that those words mean merely for the purpose of saving the mother from instant death. There are cases, we are told, where it is reasonably certain that a pregnant woman will not be able to deliver the child which is in her womb and survive. In such a case where the doctor anticipates, basing his opinion upon the experience of the profession, that the child cannot be delivered without the death of the mother, it is obvious that the sooner the operation is performed the better. The law does not require the doctor to wait until the unfortunate woman is in peril of immediate death. In such a case he is not only entitled, but it is his duty to perform the operation with a view to saving her life....

As I have said, I think those words ought to be construed in a reasonable sense, and, if the doctor is of opinion, on reasonable grounds and with adequate knowledge, that the probable consequence of the continuance of the pregnancy will be to make the woman a physical or mental wreck, the jury are quite entitled to take the view that the doctor who, under those circumstances and in that honest belief, operates, is operating for the purpose of preserving the life of the mother.

The jury acquitted the defendant.

(*Bourne* is discussed in a note by Seaborne Davies (1938) MLR 126.) If the effect of *Bourne* is to make lawful a 'therapeutic' abortion, the question arises as to the limits at common law of this notion. As Glanville Williams wrote in his paper, 'The Law of Abortion' (1952) Current Legal Problems 128 at 136:

> The decision in *Bourne* has ameliorated the law but has not yet taken full practical effect. The medical practitioner is said to be still chary to act, except in the clearest cases, partly because he fears that public opinion may not be in favour and partly because he is not certain how far the *Bourne* decision protects him.

There were some further English cases which were considered in a leading New Zealand case. The court was asked to interpret s 183 of the Crimes Act 1961 (NZ) which adopts, in essence, the language of s 58 of the English statute.

R v Woolnough [1977] 2 NZLR 508 (NZCA)

Richmond P: Since *Bourne* there have been two further cases spaced at the intervals of 10 years in England to which we were referred by counsel. The first was *R v Bergmann* (unreported, UK, 1948, Morris J). In *Smith and Hogan's Criminal Law* (3rd edn) 273-274 the learned authors state that Morris J (as he then was) '... is reported to have said that the court will not look too narrowly into the question of danger to life where danger to health is anticipated'. The later case is *R v Newton*... In that case Ashworth J is reported as directing the jury in the following way:

> The law about the use of instruments to procure miscarriage is this: 'Such use of an instrument is unlawful unless the use is made in good faith for the purpose of preserving the life or health of the woman.' When I say health I mean not only the physical health but also her mental health. But although I have said that 'it is unlawful unless', I must emphasise and add that the burden of proving that it was not used in good faith is on the Crown ([1958]) Crim L Rev 469).

In New Zealand there is no real authority on the point. In *R v Anderson* [1951] NZLR 439 at 443, it appears to have been assumed that *Bourne's* case applied in New Zealand but the point was not really in issue. When the question arose for consideration at the first trial of Dr Woolnough, and again at the second trial, Speight J and Chilwell J accordingly had no New Zealand authority on which to found an opinion. In effect what they have done is to expand the *Bourne* test, in words at least, if not so greatly as a matter of substance, by accepting the preservation of the *health* of the mother as an alternative justification to preserving the *life* of the mother. This is the way the matter was put by Ashworth J in *R v Newton*, but Speight J and Chilwill J have in another respect qualified the test by stressing the need for an honest belief that the abortion was necessary to preserve the woman from *serious* danger to her life or physical or mental health, not being merely the normal dangers of pregnancy and childbirth. As earlier mentioned, the most fundamental criticism made by the Solicitor-General is to the effect that Speight J and Chilwell J went too far when they accepted that serious danger to the *health* of the mother could be a justification for an abortion irrespective of whether or not such danger to health carried with it a real threat to the mother's *life*...

In the present case the court is concerned only with the concept of the welfare of the mother as a justification for an abortion in the early stages of pregnancy. In that field we have the assistance of s 182(2), which at least shows that the legislature itself was positively of the view that a bona fide intention to preserve the *life* of the mother in the late stages of pregnancy would justify the procurement of her miscarriage. The narrow question, then, is whether the courts ought not, in the case of early pregnancy at least, to extend that concept to include a bona fide intention to preserve the *health* of the mother from serious harm.

I can see no sufficient reason why this should not be done. In the first place it seems to me that the 'reasonable' interpretation of preservation of the *life* of the mother which was accepted in *Bourne* is likely to be an artificial and perhaps difficult one in practice. That this is the view of some English judges appears from the gradual shift away in emphasis disclosed in the directions given to the jury by Morris J and Ashworth J in the two cases to which I have earlier referred. The textbooks favour the open acknowledgement of preservation of health as well as preservation of life as preventing an abortion from being unlawful. Reference may be made to *Glanville Williams* (op cit) 153-154 and to *Smith and Hogan* (op cit) 274. Moreover, it is important to remember that the function impliedly entrusted to the courts by s 183 is not to say who is right and who is wrong as between the extreme views held by different sections of the community as regards this highly controversial subject. Rather the courts have to do their best to draw a line at a point where the procuring of a miscarriage ceases to be merely a matter of debate, from a religious, moral or ethical point of view, and becomes activity of a kind which warrants its designation as criminal. Finally I remind myself that as at the time when the Crimes Act 1961 was enacted, after lengthy preliminary consideration by a committee and then by the late Sir George Finlay, Ashworth J's direction in *R v Newton* had not only been reported in the *Criminal Law Review* but had also been the subject of an extensive article in that same journal. All this affords some indication that our legislature was content to accept the developing views of the English judges as applicable in this country.

Woodhouse J agreed. Wild CJ dissented.

(New Zealand law is now governed by s 187A of the Crimes Act 1961 (as amended in 1977) which defines 'unlawfully'. See D B Collins *Medical Law in New Zealand* (1992) paras 7.13.9 *et seq*.)

It must be remembered that whatever the scope of the *Bourne* exception to ss 58 and 59 of the Offences Against the Person Act 1861, the legal availability of abortion was always subject to the Infant Life (Preservation) Act 1929. We shall return to this legislation later, but for the present it should be noted that it limited abortions to those where the foetus or unborn child was not 'capable of being born alive' (s 1(1)). Even though the 1929 Act was passed to close a loophole where the child was killed in the course of being born – and hence it was not 'procuring a miscarriage' or murder – it prevented doctors from 'wilfully' killing an unborn child by way of an abortion at least after 28 weeks when it was presumed to be 'capable of being born alive' (s 1(2)) and probably before if it was capable of surviving (see *infra*). The only exception was where it was 'done in good faith for the purpose only of preserving the life of the mother'. This exception was far narrower than the interpretations by the courts that we have seen of *Bourne*.

The common law is now only of historical interest in England, Wales and Scotland, where the Abortion Act 1967 applies. It remains, however, the basis for determining the legality of abortion in other jurisdictions (see eg *CES v Superclinics (Aust) Pty Ltd* (1995) 38 NSWLR 47 (NSW CA) discussed (1996) 4 Med L Rev 102 (AG)) and in Northern Ireland (see eg *Northern Health & Social Services Board v F and G* [1993] NI 268 and *Re AMNH* (1994) 2 Med L Rev 374).

2. The Abortion Act 1967

Even after these cases, what was lawful still remained uncertain. The consequences, which served as the springboard for the 1967 Abortion Act, are described in the following extract.

Glanville Williams *Textbook of Criminal Law* (2nd edn, 1983)

Bourne's acquittal did not at once produce a large increase in medical abortions. The attitude of the medical profession in general was hostile, and tragic cases continued to occur. A girl of 12, pregnant by her father, was refused an abortion. Special boarding schools were opened for expectant mothers aged from 12 upwards, in order that they might continue with their lessons while looking after their babies. Woman who had been raped, woman deserted by their husbands, and overburdened mothers living in poverty with large families, also failed to get a medical abortion. One 'liberal' hospital in London and one in Newcastle performed the operation comparatively freely, and abortions could be readily bought in Harley Street; but in general the mass of woman could only go to a 'back-street abortionist', wielding a knitting needle, syringe or stick of slippery elm, or to a skilled operator acting illegally for large fees. Some unwilling mothers-to-be used dangerous methods on themselves, or occasionally committed suicide. Although illegal abortions ran into thousands each year, convictions were comparatively few (less than a hundred a year), largely because women who had sought help of an abortionist were unwilling to give him away, but partly also because the police themselves tended not to look upon abortions as a real crime. The only people who were effectively deterred by the law were the doctors, who alone could operate safely. The problem was common to all Christian countries that started with an unqualified prohibition of abortion.

At the same time as these evils were beginning to be acknowledged, the opinion arose that a woman had the right to control her own fertility. But against the pro-abortionists was arrayed a powerful religious lobby basing itself upon the 'sanctity of life'.

The Abortion Act 1967 was a compromise measure which, while not satisfying all demands, substantially liberalised the law. In England and Scotland it superseded the case law, including *Bourne*.

The report of a committee chaired by Mrs Justice Lane described the situation before the 1967 Act.

Committee on the Working of the Abortion Act (Cmnd 5579) (1974)

The Acts of 1861 and 1929, with the new and liberal interpretation given to them by Mr Justice Macnaughten remained the law of England and Wales until the passing of the Abortion Act 1967. The number of abortions performed in reliance upon that interpretation (as distinct from those which were certainly illegal) rose; eg in 1966 in NHS hospitals alone there were 6,100 recorded abortions. Nevertheless, it was felt by many, though by no means all, concerned with the problems that there was insufficient precision in the law and that doctors and patients alike ought to have a clearer indication of when abortion was permissible. This, quite apart from the views of those who advocated a more liberal view, was why a new Act was considered to be necessary.

In 1937, a year or so before the Bourne case was tried, a Home Office and Ministry of Health Inter-Department Committee, under the chairmanship of Mr Norman Birkett, KC (later Lord Birkett) was set up to 'enquire into the prevalence of abortion, and the law relating thereto, and to consider what steps might be taken by more effective enforcement of the law or otherwise to secure a reduction of the maternal morality and morbidity arising therefrom'. The Committee of course considered the effect of the Bourne case before recommending, in 1939, that: −

the law should ... be amended to make unmistakably clear that a medical practitioner is acting legally, when in good faith he procures the abortion of a pregnant woman in circumstances which satisfy him that continuance of the pregnancy is likely to endanger her life or seriously to impair her health.

Neither the government of the day, nor any succeeding government, introduced any legislation to implement the recommendation. Various private members introduced Bills to amend the abortion law, including Mr Joseph Reeves in 1952, Mr Kenneth Robinson in 1961 and Lord Silkin in the House of Lords in 1965. Lord Silkin's measure was superseded in 1966 by Mr David Steel's 'Medical Termination Bill' which, after considerable amendment, was passed as the Abortion Act 1967, coming into force on the 27 April 1968.

The Abortion Act 1967 provided a defence to the crimes under ss 58 and 59 of the Offences Against the Person Act 1861 providing certain conditions were satisfied. The most significant was that by s 1(1):

1(1) ... two registered medical practitioners are of the opinion, formed in good faith −
(a) that the continuance of the pregnancy would involve risk to the life of the pregnant woman, or of injury to the physical or mental health of the pregnant woman or any existing children of her family, greater than if the pregnancy were terminated; or
(b) that there is a substantial risk that if the child were born it would suffer from such physical or mental abnormalities as to be seriously handicapped.

However, the 1967 Act did not affect liability for the crime of child destruction under the Infant Life (Preservation) Act 1929 when an abortion involved the destruction before birth of a child 'capable of being born alive' (s 1(1)).

Under s 1(2) of the 1929 Act evidence that a woman had been pregnant for 28 weeks or more raised a presumption that her child was 'capable of being born alive'. Dissatisfaction felt by some that this limit of 28 weeks carried the necessary implication that a child of less than 28 weeks' gestation was not 'capable of being born alive' (even though the courts interpreted the Act to apply to less mature foetuses), led to calls for the introduction of a shorter period of time. A number of Private Members' Bills were introduced by John Corrie MP in 1979 and by David Alton MP in 1987 and on a number of occasions thereafter. Corrie proposed an upper time limit of 20 weeks except in the case where the foetus would be 'seriously handicapped' when the upper limit would be 28 weeks. David Alton proposed an even more restricted upper limit of 18 weeks with certain exceptions (for the texts and comment thereon see the *First Edition*, of this book, pp 799-806A).

During the passage of the Human Fertilisation and Embryology Bill in 1990, with all its attendant controversy, the Government conceded that reform of the Abortion Act 1967 should be considered (for a discussion of the legislative process see S Sheldon *Beyond Control – Medical Power and Abortion Law* (1997), ch 6). A series of complex and alternative amendments to the 1967 Act were tabled proposing changes in both the time limits and the grounds for abortion. After a flurry of late-night voting in the House of Commons on 21 June 1990, s 37, amending s 1 of the 1967 Act, emerged. Both the House of Lords and the House of Commons subsequently confirmed what had been decided that night. Ironically, although the pressure for reform was from those who wished to see limitations introduced into the 1967 Act, s 37, in fact, has the effect of significantly liberalising the law. The amended provisions came into effect of 1 April 1991.

Section 1 of the Abortion Act 1967 now provides:

> 1 (1) Subject to the provisions of this section, a person shall not be guilty of an offence under the law relating to abortion when a pregnancy is terminated by a registered medical practitioner if two registered medical practitioners are of the opinion, formed in good faith –
> (a) that the pregnancy has not exceeded its twenty-fourth week and that the continuance of the pregnancy would involve risk, greater than if the pregnancy were terminated, of injury to the physical or mental health of the pregnant woman or any existing children of her family; or
> (b) that the termination is necessary to prevent grave permanent injury to the physical or mental health of the pregnant woman; or
> (c) that the continuance of the pregnancy would involve risk to the life of the pregnant woman, greater than if the pregnancy were terminated; or
> (d) that there is a substantial risk that if the child were born it would suffer from physical or mental abnormalities as to be seriously handicapped.
> (2) In determining whether the continuance of a pregnancy would involve such risk of injury to health as is mentioned in paragraph (a) or (b) of subsection (1) of this section, account may be taken of the pregnant woman's actual or reasonably foreseeable environment....
> (4) Subsection (3) of this section, and so much of subsection (1) as relates to the opinion of two registered medical practitioners, shall not apply to the termination of a pregnancy by a registered medical practitioner in a case where he is of the opinion, formed in good faith, that the termination is immediately necessary to save the life or to prevent grave permanent injury to the physical or mental health of the pregnant woman.

(For discussions of the Act see A Grubb [1991] Crim LR 659; J Montgomery (1991) 45 MLR 524 at 531-533 and J Murphy [1991] JSWFL 375.)

3. The grounds

Under the amended Act there are four subsections spelling out the grounds for a lawful abortion, in contrast to the two grounds under the old law. What changes have taken place?

(a) 'Risk of physical or mental injury' – s 1(1)(a)

The ground contained in this subsection in part repeats the ground most commonly relied upon for abortions under the old law. There are four features of the subsection which call for comment. First, the pregnant woman's doctor must be satisfied that the risk to her physical or mental health would be greater if the pregnancy were to continue than if it were to be terminated. What is being contrasted here in this *comparative* exercise are the risks inherent in terminating the pregnancy *now* and the relevant risks to the mother in going to full term. The risks to her need not, therefore, be greater at the time of the termination itself.

Prior to the amendment, what had to be contrasted was the risk of injury to the pregnant woman's physical or mental health or *her life*. This latter risk is now dealt with separately in sub-s 1(1)(c) which is dealt with below. What is important to notice for the moment is that the old ground could as a matter of logic always be satisfied at least during the first trimester. This is because of the so-called 'statistical argument', namely that it is always of less risk to the mother to terminate rather than to continue the pregnancy if what is being considered is the risk to her *life*. Although the risk to her life in being pregnant is low, the modern procedures used to terminate pregnancy during the first trimester pose an even lower risk. Now that *risk to life* is no longer relevant under this subsection, does the 'statistical argument' still apply when considering only the risk to the pregnant woman's health? If not, the net effect is that a doctor must rely upon the ground under sub-s 1(1)(c) if she wishes to justify the termination solely on the basis of the 'statistical' argument.

A second point to notice is what is meant by a risk to the pregnant woman's health? The subsection refers to 'physical or mental health'. The former is self-evident; the latter, however, requires further consideration.

Glanville Williams *Textbook of Criminal Law* (2nd edn, 1983)

What is meant by 'the mental health of the pregnant woman'?
...Narrowly interpreted, it may require the doctor to fear that the patient will suffer from what is commonly a mental illness, whether a psychosis or severe neurosis. This may include a depressive psychosis, and the British Medical Association recognises that termination may properly be advised on account of a 'reactive depression', which is a pathological state of hopeless despair resulting from circumstances. If the question is one of mental illness, the natural course would be to call in a psychiatrist, a specialist in mental disorder.

But 'mental health' is susceptible of a wider meaning. The definition of health advanced by the World Health Organisation is that it is 'the state of complete mental, physical and social well-being, and not merely an absence of disease or infirmity'. Gynaecologists who take this broad view do not insist upon a psychiatric opinion, but are ready to act on their own opinion of the case, backed by the family doctor.

Thirdly, so far we have concentrated upon the risk to a pregnant woman's health. Subsection 1(1)(a) also permits abortion if there is a risk of 'injury to the physical or mental health of...any existing children' of her family's which is 'greater than if the pregnancy were terminated'. Professor Glanville Williams in his *Textbook of Criminal Law (supra)* poses the question 'How can existing children be affected in health by having another brother or sister?'

Sometimes it may be reasonable to make this judgment. Consider the mother of a 'problem family'. She is living in poverty, with a large brood of children. Her husband has been in prison and has now been arrested again. Her existing children are badly cared for and play truant. Now she is pregnant once more. It may confidently be predicted that if the pregnancy is allowed to go to term, matters will be worsened for the existing children to the extent that their health may be affected. In practice, doctors who terminate on this ground generally tick it as an extra to the health of the woman.

Can the doctor take the poverty of the family into account?
Not directly, but he can if the woman's poverty, aggravated by the addition to her family, is likely to affect her health or that of her other children.

Even if this is so, the question arises as to who are 'children of the pregnant woman's family'? As in other legal contexts, the notion of 'family' can be given a variety of meanings, some broader than others. So, for example, 'children of her family' could be restricted to children born in wedlock and particularly limited to children of her current marriage. At its widest, it could extend to all children whom she has treated as part of her family. Also, the notion of a 'child' could, and perhaps should, be said to include an adult who remains dependent upon the woman and within her immediate family by reason of disability. In the case of such a disabled child, perhaps the risk of injury is easier to envisage. The arguments are examined in the following article.

A J C Hoggett 'The Abortion Act 1967' [1968] Crim LR 247

It is submitted that, for the purposes of this Act, 'family' means the sociological and not the legal unit. It thus includes not only the mother's illegitimate children living with her but also the illegitimate children of her husband by a previous mistress. Clearly the words cover adopted children but there seems no reason why they should not cover children living in the family who are adopted in all but law. 'Children of her family', it is submitted, also includes the case of the daughter of a widower when [the pregnant woman is] acting *in loco matris*. This wide interpretation of the Act seems sanctioned by the fact that reference may be made to the pregnant woman's actual environment which includes the children mentioned above. The courts have shown a tendency to interpret the words 'child of the family' in a generous fashion.

A wide interpretation is consistent with Parliament's having given an extended meaning to 'child of the family' in, for example, the Children Act 1989 (s 105). This legislation is concerned with the 'child of a family' in marriage. Of course, the Abortion Act is concerned with a child of *her* family and, therefore, an even wider view is justified.

Fourthly, s 1(2) provides that in assessing the relative risk of injury to health 'account may be taken of the pregnant woman's actual or reasonably foreseeable environment'. Does this allow a doctor to have regard to a risk of injury to health arising after she has given birth? Professor Glanville Williams in his *Textbook of Criminal Law (supra)* suggests a wide interpretation of s 1(2).

The Act refers to 'risk of injury to the health of the *pregnant* woman', and one may argue that when the child has been born the woman is no longer pregnant. Moreover, it must be 'the continuance of the pregnancy' that produces this risk, and it is perhaps slightly strange, though not impossible, to say that the burden on a mother of having to rear a child was a result of 'the continuance of the pregnancy'.

On the other hand there are two clues in the Act making it reasonably clear that the wider meaning was intended by Parliament.

1　The words just quoted are used with regard to both the health of the woman and the health of existing children of her family. If one pays regard to the health of existing children, as the Act allows, it would be illogical to do this only during the time of gestation of the new addition to the family. What was evidently intended was that existing children might be adversely affected by the extra child being born and having to be brought up by an already overburdened mother.

2　Subsection (2) provides that 'account may be taken of the pregnant woman's actual or reasonably foreseeable environment'. This is not, as has sometime been thought, a purely 'social' ground for termination, since it is related to the question of health. It does not allow the operation merely because the patient will otherwise lose her job or her husband. Still, the statutory words make it clear that the question of health is to be considered broadly. There is not much point in directing the doctor to look ahead to the woman's future environment if he is to consider only the time of pregnancy. So it is really quite clear that the Act is intended to provide for the case of the overburdened mother.

If Professor Williams is correct, and it would appear that he is, such that account may be taken of the environment in which she or the existing children will find themselves, would a termination under s 1(1)(a) be justified on the basis that a child of the other sex is desired? This, of course, is a serious problem in some ethnic communities. The birth of a boy may be more desirable. A pregnant woman may be under pressure to terminate her pregnancy once it is discovered she is carrying a girl. Alternatively, existing girl children may have their future interest including their health affected by the birth of a brother who may be treated preferentially. Leaving aside a termination based solely upon the 'statistical argument', the legality of such a termination would depend on a doctor forming the view that the pregnant woman's health or that of her female children would be put at greater risk than if she terminated the pregnancy. Given that the Act confers a wide discretion to the doctors, such a case could well fall within s 1(1)(a) providing the doctors act in good faith.

Fifthly, and perhaps most importantly, s 1(1)(a) introduces a time-limit of 24 weeks for terminations under this ground alone. The crucial issue here, therefore, is the meaning of the words 'the pregnancy has not exceeded its twenty-fourth week', ie at what point in time can it first be said that woman is 'pregnant'? Undoubtedly, the meaning of the word 'pregnant' is a matter of law for the court (see, for example, *C v S* [1987] 1 All ER 1230 at 1242, per Sir John Donaldson MR on the meaning of the phrase 'capable of being born alive' in the Infant Life (Preservation) Act 1929).

There are at least four possible points in time at which the clock could start running in calculating the 24 weeks: (A) the first day of the woman's last period; (B) the date of conception (up to 14 days later); (C) the date of implantation (up to ten days later) and (D) the first day of the woman's first missed period (about four weeks after (A)).

In England the medical profession calculates the length of gestation of a baby on the basis of (A) because it is the most certain date of any of these alternatives. Options (B) and (C), namely the date of conception and the date the fertilised egg implants into the woman, by contrast, cannot be known for certain. But there are difficulties with option (D), because although the first day of the woman's first missed period is certain, it may be quite misleading to indicate length of pregnancy where, for example, following conception during the last week of a cycle the woman does not miss the next period but only the one that follows. The date calculated on the basis of (D) could be about five weeks after conception has actually occurred.

So, when does time start to run? The law might accept the medical profession's approach in option (A) because of the certainty it would achieve. More importantly, however, it might be accepted because it is the basis upon which Parliament introduced the 24-week time-limit in s 1(1)(a). The 24-week limit (as calculated by the medical profession) represents Parliament's view of the stage of development when a foetus is capable of surviving. At this point the legislative intent is that the foetus should not be aborted except under the more restrictive grounds set out in the remainder of s 1(1). If any of the other options for starting time to run were accepted, this premise would be nullified. On that basis, in order to conform to the underlying premise that a foetus which is capable of surviving should not be aborted on the ground in s 1(1)(a), the time-limit should actually be 22 weeks or even less.

On the other hand, there are a number of arguments which suggest that options (B) or (C) are more appropriate interpretations of s 1(1)(a). First, it is wrong to adopt an interpretation which leads to the absurd conclusion that a woman is pregnant in the 14 days (approximately) between the first day of her last period and the time of conception when this is patently not the case. Secondly, the medical profession's approach exemplified in option (A) could act to the detriment of a defendant since it results in the shortest possible time for the 24-week period to run. After all, the medical profession's view is only as to when pregnancy begins and was not formulated with an eye to setting the upper time-limit for abortion. A pregnancy calculated on the basis of (A) at 25 weeks is likely, in fact, to be a case where conception and implantation will have occurred less than 24 weeks before the abortion. Ambiguities in criminal statutes should be construed in a defendant's favour and not against him, particularly when interpreting a section providing a defence to a criminal offence.

This would support one of the other alternatives: but which one? It is suggested that (C) is legally the more justifiable. It is widely recognised that the offence of procuring a miscarriage under s 58 of the Offences Against the Person Act 1861 only applies after an embryo has implanted. There is even indirect Parliamentary support for this interpretation in s 2(3) of the Human Fertilisation and Embryology Act which states that '[f]or the purposes of [HUFEA], a woman is not to be treated as carrying a child until the embryo has become implanted'. Hence, as we saw earlier, the use of contragestive birth control measures such as post-coital birth control pills and IUDs are not illegal under s 58 if they are intended to act on the woman by preventing implantation. There is some attraction to the symmetry of interpreting the Abortion Act so that the defence to the offence in s 58 operates from the point in time when that crime could first be committed, ie at implantation.

(b) 'Necessary to prevent grave permanent injury to physical or mental health' – s 1(1)(b)

This is a new ground introduced by the amendments in 1991. Its genesis is probably s 1(4) of the 1967 Act which, as we shall see, creates a justification for performing an abortion in certain situations of emergency where a doctor '... is of the opinion, formed in good faith, that the termination is immediately necessary to save the life or to prevent grave permanent injury to the physical or mental health of the pregnant woman'.

Section 1(4) does not, however, create a *ground* for performing an abortion but merely removes the need to satisfy the conditions under the Act relating to the place where the abortion is to be performed and the need for two medical opinions when a ground otherwise exists. Such abortions would have been justified under the ground in the unamended s 1(1)(a). With the amendment to s 1(1)(a) introducing a time-limit of 24 weeks, Parliament considered that where the risk to the mother was more serious than injury to her physical or mental health, abortions should not be restricted to 24 weeks. Hence, the new s 1(1)(b) (and s 1(1)(c) on 'risk to life', see below) was introduced to achieve this aim.

There are two points to notice in relation to s 1(1)(b). First, unlike s 1(1)(a) (and s 1(1)(c)) this ground for abortion does not appear to require the certifying doctors to engage in a comparison of risks between the continuation and termination of the pregnancy. What the doctors have to be satisfied of is 'that the termination is necessary'. What is involved in a determination by the doctors that the termination is 'necessary'? You will recall that the Act only requires the doctors to be satisfied of a ground 'in good faith'. Hence, they need not show that it was necessary but merely that they formed that view in good faith at the time. A termination will only be necessary, however, and the doctors could only be so satisfied, if termination was the only course available 'to prevent grave permanent injury to the physical or mental health of the pregnant woman'. Consequently, it may be insufficient for the doctors merely to be satisfied that there was such a risk to the woman or even that continuing the pregnancy involved a greater risk than termination of the pregnancy. This is because an alternative course of action may be available to deal with the danger to the pregnant woman. Only if there are no alternative courses of action which a reasonable doctor would contemplate, could it be said that a termination is 'necessary'.

The second point to notice concerns the meaning of the phrase 'grave permanent injury'. The words should be given their ordinary meaning. A court would, therefore, not interpret the phrase so as to cover transitory conditions affecting the mother's health but would not require, necessarily, that the mother's life be at risk. In a debate in the House of Lords, Mackay LC provided some guidance:

Hansard, HL vol 522, col 1039 (18 October 1990)

> An additional category already specified in the 1967 Act as a ground for emergency abortion on the opinion of one doctor is that of preventing grave permanent injury to the physical or mental health of the woman. The use of the words 'grave' and 'permanent' suggest that there is a stiff legal test to cover special situations where termination might be contemplated primarily in the interest of the pregnant woman. An example of this might be where she has severe hypertension and continuation of the pregnancy might result in permanent kidney, brain or possibly heart damage. In those circumstances the method of termination used would be selected in the best interests of the woman, but the intention would be to deliver a living baby where possible.

(c) 'Risk to life' – s 1(1)(c)

As under s 1(1)(a), this ground requires the doctors to balance the risk in continuing the pregnancy against the risk of termination. Here, the risk involved is the 'risk to the life of the pregnant woman'. On the face of it, this is restricted to circumstances where the pregnant woman's condition threatens to end her life. However, the ground only requires that the termination *reduces* the risk to her life. In other words, the doctors are not required to be satisfied that the termination will *eliminate* the risk to her life – there may exist a continuing, though lesser, risk to her life. (The termination will be justified, however, if the woman though still at risk stands a better chance of surviving than if she remains pregnant.)

A further point to notice concerns the meaning of the phrase 'risk to the *life* of the pregnant woman' (our emphasis). In *Bourne* we saw Macnaghten J gave a broad interpretation to s 1(1) of the Infant Life (Preservation) Act 1929. This provides a defence to the crime of child destruction where the unborn child is killed 'for the purpose only of preserving the life of the mother'.

> **Macnaghten J**: As I have said, I think those words ought to be construed in a reasonable sense, and, if the doctor is of opinion, on reasonable grounds and with adequate knowledge, that the probable consequence of the continuance of the pregnancy will be to make the woman a physical or mental wreck, the jury are quite entitled to take the view that the doctor who, under those circumstances and in that honest belief, operates, is operating for the purpose of preserving the life of the mother.

This broad interpretation of 'risk to life' cannot be properly applied to s 1(1)(c), since it is inconsistent with the existence of the grounds in s 1(1)(a) and (b). 'Life' must mean 'life' in the present structure of s 1(1) of the 1967 Act. That is to say that if the decision is made during the first 24 weeks of pregnancy that the woman would become a 'mental wreck', section 1(1)(a) would apply. If this determination is made after 24 weeks providing her condition amounts to a 'grave permanent injury to [her] mental health' then the abortion can be performed under s 1(1)(b), but not otherwise.

(d) 'Substantial risk' (so as to be) 'seriously handicapped' – 1(1) (d)

The final ground under the 1967 Act is contained in s 1(1)(d). This permits an abortion to be performed in cases where:

there is a substantial risk that if the child were born it would suffer from such physical or mental abnormalities as to be seriously handicapped.

Professor Williams in his *Textbook of Criminal Law (supra)* explains the basis of this ground which re-enacts the terms of what was s 1(1)(b) prior to the 1991 amendments.

It is sometimes justified for eugenic reasons, but in fact the contribution that abortion is likely to make to the betterment of man's genetic inheritance is slight. No: the argument for abortion on the fetal indication relates to the welfare of the parents, whose lives may well be blighted by having to rear a grossly defective child, and perhaps secondarily by consideration for the public purse. That this is the philosophy of the Act is borne out by the fact that it allows termination only where the child if born would be seriously handicapped, not where it is merely carrying undesirable genes.

Whereas the health grounds recognised in the Act merely enlarge on the attitude of the judge in *Bourne,* that the health of full human beings is to be preferred to the interests of the fetus in being born where the two interests conflict, the fetal ground marks a new departure. The fetus is destroyed not necessarily in its own interest (the physician need make no judgment that life will be a burden for it), but in the interest either of the parents or of society at large, though of course only upon the request of the mother.

Although argument still rages on whether abortion should be permitted merely as a matter of convenience to the woman, the fetal ground is almost universally accepted. But it is of some interest to note that anyone who does accept the fetal ground for abortion commits himself to the view that the moral status of the fetus is not the same as that of a child. For we do not permit children to be killed because they are seriously handicapped.

Professor Williams was discussing this ground as it first appeared in the Abortion Act in 1967. His point about its almost universal acceptance as a ground for abortion is supported by the fact that the wording was unchanged by the amendments in 1991. There is, however, one important point to notice. Abortion on this ground, as it *now* appears, is not subject to any time-limit, in contrast to the previous state of the law affected as it was by the Infant Life (Preservation) Act 1929 as we shall shortly see. Whether this change in the law will have impact on practice will primarily depend upon two matters: first, the extent to which some foetal abnormalities, not currently detectable early in pregnancy, in fact become detectable but only at a much later stage; and secondly, even in these cases, the extent to which doctors are prepared to perform abortions under this ground late in pregnancy.

We should now turn our attention to the meaning of the two crucial phrases – 'substantial risk' and 'seriously handicapped'. Professor Glanville Williams in his *Textbook of Criminal Law (supra)* writes:

The physician must decide whether there is a 'substantial' risk that the child if born would be 'seriously' handicapped. Advances in knowledge and medical skills make it more and more possible to attach a precise mathematical weight to the chance of the fetus being affected by genetic defects or by what happens to it in the womb. But the doctor still has to decide whether the case is sufficiently grave to justify termination. He may, of course, take the view that a relatively low risk justifies termination if the risk is of a relatively serious handicap: in common sense, the two factors are inversely related. Even when the doctor thinks that the 'fetal indication' is not itself sufficiently present, the fact that the patient is extremely depressed by worry that the child may be affected can itself be a reason for termination on the health ground.

Arguably, when Professor Williams asserts that 'a relatively low risk justifies termination if the risk is of a relatively serious handicap', he adopts an interpretation which is difficult to sustain. A risk is either 'substantial' or it is not irrespective of what degree of handicap it relates to.

A J C Hoggett 'The Abortion Act 1967' [1968] Crim LR 247

...it seems to have been assumed that 'substantial risk' was one where it was more probable than not that the child would suffer from an abnormality. This quasi-mathematical interpretation is not satisfactory since it could lead to the view that it is possible only to take into account those cases where it is known that an abnormality has at least a one in two chance of appearing. It may be possible to diagnose the presence of the abnormality with absolute certainty as in certain cases of mongolism. In other cases, there may be an equal chance that a child will suffer from an abnormality. Such is the case, for example, where a male haemophiliac is married to a haemophilia-carrier or where blood group incompatibilities exist between parents. Other examples exist. It seems wrong, in principle, to exclude cases where the risk is less than one in two. Thus the chance of a haemophilia-carrying woman having a haemophiliac son is one in four and if parents have already produced one child with phenylketonuria, the chances that a subsequent child will have the disease are again one in four.

Moreover, there are cases where for genetical or other reasons it is not possible to calculate the risk with mathematical precision. A child, born to a woman who contracts german measles during early pregnancy, has roughly a two in three chance of being affected if the disease was present in the first weeks, a one in two chance if present during weeks four to eight and a one in three chance if present eight to twelve. Again, although the genetics of such abnormalities as anencephaly, hydrocephaly and spina bifida is not fully understood, the involvement of hereditary factors is sufficiently established to have the result that many doctors would recommend an abortion where the woman had already given birth to a child so affected even though the risk is quite small. It is surely proper for a doctor to accept higher odds against an abnormality manifesting itself if its effects should be very severe.

Judgment is also complicated by the fact that there must not only be a substantial risk of abnormality but also of resultant serious handicap. It is often impossible to tell how serious the handicap will be. In the case of german measles, the child may only be suffering from cataracts amenable to treatment. There are also differing degrees of spina bifida. It has been suggested that 'seriously handicapped' means 'incapable of carrying out any normal activity'. This seems dangerously strict since a haemophiliac, for instance, is capable of many normal activities although his disease may severely limit their range.

Despite its restrictive wording, section 1(1)(b) [now s 1(1)(d)] should be liberally interpreted so as to protect the doctor who has made a difficult decision in good faith. Should it ever be necessary to interpret the words 'substantial risk' or 'seriously handicapped', for example where the risk is exactly known, then it is submitted that the test to be applied should be – could any reasonable doctor consider this a substantial risk or a serious handicap. In such cases, it may also be possible to pray in aid section 1(1)(a). For example, a woman who knows that she has had german measles may suffer six months of anxiety before birth and it may be months after the birth before it can be determined whether the child has been affected.

In its guidance to practitioners, the Royal College of Obstetricians and Gynaecologists offers the following, we would suggest helpful, advice on the statutory phrases 'substantial risk' and 'serious handicap'.

Royal College of Obstetricians and Gynaecologists *Termination of Pregnancy for Fetal Abnormality* (1996)

3.2.1 Substantial risk

'Substantial' is not defined in the Act. According to the second edition of the Oxford Dictionary (1991) it means, amongst other things 'of real significance', 'important', 'sizeable', 'fairly large', 'real' 'having real substance'. Clearly, there is room for lawyers to argue about what risks are substantial: on the other hand a risk may be substantial without satisfying the test of being more likely than not; equally the risk must be more than a mere possibility. In the context that a decision to perform an abortion because there is a substantial risk rather than a certainty of abnormality may result in the loss of a normal fetus.

3.2.1 Many fetal abnormalities can be diagnosed with near certainty. For others, such as those associated with intra-uterine infection or exposure to potentiality teratogenic drugs only a probability of abnormality can be provided. Every effort should be made to obtain a positive antenatal diagnosis of fetal abnormality when this is practicable. The medical practitioners certifying that a risk is substantial should bear in mind that the risk should also be likely to be considered substantial by informed persons with no personal involvement in the pregnancy and its outcome. Factors in the decision are:
–   the information that has been obtained from diagnostic procedures about the fetal abnormality;
–   published studies of the outcome for such a fetus, both during pregnancy, as a child and as an adult;

3.3.1 Serious handicap

The abortion law allows the termination of pregnancy at any gestation if a fetal abnormality is untreatable and would prevent survival after birth but, if there is an abnormality that would allow long term survival, the medical practitioners have to judge whether the abnormality would be likely to result in 'serious handicap'.

3.3.2 The World Health Organisation has defined disability as follows:

... any restriction or lack (resulting from an impairment) of ability to perform an activity in the manner or within the range considered normal for a human being.

In interpreting the definition, the WHO considers that:

Disability is concerned with abilities, in the form of composite activities and behaviours, that are generally accepted as essential components of everyday life. Examples include disturbances in behaving in an appropriate manner, in personal care (such as excretory control and the ability to wash and feed oneself), in the performance of other activities of daily living, and in locomotor activities (such as the ability to walk).

The WHO has a scale of the severity of disability. Only individuals with disability at the third or higher points of the scale would be considered by most people to be seriously handicapped. Points 3 and 4 are defined as follows:

3. Assisted performance. Includes the need for a helping hand (ie: the individual can perform the activity or sustain the behaviour, whether augmented by aids or not, only with some assistance from another person.)

4. Dependent performance. Includes complete dependence on the presence of another person (ie: the individual can perform the activity or sustain the behaviour, but only when someone is with him most of the time).

3.3.3 A person is only likely to be regarded as seriously handicapped if they need the support described in the WHO Points 3 and 4. However, an opinion that a particular fetal abnormality would be associated with serious handicap should be based on a careful consideration of the following factors, not all of which will be relevant in every case.

These are:

–   the probability of effective treatment, either *in utero* or after birth;
–   the probable degree of self-awareness and of ability to communicate with others;
–   the suffering that would be experienced;
–   the extent to which actions essential for health that normal individuals perform unaided would have to be provided by others;

Judgements should be cautious, recognising that it is not possible to give an authoritative view of the meaning of 'seriously handicapped' as this has not been interpreted by the courts.

Certainly, as regards 'serious handicap', the RCOG guidance takes a quite broad view in contemplating disabilities falling within WHO Point 3.

There is a further question concerning the meaning of 'seriously handicapped'. Notice that s 1(1)(d) requires that '*if born*, the child would suffer from such physical or mental abnormalities as to be seriously handicapped' (our emphasis). Does this mean that the abnormalities must constitute or amount to a handicap *at birth* or will it suffice that a latent condition exists at birth which will, *or may*, manifest itself later in life? And, if the latter, must it manifest itself during *childhood* since s 1(1)(d) refers to the 'child' suffering the serious handicap?

On one view the subsection requires that the handicap must exist at birth. As a consequence, on this view, an abortion could not be performed if the physical or mental symptoms of handicap will only manifest themselves at some later point in time.

Another view, however, can be taken of the meaning of the subsection. This would permit an abortion providing the handicap will manifest itself at some point in the future during the baby's childhood, for example. Tay-Sachs disease. However, there are two further points that require consideration. First, even if this view is correct some conditions will not manifest themselves until adulthood, for example, Huntington's disease. Although it is more difficult to interpret the section as covering this situation, once it is accepted that the handicap need not manifest itself at birth, it would seem to undermine the purpose of the provision narrowly to restrict it to childhood.

Finally, what if there is no certainty that there will be a handicap but merely a chance of inheriting the condition which will lead to handicap? There is merely a 'risk of a risk'. This does not give rise to any new problem. It is a matter of interpreting and applying the statutory phrase 'substantial risk' which we considered earlier. What, however, this last point does illustrate is that whenever there is a chance of inheriting a condition there is also a chance of inheriting a gene which merely makes the individual a carrier who will not develop the condition itself. Assuming there is a 'substantial risk' of the individual becoming a carrier, will this fall within s 1(1)(d)? In other words, can it be said that a carrier of a genetic abnormality suffers from a 'serious handicap'?

Whilst the section should be given a wide meaning to cover physical or mental disabilities which manifest themselves at any time after a child's birth, there is no justification for including carrier status alone. This is because the legislative purpose behind this ground would not be furthered. If Professor Williams is correct that the ground 'relates to the welfare of the parents whose lives may well be blighted by having to rear a grossly defective child' (see *supra*) a child who is merely a carrier would not produce this hardship. There is, of course, another purpose which *may* underlie this ground, namely to avoid the birth of children whose quality of life would be intolerable because of their handicap (see eg D Morgan 'Abortion: The Unexamined Ground' [1990] Crim LR 687). Again, if this were so a carrier could not be said to be bearing an intolerable burden merely by being a carrier even if he may face some stigma or some hard choices about reproduction may be forced upon him later in life.

4. Time limits

Prior to the amendment of the Abortion Act which came into effect on 1 April 1991, the legality of any abortion had to be considered not only in the light of the Abortion Act 1967 but also taking account of the Infant Life (Preservation) Act 1929. As originally drafted, the 1967 Act did not provide a defence to the 1929 Act (s 5(1)). As a result, it was the 1929 Act which set the upper time limit for abortions in England and Wales (but not Scotland: see K Norrie 'Abortion in Great Britain: One Act, Two Laws' [1985] Crim LR 475). It will be recalled that, until 1991, the Abortion Act itself contained no time limits.

Infant Life (Preservation) Act 1929

1 (1) Subject as hereinafter in this subsection provided, any person who, with intent to destroy the life of a child *capable of being born alive,* by any wilful act causes a child to die before it has an existence independent of its mother, will be guilty of felony, to wit, of child destruction, and shall be liable on conviction thereof on indictment to penal servitude for life.

Provided that no person shall be found guilty of an offence under this section unless it is proved that the act which caused the death of the child was not done in good faith for the purpose only of preserving the life of the mother.

(2) For the purpose of this Act, evidence that a woman had at any material time been pregnant for a period of twenty-eight weeks or more shall be *prima facie* proof that she was at that time pregnant of a child capable of being born alive.

(Our emphasis.)

The 1929 Act is now irrelevant in determining the legality of an abortion because by amendment to the 1967 Act it is now provided that:

> 5 (1) No offence under the Infant Life (Preservation) Act 1929 shall be committed by a registered medical practitioner who terminates a pregnancy in accordance with the provisions of this Act [ie, the Abortion Act 1967].

Hence, the only relevant question in determining the legality of an abortion is whether the terms of the 1967 Act as amended have been complied with.

There is one possible lacuna in the new s 5(1). On its face it only applies to a 'registered medical practitioner'. To the extent that nurses and others are involved in a termination which would, apart from s 5(1), fall foul of the 1929 Act, they seem to have no defence. There is no doubt that this is due to a parliamentary oversight.

It will be recalled that *only* s 1(1)(a) imposes a time-limit namely one of 24 weeks. While in general, therefore, the provisions of the 1929 Act may no longer be relevant in the context of a lawful abortion, there is one important point to bear in mind. Consider a civil action brought by a mother whose pregnancy pre-dated the 1991 amendments and who has given birth to a disabled child. She claims that she was negligently not given the opportunity to choose an abortion. In such a case, a defendant might argue that the disability was only discovered (or discoverable) at a time when an abortion would have been illegal under the 1929 Act. Cases of this kind, raising questions of the legality of pre-1991 abortions, may well arise for some years to come.

In these cases, the crucial legal question is the meaning of the statutory phrase 'capable of being born alive'. What the Act provides is that a foetus will *prima facie* be so regarded if it has reached 28 weeks of gestational age. The Act does not, therefore, preclude the possibility that a child may be *capable of being born alive* at an earlier gestational age. Thus, the issue is what is the precise meaning of the phrase 'capable of being born alive' and does this equate with a particular period of time? This critically important question fell to be considered in the case of *C v S* [1988] QB 135, [1987] 1 All ER 1230 (discussed in A Grubb and D Pearl (1987) 103 LQR 340). The case concerned an application by C, the father of a child carried by S, his former girlfriend, for an injunction to prevent her seeking or obtaining an abortion. At first instance, Heilbron J set out the facts, the medical testimony and the legal background.

C v S [1988] QB 135, [1987] 1 All ER 1230 (Heilbron J and CA)

Heilbron J: [Counsel for the applicant] ... submits that ... the doctor would be contravening the provisions of [the 1929 Act] and would be guilty, because he would be aborting a foetus of 18 weeks. Indeed, he further submitted that any doctor who has since 1967, or who proposed to, abort a foetus of that duration must be guilty of the offence.

Counsel did not resile from the implications of that assertion, relying for it on the terms of the 1929 Act and the statements of Mr Norris in his affidavits, particularly in that which stated that 'an unborn child of eighteen weeks gestation were it to be delivered by hysterotomy *would be* live born' (my emphasis).

The affidavits are important. They indicate very clearly the wide difference in thinking and interpretation between medical men, all of high reputation and great experience, in regard to the language used in the 1929 Act. I will now read the affidavits, so as to incorporate their explanation of certain phrases and terms into this judgment. I begin, because it was the first, with that of Mr Norris, emeritus consultant gynaecologist at St Peter's Hospital, Chertsey. He stated in para 2 of his first affidavit that 'an unborn child of eighteen weeks gestation were it to be delivered by hysterotomy would be live born'. He then went on to refer to a definition of this expression or condition by the World Health Assembly under art 23 of the Constitution of the World Health Organisation in 1976 (subsequent to both the Acts in this matter) as being –

the complete expulsion or extraction from its mother of a product of conception irrespective of the duration of pregnancy, which after such separation breathes or [and I emphasise the 'or' in his affidavit] shows any other evidence of life such as beating of the heart, pulsation of the umbilical cord or definite movement of voluntary muscle whether or not the umbilical cord has been cut or the placenta is attached.

To that affidavit Professor John Richard Newton replied. He did so, in his first affirmation, on 16 February. He said:

I am the Layson Tait Professor of Obstetrics and Gynaecology and Head of Department at the Birmingham University Medical School Queen Elizabeth Hospital Edgbaston Birmingham. I have been a Gynaecologist for twenty years and held my present position since 1979.

He had been shown a copy of Mr Norris's affidavit and asked to comment on it and in regard to para 2 he said:

I believe it confusing in the circumstances to use the words 'live born' for a foetus of 18 weeks gestation. As Mr. Norris says the term has been defined by Article 23 of the World Health Assembly in 1976. There is now produced ... a copy of a report known as 'Report on Foetal Viability and Clinical Practice' which was prepared in August 1985 by a representative committee on behalf of the Royal College of Obstetricians and Gynaecologists, the British Paediatric Association, Royal College of General Practitioners, Royal College of Midwives, British Medical Association and the Department of Health and Social Security ... I refer in particular to the twelfth page of that report in which reference is made to the recommendation of the World Health Organisation concerning perinatal statistics. The committee to which I have referred above was charged with the task of considering foetal viability and comparison is made between the World Health Organisation definition and the concept of foetal viability. As will be seen from the report the purpose behind the World Health Organisation definition was to standardise the perinatal statistics for member countries of births. The purpose behind the definition was specifically not to define independent foetal viability and the committee go on to consider that concept and I believe that to be the important concept in these circumstances. Foetal viability means that the foetus is capable of independent human existence separate from the mother.

He then refers to the contents of this report of the various prestigious colleges and associations of doctors and says:

It will be seen that in the survey of 29 neo-natal intensive care units in the United Kingdom during 1982 no foetus of less than 23 weeks survived after delivery. It is my conclusion therefore that a foetus of anything below 23 weeks cannot survive independent of its mother and has therefore no viability.

A few days later Mr Norris swore a second affidavit, in order to amplify the first. He then suggested that the period of gestation was 2, or possibly 3, weeks more than the 18 weeks which had been mentioned. He went on to explain the expression 'live born' which had been used in his first affidavit:

4 ... In case there is any ambiguity I wish to assert that in so stating I mean that in my opinion any foetus of eighteen weeks or longer gestation is capable of being born alive and that by 'alive' I mean showing real and discernible signs of life within the meaning of the World Health Organisation definition set out in my original Affidavit and of the Births and Deaths Registration Act 1926 current when the Infant Life (Preservation) Act 1929 was passed and also of the Births and Deaths Registration Act 1953 now current. Under the provisions of both these statutes such a child shall be registered as a live birth.

5. A child of eighteen or even twenty-one weeks gestational age although capable of being born alive and capable of surviving for some time outside the womb is not generally regarded by the medical profession as being viable because present paediatric skills are insufficient to assist it to remain alive for more than a limited time.

On the same day, 19 February, Professor Newton, having read the second affidavit of Mr Norris, stated in a further affidavit:

1 ... Although he uses the expression 'live born' in [his first] affidavit he does not mention, nor did I understand that he was specifically referring to the words actually appearing in an Act of Parliament namely the words 'born alive' in Section 1 Infant Life (Preservation) Act 1929. This has now been drawn to my attention and I give my comments.

2. The expression 'born alive' used in the Infant Life (Preservation) Act 1929 raises difficulties before the expiration of 28 weeks of gestation.

3. Although it is difficult to generalise, for reasons which I will refer to in paragraph 4 after 8 weeks of gestation some fetuses will exhibit some primitive fetal movement, have a primitive heart tube which contracts and the circulation has started to develop but these fetuses will be quite incapable of life separate from the mother.

4. Each individual fetus in each individual mother develops differently and at different rates.

He then refers to the difficulty of the medical assessment of the gestational period in any particular case, which must be approximate and which may be complicated, as indeed in this case, by irregular menstruation. However, there are some firm generalisations on development which could be made.

In a foetus of 18-21 weeks gestation the cardiac muscle is contracting and a primitive circulation is developing, but in my opinion lung development does not occur until after 24 weeks gestation; before this time the major air passages have been formed and there is gradual development of the bronchioles but these terminate in a blind sac incapable of gas exchanges prior to 24 weeks.

He says that a foetus of 18 to 21 weeks gestation could be delivered by hysterotomy but that would not be routinely used on such a fetus, and he describes the type of operation:

Once placental separation occurs whether the delivery has been by hysterotomy or vaginally it will not be able to respire ... What constitutes 'born alive' is controversial among the medical profession and often turns not only on medical knowledge but on the moral views of the person giving his opinion. I would mention that the development of each particular foetus in each particular mother is an individual process, the progress of which [at] any stage before 28 weeks can best be ascertained by an examination of the particular mother in question or at the very least detailed knowledge of that individual person.

With that I must entirely agree, and counsel for Mr C conceded that that must be so. It is an important aspect of this case, to which I will later refer. Professor Newton continued:

Whether or not a foetus up to 24 weeks of gestation is delivered by hysterotomy or vaginal delivery it will not be capable of surviving once the placental separation occurs. Up to 24 weeks in my opinion the lungs are incapable of sustaining life because they are not adequately developed. The development of other organs within the foetus is at an equally primitive stage incapable of sustaining life. I do not consider the indicia referred to in paragraph 3 hereof to equate with being 'alive'. I equate 'alive' with being able to sustain a separate independent existence and in my opinion this foetus is clearly not capable of being able to do until after 24 weeks of gestation.

... Counsel's case that Mr C was entitled to an injunction because a crime was threatened depended, it appears, partly, as counsel for Miss S submitted, on the extraordinary and dogmatic assertion with regard to the ability to be born alive of *every* 18-week foetus, without any personal knowledge or examination of any of these countless unborn children, partly on his interpretation of 'being born alive' and partly on the view adumbrated by counsel for Mr C that, if any doctor was intending to perform an abortion on an 18-week foetus, it would be perverse of him or her to assert other than that the foetus was capable of being born alive. Counsel, though not Mr Norris, submitted that no other interpretation of 'live born' than that of Mr Norris is within the words of the Act.

I disagree. Council for Mrs S pointed out that Mr Norris did not disagree with Professor Newton that an 18-week foetus cannot breathe and cannot even be mechanically ventilated. I would have thought that to say, as he has, that a child is live born or alive, even though it cannot breathe, would surprise not only doctors but many ordinary people.

The word 'viable' is, I believe from what I have heard in this case, sometimes used interchangeably and in a number of cases where others might use the words 'born alive'. In the United States of America, in the Supreme Court, in *Roe v Wade* 410 US 113 at 163 (1973) it was said:

With respect to the State's important and legitimate interest in potential life, the 'compelling' point is at *viability*. This is so because the foetus then presumably has the capability of meaningful life outside the mother's womb. State regulation protective of fetal life after viability thus has both logical and biological justifications. (My emphasis.)

As far as the phrase in the 1929 Act is concerned, counsel for Mr C submits, it either contains an ambiguity or the phrase is a technical one. In my view, one or both of those submissions is or are correct. That expression, in my judgment, does not have a clear and plain meaning. It *is* ambiguous. It is a phrase which is capable of different interpretations, and probably for the reason that it is also a medical concept and, as with the example of earlier days, the expertise of doctors may well be required and gratefully received to assist the court.

Even distinguished medical men have found considerable difficulties but have discovered that it is more helpful to equate that phrase with viability, possibly with the example from the parliamentary draftsman in mind.

I cannot accept counsel for the plaintiff's submission that this is not, at any rate in this court, even partly a matter of expert opinion as to the meaning of 'alive', for I have to point out that the first expert, namely Mr Norris, who produced an affidavit on that very topic was introduced by him. Professor Newton replied later.

Counsel on behalf of the Official Solicitor, acting as amicus curiae, submitted that the alleged threatened criminality raised a difficult question of interpretation and pointed out that s 5(1) of the 1967 Act itself incorporates the word 'viable' in the phrase which refers to 'protecting the life of the viable foetus', a section to which I have already referred. By that date, he argued, Parliament would no doubt be aware of the controversies over the law on abortion and it is possible that the use of that word is some indication that Parliament thought it necessary to use that particular qualifying word. I think that that is possible too, though I would not attach too much weight to the parenthesis containing that word as an aid to construction.

Perhaps it is more significant that, though the reference to a foetus of 28 weeks or more being deemed 'capable of being born alive' is referable to the burden of proof, it is probably dealing with a foetus of an age that would be known or expected to be viable in 1929.

Mr Norris, of course, does not limit his statement to a question of presumption. He goes much further and in effect makes his 18 weeks an irrebuttable presumption, thus at a stroke as it were, reducing the 28 weeks to 18.

Counsel for the Official Solicitor submitted that the court should reject Mr Norris's interpretation of 'born alive' as the minimum indicia, without breathing, possibly with circulation and minus a number of indications referred to by Professor Newton.

In considering this submission, I find Mr Norris's statements as to the inevitability of every 18-week foetus being born alive unacceptable. It is not necessary for me, nor would I want, to try to decide on affidavit evidence in a somewhat limited sphere the answer, which baffles men and women with great scientific expertise, to a very profound question. I would, however, say that I am not greatly attracted to the very limited definition relied on by Mr Norris and I do not accept it as a realistic one.

Heilbron J, however, does not seem to reach a final view on this issue since she dismissed the plaintiff's application on other grounds. On appeal, the Court of Appeal dealt squarely with the point.

Sir John Donaldson MR: We have received affidavit evidence from three doctors, none of whom has examined Miss S. Their evidence is thus necessarily directed at the stage in the development of a foetus which can normally be expected to have been reached by the 18th to 21st week. On this, as one would expect, they are in substantial agreement. At that stage the cardiac muscle is contracting and a primitive circulation is developing. Thus the foetus could be said to demonstrate real and discernible signs of life. On the other hand, the foetus, even if then delivered by hysterotomy, would be incapable ever of breathing either naturally or with the aid of a ventilator. It is not a case of the foetus requiring a stimulus or assistance. It cannot and will never be able to breathe. Where the doctors disagree is as to whether a foetus, at this stage of development, can properly be described as 'a child capable of being born alive' within the meaning of the 1929 Act. That essentially depends on the interpretation of the statute and is a matter for the courts.

We have no evidence of the state of the foetus being carried by Miss S but, if it has reached the normal stage of development and so is incapable ever of breathing, it is not in our judgment 'a child capable of being born alive' within the meaning of the 1929 Act and accordingly the termination of this pregnancy would not constitute an offence under that Act.

Stephen Brown and Russel LJJ agreed.

Is it not the case that the Court of Appeal has interpreted the 1929 Act as protecting the 'viable foetus'? (for a different view see: J Keown, "The Scope of the Offence of Child Destruction" (1988) 104 LQR 120). Even if this is so, it still leaves the question of what 'viable' means. Does it mean 'capable of surviving'? If it does, even this needs further clarification. For how long must a foetus be capable of surviving to come within this definition? The rule in homicide cases is that it is immaterial how long the person (including the newborn child) would have lived. As Glanville Williams tells us: ' ... every instance of killing is an instance of accelerating death; and even if death is hastened by as little as five minutes it is still a criminal homicide.' *(Textbook of Criminal Law (supra)* at p 378.)

Support for this wide view of 'the capacity to survive' is to be found in Heilbron J's tentative observation that 'viability ... embraces not only being born alive but surviving, for however short a time ...' (at p 1238). Would a court adopt this view when considering a foetus *in utero*? Or would a court determine that a crime was committed only where it could be shown that a foetus would have been capable of being born alive or surviving for a reasonable period of time?

The issue arose directly in the following case.

Rance v Mid-Downs HA [1991] 1 QB 587, [1991] 1 All ER 801 (QBD)

The plaintiffs were a married couple. In late 1982 or early 1983 the first plaintiff became pregnant. On 9 June 1983 when the first plaintiff was about 26 weeks pregnant she had an ultrasound scan at a hospital administered by the defendant health authority. The radiographer taking the scan thought that the scan showed a possible abnormality in the foetus and marked on her notes '??F. Spine'. Later that day she discussed her suspicions of abnormality with the consultant radiologist at the hospital, who decided that no further action should be taken because there was 'no firm evidence of abnormality'. On 13 September the baby was born and was found to be suffering from spina bifida. The plaintiffs subsequently discovered that the spina bifida may have shown up on one of the scans taken of the first plaintiff and they brought an action against the health authority and the consultant radiologist claiming that the defendants had been negligent in not ascertaining whether the foetus was abnormal when that possibility was raised by the radiographer and had thereby deprived the plaintiffs of the possibility of having the pregnancy terminated. The defendants denied negligence and contended that in any event if the abnormality had been discovered at 26 weeks it would have been an offence under s 1 of the Infant Life (Preservation) Act 1929 to have terminated the first plaintiff's pregnancy then because the termination would have taken place when the foetus was 27 weeks old and by that time the foetus was 'a child capable of being born alive' whose destruction before it had an existence independent of its mother was unlawful except where it was necessary to preserve the mother's life.

Brooke J: To interpret the intention of Parliament when it enacted the 1929 Act, I must put myself in the draftsman's chair in 1929. I must identify the historical background and the mischief which the Act was enacted to remedy and I must construe the words in dispute in the context of the Act as a whole. If the natural and ordinary meaning of the words is clear, I must give effect to them, even if I find their effect goes beyond what was needed to deal with the mischief. If that meaning is ambiguous, then I must call in aid other appropriate canons of construction to help me to identify Parliament's intention. I must also consider the effect, if any, on the construction of the 1929 Act, s 5(1) of the 1967 Act....

English law has always made a distinction between the status of a foetus or child in its mother's womb and the status of a child born alive. It is manslaughter unlawfully to kill a child born alive and murder if the requisite intent is proved. Four nineteenth century cases illustrate the approach of English judges when the termination of life occurred at or near the moment of birth. In *R v Poulton* (1832) 5 C & P 329, 172 ER 997 there was evidence that the baby had breathed but insufficient evidence that the child had ever been fully born. The jury was told by a medical expert that it frequently happened that a child was born as far as the head was concerned but that death took place before the whole delivery was complete. Littledale J directed the jury that they must be satisfied that the child had been born alive before they could convict and added (5 C & P 329 at 330, 172 ER 997 at 998):

With respect to the birth, the being born must mean that the whole body is brought into the world; it is not sufficient that the child respires in the progress of the birth.

In *R v Enoch* (1833) 5 C & P 539, 172 ER 1089 Parke J adopted this ruling when he directed the jury that the child might breathe before it was born but its having breathed was not sufficiently life to make the killing of the child murder and that there must have been an independent circulation of the child.

In *R v Brain* (1834) 6 C & P 349, 172 ER 1272 Parke J directed a jury that if a child had been wholly born, and was alive, it was not essential that it should have breathed at the time it was killed, since many children were born alive, yet did not breathe for some time after birth.

Finally, in *R v Handley* (1874) 13 Cox CC 79 Brett J was concerned with a case in which a newly born child was found dead. The umbilical cord was separated, the internal viscera were healthy and the bowels had acted soon after birth. The bladder and stomach were empty. The general effect of the medical evidence was that the child was full born, was born alive and from the inflated condition of the lungs had lived for an hour or more. Brett J directed the jury that a child was considered to have been born alive, ie whether it existed as a live child, that is to say, breathing and living by reason of its breathing through its own lungs alone, without deriving any of its living or power of living by or through any connection with the mother.

Parliament showed that it was aware of the common law approach to the concept of being alive in its legislation relating to the registration of births and deaths. For example, the statutory definition of the expression 'still-born', in s 12 of the Births and Deaths Registration Act 1926, is that it:

> ...shall apply to any child what has issued forth from its mother after the twenty-eighth week of pregnancy and which did not at any time after being completely expelled from its mother, breathe or show any other signs of life.

In 1929, therefore, the law protected the foetus in utero when it prohibited acts done unlawfully to procure a miscarriage. It protected the child which was born as a live child, breathing and living without any connection with its mother. It provided no protection, however, to the child while it was in the process of being born and before it had been completely separated from its mother, and the extinction of the child's potential life at this intermediate stage was not an offence. This lacuna in the law was identified by Talbot J when charging the grand jury at the Liverpool Assizes in June 1928 in these words:

> The law upon the matter is unsatisfactory and it is right that every appropriate opportunity should be taken to call public attention to it. It is a felony to procure abortion and it is murder to take the life of a child when it is fully born, but to take the life of a child while it is being born and before it is fully born is no offence whatever.

(Cited in the *Report of the Select Committee on the Infant (Preservation) Bill* (HL Paper (1987-88) no 50) para 8.)

I am satisfied that this was the mischief which Parliament intended to remedy when it enacted the 1929 Act. In remedying the mischief, it adopted the concept of 'born alive', which was now well understood following the direction of Brett J in *R v Handley*, and it extended the protection of the law to the child who was capable of being born alive up to the moment when it was in fact born alive and therefore qualified to receive the protection of the law of homicide. It was agreed between counsel that in the event the words used by Parliament in 1929 extended to cover not only the period of birth but also the period when the child capable of being born alive was still in its mother's womb.

Parliament gave effect to its new determination to protect the existence of the child capable of being born alive in s 1(1) of the 1929 Act. In contrast, s 1(2) of the Act was concerned with practical ways and means of giving effect to Parliament's intentions. Parliament could have chosen to resolve the difficult problem of proving in a criminal court that the child whose existence was terminated was capable of being born alive, by enacting a cut-off date, say at 28 weeks, before which there was a conclusive presumption that a child was incapable of being born alive and after which there was a rebuttable presumption that it was so capable. However, this course was not adopted. Parliament created the rebuttable presumption that a child of over 28 weeks' gestation was capable of being born alive, but it was otherwise silent on matters of evidential proof. Therefore, if the Crown succeeded in proving, to a criminal standard of proof, that a particular child of under 28 weeks' gestation had been capable of being born alive, the defendant would be convicted of an offence under the new Act if the other ingredients of the offence were proved. The difficulty was not with the concept 'capable of being born alive', but with proving to a jury's satisfaction without the help of a statutory presumption or information derived from modern technological know-how, that the child in question had had those attributes.

In my judgment the meaning of the words 'born alive' are clear, and the meaning of the words 'capable of being born alive' are also clear. The anencephalic child (who lacks all or most of the cerebral hemispheres but is capable of using its lungs) and the spina bifida child (who possesses one or more of the adverse criteria identified by Professor Lorber) is each born alive if, after birth, it exists as a live child, that is to say breathing and living by reason of its breathing through its own lungs alone, without deriving any of its living or power of living by or through any connection with its mother. For the purposes of this judgment I do not have to consider the case of life before breathing, which was referred to in *R v Brain*. Once the foetus has reached a state of development in the womb that it is capable, if born of possessing those attributes, it is capable of being born alive within the meaning of the 1929 Act. My confidence in this conclusion is strengthened by reference to *C v S* [1987] 1 All ER 1230 at 1242, [1988] QB 135 at 151. In giving the judgment of the Court of Appeal Sir John Donaldson MR rejected the proposition that a foetus between 18 and 21 weeks of age was, or might be, a child 'capable of being born alive', in these words:

> ... the fetus, even if then delivered by hysterotomy, would be incapable ever of ... requiring a stimulus or assistance. It cannot and will never be able to breathe ... if [this fetus] has reached the normal stage of development and so is incapable ever of breathing, it is not in our judgment 'a child capable of being born alive' within the meaning of the 1929 Act ...

I have taken into account the view of Heilbron J in the same case that the phrase 'capable of being born alive' does not have a clear and plain meaning and is ambiguous (see [1987] 1 All ER 1230 at 1239-1240, [1988] QB 135 at 147). However, in my judgment, the words are for all practical purposes clear and on ordinary principles of statutory construction the intention Parliament in 1929 is clear and I must give effect to it.

I do not consider that the enactment of s 5(1) of the 1967 Act ('Nothing in this Act shall affect the provisions of the Infant Life (Preservation) Act 1929 (protecting the life of the viable foetus)') changes or modifies the meaning of the 1929 Act in any way. The primary dictionary meaning of the word 'viable', which is derived from the French word 'vie', is 'capable of living'. I was also referred to *Larousse*, which shows that the primary meaning of the French word 'viable' is 'qui peut vivre'. I have allowed for the fact that the 1967 Act was derived from a private member's Bill, of which Lord Diplock commented in *Royal College of Nursing of the UK v Dept of Health and Social Security* [1981] 1 All ER 545 at 567, [1981] AC 800 at 824:

> ... maybe for that reason, it lacks that style and consistency of draftmanship both internal to the Act itself and in relation to other statutes which one would expect to find in legislation that had its origin in the office of parliamentary counsel.

However, even if I was persuaded that Parliament could alter the clear meaning of an earlier Act by this rather elliptic means – and there is certainly nothing in the excerpt from *Craies on Statute Law* (7th edn, 1971) pp 146-149 to which I was referred, to suggest that this method of 'legislative declaration' or 'parliamentary exposition' has any precedent – I do not consider that in 1967 Parliament intended to do so. In my judgment the word 'viable' was simply being used as a convenient shorthand for the words 'capable of being born alive' and I cannot discern any Parliamentary intention in 1967 to change the effect of the 1929 Act.

Counsel for the plaintiffs submitted at the beginning of his closing speech that the words 'capable of being born alive' meant 'viable', in the sense of 'capable of being born alive and surviving into old age in the normal way without intensive care or surgical intervention'. He submitted that in 1929 Parliament can only have had in mind the natural capacity given to a child to survive without artificial aids and interventions unthought of in 1929. He pointed out that any other interpretation, given the wider meaning for which he contended, introduced considerably more uncertainty. If not into old age, then what length of survival should be postulated? Why stop at 7 or 28 days? If intensive care, what degree of intensive care? The care of a specialist referral centre or a peripheral hospital? Is operative intervention to be postulated or not?

When I tested this submission in argument, he appeared to be willing to withdraw from it, and his fall-back submission was that the words entailed the concept of being alive and surviving for a reasonable period. He said that it would be for a jury to decide how long was reasonable, but he suggested that 28 days, or possibly seven days, would have been the sort of period which Parliament would have had in mind.

The posing of all these questions, and the shifting stances adopted by counsel in argument, strengthen me in my conviction that my preferred construction of the disputed words is correct. I do not believe for one moment that Parliament intended the protection it was affording to children in the course of being born to be limited to the class of healthy children originally identified by counsel and to be denied to those children whose expectation of long life was not so assured at the moment of birth. Nor do I consider, particularly in the light of the historical background to the Act, that Parliament intended the concept of 'capable of being born alive' to be left to be decided by different juries' views of what period of survival after birth should be regarded as reasonable in order to qualify the child for the protection of the Act....

[In conclusion] I am satisfied to a very high standard of proof that [the baby] would have been capable of being born alive at the time any hypothetical abortion had taken place and that abortion would therefore have been unlawful.

The impact of the decision in *Rance* was that prior to 1991 abortions were only legal, in practice, up to the 22nd to 24th week of pregnancy depending upon the development of the particular foetus.

5. Places

Section 1(3) of the 1967 Act provides:

> Except as provided by subsection (4) of this section, any treatment for the termination of pregnancy must be carried out in a hospital vested in a Primary Care Trust or the Secretary of State for the purposes of his functions under the National Health Services Act 1977 or the National Health Service (Scotland) Act 1978 or in a hospital vested in a National Health Service trust or in a place approved for the purposes of this section by the Secretary of State.

Consequently, private clinics require the approval of the Secretary of State to carry out abortions and he, in effect, operates a licensing procedure entailing an application procedure, monitoring and inspection by the Department of Health (see *Abortion Act 1967: Compendium of Guidance* (DOH) (1994)). One important feature is that specific approval is required to carry out abortions after the 20th week of pregnancy and 'late abortions', ie these after the 24th week are prohibited. The latter may only be obtained in an NHS institution.

Ordinarily, no difficulty arises since the 'treatment for the termination' either has or has not been carried out in an institution covered by sub-s (3). The development of the drug RU-486 (Mifepristone) creates problems with this provision.

Mifepristone blocks the action of the female hormone, progesterone, and causes the surface of the endormetrium to be shed. In doing this, Mifepristone can have two distinct effects. First, if taken a short time after sexual intercourse it can prevent the implantation of a fertilised egg. As such, it does not have a contraceptive effect but rather it acts as a contragestive. Importantly, by acting to prevent implantation, it is not an abortifacient (see *supra*).

Secondly, however, Mifepristone can also act to dislodge a fertilised egg which has implanted at the time the drug is taken. As such it is an abortifacient. In July 1991 Mifepristone was granted a product licence in the UK for use as an abortifacient and is marketed by its developers, Roussel, under the brand name *'Mifegyne'* (Product Licence No: PL 0109/0232).

The use of Mifepristone is regulated by the conditions of its product licence granted under the Medicines Act 1968. These, in turn, are reflected in the approved Data Sheet for *'Mifegyne'* (08 DSF 91 UK) as follows.

> Medicinal abortion using Mifepristone does not require that the woman be admitted to hospital as an in-patient. Instead, it may be prescribed within the first seven weeks of pregnancy (or nine weeks after the first day of the last monthly period); the woman should be under 35 and a fit non-smoker; 600mg of the drug should be taken (in divided doses of 200mg); the woman will be observed for at least 2 hours; following which she will be discharged home to return 36-48 hours later for the insertion of a prostaglandin vaginal pessary which ensures the termination is successful in 95% of cases. For the remaining 5% of cases surgical intervention will be necessary. While it is essential that the woman should remain under the care of a doctor, she does not have to remain in a clinic or hospital except for the initial administration and subsequent insertion of the prostaglandin pessary.

Two difficulties of interpretation of the Abortion Act arise here out of the use of Mifepristone: (1) does the 'treatment for the termination of pregnancy' take place at an NHS hospital, NHS Trust or other place approved by the Secretary of State as is required by s 1(3) of the Act? in determining this, what is the 'treatment' which must be carried out at one of these places?

Until the development of Mifepristone, legal terminations of pregnancy were, and were always intended to be, carried out in an NHS hospital or an approved clinic. The procedures involving surgery, dilatation and curettage (D & C) or by medical induction require that they are carried out in such institutions because of the need for their facilities and staff. As we have seen Mifepristone does not require that the patient be hospitalised and it was certainly contemplated that Mifepristone might be administered in a GP's surgery (see *Hansard* HC vol 174, col 1199, Kenneth Clarke). If Mifepristone were prescribed by a general practitioner in a surgery, the surgery would need to be individually approved by the Secretary of State under s 1(3) as an approved place. This would have presented a practical difficulty given the number of GP surgeries that exist. To meet this, s 1(3A) was added to the 1967 Act (by s 37 of the Human Fertilisation and Embryology Act 1990) specifically to cover the use of Mifepristone and its prescription by GPs.

Section 1(3A) provides:

1(3A) The power under subsection (3) of this section to approve a place includes power, in relation to treatment consisting primarily in the use of such medicines as may be specified in the approval and carried out in such manner as may be so specified, to approve a class of places.

As a result, the Secretary of State may approve, as a class, such places as GPs' surgeries although she does not appear to have done so to date. At present, however, it seems that Mifepristone is only licensed for use in hospitals.

Another problem still remains if Mifepristone is prescribed in an NHS hospital or approved place. What s 1(3) and 1(3A) require is that the *'treatment* for the termination of pregnancy'* must be carried out at an NHS (or Trust) hospital or approved place. If the word 'treatment' is limited in meaning to the prescription, the initial administration of the drug and the follow-up use of the prostaglandin pessary, it is clear from the conditions of the product licence that these must occur in an NHS hospital or approved place.

However, this assumes a somewhat narrow view of the meaning of 'treatment'. As we have seen, when Mifepristone is prescribed the woman will take three 200mg pills at the hospital. If, after two hours, she displays no effects she will be discharged home to return 36 to 48 hours later for the prostaglandin pessary to be inserted unless she has already aborted. Consequently, Mifepristone will affect her throughout this period. Arguably, her 'treatment' relates to the whole of this period of time during which the drug is acting on her. Such a view is entirely consistent with the case, *Royal College of Nursing of the UK v DHSS* [1981] AC 800 (see *infra*) where it is clear that the House of Lords viewed 'termination of pregnancy ... as being a process of treatment' per Lord Keith at 834).

If this wider view is right, there are two options. First, the Secretary of State could seek to approve every place under the sun where the woman might go. But this would be impracticable and, in any event, almost certainly beyond the powers conferred by s 1(3) and 1(3A). On one view, the power to approve a class of place appears to be unfettered and, therefore, approval of any class of place would seem to be within the powers given the Secretary of State under s 1(3). However, statutory powers are rarely considered by the courts to be beyond review. Certainly, the exercise of this power would be subject to judicial review and the court would require the Secretary of State to act for a purpose implicitly contemplated by the Act. If he does not, the exercise of his power under s 1(3A) will be *ultra vires*. It could be argued that the purpose of the statute is to require that any terminations that are to be performed be performed in medical environment.

Secondly, once the treatment has begun, she will have to stay in the NHS hospital or approved place until the pregnancy is terminated. This latter consequence was clearly not intended and would defeat the purpose underlying the development of Mifepristone. It would, however, appear to be the correct interpretation of s 1(3) and 1(3A), notwithstanding the assumption embodied in Sch 2 to the Abortion Regulations 1991 (SI 1991 No 499). There, the doctor performing the termination is required to notify the Chief Medical Officer, *inter alia*, of the 'date of treatment' and the 'address of place of treatment'. Both of these clearly do not contemplate that 'treatment' should be a continuing process over several days.

6. The operation of the 1967 Act

(a) The regulations

By s 2 of the Abortion Act 1967, the Secretary of State is empowered to make regulations.

> 2 – (1) The Secretary of State in respect of England and Wales, and the Secretary of State in respect of Scotland, shall by statutory instrument make regulations to provide –
> (a) for requiring any such opinion as is referred to in section 1 of this Act to be certified by the practitioners or practitioner concerned in such form and at such time as may be prescribed by the regulations, and for requiring the preservation and disposal of certificates made for the purposes of the regulations;
> (b) for requiring any registered medical practitioner who terminates a pregnancy to give notice of the termination and such other information relating to the termination as may be so prescribed;
> (c) for prohibiting the disclosure, except to such persons or for such purposes as may be so prescribed, of notices given or information furnished pursuant to the regulations.

Contravention of these regulations is, by virtue of s 2(3), a summary criminal offence. The Abortion Regulations 1991 (SI 1991 No 499), which came into effect on 1 April 1991, deal with two main areas.

(i) CERTIFICATION OF THE NECESSARY MEDICAL OPINIONS UNDER THE ACT

The Abortion Regulations 1991 in reg 3, provide as follows:

> **Certificate of opinion**
> 3 (1) Any opinion to which section 1 of the Act refers shall be certified –
> (a)   in the case of a pregnancy terminated in accordance with section 1(1) of the Act, in the form set out in Part I of Schedule 1 to these Regulations, and
> (b) in the case of a pregnancy terminated in accordance with section 1(4) of the Act, in the form set out in Part II of that Schedule.
>   (2) Any certificate of an opinion referred to in section 1(1) of the Act shall be given before the commencement of the treatment for the termination of the pregnancy to which it relates.
>   (3) Any certificate of an opinion referred to in section 1(4) of the Act shall be given before the commencement of the treatment for the termination of the pregnancy to which it relates or, if that is not reasonably practicable, not later than 24 hours after such termination.
>   (4) Any such certificate as is referred to in paragraphs (2) and (3) of this regulation shall be preserved by the practitioner who terminated the pregnancy to which it relates for a period of not less than three years beginning with the date of the termination.
>   (5) A certificate which is no longer to be preserved shall be destroyed by the person in whose custody it then is.

Schedule 1 provides two standard certificates contemplated in reg 3(1). These are colloquially known as the 'blue forms' because of their colour. Under the previous regulations the certificate was known as the 'green form' for a similar reason. We set out here Certificate A which deals with the usual case of termination of pregnancy. Certificate B, which deals with situations of emergency, is set out *infra*.

IN CONFIDENCE   **CERTIFICATE A**

ABORTION ACT 1967

Not to be destroyed within three years of the date of operation
Certificate to be completed before an abortion is
performed under Section 1(1) of the Act

I, ...

(Name and qualifications of practitioner in block capitals)

of ....

....

(Full address of practitioner)

Have/have not* seen/and examined* the pregnant woman to whom this certificate relates at

....

(full address of place at which patient was seen or examined)

on ....

and I ....

(Name and qualifications of practitioner in block capitals)

of ....

(Full address of practitioner)

Have/have not* seen/and examined* the pregnant woman to whom this certificate relates at

....

....

(Full address of place at which the patient was seen or examined)

on ....

We hereby certify that we are of the opinion, formed in good faith, that in the case

of ....

(Full name of pregnant woman in block capitals)

of ....

(Usual place of residence of pregnant woman in block capitals)

(Ring   A   the continuance of the pregnancy would involve risk to the life of
appropriate   the pregnant woman greater than if the pregnancy were
letter(s))   terminated;

               B   the termination is necessary to prevent grave permanent injury
                    to the physical or mental health of the pregnant woman;

               C   the pregnancy has NOT exceeded its 24th week and that the
                    continuance of the pregnancy would involve risk, greater than if
                    the pregnancy were terminated, of injury to the physical or
                    mental health of the pregnant woman;

               D   the pregnancy has NOT exceeded its 24th week and that the
                    continuance of the pregnancy would involve risk, greater than if
                    the pregnancy were terminated, of injury to the physical or

mental health of any existing child(ren) of the family of the pregnant woman;

E   there is a substantial risk that if the child were born it would suffer from such physical or mental abnormalities as to be seriously handicapped.

This certificate of opinion is given before the commencement of the treatment for the termination of pregnancy to which it refers and relates to the circumstances of the pregnant woman's individual case.

Signed .... Date ....

Signed .... Date ....

*Delete as appropriate   Form HSA 1 (revised 1991)

Three observations can be made here. First, the form emphasises that it is the 'opinion' of each doctor 'formed in good faith' that one or more grounds under s 1(1) exists that is important. There may be more than one basis for the abortion and the two doctors may not agree. That does not effect the legality of the procedure.

Secondly, there seems to be no requirement that either doctor should have seen the patient or examined her. Of course, usually the two doctors will be her GP and consultant gynaecologist. And, a doctor's "good faith" opinion may be challengeable in the absence of seeing and possibly, examining her.

Thirdly, there is no legal requirement that the doctor who carries out the abortion should sign the certificate. Section 1(1) of the Act provides such a doctor with a defence providing two doctors (whether or not he is one of them) have signed the certificate.

That said, although a mistaken belief by a doctor will not, of itself, lead to a conclusion that his opinion was not formed 'in good faith', a doctor's *bona fides* may in an extreme case, be successfully subjected to challenge. The only case dealing with the issue of certification is *R v Smith* [1974] 1 All ER 376.

R v Smith **[1974] 1 All ER 376, [1973] 1 WLR 1510 (CA)**

Scarman LJ: The Act, though it renders lawful abortions that before its enactment would have been unlawful, does not depart from the basic principle of the common law as declared in *R v Bourne,* namely that the legality of an abortion depends on the opinion of the doctor. It has introduced the safeguard of two opinions: if they are formed in good faith by the time the operation is undertaken, the abortion is lawful. Thus a great social responsibility is firmly placed by the law on the shoulders of the medical profession.

On 28th April 1970 at the Hayward Nursing Home a Miss Rodgers underwent an operation performed by the appellant, the initial purpose of which was to terminate her pregnancy. The prosecution's case was that when he operated, the appellant was not acting in good faith; he had not formed a bona fide opinion as to the balance of risk between termination and continuation of her pregnancy, that is to say, that its continuance would involve risk to her physical or mental health greater than if it were terminated. The appellant's defence was twofold: he said that he formed an honest opinion as to the need for an abortion, but that when he had the girl on the operating table, he found she was starting an inevitable abortion. Thus, according to him, his operation became not a termination but a facilitating and tidying up of an inevitable abortion – a natural process which had already begun. If this be the truth, the prosecution concedes that the operation would be lawful without the need of recourse to the Abortion Act 1967.

... If the jury rejected, as they did, the tale of an inevitable abortion, the sequence of events was such as to call for very careful consideration whether it was possible to believe that the appellant had formed in good faith, or at all, the opinion necessary to give him the protection of the 1967 Act. Had he, or had he not, abused the trust reposed in him by the Act of Parliament? The burden was on the prosecution to prove beyond reasonable doubt that he had. All this was faithfully explained to the jury by the recorder. We quote only one passage towards the end of the summing-up:

[The appellant] took the view that if any girl wanted her pregnancy terminated, that of itself was, if not entirely sufficient, a very powerful indication of the risk of injury to her mental health if the pregnancy continued being greater than if the pregnancy was terminated. He told you that all his actions were within the Act, so he was telling you that, though he took the view that really with every girl or woman who wanted her pregnancy terminated that was a very powerful reason for terminating it, because it may involve risk to her mental health, he still acted within the Act and balanced the risks of termination against the risks of continuation. If two doctors genuinely form an opinion in each case that they deal with that the risk of continuance is more than the risk of termination, it does not matter whether they are right or wrong in that view. If they form that opinion genuinely and in good faith, that in fact comes within the Act, and there is no guilt attached to it. You have to wonder in the case of [the appellant] whether such a view could genuinely be held by a medical man, whether it was held in the case of Miss Rodgers in particular. The only indication on the case notes about any danger to her mental or physical health was the word 'depressed', 'not willing to marry and depressed'. Those are the only words about it on the case notes. You have to ask yourselves, was there any balancing of the risks involved in allowing the pregnancy to continue and allowing the pregnancy to be terminated, or was this a mere routine abortion case? That is what you have to consider. Was a second opinion even contemplated as a necessity in this case of Miss Rodgers? If, on the very first interview when the girl was seen by [the appellant], the very first interview he had with her, he offered to operate on her the next morning, was there any real contemplation or thought that a second opinion was necessary?

These were the questions for the jury; and they have been answered adversely to the appellant. The view the jury took was one fully open to them on the evidence; and we can see no reason for the suggestion that their view was wrong or unsafe or unsatisfactory ...

(See also, *Wall v Livingston* [1982] 1 NZLR 734 (NZCA).)

(ii) COLLECTION OF DATA

The 1991 regulations require 'any practitioner' who terminates a pregnancy to notify the appropriate Chief Medical Officer (reg 4(1)). Significantly, the regulations, while requiring such notification, impose careful restrictions upon further dissemination of the notice or information by the appropriate Chief Medical Officer. These are set out in reg 5 reproduced in Chapter 8.

(b) Emergencies

So far we have considered the operation of the Act in what might be described as usual circumstances. The Act, however, makes specific provisions for emergencies in s 1(4).

1 (4) Subsection (3) of this section, and so much of subsection (1) as relates to the opinion of two registered medical practitioners, shall not apply to the termination of a pregnancy by a registered medical practitioner in a case where he is of the opinion, formed in good faith, that the termination is immediately necessary to save the life or to prevent grave permanent injury to the physical or mental health of the pregnant woman.

As a consequence of this provision, where a termination is (a) immediately necessary (b) to save the life of the mother or prevent grave permanent injury to her physical or mental health, the decision to carry out the termination can be made by one doctor alone and need not be carried out in an NHS hospital, NHS Trust hospital or other approved place. Subsection (4) does not remove the need for the single doctor to form the view in good faith that there are grounds for termination under s 1(1), specifically those set out in s 1(1)(b) or (c). This poses no problem since there is (now) virtual symmetry between the grounds in s 1(1)(b) and (c) and the wording of sub-s (4).

As regards certification in the case of an emergency, reg 3(1)(b) of the Abortion Regulations 1991 states that:

3(1) Any opinions to which section 1 of the Act refers shall be certified ...
(b) in the case of a pregnancy terminated in accordance with section 1(4) of the Act, in the form set out in Part II of [Schedule 1].

Certificate B in Sch 1 is as follows:

IN CONFIDENCE   **Certificate B**

Not to be destroyed within three years of the date of operation

ABORTION ACT 1967

**CERTIFICATE TO BE COMPLETED IN RELATION TO ABORTION
PERFORMED IN EMERGENCY UNDER SECTION 1(4) OF THE ACT**

I, ...

(Name and qualifications of practitioner in block capitals)

of ....

....

(Full address of practitioner)

hereby certify that I *am/was of the opinion formed in good faith that it *is/was necessary immediately to terminate the pregnancy of

....

(Full name of pregnant woman in block capitals)

of ....

....

(Usual place of residence of pregnant woman in block capitals)

(Ring
appropriate
number)

in order
1. to save the life of the pregnant woman; or
2. to prevent grave permanent injury to the physical or mental
    health of the pregnant woman.

This certificate of opinion is given–

(Ring
appropriate
number)

A. before the commencement of the treatment for the termination
    of the pregnancy to which it relates; or, if that is not reasonably
    practicable, then

B. not later than 24 hours after such termination.

Signed ....

Date ....
*Delete as appropriate

Notice from the wording of the certificate, which reflects reg 3(3), that in the case of an emergency where it is not reasonably practical to complete the certification before the termination, it must be completed no later than 24 hours afterwards.

(c) Conscientious objection

The Abortion Act 1967, s 4 reads as follows:

4 – (1) Subject to subsection (2) of this section, no person shall be under any duty, whether by contract or by any statutory or other legal requirement, to participate in any treatment authorised by this Act to which he has a conscientious objection:

Provided that in any legal proceedings the burden of proof of conscientious objection shall rest on the person claiming to rely on it.

(2) Nothing in subsection (1) of this section shall affect any duty to participate in treatment which is necessary to save the life or to prevent grave permanent injury to the physical or mental health of a pregnant woman.

The effect of this provision is discussed in the following.

J K Mason and A McCall Smith *Law and Medical Ethics* (5th edn, 1999)

[An] important and unfortunate result of the 1967 Act is that some discrimination takes place against doctors, and especially those seeking to become gynaecologists, who are unable to accept its wide terms. It is, to be noted that, while a doctor may, in general, refuse to take part in the abortion procedure, he remains under an obligation to advise. Such advice is subject to the normal rules of medical negligence and the conscientious objector's only recourse is, therefore, to refer his patient to another practitioner, a practice which is only marginally compatible with a strong conscience and which must damage the essential bond of trust between doctor and patient ... The doctor's conscience does not absolve him from treating a woman when the continuation of the pregnancy is life-threatening and there is of course, no right to conscience in treating the *result* of a legal abortion; these considerations apply equally to the nursing staff.

Rarely will s 4 present any legal problem or practical difficulties. Like its counterpart in s 38 of the Human Fertilisation and Embryology Act 1990 (*supra,* ch 10), it allows for dissent on the basis of 'conscience', ie a conviction or belief based upon a moral assessment rather than prejudice. It also allows the doctor (or other) to 'opt out' of some (though not all) abortions where the individual's beliefs prevent his involvement, for example, 'late' rather than 'early' abortions or one based solely upon foetal disability. To whom, however, does s 4 apply?

The scope of s 4 has only been considered by the courts on one occasion in *Janaway v Salford AHA* [1989] AC 537, [1988] 3 All ER 1079 (discussed in A Grubb [1988] CLJ 162 and [1989] CLJ 17). The central question of difficulty raised in section 4 relates to the meaning of the words 'participate in any treatment' under the Abortion Act. The situation contemplated by s 4 is one in which a person *but for* the subsection would be under a legal duty to participate in treatment under the Act. The effect of s 4 is to absolve that person of any such duty whether it be a duty owed to his employer because of the terms of his contract of employment or to his patient. While it will be perfectly obvious in most cases whether a person is being asked to participate in a termination of pregnancy and thus may rely upon s 4, some problems arise the less closely involved the person may be.

Janaway v Salford AHA [1989] AC 537, [1988] 3 All ER 1079 (HL)

Lord Keith: My Lords, the appellant, Mrs Janaway (the applicant), took up employment with the respondent health authority on 25 June 1984. She was engaged as a secretary/receptionist at Irlam Health Centre, working for a Dr Barooah. On 11 September 1984 she was asked by Dr Barooah to type a letter which had to do with referring a pregnant patient for an appointment with a consultant with a view to the latter forming an opinion as to whether the pregnancy should be terminated under the Abortion Act 1967. The applicant, a Roman Catholic holding the belief that abortion is morally wrong, refused to type the letter, which was eventually written by hand by another doctor at the health centre. On 31 October 1984 the applicant was interviewed by a personnel officer from the authority and told him that she felt entitled to refuse to type the letter, and any others concerned with termination of pregnancy, by virtue of the conscientious objection provision contained in s 4(1) of the 1967 Act, to which I shall refer later. On 7 November 1984 the personnel officer wrote to the applicant stating that her refusal to type correspondence of the kind in question amounted to a breach of the authority's disciplinary rules as being 'unjustified refusal of a lawful and reasonable instruction' and asking for a firm assurance that she would in future carry out such instructions. The applicant sent in reply a letter dated 12 November 1984 which concluded:

> ... except insofar as I stand by the protection afforded by s 4(1) of the Abortion Act [1967] I confirm that I will continue, as I have done in the past, to carry out my contractual duties as detailed in my job description.

On 27 November 1984 the applicant had a meeting, at which she reaffirmed her position, with the personnel officer and the community services administrator. On 30 November the latter wrote to her saying that legal advice had been obtained to the effect that s 4(1) of the 1967 Act did not apply to her refusal, and that her employment had been terminated from 27 November on grounds of misconduct. The applicant appealed against her dismissal to the authority's appeal tribunal, but her appeal was dismissed, and the authority formally ratified the decision on 6 February 1985.

On 17 June the applicant, with leave, applied for judicial review in the shape of an order of certiorari to quash the authority's decision of 6 February 1985 and a declaration that, by reason of her conscientious objection to typing correspondence of the kind in question, she was not under any duty to carry out such work.

The application was dismissed by Nolan J on 12 February 1985, and his decision was affirmed by the Court of Appeal (Slade, Balcombe and Stocke LJJ) ([1988] 2 WLR 442) on 18 December 1987. The applicant now appeals, with leave granted by the Court of Appeal, to your Lordship's House....

The applicant claims the protection of s 4(1). The issue in the case turns on the true construction of the words in that subsection 'participate in any treatment authorised by this Act'. For the applicant it is maintained that the words cover taking part in any arrangement preliminary to and intended to bring about medical or surgical measures aimed at terminating a pregnancy, including the typing of letters referring a patient to a consultant. The health authority argues that the meaning of the words is limited to taking part in the actual procedures undertaken at the hospital or other approved place with a view to the termination of a pregnancy.

The argument for the applicant proceeds on the lines that the acts attracting the protection afforded by s 4(1) are intended to be coextensive with those which are authorised by s 1(1) and which in the absence of that provision would be criminal. The criminal law about accessories treats one who aids and abets, counsels or procures a criminal act as liable to the same extent as a principal actor. In the absence of s 1(1) the applicant by typing a letter of referral would be counselling or procuring an abortion, or at least helping to do so, and subject to a possible defence on the principle of *R v Bourne* [1938] 3 All ER 615, [1939] 1 KB 687 would be criminally liable. Therefore any requirement to type such a letter is relieved, in the face of a conscientious objection, by s 4(1).

The majority of the Court of Appeal (Slade and Stocker LJJ) accepted the main thrust of the applicant's argument, to the effect that ss 1(1) and 4(1) are coextensive, but decided against her on the ground that her intention in typing a letter of referral would not be to assist in procuring an abortion but merely to carry out the obligations of her employment. In their view the typing of such a letter by the applicant would not be a criminal offence in the absence of s 1(1).

Nolan J, however, and Balcombe LJ in the Court of Appeal rejected the applicant's main argument. They accepted the argument for the health authority that on a proper construction the word 'participate' in s 4(1) did not import the whole concept of principal and accessory residing in the criminal law, but in its ordinary and natural meaning referred to actually taking part in treatment administered in a hospital or other approved place in accordance with s 1(3), for the purpose of terminating a pregnancy.

In my opinion Nolan J and Balcombe LJ were right to reach the conclusion they did. I agree entirely with their view about the natural meaning of the word 'participate' in this context. Although the word is commonly used to describe the activities of accessories in the criminal law field, it is not a term of art there. It is in any event not being used in a criminal context in s 4(1). Ex hypothesi treatment for termination of a pregnancy under s 1 is not criminal. I do not consider that Parliament can reasonably have intended by its use to import all the technicalities of the criminal law about principal and accessory, which can on occasion raise very nice questions about whether someone is guilty as an accessory. Such niceties would be very difficult of solution for an ordinary health authority. If Parliament had intended the result contended for by the applicant, it could have procured it very clearly and easily by referring to participation 'in anything authorised by this Act' instead of 'in any treatment [so] authorised'. It is to be observed that s 4 appears to represent something of a compromise in relation to conscientious objection. One who believes all abortion to be morally wrong would conscientiously object even to such treatment as is mentioned in sub-s (2), yet the subsection would not allow the objection to receive effect.

The applicant's argument placed some reliance on a passage in the speech of Lord Roskill in *Royal Collage of Nursing of the United Kingdom v Department of Health and Social Security* [1981] 1 All ER 545 at 577, [1981] AC 800 at 837-838:

> My Lords I read and reread the 1967 Act to see if I can discern in its provisions any consistent pattern in the use of the phrase 'a pregnancy is terminated' or 'termination of a pregnancy' on the one hand and 'treatment for the termination of a pregnancy' on the other hand. One finds the former phrase in s 1(1) and (1) (*a*), the latter in s 1(3), the former in ss 1(4) and 2(1)(*b*) and the latter in s 3(1)(*a*) and (*c*). Most important to my mind is s 4, which is the conscientious objection section. This section in two places refers to 'participate in treatment' in the context of conscientious objection. If one construes s 4 in conjunction with s 1(1), as surely one should do in order to determine to what it is that conscientious objection is permitted, it seems to me that s 4 strongly supports the wider construction of s 1(1). It was suggested that acceptance of the department's submission involved rewriting that subsection so as to add words which are not to be found in the language of the subsection. My Lords, with great respect to that submission, I do not agree. If one construes the words 'when a pregnancy is terminated by a registered medical practitioner' in s 1(1) as embracing the case where the 'treatment for the termination of a pregnancy is carried out under the control of a doctor in accordance with ordinary current medical practice' I think one is reading 'termination of pregnancy' and 'treatment for termination of pregnancy' as virtually synonymous and as I think Parliament must have intended they should be read. Such a construction avoids a number of anomalies as, for example, where there is no pregnancy or where the extra-amniotic process fails to achieve its objective within the normal limits of time set for its operation.

That case was concerned with a particular process of treatment for the termination of pregnancy carried out in hospital, important parts of which were performed not by a registered medical practitioner but by a nurse acting under his instructions.

The issue was whether the actions of the nurse were unlawful, and it was held that they were not, on the ground that what was authorised by the Act was the whole medical process resulting in termination of pregnancy and that the process was carried out by a registered medical practitioner when that was done under his supervision and in accordance with his instructions, notwithstanding that certain parts of the process were carried out by other. The House was not concerned with the meaning of the word 'participate' in s 4(1) in relation to anything other than the medical process carried out in the hospital, and then only indirectly. So Lord Roskill's words cannot be read as having any bearing on the decision of the present case.

Lords Brandon, Griffiths Goff and Lowry agreed.

The question could also arise in the case of a GP. A woman may present herself seeking a termination of pregnancy. Assuming he has a conscientious objection, what is the extent of his legal duty to her, or, putting it another way, at what point can he rely upon s 4(1)?

In the Court of Appeal, in *Janaway* Stocker LJ raised this question in the context of a doctor's refusal to certify that a ground for termination existed:

> In my view, apart from section 4(1), a doctor would be under a duty in the performance of his professional duties to certify on the green form [ie the certificate] and to take such other steps as he might consider advisable in any case in which his medical and clinical opinion was that an abortion should be performed for any of the reasons set out in the Act, or in the green form itself. Apart from section 4(1) he would be in breach of his professional duty to his patient and [where relevant] of his duty to the employing authority if he refused to do so …

In the House of Lords, Lord Keith left the point open:

> A certain amount of argument was addressed to the Abortion Regulations 1968, SI 1968/390 [see now Abortion Regulations 1991] which, inter alia, set out the form of certificate, known as 'the green form', to be signed by two registered medical practitioners in pursuance of s 1(1)(*a*) of the 1967 Act, and to the position in relation to s 4(1) of practitioners who might be required to sign such a certificate. The regulations do not appear to contemplate that the signing of the certificate would form part of treatment for the termination of pregnancy, since reg 3(2) provides:

> Any certificate of an opinion referred to in section 1(1) of the Act shall be given before the commencement of the treatment for the termination of the pregnancy to which it relates.

> It does not appear whether or not there are any circumstances under which a doctor might be under any legal duty to sign a green form, so as to place in difficulties one who had a conscientious objection to doing so. The fact that during the 20 years that the 1967 Act has been in force no problem seems to have surfaced in this connection may indicate that in practice none exists. So I do not think it appropriate to express any opinion on the matter.

Lord Keith clearly disagreed with Stocker LJ that 'participating in any treatment' extends to cover certification (ie signing the statutory form). On the face of it, the regulation referred to by Lord Keith justifies his conclusion. If this is correct that s 4(1) does not apply, it is crucial to determine this scope of the doctor's duty to his patient, ie at what point can the doctor say that he is not prepared to go further. Stocker LJ took the view that a doctor is under a legal duty to certify when he considers it medically justified. Lord Keith chose not to express a concluded view. Certainly, the doctor has a legal duty to exercise the usual due care and skill which would involve ascertaining the relevant medical facts. The woman may, after all, be in danger from the pregnancy. In the case of an emergency, the conscientious objection provision does not apply.

> 4(2) Nothing in subsection (1) of this section shall effect any duty to participate in treatment which is necessary to save the life or to prevent grave permanent injury to the physical or mental health of a pregnant woman.

Assuming, however, that there is no emergency, two questions arise. First, does the GP have a duty under his terms of service (and, therefore, implicitly to the patient) to sign the certificate and *refer* the woman to a consultant? Secondly, even if no such duty arises, does the GP have a duty again under his terms of service (and, therefore, implicitly to the patient) at least to refer his patient to another GP who, he knows, is prepared to contemplate signing a certificate?

The answer to both questions turns upon the provisions of his terms of service under Sch 2 to the NHS (General Medical Services) Regulations 1992 (SI 1992 No 635) (a similar provision exists for doctors in 'pilot schemes' covered by the National Health Service (Primary Care) Act 1997).

Paragraph 12 provides, *inter alia*, as follows:

> 12 (1) Subject to paragraphs 3, 13 and 44 a doctor shall render to his patients all necessary and appropriate personal medical services of the type usually provided by general medical practitioners.
> (2) The services which a doctor is required by sub-paragraph (1) to render shall include the following
> ...
> (d) arranging for the referral of patients, as appropriate, for the provision of any other services under the Act. ...

The provision of services involving the termination of pregnancy is one of the 'other services' under the 1977 Act (ss 1 and 3). Consequently, it is beyond argument that in answer to our second question the GP must refer in the sense of 'pass on' his patient to another doctor who he knows is prepared to refer her (including signing the appropriate form) to a consultant obstetrician with a view to performing a termination. Notice this latter use of the word 'refer' entails signing the certificate if satisfied that a ground for abortion exists. Herein lies the answer to the first question we posed. We regard the natural meaning of 'refer' and 'referral' in para 12 as covering the situation where a GP sends his patient to a consultant for further consultation. This, we would suggest, may well involve signing the certificate. Thus, it follows that the GP's duty under his terms of service, in our view, requires that, whatever his conscientious objection, he should sign the appropriate form and he is unable in this context to rely upon s 4(1) of the Abortion Act 1967.

7. The claims of others

(a) To prevent an abortion

To what extent may someone such as the father of an unborn child prevent the mother from undergoing an abortion? Given the court's attitude to the 'sanctity' of the decision-making process between doctor and pregnant woman, it is unlikely that the courts would countenance interference by others, including putative fathers. Indeed, this is the experience throughout the world.

(i) THE FATHER QUA FATHER

Paton v Trustees of British Pregnancy Advisory Service **[1979] QB 276, [1978] 2 All ER 987 (QBD)**

Sir George Baker P:...the plaintiff, who is the husband of the second defendant, seeks an injunction in effect to restrain the first defendants, a charitable organisation, and particularly his wife, the second defendant, from causing or permitting an abortion to be carried out on his wife without his consent ...

So this plaintiff must, in my opinion, bring his case, if he can, squarely within the framework of the fact that he is a husband. It is, of course, very common for spouses to seek injunctions for personal protection in the matrimonial courts during the pendency of or, indeed, after divorce actions, but the basic reason for the non-molestation injunction often granted in the family courts is to protect the other spouse or the living children, and to ensure that no undue pressure is put on one or other of the spouses during the pendency of the case and during the breaking-up of the marriage.

There was, of course, the action of restitution of conjugal rights, a proceeding which always belied its name and was abolished in 1970. It arose because in ecclesiastical law the parties could not end the consortium by agreement. In a sense the action for restitution was something of a fiction. The court ordered the spouse to return to cohabitation. If the spouse did not return then that spouse was held to be in desertion. No more could happen. The court could not compel matrimonial intercourse: *Forster v Forster* [(1790) 161 ER 504]. So matrimonial courts have never attempted the enforcement of matrimonial obligations by injunction.

The law is that the court cannot and would not seek to enforce or restrain by injunction matrimonial obligations, if they be obligations such as sexual intercourse or contraception (a non-molestation injunction given during the pendency of divorce proceedings could, of course, cover attempted intercourse). No court would even grant an injunction to stop sterilisation or vasectomy. Personal family relationships in marriage cannot be enforced by the order of a court. An injunction in such circumstances was described by Judge Mager in *Jones v Smith* [(1973) 278 So 2d 339] in the District Court of Appeal of Florida as 'ludicrous'.

I ask the question 'If an injunction were ordered, what could be the remedy?' and I do not think I need say any more than that no judge could even consider sending a husband or wife to prison for breaking such an order. That, of itself, seems to me to cover the application here; this husband cannot by law by injunctions stop his wife having what is now accepted to be a lawful abortion within the terms of the Abortion Act 1967.

The case which was first put forward to me a week ago, and indeed is to be found in the writ, is that the wife had no proper legal grounds for seeking a termination of her pregnancy and that, not to mince words, she was being spiteful, vindictive and utterly unreasonable in seeking so to do. It now appears I need not go into the evidence in the affidavits because it is accepted and common ground that the provisions of the 1967 Act have been complied with, the necessary certificate has been given by two doctors and everything is lawfully set for the abortion.

... The two doctors have given a certificate. It is not and cannot be suggested that that certificate was given in other than good faith and it seems to me that there is the end of the matter in English law. The 1967 Act gives no right to a father to be consulted in respect of the termination of a pregnancy. True, it gives no right to the mother either, but obviously the mother is going to be right at the heart of the matter consulting with the doctors if they are to arrive at a decision in good faith, unless, of course, she is mentally incapacitated or physically incapacitated (unable to make any decision or give any help) as, for example, in consequence of an accident. The husband, therefore, in my view, has no legal right enforceable at law or in equity to stop his wife having this abortion or to stop the doctors from carrying out the abortion....

Very helpfully I have been referred to American authorities. The Supreme Court of the United States has reached the same conclusion, that a husband, or an illegitimate father, has no right to stop his wife, or the woman who is pregnant by him, from having a legal abortion. In *Planned Parenthood of Central Missouri v Danforth, Attorney-General of Missouri* [(1976) 428 US 52] the Supreme Court by a majority held that the State of Missouri

> may not constitutionally require the consent of the spouse, as it specified under s 3(3) of the Missouri Act, as a condition for abortion during the first 12 weeks of pregnancy ... clearly since the State cannot regulate or proscribe abortion during the first stage when the physician and his patient make that decision, the State cannot delegate authority to any particular person, even the spouse, to prevent abortion during that same period.

It is interesting to note that the Missouri spousal consent provision would have required the husband's consent even if he was not the father.

A spousal consent provision in an English Act could not of course be challenged as unconstitutional but there is no such provision in the 1967 Act or in the Abortion Regulations 1968 to which a challenge of ultra vires could be made. There is no provision even for consultation with the spouse and reg 5 prohibits disclosure except in specified instances of which disclosure to the spouse is not one.

Counsel have been unable to discover any extant decision in those countries whose laws derive from the common law that the consent of the husband is required before an otherwise legal abortion can be performed on the wife. Counsel for the husband's researches show that in Roman law, centuries ago, the father's consent was required or otherwise abortion was a crime, but today the only way he can put the case is that the husband has a right to have a say in the destiny of the child he has conceived. The law of England gives him no such right; the 1967 Act contains no such provision. It follows, therefore, that in my opinion this claim for an injunction is completely misconceived and must be dismissed.

In *C v S* [1988] QB 135, [1987] 1 All ER 1230, the *Paton* case was applied where the father was not married to the mother. At first instance, the judge said:

> **Heilbron J:** Counsel's case on behalf of Mr C is that he has the locus standi to bring these proceedings, based on his personal interest, which he does not put as high as a legal right, and because the proposed termination encompasses, he submits, a threatened crime concerning the life of his child.
>
> If it were to be decided that there was no such threat, he concedes that he has no standing qua father, for he does not contend that as a father he has any special rights. He concedes too that a husband has no special rights qua husband, and he accepts the correctness of the decision in *Paton v Trustees of BPAS* [1978] 2 All ER 987, [1979] QB 276 in that regard.

In the Court of Appeal the Master of the Rolls said the following:

> **Sir John Donaldson MR:** ... Technically, and now in substance in the light of what counsel for Mr C has said, the questions whether a putative father has any right to be heard on an application of this nature and whether a fetus is a legal person in law capable of suing do not arise, and of course we do not rule on them. But I have also to say that, if we had been in favour of Mr C on all other points, we should have had to have given very considerable thought to the words of Baker P in *Paton v Trustees of BPAS* [1978] 2 All ER 987 at 992, [1979] QB 276 at 282 where he said:
>
> > ... not only would it be a bold and brave judge ... who would seek to interfere with the discretion of doctors acting under the [Abortion Act 1967], but I think he would really be a foolish judge who would try to do any such thing, unless possibly, there is clear bad faith and an obvious attempt to perpetrate a criminal offence.
>
> Even then, of course, the question is whether that is a matter which should be left to the Director of Public Prosecutions and the Attorney-General.
>
> So, with that addendum on behalf of the court, we dismiss the appeal.

Mr Paton took his case to the European Commission of Human Rights claiming that art 8 of the European Convention of Human Rights guaranteeing to everyone the right to 'respect for family life' gave him the right *qua* father to the injunction he sought. The Commission rejected his argument.

Paton v United Kingdom (1980) 3 EHRR 408 (EComHR)

25. In its examination of the applicant's complaints concerning the Abortion Act 1967 and its application in this case, the Commission has next had regard to Article 8 of the Convention which, in paragraph (1), guarantees to everyone the right to respect for his family life. The Commission here notes, apart from his principal complaint concerning the permission of the abortion, the applicant's ancillary complaint concerning the permission of the abortion, the applicant's ancillary submission that the 1967 Act denies the father of the foetus a right to be consulted, and to make applications, about the proposed abortion.

The Commission also observes that the applicant, who under Article 2 claims to be the victim of a violation of the right to life of the foetus of which he was the potential father, under Article 8 invokes a right of his own.

26. As regards the principal complaint concerning the permission of the abortion, the Commission recalls that the pregnancy of the applicant's wife was terminated in accordance with her wish and in order to avert the risk to her physical or mental health. The Commission therefore finds that this decision, in so far as it interfered in itself with the applicant's right to respect for his family life, was justified under paragraph (2) of Article 8 as being necessary for the protection of the rights of another person. It follows that this complaint is also manifestly ill-founded within the meaning of Article 27(2).

In 1989 the Canadian Supreme Court reached the same view in an appeal from the Court of Appeal for Quebec. The case concerned an application for an injunction by a former boyfriend Monsieur Tremblay to restrain his former girlfriend, Mlle Daiglé, from terminating her pregnancy, then in its 21st week.

Tremblay v Daigle (1989) 62 DLR (4th) 634 (Can SC)

The Court: The argument based upon 'father's rights' (more accurately referred to as 'potential father's rights) is the third and final basis on which the substantive rights necessary to support the impugned injunction might be founded. This argument would appear to be based on the proposition that the potential father's contribution to the act of conception gives him an equal say in what happens to the foetus. Little emphasis was put on the argument in the appeal. It was alluded to by several of the parties in an indirect fashion, although it does appear to have been accepted by both Viens J in the Superior Court and LeBel JA in the Court of Appeal.

There does not appear to be any jurisprudential basis for this argument. No court in Quebec or elsewhere has ever accepted the argument that a father's interest in a foetus which he helped create could support a right to veto a woman's decisions in respect of the foetus she is carrying. A number of cases in various jurisdictions outside of Quebec have considered this argument and explicitly rejected it: *Paton v British Pregnancy Advisory Service Trustees*, supra; *Medhurst v Medhurst*, supra; *Whalley v Whalley* (1981) 122 DLR (3rd) 717 (BCSC); *Mock v Brandanburg* (1988), 61 Alta, LR (2d) 235 (QB); *Doe v Doe* 314 NE 2d 128 (Mass 1974); *Jones v Smith* 278 So 2d 339 (Fla Dist Ct App 1973). We have been unable to find a single decision in Quebec or elsewhere which would support the allegation of 'father's rights' necessary to support this injunction. There is nothing in the Civil Code or any legislation in Quebec which could be used to support the argument. This lack of a legal basis is fatal to the argument about 'father's rights'.

(ii) THE FATHER QUA NEXT FRIEND OF THE UNBORN CHILD

Even if the father cannot rely upon any right of his own to seek an injunction, can he act on behalf of the unborn child to enforce *its* rights? The following cases answer that question in the negative.

Paton v Trustees of BPAS [1979] QB 276, [1978] 2 All ER 987 (QBD)

Sir George Baker P: The foetus cannot, in English law, in my view, have any right of its own at least until it is born and has a separate existence from the mother. That permeates the whole of the civil law of this country (I except the criminal law, which is now irrelevant), and is, indeed, the basis of the decisions in those countries where law is founded on the common law, that is to say, in America, Canada, Australia and, I have no doubt in others.

For a long time there was great controversy whether after birth a child could have a right of action in respect of pre-natal injury. The Law Commission considered that and produced a working paper in 1973, followed by a final report, but it was universally accepted, and has since been accepted, that in order to have a right the foetus must be born and be a child. There was only one known possible exception which is referred to in the working paper, an American case, *White v Yup* [(1969) 458 P 2d 617], where the wrongful death of an eight months viable foetus, stillborn as a consequence of injury, led an American court to allow a cause of action, but there can be no doubt, in my view, that in England and Wales, the foetus has no right of action, no right at all, until birth. The succession cases have been mentioned. There is no difference. From conception the child may have succession rights by what has been called a 'fictional construction' but the child must be subsequently born alive. See per Lord Russel of Killowen in *Elliot v Joicey* [[1935] AC 209].

The point was further elaborated by Heilbron J in *C v S* [1988] QB 135, [1987] 1 All ER 1230:

Heilbron J: As to the position of the second plaintiff and his claim that the unborn child has the locus standi to make this application, counsel produced a wealth of authorities from far and wide, some of which he cited. His research and that of his junior was extensive, but it would serve no useful purpose, nor do I propose, to refer to most of them, for they did appear to be somewhat remote from the issue whether or not the unborn child could be a party to this motion. Counsel indeed referred me to *Mullick v Mullick* (1925) LR 52 Ind App 245, a Privy Council case relating to the right of an Indian idol to participate in legal proceedings. The facts of that case were so exceptional and so far removed from anything I have to decide as to be of little assistance.

The authorities, it seems to me, show that a child, after it has been born, and only then in certain circumstances based on his or her having a legal right, may be a party to an action brought with regard to such matters as the right to take, on a will or intestacy, or for damages for injuries suffered before birth. In other words, the claim crystallises on the birth, at which date, but not before, the child attains the status of a legal persona, and thereupon can then exercise that legal right.

This also appears to be the law in a number of Commonwealth countries. In *Medhurst v Medhurst* (1984) 46 OR (2d) 263 Reid J held in the Ontario High Court that an unborn child was not a person and that any rights accorded to the fetus are held contingent on a legal personality being acquired by the fetus on its subsequent birth alive. Nor could its father, the husband in that case, act as the fetus's next friend.

A similar decision was taken in *Dehler v Ottawa Civil Hospital* (1979) 25 OR (2d) 748, quoted with approval by Reid J, and affirmed by the Ontario Court of Appeal (see (1980) 29 OR (2d) 677n).

Having cited *Paton*, the judge continued:

I agree entirely.

In his reply, counsel's final position was summarised in this way: (1) he no longer relied on the numerous succession cases but he wished to retain some reliance on the position of the unborn child in *Thellusson v Woodford* (1799) 4 Ves 227, 31 ER 117; (2) he did not claim that a child had either a right to be born or a right to life in view of the terms of the 1967 Act; but (3) he maintained that the unborn child had a right to be a party because it was the subject of a threatened crime, that is to say that of child destruction. If there was no such threat, then this claim too failed.

In my judgment, there is no basis for the claim that the fetus can be a party, whether or not there is any foundation for the contention with regard to the alleged threatened crime, and I would dismiss the second plaintiff from this suit and the first plaintiff in his capacity as next friend.

The English case law was applied by the Court of Session in the Scottish case of *Kelly v Kelly* 1997 SLT 896.

Kelly v Kelly 1997 SLT 896 (Court of Session (IH)

Lord Justice Clerk (Cullen): The pursuer in this action seeks to have his estranged wife, the first defender, interdicted "from instructing, consenting or submitting to a termination of pregnancy". He also seeks to interdict the Royal Infirmary of Edinburgh NHS Trust, the second defenders, by its servants or agents from carrying out any termination of that pregnancy ...

It is not in dispute that certificates have been given by two medical practitioners in respect of the termination of the first defender's pregnancy and by reference to para (a) of subs (1) [of the Abortion Act 1967]. The pursuer does not seek to challenge these certificates. There was a suggestion before the Lord Ordinary that they had been given on the basis of a false account of the pursuer's past behaviour which the first defender had provided to medical staff of the second defenders. However, at the hearing of the reclaiming motion this matter was not raised again ...

We come now to the main arguments which counsel presented in support of the pursuer's case for interim interdict. In the order in which they were presented they may be broken down into a number of points as follows: (i) An action of damages lay at the instance of a child's guardian, including the father of a legitimate child, in respect of wrongful injury sustained by that child while in utero. (ii) Such an injury was actionable at the instance of the child, acting though his or her guardian, and not at the instance of the mother as an individual. (iii) If such an injury created an actionable wrong, it must be a wrong not merely sounding in damages after the event but also a wrong capable of prevention by interdict in advance of the wrong occurring. (iv) In that connection the wrong which was capable of being interdicted could not be confined to one which was only capable of causing injury to, and not the death of, the child. (v) In regard to what he described as a "peripheral issue", there should be no fiction that injury to a child caused antenatally only occurs in law at the child's birth ...

At this point it may be useful for us to make a number of observations in order to concentrate attention on the core of what is in dispute. First, we have no difficulty in accepting the proposition that the remedy of interdict would be available at the instance of a person or that person's representative to prevent damage being deliberately caused to that person, being damage which, if it occurred, would sound in an award of damages in favour of that person. Secondly, *if* an abortion is an actionable wrong to the foetus as such, we agree that the father would be entitled to take proceedings on behalf of the foetus. However, the critical question is whether the abortion is or can be an actionable wrong.

The decisions on which counsel for the pursuer relied in support of point (i) clearly show that they proceeded on the basis that the child to whom the claim related had been born alive. Thus in *Elliot v Joicey* the birth of the child provided the necessary basis for the fiction that he had been born at an earlier stage. Likewise in *Hamilton v Fife Health Board* it is clear that the right to claim damages in respect of antenatal injury was dependent on the birth of the child who has been injured ...

None of the decisions to which we were referred appear to us to provide support for the view that a foetus has a legal persona, or is otherwise recognised as capable of being vested in personal rights for the protection of which the remedy of interdict may be invoked. Counsel for the pursuer submitted that none of the decisions in jurisdictions outside Scotland had answered the question – if it was legally wrong to damage the foetus, why was it not capable of being interdicted as a wrong? However, that question itself begs a further question, namely, given that a claim can be made by or on behalf of a child who has been born in respect of an injury caused by what was done before his or her birth, does it follow that injury to the foetus as such is actionable before the birth? In our opinion it does not and our answer to that question appears to be supported by the general approach which has been followed in Scotland and in other jurisdictions. Whether it is an actionable wrong to the unborn foetus for an abortion to be performed depends essentially on whether Scots law confers in the foetus a right to continue to exist in the mother's womb. Our conclusion is that Scots law recognises no such right on the foetus. It follows that no person can invoke the power of the court to vindicate such a right.

While it is sufficient for us to reach a conclusion as to the law, there are a number of considerations which, while they form no part of the reasons for our conclusion, tend to support the maintaining of the law as it is. It is sufficient to refer to two of them.

First, to recognise the right of the foetus to continue in the womb would inevitably create a conflict with the policy of the Act to enable women to exercise their right to terminate the pregnancy in accordance with its terms. We note that the case of *Paton* was the subject of an application to the European Commission of Human Rights which declared that the application was inadmissible. In the report of their decision (*Paton v United Kingdom*) the Commission rejected the proposition that art 2 of the Convention recognised an absolute "right to life" of the foetus. At para 19 they observed that this would involve a serious risk to the life of the pregnant woman: "This would mean that the 'unborn life' of the foetus would be regarded as being of a higher value than the life of the pregnant woman". In *Re F (In Utero)* May LJ at p 533 observed that to apply the principle that the interest of the child was to be predominant was bound to create conflict between the existing legal interests of the mother and those of the unborn child; that the enforcement of the wardship order against the mother would pose insuperable difficulties.

Secondly, if the foetus has the right to its own protection which could be vindicated on its behalf by interdict there would be no reason why it should be confined to cases of abortion. If such a right existed it could be used as the basis for a father taking legal action with a view to restraining the mother from some form of activity which was claimed to be harmful to the foetus – such as smoking, and certain sports and occupations. There is plainly room for conflicting views as to what would be adverse to the interests of the foetus.

In these circumstances we are of opinion that the legal proposition on which the purser's case for interdict is based is without foundation.

As will be seen, the court characterised the action as turning on whether the law 'confers on the foetus a right to continue to exist in the mother's womb'. Given the existence of the Abortion Act 1967, the answer could hardly have been an absolute 'yes'. At best it would be a limited one of 'to the extent that the abortion was not lawful under the 1967 Act'. To have concluded otherwise would have flown in the face of Parliament's view as expressed in the 1967 Act. To this extent, the issue would have become whether the abortion was lawful and whether the putative father had standing in civil proceedings to complain about, and prevent, a breach of the criminal law. In fact, the pursuer did not argue this (and see *infra* for a discussion). Also, the court approached the case on the basis that the issue was whether the foetus had *any* legal rights prior to birth. In following *Paton* and *C v S*, the court concluded it did not. The absence of legal status prior to birth and the need for 'live birth' for the law to recognise any claim by a child is undoubtedly the law in England. It is reflected in the pre-natal injury cases (discussed in ch 12) and has been emphasised by the Court of Appeal and House of Lords in a number of cases.

The legal status of the foetus arose in a different context in the case of *Re F (in utero)* [1988] Fam 122, [1988] 2 All ER 193 CA. In this case, a local authority applied to the court to make an unborn child a ward of court to protect it from what the local authority considered to be dangerous behaviour by the mother. The Court of Appeal rejected the local authority's application on two grounds.

Re F (in utero) [1988] Fam 122, [1988] 2 All ER 193 (CA)

May LJ: in the absence of authority I am driven to the conclusion that the court does not have the jurisdiction contended for. I respectfully agree with the dictum from the judgment of Baker P in *Paton v Trustees of BPAS*. I also agree with the comments made by Heilbron J in her judgment in *C v S*.

Secondly, I respectfully agree with the judge below in this case that to accept such jurisdiction and yet to apply the principle that it is the interest of the child which is to be predominant is bound to create conflict between the existing legal interests of the mother and those of the unborn child and that it is most undesirable that this should occur.

Next, I think that there would be insuperable difficulties if one sought to enforce any order in respect of an unborn child against its mother, if that mother failed to comply with the order. I cannot contemplate the court ordering that this should be done by force, nor indeed is it possible to consider with any equanimity that the court should seek to enforce an order by committal....

I have considerable sympathy with the local authority in their position on the facts of the instant case, but I am driven to the conclusion that the judge was right and that the court has no jurisdiction to ward an unborn child. If the courts are to have this jurisdiction in a sensitive situation such as the present, I think that this is a matter for Parliament and not for the courts themselves. I do not think that even if the courts were minded to extend the jurisdiction in this type of case, they could in law or in practice limit this, as counsel suggested, to having a gestation period of not less than 28 weeks.

Balcombe LJ, having cited Baker P's judgment in *Paton* and Heilbron J's judgment in *C v S*, took the view that: 'these decisions only relate directly to the legal rights of the foetus: they are not decisive of the question before us, namely, has the court power to protect a foetus by making it a ward of court?'

Balcombe LJ: Approaching the question as one of principle, in my judgment there is no jurisdiction to make an unborn child a ward of court. Since an unborn child has, ex hypothesis, no existence independent of its mother, the only purpose of extending the jurisdiction to include a foetus is to enable the mother's actions to be controlled. Indeed, that is the purpose of the present application.... Lowe gives examples of how this might operate in practice (96 LQR 29 at 30):

> It would mean, for example, that the mother would be unable to leave the jurisdiction without the court's consent. The court being charged to protect the foetus' welfare would surely have to order the mother to stop smoking, imbibing alcohol and indeed any activity which might be hazardous to the child. Taking it to the extreme were the court to be faced with saving the baby's life or the mother's it would have to protect the baby's.

> Another possibility is that the court might be asked to order that the baby be delivered by Caesarean section: in this connection see Fortin 'Legal Protection for the Unborn Child' (1988) 51 MLR 54 at 81 and the US cases cited in note 16, in particular *Jefferson v Griffin Spalding County Hospital Authority* 274 SE 2d 457 (1981). Whilst I do not accept that the priorities mentioned in the last sentence of the passage cited above are necessarily correct, it would be intolerable to place a judge in the position of having to make such a decision without any guidance as to the principles on which his decision should be based. If the law is to be extended in this manner, so as to impose control over the mother of an unborn child, where such control may be necessary for the benefit of that child, then under our system of parliamentary democracy it is for Parliament to decide whether such controls can be imposed and, if so, subject to what limitations or conditions. Thus, under the Mental Health Act 1983, to which we were also referred, there are elaborate provisions to ensure that persons suffering from mental disorder or other similar conditions are not compulsorily admitted to hospital for assessment or treatment without proper safeguards: see ss 2, 3 and 4 of that Act. If Parliament were to think it appropriate that a pregnant woman should be subject to controls for the benefit of her unborn child, then doubtless it will stipulate the circumstances in which such controls may be applied and the safeguards appropriate for the mother's protection. In such a sensitive field, affecting as it does the liberty of the individual, it is not for the judiciary to extend the law.

Staughton LJ in a short judgment relied on reasoning similar to that of Balcombe LJ. Although only May LJ expressly approved the reasoning in *Paton* and *C v S*, Balcombe LJ did not doubt these cases. He chose instead to base his decision upon grounds of policy. Of course, the policy he identifies is equally valid in cases where a father seeks to prohibit a woman from seeking and obtaining a termination of pregnancy.

In *A-G's Reference (No 3 of 1994)* [1997] 3 All ER 936, the House of Lords was concerned with the liability for murder and manslaughter of an assailant who attacked a pregnant woman causing her unborn child to be born and subsequently die. We will return to this important decision later in this chapter. Here, it suffices to say that both Lord Mustill and Lord Hope in speeches concurred in by the other Law Lords reiterated the common law rule that an unborn child had not legal personality until birth (see especially per Lord Mustill at 948).

The Court of Appeal subsequently relied upon the *A-G's Reference* and a number of other English and overseas authorities (including *Paton* and *C v S*) in *St George's Healthcare NHS Trust v S* (1998) 44 BMLR 160. The context was, as we saw earlier (*supra* ch 6), the legality of medical intervention against the wishes of a pregnant woman for the benefit of her unborn child. One issue that featured large in the arguments in favour of intervention was that the fetus was a legal person and thus justified life saving intervention. As the following extract taken from the judgment of the Court of Appeal shows, the judges rejected the premise and whilst accepting the foetus was 'not nothing', ultimately gave effect to the woman's right to self-determination and thus to refuse treatment.

St George's Healthcare NHS Trust v S, R v Collins, ex parte S (1998) 44 BMLR 160 (CA)

Judge LJ: *The status of the foetus*
...Whatever else it may be, a 36-week foetus is not nothing: if viable, it is not lifeless and it is certainly human. In *A-G's Reference (No 3 of 1994)* [1997] 3 All ER 936, [1998] AC 245

the House of Lords considered the status of the foetus before birth in the context of an allegation of murder arising when a pregnant woman was stabbed and, following premature labour, gave birth to a child who survived for 121 days before dying as a result of the stabbing. The conclusion of the Court of Appeal was that the foetus should be treated as an integral part of the mother in the same way as any other part of her body, such as her foot or her arm. This view was rejected in the House of Lords.

Lord Mustill explained the principle ([1997] 3 All ER 936 at 943, [1998] AC 245 at 255-256):

> There was, of course, an intimate bond between the foetus and the mother, created by the total dependence of the foetus on the protective physical environment furnished by the mother, and on the supply by the mother through the physical linkage between them of the nutrients, oxygen and other substances essential to foetal life and development. The emotional bond between the mother and her unborn child was also of a very special kind. But the relationship was one of bond, not of identity. The mother and the foetus were two distinct organisms living symbolically, not a single organism with two aspects. The mother's leg was part of the mother; the foetus was not … I would, therefore, reject the reasoning which assumes that since (in the eyes of English law) the foetus does not have the attributes which make it a "person" it must be an adjunct of the mother. Eschewing all religious and political debate, I would say that the foetus is neither. It is a unique organism. To apply to such an organism the principles of a law evolved in relation to autonomous beings is bound to mislead.

Lord Hope of Craighead agreed with Lord Mustill ([1997] 3 All ER 936 at 945, [1998] AC 245 at 267):

> It [the Human Fertilisation and Embryology Act 1990] serves to remind us that an embryo is in reality a separate organism from the mother from the moment of its conception. This individuality is retained by it throughout its development until it achieves an independent existence on being born. So the foetus cannot be regarded as an integral part of the mother in the sense indicated by the Court of Appeal, notwithstanding its dependence upon the mother for its survival until birth.

Accordingly, the interests of the foetus cannot be disregarded on the basis that, in refusing treatment which would benefit the foetus, a mother is simply refusing treatment for herself.

In the present case there was no conflict between the interests of the mother and the foetus: no one was faced with the awful dilemma of deciding on one form of treatment which risked one of their lives in order to save the other. Medically, the procedures to be adopted to preserve the mother and her unborn child did not involve a preference for one rather than the other. The crucial issue can be identified by expressing the problem in different ways. If human life is sacred, why is a mother entitled to refuse to undergo treatment if this would preserve the life of the foetus without damaging her own? In the United States, where such treatment has on occasions been forced on an unwilling mother, this question has been described as 'the unborn child's right to live' and 'the State's compelling interest in preserving the life of the foetus' (*Jefferson v Griffin Spalding County Hospital Authority* (1981) 274 SE 2d 457) or 'the potentiality of human life' (*Re Madyyun* (1986) 573 A 2d 1259). In *Winnipeg Child and Family Services (Northwest Area) v G* (1997) 3 BHRC 611, a decision which will need further examination, in his dissenting judgment Major J commented (at 645): 'Where the harm is so great and the temporary remedy so slight, the law is compelled to act … Someone must speak for those who cannot speak for themselves.' That said, however, how can a forced invasion of a competent adult's body against her will, even for the most laudable of motives (the preservation of life), be ordered without irremediably damaging the principle of self-determination? …

Giving the judgment of the court (in *Re MB*), Butler-Sloss LJ said ((1997) 38 BMLR 175 at 186, [1997] 2 FCR 541 at 561):

> A competent woman, who has the capacity to decide, may, for religious reasons, other reasons, for rational or irrational reasons or for no reason at all, chooses not to have medical intervention, even though the consequence may be the death or serious handicap of the child she bears, or her own death. She may refuse to consent to the anaesthesia injection in the full knowledge that her decision may significantly reduce the chance of her unborn child being alive. The foetus up to the moment of birth does not have any separate interests capable of being taken into account when a court has to consider an application for a declaration in respect of a caesarean section operation. The law does not have the jurisdiction to declare that such medical intervention is lawful to protect the interests of the unborn child even at the point of birth.

As the mother in *Re MB* was found not to have been competent, strictly speaking this question did not arise for decision and, as Butler-Sloss LJ herself recognised, the observation was obiter.

It was, however, consistent with the reasoning in a line of authorities where a husband had made an unsuccessful application to prevent an abortion being performed on his wife *(Paton v Trustees of BPAS* [1978] 2 All ER 987, [1979] QB 276 and *C v S* (1987) 2 BMLR 143, [1988] QB 135, and with *Re F (in utero)* [1988] 2 All ER 193 at 200, [1988] Fam 122 at 143 . . .

None of these authorities appears to have been cited either in *Re T* (probably because they were not strictly relevant) or in *Re S (adult: refusal of medical treatment),* referred to earlier and, although obiter, the principle encapsulated in the language used by Butler-Sloss LJ in *Re MB* reflected the existing state of the law.

A number of authorities from outside this jurisdiction were cited in the present case, which were not before the court in *Re MB*. However, it is unnecessary to go beyond the decision of the Supreme Court of Canada given on 31 October 1997 in *Winnipeg Child and Family Services (Northwest Area) v G* (1997) 3 BHRC 611.

The mother was five months pregnant and addicted to glue-sniffing. In consequence, two of her previous children had been born with permanent disability. On the basis of parens patriae jurisdiction (not available in England, nor in view of the judgment of the Supreme Court, in Canada), it was ordered that the mother should be detained for treatment prescribed by the Director of Child and Family Services. The objective was the protection of the unborn child. The Court of Appeal in Manitoba set aside the order. The Supreme Court (by a 7:2 majority) confirmed the decision of the Court of Appeal.

In a detailed judgment, McLachlin J giving the judgment of the majority observed (at 620, 622, 628):

> To permit an unborn child to sue its pregnant mother-to-be would introduce a radically new conception into the law; the unborn child and its mother as separate juristic persons in a mutually separable and antagonistic relation. Such a legal conception, moreover, is belied by the reality of the physical situation; for practical purposes, the unborn child and its mother-to-be are bonded in a union separable only by birth ... "... Judicial intervention ... ignores the basic components of women's fundamental human rights – the right to bodily integrity, and the right to equality, privacy, and dignity ... The fetus' complete physical existence is dependent on the body of the woman. As a result, any intervention to further the fetus' interests will necessarily implicate, and possibly conflict with the mother's interests. Similarly, each choice made by the woman in relation to her body will affect the fetus and potentially attract tort liability" ... the common law does not clothe the courts with power to order the detention of a pregnant woman for the purpose of preventing harm to her unborn child. Nor, given the magnitude of the changes and their potential ramifications, would it be appropriate for the courts to extend their power to make such an order.

Mr Havers invited us to follow the reasoning in the dissenting judgment delivered by Major J. We decline to do so. Quite apart from the problem that the parens patriae jurisdiction on which the dissenting judgment depended has no more validity in this jurisdiction than it does in Canada, the reasoning of the majority coincides with the approach of this court in *Re MB,* reinforced by the observations of Lord Mustill and Lord Hope in *A-G's Reference (No 3 of 1994).* In the later part of his speech Lord Mustill said ([1997] 3 All ER 936 at 948, [1998] AC 245 at 261):

> It is sufficient to say that it is established beyond doubt for the criminal law, as for the civil law *(Burton v Islington Health Authority, De Martell v Merton and Sutton Health Authority* (1992) 10 BMLR 63, [1993] QB 204) that the child en ventre sa mère does not have a distinct human personality, whose extinguishment gives rise to any penalties or liabilities at common law.

In a final observation relevant to the issues in the present case he added ([1997] 3 All ER 936 at 949, [1998] AC 245 at 262):

> The defendant intended to commit and did commit an immediate crime of violence to the mother. He committed no relevant violence to the foetus, which was not a person, either at the time or in the future, and intended no harm to the foetus or to the human person which it would become.

The reasoning which led Lord Hope to conclude that the crime of manslaughter could be committed reinforced this observation. After examining the submission based on the proposition that manslaughter could not be established where the victim of an unlawful violent act was already dead, he continued ([1997] 3 All ER 936 at 957, [1998] AC 245 at 271):

> If the person is already dead, his life is over and no further harm can be done. No act which is done to him now or in the future can be dangerous. The mens rea which a person has when doing an unlawful act to a person who is dead is not that which is required for manslaughter. So also a person who is already dead cannot be within the scope of the mens rea which the defendant has when he does an unlawful and dangerous act to someone who is alive.

He then went on to examine the 'different problem' of the foetus. He said ([1997] 3 All ER 936 at 957, [1998] AC 245 at 271):

> For the foetus, life lies in the future, not the past. It is not sensible to say that it cannot ever be harmed, or that nothing can be done to it which can ever be dangerous. Once it is born it is exposed, like all other living persons, to the risk of injury. It may also carry with it the effects of things done to it before birth which, after birth, may prove to be harmful. It would seem not to be unreasonable therefore, on public policy grounds, to regard the child in this case, when she became a living person, as within the scope of the mens rea which B had when he stabbed her mother before she was born.

At the conclusion of his speech he said ([1997] 3 All ER 936 at 960, [1998] AC 245 at 274):

> The fact that the child whom the mother was carrying at the time was born alive and then died as a result of the stabbing is all that was needed for the offence of manslaughter when the actus reus for that crime was completed by the child's death.

In essence, if the child had not been born alive she could not have been the victim of manslaughter. The language of Lord Hope demonstrates that the concept of being 'born alive', rejected in his dissenting judgment by Major J in *Winnipeg Child and Family Services,* remains undiminished.

In our judgment, while pregnancy increases the personal responsibilities of a woman, it does not diminish her entitlement to decide whether or not to undergo medical treatment. Although human, and protected by the law in a number of different ways set out in the judgment in *Re MB,* an unborn child is not a separate person from its mother. Its need for medical assistance does not prevail over her rights. She is entitled not to be forced to submit to an invasion of her body against her will, whether her own life or that of her unborn child depends on it. Her right is not reduced or diminished merely because her decision to exercise it may appear morally repugnant. The declaration in this case involved the removal of the baby from within the body of her mother under physical compulsion. Unless lawfully justified, this constituted an infringement of the mother's autonomy. Of themselves, the perceived needs of the foetus did not provide the necessary justification.

The position as regards paternal injunctions reached in English law has been reflected in other common law jurisdictions such as Australia *(A-G of Queensland (ex re Kerr) v T* (1983) 46 ALR 275 (High Ct)) and Canada *(Borowski v A-G of Canada* [1987] 4 WWR 385 (Sask CA)). In North America by recourse also to written constitutions, courts have arrived at the same result by holding that an unborn child is not protected by the constitution, for example, the United States of America *(Roe v Wade* 410 US 113 (1973)); Quebec *(Tremblay v Daigle* (1989) 62 DLR (4th) 634 (Can SC): *dubitante* on the Charter of Rights and Freedom in Canada).

Of more importance to us, in the light of the Human Rights Act 1998, is the *Paton* case in which the European Commission considered the status of the unborn child under the European Convention on Human Rights.

Paton v United Kingdom (1980) 3 EHRR 408 (EComHR)

4. The Commission, therefore, has to examine whether this application discloses any appearance of a violation of the provisions of the Convention invoked by the applicant, in particular Articles 2 and 8. It here recalls that the abortion law of High Contracting Parties to the Convention has so far been the subject of several applications under Article 25. The applicants either alleged that the legislation concerned violated the (unborn child's) right to life (Article 2) or they claimed that it constituted an unjustified interference with the

(parents') right to respect for private life (Article 8). Two applications invoking Article 2 were declared inadmissible by the Commission on the ground that the applicants – in the absence of any measure of abortion directly affecting them by reason of a close link with the foetus – could not claim to be 'victims' of the abortion laws complained of. One application, invoking Article 8, was declared admissible by the Commission, in so far as it had been brought by two women. The Commission, and subsequently the Committee of Ministers, concluded that there was no breach of Article 8. That conclusion was based on an interpretation of Article 8 which, *inter alia*, took into account the High Contracting Parties' law on abortion as applied at the time when the Convention entered into force.

5. The question whether the unborn child is covered by Article 2 was expressly left open in Application No 6959/75 and has not yet been considered by the Commission in any other case. It has, however, been the subject of proceedings before the Constitutional Court of Austria, a High Contracting State in which the Convention has the rank of constitutional law. In those proceedings the Austrian Constitutional Court, noting the different view expressed on this question in legal writings, found that Article 2(1), first sentence, interpreted in the context of Article 2, paras (1) and (2), first sentence, interpreted in the context of Article 2, paras (1) and (2), does not cover the unborn life.

6. Article 2(1), first sentence, provides: 'Everyone's right to life shall be protected by law' (in the French text: '*Le droit de toute presonne à la vie est protegé la loî*). The Commission, in its interpretation of this clause and, in particular, of the terms 'everyone' and 'life', has examined the ordinary meaning of the provision in the context both of Article 2 and the Convention as a whole, taking into account the object and purpose of the Convention.

7. The Commission first notes that the term 'everyone' ('toute personne') is not defined in the Convention. It appears in Article 1 and in Section 1, apart from Article 2(1), in Articles 5, 6, 8 to 11 and 13. In nearly all these instances the use of the word is such that it can apply only postnatally. None indicates clearly that it has any possible prenatal application, although such application in a rare case – eg under Article 6(1) – cannot be entirely excluded.

8. As regards, more particularly, Article 2, it contains the following limitations of 'everyone's right to life enounced in the first sentence of paragraph (1):

–   a clause permitting the death penalty in paragraph (1), second sentence: 'No one shall be deprived of his life intentionally save in the execution of a sentence of a court following his conviction of a crime for which this penalty is provided by law'; and

–   the provision, in paragraph (2), that deprivation of life shall not be regarded as inflicted in contravention of Article 2 when it results from 'the use of force which is no more than absolutely necessary' in the following three cases: 'In defence of any person from unlawful violence'; 'in order to effect a lawful arrest or to prevent the escape of a person lawfully detained'; 'in action lawfully taken for the purpose of quelling a riot or insurrection',

All the above limitations, by their nature, concern persons already born and cannot be applied to the foetus.

9. Thus both the general usage of the term 'everyone' ('toute personne') of the Convention (para 7 above) and the context in which this term is employed in article 2 (para 8 above) tend to support the view that it does not include the unborn.

10. The Commission has next examined, in the light of the above considerations, whether the term 'life' in Article 2(1), first sentence, is to be interpreted as covering only the life of persons already born or also the 'unborn life' of the foetus. The Commission notes that the term 'life', too, is not defined in the Convention.

11. It further observes that another, more recent international instrument for the protection of human rights, the American Convention on Human Rights of 1969, contains in Article 4(1), first and second sentences, the following provisions expressly extending the right to life to the unborn:

Every person has the right to have his life respected. This right shall be protected by law and, in general, from the moment of conception.

12. The Commission is aware of the wide divergence of thinking on the question of where life begins. While some believe that it starts already with conception others tend to focus upon the moment of nidation, upon the point that the foetus becomes 'viable', or upon live birth.

13. The German Federal Constitutional Court, when interpreting the provision 'everyone has a right to life' in Article 2(2) of the Basic Law, stated as follows:

Life in the sense of the historical existence of a human individual exists according to established biological and physiological knowledge at least from the 14th day after conception (Nidation, Individuation) ... The process of development beginning from this point is a continuous one so that no sharp divisions or exact distinction between the various stages of development of human life can be made. It does not end at birth: for example, the particular type of consciousness peculiar to the human personality only appears a considerable time after the birth. The protection conferred by Article 2(2) first sentence of the Basic Law can therefore be limited neither to the 'complete' person after birth nor to the foetus capable of independent existence prior to birth. The right to life is guaranteed to everyone who 'lives'; in this context no distinction can be made between the various stages of developing life before or between born and unborn children. 'Everyone' in the meaning of Article 2(2) of the Basic Law is 'every living human being', in other words; every human individual processing life; 'everyone' therefore includes unborn human beings.

14. The Commission also notes that, in a case arising under the Constitution of the United States, the State of Texas argued before the Supreme Court that, in general, life begins at conception and is present throughout pregnancy. The Court, while not resolving the difficult question where life begins, found that, 'with respect to the State's important and legitimate interest in potential life, the "compelling" point is at viability'.

15. The Commission finally recalls the decision of the Austrian Constitutional Court mentioned in paragraph 6 above which, while also given in the framework of constitutional litigation, had to apply, like the Commission in the present case, Article 2 of the European Convention on Human Rights.

16. The Commission considers with the Austrian Constitutional Court that, in interpreting the scope of the term 'life' in Article 2(1), first sentence, of the Convention, particular regard must be had to the context of the Article as a whole. It also observes that the term 'life' may be subject to different interpretations in different legal instruments, depending on the context in which it is used in the instrument concerned.

17. The Commission has already noted, when discussing the meaning of the term 'everyone' in Article 2 (para 8 above), that the limitations, in paragraphs (1) and (2) of the Article, of 'everyone's' right to 'life', by their nature, concern persons already born and cannot be applied to the foetus. The Commission must therefore examine whether Article 2, in the absence of any express limitation concerning the foetus, is to be interpreted:

–   as not covering the foetus at all;
–   as recognising a 'right to life' of the foetus with certain implied limitations; or
–   recognising an absolute 'right to life' of the foetus.

18. The Commission has first considered whether Article 2 is to be construed as recognising an absolute 'right to life' of the foetus and has excluded such an interpretation on the following grounds.

19. The 'life' of the foetus is intimately connected with, and cannot be regarded in isolation from, the life of the pregnant woman. If Article 2 were held to cover the foetus and its protection under this Article were, in the absence of any express limitation, seen as absolute, an abortion would have to be considered as prohibited even where the continuance of the pregnancy would involve a serious risk to the life of the pregnant woman. This would mean that the 'unborn life' of the foetus would be regarded as being of a higher value than the life of the pregnant woman. The 'right to life' of a person already born would thus be considered as subject not only to the express limitations mentioned in paragraph 8 above but also to a further, implied limitation.

20. The Commission finds that such an interpretation would be contrary to the object and purpose of the Convention. It notes that, already at the time of the signature of the Convention (4 November 1950), all High Contracting Parties, with one possible exception, permitted abortion when necessary to save the life of the mother and that, in the meanwhile, the natural law on termination of pregnancy has shown a tendency towards further liberalisation.

21. Having thus excluded, as being incompatible with the object and purpose of the Convention, one of the three different constructions of Article 2 mentioned in paragraph 17 above, the Commission has next considered which of the two remaining interpretations is to be regarded as the correct one – ie whether Article 2 does not cover the foetus at all or whether it recognises a 'right to life' of the foetus with certain implied limitations.

22. The Commission here notes that the abortion complained of was carried out at the initial stage of the pregnancy – the applicant's wife was ten weeks pregnant – under section 1(1)(a) of the Abortion Act 1967 in order to avert the risk of injury to the physical or mental health of the pregnant woman. It follows that, as regards the second of the two remaining interpretations, the Commission is in the present case not concerned with the broad question whether Article 2 recognises a 'right to life' of the foetus during the whole period of the pregnancy but only with the narrower issue whether such a right is to be assumed for the initial stage of the pregnancy. Moreover, as regards implied limitations of a 'right to life' of the foetus at the initial stage, only the limitation protecting the life and health of the pregnant woman, the so-called 'medical indication', is relevant for the

determination of the present case and the question of other possible limitations (ethnic indication, eugenic indication, social indication, time limitation) does not arise.

23. The Commission considers that it is not in these circumstances called upon to decide whether Article 2 does not cover the foetus at all or whether it recognises a 'right to life' of the foetus with implied limitations. It finds that the authorisation, by the United Kingdom authorities, of the abortion complained of is compatible with Article 2(1), first sentence because, if one assumes that this provision applies at this initial stage of the pregnancy, the abortion is covered by an implied limitation, protecting the life and health of the woman at that stage, of the 'right to life' of the foetus.

24. The Commission concludes that the applicant's complaint under Article 2 is inadmissible as being manifestly ill-founded within the meaning of Article 27(2).

Currently, then, the applicability of art 2 of the Convention to the unborn child has yet to be determined. The issue was raised, albeit to be left unresolved, in the following case.

Open Door Counselling and Dublin Well Woman v Ireland (1992) 18 BMLR 1 (ECtHR)

The applicants were, Open Door Counselling Ltd and Dublin Well Woman Centre Ltd, two non-profit-making companies incorporated under Irish law which provided non-directive counselling to woman in and around Dublin in relation to marriage, pregnancy, family planning, procreation and health matters; Bonnie Maher and Ann Downes who worked as trained counsellors for Dublin Well Woman and Mrs X and Ms Mave Geraghty who joined the Dublin Well Woman application as woman of child bearing age. Non-directive counselling was counselling which neither included advice nor was judgmental but a service essentially directed at eliciting from the client her own appreciation to her problem and her own considered choice for its solution. If a woman wanted to consider the abortion option further, arrangements were made by the applicants to refer her to a medical clinic in Great Britain and in certain circumstances travel arrangements were made for the woman. The applicants also inspected clinics in Great Britain to ensure that they operated to the highest standards.

The applicants complained of an injunction issued at the instance of the Society for the Protection of Unborn Children (Ireland) Ltd who commenced a private action which was converted into a relator action brought by the Attorney-General of Ireland. The counselling centres and their servants and agents were –

perpetually restrained from counselling or assisting pregnant women within the jurisdiction of this Court to obtain further advice on abortion or to obtain an abortion.

The Irish Supreme Court upheld the decision but varied the injunction ordering that –

the defendants and each of them, their servants or agents be perpetually restrained from assisting pregnant women within the jurisdiction to travel abroad to obtain abortions by referral to a clinic, by making for them any travel arrangements, or by informing them of the identity and location of and the method of communication with a specified clinic or clinics or otherwise.

In their application lodged with the European Commission of Human Rights on 19 August and 22 September 1988 the applicants complained that the injunction in question constituted an unjustified interference with their right to impart and receive information contrary to art 10 of the European Convention of Human Rights. Open Door, Mrs X and Ms Geraghty further claimed that the restrictions amounted to an interference with their right to respect for private life in breach of art 8 and, in the case of Open Door discrimination contrary to art 14 in conjunction with arts 8 and 10 as pro-life groups were allowed freely to disseminate anti-abortion material.

The Irish government argued both before the Commission and court that the two women of child bearing age were not 'victims' of any such infringement as might have taken place neither were the two counsellors at the counselling centre victims within the scope of art 25 of the convention. Further that, in relation to their applications in respect of arts 8 and 14, Open Door, Ms Maher, Mrs Downes, Mrs X and Mrs Geraghty in respect of all their claims and Open Door and Dublin Well Woman in respect of newly introduced evidence about the impact of the Supreme Court decision on the health of Irish women, the applicants had not exhausted their domestic remedies as required by art 26 of the convention.

The European Commission of Human Rights on 7 March 1991 declared its opinion:

(a) by eight votes to five, that there had been a violation of art 10 in respect of the Supreme Court injunction as it affected the applicant companies and counsellors:

(b) by seven votes to six, that there had been a violation of art 10 in respect of the Supreme Court injunction as it affected Mrs X and Mrs Geraghty;

(c) by seven votes to two with four abstentions, that it was not necessary to examine further the complaints of Mrs X and Mrs Geraghty under art 8;

(d) unanimously that there had been no violation of arts 8 and 14 in respect of Open Door ...

Rolv Ryssdal P:

II. Relevant domestic law and practice concerning protection of the unborn

A. Constitutional protection
28. Article 40, s 3(3) of the Irish Constitution (the Eighth Amendment), which came into force in 1983 following a referendum, reads:

The State acknowledges the right to life of the unborn and, with due regard to the equal right to life of the mother, guarantees in its laws to respect, and, as far as practicable, by its laws to defend and vindicate that right.

This provision has been interpreted by the Supreme Court in the present case, in *Society for the Protection of Unborn Children (Ireland) Ltd v Grogan* [1989] IR 753 and in *A-G v X* 15 BMLR 104 (see para 22-25 above).

B. Statutory protection
29. The statutory prohibition of abortion is contained in ss 58 and 59 of the Offences Against the Person Act 1861. Section 58 provides that:

Every woman, being with child, who, intent to procure her own miscarriage, shall unlawfully administer to herself any poison or other noxious thing or shall unlawfully use any instrument or other means whatsoever with the like intent, and whosoever, with intent to procure the miscarriage of any woman, whether she be or not be with child, shall unlawfully administer to her or cause to be taken by her any poison or other noxious thing, or shall unlawfully use any instrument or other means whatsoever with the like intent, shall be guilty of a felony, and being convicted thereof shall be liable, [to imprisonment for life] ...

Section 59 states that:

Whoever shall unlawfully supply or procure any poison or other noxious thing, or any instrument or thing whatsoever knowing that the same is intended to be unlawfully used or employed with intent to procure the miscarriage of any woman, whether she be or be not with child shall be guilty of a misdemeanour, and being convicted thereof,
...

30. Section 16 of the Censorship of Publications Act 1929 as amended by s 12 of the Health (Family Planning) Act 1979 provides that:

It shall not be lawful for any person, otherwise than under and in accordance with a permit in writing granted to him under this section.

(a) to print or publish or cause or procure to be printed or published, or
(b) to sell or expose, offer or keep for sale or
(c) to distribute, offer or keep for distribution,

any book or periodical publication (whether appearing on the register or prohibited publications or not) which advocates or which might reasonably be supposed to advocate the procurement of abortion or miscarriage or any method, treatment or appliance to be used for the purpose of such procurement.

31. Section 58 of the Civil Liability Act 1961 provides that –

the law relating to wrongs shall apply to an unborn child for his protection in like manner as if the child were born, provided the child is subsequently born alive.

32. Section 10 of the Health (Family Planning) Act 1979 reaffirms the statutory prohibition of abortion and states as follows:

Nothing in this Act shall be construed as authorising – (a) the procuring of abortion, (b) the doing of any other thing the doing of which is prohibited by section 58 or 59 of the Offences Against the Person Act, 1861 (which sections prohibit the administering of drugs or the use of any instruments to procure abortion) or, (c) the sale, importation into the State, manufacture, advertising or display of abortifacients.

C. Case law

33. Apart from the present case and subsequent developments (see paras 11-25 above), reference has been made to the right to life of the unborn in various decisions of the Supreme Court (see, for example, *McGee v A-G* [1974] IR 284, *G v An Bord Uchtala* [1980] IR 32, *Norris v A-G* [1984] IR 36).

34. In *G v An Bord Uchtala* [1980] IR 50 at 69 Walsh J stated as follows:

[A child] has the right to life itself and the right to be guarded against all threats directed to its existence, whether before or after birth … The right to life necessarily implies the right to be born, the right to preserve and defend and to have preserved and defended that life …

35. The Supreme Court has also stated that the courts are the custodians of the fundamental rights set out in the Constitution and that their powers in this regard are as ample as the defence of the Constitution requires (see *State (Quinn) v Ryan* [1965] IR 70). Moreover, an infringement of a constitutional right by an individual may be actionable in damages as a constitutional tort (see *Meskell v Córas Iompair Eireann* [1973] IR 121).

In his judgment in *People v Shaw* [1982] IR 1, Kenny J observed:

When the people enacted the Constitution of 1937, they provided (Article 40, s.3) that the State guaranteed in its laws to respect, and, as far as practicable, by its laws to defend and vindicate the personal rights to the citizen and that the State should in particular, by its laws protect as best it might from unjust attack and in the case of injustice done, vindicate the life, person, good name and property rights of every citizen. I draw attention to the use of the words 'the State'. The obligation to implement this guarantee is imposed not on the Oireachtas only, but on each branch of the State which exercises the powers of legislation, executing and giving judgment on those laws: Article 6. The word 'laws' in Article 40, s.3 is not confined to laws which have been enacted by the Oireachtas, but comprehends the laws made by judges and by ministers of State when they make statutory instruments or regulations.

FINAL SUBMISSIONS MADE TO THE COURT BY THE GOVERNMENT

38. At the public hearing on 24 March 1992 the government maintained in substance the arguments and submissions set out in their memorial whereby they invited the Court to find that there had been no breach of the convention.

AS TO THE LAW…

III. Alleged violation of art 10

53. The applicants alleged that the Supreme Court injunction, restraining them from assisting pregnant woman to travel abroad to obtain abortions, infringed the rights of the corporate applicants and the two counsellors to impart information, as well as the rights of Mrs X and Ms Geraghty to receive information. They confined their complaint to that part of the injunction which concerned the provision of information to pregnant women as opposed to the making of travel arrangements or referral to clinics (see para 20 above). They invoked art 10 which provides:

1. Everyone has the right to freedom of expression. This right shall include freedom to hold opinions and to receive and impart information and ideas without interference by public authority and regardless of frontiers …

2. The exercise of these freedoms, since it carries with it duties and responsibilities, may be subject to such formalities, conditions, restrictions or penalties as are prescribed by law and are necessary in a democratic society, in the interests of national security, territorial integrity or public safety, for the prevention of disorder or crime, for the protection of health or morals, for the protection of the reputation or rights of others, for preventing the disclosure of information received in confidence, or for maintaining the authority and impartiality or the judiciary.

54. In their submissions to the court the government contested these claims and also contended that art 10 should be interpreted against the background of arts 2, 17 and 60 of the Convention the relevant parts of which state:

'Article 2

1. Everyone's right to life shall be protected by law. No one shall be deprived of his life intentionally save in the execution of a sentence of a court following his conviction of a crime for which this penalty is provided by law ...

Article 17

Nothing in [the] Convention may be interpreted as implying for any State, group or person any right to engage in any activity or perform any act aimed at the destruction of any of the rights and freedoms set forth herein or at their limitation to a greater extent than is provided for in the Convention ...

Article 60

Nothing in [the] Convention shall be construed as limiting or derogating from any of the human rights and fundamental freedoms which may be ensured under the laws of any High Contracting Party or under any other agreement to which it is a Party.'

A. Was there an interference with the applicants' rights?

55. The court notes that the government accepted that the injunction interfered with the freedom of the corporate applicants to impart information. Having regard to the scope of the injunction which also restrains the 'servants or agents' of the corporate applicants from assisting 'pregnant women' (see para 20 above), there can be no doubt that there was also an interference with the rights of the applicant counsellors to impart information and with the rights of Mrs X and Ms Geraghty to receive information in the event of being pregnant.

To determine whether such an interference entails a violation of art 10, the court must examine whether or not it was justified under art 10, para 2 by reason of being a restriction 'prescribed by law' which was necessary in a democratic society on one or other of the grounds specified in art 10, para 2....

The restriction was accordingly 'prescribed by law'.

C. Did the restriction have aims that were legitimate under art 10, para 2?

61. The government submitted that the relevant provisions of Irish law are intended for the protection of the rights of others, in this instance the unborn, for the protection of morals and, where appropriate, for the prevention of crime.

62. The applicants disagreed, contending, inter alia, that, in view of the use of the term 'everyone' in art 10, para 1 and throughout the convention, it would be illogical to interpret the 'rights of others' in art 10, para 2 as encompassing the unborn.

63. The court cannot accept that the restrictions at issue pursued the aim of the prevention of crime since, as noted above (see para 59 above), neither the provision of the information in question nor the obtaining of an abortion outside the jurisdiction involved any criminal offence. However, it is evident that the protection afforded under Irish law to the right to life of the unborn is based on profound moral values concerning the nature of life which were reflected in the stance of the majority of the Irish people against abortion as expressed in the 1983 referendum (see para 28 above). The restriction thus pursued the legitimate aim of the protection of morals of which the protection in Ireland of the right to life of the unborn is one aspect. It is not necessary in the light of this conclusion to decide whether the term 'others' under art 10, para 2 extends to the unborn.

D. Was the restriction necessary in a democratic society?

64. The government submitted that the court's approach to the assessment of the 'necessity' of the restraint should be guided by the fact that the protection of the rights of the restraint should be guided by the fact that the protection of the rights of the unborn in Ireland could be derived from arts 2, 17 and 60 of the convention. They further contended that the 'proportionality' test was inadequate where the rights of the unborn were at issue. The court will examine these issues in turn.

1. Article 2

65. The government maintained that the injunction was necessary in a democratic society for the protection of the right to life of the unborn and that art 10 should be interpreted inter alia against the background of art 2 of the convention which, they argued, also protected unborn life. The view that abortion was morally wrong was the deeply held view of the majority of the people in Ireland and it was not the proper function of the court to seek to impose a different viewpoint.

66. The court observes at the outset that in the present case it is not called upon to examine whether a right to abortion is guaranteed under the convention or whether the foetus is encompassed by the right to life as contained in art 2. The applicants have not claimed that the convention contains a right to abortion, as such, their complaint being

limited to that part of the injunction which restricts their freedom to impart and receive information concerning abortion abroad (see para 20 above).

Thus the only issue to be addressed is whether the restrictions on the freedom to impart and receive information contained in the relevant part of the injunction are necessary in a democratic society for the legitimate aim of the protection of morals as explained above (see para 63). It follows from this approach that the government's argument based on art 2 of the convention does not fall to be examined in the present case. On the other hand, the arguments based on arts 17 and 60 fall to be considered below (see para 78 and 79 below)....

3. Articles 17 and 60

78. The government, invoking arts 17 and 60 of the Convention, have submitted that art 10 should not be interpreted in such a manner as to limit, destroy or derogate from the right to life of the unborn which enjoys special protection under Irish law.

79. Without calling into question under the convention the regime of protection of unborn life that exists under Irish law, the court recalls that the injunction did not prevent Irish women from having abortions abroad and that the information is sought to restrain was available from other sources (see para 76 above). Accordingly, it is not the interpretation of art 10 but the position in Ireland as regards the implementation of the law that makes possible the continuance of the current level of abortions obtained by Irish women abroad.

4. Conclusion

80. In the light of the above, the court concludes that the restraint imposed on the applicants from receiving or imparting information was disproportionate to the aims pursued. Accordingly there has been a breach of art 10. ...

For these reasons, the court (1) *Dismisses* by fifteen votes to eight the government's plea that Mrs X and Ms Geraghty cannot claim to be victims of a violation of the convention; (2) *Dismisses* unanimously the remainder of the government's preliminary objections; (3) *Holds* by fifteen votes to eight that there has been a violation of art 10; (4) *Holds* unanimously that it is not necessary to examine the remaining complaints; (5) *Holds* by seventeen votes to six that Ireland is to pay to Dublin Well Woman, within three months, IR £25,000 (twenty-five thousand Irish pounds) in respect of damages; (6) *Holds* unanimously that Ireland is to pay to Open Door and Dublin Well Woman, within three months, in respect of costs and expenses, the sums resulting from the calculation to be made in the remainder of the claims for just satisfaction. ...

Partly dissenting opinion of Judge Mutscher: ...I cannot follow the majority where it finds a violation of the convention in this case on the ground that the interference in question was not 'necessary in a democratic society'. I shall try to explain my position:

(a) The case under review highlights the tension which exists between two of the conditions provided for in the second paras of arts 8 to 11 of the convention, which if satisfied may render permissible interferences with the rights guaranteed under those articles, the conditions in issue here being that of a 'legitimate aim' and that of 'necessity in a democratic society'.

According to my understanding of the position, the criterion of 'necessity' relates exclusively to my understanding of the position, the criterion of 'necessity' relates exclusively to the measures which the state adopts in order to attain the (legitimate) 'aim' pursued; it therefore concerns the appropriateness and proportionality of such measures, but it in no way empowers the European organs to 'weigh up' or to call in question the legitimacy of the aim as such, in other words to inquire into whether it is 'necessary' to seek to attain such an aim (see my opinion, in which I dissented on other grounds, *Dudgeon v United Kingdom* (1981) 4 EHRR 149).

That is why I cannot accept the definition of the term 'necessary' as 'corresponding to a pressing social need', which in fact expressed the intention of the European Court to assess for itself whether it is 'necessary' for a national legislature or a national court to seek to attain an aim which the convention recognises as legitimate. (This definition is, moreover, wholly inappropriate for the assessment of the 'necessity' of a measure which is designed only to protect the legal position or the interests of an individual; but that is not the situation here.)

(b) The aim which the Irish courts were pursuing by prohibiting all 'institutionalised' activity for the provision of information concerning the possibilities of obtaining abortions in the United Kingdom (and the organisation of trips to and stays in British clinics carrying out abortions, although this was not in issue in the present application (see para 53), it was nevertheless, in my view, an inherent aspect of the activities at least of Dublin Well Woman and, in assessing the legitimacy of the aim pursued and the necessity of the alleged interference, it cannot be dissociated from the first aspect, as the contested decision of the Irish courts concerned both aspects jointly) undoubtedly falls under 'the prevention of disorder' and 'the protection of (according to Irish standards) ... morals'. I would mention further 'the protection ... of the rights of others' (of the unborn child and also of his father). Indeed I consider that to reduce the problem of the 'legitimate aim' solely to the protection of morals is to take too narrow a view of the case (see in this connection the very relevant arguments put forward by the Irish Government, para 64 et seq of the present judgment). ...

(c) I shall refrain from expressing an opinion on whether, from the point of view of legislative policy, the prohibition of and the imposition of criminal sanctions for abortion in Ireland can still be regarded as reasonable and desirable, or indeed whether the consequences of such a policy may even be pernicious.

The choice was made by the legislature, following the 1983 referendum. The introduction of art 40.3.30 of the Constitution, protecting the life of unborn children and prohibiting abortion, is merely the legislature's response to the democratically expressed will of the Irish people. I also accept that recently a number of derogations from this absolute prohibition have been allowed. That choice must be respected and is in no way contrary to the requirements of the convention, and it is not even necessary in this connection to have recourse to the notion of the margin of appreciation which the national legislature enjoys in respect of such measures.

(d) If the convention recognises as legitimate the aim (or aims) which the Irish legislation seeks to attain, it is not for the European Court to call in question that aim simply because it may have different ideas in this regard.

It remains only to examine the 'necessity', within the meaning of art 10, para 2, of the measures adopted by the Irish authorities, necessity to be assessed as explained under (a).

In my view those measures can be regarded as appropriate and as consistent with the criterion of proportionality.

There is, however, one more argument which has to be refuted in this discussion: it has been said that, in view of the fact that the women interested in having an abortion abroad were free to obtain the information they required from publications, whose distribution in Ireland was not prohibited, the ban on information services of the kind offered by the two applicant associations must inevitably be an ineffective measure, and thus no longer 'necessary'.

Nevertheless I consider there to be a considerable difference between advertisements in the press, whose circulation in a free country it is virtually impossible to prohibit, and the setting up of specific advice and information services (together with the organisation of trips to and stays in appropriate clinics in the United Kingdom which carry out abortions), so that the contested interference cannot be regarded as ineffective. Indeed it constitutes an entirely appropriate means, although evidently not 100% effective, to attain the (legitimate) aim pursued; in any event, without such a measure there was a risk that the aim in question would not be attained.

In these circumstances I do not see how the 'necessity' of the contested measure can be denied ...

Dissenting Opinion of Judges Pettiti, Russo and Lopes Rocha approved by Judge Bigi (provisional translation) ...It is our opinion that the effect of the criminal provisions in question would have been examined as if it were a typical problem of criminal law. On a general level more account should have been taken of the basis and object of the Irish legislation on the protection of life ...

The provision of the Constitution in issue (art 40.3.30) (which was not in the original text adopted in 1937) was supported by the majority of the population and adopted in a national referendum in 1983. There was a substantial majority – 67% of the votes – opposed to abortion.

This new provision concerns solely the protection and preservation of human life and does not refer to sexual morality, or to public or private morality. The issues of freedom of expression are dealt with in general under art 40.6.10(i) of the Constitution.

The judgments of the Irish courts examined only the question of the protection of human life as provided for in the Constitution

The Constitution applies without distinction to all children in their mother's womb, irrespective of whether they were conceived in our out of wedlock.

It is not correct to regard the adoption of a position on the question of abortion as simply an expression of a view on morality and sexuality.

In our opinion the court has failed to take sufficient account of the reference to 'the rights of others' in art 10 of the convention and of art 60 in relation to the provisions in the Irish legislation which afford a broader protection of rights than the convention.

The court confines itself to an assessment of the moral issues without really replying to the reasoning invoked by the government to explain why they had to conform to the Constitution.

The injunctions of the Irish courts, concerned questions related to the protection of unborn children, mothers and embryos on Irish territory with a view to preventing transactions or services which in Ireland were designed to achieve the contrary by promoting operations abroad, for which preparations were made in Ireland. In the government's opinion, these activities constituted the preparation in Ireland of an abortion carried out abroad. Under Irish law the constitutional obligation is to protect such life while the future mother is in Ireland, which in turn necessitates the adoption of measures that can be implemented on Irish territory; it in no way concerns sexual morality.

It is well known in Ireland that abortions are possible subject to various conditions in other countries and the State has not tried to conceal this information. It is important to remember that in several member states abortion remains in principle a criminal offence, albeit with numerous exceptions and derogations. What is at issue for the Irish state is the setting up in Ireland of links between private clients and clinics carrying out abortions and the doctors at such clinics in the United Kingdom. These links are established with the aim of performing an act which is contrary to the Constitution and to the decisions of the Irish courts which must conform thereto.

Had it been a question of providing persons consulting the organisations concerned with advice on important health matters, the Irish medical and hospital services could have answered the patients' queries and catered for their needs.

The majority accept that the restriction was 'prescribed by law' and that is pursued the 'legitimate aim' of protecting morals, an aspect of which is the protection in Ireland of the unborn child's right to life. They also accept that the latter protection, recognised under Irish law, is based on moral values relating to the nature of life which are reflected in the attitude adopted by the majority of the Irish people.

It was merely considerations relating to the *necessity* and the *proportionality* of the injunctions concerning the activity of the applicant agencies which led the majority to conclude that there had been a violation of art 10 of the convention; in other words they reached the conclusion that the restraints imposed are too broad and disproportionate.

In our view, the restrictions were justified and, in any event, did not overstep the bounds of what was permissible. It was by any standards a minimal interference with the right to freedom of expression – concerning the aspect of that freedom relating to the communication and receipt of information – aimed as securing the primacy of values such as the right to life of the unborn child in accordance with the principles of the Irish legal system, which cannot be criticised on the basis of different principles applied in other legal systems ...

In conclusion, we consider that the decisions of the Irish courts did not violate art 10 of the convention. ...

Separate opinion of Judge De Meyer: ... 4. It is true, equally, that the applicant associations were restrained from communicating information which was intended to help pregnant women obtain abortions outside Ireland, and thus evade the restrictions resulting from the prohibition and punishment of abortion in Ireland itself and, in particular, violate the right of unborn children to be born.

In this context, it is indeed essentially that right which is as stake, much more so than the protection of morals, and this therefore also raises serious problems from the point of view of arts 2, 17 and 60 of the European Convention on Human Rights. ...

Dissenting opinion of Judge Blayney: ... In the circumstances, the injunction could not in my opinion be said to be disproportionate. It was the only measure possible to uphold art 40.3.30. There was no other course that the court could have taken. It was inconceivable that it should refuse to grant an injunction since this would have amounted to an abdication of its duty to protect the rights of the unborn and would have fatally undermined the moral values enshrined in art 40.3.30.

I am also of the opinion that our court is precluded by art 60 of the European Convention of Human Rights from finding that there has been a breach of art 10.

Article 60 provides as follows:

Nothing in this Convention shall be construed as limiting or derogating from any of the human rights and fundamental freedoms which may be ensured under the laws of any High Contracting Party or under any other agreement to which it is a Party.

The right of the unborn to be born is clearly a human right and it is guaranteed in Ireland by art 40.3.30 of the Constitution. Under art 60 nothing in the convention is to be construed as limiting or derogating from that right. If art 10 is to be construed as entitling the applicants to give information to pregnant women so as to assist them to have abortions in England, then in my opinion it is being construed so as to derogate from the human rights of the unborn. In his judgment in the Supreme Court in *A-G at the relation of the Society for The Protection of Unborn Children (Ireland) v Open Door Ltd* (1988) IR 593 at 624, Finlay CJ said:

> I am satisfied beyond doubt that having regard to the admitted facts the defendants were assisting in the ultimate destruction of the life of the unborn by abortion in that they were helping the pregnant woman who had decided upon that option to get in touch with a clinic in Great Britain which would provide the service of abortion.
>
> The decision that the injunction constituted a breach of art 10 amounts to interpreting that article as permitting information to be given which clearly derogates from the rights of the unborn since it assists in their destruction. In my opinion art 60 precludes such a construction.
>
> The applicants in their submissions placed reliance on the fact that the information provided by them was available elsewhere, and that the injunction did not prevent Irish women from continuing to have abortions abroad. In my opinion neither of these matters has any relevance to whether or not art 60 applies. The sole issue is whether a finding that the injunction constitutes a breach of art 10 amounts to interpreting that article as derogating from the human rights of the unborn as guaranteed by the Constitution, and in my opinion it does. For this reason also, I consider that it is not possible to conclude that there has been a breach of art 10.

The reasoning of the majority and the multiple dissents and concurrences is complex (see for discussion, M Fox and T Murphy (1992) 19 JLS 454 and R Pearce (1993) 6 JSWFL 386). The status of the unborn child under the Convention, in particular, art 2 was not directly raised. The majority showed no appetite for bringing unborn children within the Convention. Some of the dissents did, however, consider that the phrase 'for the protection of others' in art 10(2) could include action taken to protect the life of the unborn child.

The importance of this point is that the English courts may, in the future, be asked to interpret the scope of the Abortion Act 1967 consistent with the Convention by virtue of the Human Rights Act 1998 (see *supra*, ch 1).

If in a subsequent case it was decided that the unborn child is, in fact, protected by art 2, this could have a variety of effects on English law. Any effect would first depend upon the point at which the court found the right to life accrued to the unborn child, for example, at conception or at the point of viability. It would also depend (even if the right had occurred) on what weight the court was prepared to give to the conflicting right to life of the pregnant woman. In our view, the court could only adopt one approach. In any apparent clash between the rights of the mother and of the unborn child, it must necessarily prefer one of these two (there is simply no room for compromise). It would undoubtedly give precedence to the right to life of the pregnant woman (see eg *A-G v X* [1992] IR 1 (Ir Sup Ct) – right to life of pregnant woman outweighed that of the unborn child under the Irish Constitution). The woman would however, have to show that a compelling circumstance existed to justify her right gaining precedence. We would adopt the language of Beetz J (with whom Estey J agreed) in *Morgentaler v R* (1988) 44 DLR (4th) 385 (Can SC) at 420-1, that 'the interest in the life or health of the pregnant woman takes precedence over the interest in prohibiting abortions, including the interest of the state in the protection of the foetus, when the continuance of the pregnancy of each female person would or would be likely to endanger her life or health ... .' On this view, most of s 1 of the Abortion Act would survive a challenge based upon the rights of the unborn child. On the other hand, terminations of pregnancy justified on the basis of the risk to the health of existing children of the pregnant woman's family would not satisfy this standard of review under the Convention. Similarly, terminations performed under s 1(1)(d) because of foetal handicap would infringe the Convention. A doctor who sought to justify termination in these circumstances would have to show that it fell within s 1(1)(a) on the basis of risk to the pregnant woman's health (on which see the approach of Kirby P in *CES v Superclinics (Aust) Pty Ltd* (1995) 38 NSWLR 47 (NSW CA) and see also *Veivers v Connolly* (1995) 2 Qd R 326 (Qld Sup Ct)).

It may be that the mothers right to make an abortion decision would be more widely protected under article 8 of the Convention as part of her 'right to respect, for [her] private and family life. Certainly, her right would be engaged as part of her 'physical and moral integrity' (see, *Costello-Roberts v UK* 19 EHRR 112, ECtHR, 25 March 1993). Article 8(2) would permit an infringement if 'in accordance with law' and which 'is necessary in a democratic society ... for the protection of ... morals, or for the protection of the rights and freedoms of others'. Here, therefore, the argument goes full circle back to the 'rights' of the unborn child and the significant 'margin of appreciation' conceded to the Legislature (see generally, D Feldman *Civil Liberties and Human Rights in England and Wales* (1993) at pp 105-115).

(iii) THE FATHER QUA PROTECTOR OF THE PUBLIC INTEREST

If it be correct that in law no rights vest in the father or the unborn child, can a father claim to prevent an abortion as protector or the public interest? The problem is one of *locus standi*. The question can only arise if the father's claim is that the abortion, if carried out, would be a criminal offence.

League for Life in Manitoba Inc v Morgentaler [1985] 4 WWR 633 (Manitoba Queen's Bench)

Kroft J: The plaintiffs, the League for Life in Manitoba Inc and Patricia Frances Soenen, are proponents of the pro-life position. I do not question that their concern is honest and deeply felt. They have, through the civil process, sued Dr Morgentaler as well as the owners and lessees of the clinic from which he operates in the city of Winnipeg, seeking first a temporary and ultimately a permanent injunction restraining them from procuring or allowing the procuring of the miscarriage of female persons in contravention of s 251 of the Criminal Code.

The right of an Attorney-General as chief law officer of the Crown to bring proceedings for enforcement of the criminal law, either on his own initiative or ex relation at the initiative of others, is of course not at issue (although, as will be indicated, the use of the civil injunction, even by an Attorney-General, is open to some question). The position of a citizen or group whose interests and status are no different than any other member of the general public is much different and much more difficult. The motion to strike out the statement of claim is first and foremost an attack on the status of the plaintiffs. Simply put, the defendants say that on the face of the material filed the plaintiffs as private citizens have no standing, and that without standing they have no right to seek injunctive or any other relief.

The question of standing in the present proceedings has two components. Firstly, it must be determined whether the nature of the interest claimed by these particular plaintiffs gives them any right to be parties to these proceedings. Secondly, it must be decided if the statement of claim reveals a justiciable or triable issue. Unless there is an interest which the court recognises, and an issue to be tried, then the defendants are correct in saying that the statement of claim and the entire proceedings should be struck out ...

There is no difficulty in defining the rules that have traditionally been applied to determine whether a citizen on his own, has sufficient standing and sufficient cause of action to permit him, through a private action, to enforce the public criminal law. Those rules were acknowledged even by counsel for the plaintiff to be quite stringent. There has, however, in recent years, been a trend toward relaxation or liberalisation. Notwithstanding the efforts of Lord Denning, the trend is less marked in Britain than in Canada, probably because we are a federal state, and now because we have the Charter of Rights.

The argument advanced on behalf of the plaintiffs was that the rules in Canada have been, by court decisions, sufficiently changed to justify a conclusion that they have standing and have a good cause of action.

When I speak of traditional rules I do not imply that they are outmoded. They have received recognition by courts of the highest level in Britain, in Canada, and elsewhere. For convenience I will list what I think to be an accurate statement of the criteria to be considered when a member of the public claims that there is a justiciable issue to be tried, and that he is entitled to a restraining order to prevent an anticipated breach of the criminal law.

1. The criminal law creates public not private rights.
2. Public rights can, in appropriate circumstances, be asserted in a civil action by the Attorney-General, as the Crown officer who represents the public; or alternatively, by an individual acting with the consent of the Attorney-General in a relator action.
3. A private individual may sue in his own name in respect of public rights if he can show that he faces the infringement of some personal right, or that he will suffer special and personal damages.

These principles were recognised in 1977 by the House of Lords in the *Gouriet* case [*Gouriet v Union of Post Office Workers* [1978] AC 435] ...

The *Gouriet* decision was one in which the British Postal Union threatened to break the law to impose an embargo on mail to South Africa. The Attorney-General refused to take action and Mr Gouriet proceeded on his own. At the Appeal Court level all three judges would have granted an interim injunction while the justiciable issue was being determined; that is, while a declaration with respect to the role of the Attorney-General was under consideration. Lord Denning, in a far more forceful way than his colleagues, was prepared to say that when an Attorney-General refuses to take action, or delays in respect to a request for a relator action, the court, in an appropriate case, can in effect overrule him, thereby giving the right to any citizen to come directly to court and ask that the criminal law be enforced. That view was explicitly overruled by the House of Lords; and it is the House of Lords which has been followed in the Canadian cases which I mentioned.

It should be noted as well that there are important distinctions between *Gouriet* and the case before us now, so that even the Court of Appeal decisions might not necessarily be applicable here. To begin with, the Attorney-General of England has refused to lay charges. In our case two sets of criminal charges have already been laid. Secondly, the majority of the English Court of Appeal, although allowing the interim injunction, did so because there was a separate issue to be tried. There is no such issue here.

Procuring an abortion contrary to s 251 of the Code is a crime in Canada. It has been declared to be such by Parliament and does not require my declaration to confirm it.

It is interesting to note that when the *Island Records* case [[1978] Ch 122] ... came before the court in England, one year after *Gouriet*, the same Lord Denning acknowledged the general law to be as I have stated it. He held that a private citizen can enforce the criminal law only where the criminal act is both an offence against the public at large, and also where, at the same time, it causes or threatens to cause special damage to a private individual. No such allegation appears in the statement of claim of the League and Ms Soenen. ...

I have given serious consideration and weight to the arguments advanced on behalf of the plaintiffs. Nonetheless, I have reached the conclusion that they do not have the status or standing to maintain their action.

In *Paton* (*supra*), Sir George Baker P referred to this point:

The law relating to injunctions has been considered recently in the House of Lords, in *Gouriet v Union of Post Office Workers*. Many passages from their Lordships' speeches have been cited. I do not propose to go through them because it is now as clear as possible that there must be, first, a legal right in an individual to found an injunction and, second, that the enforcement of the criminal law is a matter for the authorities and for the Attorney-General. As counsel for the husband concedes, any process for the enforcement of the criminal law in a civil suit must be used with great caution, if at all. The private individual may have the right only if his right is greater than the public right, that is to say, that he would suffer personally and more than the general public right, that is to say, that he would suffer personally and more than the general public unless he could restrain this offence. That proposition is not accepted by counsel for the first defendants or by counsel for the wife, and in any event it is now suggested that the proposed abortion on the wife will be other than lawful. So, it is not necessary for me to decide that question or to consider *Gouriet v Union of Post Office Workers* further.

(See also *Wall v Livingston* [1982] 1 NZLR 734 (NZCA), where it was held that a doctor who was not treating the pregnant woman lacked *locus standi* to challenge the decision of two consultants to authorise an abortion on a teenage girl).

Given that the whole force of the argument in *C v S* (*supra*) was the alleged illegality of the proposed abortion, how was it that the court was prepared to hear the plaintiff's argument? All Heilbron J had to say to the matter was:

... I have not thought it necessary to add to this already long judgment by considering another hurdle that counsel might have encountered by reason of the decisions with regard to a private individual seeking to prevent the commission of an offence by way of an injunction, following the *Gouriet* line of cases.

It is intriguing that the Court of Appeal felt inclined to hear argument (and dispose of the case) on the assumption that the father had *locus standi* with not a single reference being made to *Gouriet*. Perhaps it was one of those occasions when the Court of Appeal was tempted to issue a declaratory judgment without wishing to appear to do so?

(b) To be consulted

There is no English law which precisely covers the question of whether a woman can be obliged in law to consult another, for example, her husband or the father of the child before undergoing an abortion.

In the United States the issue came before the Supreme Court in 1992. Necessarily the context was one of the constitutionality of legislation in Pennsylvania which imposed a duty upon a woman to provide evidence that she had consulted her husband. The judges rehearse arguments which would be relevant in determining whether English law *should* impose a duty to consult and may well be relevant under the Human Rights Act 1998.

Planned Parenthood of SE Pennsylvania v Casey (1992) 112 S Ct 2791 (US Sup Ct)

At issue were five provisions of the Pennsylvania Abortion Control Act of 1982: s 3205, which required that a woman seeking an abortion give her informed consent prior to the procedure, and specified that she be provided with certain information at least 24 hours before the abortion is performed; s 3206, which mandated the informed consent of one parent for a minor to obtain an abortion, but provided a judicial bypass procedure; s 3209, which commanded that, unless certain exceptions apply, a married woman seeking an abortion must sign a statement indicating that she has notified her husband; s 3203, which defined a 'medical emergency' that will excuse compliance with the foregoing requirements; and ss 3207(b), 3214(a), and 3214(f), which imposed certain reporting requirements on facilities providing abortion services. Before any of the provisions took effect, the petitioners, five abortion clinics and a physician representing himself and a class of doctors who provide abortion services, brought this suit seeking a declaratory judgment that each of the provisions was unconstitutional on its face, as well as injunctive relief. The District Court held all the provisions unconstitutional and permanently enjoined their enforcement. The Court of Appeals affirmed in part and reversed in part, striking down the husband's notification provision but upholding the others.

O'Connor, Kennedy and Souter JJ: Some guiding principles should emerge. What is at stake is the woman's right to make the ultimate decision, not a right to be insulted by all others in doing so. Regulations which do no more than create a structural mechanism by which the State, or the parent or guardian of a minor, may express profound respect for the life of the unborn are permitted, if they are not a substantial obstacle to the woman's excise of the right to choose. See infra ... (addressing Pennsylvania's parental consent requirement). Unless it has that effect on her right of choice, a state measure designed to persuade her to choose childbirth over abortion will be upheld if reasonably related to that goal. Regulations designed to foster the health of a woman seeking an abortion are valid if they do not constitute an undue burden.

Even when jurists reason from shared premises, some disagreement is inevitable. Compare *Hodgson* 497 US ... (opinion of Kennedy J) with id ... (O'Connor J, concurring in part and concurring in judgment in part). That is to be expected in the application of any legal standard which must accommodate life's complexity. We do not expect it to be otherwise with respect to the undue burden standard. We give this summary:

(a) To protect the central right recognized by *Roe v Wade* [(1973) 410 US 113] while at the same time accommodating the State's profound interest in potential life, we will employ the undue burden analysis as explained in this opinion. An undue burden exists, and therefore a provision of law is invalid, if its purpose or effect is to place a substantial obstacle in the path of a woman seeking an abortion before the fetus attains viability.

(b) We reject the rigid trimester framework of *Roe v Wade*. To promote the State's profound interest in potential life, throughout pregnancy the State may take measures to ensure that the woman's choice is informed, and measures designed to advance this interest will not be invalidated as long as their purpose is to persuade the woman to choose childbirth over abortion. These measures must not be an undue burden on the right.

(c) As with any medical procedure, the State may enact regulations to further the health or safety of a woman seeking an abortion. Unnecessary health regulations that have the purpose or effect of presenting a substantial obstacle to a woman seeking an abortion impose an undue burden on the right.

(d) Our adoption of the undue burden analysis does not disturb the central holding of *Roe v Wade*, and we reaffirm that holding. Regardless of whether exceptions are made for particular circumstances, a State may not prohibit any woman from making the ultimate decision to terminate her pregnancy before viability.

(e) We also reaffirm Roe's holding that 'subsequent to viability, the State in promoting its interest in the potentiality of human life may, if it chooses, regulate, and even proscribe, abortion except where it is necessary, in appropriate medical judgment, for the preservation of the life or health of the mother' *Roe v Wade* 410 US, at 164-165.

These principles control our assessment of the Pennsylvania statute, and we now turn to the issue of the validity of its challenged provisions. ...

Section 3209 of Pennsylvania's abortion law provides, except in cases of medical emergency, that no physician shall perform an abortion on a married woman without receiving a signed statement from the woman that she has notified her spouse that she is about to undergo an abortion. The woman has the option of providing an alternative signed statement certifying that her husband is not the man who impregnated her; that her husband could not be located; that the pregnancy is the result of spousal sexual assault which she has reported; or that the woman believes that notifying her husband will cause him or someone else to inflict bodily injury upon her. A physician who performs an abortion on a married woman without receiving the appropriate signed statement will have his or her license revoked, and is liable to the husband for damages.

The District Court heard the testimony of numerous expert witnesses, and made detailed findings of fact regarding the effect of this statute:

> 273. The vast majority of women consult their husbands prior to deciding to terminate their pregnancy. ...
> 279. The 'bodily injury' exception could not be invoked by a married woman whose husband, if notified, would, in her reasonable belief, threaten to (a) publicize her intent to have an abortion to family, friends or acquaintances; (b) retaliate against her in future child custody or divorce proceedings; (c) inflict psychological intimidation or emotional harm upon her, her children or other persons; (d) inflict bodily harm on other persons such as children, family members or other loved ones; or (e) use his control over finances to deprive of necessary monies for herself or her children ...
> 281. Studies reveal that family violence occurs in two million families in the United States. This figure, however, is a conservative one that substantially understates (because battering is usually not reported until it reaches life-threatening proportions) the actual number of families affected by domestic violence. In fact, researchers estimate that one of every two women will be battered at some time in their life. ...
> 282. A wife may not elect to notify her husband of her intention to have an abortion for variety of reasons, including the husband's illness, concern about her own health, the imminent failure of the marriage, or the husband's absolute opposition to the abortion. ...
> 283. The required filing of the spousal consent form would require plaintiff-clinics to change their counselling procedures and force women to reveal their most intimate decision-making on pain of criminal sanctions. The confidentiality of these revelations could not be guaranteed, since the woman's records are not immune from subpoena. ...
> 284. Women of all class levels, education backgrounds, and racial, ethnic and religious groups are battered. ...
> 285. Wife-battering or abuse can take on many physical and psychological forms. The nature and scope of the battering can cover a broad range of actions and be gruesome and torturous. ...
> 286. Married women, victims of battering, have been killed in Pennsylvania and throughout the United States. ...
> 287. Battering can often involve a substantial amount of sexual abuse, including marital rape and sexual mutilation. ...

288. In a domestic abuse situation, it is common for the battering husband to also abuse the children in an attempt to coerce the wife. ...

289. Mere notification of pregnancy is frequently a flashpoint for battering and violence within the family. The number of battering incidents is high during the pregnancy and often the worst abuse can be associated with pregnancy. ... The battering husband may deny parentage and use the pregnancy as an excuse for abuse. ...

290. Secrecy typically shrouds abusive families. Family members are instructed not to tell anyone, especially police or doctors, about the abuse and violence. Battering husbands often threaten their wives or her children with further abuse if she tells an outsider of the violence and tells her that nobody will believe her. A battered woman, therefore, is highly unlikely to disclose the violence against her for fear of retaliation by the abuser. ...

291. Even when confronted directly by medical personnel or other helping professionals, battered women often will not admit to the battering because they have not admitted to themselves that they are battered. ...

294. A woman in a shelter or a safe house unknown to her husband is not 'reasonably likely' to have bodily harm inflicted upon her by her batterer, however her attempt to notify her husband pursuant to section 3209 could accidentally disclose her whereabouts to her husband. Her fear of future ramifications would be realistic under the circumstances.

295. Marital rape is rarely discussed with others or reported to law enforcement authorities, and of those reported only few are prosecuted. ...

296. It is common for battered women to have sexual intercourse with their husbands to avoid being battered. While this type of coercive sexual activity would be spousal sexual assault as defined by the Act, many women may not consider it to be so and others would fear disbelief. ...

297. The marital rape exception to section 3209 cannot be claimed by women who are victims of coercive sexual behavior other than penetration. The 90-day reporting requirement of the spousal sexual assault statute, 18 Pa Con Stat Ann s 3218(c), further narrows the class of sexually abused wives who can claim the exception, since many of these women may be psychologically unable to discuss or report the rape for several years after the incident. ...

298. Because of the nature of the battering relationship, battered women are unlikely to avail themselves of the exceptions to section 3209 of the Act, regardless of whether the section applies to them. (744 F Supp, at 1360-1362.)

These findings are supported by studies of domestic violence. The American Medical Association (AMA) has published a summary of the recent research in this field, which indicates that in an average 12-month period in this country, approximately two million women are the victims of severe assaults by their male partners. In a 1985 survey, women reported that nearly one of every eight husbands had assaulted their wives during the past year. The AMA views these figures as 'marked underestimates', because the nature of these incidents discourages women from reporting them, and because surveys typically exclude the very poor, those who do not speak English well, and women who are homeless or in institutions or hospitals when the survey is conducted. According to the AMA, '[r]esearchers on family violence agree that the true incidence of violence is probably double the above estimates; or four million severely assaulted women per year. Studies suggest that from one-fifth to one-third of all women will be physically assaulted by a partner or ex-partner during their lifetime.' AMA Council on Scientific Affairs, Violence Against Women 7 (1991) (emphasis in original). Thus on an average day in the United States, nearly 11,000 women are severely assaulted by their male partners. Many of these incidents involve sexual assault. Id, at 3-4; Shields & Hanneke, Battered Wives' Reactions to Marital Rape, in The Dark Side of Families: Current Family Violence Research 131, 144 (D Finkelhor, R Gelles, G Hataling, & M Straus eds 1983). In families where wife-beating takes place, moreover, child abuse is often present as well (Violence Against Women, supra at 12).

Other studies fill in the rest of this troubling picture. Physical violence is only the most visible form of abuse. Psychological abuse, particularly forced social and economic isolation of women, is also common (L Walker, The Battered Women Syndrome 27-28 (1984)). Many victims of domestic violence remain with their abusers, perhaps because they perceive no superior alternative (Herbert, Silver, & Ellard, Coping with an Abusive Relationship: I. How and Why do Women Stay? 53 J Marriage & the Family 311 (1991)). Many abused women who find temporary refuge in shelters return to their husbands, in large part because they have no other source of income (Aguirre, Why Do They Return? Abused Wives in Shelters, 30 J Nat Assn of Social Workers 350, 352 (1985)). Returning to one's abuser can be dangerous. Recent Federal Bureau of Investigation statistics disclose that 8.8% of all homicide victims in the United States, 1976-86, 79 Am J Public Health 595 (1989)). Thirty percent of female homicide victims are killed by their male partners (Domestic Violence: Terrorism in the Home, Hearing before the Subcommittee on Children, Family, Drugs and Alcoholism of the Senate Committee on Labor and Human Resources, 101st Cong, 2d Sess, 3 (1990)).

The limited research that has been conducted with respect to notifying one's husband about an abortion, although involving samples too small to be representative, also supports the District Court's findings of fact. The vast majority of women notify their male partners of their decision to obtain an abortion. In many cases in which married women do not notify their husbands, the pregnancy is the result of an extramarital affair. Where the husband is the father, the primary reason women do not notify their husbands is that the husband and wife are experiencing marital difficulties, often accompanied by incidents of violence (Ryan & Plutzer, When Married Women Have Abortions: Spousal Notification and Marital Interaction 51 J Marriage & the Family 41, 44 (1989)).

This information and the District Court's findings reinforce what common sense would suggest. In well-functioning marriages, spouses discuss important intimate decisions such as whether to bear a child. But there are millions of women in this country who are the victims of regular physical and psychological abuse at the hands of their husbands. Should these women become pregnant, they may have very good reasons for not wishing to inform their husbands of their decision to obtain an abortion. Many may have justifiable fears of physical abuse, but may be no less fearful of the consequences of reporting prior abuse to the Commonwealth of Pennsylvania. Many may have a reasonable fear that notifying their husbands will provoke further instances of child abuse; these women are not exempt from s 3209's notification requirement. Many may fear devastating forms of psychological abuse from their husbands, including verbal harassment, threats of future violence, the destruction of possessions, physical confinement to the home, the withdrawal of financial support and friends. These methods of psychological abuse may act as even more of a deterrent to notification than the possibility of physical violence, but women who are the victims of the abuse are not exempt from s 3209's notification requirement. And many women who are pregnant as a result of sexual assaults by their husbands will be unable to avail themselves of the exception for spousal sexual assault, s 3209(b)(3), because the exception requires that the woman have notified law enforcement authorities within 90 days of the assault, and her husband be notified of her report once an investigation begins, s 3218(c). If anything in this field is certain, it is that victims of spousal sexual assault are extremely reluctant to report the abuse to the government; hence, a great many spousal rape victims will not be exempt from the notification requirement imposed by s 3209.

The spousal notification requirement is thus likely to prevent a significant number of women from obtaining an abortion. It does not merely make abortions a little more difficult or expensive to obtain; for many women, it will impose a substantial obstacle. We must not blind ourselves to the fact that the significant number of women who fear for their safety and the safety of their children are likely to be deterred from procuring an abortion as surely as if the Commonwealth had outlawed abortion in all cases.

Respondents attempt to avoid the conclusion that s 3209 is invalid by pointing out that it imposes almost no burden at all for the vast majority of women seeking abortions. They begin by noting that only about 20 percent of the women who obtain abortions are married. They then note that of these women about 95 percent notify their husbands of their own violation. Thus, respondents argue, the effects of s 3209 are felt by only one percent of the women who obtain abortions. Respondents argue that since some of these women will be able to notify their husbands without adverse consequences or will qualify for one of the exceptions, the statute affects fewer than one percent of women seeking abortions. For this reason, it is asserted, the statute cannot be invalid on its face. See Brief for Respondents 83-86. We disagree with respondents' basic method of analysis.

The analysis does not end with the one percent of women upon whom the statute operates; it begins there. Legislation is measured for consistency with the Constitution by its impact on those whose conduct it affects. For example, we would not say that a law which requires a newspaper to print a candidate's reply to an unfavourable editorial is valid on its face because most newspapers would adopt the policy even absent the law. See *Miami Herald Publishing Co v Tornillo* 418 US 241 (1974). The proper focus of constitutional inquiry is the group for whom the law is a restriction, not the group for whom the law is irrelevant.

Respondents' argument itself gives implicit recognition to this principle, at one of its critical points. Respondents speak of the one percent of women seeking abortions who are married and would choose not to notify their husbands of their plans. By selecting as the controlling class women who wish to obtain abortions, rather than all women or all pregnant women, respondents in effect concede that s 3209 must be judged by reference to those for whom it is an actual rather than irrelevant restriction. Of course, as we have said, s 3209's real target is narrower even than the class of women seeking abortions identified by the

State: it is married women seeking abortions who do not wish to notify husbands of their intentions and who do not qualify for one of the statutory exceptions to the notice requirement. The unfortunate yet persisting conditions we document above will mean that in a large fraction of the cases in which s 3209 is relevant, it will operate as a substantial obstacle to a woman's choice to undergo an abortion. It is an undue burden, and therefore invalid ... We recognize that a husband has a 'deep and proper concern and interest ... in his wife's pregnancy and in the growth and development of the fetus she is carrying.' *Danforth,* supra, at 69. With regard to the children he has fathered and raised, the Court has recognized his 'congnizable and substantial' interest in their custody. *Stanley v Illinois* 405 US 645, 651-652 (1972); see also *Quilloin v Walcott* 434 US 246 (1978); *Caban v Mohammed* 441 US 380 (1979); *Lehr v Robertson* 463 US 248 (1983). If this case concerned a State's ability to require the mother to notify the father before taking some action with respect to a living child raised by both, therefore, it would be reasonable to conclude as a general matter that the father's interest in the welfare of the child and the mother's interest are equal.

Before birth, however, the issue takes on a very difficult case. It is an inescapable biological fact that state regulation with respect to the child a woman is carrying will have a far greater impact on the mother's liberty than on the father's. The effect of state regulation with respect to the child a woman is carrying will have a far greater impact on the mother's protected liberty is doubly deserving of scrutiny in such a case, as the State has touched not only upon the private sphere of the family but upon the very bodily integrity of the pregnant woman. Cf *Cruzan v Director, Missouri Dept of Health* 497 US, at 281. The Court has held that 'when the wife and the husband disagree on this decision, the view of only one of the two marriage partners can prevail. Inasmuch as it is the woman who physically bears the child and who is the more directly and immediately affected by the pregnancy, as between the two, the balance weighs in her favour.' *Danforth,* supra, at 71. This conclusion rests upon the basic nature of marriage and the nature of our Constitution: '[T]he marital couple is not an independent entity with a mind and heart of its own, but an association of two individuals each with a separate intellectual and emotional makeup. If the right of privacy means anything, it is the right of the *individual,* married or single, to be free from unwarranted governmental intrusion into matters so fundamentally affecting a person as the decision whether to bear or beget a child.' *Eisenstadt v Baird* 405 US, at 453 (emphasis in original). The Constitution protects individuals, men and women alike, from unjustified state interference, even when that interference is enacted into law for the benefit of their spouses.

There was a time, not so long ago, when a different understanding of the family and of Constitution prevailed. In *Bradwell v Illinois* 16 Wall 130 (1873), three Members of this Court reaffirmed the common-law principle that 'a woman had no legal existence separate from her husband, who was regarded as her head and representative in the social state; and, notwithstanding some recent modifications of this civil status, many of the special rules of law flowing from and dependent upon this cardinal principle still exist in full force in most States.' Id, at 141 (Bradley J, joined by Swayne and Field JJ, concurring in judgment). Only one generation has passed since this Court observed that 'woman is still regarded as the centre of home and family life' with attendant 'special responsibilities' that precluded full and independent legal status under the Constitution. *Hoyt v Florida* 368 US 57, 62 (1961). These views, of course, are no longer consistent with our understanding of the family, the individual or the Constitution.

In keeping with our rejection of the common-law understanding of a woman's role within the family, the Court held in *Danforth* that the Constitution does not permit a State to require a married woman to obtain her husband's consent before undergoing an abortion. 428 US at 69. The principles that guided the Court in *Danforth* should be our guides today. For the great many women who are victims of abuse inflicted by their husbands, or whose children are the victims of such abuse, a spousal notice requirement enables the husband to wield an effective veto over his wife's decision. Whether the prospect of notification itself deters such women from seeking abortions, or whether the husband, through physical force or psychological pressure or economic coercion, prevents his wife from obtaining an abortion until it is too late, the notice requirement will often be tantamount to the veto found unconstitutional in *Danforth*. The women most affected by this law – are in the gravest danger.

The husband's interest in the life of the child his wife is carrying does not permit the State to empower him with this troubling degree of authority over his wife. The contrary view leads to consequences reminiscent of the common law. A husband has no enforceable right to require a wife to advise him before she exercises her personal choices. If a husband's interest in the potential life of the child outweighs a wife's liberty, the State could require a married woman to notify her husband before she uses a postfertilization contraceptive.

Perhaps next in line would be a statute requiring pregnant married women to notify their husbands before engaging in conduct causing risks to the fetus. After all, if the husband's interest in the fetus' safety is a sufficient predicate for state regulation, the State could reasonably conclude that pregnant wives should notify their husbands before drinking alcohol or smoking. Perhaps married women should notify their husbands before using contraceptives or before undergoing any type of surgery that may have complications affecting the husband's interest in his wife's reproductive organs. And if a husband's interest justifies notice in any of these cases, one might reasonably argue that it justifies exactly what the *Danforth* Court held it did not justify – a requirement of the husband's consent as well. A State may not give to a man the kind of dominion over his wife that parents exercise over their children.

Section 3209 embodies a view of marriage consonant with the common-law status of married women but repugnant to our present understanding of marriage and of the nature of the rights secured by the Constitution. Women do not lose their constitutionally protected liberty when they marry. The Constitution protects all individuals, male or female, married or unmarried, from the abuse of governmental power, even where that power is employed for the supposed benefit of a member of the individual's family. These considerations confirm our conclusion that s 3209 is invalid.

Stevens and Blackman JJ joined in the opinion of O'Connor, Kennedy and Souter JJ as regards the spousal notification provision. Four justices, however, dissented.

Rehnquist CJ, White, Scalia and Thomas JJ: The question before us is therefore whether the spousal notification requirement rationally furthers any legitimate state interests. We conclude that it does. First, a husband's interests in procreation within marriage and in the potential life of his unborn child are certainly substantial ones. See *Planned Parenthood of Central Mo v Danforth* 428 Us at 69 ('We are not unaware of the deep and proper concern and interest that a devoted and protective husband has in his wife's pregnancy and in the growth and development of the fetus she is carrying'); id, at 93 (White J, concurring in part and dissenting in part); *Skinner v Oklahoma ex rel Williamson* 316 US at 541. The State itself has legitimate interests both in protecting these interests of the father and in protecting the potential life of the fetus, and the spousal notification requirement is reasonably related to advancing those state interests. By providing that a husband will usually know of his spouse's intent to have an abortion, the provision makes it more likely that the husband will participate in deciding the fate of his unborn child, a possibility that might otherwise have been denied him. This participation might in some cases result in a decision to proceed with the pregnancy. As Judge Alito observed in his dissent below, '[t]he Pennsylvania legislature could have rationally believed that some married women are initially inclined to obtain an abortion without their husband's knowledge because of perceived problems – such as economic constraints, future plans, or the husband's previously expressed opposition – that may be obviated by discussion prior to the abortion,' 947 F 2d, at 726 (Alito, J concurring in part and dissenting in part).

The State also has a legitimate interest in promoting 'the integrity of the marital relationship.' 18 Pa Cons Stat s 3209(a) (1990). This Court has previously recognized 'the importance of the marital relationship in our society.' *Planned Parenthood of Central Mo v Danforth* supra, at 69. In our view, the spousal notice requirement is a rational attempt by the State to improve truthful communication between spouses and encourage collaborative decisionmaking, and, thereby fosters marital integrity. See *Labine v Vincent* 401 US 532, 538 (1971) ('[T]he power to make rules to establish, protect, and strengthen family life' is committed to the state legislatures). Petitioners argue that the notification requirement does not further any such interest; they assert that the majority of wives already notify their husbands of their abortion decision, and the remainder have excellent reasons for keeping their decisions a secret. In the first case, they argue, the law is unnecessary, and in the second case it will only serve to foster marital discord and threats of harm. Thus, petitioners see the law as a totally irrational means of furthering whatever legitimate interest the State might have. But, in our view, it is unrealistic to assume that every husband-wife relationship is either (1) so perfect that this type of truthful and important communication will take place as a matter of course, or (2) so imperfect that, upon notice, the husband will react selfishly, violently, or contrary to the best interests of his wife. See *Planned Parenthood of Central Mo v Danforth* supra, at 103-104 (Stevens J concurring in part and dissenting in part)(making a similar point in the context of a parental consent statute). The spousal notice provision will admittedly be unnecessary in some circumstances, and possibly harmful in others, but 'the existence of particular cases in which a feature of a statute performs no function (or is even counterproductive) ordinarily does not render the statue unconstitutional or even constitutionally suspect.' *Thornburgh v American College of Obstetricians and Gynecologists* 476 US at 800 (White J dissenting). The Pennsylvania Legislature was in a position to weigh the likely benefits of the provision against its likely adverse effects, and presumably concluded, on balance, that the provision would be beneficial. Whether this was a wise decision or not, we cannot say that it was irrational. We therefore conclude that the spousal notice provision comports with the Constitution. See *Harris v McRae* 448 US at 325-326 ('It is not the mission of this Court or any other to decide whether the balance of competing interests … is wise social policy').

In a footnote the dissenting justices challenge the majority's view on the impact of a spousal notification provision.

In most instances the notification requirement operates without difficulty. As the District Court found, the vast majority of wives seeking abortions notify and consult with their husbands, and thus suffer no burden as a result of the provision. 744 F Supp 1323, 1360 (ED Pa 1990). In other instances where a woman does not want to notify her husband, the Act provides exceptions. For example, notification is not required if the husband is not the father, if the pregnancy is the result of a reported spousal sexual assault, or if the woman fears bodily injury as a result of notifying her husband. Thus, in these instances as well, the notification provision imposes no obstacle to the abortion decision. The joint opinion puts to one side these situations where the regulation imposes no obstacle at all, and instead focuses on the group of married women who would not otherwise notify their husbands and who do not qualify for one of the exceptions. Having narrowed the focus, the joint opinion concludes that in a 'large fraction' of those cases, the notification provision operates as a substantial obstacle … and that the provision is therefore invalid. There are certainly instances where a woman would prefer not to notify her husband, and yet does not qualify for an exception. For example, there are the situations of battered women who fear psychological abuse or injury to their children as a result of notification; because in these situations the women do not fear bodily injury, they do not qualify for an exception. And there are situations where a woman has become pregnant as a result of an unreported spousal sexual assault; when such an assault is unreported, no exception is available. But, as the District Court found, there are also instances where the woman prefers not to notify her husband for a variety of other reasons. See 744 F Supp, at 1360. For example, a woman might desire to obtain an abortion without her husband's knowledge because of perceived economic constraints or her husband's expressed opposition to abortion. The joint opinion concentrates on the situations involving battered women and unreported spousal assault, and assumes, without any support in the record, that these instances constitute a 'large fraction' of those cases in which women prefer not to notify their husbands (and do not qualify for an exception). … This assumption is not based on any hard evidence, however. And were it helpful to an attempt to reach a desired result, one could just as easily assume that the battered women situations form 100 percent of the cases where women desire not to notify, or that they constitute only 20 percent of those cases. But reliance on such speculation is the necessary result of adopting the undue burden standard.

In England, the courts would undoubtedly consider that Parliament had pre-empted any common law development by virtue of enacting a 'code' in the form of the Abortion Act 1967. The arguments, therefore, addressed by the judges in the US Supreme Court are, in fact, ones pertinent in England to legislators should it be proposed that the 1967 Act be amended to require spousal notification. In the light of the Human Rights Act 1998, it could be argued that the father's right to be consulted fell within art 8 as part of the right to respect for his right to private and family life. Likewise, it could be argued that for the court to grant such a right would interfere with the pregnant woman's right under article 8. Here, again, we see the clash of rights and the need to accommodate them. The US Supreme Court's decision is in essence a battle over this very territory.

In *Paton* (*supra*) the European Commission of Human Rights dealt with an application under art 8 of the Convention in such a case.

27. The Commission has next considered the applicant's ancillary complaint that the Abortion Act 1967 denies the father of the foetus a right to be consulted, and to make applications, about the proposed abortion. It observes that any interpretation of the husband's and potential father's right, under Article 8 of the Convention, to respect for his private and family life, as

regards an abortion which his wife intends to have performed on her, must first of all take into account the right of the pregnant woman, being the person primarily concerned in the pregnancy and its continuation or termination, to respect for her private life. The pregnant woman's right to respect for he private life, as affected by the developing foetus, has been examined by the Commission in its Report in the *Bruggemann and Scheuten* case [(6959/75) 10 DR 100, 12 July 1977]. In the present case the Commission, having regard to the right of the pregnant woman, does not find that the husband's and potential father's right to respect for his private and family life can be interpreted so widely as to embrace such procedural rights as claimed by the applicant, ie a right to be consulted, or a right to make applications, about an abortion which his wife intends to have performed on her. The Commission concludes that this complaint is incompatible *ratione mateiae* with the provisions of the Convention within the meaning of Article 27(2).

8. Involvement of others in the medical procedure

The Abortion Act 1967 only applies 'when a pregnancy is terminated by a registered medical practitioner ...' (s 1(1)). In *Royal College of Nursing of the United Kingdom v Department of Health and Social Security* [1981] 1 All ER 545, [1981] AC 800, the House of Lords interpreted this provision. Although dissenting, Lord Wilberforce sets out the medical background to the case.

Royal Colleges of Nursing of the UK v DHSS [1981] AC 800, [1981] 1 All ER 545 (HL)

Lord Wilberforce: There is an agreed statement as to the nature of this treatment and the part in it by the doctors and the nurses or midwives. Naturally this may vary somewhat from hospital to hospital, but, for the purpose of the present proceedings, the assumption has to be made of maximum nurse participation, ie that the nurse does everything which the doctor is not required to do. If that is not illegal, participation of a lesser degree must be permissible.

1. The first step is for a thin catheter to be inserted via the cervix into the womb so as to arrive, or create, a space between the wall of the womb and the amniotic sac containing the fetus. This is necessarily done by a doctor. It may, sometimes, of itself bring on an abortion, in which case no problem arises: the pregnancy will have been terminated by the doctor. If it does not, all subsequent steps except no 4 may be carried out by a nurse or midwife. The significant steps are as follows (I am indebted to Brightman LJ for their presentation):

2. The catheter (ie the end emerging from the vagina) is attached, probably via another tube, to a pump or to a gravity feed apparatus. The function of the pump or apparatus is to propel or feed the prostaglandin through the catheter into the womb. The necessary prostaglandin is provided and put into the apparatus.

*3. The pump is switched on, or the drip valve is turned, thus causing the prostaglandin to enter the womb.

4. The doctor inserts a cannula into a vein.

*5. An oxytocin drip feed is linked up with the cannula. The necessary oxytocin (a drug designed to help the contractions) is supplied for the feed.

6. The patient's vital signs are monitored; so is the rate of drip or flow.

*7. The flow rates of both infusions are, as necessary, adjusted.

*8. Fresh supplies of both infusions are added as necessary.

9. The treatment is discontinued after discharge of the fetus, or expiry of a fixed period (normally 30 hours) after which the operation is considered to have failed.

The only steps in this process which can be considered to have a direct effect leading to abortion (abortifacient steps) are those asterisked. They are all carried out by the nurse or midwife. As the agreed statement records 'the causative factor in inducing ... the termination of pregnancy is the effect of the administration of prostaglandin and/or oxytocin and not any mechanical effect from the insertion of the catheter or cannual'.

All the above steps 2 to 9 are carried out in accordance with the doctor's instructions, which should, as regards important matters, be in writing. The doctors will moreover be on call, but may in fact never be called.

On these facts the question has to be answered: has the pregnancy been terminated by the doctor; or has it been terminated by the nurse; or has it been terminated by doctor and nurse? I am not surprised that the nurses feel anxiety as to this.

The majority's view is stated in the speeches of Lord Diplock and Roskill.

Lord Diplock: My Lords, the wording and structure of [section 1 of the Abortion Act 1967] are far from elegant, but the policy of the Act, it seems to me, is clear. There are two aspects to it: the first is to broaden the grounds on which abortions may be lawfully obtained; the second is to ensure that the abortion is carried out with all proper skill and in hygienic conditions. Subsection (1) which deals with the termination of pregnancies other than in cases of dire emergency consists of a conditional sentence of which a protasis, which is a condition precedent to be satisfied in order to make the abortion lawful at all, is stated last: 'if two registered medical practitioners are of the opinion etc'. It is this part of the subsection which defines the circumstances which qualify a woman to have pregnancy terminated lawfully. ...

The requirement of the Act as to the way in which the treatment be carried out, which in my view throws most light on the second aspect of its policy and the true construction of the phrase in sub-s (1) of s 1 which lies at the root of the dispute between the parties to this appeal, is the requirement in sub-s (3) that, except in cases of dire emergency, the treatment must be carried out in a national health service hospital (or private clinic specifically approved for that purpose by the minister). It is in my view evident that, in providing that treatment for termination of pregnancies should take place in ordinary hospitals Parliament contemplated that (conscientious objections apart) like other hospital treatment, it would be undertaken as a team effort in which, acting on the instructions of the doctor in charge of the treatment, junior doctors, nurses, paramedical and other members of the hospital staff would each do those things forming part of the whole treatment which it would be in accordance with accepted medical practice to entrust to a member of the staff possessed of their respective qualifications and experience.

Subsection (1) although it is expressed to apply only 'when a pregnancy is terminated by a registered medical practitioner' (the subordinate clause that although introduced by 'when' is another protasis and has caused the differences of judicial opinion in the instant case) also appears to contemplate treatment that is in the nature of a team effort and to extend its protection to all those who play a part in it. The exoneration from guilt is not confined to the registered medical practitioner by whom a pregnancy is terminated, it extends to any person who takes part in the treatment for its termination.

What limitation on this exoneration is imposed by the qualifying phrase, 'when a pregnancy is terminated by a registered medical practitioner'? In my opinion, in the context of the Act, what it requires is that a registered medical practitioner, whom I will refer to as a doctor, should accept responsibility for all stages of the treatment for the termination of the pregnancy. The particular method to be used should be decided by the doctor in charge of the treatment for termination of the pregnancy; he should carry out any physical acts, forming part of the treatment, that in accordance with accepted medical practice are done only by qualified medical practitioners, and should give specific instructions as to the carrying out of such parts of the treatment as in accordance with accepted medical practice are carried out by nurses or other members of the hospital staff without medical qualifications. To each of them, the doctor, or his substitute, should be available to be consulted or called on for assistance from beginning to end of the treatment. In other words, the doctor need not do everything with his own hands; the requirements of the subsection are satisfied when the treatment for termination of a pregnancy is one prescribed by a registered medical practitioner carried out in accordance with his directions and of which a registered medical practitioner remains in charge throughout.

My noble and learned friend Lord Wilberforce has described the successive steps taken in the treatment for termination of pregnancies in the third trimester by medical induction; and the parts played by registered medical practitioners and nurses respectively in the carrying out of the treatment. This treatment satisfies the interpretation that I have placed on the requirement of s 1 of the Act. I would accordingly allow the appeal and restore the declarations made by Woolf J.

Lord Roskill: ... the crucial issue is whether 'a pregnancy is terminated by a registered medical practitioner' assuming, as of course I do for present purposes, that the other prerequisites of s 1(1) of the 1967 Act are also satisfied. If a narrow meaning is given to the phrase I have just quoted, then it is the nurse and not the doctor who terminates the pregnancy. If that be right the doctor and the nurse are each guilty of a separate offence against the 1861 Act, the nurse because she is carrying out an abortion when she is not a doctor and the doctor because he is attempting to carry out an abortion when he engages in the first step which is not authorised by the 1967 Act. In addition, he is aiding and abetting the nurse's offence and both, and maybe others as well, are guilty of conspiracy to infringe the 1861 Act. This is the position which the Royal College of Nursing feared might arise and which led them to institute the present proceedings on behalf of the nursing profession in order that the question whether or not their profession are, in these circumstances, entitled to the protection of the 1967 Act might be finally determined. ...

My Lords, I read and reread the 1967 Act to see if I can discern in its provisions any consistent pattern in the use of the phrase 'a pregnancy is terminated' or 'termination of a pregnancy' on the one hand and 'treatment for the termination of a pregnancy' on the other hand. One finds the former phrase in s 1(1) and (1)(*a*), the latter in s 1(3), the former is ss 1(4) and 2(1)(*b*) and the latter in s 3(1)(*a*) and (*c*). Most important to my mind is s 4, which is the conscientious objection section. This section in two places refers to 'participate in treatment' in the context of conscientious objection. If one construes s 4 in conjunction with s 1(1), as surely one should do in order to determine to what it is that conscientious objection is permitted, it seems to me that s 4 strongly supports the wider construction of s 1(1). It was suggested that acceptance of the department's submission involved rewriting that subsection so as to add words which are not to be found in the language of the subsection. My Lords, with great respect to that submission, I do not agree. If one construes the words 'when a pregnancy is terminated by a registered medical practitioner' in s 1(1) as embracing the case where the 'treatment for the termination of a pregnancy is carried out under the control of a doctor in accordance with ordinary current medical practice' I think one is reading 'termination of pregnancy' and 'treatment for termination of pregnancy' as virtually synonymous and as I think Parliament must have intended they should read. Such a construction avoids a number of anomalies as, for example, where there is no pregnancy or where the extra-amniotic process fails to achieve its objective within the normal limits of time set for its operation. ... I think that the successive steps taken by a nurse in carrying out the extra-amniotic process are fully protected provided that the entirety of the treatment for the termination of the pregnancy and her participation in it is at all times under the control of the doctor even though the doctor is not present throughout the entirety of the treatment.

Lord Keith agreed. Lords Wilberforce and Edmund-Davies dissented.

This case effectively settles questions concerning the involvement of members of a team in a hospital or clinic who are not registered medical practitioners. There remains, however, one outstanding problem which has so far attracted no attention. We referred earlier to the drug RU-486 or Mifepristone. This drug is prescribed by a doctor, dispensed by a pharmacist, but administered to herself by the pregnant woman. In this situation who *terminates* the pregnancy?

There are two possible situations which might arise. First, the termination if only completed after the woman has returned to the hospital some 36 to 48 hours later after the prostaglandin pessary has been inserted. Here, undoubtedly the termination would be *by* the doctor even if the prostaglandin were given by a nurse under his supervision (*Royal College of Nursing* case). This is not problematic for the law. However, the alternative situation that might arise is as follows.

Suppose, instead, the effects of Mifepristone occur before the woman returns to the hospital for the prostaglandin pessary. In 55% of cases bleeding (and, therefore, the potential for a 'miscarriage') occur within 48 hours of administering Mifepristone. In a proportion of cases (about 3%) termination will occur before readmission. In our view, in this situation it must be the pregnant woman and not the doctor who terminates the pregnancy. It is she who does the last voluntary act necessary to effect the termination. Legally, the situation is analogous to a case where a doctor provides the means (eg pills) for a patient to kill himself. It is the patient who commits suicide. The doctor is guilty of assisting suicide, if anything. It cannot be said that he is guilty of murder since the law regards the patient's actions as the cause of death. *Mutatis mutandis*, here the woman causes her own termination. The provisions of the Abortion Act 1967 would not be complied with. Clearly, Parliament overlooked this fundamental point when it sought to bring Mifepristone within the framework of the Abortion Act.

However, an argument which would challenge this view could be mounted on the basis of the *Royal College of Nursing* case. There, the House of Lords (by a majority of 3-2) extended 'medical practitioner' to include all acts performed by the medical team for whom the doctor is responsible. Lord Diplock stated that 'the requirements of [the Act] are satisfied when the treatment for the termination ... is one prescribed by a registered medical practitioner carried out in accordance with his directions and of which a registered medical practitioner remains in charge throughout' (at 828-829). Hence, termination by induced labour using prostaglandin was held to be a 'termination by a registered medical practitioner', and so within the 1967 Act, even though others, such as nurses, and not a doctor, carried out many of the acts.

Could this wider notion of 'termination by a registered medical practitioner' covering all action for which the doctor takes responsibility (or 'charge') help in the case of Mifepristone? In one sense, a doctor does have responsibility for the patient throughout the treatment. However, it is a different kind of responsibility from that contemplated in the *Royal College of Nursing* case. In that case the responsibility denoted the right to control those who acted on his behalf in a professional capacity. In the case of Mifepristone, the responsibility relates to the doctor's ethical and legal duty to his patient. The relationship is neither one of control nor one where the patient (in administering the drug to herself) can be said to act on the doctor's behalf or be in his charge. It is unlikely that a future court would further expand the meaning of the 1967 Act to cover the use of Mifepristone.

9. Abortion procedures raising special problems

As we saw earlier, post-coital birth control by recourse to the 'morning after pill' or an IUD (an intra-uterine device) can only be regarded in law as birth control rather than abortion provided that the procedure is carried out before a fertilised egg is implanted in the uterus and not done with the intent to procure a miscarriage. (See the discussion *supra*.)

(a) Early abortion?

More problematical for our purposes is the procedure known as menstrual extraction or aspiration. This is considered in the following article.

V Tunkel 'Abortion: How Early, How Late and How Legal?' (1979) BMJ 253

... In view of the legal uncertainties, a doctor who regularly performed menstrual extraction (a convenient but question-begging euphemism) might until recently have thought it best to play safe by complying hypothetically with the Abortion Act; although the girl's pregnancy, if any, cannot at such an early stage be diagnosed, it would be prudent to certify as for a termination, and certainly to notify if the pregnancy was subsequently confirmed histologically.

The DPP and Mr Goldthorp

One such practitioner was Mr W O Goldthorp, the Manchester consultant gynaecologist, who in an article in the *BMJ* described how he performed menstrual extractions from 10 to 18 days after a missed period. The Chief Constable of Manchester referred the matter to the Director of Public Prosecutions. Early in 1978 the DPP expressed the opinion that menstrual extraction in these circumstances was illegal, and that purported compliance with the Abortion Act made no difference. Mr Goldthorp thereupon ceased these extractions.

The DPP's opinion was based on his understanding of the Abortion Act, which gives protection to doctors 'when a pregnancy is terminated'. This was understood by the Lane Committee to exclude 'speculative' operations, done before the existence of a pregnancy could be known. To fill this gap the committee proposed that the Act be amended by adding a new subsection: 'In this Act references to termination of pregnancy include acts done with intent to terminate a pregnancy if such exists', but there has been no legislation to implement this. And since the Act in s 5(2) states categorically that 'anything done with intent to procure the miscarriage of a woman is unlawfully done unless authorised by section 1 of this Act', it seems to be a simple either/or choice. The DPP gave a further reason for his opinion: no doctor could hold the opinion in good faith, as required by the Act, that there was a risk to the woman or the child in the continuance of the pregnancy if he did not know that she was in fact pregnant.

If to some medical readers there seems an excessive literalism in these reasons it would be as well for them to realise that this is for better or worse part of our legal tradition in the interpretation of statutes. It serves to emphasise the importance of focusing on the actual words used by Parliament and not accepting some widely repeated paraphrase or believed meaning. We return to this point below. But on the question of menstrual extraction there is now further news: the DPP subsequently had his mind changed by his superiors, the Law Officers (the Attorney-General). In March 1979 they expressed the opinion (giving no reason) that what Mr Goldthorp described in his article was protected by the Abortion Act; and that Act's references to termination of pregnancy should be understood as including steps taken to terminate a pregnancy which two practitioners in good faith believe to exist.

In this unsatisfactory state of affairs it is difficult to say with confidence what the law is. If Mr Goldthorp or others have resumed these extractions there could be a test case, as the Lane Committee suggested. For the present we have the reasoned opinion of the DPP that the operations are illegal in all circumstances and the later bald statement of the Law Officers that words may be read into the Abortion Act which would make them legal. (it is perhaps worth adding that the words suggested by the Law Officers might in any event still do not confer protection, since the two practitioners do not positively 'believe a pregnancy to exist' if they merely think that there is a chance it might. The Lane Committee's amendment is much clearer; but it would take a bold judge to read that into the unamended Act.)

Would a criminal court today adopt the DPP's opinion or Law Officers' second thoughts? The answer – or rather the question – is complicated by the fact that, although anyone may bring a prosecution for abortion, the police have to inform the DPP. He is thus given an opportunity to intervene, but he is subject to the control of the Law Officers. And, while the DPP who gave the anti-Goldthorp opinion is still in the saddle, the Law Officers who overrode him changed with the Government in May. Here, then, is rich material – medical, legal, and political – for those who enjoy speculating on current affairs. But it would be well to keep in mind what we are pondering: the prospect of prosecuting highly respected medical men. Their crime (maximum penalty, life imprisonment) is their open and ethical performance, with skill and success, of routine procedures at just the time when there are medically most desirable. Should there be even a shadow of criminality over this situation?

This is not all. Even given that the Law Officers were right and there is no longer any question of these early postcoital extractions being regarded as criminal, this exemption is achieved only by complying with the Abortion Act. The effect of this is to declare all non-statutory extraction criminal where the operator thinks, even erroneously, that the woman might be pregnant. However satisfied he may be with his diagnosis of, say, amenorrhoea, would not an honest practitioner admit that there is almost always a chance that he may be mistaken, may perhaps have been misled be his patient, and that possibly she has a very early pregnancy? If he thinks that this is a possibility then even though he does not believe it to be so, he extracts intending to remove the contents of the uterus, including any conception that may be present. It would seem odd (and perhaps even insulting to the patient) to insist on certifying under the Abortion Act in such a case. But if he does not, s 58 is inescapable: '... whosoever, with intent to procure the miscarriage of any woman, whether she be or be not with child, shall lawfully use any instrument ... shall be guilty ...'. Perhaps the ultimate irony is that it is immaterial that she was never in fact pregnant at all.

The crime is committed because of his conditional intent.

To summarise: if this account of the present law is correct, it follows that in all cases where very early, undiagnosable, pregnancy is a possibility, (1) no doctor is safe to perform a menstrual extraction, for whatever reason, without complying with the Abortion Act; and possibly also – (2) even with such compliance there will still be an offence.

Since Tunkel wrote his paper, the House of Lords in the *Royal College of Nursing* case *(supra)* has given its mind to the central question which is the meaning of the words in the Abortion Act, 'when a pregnancy is terminated'. Lord Wilberforce (who dissented in the final decision) stated that:

The argument for the department is carried even further than this, for it is said that, the words 'when a pregnancy is terminated by a registered medical practitioner' mean 'when treatment for the termination of pregnancy is carried out by a registered medical practitioner'. This is said to be necessary in order to cover the supposed cases where the treatment is unsuccessful, or where there is no pregnancy at all. The latter hypothesis I regard as fanciful; the former, if it was Parliament's contemplation at all in 1967 (for failures under post-1967 methods are not in point), cannot be covered by any reasonable reading of the words.

Termination is one thing; attempted and unsuccessful termination wholly another. I cannot be persuaded to embark on a radical reconstruction of the Act by reference to a fanciful hypothesis or an improbable casus omissus.

Lord Diplock, on the other hand, took a different view:

> ... [i]f 'termination' or 'terminated' meant only the event of miscarriage and not the whole treatment undertaken with that object in mind, lack of success, which apparently occurs in 1% to 2% of cases, would make all who had taken part in the unsuccessful treatment guilty of an offence under s 58 or s 59 of the Offences against the Person Act 1861. This cannot have been the intention of Parliament.

Lord Edmund-Davies, while agreeing with Lord Diplock in his conclusion, took a somewhat different line:

> In the foreground was the submission that, were a termination of pregnancy embarked on when (as it turned out) the woman was not pregnant, the Act would afford no defence to a doctor prosecuted under the 1861 Act. And it was secondly urged that he would be equally defenceless even where he personally treated a pregnant woman throughout if, for some reason, the procedure was interrupted and the pregnancy not terminated. I have respectfully to say that in my judgment it is these objections which are themselves absurd. Lawful termination under the Act predicates the personal services of a doctor operating in s 1(3) premises and armed with the opinion of two medical practitioners. But where termination is nevertheless not achieved the appellants invite this House to contemplate the doctor and his nursing staff being prosecuted under s 58 of the 1861 Act, the charge being, of course, not the unlawful termination of pregnancy (for *ex hypothesi* there was *no* termination) but one of unlawful administering a noxious thing or unlawfully using an instrument with intent to procure miscarriage. And on *that* charge unlawfulness has still to be established and the prosecution would assuredly fail. For the circumstances predicted themselves establish the absence of any mens rea in instituting the abortive treatment, and its initial lawfulness could not be rendered unlawful either by the discovery that the woman was not in fact pregnant or by non-completion of the abortive treatment. Were it otherwise, the unavoidable conclusion is that doctors and nurses could in such cases be convicted of what in essence would be the extraordinary crime of attempting to do a *lawful* act.
>
> My Lords, it was after drafting the foregoing that I happened on the following passage in Smith and Hogan's Criminal Law (4th edn, 1978, p 346) which I now gratefully adopt, for it could not be more apposite:
>
> > ... the legalisation of an abortion must include the steps which are taken towards it. Are we really to say that these are criminal until the operation is complete, when they are retrospectively authorised, or alternatively that they are lawful until the operation is discontinued or the woman is discovered not to be pregnant when, retrospectively, they become unlawful? When the conditions of the Act are otherwise satisfied, it is submitted that [the doctor] is not unlawfully administering, etc., and that this is so whether the pregnancy be actually terminated or not.

(b) Selective reduction

Another procedure, which may arguably be an abortion, has caused controversy. This is the procedure known as 'selective reduction'. This, to quote the description of the Voluntary Licensing Authority (which regulated assisted reproduction techniques prior to 1991) in its 3rd Report (April 1988), in Annex 5:

> ... is the term used to describe the procedure whereby one or more embryos in a multiple pregnancy are selectively killed to allow others to develop. In multiple pregnancies resulting from infertility treatment the procedure is used to avoid large multiple births though the technique was originated to stop the development of abnormal embryos in a multiple pregnancy where the remainder were normal.

The potentially crucial factual distinction between this procedure and other abortions is that when selective reduction is performed the destroyed foetus may be absorbed into the mother's body and is not expelled. Is selective reduction lawful? This requires us to consider two questions: (1) does the procedure come within the offence under s 58 of the Offences Against the Person Act 1861 of acting 'with intent to procure a miscarriage'?; and, if it does, (2) would compliance with the terms of the Abortion Act 1967 render it lawful?

(i)   THE SECTION 58 ARGUMENT

Two interrelated arguments are put here to determine whether the procedure falls within s 58. First, is the medical practitioner acting with intent to procure *a miscarriage*, and secondly, is he terminating a pregnancy?

In the following article, John Keown examines the arguments and considers that the procedure may come within s 58.

I J Keown 'Selective Reduction of Multiple Pregnancy' (1987) NLJ 1165

The first argument is that there is no need to invoke the protection of the Abortion Act since selective reduction is not prohibited by s 58. The argument runs that s 58 prohibits acts done with intent to procure miscarriage; that the word 'miscarriage' presupposes the expulsion of the fetus from the uterus, and that since selective reduction, which is performed in early pregnancy, results not in the expulsion of the fetus but in its absorption by the uterus, the procedure is not caught by the section. In support of this line of argument could be cited the many definitions of 'miscarriage', both medical and legal, which refer to the expulsion of the fetus from the uterus or to the emptying of the uterus. Against this, it may be argued that such definitions are sufficiently broad to include cases of termination of pregnancy followed by fetal absorption. In any event there is no evidence (either from medical practice or from the conduct of prosecutions for criminal abortion) that these definitions exclude such cases, nor is there any reason why they should do so. On the contrary, it has long been accepted by both medical and legal authorities that 'miscarriage' pertains not to the destination of the fetal remains but to the failure of gestation.

Defining miscarriage

In 1882, for example, a leading medical dictionary defined 'miscarriage' as the 'Interruption of gestation before the fetus has become viable'. More significantly, legal authorities have defined the word sufficiently broadly to include the failure of gestation without subsequent fetal expulsion. In the Australian case of *R v Trim* [(1943) VLR 109] a case on s 62 of the Crimes Act 1928 – the equivalent of s 58 – decided by the Full Court of the Supreme Court of Victoria, Marfarlan J stated that s 62 merely required 'an intent to cause in the case of the woman in question the event of birth, carriage or bearing which would take place in the ordinary course of nature to go amiss – go wrong or fail'.

Again, Professor Glanville Williams defines the offence of abortion as follows:

Abortion (or miscarriage) ... may be deliberately induced when it is a serious crime. For legal purposes, abortion means feticide: the *intentional* destruction of the fetus in the womb, or any untimely delivery brought about with intent to cause the death of the fetus.

In addition to these broad definitions of miscarriage, which indicate that s 58 prohibits the termination of pregnancy even if the fetus is not thereafter expelled, it is relevant to point to the mischief against which the section is directed, namely, the destruction of the unborn child. As Professor Williams wrote in 1958:

both English law and the law of the great majority of the United States regard any interference with pregnancy, however early it may take place, as criminal, unless for therapeutic reasons. The fetus is a human life to be protected by the criminal law from the moment when the ovum is fertilised.

Is it also possible that a subsidiary purpose of s 58 was to protect women from the dangers of attempted abortion? Clearly, both purposes would be frustrated by an interpretation of 'miscarriage' which would allow anyone to attempt abortion provided the intention was to cause the fetus to be absorbed and not expelled.

A second argument against the need to comply with the Abortion Act 1967 is that in aborting a fetus in a multiple pregnancy the intention of the operator is not to cause the miscarriage of the woman but to ensure the better carriage of the remaining fetuses. With respect, this argument too founders on the established meaning of 'miscarriage' and on the mischief against which s 58 is directed. The section is infringed whether the woman miscarries of all the fetuses or only of one.

Another argument is explained (only to be rejected) in the following extract.

DPT Price 'Selective Reduction and Feticide: The Parameters of Abortion' [1988] Crim LR 199

The other argument put forward by fertility specialists in favour of the legality of selective reduction *per se* is that they have not by their action terminated the pregnancy. It still continues by virtue of the fact that one or more foetuses still survive. Admittedly on one interpretation of that phrase this does appear to be true, although it might be countered that the expressions multiple pregnancy and multipregnancy themselves admit the existence of more than one pregnancy. However, one should bear in mind that the words 'termination of pregnancy' do not in fact appear in the 1861 Act but in the Abortion Act 1967, ie not in the statute creating the offence but only in the statute containing an exclusion of liability. It cannot be supposed that it was the intention of Parliament when passing either Act that it should be lawful to terminate the development of a foetus or foetuses forming part of a multiple pregnancy, especially as techniques for selective termination of pregnancy are of such recent origin. Such foetuses not 'capable of being born alive' would then be denied any protection whatsoever under the criminal law. Whether the purpose of the law is seen as the protection of the mother, the protection of the foetus, or both, there can be no justification for drawing a distinction between single pregnancies and multipregnancies. The potential for life has equally been taken away, and there has additionally been a physical intrusion upon the mother.

(ii) THE ABORTION ACT ARGUMENT

The arguments of Keown and Price are compelling. However, Price's argument has further implications. If selective reduction falls within s 58 then it may only be carried out lawfully if done in compliance with the terms of the Abortion Act 1967. Until the 1990 amendments to the 1967 Act, Price's argument would have led to the conclusion that the 1967 Act did not apply. If this had been so, then the procedure could never have been performed, since 'anything done with intent to procure the miscarriage of a woman is unlawfully done unless authorised by' the 1967 Act (s 5(2)).

In an opinion appended to the Voluntary Licensing Authority's 3rd Report, John Keown puts this point as follows:

As the better view is therefore that selective reduction is caught by section 58, the doctor would be well advised to comply with the requirements of the Abortion Act 1967 to render the procedure lawful. Compliance with the Abortion Act may, however, be ineffective. This is because the Act only affords protection when, in the words of section 1(1) 'a pregnancy is terminated'. As selective reduction results in the destruction of one or more but not all the fetuses, a court might rule that it does not terminate a pregnancy, and that compliance with the Abortion Act is ineffective.

Parliament has now put the matter beyond doubt. Section 5(2) was amended by the Human Fertilisation and Embryology Act 1990 (s 37) to provide as follows:

5(2) For the purposes of the law relating to abortion, anything done with intent to procure a woman's miscarriage (or, in the case of a woman carrying more than one foetus, her miscarriage of any foetus) is unlawfully done unless authorised by section 1 of this Act and, in the case of a woman carrying more than one foetus, anything done with intent to procure her miscarriage of any foetus is authorised by that section if –
(a) the ground for termination of the pregnancy specified in subsection (1)(d) of that section applies in relation to any foetus and the thing is done for the purpose of procuring the miscarriage of that foetus, or
(b) any of the other grounds for termination of the pregnancy specified in that section applies.

Consequently, selective reduction is lawful in two situations. First, in a case where the foetus (or foetuses) fall(s) within the foetal abnormality ground under s 1(1)(d) and the foetus(es) is/are terminated. Secondly, in a case where a multiple pregnancy exists so as to give rise to the required degree of risk of injury to the mother under s 1(1)(a), (b) or (c) and any number of the foetus(es) are terminated to reduce that risk to the mother. Notice in this situation the doctor can, in effect, randomly select any (or all) the foetuses since no foetus in particular gives rise to the risk to the mother.

What s 5(2) does not allow is the selective reduction of a pregnancy solely on the ground that the fact of its being a multiple pregnancy increases the *risk to the foetuses* the mother carries. This is not a ground under s 1 of the Abortion Act.

As a footnote, it is perhaps interesting to note that s 5(2) only tackles 'the Abortion Act argument' we discussed above. It simply assumes that selective reduction constitutes a 'miscarriage' and so accepts (perhaps conclusively) the argument above in respect of s 58 of the Offences Against the Person Act 1861.

(c) Later abortions

You will recall that, under the Abortion Act as amended, terminations of pregnancy are not subject to any time-limit except when reliance is placed upon s 1(1)(a). Thus, the possibility exists that termination may be performed at a point when the foetus might survive if delivered alive. So, termination of the pregnancy need not in practice entail the death of the foetus. What, therefore, is the doctor's duty in this situation?

There are a number of ways of analysing the problem, some of which produce awkward conclusions. Consider four different situations, remembering always that the foetus had the capacity to survive:

(1) both the pregnant woman and doctor agree that the foetus should die in the process;
(2) both the pregnant woman and doctor agree that the foetus should be delivered alive, all things being equal;
(3) the pregnant woman wishes the foetus to be delivered alive but the doctor decides to cause its death in the process;
(4) the pregnant woman wishes the foetus to die in the process but the doctor decides to deliver the child alive.

The *first* situation poses no new difficulties. Providing the doctor complies with the provisions of the Abortion Act 1967, the termination will be lawful. This situation is most likely to arise if the termination is performed under s 1(1)(d) because of 'foetal abnormality'.

The *second* situation could arise where the termination is justified under s 1(1)(b) or (c) where the pregnant woman's life is at risk or in order to avoid grave permanent injury to her. Again, providing the doctor complies with the provisions of the Abortion Act 1967, the termination will be lawful.

In the *third*, albeit highly improbable situation, again, providing the Abortion Act is complied with, the termination is lawful. It is a separate question, given the different understanding of the doctor and woman as to the outcome of the procedure, whether the pregnant woman has given a valid consent in law. Arguably, knowledge that the death of the foetus will result is an essential ingredient of consent to avoid an action in battery.

The *fourth* situation could arise where the pregnant woman seeks a termination under s 1(1)(d) but the doctor, perhaps because of his beliefs, delivers the baby alive. Here, *mutatis mutandis* the same arguments in respect of battery apply. However, providing the doctor complies with the Abortion Act, there can be no question of the termination being unlawful.

It is a further question, in this fourth situation, whether as a matter of law the doctor is under a *duty* to deliver a live child, if at all possible. (The same question arises in relation to the first situation.) When the amendments to the Abortion Act were before the House of Lords, an attempt was made to introduce a provision which would have placed a *duty* on a doctor to take all reasonable steps to secure that a child is born alive when a termination is performed under s 1(1)(b), (c) or (d). However, the attempt failed. Certainly, as regards a termination under s 1(1)(d) such a duty would not sit easily with the underlying premise of the ground that the pregnant woman is carrying an *unwanted child*. Both the pregnancy and the child are undesired because of its physical or mental disability. So, it would be inconsistent for the law to recognise that a doctor had the duty to deliver the child alive. Of course, this reasoning does not necessarily apply to terminations under s 1(1)(b) and (c) where only the *pregnancy* is unwanted but not necessarily the child. However, in both cases a doctor's duty must be conditioned by the mother's consent. Consequently, he could not, in law, be under a duty to deliver the child alive if the pregnant woman did not agree.

The above analysis of late terminations assumes that all terminations of pregnancy must be brought within the Abortion Act and that, if they are not, they would constitute the offence of 'procuring a *miscarriage*' under s 58 of the Offences Against the Person Act 1861.

This assumption may require reconsideration, not least because, if it is correct, a doctor who, for example, induces labour in a pregnant woman whose pregnancy has gone to term, and thereby terminates her pregnancy, would have to justify this conduct under the 1967 Act (as amended). For, on the face of it, the induction of labour is a termination of pregnancy and, hence, falls within the Abortion Act. However, compliance with the Abortion Act is only necessary so as to avoid liability under s 58 of the Offences Against the Person Act, *viz*, the crime of 'procuring a miscarriage'. The crucial question, therefore, is what does it mean to procure a *miscarriage*? If miscarriage means 'to be delivered prematurely of a child' (*Oxford English Dictionary*), which is the traditional view, then compliance with the Abortion Ace is essential. It could also be argued that 'miscarriage' is a term to describe an early delivery, ie within say less then 24 weeks of gestation. There is some support for this in medical convention. It is, however, difficult to square with Parliament's enactment of s 1(1)(d) – which is without time limit – providing a defence to the 'miscarriage' offence in s 58. However, if miscarriage also entails the destruction (ie death) of the foetus, then induced labour, or any termination intended to produce a live birth, need not mean that the doctor has to comply with the Abortion Act because no offence would be committed under s 58 of the Offences Against the Person Act 1861 because it would not be a *miscarriage*.

This somewhat orthodox conclusion clearly flies in the face of Parliament's intention when reforming the Abortion Act 1967. While limiting terminations under s 1(1)(a) to a time-limit of 24 weeks, Parliament considered it necessary to provide for later terminations where the pregnant woman's health needs made it essential. Hence, s 1(1)(b) and (c) do not contain time-limits. In practice, in these cases there will be a live birth because only the *pregnancy* will be *unwanted* rather than the child itself. Only very exceptionally would the health needs of the pregnant woman demand that the child die in the process of terminating the pregnancy.

10. Abortion and homicide

What is the relationship between homicide and the law of abortion? In the following extract, Glanville Williams identifies the common law position at the time he wrote – 1983. The recent decision of the House of Lords in *A-G's Reference*

(No 3 of 1994) [1997] 3 All ER 936 requires a reconsideration of the second situation he contemplates – death *ex utero*.

Glanville Williams *Textbook of Criminal Law* (2nd edn, 1983)

The law protecting neonates and the unborn is not ordinarily met with in legal practice; but it is of importance for obstetric surgeons and is a matter of philosophical and human interest. It is also the subject of strongly-felt differences of moral opinion.

The definition of homicide ... requires the victim to be *in rerum natura* or 'in being', which means that he must be 'completely born alive'.

Although injuries to a fetus causing its death do not generally amount to homicide, there is a curious rule by which they can do so. If a fetus is injured in the womb and is subsequently born alive but dies as a result of the prenatal injury, this is murder or manslaughter according to the mental element. So whether the offender is guilty of the crime will sometimes depend upon whether a doctor is able to remove the fetus from the womb while it is still alive, even though it is so premature that it is doomed to die almost immediately.

In a New Jersey case, D shot a pregnant woman whose twin sons were then delivered by caesarean section (hysterotomy) but died a short time later. He was convicted of murder of the infants. Had they died in the womb it would not have been murder.

The rule also applies to illegal abortionists. In this it seems to be over-severe, for it makes what may be a purely accidental fact turn the abortionist into a murderer.

As this extract illustrates, there are two situations to consider: first, where the foetus dies *in utero*, and secondly, where the foetus dies *ex utero* (see discussion in (1995) 3 Med L Rev 320 (AG) and (1998) 6 Med L Rev 256 (AG)).

(a) Death in utero

Let us consider the situation of death *in utero* as a result of an abortion. The Supreme Court of California examined the question when interpreting the provisions of the California Penal Code in the following case.

Keeler v Superior Court of Amador County (1970) 470 P 2d 617 (Cal Sup Ct)

Mosk J: On February 23, 1969, Mrs Keeler was driving on a narrow mountain road in Amador County after delivering the girls to their home. She met petitioner driving in the opposite direction; he blocked the road with his car, and she pulled over to the side. He walked to her vehicle and began speaking to her. He seemed calm, and she rolled down her window to hear him. he said, 'I hear you're pregnant. If you are you had better stay away from the girls and from here.' She did not reply, and he opened the car door; as she later testified. 'He assisted me out of the car ... [I]t wasn't roughly at this time.' Petitioner then looked at her abdomen and became 'extremely upset.' He said, 'You sure are, I'm going to stomp it out of you.' He pushed her against the car, shoved his knee in her abdomen, and struck her in the face with several blows. She fainted, and when she regained consciousness petitioner had departed.

Mrs Keeler drove back to Stockton, and the police and medical assistance were summoned. She had suffered substantial facial injuries, as well as extensive bruising of the abdominal wall. A Caesarean section was performed and the fetus was examined *in utero*. Its head was found to be severely fractured, and it was delivered stillborn. The pathologist gave as his opinion that the cause of death was skull fracture with consequent cerebral haemorrhaging, that death would have been immediate, and that the injury could have been the result of force applied to the mother's abdomen. There was no air in the fetus' lungs, and the umbilical cord was intact.

Upon delivery the foetus weighed five pounds and was 18 inches in length. Both Mrs Keeler and her obstetrician testified that fetal movements had been observed prior to February 23, 1969. The evidence was in conflict as to the estimated age of the fetus; the expert testimony on the point, however, concluded 'with reasonable medical certainty' that the fetus had developed to the stage of viability, ie, that in the event of premature birth on the date in question it would have had a 75 percent to 96 percent chance of survival.

An information was filed charging petitioner, in Court I, was committing the crime of murder (Pen Code, s 187) in that he did 'unlawfully kill a human being, to wit Baby Girl VOGT, with malice aforethought'. ...

Penal Code section 187 provides: 'Murder is the unlawful killing of a human being, with malice aforethought'. The dispositive question is whether the foetus which petitioner is accused of killing was, on February 23, 1969, a 'human being' within the meaning of this statute. If it was not, petitioner cannot be charged with its 'murder' and prohibition will lie.

Section 187 was enacted as part of the Penal Code of 1872. Inasmuch as the provision has not been amended since that date, we must determine the intent of the Legislature at the time of its enactment. But section 187 was, in turn, taken verbatim from the first California statute defining murder, part of the Crimes and Punishment Act of 1850. (Stats 1850, ch 99, s 19, 0 231.) Penal Code section 5 (also enacted in 1872) declares: 'The provisions of this Code, so far as they are substantially the same as existing statutes, must be construed as continuations thereof, and not as new enactments'. We begin, accordingly, by inquiring into the intent of the Legislature in 1850 when it first defined murder as the unlawful and malicious killing of a 'human being'.

It will be presumed, of course, that in enacting a statute the Legislature was familiar with the relevant rule of the common law, and, when it couches its enactment in common law language, that its intent was to continue those rules in statutory form. (*Baker v Baker* 13 Cal 87, 95-96 (1859); *Morris v Oney* 217 Cal App 2d 864 at 870, 32 Cal Rptr 88 (1963).) This is particularly appropriate in considering the work of the first session of our Legislature: its precedents were necessarily drawn from the common law, as modified in certain respects by the Constitution and by legislation of our sister states.

We therefore undertake a brief review of the origins and development of the common law of abortional homicide. (For a more detailed treatment, see Means, The Law of New York concerning Abortion and the Status of the Foetus, 1664-1968: A Case of Cessation of Constitutionality (1968) 14 NYLF 411 [herinafter cited as Means]: Stern, Abortion: Reform and the Law (1968) 59 J Crim L, C & PS 84; Quay, Justifiable Abortion – Medical and Legal Foundations II (1961) 49 Geo LJ 395.) From that inquiry it appears that by the year 1850 – the date with which we are concerned – an infant could not be the subject of homicide at common law *unless it had been born alive*. Perhaps the must influential statement of the 'born alive' rule is that of Coke, in Mid-17th century: '[If a woman be quick with childe, and by a potion or otherwise killeth it in her wombe, or if a man beat her, whereby the childe dyeth in her body, and she is delivered of a dead childe, this is a great misprision [ie, misdemeanour], and no murder; but if the childe be borne alive and dyeth of the potion, battery, or other cause, this is murder; for in law it is accounted a reasonable creature, *in rerum natura,* when it is born alive.] (3 Coke, Institutes *58 (1648).) In short 'By Coke's time, the common law regarded abortion as murder only if the foetus is (1) quickened, (2) born alive, (3) lives for a brief interval, and (4) then dies'. (Means, at p 420.) Whatever intrinsic defects there may have been in Coke's work (see 3 Stephen, A History of the Criminal Law of England (1883) pp 52-60), the common law accepted his views as authoritative. In the 18th century, for example, Coke's requirement that an infant be born alive in order to be the subject of homicide was reiterated and expanded by both Blackstone and Hale. ...

We conclude that in declaring murder to be the unlawful and malicious killing of a 'human being' the Legislature of 1850 intended that term to have the settled common law meaning of a person who had been born alive, and did not intend the act of feticide – as distinguished from abortion – to be an offence under the laws of California. ...

Notes to extract

Aftermath Cal Pen Code s 187. 'Murder is the unlawful killing of a human being, *or a fetus*, with malice aforethought. ...' The words in italics were added by amendment in 1970, 'triggered' by *Keeler.*

The word 'fetus' in section 187 is interpreted to mean 'a viable unborn child'. *People v Smith* 129 Cal Rptr 498 (1976).

By contrast, the Supreme Judicial Court of Massachusetts held in *Commonwealth v Lawrence* (1989) 404 Mass 378 that the intentional killing of a *viable* foetus *in utero* could be murder at common law, reflecting the change made to the California Penal Code noted above after *Keeler.* English law would, undoubtedly, continue to reflect the long held common law position. This was recently re-affirmed by the House of Lords in *A-G's Reference (No 3 of 1994)* [1997] 3 All ER 936 (HL) per Lord Mustill at 948. The 'born alive' rule is now unassailable in England (contrast the dissenting judgment of Major and Sopinka JJ in *Winnipeg Child and Family Services (Northwest Area) v DFG* [1997] 2 SCR 925 (Can SC) – ruled 'outdated and indefensible').

(b) Death ex utero

What, however, of the situation where the abortion leads to a live birth? If the child subsequently dies as a result of the doctor's actions, even though the abortion was lawful, could this amount to murder or manslaughter of the child now 'born alive'?

To answer this question, we need to address *two* issues; first, does the doctor have the necessary *mens rea* for the crime; and, secondly, if he does, can it be said that his action is somehow lawfully justified not least because the abortion was itself lawful. It would seen somewhat perverse that a lawful abortion could nevertheless expose a doctor to criminal liability merely because the child was born rather then killed *in utero*.

Let us take the easier situation first. Suppose a doctor were to carry out an abortion intending that the foetus should be born alive and dies. On these facts, there seems little doubt that the necessary intention for murder – to kill a living person – is present and providing a causal link can be established with the doctor's actions, murder would seem to be made out. Likewise, if a doctor were to inadvertently bring about the birth of a child in a grossly negligent way, he would seem to satisfy the requirements of manslaughter following *R v Adomako* [1994] 3 All ER 79 (HL). The only remaining issue would be whether he had a defence because the abortion fell within the 1967 Act or on some other basis. We will return to this.

The more difficult situation arises where the doctor intends to kill the child *in utero* but it dies having been born. Can this be murder? Glanville Williams in the extract from his *Textbook (supra)* states that it can on the basis of a criminal law doctrine of 'transferred malice'. This has it that a defendant's intention to kill 'x' could be transferred so as to provide the *mens rea* of murder where the defendant actually (and unintentionally) kills 'y'. In this context, an intention to cause serious harm to the pregnant woman or to kill the foetus ('x') could be transferred to the child once born ('y') and so make the doctor guilty of its murder. The doctrine, and indeed its application to the unborn child, has a long pedigree in the English common law (see J Tempkin 'Pre-Natal Injury, Homicide and the Draft Criminal Code' [1986] CLJ 414). The case of *A-G's Reference (No 3 of 1994)* [1997] 3 All ER 936 has, however, revised the common law's acceptance where an unborn child is injured and dies after birth. The case was not concerned with an abortion but rather a violent assault with a knife on a pregnant woman who subsequently gave birth to her child, which died as a result of its premature birth. In the Court of Appeal, the judges equated the foetus with the mother and held that an intention to cause serious injury to her could be transferred to the child once born ([1996] 2 All ER 10). Lord Taylor CJ said:

> It is argued on behalf of the Attorney-General that the Crown can succeed in one of two ways. If the jury are satisfied that the defendant at the time when he did the act intended to kill or cause really serious bodily injury to the foetus, then it is said that this will suffice provided 'the intention is directed to a child capable of becoming a person in being' at a later date. In the alternative it is argued that an intention to kill or cause really serious bodily injury to the mother will suffice by reason of the doctrine of transferred malice.
>
> … In the eyes of the law the foetus is taken to be a part of the mother until it has an existence independent of the mother. Thus an intention to cause serious bodily injury to the foetus is an intention to cause serious bodily injury to a part of the mother just as an intention to injure her arm or her leg would be so viewed. Thus consideration of whether a charge of murder can arise where the focus of the defendant's intention is exclusively the foetus falls to be considered under the head of transferred malice, as is the case where the intention is focused exclusively or partially upon the mother herself…

When the case reached the House of Lords, the Law Lords took a different view and rejected the application of the doctrine of 'transferred malice'. First, the judges rejected the argument, accepted by the Court of Appeal, that the foetus was merely part of the mother.

Lord Mustill: ... The decision of the Court of Appeal founded on the proposition that the foetus is part of the mother, so that an intention to cause really serious bodily injury to the mother is equivalent to the same intent directed towards the foetus. This intent could be added to the actus reus, constituted (as I understand it) by the creation of such a change in the environment of the foetus through the injury to the mother that the baby would be born at a time when, as events proved, it would not survive. I must dissent from this proposition for I believe it to be wholly unfounded in fact. Obviously, nobody would assert that once the mother had been delivered of S, the baby and her mother were in any sense 'the same'. Not only were they physically separate, but they were each unique human beings, though no doubt with many features of resemblance. The reason for the uniqueness of S was that the development of her own special characteristics had been enabled and bounded by the collection of genes handed down not only by M but also by the natural father. This collection was different from the genes which had enabled and bounded the development of M, for these had been handed down by her own mother and natural father. S and her mother were closely related but, even apart from differing environmental influences, they were not, had not been, and in the future never would be 'the same'. There was, of course, an intimate bond between the foetus and the mother, created by the total dependence of the foetus on the protective physical environment furnished by the mother, and on the supply by the mother through the physical linkage between them of the nutriments, oxygen and other substances essential to foetal life and development. The emotional bond between the mother and her unborn child was also of a very special kind. But the relationship was one of bond, not of identity. The mother and the foetus were two distinct organisms living symbiotically, not a single organism with two aspects. The mother's leg was part of the mother; the foetus was not.

The only other ground for identifying the foetus with the mother that I can envisage is a chain of reasoning on the following lines. All the case law shows that the child does not attain a sufficient human personality to be the subject of a crime of violence, and in particular of a crime of murder, until it enjoys an existence separate from its mother; hence, whilst it is in the womb it does not have a human personality; hence it must share a human personality with its mother. This seems to me an entire non sequitur, for it omits the possibility that the foetus does not (for the purposes of the law of homicide and violent crime) have any relevant type of personality but is an organism sui generis lacking at this stage the entire range of characteristics both of the mother to which it is physically linked and of the complete human being which it will later become. The argument involves one fiction too far, and I would reject it ...

Lord Hope: ... The Court of Appeal held that a foetus before birth must be taken to be an integral part of the mother, in the same way as her arm or her leg. It was for this reason that they said that the requisite intent to be proved in the case of murder, if the child was subsequently born alive and then died, was an intention to kill or to cause really serious bodily injury to the mother. I am not satisfied that this is the correct approach. The creation of an embryo from which a foetus is developed requires the bringing together of genetic material from the father as well as from the mother. The science of human fertilisation and embryology has now been developed to the point where the embryo may be created outside the mother and then placed inside her as a live embryo. This practice, not now uncommon in cases of infertility, has already attracted the attention of Parliament: see the Human Fertilisation and Embryology Act 1990. It serves to remind us that an embryo is in reality a separate organism from the mother from the moment of its conception. This individuality is retained by it throughout its development until it achieves an independent existence on being born. So the foetus cannot be regarded as an integral part of the mother in the sense indicated by the Court of Appeal, notwithstanding its dependence upon the mother for its survival until birth ...

Secondly, the judges considered what the position would be if the foetus was indeed a 'separate organism'.

Lord Mustill: ... I would, therefore, reject the reasoning which assumes that since (in the eyes of English law) the foetus does not have the attributes which make it a 'person' it must be an adjunct of the mother. Eschewing all religious and political debate, I would say that the foetus is neither. It is a unique organism. To apply to such an organism the principles of a law evolved in relation to autonomous beings is bound to mislead. I prefer, so far as binding authority permits, to start afresh, and to do so by reference to the second of the arguments advanced by the Attorney General. This builds on the rules stated above by the following stages. If D struck X intending to cause her serious harm, and the blow, in fact, caused her death, that would be murder (rule 1). If she had been nursing a baby Y which was accidentally struck by the blow and consequently died, that would also be murder (rule 1 and 2). So, also, if an evil-doer had intended to cause harm but not death to X by giving her a poisoned substance and the substance was, in fact, passed on by X to the baby, which consumed it and died as a result (rule 1, 2, and 3). Again, it would have been murder if the foetus had been injured in utero and had succumbed to the wound after being born alive (rules 1, 2, 4 and 5). It is only a short step to make a new rule, adding together the malice towards the mother, the contemporaneous starting of a train of events, and the coming to fruition of those events in the death of the baby after being born alive.

My Lords, the attractions of this argument are plain, not least its simplicity. But for my part I find it too dependent on the piling up of old fictions, and too little on the reasons why the law takes its present shape ...

Having analysed the common law's approach to the *mens rea* of murder and the doctrine of transferred malice, he continued:

My Lords, the purpose of this inquiry has been to see whether the existing rules are based on principles sound enough to justify their extension to a case where the defendant acts without an intent to injure either the foetus or the child which it will become. In my opinion they are not. To give an affirmative answer requires a double 'transfer' of intent: first from the mother to the foetus and then from the foetus to the child as yet unborn. Then one would have to deploy the fiction (or at least the doctrine) which converts an intention to commit serious harm into the mens rea of murder. For me, this is too much. If one could find any logic in the rules I would follow it from one fiction to another, but whatever grounds there may once have been have long since disappeared. I am willing to follow old laws until they are overturned, but not to make a new law on a basis for which there is no principle.

Moreover, even on a narrower approach the argument breaks down. The effect of transferred malice, as I understand it, is that the intended victim and the actual victim are treated as if they were one, so that what was intended to happen to the first person (but did not happen) is added to what actually did happen to the second person (but was not intended to happen), with the result that what was intended and what happened are married to make a notionally intended and actually consummated crime. The cases are treated as if the actual victim had been the intended victim from the start. To make any sense of this process there must, as it seems to me, be some compatibility between the original intention and the actual occurrence, and this is, indeed, what one finds in the cases. There is no such compatibility here. The defendant intended to commit and did commit an immediate crime of violence to the mother. He committed no relevant violence to the foetus, which was not a person, either at the time or in the future, and intended no harm to the foetus or to the human person which it would become. If fictions are useful, as they can be, they are only damaged by straining them beyond their limits. I would not overstrain the idea of transferred malice by trying to make it fit the present case.

How does this apply in the abortion context? It is important to notice that Lord Mustill turned his face against a 'double-transfer' – first from the mother to the foetus and secondly from the foetus to the child subsequently born. He was not concerned with the case of an intention directed at the foetus itself – which was not the facts of the case – where only a 'single transfer' would be necessary, from foetus to child. As a result, it could be argued that the House of Lords has left open the very situation pertaining to the case of abortion. The solution may properly lie in the fact that the doctrine of transfer malice requires, in Lord Mustill's words, 'compatibility between the original intention and the actual occurrence' (at 949). The crime intended and that committed must be 'like' offences. The *mens rea* of a property offence cannot be transferred so as to justify conviction for a personal injury or violence offence and vice versa. Thus, an intention to kill an unborn child is not an intention to kill a live child. These are not 'like' states of minds, in the sense of relating to 'like' offences', ie s 58 and murder. On this reasoning the doctor could not be convicted of an unlawful act of manslaughter either, although there would always remain the possibility that he might bring about the death of a live child in a grossly negligent manner which would suffice for manslaughter also.

Suppose, however, that this reasoning is not accepted and transferred malice could be applied when the foetus is the object of the doctor's intention. What, if any, defence might the doctor have? In the Court of Appeal, Lord Taylor CJ offered a possible defence (*A-G's Reference (No 3 of 1994)* (1996) 2 All ER 10 at 16):

> ... Mr Hawkesworth cautioned us that conclusions adverse to the respondent's submissions might render a doctor who carried out a lawful abortion liable to conviction if the foetus was born alive as a result of a lawful abortion and then died thereafter. His reasoning was born alive as a result of a lawful abortion and then died thereafter. His reasoning was that the Abortion Act 1967, as subsequently amended only provides that a registered medical practitioner shall not be guilty of an offence under the law 'relating to abortion' and says nothing about not being liable on a charge of murder.
>
> In our judgment, Mr Hawkesworth's concerns in this regard are misplaced. A doctor who carries out an abortion in accordance with the 1967 Act is not acting unlawfully and hence, were such a doctor to be charged with murder, the charge would fail because the element that the act must be unlawful could not be made out. Just as a doctor who causes death in a bona fide surgical operation is not guilty because he does nothing unlawful, so would a doctor carrying out a lawful abortion be similarly protected ...

So, the 'killing' would not be 'unlawful' because the 'abortion' would be lawful. In his book, *Law, Ethics and Medicine* (1984), Professor Skegg anticipated this problem (at pp 23-26). Having expressed considerable doubts about the nature of any such defence, he concluded:

P D G Skegg *Law, Ethics and Medicine* (1984)

> ... if the issue first came before a court in a case involving the abortion of a pre-viable fetus, and the abortion was performed in a way that was in the best interests of the mother's health, judges would be more likely to take the view that on these facts the doctor was not guilty of murder, even if he knew that the child would not die until after it was removed from its mother's body. As the doctor would not have been guilty of any offence if the fetus had died before it was removed or expelled from its mother's body, judges would be very reluctant to accept that the doctor could be guilty of murder because the death occurred a little later. But it is only by ensuring that the child is not born alive, following an abortion, that a doctor can be certain that his conduct could not under any circumstances amount to the offence of murder.

His final remark is, of course, the practical and sensible solution. It leaves untouched, however, the analytical one. Could the solution lie in the following?

I Kennedy and A Grubb (edn) *Principles of Medical Law* (1998)

> ... the basis for the defence is not clear. (see Grubb 'Unborn Child (Pre-Natal Injury): Homicide and Abortion (1995) 3 Med L Rev 302, 308-10 (Commentary). Such a defence is analytically problematic. First, the Abortion Act 1967 does not expressly or impliedly create a defence to a charge of murder or homicide. The legislative intention behind the 1967 Act is clear from its provisions which remove criminal liability for an offence under 'the law relating to abortion' which means under the 1861 Act. (Ss 1 (1) and 6 (1) and, since 1990, under Infant Life (Preservation) Act 1929: s 5(1)) Parliament was only concerned with offences prohibiting in utero deaths. (See Skegg, PDG *Law, Ethics and Medicine* (Clarendon Press, 1984) 23-6). Secondly, murder does not require an unlawful act. What murder requires is that *the death be caused unlawfully*: but by this the law means merely not in circumstances where the defendant has a defence, for example, self-defence, provocation, diminished responsibility, etc. Murder may be committed by a wholly lawful act. The same is true for manslaughter committed by 'gross negligence' but not, of course, for 'unlawful act' manslaughter.
>
> It is suggested that the answer to the doctor's criminal liability really lies in the mother's ability in law to consent to the harm to herself—which a 'miscarriage' undoubtedly is—and to the foetus which the Abortion Act 1967, as matter of public policy in England, permits a woman to do if the termination falls within the grounds set out in section 1 of the 1967 Act. If the mother's consent is sufficient to exempt the doctor from liability under sections 20 or 18 of the Offences Against the Person Act 1861 (for serious harm caused to her) and under section 58 (for the miscarriage of the foetus), the legality of the abortion procedure is established and there is no good reason why the unintended fact that the child is born should affect that.

Returning to the earlier situation of where the doctor intends death to occur *ex utero*, if this is the basis of the defence it would not apply. The mother's consent to injury to herself and death *in utero* of the foetus may suffice but she would be unable to consent to the death of her child *ex utero*. The licence that her consent provides is, therefore, missing in this situation. Professor Skegg's concluding observation that a doctor should ensure death occurs *in utero* still holds good as the best advice.

Part III

Medical law in action

B: During life

Chapter 12

Actions for damages by children and parents arising from occurrences before birth

In this chapter we explore the way in which the general principles of medical negligence apply to the various factual situations where the alleged negligent occurrence takes place before the birth of a child (for further discussion see I Kennedy and A Grubb (eds) *Principles of Medical Law* (1998) ch 12).

We can usefully consider the factual situations under two headings, each divided into two sub-headings:

Actions by the child:
  A. pre-natal injury
  B. wrongful life
Actions by the parents:
  A. wrongful conception
  B. wrongful birth

We use these labels as convenient devices conscious of the fact that they need explanation. In short, they are terms of art, each of which describe a group of particular situations that call for the application of common principles. One area does, however, call for mention. With the developments in genetic science, actions involving disabled children will be important where there has been a failure to counsel or test, adequately or at all, for genetic conditions (see A Capron 'Tort Liability in Genetic Counseling' (1979) 79 Columbia LR 618 and L Andrews 'Torts and the Double Helix: Malpractice Liability for Failure to warn of Genetic Risks' (1992) Houston LR 149).

Actions by the child

A. PRE-NATAL INJURY

A claim for pre-natal injury arises when a child is born injured and alleges that *his injury* was caused by the negligence of another prior to his birth. The occurrence may occur prior to his conception, while *ex utero* as an embryo (ie during IVF treatment) or *in utero* (including during the process of birth).

1. The common law

(a) The background

P J Pace 'Civil Liability for Pre-Natal Injuries' (1977) 40 MLR 141

Although Blackstone was able to assert confidently that in criminal law 'Life is the immediate gift of God, a right inherent by nature in every individual, and it begins in contemplation of the law as soon as an infant is able to stir in the mother's womb' [*Commentaries* (15th edn), Vol 1, p 129], subsequent legal development in relation to the unborn child in a civil context does not wholly endorse this view. The rights of such a child are recognised at law for certain limited purposes only, eg in connection with succession to property, the Fatal Accidents Acts and certain crimes, and there was an apparent hiatus in the law which was highlighted by the national tragedy caused by the devastating effects of the drug thalidomide. This apparent gap, which the Law Commission, in August 1974, [*Report on Injuries to Unborn Children* (No 60, Cmnd 5709)] proposed should be filled by the Congenital Disabilities (Civil Liability) Bill, was suggested by the absence of any English decision on whether a tortious action would subsist at the suit of a plaintiff in respect of post-natal damage suffered as a result of pre-natal fault.

In considering whether a right of action is to be granted in such circumstances, there are at least four possible approaches which can be, and in other jurisdictions have been, adopted. The first, a fiction applied in Civil Law jurisdictions and based upon Roman Law, is that a child *in utero*, if subsequently born alive, is deemed as already born if that would be to its advantage. The second involves attributing to the child *in utero* legal personality which, in the absence of a live birth, would have important implications for both opponents and proponents of abortion law reform. The third, and biologically unsound, view is that the unborn child is merely a part of his mother and, therefore, there can be no action on his behalf, but only on behalf of his mother, if she, while pregnant, sustained injuries through another's negligence. The fourth approach takes the view that, since the tort of negligence is incomplete unless and until damage is suffered by the plaintiff, that tort is in fact completed on the live birth of the injured infant, at which time the infant has legal personality and is able to sue through his next friend, albeit that injuries were inflicted on the infant while he was *in utero*....

If the point had fallen to be decided [an English] court would doubtless have been swayed by the words of Lamont J spoken ... in the Canadian case of *Montreal Tramways v Leveille* [[1933] 4 DLR 337 at 340]: 'the great weight of judicial opinion in the common law courts denies the right of a child when born to maintain an action for pre-natal injuries'. This was a reflection of various American authorities and of the Irish case of *Walker v Great Northern Rly Co of Ireland* [(1890) 28 LR Ir 69] ... In *Montreal Tramways*, a post-*Donoghue v Stevenson* case, the court had concluded in favour of liability but this would have been of little help to an English court. There the Supreme Court of Canada had to decide whether the defendant company was liable in respect of its negligence which, the majority of the court accepted, caused a pregnant woman passenger to give birth to a child with club-feet. The action was brought under a provision of the Quebec Civil Code whereby 'Every person ... is responsible for the damage caused by his fault to another....' ... This case was not ... directly in point on the question of whether a duty of care was owed in the situation under consideration; it merely decided that in the circumstances of that case an unborn child, through the application of a fiction, was deemed to exist and so was 'another' for the purposes of the Quebec Civil Code.

An inherent and perennial difficulty in claims for pre-natal injuries, and one which was largely the reason for the one-time refusal of a right of recovery by the American courts, is the ascertainment of a causal *nexus* between the pre-natal negligence of the defendant and the post-natal harm to the child. Though Smith J's first reason for his dissent in *Montreal Tramways* was his view that the civil law fiction favoured by the majority was restricted to property questions, his second was that he doubted whether the medical evidence adduced would allow the reasonable inference that the plaintiff's club-feet resulted from the injury to the mother. Furthermore, in *Walker* a subsidiary ground advanced by O'Brien J for denying the claim was that it would be difficult to 'trace a hare lip to nervous shock, or a bunch of grapes on the face to the fright' [(1890) 28 LR Ir 69 at 81]. Obviously the difficulty of establishing a connection between the defendant's conduct and the plaintiff's injury is not a sufficient reason for denying a right of action, though, on the state of medical knowledge at the time of *Walker*, difficulties in establishing a connection would in many cases have proved insurmountable. Advances in medical science will more often show the required connection without resort to mere speculation and conjecture, although the difficulty of establishing such a connection will increase the more removed in time is the wrongful act from the accrual of the cause of action....

In *Watt v Rama* [[1972] VR 353] the Full Court of the Supreme Court of Victoria had to decide certain preliminary points of law which arose out of a car crash in which a pregnant woman had been injured by the faulty driving of the defendant. The woman driver had subsequently given birth to the plaintiff who suffered from brain damage, epilepsy and paralysis from the neck downwards. The questions which fell to be determined were whether (1) the defendant owed a duty of care not to cause injury to the unborn plaintiff; (2) he owed a duty of care to the infant plaintiff not to injure her mother; and (3) whether the damage complained of was in law too remote. For the purposes only of the determination of those questions it was *assumed* in the plaintiff's favour that the injuries sustained by her were caused by the defendant's faulty driving. Thus, at the subsequent trial of the action the ascertainment of a connection might well prove difficult.

All three members of the court, after a comprehensive investigation of judicial and academic authorities, resorted to basic tort principles, in particular the statement of the 'neighbour principle' by Lord Atkin in *Donoghue v Stevenson*. Winneke CJ and Pape J held that it was reasonably foreseeable at the time of the collision that the defendant's conduct might cause injury to a pregnant woman in the car with which he collided. Therefore, the possibility of injury on birth to the child she was carrying must also be reasonably foreseeable. This gave rise to a potential relationship capable of imposing a duty on the defendant *vis-à-vis* the child if, and when, born alive. On such birth this relationship crystallised, since it was then that the child suffered injuries as a living person and there arose a duty on the defendant to take reasonable care in relation to the child. They concluded that the answers to the questions posed by the preliminary determination they were called upon to make were: (1) yes; (2) an answer was unnecessary; and (3) no.

The third member of the court, Gillard J, reached the same conclusions but by a somewhat different route. The application of the 'neighbour principle' resulted in the finding that, on the assumed facts, the plaintiff was a member of a class which might reasonably and probably be affected by the defendant's carelessness:

> The unborn child should be included in the class of persons likely to be affected by [the driver's] carelessness since the regeneration of the human species implies the presence on the highway of many pregnant women. [*Ibid* at p 374.]

Furthermore, the defendant as a reasonable driver should have foreseen the presence of such a woman and the risk to her child, if his failure to reach the standard of a reasonably careful driver caused him to collide with and injure the mother.

All three judges emphasised that there was nothing unusual in there being a time-lag between the defendant's careless driving and the consequential damage suffered by the plaintiff, since, particularly in cases under *Donoghue v Stevenson*, the duty of care was not dependent on the existence, at the time of the defendant's fault, of a person with the right correlative to the defendant's duty to take care. This lapse of time was relevant only in relation to the child's capacity to sue.

In *Duval v Seguin* [(1972) 26 DLR (3d) 418] the High Court of Ontario recognised that there were no authorities binding upon it and, as above, Fraser J had recourse to fundamental principles of tort. ... He took the view that, applying *Donoghue v Stevenson*, an unborn child was:

> within the foreseeable risk incurred by a negligent motorist. When the unborn child becomes a living person and suffers damages [sic] as a result of pre-natal injuries caused by the negligent motorist the cause of the action is completed. A tortfeasor is as liable to a child who has suffered pre-natal injury as to the victim with a thin skull or other physical defect. [*Ibid* at p 434.]

It is to be noted that, save for Gillard J who was prepared to deem an unborn child a person in being at the time of the defendant's negligence, the judges in these cases avoided the question of whether legal status should be accorded to a foetus. The approach adopted was basically that, since damage is essential to the tort of negligence, that tort is not completed until the damage is suffered. As the damage was not suffered in both cases until the birth of the plaintiff the tort was completed at birth, at which time there was no difficulty in attributing legal personality to the live plaintiff. On this view, according to *Watt v Rama*, pre-natal damage to the foetus is merely an evidentiary fact in relation to the issue of the causation of damage at birth.

This solution requires the establishment of a causal *nexus* between the defendant's wrongful act and the plaintiff's defective condition on birth. It is a *sine qua non* of this view that there is a birth and that that birth is a live one. The factual situation in these Commonwealth cases was such that it did not require the courts to discuss the problem of the point in time at which there is a live birth and consequent legal personality.

The absence of case law in England had, as Pace points out, led the Law Commission in 1974 in its Report on 'Injuries to Unborn Children' (No 60, Cmnd 5709) to recommend legislation creating a claim for pre-natal injury. We will deal later with the Congenital Disabilities (Civil Liability) Act 1976 which applies to birth on or after 22 July 1976. It may be asked why it is important to consider the position at common law given the existence of the 1976 Act. The answer lies in the fact that claims arising from births before the Act came into force continue to be brought before the courts. There are two principal reasons. First, the limitation period for such claims only begins to run (if at all) when the child bringing the claim reaches the age of 18. Secondly, since April 1992, legal aid is (at least until they reach majority) more widely available to children who wish to bring such a claim since they are no longer assessed on the basis of their parents' income.

For ease of exposition, it is helpful to consider the legal issues by reference to the factual groupings we identified earlier: pre-conception occurrences; *ex utero* but post-conception occurrences and *in utero* occurrences. Here we will not consider the middle of these situations since IVF treatment was not available until sometime after the common law was replaced by the 1976 Act. Since most of the case law involves occurrences *in utero* we begin with that situation.

(b) *Occurrences in utero*

It was assumed or conceded by the parties in a number of cases that a *common law* claim for pre-natal injury could be brought (*Williams v Luff* (1978) 122 Sol Jo 164; *McKay v Essex AHA* [1982] QB 1166. Cf *S v Distillers Co Ltd* [1970] 1 WLR 114). One of the most important cases in medical negligence, *Whitehouse v Jordan* [1981] 1 WLR 246 (HL) involved allegations of negligence *in utero* and during the process of birth while the plaintiff child was as yet unborn .The legal difficulties for the plaintiff raised by such an allegation went unnoticed and unremarked upon throughout the litigation. It was not until the cases of *Burton v Islington HA* and *de Martell v Merton and Sutton HA* that the issue directly arose for decision by an English court.

(i)   WHERE THE CHILD IS BORN ALIVE

Burton v Islington HA and *de Martell v Merton and Sutton HA* [1992] 3 All ER 833, (1992) 10 BMLR 63 (CA)

> Each of the plaintiffs had been born with abnormalities or disabilities which they alleged had resulted from the negligent treatment of their mothers during pregnancy by medical staff at hospitals managed by the defendant health authorities. B brought an action against the health authority alleging that her abnormalities had been caused by the carrying out of a gynaecological operation on her mother while B was in utero, that the operation should not have been performed upon a pregnant woman and that the medical staff had been negligent in carrying out the operation without first ascertaining whether B's mother was pregnant. The health authority applied to strike out B's statement of claim on the ground that it disclosed no reasonable cause of action because at the time the alleged negligence occurred and the injury was caused to the plaintiff she had no legal status, being no more than an embryo, and therefore was not a legal person to whom a duty of care could be owed and had no right to sue. D was born on 5 February 1967 suffering from severe physical disabilities and issued a writ on 15 November 1988 claiming that his disabilities were attributable to negligence on the part of the medical staff who attended his mother's confinement and his birth. The statement of claim alleged that the defendants' treatment of the delivery of the plaintiff and the confinement of his mother lacked proper skill and care in respect which were foreseeably likely to result in the plaintiff being born with disabilities and that as a consequence of those defects in treatment the plaintiff had been born with his disabilities. The question whether a child had a cause of action in respect of pre-natal injury was ordered to be tried as a preliminary issue. In such case the plaintiff was born before the coming into force of the Congenital Disabilities (Civil Liability) Act 1976. In both cases the judge held that the defendants could be liable at common law to the plaintiffs for injuries inflicted on them before their birth. The defendant health authorities appealed.

> **Dillon LJ**: The court has before it two appeals which raise the same point of law, that is to say can a child who is born alive, but suffering from disabilities occasioned by negligence on the part of the proposed defendant at a time when the child was en ventre and unborn, maintain an action for damages for negligence against the defendant.

In both these cases the alleged negligence was that of the medical staff at a hospital, but, as the decided cases show, it could have arisen from a range of other contexts, for instance from negligent driving of a motor-vehicle or negligence on the part of a railway company or tramway company in respect of a train or tram in which the mother of the child was travelling as a passenger while pregnant.

The two decisions appealed from are, firstly, that of Potts J in *Burton v Islington Health Authority* (1990) 6 BMLR 13, [1991] 1 QB 638 and, secondly, that of Phillips J in *de Martell v Merton and Sutton Health Authority* [1992] 3 All ER 820…

Since we are only concerned with a point of law, the precise facts do not matter but I should indicate them briefly to show the limited scope of this decision.

In *de Martell* the plaintiff's complaint is of negligence by medical staff when the plaintiff's mother was in labour at the time of her delivery and his birth.

In *Burton* the plaintiff's complaint is of negligence by medical staff at a much earlier period – they carried out a dilation and curettage procedure at a time when the plaintiff's mother was about five weeks pregnant with the plaintiff but did not know it, and they failed to carry out any pregnancy test before the D and C procedure. It is said that they should have done so, especially as there were circumstances which might have put and should, it is said, have put experienced medical staff on inquiry. Neither case is concerned at all with the position where a child has been stillborn as a result of a third party's negligence or has, as a result of such negligence, survived birth for only a minimal period.

… [T]he appellants say that the damage in the present case was suffered by the plaintiff whilst still en ventre and therefore while not a person in the eyes of the English law. Therefore, it is said, each plaintiff, though subsequently born alive and still now surviving, cannot sue.

There are cases not in any way in doubt on this appeal which establish the general proposition that a foetus enjoys, while still a foetus, no independent legal personality – a foetus cannot, while a foetus, sue and cannot be made a ward of court: see *Paton v Trustees of BPAS* [1978] 2 All ER 987, [1979] QB 276, *Re F (in utero)* [1988] 2 All ER 193, [1988] Fam 122 and *C v S* (1987) 2 BMLR 143 [1987] 1 All ER 1230, [1988] QB 135.

There are other contexts, however, to which I shall come, in which the English courts have adopted as part of English law the maxim of the civil law that an unborn child shall be deemed to be born whenever its interests require it – or as put by Lord Westbury LC quoting from *Justinian's Digest* D1,5,7 'De Statu Hominum' in *Blasson v Blasson* (1864) 2 De GJ & SM at 670, 46 ER 534 at 536:

Qui in utero est, perinde ac si in rebus humanis esset, custoditur, *quoties de commodis ipsius partus quaertitur*…[Lord Westbury LC's emphasis].

On that basis of the civil law, the majority of the Supreme Court of Canada held in *Montreal Tramways v Leveille* [1933] 4 DLR 337 that when a child not actually born at the time of an accident was subsequently born alive and viable it was clothed with all the rights of action which it would have had if actually in existence at the date of the accident to the mother. That was a case of an accident when, by reason of the negligence of the tramway company's motor man, the infant's mother fell from a tram to the street and was injured. Two months later she gave birth to a female child who was born with club feet.

The leading judgment, expressing the majority view, was given by Lamont J. The maxim, which I have already quoted, led to the conclusion that as the child en ventre was born alive it was to be treated as having been alive while en ventre and so could claim damages for an injury at that time. The civil law applied because the case was a Quebec case and the Civil Code of Quebec is founded on the civil law. Cannon J, who delivered his judgment in French, seems to have taken a wider view since he reached the same conclusion without reliance on the maxims of the civil law or the Quebec Civil Code: 'On peut dire que son droit est né en même temps qu'elle' (see [1933] 4 DLR 337 at 367). Certain comments in relation to the problem in the judgment of Lamont J (at 345) are cited by Phillips J in his judgment in *de Martell* [1992] 3 All ER 820 at 825–826 and have been cited in other common law jurisdiction decisions since 1933.

If a child after birth has no right of action for pre-natal injuries, we have a wrong inflicted for which there is no remedy, for, although the father may be entitled to compensation for the loss he has incurred and the mother for what she has suffered, yet there is a residuum of injury for which compensation cannot be had save at the suit of the child. If a right of action is denied to the child it will be compelled, without any fault on its part, to go through life carrying the seal of another's fault and bearing a very heavy burden of infirmity and inconvenience without any compensation therefore. To my mind it is but natural justice that a child, if born alive and viable, should be allowed to maintain an action in the Courts for injuries wrongfully committed upon its person while in the womb of its mother.

The main contexts in which the maxim of the civil law above quoted has been adopted as part of English law are set out in the speech of Lord Atkinson in *Villar v Gilbey* [1907] AC 139 at 149–150. [1904-7] All ER Rep 779 at 783–784. The best known is that, where there is a gift to a class of children living at a particular date, a child en ventre sa mère at that date but later born alive will be treated as having been living at the date and thus included in the class. A child in its mother's womb is considered as absolutely born to all intents and purposes for the child's benefit. Incidentally, and irrelevantly for present purposes, that reasoning has led to the well-established conclusion that a child en ventre at a testator's death but later born alive may rank as a life in being for the purposes of the rule against perpetuities, which is a rule of public policy under English law: see *Long v Blackall* (1799) 3 Ves 486, 30 ER 1119.

More significantly the same civil law principle led Sir Robert Phillimore in the Admiralty Court in *The George and Richard* (1871) LR 3 A & E 466 at 480 to hold that a posthumous child, later born alive, ranks as a child of its father – in that case a ship's carpenter, who lost his life when his ship was blown on to the rocks and wrecked following disablement in a collision – for the purposes of Lord Campbell's Act, the Fatal Accidents Act 1846.

For my part, I think it would be open to the English courts to apply the civil law maxim directly to the situations we have in these two appeals, and treat the two plaintiffs as lives in being at the times of the events which injured them as they were later born alive, but it is not necessary to do so directly in view of the effect which the *Montreal Tramways* case has already had in the development of the common law in this field in other common law jurisdictions.

Mr Ashworth helpfully referred us to a substantial number of United States decisions. His general thesis was that the decisions from 1884 to 1945, which held that the child when born cannot recover damages for pre-natal injury, represent the pure doctrine of the common law, while all the decisions from 1946 onwards, which all took the opposite view, are to be rejected as heretical and wrong. The effect of the post-1945 decisions is that the courts of every American state have now held, as a development of the common law and despite previous decisions to the contrary, that a child can recover damages for a pre-natal injury, and even that damages can be recovered by the estate of a stillborn child.

It is wholly unnecessary to go that far in the present case and I would not for a moment suggest that the common law of England is bound or even likely to follow every twist of the development of the common law in the United States. None the less, I would be most reluctant to hold that the common law, though capable of development in this field in every other jurisdiction, has crystallised in England at a date long past – 1891 was Mr Ashworth's preferred date. It may be added that the *Montreal Tramways* case was cited and relied on in the earliest United States case of 1946, *Bonbrest v Kotz* (1946) 65 F Supp 138, where the changed view, that a child could sue, was adopted.

The main Commonwealth case from a country with a common law jurisdiction is *Watt v Rama* [1972] VR 353, a decision of the Supreme Court of Victoria in an appellate capacity which has since been accepted by other appellate courts in Australia as a correct statement of the law, that is to say the common law of Australia. That was a case which arose out of injuries in a motor accident. The leading judgment is that of Winneke CJ and Pape J. It is founded on an analysis – in my judgment, correct – of the tort of negligence by reference to decisions of the House of Lords and the Privy Council and certain Australian decisions, and it is founded also on the *Montreal Tramways* decision. The judgment says (at 358–359):

> The real question posed for our decision is not whether an action lies in respect of pre-natal injuries but whether a plaintiff born with injuries caused by the pre-natal neglect of the defendant has a cause of action in negligence against him in respect of such injuries. To this question the defendant answers 'No', because at the time of his neglect the plaintiff was not in existence as a living person, had no separate existence apart from her mother, was not capable of suing to assert a legal right, and was not a legal person to whom he could be under a duty.

There is then reference to well-known authorities like *Donoghue v Stevenson* [1932] AC 562, [1932] All ER Rep 1, *Home Office v Dorset Yacht Co Ltd* [1970] 2 All ER 294, [1970] AC 1004, *Bourhill (or Hay) v Young* [1942] 2 All ER 396, [1943] AC 92, *Watson v Fram Reinforced Concrete Co (Scotland) Ltd* 1960 SC 92 and *Grant v Australian Knitting Mills Ltd* [1936] AC 85, [1935] All ER Rep 209, and then to a South African decision which followed the *Montreal Tramways* case, *Pinchin v Santam Insurance Co Ltd* 1963 2 SA 254, and to the *Montreal Tramways* case itself. After the citations the judgment continues (at 360–361):

> Those circumstances, accordingly, constituted a potential relationship capable of imposing a duty on the defendant in relation to the child if and when born. On the birth the relationship crystallized and out of it arose a duty on the defendant in relation to the child. On the facts which for present purposes must be assumed, the child was born with injuries caused by the act or neglect of the defendant in... Whether, as a matter of expression, you say, as was

said in the case of *Watson v Fram Reinforced Concrete Co Ltd*, that this is to be explained by postulating a continuing duty, or merely projecting the relationship of duty into the future, or whether you regard it as possible to establish a breach of duty as at birth by reference to an act antecedent to the accrual of the cause of action, may be open to debate, but it has no bearing on the precise question we are called upon to answer, namely, whether the defendant owed a duty of care to the infant plaintiff.

The other judgment in the court is that of Gillard J, who reached the same conclusion. His reasoning is lengthy and perhaps not quite the same as that of the leading judgment. He has again referred to the principal English authorities and also to *Overseas Tankship (UK) Ltd v Morts Dock and Engineering Co Ltd, The Wagon Mound (No 1)* [1961] 1 All ER 404, [1961] AC 388. He says ([1972] VR 353 at 363, 374–375):

> Having emphasised these three points, it would appear that the vital matter for determination is whether at the time that the infant plaintiff avers that she suffered the *damnum*, i.e. at the date of her birth, had the defendant committed a breach of any and what duty to the infant plaintiff causing such *damnum*? In seeking an answer to this question one cannot but be influenced by a thought expressed by Lamont J, speaking for the majority of the Supreme Court of Canada in *Montreal Tramways v Leveille* [1933] 4 DLR 337 at 345 where, for the first time, it was accepted in a superior court that an infant plaintiff should be able after birth to recover damages for pre-natal injuries. [Then he refers to the passage which I have already read. I can pass on over very thorough further citations.] I now return to consider the arguments of the defendant. Each of them really turns around the theory that prior to birth the unborn child is not a *persona juridica* and, therefore, no duty of care can be or is owed to it.... In my view, there are two answers to this assertion. The first depends on the views I have already expressed. The cause of action for negligence only comes into existence when the damage is suffered. The infant plaintiff at that period on the facts assumed is, I repeat, a *persona juridica*, with capacity to institute proceedings and to whom a duty might be owed. The injury whilst *ventre sa mère* was but an evidentiary incident in the causation of damage suffered at birth by the fault of the defendant. If, in *Grant v Australian Knitting Mills Ltd* [1936] AC 85, [1935] All ER Rep 209, the plaintiff had been a babe in arms less than 12 months old, who had worn the defective singlet instead of Dr Grant, could the action had been defeated by the knitting mills proving that the mills negligently manufactured the goods before the infant plaintiff was born? It becomes clear from the expressions used by Lord Wright speaking for the Privy Council to describe the duty and its breach, the important and significant date in relation thereto was not the date of manufacture but when the damage occurred: see also *Waton v Fram Reinforced Concrete Co Ltd*....

Then a bit further on he refers to *Villar v Gilbey*, which I have mentioned, and other English or Scottish authorities in that field, including a statement of Lord Hardwicke LC in *Wallis v Hodson* (1740) 2 Atk 114 at 117, 26 ER 472 at 473:

> ... the plaintiff was *en ventre sa mère* at the time of her brother's death, and consequently a person *in rerum natura*, so that both by the rules of the common and civil law, she was, to all intents and purposes, a child...

That is of course a child for the purposes of claiming a benefit. So he comes to the conclusion at the end of further citation from the *Montreal Tramways* case that the plaintiff was entitled to maintain the action.

Phillips J in *de Martell* [1992] 3 All ER 820 at 829 was inclined to prefer the approach of Gillard J to the approach of Winneke CJ and Pape J. But both, to my mind, lead to the same conclusion and the differences between them are not, in my judgment, significant in the context of the present appeal.

The next significant decision is the decision of Fraser J at first instance in the High Court of Ontario in *Duval v Seguin* (1972) 26 DLR (3d) 418. That case also arose out of a motor accident at the time when the infant's mother was carrying the unborn child. Fraser J had the advantage of the citation of *Watt v Rama* [1972] VR 353 even though it had not then been reported. The infant was called Ann. The judge said, after referring in passing to *S v Distillers Co (Biochemicals) Ltd* [1969] 3 All ER 1412, [1970] 1 WLR 114:

> Ann's mother was plainly one of a class within the area of foreseeable risk and one to whom the defendants therefore owed a duty .Was Ann any the less so? I think not. Procreation is normal and necessary for the preservation of the race. If a driver drives on a highway without due care for other users it is foreseeable that some of the other users of the highway will be pregnant women and that a child *en ventre sa mère* may be injured. Such a child therefore falls well within the area of potential danger which the

driver is required to foresee and take reasonable care to avoid. In my opinion it is not necessary in the present case to consider whether the unborn child was a person in law or at which stage she became a person. For negligence to be a tort there must be damages [sic]. While it was the foetus or child *en ventre sa mère* who was injured, the damages sued for are the damages suffered by the plaintiff Ann since birth and which she will continue to suffer as a result of that injury. [The judge then referred to *Watt v Rama* and continued.] The reasons given in this case contain a comprehensive analysis of all the relevant cases and literature. The members of the Court held that the cause of action was not complete until after the birth of the plaintiff when the damages were suffered. Some of the older cases suggest that there should be no recovery by a person who has suffered prenatal injuries because of the difficulties of proof and of the opening it gives for perjury and speculation. Since those cases were decided there have been many scientific advances and it would seem that chances of establishing whether or not there are causal relationships between the act alleged to be negligent and the damage alleged to have been suffered as a consequence are better now than formerly. In any event the Courts now have to consider many similar problems and plaintiffs should not be denied relief in proper cases because of possible difficulties of proof. To refuse to recognize such a right would be manifestly unjust and unreasonable. In my opinion, and for the reasons I have tried to formulate, such a refusal would not be consonant with relevant legal principles as they have developed and have been applied in the last 50 years. Under the doctrine of *M'Allister (or Donoghue) v Stevenson*, and the cases cited, an unborn child is within the foreseeable risk incurred by a negligent motorist. When the unborn child becomes a living person and suffers damages as a result of prenatal injuries caused by the fault of the negligent motorist the cause of action is completed.

(See 26 DLR (3d) 418 at 433–434).

Mr Ashworth and Mr McGregor none the less submit that, so far as the common law of England is concerned, the position crystallised with the latest actual decision in the United Kingdom before the enactment of the 1976 Act, that is the decision in 1891 of the Divisional Court of the Queen's Bench Division in Ireland in *Walker v Great Northern Rly Co of Ireland* (1890) 28 LR Ir 69.

That was a case in which the mother of the infant, then pregnant with the infant, was being carried as a passenger in a train of the railway company in Co Down when she fell by the negligence, it was said, of the railway company and the infant was thereby permanently injured and born crippled and deformed. The court held on demurrer that the statement of claim disclosed no cause of action. The decision is however profoundly unsatisfactory, not least in that two, if not three, of the members of the court attached weight to the fact that the railway company as a common carrier had sold the pregnant mother one ticket and not two – a conclusion which, if valid today, would carry the consequence that a child under three who can travel without a ticket on British Railways would have no remedy against British Railways if injured by the negligence of the British Rail employees.

Potts J in *Burton's* case (1990) 6 BMLR 13 at 23, [1991] 1 QB 638 at 650 said that he derived no assistance from *Walker v Great Northern Rly Co of Ireland*. Phillips J in *de Martell* [1992] 3 All ER 820 at 825, having read the judgments in *Walker's* case, said he was not surprised at the view of Potts J. I agree with Potts J that the case is of no assistance today. Had a case of a claim by a child for damages for pre-natal injury come before the English courts in the period from 1972 to the enactment of the 1976 Act, and had it been as well argued as the present cases have been in this court, I have no doubt that the English court would have been referred to *Watt v Rama* and *Duval v Seguin* and would have preferred the views there expressed to *Walker's* case.

Mr Ashworth and Mr McGregor none the less submit either that, so far as the English common law is concerned *Walker's* case is to be preferred to any inconsistent later decision in any other jurisdiction, or that, as an action by a child for damages for pre-natal injuries had not been recognised as valid in the English courts before 1976 – the enactment of the 1976 Act – such an action could not now be allowed to develop and the English common law should be taken as being what the latest United Kingdom cases available might have indicated before 1976. It is further submitted that, as Parliament has intervened by the 1976 Act in the matter of prenatal injuries to unborn children, it should be left to Parliament to effect any further change in the law that may be thought necessary or to develop the law form where it was left by the Divisional Court in Ireland in *Walker's* case.

I do not agree. Parliament, by the 1976 Act, deliberately left these cases where the children were born before the enactment of the 1976 Act to be decided by the law in force before the passing of that Act, that is to say the common law. But that does not simply mean *Walker's* case but the law, whatever it might be, that the English court would apply in the absence of the 1976 Act in the light of all relevant authorities including decisions, so far as helpful, of other

Commonwealth jurisdictions. Moreover, the fact that Parliament by the 1976 Act deliberately refrained from legislating for cases such as these, where the child was born before the enactment of the 1976 Act, does not in any way support the view that these cases should be left for future legislation. They were left to the existing law whatever it might be held to be.

Mr Ashworth and Mr McGregor point also to the extravagant lengths, as they would put it, to which some of the United States decisions have gone and to the dangers of conflict between the mother and her child, with the child suing for damages for injuries allegedly caused by the negligence of the mother before the child's birth. If the floodgates prove to be open too wide no doubt Parliament can intervene. But I doubt very much whether there are any claims now outstanding which are not statute-barred, in respect of children stillborn before 22 July 1976 or any children born before that date, who are locked in litigation with their mothers over whether the mother tasted alcohol or followed a diet other than that recommended by the current phase of medical opinion during pregnancy.

For the reasons mentioned I would dismiss these appeals.

Balcombe and Leggatt LJJ agreed.

Claims for pre-natal injury, of course, are negligence actions. Therefore, issues of breach of duty, causation and quantum of damages can arise. There is nothing especially problematic about these issues in this context for medical law. Thus, as *Burton* and *de Martell* show, our concern here is with the threshold question of whether a duty is owed. The Court of Appeal was satisfied that a duty is owed, but without determining the precise analytical route to reach that conclusion.

The judgments of both Winneke CJ and Gillard J in *Watt v Rama* were relied upon by Dillon LJ. Phillips J in *de Martell* had preferred the approach of Gillard J, while Potts J in *B v Islington Health Authority* had preferred that of Winneke CJ. To Dillon LJ, however, 'they both ... lead to the same conclusion and the differences between them are not ... significant'.

With respect to Dillon LJ the theoretical basis on which the cause of action rests is not dealt with entirely satisfactorily. To Winneke CJ a duty attached to the defendant at the birth of the plaintiff and it was then that the defendant breached his duty. Aware of the difficulties of this approach, Winneke CJ went on to suggest that there were in fact a number of theoretical approaches available, each of which produced the result that the defendant owed a duty to the infant plaintiff, viz there was a continuing duty; the duty could be projected into the future; or a duty was breached by an act antecedent to the accrual of the cause of action. It may be interjected that each of these poses considerable theoretical difficulties. Gillard J adopted a different route. For him the cause of action in negligence only came into existence when the damage complained of was suffered. At that time the infant plaintiff had legal personality and could be owed a duty. The antecedent inquiry was merely evidence of the causation of the damage at birth. Aware, however, of the equally problematic theoretical objections to this line of reasoning, Gillard J also relied on such cases as *Villar v Gilbey* [1907] AC 139 (HL). This case reflects a long line of English authorities which have, largely in the context of property law, incorporated the civil law principle of *nasciturus* into English law.

Arguably, the civil law approach adopted in *Montreal Tramways* is the only sound basis on which to ground a cause of action for injuries sustained while *in utero*. All attempts to manoeuvre the common law's building blocks of duty, breach and damage seem at best contrived and at worst flawed. Leggatt LJ, for example, giving the third judgment in the Court of Appeal, concluded that the basis of the plaintiff's claim was that 'each was injured when at birth he or she became a legal person damaged by the prior act of the respective defendants, and that when such act was done it was reasonably foreseeable that it might result in the plaintiff being born damaged'. In deciding thus he appeared to rely on the decision of the High Court of Ontario in *Duval v Seguin* (1972) 26 DLR (3rd) 418. There, Fraser J made foreseeability that the injured woman may be pregnant the key, such that if the pregnancy was foreseeable, the plaintiff could sue for the damage suffered since birth. The difficult question of the basis on which the defendant could owe the unborn child, foreseeable or not, a duty was avoided.

Since the Court of Appeal assumed that the child suffered 'physical injury', the Court of Appeal was able to recognise that the unborn child was owed a duty and their reasoning proceeded on that basis. In fact the judges failed to analyse the real nature of the harm suffered by the child. It did not appear to cross their minds that the harm could be of any other kind. In *Burton* (1990) 6 BMLR 13 Potts J went so far as to reject the argument that the plaintiff suffered economic loss.

> **Potts J:** [counsel] made a submission concerning economic loss. As I understood it it was that at the time the plaintiff acquired legal status on birth in April 1967 the only damages recoverable by her could be for economic loss and that since a cause of action for such loss in such circumstances is not recognised by English law her statement of claim must be struck out. However, the statement of claim specifically alleges that the plaintiff was born with numerous abnormalities. On proof that such was the case the plaintiff would be entitled to be compensated for such abnormalities and their consequences, they having become manifest on birth. Thus the plaintiff's claim is essentially for damages for injury to the person and consequential loss. It is not a claim for economic loss, however that concept is defined, and I reject this submission.

A more careful analysis might cause us to consider whether this is correct. Arguably, the child's harm is purely economic, ie the loss incurred arising out of the child's disability. The disability itself is not an injury caused by the doctor unless the child was a legal person (or possibly deemed to be so) at the time of the pre-natal occurrence. Thus, any action the child may have is for economic loss. Given the English courts' reluctance to allow such claims does this mean that the court should have reached a different conclusion? Perhaps not. The woman relies upon the doctor both for her own care and that of the unborn child. The doctor who treats a pregnant woman assumes responsibility to both her *and* the unborn child. It is this 'assumption of responsibility' towards the child by the doctor which underpins the duty of care (*Henderson v Merrett Syndicates Ltd* [1995] 2 AC 145 (HL); *Williams v Natural Life Health Foods Ltd* [1998] 1 WLR 830 (HL)). Certainly, there seems no good reason for not permitting a claim by a child against a doctor in such circumstances, irrespective of the classification of the child's harm. Not to allow the claim would be a triumph of form over content. We shall deal shortly with the Australian case of *X and Y v Pal* (1991) 23 NSWLR 26, [1992] 3 Med LR 195 (NSW CA). Here it suffices to notice the way in which Clarke JA approaches the issue of duty in a claim by a child for injuries as a result of a pre-natal occurrence:

> Once it is accepted that Dr Pal owed a duty of care to his patient and that it was foreseeable that if he did not exercise due care in treating her he may cause damage to children later born to her it is difficult to see why those children should not be within the category of persons to whom the doctor was in a relevant relationship of proximity. The fundamental elements underlying his proximity relationship with his patient were assumption of responsibility and reliance. The doctor assumed the responsibility of exercising due care in the treatment of his patient and the patient relied upon him to administer that treatment with due care. Furthermore, the doctor was working in an area in which he could, if he were not careful, so damage his patient and the child she was carrying that either that child or children later born to the patient might suffer damage.

Given our argument that the pregnant woman acts as the agent of her unborn child in establishing a duty of care, can it also be said that she acts as an agent so as to affect the child's claim when her conduct is wholly or partly deleterious to the child's interests? For example, would contributory negligence by the mother affect the child's claim? More significantly for us, would the refusal of a mother to agree to treatment necessary for the health of her unborn child mean that no claim would lie against the doctor by the child subsequently born suffering harm?

One possible analysis would be that the pregnant woman owes a duty of care to her unborn child – in the way that third parties do. From this might flow two consequences. First, others may enforce that duty so as to override her refusal to avoid pre-natal injury to her unborn child. Secondly, the child's action where it is injured as a result of a pregnant woman's refusal of medical intervention is properly brought against her, rather than the doctors. The second proposition can be logically sustained even if the first is wrong. As we saw in Chapter 6, the courts will not force a competent pregnant woman to undergo medical treatment or other interventions for the benefit of her unborn child (see *Re MB (an adult: medical treatment)* (1997) 38 BMLR 175 (CA) and *St George's Healthcare NHS Trust v S* [1998] 3 All ER 673 (CA)). But does the pregnant woman owe a duty of care not to unreasonably injure her unborn child? If she does, her refusal might be a *novus actus interveniens* isolating the doctor from liability. Equally, it would be difficult to establish breach if the doctor had complied with her refusal, as he is required to do so in law. There are policy arguments for and against a maternal duty of care and, as we shall see, the Law Commission considered the balance was against liability except where the unborn child was injured when the mother was driving a car (*supra*, paras 54–63). The 1976 Act, again as we shall see, enacted this view. But, what of the common law?

The Canadian Supreme Court considered the question of a maternal duty of care in the following case. The justices articulated the public policy issues and by a majority, denied that such a duty could ever exist in law.

Dobson v Dobson; *Canadian Abortion Rights Action League et al, Interveners* (1999) 174 DLR (4th) 1 (Can SC)

An expectant mother was in a motor vehicle accident allegedly caused by her negligent driving. The plaintiff, her child, was delivered by caesarean section later the same day. While *in utero*, he had suffered serious and permanent injury from the accident. By his litigation guardian, he commenced an action for damages. An application was brought in the New Brunswick Court of Queen's Bench to determine whether the plaintiff had the legal capacity to sue for damages caused by his mother's prenatal negligence. The court held he did have capacity to sue and the decision was upheld in the Court of Appeal. The Court of Appeal limited the mother's duty to situations in which she already owed a general duty of care to others, such as a duty to drive carefully. The decision was appealed to the Supreme Court of Canada.

Cory J: *1. Privacy and Autonomy Rights of Women*
   [23] First and foremost, for reasons of public policy, the Court should not impose a duty of care upon a pregnant woman towards her foetus or subsequently born child. To do so would result in very extensive and unacceptable intrusions into the bodily integrity, privacy and autonomy rights of women. It is true that Canadian tort law presently allows a child born alive and viable to sue a third party for injuries which were negligently inflicted while *in utero*: *Montreal Tramways, supra*. However, of fundamental importance to the public policy analysis is the particularly unique relationship that exists between a pregnant woman and the foetus she carries.

(a) Overview
   [24] Pregnancy represents not only the hope of future generations but also the continuation of the species. It is difficult to imagine a human condition that is more important to society. From the dawn of history, the pregnant woman has represented fertility and hope. Biology decrees that it is only women who can bear children. Usually, a pregnant woman does all that is possible to protect the health and well-being of her foetus. On occasion, she may sacrifice her own health and well-being for the benefit of the foetus she carries. Yet it should not be forgotten that the pregnant woman – in addition to being the carrier of the foetus within her – is also an individual whose bodily integrity, privacy and autonomy rights must be protected.
   [25] The unique and special relationship between a mother-to-be and her foetus determines the outcome of this appeal. There is no other relationship in the realm of human existence which can serve as a basis for comparison. It is for this reason that there can be no analogy

between a child's action for prenatal negligence brought against some third-party tortfeasor, on the one hand, and against his or her mother, on the other. The inseparable unity between an expectant woman and her foetus distinguishes the situation of the mother-to-be from that of a negligent third party. The biological reality is that a pregnant woman and her foetus are bonded in a union. This was recognized in the majority reasons of McLachlin J in *Winnipeg*, *supra*, at pp 944–45:

> Before birth the mother and unborn child are one in the sense that "[t]he 'life' of the foetus is intimately connected with, and cannot be regarded in isolation from, the life of the pregnant woman": *Paton v United Kingdom* (1980), 3 EHRR 408 (Comm), at p 415, applied in *Re F (in utero)*, [[1988] 2 All ER 193]. It is only after birth that the fetus assumes a separate personality. Accordingly, the law has always treated the mother and unborn child as one. To sue a pregnant woman on behalf of her unborn fetus therefore posits the anomaly of one part of a legal and physical entity suing itself.

[26] It was recognized in both *Montreal Tramways*, *supra*, and *Duval*, *supra*, that the strongest argument for imposing a duty of care upon third parties towards unborn children is that tort law is designed to provide compensation for harm caused by negligence and, to a lesser extent, to deter tortfeasors. It was submitted that to deny recognition to the type of action at issue in this appeal could leave an infant plaintiff without the protection and compensation provided by tort law, solely because the defendant is his or her mother. Accordingly, it was argued that the compensatory principle should be the basis for the imposition of a similar duty of care upon expectant women.

[27] Yet, this argument fails to take into account the fundamental difference between a mother-to-be and a third-party defendant. The unique relationship between a pregnant woman and her foetus is so very different from the relationship with third parties. Everything the pregnant woman does or fails to do may have a potentially detrimental impact on her foetus. Everything the pregnant woman eats or drinks, and every physical action she takes, may affect the foetus. Indeed, the foetus is entirely dependent upon its mother-to-be. Although the imposition of tort liability on a third party for prenatal negligence advances the interests of both mother and child, it does not significantly impair the right of third parties to control their own lives. In contrast to the third-party defendant, a pregnant woman's every waking and sleeping moment, in essence, her entire existence, is connected to the foetus she may potentially harm. If a mother were to be held liable for prenatal negligence, this could render the most mundane decision taken in the course of her daily life as a pregnant woman subject to the scrutiny of the courts.

[28] Is she to be liable in tort for failing to regulate her diet to provide the best nutrients for the foetus? Is she to be required to abstain from smoking and all alcoholic beverages? Should she be found liable for failing to abstain from strenuous exercise or unprotected sexual activity to protect her foetus? Must she undertake frequent safety checks of her premises in order to avoid falling and causing injury to the foetus? There is no rational and principled limit to the types of claims which may be brought if such a tortious duty of care were imposed upon pregnant women.

[29] Whether it be considered a life-giving miracle or a matter of harsh reality, it is the biology of the human race which decrees that a pregnant woman must stand in a uniquely different situation to her foetus than any third party. The relationship between a pregnant woman and her foetus is of fundamental importance to the future mother and her born alive child, to their immediate family and to our society. So far as the foetus is concerned, this relationship is one of complete dependence. As to the pregnant woman, in most circumstances, the relationship is marked by her complete dedication to the well-being of the foetus. This dedication is profound and deep. It affects a pregnant woman physically, psychologically and emotionally. It is a very significant factor in this uniquely important relationship. The consequences of imposing tort liability on mothers for prenatal negligence raise vastly different considerations, and will have fundamentally different results, from the imposition of such liability on third parties.

[30] In *Winnipeg*, [*Child and Family Services (Northwest Area) v G (DF)* [1997] 3 SCR 925], the majority rejected an argument which sought to extend tort principles in order to justify the forced confinement and treatment of a pregnant woman with a glue-sniffing addiction, as a means of protecting her foetus. McLachlin J observed that difficult legal and social issues arise in examining the policy considerations under the second branch of the *Kamloops* test. First, the recognition of a duty of care owed by a pregnant woman to her foetus has a very real potential to intrude upon that woman's fundamental rights. Any intervention may create a conflict between a pregnant woman as an autonomous decision-maker and the foetus she carries. Second, the judicial definition of an appropriate standard of care is fraught with insoluble problems due to the difficulty of distinguishing tortious and non-tortious behaviour in the daily life of an expectant woman. Third, certain so-called lifestyle "choices" such as alcoholism and drug addiction may be beyond the control of the pregnant woman, and hence the deterrent value of the imposition of a duty of care may

be non-existent. Lastly, the imposition of a duty of care upon a pregnant woman towards her foetus could increase, to an unwarranted degree, the level of external scrutiny focused upon her. In *Winnipeg, supra*, it was held that the lifestyle choices of a pregnant woman should not be regulated because to do so would result in an unacceptably high degree of intrusion into her privacy and autonomy rights. If that is so, then it follows that negligent acts resulting from unreasonable lapses of attention, which may so often occur in the course of a pregnant woman's daily life, should not form the basis for the imposition of tort liability on mothers.

[31] On behalf of the infant respondent, it was argued that the reasoning in *Winnipeg* is not determinative because it dealt with the standing of the foetus to sue while still *in utero*. In *Winnipeg*, the foetus which sought the detention of its mother-to-be was not a legal person and possessed no legal rights. By contrast, the present action is brought on behalf of an infant born alive whose legal rights and interests vested at the moment of birth. In other words, the sole issue in this appeal is whether a child born alive – as opposed to a foetus – should be able to recover damages for prenatal negligence from every person except his or her mother. Despite the important legal distinction between a foetus and a child born alive, as a matter of social policy and pragmatic reality, both situations involve the imposition of a duty of care upon a pregnant woman towards either her foetus or her subsequently born child. To impose either duty of care would require judicial scrutiny into every aspect of that woman's behaviour during pregnancy. Irrespective of whether the duty of care is imposed upon a pregnant woman towards her foetus or her subsequently born child, both would involve severe intrusions into the bodily integrity, privacy and autonomous decision-making of that woman. Accordingly, the policy concerns raised by McLachlin J in *Winnipeg* are equally pertinent to this appeal.

[32] I am strengthened in this conclusion by the final report of the Royal Commission on New Reproductive Technologies, *Proceed with Care* (1993), vol 2, which rejected judicial interventions in pregnancy and birth. The Commission expressed its concern with these same policy issues, and recognized the need to ensure support for pregnant women and their foetuses without interfering with the privacy interests and physical autonomy of those women. It articulated its position in the following way (at pp 955–56):

> Permitting judicial intervention therefore has serious implications for the autonomy of individual women and for the status of women collectively in our society. All individuals have the right to make personal decisions, to control their bodily integrity, and to refuse unwanted medical treatment. These are not mere legal technicalities; they represent some of the most deeply held values in society and form the basis for fundamental and constitutional human rights. A woman has the right to make her own choices, whether they are good or bad, because it is the woman whose body and health are affected, the woman who must live with her decision, and the woman who must bear the consequences of that decision for the rest of her life.

[33] Thus, it was the far-reaching implications for the privacy and autonomy rights of pregnant women which caused the Commission to recommend specifically that "civil liability never be imposed upon a woman for harm done to her foetus during pregnancy" (p 964).

[34] At trial, Miller J observed that the existing jurisprudence permits recovery from third parties, and permits a child to sue his or her parents for postnatal negligence. He held that to permit an action by a child against his mother for prenatal negligence is a "reasonable progression" in tort jurisprudence. With respect, I believe that the imposition of a duty of care upon pregnant women in these circumstances cannot be characterized as a reasonable progression. Rather, in my view, it constitutes a severe intrusion into the lives of pregnant women, with attendant and potentially damaging effects on the family unit. This case raises social policy concerns of a very real significance. Indeed, they are of such magnitude that they are more properly the subject of study, debate and action by the legislature....

(d) Consequences of Recognizing this Cause of Action

[42] There are many circumstances in which the acts or failures to act of a pregnant woman may constitute negligence and result in injury to her foetus. A general social survey indicates that of all the types of accidents in which women were involved, 28 percent occurred in motor vehicles and 21 percent occurred in the home: Statistics Canada, Catalogue No 82–003, *Health Reports* (1995), Volume 7, No 2, at p 12. In addition, for hospital admissions due to unintentional falls, the place of occurrence is the home for 47 percent of the females who reported injuries: Canadian Institute for Health Information, *National Trauma Registry Report – Hospital Injury Admissions, 1995/96* (1998), at p 57. If a legal duty of care is imposed upon a pregnant woman towards her foetus or subsequently born child, such accidents, if they occur while the woman is pregnant, could be characterized as prenatal negligence and result in tort liability.

[43] Moreover, a pregnant woman will very often choose, or be compelled by economic reality, to continue her employment in order to support and maintain, or to assist in the

support and maintenance of, her family. It seems clear that imposing a legal duty of care upon a pregnant woman would inadversely affect that woman's ability to work during pregnancy. Indeed, all of the legal problems inherent in maternal tort liability for prenatal negligence, in the context of household and highway accidents, are equally apparent in the workplace setting. Statistical data indicates that, of all the accidents in which women were injured, 14 percent occurred in the course of employment: *Health Reports, supra,* at p 12.

[44] Whether it be in the household, on the roadways, or in the workplace, the imposition of a duty of care upon a pregnant woman towards her foetus or subsequently born child could render that woman liable in tort, even in situations where her conduct could not possibly affect a third party. A mother could be held liable in tort for negligent acts or defaults, which occurred while she was pregnant and alone, and which subsequently caused damages to her born alive child. This could include the careless performance of household activities – such as preparing meals, carrying loads of laundry, or shovelling snow – while alone in the home. It could include the negligent operation of any motor vehicle – be it for personal, family or work-related purposes – even if no third party could possibly be affected. A mother who injured her foetus in a careless fall, or who had an unreasonable lapse of attention in the home, at work or on the roadways, could potentially be held liable in tort for the damages suffered by her born alive child. The imposition of tort liability in those circumstances would significantly undermine the privacy and autonomy rights of women.

[45] It becomes apparent that many potential acts of negligence are inextricably intertwined with the lifestyle choices, the familial roles and the working lives of pregnant women. Women alone bear the burdens of pregnancy. Our society collectively benefits from the remarkably important role played by pregnant women. The imposition by courts of tort liability on mothers for prenatal negligence would restrict a pregnant woman's activities, reduce her autonomy to make decisions concerning her health, and have a negative impact upon her employment opportunities. It would have a profound effect upon every woman who is pregnant or merely contemplating pregnancy, and upon Canadian society in general. Any imposition of such tort liability should be undertaken, not by the courts, but by the legislature after careful study and debate.

[46]Moreover, the imposition of tort liability in this context would carry psychological and emotional repercussions for a mother who is sued in tort by her new-born child. To impose tort liability on a mother for an unreasonable lapse of prenatal care could have devastating consequences for the future relationship between the mother and her born alive child. In essence, the judicial recognition of a cause of action for maternal prenatal negligence is an inappropriate response to the pressing social issue of caring for children with special needs. Putting a mother through the trauma of a public trial to determine whether she was at fault for the injury suffered by her child can only add emotional and psychological trauma to an already tragic situation.

[47] Such litigation would, in all probability, have detrimental consequences, not only for the relationship between mother and child, but also for the relationship between the child and his or her family. Yet, family harmony will be particularly important for the creation of a caring and nurturing environment for the injured child, who will undoubtedly require much loving attention. It seems clear that the well-being of such a child cannot be readily severed from the interests of his or her family. In short, neither the best interests of the injured child, nor those of the remainder of the family, would be served by the judicial recognition of the suggested cause of action.

[48] The primary purposes of tort law are to provide compensation to the injured and deterrence to the tortfeasor. In the ordinary course of events, the imposition of tort liability on a mother for prenatal negligence would provide neither compensation nor deterrence. The pressing societal issue at the heart of this appeal is the lack of financial support currently available for the care of children with special needs. The imposition of a legal duty of care on a pregnant woman towards her foetus or subsequently born child will not solve this problem. If anything, attempting to address this social problem in a litigious setting would merely exacerbate the pain and trauma of a tragic situation. It may well be that carefully considered legislation could create a fund to compensate children with prenatally inflicted injuries. Alternatively, amendments to the motor vehicle insurance laws could achieve the same result in a more limited context. If, as a society, Canadians believe that children who sustain damages as a result of maternal prenatal negligence should be financially compensated, then the solution should be formulated, after careful study and debate, by the legislature.

2. Difficulties of Articulating a Judicial Standard of Conduct for Pregnant Women

[49] The infant respondent and certain interveners argued that a legal duty of care should be imposed upon a pregnant woman towards her foetus or born alive child. If such a duty of care is imposed upon pregnant women, then a judicially defined standard of conduct would have to be met. One intervener argued that tort liability should be imposed where a woman's

conduct fails to conform to a "reasonable pregnant woman" standard, which would apply to *all* aspects of her behaviour while pregnant. By contrast, the infant respondent argued in favour of the test put forward by the Court of Appeal in this case. This test draws a distinction between those situations in which a pregnant woman owes a "general duty of care" and those which relate to "lifestyle choices peculiar to parenthood". In the latter cases, a mother would be immune from tort liability for prenatal negligence. Another strand in the respondent's argument is that, at the very least, a mother should be held liable for all damages suffered by her born alive child as a result of prenatal injuries caused by her allegedly negligent driving. It was argued that the existence of a mandatory insurance regime for motor vehicle negligence entitles the born alive child to compensation in such cases.

[50] I believe that the courts cannot, and should not, articulate a standard of conduct for pregnant women. To do so raises all of the troubling questions posed by Cunningham J in *Stallman*, *supra* (at p 360):

> It must be asked. By what judicially defined standard would a mother have her every act or omission while pregnant subjected to State scrutiny? By what objective standard could a jury be guided in determining whether a pregnant woman did all that was necessary in order not to breach a legal duty to not interfere with her fetus' separate and independent right to be born whole? In what way would prejudicial and stereotypical beliefs about the reproductive abilities of women be kept from interfering with a jury's determination of whether a particular woman was negligent at any point during her pregnancy?

[51] For the reasons set out later, I am of the view that the various approaches advocated by the infant respondent and the interveners fail to avoid the pitfalls of a judicially defined standard of care for pregnant women. To adopt the "reasonable pregnant woman" standard involves far-reaching implications and extensive intrusions into the rights of bodily integrity, privacy and autonomy of pregnant women. The test articulated by the Court of Appeal is, I believe, inconsistent with general principles of tort law and unworkable in practice. Finally, if the existence of motor vehicle insurance is to be relied upon as the basis for imposing a legal duty of care upon pregnant women, then this solution should be enacted by the legislature. A specific and insurance-dependent rule of tort liability cannot, and should not, be created by the courts.

(a) Reasonable Pregnant Woman Standard

[52] Linked to the unpredictable impact on the privacy and autonomy rights of women lies the difficult, perhaps impossible, task of judicially defining a standard of conduct for pregnant women. An intervener argued that a mother-to-be should be held liable for all negligent behaviour causing damages to her foetus, which would be determined in accordance with a "reasonable pregnant woman" standard. An intervener submitted that, once aware of the pregnancy, a woman should be required to conform to the standard of behaviour of a "reasonably prudent expectant mother conducting herself under similar circumstances": D Santello, "Maternal Tort Liability for Prenatal Injuries" (1988), 22 *Suffolk UL Rev* 747, at p 775. This would involve an analysis of the risks associated with a given activity, the gravity of the possible injury, and the likelihood of that injury occurring. The standard of care would be reasonable rather than absolute, and thus a pregnant woman would not be expected to act as the insurer for the health of her subsequently born child.

[53] In my view, this standard is inappropriate. It raises the spectre of judicial scrutiny and potential liability imposed for "lifestyle choices". Thus, it brings into play all of the policy concerns articulated in *Winnipeg*, *supra*. For instance, it would be open to the trier of fact to determine that a "reasonable pregnant woman", who knows or has reason to know of her condition, should not smoke cigarettes or drink alcohol. Decisions involving the standard of care in tort law focus upon generally accepted norms, rather than on the individual woman. This objective standard would permit triers of fact to dictate, according to their own notions of proper conduct, the manner in which an expectant woman should behave throughout her pregnancy. Accordingly, a pregnant woman whose lifestyle conduct was under judicial scrutiny would not benefit from a truly individual standard, which takes into account her personal situation and acknowledges her autonomy.

[54] The importance of an individual standard of assessment is emphasized by the great disparities which exist in the financial situations, education, access to health services and ethnic backgrounds of pregnant women. These disparities would inevitably lead to an unfair application of a uniform legal standard concerned with the reasonable pregnant woman. In this regard, Cunningham J noted in *Stallman*, *supra*, at p 360:

> Pregnancy does not come only to those women who have within their means all that is necessary to effectuate the best possible prenatal environment: any female of child-bearing age may become pregnant. Within this pool of potential defendants are representatives of all socio-economic backgrounds: the well-educated and the ignorant; the rich and the poor; those women who have access to good health care and good

prenatal care and those who, for an infinite number of reasons, have not had access to any health care services.

[55] Tort law is concerned with the application of objective standards of reasonable behaviour to impugned conduct. It cannot adequately address the profound public policy implications raised by this appeal. Brock CJ and Batchelder J, in dissent, expressed serious doubts as to whether it is "possible to subject a woman's judgment, action, and behavior as they relate to the well-being of her fetus to a judicial determination of reasonableness in a manner that is consistent and free from arbitrary results": *Bonte, supra*, at p 468. I share those reservations.

(b) Lifestyle Choices Peculiar to Parenthood

[56] On behalf of the infant respondent, it was argued that these policy considerations, although admittedly profound, are not raised in this appeal. Rather, it was submitted that this case is only concerned with whether a mother may be liable to her born alive child for her prenatal negligence in the operation of a motor vehicle. This position was adopted by the New Brunswick Court of Appeal. Hoyt CJNB held that, because a pregnant woman who is driving owes a general duty of care to members of the public, she must owe that same duty to her subsequently born child. However, he went on to hold that, if the activity in question is "peculiar to parenthood" or involves a "lifestyle choice", then a child born alive with injuries cannot commence an action in negligence against his or her mother. A similar dividing line is described by Professor Flemings, *supra*, at p 168:

> More complex is the question of whether a child should have a claim for prenatal injury against a parent. A distinction is in order between the general duty to avoid injury which the defendant owes to all others and those peculiar to parenthood. An instance of the former is the duty to drive carefully, which even the mother at the wheel owes to her foetus. On the other hand, there is strong aversion against inquisition into alleged parental indiscretions during pregnancy, like excessive smoking, drinking or taking drugs.

Thus, Professor Fleming describes the immunity from tort liability in this context as relating to all those activities which are "peculiar to parenthood"; that is to say, those activities that relate uniquely to parenting.

[57] With respect to those who hold this opinion, I am of the view that this distinction is unworkable. It fails to confer the scope of the role of a parent. Driving is an integral part of parenting in a great many families. For instance, a parent must often drive to pick up children from school or child care, to take them to the dentist or doctor, or to hockey practice or swimming lessons. Indeed, I doubt whether any court can articulate a sound legal test, which is both theoretically coherent and workable in practice, that could effectively limit maternal prenatal liability to cases of motor vehicle negligence. Ultimately, only the legislature can create such a narrow and specific basis of tort liability.

[58] In my view, a distinction based on duties which are "peculiar to parenthood" would lead to inconsistent results. In this regard, the American cases which considered a partial abrogation of the parental immunity doctrine, which excludes acts involving the "exercise of parental authority and discretion", are instructive. Certain American courts have rejected the parental immunity exceptions because they result in arbitrary distinctions between acts unique to parenting and those that are not: *Harman by Hartman v Hartman* 821 SW 2d 852 (Mo 1991), at pp 856–57. Significantly, several American cases considered the operation of a motor vehicle to be a family activity which engaged the parental immunity doctrine. This position treated the use of an automobile as essential to the functioning of a household. In *Hogan v Hogan*, 435 NE 2d 770 (Ill App Ct 1982), it was held that driving a child to her piano lessons constituted the operation of a motor vehicle to accomplish a family purpose. Similarly, *Eisele v Tenuta*, 404 NE 2d 349 (Ill App Ct 1980), held that driving with a minor to a college was directly connected with family purposes and objectives. In *Johnson v Myers*, 277 NE 2d 778 (Ill App Ct 1972) at pp 779–80, it was stated that "[i]n a modern society the motor vehicle plays an intimate and necessary part in the accomplishment of many family purposes". This seems to be an eminently sensible conclusion which reflects the scheduling demands of contemporary society.

[59] The Court of Appeal also referred to a "general duty of care" in articulating its test for maternal tort liability. With respect, there can be no such duty owed to the public at large. As a matter of tort law, a duty of care must always be owed by one person to another. Negligence cannot exist in the abstract. There must be a specific duty owed to a foreseeable plaintiff, which is breached, in order for negligence to arise. A "general duty of care" does not exist. Accordingly, it cannot be used as a legal test for the imposition of tort liability in cases of prenatal negligence. Even if it were possible to identify readily those activities in which a woman owes a "general duty of care", this would not limit the extent of external scrutiny and control over a pregnant woman's daily life. To rely on the "general duty of care" distinction,

in order to hold that this appeal does not raise important issues of social policy, is bound to introduce a significant element of uncertainty into tort law.

[60] Moreover, it is clear that the duty of care imposed by the Court of Appeal is by no means narrow. It would impose tort liability on mothers for prenatal negligence *in all situations* in which a "general duty of care" is owed to third parties. The distinction between lifestyle choices and a so-called "general duty of care" involves a standard which can be readily applied to many areas of a pregnant woman's behaviour, most of which are not protected by insurance. The potential breadth of maternal tort liability under this test was recognized by Professor Ian R Kerr in "Pre-Natal Fictions and Post-Partum Actions" (1998), 20 *Dal LJ* 237, at pp 270–71:

> ... employing the distinction between duties owed to the general public and those peculiar to parenthood does not assist the Court in narrowing the issue in *Dobson*. In fact, it has the very opposite effect. The rule that the Court of Appeal has derived from Fleming's distinction is that *duties owed by a pregnant woman to the general public are owed to her unborn child as well*. The consequence of this rule, which seems to have gone completely unnoticed by the Court, is that it will allow a child's litigation guardian to commence actions for pre-natal injuries resulting from innumerable sorts of lifestyle choices that a pregnant woman might embrace. These would include activities such as rollerblading, shopping in a crowded mall, spraying weedkiller on her crops, sailing, lighting fireworks for her children on Canada day, or any other activity where there is risk of harm to the general public. There is nothing unique or narrow about the act of driving a car. It is just as much a lifestyle choice as any of the other activities just mentioned ...
>
> Ironically, in its attempt to shield women from inquisitions into alleged parental indiscretions such as smoking and drinking, the Court of Appeal has expanded the liability of pregnant women. [Emphasis in original.]

[61] In essence, a rule of tort law attempting to distinguish between acts of a mother-to-be involving privacy interests and those constituting common torts would of necessity result in arbitrary line-drawing and inconsistent verdicts. Simply to state that a "general duty of care" will not apply to "lifestyle choices" is to leave open the possibility that many actions taken by pregnant women will not be considered lifestyle choices for the purposes of litigation. Is drug use, if prescribed by a physician, a lifestyle choice? Is a hazardous work environment a lifestyle choice? Indeed, is it not arguable that driving while pregnant, for the benefit and welfare of the family, constitutes a lifestyle choice?

[62] In *Winnipeg, supra*, it was argued that the potential state intrusions on behalf of the foetus would be minimal because the duty of care could be defined narrowly. It was submitted that the standard should be "to refrain from activities that have no substantial value to a pregnant woman's well-being or right of self-determination" (para 38). In rejecting this test as too vague and broad, McLachlin J observed that the proposed standard raised the following intractable questions (at para 39):

> What does substantial value to a woman's well-being mean? What does a woman's well-being include? What is involved in a woman's right of self-determination – all her choices, or merely some of them? And if some only, what is the criterion of distinction? Although it may be easy to determine that abusing solvents does not add substantial value to a pregnant woman's well-being and may not be the type of self-determination that deserves protection, other behaviours are not as easily classified.

[63] Similarly the test proposed by the Court of Appeal fails to articulate a workable judicial standard for distinguishing between tortious and non-tortious conduct. Just as McLachlin J could not identify a bright line to ground liability on the basis of conduct which fails to add "substantial value to a pregnant woman's well-being", a similar difficulty is presented by a liability rule defined by behaviour involving "lifestyle choices" or conduct "peculiar to parenthood". The determination of whether a duty of care should be imposed must be made by considering the effects of tort liability on the privacy and autonomy interests of women, and upon their families, rather than by reference to a formalistic characterization of the conduct in question.

Lamer CJ, L'Heureux-Dubé, Gonthier, Iacobucci and Binnie JJ concurred.

McLachlin J also agreed with Cory J's reasoning but, in addition, together with L'Heureux-Dubé J, argued that liability would run counter to the fundamental values of liberty and equality enshrined in the Canadian Charter.

Two Justices, Major and Bastarache JJ, dissented.

Major J: [109] In my opinion, the policy concerns raised in *Winnipeg, supra*, relative to the pregnant woman and her foetus do not apply to the mother and her born alive child. This action was brought on behalf of a legal person, not a foetus. Cory J suggests that, from the perspective of a pregnant woman, the important legal distinction between her foetus and her born alive child might not appear relevant. In his view, a pregnant woman might conclude that the behavioural restrictions to which she would be subjected in either case are identical. But the compelling point of departure is that, in contrast to *Winnipeg, supra*, in this appeal the pregnant woman's perspective is not the only legally recognized perspective. It competes with the recognized perspective of her born alive child.

[110] The issue here is twofold. First, would a finding that Cynthia Dobson owes the respondent a duty of care result in additional behavioural restrictions on her while she was pregnant? If so, are those restrictions of a nature that would justify a finding that the respondent's right to commence a tort action against his mother for prenatal injuries allegedly sustained as a result of her negligent driving should give way to Cynthia Dobson's autonomy rights on policy grounds?

[111] I respectfully disagree with Cory J that sufficient policy concerns have been raised on the facts of this case to negative the child's right to sue in tort. The appellant Cynthia Dobson was already under a legal obligation to drive carefully. She owed a duty of care to passengers in her car and to other users of the highway, such as John Carter, the other motorist involved in the collision. If her negligent driving caused the collision, she will be liable to John Carter.

[112] In these circumstances, it would be unjustified to hold that the appellant should not be liable to her born alive child on the grounds that such liability would restrict her freedom of action. Her freedom of action in respect of her driving was already restricted by her duty of care to users of the highway. Hence, to acknowledge that the suffering of her born alive child, Ryan Dobson, was within the reasonably foreseeable ambit of the risk created by her negligent driving is hardly a limitation of her freedom of action. The appellant mother would not have had to take any further precautions, additional to those she was already legally obliged to take, in order to avoid liability to her born alive child.

[113] The appellant's autonomy interests are not in issue. She was not legally free to operate a motor vehicle without due care. She did not have the freedom to drive carelessly. Therefore, it cannot be said that the imposition of a duty of care to her born alive child would restrict her freedom to drive. The respondent child cannot take away from his mother a freedom she did not have...

[115] On the facts of this case, Ryan Dobson's *prima facie* right to sue in tort arises only on the same grounds and in the same way as that of the driver of the other car. In these circumstances, the appellant's freedom of action is not in issue, and the suggestion that her son's rights ought to be negatived so as to protect her freedom of action is misplaced.

[116] Where a pregnant woman already owes a duty of care to a third party in respect of the same behaviour for which her born alive child seeks to find her liable, policy considerations pertinent to the pregnant woman's freedom of action cannot operate so as to negative the child's *prima facie* right to sue. The duty of care imposed on the pregnant woman is not more onerous because of her potential liability to her born alive child.

[117] The presence of a duty of care owed to a third party in respect of the same behaviour for which her born alive child seeks to find her liable precludes a pregnant woman from arguing successfully that her freedom of action would be restricted by the imposition of a duty of care to her born alive child. A grant of immunity from tort liability rooted in policy considerations pertinent to a pregnant woman's freedom of action must necessarily rest on a showing that such freedom of action would be restricted by the imposition of a duty of care to the born alive child. No such showing seems possible where the pregnant woman's freedom of action is already restricted in the very same respect by a duty of care owed to a third party...

[119] But matters are different where the pregnant woman does *not* owe a third party a duty of care in respect of the behaviour, as, for instance, in her lifestyle choices such as smoking, drinking, and dietary and health-care decisions. That is also true of various other activities that may place the pregnant woman in harm's way. The examples range from an unhealthy work or home environment to activities as extreme as bungy jumping. In such cases, the second branch of the *Kamloops* test may prevent the imposition of a duty of care because her freedom of action is in issue and policy reasons for immunity can be adduced. The distinction is plain and is obscured only by slippery slope and flood-gate types of argument founded in an understandably emotional response to the question.

[120] Assume, for example, that another pregnant woman was a passenger in Cynthia Dobson's car. If, as a result of negligent driving, the other pregnant woman gave birth to an injured child, there is absolutely no doubt that that born alive child would have a right to sue Cynthia Dobson: see *Tramways, supra*, and *Duval, supra*. In those circumstances, policy reasons flowing from Cynthia Dobson's freedom of action capable of negativing Ryan Dobson's right to sue seem impossible to formulate. His mother's freedom of action in

respect of her driving was already restricted by the duty of care she owed to, *inter alia*, another born alive child.

[121] The example confirms that no intrusion into a pregnant woman's freedom of action can be demonstrated in cases where a duty of care owed to a third party in respect of the same behaviour forms part of the factual situation. In such cases, the pregnant woman's freedom of action is not in issue.

[122] This view of the matter has the advantage of providing a bright-line test to distinguish situations in which the pregnant woman's freedom of action is in issue from situations in which her freedom of action is not in issue. A given factual transaction either involves a duty of care to third parties or it does not. These matters are not crystal clear. But the law of tort is well equipped to distinguish between situations where duties of care are owed and situations where duties of care are not owed. In jurisprudential matters, few lines could be brighter than those situations where a pregnant woman owes to third parties a duty of care in respect of the very same behaviour of which her born alive child complains and situations where she does not owe such duty to third parties.

[123] Policy considerations flowing from a pregnant woman's autonomy interests are not operative in situations, such as the case before us, where those interests are not in issue. These situations are distinguishable from situations where those interests are indeed in issue. Therefore, there is no need to beware that, in deciding this appeal on its own facts, we will have to decide infinitely more difficult cases truly involving lifestyle choices and autonomy interests of pregnant women. On the contrary, the very depth, complexity and importance of such cases demands that they not be decided until they in fact arise before this Court.

[124] The determining question is what social policy can justify the conclusion that, as between the rights of a pregnant woman and those of her born alive child, the rights of the child should yield.

[125] The concerns formulated in *Winnipeg*, *supra*, are not sufficient to take into account the additional factor present in the instant case: the legal personality of the born alive child. At issue is the relationship between the rights of a pregnant woman and the rights of her born alive child. A one-sided emphasis on either side of this relationship necessarily misses the subject-matter it is attempting to analyse. Such an emphasis simply begs the question.

[126] That question is what social policy considerations justify the denial of a born alive child's right to recover for negligently caused physical damages. No compelling evidence, in fact no evidence, was presented that should as a matter of social policy place the child in a subservient position to that of the negligent mother.

[127] The bare assertion of social policy concerns expressly and unilaterally centred on a pregnant woman's rights are not a sufficient answer to the question whether a pregnant woman's rights should prevail over the equally recognized rights of her born alive child. It is no answer to the plaintiff in this case that unilateral concerns about a pregnant woman's competing rights are sufficient to "negative" a negligent violation of his physical integrity. His rights, too, are at stake.

[128] While the law may grant immunity from liability based on policy reasons, those reasons must be clear and compelling and are conspicuously absent in this case. The removal of the child's cause of action is extreme and it should follow that the policy reasons for doing so should be obvious and persuasive. There was no authority advanced to support the defendant's claim in this case; that is, authority that would negate a pregnant woman's legal responsibility for negligent acts against her born alive child, where the effects of those acts are reasonably foreseeable and where they violate the physical integrity of a legal person. To recall Lamont J's words in *Tramways*, *supra*, at p 464, no other plaintiff would "be compelled, without any fault on its part, to go through life carrying the seal of another's fault and bearing a very heavy burden of infirmity and inconvenience without any compensation therefor".

[129] The special relationship between a pregnant woman and her foetus is a biological fact. This biological fact is significant for the mother-defendant. But it is also deeply significant for the born alive child-plaintiff. The legal or social policy implications to be drawn from that biological fact cannot be ascertained in the absence of equal acknowledgment of the rights of the child.

[130] To grant a pregnant woman immunity from the reasonably foreseeable consequences of her acts for her born alive child would create a legal distortion as no other plaintiff carries such a one-sided burden, nor any defendant such an advantage.

[131] Aside from a pregnant woman's autonomy interests, there may be policy considerations flowing from concerns about the appropriateness of intra-familial litigation that may be sufficient to negative any child's right to sue its parents in tort. The considerations, however, must apply to all members of the defined family unit. The conclusion that such concerns only bar tort action brought by born alive children who sustained injuries while still *in utero* is not justified.

[132] As no policy concerns sufficient to negative the child's right to sue arise on the facts of this case, the born alive respondent has the legal capacity to commence a tort action against his appellant mother for prenatal injuries allegedly sustained as a result of her negligent driving.

[133] Under the direction given by the majority in *Winnipeg, supra*, it is my opinion that the removal of Ryan Dobson's right to sue in tort for negligent violations of his physical integrity lies within the exclusive purview of the legislature, subject to the limits imposed by the *Canadian Charter of Rights and Freedoms*.

[134] I would dismiss this appeal.

Bastarache J concurred.

You will notice reference to the earlier decision of the Court in *Winnipeg Child and Family Services (Northwest Area) v G (DF)* [1997] 2 SCR 925. This case concerned the power of the court under its *parens patriae* jurisdiction to make orders to protect the life or health of an unborn child from the conduct of its mother. We discussed that decision earlier in Chapter 6. In *Winnipeg* one of the arguments was that the mother owed her unborn child a duty in negligence not to unreasonably cause it in injury. The court (by a majority) rejected that argument. In *Dobson* all the justices accepted that *Winnipeg* precluded a duty of care arising where to do so would call into question 'life-style' choices of the mother. The dissenting justices, however, in *Dobson* concluded this was not the case where the injury arose out of a mother's negligent driving – when she already owed a duty of care to others. It will, of course, be quite apparent that decisions about medical treatment are *a fortiori* 'life-style' choices made in exercise of the woman's legal right to refuse and she owes no one else a duty of care in respect of that decision. All the justices in the Canadian Supreme Court would remove this area of maternal conduct from the remit of the tort of negligence.

In England, the point has never arisen for decision but notice Dillon LJ's equivocal comment in *Burton* (*supra*). Perhaps, the point will never be decided because of the Congenital Disabilities (Civil Liability) Act 1976. Despite the fact that English law does not equate mother and unborn child as one (*A-G's Reference (No 3 of 1994)* [1998] AC 245 (HL)), the legislative policy is surely the correct one. Whilst not determinative of this issue, the 'forced caesarean section' cases illuminate the court's reluctance to be drawn into possible conflicts between mother and unborn child. To recognise a maternal duty of care would do precisely that, albeit post-birth.

Returning then to the question of whether a mother as agent of the child may affect the child's claim, the conclusion based upon principle must be that it cannot. We reach this view because we would argue that the mother as agent may only act for the benefit and not to the detriment of the unborn child: an echo of the civil law doctrine of the *nasciturus*. The Law Commission, however, in its Report, *Injuries to Unborn Children* (*op cit*) recommended that the conduct of the mother should be attributed to the child and consequently affect any claim of the child.

The mother's contributory negligence

65. Our provisional conclusion as to a mother's liability to her own child led us, almost inevitably, to the opinion that a mother's own contributory negligence ought not to effect any reduction in her child's damages. On consultation many have expressed the opinion that such a rule would be grossly unfair to tortfeasors and their insurers in a fault based tort system, and that the physical fact of identification between mother and foetus during pregnancy ought to mean that the mother's own negligence should reduce the damages payable by a tortfeasor. The medical treatment and medication of a pregnant woman depends so much upon her co-operation and care for herself that the possibility of joint liability (perhaps with the mother herself most to blame) is one which cannot be ignored. In such circumstances we think it would be wrong if, perhaps for very slight carelessness in comparison with the mother's own negligence, a doctor, chemist or drug manufacturer had to compensate the child in full for his disability.

Conclusion as to the mother's contributory negligence

66. These arguments and our own change of mind as to the mother's liability to her own child lead us now to advise that a mother's negligence should be available as a partial defence to a tortfeasor where her fault has also contributed to her child's pre-natal injury.

Contractual exemption or limitation of liability: Volenti non fit injuria

67. Strict adherence to legal principle led us in our working paper to the provisional conclusion that neither an exception clause in a mother's contract nor a mother's own voluntary assumption of risk should negative or reduce a defendant's liability. On consultation the majority of those who commented upon this provisional conclusion disagreed with it. The Bar Council's memorandum most clearly expressed the contrary view to that at which provisionally we had arrived:-

> Paragraph 25 of the Working Paper raises the cognate questions of contractual exclusion or limitation of liability and *volenti non fit injuria* … In either instance, we find it difficult to evade the effects of physical identification between mother and foetus. If two women engage in a wrestling match for the entertainment of television viewers, is the child of one who was pregnant at the time entitled to sue the other for damage for assault if he is born with an incapacity traceable to the fight? And are women to be perhaps denied transport by air or sea or employment in a particular industry on the ground that it is impossible to limit liability in contract with a foetus? Moreover we think that identification of mother with foetus in contractual relations with other members of the community is socially both acceptable and desirable.

68. Added emphasis to one of these points was given by Dr OM Stone, a member of the Family Law Sub-Committee of the Society of Public Teachers of Law, who wrote: 'I think there is a real danger that what may be a remote possibility of liability to an unborn child may be seized upon as justifying refusal to enter into a wide variety of contracts or social relationships with women of any age or status'.

69. We are convinced by these arguments that our provisional conclusion was wrong. Contractual exemptions from liability are often objectionable, but we believe that the proper way to control them is to deal with them as exemption clauses, and not as a consequence of the fact that a particular claim is being brought by a child in respect of pre-natal injuries. We are at present engaged in a full study of exemption clauses, including exemptions from or limitations of liability for negligence in respect of personal injury. In our working paper on that subject we expressed the provisional view that certain exemption clauses should be made void and that others might be subjected to a judicial test of reasonableness. Our consultation on that complex subject has confirmed our provisional view that in some circumstances it may be reasonable to rely on an exemption clause. If in a particular case it would be reasonable for a defendant to rely on a contractual exemption in a claim brought by the mother with whom he contracted, we see no reason why he should not seek to rely on the same exemption in a claim brought by the child in respect of pre-natal injury. Again, if the contract with the mother purports specifically to exclude or limit liability to her unborn child we see no reason why the defendant should not be entitled to rely upon it in an action brought by the child. Clearly, if an exemption clause is void (such as a contractual exemption from liability in respect of the death of or bodily injury to a passenger in a public service vehicle) or subject to judicial control in relation to the mother it should be similarly void or subject to control in relation to the child she is bearing.

70. There is one problem with respect to contractual exemptions: that the child, unborn when the contract with the mother is made, can never be a party to the contract so that the doctrine of privity of contract will prevent the clause from binding him. If our policy that the child should be identified with the mother in relation to such provisions is right, this must constitute a new exception to the doctrine of privity of contract.

Conclusion as to contractual exemption or limitation of liability and volenti non fit injuria

71. We are convinced by the arguments of the Bar Council that our provisional conclusion was wrong and that we ought now to advise that a defendant should be able to rely upon a contractual term binding upon the mother which exempts him from or limits his liability either towards her or towards her unborn child and upon a mother's voluntary assumption of risk. While contractual exemptions from liability are often objectionable, we believe that the proper way to control them is to deal with them generally. Our present conclusion has been arrived at in the knowledge that we are at present engaged on a full study of exemption clauses and we envisage that any recommendations which we ultimately make on this subject should become applicable in cases where pre-natal injury has been caused.

(We will see later the provisions of the Congenital Disabilities (Civil Liability) Act 1976 which reflect these recommendations (*infra*). It should be noticed here, however, that as regards contractual exemption the child's claim is now only affected to the extent that the law allows for contractual exemption by virtue of the Unfair Contract Terms Act 1977.)

(ii) WHERE THE CHILD IS BORN DEAD

It would seem that no claim could be brought in English law on behalf of a child born dead. The law is discussed in the following extract.

A Whitfield 'Common Law Duties to Unborn Children' (1993) 1 Med L Rev 28

In a number of American states, recovery by a child who dies *in utero* as a result of the defendant's negligent conduct has been permitted under Wrongful Death Acts. [See, for example, *White v Yup* 45 P 2d 617 (1969) (Nev Sup Ct) and *Mone v Greyhound Lines* 331 NE 2d 916 (1975) (Mass Sup Jud Ct). Contrast, *Justus v Atchison* 565 P 2d 122 (1977) (Cal Sup Ct).] The Second Restatement of the Law of Torts, however, states: 'if the child is not born alive, there is no liability unless the applicable wrongful death statute so provides' [at para 869].

The English position, it is submitted, is that in the case of stillbirth there is no liability under statute to anyone for the following reasons…[N]o right, either of dependency or for bereavement, can arise out of the Fatal Accidents Act 1976 because death is a precondition of such rights. The courts will inevitably conclude that one who, in the eyes of the law, has never become a 'person', cannot be said to have attained life, and therefore cannot be said to have suffered death … For the same reasons there will be no claim under the Law Reform (Miscellaneous Provisions) Act 1934 which applies only 'on the death of any person' [s 1(1)].

When considering the common law position in *Burton* and *de Martell*, Dillon LJ seemed to contemplate, obiter, that a still birth may give rise to some sort of claim by the child. He stated:

I doubt very much whether there are any claims now outstanding which are not statute-barred, in respect of children still-born before 22 July 1976 or any children born before that date who are locked in litigation with their mothers over whether the mother tasted alcohol or followed a diet other than that recommended by the current phase of medical opinion during pregnancy.

This is surprising. There can be no actionable breach of duty to those born dead: before they are born they are not 'persons' and after they are born they have no legal rights. Therefore, they cannot sue.

The only claim likely to exist, therefore, is a straightforward claim for personal injuries by a parent, usually a mother, based on circumstances giving rise to a stillbirth and quantified by reference to its consequences. That was the position in *Bagley v North Hertfordshire Health Authority* [1986] NLJ Rep 1014]. Simon Brown J accepted that a statutory bereavement claim could not arise where a child was born dead, but only where a live child was tortiously killed. However, he awarded damages to the mother not only for her physical illness but also for her loss of the satisfaction of bringing her pregnancy, confinement and labour to a successful and joyous conclusion, and for the frustration of her plans to enlarge her family. By this sensible route the common law thus provides direct compensation based on the experiences and sufferings and loss of the surviving parent(s) alone.

The majority of US States allow a wrongful death action for the death of a viable unborn child. A few (about six) even allow an action where the child is not viable (see discussion in, D Meade 'Wrongful Death and the Unborn Child: Should Viability be a prerequisite for a cause of action?' (1989) 14 Journal of Contemporary Health Law and Policy 421). As Adrian Whitfield points out, English law will not follow suit because it would require the Fatal Accidents Act 1976 to be construed so as to confer legal status upon the unborn child which it clearly does not possess (*A-G's Reference (No 3 of 1994) supra*). Damages for bereavement under the 1976 Act would likewise require a 'live birth' followed by death. Nevertheless, as he states, damages for the sequelae of a still-birth have been awarded as part of the mother's personal injury claim (*Bagley*, supra. See also *Greive v Salford HA* [1991] 2 Med LR 295 (Rose J)). An action for recognised psychiatric injury could also succeed depending upon the circumstances. Hence, a medical trauma leading to still-birth might lead to foreseeable psychiatric injury to the mother and, if present or witnessing the immediate aftermath, the father under the 'secondary victim' rules (see *supra*, ch 4).

(c) Occurrence before conception

A child may be born harmed as a result of an occurrence which took place before conception rather than *in utero*. Our concern here is only with situations where an analogy may be drawn with the cases already discussed, ie where the defendant's conduct *causes* the disability or harm which the child suffers. We discuss later pre-conception occurrences which do not cause harm to the child but which, when the child is conceived, mean that the child will be born with disabilities which result from a cause independent of the defendant, ie negligent genetic counselling (see 'wrongful life' *infra*).

A Whitfield 'Common Law Duties to Unborn Children' (1993) 1 Med L Rev 28

At common law the central issue is whether there is an act or omission leading to an injury to a child as yet to be conceived which will amount to a breach of *duty to the child later born*. There are no English authorities on the point. Dicta in the judgment of Clarke JA in *X and Y v Pal* [(1991) 23 NSWLR 26 at 37; 40; 41; and 42], imply that no distinction should be drawn between children injured by pre-conception wrongs and those injured by wrongs occurring during pregnancy…

The Law Commission, while not distinguishing between types of pre-conception occurrence, gave several examples of injury which in fact fall within this category. One is where physical injury is caused to a woman's pelvis as a result of which injury is caused to her child *in utero* when it is subsequently conceived and born. Such an occurrence could be the responsibility of almost anybody whether a car driver, an employer or an assailant. A doctor too might be responsible for such an occurrence, though a better example in practice might be where an abortion is negligently performed which so weakens the uterus that it ruptures at the end of a subsequent pregnancy and injures the child during labour. Another example would be that of pre-conception exposure through chemicals or radiation which causes gene mutation and consequent disability.

In such cases, it may well be possible to show that 'but for' the occurrence complained of the children concerned would have been born in any event and would (absent the pre-conception occurrence) have been healthy. These claims are, in fact, indistinguishable legally from *Burton* and *de Martell*. The accident of timing in the negligent conduct of the defendant ought to be irrelevant. Take, for example, the case of the negligent manufacturer of a toxic nappy. On the *Burton* and *de Martell* analysis, he will be liable to a baby whose buttocks are scorched even though the baby is *in utero* at the time of manufacture [See *Grant v Australian Knitting Mills Ltd* [1936] AC 85]. It is difficult to see any justice in the defence that a similarly injured baby who was not in fact conceived at the time of manufacture should have no claim.

It should not matter, therefore, when the negligent conduct occurs, but rather liability should turn upon the nature of the plaintiff's injury. Consequently, children born disabled as a result of pre-conception occurrences would, therefore, have claims in England, subject to questions of proof and remoteness.

As you will have noticed, Adrian Whitfield refers to the New South Wales case of *X and Y v Pal* where the occurrences which were alleged to have caused the child plaintiff's harm took place before she was conceived as well as while she was *in utero*.

X and Y v Pal (1991) NSWLR 26, [1992] Med LR 195 (NSW CA)

Clarke JA: This judgment concerns two appeals by X and her daughter Y each of whom unsuccessfully sued the three respondents, who were medical practitioners, for negligence. The reason why the appellants are named in the paper as X and Y is that Allen J made an order that they should be so known in order to conceal their true identity. During the trial the parties agreed that X should be referred to as 'AA' and Y as 'CA' and for the sake of convenience I will describe them in that way.

In about January 1973, AA became pregnant. She was at that time suffering from syphilis although she was unaware of that fact. On 2 March 1973, she consulted Dr Pal, the first respondent (I shall refer to him as Dr Pal), who was an obstetrician and gynaecologist and whose patient she remained throughout her pregnancy. Prior to her confinement Dr Pal submitted her for a number of tests. However, he failed to have her screened for syphilis. On 23 October 1973, she gave birth to a child by caesarean section. At birth the child had gross hydrocephaly and other physical deformities from which he died on 22 November 1973.

Prior to the birth of her first child, AA had been referred to the third respondent, a specialist paediatrician Dr Grunseit, by Dr Pal and she saw him on 23 October prior to the caesarean section. Dr Grunseit was also present at the delivery of the child.

On 3 July 1974, AA, who had decided that she would like to change gynaecologists, saw Dr Harris, the second respondent, with a view to determining whether she was likely to encounter problems with a further pregnancy. Following the consultation she saw Dr Grunseit again. He told her that her first baby had died from toxoplasmosis and that there was no reason why she should not proceed to become pregnant again. There was some suggestion in the evidence that AA was in fact pregnant at the time she first saw Dr Harris but if she was there is no doubt that neither she nor Dr Harris knew that fact. She was first diagnosed as being pregnant on 4 September 1974 and remained under the care of Dr Harris until after the birth of CA on 27 March 1975. She was submitted for various tests by Dr Harris but at no stage was she screened for syphilis.

CA was born dysmorphic and mentally retarded. As a result of a number of tests which were carried out on CA shortly after her birth it was discovered that both CA and AA were suffering from syphilis. This discovery shocked AA who had not been aware until that time that she was suffering from syphilis. CA has continued to suffer from a number of abnormalities, the principal of which are mental retardation and disfigurement. In her action it was claimed that all of her abnormalities resulted from the negligent failure of each of the three respondents to submit her mother AA for syphilis testing.

For her part AA claimed that she suffered from nervous and emotional shock and depression as a consequence of having given birth to a deformed child who was suffering from syphilis. She also claimed that her syphilis predated her first pregnancy and that the failure of each of the doctors to ensure that testing for syphilis was carried out was negligent.

Both actions were heard by Sully J who found that each of the doctors had been negligent, in the sense that they had failed to take reasonable care, in failing to have AA screened for syphilis.

On the appeal it was common ground between the parties that if AA had been screened for syphilis before her pregnancy with CA, or within the first trimester (twelve weeks) of that pregnancy, steps could have been taken which would have ensured that CA was not affected by the disease; that CA was born with congenital syphilis and that, but for the negligence of each of the respondents, CA would not have contracted congenital syphilis…

The primary submission of senior counsel for the respondents took the following course. A cause of action in negligence is dependent upon proof of damage consequential upon the breach of a duty to take care; it follows that proof of a duty to take care is essential to the claim of negligence; further the duty must be owed to the person claiming against the allegedly careless person – except in particular cases, of which this is not one, the fact that a duty may be owed to a person other than the one claiming damages is irrelevant; importantly, the relevant duty must be in existence when the conduct said to constitute a breach of that duty occurred; at the time Dr Pal was careless CA had not been conceived; it followed that Dr Pal did not owe her a duty of care. Summarised, the submission was that the law does not recognise a duty to take care to a person conceived subsequent to the conduct said to constitute a breach of that duty.

Fleming, *The Law of Torts* 7th edn (1987) at 152, saw two problems in a claim brought by a child deformed as a consequence of negligent conduct occurring before her birth. First, the lack of legal personality and, secondly, the absence of foreseeability.

The latter is a problem to be resolved on the facts of the case just as in the more usual cases which come before the courts. In some instances it many not be possible for a plaintiff to establish this element but in others the pre-natal injury leading to a child being born deformed may be just the kind of thing which a doctor would recognise may occur if he did not use due care. Fleming postulated two ways of overcoming the problem of the absence of legal personality. One was to deem the child 'to be a person entitled on birth of the child' (when the damage occurred and the cause of action arose) and resting liability solely on foreseeability.

If one postulates the duty in terms of the class or category of persons to whom it is owed, as I believe one should, and accepts that there may be within that class persons who are not born when the careless conduct occurs there is no need to resort to artificial concepts, such as deeming, or to be unduly troubled about the child's lack of legal personality at the time of that conduct.

While in particular cases the relevant question may simply be whether it can be said that A owed a duty to B there will be other cases in which the question, more accurately phrased, is whether A owes a duty to a category of persons so that if he breaches that duty any of the persons within that category, subject to particular defences which may arise in relation to the claim being pursued, may sue. Of course, proof that a duty is owed by A to B which duty is breached by A will not, without more, give rise to a cause of action in B. That will only arise if B suffers damage as a result of the breach. In a case such as the present that damage will be suffered, or at least the law will only recognise that it has been suffered, upon the birth of the child. The fact that damage was suffered many years after the breach of duty has never been regarded as an impediment to the cause of action. Nor should, in my view, the fact that a particular plaintiff acquired legal personality (and suffered damage) years after the breach …

For my part I would … say that if the injured person falls within the class to whom the duty was owed it matters not that he was not identified, or not in existence, at the time when those acts occurred which constituted the breach of the duty to take care…

In principle therefore it should be accepted that a person may be subjected to a duty of care to a child who was neither born nor conceived at the time of his careless acts or omissions such that he may be found liable in damages to that child. Whether or not that duty will arise depends upon whether there is a relevant relationship between the careless person and the class of persons of whom the child is one…

Accordingly while it must be accepted that the fact that a person who was injured by the careless acts or omissions of another, was neither born nor conceived at the time of those careless acts or omissions may be relevant to a determination whether a relationship of proximity existed it is certainly not the only relevant consideration.

The conclusion that a child, when born, may be able to sue in respect of careless conduct occurring before the child's birth, or even conception, leads inevitably to the next question whether Dr Pal owed a duty of care to CA. Given the undemanding nature of the test of foreseeability it is not difficult to conclude that it was foreseeable that if Dr Pal was careless in his treatment of AA damage might be suffered by children later born to her: see *Wyon Shire Council v Shirt* (1980) 146 CLR 40. But, as has been made clear by a recent series of cases in the High Court (*Jaensch v Coffey* (1984) 155 CLR 549; *San Sebastian Pty Ltd v Minister Administering the Environmental Planning and Assessment Act 1979* (1986) 68 ALR 161; *Sutherland Shire Council v Heyman* and *Hawkins v Clayton*) a relevant duty of care would arise only if there existed a relationship of proximity between CA and Dr Pal. In *Cook v Cook* (1986) 162 CLR 376 at 382, it was said that a relationship of proximity operates as:

> ... an overriding control of the test of reasonable foreseeability ... It constitutes the general determinant of the categories of case in which the common law of negligence recognizes the existence of a duty to take reasonable care to avoid a reasonably foreseeable and real risk of injury to another.

Although CA complains of physical injury this is not a case in which it can be said, as it can in settled areas of the law involving direct physical injury or damage caused by negligent act, that the reasonable foreseeability of injury to CA provides an adequate indication that the relationship between CA and Dr Pal bore the requisite degree of proximity.

Where a doctor gives careless advice, or carelessly fails to ensure that specific tests are administered to a patient it is foreseeable that damage may be caused to the patient as a consequence of that carelessness. In those circumstances it is beyond dispute that there is a relevant relationship of proximity between the doctor and the patient. But it may be difficult to determine whether the doctor in question owes a duty to take care to any other persons. For instance, to take an example raised during the hearing of the appeal, if a doctor negligently failed to diagnose a child's illness as German measles so that the child continued attending school, transferred the disease to another child whose mother was then pregnant and who, as a consequence, gave birth to a child suffering from abnormalities, could that last-mentioned child sue the doctor? Given the undemanding nature of the test of foreseeability it may well be that that chain of events was foreseeable. On the other hand it is clear that there was no element of reliance by either the pregnant mother or her child on the doctor and it would be difficult suppose that he would have had such persons in contemplation when tending to his own patient...[I]t is therefore necessary to inquire whether Dr Pal as a specialist gynaecologist and obstetrician undertaking the care of AA in her confinement was placed in such a position vis-à-vis a particular category of persons that he owed to persons within that category, a duty of care. More specifically the question is whether the doctor could have reasonably foreseen that if he did not exercise due care in carrying out his functions harm might be caused to persons other than AA and, if so, whether those persons fell within a category the members of which were within a relationship of proximity with the doctor.

It seems clear to me that if Dr Pal had applied his mind to the problem he would have recognized that unless he exercised due care he could cause harm to persons intimately related to his patient and in particular the child which was then en ventre sa mère and also children who may later be born. Reference to two American cases sufficiently makes good the point that the possibility that a doctor placed in the position of Dr Pal could, if careless, do or omit to do something which caused later children of his patient to be born with defects was, while unlikely, not a remote possibility. In *Renslow v Mennonite Hospital* 367 NE 2d 1250 (1977), a blood transfusion was carelessly administered to a woman causing sensitisation of her blood which led, years later, to her first child suffering a pre-natal insult and being born with brain damage. Again in *Bergstreser v Mitchell* 577 F 2d 22 (1978) two doctors performed a caesarean section on a woman and in doing so carelessly ruptured her uterus and failed to inform her that this had occurred. As a consequence of her damaged uterus she was forced to undergo another caesarean section on her next confinement during which the baby suffered hypoxia or anoxia causing him to be born with brain damage.

Once it is accepted that Dr Pal owed a duty of care to his patient and that it was foreseeable that if he did not exercise due care in treating her he may cause damage to children later born to her it is difficult to see why those children should not be within the category of persons to whom the doctor was in relevant relationship of proximity. The fundamental elements underlying his proximity relationship with his patient were assumption of responsibility and reliance. The doctor assumed the responsibility of exercising due care in the treatment of his patient and the patient relied upon him to administer that treatment with due care. Furthermore, the doctor was working in an area in which he could, if here were not careful, so damage his patient and the child she was carrying that either that child or children later born to the patient might suffer damage.

In this context it is not difficult, in the light of my earlier conclusions, to include the child then en ventre sa mère within the category of persons to whom the duty was owed. That child would clearly be a person that Dr Pal ought to have had in contemplation and it would not accord with notions of fairness and justice or considerations of policy to exclude that child from the category. If it be necessary to assign a specific reason for including the child within the category then it is to be found in the fact that the patient was relying on the doctor to exercise reasonable care to ensure, so far as was possible, that the child was born safe and healthy. But the patient's reliance was not limited to that aspect of the treatment but extended generally to her well being and the doctor assumed the responsibility of exercising the appropriate care to ensure that, putting it generally, she was not affected in such a manner as to lead her later to give birth to deformed children. Upon this view the relevant category would include CA…

Although factors, such as the passage of time or the intervention of other medical practitioners, might serve to deny the existence of a causal connection between any breach of the duty to which an obstetrician placed in the position of Dr Pal would owe to his patient and any children later born to her and injury suffered by one or other of them, I see no reason why ordinarily the doctor should not be regarded as having been in a relationship of proximity with a category of persons including the patient and children later born to her. For these reasons I would conclude that there was a relevant relationship in this case and that Dr Pal owed a duty of care to CA which, in his failure to submit AA to syphilis testing, he breached.

Mahoney and Meagher JJA concurred.

As the court makes clear, in principle there is no distinction between pre-conception occurrences and those *in utero* which cause harm to the unborn child.

American cases have, on a number of occasions, considered liability for pre-conception occurrences: *Bergstreser v Mitchell* (1978) 577 F 2d 22 (8th Circ) (negligent rupture of uterus damaged child *in utero* subsequently conceived); *Renslow v Mennonite Hospital* (1977) 367 NE 2d 1250 and *Yeager v Bloomington Obstetrics and Gynaecology Inc* (1992) 585 NE 2d 696 (Ind CA) (negligent failure to deal with mother's sensitisation to Rh-positive, baby damaged *in utero* subsequently conceived child). Cf *Hegyes v Unjican Enterprises Inc* (1991) 286 Cal Rptr 85 (Cal CA) (no action against negligent driver who injured woman such that her subsequently conceived child sustained injuries *in utero*: no 'special relationship' existed between driver and woman). See also the observations of Clarke JA in *X and Y v Pal* (*supra*).

One further unresolved issue under the common law is where the occurrence causes harm not to the unborn child of the patient but rather to the *grandchild* or further descendant. In principle, the common law should treat this situation no differently. Of course, in fact it may be more difficult to establish a causal link between the occurrence and the subsequent harm. However, there are powerful policy considerations which may persuade a court to reject the claim not least of which is the indeterminate nature of the potential liability to future generations, as the following case illustrates.

Enright v Eli Lilly & Co (1991) 570 NE 2d 198 (NYCA)

Wachtler CJ: The question in this case is whether the liability of manufacturers of the drug diethylstilbestrol (DES) should extend to a so-called 'third generation' plaintiff, the granddaughter of a woman who ingested the drug. According to the allegations of the complaint, the infant plaintiff's injuries were caused by her premature birth, which in turn resulted from damage to her mother's reproductive system caused by the mother's in utero exposure to DES. We hold, in accord with our decision in *Albala v City of New York*, 54 NY 2d 269, 445 NYS 2d, 108, 429 NE 2d 786, that in these circumstances no cause of action accrues in favour of the infant plaintiff against the drug manufacturers.

I.

The plaintiffs in this case are Karen Enright, born August 8, 1981, and her parents, Patricia and Earl Enright. According to their complaint, the events underlying this action began more than 30 years ago, when Karen Enright's maternal grandmother ingested DES during a pregnancy which resulted in the birth of plaintiff Patricia Enright on January 29, 1960. Plaintiffs allege that because of her in utero exposure to DES, Patricia Enright developed a variety of abnormalities and deformities in her reproductive system. As a result, several of her pregnancies terminated in spontaneous abortions and another resulted in the premature birth of Karen Enright. Karen suffers from cerebral palsy and other disabilities that plaintiff's attribute to her premature birth and, ultimately, to her grandmother's ingestion of DES.

This action was commenced by Patricia and Earl Enright individually and on behalf of their daughter against several manufacturers of DES. After issue was joined, the defendants sought summary judgment dismissing the complaint. Defendants contended that the actions were barred by the Statute of Limitations and by plaintiffs' inability to identify the manufacturer of the drug ingested by Karen's grandmother. In addition, defendants argue that Karen's claims of a preconception tort presented no cognizable cause of action…

II.

The tragic DES tale is well documented in this Court's decisions and need not be recounted here (*see eg Hymowitz v Lily & Co* [(1989) 539 NE 2d 1069; 73 NY 2d 487], *Bichler v Lilly & Co* 55 NY 2d 571, 450 NYS 2d 776, 436 NE 2d 182). It is sufficient to note that between 1947 and 1971, the drug, a synthetic estrogen-like substance produced by approximately 300 manufacturers, was prescribed for use and ingested by millions of pregnant women to prevent miscarriages. In 1971, the Food and Drug Administration banned the drug's use for the treatment of problems of pregnancy after studies established a link between in utero exposure to DES and the occurrence in teen-age women of a rare form of vaginal and cervical cancer. Plaintiffs allege that in utero exposure to DES has since been linked to other genital tract aberrations in DES daughters, including malformations or immaturity of the uterus, cervical abnormalities, misshapen Fallopian tubes and abnormal cell and tissue growth, all of which has caused in this population a marked increase in the incidence of infertility, miscarriages, premature births and ectopic pregnancies.

The Legislature and this Court have both expressed concern for the victims of this tragedy by removing legal barriers to their tort recovery – barriers which may have had their place in other contexts, but which in DES litigation worked a peculiar injustice because of the ways in which DES was developed, marketed and sold and because of the insidious nature of its harm.

For example, prior to 1986, the longstanding rule in this State was that a cause of action for personal injuries caused by a toxic substance accrued and the limitations period began to run upon exposure to the substance (*see Fleishman v Lilly & Co* 62 NY 2d 888, 478 NYS 2d 853, 467 NE 2d 517, *cert, denied* 469 US 1192, 105 S Ct 967, 83 L Ed 2d 972). The Legislature, recognizing that under this rule claims for injuries caused by exposure to DES and other toxic substances were often time barred before the harmful effects of the exposure could be discovered, changed the law to provide that the limitations period in exposure cases beings to run upon discovery of the injury (*see* CPLR 214–c; L 1986 ch 682 s 2). At the same time, the Legislature revived for one year previously time-barred causes of action based on exposure to DES and four other toxic substances (L 1986 ch 682 s 4).

More recently, this Court responded to the fact that – for a variety of reasons unique to the DES litigation context – a DES plaintiff generally finds it impossible to identify the manufacturer of the drug that caused her injuries. We held that liability could be imposed upon DES manufacturers in accordance with their share of the national DES market, notwithstanding the plaintiff's inability to identify the manufacturer particularly at fault for her injuries (*see Hymowitz v Lilly & Co supra*).

III.

In the present case, we are asked to do something significantly different. We are asked, not to remove some barrier to recovery that presents unique problems in DES cases, but to recognize a cause of action not available in other contexts simply (or at least largely) because this is a DES case.

In *Albala v City of New York* 54 NY 2d 269, 271 445 NYS 2d 108, 420 NE 2d 786, *supra*, we were presented with the question 'whether a cause of action lies in favour of a child for injuries suffered as a result of a preconception tort committed against the mother'. There, the mother suffered a perforated uterus during the course of an abortion. Four years later, she gave birth to a brain-damaged child, whose injuries were allegedly attributable to the defendants' negligence in perforating the mother's uterus. We declined, as a matter of policy, to recognize a cause of action on behalf of the child, believing that to do so would 'require the extension of traditional tort concepts beyond manageable bounds' (*id* at 271–272, 445 NYS 2d 108, 429 NE 2d 786). Among other things, we were concerned with 'the staggering implications of any proposition which would honour claims assuming the breach of an identifiable duty for less than a perfect birth' and the difficulty, if such a cause of action were recognized, of confining liability by other than artificial and arbitrary boundaries (*id* at 273,

445 NYS 2d 108, 429 NE 2d 786, citing *Park v Chessin* 46 NY 2d 401, 413 NYS 2d 895, 386 NE 2d 807; *Howard v Lecher*, 42 NY 2d 109, 397 NYS 2d 363, 366 NE 2d 64).

The case now before us differs from *Albala* only in that the mother's injuries in this case were caused by exposure to DES instead of by medical malpractice. A different rule is justified, therefore, only if that distinction alters the policy balance we struck in *Albala*.

The primary thrust of plaintiff's argument and the Appellate Division's decision is that DES itself alters that balance. From the Legislature's actions in modifying the applicable Statute of Limitations and reviving time-barred DES cases and from our adoption of a market-share liability theory in *Hymowitz*, plaintiffs perceive a public policy favouring a remedy for DES-caused injuries sufficient to overcome the countervailing policy considerations we identified in *Albala*. The implication, of course, is that the public interest in providing a remedy for those injured by DES is stronger than the public interest in providing a remedy for those injured by other means – medical malpractice, for example. We do not believe that such a preference has been established.

To be sure, recent developments demonstrate legislative and judicial solicitude for the victims of DES, but they do not establish DES plaintiffs as a favoured class for whose benefit all traditional limitations on tort liability must give way. To the extent that special rules have been fashioned, they are a response to unique procedural barriers and problems of proof peculiar to DES litigation.

In the present case, however, neither plaintiffs, the Appellate Division, nor the dissent has identified any unique feature of DES litigation that justifies the novel proposition they advance – recognition of a multigenerational cause of action that we have refused to recognize in any other context. The fact that this is a DES case does not by itself justify a departure from the *Albala* rule.

Closer to the mark, though still falling short, is plaintiff's second argument. They note that *Albala* was a negligence case and that we left open the question whether a different result might obtain under a strict products liability theory because of the potentially different policy considerations in such a case (*see Albala v City of New York supra* 54 NY 2d at 274 n, 445 NYS 2d 108, 429 NE 2d 786). Having now examined the question in the context of this particular strict products liability claim, we find no basis for reaching a different conclusion than we did in *Albala*.

… the concerns we identified in *Albala* are present in equal measure here. The nature of the plaintiff's injuries in both cases – birth defects– and their cause– harm to the mothers' reproductive systems before the children were conceived – are indistinguishable for these purposes. They raise the same vexing questions with the same 'staggering implications' (*Albala v City of New York supra* 54 NY 2d at 273, 445 NYS 2d 108, 429 NE 2d 786). As in *Albala*, the cause of action plaintiffs ask us to recognize here could not be confined without the drawing of artificial and arbitrary boundaries. For all we know, the rippling effects of DES exposure may extend for generations. It is our duty to confine liability within manageable limits (*see Tobin v Grossman* 24 NY 2d 609, 619, 301 NYS 2d 554, 249, NE 2d 419; Prosser, *Palsgraf Revisited* 52 Mich L Rev 1, 27). Limiting liability to those who ingested the drug or were exposed to it *in utero* serves this purpose.

At the same time, limiting liability in this fashion does not unduly impair the deterrent purposes of tort liability. The manufacturers remain amenable to suit by all those injured by exposure to their product, a class whose size is commensurate with the risk created…

That the product involved here is a prescription drug raises other considerations as well. First, as in most prescription drug cases (*see* Vinson & Slaughter, Products Liability: Pharmaceutical Drug Cases, at 123–140), liability here is predicated on a failure to warn of dangers of which the manufacturers knew or with adequate testing should have known.

Such a claim, though it may be couched in terms of strict liability, is indistinguishable from a negligence claim (*see Wolfgruber v Upjohn Co* 72 AD 2d 59, 423 NYS 2d 95 *aff'd on opn, below* 52 NY 2d 768, 436 NYS 2d 614, 417 NE 2d 1002). Concepts of reasonable care and foreseeability are not divorced from this theory of liability, as they may be under other strict products liability predicates. Thus, the effort to distinguish this case from *Albala* is strained…

The dissent would have us believe that this case involved nothing but application of straightforward strict products liability doctrine. But this case is fundamentally different in the same way that *Albala* was fundamentally different from other negligence cases. In neither this case nor *Albala* was the infant plaintiff exposed to the defendants' dangerous product or negligent conduct; rather, both were injured as a consequence of injuries to the reproductive systems of their mothers.

We agree with the dissenter that 'like cases should be treated alike' (Dissenting opn at 397 p 561 of 568 NYS 2d p 209 of 570 NE 2d). This is not only a fundamental principle of justice, it is also the underpinning of the doctrine of stare decisis. It is, indeed, precisely why we are bound to apply the rule of *Albala* here, in the absence of some difference between the two cases upon which a principled distinction can be drawn.

The dissent, however, discounts the precedential value of *Albala* because it was based on 'policy grounds' and therefore – in the dissenter's view – 'poses no *legal bar* to recovery' (dissenting opn at 394, p 560 of 568 NYS 2d, p 208 of 570 NE 2d). That the *Albala* rule is based on policy grounds, however, should not diminish its status as a rule of law. All legal rules, including those the dissent relies upon, are policy-based.

By adhering to *Albala*, therefore, our decision today follows established law. The dissenter, on the other hand, would expand liability beyond traditional bounds in the face of precedent from this court to the contrary, and accuses the majority of usurping the legislative function by failing to do so (dissenting opn at 397, p 561 of 568 NYW 2d, 209 of 570 NE 2d). It strikes us as a unique view of the judicial role that would allow the court to expand liability at will, but require legislative action before adhering to established limits.

In sum, the distinctions between this case an *Albala* provide no basis for a departure from the rule that an injury to a mother which results in injuries to a later conceived child does not establish a cause of action in favor of the child against the original tort-feasor. For this reason, we decline to recognize a cause of action on behalf of plaintiff Karen Enright.

Judge Hancock (dissenting): What, then, are the policy reasons seen by the majority as compelling today's decision? There appear to be three. None is availing.

First, the majority cites defendants' arguments concerning the 'staggering implications' and 'rippling effects' (majority opn at 386, 387, pp 554, 555 of 568 NYS 2d, pp 202, 203 of 570 NE 2d) that a decision upholding Karen Enright's claim might have. But this sort of 'floodgates of litigation' alarum seems singularly unpersuasive in view of our Court's repeated admonitions that it is not 'a ground for denying a cause of action that there will be a proliferation of claims' and '*if a cognizable wrong has been committed that there must be a remedy, whatever the burden of the courts*' (*Tobin v Grossman* 24 NY 2d 609, 615, 301 NYS 2d 554, 249 NE 2d 419 (emphasis added); *see, Bovsun v Sanperi* 61 NY 2d 219, 231, 473 NYS 2d 357, 461 NE 2d 843; *Battalla v State of New York* 10 NY 2d 237, 240–242, 219 NYS 2d 34, 176 NE 2d 729). Beyond that, however, when defendants' arguments are applied here to urge that although claims of DES daughters should be allowed the claims of granddaughters should not be their forebodings strike a peculiarly ironic note: ie the very fact of the 'insidious nature' of DES which may make the defendants liable for injuries to a future generation is advanced as the reason why they should not be liable for injuries to that generation. Should we be saying to these defendants and other companies which manufacture drugs 'you must be careful to produce reasonably 'safe' drugs and to warn of the risks of taking such drugs but in deciding whether a drug is 'safe' you may completely ignore the havoc of a particular drug may wreck on a future generation?' I think not.

Second, the majority suggests that permitting a cause of action for Karen Enright could result in 'overdeterrence – the possibility that research will be discouraged or beneficial drugs withheld from the market' (majority opn at 388, p 556 of 568 NYS 2d, p 204 of 570 NE 2d). But in deciding whether a particular claim for injuries from DES should be sustained, the deterrence factor is inconsequential. The wrongful conduct of the drug companies in producing and marketing DES and similarly harmful products for use by pregnant women stopped more than a generation ago when the enormity of the damage from DES became known. The sole question now involves the remedy for this past wrong, not deterrence: ie whether the remedy for DES victims made possible by the Legislature in CPLR 214–c and given effect by our Court in *Hymowitz* should be withheld from a granddaughter who suffers injuries from this wrong. But even if deterrence is assumed to be a relevant issue, should we be any less concerned with deterring the development of unsafe drugs which may cause latent damage to the third generation than in the second? Again, I think not.

Finally, in what has the ring of an economic cost-benefit analysis, the majority suggests that its generational line-drawing is proper because the manufacturers' exposure to liability is 'commensurate with the risk created' (majority opn at 387, p 555 of 568 NYS 2d, p 203 of 570 NE 2d). The argument is seen at once to be at odds with the rule that on this motion to dismiss Karen Enright's complaint (CPLR 3211[a][7]) the court must accept as true her allegations that she is a member of the class of persons to whom the risk of injury was foreseeable (*see Becker v Schwartz, supra* 46 NY 2d at 408, 413 NYS 2d 895, 386 NE 2d 807). But, in any event, the statement that liability should stop at Karen's mother's generation because it 'is commensurate with the risk' is not a statement of an argument or of a legal or policy reason for a particular result. Rather, it is simply a statement of the Court's own policy determination as to where the risk – and, hence, the liability – stops. If, as the majority apparently believes, there are economic and social considerations which require that there be some arbitrary cut-off point in cases of this kind, such a statute of repose could easily be engrafted on the Toxic Torts legislation which revived the long-outlawed dormant injury claims for DES and other substances (*see* CPLR 2140–c; *see generally,* Comment, *Preconception Torts: Foreseeing the Unconceived,* 48 U Colo L Rev 621; Phillips, *An Analysis of Proposed Reform of Products Liability Statutes of Limitations*, 56 NCL Rev 663; Note, *Statutes of Limitations and the Discovery Rule in Latent Injury Claims; An Exception or the Law?* 43 U Pitt L Rev 501, 520–523). Suffice it to say, our Legislature has not chosen to cut off the claims of injured persons in Karen Enright's generation.

Simons, Kaye, Alexander and Titone JJ concurred with Wachtler CJ.

The New York Court of Appeals' decision rests upon policy factors which would be likely to influence an English court. Of course, it should be noticed that the court's earlier decision in *Albala* denied altogether a claim for a pre-conception occurrence affecting the plaintiff's mother. English law would probably recognise such an action. The *Enright* court refused (perhaps not unnaturally) to go even further in recognising liability to a second generation plaintiff.

2. Statute: Congenital Disabilities (Civil Liability) Act 1976

The 1976 Act replaces the common law for births on or after July 22, 1976. For our purposes, the relevant provisions of the Act are as follows:

1. – (1) If a child is born as the result of such an occurrence before its birth as is mentioned in subsection (2) below, and a person (other than the child's own mother) is under this section answerable to the child in respect of the occurrence, the child's disabilities are to be regarded as damage resulting from the wrongful act of that person and actionable accordingly at the suit of the child.

(2) An occurrence to which this section applies is one which –

(a) affected either parent of the child in his or her ability to have a normal, healthy child; or

(b) affected the mother during her pregnancy, or affected her or the child in the course of its birth,

so that the child is born with disabilities which would not otherwise have been present.

(3) Subject to the following subsections, a person (here referred to as 'the defendant') is answerable to the child if he was liable in tort to the parent or would, if sued in due time, have been so; and it is no answer that there could not have been such liability because the parent suffered no actionable injury, if there was a breach of legal duty which, accompanied by injury, would have given rise to the liability.

(4) In the case of an occurrence preceding the time of conception, the defendant is not answerable to the child if at that time either or both of the parents knew the risk of their child being born disabled (that is to say, the particular risk created by the occurrence); but should it be the child's father who is the defendant, this subsection does not apply if he knew of the risk and the mother did not.

(5) The defendant is not answerable to the child, for anything he did or omitted to do when responsible in a professional capacity for treating or advising the parent, if he took reasonable care having due regard to then received professional opinion applicable to the particular class of case; but this does not mean that he is answerable only because he departed from received opinion.

(6) Liability to the child under this section may be treated as having been excluded or limited by contract made with the parent affected, to the same extent and subject to the same restrictions as liability in the parent's own case; and a contract term which could have been set up by the defendant in an action by the parent, so as to exclude or limit his liability to him or her, operates in the defendant's favour to the same, but no greater, extent in an action under this section by the child.

(7) If in the child's action under this section it is shown that the parent affected shared the responsibility for the child being born disabled, the damages are to be reduced to such extent as the court thinks are equitable having regard to the extent of the parent's responsibility…

4. – (1) Reference in this Act to a child being born disabled or with disabilities are to its being born with any deformity, disease or abnormality, including predisposition (whether or not susceptible of immediate prognosis) to physical or mental defect in the future.

(2) In this Act –

(a) 'born' means born alive (the moment of a child's birth being when it first has a life separate from its mother), and 'birth' has a corresponding meaning…

(3) Liability to a child under section 1, 1A or 2 of this Act is to be regarded –

(a) as respects all its incidents and any matters arising or to arise out of it; and

(b) subject to any contrary context or intention, for the purpose of construing references in enactments and documents to personal or bodily injuries and cognate matters,

as liability for personal injuries sustained by the child immediately after its birth.…

(5) This Act applies in respect of births after (but not before) its passing, and in respect of any such birth it replaces any law in force before its passing, whereby a person could be liable to a child in respect of disabilities with which it might be born; but in section 1(3) of this Act the expression 'liable in tort' does not include any reference to liability by virtue of this Act, or to liability by virtue of any such law.

This Act is of general application. You will notice s 1(5) which sets the standard of care in actions under the statute: 'reasonable care *having due regard* to then received professional opinion'. Here we see a statutory precursor of the standard set more generally by the House of Lords in *Bolitho v City and Hackney HA* [1997] 4 All ER 771 (HL) (*supra*, ch 4)). The statute is, however, largely concerned with establishing the existence of a duty of care (ss 1(1)–(3) and 1A(1)–(2)) and what defences may be relied upon (ss 1(4), (6)–(7) and 1A(3)). In the context of medical law it is important to develop three issues: the first concerns negligent conduct before conception producing harm to a child conceived thereafter; the second concerns a child who is negligently harmed *en ventre sa mère*; the third concerns a child harmed whilst an embryo *ex utero*.

(a) Occurrences before conception

Having seen the position under the common law, it is helpful to see how the Law Commission approached the question in recommending legislation.

Report on 'Injuries to Unborn Children' Law Commission (Report No 60, 1974)

76. As we have pointed out in paragraph 33 above, one of the differences between pre-natal injury and other personal injury is that the event of occurrence resulting from a negligent act or omission happens, in the case of pre-natal injury, at a time when the plaintiff is not in existence and to someone other than himself, namely his mother, or, exceptionally and, of course, only prior to conception, his father. So far as the negligent act or omission itself is concerned, it is of no consequence that it may happen before the plaintiff exists; the present common law rules easily comprehend this possibility. If a manufacturer negligently manufactures and markets a pram it is no answer to the claim of the child under whom it collapses that he was not alive at the date of its manufacture. In the case of pre-natal injuries, however, the equivalent of the pram's 'collapse' necessarily also occurs before the plaintiff is in existence and may occur even before the plaintiff is conceived. It is this latter possibility which has caused great concern amongst those whom we have consulted.
77. We have been given examples of cases where something happening to a child's parents before its conception can lead to its being born with disabilities. An obvious example is physical injury to a woman's pelvis causing injury to a child consequently conceived and born. It is known that radiation of the reproductive organs of animals causes gene mutations and it can almost certainly do so also in man. The exposure of mother or father to radiation could cause gene mutations which might not become manifest for several generations. A claim has succeeded before the German Supreme Court for damages for pre-natal injury in the form of congenital syphilis caused by a blood transfusion given negligently to the mother before conception, the blood donor having suffered from the illness. The negligent supply of male sperm for artificial insemination would seem to be another possible source of pre-natal injury. The possibility that a contraceptive pill might prove both ineffective and damaging to the child born because of its ineffectiveness was not ruled out by our consultation with the medical profession. There are, no doubt, a number of other possible fact situations where pre-natal injury could be caused by an event happening before conception.

The 1976 Act, which seeks to implement the Law Commission's views, is discussed by Pace.

P J Pace 'Civil Liability For Pre-Natal Injuries' (1977) 40 MLR 141

[T]he Act provides that pre-conception occurrences may found a cause of action. This situation could arise when negligent X-ray treatment or defective birth-control substances affected a parent's reproductive system to such an extent that the child subsequently conceived was born disabled [s 1(2)(a)]. The child has no right of action if at the time of the occurrence either parent knew of the risk of the child being born disabled, though this does not apply if the father is the defendant or where the occurrence is coincident with or *post* conception [s 1(4)]. This poses problems since 'new embryological data … purport to indicate that conception is a "process" over time, rather than an event'. Apart from this difficulty, the point has been made that to allow recovery for pre-conception negligence would be to recognise a legal interest in *not* being conceived. If this analysis is correct then English law will recognise the validity of 'wrongful life' actions and, indeed, Tedeschi [[1966] Israel LR 513, 531] would argue that pre-conception negligence does give rise to a 'wrongful life' action:

> When a person fathers a child and infects it with a disease by one and the same act, then either the semen was already infected when it came into contact with the ovum, so that the new entity created is diseased from its conception (and this is the true meaning of congenital disease), or the single act results in paternity and in the infection of the mother, which will be transmitted from her to the infant. In the first case it is obvious that there was only one alternative to the new being, either not to exist or to exist with the disease. But in the second case as well no separation can be made between the act of the parent causing paternity and that causing the infection, as we are faced with a single act.

> The Law Commission, favouring an action in such circumstances, approached the situation on the basis that, if a child has a legal right to begin life with a sound mind and body, and this is the effect of the proposed legislation, there is a correlative duty on its parents and others to avoid producing conception where the circumstances are likely to result in the birth of a disabled child. In other words, the remedy is sought not for being born but 'for compensation for the disability resulting from the sexual intercourse'. It should also be noted that in pre-conception cases compensation would not, without the help of the fiction provided by the Act, fulfil the function, as in other areas of tort, of restoring, as far as money can, the *status quo*. The fiction is contained in section 4(3) which states that 'Liability under this Act is to be regarded … as liability for personal injuries sustained by the child immediately after its birth.'

The argument by Pace needs to be examined carefully. He suggests that in the circumstances contemplated the Act creates a claim by the child for 'wrongful life'. We will deal with this claim later in this chapter. There are, as we shall see, a number of theoretical problems in establishing such a claim. For the present, it is sufficient to notice that at the heart of such a claim is the allegation by the child that 'but for' the negligence of the defendant it would not have been born at all. Here, on the other hand, the child is complaining that the pre-conception occurrence deprived it of a normal healthy life, ie the defendant's negligence *caused* its disabilities.

This leads to a consideration of the application of s 1(2) of the Act. On its face s 1(2)(a) appears to be concerned with pre-conception occurrences while s 1(2)(b) is concerned with post-conception occurrences. However, while in general this is true, it is not accurate to interpret them as mutually exclusive. For example, the facts of a case such as *Bergstreser* – where the mother's uterus is damaged prior to conception – fall within s 1(2)(a) since the mother's 'ability' in the sense of physical capacity to have a 'normal, healthy child' is affected. Equally, the facts could fall within s 1(2)(b) since the pre-conception occurrence is a continuing one which 'affected [her] during pregnancy' such that the child is born with disabilities that it would otherwise not have.

We saw a number of unresolved problems under the common law. Does the Act provide solutions? As regards the question of whether the conduct of the mother affects the child's claim, notice the terms of s 1(4). This makes it clear that where the basis of an action is a pre-conception occurrence the child has no claim if the mother or father of the child had knowledge of the *particular risk* of the child being born disabled (unless the father is the defendant when the mother must have knowledge).

Further, for all claims (not limited only to pre-conception occurrences), the contributory negligence of a parent or a valid restriction or exclusion of liability affects the child's claim (s 1(7) and (6)).

We considered earlier the nature of the harm caused to the child and suggested it should be categorised as economic loss arising out of its disabilities. The Act, however, deems the child's harm to be a personal injury. Section 4(3) explicitly provides that an action brought under the Act shall be regarded as an action for 'personal injury sustained by the child immediately after its birth'.

Finally, we considered whether a defendant's liability could extend beyond one generation. Whatever the position at common law, a combination of s 1(3) and 4(5) makes it clear that no such claim may be brought under the Act. Liability only arises where the defendant is 'liable in tort to the parent' of the plaintiff. However, in a second-generation claim the defendant could only be liable to the plaintiff's parent under the Act and s 4(5) excludes from the definition of 'liable in tort' any 'liability by virtue of this Act'.

(b) Occurrences in utero

Section 1(2)(b) makes it clear that an occurrence *in utero* which *causes* disabilities in the unborn child will give rise to an action. Equally, the occurrence may take place during the course of birth, for example, as in *Whitehouse v Jordan* [1981] 1 WLR 246. The Act only applies, however, if it is established that the child would not have suffered the disabilities if there had not been negligence, ie, it would have been born healthy (this will be important later when we consider the 'wrongful life' action).

As we saw before, however, s 1(2)(a) and (b) are not mutually exclusive and an *in utero* occurrence will fall within s 1(2)(a) also if it affects the mother's 'ability to have a normal, healthy child'.

A claim under the Act only arises if the child is 'born alive' as defined in s 4(2)(a). Hence, no claim will arise on behalf of the child when it is still-born. The position is the same as at common law.

One situation creates a problem given the wording of s 1(2)(b). You will notice that that section requires that the occurrence be one which 'affected *the mother* during her pregnancy' (our emphasis). Unlike the situation when the occurrence arises in the course of birth, no liability appears to exist if the occurrence merely affects *the child*. Although this will not usually be problematic, because the mother will be affected, this may not always be true. For example, if a pregnant woman is exposed to x-rays which damage the child, can it be said that the mother is 'affected'. If 'affected' means 'has a detrimental consequence upon' her, then the exposure to the x-rays does not affect her at all, only the child is affected. Even if she *were* 'affected', what she would suffer would be some form of emotional distress on learning what may have happened to the child. But this will not do. This statute requires a causal connection between her being affected and the disability in the child.

Two further points, applicable to pre-and post-conception occurrences, are of interest to the medical lawyer.

The child's cause of action is a derivative one, dependent upon a breach of the duty owed to the parent although no injury need be suffered by the parent. Being derivative it also follows, as we have seen, that defences may be mounted based upon the conduct of the patient. John Eekelaar and Robert Dingwell raise, as yet, unanswered questions for medical law arising from the derivative nature of the action.

J Eekelaar and R Dingwell 'Some Legal Issues in Obstetric Practice' [1984] JSWL 258

... If a child is to recover compensation, it is now necessary to show that the defendant was 'liable in tort' to a parent of the child, although this requirement has the modification that the parent does not have to have suffered some 'actionable injury' [s 1(3)]. Nevertheless, there must still have been some breach of legal duty towards the parent.

What difference does this make to the position of a child who has been injured by negligent delivery procedures? The answer would seem to be that unless the culpable acts or omissions can also be construed as breaching a legal duty to the mother, the child has lost its remedy. It is by no means clear that all such failure can be so construed. Inexpert manipulation of forceps, inadequate use of available monitoring equipment or a failure to make a Caesarean incision at an appropriate time all appear to be wrongs which primarily affect the child's well-being rather than the mother's and outside the scope of any duty to her. It is possible that the child's position could be saved by treating any default as a breach of duty towards the mother on the grounds that injury to the child is foreseeably likely to cause her consequential emotional distress. The child's action would then be parasitic upon her actual or potential claim.

This circuitous reasoning breaks down, however, if the attendant's default is the result of undue consideration for the mother or, particularly, if it was at her insistence by rejecting available and offered treatments. It is hard to see how the attendant could be in breach of a legal duty towards the mother when he is doing what she demands. Indeed, the Act itself compels a child's claim to be reduced by the extent to which the parent had contributed to the disability and, even, to be totally excluded if this has been done in respect to the parents' own case [s 1(6)]. If a woman, for example, refuses a Caesarean section when indicated on sound professional grounds, or rejects the application of foetal monitoring, and the child subsequently goes into distress and sustains brain damage as a result of protracted labour, the child has no claim, either against the attendant (who will have committed no tort against the mother) or against the woman herself (since the 1976 Act disallows any claim by the child against its mother for ante-natal injuries unless they were incurred while she was driving) [ss 1(1) and 2].

Moreover, the abolition of an independent duty of care towards the child makes it harder for an attendant to resist a possible claim in assault if, in the child's interests, he disregards the mother's wishes in respect of procedures involving her person. The presence of such a duty would fortify any defence to such a claim founded on the principle of necessity or of using reasonable force to prevent a crime, viz negligent manslaughter of the child [Criminal Law Act 1967, s 3(1)]. Its absence may call into question the application of the law of manslaughter for grossly negligent delivery procedures.

Women's groups have shown an increasing interest in adopting the tactic of legal action as a way of enforcing demands for alternative childbirth. With the weakening of the common law defence, obstetric attendants now find themselves caught between their long-established child protection duties and a statute which appears to give greater weight to the wishes of mothers. This unenviable position for obstetric attendants does not seem to have been created intentionally. There is no indication that the Law Commission recognised the possible consequences when they recommended the reforms represented by the 1976 Act. With the agreement of the medical bodies which they consulted, the Commission accepted the proposition that 'a child born fully alive should have a right of action, accruing at birth, in respect of injury either sustained by it after conception and before birth, or resulting from injury sustained by its mother during pregnancy due to the fault of a third party' [paras 31 and 32]. The technique which they adopted for translating this right into a legal form was, however, determined largely by 'the fact of physical identification of mother and foetus'. It was thought that this could give rise to special legal problems.

The first of these was to do with the ascertainment of prospective liability. Lawyers have long considered it desirable that people entering into contractual or other relationships should be able to be reasonably confident of the possible extent of their duties. Pregnancy complicates that. Over a wide range of legal relationships, it was thought that, if potential defendants could not regulate their liability by contract with the mother, they would simply refuse to deal with women [para 68]. By making the child's action derivative from the mother's, third parties could be assured of the extent of their liability. This point does not, however, have any bearing on the problem under discussion...Until the passage of the Congenital Disabilities (Civil Liability) Act 1976...it seems that the combination of their statutory monopoly and the common law rules allowed obstetric attendants to balance the interests of mothers and children...gave them protection if they felt it necessary to defer to the latter. The monopoly shared by obstetricians and midwives was granted as a licence to represent the state as the ultimate guardian of the nation's children. Thus, while the wishes of mothers could never be lightly disregarded, they could not have the power of veto. Under the [Nurses, Midwives and Health Visitors Act 1979], this duty began with the commencement of professional attendance at any particular labour. The Congenital Disabilities (Civil Liability) Act 1976 only recognises a separate duty to the child after the moment of birth, defined as the point when the child has a life 'separate from its mother' [s 4(2)(a)]. Both medically and legally this is not a clear-cut concept, but obviously relates to a point later than the onset of labour. Before that, the attendant's first duty appears to be the care of the mother in which, clearly, deference to her wishes will be a significant feature. If, in deferring to her and giving her correct professional attention, the child is injured, the law appears to hold that this is just too bad. On the other hand, if the attendant overrides the mother's wishes in attending to the child, he would seem to be at risk of litigation....

Such arguments lead us towards concluding that the balance of policy was more or less properly struck before 1976. At the end of the day, parents should not ultimately be free to dictate the terms under which their children are born. An obstetric attendant would be well advised to listen carefully to their requests and to consider how far they could be followed consistently with sound professional practice and the child's well-being. The child is entitled to the benefits of available technological resources and professional expertise to minimise the risks of being severely prejudiced at the outset of his life. The risks of obstetric dictatorship are partially reduced by the freedom of parents to shop around licensed attendants and influence obstetric practice. The interests of the child are protected by the basic standards represented by the monopoly.

The attenuation of the attendant's duty of care by the Congenital Disabilities (Civil Liability) Act 1976 seems to run contrary to the spirit of legislative developments in the twentieth century. No convincing arguments have been produced for abrogating the common law rights of children...We believe that this aspect of the statute should be reviewed as a matter of some urgency. In the process, however, we would also draw attention to the emerging problem of the point at which child protection duties should properly begin. The new technologies of pre-natal intervention raise issues which could not have been foreseen by the drafters of the present statutes. It is important not to confound these with the perennial disputes about abortion or the relative priority of preserving the life of mother or child in extreme cases. We do not think that these have much to contribute to the circumstances we are addressing here, of routine childbirth and regularly available pre-natal intervention.

Secondly, the reference in s 1 to a 'parent' does not take account of developments having to do with infertility treatment. With these developments there appeared the phenomena of the 'gestational parent' and the 'genetic parent'. As we saw in Chapter 10, ss 27–29 of the Human Fertilisation and Embryology Act 1990 defined a parent under these circumstances. To square the circle, the 1990 Act inserted a new s 4(4A) into the 1976 Act which provides as follows:

4(4A) In any cases where a child carried by a woman as the result of the placing in her of an embryo or of sperm and eggs or her artificial insemination is born disabled, any reference in section 1 of this Act to a parent includes a reference to a person who would be a parent but for sections 27 to 29 of the Human Fertilisation and Embryology Act 1990.

Hence, a donor of gametes who has been negligently exposed to radiation such that the gametes are damaged is a 'parent' for the purposes of the child's claim under s 1.

(c) Occurrences ex utero

If an embryo is damaged prior to its being placed in a woman as part of infertility treatment (whether during its storage or use), may a child subsequently born with disability have an action under the Act?

Under s 1(2) a claim could only arise if the doctor's negligence 'affected either parent of the child in his or her ability to have a normal, healthy child' (s 1(2)(a)). Everything turns on the meaning of the word 'ability'. If 'ability' means 'physical capacity', then a claim could not be brought. If, however, 'ability' includes also the 'opportunity' to have a normal, healthy child, then a claim could be brought.

In order to resolve this problem, Parliament introduced a new s 1A into the Act when passing the Human Fertilisation and Embryology Act 1990. Section 1A provides as follows:

Extension of section 1 to cover infertility treatments
1A. (1) In any case where –
(a) a child carried by a woman as the result of the placing in her of an embryo or of sperm and eggs or her artificial insemination is born disabled.
(b) the disability results from an act or omission in the course of the selection, or the keeping or use outside the body, of the embryo carried by her of the gametes used to bring about the creation of the embryo, and

(c)   a person is under this section answerable to the child in respect of the act or omission
        the child's disabilities are to be regarded as damage resulting from the wrongful act of
        that person and actionable accordingly at the suit of the child.

(2)   Subject to subsection (3) below and the applied provisions of section 1 of this Act, a
person (here referred to as 'the defendant') is answerable to the child if he was liable in tort
to one or both of the parents (here referred to as 'the parent or parents concerned') or would,
if sued in due time, have been so; and it is no answer that there could not have been such
liability because the parent or parents concerned suffered no actionable injury, if there was a
breach of legal duty which, accompanied by injury, would have given rise to the liability.

(3) The defendant is not under this section answerable to the child if at the time the embryo,
or the sperm and eggs, are placed in the woman or the time of her insemination (as the case
may be) either or both of the parents knew the risk of their child being born disabled (that is
to say, the particular risk created by the act or omission).

(4)   Subsections (5) to (7) of section 1 of this Act apply for the purposes of this section as
they apply for the purposes of that section but as if references to the parent or the parent
affected were references to the parent or parents concerned.

In reading this provision it is important to notice that s 4(2) of the 1976 Act
provides that:

reference to embryos shall be construed in accordance with section 1 of the Human Fertilisation
and Embryology Act 1990.

Section 1A attempts to create a scheme of liability identical to that under s 1. You
will notice the provisions in s 1A(3) relating to *volenti* by either of the child's
parents, ie, in this context the couple receiving the infertility treatment (see
ss 27–29 of HUFEA 1990). Section 4(4A) does not apply to s 1A (only s 1).
Hence, 'parents' do not include any donors of gametes or embryos.

As we can see from its terms, s 1A gives a disabled child a claim when the
negligence during fertility treatment arises from 'an act or omission' related to
'selection, 'keeping' or 'use' outside the body of the genetic material. On its
face, it was intended to cover all the conventional forms of treatment, ie IVF,
GIFT and artificial insemination. Arguably, however, it fails to achieve this
comprehensive coverage. It appears that it may be limited to IVF procedures.
Notwithstanding the generality of s 1A(1)(a), s 1A(1)(b) is limited to acts or
omissions in respect of embryos or gametes that result in the creation of an embryo
ex utero which is placed in the patient. If, therefore, the negligence concerns
'selection', 'keeping' or 'use' of the gametes with which the woman is artificially
inseminated, the section will not apply. This apparent oversight is curious; it is
probably not intended and is certainly not justified. Unfortunately, short of
amending legislation the section is so clear that a court could not avoid the
conclusion we have advanced here.

There is one final point we should notice. Negligence in relation to the 'keeping'
or the 'use' of embryos (or gametes used to produce the embryo) will cause harm
to the eventual child which would otherwise not have been present. On this
analysis the child's claim is analogous to the pre-natal injury situations we have
considered so far. By contrast, negligence in the 'selection' of embryos (or gametes
used to produce the embryo) will not cause harm in this sense. Instead, the essence
of the child's claim is that its genetic material should not have been selected and
it should not, therefore, have been born at all. This, as we shall see later, is the
so-called 'wrongful life' action which presents distinct problems for the law.
(see *infra*). It is to that action that we now turn our attention.

B. WRONGFUL LIFE

A 'wrongful life' action is one brought by a child complaining of negligent conduct
prior to birth which results in its birth when had there been no negligence it

would not have been born. In short, the essence of the claim is that the child would have been better off not to be born at all. It is important to notice that the defendant in these actions does not *cause* the child's disability. Instead, the defendant fails to avert it. This may arise in three ways. *First*, the defendant may negligently advise the parent prior to conception of the risk of any child inheriting a genetic disability. *Secondly*, the negligence could arise *ex utero* in, for example, the selection of a damaged embryo for implantation during infertility treatment. *Thirdly*, the negligence may arise after conception, for example, where the doctor fails to advise the mother that she is carrying a disabled child.

Sometimes, the dividing line between a 'wrongful life' action and one for 'pre-natal injury' may be fine. For example, in one case the defendant negligently performed an abortion. The child was born as a result but sustained injuries due to the trauma. The British Columbia Court of Appeal held that the action by the child was not for 'wrongful life' because the child's injuries were caused by the defendant: *Cherry (Guardian ad litem of v Borsman* (1992) 70 BCLR (2d) 273 (BCCA)). The court stated that the doctor 'owes a duty of care to the mother to perform his task properly but at the same time owes a duty of care to the foetus not to harm it if he should fail in meeting the duty of care he owes to the mother' (at 292). The problem is that the doctor was engaged in terminating the pregnancy. The doctor had caused the injuries to the child but had he not been negligent the child would not have been born at all. Arguably, this is a 'wrongful life' action.

1. The common law

(a) The disabled child

Can a child who has been disabled from the moment of conception bring a claim? The English common law was examined by the Court of Appeal in *McKay v Essex AHA* [1982] QB 1166, [1982] 2 All ER 771.

McKay v Essex AHA **[1982] QB 1166, [1982] 2 All ER 771 (CA)**

Ackner LJ: Mary McKay was born on 15 August 1975 and is therefore $6^{1}/_{2}$ years old. Whilst in her mother's womb she was infected with rubella (German measles) and as a result she is partly blind and deaf and is apparently disabled in other respects, the details of which have not been provided to us. She alleges in her statement of claim that Dr Gower-Davies, the second defendant, owed her a duty of care when she was *in utero*. She claims that he was negligent in that he failed to treat the rubella infection, after being told that it was suspected by her mother, the second plaintiff. She contends that this can be arrested by the injection of globulins into the mother which, although it cannot reverse or ameliorate damage already done to the unborn child, can reduce the likelihood of further damage…in addition to the claims referred to above, Mary seeks to add an additional claim against the doctor. Quite apart from his alleged failure to arrest the progress of the rubella infection by a process of injections, she claims that the duty of care which the doctor owed her when she was *in utero* involved advising her mother of the desirability of an abortion, which advice, as previously stated, the mother alleges she would have accepted. She accordingly claims that she has suffered damage by 'entry into a life in which her injuries are highly debilitating, and distress, loss and damage'. She makes a similar claim, *mutatis mutandis*, against the Essex Area Health Authority by reason of their alleged negligence in relation to their handling and testing of the samples and their failure to advise the doctor of the results of any such tests as they may have performed.…

(1) *The duty.* I can consider this in relation to the claim against the doctor, since what can be said in relation to the claim made against him applies, *mutatis mutandis*, to the claim against the area health authority.

The duty alleged is the duty to take care in relation to the unborn child. Hence the first claim for failing to treat the suspected rubella by injection, so as to reduce the likelihood of further damage. Thus, the selfsame duty is relied on for prenatal injuries as would be relied on postnatally, if there was a failure to give proper treatment after the child had been born. The embryo, or fetus, is in a comparable position to the child and adult which it may ultimately become. However, in stark contrast to the plea that the doctor should have advanced the prospect of a healthy birth of the child, the additional plea, which is still based on the same duty of care to the unborn child, relies on a negligent failure to prevent its birth. The basis of this additional claim is that, had the doctor properly discharged his obligation of care *toward the unborn child*, he would have advised the mother 'of the desirability of an abortion' (para 13), which advice the mother would have accepted (para 9). Accordingly, the fetus's existence *in utero* would have been terminated. Thus, the duty of care is said to involve a duty *to the fetus*, albeit indirectly, by advice to the mother to cause its death.

I cannot accept that the common law duty of care to a person can involve, without specific legislation to achieve this end, the legal obligation to that person, whether or not *in utero*, to terminate its existence. Such a proposition runs wholly contrary to the concept of the sanctity of human life.

Counsel for the plaintiffs contends that, where it can be established that a child's disabilities are so severe that it can be properly stated that she would be better off dead, the duty of care involves the duty to terminate its life. He seeks to support this proposition by reference to *Re B (a minor) (wardship: medical treatment)* [1981] 1 WLR 1421. As Griffiths LJ has pointed out, this was an urgent application made to the Court of Appeal in vacation and the two judgments were extempore. I am quite satisfied that Templeman LJ was saying no more than that, conceding for the purpose of argument that where the life of a child is so bound to be full of pain and suffering that it could be contended that the court could, in the exercise of its wardship jurisdiction, refuse to sanction an operation to prolong its life, the case before it clearly was not such a case. I do not consider that *Re B* provides any support to counsel for the plaintiff's contention.

Counsel for the plaintiffs was constrained to concede that, if his submission was correct, then a child born with a very minor disability, such as a squint, would be entitled to sue the doctor for not advising an abortion, which advice would have been accepted, given that the risk (which fortunately did not eventuate) of serious disabilities was due to some infection which the doctor should have diagnosed. This would indeed be an odd position. Moreover, he accepted that, if the duty of care to the fetus involved a duty on the doctor, albeit indirectly, to prevent its birth, the child would have a cause of action against its mother who had unreasonably refused to have an abortion. Apart from the complicated religious and philosophical points that such an action would raise, the social implications in the potential disruption of family life and bitterness which it would cause between parent and child led the Royal Commission to conclude that such a right of action would be against public policy (see Cmnd 7054–I, para 1465).

Of course, the doctor, in accordance with his duty of care *to the mother*, owes her a duty to advise her of the rubella infection and its potential serious and irreversible effects and on the advisability of an abortion, such an operation having in such circumstances been legalised by the Abortion Act 1967. This is, however, *nihil ad rem*.

(2) *The injury and the damages.* The disabilities were caused by the rubella and not by the doctor (I ignore whether their extent could have been reduced through injections, because that is the subject of the infant's first claim). What then are her injuries, which the doctor's negligence has caused? The answer must be that there are none in any accepted sense. Her complaint is that she was allowed to be born at all, given the existence of her prenatal injuries. How then are her damages to be assessed? Not by awarding compensation for her pain, suffering and loss of amenities attributable to the disabilities, since these were already in existence before the doctor was consulted. She cannot say that, but for his negligence, she would have been born without her disabilities. What the doctor is blamed for is causing or permitting her to be born at all. Thus, the compensation must be based on a comparison between the value of non-existence (the doctor's alleged negligence having deprived her of this) and the value of her existence in a disabled state.

But how can a court being to evaluate non-existence, 'The undiscover'd country from whose bourn No traveller returns'? No comparison is possible and therefore no damage can be established which a court could recognise. This goes to the root of the whole cause of action.

Counsel for the plaintiffs has provided no answer to the damage problem. His suggestion that you assess the compensation on the basis that the doctor had caused the disabilities and then you make some discount on a basis which he could not particularise because the doctor did not cause the disabilities does not, in my judgment, advance the matter, except to tend to confirm the impossibility of making such an assessment....

Stephenson LJ: The importance of this cause of action to this child is somewhat reduced by the existence of her other claim and the mother's claims, which, if successful, will give her some compensation in money or in care.

However, this is the first occasion on which the courts of this country or the Commonwealth have had to consider this cause of action, and I shall give my reasons for holding that it should be struck out.

If, as is conceded, any duty is owed to an unborn child, the authority's hospital laboratory and the doctor looking after the mother during her pregnancy undoubtedly owed the child a duty not to injure it, and, if she had been injured as a result of lack of reasonable care and skill on their part after birth, she could have sued them (as she is suing the doctor) for damages to compensate her for the injury they had caused her in the womb. (Cf the thalidomide cases, where it was assumed that such an action might lie: eg *Distillers Co (Biochemicals) Ltd v Thompson* [1971] 1 All ER 694, [1971] AC 458.) But this child has not been injured by either defendant, but by the rubella which has infected the mother without fault on anybody's part. Her right not to be injured before birth by the carelessness of others has not been infringed by either defendant, any more than it would have been if she had been disabled by disease after birth. Neither defendant has broken any duty to take reasonable care not to injure her. The only right on which she can rely as having been infringed is a right not to be born deformed or disabled, which means, for a child deformed or disabled before birth by nature or disease, a right to be aborted or killed; or, if that last plain word is thought dangerously emotive, deprived of the opportunity to live after being delivered from the body of her mother. The only duty which either defendant can owe to the unborn child infected with disabling rubella is a duty to abort or kill her or deprive her of that opportunity.

It is said that the duty does not go as far as that, but only as far as a duty to give the mother an opportunity to choose her abortion and death. That is true as far as it goes. The doctor's alleged negligence is in misleading the mother as to the advisability of an abortion, failing to inform or advise her of its advisability or desirability; the laboratory's alleged negligence is not so pleaded in terms but the negligence pleaded against them in failing to make or interpret the tests of the mother's blood samples or to inform the doctor of their results must, like the doctor's negligence, be a breach of their duty to give the doctor an opportunity to advise the mother of the risks in continuing to let the fetus live in the womb and be born alive. But the complaint of the child, as of the mother, against the health authority, as against the doctor, is that their negligence burdened her (and her mother) with her injuries. That is another way of saying that the defendants' breaches of their duties resulted not just in the child's being born but in her being born injured or, as the judge put it, with deformities. But, as the injuries or deformities were not the result of any act or omission of the defendants, the only result for which they were responsible was for her being born. For that they were responsible because if they had exercised due care the mother would have known that the child might be born injured or deformed, and the plaintiff's pleaded case is that, if the mother had known that, she would have been willing to undergo an abortion, which must mean she would have undergone one or she could not claim that the defendants were responsible for burdening her with an injured child. If she would not have undergone an abortion had she known the risk of the child being born injured, any negligence on the defendants' part could not give either plaintiff a cause of action in respect of the child being born injured.

I am accordingly of opinion that, though the judge was right in saying that the child's complaint is that she was born with deformities without which she would have suffered no damage and have no complaint, her claim against the defendants is a claim that they were negligent in allowing her, injured as she was in the womb, to be born at all, a claim for 'wrongful entry into life' or 'wrongful life'.

This analysis leads inexorably on to the question: how can there be a duty to take away life: How indeed can it be lawful? It is still the law that it is unlawful to take away the life of a born child or any living person after birth. But the Abortion Act 1967 has given mothers a right to terminate the lives of their unborn children and made it lawful for doctors to help to abort them.

That statute (on which counsel for the plaintiff relies) permits abortion in specified cases of risks to the mother and the child. I need not read those provisions which are enacted in the mother's interest, but there is one provision relevant to the interests of the child. Section 1(1) provides:

Subject to the provisions of this section, a person shall not be guilty of an offence under the law relating to abortion when a pregnancy is terminated by a registered medical practitioner if two registered medical practitioners are of the opinion, formed in good faith…(b) that there is a substantial risk that if the child were born it would suffer from such physical or mental abnormalities as to be seriously handicapped.

That paragraph may have been passed in the interests of the mother, the family and the general public, but I would prefer to believe that its main purpose, if not its sole purpose, was to benefit the unborn child; and, if and in so far as that was the intention of the legislature, the legislature did make a notable inroad on the sanctity of human life by recognising that it would be better for a child, born to suffer from such abnormalities as to be seriously handicapped, not to have been born at all.

The inroad, however, seems to stop short of a child capable of being born alive, because the sanctity of the life of a viable fetus is preserved by the enactment of s 5(1) that 'Nothing in this Act shall affect the provisions of the Infant Life (Preservation) Act 1929 (protecting the life of the viable foetus)'.

Another notable feature of the 1967 Act is that it does not directly impose any duty on a medical practitioner or anyone else to terminate a pregnancy, though it relieves conscientious objectors of a duty to participate in any treatment authorised by the Act in all cases with one exception: see s 4 of the Act. It is, however, conceded in this case that a medical practitioner is under a duty to the mother to advise her of her right under the Act to have her pregnancy terminated in cases such as the present. There was, on the pleaded facts of this case, a substantial risk that if the child were born it would suffer such physical or mental abnormalities as to be seriously handicapped. And, from what we have been told without objection of her present mental and physical condition, that risk has become tragically actual.

There is no doubt that this child could legally have been deprived of life by the mother's undergoing an abortion with the doctor's advice and help. So the law recognises a difference between the life of a fetus and the life of those who have been born. But, because a doctor can lawfully by statute do to a fetus what he cannot lawfully do to a person who has been born, it does not follow that he is under a legal obligation to a fetus to do it and terminate its life, or that the fetus has a legal right to die.

Like this court when it had to consider the interests of a child born with Down's syndrome in *Re B (a minor) (wardship: medical treatment)* [1981] 1 WLR 1421, I would not answer until it is necessary to do so the question whether the life of a child could be so certainly 'awful' and 'intolerable' that it would be in its best interests to end it and it might be considered that it had a right to be put to death. But that is not this case. We have no exact information about the extent of this child's serious and highly debilitating congenital injuries; the judge was told that she is partly blind and deaf, but it is not and could not be suggested that the quality of her life is such that she is certainly better dead, or would herself wish that she had not been born or should now die.

I am therefore compelled to hold that neither defendant was under any duty to the child to give the child's mother an opportunity to terminate the child's life. That duty may be owed to the mother, but it cannot be owed to the child.

To impose such a duty towards the child would, in my opinion, make a further inroad on the sanctity of human life which would be contrary to public policy. It would mean regarding the life of a handicapped child as not only less valuable than the life of a normal child, but so much less valuable that it was not worth preserving, and it would even mean that a doctor would be obliged to pay damages to a child infected with rubella before birth who was in fact born with some mercifully trivial abnormality. These are the consequences of the necessary basic assumption that a child has a right to be born whole or not at all, not to be born unless it can be born perfect or 'normal', whatever that may mean.

Added to that objection must be the opening of the courts to claims by children born handicapped against their mothers for not having an abortion. For the reasons given by the Royal Commission on Civil Liability and Compensation for Personal Injury (report, vol 1; Cmnd 7054–I), cited by Ackner LJ, that is, to my mind, a graver objection than the extra burden on doctors already open to actions for negligent treatment of a fetus, which weighed with the Law Commission.

Finally, there is the nature of the injury and damage which the court is being asked to ascertain and evaluate.

The only duty of care which courts of law can recognise and enforce are duties owed to those who can be compensated for loss by those who owe the duties, in most cases, including cases of personal injury, by money damages which will as far as possible put the injured party in the condition in which he or she was before being injured. The only way in which a child injured in the womb can be compensated in damages is by measuring what it has lost, which is the difference between the value of its life as a whole and healthy normal child and the value of its life as an injured child. But to make those who have not injured the child pay for that difference is to treat them as if they injured the child, when all they have done is not taken steps to prevent its being born injured by another cause.

The only loss for which those who have not injured the child can be held liable to compensate the child is the difference between its condition as a result of their allowing it to be born alive and injured and its condition if its embryonic life had been ended before its life in the world had begun. But how can a court of law evaluate that second condition and so measure the loss to the child? Even if a court were competent to decide between the conflicting views of theologians and philosophers and to assume an 'afterlife' or non-existence as the basis for the comparison, how can a judge put a value on the one or the other, compare either alternative with the injured child's life in this world and determine that the child has lost anything, without the means of knowing what, if anything, it has gained?

Judges have to pluck figures from the air in putting many imponderables into pounds and pence. Loss of expectation of life, for instance, has been held so difficult that the courts have been driven to fix for it a constant and arbitrary figure. Counsel for the plaintiffs referred us to what judges have said on that topic in *Rose v Ford* [1937] 3 All ER 359, [1937] AC 826 and *Benham v Gambling* [1941] 1 All ER 7, [1941] AC 157. But, in measuring the loss caused by shortened life, courts are dealing with a thing, human life, of which they have some experience, here the court is being asked to deal with the consequences of death for the dead, a thing of which it has none. And the statements of judges on the necessity for juries to assess damages and their ability to do so in cases of extreme difficulty do not touch the problem presented by the assessment of the claims we are considering. To measure loss of expectation of death would require a value judgment where a crucial factor lies altogether outside the range of human knowledge and could only be achieved, if at all, by resorting to the personal beliefs of the judge who has the misfortune to attempt the task. If difficulty in assessing damages is a bad reason for refusing the task, impossibility of assessing them is a good one. A court must have a starting point for giving damages for a breach of duty. The only means of giving a starting point to a court asked to hold that there is the duty on a doctor or a hospital which this child alleges is to require the court to measure injured life against uninjured life, and that is to treat the doctor and the hospital as responsible not for the child's birth but for its injuries. That is what in effect counsel for the plaintiffs suggests that the court should do, tempering the injustice to the defendants by some unspecified discount. This seems almost as desperate an expedient as an American judge's suggestion that the measure of damages should be the 'diminished childhood' resulting from the substantial diminuation of the parents' capacity to give the child special care: see the dissenting judgment of Handler J in *Berman v Allan* 404 A 2d 8 at 15, 19, 21 (1979). If there is no measure of damage which is not unjustified and indeed unjust, courts of law cannot entertain claims by a child affected with parental damage against those who fail to provide its mother with the opportunity to end its damaged life, however careless and unskillful they may have been and however liable thy may be to the mother for that negligent failure.

If a court had to decide whether it were better to enter into life maimed or halt than not to enter it at all, it would, I think, be bound to say it was better in all cases of mental and physical disability, except possibly those extreme cases already mentioned, of which perhaps the recent case of *Croke v Wiseman* [1981] 3 All ER 852, [1982] 1 WLR 71 is an example, but certainly not excepting such a case as the present. However that may be, it is not for the courts to take such a decision by weighing life against death or to take cognisance of a claim like this child's. I would regard it on principle as disclosing no reasonable cause of action and would accordingly prefer the master's decision to the judge's.

I am happy to find support for this view of the matter in the Law Commission's Report and the Congenital Disabilities (Civil Liability) Act 1976, to which I have already referred, and is the strong current of American authority, to which we have been referred. Direct decisions of courts in the United States of American on the same topic are of no more than persuasive authority but contain valuable material and with one exception would rule out the infant plaintiff's claims in our case....

Judicial opinion expressed in the American decisions can, I think, be summarised in the following propositions: (1) though what gives rise to the cause of action is not just life but life with defects, the real cause of action is negligence in causing life; (2) negligent advice or failure to advise is the proximate cause of the child's life (though not of its defects); (3) a child has no right to be born as a whole, functional being (without defects); (4) it is contrary to public policy, which is to preserve human life, to give a child a right not to be born except as a whole, functional being, and to impose on another a corresponding duty to prevent a child being born except without defects, that is, a duty to cause the death of an unborn child with defects, (5) it is impossible to measure the damages for being born with defects because it is impossible to compare the life of a child born with defects and non-existence as a human being; (6) accordingly, by being born with defects a child has suffered no injury cognisable by law and if it is to have a claim for being so born the law must be reformed by legislation.

The current of opinion has run in favour of the fourth consideration and against the fifth consideration even to the point of dismissing it altogether. Authority for that, and for the consideration which I have formulated, is to be found in particular in the judgment of the Supreme Court of New Jersey given by Pashman J in *Berman v Allan* 404 A 2d 8 at 11–13 (1979), in the judgments of Presiding Judge Cercone and Judge Spaeth in *Speck v Finegold* 408 A 2d 496 at 508, 51 (1979) and in the judgment of District Judge Blatt in *Phillips v USA* 508 F Supp 537 at 543 (1980)....

There are indications, to which counsel for the plaintiff called our attention, that some of the judges' opinions on the sanctity of human life were influenced by the illegality of abortion in some states; but those indications do not, in my opinion, play a decisive part in their decisions or weaken their persuasive force in considering the right answer to the same question in a jurisdiction where abortion has some statutory sanction.

I do not think it matters whether the injury is not an injury recognised by the law or the damages are not damages which the law can award. Whichever way it is put, the objection means that the cause of action is not cognisable or justiciable or 'reasonable', and I can draw no distinction between the first two terms and the third as it is rather artificially used in RSC Ord 18, r 19.

The defendants must be assumed to have been careless. The child suffers from serious disabilities. If the defendants had not been careless, the child could not be suffering now because it would not be alive. Why should the defendants not pay the child for its suffering?

The answer lies in the implications and consequences of holding that they should. If public policy favoured the introduction of this novel cause of action, I would not let the strict application of logic or the absence of precedent defeat it. But, as it would be, in my judgment, against public policy for the courts to entertain claims like those which are the subject of this appeal, I would for this reason, and for the other reasons which I have given, allow the appeal...

Griffiths LJ: The child's claim for 'wrongful life' is put against the hospital by the following steps. (1) The hospital when analysing the mother's blood owed a duty of care to the fetus in her womb. This point is conceded by the hospital for the purposes of this appeal. (2) The hospital discharges that duty of care by correctly advising whether the analysis shows that the mother has been infected. (3) In breach of that duty the hospital negligently advised that the analysis showed that the mother was not infected. (4) That breach of duty caused the birth of the child because, if the hospital had correctly advised that the mother was infected, she would have decided to have an abortion. (5) As a result of being born the child has to bear the afflictions of deafness, partial blindness and some degree of mental retardation, which society and the law should concur in treating as something that should not have happened to the child and for which she would be compensated by the negligent hospital.

It can thus be seen that the child's allegation is that but for the negligence of the hospital she would not have been born; it is a result of their wrong that she has been born; hence the term 'wrongful life'. The claim is put in a similar manner against the doctor.

Whether the law should give a remedy in such circumstances has been considered by the Law Commission. They concluded that there should be no liability for wrongful life and deliberately drafted cl 1 of the Congenital Disabilities (Civil Liability) Bill to exclude any such liability. Parliament accepted that advice and enacted the material part of the Congenital Disabilities (Civil Liability) Act 1976 in precisely the same language as the Law Commission's Bill. I am unable to accept the submission of counsel for the plaintiffs that the language of s 1 does not exclude the action for wrongful life; I have no doubt that it achieves its objective.

We have referred to seven decisions of courts in the United States of America; all save one of those courts have denied a remedy for wrongful life.

The remedy has been denied on a variety of different grounds. The Law Commission were of the opinion that it would impose an intolerable burden on the medical profession because of a subconscious pressure to advise abortions in doubtful cases for fear of actions for damages. I do not myself find this a convincing reason for denying the action if it would otherwise lie. The decision whether or not to have an abortion must always be the mother's; the duty of the medical profession can be no more than to advise her of her right to have an abortion and of the pros and cons of doing so. If there is a risk that the child will be born deformed, that risk must be explained to the mother, but it surely cannot be asserted that the doctor owes a duty to the fetus to urge its destruction. Provided the doctor gives a balanced explanation of the risks involved in continuing the pregnancy, including the risk of injury to the fetus, he cannot be expected to do more, and need have no fear of an action being brought against him.

To my mind, the most compelling reason to reject this cause of action is the intolerable and insoluble problem it would create in the assessment of damage. The basis of damages for personal injury is the comparison between the state of the plaintiff before he was injured and his condition after he was injured. This is often a hard enough task in all conscience and it has an element of artificiality about it, for who can say that there is any sensible correlation between pain and money? Nevertheless, the courts have been able to produce a broad tariff that appears at the moment to be acceptable in society as doing rough justice. But the whole exercise, difficult as it is, is anchored in the first place to the condition of the plaintiff before the injury which the court can comprehend and evaluate. In a claim for wrongful life how does the court begin to make an assessment? The plaintiff does not say, 'But for your negligence I would have been born uninjured'; the plaintiff says, 'But for your negligence I would never have been born'. The court then has to compare the state of the plaintiff with non-existence, of which the court can know nothing; this I regard as an impossible task. Counsel for the plaintiffs suggested that the court should assess the damages on the assumption that the plaintiff's injury had been caused by the hospital, and then discount the damages because it had not been so caused. But he was quite unable, and I do not blame him, to suggest any principle on which the discount should be calculated.

Again, suppose by some happy chance the child is born with only a slight deformity, can it bring an action on the basis that it would have been killed in the womb if the mother had been told of the risk of greater deformity? Such a claim seems utterly offensive; there should be rejoicing that the hospital's mistake bestowed the gift of life on a child. If such claims are rejected, on what basis could a claim be brought for a more serious injury? Only, it would seem, on the basis that the state of the child is such that it were better dead than alive. But, knowing nothing of death, who is to answer this question, and what two minds will approach the answer by the same route? I regard the question as wholly outside the competence of judicial determination.

I would reject this novel cause of action because I see no way of determining which plaintiffs can claim, that is, how gravely deformed must the child be before a claim will lie? and secondly because of the impossibility of assessing the damage it has suffered.

The common law does not have the tools to fashion a remedy in these cases. If society feels that such cases are deserving of compensation, some entirely novel and arbitrary measure of damage is called for, which I agree with the American judge would be better introduced by legislation than by judges striving to solve the insoluble.

There are a number of strands of argument relied upon by the Court of Appeal in rejecting the child's claim. *First*, no duty could be owed by the doctor to the child, in particular, because it would be contrary to public policy for the doctor to owe a 'duty to the foetus to urge its destruction'. *Secondly*, the child had not suffered any damage known to the law by being born. *Thirdly*, the assessment of a child's damages would be impossible given that it would require the court 'to compare the state of the plaintiff with non-existence, of which the court can know nothing' (see also *Millar (P's curator bonis) v CICB* (1996) 44 BMLR 70 (Ct Sess (OH)).

The position at common law is by no means as straightforward or as clear as these judgments would have it. (See R Lee 'To Be or Not To Be: Is that the Question? The Claim of Wrongful Life' in R Lee and D Morgan (eds) *Birthrights: Law and Ethics at the Beginnings of Life* (1990) at p 172. See also H Teff 'The Action for Wrongful Life in England and the United States' (1985) 34 ICLQ 423.) Initially, courts in the United States adopted a similar view of the law as that set out in *McKay*. However, during the 1980s a number of jurisdictions sought to fashion a means of giving the child *some* remedy and so adopted an alternative analysis. The breakthrough occurred in the California Court of Appeal in 1980 which reviewed, only to reject, the existing body of case law.

Curlender v Bio-Science Laboratories (1980) 165 Cal Rptr 477 (Cal CA)

Jefferson J: The appeal presents an issue of first impression in California: What remedy, if any, is available in this state to a severely impaired child – generally defective – born as the result of defendants' negligence in conducting certain genetic tests of the child's parents – tests which, if properly done, would have disclosed the high probability that the actual, catastrophic result would occur?

In the first cause of action against the named defendants, plaintiff Shauna alleged that on January 15, 1977, her parents, Phillis and Hyam Curlender, retained defendant laboratories to administer certain tests designed to reveal whether either of the parents were carriers of genes which would result in the conception and birth of a child with Tay-Sachs disease, medically defined as 'amaurotic familial idiocy'. The tests on plaintiff's parents were performed on January 21, 1977, and, it was alleged, due to defendants' negligence, 'incorrect and inaccurate' information was disseminated to plaintiff's parents concerning their status as carriers.

The complaint did not allege the date of plaintiff's birth, so we do not know whether the parents relied upon the test results in conceiving plaintiff, or, as parents-to-be when the tests were made, relied upon the results in failing to avail themselves of amniocentesis and an abortion. In any event, on May 10, 1978, plaintiff's parents were informed that plaintiff had Tay-Sachs disease.

As the result of the disease, plaintiff Shauna suffers from 'mental retardation, susceptibility to other diseases, convulsions, sluggishness, apathy, failure to fix objects with her eyes, inability to take an interest in her surroundings, loss of motor reactions, inability to sit up or hold her head up, loss of weight, muscle atrophy, blindness, pseudobulper palsy, inability to feed orally, decerebrate rigidity and gross physical deformity'. It was alleged that Shauna's life expectancy is estimated to be four years. The complaint also contained allegations that plaintiff suffers 'pain, physical and emotional distress, fear, anxiety, despair, loss of enjoyment of life, and frustration…'

The complaint sought costs of plaintiff's care as damages and also damages for emotional distress and the deprivation of '72.6 years of her life'. In addition, punitive damages of three million dollars were sought, on the ground that '[a]t the time that Defendants … [tested the parents] Defendants, and each of them, had been expressly informed by the nation's leading authority on Tay-Sachs disease that said test procedures were substantially inaccurate and would likely result in disastrous [sic] and catastrophic consequences to the patients, and Defendants knew that said procedures were improper, inadequate and with insufficient controls and that the results of such a testing were likely to be inaccurate and that a false negative result would have disastrous [sic] and catastrophic consequences to the Plaintiff, all in conscious disregard of the health, safety and well-being of Plaintiff.…'

A major (and much cited) opinion considering a claim for damages by an impaired infant plaintiff and his parents is *Gleitman v Cosgrove* 49 NJ 22, 227 A 2d 689 (1967) from the New Jersey Supreme Court. The Gleitmans brought a malpractice action against Mrs Gleitman's physician for damages because the Gleitman child, Jeffrey, had been born with serious impairments of sight, speech, and hearing. Mrs Gleitman had contracted rubella (measles) during the first trimester of pregnancy (the first three months). Defendant was made aware of this fact, but failed to inform the mother-to-be of any potentially harmful consequences to her child; Mrs Gleitman was assured by him that such consequences would not occur, although it was common medical knowledge that rubella, contracted during early pregnancy, often causes the type of defects suffered by Jeffrey, who was also mentally retarded.

The majority of the *Gleitman* court barred recovery by *either* the parents or the child on two grounds: (1) the perceived impossibility of computing damages and (2) public policy. With respect to the computation of damages, the court explained that '[t]he normal measure of damages in tort actions is compensatory. Damages are measured by comparing the condition plaintiff would have been in, had the defendants not been negligent, with plaintiff's impaired condition as a result of the negligence. The infant plaintiff would have us measure the difference between his life with defects against the utter void of nonexistence, but it is impossible to make such a determination. This Court cannot weight the value of life with impairments against the nonexistence of life itself. By asserting that he should not have been born, the infant plaintiff makes it logically impossible for a court to measure his alleged damages because of the impossibility of making the comparison required by compensatory remedies' (*Gleitman, supra* 227 A 2d 689, 692).

Any decision negating the value of life directly or by implication was seen by the majority in *Gleitman* as an impermissible expression of public policy. There was considerable discussion of the legality of any abortion which would have been undertaken to prevent Jeffrey's birth. The majority referred with approval to the analysis presented in Israel Law review 513 (1966) by Tedeschi, entitled 'On Tort Liability for "Wrongful Life"'.

A vastly different view was expressed by a dissenting opinion in *Gleitman*. It was there declared that the majority 'permits a wrong with serious consequential injury to go wholly unredressed. That provides no deterrent to professional irresponsibility and is neither just nor compatible with expanding principles of liability in the field of torts' (*Gleitman, supra*, 227 A 2d 689, 703 (dis opn)). As to the impossibility of computing damages, reference was made to a statement by the United States Supreme Court in *Story Parchment Co v Paterson Co* 282 US 555, 563, 51 S Ct 248, 250, 75 L Ed 544 (1931), that difficulties encountered in computing damages cannot be permitted to justify a denial of liability. However, the reasoning and result in *Gleitman's* majority opinion have been, in the main, followed (albeit blindly in our opinion) in other jurisdictions. (See *Stewart v Long Island College Hospital* 58 Misc 2d 432, 296 NYS 2d 41 (1968) and *Dumer v St Michael's Hospital* 69 Wis 2d 766, 233 NW 2d 372 (1975).) It has also been analysed and criticised. (See Note, 55 Minn L rev 58 (1971).)

Of some significance with respect to this question is that fact that in 1973, *Roe v Wade*, 410 US 113, 93 S Ct 705, 35 L Ed 2d 147, was decided by the United States Supreme Court. The nation's high court determined that parents have a *constitutionally protected right* to obtain an abortion during the first trimester of pregnancy, free of state interference. We deem this decision to be of considerable importance in defining the parameters of 'wrongful-life' litigation.

The *Roe v Wade* case played a rather substantial part in the partial retreat from the *Gleitman* holding by the New Jersey Supreme Court majority in *Berman v Allan* 80 NJ 421, 404 A 2d 8 (1979). The Bermans, parents and child, brought suit for medical malpractice. Mrs Berman had become pregnant in her late thirties, a circumstance involving a substantial risk that the child would be born with Down's syndrome (mongolism), one of the major characteristics of which is mental retardation. Sharon Berman, the child, was so afflicted.

Amniocentesis – by that time a well established technique for discerning birth defects *in utero* – had not been suggested to the Bermans. The majority in the *Berman* court held that the *parents* had stated a cause of action, and that they could recover damages for emotional distress, but that lifetime support for Sharon could not be awarded.

But the *Berman* court rejected the concept that the infant Sharon possessed an independent cause of action. Referring to the difficulty of measuring damages in such a case, the court declared that '[n]onetheless, were the *measure* of damages our sole concern, it is possible that some judicial remedy could be fashioned which would redress plaintiff, if only in part, for injuries suffered'. Here, the majority chose to rely on public policy considerations. The *Berman* court considered that Sharon had not suffered any damage cognisable at law by being brought into existence. It was explained that '[o]ne of the most deeply held beliefs of our society is that life – whether experienced with or without a major physical handicap – is more precious than nonlife.... Sharon, by virtue of her birth, will be able to love and be loved and to experience happiness and pleasure – emotions which are truly the essence of life and which are far more valuable than the suffering she may endure. To rule otherwise would require us to disavow the basic assumption upon which our society is based. This we cannot do.' (*Berman, supra*, 404 A 2d 8, 12–13.)

The dissenting opinion in *Berman*, noting that the majority had in effect partially overruled *Gleitman*, urged complete rejection of the majority view on the ground that '[t]he child ... was owed directly, during its gestation, a duty of reasonable care from the same physicians who undertook to care for its mother – then expectant– and that duty, to render complete and competent medical advice, was seriously breached'. (*Berman, supra*, 404 A 2d 8, 15 (dis opn).) Taking cognisance of the present legality of abortions in the first trimester, the dissent perceived a duty on the part of medical practitioners to ensure that, under certain circumstances, parents-to-be had the opportunity to decide the future of their child – its existence or nonexistence. 'To be denied the opportunity – indeed, the right – to apply one's own moral values in reaching that decision [concerning the child's future], is a serious, irreversible wrong.' (*Id* 404 A 2d at p 18.)

The dissenting opinion in *Berman* expressed the cogent observation that, as for the child, '[a]n adequate comprehension of the infant's claims under these circumstances *starts with the realisation that the infant has come into this world and is here*, encumbered by an injury attributable to the malpractice of the doctors'. (*Berman, supra*, 404 A 2d 8, 19.) (Emphasis added.)

In New York ... there have been a series of decisions wrestling with 'wrongful-life' problems with the quite predictable divergent expressions by the judiciary. In only one case, however (overruled by a higher court) did the court grant recognition to a cause of action by a child so born.

In *Park v Chessin* 60 AD 80, 400 NYS 2d 110 (1977), an intermediate New York appellate court considered the following facts. The Parks had had one child born with polycystic kidney disease, a fatal hereditary ailment. The baby died. The parents consulted defendant doctors and informed them of this; assured that the condition would not reoccur, the Parks had a second child, who also had the disease but survived for a short life span of 2 and $\frac{1}{2}$ years. The court held that these facts gave both the parents and child causes of action, that 'decisional law must keep pace with explaining technological, economic and social change. Inherent in the abolition of the statutory ban on abortion...is a public policy consideration which gives potential parents the right, within certain statutory and case law limitations, *not* to have a child. This right extends to instances in which it can be determined with reasonable medical certainty that the child would be born deformed. The *breach of this right may also be said to be tortious to the fundamental right of a child to be born as a whole, functional human being*.' (*Park, supra*, 400 NYS 2d 110, 114.) (Emphasis added.)

But this view of the law also had a short life span. This decision was reviewed in *Becker v Schwartz* 46 NY 2d 401, 413 NYS 2d 895, 386 NE 2d 807 (1978) (as a companion case) and overruled. The Beckers and their mongoloid infant sought damages from medical doctors who had not, despite the mother's age when she became pregnant, warned of the danger or informed the Beckers of amniocentesis. The parents, declared *Becker*, had stated a cause of action and could recover their pecuniary loss but *not* damages for emotional distress, as the latter recovery would offend public policy. The infant plaintiffs in both *Becker* and *Park* were held to be barred from recovery because of the inability of the law to make a comparison between human existence with handicaps and no life at all. The court particularly rejected the idea that a child may expect life without deformity: 'There is no precedent for recognition at the Appellant Division of a "fundamental right of a child to be born as a whole, functional human being"...'(*Becker, supra*, 413 NYS 2d 895 at 900, 386 NE 2d 807 at 812.)

The high court in Pennsylvania issued an exhaustive opinion in 1979 concerning the various aspects of the 'wrongful-life' problem. The case was *Speck v Finegold*, – Pa Super –, 408 A 2d 496, a malpractice suit by parents and child occasioned by the birth of the child with neurofibromatosis, a seriously crippling condition already evidenced in the child's siblings. Overruling the trial court, *Speck* recognised the parents' cause of action but not that of the infant plaintiff.

We quote at length from the *Speck* court's opinion:

In the instant case, we deny Francine's [infant plaintiff] claim to be made whole. When we examine Francine's claim, we find regardless of whether her claim is based on 'wrongful life' or otherwise, there is a failure to state a legally cognisable cause of action even though, admittedly, the defendants' actions of negligence were the proximate cause of her defective birth. Her claims to be whole have two fatal weaknesses. First, there is no precedent in appellate judicial pronouncements that holds a child has a fundamental right to be born as a whole, functional human being. Whether it is better to have never been born at all rather than to have been born with serious mental defects is a mystery more properly left to the philosophers and theologians, a mystery which would lead us into the field of metaphysics, beyond the realm of our understanding or ability to solve.... [This] cause of action ...demands a calculation of damages dependent on a comparison between Hobson's choice of life in an impaired state and nonexistence. This the law is incapable of doing. [Fn omitted.] ... unfortunately ... this is not an action cognisable in law. Thus, the recognised principle, not peculiar to traditional tort law alone, that it would be a denial of justice to deny all relief where a wrong is of such a nature as to preclude certain ascertained damages, is inapposite and inapplicable here.

(*Speck, supra*, 408 A 2d 496, 508.)

Other jurisdictions, following the lead of the New Jersey and New York cases, have rejected the concept of an infant's cause of action for 'wrongful life'. (See *Elliott v Brown* 361 So 2d 546 (Ala 1978), rejecting the 'wrongful life' cause of action in that jurisdiction; see also *Jacobs v Theimer* 519 SW 2d 846 (Tex 1975), holding that the mother of a defective child had stated a cause of action for failure of the defendant physician to diagnose rubella during early pregnancy and counsel accordingly; also, recovery was allowed for those costs reasonably related to caring for the child's physical defects. The court declared that '[n]o public policy obstacle should be interposed to that recovery' (519 SW 2d 846, 849).)

Two decisions of note have involved Tay-Sachs impairment – the condition involved in the case before us. In *Howard v Lecher* 42 NY 2d 109, 397 NYS 2d 363, 366 NE 2d 64 (1977), an intermediate appellate court in New York considered an action brought by the parent to recover damages for emotional distress form the consulting physicians. In *Howard*, the child died. Denying recovery, the *Howard* majority reasoned that recognition of the parents' cause of action 'would require the extension of traditional tort concepts beyond manageable bounds'. (397 NYS 2d at 364, 366 NE 2d at 65.)

A dissenting judge in *Howard* expostulated that the issue was simply whether a patient and parent-to-be, the mother, may recover damages from her physician for the latter's negligence. He found it not unreasonable, given the present state of medical knowledge concerning genetically caused birth deformities and the procedures available for avoiding such deformities, for the law to require an attending physician to take a genealogical history of the parents, to perform any available appropriate tests indicated by such history, and inform the parents of any potential dangers so that they would be able to make an informed decision concerning continuation of pregnancy.

In *Gildiner v Thomas Jefferson Univ Hospital* 451 F Supp 692 (ED Pa 1978), the parents had been tested for Tay-Sachs; the tests indicated that amniocentesis should be performed; it was performed, but negligently; the parents were both carriers, and the infant born to them suffered from Tay-Sachs. Relying on *Gleitman v Cosgrove, supra*, 49 NJ 22, 227 A 2d 689, the federal district court held that the parents could recover damages, but the child could not. A strong public policy was perceived in allowing parental recovery: 'Tay-Sachs disease can be prevented only by accurate genetic testing combined with the right of parents to abort afflicted fetuses within appropriate time limitations. *Society has an interest in insuring that genetic testing is properly performed and interpreted.*' (*Gildiner, supra*, 451 F Supp 692, 696.) (Emphasis added.) ...

From our analysis and study, we conclude that certain general observations are appropriate concerning the decisional law in this country to date with respect to the 'wrongful life' problem.

First. For clear analysis it is important to recognise certain distinctions among the cases purportedly dealing with the 'wrongful-life' concept. One such distinction is that concerning the condition of the child involved. Surely there is a world of difference between an unwanted healthy child who is illegitimate (*Stills v Gratton* [127 Cal Rptr 652 (Cal CA)]), the unwanted tenth child of a marriage (*Custodio v Bauer* 251 Cal App 2d 303, 59 Cal Rptr 463 (1967)) and the severely deformed infant plaintiff, Shauna, in the case at bench. Illegitimacy is a status which may or may not prove to be a hindrance to one so born, depending on a multitude of other facts; it cannot be disputed that in present society such a circumstance, both socially and legally, no longer need present an overwhelming obstacle. The same is true for the simply unwanted child. We agree with the reasoning of *Zepeda* [v *Zepeda* (1963) 190 NE 2d 849 (Ill CA)] and *Stills* that a cause of action based upon impairment of status – illegitimacy contrasted with legitimacy – should not be recognisable at law *because* a necessary element for the establishment of any cause of action in tort is missing, *injury* and damages consequential to that injury. A child born with severe impairment, however, presents an entirely different situation because the necessary element of *injury* is present.

Second. The decisional law of other jurisdictions, while not dispositive of Shauna's claim pursuant to California law, is of considerable significance in defining the basic issues underlying the true 'wrongful-life' action – one brought by the infant whose painful existence is a direct and proximate result of negligence by others. That decisional law demonstrates some measure of progression in our law. Confronted with the fact that the births of these infants may be directly traced to the negligent conduct of others, and that the result is palpable injury, involving not only pecuniary loss but untold anguish on the part of all concerned, the courts in our sister states have progressed from a stance of barring all recovery to a recognition that, at least, the parents of such a child may state a cause of action founded on negligence.

We note that there has been a gradual retreat from the position of accepting 'impossibility of measuring damages' as the sole ground for barring the infant's right of recovery, although the courts continue to express divergent views on how the parents' damages should be measured, in terms of allowing recovery for both pecuniary loss and damages for emotional distress, or, in recognising one element of recovery only, but not the other.

The concept of public policy has played an important role in this developing field of law. Public policy, as perceived by most courts, has been utilised as the basis for denying recovery; in some fashion, a deeply held belief in the sanctity of life has compelled some courts to deny recovery to those among us who have been born with serious impairment. But the dissents, written along the way, demonstrate that there is not universal acceptance of the notion that 'metaphysics' or 'religious beliefs', rather than law, should govern the situation; the dissents have emphasised that considerations of public policy should include regard for social welfare as affected by careful genetic counselling and medical procedures.

We have alluded to the monumental implications of *Roe v Wade*, *supra*, 410 US 113, 93 S Ct 705, 35 L Ed 2d 147, one of which is the present legality of, and availability of, eugenic abortion in the proper case. Another factor of substantial proportions in 'wrongful-life' litigation is the dramatic increase, in the last few decades, of the medical knowledge and skill needed to avoid genetic disaster. As the author of the article in the Yale Law Journal points out (see fn 8): 'Genetic defects represent an increasingly large part of the overall national health care burden."(87 Yale Law Journal 1496.) The writer concluded that the law indeed has an appropriate function in encouraging adequate and careful medical practice in the field of genetic counselling, observing that '[t]ort law, a well-recognised means of regulating the practice of medicine, can be used both to establish and to limit the duty of physicians to fulfil this [genetic counselling] function'. (87 Yale Law Journal 1499.)

Third. Despite the cool reception accorded such 'wrongful-life' litigation, both parents and their children have continued to seek redress for the wrongs committed, presumably for a number of reasons: (1) the serious nature of the wrong; (2) increasing sophistication as to the causes, which may not with present knowledge be attributed to the fine hand of providence but rather to lack of care; and (3) the understanding that the law reflects, perhaps later than sooner, basic changes in the way society views such matters.

... We have no difficulty in ascertaining and finding the existence of a duty owed by medical laboratories engaged in genetic testing to parents and their as yet unborn children to use ordinary care in administration of available tests for the purpose of providing information concerning potential genetic defects in the unborn. The public policy considerations with respect to the individuals involved and to society as a whole dictate recognition of such a duty, and it is of significance that in no decision that has come to our attention which has dealt with the 'wrongful-life' concept has it been suggested that public policy considerations negate the existence of such a duty. Nor have other jurisdictions had any difficulty in finding a breach of duty under appropriate circumstances or in finding the existence of the requisite proximate causal link between the breach and the claimed injury; we find no bar to a holding that the defendants owed a duty to the child plaintiff before us and breached that duty.

The real crux of the problem is whether the breach of duty was the proximate cause of *an injury cognisable at law*. The injury, of course, is not the particular defect with which a plaintiff is afflicted – considered in the abstract – but it is the birth of plaintiff with such defect.

The circumstance that the birth and injury have come hand in hand has caused other courts to deal with the problem by barring recovery. The reality of the 'wrongful-life' concept is that such a plaintiff both *exists* and *suffers*, due to the negligence of others. It is neither necessary nor just to retreat into meditation on the mysteries of life. We need not be concerned with the fact that had defendants not been negligent, the plaintiff might not have come into existence at all. The certainty of genetic impairment is no longer a mystery. In addition, a reverent appreciation of life compels recognition that plaintiff, however impaired she may be, has come into existence as a living person with certain rights.

One of the fears expressed in the decisional law is that, once it is determined that such infants have rights cognisable at law, nothing would prevent such a plaintiff from bringing suit against its own parents for allowing plaintiff to be born .In our view, the fear is groundless. The 'wrongful-life' cause of action with which we are concerned is based upon negligently caused failure by someone under a duty to do so to inform the prospective parents of facts needed by them to make a conscious choice *not* to become parents. If a case arose where, despite due care by the medical profession in transmitting the necessary warnings, parents make a conscious choice to proceed with a pregnancy, with full knowledge that a seriously impaired infant would be born, that conscious choice would provide an intervening act of proximate cause to preclude liability insofar as defendants other than the parents were concerned. Under such circumstances, we see no sound public policy which should protect those parents from being answerable for the pain, suffering and misery which they have wrought upon their offspring.

In our consideration of whether the child plaintiff has stated a cause of action, we find it instructive to look first to the statutory law of this state. Our Civil Code section 3281 provides that '*[e]very person* who suffers detriment from the unlawful act or omission of another, may recover from the person in fault a compensation therefor in money, which is called damages'. Civil Code section 3282 defines detriment as 'a loss or harm suffered in person or property'. Civil Code section 3333 provides: 'For the breach of an obligation not arising from contract, the measure of damages, except where otherwise expressly provided by this Code, is the amount which will compensate for all the detriment proximately caused thereby, whether it could have been anticipated or not'.

In addition, we have long adhered to the principle that there should be a remedy for every wrong committed. 'Fundamental in our jurisprudence is the principle that for every wrong there is a remedy and that an injured party should be compensated for all damage proximately caused by the wrongdoer. Although we recognise exceptions from these fundamental principles, no departure should be sanctioned unless there is a strong necessity therefor. The general rule of damages in tort is that the injured party may recover for all detriment caused whether it could have been anticipated or not.' (*Crisci v Security Ins Co* 66 Cal 2d 425 at 433, 58 Cal Rptr 13 at 18, 426 P 2d 173 at 178 (1967).)

We have concluded that it is clearly consistent with the applicable principles of the statutory and decisional tort law in this state to recognise a cause of action stated by plaintiff against the defendants ... the extent of recovery, however, is subject to certain limitations due to the nature of the tort involved. While ordinarily a defendant is liable for all consequences flowing from the injury (*Custodio v Bauer*, *supra*), it is appropriate in the case before us to tailor the elements of recovery, taking into account particular circumstances involved (as was done in *Stills v Gratton*, *supra*).

The complaint seeks damages based upon an actuarial life expectancy of plaintiff of more than 70 years – the life expectancy if plaintiff had been born without the Tay-Sachs disease. The complaint sets forth that plaintiff's actual life expectancy, because of the disease, is only four years. We reject as untenable the claim that plaintiff is entitled to damages as if plaintiff had been born without defects and would have had a normal life expectancy. Plaintiff's right to damages must be considered on the basis of plaintiff's mental and physical condition at birth and her expected condition during the short life span (four years according to the complaint) anticipated for one with her impaired condition. In similar fashion, we reject the notion that a 'wrongful-life' cause of action involves an attempted evaluation of a claimed right *not* to be born. In essence, we construe the 'wrongful-life' cause of action by the defective child as the right of such child to recover damages for the pain and suffering to be endured during the limited life span available to such a child and any special pecuniary loss resulting from the impaired condition.

The approach in *Curlender* was subsequently modified by the Supreme Court of California in the following case.

Turpin v Sortini (1982) 643 P 2d 954 (Cal Sup Ct)

Kaus J: This case presents the question of whether a child born with an hereditary affliction may maintain a tort action against a medical care provider who – before the child's conception – negligently failed to advise the child's parents of the possibility of the hereditary condition, depriving them of the opportunity to choose not to conceive the child. Although the overwhelming majority of decisions in other jurisdictions recognise the right of *the parents* to maintain an action under these circumstances, the out-of-state cases have uniformly denied *the child's* right to bring what has been commonly termed a 'wrongful life' action. In *Curlender v Bio-Science Laboratories* (1980) 106 Cal App 3d 811, 165 Cal Rptr 477, however, the Court of Appeal, 119 Cal App 3d 690, 174 Cal Rptr 128, concluded that under California common law tort principles, an afflicted child could maintain such an action and could 'recover damages for the pain and suffering to be endured during the limited life span available to such a child and any special pecuniary loss resulting from the impaired condition' (*id*, at p 831, 165 Cal Rptr 477), including the costs of medical care to the extent such costs were not recovered by the child's parents. In the case at bar, a different panel of the Court of Appeal disagreed with the conclusion in *Curlender* and affirmed a trial court judgment dismissing the child's cause of action on demurrer. We granted a hearing to resolve the conflict....

The allegations of the complaint disclose the following facts. On September 24, 1976, James and Donna Turpin, acting on the advice of their paediatrician, brought their first – and at that time their only – daughter, Hope, to the Leon S Peters Rehabilitation Center at the Fresno Community Hospital for evaluation of a possible hearing defect. Hope was examined and tested by Adam J Sortini, a licensed professional specialising in the diagnosis and treatment of speech and hearing defects.

The complaint alleges that Sortini and other persons at the hospital negligently examined, tested and evaluated Hope and incorrectly advised her paediatrician that her hearing was within normal limits, when, in reality, she was 'stone deaf' as a result of an hereditary ailment. Hope's parents did not learn of her condition until October 15, 1977 when it was diagnosed by other specialists. According to the complaint, the nature of the condition is such that there is a 'reasonable degree of medical probability' that the hearing defect would be inherited by any offspring of James and Donna.

The complaint further alleges that in December 1976, before learning of Hope's true condition and relying on defendant's diagnosis, James and Donna conceived a second child, Joy. The complaint avers that had the Turpins known of Hope's hereditary deafness they would not have conceived Joy. Joy was born August 23, 1977, and suffers from the same total deafness as Hope.

On the basis of these facts, James, Donna, Hope and Joy filed a complaint setting forth four causes of action against defendants Sortini, the hospital, the rehabilitation center and various Does. The first cause of action, brought on behalf of Hope, seeks damages for the harm Hope has allegedly suffered as a result of the delay in the diagnosis of her condition. The second cause of action – the only cause before us on this appeal – was brought on behalf of Joy and seeks (1) general damages for being 'deprived of the fundamental right of a child to be born as a whole, functional human being without total deafness' and (2) special damages for the 'extraordinary expenses for specialised teaching, training and hearing equipment' which she will incur during her lifetime as a result of her hearing impairment. The third and fourth causes of action, brought on behalf of James and Donna, seek, respectively, special damages relating to the support and medical care of Joy to the age of majority, and general damages for emotional distress sustained by James and Donna 'attendant to the raising and caring of a totally deaf child'....

The explanation for the divergent results [in other jurisdictions] is that while courts have been willing to permit parents to recover for medical costs or – in some cases– other harms which the parents would not have incurred 'but for' the defendants' negligence, they have been reluctant to permit the child to complain when, but for the defendants' negligence, he or she would not have been born at all.

In this context the recent decisions have either concluded that the child has sustained no 'legally cognisable injury' or that appropriate damages are impossible to ascertain.... Defendants' basic position – supported by the numerous out-of-state authorities – is that Joy has suffered no legally cognisable injury or rationally ascertainable damages as a result of their alleged negligence. Although the issues of 'legally cognisable injury' and 'damages' are intimately related and in some sense inseparable, past cases have generally treated the two as distinct matters and, for purposes of analysis, it seems useful to follow that approach.

With respect to the issue of legally cognisable injury, the parties agree that the difficult question here does not stem from the fact that defendants' allegedly negligent act and plaintiff's asserted injury occurred before plaintiff's birth.

Although at one time the common law denied recovery for injuries inflicted before birth, California – in tune with other American jurisdictions– has long abandoned that arbitrary limitation. (See Civ Code, s 29; *Scott v McPheeters* 33 Cal App 2d 629, 92 P 2d 678 (1939). See generally Robertson, *Toward Rational Boundaries of Tort Liability for Injury to the Unborn: Prenatal Injuries, Preconception Injuries and Wrongful Life*, 1978 Duke LJ 1401, 1402–1413.) Thus, if Joy's deafness was caused by negligent treatment of her mother during pregnancy, or if it resulted from a tort committed upon her mother before conception (see, eg. *Renslowe v Mennonite Hospital* (1977) 67 Ill 2d 348 [10 Ill Dec 484, 367 NE 2d 1250]; *Bergstreser v Mitchell* (8th Circ 1978) 577 F 2d 22; Annot (1979) 91 ALR 3d 316), it is clear that she would be entitled to recover against the negligent party.

Joy's complaint attempts, in effect, to bring her action within the scope of the foregoing line of cases, asserting that as a result of the defendant's negligence she was 'deprived of the fundamental right of a child to be born as a whole, functional human being without total deafness....' While the *Curlender* decision did not embrace this approach to 'injury' completely – refusing to permit the plaintiff to recover for a reduced lifespan – it too maintained that the proper point of reference for measuring defendants' liability was simply plaintiff's condition after birth, insisting that '[w]e need not be concerned with the fact that had defendants not been negligent, the plaintiff might not have come into existence at all' (106 Cal App 3d at 829), and rejecting 'the notion that a "wrongful life" cause of action involves any attempted evaluation of a claimed right *not* to be born'. (Original italics.) (*Id*, at pp 830–831, 165 Cal Rptr 477.)

The basic fallacy of the *Curlender* analysis is that it ignores the essential nature of the defendants' alleged wrong and obscures a critical difference between wrongful life actions and the ordinary prenatal injury cases noted above. In an ordinary prenatal injury case, if the defendant had not been negligent, the child would have been born healthy; thus, as in a typical personal injury case, the defendant in such a case has interfered with the child's basic right to be free from physical injury caused by the negligence of others. In this case, by contrast, the obvious tragic fact is that plaintiff never had a chance 'to be born as a whole, functional human being without total deafness'; if defendants had performed their jobs properly, she would not have been born with hearing intact, but – according to the complaint – would not have been born at all.

A plaintiff's remedy in tort is compensatory in nature and damages are generally intended not to punish a negligent defendant but to restore an injured person as nearly as possible to the position he or she would have been in had the wrong not been done. (See generally Rest 2d Torts, s 901, com a; *Stills v Gratton, supra*, 55 Cal App 3d at 706, 127 Cal Rptr 652; 4 Witkin, Summary of Cal Law (8th ed 1974) Torts, s 842, p 3137 and cases cited.) Because nothing defendants could have done would have given plaintiff an unimpaired life, it appears inconsistent with basic tort principles to view the injury for which defendants are legally responsible solely by reference to plaintiff's present condition without taking into consideration the fact that if defendants had not been negligent she would not have been born at all. (See Capron, *Tort Liability and Genetic Counseling* (1979) 79 Colum L Rev 619, 654–657; Comment *'Wrongful Life': The Right Not to be Born* (1980) 54 Tulane L Rev 480, 494–497.)

If the relevant injury in this case is the change in the plaintiff's position attributable to the tortfeasor's actions, then the injury which plaintiff has suffered is that, as a result of defendants' negligence, she has been born with an hereditary ailment rather than not being born at all. Although plaintiff has not phrased her claim for general damages in these terms, most courts and commentators have recognised that the basic claim of 'injury' in wrongful life cases is '[i]n essence ... that [defendants], through their negligence, [have] forced upon [the child] the worse of...two alternatives[,] ... that nonexistence– never being born– would have been preferable to existence in [the] diseased state'. (*Speck v Finegold* 268 Pa Super 342, 408 A 2d 496, 511–512 (1979) (conc & dis opn by Spaeth J), affd (1981) 439 A 2d 110.)

Given this view of the relevant injury which the plaintiff has sustained at the defendants' hands, some courts have concluded that the plaintiff has suffered no legally cognisable injury on the ground that considerations of public policy dictate a conclusion that life – even with the most severe of impairments – is, as a matter of law, always preferable to nonlife. The decisions frequently suggest that a contrary conclusion would 'disavow' the sanctity and value of less-than-perfect human life. (See, eg, *Berman v Allan, supra*, 404 A 2d at 12–13, *Phillips v United States, supra*, 508 F Supp at 543.)

Although it is easy to understand and to endorse these decisions' desire to affirm the worth and sanctity of less-than-perfect life, we question whether these considerations alone provide a sound basis for rejecting the child's tort action. To begin with, it is hard to see how an award of damages to a severely handicapped or suffering child would 'disavow' the value of life or in any way suggest that the child is not entitled to the full measure of legal and nonlegal rights and privileges according to all members of society.

Moreover, while our society and our legal system unquestionably place the highest value on all human life, we do not think that it is accurate to suggest that this state's public policy establishes – as a matter of law– that under all circumstances 'impaired life' is 'preferable' to 'nonlife'. For example, Health and Safety Code section 7186, enacted in 1976, provides in part: 'The Legislature funds that adult persons have the fundamental right to control the decisions relating to the rendering of their own medical care, including the decision to have life-sustaining procedures withheld or withdrawn in instances of terminal condition.... The Legislature further finds that, in the interest of protecting individual autonomy, such prolongation of life for persons with a terminal condition may cause loss of patient dignity and unnecessary pain and suffering, while providing nothing medically necessary or beneficial to the patient.' This statute recognises that – at least in some situations – public policy supports the right of each individual to make his or her own determination as to the relative value of life and death. (Cf *Matter of Quinlan* (1976) 70 NJ 10 [355 A 2d 657, 662–664]; *Superintendent of Belchertown v Saikewicz* (1977) 373 Mass 728 [370 NE 2d 417, 423–427].)

Of course, in the wrongful life context, the unborn child cannot personally make any choice as to the relative value of life or death. At that stage, however, just as in the case of an infant after birth, the law generally accords the parents the right to act to protect the child's interests. As the wrongful birth decisions recognise, when a doctor or other medical care provider negligently fails to diagnose an hereditary problem, parents are deprived of the opportunity to make an informed and meaningful decision whether to conceive and bear a handicapped child. (see, eg, *Robak v United States, supra*, 658 F 2d 471 at 476; *Berman v Allan, supra*, 404 A 2d 8 at 1; *Jacobs v Theimer, supra*, 519 SW 2d 846 at 849; cf *Cobbs v Grant* (1972) 8 Cal 3d 229 at 242–243, 104 Cal Rptr 505, 502 P 2d 1.) Although in deciding whether or not to bear such a child parents may properly, and undoubtedly do, take into account their own interests, parents also presumptively consider the interests of their future child. Thus, when a defendant negligently fails to diagnose an hereditary ailment, he harms the potential child as well as the parents by depriving the parents of information which may be necessary to determine whether it is in the child's own interest to be born with defects or not to be born at all.

In this case, in which the plaintiff's only affliction is deafness, it seems quite unlikely that a jury would ever conclude that life with such a condition is worse than not being born at all. Other wrongful life cases, however, have involved children with much more serious, debilitating and painful conditions, and the academic literature refers to still other, extremely severe hereditary diseases. Considering the short life span of many of these children and their frequently very limited ability to perceive or enjoy the benefits of life, we cannot assert with confidence that in every situation there would be a societal consensus that life is preferable to never having been born at all.

While it thus seems doubtful that a child's claim for general damages should properly be denied on the rationale that the value of impaired life, as a matter of law, always exceeds the value of nonlife, we believe that the out-of-state decisions are on sounder grounds in holding that – with respect to the child's claim for pain and suffering or other general damages – recovery should be denied because (1) it is simply impossible to determine in any rational or reasoned fashion whether the plaintiff has in fact suffered an injury in being born impaired rather than not being born, (2) even if it were possible to overcome the first hurdle, it would be impossible to assess general damages in any fair, nonspeculative manner.

… We believe … however, that there is a profound qualitative difference between the difficulties faced by a jury in assessing general damages in a normal personal injury or wrongful death action, and the task before a jury in assessing general damages in a wrongful life case. In the first place, the problem is not … simply the fixing of damages for a conceded injury, but the threshold question of determining whether the plaintiff has in fact suffered an injury by being born with an ailment as opposed to not being born at all. As one judge explained: 'When a jury considers the claim of a once-healthy plaintiff that a defendant's negligence harmed him – for example, by breaking his arm– the jury's ability to say that the plaintiff has been "injured" is manifest, for the value of a healthy existence over an impaired existence is within the experience [or] imagination of most people. The value of nonexistence – its very nature– however, is not.' (*Speck v Finegold, supra*, 408 A 2d at p 512 (Spaeth J, conc & dis) affd 439 A 2d 110.)

Furthermore, the practical problems are exacerbated when it comes to the matter of arriving at an appropriate award of damages. As already discussed, in fixing damages in a tort case the jury generally compares the condition plaintiff would have been in but for the tort, with the position the plaintiff is in now, compensating the plaintiff for what has been lost as a result of the wrong. Although the valuation of pain and suffering or emotional distress in terms of dollars and cents is unquestionably difficult in an ordinary personal injury action, jurors at least have some frame of reference in their own general experience to appreciate what the plaintiff has lost – normal life without pain and suffering. In a wrongful life action, that simply is not the case, for what the plaintiff has 'lost' is not life without pain and suffering but rather the unknowable status of never having been born. In this context, a rational, nonspeculative determination of a specific monetary award in accordance with normal tort principles appears to be outside the realm of human competence.

The difficulty in ascertaining or measuring an appropriate award of general damages in this type of case is also reflected in the application of what is sometimes referred to as the 'benefit' doctrine in tort damages. Section 920 of the Restatement Second of Torts – which embodies the general California rule o the subject (see, eg *Maben v Rankin* (1961) 55 Cal 2d 139, 144 10 Cal Rptr 353, 358 P 2d 681) – provides that '[w]hen the defendant's tortious conduct has caused harm to the plaintiff … and in so doing has conferred a special benefit to the interest of the plaintiff that was harmed, the value of the benefit conferred is considered in mitigation of damages, to the extent that this was equitable'.

In requesting general damages in a wrongful life case, the plaintiff seeks monetary compensation for the pain and suffering he or she will endure because of his or her hereditary affliction. Under section 920's benefit doctrine, however, such damages must be offset by the benefits incidentally conferred by the defendant's conduct 'to the interest of the plaintiff that was harmed'. With respect to general damages, the harmed interest is the child's general physical, emotional and psychological well-being, and in considering the benefit to this interest which defendants' negligence has conferred, it must be recognised that as an incident of defendants' negligence the plaintiff has in fact obtained a physical existence with the capacity both to receive and give love and pleasure as well as to experience pain and suffering. Because of the incalculable nature of both elements of this harm-benefit equation, we believe that a reasoned, nonarbitrary award of general damage is simply not obtainable....

Although we have determined that the trial court properly rejected plaintiff's claim for general damages, we conclude that her claim for the 'extraordinary expenses for specialised teaching, training and hearing equipment' that she will incur during her lifetime because of her deafness stands on a different footing.

Although the parents and child cannot, of course, both recover for the same medical expenses, we believe it would be illogical and anomalous to permit only parents, and not the child, to recover for the cost of the child's own medical care. If such a distinction were established, the afflicted child's receipt of necessary medical expenses might well depend on the wholly fortuitous circumstances of whether the parents are available to sue and recover such damages or whether the medical expenses are incurred at a time when the parents remain legally responsible for providing such care.

Realistically, a defendant's negligence in failing to diagnose an hereditary ailment places a significant medical and financial burden on the whole family unit. Unlike the child's claim for general damages, the damage here is both certain and readily measurable. Furthermore, in many instances these expenses will be vital not only to the child's well-being but to his or her very survival. (See *Schroeder v Perkel, supra*, 432 A 2d 834 at 841.) If, as alleged, defendants' negligence was in fact a proximate cause of the child's present and continuing need for such special, extraordinary medical care and training, we believe that it is consistent with the basic liability principles of Civil Code section 1714 to hold defendants liable for the cost of such care, whether the expense is to be borne by the parents or by the child. As Justice Jacobs of the New Jersey Supreme Court observed in his dissenting opinion in *Gleitman v Cosgrove, supra*, 227 A 2d at 703: 'While the law cannot remove the heartache or undo the harm, it can afford some reasonable measure of compensation toward alleviating the financial burdens.'

Moreover, permitting plaintiff to recover the extraordinary, additional medical expenses that are occasioned by the hereditary ailment is also consistent with the established parameters of the general tort 'benefit' doctrine discussed above. As we have seen, under that doctrine an offset is appropriate only insofar as the defendants' conduct has conferred a special benefit 'to the interest of the plaintiff that was harmed'. Here, the harm for which plaintiff seeks recompense is an economic loss, the extraordinary, out-of-pocket expenses that she will have to bear because of her hereditary ailment. Unlike the claim for general damages, defendants' negligence has conferred no incidental, offsetting benefit to this interest of plaintiff. (Cf *Schroeder v Perkel, supra*, 432 A 2d at 842.) Accordingly, assessment of these special damages should pose no unusual or insoluble problems.

In sum, we conclude that while a plaintiff-child in a wrongful life action may not recover general damages for being born impaired as opposed to not being born at all, the child – like his or her parents – may recover special damages for the extraordinary expenses necessary to treat the hereditary ailment.

Mosk J: I dissent.

An order is internally inconsistent which permits a child to recover special damages for a so-called wrongful life action, but denies all general damages for the very same tort. While the modest compassion of the majority may be commendable, they suggest no principle of law that justifies so neatly circumscribing the nature of damages suffered as a result of a defendant's negligence.

As recently as 1980, the Court of Appeal unanimously decided in *Curlender v Bio-Science Laboratories* 106 Cal App 3d 811, 165 Cal Rptr 477 (1980) that a cause of action exists for a wrongful-life tort. This court subsequently denied a petition for hearing. Thus *Curlender* was, and remains, the prevailing law of California. I see no persuasive reason to either abandon its doctrine, or to dilute its effectiveness by limiting recovery to special damages.

The revised approach in *Turpin* has been taken up in two other jurisdictions (*Harbeson v Parke-Davis Inc* (1983) 656 P 2d 483 (Wash Sup Ct) and *Procanik v Cillo* (1984) 478 A 2d 755 (NJ Sup Ct)). Most notably in the latter case, the distinguished New Jersey Supreme Court, like the California Supreme Court before it, modified its earlier view, though on this occasion it expanded liability by departing from its decisions in *Berman v Allan* (1979) 404 A 2d 8 and *Gleitman v Cosgrove* (1967) 227 A 2d 689 (1967) which we have already seen in the extracts above have been relied upon consistently by other courts to deny recovery (see Teff 'The Action for "Wrongful Life" in England and the United States' (1985) 34 ICLQ 423).

Which common law analysis is more consistent with principle and policy? In our view, English law could adopt the approach which has found favour in *Turpin*, *Procanik* and *Harbeson*. To do so, the English courts could embrace the following analysis. Three issues have to be considered: what is the doctor's duty to the child? what harm known to the law does the child suffer? and what damages should be recoverable?

As regards *duty*, the doctor's duty is to inform of the risk of disability. This is a duty owed to the unborn child. But, of course, a doctor cannot inform an unborn child (or one not yet conceived). It must, therefore, be a duty to inform the mother on behalf of the child (see, by analogy, *Poynter v Hillingdon HA* (1997) 37 BMLR 192 (QBD) and *Thomson v James* (1997) 41 BMLR 144 (CA) – duty to advise parents on behalf of child). The Court of Appeal in *McKay* was, consequently, wrong to see the doctor's duty as one owed *only* to the mother such that the child could not sue. Thus, the duty would not be that contemplated by the Court of Appeal in *McKay*, namely to counsel with a view to persuading the mother to agree to an abortion. Even if that were the duty in a case like *McKay*, it could not be so in a case like *Turpin v Sortini*. There, of course, the doctor's duty arises *before* conception of the child. His duty properly to provide genetic counselling cannot possibly be seen as a duty to seek to persuade a mother to have an abortion. Thus, this situation most clearly establishes that the doctor's duty is merely to provide information.

A related strand of argument can be seen in the *McKay* case. This is that public policy dictates that the law should not, or should not be seen to, encourage abortions. On this reasoning, even if the doctor's duty is to inform the mother of the risk of disability in her unborn child, to impose a duty to provide the information is tantamount to encouraging an abortion. This strand of argument does not stand up to close analysis. *First*, the premise that public policy points in the direction identified by *McKay* need not be accepted. This is demonstrated by the New Jersey case of *Procanik v Cillo*.

Procanik v Cillo (1984) 478 A 2d 755 (NJ Sup Ct)

Pollock J: The infant plaintiff, Peter Procanik, alleges that the defendant doctors, Joseph Cillo, Herbert Langer, and Ernest P Greenberg, negligently failed to diagnose that his mother, Rosemary Procanik, had contracted German measles in the first trimester of the pregnancy. As a result, Peter was born with congenital rubella syndrome. Alleging that the doctors negligently deprived his parents of the choice of terminating the pregnancy, he seeks general damages for his pain and suffering and for 'his parents' impaired capacity to cope with his problems. He also seeks special damages attributable to the extraordinary expenses he will incur for medical, nursing, and other health care....

The Court [in *Gleitman v Cosgrove* (1967) 227 A 2d 689] denied the parents' claim for emotional distress and the costs of caring for the infant, because of the impossibility of weighing the intangible benefits of parenthood against the emotional and monetary injuries sustained by them. Prevailing policy considerations, which *included a reluctance to acknowledge the availability of abortions and the mother's right to choose to terminate her pregnancy*, prevented the Court from awarding damages to a woman for not having an abortion. Another consideration was the Court's belief that '[i]t is basic to the human condition to seek life and hold on to it however heavily burdened.' 49 *NJ* at 30, 227 A 2d 689.

In the seventeen years that have elapsed since the *Gleitman* decision, both this Court and the United States Supreme Court have reappraised, albeit in different contexts, the rights of pregnant women and their children. The United States Supreme Court has recognized that women have a constitutional right to choose to terminate a pregnancy. *Roe v Wade*, 410 *US* 113, 93 *S Ct* 705, 35 *L Ed* 2d 147 (1973). Recognition of that right by the high court subsequently influenced this court in *Berman v Allan*, *supra*, 80 *NJ* 421, 404 *A* 2d 8.

In *Berman*, the parents sought to recover for their emotional distress and for the expenses of raising a child born with Down's Syndrome. Relying on *Roe v Wade*, *supra*, 410 *US* 113, 93 *S Ct* 705, 35 *L Ed* 2d 147, the Court found that public policy now supports the right of a woman to choose to terminate a pregnancy. *Berman v Allan*, *supra*, 80 *NJ* at 431–432, 404 *A* 2d 8. That finding eliminated one of the supports for the *Gleitman* decision – *ie* that public policy prohibited an award for depriving a woman of the right to choose whether to have an abortion [our emphasis].

Here, the New Jersey court follows the reasoning we have seen in *Turpin* even though the doctor's negligence concerned his failure to provide the plaintiff's mother with information that might lead to her choose to *abort* the plaintiff.

Secondly, if public policy were as the Court of Appeal would lead us to believe in *McKay*, it would suggest that the parents' related action for 'wrongful birth' (on which see below) should not be allowed as it too would be contrary to public policy. The parent's claim *also* turns upon the doctor's failure to inform the mother and thereby deprive her of the choice of whether or not to have an abortion (see eg *Rance v Mid-Downs HA* [1991] 1 All ER 801).

Thirdly, it is surely difficult to sustain the public policy argument given the existence of the Abortion Act 1967. The fact that Parliament has made available in a given case the opportunity of an abortion, in itself destroys the public policy argument: a point made by the New Jersey court in the context of the American constitutional 'right to choose to terminate a pregnancy'.

Fourthly, of course, the *McKay* argument could have no application in a case like *Turpin* where the doctor's negligence occurs *before the plaintiff's conception*. In such a case the negligent genetic counselling deprives the parents of the choice of whether or not to *conceive* the plaintiff.

As regards the second question, namely that of what harm the child has suffered, there are two possibilities. They are that the child is *born disabled* or that it suffers *economic loss* arising out of its disability. The Court of Appeal in *McKay* chose the first option and held that it was not a harm recognised in law. The better view is that the child's loss is financial. Of course, this would bring into play the restrictive rules relating to the recovery of damages for economic loss currently imposed by the House of Lords. Even on these restrictive rules, however, there is a perfectly respectable argument that the relationship between the doctor and mother acting on behalf of the child is sufficiently close (and indeed is quintessentially one of reliance) that the nature of the child's harm is no impediment to the claim (see by analogy the reasoning of Clarke JA in *X and Y v Pal*, *supra*).

As regards the final question, namely that of damages, the Court of Appeal's insistence that damages for pain and suffering and for being disabled are incalculable is no reason for denying recovery of the child's past or future financial loss, as the American cases make clear.

It could be said, however, that the courts do not need to fashion an action by the child since the parents will have a 'wrongful birth' claim. Apart from the non-pecuniary loss of the child, the parents can recover the past and future losses needed to care for the disabled child. The 'wrongful life' action would only have practical importance if the parents' action was limited, for example, to losses up to majority. English law may not be so restricted where there is evidence to support continued care into adulthood (see *Anderson v Forth Valley Health Board* (1997) 44 BMLR 108 (Lord Nimmo Smith), see *infra*).

(b) Disadvantaged life

So far we have been concerned with cases about children born disabled. Would the common law allow any action if the complaint is that the child has been born into circumstances that are alleged to be disadvantaged but the child is otherwise whole and healthy? Early in the development of this area of tort law, the American courts rejected claims of this kind.

Williams v State of New York (1966) 223 NE 2d 343 (NY CA)

Desmond CJ: We are to decide whether the infant claimant Christine Williams (the claim of her mother Lorene Williams is not before us now) has alleged a sufficient cause of action against the State of New York. The claim asserts negligence of the State in the care and custody of the infant's mother while the latter was a patient at a State hospital for the mentally ill 'and more particularly in failing to provide adequate, sufficient and proper care and supervision over her while she was in the custody of the State and in negligently failing to protect and safeguard her health and physical body from attack and harm from others, which negligence resulted in the infant Christine Williams being conceived, being born and being born out of wedlock to a mentally deficient mother'. The theory of suit becomes clearer when we examine the paragraph where the particulars of claimant's damage are set out thus: as a result of this neglect of the State, the child has been 'deprived of property rights; deprived of a normal childhood and home life; deprived of proper parental care, support and rearing; caused to bear the stigma of illegitimacy'.

No such theory of suit has ever before, it seems, been put forward in any court anywhere (the closest being *Zepeda v Zepeda*, 41 Ill App 2d 240, 190 NE 2d 849, cert den 379 US 945, 85 S Ct 444, 13 L Ed 2d 545, of which more will be said hereafter). The Court of Claims Judge who heard the motion thought that this lack of precedent was not fatal, and that recovery of damages was possible since there had been a wrong by the State with resulting and reasonably to be anticipated harm to the child. The Appellate Division, reversing the Court of Claims and dismissing the claim, rejected the idea that there could be an obligation of the State to a person not yet conceived and, secondly, the Appellate Division held that the 'damages' are not susceptible of ascertainment, resting as they do 'upon the very fact of conception'.

Impossibility of entertaining this suit comes not so much from difficulty in measuring the alleged 'damages' as from the absence from our legal concepts of any such idea as a 'wrong' to a later-born child caused by permitting a woman to be violated and to bear an out-of-wedlock infant. If the pleaded facts are true, the State was grievously neglectful as to the mother, and as a result the child may have to bear unfair burdens as have many other sons and daughters of shame and sorrow. But the law knows no cure of compensation for it, and the policy and social reasons against providing such compensation are at least as strong as those which might be thought to favor it. Being born under one set of circumstances rather than another or to one pair of parents rather than another is not a suable wrong that is cognisable in court. The furthest reach of our law is to paternity proceedings (see Family Ct Act) and that was accomplished by statute.

In *Williams* the court relied on the following case.

Zepeda v Zepeda (1963) 190 NE 2d 849 (App Ct Ill)

Presiding Justice, Dempsey: The plaintiff is the infant son of the defendant. He seeks damages from his father because he is an illegitimate child…the defendant is the plaintiff's father; the defendant induced the plaintiff's mother to have sexual relations by promising to marry her; this promise was not kept and could not be kept because, unbeknown to the mother, defendant was already married. The complaint charges that the promise was fraudulent, that the acts of the defendant were wilful and that the defendant injured the plaintiff in his person, property and reputation by causing him to be born an adulterine bastard. The plaintiff seeks damages for the deprivation of his right to be a legitimate child, to have a normal home, to have a legal father, to inherit from his father, to inherit from his parental ancestors and for being stigmatised as a bastard.

… An illegitimate's very birth places him under a disability. It is of this that the plaintiff complains. His adulterine birth has placed him under a permanent disability. He protests not only the act which caused him to be born but birth itself. Love of life being what it is, one may conjecture whether, if he were older, he would feel the same way. As he grows from infancy to maturity the natural instinct to preserve life may cause him to cherish his existence as much as, through his next friend, he now deplores it. But be that as it may, the quintessence of his complaint is that he was born and that he is. Herein lies the intrinsic difficulty of this case, a difficulty which gives rise to this question: are there overriding legal, social, judicial or other considerations which should preclude recognition of a cause of action?

Bearing in mind that an action for damages is implicit in any wrong that is called a tort (Prosser, Law of Torts 2nd edn, sec 1, pp 2–4) it may be inconsistent to say, as we do, that the plaintiff has been injured by a tortious act and then to question, as we do, his right to maintain an action to recover for this act. This is done deliberately, however, because on the one hand, we believe that the elements of a wilful tort are presented by the allegations of the complaint and, on the other hand, we approach with restraint the creation, by judicial sanction, of the new action required by the complaint.

Recognition of the plaintiff's claim means creation of a new tort: a cause of action for wrongful life. The legal implications of such a tort are vast, the social impact could be staggering. If the new litigation were confined just to illegitimates it would be formidable. In 1960 there were 224,330 illegitimate births in the United States, 14,262 in Illinois and 10,182 in Chicago. Vital Statistics of the United States 1960, Vol 1, secs 1 2(1962). Not only are there more such births year after year (in Illinois and Chicago the number in 1960 was twice that of 1950) but the ratio between illegitimate and legitimate births is increasing. This increase is attested by a report of the Illinois Department of Public Health, released in July 1962. This report revealed that in Chicago in 1961, of the 87,989 live births 11,021 were illegitimate, a ration of eight to one. In 1951 out of 81,801 births, 5,212 were illegitimate, a ration of fifteen to one. The present Chicago ratio is twice that of the State and more than three times that of the Nation. The number of children who remain illegitimate is also of importance in estimating possible litigation. Accurate figures are not available, but a report made in October 1962 by the Illinois Public Aid Commission disclosed that in Cook County as at December 1961 there were 54,984 illegitimate children participating in the Aid to Department Children program. How many of these were born under circumstances making legitimation impossible, the report does not reveal.

That the doors of litigation would be opened wider might make us proceed cautiously in approving a new action, but it would not deter us. The plaintiff's claim cannot be rejected because there may be others of equal merit. It is not the suits of illegitimates which give us concern, great in numbers as these may be. What does disturb us is the nature of the new action and the related suits which would be encouraged. Encouragement would extend to all others born into the world under conditions they might regard as adverse. One might seek damages for being born of a certain color, another because of race; one for being born with a hereditary disease, another for inheriting unfortunate family characteristics; one for being born into a large and destitute family, another because a parent has an unsavory reputation.

The English courts did not consider this issue before the enactment of the Congenital Disabilities (Civil Liability) Act 1976. Given the approach of the court in *McKay*, there is no doubt the English common law would adopt the same course as that taken in the American cases (see also *Cowe v Forum Group Inc* (1991) 575 NE 2d 630 (Ind Sup Ct)).

2. The Congenital Disabilities (Civil Liability) Act 1976

(a) The conventional view

The 1976 Act resulted from the recommendations of the Law Commission contained in its Report No 60, *Report on Injuries to Unborn Children* (1974). In para 89 the Law Commission concluded as follows:

> **89.** We do not think that, in the strict sense of the term, an action for 'wrongful life' should lie. In the cases referred to of negligent treatment of a woman during pregnancy and the hypothetical drug preventing spontaneous abortion, had it not been for the negligence, the child would not have been born at all. To justify an action in logic, therefore, it is necessary to argue that the child would have been better off had he never existed. Nor would it be easy to assess his damages on any logical basis for it would be difficult to establish a norm with which the plaintiff in his disabled state could be compared. He never had a chance of being born other than disabled. We have given this problem the most careful consideration and have not, we think, been unduly influenced by these considerations of logic. Law is an artefact and, if social justice requires that there should be a remedy given for a wrong, then logic should not stand in the way. A measure of damages could be artificially constructed. We

react in different ways to the various situations we have postulated, but the one which is much the most likely to give rise to claims is that which arises out of medical advice. In this situation we are clear in our opinion that no cause of action should lie. Such a cause of action, if it existed, would place an almost intolerable burden on medical advisers in their socially and morally exacting role. The danger that doctors would be under subconscious pressures to advise abortions in doubtful cases through fear of an action for damages is, we think, a real one. It must not be forgotten that in certain circumstances, the parents themselves might have a claim in negligence. Similar considerations lead us to the same conclusion in respect of the negligent performance of a therapeutic abortion.

As a consequence, in *McKay* the Court of Appeal interpreted the 1976 Act as reflecting the Law Commission's conclusion. You will recall the wording of s 1(2)(b).
Section 1(2)(b) provides:

(2) An occurrence to which this section applies is one which – . . .
(b) affected the mother during her pregnancy, or affected her or the child in the course of its birth, so that the child is born with disabilities which would not otherwise have been present.

Ackner LJ in *McKay* stated that:

Subsection (2)(*b*) is so worded as to import the assumption that, but for the occurrence giving rise to a disabled birth, the child would have been born normal and healthy, not that it would not have been born at all. Thus, the object of the Law Commission that the child should have no right of action for 'wrongful life' is achieved. In para 89 of the report the commission stated that they were clear in their opinion that no cause of action should lie:

Such a cause of action, if it existed, would place an almost intolerable burden on medical advisers in their socially and morally exacting role. The danger that doctors would be under subconscious pressures to advise abortions in doubtful cases through fear of an action of damages is, we think, a real one.

This view was adopted by the Royal Commission on Civil Liability and Compensation for Personal Injury (report vol 1; Cmnd 7054–I, para 1485)....
Thus, there can be no question of such a cause of action arising in respect of births after 22 July 1976.

Stephenson and Griffiths LJJ agreed.

(b) A challenge to this view

It may be that the wording of s 1(2)(b) is such that a 'wrongful life' action cannot be brought *under the Act* in a situation like *McKay* where during the pregnancy the doctor negligently fails to advise the mother of the risk of the child being disabled. Is it the case, however, that the common law claim, which we have argued for above, could survive the enactment of the 1976 Act? Section 4(5) provides that:

4(5) – This Act applies in respect of births after (but not before) its passing, and in respect of any such birth it replaces any law in force before its passing, whereby a person could be liable to a child in respect of disabilities with which it might be born...

In *McKay*, Ackner LJ infers from this that any claim at common law (if it were to exist) has been abolished. There is, however, an alternative view.

Jane Fortin 'Is the "Wrongful Life" Action Really Dead?' [1987] JSWL 306

It is submitted that in reaching [the] conclusion [that the common law was abolished] on the interpretation of the 1976 Act, the Court of Appeal in *McKay* was unduly influenced by the Law Commission's expressed intentions and that there are alternative approaches which were not considered. It is indeed clear that neither section 1, nor indeed any part of the 1976 Act itself, refers to liability which might arise in situations where the disability itself was neither caused by nor could have been prevented by medical interventions. Nevertheless, the common law supplements this statutory omission, if as argued above, there is indeed a common law duty on the doctor to advise the foetus through its mother, of the risks of disabilities resulting, for example from infection. There is, however, a further obstacle to the acceptance of such an approach, in the form of section 4(5) of the 1976 Act which was, *inter alia*, clearly intended to counter such an argument by stating that it 'replaces any law in force before its passing, whereby a person could be liable to a child in respect of disabilities with which it might be born'. Although the Court of Appeal in *McKay* was convinced that these words precluded any wrongful life action being brought on the basis of common law principles after the operation of the Act, an alternative interpretation is possible. The provisions of section 4(5) can be avoided quite simply because, in such cases, the doctor's liability does not arise '*in respect of disabilities*' themselves, since he had no part in their cause or effect. His liability arises solely due to his failure to advise on the unborn child's potential quality of life, *in the light of those disabilities*. This approach avoids the provisions of section 4(5) of the 1976 Act and consequently, a claim for wrongful life would be sustainable under the existing common law.

Of course, this argument if correct merely preserves the common law claim for 'wrongful life' in so far as it exists. A more far-reaching argument which was not addressed by the Court of Appeal in *McKay* is that the Act itself creates a 'wrongful life' claim in situations such as arose in *Turpin v Sortini*.

Section 1(2)(a) provides that:

An occurrence to which this section applies is one which – . . .
(a) affected either parent of the child in his or her ability to have a normal, healthy child.

In a case of negligent genetic counselling it could be argued that the doctor's failure to advise the mother of the risk of her conceiving a disabled child 'affected…her *ability* to have a normal, healthy child' (our emphasis). Normally, s 1(2)(a) (as we saw earlier) is interpreted to apply to pre-conception occurrences which *cause* harm to what would be an otherwise healthy child. The doctor's negligence in that context 'affects' the parent's 'ability' in the sense of her physical capacity to have a normal, healthy child. Here, the doctor's negligence only 'affects' the parent's 'ability' in the sense of her *opportunity* to have a normal, healthy child. The word 'ability' in s 1(2)(a) could certainly be interpreted as including 'opportunity'.

On that basis, providing the negligent advice leads to the parents conceiving a disabled child which they would not otherwise have done, the child could bring a claim under s 1(2)(a). Its claim, of course, would be a 'wrongful life' action since the normal, healthy child who would otherwise have been born would have been someone else.

This interpretation of s 1(2)(a) would only go so far in that it would be limited to pre-conception occurrences. Although it could be argued that the facts of *McKay* fell within s 1(2)(a), this would be so counter to the Law Commission's (and Parliament's) intent that the court would not adopt it. Perhaps this is because post-conception cases like *McKay* necessarily raise the 'spectre' of abortions (see the Law Commission's view in para 89 above).

Further support for the argument that s 1(2)(a) of the 1976 Act should be interpreted to cover claims by a child alleging negligent genetic counselling is provided by s 1A of the 1976 Act. This provision, as we have seen, was introduced in 1990 to allow a child, born disabled as a result of negligence during its parents' infertility treatment, to bring a claim. In addition to covering situations where the child is *caused* harm by the infertility treatment, it also covers negligence in the 'selection' of the embryo that becomes the child. Here, of course, the child's claim is one for 'wrongful life' since had the selection process not been conducted negligently, the embryo would not have been selected and thus the child would not have been born. Parliament by enacting s 1A has clearly recognised a 'wrongful life' claim. Whether it appreciated this is another matter (for a narrower interpretation excluding negligence in 'the very act of choice', see I Kennedy and A Grubb (eds) *Principles of Medical Law* (1998) para 12.77). Of course, the Act deems the child's disabilities to be 'personal … injuries' (s 4(3)(b)). This does not, however, alter the reality that the policy of the law appears to have shifted from that stated in *McKay*.

Further, although the court's task in assessing damages is no easier in principle, this did not, apparently, deter Parliament. If, therefore, the courts are required to face up to the child's action when it arises from negligence *ex utero*, should they not equally do so when it arises from negligence before conception?

Actions by the parents

We have up to this point been concerned with the circumstances in which a disabled or disadvantaged child may bring a claim arising out of negligence occurring before its birth. We now turn to consider the claim a *parent* may have in respect of the birth of either a healthy child following, for example, a failed sterilisation ('wrongful conception') or a disabled child ('wrongful birth').

A. WRONGFUL CONCEPTION

We consider here the question whether parents may bring an action following the negligence which has led to the birth of a *healthy child*. The claim may arise typically in two situations – where the negligence relates to contraceptive advice or treatment (eg a failed sterilisation); or where the negligence involves a failed abortion carried out to prevent the birth of a child who would be healthy (eg under s 1(1)(a) of the Abortion Act 1967). The basis and scope of these claims requires radical reappraisal in the light of the House of Lords' decision in *McFarlane v Tayside Health Board* [1999] 4 All ER 961.

1. An action in contract

Most doctors ordinarily treat patients within the NHS and in that case no contract arises between them. Sterilisation, being elective surgery, is quite commonly practised outside the NHS in circumstances where a contract *will* arise. As in any action in contract, the ability of a party to recover in any action depends upon the terms of the contract.

Those advising doctors will undoubtedly take their lead from the two cases and so draft their terms that it would be most unlikely that an action could sound in contract if it could not sound in tort. The two cases are *Thake v Maurice* and *Eyre v Measday*. Both raise the issue of what the doctor contracts to do: in particular, whether there is a guarantee of sterility.

Eyre v Measday [1986] 1 All ER 488 (CA)

In 1978 when the plaintiff and her husband decided that they did not wish to have any more children the plaintiff consulted the defendant gynaecologist with a view to undergoing a sterilisation operation. The defendant explained to the couple the nature of the particular operation he intended to perform, emphasising that it was irreversible. He stated that the operation 'must be regarded as a permanent procedure' but he did not inform the plaintiff that there was a small risk (less than 1%) of pregnancy occurring following the operation. Consequently, both the plaintiff and her husband believed that the result of the operation would be to render her absolutely sterile and incapable of bearing further children. In 1979 the plaintiff became pregnant and gave birth to a child. The plaintiff brought an action against the defendant for damages for, inter alia, breach of contract, contending that his representation that the operation was irreversible and his failure to warn her of the minute risk of the procedure being unsuccessful amounted to a breach of the contractual term of express or implied collateral warranty, to render her irreversibly sterile. The judge dismissed her claim and the plaintiff appealed to the Court of Appeal.

Slade LJ: It is, I think, common ground that the relevant contract between the parties in the present case was embodied as to part in the oral conversations which took place between the plaintiff and her husband and the defendant at the defendant's consulting rooms, and as to the other part in the written form of consent signed by the plaintiff, which referred to the explanation of the operation which had been given in that conversation. It is also common ground, I think, that, in order to ascertain what was the nature and what were the terms of that contract, this court has to apply an objective rather than a subjective test. The test thus does not depend on what either the plaintiff or the defendant *thought* were the terms of the contract in her or his own mind. It depends on what the court objectively considers that the words used by the respective parties must be reasonably taken to have meant. It would, therefore, be of no assistance to the defendant to say that he did not intend to enter into a contract which absolutely guaranteed the plaintiff's future sterility. It would likewise be of no assistance to the plaintiff to say that she firmly believed that she was being offered a contract of this nature.

I now turn to the first of the two principal issues which I have indicated. At the start of his argument for the plaintiff counsel indicated that his primary ground of appeal would be that the effect of the contract between the plaintiff and the defendant was one by which the defendant contracted to render the plaintiff absolutely sterile. That, of course, was the effect of Peter Pain J's decision on the particular facts of *Thake v Maurice* [1984] 2 All ER 513 [reversed on appeal, [1986] 1 All ER 497, see below]. Nevertheless, on the facts of this case, I, for my part, find this contention quite impossible to sustain. It seems to me quite clear from the evidence which we have as to the conversation which took place between the plaintiff and her husband and the defendant at the defendant's consulting rooms that he explained to them that the operation which he would propose to perform on the plaintiff was an operation by way of *laparoscopic sterilisation* and that that was the method he intended to adopt and no other. Equally, that was the nature of the operation to which the plaintiff herself agreed, as is shown by the form of consent which she signed. The contract was, to my mind, plainly a contract by the defendant to perform that particular operation.

The matter may be tested in this way. Suppose that when the plaintiff had been under anaesthetic the defendant had formed the view that an even more effective way of sterilising her would be to perform a hysterectomy and had carried out that operation, the plaintiff would, of course, have had the strongest grounds for complaint. She could have said:

> I did not give you a general discretion to perform such operation as you saw fit for the purpose of sterilising me. I gave my consent to one particular form of operation. That was the operation I asked you to do and that was the operation you agreed to do.

In the end, as I understood him, counsel for the plaintiff did not feel able to press his argument on the first issue very strongly. The nature of the contract was, in my view, indubitably one to perform a laparoscopic sterilisation.

That, however, is by no means the end of the matter. The question still arises: did the defendant give either an express warranty or an implied warranty to the effect that the result of the operation when performed would be to leave the plaintiff absolutely sterile? In response to our inquiry counsel for the plaintiff helpfully listed the two particular passages in the evidence on which he relied for the purpose of asserting that there was an *express* warranty. The first was a passage where, in the course of examination by her counsel, the plaintiff said:

> We went to the consulting rooms and we saw Mr Measday and we discussed sterilisation. He told us the method that he used for sterilising was the clip. He told us once I had had it done it was irreversible.

Counsel for the plaintiff also relied on a passage in which the plaintiff was asked in chief:

> *Q.* Did he show you the clip? *A.* He showed us a clip and he also showed us the diagram and told us where the clips go on the tubes. He said once I had the operation done there was no turning back, I could not have it reversed.

Counsel for the plaintiff referred us to para 2 of the defence in the action which read as follows:

> On the 30th October 1978 the Plaintiff consulted the Defendant about an operation of sterilisation. The Defendant examined her and agreed to carry out the operation and advised her that it must be regarded as a permanent procedure. He did not warn the Plaintiff of the slight risk of failure, nor did he guarantee success.

There was thus a specific admission in the defence that the defendant advised the plaintiff that it must be 'regarded as a permanent procedure'.

In the light of these various representations or statements by the defendant, counsel for the plaintiff submitted that it was being expressly represented to the plaintiff that the effect of the operation would be to render her sterile absolutely and for ever. I, for my part, cannot accept that submission. There has been some discussion in the course of argument on the meaning of the phrase 'irreversible' and as to the relevance of the statement, undoubtedly made by the defendant to the plaintiff, that the proposed operation must be regarded as being irreversible. However, I take the reference to irreversibility as simply meaning that the operative procedure in question is incapable of being reversed, that what is about to be done cannot be undone. I do not think it can reasonably be construed as a representation that the operation is bound to achieve its acknowledged object, which is a different matter altogether. For my part, I cannot spell out any such express warranty as is asserted from the particular passages in the evidence and in the pleadings relied on by counsel for the plaintiff to support it, or from any other parts of the evidence....

The test to be applied by the court in considering whether a term can or cannot properly be implied in a contract is that embodied in what is frequently called the doctrine of *The Moorcock* (1889) 14 PD 64, [1886–90] All ER Rep 530. It is conveniently set out in 9 Halsbury's Laws (4th edn) para 355:

> A term can only be implied if it is necessary in the business sense to give efficacy to the contract; that is if it is such a term that it can confidently be said that if at the time the contract was being negotiated someone had said to the parties, 'What will happen in such a case', they would both have replied. 'Of course, so and so will happen; we did not trouble to say that; it is too clear.'

Counsel for the plaintiff, in the light of the passage in cross-examination which I have just read and in the light of all the other background of the case to which I have referred, submitted that if someone had said to the parties, 'Is it intended that the defendant should warrant that the operation will render the plaintiff absolutely sterile?', the answer of both parties must have been, 'Yes'. This, he submitted, is really the only possible inference from what had been said on both sides in the defendant's consulting rooms. He particularly drew attention to the question that he had put to the defendant, 'Would it have been reasonable for her to have gone away from your consulting rooms thinking that she would be sterilised and that would be the end of the matter?', to which the defendant replied, 'yes, it would.' Counsel for the plaintiff submitted that the defendant himself was thus acknowledging that the reasonable inference would have been as he suggested.

Applying *The Moorcock* principles I think there is no doubt that the plaintiff would have been entitled reasonably to assume that the defendant was warranting that the operation would be performed with reasonable care and skill. That, I think, would have been the inevitable inference to be drawn, from an objective standpoint, from the relevant discussion between the parties. The contract did, in my opinion, include an implied warranty of that nature. However, that inference on its own does not enable the plaintiff to succeed in the present case. She has to go further. She has to suggest, and it is suggested on her behalf, that the defendant, by necessary implication, committed himself to an unqualified guarantee as to the success of the particular operation proposed, in achieving its purpose of sterilising her, even though he were to exercise all due care and skill in performing it. The suggestion is that the guarantee went beyond due care and skill and extended to an unqualified warranty that the plaintiff would be absolutely sterile.

On the facts of the present case, I do not think that any intelligent lay bystander (let alone another medical man), on hearing the discussion which took place between the defendant and the other two parties, could have reasonably drawn the inference that the defendant was intending to give any warranty of this nature. It is true that in cross-examination he admitted that it would have been reasonable for the plaintiff to have gone away from his consulting rooms thinking that she would be sterilised. He did not, however, admit that it would have been reasonable for her to have left his consulting rooms thinking that he had given her a *guarantee* that after the operation she would be absolutely sterile; this, I think, is the really relevant point. She has to say that this would have been the reasonable inference from what he said to her and from what she and her husband said to him. But, in my opinion, in the absence of any express warranty, the court should be slow to imply against a medical man an unqualified warranty as to the results of an intended operation, for the very simple reason that, objectively speaking, it is most unlikely that a responsible medical man would intend to give a warranty of this nature. Of course, objectively speaking, it is likely that he would give a guarantee that he would do what he had undertaken to do with reasonable care and skill; but it is quite another matter to say that he has committed himself to the extent suggested in the present case.

Purchas LJ and Sir Roualeyn Cumming-Bruce agreed.

You may think that Slade LJ's discussion of the word 'irreversible' and his application of the *Moorcock* principle has an element of the unreal about it. The contract arguments were further explored in the next case, concerned, this time, with a vasectomy.

Thake v Maurice [1986] QB 644, [1986] 1 All ER 497 (CA)

The plaintiffs, a married couple did not wish to have any more children and consulted the defendant to see whether the first plaintiff could be sterilised by vasectomy. The first plaintiff signed a form stating that he consented to undergo the vasectomy operation, which was carried out by the defendant in October 1975. In 1977 the second plaintiff became pregnant but failed to recognise the symptoms until it was too late for an abortion. In 1978 she gave birth to a baby girl. The plaintiffs brought an action against the defendant claiming that their contract with the defendant was a contract to sterilise the first plaintiff and that that contract had been broken when he became fertile again, alternatively that they were induced to enter into the contract by a false warranty or innocent misrepresentation that the operation would render the first plaintiff permanently sterile, or in the further alternative that the defendant had failed to warn them that there was a small risk that the first plaintiff might become fertile again. There was no suggestion that the defendant had not performed the operation properly, and at the time of the operation it was known in medical circles that in rare cases the effect of the operation could be reversed naturally. The judge held, inter alia, that the defendant was in breach of a contract to make the first plaintiff irreversibly sterile. The defendant appealed to the Court of Appeal.

Neill LJ: It is common ground that the defendant contracted to perform a vasectomy operation on Mr Thake and that in the performance of that contract he was subject to the duty implied by law to carry out the operation with reasonable skill and care. The question for consideration is whether in the circumstances of the instant case the defendant further undertook that he would render Mr Thake permanently sterile by means of this operation.

On behalf of the plaintiffs it is conceded that the defendant never used the word 'guarantee' in relation to the outcome of the operation, but is submitted that what the defendant said and did at the consultation on or about 25 September 1975 would have led a reasonable person in the position of the plaintiffs to the conclusion that the defendant was giving a firm promise that the operation would lead to permanent sterility.

It is not in dispute that the task of the court is to seek to determine objectively what conclusion a reasonable person would have reached having regard to (a) the words used by the defendant, (b) the demonstration which he gave and (c) the form which Mr and Mrs Thake were asked to sign.

Counsel for the plaintiffs placed particular reliance on the following matters: (1) that on more than one occasion the defendant explained to the plaintiffs that the effect of the operation was 'irreversible', subject to the remote possibility of later surgical intervention, and counsel pointed out that this explanation was reinforced by the statement in the form: 'I understand that the effect of the operation is irreversible'; (2) that the defendant agreed in evidence that the word 'irreversible' would have been understood by the plaintiffs as meaning 'irreversible by God or man'; (3) that the demonstration which the defendant gave with his hands and arms and the sketch which he drew have led the plaintiffs to believe that, because a piece of the vas was to be severed and the severed ends were to be turned back, there was no possibility whatever of the channels being reunited unless some further surgery took place; (4) that the defendant stated that two sperm tests were required to ensure that the operation was successful; this statement would have strengthened the impression given to his listeners that the operation when completed would render the patient sterile.

... For my part, however, I remain unpersuaded. It seems to me that it is essential to consider the events of 25 September 1975 and the word which the defendant used against the background of a surgeon's consulting room. It is the common experience of mankind that the results of medical treatment are to some extent unpredictable and that any treatment may be affected by the special characteristics of the particular patient. It has been well said that 'the dynamics of the human body of each individual are themselves individual'.

I accept that there may be cases where, because of the claims made by a surgeon or physician for his method of treatment the court is driven to the conclusion that the result of the treatment is guaranteed or warranted. But in the present case I do not regard the statements made by the defendant as to the effect of his treatment as passing beyond the realm of expectation and assumption. It seems to me that what he said was spoken partly by way of warning and partly by way of what is sometimes called 'therapeutic reassurance'.

Both the plaintiffs and the defendant expected that sterility would be the result of the operation and the defendant appreciated that that was the plaintiff's expectation. This does not mean, however, that a reasonable person would have understood the defendant to be giving a binding promise that the operation would achieve its purpose or that the defendant was going further than to give an assurance that he expected and believed that it would have the desired result. Furthermore, I do not consider that a reasonable person would have expected a responsible medical man to be intending to give a guarantee. Medicine, though a highly skilled profession, is not, and is not generally regarded as being, an exact science. The reasonable man would have expected the defendant to exercise all the proper skill and care of a surgeon in that speciality; he would not in my view have expected the defendant to give a guarantee of 100% success.

Accordingly, though I am satisfied that a reasonable person would have left the consulting room thinking that Mr Thake would be sterilised by the vasectomy operation, such a person would not have left thinking that the defendant had given a *guarantee* that Mr Thake would be absolutely sterile.

Nourse LJ: The function of the court in ascertaining, objectively, the meaning of words used by contracting parties is one of everyday occurrence. But it is often exceedingly difficult to discharge it where the subjective understandings and intentions of the parties are clear and opposed. Here the plaintiffs understood that Mr Thake would be permanently sterile. The defendant himself recognised that they would have been left with that impression. On the other hand, he did not intend, and on the state of his knowledge he could not have intended, to guarantee that that would be the case. Both the understanding and the intention appear to them, as individuals, to have been entirely reasonable, but an objective interpretation must choose between them. In the end the question seems to be reduced to one of determining the extent of the knowledge which is to be attributed to the reasonable person standing in the position of the plaintiffs. Would he have known that the success of the operation, either because it depended on the healing of human tissue, or because in medical science all things, or nearly all things, are uncertain, could not be guaranteed? If he would, the defendant's words could only have been reasonably understood as forecasts of an almost certain, but nevertheless uncertain, outcome and his visual demonstrations as no more than explanations of how the operation would be done. He could not be taken to have given a guarantee of its success.

I do not suppose that a reasonable person standing in the position of the plaintiffs would have known that a vasectomy is an operation whose success depends on a healing of human tissue which cannot be guaranteed. To suppose that would be to credit him with an omniscience beyond all reason. But it does seem to me to be reasonable to credit him with the more general knowledge that in medical science all things, or nearly all things, are uncertain. That knowledge is part of the general experience of mankind, and in my view it makes no difference whether what has to be considered is some form of medical or surgical treatment or the excision, apparently final, of a section of the vas. Doubtless the general experience of mankind will acknowledge the certainty that a limb, once amputated, has gone forever. Such has been the observation from time immemorial of a species to whom the spectacle of war and suffering is commonplace. But where an operation is of modern origin, its effects untried over several generations, would a reasonable person, confronted even with the words and demonstrations of the defendant in this case, believe that there was not one chance in ten thousand that the object would not be achieved? I do not think that he would.

Nourse LJ's reasoning echoes that of Slade LJ in *Eyre* but equally seems to depart from the approach to contract law ordinarily adopted by the courts. The dissenting view of Kerr LJ more closely reflects the orthodox approach.

Kerr LJ: On this appeal it was common ground that the court's task was to determine objectively the terms of the contract whereby the defendant offered and agreed to operate on the male plaintiff. What would a reasonable person in the position of Mr and Mrs Thake have concluded in that regard? Was it merely that the defendant would perform a vasectomy operation subject to the duty implied by law that he would do so with reasonable skill and care? Or was it that the defendant would perform this operation so as to render Mr Thake permanently sterile? Counsel for the defendant submitted that, even if the latter was the correct objective construction of the terms of the offer made by the defendant, it was nevertheless not so understood by Mr and Mrs Thake. He said that this was merely what they believed would be the result of the operation, not what they believed the defendant had undertaken to do, and he relied on the decision of this court in *Allied Marine Transport Ltd v Vale do Rio Doce Navegacao SA, The Leonidas D* [1985] 2 All ER 796 at 804–805, [1985] 1 WLR 925 at 935–986. But in my view no such further question arises here, since it is plain on the evidence that Mr and Mrs Thake intended that Mr Thake should be rendered permanently sterile and believed that this is what the defendant had agreed to do. No submission on these lines was made below, and it would clearly have been rejected by the submission on these lines as to the objective interpretation of the offer made by the defendant once he had agreed to perform the operation.

On this issue I have reached the same conclusion as the judge. Having regard to everything that passed between the defendant and the plaintiffs at the meeting, coupled with the absence of any warning that Mr Thake might somehow again become fertile after two successful sperm tests, it seems to me that the plaintiffs could not reasonably have concluded anything other than that his agreement to perform the operation meant that, subject to two successful sperm tests, he had undertaken to render Mr Thake permanently sterile. In my view this follows from an objective analysis of the undisputed evidence of what passed between the parties, and it was also what the plaintiffs understood and intended to be the effect of the contract with the defendant.

The considerations which lead me to this conclusion can be summarised as follows. First, we are here dealing with something in the nature of an amputation, not treatment of an injury or disease with inevitably uncertain results. The nature of the operation was the removal of parts of the channels through which sperm had to pass to the outside in such a way that the channels could not reunite. This was vividly demonstrated to the plaintiffs by the defendant's pulling apart his arms and fists and turning back his wrists, as well as by a sketch. The defendant repeatedly and carefully explained that the effect of the operation was final, as the plaintiffs said again in their evidence, subject only to a remote possibility of surgical reversal, and that was the only warning which the defendant impressed on them. Subject to this and the two sperm tests of which the plaintiffs were told, designed to make sure that the operation had in fact been successful, I cannot see that one can place any interpretation on what the defendant said and did other than that he undertook to render Mr Thake permanently sterile by means of the operation. Nor can I see anything in the transcripts of the evidence which leads to any other conclusion, and the defendant himself agreed that in the context of the discussion as a whole, the word 'irreversible' would have been understood by the plaintiffs as meaning 'irreversible by God or man'. On the evidence in this case the position is quite different, in my view, from what was in the mind of Lord Denning MR in *Greaves & Co (Contractors) Ltd v Baynham Meikle & Partners* [1975] 3 All ER 99 at 103–104, [1975] 1 WLR 1095 at 1100 when he said: 'The surgeon does not warrant that he will cure the patient.' That was said in the context of treatment or an operation designed to cure, not in the context of anything in the nature of an amputation. The facts of the present case are obviously extremely unusual, but I do not see why the judge's and my conclusion on these unusual facts should be viewed by surgeons with alarm, as mentioned by the judge. If the defendant had given his usual warning, the objective analysis of what he conveyed would have been quite different.

The spate of claims arising out of failed sterilisation led to a redrafting of the standard consent forms by the Government which were adopted by the defence organisations for use in private practice. The terms of the relevant consent form now more fully explain the risks of failure.

I understand …

that the aim of the operation is to stop me having any children and it might not be possible to reverse the effects of the operation.

that sterilisation/vasectomy can sometimes fail, and that there is a very small chance that I may become fertile again after some time....

For vasectomy I understand

that I may remain fertile or become fertile again after some time.

that I will have to use some other contraceptive method until 2 tests in a row show that I am not producing sperm, if I do not want to father any children.

(*A Guide to Consent for Examination or Treatment* (1990) HC (90) 22 as amended by HSG (92) 32, National Health Service Management Executive; Appendix A(2).) Hence, claims of the sort in *Eyre* and *Thake* are unlikely to arise in the future. It should be noticed that the cases concerned the legal *duty* in contract. The claims included damages for the costs associated with the rearing of a healthy baby. This head of damage may need to be reassessed in the light of the House of Lords' decision in *McFarlane v Tayside Health Board* [1999] 4 All ER 961, denying recovery in the tort of negligence (discussed *infra*).

2. Negligence

We do not consider here the substantive law concerned with establishing a breach of duty arising out of a failed sterilisation (or abortion) or negligent advice. These we have dealt with earlier as a matter of general principle in Chapters 4 and 5.

(a) Background

Can damages be recovered for an unwanted pregnancy following a failed vasectomy or sterilisation or abortion? In particular, can a woman recover non-pecuniary loss for the pregnancy and birth of the child and can both she and her partner recover, as pecuniary loss, the costs of rearing a healthy child? Until the recent decision of the House of Lords in *McFarlane v Tayside Health Board* [1999] 4 All ER 961 (HL), both the non-pecuniary and pecuniary loss were recoverable (see discussion in B S Markesinis and S F Deakin *Tort Law* (4th edn, 1999) pp 276–278). The latter was the more contentious (see C Symmons 'Policy Factors in Actions for Wrongful Birth' (1987) 50 MLR 269). Initially, in *Udale v Bloomsbury AHA* [1983] 2 All ER 522 (Jupp J), it was held that it was contrary to public policy for the costs of rearing a healthy child to be recovered. However, subsequently, in *Thake v Maurice* [1984] 2 All ER 513 (Peter Pain J) and [1986] 1 All ER 497 (CA) recovery of such costs were permitted and this was unequivocally established by the Court of Appeal's decision in *Emeh v Kensington and Chelsea and Westminster AHA* [1985] QB 1012. The legal position was succinctly summarised by Brooke J in *Allen v Bloomsbury HA* [1993] 1 All ER 651 at 657.

Allen v Bloomsbury HA [1993] 1 All ER 651 (QBD)

Brooke J: … the principles on which damages are to be awarded have been considered a number of times by the Court of Appeal, and I was referred to all the leading cases which have been decided in the last seven years. I derive from these cases the following principles which should guide me when I consider Mrs Allen's claim.

(1) If a doctor fails to act towards his patient with the standard of care reasonably to be expected of him, and as a foreseeable result of the doctor's breach of duty a child is born whose potential for life would have been lawfully terminated but for the doctor's negligence, the law entitles the mother to recover damages for the foreseeable loss and damage she suffers in consequence of the doctor's negligence (see *Emeh v Kensington and Chelsea and Westminster Area Health Authority* [1984] 3 All ER 1044, [1985] QB 1012).

(2) A plaintiff mother is entitled to recover general damages (and any associated financial special damage) for the discomfort and pain associated with the continuation of her pregnancy and the delivery of her child, although she must set off against this claim a sum in respect of the benefit of avoiding the pain and suffering and associated financial loss which would have resulted from the termination of her pregnancy under general anaesthetic, since in the events which have happened she has not had to undergo the operation (see *Emeh's* case [1984] 3 All ER 1044 at 1056, [1985] QB 1012 at 1028 per Purchas LJ, *Thake v Maurice* [1986] 1 All ER 497 at 508, [1986] QB 644 at 682 per Kerr LJ, *Gardiner v Mounfield* (1989) 5 BMLR 1 at 5–6 per Scott Baker J).

(3) She is also entitled to damages for economic loss quite unassociated with her own physical injury which falls into two main categories: (i) the financial loss she suffers because when the unwanted baby is born she has a growing child to feed, clothe, house, educate and care for until the child becomes an adult; (ii) the financial loss she suffers because of her obligations towards her child which she would have sought to avoid (see *Emeh's* case [1984] 3 All ER 1044 at 1053, 1056, [1985] QB 1012 at 1025, 1028 per Slade and Purchas LJJ respectively; adopted and supplied by the Court of Appeal in *Thake v Maurice* [1986] 1 All ER 497, [1986] QB 644).

(4) Although the law recognises that it is foreseeable that if an unwanted child is born following a doctor's negligence a mother may suffer wear and tear and tiredness in bringing up a healthy child, the claim for general damages she might otherwise have had on this account is generally set off against and extinguished by the benefit of bringing a healthy child into the world and seeing one's child grow up to maturity (see *Thake v Maurice* [1986] 1 All ER 497 at 508, [1986] QB 644 at 682 per Kerr LJ).

(5) However, the law is willing to recognise a claim for general damages in respect of the foreseeable additional anxiety, stress and burden involved in bringing up a handicapped child, which is not treated as being extinguished by any countervailing benefit, although this head of damages is different in kind from the typical claim for anxiety and stress associated with and flowing from an injured plaintiff's own personal injuries (see *Emeh's* case [1984] 3 All ER 1044 at 1052, [1985] QB 1012 at 1022 per Waller LJ).

Whilst the legal position was reasonably clear, the analytical basis for it was not (see A Mullis 'Wrongful Conception Unravelled' (1993) 1 Med L Rev 320). A preliminary question must be whether any injury or harm at all is suffered when a pregnancy results from a failed sterilisation or vasectomy or it continues due to a failed abortion. Has the pregnant woman suffered personal injury by becoming (or remaining) pregnant? Can an unwanted pregnancy amount to an injury? Or, is the birth of a healthy child itself an injury? Or, is the real 'gist' of the action the economic loss caused to the parents in raising the child? Is the latter a claim for 'pure economic loss' or is it loss consequential upon physical injury which is recoverable? The exact nature of the harm suffered by the parents in 'wrongful conception' cases is important for two reasons. First, the nature of the injury will engage different legal approaches when considering whether a duty of care is owed to the parent(s) in respect of the loss. Claims for 'pure economic loss' are notoriously more difficult to sustain than those of physical injury or economic loss which is consequential upon such injury. Secondly, the nature of the loss may well have an impact on the applicable limitation period (three years for physical injury but with a 'discoverability' rule and six years for pure economic loss).

By and large, the analytical underpinning of 'wrongful conception' actions was ignored by the English courts but the claims were nevertheless recognised (see discussion in A Grubb (1996) 4 Med L Rev 94). But, not all judges were disinclined to delve deeper. In *Allen v Bloomsbury HA* (*supra*), Brooke J offered the following analysis:

> **Brooke J:** I am content to assume that the Court of Appeal has recognised that in the unique circumstances surrounding the breach of a doctor's duty to a pregnant woman (or a woman who may become pregnant against her wishes) she should be entitled to recover damages for the two quite distinct foreseeable heads of loss which I identified when I was analysing the principles which should guide me in this case. The first, a claim for damages for personal injuries during the period leading up to the delivery of the child, is a claim which is comparable to, thought different from, a claim for damages for personal injuries resulting from the infliction of a traumatic injury to a plaintiff by a negligent defendant. The second, a claim for the economic loss involved in the expense of losing paid employment and the obligation of having to pay for the upkeep and care of an unwanted child, is a totally different type of claim, although it may in turn be associated with a different type of claim for damages for the loss of amenity associated with bringing up a handicapped child.
>
> I realise that if Parliament does not intervene this is likely to mean that different limitation periods may apply to the two types of claim, since it is hard to see how s 11 of the Limitation Act 1980 would apply to a claim limited to the financial costs associated with the upbringing of the unwanted child since this would be, on the facts of a case like the present, a straightforward *Hedley Byrne* (see *Hedley Byrne & Co Ltd v Heller & Partners Ltd* [1963] 2 All ER 575, [1964] AC 465) type of claim for foreseeable economic loss caused by negligent advice or misstatement. However, this is not a matter I have to decide in this case.

Thus, for Brooke J there was both an action for pre-natal personal injury and consequential financial loss due to the pregnancy and also a distinct action for post-natal financial loss under the principle in *Hedley Byrne*.

In *Walkin v South Manchester HA* [1995] 4 All ER 132 (CA) – a case to which we shall return – the Court of Appeal removed Brooke J's concern that there would be two limitation periods by rejecting his analysis that there were two actions. There was only one and it was covered by the limitation period for 'personal injuries' under s 11(1) of the Limitation Act 1980 (see Commentary (1996) 4 Med L Rev 94 (AG). (For a discussion of 'wrongful conception' actions prior to *McFarlane* see, W V Horton Rogers 'Legal Implications of Ineffective Sterilisation' (1985) 5 LS 296 and A Mullis 'Wrongful Conception Unravelled' (1993) 1 Med L Rev 320.)

Of course, even if the analytical basis of these actions was clear, there would always remain the issue of whether the law would countenance parents recovering the costs of rearing a healthy child. Is the birth of a healthy child a loss to the parents at all? Should a parental decision not to terminate the pregnancy or put the child up for adoption prevent recovery of post-natal damages? Should the law countenance the parents both retaining the child and at the same time effectively passing on the financial burden to the doctor or NHS institution?

The House of Lords in *McFarlane* addressed many of these issues.

(b) McFarlane v Tayside Health Board

McFarlane v Tayside Health Board [1999] 4 All ER 961 (HL)

Mr and Mrs M had four children. In order to limit the size of their family, Mr M agreed to have a vasectomy. Six months after the operation, the consultant surgeon advised Mr M that his sperm counts were negative, and that he could dispense with contraceptive precautions during intercourse. Mr and Mrs M relied on that advice, but subsequently Mrs M became pregnant and gave birth to a healthy daughter. Mr and Mrs M brought proceedings for negligence against the health board, seeking damages for the costs of rearing the child and for the pain and distress suffered by Mrs M in carrying and giving birth to her. The Lord Ordinary dismissed both claims, holding that such damages were irrecoverable in principle. That decision was reversed by the Second Division of the Court of Session which held that Mr and Mrs M should be given the opportunity to prove their loss and damage under both heads of claim. The board appealed.

When reading the complex speeches of the Law Lords, which run to over 40 pages, it will be helpful in advance if we summarise their conclusions. The House of Lords unanimously held that the parents could not recover the costs of rearing a healthy child. Four of the Law Lords (Lords Slynn, Steyn, Hope and Millett) did so on the basis that no duty of care was owed to the parents, as it was not 'just, fair and reasonable' for such a duty to exist. The remaining Law Lord (Lord Clyde) concluded that the financial loss was not 'reasonably foreseeable' and thus was too remote. However, the Law Lords held (Lord Millett dissenting) that the woman could recover damages for her pre-natal pain and suffering and consequential financial loss.

Lord Slynn: The Lord Ordinary (Lord Gill) dismissed both claims (1997 SLT 211). He thought that as a matter of principle they were not entitled to damages. The Second Division of the Court of Session unanimously allowed a reclaiming motion. They thought that the parties should be allowed a proof before answer that if they could establish negligence they should be given the opportunity to prove the loss, injury and damage which they aver arises directly from the fact that the wife became pregnant.

The Lord Ordinary considered the pregnancy could not be equiparated with a physical injury, but that even if it could it was not an injury for which damages are recoverable. The existence of the child and the mother's happiness derived from it could not be ignored and they outweighed the pain and discomfort. As to the claim for the rearing of the child, his view was that the choice was between (a) allowing full recovery subject to issues of remoteness and (b) allowing no recovery since the value of the child outweighed the cost of maintenance. Limiting recovery to specific heads of claim which were not outweighed by the value of having the child was not acceptable, not least because of the difficulty of valuing the child's existence. His conclusion was that to allow nothing for the benefits the parents received from having a child was wrong in principle, at any rate where a healthy child is concerned:

...I am of the opinion that this case should be decided on the principle that the privilege of being a parent is immeasurable in monetary terms; that the benefits of parenthood transcend any patrimonial loss, if it may be so regarded, that the parents may incur in consequence of the child's existence; and that therefore the pursuers in a case such as this cannot be said to be in an overall position of loss. (See 1997 SLT 211 at 216.)

Accordingly, as a matter of principle, damages were not recoverable. On the other hand (at 217): '... if the benefits to the parents do not extinguish both claims, they should certainly extinguish the claim for the costs of the child's upbringing. To hold otherwise will be to give the pursuers more than compensation.' He held that as a matter of principle damages were not recoverable and that the claims could not succeed.

On appeal (1998 SLT 307) the Lord Justice Clerk (Cullen) said that the claim was for the physical and pecuniary consequences brought in train by the second pursuer's pregnancy and childbirth rather than that the child was 'harm' to the parents. As to the claim for pain and distress resulting from the pregnancy and childbirth, they did not have to be seen as 'injury' and there was no reason for thinking that the law did not recognise them as damage. To say that was cancelled out by post-natal happiness was not acceptable. As to the costs of rearing a child, he did not accept that these could not result from the defenders' negligence: keeping the child rather than arranging an abortion or an adoption did not break the chain of causation. The parents had to spend extra money because of the defenders' negligence which led to the birth of the child. They were entitled to decide not to have a child. It was unwarranted to assume that the joy of having a child in every case exceeded any monetary claim which might arise. It could not be said that the pursuers could have suffered no loss worthy of compensation. He declined to consider whether public policy prevented the claim from being brought: that was not for the court.

Lord McCluskey said:

> "Damnum" in the context of our law of reparation means a loss in the sense of a material prejudice to an interest that the law recognises as a legal interest. When there is a concurrence of injuria and damnum the person whose legal right has been invaded with resultant loss to him has a right to recover money reparation for that loss from the wrongdoer... In my view, it is sufficient to say that a woman who becomes pregnant despite her deliberate choice not to become pregnant suffers damnum and loss in the form of significant consequences for her physical condition, being consequences which she did not desire. (See 1998 SLT 307 at 313, 315–316.)

As to whether the joy to be received from the birth of a child cancelled out pain and financial loss he said (at 316–317):

> I know of no principle of Scots law that entitles the wrongdoer to say to the victims of his wrongdoing that they must look to their prospective and impalpable gains on the roundabout to balance what they actually lose on the swings ... I conclude that the benefits to the parents of having a live healthy child cannot be taken into account under any principle known to Scots law.

He too rejected 'public policy' as the criterion for deciding the issue.

Lord Allanbridge accepted that there was injuria. Once the husband was told following the vasectomy that his sperm counts were negative and that he could dispense with contraceptive precautions the damage occurred when the wife became pregnant. His claim therefore arose before the birth of the child. He too thought they should be allowed to prove the loss, injury and damage resulting from the fact that the wife became pregnant. The parents' failure to arrange abortion or adoption was not a novus actus interveniens.

The result of the judgment of the Court of Session is that the pursuers should be able to seek to prove full recovery.

Although these judgments refer to the law of Scotland (which obviously was the applicable law) it is, as I understand it, accepted that the law of England and that of Scotland should be the same in respect of the matters which arise on this appeal. It would be strange, even absurd, if they were not.

The issues raised in this case – or similar issues arising from other methods of preventing conception and birth – have arisen in cases before the courts of England and Scotland for some 20 years but have not yet been considered by your Lordships. The issues have arisen also in the courts of states of the United States, of the Commonwealth and of other European states. Counsel have referred the House to many of these cases. There is no single universally applied test. Judges have not only said (as here) in some cases all, in some cases nothing can be recovered, they have also said that the award may be for something in between....

Cases in the United States of America

The approach of courts has varied widely both in the reasoning and in the result. At one end of the spectrum is *Szekeres v Robinson* (1986) 715 P 2d 1076 where the Supreme Court of Nevada held that there should be no award of damages. The court ruled (at 1078–1079) that the birth of a healthy but unwanted child was an –

> event which, of itself, is not a legally compensable injurious consequence even if the birth is partially attributable to negligent conduct of someone purporting to be able to prevent the eventuality of a childbirth... Our decision ... simply holds that one cannot recover in tort for such an event because the constituent element of a negligence tort, namely damages, is not present here.

The court left open the possibility of a claim in contract.

At the other end of the spectrum is *Lovelace Medical Center v Mendez* (1991) 805 P 2d 603. There the Supreme Court of New Mexico, in a failed sterilisation case, said (at 612) that where the prime motivation for the sterilisation was to conserve family resources:

> ...the Mendezes' interest in the financial security of their family was a legally protected interest which was invaded by Lovelace's negligent failure properly to perform Maria's sterilisation operation (if proved at trial) and that this invasion was an injury entitling them to recover damages in the form of the reasonable expenses to raise Joseph to majority.

They also accepted that damages should generally be awarded for pain and suffering associated with pregnancy and birth. They stressed (at 613) that the '"offsetting benefits" principle applies only to the reduction of damages or the invasion of the same interest as the one that has been found'. Thus emotional benefits could not be set off against financial detriment arising from the invasion of financial security. The setting off of emotional benefits against emotional disadvantages, although theoretically possible, should not be allowed since it would lead to unseemly cases and such litigation was contrary to public policy.

In between these two ends of the spectrum there are cases where the costs of maintenance have been rejected. Thus in *Johnson v University Hospitals of Cleveland* (1989) 540 NE 2d 1370 (Ohio) it was held that parents could only recover damages for the cost of the pregnancy itself and not the expense of rearing an unwanted child. Having considered four theories – no recovery, the valuation of benefits to mitigate damages, limited damages excluding child-rearing and full recovery, the court concluded (at 1378) that the limited damages theory was to be adopted partly, as I read it, because to allow child-rearing costs would be to invite –

> unduly speculative and ethically questionable assessments of such matters as the emotional effect of a birth on siblings as well as parents, and the emotional as well as the pecuniary costs of raising an unplanned and, perhaps, unwanted child in varying family environments... The extent of recoverable damages is limited by Ohio's public policy that the birth of a normal, healthy child cannot be an injury to her parents.

In *Public Health Trust v Brown* (1980) 388 So 2d 1084 the Supreme Court of Florida, in refusing a claim for the cost of rearing a child to a woman alleging a negligently performed sterilisation operation, followed what they saw as the majority of courts in refusing such costs. They said (at 1085–1086):

> In our view, however, its basic soundness lies in the simple proposition that a parent cannot be said to have been damaged by the birth and rearing of a normal, healthy child... it is a matter of universally-shared emotion and sentiment that the intangible but all-important, incalculable but invaluable "benefits" of parenthood far outweigh any of the mere monetary burdens involved ... Speaking legally, this may be deemed conclusively presumed by the fact that prospective parent does not abort or subsequently place the "unwanted" child for adoption ... On a more practical level, the validity of the principle may be tested simply by asking any parent the purchase price for that particular youngster. Since this is the rule of experience, it should be, and we therefore hold that it is, the appropriate rule of law.

Although this approach is followed, it seems, by the majority of state courts in which limited damages are awarded, excluding rearing costs, there is another approach. That is to accept the costs of rearing a child but to set off against those costs the non-financial benefits and joys of the parents in having a child. Thus in *Sherlock v Stillwater Clinic* (1977) 260 NW 2d 169, where a claim was brought for the birth of a child following a negligently performed sterilisation of the mother, the majority members of the Supreme Court of Minnesota held (at 176), in what they described as 'at best a mortal attempt to do justice in an imperfect world', that, after valuing reasonably foreseeable expenses to be incurred in maintaining and supporting and educating the child to maturity, in order to prevent unjust enrichment 'the trier of fact will then be required to reduce these costs by the value of the child's aid, comfort and society which will benefit the parents for the duration of their lives'. That approach is obviously in conflict with what was said in the *Lovelace* case.

The Commonwealth

In *Administrator, Natal v Edouard* 1990 (3) SA 581, in a claim for breach of contract where a sterilisation of the wife did not succeed, it was held, where the sterilisation was performed for socio-economic reasons, that the father could recover for the cost of maintaining the child but he could not recover in contract for the pain and suffering of his wife. In *L v M* [1979] 2 NZLR 519 Cooke J in the Court of Appeal in New Zealand expressed the view that the cost of rearing a child did not arise directly or indirectly from the faulty procedure adopted. In *Kealey v Berezowski* (1996) 136 DLR (4th) 708 in Canada Lax J refused damages for the costs of rearing the child.

The difficulty of these issues is highlighted in *CES v Superclinics (Australia) Pty Ltd* (1995) 38 NSWLR 47. There a woman claimed damages for loss of the opportunity to terminate a pregnancy which doctors failed properly to diagnose. The trial judge dismissed the claim since any proposed abortion would have been unlawful. On grounds of public policy Meagher JA would have excluded such a claim altogether. It was inherently so difficult to assess the damages on any acceptable basis that the task should not be undertaken. Kirby A-CJ would have allowed damages both for the pain and suffering associated with the pregnancy and birth and for the costs of rearing the child, but he would have offset the value of the benefits to be derived from the birth and rearing of the child: '... a setting-off of net benefits is something to be assessed by the fact finder in a case against the net injury incurred. Each case will depend upon its own facts. Such questions can be safely committed to trial judges or juries.' (See at 77.) In the result in order to achieve a majority order he agreed with Priestley JA that the ordinary expenses of rearing the child should be excluded. Priestley JA considered (at 84):

> The point in the present case is that the plaintiff chose to keep her child. The anguish of having to make the choice is part of the damage caused by the negligent breach of duty, but the fact remains, however compelling the psychological pressure on the plaintiff may have been to keep the child, the opportunity of choice was in my opinion real and the choice made was voluntary. It was this choice which was the cause, in my opinion, of the subsequent cost of rearing the child.

Cases from other European states

In *The Common Law of Europe Casebooks, Torts* (edited by Professor W Van Gerven, Jeremy Lever QC and others (1998)) there is an analysis of cases in the French, German and Dutch courts. I do not set out the detail of these but it seems clear that in these jurisdictions also different courts have taken different views on the difficult legal and ethical issues which arose. It seems to me from this and from a valuable article by Angus Stewart QC 'Damages for the Birth of a Child' (1995) 40 JLSS 298 that the law is still developing and that there is no universal and clear approach. I refer in particular to the cases which are mentioned in *Torts* pp 88–90 in the German courts where the test to be adopted does not appear to have been finally resolved. On the basis of what is said there the French courts would appear reluctant to award damages for maintenance arising from an unwanted birth. The Hoge Raad of the Netherlands in 1997 quashed a decision of the Court of Appeal in a case based on breach of contract and held that compensation could be awarded for the expenses of raising a child born normal and healthy and that these expenses should not be reduced by evaluating the joy of having the child (see pp 161–164).

From this review it is clear that there is a wide range of opinions to consider. None is binding on your Lordships and it must be decided which of these approaches is as a matter of principle to be adopted as a rule of the law of Scotland and England.

My Lords, I do not find real difficulty in deciding the claim for damages in respect of the pregnancy and birth itself. The parents did not want another child for justifiable economic and family reasons; they already had four children. They were entitled lawfully to take steps to make sure that that did not happen, one possible such step being a vasectomy of the husband. It was plainly foreseeable that if the operation did not succeed, or recanalisation of the vas took place, but the husband was told that contraceptive measures were not necessary, the wife might become pregnant. It does not seem to me to be necessary to consider the events of an unwanted conception and birth in terms of 'harm' or 'injury' in the ordinary sense of the words. They were unwanted and known by the health board to be unwanted events. The object of the vasectomy was to prevent them happening. It seems to me that in consequence the wife, if there was negligence, is entitled by way of general damages to be compensated for the pain and discomfort and inconvenience of the unwanted pregnancy and birth, and she is also entitled to special damages associated with both extra medical expenses, clothes for herself and equipment on the birth of the baby. She does not claim, but in my view in principle she would have been entitled to prove, compensation for loss of earnings due to the pregnancy and birth. It is not contended that the birth was due to her decision not to have an abortion which broke the chain of causation or made the damage too remote or was a novus actus interveniens. If it were suggested, I would reject the contention and I see no reason in principle why the wife should not succeed on this part of the claim.

Whether the parents should be entitled as a matter of principle to recover for the costs of maintaining the child is a much more difficult question. Logically, the position may seem to be the same. If she had not conceived because of the board's negligence there would not have been a baby and then a child and then a young person to house, to feed and to educate. I would reject (had it been suggested, which it was not) that a failure to arrange adoption (like an abortion) was a new act which broke the chain of causation or which made the damage necessarily too remote. There was no legal or moral duty to arrange an abortion or an adoption of an unplanned child.

The question remains whether as a matter of legal principle the damages should include, for a child by then loved, loving and fully integrated into the family the cost of shoes at 14 and a dress at 17 and everything that can reasonably be described as necessary for the upbringing of the child until the end of school, university, independence, maturity?

The discussion in the American cases of the 'benefits rule' to which I have referred persuades me that it should not be adopted here and it is significant that it has not been adopted in many American states. Of course judges have to evaluate claims which are difficult to evaluate, including assessments as to the value of the loss of a life, loss of society or consortium, loss of a limb or a function. But to do so and to get it even approximately right if little is known of the baby or its future at the time the valuation has to be made is very difficult. It may not be impossible to make a rough assessment of the possible costs of feeding, clothing and even housing a child during the likely period of the child's life up to the age of 17 or 18 or 25 or for whatever period a parent is responsible by statute for the support of a child. But even that can only be rough. To reduce the costs by anything resembling a realistic or reliable figure for the benefit to the parents is well nigh impossible unless it is assumed that the benefit of a child must always outweigh the cost which, like many judges in the cases I have referred to, I am not prepared to assume. Of course there should be joy at the birth of a healthy child, at the baby's smile and the teenager's enthusiasms but how can these be put in money terms and trimmed to allow for sleepless nights and teenage disobedience? If the valuation is made early, how can it be known whether the baby will grow up strong or weak, clever or stupid, successful or a failure both personally and careerwise, honest or a crook? It is not impossible to make a stab at finding a figure for the benefits to reduce the costs of rearing a child but the difficulties of finding a reliable figure are sufficient to discourage the acceptance of this approach.

Accordingly, since I have rejected the Lord Ordinary's approach that nothing should be awarded at all, the choice is between awarding all costs incurred by the parents consequent upon the conception and birth of the child on the one hand and awarding damages limited to those I have already accepted, thereby excluding the cost of rearing the child.

As to this I do not accept the argument that no damages should be awarded as otherwise children will learn that their birth was not wanted and that this will have undesirable psychological consequences. An unplanned conception is hardly a rare event and it does not follow that if the conception is unwanted the baby when it is born, or the baby as it integrates into the family, will not be wanted. Nor do I attach weight to the argument that if damages claims of this kind are allowed, doctors to protect themselves will encourage late abortions. Such an event is possible but the ethical standards of the medical profession (coupled with insurance) should be a sufficient protection in such cases, which ought to be rare if proper care is taken.

The real question raised here is more fundamental. It is to be remembered on this part of the case that your Lordships are concerned only with liability for economic loss. It is not enough to say that the loss is foreseeable as I have accepted it is foreseeable. Indeed if forseeability is the only test there is no reason why a claim should necessarily stop at the date when a statutory duty to maintain a child comes to an end. There is a wider issue to consider. I agree with Mr Stewart QC (in the article to which I have referred) that the question is not simply one of the quantification of damages, it is one of liability, of the extent of the duty of care which is owed to the husband and wife.

It is to be remembered that in relation to liability the House has recognised that, in respect of economic loss, in order to create liability there may have to be a closer link between the act and the damage than foreseeability provides in order to create liability. Thus in *Caparo Industries plc v Dickman* [1990] 1 All ER 568, [1990] 2 AC 605 Lord Bridge said that there should be a relationship of 'neighbourhood' or 'proximity' between the person said to owe the duty and the person to whom it is said to be owed. That relationship depends on whether it is 'fair, just and reasonable' for the law to impose the duty. As Mr Stewart says the alternative test is to ask whether the doctor or the board has assumed responsibility for the economic interest of the claimant 'with concomitant reliance by the claimant'.

The doctor undertakes a duty of care in regard to the prevention of pregnancy: it does not follow that the duty includes also avoiding the costs of rearing the child if born and accepted into the family. Whereas I have no doubt that there should be compensation for the physical effects of the pregnancy and birth, including of course solatium for consequential suffering by the mother immediately following the birth, I consider that it is not fair, just or reasonable to impose on the doctor or his employer liability for the consequential responsibilities, imposed on or accepted by the parents to bring up a child. The doctor does not assume responsibility for those economic losses. If a client wants to be able to recover such costs he or she must do so by an appropriate contract.

This conclusion is not the result, as it is in some of the American cases of the application of 'public policy' to a rule which would otherwise produce a different conclusion; it comes from the inherent limitation of the liability relied on. A line is to be drawn before such losses are recoverable.

I would accordingly dismiss the board's appeal in respect of the claim for solatium by Mrs McFarlane and her claim for expenses caused directly and immediately by the pregnancy and birth, including medical expenses (if any) and the cost of the layette, but I would allow the board's appeal in respect of the claim for damages for the rearing of the child.

Lord Steyn: *The cost of bringing up Catherine*
… claims by parents for full compensation for the financial consequences of the birth of the healthy child have sometimes been allowed. It may be that the major theme in such cases is that one is simply dealing with an ordinary tort case in which there are no factors negativing liability in delict. Considerations of corrective justice as between the negligent surgeon and the parents were dominant in such decisions. In an overview one would have to say that more often such claims are not allowed. The grounds for decision are diverse. Sometimes it is said that there was no personal injury, a lack of foreseeability of the costs of bringing up the child, no causative link between the breach of duty and the birth of a healthy child, or no loss since the joys of having a healthy child always outweigh the financial losses. Sometimes the idea that the couple could have avoided the financial cost of bringing up the unwanted child by abortion or adoption influenced decisions. Policy considerations undoubtedly played a role in decisions denying a remedy for the cost of bringing up an unwanted child…

I will now eliminate the grounds upon which I would not decide against the parents claim for compensation for financial loss arising from the child's birth. Counsel for the health authority rightly did not argue that it is a factor against the claim that the parents should have resorted to abortion or adoption. I cannot conceive of any circumstances in which the autonomous decision of the parents not to resort to even a lawful abortion could be questioned. For similar reasons the parents' decision not to have the child adopted was plainly natural and commendable. It is difficult to envisage any circumstances in which it would be right to challenge such a decision of the parents. The starting point is the right of parents to make decisions on family planning and, if those plans fail, their right to care for an initially unwanted child. The law does and must respect those decisions of parents which are so closely tied to their basic freedoms and rights of personal autonomy.

Counsel for the health authority argued as his primary submission that the whole claim should fail because the natural processes of conception and childbirth cannot in law amount to personal injury. This is a view taken in some jurisdictions. On the other hand, it is inconsistent with many other decisions, notably where limited recovery of compensation for pain, suffering and distress is allowed. I would not follow this path. After all, the hypothesis is that the negligence of the surgeon caused the physical consequences of pain and suffering associated with pregnancy and childbirth. And every pregnancy involves substantial discomfort and pain. I would therefore reject the argument of the health authority on this point. In the alternative counsel argued that, if money spent on Catherine is regarded as a detriment to her parents, it is outweighed by the many and undisputed benefits which they have derived and will derive from Catherine. While this factor is relevant in an assessment of the justice of the parents' claim I do not regard such a 'set off' as the correct legal analysis of the position.

It is impossible to view the case simply from the perspective of corrective justice. It requires somebody who has harmed another without justification to indemnify the other. On this approach the parents' claim for the cost of bringing up Catherine must succeed. But one may also approach the case from the vantage point of distributive justice. It requires a focus on the just distribution of burdens and losses among members of a society. If the matter is approached in this way, it may become relevant to ask of the commuters on the Underground the following question: Should the parents of an unwanted but healthy child be able to sue the doctor or hospital for compensation equivalent to the cost of bringing up the child for the years of his or her minority, ie until about 18 years? My Lords, I have not consulted my fellow travellers on the London Underground but I am firmly of the view that an overwhelming number of ordinary men and women would answer the question with an emphatic No. And the reason for such a response would be an inarticulate premise as to what is morally acceptable and what is not. Like Ognall J in *Jones v Berkshire Area Health Authority* (2 July 1986, unreported) they will have in mind that many couples cannot have children and others have the sorrow and burden of looking after a disabled child. The realisation that compensation for financial loss in respect of the upbringing of a child would necessarily have to discriminate between rich and poor would surely appear unseemly to them .It would also worry them that parents may be put in a position of arguing in court that the unwanted child, which they accepted and care for, is more trouble than it is worth. Instinctively, the traveller on the Underground would consider that the law of tort has no business to provide legal remedies consequent upon the birth of a healthy child, which all of us regard as a valuable and good thing.

My Lords, to explain decisions denying a remedy for the cost of bringing up an unwanted child by saying that there is no loss, no foreseeable loss, no causative link or no ground for reasonable restitution is to resort to unrealistic and formalistic propositions which mask the real reasons for the decisions. And judges ought to strive to give the real reasons for their decision. It is my firm conviction that where courts of law have denied a remedy for the cost of bringing up an unwanted child the real reasons have been grounds of distributive justice. That is, of course, a moral theory. It may be objected that the House must act like a court of law and not like a court of morals. That would only be partly right. The court must apply positive law. But judges' sense of the moral answer to a question, or the justice of the case, has been one of the great shaping forces of the common law. What may count in a situation of difficulty and uncertainty is not the subjective view of the judge but what he reasonably believes that the ordinary citizen would regard as right ... The truth is that tort law is a mosaic in which the principles of corrective justice and distributive justice are interwoven. And in situations of uncertainty and difficulty a choice sometimes has to be made between the two approaches.

In my view it is legitimate in the present case to take into account considerations of distributive justice. That does not mean that I would decide the case on grounds of public policy. On the contrary, I would avoid those quick sands. Relying on principles of distributive justice I am persuaded that our tort law does not permit parents of a healthy unwanted child to claim the costs of bringing up the child from a health authority or a doctor. If it were necessary to do so, I would say that the claim does not satisfy the requirement of being fair, just and reasonable.

This conclusion is reinforced by an argument of coherence. There is no support in Scotland and England for a claim by a disadvantaged child for damage to him arising from his birth: see *McKay v Essex Area Health Authority* [1982] 2 All ER 771, [1982] QB 1166. Given this position, which also prevails in Australia, Trindade and Cane *The Law of Torts in Australia* (2nd edn, 1993) p 434 observe:' ... it might seem inconsistent to allow a claim by the parents while that of the child, whether healthy or disabled, is rejected. Surely the parents' claim is equally repugnant to ideas of the sanctity and value of human life and rests, like that of the child, on a comparison between a situation where a human being exists and one where it does not.' In my view this reasoning is sound. Coherence and rationality demand that the claim by the parents should also be rejected.

Two supplementary points remain to be mentioned. First, I have taken into account that the claim in the present case is based on an assumption of responsibility by the doctor who gave negligent advice. But in regard to the sustainability of a claim for the cost of bringing up the child it ought not to make any difference whether the claim is based on negligence simpliciter or on the extended *Hedley Byrne* principle. After all, the latter is simply the rationalisation adopted by the common law to provide a remedy for the recovery of economic loss for a species of negligently-performed services: see *Williams v Natural Life Health Foods Ltd* [1998] 2 All ER 577 at 581, [1998] 1 WLR 830 at 834. Secondly, counsel for the health authority was inclined to concede that in the case of an unwanted child, who was born seriously disabled, the rule may have to be different. There may be force in this concession but it does not arise in the present appeal and it ought to await decision where the focus is on such cases.

I would hold that the Inner House erred in ruling that Mr and Mrs McFarlane are entitled in principle to recover the costs of bringing up Catherine.

The claim for pain, suffering and distress

The claim for a solatium simply alleges that Mrs McFarlane became pregnant and had to undergo a pregnancy and confinement and the pain and distress of giving birth to the child. It will be recalled that I have already rejected the argument that Mrs McFarlane suffered no personal injury .The constituent elements of a claim in delict are present. The considerations of distributive justice, which militated against the claim for the cost of bringing up Catherine, do not apply to the claim for a solatium. There is nothing objectionable to allowing such a claim. And such limited recovery is supported by a great deal of authority worldwide. I would uphold it. The pleadings also allege that the wife gave up work during the later stages of her pregnancy. Counsel for the health authority concedes that if a claim for limited recovery is allowed, such an ancillary claim would also be sustainable. This consequential relief is within the spirit of the limited recovery principle and I would indorse it.

For the reasons I have given I would uphold the decision of the Inner House on this part of the claim.

Lord Hope: *The issues in this case*

... The pursuers claim that they have suffered loss, injury and damage as a result of mistaken advice following the first named pursuer's vasectomy. They aver that they received advice that the sperm counts following analysis of the samples of sperm which he provided were negative and that they could dispense with contraceptive precautions. Just over two years after they had received that advice the second named pursuer gave birth to the couple's fifth child. The pregnancy was a normal one. There were no complications, and the child Catherine is a normal, healthy child. But the pursuers had planned to have no more children. The purpose of the operation had been to limit the size of their family. They sought damages form the health board for the pain, distress and inconvenience which the second named pursuer suffered as a result of that pregnancy and giving birth. They also sought damages for financial loss involved in caring for the child after birth and rearing her during her childhood...

The mother's claim
The mother's claim can be described in simple terms as one for the loss, injury and damage which she has suffered as a result of a harmful event which was caused by the defenders' negligence. As the pregnancy in this case was a normal one and there were no complications either during or after childbirth, there was no physical event other than the conception to which the claim can be said to be attributable. The harmful event was the child's conception. It may seem odd to describe the conception as harmful. But it was the very thing which she had been told would not happen to her after the sperm tests had been carried out following her husband's vasectomy, and it was attributable directly to the defenders' negligence.

The physical consequences to the woman of pregnancy and of childbirth are, of course, natural processes. In normal circumstances they would not be considered as a harm to her or as being due to an injury. But the law will respect the right of men and women to take steps to limit the size of their family. Any objection to the claim on moral or religious grounds must be rejected, as this is an area of family life in which freedom of choice may properly be exercised. The processes of sterilisation are readily available in our hospitals to those who wish to make use of them. It seems to me that there is no reason in principle why the law should not give damages where the conception was due to the surgeon's negligence or to negligence on the part of those responsible for the tests in the laboratory.

The Lord Ordinary rejected this claim on what he described as the central point as to the value to be placed on the child's existence in any calculation of loss in respect of the pregnancy. The defenders' position, as explained in their written case, was that as pregnancy and childbirth are natural processes they cannot amount to personal injury sounding in damages. As Mr Colin Campbell QC put it in the course of his argument, the reason why damages for these consequences of the negligence are not recoverable is that pregnancy and the birth which results from it are a normal part of life. I would reject both of these arguments. The relief and joy which follow a successful delivery and all the pleasure which a child gives to the mother in so many ways during the process of upbringing are, of course, incalculable. But I know of no principle which requires that such consequences must be taken into account in the assessment of damages where a person has previously endured pain and suffering. The fact is that pregnancy and childbirth involve changes to the body which may cause, in varying degrees, discomfort, inconvenience, distress and pain. Solatium is due for the pain and suffering which was experienced during that period. And the fact that these consequences flow naturally form the negligently caused conception which has preceded them does not remove them from the proper scope of an award of damages. Many examples can be given in the field of personal injury where the natural consequences of an initial injury, such as the development of arthritic changes at the site of the injury or of post-traumatic epilepsy, are taken into account in the assessment of damages ...

I should however like to emphasise that I do not think that it would be right to regard the mother's claims for solatium and for any financial loss attributable to the pregnancy as terminating at the precise moment of the child's birth. The pleadings do not suggest that a claim is being made in this case for any discomfort, pain or distress after the delivery or for any loss of income during the period when the second named pursuer was recovering from it. But is it not difficult to imagine that there may be cases where the mother experiences physical or emotional problems after the birth or sustains loss of income during that period which is attributable to the effects upon her of the pregnancy. I would prefer to limit the scope for the recovery of damages under this head by applying the normal rules as to the remoteness of damage rather than subjecting the claim to a strict and, as I see it, unreasonable and unrealistic timetable.

The child rearing costs
This is a claim for economic loss. The first-named pursuer does not claim that he suffered nay physical or mental injury. The loss which falls to be considered under this head is the cost of rearing a normal, healthy child ...

Mr Campbell said that the proposition which lay at the heart of the defenders' argument that damages for the cost of rearing the child were not recoverable was that the defenders' negligence had not caused harm to the pursuers. He submitted that it did not follow from the fact that the pursuers did not want to incur this expense that it was recoverable. He said that the child was not herself a harmful event, that she was not productive of harm. She had been accepted willingly and lovingly into the family. She was an unplanned but no longer an unwanted child. The exercise of placing a value on the child in order to offset the benefits which she brought against the costs of her upbringing was invidious. So a line could properly be drawn at birth as to the damages which were recoverable. For the pursuers, Mrs Smith said that their claim was not inconsistent with respect of the child's life and their acceptance of her into their family. She pointed out that for them there was no choice but to accept her once they and their other children had become aware of the pregnancy. There was no question of them seeking an abortion, and it would have been unthinkable for them to have put her out for adoption once she had been born. The correct focus should be on the position in which they had placed themselves financially as a result of the conception which occurred due to the defenders' negligence.

Differing views as to the result of the weight to be attached to these arguments are to be found in the authorities. There has been, after an initial decision to the contrary, a consistent line of authority, both in England and in Scotland, to the effect that the costs of child rearing are recoverable. Some support of that view is to be found in the Commonwealth and American cases, but there is substantial support for limiting damages to the mother's claim and excluding all claims relating to the cost of the child's upbringing ...

While most judges other than the Lord Ordinary in the present case have been content to follow *Emeh*'s case, it is worth noting that in *Jones v Berkshire Area Health Authority* (2 July 1986, unreported) Ognall J expressed surprise that the law acknowledged an entitlement to damages for a healthy child and that in *Gold v Haringey Health Authority* [1987] 2 All ER 888 at 890, [1988] QB 481 at 484 Lloyd LJ agreed with this observation. In *Allen v Bloomsbury Health Authority* [1993] 1 All ER 651 at 662 Brooke J also expressed some misgivings about this line of authority. He pointed out that contemporary commentators had pointed out that the decision in *Emeh*'s case had cleared the way for potentially heavy future awards of damages for the cost of maintaining children in this class of case. He went on:

> If an unplanned child is born after a failure by a hospital doctor to exercise the standard of care reasonably to be expected of him and the child's parents have sent all their other children to expensive boarding schools for the whole of their education then it appears to me that as the law now stands a very substantial claim for the cost of private education of a healthy child of a reasonably wealthy family might have to be met from the funds of the health authority responsible for the doctor's negligence. However, if this is regarded as inappropriate on policy grounds it is, as Waller LJ pointed out in *Emeh*'s case, for Parliament, not the courts to determine policy questions; judges at first instance, at any rate, can do no more than try to identify and apply principles approved by the higher courts unless and until Parliament intervenes.

It seems to me that, despite Mrs Smith's assurance that the claim in the present case is a modest one, it is necessary to face up to the problem which Brooke J identified in *Allen*'s case. To the example which he gave of the reasonably wealthy family one might add other examples of cases where the costs of private education might be regarded as recoverable, such as that of the expatriate banker or businessman whose work required him to reside with his wife in countries where suitable facilities for education were not available or to adopt an itinerant lifestyle. It is not difficult to see that in such cases a very substantial award of damages might have to be made for the child's upbringing. Awards on that scale would be bound to raise questions as to whether it was right for the negligent performance of a voluntary and comparatively minor operation, undertaken for the perfectly proper and understandable purpose of enabling couples to dispense with contraceptive measures and to have unprotected intercourse without having children, to expose the doctors, and on their behalf the relevant health authority, to a liability on that scale in damages. It might well be thought that the extent of the liability is disproportionate to the duties which were undertaken and, consequently, to the extent of the negligence...

The question for the court is ultimately one of law, not of social policy. If the law is unsatisfactory, the remedy lies in the hands of the legislature. It can be changed by the Scottish Parliament. As to the law, it has not been suggested that the costs of rearing the child are too remote, in the sense that they were not a reasonably foreseeable consequence of the defender's negligence. For my part, I would regard these costs as reasonably foreseeable by the wrongdoer. In this respect, I differ from the approach to this problem which has been taken by my noble and learned friend Lord Clyde. But in the field of economic loss foreseeability is not the only criterion that must be satisfied. There must be a relationship of proximity between the negligence and the loss which is said to have been caused by it and the attachment of liability for the harm must be fair, just and reasonable. The mere fact that it was reasonably foreseeable that the pursuers would have to pay for the costs of rearing their child does not mean that they have incurred a loss of the kind which is recoverable ...

In *White v Chief Constable of the South Yorkshire Police* [1999] 1 All ER 1 at 31, [1998] 3 WLR 1509 at 1540 Lord Steyn said that the contours of tort law are now profoundly affected by distinctions between different kinds of damage or harm. In that case a distinction was drawn between psychiatric harm and physical injury. The wide scope of potential liability for pure psychiatric harm, and the fact that it might result in a burden of liability on defendants to so many people which was disproportionate to their tortious conduct, made it necessary for a solution to be found on what were essentially pragmatic grounds. Lord Hoffmann ([1999] 1 All ER 1 at 42, [1998] 3 WLR 1509 at 1550–1551) contrasted the ideal of a system of corrective justice with the imperfect way the law of torts works in practice – distributive justice, which gives generous compensation to some people but leaves, for various reasons, the vast majority of cases of injury and disability uncompensated. He explained ([1999] 1 All ER 1 at 48, [1998] 3 WLR 1509 at 1556–1557) that the solution which he favoured in that case, placing the police in the same position as to pure psychiatric harm as the bereaved relatives, had been informed by considerations of distributive justice. It was a practical attempt to preserve the general perception of the law as a system of rules which is fair as between one citizen and another.

How is one to apply these very general, and necessarily imprecise, principles to the present case? Their Lordships of the Second Division gave effect to the tradition civilian system of corrective justice, which provides a remedy in damages wherever it can be demonstrated that there has been a concurrence of damnum and injuria. For the reasons which I have outlined, I do not think that this approach can be reconciled with the fact that the loss claimed under this head is pure economic loss and with recent authorities in this House, which counsel on both sides were right to accept are now part of Scots law, as to the requirements which must be satisfied if damages for loss of that kind are to be recoverable. There must be a relationship of proximity, and the attachment of liability for the harm must be just, fair and reasonable.

I do not wish to place undue emphasis on the fact that the pursuers chose to keep the child. The fact is, as Mrs Smith so ably demonstrated, they had no other choice. The law is not so harsh as to drive parents, in the very difficult situation in which the pursuers found themselves, to the alternatives of abortion or placing for adoption, which, for obvious reasons, they would have found quite unacceptable. Nevertheless they are now bringing the child up within the family. There are benefits in this arrangement as well as costs. In the short term there is the pleasure which a child gives in return for the love and care which she receives during infancy. In the longer term there is the mutual relationship of support and affection which will continue well beyond the ending of the period of her childhood.

In my opinion it would not be fair, just or reasonable, in any assessment of the loss caused by the birth of the child, to leave these benefits out of account. Otherwise the pursuers would be paid far too much. They would be relieved of the cost of rearing the child. They would not be giving anything back to the wrongdoer for the benefits. But the value which is to be attached to these benefits is incalculable. The costs can be calculated but the benefits, which in fairness must be set against them, cannot. The logical conclusion, as a matter of law, is that the costs to the pursuers of meeting their obligations to the child during her childhood are not recoverable as damages. It cannot be established that, overall and in the long run, these costs will exceed the value of the benefits. This is economic loss of a kind which must be held to fall outside the ambit of the duty of care which was owed to the pursuers by the persons who carried out the procedures in the hospital and the laboratory.

For these reasons ... I would allow the appeal on this part of the pursuers' claim.

Lord Clyde: The relevance of the pursuers' claims may be considered from various points of view. One approach is that of public policy. This has played a part in the development of the law in England in dealing with cases such as the present, and more prominently and extensively in the corresponding judicial decisions in the US. But I have considerable difficulty in finding assistance towards the solution of the present problem by reference to considerations of policy. In the present context at least, what are referred to as policy considerations include elements of what may be seen as ethical or moral considerations. But whatever the label used to identify or describe them I am not persuaded that a sufficiently solid ground for decision in the circumstances of the present case can be found by searching for a reason in policy. For one thing it is difficult to find any 'policy' ground for upholding the pursuers' claim in whole or part without finding beside it a countervailing consideration which points to the propriety of disallowing the claim. This point has been developed by C R Symmons in 'Policy Factors in Actions for Wrongful Birth' (1987) 50 MLR 269. To take but one example, the 'sanctity of human life' can be put forward as a ground for justifying the law's refusal of a remedy for a wrongful conception. On the other hand, the general recognition of the importance of family planning in society and of the propriety of adopting methods of contraception including those involving a treatment designed to achieve a permanent solution, reflects the recognition that unlimited child-bearing is not necessarily a blessing and the propriety of imposing a liability on those who negligently provide such a treatment. Particularly where consideration of public policy can be invoked by both sides to the dispute, it seems to me that to proceed upon such a ground is unlikely to lead to any confident solution.

Furthermore, while it is comforting to be able to affirm that one can seen no policy reasons for not allowing a claim such as the present to succeed, that gives little basis in principle for justifying why it should succeed. And to affirm more positively that public policy requires that the claim should succeed seems to me to be coming very close to an encroachment on the responsibilities which attach to the legislature and not to the courts. The judicial function may extend beyond the interpretation of the law to the problem of applying the law to novel circumstances. But in doing so the court should have regard to existing principles. It may be that considerations of what may be referred to as policy are of assistance in determining whether the application of the law should be extended so as to create a novel liability for damages. But the problem in the present case is not truly that kind of question. It is a problem of determining the extent of the damages to which in the circumstances the defenders are liable in law …

Another approach which might be taken in dealing with the problem of a claim for a wrongful conception is that of analysing the problem in terms of the existence of a duty to compensate. The claim made by the first named pursuer is simply one for an economic loss consequent upon the alleged negligent advice. Such a claim could be approached as a matter of liability rather than damages. In such a context the concept of the proximity of the relationship between the wrongdoer and the person affected by the wrong can be usefully invoked as a means of putting reasonable limits upon the extent to which liability for economic loss following upon negligent advice is to be permitted. In a more refined way the approach may be formulated in terms of the existence of a duty to avoid causing damage of a particular kind.

My Lords, I hesitate to adopt such an approach in the present case. As I have already noted, the issued raised in the appeal is not properly one of the existence or non-existence of a duty of care. The relationship between the pursuers and the defenders is accepted as one which is sufficiently close as to constitute such a duty and an obligation to make reparation in the event of a breach of that duty. While in the case of the first named pursuer, whose only claim is for an economic loss, it may be tempting to approach the problem as one of the existence of a liability, the second named pursuer has some right of action which can be more readily recognised and I would be prepared to accept that there should be an obligation on the defenders to make reparation to her. The obligation to make reparation is, to use the words of Lord Keith of Kinkel in *Dunlop v McGowans* 1980 SLT 129 at 133, 'single and indivisible'. So also is the ground of action on which the respective claims of the pursuers proceed. Once the obligation to make reparation for some loss is predicated, it seems to me difficult to analyse the claim for maintenance of the child as a particular, and so separate, obligation. Considerations of remoteness, and conversely of proximity, can arise in different ways both in the context of the liability for wrongdoing and in the context of the damages to which the person suffering the wrong may be entitled. It seems to me desirable to preserve the distinction between remoteness in relation to injuria and remoteness in relation to damnum. The present case is concerned with the extent of the losses which may properly be claimed in the circumstances of the case, rather than with the existence or non-existence of a liability to make reparation.

I turn next to consider the question whether the pursuers have sustained any loss which the law would recognise. The extreme position advanced by the defenders is to the effect that there has not been any loss sustained by the pursuers. That was at the heart of their submission in the Inner House and it was with that issue that the court was principally concerned. One approach here is to question whether the quantification of any loss involves such speculation and uncertainty as to be beyond the ability of the court, and so for that reason to be inadmissible. But there can be no particular problem so far as the second named pursuer's claim is concerned. The assessment of solatium for the paint, inconvenience and discomfort of pregnancy and the event of a birth is plainly something which the courts can undertake albeit necessarily on a broad basis. Her particular patrimonial losses are also readily open to quantification. The argument may be at its strongest in relation to the maintenance claim. But the short answer to any argument on the impracticability of quantifying that head of loss is that courts have managed to do just that without any evident difficulty, but with a due recognition of the imponderable elements involved. The assessment of a claim such as is presented in the present case is both practicable and practised.

So far as the solatium claim was concerned the Lord Ordinary held that the pregnancy, confinement and delivery, being natural processes did not constitute an injury. But natural as the mechanism may have been, the reality of the pain, discomfort and inconvenience of the experience cannot be ignored. It seems to me to be a clear example of pain and suffering such as could qualify as a potential head of damages. The approach which commended itself to the Lord Ordinary on the maintenance costs was to the effect that the value of the child outweighed and indeed transcended any patrimonial loss which the child might create. But in attempting to offset the benefit of parenthood against the costs of parenthood one is attempting to set off factors of quite a different character against themselves and that does not seem to me to accord with principle. At least in the context of the compensation of one debt against another, like requires to be offset against like. In this analogous context of endeavouring to cancel out the maintenance claim one would still expect economic gain to be set off by economic loss. It may be that the benefit which a child represents to his or her parent is open to quantification, but there is no principle under which the law recognises such a set off. A parent's claim for the death of a child is not offset by the saving in maintenance costs which the parent will enjoy. Nor, as was noted by the discussion in the present case, is the loss sustained by a mineworker who is rendered no longer fit for work underground offset by the pleasure and benefit which he may enjoy in the open air of a public park. Furthermore, in order to pursue such a claim against the risk of such a set-off, a parent is called upon in effect to prove that the child is more trouble than he or she is worth in order to claim. That seems to me an undesirable requirement to impose upon a parent and further militates against such an approach. Indeed, the very uncertainty of the extent of the benefit which the child may constitute makes the idea of a set-off difficult or even impracticable.

A stronger argument can be presented to the effect that the obligation to maintain the child is an obligation imposed upon the parents of the child and that they will not be held to have sustained any loss caused by the defenders' negligence if, despite the negligence, they are able to meet those obligations. This seems to me to be the line of reasoning adopted by Lax J in *Kealey v Berezowski* (1996) 136 DLR (4th) 708 where, having indicated that the financial responsibilities associated with the care and upbringing of a child are the responsibilities of parents, he stated (at 739):

> In a wrongful pregnancy case, the question becomes, to what extent, if at all, the defendant's negligence impairs the plaintiff's ability to meet those responsibilities to the unplanned child or compromises the relationship of mutual support and dependency between parent and child.

He concluded (at 740):

> the particular damage sustained in this case is an unplanned and undesired pregnancy. There is no damage caused by the defendant's negligence which prevents Ashley's parents from fulfilling their responsibilities to her or compromises in any way the relationship of mutual support and dependency which, as matter of law, arose on her birth. Accordingly, the child-rearing costs in this case are not a compensable loss.

It is not suggested in the pursuers' averments in the present case that they are unable to meet the costs of maintaining the child, nor that the relationship of mutual support and dependency has been damaged by the alleged negligence. But I am not persuaded that this approach provides a sufficient basis for rejecting the maintenance claim as not constituting a loss. The approach adopted by Lax J starts from a consideration of public policy. It is on the basis that the obligation of maintenance is a matter of public policy to be imposed on the parents that he would, as it appears, allow only an inability to meet those obligations caused by the alleged negligence to enable a compensable loss to arise. As I have already stated, I do not find a sufficiently secure basis in public policy to lead to a confident solution in the present case. The reality is that there has been and will be an expenditure of money on maintenance. The pursuers claim that they are required to spend more money than they would otherwise have required to do. They have another mouth to feed.

On the assumption that the pursuers can establish that they have each sustained a loss they must also show that the loss was caused by the alleged negligence. This is yet another approach which can be taken to the problem. So far as the second named pursuers's claim for solatium immediately associated with her pregnancy is concerned, I have no difficulty in accepting the existence of a causal connection. I have, however, found the causal link with the maintenance claim far more doubtful. I have similar difficulties with the claim by the second named pursuer in respect of a loss of earning following the birth of the child, on account, perhaps, of her having to give up her employment in order to look after the child. There are several successive stages from the allegedly negligent advice before one reaches the incurring of the maintenance costs; the intercourse without protection, the conception of the child, the carrying of the child to her birth, and the acceptance of the baby as a further member of the family with all the obligations towards her which parenthood involves. The cost of the maintenance of the child seems to me to be a loss near the limits of the causal chain. But it cannot be reasonably suggested that the chain was broken by any novus actus on the part of the pursuers. The decision to keep the child, to accept into the family a baby who was originally unwanted, cannot rank as an acting on the part of the pursuers sufficient to break the causal chain. It seems to me that a sufficient causal connection can be made out.

It might be argued that the cause of the loss in respect of the maintenance costs was properly the imposition by statute of the obligation on a parent to maintain a child, so that the cause of the loss was not the alleged negligence, but the operation of the law…

It appears to me that the solution to the problem posed in the appeal with regard to the maintenance claim should be found by consideration of the basic idea which lies behind a claim for damages in delict, that is the idea of restitution. In Lord Blackburn's words in *Livingstone v Rawyards Coal Co* (1880) 5 App Cas 25 at 39:

> … you should as nearly as possible get at that sum of money which will put the party who has been injured, or who has suffered, in the same position as he would have been in if he had not sustained the wrong …

I find no difficulty in that respect with the claim for solatium by the second named pursuer. The pain which she suffered through the carrying of an unwanted child seems to me to be reasonably a subject for compensation. The damages require to be expressed in terms of money, and in so far as money can compensate for pain and suffering a form of restitution can be made. But the claim for the financial losses immediately seems more difficult. The result of the decision of the Inner House is that the pursuers have the enjoyment of a child, unintended but now not unwanted, free of any cost to themselves and maintained at the expense of the defenders. It can be argued that the result is to be justified by treating the existence of the child as a windfall which simply has to be disregarded. Alternatively it can be argued that the benefit of the child is something which either cannot in principle be taken into account or even cannot be evaluated, and accordingly the defenders should be held liable for the whole loss suffered by the pursuers without any deduction. That may seem to be a slightly more attractive proposition than the view that the benefit should altogether outweigh the loss. But that the pursuers end up with an addition to their family, originally unintended but now, although unexpected, welcome, and are enabled to have the child maintained while in their custody free of any costs does not seem to accord with the idea of restitution or with an award of damages which does justice between both parties.

The situation in the present case is a peculiar one. Without surrendering the child the pursuers cannot realistically be returned to the same position as they would have been in had they not sustained the alleged wrong. But it cannot reasonably be claimed that they should have surrendered the child, as by adoption, or, far less, by abortion, so as to achieve some kind of approximation to the previous situation, even if such courses were available or practicable. There is no issue here of mitigation of damages. But while it is perfectly reasonable for the pursuers to have accepted the addition to their family, it does not seem to me reasonable that they should in effect be relieved of the financial obligations of caring for their child. That seems to me to be going beyond what should constitute a reasonable restitution for the wrong done.

The restitution which the law requires is a reasonable restitution. As was recognised in *Allan v Greater Glasgow Health Board* (1993) 1998 SLT 580 at 585 the eventual question is ' … whether what is sought by way of reparation can be regarded as reasonable having in mind the particular circumstances of the particular case.' In the present case we are concerned critically with a claim for an economic loss following upon allegedly negligent advice. In such a context I would consider it appropriate to have regard to the extent of the liability which the defenders could reasonably have thought they were undertaking. It seems to me that even if a sufficient causal connection exists, the cost of maintaining the child goes far beyond any liability which in the circumstances of the present case the defenders could reasonably have though they were undertaking.

Furthermore, reasonableness includes a consideration of the proportionality between the wrongdoing and the loss suffered thereby. The cost of maintaining a child may vary substantially in different circumstances. Counsel for the respondents sought to stress the modesty of the likely level of award in the present case. But once it is accepted that the cost of private education may be included in appropriate cases, as was the case, for example, in *Benarr v Kettering Health Authority* (1988) 138 NLJ 179 a relatively much more substantial award could be justified. The fact that the quantification admits the possibility of very significant differences in the level of award remains and I find it difficult in the context of a claim such as the present to accept that there would be any reasonable relationship between the fault and the claim such as would accord with the ideal of restitution. That the expense of child rearing would be wholly disproportionate to the doctor's culpability has been recognised in the American jurisprudence as one factor supporting the rule of limited damages (see *Johnson v University Hospitals of Cleveland* (1989) 540 NE 2d 1370 at 1375–1376). The solution of allowing limited damages has received considerable support in America and I consider that that solution provides the proper measure of restitution in the circumstances of the present case.

I would accordingly allow the appeal to the extent of excluding from probation the claim for any loss of wages by the second named pursuer as a result of the birth of the child, and the claim by both pursuers for additional costs in caring for, feeding and clothing and maintaining the child, and the expenses in the layette. That leaves solely the claim by the second named pursuer for solatium.

Lord Millett: The contention that the birth of a normal, healthy baby 'is not a harm' is not an accurate formulation of the issue. In order to establish a cause of action in delict, the pursuers must allege and prove that they have suffered an invasion of their legal rights (injuria) and that they have sustained loss (damnum) as a result. In the present case the injuria occurred when (and if) the defenders failed to take reasonable care to ensure that the information they gave was correct. The damnum occurred when Mrs McFarlane conceived. This was an invasion of her bodily integrity and threatened further damage both physical and financial. Had Mrs McFarlane miscarried, or carried to full term only to be delivered of a still-born child, it is impossible to see on what basis she could have been denied a cause of action, though the claim would have been relatively modest. The same would apply if Mr and Mrs McFarlane had adhered to their determination not to have another child and had proceeded to restore status quo ante by an abortion. Damages would be recoverable for the pain and distress involved as well as for any expenses incurred. The issue, therefore, is not whether Catherine's birth was a legal harm or injury, that is to say, whether the pursuers have a completed cause of action, but whether the particular heads of damage claimed, and in particular the costs of maintaining Catherine throughout her childhood, are recoverable in law.

I do not think that the solution is to be found in a process of categorisation, whether of the nature of the delict or the loss in respect of which damages are claimed. It is true that the claims in the present case are brought under the extended *Hedley Byrne* principle (see *Hedley Byrne & Co Ltd v Heller & Partners Ltd* [1963] 2 All ER 575, [1964] AC 465). But I agree with my noble and learned friend Lord Steyn that it should not matter whether the unwanted pregnancy arises from the negligent supply of incorrect information or from the negligent performance of the operation itself. It is also true that the claim for the costs of bringing up Catherine is a claim in respect of economic loss, and that claims in delict for pure economic loss are with good reason more tightly controlled than claims in respect of physical loss. But I do not consider that the present question should depend on whether the economic loss is characterised as pure or consequential. The distinction is technical and artificial if not actually suspect in the circumstances of the present case, and is to my mind made irrelevant by the fact that Catherine's conception and birth are the very things that the defenders' professional services were called upon to prevent. In principle any losses occasioned thereby are recoverable however they may be characterised. Moreover the distinction has no moral content, and while ostensibly relied upon by some of those who have rejected the claim it can in reality have played no part in their belief that it would be morally wrong to accede to it.

I am not persuaded by the reasoning of Lax J in *Kealey v Berezowski* (1996) 136 DLR (4th) 708 at 739–740 where he appears to have held that the parents sustain no loss if their ability to discharge their obligations to maintain the child is not impaired. Quite apart from the fact that their ability to discharge their obligations to their other children must be reduced, the argument does not meet the way the parents put their claim .They do not claim that they have sustained loss by the impairment of their ability to discharge their existing liabilities. They claim that they have sustained loss by the incurring of an additional liability.

I am also not persuaded by the argument that the remedy is disproportionate to the wrong. True, a vasectomy is a minor operation, while the costs of bringing up a child may be very large indeed, especially if they extend to the costs of a private education. But it is a commonplace that the harm caused by a botched operation may be out of all proportion to the seriousness of the operation or the condition of the patient which it was designed to alleviate. I am, however, more impressed by a different though related consideration. I have no doubt that it would be generally regarded as unacceptable (and probably unethical) for a surgeon to seek by contract to limit the damages for which he might be liable for his professional negligence. But I suspect that most people would regard it as reasonable for a surgeon who performed a sterilisation to attempt to exclude liability for the costs of bringing up a child whose birth he negligently failed to prevent. People would instinctively feel that there was a difference even though they might have difficulty in articulating it. But they would surely dismiss as irrelevant the facts that in the latter case the loss was purely financial or that the operation was both simple and inexpensive.

The reasons why the parents initially sought to avoid childbirth have sometimes been treated as material. I apprehend that, if material at all, they must be decisive. It will be recollected that Mr and Mrs McFarlane wanted no more children because they 'considered their family to be complete'. But suppose that they had been advised not to have any more children because there was a serious risk to Mrs McFarlane's life or of the birth of a defective child? The obvious remedy would be to have recourse to a lawful termination. But suppose that Mr and Mrs McFarlane were strongly opposed to abortion, and could not in conscience resort to one. Suppose further that, to their great joy and relief, childbirth was uneventful and the baby was entirely normal. It would seem to be absurd to allow a claim for the costs of bringing up the child in these circumstances. Recovery has been denied in a number of such cases in the United States when the feared harm did not materialise: see for example *Hartke v McKelway* (1983) 707 F 2d 1544.

But if the costs of bringing up the child are to be disallowed in that case and allowed in this, then the distinguishing feature must lie in the parents' motivation. I would be reluctant to go down this path. In the first place, there are more than the two cases to consider. The parents may have sought to guard against the risk of endangering the mother's life or the birth of a defective child, when presumably recovery would be denied. They may have agreed to sterilisation because they could not afford another child, when presumably recovery would be allowed. Or they may simply have decided that enough was enough, as in *Kealey*'s case, where the mother sought sterilisation because 'this body wasn't having any more children' (see (1996) 136 DLR (4th) 708 at 733). The present case appears, at least at first sight, to fall into this third category. Is recovery to be denied because Mr and Mrs McFarlane do not allege in terms that they could not afford another child? Or is it to be allowed because they were not motivated by genetic or therapeutic considerations? Neither principle nor policy indicates the answer.

In the second place, there are great difficulties both evidential and conceptual in this approach. The parents' motives may have been mixed and their primary motives hard to discern and, as I have already pointed out, many not have been identical. Moreover, they are unlikely to have been communicated to those responsible for performing the operation. It is enough for them to know that their patients wanted no more children; they have no need to know their reasons and it would be impertinent of them to enquire. It is difficult to justify a rule which would make their liability depend on facts which were unknown to them and which are, to put it crudely, none of their business.

It is unnecessary to consider all the various reasons which have been advanced in the cases for denying recovery of the child rearing costs. It is sufficient to examine the two principal grounds upon which such claims have been dismissed, together with the contrary arguments. First, it is said that the birth of a healthy baby is not a harm but a blessing. It is 'a priceless joy' and 'a cause for celebration'; it is 'not a matter for compensation'. Secondly, it is said that the costs of bringing up the child are not the result of his birth but of the parents' deliberate decision to keep the child and not to have an abortion or to place the child for adoption.

In an often cited passage in *Public Health Trust v Brown* (1980) 388 So 2d 1084 at 1085–1086 the court observed:

> ... a parent cannot be said to have been damaged by the birth and rearing of a normal, healthy child. Even the courts in the minority recognize…that the costs of providing for a child must be offset by the benefits supplied by his very existence…But it is a matter of universally-shared emotion and sentiment that the intangible but all-important, incalculable but invaluable "benefits" of parenthood far outweigh any of the mere monetary burdens involved … Speaking legally, this may be deemed conclusively presumed by the fact that a prospective parent does not abort or subsequently place the "unwanted" child for adoption…On a more practical level, the validity of the principle may be tested simply by asking any parent the purchase price for that particular youngster.

The decision was followed in *Cockrum v Baumgartner* (1983) 447 NE 2d 385 where the case law in the United States was extensively reviewed by the Illinois Supreme Court.

The basis for the suggested presumption may leave something to be desired, for in truth the failure to have an abortion or to place the child for adoption is no evidence that the parents themselves regard the child as being, on balance, beneficial. Many people have strong moral objection to abortion and would not countenance it even if it were lawful; while adoption is often not a realistic option. But I am persuaded of the truth of the general proposition. There is something distasteful, if not morally offensive, in treating the birth of a normal, healthy child as a matter for compensation.

I cannot accept that the solution lies in requiring the costs of maintaining the child to be offset by the benefits derived from the child's existence. I agree with Lord McCluskey that the placing of a monetary value on the birth of a normal and healthy child is 'as difficult and unrealistic as it is distasteful'. In truth is provides no solution to the moral problem. The exercise must either be superfluous or produce the very result which is said to be morally repugnant. If the monetary value of the child is assessed at a sum in excess of the costs of maintaining him, the exercise merely serves to confirm what most courts have been willing to assume without it. On the other hand, if the court assesses the monetary value of the child at a sum less than the costs of maintaining him it will have accepted the unedifying proposition that the child is not worth the cost of looking after him. Accordingly I agree with the view of all the judges below that the choice is between allowing no recovery on the basis that the benefits must be regarded as outweighing any loss, and allowing full recovery on the basis that the benefits, being incalculable and incommensurable, must be left out of account.

The contention that the birth of a healthy baby is a blessing and not a matter for compensation has been countered by three main arguments. The first distinguishes between the birth of the child and the financial consequences of the birth. The distinction is most clearly put by Kirby A-CJ (addressing a different point) in *CES v Superclinics (Australia) Pty Ltd* (1995) 38 NSWLR 47 at 75:

> In most such cases, it was not the child as revealed which was unwanted. Nor is the child's existence the *damage* in the action. The birth of the child is simply the occasion by which the negligence of the respondents manifests itself in the economic injury to the parents. It is the economic damage which is the principal unwanted element, rather than the birth or existence of the child as such. (Kirby A-CJ's emphasis.)

This is correct as far as it goes, but it does not take us very far. As I have already pointed out, the issue is not whether the birth of the child is harmful but whether the costs of maintaining the child are recoverable. The difficulty arises from the fact that the birth of the child and the financial consequences of his birth are inseparable. When parents reluctantly decide that they cannot afford a further child, they know that they can only avoid the expense by not having one. If they can prevent the conception of another child, they can avoid the costs of maintaining him. They will also avoid the distress involved in contemplating the possibility of abortion or adoption. They undergo sterilisation in order to prevent conception. Their purpose (as distinct from their motives) in undergoing sterilisation is to prevent conception, not to avoid its consequences.

The second argument is to deny that the birth of a healthy baby is always and in all circumstances a blessing and not a harm. This is undeniable. Oedipus is perhaps the prime example of this, though I doubt whether even the strongest supporters of full recovery would have awarded his unfortunate parents damages for all the predictable (because predicted) consequences of his birth. In ordinary life, however, the birth of a healthy and normal baby is a harm only because his parents, for whatever reason, choose to regard it as such.

The third argument takes advantage of this very fact. It insists that the parents are the best judges of where their interests lie. They should not be treated as receiving a benefit when it is one they have deliberately decided to forego. The point is forcibly put by Pearson J dissenting in *Public Health Trust v Brown* (1980) 388 So 2d 1084 at 1087 in language approved by Kirby A-CJ in his dissenting judgment in *CES v Superclinics (Australia) Pty Ltd* (1995) 38 NSWLR 47 at 74:

> [t]here is a bitter irony in the rule of law announced by the majority. A person who has decided that the economic or other realities of life far outweigh the benefits of parenthood is told by the majority that the opposite is true.

This is true, but it does not follow that the costs of bringing up the child are recoverable. The admissibility of any head of damage is a question of law. If the law regards an event as beneficial, plaintiffs cannot make it a matter for compensation merely by saying that it is an event they did not want to happen. In this branch of the law at least, plaintiffs are not normally allowed, by a process of subjective devaluation, to make a detriment out of a benefit.

I turn next to examine the argument that the costs of bringing up a child are not the result of his birth but of the parents' deliberate decision to keep him and not have an abortion or place him for adoption. As I have already mentioned, the defenders do not allege that Mr and Mrs McFarlane should have mitigated their loss by taking either of these steps. Abortion would probably have been unlawful, while adoption is not a realistic option for parents of four young children who have watched their mother carry a child to full term and learned of her safe delivery. Are they to be told that their parents have given their little sister away because they cannot afford to keep her? But I would go further. I regard the proposition that it is unreasonable for parents not to have an abortion or place a child for adoption as far more repugnant than the characterisation of the birth of a healthy and normal child as a detriment. I agree with Slade LJ in *Emeh v Kensington and Chelsea and Westminster Area Health Authority* [1984] 3 All ER 1044 at 1053, [1985] QB 1012 at 1024 that save in the most exceptional circumstances (which it is very hard to imagine) it can never be unreasonable for parents or prospective parents to decline to terminate a pregnancy or the place the child for adoption.

The present argument is different. It is that, however reasonable, the parents' decision to keep the child breaks the chain of causation. The point is well expressed by Priestley JA in *CES v Superclinics (Australia) Pty Ltd* (1995) 38 NSWLR 47 at 84–85:

> The point in the present case is that the plaintiff chose to keep her child. The anguish of having to make the choice is part of the damage caused by the negligent breach of duty, but the fact remains, however compelling the psychological pressure on the plaintiff

may have been to keep the child, the opportunity of choice was in my opinion real and the choice made was voluntary. It was this choice which was the cause, in my opinion, of the subsequent cost of rearing the child…Putting the matter another way, in my opinion…the defendant's negligence should not, as a matter of ordinary commonsense and experience, be regarded as a cause of the ordinary expenses of rearing a child that [its] parent has chosen to bring up. The plaintiff, having chosen to keep the child in the human way that as I have said I think most people in the community would approve of, is not entitled to damages for the financial consequences of having made that difficult but ordinary human choice.

I find the conclusion more attractive than the route by which it is reached. If the parents have a choice, it is one they should never have been called upon to make. But there is no choice if there is no realistic alternative. It would be better to substitute the word 'decision', but even this is not necessarily appropriate. It is doubtful whether Mr and Mrs McFarlane made any conscious decision to keep Catherine. It is more likely that they never even contemplated an alternative. The critical fact is that they have kept her, not that they deliberately chose or decided to do so. It is, of course, that fact which inevitably involved them in the responsibility and expense of bringing her up. But I cannot accept the proposition that this has broken the chain of causation. Catherine's conception and birth, and the restoration of the status quo by abortion or adoption, were the very things that the defenders were engaged to prevent. If conception and birth occurred, they inevitably had financial consequences. The costs of bringing her up are no more remote than the costs of an abortion or an adoption would have been. In each case the causal connection is strong, direct and foreseeable.

Nevertheless I am persuaded that the costs of bringing Catherine up are not recoverable. I accept the thrust of both the main arguments in favour of dismissing such a claim. In my opinion the law must take the birth of a normal, healthy baby to be a blessing, not a detriment. In truth it is a mixed blessing. It brings joy and sorrow, blessing and responsibility. The advantages and the disadvantages are inseparable. Individuals may choose to regard the balance as unfavourable and take steps to forego the pleasures as well as the responsibilities of parenthood. They are entitled to decide for themselves where their own interests lie. But society itself must regard the balance as beneficial. It would be repugnant to its own sense of values to do otherwise. It is morally offensive to regard a normal, healthy baby as more trouble and expense than it is worth.

This does not answer the question whether the benefits should be taken into account and the claim dismissed or left out of account and full recovery allowed. But the answer is to be found in the fact that the advantages and disadvantages of parenthood are inextricably bound together. This is part of the human condition. Nature herself does not permit parents to enjoy the advantages and dispense with the disadvantages. In other contexts the law adopts the same principle, It insists that he who takes the benefit must take the burden. In the mundane transactions of commercial life, the common law does not allow a man to keep goods delivered to him and refuse to pay for them on the ground that he did not order them. It would be far more subversive of the mores of society for parents to enjoy the advantages of parenthood while transferring to others the responsibilities which it entails.

Unlike your Lordships, I consider that the same reasoning leads to the rejection of Mrs McFarlane's claim in respect of the pain and distress of pregnancy and delivery. The only difference between the two heads of damage claimed is temporal. Normal pregnancy and delivery were as much an inescapable was its inevitable consequence. They are the price of parenthood. The fact that it is paid by the mother alone does not alter this.

It does not, however, follow that Mr and Mrs McFarlane should be sent away empty-handed. The rejection of their claim to measure their loss by the consequences of Catherine's conception and birth does not lead to the conclusion that they have suffered none. They have suffered both injury and loss. They have lost the freedom to limit the size of their family. They have been denied an important aspect of their personal autonomy. Their decision to have no more children is one the law should respect and protect. They are entitled to general damages to reflect the true nature of the wrong done to them. This should be a conventional sum which should be left to the trial judge to assess, but which I would not expect to exceed £5,000 in a straightforward case like the present.

In addition, Mr and Mrs McFarlane may have a claim for special damages. A baby may come trailing clouds of glory, but it brings nothing else into the world. Today he requires an astonishing amount of equipment, not merely the layette but pushchair, car seat, carry cot, high chair and so on. The expense of acquiring these is considerable, but in my opinion it is not recoverable. It falls into the same category as the costs of maintaining the baby. But most parents keep such items, bought for their first child, to await the arrival of further children. If Mr and Mrs McFarlane disposed of them in the belief that they would have no more children, the cost of replacing them should be recoverable as a direct and foreseeable consequence of the information they were given being wrong.

At the outset we remarked that the speeches in *McFarlane* were complex and, having read them, you will no doubt agree. The speeches do, however, have much in common as well as differing in some of the reasoning and the implications for future cases. We will analyse the decision in two stages: first, we will consider the arguments and reasoning of the Law Lords; secondly, we will consider the implications for future cases (for an excellent analysis of *McFarlane* see, JK Mason, 'Unwanted Pregnancy: A Case of Retroversion?' (2000) 4 ELR 191).

(i)   ANALYSING *McFARLANE*

First, all the judges characterise the injury suffered by a woman as a result of an unwanted pregnancy as personal or physical injury. This was the conclusion reached by the Court of Appeal in *Walkin v South Manchester HA* [1995] 4 All ER 132 (CA). In *Walkin*, Auld LJ stated:

> In my view, the failure of the attempt to sterilise Mrs Walkin was not in itself a personal injury. It did her no harm; it left her as before (see *Naylor v Preston Area Health Authority* [1987] 2 All ER 353 at 363, [1987] 1 WLR 958 at 971 per Donaldson MR, a vasectomy case). However, it seems to me that the unwanted conception, whether as a result of negligent advice or negligent surgery, was a personal injury in the sense of an 'impairment'…
>
> The resultant physical change in her body resulting from conception was an unwanted condition which she had sought to avoid by undergoing the sterilisation operation.

Likewise, Neill LJ stated:

> …the personal injury is the impairment of the mother's physical condition by the unwanted pregnancy and that the cause of action arises at the moment of conception.

Roch LJ whilst agreeing, was a little more circumspect:

> Counsel for the appellant conceded that conception followed by a normal pregnancy and the birth of a healthy child amounts to personal injuries …
>
> I have some difficulty in perceiving a normal conception, pregnancy and the birth of a healthy child as any disease or any impairment of a person's physical or mental condition in cases where the only reasons for the pregnancy and subsequent birth being unwanted are financial … I respectfully agree with Neill and Auld LJJ that the injury must be the moment of conception.

Whatever the difficulties with this view (see Commentary (1996) 4 Med L Rev 94 (AG)), it clearly now represents the law.

(In other contexts a 'wanted pregnancy' may not be a personal injury, for example, where a woman wishes to become pregnant after her partner has been sterilised: see per Neill and Roch LJJ in *Walkin* and see also, *R v Croydon HA* (1997) 40 BMLR 40 (CA)).

Secondly, for the majority of the Law Lords it followed from this that the woman was entitled to recover damages for her *pre-natal non-pecuniary loss* and also consequential financial loss, for example, loss of earnings if she had given up work whilst pregnant. As we shall see later, some judges would have gone further and allowed damages for the immediate financial (and physical) *post-natal* consequence of the birth. Lord Millett dissented on this point although he would have awarded a conventional sum for interference with the parents 'personal autonomy' in losing the freedom to limit the size of the family. No legal basis is given for this novel approach and it is difficult to justify within the tort of negligence.

Thirdly, the Law Lords accepted that the rearing costs claimed by the parents amounted to pure economic loss. Clearly, this was correct as regards Mr McFarlane as he had not suffered any personal injury, only his wife had. However, it would have been no different if the negligence lay not in advising the parties but rather in 'botching' the vasectomy operation. Although this would be personal injury to Mr McFarlane, the costs of rearing the child would not be 'immediately and directly consequential' upon it (*Spartan Steel & Alloys Ltd v Martin & Co (Contractors) Ltd* [1973] QB 27 (CA)) and thus would be irrecoverable. A man's claim would, of course, have been unquestionably for 'pure economic loss' and irrecoverable where a failed sterilisation was performed upon a woman. As regards the financial loss to Mrs McFarlane, however, that might have fallen within the rule for 'parasitic' recovery in *Spartan Steel*. In fact, only Lord Millett seemed to consider this a possibility. In any event, as Lord Millett acknowledged, the categorisation was irrelevant. The issue was whether it was 'just, fair and reasonable' to award damages for rearing a healthy child. Lord Clyde disagreed and decided the case on the basis that the loss was not reasonable or foreseeable.

There was no question in *McFarlane* that there was a sufficiently close relationship for there to be 'proximity' between the doctor and the patients. This may not always be so (see *infra*). Why was it not 'just, fair and reasonable'? Both Lord Hope and Lord Steyn referred to, and relied upon, notions of distributive and corrective justice. As regards the former, Lord Steyn referred to the fact that a child could not bring a 'wrongful life' action and so it would be incongruous to allow the parents' claim in *McFarlane*. But even if 'distributive justice' is a mechanism the courts should use to determine liability issues, Lord Steyn is comparing 'apples with oranges'. As we have seen, the child cannot bring a 'wrongful life' claim, but the parents (as we shall see) can recover for the birth of a disabled child. There may be differences between the parents' actions in the situations which might lead to different legal outcomes. But, if the crude tool of distributive justice first wealded in *White v Chief Constable of the South Yorkshire Police* [1999] 1 All ER 1 (HL) is to be used, it is the parental claims that must be compared.

As regards corrective justice, Lord Hope considered that the scale of any such claim was disproportionate to the minor procedure and error that had been undertaken. The judges remarked on the fact that actions could involve large claims for private education or the like (as in *Benarr v Kettering HA* [1988] NLJR 174) and this troubled them. Lord Millett expressly disagreed, correctly in our view, as this may often be the situation, for example, where a minor driving error causes very serious personal injury or a minor surgical slip in a hospital results in catastrophic injuries. In these instances, proportionality is not a prerequisite for liability. Why here?

Lord Slynn referred to the fact that the doctor had not assumed responsibility for the economic losses. This is curious and smacks more of 'proximity' than anything else.

More plausibly, there is a common theme running through the Law Lords' speeches and it is that there is an inherent unfairness in allowing recovery of rearing costs if no account is taken of the benefits of a healthy child. But, this calculation is impossible since the latter cannot be calculated. Therefore, no damages under this head should be recovered. Lord Steyn expressed it in terms of perceived public opinion – the traveller on the Underground – and the judges emphasised the moral repugnance of calculating the benefits and burdens of parenthood. Lord Millett went further and held that the birth of a healthy child must be a 'blessing' regardless of how it is perceived by the actual parents.

What is particularly curious about *McFarlane* is not the result which, as the English and foreign case law shows, is defensible but that the judges' approach was somehow thought to be different from the 'public policy' analysis that had previously been deployed in the case law. Lord Steyn, for example, stated that his approach avoided the 'quick sands' of public policy. This is very hard to see. The judges were, on the whole, engaging in the very balancing exercise undertaken under the guise of 'public policy' in the earlier cases. For example, Lord Steyn stated that 'the law of tort has no business to provide remedies consequent upon the birth of a healthy child, which all of us regard as a valuable and good thing'. He also considered the action to be 'repugnant to ideas of the sanctity and value of human life'. Dress these issues up as you like, but they remain the same whatever the label.

(ii) IMPLICATIONS FOR FUTURE CASES

There are a number of situations to consider.

First, in a case such as *McFarlane*, what damages precisely may be claimed? The judges, unfortunately, were not wholly clear. All would allow general damages for pain and suffering during pregnancy and at delivery. Lord Hope would also include damages for physical or emotional problems, such as post-natal depression, arising from the birth. But, thereafter, there were differences of opinion. Lords Slynn, Steyn and Hope would allow recovery of financial loss consequent upon the pregnancy; Lord Clyde was unclear on this. But Lords Slynn and Hope would also allow recovery of financial loss directly attributable to the birth, for example, loss of income whilst convalescing after delivery. Recovery would be governed by the rules of remoteness. Lord Slynn (but not Lord Hope) would include within this category the costs of the layette.

The arguments deployed by the judges would seem to permit a distinction to be drawn between financial losses *directly connected* with the pregnancy and birth and, on the other hand, rearing costs. The former do not engage the concerns which ultimately lead the judges to reject recovery of the latter.

Secondly, it will be irrelevant in a future case what the motivation for the vasectomy or sterilisation was. In *McFarlane*, the judges were unclear what the McFarlanes had told the doctor about their reasons for the procedure. Lord Millett thought it irrelevant in any event. Whether the doctors think the patient wishes a sterilisation or vasectomy for financial or other family or personal reasons cannot affect the arguments used by the judges. If relevant at all, it must be to the issue of 'proximity' and assumption of responsibility. It will always not be 'just, fair and reasonable' to impose the relevant duty of care.

Thirdly, what of a claimant's failure to terminate her pregnancy once she is aware of it. Could this be a *novus actus interveniens* such that all her losses thereafter are irrecoverable? Of course, this argument is only possible if an abortion would legally have been available (see *Rance v Mid-Downs HA* [1991] 1 All ER 801 (a 'wrongful birth' case)). If available, however, must a mother undergo an abortion?

Emeh v Kensington and Chelsea and Westminster Area Health Authority [1985] QB 1012, [1984] 3 All ER 1044 (CA)

The plaintiff, the mother of three normal children, had an abortion to terminate a fourth pregnancy and at the same time a sterilisation operation to prevent further pregnancies. The operation was performed negligently by two doctors employed by the defendant health authority and some months later the plaintiff again became pregnant, although she did not discover the fact until she was some 20 weeks' pregnant. She then decided that because she did not want any more operations she would not have another abortion but would continue with the pregnancy. She later gave birth to a child which was congenitally abnormal. She brought an action against the health authority claiming damages for, in particular, her own loss of future earnings, maintenance of the child, and pain, suffering and loss of amenity, including the extra care which the child would require. The trial judge held that the plaintiff's refusal to have an abortion was so unreasonable as to amount to a novus actus interveniens or a failure to mitigate damage and eclipse the negligence for which the health authority was responsible. The judge accordingly limited the award of damages to compensation for the plaintiff's pain and suffering up to the time she discovered the pregnancy and the pain and inconvenience of undergoing a second sterilisation operation. The plaintiff appealed.

Slade LJ: The judge, in saying that her failure to obtain an abortion was so unreasonable as to eclipse the defendants' wrongdoing, was, I think, really saying that the defendants had the right to expect that, if they had not performed the operation properly, she would procure an abortion even if she did not become aware of its existence until nearly 20 weeks of her pregnancy had elapsed.

I do not, for my part, think that the defendants had the right to expect any such thing. By their own negligence, they faced her with the very dilemma which she had sought to avoid by having herself sterilised.

For the reasons which I have attempted to give, I think that they could, and should, have reasonably foreseen that if, as a consequence of the negligent performance of the operation, she would find herself pregnant again, particularly after some months of pregnancy, she might well decide to keep the child. Indeed, for my part I would go even a little further. Save in the most exceptional circumstances, I cannot think it right that the court should ever declare it unreasonable for a woman to decline to have an abortion, in a case where there is no evidence that there were any medical or psychiatric grounds for terminating the particular pregnancy. And no such evidence has been drawn to our attention relating to this particular pregnancy of the plaintiff in the present case.

Waller LJ: Can it be said that the plaintiff's conduct was so unreasonable as to eclipse the defendants' wrongdoing? In *McKew v Holland & Hannen & Cubitts (Scotland) Ltd* [1969] 3 All ER 1621 at 1624 Lord Reid, dealing with rather different facts but in considering an argument concerning the chain of causation, said:

> But I think it right to say a word about the argument that the fact that the appellant made to jump when he felt himself falling is conclusive against him. When his leg gave way the appellant was in a very difficult situation. He had to decide what to do in a fraction of a second. He may have come to the wrong decision; he probably did. But if the chain of causation had not been broken before this by his putting himself in a position where he might be confronted with an emergency, I do not think that he would put himself out of court by acting wrongly in the emergency unless his action was so utterly unreasonable that even on the spur of the moment no ordinary man would have been so foolish as to do what he did.

That speech of Lord Reid was concurred in by Lord Guest and Lord Upjohn.

So the degree of unreasonable conduct which is required is, on Lord Reid's view, very high. In my opinion, on the findings of the judge, even as they were, I would be disposed to say that this conduct on the part of the plaintiff was not so unreasonable as to eclipse the defendant's wrongdoing. But when there is taken into account, first of all, the judge's misunderstanding of the earlier part of the plaintiff's evidence concerning dates, when she was in fact entirely truthful, and, secondly, when one sees no reference was paid by the judge to the difference between a 20-week pregnancy and an 8-week pregnancy, it would seem that, when the plaintiff decided to have the baby and, having made that decision, she then decided to sue the defendants, her conduct could not be described as utterly unreasonable. Especially when one bears in mind that she had an argument with her husband about it, he apparently wanted her to have an abortion (and the judge accepted that evidence) that makes her decision all the more understandable.

I would therefore come to the conclusion that that finding of the judge, namely her failure to undergo an abortion was so unreasonable as to eclipse the defendants' wrongdoing, is incorrect, and that the pleas of *novus actus*, or the failure to take steps to minimise the damage (in whatever way the matter is put), fails.

Purchas LJ: For my part, however, I would respectfully agree with what has fallen from Slade LJ, that it would be intolerable if a defendant, admittedly by his own admission standing charged with negligence of a professional character and having, through that negligence, placed the plaintiff in a position in which a choice or decision had to be made, was able closely to analyse that decision so as to show that it might not have been the right choice, and could thereby escape his liability.

I find it unacceptable that the court should be invited to consider critically in the context of a defence of *novus actus interveniens* the decision of a mother to terminate or not her pregnancy which has been caused by the defendants' negligence. I am satisfied that taking the features of this case as highly as one can against the plaintiff, namely that on 19 January she knew or had reason to suspect she was pregnant, her decision cannot be questioned. Although the judge put her term of pregnancy at as short a period as $16^1/_2$ weeks, it must be recalled that from the notes of her general practitioner he recorded and communicated to her a pregnancy period of 18 to 20 weeks. The judge, in coming to his conclusion on a break in the chain of causation, studies the professional evidence of Sir John Dewhurst, and considered the risks and inconvenience and discomfort of a further operation, matters which would not have been in the mind of the plaintiff at all in fact, and discounted her evidence, which he quoted in his judgment and then found not to be established because of his view of the motive of the plaintiff. Those were matters which, in my judgment, were not relevant to the decision within the objective test which the judge had taken from the textbook. They are decisions whether or not the plaintiff might have acted reasonably or not, in mitigation of damage, but in my judgment they certainly have no relevance to the more formal decision whether or not the chain of causation has been broken or at all.

What are the judges saying here? Slade LJ's statement beginning 'save in the most exceptional circumstances…' is difficult to fathom. He appears to mean that if there was evidence of medical or psychiatric grounds for an abortion, the woman's refusal might be deemed to be unreasonable. Of course, there may not be *medical* grounds for an abortion but there must be psychiatric (or at least psychological) grounds for the abortion to fall within s 1(1)(a) of the Abortion Act 1967. So, what situation is he contemplating? Most abortions? Surely not, and *Emeh* itself would be questionable. And, further, assuming these grounds do not exist, when will the most exceptional circumstances arise? Certainly, a religious or moral view that precludes a woman from seeking an abortion is not an unreasonable decision. Also, both Waller and Purchas LJJ leave open the possibility of the mother's decision being deemed unreasonable; since they decide the case on the basis that the plaintiff's pregnancy was well advanced at the relevant time.

The judges in *McFarlane* were more emphatic. Both Lord Steyn and Lord Millett found it difficult to imagine circumstances in which the woman's decision could be challenged. Lord Steyn said he could 'not conceive of any circumstances' where the decision not to have an abortion could be questioned. This now seems to be an argument doomed to failure.

Fourthly, to whom is the limited duty of care owed? Clearly, a duty would be owed to the wife or sexual partner of the patient where they were treated and advised together (see *Thake v Maurice* [1986] QB 644). This seems to have been the situation in *McFarlane* itself. Likewise, a *known* sexual partner (whether married to the patient or not) would be foreseeable (and the necessary assumption of responsibility inferred) and would fall within the duty of care if she subsequently became pregnant. What, however, of a future sexual partner who believes the patient to be infertile as a result of a vasectomy? The issue arose in the following case.

Goodwill v BPAS [1996] 2 All ER 161 (CA)

In 1985 M, who later had sexual intercourse with the plaintiff, underwent a vasectomy operation arranged by the defendant pregnancy advisory service. The defendants advised M that the operation had been successful and that he would not need to use contraception in future. In 1988, the plaintiff commenced a sexual relationship with M. Having been told by him that he had had a vasectomy and of its purported success and permanency, and having consulted her own doctor, who assured her that the chances of her becoming pregnant by M were minute, the plaintiff did not use any form of contraception in their relationship and nor did M. In 1989 the plaintiff became pregnant by M and later gave birth to a daughter. She brought an action against the defendants, claiming damages for the expenses of the birth, the cost of bringing up her daughter and loss of income arising from her reduced working hours. The county court judge dismissed an application by the defendants to strike out the action on the grounds that it disclosed no reasonable cause of action and was frivolous, vexatious or an abuse of the process of the court. The defendants appealed. The plaintiff contended that, although the case did not fall within an established category of negligence, the plaintiff should, by applying the incremental approach to negligence, be afforded a remedy in tort by analogy with established categories.

Peter Gibson LJ: Miss Booth put her case on duty of care in this way. A, a doctor, voluntarily agrees to provide a service for B, which includes performing an operation and giving informed advice about the possible consequences of that operation. The purpose of that operation is to render B permanently sterile. It is reasonably foreseeable and accepted that the doctor owes a duty of care to that person's current partner. It is further foreseeable in today's society that the patient may have sexual relations with another partner. It is therefore merely an incremental extension of the law to extend to that partner the duty owed by A to B when A provides the service for B.

In support of that submission Miss Booth referred to the familiar remarks of Lord Morris in *Hedley Byrne & Co Ltd v Heller & Partners Ltd* [1963] 2 All ER 575 at 594, [1964] AC 465 at 502–503:

> My lords, I consider that it follows and that it should now be regarded as settled that if someone possessed of a special skill undertakes, quite irrespective of contract, to apply that skill for the assistance of another person who relies on such skill, a duty of care will arise. The fact that the service is to be given by means of, or by the instrumentality of, words can make no difference. Furthermore, if, in a sphere in which a person is so placed that others could reasonably rely on his judgment or his skill or on his ability to make careful inquiry, a person takes it on himself to give information or advice to, or allows his information or advice to be passed on to, another person who, as he knows or should know, will place reliance on it, then a duty of care will arise.

In *Henderson v Merrett Syndicates Ltd, Hallam-Eames v Merrett Syndicates Ltd, Hughes v Merrett Syndicates Ltd, Arburthnott v Feltrim Underwriting Agencies Ltd, Deeny v Gooda Walker Ltd (in liq)* [1994] 3 All ER 506 at 518–519, [1995] 2 AC 145 at 178 Lord Goff referred to that passage and to certain others from the speech of Lord Devlin in *Hedley Byrne* as stating the governing principles.

Miss Booth also relied on *White v Jones* [1995] 1 All ER 691, [1995] 2 AC 207 as providing an example of an analogous situation in which a duty of care has been recognised. In that case a solicitor who was instructed to prepare a will but delayed in carrying out his instructions was held to owe a duty of care to the intended beneficiaries. She submitted that a woman who had a sexual relationship with Mr MacKinlay is in an analogous position to the intended beneficiaries under the will, because just as the solicitor was employed to confer a benefit (in the form of bequests) on a particular class of people (the beneficiaries), so the doctor is employed to confer a benefit (not getting pregnant) on a particular class of people (women who have sexual relationships with Mr MacKinlay). I admire the ingenuity of the suggested analogy, but I have to say that I am wholly unpersuaded that the analogy is real.

It must be recognised that *White v Jones* belonged to an unusual class of cases. A remedy in tort was fashioned to overcome the rank injustice that the only persons who might have a valid claim (the testator and his estate) had suffered no loss and the only persons who had suffered a loss (the disappointed beneficiaries) had no claim. I do not see any comparable injustice in the present case. On the contrary, it might be said that to give a remedy to the plaintiff against the defendants in the circumstances of the present case would not be fair, just or reasonable. The doctor who performs a vasectomy on a man on his instructions cannot realistically be described as employed to confer a benefit on the man's sexual partners in the form of avoiding pregnancy. Still less can he be so described when he is giving advice on tests after the operation. The doctor is concerned only with the man, his patient, and possibly that man's wife or partner if the doctor intends her to receive and she receives advice from the doctor in relation to the vasectomy and the subsequent tests. Whether the avoidance of pregnancy is a benefit or a disadvantage to a sexual partner of the man will depend on her circumstances. If the existence of that partner is known to the doctor and the doctor is aware that she wishes not to become pregnant by the man and the vasectomy is carried out to meet her wish as well as the man's wish, it may be said that the doctor is employed to confer that benefit on her. But that is not this case. In any event, in this case no complaint is made of the vasectomy: it is only the advice following the vasectomy that the doctor gave the man that is the subject of complaint. I cannot accept that the present is a *White v Jones* type of case at all.

Miss Booth also drew our attention to *Thake v Maurice* [1986] 1 All ER 497, [1986] QB 644, which is the case closest to the present one on its facts. That was a successful action in contract and in tort by a husband an wife whom the defendant surgeon had failed to warn of the slight risk that the husband's vasectomy might not leave him permanently sterile. But in that case advice on the husband's vasectomy was given directly to him and his wife, and both signed forms consenting to the vasectomy. There could be no doubt therefore but that a duty of care was owed by the surgeon to the wife when the surgeon advised the husband and the wife that they might reasonably take no further contraceptive precautions.

In my judgment, for the plaintiff to have a sustainable case in negligence against the defendants in respect of a financial loss arising from reliance on advice given by the defendants, it must appear that arguably the governing principles laid down in the *Hedley Byrne* case [1963] 2 All ER 575, [1964] AC 465 are satisfied. The words of Lord Oliver in *Caparo Industries plc v Dickman* [1990] 1 All ER 568 at 589, [1990] 2 AC 605 at 638 have been taken by this court to be a clear statement of the guidance to be obtained from *Hedley Byrne* on the proximity or relationship which must exist between the giver of the advice and the person who acts on it if there is to be a cause of action in negligence (see *James McNaughton Papers Group Ltd v Hicks Anderson & Co (a firm)* [1991] 1 All Er 134 at 143, [1991] 2 QB 113 at 124 and *Holt v Payne Skillington* (1995) Times, 22 December). Lord Oliver said:

What can be deduced from the *Hedley Byrne* case, therefore, is that the necessary relationship between the maker of a statement or giver of advice (the adviser) and the recipient who acts in reliance on it (the advisee) may typically be held to exist where (1) the advice is required for a purpose, whether particularly specified or generally described, which is made known, either actually or inferentially, to the adviser at the time when the advice is given, (2) the adviser knows, either actually or inferentially, that his advice will be communicated to the advisee, either specifically or as a member of an ascertainable class, in order that it should be used by the advisee for that purpose, (3) it is known, either actually or inferentially, that the advice so communicated is likely to be acted on by the advisee for that purpose without independent inquiry and (4) it is so acted on by the advisee to his detriment. That is not, of course, to suggest that these conditions are either conclusive or exclusive, but merely that the actual decision in the case does not warrant any broader propositions.

Of these conditions, I need only fasten on (3), although I am extremely dubious on the plaintiff's pleadings as to the satisfaction of conditions (2) and (4). How the defendants knew or should have known that their advice would be communicated to the plaintiff and relied upon by her as (according to the pleadings) a warranty of permanent infertility when she did not meet, or commence a sexual relationship with, Mr MacKinlay until three years later, it is not apparent. It is not pleaded that the advice was in a form showing that the defendants expected or intended its communication to Mr MacKinlay's sexual partners, nor is it pleaded that Mr MacKinlay alerted the defendants that he would be passing on the advice to his sexual partners. However, no particulars were sought of the factual allegation of knowledge in this respect and, confined as we are under this head to the pleadings, I would not decide the case on this ground. I am equally doubtful that the pleadings make the allegation that the plaintiff acted upon the advice without independent inquiry, when the pleading merely alleges that the plaintiff was induced by and relied on knowledge obtained from the statement of Mr MacKinlay that he had had a vasectomy and could not have any more children and does not link Mr MacKinlay's words with the advice in the letter of 2 April 1985. But in any event I do not see how condition (3) is satisfied. It is not alleged nor could it reasonably be alleged that the defendants knew that their advice when communicated to the plaintiff was likely to be acted upon by her without independent inquiry. The defendants could know nothing about the likely course of action of future sexual partners of Mr MacKinlay.

In my judgment on the plaintiff's pleadings the defendants were not in a sufficient or any special relationship with the plaintiff such as gives rise to a duty of care. I cannot see that it can properly be said of the defendants that they voluntarily assumed responsibility to the plaintiff when giving advice to Mr MacKinlay. At that time they had no knowledge of her, she was not an existing sexual partner of Mr MacKinlay but was merely, like any other woman in the world, a potential future sexual partner of his, that is to say a member of an indeterminately large class of females who might have sexual relations with Mr MacKinlay during his lifetime. I find it impossible to believe that the policy of the law is or should be to treat so tenuous a relationship between the adviser and the advisee as giving rise to a duty of care, and there is no analogous situation recognised as giving rise to that duty.

Thorpe LJ: I agree that the defendant is entitled to succeed on the application of 25 January 1995 on both its grounds for the reasons given by Peter Gibson LJ.

Viewing the plaintiff's case as pleaded, it does not survive the application of the six tests suggested by Neill LJ in *James McNaughton Papers Group Ltd v Hicks Anderson & Co (a firm)* [1991] 1 All ER 134 at 144, [1991] 2 QB 113 at 125. In particular, to use the terminology of the third test, the plaintiff as advisee is not entitled to look to the third party and through him to the adviser for guidance. Indeed, use of that terminology only serves to demonstrate how tenuous is the relationship between the plaintiff and the defendant. The reality is that the doctor advised Mr MacKinlay. They are in reality the adviser and the advisee. The plaintiff is no nearer the doctor adviser than one who some three and half years after the operation commenced a sexual relationship with his patient. Equally, the class to which the plaintiff belongs is in my judgment potentially excessive in size and uncertain in character. Thirdly, the state of knowledge of the adviser militates against the plaintiff. The doctor in the circumstances regards himself as advising the patient and, if a married man, the patient's wife. It cannot be said that he knows or ought to know that he also advises any future sexual partner of his patient who chance to receive his advice at second hand. Presented with such a set of facts a doctor is entitled to scorn the suggestion that he owes a duty of care to such a band so uncertain in nature and extent and over such an indefinite future span. Finally, I consider that the plaintiff fails the test of reliance. In reality a woman exploring the development of a sexual relationship with a new partner takes much on trust before experience corroborates or exposes his assurances. Her responsibility is to protect herself against unwanted conception and to take independent advice on whatever facts he presents. Thus I conclude that on an analysis of the pleadings alone the plaintiff's claim discloses no reasonable course of action.

I also conclude that a further analysis of the pleadings and the exchanged witness statement entitles the defendant to succeed on the second ground. The plaintiff's statement is commendable for its candour, but it is fatal to her case in that it establishes the following important facts. (1) In about April 1988 at the commencement of the sexual relationship and when protected by a coil the plaintiff sought independent medical advice. (2) Her doctor informed her that there was an extremely remote chance of conception despite her partner's vasectomy. Nevertheless she had the coil removed. (3) On 4 April 1989 she consulted her doctor thinking that she might be pregnant but accepted his advice that she possibly had an ovarian cyst. (4) On 21 June when informed of her pregnancy she was relieved and pleased. Subsequently she quailed at the consequences but, although termination was still medically open, she could not accept it psychologically and emotionally. Accordingly she elected to go on to give birth. Those facts simply demonstrate how far-fetched is this claim.

Both judges were, quite obviously, highly sceptical of actions by sexual partners of patients. It seems that the duty is owed only to the patient 'and possibly his wife or partner if the doctor intends her to receive and she receives advice form the doctor in relation to the vasectomy' (per Peter Gibson LJ at 167). Thorpe LJ spoke only of the patient and, if married, his wife (at 170). All future sexual partners would be excluded, as would an existing one unless the doctor is taken to be advising them directly (they are present) or indirectly (because they are known) (on the latter see per Peter Gibson LJ at 167).

Goodwill was, however a curious case even before *McFarlane* (see I Kennedy and A Grubb (eds) *Principles of Medical Law* (1998) paras 5.65–5.68). As a result of that decision, it is certainly wrongly decided in respect of the woman's financial loss in raising the child. It remains of interest only in relation to loss or damage arising from the fact of being pregnant. As the characterisation of the plaintiff's damage was crucial to the line of authority cited to, and relied upon by the court, namely cases concerned with economic loss caused by negligent auditors, it is not clear that these decisions would assist in determining whether an action lay for the physical consequences to a partner of a failed vasectomy. It seems likely, however, that the courts would limit the range of potential plaintiffs even for physical injury and its consequences in these circumstances. It is doubtful whether a doctor 'undertakes' any obligation to an unknown future sexual partner. In any event, the really important point in *Goodwill* was the plaintiff's own actions. She did not rely upon the doctor in any way. She sought her own advice from her GP and ran the risk of pregnancy. Herein lies the answer to the 'proximity' issue. Future sexual partners *ought* not to rely upon earlier advice (or whatever) about their partner's fertility. This is a matter of personal responsibility. Limiting liability to those within the 'zone of knowledge' of the doctor at the time of the treatment is both reasonable and good policy. The plaintiff in *Goodwill* fell outside it.

Fifthly, what will be the position if the child which is born is not healthy but disabled as in the earlier case of *Emeh*? Only Lord Steyn alluded to this and at the end of his speech he merely stated that 'the rule may have to be different'. No doubt it would, since the arguments about moral repugnance and the perceived demand of corrective and distributive justice will be much weaker (but notice Lord Steyn's argument about coherence and *McKay v Essex AHA* (*supra*), which points in the opposite direction). The courts are likely to allow recovery here but they will almost certainly require a deduction to be made, equivalent to the non-recovery in *McFarlane*, so as to allow only the *additional costs* associated with the disability (see *infra* for 'wrongful birth' claims).

Finally McFarlane was a delict (or tort) case. Would the same conclusion have been reached if the claim had been in contract? Lord Steyn left the matter open. Lord Slynn stated that '[i]f a client wants to be able to recover such costs he or she must do so by an appropriate contract'. Of course, it is imaginable that a contract could expressly stipulate for liability to extend to the rearing costs of a healthy child. It is, however, most unlikely in practice. The issue in the case law, as we saw, was the nature of the contractual duty: as in negligence or the more onerous guarantee. Whichever it is does not affect whether the rearing costs are recoverable. They either are or they are not. Here, the court could not rely on the 'just, fair and reasonable' liable for the policy arguments but it could, as has been suggested, just as easily accommodate them under the rubric of public policy as in the contract cases of *Thake v Maurice* and *Emeh* itself. Result: the same.

B. WRONGFUL BIRTH

The term 'wrongful birth' refers to a claim brought by the parents of a child *born disabled* as a consequence of negligence before its birth. As you will see, this action arises out of the same circumstances as the 'wrongful life' claim of a child which we discussed earlier. As with the 'wrongful life' claim, therefore, the breach of duty may occur before conception (eg negligent genetic counselling), *ex utero* (eg negligence during infertility treatment) or *in utero* (eg negligent failure to diagnose the child's disabilities).

In England no cases directly analyse the basis for the parent's 'wrongful birth' claim. However, a number of decisions have recognised the claim without raising any doubts as to its validity (eg *Rance v Mid-Downs HA* [1991] 1 All ER 801 (Brooke J); *Salih v Enfield HA* [1991] 3 All ER 400 (CA); *Fish v Wilcox* [1994] 5 Med LR 230 (CA)).

A model for analysis which an English court might well adopt is provided by the following decision of the Washington Supreme Court.

Harbeson v Parke-Davis Inc (1983) 656 P 2d 483 (Wash Sup Ct)

Pearson J: Plaintiff Leonard Harbeson has at all material times been a member of the United States Air Force. In 1970, while Mr Harbeson was stationed at Malstrom Air Force Base, his wife Jean conceived their first child. In December 1970, Mrs Harbeson learned, after suffering a grand mal seizure, that she was an epileptic. To control Mrs Harbeson's seizures, physicians at the Air Force Base prescribed Dilantin, an anticonvulsant drug, which was the first choice of doctors in the treatment of epilepsy. Mrs Harbeson took Dilantin during the remainder of her pregnancy and in march 1971 gave birth to Michael, a healthy and intelligent child.

After Michael's birth, Mrs Harbeson was transferred to McChord Air Force Base, near Tacoma. The medical facility serving the base was Madigan Army Medical Center. In May 1972, Mrs Harbeson went to Madigan for evaluation and treatment of her epilepsy. A neurologist at Madigan prescribed Dilantin to control her seizures. Between November 1972 and July 1973, the Harbesons informed three doctors at Madigan that they were considering having other children, and inquired about the risks of Mrs Harbeson's taking Dilantin during pregnancy. Each of the three doctors responded that Dilantin could cause cleft palate and temporary hirsutism. None of the doctors conducted literature searches or consulted other sources for specific information regarding the correlation between Dilantin and birth defects. The Harbesons relied on the assurances of the Madigan doctors and thereafter Mrs Harbeson became pregnant twice giving birth to Elizabeth in April 1974, and Christine in May 1975. Throughout these pregnancies, Mrs Harbeson continued to take Dilantin as prescribed by the Madigan doctors…Elizabeth and Christine have been diagnosed as suffering from 'fetal hydantoin syndrome'. They suffer from mild to moderate growth deficiencies, mild to moderate development retardation, wide-set eyes, lateral ptosis (drooping eyelids), hypoplasia of the fingers, small nails, low-set hairline, broad nasal ridge, and other physical and developmental defects. Had Mr and Mrs Harbeson been informed of the potential birth defects associated with the use of Dilantin during pregnancy, they would not have had any other children…

Wrongful birth
The epithet wrongful birth has been used to describe several fundamentally different types of action. See Annot, *Tort Liability for Wrongfully Causing One to be Born*, 83 ALR 3d 15 (1978). Many of the actions once entitled wrongful birth are now referred to as wrongful conception and wrongful pregnancy actions. *Phillips v United States*, 508 F Supp 544, 545 n1 (DSC 1981); Rogers, *Wrongful Life and Wrongful Birth: Medical Malpractice In Genetic Counseling and Prenatal Testing*, 33 SCL Rev 713, 739–41 (1982). A recent definition of a

wrongful birth action is an action brought by the parents against a physician [who] failed to inform [them] of the increased possibility that the mother would give birth to a child suffering from birth defects…[thereby precluding] an informed decision about whether to have the child.

(Footnotes omitted.) Comment, *Berman v Allan*, 8 Hofstra L Rev 257, 258 (1979), cited in *Phillips*, at 545 n 1.

Such an action was recognised by the New Jersey Supreme Court in *Schroeder v Perkel*, 87 NJ 53, 432 A 2d 834 (1981). Mr and Mrs Schroeder had two children, both of whom suffered from cystic fibrosis, a fatal genetic disorder. It was not until Mrs Schroeder was 8 months pregnant with their second child that the Schroeders learned they were carriers of the recessive gene which causes the disorder. They claimed that defendant paediatricians were negligent in failing to make an earlier diagnosis of cystic fibrosis in their first child. Had they known earlier of the condition, the Schroeders would either avoided the conception of their second child, or terminated the pregnancy. The basis of their claim, therefore, was that 'they were deprived of an informed choice of whether to assume the risk of a second child'. 87 NJ at 57, 432 A 2d 834. The New Jersey Supreme Court recognised the cause of action and held that the parents could recover the extraordinary medical expenses of raising the second child.

Schroeder is a paradigm wrongful birth case. The parents brought an action for the birth of a defective child. They claimed that defendant physicians had breached a duty to inform them of the risk of the child's being born defective. They claimed that had they known of this risk they would have prevented the birth of the child by contraception or abortion. They claimed that defendants' failure to inform was a proximate cause of the birth of the claim and that the birth was an injury compensable in damages.

Although the definition we refer to above comprehends the *Schroeder* action, it excludes the cause of action recognised in a similar case, *Speck v Finegold*, 497 Pa 77, 439 A 2d 110 (1981). Mr Speck suffered from neurofibromatosis, a disorder caused by a genetic defect. After having two children who suffered from the disorder, Mr Speck decided to undergo a vasectomy. The vasectomy was unsuccessful, and Mrs Speck became pregnant. Mr and Mrs Speck decided to terminate the pregnancy. The abortion was unsuccessful, and Mrs Speck gave birth to a daughter who suffered from neurofibromatosis.

The court allowed the parents a cause of action to recover expenses attributable to the birth and rearing of their daughter. There appears to be no reason to exclude the action in *Speck* from the definition of wrongful birth. Like *Schroeder*, it is founded upon the birth of a defective child. The parents of the child alleged defendants breached a duty of care in performing the vasectomy and abortion procedures. Had these procedures been successful, they would have prevented conception or birth of the child. The parents alleged defendants' breach was a proximate cause of the birth, and that birth was an injury to the parents, compensable in damages.

Both *Schroeder* and *Speck* recognise the right of parents to prevent the conception or birth of children suffering defects. They recognise that physicians owe a duty to parents to preserve that right. Physicians may breach this duty either by failure to impart material information or by negligent performance of a procedure to prevent the birth of a defective child. The parents' right to prevent a defective child and the correlative duty flowing from that right is the heart of the wrongful birth action.

For the purposes of the analysis which follows, therefore, wrongful birth will refer to an action based on an alleged breach of the duty of a health care provider to impart information or perform medical procedures with due care, where the breach is a proximate cause of the birth of a defective child. We do not in this opinion address issues which may arise where the birth of a healthy child is allegedly caused by a breach of duty owed to the parents. Such actions are referred to as wrongful conception or wrongful pregnancy, rather than wrongful birth. See generally, *Phillips*, at 545 n 1. Other jurisdictions have consistently treated such actions as different from, although related to, wrongful birth. We do likewise.

Having defined the scope of our inquiry, we now consider whether the wrongful birth action should be allowed in this state.

First, we measure the proposed wrongful birth action against the traditional concepts of duty, breach, injury and proximate cause. The critical concept is duty. The core of our decision is whether we should impose upon health care providers a duty correlative to the parents' right to prevent the birth of defective children.

Until recently, medical science was unable to provide parents with the means of predicting the birth of a defective child. Now, however, the ability to predict the occurrence and recurrence of defects attributable to genetic disorders has improved significantly. Parents can determine before conceiving a child whether their genetic traits increase the risk of that child's suffering from a genetic disorder such as Tay-Sachs disease or cystic fibrosis. After conception, new diagnostic techniques such as amniocentesis and ultrasonography can reveal defects in the unborn fetus. See generally, Peters and Peters, *Wrongful Life: Recognising the Defective Child's Right to a Cause of Action*, 18 Duq L Rev 857, 873–75 (1980). Parents may avoid the birth of the defective child by aborting the fetus. The difficult moral choice is theirs. *Roe v Wade* 410 US 113, 93 S Ct 705, 35 L Ed 2d 147 (1973). We must decide, therefore, whether these developments confer upon potential parents the right to prevent, either before or after conception, the birth of a defective child. Are these developments the first steps towards a 'Fascist-Orwellian societal attitude of genetic purity', *Gildiner v Thomas Jefferson Univ Hosp* 451 F Supp 692, 695 (EDPa 1978), or Huxley's Brave New World? Or do they provide positive benefits to individual families and to all society by avoiding the vast emotional and economic cost of defective children?

We believe we must recognise the benefits of these medical developments and therefore we hold that parents have a right to prevent the birth of a defective child and health care providers a duty correlative to that right. This duty requires health care providers to impart to their patients material information as to the likelihood of future children being born defective, to enable the potential parents to decide whether to avoid the conception or birth of such children. If medical procedures are undertaken to avoid the conception or birth of defective children, the duty also requires that these procedures be performed with due care. This duty includes, therefore, the requirement that a health care provider who undertakes to perform an abortion uses reasonable care in doing so. The duty does not, however, affect in any way the right of a physician to refuse on moral or religious grounds to perform an abortion. Recognition of the duty will 'promote societal interests in genetic counseling and prenatal testing, deter medical malpractice, and at least partially redress a clear and undeniable wrong'. (Footnotes omitted.) Rogers, *Wrongful Life and Wrongful Birth: Medical Malpractice in Genetic Counseling and Prenatal Testing*, 33 SCL Rev 713, 757 (1982) (hereinafter cited as Rogers).

We find persuasive the fact that all other jurisdictions to have considered this issue have recognised such a duty. These decisions are conveniently collected in Rogers, at 739–52, and we need not list them here.

Having recognised that a duty exists, we have taken the major step toward recognising the wrongful birth action. The second element of the traditional tort analysis is more straightforward. Breach will be measured by failure to conform to the appropriate standard of skill, care, or learning. RCW 4 24 290; RCW 7 70 040. *Gates v Jensen* 92 Wash 2d 246, 595 P 2d 919 (1979).

More problematical is the question of whether the birth of a defective child represents an injury to the parents. The only case to touch on this question in this state did not resolve it. *Ball v Mudge* 64 Wash 2d 247, 250 391 P 2d 201 (1964). However, it is an inevitable consequence of recognising the parents' right to avoid the birth of a defective child that we recognise that the birth of such a child is an actionable injury. The real question as to injury, therefore, is not the existence of the injury, but the extent of that injury. In other words, having recognised that the birth of the child represents an injury, how do we measure damages? Other courts to have considered the issue have found this question troublesome. In particular, the New Jersey Supreme Court has taken a different approach to the question on each of the three occasions it has confronted it. In *Gleitman v Cosgrove* 49 NJ 22, 227 A 2d 689 (1967), the court rejected the wrongful birth action altogether. One of the reasons for the rejection was the difficulty in measuring damages. When the court next considered the issue in *Berman v Allan* 80 NJ 421, 404 A 2d 8 (1979), it upheld an action for wrongful birth and permitted damages for mental anguish. However, the court refused to allow damages to compensate for the medical and other costs incurred in raising, educating, and supervising the child. The court retreated from this position in the third case, *Schroeder v Perkel* 87 NJ 53, 432 A 2d 834 (1981), and allowed the parents damages for certain medical expenses related to the child's affliction.

Other courts to have considered the issue exhibit widely divergent approaches. Comment, *Wrongful Birth Damages, Mandate and Mishandling by Judicial Fiat* 13 Val U L Rev 127 (1978); Rogers, at 750–51.

More certain guidance than that provided by decisions of other jurisdictions on the issue of damages is provided by the Legislature in RCW 4 24 010. This statute provides that, in an action by parents for injury to a child, compensation may be recovered for four types of damages: medical, hospital, and medication expenses, loss of the child's services and support, loss of the child's love and companionship, and injury to the parent-child relationship. Recovery of damages for loss of companionship of the child, or injury or destruction of the parent-child relationship is not limited to the period of the child's minority. *Balmer v Dilley* 81 Wash 2d 367, 502 P 2d 456 (1972). We have held that this section allows recovery for parental grief, mental anguish and suffering. *Hinzman v Palmanteer* 81 Wash 2d 327, 501 P 2d 1228 (1972). The statute is not directly in point because a wrongful birth claim does not allege injury to the child as the cause of the parents' injury; rather it alleges the birth of the child is the cause of the injury. Nevertheless, the statute reflects a policy to compensate parents not only for pecuniary loss but also for emotional injury. There appears to be no compelling reason that policy should not apply in wrongful birth actions. Accordingly, we hold that recovery may include the medical, hospital, and medication expenses attributable to the child's birth and to its defective condition, and in addition damages for the parents' emotional injury caused by the birth of the defective child. In considering damages for emotional injury, the jury should be entitled to consider the countervailing emotional benefits attributable to the birth of the child. Restatement (Second) of Torts s 920 (1977). Rogers, at 751–52; *Eisbrenner v Stanley*, 106 Mich App 357, 308 NW 2d 209 (1981); *Kingsbury v Smith*, 442 A 2d 1003 (1982).

The final element to be considered is whether a breach of duty can be a proximate cause of the birth of the child. Proximate cause must be established by, first, a showing that the breach of duty was a cause in fact of the injury, and, second, a showing that as a matter of law liability should attach. *King v Seattle*, 84 Wash 2d 239, 249, 525 P 2d 228 (1974). Cause in fact can be established by proving that but for the breach of duty, the injury would not have occurred. *King v Seattle, supra*. The legal question whether liability should attach is essentially another aspect of the policy decisions which we confronted in deciding whether the duty exists. We therefore hold that, as a matter of law in wrongful birth cases, if cause in fact is established, the proximate cause element is satisfied. This conclusion is consistent with the decisions of those other jurisdictions which have accepted wrongful birth actions, eg *Robak v United States* 658 F 2d 471 (7th Circ 1981).

The action for wrongful birth, therefore, fits within the conceptual framework of our law of negligence. An action in negligence claiming damages for the birth of a child suffering congenital defects may be brought in this state.

The parents may therefore recover damages for the wrongful births of Elizabeth and Christine. These damages may include pecuniary damages for extraordinary medical, educational, and similar expenses attributable to the defective condition of the children. In other words, the parents should recover those expenses in excess of the cost of the birth and rearing of two normal children. In addition, the damages may compensate for mental anguish and emotional stress suffered by the parents during each child's life as a proximate result of the physicians' negligence. Any emotional benefits to the parents resulting from the birth of the child should be considered in setting the damages.

The case law and arguments were analysed in the following Scottish decision.

Anderson v Forth Valley Health Board (1997) 44 BMLR 108 (Ct Sess (OH))

The pursuers were the parents of two sons who had been suffering from muscular dystrophy. They sought damages from a health board on the basis that the doctors for whom the board were responsible had failed in their duty to give proper advice and information about genetic risks and had failed to refer the pursuers to genetic counselling. Had this been done, it was averred, a genetic disorder affecting the first pursuer would have been discovered and she and the second pursuer would have terminated any male pregnancies. Damages were claimed for: (1) anxiety, upset and distress; and (2) patrimonial loss, including the first pursuer's lost earnings, the second pursuer's loss of opportunity to earn overtime, and the expenses caused by the need to employ carers to help look after the children throughout their lives. The defenders argued that the pursuers had suffered no loss, since the benefits of a child always outweighed any losses, that there were public policy considerations against a claim based on the failure to terminate a pregnancy, that the costs of rearing the children were pure economic losses and irrecoverable as a consequence, and that any damages for the costs of upbringing should be limited to the extent of the child's childhood.

Lord Nimmo Smith: Junior counsel for the first defenders submitted that the damages sought by the pursuer fell under two separate heads, namely solatium for the non-patrimonial loss suffered by each pursuer, and reparation for the financial costs arising from the provision made by the pursuers for the care of the children; and that the financial costs did not arise from any personal injury suffered by either pursuer. The action was predicated on the basis that apart from the alleged wrong of the defenders, the pregnancies would have been terminated and neither child would have been born. He then outlined nine main submissions, which were not in these terms. (1) The birth of a child, whether handicapped or not, is not a loss under the law of Scotland. (2) In the law of Scotland no damages are recoverable for the birth of a child because in such a case damages cannot operate as restitution. (3) Public policy should operate to exclude any claim based on a failure to terminate a pregnancy. (4) The costs associated with caring for the children are pure economic loss which was not encompassed by any duty of care on the first defenders. (5) Damages for upset and loss of amenity arising from the condition of another person are not recoverable under Scots law. (6) In any event, the claims for the financial costs of supporting the children must end when each child attains majority. (7) In any event, the claim for the expenditure on the children should be confined to the extra costs associated with each child's disability. (8) There is an element of double-counting in the averments relating to wage loss. (9) The first pursuer's claim in connection with an injury to her elbow is too remote. (10) The claim arising from the vasectomy carried out on the second pursuer is too remote …

In forming my opinion on the reasons advanced to me for dismissal of the action at this stage, there are a number of matters which I bear in mind. First, to adopt the American categorisation, this is a 'wrongful birth' case. 'Wrongful birth' and 'wrongful conception' cases appear to me to give rise to broadly similar considerations, in that they are both claims for damages allegedly suffered by persons to whom a duty of care is said to have been owed by the defenders in the provision of medical services to them, and which would not have happened but for the alleged negligence resulting in the birth or conception, as the case may be. 'Wrongful life' claims by or on behalf of children, in which it is alleged that but for the negligence of the defenders the children would not have been born, seem to me to fall into an entirely separate category. The reasons for this are clear enough, given the difficulties in the proposition that a duty of care can be owed to someone, who if reasonable care had been exercised, would never have been born; and in compensating someone for the state of non-existence of which, ex hypothesi, he has been deprived. I am not aware of any 'wrongful life' case in which damages have been awarded, and if such a case came before a Scottish court I would expect the same result as in cases such as *McKay v Essex Area Health Authority* [1982] 2 All ER 771, [1982] QB 1166: see Lord Osborne's opinion in *Millar (P's Curator Bonis) v Criminal Injuries Compensation Board* (1996) 44 BMLR 70, 1997 SLT 1180. But I do not think that any conclusions can be drawn from this for the purpose of considering 'wrongful birth' and 'wrongful conception' cases.

A further consideration is that, prima facie, the abortion of either foetus would have fallen within the scope of s 1(1) of the Abortion Act 1967 and would accordingly have been lawful. Abortion is a subject which gives rise to moral, religious and political controversy. It seems to me that, at least in the present state of the law, it is not open to a court to base its judgment, expressly or by implication, on such considerations. These are properly for Parliament to address – just as it has already addressed them in passing the 1967 Act – if and when the topic of abortion next comes before it. In the meantime, as I see it, the only proper course for me is to take this aspect of the law as I find it, and to approach this case on the basis that the course of action desiderated by the pursuers would have been lawful, and expressly to disregard any other consideration. If it be thought that the pursuit of such a lawful course of action results in consequences which are objectionable to the extent that the relative statute ought to be amended or its operation restricted so as to exclude claims such as the present, then that likewise is a matter for Parliament. In saying this, I am entirely in agreement with the views expressed in the passage I have quoted from the speech of Lord Scarman in *McLoughlin v O'Brian* [1982] 2 All ER 298 at 310, [1983] 1 AC 410 at 430, particularly when he said that the court's function is to adjudicate according to principle, leaving policy curtailment to the judgment of Parliament. I recognise that there are well-established legal rules which derive their authority from public policy considerations, and which may be regarded as embodying principles; but I think that courts, and particularly judges at first instance, should be on their guard against the formulation of 'principles' which are said to be based on public policy considerations, but are truly no more than individual a priori value judgments.

I take as my starting-point the well-established principles derived from Lord Atkin's discussion in *Donoghue (or McAlister) v Stevenson* [1932] AC 562, 1932 SC (HL) 31 as to the circumstances which give rise to a duty of care. It is not in dispute that duty of care may be owed to their patients by persons such as the present defenders in the provision of medical services. Although it is only averred that the first pursuer's vasectomy came to be discussed and performed, I have no difficulty in accepting the idea that a duty of care was owed as much to him as to her by the defenders in the provision of the services referred to on record. They were at all material times a married couple, each of whom would be directly affected by the provision of, or the failure to provide, services relating to pregnancy, childbirth, abortion and contraception. Obviously, the first pursuer would be the one who directly underwent such processes, apart from the second pursuer's vasectomy. But at least to the extent that it could reasonably be expected that the second pursuer would be involved to a significant degree, both physically and financially, in the care and upbringing of any child, I can see no reason why in the provision of services, particularly those associated with the taking of decisions between abortion and childbirth, the defenders should not be regarded as having owed a duty of care as much to the second pursuer as to the first. According to the pursuers' averments, enough information was provided to the defenders at various times to have led, if reasonable care had been exercised by them, to the provision of genetic counselling, which in turn would have resulted in the abortion of each of the two foetuses rather than the birth of the two boys. Such a course of action would, as I have said, have been lawful in terms of the Abortion Act 1967. While a number of policy considerations may have underlain the Act, it may be taken from its terms that one of them is the prevention of the birth of children suffering from such physical and mental abnormalities as to be seriously handicapped. (It is because the terminology of the Act that in the submissions of counsel and in this opinion expressions such as 'handicapped children' are used.) While the Act does not expressly say so, it may, I think, be taken from it provisions that the birth of a child so handicapped may be regarded as a harmful event for those immediately affected by his existence, who would in the ordinary course be his parents. This being so, I can see no reason why the course of action desiderated by the pursuers, which according to them would have resulted in the abortion of two foetuses, should not be regarded as having as its purpose, inter alia, the prevention of events harmful to the pursuers which were or ought to have been within the contemplation of the defenders and which, if they had exercised reasonable care, would not have happened.

While I was addressed at length on behalf of the defenders on the proposition that the consequences to his parents of the birth of a handicapped child were to be regarded as 'pure economic loss', I am unable to accept this. It is sufficient to refer to the pursuers' pleadings which set out in some detail the direct adverse impact on each of them of the births of the boys, which have produced what I would regard as a complex of consequences, very different from pure economic loss. I can see no good reason not to treat the pursuers, if their averments are proved, as having suffered personal injuries in the conventional sense, in respect of which damages would be awarded under the usual heads of solatium and patrimonial loss. I agree, in this regard, with the Court of Appeal's analysis in *Walkin v South Manchester Health Authority* (1995) 25 BMLR 108, [1995] 1 WLR 1543. In any event, if the financial consequences of the boys' births are to be regarded as pure economic loss, I can see no good reason why, in the above circumstances, the *Caparo* tests should not be regarded as satisfied. I need say no more about the tests of reasonable foreseeability and proximity, and in so far as the losses are said to be the direct result of events which the services provided by the defenders would, on the pursuers' averments, have prevented had reasonable care been exercised, I can see no good reason why it should not be regarded as fair, just and reasonable that the defenders should be made to compensate the pursuers for those losses.

This brings me to the question whether I am bound to proceed on the basis at this stage that the pursuers have suffered no loss of which they are entitled to compensation. I take as my starting point the principle that can be derived from *Livingstone v Rawyards Coal Co*, and many other cases, that the purpose of compensation is to put a pursuer, so far as money can do so, in the position in which he or she would probably have been but for the alleged negligence. This involves comparing what has in fact happened with what would probably have happened if there had been no negligence, and attempting to put a money figure on the difference in a way which does justice to both parties. I do not think that 'value' is a concept which affords any assistance in this exercise. An award to parents for the loss of a child is not arrived at by asking for what price they would have sold the child, and in my view the same applies to the converse situation. The birth and upbringing of a child no doubt bring both advantages and disadvantages, both happiness and distress: and most people most of the time would regard the former as outweighing the latter. But it seems to me to be a question of fact and degree in the circumstances of any particular case where the balance rests. It may be regarded as being within the range of reasonable responses to the birth of a child that in one case his parents may accept it as an unmixed blessing, or at least as an event which on the whole is to be welcomed, while in another it is seen as nothing less than an unmitigated disaster. These are necessarily subjective reactions, so the fact that one set of parents reacts to a birth in a way in which others might not should not be determinative either way of an entitlement to damages. This is essentially a jury question, and I can identify no reason in principle for excluding from the range of options open to a jury an award of damages arising from the birth of a child if the parents have in fact suffered what may be regarded as adverse consequences. The emphasis in a case of this kind is on what the parents have suffered overall, after account is taken of the whole impact on them of the birth of a handicapped child, which in many cases will include pleasure in the child and satisfaction in the care they are able to provide. Their distress may be tempered by these factors. This observation applies to healthy as much as to handicapped children, though in the latter case it is perhaps easier to identify loss where, as here, the claim is related to the additional burden, both emotional and financial, of caring for a handicapped child whose birth could have been prevented. I do not think that there is any justification for, in effect, imposing on parents who claim to be able to prove that they have, on balance, suffered adverse consequences as the result of the birth of a child, a value-judgment that the 'value' of the child must always outweigh these consequences in the assessment of compensation, or indeed that the concept of 'value' has any part to play in the assessment of compensation. To do so appears to me to amount to little more than an assertion, without legal foundation, that they are morally wrong to feel as they do.

While my views are supported to some extent by decisions of the American courts, I have not been strongly influenced by these decisions, because I do not know the whole range of factors of which a judge in any particular state feels entitled to take account, and how much scope may be permitted for the making by an elected judge of a decision based on personal opinions. In England, the case of *Emeh v Kensington and Chelsea and Westminster Area Health Authority* [1984] 3 All ER 1044, [1985] QB 1012 follows principles which are common to both England and Scotland, and although the decision for the Court of Appeal in that case is not of course binding on me, I find it highly persuasive. I agree with the views expressed by Lord Cameron in *Allan v Greater Glasgow Health Board* (1993) 17 BMLR 135, 1998 SLT 580 to the effect that *Emeh*'s case incorporates principles which can be found in the Scots law of delict, and I have no hesitation in following his approach in treating a claim of this kind as being governed by straightforward principles. And I regret that I must therefore disagree with Lord Gill's decision in *McFarlane v Tayside Health Board* 1997 SLT 211 for the reasons given above. In my opinion no sound argument has been advanced for dismissal of the action at this stage, and the appropriate course is to allow a proof before answer.

I can deal quite briefly with the subordinate submissions expressed to me about various aspects of the damages claimed. As I have said, it appears to me that the pursuers are claiming damages for a complex of consequences arising from the birth of the boys, in respect of which awards may be made under the heads of solatium and patrimonial loss. The claim for solatium arises from all the non-patrimonial harm they say they have suffered, of which there are a number of aspects.

Dealing first with the question of patrimonial loss, the pursuers have disclaimed any intention of claiming for more than the additional costs associated with the children's disabilities, and during the course of the debate it came to be accepted that their pleadings are confined to a claim for additional costs. These additional costs include the costs of providing for the care of the children by others. As I understand it, the pursuers claim that the extent of the children's disabilities is likely to be such as to require the provision of care by the pursuers themselves and by persons employed for that purpose. In my view, the correct test in considering future care costs is whether what is proposed is reasonable, and, if so, whether the relative expense is likely to be incurred. I do not think that the existing resources of the pursuers should operate as a limiting factor any more in this case than in the case of a seriously injured pursuer who is likely to require to pay for the provision of care in the future. Nor do I think that care costs should be limited by reference to the pursuers' obligation to aliment their children or by the cessation of that obligation if and when each of them attains the age of maturity. The claim for care costs arises, as I see it, from the natural bond between parent and child, an aspect of which is the parents' desire to care for the child. Subject to questions of the reasonableness of the consequent expenditure, which must depend on the circumstances, I can see no reason at this stage to suppose that it was not within the parties' contemplation that if the children were born suffering from disabilities the natural response of the pursuers would be to make reasonable provision for their care throughout the children's lives. Given the explanation that the averment relating to the injury to the first pursuer's elbow is intended to do no more than act as an illustration of the physical difficulties of providing care for the children and the consequent need to obtain assistance, I regard this averment as sufficiently relevant for proof. Likewise, the averment relating to the second pursuer's vasectomy is not, I was told, intended to do more than constitute an aspect of the distress suffered by the pursuers in contemplating a future in which, according to them, but for the negligence of the defenders, they would have attempted to have normal, healthy children. This again appears to me to be sufficiently relevant for proof.

Notice that the judge held that both parents were owed a duty of care.

The courts' analysis in *Harbeson* and *Anderson* raises the traditional issues found in any negligence action: duty, breach, causation, harm and damages. As we saw, each of these requires special consideration where what is complained of is the birth of a child. Much of the analysis required in respect of the action for 'wrongful birth' is the same as that for actions for 'wrongful conception', which we saw earlier: in particular, arguments concerning 'duty', 'the nature of the harm' suffered and 'causation'. Here, of course, we are concerned with the birth of a *disabled* child and, therefore, the public policy arguments raised in cases such as *Udale*, *Thake* and *Emeh*, pose no obstacle to the recovery of damages as the judge made plain in *Anderson*.

There are, however, a number of points that we should advert to. *First*, you will notice that the court in *Harbeson* did not allow the parents to recover the costs of raising a normal healthy child but only those associated with its disability, ie the extraordinary financial costs and the parents' 'mental anguish and emotional stress'. In England, the courts could allow *all* the reasonable foreseeable costs of raising the child. The judge in *Anderson* was only asked to award the extra costs. Unlike the situation we considered under 'wrongful conception' actions, the negligence here will be directly related to the child's disability – that will be why the genetic advice was sought or the abortion carried out. Thus, the doctor will have the child's disability within his contemplation (for a contrary decision after *McFarlane*, see *Rand v East Dorset HA* [2000] Lloyd's Rep Med 181 (Newman J) – only costs related to disability recoverable).

Notice also that in *Anderson* these damages were not restricted to the minority of the child. It would be reasonable to expect the parents to care for a disabled child into adulthood (see also, *Nunnerley v Warrington HA* [2000] Lloyd's Rep Med 170 (Morrison J) – costs of care of child into adulthood recoverable).

Further, the mother's claim for the latter would be consequential on her physical injury. Upon what basis could the father claim damages for psychiatric or emotional injury? Since he suffers no physical injury, his action can only succeed if he falls within the 'secondary victim' rules in the *McLoughlin/Alcock* cases. As such, his claim would be restricted to psychiatric injury caused by the shock of discovery by witnessing the disabled condition of his child. Damages for the 'wear and tear' of bringing up such a child could not be recovered (contrast, however, *McLelland v Greater Glasgow Health Board* (1998) Times, 14 October.

Secondly, albeit in unusual circumstances, an English court would refuse to allow a claim for the ordinary costs of rearing the disabled child which would be incurred by any parent if it could be established that the parents would, in any event, have gone on to have a further healthy child (see *Salih v Enfield HA*[1991] 3 All ER 400 (CA) but contrast *McLelland v Greater Glasgow Health Board* (1998) Times, 14 October).

Thirdly, we have already seen when considering claims arising from 'wrongful conception', that the Court of Appeal in *Emeh* was asked to consider the argument that the mother faced with the knowledge of her pregnancy ought to have had an abortion. We saw that the court gave this argument short shrift. In a 'wrongful birth' claim where the negligence occurs before conception (eg during genetic counselling) the argument could be made that if the child's disability is subsequently discovered during the mother's pregnancy she ought to have an abortion. The argument has more force to it here. If there is a 'substantial risk that if the child were born it would suffer from such physical or mental abnormalities as to be seriously handicapped', then an abortion would be available under s 1(1)(d) of the Abortion Act 1967 throughout the duration of the pregnancy. It is unlikely, however, that the court even in these circumstances would impose, what is in effect, an obligation to undergo an abortion. To do so would impose upon the mother the unenviable 'choice' of bearing the burden of paying for the child's upkeep or undergoing an abortion.

Chapter 13

Products liability

Background

The area of products liability is a large and specialised one. The reader is referred to a number of specialist books: Miller and Lovell *Products Liability and Safety Encyclopaedia* (1979); Stapleton *Product Liability* (1994); C Hodges (ed) *Products Liability – European Laws and Practice* (1993). Our concern here is with products liability in the provision of medical services. When may patients claim damages for injuries caused by a dangerous product? As we shall see, there are a number of possibilities: in *contract* for breach of warranty, in *negligence* for an unreasonably unsafe product, or under the *Consumer Protection Act 1987* for a 'defective' product.

Not all of these claims will be available in a particular situation. As we shall see, actions in contract will not arise within the NHS but may when the product is supplied in private health care or if, unusually, payment is made within the NHS.

What, then, are we talking about when we say 'products' in the context of medical services? There are really *two* types of product that need to be considered: *medicinal products* (drugs) and *medical devices*. The nature of the former is obvious. The latter, however, may not be but is an ever increasing category, including, for example, prostheses, contact lens, pacemakers, heart valves and wheelchairs. As these few examples show, some devices may be supplied and implanted into the patient's body others may function as external diagnostic monitoring or support aids.

By and large, the liability issues in relation to these two types of product are in principle the same. The control or regulation of them, by contrast, is not. The manufacture, sale and provision of medicinal products has been regulated by a licensing system since the 1960s (Medicines Act 1968). For medical devices, however, formal regulation occurred first in 1993 and then only to a limited extent (see Active Implantable Medical Devices Regulations 1992 (SI 1992 No 3146) as amended). Wider regulation, as we shall see, was introduced in 1995 (see Medical Devices Regulations 1994 (SI 1994 No 3017)). We will return briefly to the licensing schemes shortly.

Compensation claims for dangerous products are not new but have begun to feature more prominently in recent years. Many of these actions have thrown up difficulties and highlighted limitations in court procedures because of the number of claimants that may sue. Products have, of course, the potential to have a widespread effect injuring many individuals. The so-called 'mass tort' cases in England have led to 'creative' procedural devices involving 'test cases' and 'lead representative' actions and other ingenious procedural devices because English law does not permit 'class actions' (for a discussion, see K Oliphant 'Innovations in Procedure and Practice in Multi-Party Medical Cases' in A Grubb (ed) *Choices and Decisions in Health Care* (1993) pp 183–203; see also P Ferguson *Drug Injuries and the Pursuit of Compensation* (1996), ch 10). Pamela Ferguson provides a description.

Pamela R Ferguson *Drug Injuries and the Pursuit of Compensation* (1996)

2. Infamous Products
Some pharmaceutical products which have been marketed in Britain and/or in the United States of America have become notorious. These include thalidomide, Diethylstilbestrol (DES), intrauterine devices such as the Dalkon Shield, and certain vaccines.

(A) THALIDOMIDE
Thalidomide, which led to "the greatest drug tragedy of our time" ('*The Thalidomide Children and the Law*' Report by the Sunday Times (London, Andre Deutsch, 1973) Preface p 7), was discovered in 1953 by Ciba, a West German pharmaceutical company. Preliminary animal tests indicated that the drug had little pharmacological effect, so the company did not continue with its development. Thereafter, Chemie Gruenenthal, also a German company, marketed the drug as a sedative and allowed other companies to produce and sell thalidomide using their own brand names. It has been estimated that over one million people in West Germany took this sedative per day. The first report of suspected damage to the foetus was published in that country in 1961. The most notorious of the injuries caused by thalidomide are "phocomely" and "amely" (incomplete development, and absence of the limbs). A study conducted in the 1940s had found one case of shortened or missing limbs in four million births. During the 1960s thalidomide had been taken by so many women that virtually every paediatric clinic in Germany had at least one child born in this way (Teff and Munro '*Thalidomide: The Legal Aftermath*' (Farnborough, Hants, Saxon House, 1976) p 5); in Hamburg alone there were 50 phocomelia births in one year.

Thalidomide was marketed in Britain by Distillers Co. (Biochemicals) Ltd as a treatment for morning-sickness. Distillers advertised the drug as one which could "be given with complete safety to pregnant women and nursing mothers without adverse effect on mother or child" (Dworkin, '*Pearson: Implications for Severely-Handicapped Children and Products Liability*', Part V, Chap 3, in Allen, Bourne and Holyoak, '*Accident Compensation after Pearson*' (1979)). In December 1961 a British doctor wrote to *The Lancet*, noting that there appeared to be an increasing number of limb malformations in children whose mothers had been taking thalidomide during pregnancy (McBride, '*Thalidomide and Congenital Abnormalities*' (1961) The Lancet, p 1358).

Of the 430 British children who were injured by thalidomide, 62 of them attempted to sue Distillers. An out of court settlement was reached in 1968 but a second legal action was started in 1971. This resulted in a lump sum of £3.5 million being offered to all the claimants by the company. Public pressure forced Distillers to increase this, ultimately to £20 million. Most of this money was placed in a trust fund. It is expected that this fund will be exhausted within the next 15 years and the thalidomide victims, many of whom now have their own families, have recently succeeded in persuading Guinness, Distiller's successor company, to provide more compensation.

(B) DIETHYLSTILBESTROL (DES)
Described as "America's Thalidomide", Diethylstilbestrol is a synthetically produced oestrogen which was first synthesised in Britain in 1937 ((1981) BMJ 282 p 1536). In 1947 the American Food and Drug Administration (FDA) licensed the drug for the prevention of early miscarriage. It seems, however, that DES may actually have *increased* the likelihood of complications in pregnancy. It was also responsible for causing a rare form of vaginal and cervical cancer in the daughters of women who took the drug during pregnancy. It is suspected of having increased the incidence of genital tract abnormalities in the male off-spring of these women, and to be responsible for an increased risk of breast cancer in the women themselves.

Three to four million women in the United States of America ingested DES and between 20,000 and 100,000 babies were exposed to the effects of this drug each year for 20 years. It has also been taken by about 8,000 British women and a DES Action Group has been established to co-ordinate their claims for compensation.

It is normally essential for a plaintiff in a product liability suit to establish that the defendant was the manufacturer responsible for producing the drug which is alleged to have caused injury. When DES was first synthesised in 1937 no patent was applied for and as a result more than 300 companies have produced this drug. It has therefore been very difficult for a plaintiff to establish that the DES which was prescribed to her mother 15 to 20 years previously was manufactured by a particular pharmaceutical company. Legal Aid was granted in England to allow this to be investigated. Unfortunately, many of the doctors who prescribed the drug have since died and their records and those of pharmacists and drug companies have been lost or destroyed.

(C) INTRAUTERINE DEVICES
About 7 per cent of British women currently use intrauterine contraceptive devices. This has however been a prominent area of product liability, particularly in the United States.

i. The Dalkon Shield. The Dalkon Shield became one of the most litigated products in pharmaceutical history; it was described as "a deadly depth charge in [women's] wombs, ready to explode at any time" (per Judge Miles Lord; see Mintz, '*At Any Cost: Corporate Greed, Women and the Dalkon Shield*' (N.Y. 1985). It was manufactured in America by A H Robins Co, which began selling the Shield in 1971 and continued doing so until the mid 1970s. Within that time 4.5 million Shields had been inserted in American women and the device had been marketed in 80 countries. It has been estimated that about one in 20 women became pregnant while using this contraceptive device. The Shield is alleged to have caused pelvic inflammatory disease (an infection which damages the reproductive capacity of many women), and to have caused spontaneous miscarriages and ectopic pregnancies in others.

Robins suspended sales of this IUD on June 28, 1974 after the American Food and Drug Administration expressed concern over the incidence of spontaneous septic abortions in Shield users. The Shield caused 200 such miscarriages within its first four years on the market. By 1985 Robins had paid out about $368 million in compensation and it was calculated that it would require to pay out more than $1 billion to meet future liabilities. The company declared bankruptcy in 1986, by which time it had paid out $21 million in legal expenses (for litigation associated with the device see *In re A H Robins Co*, 406 F Supp 650; 419 F Supp 710 (1976), 438 F Supp 942 (1977); 453 F Supp 108 (1978, 505 F Supp 211 (1981); 570 F Supp 1480 (1983). Judge Miles W. Lord charged the Robins executives that:

> [N]one of you has faced up to the fact that more than nine thousand women have made claims that they gave up part of their womanhood so that your company might prosper. It is alleged that others gave their lives so you might so prosper. And there stands behind them legions more who have been injured but who have not sought relief in the courts of this land ... The only conceivable reasons you have not recalled this product are that it would hurt your balance sheet and alert women who already have been harmed that you may be liable for their injuries. (See Mintz, op. cit pp 265–267)

In Britain almost 9,000 women have attempted to claim compensation from the Robins Company. Although Robins had set up a trust fund of £1.5 billion it had offered some women as little as £440.

ii. Other IUDs. The Dalkon Shield is not the only intrauterine device to have been associated with serious side effects. In 1985 an American woman who required to have a hysterectomy as a result of using the Lippes Loop IUD was awarded $563,000. (*Beyette v. Ortho Pharmaceuticals Corporation Case* No. 82-71670 E D Mich 1985) The Coper-7 IUD also came under attack and has now been withdrawn from the market by GD Searle, its manufacturers. It has been suggested that this IUD was targeted at a less than suitable market (young, nulliparous women) and that the information leaflets provided to doctors failed to describe the risks of infection in an appropriate manner. Pretl and Osborne have stated:

> Although in the estimation of many gynaecologists, the IUD when properly used and monitored may be the contraceptive of logical choice for many women, the industry's mishandling of testing and marketing has prompted litigation as a result of which virtually no market exists in the United States today for any IUD. (Pretl and Osborne, "*Trends in US Drug Product Liability – the Plaintiff's Perspective*" Chap 9 in Howells ed, '*Product Liability, Insurance and the Pharmaceutical Industry*')

(D) VACCINES
Although there are no compulsory vaccination programmes in Britain, the Department of Health does recommend that children be immunised against diphtheria, tetanus, poliomyelitis, tuberculosis, measles and whooping cough (pertussis), and that female children be vaccinated against rubella. In 1963 the government established a Joint Committee on Vaccination and Immunisation to advise the Health Ministers of any medical aspects of these immunisation procedures. Critics of childhood immunisation programmes have argued that a rise in childhood asthma and allergies could be due to the fact that vaccinations cause a lower general immunity. Some doctors have also suggested that the natural immunity achieved from actually catching the disease is greater than that attained from immunisation.

Whooping cough is a common infection of the respiratory tract. It can cause breathing difficulties in children, as well as complications such as pneumonia and bronchitis. Convulsions leading to a loss of consciousness and, in rare cases, epilepsy or permanent brain damage, have also been associated with pertussis. Children who are not immunised run a risk of contracting whooping cough which is greater than one in six.

Many parents came to believe that the pertussis vaccine could itself cause similar, serious side effects, and the Association of Parents of Vaccine Damaged Children (APVDC) was formed in the early 1970s. Many members of the medical profession were also of this opinion. Following the first allegations that the whooping cough vaccine could induce brain damage, immunisation rates fell by one third. These rates have since increased to 73 per cent but this means that more than one in five British children are still not being immunised.

Pertussis is not the only vaccine which has been linked to iatrogenic injury. The immunisation against rubella can cause arthritis in between 9 and 14 per cent of females. (See "*Joint Problems and MMR vaccination*" Medical Monitor May 8, 1992, p 34.) The safety of the vaccine used to protect children from measles has also been questioned; paralysis and seizures have been alleged to have resulted from this vaccine and this vaccine has been linked to the development of inflammatory bowel diseases, including Crohn's disease. Two vaccines (Pluserix-MMR and Immravax) were withdrawn by the government in September 1992 after it was found that they could cause meningitis.

Concerns over vaccine injury led the Pearson Commission to recommend a system of State compensation for vaccine induced injury in children, (see Chaps 25–27 of the Pearson Report '*Royal Commission on Civil Liability and Compensation for Personal Injury*' (mnd. 7054, 1978) which in turn led to the Vaccine Damage Payments Act 1979.

JABS (Justice, Awareness and Basic Support) is a self-help group which continues to campaign for compensation for persons injured by vaccinations. More than 450 families have contacted the group.

3. Recent Drug Litigation

(A) THE BENZODIAZEPINES

The benzodiazepines are a group of chemically related hypnotics, sedatives, anxiolytics (anxiety reducing drugs) and anticonvulsants. At one time benzodiazepines were among the top five drugs prescribed in most Western countries and 16 million NHS prescriptions were issued for this group of drugs in Britain in 1992, at a cost of £14 million. (Sweeney, "*Should you be on Drugs?*" The Times, March 29, 1994) According to Parish:

> Throughout the seventies and into the eighties millions of prescriptions for benzodiazepine tablets and capsules were issued to patients. Some doctors applied little or no control over their supply, and many patients were kept on benzodiazepine anti-anxiety drugs for years on end, often for a disorder that did not need treating with such drugs in the first place. Unfortunately, some of these patients became dependent on their benzodiazepines. (Parish, '*Medical Treatments: The Benefits and Risks*' (London, Penguin Books, 1991) p 607.)

One person in six can become addicted to these tranquillisers after taking a normal dose for six months, and one person in three may be addicted after a year. According to the Council for Involuntary Tranquilliser Addition (CITA) there are about three million people in Britain who are addicted to sleeping pills and tranquillisers, some of whom may have been taking their medication for 30 years. It is ironic that the benzodiazepines were introduced as a safer alternative when the addictive nature of barbiturates was discovered.

In 1988 several hundred patients began to attempt to obtain compensation from the manufacturers of these tranquillisers, claiming that the latter had not warned the medical profession of the dangers of addition. It was also alleged that some doctors had not passed on to their patients those warnings which were provided. Among the benzodiazepine group of drugs particular attention was focused on Ativan, Valium, Librium and Hancion.

i. Ativan (lorazepam). Ativan is one of the best known benzodiazepines. Wyeth Laboratories, its manufacturer, faced suit by hundreds of persons who had become addicted to that drug. They alleged, *inter alia*, that the manufacturer ought to have warned doctors that this tranquilliser should only be prescribed for a limited duration. In July 1990 the Scottish Legal Aid Board approved applications for Legal Aid in six cases and in April 1991 a test case was started and 2,000,000 pages of documents from Wyeth were recovered by the pursuer. (*McInally v John Wyeth Ltd* 1992 SLT 344.) This case was listed to await the outcome of similar claims in England. One million people are still regularly taking Ativan, although it is now prescribed only in "exceptional" circumstances and for short periods.

ii. Librium (chlordiazepoxide) and Valium (diazepam). Most of the people who are now in a position of dependence on these drugs will have been first prescribed them many years ago.

Librium came on the market in 1960 and Valium in 1963. Valium is among the 20 best selling drugs in the world. More than 1,000 people formed a co-ordinated action committee to sue the manufacturers of these drugs.

iii. Halcion (triazolam). Dr Graham Dukes, formerly a doctor with the World Health Organisation, has called the Halcion affair "one of the worldwide drug scandals of the century". This tranquilliser was alleged to cause dramatic mood changes and violent behaviour. It was manufactured by Upjohn Company and was its second best-selling drug, with annual sales of about £143 million. In the United States Mrs Ilo Grundberg succeeded in obtaining damages from Upjohn (*Grundberg v Upjohn Co* (CD Utah, 1991) B7 FRD 372). She had been charged with the murder of her 83 year old mother but the charges were withdrawn after a Utah court accepted evidence from two psychiatrists who testified that Mrs Grundberg had been "involuntarily intoxicated" due to her consumption of Halcion at the time of the killing. She then sued the company for causing her to kill her mother. The civil case settled out of court and the amount of damages remains undisclosed, but it has been suggested that the figure could be $6–8 million. In May 1992 the FDA concluded its investigation into Halcion's safety. It decided not to ban the drug but ordered Upjohn to provide stronger warning information to patients as to its potential side effects.

There were 402 reports of adverse reactions to Halcion made to the British Committee on Safety of Medicines between 1978 and 1991 and the Department of Health finally decided to ban this drug in October 1991. It has been estimated that 600,000 people were using Halcion at the time of its banning, and that in excess of two million prescriptions were written for it in 1989. Upjohn has been informed by the licensing authority that its revocation of Halcion's licence is permanent.

The only personal injury suits which are now proceeding against Wyeth, Roche and Upjohn in relation to Ativan, Valium and Halcion, respectively, are being privately funded, since Legal Aid has been withdrawn in respect of all three actions.

(B) HUMAN INSULIN

More than 400 diabetics considered taking legal action on the basis of the alleged side effects of some human insulins, such as Humulin. The Law Societies of England and Scotland both established action groups to co-ordinate their claims (McKeone, *"Plaintiffs proliferate in insulin action"* (1991) LSG 88: 31 p 7). The change from animal to human insulin was alleged to have caused severe adverse reactions including sudden blackouts. More than 80 per cent of Britain's 200,000 insulin takers had been prescribed human insulin in preference to animal insulin (McKeone, *"Solicitors prepare for lengthy battle on human insulin"* (1991) LSG 88: 29 p 4). The British Diabetic Association distributed a questionnaire to patients, asking whether they had been adversely affected by the change in insulin. About half of all respondents felt that their condition had deteriorated on human insulin (Pickup, *"Human insulin"* (1989) BMJ, 299 p 991).

Many doctors switched their patients from animal to human insulin because of rumours that the former type of insulin might not be available for very much longer. Insulin manufacturers have now given assurances that they will continue to make beef and porcine insulin. The lack of warning of hypoglycaemia was not the only side effect which was alleged for human insulin; some diabetics claimed that it caused them to develop multiple sclerosis. It was also suggested that the use of human insulin caused an increase in the number of deaths in young diabetics. (Gale, *"Hypoglycaemia and human insulin"* (1989) The Lancet, p 1264.) It was claimed that the manufacturer's own scientists knew that there could be problems with Humulin:

> It acted faster to reduce blood sugar and the symptoms it produced were so different that patients might not realise their blood sugar was getting dangerously low. (*"Synthetic Insulin Scare"* Channel 4 news, Oct 11, 1989, per Andrew Veitch (transcript).)

A study by Teuscher and Berger had supported this (*"Hypoglycaemia unawareness in diabetics transferred from beef/porcine to human insulin"* (1987) The Lancet, ii p 382), but their findings have been accused of "bias in patient selection" and therefore "inconclusive" (Hepburn and Frier '*Hypoglycaemic unawareness and human insulin*" (1989) The Lancet, p 1394). More recently, a study of patients who had previously reported loss of awareness with human insulin concluded that " ... the use of human insulin carries no specific risk of altered awareness of hypoglycaemia." (Patrick, Bodner et al *"Human insulin and awareness of acute hypoglycaemic symptoms in insulin-dependent diabetes"* (1991) The Lancet, p 528 at p 531.) The steering committees in both England and Scotland were unable to find medical experts willing to support these claims (many doctors who specialise in diabetes had been hired as potential expert witnesses by the drug companies), and have now been disbanded.

(c) MYODIL

Manufactured by Glaxo, Myodil was a yellow dye which was injected into the spinal cavity prior to X-ray. It was alleged to have caused arachnoiditis – inflammation of the membranes covering the nerve roots within the spinal cord. There is no known cure for this condition. Myodil had been used in Britain since 1944 despite the fact that a large number of medical papers had been published from the 1950s onwards, linking its use to the later development of arachnoiditis. It was withdrawn in Sweden in the 1950s following the publication of these papers but remained in use in Britain until voluntarily withdrawn by Glaxo in 1987. Safer dyes have been available since 1977.

It had been estimated that the risk to a patient of developing arachnoiditis following a Myodil X-ray was 2 or 3 per cent. Such a risk might be thought to be acceptable since few medical procedures are entirely risk free. It must be remembered, however, that Myodil was only a diagnostic tool; in itself, it did not alleviate the back pain of patients on whom it was used. In fact, it has transpired that some of the people who were injected with this dye had nothing wrong with their backs. More than 3,600 patients alleged that the company was negligent in its testing of the dye and that it continued to manufacture Myodil when it became aware, of after it *ought* to have become aware, of the risks the dye posed. The Myodil cases were settled by Glaxo on July 31, 1995 for an *ex gratia* payment of £7 million; the company has not accepted liability.

(d) OPREN (BENOXAPROFEN)

Opren was a non-steroidal anti-inflammatory drug (NSAID) used in the treatment of arthritis. When first promoted by its Swiss manufacturer, Eli Lilly, Opren was hailed as a "wonder drug" and soon the British Health Service was spending £9 million each year on this one drug. The first benoxaprofen death was reported in the *British Medical Journal* in January 1982. In the following month its manufacturer received two reports of fatal cholestatic jaundice and by August of that year 10 more fatalities had been noted in the medical literature. The drug proved to be particularly lethal to the elderly and 61 people died before the British CSM suspended the drug's licence. 3,500 side effects were reported in total and some of Opren's non-fatal adverse effects, such as phototoxicity, (an acute and painful sensitivity to sunlight) were unique to that drug. It was marketed in the United States at Oraflex in April 1982 but was withdrawn within four months due to the British fatalities. It has now been withdrawn worldwide by the company.

In December 1987 many of the British plaintiffs agreed to accept an out-of-court settlement with Eli Lilly in which claimants would receive a share of £2.275 million. The maximum amount any individual will have received under this scheme is likely to have been between £7,000 and £8,000. The average claimant will have received only £2,000 or £3,000. This is in contrast to the situation in the United States of America, where one plaintiff alone was awarded $6 million against the company (*Borom v Eli Lilly and Co* (1983) reported in Patterson, ed. *'Drugs in Litigation: Damage Awards Involving Prescription and Nonprescription Drugs'* (Virginia, The Michie Company, 1992) p 49).

(e) ORAL CONTRACEPTIVES

Several women who allege that they have been injured by oral contraceptives are contemplating suing the manufacturers of these products. The women have suffered from pulmonary embolisms, which is a recognised risk of the Pill. They are claiming that the manufacturers ought to have provided clearer warnings of these risks (see, Aitkenhead, "*A hard pill to swallow*" The Independent, May 1, 1995 pg 21). Concern has also arisen over the increased risk of thrombosis associated with certain makes of the Pill, known as "mini Pills" (Laurence "*Doctors urge women on 'unsafe' Pill not to panic*" The Times, Oct 20, 1995).

To this list could be added the litigation by patients who contracted HIV or haemophilia from blood or blood products (see eg *Re HIV Litigation* (1990) 41 BMLR 171 (CA)) and by those who contracted new variant Creutzfeldt-Jakob Disease (n-CJD) from human growth hormone (see eg *N v Medical Research Council* [1996] 7 Med LR 309 and *The Creutzfeldt-Jakob Disease Litigation* (1997) 41 BMLR 157 (Morland J)).

Regulation

Before we turn to consider in detail the liability issues, we should look briefly at the regulatory schemes for medicinal products and medical devices. The two systems are different, as we shall see. However, each has at its centre a national 'competent authority' as regulator. For medicinal products this is the 'Medicines Controls Agency' and for medical devices it is the 'Medical Devices Agency'. Both act on behalf of the relevant Government Ministers upon whom the responsibility is placed by the legislation.

A. MEDICINAL PRODUCTS

The regulation covers manufacture (including research and testing), marketing and sales. Here we consider primarily the regulation of manufacturers of medicinal products, in practice this usually means pharmaceuticals. The supply (including prescription), sale and administration of pharmaceuticals is also regulated by the Medicines Act 1968 and the large numbers of statutory instruments made under it. Hence some drugs are generally available for purchase – 'over-the-counter' (OTC) drugs, others are only available through a pharmacist – 'pharmacy medicines', others are only available by prescription – 'prescription only medicines' (POMs). Likewise, who may prescribe drugs is restricted usually to doctors but midwives and nurses may do so in some circumstances (The Medicinal Products: Prescription by Nurses etc Act 1992). The detail of this regulation is not covered here (see *Review of Prescribing, Supply and Administration of Medicines* (DOH), March 1999). A brief overview is offered by Jonathan Montgomery.

Jonathan Montgomery *Health Care Law* (1997)

The legislation introduces a number of provisions aimed to ensure that medicines are used safely and for licit purposes. The UKCC has usefully categorized four stages in the therapeutic use of medicines; prescription, dispensation, administration, and patient acceptance (United Kingdom Central Council for Nursing, Midwifery and Health Visiting, '*Administration of Medicines*' (London: UKCC, 1986)). The last is primarily regulated by the law of consent. Administration is generally regulated by malpractice law. Certain controlled drugs may only be administered by or under the direction of medical and dental practitioners (Misuse of Drugs Regulations 1985, SI 1985 No 2066, r 7), but the actual administration is not restricted to professionals. The dispensation stage covers the process by which drugs are released for use, ceasing to be subject to any storage requirements that applied (depending on the class of drug in question). This section explains the way in which drugs are classified, and the significance of the different classifications.

Drugs are divided into a number of categories. Under the Medicines Act 1968, there is a threefold distinction into (a) prescription-only medicines, (b) medicines that can only be supplied by a pharmacist (but which can be dispensed without a prescription), and (c) general-list medicines (which need not be obtained through a pharmacist). The Misuse of Drugs Act 1971, which is primarily concerned with the control of illicit drug use, creates three categories of controlled drugs, known as classes A, B, and C. More importantly for the health context, controlled drugs are further classified by the Misuse of Drugs Regulations 1985, which places them into one of five schedules (Ibid.). Schedule 1 drugs are not used for medicinal purposes. Schedule 2 drugs include opiates and major stimulants, such as amphetamines. Schedule 3 drugs include most barbiturates, and some minor stimulants. Schedule 4 contains benzodiazepine tranquillizers. Schedule 5 contains preparations of controlled drugs where there is minimal risk of abuse.

Drugs from Schedules 2 and 3 can only be dispensed on prescription. To be valid, a prescription has to be written in ink, or some other indelible material, dated, and signed by the prescriber (Medicines (Products other than Veterinary Drugs) (Prescription Only) Order 1983, SI 1983 No 1212, as amended). The name and address of the person for whom it is prescribed must be set out, together with the dosage to be taken. If the patient is under 12 years of age, his or her age must also be recorded. Where a controlled drug is prescribed, the prescription must be handwritten personally by the prescriber (otherwise it may be written by means of carbon paper). Where a drug from Schedules 1 to 3 of the Misuse of Drugs Regulations 1985 is prescribed, the dosage must be written in both figures and words to avoid errors.

There are also requirements as to the storage of controlled drugs and record-keeping. There must be a special register, in the form of a bound book (a card index will not suffice) for controlled drugs in Schedules 1 and 2 of the 1985 Regulations. An entry must be made every time such a drug is obtained or supplied, recording the person from whom it was obtained or to whom it was supplied, the quantity involved and the form in which the drug was transferred. Regulations on the safe custody of controlled drugs apply to those in Schedules 1, 2, and 3. Such drugs must be kept locked away (Misuse of Drugs (Safe Custody) Regulations 1973, SI 1973 No 798, as amended, Sch 12. There is an exception for certain specified liquid preparations).

Regulation of the use of drugs centres on the legal power to prescribe. The use of those drugs which are not available on prescription is not regulated beyond the licensing system. That deals with the availability of drugs on a general basis. Prescription-only medicines are restricted to those patients that a health professional has identified as an appropriate recipient. Such medicines may only be dispensed under a prescription, made usually only by a medical practitioner or dentist. Limited provision has also been made for prescription by and use under the direction of midwives, occupational health nurses, and practice nurses (through regulations made under s 58 of the Medicines Act 1968, as amended). Midwives may possess and use specified controlled drugs under a 'midwives supply order', which must be signed by a doctor or by their supervisor of midwives (Medicines (Products other than Veterinary Drugs) (Prescription Only) Order 1983, Medicines (Products other than Veterinary Drugs) (Prescription Only) Order 1983 (supra), Sch 3, Pts I and III; Misuse of Drugs Regulations 1985 (supra)). Occupational health nurses may use prescription-only medicines without immediate directions provided that they do so only in circumstances specified in writing by a medical practitioner (Medicines (Products other than Veterinary Drugs) (Prescription Only) Order 1983 supra art 9 and Sch 3, Pt III, para 5). Certain district nurses and health visitors, whose registration with the UKCC is annotated to show that they are qualified to do so, may prescribe drugs under a limited formulary (*Ibid.* art 2, Sch 1A; NHS (Pharmaceutical Services) Amendment Regulations 1996, SI 1996 No 698, r 8). Ambulance paramedics are also able to use certain prescription-only medicines (Medicines (Products other than Veterinary Drugs) (Prescription Only) Amendment No. 2 Order 1992 (supra)). Special restrictions exist on the prescription of medicines for drug addicts (Misuse of Drugs (Notification of and Supply to Addicts) Regulations 1973, SI 1973 No 799).

Finally, mention needs to be made of the use of unlicensed products by doctors for individual patients. Under section 9 of the Medicines Act the usual licensing requirements are waived where a doctor or dentist uses a drug specially prepared or imported for a particular patient. This is usually known as use on a 'named patient basis'. This enables doctors to use drugs that have not yet been licensed, or to use licensed drugs in a new way that is not within the scope of the product licence. This may mean use in a different form, dosage, or with a different mode of administration. It may mean using the drug for a patient who falls outside the group for which the drug is licensed (for example using the drug for children or pregnant women when the drug has only been licensed for use in non-pregnant adults).

An outline of the regulatory system for the manufacture of drugs and pharmaceuticals (strictly, 'medicinal products') is as follows.

Pamela R Ferguson *Drug Injuries and the Pursuit of Compensation* (1996)

3. The History of Regulation

The potential of pharmaceutical products to cause harm has long been recognised; in 1747 a Select Committee of the House of Commons heard evidence of the poor quality of drugs, the incompetence of pharmacists and the lack of power of the authorities to order drugs which were found to have been adulterated to be destroyed (Report from the Select Committee on Examination of Drugs, to Prevent Adulteration (1747) Journals (H.C.) 25, 592). It was not, however, until the middle of the nineteenth century that there were legal restrictions governing the sale of drugs. Until 1843, when the Pharmaceutical Society of Great Britain was granted a charter of incorporation, any person could claim to be a pharmacist or chemist (the Pharmacy Act 1852 empowered the Society to set examinations and issue certificates. Only members of the Society could lawfully describe themselves as 'pharmaceutical chemists').

In 1914 a House of Commons Select Committee on Patent Medicines reported that, with the exception of mixtures which contained scheduled poisons, the law was powerless to prevent anyone from obtaining any drug, or preparing any compound. Nor were there any laws which prohibited the advertising of these preparations, even where extravagant claims were made as to their curative powers (Report of the Select Committee on Patent Medicines (1914) 414, ix, 1 p ix).

As a result, the Committee recommended that a manufacturer should be required to provide an account of the composition of its "medication", along with any therapeutic claims being made about the compound. This would be assessed by a special committee, which could authorise the marketing of such preparations. It is unfortunate that these recommendations were not acted upon until the 1960s, and that it took the thalidomide tragedy to galvanise the government into action.

Three years after the thalidomide tragedy the Sainsbury Committee was established to consider the relationship between the NHS and the Pharmaceutical Industry (Report of the Committee of Enquiry into the Relationship of the Pharmaceutical Industry with the National Health Service, 1965–1967 London, HMSO 1967). This Committee considered that about two-thirds of all drugs which were on the market at the time were therapeutically effective. The remaining one-third was described as "undesirable".

4. European Controls

Many of the British regulations are based on European directives. According to the European Commission itself "… the pharmaceutical industry is the sector most extensively covered by Community legislation." (Background Report: The European Medicines Evaluation Agency, ISEC/B23/94 Dec 1994.) This began with Directive 65/65, which provided that no medicinal product could be placed on the market in a Member State unless it had received authorisation from the competent authority in that state. The competent authority for Britain is the "licensing authority", the operation of which is described, below. A European Medicines Evaluation Agency (EMEA) was established in 1993. The EMEA has two sub-committees, the Committee for Veterinary Medicinal Products (CVMP) and the Committee for Proprietary Medicinal Products (CPMP) (see Dir 75/318). Member States must ensure that a medicinal product is withdrawn from the market if it is shown to be harmful under normal conditions of use, has no therapeutic efficacy or that its qualitative or quantitative composition is not as declared (Dir 75/319 [1975] OJ L147/13). The provisions of existing Directives were extended in 1989 such that blood products, vaccines, sera, toxins and allergens are now within the ambit of the regulatory process (see Dir 89/341; 89/342; and 89/391).

Most Member States consult the CPMP before withdrawing a drug from their home market. Since January 1995 authorisation of a product by the CPMP will be valid in all Member States. It is too soon to assess the impact of this, but it seems likely that companies will generally opt for the centralised procedure in future, since this will be cheaper than applying for a separate licence from each Member State.

5. The Medicines Act 1968

The 1968 Act establishes general policies in relation to the manufacture, testing and marketing of pharmaceutical products, the details of which are fleshed out by numerous statutory instruments. Given that the Misrepresentation Act 1967 and the Trade Descriptions Act 1968 were passed shortly before this, it has been suggested that the Medicines Act was part of a "consumer movement" aimed at decreasing the consumer's "vulnerability in the face of dubious marketing techniques" (Teff, *"Regulation under the Medicines Act 1968: A Continuing Prescription for Health"* (1984) Modern Law Review, 47, p 303, at pp 306–307).

The Act established a licensing authority, (s 6. The relevant Secretaries of State and Health and Agriculture Ministers who make up the licensing authority are defined in s 1(1)) and empowered it to appoint a Medicines Commission (s 2(1) see also the Medicines Commission and Committees Regulation 1970 (SI 1970 No 746)). In turn, the Commission set up a number of committees, including the Committee on Safety of Medicines (CSM) (by virtue of s 4 of the Act). The CSM provides the licensing authority with advice with respect to the safety, quality and efficacy of medicinal products. The licensing authority was authorised by the 1968 Act to make regulations governing the manufacture, testing and marketing of drugs. Regulations also control their labelling, advertising and packaging. It is a criminal offence to sell, distribute, import or export any medicinal product without a product licence (s 7) and no medicinal product can be manufactured without a manufacturer's licence (s 8(2), ss 9 and 10 provide exceptions to this for doctors, dentists, veterinary surgeons and pharmacists). Detailed as the regulations are, they do not provide a complete picture of the extent of government control since they are supplemented by "administrative directions", published in the Medicines Act Information Letters (MAIL). The Medicines Control Agency (MCA) which is an executive agency of the Department of Health, took over responsibility for all drug licensing and inspection in 1989.

(A) PRODUCT LICENCES

In determining whether or not to grant a licence for a new drug the licensing authority must consider its safety, efficacy and quality (s 19). A product licence lasts for five years, after which a manufacturer will require to submit an application for its renewal (s 24(1)). A company may not alter its method of manufacture, route of administration or recommended therapeutic uses for a drug unless it has first obtained authorisation from the licensing authority. Licensing applications require to be supported by scientific evidence, which in practice can amount to "as many as 250 or more volumes, each containing two or three hundred pages of text or tables" (Fowler, "*Careers in Drug Regulatory Authorities*" Chapter 23 of Stonier, Discovering New Medicines: Careers in Pharmaceutical Research and Development (John Wiley and Sons, 1994) p 242).

If the authority decides not to accept a submission from a pharmaceutical company in respect of a new drug, it must advise the company of its reasons for rejecting the application, and does so by means of a "section 21(1)" letter. The company may appeal against this decision, and in doing so need only address the points queried in that letter.

Marketing authorisation is required for all new products, including those which are the generic equivalent of an existing product. Fresh authorisation is required if an existing product is to be marketed for a new application. It is the regulatory authorities which decide on the classification of a new product – whether it can be marketed to the general public, whether it can only be sold under the supervision of a pharmacist, or whether it requires to be acquired by a doctor's prescription. More than half of all applications for a product licence are refused (Collier, "*Licensing and Provision of Medicines in the UK: an Appraisal*" (1985) The Lancet, pp 377–381; and the study of UK product licence applications by Rawlins and Jeffreys, (1991) pp 223–225 giving a rejection rate of 60 per cent for licence applications) and it takes almost two years, on average, for an application for a new chemical entity to be processed. An insight into the licensing processes occurred in 1989 when the CSM was taken to court by a disgruntled pharmaceutical company. Organon, the manufacturers of Bolvidon (an antidepressant), wanted to lead evidence before the CSM that its drug was safer than others. The company claimed that Bolvidon had a lower toxicity than other anti-depressants, hence was less likely to be fatal if an overdose was taken. The CSM had ruled that the safety or otherwise of a drug in an overdose situation was not relevant in assessing its safety, and refused to allow the evidence to be heard.

This was overturned by the Divisional Court and ultimately by the Court of Appeal. The latter held that, in assessing the risks and benefits of a drug, account could be taken of the risks attaching to misuse of the drug (see *R v DHSS and Others, ex p Organon Laboratories* [1990] 2 CMLR 49 [1990] COD 272). Mustill LJ held that the object of the Medicines Act 1968 was to promote public health and safety, and that the Act should be construed in a way which was favourable to the attainment of that object. He further held that the licensing authority was entitled to take into account the risk associated with other drugs for the same purpose (by virtue of s 28(3)(g)). It would seem to follow from this that the CSM would be entitled to recommend the removal of a drug from the market, purely on the basis that there exists another drug which, after comparison of the risks and benefits of the two drugs have been made, is regarded as being safer.

(B) LEAFLETS AND LABELLING

Section 85 allows regulations to be made in respect of the labelling of containers and packaging. The purpose of such regulations is to ensure that drugs are "correctly described and readily identifiable" and that "any appropriate warning or other appropriate information or instruction is given" (s 85(2)(a) and (b)). Section 86 applies to leaflets. A leaflet need not be supplied with a product if all relevant information can be contained in the packaging itself. As a result of a recent European Directive all drugs, whether obtained with or without a prescription, must include the following information (see Dir 92/27/EEC (L113/8)).

(a) the name of the product, its active ingredients, pharmaceutical form, pharmo-therapeutic group, the manufacturer's name and address, and details of the holder of the marketing authorisation;

(b) the therapeutic indications for the product;

(c) any information which is necessary before taking the product. This includes information on precautions for use and any contraindications;

(e) all necessary and usual instructions for proper use;

(f) a description of the side effects which can occur under normal use and, if necessary, the action to be taken, as well as an express invitation to communicate any undesirable effect which is not mentioned in the leaflet, to the patient's pharmacist or doctor;

(g) warning and storage precautions, and the expiry date as indicated on the label.

The information must be clearly legible and understandable. It must be indelible and in the language of the country in which the product is being sold. Member States are free to require manufacturers to include additional information, such as the price. These provisions apply to all new drugs put in circulation after January 1, 1994 and to existing products when their licences come up for renewal. Contraventions of these labelling requirements is a criminal offence (s 86(2)).

(C) THE PROVISION OF INFORMATION TO DOCTORS

Pharmaceutical manufacturers are required to provide doctors with information about prescription drugs (s 96 of the Medicine Act 1968). A manufacturer may not send advertisements or make any representations about its product to a member of the medical profession unless it has sent the doctor a copy of the product's data sheet within the preceding 15 months (Medicine (Data Sheet) Regs (SI 1972 No 2076). These data sheets may be consulted by doctors when they are deciding which particular drug to prescribe and must include details of any risks and contra-indications. Doctors may also refer to other sources of information such as the *Monthly Index of Medical Specialities* (MIMS) or the *British National Formulary* (BNF).

MIMS does not give detailed information about contra-indications and side effects, and is therefore of less use than the Data Sheets.

(D) POST-MARKETING CONTROLS

The regulation of the pharmaceutical industry does not cease once a product is marketed. Standards of Good Manufacturing Practice (GMP) are agreed between the licensing authority and the pharmaceutical industry, and members of the Medicines Inspectorate of the MCA visit the premises of manufacturers and wholesale dealers "to examine in detail how companies' products are made, controlled, stored and distributed" (Fowler, *supra* p 243). It is also a licensing condition that a company has adequate procedures for prompt recall of its products, should this become necessary (Medicines (Standard Provisions for Licences and Certificates) Regs (SI 1971 No 972) para 6 of Pt I of Sched 1 as amended by Medicines (Standard Provisions for Licensing and Certificates) Amend Regs (SI 1992 No 2846).

6.   The Detection of Adverse Reactions

(A) THE MANUFACTURER'S DUTY TO REPORT

Drug companies must report any adverse reactions discovered during their clinical trials (Sched 1, Pt II reg 3(2) para 2). All adverse reactions must be reported, whether major or minor. Any reaction which occurs during a clinical trial held in another country must also be reported. One condition of the granting of a new product licence is that the manufacturer has a system for detecting adverse reactions which are discovered once the drug is marketed (see the Medicines (Standard Provisions for Licences and Certificates) Regs (SI 1971 No 972)). A manufacturer must maintain a record of each adverse reaction which is reported to it. Such reactions must be reported within a month of receipt. Reactions which are fatal, sufficiently severe to interfere with a patient's normal activities, or which are unusual must be reported, as must any reaction which may be an example of possible drug interaction, or which involves congenital abnormalities, endocrine disturbances, fertility effects, haemorrhaging, jaundice (however mild), ophthalmic signs or symptoms, severe CNS effects, severe skin reactions after an injection or topical application, and reactions in pregnant women.

It has been estimated that the CSM receives approximately 20,000 ADR reports each year (see (1991) PLI p 175). It also receives copies of the "Death entry" supplied by the Office of Population Census and Surveys, which provides the information which is contained in death certificates (Griffin and Weber, "*Voluntary systems of adverse reaction – Part I*" (1985) Adv Drug React Ac Pois Rev 4 pp 213–230, at p 217). In November 1991 it was announced that the Medical Control Agency had developed "the world's fastest and most sophisticated system for monitoring adverse drug reactions" (PLI *supra*). The Adverse Drug Reactions On-line Information Tracking system (ADROIT) is able to process reports of adverse reactions in days, rather than in weeks. These reports come from doctors, dentists and coroners. About 70 per cent of reports come from GPs, 15 per cent from hospital doctors, and the remainder are reported mainly by the pharmaceutical companies themselves.

(B) THE "YELLOW CARD" SCHEME

Referred to as "the cornerstone of drug safety monitoring" (Talbot, "*Spontaneous reporting*" Chap 4 in Drug Safety: A Shared Responsibility (Glaxo Group Research, Churchill Livingstone, 1991) p 38), the Yellow Card Scheme is used for the spontaneous reporting of Adverse Drug Reactions by doctors. This system was established by Sir Derrick Dunlop, then chairman of the Committee on Safety of Drugs (later, the CSM) in 1964. He asked doctors to report "any untoward condition in a patient which might be the result of drug treatment" (Balfour, "*How to report suspected adverse drug reactions (ADRs)*" Chap 8 in Drug Safety: A Shared Responsibility p 7). The cards are now included as part of doctors' prescription pads.

The success stories of the Yellow Card system include the discovery that jaundice could be caused by halothane, thrombo-embolism by oestrogens, and liver damage by ibufenac. In relation to halothane, it was been argued that:

> the unravelling of the reported association between halothane and jaundice was a masterly use of adverse reaction data derived from the yellow cards. (Griffin and Weber, "*Voluntary systems of Adverse reaction reporting – Pt I*" (1985) Adv Drug React Ac Pois Rev pp 213–230 at p 228.)

Other successes have linked Aldomet (methyldopa) with hepatitis, and Hypovase (prazosin) with a loss of consciousness (ibid p 227).

The CSM publishes *Current Problems* every three months, advising pharmacists, doctors and dentists of potential danger areas. If it is felt that doctors need to be advised of a particular adverse reaction more quickly than this then a "Dear Doctor" letter may be used.

You will notice that there is also post-marketing regulation or pharmacovigilance provisions in the scheme. In order to obtain a product licence, a manufacturer will subject the potential pharmaceutical product to rigorous testing. Indeed, it is a requirement of the regulatory system. You will recall that the MCA must be satisfied of the product's 'safety, efficiency and quality' (Medicines Act 1968, s 19). In addition to the general legal issues raised by research on humans (on which see *infra*, ch 14), pharmaceutical or drug trials are regulated under the Medicines Act 1968 (and its subordinate legislation) when patients are involved. Jonathan Montgomery helpfully summarises how the system works.

Jonathan Montgomery *Health Care Law* (1997)

... Drug trials fall into a number of phases. It will be usual to begin with animal studies, regulated under the Animals (Scientific Procedures) Act 1986. The first step involving human subjects (phase I trials) will be to determine the levels at which the drug can be tolerated. These will be carried out on healthy volunteers rather than patients. They are not regulated by the Medicines Act 1968, because until a drug is used on patients it is not a medicinal product within the terms of the Act. They are, however, subject to the controls provided by local research ethics committees (for research carried out in the NHS) and by the law of consent ...

In phase II trials, the drug is tested to see whether it has clinical effects at the dosage identified as tolerable in phase I. If the drug has potentially useful effects, then phase III trials are used to compare its benefits with existing treatments. At phases II and III, trials will be unlawful without the appropriate licence (or exemption) because the drug cannot lawfully be manufactured without it.

Trials that are sponsored by a drug company can only go ahead either under a clinical trial certificate (CTC) or under the exemption scheme (CTX) (Medicines Act 1968, s 31). To obtain a trial certificate, the manufacturer needs to apply to the Medicines Control Agency. Detailed toxicological and pharmacological data must be produced to show that the trial is not likely to involve risk to the research subjects (Medicines Act 1968, s 31; Medicines (Standard Provisions for Licences and Certificates) Regulations 1971, SI 1971 No 972, as amended, Pt II). The exemption scheme permits trials to go ahead for three years on the basis of much more limited information, provided that the drug company produces a certificate signed by a registered medical practitioner who is satisfied of the accuracy of the information and that it is reasonable for the trial to be undertaken (Medicines (Exemptions from Licences) (Clinical Trials) Order 1995 SI 1995 No 2808; Medicines (Exemptions from Licences and Certificates) (Clinical Trials) Order 1995, SI 1995 No 2809).

Where a trial is not arranged by a drug company, but is to be carried out independently by a doctor or dentist, then a further exemption exists, known as the DDX. This is available where the drug is used within an existing product licence, trial certificate, or exception, or is supplied by the manufacturer solely for the purpose of the trial, provided that the Medicines Control Agency has been notified of the product, use, and the details of the supplier (Medicines (Exemption from Licences) (Special Cases and Miscellaneous Provisions) Order 1972, SI 1972 No 1200, art 4).

If trials indicate that the drug may be useful, the drug company will seek a product licence from the Medicines Control Agency. This is necessary because it is unlawful to import, market, sell, or supply a medicinal product without a licence. To acquire such a licence, applicants have to specify the use to which the medicine is to be put, including proposed dosage, and methods and routes of administration. Details of experiments (laboratory and clinical) that the applicants believe to be relevant to the safety, quality, and efficacy of the product must be provided. So must details of the manufacturing process, including quality-control mechanisms. Specimens or mock-ups of containers, packaging, and leaflets must also be made available (Medicines (Applications for Product Licences and Clinical Trial and Animal Test Certificates) Regulations 1971, SI 1971 No 973 as amended) ...

It is also possible for drugs to remain the subject of trials after licensing. Such trials are known as phase IV trials. Provided the trial involves using the drug within its product licence, no further approval is required from the Medicines Control Agency so long as it is notified of the trial and proper arrangements exist for reporting adverse reactions (Exemptions from Licences (Clinical Trials) Order 1974, SI 1974 No 498). ...

B. MEDICAL DEVICES

Since 14 June 1998, all medical devices must comply with the Medical Devices Directive (93/42/EEC). On that date, the Medical Devices Regulations 1994 (SI 1994 No 3017) came into force. Manufacturers of devices must comply with the directive and obtain a 'CE mark' before placing the device on the market for the first time. A 'medical device' means the following:

NHS Executive *Medical Devices Directive* Executive Letters, EL (95) 5 (EL 985) 23 January 1998

Annex

1.   DEFINITION

1.1 **Medical Device** means an instrument, apparatus, appliance, material or other article, whether used alone or in combination, together with any software necessary for its proper application, which—
is intended by the manufacturer to be used for human beings for the purpose of—
diagnosis, prevention, monitoring, treatment or alleviation of disease
diagnosis, monitoring, treatment, alleviation of or compensation for an injury or handicap
investigation, replacement or modification of anatomy or of a physiological process, or control of conception; and does not achieve its principal intended action in or on the human body by pharmacological, immunological or metabolic means, even if it is assisted in its function by such means.

and a 'manufacturer' means

1.2 **Manufacturer** means "the person who is responsible for the design, manufacture, packaging and labelling of a device before it is placed on the market under his own name, regardless of whether these operations are carried out by that person himself or on his behalf by a third party".

The 1994 regulations apply to all devices marked on or after 14 June 1998 unless they are custom-made devices or are intended for clinical investigation only and are labelled as such or are in vitro diagnostics (there are transitional provisions allowing devices manufactured pre-14 June 1998 to be used without a CE mark providing they are put into service before 13 June 2001). The system seeks to impose requirements for safety and product performance. There is also a vigilance system, which entails an obligation on a 'manufacturer' to report adverse incidents or events. The regulatory body in the UK is, as we saw before, the Medical Devices Agency.

The regulatory scheme is different from that for 'medicinal products' and is discussed in more detail in the following extract.

Diane Longley 'Who is Calling the Piper? Is there a Tune? The New Regulatory Systems for Medical Devices in the United Kingdom and Canada' (1998) 3 Med L Int 319

THE INTRODUCTION OF EUROPEAN REGULATION

Until fairly recently there was no *specific* legislation in the United Kingdom controlling the production and marketing of most medical devices. The Department of Health operated a voluntary manufacturer registration and product approval scheme for certain devices used by the National Health Service (NHS), and health service purchasers were encouraged to enquire whether products complied with relevant standards before placing any orders. These provisions were backed by long-standing procedures for the reporting of any adverse incidents by device users to the National Reporting and Investigation Centre, a part of the then Medical Devices Directorate within the Department of Health. Information resulting from these schemes was for the most part kept within the UK and only occasionally was it considered necessary to share it with other countries, including those of Europe.

This is now changing. Primarily as an integral part of the European single market initiative these voluntary arrangements are in the process of being replaced, as a result of a series of three European Directives, by a more comprehensive statutory system which will eventually cover *all* medical devices used in the UK. The Directives are intended progressively to replace the former national systems of each member state of the European Union. Under the latter, manufacturers often had to satisfy several, very different sets of requirements in order for their products to be marketed widely in Europe. The aim of the new scheme is to bring the medical devices industry under the same legislative control throughout Europe by the harmonisation not only of safety requirements but also of technical standards.

The Directives, each of which has a defined scope, set out certain essential requirements to which all devices must comply before being placed on the market, and lay down procedures for checking product compliance. Broadly, devices must not compromise the health or safety of patients, users and, where applicable, others. They must also attain the performance which is intended and claimed for them by manufacturers. Any risks associated with their use must be judged to be acceptable by informed clinical opinion, when weighed against their benefit. Devices which are deemed to meet these requirements are entitled to carry the CE (Communauté Européan) marking which then enables them to be made freely available throughout member states. Eventually, except for certain clearly defined exceptions, the sale of medical devices which do not bear the CE marking will be prohibited in the Community.

The first Directive, the *Active Implantable Medical Devices Directive* (90/385/EEC 20 June 1990; Implemented in the UK by the Active Implantable Medical Devices Regulations 1992 (SI 1992 No 3146) later amended by the Active Implantable Medical Devices (Amendment and Transitional Provisions) Reg 1995 (SI 1995 No 1671)) which covers all powered implants intended to remain in the human body came into effect in the UK at the beginning of 1993 with a two year transition period. Since the start of 1995 all active implantable devices, unless custom-made or undergoing clinical investigation, have had to carry the CE mark when placed on the market.

The second, the *Medical Devices Directive* (MDD) (93/42/EEC 14 June 1993). Implemented in the UK by the Medical Devices Reg. 1994 (SI 1994 No 3017) (Pursuant the Consumer Protection Act 1987), which covers the wide range of more general devices came into effect on 1 January 1995 and had a transitional period which came to an end in June this year. During that time manufacturers were able to choose whether to follow either former national controls or the requirements of the new regulations. However, the majority chose the latter.

The third Directive, the *In Vitro Diagnostic (IVD) Medical Devices Directive*, which is intended to cover reagents and apparatus for the in-vitro examination of substances and tissue derived from the human body to determine, for example, the state of health of a patient or discover any congenital abnormality had been expected to come into force in 1997, but is still under negotiation. The delay has occurred because some Member States consider that tighter controls should be introduced for certain 'high risk' products" and there are differing views on the most appropriate way to control materials derived from human tissue. ...

'The new approach', embodied in the medical devices Directives, limits legislative measures to the setting out of essential health and safety requirements only, which, allied to the parallel development of European standards, are intended to form a sound basis for the mutual recognition of products between member states. The general MDD, for example, rather than stipulating common rules to which all products must conform, sets out fourteen essential requirements or basic principles (Annex 1 93/42/EC). Manufacturers are obliged to ensure that these essential requirements are met in relation to each product and standards are designed to assist them demonstrate compliance and facilitate inspection to check that conformity.

Although manufacturer adherence to European standards is regarded as voluntary, once a proposed standard has been approved by the European Committee for Standardisation (CEN) or the European Committee for Technical Standardisation (CENELEC) and adopted by the Commission, there is a presumption that it complies with the essential requirements of the relevant Directive. Member states must then accept goods which demonstrate conformity to it (Medical Devices Directive 93/42/EEC Art 5). In effect, such standards can be regarded as akin to regulations. Manufacturers are free to produce goods to other specifications, but the 'streamlined route' to acceptance will not then be open to them and they will have the burden of demonstrating compliance with basic principles.

The overall aim of the present approach to harmonisation – via standards closely allied to essential, though broad, regulatory requirements – is to provide a reasonably flexible regime which will preclude any stifling of innovation in either the development of new products or modification of existing ones. As long as safety principles are adhered to – taking account of the acknowledged state of the art, solutions adopted for the design and construction of devices are for manufacturers alone. (Ibid. General Requirements (2).)

The emphasis on flexibility is reflected at the national regulatory level. Member States are able to retain or develop their own administrative systems by reference to common requirements and procedures, at the same time as being required to recognise the validity of that of the others; mutual recognition being encapsulated in the CE authorisation ...

THE EUROPEAN SYSTEM IN THE UK

Responsibilities of Competent Authorities

In effect the medical devices Directives envisage a hierarchical or pyramidal audit structure. In each Member State a competent authority is expected to implement the requirements of the Directives, ensure compliance, evaluate adverse incidents and carry out pre-clinical assessments of devices intended for clinical investigation. In the UK the functions of the competent authority, although ultimately the responsibility of Secretary of State for Health, is in practice delegated to the Medical Devices Agency (MDA) which is responsible for ensuring the safety, quality and efficacy of medical devices. This body, formerly known as the Medical Devices Directorate, had already accumulated wide experience in the field of medical device standards and evaluation when it was established as an executive agency of the Department of Health in September 1994 as part of the British government's Next Steps programme. That experience had enabled the Agency to play a key part in the negotiations and drafting of the European Directives.

In line with the evolution of governing forms and techniques commonly referred to as new public management (NPM) the MDA has been required to adopt many practices familiar to those in the private sector including 'a focus on customer service, the exercise of personal responsibility by individual managers, understanding of cost activities, providing value for money ... .' (A Kent, Chief Executive, MDA Annual Report and Accounts 1996–1997 p 9.)

The move in the UK from the voluntary control of *some* medical devices to the mandatory regulation of *all* devices has proved to be a major and far reaching change for the Department of Health, the pace of which seems unlikely to slacken for some time. To ensure that medical devices meet appropriate standards of safety, quality and performance in complying with the relevant Directives the MDA has to work with users, manufacturers and legislators and facilitate co-operation between them. Accordingly it is engaged in several key activities: audit of the quality assurance systems of medical device manufacturers and publication of a register of approved companies; investigation of adverse incidents; evaluation of medical devices and publication of reports; advising ministers, the Department of Health, the NHS and other health care providers, and manufacturers; contributing to the setting of safety and performance standards at national, European and international levels; and the introduction and enforcement of statutory controls throughout the UK. (Medical Devices Agency Framework Document p 5.)

To the latter end the MDA has produced a number of comprehensive and laudably comprehensible Bulletins to steer manufacturers, health care providers and others through the complexities of the Directives and UK regulations which implement them. Committed to the governments' Citizens' Charter, deregulation initiative (Working with Businesses: a code for enforcement agencies. Department of Trade and Industry, 1993) and Better Regulation programme, the MDA has also published a Code of Practice on Enforcement which provides information and guidance to the medical device industry on the role and duties of the Competent Authority, as well as laying down the minimum level of standards of service to be expected by MDA customers.

Beside standards, the Code adverts to the provision of information and openness, consultation and communication, courtesy and helpfulness, minimisation of compliance costs and the establishment of an effective complaints system. The Code is expected to be of benefit to the public, as well as manufacturers, by ensuring that regulations achieve their intended purpose and protection is improved, not to mention the reduction of the burden on taxpayers! Although there is no appeal from a refusal by the MDA to allow the CE mark to be affixed, the Code has introduced a complaints system for resolution of grievances about the handling of manufacturers' enquiries. Although the Code is specifically stated not to carry any legal status, (Code of Practice on Enforcement p 5) it is certainly arguable that it would be taken into account in any grievance with the MDA that went to litigation (Annual Report 1996/7 p 18. See also *R v North Derbyshire Health Authority, ex parte Fisher* [1997] 8 Med LR 327) as the decisions of the MDA are amenable to judicial review. Furthermore, the operation of the MDA comes within the jurisdiction of the Parliamentary Ombudsman.

Notified Bodies

Much of the work of monitoring compliance by manufacturers and their products with the requirements of the Directives is carried out by third parties. These are independent certification organisations, known in Europe as Notified Bodies, which are approved by the

Competent Authorities and notified to the European Commission and other member states (93/42/EC, Article 16 and Annex XI).

Criteria for the selection of Notified Bodies are designed to ensure impartiality and expertise and those bodies selected are audited periodically to ensure these are maintained. If standards fall, Notified Body status may be withdrawn. In the UK there are nine Notified Bodies responsible for monitoring manufacturers of moderate to high risk devices, all of which were audited by the MDA during 1996/7.

The methods that manufacturers must use to demonstrate that devices comply to essential requirements are known as conformity assessment procedures. They depend on which Directive is applicable and are relative to the risk classification of the device. Notified Bodies can be designated to monitor one or more of these procedures, or this approval may be restricted to a specific type of device. Conditions of designation have to be notified to the European Commission. While a Notified Body is permitted to sub-contract some testing and auditing activity it remains responsible for ensuring the competence of its sub-contractors.

So as not to contravene EC law and the principles of the single market manufacturers are free to apply to any Notified Body capable of carrying out the desired conformity assessment procedures in *any* member state. This flexibility has given rise to some safety concerns as there has been criticism of the standards and experience of a number of Notified Bodies approved within some Member States. As a consequence, the UK MDA has been instrumental in setting up a European Working Group on the designation and surveillance of Notified Bodies (Annual Report 1996/7 p 20). The aim is to raise standards to a more consistently high level and so prevent an undermining of confidence and ultimately the usurpation of the regulatory system by less scrupulous manufacturers who might deliberately select Notified Bodies with a reputation for being less rigorous in carrying out their duties.

Similar concerns can also be expressed in relation to competent authorities. Although not readily articulated in public, there is a very real doubt that every member state possesses the necessary expertise and is of equal competence regarding the implementation and overseeing of the operation of the regulatory requirements of the medical device directives. As pertinently, uncertainty can be raised about the degree of commitment and priority given to implementation by some member states. The implications of this issue will be discussed further in relation to the proposed mutual recognition agreement between the European Union and Canada.

Classification of Devices

In an attempt to match the level of control to the degree of risk inherent in a device the general MDD establishes four categories of product; 1, 11a, 11b and 111, the latter being the category of highest risk. Categorisation is largely dependent on the purpose of the device and is backed by a series of rules which set out the criteria. Rather than listing products, which would be likely to require constant updating, these are broad statements relating to factors such as function, properties and parts of the body treated. These tend to be more flexible and able to accommodate new developments in medical technology.

In accordance with the accent on self-regulation currently inherent in European administration, manufacturers initially determine the classification of their products, select, where required, a relevant Notified Body to confirm this and carry out the appropriate conformity assessment procedure. In the event of disagreement, either party may refer the matter to the Competent Authority for a decision. If doubt still exists the European Commission, acting in conjunction with a Regulatory Committee composed of experts from member states, may be approached for a ruling.

As already noted, the difference between each class of device is reflected in the increasing scrutiny engendered in the required conformity assessment procedure. Conformity procedures for Class 1 devices; those considered to be of least risk, can be carried out as a general rule under the responsibility of the manufacturer. For class 11a devices the intervention of a Notified Body is compulsory at the production stage. For classes 11b and 111, which constitute a higher risk potential, inspection by a Notified Body is required with regard to device design, in addition to their manufacture. Class 111, which is set aside for the most critical devices, necessitates explicit, prior authorisation with regard to conformity.

Clinical Investigation

With the exception of class 1, and especially in the case of higher risk devices, manufacturers have to supply clinical data on the safety and effectiveness of the device (Annex VIII; which sets out the information required and Annex X on the clinical evaluation process. 93/42/EC) in order to justify the affixing of the CE mark. This may be done in either of two ways. Manufacturers may design a protocol and carry out a clinical investigation to verify the performance of the device under normal conditions and assess any undesirable side-effects against benefits. Alternatively, data may be compiled from current scientific literature on the performance and safety of the device, accompanied by a written, critical evaluation of this literature. This latter method is particularly useful where a device has been in established use prior to the implementation of the EC directives and a full clinical investigation would be unwarranted.

Applications to carry out a clinical trial must be made to the competent authority at least 60 days before it is due to begin and may only proceed if no objection is raised during that time. It is the responsibility of the manufacturer to submit the necessary documentation, as the clinical investigators within health care institutions normally have no direct contact with the MDA. There is no equivalent to the 'named patient' special supply of devices on prescription, as there is for pharmaceuticals, but there are provisions for custom-made devices.

All clinical trials of devices must be carried out in accordance with the Declaration of Helsinki and must have the approval of the local research ethics committee (LREC) for the area in which the research is to be carried out. This must be sought prior to notification to the MDA, as manufacturers are required to submit a copy of LREC approval with the protocol of the proposed trial. This differs from the procedure for clinical trial applications for medicines where a CTX certificate must usually be obtained from the Medicines Control Agency *prior* to consideration by an LREC. However, the MDA has the power to overrule LREC approval on the grounds of public health or safety (MDA 1997 EC Medical Devices Directives and LRECs/MRECs) but cannot overturn an LREC decision that the proposed trial is unethical. Clinical investigations of devices already carrying the CE mark do not require notification to the Competent Authority, unless the manufacturer is proposing a use for the device which differs from that already sanctioned.

Re-categorisation

Clearly, the provisions described here only briefly are complex, requiring careful consideration and close monitoring by national authorities. In the UK the transition to the new European system has been further complicated by the fact that the general Medical Devices Directive has brought within its scope some products originally subject to the medicines control regime (Medicines Act 1968 s 104 and Directive 65/65/EEC), and has also affected the status of devices which incorporate, or are used to administer, medicinal products and substances. Consequently, this has entailed some re-categorisation of a number of products, causing some confusion and necessitating the enactment of additional legislation (The Medical Devices (Consequential Amendments – Medicines) Regulations 1994 (SI 1994 No 3119 removes a range of products from medicines control)).

In order to decide whether the medical devices or medicines regulatory scheme applies, the intended purpose of the product, including the way it is presented and the method by which its principal action is achieved, is taken into account. The principle purpose of a medical device is typically fulfilled by a physical means: mechanical action, physical barrier, replacement of, or support to, organs or body functions. By comparison, the action of a medicinal product is typically achieved by a pharmacological, immunological or metabolic means. Medical devices may of course be aided in their functions by such means, but only where these are paramount will the product be regarded as medicinal. A substance administered for diagnostic purposes may also be considered to be a medicinal product.

The main groups of products affected by the transition of control are wound dressings, absorbable surgical materials, including sutures and bone cements, interuterine devices (IUD) and contact lens care products, as well as some dental products (MDA Bulletin 17 1995). While the MDA has issued guidelines to try to clarify classification, some products remain under review and others may still give rise to uncertainty. For example, IUDs which incorporate a chemical action come under the auspices of medical device regulation, IUDs with a hormonal action come under the control of the Medicines Agency. Only in the latter is the primary purpose regarded as a drug delivery system.

Where devices administer medicinal products, but are incorporated into a single product so that this is used exclusively in the given combination and is not reusable, medicines control applies (Directive 65/65/EEC) to the product as a whole, but the safety and performance of the device part of the product must comply with the MDD. On the other hand, devices which incorporate an integral substance, which if used separately would be considered to be a medicinal product and which acts on the body ancillary to the device, is subject to medical device regulation as a whole. However the quality and usefulness of the medicinal substance must be verified by methods relating to the testing of proprietary medicines. Under the classification rules set out in the general MDD such a device fails into Class 3 and the notified body carrying out the relevant conformity assessment must consult the drug regulatory authority about its quality and effectiveness. Thus products requiring dual regulation have a potential to throw the system into uncertainty. This may well be exacerbated in the future if a proposed directive on Biocidal Products, which is likely to overlap both medicines and device regulation, comes in to force.

Post marketing surveillance

The Department of Health has for some time operated a voluntary system under which those *using* a device report any problems for investigation by MDA staff. Under the new European scheme the emphasis is on *producer* reporting. The Directive requires manufacturers – taking account the nature and risks of the product – to put procedures in place to enable systematic review of the performance of their devices in the post market phase and take corrective action where needed. It is mandatory that they notify any adverse incidents to the competent authorities immediately they come to their knowledge. There is thus a legal requirement to report any malfunction or deterioration in the characteristics or performance of the device which might lead, or might have led, to the death of a patient or user, or to a serious deterioration in health. This includes any inadequacies in labelling or instructions that might have or have had such an effect. Where a manufacturer is systematically recalling a particular type of device the manufacturer must report the technical or medical reason for the recall. Failure to comply with these provisions is a criminal offence.

The objective is to minimise risks to health and safety of patients, users and others by reducing the likelihood of the same type of serious incident involving medical devices being repeated at different times throughout the Community. This aim is lent support by a number of means: the evaluation of reported incidents by Member States, the dissemination of information which could be used to prevent a reoccurrence of the incident or alleviate the consequences and, where appropriate, modification of the device or withdrawal from the market.

Adverse incident reports are generally confidential until the outcome of investigation when information necessary to prevent further incidents is disseminated to health care providers and others. Investigation of any incident will normally be expected to be carried out by manufacturer, with the Competent Authority monitoring progress. Any resultant changes to the device require the agreement of the latter and any necessary post-investigative action or withdrawal from the market must be notified to other member states and the European Commission which 'polices' the situation.

Under a safeguard clause, if a member state ascertains that a device – which has been correctly installed, maintained and used – may compromise health and safety it is under an obligation to take all appropriate interim measures to withdraw it from the market or restrict it being put into use. When informing the Commission member states must give reasons for their action. In particular, the report must indicate whether there has been a failure to meet essential requirements, incorrect application of standards or short-comings in the standards themselves. If, after consultation, the Commission finds the action of a Member State justified, other member states are informed and appropriate action taken regarding the CE mark. Where withdrawal is attributed to defects in standards the matter must be referred to the Committee on Standards and Technical Regulations within two months.

As the UK regulations have taken effect, arrangements for the reporting of adverse incidents in the UK has also changed. However, as Member States are also permitted to take account of adverse reports from other sources, the MDA took the decision to enhance and continue their current *user* reporting system and not place total reliance on *manufacturer* notification.

In the UK advice on adverse incidents to health bodies can take several forms; hazard and safety notices, technical notes, 'dear doctor' letters, professional letters from the Chief Medical Officer and executive letters from the NHS Executive. Usually, however, these will only come into play where manufacturers fail to sort out difficulties for themselves. In addition there are a number of registers for certain devices which carry a serious risk to health such as heart valves, pacemakers, and hydrocephalus shunts, to enable patients to be traced if necessary.

One of the most fundamental difficulties for MDA surveillance is that whilst adverse incidents have steadily increased, investigation resources have not. The result is that resources are having to be concentrated in the areas of highest hazard and the proportion of incidents or defects referred to manufacturers for investigation is likely to continue to increase. Potentially, this may have some implications for decisions about liability, but it is clearly sometimes the case that the manufacturer is the only body to possess adequate facilities to test the relevant device.

The MDA role is proactive as well as reactive and the agency is currently looking at the development of more clinically meaningful data collection through its programme of product evaluation. The purpose of this is not only the fundamental one of public health protection through identification of unsafe or poorly performing devices, which then informs clinical management and NHS purchasing decisions, but is also to facilitate evaluation, and hence evolution, of the UK regulatory system itself.

To this end, beside the publication of product evaluation reports, the MDA has undertaken a number of customer surveys of hospital and general practice staff in specified areas. This feedback has indicated a high level of satisfaction with the UK system, but highlighted some shortcomings in the content of evaluation reports and in customer service. In response, and after consultation, the MDA has introduced training for customer service staff and set up a Helpline. Information on technical advances and evidence emerging from on-going evaluations in a number of fields is also to be provided more regularly to medical device purchasers and users. …

(See now also The *In Vitro* Diagnostic Medical Devices Regulations 2000 (SI 2000 No 1315) – implementing Directive 98/79/EC on *in vitro* diagnostic medical devices.)

Contract

A patient injured by a medical product may have an action for breach of contract against a supplier such as a doctor or pharmacist – though not a manufacturer, with whom he is very unlikely to have a contractual relationship. However, within the NHS the scope for such actions is extremely limited, as it is generally accepted that there is no contract between the patient and supplier, whether doctor or pharmacist. Actions for breach of contract will, therefore, really feature only in the context of the provision of private treatment.

The legal framework is set out by Professor Teff in the following extract.

H Teff in I Kennedy and A Grubb (eds) *Principles of Medical Law* (1998)

14.08   Historically, the boundaries of liability for injurious products largely derive from the law on sales warranties. Since, under the doctrine of privity, the seller of a defective product is contractually liable only to the buyer (*Dunlop Pneumatic Tyre Co.* [1991] 2 Med LR 169; Oliphant, K 'Innovations in Procedure and Practice in Multi-Party Medical Cases in Grubb, A (ed) 'Choices and Decisions in Health Care' (Chichester, 1993) in practice contract has limited relevance to claims for harm caused by medicinal products. Pharmaceutical companies very rarely have a contractual relationship with consumers for the supply of goods, unless they are private patients buying medical equipment direct from the manufacturer. Patients injured by the more potent drugs will usually have obtained them through NHS prescription. In such circumstances there is no contract with the prescribing doctor, or with the pharmacist, who is statutorily obliged to dispense drugs on presentation of a prescription and payment of any fixed charge. (*Pfizer Corp v Ministry of Health* [1965] AC 512, 535–6, per Lord Reid; *Appleby v Sleep* [1968] 1 WLR 948, 954–5.) A pharmacist could however be liable in contract for injury caused by privately prescribed drugs or by non-prescription medicines sold over-the-counter. Equally, a doctor or hospital supplying drugs or other medical materials privately could be contractually liable.

1. General Principles of Liability

14.09   Sales of medicinal products, being subject to the common law and statutory principles generally applicable to consumer sales, can give rise to liability for innocent misrepresentation (Misrepresentation Act 1967, s 2(1)) or breach of contract. In addition to grounding a claim for the breach of any express or implied terms at common law, such transactions are subject to the implied terms of the Sale of Goods Act 1979 (hereafter the SGA 1979), which in essence consolidates the Sale of Goods Act 1893. Thus the seller can be held liable if the goods sold do not correspond with their description (s 13(1)), or do not meet the 'quality conditions', either because they are not of 'satisfactory quality' (Sale and Supply of Goods Act 1994, s 1) or not fit for their particular purpose. Liability for breach of the implied terms is 'strict', there being no need to prove fault or negligence on the part of the vendor (*Frost v Aylesbury Dairy Co Ltd* [1905] 1 KB 608, CA. See also *Kendall (Henry) and Sons (a firm) v William Lillico and Sons Ltd* [1969] 2 AC 31, 84, per Lord Reid; *Vacwell Engineering Co Ltd v BDH Chemicals Ltd* [1971] 1 QB 88). There are comparable provisions regarding contracts for services in the course of which goods are 'supplied', in the Supply of Goods and Services Act 1982 (hereafter the SGSA).

14.10   Where a medicinal product is defective because of a manufacturing fault there may be a breach of the implied condition of satisfactory quality, namely, that the goods 'meet the standard that a reasonable person would regard as satisfactory' (Sale of Goods Act 1979, s 14 (2A) and (2B), as amended by the Sale and Supply of Goods Act 1994, s 1). For such liability to arise, there is no need for the buyer to have relied on the seller's skill or judgment. In principle this provision could also ground liability for unforeseen side effects resulting from defective design. However, it might be deemed unreasonable to expect drugs not to present any such dangers, and it would often be difficult to demonstrate that unavoidable risks of a powerful drug are incompatible with 'satisfactory quality'.

14.11　As regards fitness for purpose, inability of the seller to detect an unforeseen side effect is not in principle a defence (*Aswan Engineering Establishment Co v Ludpine Ltd* [1987] 1 WLR 1, CA). However, 'where the circumstances show that the buyer does not rely, or that it is unreasonable for him to rely, on the skill or judgment of the seller …', the implied condition is inapplicable (Sale of Goods Act 1979, s 14(3)). The onus is on the seller to show that there was no such reliance. Thus a dispensing pharmacist might be able to show that the implied condition was negated by a private patient's reliance on the judgment of the prescribing doctor. In addition, no liability arises in respect of the buyer's unexpected sensitivity unless it has been expressly or impliedly made known to the seller (*Griffiths v Conway (Peter) Ltd* [1939] 1 All ER 685, CA (sale); cf *Ingham v Eves* [1955] 2 QB 366, CA (work and materials). A pharmacist would therefore not normally be liable if unaware of a customer's abnormal condition or allergy (for constructive knowledge, see Atiyah, P, Sale of Goods (9th edn Adams, J) (London, 1995), 168).

14.12　Since both of the 'quality conditions' refer to 'the goods supplied under the contract', liability can arise in respect of packaging, containers, and instructions which render goods of unsatisfactory quality and/or unfit for their particular purpose(s) (*Vacwell Engineering Co Ltd v BDH Chemicals Ltd* [1971] QB 88; *Wormell v RHM Agriculture (East)* [1987] 1 WLR 1091, CA). However, the mere fact that a drug is potentially harmful will not ground liability if it is safe when taken according to the instructions.

14.13　Unlike the condition as to description, the quality conditions apply only to goods sold 'in the course of a business' (Sale of Goods Act, s 14(2), (3)). This expression would appear to cover transactions undertaken by a private hospital. The position with regard to NHS hospitals is less clear. A statutory provision making records relating to a 'business' admissible in criminal proceedings has been held not to apply to the medical records of an NHS hospital (Criminal Evidence Act 1965, s 1(1)(4); *R v Crayden* [1978] 1 WLR 604, 609 CA), on the ground that its commercial functions were ancillary to its main purpose. However, under legislation concerned to promote consumer protection, which defines a 'business' to include a 'profession' and the activities of a 'public authority' (Sale of Goods Act, s 61(1)), there is a strong case for regarding the commercial transactions of NHS hospitals (*a fortiori* if they are Trusts), as taking place 'in the course of a business' (see *Davies v Summer* [1984] 1 WLR 1301, HL) …

4. Contracts Involving the Supply of Products: Supply or Services?

14.18　Where a contract for private medical treatment is exclusively for the provision of services, at common law a doctor who has not been negligent will not normally be liable for injury. (Nathan, Lord, '*Medical Negligence*' (London, 1957) 10–11.) Similarly, under the SGSA, there is an implied term that the supplier need do no more than carry out such services with 'reasonable care and skill'. (SGSA, s 13.) If, for example, an operation on a private patient for sterilisation has been unsuccessful, in the absence of negligence there will be no breach of contract unless the doctor has guaranteed a successful outcome. (*Eyre v Measday* [1986] 1 All ER 488, CA; *Thake v Maurice* [1986] QB 644; cf *Grey v Webster* (1985) 14 DLR (4th) 706 (NBCQB).) When, however, a doctor supplies or administers drugs or other medical materials to a private patient, as when giving an injection or anaesthetic, or applying an ointment, it may not be clear whether the contract is primarily for the provision of services or for the supply of medicines. The same problem can arise when a private doctor (or hospital) supplies medical equipment, such as a prosthesis or other medical device. Even when such products are supplies, the doctor's professional role in diagnosis, advice and/or treatment will commonly be regarded as a dominant feature of the transaction, so that it is not viewed as comparable to a contract of sale. (Benjamin's Sale of Goods (London, 1992, 4th edn para 1-046. And see Nathan Medical Negligence (London, 1957), 19. Cf case 353/85 *Commission v United Kingdom* [1988] STC 251.)

14.19　However, at common law, a contract which in substance is for the supply of work and materials may contain implied terms analogous to those applicable to sales. (*Samuels v Davis* [1943] KB 526, CA; *Dodd v Wilson* [1946] 2 All ER 691.) More importantly, when goods are supplied (or administered) 'in the course of a business', (SGSA, ss 4, 9 and 18(1)) either by way of transfer, as in the case of drugs, prosthetics, dentures, and injections, or hire, as in the temporary use of splints or crutches, the contract would now be subject to the strict liability provisions of the SGSA. Essentially, as regards the quality and fitness for purpose of any such 'goods', these provisions replicate the SGA s 14(2) and s 14(3) in respect of goods 'transferred' (SGSA, s 4) or 'hired' (SGSA, s 9) to the patient. In practice, most medical contracts for work and materials involve transfer, as the patient becomes the owner of the materials used. In some instances of temporary use, however, however, the contract will be one of hire.

One point should be noted. There is no doubt that most 'medicinal products' and 'medical devices' will fall within the 1979 and 1982 Acts as 'goods', whether supplied alone or as part of medical services. However, there is uncertainty over whether human material such as organs, blood or gametes (sperm and eggs) are properly characterised as 'goods'. The same issue arises under the Consumer Protection Act 1987. It is in relation to the 1987 Act that the issue is most likely to come before a court in England, given the limited potential for contract claims in the NHS and so we defer discussion of the issue until then (*infra*).

Negligence

A. MANUFACTURER

We are concerned here principally with the liability of a manufacturer of a dangerously defective product. The liability of the doctor (or pharmacist) who supplied it is a question of establishing medical negligence which we have already discussed. Of course, in essence, the two actions – both in the tort of negligence – are the same. The patient is required to prove that the manufacturer owed her a *duty of care*, that the duty was *breached*; and that the breach *caused* the injury.

Here we concentrate on questions that, if not unique in product cases, are especially important, difficult or complex.

First, who owes the patient a duty of care? *Donoghue v Stevenson* [1932] AC 562 established that a manufacturer does owe such a duty for a dangerous product and the general rule applies to medical products. Secondly, liability is dependent upon proof of fault, ie negligence. What is the standard of care? What relevance do industry standards have? And will it be conclusive that the manufacturer has complied with a legislative requirement or one imposed by the MCA or MDA?

H Teff in I Kennedy and A Grubb (eds) *Principles of Medical Law* (1998)

2. The Standard of Care

14.25   In general terms, manufacturers are under an obligation to exercise such care as is reasonable in all aspects of the production process under their control. Liability may arise from inadequate care in matters as diverse as research and design, manufacture, presentation, and instructions for use, including warnings about risks (*Cartwright v. GKN Sankey Ltd* [1972] 2 Lloyd's Rep 242, 259, CA; *Deviez v Boots Pure Drug Co Ltd* (1962) 106 SJ 552). Determining the requisite standard has sometimes been described as an exercise in cost-benefit analysis, centring on such well-established negligence criteria as magnitude of risk, probability of harm, the burden of taking adequate precautions, and the social utility of the defendant's conduct.

14.26   The attempt, in essence, to establish where the balance of social interest lies can be unusually difficult in the case of medicinal products, the full risks and benefits of which may not become apparent for many years, if at all. The anticipated utility of any given drug, and the advantages of its early availability, may or may not be outweighed by its potential for harm. The benefits of elaborate safety precautions may or may not outweigh the inhibiting effects of innovation of cost and delay. A marginally more effective new drug may be inherently less safe than available alternatives (see *Nicholson v John Deere Ltd* (1986) 34 DLR (4th) 542, 549 (Ont HC)). Many otherwise valuable drugs present a significant risk to a minority of the public, and it has been suggested that a product which is safe for most people should be considered dangerous 'if it might affect other users who had a higher degree of sensitivity than normal, so long as they were not altogether exceptional' (*Board v Thomas Hedley* [1951] 2 All ER 431, 432, CA per Denning LJ).

(i) Common Practice

14.27　Whether or not the defendant's conduct is deemed negligent is judged by reference to the prevailing state of scientific and technical knowledge (*Vacwell Engineering Co v BDH Chemicals* [1971] 1 QB 88). Conformity with industry standards or custom, though prima facie evidence of reasonable prudence on the part of a manufacturer (cf *R v British Pharmaceutical Industry Assoc Code of Practice Committee*, The Independent, 1 Nov 1990), is not dispositive (*Morris v West Hartlepool Navigation Co* [1956] AC 552). A general indication of what constitutes appropriate pre-marketing research for pharmaceutical products is contained in the guidelines produced by the regulatory authorities (the Licensing Authority and its advisory bodies) and the industry (the Code of Practice for the Pharmaceutical Industry). However, compliance with recommended testing procedures, for example, is not ipso facto a defence in any given case. Non-compliance with accepted practice would be strong, though not conclusive, evidence of negligence (*Chin Keow v Government of Malaysia* [1967] 1 WLR 813, PC). Similarly, the views of expert official committees are relevant but not determinative (*Thompson v Johnson and Johnson Pty Ltd* [1990] 3 Med LR 148, 171–2 (SC of Victoria App Div).

(ii) Compliance With Statutory Provisions

14.28　Even full compliance with statutory requirements does not conclusively preclude liability for negligence at common law (*Bux v Slough Metals Ltd* [1973] 1 WLR 1358, CA). Hence the issue of a product licence does not automatically constitute a defence to a claim (cf 65/65/EEC OJ 22, 9 Feb 1965, 369). However, the courts would be loath to impose a standard of care that effectively penalised compliance with specific, statutorily prescribed, standards (*Budden v BP Oil and Shell Oil* (1980) 124 SJ 376, CA) and they would be reluctant to hold negligent a manufacturer who had been granted a product licence for a drug after having disclosed to the Licensing Authority all the information deemed relevant to its safety (cf *Donoghue v Stevenson* [1932] AC 562; *Daniels and Daniels v R White & Sons Ltd and Tarbard* [1938] 4 All ER 258).

Thirdly, in respect of what is that duty to be owed? In products cases, it is helpful to consider the following categories: (1) manufacturing defects; (2) design defects; (3) marketing defects; and (4) post-marketing failures.

H Teff in I Kennedy and A Grubb (eds) *Principles of Medical Law* (1998)

(iii) Manufacturing Defects

14.29　Defects arising from error in the manufacturing process are relatively rare in the pharmaceutical industry. Examples would include a failure to combine ingredients in the correct propositions, excessive potency and toxicity, the presence of some impurity or foreign body, and deterioration of the product from contamination or faulty packaging. Though the full burden of proof is formally on the plaintiff, once it has been proved that there is a defect in the product which probably did not occur after it had left the manufacturer's control, there is an 'inference of negligence' akin to *res ipsa loquitur*, if not tantamount to automatic liability (*Lockhart v Barr* 1943 SC (HL) 1). In fact, the stronger the evidence that the defendant has a careful quality control system, the more likely it is that a particular defect will be attributed to negligence in the production process (*Grant v Australian Knitting Mills Ltd* [1936] AC 85, 101; *Hill v James Crowe (Cases) Ltd* [1978] 1 All ER 812, 816). In principle, if manufacturers have an appropriate system for ordering raw materials and components and adequate testing and inspection procedures, they will not incur liability for the negligence of an independent contractor (*Taylor v Rover Co* [1966] 1 WLR 1491), though occasionally the manufacturer's duty has been treated as non-delegable (*Winward v TVR Engineering Ltd* [1986] BTLC 366, CA).

(iv) Design Defects

14.30　Manufacturers are liable for harm caused by their failure to take reasonable care to ensure that a product has been safely designed (*Hindustan Steam Shipping Co Ltd v Siemens Bros & Co* [1955] 1 Lloyd's Rep 167). Though they cannot, by definition, be liable in negligence for not knowing about undiscoverable defects, some cases have suggested that a high standard of care is expected, especially in the research that goes into the design of intrinsically dangerous and novel products. However, though the manufacturer is under a duty to keep abreast of medical and scientific discoveries, proof that design defects are attributable to negligence is often elusive, and seldom more so than in the case of medical products (*Stokes v Guest, Keen and Nettlefold (Bolts and Nuts) Ltd* [1968] 1 WLR 1776, 1783).

14.31   A major obstacle to proof of negligence in medical products litigation is that what counts as 'knowledge' can be both intrinsically problematic and complicated by the fact that scientists and medical researchers may legitimately hold conflicting views. There will often be a grey area between speculation, hypothesis, or information, on the one hand, and 'hard' knowledge on the other, and the courts are mindful of the need to guard against hindsight (*Roe v Minister of Health* [1954] 2 QB 66, 86, CA per Denning LJ). Also, though 'the law requires even pioneers to be prudent' (*Independent Broadcasting Authority v EMI Electronics Ltd and BICC Construction Ltd* (1980) 14 Build LR, 1, HL, 28 per Lord Edmund-Davies), it also reflects the importance attached to innovation. In determining the level of acceptable risk for new drugs, allowance will be made for the fact that they need to be potent to be useful and that there are practical limits on discovering risks at the stage of pre-market testing on relatively small populations in animal studies and clinical trials. By contrast with the approach of the courts towards manufacturing defects, a previous good design safety record is of distinct evidential value to the defendant.

(v) Marketing Defects

(a)   Warnings and Instructions

14.32   An important aspect of due care in the supply of products is the provision of adequate instructions for their use and, where necessary, of warnings about risks of which the defendant has actual or constructive knowledge. 'Failure-to-warn claims are now the most common form of litigated product case in the US.' (Stapleton, J '*Product Liability*' (London, 1994) 252.) Since the manufacturer is required to make available such information as will enable products to be used safely (*Kubach v Hollands* [1937] 3 All ER 907), any warnings must be readily intelligible and commensurate with risks, bearing in mind that informing the medical profession normally suffices in respect of prescription medicines. Risks, in turn, must not be minimised by promotional material (*Watson v Buckley, Osborne, Garrett & Co Ltd* [1940] 1 All ER 174. By virtue of an EC Directive on labels and leaflets, the provision of package leaflets for human medicinal products is now obligatory, unless all the required information is on the pack or label: Council Directive 92/27/EEC, OJ). The manufacturer would normally be expected to warn of a drug's inherent and irreducible risks, though there is no duty to warn of a danger which is either patent or a matter of common knowledge (*Farr v Butters Bros & Co* [1932] 2 KB 606, CA). There can, however, be liability for injury resulting from reasonably foreseeable misuse which has not been reasonably warned against (*Hill v James Crowe (Cases) Ltd* [1978] 1 All ER 812). A warning or instructions may also be needed where the danger is known to the user, but not the means of avoiding the risk. At the same time, the manufacturer may have regard to such factors as the remoteness of any danger and the possibility of causing needless alarm (*Thompson v Johnson & Johnson Pty Ltd* [1990] 3 Med LR 148 (SC of Victoria, App Div) (tampons and toxic shock syndrome). Where there has been a total failure to warn there is little scope for defences such as contributory negligence (but see *Devilez v Boots Pure Drug Co* (1962) 106 SJ 552) or volenti, since the user will normally have been unaware of any danger. In principle, there is some scope for them where an inadequate warning has been given.

(b)   Allergic Reactions

14.33   Particular difficulties surround the issue of allergic reactions. If a manufacturer knows or ought to know of the danger, in appropriate circumstances a warning would be required for the benefit of a vulnerable minority (*Ingham v Emes* [1955] 2 QB 366, CA). In the United States, courts have often relied on the 'narrow formulaic requirement that a certain percentage of persons must suffer an allergic reaction from the product before the manufacturer will be held liable' (Rogerson, C and Trebillock, M '*Products and the Allergic Consumer: A Study in the Problems of Framing an Efficient Liability Regime*' (1986) 36 UTLJ 52, 57). However, in any given case, whether or not failure to warn is reasonable could involve consideration of such factors as the severity of the consequences, the social value of the product, the availability of substitutes, and the plaintiff's access to information about allergy (Miller, C and Lovell, P '*Product Liability*' (London, 1977) 324–6) ...

(vi) Continuing Duty Of Care

14.35 If, after its potential for harm had become apparent, a marketed product caused injury, there could be liability in negligence for not having modified it or made its availability subject to a suitable warning (*Wright v Dunlop Rubber Co Ltd* (1972) 13 KIR 255, 272 CA), for not having removed it from the market and, it would seem, for not having warned previous purchasers. As regards prescription drugs, it would be negligent not to take reasonable steps to warn prescribing doctors (*Hollis v Dow Corning Corp* (1995) 129 DLR (4th) 609 (SCC)) and presumably in certain instances not to issue public warnings (*Buchan v Ortho Pharmaceuticals (Canada) Ltd* (1986) 25 DLR (4th) 658, 667, 578 (Ont CA)). To this end, manufacturers need proper procedures for monitoring adverse reactions and product recall (*McCain Foods Ltd v Grand Falls Industries Ltd* (1991) 80 DLR (4th) 252 (NBCA)).

Fourthly, two particular points arise in relation to warnings.

1. The 'learned intermediary' rule

Although duty is owed to the patient, in the case of warnings courts in other jurisdictions have held that the duty will be discharged by warning the doctor. This is known as the 'learned intermediary rule'. The basis for the rule is that it is for the doctor to decide whether to prescribe a drug and, if he does so, what information to provide to the patient. In respect of the latter, any failure to do so will be the basis for a medical negligence action against the doctor rather than a products' liability action against the manufacturer. The rule is, of course, only applicable in the case of drugs or devices prescribed or provided by the doctor. It can have no relevance where the drug is available at a pharmacy whether as an 'OTC' or 'pharmacy only' drug. There can be no expectation of an expert intermediary in these instances. While there is no English authority for the 'learned intermediary rule' in pharmaceutical cases, it has been applied in an analogous situation (see *Holmes v Ashford* [1950] 2 All ER 76 (CA) – sufficient for manufacturer to warn hairdresser about properties of a dye). It would undoubtedly be applied by an English court. The rule will not apply, however, where there is no prospect of an expert intervening and an exercise of clinical judgment in respect of *this* patient, for example, in cases of mass immunisation *Reyes v Wyeth Laboratories* (1984) 498 F 2d 1264 (5th Cir CA)) or repeat prescriptions for contraceptive pills (*MacDonald v Ortho Pharmaceuticals Corp* (1985) 475 NE 2d 65 (Mass Sup Jud Ct)).

2. Causation

In any negligence action the claimant must establish that he would not have suffered the injury 'but for' the defendant's negligence (see *supra*, chs 4 and 5). In the context of a manufacturer's failure to warn a doctor (as the 'learned intermediary'), this means that the patient must prove either that the doctor would not have prescribed the drug or that he would have warned the patient who would have decided not to agree to use it. The issues of a 'post-marketing' duty to warn, the 'learned intermediary' rule and causation were examined by the Canadian Supreme Court in a case concerned with a ruptured breast implant.

Hollis v Dow Corning Corp (1995) 129 DLR (4th) 609 (Can Sup Ct)

In 1983, implants, manufactured by the defendant corporation, were implanted in the plaintiff's breasts by a surgeon. One of the implants ruptured, requiring removal and further surgery. The literature accompanying the product warned of rupture during surgery, but not of post-surgical rupture except from abnormal squeezing or trauma. The plaintiff brought an action for damages against the manufacturer and the surgeon, succeeding at trial against the manufacturer on the basis of *res ipsa loquitur*. The action against the surgeon was dismissed. On appeal to the British Columbia Court of Appeal, the manufacturer's appeal was dismissed, but on the ground that, though not negligent in the manufacture of the product, it was liable for failure to warn, since the evidence showed that, by 1983, it had received reports of about 50 cases of ruptures. The plaintiff's appeal against the surgeon was allowed and a new trial ordered.

On further appeal by the manufacturer to the Supreme Court of Canada, **held**, dismissing the appeal, the manufacturer had a duty to warn the medical profession of potential dangers, including those coming to its notice after manufacture and distribution of the product

La Forest J: *Analysis*

[18] The sole issue raised in this appeal is whether the Court of Appeal erred in finding Dow liable to the respondent Ms Hollis for failing adequately to warn the implanting surgeon, Dr Birch, of the risk of a post-surgical implant rupture inside Ms Hollis' body. The appellant Dow does not contest Bouck J.'s factual finding that Ms Hollis' seven-year surgical ordeal caused her great physical and psychological pain, residual scarring on her breasts, and a loss of past and future income. However, Dow submits that it was not responsible for Ms Hollis' injuries. In support of this submission, Dow argues, first, that the warning it gave Dr Birch was adequate and sufficient to satisfy its duty to Ms Hollis, and second, that even if it did breach its duty to warn Ms Hollis, the breach was not the proximate cause of her injuries.

[19] For the reasons that follow, it is my view that the Court of Appeal reached the correct conclusion and that the appeal should be dismissed. Since Dow does not challenge the trial judge's findings concerning Ms Hollis' injuries, I will concentrate on the issues of duty and causation which form the basis for Dow's submissions in this appeal. In the first part of these reasons, I will address the question whether Dow breached its duty to warn, and the related question whether Dow can rely on the so-called "learned intermediary" rule to absolve itself of liability. In the second part, I will consider whether Dow's failure to warn was a proximate cause of Ms Hollis' injuries.

1.   Dow's duty to warn and the "learned intermediary" rule

(a)   The general principles

(i)   The duty to warn

[20] It is well-established in Canadian law that a manufacturer of a product has a duty in tort to warn consumers of dangers inherent in the use of its product of which it has knowledge or ought to have knowledge. The principle was enunciated by Laskin J (as he then was), for the court, in *Lambert v Lastoplex Chemicals Co* (1971), 25 DLR (3d) 121 at pp 124–5, [1972] SCR 569, where he stated:

> Manufacturers owe a duty to consumers of their products to see that there are no defects in manufacture which are likely to give rise to injury in the ordinary course of use. Their duty does not, however, end if the product, although suitable for the purpose for which it is manufactured and marketed, is at the same time dangerous to use; and if they are aware of its dangerous character they cannot, without more, pass the risk of injury to the consumer.

The duty to warn is a continuing duty, requiring manufacturers to warn not only of dangers known at the time of sale, but also of dangers discovered after the product has been sold and delivered: see *Rivtow Marine Ltd v Washington Iron Works* (1973), 40 DLR (3d) 530 at pp 536–7, [1974] SCR 1189, [1973] 6 WWR 692, *per* Ritchie J. All warnings must be reasonably communicated, and must clearly describe any specific dangers that arise from the ordinary use of the product: see, for example, *Setrakov Construction Ltd v Winder's Storage & Distributors Ltd* (1981), 128 DLR (3d) 301, 12 MVR 49, 11 Sask R 286 (CA); *Meilleur v UNI—Crete Canada Ltd* (1985), 32 CCLT 126, 30 ACWS (2d) 181 (Ont HCJ); *Skelhorn v Remington Arms Co* (1989), 69 Alta LR (2d) 298, 99 AR 22, 17 ACWS (3d) 148 (CA); *McCain Foods Ltd v Grand Falls Industries Ltd* (1991), 80 DLR (4th) 252, 116 NBR (2d) 22, 27 ACWS (3d) 542 (CA).

[21] The rationale for the manufacturer's duty to warn can be traced to the "neighbour principle", which lies at the heart of the law of negligence, and was set down in its classic form by Lord Atkin in *Donoghue v Stevenson*, [1932] AC 562 (HL). When manufacturers place products into the flow of commerce, they create a relationship of reliance with consumers, who have far less knowledge than the manufacturers concerning the dangers inherent in the use of the products, and are therefore put at risk if the product is not safe. The duty to warn serves to correct the knowledge imbalance between manufacturers and consumers by alerting consumers to any dangers and allowing them to make informed decisions concerning the safe use of the product.

[22] The nature and scope of the manufacturer's duty to warn varies with the level of danger entailed by the ordinary use of the product. Where significant dangers are entailed by the ordinary use of the product, it will rarely be sufficient for manufacturers to give general warnings concerning those dangers; the warnings must be sufficiently detailed to give the consumer a full indication of each of the specific dangers arising from the use of the product. This was made clear by Laskin J. in *Lambert, supra*, where this court imposed liability on the manufacturer of a fast-drying lacquer sealer who failed to warn of the danger of using the highly explosive product in the vicinity of a furnace pilot light. The manufacturer in *Lambert* had placed three different labels on its containers warning of the danger of inflammability. The plaintiff, an engineer, had read the warnings before he began to lacquer his basement floor and, in accordance with the warnings, had turned down the thermostat to prevent the furnace from turning on. However, he did not turn off the pilot light, which caused the resulting fire and explosion. Laskin J. found the manufacturer liable for failing to provide an adequate warning, deciding that none of the three warnings was sufficient in that none of them warned specifically against leaving pilot lights on near the working area. At p. 125, he stated:

> Where manufactured products are put on the market for ultimate purchase and use by the general public and carry danger (in this case, by reason of high inflammability), although put to the use for which they are intended, the manufacturer, knowing of their hazardous nature, has a duty to specify the attendant dangers, which it must be taken to appreciate in a detail not known to the ordinary consumer or user. A general warning, as for example, that the product is inflammable, will not suffice where the likelihood of fire may be increased according to the surroundings in which it may reasonably be expected that the product will be used. The required explicitness of the warning will, of course, vary with the danger likely to be encountered in the ordinary use of the product.

[23] In the case of medical products such as the breast implants at issue in this appeal, the standard of care to be met by manufacturers in ensuring that consumers are properly warned is necessarily high. Medical products are often designed for bodily ingestion or implantation, and the risks created by their improper use are obviously substantial. The courts in this country have long recognized that manufacturers of products that are ingested, consumed or otherwise placed in the body, and thereby have a great capacity to cause injury to consumers, are subject to a correspondingly high standard of care under the law of negligence: see *Shandloff v City Dairy*, [1936] 4 DLR 712 at p 719, [1936] OR 579, [1936] OWN 531 (CA); *Arendale v Canada Bread Co*, [1941] 2 DLR 41 at pp 41–2, [1941] OWN 69 (CA); *Zeppa v Coca-Cola Ltd*, [1955] 5 DLR 187 at pp 191–3, [1955] OR 855, [1955] OWN 885 (CA); *Rae and Rae v T Eaton Co (Maritimes) Ltd* (1961), 28 DLR (2d) 522 at p 535, 45 MPR 261 (NSSC); *Heimler v Calvert Caterers Ltd* (1975), 56 DLR (3d) 643 at pp 643–4, 8 OR (2d) 1 (CA). Given the intimate relationship between medical products and the consumer's body, and the resulting risk created to the consumer, there will almost always be a heavy onus on manufacturers of medical products to provide clear, complete and current information concerning the dangers inherent in the ordinary use of their product.

[24] I pause at this point to observe that there is an important analogy to be drawn in this context between the manufacturer's duty to warn and the doctrine of "informed consent" developed by this court in recent years with respect to the doctor-patient relationship. In *Hopp v Lepp* (1980), 112 DLR (3d) 67 at pp 69–71, 81–2, [1980] 2 SCR 192, 13 CCLT 66, and *Reibl v Hughes* (1980), 114 DLR (3d) 1 at pp 5–6, [1980] 2 SCR 880, 14 CCLT 1, this court decided that physicians have a duty, without being questioned, to disclose to a patient the material risks of a proposed procedure, its gravity, and any special or unusual risks, including risks with a low probability of occurrence, attendant upon the performance of the procedure: see also *Ciarlariello v Schacter* (1993), 100 DLR (4th) 609, [1993] 2 SCR 119, 15 CCLT (2d) 209. The principle underlying "informed consent", as Laskin CJC explained in *Hopp, supra*, at p 70, is the "right of a patient to decide what, if anything, should be done with his body"; see also *Schloendorff v Society of New York Hospital*, 105 NE 92 (NYCA 1914), *per* Cardozo J. The doctrine of "informed consent" dictates that every individual has a right to know what risks are involved in undergoing or forgoing medical treatment and a concomitant right to make meaningful decisions based on a full understanding of those risks. As Robinson J. observed in *Canterbury v Spence*, 464 F2d 772 (DC Cir 1972) at p 780:

> True consent to what happens to one's self is the informed exercise of a choice, and that entails an opportunity to evaluate knowledgeably the options available and the risks attendant upon each. The average patient has little or no understanding of the medical arts, and ordinarily has only the physician to whom he can look for enlightenment with

which to reach an intelligent decision. From these almost axiomatic considerations springs the need, and in turn the requirement, of a reasonable divulgence by physician to patient to make such a decision possible.

[25] In my view, the principles underlying the doctrine of "informed consent" are equally, if not more, applicable to the relationship between manufacturers of medical products and consumers than to the doctor-patient relationship. The doctrine of "informed consent" was developed as a judicial attempt to redress the inequality of information that characterizes a doctor-patient relationship. An even greater relationship of inequality pertains both between the manufacturer of medical products and the consumer and, to a lesser degree, between the manufacturer and the doctor. In contrast to the doctor-patient relationship, where the patient can question the doctor with respect to the risks and benefits of particular procedures and where doctors can tailor their warnings to the needs and abilities of the individual patients, the manufacturer-consumer relationship is characterized primarily by a lack of direct communication or dialogue. This lack of dialogue between manufacturer and consumer creates, as Patricia Peppin notes in "Drug/Vaccine Risks: Patient Decision-Making and Harm Reduction in the Pharmaceutical Company Duty to Warn Action" (1991), 70 Can. Bar Rev. 473 at p. 474, a relationship of complete dependency between manufacturer and patient. She explains the relationship in the following terms:

> The patient is dependent both on the company and on the doctor to provide sufficient information for an informed decision to be made, as well as for treatment to heal the body, prevent a disease or palliate the pain. Dependency characterizes the relationship between vulnerable patient and the experts who exercise control over the patient's bodily fate. The physician's relationship with the pharmaceutical company also exhibits a dependency of the doctor, because of his or her limited pharmaceutical knowledge, on the company's information; but the relationship is also one in which the physician is courted through the company's marketing efforts and one in which the doctor is immune from physical pain and vulnerability.

> Another element of the context within which the legal principles operate is the widespread use of pharmaceutical products apparently unaccompanied by significant public knowledge of the inherent risks.

A similar observation was made by Robins JA in *Buchan v Ortho Pharmaceutical (Canada) Ltd* (1986) 25 DLR (4th) 658, 32 BLR 285, 12 OAC 361, which involved a suit by a woman against the Ortho pharmaceutical company after that woman had suffered a stroke from the use of Ortho's Novum oral contraceptives. In finding Ortho liable for failing to warn consumers about the risk of stroke inherent in the use of the contraceptives, Robins JA made the following observations, at p 686:

> As between drug manufacturer and consumer, the manufacturer is a distant commercial entity that, like manufacturers of other products, promotes its products directly or indirectly to gain consumer sales, sometimes, as in this case, accentuating value while underemphasizing risks. Manufacturers hold an enormous informational advantage over consumers and, indeed, over most physicians. The information they provide often establishes the boundaries within which a physician determines the risks of a possible harm and the benefits to be gained by a patient's use of a drug.

[26] In light of the enormous informational advantage enjoyed by medical manufacturers over consumers, it is reasonable and just to require manufacturers, under the law of tort, to make clear, complete and current informational disclosure to consumers concerning the risks inherent in the ordinary use of their products. A high standard for disclosure protects public health by promoting the right to bodily integrity, increasing consumer choice and facilitating a more meaningful doctor-patient relationship. At the same time, it cannot be said that requiring manufacturers to be forthright about the risks inherent in the use of their product imposes an onerous burden on the manufacturers. As Robins JA explained in *Buchan*, *supra*, at p 687, "drug manufacturers are in a position to escape all liability by the simple expedient of providing a clear and forthright warning of the dangers inherent in the use of their products of which they know or ought to know".

(ii) The "learned intermediary" rule

[27] As a general rule, the duty to warn is owed directly by the manufacturer to the ultimate consumer. However, in exceptional circumstances, a manufacturer may satisfy its informational duty to the consumer by providing a warning to what the American courts have, in recent years, termed a "learned intermediary". The "learned intermediary" rule was first elaborated in *Sterling Drug, Inc v Cornish*, 370 F2d 82 (8th Cir 1966), a suit brought by a patient blinded after taking the drug chloroquine phosphate. The rationale for the rule was outlines by Wisdom J in

Reyes v Wyeth Laboratories, 498 F2d 1264 (5th Cir 1974) at p 1276; *cert. denied* 419 US 1096 (1974), a suit against a manufacturer of oral polio vaccine, in the following terms:

> Prescription drugs are likely to be complex medicines, esoteric in formula and varied in effect. As a medical expert, the prescribing physician can take into account the propensities of the drug, as well as the susceptibilities of his patient. His is the task of weighing the benefits of any medication against its potential dangers. The choice he makes is an informed one, an individualized medical judgment bottomed on a knowledge of both patient and palliative. Pharmaceutical companies then, who must warn ultimate purchasers of dangers inherent in patent drugs sold over the counter, in selling prescription drugs are required to warn only the prescribing physician, who acts as a "learned intermediary" between manufacturer and consumer.

The rule was later reaffirmed and developed in a series of American cases during the 1970s and 1980s involving the liability of manufacturers of prescription drugs: see, for example, *Schenebeck v Sterling Drug, Inc*, 423 F2d 919 (8th Cir 1970); *Hoffman v Sterling Drug, Inc*, 485 F2d 132 (3rd Cir 1973); *Dunkin v Syntex Laboratories, Inc*, 443 F Supp 121 (W D Tenn 1977); *Lindsay v Ortho Pharmaceutical Corp*, 637 F2d 87 (2d Cir 1980); *Timm v Upjohn Co*, 624 F2d 536 (5th Cir 1980); *cert denied* 449 US 1112 (1981); *Stanback v Parke, Davis & Co*, 657 F2d 642 (4th Cir 1981); *Walker v Merck & Co*, 648 F Supp 931 (MD Ga 1986); *affirmed* 831 F2d 1069 (11th Cir 1987); *Plummer v Lederle Laboratories*, 819 F2d 349 (2d Cir 1987). In Canada, the rule was first considered in an *obiter* passage by Linden J in *Davidson v Connaught Laboratories* (1980), 14 CCLT 251 (Ont HCJ) at p 274, and later applied by a five-member panel of the Ontario Court of Appeal in *Buchan, supra*.

[28] While the "learned intermediary" rule was originally intended to reflect, through an equitable distribution of tort duties, the tripartite informational relationship between drug manufacturers, physicians and patients, the rationale for the rule is clearly applicable in other contexts. Indeed, the "learned intermediary" rule is less a "rule" than a specific application of the long-established common law principles of intermediate examination and intervening cause developed in *Donoghue v Stevenson, supra*, and subsequent cases: see, for example, *Holmes v Ashford*, [1950] 2 All ER 76 (CA) at p 80. Generally, the rule is applicable either where a product is highly technical in nature and is intended to be used only under the supervision of experts, or where the nature of the product is such that the consumer will not realistically receive a direct warning from the manufacturer before using the product. In such cases, where an intermediate inspection of the product is anticipated or where a consumer is placing primary reliance on the judgment of a "learned intermediary" and not the manufacturer, a warning to the ultimate consumer may not be necessary and the manufacturer may satisfy its duty to warn the ultimate consumer by warning the learned intermediary of the risks inherent in the use of the product.

[29] However, it is important to keep in mind that the "learned intermediary" rule is merely an exception to the general manufacturer's duty to warn the consumer. The rule operates to discharge the manufacturer's duty not to the learned intermediary, but to the ultimate consumer, who has a right to full and current information about any risks inherent in the ordinary use of the product. Thus, the rule presumes that the intermediary is "learned", that is to say, fully apprised of the risks associated with the use of the product. Accordingly, the manufacturer can only be said to have discharged its duty to the consumer when the intermediary's knowledge approximates that of the manufacturer. To allow manufacturers to claim the benefit of the rule where they have not fully warned the physician would undermine the police rationale for the duty to warn, which is to ensure that the consumer is fully informed of all risks. Since the manufacturer is in the best position to know the risks attendant upon the use of its product and is also in the best position to ensure that the product is safe for normal use, the primary duty to give a clear, complete, and current warning must fall on its shoulders.

(b) Application of the general principles to the case at bar

[30] The first question to be answered in this appeal is whether Dow owed Ms Hollis a duty to warn her that the Silastic implant could rupture post-surgically insider her body and, if so, whether Dow satisfied that duty. In light of the foregoing jurisprudence, it is clear that the answer to this question depends on the answers to two subsidiary questions. First, did Dow have a duty to warn Ms Hollis directly, or could it satisfy its duty to warn her by warning a "learned intermediary", namely, Dr Birch? Second, assuming that Dow could properly discharge its duty to Ms Hollis by warning Dr Birch, did Dow adequately warn Dr Birch of the risk of post-surgical rupture in light of its state of knowledge at that time?

[31] Turning to the first of these questions, it is my view that the "learned intermediary" rule is applicable in this context, and that Dow was entitled to warn Dr Birch concerning the risk of rupture without warning Ms Hollis directly. A breast implant is distinct from most manufactured goods in that neither the implant nor its packaging are placed directly into the

hands of the ultimate consumer. It is the surgeon, not the consumer, who obtains the implant from the manufacturer and who is therefore in the best position to read any warnings contained in the product packaging. In this respect, breast implants are, in my view, analogous to prescription drugs, where the patient places primary reliance for information on the judgment of the surgeon, who is a "learned intermediary", and not on the manufacturer: see *Buchan, supra*, at pp 668–70. They are not analogous to oral contraceptives, with respect to which many American courts have recently imposed a direct duty to warn, because direct warnings from manufacturers of breast implants are simply not feasible given the need for intervention by a physician: see *MacDonald v Ortho Pharmaceutical Corp*, 475 NE2d 65 (Mass JC 1985) at p 70; *cert denied* 474 US 250 (1985); *Buchan, supra*, at pp 668–70. In this respect, I observe that it is not, and has never been, Dow's practice to send warnings concerning their breast implants directly to patients. Although Dow includes product information with its implants, the implants are sold only to doctors or medical establishments, who are expected to pass this information on to their patients. In light of this fact, I conclude that a manufacturer in Dow's position can discharge its duty to the ultimate consumer by giving the treating surgeon clear, complete and current information concerning any general and specific risks that arise from the ordinary use of the product.

[32] However, the mere fact that the "learned intermediary" rule is applicable in this context does not absolve Dow of liability. As I mentioned earlier, the "learned intermediary" rule presumes that the intermediary is fully apprised of the risks, and can only provide shelter to the manufacturer where it has taken adequate steps to ensure that the intermediary's knowledge of the risks in fact approximates that of the manufacturer. Thus, the second, and more important, question to be resolved is whether Dow fulfilled its duty to Ms Hollis by adequately warning Dr Birch of the risk of post-surgical rupture of the implant.

[33] Although Bouck J declined to rule on this issue, a majority of the Court of Appeal found that Dow's warning to Dr Birch was inadequate. In my view, the Court of Appeal was correct in reaching this conclusion. ...

2.   *Did Dow's breach of the duty to warn cause Ms Hollis' injury?*

[43] Dow raises two distinct causation issues in this appeal. The first is whether Ms Hollis would have elected to have the operation if she had been properly warned of the risk by Dr Birch. Dow submits that a reasonable woman in Ms Hollis' position would have consented to the surgery despite the risk and, on this basis, argues that its failure to warn was not the proximate cause of Ms Hollis' injury. The second issue Dow raises is whether Dr Birch would have warned Ms Hollis if he had been properly warned by Dow of the risk. Dow submits that Ms Hollis had the onus of establishing that Dr Birch would not have warned Ms Hollis even if fully apprised by Dow of the risk and, once again, argues that its failure to warn cannot be the proximate cause of her injuries. Counsel for Ms Hollis sought to meet the first issue on a factual basis alone. As to the second issue, however, he contested as well the underpinnings of Dow's argument, which as will appear raises more substantial legal issues. I shall accordingly approach the issues on that basis.

(a)   *Would Ms Hollis have consented to the operation even if properly warned of the risk?*

(i)   *The appropriate test*

[44] In determining whether Ms Hollis would have consented to the operation had she been properly warned by Dr Birch of the risk of rupture, Prowse JA applied the modified objective test developed by this court in *Reibl, supra*, which involved a negligence action by a patient against a surgeon for failing to warn him of the risk of paralysis entailed in elective surgery performed by that surgeon. The test applied by Prowse JA was as follows: would a reasonable woman in Ms Hollis' particular circumstances have consented to the surgery if she had known all the material risks? I note, however, that in *Buchan, supra*, at pp 685–7, Robins JA found the *Reibl* test to be inapplicable to products liability cases, and instead applied a subjective test. Robins JA's rationale deserves to be quoted at length:

> The considerations applicable to and the responsibilities involved in a doctor-patient relationship differ markedly from those of a manufacturer-consumer relationship. As between doctor and patient, there is a direct and intimate relationship in which the relative advantages and disadvantages of a proposed medical treatment, including the taking of a drug, can be considered, discussed and evaluated. As between drug manufacturer and consumer, the manufacturer is a distant commercial entity that, like manufacturers of other products, promotes its products directly or indirectly to gain consumer sales, sometimes, as in this case, accentuating value while underemphasizing risks. Manufacturers hold an enormous informational advantage over consumers and, indeed, over most physicians. The information they provide often establishes the boundaries within which a physician determines the risks of possible harm and the benefits to be gained by a patient's use of a drug. Manufacturers, unlike doctors, are not

called upon to tailor their warnings to the needs and abilities of the individual patient, and, unlike doctors, they are not required to make the type of judgment call that becomes subject to scrutiny in informed consent actions.

When a manufacturer's breach of the duty to warn is found to have influenced a physician's opinion as to the safety of a drug thereby contributing to the physician's non-disclosure of a material risk and the consumer's ingestion of the drug, the manufacturer is not entitled to require the injured consumer to prove that a reasonable consumer in her position would not have taken the drug if properly warned. At this juncture, the case stands on no different footing than the usual products liability case in which there is no question of the intervention of an intermediary, and should be treated as such. The manufacturer has put a product on the market without proper warning. The likelihood that the consumer will take the drug without knowledge of its potential risks is a foreseeable consequence of the breach of the duty to warn. Whether the particular consumer would have taken the drug even with a proper warning is a matter to be decided by the trier of fact on all of the relevant evidence.

In my opinion, it was open to the trial judge, viewing the evidence as he did, to credit the plaintiff's testimony that she would not have taken the pill had she been told of the danger of stroke, and to determine the causation issue accordingly. Whether a so-called reasonable woman in the plaintiff's position would have done likewise is beside the point.

Robins JA also addressed the argument that the imposition of a subjective standard would place an undue burden on drug manufacturers. He rejected this argument for the following reason, at p 687:

The suggestion that the determination of this causation issue other than by way of an objective test would place an undue burden on drug manufacturers is answered by noting that drug manufacturers are in a position to escape all liability by the simple expedient of providing a clear and forthright warning of the dangers inherent in the use of their products of which they know or ought to know. In my opinion, it is sound in principle and in policy to adopt an approach which facilitates meaningful consumer choice and promotes market-place honesty by encouraging full disclosure. This is preferable to invoking evidentiary burdens that serve to exonerate negligent manufacturers as well as manufacturers who would rather risk liability than provide information which might prejudicially affect their volume of sales.

[45] In my view, the rationale given by Robins JA for a subjective test is compelling and justifies the adoption of the subjective test in cases of this nature. The most serious concern raised by the application of a subjective test is that the plaintiff, with the benefit of hindsight, will always claim that she would not have used the product if she had been properly warned. In *Reibl, supra*, at pp 15–16, Laskin CJC elaborated upon this concern in the following terms:

An alternative to the subjective test is an objective one, that is, what would a reasonable person in the patient's position have done if there had been proper disclosure of attendant risks. The case for the objective standard has been tersely put in the following passage from a comment in 48 NYUL Rev 548 (1973), at p 550, entitled "Informed Consent— A Proposed Standard for Medical Disclosure":

Since proximate causation exists only if disclosure would have resulted in the patient's foregoing the proposed treatment, a standard must be developed to determine whether the patient would have decided against the treatment had he been informed of its risks. Two possible standards exist: whether, if informed, the particular patient would have foregone treatment (subjective view); or whether the average prudent person in plaintiff's position, informed of all material risks, would have foregone treatment (objective view). The objective standard is preferable, since the subjective standard has a gross defect: it depends on the plaintiff's testimony as to his state of mind, thereby exposing the physician to the patient's hindsight and bitterness.

It could hardly be expected that the patient who is suing would admit that he would have agreed to have the surgery, even knowing all the accompanying risks. His suit would indicate that, having suffered serious disablement because of the surgery, he is convinced that he would not have permitted it if there had been proper disclosure of the risks, balanced by the risks of refusing the surgery.

[46] Although the concern raised by Laskin CJC is valid and should continue to be applied in a doctor-patient relationship, in a suit against a manufacturer for failure to warn this concern

can be adequately addressed at the trial level through cross-examination and through a proper weighing by the trial judge of the relevant testimony. While this difference between the type of proof required in the two kinds of actions may seem anomalous, it is amply justified having regard to the different circumstances in which the relevant duties arise, and the consequent difference in the nature of these duties. As Robins JA intimated in *Buchan*, the duty of the doctor is to give the best medical advice and service he or she can give to a particular patient in a specific context. It is by no means coterminous with that of the manufacturer of products used in rendering that service. The manufacturer, on the other hand, can be expected to act in a more self-interested manner. In the case of a manufacturer, therefore, there is a greater likelihood that the value of a product will be overemphasized and the risk underemphasized. It is, therefore, highly desirable from a policy perspective to hold the manufacturer to a strict standard of warning consumers of dangerous side-effects to these products. There is no reason, as in the case of a doctor, to modify the usual approach to causation followed in other tortious actions. Indeed the imbalance of resources and information between the manufacturer and the patient, and even the doctor, weighs in the opposite direction. Moreover, it is important to remember that many product liability cases of this nature will arise in a context where no negligence can be attributed to a doctor. It would appear ill-advised, then, to distort the rule that is appropriate for claims against a manufacturer simply because of an apparent anomaly that results in cases where a doctor is also alleged to have been negligent.

(ii)   The application of the test to the facts of the case at bar
[47] In my view, there was sufficient evidence adduced at trial to satisfy the subjective *Buchan* test.
… [52] I, therefore, conclude that Ms Hollis would not have opted for the surgery had she known of all the attendant risks.

(b)   Would Dr Birch's conduct have been the same whether or not Dow was in breach of the duty to warn?
[53] The second causation issue *raised by Dow* is whether Dr Birch would have warned Ms Hollis of the risk of rupture if Dow had properly warned Dr Birch about that risk. Dow argues that there is no direct causal link between its breach of the duty to warn and Ms Hollis' injury because, in 1983, Dr Birch was aware of the risk of implant rupture but did not make a habit of warning his patients about that risk. In support of this argument, Dow relies on Dr Birch's testimony at trial that, in 1983, he was warning only 20% to 30% of his patients of implant rupture, and that, in determining the nature and scope of his warnings to patients, he relied more on the articles he read in medical journals than on manufacturer's warnings.
[54] It is right to say, however, that the trial judge found that in 1983 the average plastic surgeon in British Columbia did not in fact know about the possibility that rupture of Silastic implants could be a factor of any significance. This finding is supported and amplified by the fact that after Dow began circulating its more extensive 1985 warning and knowledge of the risk of rupture in the medical community became more prevalent, Dr Birch adapted his practice accordingly, and by 1989 he was warning all his patients of the risk of rupture.
[55] I do not propose to enter further into or assess these factors. I say this because, while Dow is correct in submitting that there was some ambiguity at trial concerning Dr Birch's warning practices in 1983, Dow's argument is based upon the assumption that to succeed in her claim against Dow Ms Hollis must prove that Dr Birch would have warned her if Dow had properly warned Dr Birch. I do not think this assumption is well founded. Ms Hollis, it will be remembered, demonstrated that Dow had breached its duty to warn her of the risk of rupture, that she would not have undergone the medical procedure if she had been fully informed of the risks, and that she suffered injury from the rupture. Had Dr Birch been adequately warned but had not passed on the information to Ms Hollis, Dow would, it is true, have been absolved of liability by virtue of the learned intermediary doctrine. But I fail to see how one can reason from this that, for Dow to be liable, Ms Hollis must now establish that Dr Birch would have informed her if he had known. To require her to do so would be to ask her to prove a hypothetical situation relating to her doctor's conduct, one, moreover, brought about by Dow's failure to perform its duty. While the legal and persuasive onus in a negligence case generally falls on the plaintiff, I do not see how this can require the plaintiff to prove a hypothetical situation of this kind.
[56] The reasoning in this court's decision in *Cook v Lewis*, [1952] 1 DLR 1, [1951] SCR 830, is helpful in this context. In that case, the plaintiff was shot by one of two members of a hunting party. The jury had found that the plaintiff had been shot by one of the two hunters, and that both of the hunters had been negligent in shooting in the plaintiff's direction, but were unable to say which hunter's bullet had actually hit the plaintiff. On this basis, the jury exculpated both defendants from negligence. This court set aside the jury finding and ruled that, once the plaintiff had proved that he had been shot by one of the defendants, the onus was on the defendants to establish absence of negligence. Unless they

could exculpate themselves both would be liable. In a concurring judgment setting forth his reasons for reversing the burden of proof, Rand J made the following remarks, at pp 4–5, that serve to illuminate the present discussion:

> *What, then, the culpable actor has done by his initial negligent act is, first, to have set in motion a dangerous force which embraces the injured person within the scope of its probable mischief; and next, in conjunction with circumstances which he must be held to contemplate, to have made more difficult if not impossible the means of proving the possible damaging results of his own act or the similar results of the act of another.* He has violated not only the victim's substantive right to security, but he has also culpably impaired the latter's remedial right of establishing liability. By confusing his act with environmental conditions, he has, in effect, destroyed the victim's power of proof.
>
> The legal consequence of that is, I should say, that the onus is then shifted to the wrongdoer to exculpate himself; it becomes in fact a question of proof between him and the other and innocent member of the alternatives, the burden of which he must bear. *The onus attaches to culpability, and if both acts bear that taint, the onus or prima facie transmission of responsibility attaches to both, and the question of the sole responsibility of one is a matter between them.*

(Emphasis added.)

[57] In my view, a close analogy can be drawn between *Cook* and the case at bar. The facts on the record demonstrate that Ms Hollis was inadequately warned of the possibility that the breast implants manufactured by Dow and surgically implanted by Dr Birch could rupture. While the victim's power of proof has not been destroyed in the same sense as in the hunting party case, it has been seriously undermined in that the plaintiff is, on Dow's contention, called upon to prove what a doctor would have done in a hypothetical situation. It must be kept in mind that the governing principle in a case of this nature is informed consent, namely, the right of the patient to be fully informed by the manufacturer of all material risks associated with the use of a medical product. It is clear from the record that Ms Hollis' right to informed consent was not respected in this case. We know that Dow's failure to warn was a cause of her injury; whether Dr Birch's actions in the hypothetical situation posited by Dow might also have been a cause is not a matter for Ms Hollis to prove. Ms Hollis, who was in a position of great informational inequality with respect to both the manufacturer and the doctor, played no part in creating the set of causal conditions leading to her injury. Justice dictates that she should not be penalized for the fact that had the manufacturer actually met its duty to warn, the doctor still might have been at fault.

[58] I observe that the Ontario Court of Appeal in *obiter* in *Buchan, supra*, has adopted a somewhat similar approach to causal analysis in cases of this nature. There Robins JA had this to say, at p 682:

> Once the breach of duty to warn prescribing physicians has been established, I think it fair and reasonable to presume that the inadequacy of the warning was a contributing cause of the ingestion of the drug. *It ought not be incumbent on a plaintiff to prove as part of her case what her doctor might or might not have done had he been adequately warned.* One can assume that a doctor would not ignore a proper warning or fail to disclose a material risk or otherwise act negligently. Even if the evidence were to indicate that the doctor was negligent, the manufacturer would not be shielded from liability if such negligence were a foreseeable consequence of the breach of duty to warn. The presumption may, of course, be rebutted if the defendant comes forth with evidence that despite the inadequacy of the warning the doctor's conduct towards his patient would have been the same whether or not the manufacturer was in breach of the duty …

(Emphasis added.)

[59] In the last sentence of this statement, Robins JA refers to the possibility that the manufacturer might be able to adduce evidence that the doctor's conduct might have been the same whether or not the manufacturer was in breach of its duty. I should say that whatever effect this may have regarding the apportionment of liability between the doctor and the manufacturer in the event that the doctor is also found to be negligent, it in no way absolves the manufacturer from liability to the plaintiff, except in cases where some extraneous conduct by the doctor would have made the failure to give adequate warning irrelevant. But that is not this case. In sum, in a case like the present, I see no reason why in establishing the liability of the manufacturer the law should adopt a rule requiring the plaintiff to delve into what the doctor might have done.

[60] Simply put, I do not think a manufacturer should be able to escape liability for failing to give a warning it was under a duty to give, by simply presenting evidence tending to

establish that even if the doctor had been given the warning, he or she would not have passed it on to the patient, let alone putting an onus on the plaintiff to do so. Adopting such a rule would, in some cases, run the risk of leaving the plaintiff with no compensation for her injuries. She would not be able to recover against a doctor who had not been negligent with respect to the information that he or she *did* have; yet she also would not be able to recover against a manufacturer who, despite having failed in its duty to warn, could escape liability on the basis that, had the doctor been appropriately warned, he or she still would not have passed the information on to the plaintiff. Our tort law should not be held to contemplate such an anomalous result.

[61] As I see it, the plaintiff's claim against the manufacturer should be dealt with in accordance with the following rationale. The ultimate duty of the manufacturer is to warn the plaintiff adequately. For practical reasons, the law permits it to acquit itself of that duty by warning an informed intermediary. Having failed to warn the intermediary, the manufacturer has failed in its duty to warn the plaintiff who ultimately suffered injury by using the product. The fact that the manufacturer would have been absolved had it followed the route of informing the plaintiff through the learned intermediary should not absolve it of its duty to the plaintiff because of the possibility, even the probability, that the learned intermediary would not have advised her had the manufacturer issued it. The learned intermediary rule provides a means by which the manufacturer can discharge its duty to give adequate information of the risks to the plaintiff by informing the intermediary, but if it fails to do so it cannot raise as a defence that the intermediary could have ignored this information. I observe that a number of courts in the United States have reached a similar conclusion. In *McCue v Norwich Pharmaceutical Co*, 453 F.2d 1033 (1st Cir 1972) at p 1035, for example, the Court of Appeal for the First Circuit stated:

> Even if a physician's carelessness may have taken a form not specifically anticipated, defendant should not escape liability so long as its failure to give an adequate warning may have contributed thereto. ... *[H]aving put a dangerous drug on the market without adequate warning defendant cannot be heard to say that the physician night have disregarded a proper one.*

(Emphasis added.) See also *Sterling*, *supra*, and *Hamilton v Hardy*, 549 P2d 1099 (Col CA 1976).

Conclusion

[62] On the basis of the foregoing, it is my view that Dow breached its duty to warn Dr Birch concerning the risks of post-surgical rupture in the Silastic implant and because of this failure to warn is liable to Ms Hollis for her injuries. Accordingly, I would dismiss the appeal ...

L'Heureux-Dubé, Gonthier, Cory and Iacobucci JJ concurred.

The court's survey of the common law in Canada, America and England is instructive. The court held that a manufacturer had a continuing duty to consumers in relation to its products which it discovers are dangerous after sale. That duty may entail an obligation to warn once the dangers become known. In the case of medicinal products, that duty will often be discharged by warning a 'learned intermediary'. Of course, the court was considering a duty to patients who had already received the implants. The duty might well also entail removing the product from circulation if it was unreasonably dangerous. All of this is, of course, consistent with the manufacturer's obligations in respect of post-marketing surveillance imposed by the legislation governing medicinal products and medical devices.

On the causation question, a majority of the court applied a 'subjective test': would the patient have consented to the operation if properly warned? The conclusion was that she would not. This is undoubtedly the approach an English court would take although, as in medical negligence cases, it would see the 'reasonableness' of the patient's response as a useful 'yardstick' in judging the credibility of the patient (see *Smith v Barking, Havering and Brentwood HA* [1994] 5 Med LR 285, and *supra*, ch 5). Sopinka and McLachlin JJ dissented and applied a 'reasonable person' test as is applied in Canada in negligence actions against *doctors* for a failure to warn. (The Supreme Court (including La Forest J) reaffirmed the latter in the subsequent case of *Arndt v Smith* [1997] 2 SCR 539 and Commentary (1998) 6 Med L Rev 126 (IK).) English law adheres to the formal rubric of the subjective test with an 'objective' element to test credibility (*O'Keefe v Harvey-Kemble* (1998) 45 BMLR 74 (CA)). The minority rejected the 'subjective approach' because it:

> **Sopinka J:** ... fails to take into account the inherent unreliability of the plaintiff's self-serving assertion. It is not simply a question as to whether the plaintiff is believed. The plaintiff may be perfectly sincere in stating that in hindsight she believed that she would not have consented to the operation. This is not a statement of fact that, if accepted, concludes the matter. It is an opinion about what the plaintiff would have done in respect of a situation that did not occur. As such, the opinion may be honestly given without being accepted. In evaluating the opinion, the trier of fact must discount its probity not only by reason of its self-serving nature, but also by reason of the fact that it is likely to be coloured by the trauma occasioned by the failed procedure. For this reason, the most reliable approach in determining *what would in fact have occurred* is to test the plaintiff's assertion by reference to objective evidence as to what a reasonable person would have done.

The majority saw a difference between the manufacturer-patient relationship on the one hand, and the doctor-patient relationship, on the other. The former required that the patient should not be put to the burden of establishing the *reasonableness* of their choice whether or not to consent, the latter did. In England, the exception in *Dow Corning* would not need to be justified, since the rationale of the minority is rejected and the 'subjective approach' is the rule anyway.

Perhaps more interesting is the court's approach to the causation question if the doctor would not have warned anyway. The majority did not apply the 'but for' test, since they concluded that the patient could succeed *even if* the warning would probably not have been passed on by the doctor to the patient and, it must be added, could have led the patient to refuse the procedure. La Forest J is unperturbed by his departure from the normal rule. It would be too onerous to expect a patient to prove what a doctor would have hypothetically done. Sopinka J (for the dissenting justices) disagreed. The patient must prove that the breach was a *sine qua non* of the injury, otherwise the burden of proof would be inappropriately shifted to the defendant manufacturer.

Sopinka J:
[72] In determining the second causation issue of whether Dr Birch would have warned Ms Hollis of the risk of rupture if Dow had properly warned Dr Birch about that risk, La Forest J. proposes to eliminate the fundamental requirement of tort law that the plaintiff shall establish causation in order to prove the defendant's liability. Once Ms Hollis demonstrated that Dow had breached its duty to warn of the risk of rupture, La Forest J. would hold that the plaintiff's burden of proving her case had been discharged, and that any possibility that Dr Birch would have *failed* to pass on any warning is nothing more than a question of apportionment. This approach runs counter to well-established tort principles. Simply put, in order to establish liability, the plaintiff must show not only a breach of duty by the defendant, but also that the breach in question was the *cause* of the plaintiff's injury.

[73] In the instant case, this burden applies to require the plaintiff to show that her injuries would not have occurred had Dow discharged its duty to warn Dr Birch of any dangers inherent in the implants. In other words, Ms Hollis must show that her doctor would have warned her of any dangers that had been brought to his attention and that if warned she would have refused the operation. Absent this form of proof, it cannot be said with any degree of certainty that the failure of Dow to warn physicians was *the cause* of the unfortunate injuries suffered by Ms Hollis.

[74] Professor John G. Fleming, in *The Law of Torts*, 8th ed. (Sydney: Law Book Co., 1992), at p. 143, explains the necessity of a factual finding of a cause and effect relationship between the defendant's breach of duty and the plaintiff's injury as follows:

> If such a causal relation does not exist, that puts an end to the plaintiff's case: to impose liability for loss to which the defendant's conduct has not *in fact* contributed would be incompatible with the principle of individual responsibility on which the law of torts has been traditionally based.

(Emphasis in original.)

[75] If Dr. Birch would not have passed on information from Dow to Ms Hollis, Dow's failure to provide the warning cannot be said to have contributed to Ms Hollis' injury. Liability cannot be based on failure to take measures which would have no effect and be pointless.

[76] The absence of cause cannot be finessed by sweeping it under the apportionment rug as suggested by my colleague. A finding of causation is a prerequisite to apportionment. Apportionment is authorized only in the circumstances mandated by the *Negligence Act*, R.S.B.C. 1979, c. 298, where the damage or loss is *caused* by the fault of two or more persons.

[77] My colleague refers to a number of cases, such as *Cook v Lewis*, [1952] 1 DLR 1, [1951] SCR 830; *Snell v Farrell* (1990), 72 DLR (4th) 289, [1990] 2 SCR 311, 4 CCLT (2d) 229, and *Buchan, supra*, which either reversed or relaxed the ordinary burden which rests on the plaintiff to prove causation. Those cases do not support treating causation as irrelevant. Indeed, they start with the premise that causation is a fundamental principle and address whether the plaintiff's ordinary burden should be eased. Not only is the requirement that causation be established fundamental to the law of torts, but, as well, the principle that the burden of proof of causation generally rests with the plaintiff is also well-entrenched ...

[80] ... the burden of proof is properly reversed where the defendant has somehow participated in destroying the means of proving the case against it or where the defendant somehow controls the relevant evidence. Only within this limited sphere of cases is the plaintiff partially relieved of the burden of proving causation. In this case, there is neither any suggestion of a tortious destruction of the means of proof nor does the evidence lie peculiarly in the control of the defendant Dow. On the contrary, the issue in question is largely dependent on the evidence of Dr Birch. Both Ms Hollis and Dow have equal access to the evidence of Dr Birch. Indeed, in this situation, the physician is likely to be inclined to favour his patient, the plaintiff. It is not in the interests of the physician to assert that he would not have passed on a warning that the manufacturer was duty-bound to give him for the benefit of the plaintiff. As the means of proving causation remains available to the plaintiff, it would be inconsistent with *Snell* to reverse the burden of proof. As a result, the burden of proving causation remains on the plaintiff in this case. In order to discharge the burden in question, the plaintiff must adduce evidence that her doctor would have warned her of any dangers associated with breast implants had those dangers been brought to his attention by the defendant.

[81] An alternative method of obviating the plaintiff's burden of proof was suggested by the Court of Appeal in *Buchan*. In that case, the court expressed the view that a "rebuttable presumption" exists such that a plaintiff in Ms Hollis' position need not establish all elements of causation. According to the court, at p. 682:

> Once the breach of duty to warn prescribing physicians has been established, I think it is fair and reasonable to presume that the inadequacy of the warning was a contributing cause of the ingestion of the drug. It ought not to be incumbent on a plaintiff to prove as part of her case what her doctor might or might not have done had he been adequately warned. One can assume that a doctor would not ignore a proper warning or fail to disclose a material risk or otherwise act negligently. Even if the evidence were to indicate that the doctor was negligent, the manufacturer would not be shielded from liability if such negligence were a foreseeable consequence of the breach of duty to warn. The presumption may, of course, be rebutted if the defendant comes forth with evidence that despite the inadequacy of the warning the doctor's conduct towards his patient would have been the same whether or not the manufacturer was in breach of the duty.

Based on this approach, the plaintiff need not prove that her doctor would have warned her of any dangers *unless the defendant presents some evidence* tending to show that the doctor may not have in fact passed along the appropriate warning. The burden on the defendant is discharged where sufficient evidence is adduced to *raise the issue* of causation. This is an "evidential" burden of proof, which has been described by Professor Colin Tapper in *Cross on Evidence*, 7th ed. (London: Butterworths, 1990), at p. 113, as:

> ... the obligation to show, if called upon to do so, that there is sufficient evidence to raise an issue as to the existence or non-existence of a fact in issue, due regard being had to the standard of proof demanded of the party under such obligation.

Thus, the rebuttable presumption referred to in *Buchan* merely requires the defendant to furnish sufficient proof to raise a question of whether or not the "learned intermediary" would have passed a warning along had one been provided by the manufacturer. Where this nominal burden has been discharged, the ultimate burden of proving causation remains on the plaintiff, requiring her to show that any warnings received by Dr Birch would have been passed along.

[82] If the burden of proof were reversed as proposed in *Cook v Lewis*, it would not operate against the defendant if there was sufficient evidence to raise the issue of causation.

In that event, the trier of fact would be obliged to weigh the evidence. The burden of proof would only be applied if the trier of fact were unable to come to a determinate conclusion: see *Cross on Evidence*, *supra*, at pp. 112–13, and *McCormick on Evidence*, 3rd ed. by Edward W. Cleary, general editor (St. Paul: West Publishing, 1984), at p. 947.

[83] Whether one applies the presumption in *Buchan* or reverses the burden of proof as in *Cook v. Lewis*, I am of the view that there was abundant evidence in this case to raise the issue and it was conflicting. ...

There are shades here of the House of Lords' approach to causation in *Bolitho v City of Hackney HA* [1997] 4 All ER 771 (HL) (discussed *supra*, ch 4). But only superficially. There, the House of Lords refused in principle to allow the defendant to rely upon its own actions which would themselves have been negligent. In *Dow Corning*, however, it was not the actions of the defendant, but of the doctor, and the majority's approach is not dependent upon the doctor's (hypothetical) failure to warn itself being negligent. In other words, the manufacturer could be liable despite the fact that the doctor (a third party) without any negligence would have failed to pass on the warning. Surely, the defendant's negligence was only a *causa causans* in these circumstances. What is the policy basis for liability in these circumstances? This is a further two steps away from the 'but for' test than even the House of Lords' sanctioned in *Bolitho*.

B. THE REGULATORY AUTHORITIES

Could the regulatory bodies such as the MCA and MDA be sued for a defective and dangerous product which injures patients? There are considerable, probably insurmountable, difficulties first in establishing a duty of care owed to an individual patient and secondly in proving a breach of that duty. Certainly, there would be no liability for breach of statutory duty. The courts would not find that Parliament intended to create a civil action for damages for breach of duty under the Medicines Act 1968 or the Medical Devices Regulations. Indeed, the former expressly denies the existence of such an action (see s 133(2)).

The possibility of an action in negligence is discussed in the following extract.

Anthony Barton 'The basis of liability of the licensing authority and its advisers under the Medicines Act 1968 to an individual' in Sir Abraham Goldberg and Ian Dodds Smith (eds) *Pharmaceutical Medicine and the Law* (1991)

The liability in negligence of public bodies such as licensing, regulatory, or planning authorities to the individual has been examined recently in numerous cases; the cases fall into two broad categories:
1.   Where the public body has affected the plaintiff directly by its alleged wrong.
2.   Where the public body is alleged to have been negligent in the regulation of licensing or approval of the act of a third party which has caused damage to the plaintiff.
The liability of the licensing authority to an individual in respect of a medicinal product falls into the second category. These cases present a novel development in the law of negligence:

As any proposition which relates to the duty of controlling another man to prevent his doing damage to a third deals with the category of civil wrongs of which the English courts have hitherto had little experience it would not be consistent with the methodology of the development of the law by judicial decision that any new proposition should be stated in wider terms than are necessary for the determination of the present appeal. Public policy may call for the immediate recognition of a new sub-category of relations which are the source of a duty of this nature additional to the sub-category described in the established proposition, but further experience of actual cases would be needed before the time became ripe for the coalescence of sub-categories into a broader category of relations giving rise to the duty, such as was effected with respect to the duty of care of a manufacturer of products in *Donoghue v Stevenson* ... Nevertheless, any new sub-category will form part of the English law of civil wrongs and must be consistent with its general principles. (Per Lord Diplock in *Dorset Yacht Co v Home Office* at p. 1064).

Twenty years of further experience of actual cases has provided little assistance in determining such cases and indeed the courts now approve a piecemeal approach rather than a coalescence. Some assistance as to whether a duty of care is owed by a public authority may be provided by consideration of the statute by which the authority derives its duties and powers. This is the so-called 'statutory purpose' test (*Dutton v Bognor Regis UDC*, [1972] 1 QB 373; *Anns v Merton, Governors of the Peabody Donation Fund v Sir Lindsey Parkinson Ltd*, [1985] AC 210).

> The purpose for which the powers … have been conferred on the [public body] is not to safeguard [the plaintiffs] against economic loss resulting from their failure to comply … . It is in my opinion to safeguard the occupiers of houses … and also members of the public generally, against dangers to their health. … (per Lord Keith in *Peabody* at p. 241).

Thus, in determining the justice and fairness of imposing a duty of care, the court examines, *inter alia*, the statutory purpose for which the public body derives its authority. The powers, duties and the intended class to be protected are considered. The nature of the duty allegedly breached would have to be closely related to the purpose of the power. The statutory purpose of the Medicines Act 1968 has been judicially considered:

> The licensing authority are advised by experts in the field of medicinal products. The information available to the licensing authority consists of the knowledge obtained by these experts based on long experience, the information in published literature and, over the years, the vast amount of information provided by large numbers of applicants for product licences … . The principal task of the licensing authority is to protect the public … . The licensing authority cannot discharge its duty to safeguard the health of the nation. … without having recourse to all the information available to the licensing authority … when carrying out any function imposed upon the licensing authority by the Act of 1968 in the interests of the public. (Per Lord Templeman, *Regina v Licensing Authority, ex p Smith Kline, (HL)* [1990] 1 AC 64 at p. 103).

The Council of the European Community has promulgated a Directive (65/65 EEC) on the approximation of provisions laid down by law, regulation or administrative action relating to proprietary and medicinal products. The provisions of this Directive, as amended and amplified from time to time by subsequent Directives, became binding on the UK on 1 January 1973, and must be performed and observed by the licensing authority. The Directive of 1965 recited, *inter alia*:

> … the primary purpose of any rules concerning the production and distribution of proprietary medicinal products must be to safeguard public health; …

The purpose of the Medicines Act 1968 appears consistent with this Directive. It seems that the statutory purpose of the Act is, in broad terms, concerned with the safety and licensing of medicinal products. A duty of care, by this test, would appear to be owed to the class of patients as a whole rather than individually.

Recently, the courts have demonstrated the new conservative and restrictive approach in imposing a duty of care on public bodies. It is regarded as undesirable for a public body exercising its typical functions of government in the general public interest to be liable to an unnamed, unidentified and smaller class of the public in failing adequately to regulate wrongful acts of a third party. Furthermore, the degree of control of the government body over the third party must be related to the duty owed. Generally, in respect of government bodies, such control is usually not sufficient to give rise to liability. If such liability were desirable on policy grounds, the court has indicated that it is a matter for the legislature, which is better suited than the judiciary to weigh up competing policy considerations (*Hill v Chief Constable of West Yorkshire* (CA) [1988] 1 QBD 60; *Yuen Kun Yeu v A-G of Hong Kong* (PC) [1988] AC 175; *Davies v. Radcliffe* (PC) [1990] 2 All ER 563).

It is at this stage that it is necessary, before concluding that a duty of care should be imposed, to consider all the relevant circumstances. One of the considerations … is the fear that a too literal application of a well-known observation of Lord Wilberforce in *Anns v. Merton London Borough Council* … , may be productive of a failure to have regard to, and to analyse and weigh, all the relevant considerations in considering whether it is appropriate that a duty of care should be imposed. Their Lordships consider that question to be of an intensely pragmatic character, well suited for gradual development but requiring most careful analysis …

In all the circumstances, it must be a serious question for consideration whether it would be appropriate to impose liability in negligence in these cases, or whether it would not rather be in the public interest that citizens should be confined to their remedy, as at present, in those cases where the minister or public authority has acted in bad faith. (per Lord Keith in *Rowling v Takaro* p. 501 and p. 503).

More recently, the House of Lords has considered whether a public body owes a duty of care to an individual and, as the question was *obiter*, their Lordships were expressly silent:

[There] may be cogent reasons of social policy for imposing liability on the authority. But the shoulders of a public body are only 'broad enough to bear loss' because they are financed by the public at large. It is pre-eminently for the legislature to decide whether these policy reasons should be accepted as sufficient for imposing on the public the burden of providing compensation for private financial losses. If they do so decide, it is not difficult for them to say so. (Per Lord Bridge in *Murphy v Brentwood District Council* (HL) [1990] 2 All ER 908 at p. 931.)

Although the case of alleged negligence by the licensing authority for medicinal products has not been tested in the courts, consideration of previous cases indicates their reluctance to create a new category of liability and that, in any case, the balance of interest would fall such that the public interest is favoured rather than the individual interest.

Most recently, the liability of government bodies was considered in *Re HIV Haemophiliac Litigation*, (Court of Appeal, 20 September 1990). The defendants included the Department of Health. The question arose as to the validity of the causes of action, namely negligence and breach of statutory duty. It was considered that the plaintiffs had 'made out at least a good arguable claim in law based upon common law negligence'. Dicta suggest that this term was not to be taken to be an indication of the merits of the plaintiffs' claim, but rather than as a matter of law a minimum threshold had been achieved.

Breach of duty of care
Breach of duty is a mixed question of law and fact, and its determination requires factual investigation. The licensing authority under the Medicines Act 1968 is responsible for the grant, renewal, variation, suspension and revocation of licences and certificates (Section 6). It is a body of ministers consisting of, *inter alia*, the 'health ministers'. The CSM was established to 'give advice with respect to safety, quality or efficacy' of medicines and to promote 'the collection and investigation of information relating to adverse reactions for the purpose of enabling such advice to be given' (Section 4). Where a body has been professionally advised in reaching a decision, it is able to delegate that duty and reasonably discharge that duty thereby (*Dunlop v Woollahra Municipal Council*). Presumably, such is the position where the licensing authority has been advised by the CSM. The delegation is of itself reasonable, and the reliance upon the Committee's advice will be difficult to characterise as negligent. Furthermore, there may be semantic difficulties in finding a body such as the CSM to be in breach of duty. Under the 'Bolam' test, an act is deemed not to be negligent if it is consistent with a recognised but minority body of responsible medical opinion (*Bolam v Friern Hospital Management Committee* [1957] 2 All ER 118). By its very composition, the CSM is such a responsible body of medical opinion. For this reason, a claim in negligence against its members will face fundamental difficulties.

Causation
Causation is a pure question of fact involving application of the 'but for' test. Legal causation is determined thus: but for the act complained of, would the loss have occurred? In medical litigation it is the proof of causation, above all, which may cause greatest difficulty to a plaintiff. The courts have shown a reversion to the rigorous application of the 'but for' test (*Wilsher v Essex Area Health Authority* (HL) [1988] AC 1074).

Remoteness of damage in law
The courts have recently reasserted the principle that for damages to be recoverable in negligence it must be related to physical injury (*Murphy v Brentwood District Council*). Medical litigation cases by their very nature involve personal injury, and this restriction does not generally present a difficulty. However, where a pharmaceutical company seeks damages for the wrong decision of the licensing authority, such loss as it has suffered can usually be formulated only in terms of economic loss. Accordingly, the recovery of such loss is likely to be difficult.

The difficulties of succeeding in such actions have been reinforced by the more recent decisions of the House of Lords in *X (minors) v Bedfordshire CC* [1995] 3 All ER 353 and *Stovin v Wise* [1996] 3 All ER 801. (See also *Danns v Department of Health* [1998] PIQR P226 (CA) and Commentary (1998) 6 Med L Rev 371 and *supra*, ch 4; see further I Kennedy and A Grubb (eds) *Principles of Medical Law* paras 14.42–14.47.) There might be liability where central Government bodies are directly involved in the provision of the product (see eg *N v UK Medical Research Council* [1996] 7 Med LR 309 (CJD transmitted through growth hormone)). However, the nature of the licensing process and the role of the MCA and MDA is such that a court is unlikely to find a proximate relationship with a particular individual or that it is 'just, fair and reasonable' to impose a duty of care (see A Grubb and D Pearl *Blood Testing, AIDS and DNA Profiling* (1990) pp 103–107 – considering liability for importing blood/blood products infected with HIV; and P Ferguson *Drug Injuries and the Pursuit of Compensation* (1996) ch 6).

C. CAUSATION

The principles of causation that we saw earlier (*supra*, ch 4) are applicable in products liability actions just as they are in cases of medical negligence. Actions involving drugs and vaccines have, however, thrown up particularly difficult factual problems of identifying whether the product did cause the patient's injury or whether it resulted from some other source (eg *Kay v Ayrshire and Arran Health Board* [1987] 2 All ER 417 (HL) – overdose of penicillin; *Loveday v Renton* [1990] 1 Med LR 117 (Stuart-Smith LJ) – pertussis vaccine). In nature, the problems faced by claimants are no different from those found in many types of action. The claimants' difficulties often lie in the limits of scientific evidence of 'cause and effect' and the courts' necessary reliance on expert evidence to make a determination of 'what caused the claimant's injury' (see R Goldberg 'Causation and Medicinal Products – A Legal and Probability Analysis' (1996) 4 Consumer LJ 57 and R G Lee 'Vaccine Damage: Adjudicating Scientific Dispute' in G Howells (ed) *Product Liability, Insurance and the Pharmaceutical Industry: An Anglo-American Comparison* (1991) p 52).

Usually, the causation inquiry is a 'what did it' story: was it the drug or was it something else? In products liability cases involving drugs, however, the inquiry may be a 'who dunnit' story. It may be clear on the evidence that the patient was injured by a particular drug but it may be unclear who manufactured the drug. This can arise because of the generic drug market whereby, once the patent term has expired, other manufacturers other than the original developer may market identical generic drugs. The patient may not know whose drug he took or he may have taken a number of manufacturer's drugs over a time. In America, there has been a considerable amount of litigation where this has been the issue. Many American courts have adopted innovative approaches to causation in order to find for a claimant even though it is impossible to prove that the defendant's drug (rather than another manufacturer's drug) injured him. The most well-known development is so-called 'market-share' liability invoked by the Californian Supreme Court in *Sindell v Abbott Laboratories* (1980) 607 P 2d 924. But there are others, and they are discussed in the following extract.

Pamela R Ferguson *Drug Injuries and the Pursuit of Compensation* (1996)

... problems of identifying the appropriate defendant have arisen in America in cases involving Diethylstilbestrol. More than 300 companies manufactured this drug at some time, although about one-third of these have ceased to operate. It has been suggested that "pharmacists commonly filled prescriptions for a designated brand of DES with whatever brand they happen to have on hand" (Schreiber and Hirssh, *"Theories of Liability Applied to Overcome the Unique 'Identification Problem' in DES Cases"* (1985) Medicine and Law, 4, 337 at 338). Several American states have refused to apply traditional rules of tort law to these cases, and have argued that product liability law should adapt to accommodate victims who are faced with such difficult problems of proof. The question raised by the DES cases has been described as follows:

> may a plaintiff, injured as a result of a drug administered to her mother during pregnancy, who knows the type of drug involved but cannot identify the manufacturer of the precise

product, hold liable for her injuries *a maker of a drug produced from an identical formula*? (*Sindell v Abbott Laboratories*, 607 P2d 924 (1980) per Justice Mosk.)

Some American courts have answered this question in the affirmative, and have devised several novel theories of liability in an attempt to overcome these difficulties (see Fern and Sichel, "*Evolving Tort Liability Theories: Are They Taking the Pharmaceutical Industry into an Era of Absolute Liability?*" (1985) St Louis University Law Journal, 29, 763).

In *Hall v EI Du Pont De Nemours & Co* (345 F Supp 353 (EDNY 1972)) the 13 plaintiffs were children who had been injured in incidents involving blasting caps. The children were from 10 different states and the injuries occurred during 12 unrelated incidents. However, the court allowed the plaintiffs to sue all six cap manufacturers under a theory of joint liability, since the particular cap manufacturer could not be identified and the defendants had all followed national safety standards. The case illustrates the doctrine of Enterprise Liability. This theory may be applied if it can be shown that the defendants acted essentially in concert, and that their safety requirements were determined by a trade association of the industry. It is a prerequisite that the industry consists of only a few members, virtually all of whom are cited as defendants.

In relation to pharmaceutical products, the Enterprise Liability theory was proposed in the case of *Collins v Eli Lilly & Co* (342 NW 2d 37 (1984)). The plaintiff's mother was given DES during her pregnancy and the plaintiff had developed adenocarcinoma. This had required removal of her uterus and part of her vagina. She was attempting to sue 17 parties, alleging that they had each produced or marketed DES at the relevant time. The Enterprise Liability approach was, however, rejected by the court in this case. As already noted, hundreds of different drug companies had been responsible for manufacturing DES and it was felt to be unreasonable to assume that the 17 defendants had jointly controlled the risk of injury.

(B) ALTERNATIVE LIABILITY

This was a second theory proposed in *Collins*. The leading authority here is *Summers v Tice* (33 Cal 2d 80, 194 P2d 1 (1948)) in which the plaintiff was shot in the eye by one of two negligent hunters. Both hunters had fired in the direction of the plaintiff but the latter was unable to ascertain which of the two had fired the actual shot which caused his injury. The Alternative Liability theory placed the onus on each defendant to show that he was not responsible. This principle is now contained in the Second Restatement of Torts, which states:

> Where the conduct of two or more actors is tortious, and it is proved that harm has been caused to the plaintiff by only one of them, but there is uncertainty as to which one has caused it, the burden is upon each actor to prove that he has not caused the harm. (s. 433B(3).)

It has been argued that the principle in *Summers v Tice* is a sound one:

> ... it is fairer that the burden of identification be borne by the wrongdoers rather than their victim when it is their multiplicity alone which precludes the latter from identifying the responsible culprit. (Hart and Honore, '*Causation in the Law*' (OUP, 2nd ed, 1985) p 424.)

The Alternative Liability theory has been used successfully in some DES actions but has been rejected in the majority of cases. One principle behind the theory is that the defendants are in a better position than the plaintiff to identify the negligent party or the source of the injury. In many DES cases even the defendants have encountered problems in recovering vital information. Furthermore, in *Summers v Tice* both hunters were cited as co-defendants by the plaintiff. In many DES suits the plaintiff is attempting to sue a large number of manufacturers or suppliers, but all potential defendants are not before the court. This has proved fatal in a number of cases (see *Sindell v Abbott Laboratories*, 26 Ca 3d 588), since the Restatement of Torts provides that all potential tortfeasors must be before the court before the burden of proof can shift from plaintiff to defendants. In general, the DES cases in which the Alternative Liability theory has been successful are those where the plaintiff has attempted to sue all the companies which manufactured DES at the relevant time (this was the position in the case of *Abel v Eli Lilly & Co* 343 NW 2d 164 (1979)).

(C) CONCERTED ACTION

Similar to the idea of Enterprise Liability is the theory of "Concerted Action". This was also proposed in the *Collins* case. According to this theory:

> All those who, in pursuance of a common plan or design to commit a tortious act, actively take part in it, or further it by cooperation or request, or who lend aid or encouragement to the wrongdoer, or ratify and adopt the wrongdoer's acts done for their benefit, are equally liable. (Prosser and Keaton, On Torts (St Paul, Minn, West Publishing Co, 5th ed, 1984) p 323.)

The plaintiff must demonstrate that there was some agreement, express or implicit, among the defendants. By virtue of section 876 of the Second Restatement of Torts:

> For harm resulting to a third person from the tortious conduct of another, one is subject to liability if he:
>
> (a)   does a tortious act in concert with the other pursuant to a common design with him, or
>
> (b)   knows that the other's conduct constitutes a breach of duty and gives substantial encouragement to the other … or
>
> (c)   gives substantial assistance to the other in accomplishing a tortious result and his own conduct, separately considered, constitutes a breach of duty to the third person.

Liability based on this theory has been imposed by some states in DES litigation. In *Bichler v Eli Lilly & Co* (79 App Div 2d 317, 436 NYS 2d 625 (App Div 1981) 55 NY 2d 571, 450 NYS 2d 776, 436 NE 2d 182 (1982)) the "concerted action" was based on:

> … the original cooperation by the twelve manufacturers (which included Lilly) and pooling of information, the agreement on the same basic chemical formula, and the adoption of Lilly's literature as a model for package insets for joint submission to the FDA … (Ibid. 436 NYS 2d 625, at 633.)

It was argued in *Collins* that the defendant manufacturers had acted in concert since each had relied upon the tests of its fellow producers and had derived advantage from the promotional activities and advertising of the others. This argument was rejected by the court on the basis that the defendants' activities were more in the nature of parallel conduct than concerted action.

Similarly, in the case of *Sindell v Abbott Laboratories* (26 Cal 3d 588, 607 P2d 924, 163 Cal Rptr 132 (1980)) the court stated:

> What the [plaintiff's] complaint appears to charge is defendants' parallel or initiative conduct in that they relied upon each others' testing and promotion methods. But such conduct describes a common practice in industry: a producer avails himself of the experience and methods of others making the same or similar products. Application of the concept of concert of action to this situation would expand the doctrine far beyond its intended scope and would render virtually any manufacturer liable for the defective products of an entire industry, even if it could be demonstrated that the product which caused the injury was not made by the defendant. (Ibid. 26 Cal. 3d at 605.)

(D) MARKET SHARE LIABILITY

The three theories which have been looked at so far were already recognised by the law at the time of the DES litigation. A fourth theory which has gained some acceptance in DES litigation is that of "Market Share" liability. This was a novel theory of liability, invented by some American courts specifically to assist DES plaintiffs. The theory was successfully applied in the case of *Sindell v Abbott Laboratories*, mentioned above. The plaintiff attempted to sue 11 named and 100 unnamed pharmaceutical companies. Ultimately, the Supreme Court of California held that she had a valid cause of action against five of the companies, the Upjohn Company; ER Squibb & Co; Eli Lilly; the Rexall Drug Company and Abbott Laboratories.

The Market Share theory requires a plaintiff to demonstrate that the defendants were responsible for a substantial share of the drug market. Each defendant must then show that it did not produce the particular drug which was responsible for the plaintiff's injury (it has been held that a manufacturer who had 10 per cent of the DES market did not have a sufficiently large "Market Share" to be subject to this form of liability – see *Murphy v ER Squibb & Sons* (1985) (1985) 40 Cal 3d 672, 221 Cal Rptr 447, 710 P 2d 247). Each manufacturer which fails to demonstrate this is liable to pay a percentage of the compensation awarded to the plaintiff, and this percentage is dependant on the share of the market for which the company was responsible at the relevant time (that is, at the time when the plaintiff's injury or loss occurred). A defendant may bring other producers of the drug into the action as co-defendants (*Smith v Cutter Biologicals Incorporated* 823 P 2d 717 (Han 1991)).

The reasoning in *Sindell* was rejected in the later cases of *Mizell v Eli Lilly & Co* (526 F Supp 589 (DSC 1981)), *Ryan v Eli Lilly & Co* (514 F Supp 1004 (DSC 1981)) and in the *Collins* case itself. One major reason for this was the recognition that in any particular case none of the companies being sued might have actually been responsible for producing the drug which caused the plaintiff's injuries.

Where a Market Share liability approach is accepted, this may allow a plaintiff to claim punitive damages from the defendants. In the case of *Morris v Parke-Davis & Co* (573 F Supp 1324 (CD Cal 1983)) the plaintiff could not identify the manufacturer of the DTP vaccine which had caused his brain damage. In allowing the plaintiff to seek punitive damages from all five defendants the court stated:

> If manufacturers act with conscious disregard for human safety, they should not be allowed to escape punitive damages simply because the nature of their activity makes it impossible to identify which of them is responsible for the resulting harm. (Quoted in Vinson and Slaughter, eds, '*Product Liability: Pharmaceutical Drug Cases*' 1988 p 286.)

(E) RISK CONTRIBUTION

A further theory which has been developed by some American courts can be described as one of "Risk Contribution". This does not require the plaintiff to raise suit against all possible defendants, but rather to act against some of the potential tortfeasors, only. The injured party requires to show that the defendants manufactured the type of drug involved. It is still open to each of the defendants to prove that it did not produce the particular DES in question. The theory is an amalgam of the "Market Share" and "Alternative Liability" theories, and was applied in the case of *Martin v. Abbott Laboratories* (689 P. 2d 368 (Wash. 1984)). The criteria which the plaintiff requires to meet are similar to those specified in the *Collins* case. However, the defendants in *Collins* may have been found jointly liable for the total amount of the plaintiff's loss, despite the fact that all potential tortfeasors might not have been before the court. In *Martin's* case the court determined that the defendants could only be found liable for a percentage of the plaintiff's compensation, equivalent to their percentage share of the market at the time. Hence a plaintiff who sues manufacturers who were responsible for 60 per cent of the market will recover only 60 per cent of the compensation that would otherwise be due.

More recently, the New York Court of Appeals in *Hymowitz v Eli Lilly & Co* (1989) 539 NE 2d 1069 went further and imposed liability on a manufacturer even where it could show it had not actually produced the drug which injured the patient. The judgment of the court, given by the (then) Chief Justice, traces the developments in other US jurisdictions only to reject them for an even more radical approach.

Mindy Hymowitz v Eli Lilly & Co (1989) 541 NYS 2d 941 (NY CA)

Wachtler CJ: Plaintiffs in these appeals allege that they were injured by the drug diethylstilbestrol (DES) ingested by their mothers during pregnancy. They seek relief against defendant DES manufacturers. While not class actions, these cases are representative of nearly 500 similar actions pending in the courts in this state; the rules articulated by the Court here, therefore, must do justice and be administratively feasible in the context of this mass litigation. With this in mind, we now resolve the issue twice expressly left open by this Court, and adopt a market share theory, using a national market, for determining liability and apportioning damages in DES cases in which identification of the manufacturer of the drug that injured the plaintiff is impossible (see, *Kaufman v Lilly & Co*, 65 NY2d 449, 456; *Bichler v Lilly & Co*, 55 NY2d 571, 580).

The present appeals are before the Court in the context of summary judgment motions. In all of the appeals defendants moved for summary judgment dismissing the complaints because plaintiffs could not identify the manufacturer of the drug that allegedly injured them … In a products liability action, identification of the exact defendant whose product injured the plaintiff is, of course, generally required (see, e.g., *Morrissey v Conservative Gas Corp*, 285 AD 825, affd 1 NY 2d 741; Prosser & Keeton, Torts § 103, at 713 [5th ed]). In DES cases in which such identification is possible, actions may proceed under established principles of products liability (*Bichler v Lilly Co*, supra at 579). The record now before us, however, presents the question of whether a DES plaintiff may recover against a DES manufacturer when identification of the producer of the specific drug that caused the injury is impossible.

A.

As we noted in *Bichler v Lilly Co* (supra at 580, n5), the accepted tort doctrines of alternative liability and concerted action are available in some personal injury cases to permit recovery where the precise identification of a wrongdoer is impossible. However, we agree with the near unanimous views of the high state courts that have considered the matter that these doctrines in their unaltered commonlaw forms do not permit recovery in DES cases (see, e.g., *Sindell v Abbott Labs*, supra; *Collins v Lilly & Co*, 116 Wis2d 166; *Martin v Abbott Labs*, supra; but see, *Abel v Lilly & Co*, 418 Mich 311 [held that there was a question of fact presented as to alternative liability and concerted action]).

The paradigm of alternative liability is found in the case of *Summers v Tice* (33 Cal 2d 80). In *Summers* (supra), plaintiff and the two defendants were hunting, and defendants carried identical shotguns and ammunition. During the hunt, defendants shot simultaneously at the same bird, and plaintiff was struck by birdshot from one of the defendants' guns. The court held that where two defendants breach a duty to the plaintiff, but there is uncertainty regarding which one caused the injury, "the burden is upon such actor to prove that he has not caused the harm" (Restatement [Second] of Torts § 433B[3]; *Bichler v Lilly & Co*, supra at 580, n5; cf., *Ravo v Rogatnick*, 70 NY2d 305 [successive tortfeasors may be held jointly and severally liable for an indivisible injury to the plaintiff]). The central rationale for shifting the burden of proof in such a situation is that without this device both defendants will be silent, and plaintiff will not recover; with alternative liability, however, defendants will be forced to speak, and reveal the culpable party, or else be held jointly and severally liable themselves. Consequently, use of the alternative liability doctrine generally requires that the defendants have better access to information than does the plaintiff, and that all possible tortfeasors be before the court (see, *Summers v Tice*, supra at 86; Restatement [Second] of Torts §433B, comment h). It is also recognized that alternative liability rests on the notion that where there is a small number of possible wrongdoers, all of whom breached a duty to the plaintiff, the likelihood that any one of them injured the plaintiff is relatively high, so that forcing them to exonerate themselves, or be held liable, is not unfair (*Sindell v Abbott Labs*, supra at 139).

In DES cases, however, there is a great number of possible wrongdoers, who entered and left the market at different times, and some of whom no longer exist. Additionally, in DES cases many years elapse between the ingestion of the drug and injury. Consequently, DES defendants are not in any better position than are plaintiffs to identify the manufacturer of the DES ingested in any given case, nor is there any real prospect of having all the possible producers before the court. Finally, while it may be fair to employ alternative liability in cases involving only a small number of potential wrongdoers, that fairness disappears with the decreasing probability that any one of the defendants actually caused the injury. This is particularly true when applied to DES where the chance that a particular producer caused the injury is often very remote (*Sindell v Abbott Labs*, supra at 603; *Collins v Lilly & Co*, supra at 184). Alternative liability, therefore, provides DES plaintiffs no relief.

Nor does the theory of concerted action, in its pure form, supply a basis for recovery … as the present record reflects, drug companies were engaged in extensive parallel conduct in developing and marketing DES (see, id. at 585). There is nothing in the record, however, beyond this similar conduct to show any agreement, tacit or otherwise, to market DES for pregnancy use without taking proper steps to ensure the drug's safety. Parallel activity, without more, is insufficient to establish the agreement element necessary to maintain a concerted action claim (*Sindell v Abbott Labs*, supra at 605; *Collins v Lilly & Co*, supra at 85; *Martin v Abbott Labs*, supra at 599). Thus this theory also fails in supporting the action by DES plaintiffs.

In short, extant common law doctrines, unmodified, provide no relief for the DES plaintiff unable to identify the manufacturer of the drug that injured her. This is not a novel conclusion; in the last decade a number of courts in other jurisdictions also have concluded that present theories do not support a cause of action in DES cases. Some courts, upon reaching this conclusion, have declined to find any judicial remedy for the DES plaintiffs who cannot identify the particular manufacturer of the DES ingested by their mothers (see, *Zafft v Lilly & Co*, 67 SW2d 241 [Mo] [en banc]; *Mulcahy v Lilly & Co*, 386 NW2d 67 [Iowa] [stating that any change in the law to allow for recovery in non-identification DES cases should come from the legislature]). Other courts, however, have found that some modification of existing doctrine is appropriate to allow for relief for those injured by DES of unknown manufacture (e.g., *Sindell v Abbott Labs*, supra; *Collins v Lilly & Co*, supra; *Martin v Abbott Labs*, supra).

We conclude that the present circumstances call for recognition of a realistic avenue of relief for plaintiffs injured by DES. These appeals present many of the same considerations that have prompted this Court in the past to modify the rules of personal injury liability, in order "to achieve the ends of justice in a more modern context" (see, *People v Hobson*, 39 NY2d 479, 489; *Codling v Paglia*, 32 NY2d 330, 341), and we perceive that here judicial action is again required "to overcome the inordinately difficult problems of proof" caused by contemporary products and marketing techniques (see, *Bichler v Lilly & Co*, supra at 579–580 [quoting *Caprara v Chrysler Corp*, 52 NY2d 114, 123]).

Indeed, it would be inconsistent with the reasonable expectations of a modern society to say to these plaintiffs that because of the insidious nature of an injury that long remains dormant, and because so many manufacturers, each behind a curtain, contributed to the devastation, the cost of injury should be borne by the innocent and not the wrongdoers. This is particularly so where the legislature consciously created these expectations by reviving hundreds of DES cases. Consequently, the ever-evolving dictates of justice and fairness, which are the heart of our common-law system, require formation of a remedy for injuries caused by DES (see, *Woods v Lancet*, 303 NY 349, 355; see, also, Kaye, The Human Dimension in Appellate Judging: A Brief Reflection on a Timeless Concern, 73 Cornell L. Rev. 1004).

We stress, however, that the DES situation is a singular case, with manufacturers acting in a parallel manner to produce an identical, generically marketed product, which causes injury many years later, and which has evoked a legislative response reviving previously barred actions. Given this unusual scenario, it is more appropriate that the loss be borne by those that produced the drug for use during pregnancy, rather than by those who were injured by the use, even where the precise manufacturer of the drug cannot be identified in a particular action. We turn then to the question of how to fairly and equitably apportion the loss occasioned by DES, in a case where the exact manufacturer of the drug that caused the injury is unknown.

B.
The past decade of DES litigation has produced a number of alternative approaches to resolve this question. Thus, in a sense, we are now in an enviable position; the efforts of other courts provided examples for contending with this difficult issue, and enough time has passed so that the actual administration and real effects of these solutions now can be observed. With these useful guides in hand, a path may be struck for our own conclusion ...

A narrower basis for liability, tailored more closely to the varying culpableness of individual DES producers, is the market share concept. First judicially articulated by the California Supreme Court in *Sindell v Abbott Labs* (supra), variations upon this theme have been adopted by other courts (see, *Collins v Lilly & Co.*, supra; *Martin v Abbott Labs*, supra). In *Sindell v Abbott Labs* (supra), the Court synthesized the market share concept by modifying the *Summers v Tice* (supra) alternative liability rationale in two ways. It first loosened the requirement that all possible wrongdoers be before the court, and instead made a "substantial share" sufficient. The court then held that each defendant who could not prove that it did not actually injure plaintiff would be liable according to that manufacturer's market share. The court's central justification for adopting this approach was its belief that limiting a defendant's liability to its market share will result, over the run of cases, in liability on the part of a defendant roughly equal to the injuries the defendant actually caused (id. at 612).

In the recent case of *Brown v Superior Court* (44 Cal 3d 1049), the California Supreme Court resolved some apparent ambiguity in *Sindell v Abbott Labs*, and held that a manufacturer's liability is several only, and, in cases in which all manufacturers in the market are not joined for any reason, liability will still be limited to market share, resulting in a less than 100% recovery for a plaintiff. Finally, it is noteworthy that determining market shares under *Sindell v Abbott Labs* proved difficult and engendered years of litigation. After attempts at using smaller geographical units, it was eventually determined that the national market provided the most feasible and fair solution, and this national market information was compiled (see, *In re Complex DES Litigation*, No. 830/109 Cal Super Ct).

Four years after *Sindell v Abbott Labs*, the Wisconsin Supreme Court followed with *Collins v Lilly & Co* (116 Wis 2d 166). Deciding the identification issue without the benefit of the extensive California litigation over market shares, the Wisconsin court held that it was prevented from following *Sindell* due to "the practical difficulty of defining and proving market share" (id. at 189). Instead of focusing on tying liability closely to the odds of actual causation, as the *Sindell* court attempted, the *Collins* court took a broader perspective, and held that each defendant is liable in proportion to the amount of risk it created that the plaintiff would be injured by DES. Under the *Collins* structure, the "risk" each defendant is liable for is a question of fact in each case, with market shares being relevant to this determination (id. at 191, 200). Defendants are allowed, however, to exculpate themselves by showing that their product could not have caused the injury to the particular plaintiff (id. at 198).

The Washington Supreme Court, writing soon after *Collins v Lilly & Co*, took yet another approach (see, *Martin v Abbott Labs*, 102 Wash 2d 581). The *Martin* court first rejected the *Sindell* market share theory due to the belief (which later proved to be erroneous in *Brown v Superior Court* [supra]) that California's approach distorted liability by inflating market shares to ensure plaintiffs of full recovery (id. at 601). The *Martin* court instead adopted what it termed "market share alternative liability," justified, it concluded, because "[e]ach defendant contributed to the risk of injury to the public, and consequently, the risk to individual plaintiffs" (id. at 604).

Under the Washington scheme, defendants are first allowed to exculpate themselves by proving by the preponderance of the evidence that they were not the manufacturer of the DES that injured plaintiff. Unexculpated defendants are presumed to have equal market shares, totalling 100%. Each defendant then has the opportunity to rebut this presumption by showing that its actual market share was less than presumed. If any defendants succeed in rebutting this presumption, the liability shares of the remaining defendants who could not prove their actual market share are inflated, so that the plaintiff received a 100% recovery (id. at 605–606). (The actual operation of this theory proved more mathematically complex when the court was presented with the question of what to do about unavailable defendants. Recognizing that the possibility of abuse existed when defendant implead unavailable defendants, who would then be assumed to have had an equal share of the market, the court placed the burden upon appearing defendants to prove the market share of the absent ones (*George v Parke-Davis*, 107 Wash 2d 584). If this can be proved, the plaintiff simply cannot recover the amount attributable to the absent defendant, and thus recovery in the case is less than 100%. If the market share of the absent defendant cannot be shown, the remaining defendants who cannot prove their market shares have their shares inflated to provide plaintiff with full recovery. Finally, if all appearing defendants can prove their market shares, their shares are never inflated, regardless of whether the market share of a non-appearing defendant can be proved or not; thus, in this situation, the plaintiff again will not recover her full damages (id.).) The market shares of defendants is a question of fact in each case, and the relevant market can be a particular pharmacy, or county, or state, or even the country, depending upon the circumstances the case presents (*George v Parke-Davis*, supra).

Turning to the structure to be adopted in New York, we heed both the lessons learned through experience in other jurisdictions and the realities of the mass litigation of DES claims in this State. Balancing these considerations, we are led to the conclusion that a market share theory, based upon a national market, provides the best solution. As California discovered, the reliable determination of any market smaller than the national one is not practicable. Moreover, even if it were possible, of the hundreds of cases in the New York courts, without a doubt there are many in which the DES that allegedly caused injury was ingested in another State. Among the thorny issues this could present, perhaps the most daunting is the spectre that the particular case could require the establishment of a separate market share matrix. We feel that this is an unfair, and perhaps impossible burden to routinely place upon the litigants in individual cases.

Nor do we believe that the Wisconsin approach of assessing the "risk" each defendant caused a particular plaintiff, to be litigated anew as a question of fact in each case, is the best solution for this State. Applied on a limited scale this theory may be feasible, and certainly is the most refined approach by allowing a more thorough consideration of how each defendant's actions threatened the plaintiff. We are wary, however, of setting loose, for application in the hundreds of cases pending in this State, a theory which requires the factfinder's individualized and open-ended assessment of the relative liabilities of scores of defendants in every case. Instead, it is our perception that the injustices arising from delayed recoveries and inconsistent results which this theory may produce in this State outweigh arguments calling for its adopting.

Consequently, for essentially practical reasons, we adopt a market share theory using a national market. We are aware that that the adoption of a national market will likely result in a disproportion between the liability of individual manufacturers and the actual injuries each manufacturer caused in this State. Thus our market share theory cannot be founded upon the belief that, over the run of cases, liability will approximate causation in this State (see, *Sindell v Abbott Labs*, supra at 612). Nor does the use of a national market provide a reasonable link between liability and the risk created by a defendant to a particular plaintiff (see, *Collins v Lilly & Co*, supra; *Martin v Abbott Labs*, supra). Instead, we choose to apportion liability so as to correspond to the overall culpability of each defendant, measured by the amount of risk of injury each defendant created to the public at large. Use of a national market is a fair method, we believe, of apportioning defendants' liabilities according to their total culpability in marketing DES for use during pregnancy. Under the circumstances, this is an equitable way to provide plaintiffs with the relief they deserve, while also rationally distributing the responsibility for plaintiffs' injuries among defendants.

To be sure, a defendant cannot be held liable if it did not participate in the marketing of DES for pregnancy use; if a DES producer satisfies its burden of proof of showing that it was not a member of the market of DES sold for pregnancy use, disallowing exculpation would be unfair and unjust. Nevertheless, because liability here is based on the overall risk produced, and not causation in a single case, there should be no exculpation of a defendant who, although a member of the market producing DES for pregnancy use, appears not to have caused a particular plaintiff's injury. It is merely a windfall for a producer to escape liability solely because it manufactured a more identifiable pill, or sold only to certain drugstores. These fortuities in no way diminish the culpability of a defendant for marketing the product, which is the basis of liability here. (Various defendants argue here that although they produced DES, it was not sold for pregnancy use. If a defendant was not a member of the national market of DES marketed for pregnancy, it is not culpable, and should not be liable. Consequently, if a particular defendant sold DES in a form unsuitable for use during pregnancy, or if a defendant establishes that its product was not marketed for pregnancy use, there should be no liability. From the record before the Court here, however, the facts are not developed well enough to establish that any defendants were not in the national market of DES sold for pregnancy use. Thus summary judgment cannot at this time be granted on this issue as to any defendants.)

Finally, we hold that the liability of DES producers is several only, and should not be inflated when all participants in the market are not before the court in a particular case. We understand that, as a practical matter, this will prevent some plaintiffs from recovering 100% of their damages. However, we eschewed exculpation to prevent the fortuitous avoidance of liability, and thus, equitably, we decline to unleash the same forces to increase a defendant's liability beyond its fair share of responsibility. (The dissenter misapprehends the basis for liability here. We have not by the backdoor adopted a theory of concerted action. We avoided extending this theory, because its concomitant requirement of joint and several liability expands the burden on small manufacturers beyond a rational or fair limit. This result is reached by the dissent, not by the majority, so that criticism on this front is misplaced.)

We are confronted here with an unprecedented identification problem, and have provided a solution that rationally apportions liability. We have heeded the practical lessons learned by other jurisdictions, resulting in our adoption of a national market theory will full knowledge that it concedes the lack of a logical link between liability and causation in a single case. The dissent ignores these lessons, and, endeavoring to articulate a theory it perceives to be closer to traditional law, sets out a construct in which liability is based upon chance, not upon the fair assessment of the acts of defendants. Under the dissent's theory, a manufacturer with a large market share may avoid liability in many cases just because it manufactured a memorably shaped pill. Conversely, a small manufacturer can be held jointly liable for the full amount of every DES injury in this State simply because the shape of its product was not remarkable, even though the odds, realistically, are exceedingly long that the small manufacturer caused the injury in any one particular case.

Therefore, although the dissent's theory based upon a "shifting the burden of proof" and joint and several liability is facially reminiscent of prior law, in the case of DES it is nothing more than advocating that bare fortuity be the test for liability. When faced with the novel identification problem posed by DES cases, it is preferable to adopt a new theory that apportions fault rationally, rather than to contort extant doctrines beyond the point at which they provide a sound premise for determining liability.

Mollen J dissented, rejecting liability when a defendant could prove his drug was not taken by the patient.

Mollen J: I respectfully disagree with the majority's conclusion that there should be no exculpation of those defendants who produced and marketed DES for pregnancy purposes, but who can prove, by a preponderance of the evidence, that they did not produce or market the particular pill ingested by the plaintiff's mother. Moreover, in order to ensure that these plaintiffs receive full recovery of their damages, as they are properly entitled to by any fair standard, I would retain the principle of imposing joint and several liability upon those defendants which cannot exculpate themselves ... none of the jurisdictions which have adopted varying theories of collective liability in DES cases, has refused to permit exculpation of those defendants which have been able to prove that they could not have produced or marketed the pill which caused the particular plaintiff's injuries, thereby recognizing that to preclude exculpation would directly and unnecessarily contravene the established common law tort principles of causation (see, *Sindell v Abbott Labs*, supra; *Collins v Lilly & Co*, supra; *Martin v Abbott Labs*, supra; *Abel v Eli Lilly Co*, supra; *McCormack v Eli Lilly & Co*, supra; see also, *Burnside v Abbott Labs*, 351 Pa S 264).

Clearly, the development and underlying purpose of the various concepts of liability in DES cases has been to provide a means whereby the plaintiffs, who cannot identify the actual manufacturer of the pill ingested by their mother, are alleviated of the traditional burden of proof of causation and to shift that burden to the defendants. The various theories of collective liability which have been adopted in the several jurisdictions in an effort to provide plaintiffs with a means to recovery for their injuries, were not intended to, and did not, provide DES plaintiffs with an unprecedented strict liability cause of action. However, the majority herein, by precluding exculpation of those defendants in DES cases who produced DES for pregnancy purposes but who can establish, by a preponderance of the evidence, that they did not and could not have produced or marketed the pill which caused the plaintiff's injuries, has created such a radical concept and purports to limit it to DES claims. In the majority's view, the defendant's liability in DES cases is premised upon the overall risk of injury which they created to the public at large in producing and marketing DES for pregnancy purposes and, therefore, exculpation of those defendants who can establish that the plaintiff's mother did not ingest their pill, would be inconsistent with the overall risk theory of liability. By taking this view, however, the majority, while stating that it is adopting a market share theory of liability, is, in essence, despite its disclaimer of doing so, adopting a concerted action theory of liability, but has eliminated therefrom the requirement that the plaintiffs establish that the defendants tacitly agreed to produce and market DES for pregnancy use without proper testing and without adequate warnings of the potential dangers involved.

Such a result, represents a radical departure from fundamental tenets of tort law and is unnecessarily unfair and inequitable to the defendants who have proven, or can prove, that they did not produce the pill which caused the injury. Moreover, this result is directly contrary to the majority's own statement that it is rejecting the "conscious parallelism" theory utilized in *Bichler v Eli Lilly & Co* (79 AD2d 317, affd 55 NY2d 571), because, as stated by the majority therein, "(p)arallel behavior, the major justification for visiting liability by the product of one manufacturer upon the head of another under this analysis, is a common occurrence in industry generally. We believe, therefore, that inferring agreement from the fact of parallel activity alone improperly expands the concept of concerted action beyond a rational or fair limit; among other things, it potentially renders small manufacturers in the case of DES and in countless other industries, jointly liable for all the damages stemming from the defective products of an entire industry" (slip opinion, p 12).

I fully concur with the above stated position of the majority and thus, I cannot agree that the imposition of liability of drug companies, in this case DES manufacturers, solely upon their contribution, in some measure, to the risk of injury by producing and marketing a defective drug, without any consideration given to whether the defendant drug companies actually caused the plaintiff's injuries, is appropriate or warranted. Rather, I would adopt a market share theory of liability, based upon a national market, which would provide for the shifting of the burden of proof on the issue of causation to the defendants and would impose liability upon all of the defendants who produced and marketed DES for pregnancy purposes, except those who were able to prove that their product could not have caused the injury. Under this approach, DES plaintiffs, who are unable to identify the actual manufacturer of the pill ingested by their mother, would only be required to establish, (1) that the plaintiff's mother ingested DES during pregnancy; (2) that the plaintiff's injuries were caused by DES; and (3) that the defendant or defendants produced and marketed DES for pregnancy purposes. Thereafter, the burden of proof would shift to the defendants to exculpate themselves by establishing, by a preponderance of the evidence, that the plaintiff's mother could not have ingested their particular pill. Of those defendants who are unable to exculpate themselves from liability, their respective share of the plaintiff's damages would be measured by their share of the national market of DES produced and marketed for pregnancy purposes during the period in question.

I would further note that while, on the one hand, the majority would not permit defendants who produced DES for pregnancy purposes to exculpate themselves, the majority at the same time deprives the plaintiffs of the opportunity to recover fully for their injuries by limiting the defendants' liability for the plaintiff's damages to several liability. In my view, the liability for the plaintiff's damages of those defendants who are unable to exculpate themselves should be joint and several thereby ensuring that the plaintiffs will receive full recovery of their damages. In addition to being fair to the DES plaintiffs, the imposition of joint and several liability is consistent with that portion of the revival statute which specifically exempted DES claims from those provisions which provide, with certain exceptions, for several liability of joint tortfeasors (see, L. 1986, ch. 652, § 12; CPLR § 1600 et seq.). Moreover, in order to ease the financial burden on the specific defendants named in the lawsuit, the defendants would have the option of seeking contribution from their fellow defendants for damages in excess of each defendant's particular market share, and a defendant should be permitted leave to implead those DES manufacturers who the plaintiff has not joined, in order to ensure, where possible, full contribution (see, e.g., *Dole v Dow Chemical Co*, 3D NY2d 143). Admittedly, adherence to joint and several liability could result in a disproportion between a defendant's potential liability for the damages suffered by the plaintiff and defendant's actual national market share; however, the opportunity to present exculpatory evidence reduces the risk of imposing liability on innocent defendants.

The application of the aforesaid principles, although somewhat innovative and a modification of traditional tort law, (i.e., the burden of proof is on the plaintiff to prove proximate causation) would, in view of the exigent circumstances, be in furtherance of a valid public policy of imposing the burden of bearing the cost of severe injuries upon those who are responsible for placing into the stream of commerce the causative instrumentality of such injuries. Adherence to this principle would not be too dissimilar from the accepted doctrine of res ipsa loquitur which provides, in essence, that where an instrumentality which caused the plaintiff's injuries was in the exclusive control of the defendant and the accident which occurred is one which would not ordinarily happen without negligence, these facts are sufficient to justify an inference of negligence and to shift the burden upon the defendant of coming forward with an explanation (see, e.g., *Galbraith v Busch*, 267 NY 30, 234; Richardson, *Evidence* § 93, p 68 [Prince 10th ed]). Thus, this approach, unlike that taken by the majority, does not represent an unnecessary and radical departure from basic principles of tort law. By characterizing this approach as nothing more than advocating that bare fortuity be the test for ability (slip opinion p 19, n 3) the majority fails to perceive that this is no more and no less than a basic principle of tort law; i.e., a plaintiff may not recover for his or her injuries from a defendant who could not have caused those injuries. When the majority eliminates this fundamental causative factor as a basis for recovery, it effectively indulges the act of judicial legislating. I would further note that if the Legislature had intended to adopt this radical approach which is at total variance with traditional tort law, it could readily have done so when it enacted the revival statute for, among others, DES Plaintiffs. Its refusal to do so can certainly not be deemed to be an invitation to this Court to assume the legislative role.

Two questions remain. First, are there any limits to the application of 'market share' liability? Secondly, is an English court likely to adopt it?

Andrew Grubb and David S Pearl *Blood Testing, AIDS and DNA Profiling* (1990)

The rationale of the *Sindell* case is that manufacturers who have placed upon the market *identical products which are dangerous* should not be able to escape liability because of the difficulties of proof facing a plaintiff in showing which manufacturer produced the particular product. Liability is imposed for *creating a risk of harm*, a risk which is common to all the products, and manufacturers should bear their share of the total harm that all the products will inflict on the community. In this way, 'each manufacturer's liability for an injury would be approximately equivalent to the damage caused by DES it manufactured' (*Sindell v Abbott Laboratories* (1980) 607 P 2d 924 (Cal SC) 938).

As a result, the policies underlying 'market share' liability may be inapplicable where the product is not uniformly dangerous, for example in the case of the combined diphtheria–pertussis–tetanus or DPT vaccine (*Shackil v Lederle Laboratories* (1989) 561 A 2d 511 (NJ SC)), or asbestos (*Thompson v John-Manville Corp* (1983) 714 F 2d 581 (5th Cir)). If it were, each manufacturer's liability could not be based upon the risk they have created to the community simply by looking at their 'market share' alone but would require the court also to take account of the degree of risk created by their *particular* product (see for example, ibid at p 583). The logic of 'market share' liability disappears in this situation ...

In any event, there is little to suggest that English Courts are prepared to innovate in the area of causation to assist injured plaintiffs. Indeed, 'market share' liability is not accepted in some US jurisdictions (*Mulcahy v Eli Lilly* (1986) 386 NW 2d 67 (Iowa SC)). In England, the House of Lords has rejected theories of liability based upon increased risk of harm to the plaintiff and has reaffirmed the traditional 'all-or-nothing' approach of the common law (*Wilsher v Essex Area Health Authority* [1988] AC 1074, [1988] 1 All ER 871 and *Hotson v East Berkshire Area Health Authority* [1987] AC 750, [1987] 1 All ER 210).

An English court is also unlikely to adopt a 'market share' approach to causation because of the problems associated with it and would probably consider that any such developments must come, if at all, from Parliament (*Wilsher*, op cit, per Lord Bridge at p 883).

On the latter question, Pamela Ferguson (*supra*) points out that British judges are much less inclined to 'devis[e] novel methods of liability' (at p 144). She concludes:

... Causation therefore provides a minimum link between plaintiff and defendant. In cases such as *Hymowitz*, however, the connection between defendant and plaintiff is highly tenuous; we can say only that the former was responsible for producing a drug which is of a similar type to that which injured the latter. Alternatively, we could describe the relationship as being that the former has produced a product which is likely to have injured several members of a class of people, and that while the plaintiff was not one of those injured by the defendant's product, she was a member of a class of injured people, and is thus deserving of compensation. Once this minimal link of a causative relationship between the parties is breached, then one must question why it is that the defendant manufacturer is to be held responsible for compensating the plaintiff, rather than some other person or body. It may be said to be a form of "rough justice", in that the defendant has caused injury, hence ought to pay for its actions, while the plaintiff has been injured and ought to be compensated. It is submitted, however, that in cases such as *Hymowitz* the link between the defendant and the plaintiff has become so tenuous that a preferable option might be to acknowledge that tort law is not necessarily the best method of reallocating funds in such circumstances. ...

We shall return to the final point later in this chapter. Finally, it should be noted that in 1992, the Dutch Supreme Court rejected 'market share' liability in a DES case (Hrl October 9, 1992 Rvde W 1992, nt 219). Instead, the court applied the 'alternative liability' doctrine (under s 6:99 of the Dutch Civil Code) to make each manufacturers of DES jointly and severally liable (see J G Teulings (1994) 110 LQR 228 and

L Bergkamp 'Compensating Personal Injuries Caused by DES: "No Causation Liability" in the Netherlands' (1994) 1 European Journal of Health Law 35).

Consumer Protection Act 1987

Until 1987, the two bases for a products liability claim were breach of contract and negligence. The former suffered from the limitation that only those 'privy' to the contract could sue; the latter required proof of negligence which was often problematic. The 1960s and 1970s saw the climate change both domestically and in Europe such that there was a drive to reform (and harmonise in Europe) laws for compensating those who suffered injury through defective products. The move was in large part sparked by the Thalidomide drug disaster in the 1960s. The way forward was seen as a shift from 'fault-based' liability to strict liability where the manufacturer was required to carry the risk of his product causing injury: as he was the best 'loss carrier', he could 'internalise' his costs. Eventually, this led to the adoption by the European Union of a harmonising Directive on *Products Liability* in 1985 (85/374/EEC).

The Consumer Protection Act 1987, Pt II is intended to give effect to the European Products Liability Directive. The Act imposes strict liability (s 2) for defective products (s 3) upon producers (including manufacturers) and suppliers where the product causes physical injury (including death) or property damage (s 5). There are a number of defences to an action (s 4), particularly important in drug and medical product cases is the so-called 'development risks' defence (s 4(1)(e)). The Act came into effect on 1 March 1988 and only applies to a product put into circulation after that date (s 50(7)). Actions must be brought within the usual limitation period under the Limitation Act 1980, ie three years of the personal injury or its 'discoverability' (s 11A, Limitation Act 1980). However, unlike other actions for personal injury such as negligence, there is a long-stop time limit of ten years beginning with the date when the product was first put into circulation (s 11A(3)).

To date, almost ten years after the Act came into force, there have been no decided cases under the 1987 Act. It has, nevertheless, been relied upon in at least two: *AB v South West Water Services Ltd* [1993] QB 507 (CA) – contaminated water; claims by haemophiliacs infected with hepatitis-C from blood products.

In what follows, we concentrate on those aspects of the 1987 Act which are of particular interest for medical products (for broader discussions see: J Stapleton *Products Liability* (1994); A Clark *Products Liability* (1989)).

A. WHO CAN BE LIABLE?

This is dealt with in s 2 of the Act.

Liability for defective products

2.—(1) Subject to the following provisions of this Part, where any damage is caused wholly or partly by a defect in a product, every person to whom subsection (2) below applies shall be liable for the damage.

(2) This subsection applies to—

(a) the producer of the product;

(b) any person who, by putting his name on the product or using a trade mark or other distinguishing mark in relation to the product, has held himself out to be the producer of the product;

(c) any person who has imported the product into a member State from a place outside the member States in order, in the course of any business of his, to supply it to another.

(3) Subject as aforesaid, where any damage is caused wholly or partly by a defect in a product, any person who supplied the product (whether to the person who suffered the damage,

to the producer of any product in which the product in question is comprised or to any other person) shall be liable for the damage if—

(a) the person who suffered the damage requests the supplier to identify one or more of the persons (whether still in existence or not) to whom subsection (2) above applies in relation to the product;

(b) that request is made within a reasonable period after the damage occurs and at a time when it is not reasonably practicable for the person making the request to identify all those persons; and

(c) the supplier fails, within a reasonable period after receiving the request, either to comply with the request or to identify the person who supplied the product to him.

(4) Neither subsection (2) nor subsection (3) above shall apply to a person in respect of any defect in any game or agricultural produce if the only supply of the game or produce by that person to another was at a time when it had not undergone an industrial process.

(5) Where two or more persons are liable by virtue of this Part for the same damage, their liability shall be joint and several.

(6) This section shall be without prejudice to any liability arising otherwise than by virtue of this Part.

Hence, the principal liability is that of the 'producer'. While a 'supplier' may also be liable, he can escape liability by identifying his supplier or the producer to the claimant.

'Producer' is defined in s 1(2) as follows:

(2) In this Part, except in so far as the context otherwise requires— ...

"producer", in relation to a product, means—

(a) the person who manufactured it;

(b) in the case of a substance which has not been manufactured but has been won or abstracted, the person who won or abstracted it;

(c) in the case of a product which has not been manufactured, won or abstracted but essential characteristics of which are attributable to an industrial or other process having been carried out (for example, in relation to agricultural produce), the person who carried out that process;

"product" means any goods or electricity and (subject to subsection (3) below) includes a product which is comprised in another product, whether by virtue of being a component part or raw material or otherwise; and

"the product liability Directive" means the Directive of the Council of the European Communities, dated 25th July 1985, (No. 85/374/EEC) on the approximation of the laws, regulations and administrative provisions of the member States concerning liability for defective products.

This definition would obviously cover the manufacturer of a drug or medical device. It would also cover someone who 'abstracted' a substance not manufactured, for example, blood, semen or other body tissue (subject to there being 'products' under the Act, on which see below).

'Supply', and hence a 'supplier' is defined in s 46 of the Act and includes someone who sells the product and, importantly, for us someone 'providing the goods in or in connection with [the] performance of any statutory function' (s 46(1)(e)). Within the NHS, as we have seen, 'sales' rarely occur. However, a pharmacist, doctor, NHS Trust or other who 'provides' a defective product within the NHS will be a 'supplier' and could only escape liability by identifying an earlier party in the chain of supply (see A Grubb and D Pearl *Blood Testing, AIDS and DNA Profiling* (1990) pp 136–137).

B. LIABILITY FOR WHAT?

As s 2(1) makes clear (*supra*), liability is for personal injury or death caused 'wholly or partly by a defect in a product'.

What, then, is 'a product' and when will it be 'defective'? Section 1(2) defines 'product' to mean:

any goods ... and includes a product which is comprised in another product, whether by virtue of being a component part or raw material or otherwise.

In turn, s 45(1) states that 'goods' includes 'substances' and 'substance' means 'any natural or artificial substance'. Clearly, there will be no definitional problem with drugs or medical devices such as contact lens, prostheses etc. The question arises, however, whether parts of the human body (such as organs) or substances derived from it (such as blood or gametes) are 'products' under the Act. On a literal reading of s 45(1) they would seem to be covered.

The following extract discusses the issue in the context of liability for HIV infected blood.

Andrew Grubb and David S Pearl *Blood Testing, Aids and DNA Profiling* (1990)

A number of English cases concerned with the Sale of Goods Act 1979 have drawn a distinction between a contract purely for the supply of goods (and hence within the legislation) and a contract where the supply of goods is merely incidental to the provision of a service (and hence not within the legislation).

The distinction is, at least superficially, attractive. Two cases either side of the line illustrate the service/goods dichotomy. In *Robinson v Graves* ([1935] 1 KB 579) it was held that a contract commissioning a portrait from an artist was not a contract for the sale of goods since the substance of the contract was that:—

> ... skill and labour [had] to be exercised for the production of the article and that it is only ancillary to that that there will pass from the artist to his client or customer some materials additional to the skill involved in the production of the portrait ... (Ibid, per Greer LJ at p 587.)

On the other hand, in *Lee v Griffin* ((1861) 1 B & S 272) a contract for the manufacture of a set of false teeth was held to be a contract for the sale of goods.

How can these cases assist in the context of the supply of blood or blood products? The provision of blood within the NHS by a doctor of a hospital involves, of course, a considerable element of professional skill because the supply is part of the treatment of a patient. In this sense, the supply of blood is incidental to the exercise of that professional skill. The transaction, as a whole, is properly viewed as the provision of services rather than the supply of goods (see *Dodd v Wilson* [1946] 2 All ER 691). The supply is so integral to the medical service that is undertaken by the health carers that it would be wrong to isolate the provision of goods from the overall transaction.

While factually this interpretation of the Act is possible, we do not believe that the Act should be interpreted in this way. The distinction between 'goods' and 'services' cannot be made in isolation. Except in the case of the supply of 'pure' services, a judicial choice has to be made in selecting one or other categorisation. This can only be done in the light of the legislative intent behind the 1987 Act and the relevant policy consideration of whether blood *should* be seen as the supply of 'goods'.

(i) *Legislative intent*
As regards legislative intent, Parliament has not distinguished between contracts for the sale of goods and contracts combining the provision of services with the supply of goods. The Supply of Goods and Services Act 1982 establishes 'contractual strict liability' through the imposition of similar warranties of fitness for purpose and quality in consumer contracts of both types (in Part I of the Act; s 2 (title), s 4 (quality and fitness for purpose). See also ss 3 and 5). It would seem that only the provision of 'pure' services is excluded from the ambit of the 1987 Act, which imposes a strict liability in tort (see *Luxmoore-May v Messenger May Baverstock* [1990] 1 All ER 1067 (CA); see also *Bolam v Friern Hospital Management Committee* [1957] 2 All ER 118, [1957] 1 WLR 582).

(ii) *Policy*
A related argument derives from a development in the US case law. A number of US jurisdictions have refused to apply the principles of strict liability to the supply of infected blood or blood products. The classic illustration is the case of *Perlmutter v Beth David Hospital* ((1954) 123 NE 2d 792 (NYCA). The plaintiff received a blood transfusion infected with the hepatitis virus and he subsequently developed the disease. The plaintiff sued the hospital where the transfusion had been carried out, under the New York sales law, on the basis of a breach of an implied warranty that the blood was of merchantable quality. The New York Court of Appeals rejected the plaintiff's action. The court held that the supply of blood was a service and did not involve the sale of a product, which was necessary under the legislation. The court stated that (Ibid. at p 795):

The supply of blood was entirely subordinate to [the hospital's] paramount function of furnishing trained personnel and specialized facilities in an endeavour to restore the plaintiff's health. It is not for blood ... for which the plaintiff bargained, but the wherewithal of the hospital staff and the availability of hospital facilities to provide whatever medical treatment was considered advisable. The conclusion is evident that the furnishing of blood was only very secondary to the services provided by the hospital.

It can be seen that, as with the English cases we noted earlier, the court uses the 'goods'/ 'service' dichotomy to avoid imposing strict liability upon a hospital. The factual distinction, however, means that blood banks or manufacturers of blood products are subject to strict liability, since there is no service element in their activities. But it is not that simple; the factual distinction in itself does not determine whether strict liability applies. If it did it would not explain why some courts have not applied strict liability in the case of manufacturers (*Kozup v Georgetown University* (1988) 851 F 2d 437 (DC CIR.)) and, on the other hand why some courts have applied strict liability to hospitals (*Cunningham v MacNeal Memorial Hospital* (1970) 266 NE 2d 879 (Ill SC); *Brody v Overlook Hospital* (1972) 296 A 2d 668 (NJ App Ct); affirmed on appeal (1975) 332 A 2d 596 (NJ SC)).

In truth, whether judges in the US have applied the regime of strict products liability to infected blood has reflected an evaluation of a number of policy factors which influence the determination of whether strict liability is appropriate. Underlying this approach has been a rejection of the policy grounds normally justifying the imposition of strict liability. It is policy considerations which have led the legislatures of most US states to enact what are known as 'blood shield' statutes which deem the provision of blood or its products to be a service and not a sale of goods for all purposes including strict products liability. These statutes were enacted either during the 1970s to deal with the hepatitis infection cases then coming before the courts or more recently to deal with the AIDS cases. The overwhelming view is that the 'blood shield' statutes protect all professionals involved in the supply of blood from strict liability actions.

Principally two arguments have been influential in the US – first, the need for a profit motive and secondly, the great public utility and benefit derived from the supply of blood or its products to patients.

In the case law, central to the imposition of strict liability is an acceptance of the argument that strict liability is concerned with shifting the burden of loss caused by a defective product from an injured innocent individual to a manufacturer who has put the product in the market place for profit. Hence, with one or two exceptions, the courts have made commercial dealers in blood subject to strict liability. US products liability requires the *sale* of a product for an action to lie.

Although this underlying policy might be attractive in the UK it is difficult to sustain in view of two specific provisions in the 1987 Act which strongly suggest that the Act is not restricted to profit making 'supplies' of defective products. First, the definition of 'business' includes the activities of local authorities and other public bodies (s 45(1)). Secondly, as we have seen, the definition of 'supply' under s 46(1)(e) includes 'providing ... goods in or in connection with the performance of any statutory function'. This latter provision is not restricted to a function which is profit making. Clearly most activities of public bodies and the performance of their statutory functions will not involve a profit motive. The only contrary indication is s 4(1)(c) of the Act which provides a defence where the product is supplied 'otherwise than in the course of a business' and, if the defendant is a 'producer', he has not produced it for profit. However, the defence does not apply to the supply of blood in the NHS even if no profit element exists. Although the second part of the defence is satisfied (the blood will not have been 'produced' for profit), the activities of the health authority are 'business' activities under s 45(1), and thus the supply would not be 'otherwise than in the course of business' as required by the first part of the defence.

The second reason has, perhaps, exhibited the greater influence over American courts and legislatures. Undoubtedly, the provision of blood or blood products serves a vital public need in the treatment of the sick. The overwhelming utility this represents is often a central justification for excluding strict liability and it applies regardless of the motive of the supplier; hence the legislative exclusion of *all* blood suppliers under the 'blood shield' statutes. This policy argument cannot be ignored, but it is suggested that an English court would not use it to exclude *in limine* a claim under the 1987 Act by a patient infected with HIV through blood. Instead, the court would take account of the great utility of the service offered by the NHS in deciding whether infected blood is 'defective' under the Act.

The recent Canadian case of *ter Neuzen v Korn* (1995) 127 DLR (4th) 577 considers the question of whether the supply of HIV infected semen falls within legislation dealing with the sale of 'goods' or within a common law warranty. We saw the case earlier (*supra*, ch 4). Here we set out the judgment of Sopinka J (with whom all the other justices of the Canadian Supreme Court agreed as on this point) concluding that artificial insemination was not covered by the Act.

ter Neuzen v Korn (1995) 127 DLR (4th) 577 (Can Sup Ct)

The plaintiff was infected with the human immunodeficiency virus (HIV) as a result of artificial insemination by the defendant physician in January, 1985. The risk of infection from artificial insemination was not widely known in North America until mid-1985, when the defendant discontinued his program. In January, 1985, no test was available in Canada for the detection of HIV in semen or blood. The defendant physician recruited and screened semen donors according to standard practice across Canada at that time. The trial judge directed the jury that it was open to them to find the general practice to be negligent and they did so find. The trial judge also directed the jury that if the contract between the plaintiff and the defendant was primarily for goods, as opposed to services, the *Sale of Goods Act*, R.S.B.C. 1979, c. 370, would apply and that any common law warranty in a contract for medical services would mirror requirements not to be negligent. The trial judge did not instruct the jury as to the upper limit of non-pecuniary damages. The jury found the defendant negligent and awarded $883,800 in damages, including $460,000 in non-pecuniary damages. The defendant appealed to the British Columbia Court of Appeal, which allowed the appeal and ordered a new trial, holding that this was not a case in which the jury acting judicially could find the common practice of competent Canadian practitioners to be negligent; no common law warranty applied and the non-pecuniary damages exceeded the upper limit.

Sopinka J: ... *Warranty under the Sale of Goods Act*
[67] In order for the *Sale of Goods Act* to apply, a contract must primarily be for the purpose of selling goods. If the sale of a good is merely incidental to what is primarily a contract for services, then the statute will not imply a warranty. As Legg J. observed in *Gee v. White Spot Ltd.* (1986), 32 D.L.R. (4th) 238, 7 B.C.L.R. (2d) 235 (S.C.), in order to come within the *Sale of Goods Act*, a contract need not be one exclusively for the sale of goods. However, the sale of a good must be the primary purpose of the contract. Whether a contract is primarily one for the sale of goods or primarily one for services depends upon the essential character of the agreement. As G.H.L. Fridman wrote at p. 25 of *Sale of Goods in Canada*, 2nd ed. (Toronto: Carswell, 1979):

> ... if the primary object of the contract is the transference of property in something which was not originally the property of the "buyer", the contract will be one of sale of goods: but if the primary purpose of the parties is the performance of certain work, or the provision of services, incidentally to which the property in goods is to pass from one party to the other, the contract will not be one of sale of goods.

[68] Thus, the preliminary question that arises is whether the AI procedure performed by the respondent primarily involved a contract for the sale of semen, or was it primarily a contract for medical services. If the procedure is properly characterized as the latter, then the appellant's argument under the *Sale of Goods Act* must fail. As the Court of Appeal did, I intend to address this issue assuming that there was in fact a sale of semen between the appellant and respondent. However, I note that it is not entirely clear that this was the case ...
[71] The jury correctly concluded that the contract to perform the AI procedure on the appellant was primarily a contract for medical services and not a sale of semen. To hold otherwise would be to distort the true nature of the whole agreement between the parties. The provision of the semen was obviously an important component to the AI procedure; however the primary reason the appellant went to a gynaecologist was for professional medical services and expertise. As the respondent argues, he provided medical services to the appellant in order to assist her to become pregnant by way of artificial insemination. Although donor semen was a necessary component of this process, the contract was not primarily for a sale of semen.
[72] It is not relevant that the actual AI procedure was relatively simple and quick. The appellant still relied on the respondent's expertise in the screening process for donors, the collection of the semen, the insemination procedure itself, an the provision of medical advice and information concerning any risks and the possibility of success of the AI procedure. It cannot be contended that the contract was one primarily for the sale of semen such as to attract the application of the *Sale of Goods Act*.

(3) Warranty implied by the common law
[73] The fact that the contract was primarily one for services does not end the possibility that there was an implied warranty that the semen would not be contaminated with HIV. The appellant also bases her claim under the common law by virtue of which a warranty may be implied in a contract for goods and services ...

[76] In England, strict liability is imposed for implied warranties of fitness for defective products supplied under contracts for work and materials as well as under contracts for sale. The purchaser has a remedy against the business seller, even absent negligence. The seller can always recover, up the chain of production, from the manufacturer … *Young & Marten Ltd v McManus Childs Ltd*, [1969] 1 A.C. 454 (H.L.) dealt with contractors who were building a house and subcontracted the roofing work. The roofing tiles which were used contained a latent defect which was not apparent upon inspection. As a result, the contractor suffered damages and claimed that there was an implied warranty of quality or fitness. Lord Reid observed that, in such cases where there is no evidence of negligence by the manufacturer, unless the owners of the house could recover from the subcontractor, they would be without a remedy. However, if the subcontractors were held liable, they could generally recover from the manufacturer under the *Sale of Goods* legislation. The court adopted the general rule which was laid down by du Parcq J. in *G.H. Myers*. Lord Reid also made the following relevant observations (at p. 468):

It appears to me that less cogent circumstances may be sufficient to exclude an implied warranty of quality where the use of spare parts is only incidental to what is in essence a repairing operation where the customer's main reliance is on the skill of the tradesman, than in a case where the main element is the supply of an article, the installation being merely incidental.

[80] In the result, the court affirmed that, in the circumstances of that case, the common law implied a warranty and the subcontractor was liable for the defective tiles. It was not conclusive that there was an element of services along with the supply of goods.

[81] The principles espoused in the English case law have also been adopted in Canada … Thus, unlike the *Sale of Goods Act*, such warranties are equally applicable to contracts for the provision of work and materials. Secondly, unless the circumstances of the case are sufficient to exclude the warranty, there will be an implied term "that the materials will be reasonably fit for the purposes for which they were intended" (p. 266).

[83] Accordingly, it is apparent that apart from the *Sale of Goods Act*, a court must consider whether a common law warranty of fitness and merchantability should be implied into the contract which includes services as well as the provision of materials. However, such a warranty will not be implied in all circumstances. The court must examine the specific nature of the contract and the relationship between the parties in order to assess whether it was the intention of the parties that such a warranty be implied …

[84] It is important to note that a rationale for implying warranties in contracts of goods and services is that a supplier of goods generally has recourse against the manufacturer under the *Sale of Goods Act* as a result of the statutory conditions imposed. Thus, one can always proceed up the chain of production and ultimately recover from the one who should bear responsibility for the production of faulty goods. From time to time, the supplier will be unable to recover from the manufacturer, for example, owing to insolvency or limitation periods. However, arguably it is better that the purchaser be compensated and the supplier occasionally bear the cost of defects than leaving the consumer without a remedy. It is important to keep this policy rationale in mind when considering whether such a warranty should be implied in the context of this case, which deals with biological substances.

[85] Thus, the question that must be addressed in this appeal is whether, in the circumstances of this case, where there is a contract to conduct a medical procedure involving the use of biological material (semen), it is appropriate to imply a term that the semen was warranted to be without any defects (HIV) contamination. Secondly, if it is appropriate to imply a term in the contract for medical services was the trial judge correct in holding that the respondent only warranted to take reasonable care to ensure that semen would not be used if it were contaminated with any STDs. In this regard, one must consider whether the nature of the contract at issue in this appeal is analogous to the commercial contracts which were dealt with in the English and Canadian cases discussed above. It is important to address any policy considerations and the implications of imposing warranties in these circumstances.

[86] In answering these difficult questions, it is useful to survey some of the American jurisprudence which has dealt with this issue more frequently, in the context of warranties for the supply of blood. In my view, these cases are directly analogous to the supply of semen in an AI practice.

[87] The leading American authority on this issue, which has been followed many times subsequently, is *Perlmutter v Beth David Hospital*, 123 N.E.2d 792 (N.Y. 1954). In that case, a patient received a blood transfusion during the course of a medical procedure performed at the hospital. The blood contained jaundice viruses and as a result the plaintiff became infected. There was no question of any negligence on the part of the hospital as there were no means available for detecting the contamination in the blood. The plaintiff sought recovery under the *Sales Act* arguing that there was an implied warranty that the blood would be fit for its purpose and of merchantable quality. The issue turned on whether the transaction constituted

a sale under the legislation. It must be observed at this point that the plaintiff did not argue that there was an implied warranty under the common law for material supplied under a contract for service and material. None the less, much of the discussion on the *Sales Act* is relevant to the case at bar.

[88] The majority of the court examined the nature of the contract between the hospital and held (at p. 794):

> The essence of the contractual relationship between hospital and patient is readily apparent; the patient bargains for, and the hospital agrees to make available, the human skill and physical material of medical science to the end that the patient's health be restored.

> Such a contract is clearly one for services, and, just as clearly, it is not divisible. Concepts of purchase and sale cannot separately be attached to the healing materials – such as medicines, drugs, or, indeed, blood – supplied by the hospital for a price as part of the medical services it offers. That the property or title to certain items of medical material may be transferred, so to speak, for the hospital to the patient during the course of medical treatment does not serve to make each such transaction a sale. "'Sale' and 'transfer' are not synonymous", and not every transfer of personal property constitutes a sale. ... It has long been recognized that, when service predominates, and transfer of personal property is but an incidental feature of the transaction, the transaction is not deemed a sale within the Sales Act.

[89] It should be observed that the majority focused on the sharp distinction between a contract of sale and one for services that exists in this context. While this is important for determining whether sale of goods legislation is applicable, it is not as crucial in the context of implied warranties under the common law which are also available for contracts of service where a good is furnished. None the less, the remarks in *Perlmutter* are highly relevant since, as was noticed by Lord Reid in *Young & Marten Ltd.*, it will be less likely that such a warranty will be implied in a contract which is primarily for services where the transfer of the good is merely incidental.

[90] In *Perlmutter*, it was held that the supplying of blood was entirely subordinate to the main purpose of the hospital, which was providing trained professionals and specialized facilities to care for the patient's health. The patient does not bargain for blood. Rather, it is the skill of the medical staff and the facilities which is sought. Fuld J. concluded that supplying the blood was entirely incidental to the services performed. In my view, the same can be said of the semen in the present case, as I discussed earlier in respect of the *Sale of Goods Act*.

[91] In examining the nature of the contract at issue, Fuld J. noted some of the policy considerations which are relevant in this context. At p. 795, the following was observed:

> If, however, the court were to stamp as a sale the supplying of blood – or the furnishing of other medical aid – *it would mean that the hospital, no matter how careful, no matter than the disease-producing potential in the blood could not possibly be discovered, would be held responsible, virtually as an insurer, if anything were to happen to the patient as a result of "bad" blood* ...

(Emphasis added.)

[92] Although these comments were made in the context of sale of goods legislation, they apply equally to the situation of an implied warranty under common law. In either situation, a medical practitioner would be held strictly liable for the biological products employed in the medical procedures, notwithstanding that it may be impossible for the doctor to detect any risks. This would have the effect of making physicians insurers of the biological substances that are used in medical procedures.

[93] While it is true that the primary purpose of the implied warranty is to hold the supplier of goods liable notwithstanding the absence of negligence, different considerations apply in the context of the medical profession than in the ordinary commercial context. As Fuld J. observed (at p. 795):

> The art of healing frequently calls for a balancing of risks and dangers to a patient. Consequently, if injury results from the course adopted, where not negligence or fault is present, liability should not be imposed upon the institution or agency actually seeking to save or otherwise assist the patient.

[94] Furthermore, it should be noted that unlike in the ordinary commercial context, the doctor cannot trace the liability back to the initial manufacturer. Biological products are not manufactured goods in the same sense as commercial goods. The underlying rationale for the strict liability imposed under the *Sale of Goods Act* or by virtue of an implied warranty at common law does not apply to goods which are not manufactured in the ordinary sense.

Absent negligence on the part of the donor (for example, if he knew he had AIDS), one would hardly expect that the respondent, in the present case, could recover from the donor for the semen contaminated with HIV, either under the *Sale of Goods Act* or under an implied warranty at common law. This is unlike a commercial contract where it would be open to a supplier to sue the manufacturer, even absent negligence on its part.

[95] Moreover, it must be recognized that biological products such as blood and semen, unlike manufactured products, carry certain inherent risks. In some ways, these substances are inherently dangerous, although they are essential to medical procedures. Whether a doctor is trying to save a patient's life via a blood transfusion, or is simply attempting to assist a patient to become pregnant by AI, the physician cannot control the safety of these products beyond exhibiting the reasonable care expected of a professional to ensure that the biological substance is free from harmful viruses. By contrast, in the commercial world, the manufacturer has control over the goods. If they cannot be manufactured to be safe, then the products ought to be removed from the market. In medicine blood is essential to a variety of procedures in order to save lives. While arguably, AI is not in the same category as other life-saving techniques, it is none the less a very important medical procedure. As long as the entire procedure does not amount to an unreasonable risk such that it ought not to be offered at all, the patient is entitled to weigh those risks and elect to proceed.

[96] In *Fisher v Sibley Memorial Hospital*, 403 A.2d 1130 (D.C. 1979), an action was commenced for injury suffered when a patient contracted hepatitis after a blood transfusion supplied by the hospital. It was not possible to detect the virus in the blood. The Court of Appeal held that the theories of implied warranty and merchantability and strict liability in tort had no place in the context of a hospital furnishing blood. At pp. 1132–3, Gallagher J. held as follows:

> The activities involved in the transfusion of whole blood, a component of the living body, from one human being to another may be characterized as sui generis in that the sequence of events involve acts common to legal concepts of both a sale and a service. Moreover, it seems to us that under the facts in the case before us *it would be unrealistic to hold that there is an implied warranty as to qualities of fitness of human blood on which no medical or scientific information can be acquired and in respect to which plaintiff's physician has the same information, knowledge, and experience as the supplier.*

(*Balkowitsch v. Minneapolis War Memorial Blood Bank, Inc.*, 270 Minn. 151, 132 N.W.2d 805, 811 (1965).)

> We agree with those courts which hold that the furnishing of blood is more in the nature of a service than of a sale of goods. Treating blood transfusions as an incidental service performed by hospitals comports with reality, and with the policies underlying merchantability liability. *Although theoretically a seller's inability to discover defects in the goods he sells is not relevant to a warranty cause of action, we cannot ignore the difficulty of detecting hepatitis in blood given the current state of medical knowledge.* To characterize as a sale the supplying of blood would mean that the hospital, no matter how careful, would be held responsible, virtually as an insurer, if the patient were harmed as a result of impure blood. *After balancing the safety of the individual with the interests of the hospital (in light of the absence of an adequate test to determine the presence of hepatitis in the blood) and the public interest in assuring the ready availability of blood for medical treatment, we are reluctant to extend ... merchantability liability to a nonsale transaction by analogy or by characterizing the transaction as a sale.*

(Emphasis added.)

[97] The court was of the view that it was unnatural to force a blood transfusion into the commercial sales mould since the main object of the hospital is health care and treatment. It was also noted that blood products are "unavoidably dangerous" (p. 1134) and the patient relies on the doctor's skill rather than any warranties of fitness.

[98] I also find the case of *St. Luke's Hospital v Schmaltz*, 534 P.2d 781 (Colo. 1975), to be persuasive. That case also involved a blood transfusion resulting in the patient contracting hepatitis. The court followed the reasoning in *Perlmutter* and rejected the imposition of strict liability in tort or on the basis of a warranty due to policy considerations. It was held that a realistic view of the relationship between a hospital and a patient is not that of a commercial transaction where a good is sold for a price. Rather, the patient bargains for the skill and materials of medical science in order to care for the patient's health. It is simply not realistic to view the furnishing of blood as a sale of a product.

[99] Although the majority of American cases have followed *Perlmutter*, a few have criticized the policy analysis conducted. For example, in *Cunningham v MacNeal Memorial Hospital*, 266 N.E.2d 897 (Ill. 1970), the court again considered the situation of a patient who contracted hepatitis through a blood transfusion. The court rejected the idea that an

implied warranty did not arise because no "sale" was involved. Notwithstanding that blood is not a manufactured article of commerce, the court considered it a product which is distributed for consumption. The blood was sold in a container and the court felt it was unreasonable not to conclude that there was a sale of goods which was divisible from the contract for services.

[100] However, the vast majority of American cases have agreed that the policy considerations dictate that, in the context of the provision of medical services, medical professionals should not be held strictly liable under warranty for goods used in the provision of those services. In my view, the reasoning of the majority in *Perlmutter*, and the line of cases which follow it, is more apt in the Canadian context with respect to implied warranties at common law. Although, the American decisions did not deal with exactly this issue, the remarks made with respect to warranties under sale of goods legislation provide support for the view that it is inappropriate to imply a warranty in these circumstances under the common law.

[101] I am, therefore, in agreement with the Court of Appeal's conclusion in the present case that it would be inappropriate to imply a warranty of fitness and merchantability in the circumstances of this case. As Cory J.A. observed in *G. Ford Homes*, courts should be very wary about implying terms of contracts and there may be circumstances which ought to exclude such a warranty. In the present case, the action against the respondent for injury resulting from the AI procedure should be confined to negligence. I would adopt the following conclusion of the Court of Appeal at pp. 517–18:

> In the face of the American experience, we are unable to identify any policy reason why a physician should face stricter liability for "goods" which are furnished to a patient in the course of medical service than he or she would be for any lack of professional care and skill which must be brought to every healing or treating engagement.

[102] I note that even if I am wrong in my conclusion that a warranty should not be implied in the circumstances of this case, I would hold, as the trial judge did, that any warranty would simply be to take reasonable care. In other words, if the parties intended that there be any contractual warranty, the nature of the warranty in this case would simply be to the effect that the respondent exercise diligence and care in performing the AI and selecting the donors. The contract was primarily one for medical services and parties would not have contemplated that the respondent would warrant the success of the procedure nor that the semen would not be contaminated with an STD. As the trial judge stated, the respondent "undertakes to meet the standards of a reasonably competent person practising in his field". It would be unreasonable to hold the respondent to any higher standard.

[103] In the result, the appellant's argument that there was an implied warranty at common law that the donor's semen would not be infected with HIV must also fail.

La Forest, Gonthier, Cory, McLachlin and Iacobucci JJ concurred.

The legislative context in England for 'sales' may be quite different, since the Supply of Goods and Services Act 1982 applied warranties to both the supply of 'goods' and of 'goods and services' (ss 4, 9 and 18(1)). Of course, the same policy arguments might drive an English court to characterise the 'supply' as one of a 'service' only and hence subject to the implied term of 'reasonable skill and care' (s 13). This is the same debate relevant to the application of the 1987 Act. A similar policy is inherent in the US cases, which rely upon 'comment k' to the *Restatement (2d) of Torts* to exclude 'blood' from the strict liability regime.

Andrew Grubb and David S Pearl *Blood Testing, AIDS and DNA Profiling* (1990)

… the US courts usually do not impose strict liability where infection is transmitted through blood. The great utility of blood or blood products in the treatment of patients has led almost all courts not to apply strict liability in this area. The courts have done so on two grounds. The first, which we have already examined, is that the provision of blood is a service and not the sale of a product. Most legislatures have enacted provisions to ensure this. Secondly, the courts apply *Comment k* to the Restatement (2d) of Torts which exempts *unavoidably unsafe* products from strict liability. For example, *Comment k* is normally applied to prescription drugs because as a class (*Brown v Superior Court* (1988) 751 P 2d 470 (Cal Sup Ct)) or in individual instances (*Feldman v Lederle Laboratories* (1984) 479 1 2d 374 (NJ Sup Ct)) the benefits of the drug far outweigh their inherent risk of harming patients. As a consequence, a judge determines as a threshold question whether to leave a strict liability action to a jury. If a judge decides that a product, such as a drug, is unavoidably dangerous, then the manufacturer's liability turns upon proof of negligence in the design of the drug or in a failure to warn the user of the inherent danger of the drug. Liability in the latter case is also generally considered to be founded in negligence.

The application of *Comment k* can be seen in two cases. In *Belle Bonfils Memorial Blood Bank v Hansen* ((1983) 665 P 2d 118 (Cdo Sup Ct)) the Colorado Supreme Court held that a blood bank could not be strictly liable for blood which contained the Hepatitis non-A, non-B virus (now identified as Hepatitis C) which infected the plaintiff after a blood transfusion. The court identified a number of elements that a manufacturer must prove to fall within *Comment k*. First, the product's utility must greatly outweigh the risk created by its use. The product must carry a 'unique and profound benefit'. Secondly, the risk must be a known risk. Thirdly, the product's benefits must not be achievable in another manner. Fourthly, the risk must be unavoidable under the present state of knowledge. Finally, the product must have been properly manufactured and accompanied by an adequate warning of the danger. Since hepatitis non-A, non-B, could not be detected in blood at the time of the plaintiff's transfusion and the risk of transmission was known, the court concluded that on proof of the other requirements of *Comment k* the defendant would not be strictly liable (*Hines v St Joseph's Hospital* (1974) 527 P 2d 1075 (NM CA)).

The *Belle Bonfils* case was applied in *Miles Laboratories v Doe* ((1989) 556 A 2d 1107 (Md CA)) when the blood carried HIV infection. Here, however, the court extended the scope of 'unavoidably unsafe' products to those where the risk of infection is unknown. The court accepted that the rationale of cases such as *Belle Bonfils* should apply to a blood product which had been given to the plaintiff in 1983 – before the risk of HIV infection was even appreciated. The court concluded that the compelling necessity for blood products ordinarily outweighed the risk in blood transfusions: (Ibid, at p 1121 per Murphy CJ.)

> Taking into account the absolute necessity for a continuously adequate supply of blood and blood products, that these substances are not merely useful but essential to life and health, that it was not known in 1983 that the AIDS virus was transmitted through blood, and there being no scientific test by which to detect the presence of the AIDS virus when the blood was administered in this case, we think that a blood clotting factor concentrate sold in such circumstances ordinarily is "unavoidably unsafe" as a matter of law ... In other words, considering the unique nature of blood as a lifesaving, life-sustaining substance without any apparent substitutes ... [*Comment k* is] ... applicable ...

(For discussion of strict liability for the supply of gametes in Gland, see K Stern 'Strict Liability and the Supply of Donated Gametes' (1994) 2 Med L Rev 261.)

Turning to the second question of when a product will be 'defective', s 3 provides as follows:

Meaning of "defect"
3.—(1) Subject to the following provisions of this section, there is a defect in a product for the purposes of this Part if the safety of the product is not such as persons generally are entitled to expect; and for those purposes "safety", in relation to a product, shall include safety with respect to products comprised in that product and safety in the context of risk of damage to property, as well as in the context of risks of death or personal injury.
(2) In determining for the purposes of subsection (1) above what persons generally are entitled to expect in relation to a product all the circumstances shall be taken into account, including—
(a) the manner in which, and purposes for which, the product has been marketed, its get-up, the use of any mark in relation to the product and any instructions for, or warnings with respect to, doing or refraining from doing anything with or in relation to the product;
(b) what might reasonably be expected to be done with or in relation to the product; and
(c) the time when the product was supplied by its producer to another;
and nothing in this section shall require a defect to be inferred from the fact alone that the safety of a product which is supplied after that time is greater than the safety of the product in question.

Following the pattern previously adopted when discussing negligence, the product can be said to be defective in respect of its manufacture, or its design, or because it is not safe having regard to any warnings or directions (or the absence thereof).

Negligence looks to the conduct of the manufacturer (or other) and asks whether he was careless in the light of the foreseeable risks at the time. Strict liability, by contrast, is concerned with the condition of the product and asks whether it is defective. If negligence theory requires a manufacturer to use technology that was available at the time of manufacture, to design according to a reasonable risk/benefit ratio or to warn of risks which were known (or should have been) at the time, a theory of strict products liability should require more. Complying with the so-called 'state of the art' at the time of manufacture ought not to suffice to excuse a manufacture in the design defect case. Warning only about risks that were known (or reasonably capable of being known) also should not be sufficient. Strict liability should, on one view, require, for example, that a manufacturer warn about even *un*knowable risks (an impossibility but required by the logic of strict liability) and perhaps (though less likely) that he be liable even though he complied with the state of the art. As Lord Scarman stated in the course of the debate in the House of Lords on the Act: '[i]f you introduce the "state of the art" defence, you are really introducing negligence or fault by the back door' (414 HL Deb, col 1427). How does the 1987 Act apply to medical products? First, s 3(1) is concerned with *unsafe or dangerous* products rather than ones which are defective in *quality* alone. Secondly, the product must not be as safe 'as persons generally are entitled to expect'. Thirdly, in reaching a determination on this statutory test, the court is required to have regard to 'all the circumstances', including its packaging, any warnings or instructions, its foreseeable use and the time it was first supplied (s 3(2)). As regards the final matter, the fact that the product is now marketed in a safer way should not lead to an inference that it was defective at the time of supply.

The application of the 1987 Act and its definition of 'defect' is considered in the following extract, concerned with the liability for HIV-infected blood. As you read it, you will see reference to a number of US derived concepts: 'the consumer expectation test', the 'risk/utility test' and 'the development risks defence'.

Andrew Grubb and David S Pearl *Blood Testing, AIDS and DNA Profiling* (1990)

… The crucial question is whether blood or blood products which are infected with HIV are 'defective' under the Act. In particular, are 'persons … generally entitled to expect' blood not to carry the HIV infection? The 1987 Act only applies to the 'supply' of a product, ie a blood transfusion, which occurs after 1 March 1988. As we have already seen, blood has been tested for HIV antibodies since October 1985. Blood products have been heat treated with, it would appear, complete success since that date also. Consequently, in practical terms, the Act can only apply where:

1. A *failure in the system* has allowed infected blood to go undetected;
2. HIV-2 has infected the patient because an *HIV-2 test is not employed*;
3. The blood *falsely tests negative* because the importance (or duration of) the silent infection period is not appreciated;
4. Some, as yet, *unidentified risk of infection causes the patient's injury* – for example, an HIV-3 infective agent which is not tested for or, in the case of blood products, which is unaffected by the heat treating process.

Except for the first of these situations, it is very unlikely that an action could be successfully brought under the 1987 Act. These situations raise a number of basic questions relating to the construction and scope of the Act's provisions. Will an action lie under the Act where:

(a) it is known in general terms that blood carries a risk of infection but its presence cannot be detected, and therefore determined, in any particular unit of blood ('the known but undiscoverable risk');

(b) as in (a) there is a known risk in general terms that blood carries a risk of infection and its presence could be detected, but this is not done because of cost and the low risk perceived ('the cost/benefit, risk/utility question');

(c) it is not known that there is a risk of infection in blood and that risk could not be known in the current state of scientific knowledge ('the unknowable risk' or 'development risks' defence)?

The test of 'defect' in s 3(1) of the 1987 Act is similar to the 'consumer expectation' test used by some US courts in products liability cases. Section 402A of the highly influential Restatement (2d) of Torts recognises a strict liability action for the sale of a 'defective product' which is 'unreasonably dangerous'. Both of these terms are explained in the *Comments* which accompany s 402A in terms of the expectations of consumer safety. For example, the latter is defined in *Comment i* as meaning '… dangerous to an extend beyond that which would be contemplated by an ordinary consumer who purchases [the product] with the ordinary knowledge common to the community as to its characteristics.' Consequently, the Act creates an objective standard of defect. By using the phrase 'persons generally', it requires an assessment by the court of whether a reasonable man would expect the product to be safer than it was. In determining this, the Act does not look simply to the degree of safety that the average man on the street would expect. The test is intended to be normative and not merely descriptive of the state of public expectation. Section 3(1) does not speak of what 'persons generally expect' but, instead, what 'persons generally are *entitled* to expect' (our emphasis).

(a) 'Defect' and system failure
The 'consumer expectation' test remains important in most American jurisdictions in cases where a manufacturing defect is alleged, for example, where a product is flawed in the manufacturing process. Consumer expectations can be judged against the remaining unflawed products. The standard is set by the manufacturer and the consumer's frustrated expectations are clearly seen when the product dangerously fails to live up to those expectations.

Consequently, where there is a failure in the blood testing system, this is the clearest example of liability arising under the Act. Indeed, if a strict liability regime is to have any application at all, it must do so where there has been a systems failure that results in a dangerous product. Blood will not be as safe as 'persons generally are entitled to expect' under s 3(1) of the 1987 Act if it is infected because the Blood Transfusion Service fails (for what ever reason) to test the blood or tests the blood and mixes up the results so that the blood is not discarded. If a reasonable person has any expectation about the safety of blood, it will be that the blood has been tested to the usual extent currently employed. In this situation, these expectations will be frustrated.

Liability under the 1987 Act adds little since, in any event, a court would almost certainly categorise this sort of systems failure as careless (for example *Grant v Australian Knitting Mills* [1936] AC 85).

The court would probably apply the maxim *res ipsa loquitur* to infer carelessness (see *Henderson v Jenkins* [1970] AC 282, [1969] 3 WLR 732). Before leaving this example, we have to consider the effect of s 4(1)(e) of the 1987 Act. Section 4(1)(e) provides a defence if:

> ... the state of scientific and technical knowledge at the relevant time was not such that a producer of products of the same description as the product in question might be expected to have discovered the defect if it had existed in his products while they were under his control.

This section creates what has become known as the 'development risks' defence (see Newdick, '*The Development Risk Defence of the Consumer Protection Act 1987*' [1988] CLJ 455). Usually, the defence, if established, operates where the risk of harm in a product could not have been known by the manufacturer. Again, usually the inability to discover the risk will arise from the inadequacy of scientific research at that time. The defence is most commonly associated with pharmaceutical products where unforeseeable risks are most likely to arise. Under s 4(1)(e) proof by the defendant manufacturer that manufacturers of similar products would not have discovered the defect gives rise to a defence. As a consequence, unlike the more objective provision of the directive, the Act 'comes very close to a traditional negligence formula.' (See Winfield and Jolowitz on Tort (1989, 13th edn) at p 258.)

The wording of s 4(1)(e) probably goes further than the normal understanding of the development risks defence. It would also give rise to a defence where it is known that a product may be defective but the manufacturer cannot discover whether or not that is the case. In other words, the known but undiscoverable risk is also covered. Suppose that the reason why blood contains HIV infection is not because the process has exceptionally broken down through the fault of a technician. Instead, the infection is present because of the known risk that the testing process statistically will fail in a given number of instances but it is impossible to know which particular tests have produced false negatives. If, as seems likely, the words 'scientific' and 'technical' can be read disjunctively in s 4(1)(e) of the 1987 Act, then it could be argued that '... technical knowledge ... was not such that a producer ... [of blood] ... might be expected' to discover the HIV infection. A close similarity can be seen with quality control failures in manufacturing processes which, it has been argued, fall within s 4(1)(e). The problem is that if the defence under the Act applies it puts the manufacturer in a better position than in a negligence action where failures in quality control would not excuse.

It would be a curious result if the law of negligence was stricter than the strict liability regime under the Act (see Newdick (supra) at 469–473).

(b) 'Defect' and HIV-2 testing-the known risk
What if the infection is due to the failure to test for the distinct HIV-2 infection?

We assume at this point that the risk of HIV-2 infection is known and that other reasons lead to a failure to test and detect its presence in the blood. It is difficult to state precisely when this knowledge was acquired. However, it seems clear that the risk was probably known by 1 March 1988 when the Consumer Protection Act came into force. If the risk were unknown and unknowable in the current state of scientific knowledge then a different issue arises, which is discussed below, in relation to 'development risks'.

Are 'persons ... generally entitled to expect' that blood is free from infection even in this situation? It is not easy to answer this question. What are society's expectations of blood safety? Like pharmaceutical products, blood is an inherently dangerous product. Surely, there can be no certainty of safety? Even if society does believe that blood is safe from infection since October 1985, are they 'entitled' to have that expectation, if it is not feasible or practical to remove all risk of harm from blood? Is a court entitled to take account of these factors in applying the words of s 3(1) of the 1987 Act? On the face of it, the 'consumer expectations' test of the Act requires an intuitive response of society's expectations without regard to why the product was dangerous. As we have already noted, strict liability is concerned with the condition of the product, not with evaluating the propriety of the manufacturer's conduct. The distinction may not, however, be so clear cut.

Applying a consumer expectation test has proved difficult in other than simple cases in the US. Not only is there a difficulty in interpreting s 3 of the Act, but as the US experience shows, the test it adopts has limitations. First, in design defect cases where all the manufactured products are alike and the argument is that they are all defective, there is no easy standard against which to measure a consumer's expectation. The court applies its own intuitive, and therefore largely subjective, assessment of society's expectations (see *Turner v General Motors Corp* (1979) 584 SW 2d 844 (Texas SC); *Lester v Magic Chef Inc* (1982) 641 P 2d 353 (Kan SC) (Praeger J dissenting)). Equally, in complex design and warning defect cases, consumers will rarely have any specific expectations of safety (see for example, *Knitz v Minister Mach Co* (1982) 432 NE 2d 814). Secondly, where a dangerous defect is 'obvious and patent', a consumer can have no expectation of greater safety, because the danger is apparent from the product itself. Thirdly, a manufacturer could avoid a strict liability claim by making the danger apparent by warning about it. The consumer expectation test does not allow for the possibility that the court could hold that the manufacturer is strictly liable because the product is 'defective' (or 'unreasonably dangerous') even with a warning or an 'obvious and patent' danger, ie the design should be improved or the product not marketed. In an attempt to overcome these difficulties, many US courts have either replaced or, at least, supplemented (*Baker v Lull Engineering Co* (1978) 573 P 2d 443 (Cal SC)) the 'consumer expectation' test by a different test to determine whether a product is 'defective' or 'unreasonably dangerous'. The courts have developed the 'risk/utility' test. This approach requires the court, in rough terms, to balance the risks of the product against its utility and the cost and ease of producing a safer design. Only if the risks outweigh the utility, etc, will the product be defective. This, of course, is the same process used to determine whether a defendant's conduct is careless (ie in breach of duty) in a negligence action. However, one difference remains between negligence and strict liability. In a negligence action, the court balances the known or *reasonably foreseeable* risk inherent in the defendant's conduct against the utility of it. There can be no liability for conduct which creates an unknown and an unknowable risk of harm. In a strict liability action the manufacturer is *deemed to know* of the risk and the existence of the danger. In *Phillips v Kinwood* ((1974) 525 P 2d 1033, at p 1036), the Oregon Supreme Court explained it thus:

> A dangerously defective article would be one which a reasonable person would not put into the stream of commerce *if he had knowledge of its harmful character*. The test, therefore, is whether the seller would be negligent if he sold the article *knowing of the risk involved*. Strict liability imposes what amounts to constructive knowledge of the condition of the product.

In applying the terms of s 3(1) of the 1987 Act, the judges could attempt to intuitively determine 'consumer expectations' even when to do so is difficult and, perhaps, impossible. Alternatively, the courts could accept that the words of s 3 are 'simply a semantic veneer covering what in reality is a cost-benefit.' Expectations of safety cannot be quantified without having regard to the cost, practicality and the technology available, etc, to make the product safer along with the utility and benefits to be derived from the marketing of the product. It must be relevant to know what could have been done and how difficult and costly it would have been to do it when deciding whether the product is safe enough. Of course, this evidence would not be conclusive, only relevant. The Act adopts in form a 'consumer expectation' test, but in reality it requires a 'risk/utility' or 'cost/benefit' analysis to be undertaken.

It follows that in applying the 1987 Act, a court's reasoning in deciding whether blood infected with HIV-2 is defective will involve precisely the same process that would arise in a negligence action. A conscious decision not to test for HIV-2 will have to be justified on the grounds of, for example, feasibility, cost and the low level of risk seen in the light of the great utility of blood and blood products to patients.

One further point concerns the question of warnings. In determining whether a product is defective, s 3(2) requires the court to have regard to:

> ... any ... warnings with respect to, doing or refraining from doing anything with or in relation to the product.

A warning may lead a court to decide that the product is as safe as can be expected. A product such as blood has great benefits in its use (ie its utility is high) but it carries a known risk of infection which cannot be detectable or eliminated. In these circumstances, providing a warning of the risk is given then the product will not be defective under the Act. Just as we saw in the case of a negligence action, the warning should be given to the patient's doctor as the 'learned intermediary'. It will then be a matter for his professional judgment whether he passes the warning on to the patient. A negligent failure to do so may give rise to a malpractice action but no action will lie under the Act.

The third situation – 'the unknowable risk' – raises the issue of the 'developments risk defence'. This is provided for in s 4(1)(e) of the Act.

4.—(1) In any civil proceedings by virtue of this Part against any person ("the person proceeded against") in respect of a defect in a product it shall be a defence for him to show—...

(e) that the state of scientific and technical knowledge at the relevant time was not such that a producer of products of the same description as the product in question might be expected to have discovered the defect if it had existed in his products while they were under his control; or

This provision may be crucial in many products liability cases concerning pharmaceuticals. Since the manufacturer will argue that they did not know of the risk, *nor could they*. The latter would excuse them in a negligence action but will it in a strict liability; claim under the 1987 Act? Returning to the liability for HIV infected blood, we see the following discussion.

Andrew Grubb and David S Pearl *Blood Testing, AIDS and DNA Profiling* (1990)

Blood may remain infected because the risk of 'silent infection' is not appreciated. Equally, if we return to the previous example, blood could be infected with HIV-2 because, at the time, the existence of HIV-2 was unknown and hence before a test to identify the presence of HIV-2 was developed. In both these situations, or where some as yet unidentified (and unknown) risk such as a further HIV strain, materialises and infects an individual, no action will lie under the Act. Two different analyses will lead to this conclusion. The first looks to whether a product, here blood, can be 'defective' if it carries within itself an *unknowable* risk of harm; the second assumes that the product is 'defective' but looks instead to the scope of the 'development risks' defence under s 4(1)(e) of the 1987 Act.

Turning to the first of these, will blood which carries an unknowable risk of harm be defective? Are 'persons generally ... entitled to expect' that a product will not carry an unknowable risk of harm? It is certainly possible that a reasonable consumer might *expect* a product not to contain any hidden risks which cannot be detected. A product may appear to be safe. The manner in which a product is marketed together with any indications of its safety and the specific warnings accompanying it may leave the reasonable consumer with the expectation that the product is safe or, at least, safe except for problems stated in the warnings (See the approach of the Missouri Supreme Court in *Elmore v Owens-Illinois* (1984) 673 SW 2d 434). But, it is unlikely that a court, applying the words of s 3(1), would decide that a reasonable consumer is *entitled* to expect this impossible level of safety.

It is not unthinkable that a manufacturer should be liable for unknowable risks. In the US, in cases of manufacturing and design defect, manufacturers are usually deemed to know the inherent risk of their product, even if that was unknowable at the time of distribution (*Phillips v Kinwood Machine Co* (1974) 525 P 2d 1033 (Or Supp Ct) (design defect)).Indeed, it is precisely because a plaintiff does not have to prove that the manufacturer knew or ought to have known of the risk, that the US courts have ensured that strict liability and negligence are distinguished when both causes of action ultimately require a cost/benefit or risk/utility analysis. In strict liability, the test is whether a 'reasonable manufacturer' would have manufactured the product in the light of the risk that is now known to be inherent in it. However, in the area of warnings, the courts have imposed liability only if the manufacturer knew or ought to have known of a risk and failed to warn the consumer of it. Because this fails to distinguish negligence and strict liability, other courts have held that a product is defective if a manufacturer fails to warn of a risk that he could not have known about (*Beshada v John-Manville Products Corp* (1982) 447 A 2d 539 (NJ Sup Ct) (duty to warn of unknowable risk inherent in asbestos)). This approach is very much the minority view in the US and several influential decisions have rejected it, at least, in the context of products which are inherently dangerous such as pharmaceutical products and, perhaps, blood itself (*Feldman v Lederle Laboratories* (1984) 479 A 2d 347 (NJ Sup Ct) (Pharmaceuticals); *Brown v Superior Court* (1988) 751 P 2d 470 (Cal Sc)) (Pharmaceuticals).

Under the Act, however, there are conflicting indications as to whether a product which has an inherent unknowable risk is 'defective'. Section 3(2)(c) of the 1987 Act suggest that it will not be. It states that the court must have regard to '… the time when the product was supplied by its producer to another' in determining whether the product is defective. In other words the Act encourages a 'foresight and not a 'hindsight' approach when evaluating the expectations of 'person generally' under s 3(1). Consequently, perhaps consumers are 'entitled to expect' safety from risks which are known or could reasonably be known.

There are problems with this view. If it is correct, liability under the Act is indistinguishable form liability in negligence. Once foresight of risk is allowed to dominate a determination of 'defect', negligence and strict liability merge. The US courts, realising this, have applied a 'hindsight test'. Could it have been Parliament's intention in passing the Act to add nothing to the law of negligence? The whole purpose behind the legislation was the intention to impose liability even where fault, ie negligence, could not be established. A hindsight approach to risks is, therefore, more appropriate. Logic also supports this view. If a product with an unknowable risk is not defective, the 'development risk' defence under s 4(1)(e) would be wholly unnecessary.

In the result, we take the view of the law that 'persons generally' might be entitled to expect in certain circumstances that a product is free even from unknowable dangers. It does not follow, of course, that a product will be defective simply because an unknowable danger subsequently harms someone. It would still be necessary to prove that the unknowable risk in the product outweighed its utility. However, it is very unlikely that blood would be defective under this test. The utility of blood, ie the obvious benefits to patients coupled with the absence of any less dangerous alternative to blood which could be substituted for it, are likely to lead a court to the conclusion that the blood is not defective.

Even if this were not so, the 'development risks' defence in s 4(1)(e) would provide the blood suppliers with a defence. An unknowable risk of infection would come within the statutory words that '… the state of scientific … knowledge … was not such that a producer of … [blood] … might be expected to have discovered the [infection] …' Indeed, these words would appear to go further and also cover the situation where the infection in the blood is not *reasonably discoverable*. Unlike the wording of the Directive upon which it is based, s 4(1)(e) of the 1987 Act looks to the discoverability of a risk within the manufacturing community in question. The only distinction between this and liability in negligence is that in the latter the plaintiff has to prove that a particular risk was reasonably discoverable, while under the Act the burden of proving the negative, that the risk was *not reasonably discoverable*, is placed upon the manufacturer.

You will see at the end of this extract reference to art 7(e) of the Directive whose wording is different from s 4(1)(e). The former provides for a defence where:

… the state of scientific and technical knowledge at the time when he put the product into circulation was not such as to enable the existence of the defect to be discovered …

The directive seems to embody a tougher standard than does the apparently 'community-orientated' standard in s 4(1)(e). The 'development risks' defence has been the most controversial part of the 1987 Act. The UK did not have to implement art 7(e) at all. In fact, most states have expect for Finland and Luxembourg (France has yet to do so). However, Germany and Spain exclude pharmaceuticals from their national equivalent (see generally, C Hodges (ed) *Products Liability: European Laws and Practice* (1993)).

Its place in the Directive and 1987 Act owes much to the lobbying of the pharmaceutical industry that considered without it innovation would be stifled. Some have argued that the Act has correctly implemented the Directive (see C Newdick 'The Development Risk Defence of the Consumer Protection Act 1987' [1988] CLJ 455). A different argument would be that s 1(1) requires that the 1987 Act be interpreted consistently with the directive when it states that the Act 'is necessary in order to comply with the product liability Directive *and shall be construed accordingly*' (emphasis added). The European Commission took proceedings against the UK Government for failure to properly implement art 7(e). In *Commission v UK* (Case C-300/95) [1997] All ER (EC) 481, the European Court of Justice dismissed the proceedings for this very reason. The court also offered its own interpretation of the Directive (and, of course, the 1987 Act) and, in so doing, has toughened up the apparent meaning of s 4(1)(e) of the 1987 Act. The court's reasoning is discussed in the following extract.

Christopher Hodges 'Development Risks: Unanswered Questions' (1998) 61 MLR 560

Infringement proceedings, commenced under Article 169 of the EC Treaty, alleging that the UK had failed properly to implement the Directive, were dismissed by the Court of Justice on 29 May 1997 (Case C-300/95, *Commission of the European Communities v United Kingdom of Great Britain and Northern Ireland*). The Court's reasoning was partly procedural and partly substantive. On the procedural side, the Commission had failed to prove its claim that the result intended by Article 7(e) of the Directive would clearly not be achieved in the UK's domestic legal order. There was nothing in the material produced to the Court to suggest that courts in the United Kingdom would not interpret section 4(1)(e) in the light of the wording and the purpose of the Directive so as to achieve its result, particularly because section 1(1) of the Consumer Protection Act expressly imposes such an obligation on the national courts. There was, for example, an absence of any decision of a UK court on the meaning of section 4(1)(e), which would show that the defence was being applied incorrectly.

The presumption of the producer's knowledge
Various issues are raised by the UK's wording. First, to what extent must the unknown risk which has caused the injury be objectively or subjectively discoverable by the producer? On the face of the Directive's wording, the test is entirely objective and capable of a yes or no answer: was the scientific and technical knowledge such that the defect could be discovered? Yet on the face of the UK wording, it might be thought that the test is more subjective and favourable to a producer: might another producer of the same product be expected to have discovered the defect? There is also a significant question as to the extent to which discoverability is strictly objective or to include some element of reasonableness. Consideration of these issues shows that the problem is not with the UK wording but with the wording of the defence in the Directive. The concepts deployed in the Directive simply do not fit the reality of the discovery of product safety issues.

The Court rejected the Commission's submission that the UK defence depends on the subjective knowledge of a producer taking reasonable care in the light of the standard precautions taken in the industrial sector in question – ie a negligence approach rather than a strict liability approach.

The reference in section 4(1)(e) to another producer of the same product might be thought to limit to a particular industrial sector first the relevant state of technical and scientific knowledge and secondly the discoverability of the defect. Such considerations, say the UK's critics, come dangerously close to importing the reasonableness standard of negligence by concentrating on the activities of a limited class of manufacturers rather than on the objective concepts of the state of knowledge, discoverability and defect.

The Advocate General thought that the industrial sector concerned had no relevance to the state of scientific and technical knowledge but did have relevance in relation to discoverability:

It should first be observed that, since [Article 7(e)] refers solely to the 'scientific and technical knowledge' at the time when the product was marketed, it is not concerned with the practices and safety standards in use in the industrial sector in which the producer is operating. In other words, it has no bearing on the exclusion of the manufacturer from liability that no-one in that particular class of manufacturer takes the measures necessary to eliminate the defect or prevent it from arising if such measures are capable of being adopted on the basis of the available knowledge.

Other matters which likewise are to be regarded as falling outside the scope of Article 7(c) are aspects relating to the practicability and expense of measures suitable for eliminating the defect from the product. Neither, from this point of view, can the fact that the producer did not appraise himself of the state of scientific and technical knowledge or does not keep up to date with developments in this area as disclosed in the specialist literature, be posited as having any relevance for the purpose of excluding liability on his part. I consider, in fact, that the producer's conduct should be assessed using the yardstick of the knowledge of an expert in the sector (Case C-300/95 Commission v. UK).

Without elaborating, the Court endorsed the Advocate General's conclusion in holding that:

> ... Article 7(c) is not specifically directed at the practices and safety standards in use in the industrial sector in which the producer is operating, but unreservedly, at the state of scientific and technical knowledge, including the most advanced level of such knowledge, at the time when the product in question was put into circulation. (Ibid, Judgment of 29 May 1997, para 26.)

It might be said that the UK reference to a producer of similar products in fact reinforces rather than undermines the objectivity of the defence by making it clear that the test does not relate to the subjective ability to apply that state of knowledge of the particular producer nor his subjective ability to apply that state of knowledge and deduce or discover that the defect was present in his product. The court confirmed that the defence does not contemplate the state of knowledge of which the producer in question actually or subjectively was or could have been apprised, but the objective state of scientific and technical knowledge, including the most advanced level of such knowledge, of which the producer is presumed to have been informed. It would, therefore, seem that the Court rejected the UK's submission that the state of scientific and technical knowledge does not refer to what the producer in question actually knows or does not know, but to the state of knowledge which producers of the class of the producer in question, understood in generic sense, may objectively be expected to have. Thus, it now seems that if the state of scientific and technical knowledge in a particular industrial sector would not have led to discovery of the defect, but more advanced knowledge in another sector or in the academic community which was not available to the first sector would have led to discovery, the defence cannot succeed. The implicit policy consideration here is to encourage producers to maintain the highest standards of vigilance in relation to identifying and applying scientific and technical information. Such an approach does, however, prompt the question about whether the standard set by the defence is so high that it could ever succeed in practice. If that were the case, the policy of apportionment of risk would have failed to have been implemented by the defence.

Knowledge must be accessible

In one important respect, however, the Court of Justice has limited the severity of the defence. The Advocate General had pointed out that there exist major differences in the accessibility of scientific and technical knowledge. He adopted the example of the difference between a study of a researcher in a university in the United States published in an international English language journal and similar research carried out by an academic in Manchuria published in a local scientific journal in Chinese which is not circulated outside the boundaries of the region. He thought that it was unrealistic and unreasonable to take the view that the study published in Chinese has the same chances as the other of being known to a European product manufacturer.

Without referring to this reasoning the Court of Justice held that it is implicit in the wording of Article 7(e) that the relevant scientific and technical knowledge must have been *accessible* at the time when the product in question was put into circulation. The Court accepted that the Directive 'raises difficulties of interpretation' in relation to deciding the question of accessibility. The Advocate General went so far as to adopt a dyed-in-the-wool reasonableness test, such as that adopted in negligence and which in theory has no place in strict liability:

> ... the state of knowledge must be construed so as to include all data in the information circuit of the scientific community as a whole, bearing in mind, however, on the basis of a reasonableness test the actual opportunities for the information to circulate. ...
> ... it must therefore be proved, in order to exclude liability on the part of the producer, that it was impossible, in the light of the most advanced scientific and technical knowledge objectively and reasonably obtainable and available, to consider the product was defective.
> (Ibid, Opinion of Advocate General Tesauro of 23 January 1997 paragraphs 23 and 26.)

What knowledge should a producer act on?

The reality is that both scientific and technical knowledge are dynamic: they develop constantly. Evolving scientific knowledge, particularly in relation to innovations, may be viewed as a mass of facts, hypotheses and opinions held by a potentially large number of scientists who each have greater or lesser expertise in and understanding of the subjects involved. The state of scientific and technical knowledge may well consist of many inconsistent or even incorrect facts and views of individuals. The Advocate General recognised this:

> The progress of scientific culture does not develop linearly in so far as new studies and new discoveries may initially be criticized and regarded as unreliable by most of the

scientific community, yet subsequently after the passage of time undergo an opposite process of 'beatification' whereby they are virtually unanimously endorsed. It is therefore quite possible that at the time when a given product is marketed, there will be isolated opinions to the effect that it is defective, whilst most academics do not take that view. The problem at this juncture is to determine whether in such a situation, that is to say, where there is a risk that is not certain and will be agreed to exist by all only *ex post*, the producer may still rely on the defence provided for in Article 7(e) of the Directive.

In my view, the answer to this question must be in the negative. In other words, the state of scientific knowledge cannot be identified with the views expressed by the majority of learned opinion, but with the most advanced level of research which has been carried out at a given time. (Ibid. Opinion of Advocate General Tesauro of 23 January 1997 paragraph 21).

The Court of Justice adopted without analysis or explanation the view that, to establish the defence, the producer must prove that the defect was undiscoverable on the basis of the most advanced level of scientific and technical knowledge. The problem is that this approach does not accord with the reality of scientific and technological knowledge, nor of product development and the monitoring and improvement of product safety. The scientific method involves the observation of phenomena and the development and testing of hypotheses. The process of scientific discovery involves observation, recording, speculation, deduction, demonstration and replication before deductions can be made as to absolute knowledge and certainty. On one view, any of these states of 'knowledge' would apparently enable the existence of the defect to be discovered. For example, knowledge of certain observations would, in the mind of an experienced scientist, trigger a line of inquiry involving the need for more research, perhaps even by applying standard techniques, which would have led to the discovery of the defect. Scientific creativity involves the application of judgment, reason and selectivity. Failure to follow up a line of inquiry is an issue of conduct which might by judged in negligence, but it is suggested that it is going too far under strict liability to discovery of further knowledge which does not exist at the time.

Knowledge of certain scientific facts does not necessarily imply that a particular fact about a product (about a particular defect) would, at the time and without hindsight, have been scientifically known or understood, even if the initial state of knowledge did in fact subsequently lead to the knowledge of the defect and such later knowledge might be said by some scientists – but perhaps not by others – to have been discoverable at the earlier time. If, with hindsight, it would have been a theoretical possibility – however low – of someone discovering the defect in the product, then, on a literal reading, the defence fails. This approach must be wrong. Facts and data may be known about a product but that may not mean that there may be sufficient understanding at the appropriate time about their significance as to enable the defect to be discovered. Reassessment of the same facts at a later time, whether by the same or a different brain or process, may lead to a different conclusion being 'discovered' from that which is justified earlier. The benefit of hindsight cannot be overlooked.

Verification of whether a defect was in fact discoverable requires one to consider its probability, having regard to all available scientific knowledge including that derived from research. The concept of reasonableness must regulate discoverability: knowledge of certain observed facts at the time the product was put into circulation does not imply that all conclusions which might subsequently be postulated, deduced or proved from those facts are 'discoverable' at that time. Stapleton has argued forcefully that there is no logical distinction between the case where the defect was absolutely undiscoverable and the case where it was discoverable only be extraordinary means.

It seems meaningless and absurd for the law to seize upon the instant when one particular individual might have the suspicion, speculation or 'hunch' of a connection which much later is shown to have had substance … To give the defence substance then it must protect in cases of defects which could only be discovered, if at all, by extraordinary means. The manufacturer would only be liable for reasonably discoverable defects … a half-way house between 'reasonably discoverable' and 'absolutely discoverable' is not workable … (J Stapleton *Product Liability* (London, Butterworths, 1994) 242.)

The Court rejected a test of discoverability based on the views expressed by the majority of learned opinion at a particular time. Instead, it demands the most advanced level of research which has been carried out. What on earth does that mean? Where expert views differ, the most advanced is to prevail, notwithstanding the fact that it might be a minority opinion. Is it not highly likely that views would also differ on what knowledge in the most advanced? This test merely invites further expert disagreement and is of little assistance to court.

The reality is that the Court's attempt to interpret the Directive in this respect is bound to lead to difficulties since the conceptual approach of the Directive does not fit reality. In reality, a manufacturer needs to consider the safety in use of his product in the light of available techniques and knowledge. He has no option but to accept the prevailing state of knowledge, which in some circumstances may mean the majority view. If there is a minority view that the product might have a certain defect but the majority view is that this is incorrect, the law would seem to be that the producer is obliged to design the defect out, to warn against it or to change his manufacturing processes. Yet he remains unable to identify the defect. He might be faced with enormous cost in warning against a plethora of hypothetical defects, which would undermine the impact of genuine warnings.

An example might help. The summary of product characteristics of a medicinal product might state the state of the latest knowledge on the actual incidence and severity of a particular adverse reaction which has been associated with the product. There might be a minority opinion amongst academics that the incidence and severity is much higher and this might be supported by published research. What should the manufacturer say in his product information? Should he speculate? The minority view might be disproved by further research. His ability to make any amendment is in fact limited since the wording of summaries of product characteristics is subject to approval by a competent authority and cannot be changed without the authority's consent (Directive 92/27/EEC, Directive 65/65/EEC Article 4a and Others). The experience is that the authorities are unlikely to permit wording based on minority but unaccepted theories. This issue leads on to the problem of methodology.

Is knowledge of methodology scientific and technical knowledge?

The basic problem with the defence is that a literal concept of *undiscoverability* is an unworkable test. The truth is that *any* defect can be discovered prior to marketing given sufficient testing. Such testing simply requires time and money – however inimical to the wider public interest in striking a balance between shoddy research and inordinate delay in bringing potentially useful products to market. In this context it is important to note that the concept of scientific and technical knowledge refers to knowledge of more than accepted scientific and technical facts (eg high voltage electricity is dangerous) from which a deduction can be made. The concept also includes scientific *methodology*.

Scientific and technical knowledge includes knowledge of techniques by which the level of safety of a product in use may be tested and verified, and defects discovered. The issue, however, is how much testing it is reasonable to expect the producer of an innovative product to undertake pre-marketing. Community policy recognises ethical, commercial and social limitations on the extent of pre-market testing. The fact that the safety of products must be continuously evaluated throughout their lifetime is recognised by the post-marketing obligations contained in many regulatory Directives, such as Directive 92/59/EEC on general product safety and the pharmacovigilance system of Regulation EC 2309/93. This reflects acceptance of the fact that research continues and pre-marketing research often only allows an estimate of risk to be made. The defence is very difficult to apply consistently with the recitals to the Directive to products for which unidentified and unwanted hazards are to be expected but cannot be discovered by reasonable testing in advance of marketing and reasonable post-marketing monitoring.

At the time at which a product is placed on the market, it may will be discoverable that it has certain defects which are as yet unidentified or unquantified but which would be discovered given further testing. For example it is known that every medicine has an adverse reaction profile. What is not known in the early stages of its marketed life is the precise identification, incidence or severity of particular adverse reactions. The identification of this information is precisely why the pharmacovigilance system is enacted as a regulatory obligation. It would be quite irrational for methodology to be equated with scientific and technical knowledge for the purposes of Directive 85/374/EEC.

At first sight, the test in the defence seems to be whether the defect could have been discovered by any human, using, it is implied, all available powers of logic, data and techniques. Relevant techniques might include the most sophisticated information technology, computing, testing and monitoring in use. Clearly, if this analysis is correct, the standard set by the defence is very high. It would only succeed in very rare circumstances, if ever. It requires all producers to adopt the very highest contemporary standard of methodology. Given that many innovations are discovered by small and medium enterprises, is it reasonable to expect all enterprises to adopt the same highest possible standard, irrespective of resources and cost?

These considerations undermine the credibility of this defence. The charge against the wording of the defence in the Directive is, therefore, that it is not capable of being interpreted in practice. It is unworkable on a literal reading and requires interpretation if it is to reflect the policy objective of protecting innovation. Several leading scholars agree that the defence must be interpreted as including a requirement of reasonableness in relation to both the state of knowledge and to discoverability.

Development risks are about reasonable discoverability ...[the issue] does not relate to the preclusion of known hazards but to the question of whether unknown hazards ought to have been discovered (A.M. Clarke '*Product Liability*' (London: Sweet and Maxwell 1989) 151). ...

The court's adoption of the 'accessibility test' of the Advocate General is puzzling. It seems to introduce a 'reasonableness' test akin to negligence in resolving the 'discoverability' of the defect. It would run counter to the Directive itself and to the overall flavour of the judgment. In a reply to Chris Hodges' comment, Mildred and Howells offer an alternative reading of the case which is less destructive of the core notion of strict liability.

Mark Mildred and Geraint Howells 'Comment on Development Risks: Unanswered Questions' (1998) 61 MLR 570

... The question, however, is whether the defect was discoverable at a certain point of time by the virtue of the then state of scientific and technical knowledge. The difficulty (unresolved by the Court of Justice) is the meaning of 'state'. The choice may be between requiring the knowledge leading to the defect to be available as a whole or to be available in its component parts with the logical or empirical connection remaining to be made. It was no part of the Commission's case before the Court that the producer should be fixed with 'knowledge' contained in unpublished material. It is submitted that, given the imposition on the consumer of the burden of proving the existence of the defect as a condition precedent to the invocation of the defence, the purpose of the Directive is best achieved by allowing the existence of the component parts (which could be assembled into knowledge of the defect) to defeat the defence. The introduction of the qualification of accessibility is both gratuitous and illogical: if the knowledge (albeit inaccessible to the producer) existed ie had been discovered, how could the means to enable it to be discoverable not have been available?

The existence of powerful computerised databases will allow the producer to satisfy itself of the nature of published knowledge in the various fields of knowledge before putting a product into the production stage and again before putting it into circulation. Since they will be available without regard to the industrial sector within which the producer works there is no reason to confine discoverability by accessibility to a particular sector ... the test of discoverability made explicit in the Directive should be objectified as far as possible and the defence itself given as narrow a meaning as is consistent with the requirement that the producer be fixed only with knowledge which is accessible to it (paragraphs 26–29 of the Judgment: [1997] All ER (EC) 481, 494–495). The imposition of the requirement of accessibility (perplexing as it is) appears from the context to go to the question of publication rather than the resources of the actual producer. As the ECJ itself said: '... art 7(e) is not specifically directed at the practices and safety standards in use in the industrial sector in which the producer is operating ...' (Ibid para 26) ...

(For further discussion of the 'development risks' defence, see C Newdick (1991) 20 Anglo AM-LR 309; Stoppa (1992) 12 LS 210.)

C. DEFENCES

We have already seen perhaps the most important defence to an action under the 1987 Act, namely the 'developments risk' defence. The remaining defences are contained in s 4 of the 1987 Act. In addition, s 6(4) applies the Law Reform (Contributory Negligence) Act 1945 to actions under the 1987 Act so that a person's contributory negligence allows the court to reduce his damages.

Section 4, leaving out the 'development risk' defence, provides as follows:

Defences

4(1) In any civil proceedings by virtue of this Part against any person ("the person proceeded against") in respect of a defect in a product it shall be a defence for him to show—

(a) that the defect is attributable to compliance with any requirement imposed by or under any enactment or with any Community obligation; or

(b) that the person proceeded against did not at any time supply the product to another; or

(c) that the following conditions are satisfied, that is to say—

(i)   that the only supply of the product to another by the person proceeded against was otherwise than in the course of a business of that person's; and

(ii) that section 2(2) above does not apply to that person or applies to him by virtue only of things done otherwise than with a view to profit; or

(d)   that the defect did not exist in the product at the relevant time or ...

(f)   that the defect—

(i)   constituted a defect in a product ("the subsequent product") in which the product in question had been comprised; and

(ii) was wholly attributable to the design of the subsequent product or to compliance by the producer of the product in question with instructions given by the producer of the subsequent product.

(2) In this section "the relevant time", in relation to electricity, means the time at which it was generated, being a time before it was transmitted or distributed, and in relation to any other product, means—

(a)   if the person proceeded against is a person to whom subsection (2) of section 2 above applies in relation to the product, the time when he supplied the product to another;

(b)   if that subsection does not apply to that person in relation to the product, the time when the product was last supplied by a person to whom that subsection does apply in relation to the product.

Two aspects of s 4 merit comment. First, s 4(1)(c) seeks to provide a defence where, *inter alia*, the supply is by way of gift. The defence applies where it is done 'otherwise in the course of a business' *and* the defendant is not a 'producer' or if he is , he is acting 'otherwise than with a view of to profit'. The defence does not cover 'supply' by a doctor or hospital within the NHS since s 45(1) states 'business' included a 'profession' and the activities of a 'public authority'. More arguable is whether a pharmaceutical company is covered when providing promotional samples or supplies as part of a clinical trial. The better view is that the pharmaceutical company cannot rely on the defence. The supply is 'in the course of [their] business' (s 4(1)(c)(i)). What else is it? In any event, they are the 'producer' of the product and it is being supplied 'with a view to profit' (s 4(1)(c)(ii)) albeit not immediate profit, but by way of future sales.

Secondly, s 4(1)(a) may be relevant in the pharmaceutical or medical device context. Pamela Ferguson discusses it.

Pamela R Ferguson *Drug injuries and the Pursuit of Compensation* (1996)

... The 1987 Act provides that it is a defence for a producer to show that the defect "... is attributable to compliance with any requirement imposed by or under any enactment." (s 4(1)(a)). This compliance must be with a statutory requirement or Community obligation, and must be mandatory, hence observance of British Standards or a Trade Practice Code will not be a defence. The fact that a producer has complied with these regulations is not of itself a defence; the defence is only available where the defect is *attributable* to compliance with the regulations. Hence the defendant must show that the product's defective condition is due to the fact that it required to conform to a particular regulation.

Numerous regulations relating to pharmaceutical products have been made under the Medicines Act 1968. The ABPI stated in its evidence to the Pearson Commission that it did not regard approval of a new product by the Committee on Safety of Medicines as diminishing the responsibility of its members for any defects in their products (The Royal Commission on Civil Liability and Compensation for Personal Injury (1978 Cmnd 7054) ("The Pearson Report") para 1260). Pearson approved of this and recommended that there should be no defence of "official certification", as such. This defence might, however, be used where a manufacturer has asked the licensing authority to allow a particular side effect to be mentioned in a patient information leaflet, but the authority has refused to agree to this. ...

As Chris Hodges points out in *Product Liability: European Laws and Practice* (*supra*) at para 2-062: reliance on the defence 'is likely to be rare, such as where a particular design change is required or particular wording required in product information such as a warning' (eg the Medicines (Labelling) Amendment Regulations 1992 (SI 1992 No 3273) and the Medicines (Leaflets) Amendment Regulations 1992 (SI 1992 No 3274) both as amended by SI 1994 No 104).

Vaccine damage scheme

The Royal Commission on *Civil Liability and Compensation for Personal Injury* (1978 Cmnd 7054) ('The Pearson Report') argued that children and adults who had suffered injury as a result of vaccination for the good of the community should recover compensation on a strict liability basis rather than requiring them to prove fault.

1407 For those children who can be shown to have been victims of vaccine damage, we consider that there is a case for an additional remedy in the field of tort.

1408 Under the present law, an action in tort against a doctor who performs a vaccination in the recognised circumstances and using the recognised methods would be unlikely to succeed since he could not be said to be acting outside the bounds of proper practice, and would not be negligent. We are not aware of any successful actions. We think an alternative remedy should be made available. Where vaccine damage can be proved to have followed from medical procedures recommended by the Government or a local authority, those who suffer serious and lasting damage should be entitled to bring an action in tort for damages against the Government or the authority concerned. This would normally apply only to children, but we think that adults should also be included, in order to cover those exceptional circumstances in which the Government or a local authority might recommend adults to be vaccinated in the public interest.

1409 We think that the basis of liability should not be fault but should be strict, that is to say that, where a plaintiff can show on the balance of probabilities that the injury suffered was attributable to the administration of a vaccine on the recommendation of the Government or a local authority, he should be entitled to compensation. Subject to these matters of causation and fact, there should be no defences.
We reach these conclusions because vaccination is recommended by the state for the benefit of the community; and where it causes injury the state ought to provide compensation, as part of the cost of providing protection for the community as a whole.

1410 We are conscious of the view that special compensation provision for vaccine damage might act as a deterrent to vaccination, on the grounds that it would imply that there must be a real danger. But there is also the opposite view, which we share, that the Government must be confident about vaccination before it would make such provision. We naturally hope that any increase in litigation resulting from our recommendations, and any attendant publicity, will not have an adverse impact on the future vaccination programme.

1411 We are aware that proof of causation could pose problems for the courts. The convulsions which may be symptomatic of damage by whooping cough vaccine, for example, can also occur naturally, and we are aware of no clinical tests which could distinguish the one from the other. Nevertheless, we see no need to suggest that the courts should adopt a different approach to the proof of causation than that of assessing the balance of probabilities as in the case of other tort actions. No doubt case law would develop on this difficult matter.

1412 We are also aware that the courts would need to assess what is severe damage if, as we propose, a remedy in strict liability is to be confined to such cases.

1413 We recommend that the Government, or the local authority concerned, should be strictly liable in tort for severe damage suffered by anyone (adult or child) as a result of vaccination which has been recommended in the interest of the community.

Following the Pearson Report the Government enacted an 'interim scheme' in the Vaccine Damage Payments Act 1979. The Act and its 'interim scheme' remains in force 20 years later. Writing in 1978, Professor Gerald Dworkin described the main provisions of the Act.

Gerald Dworkin 'Compensation and Payments for Vaccine Damage' (1978) Journal of Social Welfare Law 330

The main provisions of the Vaccine Damage Payments Act, which is now in operation, may be summarised briefly;
(1) Claims may be made for payments of £10,000 for the benefit of persons severely disabled as a result of vaccination against a range of diseases, at present prescribed as diphtheria,

tetanus, whooping cough, polio, measles, rubella, tuberculosis and smallpox (if the vaccination was given before August 1971 when it ceased to be offered as routine procedure in early childhood).

(2)   The range of claimants is extended to include persons severely disabled as a result of vaccinations given to a mother before birth and in certain cases to persons contracting a disease through contact with a third person who had been vaccinated against it.

(3)   A person is severely disabled if he is at least 80 per cent disabled for the purposes of the Social Security Act 1975.

(4)   Provided that the claimant survived both May 9, 1978, and the age of two, claims can be made in respect of vaccinations carried out since the inception of the National Health Service in July 1948.

(5)   Apart from vaccination against polio or rubella, the scheme applies to vaccinations given to persons under 18 or at the time of an outbreak of the disease in the United Kingdom.

(6)   Claims are determined on behalf of the Secretary of State and there is provision for an independent medical tribunal to review matters such as the extent of disablement and the question of causation, which is expressly stated shall be determined "on the balance of probability."

(7)   Payments under the Act are without prejudice to other civil proceedings but a court must set off a payment against any damages which a court awards in respect of disablement. It was also stated extra-legally in debate that, for the purposes of social security benefits, the Supplementary Benefits Commission would ignore the £10,000 payment to a child; but if the payment is made to an adult it will be taken into account although sympathetic consideration will be given to special circumstances. It was also suggested that the £10,000 would be taken into account for legal aid purposes.

Subsequently, the Act has been amended so that the maximum payment is now £40,000 (Vaccine Damage Payments Act 1979 Statutory Sum Order 1998 (SI 1998 No 1587)). Also, the Act now covers vaccination against Haemophilius type b infection (hib) (SI 1995 No 1164).

The scheme is not beyond criticism.

Robert G Lee 'Vaccine Damage: adjudicating scientific dispute' in Geraint G Howells (ed) *Product Liability, Insurance and the Pharmaceutical Industry: An Anglo-American Comparison* (1991)

… There are a number of obvious criticisms …

1   The sum of compensation is not even close to the figure which would be awarded at common law (it began at £10,000 and is currently set at £20,000) (the point is still well made even though the figure is now £40,000);

2   the rule of 80 per cent disability seems high and arbitrarily fixed;

3   the award of a lump sum payment has led to handicapped children being deprived of other means-tested benefits (contrary to government assurances).

However, the greatest of all problems at tribunal level, has been that of causation. The number of applicants has been far larger than predicted, although of course some claims may have been purely speculative. Nonetheless, an estimate based on awards would indicate that brain damage occurred between 1958 and 1981 with a frequency of about 1:25,000 children receiving pertussis vaccination. Nonetheless, failure rates are high. By February 1984, by which time most claims had been heard, only thirteen per cent of initial determinations had led to awards. Of the claims rejected, about half went to appeal, and in seventy-two per cent of appeals, no awards were made, the appeal being rejected (Hansard, H.C., 2 March 1982, col. 123). Success rates before different regional tribunals vary enormously. Figures show that a claimant is twice as likely to succeed before the Nottingham tribunal than before the Edinburgh tribunal (Ibid, col. 122). Clearly, the wide variations here reflect divisions of medical opinion probably as to the frequency with which vaccine damage (as defined) occurred. Nonetheless, the scheme indicates that a number of eminent physicians have a sufficient acceptance of the phenomenon of vaccine-induced brain damage that they undertook the task of assessing individual assertions of such a medical condition …

In June 2000, the Government announced it was increasing payments under the Scheme to £100,000, decreasing the 80% disability criterion to 60% and allowing claims by children up to the age of 18.

Chapter 14

Research

Introduction

It is a truism that for medical practice to develop and improve in any systematic and ordered way research must be carried out. It is equally a truism that such research must include research on human beings whether they are patients or are healthy.

When we speak of research we adopt the analysis set out in Nicholson (ed) *Medical Research with Children* (1986) (at pp 24–26):

> *Research* may be defined as in the *Shorter Oxford English Dictionary*: 'An investigation directed to the discovery of some fact by careful study of a subject; a course of critical or scientific inquiry'. The second part of that definition is more useful when considering medical research because of the potential confusion, posed by the use of the word 'investigation' in the first part. 'Investigation' tends to be used more specifically in medical practice to denote the ascertainment of a particular anatomical, biochemical, or physiological value in a patient. Examples of such 'investigations' are a chest X-ray, the measurement of the haemoglobin level in blood, or lung function tests. In our discussions, however, 'research' was seldom used by itself, without some other word attached. Phrases such as 'research project', 'research procedure', or 'therapeutic research' were used more frequently.
>
> A *research project* is a systematic enquiry designed to contribute to generalisable knowledge. It is important to emphasise that it is systematic in design and execution, and requires honest and accurate recording of all information obtained. A speculative or haphazard attempt at a new therapy, for instance, cannot be regarded as a research project.
>
> A *research intervention* is a specific act performed on a research subject during the course of a research project. Such an intervention may involve the performance of an investigation. used in the medical sense noted above, such as the taking of a blood sample or the measurement of lung function tests, or even simply weighing the subject. Alternatively, an intervention might be manipulation of the subject's diet, or the giving of a substance.
>
> Research interventions may be either *invasive* or *non-invasive*. Essentially, any activity, part or all of which involves an entrance of any sort into a subject's body, is invasive. For instance, urine may be collected by both invasive and non-invasive techniques. If a urine bag is attached to an infant to collect urine voided normally, that is a non-invasive intervention, even though it may cause the infant some discomfort. If on the other hand the urine is collected by supra-pubic aspiration – that is, by passing a needle through the abdominal wall into the bladder and withdrawing some urine – the intervention is invasive. The borderline between invasive and non-invasive may sometimes be difficult to ascertain. Swabbing the skin so as to obtain a sample of bacteria growing thereon is a non-invasive intervention; swabbing the throat for similar purposes, while not involving the breaking of any skin or tegument, should be regarded as an invasive intervention.
>
> Some research projects do not involve any interventions and consist only in *observation*. The *Concise Oxford Dictionary* defines an observation as 'accurate watching and noting of phenomena as they occur in nature with regard to cause and effect or mutual relations', and it is in that sense that 'observation' has been used in this report. In medical research such 'accurate watching' might just be of the colour of a subject's skin, or the size of the pupils of his eyes. Were the pulse to be measured by feeling it at the wrist, that would constitute an intervention rather than an observation. Pure observation is an activity more commonly found in psychological research, particularly that undertaken by human ethologists, when the behaviour of one or more subjects is observed and recorded.

Our concern here is with research interventions as defined. As the law stands, no legal complaint can arise from observational research as described.

Research on human beings has undoubtedly been carried out in one way or another as long as there has been medicine. As Carolyn Faulder, in her book *Whose Body Is It?* (1985), puts it (pp 64–65):

> Few people would seriously argue that doctors are wrong to want to increase their understanding of the human body and the ills to which it is prone. Doctors want to be able to do the best they can for their present patients and they would like to do even better for future patients. *We* want them to find the cure for cancer and other serious diseases and to help us to live longer and healthier lives. *We* expect them to give us the best available treatment. *We* want to feel safe in their hands, reassured that whatever they suggest to us is backed by sound scientific knowledge and that our welfare is their first consideration. We want it all, but medical advance is impossible without research and experimentation – and some of that experimentation must be done on human beings.
>
> In a sense all medical treatment is experimental. However well tried a particular therapy may be, the doctor can never be entirely sure how the individual patient will respond. Far more experimental is any treatment which is offered to patients simply because the doctor believes it works, even though it may never have been put to the test in a comparison with a control group of patients who either are not getting the treatment or are being offered an alternative.

By the end of the nineteenth century, as Faulder (*op cit*) writes (pp 62–64):

> New treatments were proliferating and it became increasingly apparent to the more scientifically minded members of the profession that clinical observation and judgment, although valuable, was too easily distorted by prejudice and personal bias to be reliable. What was needed was some more objective method of verification. The first trial by numbers was done in the early nineteenth century by a Frenchman, Professor Pierre-Charles-Alexandre Louis, who was able to demonstrate the uselessness of blood-letting by comparing the results of large numbers of cases.
>
> However, it was not until well into this century that controlled clinical trials began to be accepted as a method of scientific evaluation. And it was not until after the Second World War that the principle of randomisation was introduced into clinical research. This concept of random allocation was described by its innovator, the statistician Sir Ronald Fisher, who first used it in studies of agricultural crop production, as the primary principle of experimental design. It was another eminent statistician, Sir Austin Bradford Hill, who initiated its use in medical research with the historical trial in 1946 of the antibiotic Streptomycin for tuberculosis. Very simply, randomisation operates on the 'toss of a coin' principle: subjects suffering from a particular illness at the same stage are randomly allocated to different groups for different treatments and then carefully observed and followed up to compare the results. Its purpose is to eliminate any element of human or accidental bias in selecting patients for treatment which would distort the assessment of the results. Clinical trials using this principle of randomisation are called randomised controlled trials [RCT]…
>
> That RCTs have become so widely used is probably due as much as anything to the pithy monograph extolling their virtues written by Dr Archibald Cochrane in the early seventies. He advocated not merely that they were efficient for testing new treatments but that they provided a cost-effective method for testing traditional procedures, many of them outdated and illogical, which the NHS was finding difficulty in discarding. He urged that even simple measures, like when a patient should be got out of bed after surgery, should be put to the test by this rigorous method.
>
> Since then RCTs have been considerably developed and refined and they are now extensively used to test new drugs, surgical techniques, radiotherapy, screening procedures, alternative methods of delivering medical care and a host of other medical interventions.

Faulder asserts that (p 64):

> This means that although only a relatively small percentage of patients actually receiving medical treatment are doing so in a trial (approximately 10 per cent), there are many more of us drawn from the so-called healthy population who may be involved in a trial, with or without our knowledge. For example, a trial testing different methods of counteracting hypertension or a new way of offering a screening service, say for cervical cancer, can be done on a regional basis throughout the community. Very often in such trials neither of the comparison groups taken out of a selected population will be aware that they are being monitored in a study.

Faulder goes on to identify types of research on humans as follows (pp 65–66):

> … there is the non-therapeutic trial which is carried out on healthy volunteers who will get no personal benefit from the experiment but who offer their bodies, or their minds, to test a hypothesis, the effects of a drug or perhaps a psychological theory. The second form of

human experimentation, or study, as doctors prefer to call it, is that done on patients with a particular illness or condition in clinical trials to compare the merits of different treatments. This type of clinical research combined with professional care enables doctors who are genuinely uncertain about which treatment they should be offering to their patients to feel secure that those who get the new treatment will be carefully monitored and that the final judgment of the results does not rely on their opinion alone.

Both forms of research contemplate the use of controls, that is, as Nicholson (ed) in *Medical Research with Children* (1986) (p 31) explains, 'controls are subjects who are used for the purposes of comparison. In a trial of a new drug, for instance, the subjects may… receive either the drug or an inert substance, a placebo. Those receiving the placebo act as controls, since they will come under all the same influences – whether pathological, environmental or psychological – as the subjects, except for the influence of the drug that is on trial'.

In the case of *clinical* trials, as Faulder adds (p 66): '[a] control group of patients in a clinical trial receives the "best standard therapy" and is used as a measure of comparison with another group of patients allotted to the new treatment under study.'

Finally, Carolyn Faulder identifies (p 66):

… three provisos [which] are fundamentally important in the ethical conduct of any trial using human subjects and [which] should be equally well understood by both categories of participants – patients/volunteers and doctors.

These are:
- Provided that the patients or volunteers who participate in all these types of experiments are fully informed and freely give their consent, they are not being used as guinea pigs.
- Provided that the trials are well designed and conform to the conditions prescribed in the Declaration of Helsinki, they are a reliable and ethical way of conducting medical research.
- Provided that the doctors who participate in a trial always put the welfare of their individual patients before the interests of science and society, they can be sure that they are caring for their patients according to the highest medical and ethical standards.

A. THE NUREMBERG TRIALS

Undoubtedly, the greatest incentive to regulate research on human beings was the awareness of, and revulsion at, what had been done in the name of medical research during World War II. Jay Katz in his book *Experimentation with Human Beings* (1972) sets out the major elements of the trial of Dr Karl Brandt and others before the Nuremberg Military Tribunals (pp 292–306):

1. Indictment
The United States of America, by the undersigned Telford Taylor, Chief of Counsel for War Crimes, duly appointed to represent said Government in the prosecution of war criminals, charges that the defendants herein participated in a common design or conspiracy to commit and did commit war crimes and crimes against humanity, as defined in Control Council Law No 10, duly enacted by the Allied Control Council on 20 December 1945…

Count Two [and Three] – War Crimes [and Crimes against Humanity]

Between September 1939 and April 1945 all of the defendants herein unlawfully, wilfully, and knowingly committed war crimes [and crimes against humanity], as defined by Article II of Control Council Law No 10, in that they were principals in, accessories to, ordered, abetted, took a consenting part in, and were connected with plans and enterprises involving medical experiments without the subjects' consent, upon [German civilians and] civilians and members of the armed forces of nations then at war with the German Reich… in the course of which experiments the defendants committed murders, brutalities, cruelties, tortures, atrocities, and other inhuman acts. Such experiments included, but were not limited to the following:

High-altitude experiments. From about March 1942 to about August 1942 experiments were conducted at the Dachau concentration camp, for the benefit of the German Air Force, to investigate the limits of human endurance and existence at extremely high altitudes. The experiments were carried out in a low-pressure chamber in which the atmospheric conditions and pressures prevailing at high altitude (up to 68,000 feet) could be duplicated. The experimental subjects were placed in the low-pressure chamber and thereafter the simulated altitude therein was raised. Many victims died as a result of these experiments and others suffered grave injury, torture, and ill-treatment...

Freezing experiments. From about August 1942 to about May 1943 experiments were conducted at the Dachau concentration camp, primarily for the benefit of the German Air Force, to investigate the most effective means of treating persons who had been severely chilled or frozen. In one series of experiments the subjects were forced to remain in a tank of ice water for periods up to 3 hours. Extreme rigor developed in a short time. Numerous victims died in the course of these experiments. After the survivors were severely chilled, rewarming was attempted by various means. In another series of experiments, the subjects were kept naked outdoors for many hours at temperatures below freezing. The victims screamed with pain as parts of their bodies froze.

Malaria experiments. From about February 1942 to about April 1945 experiments were conducted at the Dachau concentration camp in order to investigate immunization for and treatment of malaria. Healthy concentration-camp inmates were infected by mosquitoes or by injections of extracts of the mucous glands of mosquitoes. After having contracted malaria the subjects were treated with various drugs to test their relative efficacy. Over 1,000 involuntary subjects were used in these experiments. Many of the victims died and others suffered severe pain and permanent disability.

Sulfanilamide experiments. From about July 1942 to about September 1943 experiments to investigate the effectiveness of sulfanilamide were conducted at the Ravensbrueck concentration camp for the benefit of the German Armed Forces. Wounds deliberately inflicted on the experimental subjects were infected with bacteria such as streptococcus, gas gangrene, and tetanus. Circulation of blood was interrupted by tying off blood vessels at both ends of the wound to create a condition similar to that of a battlefield wound. Infection was aggravated by forcing wood shavings and ground glass into the wounds. The infection was treated with sulfanilamide and other drugs to determine their effectiveness. Some subjects died as a result of these experiments and others suffered serious injury and intense agony...

Epidemic jaundice experiments. From about June 1943 to about January 1945 experiments were conducted at the Sachsenhausen and Natzweiler concentration camps, for the benefit of the German Armed Forces, to investigate the causes of, and inoculations against, epidemic jaundice. Experimental subjects were deliberately infected with epidemic jaundice, some of whom died as a result, and others were caused great pain and suffering...

Spotted fever [typhus] experiments. From about December 1941 to about February 1945 experiments were conducted at the Buchenwald and Natzweiler concentration camps, for the benefit of the German Armed Forces, to investigate the effectiveness of spotted fever and other vaccines. At Buchenwald numerous healthy inmates were deliberately infected with spotted fever virus in order to keep the virus alive; over 90 percent of the victims died as a result. Other healthy inmates were used to determine the effectiveness of different spotted fever vaccines and of various chemical substances. In the course of these experiments 75 percent of the selected number of inmates were vaccinated with one of the vaccines or nourished with one of the chemical substances and, after a period of 3 to 4 weeks, were infected with spotted fever germs. The remaining 25 percent were infected without any previous protection in order to compare the effectiveness of the vaccines and the chemical substances. As a result, hundreds of the persons experimented upon died...

Experiments with poison. In or about December 1943, and in or about October 1944, experiments were conducted at the Buchenwald concentration camp to investigate the effect of various poisons upon human beings. The poisons were secretly administered to experimental subjects in their food. The victims died as a result of the poison or were killed immediately in order to permit autopsies. In or about September 1944 experimental subjects were shot with poison bullets and suffered torture and death...

Between June 1943 and September 1944 the defendants Rudolf Brandt and Sievers... were principals in, accessories to, ordered, abetted, took a consenting part in, and were connected with plans and enterprises involving the murder of civilians and members of the armed forces of nations then at war with the German Reich and who were in the custody of the German Reich in exercise of belligerent control. One hundred [and] twelve Jews were selected for the purpose of completing a skeleton collection for the Reich University of Strasbourg. Their photographs and anthropological measurements were taken. Then they were killed. Thereafter, comparison tests, anatomical research, studies regarding race, pathological features of the body, form and size of the brain, and other tests, were made. The bodies were sent to Strasbourg and defleshed.

2. Opening statement of the prosecution by Brigadier General Telford Taylor

I turn now to the main part of the indictment and will outline at this point the prosecution's case relating to those crimes alleged to have been committed in the name of medical or scientific research... What I will cover now comprehends all of the experiments charged as war crimes ... and as crimes against humanity... the indictment...

A sort of rough pattern is apparent on the face of the indictment. Experiments concerning high altitude, the effect of cold, and the potability of processed sea water have an obvious relation to aeronautical and naval combat and rescue problems. The mustard gas and phosphorous burn experiments, as well as those relating to the healing value of sulfanilamide for wounds, can be related to air-raid and battlefield medical problems. It is well known that malaria, epidemic jaundice, and typhus were among the principal diseases which had to be combated by the German Armed Forces and by German authorities in occupied territories.

To some degree, the therapeutic pattern outlined above is undoubtedly a valid one, and explains why the Wehrmacht, and especially the German Air Force, participated in these experiments. Fanatically bent upon conquest, utterly ruthless as to the means or instruments to be used in achieving victory, and callous to the sufferings of people whom they regarded as inferior, the German militarists were willing to gather whatever scientific fruit these experiments might yield.

But our proof will show that a quite different and even more sinister objective runs like a red thread through these hideous researches. We will show that in some instances the true object of these experiments was not how to rescue or to cure, but how to destroy and kill. The sterilization experiments were, it is clear, purely destructive in purpose. The prisoners at Buchenwald who were shot with poisoned bullets were not guinea pigs to test an antidote for the poison; their murderers really wanted to know how quickly the poison would kill. This destructive object is not superficially as apparent in other experiments, but we will show that it was often there.

Mankind has not heretofore felt the need of a word to denominate the science of how to kill prisoners most rapidly and subjugate people in large numbers. This case and these defendants have created this gruesome question for the lexicographer. For the moment we will christen this macabre science 'thanatology', the science of producing death. The thanatological knowledge, derived in part from these experiments, supplied the techniques for genocide, a policy of the Third Reich, exemplified in the 'euthanasia' program and in the widespread slaughter of Jews, gypsies, Poles, and Russians. This policy of mass extermination could not have been so effectively carried out without the active participation of German medical scientists...

The experiments known as 'high-altitude' or 'low-pressure' experiments were carried out at the Dachau concentration camp in 1942. According to the proof, the original proposal that such experiments be carried out on human beings originated in the spring of 1941 with a Dr Sigmund Rascher. Rascher was at that time a captain in the medical service of the German Air Force, and also held officer rank in the SS. He is believed now to be dead.

The origin of the idea is revealed in a letter which Rascher wrote to Himmler in May 1941 at which time Rascher was taking a course in aviation medicine at a German Air Force headquarters in Munich. According to the letter, this course included researches into high-altitude flying and

considerable regret was expressed at the fact that no tests with human material had yet been possible for us, as such experiments are very dangerous and nobody volunteers for them. (1602-PS.)

Rascher, in this letter, went on to ask Himmler to put human subjects at his disposal and baldly stated that the experiments might result in death to the subjects but that the tests theretofore made with monkeys had not been satisfactory.

Rascher's letter was answered by Himmler's adjutant, the defendant, Rudolf Brandt, who informed Rascher that – '...Prisoners will, of course, gladly be made available for the high-flight researches.'

...The tests themselves were carried out in the spring and summer of 1942, using the pressure chamber which the German Air Force had provided. The victims were locked in the low-pressure chamber, which was an airtight ball-like compartment, and then the pressure in the chamber was altered to simulate the atmospheric conditions prevailing at extremely high altitudes. The pressure in the chamber could be varied with great rapidity, which permitted the defendants to duplicate the atmospheric conditions which an aviator might encounter in falling great distances through space without a parachute and without oxygen.

... The first report by Rascher was made in April 1942, and contains a description of the effect of the low-pressure chamber on a 37-year-old Jew. (1971-A-PS.) I quote:

The third experiment of this type took such an extraordinary course that I called an SS physician of the camp as witness, since I had worked on these experiments all by myself.

It was a continuous experiment without oxygen at a height of 12 kilometres conducted on a 37-year-old Jew in good general condition. Breathing continued up to 30 minutes. After 4 minutes the experimental subject began to perspire and wiggle his head, after 5 minutes cramps occurred, between 6 and 10 minutes breathing increased in speed and the experimental subject became unconscious; from 11 to 30 minutes breathing slowed down to three breaths per minute, finally stopping altogether.

Severest cyanosis developed in between and foam appeared at the mouth.

At 5 minute intervals electrocardiograms from three leads were written. After breathing had stopped Ekg (electrocardiogram) was continuously written until the action of the heart had come to a complete standstill. About 1/2 hour after breathing had stopped, dissection was started...

Another series of experiments carried out at the Dachau concentration camp concerned immunization for and treatment of malaria. Over 1,200 inmates of practically every nationality were experimented upon. Many persons who participated in these experiments have already been tried before a general military court held in Dachau, and the findings of that court will be laid before this Tribunal. The malaria experiments were carried out under the general supervision of a Dr Schilling, with whom the defendant Sievers and others in the box collaborated. The evidence will show that healthy persons were infected by mosquitoes or by injections from the glands of mosquitoes. Catholic priests were among the subjects. The defendant Gebhardt kept Himmler informed of the progress of these experiments. Rose furnished Schilling with fly eggs for them, and others of the defendants participated in various ways which the evidence will demonstrate.

After the victims had been infected they were variously treated with quinine, neosalvarsan, pyramidon, antipryrin, and several combinations of these drugs. Many deaths occurred from excessive doses of neosalvarsan and pyramidon. According to the findings of the Dachau court, malaria was the direct cause of 30 deaths and 300 to 400 others died as the result of subsequent complications...

From December 1941, until near the end of the war, a large program of medical experimentation was carried out upon concentration camp inmates at Buchenwald and Natzweiler to investigate the value of various vaccines. This research involved a variety of diseases – typhus, yellow fever, smallpox, paratyphoid A and B, cholera, and diphtheria...

The general pattern of these typhus experiments was as follows. A group of concentration camp inmates, selected from the healthier ones who had some resistance to disease, were injected with an anti-typhus vaccine, the efficacy of which was to be tested. Thereafter, all the persons in the group would be infected with typhus. At the same time, other inmates who had not been vaccinated were also infected for purposes of comparison – these unvaccinated victims were called the 'control' group. But perhaps the most wicked and murderous circumstance in this whole case is that still other inmates were deliberately infected with typhus with the sole purpose of keeping the typhus virus alive and generally available in the bloodstream of the inmates...

The 20 physicians in the dock range from leaders of German scientific medicine, with excellent international reputations, down to the dregs of the German medical profession. All of them have in common a callous lack of consideration and human regard for, and an unprincipled willingness to abuse their power over the poor, unfortunate, defenseless creatures who had been deprived of their rights by a ruthless and criminal government. All of them violated the Hippocratic commandments which they had solemnly sworn to uphold and abide by, including the fundamental principle never to do harm – '*primum non nocere*'.

Outstanding men of science, distinguished for their scientific ability in Germany and abroad, are the defendants Rostock and Rose. Both exemplify, in their training and practice alike, the highest traditions of German medicine. Rostock headed the Department of Surgery at the University of Berlin and served as dean of its medical school. Rose studied under the famous surgeon, Enderlen, at Heidelberg and then became a distinguished specialist in the fields of public health and tropical diseases. Handloser and Schroeder are outstanding medical administrators. Both of them made their careers in military medicine and reached the peak of their profession. Five more defendants are much younger men who are nevertheless already known as the possessors of considerable scientific ability, or capacity in medical administration. These include the defendants Karl Brandt, Ruff, Beiglboeck, Schaefer, and Becker-Freyseng.

A number of others such as Romberg and Fischer are well trained, and several of them attained high professional position. But among the remainder few were known as outstanding scientific men. Among them at the foot of the list is Blome who has published his autobiography entitled 'Embattled Doctor' in which he sets forth that he eventually decided to become a doctor because a medical career would enable him to become 'master over life and death'...

I intend to pass very briefly over matters of medical ethics, such as the conditions under which a physician may lawfully perform a medical experiment upon a person who has voluntarily subjected himself to it, or whether experiments may lawfully be performed upon criminals who have been condemned to death. This case does not present such problems. No refined questions confront us here.

None of the victims of the atrocities perpetrated by these defendants were volunteers, and this is true regardless of what these unfortunate people may have said or signed before their tortures began. Most of the victims had not been condemned to death, and those who had been were not criminals, unless it be a crime to be a Jew, or a Pole, or a gypsy, or a Russian prisoner of war.

Were it necessary, one could make a long list of the respects in which the experiments which these defendants performed departed from every known standard of medical ethics. But the gulf between these atrocities and serious research in the healing art is so patent that such a tabulation would be cynical.

These experiments revealed nothing which civilized medicine can use. It was, indeed, ascertained that phenol or gasoline injected intravenously will kill a man inexpensively and within 60 seconds. This and a few other 'advances' are all in the field of thanatology...

Apart from these deadly fruits, the experiments were not only criminal but a scientific failure. It is indeed as if a just deity had shrouded the solutions which they attempted to reach with murderous means. The moral shortcomings of the defendants and the precipitous ease with which they decided to commit murder in quest of 'scientific results', dulled also that scientific hesitancy, that thorough thinking-through, that responsible weighing of every single step which alone can insure scientifically valid results. Even if they had merely been forced to pay as little as two dollars for human experimental subjects, such as American investigators may have to pay for a cat, they might have thought twice before wasting unnecessary numbers, and thought of simpler and better ways to solve their problems. The fact that these investigators had free and unrestricted access to human beings to be experimented upon misled them to the dangerous and fallacious conclusion that the results would thus be better and more quickly obtainable than if they had gone through the labour of preparation, thinking, and meticulous preinvestigation.

A particularly striking example is the sea-water experiment. I believe that three of the accused... will today admit that this problem could have been solved simply and definitively within the space of one afternoon. On 20 May 1944 when these accused convened to discuss the problem, a thinking chemist could have solved it right in the presence of the assembly within the space of a few hours by the use of nothing more gruesome than a piece of jelly, a semipermeable membrane and a salt solution, and the German Armed Forces would have had the answer on 21 May 1944. But what happened instead? The vast armies of the disenfranchised slaves were at the beck and call of this sinister assembly; and instead of thinking, they simply relied on their power over human beings rendered rightless by a criminal state and government...

Who could German medicine look to to keep the profession true to its traditions and protect it from the ravaging inroads of Nazi pseudo-science? This was the supreme responsibility of the leaders of German medicine – men like Rostock and Rose and Schroeder and Handloser. That is why their guilt is greater than that of any of the defendants in the dock. They are the men who utterly failed their country and their profession, who showed neither courage nor wisdom nor the vestiges of moral character....

3. Extracts from argumentation and evidence of prosecution and defense

a.   Testimony of defense expert witness Dr Franz Vollhardt
Direct examination.
Dr Marx: Please, would you briefly tell the Tribunal what your scientific activities have been and in what special field you have taken a particularly great interest, and since when?
Witness Vollhardt: I am Professor of Internal Medicine at Frankfurt and predominantly I have dealt with the questions of circulation, metabolism, blood pressure, and kidney diseases....
Q: Which foreign academies and foreign societies have you been a member of?...
A: I am Honorary Doctor of the Sorbonne, Paris, of Goettingen and Freiburg; and as far as societies are concerned, there are a lot of them, Medical Society of Edinburgh, at Geneva, at Luxembourg. I am an Honorary Member of the University at Santiago, and so on and so forth....
Q: Now, Professor, have you sufficient insight into the planning and carrying out of the so-called sea-water experiments to give an expert opinion on that subject?...
A: I think that scientifically speaking the planning was excellent and I have no objection to the entire plan. It was good to add a hunger-and-thirst group because we know by experience that thirst can be borne less well than hunger, and if people are suffering from hunger and thirst too, they do not suffer from hunger, but do suffer from thirst; and that resembles what shipwrecked persons would be subjected to because they only suffer from thirst. It was excellent that Wofatit was to be introduced into the experiments too, although it was expected from the beginning that this wonderful discovery would show its value....
Q: Could the aim of these experiments have been achieved with a semipermeable membrane?

A: I don't understand how one can imagine this. What we are concerned with is the question of how long the human body can survive without water and under the excess quantity of salt. Now, that is subject to the water content of the body and it depends first of all, upon whether water is only used by the intermediary tissues or whether the cell liquid too is being used up. In the latter case, there is a danger which becomes apparent through excess potassium quantities, and this was also continuously observed and checked during such experiments, and there were no excess potassium quantities such as can be expected after 6 days.

Q: Nor would it be right to say that these experiments were not planned scientifically and medically, is that correct?

A: Absolutely not.

Q: Could they have been planned differently?

A: I couldn't imagine how.

Q: Were these experiments in the interests of active warfare, or in the interests of the care of shipwrecked sailors or soldiers?

A: The latter.

Q: In other words, for aviators and sailors who were shipwrecked or might be shipwrecked?

A: Towards the end of the war there was an increase in the number of pilots shot down as well as of shipwrecked personnel, and it was, therefore, the duty of the hygiene department concerned to consider the question of how one could best deal with such cases of shipwrecked personnel...

Q: Now, Professor, the experiments we were talking about; did they have a practical valuable aim and did they show a corresponding result?

A: Yes, that is correct. For instance an important observation was made which Eppinger had expected; he wanted to see if the kidneys did concentrate salt under such extreme conditions to an even higher extent than one expected previously. One thought that it would be something like 2.0 percent but 2.6 or 2.7 percent and record figures of 3.0, 3.5, 3.6 and 4 percent are shown, so that the fortunate man who is in a position to concentrate 3.6 percent or 4 percent of salt would be able to live on sea water for quite a long period....

Finally, one unsuspected fact was shown which may be connected with this, and that is that the drinking of small quantities of sea water up to 500 cc given over a lengthy period turned out to be better than unalleviated thirst....

Q: So, you think that the result of these experiments is not only of importance in war-time, but is also of importance for the problems of seafaring nations?

A: Quite right, it is a wonderful thing for all seafaring nations.

b.   Final plea for defendant Joachim Mrugowsky...

The case with the typhus experiments is different. No order was given to kill a man in order to obtain knowledge. But the typhus experiments were dangerous experiments. Out of 724 experimental persons, 154 died. But these 154 deaths from the typhus experiments have to be compared with the 15,000 who died of typhus every day in the camps for Soviet prisoners of war, and the innumerable deaths from typhus among the civilian population of the occupied eastern territories and the German troops. This enormous number of deaths led to the absolute necessity of having effective vaccines against typhus in sufficient quantity. The newly developed vaccines had been tested in the animal experiments as to their compatibility....

The Tribunal will have to decide whether, in view of the enormous extent of epidemic typhus, in view of the 15,000 deaths it was causing daily in the camps for Russian prisoners of war alone, the order given by the government authorities to test the typhus vaccines was justified or not. If the answer is in the affirmative, then the typhus experiments at Buchenwald were not criminal, since the prosecution did not contest that they were carried out according to the rules of medical science....

c.   Testimony of defendant Gerhard Rose

Direct examination...

Dr Fritz: What do you know about the reasons for this protest (against experiments) being ignored and the typhus experiments being carried out in spite of it?...

Defendant Rose: The Buchenwald experiments (with typhus vaccine) had four main results. First of all, they showed that belief in the protective effect of Weigl vaccine was a mistake, although this belief seemed to be based on long observation. Secondly, they showed that the useful vaccines did not protect against infection, but almost certainly prevented death, under the conditions of the Buchenwald experiments. Thirdly, they showed that the objections of the biological experts to the vitelline membrane vaccines and to the lice vaccines were unjustified, and that vitelline membrane, rabbit lungs, and lice intestines were of equal value. We learned this only through the Buchenwald experiments. This left the way open to mass production of typhus vaccines.

The Buchenwald experiments showed in time that several vaccines were useless; First, the process according to Otto and Wohlrab, the process according to Cox, the process of

Rickettsia Prowazeki murina, that is, vaccine from egg cultures; secondly, the vaccines of the Behring works which were produced according to the Otto process, but with other concentrations; finally the Ipsen vaccines from mouse liver. The vaccines of the Behring works were in actual use at that time in thousands of doses. They always represented a danger to health. Without these experiments the vaccines, which were recognized as useless, would have been produced in large quantities because they all had one thing in common: their technical production was much simpler and cheaper than that of the useful vaccines. In any case, one thing is certain, that the victims of this Buchenwald typhus test did not suffer in vain and did not die in vain. There was only one choice, the sacrifice of human lives, of persons determined for that purpose, or to let things run their course, to endanger the lives of innumerable human beings who would be selected not by the Reich Criminal Police Office but by blind fate....

d.   Testimony of prosecution expert witness Dr Andrew C Ivy
Direct examination...
Mr Hardy: It is your opinion, then, that the state cannot assume the moral responsibility of a physician to his patient or experimental subject?
   Witness Dr Ivy: That is my opinion.
   Q: On what do you base your opinion? What is the reason for that opinion?
   A: I base that opinion on the principles of ethics and morals contained in the oath of Hippocrates. I think it should be obvious that a state cannot follow a physician around in his daily administration to see that the moral responsibility inherent therein is properly carried out. This moral responsibility that controls or should control the conduct of a physician should be inculcated into the minds of physicians just as moral responsibility of other sorts, and those principles are clearly depicted or enunciated in the oath of Hippocrates with which every physician should be acquainted.
   Q: Is the oath of Hippocrates the Golden Rule in the United States and to your knowledge throughout the world?
   A: According to my knowledge it represents the Golden Rule of the medical profession. It states how one doctor would like to be treated by another doctor in case he were ill. And in that way how a doctor should treat his patients or experimental subjects. He should treat them as though he were serving as a subject.
   Q: Several of the defendants have pointed out in this case that the oath of Hippocrates is obsolete today. Do you follow that opinion?
   A: I do not. The moral imperative of the oath of Hippocrates I believe is necessary for the survival of the scientific and technical philosophy of medicine....

e.   Closing brief for defendant Siegfried Ruff...
Experiments which time and again have been described in international literature without meeting any opposition do not constitute a crime from the medical point of view. For nowhere did a plaintiff arise from the side of the responsible professional organization, or from that of the administration of justice, to denounce as criminal the human experiments described in literature. On the contrary, the authors of those reports on their human experiments gained general recognition and fame; they were awarded the highest honours; they gained historical importance. And in spite of all this, are they supposed to have been criminals? No! In view of the complete lack of written legal norms, the physician, who generally knows only little about the law, has to rely on and refer to the admissibility of what is generally to be admissible all over the world.
   The defense is convinced that the Tribunal, when deciding this problem without prejudice, will first study the many experiments performed all over the world on healthy and sick persons, on prisoners and free people, on criminals and on the poor, even on children and mentally ill persons, in order to see how the medical profession in its international totality answers the question of the admissibility of human experiments, not only in theory but also in practice.
   It is psychologically understandable that German research workers today will, if possible, have nothing to do with human experiments and will try to avoid them, or would like to describe them as inadmissible even if before 1933 they were perhaps of the opposite opinion. However, experiments performed in 1905–1912 by a highly respected American in Asia for the fight against the plague, which made him famous all over the world, cannot and ought not to be labelled as criminal because a Blome is supposed to have performed the same experiments during the Hitler period (which, in fact, however, were not performed at all); and experiments for which, before 1933, a foreign research worker, the Englishman Ross, was awarded the Nobel Prize for his malaria experiments, do not deserve to be condemned only because a German physician performed similar experiments during the Hitler regime...

f.   Testimony of prosecution expert witness Dr Andrew C Ivy
Cross-examination...
Dr Sauter: Witness, you spoke yesterday of a number of experiments carried out in the United States and in other countries outside Germany. For example, pellagra, swamp fever.

beri-beri, plague, etc. Now, I should like to have a very clear answer from you to the following question. In these experiments which you heard of partly from persons involved in them and partly from international literature, did deaths occur during the experiments and as a result of the experiments or not? Professor, I ask you this question because you said yesterday that you examined all international literature concerning this question, and, therefore, have a certain specialized knowledge on this question.

Witness Dr Ivy: I also said that when one reviews the literature, he cannot be sure that he has done a complete or perfect job.

So far as the reports I have read and presented yesterday are concerned, there were no deaths in trench fever. There were no deaths mentioned, to my knowledge, in the article on pellagra. There were no deaths mentioned. to my knowledge, in the article on beri-beri, and there were no deaths in the article, according to my knowledge, in Colonel Strong's article on plague. I would not testify that I have read all the articles in the medical literature involving the use of human beings as subjects in medical experiments.

Q: And, in the literature which you have read, Witness, there was not a single case where deaths occurred? Did I understand you correctly?

A: Yes, in the yellow fever experiments I indicated that Dr Carroll and Dr Lazare died.

Q: That is the only case you know of?

A: That's all that I know of....

g.   *Testimony of defendant Gerhard Rose*
Cross-examination...

Mr McHaney: Now, would the extreme necessity for the large-scale production of typhus vaccines and the resultant experiments on human beings in concentration camps have arisen had not Germany been engaged in a war?

Defendant Rose: That question cannot simply be answered with 'yes' or 'no'. It is, on the whole, not very probable that without the war typhus would have broken out in the German camps, but it is not altogether beyond the bounds of possibility because in times of peace too typhus has broken out in individual cases from time to time. The primary danger in the camps is the louse danger, and infection by lice also occurs in times of peace. If typhus breaks out in a camp that is infected with lice, a typhus epidemic can arise in peacetime too, of course.

Q: But Germany had never experienced any difficulty with typhus before the war. Isn't that right?

A: Not for many decades, no.

Q: You stated that nine hundred persons were used in Dr Strong's plague experiments?

A: Yes, I know that number from the literature on the subject.

Q: What is the usual mortality in plague?

A: That depends on whether it is bubonic plague or lung pest. In one, namely, bubonic plague, the mortality can be as high as sixty or seventy percent. It also can be lower. In lung pest, the mortality is just about one hundred.

Q: How many people died in Dr Strong's plague experiments?

A: According to what his report says, none of them died, but this result could not have been anticipated because this was the first time that anyone had attempted to inoculate living plague virus into human beings, and Strong said in his first publication in 1905 that he himself was surprised that no unpleasant incidents occurred and that there was only severe fever reaction. That despite this unexpectedly favorable outcome of Strong's experiments the specialists had considerable misgivings about this procedure can be seen first of all from publications where that is explicitly stated; for example, two Englishmen say that, contrary to expectations, these experiments went off well but nevertheless this process cannot be used for general vaccination because there is always the danger that, through some unexpected event, this strain again becomes virulent. Moreover, from other works that Strong later published it can be seen that guinea pigs and monkeys that he vaccinated with this vaccine died not of the plague, but of the toxic effects of the vaccine. All these difficulties are the reason why this enormously important discovery, which Koller and Otto made in 1903, and Strong in 1905, has only been generally applied, for all practical purposes, since 1926. That is an indication of the care and fear with which this whole matter was first approached, and Strong could not know ahead of time that his experiments would turn out well. I described here the enormous concern that Strong felt during all these months regarding the fact that that might happen which every specialist feared, viz, that the virus would become virulent again. That is an enormous responsibility.

Q: Be that as it may, nobody died. That is a fact, isn't it?

A: If anyone did die, the publications say nothing about it. There were deaths only among the monkeys and guinea pigs that are mentioned in the publication. If human beings died, there is no mention in the publication. It is generally known that if there are serious accidents in such experiments as this, they are only most reluctantly made public....

NOTE
Leo Alexander, 'Medical Science under Dictatorship' 241 *New England Journal of Medicine* 39, 43 (1949)....

[A] series of experiments gave results that might have been an important medical contribution if an important lead had not been ignored. The efficacy of various vaccines and drugs against typhus was tested at the Buchenwald and Natzweiler concentration camps. Prevaccinated persons and non-vaccinated controls were injected with live typhus rickettsias, and the death rates of the two series compared. After a certain number of passages, the Matelska strain of typhus rickettsia proved to become avirulent for man. Instead of seizing upon this as a possibility to develop a live vaccine, the experimenters, including the chief consultant, Professor Gerhard Rose, who should have known better, were merely annoyed at the fact that the controls did not die either, discarded this strain and continued testing their relatively ineffective dead vaccines against a new virulent strain. This incident shows that the basic unconscious motivation and attitude has a great influence in determining the scientist's awareness of the phenomena that pass through his vision.

4. Final plea for defendant Karl Brandt by Dr Robert Servatius...
It is contended that the state finds its limits in the eternal basic elements of law, which are said to be so clear that anyone could discern their violation as a crime, and that loyalty to the state beyond these limits is therefore a crime. One forgets that eternal law, the law of nature, is but a guiding principle for the state and the legislator and not a counter-code of law which the subject might use as a support against the state. It is emphasized that no other state had made such decisions up to now. This is true only to a certain extent. It is no proof, however, that such decisions were not necessary and admissible now. There is no prohibition against daring to progress.

The progress of medical science opened up the problem of experiments on human beings already in the past century, and eventually made it ripe for decision. It is not the first time that a state has adopted a certain attitude with regard to euthanasia with a change of ideology.

Only the statesmen decide what is to be done in the interests of the community, and they have never hesitated to issue such a decision whenever they deemed it necessary in the interest of their people. Thereupon their rules and orders were carried through under the authority of the state, which is the basis of society.

Inquisition, witch trials, and revolutionary tribunals have existed in the name of the state and eternal justice, and the executive participants did not consider themselves criminals but servants of their community. They would have been killed if they had stood up against what was believed to be newly discovered eternal justice. What is the subject to do if the orders of the state exceed the customary limits which the individual himself took for inviolable according to tradition?

What did the airman think who dropped the first atomic bomb on Hiroshima? Did he consider himself a criminal? What did the statesmen think who ordered this atomic bomb to be used? We know from the history of this event that the motive was patriotism, based on the harsh necessity of sacrificing hundreds of thousands to save their own soldiers' lives. This motive was stronger than the prohibition of the Hague Convention, under which belligerents have no unlimited right in the choice of methods for inflicting damage on the enemy.

'My cause is just and my quarrel honorable', says the King. And Shakespeare's soldier answers him: 'That's more than we know.' Another soldier adds: 'Ay, or more than we should seek after; for we know enough if we know we are the king's subjects; if his cause be wrong, our obedience to the king wipes the crime out of us.'

It is the hard necessity of the state on which the defense for Karl Brandt is based against the charge of having performed criminal experiments on human beings.

Here also – in addition to the care for the population – the lives of soldiers were at stake. soldiers who had to be protected from death and epidemics. In Professor Bickenbach's experiment, the issue was the lives of women and children who without 45 million gas masks would have been as unprotected against the expected gas attack as the Japanese were against the atomic bomb. Biological warfare was imminent, even praised abroad as cheaper and more effective than the atomic bomb.

The prosecution opposes to this necessity the condition of absolute voluntariness.

It was a surprise to hear from the expert Professor Ivy that in the penitentiaries many hundreds of volunteers were pressing for admission to experiments, and that more volunteered than could be used. I do not want to dispose of this phenomenon with irony and sarcasm. There may be people who realize that the community has the right to ask them for a sacrifice. Their feelings of justice may tell them that insistence on humanity has its limits. If humanity means the appeal to the strong not to forget the weak in the abundance of might and wealth, the weak should also make their contribution when all are in need.

But what if in the emergency of war the convicts, and those declared to be unworthy to serve in the armed forces, refuse to accept such a sacrifice voluntarily, and only prove an asocial burden to state and community and bring about the downfall of the community? Is not compulsion by the state then admissible as an additional expiation?

The prosecution says 'No.' According to this, human rights demand the downfall of human beings.

But there is a mixture of voluntariness and compulsory expiation, 'purchased voluntariness'. Here the experimental subject does not make a sacrifice out of conviction for the good of the community but for his own good. The subject gives his consent because he is to receive money, cigarettes, a mitigation of punishment, etc. There may be isolated cases of this nature where the person is really a volunteer, but as a rule it is not so.

If one compares the actual risk with the advantage granted, one cannot admit the consent of these 'voluntary prisoners' as legal, in spite of all the protective forms they have to sign, for these can only have been obtained by taking the advantage of inexperience, imprudence, or distress.

Looking through medical literature, one cannot escape the growing conviction that the word 'volunteer', where it appears at all, is used only as a word of protection and camouflage; it is hardly ever missing since the struggle over this problem became acute.

I will touch only briefly on what I have explained in detail in my closing brief. No one will contend that human beings really allowed themselves to be infected voluntarily with venereal disease; this has nowhere been stated explicitly in literature. Cholera and plague are also not minor inconveniences one is likely to undergo voluntarily for a trifle in the interest of science. Above all, it is not customary to hand over children for experimental purposes, and I cannot believe that in the 13 experiments carried out on a total of 223 children, as stated in Document Karl Brandt 117... the mothers gave their consent. Would not the mothers have deserved the praise of the scientist for the sacrifice they trustfully made in the interest of science, praise which is otherwise liberally granted to real volunteers in reports on experiments?

Is it not likely to have been similar to the experiments carried out by Professor McCance? The German authorities who condemn the defendants in a particularly violent form have no objection to raise here against the order to hand over weakling children to a research commission for experimental purposes. The questionnaires which the Tribunal approved for me in order to get further information about this matter have not been answered as the higher authorities did not give permission for such statements to be made. This silence says enough; it is proof of what is supposed to be legal today in the line of 'voluntariness'.

It is repeatedly shown that the experiments for which no consent was given were permitted with the full knowledge of the government authorities. It is further shown that these experiments were published in professional literature without meeting any objection, and that they were even accepted by the public without concern as a normal phenomenon when reports about them appeared in popular magazines.

This happens at a time when the same press is stigmatizing as crimes against humanity the German experiments which were necessary in the interests of the state. Voluntariness is a fiction; the emergency of the state hard reality.

In all countries experiments on human beings have been performed by doctors, certainly not because they took pleasure in killing or tormenting, but only at the instigation and under the protection of their state, and in accordance with their own conviction of the necessity for these experiments in the struggle for the existence of the people....

5. Final statements of the defendants...

a. *Final statement of defendant Siegfried Handloser...*

More than 150 years ago, the motto and guiding principle created for German military doctors and their successors was 'Scientiae, Humanitati, Patriae' (for Science, Humanity, and Fatherland). Like the medical officers in their entirety I also have remained true to that guiding principle in thought and in deed. Realizing the outcome of the events of these recent times, may the joint endeavors of all the nations succeed in avoiding in future the immeasurable misfortune of war, the dreadful side of which nobody knows better than the military doctor.

b. *Final statement of defendant Gerhard Rose...*

Everyone who, as a scientist, has an insight into the history of dangerous medical experiments, knows with certainty the following fact. Aside from the self-experiments of doctors, which represent a very small minority of such experiments, the extent to which subjects are volunteers is often deceptive. At the very best they amount to self-deceit on the part of the physician who conducts the experiment, but very frequently to a deliberate misleading of the public. In the majority of such cases, if we ethically examine facts, we find an exploitation of the ignorance, the frivolity, the economic distress, or other emergency on the part of the experimental subjects. I may only refer to the example which was presented to the Tribunal by Dr Ivy when he presented the forms for the American malaria experiments.

You yourselves, gentlemen of the Tribunal, are in a position to examine whether, on the basis of the information contained in these forms, individuals of the average education of an inmate of a prison can form a sufficiently clear opinion of the risks of an experiment made with pernicious malaria. These facts will be confirmed by any sincere and decent scientist in a personal conversation, though he would not like to make such a statement in public….

6. Judgment…

Beals, Sebring, Crawford, JJ:… Judged by any standard of proof the record clearly shows the commission of war crimes and crimes against humanity substantially as alleged in counts two and three of the indictment. Beginning with the outbreak of World War II criminal medical experiments on non-German nationals, both prisoners of war and civilians, including Jews and 'asocial' persons, were carried out on a large scale in Germany and the occupied countries. These experiments were not the isolated and casual acts of individual doctors and scientists working solely on their own responsibility, but were the product of coordinated policy-making and planning at high governmental, military, and Nazi Party levels, conducted as an integral part of the total war effort. They were ordered, sanctioned, permitted, or approved by persons in positions of authority who under all principles of law were under the duty to know about these things and to take steps to terminate or prevent them.

The great weight of the evidence before us is to the effect that certain types of medical experiments on human beings, when kept within reasonably well-defined bounds, conform to the ethics of the medical profession generally. The protagonists of the practice of human experimentation justify their views on the basis that such experiments yield results for the good of society that are unprocurable by other methods or means of study. All agree, however, that certain basic principles must be observed in order to satisfy moral, ethical, and legal concepts:

1. The voluntary consent of the human subject is absolutely essential.

This means that the person involved should have legal capacity to give consent; should be so situated as to be able to exercise free power of choice, without the intervention of any element of force, fraud, deceit, duress, over-reaching, or other ulterior form of constraint or coercion; and should have sufficient knowledge and comprehension of the element of the subject matter involved as to enable him to make an understanding and enlightened decision. This latter element requires that before the acceptance of an affirmative by the experimental subject there should be made known to him the nature, duration, and purpose of the experiment; the method and means by which it is to be conducted; all inconveniences and hazards reasonably to be expected; and the effects upon his health or person which may possibly come from his participation in the experiment.

The duty and responsibility for ascertaining the quality of the consent rests upon each individual who initiates, directs, or engages in the experiment. It is a personal duty and responsibility which may not be delegated to another with impunity.

2. The experiment should be such as to yield fruitful results for the good of society, unprocurable by other methods or means of study, and not random and unnecessary in nature.

3. The experiment should be so designed and based on the results of animal experimentation and a knowledge of the natural history of the disease or other problem under study that the anticipated results will justify the performance of the experiment.

4. The experiment should be so conducted as to avoid all unnecessary physical and mental suffering and injury.

5. No experiment should be conducted where there is an *a priori* reason to believe that death or disabling injury will occur; except, perhaps, in those experiments where the experimental physicians also serve as subjects.

6. The degree of risk to be taken should never exceed that determined by the humanitarian importance of the problem to be solved by the experiment.

7. Proper preparations should be made and adequate facilities provided to protect the experimental subject against even remote possibilities of injury, disability, or death.

8. The experiment should be conducted only by scientifically qualified persons. The highest degree of skill and care should be required through all stages of the experiment of those who conduct or engage in the experiment.

9. During the course of the experiment the human subject should be at liberty to bring the experiment to an end if he has reached the physical or mental state where continuation of the experiment seems to him to be impossible.

10. During the course of the experiment the scientist in charge must be prepared to terminate the experiment at any stage, if he has probable cause to believe, in the exercise of the good faith, superior skill, and careful judgment required of him that a continuation of the experiment is likely to result in injury, disability. or death to the experimental subject.

Of the ten principles which have been enumerated our judicial concern, of course, is with those requirements which are purely legal in nature – or which at least are so clearly related to matters legal that they assist us in determining criminal culpability and punishment. To go beyond that point would lead us into a field that would be beyond our sphere of competence. However. the point need not be laboured. We find from the evidence that in the medical experiments which have been proved, these ten principles were much more frequently honored in their breach than in their observance. Many of the concentration camp inmates who were the victims of these atrocities were citizens of countries other than the German Reich. They were non-German nationals, including Jews and 'asocial persons', both prisoners of war and civilians, who had been imprisoned and forced to submit to these tortures and barbarities without so much as a semblance of trial. In every single instance appearing in the record, subjects were used who did not consent to these experiments; indeed, as to some of the experiments, it is not even contended by the defendants that the subjects occupied the status of volunteers. In no case was the experimental subject at liberty of his own free choice to withdraw from any experiment. In many cases experiments were performed by unqualified persons; were conducted at random for no adequate scientific reason, and under revolting physical conditions. All of the experiments were conducted with unnecessary suffering and injury, and but very little, if any, precautions were taken to protect or safeguard the human subjects from the possibilities of injury, disability, or death. In every one of the experiments the subjects experienced extreme pain or torture, and in most of them they suffered permanent injury, mutilation, or death, either as a direct result of the experiments or because of lack of adequate follow-up care.

Obviously all of these experiments involving brutalities, tortures, disabling injury, and deaths were performed in complete disregard of international conventions, the laws and customs of war [and] the general principles of criminal law as derived from the criminal laws of all civilized nations... Manifestly human experiments under such conditions are contrary to 'the principles of the law of nations as they result from the usages established among civilized peoples, from the laws of humanity, and from the dictates of public conscience'....

There is some evidence to the effect that the camp inmates used as subjects in the first series submitted to being used as experimental subjects after being told that the experiments were harmless and that additional food would be given to volunteers. But these victims were not informed that they would be artificially infected with a highly virulent virus nor that they might die as a result. Certainly no one would seriously suggest that under the circumstances these men gave their legal consent to act as subjects. One does not ordinarily consent to be the special object of a murder, and if one did, such consent would not absolve his slayer....

[Sixteen of the twenty-three defendants were found guilty of war crimes and crimes against humanity. Seven, including Karl Brandt, Rudolf Brandt, and Joachim Mrugowsky, were sentenced to death by hanging; the other nine, including Siegfried Handloser and Gerhard Rose, to imprisonment varying from ten years to life.]

The ten principles set out in the above judgment have become known as the Nuremberg Code. It is sometimes thought that they constitute the first modern attempt to lay down the principles upon which research is to be conducted. Nicholson (ed), however, points out in *Medical Research with Children* (1986) that (p 154):

The first modern guidelines for the conduct of clinical research were produced by the German Ministry of the Interior in 1931... They were produced in response to frequent allegations, in both the German Press and Parliament, of unethical conduct by doctors during the previous decade. At that time Germany had a thriving chemical industry, collaboration with which had enabled researchers to develop the first chemotherapeutic agents for infections such as malaria, trypanosomiasis, and leishmaniasis, and led to animal trials of Prontosil, the first sulphonamide, in 1933. Howard-Jones suggests that doctors may well not have been 'sufficiently critical in exploiting the multiplicity of new remedies' placed at their disposal. In the midst of the public debate. the Berlin Medical Board suggested that there should be an official body to regulate all proposed experiments on humans: it seems likely that this was the first time that peer review of modern clinical research had been suggested. Little came of the suggestion, however.

Obviously, these earlier guidelines proved irrelevant once the Nazis embarked upon the kind of investigation mentioned in the *Brandt* trial.

B. THE HELSINKI DECLARATION

The Nuremberg Code represented the basis on which civilised society was expected to conduct itself until it was supplemented by the Declaration of Helsinki of the World Medical Association in 1964 (as amended).

It is the mission of the medical doctor to safeguard the health of the people. His or her knowledge and conscience are dedicated to the fulfilment of this mission.

The Declaration of Geneva of the World Medical Association binds the physician with the words, 'The health of my patient will be my first consideration', and the International Code of Medical Ethics declares that 'A physician shall act only in the patient's interest when providing medical care which might have the effect of weakening the physical and mental condition of the patient'.

The purpose of biomedical research involving human subjects must be to improve diagnostic, therapeutic and prophylactic procedures and the understanding of the aetiology and pathogenesis of disease.

In current medial practice most diagnostic, therapeutic or prophylactic procedures involve hazards. This applies especially to biomedical research.

Medical progress is based on research which ultimately must rest in part on experimentation involving human subjects.

In the field of biomedical research a fundamental distinction must be recognised between medical research in which the aim is essentially diagnostic or therapeutic for a patient, and medical research, the essential object of which is purely scientific and without implying direct diagnostic or therapeutic value to the person subjected to the research.

Special caution must be exercised in the conduct of research which may affect the environment, and the welfare of animals used for research must be respected.

Because it is essential that the results of laboratory experiments be applied to human beings to further scientific knowledge and to help suffering humanity, the World Medical Association has prepared the following recommendations as a guide to every physician in biomedical research involving human subjects. They should be kept under review in the future. It must be stressed that the standards as drafted are only a guide to physicians all over the world. Physicians are not relieved from criminal, civil and ethical responsibilities under the laws of their own countries.

I. Basic principles

(1) Biomedical research involving human subjects must conform to generally accepted scientific principles and should be based on adequately performed laboratory and animal experimentation and on a thorough knowledge of the scientific literature.

(2) The design and performance of each experimental procedure involving human subjects should be clearly formulated in an experimental protocol which should be transmitted for consideration, comment and guidance to a specially appointed committee independent of the investigator and the sponsor provided that this independent committee is in conformity with the laws and regulations of the country in which the research experiment is performed.

(3) Biomedical research involving human subjects should be conducted only by scientifically qualified persons and under the supervision of a clinically competent medical person. The responsibility for the human subject must always rest with a medically qualified person and never rest on the subject of the research, even though the subject has given his or her consent.

(4) Biomedical research involving human subjects cannot legitimately be carried out unless the importance of the objective is in proportion to the inherent risk to the subject.

(5) Every biomedical research project involving human subjects should be preceded by careful assessment of predictable risks in comparison with foreseeable benefits to the subject or to others. Concern for the interests of the subject must always prevail over the interests of science and society.

(6) The right of the research subject to safeguard his or her integrity must always be respected. Every precaution should be taken to respect the privacy of the subject and to minimise the impact of the study on the subject's physical and mental integrity and on the personality of the subject.

(7) Physicians should abstain from engaging in research projects involving human subjects unless they are satisfied that the hazards involved are believed to be predictable. Physicians should cease any investigation if the hazards are found to outweigh the potential benefits.

(8) In publication of the results of his or her research, the physician is obliged to preserve the accuracy of the results. Reports of experimentation not in accordance with the principles laid down in this Declaration should not be accepted for publication.

(9) In any research on human beings. each potential subject must be adequately informed of the aims, methods, anticipated benefits and potential hazards of the study and the discomfort it may entail. He or she should be informed that he or she is at liberty to abstain from participation in the study and that he or she is free to withdraw his or her consent to participation at any time. The physician should then obtain the subject's freely-given informed consent, preferably in writing.

(10) When obtaining informed consent for the research project the physician should be particularly cautious if the subject is in a dependent relationship to him or her or may consent under duress. In that case the informed consent should be obtained by a physician who is not engaged in the investigation and who is completely independent of this official relationship.

(11) In case of legal incompetence, informed consent should be obtained from the legal guardian in accordance with national legislation. Where physical or mental incapacity makes it impossible to obtain informed consent, or when the subject is a minor, permission from the responsible relative replaces that of the subject in accordance with national legislation.

Whenever the minor child is in fact able to give a consent, the minor's consent must be obtained in addition to the consent of the minor's legal guardian.

(12) The research protocol should always contain a statement of the ethical considerations involved and should indicate that the principles enunciated in the present Declaration are complied with.

II. *Medical research combined with professional care*

(Clinical research)

(1) In the treatment of the sick person, the physician must be free to use a new diagnostic and therapeutic measure, if in his or her judgment it offers hope of saving life, re-establishing health or alleviating suffering.

(2) The potential benefits, hazards and discomfort of a new method should be weighed against the advantages of the best current diagnostic and therapeutic methods.

(3) In any medical study, every patient – including those of a control group, if any – should be assured of the best proven diagnostic and therapeutic method. This does not exclude the use of insert placebo in studies where no proven diagnostic or therapeutic method exists.

(4) The refusal of the patient to participate in a study must never interfere with the physician-patient relationship.

(5) If the physician considers it essential not to obtain informed consent, the specific reasons for this proposal should be stated in the experimental protocol for transmission to the independent committee (I.2).

(6) The physician can combine medical research with professional care, the objective being the acquisition of new medical knowledge, only to the extent that medical research is justified by its potential diagnostic or therapeutic value for the patient.

III. *Non-therapeutic biomedical research involving human subjects*

(Non-clinical biomedical research)

(1) In the purely scientific application of medical research carried out on a human being, it is the duty of the physician to remain the protector of the life and health of that person on whom biomedical research is being carried out.

(2) The subjects should be volunteers – either healthy persons or patients for whom the experimental design is not related to the patient's illness.

(3) The investigator or the investigating team should discontinue the research if in his/her or their judgment it may, if continued, be harmful to the individual.

(4) In research on man, the interest of science and society should never take precedence over considerations related to the well-being of the subject.

Revision of the Declaration is currently being contemplated. The proposed revision is extensive and controversial (for text see, (1999) 147 Bull Med Eth 18–22).

C. THE IMPACT OF HELSINKI

Despite the Declaration of Helsinki, in 1964 Beecher could still write his seminal paper in the *New England Journal of Medicine:*

H Beecher 'Ethics and Clinical Research' (1966) 274 New Eng J Med 1354

Nearly everyone agrees that ethical violations do occur. The practical question is, how often? A preliminary examination of the matter was based on 17 examples, which were easily increased to 50. These 50 studies contained references to 186 further likely examples, on the average 3.7 leads per study; they at times overlapped from paper to paper, but this figure indicates how conveniently one can proceed in a search for such material. The data are suggestive of widespread problems, but there is need for another kind of information, which was obtained by examination of 100 consecutive human studies published in 1964, in an excellent journal; 12 of these seemed to be unethical. If only one quarter of them is truly unethical, this still indicates the existence of a serious situation. Pappworth, in England, has collected, he says, more than 500 papers based upon unethical experimentation. It is evident from such observations that unethical or questionably ethical procedures are not uncommon....

Known effective treatment withheld

Example 1. It is known that rheumatic fever can usually be prevented by adequate treatment of streptococcal respiratory infections by the parenteral administration of penicillin. Nevertheless, definitive treatment was withheld, and placebos were given to a group of 109 men in service, while benzathine penicillin G was given to others.

The therapy that each patient received was determined automatically by his military serial number arranged so that more men received penicillin than received placebo. In the small group of patients studied 2 cases of acute rheumatic fever and 1 of acute nephritis developed in the control patients, whereas these complications did not occur among those who received benzathine penicillin G.

Example 2. The sulfonamides were for many years the only antibacterial drugs effective in shortening the duration of acute streptococcal pharyngitis and in reducing its suppurative complications. The investigators in this study undertook to determine if the occurrence of the serious nonsuppurative complications, rheumatic fever and acute glomerulonephritis, would be reduced by this treatment. This study was made despite the general experience that certain antibiotics, including penicillin, will prevent the development of rheumatic fever.

The subjects were a large group of hospital patients; a control group of approximately the same size, also with exudative Group A streptococcus, was included. The latter group received only non-specific therapy (no sulfadiazine). The total group denied the effective penicillin comprised over 500 men.

Rheumatic fever was diagnosed in 5.4 percent of those treated with sulfadiazine. In the control group rheumatic fever developed in 4.2 percent.

In reference to this study a medical officer stated in writing that the subjects were not informed, did not consent and were not aware that they had been involved in an experiment, and yet admittedly 25 acquired rheumatic fever. According to this same medical officer *more than 70* who had had known definitive treatment withheld were on the wards with rheumatic fever when he was there.

Example 3. This involved a study of the relapse rate in typhoid fever treated in two ways. In an earlier study by the present investigators chloramphenicol had been recognized as an effective treatment for typhoid fever, being attended by half the mortality that was experienced when this agent was not used. Others had made the same observations, indicating that to withhold this effective remedy can be a life-or-death decision. The present study was carried out to determine the relapse rate under the two methods of treatment; of 408 charity patients 251 were treated with chloramphenicol, of whom 20, or 7.97 percent, died. Symptomatic treatment was given, but chloramphenicol was withheld in 157, of whom 36, or 22.9 per cent died. According to the data presented, 23 patients died in the course of this study who would not have been expected to succumb if they had received therapy....

Physiologic studies

Example 5. In this controlled, double-blind study of the hematologic toxicity of chloramphenicol, it was recognized that chloramphenicol is 'well known as a cause of aplastic anemia' and that there is a 'prolonged morbidity and high mortality of aplastic anemia' and that 'chloramphenicol-induced aplastic anemia can be related to dose...' The aim of the study was 'further definition of the toxicology of the drug'...

Forty-one randomly chosen patients were given either 2 or 6 gm of chloramphenicol per day; 12 control patients were used. 'Toxic bone-marrow depression, predominantly affecting erythropoiesis, developed in 2 of 20 patients given 2.0 gm and in 18 of 21 given 6 gm of chloramphenicol daily.' The smaller dose is recommended for routine use.

Example 6. In a study of the effect of thymectomy on the survival of skin homografts 18 children, three and a half months to eighteen years of age, about to undergo surgery for congenital heart disease, were selected. Eleven were to have total thymectomy as part of the operation, and 7 were to serve as controls. As part of the experiment, full-thickness skin homografts from an unrelated adult donor were sutured to the chest wall in each case. (Total thymectomy is occasionally, although not usually part of the primary cardiovascular surgery involved, and whereas it may not greatly add to the hazards of the necessary operation, its eventual effects in children are not known.) This work was proposed as part of a long-range study of 'the growth and development of these children over the years'. No difference in the survival of the skin homograft was observed in the 2 groups....

Example 8. Since the minimum blood-flow requirements of the cerebral circulation are not accurately known, this study was carried out to determine 'cerebral hemodynamic and metabolic changes... before and during acute reductions in arterial pressure induced by drug administration and/or postural adjustments'. Forty-four patients whose ages varied from the second to the tenth decade were involved. They included normotensive subjects, those with essential hypertension and finally a group with malignant hypertension. Fifteen had abnormal electrocardiograms. Few details about the reasons for hospitalization are given.

Signs of cerebral circulatory insufficiency, which were easily recognized, included confusion and in some cases a nonresponsive state. By alteration in the tilt of the patient 'the clinical state of the subject could be changed in a matter of seconds from one of alertness to confusion, and for the remainder of the flow, the subject was maintained in the latter state'. The femoral arteries were cannulated in all subjects, and the internal jugular veins in 14.

The mean arterial pressure fell in 37 subjects from 109 to 48 mm of mercury, with signs of cerebral ischemia. 'With the onset of collapse, cardiac output and right ventricular pressures decreased sharply.'

Since signs of cerebral insufficiency developed without evidence of coronary insufficiency the authors concluded that 'the brain may be more sensitive to acute hypotension than is the heart'...

Studies to improve the understanding of disease

Example 14. In this study of the syndrome of impending hepatic coma in patients with cirrhosis of the liver certain nitrogenous substances were administered to 9 patients with chronic alcoholism and advanced cirrhosis; ammonium chloride, diammonium citrate, urea or dietary protein. In all patients a reaction that included mental disturbance, a 'flapping tremor', and electroencephalographic changes developed. Similarly signs had occurred in only 1 of the patients before these substances were administered.

> The first sign noted was usually clouding of the consciousness. Three patients had a second or a third course of administration of a nitrogenous substance with the same results. It was concluded that marked resemblance between this reaction and impending hepatic coma implied that the administration of these [nitrogenous] substances to patients with cirrhosis may be hazardous...

Example 18. Melanoma was transplanted from a daughter to her volunteering and informed mother, 'in the hope of gaining a little better understanding of cancer immunity and in the hope that the production of tumor antibodies might be helpful in the treatment of the cancer patient'. Since the daughter died on the day after the transplantation of the tumor into her mother, the hope expressed seems to have been more theoretical than practical, and the daughter's condition was described as 'terminal' at the time the mother volunteered to be a recipient. The primary implant was widely excised on the twenty-fourth day after it had been placed in the mother. She died from metastatic melanoma on the four hundred and fifty-first day after transplantation. The evidence that this patient died of diffuse melanoma that metastasised from a small piece of transplanted tumor was considered conclusive.

Technical study of disease

Example 19. During bronchoscopy a special needle was inserted through a bronchus into the left atrium of the heart. This was done in an unspecified number of subjects both with cardiac disease and with normal hearts.

The technique was a new approach whose hazards were at the beginning quite unknown. The subjects with normal hearts were used, not for their possible benefit but for that of patients in general....

Example 21. This was a study of the effect of exercise on cardiac output and pulmonary-artery pressure in 8 'normal' persons (that is, patients whose diseases were not related to the cardiovascular system), in 8 with congestive heart failure severe enough to have recently required complete bed rest, in 6 with hypertension, in 2 with aortic insufficiency, in 7 with mitral stenosis, and in 5 with pulmonary emphysema.

Intracardiac catheterization was carried out, and the catheter then inserted into the right or left main branch of the pulmonary artery. The brachial artery was usually catheterized; sometimes, the radial or femoral arteries were catheterized. The subjects exercised in a supine position by pushing their feet against weighted pedals. 'The ability of these patients to carry on sustained work was severely limited by weakness and dyspnea.' Several were in severe failure. This was not a therapeutic attempt but rather a physiologic study.

Bizarre study

Example 22. There is a question whether ureteral reflux can occur in the normal bladder. With this in mind, vesicourethrography was carried out on 26 normal babies less than forty-eight hours old. The infants were exposed to x-rays while the bladder was filling and during voiding. Multiple spot films were made to record the presence or absence of ureteral reflux. None was found in this group, and fortunately no infection followed the catheterization. What the results of the extensive x-ray exposure may be, no one can yet say.

Comment on death rates
In the foregoing examples a number of procedures, some with their own demonstrated death rates, were carried out. The following data were provided by 3 distinguished investigators in the field and represent widely held views.
Cardiac catheterization: right side of the heart, about 1 death per 1,000 cases; left side, 5 deaths per 1,000 cases. 'Probably considerably higher in some places, depending on the portal of entry.' (One investigator had 15 deaths in his first 150 cases.) It is possible that catheterization of a hepatic vein or the renal vein would have a lower death rate than that of catheterization of the right side of the heart, for if it is properly carried out, only the atrium is entered en route to the liver or the kidney, not the right ventricle, which can lead to serious cardiac irregularities. There is always the possibility, however, that the ventricle will be entered inadvertently. This occurs in at least half the cases, according to 1 expert – 'but if properly done is too transient to be of importance'.
Liver biopsy: the death rate here is estimated at 2 to 3 per 1,000, depending in considerable part on the condition of the subject.
Anesthesia: the anesthesia death rate can be placed in general at about 1 death per 2,000 cases. The hazard is doubtless higher when certain practices such as deliberate evocation of ventricular extrasystoles under cyclopropane are involved.

In England, as Nicholson (ed) points out in *Medical Research with Children* (p 4):

1967 saw the publication of the first report of the Royal College of Physicians 'Committee on the supervision of the ethics of clinical investigations in institutions', which also recommended that every hospital or institution in which clinical research was undertaken should have a group of doctors that 'should satisfy itself of the ethics of all proposed investigations'. In the same year, M H Pappworth published his book *Human Guinea Pigs*, which detailed several hundred reports of medical experiments that he considered unethical, most of which had been carried out either in the United Kingdom or in the United States of America. He proposed that 'research committees', each with at least one lay member, should be established in every region to review the ethics of proposed investigations, and that, by law, they should be responsible to the General Medical Council.
  Over the next few years many hospitals in the United Kingdom did establish ethics committees to review proposed clinical research investigations. Even to this day, however, there is no statutory duty on health authorities. boards of governors, or other hospital managers to set up such research ethics committees and, indeed, some have not yet done so. At the request of the Chief Medical Officer of the Department of Health and Social Security (DHSS) in 1973, the Royal College of Physicians committee again made recommendations, [*Supervision of the Ethics of Clinical Research Investigations*] suggesting principally (1) that all proposals for clinical research investigations should be referred to the appropriate ethics committee for approval, and (2) that there should be a lay member on each research ethics committee. The DHSS finally published an advisory circular in 1975 [*Supervision of the Ethics of Clinical Research Investigations and Fetal Research* (1975) HSC (IS) 153] confirming the 1967 and 1973 recommendations of the Royal College of Physicians, but without giving them the force of statute.

The concern over the conduct of research remains; for example the judicial inquiry under Judge Cartwright into *Allegations Concerning the Treatment of Cervical Cancer at National Women's Hospital* (July 1988) in New Zealand (for a discussion see A V Campbell 'A Report from New Zealand: An "Unfortunate Experiment"' (1989) Bioethics 59).

D. TERMINOLOGY

Traditionally, any analysis of the law and ethics concerning research on human beings has drawn a distinction between therapeutic and non-therapeutic research. Unless carefully analysed these terms may lead to confusion. Thus, it is important at the outset to understand what is meant by them before embarking on any examination of the law.

The Institute of Medical Ethics in its Working Party Report, *Medical Research with Children* (1986) defines the distinction between these terms and illustrates it as follows (pp 33–36):

> The central point is that since therapy is distinguished from research by the intention of the person doing it, research can never be, in itself, therapy.
>
> Therefore the distinction has to be that *therapeutic research* is research consisting in an activity which has also a therapeutic intention, as well as a research intention, towards the subjects of the research, and *non-therapeutic research* is research activity which has not also a therapeutic intention.
>
> A therapeutic intention is to have as one's purpose therapy…
>
> This definition of the distinction between therapeutic and non-therapeutic research was approved by the working group because it makes clear the dual intent of therapeutic research. It was also argued, however, that such dual intent was unlikely or even impossible; a researcher would always have the primary intent of gaining new knowledge. Such a suggestion seems improbable, however: in reality, a researcher would be using his clinical and therapeutic acumen in the interests of the research element of his activity, at the same time as using his research skills for the clinical benefit of his research subject. If one invites friends round for dinner, one has the dual intent of feeding them and talking with them: it would indeed be a strange occasion if one fed them only without saying a word the whole evening: or vice versa!
>
> One research proposal examined by the working group illustrates both the need in some circumstances to decide whether a project is therapeutic or non-therapeutic, and the difficulties that may be met in so deciding. The proposal had been submitted to the working group by the chairman of a research ethics committee which had been in difficulty when trying to decide whether or not to approve the proposal.
>
> The purpose of the project was to study water fluxes in sick pre-term infants and to assess in particular the insensible water gain from humidifiers attached to artificial ventilators, and the insensible water loss from the lungs and skin. Ten infants requiring artificial ventilation for hyaline membrane disease would be studied. In such infants, water balance is very important in determining the development of several potentially fatal complications, but little is known about insensible water gain or loss from the expiratory tract in particular. In the study, deuterium oxide, heavy water or D_2O, would be added to the humidifier water in the artificial ventilator. Its accumulation in the neonate could then be followed by measuring the proportion of D_2O to ordinary water. H_2O, in blood samples taken sequentially. These blood samples would be very small, since only five microlitres (about one-twentieth of a drop) of blood would be required in order to measure D_2O by mass spectrometry; they would be taken – over a period of three days, and with no discomfort – from an umbilical arterial catheter, which is usually inserted when infants are artificially ventilated.
>
> The problem that has arisen with this proposal concerned the obtaining of parental consent. The policy in the special baby care unit where the proposed project would be undertaken was not to obtain informed consent for this type of study. The researchers therefore proposed to dispense with informed consent, while the research ethics committee thought that it should be obtained.
>
> One reason why it is necessary to establish whether such a project is therapeutic or non-therapeutic is a legal one. The removal of blood samples from the infants would be an assault unless consent had been given. Although there is no specific statement of the law in such circumstances, it is likely that the courts would always regard unconsented invasive non-therapeutic research as unlawful. They might take a somewhat more lenient view of unconsented therapeutic research, though not necessarily.
>
> The basic difficulty in considering whether or not this project is therapeutic research is to decide whether there is a therapeutic intention towards the infant subjects. It is essential to provide humidified air to infants on artificial ventilators: one argument therefore states that the addition of D_2O to humidifier water merely alters slightly one therapeutic activity without in any way altering the therapeutic intention. It is a necessary part of medical practice to examine the results of therapies that are used in order that they may be improved: such assessment of a therapy is inevitably therapeutic research.
>
> Another view would suggest that the addition of D_2O to humidifier water is not a necessary part of therapy, and is not intended, in itself, to be therapy. The taking of additional blood samples – even though they amount to a very small total quantity – is not a therapeutic activity; the researchers have not stated how soon the measurements of D_2O might be made, and nowhere in their protocol have they suggested that the measurements might be used to improve the control of water balance in the infant subjects. The project is therefore designed

to gain physiological knowledge, and there is no therapeutic intention towards the infant subjects in the proposed activities that are additional to standard therapy.

The problem of deciding which argument is correct seems finally to be insoluble. In terms of the definitions adopted by the working group… it is possible, however, to conclude that this is a therapeutic research project since the researchers have both a therapeutic intention, in humidifying the air supplied by the ventilators, and a research intention. It is not suggested that the definitions adopted by the working group will solve all the problems with which research ethics committees are in practice faced. The researchers in the anorectal manometry project, for instance, had no therapeutic intention towards the controls that they used. To identify the controls as taking part in therapeutic research because there was a therapeutic intention towards the subjects of the research project seems invidious and inherently inequitable. In some circumstances it may then be important to abandon attempts to describe a whole research project as either therapeutic or non-therapeutic, and to consider instead the nature of the actual procedures undertaken. In this case, the subjects had therapeutic interventions performed on them, while the controls had non-therapeutic interventions performed.

The definitions adopted by the working group allow firm conclusions to be reached about some other projects mentioned earlier. When the Willowbrook experiments started, there was no therapeutic intention in them towards the handicapped subjects, although some benefits may have accrued to them incidentally. By the working group's definitions, they were therefore non-therapeutic research projects. On the other hand, the comparative trials of treatment regimes for leukaemia and other malignancies were and are therapeutic research, since there has always been a therapeutic intention towards each of the subjects. even when the major benefits would probably fall to later cohorts. The definitions also obviate the need for such complicating expressions as 'partly therapeutic', that have been suggested to describe an intervention such as the taking of an additional two millilitres of blood for a research purpose, when a blood specimen is to be taken anyway as part of therapy. Since the act of taking the blood sample has both a therapeutic and a research intention, the act is therapeutic – by definition.

Professor Richard Hare, a member of the Working Party, in his paper 'Little Human Guinea Pigs' in M Lockwood (ed) *Moral Dilemmas in Modern Medicine* (1985), states that: 'therapeutic research is thus an activity which has both aims [therapy and research]; non-therapeutic research is an activity which has only a research and not a therapeutic aim'. We would suggest some caution is necessary before adopting this approach. It is acceptable if therapeutic research is taken to mean that the intention to carry out therapy and research *relates to the same activity*. It is problematic if it seeks to suggest that once engaged on therapy, anything done thereafter by way of research, though unconnected with the therapy, qualifies as therapeutic research.

The Institute's Working Party drew attention to one further term which warrants consideration in any examination of the regulation of research, namely, *innovative therapy* (pp 36–37).

Innovative therapy consists in the performance of a new or non-standard intervention as all or part of a therapeutic activity and not as part of a formal research project.

Innovative therapy may therefore be quite haphazard, starting just when a doctor has a bright idea that he wants to try out. If the bright idea seems to be any good, then innovative therapy can become research as soon as the bright idea is examined in a systematic manner. Much innovative therapy is surgical in nature, since surgeons often try out modifications to existing surgical procedures and occasionally try out new operations. It is rare for these modifications or new operations to be undertaken as part of a formal research project and they have not in general been subject first to peer review or review by a research ethics committee. Another sort of innovative therapy would be the introduction of new instruments, if these were not formally compared with existing ones. Innovative therapy is comparatively rare in the use of medicines, but it can still occur. A doctor may decide that a drug that is already available for the treatment of one disease might be useful in the treatment of another, and he is at liberty within the limits of his professional expertise to go ahead and try it. One example a few years ago was the use of injectable phenothiazine drugs. These were introduced to help in the treatment of schizophrenia, their value being that a schizophrenic could have his illness controlled by a monthly injection. Doctors looking after mentally handicapped children with severe behaviour disturbances realized that these drugs might help: it was found that monthly injections of quite small doses produced considerable improvement in the behaviour of the few children in whom the drugs were tried. It was then decided to set up a controlled trial to discover whether the results were real: ie what started as innovative therapy became therapeutic research as the trial was set up, and the haphazard procedures became formalised.

In our view, the Working Party was right to draw attention to innovative therapy and highlight the fact that it may consist in doing the same things with the same intentions as researchers may do, but without any of the constraints associated with the proper conduct of research. To the extent that the intention is to acquire knowledge and not solely to care for the patient it is our view that innovative therapy should be subject to the same regime of control that attends research properly so-called (see also, Royal College of Physicians *Guidelines on the Practice of Ethics Committees in Medical Research Involving Human Subjects* (3rd edn, 1996), at para 6.4 and 6.5).

The regulation of research

Research on animals has been regulated by law since the Cruelty to Animals Act 1876. (The current law is contained in the Animals (Scientific Procedures) Act 1986: see generally, G Langley (ed) *Animal Experimentation: The Consensus Changes* (1989)). In contrast, there has never been any statute specifically regulating the conduct of research on human beings. You may think this is not atypical of the state of affairs in the United Kingdom. This is not to say that medical research is unregulated, because it is. In particular a system of local and regional ethics committees (LRECs and MRECs) review research protocols before research on humans may be carried out in the NHS. We shall return to examine this extra-statutory regulation in some detail below. Before doing so, however, we should notice that there are a number of areas of medical research to which specific regulatory regimes apply in addition to the LREC/MREC system.

In Chapter 10 we saw how research on human embryos is controlled by the Human Fertilisation and Embryology Act 1990 and requires a licence from the Human Fertilisation and Embryology Authority to be legal. Of course, unless one takes a particular view about the moral and legal status of embryos, this does not involve research on human subjects. Similar claims could be made in respect of research on foetuses (especially dead foetuses) or foetal material. Here there is no discrete regulatory regime though there is a specific Code of Practice specific to this research which is to be applied by LRECs/MRECs (see *Review of the Guidance on Research Use of Fetuses and Fetal Material* (Cmnd 762) (1989) (Polkinghorne Committee)). We discuss such research later in Chapter 15.

In three areas specific regulation does exist: (a) medicinal products; (b) gene therapy; and (c) xenotransplantation.

As regards medicinal products, the Medicines Act 1968 regulates clinical trials on patients (but not health volunteers) of unlicensed medicinal products. This is part of the licensing system for the manufacture, supply or sale of such products contained within the 1968 Act and EU Directives (see eg EC Dir 65/65/EEC as amended and Reg (EEC) 2309/93). The essence of the system is one of notification and prior approval of clinical trials involving drugs by the UK Medicines Control Agency.

I Dodds-Smith 'Clinical Research' in C Dyer (ed) *Doctors, Patients and the Law* (1992)

Regulatory approval
While there is no specific legislation regulating how a clinical trial in the UK must be conducted, there is provision for notification or approval by the licensing authority (the UK

Health Ministers and Agriculture Ministers) of clinical trials prior to their commencement. This is done through the Medicines Control Agency.

Phase II and Phase III trials and pharmaceutical companies

Under the terms of the Medicines Act 1968 a supplier of an unlicensed medicinal product intended to be used in a trial in the UK involving *patients* must (unless he is already the holder of a product licence which authorises the trial) first apply for a clinical trial certificate – a CTC. A CTC (effective for two years but renewable) may be granted only after detailed pharmaceutical and toxicological data regarding the drug in question have been provided and assessed by the licensing authority (often with advice from an expert advisory committee) as not likely to involve serious risk to trial subjects. This can be a rigorous and lengthy procedure. Fortunately since the passing of an order in 1981 it has not been necessary in every case to apply for a CTC. The order introduced a scheme under which suppliers may be exempted from the need to hold a CTC for a new product for three years, provided certain undertakings are given and the licensing authority finds no objection. This is a form of negative clearance involving no assessment of the data and cannot be taken therefore as an indication of positive approval or that the licensing authority considers the proposed trial safe.

Doctors and dentists

Doctors and dentists conducting their own trials are exempt in some circumstances from the requirements to hold licences and certificates. Where a clinical trial in patients is to be initiated and conducted by a doctor or dentist *other than* under arrangements made by or with the manufacturer or supplier, there is no requirement for a CTC provided that certain conditions are met. This exemption is generally referred to as the 'DDX' provision. In order to qualify the doctor or dentist must show:

(i) that the seller or supplier of the product is selling or supplying it 'exclusively for the purposes of the trial', or if not, insofar as it is also sold or supplied for other purposes, these are covered by a product licence or certificate or under an exemption.

(ii) that the clinical trial is 'not to be carried out under arrangements made by or on behalf of' the product's manufacturer, seller, supplier or the person responsible for its composition.

(iii) that the doctor or dentist has notified the licensing authority of the trial, specifying the product, its use and the supplier's details.

In such cases the company supplier or seller is not required to have a product licence or a CTC.

The order means, for example, that if a doctor wishes to carry out trials on a drug which is licensed for certain indications but the trial is designed to investigate the use of the product in different indications, he would need to apply for a DDX. The manufacturer of the product would be supplying the doctor for the purposes of the trial. However, the manufacturer may also be supplying quantities of the drug to the same practitioner for use in its licensed indications, in which case those supplies must be covered by a product licence or an exemption provided by the Act.

To qualify for the DDX exemption, the trial must be the practitioner's responsibility and on his initiative. A DDX should not be sought where the trial is in reality to be carried out to the manufacturer's or supplier's design or at his desire, in which case a CTC or CTX should be obtained by the manufacturer or supplier.

It is not unusual for new drugs to be the subject of trials after licensing (Phase IV). A requirement for some form of subsequent monitoring of a newly licensed drug can often be made a term of the product licence. If a doctor is carrying our his own study with a licensed product and the study involves using the product for the indications for which it is licensed, the trial needs no regulatory approval provided that notification has been given to the licensing authority and proper arrangements made for reporting adverse reactions. This provision would cover trials instigated by doctors whether within general practice or working within hospitals or clinics.

(For the situation as regards 'medical devices', see C Hodges 'European Regulation of Medical Devices' in J O'Grady, I Dodds-Smith, N Walsh and M Spencer (eds) *Medicines, Medical Devices and the Law* (1999) – no prior approval system but provision of data on clinical evaluation carried out in accordance with Helsinki Declaration – 90/385/EEC and 93/42/EEC and the Medical Device Regulations 1994 (SI 1994 No 3017) and the Active Implantable Medical Device Regulations 1992 (SI 1992 No 3146) as amended. See *supra* ch 13).

In relation to gene therapy, the Government established the Gene Therapy Advisory Committee (GTAC) in 1993, following the recommendations of the

Clothier Committee on the *Ethics of Gene Therapy* (CMJ 1788 1992). The background is set out in the Clothier Report as follows:

Report of the Committee on the Ethics of Gene Therapy (Cm 1788) (1992)

2.14. The prospect of gene therapy is obviously attractive if it can make good the genetic defects responsible, and thereby cure or alleviate disorders in which the outcomes are so dismal. Moreover, the effective introduction of gene therapy into medical practice would also serve to augment and enhance the choices that may face parents who are at high risk of transmitting a serious disorder to their children.

2.15. Gene therapy has wider possibilities for medical practice than the correction of single gene disorders. For example, it is being investigated as a possible new approach to the management of a wide spectrum of diseases, ranging from infections such as AIDS to cancer, and it is being studied as a means of strengthening the body's immune response to viral infections. Various approaches are being used which require the insertion of genes into particular cell populations in an attempt to counter some of the basic changes in cells which lead to them becoming cancerous. Gene therapy is also being explored for the management of chronic diseases such as diabetes. The requirements for demonstration of the effectiveness of this approach in animal systems, and the clear demonstration of its safety, will follow the same principles as those set out for the use of gene therapy to correct single gene disorders.

Normal human characteristics

2.16. Normal variations in human characteristics such as personality, intelligence and physique may also be explained by the inheritance of multiple genes and their interaction, together with environmental influences. We are alert to the profound ethical issues that would arise were the aim of gene modification ever to be directed to the enhancement of normal human rights.

Gene therapy

2.17. Some genes have been isolated, together with the associated DNA sequences which are required to regulate their working in the cell. They have been replicated and their structures and functions studied. Such isolated genes have been inserted into living cells cultivated in the laboratory, which then produce the protein for which the inserted gene carries the code (ie the gene is *expressed*). Isolated genes have also been inserted experimentally into animals and shown to work. This has been applied for practical purposes; for example, human genes have been used in sheep to achieve production of the protein needed to treat haemophilia. It is now possible to insert appropriate human genes into selected cells of patients with specific genetic disorders. These developments have opened the way to gene therapy.

Scientific requirements for gene therapy

2.18. If gene therapy of a particular disorder is to be achieved a number of requirements must be met:

(a) The gene must have been isolated and be available for therapeutic use.
(b) Something must be known of the function of the gene, so that treatment can be sensibly designed.
(c) It must be known which tissues and cell types need to express the gene and when, during development, its expression is required.
(d) The genetic sequences that control the function of the gene, for example by switching it on and off, must be known and have been isolated. If gene therapy is to work it is clearly important that the product of the gene is made in the right cells, in the right amounts and at the right time. Too much or too little of the gene product, or its production in the wrong cells, or at the wrong time during development, could be harmful.
(e) There must be means available for getting the gene, and its controlling elements, into the right cells and under the right control. Conversely, the gene must be prevented from getting into the wrong cells, or to the wrong place within a cell, or from spreading to other tissues, or even to other individuals, any of which might cause harm.
(f) Means must be available for monitoring the efficacy and safety of the treatment, for a long time.

These requirements are discussed in more detail in the following paragraphs.

2.19. As we said, genes contain the recipes that cells use to make particular proteins. It is obviously important that the genetic recipe should be correct, so that the right protein is made; and just as important that the gene should be expressed at the right time. There are elaborate genetic signals, not yet well understood, which regulate whether particular genes are switched on or off at particular times of development and in particular cells or tissues. This 'gene control' must be satisfactorily preserved if a transplanted gene is to work effectively.

2.20. For a transferred gene to do any good it must clearly be targeted into the cells which need it. If a particular gene is essential for the proper function of the liver there is little point in placing it into the hair root cells. It is necessary, therefore, to know in which tissues the gene is required and how to ensure that it gets there.

2.21. Gene therapy could be attempted by seeking to correct part of an abnormal gene to make it functional again; or by removing the abnormal gene and replacing it with a normal one; or by simply inserting a normal gene, so that the necessary gene product is made, while leaving the abnormal gene in place within the cells. At this very early stage of gene therapy research, the last of these approaches, although the least elegant, is likely to be the most practicable, because the technical means for inserting genes into cells are already at hand whereas the means for removing existing genes from cells are much less advanced.

2.22. The inserted gene must be integrated somewhere within the cells being treated, in such a way that it becomes part of the genetic constitution of those cells and is transmitted to the cellular progeny each time the cells divide. Ideally it should be inserted precisely in place of the abnormal gene, and be subject to the same cellular environment and cellular controls as in the natural state. In practice this may be very difficult to achieve, current methods merely allowing the gene to be inserted at any random site within the genetic material of the cell. The majority of genes apparently function satisfactorily following insertion in this way. There is, however, the danger that such random insertion may lead to inappropriate control of the gene – of where, when and how much of the gene product is expressed. It is also possible that the random insertion may actually disrupt some other genetic function, with unwanted consequences.

2.23. Even within a single tissue there are many different types of cell. For example, in blood there are red blood cells and many different kinds of white blood cell. Normally these cells undergo constant replacement and renewal. This biological maintenance programme depends upon the presence of a very small number of *stem cells* whose function it is to generate new cells. If genes are placed in cells other than stem cells their effect will last only for as long as those treated cells survive. As they are replaced the effect of gene therapy will be lost. To avoid this it is necessary to target gene therapy at the stem cells, so that the new cells being formed have the correcting gene in place. This is made difficult because stem cells are few and in many tissues they cannot be easily identified.

Somatic cell gene therapy
2.24. Making good a defective gene in the body cells where it is needed is known as somatic cell gene therapy. The aim is to provide the right genetic information, under proper control, in precisely those cells which need it for their normal function. Ideally, the effect should be permanent so that no further therapy is required. It should also be permanent in the sense that the inserted gene is securely lodged. If successful, therapy would make good the genetic defect in the treated cells and tissues of the individual, although the abnormal gene would still be present in other tissues. This is unlikely to matter provided the abnormal gene product has no effect, or, if it is actually harmful, is not used. However, the germ cells, which give rise to sperm or ova, would retain the defective form of the gene, with the possibility of its transmission to future generations.

Methods of gene therapy
2.25. Our interest in the methods available for inserting genes into living cells turns on their safety and effectiveness. Genes can be inserted into cells directly by physical techniques or by using a biological vehicle for delivery. At present, delivery employing suitably modified viruses seems most promising. Viruses are fashioned by nature to enter cells and to insert their own genetic material. Some viruses can be modified to carry genetic material different from their own, and insert it into host cells, and thus provide a technique for gene modification therapy. So far it has been possible only to supplement a defective gene, not to replace it; neither is it yet possible to lodge a gene precisely where it would naturally be. Nonetheless, this approach may well be effective in selective disorders. In time it may be feasible to harness the natural process of *recombination* which allows formation of new combinations of genes.

Germ line gene therapy
2.26. In order to remove the threat to future generations of a defective gene it would be necessary to correct the defect in the germ cells, which give rise to ova and sperm. This is known as germ line gene therapy. Because little is known about the possible consequences and hazards, and any harm to future generations would take a long time to discover and deal with, this application of gene therapy needs to be considered quite separately from somatic cell gene therapy.

Possible dangers of gene therapy
2.27. Among the possible dangers of gene therapy are, therefore, that:

(a) It might not work, in which case the patient will have undergone the procedure without benefit.
(b) The correcting gene might be inserted into the wrong cell type, or be expressed inappropriately, either in the wrong amount or at the wrong time during development. The therapy might then do more harm than good.
(c) The gene might be inserted in such a way as to cause a new mutation, by disrupting some other gene or its means of control. This might initiate a new genetic disease, or perhaps an uncontrolled multiplication of cells which could lead to cancer.
(d) If the means of inserting the gene were faulty, it is conceivable although in the present state of knowledge improbable, that the gene, or parts of it, might emerge from the cells and be "infective", moving to other somatic cells or germ line cells, or even to other individuals. This might cause harm to the treated patient and to others.

These factors which bear on the effectiveness and safety of gene therapy must all be taken carefully into account when proposals for gene therapy are considered.

The techniques of gene therapy are undoubtedly new. New therapeutic procedures need to be rigorously tested in order to ensure that they are beneficial and safe. Research on human subjects raises its own concerns about the rights of patients and others who are being used as 'guinea pigs'. The Clothier Committee considered whether gene therapy was research (*op cit*, paras 3.9–3.10):

3.9. The initial use of gene therapy will clearly be a digression of this sort from ordinary medical practice. Indeed, the establishment of this Committee acknowledged concerns that gene therapy is perceived as different, both in its nature and possible consequences, from treatments used hitherto in medical practice, including those already applied to the treatment of genetic disorders. The prospect has raised the question whether gene therapy should be subject to more than the usual constraints which direct ordinary medical practice and innovation, or even those which at present govern medical research.

3.10. Our discussions and enquiries confirmed our tentative view, that, notwithstanding the primary intention to benefit an individual patient, gene therapy should initially be regarded as research involving human subjects, and governed by requirements at least as exacting as those which at present applied to that kind of research. Accordingly, any proposal to conduct gene therapy should be subject to approval following authoritative ethical review, which includes critical scrutiny of its medical and scientific merit, the legal implications, and wider public concerns. It should also be subject to conditions laid down for the conduct and oversight of therapy and evaluation and reporting of the outcome. In what follows we consider the detailed basis of this view and the means by which it may be given force. This position is in keeping with the general view that any marked change in medical practice should be subject to the discipline of scientific, medical and ethical appraisal before its introduction.

As we have seen, the Clothier Report identified a number of dangers inherent in gene therapy. The committee considered whether gene therapy of either kind should be permitted and, if so, how it should be regulated. The committee recommended that germ line therapy should be banned. By contrast, the committee recommended a regulatory framework for permitting somatic cell therapy. Many of the recurring themes of medical law were considered by the committee in their deliberations, (*op cit* paras 4.1–6.4):

Purpose of somatic cell gene therapy
4.1. The purpose of somatic cell gene therapy in an individual patient is to alleviate disease in that individual, and that individual alone. There would be no intention to modify the gene in the germ line. We consider that the development of safe and effective means of gene modification for this purpose is a proper goal for medical science, and we recommend that the necessary research should continue.

Initial application of somatic cell gene therapy
4.2. A new treatment yet unproven in human subjects should only be contemplated when the potential benefits outweigh possible harm, including inadvertent harm, to the patient, and to others, and any discomfort and distress that might accompany treatment. It is evident that this position is now being reached in respect of gene therapy for a number of serious genetic disorders. Somatic cell gene therapy may hold great potential benefit for some patients, but it may also carry risks which are more than minimal. Therefore, to ensure that the benefits are assessed and the risks are identified as expeditiously as possible, we recommend that

somatic cell gene therapy should, for the present, be conducted according to the discipline of research.

4.3. The first candidates for gene therapy should be patients who are suffering from a disorder which is life-threatening, or causes serious handicap, and for which treatment is unavailable or unsatisfactory; but which has not already progressed so far as to reduce significantly the potential for benefit. Therapy should hold promise of bringing about a remission in the advance of the disorder whilst sparing the patient any unduly adverse consequences of treatment. To achieve most benefit, by preventing suffering, impaired development and irreversible damage, gene therapy should be considered at the earliest possible stage in the course of the disorder. A patient who had already suffered irreversible tissue and organ damage would be subject at best to only partial relief by gene therapy. Among those disorders to which gene therapy might be applicable are some which lead to irreversible and cumulative effects from early childhood, and even before birth. In such instances therapy must be given correspondingly early in life.

4.4. The basic structures and organs of the body are formed during the first few weeks after fertilisation. If, because of a genetic defect (or, indeed, any other adverse influence), this early development has been impaired it is unlikely that any resulting structural fault could be corrected except by surgery. This state of affairs naturally leads to the consideration of interventions that might be possible in the very earliest stages of life, soon after fertilisation. There are many technical problems to be overcome, and there would need to be clear safeguards for the mother; but we see no objection in principle to such a procedure provided it takes place after differentiation of the germ line cells, which has occurred by five weeks after fertilisation.

Somatic cell gene therapy research

4.5. The normal rules which govern research in human subjects and the requirements for prior ethical approval of research and its subsequent oversight, which have been considered ...should apply to somatic cell gene therapy. When a patient who is the subject of such research stands to benefit directly from participation it is properly described as therapeutic research.

4.6. A decision on whether gene therapy research should proceed must depend on the careful prior assessment of the balance of potential benefits and risks for the individual patient. This assessment must draw on knowledge of the genetic basis of the disorder, its pathological effects and clinical course. It will call for evidence of adequate experience of gene modification in experimental systems using isolated cells and laboratory animals, and must incorporate a judgment on the possible consequences of the proposed treatment. The risks to the patient will largely depend on the safety of procedures for introducing genes into cells therapeutically, and the effects, both immediately and in the long term. Safety must be a foremost consideration when proposals to conduct gene therapy are made. Intrusions on privacy, too, are an inevitable accompaniment of such pioneering procedures and the long term follow-up that is necessary.

4.7. In their joint statement the European Medical Research Councils brought out clearly the technical complexity of the procedures used in gene modification. Undesirable consequences (to which we have drawn attention...) might include genetic modification of the germ line, and its effects in progeny; modification of somatic cells other than those which have been targeted; interference with the normal working of modified cells; cancerous changes in cells of the population modified; and changes induced by the insertion process.

4.8. The crucial first step in ethical review is a careful assessment of the scientific merits of the proposal, the competence of those wishing to carry out gene therapy, and the potential benefits and risks in each particular instance for which a proposal is made. This assessment should include a critical examination of the arrangements to be made for the conduct of therapy and subsequent monitoring. It will necessarily call upon an uncommon degree and range of scientific and medical expertise, encompassing a deep knowledge of molecular biology, of experimental work in gene manipulation, and close familiarity with the molecular basis and clinical features of the disorder under consideration. No existing body is constituted for these tasks. Accordingly we recommend that a supervisory body with the necessary collective expertise, experience and authority be set up, having the responsibility for making such assessments in conjunction with ethical review. We also recommend that any proposal for gene therapy must be approved by this body as well as by a properly constituted local research ethics committee (LREC).

4.9. There is a duty to identify and assess promptly any adverse consequence of gene therapy for the patient, both in the aftermath of treatment and in the long term. This duty does not end with the death of the patient. To verify that therapy has not inadvertently affected offspring and successive generations monitoring should extend at least into the next generation. Indeed, insofar as it is possible, monitoring should continue over several generations. Therefore, those conducting such research have a duty not only to maintain adequate records but also to ensure that an effective monitoring system is in place. It will require that a register be set up, and carefully maintained, with safeguards to protect confidentiality. We recommend that the necessary arrangements are made before the therapy begins. A complementary duty is to obtain the reliable commitment of patients, and their families, to participate in extended follow-up. During the process of informing and counselling, and obtaining consent, the patient should learn of the need for such follow-up and understand the reasons for it. The patient should also be made aware that although follow-up might be intrusive and burdensome the doctors accept a duty to minimise these effects.

4.10. Accordingly, the conditions which must be satisfied when gene therapy research is proposed are that:

(a) There must be sufficient scientific and medical knowledge, together with knowledge of those proposing to undertake the research, to make sound judgments on:
   (i)   the scientific merit of the research;
   (ii) its probable efficacy and safety;
   (iii) the competence of those who wish to undertake the research; and
   (iv) the requirements for effective monitoring.

(b) The clinical course of the disorder must be known sufficiently well for the investigators and those entrusted with counselling to:
   (i)   give accurate information and advice; and
   (ii) assess the outcomes of therapy.

Consent to research

4.11. A prior ethical requirement of research involving patients is the consent of the individual subject. Consent implies that sufficient information has been given, in a form that is understood, to enable that individual to make a voluntary decision to participate or not. Because gene therapy has novel, complex and possibly far-reaching aspects we are concerned to ensure that the patient is enabled to take these fully into account when giving consent. It is important that serious attention be given not only to the content of the information given to the patient but also to the way in which it is conveyed. Above all, care must be taken to ensure that the patient has understood the risks, benefits and obligations, and has the fullest possible information. Independent advice, not aimed at obtaining consent, should ideally be provided by someone unconnected with the research or therapeutic team and well versed in the implications of gene therapy.

4.12. We foresee the possibility that a competent adult, in whom the disorder had progressed to a stage at which there was little prospect of direct benefit from therapy, might nevertheless consent to participate in non-therapeutic research – for the collective human benefit that the research should be designed to yield. For such research to be ethical it must be to assess the consequences of the procedure, by measurement or detection of changes within the body, or their absence, even if there were to be no discernible clinical benefit. We conclude that participation by a competent adult in such research is acceptable.

4.13. Children with genetic diseases are likely to be among the first candidates for gene therapy. The special problems to be faced when children are the subjects of research have been examined in existing guidelines. The foremost consideration must be the best interests of the child, and in this respect somatic cell gene therapy raises no new ethical issue.

Confidentiality of genetic information

4.14. Clear principles govern the confidentiality of personal health information obtained within the National Health Service (NHS), the use of such information, and the circumstances in which it might be disclosed. They are set out in guidance '*Confidentiality, Use and Disclosure of NHS Information*' which is to be issued shortly. The guidance takes account of the ethical obligations of health professionals towards protecting the confidentiality of personal health information.

4.15. The duty of confidentiality is by no means absolute; it is balanced by a duty of disclosure. The tension is heightened when the special qualities of genes and genetic events give rise to different and possibly conflicting, interests of kindred, including those yet unborn, who share, or might share, the same genes. For example, an individual might be the source of genetic information which is important to relatives. It might be important to their health care, decisions on parenthood, or like plans which might be influenced by known health risks. Conversely, information which is important to a particular individual might only be obtainable from relatives. These factors have a bearing on the confidentiality of such information and the circumstances in which it might be disclosed. Similar considerations also lead to the question of just what genetic information should be sought from any individual. These issues are already familiar to clinical geneticists, who are guided in their practice by evolving codes on the circumstances in which the boundaries of confidentiality may be extended beyond the individual to include kindred. Therefore, when consent to treatment is sought, which in the case of a child will be from the parents or guardians or other persons who may legally be in a position to give consent on behalf of the child, the possible need for subsequent disclosure of personal health information should be discussed.

4.16. In the case of a child, the parents or others giving consent should first be told that the duty of confidentiality is to the child and, whatever their wishes, that it is in the child's best interests, at the proper time, to know its own clinical history. There might also be a duty, as stated above, to disclose the information to others, including those of subsequent generations.

Gene therapy and the essence of humanity
4.17. The total complement of genes which are found in the human population, the human *gene pool*, is the source of human genetic variability. From it is drawn the parental contribution to the unique endowment of genes possessed by each individual human being, or by identical twins. The interaction of these genes and external influences throughout life confers the quality of humanness, a quality that in each individual is characterised, in part, by variants which determine human differences, and contributes to the collective quality we call humanity.
4.18. This is the background against which we have considered the origin of material that might be used in gene therapy. So far as we can see the genes used in therapy will come from a human source. Should it ever become clinically necessary to use genes which have been derived from any species other than man we believe that such use would in no way impair the humanness of an individual who received the gene. The change conferred would be no different in kind from that resulting from any medical intervention which introduced tissue from other individuals; for example, an organ transplantation, or blood transfusion; or, indeed, from another species, as in the case of pig's [sic] heart valves, which are commonly used to replace defective valves in the human heart.

Preclinical experimental procedures
4.19. We are sensitive to issues raised by the use of laboratory animals in genetic experiments that precede therapy in patients. These issues are common to all experimentation in animals. They concern the welfare of such animals, which is a responsibility of the Home Office. However, the types of procedures used in preclinical genetic studies raise no new problem either in substance or scale.
4.20. The safety of procedures for gene manipulation is a responsibility of the Advisory Committee on Gene Manipulation (ACGM). ACGM was established in 1984 by the Health and Safety Commission and is primarily responsible for advising on health and safety at work issues, for which the Health and Safety Commission is responsible to the Secretary of State for Employment. ACGM is also able to advise the Health, Agriculture, Environment, Industry and Northern Ireland Ministers on such other matters relating to genetic manipulation as may be referred to those ministers, and to offer comment on the technical or scientific aspects of any new developments in genetic manipulation which may have implications for their departments. We do not foresee any new problems in this respect but, nevertheless, we recommend that the attention of ACGM be drawn to our report.

Costs
4.21. We are not charged with concern for the allocation of national resources as between different kinds of illness, groups of patients, or particular therapies. These are political questions, and the priorities, when resources are limited, must be decided by those entrusted with the provision of health care, guided by the national will as expressed through Parliament. We do, however, draw attention to the high costs of treatment and care of patients who are afflicted with chronic disorders of genetic origin which are severely disabling. These financial and human costs are not borne by health services alone, but also by other agencies, and by families themselves. In the event of the potential benefits of gene therapy being realised, these costs should be set against the costs of therapy and the provision of services and access to them, and savings that alleviation of these diseases may bring.

Limits to somatic cell gene therapy
4.22. We are firmly of the opinion that gene therapy should at present be directed to alleviating disease in individual patients, although wider applications may soon call for attention (see 2.15). In the current state of knowledge it would not be acceptable to use gene modification to attempt to change human traits not associated with disease. In addition, whilst we recognise that many selective influences, whether random, accidental, or caused by medical interventions, result in changes to the total human gene pool, we hold the general view that human genetic variability and diversity are precious and should be protected.

Conclusion
4.23. We conclude that the development and introduction of safe and effective means of somatic cell gene modification, directed to alleviating disease in individual patients, is a proper goal for medical science. Somatic cell gene therapy should be regarded, at first, as research involving human subjects and we recommend that its use be conditional upon satisfactory scientific, medical and ethical review. Although the prospect of this new therapy heightens the familiar ethical concerns which attend the introduction of any new treatment, we conclude that it poses no new ethical problems. However, in view of the scientific and medical complexity of this treatment and the need for a most careful assessment of the

therapy proposed in each instance, and subsequent long term monitoring, we recommend that a new supervisory body should be set up and charged with these tasks...

Germ Line Gene Therapy

5.1. The purpose of gene modification of sperm or ova or cells which produce them would be to prevent the transmission of defective genes to subsequent generations. Gene modification at an early age of embryonic development, before differentiation of the germ line, might be a way of correcting gene defects in both the germ line and somatic cells. However we share the view of others that there is at present insufficient knowledge to evaluate the risks to future generations, to which we have already pointed.

5.2. We recommend, therefore, that gene modification of the germ line should not yet be attempted. For couples identified as being at risk of bearing a child with a serious genetic disorder, embryonic diagnosis and selective implantation of an unaffected embryo would provide another way of achieving the same end without incurring the unknown risks of germ line modification. (See 4.3–4.4.) Moreover, this approach offers the prospect of avoiding genetic disorders which result in structural fetal abnormalities.

Supervision of Gene Therapy

Expert Supervisory Body

6.1. Among our tasks were: to invite and consider proposals from doctors wishing to use such treatment on individual patients; and to provide advice to United Kingdom Health Ministers on scientific and medical developments which bear on the safety and efficacy of human gene modification. An assessment of the safety and efficacy of gene therapy, and of the design, content and conduct of research involving patients, depends upon technical, scientific and medical expertise which only a minority of members of this Committee possess. Similar expertise is required in this field to provide advice to Ministers. During consultation we encountered much support for the setting up of a new expert group. Local research ethics committees (LRECs), in particular, wished for a national body to which they could look for advice when proposals to conduct gene therapy research were submitted to them for ethical review. Moreover, we have come to the conclusion that continuing supervision of gene therapy is necessary. No existing body is constituted for these tasks. Consideration of particular proposals for research is excluded from the tasks envisaged for the Nuffield Bioethics Council which was set up during 1991. Therefore, to discharge the second part of our remit, we recommend the establishment of a new expert supervisory body [4.8].

6.2. We recommend that this supervisory body should be of sufficient standing to command the confidence of LRECs, and of the public, the professions and of Parliament. It should have a responsibility for:

(1) advising on the content of proposals, including the details of protocols, for therapeutic research in somatic cell gene modification;
(2) advising on the design and conduct of the research;
(3) advising on the facilities and service arrangements necessary for the proper conduct of the research;
(4) advising on the arrangements necessary for the long term surveillance and follow-up of treated patients;
(5) receiving proposals from doctors who wish to conduct gene therapy in individual patients and making an assessment of:
    (a) the clinical status of the patient;
    (b) the scientific quality of the proposal, with particular regard to the technical competence and scientific requirements for achieving therapy effectively and safely;
    (c) whether the clinical course of the particular disorder is known sufficiently well
       –   for sound information, counselling and advice to be given to the patient (or those acting on behalf of the patient)
       –   for the outcomes of therapy to be assessable;
    (d) the potential benefits and risks for the patient of what is proposed;
    (e) the ethical acceptability of the proposal.

In the light of this assessment the expert supervisory body should make a recommendation on whether the proposal should be approved, and if so on what, if any, conditions. The supervisory body should also have a responsibility for:

(6) acting in co-ordination with LRECs;
(7) acting as a repository of up-to-date information on research in gene therapy internationally;
(8) setting up and maintaining a confidential register of patients who have been the subjects of gene therapy;
(9) oversight and monitoring of the research;
(10) providing advice to Health Ministers in the United Kingdom, on scientific and medical developments which bear on the safety and efficacy of human gene modification.

6.3. We recommend that any proposal for gene therapy must be approved by this body as well as by a properly constituted LREC.

6.4. Decisions on a therapeutic intervention for an individual should be made promptly, and the new arrangements should not cause unnecessary delay to the consideration of proposals. Therefore, we recommend that anyone wishing to conduct such research should submit proposals simultaneously to LRECs and the new supervisory body.

Whilst GTAC has no statutory basis, its approval must be obtained before gene therapy research is conducted on humans. At present, GTAC will only consider somatic gene therapy (which affects only the individual concerned) and not germ line gene therapy (which may affect future generations). This is in line with the Clothier Committee's recommendation (*op cit*, para 5.2) (for GTAC's procedures, see *Evidence on Making Proposals to Conduct Gene Therapy Research on Human Subjects* (GTAC 1994)).

The final area we should notice is xenotransplantation, ie the transplantation of viable animal tissue into humans such as pig hearts or kidneys or pancreatic cells. In January 1997 the Government's Advisory Group on the Ethics of Xenotransplantation reported (*Animal Tissue into Humans*). Thereafter, the Government set up the UK Xenotransplantation Interim Regulatory Authority (UKXIRA) charged, *inter alia*, with the task of advising the Secretary of State for Health whether to allow such procedures. Whilst UKXIRA, like GTAC, has no statutory basis, no xenotransplantation procedures may take place within the NHS without the Secretary of State's written approval following advice from UKXIRA: see HSC 1998/126 announcing binding Directions on Health Authorities and NHS Trusts. We discuss in Chapter 15 issues arising from xenotransplantation (for UKXIRA's procedures, see *Guidance on Making Proposals to Conduct Xenotransplantation on Human Subjects* (UKXIRA, 1998)).

We should now turn to consider in detail the general regulatory framework for research on humans.

A. LRECS

In 1991 the Department of Health issued Guidelines on *Local Research Ethics Committees*. The accompanying NHS Executive letter (HSG (91)5) sets out the objectives of the guidelines and action required of NHS bodies.

Every health district should have a local research ethics committee (LREC) to advise NHS bodies on the ethical acceptability of research proposals involving human subjects. District Health Authorities are responsible for establishing and maintaining LRECs, in consultation with NHS bodies in their districts. The booklet 'Local Research Ethics Committees' gives detailed guidance on:
- the establishment and function of LRECs, and the administrative framework within which they work (Chapter 2);
- the ethical principles to which LRECs should have regard (Chapter 3);
- particular groups as research subjects (Chapter 4).
Responsibility for deciding whether a research proposal should proceed, within the NHS, lies with the NHS body under whose auspices the research would take place.

Action
NHS bodies should take into account the following specific requirements:
- As soon as possible and no later than 1 February 1992, each District Health Authority should establish an LREC (or, exceptionally, more than one) and provide it (or them) with adequate administrative support.
- Any NHS body asked to agree a research proposal falling within its sphere of responsibility should ensure that it has been submitted to the appropriate LREC for research ethics approval:
  - district health authorities, about research within their hospitals or community health services, or in private sector providers under contract to the DHA;
  - special health authorities, about research within their units;
  - family health services authorities, about research involving general medical, general dental, or other family health services;
  - NHS trusts, about research within the units they control;

and should take the LREC's advice into account before deciding whether the research project should go ahead. Projects which do not have LREC approval must not be agreed.

The guidelines contemplate as the principal regulatory mechanism the creation of what are called Local Research Ethics Committees (LRECs) whose task is to consider research protocols and advise the relevant NHS body. It will be realised, of course, that the guidelines relate only to research conducted within the NHS. LRECs may, by agreement, consider the proposals of researchers outside the NHS. The guidelines apply to all research involving human subjects within the NHS, including studies restricted to patient records or biological material (see para 1.3 below. Contrast, *Guidelines on the Practice of Ethics Committees in Medical Research Involving Human Subjects* (3rd edn, 1996), RCP at Appendix B).

1.1. Medical research is important, and the NHS has a key role in enabling it. The approval of research projects is an important management responsibility involving the availability of resources, financial implications, and ethical issues. Such considerations are generally best left to the local management team, but on ethical issues they need to take into account independent advice. The purpose of a local research ethics committee is to consider the ethics of proposed research projects which will involve human subjects, and which will take place broadly within the NHS. The LREC's task is to advise the NHS body under the auspices of which the research is intended to take place. It is that NHS body which has the responsibility to decide whether or not the project should go ahead taking account of the ethical advice of the LREC. For convenience, local research ethics committees are normally organised on a health district basis, but they exist to advise any NHS body. They are not in any sense management arms of the District Health Authority.

1.2. The NHS bodies which will look to an LREC for advice on the ethics of proposed research projects are therefore:
–   district health authorities (in respect of research taking place within their hospitals or community health services or in private sector providers under contract to the DHA)
–   special health authorities (in respect of research taking place within their units)
–   family health services authorities (in respect of research involving general medical, general dental, or other family health services)
–   NHS trusts (in respect of research taking place within the units they control).

1.3. An LREC must be consulted about any research proposal involving:
–   NHS patients (ie subjects recruited by virtue of their past or present treatment by the NHS) including those treated under contracts with private sector providers
–   fetal material and IVF involving NHS patients
–   the recently dead, in NHS premises
–   access to the records of past or present NHS patients
–   the use of, or potential access to, NHS premises or facilities.

1.4. No NHS body should agree to such a research proposal without the approval of the relevant LREC. No such proposal should proceed without the permission of the responsible NHS body. These requirements apply equally to researchers already working within the NHS and having clinical responsibility for the patients concerned, as they do to those who have no other association with the NHS and its patients, beyond the particular research project.

1.5. The relevant LREC in each case is normally that constituted in respect of the health district within the area of which the research is planned to take place. Special arrangements apply to multi-centre research, and these are referred to in Chapter 2 paragraph 18.

1.6. By agreement an LREC may also advise on the ethics of studies not involving NHS patients, records or premises, carried out for example by private sector companies, the Medical Research Council or universities.

ESTABLISHMENT

2.1 Although the LREC exists to provide independent advice to any NHS body within the geographical area of a health district, it is necessary for one of the NHS bodies to take the responsibility for establishing the LREC, and for providing its administrative support. This task falls to the District Health Authority. However each DHA should consult all the NHS bodies which are likely to use the LREC before establishing it.

2.2 It does not follow, however, that the members of the LREC are in any way representative of, nor beholden to, any of the NHS bodies which collaborate in its establishment, nor that the LREC as a whole is an arm of the management of any of them. The object of consultation is to ensure that all the NHS bodies which will use the LREC should have confidence in its ability to provide sound research ethics advice.

2.3 In exceptional circumstances it may be appropriate to establish two LRECs in one District. An example of this might be where there is a particularly high burden of work, perhaps originating from two distinct research centres within the locality. In such a case the DHA should secure agreement from all the relevant NHS bodies concerning the respective responsibilities of the LRECs, and should ensure that the administrative arrangements enable both to work together effectively.

MEMBERSHIP
2.4 An LREC should have eight to twelve members. This should allow for a sufficiently broad range of experience and expertise, so that the scientific and medical aspects of a research proposal can be reconciled with the welfare of research subjects, and broader ethical implications.

2.5 Members should be drawn from both sexes and from a wide range of age groups. They should include:

- hospital medical staff
- nursing staff
- general practitioners
- two or more lay persons.

2.6 Despite being drawn from groups identified with particular interests or responsibilities in connection with health issues, LREC members are not in any way the representatives of those groups. They are appointed in their own right, to participate in the work of the LREC as individuals of sound judgement and relevant experience.

2.7 The health professionals should include those occupied chiefly in active clinical care as well as those experienced in clinical investigation and research. As well as consulting the relevant NHS bodies in connection with health professional appointments DHAs should consult local professional advisory committees and relevant health professional associations. Lay members should be appointed after consultation with the Community Health Council. At least one lay member should be unconnected professionally with health care and be neither an employee nor adviser of any NHS body.

CHAIRMAN AND VICE-CHAIRMAN
2.8 After consultation with the relevant NHS bodies the DHA should appoint a chairman and vice-chairman from amongst the members of the committee. At least one of these posts should be filled by a lay person.

PERIOD OF APPOINTMENT
2.9 Members should serve on LRECs for terms of three to five years. Terms of appointment may be renewed. but normally not more than two terms of office should be served consecutively.

CO-OPTION
2.10 The LREC should, on its own initiative, seek the advice of specialist referees, or co-opt members to the committee. so as to cover any aspect, professional, scientific or ethical, of a research proposal which lies beyond the expertise of the existing members.

LEGAL LIABILITY
2.11 Concern has been expressed by some LREC members that they may be legally liable for injury caused to patients participating in research projects. DHAs will wish to advise appointees on these matters. Legal advice available to the Department of Health is that there is little prospect of a successful claim against an LREC member for a mishap arising from research approved as ethical by the LREC. Any such claim would lie principally against the researcher concerned, and against the NHS body under the auspices of which the research took place. The principal defendants should seek to have any claim against an LREC member struck out. Those members of an LREC who are employees of an NHS body are already covered by NHS indemnity arrangements. The DHA should also bear any costs in the case of other LREC members unless the member concerned is guilty of misconduct or gross lack of care in the performance of his or her duties and provided that, if any claim is threatened or made, the member notifies the DHA and assists it in all reasonable ways. If necessary, the DHA may give the following undertaking to this effect to LREC members who are not employees of an NHS body:

We confirm that the DHA will take full responsibility for all your actions in the course of the performance of your duties as a member of the LREC other than those involving bad faith, wilful default or gross negligence: you should, however, notify the DHA if any action or claim is threatened or made, and in such an event be ready to assist the authority as required.

DHAs should keep a record of which LREC members are covered by virtue of their NHS employment and which are not.

WORKING PROCEDURES

2.12 The LREC should always be able to demonstrate that it has acted reasonably in reaching a particular decision. When research proposals are rejected by the LREC, the reasons for that decision should be made available to the applicant. Good standing orders and accurate record keeping are important. Standing orders should be drawn up by the DHA covering frequency of meetings and working methods. Conducting business by post or telephone should be discouraged and the situations in which chairman's action can be taken should be clearly described.

KEEPING A REGISTER

2.13 The LREC should keep a register of all the proposals which come before it. The register should include the name and address of the organisation carrying out the research; names and qualifications of the research team; details of the premises in which the research will be conducted; medical support and other facilities available; a brief description of what is required of the research subjects and confirmation of compliance with any other guidelines (such as RCP or ABPI). This register would not normally be available for public consultation but should be open to the relevant NHS bodies for management purposes.

FOLLOWING UP

2.14 Once the LREC has approved a proposal, the researcher should be required to notify the committee, in advance, of any significant proposed deviation from the original protocol. Reports to the committee should also be required once the research is underway if there are any unusual or unexpected results which raise questions about the safety of the research. Reports on success (or difficulties) in recruiting subjects may also provide the LREC with useful feedback on perceptions of the acceptability of the project among patients and volunteers.

CONFIDENTIALITY OF PROCEEDINGS

2.15 LREC members do not sit on the committee in any representative capacity and need to be able to discuss the proposals which come before them freely. For these reasons LREC meetings will normally be private and the minutes taken will be confidential to the committee.

PRODUCING AN ANNUAL REPORT

2.16 Each year the LREC should submit a report to the DHA, and copies should be sent to all the NHS bodies which the LREC exists to advise, and to the CHC. The names of committee members, the number of meetings held and a list of proposals considered (including whether they were approved, approved after amendment, rejected or withdrawn) should be included. This report should be available for public inspection.

ADVICE TO NON-NHS BODIES

2.17 Not all medical research involving human subjects takes place within the NHS. Even where there is *no* NHS involvement of any kind, the body conducting the research should be encouraged to submit its proposals to the LREC for advice. In such cases, the LREC should report to the DHA the cost of its work so that the cost can be recovered from the outside body conducting the research. The LREC must also seek a full indemnity from the outside body against the possibility of future legal action.

MULTICENTRE RESEARCH

2.18 Each LREC is free to arrive at its own decision when considering a proposal which is planned to take place in more than one area. It would, however, obviously be sensible – in the interests of eliminating unnecessary delay and of ensuring that similar criteria are used to consider a proposal – that committees should arrive at a voluntary arrangement under which one LREC is nominated to consider the issue on behalf of them all. Health authorities should positively encourage networks for neighbouring LRECs so that such co-operation is more easily achieved.

It should be noted at the outset that in law there is no obligation on a Health Authority, an NHS Trust hospital, a pharmaceutical company or other such body to set up a Research Ethics Committee when involved in research on patients or healthy volunteers. The Department of Health's Circular requires Health Authorities to set up Research Ethics Committees, but by virtue of its being in a Circular, rather than legislation or a direction under s 17 NHS Act 1977, this is not a formal legal requirement. Further, there is no obligation in law on a potential researcher to submit a protocol to an Ethics Committee for review and approval.

Thus, any authority which an Ethics Committee wields is informal and extra-legal. Such authority should not, however, be minimised. As regards the NHS in England and Wales, the Department of Health's Circular places a clear duty on HAs to appoint them and thereby endows them with considerable status. Those who fund research ordinarily stipulate that research, to be funded, must be approved by an Ethics Committee. Researchers within the NHS will be denied access to patients without such approval according to the Circular. Finally, research results may not be published, at least in British journals.

B. MRECS

You will notice reference in the DoH's guidance to 'multicentre research' ie where the research is to be carried out at a number of research centres. Here complications arise and generate multiplicity of applications to different LRECs, some of whom may not allow the research to go ahead or others that may do so on different conditions. In order to deal with such difficulties, from 1 July 1997 the DoH established Multi-Centre Research Ethics Committees (MRECs) on a regional basis in England and one for each of Wales, Scotland and Northern Ireland. The structure of the MREC system and the functions of the committees is set out in *Ethics Committee Review of Multi-Centre Research – Establishment of Multi-Centre Research Ethics Committees* (HSG (97)23).

The system applies where the research will be carried out within five or more LRECs geographical boundaries (para 10). Local arrangements for one LREC to review a research proposal on behalf of others may still be applied, under para 2.18 of the LREC guidance, where less than five centres are involved.

Department of Health *Ethics Committee Review of Multi-Centre Research; Establishment of Multi-Centre Research Ethics Committees* (1997) HSG (97)23

Introduction
2. The system will cover all multi-centre research in the NHS, including clinical trials; records-based, qualitative and Health Services economic research; and surveys; and be able to advise on health-related non-NHS research.
3. LRECs will retain autonomy in recommending whether the research should go ahead locally and will remain accountable to Health Authorities (HAs) for decisions affecting their local populations.

The New System 3
4. A system of Multi-centre Research Ethics Committees (MRECs) will be set up. An MREC will be an advisory body providing independent advice on the science and general ethics of multi-centre research proposals. One MREC will be set up in each of the English regions and one each in Wales, Scotland and Northern Ireland. Regional arrangements will be consistent with this guidance; and MRECs' consideration of research proposals must be consistent with guidance to LRECs (see Local Research Ethics Committees, Chapter 3) (HSG (91)15 Department of Health, August 1991).
5. Each multi-centre research protocol will be considered by one MREC only – usually the one in the region in which the principal researcher is based. That MREC'S advice will be given to LRECs in every locality involved, not just those within its host part of the United Kingdom.
6. Once MREC approval has been obtained LRECs in every locality involved will have the opportunity to accept or reject the protocol for local reasons but will not be allowed to amend it. LRECs may occasionally need to seek purely locally applicable amendments which do not affect the integrity of the protocol, for example information sheets and consent forms

in minority languages. They should only do so when essential. LRECs will be asked to notify their decisions to the designated MREC within a specified timescale, and in particular give reasons if they refuse a proposal. Thus the system will incorporate an additional safeguard which could bring to the attention of an MREC any major points that had possibly been missed in its consideration of the scientific and wider ethical aspects. The MREC will be obliged to consider any such points.

7. The system will involve rigorous scrutiny of each protocol by the relevant MREC, including, where necessary, detailed discussion with the principal researcher and/or expert advisers. It will allow LRECs scope to discuss local matters pertaining to MREC-approved protocols with the local and/or principal researcher (where the latter can help expedite clearance).

8. MRECs will expect to receive protocols which have already been subject to scientific critique (although exceptions will be permitted if there is a satisfactory explanation). They will be required to take account of such critiques.

MREC members are appointed for three to five years and may be reappointed for a further term (para 13). As regards the membership, the guidance states (para 11):

11. Each MREC will have a broad range of experience and expertise with members reflecting a mix of gender, age and ethnic background, drawn from across the region. They will include hospital medical staff, nursing staff, general practitioners, other NHS professional staff and lay persons. The health professionals should include those occupied chiefly in active clinical care as well as those experienced in clinical investigation and research. Experienced LREC members will be likely to be suitable candidates. At least a third (but no more than six in total) of the membership will be lay. Simultaneous membership of an MREC and an LREC will be permissible.

The detail of the procedure can be found in the DoH guidance, HSG(97)23. Common application forms have been devised by the DoH (see C Foster (ed) *Manual for Research Ethics Committees* (1997) III.49) and standard operating procedures developed, not just for MRECs but also for LREC (see C Bendall *Standard Operating Procedures for Local Research Ethics Committees* (1994)).

The relationship between MRECs and LRECs is dealt with in the guidance. As we saw, a LREC must approve a protocol for research within its geographical remit before research can take place. It may reject the application but it cannot amend the substance of the protocol other than to take account of purely local matters (para 6). In other words, the LREC may not approve with amendments an MREC approved protocol by imposing conditions or requirements based upon its different view of the ethics of the proposal. The LREC must 'take it or leave it'. Local amendments must not 'affect the integrity of the protocol' but may require, for example, information sheets or consent forms to be in minority languages prevalent in its area. If the LREC has major ethical or scientific concerns it must, when refusing approval, inform the MREC of its decision with reasons and the MREC will then have an opportunity to consider whether these matters were overlooked or given insufficient attention when granting earlier approval.

As the system began to operate, it became clear that all was not clear about the relationship between MRECs and LRECs. In order to clarify matters, the DoH has twice issued letters to MRECs and LRECs. The first of these, from the Chief Medical Officers of Scotland and England (1997; set out at (1998) 134 Bull Med Eth 18–19), emphasises the need for use of standard application forms by MRECs (as required by HSG(97)23) and their subsequent use for LREC approval. It also emphasises that the LREC may not request changes to the research protocol approved by the MREC. The second letter, from the Chief Scientific Officer at the Scottish Office (adopted in England and Wales), provides more detailed guidance on the role and workings of LRECs considering protocols already approved by a MREC.

A J M Palmer 'Review: Research Ethics Committee Update' (1998)138 Bull Med Eth 14

Refusal of local permission is the exception but due consideration of suitability of the local researcher and research site is extremely important in maintaining the overall quality of ethical review of research. There is a need for a uniform process for local review which gives minimum additional burden to LRECs and to researchers but prevents the delay in review which is proving unacceptable.

Current advice is that "Chairman's action" does not meet the proposed requirements for clinical trials generating data that are intended to be submitted to the regulatory authorities. A model process recommended by a number of LRECs has been considered and found acceptable to the regulatory authorities. All LRECs are now asked to adopt the following 'Executive Sub-Committee' process to deal with MREC approved applications which cannot be considered by Chairman's action.

A. The LREC "Executive Sub-Committee" process for dealing with MREC approved applications

The LREC should establish a standing Executive Sub-Committee specifically to consider MREC-approved applications.

The entire Sub-Committee should consist of any number of members the LREC deems appropriate, but the quorum for a meeting shall be at least two members. For purposes of this Sub-Committee, the LREC administrator cannot be regarded as a member of the LREC.

On receipt of an MREC approved application from a local researcher the Administrator will advise the LREC Chairman (or if he is unavailable the Vice-Chairman) who will call a meeting of the Executive Sub-Committee within two weeks. The need for only two members to act in this capacity should always make this possible. He will also indicate whether he wishes the local researcher to be present.

Notice of intention to hold a Sub-Committee meeting shall be communicated to its members (and to the applicant) by the Administrator.

The Chair at the Sub-Committee Meeting will be taken by the LREC Chairman, or in his absence the Vice-Chairman, or – in the case of unavailability of either Chairman or Vice-Chairman – by a member previously appointed by the Chairman (or in his absence the Vice-Chairman).

The meeting and the decision of the Executive Sub-Committee will be minuted and communicated in writing to the researcher within five working days. Rejection of the application can only be for local reasons and must be accompanied by a full explanation for this decision. A copy of the approval or rejection letter should be sent to the administrator of the relevant MREC.

An approved decision by the Executive Sub-Committee does not require subsequent ratification by the full LREC and the local researcher may start the research on receipt of the approval letter, subject to having already obtained the necessary permission of any local NHS management, e.g. the Trust's R&D Director acting on behalf of the Chief Executive. The decision of the Executive Sub-Committee will be reported to the next meeting of the LREC.

All correspondence and minutes should include the LREC reference number, the MREC reference number, the title of the study and any study reference number relating to the regulatory authorities.

B. What issues is the executive Sub-Committee asked to consider on behalf of the LREC?

i. *The suitability of the local researcher.* LRECs are very experienced at considering whether the qualifications and grade of a local researcher (as described in Annex D to the application form) are adequate to support approval to undertake the supervision of the research as described in the MREC application form itself. As with purely local applications, they will wish to consider any local intelligence about both competence and capacity, particularly in respect of the total number of projects being undertaken simultaneously by an individual.

ii. *The suitability of the site.* LRECs will be familiar with their local clinical environment and facilities. If there are special concerns, not covered by the standard paperwork used, they might make these specific enquiries of the local researcher prior to or at the Sub-Committee meeting. The minutes and the subsequent correspondence will need to reflect this.

iii. *The suitability of the subjects.* LRECs are best placed to consider whether their local population is an appropriate one for the new research study. The portfolio of research activity in a location reflects the interests of the local researchers, and the Sub-Committee will, from its own LREC database, have access to *the* necessary information to allow them to decide if the local population should be exposed to further recruitment in a particular research area.

iv. *The Patient Information Sheet and Consent-form.* These will already have undergone ethical review by the MREC and any changes necessary from an ethical standpoint will already have been made to their content prior to ethical approval. The MREC will have had regard both to the needs and rights of the research subject and to the requirements of the regulatory bodies. The LREC Executive Sub-Committee will now need to check that local information (such as contact numbers and addresses) are appropriately inserted. They may also advise on whether the PIS and Consent form need to be produced in languages other than English. No other changes may be requested to the PIS or consent form, as doing so affects the integrity of the protocol.

v. The Sub-Committee is not required to make any further observations on the application.

The working of the MREC system is the subject of a review by the Department of Health.

C. LEGAL ACCOUNTABILITY OF RECS

Once a Research Ethics Committee constitutes itself and reviews research proposals, though it has no legal standing, it takes on legal duties. These duties derive from the central purposes of the Committee: to protect research subjects and maintain proper standards of practice in research, while ensuring that valid and worthwhile research is carried out. (For a discussion, see *Discussion Paper on Legal Liability, Insurance and Indemnity Arrangements for Institutional Ethics Committees*, Australian National Health and Medical Research Council (November 1993).) It is important, of course, to notice the more limited side of LRECs (and their members) when considering a protocol already approved by a MREC. However, it is difficult to see how an LREC could be absolved of its duty to reject an approved protocol if it considered it unethical whatever the DoH's guidance states.

The single most important legal duty imposed on the Committee is to address those issues which are relevant to any decision about a research proposal before deciding whether or not to approve it. More accurately, this duty is imposed on Committee members, since the Committee as a Committee has no separate legal identity. We shall consider later the question of legal liability which members may incur for breach of this duty.

To comply with their duty, Committee members must satisfy themselves on a number of matters. These include, as reflected in the forms of application for approval of research projects now commonly used, consideration of the following:

(a) on examination of the question to be answered and the outline of the research, that the research project is scientifically sound;

(b) whether the research is, by reference to the intention of the researcher, therapeutic or non-therapeutic, since the law places greater limits on the pursuit of non-therapeutic research out of concern to protect the research subject. In this context and generally it may be advisable to seek assurance that the proposal complies with the law;

(c) that the duration of the project is stated and is reasonable given the aims;

(d) that in the context of therapeutic research the risks to the subject which may be involved in the research can be justified by reference to the intended aims, both as regards the care of the patient and the advancement of knowledge;

(e) that any discomfort suffered by a subject of research is not greater than necessary and commensurate with the intended benefit, and that where the research is non-therapeutic, the risk to the subject is no more than minimal;

(f) that the investigator is suitably qualified and experienced;

(g) that the premises on which the research is to be conducted are adequate and that medical supervision, if appropriate, is available;

(h) that consent is to be obtained (except in exceptional circumstances), that the method of obtaining consent is appropriate and that any money to be paid to a volunteer does not serve as an inducement to persuade an otherwise unwilling person to participate;

(i) that, where appropriate and with the consent of the subject, contact is to be established with the subject's GP, such that anyone who refuses contact with his GP should be rejected as a research subject;

(j) that proper procedures exist to ensure medical confidentiality;

(k) that, where a drug is to be used, the legal status of the drug is established;

(l) that arrangements for compensation in the case of mishap and injury exist;

(m) that appropriate procedures exist for monitoring the progress of the research;

(n) that particular care is taken, especially as regards consent, in the case of research subjects who may be particularly vulnerable, eg children, elderly, mentally ill, mentally handicapped, students, employees, and the unemployed.

The legal duty of a member of an Ethics Committee is, at its most general, to behave as a reasonable member of such a Committee. In the absence of any legal guidance it is a matter for debate what the law would require of a reasonable

Committee member. Arguably, the duties set out above could, with some variation depending on the circumstances, be held to define what is reasonable.

Thus, failure on the part of a Committee member to satisfy himself on any of these questions may render him liable to a legal claim in negligence at the suit of a research subject if the research subject suffers harm as a consequence. (Obviously, the Committee member will not be in breach of his duty if a subject is harmed through the carelessness of the researcher.) Notice, however, that the law does not require the Committee member to get things right. Rather, as has been said, the obligation is to behave reasonably. Clearly, the expertise of the member may limit what he can do, but the law is likely to require that any reasonable member finding a matter on which he is unsure, should seek advice, (subject to the constraints of confidentiality), and may not simply remain in a state of ignorance. Further attempts to particularise what is reasonable may not be helpful, since much will depend on the facts of any particular case, and the resources and backgrounds of the particular Committee (subject, of course, to the proviso that a certain basic minimum of resources must be available). For example, the obligation to satisfy themselves that proper arrangements exist for compensation in the event of injury may appear onerous to many members who would argue that they are not specialists in insurance and finance. The response may be that their duty is to make reasonable inquiry, to ascertain, in other words, that compensation has been raised with the subject and that some provision has been made. To expect more of members may be unreasonable.

As has been said, liability would be personal. Thus, each Committee member must, if he is to serve on a Committee, make all reasonable efforts to comply with these various duties. If unable to do so, despite his reasonable efforts, the wise course would be to resign so as to avoid incurring possible liability. Notice that members who serve on the Committee as nominees of a Health Authority, Company, or some such body, which employs them, will be indemnified by their employer if sued in negligence (see DoH guidance on LREC, *op cit*, at para 2.11). This will not assist the member who serves in a personal capacity and has no employer to look to. Such members are well advised to seek some formal arrangement as to indemnity in the case of being sued, as a condition of agreeing to serve (see, *NHS Indemnity, Arrangements for Handling Clinical Negligence Claims Against NHS Staff*, HSG (96)48 at Annex A, 15).

The views expressed here concerning legal liability are not supported unanimously (but see *Weiss v Solomon* (1989) 48 CCLT 280 (Qu Sup Ct) – hospital liable for negligence of research committee). The Department of Health's Circular relating to LRECs, however, somewhat grudgingly supports the view expressed (see para 2.11, *supra*). In relation to members of MRECS, the DoH guidance, HSG (97)23 repeats the view that a claim would most probably be against the researcher or NHS body where the research was being carried out. Somewhat differently from its earlier view, however, it states that the Secretary of State for Health would be most likely sued as he, rather than any Health Authority or Trust, has set up the MREC and which is accountable to him (para 22). This liability must be based upon a non-delegable primary duty and is problematic (see, *supra*, ch 4 and extract below).

Professor Margaret Brazier examines the legal problems surrounding any claim in negligence in this context.

M Brazier 'Liability of Ethics Committee and Their Members' (1990) PN 186

A patient injured by what he believes to be a wrongly authorised trial will sue in negligence. Against whom will he serve his writ? The ethics committee itself lacks the necessary legal personality to be a defendant in a civil action....

Any action in respect of the committee's decisions... will lie against [the health] authority. The plaintiff, of course, is free to sue any or all of the members of the committee individually as well. But would it be worth his while? As he has a right of action against the authority, why bother to pursue probably impecunious committee members? And, as we shall see later, any action against an individual member would generate even more formidable problems of proving negligence than is the case in an action against the district health authority.

Patients suing non-NHS Committees may find it a little harder to identify a clearly solvent defendant and so may be more likely to resort to an action against individual committee members. The private hospital or drug company ethics committee itself has no corporate status. It has no legal personality enabling the committee as an entity to be sued. It is less clear than in the case of the NHS whether a 'private' ethics committee can be seen as simply an organ of the relevant institution, so that the hospital or company could be sued as responsible for a tortious act of its own, albeit made on its behalf by the committee. Consider, for example, a committee appointed by a company which exists solely to provide drug testing services for the pharmaceutical industry. It may well be argued that the company undertakes a duty of care to each and every volunteer recruited for trials and discharges that duty in part via the scrutiny of trials by its ethics committee. Similarly when a private hospital or clinic sets up an ethics committee to scrutinise either clinical trials or treatment, it may be argued that the hospital is in breach of the duty it undertakes to all patients admitted for treatment if 'its' ethics committee wrongfully approves a trial or treatment. But the case for direct liability on the part of the private sector institution is not as clearcut as the case for liability on the part of the health authority within the NHS. A patient might well be advised to join individual members of private sector ethics committees as defendants 'just in case'.

In no case, of course, is the health authority, private hospital or company vicariously liable for any tort committed by individual committee members. The public authority or corporate defendant will have to be found to be in breach of a direct and primary duty to the patient or volunteer. [Without such a primary duty obviously the health authority or private institution can thus not be sued by the patient or volunteer. For discussion of the potential to extend primary, non-delegable duties beyond the ambit of *Cassidy v Ministry of Health*, see *Street on Torts* (8th edn) 1988 at pp 543–59.] A local research ethics committee will include hospital medical staff and nursing staff who are employees of the authority. In their role as ethics committee members they are not acting in the course of their employment, and so the authority is no more vicariously liable for them than for their colleagues who are lay members or local general practitioners. Medical practitioners serving on ethics committees may well be covered against liability by their medical protection organisation. Other members should consider asking for an indemnity from the district health authority against any liability in tort arising from membership of an ethics committee...

A plaintiff suing any health authority or private sector institution on the grounds that its ethics committee wrongfully sanctioned a trial or treatment faces a series of difficulties proving breach of duty and causation...

[W]ould... the ethics committee also commit a tort if they had authorised the trial knowing that no valid consent would be obtained from a patient or volunteer? The first line of attack against the committee would be to argue that the committee, and its members, are joint tortfeasors with the clinician. By authorising a battery the committee shares responsibility for that battery. That argument has been pursued in the USA where Elizabeth Bouvia contended that the ethics committee which endorsed doctors' decisions to go on feeding her artificially against her will shared their liability for battery.

The alternative course is for the plaintiff to allege negligence against the committee. He would argue that to authorise a trial which entailed a battery by the clinician was negligent. The complexity of 'medical battery' and the application of *Chatterton v Gerson* and *Sidaway* confuses lawyers. Not many ethics committees of any type have lawyer members. How would a court decide whether a reasonable ethics committee would/should have noted the potential illegality in the trial? What would be the relevance, if any, of the Declaration of Helsinki, which states that in certain circumstances it is ethical not to obtain consent from patients in therapeutic research programmes? A plaintiff surmounting these hurdles in an action for negligence would finally have to prove that had the ethics committee acted properly and required a valid consent to participation in the trial, he would have refused his consent. Otherwise he fails to prove that 'but for' the committee's negligence, he would never have suffered the relevant injury.

When the patient's grievance is not that he did not agree to take part in the trial, but rather that the committee should never have authorised such a dangerous trial, proving breach of duty is even more problematic. Consider this (as far as I know) hypothetical trial. An obstetrician wishes to conduct a controlled trial to assess the need for Caesarian section in women with mild to moderate *placenta praevia*. Women are, with their consent, randomly allocated to caesarian and non-caesarian groups. Several women allowed to go into labour suffer devastating haemorrhages and lose their babies. Whether the obstetrician was negligent depends on expert evidence from obstetricians as to whether in embarking on the trial at all the defendant conformed to a responsible body of professional opinion. It does not follow that proving the obstetrician was negligent means the ethics committee was negligent too. Applying the *Bolam* test to ethics committees requires evidence from expert ethicists. Would a properly informed and conducted committee have discovered the dangers of, and/or lack of merit in the trial? The relevant experts may be chairpersons of other ethics committees.

Suing a health authority or private sector body for the negligence of its ethics committee creates enough problems of proving breach of duty; suing an individual member might be a nightmare. What is the relevant standard of care? Sued personally each member can only be responsible for his or her own negligence....

Suppose the committee approves a trial any responsible medical practitioner should have recognised as unmeritorious and unacceptably dangerous. [Would a lay member be] exonerated because no reasonable lay member could have seen the danger while medical colleagues are held liable? By contrast, if the committee approves a trial [the lay member] should have realised entailed a battery, [is he] liable in negligence while they are exculpated? The 'reasonable member of the ethics committee' is a myth, unless some compromise figure knowing a bit of everything is constructed. Perhaps the test should be not was the decision reasonable, but was the procedure reasonable? Did each member assess the project conscientiously and seek to ensure the project was accurately and thoroughly reviewed? In that case maybe missing a meeting for no good reason might be negligent, as might reviewing the proposals at 1.00 a.m. after a lengthy dinner engagement!

Finally a plaintiff suing in respect of a drug trial faces again the bugbear of causation. If the drug is experimental, the lack of documentation as to its effects may make it difficult to prove the drug caused the injury complained of. So far, the House of Lords has been entirely unsympathetic to pleas to infer causation in medical negligence claims.

As we shall see shortly, in Ireland research is regulated by statute (see generally, D Tomkin and P Hanafin, *Irish Medical Law* (1995), ch 10 and especially pp 213–4). In an amendment to the original statutory scheme (Control of Clinical Trials Act 1987) a provision was introduced in 1990 in the Control of Clinical Trials and Drugs Act 1990 to grant, *inter alia*, immunity from liability to ethics committees and their members. Section 5(1) provides:

5. (1) No action or other proceeding shall lie or be maintainable (except in the case of wilful neglect or default) against –
(a) ...
(b) ...
(c) an ethics committee or any member thereof.

Apart from possible liability in tort, is there any other system of legal accountability? There are a further cluster of duties imposed on Research Ethics Committees, the precise nature of which is unclear. They undoubtedly reflect ethical concerns. What legal standing, if any, they have is problematical. It may be that failure to observe them could result not in the personal liability of a member but in a court being asked to examine by way of judicial review a decision of the Committee with a view to declaring it invalid. The consequence would be that any authority for the research given by the Committee would be null.

Before we turn to consider these duties, we should examine whether it is correct that in principle an REC is amenable to judicial review. As we have seen, RECs are not creatures of statute. However, the courts have extended the scope of judicial review to include non-statutory bodies and functions providing the body is exercising a public function (*R v Panel on Take Overs and Mergers, ex p Datafin plc* [1987] QB 815). Subsequently, in one case it was assumed by a court that an REC was amenable to judicial review (*R v Ethical Committee of St Mary's Hospital (Manchester), ex p H* [1988] 1 FLR 512). Given the fact that the Government has adopted LRECs as the institution to perform an important public role, there is little doubt that the court would entertain an application for judicial review. The point is almost beyond doubt in the case of MRECs which are mandatory (as is the submission of multi-centre applications to them) and are accountable to the Secretary of State (HSG (97)23 at para 14).

Standard operating procedures have now been drawn up for LRECs by the DoH and are adopted by MRECs. These set out the constitution, proper practices and procedures and working methods of RECs (*Standard Operating Procedures for Local Research Ethics Committees* (1994)). These are likely to set the 'bench mark' for the courts when examining the conduct of RECs. Returning to consider the public law obligations of a REC, the first duty is the duty of the Committee to act within the terms of reference and scope established by the formal mechanism by which it came into being.

The second duty is to be properly constituted. This does not refer to the vexed question of membership, ie whether particular constituencies should be represented or what is the proper balance between health-care professionals and others. Instead it refers to the need to have rules concerning, for instance, the nomination and selection of members, their period of office, the terms on which they serve, the selection of a chair, the minimum and maximum size of the Committee, what constitutes a quorum and the power to co-opt members from time to time.

Thirdly, the Committee has a duty to establish proper working procedures or Standing Orders, as they are sometimes called. These should include, *inter alia*, establishing rules concerning:

(i)   frequency of meetings;
(ii)   preparation of agenda and minutes;
(iii) development of a standard application form;
(iv)   distribution of papers prior to meetings;
(v)   the scope of Chairman's action;
(vi)   confidentiality;
(vii) conflicts of interest in members as regards applicants or applications;
(viii) delegation of tasks to sub-committees, and the consequent relationship between the Committee and such sub-committees;
(ix)   the maintenance of a register of all research proposals and all action taken regarding them;
(x)   the basis of decision-making, ie bare majority, 2/3 majority, etc and any special rules on decisions concerning types of research projects, eg on the vulnerable;
(xi)   procedures for recording in writing the decisions of the Committee;
(xii) procedures for reporting adverse occurrences;
(xiii) giving reasons for decisions.

There is very considerable uncertainty as to whether these are in fact *legal* duties. Furthermore, even if some are, others (the more trivial or detailed) may not be. The legal criterion which a court would apply is that of 'fairness', or 'natural justice', ie is the Committee acting in a way which meets these criteria?

Finally, the Committee, so as to demonstrate that it is acting properly and responsibly, has a duty to submit itself to public scrutiny by rendering an account periodically of its conduct. This is best achieved as regards the general public by producing and publishing an annual report with sufficient detail to allow scrutiny. As regards the research community, this is best achieved by providing, in addition to any annual report, reasoned responses to any inquiry or complaint it may receive.

This extra-statutory approach to the regulation of research is common to most European countries (though not America). There is, however, another approach.

C Hodges 'Harmonisation of European Controls over Research: Ethics Committees, Consent, Compensation and Indemnity' in A Goldberg and I Dodds (eds) *Pharmaceutical Medicine and the Law* (1991)

It is relevant to contrast the approach taken in the recent French, Irish and Spanish legislation on clinical research [France: Law on the Protection of Persons Undergoing Biomedical Research, 1988, 1990, 1991; Republic of Ireland: Control of Clinical Trials Act, 1987, 1990; Spain: Medicaments Law 1990], which all provide that permission to carry out research is under the control of the Minister of Health but that the opinion of an ethical committee must first be obtained. The French legislation is supplemented by detailed decrees and a fixed regional network of ethics committees. Under none of these systems is there a requirement for continued monitoring by the committees or for adverse reactions to be reported to them: their role appears to cease after initial approval has been given (subject to possible reconsideration of amendments to the protocol) and regulatory responsibility passes to the regulatory authorities....

[T]he French law specifies that each regional advisory committee shall consist of 12 permanent members, each of which is to have a specific specialisation. There are to be four researchers, one GP, two pharmacists, and one each of a nurse, a person qualified in ethical matters, a person active in the social field, a psychologist and a lawyer. Each member shall also have an alternate. At least six members must be present for a valid decision to be made, four of whom must be from particular categories of specialisation. Members are chosen at random from a list of candidates drawn up by the regional government on nominations from relevant bodies. The members receive no remuneration but their expenses are defrayed. The French law also specifies that all places where healthy volunteer research is to be carried out must be authorised by the regional government.

The French legislation is therefore extremely detailed. This is not the case with the Irish legislation, since there is little call for permanent ethics committees to be established there on a regional basis. For each individual trial, the membership of a proposed committee has to be submitted to the minister, who will approve it if he considers

that the committee... is competent to consider the justification for conducting the proposed clinical trial and the circumstances under which it is to be conducted. [Control of Clinical Trials Act 1987, s 8(1).]

The composition of the committee may at any time be changed with the approval of the minister. [*ibid*, s 8(5)] Non-statutory guidelines encourage the selection of committees to include lay, legal and business representation as well as medical and paramedical expertise.

The Spanish law is a little more detailed, specifying that ethics committees

should be constituted, at least, by an interdisciplinary team made up of medical doctors, hospital pharmacists, clinical pharmacologists, nursing personnel and persons unrelated with health professionals of which, at least one shall be a jurist. [Medicaments Law 25/1990, Title 3, Article 64.3]...

The French, Irish and Spanish legislation provides that the ultimate decision on an application rests with the minister. [Control of Clinical Trials Act, 1987, Section 4; Law on the protection of persons undergoing biomedical research, Article L.209–12; Medicaments Law 25/1990, Article 65.] Curiously, neither the French nor Irish legislation specifies any criteria on which the minister may exercise his power – there is not even a reference to the Declaration of Helsinki. This is in contrast to the extensive criteria specified in that legislation for consideration by an ethics committee. The Spanish law, however. does specify that clinical trials must:

– only be undertaken after sufficient scientific data are available which guarantee that the risks are reasonable;
– be conducted in accordance with the Declaration of Helsinki;
– only be commenced if there is reasonable doubt as to the efficacy and safety of the matter to be tested. [Medicaments Law 25/1990, Article 60]...

As far as procedure is concerned, positive ministerial approval is required in Ireland, within 12 weeks of the application and after consultation with the National Drugs Advisory Board. In France, there is a negative approval system on a similar basis to the UK CTX system: the sponsor forwards a letter of intent to the minister together with the opinion of the committee. Spain requires positive authorisation by the Ministry of Health and Consumption, but the law also establishes a negative approval system under which the ministry has 60 days to object in the case of further similar trials of a product for which one clinical trial has already been approved, and of trials for new dosages or indications of medicines already licensed. [*Ibid*, Article 65.]

(For recent legislation in Europe: see, Medical Research Involving Human Subjects Act 1999 (Netherlands) and Medical Research Act 1999 (Finland) – for text see (1999) 152 Bull Med Eth 13 and (2000) 155 Bull Med Eth 7 respectively.)

Therapeutic research

There are at least three situations in which therapeutic research may be carried out:

(1) a doctor tests the efficacy of a new treatment where none had previously been available and the patient would have received ordinary nursing care, symptomatic relief but nothing else;

(2) a doctor tests the efficacy of a new treatment as against other established forms of treatment;

(3) a doctor tests treatments A, B and C (all of which are established) because it has not been established which is the most efficacious.

All of these types of research can be generically described as 'clinical trials'. They can be carried out in a variety of ways which are the subject of considerable scientific dispute, for example the allocation of the patient to one treatment or another may, or may not, be *random*. As we shall see, the use of randomisation calls for particular examination.

Before considering in detail the law applicable to clinical trials, it is important to make a general point. Since clinical trials entail a doctor-patient relationship, the general law concerning the duty of the doctor to act in the best interests of his patient and not to harm him applies. This has certain consequences for the conduct of trials.

First, if the trial consists in testing a new treatment, the doctor must have reasonable grounds for believing that the new treatment may be efficacious. For example, all necessary and appropriate research on animals and other studies must have been carried out.

Secondly, patients not receiving any new treatment which is the subject of the trial (ie those in the 'control' group) must receive the best available established treatment.

Thirdly, the trial must contain an appropriate mechanism (a 'stopping rule') whereby it may be discontinued if (a) a new treatment proves less beneficial than established treatment; or (b) a new treatment proves more beneficial than existing therapies or the best available other; or (c) therapy A shows a marked benefit over therapies B and C or vice versa (see for a description, W A Silverman, *Human Experimentation* (1986), ch 9).

In addition to these general propositions derived from the doctor's general duty to his patient, the law relating to the conduct of clinical trials is, in effect, the law relating to consent. (For issues concerned with confidentiality and data protection see, *supra* chs 7 and 8 respectively.)

A. THE COMPETENT PATIENT

1. Competence

We have already analysed the meaning of 'competence'. The only additional point which needs to be made here relates to the applicability of s 8(1) of the Family Law Reform Act 1969. This provision, you will recall, states that:

> the consent of a minor who has attained the age of 16 to any surgical, medical or dental treatment which, in the absence of consent, would constitute a trespass to his person, shall be as effective as it would be if he were of full age...

The question to be considered is whether therapeutic research is 'treatment' within the Act, so that a person over the age of 16 is *prima facie* competent. Arguably, therapeutic research, because it entails two intentions – to treat and to do research – is more than 'treatment' within the Act, such that the power to consent would remain with the proxy until the minor reaches majority, ie 18, unless found to be competent as explained in the *Gillick* decision. On this analysis, a minor between 16 and 18 years of age would not *prima facie* be competent to consent to therapeutic research. Furthermore in applying *Gillick*, a relatively high standard of comprehension by the minor would have to be shown since therapeutic research entails research on a *sick* minor. It could be said that the law would protect such a minor from consenting save when the illness and the research were trivial because a court might well find any given minor lacked the necessary maturity to consent. This analysis would apply, perhaps, with even greater force, to a minor under 16. (See *Local Research Ethics Committees* (1991) HSE (91)5, paras 4.1– 4.4 endorsing the view expressed above.) (For further guidance on children's consent to research, see: *The Ethical Conduct of Research on Children* (1991), MRC; *Guidelines for the Ethical Conduct of Medical Research Involving Children* (1992), British Paediatric Association; *Guidelines on the Practice of Ethics Committees in Medical Research Involving Human Subjects* (1996), RCP.)

The concern for the competence of the patient is not, of course, limited to the minor. Therapeutic research on adults equally contemplates research on a sick person. The law would insist that those contemplating research satisfy themselves that in assessing a patient's competence to volunteer they have taken account of the possible effect of such factors as pain, other medication and other therapies.

2. Voluntariness

We have already considered the law concerning voluntariness (*supra*, ch 5). It is easy to state that the law requires that a patient truly must volunteer his consent. It is quite another thing to ensure that this is so.

The point is well put by the US President's Commission in its 1982 Report 'Making Health Care Decisions' (pp 66–68).

…Blatant coercion may be of so little concern in professional-patient relationships because, as physicians so often proclaim, it is so easy for health professionals to elicit a desired decision through more subtle means. Indeed, some physicians are critical of the legal requirement for informed consent on the grounds that it must be mere window dressing since 'patients will, if they trust their doctor, accede to almost any request he cares to make'. On some occasions, to be sure, this result can be achieved by rational persuasion, since the professional presumably has good reasons for preferring a recommended course of action. But the tone of such critics suggests they have something else in mind: an ability to package and present the facts in a way that leaves the patient with no real choice. Such conduct, capitalising on disparities in knowledge, position, and influence, is manipulative in character and impairs the voluntariness of the patient's choice.

Manipulation has more and less extreme forms. At one end of the spectrum is behaviour amounting to misrepresentation or fraud. Of particular concern in health care contexts is the withholding or distortion of information in order to affect the patient's beliefs and decisions. The patient might not be told about alternatives to the recommended course of action, for example, or the risks or other negative characteristics of the recommended treatment might be minimised. Such behaviour is justly criticised on two grounds: first, that it interferes with the patient's voluntary choice (and thus negates consent) and, second, that it interferes with the patient's ability to make an informed decision. At the other end of the spectrum are far more subtle instances: a professional's careful choice of words or nuances of tone and emphasis might present the situation in a manner calculated to heighten the appeal of a particular course of action.

It is well known that the way information is presented can powerfully affect the recipient's response to it. The tone of voice and other aspects of the practitioner's manner of presentation can indicate whether a risk of a particular kind with a particular incidence should be considered serious. Information can be emphasised or played down without altering the content. And it can be framed in a way that affects the listener – for example 'this procedure succeeds most of the time' versus 'this procedure has a 40 percent failure rate'. Health professionals who are aware of the effects of such minor variations can choose their language with care, if, during discussion with a patient. they sense any unintended or confused impressions being created, they can adjust their presentation of information accordingly.

Because many patients are often fearful and unequal to their physicians in status, knowledge, and power, they may be particularly susceptible to manipulations of this type. Health care professionals should, therefore, present information in a form that fosters understanding. Patients should be helped to understand the prognosis for their situation and the implications of different courses of treatment. The difficult distinction, both in theory and in practice, is between acceptable forms of informing, discussion, and rational persuasion on the one hand, and objectionable forms of influence or manipulation on the other.

Since voluntariness is one of the foundation stones of informed consent, professionals have a high ethical obligation to avoid coercion and manipulation of their patients. The law penalises those who ignore the requirements of consent or who directly coerce it. But it can do little about subtle manipulations without incurring severe disruptions of private relationships by intrusive policing, and so the duty is best thought of primarily in ethical terms.

An English court would approach the issue of whether any particular individual's consent was voluntarily given, as did the Court of Appeal in *Freeman v Home Office (No 2)* [1984] 1 All ER 1036 at 1044–5 (see *supra*, ch 5), as a matter of fact rather than a matter of law.

3. Information

The proposition that the patient must be adequately informed to make any consent to therapeutic research valid poses the question, what legal action would lie if the patient was not so informed? We have discussed already the relationship between the torts of battery and negligence and the adequacy of information given to patients (*supra*, ch 5). We will not rehearse the general points here. We must, however, ask whether in the specific context of therapeutic research any failure adequately to inform a patient would render the doctor liable to an action in battery or negligence.

(a) Battery

One view, and it is ours, is that where there is a dual intention on the part of the doctor, ie to treat *and* to conduct research, any failure to inform the patient concerning *both* of these intentions and their possible consequences would amount in law to a battery. This is because in the absence of such knowledge the patient will have assented to a procedure which is materially different in its nature from that which the doctor intends to carry out. To put it another way, research adds a further component to the quality of the consent that the law requires.

The law does not require people to volunteer and will provide a remedy to the patient against the doctor who conscripts him, the remedy being in battery to demonstrate the law's concern for the rights of the patient. Indeed, arguably the failure to disclose the intention to conduct research would amount to fraud sufficient to vitiate any consent which might otherwise be valid. If this is the law, that failure to inform is a battery, then what must the doctor do to act lawfully? In short, the answer must be that the doctor must make explicit his intention to carry out research. A court may insist on the patient being informed of three particular matters in addition to this generalised intention. Each of them is an aspect of those interests of the patient which the law of battery seeks to protect. The patient must be informed: (1) that he may refuse to take part in the research project or may at any time withdraw from the research and that in either case if he does so he will suffer no adverse consequences in terms of the treatment he will then receive; (2) that the nature of the research may be such that he may be a member of a control group in a trial which is intended to evaluate the efficacy of a new therapy; (3) that the trial is a randomised controlled trial (RCT) if it be such.

As regards (2), one consequence of being a member of a control group could be that the patient does not receive the form of treatment which subsequently proves to be the more efficacious. To meet this ethical difficulty researchers ordinarily would be expected to provide for periodic examination of the emerging data. It is our view that a patient's consent is not informed for the purpose of the tort of battery unless he is made aware of this periodic review.

As regards (3), randomisation means that a treatment regime is assigned to a patient randomly without regard to the particular circumstances of that patient, his needs, his preferences or the preferences of his doctor. Again, it is our view that a patient may volunteer for such a trial but his consent is only valid if he is given the opportunity of knowing it is randomised and he is aware of what this means.

(b) Negligence

Putting aside the question of whether a battery action would lie, what is the duty of the doctor, looking now to the tort of negligence? Is the doctor merely obliged to conform with what we have seen to be his duty of care as regards information in cases of treatment? Or are there additional obligations placed upon him by virtue of his dual intentions?

If the general duty were all that was required it would mean that in undertaking clinical trials a doctor would be held to the duty as explained in *Sidaway*. We have seen that this gives considerable weight to the views of the medical profession (*supra*, ch 5). Does *Sidaway* apply to clinical trials? One view is that *Sidaway* is limited to circumstances in which the doctor's only intention is to treat the patient and does not extend to cases of dual intention. This is because if we look to the majority views in *Sidaway*, the primary reliance on what doctors would do as a professional body has no relevance when what is being considered is research. Whether or not it is proper to engage in research is a matter of public policy and not professional opinion. That being so, what amounts to proper disclosure is a matter of law for the courts.

If we look at Lord Scarman's speech, as perhaps we would be entitled to in this context, we would say that ordinarily the doctor must advise the patient that he is involved in a clinical trial and what this entails. We would further say that Lord Scarman's recourse to the 'therapeutic privilege' as justifying non-disclosure of information does not apply to information relating to the fact that the patient is in a clinical trial and what that entails. To argue that a doctor need not tell a patient that he is in a clinical trial since this would mean that he had to be told of other things concerning his condition, would be to use one justifiable non-disclosure as support for an entirely distinct non-disclosure. Arguably this puts the cart before the horse! If the patient's interests require that he not be informed of certain matters concerning his condition for the purposes of his treatment, this is an argument against using him in a clinical trial rather than serving to justify his use and the subsequent non-disclosure of this to him.

If the above view, that *Sidaway* and its reliance upon professional opinion does not govern the conduct of clinical trials, is right, what does the law of negligence say is the doctor's duty as regards disclosing information? In our view, the law would demand disclosure of the following (bearing in mind that the term 'disclosure' refers not only to the volunteering of information but also to the truthful answering of any questions asked):

(1) The information which we earlier considered essential so as to avoid a claim in battery;
(2) The information which apprises the patient of the *material risks* associated with the research.

What does 'material' mean in this context? The meaning given to it in cases of informed consent to treatment in North America is that, a risk is material if it would be judged to be so by a *reasonable patient*. Here, where we are discussing an intention to carry out research, a good argument exists for saying that it should be those risks of which the *particular patient* volunteering for the research would wish to be informed.

In *Halushka v University of Saskatchewan* (1965) 52 WWR 608 at 616, Hall JA said:

> There can be no exceptions to the ordinary requirements of disclosure in the case of research as there may well be in ordinary medical practice. The researcher does not have to balance the probable effect of lack of treatment against the risk involved in the treatment itself. The example of risks being properly hidden from a patient when it is important that he should not worry can have no application in the field of research. The subject of medical experimentation is entitled to a full and frank disclosure of all the facts, probabilities and opinions which a reasonable man might be expected to consider before giving his consent.

Even the objective reasonable patient test may not go far enough when we are considering therapeutic research. Any risk which the particular patient might consider relevant would be a more appropriate legal standard (see *infra*, non-therapeutic research and *Weiss v Solomon* (1989) 48 CCLT 280 (Que Sup Ct) – court imposed the most exacting duty of disclosure, including the duty to disclose even rare or remote insts of serious consequences).

(3) The information, in addition to any risks, which is material to allow the patient to make an informed decision.

Here we have in mind such information as the fact that the patient may have to undergo additional (and perhaps discomforting) tests; may have to stay in hospital when otherwise he would be at home; may have to visit the hospital more frequently for tests and other such inconveniencing circumstances associated with the research.

The importance of disclosure of information to research subjects is emphasised by the General Medical Council in its guidance, *Seeking Patients' Consent: The Ethical Considerations* (1998).

> 36. You must take particular care to be sure that anyone you ask to consider taking part in research is given the fullest possible information, presented in terms and a form that they can understand. This must include any information about possible benefits and risks; evidence that a research ethics committee has given approval; and advice that they can withdraw at any time. You should ensure that participants have the opportunity to read and consider the research information leaflet. You must allow them sufficient time to reflect on the implications of participating in the study. You must not put pressure on anyone to take part in research. You must obtain the person's consent in writing. Before starting any research you must always obtain approval from a properly constituted research ethics committee.

Further explicit recognition of the need for disclosure of information is found in the International Conference on Harmonisation *Guideline for Good Clinical Practice* (1996).

4.8 Informed Consent of Trial Subjects

4.8.1 In obtaining and documenting informed consent, the investigator should comply with the applicable regulatory requirement(s), and should adhere to GCP and to the ethical principles that have their origin in the Declaration of Helsinki. Prior to the beginning of the trial, the investigator should have the IRB/IEC's written approval/favourable opinion of the written informed consent form and any other written information to be provided to subjects.

4.8.2 The written informed consent form and any other written information to be provided to subjects should be revised whenever important new information becomes available that may be relevant to the subject's consent. Any revised written informed consent form, and written information should receive the IRB/IEC's approval/favourable opinion in advance of use. The subject, or the subject's legally acceptable representative should be informed in a timely manner if new information becomes available that may be relevant to the subject's willingness to continue participation in the trial. The communication of the information should be documented.

4.8.4 None of the oral and written information concerning the trial, including the written informed consent form, should contain any language that causes the subject or the subject's legally acceptable representative to waive or to appear to waive any legal rights, or that releases or appears to release the investigator, the institution, the sponsor, or their agents from liability for negligence.

4.8.5 The investigator, or a person designated by the investigator, should fully inform the subject or, if the subject is unable to provide informed consent, the subject's legally acceptable representative, of all pertinent aspects of the trial including the written information given approval/favourable opinion by the IRB/IEC.

4.8.6 The language used in the oral and written information about the trial, including the written informed consent form, should be as non-technical as practical and should be able to be understandable to the subject, or the subject's legally acceptable representative and the impartial witness, where applicable.

4.8.7 Before informed consent may be obtained, the investigator, or a person designated by the investigator, should provide the subject or the subject's legally acceptable representative ample time and opportunity to inquire about details of the trial and to decide whether or not to participate in the trial. All questions about the trial should be answered to the satisfaction of the subject or the subject's legally acceptable representative.

4.8.8 Prior to a subject's participation in the trial, the written informed consent form should be signed and personally dated by the subject or by the subject's legally acceptable representative, and by the person who conducted the informed consent discussion.

4.8.9 If a subject is unable to read or if a legally acceptable representative is unable to read, an impartial witness should be present during the entire informed consent discussion. After the written informed consent form and any other written information to be provided to subjects is read and explained to the subject or the subject's legally acceptable representative, and after the subject or the subject's legally acceptable representative has orally consented to the subject's participation in the trial and, if capable of doing so, has signed and personally dated the informed consent form, the witness attests that the information in the consent form and any other written information was accurately explained to, and apparently understood by, the subject or the subject's legally acceptable representative, and that informed consent was freely given by the subject or the subject's legally acceptable representative.

4.8.10 Both the informed consent discussion and the written informed consent form and any other written information to be provided to subjects should include explanations of the following:
(a) That the trial involves research.
(b) The purpose of the trial.
(c) The trial treatment(s) and the probability for random assignment to each treatment.
(d) The trial procedures to be followed, including all invasive procedures.
(e) The subject's responsibilities.
(f) Those aspects of the trial that are experimental.
(g) The reasonably foreseeable risks or inconveniences to the subject and, when applicable, to an embryo, foetus, or nursing infant.
(h) The reasonably expected benefits. Where there is no intended clinical benefit to the subject, the subject should be made aware of this.
(i) The alternative procedure(s) or course(s) of treatment that may be available to the subject, and their important potential benefits and risks.
(j) The compensation and/or treatment available to the subject for participating in the trial.
(k) The anticipated prorated payment, if any, to the subject for participating in the trial.
(l) The anticipated expenses, if any, to the subject for participating in the trial.
(m) That the subject's participation in the trial is voluntary and that the subject may refuse to participate or withdraw from the trial, at any time, without penalty or loss of benefits to which the subject is otherwise entitled.
(n) That the monitor(s), the auditor(s), the IRB/IEC, and the regulatory authority(ies) will be granted direct access to the subject's original medical records for verification of clinical trial procedures and/or data, without violating the confidentiality of the subject, to the extent permitted by the applicable laws and regulations and that, by signing a written informed consent form, the subject or the subject's legally acceptable representative is authorising such access.
(o) That records identifying the subject will be kept confidential, and to the extent permitted by the applicable laws and/or regulations, will not be made publicly available. If the results of the trial are published, the subject's identity will remain confidential.
(p) That the subject or the subject's legally acceptable representative will be informed in a timely manner if information becomes available that may be relevant to the subject's willingness to continue participation in the trial.
(q) The person(s) to contact for further information regarding the trial and the rights of trial subjects, and whom to contact in the event of trial-related injury.
(r) The foreseeable circumstances and/or reasons under which the subject's participation in the trial may be terminated.
(s) The expected duration of the subject's participation in the trial.
(t) The approximate number of subjects involved in the trial.

4.8.11 Prior to participation in the trial, the subject or the subject's legally acceptable representative should receive a copy of the signed and dated written informed consent form and any other written information provided to the subjects. During a subject's participation in the trial, the subject or the subject's legally acceptable representative should receive a copy of the signed and dated consent form updates and a copy of any amendments to the written information provided to subjects.

Adherence is in practice, required by regulatory authorities in the European Union and America. The GCP Guidelines are not in themselves law, although they serve as the basis for the conduct of research by most major enterprises engaged in medical research, ie where medicinal products are involved. These guidelines replace those issued in the European Union by the Committee on Proprietary Medicinal Products in 1991 and, of course, have a wider application geographically. In July 1991 Directive 91/507/EEC (having to do with the harmonisation of the laws on the licensing and testing of medicinal products) required Member States to implement its provisions by 1 January 1992. This has been effected through the Medicines (Applications for Grant of Product Licences – Products for Human Use) Regulations 1993 (SI 1993 No 2538) which came into force on 29 November 1993 (see also, Medicines for Human Use (Marketing Authorisations Etc) Regulations 1994 (SI 1994 No 3144)). *Inter alia*, paragraph 1.1 of Part 4 of the Annex to the Directive provides that:

> All phases of clinical investigation, including bioavailability and bioequivalence studies, shall be designed, implemented and reported in accordance with *good clinical practice* (our emphasis).

It is a matter of conjecture whether the reference to 'good clinical practice', without this phrase being given any specific prominence or meaning, represents an incorporation by reference of the earlier European Guidelines on GCP. It seems unlikely that the reference could be construed to incorporate the *subsequent* international guidelines. The proposed EU Directive on 'good clinical practice' would, however, put the matter beyond doubt whose terms, once agreed, would in time become binding on all EU members including the United Kingdom (see (1998) 135 Bull Med Eth 6–11 and (1999) 148 Bull Med Eth 3–4: original draft and subsequent proposed amendments). If the Guidelines or their international successor are part of the Directive, then it may be thought that English law will have been extended even beyond what in our view represents the common law. One oddity of the Guidelines on GCP is the reference in paragraph 4.8.1 to the Helsinki Declaration. You will recall that the Helsinki Declaration, while requiring informed consent as a 'basic principle', in II.5 provides that in certain circumstances it may be dispensed with. The traditional interpretation of this exception is that it applies when the doctor does not wish to tell the patient what is wrong with him because such information, in the view of the doctor, would be deleterious to the patient's best interests. The logic is that if the doctor chooses not to tell the patient about his condition, *a fortiori* the doctor cannot ask for permission to involve that patient in research on his condition. We have already seen that this position is legally untenable in England. Furthermore, it sits ill with the remainder of the Guidelines on GCP and the importance they give to informed consent. Therein lies the oddity.

By contrast to the position in England, American law has gone much further in prescribing a framework for regulating research, not least as regards informed consent. By way of introduction, the history leading to regulation is described in the following.

Furrow, Greaney, Johnson, Jost and Schwartz *Health Law* (1995) vol 2

> In the United States research has... been tainted by racially and politically motivated choices of subject for medical investigation. Indeed, one of the defenses raised at the Nazi war trials was that there was no relevant distinction between what the Nazi physicians did and the contemporaneous American practice of using conscientious objectors and prisoners (including 'political' prisoners, such as those convicted of treason) as subjects in research designed to improve America's military strength. The argument that the United States applied a double standard that condemned only Nazi research is bolstered by the fact that there was no effort to seek retribution against Japanese experimenters who were doing work with serious implications for biological warfare, but who cooperated with the United States after their capture.

The most famous twentieth century American breach of research ethics was the Tuskegee Syphilis Study. In this study, hundreds of poor African American men in the South were studied so that the research agency, the United States Public Health Service, could develop an understanding of the natural history of syphilis. Poor rural African Americans were chosen as subjects because of the difficulty they might have in seeking treatment for syphilis and because it was thought that African Americans, who were considered naturally more sexually active and physically and mentally weaker than whites, would be more likely to benefit from the outcome of the study. The natural history of the disease could be discovered only if any treatment provided to the subjects were ineffective. The United States Public Health Service continued this research for some forty years. Even when penicillin, the first truly effective treatment for syphilis, became available, the Public Health Service physicians failed to offer that treatment to most of their subjects. and many were regularly discouraged from getting other forms of treatment. The study came to public light in 1972 and was the topic of federal administrative and Congressional hearings in 1973. While participants in the study successfully sued the Public Health Service for compensation, no criminal actions arose out of the case.

The Tuskegee Syphilis Study is not unique as an example of American medical research failing to respect individual subjects. Other publicized cases include the Jewish Chronic Disease Hospital case, in which live cancer cells were injected into patients without their knowledge, and the Willowbrook State Hospital hepatitis study, in which children admitted to a state hospital rife with hepatitis were given the disease as a condition of admission. In each of these cases, as in the Nazi experiments, the only authorities determining whether the subjects were properly selected were the medical investigators themselves. In addition, in early 1994 the United States government began to reveal previously witheld information about radiation studies, conducted over the course of decades, some of which were carried on without the consent, or even the knowledge, of those who were made subjects of the studies.

The first formal federal policy requiring outside review of research involving human subjects was imposed in 1966 by the Public Health Service upon those seeking grants from it. The 1966 policy required prior consideration of 'the risks and potential medical benefits of the investigation' before a protocol could be submitted to the Public Health Service.

In 1974, one year after the public disclosure of the Tuskegee Syphilis Study, Congress enacted the National Research Act establishing the National Commission for Protection of Human Subjects of Biomedical and Behavioral Research, which was to 'conduct a comprehensive investigation and study to identify basic ethical principles' that should underlie the conduct of human subjects research. That Commission was also to develop procedures to assure that the research would be consistent with those ethical principles and to recommend guidelines that could apply to human subjects research supported by the Department of Health, Education and Welfare. In recognition of the interdisciplinary nature of the issue, the Act also required the establishment of institutional review boards (IRBs) at institutions under contract with the Department of Health, Education and Welfare.

By 1975, when the Department of Health, Education and Welfare issued its 'Policy for the Protection of Human Research Subjects', virtually every university, medical school, and research hospital had established IRBs which operated within the requirements of both federal and state regulations. The federal regulations were revised by what had become the Department of Health and Human Services (DHSS) in 1981 to remove the necessity of IRB reviews from some low-risk research and to provide for informal consent procedures in some cases. Every year in the United States, hundreds of IRBs will review thousands of research protocols. No research involving human subjects funded by the Department of Health and Human Services – and virtually no other research involving human subjects – may be carried out at an institution without that institution's IRB approval.

The current regulations on 'Protection of Human Subjects' (1990) 45 CFR provide in paras 46.116 and 46.117:

§ 46.116 General requirements for informed consent

Except as provided elsewhere in this or other subparts, no investigator may involve a human being as a subject in research covered by these regulations unless the investigator has obtained the legally effective informed consent of the subject or the subject's legally authorized representative. An investigator shall seek such consent only under circumstances that provide the prospective subject or the representative sufficient opportunity to consider whether or not to participate and that minimize the possibility of coercion or undue influence. The information that is given to the subject or the representative shall be in language understandable to the subject or the representative. No informed consent, whether oral or written, may include any exculpatory language through which the subject or the representative is made to waive or appear to waive any of the subject's legal rights, or releases or appears to release the investigator, the sponsor, the institution or its agents from liability for negligence.

(a) Basic elements of informed consent. Except as provided in paragraph (c) or (d) of this section, in seeking informed consent the following information shall be provided to each subject:

(1)   A statement that the study involves research, an explanation of the purposes of the research and the expected duration of the subject's participation, a description of the procedures to be followed, and identification of any procedures which are experimental;

(2)   A description of any reasonably foreseeable risks or discomforts to the subject;

(3)   A description of any benefits to the subject or to others which may reasonably be expected from the research;

(4)   A disclosure of appropriate alternative procedures or courses of treatment, if any, that might be advantageous to the subject;

(5)   A statement describing the extent, if any, to which confidentiality of records identifying the subject will be maintained;

(6)   For research involving more than minimal risk, an explanation as to whether any compensation and an explanation as to whether any medical treatments are available if injury occurs and, if so, what they consist of, or where further information may be obtained;

(7)   An explanation of whom to contact for answers to pertinent questions about the research and research subjects' rights, and whom to contact in the event of a research-related injury to the subject; and

(8)   A statement that participation is voluntary, refusal to participate will involve no penalty or loss of benefits to which the subject is otherwise entitled, and the subject may discontinue participation at any time without penalty or loss of benefits to which the subject is otherwise entitled.

(b) Additional elements of informed consent. When appropriate, one or more of the following elements of information shall also be provided to each subject:

(1)   A statement that the particular treatment or procedure may involve risks to the subject (or to the embryo or fetus, if the subject is or may become pregnant) which are currently unforeseeable;

(2)   Anticipated circumstances under which the subject's participation may be terminated by the investigator without regard to the subject's consent;

(3)   Any additional costs to the subject that may result from participation in the research;

(4)   The consequences of a subject's decision to withdraw from the research and procedures for orderly termination of participation by the subject;

(5)   A statement that significant new findings developed during the course of the research which may relate to the subject's willingness to continue participation will be provided to the subject; and

(6)   The approximate number of subjects involved in the study....

(d) An IRB may approve a consent procedure which does not include, or which alters, some or all of the elements of informed consent set forth above, or waive the requirements to obtain informed consent provided the IRB finds and documents that:

(1)   The research involves no more than minimal risk to the subjects;

(2)   The waiver or alteration will not adversely affect the rights and welfare of the subjects;

(3)   The research could not practicably be carried out without the waiver or alteration; and

(4)   Whenever appropriate, the subjects will be provided with additional pertinent information after participation.

(e) The informed consent requirements in these regulations are not intended to preempt any applicable federal, state, or local laws which require additional information to be disclosed in order for informed consent to be legally effective.

(f)   Nothing in these regulations is intended to limit the authority of a physician to provide emergency medical care, to the extent the physician is permitted to do so under applicable federal, state, or local law.

§ 46.117 Documentation of informed consent

(a) Except as provided in paragraph (c) of this section, informed consent shall be documented by the use of a written consent form approved by the IRB and signed by the subject or the subject's legally authorized representative. A copy shall be given to the person signing the form.

(b) Except as provided in paragraph (c) of this section, the consent form may be either of the following:

(1)   A written consent document that embodies the elements of informed consent required by § 46.116. This form may be read to the subject or the subject's legally authorized representative, but in any event, the investigator shall give either the subject or the representative adequate opportunity to read it before it is signed; or

(2)   A 'short form' written consent document stating that the elements of informed consent required by § 46.116 have been presented orally to the subject or the subject's legally authorized representative. When this method is used, there shall be a witness to the oral presentation. Also, the IRB shall approve a written summary of what is to be said to the subject or the representative. Only the short form itself is to be signed by the subject or the

representative. However, the witness shall sign both the short form and a copy of the summary, and the person actually obtaining consent shall sign a copy of the summary. A copy of the summary shall be given to the subject or the representative, in addition to a copy of the 'short form.'

(c) An IRB may waive the requirement for the investigator to obtain a signed consent form for some or all subjects if it finds either:

(1) That the only record linking the subject and the research would be the consent document and the principal risk would be potential harm resulting from a breach of confidentiality. Each subject will be asked whether the subject wants documentation linking the subject with the research, and the subject's wishes will govern; or

(2) That the research presents no more than minimal risk of harm to subjects and involves no procedures for which written consent is normally required outside of the research context.

It should be noted that the regulations do no apply to 5 categories of low risk research, in particular, retrospective studies on patient records or biological material (45 CFR 46.101(b)).

4. Limits of research

As with treatment, the permissible limits of therapeutic research are measured in law by reference to a risk-benefit ratio. A patient may only be exposed in the course of treatment to risks which can be demonstrated to bring with them the likelihood of greater benefit. Clearly, the more severe the patient's illness the greater are the risks which can lawfully be taken in treating him if a real probability of benefiting him exists. Similarly, in the context of therapeutic research the risks which research might expose the patient to (even without his knowledge) must be demonstrably outweighed by the expected benefits.

Prima facie, however, concern for the relationship between risk and benefit is of greater importance in the regulation of research which is non-therapeutic or which involves those who are incompetent to consent. We will consider this in greater detail later. When the research is therapeutic and the patient is competent it will ordinarily be left to the patient to determine the risk-benefit ratio for himself – having, of course, been properly informed.

A further question needs to be examined. Is the doctor limited in the form of research to be employed in that he may not involve his patient in a randomised controlled trial? The question arises because randomisation, as we have seen, entails assigning a patient to a treatment category without reference to the patient's particular circumstances or preferences or, indeed, the doctor's preferences. For example, a patient may prefer fewer hospital visits or interventions but because he is in an RCT will not be able to have his preference respected. Being involved in an RCT requires that he waive his preferences. Provided he is informed of the implications of randomisation and agrees to be part of the trial this will not create a legal problem. Also, the doctor may prefer one form of treatment rather than another when two are being compared but may as a consequence of the trial have to offer what, to him, is less preferable. The apparent answer is that if the patient is apprised of all that is involved in being in a randomised controlled trial then his consent is properly informed. The law may not, however, be so simple. It will be clear from the brief description of randomisation that it may involve the patient in waiving the doctor's duty to act in his best medical interests. It is undoubtedly in the patient's best medical interests to have a doctor who is confident that the treatment he is offering is the best for the patient. If the doctor does not believe this (and *a fortiori* if the trial is 'double blind'), the patient may become aware of his doctor's lack of confidence and consequently lose confidence in his treatment himself. This is an illustration of what a number of commentators identify as an inevitable conflict of loyalties intrinsic, in particular, in RCTs. (See eg A Schafer 'The Ethics of the Randomised Clinical Trial' (1982) 307 New Eng J Med 719.)

Even if such a conflict is not *inevitable* in RCTs, the possibility nevertheless exists. This being so, the argument is that in law a patient who is ill should as a matter of public policy be prevented from absolving the doctor from his duty to do his best for his patient.

B. THE INCOMPETENT PATIENT

1. Children

Can a proxy, who will usually be a parent, consent to therapeutic research on an incompetent child?

If we address the three issues which we have identified as significant, it goes without saying first of all that the consent of the proxy must be voluntarily given. A court would, of course, be vigilant to ensure that consent by, for example, a parent was not obtained by improper pressure. An example of this could be where a child would only receive otherwise available treatment *if* it was entered into a clinical trial. There may be circumstances where treatment is *only* available as part of a trial, ie when no accepted treatment currently exists. In such a case the offering of treatment only on these terms would not amount to unlawful pressure.

As regards the information which (now) the proxy and not the patient must be given, the doctor must make *at least* as full a disclosure as the law would require him to give to the competent patient. Arguably, the law would also require the doctor to disclose to the proxy that information which materially affects the proxy in his continued care of the child, for example the consequences for the proxy of the participation of the child in the trial or of the occurrence of a risk entailed in the trial *for the proxy.*

Finally, as regards the limits of the proxy's authority to consent, since we are considering *therapeutic* research these must fundamentally reflect the risk-benefit ratio of participation in the trial. The proxy must be satisfied that on a reasonable assessment of this ratio, it is in the best interests of the child to participate.

What about RCTs? Is there, however, a difference for participation in a trial which involves randomisation? *Prima facie* it would appear that randomisation would be legally acceptable because the proxy can be informed of what it involves. But, since randomisation entails a possible conflict of loyalties for the doctor it could be said that a proxy was not acting in the child's best interests in consenting to a child's participation in an RCT. Indeed, can it *ever* be in a child's best interests to waive the doctor's duty to do his best for his patient?

One further point is worth noting. Clearly as a matter of considerate decision-making by the proxy and good medical practice, the *assent* of the child should be sought and obtained when it can be meaningfully given. If the child refuses to assent, however, a court would not find that involvement of the child was unlawful providing the procedure was in the child's 'best interests'. (See *Guidelines for the Ethical Conduct of Medical Research Involving Children* (British Paediatric Association) 1992, ch 6.)

2. Adults

Any valid consent in the case of an incompetent adult would have to come from someone other than the patient. We have seen, however, that even in the context of treatment, without specific statutory authority the law does not empower anyone to consent as a proxy. You will recall (in Chapter 6) that the House of Lords in *Re F (a mental patient: sterilisation)* [1990] 2 AC 1 developed the doctrine of necessity so as to provide the legal basis for the treatment of incompetent adults. As a consequence, a doctor may treat such a patient provided that it is in the patient's best interests to do so. Does the approach in *Re F* apply to therapeutic research? The prevailing view, as the following commentator indicates, is that the analysis in *Re F* does apply to therapeutic research.

C Hodges 'Legal and Ethical Issues in Research in the United Kingdom: Children, the Elderly and the Mentally Incapacitated' (1992) 6 Pharmaceutical Medicine 309

Re F concerned treatment, not research. so a definitive legal statement in relation to research is, therefore, not available. Since the case concerned the sterilization of a mentally handicapped woman, it will immediately be seen that by defining the 'best interests' of the patient as to save life, or to ensure improvement, or to prevent deterioration in physical or mental health, all non-therapeutic research and possibly even some therapeutic research, such as giving a placebo, might be illegal if the same interpretation of the phrase 'best interests' were to be applied in research. The decision established what is referred to as a 'doctrine of necessity' for treatment without consent. The necessity is, or course. that of the individual patient rather than society, or any other individual. However, both the RCP [*Research Involving Patients* (1990) para 7.34] and MCR [*The Ethical Conduct of Research on the Mentally Incapacitated* (1991) para 7.2.2] consider that the 'best interests' principle should equally apply when the treatment in question is still in the research phase.

You will notice that Christopher Hodges refers to the MRC's Working Party Report on *Research on the Mentally Incapacitated* (1991) chaired by Mrs Renee Short. Paragraphs 7.2.2 and 7.2.4 offer the following analysis:

7.2.2 While the judgment in *Re F* concerned conventional medical treatment and not research, we agree with the conclusion of the RCP 1990 Report 'Research Involving Patients', that the principle enunciated should equally apply when the treatment in question is still in the research phase. An experimental medicinal procedure may be the only appropriate therapy and provided the relevant health professional acts with proper skill and care and in the best interests of the patient, neither liability for trespass nor negligence should arise…
7.2.4 We are clear that, provided the necessary safeguards are in place, the ethical grounds for including mentally incapacitated people in therapeutic research (and indeed for not denying them the opportunity to participate in research that offers the prospect of improving their health) are so great, that it would be contrary to accepted good practice to be deterred by the comparative lack of clarity surrounding the legal position. However, it may be prudent for doctors contemplating special categories of treatment of a serious and irreversible nature in a research context to consider whether it is appropriate to seek endorsement of their actions by the court, no doubt in consultation with the relevant ethics committee.

We agree in principle with the analysis suggested by Christopher Hodges and the MRC. We saw above that it is lawful for a proxy to consent to therapeutic research on a child. Obviously, the proxy must act in the best interests of the child and be satisfied that the risk-benefit ratio is in the child's favour. If it were unlawful to conduct therapeutic research on an incompetent adult, the adult would be in a worse position as a matter of law than a child. This is because any proposed therapeutic research though it carries risks, must, to be lawful, also carry an expected benefit. The adult would, consequently, be denied by law this chance of a benefit.

Therefore, in our view, a court would decide that the law is as follows: an incompetent adult may be the subject of therapeutic research where that research would be justified in the case of a competent adult (ie, in his 'best interests') provided that the researcher has satisfied an appropriately constituted LREC as to the scientific validity of the proposed research and the need for, and the ethical propriety of, such research. The European Convention on Human Rights and Biomedicine (November 1996) contains specific provisions dealing with research on incompetent patients whether children or adults. Article 17, para 1 provides as follows:

Article 17. (Protection of persons not able to consent to research)
1. Research on a person without the capacity to consent as stipulated in Article 5 may be undertaken only if all the following conditions are met:
    i   the conditions laid down in Article 16, sub-paragraphs i) to iv) are fulfilled;
    ii   the results of the research have the potential to produce real and direct benefit to his or her health;

iii   research of comparable effectiveness cannot be carried out on individuals capable of giving consent;

iv   the necessary authorisation provided for under Article 6 has been given specifically and in writing, and,

v   the person concerned does not object.

You will notice the references to arts 5 and 16. Article 5 is concerned with obtaining the 'free and informed consent' of a patient prior to an interventions. Article 6 is concerned with proxy consent for incompetent patients (see *supra*, ch 1). Article 16 provides protection for research subjects in general. It applies both to research on competent and incompetent individuals. It provides as follows:

Article 16. (Protection of persons undergoing research)
Research on a person may only be undertaken if all the following conditions are met:

i   there is no alternative of comparable effectiveness to research on humans;

ii   the risks which may be incurred by that person are not disproportionate to the potential benefits of the research;

iii   the research project has been approved by the competent body after independent examination of its scientific merit, including assessment of the importance of the aim of the research, and multidisciplinary review of its ethical acceptability;

iv   the persons undergoing research have been informed of their rights and the safeguards prescribed by law for their protection.

v   the necessary consent as provided for under Article 5 has been given expressly, specifically and is documented. Such consent may be freely withdrawn at any time.

Article 17, para 1, therefore, allows for therapeutic research on incompetent patients under the stipulated conditions which largely reflect the position in English law. Notice art 17(1)(ii) and (iii) in particular requiring the potential for 'real and direct benefit' to the individual's health and that the research could not be conducted on competent individuals as effectively. Thus, art 17 allows for research on a medical condition found in children or in incompetent adults, for example, Alzheimer's Disease, and which requires involvement of those individuals to test the particular treatment or procedure.

You will have noticed that the MRC's Working Party Report (*op cit*) suggests that it would be 'prudent' to obtain the court's approval where the intervention is of 'a serious and irreversible nature'. While such caution was understandable in the aftermath of *Re F*, subsequent decisions of the High Court have cast doubt on the need to involve the court where what is contemplated is therapeutic (see *supra*, ch 6). Although the cases do not specifically concern therapeutic *research*, the import is clear, namely that where it is proposed to *treat* the patient in his 'best interests' recourse to the court is not essential (see, for example, *Re H (mental patient)* (1992) 9 BMLR 71).

Non-therapeutic research

You will recall that here we are concerned with research where the researcher has only one intention, ie to obtain information through systematic inquiry so as to contribute to generalisable knowledge. There is no intention to treat the person who is the subject of the research.

There are two categories of persons upon whom non-therapeutic research may be carried out: patients and the healthy.

A. PATIENTS

We can perhaps deal shortly with patients. Ordinarily, a doctor's duty to care for his patient would preclude his engaging in non-therapeutic research on such a person. This is because it would ordinarily be difficult to show that it was in the best medical interests of the patient to be exposed to additional interventions which carry risks and which are not designed to aid in his treatment.

There may be, of course, circumstances in which a patient with a minor illness may volunteer to take part in non-therapeutic research. If the proposed research carries no demonstrable risk of harm to the patient nor will it affect deleteriously the patient's condition, then it may be that the patient may lawfully be party to non-therapeutic research. In our view, however, the evidence of absence of risk would have to be clear and compelling. In such a (rare) case the legal position of the patient will be the same as that of the healthy volunteer which we now turn to consider.

B. HEALTHY VOLUNTEERS

We noticed in the context of therapeutic research that there are some basic conditions to be met in any clinical trial. Equally, this is so in the conduct of non-therapeutic research. In addition to those points made earlier (see *supra*) which are relevant here also, the following conditions must also be observed:

(1) the doctor must obtain an appropriate medical history from the volunteer so as to ensure that the proposed procedure carries no increased risk in the light of that history;
(2) the doctor must obtain the permission of the volunteer to inform his family doctor that he is participating in a trial and should obtain from that doctor any relevant medical details about the volunteer;
(3) the doctor must satisfy himself that the volunteer is not participating in any other trial contemporaneously nor engaging in other conduct, eg an intention to drive home in certain circumstances, whereby the volunteer's health may be put at risk;
(4) the doctor must have available all appropriate medical equipment to meet any foreseeable eventuality arising out of the trial, eg in appropriate circumstances resuscitation equipment;
(5) the doctor must ensure that the volunteer is prepared to keep him informed of any changes in the volunteer's circumstances.

A failure to fulfil any of these obligations could well expose the doctor to liability in negligence if any harm ensues. Beyond these general points, as with therapeutic research, the central legal issue warranting analysis is consent. If a valid consent is not obtained then liability in battery or negligence may arise.

1. The competent volunteer

(a) Competence

As we have seen before, the common law looks to the understanding and maturity of an individual in determining competence. Just as with therapy, an adult would *prima facie* be presumed competent to volunteer for non-therapeutic research.

In the case of children, we have seen that s 8(1) of the Family Law Reform Act 1969 deems children between the ages of 16 and 18 to be competent to consent to treatment to the same extent as an adult. The Act has no application to non-therapeutic research since its wording is limited to 'surgical, medical or dental *treatment'* (our emphasis) (see *Re W (a minor) (medical treatment)* [1992] 4 All ER 627, (CA) at 635 per Lord Donaldson MR and at 649 per Nolan LJ). The capacity of a child under 18 to consent to non-therapeutic research is, therefore, governed by the common law.

As we saw earlier, it is our view that the approach of the House of Lords in *Gillick* is applicable to therapeutic research. In our view this is equally true of non-therapeutic research. A child (under the age of 18) who has the capacity to understand what is involved in the research may be able to give a valid consent. The capacity of a child will, therefore, depend upon his or her understanding and maturity.

As we saw in relation to therapeutic research, this is likely to be a relatively high standard of comprehension. Since non-therapeutic research lacks any potentially beneficial consequences for the child and may indeed carry a risk of harm, in our view the law would require an even greater level of comprehension for this type of research.

(b) Voluntariness

A court would analyse the voluntariness or otherwise of a healthy volunteer in accordance with the principles we have already seen in the context of therapeutic research, relying principally on the dictum of Lord Donaldson MR in *Freeman v Home Office (No 2)* (*supra*, ch 5). In short, it will be a matter of fact in every case. The matter which may be of primary concern is the possibility of exploitation of persons who may 'volunteer' for research because of some felt pressure. Pressure can come in a number of forms. There is the obvious case of financial inducements and the effect they may have on the financially disadvantaged (see *Local Research Ethics Committees* (HSG (91)5) paras 3.15–3.16: 'payment in cash or kind to volunteers should only be for expense, time and inconvenience reasonably incurred'. See also Royal College of Physician's Report, *supra*, paras 17.1–17.3.) The less obvious case, perhaps, is what some have called 'contextual duress' when, for example, a student 'volunteers' to participate in research at the 'invitation' of his teacher, or an employee at the behest of his employer, or a junior colleague at the behest of the leader of the research team, or any person who is a junior or subordinate member of a hierarchically structured group. As Professor Gerald Dworkin points out in 'Law and Medical Experimentation' (1987) 13 Monash ULR 189 at 204:

> It does not follow that financial inducements should destroy the voluntary nature of all responses, yet where students and out of work youths are offered significant sums of money to test new drugs, as happened in London recently, the nature of consents and inducements should be examined very carefully. In defining the use of such volunteers it was argued that there was nothing unethical in paying volunteers to test new drugs so long as they were fully informed of any possible risks; and a further justification was put forward that there was a non-fault compensation scheme in case anything went wrong. This does seem to miss the point: volunteers certainly can give informed consent to properly conducted research procedures, but even informed consent can be involuntary.

Particularly problematical is the position of prisoners who may have been told repeatedly that their sentence or conditions of imprisonment will not be affected but may none the less volunteer because (they think) their chances of parole, for example, may be improved.

In all such cases the law will begin with the premise that a competent adult is free to do what he wishes and must be assumed to have acted voluntarily if he participates. Thus, these particular examples and classes of person will not be treated any differently by the law. Professor Somerville weighs the arguments well concerning the use of prisoners in research in *Consent to Medical Care* (1980), pp 96–98:

> ...there is at least one commentator who believes that one is never, under any conditions, justified in using these persons as research subjects. Bronstein argues that the distinguishing and prohibitive element in the use of prisoners as subjects, is the involvement of the state and the necessary rights it has over the prisoners' bodies simply by virtue of the fact of imprisonment [AE Sabin, AJ Bronstein, WN Hubbard, 'The Military/The Prisoner', in 'Experiments and Research with Humans: Values in Conflict'. National Academy of Sciences,

Academy Forum, Washington, 1975, p 127, per Bronstein, at pp 130–5]. He makes the thought-provoking statement that '[i]t is not so much the actual, occasional abuse of captive human subjects, but the potential for abuse which concerns [him]'. Thus it is not necessary to show abuses to invalidate experimentation in prisons, because the 'potential for abuse' is sufficient to do this. It is important to consider these matters because it makes one realise that a discussion of 'informed' consent in relation to the use of prisoners as research subjects is not enough, as there may be a duty to not even request the prisoner's consent to participation in the experiment. Kilbrandon states this in a very effective way when he says that to put a man in prison is to deprive him of a large number of consents, therefore it is distasteful to confer on him a consent which is not for his own benefit [Lord Kilbrandon, 'Final Discussion', in Wolstenholme and O'Connor (eds), CIBA Foundation symposium, 'Ethics in Medical Progress: with special reference to transplantation' p 202 at 205].

An argument contrary to the above views advocating prohibition of medical experiments on prisoners or only allowing it under much more restrictive conditions than apply to the unconfined population, is that prisoners should not be deprived of any more rights that accrue to other members of society, than absolutely necessary. One such right is that of personal inviolability of both mind and body, any exceptions normally depending on consent. And thus the corollary, the right to consent and the right not to consent. For reasons quite apart from medical experimentation, for instance to give a legal right of action against brutality in prisons it may be important to retain for prisoners these rights to inviolability, and to consent, and not to consent. Therefore, in the context of medical treatment or research, the right to consent should not be abrogated for fear that the rights associated with it, that of inviolability and the right not to consent, will also be affected. Rather its exercise must be safeguarded. This is expressed by Ramsey in the following words: 'I am one who happens to believe that prisoners have not been and should not be drummed out of the human race. They ought, therefore, not to be excluded in principle from the community of risk-filled human consent to good purposes, even if the needed practical protections for them are so formidable as to prohibit the general use of prisoners in medical research.' [P Ramsey, 'The Ethics of a Cottage Industry in an Age of Community and Research Medicine' NEJM 284(13) 700 (1971) at 705.]

It may be that if research participation is seen as a privilege, it should not be allowed because distribution of this privilege can become a coercive tool in the hands of wardens and prison authorities, thus affecting the voluntariness of prisoners' consent. This is related to another reason for not allowing research on prisoners. It is that the attitude of prison staff towards prisoners often leaves much to be desired and may amount to coercion to consent, or even ignores, in all but theory, the necessity for free and informed consent. For instance, with respect to prisoner experimentation, a warden at Montana State Prison stated: 'we want our prison to be a living laboratory for the people of Montana... There should be no conflict in offering *our* physical and human resources [prisoners] to other disciplines...'

Further, some arguments put forward in support of prison experimentation rely on the *control factor* inherent in imprisonment, as an advantage justifying research on prisoners taking place. But these arguments themselves provide further arguments *against* using prisoners, because they raise serious doubts about the validity of the consent given. Examples of such reasoning are that it is beneficial for experimental purposes to be able to totally control the subjects, and the experimentation and the rewards it offers may themselves augment the effective power of the prison authorities over prisoners. Newman found a reason given to justify the use of prisoner subjects was the doubtful altruism that wardens, as public officials, were interested in promoting science and, perhaps more realistically if still not acceptable, in promoting a research programme which helps the training and education of prisoners [RW Newman. 'The Participation of Prisoners in Clinical Research', in Ladimer and Newman eds 'Clinical Investigation in Medicine: Legal Ethical and Moral Aspects' at 467]. Both these words, training and education, may be used in their genuine sense, but may also be euphemisms for establishing and justifying a more effective system of control of prisoners, without corresponding educative benefit to them. Thus the very advantage of using prisoners – their availability, the convenience they offer as subjects, the ease with which they can be controlled – are precisely the factors throwing doubt on the validity of their consent and weighing against their participation in medical research.

(c) Information

We set out all the relevant legal points relating to the duty to disclose when we considered therapeutic research (*supra*): that research is being carried out; that the volunteer may withdraw at any time without adverse consequences; the form of the research, eg that it is an RCT; the need for the disclosure of material risks and information; answering any questions truthfully. We would only add one point. In the context of research on healthy volunteers we have no doubt that the courts would adopt a *subjective test* of materiality which would require disclosure of all information which the particular volunteer would want to know.

Contrast the following decision of the Saskatchewan Court of Appeal.

Halushka v University of Saskatchewan (1965) 52 WWR 608 (Sask CA)

Hall JA: The appellants, Wyant and Merriman, were medical practitioners employed by the appellant, University of Saskatchewan....

The respondent, a student at the University of Saskatchewan, had attended summer school in 1961. On August 21, 1961, he went to the employment office to find a job. At the employment office he was advised that there were no jobs available but that he could earn $50 by being the subject of a test at the University Hospital. The respondent said that he was told the test would last a couple of hours and that it was a 'safe test and there was nothing to worry about'.

The respondent reported to the anaesthesia department at the University Hospital and there saw the appellant, Wyant. The conversation which ensued concerning the proposed test was related by the respondent as follows:

> Dr Wyant explained to me that a new drug was to be tried out on the Wednesday following. He told me that electrodes would be put in both my arms, legs and head and then he assured me that it was a perfectly safe test, it has been conducted many times before. He told me that I was not to eat anything on Wednesday morning that I was to report at approximately nine o'clock, then he said it would take about an hour to hook me up and the test itself would last approximately two hours, after the time I would be given fifty dollars, pardon me, I would be allowed to sleep first, fed and then given fifty dollars and driven home on the same day.

The appellant, Wyant, also told the respondent that an incision would be made in his left arm and that a catheter or tube would be inserted into the vein.

The respondent agreed to undergo the test and was asked by the appellant, Wyant, to sign a form of consent. This form, entered as Ex D1, reads as follows:

Intensive Care 460–57–2

Halushka, Walter
72756 Jan 2'40 MR.
Dr. Nanson

Consent for tests on volunteers

I, Walter Halushka, age 21 of 236 – 3rd Street Saskatoon hereby state that I have volunteered for tests upon my person for the purpose of study of

Heart & Blood Circulation Response under General Anaesthesia

The tests to be undertaken in connection with this study have been explained to me and I understand fully what is proposed to be done. I agree of my own free will to submit to these tests, and in consideration of the remuneration hereafter set forth, I do release the chief investigators, *Dr G M Wyant and J E Merriman* their associates, technicians, and each thereof, other personnel involved in these studies, the University Hospital Board, and the University of Saskatchewan from all responsibility and claims whatsoever, for any untoward effects or accidents due to or arising out of said tests, either directly or indirectly.

I understand that I shall receive a remuneration of $50.00 for each test...
Witness my hand and seal.

[Sgd.] WALTER HALUSHKA
[Sgd.] IRIS ZAECHTOWSKI (Witness)
Date: Aug 22/61

The respondent described the circumstances surrounding the signing of D1, saying:

> He then gave me a consent form, I skimmed through it and picked out the word 'accident' on the consent form and asked Doctor Wyant what accidents were referred to, and he

gave me an example of me falling down the stairs at home after the test and then trying to sue the University Hospital as a result. Being assured that any accident that would happen to me would be at home and not in the Hospital I signed the form.

The test contemplated was known as 'The Heart and Blood Circulation Response under General Anaesthesia', and was to be conducted jointly by the appellants, Wyant and Merriman, using a new anaesthetic agent known commercially as 'Fluoromar'. This agent had not been previously used or tested by the appellants in any way.

The respondent returned to the University Hospital on August 23, 1961, to undergo the test. The procedure followed was that which had been described to the respondent and expected by him, with the exception that the catheter, after being inserted in the vein in the respondent's arm, was advanced towards his heart. When the catheter reached the vicinity of the heart, the respondent felt some discomfort. The anaesthetic agent was then administered to him. The time was then 11:32 am. Eventually the catheter tip was advanced through the various heart chambers out into the pulmonary artery where it was positioned.

The appellants, Wyant and Merriman, intended to have the respondent reach medium depth of surgical anaesthesia. However, an endotracheal tube which had been inserted to assist the respondent in breathing caused some coughing. In the opinion of the appellant, Wyant, the coughing indicated that the respondent was in the upper half of a light anaesthesia – on the verge of waking up. At 12:16 pm, therefore, the concentration of the mixture of the anaesthetic was increased. The respondent then descended into deeper surgical anaesthesia.

At about 12:20 pm there were changes in the respondent's cardiac rhythm which suggested to the appellants, Wyant and Merriman, that the level of the anaesthetic was too deep. The amount of anaesthetic was then decreased, or lightened.

At 12:25 pm the respondent suffered a complete cardiac arrest.

The appellants, Wyant and Merriman, and their assistants took immediate steps to resuscitate the respondent's heart by manual massage. To reach the heart, an incision was made from the breastbone to the line of the arm-pit and two of the ribs were pulled apart. A vasopressor was administered as well as urea, a drug used to combat swelling of the brain. After one minute and 30 seconds the respondent's heart began to function again.

The respondent was unconscious for a period of four days. He remained in the University Hospital as a patient until discharged 10 days later. On the day before he was discharged, the respondent was given $50 by the appellant, Wyant. At that time the respondent asked the appellant, Wyant, if that was all he was going to get for all he went through. The appellant said that $50 was all that they had bargained for but that he could give a larger sum in return for a complete release executed by the respondent's mother or elder sister.

As a result of the experiment, the appellants concluded that as an anaesthetic agent 'Fluoromar' had too narrow a margin of safety and it was withdrawn from clinical use in the University Hospital.

The respondent brought action against the appellants, basing his claim for damages on two grounds, namely, trespass to the person and negligence....

The main issue before the jury concerning the respondent's claim of trespass to the person was that of consent....

It was on the basis of the ordinary physician-patient relationship that the learned trial judge charged the jury on the matter of consent. In dealing with this part of the case he said:

> In the circumstances of this case I will say that before signing such a document the plaintiff was entitled to a reasonably clear explanation of the proposed test and of the natural and expected results from it.

In my opinion, the duty imposed upon those engaged in medical research, as were the appellants, Wyant and Merriman, to those who offer themselves as subjects for experimentation, as the respondent did here, is at least as great as, if not greater than, the duty owed by the ordinary physician or surgeon to his patient. There can be no exceptions to the ordinary requirements of disclosure in the case of research as there may well be in ordinary medical practice. The researcher does not have to balance the probable effect of lack of treatment against the risk involved in the treatment itself. The example of risks being properly hidden from a patient when it is important that he should not worry can have no application in the field of research. The subject of medical experimentation is entitled to full and frank disclosure of all the facts, probabilities and opinions which *a reasonable man* (our emphasis) might be expected to consider before giving his consent.... The respondent was not informed that the catheter would be advanced to and through his heart but was admittedly given to understand that it would be merely inserted in the vein in his arm. While it may be correct to say that the advancement of the catheter to the heart was not in itself dangerous and did not cause or contribute to the cause of the cardiac arrest, it was a circumstance which, if known, might very well have prompted the respondent to withhold his consent. The undisclosed or

misrepresented facts need not concern matters which directly cause the ultimate damage if
they are of a nature which might influence the judgment upon which the consent is based.

The court dismissed the appeal.

In our view, Hall JA's reference to the 'reasonable man' standard does not go
far enough. English law would insist upon a subjective standard (see the
subsequent case in Canada of *Weiss v Solomon* (1989) 48 CCLT 280 (Qu Sup Ct)
requiring the 'highest possible' standard of disclosure; discussed by B Freedman
and K Glass (1990) 18 Law, Medicine and Health Care 395).

(d) Limits

We are considering here the limits imposed by law to that which a healthy
volunteer may consent, such that any consent given thereafter is invalid.

A competent person may, of course, agree to expose himself to a variety of
risks. Indeed, society approves of this, eg by encouraging sport. But the example
of sport is informative, for boxing matches which are inevitably risky encounters
may lawfully be engaged in; prize fights, however, are unlawful despite the
apparent consent of the participants. So it is with non-therapeutic research. A
person *can* lawfully take some risks with his body by volunteering for non-
therapeutic research but the law would impose certain limits as a matter of public
policy. Nicholson (ed) (*op cit*) sets out in table form risk equivalents, ie an 'attempt
to find equivalence between different scales of risks and the statistical probabilities
of certain adverse events' (p 119).

Table 5.6 Risk equivalents

British definition	Negligible	Minimal	More than minimal
American definition	Minimal	Minor increase over minimal	Greater than minor increase over minimal
Risk of death	less than 1 per million	1 to 100 per million	Greater than 100 per million
Risk of major complication	less than 10 per million	10 to 100 million	Greater than 1000 per million
Risk of minor complication	less than 1 per thousand	1 to 100 thousand	Greater than 100 per thousand

Referring to this table he states that (p 120):

...the overall risks of non-therapeutic research... would lie in the category 'minor increase
over minimal' for both major and minor complications. It seems perfectly acceptable to
subject adults, who have given informed consent, to such a level of risk.

The American term 'minimal risk' equivalent to the British term 'negligible risk'
is defined in the HHS Regulations on the Protection of Human Research Subjects
in 1990 as (para 46.102 (g)):

(g) 'Minimal risk' means that the risks of harm anticipated in the proposed research are not
greater, considering probability and magnitude, than those ordinarily encountered in daily
life or during the performance of routine physical or psychological examinations or tests.

We agree that the limit suggested by the relevant guidelines and Nicholson (ed) is probably that which a court would endorse. The implication of such a view is, of course, that any research on a healthy volunteer which on the basis of existing knowledge properly analysed poses a risk which is more than a 'minor increase over minimal' would in law amount to a battery and even, possibly, a crime in appropriate circumstances.

2. The incompetent volunteer

Here, we are considering the circumstances under which an incompetent individual may lawfully be volunteered for non-therapeutic research.

(a) Children

There are two issues which need to be considered: who, if anyone, can lawfully volunteer a child for non-therapeutic research and if anyone can, what are the limits to what the child can be volunteered for? We will consider these issues together.

In a seminal article in 1978, Professor Gerald Dworkin explained the background.

G Dworkin 'Legality of Consent to Nontherapeutic Medical Research on Infants and Young Children' (1978) 53 Archives of Disease in Childhood 443

> For some years the view of lawyers advising the medical profession has been that such... research is unlawful. This is a view expressed. for example, by Speller, [Speller, S R (1971) *Law Relating to Hospitals and Kindred Institutions*, 5th ed. pp 144–145. H K Lewis, London.] the Medical Research Council, [Medical Research Council (1964). Responsibility in investigations on human subjects, *British Medical Journal*, 2, 178–180.] the Medical Protection Society, [Leahy Taylor, J (1975). Ethical and legal aspects of non-therapeutic clinical investigation, *Medico-Legal Journal*, 43, 53–68.] the Medical Defence Union, [Pratt, H (1977). Research on infants, *Lancet*, 1, 699; 1052.] Sir Harvey Druitt (a former Treasury Solicitor), [Curran, W J and Beecher, H K (1969), Experimentation in children; a reexamination of legal and ethical principles, *Journal of the American Medical Association*, 210, 77–83.] Sir George Godber (a former Chief Medical Officer to the Department of Health and Social Security (DHSS)) [Godber, G (1974). Discussion. Symposium on Constraints on the Advance of Medicine, *Proceedings of the Royal Society of Medicine*, 67, 1311.] and to the DHSS itself. The authority for this view rests on general legal principle rather than on any specific rule or ruling. Thus, the general philosophy of the law is that parents are under a duty to look after a child's interests and so any nontherapeutic procedures cannot be justified.

He ended his article with the following bold conclusion (at p 445):

> It is submitted that it is quite proper for those medical bodies which give guidance to the profession to change their present uncertain statements as to the law and replace them with a much clearer guide to the effect that 'although there is as yet no clear legal authority, it appears that it is lawful to conduct nontherapeutic research procedures on infants and young children provided the following requirements are strictly observed:
> (a) the design, details. and ethical criteria of the research are approved by the appropriate ethical committee;
> (b) there is voluntary, informed, parental consent; and
> (c) there is no, or a minimal, risk'.

By 1987, when Professor Dworkin wrote his paper 'Law and Medical Experimentation' (1987) 13 Monash ULR 189, there had grown up a considerable volume of scholarship which tended to support his previous view. For example, we have referred on several occasions to the Working Group set up by the Institute of Medical Ethics whose report was published in 1986 entitled *Medical Research with Children*. In Chapter 5 on 'Risks and Benefits in Research on Children', Nicholson (ed) writes (p 120):

After a long debate. the working group agreed unanimously, however, that it was not acceptable to subject children, for whom only a proxy consent was available, to even a minor increase over minimal risk in non-therapeutic research. In other words, non-therapeutic research on children, regardless of possible benefits, can only be undertaken ethically if the risks of the procedures involved are in the 'minimal' category.

Furthermore, the climate of opinion and the popular understanding of what was involved had changed. Still Professor Dworkin (*supra*) was cautious in analysing the law (pp 198–203):

There is a widespread agreement that it is ethical, in some circumstances, to carry out non-therapeutic research with children. The fourth International Summit Conference on Bioethics, held in Canada in April 1987, summarised the generally accepted controlling conditions: 'The specific project must be approved by a research ethics committee; all needed knowledge must have been obtained through research with adults or animals; there must be no valid alternative to the use of children in the research; a valid proxy consent (by family, guardians, ombudsman, those with power of attorney or others) must have been obtained for each research subject; and to the extent possible, the child should have given assent.' Is this ethical statement, however, reflected in the law?

The 'best interests' of the child approach
For a long time, in England, the advice given to the medical profession was that non-therapeutic research upon young children was unlawful. The Medical Research Council stated that '…in the strict view of the law parents and guardians of minors cannot give consent on their behalf to any procedures which are of no particular benefit to them and which may carry some risk of harm'. The authority for all this rested on general legal principle, rather than on any specific rule or ruling. Since the general philosophy of the law is that parents and guardians are under a duty to look after a child's interests, it seems to follow that non-therapeutic procedures cannot be justified.

Thus, in the well known case of *Wellesley v Duke of Beaufort* [(1827) 2 Russ 1] Lord Eldon, when exercising the Crown's power as *parens patriae*, showed that: 'it has always been the principle of this Court not to risk the incurring of damage to children… which it cannot repair, but rather to prevent the damage being done'. The American Supreme Court, admittedly in a different context, expressed the view that:

parents may be free to become martyrs themselves. But it does not follow [that] they are free, in identical circumstances, to make martyrs of their children before they have reached the age of full and legal discretion when they can make that choice for themselves. [*Prince v Massachusetts* (1944) 321 US 158 at 170.]

Recent developments in the law relating to sterilisation emphasise the courts' concern to safeguard the 'best interests' of incompetent subjects, although the extent to which courts should go in giving effect to those interests has varied in different jurisdictions. Thus, the Supreme Court of Canada refused to sanction a 'non-therapeutic' sterilisation of a mentally retarded girl even though it was said to be in her best interests, because it felt that the legislature was better equipped to decide such an important policy matter [*Re Eve* (1986) 31 DLR (4th) 1] whereas the House of Lords, scorning the value of the therapeutic/non-therapeutic distinction in this context, took a more robust view of its role and authorised the sterilisation of a 17 year old girl 'in her best interests'. [*Re B (a minor)* [1987] 2 All ER 206.] It would not have acted on a lower criterion than the best interests of the child; and other dicta also emphasise the parental duty to apply this standard. [*Gillick v West Norfolk and Wisbech AHA* [1985] 3 All ER 432, per Lord Templeman.]

Thus, there is at least an arguable case in favour of the view that proxy consent cannot be given for non-therapeutic research. But a total ban would be Draconian and certainly out of line with national and international ethical codes. Accordingly, it becomes necessary to look for an alternative view of the law.

Alternative views

(a) Distorting the concept of 'therapy'
Some of the views advanced have been unprepossessing. One extreme approach turned on the therapeutic/non-therapeutic distinction. If the concept of 'therapeutic' could be widened, then the scope for proxy consent would be increased. For example, the World Health Organisation defines 'health' as a state of complete physical, mental and *social* well-being

and not merely the absence of disease or infirmity. Accordingly, it could be argued that carefully considered proxy consents for clinical research are exercises in social responsibility which could benefit the future well-being of the volunteered subject since one can reasonably expect a child in later life to identify with the objects of the research. This smacks very much of the 'ends justifying the means', and is not attractive as a legal argument. Yet similar semantic arguments have been upheld.

For example, the early kidney transplantations could only be effected between very close relatives and American courts were asked to consider the legality of such transplantations from infant donors to twin donees, in cases where the ages of the sets of twins ranged from 14 to 19. Evidence was advanced that each donor twin and the parents had been fully informed of the nature of the operation and had given voluntary informed consents and psychiatrists testified that if the operations were not performed and the sick twins were to die, the healthy potential donor twins could suffer 'grave emotional impact' for the remainder of their lives. The operations were accordingly adjudged 'therapeutic': they were necessary for the continued good health and future well-being of, and conferred benefits upon, the donors as well as upon the donees.

Understandably, there are many who view such artificial attempts to distort descriptive terminology with distaste. For example, one Canadian court which was looking for a 'therapeutic' reason for ordering a hysterectomy to be performed on a seriously retarded child, found that reason in the child's alleged phobic aversion to blood which, it was feared, would seriously affect her when her menstrual periods began. Accordingly, sterilisation was authorised. The Supreme Court of Canada stated that whilst sterilisation may, on occasion, be necessary as an adjunct to treatment of a serious malady, there was no room for subterfuge and [that] that decision was, at best, dangerously close to the limits of the permissible. [*Re Eve supra*, commenting on *Re K and Public Trustee* (1985) 19 DLR (4th) 255 (BC CA).]

(b) The concept of 'substituted judgment'
Another concept which is creeping into American case-law in contrast to the traditional 'best interests' approach to proxy consent is that of 'substituted judgment'. The proxy, or court, does not attempt to decide what is in the 'best interests' of the patient, but rather what decision would be made by the individual if he were competent. The court 'dons the mental mantle of the incompetent and substitutes itself as nearly as possible for the individual in the decision-making process'. [*Superintendent of Belchertown State School v Saikewicz* (1977) 370 NE 2d 417.] It is one of those strange doctrines which was used in England in the early nineteenth century in connection with the administration of the estates of incompetent persons, [*Ex p Whitbread* (1816) 2 Mer 99] forgotten, and then rediscovered recently by American courts. It has been raised in cases involving incompetent persons to help establish whether, for example, to consent to the withdrawal of life support systems or to certain unusual or controversial types of medical treatment, such as shock therapy or psychosurgery.

It is a controversial concept, not the least because of the inherent difficulties of attempting to assess what an incompetent patient would have decided were he competent, whether that assessment should be subjective or objective and, if objective, how it can really differ from a 'best interests' approach. No court has yet been called upon to authorise its use in connection with clinical research. although it was raised in *Kaimowitz v Michigan Dept of Mental Health* [(1973) 42 USLW 2063] where it was held, understandably, that no proxy consent could be given for experimental psychosurgery. It is unlikely to be of much help in the current debate.

(c) The 'not against the interests of the child' approach
The most likely approach is to reconsider more carefully the emphasis which the legislature and the courts understandably place upon the need for proxies only to act in the best interests of the child or other incompetent person.

Most of these statements have been made in contexts quite different to those of non-therapeutic clinical research. Although much welfare legislature does stress that the welfare of a child is 'paramount', other provisions refer to the welfare of a child being the *first* consideration. 'First consideration', of course, suggests that there are other considerations which can be balanced by a parent against the best interests of the child, and indeed override it. And where a court has to carry out these tasks it usually has to act as a 'judicial reasonable parent'.

The balancing of various interests can best be seen in ward of court cases. For example, in *Re X (a Minor)* [[1975] 1 All ER 697] the defendants proposed to publish a book describing the depraved behaviour of the deceased father of a 14 year old girl. It was accepted that if she were to read the book or hear about it from others, it would be *psychologically* grossly damaging to her. The Court of Appeal, in exercising its wardship jurisdiction, was not prepared to allow the interests of the child to prevail over the wider interest of freedom of publication. It is not correct to say 'that in every case where a minor's interests are involved, those interests are always paramount and must prevail... The court is required to do a difficult balancing act'. Here the court found the scale tipped heavily in favour of publication and against the minor.

Perhaps the most relevant analogy, however, concerns the power to take blood tests from children in paternity actions. Here, the conflict is between the interests of the child and that of doing justice. In 1970 the House of Lords considered a case [*S v S* [1970] 3 All ER 107] where an official guardian had objected to a blood test on a child in paternity proceedings on the ground that this intrusive procedure was not for the child's benefit. This argument was not accepted by the court, and statements abound in the judgments that the benefit of the child is not always an adequate criterion. Lord Reid analysed the situation clearly: first, he proclaimed the principle of physical integrity as: 'There is no doubt that a person of full age and capacity cannot be ordered to undergo a blood test against his will.... The real reason is that English law goes to great lengths to protect a person of full age and capacity from interference with his personal liberty.' Secondly, he struck a blow against one modern theory of children's rights by denying them an absolute right to physical integrity as against their parents: 'But the position is very different with regard to young children. It is a legal wrong to use constraint on an adult beyond what is authorised by statute or ancient common law powers connected with crime and the like. But it is not and could not be a legal wrong for a parent or person authorised by him to use constraint to his young child provided it is not cruel or excessive.' Thirdly, such a power goes beyond simple domestic situations such as chastisement: 'It seems to me to be impossible to deny that a parent can lawfully require that his young child should submit to a blood test. And if a parent can require that, why not the court?' And fourthly, a move away from the 'best interests' approach:

> Surely a reasonable parent would have some regard to the general public interest and would not refuse a blood test unless he thought that would clearly be against the interests of the child?... I would hold that the court ought to permit a blood test of a young child to be taken unless satisfied that this would be against the child's interest.

Thus, there seems to be strong authority for saying that in some cases the 'best interests of the child' approach can give way to a rule that a parent should not do anything 'clearly against the interests' of the child. This certainly makes sense. In real life, reasonable parents cannot, and should not, always opt for that activity which presents the least physical risk to the child. Children must be allowed to run risks: climbing trees, riding bicycles, playing 'rough' sports, where the statistical risks may far outweigh anything involved in properly conducted clinical research. Medical procedures involving slight risks, for example vaccinations, occur daily where the benefit may be primarily for other children and the community. Thus, a reasonable and socially responsible parent might think that there was merit in taking the social interest into account and contributing to medical research, provided always that the risk to the child was 'minimal'.

This view of the law accords with the ethical codes and is now being acted upon by the medical profession. Unfortunately, however, the law is not clear beyond all reasonable doubt. A blind development of the 'best interests' approach could box the law into an inflexible position. This appears to have happened in South Australia. The *Consent to Medical and Dental Procedures Act* 1985, which was passed presumably to clarify the law relating to teenage girls receiving contraceptive help from doctors, follows the *Gillick* line providing that a minor under 16 has full capacity to consent to medical procedures if two practitioners are of the opinion first, that the minor is capable of understanding the nature and consequences of the procedure; and secondly, that 'the procedure is in the best interests of the health *and* well-being of the minor'. It also provides for parental proxy consent, which presumably must be exercised subject to similar restraints. This would seem to authorise a 'medical procedure', which is defined as 'any procedure carried out by, or pursuant to directions given by, a medical practitioner' [section 4] only if it complies with the best interests rule; in which case it would be difficult to argue that the scope for non-therapeutic research can be wider. Does that mean that, inadvertently, all clinical research on children under 16 has been ruled out?

There seems to be a strong case for general legislative consideration, and clarification, of the power to give proxy consent for the purposes of research on children.

You will notice that Professor Dworkin in the penultimate paragraph of his paper refers to the 'ethical codes' and the responses of the medical profession. In its 1992 *Guidelines for the Ethical Conduct of Medical Research Involving Children* (at p 4) the British Paediatric Association makes the case for non-therapeutic research on children but limits it to situations where the child is not exposed to more than a minimal risk.

Medical research involving children is an important means of promoting child health and wellbeing. Such research includes systematic investigation into normal childhood development and the aetiology of disease, as well as careful scrutiny of the means of promoting health and of diagnosing, assessing and treating disease. It is also important to validate in children the beneficial results of research conducted in adults.

Research with children is worthwhile, if each project:

– has an identifiable prospect of benefit to children;
– is well designed and well conducted;
– does not simply duplicate earlier work;
– is not undertaken primarily for financial or professional advantage;
– involves a statistically appropriate number of subjects;
– and eventually is to be properly reported...

Ultimately, the BPA concludes (at p 9):

It would be unethical to submit child subjects to more than minimal risk when the procedure offers no benefit to them, or only a slight or very uncertain one.

This view is reflected in the Guidelines published by the Royal College of Physicians (*Guidelines on the Practice of Ethics Committees in Medical Research Involving Human Subjects* (1996) para 8.7) and the Medical Research Council (*The Ethical Conduct of Research on Children* (1991)).

(b) Adults

The first criterion which must be satisfied in law is that there is a real and justified need for research on *incompetent* adults, ie that the knowledge sought may not be discovered from research on competent consenting adults. This is only a particular illustration of the general legal principle that the law seeks to protect the vulnerable. Satisfying this criterion by no means implies that it is lawful thereafter to carry out non-therapeutic research. Indeed, it would appear that such research cannot lawfully be carried out. There is no one who, in law, can authorise it as a proxy. Even the court if it were to have a *parens patriae* power could not authorise such research since the power exists specifically for cases where 'some care should be thrown round [the ward]' (*Wellesley v Duke of Beaufort* (1827) 38 ER 236 at 243). Also, of course, the approach of the House of Lords in *Re F* would not assist since non-therapeutic research could not be said to be in the '*best* interests' of the incompetent adult. If, however, the law does not permit any non-therapeutic research on an incompetent adult, the curious situation would arise that such research may be permissible in the case of children but not in the case of adults. This apparent anomaly could be explained by noticing that in the case of children the parent can act as the protector of the child's interests whereas no such person exists in the case of the adult.

Whatever the legal position, it is undoubtedly the case that there has been a shift in thinking about the ethics of non-therapeutic research on the incompetent adult.

MRC *The Ethical Conduct of Research on the Mentally Incapacitated* (1991)

6.3 Non-therapeutic research

6.3.1 Because it might infringe the rights of a group which society should take particular care to protect, the participation of people who cannot consent in non-therapeutic research raises more complex ethical issues. We do not seek to argue that a mentally incapacitated person's participation in non-therapeutic research is directly in his interests. But we recognise that there are circumstances in which it is important to gain knowledge which may be of benefit to mentally incapacitated people in general and which can only be acquired as a result of research which involves those who are unable to consent.

6.3.2 We therefore believe that there is a strong case for including those unable to consent in such research, but it is essential that the safeguards listed at 6.1.3 are observed, and that those included are placed at no more than negligible risk of harm.

6.3.3 The degree of risk involved in a project should be given particularly careful scrutiny by the LREC when mentally incapacitated people are to be included. There have been various attempts to describe and define degrees of risk. We use the term negligible risk to mean that the risks of harm anticipated in the proposed research are not greater, considering the probability and magnitude of physiological or psychological harm or discomfort, than those ordinarily encountered in daily life or during the performance of routine physical or psychological examination or tests. Examples of procedures involving negligible risk would include the observation of behaviour, non-invasive physiological monitoring, physical examinations, changes in diet and obtaining blood and urine specimens...

6.3.4 We are clear that participation in such research of an individual unable to consent can only be ethical if a relative, friend or person acceptable to the LREC and not directly involved in the research agrees that participation would place that individual at no more than negligible risk of harm and is therefore not against that individual's interests.

Paragraph 6.3.2 refers back to para 6.1.3. This states:

6.1.3 At the same time, there is agreement on the need for strict safeguards for such research. In particular:
– those unable to consent should take part in research only if it relates to their condition and if the relevant knowledge could not be gained by research in persons able to consent
– all projects must be approved by the appropriate LRECs
– the inclusion of an individual unable to consent should be subject to the agreement of an informed, independent person acceptable to the LREC that that individual's welfare and interests have been properly safeguarded
– those included in the research do not object or appear to object in either words or action.

(See also Royal College of Physicians, *op cit* paras 8.9–8.17.)

The current law, however, is probably more restrictive in its approach, given the law's commitment to the criterion of 'best interests'. Nevertheless, both the European Convention on Human Rights and Biomedicine (1996) and the English Law Commission (1995) contemplate research of incompetent patients and others in specified circumstances.

Article 17, para 2 of the Convention provides as follows:

17(2) Exceptionally and under protective conditions prescribed by law, where the research has not the potential to produce results of direct benefit to the health of the person concerned, such research may be authorised subject to the conditions laid down in paragraph 1, sub-paragraphs i), iii), iv) and v) above, and to the following additional conditions:
  i. the research has the aim of contributing, through significant improvement in the scientific understanding of the individual's condition, disease or disorder, to the ultimate attainment of results capable of conferring benefit to the person concerned or to other persons in the same age, category or afflicted with the same disease or disorder or having the same condition.
  ii. the research entails only minimal risk and minimal burden for the individual concerned.

You will recall earlier (*supra*) the requirements of para 1 concerned with *therapeutic* research and incompetent individuals. Paragraph 2 disapplies the need for there to be 'potential to produce real and direct benefit' to the health of the individual and substitutes these two stringent conditions. Notice the research must have the aim of producing 'significant' scientific advance into a condition, disorder etc of the individual and, if not capable of benefiting him, would be capable of benefiting like individuals in the future. Thus, this does not licence the involvement of incompetent health 'volunteers'. Notice also the limited risk to which the individual may be exposed – 'minimal work' and 'minimal burden'.

In its Report, *Mental Incapacity* (No 231 1995), the Law Commission put the case for non-therapeutic research on incompetent adults and proposed a statutory scheme providing protection to individuals undergoing such research.

Law Commission '*Mental Incapacity*' (Report No 231 1995)

6.31 We suggested in our consultation paper (Consultation Paper No 129, para 6.28) that the balance of expert opinion favours the participation of people unable to consent in even non-therapeutic research projects, subject to strict criteria. The majority of our consultees argued that there is an ethical case for such participation. This case turns on the desirability of eradicating painful and distressing disabilities, where progress can be achieved without harming research subjects. The wide range of guidance and expert commentary on this matter shows a striking degree of consensus over the factors which make non-therapeutic research ethical (see, eg, the Royal College of Physicians, 'Research Involving Patients' (1990) paras 7.41 and 7.65), and we remarked a similar consensus in the responses submitted to us on consultation. In summary, the consensus appears to be that non-therapeutic research involving participants who cannot consent is justifiable where (1) the research relates to the condition from which the participant suffers, (2) the same knowledge cannot be gained from research limited to those capable of consenting, and (3) the procedures involve minimal risk and invasiveness. The recommendations which follow are intended to resolve the unacceptable anomaly that projects of this type, assessed by those with appropriate scientific and ethical expertise as being important and meritorious, in fact involve actionable unlawful conduct by the researchers. At the same time, our recommendations will place necessary protections for the participant without capacity on a statutory footing.

We recommend that research which is unlikely to benefit a participant, or whose benefit is likely to be long delayed, should be lawful in relation to a person without capacity to consent if (1) the research is into an incapacitating condition with which the participant is or may be affected and (2) certain statutory procedures are complied with. (See paras 6.33–6.37), (Draft Bill, clause 11(1).)

6.32 Special considerations may apply in relation to the testing of medicinal products. The UK has implemented (The Medicines (Applications for Grant of Product Licences – Products for Human Use) Regulations 1993 (SI 1993 No 2538) a European Directive on the licensing and testing of medicinal products. The Directive requires compliance with "good clinical practice" (Commission Directive 91/507/EEC (OJ L 270, 26.9.91, p 32) Annex, Part IV, para 1.1). In 1991 the European Commission issued guidelines on "Good Clinical Practice for Trials on Medicinal Products in the European Community", one of the guidelines being that "consent must always be given by the signature of the subject in a non-therapeutic study". (Commission of the European Communities EC 43 1990–91, para 1.14.) If "good clinical practice" in the 1991 directive means good clinical practice as defined in the 1991 guidelines, then the directive forbids any non-therapeutic product research involving a participant without capacity to consent. One leading text book on medical law concludes that the meaning of "good clinical practice" in the directive is "a matter of conjecture". (I Kennedy and A Grubb, *Medical Law:* Text with Materials (2nd ed 1994) p 1048.) Our own view is that it is not restricted to those matters set out in the 1991 guidelines and we understand that the Department of Health shares this view. In relation to those participants who lack capacity, our recommendations are designed to put good clinical practice on a proper legal footing.

A Mental Incapacity Research Committee
6.33 The Department of Health has instructed District Health Authorities to set up Local Research Ethics Committees (LRECs) "to advise NHS bodies on the ethical acceptability of research proposals involving human subjects" (NHS Management Executive HSG (91)5, which has the status of Department of Health guidelines). LRECs have no legal standing, a decision by a LREC does not make a researcher's actions lawful, and statute cannot enable a non-statutory body to achieve such an end. In the consultation paper (Construction Paper No 129, para 6.29) we suggested that a judicial body should have power to make a declaration that proposed research involving persons without capacity would be lawful. Courts and the adversarial process, however, are not well adapted to cases where there are no opposing parties to present evidence. Ordinary judges will have no relevant scientific expertise. Instead, therefore, we recommend that a new statutory committee should be established. This will supplement the "extra-legal" checks and balances which already exist, avoiding duplication of valuable time and effort.

We recommend that there should be a statutory committee to be known as the Mental Incapacity Research Committee. (Draft Bill, clause 11(2).)

6.34 A non-therapeutic research procedure should only be lawful in relation to a person who is without capacity to consent if the new Mental Incapacity Research Committee approves the research. Although most research which would otherwise be unlawful will be "medical" in the broadest sense, we do not suggest that the remit of the committee should be expressly limited to medical research. The criteria to be applied by the committee should be set out in statute. They all refer to the one particular issue of participants without capacity. Wider scientific questions will still be investigated by the relevant funding bodies. If NHS patients are involved, then the ethical advice of the LREC will be required before the Department of Health guidance will be satisfied.

We recommend **that the committee may approve proposed research if satisfied:**

(1) that it is desirable to provide knowledge of the causes or treatment of, or of the care of people affected by, the incapacitating condition with which any participant is or may be affected,

(2) that the object of the research cannot be effectively achieved without the participation of persons who are or may be without capacity to consent, and

(3) that the research will not expose a participant to more than negligible risk, will not be unduly invasive or restrictive of a participant and will not unduly interfere with a participant's freedom of action or privacy. (Draft Bill, clause 11(3).)

6.35 The draft Bill makes provision for the composition and procedures of the committee (Draft Bill, Sch 2).

Protection for the individual participant

6.36 It is not realistic or practicable for the individual participation of a person without capacity in a particular project to be referred to the special statutory committee for approval. The committee's role is to approve the research protocol, and we anticipate this involving documentary submissions in most cases. There is, however, a need for a separate and individualised independent check to confirm whether any particular proposed participant should indeed be brought into the project. Our recommendations therefore involve a two-stage process. By way of example, researchers obtain the committee's approval to a project which envisages tests on those with advanced Alzheimer's Disease. The researchers should not then be under the impression that this approval means they may involve in their project all the residents of a particular nursing home who have been diagnosed as suffering from Alzheimer's Disease without the need for any further permission. They must approach each of these proposed participants as an individual. They must ask whether this particular person does indeed have the capacity to consent to what is proposed. It may be that an explanation in simpler or more appropriate terms would be quite comprehensible to the person, especially if given by a person familiar to him or her. If, however, it appears that the proposed participant is without capacity to consent to what is proposed then an independent check is required, and we describe the nature of this check below.

6.37 In most cases the appropriate person to carry out an independent check will be a registered medical practitioner who is not involved in the research project. This need not be an independent doctor appointed to consider such matters by the Secretary of State (as recommended in relation to "second opinion category" treatments) (see paras 6.7–6.8). The important point is simply that this doctor should not be involved with the proposed research. The doctor who knows the person best, by virtue of having responsibility for his or her general medical care, will often be the best candidate. An attorney with express authorisation from a donor should, however, be able to consent on the donor's behalf. Similarly, a court-appointed manager may have express authority to give such consent. In some cases the court itself may have made it clear whether the person concerned may participate in non-therapeutic research. In none of these situations need the "second opinion" doctor be involved. There will also be some rare cases where the research protocol does not contemplate any direct contact between researcher and participant. These might involve covert observation or photographing, or the inspection of written records. In such cases, the broad ethical issues still have to be weighed by the committee but there is no purpose in anyone else looking at individual circumstances. The committee should therefore have the power to designate a project as one which does not involve direct contact with participants, with no second-stage check then required.

We recommend **that, in addition to the approval of the Mental Incapacity Research Committee, non-therapeutic research in relation to a person without capacity should require either:**

(1) court approval,

(2) the consent of an attorney or manager,

(3) a certificate from a doctor not involved in the research that the participation of the person is appropriate, or

(4) designation of the research as not involving direct contact. (Draft Bill, clause 11(1)(c) and (4).)

6.38 Where the court, an attorney, a manager or an independent doctor is considering the question of a particular individual participating in a project then regard should be had to the factors in the best interests checklist (Draft Bill, clause 11(5) and clause 3(2)).

6.39 In accordance with the recommendations we have made elsewhere in this report, there should be a clear prohibition against anything being done to a research participant if he or she objects to what is being done. Equally, in the event that a person has made an effective advance refusal to participate in a non-therapeutic research project then no approval of the committee or third party's confirmation would have any effect (Draft Bill, clause 11(6)).

In its Green Paper, *Who Decides*? (Cm 3803, 1997), the Lord Chancellor's Department remained open to permitting non-therapeutic research on incompetent adults subject to safeguards (paras 5.35–5.39) but doubted the need for the Mental Incapacity Research Committee as a necessary protection over and above the existing system of LRECs and MRECs (para 5.41). The Government has now decided not to bring forward legislation dealing with research on incompetent adults: *Making Decisions* (Cm 4465), LCD 1999, para 12.

You will notice reference in the Law Commission's Report (para 6.32) to the European GCP Guidelines. We referred to these earlier (*supra*). While para 1.13 permitted in limited circumstances *therapeutic* research on the incompetent if certain safeguards are observed, para 1.14 provided:

> 1.14 Consent must always be given by the signature of the subject in a non-therapeutic study, ie when there is no direct clinical benefit to the subject.

It could not be clearer from this paragraph that the European Guidelines prohibited non-therapeutic research on incompetent adults. We saw earlier the discussion about whether the Medicines (Applications for Grant of Product Licences – Products for Human Use) Regulations 1993, (SI 1993 No 2538) had incorporated by reference the EC GCP Guidelines and the subsequent ICH Guideline which came into effect in January 1997.

Importantly, the ICH *Guidelines for Good Clinical Practice* (1996) do not contain an absolute prohibition on non-therapeutic research on incompetent subjects. Paragraph 4.8.13 sets out the usual position of the need for written informed consent:

> 4.8.13 Except as described in 4.8.14, a non-therapeutic trial (ie a trial in which there is no anticipated direct clinical benefit to the subject), should be conducted in subjects who personally give consent and sign and date the written informed consent form.

However, para 4.8.14 provides for an exception:

> 4.8.14 Non-therapeutic trials may be conducted in subjects with consent of a legally acceptable representative provided the following conditions are fulfilled:
> (a) The objectives of the trial can not be met by means of a trial in subjects who can give informed consent personally.
> (b) The foreseeable risks are low.
> (c) The negative impact on the subject's well-being is minimised and low.
> (d) The trial is not prohibited by law.
> (e) The approval/favourable opinion of the IRB/IEC is expressly sought on the inclusion of such subjects, and the written approval/favourable opinion covers this aspect.
> Such trials, unless an exception is justified, should be conducted in patients having a disease or condition for which the investigational product is intended. Subjects in these trials should be particularly closely monitored and should be withdrawn if they appear to be unduly distressed.

Leaving aside the difficulty in English law of the notion of 'legally acceptable representative', these guidelines are largely in tune with the terms of the European Convention and the Law Commission's proposal that we have just seen.

Ultimately, at least in the context of research involving medicinal products, the proposed EU Directive on Clinical Trials will determine the legality of such trials when approved and in force in the European Union (for a discussion of European developments: see D Sprumont 'Legal Protection of Human Research Subjects in Europe' (1999) 6 European J of Health Law 25).

That such research may take place remains highly controversial and there is unlikely to be any consensus reached, whatever position is taken by the Lord Chancellor in any future legislation concerned with mentally incapacitated adults (see now, *Making Decisions, supra*).

The same depth of concern arose in New Zealand after Judge Cartwright's Report into *Allegations Concerning the Treatment of Cervical Cancer at the National Women's Hospital* (1988). As a result s 10 of the New Zealand Bill of Rights Act 1990 provides that:

10. Right not to be subjected to medical or scientific experimentation. – Every person has the right not to be subjected to medical or scientific experimentation without that person's consent.

The clear and intended effect of s 10 is to outlaw medical research on those not competent to consent for themselves.

Compensation

We are not concerned here with legal actions brought by participants in research who have been injured through some fault or misdeed on the part of the researcher. Instead, we are concerned with the question that has increasingly occupied the attention of medical researchers, commentators and the Government: if a participant in a trial, whether patient or healthy volunteer, suffers harm in some way related to the trial and has need for compensation, should there be some method of compensation available to him in circumstances where the existing forms of legal liability (eg negligence and under the Consumer Protection Act 1987) do not apply? The Government's involvement through the Department of Health in this question arose from the public concern following the deaths of two students (one in Cardiff and the other in Dublin) in 1985 who were healthy volunteers in drug trials.

The argument raised is that society gains through the willingness of some to participate in research and society should be prepared, therefore, to provide for any casualties of such research rather than leave them to the vagaries of litigation and the existing social security system. This argument was put by the Royal Commission on Civil Liability and Compensation for Personal Injury (Cmnd 7054) in 1978 and is reflected in their recommendation (paras 1339–1341).

Volunteers for medical research

1339 People may volunteer to take part in research or clinical trials of new forms of treatment or new drugs. Strict precautions are imposed, including the screening of experiments by medical ethical committees. Nevertheless the Medical Research Council stated in their evidence to us:

despite the exercise of the highest degree of care and skill by the medical investigator concerned, death or a personal injury which was quite unforeseen and indeed quite unforeseeable might be suffered by a person who volunteers to participate in such an investigation. For example, a volunteer taking part in a recent trial of live attenuated influenza vaccine developed a neurological lesion shortly after the administration of the vaccine – the first known neurological sequela to any attenuated influenza virus despite the fact that many hundreds of thousands of such inoculations had been given during the preceding ten years; a causal connection between the administration of the vaccine and the neurological lesion could neither be proved nor disproved. In such a situation, the Medical Research Council would seek authority to make an *ex gratia* payment from public funds to the volunteer or his dependants and such a payment has been approved for the volunteer who developed the lesion in question.

Patients undergoing clinical trials
1340 Patients as well as healthy volunteers may be asked if they will agree to accept a new form of treatment in the interests of research. If a patient is given such treatment, and through it suffers injury, or a worsening of his condition which would not have been expected with conventional treatment, he is in the same position as a healthy person volunteering to take part in research.
1341 We think that it is wrong that a person who exposes himself to some medical risk in the interests of the community should have to rely on *ex gratia* compensation in the event of injury. We recommend that any volunteer for medical research or clinical trials who suffers severe damage as a result should have a cause of action, on the basis of strict liability, against the authority to whom he has consented to make himself available.

In the years since these recommendations, no progress has been made towards providing compensation for research subjects. What has emerged instead is a series of recommendations from bodies such as the Royal College of Physicians and the Association of the British Pharmaceutical Industry (ABPI). In addition, the Department of Health's Guidance on LRECs refers to arrangements for compensation. Despite their existence, these recommendations are no more than that. You will see that a feature of the approach adopted by the ABPI is to seek to endow their arrangements with some semblance of legal form through the device of a contract between the researcher and the research subject in the case of healthy volunteer studies. The ABPI scheme is described by Christopher Hodges in the following extract.

C Hodges 'Harmonisation of European Controls over Research: Ethics Committees, Consent, Compensation and Indemnity' in A Goldberg and I Dodds-Smith *Pharmaceutical Medicine and the Law* (1991)

> In the UK the provision of compensation for research injury is left to a non-statutory regime, dependent merely upon whether or not the sponsor and/or contract research house [ie, a company not a member of the ABPI] in fact abide by the ABPI guidelines. Curiously, the DoH Guidelines are entirely silent on the advisability of or any requirement for adherence to the ABPI guidelines. Different ABPI guidelines cover different types of research:
>
> *Non-patient human volunteers: 1988 ABPI guidelines*
> The relationship between the volunteer and the sponsor should be governed by the terms of a written contract included in the consent form which the volunteer signs to signify his agreement to take part in the study. The ABPI guidelines state:
>
>> 11.7 The agreement should clearly record the obligation the pharmaceutical company or research establishment has accepted in terms of financial rewards for participation and compensation in the event of injury. In particular, the volunteer should be given a clear commitment that in the event of bodily injury he will receive appropriate compensation without having to prove either that such injury arose through negligence or that the product was defective in the sense that it did not fulfil a reasonable expectation of safety. The agreement should not seek to remove that right of the volunteer, as an alternative, to pursue a claim on the basis of either negligence or strict liability if he is so minded.
>> 11.8 Where pharmaceutical companies sponsor studies to be performed in outside research establishments, the responsibility for paying compensation should be clarified and reflected in the contractual documentation with the volunteer. Where the sponsor company is to provide the undertaking regarding compensation, it is recommended that the sponsor company enters into an unqualified obligation to pay compensation to the volunteer on proof of causation, having previously protected its rights to recourse against the research establishment in its agreement with that establishment, to cover the position where the negligence of its contractor may have caused or contributed to the injury to the volunteer. A volunteer can reasonably expect that compensation will be paid quickly and that any dispute regarding who will finally bear the cost of the compensation paid to him will be resolved separately by the other parties to the research.
>
> A model agreement is attached to the guidelines, in which the relevant clauses read:

8(iii) In the event of my suffering any significant deterioration in health or well-being caused directly by my participation in the study, compensation will be paid to me by the company. (iv) The amount of such compensation shall be calculated by reference to the amount of damages commonly awarded for similar injuries by an English court if liability is admitted, provided that such compensation may be reduced to the extent that I, by reason of contributory fault, am partly responsible for the injury (or where I have received equivalent payment for such injury under any policy of insurance effected by the company for my benefit)…

Negligence by an investigator is therefore irrelevant as far as a claim by an injured party for compensation is concerned. He is to be paid forthwith by the sponsor, who may then have a claim against the investigator (and the contractual documentation between them should provide for this). There is also a provision for arbitration in the event of a dispute over payment of compensation.

In 1986, the RCP criticised the fact that compensation for injury suffered as a result of research conducted in and sponsored by universities, NHS hospitals, the Medical Research Council and other similar establishments is not covered by any guideline commitment but is dependent on an *ex gratia* payment.

> We believe that universities and other institutions should make binding commitments to provide compensation, because we consider it unacceptable that a healthy volunteer should have to rely on an *ex gratia* payment.

Patient volunteers: 1991 ABPI guidelines
The 1983 guidelines were revised in 1991 in the light of developing considerations, especially the 1990 Report of the RCP's Working Party, *Research involving patients*. The relationship between the sponsor and subject is, in the case of [research on patients for whose condition the treatment is intended], not contractual and the guidelines state that the sponsor's assurance to abide by them is 'without legal commitment'.

> 1.2 Compensation should be paid when, on the balance of probabilities, the injury was attributable to the administration of a medicinal product under trial or any clinical intervention or procedure provided for by the protocol that would not have occurred but for the inclusion of the patient in the trial.
> 1.3 Compensation should be paid to a child injured *in utero* through the participation of the subject's mother in a clinical trial as if the child were a patient-volunteer with the full benefit of these guidelines.
> 1.4 Compensation should only be paid for the more serious injury of an enduring and disabling character (including exacerbation of an existing condition) and not for temporary pain or discomfort or less serious or curable complaints.
> 1.5 Where there is an adverse reaction to a medicinal product under trial and injury is caused by a procedure adopted to deal with that adverse reaction, compensation should be paid for such injury as if it were caused directly by the medicinal product under trial.
> 1.6 Neither the fact that the adverse reaction causing the injury was foreseeable or predictable, nor the fact that the patient has freely consented (whether in writing or otherwise) to participate in the trial should exclude a patient from consideration for compensation under these guidelines, although compensation may be abated or excluded in the light of the factors described in paragraph 4.2 below.
> 1.7 For the avoidance of doubt, compensation should be paid regardless of whether the patient is able to prove that the company has been negligent in relation to research or development of the medicinal product under trial or that the product is defective and therefore, as the producer, the company is subject to strict liability in respect of injuries caused by it.…
> 4.1 The amount of compensation paid should be appropriate to the nature, severity and persistence of the injury and should in general terms be consistent with the quantum of damages commonly awarded for similar injuries by an English court in cases where legal liability is admitted.
> 4.2 Compensation may be abated, or in certain circumstances excluded, in the light of the following factors (on which will depend the level of risk the patient can reasonably be expected to accept):
> 4.2.1 the seriousness of the disease being treated, the degree of probability that adverse reactions will occur and any warnings given;
> 4.2.2 the risks and benefits of established treatments relative to those known or suspected of the trial medicine.
> This reflects the fact that flexibility is required given the particular patient's circumstances. As an extreme example, there may be a patient suffering from a serious or life-threatening disease who is warned of a certain defined risk of adverse reaction. Participation in the trial is then based on an expectation that the benefit/risk ratio

associated with participation may be better than that associated with alternative treatment. It is, therefore, reasonable that the patient accepts the high risk and should not expect compensation for the occurrence of the adverse reaction of which he or she was told.

There is provision for arbitration by an independent expert in the event of any difference of opinion.

Compensation is excluded, however, where
1. The product failed to have its intended effect.
2. The injury was caused by another licensed medicinal product which was administered as a comparison with the product under trial.
3. A placebo has failed to provide a therapeutic benefit.

Compensation should not be paid, or should be abated, to the extent that the injury has arisen through:
1. A significant departure from the agreed protocol.
2. The wrongful act or default of a third party, including a doctor's failure to deal adequately with an adverse reaction.
3. Contributory negligence by the patient.

None of these exclusions represents a departure from the 1983 guidelines, except perhaps for the first, that 'the product failed to have its intended effect', which may have been implicit before.

The approach set out in these guidelines is a logical application of legal principles. The subject is given the considerable benefit of not having to prove negligence, but the guidelines do not constitute a 'no-fault' compensation scheme because of the applicability of rules on causation, most notably in the exclusions. The subject is also at a disadvantage because there is no legal commitment to pay by the sponsor. The RCP criticised the 1983 guidelines for this reason, and recommended that there should be a contractual commitment to compensate patient volunteers, perhaps with the investigator acting as the company's agent for this limited purpose. The ABPI did not adopt this view in its 1991 revision. The matter is certainly not susceptible to a simple answer, since the imposition of a contractual relationship on a treatment situation which is not normally contractual is not a simple matter, either for reasons of achieving universality or practicability, or from the point of view of effecting an alteration in the nature of the patient-doctor relationship, with the potential for conflict that exists here. The ABPI would point to the absence of any practical problem over compensation which needs to be resolved: research injuries are fortunately extremely rare and companies are generally well aware of the need to avoid adverse criticism. In practice, the guidelines might therefore be interpreted liberally in any given case.

It is interesting to note that although the RCP recommended that compensation should be paid for *involvement* in research and not confined to injury due to a treatment under test itself (which the ABPI has adopted) and also to injury due to withholding active treatment (which the ABPI has not adopted), it did *not* recommend that compensation should be paid for injury due to a standard medicine used for comparison or to failure of a treatment to have its hoped for or intended effect. A strong case could, however, be made that these exclusions and the exclusion of placebo-induced injury should all be compensated. Again, it is possible that in practice a company might be well advised to avoid any unduly restrictive stance.

In its report of 1990, the RCP criticised the fact that patients injured in publicly funded research have to rely on an *ex gratia* and *ad hoc* system:

> ...patients... [should be] compensated on an agreed basis which should be made clear to them before they consent... The absence of [a policy to compensate] should be treated as a material fact to be disclosed by the investigator to the patient.

The Department of Health's Guidelines (*op cit*) refer to compensation somewhat shortly and inconclusively.

3.17 Arrangements for compensation in the event of a research subject being harmed, whether by negligence or not, will vary according to what type of body is sponsoring the research proposal. The LREC should ensure that those who agree to participate in research which may involve some risk, whether as patients or healthy volunteers, are told at the outset what arrangements will apply in their case. The LREC should seek evidence from the sponsor that these arrangements have adequate financial backing.
3.18 NHS bodies are not empowered to offer advance indemnity to participants in research projects. A person suffering injury as a result of having taken part in research would be able to pursue a claim for negligence through litigation. Each case would of course have to be considered on its merits.

3.19 Private sector companies sponsoring research are usually able to ensure that effective provision is made to compensate any research subject whose health may be affected. To this end LRECs should seek confirmation that any such company conducting or sponsoring a patient or healthy volunteer study accepts responsibility for compensation and provides details of the basis on which it will be provided i.e. causation, fault etc, plus evidence of their ability to fulfil it.
3.20 Volunteers must therefore be told in advance of all known risks and be made aware that there could also be unforeseen risks and of the possible difficulties in obtaining compensation.

The terms of para 3.18 have been widely criticised since they offer no assurance that compensation will be available. The explanation lies in the established practice of the Treasury which does not permit Government bodies to act as insurers. Subsequently, further guidance has been given by the Department of Health in HSG (96)48, *Arrangements for Handling Clinical Negligence Claims Against NHS Staff*. NHS staff are covered for negligence claims arising out of clinical trials whether involving patients or health volunteers. The guidelines also recognise that in exceptional circumstances an *ex gratia* payment may be made of up to £50,000 for non-negligent harm suffered during a clinical trial.

Annex B to HSG (96)48 sets out a scheme for indemnity for clinical studies sponsored by pharmaceutical companies.

Annex B Indemnity for Clinical Studies Sponsored by Pharmaceutical companies

Section One
1. Clinical research involving the administration of drugs to patients or non-patient human volunteers is frequently undertaken under the auspices of Health Authorities or NHS Trusts.
2. When the study is sponsored by a pharmaceutical company, issues of liability and indemnity may arise in case of injury associated with administration of the drug or other aspects of the conduct of the trial.
3. When the study is not sponsored by a company but has been independently organised by clinicians, the NHS body will carry full legal liability for claims in negligence arising from harm to subjects in the study.
4. The guidance in Section 2 and the Appendix has three purposes:
to ensure that NHS bodies enter into appropriate agreements which will provide indemnity against claims and proceedings arising from company-sponsored clinical studies;
to ensure that NHS bodies, where appropriate, use a standard form of agreement (Appendix) which has been drawn up in consultation with the Association of the British Pharmaceutical Industry (ABPI);
to advise Local Research Ethics Committees (LRECs) of the standard form of agreement.

Section Two
1. A wide variety of clinical studies involving experimental or investigational use of drugs is carried out within NHS bodies. This includes studies in patients (clinical trials) and studies in healthy human volunteers. They may involve administration of a totally new (unlicensed) drug (active substance or 'NAS') or the administration of an established (licensed) drug by a novel route, for a new therapeutic indication, or in a novel formulation or combination . . .
4. Participants in a clinical study may suffer adverse effects due to the drug or clinical procedures. The appendix to this annex is a model form of agreement between the company sponsoring a study and the NHS body involved, which indemnifies the authority or trust against claims and proceedings arising from the study. The model agreement has been drawn up in consultation with the Association of the British Pharmaceutical Industry (ABPI).
5. This form of indemnity will not normally apply to clinical studies which are not directly sponsored by the company providing the product for research, but have been independently organised by clinicians. In this case, the NHS body will normally carry full legal liability for any claims in negligence arising from harm to subjects in the study.
6. The NHS body will also carry full legal liability for any claims in negligence (or compensation under the indemnity will be abated) where there has been significant non-adherence to the agreed protocol or there has been negligence on the part of an NHS employee, for example, by failing to deal adequately with an adverse drug reaction.
7. The form of indemnity may not be readily accepted by sponsoring companies outside the UK or who are not members of the ABPI. NHS bodies should, as part of their risk management, consider the value of indemnities which are offered and consider whether companies should have alternative arrangements in place.

8. Several health authorities and trusts have independently developed forms of indemnity agreement. However, difficulties have arisen when different authorities have required varying terms of indemnity and this has, on occasion, impeded the progress of clinical research within the NHS. Particular difficulties may arise in large multi-centre trials involving many NHS bodies when it is clearly desirable to have standardised terms of indemnity to provide equal protection to all participants in the study.

9. Responsibility for deciding whether a particular company-sponsored research proposal should proceed within the NHS rests with the Health Authority or Trust within which the research would take place, after consideration of ethical, clinical, managerial, financial, resource, and legal liability issues. The NHS body is responsible for securing an appropriate indemnity agreement and should maintain a register of all clinical studies undertaken under its auspices with an indication whether it is a company-sponsored study and, if so, with confirmation that an indemnity agreement is in place. If for any reason it is considered that the model form of indemnity is not appropriate or that amendments are required, the NHS body involved should seek legal advice on the form or amendments proposed.

10. Even when the model form of indemnity is agreed, the NHS body should satisfy itself that the company sponsoring the study is substantial and reputable and has appropriate arrangements in place (for example insurance cover) to support the indemnity. The NHS body will carry full liability for any claims in negligence if the indemnity is not honoured and there is not supporting insurance.

11. Where a clinical study includes patients or subjects within several NHS bodies, for example in a multi-centre clinical trial, it is necessary for each Authority or Trust to complete an appropriate indemnity agreement with the sponsoring company.

12. Where independent practitioners, such as general medical practitioners, are engaged in clinical studies, Health Authorities should seek to ensure that such studies are the subject of an appropriate indemnity agreement. It is good practice for the GP to notify the Health Authority of his participation in any clinical study.

13. Clinical investigators should ensure that details of any proposed research study are lodged with the appropriate NHS body and should not commence company-sponsored research unless an indemnity agreement is in place.

14. Local Research Ethics Committees (LRECs) provide independent advice to NHS and other bodies and to clinical researchers on the ethics of proposed research projects that involve human subjects [HSG(91)5]. Clinical investigators should not commence any research project involving patients or human volunteers without LREC agreement. Acceptance of the ABPI guidelines and the terms of the model indemnity agreement should normally be a condition of LREC approval of any pharmaceutical company sponsored project.

The indemnity agreement contemplates payment to the NHS body for any negligence claims arising from adverse effects of the drug being tested and also required the 'sponsor' to operate 'in good faith' the ABPI guidelines for non-negligent compensation to patients and healthy volunteers that we saw earlier.

The current position could be regarded as less than satisfactory, especially given the altruism of those who take part in research. Some other European countries regard the making of proper provision for compensation of such importance that legislation is demanded. The position is discussed by Christopher Hodges in his paper in *Pharmaceutical Medicine and the Law* (*op cit*).

In Germany, drug manufacturers are subject to an insurance based compensation system with absolute liability. [German Federal Drug Law 1976 sections 1, 2, 84–94]...

The German Drug Law specifies that insurance must be held which must stand in appropriate relation to the risks involved in the clinical trial and in the case of death or permanent disability must total at least DM 500,000. [*Ibid* section 40.]

The recent legislation in Ireland, France and Spain also provides for consideration of insurance. Under a French decree a sponsor has to hold quite a high level of insurance: cover of at least FFr 5 million per victim, FFr 30 million per research protocol and FFr 50 million for all claims made in an insurance year must be held until 10 years after the end of the research. [French Decree No. 91–440 of 14 May 1991.] The Irish Act is silent on the question of the basis of compensation. It provides merely that the sponsor and investigator must establish to the satisfaction of the minister in advance of each trial on a case by case basis that they have sufficient security to provide for payments of damages on their own behalf if they are personally negligent. [Control of Clinical Trials Act 1987, section 10 (as amended)] This does not give rise to an obligation to pay compensation as such, on any basis. 'Security' is defined as including a contract of insurance, a contract of indemnity, a guarantee, a surety, a warranty and a bond. [Control of Clinical Trials and Drugs Act 1990, section 3 amending section 10 of the 1987 Act.] Neither the Spanish law nor the Irish legislation and guidelines mention any financial sums or limits. However the Spanish law does include some interesting provisions. [Ley Del Medicamento 25/1990, Article 62.] First, a trial can only be started if 'insurance covering the damages' is in place. This presumably refers to damages which might be awarded by a Spanish court, but up to what level? Compensation for many injuries might be awarded at a trivial level, but equally it might be the case that very high damages might be awarded in individual cases. Although regulations might be made under the Spanish law which set further guidelines, the approach seems to be to leave the risk with the promoter, chief researcher and owner of the hospital or centre in question, since the law specifically provides that these people shall be severally liable without proof of fault if the insurance does not cover the damages. It is, of course, inherent in this approach that the appropriate level of damages should be set by a court: there is no specific arbitration or mediation procedure under the law, unlike the approach under the UK ABPI guidelines. The Spanish law does, however, assist the injured research subject by reversing the burden of proof in his favour for injuries which occur during the trial or within one year after its termination.

Recurrent questions arise in relation to compensation for injury as to who should bear the responsibility for compensation in the event of the subject suffering injury which might not be attributable to the compound under research. The French statute and the various ABPI guidelines attempt to deal with this point, but are perhaps not entirely successful.

The provisions of the French law relating to compensation essentially place the responsibility for compensation on the sponsor, whether in non-therapeutic or therapeutic research, irrespective of the negligence of the investigator, although the wording in the latter case is ambiguous:

> In the case of biomedical research with no direct benefit to the individual, the sponsor, even when not at fault, takes responsibility for the compensation of any harmful effects of the research on a person undergoing it, notwithstanding the possible action of a third party or the voluntary withdrawal of the person who initially consented to undergo the research.
>
> In the case of biomedical research with direct benefit to the individual, the sponsor takes responsibility for the compensation of any harmful effects of the research on a person undergoing it, unless he proves that such adverse effects are not attributable to his or any participating party's action, notwithstanding the possible action of a third party or the voluntary withdrawal of the person who initially consented to undergo the research.
>
> In all biomedical research, the sponsor shall take out insurance covering his and any other participating party's liability as it results from this article, irrespective of the relationship between the sponsor and the participating parties. The provisions of this article are binding on all parties. [Law on the Protection of Persons Undergoing Biomedical Research, Article L.209–7.]

The essential burden of compensation is therefore firmly on the sponsor. In the case of research in healthy volunteers, the burden is absolute and negligence of an investigator is, at least as between sponsor and subject, irrelevant. However, the provisions of the second paragraph, dealing with research on patients, are somewhat ambiguous as to the extent to which proof of the action of a third party excuses the sponsor.

Innovative therapy

We have already commented upon the notion of 'innovative therapy' and its relationship with research. We reached the conclusion (*supra*) that where the doctor's intention is to acquire knowledge and not merely to care for his patient, the constraints normally associated with the conduct of research should apply. There is, of course, a scientific as well as a moral and legal basis for this view. The pursuit of knowledge is best conducted in a systematic fashion. Bad science is bad ethics. Innovative therapy should properly be regarded as one of two things: either *research*, with all that flows therefrom; or *therapy*, where the sole intention is to care for the particular patient involved. Consequently, the law does not inhibit development. It says, however, that any development must be defended as research or justified as appropriate albeit innovative therapy, against the background of a possible claim in negligence.

Pursuing the point concerning a claim in negligence relating to the performance of the procedure, we must take as our point of departure *Hunter v Hanley* 1955 SC 200. In that case, you will recall, Lord Clyde said:

> It follows from what I have said that in regard to allegations of deviation from ordinary professional practice... such a deviation is not necessarily evidence of negligence. Indeed it would be disastrous if this were so, for all inducement to progress in medical science would then be destroyed. Even a substantial deviation from normal practice may be warranted by the particular circumstances. To establish liability by a doctor where deviation from normal practice is alleged, three facts require to be established. First of all it must be proved that there is a usual and normal practice; secondly it must be proved that the defender has not adopted that practice; and thirdly (and this is of crucial importance) it must be established that the course the doctor adopted is one which no professional man of ordinary skill would have taken if he had been acting with ordinary care.

In the later care of *Landau v Werner* (1961) 105 Sol Jo 1008 (CA), Sellers LJ stated that:

> A doctor might not be negligent if he tried a new technique but if he did he must justify it before the Court. If his novel or exceptional treatment had failed disastrously he could not complain if it was held that he went beyond the bounds of due care and skill as recognised generally.

These cases illustrate the desire of the courts to allow doctors some discretion so as to develop medical practice while wishing to set proper limits to the extent to which they may go. Notice the following words of Hunter J in *Brook v St John's Hickey Memorial Hospital* (1978) 380 NE 2d 72 (Sup Ct Ind):

> Too often courts have confused judgmental decisions and experimentation. Therapeutic innovation has long been recognised as permissible to avoid serious consequences. The everyday practice of medicine involves constant judgmental decisions by physicians as they move from one patient to another in the conscious institution of procedures, special tests, trials and observations recognised generally by their profession as effective in treating the patient or providing a diagnosis of a diseased condition. Each patient presents a slightly different problem to the doctor. A physician is presumed to have the knowledge and skill necessary to use some innovation to fit the peculiar circumstances of each case.

If doctors are to be given some leeway but not encouraged to leap too far into the dark there must be some criterion in law to which the doctor can refer. The notion of 'minimal risk' may be of assistance, or would such a criterion unnecessarily inhibit the doctor from trying new techniques outside the ambit of systematic research? Consider the following case which arose in the United States.

Karp v Cooley (1974) 493 F 2d 408 (US CA, 5th Cir)

Bell J: Medical history was made in 1969 when Dr Denton A Cooley, a thoracic surgeon, implanted the first totally mechanical heart in 47-year-old Haskell Karp. This threshold orthotopic cardiac prosthesis also spawned this medical malpractice suit by Mr Karp's wife, individually and as executrix of Mr Karp's estate, and his children, for the patient's wrongful death....

There is no dispute that prior to entering St Luke's Episcopal Hospital in Houston on March 5, 1969, Haskell Karp had a long and difficult ten-year history of cardiac problems. He suffered a serious heart attack in 1959 and was hospitalised for approximately two months because of diffuse anterior myocardial infarction. He had incurred four heart attacks, thirteen cardiac hospitalisations and considerable medical care culminating in the insertion of an electronic demand pacemaker in May, 1968. Subsequent hospitalisation in September and October, 1969 occurred, and finally the decision was made to seek the assistance of Dr Cooley.... [Dr Cooley testified]:

> I told [Mr Karp] we had no heart donor available, had no prospect of one... I told him that there was a possibility that we had a device which would sustain his life in the event that he would die on the operating table. We had a device which would sustain his life. hopefully, until we could get a suitable donor. I had told him that I did not know whether it would take a matter of hours or days, weeks, or maybe not at all, but it would sustain his life and give us another possibility of salvaging him through heart transplantation.

Dr Cooley said he did not recall who was present when these discussions began. Dr Cooley described his discussion of this device:

> I told him that it was a heart pump similar to the one that we used in open-heart surgery; that it was a reciprocating-type pump with the membrane, in which the pumping element never became in contact with the bloodstream; that it was designed in such a manner that it would not damage the bloodstream or it would cause minimal damage to the bloodstream; that it would be placed in his body to take over the function of the dead heart and to propel blood throughout his body during this interim until he could have a heart transplant.... I told him this device had not been used in human beings; that it had been used in the laboratory; that we had been able to sustain the circulation in calves and that it had not been used in human beings. It had been used on the bench in what we call *in vitro* experiments, *in vitro* as opposed to *in vivo*.... I told him it had been tested in the laboratory, it had not been used in a human being, but I was confident that it would support his circulation.... I told him that we had been successful in keeping an animal alive for more than forty hours with the device, but that this was a calf. It was a 300-pound animal in which the demands on the pump were far greater than they would be in the human body, and that I was reasonably confident that this device would sustain his life until we could get a heart transplant. But no guarantees were made at all.

Dr Cooley admitted he and Mr Karp did not discuss the number of animals in which the device had been tested, nor whether the animals sustained damage to their bodies by the use of his pump.

Asked by appellants' counsel whether he described it as a heart-lung pump similar to that used in other open heart surgeries, Dr Cooley said, 'I told him it was a pump. I didn't tell him it was a lung. I told him it was an artificial heart, that it was a pump which would replace temporarily the heart.'...

According to the anaesthesia record,... Mr Karp was brought into the operating room at about 1:15 pm. When Dr Keats saw Mr Karp at that time he believed Mr Karp's death to be imminent. Dr Keats said Mr Karp was in great distress; he was having difficulty breathing, shortness of breath and he was pale and sweating. Dr Keats said he hurriedly got Mr Karp on the operating table, started giving him oxygen, and put him to sleep as rapidly as possible so that they could put a tube in his windpipe to assist his breathing. Dr Keats then sent word to Dr Cooley that they 'had better go ahead with the operation as expeditiously as possible, otherwise the patient may not last long enough to have the operation'.... Dr Cooley says Mr Karp was near death when he entered the operating room, 'mottled and blue'. He said he felt Mr Karp was 'virtually moribund' at that time.

The operation was then begun with Dr Cooley as chief surgeon, Dr Liotta as first assistant, Dr Grady Hallman as second assistant, and Dr Keats as anaesthesiologist. [Dr Cooley] said that he opened the pericardium and that as a result of a very feeble heart action the heart pump was started as quickly as possible. Dr Keats remembers that as Mr Karp's heart became visible 'it was a very large heart that filled the entire surgical field'. Dr Cooley said that the heart was functioning very feebly, was virtually noncontractile and could not support Mr Karp. After Mr Karp had been on the heart-lung or heart oxygenator a sufficient time to get his heart going again an incision was made in the left ventricle. Dr Cooley said that Mr Karp had scar tissue circumferentially around the inside of his left ventricle, that his entire interventricular septum was one solid piece of scar tissue, the anterior ventricle was almost completely displaced by scar tissue, and there was an aneurysm on the posterior aspect of the ventricle....

Although Dr Cooley said the situation was then 'virtually hopeless', he began to do what he could with the resection procedure. He excised the most severely damaged part of the ventricular myocardium in his repair of the left ventricle. Because of the extensive scarring it was necessary to excise part of the right ventricle. In completing this complicated repair it was then necessary to sew the partition back to the right ventricle. and sew the left ventricle back to them. Dr Cooley said that Mr Karp did not have an anterior aneurysm but that the anterior myocardium was diffusely dilated. He added that it was very difficult to differentiate between a dilated scarred heart and an aneurysm. He described the nonfunctioning large area on the left ventricle as having a paradoxical motion and a ballooning out effect. He compared the size of the balloon to a cantaloupe. He said there was no threat of break or rupture in lesions like this; that he had never seen one rupture; and that he never told a patient a ventricular aneurysm would burst.

It is to be noted here that although Mrs Karp testified her husband had appeared normal on the day of the surgery, there is no lay or expert testimony other than that Mr Karp was near death at the time of the operation.

According to Dr Hallman, the repair described above was done in the manner that cardiovascular surgeons normally go about performing this operation. However, Dr Hallman said that due to the extensive scarring of the heart, there simply was not sufficient healthy heart muscle remaining to form an efficient pump to support Mr Karp's life. Dr Hallman,

Dr Keats and Dr Cooley all testified that at this point, that is after the attempted resection, Mr Karp was again faced with imminent death.

Dr Cooley said that it took about 20 minutes to make the resection repair. He said that after the repair the clamp was taken off the ascending aorta to attempt to restart the myocardium. He stated that there was fibrillation and that he attempted an electrical countershock at least once. He stated that there was a sinus type or nodal rhythm at that point but that the rhythm contraction was too weak to support life due to the fact that there simply was too much scar tissue in the heart. Dr Hallman testified that some thirty minutes elapsed between the end of the repair and the decision to remove the heart. Mr Karp's heart was then removed and the mechanical device was inserted. Dr Cooley said that the mechanical heart functioned very well and Mr Karp responded to stimulation within 15 or 20 minutes after the incision was closed. His blood pressure was well sustained according to Dr Cooley and he showed signs of cerebral activity. Dr Keats said that Mr Karp was amazingly well following the operation, that the records reflect that he was responding reasonably to commands within 20 minutes post-operatively. Dr Keats testified that the endocracheal [sic] tube was removed about 1:20 am, and that he saw Mr Karp some time the next morning at which time he was responsive and could communicate.

After the mechanical heart had been inserted, Dr Cooley said he went to Mrs Karp and told her that the wedge procedure had been unsuccessful; that he had proceeded with the use of the mechanical device and that they were going to try to get a donor. The transplant operation was performed on the morning of April 7, 1969, approximately 64 hours after the mechanical device had been implanted in Mr Karp. He died the next day, April 8, 1969, some 32 hours after the transplant surgery....

Suits charging failure by a physician adequately to disclose the risks and alternatives of proposed treatment are not innovations in American law. They date back a good half-century, and in the last decade have increased in number.

...Physicians and surgeons have a duty to make a reasonable disclosure to a patient of risks that are incident to medical diagnosis and treatment. True consent to what happens to one's self is the informed exercise of a choice, and that entails an opportunity to evaluate knowledgeably the options available and the risks attendant upon each. From these general principles, however, the focus in each individual case must necessarily relate back to what the physician said or failed to say and what the law requires him to say.

The Texas standard against which a physician's disclosure or lack of disclosure is tested is a medical one which must be proved by expert medical evidence of what a reasonable practitioner of the same school of practice and the same or similar locality would have advised a patient under similar circumstances.... As we understand appellants' contention, it is that Mr Karp was not told about the number of animals tested or the results of those tests; that he was not told there was a chance of permanent injury to his body by the mechanical heart, that complete renal shutdown could result from the use of the prosthesis, that the device was 'completely experimental', and that Dr Cooley failed to tell Mr Karp that Dr Beazley had said Mr Karp was not a suitable candidate for surgery. Nine physicians testified, but none suggested a standard of disclosure required by Texas law under these circumstances. Appellants argue Dr Cooley himself set the standard requiring the disclosure of Dr Beazley's evaluation. Texas law does permit the defendant doctor to establish the standard of disclosure, but Dr Cooley's testimony says no more than that what is a reasonable medical practice is a question of medical judgment. Dr Cooley's admitted failure to tell Mr Karp of Dr Bearley's March 6 notation is of no import; Dr Leachman testified he did not think the notation made any difference. The March 6 notation, made during the course of an initial evaluation, was in Dr Beazley's view not a medical opinion but a reservation about the psychological or emotional acceptance of less than a perfect result.

What is missing from the evidence presented is the requisite expert testimony as to *what* risks under these circumstances a physician should disclose.

...What is significant then is what Mr Karp was told, and Mrs Karp's testimony is relevant only to the extent that it evidences what Mr Karp was told when she was present. Dr Cooley's undisputed testimony is that he began discussing with Mr Karp the proposed wedge excision and the alternative procedure of a mechanical heart as a stop-gap to a transplant about a week before the April 4 operation. He said he next talked with Mr Karp the evening of April 2. The consent form was prepared on April 3 and although there is a dispute as to *when* it was signed, there is no question it was signed by Mr Karp. Thus it was against the backdrop of at least two conversations with Dr Cooley, at which Mrs Karp was not present, that Mr Karp was presented and signed the consent document. The consent form is consistent with Dr Cooley's testimony of what he told Mr Karp. Although not necessarily conclusive, what Haskell Karp consented to and was told is best evidenced by this document. It is of considerable import that each step of the three-stage operation, objected to due to an alleged lack of informed consent, was specifically set out in the consent document signed by the patient....

Appellants have not introduced evidence required by Texas law to show a lack of Karp's informed consent or of breach of Dr Cooley's duty to adequately apprise Karp of the nature and risks of the operation that warrant... submission of this issue to the jury....

To meet the proper standard of medical care, the physician must possess a reasonable degree of skill and exercise this skill with ordinary care and diligence. A specialist like Dr Cooley is bound to exercise the degree of skill and knowledge that is ordinarily possessed by similar specialists. As with the doctrine of informed consent, supra, plaintiffs are obligated under Texas law to produce expert medical testimony to establish a medical standard of conduct, deviation from that standard and proximate cause. Appellants again assert Dr Cooley testified to the established standard and that he did not meet it. The apparent theory is that Dr Cooley was negligent in proceeding with the wedge resection when he said it could not be beneficial. This language, however, cannot be considered alone as a standard, even if it were construed to be one; rather, it must be read in the context of his total testimony, which in no wise establishes negligence. Appellants also failed to raise a fact issue on the proximate cause question.... Since the expert testimony failed to evidence that there were negligent acts or omissions by defendants or that any of their acts or omissions were a proximate cause of Mr Karp's death, a directed verdict for both defendants was proper....

Appellants contend that the trial court erred in directing a verdict on the issue of experimentation. They acknowledge that no Texas case has expressly dealt with a cause of action based on experimentation, but assert that our court's decision in *Bender v Dingwerth* suggests that the decision as to what is actionable experimentation should be left to a jury. We do not agree.

A Texas court bound in traditional malpractice actions to expert medical testimony to determine how a reasonably careful and prudent physician would have acted under the same or similar circumstances would not likely vary that evidentiary requirement for an experimentation charge. This conclusion is also suggested by the few reported cases where experimentation has been recognised as a separate basis of liability. The record contains no evidence that Mr Karp's treatment was other than therapeutic and we agree that in this context an action for experimentation must be measured by traditional malpractice evidentiary standards. Whether there was informed consent is necessarily linked to the charge of experimentation, and Mr Karp's consent was expressly to all three stages of the operation actually performed – each an alternative in the event of a preceding failure. As previously discussed, appellants have not shown an absence of Mr Karp's informed consent. Causation and proximate cause are also requisite to an actionable claim of experimentation. Even if Dr DeBakey's testimony, as discussed subsequently, were admitted and did establish a standard and a departure from that standard in using this prosthetic device, substantial evidence... on causation and proximate cause simply is not reflected in the record. That alone would warrant the directed verdict on this issue....

We cannot conclude that the trial court's decision to exclude Dr DeBakey's testimony was clearly erroneous. His testimony would have shown at most that, in his opinion, the pump tested under his supervision was not ready for use in humans and that he would not have recommended its use. He may have demonstrated that the animals tested with a prosthetic device at Baylor died of renal failure, but he refused to state that the prosthetic heart used in those experiments was the reasonable medical probable cause of the renal failure. He repeatedly declined to give an opinion regarding the pump used in Mr Karp stating only that the Karp pump was similar to the ones developed under his supervision. He declined to answer the only hypothetical question propounded, even though he had examined at the court's request Karp's medical records, since he had not personally examined Mr Karp. While it is conceivable that relevance *might* have been established between Dr DeBakey's experiments and conclusions regarding his mechanical heart and the Karp device and its use, the record does not supply the link. Further, because of the absence of evidence on proximate cause on the informed consent and experimentation issues, Dr DeBakey's testimony, even if admitted, would not change the requirement... to direct a verdict for defendants. We therefore do not disturb the trial court's determination.

As you can see, this case also points us to another aspect of liability in negligence which warrants analysis in the context of innovative therapy. What must the doctor disclose to the patient so as to comply with his legal duty and thereby obtain a valid consent?

In the case of *Zimmer v Ringrose* the Alberta Court of Appeal appears to draw a distinction between the information which must be disclosed on the one hand if the case is one of research and on the other, if it is a case of innovative therapy.

Zimmer v Ringrose (1981) 124 DLR (3d) 215 (Alt CA)

The plaintiff underwent an ineffective silver nitrate sterilisation operation. The defendant did not indicate to her that the procedure was not generally accepted in the medical community. The plaintiff subsequently became pregnant and underwent an abortion. The plaintiff sued the defendant, *inter alia*, in negligence for damages to compensate her for her injuries.

Prowse JA: I would not impose upon the appellant the duty of disclosure owed by a medical researcher to the subject of his experiment. The scope of this duty was described by Hall JA in *Halushka v University of Saskatchewan et al.* (1965) 53 DLR (2d) 436 at 443–4, 52 WWR 608 at 616:

> ...the duty imposed upon those engaged in medical research... to those who offer themselves as subjects for experimentation... is at least as great as, if not greater than, the duty owed by the ordinary physician or surgeon to his patient.... The subject of medical experimentation is entitled to a full and frank disclosure of all the facts, probabilities and opinions which a reasonable man might be expected to consider before giving his consent.

In the case of a truly 'experimental' procedure, like the one conducted in *Halushka v University of Saskatchewan*, no therapeutic benefit is intended to accrue to the participant. The subject is simply part of a scientific investigation designed to enhance human knowledge. By contrast, the sterilisation procedure performed by the appellant in this case was directed towards achieving a therapeutic end. By means of a successful sterilisation, the respondent could avoid the occurrence of an unwanted pregnancy and the adverse health problems associated with it. In my opinion, the silver nitrate method was experimental only in the sense that it represented an innovation in sterilisation techniques which were relatively untried. According to the testimony of the respondent's expert witness, the procedure itself could not be dismissed out of hand as being medically untenable. Indeed, his primary criticism of the method appears to have been the absence of adequate clinical evaluation. To hold that every new development in medical methodology was 'experimental' in the sense outlined in *Halushka v University of Saskatchewan* would be to discourage advances in the field of medicine. In view of these considerations, the application of the standard of disclosure stated in the *Halushka* case would be inappropriate in this instance.

In the case at bar, the medical procedure performed was one to which the respondent had consented. Mrs Zimmer understood the nature of the silver nitrate technique and agreed to undergo that method of sterilisation. Consequently, the appellant is not liable for battery. However, the evidence does raise the question of negligence.

At trial, Macdonald J found that there was no comparison given by the appellant between his method and other methods of effecting sterilisation. As a result, the respondent had no opportunity to measure the risks involved in the silver nitrate method against those involved in other forms of sterilisation. Furthermore, the appellant failed to apprise Mrs Zimmer of the fact that the silver nitrate technique had not been approved by the medical profession. A reasonable practitioner would have made such a disclosure for he would have realised that this information would likely influence his patient's decision whether to undergo the procedure. In view of his failure to satisfy this duty of care, I must conclude that the appellant's conduct was indeed negligent.

It should be emphasised that the problem here was not that the doctor was utilising an innovative technique but rather that he breached the duty of care imposed upon him by the doctor-patient relationship. A physician is entitled to decide that the situation dictates the adoption of an innovative course of treatment. As long as he discharges his duty of disclosure, and is not otherwise in breach of his duties of skill and care, eg, has not negligently adopted the procedure given the circumstances, the doctor will not be held liable for implementing such a course of treatment.

There is currently no English case which has specifically addressed this issue. Of course, since *Reibl v Hughes* the *Halushka* standard is now the standard for treatment. In England a court would begin its analysis of the extent of the duty to disclose with the House of Lords decision in *Sidaway*. One case may be instructive. As it happens, *Sidaway* did not serve as the basis for the court's analysis in this case. This may be explicable, however, on the ground that the court considered a statutory provision which seems to contemplate an action in battery in the case of non-compliance with the Act.

R v Mental Health Act Commission, ex parte X (1988) 9 BMLR 77 (Div Ct)

Stuart-Smith LJ: The applicant is a young man of 27. Unhappily he is a compulsive paedophile. This had led him into trouble with the courts, such that over the past ten years or so he has been convicted of 16 offenses of indecency or indecent assault on young boys under the age of 16. On three occasions he has served custodial sentences. He was released from a two year sentence on 19th September 1986. His evidence is that while in prison he had determined to try and change his ways; but he realised that he needed medical help in doing so. Within days of his release he consulted Dr Silverman, who is consultant psychiatrist at Ealing Hospital and has had considerable experience in dealing with sexual deviation and sex offenders. Dr Silverman prescribed treatment by means of Cyproterone acetate which is an antiandrogen. Despite increasing doses the drug was not successful in suppressing the applicant's sexual urges.

…The applicant was afraid that he might re-offend again [sic] and also afraid about the high dosage he was receiving. He was therefore anxious to see if Dr Silverman could prescribe some more effective drug. Dr Silverman made enquiries both from a distinguished endocrinologist and ICI, the manufacturers of the drug, Goserelin, which they manufactured under the trade name Zoladex.

Goserelin is manufactured for the treatment of cancer of the prostate, but it operates by reducing the testosterone to castrate levels, which apparently allows a tumour to regress. As a result of his enquiries Dr Silverman concluded that Goserelin might be a suitable and safer treatment for the applicant. He explained to the applicant how it worked and gave him the ICI data sheet. The applicant was enthusiastic to receive it.

The treatment consists of a monthly subcutaneous injection of an implant into the abdomen. The implant is a small solid cylindrical depot 1 cm long and 1 mm in diameter. The cylinder is composed of polymer and degrades over the ensuing month, gradually releasing the drug. The applicant received the first injection on 8th July 1987. Within a short time the applicant found that he was no longer having sexual urges and was very pleased with the result. A second injection was given on about 8th August.

Meanwhile Dr Silverman had contacted the Mental Health Act Commissioners and told them that he was treating the applicant with Goserelin and that the applicant suffered from mental disorder within the meaning of the Mental Health Act 1983. He was unsure if the treatment came within the purview of section 57 of the Mental Health Act 1983.

On 18th August three Commissioners visited Ealing Hospital and interviewed the applicant. It is clear that the Commissioners concluded that the treatment was governed by section 57 of the Mental Health Act 1983 and the applicant was capable of understanding the nature, purpose and likely effects of it and had consented to it.…

A further injection was given on 8th September 1987, but it was made clear by the Commission that no further treatment could be given… The applicant consulted his solicitors who by letter of 30th September 1987 protested that the treatment did not fall within section 57 of the Mental Health Act 1983 and that therefore the Commission had no jurisdiction in the matter.…

Section 57(2)(a) of the Mental Health Act 1983 provides: 'a registered medical practitioner appointed for the purposes of this Part of this Act by the Secretary of State (not being the responsible medical officer) and two other persons appointed for the purposes of this paragraph by the Secretary of State (not being registered medical practitioners) have certified in writing that the patient is capable of understanding the nature, purpose and likely effects of the treatment in question and has consented to it'.

A number of points should be made.… The subsection is concerned both with capacity and consent, and the Commissioners have to be satisfied on both heads.… [T]he words are 'capable of understanding' and not 'understands'. Thus the question is capacity and not actual understanding.… [I]t is capacity to understand the likely effects of the treatment and not possible side effects, however remote.

But there is a dispute between the parties as to the concept of consent and the proper test to be applied. [Counsel for the applicant] submits that this part of the Mental Health Act 1983 was passed to deal with the difficult problem when a mental patient does not have the capacity to understand the nature and likely effects of treatment, which in some cases may be irreversible, and therefore may not be able to consent as a matter of law, so that such treatment, if given, would amount to an assault. He therefore submits that the provisions of Section 57(2)(a) of the Mental Health Act 1983 are designed to meet this problem and that accordingly the question of consent should be approached in the same way that the Court considers this problem when deciding if a normal patient has consented to medical treatment. The question therefore is whether, as a matter of fact, the patient has consented or agreed to the treatment. An apparent consent will not be a true consent if it has been obtained by fraud, misrepresentation, duress or fundamental mistake; but that is the extent of the enquiry.

In support of this proposition [counsel for the applicant] relies upon *Charterton v Gerson* [1981] QB 432, [1981] 1 All ER 257, at 442 of the former report where Bristow J said:

> In my judgment what the court has to do in each case is look at all the circumstances and say 'Was there a real consent?' I think justice requires that in order to vitiate the reality of consent there must be a greater failure of communication between doctor and patient than that involved in a breach of duty if the claim is based on negligence. When the claim is based on negligence the plaintiff must prove not only the breach of duty to inform, but that had the duty not been broken she would not have chosen to have the operation. Where the claim is based on trespass to the person, once it is shown that the consent is unreal, then what the

plaintiff would have decided if she had been given the information which would have prevented vitiation of the reality of her consent is irrelevant. In my judgment once the patient is informed in broad terms of the nature of the procedure which is intended, and gives her consent, that consent is real, and the cause of action on which to base a claim for failure to go into risks and implications is negligence, not trespass. Of course if information is withheld in bad faith, the consent will be vitiated by fraud.

[Counsel for the Commission], on the other hand, submits that this test is not appropriate in a public law setting; I confess I do not follow this distinction. He submits that whether or not a patient consents is a matter for the subjective judgment of the Commissioners and they can apply any test which in their discretion they think fit. I cannot accept this. No doubt the consent has to be an informed consent in that he knows the nature and likely effect of the treatment. There can be no doubt that the applicant knew this. So too in this case, where the treatment was not routinely used for control of sexual urges and was not sold for this purpose, it was important that the applicant should realise that the use on him was a novel one and the full implications with use on young men had not been studied, since trials had only been involved with animals and older men.

The court held that the regulations made under s 57 of the Mental Health Act 1983 only applied to 'the surgical implantation of hormones for the purposes of reducing male sexual drive' and that the synthetic compound 'Goserelin' given to the applicant was neither a 'hormone' nor was it given by 'surgical implantation'. (On these issues, see P Fennell 'Sexual Suppressants and the Mental Health Act' [1988] Crim LR 660.) In a case which did not involve the Mental Health Act or some such statute, the court would be more likely to use an analysis based upon negligence.

Chapter 15

Donation and transplant of human tissue and fluids

Introduction

In this chapter we are concerned with the donation and transplantation of human tissue. In large part, we examine the legality of donation for transplantation by live donors and by the dead. The emphasis, therefore, is upon therapeutic use of organs and human tissue. However, we also deal with other uses of human tissue, for example, for research. Use of dead human *bodies* is discussed in Chapter 18. Increasingly important is the regulation of commercial exploitation of human tissue, fluids and parts, whether for research purposes or otherwise. The legal framework is far from clear, in particular whether human body parts may be conceived legally as 'property' and subject thereafter to the legal regime pertaining to 'property'. Of course, the most common situation – and one that features most prominently in the public's mind – is that of donation for transplantation. Before turning to the legal issue we set the scene in respect of the latter.

In what is probably the leading review that has been undertaken on transplantation law and practice, the authors of the King's Fund Institute Report examine the situation in the UK as follows:

B New, M Soloman, R Dingwall, J McHale 'A Question of Give and Take: Improving the supply of donor organs for transplantation' Kings Fund Institute (1994)

The UK's procurement arrangements
The following describes a typical course of events involving the transplant of a cadaver organ into a recipient. Details will vary, as will the sequence of events, but the description offers a basic indication of how the system in the UK operates.

A typical transplantation
A potential donor will typically have suffered some form of massive cerebrovascular accident, such as intracranial haemorrhage or head trauma as a result of a road accident. Initially, they would be transferred to an intensive care unit (ICU) for ventilation, diagnosis and the hoped-for recovery. However, not all patients who suffer a cerebrovascular accident will be ventilated in an ICU. Some may suffer respiratory arrest after admission to a general ward and will not be ventilated if the prognosis looks hopeless. These patients can also be suitable as organ donors.

If recovery looks unlikely for those taken to ICU for diagnosis and treatment, the relatives are informed of this possibility by intensive care staff. Then the first of two sets of brain stem death tests are performed. If this test confirms death, and if there do not appear to be any general medical contraindications to donation, the ICU staff will make a formal request for organs. The transplant co-ordinators are notified and will typically travel to the donating hospital. The co-ordinators liaise with the relatives and the intensive care team, ensuring that the relatives are handled properly and – if donation is agreed – that the necessary organisational arrangements are taken care of. After a second set of brain stem death tests is performed, between six and twelve hours after the first, and if brain stem death is confirmed, the patient is proclaimed dead. The coroner must be informed if the death is 'reportable'; occasionally this will result in the coroner denying permission to go ahead with transplantation if a post-mortem examination is necessary.

Details differ depending on how many organs are being donated, with 'multi-organ' donors entailing the most difficult co-ordination . . . For kidneys, tissue-type matching is an important part of the process and due to the number of those on national waiting lists a beneficially matched recipient will normally be available. A convention is that one kidney will usually be retained locally and the other distributed according to a national waiting list on the basis of beneficial matching. The local kidney transplant team will remove both kidneys and, if they co-operate with the convention, send the second kidney to the relevant centre elsewhere in the country.

For a multi-organ donor, the non-renal surgical teams and transplant centre are selected on a national rota basis, depending on a suitable recipient being available – if the centre at the top of the list has a suitable recipient, then their team removes the organ and the centre is moved to the bottom of the list. A central element in the co-ordinators' practical role is to liaise with the UK Transplant Support Service Authority (UKTSSA) and non-renal teams to facilitate these processes. In general, organs are not removed unless it is believed that a suitable recipient is available.

The explanation – the surgical removal of organs – takes place at the donating hospital by the transplant teams when theatre time can be arranged. For multi-organ donation, the operation takes an average of about five hours. The transplant teams then take the organs back to their transplant units to complete the transplantation.

This brief outline essentially illustrates a 'best case'. At many points in the process potential donor organs can be lost: if brain stem death tests are not undertaken, or if relatives refuse permission to remove organs, or, as has been indicated, due to the difficulties of arranging for multiple donation. Partly to ensure that such losses were minimised, transplant co-ordinators were employed and these individuals are now an integral part of the transplantation process.

The transplant co-ordinators
The first transplant co-ordinators were introduced in the UK in the late 1970s. There are now approximately sixty posts, employed by Regional Heath Authorities and working in proximity to a transplant unit. In part their role is educational: the aim is to keep all health care professionals involved in transplantation activity abreast of the best practice and latest developments relating to donor suitability and the donor referral process. Updates are provided on current successes and initiatives. Although a wide range of health professionals are targeted, it is the critical care specialists – intensivists, critical care nurses and anaesthetists – who are considered particularly important.

The educational role is complemented by practical support in the donating unit at the time of donation. It is now estimated that 70 per cent of the co-ordinators will facilitate the process in this way – the remainder liaise over the telephone . . . Typically, co-ordinators arrive on the scene at some time between the two sets of brain stem death tests. They are not therefore directly involved in the initial elements of the transplant process – performing brain stem death tests, assessing for general medical contraindications and approaching the relatives with news of death and the initial request for donation – so it is these elements which constitute important parts of training and education. However, co-ordinators have a valuable practical role. They can provide support and advice for the families and ICU staff, organise the call up and arrival of transplant teams, liaise with UKTSSA over waiting lists and tissue-type matching, and arrange theatre time. Finally, the co-ordinators consider a vital element of their job to be the follow-up, both to the ICUs and to the families of the donors.

UK's transplantation activity
Between 1980 and 1991 the number of individuals in the UK with a functioning graft as a proportion of all those on renal replacement therapy increased from 44.0 per cent to 55.3 per cent – the highest in Europe . . . This increase in the proportion with a functioning graft was matched by a reasonably steady increase in the number of cadaveric transplants performed in the UK until the 1990s. Figure 6 shows, however, that since a peak of 1732 transplants in 1989 the number has dropped to 1624 transplants in 1992. The latest data from the UKTSSA show that this has dropped further to 1562 in 1993 . . . Waiting lists have risen steadily, however, reaching a peak of 4361 people waiting for a kidney in the UK at the end of 1992.

The UK has only a small proportion of reported transplanted kidneys from live donors, currently constituting about 5 per cent of the total. Unfortunately, the United Kingdom Transplant Support Service Authority (UKTSSA) does not hold data on live donations prior to 1989, but estimates from surveys of individual transplant centres indicate that up until 1989 the proportion of all transplants from live donors was approximately 10 per cent . . . . Certainly since 1989 the number of live transplants undertaken has dropped from 118 to 91 (UKTSSA, personal communication). This reduction is at odds with the world-wide trend described earlier.

Figure 6 UK cadaveric kidney transplants performed and numbers waiting at year end, 1980–1992

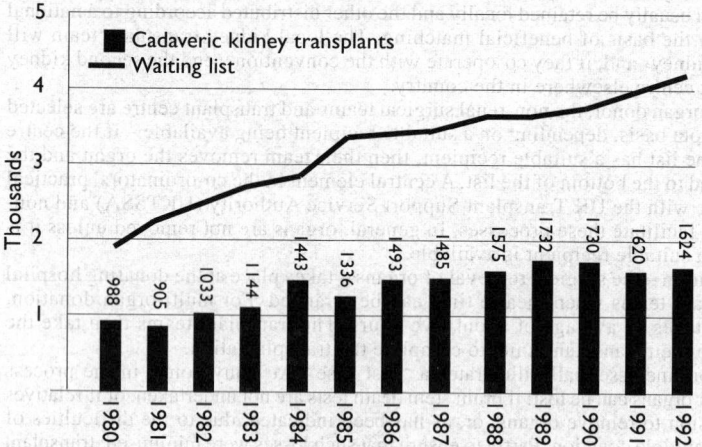

Note: Data do not include combined kidney and pancreas transplants
Sources: UKTSSA and Healthcare Parliamentary Monitor, 5 August 1991.

Activity for liver and heart transplants are shown in Figure 7. Heart transplant activity has followed the trend observed for the world total: a steady increase until the 1990s when the rate levelled off at just over 300 transplants per year. The number of liver transplants has risen more steadily, again following the world trend, reaching 506 transplants in 1992. Waiting lists for both these technologies are relatively low when compared with those for kidney transplants: those waiting for a heart at the end of 1992 numbered 325, and those for liver only 83. In the UK these data are only available as a useful estimate of need from 1990, before which they included patients on European waiting lists. On this limited evidence they are both rising: the heart waiting list stood at 239 in 1990, that for liver at 57.

Figure 7 UK and Eire heart and liver transplants, 1983–1992

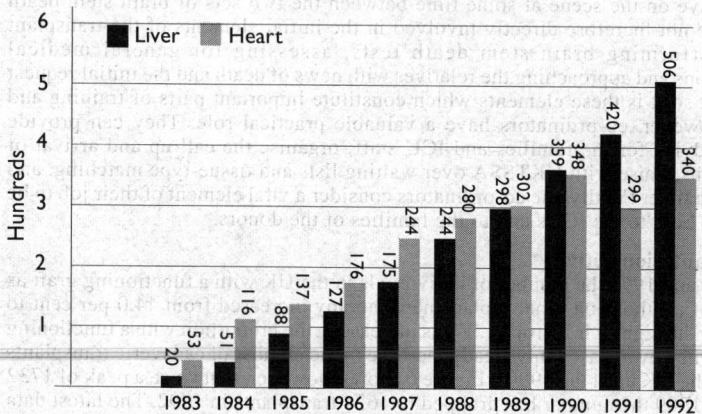

Note: Heart transplants include 'domino hearts' but not combined heart and lung.
Source: UKTSSA

The report highlights an issue that we shall return to later – the gap between supply and demand (pp 15–16):

The increases in transplantation activity during the 1980s did not succeed in guaranteeing an organ for everyone who would benefit, and for the majority of people long waits, particularly for kidneys, were the norm. The plateau in kidney transplantation has now made this situation worse. International data for those waiting for a kidney transplant are less readily available than for transplants themselves, but good data are available for the UK and some European countries. Figure 5 shows the aggregate number of kidney transplants performed from cadaveric donors, and waiting lists at the year end, in the UK and Eurotransplant region – the area covered by the Eurotransplant Foundation for co-ordinating and promoting transplantation activity in Austria, Belgium, Germany, Luxembourg and the Netherlands. The number of transplants rose from 14.7 pmp in 1989 to 30.8 pmp in 1992, but the last two years have seen a decrease in activity and, overall, the trend echoes that of world activity. However, the number of those on waiting lists continues to rise steadily. Almost 15,000 were waiting for a kidney in the six countries at the end of 1992, with the gap between those waiting and those receiving transplant growing ever wider.

Those waiting for a heart and liver do not face such a long wait, although the situation is getting worse and, of course, many die before an organ becomes available. Between 1987 and 1992 the number waiting for a heart in the Eurotransplant region has increased from 96 to 938, and for a liver from 95 to 344, though these figures include ex-German Democratic Republic patients from 1990 onwards. Transplants only increased from 392 to 753 for hearts, and from 273 to 780 for livers over the same period. Non-renal organ transplants are constrained by the availability of transplant centres and by technical aspects to a greater degree than kidneys. Ultimately, though, they depend on donors, and to that extent face the same constraint as kidney transplantation.

The problem facing the transplant community can therefore be simply stated; there are not enough organs to meet demand, and the situation is getting worse. Waiting times are long – in the UK the wait for an average patient for a kidney at the end of 1992 was two and a half years – and are getting longer. Up until recently the international transplant community might have consoled itself with the thought that at least more people were being treated, but this is, on an aggregate level, no longer the case.

Interestingly, it is not necessarily the lack of human and capital resources which is constraining kidney transplant activity. The United Kingdom has 36 centres undertaking transplantation activity during 1991 at an average of 49 transplants per centre. However, a recent review of specialist services in London recommended that to ensure a high quality of outcome transplant centres should each conduct at least 100 grafts annually, justifying a team of three or four surgeons and ensuring the economical use of nursing staff . . . They suggested that this meant that London's regions' 14 centres should be reduced to five. Furthermore these recommendations were made with a view to a maximum throughput of 600 operations as opposed to the current 480. So a reduction in current capacity would still leave plenty of room for growth if only the organs were available.

Figure 5 Total cadaveric kidney transplantation rates and waiting list figures in the UK and Eurotransplant region, 1980–1992

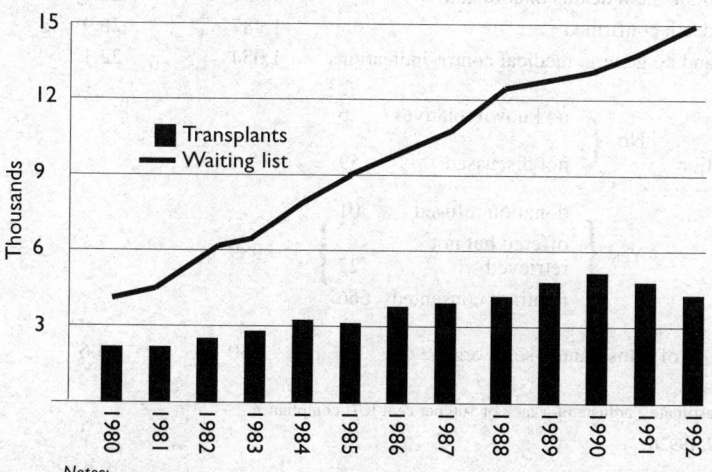

Notes:
1   Eurotransplant region consists of: Austria, Belgium, Germany, Luxembourg, Netherlands.
2   Figures exclude ex-DDR residents.
Source: As Figure 1.

The authors comment on the 'efficiency' of organ retrieval in the UK as follows (pp 28–29):

> The best estimate of how well the 'pool' is utilised in the UK is provided by the work of Sheila Gore and colleagues from the MRC Biostatistics Unit, as a result of a recommendation from the Hoffenberg committee . . . The study – henceforward referred to as the 'national audit' – undertook a confidential audit of all deaths in intensive care units in England in 1989 and 1990. It does not, therefore, include potential donors on general wards, but nevertheless provides the best evidence of how effectively potential donors in ICUs are managed in England. A brief summary of the results is presented in Table 5.
>
> One finding from the audit not reported in Table 5 was the regional variation in confirmed brain stem deaths. The researchers recommended increasing the number of brain stem death tests, but it was acknowledged that much of the variation in the number of tests undertaken could be explained by variations in the incidence of deaths from non-cranial causes. This supports the findings reported above: variations in donor rates will be due in part to variations in intracranial haemorrhage rates.
>
> Although a significant proportion of potential brain stem deaths are not tested (perhaps indicating that potential donors are lost), it has been noted that 'possibly' brain stem dead individuals can show clear general medical contraindications to organ donation, thereby rendering formal testing redundant . . . Furthermore, only six per cent of potential donors' families were not formally approached with a request for donation. Rather more significant is the number of relatives who refused permission for donation to go ahead – 30 per cent (301 from 989) of those with whom organ donation was discussed. Reducing this proportion should clearly be an important policy goal. However, it would require this proportion to be reduced to close to zero for the UK to approach the transplantation rates of Belgium, Spain and Austria. Clearly this is highly unlikely, even under a reasonably strict interpretation of presumed constant legislation.

Table 5   Estimated numbers of ICU deaths per year in various categories based on the national audit of ICUs in England, 1989 and 1990

Category	Estimated numbers	pmp
■ ICUs account for approximately 84 per cent of cadaveric solid organ donors. Estimated number of deaths in ICUs per year	13,000	
■ Number of deaths considered to 'possibly' satisfy brain stem death criteria	1,768	37.0
■ Number of brain stem deaths undertaken	1,339	28.0
■ Brain stem death confirmed	1,287	26.9
■ Confirmed and no general medical contra-indications	1,054	22.1

Organ donation offered to relatives?

No { no known relatives 6
not discussed 59

Yes { donation refused 301
offered but not retrieved 22
relatives consented 666 } 989

	Estimated numbers	pmp
■ Became donor of transplanted solid organ	650	13.6

Note: figures are estimates, adjusted for lack of 100 per cent ICU compliance

Source: Gore *et al*, 1992b

We will return to the conclusions of this Report later in the chapter when we examine reform of the law in the UK.

The living donor

A. CONSENT: THE COMMON LAW

1. Adults

The first issue that we should consider is whether an adult may, as a matter of law, validly consent to the removal of an organ for transplantation.

Jesse Dukeminier 'Supplying Organs for Transplantation' (1970) 68 Michigan Law Review 811

Mayhem is the crime of intentionally and maliciously maiming or disfiguring a person. At common law, mayhem was limited only to deprivation of such of a man's organs 'as may render him the less able, in fighting, either to defend himself or to annoy his adversary'. Included were a man's hand, his finger, his foot, his testicle, or his eye. The significance of the organs in fighting is irrelevant today, and modern statutes have extended the crime of mayhem to disfigurings in general and to the disfiguring of women as well as of men. Under modern law, it is possible to contend that surgically removing an internal organ from a person constitutes mayhem.

Again the question arises whether, if removing a kidney for transplantation is mayhem, consent by the donor is a defense to the charge. Only two cases are even remotely relevant, Coke in 1603, [1 *Coke on Littleton* para 194 at 126.6] 'a strong and lustie rogue' directed his companion to cut off the rogue's left hand so that he might get out of work and beg more effectively. Both the rogue and his companion were convicted of mayhem; consent was held to be no defense to the crime. In *State v Bass* [(1961) 130 SE 2d 481] a man wanted his fingers cut off so that he could collect insurance money. With full knowledge of the purpose, a physician deadened four fingers of the man's left hand, which were then cut off by another man using an electric saw. The physician was convicted of being an accessory to mayhem. The court held that consent of the person was no defense to the charge. Although the opinion of the court in *State v Bass* was extremely vague, the court apparently thought that cutting off the fingers was no 'benefit' to the man and that the conduct was 'antisocial'. The court did not indicate what policy propositions it assumed in its determination that insurance proceeds provided no offsetting benefits for the loss of the fingers and that the conduct was antisocial.

The Law Reform Commission of Australia's Report No 7 (1977) on 'Human Tissue Transplants' (pp 22–24) states as follows:

The common law of…England, offers no rule or principle dealing with human tissue transplants as such, nor, for that matter, with surgery as such. There is a lack of case law, and in the rare decisions when judges have spoken on the common law principles applicable to surgery, the central issues have not involved the lawfulness of the surgery, but other legal questions such as divorce, or injury during a sporting event. This has caused resort to analogy and rationalisation by some legal writers, resulting in suggestions that common law principles applicable to transplantation may be derived from consideration of recondite legal rules such as the ancient common law offence of 'maim'. More accepted and authoritative (but in the opinion of some hardly less bizarre) has been the suggestion that surgery amounts in law to 'assault and battery' (hereinafter called assault), thus falling under the law of trespass 'based on the inviolability of the person'. In extra-curial analyses of the common law both Lord Devlin [*Samples of Law Making* (1962) at 83–103] and Lord Justice Edmund Davies [(1969) 62 *Proc of Roy Soc of Med* 633] have taken this view of surgery. The opinions of such judges as these, and the lack of judicial precedent, expose the failure of the common law to provide acceptable answers to the modern medical practice of transplantation. There is little prospect of a constructive reply to the plea for reform made by Professor Daube in 1966 [*Ethics in Medical Progress* (1966) at 183]:

An operation should be treated as a positive, beneficent, admirable action from the outset, not as a lawful infliction of harm. It is a cure, and only where essential elements are lacking in a situation does it become wrongful. After all, we do not construe marital…intercourse as rape licensed by virtue of consent…

Briefly, the common law principles of assault, in their application to the transplantation of human tissue (and to surgery generally) may be seen from the following summary. First, assault amounts to a tort, or civil wrong, giving rise to a private claim for damages enforceable in the courts. Assault is also a crime, punishable by criminal process. Secondly, the common law regards all surgery as a trespass to the person but one which can be justified or defended, in the case of the tort of assault, on the basis of consent given by the patient. Thus, it will be a defence to claim for damages for assault if the surgeon proves that the patient consented to the operation. This defence, unfortunately, may not extend to the case of the emergency-unconscious patient, or the patient who lacks legal capacity (a small child or a mental patient). Worse, it may have no application at all in the case of a live donor of tissue, because, despite his consent, it cannot be said that the surgery on him is for his benefit. Thirdly, in the case of the crime of assault, at least, occasioning 'grievous bodily harm', consent of the patient or victim is no defence to a charge…

…However, the proposition that consent is no defence to a criminal charge is the general rule, and exceptions have been made to it. Presumably normal surgery would be an exception, but there is no decided case directly in point. The consent should be free and informed. The surgeon should advise the patient of all material facts relevant to the operation so that the patient may balance risk and benefit. Deception or even failure to make full disclosure may vitiate consent. The law and literature on 'consent' is extensive, requiring separate consideration of the adult patient, the child, the mentally incompetent, and the patient who is unconscious or an emergency case…

Consent to assault: What does the common law have to say to a 'normal' donor, that is to say an adult, with mental competence, properly advised, and anxious to give tissue for transplant, for example, one of two healthy kidneys? At first sight it may seem that removal of the tissue would not offend any legal principle. However, the criminal law is not entirely sympathetic to the defence of 'consent'. In addition, it cannot be said, in any normal sense, that the removal of the tissue is for the benefit of the donor. It follows that the surgeon's legal position is not easily determined.

Professor Gerald Dworkin, writing in 1970, states the following:

G Dworkin 'The Law Relating to Organ Transplantation in England' (1970) 33 MLR 353

To determine the legality of live donor transplantations it is first necessary to examine the legal basis for surgical operations generally. Under medieval law, a person committed the crime of mayhem (maim) if he so injured another as to make him less able to fight or to defend himself or to annoy an adversary. To amputate a limb, even with the victim's consent was, on the face of it, an unlawful act, since it deprived the king of a fighting man. In early Victorian times when soldiers, as part of their training, had to bite cartridges, a soldier got a dentist to pullout his front teeth to enable him to avoid training and it was thought that both were guilty of a crime. The modern law is obscure but the crime, to some extent, turns of two interconnected factors. The first is the nature of the physical harm: one person does not have a licence to mutilate or cause bodily harm to another for any purpose merely because that person has consented. The degree of bodily harm is, of course, important: the test is no longer whether it impairs or may impair the victim's ability to fight for his country, but presumably the seriousness of the harm must be of that order. 'Bodily harm…includes any hurt or injury calculated to interfere with the health or comfort of the prosecutor. Such hurt or injury need not be permanent, but must, no doubt, be more than merely transient or trifling.' The second factor involves questions of public policy. The law may permit some kinds of assault and battery but not others: the dividing line between the permissible and the impermissible is not clear but the courts have accepted and still accept the burden of safeguarding individuals even against themselves.

The relevance of this aspect of the criminal law is that it provides a basis for saying that many surgical operations are *prima facie* unlawful. Without further justification not only would operations be criminal acts, but they would also be unlawful in the civil law and surgeons might be liable to pay compensation for the consequences of their acts, even though they had exercised all reasonable care. What are the criteria, then, which convert unlawful acts into lawful surgical operations? In some countries the criminal codes absolve from responsibility persons who perform in good faith and with reasonable care and skill a surgical operation upon another person, with his consent and for his benefit, if the performance of the operation is reasonable in the circumstances. No such provision appears in any United Kingdom legislation but it is clear, of course, that surgery, within limits, is a perfectly legal activity. Sir James Fitzjames Stephen formulated the general proposition that 'everyone has a right to consent to the infliction of any bodily injury in the nature of a surgical operation upon himself' and stated that although he knew of no authority for this, the existence of surgery as a profession assumed its truth…

Professor Dworkin then identifies four conditions to be specified:

(i) *The patient must give a full, free and informed consent...*
(ii) *The operation must be therapeutic; it must be expressly for the patient's benefit.* The major distinguishing feature between surgical operations and unlawful mutilation is, of course, that all surgical operations are allegedly in the medical interests of the patient. Coke refers to a case in 1603 where 'a young and lustie rogue prevailed upon a friend to cut off his left hand, so that he might be better able to beg'. Both were found guilty of the crime of maim; today they would also be criminally liable. In the criminal codes of some countries, the provisions concerning surgical operations expressly state that they must be for the patient's benefit; in other countries this, until recently, has been accepted as being obvious.
(iii) *There must be lawful justification.* This is a relatively unexplored and open-ended requirement. Ethical and social questions are more relevant here and the courts may occasionally use this rubric to extend the law to meet new circumstances. Most surgical operations are lawful. The most obvious example of an unlawful operation is that of abortion because, apart from those cases where abortion is permissible under the Abortion Act 1967, abortions are statutory criminal offences, whether performed by doctors or unqualified persons...It is unlikely that the courts would condemn circumcision as unlawful. No doubt the ritual circumcision of Jewish infants could be upheld on grounds of religious toleration, although circumcision for non-religious reasons would have to be accepted on wider public policy grounds.
(iv) *Generally, the operation must be performed by a person with appropriate medical skills.*

Professor Dworkin goes on to examine the legality of transplantation in the context of kidney transplants.

Is it lawful to remove a kidney from a live donor?
The legality of live donor transplants turns upon whether or not the first three conditions for lawful surgical operations are satisfied.

First, is the operation therapeutic? There is no doubt that the purpose of a kidney transplant is to benefit the donee. It seems equally clear that to take a kidney from a living donor can rarely be of any benefit to him, it is arguable that the donor who is left with one healthy kidney maybe in no worse position that he is with two, since after a time the remaining kidney apparently does the work of two. Indeed, it may be that life insurance companies would accept an otherwise healthy donor as a normal risk. The difficulty, however, arises should anything happen to the solitary kidney: a kidney illness to a person with only one kidney is generally far more serious than to a person with two. A kidney transplant, then, in most cases can be of no therapeutic value to the donor.

Secondly, is there lawful justification for the surgical procedure? It has been suggested that the removal of a kidney from a healthy donor is not a maiming in the accepted sense because it is no great disability in most cases to lose one kidney. One calculation suggests that the total risk involved to the donor is 0.12 percent, divided into an immediate risk of 0.05 per cent as a post-operative accidental risk, and 0.07 per cent as the risk of any kind of accident occurring later to affect the remaining kidney. Whether or not this can be said to be a maiming, it is most certainly the infliction of bodily harm which is capable of being more than transient or trifling.

Arguments, of varying force, can be put forward to support the view that such transplants are lawfully justified. Thus, the courts have by implication recognised the legality of some kinds of homografts; for example, the practice of taking blood from donors for the purposes of blood transfusions is incapable, without more, of being legally challenged today. The position of a blood donor and a kidney donor, although in some ways similar in kind, is, however, clearly different in degree. It is difficult to categorise the blood transfusion procedure as the infliction of bodily harm of more than a trifling or transient nature.

Perhaps a closer, though by no means close, analogy is that of skin-grafting. In an American case, *Bonner v Moran* [(1941) 126 F 2d 121 (US CA DC)], a court held a surgeon liable for trespass when a fifteen-year-old boy consented to skin grafts being taken from his body for the benefit of his badly burned cousin. The basis of the decision was that the boy was not old enough to give his consent, and his parents should have done so for him. By implication, it can be argued that the court would have allowed a non-therapeutic skin-graft had the proper consent been obtained.

Another argument is that the courts should treat a volunteer in this situation in the same favourable way as rescuers. A volunteer who risks his life or exposes himself to injury, for example, in rescuing a person from a fire, is not condemned for his actions if he has acted reasonably, nor are they regarded as unlawful; instead, he may be entitled to recover damages for any injury he suffers from the person whose negligence created the dangerous situation. The courts treat rescuers favourably: 'danger invites rescue' is now an accepted phrase. If this is so, the law should look favourably on a volunteer donor so that the act would not be categorised as unlawful.

These are merely some arguments which a willing court might use if it was prepared to restate the existing law to meet new medical trends. Speaking extra-judicially, Edmund Davies LJ has said [(1969) 63 *Proc Roy Soc Med* 633 at 634] that he would

> be surprised if a surgeon were successfully sued for trespass to the person or convicted of causing bodily harm to one of full age and intelligence who freely consented to act as donor – always provided that the operation did not present unreasonable risk to the donor's life or health. That proviso is essential. A man may declare himself ready to die for another, but the surgeon must not take him at his word.

Until this issue is judicially or legislatively resolved, however, it is arguable in legal theory that the taking of a kidney from a healthy donor is normally an unlawful operation.

Thirdly, is there an informed voluntary consent? Even if the courts were to decide that live donor transplants were, within limits, lawfully justified, problems could arise in connection with the donor's consent to the removal of a kidney. In addition to all the strict requirements that the donor must be fully informed of all the relevant facts and risks, so that he can make up his own mind, difficulties may arise in those situations where the donor and donee are related. The relationship between donor and donee may be, for example, that of twins or parent and child: in these family situations the social and psychological pressures upon a person who knows that his failure to give consent will result in the death of the sick person must be very strong indeed. It may often be difficult to decide whether a consent in this situation is truly voluntary. It is true that where doctors are in doubt whether the donor's consent is in fact voluntary they may solve the problem (for the donor, at least, and his family, though not for the potential donee) by saying that the donor is medically unsuitable. Although the medical prospects are better where the blood relationship is closest, the chances of a truly voluntary consent are greater where the relationship is distant or non-existent.

Thus, our view is that *prima facie* an adult can give valid consent to the removal of an organ or other tissue for the purposes of transplantation (notice also art 19 of the European Convention on Human Rights and Biomedicine (1996)). However, in determining whether in any particular case a valid consent may have been given the law may take account of a number of factors.

First, the law will have regard to whether the tissue is regenerative (eg blood or bone marrow) or is non-regenerative (eg a kidney). (See Dukeminier and Sanders 'Medical Advances and Legal Lag: Haemodialysis and Kidney Transplantation' (1968) 15 UCLA Law Review 357.) The distinction is a factual one. Its relevance in law arguably lies in the fact that in the case of non-regenerative tissue the risks to the donor's health will ordinarily be greater (even in the case of the donor's consent of twinned organs such as kidneys) such that the law in determining the validity of the consent will scrutinise more carefully the benefit/burden ratio.

Secondly, if the tissue is not only non-regenerative but is also vital for life, eg a liver or heart, any consent would be invalid since the surgeon would commit murder.

Thirdly, it is doubtful that the donation is beneficial to the donor in that it is in his medical interests. It may be enough, however, that it does not harm him despite the normal notion that medical treatment to be lawful should be in the patient's interests, if not best interests.

As regards this third point, Peter Skegg comments, in *Law, Ethics and Medicine* (at p 36):

> …Indeed, sometimes a procedure is performed on a person in the knowledge that it will certainly be to that person's bodily detriment. This is the case when a kidney is removed from a healthy person, for transplantation into someone who is in need of it. The operation is a major one, and is not without risks. But it is not unreasonably dangerous, and the probable benefit to the recipient far outweighs the probable detriment to the donor. Hence, if called upon to deal with a case in which a kidney had been removed from a consenting adult, for transplantation into someone in need of it, the courts may confidently be expected to take the view that the operation did not amount to the offence of battery. Even though the operation causes serious bodily harm, there is clearly a good reason for it…

He continues (p 37):

> ...A court is not likely to inquire closely into whether there are good reasons for a particular intervention. There is no danger of a court attempting to decide whether there were good reasons for removing a kidney from a living donor, instead of keeping the patient on dialysis in the hope that a suitable cadaver kidney would become available...

He then concludes (p 43):

> To revert to the example of the removal of a kidney from a living person for transplantation to another: as there is a shortage of kidneys for transplantation, and as transplants from living donors are at least as successful as those from cadavers, the courts may be expected to accept that there is a 'just cause or excuse' or 'good reason', for such operations. Where consent is also present, such operations will not amount to the offence of causing grievous bodily harm.

Finally, we should notice that the Law Commission in its Consultation Paper (No 139) *Consent in the Criminal Law* (1995) accepted the conclusions of Professors Dworkin and Skegg. Without settling on any particular legal basis, the Law Commission concluded that 'there can be no doubt that, once a valid consent has been forthcoming, English law now treats as lawful operative procedures designed to remove regenerative tissue, and also non-regenerative tissue that is not essential for life' (para 8.32) (see generally *supra*, ch 5).

2. Children

Notwithstanding the development of modern anti-immunosuppressant drugs, transplants are more likely to be successful between genetically related individuals because of the increased chances of a better tissue match. Siblings, including minors, constitute, therefore, a potential class of good donors. In the UK it seems that organ donation by living children is rare, ie 'solid' organs such as kidneys or liver lobes. However, this is not so for regenerative tissue such as bone marrow donations. As regards organs, J K Mason and A McCall Smith in *Law and Medical Ethics* (5th edn, 1999) comment as follows (at pp 346–7):

> Our inquiries indicate that no currently practising British transplant surgeon would accept a live child as an organ donor; only one such instance, involving an identical twin aged 17 years, has arisen in the United Kingdom in the last 15 years. Only five living minor donors have been used in the Eurotransplant catchment area and none has been recorded in France, despite the enabling legislation; similarly, none is recorded by Scandiatransplant.

Limitations on the ability of minors to donate are not uncommon in legislative provisions. Often this is based upon a fear that where the child is incompetent, the parents will be placed in an impossible position in deciding whether to consent if the donation is necessary for the well-being (possibly life) of another child. Price and Garwood-Gowers survey the European scene as follows:

David PT Price and Austen Garwood-Gowers 'Transplantation From Minors: Are Children Other People's Medicine?' (1995) 1 Contemporary Issues in Law 1

> In a number of countries within Europe legislation specifically prohibits the use of minors as living transplant organ donors, for example, in Spain, Portugal, Finland, Greece, Romania and Russia. Outside Europe also certain national laws prohibit donation by minors, for example in Algeria, Argentina and Mexico. Various other European countries permit living donation by minors, but subject to the satisfaction of pre-conditions. In Norway a minor under 18 may donate an organ where he or she consents, where special grounds exist and where the authorisation of the guardian and the person exercising parental authority and responsibility for the care of the minor, and the Directorate of Health Services, have been obtained. In France, a minor may only donate an organ to a sibling. The minor's legal representative must consent and the authority

of a committee of three experts be given. The views of the minor have to be sought wherever possible and the donation may not proceed where the minor objects. In Denmark, a competent minor may donate subject only to parental consent also having been given. Outside Europe certain countries have similar legal regimes. In South Africa minors may donate with the consent of parents or guardians. In the Syrian Arab Republic minors may donate organs only where the donor and recipient are twin brothers and the consent of one parent or guardian is provided. In one or two jurisdictions competent minors may donate without further pre-requisites being satisfied, for example, Turkey.

Laws relating to the donation of regenerable tissue of minors are sometimes more permissive. For example, although the donation of organs by minors is prohibited in Greece and Russia, the donation of bone marrow by minors is permitted, similarly all renewable tissue in Finland, subject to conditions. Laws relating to blood donation by minors vary significantly. In some jurisdictions, such as Romania and Algeria this is prohibited, whilst in others a minor can donate subject to his or her agreement and parental consent. In Italy, a minor aged under 18 can donate platelets and leucocytes, but not whole blood or plasma, subject to parental, or judicial curator, consent.

Similar concerns have led to restrictions in Canada and Australia. As regards Canada, Ellen Picard and Gerald Robertson comment as follows:

Ellen I Picard and Gerald B Robertson *Legal Liability of Doctors and Hospitals in Canada* (3rd edn, 1996)

In most provinces the legislation makes no provision for *inter vivos* donation of non-regenerative tissue by a minor, and this effectively rules out such a procedure, because *inter vivos* transplantation can only be done in accordance with the Act and not otherwise. (The Human Tissue Gift Act, R.S.A. 1980, s 3(2)). However, a few provinces have recently amended their legislation to permit *inter vivos* donation of non-regenerative tissue by minors aged 16 years or over (Human Tissue Act, RSM 1987 s 10(1); Human Tissue Gift Act R.S.O. 1990, s 3(1); Human Tissue Donation Act, S.P.E.I., 1992, s 6(1)). In some provinces this is subject to a number of conditions and limitations; for example, the parents must consent (*Ibid* s 10(2)(b)), the proposed recipient must be a member of the donor's immediate family (Human Tissue Act, R.S.M. 1987 s 10(2)(c)), and an independent assessment must be conducted (Human Tissue Donation Act S.P.E.I. 1992, ss 6(3)).

Three provinces – Manitoba, (Human Tissue Act, RSM, 1987 s 11), P.E.I. (Human Tissue Donation Act, S.P.E.I. 1992 ss 6, 7), and Quebec (Civil Code of Quebec, art 19) – have amended their legislation to permit the removal of regenerative tissue from children, subject to a number of restrictions and safeguards.

As regards Australia, John Devereux summarises the state legislation first as regards *regenerative* and then *non-regenerative* tissue as follows:

John Devereux *Medical Law: Text, Cases and Materials* (1997)

All jurisdictions (except the Northern Territory) provide for the removal of regenerative tissue from children. However, this must only be for the purpose of transplantation into the body of a parent or sibling. In Western Australia, Tasmania and the Australian Capital Territory, this is extended to include transplantation into the body of a relative.

Consent may be given in writing by a parent of the child, following medical advice as to the nature and effect of the removal, which must be furnished to, and understood by, both parent and child.

In all jurisdictions except South Australia and Western Australia, an accompanying certificate must be provided by a designated officer or medical practitioner which typically must restate the terms of the consent and:
*   that the requisite medical advice was duly furnished;
*   the consent was given in his or her presence;
*   the parent was of sound mind and freely gave the consent;
*   that the child understood the nature and effect of the tissue removal and transplantation;
*   the child was in agreement with the proposed procedure.

In Queensland, a cooling-off period of 24 hours is additionally required.

In South Australia, the tissue removal must be approved by a ministerial committee.

Only Victoria and Queensland make provision for removal of regenerative tissue from a child who does not, due to his or her age, understand what is going on. These States provide that the relevant designated officer or medical practitioner additionally certify that they are of the opinion that the proposed recipient family member is in danger of dying without the transplant. In

Queensland, there is the added proviso, which must also be certified, that the risk to the donor child is minimal . . .

The Australian Capital Territory is the only jurisdiction which makes provision for the removal of non-regenerative tissue from a child. All other jurisdictions forbid it, expressly or impliedly.

In the Australian Capital Territory, the tissue removal may only take place when a family member is in danger of dying without a transplant and both parents of the child consent to the procedure. These two requirements must be incorporated into a certificate given by the relevant medical practitioner, which also contains the other declarations noted above. The matter must then be referred to a ministerial committee for decision. Where only one parent is available, the matter may still be referred to the committee.

In England, as we shall see, there is no directly relevant legislation. What, then, is the law? Can a child in his own right ever in law consent to donate an organ or tissue to another? (See, generally, DPT Price and A Garwood-Gowers 'Transplantation From Minors: Are Children Other People's Medicine?' (1995) 1 Contemporary Issues in Law 1.) In the absence of any statutory guidance, two views of the common law may be advanced. The first would mirror the analysis in *Gillick*; the second would suggest that there are some things to which a child may not in law consent and thereby equates competence with majority or some other particular cut-off point.

If we take the second view first, not only does this apparently fly in the face of *Gillick* but it also poses problems for a traditional common law approach which does not rely on particular cut-off points. Granted that there may be a distinction between the situation of transplantation and *Gillick* in that here the intervention may not be 'treatment' in the narrow sense of *obviously* benefiting the child; none the less there seems no reason to limit *Gillick* to that sort of procedure. Furthermore, it leaves unclear what the particular cut-off point would be. The age of 16 seems to have no particular relevance because s 8(1) of the Family Law Reform Act 1969 would only put the matter beyond doubt if every donation by a child was indisputably seen as 'treatment'.

In fact, very few donations can be seen as treatment even given a liberal interpretation of that term (see *Re W (a minor) (medical treatment)* [1992] 4 All ER 627 at 647 per Nolan LJ). But yet, can it be said that a donation of blood by a 17-year-old highly intelligent person, which is unlikely to attract the description 'treatment', is unlawful in every case? If our legal instinct leads us to answer 'no', then we must look elsewhere for a guiding principle. What of the attainment of the age of 18, the only other candidate? Why should the attaining of majority be relevant? Can it be the case that, until majority, every donation is unlawful? Our example of the 17-year-old blood donor, which admittedly is proposed without authority, suggests otherwise.

This takes us back to our first view that the *Gillick* decision would also be relevant in this context, ie that the competence in law of a child must turn on the child's capacity to understand or comprehend the proposed procedure. This would produce the conclusion that the validity of the child's consent will turn on such factual questions as the seriousness of the intervention, the degree of risk intrinsic in the procedure, the long-term implications for the donor and so on. It may be, therefore, that it would be a rare child whom the law would find competent to consent to the donation of a kidney as against the donation of blood (see *Re W, supra,* per Lord Donaldson MR at 635). But the law has no hard and fast rule.

3. Parents, the court and others

The question here is the extent in law to which a proxy, usually a parent, can volunteer a child as the donor of an organ or other tissue. In analysing the legal regime regulating the proxy's authority, a significant factor must be the seriousness of the procedure involved and its consequences. Removal of a kidney calls for more careful deliberation than perhaps the removal of a small quantity of skin or blood. Removal of bone barrow, which may be a painful process carrying certain risks but which is less serious in its consequences than the removal of a kidney since it regenerates, falls somewhere between these.

We have already seen the general approach adopted by the law in analysing the authority of the proxy (*supra*, ch 6) in our discussion of the general law of consent, specifically in cases such as *Bonner v Moran* (1941) 126 F 2d 121; *Hart v Brown* (1972) 289 A 2d 386; *Strunk v Strunk* (1969) 445 SW 2d 145; *Curran v Bosze* (1990) 566 NE 2d 1319 (Ill Sup Ct) and the important English case of *Re Y (mental patient: bone marrow donation)* [1996] 2 FLR 787, [1997] Fam 110 (Connell J). The cases make two points. First, if the legal test is 'best interests' of the incompetent donor, then they appear to identify a doubtful notion of benefit, ie the psychological and emotional benefits derived from altruism. Secondly, if the courts are not adopting this approach then are they introducing another test, that the proxy may consent to that which is 'not against the interests' of the incompetent donor. This would allow the proxy to consent to a wider range of interventions, including some tissue donations. But, it is doubtful whether this would be so where the procedure involves other than minimal risk, ie kidney rather than blood donation.

Where an incompetent person is an adult, we have seen that the law does not empower anyone to consent to treatment regarding that adult. *A fortiori*, this would apply to decisions regarding the removal of healthy tissue. Further, we have seen that the court has no power to consent as *parens patriae* to treatment; *a fortiori* to the removal of healthy tissue. Thus, the question is whether the removal of tissue for transplantation would fall within the approach of the House of Lords in *Re F*, ie as being in the person's 'best interests'.

There is little doubt that if this were the test applied, removal of tissue from an incompetent adult for transplantation would be unlawful. It is an open question, therefore, whether the analytical strategy referred to above as regards children, namely resort to a test of 'not against the interests' of the incompetent represents the law.

Given the nature and the context of organ or tissue donation from an incompetent adult or child, it is likely that the courts will either require (in the case of the child) or consider it desirable (in the case of an adult), that any case in which donation is contemplated should be brought before the court. We discussed this earlier (*supra*, ch 6) where it will be recalled that Neill LJ and Lord Bridge in *Re F* specifically mentioned 'live organ donation' as just such a situation (see also *Re W (a minor) (medical treatment)* [1992] 4 All ER 627 at 648–669 per Nolan LJ). Subsequently, in *Re Y (mental patient: bone marrow donation* [1997] Fam 110 at 116, Connell J stated that the court's prior sanction was required in the case of bone marrow donation (a regenerative tissue) by an incompetent adult (see *supra*, ch 6).

Finally, we should note the provisions of the European Convention on Human Rights and Biomedicine. Article 20 recognises that, 'exceptionally', an organ or tissue may be removed from an incompetent adult or child.

Article 20. (Protection of persons not able to consent to organ removal)
1.　No organ or tissue removal may be carried out on a person who does not have the capacity to consent under Article 5.
2.　Exceptionally and under the protective conditions prescribed by law, the removal of regenerative tissue from a person who does not have the capacity to consent may be authorised provided the following conditions are met:
　i.　there is no compatible donor available who has the capacity to consent.
　ii.　the recipient is a brother or sister of the donor,
　iii.　the donation must have the potential to be life-saving for the recipient,
　iv.　the authorisation provided for under paragraphs 2 and 3 of Article 6 has been given specifically and in writing, in accordance with the law and with the approval of the competent body,
　v.　the potential donor concerned does not object.

As you will see, the 'exception' to the general prohibition in para 1 is very specific. In particular, the recipient must be a 'brother or sister of the donor'. This limitation does not feature explicitly in English law following *Re Y (supra)*. However, it may be implicit, and be the usual circumstance, given the approach of Connell J in *Re Y* on the need for a 'close knit family' sufficient to show adequate detriment to the donor of losing the relative. Notice that the donor, although not competent, must not object. This would undoubtedly be reflected in an English court's approach in evaluating the 'best interests' of the incompetent donor. Finally, you will see that para 2(iv) requires that consent ('authorisation') be given under art 6 (ie by a recognised proxy) and 'with the approval of the competent body'. The latter would reflect the requirement in *Re Y* to seek court approval before proceeding. It is also reflected in the Law Commission's proposals for reform of the law relating to incapacitated adults in its Report No 231 *Mental Incapacity* (1995) in relation to donation of non-regenerative tissue and bone marrow (para 6.5). It is arguable that any reform should go further and require court approval for donation of *any* tissue (see *Who Decides?* (LCD Consultation Paper) (1997 Cm 3803), para 5.13 but see *supra*, ch 6 for the Government's most recent proposals).

B. CONSENT: STATUTORY LIMITATIONS

The Human Organ Transplants Act 1989 limits the scope of donation by living donors of organs for transplantation by setting restrictions on transplants between persons who are not 'genetically related'.

There are two matters of definition that we should address at the outset.

1. 'Organ'

The Act applies only to 'organs'. Section 7(2) of the Act states that:

> 7(2)...'[O]rgan' means any part of a human body consisting of a structured arrangement of tissues which, if wholly removed, cannot be replicated by the body.

It is clear that under the Act the statutory meaning of 'organ' is intended to be a term of art which may not be coterminus with the medical definition of organ. It would appear that the intention of the legislature was to distinguish between parts of the body which are capable of regeneration and those which are not. Blood, skin, semen, bone marrow and hair are examples of regenerative parts of the body. On the other hand, the heart, kidneys, liver, pancreas and lungs are examples of non-regenerative parts of the body.

The statutory definition is not, however, without its difficulties. First, an organ must consist of 'a structured arrangement of tissues' and must be a 'part of a human body'. While this causes no difficulties in obvious cases of a solid mass of tissue, such as the heart, it is not entirely clear whether bodily fluids come within the statutory (though not medical) definition of 'organ'. Generally, bodily 'tissue' is understood within the medical profession to relate to the epithelial (eg skin), connective (eg cartilage or muscle) or nervous (eg a nerve) tissues. These tissues are structured in the sense that they consist of an aggregation of cells in an interwoven fabric or network. Semen or ova would not fall within this meaning. Similarly, blood and bone marrow though consisting of an aggregation of cells are not structured in that way.

The second difficulty concerns that aspect of the definition of 'organ' which requires that the part of the body in issue 'if wholly removed', cannot be 'replicated by the body'. Clearly, these words were intended to capture the essence of the non-regenerative nature of the body part. To a large extent, s 7(2) succeeds. Where the part removed is the whole of the organ (used in the medical sense) and that part cannot be replicated (ie replaced) by the body, no difficulty arises; the part is 'an organ' within the Act. A problem arises, however, when the 'part' removed is a part of an organ (used in the medical sense). The best example would be the removal of a part (ie the lobe) of a liver. Is the removal of a part of an organ (used in the medical sense) covered by the Act? Clearly the phrase 'part of a human body' can include a part of an organ (used in the medical sense). The lobe of a liver is as much a 'part of a human body' as is the liver itself. The difficulty is that s 7(2) requires that the 'part', if 'wholly removed', will not regenerate. In the case of the lobe of a liver this will not be so if the 'part' which has to be visualised as not regenerating if wholly removed is the 'part' which is removed, ie the lobe, since the lobe can regenerate. If, however, the 'part' which has to be visualised as not regenerating if wholly removed is the liver itself, then it will be covered by the Act because if wholly removed the liver will not regenerate. This latter interpretation is difficult to sustain. Nevertheless, it has been assumed that removal of a liver lobe would be covered by the Act (see the forms issued to comply with The Human Organ Transplants (Supply of Information) Regulations 1989 (SI 1989 No 2108)).

This view could only be justified if the word 'part' in s 7(2) is interpreted in this sort of case as referring to the organ (used in the medical sense) of which the removal portion is itself a part. Hence, to bring the removal of portion of an organ (used in the medical sense) within the Act, we are required first to consider that portion as a 'part of a human body' under s 7(2) and then give these words a different meaning as referring to the totality of the organ (used in the legal sense) as regards which regeneration cannot occur. This is an interpretation which defies common sense.

However, the better interpretation equally has its difficulties. If 'part of a human body' refers to the portion removed, the words 'if wholly removed' have no sense at all. This is because the intention will always be to remove the whole of the relevant portion. The Act, therefore, merely asks whether the part will regenerate 'if removed'. The word 'wholly' adds nothing. Thus, if the portion removed, as in the case of the lobe of the liver, will regenerate then the removal for transplantation of a portion, though it be a part of the body and therefore an organ, will not be within the Act because *it* will regenerate when it is removed.

Furthermore, if the Act were interpreted to capture cases such as a liver lobe transplant, that interpretation would have unexpected effects. For example, skin transplants will be covered because even if only some skin is removed and that will regenerate, looking at the totality of the skin, if 'wholly removed' *this* will not regenerate. Thus, skin and liver lobe transplants are either both covered by the Act, or neither is covered. Parliament, however, only intended to include the latter.

During the progress of the Bill through the House of Commons the important question arose as to whether the Act would apply to human gametes, ie sperm and ova, or, indeed, human embryos. As we have already seen in Chapter 10, the Human Fertilisation and Embryology Act 1990 creates a regulatory framework in this area. In particular, it deals with payment for human gametes and embryos and the donation of them. If the 1989 Act applies also to them, there will be a clear conflict between the two statutory regimes which was not Parliament's intention (see Parl Deb (HC) (2nd Reading Ctte) 16 May 1989 at p 38). Although it has been suggested otherwise (Price and Mackay, 'The Trade in Human Organs' (1991) NLJ 1272 at 1273), it is plain that the 1989 Act does not apply for the following reasons. First, human gametes and embryos do not fall within the definition of 'organ' under s 7(2). As regards human gametes, they are not 'a structured arrangement of tissues', being unicellular. As regards embryos, even if they are this, they are not 'any part of a human body'. Secondly, it may be stretching the language of the 1989 Act too far to describe a 'transplant' the removal and donation of human gametes and embryos by a process which is, in fact, an implant. A transplant involves replacement of that which existed.

2. 'Genetically related'

The second matter of definition we should note concerns the phrase 'genetically related'. Section 2 provides:

2. – (1) Subject to subsection (3) below, a person is guilty of an offence if in Great Britain he –
(a) removes from a living person an organ intended to be transplanted into another person; or
(b) transplants an organ removed from a living person into another person,
unless the person into whom the organ is to be or, as the case may be, is transplanted is genetically related to the person from whom the organ is removed.
   (2) For the purposes of this section a person is genetically related to –
(a) his natural parents and children;
(b) his brothers and sisters of the whole or half blood;
(c) the brothers and sisters of the whole or half blood of either of his natural parents; and
(d) the natural children of his brothers and sisters of the whole or half blood or of the brothers and sisters of the whole or half blood of either of his natural parents;
but persons shall not in any particular case be treated as related in any of those ways unless the fact of the relationship has been established by such means as are specified by regulations made by the Secretary of State.

For the purposes of the Act, you will see that the phrase 'genetically related' is, under s 2(2), a term of art. Only certain relatives fall within the definition. Grandparents and grandchildren, for example, are excluded. Spouses equally are excluded. The following diagram reflects those who are 'genetically related' under the Act to 'X', the donor or recipient of the transplanted organ.

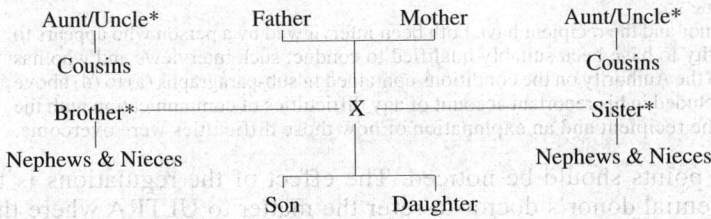

*includes 'of the half-blood' (s 2(2)(c) and (d))

If s 2 imposes restrictions upon transplants between genetically unrelated persons, how is the genetic relationship to be established? Section 2(2) requires that 'the fact of the relationship has been established by such means as are specified by regulations made by the Secretary of State'. The Human Organ Transplants (Establishment of Relationship) Regulations 1989 (SI 1989 2107) provide for testing by approved testers using 'appropriate tests', ultimately including DNA profiling, as set out in detail in reg 2 of the regulations. Unless the relationship has been so established an offence will be committed under s 2(1) by the doctors involved in the removal for transplant of an organ or the transplant itself.

3. ULTRA

Despite this, s 2(3) of the Human Organ Transplants Act 1989 provides as follows:

2. (3) The Secretary of State may by regulations provide that the prohibition in subsection (1) above shall not apply in cases where –
(a) such authority as is specified in or constituted by the regulations is satisfied –
   (i) that no payment has been or is to be made in contravention of section 1 above; and
   (ii) that such other conditions as are specified in the regulations are satisfied; and
(b) such other requirements as may be specified in the regulations are complied with.

This provision allows the Secretary of State to provide a mechanism for allowing transplants between genetically unrelated persons. As can be seen, this mechanism can only come into play if the prior condition – which is a central feature of the Act – is satisfied, namely that there has been no commercial dealing in the organ (for a discussion of s 1 of the 1989 Act see *infra*).

The Human Organ Transplants (Unrelated Persons) Regulations 1989 (SI No 2480) create an authority called the Unrelated Live Transplant Regulatory Authority (ULTRA). Regulation 3 provides as follows:

3. – (1) The prohibition in section 2(1) of the Act (restriction of transplants between persons not genetically related) shall not apply in cases where a registered medical practitioner has caused the matter to be referred to the Authority and where the Authority is satisfied: –
(a)   that no payment has been, or is to be, made in contravention of section 1 of the Act;
(b)   that the registered medical practitioner who has caused the matter to be referred to the Authority has clinical responsibility for the donor; and
(c)   except in a case where the primary purpose of removal of an organ from a donor is the medical treatment of that donor, that the conditions specified in paragraph (2) of this regulation are satisfied.
  (2) The conditions referred to in paragraph (1)(c) of this regulation are:–
(a)   that a registered medical practitioner has given the donor an explanation of the nature of the medical procedure for, and the risk involved in, the removal of the organ in question;
(b)   that the donor understands the nature of the medical procedure and the risks, as explained by the registered medical practitioner, and consents to the removal of the organ in question;
(c)   that the donor's consent to the removal of the organ in question was not obtained by coercion or the offer of an inducement;
(d)   that the donor understands that he is entitled to withdraw his consent if he wishes, but has not done so;
(e)   that the donor and the recipient have both been interviewed by a person who appears to the Authority to have been suitably qualified to conduct such interviews and who has reported to the Authority on the conditions contained in sub-paragraphs (a) to (d) above and has included in his report an account of any difficulties of communication with the donor or the recipient and an explanation of how those difficulties were overcome.

The following points should be noticed. The effect of the regulations is to require the potential donor's doctor to refer the matter to ULTRA where the parties are not proved to be 'genetically related' under the Act. Further, ULTRA has to be satisfied on three questions, the first of which is that no payment has been made in contravention of s 1. The second is that (by reg 3(1)(b)) the referring doctor is the doctor who 'has clinical responsibility for the donor'. What does this phrase mean? Clearly it is intended that it should refer to the surgeon who would be responsible for removing the organ. The form of words is odd since at the time of referral to ULTRA the surgeon may not yet have assumed any 'clinical responsibility' for the would-be donor.

The third question is that certain conditions set out in the regulations are satisfied. This is subject to the exception where the 'primary purpose of removal of an organ from a donor is the medical treatment of that donor'. This recognises the medical fact that when a patient undergoes a lung transplant it is customary to remove his heart also. The heart, if healthy, is then available for transplant to another. The conditions specified in the regulations, the object of which is to prevent a would-be donor from being exploited, has no relevance in this special situation (see HC(90) 7, para 10 referring to 'a domino transplant').

The conditions (set out in reg 3(2)) are relatively self-explanatory but call for some comment. The doctor referred to in reg 3(2)(a) and (b) may, in practice, not be the surgeon who has 'clinical responsibility for the donor'. This view that they need not be the same follows from the phrase '*a* registered medical practitioner' (our emphasis) in reg 3(2)(a). Proper recognition is thereby given to variations in practice as to which doctor in the team actually explains the procedure to, and obtains consent from, the donor. Secondly, reg 3(2)(a) to (d) when read together provide the code for obtaining a valid consent from an organ donor. Two important variations from the general law are worthy of note. Unlike the general law, reg 3(2)(a) imposes upon a doctor *the obligation* to advise the donor of 'the risk (sic) involved in, the removal of the organ'. There is no room here for an application of the *Bolam* test. Further, reg 3(2)(b) requires that the donor '*understands* the nature of the medical procedure and the risks' (our emphasis). The general law probably requires no more than that the doctor should have reasonable grounds to believe either that the patient has the capacity to understand what he is told (or knows) or, possibly, that he has in fact understood it. Whichever view is correct (and it is not clear), the general law certainly does not require that a patient should *actually understand* the information. The difference here may be that we are not concerned with the treatment of a patient and therefore the law may require more from the doctor.

A very significant consequence of reg 3(2) of the regulations is that the requirement of explicit consent based upon understanding by the donor means that an incompetent person (whether child or adult) who is not 'genetically related' to the intended recipient of the organ cannot be an organ donor.

Given the lack of clarity in the common law (as we have seen), as to whether an incompetent (who for these purposes would have to be genetically related) can legally be an organ donor, it may well be that a court would be guided by the prohibitions in the regulations and apply them *mutatis mutandis* so as to have a further reason for holding that all incompetents cannot legally be organ donors.

Next, why did Parliament distinguish between donations between genetically related persons and those who are not? The explanation offered by the then Parliamentary Under Secretary of State for Health, in the House of Commons (HC Deb, 6 July 1989) during the passage of the Bill was as follows:

> The Bill already excludes genetically related people from scrutiny by the authority. A reason for that is that the existence of a close genetic relationship can be verified with a high degree of accuracy by laboratory testing. In this country, the vast majority of life transplants would be covered by that exemption, as close family members are both more likely to come forward to offer themselves as donors and to prove compatible, in the medical sense.
>
> Under the Bill, the existence of a genetic relationship would be verified in each case in an objective way by such testing. Appropriate tests may have already been carried out in the process of trying to establish the compatibility of the donor and would-be recipient, the existence of some kind of relationship or personal tie is more difficult to establish. Unfortunately, we cannot rule out the possibility of non-genetic 'relationships' being formed solely for the purpose of the operation or of pressure – economic or otherwise – being brought to bear upon a donor to submit to a transplant operation.
>
> For those reasons, it is intended that the authority will consider the available evidence in each case where no genetic relationship has been established, before giving an independent decision on whether an offer of donation is altruistic. However, the fact that the authority will scrutinise all cases of live donation between non-related persons does not imply the unnecessary obstacles will be placed in the way of transplants between spouses or 'in law' relations.

As this makes plain, Parliament was concerned that the donation be entirely altruistic and presumes that this will be so in the case of those who are 'genetically related' whereas it may not be otherwise. It is fair to ask, however, if the key to altruism is close family ties, why should a spouse (or, indeed, long-term partner) be treated as a stranger? Furthermore, grandparents and grandchildren *are* genetically related and may surely be presumed to act as altruistically as those included within the Act, yet they too are excluded as if they were strangers. It cannot be that a grandparent is necessarily too old to be a donor because someone may be a grandparent at 40!

By contrast, if altruism is the key, why should Parliament restrict unregulated donation to the genetically related? It could be said that intra-family donations may well be the product of severe social pressure ('coercion') rather than altruism (notice the wording of reg 3(2)(c) of the regulations set out above). In some jurisdictions, as we have seen, legislation prohibits the removal of non-regenerative tissue (and sometimes even regenerative tissue) from a minor for the purpose of transplantation, recognising the danger of pressure within the family.

C. THE AGREEMENTS TO DONATE

An initial point that we should notice is that we are not concerned here with these arrangements which are covered by the Human Fertilisation and Embryology Act 1990, that is arrangements having to do with infertility and involving eggs, sperm or embryos.

As regards the arrangements we are concerned with in this chapter, there will, ordinarily, be two distinct agreements. The first will be between the donor and a doctor or other agency involved in the removal and storage of the tissue or organ or, possibly, directly between the donor and the intended recipient ('the donation agreement'). An example of the latter where there will not be a doctor or other agency involved may be the case of sperm donation.

The second agreement will be between the doctor or storage institution and the recipient ('the transfer agreement').

1. The Human Organ Transplants Act 1989

The validity of an agreement to donate or transfer any organ to a patient must now take account of the Human Organ Transplants Act 1989. By s 1 commercial dealings in human organs are prohibited. The government took swift action because of concerns about possible trafficking in human organs and, in particular, the so-called 'kidneys for sale' case. In that case, the General Medical Council found three doctors guilty of 'serious professional misconduct' for having been involved in arrangements to buy organs for transplantation.

Section 1 provides:

Prohibitions of commercial dealings in human organs

1. (1) A person is guilty of an offence if in Great Britain he –
   (a) makes or receives payment for the supply of, or for an offer to supply, an organ which has been or is to be removed from a dead or living person and is intended to be transplanted into another person whether in Great Britain or elsewhere;
   (b) seeks to find a person willing to supply for payment such an organ as is mentioned in paragraph (a) above or offers to supply such an organ for payment;
   (c) initiates or negotiates any arrangement involving the making of any payment for the supply of, or for an offer to supply, such an organ; or
   (d) takes part in the management or control of a body of persons corporate or unincorporated whose activities consist of or include the initiation or negotiation of such arrangements.
   (2) Without prejudice to paragraph (b) of subsection (1) above, a person is guilty of an offence if he causes to be published or distributed, or knowingly publishes or distributes, in Great Britain an advertisement –
   (a) inviting persons to supply for payment any such organs as are mentioned in paragraph (a) of that subsection or offering to supply any such organs for payment; or
   (b) indicating that the advertiser is willing to initiate or negotiate any such arrangement as is mentioned in paragraph (c) of that subsection.

(a) The scope of section 1

There are three types of conduct which are made criminal by this provision. The offences are committed whether the organ is removed from a dead or living person provided that there is an intention that it be used for transplantation.

(i) 'PAYMENT' FOR 'SUPPLY'

The first offence relates to making or receiving payment for the supply of an organ (s 1(1)(a)) or offering to supply (s 1(1)(b)). Of particular importance here is the meaning of the words 'supply' and 'payment'. Clearly, the provision of an organ by a donor is covered. But what of the surgeon who removes the organ and the surgeon, if different, who transplants the organ into the patient? Do either of these 'supply' an organ within s 1(1)(a)? It could be argued that both 'supply' in the sense that they *provide* an organ by their conduct. A better view is, however, that only a donor supplies an organ within the Act. Support for this view is found in s 1(1)(b), which seems to limit the supplier to the donor because it is an offence directed at the donor. (It could be said that a supplier could also be someone (or an institution) who holds organs in a tissue bank). If the surgeon who removes or transplants an organ were a 'supplier', the consequence would be *prima facie* that the surgeon in the private sector could not be paid for doing his job. As regards the removal of an organ, however, the surgeon would not commit an offence in that the word 'payment' is defined in s 1(3) so as to exclude 'payment for…the cost of removing'. No reference is made to payment for the cost of transplanting but the surgeon in private practice who transplants rather than removes ought not to be in any worse position. Consequently, 'supply' must be restricted to the action of the donor.

There are a number of implications that flow from this interpretation. What is the purpose behind the exclusion from the Act in s 1(3) of payments for 'defraying' or 'reimbursing':

(a) the cost of removing, transporting or preserving the organ to be supplied.

Clearly, Parliament did not intend that payments received or made and relating to the removal of an organ should fall within the Act. The assumption seemed to be that they needed to be explicitly excluded. As we have seen, however, the limited meaning of 'supply' excludes anything to do with the removal in any event. Thus s 1(3)(a) is superfluous as regards the 'remover'. It would still apply, however, so as to permit an intermediate 'supplier' such as the UKTSSA to cover its costs.

Given its existence, however, s 1(3) raises the difficulty that Parliament was concerned to exclude only costs associated with removal, etc and not with transplanting. Does this mean that payment to the transplant surgeon for his services is a crime? The answer would be 'yes' unless the limited meaning of supply is correct, ie that only the donor (or intermediary) supplies. Once this limited meaning is accepted the fact that payment for transplant is not excluded from the meaning of 'payment' is irrelevant.

Finally, it is worth noting that s 1(3)(b) excludes certain payments to the donor from the Act. It provides as follows:

(3) In this section 'payment' means payment in money or money's worth but does not include any payment for defraying or reimbursing – …
(b) any expenses or loss of earning incurred by a person so far as reasonably and directly attributable to his supplying an organ from his body.

Thus, the donor's medical costs may not be met by the transplant recipient or other as this would be 'payment in…money's worth' (compare the situation for donation of eggs (*supra*, ch 10), and in relation to surrogacy, (*supra*, ch 10). Notice, only 'expenses' or 'loss of earnings' *incurred* so far as reasonable etc fall outside the statutory definition of 'payment'. Hence, it would seem to cover only 'out of pocket' losses by way of reimbursement. It would not allow, therefore, payment of a 'hypothetical salary' to cover the time etc involved in donating.

(ii) 'BROKERING'

The second offence created by s 1 relates to what, in essence, could be described as 'brokering' (s 1(1)(b), (c) and (d)). The Act is very broadly drawn so as to catch a wide range of activities which would lead to commercial dealings in organs. Hence, those who seek a donor willing to supply an organ for payment or those who initiate or negotiate an arrangement involving the supply of such an organ, will all commit criminal offences. Curiously, the Act goes even further by making it a criminal offence to initiate or negotiate an arrangement for what can only be described as an option on such an organ. This is the only meaning that can be given to that part of s 1(1)(c) which makes it a crime to initiate or negotiate 'any arrangement involving the making of any payment…for an offer to supply, such an organ'.

(iii) 'ADVERTISING'

The third offence relates to advertising for, or to be, a donor in return for payment. Section 1(4) gives the word 'advertisement' a wide meaning such that it includes 'any form of advertising', whether permanent or not, and whether oral or in writing. Also, the Act includes advertisements directed to the public at large, a section of the public or, it seems, to selected individuals.

(iv) GENERALLY

Two general points relating to all the offences must be made. First, as regards s 1(1), the Act does not explicitly identify what state of mind (*mens rea*) is required for the offences. Undoubtedly, *mens rea* would be required notwithstanding that the offences are only triable summarily with a maximum sentence of three months' imprisonment. A court would probably require an 'intention' to do the prohibited conduct.

Secondly, an attempt or conspiracy to commit one of the offences under the Act would also be a crime under the Criminal Attempts Act 1981 and the Criminal Law Act 1977.

(b) A counter-view on commercial dealings

The UK Government's response in 1989 reflected a widespread antipathy towards the notion of commerce, eg the Guidelines of the British Transplantation Society (1985) the Resolution of the Council of Ministers of the European Community (art 9, Resolution (78) 29) (for the text of these see *First Edition*, pp 1003–1007). The arguments concerning commercialisation were rehearsed as long ago as 1970 (see J Dukeninier 'Supplying Organs for Transplantation' (1970) 68 Michigan Law Review 811, referred to in *Second Edition* at pp 1095–1097).

An interdisciplinary expert group, the International Forum for Transplant Ethics, has challenged the public policy position enshrined, for example, in the Human Organ Transplants Act. Their discussion concerns kidneys but is of more general application.

J Radcliffe-Richards *et al* 'The Case for Allowing Kidney Sales' (1998) 351 The Lancet 1950

When the practice of buying kidneys from live vendors first came to light some years ago, it aroused such horror that all professional associations denounced it and nearly all countries have now made it illegal. Such political and professional unanimity may seem to leave no room for further debate, but we nevertheless think it important to reopen the discussion.

The well-known shortage of kidneys for transplantation causes much suffering and death. Dialysis is a wretched experience for most patients, and is anyway rationed in most places and simply unavailable to the majority of patients in most developing countries. Since most potential kidney vendors will never become unpaid donors, either during life or posthumously, the prohibition of sales must be presumed to exclude kidneys that would otherwise be available. It is therefore essential to make sure that there is adequate justification for the resulting harm.

Most people will recognise in themselves the feelings of outrage and disgust that led to an outright ban on kidney sales, and such feelings typically have a force that seems to their possessors to need no further justification. Nevertheless, if we are to deny treatment to the suffering and dying we need better reasons than our own feelings of disgust.

In this paper we outline our reasons for thinking that the arguments commonly offered for prohibiting organ sales do not work, and therefore that the debate should be reopened. Here we consider only the selling of kidneys by living vendors, but our arguments have wider implications.

The commonest objection to kidney selling is expressed on behalf of the vendors: the exploited poor, who need to be protected against the greedy rich. However, the vendors are themselves anxious to sell and see this practice as the best option open to them. The worse we think the selling of a kidney, therefore, the worse should seem the position of the vendors when that option is removed. Unless this appearance is illusory, the prohibition of sales does even more harm than first seemed, in harming vendors as well as recipients. To this argument it is replied that the vendors' apparent choice is not genuine. It is said that they are likely to be too uneducated to understand the risks, and that this precludes informed consent. It is also claimed that, since they are coerced by their economic circumstances, their consent cannot count as genuine.

Although both these arguments appeal to the importance of autonomous choice, they are quite different. The first claim is that the vendors are not competent to make a genuine choice within a given range of options. The second, by contrast, is that poverty has so restricted the range of options that organ selling has become the best, and therefore, in effect, that the range is too small. Once this distinction is drawn, it can be seen that neither argument works as a justification of prohibition.

If our ground for concern is that the range of choices is too small, we cannot improve matters by removing the best option that poverty has left, and making the range smaller still. To do so is to make subsequent choices, by this criterion, even less autonomous. The only way to improve matters is to lessen the poverty until organ selling no longer seems the best option; and if that could be achieved, prohibition would be irrelevant because nobody would want to sell.

The other line of argument may seem more promising, since ignorance does preclude informed consent. However, the likely ignorance of the subjects is not a reason for banning altogether a procedure for which consent is required. In other contexts, the value we place on autonomy leads us to insist on information and counselling, and that is what it should suggest in the case of organ selling as well. It may be said that this approach is impracticable, because the educational level of potential vendors is too limited to make explanation feasible, or because no system could reliably counteract the misinformation of nefarious middlemen and profiteering clinics. But even if we accepted that no possible vendor could be competent to consent, that would justify only putting the decision in the hands of competent guardians. To justify total prohibition it would also be necessary to show that organ selling must always be against the interests of potential vendors, and it is most unlikely that this would be done.

The risk involved in nephrectomy is not in itself high, and most people regard it as acceptable for living related donors. Since the procedure is, in principle, the same for vendors as for unpaid donors, any systematic difference between the worthwhileness of the risk for vendors and donors presumably lies on the other side of the calculation, in the expected benefit. Nevertheless the exchange of money cannot in itself turn an acceptable risk into an unacceptable one from the vendor's point of view. It depends entirely on what the money is wanted for.

In general, furthermore, the poorer a potential vendor, the more likely it is that the sale of a kidney will be worth whatever risk there is. If the rich are free to engage in dangerous sports for pleasure, or dangerous jobs for high pay, it is difficult to see why the poor who take the lesser risk of kidney selling for greater rewards – perhaps saving relatives' lives, or extricating themselves from poverty and debt – should be thought so misguided as to need saving from themselves.

It will be said that this does not take account of the reality of the vendors' circumstances: that risks are likely to be greater than for unpaid donors because poverty is detrimental to health, and vendors are often not given proper care. They may also be underpaid or cheated, or may waste their money through inexperience. However, once again, these arguments apply far more strongly to many other activities by which the poor try to earn money, and which we do not forbid. The best way to address such problems would be by regulation and perhaps a central purchasing system, to provide screening, counselling, reliable payment, insurance, and financial advice.

To this it will be replied that no system of screening and control could be complete, and that both vendors and recipients would always be at risk of exploitation and poor treatment. But the evidence we have shows that there is much more scope for exploitation and abuse when a supply of desperately wanted goods is made illegal. It is, furthermore, not clear why it should be thought harder to police a legal trade than the present complete ban.

Furthermore, even if vendors and recipients would always be at risk of exploitation, that does not alter the fact that if they choose this option, all alternatives must seem worse to them. Trying to end exploitation by prohibition is rather like ending slum dwelling by bulldozing slums: it ends the evil in that form, but only by making things worse for the victims. If we want to protect the exploited, we can do it only by removing the poverty that makes them vulnerable, or, failing that, by controlling the trade.

Another familiar objection is that it is unfair for the rich to have privileges not available to the poor. This argument, however, is irrelevant to the issue of organ selling as such. If organ selling is wrong for this reason, so are all benefits available to the rich, including all private medicine, and, for that matter, all public provision of medicine in rich countries (including transplantation of donated organs) that is unavailable in poor ones. Furthermore, all purchasing could be done by a central organisation responsible for fair distribution.

It is frequently asserted that organ donation must be altruistic to be acceptable, and that this rules out payment. However, there are two problems with this claim. First, altruism does not distinguish donors from vendors. If a father who saves his daughter's life by giving her a kidney is altruistic, it is difficult to see why his selling a kidney to pay for some other operation to save her life should be thought less so. Second, nobody believes in general that unless some useful action is altruistic it is better to forbid it altogether.

It is said that the practice would undermine confidence in the medical profession, because of the association of doctors with money-making practices. That, however, would be a reason for objecting to all private practice; and in this case the objection could easily be met by the separation of purchasing and treatment. There could, for instance, be independent trusts to fix charges and handle accounts, as well as to ensure fair play and high standards. It is alleged that allowing the trade would lessen the supply of donated cadaveric kidneys. But although some possible donors might decide to sell instead, their organs would be available, so there would be no loss in the total. And in the meantime, many people will agree to sell who would not otherwise donate.

It is said that in parts of the world where women and children are essentially chattels there would be a danger of their being coerced into becoming vendors. This argument, however, would work as strongly against unpaid living kidney donation, and even more strongly against many far more harmful practices which do not attract calls for their prohibition. Again, regulation would provide the most reliable means of protection.

It is said that selling kidneys would set us on a slippery slope to sell vital organs such as hearts. But that argument would apply equally to the case of the unpaid kidney donation, and nobody is afraid that that will result in the donation of hearts. It is entirely feasible to have laws and professional practices that allow the giving or selling only of non-vital organs. Another objection is that allowing organ sales is impossible because it would outrage public opinion. But this claim is about western public opinion: in many potential vendor communities, organ selling is more acceptable than cadaveric donation, and this argument amounts to a claim that other people should follow western cultural preferences rather than their own. There is, anyway, evidence that the western public is far less opposed to the idea, than are medical and political professionals.

It must be stressed that we are not arguing for the positive conclusion that organ sales must always be acceptable, let alone that there should be an unfettered market. Our claim is only that none of the familiar arguments against organ selling works, and this allows for the possibility that better arguments may yet be found.

Nevertheless, we claim that the burden of proof remains against the defenders of prohibition, and that until good arguments appear, the presumption must be that the trade should be regulated rather than banned altogether. Furthermore, even when there are good objections at particular times or in particular places, that should be regarded as a reason for trying to remove the objections, rather than as an excuse for permanent prohibition.

The weakness of the familiar arguments suggests that they are attempts to justify the deep feelings of repugnance which are the real driving force of prohibition, and feelings of repugnance among the rich and healthy, no matter how strongly felt, cannot justify removing the only hope of the destitute and dying. This is why we conclude that the issue should be considered again, and with scrupulous impartiality.

What would such a world look like? You will notice Radcliffe-Richards *et al*'s reference to 'regulation and perhaps a central purchasing system'. Professor John Harris, a philosopher, has proposed and defended a scheme.

John Harris *Clones, Genes and Immortality: Ethics and the Genetic Revolution* (2nd edn, 1998)

What difference would commerce make? Again the main danger is exploitation. If exploitation can be ruled out then again the choice between commercial and non-commercial schemes would be a matter of public policy. If, however, the shortfall in donor bodily products could not be made up by a voluntary scheme, this might well provide arguments for financial incentives. We accept (perhaps we should not) substantial occupational risks for many people with substantially less moral justification than would be available to those selling organs to save the lives of others. It is not clear that the risks of tissue or organ sale are substantially greater than occupational hazards of other sorts, or that they are more vitiated by the financial interests involved than are the sale of services.

Safeguards

Of course if the sale of donor organs is to be permitted, it would need to be carefully regulated and questions about the level of remuneration and safeguards against wrongful exploitation must be carefully considered. In the recent United Kingdom case in which Dr Raymond Crockett was removed from the medical register for taking part in the sale of kidneys, allegations were made that the donors had not consented and indeed did not even know that their kidneys were to be removed. One Turkish donor, Mr Ahmet Koc, was reported as thinking 'he was undergoing a medical examination for [a] job but in fact he was operated on and a kidney removed'. However, later the Turkish courts chose not to believe this story and he was given a suspended sentence in Turkey for trafficking in organs when 'it was found he had advertised his kidney in a newspaper'.

It is difficult to know whether those who sell their organs would be wrongfully exploited or not. Leaving aside issues of autonomy and consent, the idea of exploitation seems here to imply some conception of a fair price. In so far as we do not know what a fair price for live donor organs would be, we have no reason to suppose that a particular price is unfair. For the allegation that a particular rate is exploitative presupposes either a fair price or at least a 'market rate'.

There is of course a certain problem for those who object to such sales of organs on the grounds of exploitation of the vendor and who use some conception of a market price. For they seem to be involved in the following problem: to deem a certain price exploitative (presumably of the donor – although an unduly high price exploits purchasers) and consequently to restrict sales prevents the formation of a 'market-place' and hence the establishing of the very 'market price' presupposed by judgments that a particular price is too low and hence exploitative!

Here again, even if we could be confident that in a particular case there was exploitation of the vendor this would not of itself show the transaction to be morally objectionable. We would need to know much more. If the decision to sell was not autonomous, then this would surely and clearly constitute a moral objection to the practice even at the cost of the life of the victim. But if the exploitation was merely a question of under-payment I doubt whether this would be sufficient grounds to ban the practice as a whole. Financial adjustments and compensation could always be arranged.

Here I have been concerned with the question of whether or not, in principle, the sale of human tissue and organs is ethically questionable. The practical implementation of a commercial scheme would of course require careful planning and detailed safeguards.

Because of the immense difficulties in the way of doing this successfully I would hope that sufficient donor organs could be obtained non-commercially. However, where this is unlikely to prove possible we should, it seems to me, consider alternatives.

Sketch for an ethically defensible market in organs

I now offer for consideration one possible commercial scheme which might work to make up the shortfall in live donor organs and tissues required for therapeutic purposes. Any such scheme must be morally defensible: it should have built into it safeguards against wrongful exploitation and show concern for the vulnerable, as well as taking into account considerations of justice and equity. If all this can be done then a market in human body products will be shown to be, at the very least, not *prima facie* unethical.

'Monopsony'

One way of attending to this need for prudent regulation would be to establish a monopsony, that is 'a situation where only one buyer exists for the products of several sellers'. The one legitimate purchaser in the marketplace would be required to take on responsibility for ensuring equitable distribution of all organs and tissues purchased. This would prevent the rich using their purchasing power to exploit the market at the expense of the poor. The monopsonist would also have other obligations, such as ensuring correct tissue typing to maximize histocompatibility and so minimize graft rejection, and screening for diseased or otherwise hazardous organs and tissues (eg AIDS-infected blood, etc).

In the United Kingdom, the National Health Service might be ideally suited as our lone purchaser. The NHS or a comparable monopsonistic purchaser would purchase live organs and tissues just as it does other goods, eg kidney dialysis machines. It would then make them available as needed at no direct cost to the recipient.

Pricing Policy

There may be a problem here with pricing policy. In effect, the monopsonist is responsible for the running of the scheme. Should it also be permitted to set the prices of various organs and tissues which it is interested in purchasing? Leaving the pricing of organs to the judgment of the purchaser within a particular market place introduces the possibility of a conflict of interests. If the monopsonist were not only to act as purchaser, but also held responsibility for setting the price of what it purchased, it is not unlikely that it would attempt to set prices as low as possible so as to conserve its resources. However, this would be counterbalanced by the need to provide sufficient incentives to attract would-be organ vendors.

This latter point may provide an option for a mechanism of rigid or fixed prices. It might be thought that in a monopsonistic market there is no possibility for a free-market pricing mechanism. However, it must not be forgotten that the monopsonist is under pressure to purchase, this pressure resulting from the need for organs: if the purchaser is responsible for supplying patients with organs, and if there is a demand from the public for such provision, the purchaser will have an obligation to provide organs and a powerful motive for discharging the obligation. This affords the would-be vendor a degree of bargaining power over the price she can demand for her organ. There is an analogy here with the National Health Service purchasing drugs and other equipment in the current system: in the UK, even prior to growth of private-sector health care, the position of the National Health Service as the lone major purchaser of pharmaceuticals did not afford it the power to dictate the prices of the drugs it purchased.

Justice

It seems only right that those who contribute to the scheme and run the risks involved in organ supply, however small these risks may be, should also be in a position to benefit from the scheme if they one day require an organ. They should be able to benefit personally and also by knowing that their friends and family will also benefit by being eligible for organs should they require them. This constitutes a further argument for confining the marketplace to a geo-political area within which all will stand to benefit from the contributions of any.

Confining the marketplace

Where payment for organs occurs in the world, whether legally or illegally within a certain jurisdiction, there is a common thread that represents an undesirable effect of the market. It does not seem to be an over-generalization to say that usually the organ vendors come from 'underdeveloped' or 'developing' nations and that, while those who purchase organs may be the wealthy within those nations, because of the disparity in wealth between these and the 'developed' nations (and because, as a general rule, where they exist, laws against commerce in organs are less strictly enforced in these nations than in the developed nations), organ purchasers tend more often to be from the latter. Thus it is not surprising that in a recent scandal in the United Kingdom, the kidneys removed from the four Turks for payment were used for transplantation in patients at a private hospital in the United Kingdom. In that case, Mr Roger Henderson QC, counsel for the General Medical Council (the United Kingdom's regulatory authority for doctors), was reported as saying that '[t]here were great differences in wealth, health and understanding between rich and poor countries which created circumstances in which the rich could prey on the poor unless steps were taken to prevent it'.

One way of preventing rich nations preying on poor ones would be to confine the marketplace, perhaps to a particular nation state, but just as reasonably to a regional bloc of states. We could thus imagine various marketplaces facilitating commerce in live organs and tissues whilst restricting such commerce to the member states of a customs union, say, or a common market. Several such blocs which might lend themselves readily to our purpose already exist worldwide: in Europe, the EU (European Union); in South America, LAFTA (Latin American Free Trade Area), CACM (Central American Common Market), and ACM (Andean Common Market and Community); in the Caribbean, CARICOM (Caribbean Economic Community); in Africa, UDEAC (Union Douanière et Economique de l'Afrique Centrale), EAC (East African Community), CEAO (Communauté Economique de l'Afrique de l'Ouest), and ECOWAS (Economic Community of West African States); and in South-East Asia, ASEAN (Association of South-East Asian Nations). To prevent conflicts of interest, the monopsonist in any one bloc should not be an institution of any particular member state of that bloc.

Confining the marketplace also gets over the problem of organ vendors, or their families, not being eligible as organ recipients because they do not reside in the catchment area of a health service managed by the relevant monopsonist.

There may be a further reason for confining the marketplace, perhaps not a very charitable one but one which operates at a practical level and has some rough justice about it. We mention it here for what it is worth. It was reported in September 1990 that of 130 patients from the United Arab Emirates and Oman who had purchased kidneys for transplantation from living unrelated 'donors' in Bombay, India, 24 had died within one year of transplantation. Various reasons for this unusually high mortality rate can be postulated, including poor conditions and facilities in Bombay, and the condition of blood products and the purchased kidneys themselves. Three of the patients became seropositive for hepatitis B during follow up in their home countries, and four were found to be HIV seropositive having tested negative for HIV antibody prior to transplantation. While all blood is routinely tested for HIV in Oman and the UAE, only 5 per cent is checked in Bombay. Thus confining of the marketplace would not only prevent depredation of poor states by richer ones, but could also ensure that anyone who has sold her healthy organ into the scheme can expect the same standard of service as the person who received her organ should she later come to need a transplant herself. It seems equitable that organ recipients (or vendors for that matter) of similar age and health within the same marketplace should not face different levels of risk for the same operation.

Human organs in vivo as capital
Consider one particular worry concerning commerce in human biological materials which has been voiced by Lori B. Andrews, '[A]llowing payment to living persons for solid organs could lead society to view the poor as suddenly having capital and consequently being ineligible for welfare payments.' The legislation that introduced a monopsonistic market would have to rule this out as effectively coercing the poor into donation. It is worth emphasizing that nothing we have said rules out altruistic donation as a mode of organ procurement alongside a commercial scheme – we would not wish to discourage donation. If the individual chooses to *donate*, rather than *sell* her kidney, it would be unjust for that individual to be penalized for doing so.

The situation changes only when the individual avails herself of the option to sell her organs. Depending on the price she has been paid for her organ, she might then be liable to a loss of welfare benefits and also to tax. While we note this as a possibility, our suggestion at both a practical and ethical level would be to exempt the profits from organ and tissue sale from tax and also from benefit reduction – an added incentive to sell and a recognition of the residual altruism involved. It should be recognized that when a person sells an organ she acts both selfishly, in advantaging herself, *and* altruistically in providing a public service.

Free market or regulation?
Whether there should be a free market with prices being set by the market or whether the price of body products should be nationally or internationally agreed is a further question, and one I raise only to ignore. We can imagine a price for organs at which there were no donors who would not have been voluntary donors, and we can imagine prices at which substantially greater numbers of donors would come forward. On the other hand of course there are clearly prices which few potential purchasers could afford and prices which most could afford. There is a clear sense in which while would-be purchasers are necessarily vulnerable, would-be donors are only contingently so.

Since it is desirable that those whose lives are at risk should be saved but no more lives be put at risk than is necessary to maximize lives saved, we should adopt the scheme which would have this effect. Which this is I have no idea.

Who is more vulnerable?
It is important to be clear about just what is and is not being asserted here and so I must re-emphasize a point made briefly already.

One question we should press here is, who is more vulnerable, who is more in need of our protection? If we ask this question we might see the ethics of commercial transplantation in a different light. The dying people who need transplants are also entitled to our concern, respect, and protection: they do not wish to die. Those who would choose to sell organs are volunteers to a small but significant risk. Is it morally preferable to condemn one group of citizens to certain death rather than offer incentives (temptations if you like) to another group to run risks? Isn't it rather better to protect the most vulnerable by permitting another group to choose whether or not to run a risk in the hope of both benefiting their fellow human beings and benefiting themselves financially?

Is a society which allows 20,000 people a year to die for want of donor organs a better society than one which saves those lives by allowing other citizens to run small risks to prevent such deaths and which pays the citizens for so doing?

In a sense we already live in such a society. Any society which maintains rescue services and pays rescue personnel to run risks *is such a society*. When a society maintains fire services, police and ambulance services, military 'defence' forces, and even health professionals it accepts that it will call upon such personnel to run risks, including risks of death in the public interest and it accepts that such people should be paid for so doing whether or not they are volunteers.

(For further detail on his scheme, see C Erin and J Harris 'A Monopsonistic Market' in I Robinson (ed) *The Social Consequences of Life and Death under High Technology Medicine* (1994) at pp 134–157.)

The UK Government is most unlikely to contemplate a change in the law which can, in any event, be defended for example, as preventing an unjustified violation of body integrity: see S Wilkinson and G Garrard 'Bodily Integrity and the Sale of Human Organs' (1996) 22 JME 334. Article 21 of the European Convention on Human Rights and Bioethics (1996) states tersely: 'The human body and its parts shall not, as such, give rise to financial gain.' It is clear European policy, therefore, to outlaw organ sales: see *Explanatory Report*, January 1997 at para 132 (see also reproduced in Draft Protocol on Transplantation of Organs and Tissues of Human Origin, February 1999, art 19).

2. Agreements not affected by the 1989 Act

It is important to recognise that there are two distinct types of arrangement to consider. They are non-commercial arrangements to donate tissue or other bodily materials including that covered by the 1989 Act (ie 'organs' as defined in s 7(2)) and commercial arrangements to donate tissue or other bodily materials not falling within the definition of 'organ' under the 1989 Act.

(a) Non-commercial arrangements

Reminding ourselves that there are two distinct arrangements in play – 'the donation agreement' and 'the transfer agreement' – what we are concerned with here is whether these agreements are valid gifts. As regards the *donation agreement*, its validity will depend upon considerations of public policy involving such issues as consent which we explored earlier in Chapter 5? As regards the *transfer agreement*, there would seem to be no reason why such an agreement would not be valid as a gift if intended for the treatment of a patient.

In relation to both agreements if they be valid gifts, clearly any conditions in the gift (such as, that the tissue be transplanted into a particular person) have to be complied with. Of course, any legal redress in this situation which the donor may seek would depend on a civil action being available to him which, in turn, would appear to depend upon there being some form of proprietorial claim over the tissue (see *infra*).

If these arrangements can only be categorised as gifts, are there any ways in which they may be enforced by the intended *recipient*? As regards the donation agreement this very question arose in the US case of *McFall v Shimp* (1978) 10 Pa D&C (3d) 90. Russell Scott describes the background to the case.

R Scott *The Body as Property* (1981)

Robert McFall of Pittsburgh, Pennsylvania, was overwhelmed by the symptoms of aplastic anaemia in June 1978. A nightmare began for the thirty-nine-year-old bachelor when he began to develop bruises after bumping into objects during his work installing insulation materials in confined spaces in buildings. The bruises would not go away, and soon he began to have nose bleeds that continued for hours at a time. He went to a local hospital in suburban Pittsburgh, where the doctors diagnosed aplastic anaemia, a rare, almost certainly fatal disease of the bone marrow and blood. The prospects of death after contracting this disease have been put by some medical studies at 90 percent with an average survival period somewhere between three and four months. There is only one real source of cure, and that is a transplant of compatible bone marrow. This transplant gives a good expectation of complete recovery. Without it, the patient must expect to die.

The statistical likelihood of finding compatible bone marrow is almost one in sixty thousand. There are as yet no computerised banks containing comprehensive national tissue information (though in some parts of the world, for example, at Westminster Hospital in London, computerised tissue banks are being built up and already contain information about thousands of prospective donors). On the other hand, the prospect of finding tissue compatibility inside a family is far higher, and increases with the closeness of the relationship.

Robert McFall had three brothers and three sisters. They had all gone their separate ways following their mother's death in 1949, and there had been little family communication after that time. By means of computer checks through driver's licence records, they were all traced, and agreed to submit to tissue-typing tests. None of them turned out to be a compatible donor. It was then decided to enquire whether a first cousin of McFall, David Shimp, a crane operator in a steel mill, would agree to be tested. Shimp was aged forty-three and married. When both men were younger they had gone to camps together and had shared many experiences.

Shimp agreed to undergo a preliminary test but did not bother to tell his wife. The test proved to be positive, suggesting that Shimp's bone marrow would be a perfect match for Robert McFall. A second test was arranged, but Shimp cancelled the appointment. He had changed his mind, and from that time onward refused to have anything more to do with the affair. According to reports, Shimp said his wife was angry that he had taken the test without discussing it with her, and wanted him to discontinue his participation. His mother had expressed the same wish. One report said that Shimp had been influenced by a dream that if he went into hospital for the bone marrow removal, he would never come out. Friends and other relatives put great pressure on him to proceed with the tests, but he would not budge. It was even said that he considered bringing legal proceedings to stop harassment, because the story had gotten into the hands of the media, which gave it considerable publicity. However, it was Robert McFall who first resorted to the courts.

In the last week of July, McFall sued David Shimp in Allegheny County Court, Pennsylvania, asking for an order that would compel Shimp to submit to further tests, and eventually to the removal of a quantity of his bone marrow for transplant to McFall. Time was now all-important for McFall, and the normal delay of court hearings too risky. His lawyers asked for an urgent preliminary injunction, which, if granted, would direct Shimp forthwith to undergo the further tests. In this atmosphere events moved rapidly, and *McFall v Shimp* was dealt with and disposed of on July 25 and 26 by the Civil Division of the Allegheny County Court, Judge John P Flaherty, Jr, presiding.

The plaintiff's brief was a document of originality and persuasion, skilfully prepared by his attorney, John W Murtagh, Jr. Its opening words went straight to the heart of the matter, posing for determination an issue as profound as any that could be put to a court of law. The judge was asked, in so many words, to determine whether society may overrule a citizen's claim to an absolute right to his bodily security in order to save the life of one of its members. The brief submitted, for reasons it set out in detail, that the answer is and must be 'yes'. It then tackled some of the medical questions, asserting that the removal procedure was medically safe, would at most result in minor and temporary discomfort, and would deprive the defendant of nothing but his time because bone marrow is a regenerative tissue that promptly replaces itself.

McFall's lawyers had found no precedent or comparable case that could directly assist the court, and the judge himself later commented that 'a diligent search has produced no authority'. Accordingly, the claim for legal relief was put in fundamental terms, based on morality, ethics, custom, scholarly legal pronouncements, and judicial opinion…

McFall's case then cited some well-known circumstances in which bodily integrity is lawfully disregarded because of overriding social considerations: public health requirements for vaccination and quarantine; criminal law powers to take hair, blood, clothes, and semen; marriage law requirements of blood tests; defence law requirements of military service; and compulsory assistance to law enforcement officers in emergencies. To these McFall sought to add his own case as representing a new category. To demonstrate that the court could, by reference to principle and precedent, extend the law in this fashion if it wished, the plaintiff produced the fruits of some extremely original research.

Power to make an order of the kind requested was traced back some seven hundred years from the Allegheny County Court, through the Pennsylvanian and United States legal systems, to the ancient English Courts of Chancery and the powers to dispense justice granted to those courts in the reign of King Edward I. This English king ascended his throne in the year 1272, and in the thirteenth year of his reign, Parliament passed the statute now known as the second Statute of Westminster. It contained the following provision: 'Whensoever from thenceforth a writ shall be found in the Chancery, and in a like case falling under the same right and requiring a like remedy, no precedent of a writ can be produced, the Clerks in Chancery shall agree in forming a new one; lest it happen for the future that the Court of our lord the king be deficient in doing justice to the suitors'…

The question was whether Robert McFall's claim should be recognised by the courts, and whether the law should regard David Shimp as having a duty towards him. 'Has the duty the Plaintiff seeks to impose upon the Defendant ever been recognised in law or equity?' asked the brief. In support of an affirmative answer, reliance was next placed upon the so-called Rescue Cases.

The legal principle of rescue recognises the social duty of a citizen to act positively to attempt to rescue another who is in personal danger. A yachtsman may be found to have a positive duty to try to save a drowning man. American and British laws have not favoured the rescue concept and have been reluctant to equate moral with legal obligation. Generally speaking, their approach has been to recognise that certain relationships should produce legal duties and obligations, for example, the relationship of doctor and patient. They have been slow to build specific legal duties on the foundation of general moral concepts, particularly when this might result in conflict with 'individualist' philosophy. In the words of one American judge, 'common law courts have been reluctant to impose affirmative duties on individuals even in situations in which most people would feel under a moral obligation to act'...

McFall's lawyer claimed that in recent years American and English lawmakers had undergone some change of heart. Examples were provided of the 'ebbing of the strongly individualist philosophy of the early common law', and of cases in which courts had countenanced exceptions to the general rule that refuses to impose a duty to rescue. On the subject of yachtsmen, he was able to point to a decision in which a court held that a yacht owner whose guest fell overboard was under a positive duty to rescue the guest. He put to the court that it was possible to detect a growing Anglo-American acceptance of the principle that legal consequences should attach to conduct that displays indifference to the peril of a stranger. On McFall's behalf, he also put forward and supported a model set of standards proposed in 1965 by a prominent advocate of the rescue principle. These standards, which did not reach the statute book, contained specific suggestions for the provision of medical aid by means of blood transfusion. The basic proposal was that a person should have a legal duty to attempt rescue whenever another was in imminent danger and the first person was the only practical source of help. The duty would apply only if the danger would lead to substantial harm to person or property, and the risk to the rescuer would be 'disproportionately' less than the prospective harm. On the subject of blood transfusion, no objection was seen to a general rule that citizens should be placed under a community duty to give blood. The drafter urged that, at the very least, any blood donor could logically be placed under a duty to continue to give blood, for by giving his tissue in the first place, he indicated that his bodily security was 'subordinated to some other interest'; it was accepted, however, that a person opposed to blood transfusion should not normally be held liable for failure to give blood even if it resulted in loss of life. When these standards were formulated in 1965, the safe removal of bone marrow had not appeared as a lifesaving procedure, but presumably the same philosophy of compulsory donation could be applied to bone marrow donation, and to any other body tissue or organ which, as medicine develops, may be removed without impairing a person's health or well-being. It should not be forgotten in considering this argument that right now a person with one healthy kidney is as acceptable to life insurance companies as a person with two.

The plaintiff's brief argued that Shimp's behaviour in undergoing the first test had placed him in the same position as the blood donor who has previously given blood. By permitting himself to be tissue-typed and by demonstrating a four-tissue match with his cousin, he had obligated himself to continue. The brief claimed that Shimp had 'cruelly abandoned the Plaintiff after the Plaintiff was allowed to hope for a successful end to his ordeal', and should be compelled to continue to offer aid because the plaintiff had thereby been exposed to the risk of greater harm: McFall's chances of cure had been diminished due to the delays caused by Shimp's initial embarkation on a programme of assistance and his later refusal to proceed.

The brief ended with the plea that the court, as the voice of society, should not in the name of the defendant's bodily security abandon Robert McFall to a short, medically dominated life and certain death. 'Our noblest tradition as a free people and our common sense of decency, society and morality all point to the proper result in this case. We respectfully suggest that it is time our law did likewise.'

On July 25, 1978, in a preliminary hearing, Judge Flaherty had to decide whether Robert McFall had disclosed any kind of legal case at all and whether David Shimp had an obligation even to offer a defence. He considered the matter and heard medical evidence of the plaintiff's low chance of survival, the 'minimal risks' in bone marrow removal, and the fact that the plaintiff would have at least a 50 percent chance of cure after a transplant from the defendant. The judge then directed that Shimp's attorney file a brief setting out the reasons why he should not be ordered to give the bone marrow. A hearing was fixed for the next day. McFall had negotiated his first legal hurdle.

The essence of Shimp's defence was contained in his attorney's argument that the law of Pennsylvania did not impose upon him any duty to help his cousin. Whatever had been said about 'minimal risks' of bone marrow donation, the fact remained that the risks existed, and it could be dangerous. Though it is regarded medically as safe, bone marrow removal involves general anaesthetic and extraction of the marrow from the pelvic bone by means of a specially designed needle, which may be inserted as many as two hundred times in order to obtain the required quantity. This process can have a strong psychological effect upon the donor, particularly if he has a fear of surgery, or a fear of losing part of his body, and can cause him to develop hostility towards the recipient. Even if no risk existed, his client was still under no legal obligation to come to anybody's aid, said Shimp's attorney. Finally, he said, McFall's claim was suspect because it rested upon a view of what the law ought to be, not upon the reality of the law as it then was.

McFall v Shimp (1978) 10 Pa D&C (3d) 90 (Ct Comm Pl, Pa)

Flaherty J: The plaintiff, Robert McFall, suffers from a rare bone marrow disease and the prognosis for his survival is very dim, unless he receives a bone marrow transplant from a compatible donor. Finding a compatible donor is a very difficult task, and limited to a selection among close relatives. After a search and certain tests, it has been determined that only the defendant is suitable as a donor. The defendant refuses to submit to the necessary transplant, and before the Court is a request for a preliminary injunction which seeks to compel the defendant to submit to further tests, and, eventually, the bone marrow transplant.

Although a diligent search has produced no authority, the plaintiff cites the ancient statute of King Edward I, *St Westminster* 2, 13 Ed 1, c 24, pointing out, as is the case, that this Court is a successor to the English Courts of Chancery and derives power from this statute, almost 700 years old. The question posed by the plaintiff is that, in order to save the life of one of its members by the only means available, may society infringe upon one's absolute right to his 'bodily security'?

The common law has consistently held to a rule which provides that one human being is under no legal compulsion to give aid or to take action to save that human being or to rescue. A great deal has been written regarding this rule which, on the surface, appears to be revolting in a moral sense. Introspection, however, will demonstrate that the rule is founded upon the very essence of our free society. It is noteworthy that counsel for the plaintiff has cited authority which has developed in other societies in support of the plaintiff's request in this instance. Our society, contrary to many others, has as its first principle, the respect for the individual, and that society and government exist to protect the individual from being invaded and hurt by another. Many societies adopt a contrary view which has the individual existing to serve the society as a whole. In preserving such a society as we have it is bound to happen that great moral conflicts will arise, and will appear harsh in a given instance. In this case, the Chancellor is being asked to force one member of society to undergo a medical procedure which would provide that part of that individual's body would be removed from him and given to another so that the other could live. Morally, this decision rests with the defendant, and, in the view of the Court, the refusal of the defendant is morally indefensible. For our law to *compel* the defendant to submit to an intrusion of his body would change every concept and principle upon which our society is founded. To do so would defeat the sanctity of the individual, and would impose a rule which would know no limits, and one could not imagine where the line would be drawn.

This request is not to be compared with an action at law for damages, but rather is an action in equity before a chancellor, which in the ultimate, if granted, would require the forcible submission to the medical procedure. For a society, which respects the rights of *one* individual, to sink its teeth into the jugular vein or neck of one of its members and suck from it sustenance for *another* member, is revolting to our hard-wrought concepts of jurisprudence. Forcible extraction of living body tissue causes revulsion to the judicial mind. Such would raise the spectre of swastika and the Inquisition, reminiscent of the horrors this portends.

This Court makes no comment on the law regarding the plaintiff's right in an action at law for damages, but has no alternative but to deny the requested equitable relief. An Order will be entered denying the request for a preliminary injunction.

McFall concerns the enforcement of the *donation agreement*. As far as the *transfer agreement* is concerned, there can be no question of the law specifically enforcing an agreement to transplant tissue or an organ into a patient by analogy to the traditional ground that equity will not enforce a contract for personal services.

This disposes of one aspect of enforcing the transfer agreement: there is, however, another issue to consider. Could a donee seek through the law to enforce the transfer to him of the tissue of other bodily material *once removed* from the donor? The answer must be that this would be a case of an imperfect gift. Assuming the tissue is property, delivery, actual or constructive, would not have taken place and, therefore, the donee would have no cause of action.

(b) Commercial arrangements outside the 1989 Act

The existence of the 1989 Act does not preclude the possibility of commercial dealings in tissue and other body material not covered by the statutory definition of 'organ'. We have already discussed the threshold issue of public policy, *viz* whether commercial agreements should be lawful. Here it is important to notice that a court might be influenced by the fact that Parliament appears to have deliberately refrained from legislating as regards certain material by adopting a limited definition of 'organ'. Therefore, the court should be slow to legislate judicially where Parliament has chosen not to. Further, the material we are concerned with here will be regenerative and usually will be bodily fluids such as blood. The public policy arguments against commercial dealings which we saw earlier, are less powerful in this context.

On the assumption that commercial dealings are not proscribed by law, the remaining question is what would be the terms of any such contracts. The terms may be implied by law as well as being expressly agreed between parties. Consideration of implied terms, of course only becomes important as regards the *transfer agreement*.

We discuss this 'products liability' issue in detail in Chapter 13. Here, it suffices to remind ourselves of the basic contractual framework. Do the provisions of the Sale of Goods Act 1979 and of the Supply of Goods and Services Act 1982 apply? Both the 1979 and the 1982 Acts apply only where the supplier of the goods or service acts 'in the course of a business'. It seems clear that the activities of a private hospital, blood bank or the like would constitute a 'business'. (So, too, would the activities of an NHS hospital or Trust were it to contract with the donee: see s 18(1) of the 1982 Act.) If so, should the transfer agreement be categorised as a contract for the supply of *goods* or *services*? Since the 1982 Act, identical terms will be imposed into a contract for the supply of goods or goods linked to services (ss 2–5). Only if the contract is entirely one for services would the obligation under the contract be simply one to exercise reasonable care and skill (ss 5, 13). The better view is that the contracts under discussion here would fall within the 1982 Act as being a contract for the supply of goods *and* services.

D. PROPERTY RIGHTS OVER TISSUE AND OTHER BODILY MATERIAL

At a number of points in our discussion so far, it has been assumed tacitly that tissue and other bodily materials when removed can legally be categorised as *property* amenable to ownership, or at least, the assertion of rights over it. If this assumption be correct, a new set of issues emerges for discussion. These have to do with the rights of the person from whom the tissue is removed and any other party dealing with it to exercise some control over its use and, perhaps, be entitled to a part (or the whole) of any financial gain made through its use.

We saw in Chapter 10 that dealing with human ova, sperm and embryos is regulated by the Human Fertilisation and Embryology Act 1990. Control of these turns upon the terms of the legislation and not (in all probability) upon questions of property. Here, we are concerned with other body parts or material. The sort of circumstances the law must address include the following: the use by a pathologist of a piece of tissue removed for histological analysis, the retention of excised material so as to develop an archive for teaching and research and the use of excised material as part of the process of producing a new therapeutic agent.

Some of these uses may be self-evident, others are not. In particular, developments in molecular biology involving the creation of immortal cell-lines and the extraction of pluripotent stem-cells were until recently pure science fiction. The Nuffield Council on Bioethics in its report, *Human Tissue: Ethical and Legal Issues* (1995), describes some important issues beyond transplantation.

Nuffield Council on Bioethics *Human Tissue: Ethical and Legal Issues* (1995)

Tissue replacement
5.9 Tissue engineering is an advancing science that unites the principles of biology and engineering in the development of tissue substitutes that restore, maintain or improve

anatomical or physiological function. Research investigators have already attempted to develop substitutes for almost every mammalian tissue. Many of the components used in tissue engineering are of human origin, although some are artificial. Appendix 5, while not exhaustive, lists some of these developments.

5.10 Strategies for tissue replacement as an alternative to tissue transplantation include the use of:

- tissue inducing substances, such as human growth factors, to stimulate the growth of replacement cells or tissue. An example is the use of erythropoietin to stimulate the production of red blood cells as an alternative to blood transfusion (paragraph 5.5).
- isolated cells or cell substitutes. Fetal nerve cells, for example, may be transplanted into the brains of patients suffering from Parkinson's disease. The fetal cells release the neurotransmitter dopamine that is deficient in Parkinson's disease patients. The use of cell free haemoglobin as a substitute for blood transfusion is another example (paragraph 5.5).
- cells placed on or within artificial supporting matrices to form tissue masses or constructs which can be implanted. Techniques are being developed in which liver cells are contained within an artificial matrix. If successful, such artificial tissue could provide an alternative to liver transplants. For skin grafts, a supporting matrix alone can be used to stimulate the growth of the patient's own blood vessels and cells.

Research studies of human tissue and cells

5.11 Excised organs, tissue slices or snips and isolated cells may be kept viable for a limited time under experimental conditions and used for research purposes. The research may involve fundamental studies of tissue function: of gaseous exchange in the lung, for example, or the transport of substances across the placenta. Applied research may make use of infected or diseased tissue: studies of white blood cells infected with the HIV virus, or of blood vessels affected by atherosclerosis are examples.

5.12 Human tissue is used in the discovery and the development of medicines. Much of this research is performed by pharmaceutical companies. Isolated tissue may be exposed to potential medicines intended to exert a specific effect and the response of the tissue measured. The liver has an important function in breaking down drugs and toxic substances and eliminating them from the body. So studies of sections of human liver, or of isolated liver cells, are important for determining the fate of a new medicine in the liver, its toxicity and how fast it is eliminated from the body, before the medicine is tried on healthy volunteers.

Diagnosis using cells

5.13 Cells of the blood, bone marrow, amniotic fluid and chorionic villi may be cultured for analysis of the chromosomes or DNA for diagnosis of disorders such as Down's syndrome, cystic fibrosis and leukaemia.

5.14 Unmodified human cells survive under artificial conditions for only a few generations. If modified by chemical treatment or incorporation of tumorigenic viruses, cells can be made to grow continuously as 'immortal' cell lines. Some cell lines of human origin originated many years ago from the cells of malignant tumours. Some cell lines are commercially available, others are prepared by individual laboratories for specific purposes. One advantage of cell lines is that they can be used to produce large numbers of cells, and their various components. This reduces the need to collect quantities of fresh tissue. Examples of the increasing use of human cell lines for the production of therapeutic products and in medical research include:

- fundamental studies of cell behaviour and function. An example is the use of cell lines for researching the mechanisms by which cells repair the DNA damage caused by radiation;
- applied research to develop new therapeutic agents such as antiviral or anticancer medicines and to study their effects and their possible interactions with other medicines. An important element of such research is the toxicity testing of new medicines. This is one situation where the use of human cell lines may be more appropriate than the use of animals. The human lymphocyte assay, for example, is used in measuring the mutagenic potential of new medicines;
- the production of therapeutically active substances on exposure to toxins or infectious agents. These substances can be collected and manufactured as medicines. For example, the interferons produced by cells when they are exposed to viruses can be used to treat leukaemia or hepatitis;
- the propagation of human viruses that are then used to make vaccines. The production of rubella vaccine from human fetal cell lines is an example.

Studying subcellular components

5.15 Human tissue and cells can be used to isolate subcellular components for medical or biological research. Microsomes, for example, are small subcellular structures that, when isolated from liver cells, can be used to investigate the breakdown of new medicines. Perhaps the most important subcellular component, however, is the genetic material of cells, which is being used increasingly for research.

5.16 The isolation of genes coding for specific proteins has proved a powerful method for investigating the basic mechanisms underlying different biological processes, whether normal or diseased. Isolation and study of the cystic fibrosis gene, for example, indicated that it codes for a protein required for the transport of chloride ions across cell membranes. The absence of this transport in the lungs of cystic fibrosis patients accounts for the accumulation of sticky mucus in the lungs. Current research is working towards treating inherited disorders of this kind by somatic cell gene therapy which involves delivering corrective DNA to the affected tissue.

5.17 The insertion of foreign genes, which may be of human origin, into animals produces so-called transgenic animals. Transgenic animals can provide models for the study of some human diseases. Transgenic mouse strains which develop cystic fibrosis, for example, are used to test the use of gene therapy as a potential new treatment for the disease. Transgenic animals producing human proteins may eventually form a source of animal organs and tissue for transplantation or reconstructive surgery which are less susceptible to rejection than tissue from unmodified animals.

5.18 Human genes may be isolated and incorporated into microbial cells such as bacteria or yeast which are then grown in large scale biotechnology facilities to produce important medicines such as insulin, growth hormone, and erythropoietin.

Pathological examination, archiving and storage

5.19 The importance of this range of uses of human tissue is difficult to over estimate in modern biomedical practice. Almost all human tissue removed during surgical intervention or taken at autopsy is examined diagnostically by a pathologist.

5.20 The tissue, which may be fresh or fixed, is first examined macroscopically. Then representative blocks are taken, embedded in wax, cut into thin sections, mounted on glass slides, stained and examined using the microscope. The primary purpose of this histopathological examination is to establish or to confirm the diagnosis. In the case of malignant disease, the degree of spread can be ascertained. Progress, either of disease or its treatment, can be measured in certain conditions by examination and comparison of serial biopsy specimens.

5.21 These stained microscope slides and the blocks from which they were made, together with stained slides from cytological examinations (for example, for cervical cytology) must be stored so that they are available for re-examination or review as part of good practice in histopathology laboratories. Some stained blood or bone marrow films for haematological examination are also stored in this way, as are some slides made in the course of cytogenetic diagnosis. The collection, with its attendant documentation, forms the pathological archive and is a cardinal resource, not only in diagnosis and management of individual patients, but in undergraduate and postgraduate teaching and education, research, review and scholarship. Pathological archives are large; a hospital dealing with 10,000 specimens of tissue a year will generate around 25,000 blocks and some 40,000 slides. The University Department of Morbid Anatomy at the Royal London Hospital has around 4,500,000 slides, 1,500,000 blocks and 10,000 wet specimens in store.

5.22 By study of the archive, pathologists can arrive at conclusions about the natural history of a disease by obtaining a view of how it behaves in many individuals. Such study of pathological archives confirmed the link between exposure to asbestos and lung disease. By this method new varieties of tumours within a particular classification have been identified behaving either less or more aggressively. This information will, in turn, inform therapeutic choice when a new patient presents; it may minimise the extent of surgery if experience has shown that radical procedures are unnecessary or ineffective, or it may indicate the need for more radical intervention if the prognosis has proved poor with conservative therapy in the past. This approach also allows the evaluation of the effectiveness of different medicines used to treat diseases. Molecular biological methods applied to material stored many decades previously may provide genetic information and historical evidence of early occurrence of particular viral infections.

5.23 The archive is essential in quality control and assurance. The slides are a permanent record that can be checked by independent experts in the interests of peer audit review and quality assurance. The archive may be reviewed when individual diagnoses are queried, as has proved necessary, for example, in the difficult area of cervical screening of women. Large sections of the pathological archive are occasionally reviewed where mistakes are thought to have occurred. In the United Kingdom, for instance, reviews of diseased bone samples have recently been performed.

5.24 Thus, collectively and for individual patients, careful record keeping relevant to the histopathological archive allows definition of the natural history of disease, permits identification of new disease entities, establishes the efficacy, or sometimes, the failure of treatment and permits reassessment of management if unexpected features are encountered.

5.25 In all pathological archives the material is stored anonymously, being identified by laboratory number. Thus, if the material is to be used for research purposes anonymity is readily assured, but patient identity can be established by the pathologist from the confidential diagnostic records, if the research reveals information of relevance to the treatment of the patient.

(For a discussion of intellectual property issues, see: Nuffield Council on Bioethics *Human Tissue: Ethical and Legal Issues* (1995) ch 11; L Bently and B Sherman 'The Ethics of Patenting: Towards a Transgenic Patent System' (1995) 3 Med L Rev 275.)

1. The nature of property rights

What, then, is the legal framework for thinking about control over tissue or other body material which has been excised? One framework would be to look to that which governs the *removal* of tissue? This we have already seen in relation to the living donor. It is the common law of consent. Notice the Human Organ Transplants Act 1989 is only relevant where an 'organ' is to be removed and it is to be used for *transplantation*. Thus, removal would be lawful if the individual consent to it or, if incompetent (or a child), the removal was lawful being in that individual's 'best interests'. We have already examined this earlier in the chapter.

This framework, however, has little to do with *control* of subsequent use of the tissue by the donor. The donor's argument would have to be that the use was unexpected and of which the donor was unaware such that his or her consent to its removal was invalid. Such an argument would succeed if the donor, as a consequence, did not understand the 'nature and purpose' of the removal of the tissue ('the touching') and the removal would be a battery. For example, a person who thought the tissue was being removed as part of his treatment when in truth it was not because it was for research purposes may not have given a valid consent (see *infra*). Of course, even here the individual fails to gain 'control' over the excised tissue. And, in any event, the argument has limited importance, since it would not assist where the use was of leftover tissue removed for therapeutic purposes. Providing the person was aware that the removal was for such purposes, there could be no battery based upon subsequent (mis)use of the tissue. The legal framework that focuses upon the removal is therefore of limited – or no – importance when the issue concerns the subsequent use of excised tissue.

An alternative framework would be, as has been suggested earlier, that of property. Property law would, by contrast, have something to say about subsequent 'use' and 'control' of tissue (and other bodily material) removed from a living person. Even if it applies, there is still much to be decided, as we shall see. Who may claim proprietary rights over the tissue? The donor? Others who obtain the tissue or improve it in some way? Before we address these questions, it would be helpful to examine briefly what the legal institution of 'property' means. One of us does so in the following extract.

A Grubb 'I, Me, Mine': Bodies, Parts and Property (1998) 3 Med L Int 299

Property is a 'legal and social institution governing the use of most things and the allocation of some items of social wealth' (JW Harris '*Who Owns My Body*' (1996) 16 OJLS 55). Every western society has a system of property and a legal system that allows for its enjoyment, its transfer and to permit control over it to the exclusion of others. In general, one can say that the rules of private property operate to distribute in society those resources which are valuable and for which there is greater demand than supply. They assign to individuals rights in, and over, these resources. The importance of property to societies is signified by the fact that historically property laws have featured more prominently in western legal systems, particularly English law, than say have laws relating to the person. Clarity, comprehensiveness and certainty have been the key features that property law systems have strived for. English law's rules are immensely complex and diverse and often rooted in their medieval legal origins. We distinguish between *real* property (land in effect), *personal* property (tangible things such as chattels and intangible things such as debts or other choses in action) and intellectual property (for example, patents and copyright).

It is, however, important to understand the notion of 'property' in English law. It is used in two senses: one descriptive of the 'thing' itself, the other of an individual's relationship with the 'thing'. A statement to the effect that 'apples, dogs, books and land are property' illustrates the first usage. Contrariwise one could state: 'ideas, human beings and information are not property'. These statements tell us nothing about the relationship of the 'things' with any individual or group of individuals and, in particular, the law's position on that. It is the second sense of property that serves that function. Thus, we might use language which asserts 'rights' over the 'thing' in question: 'That apple is mine', 'I own Rover, the dog' and 'I am the tenant of that flat or its my freehold you are talking about'. The latter – like 'John is in possession of the book I loaned him' – demonstrates that more than one person my assert 'rights' over a 'thing' and hence claim that they have 'property' in it. We could say 'I' *own* the book and 'John' has *possession* of it. Both describe a relationship with the book and both legal notions may, in fact will, give rise to rights over the book, albeit that they will be slightly different.

Concurrent and relative claims to 'property' in a thing, especially if it is land, are very common in English law. We describe individuals as *owning* property, by which we usually mean exercising complete (or near enough) dominion over the thing (see A M Honoré, 'Ownership' in *Oxford Essays in Jurisprudence*, First Series (ed) A G Guest (1961) p 107). We also speak of individuals being in *possession* of property (see D R Harris, 'The Concept of Possession in English Law' *ibid*). Whilst an owner may well be in possession of a thing, others may possess property, be entitled to enjoy it and look to the law's protection against interference with that enjoyment. In other words, possession may entail 'property' interests over a thing, albeit of lesser kind (relatively speaking) than is attached to ownership. In fact, English law, unlike civilian systems, pays little heed to the notion of absolute title (or dominion) and is more concerned with protecting the 'rights' of a possessor; only usually bothering about ownership as a 'trump' in disputes with other less entitled possessors.

'Property' in the sense of describing the relationship between a thing and an individual generates a range of legal rules governing the relationship. There is no definitive catalogue which can be drawn up but one might offer the following as plausible categories of rules describing the 'thing-person' relationship (see J W Harris *op cit* pp 59–62). First, there are what might be termed *user entitlements*; rules which allow a person to exploit or enjoy the thing perhaps even commercially. Secondly, there are rules conferring *exclusionary control* over the thing. Trespassory rules preventing others dealing with the thing: exemplified by the call to 'stay off my land' or 'leave my dog alone'. Thirdly, there are rules conferring *dispositional liberties*, allowing transfer by, for example, gift or selling. All of these are, in some part at least, essential requirements for an individual to have 'property' in a thing. However, they do not necessarily mean that the rules have the same content when applied to different individuals in relation to the same thing. So, in the example where 'John is in possession of my book' because I have loaned it to him, John has the current right to enjoy my book (a user entitlement) and he also has the right to prevent others (apart from me) from interfering with that entitlement by virtue of his lawful possession of the book (exclusionary control). He does not, however, have the ability to lawfully transfer the book to another. I, however, do not have a current user entitlement because I have temporarily exercised my dispositional liberty to loan by way of bailment my book to John. I can, however, by virtue of my ownership of the book decide to transfer the book to another by gift or sale. I can also chose to consign the book to the rubbish tip or simply destroy it.

Equally these types of rule do not mean that the rules bear the same content when applied to different 'things'. Hence, there may be limitation rules which restrict the person's 'user entitlement', for example, the law of nuisance, planning laws, laws prohibiting cruelty to animals or which allow for compulsory expropriation of the property. There may be rules which limit an individual's ability to dispose of the thing, for instance, by restricting sales and allowing only transfers for non-value or, in exceptional circumstances, preventing alienation altogether, although this is rare.

II.   Property: The Human Body

Does an individual have any 'property' rights in or over his body or its parts or tissue derived from it? Can anyone else acquire 'property' over another's body, its parts or tissue derived from it? Upon the answers to these questions may turn whether a person can control the use of his tissue or body parts; his ability to share in any commercial exploitation of his genetic material; and the rights of others to protect the body parts and tissue from interference by others. The questions are particularly important today as developments in the medical and other sciences increasingly permit and create therapeutic uses for human bodily material. The demands for scientific study on body samples and the storage and archiving of tissue and fluids have focused attention on who can control and exploit the material. Anatomical specimens exist in museums and medical exhibits can be found in hospitals and elsewhere. The questions are, in themselves, not new. Indeed, the problem of 'body ownership' have existed for sometime as body material has long been useful. The first kidney transplant was in 1954 but corneal grafting occurred earlier and it has been claimed that successful bone transplants were carried out as early as the late 19th Century (see R Scott, *The Body as Property*, (1981)). Blood transfusions date back to the 17th century (see R M Titmuss, *The Gift Relationship* (1997) Ch 5). Even longer, scientists and doctors have used dead bodies for the purposes of teaching and studying anatomy (see R Richardson '*Death, Dissection and the Destitute*' (1988)).

1.   Body Ownership Language

It is a commonly felt connection that all that is 'I' is also 'Mine' and somehow belongs to 'Me'. Equally, the sense of 'it's mine' continues even after a body part or tissue has been taken from an individual. Who can forget Tony Hancock's indignant assertion when he said in the *Blood Donor*:

> Well of course it's got something to do with me, it's my blood...Well all right – was. But you can't expect my interest in it to cease just because you've got it.

The language of 'body ownership' is part of everyday speech and culture. Tony Hancock's diatribe exemplifies that. We are all familiar with the self-assertion to another of: 'It's my body and I'll do what I want with it' or 'You don't own me!'. Jim Harris has argued that this is no more than rhetoric and we do not actually mean what we say; anymore than we would, if asked to explain, say that 'this is my child' is to assert a property interest in a son or daughter (J W Harris, *op cit* at 62–65). It is, instead, really about asserting a freedom to be left alone – a personal, rather than property, right – reflected in the law requiring consent to a touching. Nevertheless, some political philosophers have argued that individuals do have 'property' in their bodies which they, as a result, own. The arguments date back to such philosophical luminaries as John Locke and John Stuart Mill. They have done so, largely, to argue for rights over the so-called 'fruits of labour' such as work. The argument of self-ownership is based upon the follow line of reasoning: if an individual is not a slave (and none of us is), nobody else owns my body, therefore I must own myself and everything that it produces. As Jim Harris explains (J W Harris, *op cit* at p 68):

> Starting with the premise of self-ownership, ownership of the fruits of my labour follow automatically. My body is the tree; my actions are the branches; and the product of my labouring activities is the fruit.

A number of modern philosophers have followed the Locke/Mill line and some, most famously Robert Nozick, have taken it further to develop a liberal attack on taxation and redistribution of wealth as being an unjustified assault upon an individual's self-owned 'labours' (Robert Nozick *Anarchy, State and Utopia* (1974)). The premise explicit in this view has been criticised as a 'spectacular non sequitur': just because I am not a slave and nobody else owns me, does not mean that I do (J W Harris, *op cit* at 71–3). Whatever the results of the philosophical musings, the law is otherwise. Not only does no-one else own my body, neither do I. Legal conceptions of 'property' do not extend to ownership of another or self-ownership. This is not to say that a person cannot assert property interests in parts or tissue that were part of his body or that property interests cannot be claimed over a dead body or its parts.

(For a discussion of the institution of property, see: J Harris *Property and Justice* (1996); S R Munzer *A Theory of Property* (1990).)

2.   Property rights in body parts

Professor Bernard Dickens picks up the arguments in an important article.

Bernard M Dickens 'The Control of Living Body Materials' (1977) 27 University of Toronto Law Journal 142

A.   *THE SOURCE'S INCHOATE TITLE*

The positive functions of control of a live person's separated body materials are to serve his interests as a human being, paying due regard to his autonomy and confidentiality, and in part to apply the means of acquisition of body materials to the uses that can be made of them, consistent with communal approval or tolerance. Negatively, the function of control is to give the human source preventive or remedial power over detrimental use of his body materials. It may be proposed that the donor's autonomy is served by providing for his indicated wishes and preferences to prevail posthumously as to the disposition of his body materials, and the law should make comparable provision for disposition during his lifetime. The legal principles that may be applied to this cause require identification, however, and no single principle may necessarily be derived from the different means of acquisition of body materials, nor govern the variety of their uses.

A philosophical approach to the origination from a living body of independently tangible material or of fluids capable of isolation may be to consider them *res nullius*, that is, corporeal items in the legal ownership of nobody. They might be reduced into possession by the first person to obtain physical control who intend to exercise control over them, in accordance with the test of classical jurisprudence. This prescription of possession from which ownership may be inferred would by definition afford the human source no prior interest. In a sophisticated legal system where personal property rights are highly developed, the list of items constituting *res nullius* is short. The concepts of property and ownership have tended to be pragmatic, evolving in response to the economic or spiritual recognition of objects as having value; 'property' describes a valuable right or interest in a thing, moreover, rather than the thing itself. In pre-history, for instance, when humans could survive only where land, natural crops, wild animals, and game were available without the application of systematic labour to agriculture and hunting or trapping, they had no value, and were not considered ownable. Use may expose scarcity, however, scarcity begets value, and value is concretized in property. Value is both material (or economic) and superstitious (including sentimental and spiritual), but it is only in recent times that separated body materials have become capable of a use that gives them value, whether for sale or for philanthropic dedication. Even in the case of cadavers, their employment in medical education occurred on a significant scale only when medicine evolved the conceit of being scientific, which happened after the common law had largely exhausted its capacity for free growth, so that creative legal use of cadavers required the formulation of legislation, namely anatomy acts.

No theoretical limit can be set to how far the law may go in recognizing new property interests. Materials as abstract as gas can be possessed and stolen, as may electricity, and vibration has been treated as an 'object' in trespass and possibly nuisance law. In 1940 it was observed that 'Atmospheric or etheric vibrations, in the form of radiated waves, have become one of the most important forces in the world, and at any moment a legal question may arise whether they are capable of property or possession.' While 'Knowledge or ideas, as such, do not constitute property,' the mode of expression of an idea can attract copyright protection. Thus, a person's interest in producing the electrochemical activity that can be monitored in his brain may in the future be analysed in terms of property, rather than of privacy, and as, for instance, a meditative or creative technique, may become comparable to intellectual, literary, and industrial property.

The characterization of separated body materials as *res nullius* may serve the interests of neither the human source nor others. To suggest that material immediately passes into the absolute ownership of the hospital or physician undertaking or supervising its removal and intending to appropriate it might defeat the source's justifiable interest in its use or disposition and the purpose of its specific donation, for instance for diagnosis, transplantation, or a particular research project. It may be inadequate regarding even body waste, of which a person will normally relieve himself as speedily and conveniently as possible compatibly with social delicacy, expecting and hoping never to hear of it again. Sanitary regulations and the general law on nuisance require one in charge of premises or land on which such waste is discharged adequately, to dispose of it...

Recognizing waste materials as *res nullius*, capable of exclusive legal control by the person first possessing them, clearly will not serve the interests of the human source. Similarly, recognition as *res nullius* of material such as a limb or digit severed from the human source in an accident or an assault may be inconsistent with his interest in its preservation for prompt surgical rejoining to his body. His claim to it should not be impaired by the chance of the item falling upon another's land or being retrieved and retained by a stranger not implicated in causing the loss. A better approach, therefore, may be to consider the human source as having an inchoate right of property in materials issuing from his body, which right he may expressly or by implication abandon to another, or similarly make prevail over a contending claim.

This may well accord to the sentimental reaction to the origination of body material in its separate state. The right is better considered inchoate than fully constituted, since the material may never in fact come under the source's notional or physical control. He may be unconscious, for instance, when it is separated, and it may be deemed abandoned, perhaps to a hospital, very soon after it is first isolated. Traditional jurisprudential tests of, for instance, intention, possession, and control as affecting ownership may more easily be preserved by considering the initial interest of the source *prima facie* a superior right to that of any other person, but a right only in prospect.

B. REMOVED AND DISCHARGED MATERIALS

In the absence of an express claim to ownership by the source of materials removed or discharged from his body, or of a necessary assumption of his best right, as in the case of an unconscious or dazed victim's interest in a severed replaceable limb, he may be required continuously to act or otherwise to show an intention to maintain his control in better repair than that of any other person. The required degree of demonstration of continuing interest will depend, of course, upon the circumstances. The analogy may be invoked of rights in international law to newly discovered territory, where it has been observed that 'an inchoate title could not prevail over the continuous and peaceful display of authority by another'. A source of materials may, for instance, set conditions upon another's possession, as when blood is donated upon condition that a contract price be paid, urine is given for diagnosis, or an eye is given for the purpose of pathologic examination, or he may give directions as to disposition.

In *Browning v Norton Children's Hospital* [(1974) 504 SW 2d 713 (Ky CA)], for instance, the court observed that 'when one consents to and authorizes an operation while a patient in hospital (*absent any specific reservation, demand, or objection* to some normal procedure), he then and thereby, in effect, accepts all the rules, regulations, and the modus operandi of that hospital' as to disposal of surgically removed tissue. The right to make specific reservation, demand, or objection that supersedes the hospital's normal practice is worthy of note. The court's additional opinion that 'Is it the duty of the surgeon to take a dismembered part of a human body into his care and custody – for the amputee? We think not,' may be discounted in favour of a later view that 'It could not be said that a person has no property rights in wastes or other materials which were once a part of or contained within his body, but which normally are discarded after their separation from the body.' Nevertheless both judgments require the patient to take the initiative to express any specific reservation, demand, or objection prior to surgery or other removal. When surgery or discharge is complete, or when a pathologist has completed inspection of the material, the assumption of abandonment may arise.

The legal inference of the source's silence and passivity is that his inchoate right to his separated body material is yielded to the hospital or other possessor, such as a hairdresser. The proposal favouring the hospital's right is based both on the policy that the hospital's potential for creative use should prevail over a presumption that the silent patient gives possession on an implied condition of destruction, and on observable practice. In *Venner v State of Maryland* [(1976) 354 A 2d 483 (Md CA)] for instance, the court noted that 'It is not unknown for a person to assert a continuing right of ownership, dominion, or control, for good reason or for no reason, over such things as excrement, fluid waste, secretions, hair, fingernails, toenails, blood, and organs or other parts of the body, whether their separation from the body is intentional, accidental or merely the result of normal body functions,' but that 'By the force of social custom, we hold that when a person does nothing and says nothing to indicate an intent to assert his right of ownership, possession, or control over such material, the only rational inference is that he intends to abandon the material.'

In practice, of course, the material usually is fit only for destruction, and nothing is gained from asking whether this reflects the prevailing intention of the patient or of the hospital…

Regarding discharged material bearing less symbolic or spiritual weight than an advanced fetus, it may accordingly be proposed that the passive human source be deemed in principle to have abandoned his legal interest in it. If it comprises 'tissue' to be used for transplantation, his consent may be required under human tissue gift laws, but use may be made for other therapy and for research and teaching without reference to him; his consent, and a fortiori his informed consent, is not required. Reference to such use in a hospital admission or consent to treatment form may be useful, however, since this might overcome problems of using material immediately upon its origination from the source, perhaps while he is still under anaesthetic or otherwise of impaired perception.

This legal position should meet at least in part the despairing complaint of Dr Hugh Fudenberg that 'In most university hospitals [in the United States] it is not possible to take excess urine that is discarded after urinalysis or the excess few drops of blood discarded after blood is drawn for a blood test and use them to work out some new tests that could then be standardized for a new diagnosis of disease without getting the written consent of the person involved.' Nevertheless, the ethical constraints upon a physician with a professional or other interest in a potential tissue recipient attending or certifying the death of a potential donor may have to be extended by analogy to cover the situation of a source's presumed abandonment of usable materials. If an attending physician is going to want such materials for a use affording the patient no therapeutic or diagnostic benefit, the patient's express consent may have to be independently sought beforehand, lest abandonment of his property may appear to have been effected by the exercise of undue influence. The rebuttable legal presumption of the physician's undue influence serves generally to redress the inequality of the doctor-patient relation, but in this case it also affords protection to both parties against the donor later suspecting that the material did not have to be removed at all, but was taken to serve the physician's research interests…

It has been seen that abandonment must be into the legal control of another, as opposed to constituting the property *res nullius*. Express abandonment to an identified volunteer may be tantamount to a gift, but both spoken or another abandonment, and in particular implied abandonment, may leave some question as to the identity of the legal recipient. Varieties of usable materials and the means of their separation differ too widely for a definitive answer, but, because of scarcity of materials and competition for their use between patients in need, and also between physicians, surgeons, and comparable health professionals, an assumption of an institutional rather than a private successor may be favoured; that is, a hospital, clinic, or laboratory rather than an individual such as a removal surgeon, inspecting pathologist, potential researcher, or, for instance, transplant surgeon. Apart from obviating problems of succession to title upon death of the individual, and reducing the effect of the legal presumption of undue influence, this will increase the likelihood that use of the scarce material will be debated in scientific and ethical terms, rather than allowing decisions to be taken according to the private or secret choice of any one person. Just how scarce resources are institutionally allocated in medicine to assist the living and to promote research is a matter of grave and occasionally vital concern, on which far more information should be made available to the public. Development of this theme lies beyond the present study, but it may be preferable in itself, and compatible with observable trends in other areas where novel property interests have become identified, that control should rest with public rather than with private agencies. Such a preference would also be compatible with anatomy acts, which tend to provide for distribution of corpses to teaching hospitals and similar institutions but not to purely private agencies.

C.   SPECIFICALLY DONATED MATERIALS

Beyond this consideration of control of materials in which the source has no further interest, except perhaps as to the choice between destruction or general use, lies the issue of the source identifying a specific use or user. This may concern material he would not otherwise release, such as a healthy kidney or his bone marrow, and those whose release is for his therapeutic, diagnostic, or cosmetic advantage, but which he does not abandon. Where he sells material such as blood, skin, or urine, he may be taken to give an absolute title in the normal way of commerce, including rights to such aspects of his confidentiality as the sale may require. This is not to say, of course, that confidentiality is necessarily sacrificed, since a sale of, for instance, semen for artificial insemination, may require confidentiality to be preserved, even to the extent of prohibiting the donor from revealing his identity. Where sale does not occur or is illegal, philanthropic dedication may similarly pass title to the appointed recipient, which may be an institution or, for instance, a named sick relative…

It is clear that donation of material for application to a specified person or purpose (such as the donor's diagnosis) would give the hospital and its personnel no proprietary interest in it, except the 'special property' or 'qualified ownership' of a bailee. The bailment relation may remain until termination by the donor's revocation or by execution in the form of prescribed application of the materials to the intended recipient or purpose. It may be, however, that property will pass when the donor totally divests himself of possession by delivering them to, or allowing acquisition by, appropriate hospital personnel, who then become bailees of the identified recipient. The labour that medical specialists may need to give to preservation of materials, and the skills they must devote to achieving effecting transfer to the recipient, may render it unsuitable to consider that the hospital or individuals concerned hold the materials for transfer as mere servants or agents of the donors or the donees. Destruction of an organ after transplantation would appear to be a personal injury, the organ being in the category of *res quae usu consumuntur*, but legal action would be more easily conceivable in negligence than in trespass to the person; indeed, trespass in the sense of interference unjustified by consent or necessity might be hard to show.

A hospital that holds as bailee an organ or other material that has been dedicated to a specific recipient or given for diagnosis or, for instance, to assist genetic counselling, but that either uses it for another recipient or purpose, or simply destroys it, would seem in principle to be liable in conversion. Action would be at the instance of the human source or the recipient, depending on which of them had the immediate right to possession of the material. A slight conceptual problem with the tort of conversion concerns the traditional remedy of pecuniary damages, however, since 'the measure of damages for conversion is the full value of the chattel so that the action, in effect, forces an involuntary purchase on the convertor'. Human tissue legislation may make active promotion of a sale 'invalid as being contrary to public policy', but clearly public policy does not prevent such 'involuntary purchase'; the difficulty raised in establishing 'the full value' in terms of market criteria or the cost of replacement. This lack of apparent value may protect the hospital from a larceny charge, but liability in conversion may remain, since 'the plaintiff is also entitled to compensation for any special damage which the law does not regard as too remote'. A quantifiable loss may be shown regarding the lost opportunity for receiving satisfaction from giving benefit to the specified recipient or cause, or for obtaining a transplant or transfusion or the benefit to the better diagnosis or counselling. Whether a potential plaintiff can show such special damage more easily by acting in conversion rather than in negligence goes to liability itself, however, whereas in conversion it goes only to the quantum of damages recoverable, giving advantage to proceedings in conversion. Since a hospital's duty as bailee generally arises only upon the owner expressly intimating his interest in the separated materials, however, an intended recipient may have difficulty acting in conversion.

An uncertain issue arises when the source expressly directs a hospital to destroy material it appropriates instead. Such instruction, if a hospital is prepared to accept it, may amount to abandonment, but a patient's need for confidentiality may give him an interest in his body material being destroyed rather than simply left at large. In principle, destruction is a right of ownership, and frustration of its exercise may amount to such interference with the right of a person entitled to possession as constitutes conversion. A claim in conversion regarding anonymous material may offend against the public interest, but a court not wishing to dismiss a claim on policy grounds, and not wishing to find for a fractious plaintiff and require the defendant hospital to pay even nominal damages and perhaps costs, could exonerate the hospital under the principle *de minimis non curat lex*.

Principles of the reasoning above would be generally applicable to materials a subject dedicates to experimentation specified, by reference to institution, project, or principal investigator, in a consent form or as understood in a verbal consent. When a project proves abortive, for instance because its early results are too adverse to subjects, because its funds fail, or because a key investigator departs, and when a project has materials surplus to its needs for completion, materials already isolated may conscientiously be used in another project without renewed consent, rather than be wasted. If consent can conveniently be sought there may be a case in ethics and etiquette for requiring the subject-donor to be approached, but the donation may be seen preferably in legal principle as a gift rather than a bailment. Conditions may be imposed upon gifts, but not if they are contrary to public policy or too inconsistent with the nature of an absolute gift. In practice, details of the research given in a consent form contribute to the informed quality of the subject's consent, and are not a guarantee of specific use. Law and ethics may coincide, however, in proscribing the deceitful use of such information to induce the donation of materials intended *ab initio* for another use.

The condition for alternative use without express consent is, however, preservation of the subject's confidentiality. No legal problem may arise in conscientious use in one project of material given for another project where data accompanying the material are anonymous. Where the subject is identifiable from data already given, however, or where further information may be required from him in person or from his medical record, confidentiality requires that his prior consent be obtained. A research subject is frequently informed expressly of his rights to withdraw from the study at any time, but withdrawal is not retrospective so as to deny either use of body materials already contributed, or access to subsequent projects in which they may anonymously serve. It may seem that giving wider circulation than was initially agreed upon with an identifiable subject to information about, for instance, his body weight, allergies, eating habits, and blood pressure, can cause him so little detriment as to fall within the legal principle *de minimis non curat lex*, but neutral physiological data may in some cases be socially sensitive, as, for instance, results of phallometric testing disclosing a male's erotic preferences.

Professor Dickens offers an argument in favour of the property analysis. Importantly, he sees the 'property' as vesting in the source but, in appropriate circumstances, those interests being transferred to the remover by abandonment or by way of gift.

It is important to notice the historical content in which the 'property' approach falls to be considered. In particular, it was assumed by the middle of the nineteenth century that it was a rule of English law that a corpse could not be the subject of property – the so-called 'no property' in a corpse rule (see *infra*, ch 18). There is no doubt that this rule influenced attitudes to the living body and its parts. The notion that excised tissue or parts should be categorised as 'property' was not easily accepted. There are very few English cases which have considered whether tissue removed from a living person can be 'property'. In *R v Welsh* [1974] RTR 478 and *R v Rothery* [1976] RTR 550, the Court of Appeal assumed that urine and blood respectively were 'property' capable of being stolen. More recently, and more significantly, in *R v Kelly* [1998] 3 All ER 741 (CA), the court held that body parts derived from corpses were 'property' capable of being stolen notwithstanding the 'no property' in a corpse rule where work and skill had resulted in the body parts acquiring different attributes. In the particular case, it was the work of anatomists. Rose LJ went, at least potentially, further when he said (at 750):

> It may be that if, on some future occasion, the question arises, the courts will hold that human body parts are capable of being property...even without the acquisition of different attributes, if they have a use or significance beyond their mere existence. This may be so, if, for example, they are intended for use in an organ transplant operation, for the extraction of DNA or, for that matter, as an exhibition in a trial.

This would represent a most significant step and it is the most explicit recognition so far that excised tissue and body parts may be property. We will return later to consider who has the property rights. You will recall Professor Dickens' view that prima facie it is the source, ie the donor/patient. Interestingly, in each of the cases we have referred to, the court assumed it was the receiver who could exercise property rights over the tissue or body substance. (For discussions of the case law in England and elsewhere, see: P Matthews 'Whose Body? People as Property' (1983) 36 CLP 193 and R S Magnusson 'Property Rights in Human Tissue' in N Palmer and E McKendrick (eds) *Interests in Goods* (2nd edn, 1998) ch 2.)

3. The *Moore* case

A decision of immense importance is that of the California Supreme Court in the following case. It concerned the commercial exploitation of cells derived from a patient's tissue to produce an immortal cell-line (the Mo-line) named after the patient, John Moore.

Moore v Regents of the University of California (1990) 793 P 2d 479 (Cal Sup Ct)

Panelli J: Our only task in reviewing a ruling on a demurrer is to determine whether the complaint states a cause of action. Accordingly, we assume that the complaint's properly pleaded material allegations are true and give the complaint a reasonable interpretation by reading it as a whole and all its parts in their context. (*Phillips v Desert Hospital Dist* (1989) 49 Ca 3d 699, 702; *Bland v Kirwan* (1985) 39 Cal 3d 311, 318; *Tameny v Atlantic Richfield Co* (1980) 27 Cal 3d 167, 170.) We do not, however, assume the truth of contentions, deductions, or conclusions of fact or law. (*Daar v Yellow Cab Co* (1967) 67 Cal 2d 695, 713.) For those purposes we briefly summarize the pertinent factual allegations of the 50-page complaint.

The plaintiff is John Moore (Moore), who underwent treatment for hairy-cell leukemia at the Medical Center of the University of California at Los Angeles (UCLA Medical Center). The five defendants are: (1) Dr David W Golde (Golde), a physician who attended Moore at UCLA Medical Center; (2) the Regents of University of California (Regents), who own and operate the university; (3) Shirley W Quan, a researcher employed by the Regents; (4) Genetics Institute, Inc (Genetics Institute); and (5) Sandoz Pharmaceuticals Corporation and related entities (collectively Sandoz).

Moore first visited UCLA Medical Center on October 5, 1976, shortly after he learned that he had hairy-cell leukemia. After hospitalizing Moore and 'withdr[awing] extensive amounts of blood, bone marrow aspirate, and other bodily substances,' Golde confirmed that diagnosis. At this time all defendants, including Golde, were aware that 'certain blood products and blood components were of great value in a number of commercial and scientific efforts' and that access to a patient whose blood contained these substances would provide 'competitive, commercial, and scientific advantages.'

On October 8, 1976, Golde recommended that Moore's spleen be removed. Golde informed Moore 'that he had reason to fear for his life, and that the proposed splenectomy operation...was necessary to slow down the progress of his disease.' Based on Golde's representations, Moore signed a written consent form authorizing the splenectomy.

Before the operation, Golde and Quan 'formed the intent and made arrangements to obtain portions of [Moore's] spleen following its removal' and to take them to a separate research unit. Golde gave written instructions to this effect on October 18 and 19, 1976. These research activities 'were not intended to have…any relation to [Moore's] medical…care]. However, neither Golde nor Quan informed Moore of their plans to conduct this research or requested his permission. Surgeons at UCLA Medical Center, whom the complaint does not name as defendants, removed Moore's spleen on October 20, 1976.

Moore returned to the UCLA Medical Center several times between November 1976 and September 1983. He did so at Golde's direction and based upon representations 'that such visits were necessary and required for is health and well-being, and based upon the trust inherent in and by virtue of the physician-patient relationship…' On each of these visits Golde withdrew additional samples of 'blood, blood serum, skin, bone marrow aspirate, and sperm.' On each occasion Moore traveled to the UCLA Medical Center from his home in Seattle because he had been told that the procedures were to be performed only there and only under Golde's direction.

'In fact, [however] throughout the period of time that [Moore] was under [Golde's] care and treatment,…the defendants were actively involved in a number of activities which they concealed from [Moore]…' Specifically, defendants were conducting research on Moore's cells and planned to 'benefit financially and competitively…[by exploiting the cells] and [their] exclusive access to [the cells] by virtue of [Golde's] on-going physician-patient relationship…'

Sometime before August 1979, Golde established a cell-line from Moore's T-lymphocytes. On January 30, 1981, the Regents applied for a patent on the cell-line, listing Golde and Quan as inventors. '[B]y virtue of an established policy…[the] Regents, Golde, and Quan would share in any royalties or profits…arising out of [the] patent.' The patent issued on March 20, 1984, naming Golde and Quan as the inventors of the cell-line and the Regents as the assignee of the patent. (U.S. Patent No. 4,438,032 (Mar. 20, 1984).)

The Regent's patent also covers various methods for using the cell-line to produce lymphokines. Moore admits in his complaint that 'the true clinical potential of each of the lymphokines [is] difficult to predict, [but]…competing commercial firms in these relevant fields have published reports in biotechnology industry periodicals predicting a potential market of approximately $3.01 Billion Dollars by the year 1990 for a whole range of [such lymphokines]…'

With the Regent's assistance, Golde negotiated agreements for commercial development of the cell-line and products to be derived from it. Under an agreement with Genetics Institute, Golde 'became a paid consultant' and 'acquired the rights to 75,000 shares of common stock'. Genetics Institute also agreed to pay Golde and the Regents 'at least £330,000 over three years, including a pro-rata share of [Golde's] salary and fringe benefits, in exchange for…exclusive access to the materials and research performed' on the cell-line and products derived from it. On June 4, 1982, Sandoz 'was added to the agreement,' and compensation payable to Golde and the Regents was increased by $110,000. '[T]hroughout this period,…Quan spent as much as 70 [percent] of her time working for [the] Regents on research' related to the cell-line.

Based upon these allegations, Moore attempted to state 13 causes of action. Each defendant demurred to each purported cause of action. The superior court, however, expressly considered the validity of only the first cause of action, conversion. Reasoning that the remaining causes of action incorporated the earlier defective allegations, the superior court sustained a general demurrer to the entire complaint with leave to amend. In a subsequent proceeding, the superior court sustained Genetics Institute's and Sandoz's demurrers without leave to amend on the grounds that Moore had not stated a cause of action for conversion and that the complaint's allegations about the entities' secondary liability were too conclusory. In accordance with its earlier ruling that the defective allegations about conversion rendered the entire complaint insufficient, the superior court took the remaining demurrers off its calendar.

With one justice dissenting, the Court of Appeal reversed, holding that the complaint did state a cause of action for conversion. The Court of Appeal agreed with the superior court that the allegations against Genetics Institute and Sandoz were insufficient, but directed the superior court to give Moore leave to amend. The Court of Appeal also directed the superior court to decide 'the remaining causes of action, which [had] never been expressly ruled upon'…

Moore also attempts to characterize the invasion of his rights as a conversion – a tort that protects against interference with possessory and ownership interests in personal property. He theorizes that he continued to own his cells following their removal from his body, at least for the purpose of directing their use, and that he never consented to their use in potentially lucrative medical research. Thus, to complete Moore's argument, defendants' unauthorized use of his cells constitutes a conversion. As a result of the alleged conversion, Moore claims a proprietary interest in each of the products that any of the defendants might ever create from his cells or the patented cell-line.

No court, however, has ever in a reported decision imposed conversion liability for the use of human cells in medical research. While that fact does not end our inquiry, it raises a flag of caution. In effect, what Moore is asking us to do is to impose a tort duty on scientists to investigate the consensual pedigree of each human cell sample used in research. To impose such a duty, which would affect medical research of importance to all of society, implicates policy concerns far removed from the traditional, two-party ownership disputes in which the law of conversion arose. Invoking a tort theory originally used to determine whether the loser or the finder of a horse had the better title, Moore claims ownership of the results of socially important medical research, including the genetic code for chemicals that regulate the functions of every human being's immune system.

Accordingly; we first consider whether the tort in conversion clearly gives Moore a cause of action under existing law. We do not believe it does. Because of the novelty of Moore's claim to own the biological materials at issue, to apply the theory of conversion in this context would frankly have to be recognized as an extension of the theory. Therefore, we consider next whether it is advisable to extend the tort to this context.

1.   Moore's Claim Under Existing Law

'To establish a conversion, plaintiff must establish an actual interference with his ownership or right of possession…Where plaintiff neither has title to the property alleged to have been converted, nor possession thereof, he cannot maintain an action for conversion.' (*Del E Webb Corpn v Structural Materials Co* (1981) 123 Cal App 3d 593, 610–611. See also *General Motors A Corpn v Dallas* (1926) 198 Cal, 365, 370.)

Since Moore clearly did not expect to retain possession of his cells following their removal, to sue for their conversion he must have retained an ownership interest in them. But there are several reasons to doubt that he did retain any such interest. First, no reported judicial decision supports Moore's claim, either directly or by close analogy. Second, California statutory law drastically limits any continuing interest of a patient in excised cells. Third, the subject matters of the Regents' patent – the patented cell-line and the products derived from it – cannot be Moore's property.

Neither the Court of Appeal's opinion, the parties' briefs, nor our research discloses a case holding that a person retains a sufficient interest in excised cells to support a cause of action for conversion. We do not find this surprising, since the laws governing such things as human tissues, transplantable organs, blood, fetuses, pituitary glands, corneal tissue, and dead bodies deal with human biological materials as objects sui generis, regulating their disposition to achieve policy goals rather than abandoning them to the general law of personal property. It is these specialized statutes, not the law of conversion, to which courts ordinarily should and do look for guidance on the disposition of human biological materials…

The next consideration that makes Moore's claim of ownership problematic is California statutory law, which drastically limits a patient's control over excised cells. Pursuant to Health and Safety Code section 7054.4, '[n]otwithstanding any other provision of law, recognizable anatomical parts, human tissues, anatomical human remains, or infectious waste following conclusion of scientific use shall be disposed of by interment, incineration, or any other method determined by the state department [of health services] to protect the public health and safety.' Clearly the Legislature did not specifically intend this statute to resolve the question of whether a patient is entitled to compensation for the nonconsensual use of excised cells. A primary object of the statute is to ensure the safe handling of potentially hazardous biological waste materials. Yet one cannot escape the conclusion that the statute's practical effect is to limit, dramatically, a patient's control over excised cells. By restricting how excised cells may be used and requiring their eventual destruction, the statute eliminates so many of the rights ordinarily attached to property that one cannot simply assume that what is left amounts to 'property' or 'ownership' for purposes of conversion law.

It may be that some limited right to control the use of excised cells does survive the operation of this statute. There is, for example, no need to read the statute to permit 'scientific use' contrary to the patient's expressed wish. A fully-informed patient may always withhold his consent to treatment by a physician whose research plans the patient does not approve. That right, however, as already discussed, is protected by the fiduciary-duty and informed-consent theories.

Finally, the subject matter of the Regent's patent – the patented cell-line and the products derived from it – cannot be Moore's property. This is because the patented cell-line is both factually and legally distinct from the cells taken from Moore's body. Federal law permits the patenting of organisms that represent the product of 'human ingenuity,' but not naturally occurring organisms. (*Diamond v Chakrabarty, supra,* 447 US 303, 309–310.) Human cell-lines are patentable because '[l]ong term adaptation and growth of human tissues and cells in culture is difficult – often considered an art…' and the probability of success is low. (OTA Rep., *supra,* at p 33.) It is this inventive effort that patent law rewards, not the discovery of naturally occurring raw materials. Thus, Moore's allegations that he owns the cell-line and the products derived from it are inconsistent with the patent, which constitutes an authoritative determination that the cell-line is the product of invention. Since such allegations are nothing more than arguments or conclusions of law, they of course do not bind us. (*Daar v Yellow Cab Co, supra,* 67 Cal, 2d at p 71.)

2. Should Conversion Liability Be Extended?

As we have discussed, Moore's novel claim to own the biological materials at issue in this case is problematic, at best. Accordingly, his attempt to apply the theory of conversion within this context must frankly be recognized as a request to extend that theory. While we do not purport to hold that excised cells can never be property for any purpose whatsoever, the novelty of Moore's claim demands express consideration of the policies to be served by extending liability (cf *Nally v Grace Community Church, supra,* 47 Cal 3d at pp 291–300; *Foley v Interactive Data, supra,* 47 Cal 3d at pp 634–700; *Brown v Superior Court,* supra, 44 Cal 3d at pp 1061–1065) rather than blind deference to a complaint alleging as a legal conclusion the existence of a cause of action.

There are three reasons why it is inappropriate to impose liability for conversion based upon the allegations of Moore's complaint. First, a fair balancing of the relevant policy considerations counsels against extending the tort. Second, problems in this area are better suited to legislative resolution. Third, the tort of conversion is not necessary to protect patients' rights. For these reasons, we conclude that the use of excised human cells in medical research does not amount to a conversion…

The extension of conversion law into this area will hinder research by restricting access to the necessary raw materials. Thousands of human cell-lines already exist in tissue repositories, such as the American Type Culture Collection and those operated by the National Institutes of Health and the American Cancer Society. These repositories respond to tens of thousands of requests for samples annually. Since the patent office requires the holders of patents on cell-lines to make samples available to anyone, many patent holders place their cell-lines in repositories to avoid the administrative burden of responding to requests. (OTA Rep, *supra,* at p 53.) At present, human cell-lines are routinely copied and distributed to other researchers for experimental purposes, usually free of charge. This exchange of scientific materials, which still is relatively free and efficient, will surely be compromised if each cell sample becomes the potential subject matter of a lawsuit (OTA Rep, *supra,* at p 52).

To expand liability by extending conversion law into this area would have a broad impact. The House Committee on Science and Technology of the United States Congress found that '49 percent of the researchers at medical institutions surveyed used human tissues or cells in their research.' Many receive grants from the National Institute of Health for this work (OTA Rep, *supra,* at p 52). In addition, 'there are nearly 350 commercial biotechnology firms in the United States actively engaged in biotechnology research and commercial product developments and approximately 25 to 30 percent appear to be engaged in research to develop a human therapeutic or diagnostic reagent…Most, but not all, of the human therapeutic products are derived from human tissues and cells, or human cell-lines or cloned genes.' (*Id,* at p 56.)…

Lucas CJ, Eagelson, Kennard and Arabian JJ concurred.

The majority remanded the case for trial on the issue of whether Moore gave a valid consent for research to be undertaken on his tissue given that the doctors owed Moore a fiduciary duty to disclose their 'personal interests unrelated to the patient's health, whether research or economic, that may affect [the doctor's] medical judgment'. Mosk J filed a powerful dissent.

Mosk J: The majority first take the position that Moore has no cause of action for conversion under existing law because he retained no 'ownership interest' in his cells after they were removed from his body. To state a conversion cause of action a plaintiff must allege his 'ownership or right to possession of the property at the time of the conversion' (*Baldwin v Marina City Properties Inc* (1978) 79 Cal App 3d 393, 410). Here the complaint defines Moore's 'Blood and Bodily Substances' to include inter alia his blood, his bodily tissues, his cells, and the cell-lines derived therefrom. Moore thereafter alleges that 'he is the owner of his Blood and Bodily Substances and of the by-products produced therefrom…' And he further alleges that such blood and bodily substances 'are his tangible personal property, and the activities of the defendants as set forth herein constitute a substantial interference with plaintiff's possession or right thereto, as well as defendants' wrongful exercise of dominion over plaintiff's personal property rights in his Blood and Bodily Substances.'

The majority impliedly hold these allegations insufficient as a matter of law, finding three 'reasons to doubt' that Moore retained a sufficient ownership interest in his cells, after their excision, to support a conversion cause of action. In my view the majority's three reasons, taken singly or together, are inadequate to the task.

The majority's first reason is that 'no reported judicial decision supports Moore's claim, either directly or by close analogy.' Neither, however, is there any reported decision rejecting such a claim. The issue is new as its source – the recent explosive growth in the commercialization of biotechnology.

The majority next cite several statutes regulating aspects of the commerce in or disposition of certain parts of the human body, and conclude in effect that in the present case we should also 'look for guidance' to the Legislature rather than to the law of conversion. Surely this argument is out of place in an opinion of the highest court of this state. As the majority acknowledge, the law of conversion is a creature of the common law. 'The inherent capacity of the common law for growth and change is its most significant feature. Its development has been determined by the social needs of the community which it serves. It is constantly expanding and developing in keeping with advancing civilization and the new conditions and progress of society, and adapting itself to the gradual change of trade, commerce, arts, inventions, and the needs of the country'. In short, as the United States Supreme Court has aptly said, 'This flexibility and capacity for growth and adaptation is the peculiar boast and excellence of the common law.'...Although the Legislature may of course speak to the subject, in the common law system the primary instruments of this evolution are the courts, adjudicating on a regular basis the rich variety of individual cases brought before them (*Rodriguez v Bethlehem Steel Corpn* (1974) 12 Cal 3d 382, 394)...

The majority's second reason for doubting that Moore retained an ownership interest in his cells after their excision is that 'California statutory law...drastically limits a patient's control over excised cells.' For this proposition the majority rely on Health and Safety Code section 7054.4 (hereafter section 7054.4). The majority concede that the statute was not meant to directly resolve the question whether person in Moore's position has a cause of action for conversion, but reason that it indirectly resolves the question by limiting the patient's control over the fate of his excised cells: 'By restricting how excised cells may be used and requiring their eventual destruction, the statute eliminates so many of the rights ordinarily attached to property that one cannot simply assume that what is left amounts to 'property' or 'ownership' for purposes of conversion law.' As will appear, I do not believe section 7054.4 supports the just quoted conclusion of the majority.

First, in my view the statute does not authorize the principal use that defendants claim the right to make of Moore's tissue, ie, its commercial exploitation. In construing section 7054.4, of course, 'we look first to the words of the statute themselves' (*Long Beach Police Officers Assn v City of Long Beach* (1988) 46 Cal 3d 736, 741), and give those words their usual and ordinary meaning (*California Teachers Assn v San Diego Community College Dist* (1981) 28 Cal 3d 692, 698).

By its terms, section 7054.4 permits only 'scientific use' of excised body parts and tissue before they must be destroyed. We must therefore determine the usual and ordinary meaning of that phrase. I would agree that 'scientific use' at least includes routine postoperative examination of excised tissue conducted by a pathologist for diagnostic or prognostic reasons (eg, to verify preoperative diagnosis or to assist in determining postoperative treatment). I might further agree that 'scientific use' could be extended to include purely scientific study of the tissue by a disinterested researcher for the purpose of advancing medical knowledge – provided of course that the patient gave timely and informed consent to that use. It would stretch the English language beyond recognition, however, to say that commercial exploitation of the kind and degree alleged here is also a usual and ordinary meaning of the phrases 'scientific use'.

The majority dismiss this difficulty by asserting that I read the statute to define 'scientific use' as 'not-for-profit scientific use', and by finding 'no reason to believe that the Legislature intended to make such a distinction.' The objection misses my point. I do not stress the concept of profit, but the concept of science: the distinction I draw is not between nonprofit scientific use and scientific use that happens to lead to a marketable by-product; it is between a truly scientific use and the blatant commercial exploitation of Moore's tissue that the present complaint alleges. Under those allegations, defendants Dr David W Golde and Shirley G Quan were not only scientists, they were also fully-fledged entrepreneurs; the complaint repeatedly declares that they appropriated Moore's tissue in order 'to further defendants' independent research and commercial activities and promote their economic, financial and competitive interests.' The complaint also alleges that defendant Regents of the University of California (hereafter Regents) actively assisted the individual defendants in applying for patent rights and in negotiating with bioengineering and pharmaceutical companies to exploit the commercial potential of Moore's tissue. Finally, the complaint alleges in detail the contractual arrangements between the foregoing defendants and defendants Genetics Institute, Inc, and Sandoz Pharmaceuticals Corporation, giving the latter companies exclusive rights to exploit that commercial potential while providing substantial financial benefits to the individual defendants in the form of cash, stock options, consulting fees, and fringe benefits. To exclude such traditionally commercial activities from the phrase 'scientific use', as I do here, does not give it a restrictive definition; rather, it gives the phrase its usual and ordinary meaning settled law requires.

Secondly, even if section 7054.4 does permit defendants' commercial exploitation of Moore's tissue under the guise of 'scientific use', it does not follow that – as the majority concluded – the statute 'eliminates so many of the rights ordinarily attached to property' that what remains does not amount to 'property' or 'ownership' for purposes of the law of conversion.

The concepts of property and ownership in our law are extremely broad. (See Civ. Code, §§654, 655.) A leading decision of this court approved the following definition: 'The term 'property' is sufficiently comprehensive to include every species of estate, real and personal, and everything which one person can own and transfer to another. It extends to every species of right and interest capable of being enjoyed as such upon which it is practicable to place a money value.' (*Yuba River Power Co v Nevada Irr Dist* (1923) 207 Cal 521, 523.)

Being broad, the concept of property is also abstract: rather than referring directly to a material object such as a parcel of land or the tractor that cultivates it, the concept of property is often said to refer to a 'bundle of rights' that may be exercised with respect to that object – principally the rights to possess the property, to use the property, to exclude others from the property, and to dispose of the property by sale or by gift. 'Ownership is not a single concrete entity but a bundle of rights and privileges as well as of obligations.' (*Union Oil Co v State Bd of Equal.* (1963) Cal 2d 441, 447.) But the same bundle of rights does not attach to all forms of property. For a variety of policy reasons, the law limits or even forbids the exercise of certain rights over forms of property. For example, both law and contract may limit the right of an owner of real property use his parcel as he sees fit. Owners of various forms of personal property may likewise be subject to restrictions on the time, place, and manner of their use. Limitations on the disposition of real property, while less common, may also be imposed. Finally, some types of personal property may be sold but not given away, while others may be given away but not sold, and still others may neither be given away nor sold.

In each of the foregoing instances, the limit or prohibition diminishes the bundle of rights that would otherwise attach to the property, yet what remains is still deemed in law to be a protectible property interest. 'Since property or title is a complex bundle of rights, duties, powers and immunities, the pruning away of some or a great many of these elements does not entirely destroy the title...' (*People v Walker* (1939) 33 Cal App 2d 18, 20 [even the possessor of contraband has certain property rights in it against anyone other than the state].) The same rule applies to Moore's interest in his own body tissue: even if we assume that section 7054.4 limited the use and disposition of his excised tissue in the manner claimed by the majority, Moore nevertheless retained valuable rights in that tissue. Above all, at the time of its excision, he at least had the right to do with his own tissue whatever the defendants did with it: ie, he could have contracted with researchers and pharmaceutical companies to develop and exploit the vast commercial potential of his tissue and its products. Defendants certainly believe that their right to do the foregoing is not barred by section 7054.4 and is a significant property right, as they have demonstrated by their deliberate concealment from Moore of the true value of his tissue, their efforts to obtain a patent on the Mo cell-line, their contractual agreements to exploit this material, their exclusion of Moore from any participation in the profits, and their vigorous defense of this lawsuit. The Court of Appeal summed up the point by observing that 'Defendants' position that plaintiff cannot own his tissue, but that they can, is fraught with irony.' It is also legally untenable. As noted above, the majority cite no case holding that an individual's right to develop and exploit the commercial potential of his own tissue is not a right of sufficient worth or dignity to be deemed a protectible property interest. In the absence of such authority – or of legislation to the same effect – the right falls within the traditionally broad concept of property in our law.

The majority's third and last reason for their conclusion that Moore has no cause of action for conversion under existing law is that 'the subject matter of the Regent's patent – the patented cell-line and the products derived from it – cannot be Moore's property.' The majority then duly offer an explanation: 'This is because the patented cell-line is factually and legally distinct from the cells taken from Moore's body.' Neither branch of the explanation withstands analysis.

First, in support of their statement that the Mo cell-line is 'factually distinct' from Moore's cells, the majority assert that 'Cells change while being developed into a cell-line and continue to change over time', and in particular may acquire an abnormal number of chromosomes. No one disputes these assertions but they are nonetheless irrelevant. For present purposes no distinction can be drawn between Moore's cells and the Mo cell-line. It appears that the principal reason for establishing a cell-line is not to 'improve' the quality of the parent cells but simply to extend their life indefinitely, in order to permit long-term study and/or exploitation of the qualities already present in such cells. The complaint alleges that Moore's cells naturally produced certain valuable proteins in larger than normal quantities; indeed, that was why defendants were eager to culture them in the first place. Defendants do not claim that the cells of the Mo cell-line are in any degree more productive of such proteins than were Moore's own cells. Even if the cells of the Mo cell-line in fact have an abnormal number of chromosomes, at the present stage of this case we do not know if that fact has any bearing whatever on their capacity to produce proteins; yet it is in the commercial exploitation of that capacity – not simply in their number of chromosomes – that Moore seeks to assert an interest. For all that appears, therefore, the emphasized fact is a distinction without a difference.

Second, the majority assert in effect that Moore cannot have an ownership interest in the Mo cell-line because defendants patented it. The majority's point wholly fails to meet Moore's claim that he is entitled to compensation for defendants' unauthorized use of his bodily tissues before defendants patented the Mo cell-line: defendants undertook such use immediately after the splenectomy on October 20, 1976, and continued to extract and use Moore's cells and tissue at least until September 20, 1983; the patent, however, did not issue until March 20, 1984, more than seven years after the unauthorized use began. Whatever the legal consequences of that event, it did not operate retroactively to immunize defendants from accountability for conduct occurring long before the patent was granted.

Nor did the issuance of the patent in 1984 necessarily have the drastic effect that the majority contend. To be sure, the patent granted defendants the exhaustive right to make, use, or sell the invention for a period of 17 years (35 U.S.C. § 154). But Moore does not assert any such right for himself. Rather, he seeks to show that he is entitled, in fairness and equity, to some share in the profits that defendants have made and will make from their commercial exploitation of the Mo cell-line. I do not question that the cell-line is primarily the product of the defendants' inventive effort. Yet likewise no one can question Moore's crucial contribution to the invention – an invention named, ironically, after him: but for the cells of Moore's body taken by defendants, there would have been no Mo cell-line. Thus the complaint alleges that Moore's 'Blood and Bodily Substances were absolutely essential to defendants' research and commercial activities with regard to his cells, cell-lines, [and] the Mo cell-line…and that defendants could not have applied for and had issued to them the Mo cell-line patent and other patents described herein without obtaining and culturing specimens of plaintiff's Blood and Bodily Substances.' Defendants admit this allegation by their demurrers, as well they should: for all their expertise, defendants do not claim they could have extracted the Mo cell-line out of thin air.

Nevertheless the majority conclude that the patent somehow cut off all Moore's rights – past, present and future – to share in the proceeds of defendants' commercial exploitation of the cell-line derived from his own body tissue. The majority cite no authority for this unfair result, and I cannot believe it is compelled by the general law of patents: a patent is not a license to defraud. Perhaps the answer lies in an analogy to the concept of 'joint inventor.' I am aware that 'patients and research subjects who contribute cells to research will not be considered inventors.' (OTA Rep, *supra*, at p 71.) Nor is such a person strictly speaking a 'joint inventor' within the meaning of the term in federal law (35 U.S.C. § 116). But he does fall within the spirit of that law. 'The joint invention provision guarantees that all who contribute in a substantial way to a product's development benefit from the reward that the product brings. Thus, the protection of joint inventors encourages scientists to cooperate with each other and ensures that each contributor is rewarded fairly…'

'Although a patient who donates cells does not fit squarely within the definition of a joint inventor, the policy reasons that inform joint inventor patents should also apply to cell donors. Neither John Moore nor any other patient whose cells become the basis for a patentable cell-line qualifies as a 'joint inventor' because he or she did not further the development of the product in any intellectual or conceptual sense. Nor does the status of patients as sole owners of a component part make them deserving of joint inventorship status. What the patients did do, knowingly or unknowingly, is collaborate with the researchers by donating their body tissue…By providing the researchers with unique raw materials, without which the resulting product could not exist, the donors become necessary contributors to the product. Concededly, the patent is not granted for the cell as it is found in nature, but for the modified biogenetic product. However, the uniqueness of the product that gives rise to its patentability stems from the uniqueness of the original cell. A patient's claim to share in the profits flowing from a patent would be analogous to that of an inventory whose collaboration was essential to the success of a resulting product. The patient was not a coequal, but was a necessary contributor to the cell-line.' (Danforth, Cells, Sales, & Royalties: The Patient's Right to a Portion of the Profits (1985) 6 Yale L & Pol'y Rev 179, 197, fns omitted, (hereafter Danforth).)

Under this reasoning, which I find persuasive, the law of patents would not be a bar to Moore's assertion of an ownership interest in his cells and their products sufficient to warrant his sharing in the proceeds of their commercial exploitation…

Having concluded – mistakenly, in my view – that Moore has no cause of action for conversion under existing law, the majority next consider whether to 'extend' the conversion cause of action to this context. Again the majority find three reasons not to do so, and again I respectfully disagree with each.

The majority's first reason is that a balancing of the 'relevant policy considerations' counsels against recognizing a conversion cause of action in these circumstances. The memo identifies two such policies, but concedes that one of them – 'protection of a competent patient's right to make autonomous medical decisions' – would in fact be promoted, even though 'indirectly', by recognizing a conversion cause of action.

The majority focus instead on a second policy consideration, ie their concern 'that we not threaten with disabling civil liability innocent parties who are engaged in socially useful activities, such as researchers who have no reason to believe that their use of a particular cell sample is, or may be, against a donor's wishes.' As will appear, in my view this concern is both overstated and outweighed by contrary considerations.

The majority begin their analysis by stressing the obvious facts that research on human cells plays an increasingly important role in the progress of medicine, and that the manipulation of those cells by the methods of biotechnology has resulted in numerous beneficial products and treatments. Yet it does not necessarily follow that, as the majority claim, application of the law of conversion in this area 'will hinder research by restricting access to the necessary raw materials,' ie, to cells, cell cultures, and cell-lines. The majority observe that many researchers obtain their tissue samples routinely and at little or no cost, from cell-culture repositories. The majority then speculate that 'This exchange of scientific materials which is still relatively free and efficient, will surely be compromised. Each cell sample becomes the potential subject matter of a lawsuit.' There are two grounds to doubt that this prophecy will be fulfilled.

To begin with, if the relevant exchange of scientific materials was ever 'free and efficient,' it is much less so today. Since biological products of genetic engineering became patentable in 1980 (*Diamond v Chakrabarty* (1980) 447 US 303), human cell-lines have been amenable to patent protection and, as the Court of Appeal observed in its opinion below, 'The rush to patent for exclusive use has been rampant.' Among those who have taken advantage of this development, of course, are the defendants herein: as we have seen, defendants Golde and Quan obtained a patent on the Mo cell-line in 1984 and assigned it to defendants Regents. With such patentability has come a drastic reduction in the formerly free access of researchers to new cell-lines and their products: the 'novelty' requirement for patentability prohibits public disclosure of the invention at all times up to one year before the filing of the patent application. (35 USC § 102(b).) Thus defendants herein recited in their patent specification, 'At no time has the Mo cell-line been available to other than the investigators involved with its initial discovery and only the conditioned medium from the cell-line has been made available to a limited number of investigators for collaborative work with the original discoverers of the Mo cell-line.'

An even greater force for restricting the free exchange of new cell-lines and their products has been the rise of the biotechnology industry and the increasing involvement of academic researchers in that industry. When scientists became entrepreneurs and negotiated with biotechnological and pharmaceutical companies to develop and exploit the commercial potential of their discoveries – as did defendants in the case at bar – layers of contractual restrictions were added to the protections of the patent law.

In their turn, the biotechnological and pharmaceutical companies demanded and received exclusive rights in the scientists' discoveries, and frequently placed those discoveries under trade secret protection. Trade secret protection is popular among biotechnology companies because, among other reasons, the invention need not meet the strict standards of patentability and the protection is both quickly acquired and unlimited in duration. (Note, Patent and Trade Secret Protection in University Industry Research Relationships in Biotechnology (1987) 24 Harv J of Legis, 191, 218–219.) Secrecy as a normal business practice is also taking hold in university research laboratories, often because of industry pressure (*id*, at pp 204–208): 'One of the most serious fears associated with university-industry cooperative research concerns keeping work private and not disclosing it to the researcher's peers…Economic arrangements between industry and universities inhibit open communication between researchers, especially for those who are financially tied to smaller biotechnology firms.'' (Howard, *supra*, 44 Food Drug Cosm LJ at p 339, fn 72.)

Secondly, to the extent that cell cultures and cell-lines may still be 'freely exchanged,' eg, for purely research purposes, it does not follow that the researcher who obtains such material must necessarily remain ignorant of any limitations on its use: by means of appropriate record keeping, the researcher can be assured that the course of the material has consented to his proposed use of it, and hence that such use is not a conversion. To achieve this end the originator of the tissue sample first determines the extent of the source's informed consent to its use – eg, for research only, or for public but academic use, or for specific or general commercial purposes; he then enters this information in the record of the tissue sample, and the record accompanies the sample into the hands of any researcher who thereafter undertakes to work with it. 'Record keeping would not be overly burdensome because researchers generally keep accurate records of tissue sources for other reasons: to trace anomalies to the medical history of the patient, to maintain title for other researchers and for themselves, and to insure reproducibility of the experiment.' (Toward the Right of Commerciality, *supra*, 34 UCLA L Rev, at p 241.) As the Court of Appeal correctly observed, any claim to the contrary 'is dubious in light of the meticulous care and planning necessary in serious modern medical research.'…

...[I]n my view whatever merit the majority's single policy consideration may have is outweighed by two contrary considerations, ie, policies that are promoted by recognizing that every individual has a legally protectable property interest in his own body and its products. First, our society acknowledges a profound ethical imperative to respect the human body as the physical and temporal expression of the unique human persona. One manifestation of that respect is our prohibition against direct abuse of the body by torture or other forms of cruel or unusual punishment. Another is our prohibition against indirect abuse of the body by its economic exploitation for the sole benefit of another person. The most abhorrent form of such exploitation, of course, was the institution of slavery. Lesser forms, such as indentured servitude or even debtor's prison, have also disappeared. Yet their specter haunts the laboratories and boardrooms of today's biotechnological research-industrial complex. It arises wherever scientists or industrialists claim, as defendants claim here, the right to appropriate and exploit a patient's tissue for their sole economic benefit – the right, in other words, to freely mine or harvest valuable physical properties of the patient's body: 'Research with human cells that results in significant economic gain for the researcher and no gain for the patient offends the traditional mores of our society in a manner impossible to quantify. Such research tends to treat the human body as a commodity – a means to a profitable end. The dignity and sanctity with which we regard the human whole, body as well as mind and soul, are absent when we allow researchers to further their own interests without the patient's participation by using a patient's cells as the basis for a marketable product.' (Danforth, *supra*, 6 Yale L & Pol'y Rev at p 190, fn omitted.)

A second policy consideration adds notions of equity to those of ethics. Our society values fundamental fairness in dealings between its members, and condemns the unjust enrichment of any member at the expense of another. This is particularly true when, as here, the parties are not in equal bargaining positions. We are repeatedly told that the commercial products of the biotechnological revolution 'hold the promise of tremendous profit.' (Toward the Right of Commerciality, *supra*, 34 UCLA L Rev at p 211.) In the case at bar, for example, the complaint alleges that the market for the kinds of proteins produced by the Mo cell-line was predicted to exceed $3 billion by 1990. These profits are currently shared exclusively between the biotechnology industry and the universities that support that industry. The profits are shared in a wide variety of ways, including 'direct entrepreneurial ties to genetic-engineering firms' and 'an equity interest in fledgling biotechnology firms' (Howard, *supra*, 44 Food Drug Cosm LJ at p 338). Thus the complaint alleges that because of his development of the Mo cell-line defendant Golde became a paid consultant of defendant Genetics Institute and acquired the rights to 75,000 shares of that firm's stock at a cost of 1 cent each; that Genetics Institute further contracted to pay Golde and the Regents at least $330,000 over 3 years, including a pro rata share of Golde's salary and fringe benefits; and that defendant Sandoz Pharmaceuticals Corporation subsequently contracted to increase that compensation by a further $110,000.

There is, however, a third party to the biotechnology enterprise – the patient who is the source of the blood or tissue from which all these profits are derived. While he may be a silent partner, his contribution to the venture is absolutely crucial: as pointed out above (pt 3, ante, but for the cells of Moore's body taken by defendants there would have been no Mo cell-line at all). Yet defendants deny that Moore is entitled to any share whatever in the proceeds of this cell-line. This is both inequitable and immoral. As Dr Thomas H Murray, a respected professor of ethics and public policy, testified before Congress, 'the person [who furnishes the tissue] should be justly compensated...If biotechnologists fail to make provision for a just sharing of profits with the person whose gift made it possible, the public's sense of justice will be offended and no one will be the winner.' (Murray, Who Owns the Body? On the Ethics of Using Human Tissue for Commercial Purposes (Jan-Feb 1986) IRB: A Review of Human Subjects Research, at p 5.)

There will be such equitable sharing if the courts recognize that the patient has a legally protected property interest in his own body and its products: 'property rights in one's own tissue would provide a morally acceptable result by giving effect to notions of fairness and preventing unjust enrichment...Societal notions of equity and fairness demand recognition of property rights. There are bountiful benefits, monetary and otherwise, to be derived from human biologies. To deny the person contributing the raw material a fair share of these ample benefits is both unfair and morally wrong.' (Toward the Right of Commerciality, *supra*, 34 UCLA L Rev, at p 229.) 'Recognizing a donor's property rights would prevent unjust enrichment by giving monetary rewards to the donor and researcher proportionate to the value of their respective contributions. Biotechnology depends upon the contribution of both patients and researchers. If not for the patient's contribution of cells with unique attributes, the medical value of the bioengineered cells would be negligible. But for the physician's contribution of knowledge and skill in developing the cell product, the commercial value of the patient's cells would also be negligible. Failing to compensate the patient unjustly enriches the researcher because only the researcher's contribution is recognized.' (*Id* at p 230.) In short, as the Court of Appeal succinctly put it, 'if the science has become science for profit, then we fail to see any justification for excluding the patient from participation in these profits.'...

The majority's second reason for declining to extend the conversion cause of action to the present context is that 'the Legislature should make that decision,' I do not doubt that the Legislature is competent to act on this topic. The fact that the Legislature may intervene if and when it chooses, however, does not in the meanwhile relieve the courts of their duty of enforcing – or if need be, fashioning – an effective judicial remedy for the wrong here alleged. As I observed above (pt 2, *ante*), if a conversion cause of action is otherwise an appropriate remedy on these facts we should not refrain from recognizing it merely because the Legislature has not yet addressed the question. To do so would be to abdicate pro tanto our responsibility over a body of law – torts – that is particularly a creature of the common law. And such reluctance to act would be especially unfortunate at the present time, when the rapid expansion of biotechnological science and industry makes resolution of these issues an increasingly pressing need.

The inference I draw from the current statutory regulation of human biological materials, moreover, is the opposite of that drawn by the majority. By selective quotation of the statutes the majority seem to suggest that human organs and blood cannot legally be sold on the open market – thereby implying that if the Legislature were to act here it would impose a similar ban on monetary compensation for the use of human tissue in biotechnological research and development. But if that is the argument, the premise is unsound: contrary to popular misconception, it is not true that human organs and blood cannot legally be sold.

As to organs, the majority rely on the Uniform Anatomical Gift Act (Health & Saf Code, § 7150 et seq, hereafter the UAGA) for the proposition that a competent adult may make a post mortem gift of any part of his body but may not receive 'valuable consideration' for the transfer. But the prohibition of the UAGA against the sale of a body part is much more limited than the majority recognized: by its terms (Health & Saf Code, § 7155, subd (a)) the prohibition applies only to sales for 'transplantation' or 'therapy'. Yet a different section of the UAGA authorizes the transfer and receipt of body parts for such additional purposes as 'medical or dental education research, or advancement of medical or dental science.' (Health & Saf Code, § 7153, subd (a)(1).) No section of the UAGA prohibits anyone from selling body parts for any of those additional purposes; by clear implication, therefore, such sales are legal. Indeed, the fact that the UAGA prohibits no sales of organs other than sales for 'transportation' or 'therapy' raises a further implication that it is also legal for anyone to sell human tissue to a biotechnology company for research and development purposes.

With respect to the sale of human blood the matter is much simpler: there is in fact no prohibition against such sales. The majority rely on Health and Safety Code 1606, which provides in relevant part that the procurement and use of blood for transfusion 'shall be construed to be, and is declared to be the rendition of a service...and shall not be construed to be, and is declared not to be, a sale...' There is less here, however, than meets the eye; the statute does mean that a person cannot sell his blood or, by implication, that his blood is not his property. 'While many jurisdictions have classified the transfer of blood or other human tissue as a service rather than a sale, this position does not conflict with the notion that human tissue is property.' (Columbia Note, *supra*, 90 Colum. L Rev at p 544, fn 76.) The reason is plain: 'No State or Federal statute prohibits the sale of blood, plasma, semen, or other replenishing tissues if taken in nonvital amounts. Nevertheless, State laws usually characterize these paid transfers as the provision of services rather than the sale of a commodity. [Para] The primary legal reason for characterizing these transactions as involving services rather than goods is to avoid liability for contaminated blood products under either general product liability principles of the [Uniform Commercial Code's] implied warranty provisions.' (OTA Rep, at p 76, fn omitted.) The courts have repeatedly recognized that the foregoing is the real purpose of this harmless legal fiction. (See, eg *Hyland Therapeutics v Superior Court* (1985) 175 Cal App 3d 509; *Cramer v Queen of Angels Hosp.* (1976) 62 Cal App 3d 812; *Shepard v Alexian Brothers Hosp* (1973) 33 Cal App 3d 606.) Thus despite the statute relied on by the majority, it is perfectly legal in this state for a person to sell his blood for transfusion or for any other purpose – indeed, such sales are commonplace, particularly in the market for plasma. (See OTA Rep, *supra* at p 121.)

It follows that the statutes regulating the transfers of human organs and blood do not support the majority's refusal to recognize a conversion cause of action for commercial exploitation of human blood cells without consent. On the contrary, because such statutes treat both organs and blood as property that can legally be sold in a variety of circumstances, they impliedly support Moore's contention that his blood cells are likewise property for which he can and should receive compensation, and hence are protected by the law of conversion...

The majority's final reason for refusing to recognize a conversion cause of action on these facts is that 'there is no pressing need' to do so because the complaint also states another cause of action that is assertedly adequate to the task; that cause of action is 'the breach of a fiduciary duty to disclose facts material to the patient's consent or, alternatively...the performance of medical procedures without first having obtained the patient's informed consent'. Although last, this reason is not the majority's least; in fact, it underlies much of the opinion's discussion of the conversion cause of action, recurring like a leitmotiv throughout that discussion.

The majority hold that a physician who intends to treat a patient in whom he has either a research interest or an economic interest is under a fiduciary duty to disclose such interest to the patient before treatment; that his failure to do so may give rise to a nondisclosure cause of action; and that the complaint herein states such a cause of action at least against defendant Golde. I agree with that holding as far as it goes.

I disagree, however, with the majority's further conclusion that in the present context a nondisclosure cause of action is an adequate – in fact, a superior – substitute for a conversion cause of action. In my view the nondisclosure cause of action falls short on at least three grounds.

First, the majority reason that 'enforcement of physicians' disclosure obligations' will ensure patients' freedom of choice. The majority do not spell out how those obligations will be 'enforced'; but because they arise from judicial decision (the majority opinion herein) rather than from legislative or administrative enactment, we may infer that the obligations will primarily be enforced by the traditional judicial remedy of an action for damages for their breach. Thus the majority's theory apparently is that the threat of such an action will have a prophylactic effect: it will give physician-researchers incentive to disclose any conflicts of interest before treatment, and will thereby protect their patients' right to make an informed decision about what may be done with their body parts.

The remedy is largely illusory. '[A]n action based on the physician's failure to disclose material information sounds in negligence. As a practical matter, however, it may be difficult to recover on this kind of negligence theory because the patient must prove a causal connection between his or her injury and the physician's failure to inform.' (Martin & Lagod, Biotechnology and the Commercial Use of Human Cells: Toward an Organic View of Life and Technology (1989) 5 Santa Clara Computer & High Techn LJ 211, 222, fn omitted.) There are two barriers to recovery. First, 'the patient must show that if he or she had been informed of all pertinent information, he or she would have declined to consent to the procedure in question.' (*Ibid.*) As we explained in the seminal case of *Cobbs v Grant* (1972) 8 Cal 3d 229, 245, 'There must be a causal relationship between the physician's failure to inform and the injury to the plaintiff. Such a causal connection arises only if it is established that had the revelation been made consent to treatment would not have been given.'

The second barrier to recovery is still higher, and is erected on the first: it is not even enough for the plaintiff to prove that he personally would have refused consent to the proposed treatment if he had been fully informed; he must also prove that in the same circumstances no reasonably prudent person would have given such consent. The purpose of this 'objective' standard is evident: 'Since at the time of trial the uncommunicated hazard has materialized, it would be surprising if the patient-plaintiff did not claim that he had been informed of the dangers he would have declined treatment. Subjectively he may believe so, with the 20/20 vision of hindsight, but we doubt that justice will be served by placing the physician in jeopardy of the patient's bitterness and disillusionment. Thus an objective test is preferable: ie, what would a prudent person in the patient's position have decided if adequately informed of all significant perils.' (*Cobbs v Grant, supra,* 8 Cal 3d 229, 245.)

Even in an ordinary *Cobbs*-type action it may be difficult for a plaintiff to prove that no reasonably prudent person would have consented to the proposed treatment if the doctor had disclosed the particular risk of physical harm that ultimately caused the injury. (See, eg, *Morganroth v Pacific Medical Center Inc,* (1976) 54 Cal App 3d 521, 534 [affirming nonsuit in a *Cobbs*-type action on ground, inter alia, of lack of proof that plaintiff would have refused coronary arteriogram if he had been told of risk of stroke].) This is because in many cases the potential benefits of the treatment to the plaintiff clearly outweigh the undisclosed risk of harm. But that imbalance will be even greater in the kind of non disclosure action that the majority now contemplate: here we deal not with a risk of physical injuries such as a stroke, but with the possibility that the doctor might later use some of the patient's cast-off tissue for scientific research or the development of commercial products. Few if any judges or juries are likely to believe that disclosure of such a possibility of research or development would dissuade a reasonably prudent person from consenting to the treatment. For example, in the case at bar no trier of fact is likely to believe that if defendants had disclosed their plans for using Moore's cells, no reasonably prudent person in Moore's position – ie, a leukemia patient suffering from a grossly enlarged spleen – would have consented to the routine operation that saved or at least prolonged his life. Here, as in *Morganroth (ibid)* a motion for nonsuit for failure to prove proximate cause will end the matter. In this context, accordingly, the threat of suit on a nondisclosure cause of action is largely a paper tiger.

The second reason why the nondisclosure cause of action is inadequate for the task that the majority assign to it is that it fails to solve half the problem before us: it gives the patient only the right to refuse consent, ie, the right to prohibit the commercialization of his tissue; it does not give him the right to grant consent to that commercialization on the condition that he share in its proceeds. 'Even though good reasons exist to support informed consent with tissue commercialization; a disclosure requirement is only the first step toward full recognition of a patient's right to participate fully. Informed consent to commercialization, absent a right to share in the profits from such commercial development, would only give patients a veto over their own exploitation. But recognition that the patient[s] [have] an ownership interest in their own tissues would give patients an affirmative right of participation. Then patients would be able to assume the role of equal partners with their physicians in commercial biotechnology research.' (Howard, *supra*, 44 Food Drug Cosm LJ at p 344.)

Reversing the words of the old song, the nondisclosure cause of action thus accentuates the negative and eliminates the positive: the patient can say no, but he cannot say yes and expect to share in the proceeds of his contribution. Yet as explained above...there are sound reasons of ethics and equity to recognize the patient's right to participate in such benefits. The nondisclosure cause of action does not protect that right; to that extent, it is therefore not an adequate substitute for the conversion remedy, which does protect the right.

Third, the nondisclosure cause of action fails to reach a major class of potential defendants: all those who are outside the strict physician-patient relationship with the plaintiff. Thus the majority concede that here only defendant Golde, the treating physician, can be directly liable to Moore on a nondisclosure cause of action: 'The Regents, Quan, Genetics Institute and Sandoz are not physicians. In contrast to Golde, none of these defendants stood in a fiduciary relationship with Moore or had the duty to obtain Moore's informed consent to medical procedures.' As to these defendants, the majority can offer Moore only a slim hope of recovery: if they are to be liable on a nondisclosure cause of action, say the majority, 'it can only be on account of Golde's acts and on the basis of a recognized theory of secondary liability, such as respondeat superior.' Although the majority decline to decide the question whether the secondary-liability allegations of the complaint are sufficient, they strongly imply disapproval of those allegations. And the majority further note that the trial court has already ruled insufficient the allegations of agency as to the corporate defendants.

To the extent that a plaintiff such as Moore is unable to plead or prove a satisfactory theory of secondary liability, the nondisclosure cause of action will thus be inadequate to reach a number of parties to the commercial exploitation of his tissue. Such parties include, for example, any physician-researcher who is not personally treating the patient, any other researcher who is not a physician, any employer of the foregoing (or even of the treating physician), and any person or corporation thereafter participating in the commercial exploitation of the tissue. Yet some or all of those parties may well have participated more in, and profited more from, such exploitation than the particular physician with whom the plaintiff happened to have a formal doctor-patient relationship at the time.

In sum, the nondisclosure cause of action (1) is unlikely to be successful in most cases, (2) fails to protect patients' rights to share in the proceeds of the commercial exploitation of their tissue, and (3) may allow the true exploiters to escape liability. It is thus not an adequate substitute, in my view, for the conversion cause of action.

Broussard J also dissented on the conversion claim.

There are a number of important points to notice about the *Moore* decision. First, the majority were greatly influenced by the legislative context in California and the sense that the policy arguments were sufficiently complex that the court should leave the recognition of property claims, if at all, to the legislature. Secondly, the court did not exclude the possibility of property claims over excised tissue altogether. They contemplated that the researcher might have such a claim and it was this irony which was highlighted in Mosk J's dissent. (We shall return to this later.) Finally, the majority emphasised that the plaintiff was seeking to assert rights over a cell-line which was markedly different from his own cells which had been removed. The cell-line was produced through the skill and ingenuity of the researcher. For the minority it did not matter that the 'end product' was different since it was derived from the plaintiff's cells. (For discussions of *Moore*, see: E R Gold *Body Parts: Property Rights and the Ownership of Human Biological Materials* (1996) ch 2; B Dickens 'Living Tissue and Organ Donors and Property Law: More on *Moore*, (1992) 8 Journal of Contemporary Health Law and Policy 73.)

The reasoning in *Moore*, and its place as part of English law, is considered in the following extract.

Gerald Dworkin and Ian Kennedy 'Human Tissue: Rights in the Body and its Parts' (1993) 1 Med L Rev 29

The majority of the Supreme Court decided that the plaintiff must be satisfied with a personal remedy and rejected the proprietary action. The arguments of the scientific community that research and development in biotechnology would be slowed down and otherwise hampered if persons were to have proprietary rights in their own tissue weighed heavily with the court: '*unencumbered* access to human tissue for research is essential to progress and public health;...these sources must remain unencumbered, and medical researchers be free to both combine these materials with tissue taken from others, and dispose of the tissues, without answering to the person from whom the tissue was taken...[If the] plaintiff is permitted to have decision making authority and a financial interest in the cell-line, he would then have the unlimited power to inhibit medical research that could potentially benefit humanity. He could conceivably go from institution to institution seeking the highest bid and, if dissatisfied, claim the right simply to prohibit the research entirely.'

Thus, the primary reason for the Court's approach was one of public policy and all the subsidiary arguments employed were designed simply to add weight to this factor. Even in terms of American law, the reasons employed, as the dissenting opinions of Broussard and Mosk JJ demonstrate, are challengable.

First, it was argued that since the case was novel and no previous decision had applied the conversion remedy to human tissue, it would be wrong for the Court to extend the law. It would have been just as valid, however, to regard tissue as personal property and simply accept that conversion should apply here as in all other property cases.

Secondly, it was maintained that in an important policy matter of this kind any extension of the law is best left for the legislature. The simple response is that, however desirable legislative consideration of this matter may be, where a court is called upon to determine a tortious dispute, it has traditionally exercised its jurisdiction to develop the law on a case-by-case basis.

The third approach was to look at the trend of related Californian legislation (for example, that dealing with the disposal of tissue and organs for transplantation) to see whether any clear policy could be discerned. The majority found, implicit in this legislation, a clear policy against persons having proprietary control over their tissue. The minority, however, disputed this.

A fourth point, emphasized by one judge, was the immortality of Moore seeking recognition of a right to *sell* his body tissue *for profit*: 'the ramifications of recognising and enforcing a property interest in body tissues is not unknown, but are greatly feared...[as was] the effect on human dignity of a marketplace in human body parts [and] the impact upon research and development of competitive bidding for such materials.' Whilst the issue of commercializing human tissue is an important general matter ripe for legislative consideration, it is less obvious that the court should take action on this matter unless it was convinced that there was an overwhelming case for it to exercise its controversial paternalistic jurisdiction to ban unacceptable conduct in the public interest. In any event, it has been pointed out that, whilst it is arguable as a matter of policy or morality that a court may ban or restrict any person from profiting from the fortuitous value that adheres in a part of the human body, this decision does not do that: it simply bars Moore, the source of the cells, from obtaining the benefit of the cells' value but permits the doctor, who obtained the cells from Moore by allegedly improper means, and others, to retain and exploit the full economic value of their 'ill-gotten' gains free of their ordinary common law liability for conversion.

It was this fear that Moore might be able to use the conversion argument to extend his remedy as far as the revenue obtained from the exploitation of the patents that led the Court additionally to disclaim any causal relationship between his cells and the patented cell line and products derived from it. Even though there was no apparent significant difference between the cells and the cell line, the Court regarded them as both *factually* and *legally* distinct. The majority concluded that the patent somehow cut off all Moore's rights; even though Moore was not claiming that he was solely entitled to the patent which had been based upon his cells but merely to some share in the commercial exploitation of the patent or products which were derived from his cells.

A fifth consideration concentrated upon the position of third parties. In particular, it was feared that a conversion remedy, which was not linked to fault, would impose liability on all those into whose hands the cells might come, whether or not the particular defendants participated in, or knew of, the inadequate disclosures that violated the patient's right to make an informed decision. In the absence of any provision safeguarding the bona fide innocent user of tissue, there is certainly a risk of liability, but this risk exists when people acquire any property from those without proper title. Those who acquire property have to be alert as to the organizations from who they obtain their material and it is likely that the fears expressed have been considerably overestimated.

Lastly, the majority of the Court concluded that not only was the conversion remedy undesirable but, in any event, it was unnecessary since Moore's *personal* remedy for breach of fiduciary duty and the failure to obtain informed consent was sufficient to protect him. To Moore, that must have seemed a curious conclusion. It was not clear what compensation Moore would have been entitled to on the basis of the personal remedy: the Court did not see fit to discuss this issue. Does an action for negligence in this context extend beyond any possible physical damage (and there was none) to any emotional distress or other personal injury to cover also the loss of any profits from the exploitation of the patent? Had Moore been informed of all the facts he might still have given his unconditional consent and he would have suffered no loss; alternatively, had he objected, there would have been no relevant exploitation of his cells and no damage; alternatively, he might have given his consent on terms that he shared in the profits and was entitled to compensation for that.

On the other hand, putting aside the limitations inherent in a negligence action, an action for breach of fiduciary duty is grounded in equity and, as will be discussed later, provides the opportunity to seek an account of profits or other restitutionary benefits. Thus, although this appears to have been the assumption, it is by no means clear that Moore would have been entitled to less than he would have been entitled to under a proprietary action. The majority of the Supreme Court may have been right that Moore would not suffer by having to rely on an action for breach of fiduciary duty, even though they assumed that this action would not threaten the research community. Arguably, however, it would be difficult to bring an action against *third parties* on the basis of the personal rather than the proprietary remedy, which would be important for all those defendants other than the doctor treating Moore.

Would Moore Have Succeeded Under English Law?

Moore might have a greater chance of success under English law were he to pursue the conversion-proprietary claim rather than the personal action. Conversion (or trover) lies where a defendant carries out some wrongful act or interference with the dominion or control of goods in the possession of another. On the basis of the earlier analysis, there is no reason to suppose that, *prima facie*, human tissue would not be regarded as 'goods'. For example, Halsbury states that 'trover may…lie for human tissue or for human remains'.

Thus, an English common law approach to the *Moore* case could proceed on the following lines. Moore's personal right to physical security ensures that nobody may take tissue from his body without appropriate prior consent. At this stage, at the most, Moore might have an inchoate right of property in his tissue which would become a full property right once it has been removed from his body. Prior to removal Moore could have expressly (for example, in an appropriately worded consent form) abandoned any material removed from his body or transferred the property to the hospital or medical authorities for destruction or for specific or general research or other purposes. It would also have been possible, though extremely unusual, for such an express transfer of any human tissue (other than an 'organ' within the meaning of the Human Organ Transplants Act 1989) to be by way of sale for some monetary or other consideration. In the absence of any express provision, it is likely that Moore's standard consent to medical treatment would carry with it an implied abandonment of discarded human tissue. Accordingly, the medical authorities would then be free to assume total property rights over the tissue without any further legal obligation to refer back, or be accountable to, Moore. In most circumstances, the mere fact that the physician failed to disclose any research or economic potential of discarded tissue is unlikely to affect the analysis: the norm of implied abandonment is likely to prevail. Thus, in the vast majority of situations, though a conversion action is technically feasible, it would not be sustainable.

The situation is likely to be different, however, in two cases. First, where the patient, or other person from whom tissue is removed, expressly addresses the question of what will, or should, happen to the tissue after its removal. On the argument advanced earlier, he would have a right to control the future of the removed tissue. In those circumstances, it is for the medical authorities to decide whether to accept the terms upon which it is to receive the tissue. If it acts inconsistently with the donor's wishes, then, *prima facie*, there is an action for conversion.

Secondly, the fact situation may be extreme. Simply to know that patients' tissue may be used for research (even *sold* to laboratories) and that in some rare cases it could have unique and valuable economic potential should not in itself be sufficient to impose an obligation upon a physician to disclose such a matter to the patient. There would have to be some element of deception. *Moore* was argued as a case of blatant deception prior to the removal of the relevant tissue. In such unusual circumstances, it is likely that the failure to disclose known information about commercial potential could be regarded as so important to the patient's decision to undergo the medical procedures as to affect the validity of Moore's consent and so justify an action against the physician for *trespass*. In any event, it is likely that an English court would be prepared to employ equitable principles in support of the patient: Moore surely must come somewhere within the equitable principles relating to 'fraud, duress or undue influence' to receive the support of equity. Moore would have the right to avoid the transaction and be free to pursue a conversion action, in addition to any other cause of action that may be available.

What, then, are the policy arguments for and against a property analysis? The *Moore* case illustrates the clash between individual rights and the needs of the community to foster medical research and, it is claimed, commercialisation of its products by researchers. For some, cases such as *Moore* raise the spectre of commercialisation of the body if patients such as *Moore* did gain financially and this is somehow wrong as violating human dignity. It is worth noting that art 21 of the European Convention on Human Rights and Biomedicine (1996) provides that: 'The human body and its parts shall not, as such give rise to financial gain.' European policy is, therefore, clear. The important words are, perhaps, '*as such*'. Thus, researchers are not precluded from gain, nor are those who use human tissue to develop tests or cultures, nor are donors precluded from recovering expenses. It is, in other words, only the direct buying and selling of tissue which is prohibited out of a respect for human dignity (see *Explanatory Report*, January 1997, paras 131–134).

The policy arguments are addressed in the US context in the following article.

B Hoffmaster 'Between the Sacred and the Profane: Bodies, Property, and Patents in the Moore Case' (1992) 7 Intellectual Property Journal 116

5. THE ARGUMENTS

(a) Human Dignity and Commercialization of the Body

Allowing Moore to benefit financially from the use of his body materials is regarded by some as violating human dignity. But how and why this might be is not easy to understand. Moore would be profiting from the use of his own body, not anybody else's body, so no comparison with slavery is apt. Moreover, people are routinely permitted to sell regenerative parts of their bodies, notably blood plasma and sperm, without moral qualm...

In addition, explicit legal restrictions on the sale of body materials are quite narrowly drawn. As Mosk J emphasized in his dissenting opinion in the Supreme Court in *Moore*, the *Uniform Anatomical Gift Act* ('UAGA') in the US prohibits receiving 'valuable consideration' for the transfer of body parts for other purposes of transplantation or therapy. Another section of the Act authorizes the transfer and receipt of body parts for other purposes such as 'medical or dental education, research, or advancement of medical or dental science,' and no section of the UAGA prohibits the selling of body parts for these additional purposes. In the context of medical therapy, lifesaving therapy in particular, the commercialization of body parts is, with good reason, morally objectionable, and this moral condemnation has acquired the force of law. But in other contexts (eg, research and education, for instance) and for other materials (eg, organs, tissues, and cells other than hearts, kidneys, livers, and bone marrow), our practices instantiate different moral attitudes toward the commercialization of the body.

Perhaps, then, it is not commercialization of the body per se that infringes dignity, but commercialization of parts, components, or aspects of the body that are constitutive or reflective of our uniqueness as human beings. Mosk J suggested this interpretation when he observed that 'our society acknowledges a profound ethical imperative to respect the human body as the physical and temporal expression of the unique human persona' (see *Moore* at 182). This view explains the dignified treatment of corpses, for example. Our empty mortal shells are powerful symbols of the unique and irreplaceable individuals who once inhabited them and accordingly deserve respect. But after death the entire body is not linked with uniqueness. Parts may be removed post mortem for the purposes of autopsy or transplantation, for instance. What parts, components, or aspects of the body are essentially and irrevocably connected with the uniqueness of persons remains unclear. Descartes thought the soul resided in the pineal gland, which has no known function and is now believed to be a vestigial sensory organ. But suppose Descartes were right. Would that mean that only the pineal gland could not be commercialized because it is the only part of our body inextricably tied to our uniqueness? In the absence of a theory of personal identity that implicates bodies, or parts thereof, in human distinctiveness, this amendment of the dignity objection is unpersuasive.

There is, however, an alternative understanding of human dignity that would permit commercialization of the body – a Kantian-inspired account, according to which what is distinctive of human beings is non-corporeal rationality. The body is not intrinsic to human dignity; instead, it is to be used in the service of the rational will, the exercise of which manifests autonomy. The following position typifies this view:

> The wisdom of the decision to sell an organ of one's body is irrelevant. It is critical...that individuals be given maximum latitude in determining their own personal destinies.

The right to freely decide is more important than the wisdom of the choice actually made.
('The Sale of Human Organs: Implicating a Privacy Right' (1987) 21 Val U L Rev 741 at 761.)

To the extent, then, that commercialization of the body would enhance or expand this species of rational autonomy, it would likewise promote dignity.

The difficulty with this position is its extremeness, for it is not clear how granting individuals 'maximum latitude in determining their own personal destinies' stops short of licence. This view is not consistent with all the moral and legal restrictions that currently exist on what people can do to, for, and with their bodies. It provides no guidance as to how or where limits are to be set, but establishing those limits is precisely the task at hand.

(b) Policy Arguments

As we have seen, the majority justices in the Supreme Court felt they were not only entitled but also bound to consider the 'policy' considerations raised by Moore's claim. Many of the policy arguments they adduce mirror objections to permitting the buying and selling of tissues and organs for transplantation. There is the worry that commercialization would impede research because it would decrease the supply of available body materials. Individuals would hold back while haggling for the highest price or negotiating the best possible deal, and the prospect of pecuniary gain would decrease the number of donations of body materials. But, as with transplantation, the genuineness of this fear is almost impossible to assess. An Office of Technology Assessment ('OTA') analysis of 'Ownership of Human Tissues and Cells' observes, for example, that '[t]he precise effect that introducing a market system would have on supply of human biologicals remains a matter of speculation.' Curiously, though, when commercialization works to the advantage of scientists, its negative impact on research is less emphasized. The possibility of obtaining patents has already begun to cast a shroud of secrecy around science and has decreased the extent to which research materials and results are freely shared among scientists. Nevertheless, allowing researchers to profit is regarded as a stimulant to science, whereas compensating sources for their materials is regarded as a depressant.

Another worry is that compensating sources would substantially increase the cost of conducting research. Simply having to pay for materials that are now free would be a significant burden. Then there are the transaction costs associated with negotiating with sources and keeping elaborate records of who contributed what. In fact, the OTA analysis holds that '[t]he transaction costs associated with paying sources…are likely to dwarf the costs of actual payments to the sources.' In reply, though, it has been noted that the very nature of this research already requires detailed record-keeping that would permit the tracing of materials to their origins. Supplementing these supply and transaction costs are potential litigation and insurance costs, as well as the cut that brokers might take should a market develop. When the funding for research is limited, and perhaps will even diminish in the future, increasing the costs reduces the amount of research that can be done. Moreover, increases in research costs would eventually be passed on and increase the cost of health care itself. Given an increasingly tight, constrained health care budget, that would mean either that fewer people would receive the care they need or that savings would have to be induced in other sectors of society.

There are also concerns about deleterious consequences at the individual level. Being able to receive money for one's bodily substances might encourage people to assess risks differently and to take risks they would not otherwise take. Moreover, the quality of the materials provided might diminish. Hepatitis and acquired immune deficiency syndrome have already been transmitted by blood products, and Creutzfeldt-Jakob disease has been transmitted by pituitary hormone preparations. But again, as the OTA Report makes clear, one can go either way with respect to issues of safety and quality:

Viewed from one perspective, commercial pressures could aggravate quality problems, while altruistic systems could help ensure good quality. On the other hand, quality may be problematic precisely because there is insufficient commercialization and because of the protection from liability that voluntarism might afford to those people responsible for procuring and dispensing human tissues and cells.

Because our knowledge is so limited and because the future is so refractory, these consequentialist concerns are intrinsically difficult to assess. The problem is compounded because the salience and the soundness of these various fears depend upon the particular configuration of a system for compensating sources. Would it be a market or a nonmarket system? Would private, nonprofit institutions be involved? What about government organizations? If the system were to contain a combination of these, and perhaps other, possibilities, what exactly would the mix be? Would compensation be prospective or retrospective? Without answers to questions such as these, policy arguments flounder. Yet the more the configuration of a compensation system is specified, the more inadequate our resources for predicting how it might operate seem. Thus, policy arguments are a slender, tenuous reed upon which to rest a resolution of this problem…

6.   THE SOCIAL CONTEXT

Allusions to the 'social context' of a problem are frequently vague and unsatisfying. Nevertheless, appreciating the contexts in which moral and legal problems arise is vital to an intelligent understanding and resolution of them. In a case such as *Moore*, pertinent contextual considerations arise at both a specific, practical level and a general, background level. The force of the former is pragmatic. Physician-researchers unquestionably should reveal their interest in working on a patient's body materials. As the majority opinion in the Supreme Court makes clear, a patient's right to self-determination would be compromised if this conflict of interest were not disclosed. That is one potential harm that disclosure avoids. But there is another potential harm that is not recognized by the Supreme Court: the possibility that standard medical or surgical procedures might be altered in order either to facilitate the taking of body tissues for research or to increase the amount of tissue collected. This kind of alteration reportedly occurs now with the procurement of human fetal tissue for research:

> Abortion and procurement procedures are sometimes altered to increase the chances of obtaining certain types of fetal tissue. It is unknown whether such modifications increase the risks of harm, discomfort, or inconvenience to women, or increase the chance that tissue is removed from living fetuses. It is also unknown whether women are informed of the modifications that will be made if they consent to donate fetal tissue. (D Vawter et al 'The Use of Fetal Tissue' (1990).)

If procedures were to be altered for the sake of obtaining research materials, the nature of the changes, the reasons for them, and the attendant risks would have to be discussed with the patient, and the patient would have to consent to the altered procedure. The need to avoid violating autonomy and the need to avoid unilaterally imposing additional risks of harm, discomfort, or inconvenience mandate that physician-researchers disclose their interest in conducting potentially lucrative research on a patient's bodily substances.

Suppose a doctor asks for permission to use a patient's excised tissue in research. In order to make a decision, the patient must be informed of the likely benefits of such research, and if one of those likely benefits is that the doctor will profit from the marketing of products derived from the research, the patient must be so apprised. But then what? What is the patient supposed to do? The patient could be asked to waive any rights that he or she might have to the resulting profits. That is what Moore was eventually asked to do. But the legitimacy of any such waiver is highly questionable. The patient is in a vulnerable position, often debilitated and with the overriding desires to put an end to pain and suffering and to regain as much health and restore as much normal functioning as possible. Now the patient is being asked to do something, not related to getting better, by a doctor from whom he or she simply wants the best possible care. When health or life is at stake, would any reasonable patient do anything that might jeopardize the attention, skill or effort of his or her doctor? Moreover, the bargaining position of the doctor is vastly superior. The doctor possesses greater knowledge and power and, most likely, greater wealth. In addition, the nature of the illness might not give the patient time to marshal resources or engage in extended negotiations. If bargaining is to occur, the situation is heavily loaded in favour of the doctor.

Two lessons emerge from these pragmatic considerations. One is that the issue of remuneration cannot be neatly severed from the issue of consent. Once patients are aware that their body substances have potential market value, they will want to know how much of whatever profit is likely to materialize they are entitled to receive. Their pecuniary interest will follow, not as ineluctably as night follows day, but just as naturally. The second point is that any attempt to determine the patient's entitlement by negotiations between a powerful doctor and a weak and possibly impaired patient who is in distressing circumstances is unfair. A different kind of resolution is needed.

The more general side to the social context consists of the legal and economic, and ultimately cultural, milieu that comprises the background to this issue. That background has changed in an important way because the US Congress has created an explicit incentive for the commercialization of the body. The nature of the change can be appreciated in light of Congress's earlier handling of the acquisition of human growth hormone ('hGH') from pituitary glands (T Murray, 'Who Owns the Body? On the Ethics of Using Human Tissue for Commercial Purposes' (1986) 8 IRB 1, at 2). Before genetically engineered growth hormone became available, hGH, needed for the treatment of children who do not themselves produce enough growth hormone, had to be extracted from the pituitary glands of cadavers. In order to put an end to what has been called the 'mad scramble to obtain pituitaries from human cadavers,' Congress created the National Hormone and Pituitary Program ('NHPP') within the National Institutes of Health (*ibid*). Until the sum was doubled in 1984, hospitals received £2 for each pituitary they provided:

> This amount was not intended as a bounty, and was merely an aid in covering the costs of removing, storing, and shipping. The NHPP in turn charged only a small handling fee for the scarce hGH. This means of obtaining pituitaries operated apart from profits and property. (*Ibid*.)

A similar policy for non-commercialization is imposed on organs and tissues to be used for transplantation by the UAGA. In the realm of research, however, the situation is now different.

Things have changed because Congress felt that the results of government-funded research were not adequately reaching the public. Prior to 1980 it was common to require that rights in inventions made in the course of government-sponsored research be assigned to the government because it was believed that 'private ownership of inventions made through public funding was contrary to the public interest.' (R Eisenbury 'Proprietary Rights and the Norms of Science in Biotechnology Research' (1987) 97 Yale LJ 177 at 182). But Congress's conception of the public interest has shifted. The *Patent and Trademark Laws Amendment Act* of 1980 now 'encourages universities to patent and license inventions made in the course of government-sponsored research.' (*Ibid* at 196.) This new policy, designed to foster dissemination through commercialization, applies to patents obtained for the products of biotechnology research. Researchers like Golde and universities like UCLA have been explicitly spurred by the federal government to patent the outcomes of their research.

This legal and economic development transforms the context in which biotechnology research occurs. The nature of the change can be illustrated by a story Murray relates about a boy who had a rare, valuable blood type associated with one of the clotting factors (T Murray *op cit* at 2–3). The boy regularly donated blood to be used for research in a medical centre, but when a pharmaceutical firm discovered that it could use his blood, he sold it to the company at a 'stiff price'. Murray's reaction to this story is absolutely right:

> The boy and his family probably felt that while it was fine to give without remuneration to a non-commercial enterprise, in the hope that some human good might come out of the research his blood made possible, he would have been a fool to give it free to a company that might profit from it. This story says something about our willingness to give gifts, even ones that involve pain, *under the right circumstances*. At the same time, it tells us that arrangements that smack of commercialism change the nature of the transaction to something quite different from a gift. (*Ibid* at 3. Emphasis added.)

As a result of the US *Patent and Trademark Laws Amendment Act*, biotechnology research not only 'smacks' of commercialism, it reeks of it. Congress has converted what once was a system predicated upon altruism into one predicated upon commercialism. The form Moore signed to consent to his splenectomy has not been made available, but it would be surprising if it did not contain the usual 'boilerplate' terms by which Moore agreed to allow his excised tissue to be used for scientific and educational purposes. Under the old, altruistic system that would be unobjectionable. Like the boy with the rare blood, Moore would be a fool to give his tissue freely to those who might profit from it. As Murray realizes, this fundamental change will not go unnoticed by the public: 'If biotechnologists fail to make provision for a just sharing of the profits with the person whose gift made it possible, the public's sense of justice is likely to be offended, and no one will be the winner.' (*Ibid* at 5.) And the deeper threat here, as Murray also points out, is that public confidence in science and the willingness to support science by, among other things, providing tissues and organs will be undermined (*ibid*).

This Congressional inducement to commercialization will gradually but irrevocably erode the moral dignity – the sacredness – that has been attached to the human body. Morality does not exist solely in the abstract – in the general norms of a philosophical system. Rather, morality is embedded in the practices of ordinary life. It is part and parcel of our personal, family, and social relationships, our legal relationships – in short, all our manifold, interlocking social exchanges. Morality affects these relationships but is, in turn, affected by them. Morality changes and progresses in reaction to the pressures created by social, cultural, economic and scientific developments. An historical example is the shift in the moral appraisal of usury:

> The early Church condemned lending at interest as a form of avarice. If one's neighbor were in need, it was wrong to demand interest before supplying his wants. The growth of commerce, however, introduced complications; the borrower was no longer 'in need', but sought capital for use in profit-making. Gradually, the ecclesiastical prohibition was qualified. Where the borrower wanted money to make more money, it seemed reasonable that the lender should share in his gains. (S Benn and R Peters, 'Social Principles and the Democratic State' (1959) at 166.)

Unless checked, a comparable transformation, instigated by the commercial pressures now unleashed by Congress, will occur with respect to the moral status of the body. Gradually it will come to seem reasonable that the prohibition on commercialization of the body be dissolved. And just as it came to seem reasonable that lenders should share in gains, so it will seem reasonable that those who provide body materials for profit-making should also share in gains. Human bodies will become profaned or debased because the commercial value they will have acquired will supplant their dignity. Kant puts this contrast nicely: 'Whatever has a value can be replaced by something else which is *equivalent*; whatever, on the other hand, is above all value, and therefore admits of no equivalent, has a dignity.' (I Kant 'Fundamental Principles of the Metaphysic of Morals' (1949) 51. Emphasis added.) When human bodies, or parts thereof, possess an equivalent in money, they lose much, if not all, of the distinctiveness that is the basis of veneration and respect. They move from the realm of the sacred to the realm of the profane.

This is not to suggest that commercialization of the body is either desirable or inevitable. The ideal situation would be to insulate the exchange of body substances as much as possible from commercialization. In Broussard J's view, for instance,

> [I]t would be wiser to prohibit any private individual or entity from profiting from the fortuitous value that adheres in a part of a human body, and instead to require all valuable excised body parts to be deposited in a public repository which would make such materials freely available to all scientists for the betterment of society as a whole. The Legislature, if it wished, could create such a system as it has done with respect to organs that are donated for transplantation. (See *Moore* at 172.)

But Congress has set society on the opposite path. Assuming that this change is irrevocable, what is to be done?

The most feasible course, practically and morally, is to recognize this reality and shape it in a way that promotes justice and mitigates potentially deleterious outcomes. That could be accomplished through the legislation of an international licensing scheme with a fixed rate of profit-sharing. Such an approach has numerous advantages. The scheme could determine an appropriate rate of compensation that would be constant across individual cases and jurisdictions. The bargaining power between doctor and patient would be equalized, and the vagaries of situations would be eliminated. Consistency would do much of the work in achieving both genuine fairness and the appearance of fairness. To the objection that any fixed rate of profit-sharing is unfair because insensitive to the demands of particular situations, it can be replied that substantial arbitrariness exists in the judicial determination of damages. Most importantly, direct commercialization of the body is mitigated:

> [A] profit-sharing plan relieves the perception that patients are 'selling' their body parts. The free market system sets a price on the body part itself, whereas the license arrangement focuses on the profits made from the product. (M Danforth, 'Cells, Sales and Royalties: The Patient's Right to a Portion of the Profits' (1988) 6 Yale L and Pol'y Rev 179, at 200.)

Professor Hoffmaster's conclusion (*op cit* at 146-147, however, is that a legislative and not judicial resolution of the problem is more appropriate:

> …because the circumstances in this case are idiosyncratic, it should not be used as a vehicle for policymaking. It is only rarely that someone's tissue or cells will have enormous prospective commercial value, that that potential value can be recognized in advance, and that research in fact develops products that realize that value. The legal saw that 'hard cases make bad law' might be trite, but it is apt here. For these reasons, then, a legislative, rather than a judicial, resolution of the problem should be sought.
>
> In a legislative forum the issue can be defined more broadly. Instead of asking whether bodies are property or whether people own their bodies, the question can be posed more generally: should people be entitled to share in profits that result from the commercialization of products developed from body materials they have relinquished? In addressing this question, one could pay attention to characteristics of more typical situations: the use of body materials that are available from an array of sources, the incorporation of body materials from many different sources into a single line of research, the way research builds incrementally on the results of previous research, and the low probability that any line of research will generate lucrative products. Policy should be developed on the basis of and for common, standard situations, not rare, exotic situations. Moreover, in a legislative arena the social context that frames the problem can be appreciated, and considerations of fairness between individual parties and of social justice can operate outside the constraints of doctrinal law.

(For further discussions of the policy and philosophical arguments, see, eg, L Andrews 'My Body My Property' (1986) 16(5) Hastings Center Report 16; ER Gold *Body Parts: Property Rights and the Ownership of Human Biological Materials* (1996); J Harris 'Who Owns My Body?' (1996) OJLS 55; M D A Freeman 'Taking the Body Seriously?' in K Stern and P Walsh (eds) *Property Rights in the Human Body* (1997) p 13.)

There is, at best, only weak authority that English law currently accepts what might be called the property approach (*Welsh, Rothery* and *Kelly, supra*). Before reaching an authoritative view a court will need, as did the Supreme Court of California in *Moore*, to take account of the policy implications of adopting the property approach. This takes us on to the next two issues. The obvious complexity of the circumstances in which the legal status of excised body material arises may persuade a court that the matter is really one for Parliament. You will recall that this was the approach endorsed by the majority in *Moore*. Although an English court may find it hard to resist this temptation, it would be unfortunate if, in this fast-moving area of medical science, the law remained in a state of uncertainty until such a time as Parliament took a view.

If courts decided to grasp the nettle, should the property approach be adopted? You will recall that the judges in *Moore* looked for guidance from existing legislation as to how the law as expressed by the legislature viewed human tissue. If the same search were undertaken by an English Court, is there any English legislation or other sources of public policy to serve as a guide? There are four legislative sources to note: the Human Tissue Act 1961; s 25 of the National Health Service Act 1977; the Human Organ Transplants Act 1989 and the Human Fertilisation and Embryology Act 1990.

None of these Acts deals explicitly with the property approach. Our concern is whether there is any underlying assumption as to the legal status of human tissue in these Acts. The Human Tissue Act 1961 only deals with disposition of human tissue on death. Even in that context, the Act creates a special statutory scheme for post-mortem donation which is not based upon notions of property. The 1961 Act, therefore, takes us no further. By contrast, s 25 of the NHS Act and the Human Organ Transplants Act 1989 appear to be based upon an implicit adoption of the property approach. Section 25 of the 1977 Act provides that:

25. Where the Secretary of State has acquired –
(*a*) supplies of human blood for the purpose of any service under this Act, or
(*b*) any part of a human body for the purpose of or in the course of providing, any such service, or
(*c*) supplies of any other substances or preparations not readily obtainable,
he may arrange to make such supplies or that part available (on such terms, including terms as to charges, as he thinks fit) to any person…

We have already analysed the provisions of the 1989 Act (*supra*) which prohibit commercial dealings in human organs for transplantation (s 1). Both of these statutory provisions assume that human tissue is amenable to transfer and disposal in that the tissue is treated as if it were a *res* albeit *extra commercium*. By far the strongest support for the property approach can be found in HUFEA. As we have seen (*supra*, ch 10), the control and disposal of human gametes and embryos rest with the donor(s) (see, principally, Sch 3). Placing control in the hands of the donor(s) reflects a reliance upon the property approach without explicitly stating it.

The combination of these statutory provisions strongly suggests a growing legislative acceptance of the property approach which a court may treat as a guide. The judgment of Rose LJ in *R v Kelly* [1998] 3 All ER 741 (CA) especially at 750 supports this conclusion.

4. Working through the property approach

Accepting the property approach, the next issue must be in whom are the proprietary rights over the excised tissue vested? In other words, whose property is the tissue? Is it the source? You will recall that this was Professor Dickens' view. On this analysis others (such as the 'remover' or 'improver') could only acquire property rights if they were transferred by gift, by sale or possibly by abandonment. An alternative analysis would see the property rights vested in the remover either at the time of removal or on acquiring possession of the part which would otherwise be *res nullius*. The three approaches are discussed in the 1995 Report of the Nuffield Council on Bioethics:

Nuffield Council on Bioethics *Human Tissue: Ethical and Legal Issues* (1995)

9.4   At common law, the issue has not been tested in English law. It is instructive to enquire why the question of a claim over tissue once removed has not received legal attention. The answer seems simple. In the general run of things a person from whom tissue is removed has not the slightest interest in making any claim to it once it is removed. This is obviously the case as regards tissue removed as a consequence of treatment. It is equally true in the case of the donation of tissue whether, for example, blood, bone marrow or an organ. The word donation clearly indicates that what is involved is a gift.

9.5   It is certainly true, of course, that an appendix or gallstone may be returned to a patient who may refer to it as **her** appendix or gallstone. But this says nothing about any legal claim she may have to the appendix. In fact, in the case of the returned appendix, one view of the legal position may be as follows: the patient consents to the operation which involves the removal of her appendix; by her consent to the operation she **abandons** any claim to the appendix; on removal the appendix acquires the status of a *res* (a thing) and comes into the possession of the hospital authority prior to disposal; in response to a request by the patient that it be returned, the hospital gives the appendix to the patient as a gift; the appendix then becomes the property of the patient.

9.6   While what has been said about the lack of interest of the patient in the fate of tissue removed from him may be true, some have enquired whether a claim to tissue which has been removed can be advanced in certain circumstances. One such circumstance is the use of fetal tissue subsequent to an abortion. Does a mother, it may be asked, have any claim to the tissue? The report of the Polkinghorne Committee did not claim to resolve the question (Polkinghorne J et al (1989) *Review of the Guidance on the Research Use of Fetuses and Fetal Material*, London's HMSO). Instead, it provided for a scheme whereby the woman has to give explicit and unconditional consent to the use of the fetal tissue before it may be used. The same scheme of consents, circumventing the need to resolve questions of property and ownership, was employed in the Human Fertilisation and Embryology Act.

9.7   But there are other circumstances in which the question posed in paragraph 9.6 may arise. In some circumstances, it could be argued, and has been by a number of commentators (eg B Dickens, 'Living Tissue and Organ Donors and Property Law', (1992) 8 Journal of Contemporary Health Law and Policy, p 73), that tissue once removed becomes the property of the person from whom it is removed. This is to say that consent to removal does not **entail** an intention to abandon. The tissue may well, in fact, be abandoned or donated, but these imply a prior coming into existence of a *res* and the exercise of rights over it. Indeed, such an analysis is logically essential, it is argued, even if the resulting property (ie a person's assertion of a property right over the new *res*), exists merely for a moment (a *scintilla temporis*). On this view the person from whom tissue is removed must have a property right in the tissue which expressly or by implication he could waive on removal so that the property passes to another. The consequence is, of course, that if the property right were not waived, it would be retained. To return to the example in paragraph 9.5, the appendix would have become (and remained) the patient's property had she not by implication waived any right to it.

9.8   The case of *Venner v State of Maryland* (1976) 354 A 2d 483 (Md CA), decided by the Court of Special Appeals in Maryland, USA, may be of assistance. Powers J held that, '*By the force of social custom…when a person **does nothing and says nothing to indicate an intent to assert his right of ownership, possession, or control over** [bodily] **material**, the only rational inference is that he intends to abandon the material*' (our emphasis). The implication of this approach is clear.

1   The legal presumption is in favour of abandonment.

2   Abandonment may be prospective.

3   Where, however, the circumstances are such that abandonment may not be presumed, it must follow that if no consent were given, or a consent expressed to be 'on terms', were given, property rights over the tissue **would not necessarily** pass but would be retained by the person from whom the tissue was removed…

9.11 So far, we have noticed the following as possible legal approaches to any claims made by the person from whom tissue is removed: either

1   consent to removal entails abandonment; or

2   on removal, property rights vest in the person from whom it is removed. It is presumed that these are abandoned, but they can be retained.

A further legal approach is to argue that tissue once removed becomes property, but at the time of its removal it is *res nullius*, ie that it belongs to no-one until it is brought under dominion (the traditional legal example is the wild animal or plant). This would reflect the traditional view of '*no property in the body*'. It would also mean that a person could not prospectively donate 'his' tissue, once removed from his body. All he could do would be to consent to the removal. If this analysis were adopted, the tissue would be the property of the person who removed it or subsequently came into possession of it. The person from whom it was removed would not, however, have any property claim to it.

9.12 The current state of English law makes it unclear (at best) which of these approaches (or another) represents the law. Interest in the validity of property claims over removed tissue has, however, been rekindled because of an awareness of circumstances in which tissue has been removed and then developed in some way so as to serve as the basis for a commercial product. The *locus classicus* is the well known *Moore* case which has already been referred to (paragraphs 2.15 – 2.16 and Appendix 1). In *Moore*, the Supreme Court of California, trying a preliminary point of law, decided that Moore had no property rights in the tissue taken from his body. Although not expressed in such a way, if we impose the language that we have employed, the court appears to have found that Moore's consent to the operation entailed an abandonment of any claims over the removed tissue. Thus, he could not assert a claim in property as the basis either for objecting to the removal of his tissue or for having a share in whatever profit was gained through its use. The issue of the validity of the consent he gave to the operation and subsequent procedures then became the focus of the case…

9.14 Of the various approaches referred to, therefore, it may be that a preferable approach for the English courts would be the following:

1   It will be entailed in any consent to **treatment** that tissue removed **in the course of that treatment** will be regarded in law as having been abandoned by the person from whom it was removed;

2   tissue removed **in circumstances other than treatment**, which is **voluntarily donated,** will be regarded as a gift. Use for purposes other than those for which consent was given could give rise to a claim on the part of the person from whom the tissue was removed. Such a claim will depend on the terms of the original consent;

3   where tissue is removed voluntarily but is intended to be kept **for the donor**, for example autologous blood donations, the donor will be able to claim the tissue by virtue of the agreement under which it is kept. (The donation of gametes and embryos is subject to a specific statutory framework of consents regulating *inter alia* the giving and withdrawing of consent to use);

4   where tissue is removed without **explicit** knowledge and consent, any claim the person from whom it was removed may have as regards the subsequent use of that tissue will turn on the validity of any general consent which may have been given, ie as to whether removal and subsequent use of the tissue could legitimately be said to be implied.

The approach of the Nuffield Council has been subject to challenge.

Paul Matthews 'The Man of Property' (1995) 3 Med L Rev 251

The Report…takes the property approach further, by proposing a very sophisticated analysis of how a patient (P), whose appendix is removed, may come to own it:

(1) P consents to removal;
(2) that consent involves the abandonment of rights in the appendix;
(3) on removal, the appendix acquires the status of a thing;
(4) the hospital authority has (lawful) possession of it, and hence has possessory rights in relation to it;
(5) P requests that the appendix be given to P;
(6) the hospital authority transfers its possessory rights and its physical possession to P. (Para 9.5).

It will be seen that this analysis depends on two things. First, a considerable legal gloss is put on very few primary facts (and in particular P's consent to the operation). Second, the analysis relies on the doctrine of abandonment. (We shall have to return to abandonment in more detail later.)

The Report (para 9.8) then goes on to set out an alternative analysis of these facts. This is, while consent to removal does not necessarily involve abandonment, it is to be *presumed in* cases where P does nothing to assert any rights over the removed tissue, ie, silence equals abandonment. If there is no abandonment, the tissue remains the 'property' of the person from whom it was removed. Of course, this is merely a yet more complex version of the original analysis. The abandonment at stage (2) is now contingent rather than certain. If it does not in fact occur, possessory rights are retained by P at stage (4), and stages (5) and (6) are unnecessary.

A so-called further approach put forward by the Report (para 9.11) is in fact yet another variation. This is that the tissue belongs to no one (is *res nullius*) when removed, and belongs to the first person to obtain possession. Hence, the prospective abandonment at stage (2) is ineffective, and what follows is essentially the first analysis again, ie, that the tissue 'belongs' to the hospital authority. Two comments may be made about this. First, there is no English authority for treating human tissue as '*res nullius*', as if it were some sort of wild animal or plant. (See dictum of Griffith C J in *Doodeward v Spence* (1908) 6 CLR 406 at 414). Second, the Report assumes (in my view wrongly), that when the doctor removes the tissue he does so independently of P, and hence he or his employer, the hospital authority, is entitled in his or its own right. I will come back to this point.

The Report discusses the merits of these various approaches, and concludes that the preferable approach is, in fact, *none* of them. Instead, the following even more sophisticated analysis is put forward: (para 9.14)

(1)   tissue removed during treatment to which the patient (P) consents is abandoned;
(2)   tissue removed otherwise than during treatment is a gift, *if* 'voluntarily donated';
(3)   tissue removed and intended to be used for the benefit of the donor will, as a result, belong to the donor;
(4)   claims to tissue removed without explicit knowledge and consent (ie, not within (1) to (3) above) must depend on how far P can be said to have impliedly consented to removal and subsequent use;
(5)   where a person cannot lawfully consent, and no one can consent on his behalf, the Report would prefer to see legislation, but, since that is unlikely, suggests that the courts rely on the notion of 'public interest'. Thus, it would be legally justified to remove and use tissue from an incompetent adult if the use was a 'justifiable use'.

It will be seen that this approach mixes property and non-property analysis.

Now all of this is very interesting, but there is a fundamental problem. To the extent that it lays down propositions of *law*, it is all dependent on drawing certain inferences of fact and intention, *not* from the circumstances of each individual case, but from one *idealised* case. Thus, for example, in *Venner v State of Maryland* ((1976) 354 A 2d 483), Powers J said that

> By the force of social custom…when a person does nothing and says nothing to indicate an intention to assert his right of ownership, possession or control over [bodily] material, the only rational inference is that he intends to abandon the material.

This may have been a proper inference to draw, in 1976, in Maryland, USA, *on the facts of the particular case*. But to say that, forever thereafter, wherever in the world it might be, whatever the state of the development of medical science, or whatever particular facts, it was 'the only rational inference' from P's silence would be foolish…what P intends or does not intend in consenting to an operation must depend on the precise circumstances. This will include the nature of the operation, the material to be used, the usefulness of such material in the current state of medical science, and so on. It cannot be laid down as a general proposition that (for example) consent to the removal of tissue necessarily entails an intent to abandon it.

And there is another reason for this conclusion. I criticised above the assumption that the doctor is entitled to assert a right to the tissue independent of P. Consider the following:

(1)   P tells his gardener to pick apples from P's trees. Once they have been picked, who owns the apples?
(2)   P engages a demolition contractor to knock down P's house. Once the house has been knocked down, who owns the bricks?
(3)   P has her long hair cut short by the hairdresser. Who owns the cut off tresses?

It is simply not self-evident that P has no claim to the apples, the bricks, and the hair. If P engages someone (whether employee or independent contractor), to perform a service which involves some action in relation to P or P's property, there is no obvious reason why without more the contractor should have a better claim to the severed products than P. If P had picked the apples, demolished the house, or cut her own hair, there would be no question. But the contractor is only P's agent to do, on P's instructions, what P cannot or will not do for him/herself. Of course, there could be an express agreement on the subject. Usually there is not, and so we must see if one can be implied. Surely, if the contractor cannot show such an (implied) agreement, then for this purpose there is not one, and P's rights are the same as if P had done the work in question. After all, *qui facit per alium facit per se*.

Why then should it be different if P engages a doctor (D) (whether privately or through the statutory entitlement of the National Health Service) to remove bodily tissue? D is performing a service for P, not independently foraging for specimens like a truffle hunter in the early morning.

To revert to the example of the removed appendix given in the Report, why is not the true analysis the following:

(1) P asks D to perform a service for him, by removing the appendix;
(2) on removal, the appendix is in P's possession via the agency of D, who is P's agent to remove it;
(3) hence P has the best right to possession of the appendix, *unless* P has agreed, or subsequently agrees, to transfer such rights to another or (possibly) to abandon it (the burden of proving this agreement lying on the person asserting it).

The fact that D is employed by someone else, for example, a health authority or NHS trust, is simply irrelevant.

You will notice the Nuffield Council's reliance upon the doctrine of abandonment in cases such as *Venner v State of Maryland* (1976) 354 A 2d 483 and the Californian Court of Appeal decision in the *Moore* case. The argument goes thus. A donor will lose the right to control where the tissue is used with his express or implied consent. Alternatively, the donor may have expressly abandoned his tissue or be deemed to have impliedly done so. The doctrine of abandonment is well known to the law of personal property. We set out the relevant case law relied upon.

Venner v State of Maryland (1976) 354 A 2d 483 (Ct of Spec App Md)

Powers J: It could not be said that a person has no property right in wastes or other materials which were once a part of or contained within his body, but which normally are discarded after their separation from the body. It is not unknown for a person to assert a continuing right of ownership, dominion, or control, for good reason or for no reason, over such things as excrement, fluid waste, secretions, hair, fingernails, toenails, blood and organs or other parts of the body, whether their separation from the body is intentional, accidental, or merely the result of normal body functions.

But it is all but universal custom and human experience that such things are discarded – in a legal sense, abandoned – by the person from whom they emanate, either 'on the spot', or, if social delicacy requires it, at a place or in a manner designed to cause the least offense to others.

By the force of social custom, we hold that when a person does nothing and says nothing to indicate an intent to assert his right of ownership, possession, or control over such material, the only rational inference is that he intends to abandon the material. When one places, or permits others to place waste material from his body into the stream of ultimate disposition as waste, he has abandoned whatever legal right he therefore had to protect it from prying eyes or acquisitive hands.

While Justice Powers recognises the general case, there are limits to the circumstances in which a court will find that tissue has been abandoned *impliedly*. This was explored in the intermediate appeal court in *Moore* when it adopted the property approach subsequently rejected by the Supreme Court.

Moore v Regents of University of California (1988) 249 Cal Rptr 494 (Cal CA)

Rothman JA: Defendants argue that even if plaintiff's spleen is personal property, its surgical removal was an abandonment by him of a diseased organ. They assert that he cannot, therefore, bring an action for conversion.

The essential element of abandonment is the intent to abandon. The owner of the property abandoned must be 'entirely indifferent as to what may become of it or as to who may thereafter possess it.' (*Martin v Cassidy* (1957) 149 Cal App 2d 106, 307 P 2d 981, quoting 1 Cal Jur 2d, Abandonment, § 2, p 2.)

'It may be said that abandonment is made up of two elements, act and intent, and the intent must be gathered from all the facts and circumstances of the case. [Citations.]' (*Paul v Gulf Red Cedar Co* (1936) 15 Cal App 2d 196, 199, 59 P 2d 183.)

The question whether the plaintiff abandoned his spleen, or any of the other tissues taken by the defendants, is plainly a question of fact as to what his intent was at the time...A consent to removal of a diseased organ, or the taking of blood or other bodily tissues, does not necessarily imply an intent to abandon such organ, blood or tissue. The only fact alleged in the complaint on the subject is that the spleen was surgically removed, and that, had plaintiff known of defendants' intentions regarding the spleen, he would not have consented to its removal at UCLA. While it may be true that many people under such circumstances would be entirely indifferent to the disposition of removed tissue, we cannot assume plaintiff shared this state of mind. Nothing in the complaint indicates that plaintiff had an intent to abandon his spleen, and we do not find that, as a matter of law, anyone who consents to surgery abandons all removed tissue to the first person to claim it. Certainly, in the example of an unconscious patient, the concept of abandonment becomes ridiculous.

In California, absent evidence of a contrary intent or agreement, the reasonable expectation of a patient regarding tissue removed in the course of surgery would be that it may be examined by medical personnel for treatment purposes, and then promptly and permanently disposed of by interment or incineration in compliance with Health and Safety Code section 7054.4. Simply consenting to surgery under such circumstances hardly shows indifference to what may become of a removed organ or who may assert possession of it. Any use to which there was no consent, or which is not within the accepted understanding of the patient, is a conversion. It cannot be seriously asserted that a patient abandons a severed organ to the first person who takes it, nor can it be presumed that the patient is indifferent to whatever use might be made of it.

An inference of abandonment is particularly inappropriate when it comes to the use undertaken by defendants involving recombinant DNA technology. Almost from the beginning, this technology has incited intense moral, religious and ethical concerns. There are many patients whose religious beliefs would be deeply violated by use of their sells in recombinant DNA experiments without their consent, and who on being informed, would hardly be disinterested in the fate of their removed tissue...

Rothman JA's thesis is that rarely (if ever) will a person be impliedly deemed to abandon his property for all purposes. Instead, he will abandon it 'on terms' to be determined in the light of the factual circumstances pertaining at the time (see also *Williams v Phillips* (1957) 121 JP 163).

There is, however, a legal difficulty. The doctrine of abandonment may not be applicable here, or at all in English law.

P Matthews 'The Man of Property' (1995) 3 Med L Rev 251

What is of more concern is that, notwithstanding the Report's reliance on it, the status of the doctrine of abandonment at all in English law is doubtful. The cases are limited and often equivocal. Two propositions cannot however be controverted. The first is that there has never been suggested to be any *general* doctrine of abandonment in English law, but at most only abandonment in individual cases for specific purposes (eg, theft, wreck, salvage, treasure trove). Secondly, in most of these cases, English law has changed its mind at least once as to whether abandonment should or should not be possible.

The most recent general common law authority on the subject is a decision of the Court of Appeal of New South Wales in 1981 (*Moorehouse v Angus and Robertson* [1981] 1 NSWLR 700). Here it was argued that leaving chattels in another's hands for many years without asking for them amounted to an abandonment. The Court declined to decide as a matter of principle whether divesting abandonment was possible at all, but held that, if it was, it required a clear and unequivocal intention to abandon, which had not been proved in this case. So if abandonment is possible, it is unlikely to be implied from general consent to an operation, even one in which tissue is necessarily to be removed.

(See further, A Hudson 'Abandonment' in N Palmer and E McKendrick (eds) *Interest in Goods* (2nd edn, 1998) ch 23.)

One final point on abandonment or consensual transfer (gift). The analysis would be impossible to apply if the donor were an incompetent adult. Only the Court of Protection could effect the gift or otherwise relinquish the interest of the donor in the tissue.

Leaving aside the possibility of gift or abandonment, you will have seen the argument that those who remove the tissue may also acquire property rights over it for the first time. There is no transfer of the source's rights; the tissue can *only* be considered the property of the 'remover' or 'improver'. The point arose directly in a post- *Moore* case in America.

US v Arora (1993) 860 F Supp 1091 (US Dist Ct)

Messitte J:

Introduction

In this civil suit for conversion and trespass, the United States contends that Doctor Prince Kumar Arora intentionally tampered with and destroyed cells in a research project at the National Institute of Health in Bethesda, Maryland. Dr Arora denies tampering and in any case responds that the Government sustained no damages by reason of the cell deaths.

The Court, sitting without a jury, received testimony and exhibits over several days and has considered the parties' post-trial briefs. On the basis of the evidence and pleadings, the Court concludes that Dr Arora did tamper with, destroy, and convert Alpha 1–4 cells; that he is liable for the cost of the flasks and materials associated with the creation of the cells as well as the reasonable value of the time it took a laboratory assistant to re-create the cells; and that, while not liable in compensatory damages for the delay he caused in the completion of the research project, he must respond in punitive damages, as to which the effect his actions had on the research project is a relevant consideration.

The Court will award the United States $450.20 in compensatory damages and $5,000.00 in punitive damages…

Questions Presented
The Court is faced with four fundamental questions in this case:
1) Did Dr Arora in fact tamper with the Alpha 1–4 cells?
2) If so, did the tampering constitute either the tort of conversion or trespass?
3) If either such tort was committed, what compensatory damages, if any, should be assessed?
4) If either tort was committed, what punitive damages, if any, are appropriate?…

[having concluded that Dr Arora did tamper with the cells the judge continued]

Was there a conversion or trespass?
A) It is not necessary to recount here the historical development of the torts of trespass and conversion, a matter more than adequately explored in Prosser and Keeton on *The Law of Torts*, 14–15 (5th ed 1984). For present purposes, it suffices to observe that the difference between the two torts is fundamentally one of degree, trespass constituting a lesser interference with another's chattel, conversion a more serious exercise of dominion or control over it. See Restatement (Second) of Torts 222A, Comment (1965).

Thus a trespass has been defined as an intentional use or intermeddling with the chattel in possession of another, Restatement (Second) of Torts 217(b), such intermeddling occurring, inter alia, when 'the chattel is impaired as to its condition, quality, or value.' *Restatement (Second) of Torts, § 218(b)*. See also *Walser v Resthaven Memorial Gardens, Inc*, 98 Md App 371, 395, 633 A 2d 466 (1993).

A 'conversion', on the other hand, has been defined as:

[A]n intentional exercise of dominion or control over a chattel which so seriously interferes with the right of another to control it that the actor may justly be required to pay the other the full value of the chattel.

Restatement (Second) of Torts, § 222A(1). See also *Staub v Staub*, 37 Md App 141, 376 A 2d 1129 (1977). Whereas impairing the condition, quality or value of a chattel upon brief interference can constitute a trespass, intentional destruction or material alteration of a chattel will subject the actor to liability for conversion. *Restatement (Second) of Torts*, § 266. See also *Kalb v Vega*, 56 Md App 656, 468 A 2d 676 (1983).

A number of factors are considered in determining whether interference with a chattel is serious enough to constitute a conversion as opposed to a trespass. These include:
a)   the extent and duration of the actor's exercise of dominion or control;
b)   the actor's intent to assert a right in fact inconsistent with the other's right of control;
c)   the actor's good faith'
d)   the extent and duration or the resulting interference with the other's right of control;
e)   the harm done to the chattel;
f)   the inconvenience and expense cause to the other.
Staub, 37 Md App at 143-144, 376 A 2d 1129, quoting Restatement (Second) of Torts, § 222A(2).

Assuming for the moment that a cell line is a chattel capable of being converted or trespassed upon, it is clear that the United States owned the Alpha 1-4 cell line and that Dr Arora's dominion or control [over] it, while brief, was total. He intended to act inconsistently with Dr Sei's right to control the cells, he did not act in good faith, and the committed the ultimate harm – he destroyed the cells. While certain easily identifiable expense was caused by Dr Arora's inappropriate acts, it is also apparent that he caused serious inconvenience to what was a critically important research project. By this analysis, if any tort was committed, it was unquestionably a conversion, not a mere trespass.

But did he convert the cell line?
In what appear to be the only cases in which plaintiffs have sought recovery for conversion of cell lines, courts have in fact held the cause of action does not lie. These cases, however, are easily distinguishable from the present case, if not subject to challenge on their own

terms. Thus, in *Moore v The Regents of the Univ. of California, et al*, 51 Cal 3d 120, 793, P 2d 479, 271 Cal Rptr 146 (1990), plaintiff Moore, while a patient at defendant hospital, had had certain blood products removed by defendant physician, which confirmed a diagnosis of hairy-cell leukemia. Defendants allegedly were aware that these blood products were of great value in a number of commercial and scientific efforts and that access to a patient whose blood contained the substances would provide significant competitive commercial and scientific advantages. Without telling plaintiff this, defendant physician removed the cells from plaintiff's body and eventually developed them for commercial purposes. Moore's suit was based in part on an alleged conversion of his body materials. In holding that Moore could not recover on a theory of conversion, the court found that Moore no longer had a property interest in the bodily materials. At least two dissenters took sharp issue with that proposition, for reasons which need not be pursued here. What is important for present purposes, however, is the distinction made by Justice Broussard in the dissenting portion of his opinion:

> If, for example, another medical center or drug company had stolen all of the cells in question from the UCLA Medical Center laboratory and had used them for its own benefit, there would be no question but that a cause of action for conversion would properly lie against the thief, and the majority opinion does not suggest otherwise. 51 Cal 3d at 153, 271 Cal Rptr 146, 793 P 2d 479.

In the context of the present case, while there is no allegation that Dr Arora stole a cell line belonging to NIH, there is the equivalent allegation that he substantially interfered with and destroyed or altered its nature.

In *Miles Inc v Scripps Clinic and Research Foundation*, 810 F Supp 1091 (SD Cal 1993) conversion of a cell line was also involved, more particularly the right to commercialize the cell line, ie to make a profit based upon it. Plaintiff pharmaceutical company alleged that a research foundation with whom it was a joint venturer had deprived it of the right to participate in the benefits of a cell line that had been developed in the joint venture. Plaintiff contended that defendant had conspired with certain employees to transfer the right to commercialize the cell line to defendant. The *Miles* court was careful to point out that the conversion claim involved was not as to the cell line itself, but rather to the right to commercialize the cell line. The court in fact found plaintiff did have a property interest in the right to commercialization of the cell line, but concluded that, by virtue of the *Moore* case, California had not recognized a cause of action for conversion of that intangible right. The court noted that plaintiff was essentially asserting a breach of contract claim …

Assuming that *Moore* was correctly decided and that *Miles* is a correct interpretation of *Moore*, it still remains true that neither contract nor patent law would cover the wrongdoing in the present case. Those areas of the law extend to cases of unauthorized use of the cells, not their intentional destruction.

The fact is that the United States Supreme Court has recognized that a living cell line is a property interest capable of protection. See *Diamond v Chakrabarty*, 447 US 303, 65 L Ed 2d 144, 100 S Ct 2204 (1980) (inventor of a genetically-engineered organism could obtain protection of ownership interests under patent laws). Other courts have likewise acknowledged the cell line's status as property, see eg *Pasteur v United States*, 814, F 2d 624 (Fed. Cir 1987) (donated cell line assumed to be property but transfer held not subject to Contract Disputes Act). The Court thus sees no reason why a cell line should not be considered a chattel capable of being converted. Indeed, if such a cause of action is not recognized, it is hard to conceive what civil remedy would ever lie to recover a cell line that might be stolen or destroyed, including one with immense potential commercial value, as this one apparently had and has. See generally Catherine M Valerio Barrad, 'Genetic Information and Property Theory,' 87 Nw U L Rev 103 (1992). The Court is satisfied, therefore, under the circumstances of this case, that the Alpha 1–4 cell line was capable of being converted and that in fact Dr Arora converted it…

Conclusion

The Court, therefore, will enter judgment on Count I, the conversion count, in favour of the United States, in the sum of $5,450.20 compensatory damages and $5,000.00 punitive damages and Defendant will also be directed to pay court costs. In light of the Court's judgment as to Count I, the Court will dismiss Count II, in trespass, as moot.

A separate Final Order of Judgment will be entered.

We have already seen Paul Matthews' rejection of the argument that human tissue is *res nullius* such that title rests in the first occupant, ie the remover – though this could be an explanation of *Arora*, given the decision in *Moore* that the source never had any proprietary rights in the cells or cell-line. Alternatively, the argument may be based upon the idea that where the 'remover' improves the tissue he thereby acquires property rights over the tissue. The Nuffield Council rely for this upon the decision of the Australian High Court in *Doodeward v Spence* (1908) 6 CLR 406 (fully discussed *infra*, ch 18). There is, however, a difficulty here also. Paul Matthews again makes the arguments.

P Matthews 'The Man of Property' (1995) 3 Med L Rev 251

The [Nuffield Council's] Report goes to some trouble to establish that the common law authorities in some circumstances establish rights of possession to human tissue, and that such rights can properly be called a species of 'ownership'...the Working Party's answer is their citation of *Doodeward v Spence* ((1908) 6 CLR 406), the Australian High Court case most discussed in this chapter. This case is said to support the proposition that:

> If some work is carried out on the body part, for example to preserve it, which changed the part, then it could acquire the characteristics of property and be subject to property rights.

Plainly, this is a view drawn from Locke's 'labour-theory' of property (J Locke, 'Two Treatises of Government' (1690) 2.5). And such a proposition, if true, might justify a no-property analysis *vis-à-vis* the patient from whom the tissue was removed, but a property analysis *vis-à-vis* the user of the tissue.

But it is doubtful that this represents the view of more than one of the three judges in the case, namely Griffiths CJ. He and Barton J held (against the dissent of Higgins J) that the plaintiff could maintain detinue for the preserved remains of a stillborn child with two heads. But Barton J only joined with Griffiths CJ *because the child had been stillborn*. He would have joined Higgins J – and the plaintiff would have lost – if it had been born alive and subsequently died. Thus the stillborn child (never having been a living person) was capable from the outset of being property; it did not *become* so only by virtue of work done. On this point Griffiths CJ was in a minority of one.

Moreover, the proposition offered up in the Report as stated is inconsistent with other principles of property law. If the remains are *res nullius*, then first occupancy is sufficient to give rights to possession which will be protected by the law. (*Case of Swans* (1592) 7 Co Rep 15b at 17b; *Blades v Higgs* (1865) 11 HLC 621 at 638). There is no need to do any *work*. If, on the other hand, someone has rights in a thing, another person acquires no superior right merely by doing work on, or 'improving', that thing (*Falcke v Scottish Imperial Insurance Co* (1886) 34 Ch D 234).

However this may be, the Report concludes that the user of tissue once removed acquires at least possessory rights 'and probably a right of ownership' (whatever that means) over it, even though the user has not, in fact, done any work on it. (We must be meant to assume that the logically prior possessory claims of the person from whom the tissue came have been defeated by one of the means referred to . . .).

Matthews' point is that the 'work/skill' exception even if good law – on which see *infra*, ch 18 – is not necessary if the tissue is *res nullius*; possession alone will do as sufficient title to control the property against inference by all others who by definition will have a lesser right to possess. The exception may make sense in the case of parts taken from 'dead bodies' in order to overcome the 'no property' rule and to make that which was not previously property into property and, at the same time, vest the concomitant rights in the 'improver'. (But note Rose LJ's broader category in *R v Kelly, supra*). It does not operate, however, as a divesting mechanism. Thus, Matthews also directs us to the further point that if the tissue is *prima facie* that of the source it will remain so, despite the expenditure of skill or work upon it by another. What we are considering here is the question of 'specification' in English law. Is Matthews correct? There is a possible contrary argument. In a case such as *Moore*, the 'property' changes in character because of the improvement. Who may assert proprietary rights over it? As one of us has commented:

A Grubb 'I, Me, Mine: Bodies, Parts and Property' (1998) 3 Med L Int 299

Is the situation one of 'accession' where the source retains property rights? (*Thomas v Robinson* [1977] 1 NZLR 385). An example would be where a new headlamp is added to a car: ownership of the headlight accedes, and is lost to the owner of the car (N Palmer and A Hudson,

'Improving Stolen Chattels' in *Interests in Goods* (1998) at 931–5.) Or is this an example of 'specification' where a *nova species* is produced and it seems that the specificator (ie, the researchers) acquires all proprietary rights over the 'new' property (see *Borden Ltd v Scottish Timber Products Ltd* [1981] Ch 25 and *Re Peachdart Ltd* [1984] Ch 131 in Palmer and Hudson). Even if the latter is the case in English law, the remover may remain liable for converting the source's property (if that what it be) prior to the specification. The calculation of damages for conversion, including what account is to be taken of the 'improvement' (ie that which generates the profit), is difficult and has been said to be 'anyone's guess'. This is not to say that the court might not entertain an equitable distribution were an account of profits sought.

(For a discussion of specification, accession and mixtures, see: N Palmer and A Hudson 'Improving Stolen Chattels' in N Palmer and E McKendrick (eds) *Interests in Goods* (2nd edn, 1998) ch 36; P Birks *ibid* ch 9; P Matthews 'Specification in the Common Law' (1981) 10 Anglo-Am LR 121.)

As this indicates, even if the researchers acquire proprietary rights, a claim in convention would still lie. This, in itself, could extinguish the source's proprietary rights over the tissue (or its product) (see Torts (Interference with Goods) Act 1977, s 5). The measure of damages is not clear (for a discussion see P Matthews [1981] CLJ 340). Dworkin and Kennedy offer the following analysis:

G Dworkin and I Kennedy 'Human Tissue: Rights in the Body and its Parts' (1993) 1 Med L Rev 29

Damages are likely to be very difficult to assess. At one extreme, he would be entitled to the normal measure of damages for conversion, which would be the value of the 'goods' *at the time of the conversion*, together with any consequential and non-remote damage. This would be unlikely to satisfy Moore: the value of his cells was negligible until they were transformed by the defendants' skill into a patented cell line and its various products. At the other extreme, he might claim some or all of the profits from the exploitation of the patent and its products, which could be regarded as the improved products of Moore's cells. In some cases of conversion, where the value of the converted goods has risen by the time of the judgment, the latter date can be used for valuation. The case law suggests that there is no hard and fast rule: it is not possible '...to attempt to lay down any rule which is intended to be of any universal application as to the date by reference to which the value of the goods is to be assessed. The method of valuation and the date of valuation will depend on the circumstances' (see *IBL v Coussens* [1991] 2 All ER 133 at 139 per Neill LJ).

Thus, the measure of damage is anyone's guess, as also would be the extent to which the work of the defendants in improving the cell-line could be taken into account in reducing the amount of compensation due to Moore. Whilst the Torts (Interference with Goods) Act 1977, section 6 provides that an allowance may be made to a defendant for any increase in the value of the goods due to expenditure or work on them by a defendant who acted in the mistaken but honest belief that he had a good title to the goods, the physician in the *Moore* case would not be able to rely upon that provision, although those who later used the tissue for research and development might well be able to do so (compare with well-known American case of *Wetherbee v Green* (1871) Mich 311).

An alternative to damages would be to seek equitable remedies such as delivery up or an account of profits or some similar equitable principle: there is considerable scope, although not in this paper, for developing arguments based upon constructive trust, unjust enrichment, and the like.

There are many examples of defendants being ordered to disgorge their profits, or a major part of them, although none appears to be directly comparable to the Moore situation. For example, in one very old and unusual case, the plaintiff was the father of baby Siamese twins who had given custody of them to the defendant who agreed to maintain the father and his family during the babies' lives, and to pay one eighth of the proceeds of displaying them. The twins died after one month and the defendant then embalmed their bodies and continued to exhibit them. The plaintiff brought equitable proceedings and the Court ordered that the bodies should be buried and that the defendant should account to the plaintiff for all the money obtained from the wrongful exploitation of these bodies (*Herring v Walround* (1682) 22 ER 870. Cited in Matthews, 'Whose Body? People as Property' (1993) CLP 193 at 220).

More recent authorities demonstrate that those who obtain patents as the result of unlawful acts may be ordered to hold the patent on trust for the person who had been wronged (*Seager v Copydex* [1967] 2 All ER 415), that some wrongdoers may be ordered by courts of equity to account for *all* the profits gained from their wrongful conduct (eg *Franklin v Giddins* (1978)

Qd R 72), and, to demonstrate the continuing flexibility of equity, even in cases of undue influence where restitution would ordinarily be ordered, the courts have been prepared to permit wrongdoers to retain a *reasonable* sum for the efforts involved in making profits (*O'Sullivan v Management Agency* [1985] 3 All ER 351).

An English court has sufficient scope to provide a robust and common sense answer to the *Moore* case: which, on these facts should provide him with something akin to a royalty for using unique property of his in circumstances where he should not be regarded as having abandoned his rights.

Picking up on this final, perhaps obviously commonsense approach, an equitable solution has been proposed.

E Scowen 'The Human Body – Whose Property and Whose Profit' (1990) 1(1) Dispatches 1

Perhaps of greater interest in the *Moore* case is the Supreme Court's decision on the ability of a person to own and control after removal his tissues and body parts. Moore argued that he continued to own his cells and hence retained the right to direct their use in potentially lucrative research and, consequently, he was entitled to the profits generated. No court had previously decided this issue. To apply the notion of ownership (and hence the tort of conversion) in this context would have been novel, and an extension of the common law. The Supreme Court refused to take this step forward.

The court agreed that for Moore to establish an action for conversion, he would have to prove he owned the excised cells or, at least, had a right to possession of them. Moore did not expect to retain possession of his cells after removal, and thus he could only sue for conversion if he retained ownership in them. The Court was influenced by a number of factors in denying this part of Moore's claim. First, there were no judicial precedents. Second, the statutory law in California strongly suggested that a patient could at best have a very limited right to control research on excised cells. Thus, in the light of this, it would be inconsistent to view Moore's cells as property at common law entailing the consequent right to control their use. Thirdly, the Court drew a distinction between the cells removed from the body and the profitable cell-line. Even if Moore could own the former, the cell-line, which was subsequently produced by the defendants, was sufficiently distinct from the original cells that Moore could not claim he owned that. Fourthly, the Court took the view that enforcing a physician's obligations to disclose his research interests and any potential for commercial exploitation sufficiently protected patients from the type of harm which Moore alleged, without the need to recognise his proprietary claim.

The decision of the Supreme Court is something of a disappointment. The dismissal of the property claim rests on somewhat slender authority. The absence of judicial precedent is quoted, but as remarked by the two dissenting judges, no case law dictated the majority's view either. The statutory law in California exerted a strong influence on the Court, but in truth is ambiguous in the present context. Although the statute regulates scientific research, it makes no mention of bodily material for commercial exploitation. Hence, the statutory provisions do not necessarily deny Moore's conversion claim.

Finally, the Court took the view that any impediment to research on human cells was against the public interest. To recognise a patient's property rights over excised body material could adversely affect research and so the grant of such rights was a matter solely for the state legislature.

If the case depends upon the statutory context in California, the impact on English law might not be significant since there is no legislative indication that an individual has only limited rights over excised bodily tissue in England. Arguably in this country, public policy points in the opposite direction (for example, see the Polkinghorne Report on the use of fetal tissue) and hence, the English courts might find the dissenting judgment of Justice Mosk more persuasive. He held that at common law a patient retained proprietary rights over excised cells unless the patient had abandoned them. Mosk J strongly rejected all the arguments pressed by the majority of the court and concluded that it would be 'inequitable and immoral' not to allow Moore a share of the profits arising from an enterprise to which his 'contribution…[was] absolutely crucial'.

As this highlights, an important reason for accepting a proprietary claim in a situation like the *Moore* case, is the underlying belief that the provider of the raw 'materials' which are commercially exploited should receive at least some share of the profit. The majority of the Court argued that if Moore succeeded in establishing a breach of fiduciary duty or a lack of informed consent this would be achieved. But, as Justice Mosk pointed out, it is unlikely for two reasons: first, in a negligence action the measure of damages is the patient's loss due to harm and not loss of profits due to improper use of his cells; secondly, the major profits, if they arise, will not primarily accrue to the doctors against whom these two actions lie, but the commercial concerns at one remove from them. Whilst the doctrine of vicarious liability might reach the profit makers if the doctors were their employees, this will not be the case in many circumstances.

Only by recognising the patient's proprietary claim could a court ensure, as equity requires, that the provider of the cells should receive a reasonable share in the profits.

It is important to note a point not developed in *Moore's* case. A proprietary claim would only entitle the patient to a share, perhaps even a small share of the profits, because equity would recognise the elements of work and skill employed in the development of a cell-line, and compensate the medical researchers accordingly. Their share might be the greater. It is arguable that the majority of the Court may have been influenced by the belief that if Moore succeeded in his proprietary claim all profits would be his or at least he could decide on any distribution.

There is, however, a practical solution. All the problems associated with the property approach might be made to go away if the practice of obtaining the donor's consent to subsequent use and exploitation were to be adopted. The Nuffield Council in its Report, *op cit*, recommends that good practice requires that explicit consent is given by donors to storage and other uses (para 13.16). It recommends that consent forms for treatment should also be amended to cover acceptable further uses of tissue removed during treatment (para 6.29.1). Of course, if the property approach is correct then the donor's consent is essential (subject to implied abandonment) if the user is to avoid liability in conversion – either to effect a gift or as an explicit intention to abandon. Alternatively, consent may be necessary to avoid a claim by the donor that his bodily integrity was invaded unlawfully. This, you will recall, was the approach of the majority in the *Moore* case. We have already discussed whether there is any basis for this approach in English law, involving as it does an extensive duty to disclose or an extension of the law of battery (*supra*, ch 5).

What the donor must consent to will, of course, depend upon the circumstances. If the use to which the tissue is to be put is of a general nature, eg archiving or teaching, then a general consent to those uses will be sufficient. This is so also if the tissue is to be used for research. Article 22 of the European Convention on Human Rights and Biomedicine (1996) enshrines the need for consent. It states:

When in the course of an intervention any part of a human body is removed, it may be stored and used for a purpose other than that for which it was removed, only if this is done in conformity with appropriate information and consent procedures.

Thus, tissue or other body parts removed during treatment could only be stored and used for that purpose if the individual had at the time (or subsequently) agreed to its storage and use, for example, for research or other specified purposes. It is not at all clear that 'appropriate information and consent procedure' permit anything other than explicit consent. Certainly, it seems unlikely that the individual's implied consent could be relied upon if this were based solely upon the premise that he can be taken to agree to any proper use. But, would it, for example, suffice that the individual had not 'opted out' when prominent notices indicated what uses might be made of excised tissue? The *Explanatory Report* to the Convention suggests that this might do in some circumstances (see *Explanatory Report*, January 1997 at para 137).

The problematic point is where the research leads or may lead to financial gain. Under the property approach if there is no consent given for the *exploitation* of the tissue, even if such exploitation was not contemplated at the time of removal, the consent is exceeded. The donor has a claim. If, however, the need for consent derives from the laws concerned with the protection of bodily integrity, it is clear that exploitation not contemplated at the time of removal would not retrospectively affect the valid consent given at the time of removal and would not, therefore, give rise to a claim.

The position is less clear if there was an undisclosed intention to exploit the tissue removed. American law tends to regard the relationship between doctor and patient as a fiduciary one thus casting upon the doctor a duty not to create a situation of conflict of interests with the patient whereby the doctor benefits at the patient's expense, unless the patient consents to the conflict arising. English law, as we have seen in Chapters 5 and 8, does not see the relationship as a fiduciary one. Hence the argument of there being a duty to disclose, as we saw, is harder to make. Unfortunately, the tissue may not be used or exploited by the doctor who treated the patient. There will not be, on any view, a fiduciary relationship between the researcher or biotechnology company and the donor. Hence, as against them, only the property approach could assist the donor (see Mosk J's views in *Moore*). (An example of resort to a framework of consents so as to avoid the need to determine the legal status of extra-corporeal bodily material can be seen in Sch 3 to the Human Fertilisation and Embryology Act 1990 (discussed *supra*, ch 10).)

E. LIABILITY IN TORT

1. Negligence

(a) Action by donee

When, if ever, can the donor of tissue or an organ, or a doctor or procurement agency, be liable to the donee who suffers harm as a consequence of the donation?

The ordinary principles of negligence apply in any possible action brought by a donee of tissue or an organ (on which see *supra*, ch 4). What may be helpful here is to notice the sorts of particular problems which arise in any possible negligence action (see generally, Kusanovich 'Medical Malpractice Liability and the Organ Transplant' (1971) 5 USFL Rev 223).

(i) AN ACTION VERSUS THE DONOR

The donor's potential liability will most probably arise from allegations of non-disclosure of a known (or knowable?) genetic problem, risk of infection or other relevant history which could cause injury to the donee. The question is what is the donor's duty of disclosure in such circumstances?

The duty of the donor might well turn on such factors as (i) knowledge that he suffers from some infection or is the carrier of a defective gene; (ii) knowledge that he has taken part in high risk activity (eg in the context of infection with HIV). Of course, if the donor intends to infect or injure the recipient then liability will fall under the rule in *Wilkinson v Downton* [1897] 2 QB 57. Such a situation is most unlikely; more likely is negligently caused harm. Whether a donor of an organ or tissue owes a duty of care to a recipient is a novel question. It must be borne in mind that the recent approach to the tort of negligence suggests that the House of Lords would be reluctant to recognise liability here (eg *Caparo Industries plc v Dickman* [1990] 2 AC 605 and *Murphy v Brentwood DC* [1991] 1 AC 398). Nevertheless, it is suggested that a donor's relationship with the recipient would be sufficiently close for there to be 'proximity' and that it would be 'just and reasonable' to impose the duty of care. Apart from the practical point we make below, it would be irrelevant whether the donation was anonymous or the donor and recipient knew (of) each other (see discussion in the context of blood donors in A Grubb and D Pearl *Blood Testing, AIDS and DNA Profiling: Law and Policy* (1990) pp 119–121).

Furthermore, even if a duty to disclose on the part of the donor were found to exist, it may still be said that the conduct of others, such as the doctors or those in a pathology laboratory, if careless, breaks the chain of causation. The better view is, however, that carelessness of this sort is reasonably foreseeable and should not therefore be held to constitute a *novus actus interveniens* (see Hart and Honoré *Causation in the Law* (2nd edn, 1985) at p 184).

This body of law, important as it is, does not entirely resolve questions of the liability of a donor to a donee in the context of the donation of body tissue or an organ. This is because what we are concerned with may differ in one significant respect from sexually transmitted disease: the tissue and organ donation may be between non-genetically related persons and thus would take place in circumstances of anonymity. In such a case, the donee cannot trace who the donor was. And, when a donee attempted to do so, the Florida court in the following case refused his application.

Rasmussen v South Florida Blood Service (1987) 500 So 2d 533 (Sup Ct Florida)

Barkett J: We have for review *South Florida Blood Service, Inc v Rasmussen*, 467 So 2d 798 (Fla 3d DCA 1985). In that decision, the district court certified the following as a question of great public importance:

> Do privacy interests of volunteer blood donors and a blood service's and society's interest in maintaining a strong volunteer blood donation system outweigh a plaintiff's interest in discovering the names and addresses of the blood donors in the hope that further discovery will provide some evidence that he contracted AIDS from transfusions necessitated by injuries which are the subject of his suit?

We answer the question in the affirmative.

On May 24, 1982, petitioner, Donald Rasmussen, was sitting on a park bench when he was struck by an automobile. He sued the driver and alleged owner of the automobile for personal injuries he sustained in the accident. While hospitalised as a result of his injuries, Rasmussen received fifty-one units of blood via transfusion. In July of 1983, he was diagnosed as having 'Acquired Immune Deficiency Syndrome' (AIDS) and died of that disease one year later. In an attempt to prove that the source of his AIDS was the necessary medical treatment he received because of injuries sustained in the accident, Rasmussen served respondent, South Florida Blood Service (Blood Service), with a *subpoena duces tecum* requesting 'any and all records, documents and other material indicating the names and addresses of the [51] blood donors'. (South Florida Blood Service is not a party to the underlying personal injury litigation, and there has been no allegation of negligence on the part of the Blood Service.)

The Blood Service moved the trial court to either quash the *subpoena* or issue a protective order barring disclosure. ...

It is now known that AIDS is a major health problem with calamitous potential. At present, there is no known cure and the mortality rate is high. As noted by the court below, medical researchers have identified a number of groups which have a high incidence of the disease and are labelled 'high risk' groups ...

As the district court recognised, petitioner needs more than just the names and addresses of the donors. His interest is in establishing that one or more of the donors has AIDS or is in a high risk group. Petitioner argues that his inquiry *may* never go beyond comparing the donors' names against a list of known AIDS victims, or against other public records (eg conviction records in order to determine whether any of the donors is a known drug user). He contends that because a limited inquiry *may* reveal the information he seeks, with no invasion of privacy, the donors' privacy rights are not yet at issue. We find this argument disingenuous. As we have already noted, the discovery rules allow a trial judge upon good cause shown to set conditions under which discovery will be given. Some method could be formulated to verify the Blood Service's report that none of the donors is a known AIDS victim while preserving the confidentiality of the donors' identities. However, the *subpoena* in question gives petitioner access to the names and addresses of the blood donors with no restrictions on their use. There is nothing to prohibit petitioner from conducting an investigation without the knowledge of the persons in question. We cannot ignore, therefore, the consequences of disclosure to nonparties, including the possibility that a donor's coworkers, friends, employers, and others may be queried as to the donor's sexual preferences, drug use, or general life-style.

The threat posed by the disclosure of the donors' identities goes far beyond the immediate discomfort occasioned by a third party probing into sensitive areas of the donors' lives. Disclosure of donor identities in any context involving AIDS could be extremely disruptive and even devastating to the individual donor. If the requested information is released, and petitioner queries the donors' friends and fellow employees, it will be functionally impossible to prevent occasional references to AIDS. As the district court recognised:

> AIDS is the modern day equivalent of leprosy. AIDS, or a suspicion of AIDS, can lead to discrimination in employment, education, housing and even medical treatment.

We wish to emphasise that although the importance of protecting the privacy of donor information does not depend on the special stigma associated with AIDS, public response to the disease does make this a more critical matter. By the very nature of this case, disclosure of donor identities is disclosure in a damaging context. We conclude, therefore, that the disclosure sought here implicates constitutionally protected privacy interests.

Our analysis of the interests to be served by denying discovery does not end with the effects of disclosure on the private lives of the fifty-one donors implicated in this case. Society has a vital interest in maintaining a strong volunteer blood supply, a task that has become more difficult with the emergence of AIDS. The donor population has been reduced by the necessary exclusion of potential blood donors through AIDS screening and testing procedures as well as by the unnecessary reduction in the donor population as a result of the widespread fear that donation itself can transmit the disease. In light of this, it is clearly 'in the public interest to discourage any serious disincentive to volunteer blood donation'. Because there is little doubt that the prospects of inquiry into one's private life and potential association with AIDS will deter blood donation, we conclude that society's interest in a strong and healthy blood supply will be furthered by the denial of discovery in this case.

In balancing the competing interests involved, we do not ignore Rasmussen's interest in obtaining the requested information in order to prove aggregation of his injuries and obtain full recovery. We recognise that petitioner's interest parallels the state's interest in ensuring full compensation for victims of negligence. However, we find that the discovery order requested here would do little to advance that interest. The probative value of the discovery sought by Rasmussen is dubious at best. The potential of significant harm to most, if not all, of the fifty-one unsuspecting donors in permitting such a fishing expedition is great and far outweighs the plaintiff's need under these circumstances. ...

We think that this reflects what an English court would decide. The point arose directly in *AB v Scottish Blood Transfusion Service* [1990] SCLR 263, (1989) 15 BMLR 91 (Court of Session (Outer House)) where Lord Morrison held that public policy (as evidenced by the certificate of the Secretary of State) demanded that the anonymity of the blood donor be preserved in the interests of maintaining a national blood transfusion service. For an analogous example of the balancing of the factors of public policy in English law, see *D v National Society for the Prevention of Cruelty to Children* [1978] AC 171, [1977] 1 All ER 589.

By contrast, some courts in the United States have held otherwise. Even then, however, they have allowed discovery of the donor's identity but have prevented contact with him or have refused to identify the donor but allowed questions to be put to him through the court (eg *Tarrant County Hospital District v Hughes* (1987) 734 SW 2d 675 (Tx CA) and *Belle Bonfils Memorial Blood Center v District Court of Denver* (1988) 763 P 2d 1003 (Colo SC). See also *PD v Australian Red Cross Society* (1993) 30 NSWLR 376 (NSWCA) – permitting disclosure providing no action brought against donor and no direct approach made: see Commentary (1994) 2 Med L Rev 110 (AG)).

(ii) AN ACTION VERSUS THE DOCTOR OR PROCUREMENT AGENCY

We are here in the realm of product liability which we discussed in detail in Chapter 13. Here we merely illustrate the legal issues. Reference should be made to the earlier discussion. The injury may arise through the transplantation of an organ or other tissue, the transfusion of blood or, indeed, the donation of gametes during medically assisted reproduction involving donated gamete(s) or embryos. In the latter instance the action may be brought by the patients or the child who may also be infected or have inherited a genetic disorder (on claims by the child, see *supra*, ch 12). The donee will be alleging negligence in carrying out the particular procedure, a failure to discover relevant medical information from the donor or the donee, not carrying out proper tests or failing to inform a donee of the risks and alternatives, in breach of the doctor's legal duty. Best practice imposes obligations on those dealing with blood, organs and tissues to screen donors adequately or test the body material itself for a whole range of infections, eg, HIV 1/2, Hepatitis B and C and CJD (see, in relation to tissue and organs: *Guidance on the Microbiological Safety of Human Tissues and Organs Used in*

Transplantation HSG 96(26)). No doubt these requirements would set as a *minimum* the legal standard of care. Of course, more may be required. (For best practice in relation to screening and testing donors of reproductive material, see HFEA *Code of Practice* (4th edn, 1998) paras 3.43–3.60.)

Kenneth Norrie illustrates some of the situations:

K Norrie 'Human Tissue Transplants: Legal Liability in Different Jurisdictions' (1985) ICLQ 442

... For example, to transfer blood taken from a hepatitis sufferer to a recipient would surely suggest liability in damages for the person responsible to ensure that the blood was uninfected. In *Ravenis v Detroit General Hospital* [234 NW 2d 411 (1975)], a claim was held competent where it was alleged that the hospital was negligent in the selection of cornea donors who were not fit within the medical standard of care of the community. Similarly, concern has lately been expressed about patients receiving blood transfusions from donors who suffer from acquired immunodeficiency syndrome (AIDS) [*semble* infected with HIV]. Since the person actually performing the operation is ultimately responsible for the recipient's health, it is with him that liability must eventually rest, though he may also share it with the physician responsible for the extraction of the donation if he is different. Giesen cites a French case in which a surgeon was held liable for transplanting a cornea into a recipient having taken it from a donor who had died from rabies. The recipient shortly afterwards also died from rabies. In this case it would appear that the transplanting surgeon was responsible not only for the transplantation, but also for the wrongful diagnosis of the donor's death as being from brain-fever. Difficulties as to who is liable to the recipient may arise if the person performing the transplant into the recipient is different from the person extracting the organ from the donor (as will generally be the case, for example, with blood transfusions). It is submitted that the determination of the person liable in such circumstances shall depend upon the extent to which the surgeon performing the transplant is entitled to rely on what he is told by the person extracting the donation. While the transplanting surgeon, being ultimately responsible for the patient's welfare, must in the general case be held liable for failing personally to ensure the suitability of the donation (just as a surgeon, being ultimately responsible for the procedure in any operation, is not entitled to rely on a swab count reported correct to him by a nurse), it is nevertheless possible to envisage circumstances in which he may escape liability. In, for example, the case of blood transfusions, it is suggested that the doctor performing the transfusion is entitled to rely on the information concerning the blood which he is given from the blood bank or persons responsible for taking the donation, because it would be unreasonable to expect him to carry out his own (repeat) tests to determine the blood group etc of the donation.

(For a discussion of the law in the United States, see *Annotation* 'Liability of hospital, physician, or other individual medical practitioner for injury or death resulting from blood transfusion' 20 ALR 4th 129.)

As Norrie notes, the questions raised here have acquired particular importance because of the spread of HIV infection. There have been a number of cases in Australia (eg *H v Royal Alexandra Hospital for Children* [1990] 1 Med LR 297 and *E v Australian Red Cross Society* [1991] 2 Med LR 303) and a large number in the US (eg *Kozup v Georgetown University* (1987) 663 F Supp 1048 (D DC) and (1988) 851 F 2d 437 (DC Cir)). For an account of developments in the law, see A Grubb and D Pearl, *Blood Testing, AIDS and DNA Profiling: Law and Policy* ((1990) ch 3). Likewise, the recent litigation concerning the transmission of Creutzfeldt – Jakob Disease (CJD) in human growth hormone, illustrates this kind of products liability litigation. (See discussion in D Crichton, R Mays and S Middlemiss 'Liability for CJD Deaths' [1998] Juridical Review 89; and for the reported case law, see *N v UK Medical Research Council* [1996] 7 Med LR 309 and *Re The Creutzfeldt-Jakob Disease Litigation* (1997) 41 BMLR 157 (Morland J).)

By way of example, we consider the HIV litigation. In the UK in *Re HIV Haemophiliac Litigation* (1990) 41 BMLR 171 (CA), 962 haemophiliacs sued the Government in negligence and for breach of statutory duty under the National Health Service Act 1977 (see *supra*, ch 4). The plaintiffs were infected with the Human ImmunoDeficiency Virus (HIV), which causes AIDS, as a result of receiving infected Factor VIII (the clotting agent) imported from America during the early 1980s.

The plaintiffs made a wide range of allegations of negligence against the Government including: (1) failure to achieve self sufficiency in UK blood products and continuing to import blood products from America; (2) failure to use heat treated blood products, a process which destroys HIV; (3) failure to screen out infected blood donors in the UK; (4) failure to use tests to detect infected donated blood; (5) failure to revoke or suspend the licences granted under the Medicines Act 1968 to commercially produced blood products from America. The action was not a trial of the plaintiffs' claims against the Government but was an application for discovery of a large number of Government documents. The documents were, on the whole, internal Government documents relating to the formulation of Government policy on the activities of, and allocation of resources to, the Blood Transfusion Service and, in addition, the importance of American blood products. The Government resisted their disclosure, claiming it was against the public interest. The main argument of the Government was that the documents were irrelevant because the plaintiffs' allegations of negligence could not be legally sustained.

The Court of Appeal held that it was impossible to say that the haemophiliacs did not have an arguable legal case in negligence against the Government. The court held that the Government could owe a duty to the haemophiliacs to exercise reasonable care in the running of the NHS so as to protect them from receiving infected blood products even though many of the plaintiffs' allegations involved challenges to the Government formulation of policy within the NHS. Where the formulation of Government policy is challenged in a negligence action the courts have been reluctant to impose legal duties on Government, regarding such issues as political and non-justiciable in the courts. The court emphasised that there would be difficulties at the trial because the claims involved 'the exercise of discretion, policy making, allocation of resources' but that at this preliminary stage of the case it could not be emphatically held that no legal action could be brought. However, the court emphasised that the trial court might, after a full consideration, decide there was no case in law.

In addition, the court also emphasised that at the trial the plaintiffs might still fail because the Court of Appeal was assuming the facts favourable to their claim at this preliminary stage. Establishing negligence might be difficult when the facts were fully investigated. As Ralph Gibson LJ said:

> [i]t may be that, at the dates alleged, the nature and gravity of the risks to the plaintiffs were not as alleged or were not known to be such; and that the alleged steps for eliminating the risk were not available, or were reasonably judged to be of inadequate utility.

As regards the plaintiffs' claims based upon a breach of statutory duty under the National Health Service Act 1977, the Court of Appeal was more circumspect about the potential success of the claim. The court took the view that the duties imposed upon the Secretary of State for Health under the Act were vague and general and not such as to 'clearly demonstrate the intention of Parliament to impose a duty which is to be enforced by individual civil action'. Ralph Gibson LJ described the plaintiffs' actions as being 'at best of uncertain validity in law'.

Nevertheless, since the plaintiffs' negligence claims were legally arguable, the court referred the case back to a judge who would decide, after inspecting the documents, whether they were 'very likely to assist' the plaintiffs and, if so, order their production. The Court of Appeal allowed the plaintiffs' claim to continue. In the words of Bingham LJ, '… the law might arguably be thought defective if it did not afford redress'.

In December 1990, the Government agreed a settlement with the plaintiffs and so the liability of the defendants was never determined. In March 1992 the

Government settled the remaining claims of plaintiffs who had been infected through blood transfusions. Hence, the legal issues which were so clearly focused in this case remain unanswered in the UK.

As this case and the litigation relating to CJD shows, there are a variety of potential bases for liability (see also *supra*, ch 13). They include the adequacy of screening donors, the existence and adequacy of procedures for testing blood and other tissue for HIV and other infection and failure to warn adequately (or at all) of the risks of transmissions. These potential bases for liability can apply, *mutatis mutandis*, to infection transmitted through other body fluids (eg semen) or tissue (eg kidneys).

(b) Action by donor

(i) AN ACTION VERSUS THE DOCTOR

Is the extent of the doctor's duty to disclose the same when the doctor is advising the donor as when he is advising the donee? As regards the genetically *unrelated* donor the matter is dealt with in the 1989 regulations (see *supra*). Failure to comply would give the donor a cause of action in negligence if he suffered harm because the court would likely regard the regulations as setting the standard for disclosure. Where the donor is genetically *related* to the intended donee the court might similarly be guided by the regulations even though they do not, strictly speaking, apply. After all, the donor is a healthy person who is being subjected to procedures of varying degrees of risk. Here, there can be no justification for withholding relevant information on medical grounds. This duty encompasses an obligation to explain the alternatives, consequences and risks and importantly may include a duty to advise about the possible psychological, as well as physical, reactions which the donor may develop after the donation.

In addition to actions based upon a failure to inform the doctor, a doctor might, of course, be sued for the negligent performance of the procedure. We are here in the realm of medical malpractice law which we have already considered in Chapter 4.

(ii) AN ACTION VERSUS A THIRD PARTY

Urbanski v Patel (1978) 84 DLR (3d) 650 (Manitoba Queen's Bench)

Wilson J: These two suits for medical malpractice were consolidated for trial. Plaintiffs Shirley and Stanley Firman, husband and wife, claim damages caused by defendants' negligence in mistakenly removing Mrs Firman's one and only kidney, whereby both their lives have been seriously disrupted. Plaintiff Urbanski, Mrs Firman's father, donated one of his own kidneys (as what father would not?) for transplant, in a vain effort to ease the disaster, and claims his own costs and other expenses associated with that operation ...

Patel admits negligence, and concedes liability to the Firmans, but denies any responsibility to Urbanski as a result of his negligent treatment of Mrs Firman ...

... Shirley Firman and her doctor decided that, all things considered, it would be just as well if there were no more children. And so, it was arranged she would undergo a tubal ligation. And, because for some time she had felt occasional abdominal discomfort (nothing specific or disabling and perhaps caused, thought her doctor, by an ovarian cyst) her operation was to include exploration for and, if found, removal of that offender.

Otherwise in good health, on April 17th Mrs Firman submitted to this procedure when, by mistake, defendant incorrectly identified a body found in the lower left quadrant of her abdomen and excised this, believing it to be an ovarian cyst.

But, it was a kidney, out of place indeed (ectopic) but a kidney none the less. Indeed, her only kidney, this being a congenital accident hitherto unknown, or even suspected. And while seemingly one can get along quite well – as had this plaintiff – with only half the normal complement of two kidneys, the situation is altogether different if the patient has none at all.

Within two days of the operation Mrs Firman had been admitted to the emergency department of the Health Sciences Centre in Winnipeg. By that time, the material removed had been correctly identified, and the total absence of any renal function was confirmed. On the day following, April 20th, the significance of this irreversible disaster was explained to the plaintiff husband and wife, and Mrs Firman was put on peritoneal dialysis …

… [A] suitable candidate may be invited to surrender one of his two kidneys to someone else who has none at all, the risk to the donor, seemingly not that great in any event, being entirely overborne by the desperate condition of the other, and the expected improvement in life-style for the donee.

Search elsewhere was finally abandoned, and in the spring of 1976 Shirley's father, the plaintiff Urbanski, volunteered one of his kidneys, implanted on May 8th. Unhappily this was not a success, and it had to be removed three days later, when of course she went back to the machine. On May 31st a cadaveric transplant was attempted, with no more success, and this was removed on June 4, 1976.

… [As for] Victor Urbanski, in its simplest terms this plaintiff says that he did no more than would any other father, faced with the obvious distress of his daughter, namely, donated one of his own kidneys so that she – who had none – may have a better chance of survival.

Defendant's plea is that this act, and the expenses attendant thereon, may not be looked upon as a foreseeable consequences of the wrong done to Shirley Firman.

That argument prevailed in *Sirianni v Anna* 285 NYS 2d 709 (1967). In that case because of the acute infection which set in after a routine hernia repair, an exploratory operation was done to see if, perhaps, the patient's condition was caused by a wound abscess or by appendicitis. In the course of this surgery a kidney was removed. And, as with Mrs Firman, that was the patient's only kidney. Dialysis was not a full answer, and his mother donated one of her kidneys, and sued for her expenses and general damages.

Her action failed, Ward, J, considering (p 712) that:

The premeditated, knowledgeable and purposeful act of this plaintiff in donating one of her kidneys to preserve the life of her son did not extend or reactivate the consummated negligence of these defendants. The conduct of the plaintiff herein is a clearly defined, independent, intervening act with full knowledge of the consequences.

Mrs Sirianni's decision to give up one of her kidneys he thought was wilful, intentional, voluntary, free from accident, and could not be laid at defendant's door. The classical tests of foreseeability and proximate cause, thought the learned Judge, precluded recovery, because the plaintiff's conduct was a clearly defined, independent, intervening act. And, since that act was independent, as well as unforeseeable, it broke the causation, and superseded defendant's negligence in removing the kidney.

But in 1963, when Mrs Sirianni's son lost his kidney, indeed in 1967 when her case was decided, the notion of organ transplant was in its infancy. We all know that not until December, 1967, did Dr Christian Barnard accomplish the first heart transplant in man. So then, Ward J, could well comment, as he did (p 713) that, 'The miracle of modern medical science seems not to be on the threshold of successfully transferring many organs from one human body to another.'

Sirianni, of course, is not binding on me. Apart from that, in studying that case one should read, too, the commentary thereon included in the very useful article 'Medical Malpractice Liability and the Organ Transplant', published with the April, 1971 issue, 5 USFL Rev 223, by Mark Kusanovich, who wrote, at pp 258–9:

Kidney transplantation is of recent origin. Thus, the date on which Sirianni's kidney was negligently removed is relevant to determine whether a contingency of transplant from a live donor was foreseeable. Apparently, the first successful human kidney transplant was performed in 1954. By 1963, 244 kidney transplants had involved live donors. But at that time the field was still very new with live donors coming from close members of the family and with some physicians discouraging donation except from identical twins. Thus, in 1963, the date of the Sirianni transplant, the question whether it was foreseeable that Sirianni, who had no twin, would receive a live organ donation was debatable. Since 1963, kidney transplantation has progressed rapidly. The statistics up to 1970 indicate that approximately 4,000 kidney transplants have been performed and registered. Therefore, it is arguable in the future that whenever disease or removal of kidneys is foreseeable, human donation will likewise be foreseeable.

In testifying before me, Dr Thomson spoke of 123 kidney transplants in Winnipeg alone; both he and Dr Fenton spoke of the many thousands performed in the United States and Europe. If not routine – because of the danger of rejection, and so worsening of the patient's chance for a successful operation by risking the build-up of antibodies – certainly I think it can fairly be said, in light of today's medicine, kidney transplant is an accepted remedy in renal failure. Certainly defendant here can hardly be heard to deny its 'foreseeability', in the dictionary sense of that word.

In other terms, the transplant, surely, must be viewed as an expected result, something to be anticipated, as a consequence of the loss of normal kidney function.

The world of medicine has progressed beyond the *ratio* in *Sirianni*, so that, given the disaster which befell Shirley Firman, it was entirely foreseeable that one of her family would be invited, and would agree, to donate a kidney for transplant, an act which accords, too, with the principle developed in the many 'rescue' cases.

American jurisprudence perhaps anticipated our own in this field, Mr Justice Cardozo's classic remarks in *Wagner v International Railway Co* 232 NY Rep 176 (1921), being penned in 1921. From that judgment, p 180:

> Danger invites rescue. The cry of distress is the summons to relief. The law does not ignore these reactions of the mind in tracing conduct to its consequences. It recognises them as normal. It places their effects within the range of the natural and probable. The wrong that imperils life is a wrong to the imperilled victim; it is a wrong also to his rescuer … The risk of rescue, if only it be not wanton, is born of the occasion. The emergency begets the man. The wrongdoer may not have foreseen the coming of a deliverer. He is accountable as if he had …

In 1935, with *Haynes v Harwood* [1935] 1 KB 146 at 156–7, Greer, LJ, accepted the American rule as stated by Professor Goodhart in the Cambridge Law Journal, vol V (1935), p 132:

> In accurately summing up the American authorities … the learned author says this (at p 196): 'The American rule is that the doctrine of the assumption of risk does not apply where the plaintiff has, under an exigency caused by the defendant's wrongful misconduct, consciously and deliberately faced a risk, even of death, to rescue another from imminent danger of personal injury or death, whether the person endangered is one to whom he owes a duty of protection, as a member of his family, or is a mere stranger to whom he owed no such special duty.' In my judgment that passage not only represents the law of the United States, but I think it also accurately represents the law of this country.

Both pronouncements were adopted by our own Supreme Court in *Corothers v Slobodian* (1974) 51 DLR (3d) 1, [1975] 2 SCR 633, [1975] 3 WWR 142, wherein Ritchie, J, disposed of the notion of *novus actus*, or 'independent' act by the rescuer, so long as the one imperilled continues in the situation which prompts rescue.

And so, defendant, I find, is answerable to Victor Urbanski.

Technical considerations behind the decision to invite him to undergo such an operation are adequately reviewed in Dr Thomson's letter of March 30, 1976, wherein the doctor presents the primacy of the woman's father as most likely source for the attempt, and the very significant advantages to Mrs Firman in the event of success. Given the situation so outlined, and the relationship between the proposed donor and donee, the man's response to the invitation is not surprising.

Following an extensive series of tests and examinations, for which he was obliged to attend the Health Sciences Centre, on May 5, 1976, Victor Urbanski was admitted to hospital, and his left kidney was removed the day following. Up and around within a day or so, he was discharged from hospital on May 14th. No involvement or abnormalities were noted on his post-operative examinations, May 31 and November 16, 1976, with the exception of some hernia problems, present before the event. Removal of the left kidney does not affect his life expectancy, and apart from the annual medical examination recommended in such cases, his life-style should not be changed by what he has undergone.

For all that, this plaintiff now has but one kidney, and stands in some prejudice, should his kidney function suffer distress by reason of illness or trauma.

For the operation itself, loss of his kidney and post-operative recovery (for which the doctors thought six weeks would suffice, although his discomfort, perhaps loss of confidence, persisted somewhat beyond that period) I would allow $5,000.

Although he operates a farm, Victor Urbanski's principal income is from his trade as a carpenter, seasonal work done in the local district. I am not persuaded there was any serious disruption of the farm; on the other hand, he lost the best part of the building season. For loss of income $3,500 is not unreasonable. Adding $150 for the cost of his several trips into Winnipeg for tests, etc, his claim is allowed at $8,650.

And finally, for Manitoba Hospital Services Commission as to medical and hospital services, drugs, etc, related to Victor Urbanski's operation, $1,906.26.

The approach of the court in *Urbanski* is not without its critics. G Robertson in 'A New Application of the Rescue Principle' (1980) 96 LQR 19 at p 20 writes:

> [The] treatment of the foreseeability question is, however, open to criticism. In regarding the issue of foreseeability as being relevant only to the question of remoteness, the court failed

to consider *whether or not the defendant owed the plaintiff a duty of care*. The defendant was unaware, until after the operation, that the patient had only one kidney, and thus he could not be expected to have foreseen, at the time of the operation, that removal of the patient's kidney would result in the need for transplantation. It follows, therefore, that since injury to the plaintiff was not reasonably foreseeable at the time of the negligent act, no duty of care was owed to him by the defendant. (Our emphasis.)

Perhaps, the most important aspect of *Urbanski* is the way in which the court treated the plaintiff's conduct as not amounting to a voluntary assumption of the risk of injury. Again, Robertson (*op cit*) explains:

The significance of *Urbanski* lies in the fact that it extends the basis for recovery in rescue cases to an entirely new type of situation. In previous cases, the rescue attempt has involved a *risk* of physical injury to the rescuer, which he has chosen, either consciously or instinctively, to ignore in going to the assistance of the person in danger. In the *Urbanski* situation, physical injury is inevitable, and it is the rescuer's conscious decision to submit to such injury that forms the basis of the rescue attempt.

Despite this distinction, the court regarded the plaintiff's claim as falling within the established 'rescue principle', and it is submitted that an English court would be likely to do the same. There is no reason why the plaintiff's claim should be prejudiced merely because the sustaining of physical injury is a necessary part, and not merely an incidental consequence, of the rescue attempt. Moreover, it is now clear … that the law affords as much protection to the rescuer who stops for reflection before making his attempt, as it does to the person who rescues on impulse: *Haynes v Harwood* [1935] 1 KB 146 at 159.

The court also concluded that the defence of *volenti* should be rejected … The plaintiff in *Urbanski* can scarcely be said to have *voluntarily* assumed the risk of injury, notwithstanding that he realised that such injury was inevitable, given the dilemma in which he had been placed by the defendant's negligent act. The plaintiff's parental feelings towards his daughter, coupled with an understandable sense of moral obligation, left him without any real choice in the matter.

The case has not been followed in the United States. In four decisions (*Sirianni v Anna* (1967) 285 NYS 2d 709; *Moore v Shah* (1982) 458 NYS 2d 33; *Ornelas v Fry* (1986) 727 P 2d 819 and *Petersen v Farberman* (1987) 736 SW 2d 441), the courts have refused to apply the 'rescue doctrine' in this type of situation.

Moore v Shah (1982) 458 NYS 2d 33 (Sup Ct NY (App Div))

Weiss J: In what appears to be a case of first impression for an appellate court, we are called upon today to determine whether the donor for a kidney transplant has a cause of action against a physician who was allegedly guilty of negligence in the diagnosis and prescribed treatment of his patient, the donee, in this case the donor's father. The complaint alleges that the negligent diagnosis and treatment caused the father's kidney failure, necessitating later transplantation. Plaintiffs would have this court extend the well-defined principles of the rescue doctrine to one whose decision to come to the aid of his father was deliberate and reflective, not made under the pressures and exigencies of an emergency situation, and significantly, at a time after defendant's alleged negligent acts. For the reasons stated, we decline to do so and affirm the order at Special Term which granted defendant's motion to dismiss the third cause of action asserted in the complaint by plaintiff Marvin Richard Moore.

The predicate for holding a defendant liable must be that a duty is owed the plaintiff, the breach of which duty is the proximate cause of plaintiff's injury (*Palsgraf v Long Is RR Co*, 248 NY 339, 162 NE 99). In order to establish the existence of such duty, a defendant must foresee that his negligence could cause injury, in this case not only to his patient, but to the patient's son as well. While questions concerning what is foreseeable are generally issues for resolution by the finder of fact, there are certain instances where only one conclusion may be drawn from the established facts and where the question of legal cause may be decided as a matter of law (*Derdiarin v Felix Contr Corpn*, 51 NY 2d 308 at 315, 434 NYS 2d 166, 414 NE 2d 666). Plaintiff contends, however, that the rescue doctrine serves to establish the requisite foreseeability between the doctor's negligence in treatment of his father and injury to himself as the rescuer (see Prosser, Torts [4th edn], § 44, p 277; see, also, *Gibney v State of New York*, 137 NY 1, 6, 33 NE 142; *Eckert v Long Is RR Co*, 43 NY 502), arguing that defendant knew or should have known plaintiff would logically be the first person to donate a kidney to his father. It is true that a wrong perpetrated upon a victim is also a wrong to his rescuer (*Wagner v International Ry Co*, 232 NY 176, 180, 133 NE 437), and that so long as the rescue is not a rash or wanton act, the rescue doctrine extends a defendant's liability to the rescuer (*Provenzo v Sam*, NY 2d 256, 296 NYS 2d 322, 244 NE 2d 26; *Wagner v International Ry Co*, 232 NY 176, 180–181, 133 NE 437, *supra*; *Lafferty v Manhasset Med Center Hosp*, 79 AD 2d 996, 1000, 435 2d 307; affd 54 NY 2d 277, 445 NYS 2d 111, 429 NE 2d 789). While plaintiff did not act compulsively or instinctively under pressures of emergency requiring the immediate action usually attendant upon rescues, there are authorities which have applied the doctrine in other than spontaneous reaction situations (see *Guarina v Mine Safety Appliance Co*, 25 NY 2d 460, 306 NYS 2d 942, 255 NE 2d 173; *Rucker v Andress*, 38 AD 2d 684, 327 NYS 2d 848; *Keith v Payne*, 164 App Div 642, 150 NYS 37). However, we find that foreseeability alone is not enough to impose liability. Since plaintiff was never defendant's patient, no duty to him originally existed. Therefore, we are here involved with a question of whether foreseeability should be employed as the sole means to create a duty where none existed before (see 2 Harper & James, Torts, § 18.2, particularly p 1027; see generally, §§ 18.3–18.5). It is obvious that extension of liability of a physician to every person who conceivably might come forward as a kidney donor could create a group beyond manageable limits. Then Associate Judge Cooke, writing for the Court of Appeals in *Pulka v Edelman*, 40 NY 2d 781, 390 NYS 2d 393, 358 NE 2d 1019, said:

> If a rule of law were established so that liability would be imposed in an instance such as this, it is difficult to conceive of the bounds to which liability logically would flow. The liability potential would be all but limitless and the outside boundaries of that liability, both in respect to space and the extent of care to be exercised, particularly in the absence of control, would be difficult of definition. (*Id* at 786, 390 NYS 2d 393, 358 NE 2d 1019.)

We agree. In order to recover, a plaintiff must be one within the 'zone of danger' (*Tobin v Grossman*, 24 NY 2d 609, 616, 301 NYS 2d 554, 249 NE 2d 419; *Palsgraf v Long Is RR* Co, 248 NY 339, 162 NE 99, *supra*). It is difficult to charge a physician with the responsibility to foresee each and every person other than his patient who might conceivably be affected by his negligence.

> A duty arises when the relationship between individuals, the asserted plaintiff and defendant, is such as to impose upon the latter a legal obligation for the benefit of the former ... 'While a court might impose a legal duty where none existed before ... such an imposition must be exercised with extreme care ..."In the absence of duty, there is no breach and therefore no liability ... (*De Angelis v Lutheran Med Center*, 84 AD 2d 17, 22, 445 NYS 2d 188).

Our research has disclosed but one reported case in which the plaintiff was an actual organ donor. In *Sirianni v Anna* 55 Misc 2d 553, 285 NYS 2d 709, where a similar factual pattern to the instant case existed, Special Term granted defendant's motion to dismiss the complaint. While this court is not bound by *stare decisis* to follow that decision, we are persuaded by subsequent cases that it was correct. Only one year ago, the Court of Appeals held that where there is no allegation that the defendant was negligent with respect to the plaintiff as opposed to the patient, the case does not fall within recognised limits to the rescue doctrine and it declined to extend existing principles of law so as to include third parties who suffer (shock) as a result of direct injury to others. (*Lafferty v Manhasset Med Center Hosp* 54 NY 2d 277, 445 NYS 2d 111, 429 NF 2d 789, citing *Tobin v Grossman* 24 NY 2d 609, 301 NYS 2d 544, 249 NE 2d 419, *supra*; *Vaccaro v Squib Corpn* 52 NY 2d 809, 436 NYS 2d 871, 418 NE 2d 386; *Becker v Schwartz* 46 NY 2d 401, NYS 2d 895, 386 NE 2d 807; *Howard v Lecher* 42 NY 2d 109, 397 NYS 2d 363, 366 NE 2d 64.) We agree with the opinion of the Appellate Division, Second Department, 'that courts should not shirk their duty to overturn unsound precedent and should strive to continually develop the common law in accordance with our changing society ... Yet, the mere potential ability to change the common law is not the same as the desirability of making a particular change ...' (*De Angelis v Lutheran Med Center*, 84 AD 2d 17, 24, 445 NYS 2d 188, *supra*.) There are serious policy considerations which militate against the recovery sought here. Our decision may best be summarised in the words of then Associate Judge Breitel in *Tobin v Grossman*, 24 NY 2d 609, 301 NYS 2d 554, 249 NE 2d 419, *supra*: 'Every injury has ramifying consequences, like the ripplings of the waters, without end. The problem for the law is to limit the legal consequences of wrongs to a controllable degree' (*id* at 619, 301 NYS 2d 554, 249 NE 2d 419). We decline here to extend the common law to create a remedy for these plaintiffs.

John Spencer in 'Tissue Donors: Are They Rescuers, or Merely Volunteers?' [1979] CLJ 45 at 46–47 justifies the decision in *Urbanski*, in the face of the considerable difficulties of principle involved, as follows:

> ... what are the unspoken factors in cases such as these which influence judges to find that consequences are or are not reasonably foreseeable? To a large extent, they are how badly the

defendant has behaved, and how meritoriously the plaintiff. It is hard to think of a more striking piece of medical negligence than removing a kidney in mistake for an ovarian cyst. And it is hard to think of a more meritorious plaintiff than the altruistic Mr Urbanski who, in the face of pain, risk and personal inconvenience, volunteered his vital organs in an attempt to repair the mistake.

Urbanski was followed in a decision of the German Federal Supreme Court on 30 June 1987, JZ 1988, 150 (see B S Markesinis *The German Law of Torts: A Comparative Introduction* (3rd edn, 1997) at pp 632–639). If an English court did follow *Urbanski* there are certain implications which might follow. Robertson (*op cit*) considers a number of them:

> ... [I]f the plaintiff in *Urbanski* had had only one kidney, would it have been 'reasonable' for him to offer this for transplantation? (a hypothetical situation, given that the medical profession would almost certainly refuse such an offer). There must come a point in such cases at which the extent of the proposed injury to the rescuer is so great as to make it unreasonable for him to decide to submit to such injury ...
>
> The *Urbanski* decision also leaves other interesting questions unanswered. For example, as mentioned above, the transplant of the plaintiff's kidney proved to be unsuccessful. What if the patient's husband had then agreed to donate one of *his* kidneys, would he have been able to recover damages from the defendant as well? If there had been several unsuccessful transplants from members of the patient's family before success was finally achieved, would all the donors have had a cause of action against the defendant? Although one might instinctively answer this question in the negative, it is difficult to see the legal grounds on which such an answer could be substantiated. Surely it is reasonably foreseeable that a kidney transplant, even successive transplants, may be unsuccessful; and that suitable members of the patient's family will continue to come forward as donors until success is achieved. Moreover, the mere fact that previous transplants have been unsuccessful does not *necessarily* mean that transplants from other donors will also fail. Thus, it may be as reasonable for the last in the succession of donors, as it is for the first, to come to the assistance of the patient.
>
> Secondly, the court in *Urbanski* was obviously influenced by the father/daughter relationship that existed between rescuer and rescuee. Would the court's decision have been the same if the rescuer had been a complete stranger, inspired by altruistic rather than parental sentiment? Although such transplants are presently uncommon in most countries, the point is not without legal significance. It would seem unreasonable to make the outcome of the plaintiff's claim depend on the existence of a special relationship between himself and the rescuee. Whether the rescuer is a relation of the rescuee or a mere stranger, he should be entitled to compensation if he acts reasonably, out of a genuine desire to assist a person who has been placed in danger due to the defendant's negligence. Certainly, this has been the approach adopted in previous cases: see, for example, *Chadwick v British Railways Board* [1967] 2 All ER 945, [1967] 1 WLR 912. However, it is thought unlikely that courts would be willing to extend this approach to the *Urbanski* situation. One suspects that policy considerations, possibly couched in terms of the defence of *volenti*, would weigh heavily against the plaintiff. In a country which frowns upon payment even to blood donors, the possibility of a non-relative receiving compensation, albeit from a negligent defendant, for the voluntary act of donating a kidney is one which courts would be unlikely to encourage.

Spencer (*op cit*) does not accept Robertson's final point. He states:

> It is inconceivable that anyone not closely connected with Mrs Firman would have succeeded in a claim. Perhaps the decision can be seen as part of a general recognition by the courts that members of a family feel morally obliged to do more for each other than they are legally required to do, and a consequential willingness to compensate them, directly or indirectly, when they do it ...

(For a discussion of the liability of doctors to non-patients, see *supra*, ch 4.)

2. The Consumer Protection Act 1987

We have discussed the application of the Consumer Protection Act 1987 earlier (see ch 13) and, in particular whether the strict liability regime of that Act for 'defective products' could be applied to tissue or an organ which caused harm to the donee.

The dead donor

A. INTRODUCTION

Whilst donation by living persons has increased in recent years, the vast majority of donations comes from the dead or cadavers. Gerald Dworkin writes as follows:

G Dworkin 'The Law Relating to Organ Transplantation in England' (1970) 33 MLR 353

Because of the practical difficulties of obtaining organs from live donors, medical attention was directed to the possibility of obtaining organs from the bodies of dead donors. The practical advantages are obvious: the donor, once pronounced dead, is not exposed to any of the hazards which face the live donor; in some cases, such as heart or liver transplants, it is not possible to take organs from live donors; and the potential supply of organs from cadavers is much greater than from live volunteers. Practical difficulties also exist: until recently, although eyes could be 'kept' for several hours after death all other organs had to be taken and used with an hour of death; even with rapid medical progress it will be desirable for some time to come to perform the operation as soon as possible after the death of the donor.

... The existing law
(a) *Common law*. The common law position concerning corpses is curious but relatively well established. A corpse cannot ordinarily be the subject of ownership. Usually the executor or next-of-kin will have lawful possession of the body and there is a duty to arrange for burial at the earliest opportunity. It follows that, at common law, a man cannot by his will, or otherwise, legally determine what shall happen with his body after his death, although in most cases his wishes concerning the disposal of his body will be observed. That does not, of itself, authorise organs to be taken from corpses for the purpose of transplantation.

(b) *Statute*. The need for human bodies for medical purposes is not new: bodies have always been required for anatomical teaching and research. But any attempt on the part of persons in possession of a body to sell it, even for the purpose of dissection, was unlawful; the bodies of persons convicted of murder were alone capable of being used for dissection. The scandals of body-snatching and the publicity of the murder trial of Burke and Hare led to the passing of the Anatomy Act 1832, which enabled bodies to be supplied legally to medical schools for the purpose of anatomical examination. The demand for corpses was then successfully met for over a century.

It is only in recent times that the medical profession realised that the law relating to cadavers was far too restrictive. The successful development of the corneal graft operation focused attention on the lack of supply of eyes and the inability of potential donors to bequeath their eyes for such purposes. In a little debated, but carefully prepared, piece of legislation the Corneal Grafting Act 1952 (the wording of which to some extent followed the Anatomy Act 1832) was passed authorising the use of eyes of deceased persons for therapeutic purposes. This Act quickly proved to be too narrow, for it did not enable any other part of the body to be removed. However, once this kind of provision was on the statute book, it was much easier to extend it. The Human Tissue Act 1961 at present governs the English law relating to cadaver transplantation.

We return to the legal issues surrounding the use of whole dead bodies, for example for anatomy, again in Chapter 18.

B. THE HUMAN TISSUE ACT 1961

The Human Tissue Act 1961, s 1 (as amended) provides:

1. – (1) If any person, either in writing at any time or orally in the presence of two or more witnesses during his last illness, has expressed a request that his body or any specified part of his body be used after his death for therapeutic purposes or for purposes of medical education or research, the person lawfully in possession of his body after his death may, unless he has reason to believe that the request was subsequently withdrawn, authorise the removal from the body of any part or, as the case may be, the specified part, for use in accordance with the request.

(2) Without prejudice to the foregoing subsection, the person lawfully in possession of the body of a deceased person may authorise the removal of any part from the body for use for

the said purposes if, having made such reasonable enquiry as may be practicable, he has no reason to believe –

(a) that the deceased had expressed an objection to his body being so dealt with after his death, and had not withdrawn it; or

(b) that the surviving spouse or any surviving relative of the deceased objects to the body being so dealt with.

(3) Subject to subsections (4) and (5) of this section, the removal and use of any part of a body in accordance with an authority given in pursuance of this section shall be lawful.

(4) No such removal shall be effected except by a fully registered medical practitioner, who must have satisfied himself by personal examination of the body that life is extinct.

(4A) No such removal of an eye or part of an eye shall be effected except by –

(a) a registered medical practitioner, who must have satisfied himself by personal examination of the body that life is extinct; or

(b) a person in the employment of a health authority, Primary Care Trust or NHS trust acting on the instructions of a registered medical practitioner who must, before giving those instructions, be satisfied that the person in question is sufficiently qualified and trained to perform the removal competently and must also either –

(i) have satisfied himself by personal examination of the body that life is extinct, or

(ii) be satisfied that life is extinct on the basis of a statement to that effect by a registered medical practitioner who has satisfied himself by personal examination of the body that life is extinct.

(5) Where a person has reason to believe that an inquest may be required to be held on any body or that a post-mortem examination of any body may be required by the coroner, he shall not, except with the consent of the coroner, –

(a) give an authority under this section in respect of the body; or

(b) act on such an authority given by any other person.

(6) No authority shall be given under this section in respect of any body by a person entrusted with the body for the purpose only of its interment or cremation.

(7) In the case of a body lying in a hospital, nursing home or other institution, any authority under this section may be given on behalf of the person having the control and management thereof by any officer or person designated for that purpose by the first-mentioned person.

(8) Nothing in this section shall be construed as rendering unlawful any dealing with, or with any part of, the body of a deceased person which is lawful apart from the Act.

1. Authorisation of removal

By way of preliminary it should be noticed that the donation may be for one (or more) of *three* purposes: *therapeutic, medical education* or *research*. Clearly more than transplantation is contemplated. Usually these terms will not cause difficulty. It would be unduly restrictive to read "medical education" too narrowly. It should be taken to include education of health professionals in general, for example, nurses etc (see PDG Skegg, "The Use of Corpses for Medical Education and Research: The Legal Requirements" (1991) 31 Medicine, Science and Law 345 at 346–347). Also, it does not seem that 'research' is restricted to *medical* research although instances where it will not be so must be exceedingly rare.

(a) Donation under section 1(1)

The requirements to be satisfied are as follows:

(i) request by deceased prior to death;
(ii) in the appropriate form;
(iii) no withdrawal of request;
(iv) life is extinct;
(v) an authorisation within s 1(1):
  – by a person lawfully in possession;
  – concerning the removal of that specified in s 1(1).

In considering these requirements it is important to notice that the drafting of the Act gives rise to a number of problems of interpretation but there are no cases to assist us.

(i)   REQUEST BY DECEASED

To be valid the request must have been made by a competent person. The precise nature of competence is not specified in the Act. An analogy may be drawn with capacity to make a valid will. Cockburn CJ put it as follows in *Banks v Goodfellow* (1870) LR 5 QB 549 at 567:

> ... [H]e ought to be capable of making his will with an understanding of the nature of the business in which he is engaged, a recollection of the property he means to dispose of, of the persons who are the objects of his bounty, and the manner in which it is to be distributed between them. It is not necessary that he should view his will with the eye of a lawyer, and comprehend its provisions in their legal form. It is sufficient if he has such a mind and memory as will enable him to understand the elements of which it is composed, and the disposition of his property in its simple forms.

An English court could insist upon this level of comprehension. Perhaps the better approach would be that which we suggested as regards making a valid request under the Data Protection Act 1998 (*supra*, ch 7). In *Re K* [1988] Ch 310, [1988] 1 All ER 358, Hoffmann J asked the question whether a power of attorney created under the Enduring Powers of Attorney Act 1985 was 'valid if the donor understood the nature and effect of an enduring power of attorney notwithstanding that she was at the time of its execution incapable by reason of mental disorder of managing her property and affairs' (at 360–361). He concluded that: '[I]n principle ... an understanding of the nature and effect of the power [ie the transaction] was sufficient for its validity' (at 361).

A related question is whether the provisions of the Wills Act 1837, s 7 requiring that the testator be 18 or over, would be applicable by analogy here? David Lanham argues otherwise, and we agree.

D Lanham 'Transplants and the Human Tissue Act 1961' (1971) 11 Med Sci Law 16

> There is no mention in the Act of any age limit within which it is possible to make a request. At the committee stage in the House of Commons Mr Page raised the problem of the age of consent. He asked whether a request by a teenager would be sufficient under the section and suggested a provision that a request could be made on behalf of very young children by the guardian (HC Deb, Vol 643, col 839). The Ministry of Health in a brief reply (*ibid.*, col 846) said that there was no age limit. No special provision was made to cover the position of very young children. The solution is probably that if a child is old enough to understand the position sufficiently to make the request, the request is valid for section 1(1). If the child is not old enough, section 1(1) will not be applicable and authorisation will have to be made under section 1(2).

That a competent child may make a request is recognised in the Department of Health's *Code of Practice for the Diagnosis of Brain Stem Death* (1998). Paragraph 8.10, so far as relevant, provides:

> **8.10 Children.** It will be unusual for a child to have requested in advance that his organs or tissue be used for transplantation. In such a case, however, providing the child is of an age when it is reasonable to believe he or she would have understood what that involved, the designated person is entitled to authorise removal in accordance with the request as if the child were an adult. Even where the child has made such a request, enquiry should be made to the parents as a matter of good practice.

Acting on a child's request is not, of course, without its difficulties. Price and Garwood-Gowers comment as follows and suggest an alternative which would require the legislation to be amended.

David P T Price and Austen Garwood-Gowers 'Transplantation from Minors: Are Children Other People's Medicine? (1995) 1 Contemporary Issues in Law 1

However, there are difficulties attached to the notion of competence in this context. In the scenario of ordinary medical procedures being recommended to a patient, the patient has to make a decision in the presence of the health professional(s) concerned and competence can be assessed at that point. With regard to a request to donate after death this decision may be made privately at any time by the completion and signing of a donor card for instance. It is the signatory's competence at that moment which is crucial. Any assessment of competence would presumably have to be made retrospectively in such a situation. But how could this be reliable? Even if relatives could help in providing evidence of his/her general competence at that time this might not be sufficient and anyhow such an enquiry would have to be conducted speedily in order for a body organ to remain viable.

The above difficulties lean us toward the desirability of a fixed age in this context, in the interests of certainty and reliability. This age should be fixed below the age of majority. Indeed, the age of consent for medical treatment is generally 16. The age for transplant purposes ought to be 16 or less – the view taken by these authors is that it should be fixed at 14, as for living organ donation. The advantage would be further promotion of respect of autonomy. The wishes and preferences of adolescents would generally determine the fate of their bodies after death rather than solely those of relatives, hospital administrators and health professionals. Fourteen year olds and over would be presumed to be competent, whereas a test of Gillick competence would place the burden on those representing the deceased minor to establish the competence of the minor at the time of the decision to allow his/her organs to be removed after death – a potentially difficult thing to satisfy.

Whilst the need for certainty which they identify is desirable and is found, for example, in the Wills Act 1831, which requires that the testator must be 18 (s 7), the difficulty they identify may not be insuperable and is no different from that which arises when the validity of an advance refusal of medical treatment is in issue (see *supra*, ch 5). Perhaps, the recommendation in the DoH *Code of Practice* to consult the relatives provides some assistance in practice.

(ii) APPROPRIATE FORM

Given that the request may be made in writing, some concern has been expressed as to whether a printed card (a donor card) comes within the terms of the Act. It may well be that Parliament had in mind that the request be written by hand. However, such a narrow view (excluding all cases of printed requests) would probably be rejected by a court as out of touch with modern society. The British Transplant Society took the view that in addition to amending s 1(2) of the Act (on which see *infra*), the following new subsection should be added:

For the avoidance of doubt in the interpretation of this section it is hereby declared:
... that a printed but personally signed donor card or other document, is 'in writing' for the purpose of subsection 1 of this section.

A further question is whether the request in writing must be signed. Again the statute is silent on the matter. Arguably the purpose of the statute would be defeated if a court interpreted 'in writing' as demanding a signature. Inclusion on the NHS Organ Donor Register, a computer database, would suffice for the Act's requirement.

Finally, if the request is made orally it must be made in the presence of two or more witnesses and during the 'last illness' of the deceased. Ordinarily this would pose problems of interpretation but since the request only falls to be considered after death, hindsight will often resolve the question. 'Last illness' must, of course, refer to the illness which resulted in, or contributed to, the death. The point is that the request was made in contemplation of death. It seems reasonable, therefore, to interpret the provision as requiring that the deceased knew, at least, of his illness if not of its prognosis. He need not necessarily, be on his 'death bed'. Equally, it would not suffice if the request was made during an illness which, as a matter of fact, the deceased recovered from, only to die from an unrelated event, for example, in a road accident.

(iii) WITHDRAWAL OF REQUEST

Lanham in 'Transplants and the Human Tissue Act 1961' (*op cit*) at p 7, writes as follows:

> If the person who is lawfully in possession of the body has reason to believe that the request has been withdrawn, he is not permitted to authorise the removal and use of the body in accordance with the request. No form of withdrawal is specified, so that the request can be withdrawn orally even if it was given in writing. Nor if the withdrawal is oral need it be made in the presence of two witnesses. It will only operate, however, if it is communicated in some way to the person who becomes the person lawfully in possession of the body, since the original request is effective unless the person lawfully in possession does have reason to believe that the request has been withdrawn. If the patient changes his mind again after withdrawing the request, he must presumably renew his request in writing or in the presence of two or more witnesses. There appears, however, to be no duty upon the person lawfully in possession to make inquiries about whether a request once given had been withdrawn ... It is presumably for any person knowing of the withdrawal to acquaint the person lawfully in possession of the body with the fact of withdrawal.

We agree with Professor Lanham's analysis and would add some further points. First, s 1(1) does not indicate whether the withdrawal must have been made whilst the deceased was competent. Can a competent request be 'withdrawn' by an incompetent individual? Logically, of course, it cannot. As we indicated earlier, a 'request' must be made by a competent person because otherwise it is legally not a valid request at all. The same must go for a 'withdrawal'.

Secondly, the views of the deceased's relatives or their objections to removal of the body part are irrelevant under s 1(1) except to the extent that they communicate to the person lawfully in possession that the deceased withdrew his request. As the DoH *Code of Practice* points out, it will nevertheless be good practice to consult the relatives or partner. Paragraph 8.2 of the *Code* provides:

> ... If a relative or partner objects despite the known request by the patient, staff will need to judge according to the circumstances of the case whether it is wise to proceed with organ removal. Staff need to consider the feelings of relatives, who may be under great stress, so that in practice any objections raised by relatives usually take priority over donor's wishes.

Finally, s 1(1) does not require that the person lawfully in possession should know for certain that the deceased's request was withdrawn. Section 1(1) only requires that he must not have 'reason to believe' that it was withdrawn. It would be sufficient if the person lawfully in possession had evidence that should lead him to conclude that the deceased's request was withdrawn, ie actual knowledge of facts which would lead a reasonable person to that conclusion.

(iv) LIFE IS EXTINCT

The obvious importance of this is reflected in the fact that there is a further specific provision in s 1(4) that death be established by personal examination of the body by the transplant surgeon. The only exception to this is found in s 1(4A), which was added by the Corneal Tissue Act 1986. This allows for the removal of eyes (or parts of eyes) by an appropriately qualified employee of a Health Authority, Primary Care Trust or NHS Trust where he acts on the instructions of a doctor who has satisfied himself by personal examination that the person is dead and has told the technician.

Prima facie this means that the death of the donor should first be established by those caring for the patient/donor using the established criteria and procedures for determining death (see *infra*, ch 18). Then, for a second time, death must be determined to have occurred by the transplant surgeon. Because of the development of ventilators and other means of life-support, the determination of death is not incompatible with the continued presence of heartbeat and respiration (see *infra*, ch 18). This gives rise to the so-called 'beating heart cadaver' whereby an organ can be removed from a corpse, the heart and respiration of which is artificially maintained after the declaration of death so as to preserve the organ's viability prior to transplant.

The Act requires the transplant surgeon to be satisfied by 'personal examination' of the body. On the face of it, he could only be satisfied that 'life is extinct' in such a case if he carries out the 'brain-stem' tests himself or witnesses them being carried out. It would not be sufficient if he acted on the 'say so' of the patient/donor's carers alone. The DoH *Code of Practice* is slightly more ambiguous and states that he must reach his determination 'on the basis of his examination, and the results of any tests diagnostic of brain-stem death made by other doctors' (para 9.4). This could mean that he should carry out the second set of tests required to determine 'brain-stem' death (see *infra*, ch 18). However, it cannot be so because the *Code* requires that the diagnosis of death be made by competent practitioners who are 'not members of the transplant team' (para 3.3). The transplant surgeon's task must, therefore, be to carry out a third set of tests ('the personal examination of the body') which, if consistent with a diagnosis of 'brain-stem' death, and when taken with the earlier sets of tests, may lead him to be satisfied that 'life is extinct'.

(v) AN AUTHORISATION WITHIN SECTION 1(1)

I. 'Lawfully in possession'

The authorisation for the removal of an organ must be given by a person lawfully in possession of the corpse. The meaning of this phrase is explained by David Lanham:

D Lanham 'Transplants and the Human Tissue Act 1961' (1971) 11 Med Sci Law 16

It is almost commonplace knowledge that in general a dead body cannot be owned. This means that at common law a body cannot be stolen. The law does, however, recognise a right to possession of a dead body and is prepared to protect that possession. Possession is one of the most difficult concepts of the law and it is perhaps not surprising that there has been some doubt as to its meaning under the Human Tissue Act 1961.

The leading case of possession of a dead body is *Williams v Williams* (1882) 20 Ch D 659 where Kay J held that the deceased's executors were lawfully entitled to the possession of his body. If the deceased has died intestate, his administrators will then be entitled to possession. In *R v Fox* (1841) 2 QB 246 the executors were able to enforce their right to possession against a gaoler who refused to deliver up the body of a deceased prisoner unless the executors first satisfied certain claims made by the gaoler against the deceased. But the fact that the executors or administrators have a better right than the person in whose custody the body is does not mean that the latter person is not lawfully in possession until the executors claim their right.

That person other than the executors or administrators might lawfully be in possession of the body was recognised in *R v Feist* (1858) Dears & B 590 where it was held that the master of a workhouse was a person having lawful possession of the body of a deceased pauper for the purposes of permitting the body to undergo anatomical examination under the Anatomy Act 1832. The case has been criticised (see *Russell on Crime*, 12th edn, p 1419) on the ground that the master of the workhouse was merely the servant of the poor law authority and that possession of the workhouse was in the latter body. Even if the criticism is valid it does not affect the principle that a person other than the executor or administrator may be lawfully in possession of a dead body.

If it be accepted that a person other than the executor may be lawfully in possession of a dead body certain cases at common law indicate the persons who are in possession in different circumstances. In *Williams v Williams* (*supra*) the executors' right to possession of the body was linked with the responsibility for its burial. In the cases below responsibility for burial was established, and by parity of reasoning those under the duty to bury must have had the right to possession of the body.

In *Ambrose v Kerrison* (1851) 10 CB 776 it was held that a husband was under a duty to dispose of the body of his deceased wife even though he was separated from her. Jarvis CJ expressly likened the position of the husband to that of an executor. The case was followed in *Bradshaw v Beard* (1862) 12 CBNS 344. It was held in *R v Vann* (1851) 2 Den 325 that a father was under a duty to dispose of the body of his deceased child if he had the means to do so, and in *R v Stewart* (1840) 12 Ad & El 773 it was said that every householder in whose house a person died was bound to arrange for the burial of the body.

As might be expected, any statement of general principles is lacking in the cases referred to above. it is submitted, however, that the person who has actual physical custody of the body has lawful possession (and the duty of disposal) of it until someone with a higher right (eg an executor or parent) claims the body. Though in no way authoritative in court, the following statement in *Hansard*, HC Deb Vol 643, col 835, seems to represent the law: 'In the absence of executors there is a common law duty to see that the body is buried and the person lawfully in possession is normally the occupier of the premises where the body lies, or the person who has the body.'

One particular aspect of very great importance in the present context is the legal position when a person dies in hospital. When the Human Tissue Bill was passing through Parliament it was said that 50 per cent of the deaths in this country occur in hospital. It would appear on the general principles discussed above that where a person dies in hospital the hospital management committee or board of governors are legally in possession of the body until someone with a better title to possession (eg an executor) claims it. When the Bill was in committee in the House of Commons, an amendment was moved to make it clear beyond any doubt that where a body lay in a hospital the person having control of the management of the hospital was lawfully in possession. The Government resisted the amendment on the ground that it might be interpreted as giving the hospital authorities a right to possession enforceable against executors. (HC Deb, Vol 643, col 836.) Nonetheless it seems clear at common law that the hospital authorities are lawfully in possession of the body and this position is impliedly confirmed by section 1(7) of the 1961 Act – 'In the case of a body lying in a hospital, nursing home or other institution, any authority under this section may be given on behalf of the person having the control and management thereof by any officer or person designated for that purpose by the first-mentioned person.' This provision clearly assumes that the hospital authorities are normally in possession of a body lying in hospital and provides a convenient system whereby a designated person (eg the medical superintendent) may carry out the function of the person lawfully in possession. …

Despite the seemingly overwhelming case for arguing that the hospital authority is capable of being lawfully in possession of the deceased's body, Dr Addison, in his letter to the *British Medical Journal* [(1968) 1 Br Med J 516] says that the Medical Defence Union has been advised by leading counsel that, save in the exceptional case, the hospital where a patient dies is not lawfully in possession of the body for the purposes of the Act. It is respectfully suggested that, at least in the context of the road accident victim, counsel is wrong.

The strongest case is one in which the person who dies in hospital dies intestate and without a spouse or relatives. In such a case there is no one at the time of death with a better right to possession than the hospital and it cannot be doubted that the hospital is lawfully in possession of the body. But even if there is someone with a better right to possession than the hospital, it does not follow that he is in possession as soon as the patient dies. Suppose the patient has made a will naming executors. The executors will have a better right to possession than the hospital, but at the time of the patient's death they may not even know that there is a body over which they have a right to possession. Without knowledge they cannot have the intention to possess and so one of the elements normally required for the acquisition of possession is missing. The same holds true if the person leaves a widow or other surviving relatives. The cases where a person possesses objects of which he has no knowledge but which are contained in his property (eg *Elwes v Brigg Gas Co* (1886) 33 Ch D 562) are not in point and do not invalidate the general rule requiring *animus possidendi*. If Professor Woodruff's statement that many grafts are lost because next-of-kin cannot be contacted in time is right, cases in which the executors or relatives cannot be found in time can hardly be regarded as 'exceptional'. At the very least until the executors or relatives know about the death, the hospital must be regarded as lawfully in possession of the body.

In other cases there is more room for argument. Presumably the mere fact that the executors or relatives know about the death is not enough to vest possession in them. There must be an intention to possess. Furthermore that intention must presumably be communicated to the hospital, since intention by itself does not constitute possession: see *Salmond on Jurisprudence* (11th edn, p 322).

But once a person with a better right of possession communicates his intention to possess to the hospital, the hospital's authority under the 1961 Act ceases. If, as is almost certainly the case, the hospital recognises that person's right to possession, the latter becomes the possessor. While the body remains in the hospital, the hospital may also be in possession but since there will be another person lawfully in possession, his consent will be a necessary condition to the giving of authority under the Act. If on the other hand the hospital were to refuse to recognise the executor's or relative's rights (a situation which seems most unlikely), the hospital and not the executors or relatives would remain in possession, but the hospital would not then be lawfully in possession, and once again the hospital's powers under the Act would cease.

Finally, one class of person who might be regarded as lawfully in possession of the body is specifically denied the right of granting authority under the Act. Section 1(6) provides that: 'No authority shall be given under this section in respect of any body by a person entrusted with the body for the purpose only of its interment or cremation.' Accordingly, a funeral undertaker is not able to give authority as a person lawfully in possession of the body.

We agree with this analysis and the DoH *Code of Practice* (1998) confirms the view expressed by Professor Lanham (for a discussion of the 'right to possess' a body for the purposes of disposal, see *infra*, ch 18). Paragraph 5.2 provides as follows:

5.2 Person Lawfully in Possession of Body in Hospital. Under the Human Tissue Acts only the person lawfully in possession of a body or his designate can authorise the removal of organs or tissue from a body. This authorisation may be given orally. Where a dead body is in an NHS hospital or other institution, the person with control and management of the hospital or institution (such as an NHS Trust) is the person lawfully in possession of the body until such time as it is claimed by the person who has the right to possession of it for the purposes of disposal (usually the executor, administrator or next of kin of the patient) or, by reason of their statutory obligations, the Coroner or Procurator Fiscal.

The *Code* in para 5.2 goes on to recognise that a specific delegation must occur within the NHS by, for example, an internal protocol and this may include delegation to an appropriate group such as consultant clinicians in intensive care units:

The person lawfully in possession of the body has powers and duties in connection with the removal of organs. The Acts empower a health services body (whether Health Authority or NHS Trust) to designate any officer or person to act on its behalf. This Code of Practice will assume that the health services body has delegated its power in this way to an appropriate person (or persons) who will be readily available, for example the consultant clinician in charge of the patient, who will hereafter be referred to as 'the **designated person**'.

One final point: it will be noticed that the statute states that the person 'lawfully in possession' *may* authorise. It is clear, therefore, that the donor's expressed request need not necessarily be complied with, since the person lawfully in possession retains an absolute discretion. This must be right since there will be circumstances in which it would be undesirable to remove any tissue, whatever the donor's wishes.

II. Removal of that specified in section 1(1)

It will be noted that there is a discrepancy in the wording of s 1(1) between what the donor may have requested and what the person 'lawfully in possession' may authorise. The Human Tissue Act 1961, s 1(1) states (our emphasis):

1. – (1) If any person, either in writing at any time or orally in the presence of two or more witnesses during his last illness has expressed a request that *his body or any specified part of his body* be used after his death for therapeutic purposes or for purposes of medical education or research, the person lawfully in possession of his body after his death may, unless he has reason to believe that the request was subsequently withdrawn, authorise the removal from the body of *any part or, as the case may be the specified part*, for use in accordance with the request.

The upshot would appear to be that, although no problems arise in relation to transplantation where by definition only 'parts' will be removed and used, the donor may, under s 1(1), purport to leave 'his body' for purposes of medical education and research but the person lawfully in possession may only authorise the removal and use of 'part(s)' of his body. (For discussion of the use of whole bodies for educational and research purposes, see ch 18, *infra*.)

(vi) CONSENT OF THE CORONER

D Lanham 'Transplants and the Human Tissue Act 1961' (1971) 11 Med Sci Law 16

An inquest may be required where there is reasonable cause to suspect that the deceased died either a violent or unnatural death or a sudden death of which the cause is unknown or has died in prison or in such place or circumstances as to require an inquest in pursuance of any Act: [Coroners Act 1988, s 8(1)]. In the case of a sudden death of which the cause is unknown the coroner may, as an alternative, order a post mortem examination: [Coroners Act 1988, s 19] ...

The importance of these provisions in relation to organ transplants is that in practice the victims of motoring accidents may constitute an important category of potential donors and that this is the kind of case in which the coroner's consent is necessary. The attitude of coroners is therefore of great significance. In the nature of things there is no reported case giving guidance on how coroners ought to exercise their discretion.

... First, the Act itself does not state any absolute bars to the coroner's granting consent. It may be that for practical reasons it will not be possible to obtain organs from a victim of homicide in time for transplantation because of the desirability of preserving the body so far as possible intact for the post mortem examination. But there may be cases where the investigation of the causation of the injuries would in no way be impeded by the removal of organs unconnected with the injuries (eg, where the kidneys are removed in the case of fatal head injuries) and in such circumstances a coroner might be prepared to give consent. Secondly, the meaning of 'consent' is not entirely clear. An express prior consent to the removal of organs from a specified dead body is obviously adequate. But can the coroner give a general consent in advance? Can he, for instance, notify the hospitals in his area that 'in the following circumstances ... I consent to the removal of the following organs ... from any dead body over which I have jurisdiction'? Alternatively, can he delegate to his pathologist the power to give consent in certain defined circumstances? Generally when a statute confers on a public officer or body a discretion to consent to a certain course of action the discretion must be exercised on a specific application for consent and a general statement of policy is not regarded as an exercise of the discretion. ...

... Again, a person or body given discretionary powers by Parliament is generally expected to exercise those powers himself and not to delegate their exercise. But neither of these rules is absolute. A body given a discretion may sometimes 'in the honest exercise of its discretion, adopt a policy and announce it to those concerned, so long as it is ready to listen to reasons why, in an exceptional case, that policy should not be applied'; see *Schmidt v Secretary of State* [1969] 2 Ch 149 at 169. Furthermore, in one of the leading cases on delegation, *Vine v National Dock Labour Board* [1957] AC 488, Lord Somervell, far from stating an absolute rule against delegation, said (at p 512) 'In deciding whether a "person" has power to delegate one has to consider the nature of the duty and the character of the person.' For a case which illustrates the fact that the rule against delegation is not absolute see *Osgood v Nelson* (1872) LR 5 HL 636. These cases are, like those in which the general rules about fettering discretion and non-delegation are discussed, far removed from the question of the coroner's jurisdiction but it is thought they may be used to support the very beneficial practice whereby coroners give general advance consent. Provided that the coroner's policy clearly achieves the purpose of section 1(5) – to preserve relevant evidence – there is every reason why the law should recognise the legality of the practice.

In a Home Office Circular (No 65 of 1977) guidance is given to coroners in relation to organ transplants. It is discussed in the leading text on coronial law.

P Matthews and J Foreman (eds) *Jervis on the Office and Duties of Coroners – with Forms and Precedents* (11th edn, 1993)

6–57 ... the Home Office has given guidance on the circumstances in which a coroner should delay or refuse giving his consent to removal of material. The Home Office view is that, since a coroner is an impartial legal officer, he should never refuse consent on moral or ethical grounds, but only where his own functions or other legal considerations are involved. Specifically, the Home Office considers only three cases in which refusal would be proper:

(1) Where the material, consent to removal of which is sought, would have an evidential value in later criminal proceedings which the coroner is aware might take place;

(2) where death is thought to have been caused, wholly or partly, by some malfunction in the organ or other material itself;

(3)   where the coroner's own enquiries might be obstructed by such removal.

6–58   In the nature of things, material having evidential value in later criminal proceedings is likely to be damaged in some way, and thus cases where removal of such material for transplantation is sought will be few and far between. Similarly an organ which is defective and has caused the death is unlikely to be a desirable candidate for transplant. In practice, therefore, the only objection to consent which the coroner will normally be able to put forward consistently with the Home Office guidance is that in category (3) above. To the extent that this does not overlap with the other two categories, it seems to cover logistical problems (such as the need for a post-mortem examination) rather than medical or legal ones. In considering whether to object under this heading to the removal of organs, the coroner may need to consult with the pathologist and the doctor(s) who cared for the deceased before his death.

6–59   Although the coroner's discretion to consent or not appears to be absolute, in the sense that there is no appeal from his decision, there is little doubt that, as with any other coronial decision, it will be subject to judicial review (para 19-22). The court in a proper case could quash the coroner's decision, but not (of course) substitute its own. If a coroner persisted in making perverse decisions, the only solution would appear to be to remove him for misbehaviour (para 3-15).

(b) Donation under section 1(2)

The Human Tissue Act 1961, s 1(2) provides:

> Without prejudice to the foregoing subsection, the person lawfully in possession of the body of a deceased person may authorise the removal of any part from the body for use for the said purposes if, having made such reasonable enquiry as may be practicable, he has no reason to believe –
> (a) that the deceased had expressed an objection to his body being so dealt with after his death, and had not withdrawn it; or
> (b) that the surviving spouse or any surviving relative of the deceased objects to the body being so dealt with.

The requirements to be satisfied under s 1(2) are largely those already considered, ie the requirements relating to: (a) the persons lawfully in possession; (b) the need for a deceased person; (c) removal of only a part or parts of the body.

There are, in addition, other requirements which only arise in s 1(2). These relate to the following statutory words:
(i)   'having made such reasonable enquiry as may be practicable';
(ii) 'the person lawfully in possession has no reason to believe …';
(iii) 'that the deceased has (not) expressed an objection';
(iv) 'that the surviving spouse or any surviving relative …';
(v)   'that the surviving spouse or any surviving relative "*objects*"';
These are considered separately below.

(i)   'HAVING MADE SUCH REASONABLE ENQUIRY AS MAY BE PRACTICABLE'

Professor Peter Skegg examines this requirement in the following paper.

P Skegg 'Human Tissue Act 1961' (1976) 16 Med Sci Law 197

Had it been so desired, s 1(2) could easily have specified that the person lawfully in possession of the body should never authorise the removal of parts of it unless the surviving spouse, and any relatives of the deceased, had agreed to this being done. But s 1(2) imposes no such requirement. Nor does it require the person lawfully in possession of the body to make all possible enquiries whether there is a relevant objection. He need only make 'such reasonable enquiry as may be practicable'.

If the requirement of reasonable enquiries stood on its own, there could clearly be considerable discussion of the extent to which the impracticability of an enquiry should be given weight in determining whether that enquiry was 'reasonable'. However, as s 1(2) requires, not the making of all reasonable enquiries, but only 'such reasonable enquiry as may be practicable', that consideration need not be pursued at this stage. Putting aside the issue of practicability, what enquiries are reasonable?

In determining whether the person lawfully in possession of the body has made reasonable enquiries, some weight must clearly be given to the resources – both in terms of finance and manpower – available to him, and to the other claims on those resources. Where a hospital authority is the person lawfully in possession of a body, it is clearly not reasonable for all other administrative activities to cease for a day, while staff assist in an enquiry as to whether any one of the dozens of traceable relatives of the deceased has any objection to the removal of a pituitary gland for research purposes, or an eye for corneal transplantation. Where the newly bereft spouse or parent is the person lawfully in possession of the body, he or she can hardly be expected to spend many hours telephoning distant relatives, with whom they may have had no contact for years, enquiring whether they have any objection to the removal of a specimen from the body of the deceased spouse or child.

Another factor which should be taken into account in determining the reasonableness of an enquiry is its likely utility. An enquiry would not be unreasonable because every available colleague or friend of the deceased has not been contacted, to enquire whether the deceased ever expressed an objection to the use of his body for the envisaged purpose. Although it is possible that any one of them may recall some relevant statement of the deceased, the likelihood of the enquiry producing relevant information would normally be so slight that it would not be unreasonable to omit to make it.

A third consideration in determining whether it is reasonable to enquire of a particular person is that person's age and his physical and emotional condition. It would surely be unreasonable to enquire of young children, or of someone who was critically ill as a result of the accident in which the potential donor died. It would probably also be considered unreasonable to approach a severely distressed spouse or relative, whose health could be detrimentally affected in consequence of an enquiry.

In determining what amounts to a reasonable enquiry, a court would undoubtedly give considerable weight to accepted attitudes concerning what is a reasonable enquiry. In practice, it is widely accepted that a reasonable enquiry normally requires no more than enquiring of either the spouse or a close relative whether he or she has reason to believe that the deceased had expressed an objection, or whether some other person, whose objection is relevant, objects. Even where a more extensive enquiry is practicable, this enquiry is generally regarded as reasonable (see eg HSC (IS) 156, para 11). Given this consensus, it is unlikely that a court would take a different view.

As already stressed, s 1(2) does not require the making of all reasonable enquiries. It requires only 'such reasonable enquiry as may be practicable'. The crucial issue is whether, in determining the practicability of an enquiry, it is permissible to take account of the time within which the part must be removed if it is to be of use for the desired purposes. The Long Title of the Act indicates that the main purpose of s 1 was 'to make provision with respect to the use of parts of bodies of deceased persons for therapeutic purposes and purposes of medical education and research'. The purpose of s 1(2) is not simply to allow the relative to object if he so wishes ... If it was, it would require that the person lawfully in possession of the body contact every relative and enquire whether he or she objects. As it stands, s 1(2) attempts a compromise between the interests of the parties specified and the interests of those who may benefit from the use of parts of the body. For this reason, it requires only 'such reasonable enquiry as may be practicable'. In determining the practicability of an enquiry, there is no warrant for excluding from consideration the time within which a part must be removed if it is to be of use for the intended and approved purpose. Indeed, this factor will sometimes be crucial. For example, when it is desired to remove a kidney for transplantation from a body which is not being maintained on a ventilator, it will not be practicable to make as extensive enquiries as when it is desired to remove a bone for the purpose of medical education. This is because a kidney which is left in a body for more than an hour after the cessation of respiration and circulation becomes irreversibly damaged.

The issue of whether it is permissible to take account of the time available in determining the practicability of an enquiry is closely related to, but distinct from, one other issue. This is whether the person lawfully in possession may ever give his authority without making any enquiry, on the grounds that no enquiry was both reasonable and practicable. On one view, s 1(2) requires that at least some enquiry always be made before the person lawfully in possession of the body may authorise the removal. But on another view, an enquiry need only be made if it is both reasonable and practicable to make one. On this interpretation, if no enquiry was both reasonable and practicable the person lawfully in possession of the body could still give his authority, if he had no reason to believe that there was a relevant objection. In such circumstances, s 1(2) would operate like its predecessor in the Corneal Grafting Act 1952, where there was no obligation to make an enquiry in any circumstances. If a choice must be made between these two approaches, the second seems preferable. But it may be questioned whether in practice any choice is necessary. It is difficult to envisage a situation where at least some enquiry is not both reasonable and practicable. Extensive enquiries are clearly impracticable in the case of an accident victim who is brought into hospital dead, and whose kidneys must be removed within a very short time if they are to be of use for transplantation. However, at the very least, it is always both reasonable and practicable to enquire whether the deceased is carrying on his person any indication that he expressed an objection to the proposed use of his body.

Notice the interpretation given to the important word 'practicable'. Professor Gerald Dworkin argues otherwise.

G Dworkin 'The Law Relating to Organ Transplantation in England' (1970) 33 MLR 353

… The only guidance given to the hospital is that it may act provided it has made such reasonable inquiry as may be practicable. … [The argument that] it would not be practicable to spend too long trying to trace relatives since the body must be used within a short time after death would not be decisive. The practicability of the inquiry must relate to the steps taken to trace the relatives not to the practicability of using the body, since the basis of the provision is to allow the relative to object if he so wishes. Where a close relative is available and does not object then the medical authorities are on slightly safer ground in proceeding in spite of the possibility that other relatives who were within the range of immediate contact and who were not consulted might object and claim that the use of the body was unlawful. It is clear, however, that a hospital will rarely be in a position to guarantee that it has made all reasonable inquiries if the body is used within a few hours of death.

On balance, in our view Professor Dworkin's view of the likely interpretation of the word 'practicable' more closely reflects the intent behind, and the structure of, s 1(2).

The DoH *Code of Practice* (1998) seeks to give guidance on the scope of the duty to enquire. Paragraph 8.8 states:

8.8 … In most instances it would be sufficient to discuss the matter with any one relative who has been in close contact with the deceased, determining whether there is reason to believe that any other relative or partner would be likely to object. There is no need to establish a lack of objection from all relatives before authorising the removal of organs.

Professor Skegg in his article argues that in some circumstances it would be permissible to give an authorisation under s 1(2) without making *any* inquiries. This is acknowledged in the DoH *Code of Practice* (1998), correctly we would suggest.

8.9 Authorisation in the Absence of Relatives. If a donor's relatives are unavailable it would be impracticable to ask them and if they were, for example, young children or very seriously ill it would generally be unreasonable to do so. In such circumstances the *designated person* can proceed to give authorisation if there is no reason to believe that there is a relevant objection but a note of the enquiries made should be entered on the transplantation check list … In those rare occasions where there are no existing relatives, the relatives cannot be traced or the potential donor is unidentified, removal of organs may be authorised by the person lawfully in possession of the body. If the responsible authority has delegated this responsibility to the clinical consultant in charge of the patient's care it is good practice to discuss the issue of organ removal with an appropriate colleague.

(ii) 'THE PERSON LAWFULLY IN POSSESSION HAS NO REASON TO BELIEVE …'

These words may call for a somewhat different interpretation in sub-s (2) than in sub-s (1). As regards sub-s (2), there can be no doubt that the person lawfully in possession is under a duty to inquire so as to enable him to conclude that there is no reason to believe that an objection has not been made (or would not be made). Subsection (1) makes no specific reference to an 'inquiry' such that it is less clear there that having 'a reason to believe' involves the obligation to seek out information. In contrast to s 1(2), therefore, it is our view that under s 1(1) the person lawfully in possession of a body can act provided he does not have actual (or possibly, constructive) knowledge that a request has been withdrawn from the information already available to him. Notice that the Act does not require that the person 'lawfully in possession' should personally inquire of the relatives. This will normally be done by others, nurses and transplant co-ordinators. It suffices that the person 'lawfully in possession' is satisfied that such inquiries have been properly carried out (see DoH *Code of Practice* (1998) para 8.3).

(iii) 'THAT THE DECEASED HAS (NOT) EXPRESSED AN OBJECTION'

The short point here is that the statute is silent as to the form in which the objection must be expressed. It could be argued that a written objection is required for the sake of certainty. However, as we have seen, wherever writing was thought necessary by Parliament it was so stated, eg a written request in s 1(1).

Any objection by the deceased must have been actually 'expressed' in order to fall within s 1(2)(a). Potential objection is not contemplated, it would seem. However, a different view is apparently taken in the DoH *Code of Practice* (1998). In paragraph 8.9 it is stated:

Cases when a potential donor's views about organ removal cannot be established and the relatives cannot be contacted are exceptional, but it is reasonable to assume in such cases that if a donor has belonged to a religious group which objects to the removal of organs from the body, he himself would have objected.

Seen as a matter of 'good practice', this may well be appropriate. Seen as a legal impediment to authorisation by the person 'lawfully in possession', it is more problematic as no objection was 'expressed' by the deceased. It seems he only *would have* objected if asked. Only if an inference could be drawn that he must have expressed an objection because of his religious beliefs would this be an objection falling within s 1(2)(a).

Finally, notice the objection by the deceased under s 1(2)(a) (or by the surviving spouse or relatives under s 1(2)(b)) may be general or specific. Thus, it may relate to the removal of all (or specific) parts of the body. Also, it may be an objection to removal for any of the stated purposes (therapeutic, education or research) or for a specific use, for example, research.

The person 'lawfully in possession' may only authorise removal consistently with the objection that the deceased (or others) have expressed.

(iv) 'THAT THE SURVIVING SPOUSE OR ANY SURVIVING RELATIVE (HAS NOT OBJECTED)'

Usually it will be legally and factually clear who are the deceased's surviving spouse and relatives. Obviously, widows, widowers and the parents of dead children are covered.

Peter Skegg 'Human Tissue Act 1961' (1976) 16 Med Sci Law 197

… The Act does not provide any definition of 'relative', but the separate reference to 'any surviving spouse' lends support to the view that in this context 'relative' does not include persons to whom the deceased was related only by marriage. The courts have given a restrictive interpretation to 'relative' or 'relation' when used by a testator in his will (see eg *Anon* (1716) 1 P Wms 327; *Eagles v Le Breton* (1873) 42 LJ Ch 362 at 363; *Re Bridgen, Chaytor v Edwin* [1938] Ch 205 at 208–210). However, this is because 'else it would be uncertain; for the relation may be infinite' (*anon, supra*), and it would be unwise to assume that 'relative' would be interpreted in a limited sense in this context. The original Memorandum on the Act advised hospital authorities of the Minister's opinion that the word should be interpreted in its widest sense, to include those who claim quite a distant relationship with the deceased (HM (61) 98, para 8). The recent Guidance Circular was more equivocal. It simply advised that there are 'some circumstances' in which 'relative' should be interpreted 'in the widest sense, eg to include those who although claiming only a distant relationship are nevertheless closely connected with the deceased' (HSC (IS)

156, para 11). In fact, there is no warrant for interpreting the word differently according to the circumstances. The Circular appears to confuse the issue of who is a relative with the issue of whether it is reasonable and practicable to enquire of a particular relative.

Professor Skegg must be correct and the 1998 *Code of Practice* (para 8.8) which replace the HSC referred to, is, it is suggested, addressing the scope of the obligation to inquire (see *supra*).

Whatever breadth of meaning is given to 'relative' it cannot, however, cover the deceased's unmarried partner of whatever gender. Of course, consultations with them may be good practice and appropriate (see DoH *Code of Practice* (1998) para 8.4). Their personal objection to the donation would be irrelevant under the Act. If, however, they provide information that the deceased did object then this will prevent the person lawfully in possession giving authorisation inconsistent with the objection: who communicates this to him is unimportant.

(v) 'OBJECTS'

Peter Skegg in his paper 'Human Tissue Act 1961' (*op cit*) analyses this requirement:

> It has been said that, 'You cannot consent to a thing unless you have knowledge of it' (*Re Caughey, ex p Ford* (1876) 1 Ch D 521 at 528 per Jessel MR). Similarly, it could be said that a person cannot object to something being done unless he is aware of the proposal to do it (cf. *R v Feist, supra*). But it may also be argued that a person can have a sufficiently clear and consistent attitude to certain conduct for it to be said that he 'objects' to it, even though he is ignorant of a particular proposal to act. Even on this broader interpretation of 'objects', there would still be many people who could not be said to object, even though on being informed of a particular proposal they might well object. The problem in practice is that the person lawfully in possession of the body could not know into which category of actual or potential objector a spouse or relative came. At present, it would be wise to act as if s 1(2)(b) read 'objects *or* would object', rather than simply 'objects'.

This view that s 1(2)(b) contemplates *potential* objection by the surviving spouse or relatives is to be preferred, notwithstanding Professor Skegg's more narrow reading of the statute in other contexts. (Contrast an objection by the deceased under s 1(2)(a) – '*expressed* an objection', *supra*).

2. Failure to comply with the Human Tissue Act 1961

All that has gone before in our analysis of the Human Tissue Act 1961 rests in part, at least, on the assumption that someone aggrieved at a failure properly to comply with the terms of the Act can in law do something about it. Curiously, this is at the same time the most important question and yet the most neglected. It is commonly assumed that if the Act is not complied with 'something can be done', but we must examine this premise closely.

(a) Criminal law

(i) THE COMMON LAW

Peter Skegg 'Liability for the Unauthorized Removal of Cadaveric Transplant Material' (1974) 14 Med Sci Law 53

> It has long been established that it is a common law crime to prevent the disposal of a corpse by detaining it for a claim upon a debt (*R v Scott* (1842) 2 QB 248) or by selling it when retained and employed to bury it (*R v Cundick* (1822) Dow & Ry NP 13). As it seems that there is a more general offence of preventing the lawful disposal of the body (see *R v Young* (1784) 4 Wentworth's System of Pleading 219, which appears to be the case referred to in *R v Lynn; R v Hunter* [1974] QB 95) the question arises whether, by removing transplant material, a donor could be said to

prevent the disposal of the body. If the removal involved the retention of the whole body, despite the request of the person entitled to possession that the body be delivered up to him, then the doctor would almost certainly incur liability. However, so long as that which was available for disposal was recognizable as the body of the deceased it is doubtful whether the unauthorized retention of internal parts of the body could be said to prevent the disposal of the body. Doctors often retain parts of bodies after post-mortem examinations – indeed, where sufficient material is retained after an official post-mortem examination, coroners sometimes permit the disposal of the corpse before inquiries into the death are completed. It does not appear to have been suggested that by retaining parts of a body a doctor prevents the disposal of the corpse. The unauthorized removal and retention of transplant material would, therefore, be unlikely to amount to a common law crime of preventing disposal of the body, much less to the narrower statutory crime of wilfully obstructing a burial (Burial Laws Amendment Act 1880, s 7).

There are *dicta* to the effect that the common law will not allow any indecent interference with the bodies of the dead (eg, *Foster v Dodd* (1866) LR 1 QB 475 at 485). The cases along these lines have all concerned interferences with bodies after burial, but the courts might well hold that certain interferences with dead bodies at any earlier stage also constitute a common law crime. Touching of a sexual nature and pointless mutilation might be held to amount to such a crime. For the present purpose, the important question is whether unauthorized interferences with an unburied corpse for medical purposes would amount to a common law crime. Although the means by which bodies used to be acquired for the practice of anatomy were sometimes unlawful, there is reason to believe that the practice of anatomy was itself perfectly lawful at common law (Anatomy Act 1832, Preamble; *R v Price* (1884) 12 QBD 251 at 252, 253; *R v Feist* (1858) Dears & B 590 at 594–5, *in arguendo*). This being so, the very much more limited interference with a body involved in the removal of organs or tissues for transplantation, should not amount to any common law crime of indecent or improper interference with a corpse.

Arguably, the last suggestion of Professor Skegg can be dealt with by noticing that the transplant doctor will lack the necessary intention to act indecently (for a discussion of the legality of anatomy, see *infra*, ch 18).

(ii) UNDER THE ACT

The Human Tissue Act 1961 does not itself provide for any sanction for failure to comply with its terms. However, the suggestion has been put that the ancient crime of disobedience of a statute may be relevant, which is a common law crime.

R v Lennox-Wright [1973] Crim LR 529 (CCC)

HH Judge Lawson QC: The defendant, who had taken and failed two medical examinations abroad, gained admission to the ophthalmic department of an English hospital by means of false representations, and a forged document which purported to show that he had qualified as an MD of Louvain University in Belgium.

In the course of his work at the hospital, he removed the eyes from a dead body for their further use in a different hospital. He was charged *inter alia*, with (after amendment): 'Doing an act in disobedience of a statute by removing parts of a dead body, contrary to section 1(4) of the Human Tissue Act 1961'.

The Human Tissue Act 1961, makes provision for the use of parts of bodies of deceased persons for therapeutic purposes and purposes of medical education and research and with respect to the circumstances in which the removal of parts of a body may be carried out. Section 1(4) of the Act provides that: 'No such removal shall be effected except by a fully registered medical practitioner, who must have satisfied himself by personal examination of the body that life is extinct'.

On a motion to quash the count it was contended by the defence that the Act was merely regulatory and created no offence; and that the Act provided no punishment for contravening section 1(4).

Held, (1) The law was well settled that if a statute prohibits a matter of public grievance to the liberties and securities of the subject or commands a matter of public convenience (such as repairing of highways or the like) all acts or omissions contrary to the prohibitions or command of the statute are misdemeanours at common law punishable by indictment unless such method manifestly appears to be excluded by statute. (2 Hawkins, c 25, s 4; *R v Hall* [1891] 1 QB 747; *R v Wright* (1841) 9 C & P 754.) See paragraph 6 of *Archbold*.

(2) It followed that the punishment was governed by the common law and therefore an unlimited term of imprisonment or an unlimited fine could apply.

Professor Sir John Smith in his Commentary [1973] Crim LR 529 wrote:

> According to Stephen, *Digest of the Criminal Law*, Art 152: 'Every one commits a
> misdemeanour who wilfully disobeys any statute of the realm by doing any act which it
> forbids, or by omitting to do any act which it requires to be done, and which concerns the
> public or any part of the public, unless it appears from the statute that it was the intention of
> the Legislature to provide some other penalty for such disobedience.'
>
> It is usual at the present day for Parliament, when it intends to create a criminal offence,
> expressly so to provide and to lay down a maximum punishment for the offence. So common
> is this practice that it might be thought that, when Parliament does not provide in express
> terms for a criminal sanction at the present day, none is intended. This is particularly so
> since the effect of applying the principle stated above is that the offence is a misdemeanour
> triable on indictment and punishable with fine and imprisonment at the discretion of the
> court.

Section 1(8) of the Human Tissue Act provides:

> Nothing in this section shall be construed as rendering unlawful any dealing with, or with
> any part of, the body of a deceased person which is lawful apart from this Act.

Is the effect of s 1(8) that even if *R v Lennox-Wright* is correct, *viz* that there is a
common law crime of failing to obey a statute, it has no application to the Human
Tissue Act? Now the matter seems beyond dispute, since the case of *R v Horseferry
Road Justices, ex p Independent Broadcasting Authority* [1987] QB 54, [1986]
2 All ER 666 shows that the ancient crime does not have much life, if any, left in
it and certainly does not apply in the case of the Human Tissue Act.

R v Horseferry Road Justices, ex parte Independent Broadcasting Authority [1987] QB 54, [1986] 2 All ER 666 (Div Ct)

Lloyd LJ: In 1976 the Law Commission in their Report on Conspiracy and Criminal Law Reform
(HC Paper (1975–76) no 176) p 140 para 6.1 described the 'doctrine' of contempt of statute as
obsolete, but not dead. They recommended that the doctrine be abolished (p 142, para 6.5):

> In essence [they said] this is a matter of statutory construction; and the modern approach
> would, we think, be to ask whether, in the absence of an express provision making
> particular conduct an offence, there was any intent by Parliament to penalise that conduct.
> The answer today, we suggest, would always be in the negative ...

In *Maxwell on the Interpretation of Statutes* (12th edn, 1969) pp 334–335 it is said that the
procedure by way of indictment for breach of a statutory duty is never used today.

How then does the matter stand? The one thing which to my mind emerges clearly from all
the authorities to which I have referred and in particular from the qualification in *Hawkins*,
'unless such method of proceeding do manifestly appear to be excluded', is that it is a question
of construction in each case whether a breach of statutory duty for which Parliament has
provided no remedy creates an offence or not. Among the factors which will have to be
considered are: (i) whether the duty is mandatory or prohibitory; (ii) whether the statute is
ancient or modern; for in ancient statutes it was far more common than it is today for no
offence to be defined, but to leave enforcement, for example, to a common informer; and
(iii) whether there are any other means of enforcing the duty. In the case of a mandatory duty
imposed by a modern statute, enforceable by way of judicial review, the inference that
Parliament did *not* intend to create an offence in the absence of an express provision to that
effect is, nowadays, almost irresistible.

Counsel for the IBA urged us to hold that *R v Price* (1840) 11 Ad & El 727, 113 ER 590,
Rathbone v Bundock [1962] 2 All ER 257, [1962] 2 QB 260 and *R v Lennox-Wright* [1973]
Crim LR 529 were wrongly decided, if they cannot be distinguished. He argued that the rule
as stated in *Hawkins* has ceased to exist: cessante ratione legis, cessat lex ipsa. I do not find
it necessary to go that far; for, as I have said, the 'rule' or 'doctrine' never was more than a
rule of construction. It is not a substantive rule of law. The only difference between today
and 1716, when *Hawkins* was first published, is that it is easier to infer in the case of a
modern statute that Parliament does not intend to create an offence unless it says so. There is
no longer any presumption, if indeed there ever were, that a breach of duty imposed by
statute is indictable. Nowadays the presumption, if any, is the other way; although I would
prefer to say that it requires clear language, or a very clear inference, to create a crime.

(See further, P D G Skegg 'Criminal Liability for the Unauthorized Use of Corpses for Medical Education and Research' (1992) 32 Medicine, Science and the Law 51 at 52–53 and I Kennedy *Treat Me Right* (1991) ch 11, especially pp 230–233.)

(b) Tort liability

Professor Skegg examines this in the following extract:

Peter Skegg 'Liability for the Unauthorized Removal of Cadaveric Transplant Material' (1974) 14 Med Sci Law 53

There do not appear to be any reported English cases in which a plaintiff has recovered damages for an unauthorized interference with a corpse. Nor are there any established torts which are obviously applicable to such conduct.

The English courts have not recognized any property interest in a corpse (*Dr Handayside's* case (C 18), 1 Hawk. PC 148, n 8, 2 East PC 652; *R v Sharpe* (1857) Dears & B 160 at 163; *Williams v Williams* (1882) 20 Ch D 659 662–3, 665; *R v Price* (1884) 12 QBD 247 at 252); so the unauthorized removal of cadaveric transplant material would not give rise to an action in trespass to goods, conversion, or detinue (see, eg, *Dr Handayside's* case, also *Hamps v Darby* [1948] 2 KB 311 at 319, 320, 322, 328). The tort of negligence would very rarely be applicable, for the doctor would not normally owe a duty of care to the person aggrieved by the unauthorized removal (see the comments on *Owens v Liverpool Corpn* [1939] 1 KB 394 in *Bourhill v Young* [1943] AC 92 at 100, 105, 110, 116). In the rare cases where the doctor did owe such a duty, knowledge of the unauthorized removal would be unlikely to cause nervous shock, or to harm health. The innominate tort of intentional acts calculated to cause bodily injury (see *Wilkinson v Downton* [1897] 2 QB 57; *Janvier v Sweeney* [1919] 2 KB 316) would rarely, if ever, apply.

Although the courts have not recognized any property interests in the corpse of a human being, they have recognized that the person under a duty to dispose of the body has a right to possession for that purpose (eg, *R v Fox* (1841) 2 QB 246). On the principle *ubi jus ibi remedium*, an intentional and unauthorized interference with this right should render the interferer liable, at the suit of the person entitled to possession. Recovery was permitted in one Canadian case (*Edmonds v Armstrong Funeral Home Ltd* [1931] 1 DLR 676), where a doctor had made an unauthorized post-mortem examination of the corpse. The unauthorized removal of transplant material would probably also be actionable. There would not be any need to prove actual damage, although the measure of damages would obviously be greater if the plaintiff could show that he suffered in consequence of the interference. Of course, in many cases the unauthorized interference would not come to the notice of the potential plaintiff and, even if it did, it might be difficult for him to establish that he was the person entitled to possession of the corpse. If the potential plaintiff had consented to the removal of the transplant material, and the doctor had complied with any conditions he expressly or impliedly laid down, it would not be open to him to recover damages on the ground of interference with his right to possession. The fact that the doctor did not comply with the provisions of the Human Tissue Act 1961 would be irrelevant.

(See further, P D G Skegg 'Liability for the Unauthorized Removal of Cadaveric Transplant Material: Some Further Comments' (1977) 17 Med Sci Law 123.)

Professor Skegg is more optimistic about tort liability than are we (for further discussion, see *infra*, ch 18). Clearly, the deliberate removal of an organ outside the provisions of the Human Tissue Act 1961 could give rise to an action if it was intended ('calculated') to cause harm to the deceased's relatives. So much would follow from an application of *Wilkinson v Downton* [1897] 2 QB 57. Beyond that, however, any action could only be for infringement of the right to possession for the purposes of disposal of the body or in the tort of negligence where the only harm in practical terms will be psychiatric injury.

Could an infringement of the 'right' give rise to an action? One problem would, of course, be that the removal of an organ would not necessarily prevent the burial of the body in any real sense. Hence, it could be argued that, unlike keeping the whole body, for example, for anatomy, the transplant situation is not even an infringement of the right to possess the body for burial. However, leaving that aside, it could be argued that an intentional interference may be actionable (see

P D G Skegg and I Kennedy (1995) 3 Med L Rev 22 at 223). There is, it has to be said, no indication of such an action in the English case law.

As regards a negligent interference, American courts have contemplated such an action (see *Mackey v US* (1993) 8 F 3d 826 (DCC CA) and Commentary (1995) 3 Med L Rev 222 (IK)). Again, English law gives no indication but it is likely that the courts would wish to develop such claims within the confines of the framework for recovering negligently inflicted psychiatric injury (for a US case, see *Gonzalez v Metro Dade City Health Trust* (1995) 651 So 2d 673 (Fla Sup Ct) and Commentary (1996) 4 Med L Rev 216 (AG)). The limiting requirements applied by the House of Lords in *McLoughlin v O'Brian* [1983] 1 AC 410 and *Alcock v Chief Constable of the South Yorkshire Police* [1992] 1 AC 310 make it unlikely that the deceased's relatives would have a claim as 'secondary victims' unless, rather exceptionally, they were to witness the procedure. To have learnt of the unauthorised removal of an organ would not be sufficient to establish 'proximity' under the *McLoughlin/Alcock* rules. The relatives would not, of course, count as 'primary victims' regardless of their involvement in the events surrounding the death of the relative. They would have to be personally *at risk* from the procedure itself – which would not be the case (see *White v Chief Constable of the South Yorkshire Police* [1999] 1 All ER 1 (HL)).

Improving the supply of organs for transplantation

A. INTRODUCTION

It is widely perceived that there is a shortage of organs for transplantation in this country, as we saw earlier. In this section, we examine how that shortage may be overcome. The background is discussed in the following extract of a working group of the Royal Colleges chaired by Sir Raymond Hoffenberg:

Report of the Working Party on the 'Supply of Donor Organs for Transplantation' (1987)

Transplantation of the kidneys and other organs has been one of the great advances of the last quarter of a century. There is much public interest and support. Most people are prepared to give organs in appropriate circumstances, yet there is a shortfall in organ supply and a growing list for transplants. For kidneys this has risen from 2,500 to 3,500 in the last five years. The waiting lists for heart transplants, liver transplants and corneal grafts have doubled in the last two years. We, a working party from the Conference of Medical Royal Colleges and their Faculties in the UK, have been asked by the Department of Health and Social Security to find out why there is a shortfall and to make recommendations to remedy this. ...

It has been estimated that about 4,000 brain stem deaths occur each year in the United Kingdom. In 1986, 800 donors provided 1,600 kidneys and in the same year there were 200 heart, 120 liver and about 1,500 corneal donations. In the first quarter of 1987 kidney donation fell by 19.1% in comparison with the same period in 1986. Heart donations increased by 37% and liver donations by 10%, showing that there were more multiple donations from a smaller number of donors.

There are insufficient kidneys to meet the needs of those waiting for renal transplantation and for those who in succeeding years will develop renal failure. About 2,500 people start dialysis each year and this could rise to around 4,000. The projected need for kidneys, therefore, is at least 2,500 and might be as high as 4,000 each year. This could be achieved if a higher proportion of those with brain stem death were to become donors. The cost savings to the health service of a kidney transplant have recently been estimated at £30,000, this being the amount that would otherwise be spent on chronic dialysis. ...

Reasons for the shortfall

1) Lack of medical experience and knowledge
Most doctors will have little experience of brain stem death and of requesting organ donation. Knowledge of the criteria for brain stem death, of the arrangements for transplantation and of the benefit of transplantation is not universal. Skill and sensitivity in the approach to

bereaved relatives is variable. As a result there may be a reluctance to diagnose brain stem death and a failure to ask for organ donation. Some hospitals seldom provide organs for transplantation, yet when a sympathetic and experienced person talks with the relatives, permission is likely to be granted. Some hospitals have obtained 90% agreement to donation.

2)   *Doubt about the success of the transplant programme*
This should no longer be entertained since the benefits of transplantation to the majority of recipients are proven. The three-year survival rate of kidney transplants is now commonly in excess of 75%, for hearts about 75% at one year and for livers 70% at one year. The actuarial patient survival statistics for kidney recipients show a better prognosis than is experienced by patients with gastrointestinal cancer, stage II carcinoma of the breast and carcinoma of the prostate, for example. Patients with kidney transplants have been recorded to survive in good health for 25 years, liver transplants for 16 years, heart transplants for 15 years and pancreas transplants for 8 years. Lung transplants have survived up to 3 years. With improvements in tissue matching and immunosuppression in more recent years, more patients with organ transplants can be expected to survive with their transplant for long periods of time, if not for the term of their natural life. For the failing heart, liver and lung, transplantation may be the only option. For the failing kidney, transplantation provides a better quality of life at lower cost than dialysis. The public is well aware of the benefits of transplantation in adults and in children.

3)   *Doubt about the criteria for brain stem death*
The BBC Panorama programme of 1980 which cast doubt on the criteria was followed by a fall in the number of organ donations, but this has since risen and an increase of about a third followed the BBC 'That's Life' programme in 1985. In the three months since the publication of articles on brain stem death in the Sunday Times at the end of 1986, there has been a 19.1% fall in the number of kidney donations.

We have taken evidence from a physician and from an anaesthetist who are opposed to the removal of organs from heart-beating donors. They accept that the fulfilment of the criteria for brain stem death does permit withdrawal of ventilation but they believe that death only occurs when circulation and respiration cease. Further refinement of tests of brain stem function would not satisfy them that death had occurred before the heart stops beating. The difference between our views and theirs is in the concept of when death occurs.

We are convinced that the criteria for brain stem death are adequate and believe that once the brain stem is dead, sentient existence is no longer possible and that the person is dead. We do not think that electro-encephalography, four-vessel arteriography, doppler or isotope studies of cerebral blood flow would give further useful information.

We accept that a small minority of doctors and some members of the public have reservations about that concept of brain stem death despite full explanation, and that patients and their relatives must always be free to decline consent to organ donation.

The Society of British Neurological Surgeons at its meeting in April 1987 unanimously supported the view that the clinical criteria for the diagnosis of brain stem death were entirely satisfactory. There is overwhelming informed professional opinion that ventilation after death does no more than allow the heart to beat, so maintaining circulation. This makes possible the donation in good condition of kidneys, heart, lung, liver and pancreas.

4)   *Demand for intensive care beds*
It is not possible to transfer to intensive care units all those who might become brain stem dead. Transfer and treatment should be in the interest of the patient. A possible exception is when relatives have particularly requested organ donation. If there is an insufficient number of staffed intensive care beds for all those who require intensive care, organ donation will be reduced. Many clinicians in charge of intensive care units agree that given more beds, equipment and staff, more potential donors could be managed.

5)   *Constraints of time*
It may take several hours to discuss matters with bereaved relatives and to make the arrangements for organ donation with a transplant team.

6)   *Limited theatre time*
Because of pressure an operating theatres for other emergencies, there may be reluctance to embark upon organ removal, especially more lengthy multiple organ retrieval, which may occupy a theatre for several hours. The disruption to the donor hospitals' routine has been a significant disincentive to further referral of donors in some hospitals.

7)   *Cost*
There is no rational basis for financial arguments against procurement. As clinical budgeting takes hold, there will be greater awareness both of the costs of removing organs and the cost savings to the health service of a successful transplant.

8)   Medico-legal constraints
We have found general praise for the attitude and helpfulness of coroners. Seldom has the need for a coroner's post mortem examination prevented the donation of organs.

A number of options have been proposed to increase the availability of organs for transplantation. Some involve little more that improvements in current practice, for example, in intensive care units and in the dissemination of donor cards and the NHS Donor Register. Others are more, or even more, radical. These, by and large, would involve changes in the law in this country. Examples would be a legislative requirement of 'required request', ie imposing an obligation on those in ICUs to ask the relatives of the deceased for permission to remove organs and moving to an 'opting out' system of presumed consent. Most radical would be to see dead bodies as 'public property', from which organs could be removed *despite* the objections of the deceased or the relatives.

We now turn to look at these possibilities in detail.

B. IMPROVING CURRENT PRACTICE

Much has been done in recent years to improve the co-ordination of organ donation throughout the United Kingdom and Europe. In the UK a system of transplant co-ordinators has developed and a Special Health Authority, the United Kingdom Transplant Support Service Authority (UKTSSA) has been created to oversee the organisation of transplantation in the UK.

The system is described in the Department of Health's *Code of Practice for the Diagnosis of Brain Stem Death* (1998).

GUIDELINES FOR THE MANAGEMENT OF POTENTIAL ORGAN AND TISSUE DONORS

6.   Introduction

The purpose of this section is to explain and provide guidelines on the sequence of events leading to organ or tissue donation by a patient pronounced brain stem dead.

Over the last decade the Transplant Coordinator has played a central role in these events. Transplant Coordinators are usually, but not invariably, based at large transplant centres and fulfil several important functions. A network of Transplant Coordinators now covers all the NHS hospitals in the UK. The local Transplant Coordinator is thus the contact individual to whom all potential organ donors should be referred. Subsequently, the Transplant Coordinator establishes contact, usually in person, with the donor hospital, the relevant doctors and nurses responsible for the care of the potential donor and also the relatives, partner or carers of the donor. At the appropriate time the opinions of the relatives, partners and carers with regard to organ and tissue donation is usually ascertained by the Coordinator following full discussion of the issues. This procedure will be made easier if the Coordinator contacts the United Kingdom Transplant Support Service Authority (UKTSSA) and finds out from the NHS Organ Donor Register whether or not the potential donor was registered as willing to donate all, or some, of his or her organs for transplantation.

UKTSSA is a Special Health Authority responsible, among other things, for the matching, allocation and distribution of organs donated for transplant. As part of this function, UKTSSA maintains the National Transplant Database which contains details of all potential organ transplant recipients in the UK and Republic of Ireland. The UKTSSA is directly linked to transplant centres in the UK and Republic of Ireland through a communications link, and is responsible for liaison directly with Coordinators at transplant centres nationwide to ensure that all potential donor organs are allocated to the patients on the waiting list who can most benefit from them. If organ donation is to proceed, the Transplant Coordinator makes contact with the UKTSSA, and coordinates the arrangements with the surgical teams responsible for organ removal.

7.   Transplant Coordinator

7.1 Contact. The Transplant Coordinator will usually be contacted by medical or nursing staff from the Intensive Therapy Unit or ward on which the patient is being nursed. If there are difficulties in contacting the local Coordinator, contact should be made either directly with the local transplant unit or with the United Kingdom Transplant Support Service Authority (UKTSSA), telephone:

0117 975 7575, who will identify and inform the local transplant unit. The local Transplant Coordinator will usually inform the UKTSSA and the local transplant unit.

7.2 Protocol and Records. The local Transplant Coordinator will provide protocols to be followed when a potential donor is identified. If no local protocols are available, national protocols may be obtained from the United Kingdom Transplant Coordinator's Association (UKTCA), telephone: 0191 213 1674.

7.3 Initial Assessment. If there is any doubt about the suitability of the patient for organ donation this can be discussed by the Transplant Coordinator by telephone. If this initial assessment indicates that the patient is unsuitable for organ donation the relatives will not need to be approached. Otherwise the coordinator will attend the ward on which the patient is being nursed to carry out an initial assessment of the potential donor, collating all clinical details relevant to organ donation.

8. The Relatives

It remains important that relatives, partners and carers be kept fully informed of the clinical state of the patient and decisions regarding management.

8.1 Contact With Relatives, Partners and Carers. The Transplant Coordinator would not normally discuss the possibility of organ donation until the diagnosis, prognosis and concept of brain stem death have been discussed by medical and nursing staff on the ward. Only when relatives indicate, before brain stem death has been formally diagnosed, a willingness that organs be donated would it be reasonable for the coordinator to discuss matters at that stage.

8.2 Prohibition on Payment for Organs. The Human Organ Transplants Act 1989 prohibits commercial dealing in organs including non-regenerative tissue. It is a criminal offence to make or receive payment in return for supplying an organ from a dead or living person and intended for transplantation. It is also an offence to broker or negotiate an arrangement involving such payment or to advertise for donors who will be paid. Payment includes money or its equivalent but does not include payment covering the costs of removing, transporting or preserving an organ or reasonable expenses or loss of earnings paid to a donor.

9.   Retrieval of Organs and Tissue

When brain stem death is confirmed, the Transplant Coordinator is responsible for obtaining authorisation for organ removal either orally or, preferably, in writing but must in any case ensure that a proper record is kept of the views of relatives.

9.1 The Local Transplant Team. The Coordinator will inform the local transplant team responsible for the retrieval of organs and inform UKTSSA for the provisional allocation of organs.

9.2 Practical Details. The Coordinator arranges for the practical procedures involving theatre time, anaesthetic support, the retrieval team and the donor ITU or ward.

9.3 Screening Tests. In accordance with HSG (96) 26 'Guidance on the Microbiological Safety of Human Tissue and Organs used in Transplantation', the Transplant Coordinator organises those necessary virological and bacteriological screening tests and arranges tissue screening where relevant. It is also important to exclude, as far as possible, evidence for malignant disease in the donor. There may be differing requirements in this respect for certain tissues eg corneas.

9.4 Organ Retrieval and Transplant. Before removing organs or tissue, the surgeon must personally examine the body of the potential donor and on the basis of his examination, and the results of any tests diagnostic of brain stem death made by other doctors, he must be satisfied that the potential donor is dead. Eyes may be removed by an appropriately qualified and trained person who is not a doctor, but not until a doctor who has personally examined the body has stated that the potential donor is dead. When the results of the virological and bacteriological screening are to hand, the Coordinator advises the UKTSSA and the Transplant Units of the results and organ retrieval is undertaken where appropriate. Although it is reasonable to proceed with organ removal expeditiously following certification of brain stem death and receipt of appropriate authorisation for organ removal, organs must not be transplanted until microbiological safety to do so has been established.

10. Transplant Arrangements

The Transplant Coordinator will contact the UKTSSA and the Recipient Transplant Unit to organise organ transplantation.

11. Tissue Banking

The Transplant Coordinator may, with appropriate authorisation from the person lawfully in possession of the body, arrange for tissues such as cornea, bone, skin and heart valves to be retrieved and stored for future clinical use. These tissues can be retrieved from an organ donor up to 48 hours after circulatory arrest. When such tissues are to be stored, the Transplant Coordinator must organise liaison with the relevant tissue bank.

In a seminal report, the King's Fund Institute has examined the current system:

B New, M Solomon, R Dingwall, J McHale *A Question of Give and Take: Improving the Supply of Donor Organs for Transplantation* (1994) King's Fund Institute

The final means of improving current practice in relation to all organs is to extend the transplant co-ordinator network. There appears to be two approaches. In the UK the transplant co-ordinators are organised at the regional level, work in proximity to transplant centres and consist of full-time staff predominantly from a nursing background. Similar systems operate in the Eurotransplant countries, although Germany has a majority of doctors . . . One could simply expand the number of co-ordinators employed in this way. A rather more ambitious alternative would be to adopt the approach utilised in Spain, and described in Box 5.

THE SPANISH TRANSPLANT CO-ORDINATOR NETWORK

The Spanish national co-ordinating organisation, ONT (Organizacion Nacional de Trasplantes), and the system of co-ordinators was only 'consolidated' in 1990 (Matesanz, 1991). Transplant co-ordinators are organised on a two tier basis with a regional co-ordinator in each of the fifteen regions, and 118 teams working at the local donating hospital level. This means that every major hospital with ICU facilities has a co-ordinating team attached. The team may have one, two or three members, consisting of a combination of doctors and nurses. All the doctors and one third of the nursing staff on these teams are part-time, the rest of their time is spent working in their specialty – see Figure 17.

The most important element of this system is that the co-ordinators, key agents in the procurement process, are employed at all the donating hospitals and not just those which have a transplant unit. Furthermore, the majority of the local co-ordinators work only part of their time as co-ordinators, the remainder of their time spent in specialty work, predominantly in intensive care or nephrology. The combined effect is for intensive care and nephrological work in Spain to be directly integrated into the organ procurement process. As indicated by the discussion of the UK transplant co-ordinators, education and liaison with intensive care staff is of prime importance. In Spain this process can be more or less continuous with units having dedicated part-time or whole time staff on site. Under such a system, local hospitals without transplant units are likely to be sympathetic and well-informed as to the needs and importance of the transplant procurement process.

The evidence for the effect such a system has had on transplant activity is not conclusive, but nevertheless strongly suggests a positive impact. As indicated in the box, the system was fully implemented as late as 1990. Since then the number of co-ordinator teams increased from 56 to 118. Figure 18 shows the Spanish kidney transplant activity from 1980 until 1992. It appears that after a steady increase until the mid-1980s, activity levelled off between 1986 and 1989. From 1990 until 1992, however, there has been a remarkable increase. It certainly looks as though the implementation of the national network of co-ordinators and their expansion was accompanied by a substantial increase in transplantation activity.

Such evidence cannot be conclusive – there may well have been other factors at work, such as improved publicity or worsening road traffic accident rates. Furthermore, caution should be exercised in assuming that the UK would be able to emulate the overall transplant rate for similar reasons – this country already has a national co-ordinating system and our road death rate is low and falling. It should also be noted that ICU staff trained for the needs of the transplant community would constitute a break with the tradition of clear separation between the curative/therapeutic role of ICU staff and the procurement role of the co-ordinators. It would be vital that no confusion of these roles should result, leading to ethical concerns as to the motivation of the ICU staff.

Nevertheless, the arrangements in Spain, quite possibly designed with the benefit of being able to observe the failings of other systems, appear worthy of close attention and, if nothing else, they certainly allowed the Spanish transplant community to take full advantage of the opportunities presented to them. Spain now has the second highest rate of cadaveric kidney transplantation in the world. The introduction of such a policy would not necessitate a wholesale reform of the UK's co-ordinator network. If further resources were to become available they could be spent on part-time co-ordinators in local hospitals with major ICUs. Where more than one co-ordinator now works full-time in a single centre, individuals could be redeployed.

Even if these developments were not to influence greatly the effectiveness of current practice in the UK, they may still have an important function in supporting future reforms. The closer integration of the transplant community and the major donating hospitals is likely to be an important precondition for the potential for success of many of the proposals outlined below. Many of these options rely on non-transplant staff being particularly well motivated and instructed in the particular procedures concerned.

Figure 18 Spanish kidney transplant activity, 1980–1992

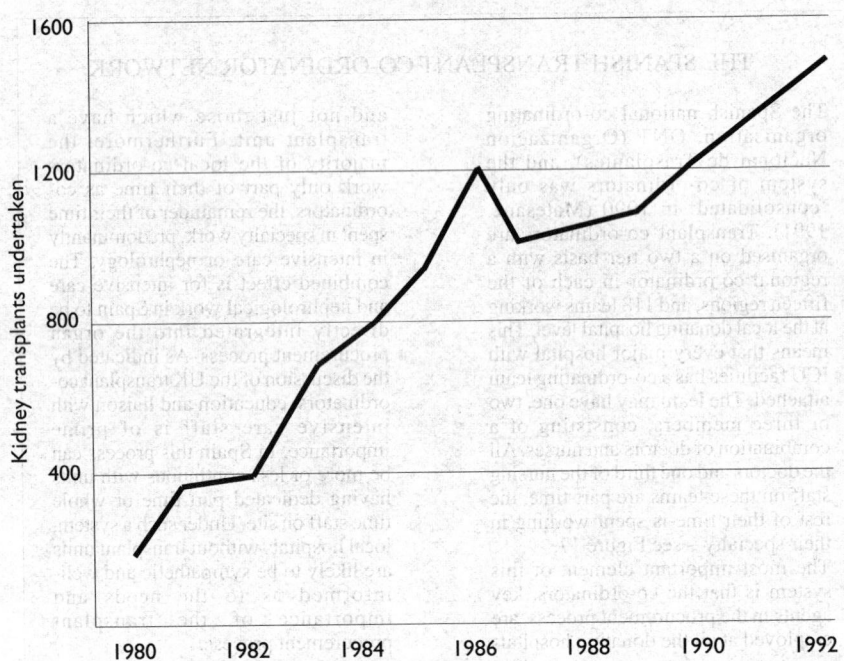

Source: Organizacion Nacional de Trasplantes.

Further practical measures were also considered in the report (pp 47–50):

Improving technical and logistical procedures
It has been suggested that technical and logistical procedures can be improved by:
- increasing the number of brain stem death tests;
- reducing the number of general medical contraindications; and
- improving the organisation of multi-organ donation.

Brain stem death testing
The first possibility – suggested by the findings of the national audit – is to increase the number of individuals who undergo brain stem death tests when they 'possibly satisfy' brain stem death criteria. Researchers have estimated that by reducing the non-performance of these tests

the number of offered donors could be increased by a modest proportion . . . However, it is likely that the audit picked up many 'possible' brain stem deaths in a technical sense – they would have satisfied the particular criteria involved – but because ICU staff were aware of overwhelming medical contraindications the tests were not actually undertaken . . . If this is true, then the potential for improvement may be rather limited. Nevertheless, it is clearly important for brain stem death tests to be undertaken whenever there is the possibility of a suitable donor.

The more likely means of achieving increased brain stem death tests is not to concentrate on those already in ICUs, but to test those potential donors who would have died outside the ICU on general and surgical wards or in the Accident and Emergency department, by 'electively' admitting them to an ICU and placing them on a ventilator. Such a system of elective ventilation is discussed further below.

Medical contraindications
A second potential improvement involves a better understanding of the general medical contraindications to donation. Whereas it is undoubtedly true that overwhelming septicaemia, for example, will clearly indicate unsuitability, intensive care staff may not always be aware of the precise range of contraindications. In an interim report of the national audit it was found that, of 47 potential donors with specified general medical contraindications, only 10 donors were discussed with the transplant team and the co-ordinators . . . As transplantation techniques improve, so the range of potential donors widens. For example, extremes of age are often no longer considered to be general contraindications.

However, in a follow-up to the national audit, transplant surgeons considered that in only 6 per cent of cases where a brain stem dead patient was listed as having general medical contraindications, were the kidneys actually transplantable. The liver was transplantable in only 1 per cent of these cases, and in no cases were the heart or lungs considered transplantable. The follow-up study concluded that it was 'reassuring that ... so few transplantable organs were missed' . . .

Improving arrangements for the multi-organ donor
A final set of improvements to current practice relate to logistical difficulties, or circumstances which lead to the non-use of otherwise suitable organs. Such difficulties apply more to the non-renal organs, with kidneys almost always successfully transplanted into a suitable recipient. For other organs, the situation is rather more problematic. Non-renal organs deteriorate faster than kidneys and many more are unsuitable by the time of the transplant operation; suitable recipients are fewer in number; non-renal transplant units are less common and transplant teams are occasionally not available or have to travel long distances; and lack of theatre time may also militate against non-renal explanation.

One example of how some of these problems can be addressed is provided by an initiative from Addenbrooke's Hospital, Cambridge, which seeks to simplify the multi-organ donor procurement process . . . Traditionally, each organ requires its own team, often requiring large distances to be travelled by the teams and entailing feats of organisation by the co-ordinator. Under the scheme, a combination of staff from liver and heart transplant centres form a single surgical team trained and available for the removal of all solid organs. Once stored, the organs are shipped to their allotted destinations. Not only does this reduce the possibility for losing organs due to logistical difficulties, but it should significantly reduce the inconvenience caused to the donating hospital by large numbers of medical personnel arriving with little warning, and the

> possibility of five separate surgical teams in the operating theatre, sometimes unknown to one another and speaking different languages . . .

It has been suggested that the impact of this practice has had a deleterious effect on the whole process of organ donation, and may even have had an influence on the levelling off of donation rates. A single case of insensitivity from a travelling surgeon could be enough to provoke resistance among ICU staff to future co-operation in the procurement and management of donors. The Cambridge scheme is now to be implemented throughout the UK.

Reducing relatives' refusal and non-discussion
A second set of improvements to current practice relates to methods aimed at reducing the extent to which relatives' consent is withheld. As discussed earlier, this is by far the most significant cause of the non-use of otherwise suitable organs. Three options present themselves:
- improved dissemination of donor cards;
- reductions in the refusal rate of those with whom discussion takes place;
- reduction in non-discussion with relatives.

Improved dissemination of donor cards
The first option involves improved dissemination of the donor card. Initiated in 1971 as a private enterprise, and relating at first only to kidneys, it was soon adopted by the DHSS and developed as a national policy. Since its inception it is estimated that an average of 10 million cards have been distributed every year. Little is known about the precise destination of the

cards – they are supplied to charities, GPs' surgeries, libraries, police stations and hospitals – but at least three million per year are issued with the driving licence by DVLC.

The impact of the card operates in two ways. First, it is a direct signal to those who are in possession of the body, and to relatives, that the deceased individual wanted to donate their organs. Second, it acts indirectly: as an instrument of publicity, a focus for debate and a symbolic indication to family members of an individual's intention whilst alive.

For the card to have a direct impact, it must be found on the body of the deceased at or shortly after the time of death. Although 70 per cent of the UK population are actively in favour of donating their own organs, only 20 per cent or so usually carry a donor card, as the discussion of public opinion in Chapter 3 indicated. It is reported that significantly less than 20 per cent of potential donors have cards which are actually found on their person at the time of death. Unfortunately, such evidence can only be anecdotal since data on possession of a donor card at death are not recorded, and neither was this information sought in the national audit. The fact that there are no recorded cases of relatives refusing donation in the face of a donor card (a legally unnecessary, but nevertheless universally observed, practice), might lead one to think that substantially increased possession of the card would improve donation rates.

The achievement of such a goal, however, would require significant improvements in the card-carrying habits of the British public, and, furthermore, among those members who would otherwise have organ donation refused by their relatives. Merely increasing the carrying of cards among those members of the public whose families already approve donation is of relatively little value. So, since 70 per cent approval is reported for organ donation it is tempting to expend resources in an attempt to ensure that this proportion of the population always carries a card. But if they are the same proportion who already consent to donation – 70 per cent of potential donors' families consented to donation in the national audit – then this increased card carrying could quite possibly have no impact at all on the donation rate.

The task is to achieve card carrying by those members of the public whose families would otherwise have refused consent, a far more difficult proposition, and one for which it is particularly hard to design an appropriate dissemination strategy. The Departments of Health and Transport have arranged for all new and renewed driving licences to contain a box to record the holder's willingness to donate, which will go some way toward solving the problem of lost or mislaid cards. This is a laudable strategy but does little to overcome the problem of targeting the appropriate groups.

Irrespective of these difficulties, the second, indirect, way in which the card has an impact – as a means of raising public awareness – should not be underestimated. The policy of voluntarism as exemplified by the donor card may have reached the limits of its potential as a direct means of influencing refusal rates. But it is still a valuable symbolic reminder of the shortage of organs, and probably lies behind the high degree of public awareness of this issue.

Reducing refusal rates by other means
The second option, notwithstanding the donor card, is to reduce the rate at which relatives refuse permission. Within the current legal framework, one means of reducing refusal rates is to encourage a more skilled, sympathetic and persuasive contact with the deceased's relatives by intensive care staff. The chief difficulty is the stressful and emotional context in which such an approach has to be made. The intensive care staff will almost invariably make the first contact once it is suspected that brain stem death is a possibility, and so their training is of the utmost importance. Prompt utilisation of transplant co-ordinators is also desirable. The extent to which such improvements can contribute to a significant reduction in the 30 per cent refusal rate is open to debate, however.

Another strategy has demonstrated rather more measurable benefits. Publicity campaigns have long been associated with attempts to improve donation rates, and there is some evidence of their success. Ironically, the most infamous example is of adverse publicity: the fall-off in donation rates after the Panorama television programme of October 1980 entitled 'Are the donors really dead?'. Other campaigns have appeared to have a positive impact. Lewis and Snell (1986) reported a 42 per cent increase in donation rates which coincided with a six month campaign by the DHSS in 1984 to advertise the merits of the kidney donor card. Gore *et al.* (1991) reported a significant drop in refusal rates by relatives – from 30 to 22 per cent – during a period of 'intense, positive publicity about transplantation' during October–November 1989.

The evidence is not conclusive, however. The 1984 campaign coincided with the introduction of the drug cyclosporin which greatly improved the effectiveness of transplantation and certainly would have encouraged greater activity regardless of donation rates. A recent television campaign conducted by the Department of Health during March 1993 appears to have had no effect on donation rates, according to provisional data from the UKTSSA (1994), even though a preliminary evaluation of the campaign reported improved discussion within families (Department of Health communication, 1993). The data show that the number of cadaveric kidney transplants have dropped to their lowest level since 1987, and the number of donors is 4 per cent lower than in 1992.

Furthermore such campaigns are expensive – the March 1993 event cost £1.5 million (UKTSSA, 1993b) – and temporary in their impact – the refusal rates recorded by Sheila Gore and colleagues soon returned to their pre-campaign level of around 30 per cent. Although useful in sustaining public awareness of the issues at stake, it does not appear that publicity campaigns are a cost-effective means of improving on current levels of donation in the long-term.

Reducing non-discussion
A small number of relatives are not asked if they are willing to agree to donation at all. Although small – only 6 per cent of contacted families had no discussion – such a proportion is still significant. Indeed, it has been suggested that some form of required request legislation – whereby doctors would have to make a request for every suitable potential donor – may be appropriate, and this is discussed later in this chapter. However, apart from the emotional burden this places on the medical staff, it is likely that many of those who were reported as having no discussion either clearly objected without prompting, or it was brought to the attention of the medical staff in some other way that they would refuse.

You will notice the reference in the report to donor cards. These are, of course, well known if not extensively used. Since the report was published, the NHS Organ Donor Register has been set up which allows an individual to 'opt in' (ie under s 1(1) of the 1961 Act) by the inclusion of his or her name on a centralised computer which may be more easily accessed by the transplant team (for a discussion of this possibility, see *A Question of Give and Take* (*op cit*) p 54.)

You will also notice reference to approaches to the deceased's relatives. We will return to this under 'required request' shortly.

A further possibility would be to increase the supply of organs from *living* donors. This was supported by the Report of the King's Fund Institute (*op cit*) pp 666–668 providing proper safeguards were taken to prevent improper pressure to donate being applied. Also, the *Advisory Group on the Ethics of Xenotransplantation* (1996) favoured development.

Advisory Group on the Ethics of Xenotransplantation (1996)

IMPROVING THE SUPPLY OF LIVING DONORS

5.21 Experience from other countries suggests that it may also be possible to increase the contribution made through live donation. This is regulated by the Human Organ Transplants Act 1989. Thus, amendment of the Act would be necessary to take forward some of the following measures (for example, the sale of organs). Most living donors are genetically related to the intended recipients. Where donation between unrelated persons is proposed, particular controls are applied through the Unrelated Live Transplant Regulatory Authority (ULTRA).

5.22 Live kidney donation is well-established and transplant survival rates exceed those for cadaver organs. In 1995, 8.5% of transplants were from living donors (2.6 per million population). Varying live donation rates across regions in Britain and internationally [noted by the UKTSSA] suggests that there may be some potential for increases in regions with lower rates. Norway, for example, performs far more live related or living donor transplants than any other country (17pmp). Even a small increase in live donation rates could have a considerable impact. However, live donation is not without problems. Adverse psychological effects have been reported in donors, some of whom may, for example, have felt pressured into donating an organ.

5.23 Live partial-liver donation is also possible for transplant into children and a limited programme has started in the UK. The US has also had some experience of live lung-lobe donation to children. This depends on two adult donors (usually parents) donating lobes for transplantation. However, there is the possibility of significant morbidity in the donors and this, combined with the knowledge that even with live lung-lobe donation, chronic rejection may well occur resulting in only medium term survival, mitigates against expansion of the programme.

5.24 Thirdly, there is, in principle, the option of a market in organs. Currently it is illegal to trade in organs (usually, this would involve the sale of someone's kidney). In 1989 it was found that some Turkish people had been brought to the UK and paid to have a kidney removed and transplanted into patients in a private London hospital. Legislation (the Human Organ Transplants Act 1989) was then enacted to make such trade in organs illegal. Doctors who become involved in such trade are also likely to be found guilty of serious professional misconduct and suffer censure.

5.25 Having reviewed the various options, we conclude that some expansion of the live related transplant programme is possible, although this would not be without its difficulties.

C. NEW PROCEDURES WITHIN THE CURRENT LAW

We are here concerned with, first, the practice of so-called 'elective ventilation' (EV) or 'non-therapeutic ventilation' and, secondly, the use of non-heart-beating donors (NHBDs).

1. Elective ventilation

The practice was developed at the Royal Devon and Exeter Hospital (see Feest, Riad, Collins *et al* 'Protocol for Increasing Organ Donation after Cerebrovascular Deaths in a District General Hospital' (1990) 335 Lancet 1133).

The practice and its implications is discussed in the King's Fund Institute Report.

B New, M Solomon, R Dingwall, J McHale *A Question of Give and Take: Improving the Supply of Donor Organs for Transplantation* **(1994) King's Fund Institute**

A protocol has been developed at the Royal Devon and Exeter Hospital, designed to ensure that patients dying of cerebrovascular accident are managed by transfer to ICU so that their organs could be retrieved – see Box 7.

THE EXETER PROTOCOL

There is no age limit for organ donation, patients over the age of 70 years may be suitable.

Criteria for identification of patients with intracranial vascular accidents as potential organ donors:
*   Characteristic mode of onset: sudden with rapid development of coma
*   Progressive decline in conscious level
*   Deep coma: lack of withdrawal response to painful stimuli
*   Intracranial vascular accident confirmed by CT scan is desirable

THE ICU REGISTRAR SHOULD BE INFORMED WHEN A PATIENT IS ADMITTED IN DEEP COMA

Exclusions:
Reversible causes of coma

Procedure – this sequence of events must be strictly observed:
*   Junior medical staff discuss case with consultant concerned
*   Consultant or nominee discuss suitability of patient with member of transplant team
*   If patient is suitable, discuss with consultant in charge of ICU
*   If all are agreed, consultant physician or nominee should approach relatives

Approach to relatives
Discussion with the relatives will need to include:
*   The physician's belief that the patient is unlikely to recover
*   A request for organ donation
*   The need for transfer to ICU as the appropriate place for management of organ donation
*   The possibility of the patient being removed from ICU to a ward if he or she ceases to be suitable as a donor

Management in ICU
Degree of intensive treatment is for discussion between consultant physician and consultant in ICU

Sources: Feest *et al.*, 1990; Collins, 1992

The protocol began on 1st May 1988 and over the next 19 months the team estimated that eight patients who would otherwise have been missed became donors. When these individuals were added to those who had become donors without reference to the protocol the study team estimated that the donor rate (individual donors) pmp per year increased from 19.8 to 37.5 – or 75 kidneys pmp, more than two and a half times the national average . . . . Since then, the team members have reassessed their estimate downwards, with, over a four year period, 13 from 39 donors coming from the protocol . . . This still represents an increase of 50 per cent over a non-protocol system.

It may be that this increase would not be easy to reproduce nationwide. Furthermore, the number of extra donors is small in absolute terms and therefore the reported increases are likely to be outside confidence limits for statistical significance . . . although this claim has been challenged. Nevertheless, even if the national increase were substantially less than that estimated by the Exeter team, it would still represent a significant increase in donor rates. A study similar to the English national audit but undertaken in Wales and including deaths outside the ICUs, came to similar conclusions about the opportunities presented by elective ventilation:

> the supply of donor organs ... could be increased by altering the management of patients aged 50–69 dying in general medical wards, in particular by increasing the number ventilated . . .

Effect on ICU workload

The protocol is not without its critics. The most common criticism is that elective ventilation would cause a large increase in the workload of ICUs which they would not be able to accommodate, and possibly make it more difficult for those in immediate danger of losing their life to gain access to a bed . . . How much strain is, in fact, likely to be placed on ICUs?

The best estimate of the current availability of ICU facilities – namely, the ratio of occupied to staffed ICU beds – comes from a census survey conducted in 1989 over two days: Sunday 5th and Tuesday 7th of November . . . 187 of the 226 ICUs contacted responded. The survey found that, at 3pm on Tuesday 7th November, the mean number of staffed beds was 4.4 and the mean number of occupied beds was 3.6. In yearly terms, this translates into an average of 1314 occupied bed days out of 1606 staffed bed days. ICUs are clearly under pressure and have little leeway for admitting increased numbers of patients, a proposition supported by a more recent audit . . . Furthermore, 40 per cent of the units had fewer than four staffed beds, and only a third of these were able to accept new admissions. Of the larger units, only just over one half were able to do the same.

But what difference would a national policy of elective ventilation make? At Exeter – and this is likely to be an over-estimate – the team found on average three donors per year from the protocol from a population of 303,000. This translates into 10 donors pmp per year. The 277 ICUs in England . . . serve a population of 47.8 million, which means that, at best, there would be 478 extra donors to be found nationwide, an average of just under two per unit. Let us assume an upper limit of three per unit for the purposes of this discussion.

How long would these donors spend in an ICU bed? No electively ventilated donors should spend more than 48 hours in the ICU according to the Exeter experience, and this can be written into the protocol. Thus if donors turn out not to be suitable or do not continue to respiratory arrest, then they should be removed from the ICU. One donor in Exeter spent 127 hours in the ICU, but personal communication with staff from the hospital has confirmed that this would not be normal practice and only occurred because there was no pressure on ICU beds at the time. Indeed, all but two of the donors in the initial report of the protocol were in the ICU for less than 24 hours . . . Let us estimate two bed days per donor as the highest likely average length of stay.

Thus, on the most extreme estimate, units will, on average, have to accommodate three electively ventilated donors per year spending a total of six bed days in the unit. This would be in addition to the current mean occupancy rate of 1,314 bed days – an increase of 0.46 per cent. 470 extra donors constitutes an increase of 66 per cent on the English donor rate for 191, but is likely to increase ICU workload by less than 1/100th of that proportion. Whilst it is acknowledged that these average figures hide the fact that some units will be at full capacity, and therefore entirely unable to contribute to the policy, this analysis draws attention to the relatively small impact such a policy would have on the intensive care community, whilst having a potentially enormous impact on transplant activity.

Conclusion

Further evidence on the potential effectiveness of elective ventilation is required notwithstanding the results reported above. The Exeter study was small and involved clinicians from a number of different specialties collaborating successfully on a single site. These conditions would not be the norm nationally, since, for example, most ICUs occupy a site without a transplant unit.

(a) Is it lawful?

Is elective ventilation lawful? The answer is almost certainly that it is not. The procedure cannot be demonstrated to be in the patient's 'best interests'. Jean McHale examines this question.

J V McHale 'Elective Ventilation – Pragmatic Solution or Ethical Minefield?' (1995) 2 Professional Negligence 23

The legality of elective ventilation

Generally, before medical procedures are undertaken the consent of a patient must be obtained. Without it the doctor risks a prosecution for the crime of assault and a tort action in battery. However, if for example the patient's mental faculties are impaired he may be unable to give consent himself. In this situation treatment may still be given if the doctor caring for the patient determines that it is in the patient's best interests to do so. The extent to which the power to treat in 'best interests' extends to non-therapeutic procedures such as elective ventilation remains uncertain. It is questionable whether a court would be prepared to hold that elective ventilation is in the best interests of the patient. Elective ventilation has the effect of prolonging the life of the patient in a situation in which no recovery is possible. The House of Lords has held that the continuation of treatment where that treatment is clearly hopeless is unlawful. In *Airedale NHS Trust v Bland* Lord Browne-Wilkinson stated that:

> If there comes a stage where the responsible doctor comes to the reasonable conclusion (which accords with a responsible body of medical opinion) that further continuance of an intrusive life support system is not in the best interests of the patient, he can no longer lawfully continue that life support system: to do so would constitute the crime of battery and the tort of trespass to the person.

Kennedy and Grubb commenting on the *Bland* case and referring to medical procedures undertaken with a view to transplantation suggest that if Lord Browne-Wilkinson's comments are a correct statement of the existing law then procedures such as elective ventilation are currently unlawful.

However, it has been suggested that while certain non-therapeutic procedures may not be in the patient's best interests, never the less they may be justifiable if there is a strong public policy reason why the procedure should be undertaken and if they are not against the patient's best interests. For example, it has been argued that the inclusion of a mentally incompetent adult in a non-therapeutic trial which only posed a minimal risk would not be against a patient's best interests. The public interest would support such a trial going ahead.

This argument has not yet been tested in the courts. But even if the courts were to accept that certain non-therapeutic procedures should be performed on mentally incompetent adults that does not mean that they would sanction elective ventilation. At present there is disagreement as to whether elective ventilation is 'not against' the best interests of a patient. Firstly, elective ventilation might be said to deny the patient a right to a peaceful and dignified death. Their last hours are spent in the hustle and bustle of the intensive care unit wired up to invasive machinery rather than in a quiet ward. There is also a risk that when the ventilator is switched off the patient will not be brain stem dead but will be found to be in a persistent vegetative state. The patient will have had their life prolonged due to elective ventilation, and there is a risk too that ventilating the patient may have precipitated the persistent vegetative state. The veracity of these claims cannot be established at present because all elective ventilation has been halted due to the fear it is unlawful.

Even if we can be satisfied that elective ventilation is not against the interests of an individual patient can it really be said that it is in the interests of the public as a whole? Routh argues that intensive care units are established with the aim of saving lives and to use them to undertake elective ventilation is an unjustifiable departure from this principle. The Kings Fund, in response to this, commented that:

> specialities in a health service should not operate parochially. If the skills of intensivists can be used to save life in ways which happen to differ radically from previous practice, then this is in itself not sufficient reason for resisting change.

This may be the case but questions will be asked whether elective ventilation is the most effective use which can be made of medical resources. If intensive care units are used for elective ventilation does this mean that other patients will not receive treatment? The Kings Fund Report suggested that the evidence indicated that the benefits of elective ventilation outweighed any disadvantages. They quote statistics indicating that use of elective ventilation could lead to 470 extra donors each year – 66 per cent increase on 1991 donation figures but that it would lead to an increase in the workload of intensive care units of less than 1/1000th of that proportion?

Under existing law there is the possibility that if a patient had indicated by an advance directive that if they fell into a hopeless condition they would agree to be electively ventilated prior to transplantation then that wish should be honoured. The courts have recently indicated that they would be prepared to recognise advance directives. But whether the courts would uphold a directive which requested that elective ventilation be given is unclear. English law has never recognised an individual as having an absolute right to do what they will with their own body and as noted above there was opposition in the *Bland* case to preserving life at all costs. Nevertheless a court might be influenced in upholding a directive by the fact that in giving effect to the wishes of the deceased their life would not be prolonged unduly – patients are ventilated for no more than 48 hours. The court might also take into account that giving effect to the wishes of the patient would also facilitate organ transplantation which may be regarded as a socially desirable activity.

McHale 'flies two kites' in the extract: (1) the 'not against the interests' test; and (2) the use of an advance directive. We have seen that the former test has little support in the English case law (see *supra*,ch 6). It does not, in our view, progress the legal argument under the common law any further. We shall see shortly, however, that it may be important in determining the ethical basis for EV and hence any reform of the law.

The second 'kite' of McHale's is more intriguing. There is no doubt that advance directives can be legally valid in England (see *infra*, ch 16). Generally, they are concerned with *refusals* of treatment so that the (now) incompetent patient may refuse in advance medical treatment or intervention which others might in the circumstances deem to be in his 'best interests'. By contrast, in EV the advance directive would be one that would *consent* to an intervention that would not otherwise, we shall assume, be in his 'best interests'. Clearly, advance consents have some legal effect. Otherwise all consents to surgery under general anaesthetic would be invalid. The issue here is whether a patient's advance consent could 'trump' what would otherwise be the doctor's duty to act in his best interests, which would be, we can assume, not to carry out the EV procedure. There is no obvious solution to this which can be easily divined from the existing case law in England. Ultimately, it must be a matter of public policy. Arguably, since a competent patient may act contrary to his own best interests, at least within limits, for good reason so as, for example, to donate a non-essential organ (see *supra*), a patient may *in advance* license an EV procedure for precisely the same purpose. A contrary view would have it that the individual possesses a negative right to protect his bodily integrity but does not have the positive right to override the normal duty of others to act in his 'best interests'. The strongest argument for this is that an advance refusal does not require others to act against the patient's 'best interests' since the refusal redefines those interests from the patient's perspective. On balance, we consider the latter view to best represent English law at present.

Of course, advance consents in EV situations may not be terribly practical. First, advance directives are not widely used in any event. Secondly, the directive would have to be very specific in order to be 'clear' and 'applicable' to the circumstances of EV (see *infra*, ch 16). In practice, this may make the possibility unlikely.

A further argument has been made that EV is lawful. This argument avoids the pitfalls of the 'best interests' test by claiming that a patient under the 'Exeter Protocol' is already dead. Thus, the legality has to be judged only by the law applicable to dealings with dead bodies (see *infra*, ch 18).

Professor David Price analyses this argument in the context of 'brain-stem death' (on which see *infra*, ch 18).

David P T Price 'Organ Transplant Initiatives: the Twilight Zone' (1997) 23 Journal of Medical Ethics 170

By contrast with the majority view across all disciplines, the clinicians who developed the Exeter protocol argue that the process of dying is not prolonged by EV, as the patient is already dead – one is ventilating a corpse. The basic disagreement here might seem to be founded on a dispute as to the meaning of death itself, whereas this is not in fact so, only brain death is in issue – it is not possible to rely on traditional cardiopulmonary criteria when the natural functioning of the heart and lungs is obscured by the intervention of the ventilator. Moreover, the clinicians themselves do not purport to be relying on "cardiopulmonary death". Riad, from Exeter, has said "The procedure causes no harm to the patient as ventilation is instituted at the time of respiratory arrest *which is the consequence of brain death*. ... Therefore it is important not to institute EV before respiratory arrest" (Riad, H 'The Exeter Protocol for elective ventilation: British Transplantation Society News Letter 1994). Such a sequence of events is explicitly referred to in the Memorandum on the Diagnosis of Death attached to *Cadaveric*

Organs for Transplantation (1983) issued by the Conference of the Medical Royal Colleges: "In a minority of cases, brain death does not occur as a result of the failure of other organs or systems but as a direct result of severe damage to the brain itself from, perhaps, a head injury or a spontaneous intracranial haemorrhage. Here the order of events is reversed: instead of the failure of such vital functions as heart beat and respiration eventually resulting in brain death, brain death results in the cessation of spontaneous respiration: this is normally followed within minutes by cardiac arrest due to hypoxia. If however oxygenation is maintained by artificial ventilation, the heart beat can continue for some days, and haemoperfusion will for a time be adequate to maintain function in other organs, such as the liver and kidneys". Supporters of the Exeter protocol argue that cessation of respiration is (necessary and sufficient) evidence that the patient has *already* succumbed to brain death – the question is whether this is so. …

Riad and Nicholls have said "The dilemma is that there is a difference between the diagnosis of death and the timing of death. We believe we ventilate patients at the moment of death, even though we diagnose death only by formal testing for brain stem death some hours later" (Riad H, Nicholls A 'Elective ventilation of potential organ donors' British Medical Journal 1995, 310: 714–5). The King's Fund Report also noted that in this context the *actual* point of death might have been the same (where cessation of respiration precedes brain death and when it occurs as a consequence of brain death), but the point of *confirmation* of death is not – as the electively ventilated patient is not officially confirmed as being dead until two sets of brain stem death tests have been performed. Jones, however, has said "Nor can one escape this dilemma by seeking to differentiate between the diagnosis of death and the timing of death. To say that patients are ventilated 'at the moment of death, even though we *diagnose* death only by formal testing for brain stem death some hours later' merely shifts the ground as to the 'determination' of death. There must be some agreed criteria for determining the moment of death – that is, the doctors must have grounds for being able to say that 'this patient is dead' and this in itself entails a process of diagnosis. It is simply that this diagnosis does not comply with the strict criteria laid down for determining 'formal' brain stem death" (Jones M 'Elective ventilation of potential organ donors: The Legal Background' British Medical Journal 1995; 310: 717–18). The potential dichotomy nevertheless exists between the time of death and the diagnosis/confirmation of death, although this has no significance in everyday cases. The diagnosis of brain death is in one sense inevitably retrospective, death has already occurred at a point in time which is unknown and unknowable …

Despite certain views to the contrary, it seems that there is no mandatory legal requirement at present that a person cannot be declared brain (stem) dead unless the recommendations of the report of the medical royal colleges – ie the code of practice – have been complied with in their entirety. The code of practice, although highly influential, does not have the force of law.

Kennedy and Grubb have previously analysed the likely legal position if a patient were declared dead according to brain stem criteria but without the code of practice having been fully adhered to. They believe the answer is contingent upon whether a mistake was made as regards the exclusion of certain pre-conditions (for example, drugs, hypothermia, etc), a failure to perform all the relevant tests, or whether the tests were just not repeated. They are of the opinion that with respect to the first matter the court would simply decide, as a matter of fact, whether the patient was nevertheless dead. On the second issue they state that "We take the view that a court, in the absence of evidence of irresponsible behaviour by the doctor, would be reluctant to find that the patient was not dead at the time asserted". On the latter issue they suggest that if the tests were confirmatory the courts would be likely to find that the death occurred after the completion of those tests on the *first* occasion. The cases cited above appear to bear them out. Confirmation is evidence that death has already occurred, reinforcing the dichotomy between the time of death and the date of recording of death. Indeed, the time of confirmation is capable of manipulation for specific ends and therefore should not be invariably tied to the *time* of death. Although no brain stem death "tests" are seemingly carried out at all prior to EV, a thorough diagnosis of the person's condition is conducted and many of the same contra-indications for brain stem death are ruled out, for example, reversible causes of coma. There must be some possibility that a court would find that an electively ventilated patient *was* already dead when ventilation was commenced where (i) there was confirmation of the loss of ability for spontaneous respiration and (ii) later performed brain stem death tests proved positive – especially where these were performed almost immediately after the patient was ventilated. However, if one of the concerns is that EV protocols may lead to patients being induced into a PVS state, then certainty regarding the moment of death seems rather dubious – although currently we do not know how great this risk is or whether it is even a true risk at all, because of the moratorium on EV itself.

… the dichotomy between the diagnosis of death and the time of death requires clarification. If a patient is not actually dead until two sets of brain stem death tests are carried out, as the code suggests, then the patient is still alive up until that point. No procedures should therefore be carried out which are not in the patient's best interests, such as those designed solely to preserve the viability and quality of a potential transplant organ. This would fall foul of the same proscription as EV, ie that it constitutes an unlawful battery. If the second set of tests are confirmatory instead, then such procedures may be permissible, because the individual is dead.

The latter view may, as we shall see, represent English law (see *infra*, ch 18). Notwithstanding these arguments, the present position in England is that the Department of Health has effectively outlawed EV procedures where ventilation is undertaken not for the patient's own benefit: see 'Identification of Potential Donors of Organs for Transplantation' NHS Executive, HSG (94)41. See also DoH *Code of Practice* (*supra*) para 4.3.

(b) Should EV be allowed?

The arguments about whether elective ventilation should be permitted were addressed in the King's Fund Institute Report.

B New, M Solomon, R Dingwall, J McHale *A Question of Give and Take: Improving the Supply of Donor Organs for Transplant* **(1994) King's Fund Institute**

> The possibility that the procedure is unlawful does not automatically imply that it is unethical. Ethical objections deserve analysis in their own right, and they have been arranged under three headings. Elective ventilation:
> * impedes traditional ICU work;
> * is against the best interests of the patient;
> * offends the dignity of the dying process.
>
> **Impedes traditional ICU work**
> The first criticism stems from the fact that 'a policy to initiate supportive care of a patient when it is known that it will not benefit that patient in any way is very different from the traditional approach' (G Routh (1992) 'Elective ventilation for organ donation – the case against', Care of the Critically ill, 8, 60–61). The objection appears to be that ICU resources should be solely devoted to the saving and prolongation of life, and that their use for any other purpose, such as the preservation of cadavers for organ removal, should only be undertaken when the initial purpose was one of rescue and life extension.
> Let us first assume that there is an unlimited supply of intensive care beds. Is there an ethical case for resisting the use of ICU facilities under these circumstances? To do so would be to make an ethical distinction between the direct and indirect saving and extension of life, and this does not seem reasonable. An electively ventilated patient is quite clearly a means of saving other lives and reducing other suffering, albeit only as the first link in a chain which results in a transplanted organ. However, specialties in a health service should not operate parochially. If the skills of intensivists can be used to save life in ways which happen to differ radically from previous practice, then this is in itself not sufficient reason for resisting that change.
> If it is appropriate in principle to use intensive care facilities purely to expedite organ retrieval, why in practice is it still resisted? Unlike the debate surrounding changing the law to one of presumed consent, where the individual concerned is already occupying a bed in the ICU, electively ventilating a potential donor would mean that an accident victim with a good chance of survival might be denied treatment. This is highly unlikely in practice; more likely is a situation whereby
>
> > a decision has to be made whether or not to discontinue ventilation on the potential donor when the family have agreed to and expect him to become a donor (ibid).
>
> Notwithstanding the evidence cited earlier that the average increase in an ICU's workload would be small, cases such as that described above are bound to occur if elective ventilation becomes a national policy. Is it ethical to allow for the possibility of such an event?
> The question is, rather, whether it is reasonable to allow for the possibility of unpalatable choices. As things stand, any reasonably busy ICU may not be able to cope with a sudden influx of two or three seriously injured individuals – choosing between those who can benefit from care is a common problem for those working in the NHS. Having to decide to remove an electively ventilated patient to free a bed will certainly not be welcomed by ICU staff. But it is a circumstance made necessary by an attempt to provide potentially life-saving organs for others. The alternative is to leave an available bed potentially unused when it could be providing the means for securing additional organs. This would seem harder to defend ethically.

Against the best interests of the patient
There is a perception among some in the intensive care community that elective ventilation causes death to be 'postponed' when there are no clinical grounds for so doing:

> deliberately prolonging a patient's dying is unacceptable for any reason (Park et al (1993) 'Organ donation' BMJ, 306, 145).

Such procedures constitute poor medical practice and erode the confidence which the public has in the medical profession. Relatives may be forgiven for being confused and distressed by a process which simultaneously informs them that a loved one is sure to die whilst taking the individual in question to a department which is devoted to attempts at saving life. Perhaps the most serious scenario involves a prospective donor failing to satisfy brain stem death criteria and remaining in a persistent vegetative state after ventilation is stopped (Routh (1992) op cit). This scenario is one which is recognised by proponents of elective ventilation as deserving serious consideration (C H Collins (1992) 'Elective Ventilation for organ donation – the case in favour', Care of the Critically ill, 8, 57–59). It offers the prospect of a real prolongation of a 'living death' and all the associated grief of the relatives.

Leaving aside the possibility of misdiagnosis for a moment, the accusation that death is being prolonged is strongly refuted by doctors who developed the Exeter protocol. They argue that the point of death is no different whether one adopts the protocol or not:

> ... such patients die when breathing ceases; elective ventilation does not prolong the act of dying, for one is ventilating a corpse (A Nicholls and H Riad (1993) 'Organ donation' BMJ, 306, 517–518).

The difference between the electively ventilated patient and those dying on general wards is twofold. First, the electively ventilated patient is transferred to ICU whilst still alive. Second, the official confirmation of death, after the second set of brain stem death tests, is made somewhat later than if the patient died on the general ward. The actual point of death, however, will have been the same in either case, since artificial ventilation is only initiated once respiratory arrest has taken place (although there is a view that death may be postponed for a short period of time). The legal controversy stems from the fact that this intervention is not in the patient's interests, and he or she is in no position to consent to it.

But is this situation ethically unacceptable? The Exeter protocol only considers those patients in deep coma with 'lack of withdrawal response to painful stimuli'. Even though the patient is placed on a ventilator when this is not for their own benefit, the procedure does not cause distress. Even if the moment of brain stem death can be shown to have been postponed for a short period in the electively ventilated patient, this does not automatically indicate that the patient's interests have been abused. And the fact remains that other patients stand to benefit.

However, a mistaken diagnosis is another matter. Although there are no reported cases, it is possible that respiratory arrest coupled with elective ventilation could result in the patient remaining in a persistent vegetative state. Brain stem death would not have occurred in such a patient and the concern is that in some way elective ventilation confounds the original diagnosis. Patients in a persistent vegetative state do not recover, and so such an outcome would clearly not be in the patient's interest. This assessment was recently reinforced by the high court ruling on Tony Bland, left in a persistent vegetative state after the Hillsborough football stadium disaster (*Airedale NHS Trust v Bland* [1993]). If elective ventilation directly caused significant numbers of such patients, it would render the procedure unethical.

The only way to establish whether this possibility is a real one is to undertake a large-scale randomised study. PIVOT, the proposed research mentioned in Chapter 4, includes a randomisation element which would allow an assessment of the validity of this concern. But before this element of the study can go ahead the legal position must be resolved; as matters stand, the law prevents such research.

Offends the dignity of the dying process
The desire for a painless, dignified and peaceful death is deeply rooted into many of the world's cultures. Respect for the corpse is of symbolic importance, and the funeral constitutes a fundamental rite of passage. Intensive care staff must deal with these issues more than most and it is perhaps unsurprising that views such as these are commonly heard:

> I take exception to the idea ... that we should scout around the wards, look for patients about to die and take them to the Intensive Care Unit, intubate them and ventilate them until they are brain dead so that their organs can be used for the purposes of transplantation.

There is a belief that the 'good death' is becoming a thing of the past, and that we are in danger of undermining the dignity of the dying process. Although the passage quoted above from an eminent intensivist may somewhat caricature the process described by clinicians in Exeter (T G Feest et al (1990) 'Protocol for increasing organ donation after cerebrovascular deaths in a district hospital The Lancet, 335, 1133–1135). It has a serious message. Moving individuals with no hope of recovery from one department to another and attaching ventilatory equipment could well be viewed as deeply undignified.

Those who developed the Exeter protocol were quite clear that the process should not be initiated without the relatives' understanding and agreement. This should clearly apply in all units where elective ventilation is introduced.

But it may still be argued that such procedures prevent the 'good death' in a more fundamental sense, regardless of how the relatives feel. A peaceful and dignified departure of the spirit and soul, whatever one's religious beliefs, is simply not possible if one's mortal remains are being moved from pillar to post. Such an assertion is not, in the final analysis, refutable. But we should remind ourselves that acceptable modes of dying change with changing cultures and technologies. A century ago the notion of dying whilst attached to various forms of machinery would no doubt have seemed undignified to some. As the rationales for new practices are understood, new contexts for dying become acceptable. It may not be long before actively managing death to save other lives is as 'good' and dignified a form of dying as any other.

Concluding comment
The only significant ethical concern with elective ventilation relates to the possibility of increased numbers of patients in a persistent vegetative state. A study which would resolve this issue has been postponed because the procedure appears to be unlawful. However, the ethical grounds for this unlawfulness can only be established by conducting the study. This 'Catch-22' situation is clearly unsatisfactory and requires resolution.

(For further discussion arguing in favour of EV, see A Shaw, 'Non-therapeutic (Elective) Ventilation of Potential Organ Donors: The Ethical Basis for Changing the Law' (1996) 22 Journal of Medical Ethics 72.)

In its report on *Mental Incapacity* (No 231, 1995), the Law Commission proposed a mechanism whereby EV could be permitted in the future.

Law Commission *Mental Incapacity* (Report No 231, 1995)

6.26 We did not invite specific views on either elective ventilation or genetic screening in our consultation papers. While the expert reports referred to above suggest that there is a case for legalising both procedures, none of the comments which have been made to us by respondents allow us to be confident that the case has been made out. We are, however, persuaded that there may come a time when Parliament could be confident that a procedure which was not intended to be in the best interests of a person without capacity to consent to it should nevertheless be rendered lawful. We therefore consider that the Secretary of State should have power to introduce such a change in the law, after consultation and subject to an affirmative resolution by each House of Parliament.

We recommend that the Secretary of State may make an order providing for the carrying out of a procedure in relation to a person without capacity to consent if the procedure, although not carried out for the benefit of that person, will not cause him or her significant harm and will be of significant benefit to others. (Draft Bill, clause 10(4).)

If any procedures are designated by the Secretary of State in future, there should (in accordance with the recommendations made elsewhere in this report) still be a clear prohibition against things being done to a person who objects or to a person who has made an applicable advance refusal (Draft Bill, clause 10(5)).

In *Who Decides?* (Cm 3803, 1997), the Lord Chancellor's Department sought views on this recommendation (see paras 5.31–5.34) but has subsequently decided not to take the matter further: *Making Decisions* (Cm 4465) 1999 (see *supra*, ch 6).

2. Non-heart beating donors

The practice is described by Professor David Price in the following extract. As he points out, the use of NHBDs for transplantation is a 'throw-back' to the era before patients were maintained on ventilators in ICUs.

David P T Price 'Contemporary Transplantation Initiatives: Where's the Harm in Them?' (1996) 24 Journal of Law, Medicine and Ethics 139

In the 1980s, new NHBD protocols of two distinct types were implemented worldwide, although both rely on death confirmed by traditional cardiopulmonary criteria. The first type involves the removal of organs immediately after death, the preeminent example being the University of Pittsburgh Medical Center Protocol (the Pittsburgh Protocol). The second involves the perfusion and cooling of kidneys immediately following death and subsequent organ removal. Protocols of this type have sprung up in Holland, Great Britain (for example, at Leicester General Hospital), Italy, France, Spain, Japan, and the United States (for example, the Regional Organ Bank of Illinois).

All these initiatives are designed to minimize warm ischemia time during which organs sustain damage due to the interruption of blood supply, thus affecting their viability for transplantation …

The Pittsburgh NHBD Protocol seeks to control the time and place of death of patients (with a wide range of clinical conditions) who are expected to die shortly and who are dependent on life-sustaining treatment, for example, mechanical ventilation. After such a patient or his/her surrogate(s) has agreed to withdrawal of further life-sustaining measures and, on a separate occasion, the patient or the family have requested organ donation, life-support is withdrawn and the organs removed immediately following death. NHBD perfusion protocols seek to avoid organ deterioration by cooling the organs while still inside the body, immediately following death, but prior to removal. These are essentially temporary measures initiated in most instances to allow sufficient time for authorization for organ donation to be obtained. Typically, an incision is made in the patient's groin, a catheter inserted into the femoral artery, and perfusion carried out. Unlike the alternative form of NHBD protocol (for instance, Pittsburgh) … , in some instances neither the deceased nor the family has previously authorized the procedures to be carried out. By contrast with EV, NHBD protocols have a relatively long history. NHBDs were in fact the main source of organ donation prior to the acceptance and use of heart-beating donors in the 1970s, and their use is on the increase once more.

What are the legal issues here? There are two. First, are such patients dead? This is a prerequisite, as we saw, to the application of the Human Tissue Act 1961. Secondly, is the perfusion procedure lawful?

As to the question of 'death', Professor Price comments as follows:

David P T Price 'Organ Transplant Initiatives: the Twilight Zone' (1997) 23 Journal of Medicine Ethics 170

Under the Pittsburgh protocol, organs are removed immediately the patient is shown to be apnoeic and unresponsive for two minutes to one of three electrocardiographic criteria, ie ventricular fibrillation, electric asystole or electromechanical dissociation. Typically though, the medical literature describing NHBD protocols is less than full and explicit as to *how* and *when* death is determined according to cardiopulmonary criteria. In Tokyo, cooling *in situ* is commenced "immediately after cardiac arrest", whilst at King's College, Dulwich organs are removed "up to 45 minutes after the heart has stopped beating". Unlike EV, NHBD protocols involve a choice between competing concepts of death, not just varying criteria for the same concept of death. As Mason and McCall Smith state, "If we are to accept the concept of 'brain death' as argued below, we should treat the person in irreversible cardiorespiratory failure as dying rather than dead – for the true agonal period in natural death is that which lies between cardiac arrest and cerebral failure" (Mason J, McCall Smith A *Law and Medical Ethics* London, 1994, 281). According to this perspective, failures of respiration and heartbeat are relevant only because they will *lead*, in some cases, to death.

The primary reliance under NHBD protocols is upon irreversible loss of cardiopulmonary function as the *standard* of death, not simply as evidence of brain death. It is well known that the brain stem (and *a fortiori* the whole brain) will only cease to function after loss of cardiac function and oxygen deprivation lasting for some minutes – certainly more than the two minutes stipulated by the Pittsburgh protocol. But even assuming that there is an independent alternative cardiopulmonary standard of death, it is not clear that such patients are dead even according to this standard. The primary problem here is the difficulty in establishing that the cessation of respiration and heartbeat was *irreversible* – which is an explicit and invariable legislative stipulation. For many, two minutes of asystole is insufficient to establish that spontaneous auto-resuscitation will not occur. In addition, the Pittsburgh protocol excludes the possibility of interventions that could restart the heart (artificial resuscitation is withheld by virtue of the joint decision of doctors and relatives).

A nebulous concept

But is irreversibility *properly* a facet of legal or ethical standards of death, and if so, what does it convey? Necessarily, reversibility requires the benefit of some significant degree of hindsight, which such protocols may partially preclude in the quest to preserve the viability of organs for transplantation. However, although reversibility is undoubtedly a nebulous and problematic concept, as has been noted by numerous commentators in this journal, it is not for that, or any other, reason dispensable either legally or ethically. Moreover, the notion of reversibility based upon what is "ethically significant", as suggested by Tomlinson, is dubious. Our duties to the living may dictate whether someone "will die" but they cannot determine whether a person "is dead" ie whether we *could* have reversed it, not whether we *should* have reversed it. Inevitably irreversibility is relative and linked to time and culture, but this is not to say that death is relative as between individuals of the same culture and at the same relevant time.

Cole argues that the notion of irreversibility is superfluous because it is out of line with the "ordinary concept" of death, which is based on the loss of a *natural* capacity to resume (cardiopulmonary) function, and that consequently such a notion should not form any part of a legal definition of death. This is surely implausible, since our lives are supported by all manner of non-natural means, some temporary some permanent. None the less, would it not be plausible instead *to link* the notion of reversibility with the notion of natural functioning? Although we surely would not say that a person was dead simply on account of cardiac arrest when we could restore respiration and circulation by artificial means, we would surely not assert either that all individuals were alive until the point where artificial means could not even cause the lungs to inflate or the blood to circulate? It can be sensibly conceived that a person is dead when the functions of the body are being *wholly driven* by technology, ie such measures are not even *assisting* the natural functioning of the body, either temporarily or permanently. At the point where loss of cardiac and respiratory function produces brain stem death the individual ceases to live regardless of extended mechanical "existence" – there is no integrated functioning of the body, and no consciousness, from that moment. The point of brain death is therefore the critical point in time whether loss of cardiac function and respiration is an end in itself or only the catalyst for loss of brain function. Catherwood argued in this journal that "Dying is not an irreversible process, until that process gets to a point where our available technology cannot help" (Catherwood, J 'Rosencrantz and Guildenstern are dead'? Journal of Medical Ethics 1992: 18: 34–9). In so doing he is question-begging in using the word "help". Helped to do what? If lung functioning can be mechanically sustained even where the patient has suffered brain stem death, is he/she "helped" or is he/she already dead?

Ironically, although NHBD protocols are explicitly stated to be founded on cardiorespiratory criteria, after a certain period of time has elapsed artificial ventilation is applied in many instances as well as cardiac massage. This appears to prove that the cessation was *not* irreversible. However, in fact this procedure implicitly relies on the notion of irreversibility propounded above. If not, such donors are simply not "non-heart-beating" at all! As it is imperative to rely on the death of the brain, the issue is simply what evidence is required to establish that such brain death has occurred. There is no dichotomy between heart-beating and non-heart-beating donors. Cardiopulmonary cessation is evidence of death, not death itself ...

I have argued that death is only brain death but that in any event the important point in time under *any* standard of death is the point of brain stem death, as only then would cardiorespiratory failure be irreversible. Where brain death *follows* cardiorespiratory failure a period of time must be agreed upon beyond which it is considered that the brain stem cannot have survived. A consensus apparently developed at a recent symposium of transplantation experts in Maastricht, that at least ten minutes should have elapsed without cardiopulmonary function before a potential NHBD is pronounced dead (Maastricht Symposium on non-heart beating donors Transplantation Proceedings 1995; 27; 5: 2891–2939). The consultants to the President's Commission incidentally also advised that at least ten minutes of proven lack of circulation to the brain was necessary (Presidents Commission for the Study of Ethical Problems in Medicine and Biomedical and Behavioral Research 'Guidelines for the determination of death. Defining Death' Washington 1981).

(On the legal approach to 'brain-stem death', see *infra*, ch 18.) As to the propriety of the perfusion procedure, the authors of the King's Fund Institute Report (*op cit*) concluded (at p 66) that: 'Such a small scale procedure may prove ethically acceptable.' They concluded, however, that in law this would not be an unreasonable mutilation of a corpse. We discuss the use of dead bodies and the law relating to that in Chapter 18. Price, again, summarises the argument from an ethical perspective.

David P T Price 'Contemporary Transplantation Initiatives: Where's the Harm in Them?' (1996) 24 Journal of Law, Medicine and Ethics 139

In considering the ethical acceptability of *in situ* perfusion of organs, we must ask whether cutting into a corpse can constitute a harm to the (now dead) individual, and, if so, what *kind* of harm? It has been asserted *inter alia* by Youngner that it is impossible to inflict harm on a dead patient. Our views here, though, will probably be significantly influenced by our attitudes to the "self" when a person has died. The LRC of Canada commented that "[u]nder one view, persons are seen as inseparable from their bodies. Consequently, the dignity of the human body is inseparable from the dignity of the person. This nexus survives death, because the body symbolizes the person who once lived." The manner of treatment after death has historically been regarded as at least partially reflective of the respect, or lack of it, accorded to the once living individual. In the nineteenth century, for instance, public dissection of the legally executed cadaver was viewed as an ingredient of the punishment itself. In this context, loss of dignity is unrelated to actual or surrogate psychological suffering or awareness. It reflects on the once living person.

Philosophers have long debated whether a dead person can be morally harmed. Views differ. Some, such as Ernest Partridge, contend that the dead have no interests and are consequently beyond harm or benefit (E Partridge, 'Posthumous Interests and Posthumous Respect' Ethics, 91 (1981) at 243–44). By contrast, Bonnie Steinbock convincingly asserts that the common saying that the dead are beyond harming refers ... to the fact that the dead cannot be hurt, angered or distressed. But, their surviving interests can be defeated, and when this happens, the subject of posthumous harm is the antemortem person, for it is the antemortem person who cared about what would happen after he died. (B. Steinbock, *Life Before Birth: The Moral and Legal Status of Embryos and Fetuses* (New York: OUP, 1992) p 16).

The difficulty is isolating which interests survive the interest-bearer's death. Desires, wants, and aims are crucial to the concept of interests, and the vast majority of us have legitimate wishes, desires, and wants concerning what happens to our corpse which can be thwarted by others or events.

Moreover, some aspirations can *only* be fulfilled after our deaths, for example, the posthumous disposal of one's property by will. Raymond Belliotti argues that only if the object of our interests and desires *is* (not simply believed to be) realized, are those interests and desires fulfilled. Thus, despite Russell Scott's remark that the "very idea of applying the notion of personal autonomy to a corpse is absurd; at most, personal autonomy is only artificially extended beyond death," (R Scott *The Body as Property* (New York: Viking Press (1981) at 260)) notions of autonomy *can* seemingly stretch beyond the point of death; but it is not the corpse's autonomy but that of the former living person represented by the corpse. The LRC of Canada suggested that respecting the wishes of a person about treatment of their body after death gives rise to a "fuller sense of autonomy."

Questions also arise about the interests of others. The LRC of Canada stated that

> [m]inimally invasive experimentation or medical education techniques may not disfigure or mutilate the newly dead or otherwise violate their bodily integrity. However, even marginally invasive techniques such as intubation might be considered an indignity or mistreatment, if consent is not obtained from a family that considers such techniques offensive, outrageous or violative of religious beliefs.

The difficulty here is balancing the harms and possible aspirations in the absence of such consent. The right to permit use of a deceased loved one's organs for transplantation is viewed by many as an important psychological and emotional issue at such a distressing time – it can even form part of the grieving process. Cutting into a corpse may be perceived as mutilation from a purely physical perspective; but it may also be viewed as the preservation of rights of autonomy from another – an issue on which I expand below. Without implementing NHBD cooling protocols, some of these other interests and values may not be effectuated. Moreover, even if relatives are wronged by these procedures, this would only amount to "offense" (in Feinberg's terminology), which is of a lesser order of importance than "harm" in the overall scale of wrongs and may therefore have to be "weighed in the balance." (J Feinberg, *Harm to others* (Oxford: OUP, 1984) at 34).

D. CHANGING THE LAW

Here we consider four options: (1) clarifying the existing law; (2) presumed consent; (3) required request; and (4) removal without permission.

1. Clarifying the 1961 Act

As we saw, there are a number of ambiguities in the 1961 Act which generate uncertainty over its application in practice. It can be argued that, in itself, this contributes to problems in obtaining organs for transplantation.

The most extensive review of the Human Tissue Act with a view to clarifying its provisions within the framework of a system of 'opting in' was attempted by the British Transplantation Society.

British Transplantation Society Report (1975)

The Committee agreed that, in view of the unhelpful interpretations of the Human Tissue Act which persist in some quarters, statutory clarification of the Act was desirable.
The existing s 1(2) ... should be repealed, and the following provision substituted:

Without prejudice to the foregoing subsection, the person lawfully in possession of the body of a deceased person may authorise the removal of any part from the body for use for the said purpose if, *having made such inquiry as is both reasonable and practicable in the time available*, he has no reason to believe that the deceased had expressed an objection (which he was not known to have withdrawn) to his body being so dealt with after his death.
Provided that authorisation shall not be given under this subsection if the person lawfully in possession of the body has reason to believe that the surviving spouse or any surviving relative of the deceased objects to the body being so dealt with.

In addition there should be a new subsection, providing that:

For the avoidance of doubt in the interpretation of this section, it is hereby declared:

(a) That the hospital authority is the person in possession of the body of a deceased person lying in the hospital, and that this possession is lawful until such time as the hospital authority fails to comply with a request for possession of the body, made by the person who has the right to immediate possession of it.
(b) That a printed but personally signed "donor card", or other document, is "in writing" for the purpose of subsection 1 of this section.
(c) The "time available", for the purpose of an inquiry under subsection 2 of this section, extends only until the moment at which steps must be taken to remove the part of the body, if it is to be suitable for the therapeutic or other purpose in question.

The effect of these provisions would be to overcome the unfortunate (and, it is thought, unjustified) doubts concerning the interpretation of 'such reasonable inquiry as may be practicable' and 'person lawfully in possession of the body' under the present law, and to prevent any doubts arising over the interpretation of 'in writing'.
Only in one respect does the suggested amendment seek to alter what the Committee understands to be the current legal position. Though authorisation could not be given under the proposed s 1(2) if the person lawfully in possession of the body had reason to believe that the spouse or any relative of the deceased objected, he would no longer be under a duty to make enquiries as to whether they did object. He would, however, invariably approach the closest available relatives, in the course of making 'such inquiry as is both reasonable and practicable' to determine whether the deceased had expressed an objection. They would thus have the opportunity of making known their own (or others') objections. This change would represent a reversion to the legal position of the spouse and relatives under the Corneal Grafting Act, 1952, which was very much more satisfactory in this respect.
Some members of the Committee favoured a more radical amendment of the Human Tissue Act. But in view of the failure of more radical proposals to make progress through Parliament, and in view of the general consensus among surgeons that it would be undesirable to remove organs for transplantation in the face of objections from the spouse of relatives, it was decided to press for a limited amendment.

2. Presumed consent

One possible reform to the UK legislation which has been suggested would move from an 'opting in' system to one of 'opting out'. Thereby, the deceased's consent to organ donation would be presumed unless he or she had objected prior to their death.
The most well-known system of presumed consent is that in Belgium. In 1986 Belgium enacted legislation adopting an 'opting out' system, the Law of 13 June 1986 on the removal and transplantation of organs (*Moniteur belge*, 14 February 1987, No 32, pp 2129–2132).

Removal after death
10. – (1) Organs and tissues for transplantation, and for the preparation of therapeutic substances in accordance with the conditions laid down in Section 2, may be removed from the body of any person recorded in the Register of the Population or any person recorded for more than six months in the Aliens Register, unless it is established that an objection to such a removal has been expressed.

It shall be a requirement, in the case of persons other than those mentioned above, that they have explicitly expressed their consent to the removal.

(2) Only a person who has attained 18 years of age and is capable of making known his wishes may express the objection provided for in subsection 1.

If a person has not attained 18 years of age but is capable of making known his wishes, the objection may be expressed either by him or, during his lifetime, by his close relatives living with him.

If a person has not attained 18 years of age and is incapable of making known his wishes, the objection may be expressed during his lifetime by his close relatives living with him.

If a person is incapable of making known his wishes by reason of his mental condition, the objection may be expressed during his lifetime by any legal representative or guardian for the time being he may have, failing which, by his closest relative.

(3) The Crown shall make provision for a method of expressing an objection to the removal for the donor or the persons referred to in subsection 2.

For this purpose, the Crown shall be empowered, under the conditions and in accordance with the rules laid down by it:

(*a*)   at the request of the person concerned, to have the objection made known through the Services of the National Register;

(*b*)   to regulate access to this information, so that the physicians carrying out the removal can be informed of the objection.

(4) A physician may not proceed to carry out the removal;

1.   If an objection has been expressed in the manner provided for by the Crown;

2.   if an objection has been expressed by the donor in another manner that has nevertheless been communicated to the physician; or

3.   if a close relative has communicated his objection to the physician. This objection may not override the expressed wishes of the donor.

'Close relative' means a relative up to the first degree of, or the spouse residing with, the donor.

(The law is discussed in H Nys (ed) *International Encyclopaedia of Laws: Medical Law* H Nys, 'Belgium', paras 372–401.) Presumed consent legislation, including that in Belgium, is discussed in the King's Fund Institute Report (at pp 56–59):

B New, M Solomon, R Dingwall, J McHale *A Question of Give and Take: Improving the Supply of Donor Organs for Transplantation* (1994) King's Fund Institute

Presumed consent schemes have been introduced into many countries, although attempts to enact such legislation in the UK have always failed, the latest being the Transplantation of Human Organs Bill 1993. The international legislation falls into several categories. The purest version of the law allows automatic removal except in a situation in which the deceased has expressed an objection during his or her lifetime. This 'strict' type of presumed consent procedure applies in Austria where organs can be removed

provided in his or her life, the person concerned has not expressed an objection. The views of close relatives are not taken into account (Conference of European Health Ministers, 1987b).

A slightly less strict version of presumed consent operates in Belgium where, if there is no explicit objection by the deceased, the relatives are allowed to object but the medical profession are under no obligation to seek their views. The relatives must initiate the process under these circumstances.

Other, still weaker, schemes allow removal unless the deceased has made an explicit or informal objection at any time. Such a formulation of the law effectively requires that the relatives are consulted in order to glean the wishes of the deceased. Although it is formally the views of the deceased whilst alive which are being sought, such schemes allow the relatives to object on the deceased's behalf. France and Spain operate presumed consent legislation of this kind.

Finally, a scheme in operation in Singapore provides for the automatic exclusion of certain categories of potential donor, including non-citizens and Muslims. Muslims can, however, donate their organs if they wish, by pledging their organs whilst alive or if their relatives consent.

In this chapter the evidence of the law's efficacy will be examined. Since the hypothesised effect of presumed consent laws in high transplanting nations can be confounded by road deaths, for example, a more appropriate approach is to examine the affect of introducing a law on the trend of procurement activity in a single country.

Does presumed consent work? Belgium
Belgium enacted presumed consent legislation in June 1986 in the middle of a period of sustained and steady growth in kidney transplantation across Europe. Figure 20 shows the number of available kidneys (equivalent to the number transplanted by country of origin,

thus adjusting for import and export flows) between 1980 and 1992 in the UK and four Eurotransplant region countries.

Figure 20 Available kidneys in the UK and Eurotransplant region, 1980–1992 (pmp)

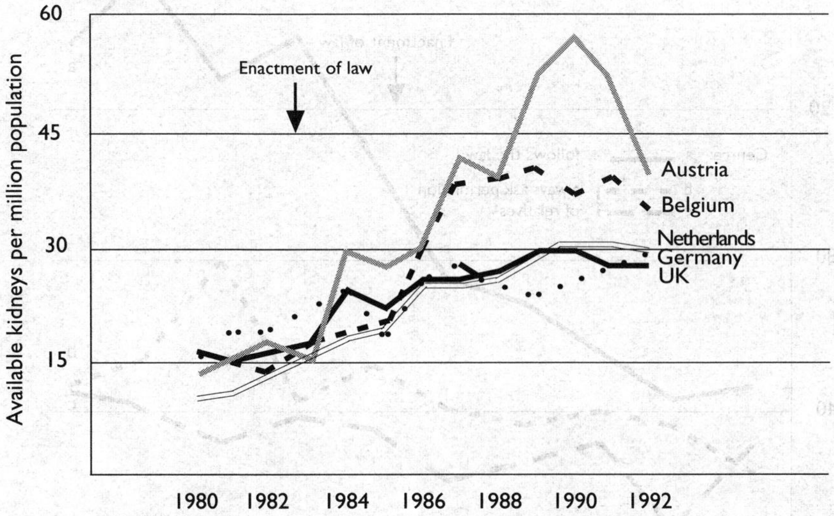

Note: 'Available kidneys' refers to the number of transplanted kidneys derived from a particular country, but possibly transplanted abroad.
Source: As Figure 1.

Belgium did increase the number of available kidneys by a significant margin during 1987 – a rise of 37 per cent over the year before – and this does not seem to be simply the continuation of an earlier trend. Furthermore, neither the UK, Germany nor the Netherlands experienced a similar increase in the same year. On the other hand, Austria did experience a similar increase, drawing attention to the fact that the effect experienced in Belgium could have been as a result of other factors (Austria did not introduce similar legislation in the same year having done so in 1982, formalising a 200 year tradition of routinely utilising the corpse for medical purposes). For instance, the publicity devoted to the organ donation issue whilst the law was being debated could itself have promoted a greater willingness to donate on the part of the public and a more informed attitude on behalf of ICU staff. It has also been noted that the number of transplant co-ordinators increased at around this time, and that the law formalised systems of reimbursement so that donating hospitals could be sure that they would receive the appropriate payment for managing the donor.

These objections are inconclusive, however. One would expect a 'publicity effect' to subside. The increase in the number of co-ordinators was likely to be as much a result of the increased number of donors as the cause of it. And the law merely formalised payment systems which operated successfully for the majority of hospitals beforehand. But perhaps the best evidence is provided by Figure 21.

The chart shows the difference between centres which always asked permission, and the centre which 'followed the law'. It is clear that the influence of publicity, co-ordinators and payment systems had no effect in those centres where relatives' permission is always sought. It certainly seems as though the law had an independent effect on kidney retrieval where its provisions were adopted.

In any time-series analysis 'concurrent interventions' such as those described above will always make it difficult to prove the causal influence of the intervention in question, in this case a law. On balance, though, the evidence suggests that the introduction of presumed consent in Belgium had a significant impact on the availability of organs.

Does presumed consent work? Singapore
Singapore also introduced presumed consent legislation after a long period of transplant activity under an 'opting-in' system. The number of transplants undertaken in Singapore are relatively small and so were not included in the international analysis. Nevertheless, the development of kidney transplantation over time has some interesting features as shown in Figure 22.

Figure 21 Kidney retrieval in three different centres in Belgium, 1981–1990

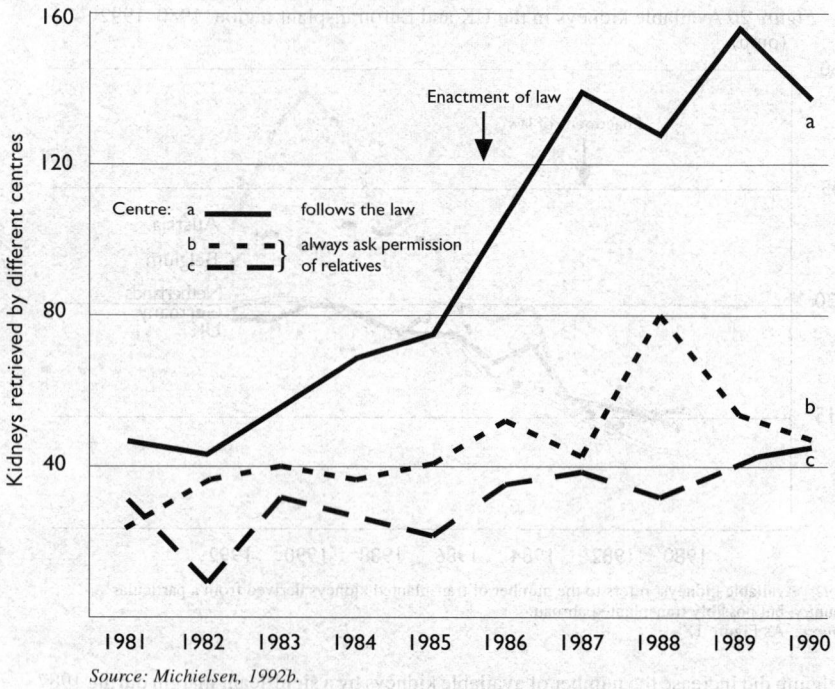

Source: Michielsen, 1992b.

Figure 22 Cadaveric kidney transplants in Singapore, 1970–1990

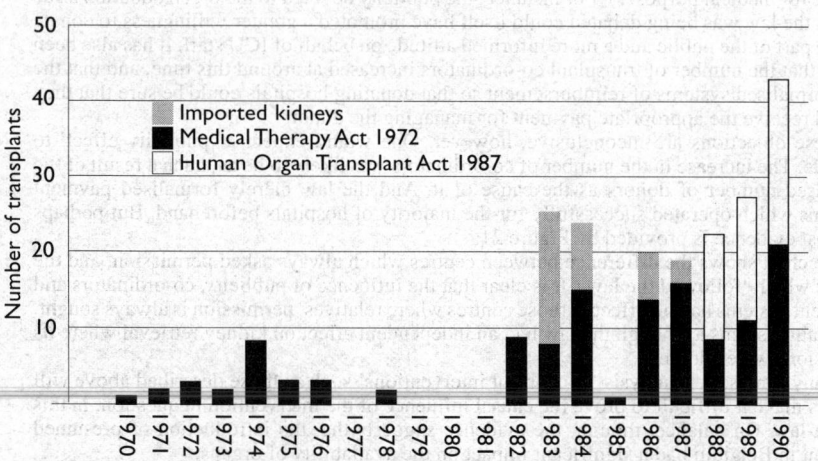

Note: All cadaveric transplants performed in Singapore are displayed. This includes voluntary donation of kidneys under the Medical (Therapy, Education and Research) Act 1972 (opting-in), kidneys imported from Europe and North America and kidneys procured under the Human Organ Transplant Act 1987 (presumed consent).
Source: Soh *et al.*, 1991.

Between 1970 and 1982 only 30 cadaveric kidneys were transplanted, constituting an average of approximately 0.9 pmp per year, clearly inadequate by any international standards. In an attempt to increase this level of activity, kidneys were imported from Europe and North America – transplants from this source are shown by the light shaded area. The initial success of this policy was short lived when it became clear that the one-year graft survival of these kidneys was poor, probably as a result of the prolonged 'cold ischaemia' times involved.

In 1987, the Human Organ Transplant Act was introduced incorporating the provisions described above. The number of transplants undertaken in 1988–90 increased significantly over the 'non-import' total of the previous years, imports being discontinued in 1988. Some analyses – including that represented in Figure 22 – have attempted to isolate exactly the number of kidneys procured under the new law compared with the number obtained under the old opting-in legislation, which still applied for those wishing to pledge their organs. However, such an analysis will underestimate the number of voluntary pledges, since it cannot be known for certain how many families would have consented given the chance. Nevertheless, the evidence from Singapore adds to that from Belgium as to the efficacy of presumed consent legislation.

Is such a law acceptable ethically and as a matter of public opinion? The ethical arguments are considered in *A Question of Give and Take* (*op cit* at 61–63):

Article 10 of the Council of Europe's recommendations on organ donation issued in 1978 provided that:

no removal must take place where there is explicit or presumed objection on the part of the deceased, in particular taking into account his religious and philosophical convictions (Council of Europe (78) 29).

In 1987 another Conference of European Health Ministers came down in favour of the promotion of cadaver organ donation. However, Article 10 of the earlier resolution was rewritten to provide that removal may take place only where there is consent on behalf of the deceased – although this consent could be 'presumed' in the absence of express objection. This change in emphasis left the question of whether a presumed consent or an opting-in policy was to be adopted to the individual nation.

There appear to be four ethical issues relating to implementing presumed consent legislation relating to:

- the wishes of the individual;
- the sensibilities of the relatives;
- trust in the medical profession;
- good medical practice.

The wishes of the individual

The first concern would be most serious in the context of 'routine salvaging', a system whereby one could not 'opt-out'. Should routine salvaging be allowed? It has been noted that in many areas of legislation the general public interest takes priority over the wishes of the individual . . . There is a public interest in ensuring an efficient supply of organs. Once dead, why should a person's wishes be respected? This type of argument is open to the objection that it is insensitive to the wishes of deceased. In our society the wishes of the dead are respected by, for example, giving legal force to the declarations made in their last will and testament.

More commonly, individuals are given the opportunity to 'opt-out' under presumed consent legislation. Although less serious, the concern remains that individual wishes would be ignored. The Hoffenberg Committee commented that there was a danger that organs would be removed when this was not the wish of the person whilst alive (R Hoffenberg (1987) Report of the Working Party on the Supply of Donor Organs for Transplantation' DHSS, London). Persons may feel pressurised into not opting-out because it might be seen as socially unacceptable. Others may be ignorant of the law or unable to understand it – vulnerable groups would be most at risk. In a multi-cultural society, the risk of ignoring the implicit wish of individuals with strong religious beliefs is particularly serious. No presumed consent legislation can possibly guarantee that the wishes of all concerned will be respected.

The sensibilities of the relatives

If concern would be felt by those now living with strong beliefs about the proper procedure for their body after death, distress could certainly be caused to family members who wished to grieve without the knowledge or suspicion that the body of a loved one was being 'mutilated' – particularly if donation was conducted only under a 'presumption' that the deceased had given consent. The Conference of European Health Ministers (1987) commented that,

the role of the family in deciding on organ removal is much more important in cases of presumed consent than in cases of express consent. In the latter case the sentimental objections of the family have to be weighed against the legal rights of the deceased who has willed the organ donation. In the case of presumed consent the family's express objection weighs more heavily against the presumed consent of the deceased ... In practice therefore whether consent is express or presumed, the final decision rests to a very large extent with the family of the deceased ...

It is worth noting, however, that the sensibilities of families are not taken into consideration in the case of a coroner's autopsy. In England in the early 1980s 'some 20 per cent of persons dying ... [were] subject to a medico-legal autopsy'. In other words, a large number of deceased individuals are subjected to invasive surgery, without the need for consent, to satisfy social imperatives. What is more, society sanctions such investigations only as a means of establishing cause of death or to help in the solving of a crime – lives are not directly at stake. The ethical distinction which supports the coroner's autopsy but denies the donation of organs unless consent is provided, is by no means clear.

Trust in the medical profession
Both these possible consequences – ignoring individual rights and offending the family's feelings – could have an impact on trust and respect for the medical profession. Whilst presumed consent may, in the short run, furnish more organs for transplants, in the long run its systematic effect on the institutions of medical care could be depressing and corrosive of that trust upon which doctor-patient relationships depend. And, even in the short run, public controversy can adversely affect donation rates. Furthermore, doctors may be unwilling to override the wishes of nearest relatives regarding organ donation, blunting the impact of the schemes.

Good medical practice
There may also be certain medical risks in removal without consent. In October 1979 a woman who died suddenly in France had her corneas transplanted. Unfortunately, the recipient contracted rabies. It was later revealed that the donor had contracted rabies when bitten by a dog in Egypt shortly before her death. Her family knew this and had they been asked they would have been able to pass on this information to the medical team.

Can presumed consent legislation be ethical?
If a presumed consent scheme were to be introduced certain questions would need to be addressed. Would all organs be covered by a presumed consent scheme? Should organs be made available simply for clinical transplant or also for experimentation purposes? Should certain vulnerable groups of patients be excluded from routine removal? The 1969 Renal Transplantation Bill, an attempt to introduce a limited form of presumed consent, provided exclusions for persons who, at the time of death, were suffering from mental illness or mental handicap, minors, those over 65, prisoners and permanent residents in institutions for the aged, disabled or handicapped.

It may also be necessary for a statutory definition of death to be enacted. This would, as was noted earlier, prove a difficult and controversial task. Presumed consent would also have to be accompanied by massive publicity in order that members of the public were made aware of their opportunity to opt out. In addition the legislators would need to address themselves to the question of who should have ownership and control of the cadaver and of the organs.

However, it may be that many of these ethical objections can be overcome by sufficiently carefully drafted legislation. Individual rights can be safeguarded by means of computer registries and exclusions of certain categories of individual. The sensibilities of the relatives can be safeguarded by allowing them to initiate an objection which must be respected. The position of the medical profession is protected by allowing the individual clinician to decide how and when to utilise the law's provisions. Such a law would also allow for donation under circumstances whereby the relatives, at a moment of grief, do not wish to discuss the possibility, but would otherwise normally be in favour of donation.

Nevertheless, unless the medical profession broadly supports the implementation of presumed consent legislation there is a serious danger that transplantation will be brought into disrepute by the controversy which would ensue. ... This in turn may corrode the public's trust in doctors and medicine. The best way forward is for the debate to continue until those who would have to work within a new law are satisfied that their reservations have been addressed.

What of public opinion? As part of their work, the authors of the King's Fund Report commissioned a national survey by the Office of Population Censuses and Surveys in 1992 (see, *op cit*, ch 3 for the methodology and detail). One issue addressed was that of 'presumed consent' (at p 43):

In view of the current debate about the possibility of a change to a system of presumed consent, three British surveys in 1992 asked people for their views about this proposal. A summary of the results is shown in Table 9.

Table 9 Attitudes to presumed consent

%	OPCS	DoH	BKPA
In favour	40	46	61
Against	48	43	30
Other (neutral or don't know)	12	11	10

One in five of respondents to the OPCS survey were 'definitely' in favour of introducing presumed consent in Britain. A similar proportion was 'possibly' in favour. However, slightly more people (48 per cent) were against the proposal than in favour. The DoH survey, on the other hand, found slightly more people were in favour of the suggestion than against, although the difference was minimal. Overall, the small differences between the numbers for and against in these two surveys suggest that public opinion in Britain is split roughly evenly over the issue of presumed consent.

However, the result from the BKPA survey, suggesting that twice as many people in Britain favour 'opting-out' (as it was termed in this survey) than oppose it, appears to paint a different picture. One possible explanation of this difference is the precise wording of the question. In both the OPCS and DoH surveys, the proposed new arrangements were described and contrasted with the present system. People were then asked the question whether they were for or against the new system just described. In contrast, respondents to the BKPA survey were simply asked:

Would you approve or disapprove if the kidneys of anyone who had just died could be used unless they had 'opted-out', that is, stated that this must not be done?

The emphasis in this question is more on the use of organs, as opposed to the actual process of registering an objection to 'opt-out'. By describing the situation of someone 'who had just died', the question may tend to prompt people to imagine a scene in a hospital. In this case, therefore, respondents might be more likely to be in favour of any proposal which increased the likelihood of actual donation. In contrast, the questions in the other two surveys focus on the process of 'opting-out' while the potential donor is still alive, and make more explicit the change from the existing system. It might be argued, therefore, that responses to these questions are slightly more considered and based on a more complete account of the proposed change and its implications for potential donors. It may also be the case that responses specifically for kidney donation differ from those regarding organ donation more generally.

It is possible to make comparisons with opinions in two other countries. In the USA, 39 per cent of respondents were in favour of presumed consent and 52 per cent were against. This is broadly similar to the balance of opinion in the OPCS survey. In Holland, 24 per cent of respondents preferred changing to a system of 'opting-out', while 75 per cent wanted to keep their present system of 'opting-in'. So it seems that British people, in their collective ambivalence, are not as opposed to presumed consent as the Dutch.

In summary, public opinion in Britain appears to be divided over the issue of presumed consent. However, it is difficult to predict exactly how public opinion might change after the introduction of any new legislation in the future.

No Bill advocating 'opting out' or any other major reform has reached the statute book in England. The latest dismissal of the idea of 'opting out' is contained in the Report of the Working Party on the Supply of Organs for Transplantation, chaired by Sir Raymond Hoffenberg (*op cit*) p 6:

We have been told that an *Opting Out* Scheme might increase donations by allowing organs to be removed after brain stem death from those who had not recorded an objection, but we do not recommend this. There would be a risk that organs might be removed when this had not been the wish of the person or their relatives. It does not in itself enlist the co-operation of doctors. We would prefer organ donation to be seen as a positive gift with the consent of relatives who in practice would always be approached.

By contrast, in the King's Fund Report (*op cit*), a scheme for UK legislation encompassing presumed consent is proposed (at p 64):

AN ETHICAL PRESUMED CONSENT LAW FOR THE UK?

A mixture of the Belgian presumed consent legislation of 1986 and that instituted in Singapore in 1988 could provide an ethically acceptable legal framework for the UK. Such a law would have to include the following elements, in the light of the discussion in the text.

- The opportunity for individual members of society to register their objection and to 'opt-out'. This should be made as easy as possible, and be accompanied by substantial ongoing publicity so that future generations would be aware of the 'default' position.

- The opportunity for sections of society to be automatically excluded – to be 'presumed objectors'. These might include religious groups, such as Muslims or orthodox Jews, as well as the mentally ill or handicapped and other vulnerable groups.

- The family should be provided with the right to initiate an objection and withhold donation in the absence of explicit pledges on behalf of the deceased. This would protect the sensibilities of those families with particularly strong feelings. Doctors would not be obliged to request permission, however.

- The medical profession should be given clear responsibility for implementing the law in the way they see fit on a case by case basis. No compulsion or penalty for failing to act should be involved.

These comprise the broad principles which should guide any presumed consent legislation; the details would obviously need careful debate and drafting. Nevertheless, the Belgian and Singaporean experience has provided us with valuable guidance on workable, ethical legislation.

(For a recent plea for reform of the law, see I Kennedy, R Sells, A Daar *et al* 'The Case for "Presumed Consent" in Organ Donation' (1998) 351 Lancet 1650 and BMA *Organ Donation in the 21st Century* (2000).)

3. Required request

Arthur Caplan 'Organ Procurement: It's Not in the Cards' (1984) 14(5) Hastings Center Report 9

One key factor emerges from both the French and the American experience: the major obstacle to organ procurement is the failure to ask family members about organ donation. French physicians are entitled by law to take tissues without asking anyone but are unwilling to do so. American physicians are entitled by the Uniform Anatomical Gift Act to take tissues from those who sign donor cards but they are unwilling to do so. Whether or not one believes that the wishes of the family should supersede either the wishes of the public, as in France, or the wishes of the individual, as in the United States, in fact both countries always treat the family as the final authority insofar as the disposition of the dead is concerned.

The respect accorded family members' wishes in these two large and medically sophisticated nations would seem to dictate the kind of public change that has the greatest chance of alleviating the shortage in cadaver donors. The French experience indicates that the only practical policy options are those that recognise and respect the role of family members in participating in decisions about cadaver donation. The weak version of required request acknowledges the role of family members, while at the same time ensuring that an optimal environment exists for eliciting organ donations.

Physicians, nurses, or other hospital personnel should be required to inquire whether available family members will give their consent to organ donation. This could be accomplished by modifying the current legal process for declaring death in all states to include a provision requiring that a request concerning organ donation be made to available family members by a party not connected with the determination of death. When family members are not available, organs would be removed only if a donor card or other legal document were present. Or, hospital accreditation requirements could be revised to include a provision mandating that at death the families of potential donors be approached about their willingness to consent.

... People must be asked to act if their altruistic motivations are to make a significant difference in helping those in need.

Cadaver organ donation is, whether we like it or not, a family matter. Families should be given every opportunity to act upon their desire to transform the tragedy of death into the gift of life. But they must be asked. If our society were to institute a policy of weak required request, those who are, according to the public opinion polls, willing to give would have a maximal opportunity to do so. We should not allow our concern for the rights and values of the individual to blind us to policy options that can accommodate both individual autonomy and community good.

An example of legislation in the United States can be seen in a 1985 amendment to the New York Public Health Law.

4351. 1. Where, based on accepted medical standards, a patient is a suitable candidate for organ or tissue donation, the person in charge of such hospital, or his designated representative, other than a person connected with the determination of death, shall at the time of death request any of the following persons, in the order of priority stated, when persons in prior classes are not available and in the absence of (1) actual notice of contrary intentions by the decedent, or (2) actual notice of opposition by a member of any of the classes specified in paragraph (*a*), (*b*), (*c*), (*d*), or (*e*) hereof or (3) other reason to believe that an anatomical gift is contrary to the decedent's religious beliefs, to consent to the gift of all or any part of the decedent's body for any purpose specified in article forty-three of this chapter:
(*a*) the spouse;
(*b*) a son or daughter twenty-one years of age or older;
(*c*) either parent;
(*d*) a brother or sister twenty-one years of age or older;
(*e*) a guardian of the person of the decedent at the time of his death.
Where said hospital administrator or his designee shall have received actual notice of opposition from any of the persons named in the subdivision or where there is otherwise reason to believe that an anatomical gift is contrary to the decedent's religious beliefs, such gift of all or any part of the decedent's body shall not be requested. Where a donation is requested, consent or refusal need only be obtained from the person or persons in the highest priority class available.
2. Where a donation is requested, said person in charge of such hospital or his designated representative shall complete a certificate of request for an anatomical gift, on a form supplied by the commissioner [for health]. Said certificate shall include a statement to the effect that a request for consent to an anatomical gift has been made, and shall further indicate thereupon whether or not consent was granted, the name of the person granting or refusing the consent, and his or her relationship to the decedent. Upon completion of the certificate, said person shall attach the certificate of request for an anatomical gift to the death certificate required by this chapter or, in the city of New York, to the death certificate required by the administrative code of the city of New York.
3. A gift made pursuant to the request required by this section shall be executed pursuant to applicable provisions of article forty-three of this chapter.
4. The commissioner shall establish regulations concerning the training of hospital employees who may be designated to perform the request, and the procedures to be employed in making it.
5. The commissioner shall establish such additional regulations as are necessary for the implementation of this section.

(See further on the position in the US, Daphne Sipes 'Requesting Organ Donations: A New State Approach to Organ Transplants' (1987) 8 Health Law in Canada 39.)
In the UK, not only legislation but even the idea of a 'legally required request' was rejected by the Hoffenberg Working Party (*op cit*):

We have considered *legally required request*. In the USA, 30 States have in the past two years enacted legislation requiring either that the hospital administrator or his designee should ask for the gift of organs, or that protocols are established for requesting the gift. In a smaller number of States there are penalties for non-compliance by fine or loss of licence. We agree with the Society of British Neurological Surgeons and with some others who have given evidence to us that the establishment of the above procedures for referral with an effective audit would be preferable to legally required request.

This seems a rather perfunctory rejection of the notion of a legally 'required request'. It could be said that the Working Party was more concerned with legal sanction against doctors who do not 'request' as a statute would require, rather than with the notion of required request *per se*.

Nevertheless, there are dangers of enacting such a law as is pointed out in the King's Fund Report (*op cit*) (at p 63):

> Doctors and relatives may find the system distressing, though for rather different reasons than those relating to presumed consent. Doctors may be put under pressure to find that donors are suitable candidates for donation with implications for the diagnosis of brain stem death. Unlike presumed consent legislation, required request prescribes actions. It does not in general allow for the doctor to decide on a case by case basis the proper approach. In some circumstances it may be quite clear that requesting organ donation may be insensitive to the needs of the family. To suggest to relatives that organ donation is a gift of life is to play upon their emotions and guilt feelings at the time of their loved one's death.
>
> There is also a danger that respect for donors may be eroded in the constant search for organs and this may have long term implications for public confidence in the medical team and the organ donation process. In general it seems clear that required request's prescriptive nature, and the associated problems of enforceability, mean that it is ethically unsustainable. There is also little evidence that it would be effective in improving the supply.

As regards the final point, the King's Fund Report makes the following observation (at p 60):

> While there was an initial increase in the availability of organs, over time the schemes do not appear to have had a major impact. One reason for this, it is suggested, is the lack of institutional commitment to ensuring that the required request procedures are followed. The United States experience illustrates that simply to enact required request legislation is not enough. It is vital to have adequately trained and qualified personnel.
>
> As one organ procurement official observed:
>
> > if you simply ask relatives about organ donation by simply citing the law the consent rate is zero.
>
> Another reason suggested for the lack of dramatic impact of required request is that doctors find organ procurement time consuming and emotionally demanding. It is questionable whether statutory enactment of required request would have a significant impact. The national audit found that only 6 per cent of relatives in the UK are not approached when an otherwise potential donor is on a ventilator, and many of these would probably have communicated their unwillingness to consider donation by other means.

4.   Without permission

The most radical reform would be to dispense altogether with the need for consent by the deceased or relatives and to permit the taking of organs even if there was objection. We saw this referred to in the King's Fund Institute Report earlier. The arguments for this were put by Professor Jesse Dukeminier in an important article in 1970.

Jesse Dukeminier 'Supplying Organs for Transplantation' (1970) 68 Michigan Law Review 811

Removal of cadaver organs regardless of objection
A recent analysis of the problem of supplying organs resulted in the suggestion that legislation be enacted to authorise the removal, with or without consent, of cadaver organs useful for transplantation. The ethical basis for this solution to the problem of organ supply is that saving human life is paramount to all other policies and that no one has the right to deny another the chance to live.

Today, in disposing of the dead, the principle of protecting life requires that a coroner perform an autopsy on a body when homicidal behaviour is suspected, even though the next of kin objects. Courts have uniformly held that the rights of the decedent and next of kin are subordinate to the paramount public interest in apprehending killers. In these circumstances the autopsy may be held without the consent of the next of kin or even over his positive objection. Catching a murderer both prevents further homicidal behaviour by the man apprehended and deters homicidal behaviour by others. The overriding principle is protecting the lives of the survivors. ....

If one accepts the view that saving human life requires the removal of useful cadaver organs regardless of the wishes of the decedent or next of kin the question arises whether a statute effectuating that policy would run foul of any constitutional provisions prohibiting the taking of property without compensation. One recent study concludes that such a statute would constitute a taking of the property of the next of kin, who would have to be paid compensation for the cadaver organs. That conclusion, however, is erroneous. Even accepting the highly questionable assumption that it is appropriate to classify the next of kin's interest in a cadaver as a property right, the next of kin's claim does not become an 'interest' in property until the death of the decedent. At any time prior to the occurrence of that event, the potential interest may be abolished without paying compensation, as may be seen by an analysis of the law relating to the closely analogous cases of a right of dower or an expectancy of an heir. While the decedent is alive, these rights are contingent upon surviving the decedent; in legal parlance, dower remains inchoate, and the expectancy of an heir is not recognised as an interest or right at all. Inchoate dower may be abolished without violating the Constitution. Indeed almost a hundred years ago the Supreme Court [*Rendall v Kreiger* (1874) 90 US (23 Wall) 137, 148] declared:

> [Dower] is wholly given and the power that gave it may increase, diminish, or otherwise alter it, or wholly take it away. It is upon the same footing with the expectancy of heirs, apparent or presumptive, before the death of the ancestor. Until that event occurs the law of descent and distribution may be moulded according to the will of the legislature.

Thus, by analogy to inchoate dower or to the expectancy of an heir, it may be concluded that the rights of the next of kin to control the cadavers of persons living can be changed or abolished without paying any compensation.

It might also be thought that the decedent has an interest in what is done with his body, but the common-law rule is that there is no property in a dead body and that consequently a man cannot by will dispose of his body. If, however, cadaver organs are deemed to be property, compensation for their taking is not required, since succession to a man's property at death can be changed, and perhaps even abolished, by a legislature without violating the Constitution.

> Rights of succession to the property of a deceased, whether by will or by intestacy, are of statutory creation, and the dead hand rules succession only by sufferance. Nothing in the Federal Constitution forbids the legislature of a state to limit, condition, or even abolish the power of testamentary disposition over property within its jurisdiction. [*Irving Trust Co v Day* (1942) 314 US 556 562]

State supreme courts, with the exception of that of Wisconsin, agree that the power to dispose of property by will may be controlled by the legislature, subject only to the constitutional guarantees of equal protection and due process of law. These broad statements may not be wholly reliable, inasmuch as the power of the legislature to abolish testation has never been directly tested. Yet if the state can take by taxation a percentage of a man's property at death in order to raise revenue and to break up great fortunes, it is difficult to find any reason why the state cannot constitutionally take a specific item, such as a kidney, to save a human life.

Moreover, if organs are treated as property of the decedent, the decedent may have no power to order destruction of his organs by burial or cremation so long as the organs have value. It has been held in a number of cases that a direction to destroy one's own property at death is against public policy and is therefore void. Although these cases could provide the basis for an argument that permitting the destruction of valuable human organs to satisfy a decedent's wish is against public policy, courts today probably would not accept such an argument. Thinking of a cadaver as a valuable resource is still too startling; but as organ transplants become very successful courts may become more receptive to the argument.

It is, however, extremely troublesome to use property terms in the litany of justification for the taking of cadaver organs, for cadaver organs are not property in any conventional sense. Under modern law the next of kin is given a cause of action for unauthorised dissection, and courts have sometimes characterised this right in the next of kin as a property or a quasi-property right. But as Dean Prosser points out, 'it is in reality the personal feelings of the survivors which are being protected under a fiction likely to deceive no one but a lawyer' [*The Law of Torts* 51 (3d edn, 1964)]. Even if the fiction is accepted for purposes of unauthorised dissection cases, the answer to the question whether the rights are property rights for purposes of the Constitution should not turn upon a characterisation made by state courts in such an entirely different context. In determining the constitutionality of legislation authorising the removal of cadaver organs regardless of objection it is inappropriate to begin the analysis by accepting a characterisation of cadaver organs as property. As Justice Jackson said some years ago with reference to another claim of a constitutionally protected 'property right'. 'We cannot start the process of decision by calling such a claim as we have here a "property right"; whether it is a property right is really the question to be answered.' [*United States v Willow River Power Co* (1945) 324 US 499 at 502]

In striking a balance between the interests of the public and the desires of the decedent and the survivors, legislatures have already subordinated the interests of the decedent and survivors to the public interest in saving human life, to interests of public health and convenience, and to the economic welfare of undertakers, employers, and insurers. In view of that background, it would surely be odd to find that the fourteenth amendment forbids subordinating the interest of the decedent and next of kin to the public interest in saving the life of a human being.

The arguments have been taken up more recently by Professor John Harris, a philosopher, who argues that dead bodies should be in the public domain.

John Harris *Clones, Genes, and Immortality* (2nd edn, 1998)

The solution to the problem of sensibilities is of course to determine that cadavers, like the foreshore, belong to the state and that therefore neither relatives nor the former 'owners' of the cadavers would have any binding interest in their fate. People would, I believe, soon get used to the idea, particularly if there was a concerted campaign of education and argument, and the automatic public ownership of dead bodies and their bodily products would remove the need to interpose intrusive requests between people and their grief.

Indeed it seems clear that the benefits from cadaver transplants are so great, and the reasons for objecting so transparently selfish or superstitious, that we should remove altogether the habit of seeking the consent of either the deceased or relatives. This we already do when post-mortem examinations are ordered without any consents being required and despite the fact that these too involve interference with the dignity of a dead body and the removal (albeit temporarily) of organs. It has always seemed to me curious that the state can order a post-mortem examination to satisfy its curiosity about the cause of death, but not order cadaver transplants in order to save the lives of living citizens. Of course, post-mortems are not usually ordered out of simply curiosity, there are public safety and public policy considerations. It is important that the cause of death be known in case the same cause represents a further danger to the community, whether that danger be in the form of a disease or contagion, or in the form of a possible murderer at large. But again related but more powerful considerations weigh in favour of public ownership of cadavers ...

This is, to say the least, a controversial position and not one which is likely to find its way on to the legislative agenda of any UK Government in the near future. Indeed, it would not reflect contemporary European public policy. Article 16 of the Draft Protocol on *Transplantation of Organs and Tissues of Human Origin* (1999) provides the deceased (but not the relatives) with a veto on the removal of tissue or organs for transplantation.

E. XENOTRANSPLANTATION

One source of organs which we have not considered so far is animals. Xenotransplantation has been mooted as a significant remedy to the shortage of some organs and tissues. In particular, pigs are seen as a potential source of such material for transplantation. Xenotransplantation raises a number of issues for the law which we discuss elsewhere, for example, the regulation of research and the obligations owed to a research subject (see *supra*, ch 14). The practice also raises questions about the use of animals for human ends and also scientific (and ultimately ethical) issues about the risks involved of transmitting pathogens to recipients and possibly the wider public. We do not discuss these issues in detail here (see M Fox 'Animal Rights and Wrongs: Medical Ethics and the Killing of Non-Human Animals' in R Lee and D Morgan (eds) *Death Rites: Law and Ethics at the End of Life* (1994) p 131; W Cartwright 'The Pig, the Transplant Surgeon and the Nuffield Council' (1996) 4 Med L Rev 250: M Fox and J McHale 'Xenotransplantation: The Ethical and Legal Ramifications' (1998) 6 Med L Rev 42).

The Government's *Advisory Group on the Ethics of Xenotransplantation* (1996) examined the ethical, scientific, legal and public policy issues raised by xenotransplantation (see recommendations 34–56, *infra*). We set out here in full the summary of its main conclusions and recommendations.

Advisory Group on the Ethics of Xenotransplantation (1996)

1   The **Advisory Group on the Ethics of Xenotransplantation** was appointed by the Secretary of State for Health with the following terms of reference:

In the light of recent and potential developments in xenotransplantation, to review the acceptability of and ethical framework within which xenotransplantation may be undertaken and to make recommendations.

2. Xenotransplantation is the transplant of tissue (including solid organs) between species. We are primarily concerned with xenotransplantation in the context of the use of non-human animals to provide tissue for transplant to humans. Interest in xenotransplantation has been reawakened by scientific developments which seek to enable humans to tolerate animal tissue (specifically that of the pig) by modifying the genetic make-up of the pig through the addition of particular human genes.

3. We use the word tissue to refer to solid organs and other tissue. We use the word animal to refer to non-human animals. We describe animals from which tissue is taken as **source animals**.

4. Our assessment of the ethical acceptability of xenotransplantation involves a two stage process: first whether this use of animals is unacceptable under any circumstances; secondly whether it may be acceptable under certain circumstances and, if so, what circumstances make it so. Our response to this second question led us to identify the benefits which xenotransplantation could bring and to weigh them against the possible harms, whether to animals, patients or the wider population.

5. Our main conclusion is that it is not currently acceptable to move to trials involving humans due to the lack of knowledge at the present time concerning aspects of physiology, immunology and the risk of infection (see paragraph 16, 17 and 20). We also recommend that a National Standing Committee should be established to oversee the development of xenotransplantation. Any applications to undertake trials would have to be approved by this Committee (see paragraph 47). The Committee should be established by law.

6. We reached these conclusions concerning the ethical acceptability of xenotransplantation as follows:
   - we recognise that some may regard all use of animals as wrong regardless of any potential benefits;
   - we do not adopt this position, but rather a weighing of benefit versus harm;
   - we consider that benefits to patients and the wider population may flow from the development and introduction of xenotransplantation;
   - we consider that any benefits must, however, be set against the possibility of harm arising.

7. Animals vary a great deal in their abilities and mental capacities and presumably in their capacity for suffering. The non-human primates (hereafter, primates), including chimpanzees and baboons, are at the higher end of this scale, and have close affinities with humans. We consider that these animals can be distinguished from other animals not least by virtue of their greater self-awareness and mental capacity. We consider that these features increase their capacity for suffering, particularly given the conditions under which source animals would be kept in order to ensure proper controls (eg biosecure and isolated accommodation). **We therefore conclude that it would be ethically unacceptable to use primates as source animals for xenotransplantation, not least because they would be exposed to too much suffering** [Para 4.28].

8. But primates are also involved in the **research** being carried out into xenotransplantation, primarily as recipients of tissue transplanted from pigs. We regard such research as being necessary to protect the interests of potential patients. Can this use in research be justified? A primate used for research purposes may (indirectly) provide benefit for a large number of humans, due to the information generated from the research. Thus, the ratio of benefit to humans against harm to the primate may provide an ethical basis for the use of primates in research. By contrast, a primate used as a source animal could only benefit one or at best a very small number of humans. Further, the conditions which would prevail for primates to be used in research would not be those which prevail for source animals. We recognise the case for such research to take place and note that such research is currently permitted under the provisions of the Animals (Scientific Procedures) Act and thus: **We conclude that it would be ethically acceptable to use primates in the research into xenotransplantation, but only where no alternative method of obtaining information exists and this use should be limited so far as is possible** [Para 4.29].

9. The pig is attracting the most interest as a potential source animal. We ask whether the use of this animal as a source for xenotransplantation is similarly ethically unacceptable? **We conclude that the use of the pig for xenotransplantation may be ethically acceptable. We conclude further, however, that the acceptability lies in balancing the benefit to humans against the harm both to the pig and to humans** [Para 4.30].

10. This conclusion entails an analysis which weighs not only the benefits to humans against the harm done to the pig, but also the benefits to individual patients against the potential harm both to those patients and to the wider human population. The various harms which are

intrinsic to xenotransplantation include the effects on the animal of genetic modification and the effects on the human of transplantation of animal tissue, the possible suffering of patients, the possible suffering of animals, and the potential harm caused by diverting attention away from other areas of research and resources towards this treatment.

11. The pigs intended for use in xenotransplantation are genetically modified. **We take the view that some degree of genetic modification is ethically acceptable providing that there is a concomitant benefit to humans and that the pig neither suffers unduly nor ceases recognisably to be a pig** [Para 4.36].

12. Further genetic modification of animals may be proposed over the coming years. **We take the view that there are limits to the extent to which an animal should be genetically modified and that constant monitoring both of animals which have been modified, so as to assess effects, and of proposed genetic modifications must take place** [Para 4.39].

13. There is a general misgiving about transplanting animal tissue into humans and, in particular, concern about transplantation of certain tissues. **We take the view that the procedures currently proposed do not go beyond acceptable limits and, further, that the criterion for evaluating the ethical acceptability of xenotransplants depends on the function performed by the tissue involved** [Para 4.43].

14. However, further developments may raise concerns. **We take the view, therefore, that new developments should be monitored to ascertain whether they appear to go beyond what may be acceptable limits** [Para 4.44].

15. There remain medical risks which may result from xenotransplantation, related to physiology (the functioning of the tissue), immunology (the possible rejection of the tissue), and infection (transmitted from the animal through the tissue to the patient and possibly the wider population).

16. **We conclude that the evidence on transplant function, organ growth and the functioning of the recipient's immune system within the transplant is too limited, at the current time, to justify a move to clinical trials. We recommend that further research should be carried out and analysed before such trials can take place. We note that some of this research may involve the use of primates and must therefore be read in the light of the recommendations we have made about their use** [Para 4.50].

17. **We consider that the evidence on immunological rejection is too limited, at the current time, to justify a move to clinical trials. We recommend that further research should be carried out to investigate more fully the rejection processes associated with xenotransplantation and to determine an effective and acceptable immunosuppression regimen** [Para 4.52].

18. As regards the risks of infection, these vary between infectious agents. **We consider that it is ethically acceptable to take the risks of infection associated with fungi, parasites, bacteria and prions provided that source animals are maintained in conditions which aim to minimise the risk of infection and provided that any infections which arise are monitored. We accordingly recommend that such conditions are established for animals reared for use in xenotransplantation** [Para 4.55].

19. Prion-related diseases can remain latent for long periods of time and it is currently only possible to positively identify their presence after death. **We further recommend, therefore, that with regard to prion-related diseases, there should be a programme of culling of sentinel pigs over a wide age range to test for neuropathological changes** [Para 4.56].

20. Viruses cause the most concern particularly as it is possible that there are a number of porcine viruses which have not yet been identified. **We conclude that there is insufficient knowledge about the known viruses to make it safe to proceed to clinical trails at the current time. We recommend that further research should be carried out on known viruses, including the porcine retroviruses, cytomegalovirus (CMV) and circovirus, before clinical trials may be considered** [Para 4.58].

21. Given that there are likely to be other pathogens which have not yet been identified, we asked ourselves whether it would **ever** be ethically acceptable to proceed with xenotransplantation. **We conclude that, at the stage when it is considered that a full investigation of potential infection risks has been carried out, and the risks have been shown to be within tolerable margins, it would be ethically acceptable to proceed. This is subject to there being a system in place to monitor the emergence of any unusual disease or any unknown pathogens and to require, as a consequence, that appropriate additional research be completed in a proper fashion** [Para 4.63].

22. We attach importance to infection control and monitoring arrangements. It would be important to maintain infection control standards in the animal facilities. **We recommend that such standards be designed and agreed and further recommend that animal facilities be monitored to ensure that these standards are observed** [Para 4.66].

23. The transport of animals (or of tissue) between sites and the removal of tissue are points in any production process where biosecure conditions might more easily be breached. **We**

recommend that particular attention be paid to these, in terms of both, establishing and monitoring standards [Para 4.67].

24. There is one further issue relating to the risk of infection. We are not aware of any assessment of the risks to animals through the mutation of animal pathogens in human hosts and **we recommend that this issue should be considered further** [Para 4.70].

25. We have recommended that a range of investigations be undertaken with the aim of providing further information on the physiological, immunological and infection effects of xenotransplantation. **We recommend that this programme should be co-ordinated, so far as is possible, and the results monitored and assessed with a view to determining whether further research is needed and whether clinical trials are acceptable** [Para 4.71].

26. There is a limit to the information which may be provided through trials on primates. **We recommend that those who have responsibility for co-ordinating the programme should do so with particular regard to this point** [Para 4.72].

27. Infection control arrangements in animal facilities may cause some degree of harm to the animals. Our concerns relate to the procedures involved in the xenotransplantation production process; to the infection-free environment, including monitoring arrangements; to some specific restrictions on the movement of pigs; and to the potential wastage of animals.

28. The procedures which would take place in a xenotransplantation production process and which would cause us concern are:
    - the removal, and then replacement, of eggs from sows under anaesthesia (so that the human gene may be micro-injected into the egg).
    - hysterectomy and removal of the piglets from the sow.
    - the serial tissue sampling which takes place to test for genetic modification and for infectious agents.

    However, these are intrinsic parts of the programme and are currently unavoidable. Although these procedures are *currently* unavoidable, every effort should be made to minimise suffering through development of alternative techniques.

29. Tissue will be removed from the animal under appropriate anaesthesia and, usually, the animal will be killed immediately. However, the sequential removal of tissue is a possibility. **We conclude that the sequential removal of solid organs is ethically unacceptable and further, we take the view that the sequential removal of any tissue is ethically unacceptable** [Paras 4.93–4.94]. We exclude here the taking of blood and tissue for monitoring purposes.

30. Controlled environments, such as specific pathogen free conditions, may raise specific concerns about animal welfare. For example, there may be a lack of rooting or bedding material, low levels of natural light and possible social isolation. **We recommend that such issues be addressed in the design of SPF facilities for xenotransplantation to determine whether improvements can be made** [Para 4.95].

31. We are also concerned, specifically, about the use of farrowing crates. This, of course, is not unique to xenotransplantation and we recognise that there is currently no practical alternative available. **We recommend that research to establish appropriate alternatives to farrowing crates should be encouraged** [Para 4.96].

32. The issue of **wastage** of pigs arises at various points in the process of producing pigs for xenotransplantation. **We recommend that wastage rates be monitored closely during any future development of xenotransplantation** [Para 4.97].

33. Research into aspects of xenotransplantation will continue for some considerable time, including the transplantation of pig tissue to primates. **We therefore take the view that further research involving primates should be kept to the minimum necessary, and that, wherever appropriate, other means of generating reliable information be used. We also recommend that the welfare of the animals used should be closely monitored and supervised** [Para 4.98].

34. We conclude, generally, that: **from the point of view of animal welfare, the use of pigs for xenotransplantation is ethically acceptable as long as continued efforts are made to avoid or minimise the harm caused** [Para 4.99].

35. We are concerned that resources for xenotransplantation are allocated fairly and justly and with regard to alternative services. **We recommend therefore that the National Specialist Commissioning Advisory Group (NSCAG) consider the purchase of the various xenotransplantation services, should their development reach the stage at which central support for the treatment costs might be appropriate during clinical evaluation. NSCAG could also consider the purchase of xenotransplant services, should they become established, but not widely provided, services. We further recommend that in its considerations, the NSCAG should take account of the various concerns which we have expressed in this Report** [Para 4.106].

36. Xenotransplantation may have a detrimental effect on the allotransplantation programme in that public perception of its success, or otherwise, could affect the supply of human

organs. Our concern relates to the risk of reducing the supply. **We accordingly recommend that consideration be given to means of educating the public about xenotransplantation** [Para 4.110].

37. The advent of xenotransplantation may also affect the development of other therapies, should investment be directed at it rather than more generally. **We take the view that Government, through the relevant mechanisms, should ensure that research into therapeutic responses for those whose conditions currently call for transplantation, in addition to xenotransplantation, is adequately supported** [Para 4.112].

38. The assessment of the ethical acceptability of xenotransplantation also depends on the existence and availability of other therapies. If there are no such therapies, xenotransplantation would appear to have the advantage. However, if such therapies exist, or could be developed in the relevant timescale, it becomes more difficult ethically to make the case for xenotransplantation. No unique benefit would flow from it to outweigh the ethical concerns which are intrinsic to it.

39. Allotransplantation is currently the treatment of choice for those patients who could benefit from xenotransplantation, but the allotransplant programme is restricted due to the shortage of organs and other tissue. We asked ourselves whether this programme could be improved. **We conclude that more organs, and other tissue, *could* be obtained from cadaveric donors.** This could be achieved primarily through continued attention to improving management of the organ retrieval system and to training those involved. **We recommend that due attention continue to be given to improving donation rates** [Para 5.19].

40. Further options for increasing the availability of cadaveric organs and tissue would exist, should there be changes in UK law. **We do not, however, recommend such changes.** We are not convinced that they are justified on the basis of current evidence. **We recommend, however, they be kept under review** [Para 5.20].

41. There appears to be potential for therapies other than xenotransplantation to be developed in response to the conditions currently requiring transplantation, in particular, artificial organs and somatic cell gene therapy. **We recommend that appropriate means be found to support and encourage continued research into the development and application of gene therapy and artificial organs** [Para 5.40].

42. Health promotion measures and preventive medicine might assist in avoiding the need for transplantation. There seems to be some potential for such measures to make some impact. However we emphasise that some of the relevant medical conditions are not amenable to these measures. We nevertheless **recommend that such measures should continue to be pursued** [Para 5.49].

43. We conclude that there are indeed other procedures, either in existence (such as health promotion methods) or in development (such as artificial organs) which may provide alternatives to xenotransplantation. We repeat that such methods must be pursued in tandem with xenotransplantation. We do not consider that it is possible to predict, at the present time, which therapies are most likely to meet the needs of the patients whose conditions currently call for transplantation. We consider that these means of meeting the needs of patients must be explored as they potentially offer the benefits of xenotransplantation without some of its inherent harms.

44. We have outlined a number of conditions in paragraphs 11–37. **We conclude that only if the conditions which we have outlined are met could xenotransplantation be considered to be ethically acceptable** [Para 6.2]. These conditions include the prohibition of primates as a source species, conditions designed to minimise the risks to the patient and the wider population, and conditions designed to minimise the harms to the animal.

45. What we are concluding, in effect, by those of our conditions which refer to the state of scientific knowledge, is that current knowledge is not yet such as to allow us to support the introduction of xenotransplantation at the present time. Given the constantly changing nature of science, the conditions we have established are necessarily conditions arising from what we currently know. They are, therefore, necessary but not sufficient conditions [Para 6.7].

46. We therefore conclude that some mechanism should be put in place to ensure that these conditions are met and that no research into xenotransplantation involving humans should be carried out until there is evidence that these conditions have been met. We also note that any approval of clinical trials would not presuppose a move to a therapeutic programme. The outcomes of clinical trails, for each proposed xenotransplant therapy, should be carefully assessed before any such move to a therapeutic programme is contemplated. There is also a clear need for the progress of clinical trials to be closely monitored and to be stopped, should it be thought appropriate in the light of adverse effects. Similarly, any therapeutic programme must be monitored and discontinued if thought appropriate in the light of adverse effects [Para 6.8].

47. We therefore **conclude that a Standing Committee on xenotransplantation is required to monitor and review these matters and accordingly recommend the establishment**

of such a committee. **We further recommend that such a Committee should have a national role and that it should be established by primary legislation** [Para 6.9].

48. The second element in our terms of reference concerns the nature of any ethical framework within which xenotransplantation, were it to proceed, could ethically be undertaken. The development of this framework involves consideration of the further ethical concerns which arise, should xenotransplantation proceed to involve humans, first, in clinical trials, and potentially, in therapeutic programmes. Consideration of the framework also involves consideration of the current legal framework and discussion of the responsibilities of the proposed National Standing Committee.

49. The further ethical considerations which arise relate to the patient, the professionals who would be involved, the clinical sites in which xenotransplantation procedures would take place and our recognition of the ethical difficulties which xenotransplantation poses.

50. One issue is whether children and those incapable of giving valid consent should be considered for inclusion in clinical trials. **We recommend that children should not be included in trials, at least until all the initial concerns about safety and efficacy have been satisfactorily resolved. We take the same view as regards those incapable of giving valid consent** [Para 7.7].

51. Consent is an exceptionally complex concept from both an ethical and legal standpoint. We are content to conclude here that the principles ordinarily applied both in the context of therapeutic research and treatment should equally apply to xenotransplantation. However, there are certain particular issues which are raised by xenotransplantation and which call for particular comment. **We recommend that they should be incorporated into any consent arrangements, so that the patient may be properly informed** [Para 7.11].

52. We note the need of the patient to assimilate a considerable volume of information, as part of the consent process. **We recommend that a system of counselling, independent of the transplant team, should be in place and that prospective xenotransplant recipients should have access to it, both before any clinical trial and if judged appropriate, subsequently, should any xenotransplant programme be established** [Para 7.13].

53. The potential psychological and social effects of xenotransplantation are an issue of potential significance and on which there is little evidence. **We recommend that the psychological effects of xenotransplantation should be kept under review and that consideration should be given to funding research into these effects** [Para 7.14].

54. Some patients, for whatever reason, might choose not to opt for a xenotransplantation procedure. **We recommend that patients who choose not to opt for xenotransplantation should not be penalised in any way in their medical care** [Para 7.15].

55. The relatives of patients who would be undergoing a new and untried form of treatment also deserve consideration. **We recommend that the clinical site where the xenotransplantation procedure takes place should address the needs of relatives as well as the needs of patients** [Para 7.20].

56. A variety of professionals would be involved in xenotransplantation such that a wide variety of related issues would need to be addressed. These include their training needs and the consequent provision of training and the complementary nature of the roles of the professions involved. **We recommend that these issues be addressed as a matter of priority, taking advice from interested professional groups** [Para 7.25].

57. We also consider registration of those who would be involved with the source animals to be important. The Institute of Animal Technology produces guidelines which apply to Registered Animal Technicians. The British Veterinary Nursing Association produces similar guidelines for Veterinary Nurses. **We consider that such guidelines (currently non-statutory) should apply to all animal technicians and veterinary nurses involved in xenotransplantation, together with an appropriate system of monitoring compliance with them** [Para 7.24].

58. We recognise that, as in the rest of the population, the views of the professionals in veterinary and human health care will vary. **We consider that those whose work may involve them in xenotransplantation must be given information about xenotransplantation and its effects, so that they are able to make a personal decision** about their involvement. **Further, we take the view that any person in such a situation should have the right to "opt-out" of this work without prejudice to career or employment.** This right should be protected by legislation [Para 7.26].

59. It is clear from the above that any clinical site where xenotransplantation took place would have a range of responsibilities to fulfil. **We recommend that those clinical sites in which it may be proposed that xenotransplantation should take place be assessed at the early clinical trial stage. We further recommend that any assessment should be based on the conditions which we have outlined** [Para 7.28].

60. We have concluded that the conditions which we have outlined are such that they should be backed by primary legislation. If a legal framework (whether in one law or a combination of laws) were to exist which could serve the needs which we have identified, this would

obviate the need to recommend primary legislation. However, we conclude that, although there are provisions in current legislation which address many of our concerns, they do not entirely meet the needs which we have identified. As a consequence, **we recommend that a comprehensive statutory framework of regulation be put in place, taking account of and drawing upon existing law wherever it is relevant and appropriate** [Para 8.4].

61. **We further recommend that such legislation should, among other things, ensure that the animals involved in xenotransplantation are brought and remain within the provisions of the Animals (Scientific Procedures) Act 1986 (ASPA) by appropriate amendments** [Para 8.35].

62. We have recognised that the Animals (Scientific Procedures) Act can meet a number of our concerns about animal welfare and that a well-established and highly regarded system of inspection exists. But xenotransplantation would raise new issues and **we therefore recommend that an appropriate code of practice be issued under ASPA and that this should take into account the concerns which we have expressed** [Para 8.36].

63. We have already noted it is possible that biosecure conditions be breached during the transport of tissue or animals. **We therefore recommend that the movement of tissue be brought within regulatory control in the primary legislation which we propose** [Para 8.45].

64. We consider that any proposed use for food of animals which are part of any xenotransplantation programme should be regulated. The EC Novel Foods Regulation meets our concerns on this point but we note that labelling may not be required for those animals which are the product of a xenotransplantation programme but are not genetically modified. **We recommend that consideration should be given to whether such animals should be used as food and, if so, whether labelling on food produced from them is required** [Para 8.49].

65. We considered both domestic and European legislation which relates to medicines and medical devices. We have noted the highly regarded regulatory structures which exist under such legislation. However, it is our opinion that these could not be said, beyond significant doubt, to apply to xenotransplantation and that, therefore, the existing legal framework is inadequate to answer our concerns about risks to patients and to the wider population arising from tissue from animals which are part of a xenotransplantation programme. **We recommend that the legislation which we propose take account of these regulatory structures so as to ensure that a similar structure is put in place to regulate any procedure involving xenotransplantation** [Para 8.67].

66. We consider that clinical trials of xenotransplantation procedures should be considered to be "medical research". **We recommend that the approval and monitoring of such trials should be conditional on the approval of and monitoring by the National Standing Committee** which we propose [Para 8.74].

67. We have expressed the view that there are potential limits to the ethical acceptability of the genetic modification of animals for the purposes of xenotransplantation and to the animal tissue which may be transplanted into humans. **We recommend the National Standing Committee monitor developments and examine any which could cause public concern** [Para 8.75].

68. It is possible that the private sector may wish to undertake xenotransplantation. **We recommend that guidance be issued to Health Authorities that the prior approval of xenotransplantation procedures by the National Standing Committee should be regarded as a condition for obtaining or remaining registration under Part II of the Registered Homes Act 1984. We further recommend that any new primary legislation on xenotransplantation should seek to ensure that similar conditions apply for independent facilities as for NHS hospitals** [Para 8.77].

69. Developments in xenotransplantation are taking place around the world and several different groups, including the Food and Drug Administration in the United States and the World Health Organisation, are developing guidelines. **We recommend that appropriate account be taken of international developments and that there should be liaison with the EC and with other Member States and with appropriate international organisations, particularly in the framing of appropriate legislation and regulations** [Para 8.85].

70. We have concluded that new, specific, primary legislation to regulate xenotransplantation is required in the interests of patients, public health and animal welfare. We recognise, however, the pressure on Parliamentary timetables. **We therefore recommend, as an interim measure only, that our recommendations, particularly with regard to the National Standing Committee, are taken forward on a non-statutory basis until such time as legislation can be brought forward.** Such an interim body should not be regarded as a substitute for legislation [Para 9.2].

71. **We recommend that the National Standing Committee should have overall national responsibility for overseeing the development of xenotransplantation; that is, the transplant of viable, replicating, animal tissue into humans.** Its role will cover, broadly, the **setting of standards** for continued research into and, if appropriate, the introduction of xenotransplantation, and **ensuring their implementation.** Given the range of expertise which would necessarily be represented on such a Committee it could additionally be responsible for a range of related, additional, functions. The Committee would be charged with ensuring that the recommendations contained in this Report are implemented [Para 9.3].

72. As regards overseeing the development of xenotransplantation, **we further recommend that in carrying out its responsibilities, the National Standing Committee should work with other interested bodies in an appropriate way so as to co-ordinate the work being undertaken, thus minimising duplication, and to call upon the skill and expertise necessary to undertake its role successfully** [Para 9.6].

73. We note that the Animal Procedures Committee does not directly consider each of the many licence applications made. **We recommend that the Home Secretary treat xenotransplantation as a special case, and request the APC to consider which mechanisms may be needed to deal in a co-ordinated manner with all applications which involve xenotransplantation** [Para 9.8].

74. We see a need for close liaison between the National Standing Committee on Xenotransplantation and the Animal Procedures Committee. **We accordingly recommend that the National Standing Committee should act in co-ordination with the Animal Procedures Committee and measures to achieve this should be addressed as a matter of urgency.** [Para 9.9].

75. We have argued that the National Standing Committee should approve any applications for clinical research involving xenotransplantation but we also recognise the role of Local Research Ethics Committees. Thus, we **recommend that the National Standing Committee should co-ordinate its activities with those of LRECs.** We further **recommend that any proposal for research into xenotransplantation which involves humans must be approved by the National Standing Committee prior to approval by a properly constituted LREC.** We also **recommend that the arrangements for the co-ordinated working of the proposed National Standing Committee with LRECs should be addressed as a matter of urgency and further that these arrangements should seek to minimise the problems of delay and bureaucracy** [Para 9.10].

76. **We recommend that the proposed National Standing Committee should be funded by, and be under the aegis of the appropriate UK Government Departments** [Para 9.12].

77. We have recommended that, as a temporary measure, the National Committee should be set up on an interim basis. **We recommend that such a committee be supported by some means of control, through, for example, appropriate guidance to LRECs, and that the Committee should be empowered, where necessary, to bring matters of concern to the attention of Ministers** [Para 9.14].

The Government in January 1997 announced its broad agreement with the report but sought further consultation on some issues (see *The Government Response to 'Animal Tissue into Humans'* (January 1997)). In particular, the Government announced the setting up of the UK Xenotransplantation Interim Regulatory Authority (UKXIRA) to oversee xenotransplantation. The UKXIRA is charged with the role of evaluating 'aspects of safety, ethics and efficacy' of xenotransplantation. In July 1998, the Secretary of State issued Directions to NHS bodies requiring his prior approval before treatments involving xenotransplantation are commissioned or offered (HSC 1988/126). Any trial or procedure involving xenotransplantation into humans must first be approved by UKXIRA together with any other relevant approval from an appropriate ethics committee, the Gene Therapy Advisory Committee (GTAC) and the involvement of the Medicines Control Agency (MCA) or Medical Devices Agency (MDA) if appropriate. Authorisation under the Animals (Scientific Procedures) Act 1986 would also be required in relation to the use of the animals. The Government produced an accompanying document, *Guidance on Making Proposals to Conduct Xenotransplantation on Human Subjects* (1998). Thereby, a quasi-legislative scheme for carrying forward xenotransplantation was set up, including a detailed procedure with guidance for making applications to UKXIRA.

Use of foetuses and foetal tissue

In this section we are concerned with use of foetal tissue principally for transplantation but also for research (for the use of dead bodies generally, see *infra*, ch 18).

A. THE BACKGROUND

The following article by Professor Raanan Gillon sets the scene:

Raanan Gillon 'Editorial' (1988) 296 BMJ 1212

Ethics of fetal brain cell transplants

In analysing the ethical issues provoked by the technique of transplanting fetal brain cells into the brains of patients with Parkinson's disease ... it may be helpful to consider the various affected parties within the framework of four widely acceptable moral considerations: respect for people and their autonomy, beneficence (doing good), non-maleficence (avoiding doing harm), and justice (fairness in distribution of resources, in respect for rights, and in respect for morally acceptable laws). Such analysis is benefited by discussion on this subject at Britain's first multidisciplinary conference on philosophy and ethics in reproductive medicine, which was held [in April 1988] in Leeds.

Obligations to the recipients of the fetal brain cells seem well met. Thus, as the conference heard from Dr Richard West, chairman of the ethics committee that approved the research, the committee followed the standard research ethics committee guidelines of the Royal College of Physicians. Theoretical considerations, animal research, and preliminary results of clinical research abroad had shown a reasonable prospect of benefiting the severely affected patients (beneficence) with an acceptably low risk of harming them (non-maleficence). The requirement of adequately informed consent respected their autonomy, and no justice considerations were infringed either in terms of fair distribution of resources or infringement of the subject's rights; and the procedures were legally acceptable.

Moral qualms were expressed at the conference about the women whose aborted fetuses were used. Although such women signed consent forms disclaiming any views on the disposal of the fetus, some participants vigorously argued that the women concerned ought to be given more explicit information if the fetal tissues might be used for transplantation or other research and their specific unpressured consent obtained. On the other hand, a woman lawyer argued that not to be satisfied with an adult woman's signature disclaiming views on disposal of the fetus smacked of patronising sexism. In addition, such women might be benefited by being told the outcome, where successful, of any use made of fetal tissues, as proposed by the Conference of Medical Royal Colleges for transplantation.

The women's welfare might be adversely affected if special and more risky abortion techniques were used in order to preserve the fetal brains for transplantation. Furthermore, if such use became widespread women might be increasingly exploited by commercial or other pressures to become pregnant to provide aborted tissues. But given suitable controls to prevent such problems no insuperable moral objections seemed to arise from the perspective of the pregnant women. Their autonomy could be respected, they could be benefited with low probability of harm, their rights could be respected, and they could actually contribute to greater distributive justice by permitting their fetuses to be used to benefit others medically; and provided the abortions are carried out according to the requirements of the Abortion Act the procedures are lawful.

But is the Abortion Act a morally acceptable law? The main ethical objections offered at the conference concerned precisely that question in relation to the third affected party, the aborted fetuses. One of the main speakers, Miss Pamela Sims, a consultant obstetrician and gynaecologist and moral opponent of abortion, argued that, since abortion and the Abortion Act were morally unacceptable, using fetal parts for transplantation after abortion was also morally unacceptable – 'the end cannot justify the means'.

Clearly if the fetus is to be accorded full moral status destroying it for the benefit of others would be unacceptable: but, as the ethics committee reportedly reasoned, it was not for its members to deploy their personal moral reservations about abortions in coming to their decisions. It, like the Peel Committee, to whose advice it had scrupulously adhered, started from the presumption that abortions were to be carried out. The moral question then becomes: *given* that abortions have been carried out is it morally acceptable to use fetal tissues to benefit others? The relevant means here, as philosopher Jenifer Jackson pointed out, was the transplantation of tissues from already aborted fetuses, and those means could be morally acceptable even to those who believed the abortions themselves and the Abortion Act to be morally wrong, Dr Wendy Greengross, general practitioner and member of the Warnock Committee, illustrated the point succinctly – the fact that a brain dead man on a respirator had been murdered would not morally prohibit using his organs for transplantation.

Finally, are the interests of society threatened by this development? Some concern was expressed at the conference that ethics committees were able locally to make socially controversial decisions including decisions about 'human brain transplants' with only one lay member on the committee and without any of the members having had any formal training in ethical analysis. Ms Jean Robinson, a lay member of the General Medical Council, vigorously argued that there should be a minimum of two lay members on an ethics committee, which should always be prepared to justify its decisions to the public (as it had in this case). Several of the foreign visitors found it peculiar that no national bioethics committee had been established, at least to provide analysis and advice on particularly contentious or difficult medicomoral issues. Such a committee, if also charged to anticipate developments in bioethics, would provide a foothold on the 'slippery slope' about which Miss Sims warned the conference.

Necessarily, there is a linkage between use of foetal tissue for these purposes and research since by its very nature the former entails the latter. (For the use of foetal reproductive material, see Human Fertilisation and Embryology Act 1990, s 3A (prohibiting use for fertility treatment) and *supra*, ch 10.)

B. IS IT LAWFUL?

We are here concerned with the use of the tissue from a dead foetus. We do not discuss here the regulation of the disposal of the remains of stillborn babies (ie, those of at least 24 weeks gestation) and other foetuses (see Davies: *Law of Burial, Cremation and Exhumation* (1993) (ed) D Smale, pp 14–20).

Since the tissue is harvested only when the foetus is *ex utero* as a consequence of an abortion (or still birth), the legal problem only concerns the 'legality of the means' whereby the death was brought about. It would be otherwise if it were proposed to use tissues from a foetus which would be capable of surviving *ex utero*. In such a case, no tissue could be used until the foetus died naturally and clearly any attempts to bring about its death would be either child destruction (if it did not fall within s 1(1)(b)–(d) of the Abortion Act 1967) or homicide depending upon whether the foetus yet had an 'existence independent of its mother'. Some objections have been raised against the possibility of a woman becoming pregnant by her spouse or partner solely with the intention of aborting the foetus and thereby providing tissue for transplant into the spouse or partner. Apart from possible ethical objections, are there legal objections to this? There may be, of course, principally objections under the Abortion Act if it were properly applied. In addition, there may be an argument that their conduct so offends against public policy as to amount to a crime, ie conduct calculated to outrage public decency – if this be a crime in itself. If, however, as may be the case, the crime consists only in conspiracy to outrage public decency, a charge could only be brought if the couple were not married (see G Williams *Textbook of Criminal Law* (2nd edn, 1983) at p 432).

On the assumption that the above legal conditions are satisfied, it was recommended, as we shall see below, by the Polkinghorne Committee (Cm 762, 1989) that the consent of the mother be obtained before the foetal tissue may be used. Is this a legal requirement? One argument might be that the mother's (or indeed father's) agreement is required because they may object to the donation under s 1(2) of the Human Tissue Act 1961. This would indeed be correct if the foetus was a 'deceased person'. However, to be a 'deceased person' it must before its death have been a 'person' in law. It will not be, of course, if it died before birth (see *A-G's Reference (No 3 of 1994)* [1997] 3 All ER 936 (HL)) and the gestational age would be irrelevant. Only if it were 'born alive' would the foetus count as a legal 'person'. The common law requires that the child should have 'an existence independent of its mother'. This entails that it is wholly extruded from the mother's body (*R v Poulton* (1832) 5 C & P 329) although not necessarily physically separated. The case law dating back to the nineteenth century is unclear (see S B Atkinson 'Life, Birth and Live Birth' (1904) 20 LQR 134). There, we see the need for an independent circulation (*R v Enoch* (1833) 5 C & P 539), that it had breathed (*R v Handley* (1874) 13 Cox CC 79) or, at least, was able to breathe through its own lungs (*R v Brain* (1834) 6 C & P 349). All of these would exclude early foetuses born 'alive' from the protection of the law of homicide once fully expelled from their mother (see *Rance v Mid-Downs HA* [1991] 1 All ER 801 at 816 per Brooke J). The better view is that expressed by Professor Glanville Williams in the first edition of his authoritative *Textbook of Criminal Law* (1978) at p 263 that an aborted foetus is "a person ... no matter how short the period of gestation". The crucial issue in applying the Human Tissue Act 1961 would, therefore, be whether the foetus was 'alive'. Personhood, for the law, is not, therefore, dependent upon gestational age.

Beyond this, consent can only be a *legal* requirement if the mother retains some proprietary rights in or over the foetus, or, the use of the tissue constitutes an invasion of her bodily integrity (as we discussed earlier). (For an insightful discussion from an American perspective see J A Robertson 'Fetal Tissue Transplants' (1988) 66 Washington University Law Quarterly 443.)

In *Doodeward v Spence* (1908) 6 CLR 406 the Australian High Court held that there could be proprietary interests in a stillborn child (for a full discussion, see *infra*, ch 18). Even leaving aside the fact that this is not an English case, how the case helps us to understand English law is uncertain. Griffith CJ held that the 'no property' in a corpse rule did not apply because 'work and skill' had been expended upon it by preserving it in spirits in a bottle. This differentiated it from 'a mere corpse awaiting burial' and conferred upon the artificer property interests. Griffith CJ's reasoning would not assist in the situation we are contemplating for two reasons. First, the dead foetus will remain 'a mere corpse awaiting burial' since it will remain unchanged prior to the removal of any tissue. Secondly, for Griffith CJ it was the person who changed the nature of the foetus, rather than the mother, who acquired proprietary interests over it. Barton J agreed with Griffith CJ but for different reasons. For him, the 'no property rule' did not apply since a stillborn was not a 'person', having never been alive. This is, of course, more helpful where the foetus dies *in utero*, however, he too saw the proprietary interests thereafter vest in the doctor, who acquired it after birth, *not the mother*. The third member of the Australian High Court, Higgins J, rejected both lines of argument and applied without qualification the 'no property' rule to a dead foetus. Thus, the law remains uncertain whatever the Polkinghorne Committee considered 'best practice' (see further, *infra*, ch 18).

C. REGULATION

In 1972 guidance was issued on the use of foetuses and foetal tissue as a result of the Report of the Advisory Group, *The Use of Fetuses and Fetal Materials for Research* (1972) under the chairmanship of Sir John Peel. The report contained a recommended *Code of Practice*. Advances is scientific knowledge and medical research lead to the setting up of a committee to produce a *Review of the Guidance on the Research Use of Fetuses and Fetal Material* (Cm 762) under the chairmanship of Sir John Polkinghorne, which reported in 1989. The committee reviewed the ethical basis for using foetal tissue, proposed an ethical framework for its use and prepared a *Code of Practice*.

Review of the Guidance on the Research Use of Fetuses and Fetal Material (Cm 762), (1989)

Ethical basis

2.1. Central to all ethical considerations relevant to our inquiry is the moral status enjoyed by the human fetus *in utero* and *ex utero* (see definition at 1.5). This was also a question considered by the Warnock Committee whose approach we have found helpful. That Committee was concerned with the embryo at an earlier stage of development than the fetuses which are our concern. It gave the following response to the question of the moral status of the embryo:

> Although the questions of when life or personhood begin appear to be questions of fact susceptible of straightforward answers, we hold that the answers to such questions in fact are complex amalgams of factual and moral judgments. Instead of trying to answer these questions directly we have therefore gone straight to the question of *how it is right to treat the human embryo*. We have considered what status ought to be accorded to the human embryo, and the answer we give must necessarily be in terms of ethical or moral principles. (Paragraph 11.9 p. 60).

2.2. The Warnock Committee agreed that "the embryo of the human species ought to have a 'special status' " and it went on to recommend that "the embryo of the human species should be afforded some protection in law" (p. 63). The special status thus discussed must, *a fortiori* apply to the more developed fetus with which we are concerned. The Warnock Committee recognised that its views would have some significant impact upon the recommendations of the Peel Report, commenting in a footnote:

> *Aborted embryos*
> The focus of this chapter is on the very early human embryo. Almost all of these embryos will result from *in vitro* fertilisation, although some might be obtained from uterine lavage. We are conscious, however, that there are other whole live embryos and fetuses of greater gestational age, which may become available for research following termination of pregnancy. We recognise that both abortion and the Code of Practice contained in the report on "The Use of Fetuses and Fetal Material for Research" (The Peel Report) are very much outside our terms of reference. Nevertheless it seems to us totally illogical to propose stringent legislative controls on the use of very early human embryos for research, while there is a less formal mechanism governing the research use of whole live embryos and fetuses of more advanced gestation. Although we understand that these mechanisms have worked well, we consider there is a case for bringing any research that makes use of whole live aborted embryos or fetuses – whether obtained from *in vitro* fertilisation, uterine lavage, or termination of pregnancy – within the sort of legislative framework proposed in this report. We suggest that this be given urgent consideration. (Paragraph 11.18 p. 64).

2.3. Our approach in this Report lays less stress upon legislation. We do not believe that legislation would allow the flexibility which may be needed in the light of developing knowledge and experience. We are reinforced in this view by our understanding that there has been a careful observance of the Peel Code since its introduction. No claimed breaches of the Code have been brought to our attention in the evidence submitted to the Committee. We therefore feel that it is best to proceed, where possible, by means of ethical guidelines and a Code of Practice accepted and implemented by the professions involved. We set out these guidelines, together with a suggested Code of Practice, at the conclusion to this report.
2.4. Central to our understanding is the acceptance of a special status for the living human fetus at every stage of its development which we wish to characterise as a profound respect based upon its potential for development into a fully-formed human being. The living fetus is not to be treated instrumentally as a mere object available for investigation or use. That respect carries over in a modified fashion to the dead fetus, in a way analogous to the respect we afford to a human cadaver on the basis of its having been the body of a human person. In accordance with this profound respect due to the human fetus based on its potential development, we are unable to accept the implication of the Peel Report that there is a category of pre-viable fetus, of less than 20 weeks gestational age whose early stage of development would permit its being used for research or other purposes, without the requirement that it lacks the signs of life. We do not question that there is some enhancement of the necessary degree of respect as the fetus develops. However, whatever view is taken on the recommendation of the Warnock Committee in relation to embryos of age less than 14 days, we find ourselves in agreement as regards the treatment of the live fetus beyond that age (see 1.4). Accordingly, in the case of the live whole fetus at least beyond 14 days after fertilisation, whether inside or outside the womb, we recommend that research or other use should only take place under the conditions set out in 3.2. which are derived from those applicable to research on fully-developed human subjects.
2.5. The terms of reference of this Committee do not invite it to review policy, practice or legislation relating to abortion. Nevertheless, most of the fetal tissue whose potential use is our concern is likely to have become available as a result of therapeutic abortions. A number of submissions have suggested to us that the act of so inducing abortion is one of such moral reprehensibility that it taints beyond acceptability any possible beneficial use of the fetal

material so obtained. In the opinion of those who hold this view it is only morally permissible to consider the use of tissue from spontaneously aborted fetuses.

2.6. The Committee has given this opinion careful consideration but it is unable to share it. In making that judgment the Committee does not rely solely on the legality of abortion performed under the 1967 Act: for the legal and the moral are distinct and only partially overlapping categories. We recommend that great care should be taken to separate the decisions relating to abortion and to the subsequent use of fetal tissue (see Chapter 5). In these circumstances the carry-over of a moral taint would seem arguable only if the initial act were one of very great moral turpitude. Most people will acknowledge the moral seriousness of terminating the existence of a fetus, with its potential of growth into a fully-developed human being, but in the circumstances envisaged by the 1967 Act this grave step is permitted only in situations where there are also other serious moral issues to be considered, such as those arising from concern for the health of the mother.

2.7. The situation then is one in which a number of possible conflicting moral factors are involved. We do not believe that in circumstances of such moral complexity it is right to regard the termination of pregnancy as inevitably so heinous that any subsequent use of the fetal tissue thereby made available is morally disqualified. We recognise, of course, that in particular cases there may be differing views about whether the conflicting moral factors have been correctly weighed. We do not accept, however, that this would allow as general conclusions either that the termination of pregnancy is inevitably wrong or that as a consequence it compounds this wrongfulness to contemplate even the beneficial use of fetal tissue.

2.8. Rather similar considerations apply to an issue in relation to consent for the use of fetal tissue which has also been put to us in a number of submissions. The use of fetal tissue from terminations of pregnancy has been justified by analogy with the use of human organs which have become available as a result of morally questionable circumstances, such as careless accident or even murder. However, it has been suggested that this analogy is imperfect since in the case of abortions the one who consents to the use of the material (the mother) is also the one who has brought about its availability by her decision to seek the termination of the existence of her fetus. Some have argued that this decision abrogates the mother's subsequent rights in relation to her fetus. Again, this is an opinion to which the Committee has given careful consideration, but once more it is one that we are unable to accept. Because abortion is a decision of moral ambiguity and perplexity for many, reached only through a conflict of considerations, it seems too harsh a judgment of the mother's relation to her fetus to suppose that she is no longer in a special position with regard to it, following an abortion.

2.9. It is clear that in the case of fetuses which are spontaneously aborted some of the perplexities discussed in the previous paragraphs do not arise. It has been put to us in a number of the submissions received that this would afford a moral acceptability to the use of fetal tissue thus derived which would not be present in tissue derived from a therapeutic abortion. In our view there is not this moral distinction. We recommend that fetal tissue which has become available following spontaneous abortion or death *in utero* should be dealt with in the same way as tissue which is derived from the therapeutic abortion. Since we do not accept that material available from therapeutic abortion carries a moral taint, it follows that the potential recipient of a fetal tissue transplant does not have the right to insist on knowing whether the tissue originates from a spontaneous abortion or from a termination.

Conscientious objection to the use of fetal tissue

2.10. We have been able to reach these conclusions unanimously but we recognise that there are differing ethical views, held by substantial numbers of those concerned with such matters and legitimately reached after careful consideration of the issues. It is of particular importance that account should be taken of the variety of views that may be held by people who may be directly involved in work with fetal tissue, for example, members of the medical and nursing professions.

2.11. We considered whether members of these professions should be under any duty to participate in the use of fetal tissue for research or therapy. The Peel Committee had recommended that "no member of staff should be under any duty to participate in research … if he or she has conscientious objection" (Paragraph 43). The evidence we received from the nursing professions was not conclusive. Because of the ethical delicacy of the issues and the high degree of public concern about them we endorse Peel's recommendation and extend it to include therapy. Accordingly, we recommend that no member of the medical or nursing staff should be under any duty to participate in research or therapy using the fetus or fetal tissue if he or she has conscientious objection. This right of non-participation applies only to actions using tissue, eg an operation involving its transplantation, and not to the prior or subsequent care of a patient thus treated. A paragraph to this effect is included in our Code of Practice.

Ethical practice

3.1. We have been unable to accept the distinctions set out in the Peel Report between fetuses which show signs of life but which are of different gestational ages (2.4). A fetus is entitled to respect, according it a status broadly comparable to that of a living person. Thus the relevant categories of ethical significance are "alive" and "dead". The category of "pre-viable", used in the Peel Report, is not of ethical relevance.

3.2. In keeping with that respect, the declared intention to abort a fetus does not of itself abrogate that status. It follows that in general, with the exception of abortion permitted under the 1967 Abortion Act, intervention on a living fetus *in utero* or *ex utero* should carry only minimal risk of harm or, if a greater risk than that is involved, the action is, on balance, for the benefit of the fetus. In the case of the fetus *in utero* these considerations have, of course, to be weighed against consideration of the well-being of the mother. As regards trial procedures carrying greater than minimal risk (eg the trial of diagnostic procedures for seriously disabling conditions in the fetus), but which may be of great potential benefit to the group to which the subject of the trial belongs, the delicate ethical issues must be considered in a manner broadly similar to the way such issues are considered for children and adults.

3.3. It must follow that it is unethical to administer drugs or carry out any procedures during pregnancy with the deliberate intent of ascertaining whether or not they might harm the fetus. We recommend that all clinical research into techniques for terminating pregnancy must take place within the period of and as part of the process of termination . . .

The dead fetus: legal and moral status

3.8. We should at this stage emphasise that while in the uterus the fetus is not a legal person. If the fetus is born and lives *ex utero*, even if only for a short time, it then becomes a legal person and the general law applicable to children applies.

3.9. The consequence of the above is that in considering the use for transplantation or research of tissue from fetuses whose death occurs *in utero* the provisions of the Human Tissue Act 1961 relating to consent are not relevant, since they refer to removal of tissue from deceased persons. It may be that no consent is required in law.

3.10. However, legal considerations alone are too narrow for our purpose. We have already asserted sufficiently strongly our view of the primacy of ethical considerations and on that basis we consider that the mother's consent should always be obtained. We therefore recommend that, even if not required by law, the consent of the mother should be obtained if the fetus or fetal tissue is to be used. This applies whether the tissue is derived from a termination (where we have discussed the mother's rights at 2.8) or from a spontaneous abortion.

Neural tissue

3.11. When transplantation of brain tissue is involved, some anxieties have been expressed about whether this would constitute any degree of "personality transfer" between donor and recipient. We do not believe that this is conceivable in relation to the small fragments of tissue currently used but we recommend a cautious approach in the light of current knowledge. We recommend that in the case of nervous tissue only isolated neurones or fragments of tissue should be used for transplantation. We also recommend that this particular guidance should be kept under close review with consideration being given to the ethical implications, as well as the scientific merits, of any new use being proposed.

Contents of the uterus other than the fetus

3.12 The Peel Report described the contents of the uterus resulting from pregnancy, excluding the fetus ie the placenta, fluid and membranes, as "fetal material". We are inclined to refer to such items, together with the umbilical cord, as "contents of the uterus". The special status which we attach to the fetus stems from its potential for development into a fully-formed human being. No such potential is present in material such as the placenta, and we consider that attempts to invest it with any special status devalue the notion of respect, which very properly attaches to the fetus itself. It follows that subsequent remarks in this report about particular ethical considerations relating to the human fetus should not generally be taken as applying to the other contents of the uterus.

3.13. If the use of these other contents of the uterus requires that tests be carried out to detect the presence of transmissible disease (eg HIV or hepatitis) then we recommend that the consent of the mother should be obtained in the same way as if the test was being carried out on fetal tissue. Consent is discussed more fully in Chapter 6 and the particular conditions imposed by testing for disease at 6.9. However, subject to the conditions mentioned there, and the financial controls mentioned in Chapter 8, the contents of the uterus, other than the fetus, may be used for research or therapy.

Separation of the supply of fetal tissue from its use

4.1. We have taken the view that, whatever one's ethical opinion about abortion itself, it does not follow that morally there is an absolute prohibition on the ethical use of fetuses or fetal tissue from lawful abortion. We have argued that the termination of pregnancy and the subsequent use of fetal tissue should be recognised as separate moral questions and we regard it as of great importance that the separation of these moral issues should be reflected in the procedures employed. Accordingly, we have recommended that great care should be taken to separate the decisions relating to abortion and to the subsequent use of fetal material. The prior decision to carry out an abortion should be reached without consideration of the benefits of subsequent use. The generation or termination of pregnancy to produce material for research or therapy is unethical.

4.2. It has been argued that knowledge of the use of fetal tissue could influence mothers' decisions to have their pregnancies terminated. It has been suggested that the use of fetal tissue could place women under pressure when reaching a decision or result in more abortions taking place. It has even been put to us that someone could become pregnant in order to make a fetus available for medical use. In our view, pregnancy undertaken to such an end would be an ethically unacceptable use of the fetus as an instrument (treating it as a "thing"). It is not possible fully to discern people's motivations, but it is possible to limit the degree to which morally dubious wishes can be implemented. To this end we recommend, not only the separation of the decisions relating to abortion and the subsequent use of fetal tissue, but also procedures which will make it impossible for a mother to specify that fetal tissue, which she makes available, should be used in a particular way.

Method and timing of terminations and the use of fetal tissue

4.3. It has been put to us that knowledge of the potential use of fetal tissue could affect, not only the number of abortions taking place, but also their method and timing. For example, for transplantation purposes there might be a need for fetal tissue from second trimester fetuses, while it is normally in the mother's interest that the termination should be carried out as early in the pregnancy as possible. It will often be the case that abortion by one method will be safer for the mother but abortion by a different method may be more suitable for certain research purposes. Such considerations in our view have no place in treatment or care. We recommend that the management of the pregnancy of any mother should be dictated by her health care needs alone, and this will include the method and timing of an abortion. Similarly, we recommend that the clinical management of a mother whose fetus dies *in utero*, or who has a spontaneous abortion, should not be influenced by consideration of the use to which the fetus might be put.

Inducements

4.4. We consider that offering any kind of inducement to, or pressure on, a mother to let her fetal tissue be used is ethically unacceptable. The Peel Code prohibited "monetary exchange for fetuses or fetal material" but this is not quite enough. In the first place financial inducements can come in ways more subtle than a simple monetary exchange (for example, by the remission of fees). Secondly, an inducement may be indirect, perhaps being offered to the institution where the abortion takes place rather than to the woman. For example, where extra facilities were offered to the clinic or staff at the same time as fetal tissue was being supplied, it would be difficult to resist the conclusion that an exchange was taking place. Equally there should be no pressure to supply associated items eg placentae. Financial controls are discussed more fully in Chapter 8.

We have taken the view that the effective way to prevent improper inducements is for potential recipients of fetal tissue to be unable to contact potential donors or exert influence in any way, and we discuss in Chapter 5 how this may be achieved.

Women who wish to let the method and timing of termination be influenced by the use of fetal tissue

4.5. We concluded at 2.8 that a woman who has consented to an abortion should be consulted on whether her fetal tissue may be used. It has been suggested to us that the mother should similarly be able to control the manner of that subsequent use, for the greatest public benefit. Separation, as described above, aims to put the mother beyond the influence of those, such as users of fetal tissue, whose interests might conflict with hers. However, it may be the mother herself who requests that the timing and method of her abortion should be dictated by factors other than her own health. It has been suggested that the distress of a woman undergoing an abortion might be alleviated by her knowledge that the fetal tissue was to be put to beneficial use.

4.6. We have given careful consideration to these points but ultimately we are not persuaded by them. In our view the arguments for separation are of such ethical importance that they outweigh those for allowing the mother to make any direction regarding the use of her fetus or fetal tissue. Any system which made it possible for a mother to direct the specific use of fetal tissue could not be combined with the effective separation of the prior decision to terminate pregnancy and the process of abortion from the subsequent use of fetal tissue. Furthermore, a woman who has no knowledge of what will actually happen to the fetus or fetal tissue will be less likely to let the possibility of beneficial use of tissue influence her decision to have an abortion. In consequence, in addition to our recommendation that the mother should not be able to specify that fetal tissue which she makes available should be used in a particular way, we recommend that the mother should not know whether the fetus will be used at all, and we incorporate a provision to this effect in our Code of Practice . . .

Consent

6.1. In earlier chapters we have given our view that the use of fetal tissue always requires the mother's consent, although we have recognised that it will not normally be a legal requirement.

6.2. Discussion of consent has been affected by the consideration that a woman undergoing an abortion may be distressed if she has to consider too closely the possibility of her fetus being used for research or transplantation. The Peel Committee had this in mind when reaching the form of words, in their code, at Paragraph 3.ii that there should be "no known objection on the part of the parents." We regard this as insufficient. We are conscious of the need to avoid distress but are even more strongly opposed to formulations which disguise the reality of what is to take place. Distress will be caused to the mother if she later feels that she did not know what was going to happen to her fetus.

6.3. We recommend that positive explicit consent should be obtained from mothers to the use of the fetus or fetal tissue. We see the process of consent as requiring the mother to be counselled and given all the information, in a form that is comprehensible, to enable her to make a proper judgment of whether or not to allow the fetus to be used for research and therapy, including transplantation. This may take the form of an information sheet which might be supplemented with discussion. The information will have to be general because it must embrace all uses to which the fetus may be put.

Timing of consent

6.4. In the case of spontaneous abortion or where the death of the fetus occurs *in utero*, consent will clearly be sought after the death of the fetus, although the precise timing will be dictated by the need to minimize distress.

6.5. In the case of therapeutic abortion, we recommend that consent to the use of fetal tissue should be distinct from, and subsequent to, consent to termination of pregnancy, although both consents could be obtained on the same occasion. It has been suggested that, for the two decisions to be separated in a genuine way, consent to the use of the fetus should take place after the termination. Otherwise, the very fact of asking the woman to consent to the use of the fetus or fetal material before she has actually undergone the abortion may override any final misgivings she may have and may persuade her to choose a method and timing of the abortion which maximises the potential for use of the fetus or fetal materia. We have given this careful consideration but we are not persuaded that this is desirable. It is impossible to prevent mothers giving thought to the possibility of research and transplantation before the abortion takes place, even if their consent is not sought until later. In many cases there would be no significant difference in separation by having consent after the operation. Furthermore, the validity of any consent the woman gave immediately following the termination of pregnancy would be seriously in doubt because of the effects of anaesthesia and other surrounding circumstances, such as the need for haste in making the material available. There would therefore be difficulty in obtaining consent which could fairly be regarded as valid.

6.6. The question of subsequent use of the fetus must not be introduced by those responsible for counselling the mother until she has decided to have her pregnancy terminated and given her consent to that operation. It is, of course, impossible to prevent the mother introducing the subject, and putting questions about the method and timing of abortion in relation to subsequent use. However, since it will not be permissible to given any indication of the use to which any particular fetus might be put, or even if it will be used at all, it will not be possible to give advice of this kind.

6.7. Having established the mother's position in this area, we considered whether the consent of anyone else was desirable or necessary. The father's case for being consulted would depend, as does the mother's, on respect rather than on the law. (It should be noted that his consent is not held necessary for the termination of pregnancy.) While the father's involvement may be desirable for a number of reasons – for example, he may know of some genetically transmitted disease or test on fetal tissue may reveal a finding of potential significance to him – we belief that his relationship with the fetus is less intimate than that of the mother. We recommend that, although it may be desirable, the father's consent should not be a requirement for the use of fetal tissue and he should not have the power to forbid research or therapy making use of fetal tissue.

Mothers who cannot give valid consent

6.8. In the case of mothers who are considered unable to give valid consent to the termination of a pregnancy, consent to the use of the fetus or fetal material for research or transplantation should be sought from the person (usually a parent) who has authority to consent to termination. Again, this is out of respect for the feelings of the mother as represented by her proxy, rather than any requirement of law. The use of material from such mothers should in general be avoided unless there are important and special reasons to do so.

Procedures for screening for transmissible disease

6.9. Testing the fetus or the mother for infections such as HIV or hepatitis will be required for a number of procedures including transplantation. Such test, whether carried out on the fetus, placenta, or on the mother herself, may have grave implications for the mother and her consent is, therefore, necessary. There is much current discussion of how such consent should be obtained, particular as regards testing for HIV antibody. We therefore recommend that the best current practice and guidance should be followed, in a manner which ensures that valid consent is obtained and the principles of separation are maintained. Since we have concluded, in discussing the separation issue, that the mother should be ignorant of the use to which her fetus will be put, we recommend that at the time of being asked to consent to the use of fetal tissues, consent should also be sought to testing for disease, with specific mention of HIV.

The use of the fetus or fetal tissue for specific purposes

6.10. Our attention has been drawn to the distress which may be caused by the use of the fetus or fetal tissue for teaching purposes without the mother having been consulted or having given her permission. We do not believe that this issue comes strictly within our terms of reference, but we think it is a clear implication of the ethical attitude adopted in this Report that valid and appropriately informed consent should always be obtained.

6.11. We recognize that there may be patients who would be prepared to consent to the release of tissue either for research or for transplantation, but not for both, or who would only object to the use of tissue for teaching purposes. We have concluded, however, that to allow for such preferences would be too great a breach of our principle that a mother should not be able to direct that the fetus be used in a specific way. Explicit consent for all these purposess should, therefore, be obtained on all occasions.

Disposal of the fetus (mothers who do not wish to participate in research and transplantation)

6.12. Although this may be outside our terms of reference, we would like to put on record our belief that on general ethical grounds of respect, all mothers (whether participating in the provision of fetal tissue or not) should be given the opportunity clearly to express their wishes about the eventual disposal of the dead fetus, and that these wishes should, wherever possible, be respected.

Elements to be included in any consent form

6.13. For consent to be valid, adequate information must be provided to the patient, who must have an opportunity to reflect on her decision. It is only after the patient has had the opportunity to make an informed and considered decision that her signature should be sought for a consent form.

6.14. Any consent should take account of the following:

1. No specific reference should be made to any particular research or therapy nor any suggestion made that any use will, in fact, take place. It should be confirmed that any use will be strictly controlled and restricted to purposes for which tissue of this kind is necessary for medical benefit.
2. The mother should be assured that appropriate measures will be taken to prevent her being identified by anyone, apart from those attending her.
3. The need to test for HIV and other conditions must be explained, with counselling according to current guidelines.
4. The mother's explicit consent must be obtained to the use of fetal tissue in research, therapy and teaching.
5. The mother should be asked to relinquish any property rights. This topic is discussed at 8.4.

The *Code of Practice* proposed by the Polkinghorne Committee, and subsequently adopted within the NHS, is as follows:

Code of practice on the Use of Fetuses and Fetal Material in Research and Treatment

Figures in brackets refer to the relevant paragraph in the text of the Report. In this Code *fetus* means the embryo or fetus from implantation until gestation ends and, unless qualified by the words *in utero*, includes the fetus outside the womb. (1.3)

1. Treatment of the fetus

1.1. Two categories of fetus are recognised:

(a) The *live* fetus, whether *in utero* or *ex utero*, which should be treated on principles broadly similar to those which apply to treatment and research conducted with children and adults. (2.4, 3.2)

(b) The *dead* fetus. The determination of death shall be by reference to the absence of vital functions, as indicated by the absence of spontaneous respiration and heartbeat after consideration of possibly reversible factors, such as the effects of hypothermia in the fetus, or of drugs or metabolic disorders in the mother. This determination shall be made or confirmed by a doctor responsible for the clinical management of the mother and the fetus and not involved with the subsequent unconnected use of fetal tissue. (3.7)

Only tissue from the dead fetus is ethically available for use in therapy.

1.2. It is unethical to administer drugs or carry out any procedures during pregnancy with the intent of ascertaining whether or not they might harm the fetus. (3.3)

1.3. In the case of nervous tissue only isolated neurones or fragments of tissue may be used for transplantation. (3.11)

2. Contents of the uterus other than the fetus

The contents of the uterus resulting from pregnancy other than the fetus (ie the placenta, fluid and membranes) may be used for research or therapeutic purposes subject to the conditions relating to screening at section 4.5 of this Code and those relating to finance at section 7. (3.12)

3. Separation of the supply of fetal tissue from the practice of research and therapy

3.1. The decision to carry out an abortion must be reached without consideration of the benefits of subsequent use. The generation or termination of pregnancy to produce suitable material is unethical. (4.1)

3.2. The management of the pregnancy of any mother should not be influenced by use of the fetus in research or therapy. In this context, management of the pregnancy should be taken to include:
(a)   the method and timing of an abortion;
(b)   the clinical management of a mother whose fetus dies *in utero* or who has a spontaneous abortion.

3.3. No inducements, financial or otherwise, should be put to the mother or to those who are in a position to influence her decision to have her pregnancy terminated, or to allow fetal tissue to be used. (4.4)

3.4. The mother should not be informed of the specific use which may be made of fetal tissue, or whether it is to be used at all. (4.2, 4.6)

3.5. Those involved in the process of abortion and responsible for the clinical care of the mother should not knowingly be involved in research on the fetus or fetal tissue collected. Dissection of the dead fetus, research on it, or transplantation of fetal tissue should, when practicable, be on separate premises and certainly not in the same room. However, ethically acceptable exceptions to this degree of separation occur when research is concerned with the investigation of cases of fetal death *in utero* or spontaneous abortion, or analogous post-mortem concerns arising from previous medical history. (5.7)

3.6. *The source* must keep records indicating the next destination of any fetal tissue which is released for purposes of research or therapy, and it should have a means of satisfying itself that anyone to whom tissue is sent has satisfied the requirements of this Code. The mother's identity should not be revealed when fetal tissue is released, although some coding will be necessary which will enable her to be traced by those responsible for her clinical management, should relevant information come to light through examination of the fetal tissue. (5.3)

3.7. Any *intermediary* or tissue bank which receives or passes on fetal tissue must keep a record of the destination and origin of all tissue and not reveal details of the identity of the source to the user and *vice versa*. (5.4)

3.8 On the same principle the *user* should be able to satisfy itself that any material it receives has been procured in accordance with the requirements of this Code. It must keep records indicating the proximate source of any fetal tissue and the use to which it is put, but should not reveal details of the use to the source. (5.5)

3.9. Details about a fetus (eg gestational age) which might be of significance for research but could not be used for identification may be released by the source, but it is not acceptable for the source to be approached with requests for fetuses with particular characteristics. (5.6)

4.   Consent

4.1. The written consent of the mother must be obtained before any research or therapy involving the fetus or fetal tissue takes place. Sufficient explanation should be offered to make the act of consent valid. (6.3)

4.2. Consent to the termination of pregnancy must be reached before consent is sought to the use of fetal tissue, and without reference to the possibility of that use. Provided the question of use is not introduced until consent to the termination of pregnancy has been obtained, it is permissible to deal with the two issues on the same occasion. (6.5)

4.3. It may be desirable to consult the father since, for example, tests on fetal tissue may reveal a finding of potential significance to him, and because he may have knowledge of a transmissible or hereditary disease, but his consent shall not be a requirement nor should he have the power to forbid research or therapy making use of fetal tissue. (6.7)

4.4. In the case of spontaneous abortions (or where death of the fetus has occurred *in utero*) consent to use fetal tissue should preferably be sought only after the fetus has died. (6.4)

4.5 Consent should be obtained from the mother to tests if any screening is to take place for transmissible disease or if any procedure is contemplated which could have similar consequences for the mother and affect her clinical management. Any such tests, and the counselling to accompany them, should be conducted according to the best current practice and guidance, in a manner which ensures that the principles of separation are maintained. (6.9)

5. Conscientious objection

No member of the medical or nursing staff should be under any duty to participate in research or therapy involving the fetus or fetal tissue if he or she has conscientious objection. This right of non-participation does not extend to the prior or subsequent care of a patient thus treated. (2.11)

6. Ethics committees

All research or therapy of an innovative character involving the fetus or fetal tissue should be described in a protocol and be examined by an ethics committee. Projects should be subject to review until the validity of the procedure has been recognised by the committee as part of routine medical practice. The ethics committee has a duty to examine the progress of the research or innovative therapy (eg by receiving reports). It should have access to records and be able to confirm that the material is in fact being used for the purpose set out in the protocol. It should also be able to examine the record of any financial transactions involving fetal tissue. Before permitting research the ethics committee must satisfy itself (7.4):

(a)   of the validity of the research or use proposed;

(b)   that the objectives of the proposed use cannot be achieved in any other way;

(c)   that the researchers or clinicians have the necessary facilities and skill.

7. Finance

There should be no monetary exchange for fetuses or fetal tissue. Profit from any dealing in fetal tissue or the other contents of the uterus is unethical. (8.1, 8.3)

D. TWO COMMENTS ON POLKINGHORNE

You will notice that, in its report, the Polkinghorne Committee address two important issues: (1) consent to use; and (2) the separation of the abortion decision from use of the tissue. John Keown critically examines these parts of the report in the following extract:

John Keown 'The Polkinghorne Report on Fetal Research: Nice Recommendations, Shame About the Reasoning' (1993) 19 Journal of Medical Ethics 114

II. Consent

The Peel Code drew criticism for not requiring the informed consent of the mother to the use of her fetus. Polkinghorne's recommendations meet this criticism and, it is submitted, properly respect the mother's interests in the fate of her fetus. However, the report is nevertheless open to criticism, firstly for omitting to answer satisfactorily certain objections to any requirement of maternal consent and, secondly, for its reasoning rejecting the case for a requirement of paternal consent or, at least, consultation.

1.   MATERNAL CONSENT

The committee rejected the argument that allowing the mother to consent to the use of the fetus is like asking a murderer to consent to the use of his victim. It preferred the view that because abortion is a decision of 'moral ambiguity and perplexity to many, reached only through a conflict of considerations' it was too harsh a judgment of the mother's relation to her fetus to suppose that she was no longer in a 'special position' with regard to it ('*Review of the guidance on research use of fetuses and fetal material*' London: Her Majesty's Stationary Office, 1989: CM 762, para 2.8).

However, the committee did not address the associated objection that, although the mother's proxy consent to research on her child is normally required, this is because it is presumed that she has the best interests of the child at heart, and that this presumption does not apply in the case of the mother who has decided to reject the child by abortion, at least for other than a grave reason.

Professor Ramsey concludes, with reference to research on the living pre-viable fetus, that it is 'morally outrageous ... to designate women who elect abortion for comparatively trivial reasons, or for social convenience or economic betterment, to the socially responsible role or ascribe to them the decisional competence and deputyship to say whether the abortus should or should not be used in medical experimentation' (Ramsey P. *The ethics of fetal research* New Haven + London: Yale University Press, 1975: 95).

This objection has been extended by Bopp and Burtchaell to the dead fetus. 'The very agents of someone's death are surely disqualified to act on the behalf or in the stead of the victim – disqualified as a man who has killed his wife is morally disqualified from acting as her executor'. They add that if the mother is to be regarded not as the guardian of the fetus but as its next-of-kin, this is an 'ominous innovation: that within one's lifetime another person be legally permitted to assume authority, not as a protector exercising protective care, but as a survivor acting in her own interests' (National Institutes of Health *Report of the human fetal tissue transplantation research panel* Bethesda, Maryland: National Institutes of Health, 1988: 58–59).

Whether this would be such an 'ominous innovation' is, however, open to question: would it differ from asking a wife shortly before the death of her husband if she had any objection to his organs being transplanted? In relation to the living fetus, by contrast, Ramsey's point appears to have some force: should the committee not have considered whether the woman who has aborted the fetus is an appropriate person to safeguard its interests?

2.   PATERNAL CONSENT

In rejecting a requirement of paternal consent, the committee states that the father's case for being consulted rests, as does that of the mother, on respect rather than on the law and that his consent is not required for an abortion. Both of these statements are open to criticism, the first for being inaccurate, the second for being irrelevant.

First, if the fetus dies after live birth then, as the Peel Code recognises, the Human Tissue Act 1961 applies. This Act makes provision for the use of parts of the body for therapy or research and allows the person lawfully in possession of the body to authorise the use of the body for these respective purposes provided that he or she, having made such reasonable enquiry as may be practicable, has no reason to believe that any surviving relative of the deceased objects to such use. Consequently, the absence of paternal consultation could result in the removal of fetal tissue not being authorised by the Act.

Secondly, while it is true that the father's consent is not required for an abortion the relevance of this is not explained. It certainly does not follow that because the father is denied a veto on abortion he should therefore be denied a veto on the use of the abortus.

One argument for his involvement is that tests on the fetus may have implications for him. The committee, while acknowledging this, nevertheless concludes that his consent should not be required because his relationship with the fetus is 'less intimate' than that of the mother, a conclusion which is both vague and a *non sequitur*.

What is meant by 'less intimate'? Does it imply that the mother is more concerned than the father about the disposal of the fetus? If so, where is the evidence for this assumption?

Even if it were true, why should it override the desirability of consulting the father because of his relationship to the fetus and because tests on the fetus may have implications for him? No reason is given. It is surely one thing to assert that the mother has a stronger claim to be consulted that the father, but quite another to conclude that recognition of her claim is incompatible with recognition of his.

Finally, it is noteworthy that in the US the Uniform Anatomical Gift Act, enacted in all the states, requires the consent of one parent and the non-objection of the other, and that the guidelines on fetal research issued by the National Commission for the Protection of Human Subjects of Biomedical Research require the consent of the mother and non-objection of the father.

III. The principle of 'separation'

Apart from meeting some of the central objections to the Peel Code, the new code makes additional recommendations intended to improve the regulation of the use of fetal tissue. A cardinal aim of the code is to separate the decision to terminate a pregnancy from the decision to allow the use of the resulting fetal tissue:

> The decision to carry out an abortion must be reached without consideration of the benefits of subsequent use. The generation or termination of pregnancy to produce suitable material is unethical (*Review of the guidance on research use of fetuses and fetal material* (op cit) para 3.1).

The code adds that the management of the mother's pregnancy should not be influenced by the prospective use of the fetus (ibid., para 3.2) and that no inducements should be offered to the mother to abort or allow the fetus to be used (ibid., para 3.3). Nor should she be informed of the specific use which may be made of fetal tissue, or whether it is to be used at all (ibid., para 3.4).

1. COMPLICITY IN PAST ABORTIONS

The committee rejects the arguments that abortion is so immoral that it taints beyond acceptability any beneficial use of the fetal material so obtained. It concludes that this would only be arguable if the abortion were an act of 'very great moral turpitude' and that in the circumstances envisaged by the Abortion Act 1967 abortion is only permitted where there are other serious moral issues to be considered, such as concern for the health of the mother (ibid., para 2.6). It observes that in circumstances of such moral complexity, it is not right to regard abortion as inevitably so heinous that any use of the fetal tissue gained thereby is immoral and adds that although in particular cases there may be disagreement about whether the moral factors have been properly weighed this does not allow as general conclusions either that abortion is generally wrong or that as a result the beneficial use of fetal tissue compounds this wrongfulness. It also points out that the use of fetal tissue has been justified by analogy with the use of organs which become available as the result of a careless accident or even murder (ibid., para 2.7–2.8).

This discussion of moral complicity is unsatisfactory. It is not clear why the committee rejects the argument from complicity: is it because abortion is not an act of 'very great moral turpitude' or is it because, even if it is, use of the resultant tissue does not amount to complicity? If the former, then the committee's apparent assumption that abortions carried out (ostensibly) under the Abortion Act 1967 are not immoral surely requires justification, particularly in the light of evidence indicating that the bulk of abortions are performed for social rather than health reasons and of the admission by the Act's promoter that abortion is being used as a contraceptive.

If, alternatively, the committee rejects the argument from complicity on the ground that use of fetal tissue is no more immoral than the use of the corpse of a murder victim, should not the committee have considered whether a truer analogy would have been with *institutionalised* homicide? As LeRoy Walters has written:

> If a particular hospital became the beneficiary of an organised homicide-system which provided a regular supply of fresh cadavers, one would be justified in raising questions about the moral appropriateness of the hospital's co-operation with the suppliers.

Similarly, would not a doctor in Nazi Germany who was regularly supplied for his research with the corpses of gassed Jews incur moral guilt for complicity in the systematic atrocities from which his work benefited? Such analogies may or may not be persuasive, but did they not merit consideration by the committee?

The committee goes on to conclude that, since it does not accept that fetal material resulting from an induced abortion is morally tainted, the recipient has no right to know whether it is the result of a spontaneous or induced abortion (ibid., para 2.9), although medical and nursing staff should have a right of conscientious objection to participation in the use of fetal material for research or therapy (ibid., para 2.11). If, however, there is no moral taint attaching to the fetal material, it is not clear why staff should have a right to refuse nor why, if staff have that right, patients should not.

2. COMPLICITY IN FUTURE ABORTIONS

A no less trenchant objection to the use of fetal tissue, which is again dealt with less than convincingly by the committee, has been well made by Bopp and Burtchaell, namely, that fetal use may not only entail complicity in abortions which produced the fetuses but may also involve complicity in the future abortions it may encourage.

(a) Aborting in order to produce fetal tissue

The new code's attempt to separate the decision to abort from that to use the resulting fetal tissue reflects the committee's belief that it is unethical to allow the prospect of the use of fetal tissue to encourage abortion. The report asserts that abortion and the use of fetal tissue thereby obtained are 'separate moral questions' and that it is of great importance that this should be reflected in the procedures employed (ibid., para 4.1). It adds that the generation of a pregnancy to provide tissue would be unethical as it would involve treating the fetus as a thing. The report consequently recommends the separation of the decisions to terminate pregnancy and to use the resulting tissue, and the creation of procedures which will make it impossible for the woman to specify that the tissue should be used in a particular way (ibid., para 4.2).

The report's reasoning seems inconsistent. In particular, it is difficult to see why the report takes such pains to separate the decision to abort from that to use the material when it does not regard abortion as immoral in the first place. Although the report is unclear about the circumstances in which abortion is unethical, it rejects the view that abortion is always immoral. It states that the destruction of the unborn fetus is permitted under the Abortion Act 1967 'only in situations where there are also other serious moral issues to be considered, such as those arising from concern for the health of the mother' (ibid., para 2.6); that the situation is one in which a number of possible conflicting moral factors are involved and that the fact that there may be differing views about whether these factors have been correctly weighed does not mean that abortion is inevitably wrong (ibid., para 2.7); and that abortion is 'a decision of moral ambiguity and perplexity for many, reached only through a conflict of considerations' (ibid., para 2.8).

Yet, if abortion in the interests of the woman's health is morally acceptable, it is surely inconsistent to conclude that an abortion to provide tissue is not justifiable in the service of those same interests. A clear example would be where the tissue is required to treat an illness of her own. But is there any reason why her health could not benefit even if the tissue were required for another, particularly her child, spouse or parent? It is noteworthy, in view of the committee's reference to the Abortion Act 1967, that such abortions would be as lawful as any other abortions performed in the interests of the woman's health. Indeed, the Act specifically permits abortion in cases where the risk to the health of any existing children from continuing the pregnancy is greater than the risk from terminating it (Abortion Act 1967 section 1(1)(a)). Further, it may well be that an abortion to provide tissue for another is, not least because of its altruistic motive, a weightier reason than a number of others currently accepted by many as ethical.

As Robertson points out, the morality of abortion to provide tissue for the woman or another 'depends on the value placed on early fetuses and on the acceptable reasons for abortion'. He concluded: 'There is no sound ethical basis for prohibiting this sacrifice of the fetus when its sacrifice to end an unwanted pregnancy or pursue other goals is permitted' (Robertson, J. A. 'Rights, Symbolism and public policy in fetal tissue transplants' Hastings Center Report 1988: 18:5).

(b) Conceiving in order to produce fetal tissue
Nor is it clear why, if abortion is ethical, it is unethical to generate a pregnancy in order to provide tissue. The report claims that this would be to treat the fetus instrumentally but omits to explain how this is any different from aborting the fetus in the interests of the mother's health. Surely a fetus which is destroyed in order to promote the woman's health is being used no less instrumentally – as a means to an end – than one generated and terminated for that purpose (ibid.).

(c) Abortion, research and moral consistency
If abortion in the interests of the woman's health is ethical, and a termination of a pregnancy is carried out in the interests of the woman's health, then it is *ex hypothesi* ethical whether its purpose is to provide tissue (whether for herself or another) or not, and whether the fetus was deliberately generated for that purpose or not. Indeed, is the threat to a woman's health from continuing a pregnancy which she generated solely to provide tissue not likely to be even greater than that from continuing a pregnancy which was either originally wanted or simply unplanned?

All this is not to disagree with the committee's opposition to the deliberate destruction of a fetus to provide tissue, whether generated for this purpose or not. On the contrary, it is submitted that its opposition is wholly warranted. But it is submitted that it is only possible to hold this position *consistently* if abortion for other purported justifications, such as preserving the woman's health, is equally opposed. Indeed, would such a position not be more in harmony with the committee's assessment of the moral status of the fetus?

The report concludes that the fetus, because of its potential for development into a fully developed human being, merits a 'special status' and 'profound respect', and it recommends that, in the context of research, it be treated according to principles broadly similar to those which apply to children and adults. These principles, as contained in the Declaration of Helsinki, emphasise that the interests of the individual take precedence over the interests of science and society.

If being subjected to harmful research or being aborted to produce tissue is inconsistent with 'profound respect' and with principles 'broadly similar' to those adopted at Helsinki, why is abortion for other reasons not also inconsistent with them?

The counter-argument that in the context of abortion the interests of the fetus may conflict with those of the mother surely fails, for such conflict (whether between the fetus and the mother and/or others) may equally exist in the context of research and therapy.

In short, if the committee's principles rule out harmful research and abortion to produce tissue, it is difficult to see why they do not also rule out abortion for other reasons. Conversely, if they do not rule out abortion for other reasons, it is difficult to see why they rule out harmful research and abortion to produce tissue.

We have examined the legal issue of consent to use earlier. Professor John Robertson provides an account of the issue of separation as follows and reaches a permissive conclusion.

John A Robertson *Children of Choice: Freedom and the New Reproductive Technologies* (1994)

Does Use of Fetal Tissue Encourage Abortion?

Would use of tissue from abortions that are already occurring encourage women to abort? The opponents of federal funding claimed that therapeutic uses of aborted fetuses will make it easier for women who are ambivalent about ending a pregnancy to do so, if they know that the tissue will be donated to save lives. They also think that rules designed to insulate the abortion decision from use of the resulting tissue are unworkable.

This position is evident in Secretary Sullivan's reasons for continuing the moratorium against federal funding of fetal tissue research:

> I am persuaded that one must accept the likelihood that permitting the human fetal research at issue will increase the incidence of abortion across the country. I am particularly convinced by those who point out that most women arrive at the abortion decision after much soul searching and uncertainty. Providing the additional rationalization of directly advancing the cause of human therapeutics cannot help but tilt some already vulnerable women toward a decision to have an abortion.

Evidence for this position, however, is difficult to find. At issue is what motivates women to terminate pregnancy. The NIH Advisory Panel heard evidence that the primary factor in a woman's decision to have an abortion was the fact that the pregnancy was unwanted. While a significant number of women undergoing abortion experience ambivalence, and a minority of them might even change their mind several times before the abortion, the key factor remained whether the pregnancy, in light of the totality of their circumstances, was wanted. Accordingly, the panel concluded that a request shortly before the abortion occurred for consent to use the resulting tissue for anonymous use in transplantation research or therapy would not lead women not otherwise willing to do so. Donation might, of course, make them feel somewhat better about their abortion experience, but given the separation of the abortion decision and the request to donate, and the fact that donation is anonymous and uncompensated, it is reasonable to think that fetal tissue transplants will not affect the abortion decision itself.

Secretary Sullivan and his allies, in taking a different view, did not always distinguish what is importantly at stake here. His argument basically was that tissue donation will provide an "additional rationalization" for abortion which "cannot help but tilt some already vulnerable women toward a decision to have an abortion." But this assumes that they will know and expect to be asked to donate fetal tissue before they have finally decided to have an abortion. Both the NIH Advisory Panel and Congress had made clear that the decision to abort must come first. Only after the woman has signed the consent for the abortion and is present in the clinic where the procedure will be done may she then be asked to donate tissue. While a few women might still have not gone through with the abortion at this point but for the request to donate, there is no reason to think that this number will be significant. Moreover, there is no particular reason to think that general public awareness that fetal tissue is obtained from abortions will, by assuaging ambivalence before a pregnant woman reaches the clinic, greatly increase the number of abortions.

In the absence of data, however, there is no clear empirical way to resolve the question. One can only make a judgment about which scenario about a pregnant woman's decision-making process appears to be more accurate. The proponents of fetal tissue use cannot prove that there will never be a woman for whom the possibility of donating, even anonymously will not be the determinative factor in her decision to abort. A few woman who are highly ambivalent about aborting may decide to abort because the prospect of donation makes the abortion just palatable enough to be undergone.

Opponents, on the other hand, fail to recognize that the number of women so affected will be vanishingly small. The chance to help science or unidentified, anonymous patients may make women who abort and donate tissue feel better, but this factor is unlikely to be determinative in the vast majority of cases. Surely it is more reasonable to believe that the wanted or unwanted status of the pregnancy and the woman's marital, social, economic, and physical situation will dwarf whatever effect the possibility of anonymous tissue donation for research or therapeutic purposes would have. Whether a pregnancy is wanted or not will continue overwhelmingly to determine whether an abortion occurs.

Because it is reasonable to assume that a very small number of additional abortions might occur if fetal tissue from induced abortions is used, the controversy is really over what public policy stance to take if even a small number of abortions occur because tissue will be donated. Proponents of use argue that the increase is nonexistent or so small as to be *de minimis*. Opponents, on the other hand, argue that any increase in abortions as a result of federal funding, no matter how small, is unacceptable.

The opponent's position, however, seems inconsistent with their position on other policy issues in which there is a small risk that some lives will be lost. For example, they do not oppose public funding of new bridges and highways or FDA approval of new drugs, despite the clear statistical risk that some lives will be lost as a result. Nor do they oppose the sale of guns and knives, even though some unknown number of persons will intentionally kill others as a result. Rather than demand a zero level of risk of loss of life with regard to these policies, fetal tissue opponents tolerate the risks because they are so relatively small and important public purposes are served. With abortion and fetal tissue donation, however, the slight magnitude of the threat to fetuses counts not at all. For them even enormous benefits to long-suffering patients and families cannot justify a small risk that a few additional abortions might occur, despite careful efforts to insulate tissue donation from the decision to abort.

Conception and Abortion to Obtain Tissue

Despite these differences, both proponents and opponents of fetal tissue transplants share the view that abortion for the purpose of obtaining tissue is undesirable and should not be encouraged. As noted, the NIH Advisory Panel, like other advisory bodies, most ethical commentators, and federal law have built in safeguards to prevent abortion solely to obtain tissue for transplant ...

Would it be wrong to abort an existing pregnancy to obtain the needed tissue for that person? Would it be wrong to conceive in order to produce a pregnancy that could be aborted to get needed tissue? Let us distinguish the situation where the woman is already pregnant from the situation where she conceives in order to procure tissue by abortion.

THE WOMAN IS ALREADY PREGNANT

If the woman is already pregnant, the right to avoid procreation by ending pregnancy to help a loved one is at issue. But for the family member's need, the woman would have gone to term with the pregnancy. She is now choosing to abort, not because she does not wish to parent, but because she finds the needs of the family member more pressing than her interest in having this particular offspring.

The ethical acceptability of such an act depends on the acceptability of abortion generally. If early abortion is ethically permissible, the particular reasons why the pregnancy is unwanted should not ordinarily affect the ethical acceptability of abortion. The woman's decision that the burdens of gestation and/or child rearing are too great is respected because she is in the best position to assess those burdens and because early fetuses are too neurologically immature to have interests in their own right . . . [A]borting previable fetuses does not harm or wrong them, since they are insufficiently developed to experience harm. The symbolic impact of abortion on respect for human life is outweighed by the pregnant woman's interests in avoiding the burdens of pregnancy.

If abortion is acceptable to avoid those burdens, it is difficult to see why abortion is any less acceptable when the pregnancy becomes unwanted because abortion will provide the opportunity to save a loved one in need. Although a deliberate sacrifice of the fetus occurs, the sacrifice is occurring for a reason that is at least as strong, if not stronger than abortion to avoid unplanned or unwanted motherhood.

On the other hand, if abortion is deemed morally impermissible, then abortion to procure tissue to save a life would be as well. However, if abortion is viewed as morally impermissible except in very exceptional circumstances, such as to protect the mother's life or health, in cases of rape or incest, or severe genetic deformity, the abortion to procure tissue could be supported. The need to save another's life seems to be equivalent in gravity to those exceptional circumstances.

Of course, aborting a wanted pregnancy to prevent severe neurologic disease in oneself or one's family poses an excruciating dilemma. An otherwise wanted fetus will be sacrificed to save a parent, spouse, sibling, or child who already exists. Such a tragic choice will engender loss or grief whatever the decision. However, unless one is against abortion in most or all circumstances, one cannot say that the choice to abort is ethically impermissible. There is no sound ethical basis for prohibiting this sacrifice of the fetus when its sacrifice to end an unwanted pregnancy or avoid other burdens is permitted ... if the jurisdiction otherwise accepted abortion for compelling reasons, banning abortions to obtain tissue to save a family member's life would be difficult to justify independently. It would seem to be as compelling, if not more so, than other reasons for abortion. If the fear is that some women will be coerced or pressured into abortions by family members, ways to minimize that danger without preventing all abortions to procure tissue could be devised.

CONCEIVING AND ABORTING FOR TRANSPLANT PURPOSES

When a woman not yet pregnant seeks to conceive in order to abort and provide tissue for transplant, the issues raised are slightly different because the right to conceive, as well as the right to abort, is implicated. It is a clearer case of using one's reproductive capacity for nonreproductive purposes than is aborting an existing pregnancy to obtain tissue. The right to procreate is not involved, because no intention to have and rear children exists. Rather, the issue is whether one may take the first steps toward procreation when there is no intent to complete the process.

Would such a practice be ethical? Again, the question depends on the perceived acceptability of abortion. If abortion to obtain tissue for transplant is acceptable if a pregnancy otherwise existed, no greater harm occurs to the fetus conceived expressly to be aborted. Since there is no greater harm to the fetus, the difference seems to be a symbolic one, akin to creating embryos solely for research or creating and transferring many embryos to the uterus when selective reduction of a multifetal pregnancy is likely to ensue.

Deliberate creation with intent to abort may have greater symbolic significance, however, because it denotes a greater willingness to use fetuses as a means to serve other ends. However, aborting when already pregnant to procure tissue for transplant or because the pregnancy is unwanted also denotes a willingness to use the fetus as a means to other ends. As long as abortion of an existing pregnancy for transplant purposes is ethically accepted, people might reasonably conclude – as they could with creation of embryos solely for research – that the additional symbolic devaluation of human life through deliberate creation and destruction of prenatal life is negligible, and thus is insufficient to outweigh the substantial gain to transplant recipients that deliberate creation provides.

In sum, deliberate creation of fetuses to be aborted for tissue procurement is more ethically complex and defensible than its current widespread dismissal would suggest. Such a practice is, of course, not in itself desirable, but in a specific situation of strong personal or familial need may be ethically justified. Persons who rationally compare the competing concerns may well conclude that in some circumstances, with safeguards to protect women from coercion or exploitation, the use of one's reproductive capacity to obtain fetal tissue for transplant should be ethically and legally acceptable. When the need for such abortions arises, this issue should be fully debated and not dismissed out of hand as ethically unacceptable.

Part III

Medical law in action

C: The end(ing) of life

Chapter 16

The end(ing) of life: the competent patient

In this chapter we are concerned with the legal effect of decisions by *competent* patients concerning the end (or ending) of their life. We discussed in Chapter 5 the legal concept of competence and say no more about that here other than to assume the patient is competent according to the appropriate legal test. We will divide our analysis of the law into two parts. *First*, we will consider decisions taken about current treatment to be carried out (or not) while the patient remains competent. *Secondly*, we will consider decisions taken about future treatment to be carried out (or not) at a time when the patient is no longer competent.

Contemporaneous decisions

A. REFUSING TREATMENT

1. The right to refuse

As we saw in Chapter 6, English law recognises the general principle that a competent patient is entitled to refuse treatment, even life-sustaining treatment. As we saw, the courts seem persuaded that there ought to be an exception to this: the competent minor (*Re W (a minor) (medical treatment)* [1992] 4 All ER 627 (CA)). In Chapter 6 we criticised the creation of this exception. Here, we are concerned with the situations falling within the general principle rather than the exception. We extensively considered this issue in Chapter 6 and the reader is referred to the material.

It suffices for our purposes to refer to the statements of Lord Donaldson MR in *Re T (adult: refusal of medical treatment)* [1992] 4 All ER 649 at 652–653 (CA) and Lords Keith (at 860), Goff (at 866), Browne-Wilkinson (at 881–2) and Mustill (at 889) in *Airedale NHS Trust v Bland* [1993] 1 All ER 821 (HL). In essence they accept, as Lord Keith put it in *Bland*, that '…a person is completely at liberty to decline to undergo treatment, even if the result of his doing so will be that he will die' (at 860). More recently the Court of Appeal stated in *St George's Healthcare NHS Trust v S* [1998] 3 All ER 673 (CA) at 685 per Judge LJ:

> Even when his or her own life depends on receiving medical treatment, an adult of sound mind is entitled to refuse it. This reflects the autonomy of each individual and the right of self determination.

The approach of the English courts reflects that of courts in North America: *Nancy B v Hôtel-Dieu de Québec* (1992) 86 DLR (4th) 385 (Que Sup Ct) (Canada) and, for example, *McKay v Bergstedt* (1990) 801 P 2d 617 (Nev Sup Ct). The *Bergstedt* case is instructive in that it reviews the US cases and thereby rehearses the anxieties found in them, particularly concerning the state's interests in *preserving life* and *preventing suicide* (for an earlier discussion, see *supra*, ch 6).

McKay v Bergstedt **(1990) 801 P 2d 617 (Nev Sup Ct)**

Steffen J: Kenneth Bergstedt was a thirty-one-year-old mentally competent quadriplegic who sought to vindicate on appeal the lower court's decision confirming his right to die…

FACTUAL BACKGROUND

At the tender age of ten, Kenneth suffered the fate of a quadriplegic as the result of a swimming accident. Twenty-one years later, faced with what appeared to be the imminent death of his ill father, Kenneth decided that he wanted to be released from a life of paralysis held intact by the life-sustaining properties of a respirator. Although Kenneth was able to read, watch television, orally operate a computer, and occasionally receive limited enjoyment from wheelchair ambulation, he despaired over the prospect of life without the attentive care, companionship and love of his devoted father.

The limited record before us reflects substantial evidence of facts relevant to the proceedings below and material to the framework upon which the resolution of this appeal is constructed. First, a board-certified neurosurgeon determined that Kenneth's quadriplegia was irreversible. Second, a psychiatrist examined Kenneth and found him to be competent and able to understand the nature and consequences of his decision. Third, Kenneth arrived at his decision after substantial deliberation. Fourth, Kenneth's trusted and devoted father understood the basis for his son's decision and reluctantly approved. Fifth, although Kenneth's quadriplegia was irreversible, his affliction was non-terminal so long as he received artificial respiration.

Kenneth thus petitioned the district court as a non-terminal, competent, adult quadriplegic for an order permitting the removal of his respirator by one who could also administer a sedative and thereby relieve the pain that would otherwise precede his demise. Kenneth also sought an order of immunity from civil or criminal liability for anyone providing the requested assistance. Additionally, he petitioned the court for a declaration absolving him of suicide in the removal of his life-support system.

In ruling, the district court determined that Kenneth was a mentally competent adult fully capable of deciding to forgo continued life connected to a respirator. The court also found that he understood that the removal of his life-support system would shortly prove fatal.

In concluding that Kenneth had a constitutional privacy right to discontinue further medical treatment, the court also ruled that given Kenneth's condition, judicial recognition of the primacy of his individual rights posed no threat to the State's interest in preserving life, adversely affected no third parties, and presented no threat to the integrity of the medical profession. The district court thus concluded that Kenneth was entitled to the relief sought.

DISCUSSION

I

Our research revealed five cases involving decision by competent adults to discontinue the use of life-support systems. Three of the five cases were brought by petitioners who were terminally ill. The other two actions, like the instant case, involved non-terminal, competent adults who were dependent upon artificial life-support systems. Relief was granted in each of the five cases, albeit posthumously in two of the cases where petitioners had died before their appeals were decided.

One of the verities of human experience is that all life will eventually end in death. As the seasons of life progress through spring, summer and fall, to the winter of our years, the expression unknown to youth is often heard evincing the wish to one night pass away in the midst of a peaceful sleep. It would appear, however, that as the scientific community continues to increase human longevity and promote 'the greying of America', prospects for slipping away during peaceful slumber are decreasing. And, for significant numbers of citizens like Kenneth, misfortune may rob life of much of its quality long before the onset of winter.

Because many individuals find themselves facing a terminal condition susceptible to indefinite suspension by medical intervention, the question arises with increasing frequency and fervor concerning the extent to which persons have the right to refuse an artificial extension of life. Courts considering the question have basically agreed that the answer is to be found in the balancing of interests between the person in extremis and the State. On the one hand is the interest of the individual in determining the extent to which he or she is willing to have a devastated life continued artificially or by radical medical treatment. On the other hand, courts agree that the State has several interests of significance that must be weighed in determining whether the rights of the individual should prevail. Those interests have generally been defined as: (1) the interest of the State in preserving the sanctity of all life, including that of the particular patient involved in a given action; (2) the interest of the State in preventing suicide; (3) the interest of the State in protecting innocent third persons who may be adversely affected by the death of the party seeking relief; and (4) the State's interest in preserving the integrity of the medical profession…

Under the common law, 'no right is held more sacred, or is more carefully guarded…than the right of every individual to the possession and control of his own person, free from all restraint or interference of others, unless by clear and unquestionable authority of law.' *Cruzan v Director, Missouri Department of Health* 110 S Ct 2841, 2846 (1990) (quoting *Union Pacific R Co v Botsford*, 141 US 250, 251 (1891)). Continuing, the *Cruzan* court declared that 'this notion of bodily integrity has been embodied in the requirement that informed consent is generally required for medical treatment'. Id. The corollary embodied in the right of informed consent is the right to refuse the proffered medical treatment or regimen irrespective of consequences. See *Bartling*, 163 Cal App 3d at 194. Obviously, if a patient is powerless to decline medical treatment upon being properly informed of its implications, the requirement of consent would be meaningless. We nevertheless agree with other courts which have held that the right to refuse medical treatment is not absolute. See *Satz v Perlmutter*, 362 So 2d 160, 162 (Fla App 1978); *State v McAfee*, 385 SE 2d at 652; *Cruzan, by Cruzan v Harmon*, 760 SW 2d 408, 421 (Mo 1988) (en banc); *Matter of Farrell*, 529 A 2d at 410. Courts have consistently balanced the fundamental right of the individual to refuse medical treatment against the four State interests enumerated above. See eg, *Bouvia v Superior Court*, 179 Cal App 3d 1127 (Cal Ct App 1986); *Bartling v Super Ct* (Glendale Adven Med), 163 Cal App 3d at 186; *Satz v Perlmutter*, 362 So 2d at 160; *State v McAfee*, 385 SE 2d at 651; *Superintendent of Belchertown v Saikewicz*, 370 NE 2d 417 (Mass 1977); *Cruzan, By Cruzan v Harmon* 110 S Ct at 2841; *Matter of Farrell*, 529 A 2d at 404…

II

Turning, as we must, to the legitimate interests of the State, we now balance those interests against Kenneth's…common law right of self-determination, and we do so for decisional purposes despite Kenneth's death.

I. The interest of the State in preserving life. The State's interest in preserving life is both fundamental and compelling. Indeed, it constitutes a basic purpose for which governments are formed. Nevertheless, the State's interest in the preservation of life is not absolute. For example, State-sponsored executions may constitute an exception to the duty to preserve life for a complex of reasons ranging from an emphasis on the value of the lives of innocent victims to the necessity of maintaining an orderly society where the quality of life is of pre-eminent concern. Moreover, as the quality of life diminishes because of physical deterioration, the State's interest in preserving life may correspondingly decrease. However, the State's attenuated interest does not evince a lesser appreciation for the value of life as the physical being deteriorates, but rather a recognition of the fact that all human life must eventually succumb to the ageing process or to intervening events or conditions impacting the health of an individual. Moreover, an interest in the preservation of life 'at all costs' is demeaning to death as a natural concomitant of life. Despite its frightening aspects, death has important values of its own. It may come as welcome relief to prolonged suffering. It may end the indignities associated with life bereft of self-determination and cognitive activity. In the mind of some, it may satisfy longings for loved ones preceding them in death. In short, death is a natural aspect of life that is not without value and dignity.

Courts have recognized that persons may reach a condition of life where the individual preference for a natural death may have greater primacy that the State's interest in preserving life through artificial support systems. Although we would have stated it differently, the court in *Matter of Conroy*, 486 A 2d 1209 (NJ 1985), declared that 'in cases that do not involve the protection of the actual or potential life of someone other than the decision-maker, the state's indirect and abstract interest in preserving the life of the competent patient generally gives way to the patient's much stronger personal interest in directing the course of his own life.' Id. At 1223. We do not view the State's interest in preserving the life of a competent patient as either abstract or indirect. It remains, in our view, not only compelling and fundamental, but focused and direct as well. The State's interest in preserving all human life, including that of the particular patient, should not be suspended or minimized under any conditions. We nevertheless agree with the court in *Satz v Perlmutter* that 'there can be no doubt that the State does have an interest in preserving life, but… 'there is a substantial distinction in the State's insistence that human life be saved where the affliction is curable, as opposed to the State interest where, as here, the issue is not whether, but when, for how long and at what cost to the individual [his] life may be briefly extended'. *Perlmutter*, 362 So 2d at 162 (quoting from *Superintendent of Belchertown v Saikewicz*, 370 NE 2d 417, 425–26 (Mass 1977)). In *Perlmutter*, however, the competent adult patient was terminally ill with a prognosis of a short remaining life even while connected to a respirator. The *Perlmutter* ruling is therefore of limited value to the instant case.

In both *Bouvia* and *Bartling* the adult patients were, as here, non-terminal and competent… Although we may have a difference of opinion over some of the statements…from *Bouvia*, we do believe that at some point in the life of a competent adult patient, the present or prospective quality of life may be so dismal that the right of the individual to refuse treatment or elect a discontinuance of artificial life-support must prevail over the interest of the State in preserving life. In instances where the prospects for a life of quality are smothered by physical pain and suffering, only the sufferer can determine the value of continuing mortality. We therefore conclude that in situations involving adults who are: (1) competent; (2) irreversibly sustained or subject to being sustained by artificial life-support systems or some form of heroic, radical medical treatment; and (3) enduring physical and mental pain and suffering, the individual's right to decide will generally outweigh the State's interest in preserving life.

On the assumption that Kenneth would survive the issuance of this opinion, we reviewed his record carefully in an effort to sensitively analyse the circumstances under which he lived and the reasons that prompted him to seek a judicial imprimatur of his decision to disconnect his respirator. It appears that Kenneth's suffering resulted more from his fear of the unknown than any source of physical pain. After more than two decades of life as a quadriplegic under the loving care of his parents, Kenneth understandably feared for the quality of his life after the death of his father, who was his only surviving parent. Although Kenneth completed elementary and high school through private tutoring, study and telephone communication with his teachers, and wrote poetry and otherwise lived a useful and productive life, his physical condition was dire. His quadriplegia left him not only ventilator-dependent, but entirely reliant on others for his bodily functions and needs. His limited sources of entertainment, including reading, watching television and writing poetry through the oral operation of a computer, also required the attentive accommodations of others. Since the death of his mother in 1978, all of these services were provided by his father and attending nurses occasionally called to the home.

It thus appears, and the record so reflects, that Kenneth was preoccupied with fear over the quality of his life after the death of his father. He feared that some mishap would occur to his ventilator without anyone being present to correct it, and that he would suffer an agonizing death as a result. In contemplating his future under the care of strangers, Kenneth stated that he had no encouraging expectations from life, did not enjoy life, and was tired of suffering. Fear of the unknown is a common travail even among those of us who are not imprisoned by paralysis and a total dependency upon others. There is no doubt that Kenneth was plagued by a sense of foreboding concerning the quality of his life without his father.

Someone has suggested that there are few greater sources of fear in life than fear itself. In Kenneth's situation it is not difficult to understand why fear had such an overriding grasp on his view of the quality of his future life. Given the circumstances under which he labored to survive, we could not substitute our own judgment for Kenneth's when assessing the quality of his life. We therefore conclude that Kenneth…enjoyed a preeminent right under the common law to withdraw his consent to a continued medical regimen involving his attachment to a respirator. In so ruling, we attach great significance to the quality of Kenneth's life as he perceived it under the particular circumstances that were afflicting him…

2. *The interest of the State in preventing suicide.* Controversy continues to rage over this semantics-laden issue. Opponents of Kenneth's position describe it in terms of a State-sponsored suicide. Our research reveals no court declaring it so. We nevertheless recognize the controversy as a healthy concern for the value of an individual life.

The dictionary definition of suicide is 'the act or an instance of taking one's own life by a person of years of discretion and of sound mind; one that commits or attempts self-murder.' Webster's Third New International Dictionary (1968). As we will attempt to show, Kenneth harbored no intent to take his own life, voluntarily or otherwise. He did not seek his own destruction and he most certainly eschewed self-murder, a fact made evident by his petition to the district court for an order declaring that the exercise of his right to decide would not amount to an act of suicide.

It is beyond cavil in one sense, that Kenneth was taking affirmative measures to hasten his own death. It is equally clear that if Kenneth had enjoyed sound physical health, but had viewed life as unbearably miserable because of his mental state, his liberty interest would provide no basis for asserting a right to terminate his life with or without the assistance of other persons. Our societal regard for the value of an individual life, as reflected in our Federal and State constitutions, would never countenance an assertion of liberty over life under such circumstances.

It must nevertheless be conceded, as noted above, that death is a natural end of living. There are times when its beckoning is sweet and benevolent. Most would consider it unthinkable to force one who is racked with advanced, terminal, painful cancer to require a therapy regimen that would merely prolong the agony of dying for a brief season. In allowing such a patient to refuse therapy could it seriously be argued that he or she is committing an act of suicide?

The informed consent doctrine presupposes that persons faced with difficult medical decisions that will, at best, substantially alter the quality of their future lives, may elect to refuse treatment and let the processes of nature take their course. Few would conclude that exercising the right to refuse treatment would be tantamount to suicide. Such persons have not sought to contract the disease or condition that threatens both the quality and duration of their lives. Rather, they have evaluated their circumstances and determined that a future sustained by radical medical treatment or artificial means and entailing a drastic decrease in the quality of their lives, is not a valued alternative despite its effectiveness in extending life or delaying death. Moreover, we see no difference between the patient who refuses treatment and the one who accepts treatment and later refuses its continuance because of a resulting loss in the quality of life.

The primary factors that distinguish Kenneth's type of case from that of a person desiring suicide are attitude, physical condition and prognosis. Unlike a person bent on suicide, Kenneth sought no affirmative measures to terminate his life; he desired only to eliminate the artificial barriers standing between him and the natural processes of life and death that would otherwise ensue with someone in his physical condition. Kenneth survived artificially within a paralytic prison from which there was no hope of release other than death. But he asked no one to shorten the term of his natural life free of the respirator. He sought no fatal potions to end life or hurry death. In other words, Kenneth desired the right to die a natural death unimpeded by scientific contrivances.

Justice Scalia's concurring opinion in *Cruzan* suggests that 'insofar as balancing the relative interests of the State and the individual is concerned, there is nothing distinctive about accepting death through the refusal of 'medical treatment', as opposed to accepting it through the refusal of food, or through the failure to shut off the engine and get out of the car after parking in one's garage after work.' *Cruzan*, 110 S Ct at 2862. We respectfully disagree with the learned justice. The distinction between refusing medical treatment and the other scenarios presented by Justice Scalia is the difference between choosing a natural death summoned by an uninvited illness or calamity and deliberately seeking to terminate one's life by resorting to death-inducing measures unrelated to the natural process of dying.

Impliedly, Justice Scalia's last two hypotheticals involved persons who were ambulatory and able to survive without artificial intervention. If they were physically healthy, society's respect for human life demanded that the State prevent, if possible, their deaths by suicide. There was no need to present either person with life-extending medical options, and both enjoyed the prospect of mental rehabilitation that might restore the will to live. There is a significant distinction between an individual faced with artificial survival resulting from heroic medical intervention and an individual, otherwise healthy or capable of sustaining life without artificial support who simply desires to end his or her life. The former adult, if competent, exercises a judgment based upon an assessment of the quality of an artificially maintained life vis-à-vis the quality of a natural death. Conversely, the latter acts from a potentially reversible pessimism or mental attitude concerning only the quality of life.

We are not deciding competing interest between a non-existent right to choose suicide and the interest of the State in preserving life. The State's interest in the preservation of life relates to meaningful life. Insofar as this State's interest is concerned, the State has no overriding interest in interfering with the natural processes of dying among citizens whose lives are irreparably devastated by injury or illness to the point where life may be sustained only by contrivance or radical intervention. In situations such as Kenneth's, only the competent adult patient can determine the extent to which his or her artificially extended life has meaning and value in excess of the death value.

Other courts have consistently agreed that rejecting treatment in the form of artificial life-support systems is not a euphemistic exercise in suicide. See, eg, *Bouvia v Superior Court*, 179 Cal App 2d at 1144; *Bartling v Superior Court*, 163 Cal App 3d at 196; *Floody v Manchester Memorial Hosp*, 482 A 2d 713, 720 (Conn Super Ct 1984); *Satz v Perlmutter*, 362 So 2d at 162–63; *State v McAfee*, 385 SE 2d at 652 (by implication); *Brophy v New England Sinai Hosp*, 497 NE 2d 626, 638 (Mass 1986); *Matter of Farrell*, 529 A 2d at 411; *Matter of Storar*, 420 NE 2d 64, 71 (NY 1981); *Leach v Akron General Medical Center*, P 2d 738, 743 (Wash 1983). However, we do not necessarily agree with the analysis of other courts on the subject. For example, the court in *Bouvia* concluded that 'the trial court seriously erred by basing its decision on the 'motives' behind Elizabeth Bouvia's decision to exercise her rights. If a right exists, it matters not what 'motivates' it exercise.' *Bouvia*, 179 Cal App 3d at 1145. In the first place, as we have already seen, the 'right' is not absolute. It must be balanced against the previously enumerated interests of the State. Secondly, because the State has an interest in both preserving life and preventing suicide, the circumstances under which the individual seeks to exercise his liberty interest or common law right of refusal must be considered. Part of the complex of circumstances to be considered relates to the attitude or motive of the patient. To a large extent, a patient's attitude or motive may be judged from such factors as severity of physical condition, diagnosis, prognosis, and quality of life. If a competent adult is beset with an irreversible condition such as quadriplegia, where life must be sustained artificially and under circumstances of total dependence, the adult's attitude or motive may be presumed not to be suicidal. In our view, there is a substantial difference between the attitude of a person desiring non-interference with the natural consequences of his or her condition and the individual who desires to terminate his or her life by some deadly means either self-inflicted or through the agency of another.

As medical science continues to develop methods of prolonging life, it is not inconceivable that a person could be faced with any number of alternatives that would delay death and consign him or her to a living hell in which there is hopelessness, total dependence, a complete lack of dignity, and an ongoing cost that would impoverish loved ones. The State's interest in preserving life and preventing what some may erroneously refer to as suicide does not extend so far.

Kenneth did not wish to commit suicide. He desired only to live for as long as the state of his health would permit without artificial augmentation and support. Society has no right to force upon him the obligation to remain alive under conditions that he considered to be anathema. To rule otherwise would place an unwarranted premium on survival at the expense of human dignity, quality of life, and the value that comes from allowing death a natural and timely entrance…

*3. The interest of the State in protecting innocent third persons…*This State interest was simply not implicated in Kenneth's request.

4. The State's interest in preserving the integrity of the medical profession. In *Matter of Farrell*, the competent adult patient was a thirty-seven-year-old woman who was terminally ill with amyotrophic lateral sclerosis (Lou Gehrig's disease). Although Kathleen Farrell died before her appeal was decided, the *Farrell* court nevertheless determined that 'medical ethics create no tension in this case. Our review of well-established medical authorities finds them in unanimous support of the right of a competent and informed patient such as Mrs Farrell to decline medical treatment'. *Matter of Farrell*, 529 A 2d at 411–12 (discussing authorities). We deem it unnecessary to quote from medical authorities to further support the conclusion reached in *Farrell*. The State has an unquestioned duty to see that the integrity of the medical profession is preserved and that it is never allowed to become an instrument for the selective destruction of lives deemed to have little utility.

Despite the medical profession's healing objectives, there are increasing numbers of people who fall in the category of those who may never be healed but whose lives may be extended by heroic measures. Unfortunately, there are times when such efforts will do little or nothing more than delay death in a bodily environment essentially bereft of quality. Under such conditions or the reasonably likely prospect thereof, the medical profession is not threatened by a competent adult's refusal of life-extending treatment. The President's Commission, established by Congress in 1978, and consisting of doctors, ethicists, lawyers, theologians and others, concluded:

> The voluntary choice of a competent and informed patient should determine whether or not life-sustaining therapy will be undertaken, just as such choices provide the basis for other decisions about medical treatment. Health care institutions and professionals should try to enhance patients' abilities to make decisions on their own behalf and to promote understanding of the available treatment options…Health care professionals serve patients best by maintaining a presumption in favor of sustaining life, while recognizing that competent patients are entitled to choose to forego any treatments, including those that sustain life.

President's Commission for the Study of Ethical Problems in Medicine and Biomedical and Behavioral Research, Deciding to Forgo Life-Sustaining Treatment, p 3 (US Gov't Printing Office 1983).

We are of the opinion that Kenneth's request to be relieved of his connection to a respirator did not present an ethical threat to the medical profession. Because a competent adult would have enjoyed a qualified…common law right to refuse a life-sustaining attachment to a respirator in the first instance, there is no reason why such an adult could not assert the same rights to reject a continuation of respirator-dependency that has proven too burdensome to endure…

IV

If Kenneth had survived the date of the issuance of this opinion, we would have confirmed his right to discontinue his artificial life-support system…

Young CJ, Rose and Mowbray JJ agreed. Springer J dissented.

It is important to notice that in England the court in *Re T* recognised that the right to refuse life-sustaining treatment applied to all competent adult patients and not merely those who were terminally ill. Cases such as *Re T* and *Bergstedt* raise more starkly the argument that the patient is seeking to commit suicide. The affirmation of the right to refuse treatment in *Re T* indicates that the Court of Appeal must have have been committing suicide. Curiously, however, the judges did not expressly refer to the point. Subsequently, in *Bland* Lord Goff (at 866) made the point explicitly.

Lord Goff: I wish to add that, in cases of this kind, there is no question of the patient having committed suicide, nor therefore of the doctor having aided or abetted him in doing so. It is simply that the patient has, as he is entitled to do, declined to consent to treatment which might or would have the effect of prolonging his life, and the doctor has, in accordance with his duty, complied with his patient's wishes.

See further *Secretary of State for the Home Dept v Robb* [1995] 1 All ER 677 (Thorpe J). (For a detailed discussion of the relationship between refusal of life-saving treatment and suicide see *supra*, ch 6 and M Otlowski, *Voluntary Euthanasia and the Common Law* (1997) at 65–86 and D P T Price 'Assisted Suicide and Refusing Medical Treatment: Linguistics, Morals and Legal Contortions' (1996) 4 Med L Rev 270.)

2. Limits on the right to refuse

We have already seen that the cases in the United States seek to place limits on a patient's freedom of decision by reference to various state interests (see also the discussion of Thorpe J in *Secretary of State for the Home Dept v Robb* [1995] 1 All ER 677 at 682, *supra* ch 6). From *Bergstedt* we have learned that the state's interest in preventing suicide cannot stand as a limitation. As regards the state's interest in preserving life, save in the problematic case of the competent minor, reference to such an interest is incoherent if the law already recognises, as it does, the competent patient's right to make his own decisions including the refusal of life-sustaining treatment. As regards the state's interest in protecting innocent third parties, this is a deeply problematic limit, as we saw in the context of the pregnant woman in cases such as *Re AC* (1990) 573 A 2d 1235 (DC CA) and *St George's Health Care NHS Trust v S* [1998] 3 All ER 673 (CA): see ch 6, *supra*.

The last of the state interests mentioned in cases such as *In the Matter of Conroy* (*infra*, ch 17) and *Bergstedt* is that of 'safeguarding the integrity of the medical profession'. In so far as this goes beyond asking them to be involved in suicide and act illegally, the New Jersey Supreme Court in a subsequent case of *Re Farrell* (1987) 529 A 2d 404, stated:

> **Garibaldi J:** Even as patients enjoy control over their medical treatment, health-care professionals remain bound to act in consonance with specific ethical criteria. We realise that these criteria may conflict with some concepts of self-determination. In the case of such a conflict, a patient has no right to compel a health-care provider to violate generally accepted professional standards. Cf *President's Commission Report*…at 44. ('A health care professional has an obligation to allow a patient to choose from among medically accepted treatment options…or to reject all options. No one, however, has an obligation to provide interventions that would, in his or her judgment, be countertherapeutic.')

The obscure nature of this limitation is illustrated in *Brophy v New England Sinai Hospital* (1986) 497 NE 2d 626. The Supreme Judicial Court of Massachusetts recognised the right of an incompetent patient in a persistent vegetative state to refuse artificial hydration and nutrition albeit that the right had to be exercised by a proxy on the patient's behalf. However, the court did not require the hospital, in which Brophy was, to desist from these interventions.

> **Liacos J:** The hospital argues that it has no constitutional, statutory, or common law right to deny nutrition and hydration to Brophy so as to bring about his death. The probate judge held that the hospital and its medical staff 'should not be compelled to withhold food and water to a patient, contrary to its moral and ethical principles, when such principles are recognised and accepted within a significant segment of the medical profession and the hospital community'. We agree. Neither GL c 111, §70E (1984 ed), the Massachusetts patients' rights statute, the doctrine of informed consent, nor any other provision of law requires the hospital to cease hydration and nutrition upon request of the guardian. There is nothing in *Superintendent of Belchertown State School v Saikewicz*, 373 Mass 728, 370 NE 2d 417 (1977), and its progeny which would justify compelling medical professionals, in a case such as this, to take active measures which are contrary to their view of the ethical duty towards their patients. See *Brandt v St Vincent Infirmary*, 287 Ark 431, 701 SW 2d 103,

106–107 (1985). There is substantial disagreement in the medical community over the appropriate medical action. It would be particularly inappropriate to force the hospital, which is willing to assist in a transfer of the patient, to take affirmative steps to end the provision of nutrition and hydration to him. A patient's right to refuse medical treatment does not warrant such an unnecessary intrusion upon the hospital's ethical integrity in this case.

It is at best curious that a patient's right to refuse an offer of treatment should be subject to his finding a doctor who is prepared to comply with his request. There was another hospital willing to accept Brophy on his terms. Likewise, in *Secretary of State for the Home Dept v Robb* [1995] 1 All ER 677, Thorpe J found this interest a difficult one. In a case concerned with the force feeding of a hunger-striker in prison, he stated (at 682):

> **Thorpe J:** The third consideration of maintaining the integrity of the medical profession is one that I find hard to recognise as a distinct consideration. Medical ethical decisions can be acutely difficult and it is when they are at their most acute that applications for declaratory relief are made to the High Court. I cannot myself see that this is a distinct consideration that requires to be set against the right of self-determination of the individual.

There is one further question concerning the limits of a patient's refusal: can it in law extend to forbidding nurses to carry out the regular activities of washing and changing and otherwise supervising the patient's general hygiene (ie 'nursing care')? In the unlikely event that a patient 'turns his head to the wall' and forbids anyone to have anything to do with him, are the nurses so bound? Would this not be a clear example of a situation where the interests of others, whether health care professionals or other patients whose health might be compromised by complying with the request, would prevail over the patient's? This would mean that the patient could be bathed, cleaned and looked after against his wishes. The justification in law would rest in public policy. The same arguments would not apply, however, where what was being considered was not 'nursing care'.

The view expressed here was followed by the Law Commission in its Report, *Mental Incapacity* (No 231, 1995) in its recommendations concerning advance refusals of treatment.

Law Commission *Mental Incapacity* (Report No 231) (1995)

Exclusion of 'basic care'

5.34 In the consultation paper we proposed that an advance directive should never be effective in refusing either pain relief or basic care. (Consultation Paper No 129, para 3.34.) On consultation, there was general agreement to the proposition that a patient's right to self-determination could properly be limited by considerations based on public policy. A number of respondents highlighted the effect on staff and other patients if patients were to have power to refuse in advance even the most basic steps to ensure comfort and cleanliness. One respondent argued that since a patient with capacity can refuse all types of treatment the same rule should apply to those making anticipatory refusals, but this minority view did not appeal to us. (Ibid, para 3.25 n 77.) We were grateful for the assistance of the BMA on the details of the proposed exclusion clause. We accept that patients with capacity regularly refuse certain types or levels of pain relief because they prefer to maintain alertness, and we prefer now to refer only to the alleviation of severe pain. We have also replaced reference to 'spoon-feeding' with reference to direct oral feeding, to cater for the administration of nutrition and hydration by syringe or cup. Our proposed definition of 'basic care' reflects a level of care which it would be contrary to public policy to withhold from a patient without capacity.

We recommend that an advance refusal of treatment should not preclude the provision of 'basic care', namely care to maintain bodily cleanliness and to alleviate severe pain, as well as the provision of direct oral nutrition and hydration. (Draft Bill, clause 9(7)(a) and (8).)

(See also the BMA's view in *Advance Statements About Medical Treatment* (1995) para 5.1.)

Of course, neither the Law Commission nor the BMA were concerned with contemporaneous refusals by competent patients, but in our view the law is the same. The Law Commission's proposals would, however, exclude the provision of 'basic care' from the doctor's 'general authority' where force would be necessary in the face of the patient's objection (see cl 5(1)(a) of the Draft Mental Incapacity Bill). Subject, that is, to taking 'steps necessary to avert a substantial risk of serious harm to the person concerned'. The BMA takes a slightly different view, allowing for 'objection' to even oral feeding (*op cit*, at para 2.3). In our view, in this instance the law could countenance the use of reasonable force in the face of a competent refusal on the grounds of public policy where the patient's life was at risk or there was a serious danger of irreparable and serious harm to the individual.

B. REQUESTING TREATMENT

The patient, as we have seen, may absolve the doctor from his duty to provide any particular treatment by refusing that treatment. The question which remains is whether the patient may demand that the doctor exceed what would ordinarily be regarded as his duty. Admittedly, the doctor's duty contemplates the exercise of appropriate discretion, but is there a point at which the doctor is not obliged to comply with the requests or demands of his patient?

There are three issues which come to mind. The first is when the patient requests or demands a form of care which the doctor in the exercise of reasonable medical judgment determines is futile, in that it will be of no benefit of any kind to the patient. As in all cases where a doctor has formed a reasonable and responsible clinical judgment that treatment is not called for, the law will not second-guess him by ordering him to provide the treatment (see eg *Re J (a minor) (wardship: medical treatment)* [1992] 4 All ER 614 (CA) discussed *supra*, ch 6). Of course, if there is some element of benefit but only at considerable cost, it is for the competent patient to be given the choice whether to opt for it or not, but this is not what we are considering here.

The second issue is more problematical. Some would argue that a doctor's duty to his patient is circumscribed by his duty to society. They would draw the implication that a doctor, in deciding whether to offer or provide a particular treatment, should consider the effect that his decision will have on overall resources. The Archbishop of Canterbury, in his Edwin Stevens lecture at the Royal Society of Medicine in 1976 (70 Proc Roy Soc Med 80), wrote:

> The doctor has a responsibility – an accountability – to the patient and the patient's family under his immediate care. But he has also a responsibility to the other patients in the long waiting queue. He has a further responsibility – to the Government, or, to put it more personally but none the less accurately, to his fellow tax-payers who provide the resources to keep the National Health Service going. The question arises as to whether some kind of consensus – I had almost said some kind of ethic – can emerge on the distribution of resources as between one part of the Health Service and another. A free-for-all could be disastrous.

What view would a court take? In our view, a court would decide that it is not the responsibility of a doctor caring for a particular patient to consider the interests of others. The fact that the patient is dying is of no consequence here. Only if the treatment is otherwise uncalled for, as being futile, would the doctor be justified in ignoring the patient's request or demand. As Robert Veatch has pointed out in his book *A Theory of Medical Ethics* (1981), it is not for the doctor to do other than care for his patient's interests (see eg pp 281–287). To ask him to do more is to ask him to adopt an impossibly bifurcated moral position. Support for this view may be found in the dictum of Lord Browne-Wilkinson in *Bland* where he said (at 879):

it is not legitimate for a judge in reaching a view as to what is for the benefit of the one individual whose life is in issue to take into account the wider practical issues as to allocation of limited financial resources or the impact on third parties of altering the time at which death occurs.

1. Doctor-assisted death

At the outset we should distinguish between the situation in which a doctor is asked to assist the patient in bringing about his death (aiding and abetting suicide) and where the doctor is asked to kill the patient ('mercy killing'). The current legal position is explained by Professor Glanville Williams.

Glanville Williams *Textbook of Criminal Law* (2nd edn, 1983)

A person cannot consent to his own death. The rule is not based upon utilitarian considerations even though these may sometimes buttress it. It is a theocratic survival in our predominantly secular law; and religious ('transcendental') arguments are still its main support.

What is the difference between killing a person with his consent and assisting his suicide? The first is generally murder, while the second is the statutory offence [under s 2 of the Suicide Act 1961]. The distinction between them is the distinction between perpetrators and accessories. If a doctor, to speed his dying patient's passing, injects poison with the patient's consent, this will be murder; but if the doctor places the poison by the patient's side, and the patient takes it, this will be suicide in the patient and the doctor's guilt will be of the abetment offence under the Suicide Act (not abetment in murder). Although this is the theoretical distinction, a case of consent-killing is occasionally reduced to one of assisting suicide.

The distinction may be thought to have no moral relevance, since the doctor assists the patient's death in both cases. But one or two points may be made. If V asks D to help him to die, D may reasonably say: 'I do not approve of what you propose, and will not do the job for you. But you are entitled to act on your own responsibility; and since you are ill and cannot obtain the means of suicide yourself, I do not mind supplying them to you.' Besides this, the fact that the patient takes the poison with his own hand helps to allay fears that perhaps he did not really consent. Suicide is more clearly an act of self-determination than consent to be killed, and requires greater strength of purpose.

The question may again be asked whether there is any social value in denying the doctor's right to help his patient in this way in terminal cases. Several unsuccessful attempts have been made to change the law, but they have foundered because of the united opposition of the churches and of the medical profession itself. Doctors fear that if they were given the legal power to terminate their patient's lives, although with consent, they would lose the confidence of their patients.

You will notice the reference by Professor Williams to the Suicide Act 1961, s 2(1), which provides as follows:

A person who aids, abets, counsels or procures the suicide of another, or an attempt by another to commit suicide, shall be liable on conviction on indictment to imprisonment for a term not exceeding fourteen years.

(a) The current law

Will a doctor who provides a patient with the means to bring about his own death be guilty of an offence under s 2(1) of the Suicide Act 1961? There are two questions to be resolved. First, does the doctor 'aid, abet, counsel or procure' the suicide of the patient? Secondly, does the doctor have the necessary state of mind required under s 2(1)? Both of these questions were considered in the following case, albeit one not involving a doctor.

A-G v Able [1984] 1 All ER 277, [1984] QB 795 (QBD)

The executive committee of a society which existed to promote voluntary euthanasia published a booklet entitled 'A Guide to Self-Deliverance' and sold it on request to members of the society aged 25 and over. Some 8,000 copies were distributed in that manner. The booklet's expressed aims were to overcome the fear of dying and to reduce the incidence of unsuccessful suicides. The booklet set out in detail several methods of what it termed 'self-deliverance' but could have deterred some people from committing suicide. The society took the view that the booklet would not encourage suicide and that it was in the public interest to make the advice it contained available to those persons who requested the booklet. The Attorney General, however, took the view that distribution of the booklet constituted an offence under s 2(1) of the Suicide Act 1961, but because he wished to avoid prosecuting members of the society's executive committee, who were respectable persons and had issued the booklet out of genuine and strongly-held beliefs, he applied in civil proceedings for declarations that the future supply of the booklet to persons who were known to be, or were likely to be, considering or intending to commit suicide constituted the offence of aiding, abetting, counselling or procuring the suicide of another, contrary to s 2(1) of the 1961 Act, if after reading the booklet such a person committed or attempted to commit suicide, that constituted an attempt to commit an offence under s 2(1) even where such person after reading the booklet did not commit or attempt suicide. The respondents, who were members of the society's executive committee, submitted that it was inappropriate to grant the declaratory relief sought.

Woolf J: A starting point [for considering whether declaratory relief should be granted] must be the terms of s 2(1) of the 1961 Act itself. The intent of the subsection is clear. Section 1 of the Act having abrogated the criminal responsibility of the suicide, s 2(1) retains the criminal liability of an accessory at or before the fact. The nature of that liability has, however, changed. From being a participant in an offence of another, the accessory becomes the principal offender. This has the result that to attempt to 'aid, abet, counsel or procure the suicide of another, or an attempt by another to commit suicide' can be an offence even if the person concerned does not attempt to commit suicide: see *R v McShane* (1977) 66 Cr App Rep 97 and s 3 of the Criminal Attempts Act 1981. This is of significance in relation to the present issues because if the distribution of the booklet amounts to an offence under s 2(1) of the 1961 Act when the person to whom the booklet is distributed commits suicide or attempts to commit suicide, then the distribution to that person, if there is no attempt to commit suicide, could be an attempt to commit an offence under s 2(1) in the appropriate circumstances.

This being the general effect of s 2(1), the issue can be confined to considering whether distributing the booklet to someone who commits suicide or attempts to commit suicide makes the distributor 'an accessory before the fact' to the suicide or attempted suicide, the position so far as the distributor is concerned being exactly the same as it would be if either suicide or attempted suicide was still a criminal offence...

The editor of *Russell on Crime*...provides assistance as to what is the 'bare minimum' which is necessary to constitute a person an accesory before the fact. It is stated (p 151):

...the conduct of an alleged accessory should indicate (a) that he knew that the particular deed was contemplated, and (b) that he approved of or assented to it, and (c) that his attitude in respect of it in fact encouraged the principal offender to perform [and I would here add 'or attempt to perform'] the deed.

In relation to the first minimum requirement, those responsible for publishing the booklet, because of its terms, would almost certainly know that a significant number of those to whom the booklet was intended to be sent would be contemplating suicide. They would not know precisely when, where or by what means the suicide was to be effected, if they took place, but this does not mean that they cannot be shown to be accessories. As Lord Parker CJ said in *R v Bainbridge* [1959] 3 All ER 200 at 202, [1960] 1 QB 129 at 134:

...if the principal does not totally and substantially vary the advice or the help and does not wilfully and knowingly commit a different form of felony altogether, the man who has advised or helped, aided or abetted, will be guilty of an accessory before the fact.

As the judge had directed the jury in that case: 'It must be proved he knew the type of crime which was in fact committed was intended.'

In relation to the second requirement, if the recipients of the booklet committed or attempted to commit suicide, the contents of the booklet indicate that the publishers approved or assented to their doing so. To conclude otherwise is inconsistent with the whole object of the booklet, which is to assist those who feel it necessary to resort to self-deliverance.

I turn, therefore, to the final minimum requirement. I have no doubt that, in the case at least of certain recipients of the booklet, its contents would encourage suicide. Ignorance how to commit suicide must by itself be a deterrent. Likewise, the risks inherent in an unsuccessful attempt must be a deterrent. The contents of the booklet provide information as to methods which are less likely to result in an unsuccessful attempt. This assistance must encourage some readers to commit or attempt to commit suicide. This is clearly appreciated by the publishers, thus their care to control the persons to whom the booklet is to be sold and their advice as to the safe keeping of the booklet...

The fact that the supply of the booklet could be an offence does not mean that any particular supply is an offence. It must be remembered that the society is an unincorporated body and there can be no question of the society committing an offence. Before an offence under s 2 can be proved, it must be shown that the individual concerned 'aided, abetted, counselled or procured' a suicide or an attempt at suicide and intended to do so by distributing the booklet. The intention of the individual will normally have to be inferred from facts surrounding the particular supply which he made. If, for example, before sending a copy of the booklet, a member of the society had written a letter, the contents of which were known to the person sending the booklet, which stated that the booklet was required because the member was intending to commit suicide, then, on those facts, I would conclude that an offence had been committed or at least an attempted offence contrary to s 2 of the 1961 Act. However, in the majority of cases, a member requesting the booklet will not make clear his intentions and the supply will be made without knowledge of whether the booklet is required for purposes of research, general information, or because suicide is contemplated. Is it, therefore, enough that in any particular case the person responsible for making the supply would appreciate that there is a real likelihood that the booklet is required by one of the substantial number of members of the society who will be contemplating suicide? It is as to this aspect of the case that there is the greatest difficulty and little assistance from the authorities.

Counsel on behalf of the respondents contends that before a person can be an accessory, there must be a consensus between the accessory and the principal, and there can be no consensus where the alleged accessory does not even know whether the principal is contemplating (in this case) suicide. As, however, is pointed out in Smith and Hogan *Criminal Law* (4th edn, 1978) while counselling implies consensus, procuring and aiding do not. The authors say (p 116):

> ...the law probably is that: i) 'Procuring' implies causation but not consensus, ii) 'abetting' and 'counselling' imply consensus but not causation and iii) 'aiding' requires actual assistance but neither consensus nor causation.

As a matter of principle, it seems to me that, as long as there is the necessary intent to assist those who are contemplating suicide to commit suicide if they decide to do so, it does not matter that the supplier does not know the state of mind of the actual recipient. The requirement for the necessary intent explains why in those cases where, in the ordinary course of business, a person is responsible for distributing an article, appreciating that some individuals might use it for committing suicide, he is not guilty of an offence. In the ordinary way, such a distributor would have no intention to assist the act of suicide. An intention to assist need not, however, involve a desire that suicide should be committed or attempted.

In this connection, I must refer to *R v Fretwell* (1862) 9 Cox CC 152. In that case the Court of Criminal Appeal decided that the mere provision of the means of committing a crime is not sufficient to make the provider guilty as an accessory. In giving the judgment of the court, Erle CJ said (at 154):

> In the present case the prisoner was unwilling that the deceased should take the poison; it was at her instigation and under the threat of self-destruction that he procured it and supplied it to her; but it was found that he did not administer it to her or cause her to take it. It would be consistent with the facts of the case that he hoped she would change her mind; and it might well be that the prisoner hoped and expected that she would not resort to it.

While I accept that this reasoning does not accord with mine, I do not regard the case as requiring me to come to a different conclusion from that which I have indicated. That case is inconsistent with *National Coal Board v Gamble* [1958] 3 All ER 203, [1959] 1 QB 11 and I regard it as confined to its own facts, for the reasons indicated in Smith and Hogan *Criminal Law* (4th edn, 1978, pp 120, 121).

Counsel for the respondents points out, and this I accept, that in some cases the booklet, far from precipitating someone to commit suicide, might have the effect of deterring someone from committing suicide when they might otherwise have done so. In such circumstances, he submits, it would be quite nonsensical to regard the supply of the booklet as being an attempted offence contrary to s 2 of the 1961 Act. I agree, though I recognise that on one approach the result would be different. The reason why I agree with the submission is because, in such a case, the booklet has not provided any assistance with a view to a contemplated suicide. Such assistance is necessary to establish the actus reus for even the attempted offence.

There will also be cases where, although the recipient commits or attempts to commit suicide, the booklet has nothing to do with the suicide or the attempted suicide; for example, a long period of time may have elapsed between the sending of the booklet and the attempt. In such a case, again, I would agree with counsel for the respondents that there would not be a sufficient connection between the attempted suicide and the supply of the booklet to make the supplier responsible. This does not mean that it has to be shown that the suicide or attempted suicide would not have occurred but for the booklet. However, if 'procuring' alone is relied on, this may be the case. As Lord Widgery CJ stated in *A-G's Reference (No 1 of 1975)* [1975] 2 All ER 684 at 686–687, [1975] QB 773 at 779–780:

> To procure means to produce by endeavour. You procure a thing by setting out to see that it happens and taking the appropriate steps to produce that happening…You cannot procure an offence unless there is a causal link between what you do and the commission of the offence…

However, you do not need to procure to be an accessory and the same close causal connection is not required when what is being done is the provision of assistance.

I therefore conclude that to distribute the booklet can be an offence. But, before an offence can be established to have been committed, it must at least be proved (a) that the alleged offender had the necessary intent, that is, he intended the booklet to be used by someone contemplating suicide and intended that that person would be assisted by the booklet's contents, or otherwise encouraged to take or to attempt to take his own life; (b) that while he still had that intention he distributed the booklet to such a person who read it; and (c) in addition, if an offence under s 2 of the 1961 Act is to be proved, that such a person was assisted or encouraged by so reading the booklet to take or to attempt to take his own life, otherwise the alleged offender cannot be guilty of more than an attempt.

If these facts can be proved, then it does not make any difference that the person would have tried to commit suicide anyway. Nor does it make any difference, as the respondents contend, that the information contained in the booklet is already in the public domain. The distinguishing feature between an innocent and guilty distribution is that in the former case the distributor will not have the necessary intent, while in the latter case he will.

However, in each case it will be for a jury to decide whether the necessary facts are proved. If they are, then normally the offence will be made out. Nevertheless, even if they are proved, I am not prepared to say it is not possible for there to some exceptional circumstances which means that an offence is not established.

Of course, this case is concerned with the publication of a book rather than a doctor providing the means for a particular patient to end his life. The importance of the case, however, lies in Woolf J's identification of what constitutes the elements of the offence which, as you will have seen, he lists at the end of his judgment. The reservation Woolf J expresses concerning proof of the existence of these elements when the case concerned a book issued to the public at large would not trouble a jury in the case of a particular doctor advising or helping a particular patient for a known purpose (for a discussion of *Able*, see K J M Smith 'Assisting in Suicide – The Attorney-General and the Voluntary Euthanasia Society' (1983) Crim L Rev 579).

Margaret Otlowski summarises the implications for doctors.

Margaret Otlowski *Voluntary Euthanasia and the Common Law* (1997)

> To establish a person's guilt as an aider and abettor, it is necessary to show that the person was intentionally assisting or encouraging the commission of the act in question or that he or she was at least ready to assist if required. The prohibition on 'aiding and abetting' suicide is of direct relevance in the medical context since a doctor who, at a patient's request, provides the means of committing suicide is, without doubt, aiding the patient's suicide. In many cases, there would be little difficulty in establishing that the doctor thereby intended to assist the patient to commit suicide (even though the doctor may have hoped that the patient would not do so) and that the patient was in fact assisted or encouraged in taking, or attempting to take his or her own life. In circumstances where the doctor has provided the patient with information and advice, for example, regarding the toxicity of drugs and what would amount to a lethal dose, the doctor's conduct may also attract liability on the basis of 'counselling' (eg Canada – Criminal Code 1985 s 241(a)) or even 'procuring' the patient's suicide (Australia – NT Criminal Code 1983 s 168(b), Qld Criminal Code 1995 s 108(a), WA Criminal Code 1913 s 288(1); New Zealand – Crimes Act 1961 s 179(a)). Once the basis for liability for assisted suicide is made out under the statutory prohibition, the special features which arguably set a doctor's conduct apart from other forms of criminal conduct are irrelevant. Thus, as was seen in the preceding chapter in relation to a doctor's liability for murder, the fact that the doctor was acting *bona fide* and that assistance was provided at the request of the patient within the context of a doctor/patient relationship would not exculpate a doctor from criminal liability. Furthermore, it would be irrelevant that the patient was in a terminal condition and that the patient's death was in any event imminent.

Much will, therefore, turn upon a jury's view of the facts were a doctor to be charged with the offence – although lenient directions to juries are not unknown. Again, Otlowski (*op cit*) illustrates this, albeit not in the context of a doctor, in the case of *R v Chard* (1993) Times, 23 September.

> ...there have been instances in England where prosecutions have been brought for assistance in suicide. One such case was *R v Chard* The Times, 23 Sept. 1993 in which the defendant was prosecuted for having provided the deceased with paracetamol pills at her request which she subsequently used to commit suicide. The defendant had given evidence that it had been the deceased's wish to have the option, if she so decided, of taking her own life. Judge Pownall QC of the Old Bailey directed the jury to find the defendant not guilty, finding that there was no evidence to support the charge of aiding and abetting suicide. His Honour held that the defendant had only provided her with an option of taking her own life and that is not enough. Whilst this decision may potentially be seen as a liberalization of the law, caution must be exercised in not overstating the relevance of the individual cases which come before the courts by way of prosecution, particularly in the context of a prosecution of a person who has assisted another to die – the interpretation of the law in such cases is often influenced by considerations of sympathy and leniency to the defendant.

(b) Changing the law

It has been increasingly argued that the law relating to doctor-assisted suicide should be changed. In its present form, it is said, it means that patients are denied control over their own death, when they are unable to help themselves and where the doctor is the only real and reliable source of help. The argument continues that they are thus condemned to suffer, since withdrawal of treatment may not bring about their death, and doctors may be made helpless onlookers (or forced surreptitiously to kill the patient, see *infra*).

Professor Robert Weir puts the arguments for and against what he calls physician-assisted suicide.

R Weir 'The Morality of Physician-Assisted Suicide' (1992) 20 Law, Medicine & Health Care 116

> In March, 1989, 12 physicians published an article on the provision of care to hopelessly ill patients. Unfortunately, many of the substantive points in that article received insufficient attention from readers because the authors' call for appropriate, continually adjusted care for terminally ill patients was overshadowed by a portion of the document in which ten of the authors agreed that 'it is not immoral for a physician to assist in the rational suicide of a terminally ill person.' [Wanzer et al 'The Physician's Responsibility Towards Hopelessly Ill Patients: A Second Look' (1989) New Engl J Med 320.]
>
> In June, 1990, Jack Kevorkian, a retired pathologist in Michigan, gained international media attention by enabling Janet Adkins, a woman in the early stage of Alzheimer's disease, to terminate her life with the help of his 'suicide machine.' The features of the case were so unusual that physicians, ethicists, and attorneys in health law who were interviewed by journalists were unanimous in judging this particular act of physician-assisted suicide deplorable.
>
> In March 1991, Timothy Quill, an internist in New York, published a detailed account of the suicide of one of his patients identified only as 'Diane,' a patient with acute myelomonocytic leukemia who requested and received his assistance in killing herself with an overdose of barbiturates. Given the features of this particular case, some of the professionals in medicine, ethics, and law interviewed by the media judged Dr Quill's action to have been morally acceptable, even if against the law in New York.
>
> The issue of physician-assisted suicide (PAS) is not limited to these well-publicized examples. The American Hospital Association estimates that many of the 6,000 daily deaths in the United States are orchestrated by patients, relatives, and physicians, although how many of these deaths are assisted suicides is unknown. In a 1990 *New York Times*-CBS poll, taken two weeks after the initial publicity of the Adkins case, 53 percent of the respondents said that physicians should be allowed to assist a severely ill person in terminating his or her own life. Moreover, PAS is beginning to be addressed as a separate ethical issue in the medical literature, without being lumped together with the related but different issue of voluntary euthanasia.

The legal status of PAS is also being tested in an unprecedented manner. The Hemlock Society, having failed three years ago to get 'The Humane and Dignified Death Act' on the ballot in California, successfully worked with a coalition called Washington Citizens for Death with Dignity to get Initiative 119 on the ballot in Washington in November, 1991. The wording of this initiative, using language that blurs the differences between PAS and voluntary euthanasia, simply asked voters: 'Shall adult patients who are in a medically terminal condition be permitted to request and receive from a physician aid in dying'?

Given these events, the time has come for a serious discussion of the morality and legality of physician-assisted suicide. I hope to contribute to that discussion by first analyzing the concept of assisted suicide and describing the diversity of possible legal responses to acts of PAS. I will then provide an ethical analysis of PAS by discussing the cases of Janet Adkins and 'Diane', sorting out the competing ethical arguments about this issue, and making some recommendations for professional practice and public policy.

The concept of assisted suicide
As is true for all suicides, an assisted suicide involves someone (a person outside a clinical setting, or a patient in a clinical setting) who has suicidal motives, intends to die, does something to cause his or her death, and is non-coerced in deciding to kill himself or herself. However, in contrast to 'normal' suicides, an assisted suicide requires aid from a physician, a relative or friend of the person wanting to commit suicide, or some other person who carries out the role of 'enabler'. The enabler can assist the suicidal person in any number of ways: by supplying information (eg, from the Hemlock Society) on the most effective ways of committing suicide, purchasing a weapon of self-destruction, providing a lethal dose of pills or poison, giving the suicidal person encouragement to carry out the lethal deed, or helping in the actual act of killing (eg, by helping the person take the pills, pull the trigger of a gun, close the garage doors, or turn on the gas). Also in contrast to suicide, an act of assisted suicide is an illegal act in many jurisdictions, punishable by fines and-or short-term imprisonment...

The case against physician-assisted suicide
Making a case for an ethical position, especially one that is contrary to traditional moral thinking and current law, requires an analysis of competing arguments and an effort to be as persuasive as possible. I now turn to that dual task by first examining five ethical arguments, some with variant themes, that are sometimes advanced against physician participation in assisted suicide.

(1)   The medical profession is committed to healing
The most common argument against PAS has two variants, both of which are based on the view that physicians constitute a unique profession that is defined, at least in part, by a traditional group morally stipulating standards of care and of behavior by members of the group. One version of this argument involves a direct appeal to the Hippocratic Oath, dating from the fourth century BC. In particular, current opponents of PAS appeal to the portion of the oath that declares: 'I will neither give a deadly drug to anybody if asked for it, nor will I make a suggestion to this effect.'

The second, more general version of this argument emphasizes the centrality of healing in defining who physicians are and what they do in their professional role. For some persons who advocate this view of medicine, the notion that physicians might, even in rare instances, assist patients to commit suicide is automatically and without exception ruled out of bounds for any member of the medical profession. As stated by David Orentlicher, 'Treatment designed to bring on death, by definition, does not heal and is therefore fundamentally inconsistent with the physician's role in the patient-physician relationship.' [(1989) 262 JAMA 1844.]

(2)   Physicians should not cause death
A related argument asserts that there is no difference between PAS and voluntary euthanasia. Once a physician moves beyond abating life-sustaining treatment, so the argument goes, it does not really matter whether the physician's participation in helping to hasten the patient's death at the patient's request is by prescribing barbiturates or by injecting a lethal agent. Both acts 'encourage doctors to use their skills to kill their patients.' According to Leon Kass, there is little difference between a physician's role as an accomplice to death or as an agent of death: assisting in a patient's death 'is as much in violation of the venerable proscription against euthanasia as were the physician to do it himself.'

(3)   Patients should not request physician-assisted suicide
This argument also has two variants, both of which address the moral responsibility of patients in the relationships they have with physicians. One version, the simpler of the two, states that patients should never ask their physicians to help them commit suicide, given that (a) many persons regard suicide as an immoral act and (b) physician participation in enabling that act of self-destruction to occur may constitute criminal action.

The second version of this argument is based on the difference between negative and positive moral rights, as these rights apply to the relationship between a patient and that patient's physician. A decision made by a patient to forgo mechanical ventilation, feeding tubes, or some other life-sustaining treatment involves the *negative* right (or liberty right) of treatment refusal. A correlate of this negative right is the obligation of the patient's physician not to interfere with or thwart that negative right unless the physician has some overriding obligation of another sort.

By contrast, a request by a patient for a physician's assistance in committing suicide can be interpreted as involving a *positive* right (or welfare right), or at least a claim to that effect. The difference is important: the patient does not merely request to be left alone by the physician, but tries to impose a moral obligation on the physician to help the patient accomplish the desired end of self-destruction. That claim, whether based on merit or need, is weak, and certainly need not be regarded as imposing an obligation on the physician who receives it.

(4) Physician-assisted suicide would lead to mistrust and abuses

This view, a form of the 'slippery slope' argument, projects two unfortunate consequences that would follow from the widespread acceptance and/or legalization of PAS. One of these consequences would be damage to the relationship of trust that, one hopes, exists between patients and their physicians. According to David Orentlicher, even a discussion of assisted suicide could damage the patient-physician relationship in two different ways: it could raise questions in the patient's mind about the value the physician attaches to the patient's present life of disability and suffering, and it could raise doubts in the patient's mind about the physician's commitment to provide effective treatment for the patient's current medical conditions. Either way, a physician's willingness even to discuss the possibility of assisted suicide 'might seriously undermine' the patient's trust in the physician.

The other consequences, that of abuses by physicians in assisting patients to commit suicide, would be equally serious. As vividly illustrated by the actions of Jack Kevorkian, some physicians would undoubtedly agree to help patients kill themselves without determining whether a given patient is clinically depressed, whether appropriate other medical opinions have been secured, whether the request for help is necessary, whether alternatives to assisted suicide have been explored, or whether relatives and friends who would be psychologically harmed by an unexpected suicide are aware of what may happen.

The fact that 'Diane's' case was handled in a better manner is of little comfort, according to this argument, since it merely demonstrates that virtually all cases of PAS involve physicians acting alone, with no scrutiny from their peers, the courts, or anybody else.

(5) Physician-assisted suicide is unnecessary

Patients turn to their physicians for help in committing suicide for any number of reasons. Chief among these reasons is a desire to avoid the prolonged pain and suffering, both physician and psychological, often involved in the course of a chronic and/or terminal condition. Frequently having witnessed the long, painful deaths of relatives in hospital settings, patients sometimes ask their physicians to help them avoid the same fate. Concerned that physicians will be unable to control the pain or effectively manage the symptoms of their chronic medical conditions, they conclude that suicide, perhaps requiring assistance from a physician or someone else, is their only alternative.

Such reasoning is wrong, according to advocates of hospice programs. In this argument, the availability of hospice care throughout the country precludes the need for patients to seek suicide, thus making the participation of physicians in assisting suicide unnecessary. Some physicians may, out of ignorance regarding effective pain control, 'agree with patients that their suffering is intolerable and worthy of assisted suicide when in fact the pain may be easily treatable.' A preferable altlernative is for physicians to learn how to relieve patients' pain more effectively, manage the symptoms of their conditions more appropriately, and assure them that prolonged suffering need not be the fate that awaits them.

Do these five arguments, taken single or as a collective argument, make a persuasive case that physicians should never agree to assist their patients in committing suicide? I think not, for the following reasons. Critics of PAS who use the first argument take an undeniably important, defining feature of the medical profession, but emphasize it to the exclusion of other ways of describing who physicians are and what they do professionally. Healing the sick and injured is surely one of the goals of medicine, but not in isolation from other appropriate medical goals. Preventing disease, saving and prolonging lives, relieving pain and suffering, ameliorating disabling conditions, and avoiding undue harm to patients are also important goals that represent defining features of medicine as a profession.

Some of these goals of medicine, it is important to note, are appropriate even when patients cannot be healed – and even when some patients turn to their physicians for help in putting an end to an existence they have come to regard as intolerable. The achievement of these appropriate medical goals is more important than a literal adherence to an ancient oath whose religious and moral framework is of such limited relevance to contemporary medicine that the oath is frequently altered when used in medical school convocations and increasingly replaced entirely by other kinds of oaths, including those written by medical students themselves.

The second argument, the one equating PAS with voluntary euthanasia, is simply misplaced in the debate over PAS. It is true, of course, that euthanasia has for centuries been regarded as contrary to morally responsible medical practice, but the intentional killing of patients is not the ethical issue involved in PAS. Physicians do not cause the deaths of patients in these cases; the patients cause their own deaths, a legal act in all 50 states, subsequent to receiving some type of enabling help from their physicians. Thus critics of PAS who assert that physicians are thereby killing patients are either (a) mistaken about the differences between assisted suicide and voluntary euthanasia or (b) intentionally blurring the differences between these two acts to score points with the emotive language of 'killing'.

The third argument is largely true, in my view, because it appropriately indicates that patients should not make unreasonable demands on physicians. Patients should be hesitant to try to involve their physicians in acts of assisted suicide, just as any of us should refrain from encouraging other persons to participate in actions that may be contrary to their value systems. Equally important, when patients with chronic, progressively deteriorating, or terminal conditions do ask their physicians for help in committing suicide, they should understand that they have no justifiable reason for thinking that their physicians are obligated to render such help. Physician-assisted suicide should be motivated by compassion for a patient, not a misplaced sense of moral obligation.

The last two arguments, the ones stating that PAS is dangerous and unnecessary, are only partially true. Abuses in the name of physician-assisted suicide will undoubtedly take place in the future, as they undoubtedly already do. Whether the abuses will be greater than at present is impossible to say. What is possible to say, however, is that PAS seems to be both necessary and morally justifiable in rare cases and, if handled correctly by morally responsible physicians, need not threaten the foundation of trust that is crucial to patient-physician relationships.

The occasional necessity of PAS is illustrated by the case of 'Diane', who requested assistance from Timothy Quill in terminating her life even though she was receiving appropriate medical care as a hospice patient. Unfortunately, even hospice care fails, for some patients, to provide them with sufficient personal control over the terminal phase of their lives. 'Diane's' case also suggests that a patient's level of trust in a physician may be increased, not undermined, when a caring physician indicates a reluctant willingness to help the patient bring her or his life to an end.

The case for physician-assisted suicide
Having provided this critical assessment of arguments against PAS, I will now put forth five arguments that may prove to be persuasive in justifying some cases of physician participation in assisted suicide. Taken together, the arguments claim that PAS is occasionally justifiable as a compassionate way for physicians to respond to current medical reality by alleviating patient suffering, optimizing patient control, and minimizing harm to the patient and other persons important to the patient. Taken individually, the arguments suggest that physicians should, in rare cases, consider assisting their patients to commit suicide, for any of five reasons.

(1) To respond to current medical reality
Change is a regular part of medicine, whether the change takes the form of new diagnostic tools, new research discoveries, new victories over old diseases, new diseases, new health problems, new drugs, new life-sustaining technologies, or new concerns over matters pertaining to bio-medical ethics, health economics, and health law. Change is surely a factor in the medical problems that patients bring their physicians, with adult patients now presenting more medical problems that are chronic or degenerative in nature than ever before. Added to this factor is another one: patients are living increasingly longer lives, with the combination of chronic medical conditions and extended life expectancy representing the distinct possibility, for some persons, that remaining alive will be regarded as offering nothing other than more disability, more financial and personal hardship, and more suffering.

The good news is that many adults are now capable, with the help of pharmacological and technological advances in medicine, of having long lives with a remarkable health status that would have been unachievable earlier in this century and unimaginable before that. The bad news is that some adults are caught in an existential situation dominated by intractable pain, severe disability, progressive dementia, a deteriorating neurological condition, a terminal condition, or some combination of these that makes life seem not to be worth living. An unknown number of these persons decide that death is a preferable option to the suffering that life holds for them and, for their own personal reasons, ask their physicians to help them end the suffering.

It is this part of medical reality – the realistic limits of physicians to heal all their patients and effectively relieve suffering – that represents the ethical core of the debate over PAS. Rather than quoting a passage from the Hippocratic Oath about what physicians cannot do for their patients, contemporary physicians should address medical reality as it currently exists in their patients – some with terminal conditions, and an increasing number with chronic and degenerative diseases – and consider again what they might do for that small minority of patients who find their lives to be intolerable and who, perhaps as a last resort, turn to their physicians for help in bringing about death.

(2) *To alleviate patient suffering*

Virtually anyone who is ill suffers from time to time. For some patients, suffering is primarily physical in nature, with the particular forms of suffering including nausea, dyspnea, fever, hunger, thirst, diarrhea, and pain. For other patients, suffering is partially or perhaps primarily psychological in nature, with individuals experiencing anxiety, depression, denial, loneliness, helplessness, anger, and fear. Much of this suffering, whether physiological or psychological in nature, can be effectively managed with emphathic support, medications, various other medical and surgical interventions, nursing care, psychological counseling, stress-reduction techniques and rest.

But for Janet Adkins, 'Diane', and an unknown number of other patients, the multiple efforts made by themselves, their families and friends, and their physicians to alleviate their suffering ultimately do not work. Janet Adkins, it seems, experienced substantial psychological suffering brought on by thoughts about the losses she had already experienced (she could no longer read literature or play the piano). Additional psychological suffering was undoubtedly created by the anxiety and fear of wondering what her remaining years with Alzheimer's disease would be like for herself and her family.

'Diane' experienced the physical suffering caused by her disease-related bone pain, weakness, infections, fatigue, and fever, but she preferred this suffering to the suffering she would have experienced through hospitalization, chemotherapy, radiation therapy, and bone marrow transplantation. In addition, she seems to have experienced substantial psychological suffering that included anger at an insensitive oncologist, anxiety over losing control of her living and dying, fear about her increasing discomfort and dependence, fear about additional pain, and an overwhelming sense of injustice regarding the leukemic condition that struck her soon after she had conquered her other health problems.

The ethical challenge that is presented to physicians by such cases is direct and sharp: should I, having exhausted all other therapeutic possibilities, respond affirmatively to a request for help made by one of my patients? Should I, with the intention of alleviating the life-ruining suffering that my patient is experiencing, be willing to assist the patient in committing suicide? In at least some cases, the appropriate answer is yes.

(3) *To optimize patient control*

The desire to have control over one's living, dying, and death is a factor in assisted suicide cases that matches the desire for suffering to be ended. Janet Adkins was willing to travel from Portland to Seattle for experimental treatment, then to fly (with her husband) to Detroit to make use of the 'suicide machine' in order to end her life before it was ravaged further by Alzheimer's disease. Although legitimate questions have been raised about her mental status at the time, there seems to be little doubt that, if she was still autonomous in the days before her death, her choice to kill herself was a choice to control her destiny instead of permitting her disease to control her.

The desire for personal control is even clearer in 'Diane's' case. Quill states that 'Diane', having overcome her earlier medical problems, 'took control of her life' and developed 'a strong sense of independence and confidence'. When she went against Quill's medical advice and the wishes of her family in refusing chemotherapy, she 'articulated very clearly that it was she who would be experiencing all the side effects of treatment'. Later, when 'Diane' knew she was dying, Quill says that it was 'extraordinarily important to 'Diane' to maintain control of herself and her own dignity during the time remaining to her' in describing his own participation in the case, Quill states that he felt he was 'setting her free to get the most out of the time she had left, and to maintain dignity and control on her own terms until her death'.

For physicians in such cases, the option of trying to optimize patient control represents the ultimate challenge of how far one is willing to go to respect the autonomy of patients. If (as seems clear in 'Diane's' case, but not Janet Adkins' case) the patient who requests assistance is autonomous, the patient is therefore capable of making an informed, deliberative, and voluntary decision regarding her or his health care. If personal control over one's living and dying is highly valued by the patient, the decisions made about health care will reflect that value. In extreme cases the desire to remain autonomous and in control sometimes includes a request for help from a physician – a request for help in exercising control over one's final exit.

(4) *To minimize harm to the patient and others*

The ethical principle of nonmaleficence has considerable importance in medicine. Throughout the history of medicine, physicians have been expected to avoid intentionally or negligently harming their patients. Given that patients are frequently harmed in a variety of ways in clinical contexts, the ethical requirement placed on physicians is that of trying to ensure that patients are not harmed on balance in the course of efforts to heal them or otherwise promote their welfare.

Traditionally, the ultimate harm to befall a patient has been considered to be death. As a consequence, two longstanding moral rules of medical practice have been derived from this professional aversion to having any intentional (or negligent) role in a patient's death: 'do not kill' and 'do not assist another person's death'.

In the great majority of cases, these moral rules continue to apply. However, patients can be harmed in several significant ways short of death, through the invasion of their important interests, the impairment of their mental or psychological welfares, physical injury, and technological abuse. Moreover, most thoughtful persons have some sort of informal ranking or other cataloging of harmful events that could take place in their lives that would represent, to them, a fate worse than death.

Janet Adkins, 'Diane', and unknown other persons have concluded that remaining alive under terrible, worsening circumstances is a fate worse than death. The important question is whether physicians should have any role in facilitating one harmful event (a patient's self-destruction) in order to help the patient avoid other harms (eg, intractable pain, progressive dementia, loss of personhood, incalculable damage to a family) that the patient regards as worse. In rare cases, the appropriate answer is affirmative, both for the sake of the patient and for persons loved by the patient.

(5) To act out of compassion
What counts as a morally responsible motive for physician participation in assisted suicide? The list of possible motives includes a desire to help the patient, an undervaluing of the quality of the patient's life, a desire to help the family emotionally and financially, a misplaced sense of duty to the patient, a desire for publicity, and so forth.

According to media accounts of the Janet Adkins case, Jack Kevorkian seems to have had several motives, including the desire for publicity in the medical profession. By contrast, Timothy Quill seems not to have been motivated by considerations other than the physical and psychological welfare of his patient and her family.

In my view, the only acceptable motive for physicians to have in enabling a patient to commit suicide is that of compassion. In many instances, of course, compassionate physicians decide, for good moral reasons, not to help patients achieve the sort of self-deliverance that they seek. In other, much less frequent instances, compassionate physicians sometimes decide that the plea for help from a patient for whom life has become intolerable is a request that cannot and should not be rejected. Either moral choice, if motivated by compassion, can be correct, depending on the facts of individual cases.

Justifiable practice and public policy
For PAS to be justifiable, several conditions have to be met. First, a morally responsible physician who is asked to assist in a suicide should determine if the patient is suffering from treatable clinical depression and, if so, recommend treatment for that condition. In addition, the physician should try to determine if the patient's pain and other suffering are, in fact, refractory to treatment.

A second condition is for the physician to determine that assisted suicide is a moral last resort, in the sense that there are no effective medical options available that are acceptable to the patient. No medical treatment is available that will reverse or cure the patient's condition, no life-sustaining treatment is being used that could be abated at the patient's request, and no intervention (even hospice care) seems to provide the relief and release the patient desperately seeks.

A third condition consists of several conversations between the physician and the patient, with at least one of the conversations including one or more of the patient's closest relatives and friends. From the physician's perspective, these conversations, whether done within a few days or over several weeks, should have several purposes: to determine that the patient is autonomous and the decision to commit suicide is rational, to recommend a second medical opinion and other appropriate professional help, to make sure that no acceptable alternatives to assisted suicide are available, to determine that the request for assistance is necessary, and to make sure that the patient's close relatives and friends are informed about the prospective suicide. The consent of the patient's family to the contemplated suicide is not required, but they should at least be aware, in general terms, of what may happen so that the psychological harm they experience will be lessened when they find out that the suicide has taken place.

Even when these conditions are met in individual cases, important questions remain as to how PAS cases should be handled in terms of public policy. How should the law respond when a physician or other person helps an individual do something that is legal in every state, when that legal activity is suicide? Should physicians who decide to assist one or more of their patients in committing suicide be criminally liable, either under a specific state statute or a state homicide law? Should assisted suicide, whether done by physicians or other persons, be decriminalized? Should PAS, along with voluntary euthanasia, be legalized as 'physician-aid-in-dying' under certain conditions?

These questions and many others regarding PAS as a matter of public policy require careful analysis and extensive discussion, much more than can be completed here. However, I have some tentative recommendations that might contribute to the discussion. A preferable alternative to the current patchwork of state laws on assisted suicide would be for the National Conference of Commissioners on Uniform State Laws (NCCUSL), working with appropriate medical groups, to develop modern legislation on PAS that might be adopted throughout the country, so that physicians practicing in any state could have greater certainty regarding the legality (or illegality) of PAS. My hope is that this new legislation will remove PAS from the criminal statutes in all states, so that physicians who decide for reasons of compassion to engage in PAS will no longer have to be secretive and deceptive with their professional colleagues about having done so.

In my view, the legal restrictions on assisted suicide should be lifted only for physicians. Given the ease with which emotionally unstable, demented, and suicidal individuals could be 'assisted' in their deaths by numerous other persons with questionable motives, the NCCUSL and/or various state legislatures may decide to maintain the legal liability attached to acts of assisted suicide when performed by persons other than physicians.

Physicians, of course, should not be given a legal blank check. Physicians who receive requests for help in committing suicide with regret and sadness, who give serious consideration to such requests only in carefully limited circumstances, and who meet the conditions for morally responsible PAS should not face legal penalties. By contrast, physicians who are irresponsible in taking requests for PAS, who fail to exercise appropriate care in working with patients seeking PAS, and who are careless in providing patients with the means of self-destruction should face penalties for such negligence, perhaps including losing their licenses to practice medicine.

One final point. The case for PAS has been developed with great reluctance, both because I wish such activity by physicians were unnecessary and because I am uncomfortable advocating an ethical position that departs from much traditional thinking about ethics in medicine. However, I am convinced that PAS is sometimes necessary, that it is an alternative not to be automatically rejected by morally responsible physicians, and that it is, in at least some instances, justifiable as the right and compassionate thing to do.

The House of Lords' Select Committee, in its report in 1994, rather dismissively, rejected all calls for reform.

House of Lords' Select Committee *Report of the Select Committee on Medical Ethics* (HL Paper 21, Session 1993–94)

ASSISTED SUICIDE

262. As far as assisted suicide is concerned, we see no reason to recommend any change in the law. We identify no circumstances in which assisted suicide should be permitted, nor do we see any reason to distinguish between the act of a doctor or of any other person in this connection.

Despite the fact that this recommendation is somewhat 'delphic' and not defended at any length, the Government unequivocally supported it in its response in 1994 to the Select Committee's Report (Cm 2553) stating (at 5):

The Government can see no basis for permitting assisted suicide. Such a change would be open to abuse and put the lives of the weak and vulnerable at risk.

The battle lines are, as a result, well and truly drawn. The Government's position is clear and the politics of legislation in this area are fraught with difficulty, given the parliamentary opposition to any change of the law which could be perceived as weakening the sanctity of human life.

Two questions of considerable importance remain. First, does the absolute prohibition on physician-assisted suicide in English law conform with the European Convention on Human Rights? Secondly, what shape might legislation take if we were to permit physician-assisted suicide in certain circumstances? Let us consider these questions in turn.

(i) HUMAN RIGHTS COMPATIBILITY

We saw in Chapter 1 that the Human Rights Act 1998, incorporating the European Convention on Human Rights, has a considerable impact upon medical law. To what extent will the Convention affect the law on physician-assisted suicide? Of course, the English courts do not have the power to disapply the provisions of the Suicide Act 1961, even if it were held to infringe the Convention (contrast the position in Canada and the United States: see, *Rodriguez v British Columbia (A-G)* (1993) 107 DLR (4th) 342 (Can SC) and *Washington v Glucksberg* (1997) 521 US 702 and *Vacco v Quill* (1997) 117 S Ct 2293 (US Sup Ct)). The English courts could, however, make a declaration of incompatibility under s 4 of the 1998 Act. More likely, the courts may try and interpret the Suicide Act 1961 restrictively in order to be consistent with the Convention as they are required to by s 3 of the 1998 Act. The issue could also be raised before the European Court of Human Rights in the usual way. What, then, are the relevant Convention provisions? Article 2 ('right to life') and art 8 ('right to respect for private and family life') seem to be the most appropriate provisions.

Article 2
1. Everyone's right to life shall be protected by law. No one shall be deprived of his life intentionally save in the execution of a sentence of a court following his conviction of a crime for which this penalty is provided by law.
2. Deprivation of life shall not be regarded as inflicted in contravention of this Article when it results from the use of force which is no more than absolutely necessary:
(a) in defence of any person from unlawful violence;
(b) in order to effect a lawful arrest or to prevent the escape of a person lawfully detained;
(c) in action lawfully taken for the purpose of quelling a riot or insurrection.

Article 8
1. Everyone has the right to respect for his private and family life, his home and his correspondence.
2. There shall be no interference by a public authority with the exercise of this right except such as is in accordance with the law and is necessary in a democratic society in the interests of national security, public safety or the economic well-being of the country, for the prevention of disorder or crime, for the protection of health or morals, or for the protection of the rights and freedoms of others.

It could be argued that art 8 is sufficiently broad that it prohibits any law which prevents a person exercising a choice, albeit through another (the doctor), to end his life unless justified under the provisions of art 8(2). By contrast, art 2 seems to prevent any relaxation in the law. We shall return to these arguments later. As it happens, a similar argument based upon s 7 of the Canadian Charter of Rights and Freedoms was considered by the Canadian Supreme Court in the following case.

Rodriguez v British Columbia (A-G) (1993) 82 BCLR (2d) 273 (Can SC)

The petitioner, 42, was suffering from amyotrophic lateral sclerosis, an incurable, progressive disease affecting the nervous system, leading to extensive muscle wasting. Victims of the disease generally die within two or three years of first diagnosis, due to wasting of the muscles used in breathing. Prior to that time, victims experience difficulty with speech, chewing and swallowing. Feeding eventually must be done by stomach tube and the victim requires total care as most bodily functions are lost. Death generally results from starvation or choking. The petitioner wished to avoid the future stress and loss of dignity caused by the prospect of such a death and she proposed to have a physician install an intravenous line containing some effective agent which, at the appropriate time, the petitioner would be able to transfer into her body by activating a switch, ending her life. She applied for an order declaring invalid s 241(b) of the *Criminal Code*, which makes aiding or abetting a suicide a criminal offence. She relied on ss 7, 12 and 15(1) of the *Canadian Charter of Rights and Freedoms*. Her application was dismissed and by a majority (McEachern CJ dissenting) the British Columbia Court of Appeal dismissed her appeal ([1993] 3 WWR 553). She appealed to the Canadian Supreme Court which, by a majority of 5–4, also dismissed her appeal.

Sopinka J: I have read the reasons of the Chief Justice and those of McLachlin J herein. The result of the reasons of my colleagues is that all persons who by reason of disability are unable to commit suicide have a right under the *Canadian Charter of Rights and Freedoms* to be free from government interference in procuring the assistance of others to take their life. They are entitled to a constitutional exemption from the operation of s 241 of the *Criminal Code*, RSC, 1985, c C–46, which prohibits the giving of assistance to commit suicide (hereinafter referred to as assisted suicide). The exemption would apply during the period that this Court's order would be suspended and thereafter Parliament could only replace the legislation subject to this right. I must respectfully disagree with the conclusion reached by my colleagues and with their reasons...

I have concluded that the conclusion of my colleagues cannot be supported under the provisions of the *Charter*...

I.   Section 7
The most substantial issue in this appeal is whether s 241(b) infringes s 7 in that it inhibits the appellant in controlling the timing and manner of her death. I conclude that while the section impinges on the security interest of the appellant, any resulting deprivation is not contrary to the principles of fundamental justice. I would come to the same conclusion with respect to any liberty interest which may be involved.

Section 7 of the *Charter* provides as follows:

> 7. Everyone has the right to life, liberty and security of the person and the right not to be deprived thereof except in accordance with the principles of fundamental justice.

The appellant argues that, by prohibiting anyone from assisting her to end her life when her illness has rendered her incapable of terminating her life without such assistance, by threat of criminal sanction, s 241(b) deprives her of both her liberty and her security of the person. The appellant asserts that her application is based upon (a) the right to live her remaining life with the inherent dignity of a human person, (b) the right to control what happens to her body while she is living, and (c) the right to be free from governmental interference in making fundamental personal decisions concerning the terminal stages of her life. The first two of these asserted rights can be seen to invoke both liberty and security of the person; the latter is more closely associated with only the liberty interest.

(a)   Life, Liberty and Security of the Person
The appellant seeks a remedy which would assure her some control over the time and manner of her death. While she supports her claim on the ground that her liberty and security of the person interests are engaged, a consideration of these interests cannot be divorced from the sanctity of lilfe, which is one of the three *Charter* values protected by s 7.

None of these values prevail a priori over the others. All must be taken into account in determining the content of the principles of fundamental justice and there is no basis for imposing a greater burden on the propounder of one value as against that imposed on another.

Section 7 involves two stages of analysis. The first is as to the values at stake with respect to the individual. The second is concerned with possible limitations of those values when considered in conformity with fundamental justice. In assessing the first aspect, we may do so by considering whether there has been a violation of Ms Rodriguez's security of the person and we must consider this in light of the other values I have mentioned...

What, then, can security of the person be said to encompass in the context of this case? The starting point for the answer to this question is *R v Morgentaler* [1988] 1 SCR 30 in which this Court struck down *Criminal Code* provisions which had the effect of preventing women access to therapeutic abortion unless they complied with an administrative scheme found to be contrary to principles of fundamental justice.

...In my view...the judgments of this Court in *Morgentaler* can be seen to encompass a notion of personal autonomy involving, at the very least, control over one's bodily integrity free from state interference and freedom from state-imposed psychological and emotional stress. In *Reference re ss 193 and 195.1(1)(c) of the Criminal Code (Man)*, [1990] 1 SCR 1123 Lamer J (as he then was) also expressed this view, stating at p 1177 that '[s]ection 7 is also implicated when the state restricts individuals' security of the person by interfering with, or removing from them, control over their physical or mental integrity'. There is no question, then, that personal autonomy, at least with respect to the right to make choices concerning one's own body, control over one's physical and psychological integrity, and basic human dignity are encompassed within security of the person, at least to the extent of freedom from criminal prohibitions which interfere with these.

The effect of the prohibition in s 241(b) is to prevent the appellant from having assistance to commit suicide when she is no longer able to do so on her own. She fears that she will be required to live until the deterioration from her disease is such that she will die as a result of choking, suffocation or pneumonia caused by aspiration of food and secretions. She will be totally dependent upon machines to perform her bodily functions and completely dependent upon others. Throughout this time, she will remain mentally competent and able to appreciate all that is happening to her. Although palliative care may be available to ease the pain and other physical discomfort which she will experience, the appellant fears the sedating effects of such drugs and argues, in any event, that they will not prevent the psychological and emotional distress which will result from being in a situation of utter dependence and loss of dignity. That there is a right to choose how one's body will be dealt with, even in the context of beneficial medical treatment, has long been recognized by the common law. To impose medical treatment on one who refuses it constitutes battery, and our common law has recognized the right to demand that medical treatment which would extend life be withheld or withdrawn. In my view, these considerations lead to the conclusion that the prohibition in s 241(b) deprives the appellant of autonomy over her person and causes her physical pain and psychological stress in a manner which impinges on the security of her person. The appellant's security interest (considered in the context of the life and liberty interest) is therefore engaged, and it is necessary to determine whether there has been any deprivation thereof that is not in accordance with the principles of fundamental justice...

(b) The Principles of Fundamental Justice
...On the one hand, the Court must be conscious of its proper role in the constitutional make-up of our form of democratic government and not seek to make fundamental changes to long-standing policy on the basis of general constitutional principles and its own view of the wisdom of legislation. On the other hand, the Court has not only the power but the duty to deal with this question if it appears that the *Charter* has been violated. The power to review legislation to determine whether it conforms to the *Charter* extends to not only procedural matters but also substantive issues. The principles of fundamental justice leave a great deal of scope for personal judgment and the Court must be careful that they do not become principles which are of fundamental justice in the eye of the beholder only.

In this case, it is not disputed that in general s 241(b) is valid and desirable legislation which fulfils the government's objectives of preserving life and protecting the vulnerable. The complaint is that the legislation is over-inclusive because it does not exclude from the reach of the prohibition those in the situation of the appellant who are terminally ill, mentally competent, but cannot commit suicide on their own. It is also argued that the extension of the prohibition to the appellant is arbitrary and unfair as suicide itself is not unlawful, and the common law allows a physician to withhold or withdraw life-saving or life-maintaining treatment on the patient's instructions and to administer palliative care which has the effect of hastening death. The issue is whether, given this legal context, the existence of a criminal prohibition on assisting suicide for one in the appellant's situation is contrary to principles of fundamental justice.

Discerning the principles of fundamental justice with which deprivation of life, liberty or security of the person must accord, in order to withstand constitutional scrutiny, is not an easy task...

This Court has often stated that in discerning the principles of fundamental justice governing a particular case, it is helpful to look at the common law and legislative history of the offence in question (*Re BC Motor Vehicle Act* [1985] 2 SCR 486 and *Morgentaler, supra*, and *R v Swain*, [1991] 1 SCR 933). It is not sufficient, however, merely to conduct a historical review and conclude that because neither Parliament nor the various medical associations has ever expressed a view that assisted suicide should be decriminalized, that to prohibit it could not be said to be contrary to the principles of fundamental justice. Such an approach would be problematic for two reasons. First, a strictly historical analysis will always lead to the conclusion in a case such as this that the deprivation is in accordance with fundamental justice as the legislation will not have kept apace with advances in medical technology. Second, such reasoning is somewhat circular, in that it relies on the continuing existence of the prohibition to find the prohibition to be fundamentally just.

The way to resolve these problems is not to avoid the historical analysis, but to make sure that one is looking not just at the existence of the practice itself (ie, the continued criminalization of assisted suicide) but at the rationale behind that practice and the principles which underlie it.

The appellant asserts that it is a principle of fundamental justice that the human dignity and autonomy of individuals be respected, and that to subject her to needless suffering in this manner is to rob her of her dignity. The importance of the concept of human dignity in our society was enunciated by Cory J (dissenting, Lamer CJ concurring) in *Kindler v Canada (Minister of Justice)* [1991] 2 SCR 779, at p 813. Respect for human dignity underlies many of the rights and freedoms in the *Charter*.

That respect for human dignity is one of the underlying principles upon which our society is based is unquestioned. I have difficulty, however, in characterizing this in itself as a principle of fundamental justice within the meaning of s 7. While respect for human dignity is the genesis for many principles of fundamental justice, not every law that fails to accord such respect runs afoul of these principles. To state that 'respect for human dignity and autonomy' is a principle of fundamental justice, then, is essentially to state that the deprivation of the appellant's security of the person is contrary to principles of fundamental justice because it deprives her of security of the person. This interpretation would equate security of the person with a principle of fundamental justice and render the latter redundant.

I cannot subscribe to the opinion expressed by my colleague, McLachlin J, that the state interest is an inappropriate consideration in recognizing the principles of fundamental justice in this case. This Court has affirmed that in arriving at these principles, a balancing of the interest of the state and individual is required...

Wherer the deprivation of the right in question does little or nothing to enhance the state's interest (whatever it may be), it seems to me that a breach of fundamental justice will be made out, as the individual's rights will have been deprived for no valid purpose. This is, to my mind, essentially the type of analysis...which was carried out in *Morgentaler*. That is, both Dickson CJ and Beetz J were of the view that at least some of the restrictions placed upon access to abortion had no relevance to the state objective of protecting the foetus while protecting the life and health of the mother. In that regard the restrictions were arbitrary or unfair. It follows that before one can determine that a statutory provision is contrary to fundamental justice, the relationship between the provision and the state interest must be considered. One cannot conclude that a particular limit is arbitrary because (in the words of my colleague, McLachlin J) 'it bears no relation to, or is inconsistent with, the objective that lies behind' the legislation without considering the state interest and the societal concerns which it reflects.

The issue here, then, can be characterized as being whether the blanket prohibition on assisted suicide is arbitrary or unfair in that it is unrelated to the state's interest in protecting the vulnerable, and that it lacks a foundation in the legal tradition and societal beliefs which are said to be represented by the prohibition.

Section 241(b) has as its purpose the protection of the vulnerable who might be induced in moments of weakness to commit suicide. This purpose is grounded in the state interest in protecting life and reflects the policy of the state that human life should not be depreciated by allowing life to be taken. This policy finds expression not only in the provisions of our *Criminal Code* which prohibit murder and other violent acts against others notwithstanding the consent of the victim, but also in the policy against capital punishment and, until its repeal, attempted suicide. This is not only a policy of the state, however, but is part of our fundamental conception of the sanctity of human life. The Law Reform Commission expressed this philosophy appropriately in its Working Paper 28, 'Euthanasia, Aiding Suicide and Cessation of Treatment' (1982), at p 36:

> Preservation of human life is acknowledged to be a fundamental value of our society. Historically, our criminal law has changed very little on this point. Generally speaking, it sanctions the principle of the sanctity of human life. Over the years, however, law has come to temper the apparent absolutism of the principle, to delineate its intrinsic limitations and to define its true dimensions.

As is noted in the above passage, the principle of sanctity of life is no longer seen to require that all human life be preserved at all costs. Rather, it has come to be understood, at least by some, as encompassing quality of life considerations, and to be subject to certain legislative and social policy in this area is necessary in order to determine whether fundamental principles have evolved such that they conflict with the validity of the balancing of interests undertaken by Parliament.

(i)   History of Suicide Provisions

At common law, suicide was seen as a form of felonous homicide that offended both against God and the King's interest in the life of his citizens. As Blackstone noted in *Commentaries on the Laws of England* (1769), vol 4, at p 189:

> ...the law of England wisely and religiously considers, that no man hath a power to destroy life, but by commission from God, the author of it; and, as the suicide is guilty of a double offence; one spiritual, in invading the prerogative of the Almighty, and rushing into his immediate presence uncalled for; and the other temporal, against the king, who hath an interest in the preservation of all his subjects; the law has therefore ranked this among the highest crimes, making it a peculiar species of felony, a felony committed on oneself.

This is essentially the view first propounded by Plat and Aristotle that suicide was 'an offence against the gods or the state' (M G Velasquez, 'Defining Suicide' (1987), *3 Issues in Law & Medicine 37*, at p 40).

However, the contrary school of thought has always existed and is premised on notions of both freedom and compassion. The Roman stoics, for example, 'tended to condone suicide as a lawful and rational exercise of individual freedom and even wise in the cases of old age, disease or dishonor' (Velasquez, *supra*, at p 40). A more humane tone was struck by the Chancellor Francis Bacon who would have preferred leaving to the doctors the duty of lessening, or even ending, the suffering of their patients (L Depault, 'Le doit à la mort:

rapport juridique' (1974), *7 Human Rights Journal* 464, at p 467). There has never been a consensus with respect to this contrary school of thought.

Thus, until 1823, English law provided that the property of the suicide be forfeited and his body placed at the cross-roads of two highways with a stake driven through it. Burial indignities were also imposed in *ancien régime* France where the body of the suicide was often put on trial before being crucified (G Williams, *The Sanctity of Life and the Criminal Law* (1957), at p 259; Depaule, *supra*, at p 465, citing the *Ordonnance de 1670*, title XXII).

However, given the practical difficulties of prosecuting the successful suicide, most prohibitions centred on attempted suicide; it was considered an offence and accessory liability for assisted suicide was made punishable. In England, this took the form of a charge of accessory before the fact to murder or murder itself until the passage of the *Suicide Act, 1961* (UK), 9 & 10 Eliz. 2 c 60, which created an offence of assisting suicide which reads much like our s 241. In Canada, the common law recognized that aiding suicide was criminal (G W Burbidge, *A Digest of the Criminal Law of Canada* (1890), at p 224) and this was enshrined in the first *Criminal Code*, SC 1892, c 29, s 237. It is, with some editorial changes, the provision now found in s 241.

The associated offence of attempted suicide has an equally long period pedigree in Canada, found in the original *Code* at s 238 and continued substantively unaltered until its repeal by SC 1972, c 12, s 16. The fact of this decriminalization does not aid us particularly in this analysis, however. Unlike the situation with the partial decriminalization of abortion, the decriminalization of attempted suicide cannot be said to represent a consensus by Parliament or by Canadians in general that the autonomy interest of those wishing to kill themselves is paramount to the state interest in protecting the life of its citizens. Rather, the matter of suicide was seen to have its roots and its solutions in sciences outside the law, and for that reason not to mandate a legal remedy. Since that time, there have been some attempts to decriminalize assistance to suicide through private members bills, but none has been successful.

(ii)   Medical Care at the End of life
Canadian courts have recognized a common law right of patients to refuse consent to medical treatment, or to demand that treatment, once commenced, be withdrawn or discontinued (*Ciarlariello v Schacter*, [1993] 2 SCR 119). This right has been specifically recognized to exist even if the withdrawal from or refusal of treatment may result in death (*Nancy B v Hôtel-Dieu de Québec* (1992), 86 DLR (4th) 385 (Que SC); *Malette v Shulman* (1990), 72 OR (2d) 417 (CA)...

Following Working Paper 28, the Law Reform Commission recommended in its 1983 Report to the Minister of Justice that the *Criminal Code* be amended to provide that the homicide provisions not be interpreted as requiring a physician to undertake medical treatment against the wishes of a medical treatment, or to continue medical treatment when such treatment 'has become therapeutically useless', or from requiring a physician to 'cease administering appropriate palliative care intended to eliminate or to relieve the suffering of a person, for the sole reason that such care or measures are likely to shorten the life expectancy of this person' (Report 20, *Euthanasia, Aiding Suicide and Cessation of Treatment* (1983), at p 35).

The Law Reform Commission had discussed in the Working Paper the possibility of the decriminalization of assisted suicide in the following terms, at pp 53–54:

> First of all, the prohibition in [s 241] is not restricted solely to the case of the terminally ill patient, for whom we can only have sympathy, or solely to his physician or a member of his family who helps him to put an end to his suffering. The section is more general and applies to a variety of situations for which it is much more difficult to feel sympathy. Consider, for example, a recent incident, that of inciting to mass suicide. What of the person who takes advantage of another's depressed state to encourage him to commit suicide, for his own financial benefit? What of the person who, knowing an adolescent's suicidal tendencies, provides him with large enough quantities of drugs to kill him? The accomplice in these cases cannot be considered morally blameless. Nor can one conclude that the criminal law should not punish such conduct. To decriminalize completely the act of aiding, abetting or counselling suicide would therefore not be a valid legislative policy. But could it be in the case of the terminally ill?
>
> The probable reason why legislation has not made an exception for the terminally ill lies in the fear of the excesses or abuses to which liberalization of the existing law could lead. As in the case of compassionate murder, decriminalization of aiding suicide would be based on the humanitarian nature of the motive leading the person to provide such aid, counsel or encouragement. As in the case of compassionate murder, moreover, the law may legitimately fear the difficulties involved in determining the true motivation of the person committing the act.
>
> Aiding or counselling a person to commit suicide, on the one hand, and homicide, on the other, are sometimes extremely closely related. Consider, for example, the doctor

who holds the glass of poison and pours the contents into the patient's mouth. Is he aiding him to commit suicide? Or is he committing homicide, since the victim's willingness to die is legally immaterial? There is reason to fear that homicide of the terminally ill for ignoble motives may readily be disguised as aiding suicide.

In its Working Paper, the Commission had originally recommended that the consent of the Attorney General should be required before prosecutions could be brought under s 241(b). However, after negative public response, the Commission retracted this recommendation in its 1983 Report.

It can be seen, therefore, that while the Law Reform Commission of Canada [has] great sympathy for the plight of those who wish to end their lives so as to avoid significant suffering, [it was not] prepared to recognize that the active assistance of a third party in carrying out this desire should be condoned, even for the terminally ill. The basis for this refusal is twofold it seems – first, the active participation by one individual in the death of another is intrinsically morally and legally wrong, and second, there is no certainty that abuses can be prevented by anything less than a complete prohibition. Creating an exception for the terminally ill might therefore frustrate the purpose of the legislation of protecting the vulnerable because adequate guidelines to control abuse are difficult or impossible to develop.

(iii) Review of Legislation in other Countries
A brief review of the legislative situation in other Western democracies demonstrates that in general, the approach taken is very similar to that which currently exists in Canada. Nowhere is assisted suicide expressly permitted, and most countries have provisions expressly dealing with assisted suicide which are at least as restrictive as our s 241...

The relative provision of *Suicide Act 1961* of the United Kingdom punishes a person who aids, abets, counsels or procures the suicide of another or an attempt by another to commit suicide, and this form of prohibition is echoed in the criminal statutes of all state and territorial jurisdictions in Australia (M Otlowski, Mercy Killing Cases in the Australian Criminal Justice System (1993), 17 *Crim LJ* 10). The UK provision is apparently the only prohibition on assisted suicide which has been subjected to judicial scrutiny for its impact on human rights prior to the present case. In the Application No 10083/82, *R v United Kingdom*, July 4, 1983, DR 33, p 270, the European Commission of Human Rights considered whether s 2 of the Suicide Act 1961 violated either the right to privacy in Article 8 or freedom of expression in Article 10 of the *Convention for the Protection of Human Rights and Fundamental Freedoms*. The applicant, who was a member of a voluntary euthanasia association, had been convicted of several counts of conspiracy to aid and abet a suicide for his actions in placing persons with a desire to kill themselves in touch with his co-accused who then assisted them in committing suicide. The European Commission held (at p 172) that the acts of aiding, abetting, counselling or procuring suicide were excluded from the concept of privacy by virtue of their trespass on the public interest of protecting life, as reflected in the criminal provisions of the 1961 Act, and upheld the applicant's freedom of expression, recognizing

> the State's legitimate interest in this area in taking measures to protect, against criminal behaviour, the life of its citizens particularly those who belong to especialy vulnerable categories by reason of their age or infirmity. It recognizes the right of the State under the Convention to guard against the inevitable criminal abuses that would occur in the absence of legislation, against the aiding and abetting of suicide. [DR p 272.]

Although the factual scenario in that decision was somewhat different from the one at bar, it is significant that neither the European Commission of Human Rights nor any other judicial tribunal has ever held that a state is prohibited on constitutional or human rights grounds from criminalizing assisted suicide.

Some European countries have mitigated prohibitions on assisted suicide which might render assistance in a case similar to that before us legal in those countries. In the Netherlands, although assisted suicide and voluntary active euthanasia are officially illegal, prosecutions will not be laid so long as there is compliance with medically established guidelines. Critics of the Dutch approach point to evidence suggesting that involuntary active euthanasia (which is not permitted by the guidelines) is being practised to an increasing degree. This worrisome trend supports the view that a relaxation of the absolute prohibition takes us down the slippery slope.

...As is the case in Europe and the Commonwealth, however, the vast majority of those American states which have statutory provisions dealing specifically with assisted suicide have no intent or malice requirement beyond the intent to further the suicide, and those states which do not deal with the matter statutorily appear to have common law authority outlawing assisted suicide (Shaffer, *supra*, at p 352; and M M Penrose, 'Assisted Suicide: A Tough Pill to Swallow' (1993), 20 *Pepp L Rev* 689, at pp 700–701). It is notable, also, that recent movements in two American states to legalize physician-assisted suicide in circumstances similar to those at bar have been defeated by the electorate in those states. On November 5, 1991, Washington State voters defeated Initiative 119, which would have legalized physician-assisted suicide where two doctors certified the patient would die within six months and two disinterested witnesses certified the patients choice was voluntary. One year later, Proposition 161, which would have legalized assisted suicide in California and which incorporated stricter safeguards than did Initiative 119, was defeated by California voters (usually thought to be the most accepting of such legal innovations) by the same margin as resulted in Washington –54 to 46 percent. In both states, the defeat of the proposed legislation seems to have been due primarily to concerns as to whether the legislation incorporated adequate safeguards against abuse (Penrose, *supra*, at pp 708–714).

Overall, then, it appears that a blanket prohibition on assisted suicide similar to that in s 241 is the norm among Western democracies, and such a prohibition has never been adjudged to be unconstitutional or contrary to fundamental human rights. Recent attempts to alter the status quo in our neighbourhood to the south have been defeated by the electorate, suggesting that despite a recognition that a blanket prohibition causes suffering in certain cases, the societal concern with preserving life and protecting the vulnerable rendered the blanket prohibition preferable to a law which might not adequately prevent abuse.

(iv) Conclusion on Principles of Fundamental Justice

What the preceding review demonstrates is that Canada and other Western democracies recognize and apply the principle of the sanctity of life as a general principle which is subject to limited and narrow exceptions in situations in which notions of personal autonomy and dignity must prevail. However, these same societies continue to draw distinctions between passive and active forms of intervention in the dying process, and with very few exceptions, prohibit assisted suicide in situations akin to that of the appellant. The task then becomes to identify the rationales upon which these distinctions are based and to determine whether they are constitutionally supportable.

The distinction between withdrawing treatment upon a patient's request, such as occurred in the *Nancy B* case, on the one hand, and assisted suicide on the other has been criticised as resting on a legal fiction – that is, the distinction between active and passive forms of treatment. The criticism is based on the fact that the withdrawal of life supportive measures is done with the knowledge that death will ensue, just as is assisting suicide, and that death does in fact ensure as a result of the action taken. See, for example, the Harvard Law Review note 'Physician-Assisted Suicide and the Right to Die with Assistance' (1992), 105 *Harv L Rev* 2021, at pp 2030–2031.

Other commentators, however, uphold the distinction on the basis that in the case of withdrawl of treatment, the death is natural – the artificial forces of medical technology which have kept the patient alive are removed and nature takes its course. In the case of assisted suicide or euthanasia, however, the course of nature is interrupted, and death results *directly* from the human action taken (E Keyserlingk, *Sanctity of Life or Quality of Life in the Context of Ethics, Medicine and Law* (1979), a study paper for the Law Reform Commission of Canada's Protection of Life Project). The Law Reform Commission calls this distinction 'fundamental' (at p 19 of the Working Papeer).

Whether or not one agrees that the active vs passive distinction is maintainable, however, the fact remains that under our common law, the physician has no choice but to accept the patient's instructions to discontinue treatment. To continue to treat the patient when the patient has withdrawn consent to that treatment constitutes battery (*Ciarlariello* and *Nancy B*, *supra*). The doctor is therefore not required to make a choice which will result in the patient's death as he would be if he chose to assist a suicide or to perform active euthanasia.

The fact that doctors may deliver palliative care to terminally ill patients without fear of sanction, it is argued, attenuates to an ever greater degree any legitimate distinction which can be drawn between assisted suicide and what are currently acceptable forms of medical treatment. The administration of drugs designed for pain control in dosages which the physician knows will hasten death constitutes active contribution to death by any standard. However, the distinction drawn here is one based upon intention – in the case of palliative care the intention is to ease pain, which has the effect of hastening death, while in the case of assisted suicide, the intention is undeniably to cause death. The Law Reform Commission, although it recommended the continued criminal prohibition of both euthanasia and assisted suicide, stated, at p 70 of the Working Paper, that a doctor should never refuse palliative care to a terminally ill person only because it may hasten death. In my view, distinctions based upon intent are important, and in fact form the basis of our criminal law. While factually the distinction may, at times, be difficult to draw, legally it is clear. The fact that in some cases, the third party will, under the guise of palliative care, commit euthanasia or assist in suicide and go unsanctioned due to the difficulty of proof cannot be said to render the existence of the prohibition fundamentally unjust.

The principles of fundamental justice cannot be created for the occasion to reflect the court's dislike or distaste of a particular statute. While the principles of fundamental justice are concerned with more than process, reference must be made to principles which are 'fundamental' in the sense that they would have general acceptance among reasonable people. From the review that I have conducted above, I am unable to discern anything approaching unanimity with respect to the issue before us. Regardless of one's personal views as to whether the distinctions are maintained and can be persuasively defended. To the extent that there is a consensus, it is that human life must be respected and we must be careful not to undermine the institutions that protect it.

This consensus finds legal expression in our legal system which prohibits capital punishment. This prohibition is supported, in part on the basis that allowing the state to kill will cheapen the value of human life and thus the state will serve in a sense as a role model for individuals in society. The prohibition against assisted suicide serves a similar purpose. In upholding the respect for life, it may discourage those who consider that life is unbearable at a particular moment, or who perceive themsevles to be a burden upon others, from committing suicide. To permit a physician to lawfully participate in taking life would send a signal that there are circumstances in which the state approves of suicide.

I also place some significance in the fact that the official position of various medical associations is against decriminalising assisted suicide (Canadian Medical Association, British Medical Association, Council of Ethical and Judicial Affairs of the American Medical Association, World Medical Association and the American Nurses Association). Given the concerns about abuse that have been expressed and the great difficulty in creating appropriate safeguards to prevent these, it can not be said that the blanket prohibition on assisted suicide is arbitrary or unfair, or that it is not reflective of fundamental values at play in our society. I am thus unable to find that any principle of fundamental justice is violated by s 241(b)...

[Sopinka J held that s 12 of the *Charter* prohibiting 'any cruel or unusual treatment or punishment' was not infringed. Further, he assumed that s 15 prohibiting discrimination and providing for the right to equal protection by the law was infringed but was saved by s 1 of the *Charter*.]

IV. Section I

[S 1 provides that the *Charter* guarantees rights and freedoms subject 'only to such reasonable limits prescribed by law as can be demonstrably justified in a free and democratic society.'] I agree with the Chief Justice that s 241(b) has 'a clearly pressing and substantial legislative objective' grounded in the respect for and the desire to protect human life, a fundamental *Charter* value. I elaborated on the purpose of s 241(b) earlier in these reasons in my discussion of s 7.

On the issue of proportionality, which is the second factor to be considered under s 1, it could hardly be suggested that a prohibition on giving assistance to commit suicide is not rationally connected to the purpose of s 241(b)...Section 241(b) protects all individuals against the control of others over their lives. To introduce an exception to this blanket protection for certain groups would create an inequality. As I have sought to demonstrate in my discussion of s 7, this protection is grounded on a substantial consensus among western countries, medical organisations and our own Law Reform Commission that in order to effectively protect life and those who are vulnerable in society, a prohibition without exception on the giving of assistance to commit suicide is the best approach. Attempts to fine tune this approach by creating exceptions have been unsatisfactory and have tended to support the theory of the 'slippery slope'. The formulation of safeguards to prevent excess has been unsatisfactory and has failed to allay fears that a relaxation of the clear standard set by the law will undermine the protection of life and will lead to abuses of the exception. The recent Working Paper of the Law Reform Commission, quoted above, bears repeating here:

The probable reason why legislation has not made an exception for the terminally ill lies in the fear of the excesses or abuses to which liberalisation of the existing law could lead. As in the case of 'compassionate murder', decriminalisation of aiding suicide would be based on the humanitarian nature of the motive leading the person to provide such aid, counsel or encouragement. As in the case of compassionate murder, moreover, the law may legitimately fear the difficulties involved in determining the true motivation of the person committing the act. [At p 54.]

The foregoing is also the answer to the submission that the impugned legislation is overbroad. There is no halfway measure that could be relied upon with assurance to fully achieve the legislation's purpose; first, because the purpose extends to the protection of the life of the terminally ill. Part of this purpose, as I have explained above, is to discourage the terminally ill from choosing death over life. Secondly, even if the latter consideration can be stripped from the legislative purpose, we have no assurance that the exception can be made to limit the taking of life to those who are terminally ill and genuinely desire death.

I wholeheartedly agree with the Chief Justice that in dealing with this 'contentious' and 'morally laden' issue, Parliament must be accorded some flexibility. In these circumstances, the question to be answered is, to repeat the words of La Forest J, quoted by the Chief Justice, from *Tétreault-Gadoury v Canada (Employment and Immigration Commission)* [1991] 2 SCR 22 at p 44, whether the government can show that it had a reasonable basis for concluding that it has complied with the requirement of minimal impairment. In light of the significant support for the type of legislation under attack in this case and the contentious and complex nature of the issues, I find that the government had a reasonable basis for concluding that it had complied with the requirement of minimum impairment. This satisfies this branch of the proportionality test and it is not the proper function of this Court to speculate as to whether other alternatives available to Parliament might have been preferable.

It follows from the above that I am satisfied that the final aspect of the proportionality test, balance between the restriction and the government objective, is also met. I conclude, therefore, that any infringement of s 15 is clearly justified under s 1 of the *Charter*...In the result, the appeal is dismissed, but without costs.

La Forest, Gonthier, Iacobucci and Major JJ agreed with Sopinka J in dismissing the appeal.

McLachlin J: This case raises the question of whether a physically disabled patient may be precluded from obtaining medical assistance in committing suicide by reason of s 241 of the *Criminal Code* RSC 1985, c C–46,

...I have read the reasons of the Chief Justice. Persuasive as they are, I am of the view that this is not at base a case about discrimination under s 15 of the *Canadian Charter of Rights and Freedoms*, and that to treat it as such may deflect the equality jurisprudence from the true focus of s 15 – to remedy or prevent discrimination against groups subject to stereotyping, historical disadvantage and political and social prejudice in Canadian society. *R v Swain* [1991] 1 SCR 933, at p 992, *per* Lamer CJ. I see this rather as a case about the manner in which the state may limit the right of a person to make decisions about her body under s 7 of the *Charter*. I prefer to base my analysis on that ground.

I have also had the benefit of reading the reasons of my colleague Sopinka J. I am in agreement with much that he says. We share the view that s 241(b) infringes the right in s 7 of the *Charter* to security of the person, a concept which encompasses the notions of dignity and the right to privacy. Sopinka J concludes that this infringement is in accordance with the principles of fundamental justice, because the infringement is necessary to prevent deaths which may not truly be consented to. It is on this point that I part company with him. In my view, the denial to Sue Rodriguez of a choice available to others cannot be justified. The potential for abuse is amply guarded against by existing provisions in the *Criminal Code*, as supplemented by the condition of judicial authorisation, and ultimately, it is hoped, revised legislation. I cannot agree that the failure of Parliament to address the problem of the terminally ill is determinative of this appeal. Nor do I agree that the fact that medically assisted suicide has not been widely accepted elsewhere bars Sue Rodriguez's claim. Since the advent of the *Charter*, this Court has been called upon to decide many issues which formerly lay fallow. If a law offends the *Charter*, this Court has no choice but to so declare.

In my view, the reasoning of the majority in *R v Morgentaler*, [1988] 1 SCR 30, is dispositive of the issues on this appeal. In the present case, Parliament has put into force a legislative scheme which does not bar suicide but criminalizes the act of assisting suicide. The effect of this is to deny to some people the choice of ending their lives solely because they are physically unable to do so. This deprives Sue Rodriguez of her security of the person (the right to make decisions concerning her own body, which affect only her own body) in a way that offends the principles of fundamental justice, thereby violating s 7 of the *Charter*. The violation cannot be saved under s 1. This is precisely the logic which led the majority of this Court to strike down the abortion provisions of the *Criminal Code* in *Morgentaler*. In that case, Parliament had set up a scheme authorising therapeutic abortion. The effect of the provisions was in fact to deny or delay therapeutic abortions to some women. This was held to violate s 7 because it deprived some women of the right to deal with their own bodies as they chose thereby infringing their security of the person, in a manner which did not comport with the principles of fundamental justice. Parliament could not advance an interest capable of justifying this arbitrary legislative scheme, and, accordingly, the law was not saved under s 1 of the *Charter*.

Section 7 of the Charter
...It is established that s 7 of the *Charter* protects the right of each person to make decisions concerning his or her body: *Morgentaler, supra*. This flows from the fact that decisions about one's body involve 'security of the person' which s 7 safeguards against state interference which is not in accordance with the principles of fundamental justice. Security of the person has an element of personal autonomy, protecting the dignity and privacy of individuals with respect to decisions concerning their own body. It is part of the persona and dignity of the

human being that he or she have the autonomy to decide what is best for his or her body. This is in accordance with the fact, alluded to by McEachern CJBC below, that 's 7 was enacted for the purpose of ensuring human dignity and individual control, so long as it harms no one else': (1993) 76 BCLR (2d) 145, at p 164

…The question on this appeal is whether, having chosen to limit the right to do with one's body what one chooses by s 241(b) of the *Criminal Code*, Parliament has acted in a manner which comports with the principles of fundamental justice.

This brings us to the next question: what are the principles of fundamental justice? They are, we are told, the basic tenets of our legal system whose function is to ensure that state intrusions on life, liberty and security of the person are effected in a manner which comports with our historic, and evolving, notions of fairness and justice: *Re BC Motor Vehicle Act, supra*. Without defining the entire content of the phrase 'principles of fundamental justice', it is sufficient for the purposes of this case to note that a legislative scheme which limits the right of a person to deal with her body as she chooses may violate the principles of fundamental justice under s 7 of the *Charter* if the limit is arbitrary. A particular limit will be arbitrary if it bears no relation to, or is inconsistent with, the objective that lies behind the legislation. This was the foundation of the decision of the majority of this court in *Morgentaler, supra*.

This brings us to the critical issue in the case. Does the fact that the legal regime which regulates suicide denies to Sue Rodriguez the right to commit suicide because of her physical incapacity, render the scheme arbitrary and hence in violation of s 7? Under the scheme Parliament has sent up, the physically able person is legally allowed to end his or her life; he or she cannot be criminally penalized for attempting or committing suicide. But the person who is physically unable to accomplish the act is not similarly allowed to end her life. This is the effect of s 241(b) of the *Criminal Code*, which criminalizes the act of assisting a person to commit suicide and which may render the person who desires to commit suicide a conspirator to that crime. Assuming without deciding that Parliament *could* criminalize all suicides, whether assisted or not, does the fact that suicide is not criminal make the criminalization of all assistance in suicide arbitrary?

My colleague Sopinka J has noted that the decriminalization of suicide reflects Parliament's decision that the matter is best left to sciences outside the law. He suggests that it does not reveal any consensus that the autonomy interest of those who wish to end their lives is paramount to a state interest in protecting life. I agree. But this conclusion begs the question. What is the difference between suicide and assisted suicide that justifies making the one lawful and the other a crime, that justifies allowing some this choice, while denying it to others?

The answer to this question depends on whether the denial to Sue Rodriguez of what is available to others can be justified. It is argued that the denial to Sue Rodriguez of the capacity to treat her body in a way available to the physically able is justified because to permit assisted suicide will open the doors, if not the floodgates, to the killing of disabled persons who may not truly consent to death. The argument is essentially this. There may be no reason on the facts of the Sue Rodriguez case for denying to her the choice to end her life, a choice that those physiclly able have available to them. Nevertheless, she must be denied that choice because of the danger that other people may wrongfully abuse the power they have over the weak and ill, and may end the lives of these persons against their consent. Thus, Sue Rodriguez is asked to bear the burden of the chance that other people in other situations may act criminally to kill others or improperly sway them to suicide. She is asked to serve as a scapegoat.

The merits of this argument may fall for consideration at the next stage of the analysis, where the question is whether a limit imposed contrary to the principles of fundamental justice may nevertheless be saved under s 1 of the *Charter* as a limit demonstrably justified in a free and democratic society. But they have no place in s 7 analysis that must be undertaken on this appeal. When one is considering whether a law breaches the principles of fundamental justice under s 7 by reason of arbitrariness, the focus is on whether a legislative scheme infringes a particular person's protected interests in a way that cannot be justified having regard to the objective of this scheme. The principles of fundamental justice require that each person, considered individually, be treated fairly by law. The fear that abuse may arise if an individual is permitted that which she is wrongly denied plays no part at this initial stage. In short, it does not accord with the principles of fundamental justice that Sue Rodriguez be disallowed what is available to others merely because it is possible that other people, at some other time, may suffer, not what she seeks, but an act of killing without true consent. As this Court stated in *Swaine, supra*, at p 977, *per* Lamer CJ:

> It is not appropriate for the state to thwart the exercise of the accused's right by attempting to bring societal interests into the principles of fundamental justice and to thereby limit an accused's s 7 rights. Societal interests are to be dealt with under s 1 of the *Charter*, where the Crown has the burden of proving that the impugned law is demonstrably justified in a free and democratic society. In other words, it is my view that any balancing

of societal interests against the individual right guaranteed by s 7 should take place within the confines of s 1 of the *Charter*.

I add that it is not generally appropriate that the complainant be obliged to negate societal interests at the s 7 stage, where the burden lies upon her, but that the matter be left for s 1, where the burden lies on the state...

The state will always bear the burden of establishing the propriety of an arbitrary legislative scheme, once a complainant has shown it is arbitrary. It will do so at the s 1 stage, where the state bears the onus, and where the public concerns which might save an arbitrary scheme are relevant. This is precisely the way the majority judgments in *Morgentaler* treated the issues that arose there: it is the way I think the Court should proceed in this case.

It is also argued that Sue Rodriguez must be denied the right to treat her body as others are permitted to do, because the state has an interest in absolutely forbidding anyone to help end the life of another. As my colleague Sopinka J would have it: '...active participation by one individual in the death of another is intrinsically morally and legally wrong'. The answer to this is that Parliament has not exhibited a consistent intention to criminalize acts which cause the death of another. Individuals are not subject to criminal penalty when their omissions cause the death of another. Those who are under a legal duty to provide the necessaries of life are not subject to criminal penalty where a breach of this duty causes death, if a lawful excuse is made out, for instance the consent of the party who dies, or incapacity to provide: see *Criminal Code*, s 215. Again, killing in self-defence is not culpable. Thus there is no absolute rule that causing or assisting in the death of other is criminally wrong. Criminal culpability depends on the circumstances in which the death is brought about or assisted. The law has long recognised that if there is a valid justification for bringing about someone's death, the person who does so will not be held criminally responsible. In the case of Sue Rodriguez, there is arguably such a justification – the justification of giving her the capacity to end her life which able-bodied people have as a matter of course, and the justification of her clear consent and desire to end her life at a time when, in her view, it makes no sense to continue living it. So the argument that the prohibition on assisted suicide is justified because the state has an interest in absolutely criminalizing any wilful act which contributes to the death of another is of no assistance.

This conclusion meets the contention that only passive assistance – the withdrawal of support necessary to life – should be permitted. If the justification for helping someone to end life is established, I cannot accept that it matters whether the act is 'passive' – the withdrawal of support necessary to sustain life – or 'active' – the provision of a means to permit a person of sound mind to choose to end his or her life with dignity.

Certain of the interveners raise the concern that the striking down of s 241(b) might demean the value of life. But what value is there in life without the choice to do what one wants with one's life, one might counter. One's life includes one's death. Different people hold different views on life and on what devalues it. For some, the choice to end one's life with dignity is infinitely preferable to the inevitable pain and diminishment of a long, slow decline. Section 7 protects that choice against arbitrary state action which would remove it.

In summary, the law draws a distinction between suicide and assisted suicide. The latter is criminal, the former is not. The effect of the distinction is to prevent people like Sue Rodriguez from exercising the autonomy over their bodies available to other people. The distinction, to borrow the language of the Law Reform Commission of Canada, 'is difficult to justify on grounds of logic alone': Working Paper 28, *Euthanasia, Aiding Suicide and the Cessation of Treatment* (1982), at p 53. In short, it is arbitrary. The objective that motivates the legislative scheme that Parliament has enacted to treat suicide is not reflected in its treatment of assisted suicide. It follows that the s 241(b) prohibition violates the fundamental principles of justice and that s 7 is breached.

Section 1 of the Charter
A law which violates the principles of fundamental justice under s 7 of the *Charter* may be saved under s 1 of the *Charter* if the state proves that it is 'reasonable...[and] demonstrably justified in a free and democratic society'.

The first thing which the state must show is that the law serves an objective important enough to outweigh the seriousness of the infringement of individual liberties. What then is the objective of the provision of the *Criminal Code* which criminalizes the act of assisting another to commit suicide? It cannot be the prevention of suicide, since Parliament has decriminalized suicide. It cannot be the prevention of the physical act of assisting in bringing about death, since, as discussed above, in many circumstances that act is not a crime. The true objective, it seems, is a practical one. It is the fear that if people are allowed to assist other people in committing suicide, the power will be abused in a way that may lead to the killing of those who have not truly and of their own free will consented to death. It is this concern which my colleague Sopinka J underscores in saying that the purpose of s 241(b) is 'the protection of the vulnerable who might be induced in moments of weakness to commit suicide'.

The justification for s 241(b) embraces two distinct concerns. The first is the fear that unless assisted suicide is prohibited, it will be used as cloak, not for suicide, but for murder. Viewed thus, the objective of the prohibition is not to prohibit what it purports to prohibit, namely assistance in suicide, but to prohibit another crime, murder or other forms of culpable homicide.

I entertain considerable doubt whether a law which infringes the principles of fundamental justice can be found to be reasonable and demonstrably justified on the sole ground that crimes other than those which it prohibits may become more frequent if it is not present. In Canada it is not clear that such a provision is necessary; there is sufficient remedy in the offences of culpable homicide. Nevertheless, the fear cannot be dismissed cavalierly; there is some evidence from foreign jurisdictions indicating that legal codes which permit assisted suicide may be linked to cases of involuntary deaths of the ageing and disabled.

The second concern is that even where consent to death is given, the consent may not in fact be voluntary. There is concern that individuals will, for example, consent while in the grips of transitory depression. There is also concern that the decision to end one's life may have been influenced by others. It is argued that to permit assisted suicide will permit people, some well intentioned, some malicious, to bring undue influence to bear on the vulnerable person, thereby provoking a suicide which would otherwise not have occurred.

The obvious response to this concern is that the same dangers are present in any suicide. People are led to commit suicide while in the throes of depression and it is not regarded as criminal conduct. Moreover, this appeal is concerned with s 241(b) of the *Criminal Code*. Section 241(a), which prohibits counselling in suicide, remains in force even if it is found that s 241(b) is unconstitutional. But bearing in mind the peculiar vulnerability of the physically disabled, it might be facile to leave the question there. The danger of transitory or improperly induced consent must be squarely faced.

The concern for deaths produced by outside influence or depression centre on the concept of consent. If a person of sound mind, fully aware of all relevant circumstances, comes to the decision to end her life at a certain point, as Sue Rodriguez has, it is difficult to argue that the criminal law should operate to prevent her, given that it does not so operate in the case of others throughout society. The fear is that a person who does not consent may be murdered, or that the consent of a vulnerable person may be improperly procured.

Are these fears, real as they are, sufficient to override Sue Rodriguez's entitlement under s 7 of the *Charter* to end her life in the manner and at the time of her choosing? If the absolute prohibition on assisted suicide were truly necessary to ensure that killings without consent or with improperly obtained consent did not occur the answer might well be affirmative. If, on the other hand, the safeguards in the existing law, supplemented by directives such as those proposed by McEachern CJBC below are sufficient to meet the concerns about false consent, withholding from Sue Rodriguez the choice to end her life, which is enjoyed by able-bodied persons, is neither necessary or justified.

In my view, the existing provisions in the *Criminal Code* go a considerable distance to meeting the concerns of lack of consent and improperly obtained consent. A person who causes the death of an ill or handicapped person without that person's consent can be prosecuted under the provisions for culpable homicide. The cause of death having been established, it will be for the person who administered the cause to establish that the death was really a suicide, to which the deceased consented. The existence of a criminal penalty for those unable to establish this should be sufficient to deter killings without consent or where consent is unclear. As noted above, counselling suicide would also remain a criminal offence under s 241(a). Thus the bringing of undue influence upon a vulnerable person would remain prohibited.

These provisions may be supplemented, by way of a remedy on this appeal, by a further stipulation requiring court orders to permit the assistance of suicide in a particular case. The judge must be satisfied that the consent is freely given with a full appreciation of all the circumstances. This will ensure that only those who truly desire to bring their lives to an end obtain assistance. While this may be to ask more of Ms Rodriguez than is asked of the physically able person who seeks to commit suicide, the additional precautions are arguably justified by the peculiar vulnerability of the person who is physically unable to take her own life.

I conclude that the infringement of s 7 of the *Charter* by s 241(b) has not been shown to be demonstrably justified under s 1 of the *Charter*.

The Respective Roles of Parliament and the Courts

It was strenuously argued that it was the role of Parliament to deal with assisted suicide and that the Court should not enter on the question. These arguments echo the views of the justices of the majority of the Court of Appeal below. Hollinrake JA stated: '...it is my view in areas with public opinion at either extreme, and which involve basically philosophical and not legal considerations, it is proper that the matter be left in the hands of Parliament as historically has been the case' (p 177). Proudfoot JA added: 'On the material available to us, we are in no position to assess the consensus in Canada with respect to assisted suicide…I would leave to Parliament the responsibility of taking the pulse of the nation' (p 186).

Were the task before me that of taking the pulse of the nation, I too should quail, although as a matter of constitutional obligation, a court faced with a *Charter* breach may not enjoy the luxury of choosing what it will and will not decide. I do not, however, see this as the task which faces the Court in this case. We were not asked to second guess Parliament's objective of criminalizing the assistance of suicide. Our task was the much more modest one of determining whether, given the legislative scheme regulating suicide which Parliament has put in place, the denial to Sue Rodriguez of the ability to end her life is arbitrary and hence amounts to a limit on her security of the person which does not comport with the principles of fundamental justice. Parliament in fact has chosen to legislate on suicide. It has set up a scheme which makes suicide lawful, but which makes assisted suicide criminal. The only question is whether Parliament, having chosen to act in this sensitive area touching the autonomy of people over their bodies, has done so in a way which is fundamentally fair to all. The focus is not on why Parliament has acted, but on the way in which it has acted.

Remedy

I concur generally in the remedy proposed by the Chief Justice in his reasons, although I am not convinced that some of the conditions laid down by his guidelines are essential. In the case at bar, where the plaintiffs own act will trigger death, it may not be necessary to ascertain the consent on a daily basis, nor to a place a limit of 31 days on the certificate. What is required will vary from case to case. The essential in all cases is that the judge be satisfied that if and when the assisted suicide takes place, it will be with the full and free consent of the applicant. I would leave the final order to be made by the chambers judge, having regard to the guidelines suggested by McEachern CJBC below and the exigencies of the particular case.

L'Heureux-Dubé J agreed with McLachlin J's reasons for allowing the appeal.

Lamer CJ would have allowed the appeal on the basis of an infringement of s 15 of the *Charter* which protected the applicant's right to equality and this was not justified under s 1 of the *Charter*.

Cory J agreed with McLachlin J and Lamer CJ and would have allowed the appeal.

This is not the place for a detailed analysis of the constitutional arguments and framework of the Canadian *Charter*. Instead, our interest in the *Rodriguez* case is in the approach of the supreme court when faced with the policy issues so as, perhaps, to illustrate how the European Court or an English Court might approach a challenge to s 2 of the Suicide Act 1961.

The case stands in stark contrast to the approach of the House of Lords in the *Bland* case. All the Justices in *Rodriguez* accept that the policy arguments have to be considered by the court in applying the *Charter*. Both Sopinka and McLachlin JJ accept that s 241(b) infringes the patient's right under s 7 of the *Charter*. The different conclusions they reach on the outcome of the case stem, in essence, from their conflicting views as to who has the onus of proving that the infringement is justified ie, who has the better of the policy arguments for and against assisted suicide. Sopinka J sees this as a matter to be determined in large part under s 7 itself, where the onus lies on the individual; while McLachlin J sees this a matter for consideration under s 1 of the *Charter* where a heavy onus lies on the state.

You will notice Sopinka J's reliance upon the arguments that deregulation will permit abuse (ie the killing of those who do not wish to die) and that this state interest permeates the history of the Canadian provision and that of other countries around the world. In fact, in the one country where physician-assisted suicide is permitted, namely the Netherlands, the evidence does not provide proof of abuse, as we saw earlier, even though some would have us believe otherwise, Sopinka J included. McLachlan J, by contrast, recognises the dangers of abuse but believes that the state has not established that abuse cannot be prevented by permitting physician-assisted suicide in closely controlled circumstances (see below) and by the fact that Canada (as with every other country) makes it the criminal offence of murder to kill someone in such circumstances. It is worth noting that the court was only asked to review the constitutionality of that part of s 241 of the *Criminal Code* which prohibited *assisting* suicide (s 241(b)). No challenge was brought against that part, s 241(a), which prohibits *counselling* suicide.

How, then, might these arguments and competing approaches help us to understand how s 2 of the 1961 Act would stand up to scrutiny under the European Convention (for an informative discussion, see M Blake 'Physician-Assisted Suicide: a Criminal Office or a Patient's Right?' (1997) 5 Med L Rev 294). Unlike the broadly drafted s 7 of the Canadian *Charter*, art 2 of the Convention is limited to protecting an individual's right to *life*. As a consequence, it may not protect a patient's right to choose how to live or how to die. Indeed, it could be argued that to permit assisting suicide (or euthanasia) infringes art 2 regardless of the patient's consent (see D Feldman, *Civil Liberties and Human Rights in England and Wales* (1993) at 95–96 and 122–124). (It is doubtful whether art 5 dealing with 'security of the person' would apply.)

The contrary position is not, however, 'beyond the pale'. In the Irish case of *In the Matter of a Ward of Court* [1995] 2 IRLM 401, the Irish Supreme Court was concerned with the legality of withdrawing artificial hydration and nutrition for an incompetent patient 'very nearly' in a persistent vegetative state (PVS). The court declared it was lawful. One of the arguments presented to the court was that such a course of action was contrary to art 40.3.2 of the Irish Constitution, which requires the state to protect and vindicate the life of its citizens. In rejecting this argument, two judges specifically addressed the scope of the 'right to life'.

In the Matter of a Ward of Court [1995] 2 IRLM 401 (Ir Sup Ct)

Hamilton CJ: The right to life is one of the fundamental rights which under the Constitution the State guarantees in its laws to respect and, as far as practicable, to defend, vindicate and protect as best it may from unjust attack.

The sanctity of human life is recognised in all civilised jurisdictions and is based on the nature of man.

The Constitution recognises this right and grants to it the protection set forth in the Constitution. The courts have recognised that the right to life springs from the right of every individual to life.

There are many other fundamental rights, express or implied, which are acknowledged by the Constitution and which are afforded similar protection.

It has been well established by many decisions of this Court that where there exists an interaction of constitutional rights the first objective of the courts in interpreting the Constitution and resolving any problems thus arising should be to seek to harmonise such interacting rights.

As stated by the former Chief Justice, Finlay CJ, in the course of his judgment in the case of *Attorney General v X* [1992] 1 IR 1; [1992] ILRM 401, at p 57/429:

> There are instances, however…I am satisfied, as the authorities appear to establish, that there is a necessity to apply a priority of rights.

I am satisfied that in this case, if there was an interaction of constitutional rights which I was not capable of harmonising, the right to life would take precedence over any other rights.

The nature of the right to life and its importance imposes a strong presumption in favour of taking all steps capable of preserving it save in exceptional circumstances. The problem is to define such circumstances.

The definition of such circumstances must, of necessity, involve a determination of the nature of the right to life acknowledged by the Constitution.

In the course of his judgment in *G v An Bord Uchtála* [1980] IR 32, Walsh J stated at p 69 that:

> The right to life necessarily implies the right to be born, the right to preserve and defend (and to have preserved and defended) that life, and the right to maintain that life at a proper standard in matters of food, clothing and habitation.

In this statement, Walsh J clearly recognises that the right to life necessarily implies various other ancillary rights which were not individually or specifically set forth in the Constitution and he enumerated such rights as applied in the case with which he was dealing.

He further stated that:

> natural rights spring primarily from the natural right of every individual to life.

These rights include the right to live life in its fullest content, to enjoy the support and comfort of her family, to social contact with her peers, to education, to the practice of her religion, to work, to marry and have children, to privacy, to bodily integrity and to self-determination.

These rights are not however unqualified: they may be subject to the constituional rights of others and to the requirements of the common good.

They however spring from the right to life which is recognised by the Constitution.

As the process of dying is part, and an ultimate inevitable consequence, of life, the right to life necessarily implies the right to have nature take its course and to die a natural death and, unless the individual concerned so wishes, not to have life artificially maintained by the provision of nourishment by abnormal artificial means, which have no curative effect and which are intended merely to prolong life.

This right, as so defined, does not include the right to have life terminated or death accelerated and is confined to the natural process of dying. No person has the right to terminate or to have terminated his or her life or to accelerate or have accelerated his or her death…

Denham J: The right to life is the pre-eminent personal right. The State has guaranteed in its laws to respect this right. The respect is absolute. This right refers to all lives: all lives are respected for the benefit of the individual and for the common good. The State's respect for the life of the individual encompasses the right of the individual to, for example, refuse a blood transfusion for religious reasons. In the recognition of the individual's autonomy life is respected.

The requirement to defend and vindicate the life is a requirement 'as far as practicable', it is not an absolute. Life itself is not an absolute.

The State stands firmly committed to protect personal rights. These are the rights personal to the individual. Some of them are enumerated eg, life, person, good name and property. Some are unenumerated eg, right to bodily integrity, right to work, right to earn a livelihood, right to marital privacy, right of access to the courts, right to travel.

In this case, the right to life is in issue. The State, under the Constitution, must protect 'as best it may' that life from unjust attack. Thus, it also is not an absolute right, it is qualified.

Respect is given to the life of the ward. Her life is no less protected or guarded than any other person's. Her rights as a citizen stand.

As she herself cannot make the necessary decision as to the medical treatment, an easy way to deal with the matter would be to say that no decision can then be made. However, that would not be to respect her life. That would be to refuse to her the rights given to other persons. That would be to say effectively that by her incapacity to make a decision she has lost that right. It would be to regard her life as less worthy of decision. Therefore, in order to respect her life a decision should be made.

In taking that decision it must be made so as to preserve, defend and vindicate her life. In view of the constitutional requirement that life be respected, that it be protected as best it may from an unjust attack and that it be defended and vindicated as far as practicable, there is a clear constitutional presumption that the *status quo* in this case should continue. It is for the applicant on the balance of probabilities to establish that the life of the ward is best respected, protected and vindicated by the court acceding to the application.

Sanctity of life-sustaining
The right to life also encompasses the concept of the sanctity of life. It is a concept fundamental to our society. Life has a sacred value, an intrinsic worth. As Walsh J said in *Quinn's Supermarket v Attorney General* [1972] IR 1, the Constitution:

  reflects a firm conviction that we are a religious people.

That foundation is an aid in interpreting the law and the Constitution. In regard specifically to the right to life it enables the interpretation to be inclusive of a spiritual or religious component. This approach is signalled in the first words of Article 40.3.1° where the unqualified 'respect' for life is stated. In respecting a person's death we are also respecting their life – giving to it sanctity. That concept of sanctity is an inclusive view which recognises that in our society persons, whether members of a religion, or not, are all under the Constitution protected by respect for human life. A view that life must be preserved at all costs does not sanctify life. A person, and/or her family, who have a view as to the intrinsic sanctity of the life in question are, in fact, encompassed in the constitutional mandate to protect life for the common good, what is being protected (and not denied or ignored or overruled), is the sanctity of that person's life. To care for the dying, to love and cherish them, and to free them from suffering rather than simply to postpone death, is to have fundamental respect for the sanctity of life and its end.

You will notice that both judges contemplate compliance with the constitutional provision *even if* death occurs: the right to life includes a right to die with dignity. However, you will see that the Chief Justice was at pains to emphasise that the right did not extend to having one's life terminated or death accelerated. Clearly, there was no constitutional right to voluntary euthanasia and, though this is not absolutely clear, to assist in suicide. The court was, of course, only concerned with the withdrawal of treatment (and the right of a competent patient to refuse it) and, in Hamilton CJ's words, the 'natural process of dying' (at 426).

The US Supreme Court likewise has denied that there was, a 'right to assistance in committing suicide' protected by the 'liberty interest' in the Due Process Clause of the Fourteenth Amendment to the US Constitution. In *Washington v Glucksberg* (1997) 521 US 702 the Supreme Court was asked to hold unconsitutitonal a statute which prohibited assisted suicide (see also the accompanying case of *Vacco v Quill* (1997) 117 S Ct 2293, holding that prohibiting assisted suicide did not infringe the Equal Protection Clause of the 14th Amendment). Speaking for the majority of the Court, Rehnquist CJ stated:

> The Due Process Clause guarantees more than fair process, and the 'liberty' it protects includes more than the absence of physical restraint. *Collins v Harker Heights*, 503 US 115, 125 (1992) (Due Process Clause 'protects individual liberty against 'certain government actions regardless of the fairness of the procedures used to implement them'') (quoting *Daniels v Williams*, 474 US 327, 331 (1986)). The Clause also provides heightened protection against government interference with certain fundamental rights and liberty interests. *Reno v Flores*, 507 US 292, 301–302 (1993); *Casey*, 505 US at 851. In a long line of cases, we have held that, in addition to the specific freedoms protected by the Bill of Rights, the 'liberty' specially protected by the Due Process Clause includes the rights to marry, *Loving v Virginia*, 388 US 1 (1967); to have children, *Skinner v Oklahoma ex rel Williamson*, 316 US 535 (1942); to direct the education and upbringing of one's children, *Meyer v Nebraska*, 262 US 390 (1923); *Pierce v Society of Sisters*, 268 US 510 (1925); to marital privacy, *Griswold v Connecticut*, 381 US 479 (1965); to use contraception, ibid; *Eisenstadt v Baird*, 405 US 438 (1972); to bodily integrity, *Rochin v California*, 342 US 165 (1952), and to abortion, *Casey*, supra. We have also assumed, and strongly suggested, that the Due Process Clause protects the traditional right to refuse unwanted lifesaving medical treatment. *Cruzan*, 497 US at 278–279.
>
> But we have always been reluctant to expand the concept of substantive due process because guideposts for responsible decisionmaking in this unchartered area are scarce and open-ended. *Collins*, 503 US at 125. By extending constitutional protection to an asserted right or liberty interest, we, to a great extent, place the matter outside the arena of public debate and legislative action. We must therefore 'exercise the utmost care whenever we are asked to break new ground in this field,' ibid, lest the liberty protected by the Due Process Clause be subtly transformed into the policy preferences of the members of this Court, *Moore*, 431 US at 502 (plurality opinion).
>
> Our established method of substantive due process analysis has two primary features: First, we have regularly observed that the Due Process Clause specially protects those fundamental rights and liberties which are, objectively, 'deeply rooted in this Nation's history and tradition,' *id*. at 503 (plurality opinion); *Snyder v Massachusetts*, 291 US 97, 105 (1934) ('so rooted in the traditions and conscience of our people as to be ranked as fundamental'), and 'implicit in the concept of ordered liberty,' such that 'neither liberty nor justice would exist if they were sacrificed,' *Palko v Connecticut*, 302 US 319, 325, 326 (1937). Second, we have required in substantive due process cases a 'careful description' of the asserted fundamental liberty interest. *Flores*, supra, at 302; *Collins*, supra, at 125; *Cruzan*, supra, at 277–278. Our Nation's history, legal traditions, and practices thus provide the crucial 'guideposts for responsible decisionmaking,' *Collins*, supra, at 125, that direct and restrain our exposition of the Due Process Clause. As we stated recently in Flores, the Fourteenth Amendment forbids the government to infringe… 'fundamental' liberty interests at all, no matter what process is provided, unless the infringement is narrowly tailored to serve a compelling state interest.
>
> Justice Souter, relying on Justice Harlan's dissenting opinion in *Poe v Ullman*, would largely abandon this restrained methodology, and instead ask
>
> > whether [Washington's] statute sets up one of those 'arbitrary impositions' or 'purposeless restraints' at odds with the Due Process Clause of the Fourteenth Amendment….In our view, however, the development of this Court's substantive due process jurisprudence, described briefly above . . . has been a process whereby the outlines of the 'liberty' specially protected by the Fourteenth Amendment – never fully clarified, to be sure, and perhaps not capable of being fully clarified – have at least been carefully refined by concrete examples involving fundamental rights found to be deeply rooted in our legal tradition. This approach tends to rein in the subjective elements that are necessarily present in due process judicial review. In addition, by establishing a threshold requirement – that a challenged state action implicated a fundamental right –

before requiring more than a reasonable relation to a legitimate state interest to justify the action, it avoids the need for complex balancing of competing interests in every case.

Turning to the claim at issue here, the Court of Appeals stated that,

[p]roperly analyzed, the first issue to be resolved is whether there is a liberty interest in determining the time and manner of one's death,

79 F 3d at 801, or, in other words, '[i]s there a right to die?', *id*. at 799. Similarly, respondents assert a 'liberty to choose how to die' and a right to 'control of one's final days,' Brief for Respondents 7, and describe the asserted liberty as 'the right to choose a humane, dignified death,' *id*. at 15, and 'the liberty to shape death,' *id*. at 18. As noted above, we have a tradition of carefully formulating the interest at stake in substantive due process cases. For example, although *Cruzan* is often described as a 'right to die' case, see 79 F 3d at 799; post at (Stevens J, concurring in judgment) (*Cruzan* recognized 'the more specific interest in making decisions about how to confront an imminent death'), we were, in fact, more precise: we assumed that the Constitution granted competent persons a 'constitutionally protected right to refuse lifesaving hydration and nutrition.' *Cruzan*, 497 US at 279; *id*. at 287 (O'Connor J, concurring) ('[A] liberty interest in refusing unwanted medical treatment may be inferred from our prior decisions'). The Washington statute at issue in this case prohibits 'aid[ing] another person to attempt suicide,' Wash. Rev. Cod Sec. 9A.36.060(1) (1994), and, thus, the question before us is whether the 'liberty' specially protected by the Due Process Clause includes a right to commit suicide which itself includes a right to assistance in doing so.

We now inquire whether this asserted right has any place in our Nation's traditions. Here, as discussed above . . . we are confronted with a consistent and almost universal tradition that has long rejected the asserted right, and continues explicitly to reject it today, even for terminally ill, mentally competent adults. To hold for respondents, we would have to reverse centuries of legal doctrine and practice, and strike down the considered policy choice of almost every State. See *Jackman v Rosenbaum Co*, 260 US 22, 31 (1922) ('If a thing has been practiced for two hundred years by common consent, it will need a strong case for the Fourteenth Amendment to affect it'); *Flores*, 507 US at 303 ('The mere novelty of such a claim is reason enough to doubt that 'substantive due process' sustains it').

Respondents contend, however, that the liberty interest they assert is consistent with this Court's substantive due process line of cases, if not with this Nation's history and practice. Pointing to *Casey* and *Cruzan*, respondents read our jurisprudence in this area as reflecting a general tradition of 'self-sovereignty,' Brief of Respondents 12, and as teaching that the 'liberty' protected by the Due Process Clause includes 'basic and intimate exercises of personal autonomy,' *id*. at 10; see *Casey*, 505 US at 847 ('It is a promise of the Constitution that there is a realm of personal liberty which the government may not enter'). According to respondents, our liberty jurisprudence, and the broad, individualistic principles it reflects, protects the 'liberty of competent, terminally ill adults to make end of life decisions free of undue government interference.' Brief for Respondents 10. The question presented in this case, however, is whether the protections of the Due Process Clause include a right to commit suicide with another's assistance. With this 'careful description' of respondents' claim in mind, we turn to *Casey* and *Cruzan*.

In *Cruzan*, we considered whether Nancy Beth Cruzan, who had been severely injured in an automobile accident and was in a persistent vegetative state, 'ha[d] a right under the United States Constitution which would require the hospital to withdraw life-sustaining treatment' at her parents' request. *Cruzan*, 497 US at 269. We began with the observtion that, '[a]t common law, even the touching of one person by another without consent and without legal justification was a battery.' *Ibid*. We then discussed the related rule that 'informed consent is generally required for medical treatment.' *Ibid*. After reviewing a long line of relevant state cases, we concluded that

the common law doctrine of informed consent is viewed as generally encompassing the right of a competent individual to refuse medical treatment.

Id at 277. Next we reviewed our own cases on the subject, and stated that

[t]he principle that a competent person has a constitutionally protected liberty interest in refusing unwanted medical treatment may be inferred from our prior decisions.

Id. at 278. Therefore,

for purposes of [that] case, we assume[d] that the United States Constitution would grant a competent person a constitutionally protected right to refuse lifesaving hydration and nutrition.

Id. at 279; see id. at 287 (O'Connor J, cuncurring).We concluded that, notwithstanding this right, the Constitution permitted Missouri to require clear and convincing evidence of an incompetent patient's wishes concerning the withdrawal of life-sustaining treatment.

Respondents contend that, in *Cruzan*, we

acknowledged that competent, dying persons have the right to direct the removal of life-sustaining equipment, and thus hasten death,

Brief for Respondents 23, and that

the constitutional principle behind recognizing the patient's liberty to direct the withdrawal of artificial life support applies at least as strongly to the choice to hasten impending death by consuming lethal medication.

id. at 26.Similarly, the Court of Appeals concluded that

Cruzan, by recognizing a liberty interest that includes the refusal of artificial provision of life-sustaining food and water, necessarily recognize[d] a liberty interest in hastening one's own death.

79 F. 3d at 816. The right assumed in *Cruzan*, however, was not simply deduced from abstract concepts of personal autonomy. Given the common law rule that forced medication was a battery, and the long legal tradition protecting the decision to refuse unwanted medical treatment, our assumption was entirely consistent with this Nation's history and constitutional traditions. The decision to commit suicide with the assistance of another may be just as personal and profound as the decision to refuse unwanted medical treatment, but it has never enjoyed similar legal protection. Indeed, the two acts are widely and reasonably regarded as quite distinct. See *Quill v Vacco* [(1997) 117 S Ct 2293]. In *Cruzan* itself, we recognized that most States outlawed assisted suicide – and even more do today – and we certainly gave no intimation that the right to refuse unwanted medical treatment could be somehow transmuted into a right to assistance in committing suicide.

Respondents also rely on *Casey*. There, the Court's opinion concluded that 'the essential holding of *Roe v Wade* should be retained and once again reaffirmed.' *Casey*, 505 US at 846. We held, first, that a woman has a right, before her fetus is viable, to an abortion 'without undue interference from the State;' second, that States may restrict post-viability abortions, so long as exceptions are made to protect a woman's life and health; and third, that the State has legitimate interests throughout a pregnancy in protecting the health of the woman and the life of the unborn child. Ibid. In reaching this conclusion, the opinion discussed in some detail this Court's substantive due process tradition of interpreting the Due Process Clause to protect certain fundamental rights and 'personal decisions relating to marriage, procreation, contraception, family relationsips, child rearing, and education,' and noted that any of those rights and liberties 'involv[e] the most intimate and personal choices a person may make in a lifetime.'

The Court of Appeals, like the District Court, found *Casey* 'highly instructive' and 'almost prescriptive' for determining 'what liberty interest may inhere in a terminally ill person's choice to commit suicide':

Like the decision of whether or not to have an abortion, the decision how and when to die is one of 'the most intimate and personal choices a person may make in a lifetime; a choice 'central to personal dignity and autonomy'.

79 F. 3d at 813–814. Similarly, respondents emphasize the statement in *Casey* that:

At the heart of liberty is the right to define one's own concept of existence, of meaning, of the universe, and of the mystery of human life. Beliefs about these matters could not define the attributes of personhood were they informed under compulsion of the State.

Casey, 505 US at 851. Brief for Respondents 12. By choosing this language, the Court's opinion in *Casey* described, in a general way and in light of our prior cases, those personal activities and decisions that this Court has identified as so deeply rooted in our history and traditions, or so fundamental to our concept of constitutionally ordered liberty, that they are protected by the Fourteenth Amendment. The opinion moved from the recognition that liberty necessarily includes freedom of conscience and belief about ultimate considerations to the observation that 'though the abortion decision may originate within the zone of conscience and belief, it is more than a philosophic exercise.' *Casey*, 505 US at 852 (emphasis added). That many of the rights and liberties protected by the Due Process Clause sound in personal autonomy does not warrant the sweeping conclusion that any and all important, intimate, and personal decisions are so protected, *San Antonio Independent School Dist v Rodriguez*, 411 US 1, 33x–35 (1973), and *Casey* did not suggest otherwise. The history of the law's treatment of assisted suicide in this country has been and continues to be one of the rejection of nearly all efforts to permit it. That being the case, our decisions lead us to conclude that the asserted 'right' to assistance in committing suicide is not a fundamental liberty interest protected by the Due Process Clause…

He went on to add that, even if the right existed, the ban on assisted suicide was justified as being rationally related to legitimate state interests – the preservation of life, protecting the integrity and ethics of the medical profession and in protecting vulnerable groups. While all the justices agreed in the result, O'Connor J (with whom Ginsberg J agreed) left open whether any 'liberty interest' was engaged. Stevens, Souter and Breyer JJ went further and concluded that it did where the patient was terminally ill. Stevens J characterised it as 'an interest in deciding how, rather than whether, a critical threshold shall be crossed' (at 745). Souter J saw it as an aspect of the individual's interest in his 'bodily integrity' – as applied in refusal of treatment cases (at 777). Both Stevens and Souter JJ considered that the infringement was justified on the basis proposed by Rehnquist CJ. For O'Connor and Bryer JJ, however, the fact that pain-relieving drugs could be lawfully prescribed even if this were to accelerate the patient's death meant that the 'right' was not infringed. (For discussion of the Supreme Court decisions, see A Capron 'Death and the Court' (1997) 27(5) Hastings Center Report 25 and G Annas 'The Bell Tolls for a Right to Suicide' in L Emanuel (ed) *Regulating How We Die* 1998 p 203.)

So how should we understand the application of art 2 of the Convention? There are, as we have shown, arguments for limiting the application of art 2. Alternatively, art 2 may *prima facie* be infringed if assisted suicide is permitted.

It may be that, even if this is correct, it is necessary to look at whether art 2 infringes other rights of the patient protected under the Convention. If it does, the court might either be influenced in its interpretation of art 2 (and permit physician-assisted suicide with the consent of the patient in the properly regulated circumstances) or be required to order the priorities of the rights under the Convention (see, for example, the Irish Supreme Court's decision in *A-G v X* [1992] 2 CMLR 277, interpreting the constitutionally protected right to life and right to travel).

The most relevant provision of the Convention is Article 8 which, *inter alia*, protects an individual's right to respect for his private life. Article 8 has been interpreted widely as protecting a range of individual interests. Depriving patients of their choice of how to die may well fall within Article 8(1) (see M Blake, *op cit* at 307–310). This interpretation would reflect the approach of some of the US Supreme Court justices in *Washington v Glucksberg (supra)*, the Canadian Supreme Court in *Rodriguez (supra)* and the European Court's view that art 8 protects the individual's 'physical and moral integrity' (*Costello-Roberts v UK* (1993) 19 EHRR 112 at para 34). However, art 8(2) permits a breach of the right if it is 'in accordance with the law and is necessary in a democratic society…for the protection of health or morals, or for the protection of the rights and freedoms of others'. Could this save s 2 of the Suicide Act 1961? Of course, it is here that the policy arguments addressed in the Canadian Supreme Court in *Rodriguez* would surface. In particular, the issue would be whether s 2 was necessary and a proportionate response to achieve the purpose underlying it, namely the protection of human life and the prevention of abuse. The European Court of Human Rights (but *quaere* English courts) allows states a 'margin of appreciation', ie an element of legislative discretion. Again, a resolution of this issue would reflect the intellectual struggle between the Justices in *Rodriguez*. One commentator, at least, anticipates that the courts will vindicate a breach of art 8(1) under art 8(2).

Meredith Blake 'Physician-Assisted Suicide: A Criminal Offence or a Patient's Right?' (1997) 5 Med L Rev 294

…the focus will shift to the state, and to the question of whether that interference is justified for any one of the reasons enunciated in the second paragraph. If the state is not able to establish a 'legitimate aim' for the interference, then theoretically there is no need to proceed to the second question, which his resolved by asking whether the interference is in connection with a pressing social need and is proportionate to the aim pursued. (That is, whether the interference is 'necessary': *Sunday Times v UK* (Judgment of 26 April (1979) 2 EHRR 245.)

...both the Canadian Charter (section 1 of the Charter provides that it guarantees rights and freedoms subject 'only to such reasonable limits prescribed by law as can be demonstrably justified in a free and democratic society') and the American Constitution similarly safeguard state interests and a consideration of the comments of the Canadian and Northern American courts in *Rodriguez*, *Quill* and *Glucksberg* is therefore merited. The five different state interests which both of the US Supreme Court judgments in the latter two cases found to bear a 'rational relation' to the criminalisation of PAS, are reflected to some degree by the six 'legitimate aims' listed in paragraph two of Article 8. Working by analogy, it would seem that the last three of these – the prevention of disorder or crime, the protection of health or morals and the protection of the rights and freedoms of others – most closely relate to the current criminalisation of PAS.

The Supreme Court in *Quill* and *Glucksberg* obviously accepted, albeit not in these exact words, both the protection of health and the protection of the rights and freedoms of others as justifications for the criminalisation of PAS. It is difficult to foresee a different result under the European Convention. It is less easy to make an assessment of the relevance of the 'protection of morals' (*Quill* (1997) S Ct at 843). Physician-assisted suicide has quite correctly been acknowledged as an ethical, as much as a legal, issue. That, however, does not necessarily entail the existence of a state interest in protecting morals, even in the light of the fact that the protection of morals as a legitimate aim of state action has been associated with interferences stemming from the prohibition of homosexuality, abortion and publications. More instructive are those instances where the Strasbourg authorities have deferred to a state's law where a moral principle which is important to that state is being upheld by that law. In this respect, the continuing relevance of the act/omission distinction with respect to the ending of life in English law *may* count as a 'legitimate aim' for the prohibition.

It is therefore probably safe to assume that the court would recognise that the UK has one or more 'legitimate aims' for criminalising assisted suicide. However, the final issue for determination – whether an interference is 'necessary' – has been interpreted so as to allow for a more context-specific analysis, in the sense that it focuses upon the proportionality of the interference to the legitimate aim pursued (*Olsson v Sweden* (Judgment of 24 March 1988) 11 EHRR 259 at para 75).

The chances of the Strasbourg authorities conducting this sort of analysis at this stage, however, depends very much upon the role granted to the so-called 'margin of appreciation'. That concept permits varying deference to state judgment depending upon the nature of the right in issue, its importance for the individual and the nature of the activities concerned. In *Dudgeon* the court emphasised the need for strict supervision on the basis that sexual preference and activity represented the very essence of the right to respect for privacy (*Dudgeon v UK* (Judgment 22 Oct 1981) (No 45) 4 EHRR 149) (need to cite actual quote from case). This was despite the fact that the court also acknowledged that the activity invited a state interest in the protection of morals, a factor which has encouraged deference to the margin of appreciation (see *Handyside v UK* (Judgment of 7 Dec 1976) 1 EHRR 737). In this respect, it does not seem determinative of a case that the activity may provoke varying moral reactions. In *Laskey*, the court found that the interference was necessary on the basis that the activities involved the 'infliction of physical harm...' which was not 'trifling or transient' (see, *Laskey, Jaggard and Brown v UK* Application No (109/1995/615/703–705) 1997) at para 45). The fact that the harm was consented to did not change the court's opinion on the basis that it was a matter for the state concerned to determine the level of harm that should be tolerated 'since what is at stake is related, on the one hand, to public health considerations and to the general deterrent of the criminal law, and, on the other, to the personal autonomy of the individual' (ibid).

It is difficult to assess the implications of this statement for the inquiry here in that it seems to be restating the question rather than attempting to answer it. A clearer indicator of the potential weight of the margin of appreciation here is the emerging tendency in the jurisprudence to have regard to the position in other European states. The concept of 'European consensus' reflects the Strasbourg authorities' reluctance to overrule a state's decision or legislation where there is no evidence of a general trend in the Member States. In this respect it is significant that at the time *Dudgeon* was decided, Ireland was the only Member State which still had in place laws prohibiting homosexuality. In two cases concerning transexuality which went to Strasbourg, the Commission declined to find that the interference with the applicant's Article 8 rights (*Rees v UK* (Judgment 17 October 1986) 9 EHRR 56; *X, Y, and Z v UK* (1997) (75/1995/581/667) Judgment of 22 April 1997) was not necessary. In these two cases, the applicants sought a decision that the state should formally recognise their new sexual identities. It was stated in both cases that, although there was a discernible tendency in Europe towards granting this option, it had not yet reached the point where there could be said to be common ground reflecting 'the new shared values of democratic society in Europe...transsexualism is not a new condition, but its particular features have been identified and examined only fairly recently' (*X, Y and Z v UK, ibid*, para 44).

Whilst it is true that the applicants in these cases were requesting positive action by the state to recognise their right, as opposed to negative action in removing a prohibition, it is equally clear that there is not even a 'discernible tendency' evident in the Member States towards the legalisation of PAS. All, with the exception of the Netherlands, have in place some form of laws criminalising assisted suicide, and several have recently confirmed this position. In light of this it is difficult to avoid the conclusion that the state would be afforded a fairly generous margin of appreciation in assessing the necessity for the interference. In so doing, the question of the proportionality of the interference, the answer to which inherently requires a contextual analysis, would effectively not arise for discussion.

You will recall that Sopinka J in *Rodriguez* refers to a decision relating s 2 of the 1961 Act and the European Convention. In that case the European Commission (notice not the Court) rejected an attack on s 2 under arts 8 and 10 (*R v United Kingdom* (1983) 33 DR 270). But, it is important to notice whose rights were being asserted in this case. It was those of a defendant who had been convicted under s 2 for helping someone commit suicide. The arguments for recognising a patient's right under the Convention are stronger as indeed the Commission itself hints (para 13).

Finally, it is important to notice that the dissenting Justices in *Rodriguez* did not argue for complete deregulation of assisted suicide. The patient's right had to be limited in order to take account of the concerns accepted by all the judges (and found compelling by the majority). These judges proposed a constitutional exemption to the *Criminal Code* following a determination of a court, Lamer CJ deals with this most fully in his judgment adopting, in essence, the approach of McEachern CJ in the British Columbia Court of Appeal. He set out *seven* conditions:

(1) the constitutional exemption may only be sought by way of application to a superior court;
(2) the applicant must be certified by a treating physician and independent psychiatrist, in the manner and at the time suggested by McEachern CJ, [ie not more than 24 hours before the applicant's suicide is assisted] to be competent to make the decision to end her own life, and the physicians must certify that the applicant's decision has been made freely and voluntarily, and at least one of the physicians must be present with the applicant at the time the applicant commits assisted suicide;
(3) the physicians must also certify:
(i) that the applicant is or will become physically incapable of committing suicide unassisted, and (ii) that they have informed him or her, and that he or she understands, that he or she has a continuing right to change his or her mind about terminating his or her life;
(4) notice and access must be given to the Regional Coroner at the time and in the manner described by McEachern CJ [ie not less than 3 clear days before the applicant is examined by a psychiatrist];
(5) the applicant must be examined daily by one of the certifying physicians at the time and in the manner outlined by McEachern CJ [ie to ensure the applicant has not changed her mind];
(6) the constitutional exemption will expire according to the time limits set by McEachern CJ [ie 31 days from the date of the first certificate]; and
(7) the act causing the death of the applicant must be that of the applicant him or herself, and not of anyone else.

Lamer CJ in an addendum to his judgment modified the fourth condition to require, in the case of Ms Rodriguez only that 24 hours' notice be given. He did so because of the evidence of her deteriorating medical condition.

It is likely that if a court were to find s 2 of the Suicide Act infringed the Convention, it would permit Parliament to impose similar restrictions on the patient's right so as to prevent abuse and to ensure the patient consented.

One final point should be mentioned. It is not clear whether an English court could effect this limited constitutional challenge. Certainly, it could make a declaration of incompatibility that s 2 of the 1961 Act could *never* be consistent with the Convention – a most unlikely remedy. Equally, the court could determine that in the factual circumstances presented to it – eg terminally ill, competent patient for whom pain relief was unavailable – the prohibition in s 2 of the Act fell foul of the Convention. What it could not do, however, is read into s 2 a series of human rights related conditions to make it Convention-compatible in the way that Lamer CJ did in *Rodriguez*. This would go beyond the court's role of 'interpreting' the legislation to be compatible with the Convention if possible (Human Rights Act 1998, s 3) and amount to judicial legislation. The court could, of course, indicate what provisions, had they been in the statute, would have led it to conclude that the Convention was no infringed.

(ii) A LEGISLATIVE FRAMEWORK

What, then, could a legislative framework for physician-assisted suicide look like? Margaret Otlowski examines the question of reform.

Margaret Otlowski *Voluntary Euthanasia and the Common Law* (1997)

One possibility for reform with specific reference to the medical context is for the legalization of doctor-assisted suicide. Such a measure would provide legal protection to a doctor who, at the patient's request, provides the patient with the necessary assistance to commit suicide by, for example, providing the patient with the means for taking his or her life. There is, undeniably, a strong similarity between medically-administered active voluntary euthanasia and doctor-assisted suicide, though under the law as it presently stands, the legal outcomes are markedly different. Obviously, if active voluntary euthanasia is legalized, it would be logical also to legalize doctor-assisted suicide. Indeed, it would be strange if it were lawful if a doctor were to take active steps to end a patient's life, but could not, in the same circumstances, provide the patient with the means of taking his or her own life. The option being considered here, however, presupposes retention of the existing prohibition on medically-administered active voluntary euthanasia and envisages doctor-assisted suicide as the *only* legislative measure.

The possibility of legalization of doctor-assisted suicide has been advanced by a number of commentators and organizations (for an example of such a proposal, see the bill proposed for the legalization of physician assisted suicide in New Hampshire, USA 'An Act Relative to Death with Dignity for Certain Persons Suffering Terminal Illness 1992') and is seen by many as a preferable alternative to any change with regard to active voluntary euthanasia. Indeed, as noted earlier, the citizen-initiated referendum in the State of Oregon for legislation permitting physician-assisted suicide was passed by a majority of voters, whereas similar efforts in other states for more far-reaching change have failed. A number of arguments have been put forward in support of this method of reform. An obvious advantage is that patients genuinely wishing to commit suicide would have the benefit of appropriate medical information and assistance in achieving that result. This would reduce many of the risks associated with patient suicide; for example, that the patient's diagnosis and prognosis are inadequately confirmed, and that the means chosen for suicide will be unreliable or inappropriately used. From a practical point of view, the implementation of this proposal of doctors-assisted suicide would require minimal change to existing law. Most jurisdictions have legislation dealing with assisted suicide which could easily be amended to allow for doctor-assisted suicide and relation of the practice. Achieving legalization of medically-administered active voluntary euthanasia would, by comparison, inevitably be more complicated. Another advantage which is claimed in respect of this particular option is that acceptance of doctor-assisted suicide would at least provide some guarantee of the voluntariness of the patient's decision. One of the concerns often raised with regard to the legalization of active voluntary euthanasia is the difficulty in ascertaining truly voluntary consent. Where, however, the patient's death is precipitated by the patient's own act, there is some assurance that the patient genuinely desired death. It is argued that if a patient who has requested assistance in suicide becomes ambivalent about the idea, they can simply put off the final step. The situation is quite different, it is claimed, if death is brought about by the hand of the doctor: some patients would be too embarrassed or intimidated to express uncertainty to a doctor on the verge of giving a lethal injection, or would be concerned that the doctor might be hesitant to administer the injection at a later time. Another consideration which is advanced in support of doctor-assisted suicide in preference to active voluntary euthanasia is that it minimizes third party involvement. It is reasoned that where the patient is capable of performing the death-inducing act, there is no justification for others to do what that patient can do for him or herself. Further, it is argued, by minimizing the involvement of doctors, one avoids placing the responsibility of killing on others, and avoids the possible risk of emotional trauma to the person who brings death. Finally, proponents of doctor-assisted suicide point out that since this is a far less drastic proposal than the legalization of active voluntary euthanasia, it is likely to enjoy wider acceptability amongst doctors and the community generally.

Although the option of doctor-assisted suicide may be seen as preferable in some respects over the option of active voluntary euthanasia, it is not, on its own, a satisfactory legal response to the present problems with regard to medically-assisted dying. Whilst the possibility of doctor-assisted suicide may be appropriate and adequate in many cases, it does not represent a complete solution to the difficulties in this area. There will always be a proportion of patients who are physically unable to commit suicide. For others, the concept of suicide may for some reason be objectionable, yet they may willingly seek active voluntary euthanasia. If the legal response was limited to doctor-assisted suicide, these categories of individuals would not be provided for. Moreover, in cases of doctor-assisted suicide, there is also the possibility that the patient does not die as quickly as anticipated and further medical intervention is required in order to prevent a lingering death. Such intervention would not be possible if only doctor-assisted suicides were permitted.

In the event that reform of the law were to take this particular course of allowing doctor-assisted suicide, careful consideration would have to be given to the appropriate legislative model for securing such reform. In particular, it would be necessary to define the circumstances in which a doctor could lawfully assist the suicide of a patient; whether, for example, a doctor should be able to assist a person to commit suicide if that person is suffering from a terminal or incurable disease or whether a doctor should be able to assist any sane person who has determined to take his or her own life (Trowell, H 'Suicide and Euthanasia' (1971) BMJ 275). Similar problems of definition would of course also arise with attempts to legalize active voluntary euthanasia (and will be considered in more detail in that context), but in the area of suicide, special care would need to be taken to ensure that irrational suicide was not encouraged.

We shall see shortly that the Netherlands has legalised physician-assisted suicide (PAS) and voluntary euthanasia (VE). We will discuss these developments in relation to the latter. Likewise, the Northern Territory in Australia legalised both PAS and VS in the Rights of the Terminally Ill Act 1995. In 1997 the Federal Parliament in the Euthanasia Laws Act 1997 removed the power of the Northern Territory to legislate and to legalise euthanasia, thereby effectively overturning the 1995 Act. We will also return to this legislation later. As Otlowski pointed out, it would be curious to legislate and to legalise voluntary euthanasia but not physician-assisted suicide. However, the latter might be contemplated alone. One jurisdiction which has done just that is the State of Oregon in its Death with Dignity Act, first passed in 1994 and finally coming into force in late 1997. The background to the Act is discussed in the following extract, taken from a guide to the Act prepared by the State's Task Force to Improve the Care of Terminally Ill Oregonians (1998).

State of Oregon *The Oregon Death With Dignity Act: A Guidebook for Health Care Providers* (1998)

The State of Oregon provides for an initiative process through which laws may be adopted by a vote of the people. Oregon voters approved such an initiative, Measure 16, on November 8, 1994, and thereby enacted the 'Death With Dignity Act'. The statewide vote was 51% in favor and 49% opposed.

Implementation of the Act was enjoined on December 9, 1994, one day before the Act's effective date, by order of US District Judge Michael Hogan. On August 3, 1995, Judge Hogan permanently enjoined implementation of the Act, finding that it violated the Equal Protection Clause of the US Constitution. *Lee v State of Or* 819 F Supp 1429 (D Or 1995). The permanent injunction was appealed to the Ninth Circuit Court of Appeals, which ordered the injunction lifted, deciding that the plaintiffs lacked standing to challenge Oregon's law. *Lee v State of Oregon* 107 F 3d 1382 (9th Cir 1997). The plaintiff's petition for review to the United States Supreme Court was denied on October 14, 1997.

On March 7, 1996, the Ninth Circuit issued an 8–3 decision in another case challenging a Washington State statute criminalizing physician-assisted suicide. *Compassion in Dying v State of Washington* 79 F 3d 790 (9th cir 1996). The Ninth Circuit overturned the Washington criminal statute and found a constitutional right to physician-assisted suicide in the Due Process Clause of the US Constitution. The court's opinion took the unusual step of criticizing Judge Hogan's decision, the subject of an entirely separate appeal, and expressly approved the safeguards contained in Oregon's Death With Dignity Act.

On April 2, 1996, the federal Second Circuit Court of Appeals held that a New York criminal statute nearly identical to Washington State law was unconstitutional as applied to a terminally-ill, competent adult in the final stages of illness. *Quill v Vacco* 80 F 3d 716 (2d Cir 1996). Unlike the Ninth Circuit in *Compassion in Dying* the *Quill* court found no due process interest in assisted suicide. Instead, the Second Circuit concluded that New York's laws denied equal protection of the law to competent, terminally-ill persons. The court found the law's distinction between the right to refuse or to withdraw life-sustaining treatment and the assistance of a physician in hastening death to be irrational. Moreover, the court found no legitimate state interest in preserving life in the final stages of a terminal illness.

On June 26, 1997, the US Supreme Court overturned both the Second and Ninth Circuit decisions: *Washington v Glucksberg* No 95–110, and *Vacco v Quill* No 95–1858, *Glucksberg* held that there is no constitutional right to assisted suicide under the Due Process Clause. The Court emphasized the limits of patient autonomy and rejected arguments for a constitutional interest in all decisions implicating intimate or deeply personal concerns. *Quill* held that competent, terminally-ill patients are not denied equal protection of the law when physician-assisted suicide is prohibited by state law but the withdrawal or refusal of life-sustaining treatment is permitted. The Court endorsed professional and legal distinctions between physician-assisted suicide and withdrawal of life support or the 'double effect' of aggressive palliative care. Although these cases addressed state laws criminalizing physician-assisted suicide, the general approach of the court suggests that it will view state laws legalizing physician-assisted suicide, such as Oregon's Death With Dignity Act, as presenting primarily political, rather than constitutional, issues.

The 1997 Oregon Legislature enacted HB 2954, which referred repeal of the Death With Dignity Act to Oregon voters. The repeal effort was defeated on November 4, 1997, by a 60% to 40% margin.

(For further discussion, see M Otlowski *Voluntary Euthanasia and the Common Law* (1996) at pp 369–373 and for other international reforms see ch 6, *passim*.)

The Oregon Death With Dignity Act 1994

(General Provisions)
(Section 1)

127.800 §2.01. Definitions. The following words and phrases, whenever used in ORS 127.800 to 127.897, shall have the following meanings:

(1) "Adult" means an individual who is 18 years of age or older.

(2) "Attending physician" means the physician who has primary responsibility for the care of the patient and treatment of the patient's terminal disease.

(3) "Consulting physician" means a physician who is qualified by specialty or experience to make a professional diagnosis and prognosis regarding the patient's disease.

127.800 to 127.897 in order to obtain a prescription for medication to end his or her life in a humane and dignified manner.

(12) "Terminal disease" means an incurable and irreversible disease that has been medically confirmed and will, within reasonable medical judgment, produce death within six (6) months. [1995 c.3 §1.01]

(Written Request for Medication to End One's Life in a Humane and Dignified Manner)
(Section 2)

127.805 §2.01. Who may initiate a written request for medication. An adult who is capable, is a resident of Oregon, and has been determined by the attending physician and consulting physician to be suffering from a terminal disease, and who has voluntarily expressed his or her wish to die, may make a written request for medication for the purpose of ending his or her life in a humane and dignified manner in accordance with ORS 127.800 to 128.897 [1995 c 3 §2.01]

127.810 §2.02. Form of the written request.

(1) A valid request for medication under ORS 127.800 to 127.897 shall be substantially the form described in ORS 127.897, signed and dated by the patient and witnessed by at least two individuals who, in the presence of the patient, attest that to the best of their knowledge and belief the patient is capable, acting voluntarily, and is not being coerced to sign the request.

(2) One of the witnesses shall be a person who is not:

    (a) A relative of the patient by blood, marriage or adoption;

    (b) A person who at the time the request is signed would be entitled to any portion of the estate of the qualified patient upon death under any will or by operation of law; or

    (c) An owner, operator or employee of a health care facility where the qualified patient is receiving medical treatment or is a resident.

(3) The patient's attending physician at the time the request is signed shall not be a witness.

(4) If the patient is a patient in a long term care facility at the time the written request is made, one of the witnesses shall be an individual designated by the facility and having the qualifications specified by the Department of Human Services by rule. [1995] c. 3 s. 2.02.]

(5) 'Counselling' means a consultation between a state licensed psychiatrist or psychologist and a patient for the purpose of determining whether the patient is suffering from a psychiatric or psychological disorder, or depression causing impaired judgment.

(6) 'Health care provider' means a person licensed, certified, or otherwise authorized or permitted by the law of this State to administer health care in the ordinary course of business or practice of a profession, and includes a health care facility.

(7) 'Incapable' means that in the opinion of a court or in the opinion of the patient's attending physician or consulting physician, a patient lacks the ability to make and communicate health care decisions to health care providers, including communication through persons familiar with the patient's manner of communicating if those persons are available. Capable means not incapable.

(8) 'Informed decision' means a decision by a qualified patient to request and obtain a prescription to end his or her life in a humane and dignified manner, that is based on an appreciation of the relevant facts and after being fully informed by the attending physician of:

    (a) His or her medical diagnosis;

    (b) His or her prognosis;

    (c) The potential risks associated with taking the medication to be prescribed;

    (d) The probable result of taking the medication to be prescribed;

    (e) The feasible alternatives, including, but not limited to, comfort care, hospice care and pain control.

(9) 'Medically confirmed' means the medical opinion of the attending physician has been confirmed by a consulting physician who has examined the patient and the patient's relevant medical records.

(10) 'Patient' means a person who is under the care of a physician.

(11) 'Physician' means a doctor of medicine or osteopathy licensed to practice medicine by the Board of Medical Examiners for the State of Oregon.

(12) 'Qualified patient' means a capable adult who is a resident of Oregon and has satisfied the requirements of ORS Resources by rule. [1995] c 3 §2.02]

(Safeguards)
(Section 3)

128.815 §3.01. Attending physician responsibilities. The attending physician shall:

(1) Make the initial determination of whether a patient has a terminal disease, is capable, and has made the request voluntarily;

(2) Inform the patient of:

    (a) His or her medical diagnosis;

    (b) His or her prognosis;

    (c) The potential risks associated with taking the medication to be prescribed;

    (d) The probable result of taking the medication to be prescribed;

    (e) The feasible alternatives, including, but not limited to, comfort care, hospice care and pain control.

(3) Refer the patient to a consulting physician for medical confirmation of the diagnosis, and for a determination that the patient is capable and acting voluntarily;

(4) Refer the patient for counseling if appropriate pursuant to ORS 127.825;

(5) Request that the patient notify next of kin;

(6) Inform the patient that he or she has an opportunity to rescind the request at any time and in any manner, and offer the patient an opportunity to rescind at the end of the 15 day waiting period pursuant to ORS 127.840;

(7) Verify, immediately prior to writing the prescription for medication under ORS 127.800 to 127.897, that the patient is making an informed decision:

(8) Fulfil the medical record documentation requirements of ORS 127.855;

(9) Ensure that all appropriate steps are carried out in accordance with ORS 127.800 to 127.897 prior to writing a prescription for medication to enable a qualified patient to end his or her life in a humane and dignified manner. [1995 c 3 §3.01]

127.820 §3.02. Consulting physician confirmation. Before a patient is qualified under ORS 127.800 to 127.897, a consulting physician shall examine the patient and his or her relevant medical records and confirm, in writing, the attending physician's diagnosis that the patient is suffering from a terminal disease, and verify that the patient is capable, is acting voluntarily and has made an informed decision. [1995 c 3 §3.02]

127.825 §3.03. Counseling referral. If in the opinion of the attending physician or the consulting physician a patient may be suffering from a psychiatric or psychological disorder, or depression causing impaired judgment, either physician shall refer the patient for counseling. No medication to end a patient's life in a humane and dignified manner shall be prescribed until the person performing the counseling determines that the patient is not suffering from a psychiatric or psychological disorder, or depression causing impaired judgment. [1995 c 3 §3.03]

127.830 §3.04. Informed decision. No person shall receive a prescription for medication to end his or her life in a humane and dignified manner unless he or she has made an informed decision as defined in ORS 127.800 (7). Immediately prior to writing a prescription for medication under ORS 127.800 to 127.897, the attending physician shall verify that the patient is making an informed decision. [1995 c 3 §3.04]

127.835 §3.05. Family notification. The attending physician shall ask the patient to notify next of kin of his or her request for medication pursuant to ORS 127.800 to 127.897. A patient who declines or is unable to notify next of kin shall not have his or her request denied for that reason. [1995 c 3 §3.05]

127.840 §3.06. Written and oral requests. In order to receive a prescription for medication to end his or her life in a humane and dignified manner, a qualified patient shall have made an oral request and a written request, and reiterate the oral request to his or her attending physician no less than fifteen (15) days after making the initial oral request. At the time the qualified patient makes his or her second oral request, the attending physician shall offer the patient an opportunity to rescind the request. [1995 c 3 §3.06]

128.845 §3.07. Right to rescind request. A patient may rescind his or her request at any time and in any manner without regard to his or her mental state. No prescription for medication under ORS 127.800 to 127.897 may be written without the attending physician offering the qualified patient an opportunity to rescind the request. [1995 c 3 §3.07]

127.850 §3.08. Waiting Periods. No less than fifteen (15) days shall elapse between the patient's initial oral request and the writing of a prescription under ORS 127.800 to 127.897. No less than 48 hours shall elapse between the patient's written request and the writing of a prescription under ORS 127.800 to 127.897. [1995 c 3 §3.08]

127.855 §3.09. Medical record documentation requirements. The following shall be documented or filed in the patient's medical record:

(1) All oral requests by a patient for medication to end his or her life in a humane and dignified manner;

(2) All written requests by a patient for medication to end his or her life in a humane and dignified manner;

(3) The attending physician's diagnosis and prognosis, determination that the patient is capable, acting voluntarily and has made an informed decision;

(4) The consulting physician's diagnosis and prognosis, and verification that the patient is capable, acting voluntarily and has made an informed decision;

(5) A report of the outcome and determinations made during counseling, if performed;

(6) The attending physician's offer to the patient to rescind his or her request at the time of the patient's second oral request pursuant to ORS 127.840; and

(7) A note by the attending physician indicating that all requirements under ORS 127.800 to 127.897 have been met and indicating the steps taken to carry out the request, including a notation of the medication prescribed. [1995 c 3 §3.09]

127.860 §3.10. Residency requirement. Only requests made by Oregon residents, under ORS 127.800 to 127.897, shall be granted. [1995 c 3 §3.10]

127.865 §3.11. Reporting requirements.

(1) The Health Division shall annually review a sample of records maintained pursuant to ORS 127.800 to 128.897.

(2) The Health Division shall make rules to facilitate the collection of information regarding compliance with ORS 127.800 to 127.897. The information collected shall not be a public record and may not be made available for inspection by the public.

(3) The Health Division shall generate and make available to the public an annual statistical report of information collected under subsection (2) of this section. [1995 c 3 §3.11]

127.870 §3.12. Effects on construction of wills, contracts and statutes.

(1) No provision in a contract, will or other agreement, whether written or oral, to the extent the provision would affect whether a person may make or rescind a request for medication to end his or her life in a humane and dignified manner, shall be valid.

(2) No obligation owing under any currently existing contract shall be conditioned or affected by the making or rescinding of a request, by a person, for medication to end his or her life in a humane and dignified manner. [1995 c3 §3.12]

127.875 §3.13. Insurance or annuity policies. The sale, procurement, or issuance of any life, health, or accident insurance or annuity policy or the rate charged for any policy shall not be conditioned upon or affected by the making or rescinding of a request, by a person, for medication to end his or her life in a humane and dignified manner. Neither shall a qualified patient's act of ingesting medication to end his or her life in a humane and dignified manner have an effect upon a life, health, or accident insurance or annuity policy. [1995 c 3 §3.13]

127.880 §3.14. Construction of Act. Nothing in ORS 127.800 to 127.897 shall be construed to authorize a physician or any other person to end a patient's life by lethal injection, mercy killing or active euthanasia. Actions taken in accordance with ORS 127.800 to 127.897 shall not, for any purpose, constitute suicide, assisted suicide, mercy killing or homicide, under the law. [1995 c 3 §3.14]

(Immunities and Liabilities)
(Section 4)
127.885 §4.01. Immunities. Except as provided in ORS 127.890:

(1) No person shall be subject to civil or criminal liability or professional disciplinary action for participating in good faith compliance with ORS 127.800 to 127.897. This includes being present when a qualified patient takes the prescribed medication to end his or her life in a humane and dignified manner.

(2) No professional organization or association, or health care provider, may subject a person to censure, discipline, suspension, loss of license, loss of privileges, loss of membership or other penalty for participating or refusing to participate in good faith compliance with ORS 127.800 to 127.897.

(3) No request by a patient for or provision by an attending physician for medication in good faith compliance with the provisions of ORS 127.800 to 127.897 shall constitute neglect for any purpose of law or provide the sole basis for the appointment of a guardian or conservator.

(4) No health care provider shall be under any duty, whether by contract, by statute or by any other legal requirement to participate in the provision to a qualified patient of medication to end his or her life in a humane and dignified manner. If a health care provider is unable or unwilling to carry out a patient's request under ORS 127.800 to 127.897, and the patient transfers his or her care to a new health care provider, the prior health care provider shall transfer, upon request, a copy of the patient's relevant medical records to the new health care provider. [1995 c 3 §4.01]

127.890 §4.02. Liabilities.

(1) A person who without authorization of the patient wilfully alters or forges a request for medication or conceals or destroys a rescission of that request with the intent or effect of causing the patient's death shall be guilty of a Class A felony.

(2) A person who coerces or exerts undue influence on a patient to request medication for the purpose of ending the patient's life, or to destroy a rescission of such a request, shall be guilty of a Class A felony.

(3) Nothing in ORS 127.800 to 127.897 limits further liability for civil damages resulting from other negligent conduct or intentional misconduct by any person.

(4) The penalties in ORS 127.800 to 127.897 do not preclude criminal penalties applicable under other law for conduct which is inconsistent with the provisions of ORS 127.800 to 127.897. [1995 c3 §4.02]

(Severability)
(Section 5)
127.895 §5.01. Severability. Any section of ORS 127.800 to 127.897 being held invalid as to any person or circumstance shall not affect the application of any other section of ORS 127.800 to 127.897 which can be given full effect without the invalid section or application. [1995 c 3 §5.01]

(Form of the Request)
(Section 6)
127.897 §6.01. Form of the request. A request for a medication as authorized by ORS 127.800 to 127.897 shall be in substantially the following form:

REQUEST FOR MEDICATION
TO END MY LIFE IN A HUMANE AND DIGNIFIED
MANNER

I, _____am an
adult of sound mind.

I am suffering from _____which
my attending physician has determined is a terminal disease and which has been medically
confirmed by a consulting physician.

I have been fully informed of my diagnosis, prognosis, the nature of medication to be
prescribed and potential associated risks, the expected result, and the feasible alternatives,
including comfort care, hospice care and pain control.

I request that my attending physician prescribe medication that will end my life in a humane
and dignified manner.

INITIAL ONE:

_____I have informed my family of my decision and taken their opinions into
consideration.

_____I have decided not to inform my family of my decision.

_____I have no family to inform of my decision.

I understand that I have the right to rescind this request at any time.

I understand the full import of this request and I expect to die when I taken the medication
to be prescribed.

I make this request voluntarily and without reservation, and I accept full moral responsibility
for my actions.

Signed:_____

Dated:_____

DECLARATION OF WITNESSES
We declare that the person signing this request:
(a) Is personally known to us or has provided proof of identity;
(b) Signed this request in our presence;
(c) Appears to be of sound mind and not under duress, fraud or undue influence;
(d) Is not a patient for whom either of us is attending physician.

_____Witness 1/Date

_____Witness 2/Date

NOTE: One witness shall not be a relative (by blood, marriage or adoption) of the person
signing this request, shall not be entitled to any portion of the person's estate upon death and
shall not own, operate or be employed at a health care facility where the person is a patient or
resident. If the patient is an inpatient at a health care facility, one of the witnesses shall be an
individual designated by the facility.

[1995 c3 §6.01]

PENALTIES

127.990 [Formerly part of 97.990; repealed by 1993 c.767 §29]

127.995 Penalties. (1) It shall be a Class A felony for a person without authorization of the
principal to wilfully alter, forge, conceal or destroy an instrument, the reinstatement or revocation
of an instrument or any other evidence or document reflecting the principal's desires and interests,
with the intent and effect of causing a withholding or withdrawal of life-sustaining procedures
or of artificially administered nutrition and hydration which hastens the death of the principal.
(2) Except as provided in subsection (1) of this section, it shall be a Class A misdemeanor
for a person without authorization of the principal to wilfully alter, forge, conceal or destroy

an instrument, the reinstatement or revocation of an instrument, or any other evidence or document reflecting the principal's desires and interests with the intent or effect of affecting a health care decision. [Formerly 127.585]

The Act is complex. It sets out a number of *conditions for eligibility* to aid in dying and provides for a number of *safeguards* to avoid abuse and ensure that the patient's decision is genuine and voluntary. The Act is discussed in the following extract.

Alexander M Capron 'Legalizing Physician-Aided Death' (1996) 5(1) Cambridge Quarterly of Healthcare Ethics 10

The law applies only to residents of Oregon, 18 years of age or older. Although seen as a way to prevent people who want to commit suicide from flocking to Oregon, the residency requirement will not stop people from other states from availing themselves of the law, because residency is simply a matter of intention. People who come to Oregon with a plan to reside there are legal residents; anyone planning to commit suicide in Oregon could reasonably say, 'I plan to spend the rest of my life in the state.'

To qualify under the law, a patient must, in the opinion of an attending or consulting physician, have the ability to make and communicate healthcare decisions, including 'communication through persons familiar with their manner of communicating if those persons are available.' (Although that phrase is not explained in the statute, I assume it means that people who have been using some symbolic means of communication may continue to do so, as long as a reliable interpreter is available.) To be qualified to obtain a lethal prescription, the patient must also be suffering from a terminal disease, defined as is customary in these laws as 'an incurable and irreversible disease that has been medically confirmed and will, within reasonable medical judgment, produce death within six months.' The definition of terminal as a condition that will lead to death within 6 months has a peculiar bureaucratic history. While plans were being made to extend Medicare benefits to hospice care, the majority of patient then being cared for at hospices in the United States were cancer patients, for whom a life expectancy prognosis could be reasonably made. To limit access to a hospice in an actuarially sound, predictable fashion, the decision was made to define illness as a condition that would result in death within 6 months. Plainly, the major consequence of making an error in predicting death in a patient who lives beyond 6 months is confined to Medicare having to pay for more hospice services than projected. In contrast, for physician-assisted suicide, the gravity of the consequence of mispredicting the nearness of death are self-evident: an error could result in the death of someone who was not near death. And the likelihood of mistakes in prognosis is large, because predicting the time of death is always difficult and at 6 months predictions are highly unreliable, especially outside the field of cancer.

Beyond the requirements of adult age, competency, residency, and terminal disease, Section 3 of the Oregon statute contains four principal safeguards: informed decision making; medical confirmation; psychological consultation when needed; and repeated, verified oral and written requests.

In including these provisions, the Oregon drafters were responding to the complaints that critics had raised about the weak safeguards in the Washington and California initiatives. Unfortunately, the Oregon safeguards are largely illusory.

Informed Decision Making

The first of these safeguards is that the attending physician must lay the basis for a patient's informed decision. Specifically, an informed decision must encompass information, not only about the diagnosis and prognosis and the 'potential risks associated with and the probable results of taking the prescribed medication', but also about the feasible alternatives including, but not limited to, 'comfort care, hospice, and pain control'.

In a certain way, the requirement to be told the potential results of taking lethal medication appears absurd. The patient is asking for what will induce death. The requirement it borrows from the general law of informed consent is that if a patient is going to go in for an operation, he or she ought to know the kinds of things that could happen.

Although it is reasonable to require that information of this sort be provided in ordinary informed consent, it seems odd to stipulate that the potential risks be provided in the context of an assisted suicide if one thinks of death as the ultimate consequence: what more needs to be said? Yet, were information accurately given, this requirement would not be so odd because the truth of the matter is, despite the attention drawn to accidental poisonings in hospitals, physicians assist patients to take their own lives painlessly on an outpatient, self-administered basis. Simply put, not surprisingly this turns out to be an area where the manifest illegality of any experimentation means there has been no research. (A foot-note in medical history:

one of Jack Kevorkian's earliest forays into this area in the 1950s was to suggest the use of condemned prisoners for precisely this type of research.)

Thus, while it would be interesting if physicians really had to take seriously the statutory requirement that they outline potential risks, I suspect that the drafters probably did not intend that patients would be told the risks associated with assisted suicide such as, 'It is very likely that you are going to bungle this job,' or 'The medication may not work and someone is going to have to intervene and you may wind up in the Emergency Department after all because you are going to vomit up the pills.' Instead, the risk associated with assisted suicide was supposed to be, 'If you take this medication you will die.' A more relevant point is that the patient was also supposed to be told the feasible alternatives. Being advised of alternatives should not be dismissed lightly, because obviously that information is important for patient decision making. (The physician must also ask the patient to notify the next of kin of plans for an assisted death, but the request for assistance may not be denied on the grounds that the patient is unwilling or unable to comply with this requirement.)

Consultation
The second safeguard is that a consulting physician must confirm that the patient has a terminal illness, is capable, and has made a voluntary and informed decision. The problem here is that any doctor (including a pathologist like Jack Kevorkian) could qualify as an attending or consulting physician as long as that person is qualified to practice medicine in the state. Once a patient refers his or her care to a physician with the intent of having that physician aid the patient's suicide, the 'treatment' of the patient's terminal disease becomes achieving death, not curing illness. Thus, any physician inclined to set up a practice in Oregon specializing in assisting suicide could become a magnet for terminally ill patients from around the world. And the statute does not guarantee the independence of the consulting physician. Both the attending and consulting doctors could be partners in the same specialized suicide practice.

The protection against suicides induced by mental illness or depression is likewise a thin reed. On its face, the statute provides safeguards. If either the attending or the consulting physician believes the patient to be suffering from a psychiatric disorder (including depression) that impairs judgment, in the words of the statute, the patient must be referred to 'counseling'. Lethal medication may not be prescribed until a licensed consultant determines that the patient is not suffering from a disorder or depression. In fact, these safeguards may amount to very little. First, counselors need not be independent of the referring physician. Second, the statute explicitly states that a mental evaluation is necessary only when one of the physicians, who need not be trained in psychological evaluation, requires one. Moreover, physicians do not necessarily have either the training or the access to relevant information to determine whether someone is exerting coercion or undue influence as the statute prohibits. Indeed, I wonder how a physician ought to react upon learning that the children of an elderly widow support the patient's request for assisted suicide, or that they may even have been the origin of the idea by suggesting it to their mother, 'Don't you think you ought to have relief from this awful condition you're in? Why don't you ask the doctor for help?' Should physicians probe for such influences, and if they find them, do they disqualify the patient from aid-in-dying? Are such factors unacceptable, or are they merely part of what one would expect in normal family relations and perfectly consistent with a patient's being 'qualified' under the statute?

Repeated Requests
Finally, a person wishing to commit suicide must make a series of oral and written requests to that fact. At least 15 days must elapse between the patient's initial oral request and his or her request immediately preceding the physician's written prescription. Also, at some time between the first and the final oral request, and at least 48 hours before the prescription is written, the patient must execute a written request for medication witnessed by at least two people who can attest to the patient's apparent capacity to decide and to make a voluntary, uncoerced decision. Mirroring the advance directive statutes the Oregon law prescribes that (1) the attending physician may not serve as a witness and (2) at least one of the witnesses must be disinterested in the sense of not being a relative, someone entitled to a portion of the estate, or an owner or an employee of the healthcare facility where the patient resides or receives care. As part of finally verifying that 'the patient is making an informed decision' immediately before writing the prescription, the physician must offer the patient an opportunity to rescind the request.

Despite all this elaborate ritual, the statute does nothing to insure that the patient is acting voluntarily and competently at the time when the legal means are used. This is not surprising because the focus of the statute is on reassuring physicians that they are not at legal risk if they behave in a certain fashion, not on actually protecting against unjustifiable deaths. Once the prescription has been written, the presumption is that the physician's role is complete (although some physicians may choose to stay involved). And under the Oregon law no one is responsible for insuring that the patient is not depressed when he or she takes the fatal medication, or even that the patient has chosen to take it rather than having it administered by someone else who has decided (out of beneficent motives or otherwise!) that the time has come to end the patient's life.

As is typical in advance directive statutes, the Oregon Death With Dignity Act (1) protects wills and insurance policies from being affected if a person takes his or her life under the provisions of the Act (2) renders invalid any contract either to make or to rescind a request for lethal medication, and (3) penalizes falsification of a request or recession or coercion to request aid-in-dying. The statute also contains another provision typically found in laws covering the withdrawal of life support, 'Actions taken in accordance with this act shall not for any purpose constitute suicide, assisted suicide, mercy killing, or homicide under the law'. This disclaimer is clearly at odds with the official summary of the law's purpose, which includes removing criminal penalties for physician-assisted suicide. I assume the disclaimer was simply copied from the advance directive acts where the statutes have stated that withdrawal of care is not suicide, assisted suicide, or homicide. The reason that the disclaimer seemed comforting to policymakers and so was included, even though it is entirely incongruous in the context, is that it allows us to continue to claim to draw a line against anything associated with mercy killing or homicide because legalizing assisted suicide is seen, mistakenly in my view, as the more limited of these two potential developments.

Despite my skepticism about the Oregon statute on assisted suicide, were its only result to permit fully competent and rational people who are very near death to obtain the asistance of physicians in easing their passing, I would view the major issue to be whether this assistance is an appropriate role for physicians and related healthcare providers such as nurses and pharmacists. That issue is not itself inconsequential; but I am skeptical that physician-assisted suicide statutes are good public policy, precisely because I think they raise a host of other difficult issues and are not limited to that small category. While suicide itself is not a crime (attempted suicide now being regarded as a cause for a mental health intervention, not legal sanction), good reasons exist for treating aiding a suicide as a criminal act.

Of course, it is unlikely that many physicians will take advantage of the loopholes in the statute, although only a few such physicians could lead to a situation that I suspect few Oregonians had in mind when they voted for the ballot measure. In the short run, the problem might be just the opposite because, despite its implied promise of dignified death for all, the new law provides no guarantee that any particular patient or patients will be able to obtain the assistance they want to control the timing and manner of their deaths. No physician can be forced to write a prescription for legal drugs nor is any health insurance required to provide this particular service. Furthermore, although the statutory immunities for civil and criminal actions extend to nonphysicians present when a qualified patient ends his or her life, not everyone has friends and relatives willing to play this supportive role that may be essential to ensure that the end comes in a 'humane and dignified' manner as the statute promises. Thus, despite its implied promise, a statute simply cannot guarantee that we have dignity in our dying.

You will notice that Professor Capron is not uncritical of the Act. Following a year's experience of the Act being in force, the Oregon Health Division published a report in February 1999 and an article in the prestigious New England Journal of Medicine: see A Chin, K Hedber, G Higginson and D Fleming 'Legalized Physician-Assisted Suicide in Oregon – The First Year's Experience' (1999) 340 New Eng J Med 577. The report concluded that assisted suicide was being carried out safely. Fifteen patients were provided with the means to kill themselves during the first year of the Act being in force. However, the data which has been collected has been criticised as inadequate to monitor the application of the Act.

Kathleen Foley and Herbert Hendin 'The Oregon Report: Don't Ask, Don't Tell' (1999) 29(3) Hastings Center Report 37

Limited Data
The data...collected is largely epidemiological: the assisted suicide cases were divided between men and women, the median age of the patients was sixty-nine, all the patients were white, all but two of them had cancer, and the patients who chose assisted suicide were more likely to be divorced or never to have married. Physicians participating in assisted suicide are not asked to provide OHD with significant medical information about their patients. They are merely asked to check off a list on the OHD form indicating that such statutory requirements as a written request for a lethal dose of medication, a fifteen-day waiting period, and consultation with another physician have been met. Only one line is provided for both diagnosis and prognosis, although a diagnosis of terminal illness and prognosis of death within

six months are the essential requirements for assisted suicide in the state. The form does not inquire on what basis the physician made the medical diagnosis – for example, review of x-rays, written material, pathology reports, or other information. Nor are physicians asked to report on what basis they made the prognosis – what tables they have used, what experts they have consulted. The form does not even inquire as to the patient's reasons for requesting assisted suicide. The data do not make it possible to know what transpired in any particular case.

To supplement the meagre information required by formal reporting, OHD asked physicians who participated in assisted suicide to respond in person or by phone to a questionnaire that was also given to physicians of a comparison (control) group of patients who died of similar illnesses without assisted suicide. OHD does not tell us who asked the questions, what their training was, and whether any follow-up questions were asked. But the questionnaire (published on the Internet) and the report show that this effort was also flawed. Missing medical information was not asked for or provided.

In the absence of medical data, how does OHD reach its conclusion that patients received adequate end-of-life care? From the facts – derived from the physician questionnaire – that the proportion of patients who had advance directives and were enrolled in hospice programs was comparably high for both the case and comparison groups, and that neither worry about pain control nor financial concerns drove patients' requests for assisted suicide. But neither advance directives nor enrollment in a hospice program provides proof of competent assessment and treatment – the essential components of adequate care – any more than does patients' apparent silence about palliative care or financial concerns. Such figures cannot substitute for direct knowledge of patients and their illnesses. Although the physicians questioned reported that more patients requesting assisted suicide were concerned with loss of autonomy or loss of control of body functions than were those in the control group, physicians were not asked how these concerns were expressed or addressed. Without such information it is not possible to judge the adequacy of the care these patients received.

Issues in Care
Palliative Care. Under the Oregon law, when a terminally ill patient requests assisted suicide, physicians are required to point out that palliative care and hospice care are feasible alternatives. They are not required, however, to be knowledgeable about how to relieve either physical or emotional suffering in terminally ill patients. Without such knowledge, and without inquiry into why the patient requested assisted suicide, the physician cannot present feasible alternatives. Serious evaluation of the end-of-life care that such patients received would have to be conducted by physicians trained in palliative care, able and willing to inquire about the nature of the patient's illness and concerns and what was done to address them. We do not know that those at OHD administering the questionnaire had such training.

The report stresses the fact that only one of the fifteen patients expressed concern about inadequate pain control at the end of life. The report's authors believe this may reflect advances in palliative care in Oregon and the fact that the state ranks high in the use of morphine for medical purposes. Yet fifteen of the forty-three control patients were worried about end-of-life pain control, suggesting the concern is frequent among those who are terminally ill. But the figures themselves are suspect. They are based on physicians' responses long after the fact to the question whether patients volunteered such concerns about pain. The physicians did not directly ask the patients about their pain. The inadequacy of relying on physicians' perceptions of patients' experiences has long been documented, particularly with regard to pain: in numerous published studies physicians underestimated what patients were experiencing. In surveys of barriers to effective pain relief, patients reported that they did not want to use their time with their doctors to discuss pain relief but rather to discuss their treatments. This is particularly apt to be true of patients requesting assisted suicide, who if successful in persuading physicians to give them a lethal prescription would have no need to be concerned about future pain. A study surveying cancer patients with pain or depression showed how differences in their attitudes toward physician-assisted suicide would affect their choice of physicians: patients with pain reported they would change physicians if they knew their physician participated in physician-assisted suicide. Those with depression were more likely to seek out such physicians.

Surveys of family members of dying patients can provide insight into the adequacy of palliative care services. The OHD report fails to cite the recent Oregon Board of Medical Examiners (BME) survey of 475 surviving family members listed as informants from a stratified sample of Oregon death certificants for 1997; the survey showed a statewide trend of higher rates of moderate to severe pain reported by family members of patients dying in acute care hospitals throughout Oregon. The BME viewed the trend as a 'worrisome' statistic that suggested inadequate palliative care.

No data are available in the Oregon report on the major symptoms other than pain that interfere with patient quality of life and affect their sense of autonomy and control.

The Lethal Prescription. The report, however, does help settle one medical debate that went on between advocates and opponents prior to implementation of the law. Opponents of legalizing assisted suicide in Oregon pointed out that because there was no reliable information about the lethal dose of drugs for medically ill patients, physicians assisting suicide would essentially be experimenting on patients. In Dutch studies 20 percent of patients given 9 grams of barbiturates, considered a lethal dose, lived for more than three hours. Dutch doctors usually then intervened with a lethal injection, which would be illegal in Oregon. In a number of reported cases in this country, after swallowing presumed lethal doses of barbiturates patients did not die and families intervened with pillows or plastic bags. Advocacy groups denied the validity of the Dutch findings and of such accounts although recommending the 9-grant barbiturate does, which was given by Oregon physicians to fourteen of the fifteen Oregon cases. OHD notes without comment that four of the fifteen patients lived longer than three hours and one lived as long as eleven – figures that are consistent with the Dutch experience.

Economic Factors. The pitfalls that result from OHD's inadequate methodology are nowhere more apparent than in its conclusion that economic factors did not influence the choice of assisted suicide. OHD informs us that apprehensions that assisted suicide would be chosen by those 'fearful of the financial consequences of their illness' were unjustified. This may or may not be true, but the OHD is not in a position to know. The Oregon law does not ask physicians to inquire about patients' economic or social circumstances, nor does OHD require physicians to report such information.

On the basis of the physician questionnaire OHD concludes, 'None of the case patients or control patients expressed concern to their physicians about the financial impact of their illness. We found no significant difference between the case patients and the control patients with regard to insurance at the time of their death' (p 580).

The apparent lack of differences between the case and control groups is more likely to reflect the lack of sensitivity of the model and the superficiality of the data collected. It is very unusual for physicians to have a clear understanding of the financial issues facing their patients. More commonly they are unaware of patients' out-of-pocket expenses, or of other family and personal considerations. Physicians have little time to discuss these issues and patients have strong needs (out of pride) not to provide this information to clinicians. A patient requesting assisted suicide may also feel that the request is less likely to be granted if the physician feels that the patient is making the request because he or she cannot afford proper care. Yet certainly when a patient requests assisted suicide one would expect physicians to inquire about the patient's ability to afford adequate care, whether or not the patient raises the question and even though the law does not suggest that physicians do so.

Even among the insured there is compelling evidence to suggest that the cost of end-of-life care can contribute to financial hardship. In a comprehensive study of end-of-life care, more than half of the families involved in the care of a seriously ill family member reported at least one severe financial burden, ranging from loss of family savings and loss of income to changes in future educational plans or employment status. High deductibles, copayments or a coinsurance, and limits of coverage can all contribute to high out-of-pocket expenditures. Medicare covers only 83 percent of typical charges for lung cancer and 65 percent of typical charges for breast cancer; it does not reimburse for out-of-pocket drug expenses, which can be particularly burdensome. And hospice provides only limited nursing care (four hours per day) unless the patient is imminently dying.

Psychiatric Evaluation. Since Oregon is the first state to legalize suicide as a treatment for medical illness, it would seem to have a special responsibility to protect the significant numbers of patients who become suicidally depressed in response to serious or terminal illness. We now that medical illness is an important factor in 70 percent of all suicides over the age of sixty. We know also that two-thirds of all suicides and two-thirds of those requesting physician-assisted suicide are suffering from depression. Among patients requesting assisted suicide researchers have found depression to be the only factor that significantly predicts the wish for death.

Although a psychiatric evaluation is the standard of care for suicidal patients, the Oregon law does not require it in assisted suicide cases. Under the law, only if the physician believes that the patient might be suffering from a psychiatric or psychological disorder or from a depression causing impaired judgment must the physician refer the patient to a licensed psychiatrist or psychologist for counseling. Yet studies have shown that physicians are not reliably able to diagnose depression, let alone to determine whether the depression is impairing judgment. Passik noted in a study of cancer patients with moderate to severe depression that only 13 percent of clinicians identified depression in the patient population (Steven D Passik, Margaret V McDonald, William Dugan et al, 'Oncologists Recognition of Depression in Their Patients with Cancer' Journal of Clinical Oncology 16 (1998): 1594–1600).

With such facts in mind, a task force organized by the Oregon Health Sciences University to guide caregivers advised physicians to refer all cases requesting assisted suicide for psychiatric evaluation even though they are not legally required to do so (Kathleen Haley and Melinda Lee, eds, 'The Oregon Death with Dignity Act: A Guidebook for Health Care Providers' (1998)).

Does OHD monitor the process to see to it that depressed patients are adequately protected? Psychiatrists who have examined patients and found them depressed, with 'impaired judgment', are not even asked to file a report with OHD. Buried in a table but not discussed in the report is the fact that only four of the fifteen patients who requested assistance in suicide were referred for psychiatric or psychological evaluation. Since all fifteen cases went forward we must conclude that in no case was depression or any other mental illness considered to be compromising the patient's judgment.

If OHD wished to monitor the psychiatric evaluation, a trained psychiatrist or psychologist should have inteviewed both the prescribing physicians and the psychiatrists who saw the four patients who were evaluated. Questions such as those asked in a psychological autopsy would be asked: Were the reasons for requesting assisted suicide explored? How did the physician evaluate them? What was the physician's response? Was the patient depressed? What were the symptoms? Was treatment offered? What was the patient's response? What other risk factors for suicide were present, such as a family history of depression and/or suicide, alcoholism, or any past suicide attempts? What was the patient's past experience with the death of those close to him or her? Did the patient – like most suicides and assisted suicides – express any ambivalence about suicide? If so how was this expressed and how was it dealt with? Physicians inexperienced in dealing with suicidal patients tend to take requests to die literally and concretely, failing to hear this ambivalence.

It would have been valuable to compare interviews with physicians of eight additional patients who requested but did not carry out assisted suicide: six who died of their underlying illnesses without using lethal prescriptions given them and two who were still alive on 1 January 1999. This information was not obtained. Yet at least the first six are essentially dropouts in the study, a group that investigators normally wish to compare with their cases. Such patients might provide us with further insights into the complicated aspects of patient requests.

OHD might well consider that psychiatric assessment is intended under the Oregon law to deal only with the limited issue of a patient's capacity to make the decision for assisted suicide. But then at a minimum OHD would need to monitor on what basis clinicians referred patients for psychiatric evaluation and whether these decisions were appropriate. The psychiatrists approving the assisted suicide would have to be interviewed to learn how well they knew the patient, whether the patient was seen more than once, and on what basis they decided the patient was competent. When surveyed, only 6 percent of Oregon psychiatrists were confident that absent a long-term relationship with a patient they could satisfactorily determine in a single visit whether that patient was competent to commit suicide. The same survey revealed that the majority of those willing to evaluate a patient's competence for assisted suicide favor the practice, leading the investigators to conclude that 'a bias may be introduced into the competency evaluation' (p 1474). When advocacy groups, like Compassion in Dying, are shepherding the cases and the referrals, the likelihood of such bias would seem to be even greater.

Protecting Patients at the End of life-sustaining
The flaws in OHD's monitoring come in part from the problems and flaws in the Oregon law. Intolerable and unrelievable suffering – a requirement for assisted suicide in the Netherlands – is not a requirement of the Oregon law; the diagnosis of terminal illness is sufficient. The presumption and stipulation in the Oregon law that a diagnosis of a terminal illness is sufficient for assisted suicide does not encourage physicians to inquire into the source of the medical, psychological, social, and existential concerns that usually underlie such a request, an inquiry that leads patients and physicians to have the kind of discussion that often leads to relief for patients and makes assisted suicide seem unnecessary. Nor are physicians asked or required by the Oregon law to make such an inquiry. Certainly such a discussion with the patient described above would have included consideration of her fears of being artificially fed and assurance that she did not need to choose assisted suicide in order for that not to happen.

Although the questionnaire given to physicians provides three lines for them to reply to a question as to why their patients chose to request assisted suicide, if the physicians had not previously explored the matter with their patients those replies are of questionable value. That the Oregon Health Sciences University which examined the law felt it necessary to recommend that physicians ask patients why they are requesting assisted suicide suggests this weakness of the law, how unprepared Oregon physicians are to deal with it, and how unprotected Oregon patients are by it.

OHD monitoring reflects the law's predilections so that OHD seems determined not to ask the tough questions and not to ask them of the right people. Patients are not asked to complete and provide any information to the state. Over 70 percent of the patients were in hospice care but, since OHD did not interview hospice staff, hospice nurses and social workers who may have the most knowledge of the patients were given no voice in the monitoring process. And the information physicians provide is far too limited to be relevant to those wanting to understand the end-of-life care these patients receive.

The physicians who did not agree to assist in suicide are not interviewed by the OHD and on the basis of doctor-patient confidentiality cannot speak publicly about the reasons for their refusal. This is in contrast to physician advocates, some of whom talk and write publicly about the treatment. One wonders if they have their patients' permission to do so.

Fifteen cases in a year was seen as a small number and as such interpreted as indicating that the law was not likely to be abused. In such a controversial procedure, however, one might expect patients and physicians to be at first hesitant about participating. Although we do not have figures for the early years in the Netherlands when assisted suicide and euthanasia were first given legal sanction, they appear to have been practiced at first relatively infrequently. It was only after the practice became generally accepted for some years that the numbers rose significantly. Some of the early Dutch patients were advocates of assisted suicide who used their deaths partly to make a statement on behalf of a cause in which they believed. There has been some question as to whether the Oregon patients might either be advocates or disproportionately shepherded by advocacy groups to chosen physicians. The physician questionnaire partly addressed this latter concern in asking 'Was the patient specifically referred to you regarding PAS by an organization such as Compassion in Dying or the Hemlock Society?' inexplicably, OHD did not publish the answer. We know, however, from the period when those organizations thought it useful to publicize their involvement, that the first few patients were referred through them to physicians who would prescribe lethal medication...

OHD has a higher responsibility, to present what it knows and admit what it does not. The ideal solution would be for OHD to appoint a task force made up of physicians from out of the state who are experts in palliative care, psychiatry, and medicine to review the assisted suicide cases. Perhaps even to embark on a prospective study. Unless physicians are asked to report more than they are now required to under the law, and unless properly trained independent physicians can question the physicians and examine the data, we will not learn much from the Oregon experience. Nor will we be assured that patients who choose assisted suicide are receiving appropriate care at the end of life.

There are now attempts in the US Congress to pass legislation, the Pain Relief Promotion Act, at the federal level which would prevent (by criminalising) the prescription of drugs for the purpose of bringing about death which, if it became law and withstood any constitutional challenge, would make the Oregon Act unworkable.

2. Mercy killing

We are here concerned with a deliberate act done by a doctor to bring about the death of a patient at the patient's request. Our focus in the current law, its possible reform and what shape that might take. (For a discussion of the philosophical questions see the exchanges between John Harris and John Finnis in J Keown (ed) *Euthanasia Examined* (1995) pp 6, 23, 36, 46, 56 and 62. Of course, the literature is, in fact, voluminous.)

(a) The current law

The law was restated in *Airedale NHS Trust v Bland* [1993] 1 All ER 821 (HL) per Lord Goff at 867 and Lord Mustill at 890.

> **Lord Goff:** It is not lawful for a doctor to administer a drug to his patient to bring about his death, even though that course is prompted by a humanitarian desire to end his suffering, however great that suffering may be: see *R v Cox* (1992) 12 BMLR 38 per Ognall J in the Crown Court at Winchester. So to act is to cross the Rubicon which runs between on the one hand the care of the living patient and on the other hand euthanasia – actively causing his death to avoid or to end his suffering. Euthanasia is not lawful at common law.
>
> **Lord Mustill:** That 'mercy kiling' by active means is murder was taken for granted in the directions to the jury in *R v Adams (Bodkin)* [1957] Crim LR 365, *R v Arthur* (1981) Times, 5 November, (Farquharson J) and *R v Cox* [(1992) 12 BMLR 38], was the subject of direct decision by an appellate court in *Barber v Superior Court of Los Angeles County* (1983) 147

Cal App 3d 1006 and has never so far as I know been doubted. The fact that the doctor's motives are kindly will for some, although not for all, transform the moral quality of his act, but this makes no difference in law. It is intent to kill or cause grievous bodily harm which constitutes the mens rea of murder, and the reason why the intent was formed makes no difference at all...

So far as I am aware no satisfactory reason have ever been advanced for suggesting that it makes the least difference in law, as distinct from morals, if the patient consents to or indeed urges the ending of his life by active means. The reason must be that, as in the other cases of consent to being killed, the interest of the state in preserving life overrides the otherwise all-powerful interest of patient autonomy.

(See also Lord Keith at 861.)

The position taken by the judges in *Bland* reflects the tradition of the common law. The law of murder is clear. The doctor who intentionally causes the death of his patient commits the offence. Intention here means 'desire' or 'object' or knowing that death is a certain outcome (*R v Woollin* [1998] 4 All ER 103 (HL)). It is irrelevant that the patient is terminally ill and would have died shortly: it is sufficient if the patient's death is accelerated albeit by a short time. Likewise, the patient's consent or the doctor's good motives are not defences. (For a discussion of the law, see M Otlowski *Voluntary Euthanasia and the Common Law* (1996) pp 14–22 and P D G Skegg *Law, Ethics and Medicine* (1984) pp 122–131.)

The difficulty, therefore, in which doctors find themselves is that the law seems to draw a very clear line between the permissible and the impermissible. But, that line is often blurred or disappears in medical practice and, as we have seen, can be ethically dubious. In *Bland* (*op cit*) can Lord Goff accepted this (at 867):

Lord Goff: The law draws a crucial distinction between cases in which a doctor decides not to provide, or to continue to provide, for his patient treatment or care which could or might prolong his life and those in which he decides, for example by administering a lethal drug, actively to bring his patient's life to an end ...

It is true that the drawing of this distinction may lead to a charge of hypocrisy, because it can be asked why, if the doctor, by discontinuing treatment, is entitled in consequence to let his patient die, it should not be lawful to put him out of his misery straight away, in a more human manner, by a lethal injection, rather than let him linger on in pain until he dies. But the law does not feel able to authorise euthanasia, even in circumstances such as these, for, once euthanasia is recognised as lawful in these circumstances, it is difficult to see any logical basis for excluding it in others.

Lord Mustill (at 885) was equally unhappy about the distinction.

Lord Mustill: The conclusion that the declarations can be upheld depends crucially on a distinction drawn by the criminal law between acts and omissions, and carries with it inescapably a distinction between, on the one hand what is often called 'mercy killing', where active steps are taken in a medical context to terminate the life of a suffering patient, and a situation such as the present, where the proposed conduct has the aim for equally humane reasons of terminating the life of Anthony Bland by withholding from him the basic necessities of life. The acute unease which I feel about adopting this way through the legal and ethical maze is I believe due in an important part to the sensation that however much the terminologies may differ the ethical status of the two courses of action is for all relevant purposes indistinguishable. By dismissing this appeal I fear that your Lordships' House may only emphasise the distortions of a legal structure which is already both morally and intellectually misshapen. Still, the law is there and we must take it as it stands.

Lord Browne-Wilkinson (at 884) makes the same point.

Lord Browne-Wilkinson: The conclusion I have reached will appear to some to be almost irrational. How can it be lawful to allow a patient to die slowly, though painlessly, over a period of weeks from lack of food but unlawful to produce his immediate death by a lethal injection, thereby saving his family from yet another ordeal to add to the tragedy that has already struck them? I find it difficult to find a moral answer to that question. But it is undoubtedly the law and nothing I have said casts doubt on the proposition that the doing of a positive act with the intention of ending life is and remains murder.

Furthermore, the 'lethal injection' referred to by Lord Browne-Wilkinson may itself be question-begging in practice: the injection of poison is undoubtedly lethal but then so is the injection of morphine or heroin which ends a patient's life albeit that it is the final dose in a course of treatment for pain relief. We will see (*infra*, ch 17) how the law has accepted such medical practices even if the dosage leads to what has been called 'terminal sedation'. The example of a case where, all other pain relief having failed, the doctor administered poison at the request of the patient and for entirely compassionate reasons, is *R v Cox*. In this case the doctor only escaped conviction for murder because the charge of attempted murder was preferred since the patient's body had been cremated and thus, given her terminal condition, proof that the doctor caused her death was problematic.

R v Cox (1992) 12 BMLR 38 (Winchester CC)

Lillian Boyes, an elderly patient, suffered from an incurable condition. She was terminally ill and *in extremis*. She suffered great pain which could not be controlled by drugs. She repeatedly asked her consultant. Dr Cox and others to kill her. Dr Cox administered a lethal dose of potassium chloride and she died almost immediately. Dr Cox was prosecuted for attempted murder and convicted. The trial judge summed up the jury in the following terms.

Ognall J: The prosecution allege that Dr Cox attempted to murder Lillian Boyes. They say that he deliberately injected her with potassium chloride in a quantity and in a manner which had no therapeutic purpose and no capacity to afford her any relief from pain and suffering whilst alive. They submit that Dr Cox must have known that and that in truth his conduct in giving that injection was prompted solely and certainly primarily by the purpose of bringing her life to an immediate end.

Proof of murder, members of the jury, would require proof that the doctor's conduct actually caused her death. The prosecution have told you that having regard to Mrs Boyes' condition on that morning, they cannot exclude the possibility though they, no doubt, would say it was remote, that, in fact, she died of natural causes between the actual injection of potassium chloride and her death. That is before the potassium chloride took its effect. It is for that reason, because they cannot exclude that possibility, however remote, that as you know, the charge you have to make up your minds about is not one of murder but of attempted murder, and I am sure you understand.

If it is proved that Dr Cox injected Lillian Boyes with potassium chloride in circumstances which make you sure that by that act he intended to kill her, then he is guilty of the offence of attempted murder. You know, in this case, from the earliest stage that it has been admitted that he did indeed inject her intravenously with two ampoules of undiluted potassium chloride, which no doubt you remember without looking at it ever again, his note at page 70 of the medical records clearly indicates.

According to her younger son Patrick, after that injection she just, and I quote, 'faded away' within minutes. According to Staff Nurse Creasey she died, so she said, in a few minutes. Later, she said about one minute after the injection.

Thus, the giving of the potassium chloride in that form, intravenously, is admitted, as I have said. The only question, therefore, for your consideration, ladies and gentlemen, in arriving at your verdict, is this. Is it proved that in giving that injection Dr Cox intended thereby to kill his patient? In the context of this particular case, what is meant, what do I mean, as a matter of law by proof of an intention to kill? ...

We all appreciate, do we not, and certainly the evidence you have heard in this case demonstrates it, that some medical treatment, whether of a positive therapeutic character or solely of an analgesic kind, by which I mean designed solely to alleviate pain and suffering, carries with it a serious risk to the health or even the life of the patient. Doctors, as you know, are frequently confronted with, no doubt, distressing dilemmas. They have to make up their minds as to whether the risk, even to the life of their patient, attendant upon their contemplated form of treatment, is such that the risk is or is not medically justified. Of course, if a doctor genuinely believes that a certain course is beneficial to his patient, either therapeutically or analgesically, even though he recognises that that course carries with it a risk of life, he is fully entitled, nonetheless, to pursue it. If sadly, and in those circumstances the patient dies, nobody could possibly suggest that in that situation the doctor was guilty of murder or attempted murder.

And the problem, you know, is obviously particularly acute in the case of those who are terminally ill and in considerable pain, if not agony. Such was the case of Lillian Boyes. It was plainly Dr Cox's duty to do all that was medically possible to alleviate her pain and suffering even if the course adopted carried with it an obvious risk that as a side effect – note my emphasis, and I will repeat it – even if the course adopted carried with it an obvious risk that as a side effect of that treatment, her death would be rendered likely or even certain.

There can be no doubt that the use of drugs to reduce pain and suffering will often be fully justified notwithstanding that it will, in fact, hasten the moment of death, but please understand this, ladies and gentlemen, what can never be lawful is the use of drugs with the primary purpose of hastening the moment of death.

And so, in deciding Dr Cox's intention, the distinction the law requires you to draw is this. Is it proved that in giving that injection in that form and in those amounts Dr Cox's primary purpose was to bring the life of Lillian Boyes to an end?

If it was, then he is guilty. If, on the other hand, it was or may have been his primary purpose in acting as he did to alleviate her pain and suffering, then he is not guilty, and that is so even though he recognised that in fulfilling that primary purpose he might or even would hasten the moment of her death.

That is the crucial distinction in this case. In shorthand form, the question of primary purpose. It is relatively easy for me to define for you. It is, however, submitted to you that for any doctor it can be, and was in this case, extraordinarily difficult to apply. Certain it is, it must confront you, members of the jury, with a most exacting task in striving to reach, as I know you will, a true verdict according to the evidence. I have told you that if Dr Cox's primary purpose was to hasten her death, then he is guilty. In using the words 'hasten her death' I do so quite deliberately, members of the jury. It matters not how much or by how little her death was hastened or intended to be hastened. I am sure you understand. You may recall Staff Nurse Creasey agreeing with [counsel for Dr Cox] that at the time Lillian Boyes received the first injection, not the potassium chloride, but you remember the earlier one of diamorphine and diazepam, that at the time she received that first injection from Dr Cox that morning, she, Staff Nurse Creasey, considered that Lillian Boyes was only hours from death at best and possibly only minutes away.

Of course, there can be no certainty in that regard, but even if that be the case, no doctor can lawfully take any step deliberately designed to hasten that death by however short a period of time.

Of course, members of the jury, to hasten the death, not merely alleviate suffering, it brings it to an end, does it not? A dead person suffers no more. But that is not what I mean by alleviation of suffering, nor, I am confident, what you understand me to mean by it. Alleviation of suffering means the easing of it for so long as the patient survives, not the easing of it in the throes of and because of deliberate purposed killing.

You will remember Professor Blake's evidence. A doctor's duty is to alleviate suffering for so long as the patient survives but, he said, he must never kill in order to achieve relief from suffering. To shorten life intentionally as one's prime purpose, he agreed, is unlawful, even though it may be the only means of alleviating the patient's suffering or pain....

You must understand, members of the jury, that in this highly emotional situation, neither the express wishes of the patient nor of her loving and devoted family can affect the position. You will understand, and I tell you, that Lillian Boyes was fully entitled to decline any further active medical treatment and to specify that thereafter she should only receive painkillers. You remember she did that on 11th August. It is recorded in the notes and there is no doubt that that was universally respected by the doctors and nursing staff thereafter. That was her, Lillian Boyes, absolute right and doctors and nursing staff were obliged to respect her wishes.... [Dr Burne, a senior house officer] told you that he had told Lillian Boyes on that day when she had said 'no more active intervention, please, only painkillers from now on', he had said to her, in effect, these are my words but I hope they reflect what he told you he said to her: 'thus far and no further. We will stop your positive medical treatment. We will confine ourselves to giving you only analgesics, only painkillers, but we cannot accede to your request that we give you something to kill you.'

How then, members of the jury, do you test what the Crown say were Doctor Cox's intentions so as to answer that central question, namely was his primary purpose to bring her life to an end or was it, or may it have been, on the other hand, directed primarily to alleviating her pain and her suffering?

The answer is that you do so by looking at all the circumstances of this case as you find them proved. You will look at Lillian Boyes' medical history, especially in those last days up to the day she died, 16th August and, of course, especially including that day. You will look at the expert evidence form the doctors and others experienced in drugs and toxicology. And you may think it of fundamental importance, it is a matter for you, like all questions of fact, but you may think of fundamental importance to consider the nature of the substance finally injected by Dr Cox in those quantities into Lillian Boyes' body.

If you reach the certain conclusion that potassium chloride injected undiluted and intravenously as it was can only in Dr Cox's mind have been with the purpose of bringing her life to an end, then the charge is made out. Dr Cox, as you know, is a highly-qualified, experienced and respected consultant physician. What did he know of the properties and potential of potassium chloride used in this way? ...

Let me identify for your assistance, members of the jury, what I understand to be common ground. First, that in the context of this case potassium chloride has no curative properties. Second, that it is not an analgesic. It is not used by the medical profession to relieve pain. Neither this galaxy of talented medical men nor any written medical word has ever suggested otherwise. Third, that injected neat, as I shall put it, into a vein it is a lethal substance. One ampoule would certainly kill. According to Professor Blake the injection here was therefore twice that necessary to cause certain death.

Fourth, that any doctor would know that it would cause certain death and within a very or relatively short period of time. Fifth, that to inject two ampoules into Lillian Boyes intravenously would cause her death within minutes, if not seconds. Sixth, that Dr Toseland gave the unchallenged evidence that there is no clinical use of which he was aware that could account for the use of potassium chloride in this way.

Seventh, that Lillian Boyes was terminally ill. Once she had directed the doctors on the 11th August to abandon any treatment save for painkillers, it is beyond doubt that she had condemned herself to die, and within a relatively short time. To use the graphic phrase of [counsel for Dr Cox], she had signed her own death warrant....

That brings me, members of the jury, to what I shall call a fundamentally important grey area so far as the defence are concerned, and it lies as I understand it, and I hope you agree with me, it lies in the suggested effect of the lethal dose of potassium chloride during the very short time between its administration and the consequential death.

Professor Blake agreed that the probable effect of the injection was to alleviate her suffering only by bringing her life to an end. Notice: only by bringing her life to an end. But, both he and Dr Dixon spoke of the relief of pain in the one, two or five minutes before she succumbed to the effect of that fatal injection. This is a crucial area so far as the defence are concerned. You may think, members of the jury, that you should approach that form of analysis with some care.

First, because that is or may be the effect for those few minutes does not of itself mean that that was Dr Cox's primary purpose. It is highly relevant but not definitive. You must be careful to distinguish effect on the one hand and purpose on the other.

Second, it is, I suppose, members of the jury, a truism that in many cases of death there comes a time when the moribund person is on the very brink of death. It is a distressing subject but we have to look at it and it has been looked at closely in this case, has it not? There comes a time when the moribund, the inevitably dying person is on the very brink of death. You have heard as the jury in this trial evidence of the mechanics of death in this case. The heart begins to fail, the blood pressure is lowered, blood reaches the brain in progressively lower volumes, and as that occurs a deeper and deeper level of unconsciousness supervenes. Finally the heart stops, the brain is completely starved of blood and therefore oxygen and breathing ceases, and at that moment the patient is dead.

In that sense, no doubt you will at once accept that the patient's pain and suffering are indeed progressively reduced as the lethal dose takes effect, until the patient reaches the state described as dead. But, members of the jury, what you will have to ask yourselves, you may think, is this: is that as a matter of common sense and ordinary language saying any more than that even if – notice it – even if you purposely kill someone by drugging them you incidentally relieve their pain during their death-throes?

So, you may have little hesitation, ladies and gentlemen, if any hesitation, in accepting that as the patient dies and because they are dying their pain and suffering is during that time alleviated. Professor Blake and Dr Dixon told you so. The central question still remains, of course. Given that this injection of potassium chloride had the effect – note my emphasis – of alleviating her suffering as she died, was that or may it have been Dr Cox's primary purpose, or was it an incidental consequence of his proven primary purpose, namely, to hasten her death?

I come back to what Professor Blake said. I quote: 'It is probable that the effect of this injection was to alleviate suffering only by bringing her life to an end. By that means Dr Cox,' he agreed, 'kept his promise to Lillian Boyes that he would ensure that she would die in comfort'. And, of this aspect of the matter Dr Dixon said, 'If no relief can be given other than by shortening life and if the primary purpose of the doctor is to shorten life so that pain is alleviated that is not proper'.

Dr Dixon agreed that having regard to this patient's unique grave condition he, Dr Dixon, knew of no other way of controlling her pain other than by bringing her life to an end. He said that he hoped that if confronted with that situation which, as I understand he was saying mercifully he never had been, he hoped that if he were to be confronted with it he would have had the courage to do what Dr Cox did....

Having regard to all those matters the defence submit that Dr Cox adopted what [counsel for Dr Cox] describes as an unorthodox way but nonetheless a way of relieving pain and suffering. It is submitted for your consideration that however rare, even unique, it may be to describe the administration of potassium chloride in this way in this case it is fully justified and you cannot be sure that in all the circumstances his primary purpose was to kill.

(b) Reforming the law

While the House of Lords in *Bland* approved the decision in *R v Cox*, they did so less enthusiastically. The judges recognised the illogicality of distinguishing between withdrawal of the life-sustaining treatment and taking steps to kill a patient. The judges, however, considered reform of the law to be a matter for Parliament. Lord Goff (at 867) stated:

> It is, of course, well known that there are many responsible members of our society who believe that euthanasia should be made lawful; but that result could, I believe, only be achieved by legislation which expresses the democratic will that so fundamental a change should be made in our law, and can, if enacted, ensure that such legalised killing can only be carried out subject to appropriate supervision and control.

This is a constitutional argument based upon the respective roles of the courts and the legislature. It is generally, though not universally, accepted (see I Kennedy 'The Quality of Mercy: Patients, Doctors and Dying' (1994) (The Upjohn Lecture) – arguing for judicial action in response to legislative inaction). The reality is, however, that Parliament alone can change the law. All previous attempts to pass legislation in the UK to legalise 'mercy killing' or voluntary euthanasia have failed (see discussion in M Otlowski *Voluntary Euthanasia and the Common Law* (1996) pp 333–339). Politicians are naturally chary of espousing an issue which promotes such strong emotions on both sides.

The most recent 'official' review of the law can be found in the Report of the House of Lords Select Committee on Medical Ethics (HL Paper 21, Session 1993–94). In its report, the Committee set out the arguments presented to it: (1) for and against euthanasia; (2) for the introduction of a new offence of 'mercy killing'; and (3) for abolishing the mandatory life penalty for murder.

House of Lords' Select Committee on Medical Ethics, HL Paper 21, (1993–94)

SOME ARGUMENTS FOR AND AGAINST EUTHANASIA

91. In this section we summarise the arguments which witnesses deployed specifically in support of, or in opposition to, decriminalisation of euthanasia. However, much of the evidence which we have already discussed is also relevant to these arguments.

Autonomy and individuality

92. The chief argument of the VES in favour of euthanasia "is driven by modern concepts of personal autonomy, choice and the rights of the individual". They pointed out that "exceptions about the degree of control an individual may exercise over his or her own life have risen greatly" and that for many this extended to life's ending as well (p 85).

93. Professor Dworkin also emphasised the role of autonomy and individual decision-making in matters of life and death. He said "I am in favour of choice because people disagree about what kind of a death is meaningful for them. I, myself, believe that what sort of a death is right for a particular person and gives the best meaning to that person's life, largely depends on how that life has been lived, and that the person who has lived it is in the best position to make that decision" (Q 477). He advocated euthanasia as an option for those people who felt that to be kept alive in a situation which they found unacceptable would be harmful to their lives as a whole, cheapening what they had valued (Q 451). He said that many people would not wish to continue in a state of heavy sedation, if such were necessary for the control of pain, or in any form of permanent unconsciousness (Q 458). He said "what counts as suffering is ending a life, or allowing a life to linger, possibly for decades, in a form which the person whose life it is, and those closest to her or him, think is an insult, or a travesty" (Q 459). This view was supported by some of the letters from the public which we received.

94. Professor Dworkin suggested that arguments against euthanasia on the grounds that vulnerable people could be harmed by its practice, failed to recognise that other people could be harmed by a refusal to permit it (Q 452). The British Humanist Association suggested that "to refuse a considered request is to treat that person with contempt" (p 32).

95. The BMA on the other hand argued that, although denial of a right to euthanasia ran counter to the concept of autonomy and self determination, "granting the desires of some entails an unacceptable cost for others and therefore is contrary to other ethical imperatives such as the concept of justice" (p 31). HOPE also pointed out that "we live in a society that is more than just a group of autonomous individuals" and that therefore individual rights are balanced by social responsibilities (p 106). The Bishops said "A positive choice has to be made by society in favour of protecting the interests of its vulnerable members even if this means limiting the freedom of others to determine their end" (p 113). Other witnesses made the same point.

96. The Bishops also argued that the extension of autonomy to allow euthanasia would limit the autonomy of doctors, since "patients cannot and should not be able to demand that doctors collaborate in bringing about their deaths" (p 113). The SPUC said that "licence for euthanasia would quickly become a duty for health-care workers to take part in it, thereby limiting their personal autonomy and denying respect for private conscience" (p 237).

Sanctity of life

97. As we have seen, witnesses expressed a variety of views about the value of life. In addition, some witnesses argued strongly against euthanasia on specifically religious grounds. The Bishops said "Because human life is a gift form God to be preserved and cherished ... both Churches are resolutely opposed to the legalisation of euthanasia even though it may be put forward as a means of relieving suffering" (p 114). The Reformed Presbyterian Church of Ireland said "Life is to be viewed as his [God's] gift, given and taken again according to his sovereign will. It is thus not at the disposal of any human being" (p 284).

98. The VES rejected the absolute concept of sanctity of life as one to which only a minority subscribe, and to which even the major religions see exceptions in certain categories of justified killing (p 85). They suggest that "the phrase 'respect for life' may reflect the present day consensus on the matter more accurately than the absolutism of 'sanctity of life'" (p 86).

99. The British Humanist Association suggested that sanctity of life was not a principle on which legal structures should be based, since it depended on a religious outlook which not everyone shared. They suggested that "it is particularly hurtful to require someone who does not believe in God or afterlife to suffer intolerable pain or indignity in deference to a God or afterlife he does not accept" (p 28).

Public opinion

100. The VES cited both public and professional support for euthanasia, in the form of opinion polls (p 90, Q 188) and press articles. They suggested "that there is an informal humane consensus on this matter is now beyond doubt" (p 86) and that legislation is necessary "to bring the law into line with current thinking on right and wrong" (p 87). They said that the issue of euthanasia "is now too much one of public concern to be left to the traditional discretion of the medical profession behind closed doors" (p 87). Mr Ludovic Kennedy also suggested that public opinion was increasingly strong in support of euthanasia (Q 319). Professor Jennett reminded us that both the Appleton Conference and a majority of the Institute of Medical Ethics Working Party had recently declared that euthanasia could be an ethically justifiable option in certain circumstances, and drew attention to other indications of a shift in some sectors of professional opinion (pp 121, 122). Dr Tim Helme also drew attention to a number of surveys which suggested increasing support for euthanasia (pp 271, 272). He suggested there was a danger of the law falling into disrepute if it did not change to keep in line with public opinion (Q 694).

101. It must be noted however that the results of the public opinion polls which the VES and Dr Helme cited are far from decisive. As with any poll, the result produced is much influenced by the way in which the question is worded. It may be doubted whether the expression "to receive medical help to an immediate peaceful death" is readily understood to mean euthanasia; the omission of the word "immediate" from the 1993 poll (p 90) may be thought to cloud the matter still further.

Relationship between doctor and patient

102. The existence of a trusting and open relationship between doctor and patient is of particular importance when the patient is terminally ill and decisions must be made for care towards the end of life. The VES suggested that "any change making it easier for doctors openly to carry out their patients' wishes can only reinforce confidence on both sides" (p 88). Some other witnesses agreed.

103. More witnesses however felt that the relationship between doctor and patient would be undermined if the doctor was empowered to practise euthanasia, even under the strictest of controls. The BMA said "if doctors are authorised to kill or help kill, however carefully circumscribed the situation, they acquire an additional role, alien to the traditional one of healer. Their relationship with all their patients is perceived as having changed and as a result some may come to fear the doctor's visit" (p 29).

104. The Linacre Centre suggested that the practice of euthanasia would corrupt the character of doctors, and encourage them to view some patients as lacking inherent worth. This would undermine "a disposition indispensable to the practice of medicine: the willingness to give what is owing to patients just in virtue of their possession of basic human dignity" (p 172).

Advances in medical science

105. The VES cited developing medical technology as a factor fuelling support for euthanasia. "Having created the situation in which lives are routinely saved, transformed or prolonged by medical intervention, we can hardly pretend that the process of dying, and that alone, must be left to nature" (p 85). Mr Ludovic Kennedy suggested that advances in medical techniques meant that "the dominant fear today is of being denied release from a prolonged period of painful, distressing and undignified dying" (Q 319). This point was supported by a number of individual members of the public who wrote to us, particularly those who had witnessed the difficult death of a family member.

"Slippery slopes"

106. The so-called "slippery slope" argument was clearly put by the BMA. They said that "by removing legal barriers to the previously 'unthinkable' and permitting people to be killed, society would open up new possibilities of action". They said that "any moral stance founded on the permissibility of active termination of life in some circumstances may lead to a climate of opinion where euthanasia becomes not just permissible but desirable. Once active termination of life is a matter of choice for competent people, the grounds for excluding non-competent people from such treatment becomes harder to defend" (p 32). A number of other witnesses made a similar point. Sir Robert Kilpatrick observed that "one of the great problems is always to work out the implications of a change, because they may be much more far reaching than one can see". He cited abortion as an example, saying that the number of abortions performed each year far exceeded that expected at the time legislation was passed (Q 396). Dr David Cook made a similar point: "What began in 1968 as offering permission for doctors to perform abortions under certain restricted terms has now become an expectation ... that abortion is available on demand ... there has been a slippery slope when legislation about justified killing has been introduced". He also spoke of the human inclination always to go beyond any established limit (p 174).

107. The Reformed Presbyterian Church of Ireland feared that voluntary euthanasia would lead to a descent of the "slippery slope" because of the need for concurrence by the doctor. "The ultimate decisive factor is the patient's perceived quality of life – ie that his life is not worth living – not his request for death ... there is no logical reason, once voluntary euthanasia is allowed, why the practice may not be extended to cases where no request has been made, if in the doctor's judgment that is the best course of action for all concerned" (p 284).

Other arguments

108. The RCN were concerned for the wellbeing of the vulnerable. "We have daily contact with some of the most vulnerable people in society at the hardest times of their lives and we know that many of the problems that they suffer, they suffer as a result of poor resourcing. If euthanasia were an alternative then the imperative to provide the resources for those people, whether it is the education of doctors in pain control or provision of decent facilities for elderly people with physical illness, would be cut at a stroke" (Q 160).

109. A few witnesses considered that the knowledge that euthanasia was available as a last resort would comfort and reassure many patients who feared the future, though in the event few might take that option. The Voluntary Euthanasia Society of Scotland (VESS) said "the ability 'to leave by the door marked Exit', should the final need arise, gives many patients the courage to go on much longer" (p 269). On the other hand Mr Kennedy, although an advocate of euthanasia, acknowledged that "some people are really terrified that if this becomes law they will be in jeopardy" (Q 333).

110. HOPE suggested that a request for euthanasia was often not intended but "almost always expresses, How much value am I in society?" (Q 265). Ms Alison Davies suggested that the appropriate response to patients requesting euthanasia was "to help them to regain a sense of the worth of their own life, but we should not collude with their despair and hopelessness" (Q 681). The British Geriatrics Society said "although elderly severely ill patients may sometimes ask to be allowed to die, they very seldom request active procedures to ensure that they do" (p 25).

111. Dr Helme suggested that the practice of euthanasia would allow patients who so wished to be at home rather than in an institution (Q693). This was also mentioned as a benefit in some of the letters which we received.

112. A number of witnesses emphasised that the time of dying could be a positive and productive phase of life, which could be sacrificed if euthanasia were an option. The BMA said that if handled well the crisis of impending death can be a time of personal growth and

reconciliation for all those close to the dying person" (p 32). This point was also made by a number of individual members of the public in their letters to us.

113. The Evangelical Alliance and the British Evangelical Council suggested that if euthanasia were permitted the consequences of misdiagnosis would be particularly grave. "If a patient, on having a diagnosis of terminal illness, were to request and be granted euthanasia when no such condition existed, a tragedy would have occurred" (p 94).

114. The Handicap Division of the SPUC suggested that any system of criteria by which some requests for euthanasia were accepted and acted on, and others not, would demonstrate the view that certain people "are right to believe their lives are worthless" (p 249). The Division drew attention to the fact that most proponents of euthanasia would limit it "to those who are either terminally ill or incurably disabled ... This implies that sick and disabled people are "right to want to die" and "better off dead" whereas the able-bodied who express suicidal wishes are "wrong to want to die" and should be helped to value their lives" (p 248). The Linacre Centre made a similar point: "Any doctor who feels that a given patient still has a worthwhile life to live will not accede to a request for euthanasia from that patient. By contrast, it is precisely the judgment that a patient no longer has a worthwhile life which will seem to justify euthanasia" (p 162).

Imposed safeguards

115. Dr Helme set out a thorough and considered proposal for a framework in which, he suggested, euthanasia might be safely practised. He suggested that the law "could allow a more limited right to be relieved of extraordinary suffering ... a liberty to request euthanasia (rather than a right to demand it) reserved for exceptional circumstances" (ME 44). His proposal was for legislation to provide doctors who performed euthanasia with a "special defence" to criminal charges if they acted in accordance with one of two procedures. The first would involve notification in advance of the intention to perform euthanasia, and then retrospective scrutiny of the circumstances to ensure that the doctor had acted in accordance with prescribed conditions; if not, prosecution would follow. The second procedure, appropriate in cases where the doctor was more uncertain of the circumstances, would involve application to a Tribunal which would consider all the circumstances in advance of the action and make a recommendation; a doctor who performed euthanasia in accordance with a recommendation of the Tribunal would not have an automatic right to kill, but could usually expect not to be prosecuted. Dr Helme suggested that an advantage of his proposal was that, by making it clear that the practice of euthanasia was a statutorily controlled procedure quite separate from ordinary medical practice, there could be no pressure to participate on doctors who objected on grounds of conscience (Q 697).

116. The main safeguard proposed by the VES was that euthanasia should be performed only if the patient had, at least 30 days earlier, signed a declaration requesting it, and currently repeated that wish. They also suggested that where the request was prompted by treatable depression or anxiety, this should be observed and dealt with by the attending doctor (Q 192). This point was also made by Mr Kennedy (Q 323).

117. Professor Dworkin considered that it would not be possible always to be totally confident that a request for euthanasia was truly voluntary and not the result of pressure or coercion. But he suggested that a combination of legislative provision and social response could minimise the likelihood of such abuse (Q 442). If euthanasia were permitted, "the message would be one of individual responsibility ... the reason for permissive legislation is not that we collectively think that is the decent thing to do, but that we collectively want people to act out of their own conviction" (Q 455).

118. HOPE expressed doubts that society could ever be sure that a patient requesting euthanasia had made a choice that was "free, fully-informed and rational". They suggested that a patient's choice could be improperly influenced by depression, confusion, dementia, a feeling of being burdensome to others, or even by direct pressure from others (p 107). The Bishops expressed similar concern (p 113)...

"MERCY KILLING"

127. A number of witnesses considered the question whether, in the absence of any change in the law regarding euthanasia, certain types of deliberate killing should be treated differently from others. The Home Office discussed past proposals that there should be a reduced degree of culpability for "mercy killing" (p 17). Their view was that to take motive into account would give rise to argument (Q 43). They also suggested that the issue of "mercy killing" arose only infrequently, and that the courts often found diminished responsibility which enabled less stringent penalties to be imposed (p 17). The CPS told us that it was not common for relatives or health-care staff to volunteer information in cases which might be regarded as "mercy killing", so that there was often no police investigation (p 81). They also drew attention to other evidential difficulties in cases of that kind (p 82). They reiterated that even in respect of a "mercy killing" by a relative the CPS "would feel obliged under the law as it stands now ... to proceed with the matter and for it to be brought before the court as a case of murder" (p 83).

128. Statistics which the Home Office supplied (Table on p 18 and Supplementary Memorandum on p 25) show that between 1982 and 1991 "mercy killing" was an issue in 22 cases of homicide (in none of these cases was the defendant a doctor – relatives or other acquaintances of the patients were involved). In all but one of those cases (where the charge was infanticide) proceedings were begun on a charge of murder, but in only one case was a conviction for murder, and a sentence of life imprisonment, the outcome. In the other cases where a conviction resulted lesser offences were substituted and most of the sentences were for periods of probation or suspended imprisonment. These statistics suggest two possible conclusions: on the one hand it might appear that existing provisions are sufficiently flexible to allow appropriate outcomes to be achieved; on the other hand it might be suggested that the inadequacy of existing provisions is shown by the way in which the courts and prosecuting authorities apply them.

129. HOPE suggested that to introduce a new offence which took account of motive, could encourage medical misconduct (p 112). Mr Kennedy resisted the idea of a new offence of mercy killing, since it still implied an act against the will of the person whose life was ended, and so did not acknowledge the crucial voluntary element of euthanasia as he advocated it (p 132). The VES said that a new offence "would be better than nothing" failing the decriminalisation of euthanasia, but that it would be unsatisfactory because it focused on the perpetrator rather than on the wish of the patient (Q 214). Sir Stephen Brown agreed to a suggestion that it would be useful if the law provided for different degrees of killing, one of them being mercy killing (Q 312).

PENALTY FOR MURDER

130. The fact that a conviction for murder carries a mandatory life sentence has been widely debated, not least by a Select Committee of the House ('Murder and Life Imprisonment' Report of the Select Committee, Session 1988–89, HL Paper 78–I). That Committee recommended abolition of the mandatory life sentence, which would allow judges to take account in sentencing of the particular circumstances of each case. Its report set out clearly the arguments for and against the retention of the mandatory life sentence. The most important objection was that, as the crime of murder is presently defined, the mandatory sentence applies to an enormous range of offences. The Committee quoted Lord Hailsham of St Marylebone's speech in *R v Howe*, in which he said: "Murder, as every practitioner of the law knows, though often described as one of the utmost heinousness, is not in fact necessarily so, but consists in a whole bundle of offences of vastly differing degrees of culpability, ranging from brutal, cynical and repeated offences ... to the almost venial, if objectively immoral, 'mercy killing' of a beloved partner" ([1987] AC 417 at 433).

131. Among the factors which carried most weight with that Committee in reaching its decision was the weight of judicial opinion in England and Wales. The then Lord Chief Justice, Lord Lane, and 12 out of the 19 High Court and Court of Appeal judges who expressed a view were in favour of a discretionary sentence for murder. There is, in fact, a long tradition of judicial support for a discretionary sentence for murder, and the great majority of judges who took part in the vote in the House on the Murder (Abolition of Death Penalty) Bill in 1965 were in favour of a discretionary sentence.

132. Since the publication of the report on murder and life imprisonment, the House has had two opportunities to consider the law in this area. The first was in the debates on the Criminal Justice Bill in 1991. An amendment to that bill which provided that, in future, no court should be required to sentence a person convicted of murder to imprisonment for life was carried against the Government by a large majority. Among the supporters of the amendment were two former Lord Chancellors, the Lord Chief Justice, the Master of the Rolls and five Lords of Appeal. The amendment was overturned by the House of Commons voting strictly on party lines. The second attempt in recent years to abolish the mandatory life sentence was in a Private Member's Bill, introduced by Lord Ashley of Stoke. This was given a Second Reading on 8 February 1993, when the only speaker against the bill was the Government spokesman. With only a single dissentient, the bill also completed its later stages and was sent to the Commons. In the debates on both of these bills, the main argument put forward by the Government was that murder is a "uniquely heinous crime".

133. Most recently, an independent committee chaired by Lord Lane has repeated the call for abolition of the mandatory life sentence. That Committee concluded that it was "wrong to require judges to sentence all categories of murderer in the same way, regardless of the particular circumstances of the case" and "wrong to require the distinction between the various types of murder to be decided (and decided behind the scenes) by the Executive". It suggested that one advantage of a change in the law would be to "make it unnecessary for unsavoury devices to be adopted to evade the difficulties posed by the mandatory life sentence", the charge of manslaughter on the grounds of diminished responsibility being the prime example.

134. In evidence to us, the Home Office repeated their view that "the period of time spent in custody varies greatly from case to case and that in practice the system is flexible enough to ensure that custody is not unjustifiably prolonged" (p 17). However in 1990 and 1991 no prisoner convicted of murder served less that six years of a mandatory life sentence.

135. The VES reiterated the case for change. They said that the "crudity of the mandatory sentence ... in no way reflects the enormous moral gulf which in reality separates the aggressive murder from the "mercy killing" carried out in response to a sufferer's own wish" (p 87). They also argued that "the present rigidity of the law has led to hypocritical and degrading pleas which obscure the true facts of cases" (p 87) although when asked to explain this they gave few details (Q 205 and footnote).

In its conclusions, the Select Committee rejected calls for changes in the law to allow voluntary euthanasia and for a new crime of 'mercy killing':

VOLUNTARY EUTHANASIA

236. The right to refuse medical treatment is far removed from the right to request assistance in dying. We spent a long time considering the very strongly held and sincerely expressed views of those witnesses who advocated voluntary euthanasia. Many of us have had experience of relatives or friends whose dying days or weeks were less than peaceful or uplifting, or whose final stages of life were so disfigured that the loved one seemed already lost to us, or who were simply weary of life. Our thinking must inevitably be coloured by such experience. The accounts we received from individual members of the public about such experiences were particularly moving, as were the letters from those who themselves longed for the release of an early death. Our thinking must also be coloured by the wish of every individual for a peaceful and easy death, without prolonged suffering, and by a reluctance to contemplate the possibility of severe dementia or dependence. We gave much thought too to Professor Dworkin's opinion that, for those without religious belief, the individual is best able to decide what manner of death is fitting to the life which has been lived.

237. Ultimately, however, we do not believe that these arguments are sufficient reason to weaken society's prohibition of intentional killing. That prohibition is the cornerstone of law and of social relationships. It protects each one of us impartially, embodying the belief that all are equal. We do not wish that protection to be diminished and we therefore recommend that there should be no change in the law to permit euthanasia. We acknowledge that there are individual cases in which euthanasia may be seen by some to be appropriate. But individual cases cannot reasonably establish the foundation of a policy which would have such serious and widespread repercussions. Moreover dying is not only a personal or individual affair. The death of a person affects the lives of others, often in ways and to an extent which cannot be foreseen. We believe that the issue of euthanasia is one in which the interest of the individual cannot be separated from the interest of society as a whole.

238. One reason for this conclusion is that we do not think it possible to set secure limits on voluntary euthanasia. Some witnesses told us that to legalise voluntary euthanasia was a discrete step which need have no other consequences. But as we said in our introduction, issues of life and death do not lend themselves to clear definition, and without that it would not be possible to frame adequate safeguards against non-voluntary euthanasia if voluntary euthanasia were to be legalised. It would be next to impossible to ensure that all acts of euthanasia were truly voluntary, and that any liberalisation of the law were not abused. Moreover to create an exception to the general prohibition of intentional killing would inevitably open the way to its further erosion whether by design, by inadvertence, or by the human tendency to test the limits of any regulation. These dangers are such that we believe that any decriminalisation of voluntary euthanasia would give rise to more, and more grave, problems than those it sought to address. Fear of what some witnesses referred to as a "slippery slope" could in itself be damaging.

239. We are also concerned that vulnerable people – the elderly, lonely, sick or distressed – would feel pressure, whether real or imagined, to request early death. We accept that, for the most part, requests resulting from such pressure or from remediable depressive illness would be identified as such by doctors and managed appropriately. Nevertheless we believe that the message which society sends to vulnerable and disadvantaged people should not, however obliquely, encourage them to seek death, but should assure them of our care and support in life.

240. Some of those who advocated voluntary euthanasia did so because they feared their lives were being prolonged by aggressive medical treatment beyond the point at which the individual felt that continued life was no longer a benefit but a burden. But, in the light of the consensus which is steadily emerging over the circumstances in which life-prolonging treatment may be withdrawn or not initiated, we consider that such fears may increasingly be allayed. We welcome moves by the medical professional bodies to ensure more senior oversight of practice in casualty departments, as a step towards discouraging inappropriately aggressive treatment by less experienced practitioners.

241. Furthermore, there is good evidence that, through the outstanding achievement of those who work in the field of palliative care, the pain and distress of terminal illness can be adequately relieved in the vast majority of cases. Such care is available not only within hospices: thanks to the increasing dissemination of best practice by means of home-care teams and training for

general practitioners, palliative care is becoming more widely available in the health service, in hospitals and in the community, although much remains to be done. With the necessary political will such care could be made available to all who could benefit from it. We strongly commend the development and growth of palliative care services...

259. We have considered suggestions that, although deliberate killing should remain a criminal offence, killing to relieve suffering (that is deliberate killing with a merciful motive) should not be murder but that a new offence of "mercy killing" should be created. At present the offence of murder embraces acts of deliberate killing which vary enormously in their character and which most people would agree vary "in degree of moral guilt". (Report of the Committee on the Penalty for Homicide, Prison Reform Trust, London 1993, page 21). The significant question however is whether the law could or should make a distinction between them.

260. We consider that it should not. To distinguish between murder and "mercy killing" would be to cross the line which prohibits any intentional killing, a line which we think it essential to preserve. Nor do we believe that "mercy killing" could be adequately defined, since it would involve determining precisely what constituted a compassionate motive. For these reasons we do not recommend the creation of a new offence...

As regards abolishing the mandatory life sentence for murder, however, the Select Committee was in favour.

PENALTY FOR MURDER

261. Pressure for a new offence of "mercy killing" arises mainly because of the perceived injustice of the mandatory life sentence for murder. We strongly endorse the recommendation of a previous Select Committee ('Murder and Life Imprisonment Report of the Select Committee', Session 1988–89, HL Paper 78–I) that the mandatory life sentence should be abolished. This would enable the judicial process to take proper account of the circumstances of a case and the motives of the accused. It would avoid the law being brought into disrepute either by the mandatory imposition of a life sentence in respect of an act which was widely thought to be compassionate and (by some) arguably justifiable, or by the inappropriate substitution of lesser charges where it was expected that a jury would not convict for murder because of the mandatory life sentence. It would also give scope for an effective life sentence to be imposed where the circumstances made it appropriate...

In its response, the Government agreed with the Select Committee's view and turned its face against any reform (Cm 2553, 1994). As regards euthanasia, the Government stated it was its 'firm view that the deliberate taking of life should remain illegal' (p 1). As regards the introduction of a new offence of 'mercy killing', the Government said to do so 'would undermine the law's uncompromising attitude towards deliberate killing and might bring with it many of the dangers associated with the legislation of euthanasia' (p 5). As for the mandatory life sentence for murder, that should stay to '[mark] the unique nature of the offence of murder' (p 5).

The likelihood is, therefore, that the law will remain as it is and the doctor faced with a patient *in extremis* and asking to die will have to resort to the 'double speak' of purporting to relieve pain while bringing about death, making sure that the agent bringing about the death is one recognised by other doctors as a pain-reliever.

What, then, are the possible reforms and arguments for and against them? We should consider first the introduction of an offence of '*mercy killing*' and secondly the *legalisation* of voluntary euthanasia.

(i) AN OFFENCE OF 'MERCY KILLING'

As we saw earlier, the introduction of a lesser offence of 'mercy killing' or recognising the latter by way of reducing murder to manslaughter rather as is currently the case for provocation and diminished responsibility, has been rejected both by the Criminal Law Revision Committee in its 1980 Report on *Offences Against the Person* (14th Report, Cmnd 7844, para 115) and most recently by the House of Lords Select Committee on Medical Ethics in 1994 (*op cit*) and the Government (*op cit*). The issue is discussed in the following extract, where it is pointed out that in the medical context this may not be the better reform option.

Margaret F A Otlowski *Voluntary Euthanasia and the Common Law* **(1997)**

One possible direction for change would be to establish lesser penalties for mercy killing. This could be achieved in a number of ways. One possibility is for the creation of a separate offence for compassionate murder with a lower penalty than for murder. This would enable the courts to take account of the motive of the defendant in determining liability. A proposal along these lines has been supported by a number of commentators and agencies (eg Meyers, D, '*The Human Body and the Law*' (Chicago, 1970) 155), and has the advantage that the offender is charged with a specific offence other than murder and is liable to a lesser punishment (Law Reform Commissioner Victoria, Working Paper No 8, 'Murder: Mental Element and Punishment' (1984) 27). An alternative possibility is for the introduction of a sentencing discretion allowing for the reduction, or even setting aside, of penalties in cases of homicide prompted by compassionate motives. These two proposals are similar to the position in a number of European countries, where the actor's motive is a critical factor in determining culpability. For example, in both Switzerland and Germany, compassionate killing does not come within the classification of murder but rather manslaughter (see Articles 211 and 212 of the German Penal Code and Article 63 of the Swiss Penal Code). Moreover, in determining the appropriate punishment, the courts are required to take into account the defendant's motive which may justify a reduction in sentence. (See Article 213 of the German Penal Code and Article 64 of the Swiss Penal Code). In circumstances where the killing took place at the victim's request, it falls within a separate category of 'homicide upon request' which attracts a lesser penalty than murder (See Art 216 of the German Penal Code and Article of the Swiss Penal Code). These factors, either singly or in combination, operate to provide considerable leniency in the treatment of mercy killers in these jurisdictions.

A further possibility is for the creation of a new defence which would reduce the offence from murder to manslaughter. The onus would rest upon the defendant to adduce evidence in support of the defence, and if established, the defendant would be convicted of manslaughter rather than murder. Some commentators have favoured one or more of the foregoing solutions on the grounds that they represent an appropriate compromise. They acknowledge that cases of euthanasia are generally considered less reprehensible than ordinary acts of homicide and therefore deserving of special treatment, yet do not go so far as to formally endorse euthanasia by legalization.

Whilst the implementation of any of these reforms would arguably be an improvement on the present unsatisfactory situation, these proposals are not the appropriate solution to the particular difficulties in the area of medically administered active voluntary euthanasia. The main objection to all of the foregoing proposals in this context is that doctors remain at risk of criminal liability if they engage in the practice. It may, admittedly, be a liability for some lesser offence than murder, or the penalty may be nominal, depending on which proposal is implemented and the form in which it is introduced. The fact remains, however, that doctors who perform active euthanasia at the patient's request would still potentially be exposed to criminal prosecution. One must bear in mind that these particular proposals were not intended to deal specifically with the issue of active voluntary euthanasia in the medical context, but rather were directed generally at compassionate or mercy killings which may arise in a whole range of circumstances. This accounts for the limited nature of these proposals, seeking simply to diminish the liability of the defendant, rather than providing complete immunity ... reforms which are directed generally at mercy killings are not the appropriate solution for the particular difficulties raised by the issue of active voluntary euthanasia in the medical context. This is because mercy killing performed by family or friends on the one hand, and medically-administered active voluntary euthanasia on the other, are quite different in nature and involve quite distinct issues. Whilst there is a widespread desire to show leniency to mercy killers few would contend that such offenders should completely escape liability. In the medical context, however, where a doctor acts *bona fide* at the request of a patient and performs active euthanasia, there is a case for saying that a doctor should be protected from incurring criminal liability, provided he or she has acted in accordance with acceptable criteria. The present problems which confront the law with regard to active voluntary euthanasia, therefore, require specialized attention, and the discussion which follows will be confined to this area.

Significantly, many of the objections which have been advanced against the various proposals for change with regard to compassionate or mercy killing do not apply with the same force to medically-administered active voluntary euthanasia. For example, concerns have been raised about the difficulties in establishing the real motives behind a killing in circumstances where the killer may have acted out of mixed motive; partly motivated by compassion for the patient, but also, in part, driven by a desire to put an end to a difficult family situation or to gain some material benefit from the patient's death (eg Law Reform Commission of Canada, Working Paper Euthanasia, Aiding Suicide and Cessation of Treatment'). More general concerns have also been expressed about the possibility of abuse of any liberalization of the law, with for example, *mala fide* murders being committed and disguised as compassionate murders (ibid). However, compared with the more general mercy killing situation, it is reasonable to assume that doctors, operating under their professional codes of practice, are less likely to have some ulterior motive in hastening the death of the patient.

(ii) LEGALISING VOLUNTARY EUTHANASIA

The arguments in favour of voluntary euthanasia are materially the same as those we saw earlier in Professor Weir's article concerning doctor-assisted suicide. You will recall that the two principal arguments are the patient's right of self-determination and the doctor's (and society's) duty to behave with compassion. In her seminal book, Margaret Otlowski presents the arguments under *seven* headings.

Margaret F A Otlowski *Voluntary Euthanasia and the Common Law* (1997)

A. Self-Determination: An Argument from Liberty

The main argument in support of the legalization of active voluntary euthanasia is based on the principle of autonomy or the right to self-determination. According to this principle, each person has value and is worthy of respect, is the bearer of basic rights and freedoms, and is the final determinant of his or her destiny. Proponents argue that an individual who has decision-making capacity, has the right to control his or her own body and should be able to determine how and when he or she will die as long as this does not interfere with the rights of others. It is this human self-determination, the capacity of individuals to choose and pursue their particular life-plan, which is said to give persons their special moral status and is an essential component of the dignity that attaches to rational personhood.

Proponents argue that maintenance of the present legal prohibition on active voluntary euthanasia is an unjustifiable infringement of the liberty of those persons who would choose to be killed (Euthanasia Society, '*A Plan for Voluntary Euthanasia*' Revised edn (London, 1962) 5–9). It has been argued that to deny active voluntary euthanasia is a form of tyranny; an attempt to control the life of a person who has his or her own autonomous view about how that life should go, and that this constitutes and ultimate denial of respect for persons (Harris, J, 'Euthanasia and the Value of Life' in Keown, J (ed), '*Euthanasia Examined, Ethical, Clinical and Legal Perspectives*' (Cambridge, 1995) 6, 19)). According to proponents of euthanasia, in order to uphold the patient's interest in self-determination, doctors should be free to act upon the request of an informed and mentally capable patient for active voluntary euthanasia without fear of criminal liability.

If the principle of self-determination is accepted as the appropriate foundation for the legalization of active voluntary euthanasia there would be no need objectively to examine quality of life considerations – indeed, it would be quite inappropriate to do so. Any attempt to impose a qualitative assessment of the patient's life as a basis for active euthanasia would be a violation of the requirement of justice and would be completely contrary to the principle of patient autonomy. Different patients will inevitably have different goals and values which can best be respected by giving effect to the patient's interest in self-determination and allowing the patient to make decisions based on his or her own quality of life assessment. Thus, subject to any requirements of enabling legislation, the sole consideration should be the patient's choice, based on the patient's *subjective* assessment of his or her circumstances whether motivated by a fear of pain, suffering, dependency, or other causes.

Further, it must be understood that strict adherence to the notion of self-determination necessarily dispels any reliance upon utilitarian principles as a basis for active euthanasia. The arguments of some proponents for the legalization of active euthanasia rest on a form of utilitarian humanism which demands the decriminalization of certain acts of euthanasia and suicide. On pure utilitarian principles, active euthanasia would be justified in circumstances where the patient, and persons involved in the care of the patient, are suffering a balance of pain over pleasure and where the killing of the patient would, on utilitarian calculations, produce the greatest good for the greatest number. However, this reveals a fundamental weakness in utilitarian arguments as a basis for strictly voluntary euthanasia, in that they apply with equal force to cases of involuntary euthanasia – a practice which must be unequivocally deplored. According to utilitarian principles, provided there is a balance of pain over pleasure, active euthanasia would be justified if it could maximize benefits overall, regardless of whether the patient can or would give consent. Thus, the interests of the individual patient are subordinated to the interests of the majority. Because of this possible manipulation of utilitarian arguments towards non-voluntary and involuntary euthanasia, utilitarianism ought to be rejected as a moral theory justifying active voluntary euthanasia. In contrast, however, the autonomy-based principle of self-determination, essentially anti-utilitarian in nature, is not susceptible to the same arguments for extension to non-voluntary or involuntary forms of killing, and therefore constitutes the only acceptable basis for the legalization of active voluntary euthanasia.

B. The Patient's Right to Refuse Treatment: Is there a Morally Valid Distinction between Passive and Active Euthanasia?

In support of arguments based on the patient's interest in self-determination, proponents frequently draw attention to the inconsistency of the present law which permits a patient to induce an earlier death by refusing treatment, yet categorically prohibits a patient from seeking active assistance in dying (Kuhse, H, 'Euthanasia – Again' (1985) 142 MJA 610, Winkler E, 'Reflections on the State of Current Debate over Physician-Assisted Suicide and Euthanasia' (1995) 9 Bioethics 313)…

Proponents argue that if the law recognizes the patient's autonomy and self-determination as justification for passive euthanasia, it is logically inconsistent to refuse to recognize the same interests as a justification for active euthanasia (Kuhse, ibid). This argument, based on the inconsistency of the present law, derives significant support from the claim by many philosophers and ethicists that there is no morally relevant difference between passive euthanasia – deliberately letting a patient die – and active euthanasia – the killing of a patient; both involve the intentional termination of life. Moreover, it is argued that to deny active assistance to a patient who seeks it, is not only an infringement of that person's interest in self-determination, but may also be contrary to the patient's 'best interests', since the alternative of letting die may be neither swift nor painless (Kuhse, ibid). Furthermore, since not all terminal or incurable patients are dependent on life-sustaining treatment, they do not all have the option of inducing death by refusing treatment, except perhaps by slowly starving and dehydrating themselves to death. It could, therefore, be argued that the present law is discriminatory in its operation since it does not offer to all patients the same opportunity of inducing an earlier death.

Whilst many commentators support the view that there is no morally relevant difference between active and passive euthanasia, others have argued for the retention of the distinction. Some commentators have sought to defend the validity of the distinction on moral grounds arguing that a morally relevant difference exists which justifies maintenance of the prohibition against active euthanasia or 'killing' (eg Keyserlingk, E, 'Sanctity of Life or Quality of Life in the Context of Ethics, Medicine and Law' (Ottawa, 1979) 123–6, Beauchamp, T, 'A Reply to Rachels on Active and Passive Euthanasia' in Beauchamp, T and Perlin, S (eds) Ethical Issues in Death and Dying (1978) 246–58). Others have claimed that irrespective of philosophical arguments, a distinction is discernible in practice in view of the willingness of doctors to allow patients to die, contrasted with their intuitive opposition to active voluntary euthanasia (Gillett, G, 'Euthanasia, Letting Die and the Pause' (1988) 14 J Med Ethics 61). This claim can, however, be quickly countered on the basis that it purports to treat a value judgement as evidence and, furthermore, suggests that there is unanimity within the medical profession on the issue of active euthanasia which is clearly not the case. What this alleged distinction does reveal is that there is an element of self-deception operative here which may assist doctors in justifying their conduct in permitting patients to die.

There are others still, including the influential President's Commission for the Study of Ethical Problems in Medicine and Biomedical and Behavioural Research, in its Report Deciding to Forgo Life-Sustaining Treatment, who are prepared to acknowledge that the distinction between acts and omissions leading to death is not of itself morally relevant, yet nevertheless argue for maintenance of the current prohibition of active voluntary euthanasia on practical grounds (President's Commission for the Study of Ethical Problems in Medicine and Biomedical and Behavioural Research, 'Deciding to Forgo Life-Sustaining Treatment: A Report on the Ethical, Medical and Legal Issues in Treatment Decisions (Washington, 1983) 65–73). For example, concern is frequently expressed about the irrevocability of active euthanasia, allowing no opportunity for a change of mind or to correct mistakes, but the most serious concerns stem from a fear of abuse and other negative social consequences if active voluntary euthanasia were to be legalized.

There is no doubt at all that the existing prohibition on active voluntary euthanasia places significant limits on the self-determination of some patients. This has been recognized by many of those resisting legalization yet has not been seen as sufficient justification for any change to the present law. A prime example of this approach is to be found in the Report of the President's Commission. The commission acknowledged that policies prohibiting direct killing may conflict with the important value of patient self-determination but nonetheless went on to find this limitation on individual self-determination to be an acceptable cost of securing the general protection of human life (ibid at 73).

This reasoning is open to criticism. Particularly if one accepts the force of the argument that there is no intrinsic moral difference between active and passive euthanasia, there appears to be no valid justification for refusing to uphold the patient's self-determination in cases of active voluntary euthanasia. The practical arguments against the legalization of active voluntary euthanasia (for example, the possibility of error and abuse) can be adequately addressed through the introduction of appropriate regulation and safeguards and do not justify undermining the patient's right of self-determination. The only acceptable limitation on the patient's right to make decisions for him or herself is the requirement that the patient has decision-making capacity and is in a position to make an informed choice.

Analogy with suicide

Another argument frequently advanced in support of legalization of active voluntary euthanasia proceeds by way of analogy to the law of suicide. The argument begins with the proposition that since it is not unlawful for a person to commit or attempt to commit suicide, the law, implicitly at last, recognizes the right of an individual to take his or her life. From this premise it is argued that if an individual does have the right to take his or her life, he or she should be able to seek the assistance of others in achieving this end.

A right to commit suicide?

Some commentators have argued for a moral right to commit suicide, at least in some circumstances (eg Battin, M, 'Suicide: A Fundamental Human Right?' in Battin, M and Mayo, D (eds), 'Suicide: The Philosophical Issues' (New York, 1980) 267–285). The real issue, however, for the purposes of the present discussion, is whether an individual has a *legal right* to do so. The answer to this question must be in the negative, particularly in view of the continuing prohibition on assisting suicide and the laws which uphold intervention in the suicide of another. The most accurate assessment of the current position is that the decriminalization of suicide and attempted suicide has not created any positive or legally enforceable *right* to commit suicide – it has merely given persons the *liberty*, subject to certain constraints, of choosing to end their own lives without thereby incurring criminal liability. It could, nevertheless, still be argued that if persons are generally at liberty to commit suicide, they should also be free to seek the assistance of others in achieving their aim and, if necessary, to authorize another to take active steps to bring about their death. Further to this argument, if a third person complies with a request for assistance that person ought not be penalized since they are simply facilitating what the individual is at liberty to do. It must be emphasized that this argument does not necessarily entail general endorsement of suicide and suicide assistance. In many instances, suicidal persons are psychologically disturbed and should be prevented from implementing their plan. There are, however, cases where the choice of death is rational and where it would be entirely inappropriate to intervene, for example, in circumstances where a terminal or incurable patient seeks death as a relief from his or her suffering.

Significance of third party involvement

On the assumption that there is some validity in the analogy between suicide and active voluntary euthanasia, a crucial question which needs to be addressed is what significance, if any, should be attached to the fact that active voluntary euthanasia involves the direct assistance of a third party? Some commentators have argued that an important distinction exists between suicide on the one hand, which is an autonomous and self-regarding act, and assisted suicide or active voluntary euthanasia on the other, which requires the involvement and assistance of a third party (Callahan, D, 'Can We Return Death to Disease?' (1989) 19 Hastings Center R 4, 5). This third party involvement, they argue, constitutes a crucial difference because the conduct changes from being a purely private act to a form of public action with ramifications extending beyond the parties involved. Moreover, if it is based on dignity of human freedom and self-determination, then it is inconsistent to ask someone else to assist (Linacre Centre, Report of a Working Party '*Euthanasia and Clinical Practice: Trends, Principles and Alternatives*' (1992)). However, this objection ignores the practical realities of patients *in extremis* who are often physically unable to secure the means to a quick and easy death and may even be unable to self-administer the fatal dose if it were made available to them. It also disregards persons who are unable to commit suicide due to physical disability. On humanitarian grounds, it could be argued that it would be more compassionate and humane to assist those who wish to die but who are unable to kill themselves unaided by either directly administering active voluntary euthanasia or providing medical assistance in suicide to ensure that death is assured and achieved in a dignified manner.

Whilst it is conceded that the involvement of third parties in cases of doctor-assisted suicide and active voluntary euthanasia does differentiate these cases from autonomous suicide, it is disputed that this significantly alters the character of the acts to such a degree that they should necessarily be prohibited. The more relevant consideration is whether the patient has requested assistance. If the choice of death represents an exercise in patient autonomy and self-determination, this choice ought to be respected and it should be permissible to assist the patient in achieving his or her aim. The debate regarding third party involvement does, however, draw attention to the need also to respect the autonomy of others in dealing with a patient who seeks death.

Autonomy of others
According to accepted principles of autonomy and liberty, individuals should be free to pursue their own life choices, provided that this does not violate the rights of any third parties. In promoting the self-determination and autonomy of the patient, care must be taken no to interfere with the autonomy of others. In particular, doctors should not be required to abdicate their autonomy in favour of that of the patient. The position of third parties, and their right to remain free of involvement in the practice of active euthanasia, can be ensured by making it clear under any legislation permitting active voluntary euthanasia that doctors are under no *duty* to perform active euthanasia at the request of a patient, but may, in appropriate circumstances, be free to do so if they choose.

A right to die?
Any attempt to analyse whether there is a 'right to die', or whether such a right should exist encounters enormous difficulties. To begin with, the popular notion of a right to die is virtually meaningless in view of the fact that, ultimately, death is inevitable for everyone. Moreover, the right to die is ambiguous in that it can mean anything from a right not to be kept alive against one's will to a more positive right to seek assistance to die. For the purposes of the present discussion, it will be assumed that the expression 'right to die' is intended to convey a right to active assistance in bringing about one's death …

Should there be a right to die?
If one accepts the principle of self-determination as the basis for active voluntary euthanasia, it remains to be determined what legal status should be given to the patient's interest in choosing an earlier death. In particular, it must be decided whether patients *should* have a right to die. In this context, an important distinction must be drawn between the right to die as expressed in terms of a basic human right (although not necessarily legally enforceable) and a legal right. The recognition of the right to die as a human right would create duties on the part of the State (for example, in relation to the amendment of its laws which prohibit doctors from giving assistance in dying); it would not confer on individuals any legally enforceable right to active voluntary euthanasia or impose any obligation on doctors to participate in its administration.

The situation is more problematic where the right to die is expressed in terms of a legally enforceable right. Apart from problems of definition, there are potential difficulties in adopting a strict rights-based model as the basis for legalization of active voluntary euthanasia. Although the notion of 'rights' is expansive and, in its wider sense, can be used to encompass a variety of legal concepts, strictly speaking, rights (as distinct from liberties or privileges) are correlative with duties. Thus, the creation of any *right* to active euthanasia tends to imply a corresponding *duty* on the part of someone to become actively involved in bringing about death, although it is acknowledged that a right could conceivably be framed in a way which avoids the imposition of a duty on any particular person. For example, a 'right' to assistance could be created, but at the same time allowing conscientious objection for those doctors who are opposed to providing such assistance. Certainly in the US constitutional context, the courts have already indicated that the recognition of a constitutional right to physician-assisted suicide does not entail any duty on the part of the doctor (see the decision of the majority of the US Court of Appeals for the Ninth Circuit in the case of *Compassion in Dying v State of Washington* No 94–35534 (9th Cir March 6 1996).

Another possibility is for the right to active voluntary euthanasia to be framed simply in terms of a right of one person to authorize another to kill him or her intentionally and directly but without creating a right to demand such assistance.

There is broad agreement amongst euthanasia advocates that it would be inappropriate to impose a duty on any person to take the life of another. Although such a duty would uphold the autonomy of the patient who requests assistance, it is recognized that it would be an unjustifiable interference with the autonomy of others. It is primarily to avoid the implication of any such duty and the resulting infringement of the autonomy of third parties that a strictly rights-based model has been widely rejected as an appropriate basis for the legalization of active voluntary euthanasia.

Self-determination and the liberty to choose an earlier death
The dilemma which confronts us is to find some way to give effect to the autonomy and self-determination of the patient, but, at the same time, to protect the autonomy of others. This dilemma can best be resolved by holding that the patient's right of self-determination does not necessarily translate into an enforceable legal *right* to demand assistance to die. The patient's interest in self-determination can be appropriately protected by recognizing a *liberty*, to choose an earlier death and have the assistance of a doctor to bring it about. If the patient's interest is expressed in terms of a liberty rather than a legal right it would not be legally enforceable and would not create any duties upon others to accede to a patient's request for death. Thus, a doctor willing to assist would be *permitted* to perform active euthanasia at the request of a patient without being under any duty to do so. The creation of a liberty would

nevertheless be significant in that persons desiring active voluntary euthanasia would not be restrained from exercising that choice, and provided they have a doctor willing to comply with their request, they may lawfully secure a quick and painless death. Indeed, the mere knowledge that active voluntary euthanasia is available in the event that suffering becomes unbearable would in many instances be sufficient to put patients in control and remove the fear of having to endure intolerable pain or other distress.

It is clear from the foregoing analysis that the principle of self-determination is central to the case for legalization of active voluntary euthanasia. Consideration will now turn to a number of other arguments which support the case for legalization.

C. Prevention of Cruelty: An Argument from Mercy

Another argument, which is a cornerstone of the case for the legalization of active voluntary euthanasia, is the need to alleviate pain and suffering and to prevent cruelty. Proponents argue that to maintain the legal prohibition on active voluntary euthanasia amounts to cruel and degrading treatment and that cruelty is an evil which must be avoided so far as possible. They argue that in circumstances where there is no reasonable prospect of meaningful recovery, considerations of commonsense and compassion demand that patients should be allowed a merciful release from prolonged and useless suffering. Further, as noted earlier, reliance on the passive form of euthanasia will not necessarily guarantee a swift and painfree death. If active voluntary euthanasia were legalized, doctors would be able to comply with a patient's request to die and the merciful and kindly treatment of patients would be promoted.

A potential conflict exists between the duty to prevent cruelty and relieve suffering, and the doctor's duty to save life. This conflict can best be resolved by holding that where a patient has voluntarily requested active euthanasia, the greater duty is to accede to the patient's request and avoid unnecessary suffering. Although legalizing active voluntary euthanasia would not totally eliminate all pain and suffering associated with terminal illness, it would significantly reduce the burden on patients by placing the power to end a miserable existence under the patient's own control. This empowerment of the individual may in turn improve the quality of the remaining time, and may in fact assist the patient to live longer, confident in the knowledge that assistance is available if needed.

The argument from prevention of suffering and cruelty has been more positively stated by Kohl who has advocated the principle of 'beneficent euthanasia' (see Kohl, M, *'The Morality of Killing: Sanctity of Life, Abortion and Euthanasia* (London, 1974) 106). Kohl argues that active euthanasia is 'kind' treatment, and since society and its members have a *prima facie* obligation to treat members kindly, it follows that beneficent euthanasia is a *prima facie* obligation. It should be noted that Kohl supports not only active voluntary euthanasia but also non-voluntary euthanasia in some circumstances. Nevertheless, the value of Kohl's contribution to the debate has been to highlight that active euthanasia is a means of minimizing suffering and maximizing kind and loving treatment of patients. However, for the reasons outlined above, the notion of a *prima facie* obligation to provide euthanasia must be rejected, at least in so far as it implies that a *duty* is cast upon any particular individual to perform an act of euthanasia.

Opponents of euthanasia have sought to undermine arguments based upon the prevention of cruelty and need for merciful treatment by suggesting that the concepts of 'mercy' and 'prevention of cruelty' are flexible, capable of differing interpretations, and that this may, with time, result in an ever-increasing category of candidates for active euthanasia (eg Dyck, A, 'A Good Samaritan Ideal and Beneficent Euthanasia: Conflicting Views of Mercy' (1975) 42 Linacre Q 176, 180–1). Further, it is claimed that the concern of proponents is often not with the pain and suffering of the patient but of the family, relatives, and friends who must witness that patient's last days. However, these arguments have no validity in the present context of a proposal for active *voluntary* euthanasia which is firmly based on the fundamental principle of self-determination. The crucial issue is not whether the doctors believe it would be merciful to terminate life, or the need to relieve the understandable anguish of loved ones, but whether the patient seeks active euthanasia as a release from his or her suffering.

D. Promotion of Human Dignity

Closely related to the foregoing arguments based on self-determination and the prevention of cruelty is the argument that legalization of active voluntary euthanasia is necessary in order to promote human dignity. Proponents argue that the notion of human dignity demands that individuals have control over significant life decisions, including the choice to die, and that this control is acknowledged and respected by others. This argument is well encapsulated by Fletcher where he states that 'to prolong life uselessly, while the personal qualities of freedom, knowledge, self-possession and control, and responsibility are sacrificed, is to attack the moral status of a person (*'Morals and Medicine'*, (Princetown, New Jersey, 1979) at 191).

Advances in medical technology have greatly increased the capacity of the medical profession to prolong life. In many cases, however, death can be merely forestalled and patients may face the prospect of a prolonged and agonizing death. For many patients, the principal fear is not of pain or even death itself, but of loss of control of bodily and mental functions and the resulting helplessness and dependence on others – in short the depersonalization of the dying. Patients may understandably wish to spare themselves and their loved ones the indignity of a prolonged death and creeping mental and physical deterioration. Indeed, it is this concern for the circumstances of one's dying that has largely fuelled the campaign for 'death with dignity' and has led to the introduction in some jurisdictions of 'natural death' legislation giving legal effect to living wills and legislation providing for the appointment of enduring powers of attorney to make health care decisions.

The present law permits passive euthanasia, but this will not guarantee a patient a humane and dignified death. On the contrary, a 'natural death' achieved by the refusal of treatment may be particularly unpleasant and undignified. According to proponents, preservation of human dignity can only be assured with the acceptance of active voluntary euthanasia, and the recognition of the liberty of the individual to determine the manner and timing of his or her death...

E. What is Morally Right Should be Made Legally Permissible

Another argument advanced by some proponents, is that since active voluntary euthanasia is acknowledged by many to be *morally* right, it should be made *legally* permissible. In furtherance of this argument, attention is drawn to the conflicting demands placed on individual doctors faced with a request for active euthanasia; on the one hand, the desire to act mercifully and relieve the patient's suffering and on the other, the concern to be law-abiding and avoid violation of the criminal law. Proponents argue that this places doctors in an intolerable situation and that society has a duty to make legally permissible conduct that is merciful and widely recognized as morally right.

It is certainly true that despite the forceful objections of some commentators, there has been widespread support from a variety of sources for the view that in certain circumstances, active voluntary euthanasia is morally justified. Subject to possible negative consequences which may flow from the legalization of active voluntary euthanasia, which will be dealt with below, a strong argument can be made that the law should reflect prevailing morality...

One possible counter-argument which will be dealt with more fully in the context of the case against legalization is that an important distinction exists between the morality of the individual case and the appropriateness of developing a public policy permitting active voluntary euthanasia. In fact, many opponents of legalization are prepared to concede the morality of active voluntary euthanasia in exceptional circumstances, but vigorously reject the introduction of legislation to cover such cases which would institutionalize the practice. The validity of this position in turn depends on an assessment of the practical objections to the legalization of active voluntary euthanasia which will be undertaken later in this chapter.

F. Formalize Current Practices

A further argument in support of the legalization of active voluntary euthanasia is that we need to formalize existing practices. There are two separate aspects of this argument: first, the argument that since the practice of active euthanasia already occurs, we need to institutionalize and regulate that practice with the adoption of proper safeguards in order to protect against the risk of abuse; and secondly, that the practice should be legalized to overcome existing discrepancies between legal theory and practice. Both of these arguments will now be considered in turn.

The need to regulate and protect against abuse

... [A]vailable evidence ... indicates that some doctors, at least, are already involved in the practice of active voluntary euthanasia even though this contravenes the criminal law. As many of the opponents of legalization have pointed out, the mere fact that the law is being broken is not of itself a valid ground for legal change. There are, however, certain difficulties inherent in the present situation which call for a re-evaluation of the prohibition of active voluntary euthanasia. Because the practice is presently illegal, it is performed covertly leaving little opportunity for consultation or regulation. It was also noted that even where fellow doctors became aware of a doctor's involvement in active voluntary euthanasia, they are likely to maintain secrecy and not report their colleague to the legal authorities. Decisions are more likely to be made on the basis of the participating doctor's own conscience and his or her willingness to take risks rather than the compelling nature of the patient's request. Particularly in light of the paternalistic nature of the medical profession, this may result in a situation where active euthanasia is performed by a doctor on the basis of what he or she perceives to be the patient's best interests, but without the express consent of the patient. There is, in fact already evidence which suggests that in the hidden practice of euthanasia as it exists, active euthanasia is not always performed at the request of the patient (eg the findings of Stevens, C, and Hassan, R, 'Management of Death, Dying and Euthanasia: Attitudes and Practices of Medical Practitioners in South Australia' (1994) 20 J Med Ethics 41). This is clearly contrary to the fundamental principle of self-determination and the requirement of voluntariness in the practice of active euthanasia. Further, since some doctors may be more willing than others to contravene the criminal law, the option of active euthanasia is not presently available to all patients, thereby causing potential injustice to some.

The essence of the proponents' argument is that if the practice already occurs, it is preferable for it to be legalized and brought out into the open in order that appropriate safeguards can be implemented to protect against abuse. There is good reason to believe that the risk of abuse and idiosyncratic decision-making would be reduced if a form of active voluntary euthanasia was legally available and the need for secrecy was overcome. If a lawful means is established for doctors assisting patients to die which, subject to certain conditions, provides an immunity from criminal liability, it stands to reason that doctors would prefer to seek the protection of the law by complying with its terms rather than take the risk of incurring serious criminal liability. Legalization of active voluntary euthanasia would promote open discussion of the issues and would thereby contribute to the quality of decision-making. Legalization would also ensure that active voluntary euthanasia would be an option available to all patients subject only to the right of a doctor to decline to become involved in the practice. Patient self-determination would thereby be promoted.

The need to overcome discrepancies between legal theory and practice
The second part of the proponents' arguments concerns the need to overcome existing discrepancies between legal theory and practice. Proponents point out that even though there is evidence to suggest that some doctors are engaged in the practice of active voluntary euthanasia which constitutes murder, if one has regard to the realities of the law in practice, it is unlikely that a doctor would be prosecuted, or if prosecuted, that he or she would be convicted. From this premise, they argue that the law in operation in effect condones the practice of active voluntary euthanasia. Proponents go on to assert that the present disparity between legal theory and the law as it operates in practice is unsatisfactory, engendering cynicism and disrespect for the law (this is demonstrated through the prosecution and conviction of Dr Cox). Further, it is argued, that whilst it is most unlikely that a doctor would be prosecuted and convicted, there is, nevertheless, no guarantee of this; indeed, the very informality of the present situation invites arbitrary and capricious results. Moreover, it is argued to be unsatisfactory that doctors who are acting *bona fide* and at the request of the patient should be exposed to the risk of prosecution. Thus, proponents are of the view that active voluntary euthanasia ought to be legalized in order to close the gap between legal theory and practice, and to ensure that doctors who perform active voluntary euthanasia are not vulnerable to criminal prosecution.

The problems which stem from the present disparity between law and practice are serious and constitute good cause to re-evaluate the present criminal law prohibition on active voluntary euthanasia. A strong case can be made out that legalization of the practice is necessary in order to overcome these difficulties and to provide legal guidance for the making of medical and ethical decisions regarding the termination of life.

Arguments have also been advanced against legislating to overcome the present discrepancies between law and practice. It has, for example, been argued that notwithstanding the occasional contravention of the law, the existing prohibition plays an important part at the macro or social level in preventing many more cases of active euthanasia, a significant proportion of which would be non-voluntary and which would not in any event be legalized. Significantly, though, those who seek to make these arguments are not suggesting that in all cases where the prohibition on active voluntary euthanasia is ignored the law should be invoked to prosecute; they acknowledge that although conduct may be illegal, in some circumstances at the level of the individual case prosecution is inappropriate....

For present purposes, it can be stated that there is no evidence that the legalization of active voluntary euthanasia would lead to an increase in active non-voluntary or involuntary euthanasia; these forms of euthanasia are currently prohibited by the criminal law and would remain so.

G. Public Demand and Support for Active Voluntary Euthanasia

The case for legalization is further bolstered by evidence of growing public demand and support for active voluntary euthanasia. Opinion polls have been periodically conducted in the United Kingdom, the USA, Canada, and Australia to gauge public attitudes to whether active voluntary euthanasia ought to be legalized, and the results of these polls indicate increasing public support for its legalization (Waller, S, 'Trends in Public Acceptance of Euthanasia Worldwide' (1986) 1 Euthanasia Rev 33).

Opponents have been quick to challenge the relevance of such polls. At one level, they are critical of the manner in which the polls are conducted, particularly the way in which questions are framed (BMA Working Party report '*Euthanasia: Report of a Working Party to Review the British Medical Association's Guidance on Euthanasia*' (London, 1988) 46). It has also been argued that care needs to be taken with how such polls are to be interpreted. Attention has been drawn to inconsistencies within the same surveys and to the fact, in the light of the

US citizen-initiated referendum experience, that poll results have not always been an accurate predictor of legislative outcomes (Somerville, 'The Song of Death: The Lyrics of Euthanasia' (1993) 9 J Contemp Health Law & Policy 1, at 21). More fundamentally, however, some opponents have challenged the relevance of opinion polls in shaping law and public policy, arguing that it is not necessarily appropriate to base the law on the opinion of the majority. (BMA '*Euthanasia*' (supra)). There is, they argue, no guarantee that the opinions polled are based on an informed understanding of the issues, and even if opinions are informed and valid, opponents question whether the moral worth of an argument is to be judged by the number of those who subscribe to it.

Apart from the opinion polls, further evidence of public support and demand for legalization of active voluntary euthanasia is to be found in the emergence and growth in all jurisdictions of voluntary euthanasia societies actively campaigning for reform of the law in this area. Moreover, the issue of active voluntary euthanasia has increasingly been brought before the public by the media, and the community response has generally been favourable.

Whilst it is, admittedly, very difficult accurately to assess the state of public opinion, available evidence regarding opinion polls and the growth of the voluntary euthanasia movement would appear to indicate that there is significant and increasing public demand and support for legalization. Since the role of the law is, at least in part, to meet the real needs of the community, evidence of public demand and support for legalization of active voluntary euthanasia can only operate to strengthen the case for reform. More detailed consideration will be given to the relevance of public opinion and the role of the law later in this chapter.

Another consideration which should be noted concerns the implications of a legalized form of active voluntary euthanasia for mercy killings generally. Mercy killings or assisted suicides in the family context arise quite frequently, often in circumstances where a loved one has persistently begged for assistance to die. If active voluntary euthanasia were an option legally available in such circumstances, it would be likely to reduce the occurrence of such family mercy killings which are inevitably performed inexpertly, often by crude and undignified means, and result in serious criminal liability for the mercy killer, although in many cases, mitigated by the leniency of the criminal justice system. Clearly it is preferable to ensure that where possible, a professional medical assessment is made and that the patient's death is brought about in accordance with specified safeguards for the performance of active voluntary euthanasia.

In large part the arguments against voluntary euthanasia mirror those advanced against doctor-assisted suicide and are a mixture of the principled and the pragmatic.

The principled arguments are canvassed by the Linacre Centre in its submission to the House of Lords Select Committee on Medical Ethics and reproduced in L Gormally (ed) *Euthanasia, Clinical Practice and the Law* (1994).

L Gormally (ed) *Euthanasia, Clinical Practice and the Law* (1994)

1. Sanctity of Life and Autonomy

Central to the concerns of the Select Committee are the questions: What may justify decisions and courses of conduct intended to bring about a person's death? And: Can such decisions and conduct be justified by either the wishes or the best interests of the person to be killed? These questions are nowadays apt to give rise to talk of a conflict between respect for the sanctity of human life and respect for autonomy (self-determination). Accordingly, it seems appropriate to begin with a consideration of the significance and grounding of these moral requirements and of their precise implications for certain central issues in medical practice.

1.1 Justice and the Sanctity of Life

1.1.1. The Sanctity of Life

In the Christian tradition the idea of the sanctity of life was employed exclusively of *human* life, to assert its inviolability, ie the entitlement of any human being to protection from unjust attack. So employed the idea connotes the specific grounds for such inviolability, namely that human life possesses an intrinsic dignity and value because created by God in his own image (Genesis 1:26) for the distinctive destiny of sharing in God's own life. A significant body of theological reflection on this revealed doctrine analysed the meaning of the image of God (imago Dei) in terms of the distinctive *capacity for rational existence* inherent in man's nature. It is in the nature of human beings to possess the capacity to develop both the ability to understand what is truly good and the ability to be moved by the desire for what is good. The authentic development of these abilities can lead us into a life of self-giving love which mirrors the very life of God: being made in the image (imago) of God, we are able to acquire his likeness (similitudo), an achievement which is the proper fulfilment of a human life.

Traditional understanding of the sanctity of human life, set in its original theological context, may be summarised in three points:

(1) The notion of the sanctity of life explained why certain reasons for killing human beings were inadmissible precisely because incompatible with the distinctive dignity human beings possess. Allowing for certain justifications of killing which were thought compatible with recognition of human dignity, the core of the principle of the sanctity of human life was formulated in the requirement that one ought never intentionally to kill the innocent (that is, one ought never to adopt any course of action or omission intended to terminate the life of an innocent human being).

(2) The distinctive dignity of human beings belongs to them in virtue of a radical capacity inherent in their nature. Since it belongs to them in virtue of their *nature* it belongs to all human beings equally.

(3) The rational abilities that human beings characteristically develop (in virtue of the radical natural capacity for such development) may be exercised in ways which are consistent or inconsistent with the fulfilment which is proper to human beings. To choose and to act in ways which are inconsistent with our proper fulfilment is to choose and to act at variance with the *point* of the radical capacity in virtue of which we possess dignity. But to act in ways at variance with human dignity is not to lose human dignity: for there remains the ability to repent of bad choices and to give a right direction to a hitherto disordered life.

1.1.2 Sanctity of Life, Human Dignity and Justice

In modern Western societies the theological understanding of human dignity has been transformed into secularised doctrines of the equal dignity of all citizens, doctrines which are the basis of what is sometimes called the 'politics of universalism', which insists on the *equal* basic rights and entitlements of citizens. Secularised doctrines of human dignity need to provide (a) some account of what underpins the claim that human beings possess dignity, and (b) some account of what is required if choice and action are to be consistent with human dignity. In what follows some of the accounts which are on offer in our society will be assessed with particular reference to the adequacy of the answers they offer to the question of when killing is justified. A correct answer to this question is clearly fundamental to an understanding of justice in society, and to the criminal law, since protection from being unjustifiably killed is a precondition of enjoying whatever rights an individual may have.

1.1.3 Contemporary denials that human worth and dignity belong to all human beings.

The traditional belief in equal human dignity, both in its religious and secularised versions, is denied by a number of influential voices in our society. The understandings they offer of the basis for attributions of human dignity entail that dignity does not belong to all human beings. Broadly speaking, possession of human dignity is said by these thinkers to depend on two requirements: (a) on a human being having developed presently exercised psychological abilities for understanding, choice and rational communication; and (b) on a human being actually exercising such abilities in the enjoyment of an acceptable quality of life. The precise relevance of the first requirement is variously explained.

1.1.3(i) A characteristic explanation of the unequal value of human lives

A number of thinkers begin from the assertion that human beings are not equal in possessing basic dignity (and the value such dignity imports); they regard belief in the equal and distinctive dignity of human beings as a manifestation of an irrational prejudice (sometimes labelled 'speciesism'). Rather, they say, a human life has value only in so far as the person whose life it is is in a position to value things and projects and activities and does value them. This means that if one does not possess the developed mental abilities to make it possible for things to seem valuable to one then there is no account one can give of one's life having value. Human beings who do not possess the mental capacities to make things better *to them* do not *in themselves* matter.

On this account a human being can *give* worth and dignity to his life in so far as he is able to maintain a sense of things and projects being worthwhile and valuable. The corollary of this account of what it is for a human life to have value is that those lacking the mental abilities to confer value on their own lives must depend on others to attach value to their lives. This means, for example, that if those one would normally expect to value the life of an unborn child (the child's parents) or the life of a senile parent (his or her children) do not themselves account that life valuable, then not only is there unlikely to be a social basis for treating that life as valuable, but there is no account to be given of its value.

1.1.3.(ii) Warnock and Dworkin

The requirement that a human being possesses presently exercisable abilities in order to possess dignity or distinctive value underlies the distinction Mary Warnock makes between 'simply being alive' and 'the specifically human consciousness of having a life to lead'. Only those enjoying such consciousness, and having the abilities responsibly to lead their lives, possess a distinctive value; and it is only the possession of that consciousness which explains the gravity of killing certain human beings. For humans with some idea of having lives of their own to live, for which they are responsible, 'dying, or being killed, is a different matter from the mere cessation of life'. Those, on the other hand, who are 'simply alive', who have merely 'biological life', cannot have lives with distinctive significance, value or dignity (Mary Warnock 'The Uses of Philosophy' Oxford: Blackwell Publishers 1992, at pp 22–23).

Despite immediate appearances, a similar distinction and a similar conclusion are also basic to Ronald Dworkin's more complex reflections on human worth and dignity and his explanation of why there should be extensive liberty for medicalised killing of innocent human beings. Professor Dworkin claims that almost all citizens have a shared ideal of wishing to honour the conviction that human life is sacred. He himself speaks of human life being intrinsically valuable and sacred, and formally rejects the view that nothing is valuable unless someone wants it or needs it to get what he wants (Ronald Dworkin, 'Life's Dominion' London: Harper Collins 1993, p 69). But he also considers that one reasonable 'interpretation' of this value and sacredness of human life is the 'liberal' view that 'life's inherent value ... depends on the intrinsic importance of human creative investment' in it; that is, on what people 'make of their own lives' so that the life which is sacred and inviolable is not 'biological life' but the 'human life ... created ... by personal choice, training, commitment and decision' (ibid at pp 157, 93). So Dworkin's own (liberal) view is that a person suffering from Alzheimer's dementia

> is no longer capable of the acts or attachments that can give it [life] value. Value cannot be poured into a life from the outside; it must be generated by the person whose life it is, and this is no longer possible for him. (*ibid* at p 230.)

On Dworkin's view, while some locate the 'transcendentally important source of ... sacred value' in 'biological life', others (like himself) think the source of that value lies in the exercisable abilities, especially for rational control of one's life, in virtue of which people can give the shape and significance they wish to their lives.

It is clear, then, that Dworkin's talk about the 'shared ideal of sanctity of life' is *practically* empty. The ideal can guide no one's deliberations until it is given content by 'interpretation'; the interpretations which ground competing claims about right conduct and just law are *contradictory*; and Dworkin's conclusions coincide with the position favoured by Warnock. The contest which he professed to expel with his talk of consensus about life's sacredness returns with undeniable vigour in the struggle between the thesis (which he dubs 'conservative' but which in many periods and cultures has been recognised as radical and transforming) that human life has dignity even in the most undeveloped human beings or in those severely disabled by disease or decrepitude, and the thesis (which he approvingly dubs 'liberal') which accords to the relatively powerful lethal dominion over the relatively weak. This is a struggle in which the law simply cannot be neutral without abdicating its claim to uphold basic justice, the state's most fundamental duty to protect the lives of innocent citizens against deliberate extinction at the hands of others.

One does not have to rely on religious premises to see that the understanding of human worth advocated by Baroness Warnock and Professor Dworkin, precisely because it is a direct attack on the principle of the basic equality-in-dignity of human beings, is radically subversive of justice. A secularised doctrine of human dignity needs to be consistent with our fundamental intuitions about justice.

1.1.4 The Basis of Human Dignity and Justice

What are the implications for justice of the kind of understanding of the worth and dignity of human life proposed by Warnock and Dworkin and similar thinkers who would like to see a radical revision of our homicide laws? Common to their positions is the requirement (explicit or implicit) that human beings possess *presently exercisable abilities* in order to be counted subjects of justice, and specifically to be counted among those entitled not to be killed intentionally without just reason. For such exercisable abilities are necessary if one is to find value in objects or projects, or to entertain some idea or have a life of one's own for which one is responsible (Warnock), or if one is to be well placed 'to make something' of one's life, thus having a 'life in earnest' whose 'sacredness' might count for something in any competition with the 'investments' which someone else has made in his own life (Dworkin).

The rational abilities necessary to these activities are various, and come in varying degrees in human beings. If actual possession of such abilities is a necessary condition of the claim to be treated justly, questions will have to be faced about precisely *which* abilities must be possessed, and how developed they must be before one enjoys this claim to be treated justly. And these questions could be answered only by *choosing* which to count as the relevant abilities and precisely how developed they must be to count. But any such line-drawing exercise is necessarily arbitrary. A distinction between A and B, where A and B fall on either side of a line determining some minimal level of proximate capacity for the exercise of an ability, will not admit of reasoned defence when what is at issue is whether A and B are subjects of justice. If A qualifies for just treatment, B will fail to qualify even though there is very little difference in the degree to which he possesses the relevant abilities.

Arbitrary choices may be reasonable and unavoidable in determining some entitlements (such as the requirement that one must have been a member of a club for three years in order to enjoy certain benefits). But if one's understanding of human worth and dignity commits one to being arbitrary about who are to be treated justly (ie about who are the very *subjects* of justice) it is clear that one lacks what is recognisable as a framework of justice. For it is incompatible with our fundamental intuitions about justice that we should determine who are the subjects of justice by arbitrary choice. The need for a non-arbitrary understanding of who are the subjects of justice requires us to *assume* that *just treatment is owing to all human beings in virtue of their humanity.*

This indispensable assumption is also intrinsically reasonable. It is true that the distinctive dignity and value of human life are *manifested* in those specific exercises of developed rational abilities in which we achieve some share in such human goods as truth, beauty, justice, friendship and integrity. But the necessary rational abilities are acquired in virtue of an underlying or radical capacity, *given with our nature as human beings,* for developing precisely such abilities. Yet it should be clear that the dynamic development of this radical natural capacity is not directed to the acquisition of rational abilities for them to be exercised in just any fashion. Our abilities to know and choose are not properly exercised by, for example, believing falsehood or choosing to act unjustly, any more than our abilities to see and to walk are properly exercised in double-vision and tripping over obstacles. The nature in virtue of which we come to acquire rational abilities has its proper fulfilment then, in exercises of rational abilities in which we recognise worth and dignity. But if it is characteristic of the nature of human beings to acquire abilities which are properly exercised in ways which are inherently valuable, then it is reasonable to hold that there is an inherent value or dignity in the nature we share in common, and seriously unreasonable (and radically subversive of justice) to judge that the lives of some human beings lack inherent value because those human beings lack certain presently exercisable psychological abilities.

1.1.5 Dualism and the false valuation of human life

It is clear enough from the brief descriptions offered above that Warnock's and Dworkin's accounts of which human lives possess worth rest on contrasting what they term the condition of 'simply being alive' or possessing mere 'biological life' with the condition involved in 'having a life' (on which worth depends). Discussing obligations to patients in a persistent vegetative state in his essay 'The Right to Death' Dworkin writes:

> ... nothing in the idea that life has intrinsic importance ... can justify a policy of keeping permanently comatose people alive. The worth of their lives – the character of the lives they have led ... cannot be improved just by keeping the bodies they used to inhabit technically alive. ('The Right to Death', 'The New York Review of Books' 31 January, 1991, pp 14–17, at p 17c.)

Here we have a contrast between, on the one hand, a personal life (a life which a person has consciously led, to which value attaches), and, on the other, the ongoing biological life of a body which for some stretch of its existence may be inhabited by a person ('may be', because according to some of these thinkers some human bodies may never have truly 'personal' inhabitants).

The dualism left clear traces in the judgements in *Airedale NHS Trust v Bland*, in which a distinction was made between Tony Bland himself and his body; eg 'his spirit has left him and all that remains is the shell of his body' (Brown P); 'his body is alive, but he has no life ... He is alive but has no life at all' (Hoffmann LJ, consciously echoing Dworkin).

A dualism 'which thinks of the body as if it were some kind of habitation for and instrument of the real person, is defended by few philosophers ... It renders inexplicable the unity in complexity which one experiences in everything one consciously does. It speaks as if there were two things ... a non-bodily person and a non-personal living body. But neither of these can one recognise as oneself. One's living body is intrinsic, not merely instrumental, to one's personal life. Each of us has a human life (not a vegetable life plus an animal life plus a personal life); when it is flourishing that life includes all one's vital functions including speech, deliberation and choice; when gravely impaired it lacks some of those functions without ceasing to be the life of the person so impaired.' (J M Finnis, 'Bland Crossing the Rubicon?' (1993) LQR 329–37.)

Living human beings are organisms. On a non-dualistic view the unified life of the human organism is throughout *human*. There is not some separable organic substrate, the life of which is 'purely biological', and to which some personal subject, whose life is uniquely manifested in psychological activities, may be attached. The life that is exhibited in thinking is the *very same life* that is manifested in respiration and heartbeat. To cease to be able to think is to lose an ability, not to lose one's life.

The rejection of (anthropological) dualism is important to recovering an appreciation of the inherent dignity of every human life. There is a fundamental conflict between the position of those who acknowledge a value and dignity in human beings *given with their humanity* and the position of those who think that value and dignity belong to a life *only* in so far as a person is in control of his life and can give it a valued meaning. The latter position is not reasonable. It fails to acknowledge the value of the radical natural *capacity to develop abilities* to find meaning in life, and the dignity of the nature in which that radical capacity inheres. And it fails to acknowledge that the developed abilities find their fulfilment not in just any way of life which one can be said to be in control of but in a way of life in which one submits, for example, to the claims of truth and justice. And one is not in control of what counts as true and just. To attach value and dignity exclusively to autonomous control is to have blinded oneself to the true source of the basic value and dignity in a human life.

It is of considerable importance to note one implication of the inseparability of recognising someone's human dignity and recognising his status as a subject of justice. Since denial of the former entails denial of the latter, our practical reasoning should never involve us in judgements which amount to the denial of the inherent worth or dignity of a human being. The basic human dignity of the other is an *ineliminable* consideration when we deliberate about how we should treat him.

1.1.6 Justice and the Sanctity of Life Ethic Recovered

1.1.4 and 1.1.5 have argued for the necessity and reasonableness of attributing a fundamental worth and dignity to *every* living human being if we are to have a defensible understanding of justice. In so doing we have recovered from contemporary criticism, without benefit of religious premises, the basic truth about human worth and dignity which shapes the content of a sanctity of life ethic.

1.2 Justice and Killing

1.2.1. Killing for reasons incompatible with recognition of human dignity

Anyone who causes the death of another human being with intent to do so (ie who intentionally kills by 'act' or omission) acts on the basis that there is some reason for thinking that the person killed should have died. Quite generally what one does intentionally is identified by reference to one's *chosen purpose* in acting (under that description which makes clear its perceived desirability) and the *means* which are chosen (under that description which makes clear their perceived relevance to the achievement of one's purpose). Both of these must feature in any adequate statement of why one is acting, ie in any adequate statement of one's *reasons* for doing precisely what one is doing.

It is clear that one can intentionally bring about someone's death by an omission which is intended to bring about death: one can want someone dead and one can bring it about that he dies precisely by choosing to omit to do what one *could* (and otherwise would) have done to keep him alive. When what one omits with such an intention to terminate life is not merely something one could have done but something one had a *duty* to do, then the law has rightly regarded such intentional omissions bringing about death as murder (*R v Gibbins and Proctor* (1918) 13 Criminal Appeal Reports 134). There is no morally significant *general* distinction to be made between killing and letting die, and any attempt to rely on such a distinction is intellectually perilous. One may let a patient die for perfectly sound reasons (see 2.2 below), but one may also 'let a patient die' for unacceptable reasons, including the absolutely unacceptable reason that one wants (however reluctantly) to hasten his death.

Both omissions contrary to duty which intentionally bring about someone's death and actions which intentionally cause death raise two questions which the person responsible should answer:
– Why was it that X should die?
– What entitled you to bring about the death?
Distinguishing between acceptable and unacceptable answers to the first question is the most fundamental task in determining what is justifiable killing.

Since it is in virtue of the worth and dignity which attaches to our humanity that we establish to *whom* justice is owing, recognition of that dignity is the precondition of human beings treating each other properly. That being so, any purported justification of killing must at the very least be *consistent* with recognising the dignity of every human being. What is *absolutely* excluded, therefore, is bringing about another's death for *reasons* incompatible with recognising the dignity of the person killed.

As we have already remarked, at the beginning of this subsection, the relevant reasons are identified in the description of one's intended course of action which identifies the perceived desirability of one's goal/purpose and the perceived relevance to one's goal of one's chosen means.

This general account of which causations of death are absolutely excluded by recognition of the basic worth and dignity of every human life (viz those *intentional* causations decided upon for reasons incompatible with the recognition of human dignity) makes intelligible the *moral* significance of the distinction between intentional (intended) and (merely) foreseen causation of death. When death is merely foreseen, one's causing it does not feature among the reasons one has for acting, and so is not chosen whether as end or as means (and thus is not intended). Many worthwhile activities, entirely consistent with recognition of human dignity, would be made impossible if all foreseeable causation of death were forbidden (examples would be: high-risk surgery, the giving of opiates for pain control in doses likely to hasten death, high-risk sports).

It is clear that one of the motives of those who seek to show that there is no morally significant difference between intention and foresight is to make a prohibition of the intentional causation of death seem as unreasonable as an absolute prohibition of foreseen causation of death would evidently be. It should now be clear why an absolute prohibition can justifiably cover at least some intentional causations of death, namely all those the reasons for which are incompatible with recognising the basic dignity of the persons to be killed. To allow such killings would be to grant that human beings may be treated as though their dignity were irrelevant to how one chose to act towards them.

1.2.2 Euthanasia: killing incompatible with recognition of human dignity

In this section it will be argued that the core reason a person proposing to carry out euthanasia would have to identify, to make intelligible what he sees to be the desirability of causing death, is a reason for action incompatible with recognising the dignity of the person to be killed.

It ought to be evident that the killing of a person for advantage or convenience is inconsistent with recognition of that person's dignity, for the person killed is certainly not treated as of equal dignity with those advantaged by his death. Much advocacy of non-voluntary euthanasia is motivated by the thought that it is advantageous to others, in relieving them of the burdens of care for the handicapped and senile.

Purported justifications for voluntary euthanasia, however, as also for much non-voluntary euthanasia, speak of it as a *benefit* or a *good* for the patient. If the reason for saying that death is desirable *qua* benefit to the patient is to be consistent with recognising the basic worth and dignity of the patient's life, then it cannot rest on tacitly assuming (or seeking to show) that no positive value attaches to that life. That assumption *would* be made if the reason for saying that death would benefit the patient were that it would terminate a condition of negative value, depriving the patient of nothing of positive value. Justifications of that type, if they have any place at all for recognising a value attaching to our humanity (and many do not), in effect treat it as a *commensurable* and therefore *eliminable* value in calculating the overall 'worth' of a life. But to treat the basic human dignity of some human beings as an eliminable value is to proceed by denying to those human beings their status as subjects of justice

All standard justifications of voluntary euthanasia, in so far as they represent it as a benefit to the patient killed, do so in a way which is inconsistent with recognition of the basic dignity of every human being. Here are four standard patterns of justification:

(1)   One justification represents human existence as no more than the possibility of enjoying goods. A human life is a benefit in so far as it comes up to a standard of normality in the goods available in it. But if it sinks below that standard and is overtaken by evils it is overall an evil. Deliberately to end a life in that condition (if the patient asks to have it ended) is to benefit the patient.
Clearly this justification of voluntary euthanasia as a beneficial choice begins from the premise that our mere existence has no worth or value as such. So the justification is not consistent with recognising the dignity of every human being.

(2)   Sometimes an attempted justification of voluntary euthanasia will concede that human life has value, but then argue that this value can be eliminated by the realities of suffering. But if one treats the value attaching to our humanity as eliminable countervailing disvalues one denies that basic dignity belongs to every human being whatever his or her condition.

(3)   Some justifications of voluntary euthanasia start from the premise that human lives do not essentially possess a basic dignity and value. What gives a life value, it is claimed, is the ability of the person whose life it is to find value in projects, activities and relationships. Without a felt, *subjective* sense of worth and value a life lacks value. If a person is competent he is the only possible authority on whether he enjoys a subjective sense of value. If he soberly says he doesn't, his life lacks value. And those who lack presently exercisable abilities for finding value in their lives in consequence lack lives of value.
A justification of euthanasia which relies on the assumption that human lives do not *essentially* possess value straightforwardly denies the basic dignity of every human being.

(4)   Some proponents of voluntary euthanasia speak of recognising the dignity of the person to be killed while asserting that continued life is not in the interests of that person. But this is mystificatory rhetoric. If one says that someone's continued existence is not in the interests of that person one means that person would be better off dead, that the non-existence of that bodily person is of less disvalue than continued bodily existence. This

could be true only if continued existence is reckoned to have a negative value, for death itself can hardly be thought to have positive value. So this form of justification is inconsistent with recognition of the basic dignity of every human being.

1.3 Autonomy and Killing

It will be said that the above argument against euthanasia, both voluntary and non-voluntary, is narrow-minded in basing itself exclusively on a doctrine of equal human dignity. It will be argued that at least in respect of voluntary euthanasia there is a case to be answered in its favour based on a right to personal autonomy. As already noted, there is much talk of 'conflicting moral principles of the sanctity of life and the right to personal autonomy'. (See para 2 of Special Report (9 March 1993) from the Select Committee of the House of Lords on Medical Ethics, echoing observations in the Judgements in *Bland*), and of the need to balance their differing claims. A reasoned assessment of such talk must depend on what kind of claims in the name of autonomy are well-grounded, and more particularly on whether 'a right to personal autonomy' ever reasonably overrides what is required by recognition of human dignity. Something, therefore, needs to be said in general terms about autonomy and a 'right to personal autonomy', and about its relation to the normative constraints on killing imposed by recognition of human dignity.

1.3.1 Autonomy and a 'Right' to Personal Autonomy

The words 'autonomy' and 'autonomous' are used in respect of a capacity, a condition and a right.

To be autonomous, as the word implies, is to be self-governed or self-directed or self-determining in the conduct of one's life; that is the condition. 'Autonomy' is used of the capacity to be self-directed in the conduct of one's life. 'Respect for autonomy' involves respect at least for this capacity. 'A right to autonomy' must be a right to at least *some* exercise of the capacity for self-direction in one's life. But what exercise of the capacity? The answer we give to that question must surely depend on the understanding we have of the value of autonomy.

Some semi-popular talk about autonomy and the right to have one's autonomy respected seems to suggest that what people value is doing what they want (in the sense of acting on the wants, wishes and desires they *happen* to have) as distinct from having to do what someone else wants.

But it seems fairly clear that the ability to do what one *happens* to want to do is not sufficient for self-government in the conduct of one's life. Someone whose condition is one of wanton self-indulgence does what he happens to want to do. What is valued in the capacity for self-government is at the very least our ability to evaluate our desires and to act selectively in accordance with our evaluations.

But will action in accordance with *any* kind of evaluation count as an exercise of autonomy? Our answer to this question will depend on what we think the point of self-government or self-direction is.

The capacity for self-government is properly exercised and developed with a view to the flourishing or well-being of the person who possesses it, and of the communities to which that person properly belongs in friendship and justice. If so exercised it is indeed an aspect of that flourishing. In what way is it an aspect?

Human happiness or well-being is not left to be wholly a matter of luck, or of grace which does not require willing cooperation; what we make of ourselves (our character) makes an important difference to whether or not we flourish as human beings. And our characters are decisively shaped by our chosen actions: these do not merely bring about effects external to us, they also serve to form our dispositions. A person's exercise of choice will in this way inescapably make for well-being or misery in his life.

So there is a clear case for valuing human choice, and hence for valuing the exercise of autonomy, precisely in so far as it serves to form in us those dispositions which are conducive to human flourishing.

People differ in their views on how wide an exercise of the capacity for self-direction should be respected. One very important factor in determining those differing views is whether or not one believes there is human knowledge of moral truths, that is, knowledge of the objective requirements we need to meet if we are to flourish as human beings.

If there is such knowledge, then it is clear why we should value the exercise of choice in conformity with that knowledge: for evidently that would be an exercise of autonomy which makes for human flourishing. But it would not be obvious why we should value exercises of autonomy at variance with the objective requirements of human flourishing.

Still, if there is to be choice one has to allow not just for the possibility but also for the reality of erroneous choices. So, necessarily, respect for autonomy must leave scope for *some* erroneous choices. But it does not follow that any and every exercise of choice is to be respected. We need to bear in mind why this capacity is to be valued; and if our choices seriously undermine in us the capacity to flourish as human beings, and a *fortiori* if they aim to damage aspects of this capacity in others, there is no reason of moral principle why those choices should be respected.

1.3.2 Autonomy and the Justification of Voluntary Euthanasia

Can a right to autonomy be invoked to justify voluntary euthanasia? It is important to recognise how limited a role in justification the actual request to be killed can play. Certainly the mere fact of a request in itself provides little reason for a doctor to kill a patient. Can we envisage a doctor thinking it justifiable to kill a patient just because the patient has asked to be killed? Hardly. Indeed, we can envisage many circumstances in which doctors who are not opposed in principle to euthanasia would refuse requests; as when they think the request is prompted by an erroneous view of the prognosis, or by some relievable depression, or by circumstances which can be readily changed. Any doctor who feels that a given patient still has a worthwhile life to live will not accede to a request for euthanasia from that patient. *By contrast, it is precisely the judgement that a patient no longer has a worthwhile life which will seem to justify euthanasia.* The role of this judgement in justifying euthanasia is not altered by the different grounds a doctor may have for arriving at it. Sometimes it will seem true on the basis of evidence which the doctor can independently take stock of: pain, degeneration, depression, wretched circumstances. At other times the judgement will be clinched in the doctor's mind only by what the patient asserts: that his life is no longer worth living.

A doctor, minded to think that at bottom a human life can have value only if the person whose life it is consciously finds value in it, may well accept, in the presence of some corroborative evidence, a patient's judgement that his life has irrevocably lost value and dignity. But that fact about the doctor's background reasoning is not a ground for thinking that the doctor is not himself responsible for the judgement that this patient no longer has a worthwhile life. For it is *this* judgement which will make it appear to *him* that a choice to bring about the patient's death is a beneficent choice.

Notwithstanding, then, that the killing which carries out voluntary euthanasia is requested, the justification of that killing rests centrally on the contention that the patient no longer has a worthwhile life. *But precisely that contention is inconsistent with recognising the continuing worth and dignity of the patient's life.*

In any apparent conflict between, on the one hand, the requirement that we do not deny equal human dignity and respect for the sanctity of human life and, on the other, the putative claims of respect for autonomy, the principle of the sanctity of human life must always trump those claims. For recognition of equal human dignity is fundamental to recognition of all human beings as subjects of justice.

There is no authentic conflict between rightly respecting the sanctity of human life and rightly respecting autonomy. The exercise of human autonomy in giving shape, direction and character to a human life is not a source of value and dignity which is properly at *odds* with the fundamental source of human worth and dignity in human nature itself. For, as we saw (1.1.4), what makes it reasonable to recognise human nature as the source of our basic worth and dignity as human beings is the fact that our nature in its development is intrinsically directed to human fulfilment and human good. And what best makes sense of the ideal of respect for autonomy is the role played by free choice in the achievement of that fulfilment to which our nature is directed; for self-determining choice is integral to that achievement. But if the moral significance of autonomy is to be understood in that way, then the value of autonomy is derivative from, and reflective of, that which gives value to our humanity. So it should be clear that the claims of autonomy cannot properly extend to choices which are inconsistent with recognising the basic worth and dignity of every human being.

1.3.3 Autonomy and the Justification of Non-Voluntary Euthanasia

It is sometimes said that debility, degeneration and dependency experienced by those who have become permanently incompetent, or the undignified way in which (sometimes unavoidably) they are treated, are inconsistent with the meaning and character they had given to their lives while competent. It is then claimed, or insinuated, that this meaning and character have been the exclusive source of dignity in the lives of many such people so that their present condition should be recognised as completely depriving them of dignity. For this reason, therefore, it would be beneficent to put an end to their lives.

Sufficient has already been said to show that such a line of reasoning provides no defensible ground for euthanasia of the incompetent who were formerly competent. As many of those nurses and others who care for such persons know, and testify to by their dispositions and acts of solidarity, communion or friendship with them, these people, though sadly weakened or wounded and scarcely or no longer able to exercise their autonomy, remain the very same persons they always were. Their state is in a sense undignified, but it is *not an indignity* (of the kind inflicted upon people by demeaning actions). Right down to their deaths they continue to share in the radical equality-in-dignity of all human beings.

1.4 Sanctity of Life and Autonomy: Conclusion

The teaching of Christian tradition about the sanctity of life can be recast in secular terms as a doctrine of equal basic worth and dignity. This doctrine has to be assumed if there is to be a non-arbitrary understanding of who are the subjects of justice, but the intrinsic reasonableness of the assumption can be defended.

Since we must hold all human beings to possess an ineliminable worth and dignity if they are to be recognised as subjects of justice, any justification for killing incompatible with recognising that worth and dignity is inadmissible.

Justifications of voluntary and non-voluntary euthanasia as beneficent rely *essentially* on the judgement that, overall, the present life of the person to be killed is of negative value (not worthwhile). But such a judgement is incompatible with recognising the ineliminable worth and dignity of the person to be killed. Hence intentional killing (by act or omission) for euthanasiast reasons falls under the absolute prohibition of intentional killing of the innocent (itself the core requirement of respect for the sanctity of life).

Practical arguments against voluntary euthanasia centre on the argument of abuse, mistake and coercion of patients, and the dangers of a descent on a 'slippery slope' to involuntary euthanasia. It may be a significant difference that here, unlike the situation of physician-assisted suicide, the role of the doctor is that of the 'death dealing agent' and this may increase the opportunity for abuse, error and mistake. The impact upon the medical profession of being 'agents of death' is also raised and the adverse effect that is alleged to have on the doctor-patient relationship. We have seen many of these arguments already rehearsed by the House of Lords Select Committee on Medical Ethics (*supra*) when rejecting any change in the law (see further M Otlowski *Voluntary Euthanasia and the Common Law* (*op cit*) pp 218–249). In a wide-ranging discussion focusing upon the legislative initiative in the State of Washington (Initiative 119), but also drawing on the Dutch experience – where, as we shall see, voluntary euthanasia and physician-assisted suicide are permitted in certain circumstances – Professor Margaret Battin in an important article examines the arguments concerning the risk of abuse in some detail.

Margaret Battin 'Voluntary Euthanasia and the Risk of Abuse: Can We Learn Anything from the Netherlands?' (1992) 20 Law, Medicine and Health Care 133

In general, I think it is crucial to be as clear and forthright about the issue of abuse as possible, even if one supports, as I do, the legalization of aid-in-dying.

In doing so, one must answer two central questions:
1) Will there be abuse, and if so, precisely what kind?
2) Can abuse of this sort be prevented?

It is to the second of these questions that I will be particularly attentive here. In doing so, I shall consider only the possible effects of legalizing voluntary, active, physician-performed euthanasia and physician-assisted suicide, restricted to cases in which such help is requested by competent, terminally ill patients with less than 6 months to live – that is, I shall be considering only what Initiative 119 would have legalized – but some of the arguments will clearly apply to a wider range of possible legislation as well.

Slippery-slope arguments are designed to address the first of the two questions above: *Will there be abuse, and if so precisely what kind?* Since they are predictive empirical arguments intended to show that permitting a given practice will result in abuse, the principal strategy available to counter these arguments is to show that they fail to specify what causal mechanisms will be involved, what back-ground precedents would permit such erosion, and so on. Thus opponents of legalization warn of abuse in the future, pointing to alleged current abuse in the Netherlands as evidence; supporters of legalization, on the other hand, reply that claims about abuse in Holland are unsubstantiated or exaggerated and that there is little reason to think abuse would occur in the United States. One cannot fear an analogue of the Nazi holocaust, supporters of the legislation argue, for example, because even though there are local excrescences of antisemitic, anti-Black, and other racially prejudiced political activity, it is inconceivable that a country with such strong guarantees of civil rights could permit a large-scale extermination program. Thus the argument moves back and forth between opponents and supporters, however erratically; but it remains an essentially empirical argument about the potential consequences of legalization.

It is this argument which I would like to enter here. As I have often said elsewhere, I do not think there is any compelling argument in principle to be made against voluntary active euthanasia or physician-assisted suicide, at least in specific circumstances, and I believe that on the contrary control on one's own death as far as possible is a matter of fundamental human right. However, I also think that the warnings of potential abuse require much more sensitive and careful examination than either supporters or opponents of such legislation have generally given them. Indeed, I think it is morally responsible to advocate the legalization of euthanasia and assisted suicide only if one can conscientiously argue either that abuse would not occur or that it could be prevented, and it is on this project that I would like to embark here. Conversely, I also think it is morally responsible to oppose the legalization of euthanasia and assisted suicide, given the importance of the freedom to be suppressed, only if one can show with reasonable likelihood that abuse would occur and that it could not be prevented.

Thus either way, it is crucial to consider the issue of abuse, and this is an obligation that no party to the discussion, on either side, ought to evade; the burden of proof in establishing what the consequences of the proposed legislation would be falls, in this special case, on both sides. That persons have a basic, fundamental right to control as much as they wish and as much as is possible the timing and circumstances of their own death is a claim that I shall assume here, but this assumption does not relieve us of the obligation to consider the risk of abuse. After all, if the risks of abuse are great enough, this may entail that even basic, fundamental rights of persons should be curtailed. If on the other hand the risks of abuse turn out to be small or if abuse can be prevented, then it is morally imperative that persons' basic, fundamental right to control as much as possible the circumstances of their own dying be legally recognized.

Will abuse occur?

While euthanasia is presumably practiced clandestinely virtually everywhere else, it is openly practiced only in the Netherlands. Thus our principal source of empirical information about the potential for abuse where euthanasia is effectively legal must come from the violation of statutory law, punishable in principle by imprisonment, but the lower and supreme courts have developed a series of guidelines under which euthanasia is immune from prosecution. Thus it is effectively legal and openly practiced, and it is supported by a substantial majority of public opinion. Most Dutch hospitals now have protocols governing euthanasia, and many health-care institutions, including nursing homes and hospitals, also have developed publicly stated policies concerning whether they do or do not permit the practice.

The first nationwide study in Holland on euthanasia and other medical decisions at the end of life, prepared by a commission appointed by the Dutch government (the so-called Remmelink Commission), involved detailed interviews with 405 physicians from different disciples, a questionnaire mailed to the physicians of 7000 deceased persons, and a prospective survey in which physicians interviewed in part I gave information concerning every death in their practice (a total of 2250 deaths) during the six months after the interview. This study found that about 1.8 percent of total deaths per year in the Netherlands are the result of euthanasia with some form of physician involvement and that about 0.3 percent of deaths involve physician-assisted suicide. But it also reported that in 0.8 percent of all deaths 'drugs were administered with the explicit intention to shorten the patient's life, without the strict criteria for euthanasia being fulfilled,' and it is this that has been widely interpreted in the United States to mean that 1000 patients were killed against their will. While this is a clear misinterpretation of the data in the Dutch study, fair treatment of the issue of abuse must take account of both actual and conjectural evidence from Holland.

There are several further matters to be remembered in addressing the issue of abuse. First, judgments about abuse should in principle be comparative, weighing influences on choice, adjusted for the severity of outcome, against influences on other alternative choices. Would choices of euthanasia be more or less abused than, say, choices of high-risk surgery or choices to withhold or withdraw life-sustaining treatment? After all, any of these choices can lead to death, not only choices about euthanasia. Furthermore, judgments about abuse ought not to cloak judgments about outcomes; it cannot be assumed, without further argument, that – in the kind of case at issue here – influences on a choice for euthanasia are potentially abusive while influences on a choice to stay alive are not. It is also to be remembered that there is little theoretical agreement on just what constitutes abuse: is it a distortion of voluntariness, is it the violation of a person's interests, or what?

Finally, it is important to remember that the issue of whether abuse would occur is an issue about the outcomes of policy, not about idiosyncratic acts. In every society and with regard to every kind of social policy, unstable, psychopathic, or otherwise deranged individuals commit acts which clearly constitute abuses: nurses who randomly inject patients with fatal drugs, doctors who perform deliberately damaging, unwarranted operations on patients, anaesthetists who have sex with their patients on their operation tables. Such outlier cases will occur from time to time, regardless of the type of policies in effect. To be sure, one ought not be sanguine about the occurrence of such cases, but the real issue is not so much whether such outlier cases will occur – they will, in any country, with our without legislation – but whether the legislation itself would permit or encourage such cases on a more frequent, more accepted, more 'normal' basis. Thus, the question is whether the policies at issue – the legalization of active euthanasia and of assisted suicide – would engender an abusive pattern of practice, not whether a handful of isolated, marginal cases of abuse would occur from time to time. It is 'normal' patterns of abuse that the slippery slope arguments are properly concerned with: Would family members readily and routinely manipulate patients? Would physicians generally become callous about death? Would institutions regularly force patients into euthanasia or suicide in an effort to save costs? Would prejudice against racial, age, and handicapped groups further infect these practices?

While I have no doubt that some outlier cases of abuse would occur from time to time, I do not think the general answer to these questions is yes. Nor do I think euthanasia choices would be more abused than choices of high-risk surgery or of withholding or withdrawing life sustaining treatment. Nevertheless, I will assume the contrary for the purposes of this paper, since my real concern here is whether – if such abusive patterns might be tolerated or encouraged by legalizing euthanasia and suicide – there are effective ways of preventing abuse. This is not to assume that human nature is evil or that abuse is humanly inevitable; rather, it is to assume instead that different policies and the incentives and disincentives incorporated in policy can encourage or discourage quite different patterns of practice. Thus the question is, would the legalization of euthanasia and suicide, with or without safeguards such as those proposed by Hemlock [an American society in favour of voluntary euthanasia] or those already in place in Holland, engender abuse? If so, what sort, and can such abuse be prevented even if it would otherwise occur?

Types of possible abuse

Three conceptually distinct types of abuse can be identified among the scenarios that slippery-slope arguments portray: what we might call interpersonal abuse, professional abuse, and institutional abuse. Though they are conceptually distinct, we may expect that in practice they would often be closely intertwined. Although the parallels are not exact, they also invite three rather different sorts of solutions, that is, three rather different sorts of strategies for preventing such abuses from occurring.

1. Interpersonal abuse. Chief among the varieties of interpersonal abuse, one might expect, would be that occurring in familial solutions: the resentful or greedy spouse or other family member, who maneuvers a terminally ill patient now perceived as a burden into requesting euthanasia or assistance in suicide. Such pressures might be malevolent, the product of long years of hostility; or, perhaps more likely, they might be the product of the kind of emotional exhaustion familial caregivers often experience in attending to a patient with a lengthy, deteriorative terminal illness. 'All of your suffering could be over soon,' such a family member might be expected to say – not seeing that much of the suffering is not so much the patient's but his or her own. Familial messages supporting euthanasia or suicide can of course be given in an enormous variety of ways, both explicit or inexplicit, verbal and nonverbal, and they can be conveyed by a single individual family member or by a family as a whole.

Familial messages favoring euthanasia or suicide can be comparatively weak, involving suggestion or even the mere raising of the idea; they can be stronger, including what we might variously call recommendation, urging, 'talking into,' pleading, cajoling, remonstrating, and so on; and they can be a great deal stronger, including such tactics as threats, ultimatums, lies and so on. Not all family life is harmonious, and underlying pathology can often be exacerbated by the stresses a family member's terminal illness brings. 'All right, Granny, it's time to go' is a message we can imagine being conveyed in a large variety of ways, exhibiting an entire range from the faintest suggestions to outright coercion.

2. Professional abuse. If family members will manipulate or pressure patients into choosing death in all the usual ways family members control each other's behavior, it can be further argued, physicians will have an even larger range of methods for doing so. For instance, they may give inaccurate diagnoses or unreliable prognoses. They may scare patients with predictions of pain. They may decline to offer adequate pain control which is sporadic or has undesirable side effects. They may refuse to offer other treatment which might produce symptom relief. They may 'recommend' premature death in ways that are too persuasive for the patient to resist, or they may recommend it to the family and let the family do the persuasion. Worse still, they may learn to lean on euthanasia as a kind of medical crutch, turning almost automatically to it as the solution for every treatment problem they cannot solve; even worse, they may use it as a cover for their medical mistakes. Perhaps still worse, they will become euthanasia 'enthusiasts', employing euthanasia as part of their own political programs for reforming the medical world.

To understand these claims, it is essential first to see what background assumptions make them plausible, given that it is only voluntary euthanasia and assisted suicide that would be legalized, and then only for competent, terminally ill patients with less than 6 months to live. Yet even given the comparative narrowness of this range of cases, the dire predictions so widely voiced cannot be ignored. For this reason, it is crucial to understand what is distinctive about abuse by doctors, and to some degree by nurses and other care providers as well – that is, what is distinctive about *professional* abuse in contrast to interpersonal, usually familial, abuse of the sort discussed above.

Professional abuse, understood as that range of ways in which professionals, especially physicians, might bring a patient to 'voluntarily' request euthanasia or help in suicide who would not otherwise do so, can exhibit most of the features of interpersonal, domestic abuse – suggestion, urging, manipulation, and threat aimed at one person by another – but it incorporates an additional feature: the weight of professional authority. It is the physician who holds the power in the physician/patient relationship, not only because the physician has greater knowledge of the physiological process affecting the patient and how to control them, and because the physician's social aura conveys authoritative standing to his or her role, but also because the patient is ill. Especially when it is terminal, illness can place a person in a particularly compromised position: for many patients, illness involves discomfort and pain, anxiety, fear of impending loss of one's relationships, and fear of death. Thus 'professional authority' trades on two factors: the greater weight of the physician and the compromised position of the patient. Both factors invite abuse. The nurse may also be regarded as a medical authority, particularly in situations (eg, home care) where it is the nurse who is the primary or only contact with the patient, but it is the physician whose capacity is greatest for exploiting professional authority.

Given this disparity of power in the physician/patient relationship, physicians are very well aware of their power to influence patient choices – even while preserving the appearance of obtaining informed consent. The Latinate obscurity of medical diagnosis and the overwhelming nature of too much medical information often contribute to this possibility. Thus, many physicians claim they can get patients to agree to nearly anything they propose; it is simply a matter of how the choice is framed. Just as, in the traditional example, the glass of water can be described as half empty or half full, a proposed surgical procedure with a 50/50 predicted outcome, for example, can be described as a probable success or a probable failure; a 'good chance' can mean anything from a 10 or 20 percent chance of success to 80 or 90 percent. Information can be orchestrated to emphasize benefits or to emphasize risks, even when information about both benefits and risks is actually provided. Presumably, thus, physicians would find it easy to frame choices about euthanasia or suicide in similar ways: unfavorably for patients whom they wanted to discourage, but favorably for those whom they hope to maneuver into this choice. Thus, even under legislation which protects only *voluntary* choice by competent patients, it is argued, the physician could manipulate the patient into choosing death when the patient would not otherwise have chosen it or when it is actually contrary to his or her own wishes. In all these cases, the fiction that the patient has given informed consent can be preserved; what is problematic is the way in which the physician presents the information on which the patient's choice is based.

There is a second way in which professional authority can play a substantial role in shaping patient choice. Much of the interaction, as well as the legal support, for the relationship between physician and patient is based on assumptions of *informed consent* – that is, that the patient retains the right to give or withhold consent to treatment and that in making these choices the patient is entitled to adequate information about the alternatives involved. Informed consent must be explicitly documented for specific procedures, eg surgery; it is assumed for a wide range of minor tests and procedures involved in medical care. But reliance on informed consent also reinforces power disparities in the physician/patient role and exacerbates the weight of professional authority: in informed consent, it is the physician who proposes the specific course of treatment and the patient who gets to say yes or no. But in this arrangement, it is the physician who identifies the problem, frames any suggested solution to it, and controls how many alternative solutions are proposed. The patient cannot know whether the problem could be seen in some other way or as some different sort of problem, whether other sorts of solutions could be proposed, whether in making the choice to give or withhold consent he or she is making a choice among all the reasonable alternatives, and, sometimes, whether there really is any problem at all. The agenda is, so to speak, entirely in the control of the physician. This may of course be a reasonable arrangement for consent to medical procedures which do not raise values dilemmas, but it is hardly a defensible arrangement in the case of euthanasia. Euthanasia is, after all, a quintessential 'values' issue: whether a person prefers a chance of extended life in spite of suffering or pain, or whether he or she prefers an earlier, easier end to life in order to avoid suffering and pain. If consent to euthanasia is treated in the way consent to other medical procedures is, it will be the physician's agenda, not the patient's, that is on the table for action, and to which the patient's only option is to agree or disagree. But this, of course, is fertile ground for abuse.

Furthermore, the physician's capacity to shape patient choice in euthanasia, both by selective control of information and by initial formulation of both the problem and the solution presented for consent, may be influenced not only by malevolent but also by paternalistic intentions. To be sure, there are physicians motivated by greed, prejudice, fear of malpractice action for a medical mistake, and so on. But there may also be physicians who genuinely believe that euthanasia would be in the best interests of the patient, given the pain and suffering the physician knows otherwise lies in the patient's future, and who thus may seek to influence patient choice in this direction for the patient's own sake. Of course, whether manipulation of the patient in what the physician perceives to be the patient's own interest is to be counted as abuse depends in the end on theoretical issues about the nature of paternalism and whether abuse is defined as violation of voluntary patient choice or as violation of patient interests, but the possibility of paternalistic manipulation of the patient by the physician must at least be considered among the varieties of possible abuse.

3. *Institutional abuse.* Institutional abuse will no doubt include some of the features of interpersonal abuse and also professional abuse, but it is again conceptually distinct in its central feature: it operates by narrowing the range of actual choices open to the patient. It may seem to closely resemble those forms of professional abuse in which the physician shapes the patient's choice by selectively providing information or proposing one rather than another possible course of action for consent, but it functions in a distinct way: it erects barriers so that certain choices can be made only with difficulty or cannot be made at all. It is not only that choices are shaped, but more importantly, that only certain choices are possible, while other choices are closed off. There need be nothing clandestine about this, as there may seem to be when the physician withholds specific information or selectively emphasizes some information in order to promote certain choices; in institutional abuse, in contrast with professional abuse, the policies in question are typically open and sometimes widely known, even though they may have manipulative or coercive consequences.

What are the fears, so vocally and variably expressed in the public discussions of euthanasia? They are fears about various sorts of institutions: hospitals, nursing homes, insurance companies, the government. They are fears primarily of policies which are financially motivated, seeking to cut costs in medicine by offering less care, imposing barriers, and withdrawing certain options. They are fears that hospitals will not provide certain types of care or will provide it only to some patients, that nursing homes will let the quality of care and of institutional life deteriorate to the point where it is unbearable, that insurance companies will exclude from coverage many forms of treatment and palliation which might benefit the patient, or that they will exclude some patients from coverage altogether....

Protections against abuse

The picture of possible abuse is a grim one, particularly in a society with a chaotic health care system, but it is, I think, a real risk. Yet I also think it is possible to erect protections against such abuse that can be both stable and effective. Such protections are not foolproof, and the policies and regulations in which they are incorporated are not likely to stop those who operate outside the law in any case. Nevertheless, these protections are adequate, I believe, to prevent the kind of general, large-scale, 'normal' abuse that many forms of the slippery-slope argument predict, and thus render unwarranted the large-scale limitation of patient choice that laws prohibiting euthanasia and assisted suicide represent.

These protections fall into three general categories – policies designed to protect the quality of the patient's choice, policies designed to control professional and institutional distortions of a patient's situation, and policies designed to permit the development of objective indices of abuse. Though they are to be described separately here, they will function best, of course, in concert and interactively. Indeed, I think that all or nearly all of the forms of protections described here will need to be in place to provide reliable prevention of abuse.

Policies designed to protect the quality of the patient's choice

Policies designed to protect the quality of the patient's choice must attempt to look at two things: how the patient reached that choice, and what the content of that choice is. Both raise enormous theoretical issues, requiring answers to two philosophically difficult questions, drawing on two distinct senses of the term 'rational': what must one have done to have made a 'well-chosen' or 'rational' choice? and what characteristics must the 'right' or 'best' choice, that is, the 'rational' choice, display? Nevertheless, we can intuitively discern choices that are badly made in the sense that they are the product of irrational thinking, inadequate information, undue outside influence, and so on; and we can also discern choices that seem to be, given the interests and values of the individual making them, simply bad choices for him or her to have made, regardless of how carefully they were considered. Of course, this raises enormous issues of paternalism, but we can nevertheless discern at least the broad outlines of 'badly made' and 'bad' choices. The two mechanisms discussed below attempt to protect the quality of the patient's decision in both these cases.

Psychological evaluation. Several proposals for amending the proposed aid-in-dying legislation recommend provisions for offering or requiring a psychological evaluation of the patient who requests euthanasia or assistance in suicide. Generally, such evaluations would seek primarily to identify psychopathology or other disturbances of reasoning, especially depression, which might effect the patient's capacity to reach a fully voluntary, autonomous choice; they would thus be designed to protect the patient from choosing badly. Such evaluation might routinely use standard scales of depression, such as the Beck Inventory; it might also involve interviews by the physician involved or by a consulting physician, psychologist, or psychiatrist. Such evaluation should be conducted in private with the patient, away from the influence of family members or other parties who might exert pressures of various subtle sorts. However, it cannot be too easily assumed that any evidence of depression that could be detected in this way is grounds for rejecting a request for euthanasia or assistance in suicide; depression is a natural accompaniment of terminal illness, though more pronounced in some stages of the dying process than in others, and terminal illness, while it may involve some gains in intimacy with one's loved one, is also a period of continuing loss. The routine use of psychological evaluation adapted for other situations, especially to detect depression, ought not to impose a higher standard for decision-making than for other important decisions in life; instead, it ought to be used just to identify the clearest cases of transient, *reversible* depression which may be affecting patient choice. Thus, psychological evaluation measures used in these situations – for persons diagnosed as terminally ill, with less than six months to live – must be redesigned so that the expression of thoughts about death, considerations of suicide, or the wish to die is not interpreted as *prima facie* evidence of depression and so taken to preclude voluntary choice.

Counseling. At least until recently, most counseling available in the US has been committed to the principle of suicide prevention, and would view any expression of a wish or intention to die as grounds for further treatment. In this sense, most counseling has been directive: it has been concerned to direct clients or patients towards life-affirming choices and constructive ways of resolving their problems, away from death. Furthermore, perhaps as a result of the *Tarasoff* decision [discussed *supra*, ch 3], most psychologists have understood themselves to be obligated to report serious potential harm to third parties or to the patient [*sic*], and hence obligated to take action (for instance by initiating involuntary commitment) with respect to a patient who reports a serious intention to commit suicide. In a large range of cases, these postures are entirely appropriate. But they are not appropriate in the circumstances at issue in terminal illness, especially if the patient has a legally protected right to euthanasia or assistance in suicide; here, what is in order instead is genuinely nondirective counseling, designed to help the patient discover whether his or her request for euthanasia or assistance in suicide is in fact a genuine one, carefully thought through, fully understood, and in keeping with his or her most basic values – that is, whether it is the 'right' or 'best' or 'rational' choice *for this person*. Of course the request might be a 'cry for help' or the product of external manipulation or other abuse, but it might also be a genuine product of the person's most considered, reflective choice. Any counseling offered ought to serve solely to differentiate these two, not to close off one set of options; if not, it is useless in these situations. Suicide-prevention centres and crisis hotlines have ... been particularly remiss in failing to serve that proportion of the population who may find their services most valuable: persons considering suicide (or euthanasia) as a way of responding to the prospect of deteriorative terminal illness, as well as those with severe permanent disabilities or advanced old age. Such persons, who take themselves to be considering a rational response to difficult circumstances, cannot avail themselves of services whose announced purpose, 'suicide prevention,' makes it clear that they will work to preclude such a choice, or of services whose policies require initiating involuntary commitment for persons viewed as likely to commit suicide. Rather, what is needed is counseling designed to help a patient think through the issue in 'rational suicide,' including requests for assistance or for physician-performed euthanasia. Such suicide-neutral counseling takes the request at face value and seeks to help the patient be sure he or she has considered all consequences, acknowledged his or her own emotions, and recognized all conflicts or affirmations of value such a choice might involve. Indeed, such counseling may well serve to reduce the psychopathology of such situations by allowing more open discussion of them; but it cannot do so if it is committed to pre-shaping choice.

Continuity requirement or waiting period. Some proposals have suggested that a waiting period be required between the initial request for euthanasia or assistance in suicide and the provision of these services. The clear intent behind such proposals is to ensure that the choice is stable and enduring, rather than a fleeting, transitory response to a new setback, and hence that it is an expression of the patient's true, underlying values. Other mechanisms which might be said to provide concrete evidence of the patient's values at earlier periods in life would include such instruments as a Living Will executed before the onset of the terminal illness or at an earlier point during it; some courts have considered records of or testimony about earlier comments made by the patient concerning other persons in similar circumstances. While a short waiting period (say, 24 or 48 hours) may serve as some protection against impetuous decision-making, longer waiting periods (say, a month or two) are not only artificial but have the potential to be cruel, since they postpone that very relief the patient is seeking. Paradoxically, waiting periods may also encourage some patients to make premature requests as a way of getting into the queue early. Living Wills and Durable Power of Attorney documents need not be signed under controlled circumstances, and it is sometimes argued that they do not reliably represent a patient's true choices over time, especially since the patient may be unable to correctly anticipate his or her future situation. Despite the deficiencies of waiting periods and advance directives, nevertheless, some form of protective device designed to ensure both the stability of the choice and its consonance with the patient's own values seems appropriate – provided, of course, that it does not completely preclude any possibility for the patient to change his or her mind. Notice what is *not* recommended here as a protective device: the deliberations of a committee. These can only be deliberations about the content of the patient's choice, not the patient's voluntariness in making that choice, and I do not see that a committee decision on whether the patient may or may not end his or her life protects the quality of the patient's choice. More likely, it serves to protect the institution in which the committee is based.

Policies designed to protect against professional and institutional distortion of a patient's choice
The sorts of policies considered in this section are designed to prevent both intentional and inadvertent distortion of a patient's situation and hence a patient's choices by either the physician or other health care providers or by institutions, including hospitals, nursing homes, home agencies, insurance companies, and governmental agencies.

Prohibition of fees. In remarks published before the vote on Initiative 119, Professor Albert Jonsen warned of a 'flood of persons' who would travel to Washington in order to seek euthanasia. Other voices warned of the development of 'death houses' or 'euthanasia clinics', clearly drawing on the analogy with abortion clinics, and some suggested that unscrupulous physicians would offer inducements to patients to seek such services, perhaps by advertising in the public or medical media. Remote as these predictions might seem to be, there is a simple way to prevent such traffic and the institutional stimulation of such traffic: no physician or other health care provider should be permitted to charge a fee for performing euthanasia or for providing assistance in suicide, or at least no fee beyond minimal compensation for the time actually involved. Advertising such services, at least in any way more elaborate than announcing their availability, should also be prohibited. Euthanasia is not a complex procedure, if reliable information is available to the physician about methods for performing it (as would presumably be the case if the procedure were legalized), though it may be performed in comparatively slow ways that do involve extended time. At least some physicians in the Netherlands, where euthanasia is in effect legal and where medical information about methods to be used is widely available, report that they do not accept fees, even though the procedure may be performed in a hospital or in a home, and even though, at the request of the patient, the procedure is often performed in a way that involves a long, slow induction of sleep followed by coma over a period of several hours, usually to make the transition from life to death easier for the family to watch. Dutch physicians report that they expect to remain with the patient (and the family) throughout this time, though they do not take fees for it. Similarly, to prohibit health care facilities from advertising and from charging fees for euthanasia or any closely related ancillary services, or from charging fees that would provide a profit over expenses, would preclude at least some incentives for euthanasia and for the development of a euthanasia 'trade' or market.

Documentation. A second form of protection against abuse involves extensive documentation of any procedure involving euthanasia or the provision of assistance in suicide. Such documentation, presumably to be part of the patient's medical record, would include the medical history, the prognosis, the nature of the current problem(s), the reasons for the patient's request (both the patient's stated reasons and the physician's perceptions of the patient's reasons, if different), and a record of the physician's discussions with the patient's family, if any. Also to be included in the documentation is a clear expression of the patient's choice: not merely a signed 'informed consent' to the procedure itself, but documentation of the patient's active request. This might of course take many forms – a letter, a tape-recording of the patient's voice, or witnessed statements by observers – but the central element here is documentation of the fact that euthanasia or assistance in suicide is the patient's idea, not that of the physician, the family, or the health care facility.

As a second, equally important component, the documentation should also include a record of treatment alternatives discussed with the patient, including treatment alternatives refused by the patient as well as those accepted, forms of pain relief or symptom control offered the patient, and, also equally important, any forms of treatment potentially effective for the patient's condition but excluded from coverage by insurance policies, by the health care facility's care priorities, by governmental rationing policies, and so on. Thus these three elements of documentation serve to reflect interpersonal, professional, and institutional abuse respectively.

Reporting. The performance of euthanasia or the provision of assistance in suicide should also be reportable to an appropriate external agency. At the moment, of course, there is no such designated agency, but a number of possibilities suggest themselves: for instance, the coroner (since presumably the cause of death, euthanasia, perhaps together with the disease causing the terminal condition, would be entered on the death certificate), or the Centers for Disease Control (as a keeper of mortality statistics), or the National Institutes of Health (as a federal research agency), or Health and Human Services (as the highest level of federal bureaucracy for health issues), etc. However, the natural analogy to the Dutch reporting requirement would not be immediately plausible in the US; in the Netherlands, because euthanasia is technically a violation of statutory law and the guidelines developed in lower and supreme court cases serve as a defense to prosecutions for homicide, the physician is obligated to report any occasion of euthanasia to the Ministry of Justice after the fact, where it is reviewed and prosecution undertaken if the guidelines are not met. (As is well known, only a small proportion of Dutch physicians has been doing so, though this number has been increasing in recent years.) However, if in the United States euthanasia and assistance in suicide were legal under statutory law, reporting to the Department of Justice or state-level judicial authorities would not seem immediately plausible, since technically, no crime would have been committed; perhaps, however, a reporting requirement could be inserted in the authorizing law. Whatever the agency to which report is made, what is important in preventing abuse is that detailed information about cases of euthanasia be available for review; the effectiveness of this structure would clearly also be enhanced by a substantial penalty for not reporting.

Indices of abuse. Documentation and reporting of euthanasia cases makes possible what is perhaps the most important mechanism for the control of abuse and the reliable provision of protection to patients. What is central here is the possibility of retroactive inspection on a broad scale of patterns of performance of euthanasia. As in current analyses by John Wennberg at Dartmouth and others of geographical variation in surgical procedures and other statistical assessments of medical practice, the performance of euthanasia and assistance in suicide, if documented and reported, would also be open to objective review. Review, of course, could be made at all levels and for all factors reported: by individual physician, by health care facility, by insurance carrier, by type of terminal condition, by length of association between patient and physician, by types of pain control and symptom palliation provided, by types of alternative treatment denied, by age, race, gender, handicap status, and so on. Thus many quite revealing questions could readily be answered: Do some doctors provide assistance in suicide more frequently than others? Do the patents of some nursing homes request euthanasia more frequently than the patients of others/ Are patients covered by some health insurance plans more frequently denied care for certain sorts of conditions, and are these denials listed among their reasons for choosing euthanasia? How often are spend-down provisions among the reasons for such choices? Do black patients 'choose' euthanasia more often than white? Patients with poor educations or lower incomes more often than patients with privileged backgrounds? While such data might not always be providing deliberately intolerable care, and insurance companies forcing patients into euthanasia choices by refusing to cover certain sorts of care could be tentatively identified, and further examination of specific situations then conducted by the appropriate review organizations.

Furthermore, not only would analyses of such data reveal patterns of euthanasia practice and hence probable patterns of euthanasia abuse, but there is already some basis for comparative analysis of such data. The new Remmelink Commission study from the Netherlands provides the first objective glimpse of euthanasia practice in a climate in which it is widely accepted and in which it is legally tolerated: it is now known, as we saw earlier, that about 1.8 percent of all deaths in the Netherlands are the product of euthanasia and that about 0.3 percent of all deaths involve physician-assisted suicide. Additional information about these patients is also available: for example, their average age at the time of euthanasia (62 for men, 68 for women; interestingly, Dutch physicians report very few requests from older patients); their regional location (more in urban areas); and the approximate amount of life forgone (in 70 percent of cases, more than one week; in 8 percent, more than six months). Information is also available about the reasons for their requests of euthanasia: loss of dignity (mentioned in 57 percent of cases), pain (46 percent), 'unworthy dying' (46 percent), being dependent on others (33 percent), and tiredness of life (23 percent). According to this study, in just over 5 percent of cases was pain the only reason. Furthermore, about two-thirds of initial requests for euthanasia do not end up as a serious and persistent request at a later stage of the disease, and of the serious and persistent requests, about two-thirds do not result in euthanasia or assisted suicide since, according to the study, physicians can often offer alternatives.

Information of this sort would provide an initial basis for comparison of US experience with a country in which two relevant characteristics are different. First, the Netherlands is a country in which the practice of euthanasia is widely and generally accepted, both by patients and by physicians; thus, it is a country in which the incidence of euthanasia is, presumably, not distorted by severe social discouragement. Second, it is a country in which the practice of euthanasia is uncoerced by financial considerations on the part of the patient (the Netherlands has an effective national health insurance system which provides all residents with extensive care in the hospital, nursing home, and at home); thus, it is a country in which patient choice is not constricted in at least one way common in the US. Thus, the Dutch experience can provide tentative expectations about what our own experience might be were euthanasia accepted and were it not affected by financial considerations; though of course this is a highly conjectural strategy, examining the practices in the Netherlands can at least initially provide very rough, informal guidelines for scrutinizing our own practice. If we suppose for example that, despite differences between Dutch and American culture, somewhere around 1.8 percent is the 'normal' percentage of persons dying who would choose to do so by euthanasia when that alternative is socially accepted and when it is not coerced by financial considerations, and that a tiny additional fraction would choose physician-assisted suicide, we then have an easy measure for suspecting abuse in our own society. Are, say, 10 to 20 percent of terminally ill Medicaid patients choosing suicide, but not such a high number of privately insured patients? Thirty or 40 percent of the uninsured? About one-fourth of Dutch AIDS patients die by euthanasia; is the proportion higher among AIDS patients here? Is 'pain' the reason for which a large proportion of patients are said to have chosen euthanasia? Since this is the primary reason for only 5 percent of Dutch patients choosing euthanasia, we might well suspect foul play – or its medical and bureaucratic variations, like deliberate neglect or refusal to provide adequate symptom control – if the rates in the US were much higher. Of course, these figures can hardly be treated as rigid norms, and certainly not as either quotas or ceilings; but they can give us some idea of what we might expect were we to permit the practice here, and what would be wildly out of bounds. This is not to assume that the Dutch have got it right, so to speak, and that abuse never occurs in the Netherlands; but inasmuch as there is no documented evidence that abuse is occurring (other than very rare 'outlier' cases), it is reasonable to begin with Dutch experience as a guide to what, if all went well, we might expect in the US. To be sure, these proportions might change as social attitudes change, and would no doubt increase if acceptance for self-determination in dying were to grow; they may of course also change in the Netherlands. And these proportions would of course change dramatically if Robert Kastenbaum's well-known prediction were to come true, that suicide will become the *preferred* mode of dying because it enables a person to control the time, place, and circumstances of doing so. Thus statistical analysis cannot by itself identify patterns of abuse without some further analysis of social values and trends; but it is nevertheless adapted to identify variations in pattern within a culture and across institutional and geographic lines. What the data from the Netherlands now tell us is that we should expect that euthanasia would be quite infrequent – less than 2 percent of all deaths – and that the reasons for which patients choose it do not have to do only with pain. Of the various mechanisms for protecting against abuse, it is the possibility of potential public exposure, incurring the risk of further legal action, that provides the most secure protection, provided of course the penalties for not reporting are substantial as well. It is true that many of the slippery-slope arguments warn of abuse on a vast scale, but they forget that we can easily put in place expert methods for detecting and thus preventing it.

It cannot be doubted that whenever the topic of voluntary euthanasia is broached, rational argument becomes an early casualty. The spectre of Nazism is shamelessly resorted to as an opening gambit by those opposed to any change in the law. The nuances of arguments and the realities of modern medicine tend to be ignored. Even though the prospect of legislation permitting voluntary euthanasia in this country is unlikely for some time to come, we have already seen that two other jurisdictions have liberalised their laws – the Netherlands and, for a brief time, the Northern Territory in Australia. What, if anything, can we learn from their experiences? In particular, we can see how a liberalising law might be drafted so as to provide the maximum protection to patients of abuses and to set the appropriate 'entry requirements' for voluntary euthanasia. We shall examine the approaches in these two jurisdictions separately. Particularly as regards the Netherlands, there is a rich and detailed literature on the operation of their system and our treatment is necessarily brief. (For the most detailed and thorough analysis in the English language, see J Griffiths, A Bood, H Weyers *Euthanasia and Law in the Netherlands* (1998).)

Finally, we should observe that, given the current climate of opinion, we have not in this section considered other forms of euthanasia, ie where the patient has not expressly requested to be killed – non-voluntary and involuntary euthanasia. The law in England is clear and legislative reform is unimaginable.

(iii) THE NETHERLANDS

The legal situation in the Netherlands is complicated. It is often stated that voluntary euthanasia is 'tolerated' by the prosecutional authorities. Providing certain substantive requirements ('careful practice') are followed and certain procedural steps taken (eg reporting to the coroner), prosecution will not take place but voluntary euthanasia remains illegal. As the following discussion will show, this is not a true reflection of the *legal* position. It is the Dutch Supreme Court which has recognised that a doctor who carries out voluntary euthanasia in certain circumstances is not guilty of an offence under the Dutch Criminal Code. He has a defence of 'necessity', in reality, therefore, what he did is *legal*: any prosecution is bound to fail. To say voluntary euthanasia is only 'tolerated' would be the same as saying killing in self-defence is only 'tolerated' under English law and remains illegal. To common law eyes, the defence makes the action *legal*.

So what is the position? The important provisions of the Dutch Criminal Code are as follows:

Article 40
A person who commits an offence as a result of a force he could not be expected to resist is not criminally liable.

Article 293
A person who takes the life of another person at that other person's express and earnest request is liable to a term of imprisonment of not more than twelve years or a fine of the fifth category.

Article 294
A person who intentionally incites another to commit suicide, assists in the suicide of another, or procures for that other person the means to commit suicide, is liable to a term of imprisonment of not more than three years or a fine of the fourth category, where the suicide ensues.

J Griffiths et al *Euthanasia and Law in the Netherlands* (1998)

Euthanasia is explicitly and apparently absolutely prohibited by two articles of the Dutch Criminal Code. Article 293 prohibits killing a person at his request (the offence is a 'qualified' variety of homicide, in the sense that the homicide would otherwise be murder). Article 294 prohibits assisting a suicide (suicide itself is not a crime in Dutch law).

Despite the apparently forbidding text of these provisions, the courts have held that article 40 of the Criminal Code makes a defence of justification available to a doctor charged under articles 293 and 294. The first acquittal took place in 1983 and this was upheld by the Dutch Supreme Court in the *Schoonheim* case in 1984. The Supreme Court held that a doctor could invoke the defence of justification due to necessity if, confronted by a conflict between a duty to his patient whose suffering is 'unbearable and hopeless,' and the requirements of the Criminal Code, and exercising the care required of a medical professional, his choice was 'objectively justified'. The decision in *Schoonheim* led to a series of judicial decisions in which the conditions and limitations of the defence were gradually worked out.

The opening created by the courts came in the course of the 1980s to be reflected in prosecution policy, which now offers the doctor who keeps within the accepted limits a high degree of safety from prosecution. In this sense, euthanasia in the Netherlands is no longer illegal. Contrary to the impression in much of the foreign press, legislation recently enacted by the Dutch parliament does not affect the legality of euthanasia but only the procedure for reporting it.

As far as the legal norms concerning euthanasia are concerned, the process of legalization is largely complete, and there is little controversy over the results reached. Legal developments concerning euthanasia itself will in the coming years deal essentially with fine-tuning of the existing system (the requirement of consultation with a second doctor, for example, while itself completely non-controversial, leads to complications in some cases). There are, of course, some exceptions to this generalization. An important example is the status of written euthanasia requests made by persons who later become incompetent (especially due to senile dementia); other remaining problems include such things as how to deal with persons of diminished competence and with minors. But the most important legal developments to be expected in the near future concern not the applicable norms but the system of legal control; in particular, the question whether this could not be better accomplished outside of the criminal law is being asked with increasing insistence.

What has been said of euthanasia proper does not apply to situations in which a doctor administers lethal drugs without the patient having made an explicit request, although here, too, the general contours of the emerging legal norms are becoming clear. In the case of coma patients, severely defective newborn babies, and patients in the final stages of the dying process, recent legal developments seem, as we will see in Chapter 3.3, to point the way to a generally acceptable outcome, but these matters remain far more controversial than euthanasia proper.

By contrast with the various forms of 'active termination of life' dealt with so far, pain relief and abstention account for the lion's share of all MBSL (almost 10 times as many deaths as those due to the use of lethal drugs). They have nevertheless received relatively little attention as problems of regulation of medical behaviour. Death due to the administration of pain relief in doses known to be likely to shorten life is regarded, legally as well as in medical ethics, as subject to the 'doctrine of double effect': so long as the doctor's 'primary intent' is to relieve suffering, the fact that the earlier death of the patient is also a foreseen and even welcome consequence does not, according to this doctrine, entail that the doctor 'intended' that death. The case is regarded as one of 'normal medical practice' not subject to any special regulation, rather than one of euthanasia (if there is a request) or murder (if there is not). Apart from the general rules applying to medical practice, there are no substantive or procedural protections surrounding pain relief so long as it falls within the scope of the 'doctrine of double effect'.

You will notice reference to *Schoonheim* decision of the Dutch Supreme Court in 1984. That case, together with the subsequent decisions of *Pols, Admiraal* and *Chabot*, clarified the legal bans for voluntary euthanasia. Again, Griffiths *et al* (*op cit*) explain (at pp 81–82):

On 28 September 1991 the psychiatrist Chabot, at her request, supplied Ms B with lethal drugs. She consumed the drugs in the presence of Chabot, a GP and a friend and died shortly thereafter. Chabot reported her death the same day to the local coroner as a suicide which he had assisted.

Briefly, the facts were as follows ... Ms B was 50 years old. Over a period of several years she had undergone a series of traumatic experiences that had deprived her of all desire to continue living. Psychiatric treatment had had little effect, and she had made one serious suicide attempt. She was referred to Chabot by the Association for Voluntary Euthanasia. After extensive discussions with her, he concluded that there was no question in her case of a psychiatric disorder or a major depressive episode. Her psychic traumas were in principle susceptible to psychiatric treatment (which would, however, have been long-term and with limited chance of success), but Ms B consistently declined therapy. In Chabot's opinion, Ms B was experiencing intense, long-term psychic suffering, the suffering was unbearable and hopeless for her, and her request for assistance with suicide was well-considered. He consulted a total of seven experts. Most of them agreed with his assessment of the situation and of the treatment perspectives (none of them considered it necessary to examine Ms B).

The District Court, Assen, (Tijdschrift voor Gezondheidsrecht 1993, no 42), and the Court of Appeals, Leeuwarden (ibid no 62) found the defence of necessity well-founded. On appeal, the Supreme Court reaffirmed its earlier judgments that euthanasia and assistance with suicide can be justified if

the defendant acted in a situation of necessity, that is to say ... that confronted with a choice between mutually conflicting duties, he chose to perform the one of greater weight. In particular, a doctor may be in a situation of necessity if he has to choose between the duty to preserve life and the duty as a doctor to do everything possible to relieve the unbearable and hopeless suffering of a patient committed to his care (Nederlandse Jurisprudentie 1994, no 656: 3154).

The Court rejected the argument of the prosecution that this justification is not available in the case of assistance with suicide given to a patient whose suffering is non-somatic and who is not in the 'terminal phase'. It agreed with the holding of the Court of Appeals 'that the wish to die of a person whose suffering is psychic can be based on an autonomous judgment'. However, the Court concluded that in the circumstances of the case there was insufficient proof to support the defence of necessity, since there was no statement from an 'independent medical expert who has at least seen and examined the patient himself'. Although, the Court observed, failure to consult a colleague – whether or not the latter examines the patient – does not in an ordinary case foreclose the defence of necessity, in the case of suffering that is not somatically based, evidence of consultation including actual examination of the patient is essential. The judgment of the independent colleague should cover the seriousness of the suffering and the prospects for improvement, the alternatives to assistance with suicide, and the question whether the patient's request was voluntary and well-considered, 'without [the patient's] competence being influenced by his sickness or condition'. In passing, the Court observed that 'there can in principle be no question of lack of prospect of improvement if there is a realistic alternative to relieve the suffering which the patient has in complete freedom rejected.' Chabot was found guilty of the offence of assistance with suicide (however, no punishment was imposed).

You will see reference to the substantive and procedural requirements an in particular the requirements of 'careful practice'. Griffiths *et al* (*op cit*) explain (at pp 99–107):

The requirements of a substantive and of a procedural or professional character that must be met by a doctor who carries out euthanasia or gives assistance with suicide have become fairly clear. Some of these have been formulated by the courts in the context of criminal prosecutions, others in a variety of other legal sources, in particular proposed legislation, existing legal rules, and the reports and position-papers of various organs of the medical profession. Since our interest here is in the whole of the law (including the law that is in the process of emerging), the minor differences between the various sources are not essential. The following requirements are now generally accepted:

SUBSTANTIVE REQUIREMENTS

The essential substantive conditions of legal euthanasia concern the patient's request, the patient's suffering, and the doctor-patient relationship.

1   The patient's request must, in the terms of article 293, be 'express and earnest'. Absent such a request, the behavior concerned is not euthanasia but murder. The request requirement is operationalized as follows:

   –   the request must be explicitly made by the person concerned (Tijdschrift voor Gerzondheidsrecht 1986, no 34);
   –   the request must be voluntary (not the result of undue external influence) (*Chabot* (see translation in Modern Law Review 58: 232–248, 1995) by J Griffiths);
   –   it must be well-considered: informed, made after due deliberation and based on an enduring desire for the end of life (evidenced for instance by its having repeatedly been made over some period of time);
   –   the request should preferably be in writing or otherwise recorded.

   The requirement of a voluntary and well-considered request is actually only a variant of the general requirement of informed consent required in the case of a competent patient for all medical treatment. If there is a difference in the case of euthanasia, it lies in the oft-heard suggestion that the initiative should come from the patient himself, whereas in the case of other MBSL the doctor can suggest and even recommend a given course of action.

2   The patient's suffering must be 'unbearable' [*ondraaglijk*] and 'hopeless' [*uitzichtloos*] (in the sense of 'without hope for improvement'). This requirement is further operationalized as follows:

   –   the suffering need not be physical (paint etc) nor is a somatic basis required; non-physical suffering can include such things as the prospect of inhuman deterioration [*ontluistering*] and the possibility of not being able to die in a 'dignified' way;
   –   if the patient's suffering is based on a somatic condition, other possibilities for treating the condition or relieving the suffering must have been exhausted or have been rejected by the patient (it is well-established that in such a case the patient's exercise of the right to refuse treatment does not preclude a request for euthanasia based on the resulting suffering);
   –   if the patient's suffering is not based on a somatic condition, there must be no realistic possibility of treatment (see *Chabot* case (supra)).

   It is not clear to what extent anticipation of a fate one does not want to undergo (eg confinement to a nursing home, or further mental deterioration) can by itself meet the requirement of unbearable suffering, nor whether euthanasia can be carried out on a demented patient who is not currently suffering from the dementia but who in an earlier advance directive requested it in such circumstances.

3   Only a doctor may legally perform euthanasia. In principle this should be a doctor who has an established treatment-relationship with the patient [*behandelend arts*]. No individual doctor is under an obligation to perform euthanasia, but a doctor who is conscientiously opposed should refer the patient to another doctor.

It was until recently sometimes supposed that the patient must be in the 'terminal phase' of his illness, although the Medical Association has since 1984 rejected such a requirement as medically meaningless, and the courts rejected it from the very beginning … The former Minister of Justice's more or less one-man insistence on this limitation led to a number of prosecutions in late 1993 which were at the time generally believed to have significantly reduced the willingness of doctors to report euthanasia as such. However this may be, it is clear since the decision in the *Chabot* case (ibid) … that no such limitation applies. In fact, it is possible that the person requesting euthanasia may not necessarily have to be 'ill' at all …

If for legal purposes, within the context of the defence of justification to a criminal charge, the requirement of a 'terminal phase' plays no role, it does not follow that it is irrelevant as a matter of legal policy – one of the advantages of a decriminalized approach to control over euthanasia is that it would permit a more fine-tuned approach to the considerations relevant to a doctor's behavior. In such a context, the extent to which the patient's life is shortened by euthanasia may well influence the extent, for example, to which he should insist on exploring treatment alternatives or should engage in more than the minimum consultation.

A final substantive requirement that is sometimes suggested but appears not yet to have been accorded any legal status is that euthanasia should not be performed if the patient is receiving life-prolonging treatment that has not yet been discontinued. In other words, abstinence should have priority over administration of euthanasia. The idea is essentially the same as the 'priority principle' that has been proposed in the case of termination of life without an explicit request (comatose patients, newborn babies, etc …

PROCEDURAL AND PROFESSIONAL REQUIREMENTS ('REQUIREMENTS OF CAREFUL PRACTICE')
In addition to the substantive conditions of legal euthanasia, the doctor who performs euthanasia must meet a number of procedural requirements.

1   The doctor must take adequate steps to satisfy himself with respect to the substantive requirements set out above. (Although often so formulated, it is not clear that this is really an additional requirement.)
2   He must formally consult at least one other doctor with respect to the patient's condition and life-expectancy, the available alternatives, and the adequacy of the request (voluntary, well-considered, etc).
     –   the consultant should in principle be 'independent' (not a subordinate, a member of a joint practice, a colleague in a group practice of specialists, or a doctor involved in the treatment of the patient);
     –   in the case of a patient apparently suffering from a psychiatric disorder the consulted doctor should be a psychiatrist;
     –   if the patient's suffering is of non-somatic origin, the consultant must himself examine the patient, and in other cases he should do so;
     –   the consultant should make a written report, that becomes part of the medical dossier of the patient.
     It seems in effect to be part of the consultation requirement that the consultant agree with the decision of the responsible doctor.
3   The doctor should discuss the matter with the immediate family and intimate friends [*naasten*] of the patient (unless the patient does not want this or there are other good reasons for not doing so).
4   The doctor should discuss the matter with nursing personnel responsible for the patient's care and, if a nurse is involved in the request for euthanasia or in carrying it out, she should be included in the decision-making.
5   The doctor should keep a full written record of the case (including information concerning the above elements).
6   The termination of life should be carried out in a professionally responsible way and the doctor should stay with the patient continuously – or be immediately available – until the patient dies (except possibly, for good reasons, in the case of assistance with suicide if careful arrangements are made, including the availability of the doctor if needed).
7   Death due to euthanasia may not be reported as a 'natural death' (in effect, the doctor must report himself as having committed what *prima facie* is a serious criminal offence)…

If the above requirements for the legally permissible performance of euthanasia have been clear for about the last 10 years, there has been less clarity over how, exactly, they are to be enforced. The substantive requirements for justifiable euthanasia are enforced through the criminal law. Without the patient's voluntary and well-considered request, the behavior is not a potentially justifiable case of 'euthanasia' but a *prima facie* (though, … possibly justifiable) case of murder or manslaughter. Recent prosecutions for termination of life without an explicit request (newborn babies, coma patients, and 'help in dying' …) have in fact been prosecutions for the latter two offences. If the euthanasia is not performed by a doctor, the case falls under articles 293 or 294 but is not justifiable (except perhaps under extreme circumstances). Euthanasia in the absence of unbearable and hopeless suffering is not presently regarded as legally justifiable…

It was for some time unclear to what extent conformity with the 'procedural' requirements ('requirements of careful practice') is necessary for a successful defence to a criminal charge. It seems now to be settled that deviation from these requirements does not necessarily stand in the way of an appeal to the justification of necessity. Such a development was to be expected, since it would be disproportionate to convict a doctor for homicide when the euthanasia itself was otherwise unobjectionable and what he is really accused of is inadequate consultation, record-keeping or the like. The 'requirements of careful practice' are generally enforced in medical disciplinary proceedings (although it seems that in a case of multiple violations of the 'requirements of careful practice' the courts will hold that the defence of justification is not available).

One issue, which we shall return to later, concerns the obligation of doctors to report deaths that are as a result of voluntary euthanasia. How should a doctor report such a death? Should it be certified as a 'natural death'? Griffiths *et al* (*op cit*) explain(at pp 72–73):

> In 1985 a criminal case began in Rotterdam which definitively settled this issue. The case concerned a doctor who on 15 December 1983 had ended a patient's life in a nursing home at her explicit request. He filed a death certificate stating that the cause of the patient's death had been natural. The doctor was tried for euthanasia and for submitting a false certificate (article 228(1)) of the Criminal Code …The doctor's defence to the euthanasia charge was based on the justification of necessity. The District Court agreed and found him not guilty of euthanasia. The doctor's lawyer also invoked the justification of necessity as a defence to the second charge. She argued that the doctor was in a situation of conflict of duties: on the one hand his duty to the surviving relatives and the other patients in the nursing home for whom reporting the death as a non-natural one would have entailed additional grief and agitation, on the other his duty not to file a false certificate. Confronted with the choice of two unattractive options, he chose the less harmful one. The Court did not agree. In his opinion, filing a false certificate undermines legal control of termination of life. The doctor was sentenced to a fine of 500 guilders, half of which was made conditional (Tijdschrift voor Gezondheidsrecht 1985, no 44). On appeal, the Court of Appeals, the Hague agreed with the District Court. It also rejected the defendant's reliance on his oath of secrecy: this oath gives a doctor the right to remain silent, but not to give false information (Nederlandse Jurisprudentie 1987, no 756). In December 1987 the Supreme Court upheld the decision of the Court of Appeal (Tijdschrift voor Gezondheidsrecht 1988, no 13).

Subsequently, in 1993 the Dutch legislature acted to deal with reporting of deaths. Again, Griffiths *et al* (*op cit*) (at pp 79–80) explain:

> The legislation ultimately adopted in 1993 and currently in effect was an amendment to the Law on the Disposal of Corpses. It makes a technical change in the legal status of the forms to be used for reporting the death of a patient. Pursuant to the new Law a special form was prescribed for cases of euthanasia, assistance with suicide and termination of life without an explicit request. This form consists largely of a list of 'Points requiring attention' to be covered in the doctor's report, which more or less correspond to the various elements of the 'requirements of careful practice' laid down in the case law. In this indirect way the Dutch Parliament can be said to have addressed itself to the legitimacy of euthanasia and, via a back door, to have ratified what the courts had long since done. Technically speaking, the legislation does not affect the legality of euthanasia at all.

The Dutch system is principally concerned with voluntary euthanasia and physician-assisted suicide. However, it is important to notice that the Dutch courts have gone further, extending the defence of necessity under art 40 of the Criminal Code to severely disabled babies enduring unbearable suffering (see *Prins* (1995) and *Kadijk* (1996); see Griffiths *et al*, *op cit* at Appendix II(3)).

The Dutch system is not without its critics (see, most prominently, J Keown 'The Law and Practice of Euthanasia in the Netherlands' (1992) 108 LQR 51 and 'Euthanasia in the Netherlands: Sliding Down the Slippery Slope?' in J Keown (ed) *Euthanasia Examined* (1995) p 261). It is argued that the system is 'out of control', in particular that euthanasia is not always *voluntary*, that doctors fail to report deaths under the reporting requirements and that euthanasia is resorted to at the expense of 'palliative care'. The criticisms have influenced the views of the House of Lords Select Committee on Medical Ethics (*op cit* at paras 119–126), the Canadian Supreme Court in the *Rodriguez* decision (*supra*) and the US Supreme Court in *Washington v Glucksberg* (*supra*). On what evidence are these criticisms based? Two extensive studies have been carried out by Van der Maas and colleagues for the Dutch Government in 1990 and 1995; see, respectively, Van der Maas, Van Delden and Pijnenborg *Euthanasia and other Medical Decisions Concerning the End of Life* (1992) and Van der Maas *et al* 'Euthanasia, Physician-Assisted Suicide, and Other Medical Practices Involving the End of Life in the Netherlands, 1990–1995' (1996) 335 New Eng J Med 1699; Van der Wal *et al* 'Evaluation of the Notification Procedure for Physician-Assisted Death in the Netherlands' (1996) 335 New Eng J Med 1706.

These studies and the authors' conclusions on the data are set out in the following paper critical of the Dutch practice.

Henk Jochemsen and John Keown 'Voluntary Euthanasia Under Control? Further Empirical Evidence from the Netherlands' (1999) 25 JME 16

Nineteen ninety-one saw the publication of the results of an important survey, by Professor PJ van der Maas, into end-of-life decision making by Dutch doctors in the year 1990. Despite claims to the contrary by supporters of Dutch euthanasia, this survey helped to cast serious doubt on Dutch claims that their guidelines were sufficiently strict effectively to control the practice of voluntary euthanasia (the intentional termination of patient's lives at their request) and to prevent non-voluntary euthanasia (the intentional termination of the lives of patients incapable of making a request).

The survey disclosed the widespread practice of non-voluntary euthanasia; the use of euthanasia even when doctors thought that palliative care was a viable alternative, and the common practice by doctors of illegally certifying euthanasia death as deaths by "natural causes" instead of reporting them, as required by the guidelines, to the authorities (eg Jochemsen H, 'Euthanasia in Holland: An Ethical critique of new law' JME 1994; 20: 212).

In 1996, Van der Maas and Van der Wal published the results of an extensive survey into end-of-life decisions by Dutch doctors in the year 1995. Do the results of this survey show any improvement in the degree of control over euthanasia?

1 The survey

The survey sought particularly to ascertain the incidence of intentional life-shortening by doctors; the extent to which they complied with their duty to report such cases (in accordance with a procedure dating from 1990 which was given statutory force in June 1994), and the quality of their reporting. The main purpose of the reporting procedure is to provide for possible scrutiny of the intentional termination of life by doctors and to promote careful decision making in such cases. The most important quantitative data generated by the survey are reproduced in table 1.

Before the figures are analysed, it is important to note that the only objectively verifiable figures are those concerning the total number of deaths and the total number of cases reported. All the other figures are based on the responses of the physicians concerning cases in which they said they had recently been involved.

It is no less important to stress that this paper does not question the methodology used by the researchers to obtain their data, namely, interviews with 405 physicians and postal questionnaires mailed to physicians who attended 6,060 deaths identified from death certificates. We use the researchers' own data and standardly cite their "best estimate" (though in some cases numbers have been arrived at on the basis of percentages and numbers used in the survey and, in such cases, we have rounded off the number arrived at). In other words, our paper does not take issue with the researchers' *methodology* but with their *interpretation* of the statistics it generated.

A final preliminary point is that the Dutch adopt a particularly narrow definition of "euthanasia" as the intentional shortening of a patient's life at the patient's explicit request. In other words, "euthanasia" in the Netherlands means "active, voluntary euthanasia" and does not include intentional life-shortening by omission ("passive euthanasia") or euthanasia without the patient's request (whether non-voluntary if the patient is incompetent or involuntary if the patient is competent.) For ease of exposition, the Dutch definition is followed here unless the contrary is apparent.

Table 1   *End-of-life decisions by doctors in the Netherlands 1990–1995*

	1990		1995	
Deaths in the Netherlands	129000	(100%)	135500	(100%)
Requests for euthanasia	8900	(7%)	9700	(7.1%)
Euthanasia	2300	(1.8%)	3200	(2.4%)
Assisted suicide	400	(0.3%)	400	(0.3%)
Life-terminating acts without explicit request	1000	(0.8%)	900	(0.7%)
Intensification of paint & symptom treatment	22500	(17.5%)	20000	(14.8%)
a. Explicitly intended to shorten life	1350	(1%)	2000	(1.5%)
b. Partly intended to shorten life	6750	(5.2%)	2850	(2.1%)
c. Taking into account the probability that life will be shortened	14400	(11.3%)	15150	(11.1%)
Withdrawal/withholding treatment (incl tube-feeding)	22500	(17.5%)	27300	(20.1%)
a. At the explicit request of the patient	5800	(4.5%)	5200	(3.8%)
b. Without the explicit request of the patient				
b1.Explicitly intended to shorten life	2670	(2.1%)	14200	(10.5%)
b2.Partly intended to shorten life	3170	(2.5%)	–	
b3.Taking into account the probability that life will be shortened	10850	(8.4%)	7900	(5.8%)
Intentional termination of neonates				
a. Without withholding/withdrawing treatment	–		10.00	
b. Withholding/withdrawing treatment plus administration of medication explicitly to shorten life	–		80.00	
Assisted suicide of psychiatric patients	–		2–5	

1. EUTHANASIA AND ASSISTED SUICIDE

Between 1990 and 1995 the number of requests for euthanasia increased, as did the number of requests granted. Cases of euthanasia and assisted suicide rose from 2,700 cases in 1990 to 3,600 in 1995, or from 2.1% to 2.7% of all deaths.

According to the attending physicians, there were treatment alternatives in 17% of these cases but in almost all the patients did not want them. However, in 1994, the Dutch Supreme Court held that doctors should not hasten death whenever the alternative of palliative treatment was available, at least in cases of mental suffering and the ministers of justice and health, and the Royal Dutch Medical Association (KNMG), have decided that the same restriction should apply in cases of somatic suffering. The above cases appear, therefore, to have breached this guideline.

Life was shortened by one to four weeks in 31% of euthanasia cases and 45% of assisted suicides and by more than a month in 7% of cases of euthanasia and in 30% of assisted suicides.

Physicians stated that the main reason why patients requested euthanasia was "intolerable suffering without prospect of improvement" (74%), which has become the standard terminology to describe the seriousness of the condition required by the law. But the next most common reasons were "to prevent loss of dignity" (56%) and "to prevent further suffering" (47%). It must surely be doubted whether either of these reasons, by itself, satisfies the requirement of unbearable suffering.

Interestingly, one of the most important reasons for rejecting a request for euthanasia (cited by 35% of physicians) was the physician's opinion that the patient's suffering was not intolerable.

This suggests that, despite the emphasis placed by the advocates of euthanasia on patient autonomy, the application of euthanasia is more a function of the *physician's judgment about the quality of the patient's life* than of respect for the patient's autonomy. This suggestion is fortified by the evidence about the extent to which Dutch doctors continue to terminate the lives of patients without an explicit request.

2. LIFE-TERMINATING ACTIONS WITHOUT EXPLICIT REQUEST

The survey confirms that the intentional shortening of patients' lives without explicit request remains far from uncommon. Nine hundred patients had their lives ended without explicit request in 1995, representing 0.7% of all deaths, only a slight decrease on the 0.8% so terminated in 1990. In other words, of the 4,500 (3,200 + 400 + 900) cases in which doctors admitted they actively and intentionally terminated life, one in five involved no explicit request.

The main reason for not discussing the issue with the patient was stated to be the patient's incompetence (due, for example, to dementia). But not all patients whose lives were terminated without an explicit request were incompetent. In 15% of cases where no discussion took place but could have, the doctor did not discuss the termination of life because the doctor thought that the termination of the patient's life was clearly in the patient's best interests.

Furthermore, in a third of the 900 cases, there had been a discussion with the patient about the possible termination of life, and some 50% of these patients were fully competent, yet their lives were terminated without any explicit request. (This suggests a disturbing incidence not only of non-voluntary euthanasia but also of involuntary euthanasia.)

Moreover, in 17% of the 900 cases, treatment alternatives were thought to be available by the attending physician.

The physicians thought that life was shortened by one to four weeks in 3% of cases but by more than a month in 6%. Finally, physicians had not discussed their action with a colleague in 40% of cases, with a close relative in 30% of cases, and with anyone at all in 5%.

3. INTENSIFICATION OF PAIN AND SYMPTOM TREATMENT
In 20,000 cases (according to the death certificate survey), palliative drugs were administered in doses which almost certainly shortened life. In some 2,000 of these cases the doctor explicitly intended, and in a further 2,850 cases, partly intended, to shorten life. The researchers estimate that the grey area between intending to alleviate pain and symptoms and intending to shorten life is about 2% of all deaths, the same as in 1990.

Where doctors administered palliative drugs partly in order to shorten life, they had discussed it with the patient in just over half of the cases (52%) and in only 36% of the cases was there an explicit request for life-shortening doses by the patient. The physicians stated that 86 patients (3%) with whom they had not discussed this treatment were fully competent. Moreover, in only 36% of the cases had the doctors consulted a colleague. Life was shortened by an estimated one to four weeks in 7% of cases but by more than a month in 1%.

4. WITHHOLDING/WITHDRAWING TREATMENT
In some 27,300 cases a treatment was withheld or withdrawn (in 5,200 cases at the patient's explicit request) taking into account a probable shortening of life.

However, in 18,000 of these cases (14,200 of which involved no explicit request by the patient) it was the physician's explicit intention to shorten life (though the survey does not state in how many cases the treatment was disproportionate, in which cases doctors could, had they wished, have properly withdrawn it for that reason and without intending to shorten life.)

In the majority of cases in which no discussion with the patient had taken place, the physician stated that the patient was either incompetent or only partly competent. However, in 1% of these cases (140 patients) the physician considered the patient fully competent.

In cases where treatment was withheld or withdrawn with the explicit intent to shorten life, the physician estimated that life was shortened by one to seven days in 34% of cases, by one to four weeks in 18% and by more than a month in 9%.

5. NEONATES
The survey reports that over 1,000 newborns die in the Netherlands before their first birthday and estimates that the lives of about 15 are actively and intentionally terminated by doctors. The figure of 15 seems, however, a significant underestimate.

The survey shows that in ten cases (1%) doctors administered a drug with the explicit intention of shortening life. But it also reveals a further 80 cases in which, also with the explicit intention of shortening life, doctors administered a drug and withdrew or withheld a life-prolonging treatment. In total, therefore, it appears to have been the explicit intention of doctors to shorten the lives of 90 neonates not 15.

Moreover, in no fewer than 41% of the 1,000 cases, treatment was withdrawn or withheld with the explicit intention of shortening life. In a significant proportion of these cases, life was terminated because the babies' lives were not thought bearable. Forty-five per cent of these babies were expected to live more than four weeks, and some of them more than half a year.

In around a fifth of cases in which doctors intentionally withheld or withdrew treatment with the explicit purpose of shortening life because the baby's life was thought unbearable, there had been no discussion with the parents. Doctors said that in most cases this was because the situation was so clear that discussion was unnecessary or because there was no time, though these reasons are not elaborated.

Finally, doctors reported hardly any cases of the intentional shortening of neonatal life to the authorities.

6. ASSISTED SUICIDE OF PSYCHIATRIC PATIENTS
Based on the replies of psychiatrists in respect of the year 1995, the survey estimates that although some 320 psychiatric patients explicitly request assistance in suicide annually, only

two to five are assisted to commit suicide by psychiatrists. Among psychiatrists who would never grant a request for assisted suicide on the basis of mental suffering (almost 1/3 of the respondents) "professional opinion" was cited by 88% as the most important reason. Only 2% of psychiatrists had ever assisted suicide.

This relatively restrictive approach of psychiatrists may owe not a little to the controversy generated by the case of Dr Chabot, a psychiatrist criticised by a medical disciplinary court for assisting in the suicide of a 50-year-old woman who suffered grief after the loss of her two sons.

Disclosing statistics which support a restrictive approach, the survey also indicates that of those patients not assisted in suicide, 16% committed suicide without assistance by a physician and that, of those patients still living, 35% no longer wished for death and that the death wish in a further 10% had diminished.

7. CONSULTATION

The guidelines for permissible euthanasia and assisted suicide require the doctor, before agreeing to either, to engage in a formal consultation (*consultatie*), and not merely an informal discussion (*overleg*), with a colleague.

In cases of euthanasia and assisted suicide 92% of doctors had, according to the survey, discussed the case with a colleague. In 13% of these cases, however, the discussion did not amount to a formal consultation. Consultation took place, therefore, in 79% of cases. However, other figures in the survey suggest that consultation occurred in a significantly smaller percentage of cases. For the survey indicates that consultation occurred in 99% of reported cases but in only 18% of unreported cases and that almost 60% of all cases of euthanasia and assisted suicide were not reported, from which it seems that consultation occurred in only around half of all cases.

In the cases of life-termination without explicit request, a discussion occurred in 43% of cases but in 40% this did not amount to consultation. Consequently, there was no consultation in 97% of such cases.

Moreover, even when consultation did take place, it was usually with a physician living locally and the most important reasons given for consulting such a physician were his views on life-ending decisions and his living nearby: expertise in palliative care was hardly mentioned. Further, in the overwhelming majority of cases, the first doctor had made his mind up before consulting and the doctor consulted disagreed in only 7% of cases. In short, the requirement of consultation, even when it is satisfied, hardly operates as a rigorous check on decision making.

8. REPORTING

In 1995 41% of cases of euthanasia and assisted suicide were reported to the local medical examiner, as required by the reporting procedure. While this is an improvement on the figure of 18% reported in 1990, it means that a clear majority of cases, almost 60%, still go unreported. Moreover, the survey confirms that the legal requirements are breached more frequently in unreported cases, in which there is less often a written request by the patient, a written record by the doctor, or consultation by the doctor.

The most important reasons given by doctors for failing to report in 1995 were (as in 1990), the wish to avoid the inconvenience (for the doctor and/or the relatives) of an investigation by the authorities, and to avoid the risk of prosecution (though, as the consistently tiny number of prosecutions indicates, this risk is negligible). Thirty per cent of doctors stated that they did not report because they had failed to observe the requirements for permissible euthanasia and 12% because they considered euthanasia was a private matter between doctor and patient.

II Discussion

The second survey confirms at least three disturbing findings of the first survey.

1. INCIDENCE OF INTENTIONAL LIFE-SHORTENING WITH AND WITHOUT EXPLICIT REQUEST

Like the first survey, the second indicates a sizeable incidence of intentional life-shortening by Dutch doctors. Even adopting the unusually narrow Dutch definition of euthanasia as active, of voluntary euthanasia there were no fewer than 3,200 cases in 1995 (2.4% of all deaths), an increase of almost a thousand on the 1990 total of 2,300 (1.8% of all deaths).

But if *all* cases in which doctors explicitly intended to shorten life (whether by act or omission, and whether with or without the patient's request) are included, the total rises steeply. Adding the cases of assisted suicide (400); life-termination without explicit request (900) and the intensification of pain and symptom treatment with the explicit intent to shorten life (2,000), the total more than doubles from 3,200 to 6,500.

And if to this number are added the cases of withholding or withdrawing treatment with the explicit intent to shorten life (18,000); cases in which neonates were intentionally terminated (90 cases) and psychiatric patients assisted in suicide (two to five cases), the total rises to over 24,500 cases.

2. EUTHANASIA AS AN ALTERNATIVE TO PALLIATIVE CARE

The survey's comment that "the quality of medical treatment near the end of life has improved" might not unreasonably be thought to display a certain complacency, particularly in a country which has some way to go in the provision of adequate palliative care. The high incidence of intentional life-shortening disclosed by the survey and the relative weakness of the reasons for euthanasia given in many cases by the doctors tend to suggest that euthanasia is not confined to cases of "last resort" and is at least sometimes used as an alternative to palliative care. The case of Dr Chabot, in which the defendant doctor assisted a grieving woman, whom he did not consider to be physically or mentally ill, to kill herself, and in which the Supreme Court held that such suffering could indeed justify assisted suicide, illustrates the elasticity of the requirement of "unbearable suffering".

The survey confirms that, even when doctors believe that treatment alternatives are available, they not infrequently resort to euthanasia. The opinion of the Supreme Court, the ministers of justice and health, and the KNMG, that euthanasia is impermissible when treatment alternatives are available, even if the patient refuses them, has clearly not prevented its administration in such circumstances. In a move that would make the prospect of prosecution even more remote, the then minister of justice appeared to reverse her earlier position and instructed the attorneys general that the refusal by the patient of available treatment alternatives does not render euthanasia unlawful.

3. WIDESPREAD BREACH OF THE REQUIREMENT TO REPORT

Although 41% of cases (1,466) were reported in 1995 as opposed to 18% (486) in 1990, it remains true that in both years, as in every year in between, a clear majority of cases has gone unreported. There was, in short, no official control whatever over the majority of cases of euthanasia, assisted suicide or the termination of life without explicit request.

Nor should the alleged increase in reporting be accepted uncritically. First, the second survey records an increase in cases of euthanasia between 1990 and 1995 (900 cases) almost as large as the increase in cases reported (980 cases). Secondly, if the total of 6,500 cases of active, intentional life-shortening is used, then the proportion of unreported cases rises from 59% to 77%. On the total of 24,500 cases, the proportion unreported reaches 94%.

It will be recalled that the purpose of the reporting procedure is to allow for scrutiny of the intentional termination of life by doctors and to promote observance of the legal and professional requirements for euthanasia. The undisputed fact that a clear majority of cases (59% according to the survey, at least 77% on our calculations) still goes unreported, serves only to reinforce doubts about the ability of the procedure to fulfil its purpose and to undermine Dutch claims of effective regulation, scrutiny and control. Further, even those cases which *are* reported are reported by the doctor, and one may wonder whether the doctor's report is any more likely to disclose evidence of wrongdoing than is a tax return to disclose evidence of undeclared earnings.

Replying to this critical article, a Dutch physician and bioethicist deals with three of the criticisms – lack of palliative care, cases of non-voluntary euthanasia and under reporting.

Johannes JM Van Delden 'Slippery Slopes in Flat Countries – a Response' (1999) 25 JME 22

Euthanasia and palliative care

The Netherlands are often criticised for their presumed lack of palliative care. The existence of only very few hospices in the Netherlands, for example, is often interpreted as proof of a neglect of palliative care. Although much of this criticism is based on misunderstanding and much effort is made to improve palliative care at present, Jochemsen and Keown are right when they say that the Netherlands "have some way to go in the provision of adequate palliative care". Which is, of course, also true for many other countries. But what does this mean for a moral evaluation of euthanasia?

By and large there appear to be three ways of dealing with the issue of euthanasia. The first is to reject it on the grounds that it is forbidden by the principle of respect for life. Proponents of this view often also claim that euthanasia is not necessary at all. They believe that by paying sincere and close attention to the person who requests euthanasia the "question behind the question" will surely be revealed to be something other than a request for death, and that with good palliative care extreme suffering need not remain unanswered. In this view euthanasia and palliative care are incompatible.

An alternative response to the euthanasia issue stresses the importance of compassion. From this point of view, respect for life is of paramount importance as is good palliative care. Sometimes however, supporters of this view admit that sometimes illness and dying come with such suffering that life is reduced to pointless surviving. If all other palliative measures fail, then euthanasia may be justified. The result of this view of euthanasia is the medicalisation of the end of life, since whether euthanasia is justifiable becomes largely a matter of medical discretion.

These two responses appear to differ primarily in their answer to the question: "Does intractable excruciating suffering exist"? However, even palliative care specialists will state that, unfortunately, it does. The real difference therefore, will be whether one allows the principle of respect for life to be overridden by other considerations in special circumstances.

Most proposals to regulate euthanasia follow the second view. This is also true for the official legal position in the Netherlands where a conflict of the physician's duties is the basis for not prosecuting him or her, not the granting of a patient's right. There is no right to die in the Netherlands, nor is there an obligation for the physician to comply with the request of a competent patient to die even if certain conditions are met. From an official and legal point of view, therefore, euthanasia is only tolerated as a last resort.

The reality of the Dutch euthanasia practice, however, seems to be developing in another direction, with increasing emphasis on respect for patient autonomy. This could lead to a shift to a third approach in which euthanasia is seen as a choice. Some patients do not want to live through suffering and decline even if pain can be controlled. They want autonomously to decide about how and when to die and they want their relatives to remember them as they were when they were more or less healthy. They want to step out of life before the terminal phase really starts and they want a doctor to do the lethal work.

This development is reflected in the data produced in all major studies in the Netherlands. The first nationwide study of end-of-life decisions showed that pain hardly ever was the sole reason for requesting euthanasia (Maas PJ van der, Delden JJM van, Pijnenborg L 'Euthanasia and other medical decisions concerning the end of life' Amsterdam: Elsevier, 1992). In 1992 an independent study by Van der Wal showed that in 56% of cases of euthanasia, requests were made because patients thought suffering to be pointless and in 16% because they feared the decline (Wal G van der, Eijk JThm van, Spreeuwenberg C, 'Euthanasia and assisted suicide. II. Do Dutch family doctors act prudently?' Family Practice 1992; 9: 135–40). And the 1996 report showed that many patients asked for euthanasia to prevent more suffering. The research by Cuperus-Bosma *et al*, reported elsewhere in this issue (Cuperus-Bosma *et al*, 'Assessment of physician-assisted death by members of public prosecution in the Netherlands' Journal of Medical Ethics 1999; 25: 8–15), shows that the shift to autonomy is not a matter of patients only, but also of members of the public prosecution. The investigators showed that the presence or absence of an explicit request was the most important determination of the decision whether to hold an inquest. Life expectancy and type of suffering do play a role but a less important one.

One may also predict (as an aside) that this emphasis on patient autonomy will lead to a change in the medical circumstances in euthanasia cases. At this moment cancer is by far the predominant diagnosis. The shift towards autonomy-based decisions, however, will lead to an increase in the prevalence of situations characterised by a loss of autonomy (such as in dementia or after a stroke).

This emerging sense that one does have a right to die, means that more palliative care does not necessarily lead to a decreasing incidence of euthanasia. From a sociological point of view one may be tempted to interpret the shift towards autonomy-based requests for euthanasia as a byproduct of a liberal society, with its emphasis on self-government, control and rational choice. A moral evaluation of this development, however, will depend largely on one's normative views. Jochemsen and Keown will presume that they can rest their case: their prediction of the slippery slope has come true. Others will say that more emphasis on patient autonomy fits perfectly into the process of emancipation of the patient that has been going on since the beginning of the 1970s. They might say that it is about time to start thinking about patient decisions concerning the end of life, instead of about medical ones.

The cases of non-voluntary euthanasia

The cases of non-voluntary euthanasia, described both in the 1991 and the 1996 reports, created a new dimension in the Dutch euthanasia debate. Since the middle of the 1980s, this debate had been focused on euthanasia and assisted suicide with the explicit request of the patient as central feature. This in part had been a deliberate narrowing of the discussion because it was felt that consensus was greatest for these cases. The Dutch even changed their definition of euthanasia to mean only the cases in which there was an explicit request by the patient. Thus, a possibly justifying feature (the request) was turned into a necessary condition.

The description of the non-voluntary cases has broadened the discussion again. But what does their appearance in the reports mean? Does this prove the slippery slope? For many years Dutch commentators on euthanasia only talked about cases on request and non-voluntary cases only recently became known. Thus, the impression may have risen that the Dutch began with hastening the end of life on request and ended up with non-voluntary cases.

This, however, is not necessarily true. We simply do not know whether non-voluntary euthanasia occurred less or more often in the past. What we do know is that the occurrence of non-voluntary euthanasia did not increase in the Netherlands between 1991 and 1996, and also that its prevalence is much higher in another country (Australia), which did not slide down the slope by tolerating euthanasia for years and years.

But even if they do not prove the existence of the slippery slope, the non-voluntary euthanasia cases do form a very serious problem. They are obviously not justified by the principle of respect for patient autonomy as in the third view described above, and therefore can only be tolerated (if at all) in extreme situations where life termination is really a last resort and non-voluntary euthanasia becomes "mercy-killing". It is very unlikely that this was the case in all cases described in the Dutch reports.

Underreporting

To accept euthanasia in an individual case is one thing, to accept it on a public policy level is quite something else. It is often argued that proposals to legalise euthanasia can never contain absolute safeguards (Miles S, Pappas D, Koepp R 'Considerations of safeguards proposed in laws and guidelines to legalize assisted suicide'. In: Weir Robert F, ed 'Physician-assisted suicide' Bloomington: Indiana University Press, 1997). I think this is true: there is no rule that cannot (and will not) be broken. By the way, this goes for the prohibition of drunk-driving as well. The question is whether this justifies a prohibition of euthanasia in an individual case. The Dutch tried to have it both ways by creating a public policy based on individual cases. The least one can say is that this resulted in an unsatisfactory situation of accepting and prohibiting at the same time. This created uncertainty and unclarity both for patients and physicians and probably contributed to some extent to the critical reports such as the one commented upon here (Jochemsen H, Keown J 'Voluntary Euthanasia under control? further empirical evidence from the Netherlands' Journal of Medical Ethics 1999; 25: 16–21).

Persuading the physician to bring euthanasia cases to the knowledge of the authorities is a problem for any euthanasia policy. The Dutch notification procedure helped to raise the notification rate to 41% in 1995. As is briefly discussed in the paper by Cuperus-Bosma (supra), the government has tried to diminish further the number of unreported cases by developing a new notification procedure, in which much of the assessment is done "outside of" the legal system. Since November 1, 1998, five regional multidisciplinary assessment committees have to advise the public prosecutor in all reported cases of euthanasia. The effect of this change in procedure is not clear yet.

Cuperus-Bosma *et al* hope that reducing the role of the public prosecution will lead to fewer differences in assessment and more legal equality. However, one may ask why would these committees differ less in their assessment of cases. Their strength is their opportunity to communicate with the reporting physician in a decriminalised setting and, by so doing, influence practice. Uniformity should not be their main concern.

(For a more detailed discussion of the Dutch data, see J Griffiths, A Bood, H Weyers *Euthanasia & Law in the Netherlands* (1998), chs 5 and 7.)

(iv) NORTHERN TERRITORY (AUSTRALIA)

Whilst the Dutch practice is longer-standing, it is not based upon legislative intervention to legalise voluntary euthanasia. In England, that is the only (albeit unlikely) prospect for reform (for an argument that the judges should act see, I Kennedy 'The Quality of Mercy: Patients, Doctors and Dying', Upjohn Lecture, 25 April 1994). How could such a statute be framed? The only example is the Rights of the Terminally Ill Act 1995 in the Northern Territory in Australia. The constitutionality of the Act was upheld by the Supreme Court of the Northern Territory in July 1996 (*Wake and Gondarra v Northern Territory* (1996) 109 NTR 1) but after only a brief period in force it was, in effect, repealed by the Euthanasia Laws Act 1996 passed by the Federal Parliament and which came into force in March 1997 (for a discussion of the history, see M Otlowski *Voluntary Euthanasia and the Common Law* (*op cit*) pp v–xi). In the result four individuals' lives were ended under the Act.

Rights of the Terminally Ill Act 1995 (NT)

Part 1—Preliminary

... 3. Interpretation

In this Act, unless the contrary intention appears—

'assist', in relation to the death or proposed death of a patient, includes the prescribing of a substance, the preparation of a substance and the giving of a substance to the patient for self administration, and the administration of a substance to the patient;

'certificate of request' means a certificate in or to the effect of the form in the Schedule that has been completed, signed and witnessed in accordance with this Act;

'health care provider', in relation to a patient, includes a hospital, nursing home or other institution (including those responsible for its management) in which the patient is located for care or attention and any nurse of other person whose duties include or directly or indirectly relate to the care or medical treatment of the patient;

'illness' includes injury or degeneration of mental or physical faculties;

'medical practitioner' means a medical practitioner who has been entitled to practise as a medical practitioner (however described) in a State of a Territory of the Commonwealth for a continuous period of not less than 5 years and who is resident in, and entitled under the Medical Act to practise medicine in, the Territory;

'qualified psychiatrist' means—

   (a)   a person entitled under a law of a State or Territory of the Commonwealth to practise as a specialist in the medical specialty of psychiatry;

   (b)   a specialist whose qualifications are recognised by the Royal Australian and New Zealand College of Psychiatrists as entitling the person to fellowship of that College; or

   (c)   a person employed by the Commonwealth or a State or Territory of the Commonwealth, or an Agency or authority of the Commonwealth or a State or Territory, as a specialist or consultant in the medical specialty of psychiatry;

'terminal illness', in relation to a patient, means an illness which, in reasonable medical judgment will, in the normal course, without the application of extraordinary measures or of treatment unacceptable to the patient, result in the death of the patient.

Part 2—Request for and Giving of Assistance

4. Request for assistance to voluntarily terminate life

A patient who, in the course of a terminal illness, is experiencing pain, suffering and/or distress to an extent unacceptable to the patient, may request the patient's medical practitioner to assist the patient to terminate the patient's life.

5. Response of medical practitioner

A medical practitioner who receives a request referred to in section 4, if satisfied that the conditions of section 7 have been met, but subject to section 8, may assist the patient to terminate the patient's life in accordance with this Act or, for any reason and at any time, refuse to give that assistance.

6. Response of medical practitioner, &c., not to be influenced by extraneous considerations

(1) A person shall not give or promise any reward or advantage (other than a reasonable payment for medical services), or by any means cause or threaten to cause any disadvantage, to a medical practitioner or other person for refusing to assist, or for the purpose of compelling or persuading the medical practitioner or other person to assist or refuse to assist, in the termination of a patient's life under this Act.

Penalty: $10,000.

(2) A person to whom a reward or advantage is promised or given, as referred to in subsection (1), does not have the legal right or capacity to receive or retain the reward or accept or exercise the advantage, whether or not, at the relevant time, he or she was aware of the promise or the intention to give the reward or advantage.

7. Conditions under which medical practitioner may assist

(1) A medical practitioner may assist a patient to end his or her life only if all of the following conditions are met:

   (a) the patient has attained the age of 18 years;

   (b) the medical practitioner is satisfied, on reasonable grounds, that—

      (i) the patient is suffering from an illness that will, in the normal course and without the application of extraordinary measures result in the death of the patient;

    (ii) in reasonable medical judgment, there is no medical measure acceptable to the patient that can reasonably be undertaken in the hope of effecting a cure; and

    (iii) any medical treatment reasonably available to the patient is confined to the relief of pain, suffering and/or distress with the object of allowing the patient to die a comfortable death;

(c) two other persons, neither of whom is a relative or employee of, or a member of the same medical practice as, the first medical practitioner or each other—

    (i) one of whom is a medical practitioner who holds prescribed professional qualifications, or has prescribed experience, in the treatment of the terminal illness from which the patient is suffering; and

    (ii) the other who is a qualified psychiatrist,

have examined the patient and have confirmed—

    (iii) in the case of the medical practitioner referred to in subparagraph (i)—

      (A) the first medical practitioner's opinion as to the existence and seriousness of the illness;

      (B) that the patient is likely to die as a result of the illness; and

      (C) the first medical practitioner's prognosis; and

    (iv) in the case of the qualified psychiatrist referred to in subparagraph (ii)—that the patient is not suffering from a treatable clinical depression in respect of the illness;

(d) the illness is causing the patient severe pain or suffering;

(e) the medical practitioner has informed the patient of the nature of the illness and its likely course, and the medical treatment, including palliative care, counselling and psychiatric support and extraordinary measures for keeping the patient alive, that might be available to the patient;

(f) after being informed as referred to in paragraph (e), the patient indicates to the medical practitioner that the patient has decided to end his or her life;

(g) the medical practitioner is satisfied that the patient has considered the possible implications of the patient's decision to his or her family;

(h) the medical practitioner is satisfied, on reasonable grounds, that the patient is of sound mind and that the patient's decision to end his or her life has been made freely, voluntarily and after due consideration;

(i) the patient, or a person acting on the patient's behalf in accordance with section 9, has, not earlier than 7 days after the patient has indicated to his or her medical practitioner as referred to in paragraph (f), signed that part of the certificate of request required to be completed by or on behalf of the patient;

(j) the medical practitioner has witnessed the patient's signature on the certificate of request or that of the person who signed on behalf of the patient, and has completed and signed the relevant declaration on the certificate;

(k) the certificate of request has been signed in the presence of the patient and the first medical practitioner by another medical practitioner (who may be the first medical practitioner referred to in paragraph (c)(i) or any other medical practitioner) after that medical practitioner has discussed the case with the first medical practitioner and the patient and is satisfied, on reasonable grounds, that the certificate is in order, that the patient is of sound mind and the patient's decision to end his or her life has been made freely, voluntarily and after due consideration, and that the above conditions have been complied with;

(l) where, in accordance with subsection (4), an interpreter is required to be present at the signing of the certificate of request, the certificate of request has been signed by the interpreter confirming the patient's understanding of the request for assistance;

(m) the medical practitioner has no reason to believe that he or she, the countersigning medical practitioner or a close relative or associate of either of them, will gain a financial or other advantage (other than a reasonable payment for medical services) directly or indirectly as a result of the death of the patient;

(n) not less than 48 hours has elapsed since the signing of the completed certificate of request;

(o) at no time before assisting the patient to end his or her life had the patient given to the medical practitioner an indication that it was no longer the patient's wish to end his or her life;

(p) the medical practitioner himself or herself provides the assistance and/or is and remains present while the assistance is given and until the death of the patient.

(2) In assisting a patient under this Act a medical practitioner shall be guided by appropriate medical standards and such guidelines, if any, as are prescribed, and shall consider the

appropriate pharmaceutical information about any substance reasonably available for use in the circumstances.

(3) Where a patient's medical practitioner has no special qualifications in the field of palliative care, the information to be provided to the patient on the availability of palliative care shall be given by a medical practitioner (who may be the medical practitioner referred to in subsection (1)(c)(i) or any other medical practitioner) who has such special qualifications in the field of palliative care as are described.

(4) A medical practitioner shall not assist a patient under this Act where the medical practitioner or any other medical practitioner or qualified psychiatrist who is required under subsection (1) or (3) to communicate with the patient does not share the same first language as the patient, unless there is present at the time of that communication and at the time the certificate of request is signed by or on behalf of the patient, an interpreter who holds a prescribed professional qualification for interpreters in the first language of the patient.

8. Palliative care

(1) A medical practitioner shall not assist a patient under this Act if, in his or her opinion and after considering the advice of the medical practitioner referred to in section 7(1)(c)(i), there are palliative care options reasonably available to the patient to alleviate the patient's pain and suffering to levels acceptable to the patient.

(2) Where a patient has requested assistance under this Act and has subsequently been provided with palliative care that brings about the remission of the patient's pain or suffering, the medical practitioner shall not, in pursuance of the patient's original request for assistance, assist the patient under this Act. If subsequently the palliative care ceases to alleviate the patient's pain and suffering to levels acceptable to the patient, the medical practitioner may continue to assist the patient under this Act only if the patient indicates to the medical practitioner the patient's wish to proceed in pursuance of the request.

9. Patient who is unable to sign certificate of request

(1) If a patient who has requested his or her medical practitioner to assist the patient to end the patient's life is physically unable to sign the certificate of request, any person who has attained the age of 18 years, other than the medical practitioner or a medical practitioner or qualified psychiatrist referred to in section 7(1)(c), or a person who is likely to receive a financial benefit directly or indirectly as a result of the death of the patient, may, at the patient's request and in the presence of the patient and both the medical practitioner witnesses (and where, in accordance with section 7(4) an interpreter has been used, also in the presence of the interpreter), sign the certificate on behalf of the patient.

(2) A person who signs a certificate of request on behalf of a patient forfeits any financial or other benefit the person would otherwise obtain, directly or indirectly, as a result of the death of the patient.

10. Right to rescind request

(1) Notwithstanding anything in this Act, a patient may rescind a request for assistance under this Act at any time and in any manner.

(2) Where a patient rescinds a request, the patient's medical practitioner shall, as soon as practicable, destroy the certificate of request and note that fact on the patient's medical record.

11. Improper conduct

(1) A person shall not, by deception or improper influence, procure the signing or witnessing of a certificate of request.

Penalty: $20,000 or imprisonment for 4 years.

(2) A person found guilty of an offence against subsection (1) forfeits any financial or other benefit the person would otherwise obtain, directly or indirectly, as a result of the death of the patient, whether or not the death results from assistance given under this Act.

Part 3—Records and Reporting of Death

12. Medical records to be kept

A medical practitioner who, under this Act, assists a patient to terminate the patient's life shall file and, subject to this Act, keep the following as part of the medical record of the patient:

(a) a note of any oral request of the patient for such assistance;

(b) the certificate of request;

(c) a record of the opinion of the patient's medical practitioner as to the patient's state of mind at the time of signing the certificate of request and certification of the medical practitioner's opinion that the patient's decision to end his or her life was made freely, voluntarily and after due consideration;

(d) the reports of the medical practitioner and qualified psychiatrist referred to in section 7(1)(c);

(e) a note by the patient's medical practitioner—
     (i) certifying as to the independence of the medical practitioner and qualified
          psychiatrist referred to in section 7(1)(c) and the residential and period of practice
          qualifications of the patient's medical practitioner;
     (ii) indicating that all requirements under this Act have been met;
     (iii) indicating the steps taken to carry out the request for assistance; and
     (iv) including a notation of the substance prescribed,
     and such other information, if any, as is prescribed.
   Penalty: $10,000 or imprisonment for 2 years.

13. Certification as to death

(1) A medical practitioner who, under this Act, assists a patient to end the patient's life shall be
taken to have attended the patient during the patient's last illness for the purposes of Part IV of the
Registration of Births, Deaths and Marriages Act or any provision in substitution for that Part.

(2) A death as the result of assistance given under this Act shall not, for that reason only, be
taken to be unexpected, unnatural or violent for the purposes of the definition of 'reportable
death' in the application of Part 4 of the Coroner's Act, or be a reportable death by reason only of
having occurred during an anaesthetic.

14. Medical record to be sent to Coroner

(1) As soon as practicable after the death of a patient as the result of assistance given under this
Act, the medical practitioner who gave the assistance shall report the death to a Coroner by
sending to the Coroner a copy of the death certificate under the Registration of Births, Deaths and
Marriages Act and so much of the medical record of the patient (including that required by section
12 to be kept) as relates to the terminal illness and death of the patient.

(2) As soon as practicable after the end of each financial year the Coroner shall advise the
Attorney-General of the number of patients who died as a result of assistance given under this Act
and the Attorney-General, in such manner or report as he or she thinks appropriate, shall report
the number to the Legislative Assembly.

15. Coroner may report on operation of Act

The Coroner may, at any time and in his or her absolute discretion, report to the Attorney-
General on the operation, or any matter affecting the operation, of this Act and the Attorney-
General shall, within 3 sitting days of the Legislative Assembly after receiving the report, table a
copy of the report in the Assembly.

Part 4—Miscellaneous

16. Construction of Act

(1) Notwithstanding section 26(3) of the Criminal Code, an action taken in accordance with
this Act by a medical practitioner or by a health care provider on the instructions of a medical
practitioner does not constitute an offence against Part VI of the Criminal Code or an attempt to
commit such an offence, a conspiracy to commit such an offence, or an offence of aiding, abetting,
counselling or procuring the commission of such an offence.

(2) Assistance given in accordance with this Act by a medical practitioner or by a health care
provider on the instructions of a medical practitioner is taken to be medical treatment for the
purposes of the law.

17. Certificate of request is evidence

A document purporting to be a certificate of request is, in any proceedings before a court, admissible
in evidence and is prima facie evidence of the request by the person who purported to sign it or on
whose behalf it is purported to have been signed, for assistance under this Act.

18. Effect on construction of wills, contracts and statutes

(1) Any will, contract or other agreement, whether or not in writing or executed or made before
or after the commencement of this Act, to the extent that it affects whether a person may take or
rescind a request for assistance under this Act, or the giving of such assistance, is not valid.

(2) An obligation owing under a contract, whether made before or after the commencement of
this Act, shall not be conditioned or affected by the making or rescinding of a request for assistance
under this Act or the giving of that assistance.

19. Insurance or annuity policies

The sale, procurement or issuing of any life, health or accident insurance or annuity policy or
the rate charged for such a policy shall not be conditioned on or affected by the making or
rescinding of a request for assistance under this Act or the giving of that assistance.

20. Immunities

(1) A person shall not be subject to civil or criminal action or professional disciplinary
action for anything done in good faith and without negligence in compliance with this Act,

including being present when a patient takes a substance prescribed for or supplied to the patient as the result of assistance under this Act to end the patient's life.

(2) A professional organisation or association or health care provider shall not subject a person to censure, discipline, suspension, loss of licence, certificate or other authority to practise, loss of privilege, loss of membership or other penalty for anything that, in good faith and without negligence, was done or refused to be done by the person and which may under this Act lawfully be done or refused to be done.

(3) A request by a patient for assistance under this Act, or giving of such assistance in good faith by a medical practitioner in compliance with this Act, shall not constitute neglect for any purpose of law or alone constitute or indicate a disability for the purposes of an application under section 8 of the Adult Guardianship Act.

(4) A health care provider is not under any duty, whether by contract, statute or other legal requirement, to participate in the provision to a patient of assistance under this Act, and if a health care provider is unable or unwilling to carry out a direction of a medical practitioner for the purpose of the medical practitioner assisting a patient under this Act and the patient transfers his or her care to another health care provider, the former health care provider shall, on request, transfer a copy of the patient's relevant medical records to the new health care provider.

21. Regulations

The Administrator may make regulations, not inconsistent with this Act, prescribing all matters—

(a) required or permitted by this Act to be prescribed; or
(b) necessary or convenient to be prescribed for carrying out or giving effect to this Act.

SCHEDULE
Section 7

Request for assistance to end my life in a humane and dignified manner

I have been advised by my medical practitioner that I am suffering from an illness which will ultimately result in my death and this has been confirmed by a second medical practitioner.

I have been fully informed of the nature of my illness and its likely course and the medical treatment, including palliative care, counselling and psychiatric support and extraordinary measures that may keep me alive, that is available to me and I am satisfied that there is no medical treatment reasonably available that is acceptable to me in my circumstances.

I request my medical practitioner to assist me to terminate my life in a humane and dignified manner.

I understand that I have the right to rescind this request at any time.

Signed:

Dated:

Declaration of witnesses

I declare that—
(a) the person signing this request is personally known to me;
(b) he/she is a patient under my care;
(c) he/she signed the request in my presence and in the presence of the second witness to this request;
(d) I am satisfied that he/she is of sound mind and that his/her decision to end his/her life has been made freely, voluntarily and after due consideration.

Signed: Patient's Medical Practitioner

I declare that—
(a) the person signing this bequest is known to me;
(b) I have discussed his/her case with him/her and his/her medical practitioner;
(c) he/she signed the request in my presence and in the presence of his/her medical practitioner;
(d) I am satisfied that he/she is of sound mind and that his/her decision to end his/her life has been made freely, voluntarily and after due consideration;
(e) I am satisfied that the conditions of section 7 of the Act have been or will be complied with.

Signed: Second Medical Practitioner

[Where under section 7(4) an interpreter is required to be present]

Declaration of interpreter
I declare that—
(a)   the person signing this request or on whose behalf it is signed is known to me;
(b)   I am an interpreter qualified to interpret in the first language of the patient as required by section 7(4);
(c)   I have interpreted for the patient in connection with the completion and signing of this certificate;
(d)   in my opinion, the patient understands the meaning and nature of this certificate.

Signed: Qualified Interpreter.

We do not set out here the Rights of the Terminally Ill Regulations 1996 made pursuant to s 21 of the Act, which provided some guidelines for the carrying out of voluntary euthanasia and physician-assisted suicide.

The Act created an exception to the crimes of homicide and assisting suicide contained in ss 162 (murder) and 168 (assisting suicide) of the NT Criminal Code Act 1983.

The following extract described the provisions of the Act. Notice the following: (1) patients to whom the Act applies; (2) conditions for aiding death; (3) the nature of the patient's request; and (4) record keeping and reporting procedures.

Suzanne Trollope 'Legislating a Right to Die: The Rights of the Terminally Ill Act' 1995 (NT) (1995) 3 Journal of Law and Medicine 19

The general framework of the legislation
The general framework of the legislation is to allow for a medical practitioner to assist with the termination of a patient's life upon request, where a patient has a terminal illness: s 4. The patient must be 18 years of age (s 7(1)(a)) and of sound mind (s 7(1)(h)), replacing the previous requirement that the patient be "competent" in order to make the Act consistent with the provisions of the *Natural Death Act* 1988 (NT). Also, the request for assistance must be made in writing in accordance with the "certificate of request" in the Schedule to the Act. In the original Bill there were 14 conditions which had to be met before a medical practitioner might give assistance. There are now 16: s 7. The conditions regulate the circumstances under which euthanasia may be exercised. The more significant of these are discussed in detail below.

The general scheme of the legislation is to allow a medical practitioner to assist a patient to end his or her life. Where this is done in accordance with the provisions of the Act, the medical practitioner does not incur any criminal or civil liability in respect of that action: s 20.

"Assist" is defined in four different ways: s 3. First, a medical practitioner may prescribe for the patient a substance that may be used to terminate his or her life. Secondly, a medical practitioner may prepare that substance. Thirdly, assistance may then be given for the patient to self administer the substance; or fourthly, the medical practitioner may administer the substance to the patient. In the last two cases the medical practitioner is required to remain with the patient until the death of the patient: s 7(1)(p). The patient must be examined by a second medical practitioner who must confirm the diagnosis and prognosis of the illness: s 7(1)(c)(i), (ii) and (iii). That practitioner must also be able to certify that the patient is not suffering from a treatable clinical depression: s 7(1)(c)(iv). The original Bill was amended to ensure the independence of the two medical practitioners. The second medical practitioner must not be a relative or employee of, or a member of the same medical practice as, the first medical practitioner: s 7(1)(c).

Although the definition of "assist" revolves around the preparation and use of a "substance" for administration, the proposed legislation provides no definition of what those substances might be, nor does it provide a schedule of acceptable substances. It would appear then that the choice of drug and the form which it takes (for example, injection, tablet or liquid) is entirely up to the medical practitioner concerned. The Assembly has, however, added s 7(2) which requires a medical practitioner to be guided by appropriate medical standards and "such guidelines, if any, as are prescribed, and shall consider the appropriate pharmaceutical information about any substance reasonably available for use in the circumstances".

Although the primary focus is on enabling a medical practitioner to provide assistance to a patient to terminate his or her life, it would seem that the tasks of preparing a substance of administration and the actual administration of the substance may be performed by a "health care provider". Section 16(1) provides that an action taken by a medical practitioner in accordance with the Act "or by a health care provider on the instructions of a medical practitioner" shall not constitute an offence under Pt VI of the *Criminal Code*.

"Health care provider" is defined in s 3 as including

> in relation to a patient, ... a hospital, nursing home or other institution (including those responsible for its management) in which the patient is located for care or attention and any nurse or other person whose duties include or directly or indirectly relate to the care or medical treatment of the patient.

Section 16 would therefore provide, for example, immunity against civil or criminal liability for a pharmacist who, on the instructions of a medical practitioner, prepared a lethal substance for administration. But it is suggested that s 16(1) might also allow a delegation of the medical practitioner's power to administer a substance to terminate life, not only to a "nurse" but to a person who has no medical qualifications.

To some extent, the potential difficulties of allowing a person other than a medical practitioner to assist a patient to terminate his or her life are removed by s 7(1)(p), which requires the medical practitioner to be present while assistance is given and until the death of the patient occurs.

Patients to whom the Act will apply

The Act allows a patient who is "in the course of a terminal illness" and who is "experiencing pain, suffering and/or distress unacceptable to the patient" to request that a medical practitioner give assistance to terminate his or her life: s 4.

"Terminal illness" was not specifically defined in the original Bill. From the general provisions, however, it was clear that the legislation was only to apply to an illness from which the patient was, within the reasonable judgment of a medical practitioner, likely to die within 12 months. That diagnosis was required to be confirmed by a second medical practitioner who had examined the patient.

One of the significant alterations made to the original Bill is the removal of the requirement that the "terminal illness" be one that is likely to cause death within 12 months (the previous s 6(b)). That requirement was fraught with a number of difficulties. First, it did not make clear whether the assessment of an illness as terminal and likely to cause death within 12 months was one which was to be made after all therapy has been tried and there was no remission of the disease, or whether a patient might refuse all treatment (even where there was a potential for cure) and request assistance to terminate his or her life. Secondly, the 12-month requirement imposed on a medical practitioner an assessment that was bound to be problematical. While mathematical figures provide a simple option from the drafter's point of view, they do not in the context of legislation of this nature provide clear parameters for the medical practitioner who is attempting to act within the legal framework of the legislation. As the illness was simply to be one that would be reasonably likely to cause death within 12 months, there were, foreseeably, a whole range of illnesses that might come within that definition. For example, certain coronary conditions, cystic fibrosis and AIDS are three diverse illnesses which might at some stage be likely to cause death within 12 months. No specialist qualification was required by the original provisions of the Bill, and as will be discussed later, "distress" on its own was to be an adequate ground for termination without the necessity for the patient to be experiencing pain or suffering. In such circumstances, a medical practitioner may not have felt particularly comfortable about acceding to a request for assistance to terminate a patient's life, where death was scarcely imminent and the ability to make an accurate prognosis limited.

Consequently, the original Bill was amended, in accordance with one of the recommendations of the Select Committee (Recommendation 5.3), to substitute the 12-month proviso for what was described as "a period of terminal care", that is, the time after which any medical treatment is predominantly confined to the relief of pain, suffering and/or distress, with the object of allowing the patient to die a comfortable death.

A definition of "terminal illness" is now in the Act: s 3. It is one which

> in reasonable medical judgment will, in the normal course, without the application of extraordinary measures or of treatment unacceptable to the patient, result in the death of the patient.

This definition is supplemented by s 7(1)(b), setting out one of the conditions that must be met before a medical practitioner may assist a patient to terminate his or her life. It provides:

> A medical practitioner may assist a patient to end his or her life only if all of the following conditions are met:
>
> (b) the medical practitioner is satisfied, on reasonable grounds, that—

   (i)   the patient is suffering from an illness that will, in the normal course and without
       the application of extraordinary measures, result in the death of the patient;

   (ii) in reasonable medical judgment, there is no measure acceptable to the patient that
       can reasonably be undertaken in hope of effecting a cure; and

   (iii) any medical treatment reasonably available to the patient is confined to the relief of
       pain and/or suffering with the object of allowing the patient to die a comfortable death."

Neither subs (b)(i) nor (b)(ii) appears to add any condition not already imposed by other provisions. Subsection (b)(i) is simply a restatement of the definition of "terminal illness" now contained in s 3, while subsection (b)(ii) preserves the right of the patient to refuse to accept treatment. However, subsection (b)(iii) acts as a limitation on the illnesses that might otherwise be described as "terminal", that is, that the only medical treatment reasonably available is confined to pain relief with the object of allowing the patient to die a comfortable death.

Bearing these new provisions in mind, who might be the patients for whom voluntary euthanasia might be an option?

It should be clear from what has been said that the Act does not implement a general scheme of voluntary euthanasia for all patients who may express a wish to terminate their life. It is suggested that three broad medical situations can be identified where a patient might have that desire. These are:

(i)   a patient whose life is only being sustained by life-support equipment;

(ii) a patient who is severely physically disabled due to accident or illness; and

(iii) a patient who has a terminal illness.

The patient on life support

A person may have expressed a wish that should he or she be involved, at some time in the future, in a traumatic incident whereby life can only be supported by artificial means, he or she does not desire that support. In the Northern Territory, such patients are covered by existing legislation. The *Natural Death Act* 1988 (NT) provides that a person of sound mind over the age of 18 may direct that, in the event that they suffer a terminal illness, no extraordinary measures should be taken to prolong their life. Extraordinary measures are defined as being life-support systems. According to s 3:

> 'extraordinary measures' means medical or surgical measures that prolong life, or are
> intended to prolong life, by supplanting or maintaining the operation of bodily functions
> that are temporarily or permanently incapable of independent function.

That direction must be given in writing in accordance with a form in the Regulations made under the Act and witnessed by two adults. Terminal illness is narrowly defined in that Act as one which will bring about imminent death if "extraordinary measures" are not taken, and from which there is no prospect of permanent or temporary recovery even if those extraordinary measures are taken. The provisions of the *Rights of the Terminally Ill Act* have no application to this situation.

Interestingly, the Select Committee on Euthanasia found that the passive euthanasia provisions of the *Natural Death Act* were little known and one of the Committee's recommendations (Recommendation 5.20) was that the provisions of this Act be widely publicised throughout the Northern Territory.

The patient disabled by illness or accident

A second scenario in which a person might express a desire to terminate his or her life could be that of a mentally competent person who has suffered serious injuries in an accident or who has a progressive debilitating disease or illness that has resulted in severe loss of bodily function or control or which causes severe and unrelieved pain, but which does not pose an immediate threat to life. Such a patient might express a wish that he or she does not want to continue to live under those circumstances. Neither the existing *Natural Death Act* nor the original Bill would have had application to these patients. However, amendments made to the bill at the time of passage mean that some of these patients will now have a right to request that they be assisted to terminate their life. The expansion of the Act, in terms of the categories of patients to whom it applies, is brought about by the inclusion of a definition of "terminal illness". As previously noted s 3 defines "terminal illness" as one which "in reasonable medical judgment will, in the normal course, without the application of extraordinary measures or of treatment unacceptable to the patient, result in the death of the patient". "Illness" is further defined by s 3 as including an "injury or degeneration of mental or physical faculties". There are a number of conditions which might fit that description, even though they are not illnesses that might be thought of as terminal in the usual sense of that word. A clear example would be the patient who is without kidney function and who therefore requires ongoing dialysis. If that patient were to reject dialysis or kidney transplant (as a "treatment unacceptable to [them]"), he or she would then be regarded as having an illness which "in the normal course" will result in death. The same could be said for other cases which involve organ degeneration or failure.

However, the position is not so clear in the case of progressive diseases and illnesses. Although certain diseases might fit the requirement that they will, in the normal course, result in the death of the patient, the further requirements of s 7 (the conditions under which a medical practitioner may assist a patient to terminate his or her life) appear to impose a requirement that there be some imminence of death. Section 7(b)(iii) requires the medical practitioner to be satisfied, on reasonable grounds, that "any medical treatment reasonably available to the patient is confined to the relief of pain and/or suffering with the object of allowing the patient to die a comfortable death". Presumably this requires some sense of immediacy of death. The patient who is suffering a long-term degenerative illness but whose death is in no way imminent could not be said to be receiving pain treatment "with the object of allowing [them] to die a comfortable death". The object of pain relief in those circumstances is more likely to be to maintain life as comfortably as possible.

In addition, it is further noted that the Act now includes a definition of "illness" which includes "injury or degeneration of mental or physical faculties". Therefore, those patients who have become physically or mentally disabled as a result of an accident may be assisted to terminate their life provided that they meet the threshold requirements outlined above.

The terminally ill patient
Lastly, the desire to terminate one's life might arise where a person has been diagnosed with a terminal illness in the usual sense that most people understand that phrase, that is, a condition that will bring about death regardless of available treatment.

The Act quite clearly extends a right to those patients to terminate their life and permits, though does not compel (s 5), a medical practitioner to provide assistance for them to do so.

Circumstances in which medical practitioner may give assistance
A significant amendment to the original Bill is the alteration of the circumstances in which a medical practitioner may provide assistance to terminate the patient's life. Originally the requirement was that the illness be one that "is causing the patient severe pain or suffering or distress". This provision had the potential to cause a number of difficulties both in terms of applying a consistent approach to patients and a consistency of legal approach, and in terms of the operation of the Act. It is replaced by a requirement under s 7(1)(d) that the illness be causing the patient severe pain or suffering. It is noted that a patient may request assistance to end life under s 4 where the patient is experiencing "pain, suffering and/or distress" but clearly that request cannot be acted upon unless the illness is causing the patient severe pain or suffering.

Should "distress" have remained a ground for euthanasia?
The Select Committee did not recommend the removal of distress as a separate ground. They were of the view that "the wording at Clause 6(f) to include 'pain, or suffering or distress' [was] sufficient to eliminate any ambiguity".

What, then, might have been the factors that influenced the removal of "distress" as a separate ground? As the original Bill stood, a person could be assisted to terminate his or her life on the basis that the prognosis that he or she had less than 12 months to live had caused the person severe distress. It is not difficult to imagine that a patient, given that prognosis, and perhaps advised that the progress of the disease will result in severe pain, might seek to have his or her life terminated before the onset of that pain or other unpleasant effects of the illness or medication.

It may be the case that the proposition that voluntary euthanasia is desirable to bring about a welcome relief from physical suffering from a terminal illness would receive widespread support. In his second reading speech to the Assembly, the then Chief Minister referred to a telephone poll conducted by a local newspaper, the *Sunday Territorian*, in which 80 per cent of the 576 people who registered a vote on the question "Should euthanasia be legal in the Northern Territory?" voted Yes. He also referred to a Nationwide Newspoll published in the *Australian* on 15 February 1995 that showed 81 per cent in favour of a law allowing voluntary euthanasia. The Select Committee reported that of the total submissions received by it, 72 per cent were in favour of euthanasia or the right of choice of the individual with 27 per cent opposed to the issue or the Bill itself.

However, whether society, or even a substantial sector of it, would support voluntary death as an answer to distress is perhaps questionable. Indeed, as has been already noted, the existing laws of the Northern Territory do not generally recognise that proposition. Attempted suicide remains a crime under the *Criminal Code*.

Consequently the original Bill would have created a situation where an emotionally disturbed or mentally ill patient who unsuccessfully attempted suicide could be subject to prosecution, while a "terminally ill" patient who was emotionally distressed (but not suffering severe pain) would have been given the right to be assisted to terminate his or her life.

Certainly the life of the latter is limited in any event. Nevertheless, this raised an inconsistency of policy and approach in allowing suicide and assisted suicide for some forms of emotional distress but not for others. The Select Committee dealt with this inconsistency by recommending that s 169 of the *Criminal Code* should be repealed regardless of the outcome of the euthanasia Bill, as the Northern Territory remained the only jurisdiction in Australia to retain the crime of attempted suicide. Although this recommendation has not been implemented in the current legislation, it may be that s 169 will be repealed by subsequent legislation.

It is not, perhaps, surprising that the Assembly chose to amend the Bill to remove distress as a separate ground as termination of life as an answer to emotional distress is very much at odds with the general medical and community approach which is taken towards those suffering from distress in one form or another. If people were concerned with the so-called "slippery-slope (that is, the movement from voluntary euthanasia to involuntary euthanasia), then the removal of "distress" as a ground was one way of alleviating that concern.

To allow emotional distress as a ground for termination where a patient has a terminal illness would also have been inconsistent with the position of patients identified above, upon whom no right to terminate life was to have been conferred under either existing legislation or under the original Bill. Those with a competent mind in a physically disabled body were not to be given the right to terminate their life, no matter how distressing their circumstances might be.

Another problem posed by the inclusion of distress as a separate ground was the potential difficulty in categorising distress. It would, of course, have been necessary for the distress to be experienced by the patient. It would not have been a sufficient ground to support the assistance to terminate a patient's life, that the patient no longer wished to cause distress to close relatives by prolonging his or her life. However, presumably, it would have been sufficient for the patient to have been distressed by the effect that the illness was having on close relatives, rather than by any distress that the patient is feeling as a result of pain or shortened life expectancy. Clearly this distinction would have been a fine line to draw in practice.

In addition to confining the grounds to severe pain and suffering, the addition of a new s 8 is significant. That section prohibits a medical practitioner from assisting a patient under the Act if, after considering the advice of the second medical practitioner, "there are palliative care options reasonably available to the patient to alleviate the patient's pain and suffering to levels acceptable to the patient": s 8(1). Where palliative care options have been exercised and have brought about a remission of the patient's pain or suffering but subsequently fail to continue to do so, the initial request cannot be acted upon unless the patient confirms his or her original request: s 8(2).

While it is clear that a patient has a role in the decision-making process to refuse to accept treatment for the terminal illness, by virtue of the wording of s 7(1)(b)(ii) ("no medical measure *acceptable to the patient* that can reasonably be undertaken in the hope of effecting a cure" (emphasis added)), there is a significant limitation upon the action that can follow. The patient may not be assisted to end his or her life if there are "palliative care options reasonably available to the patient to alleviate the patient's pain and suffering to levels acceptable to the patient": s 8(1). This provision would seem to exclude the possibility that a patient can reject reasonable palliative care options. However, it is noted that the pain relief must be to "levels acceptable to the patient". As this is a purely subjective assessment, a patient who has accepted palliative care but does not believe this provides sufficient relief, might be assisted to end his or her life.

Together, these amendments have effectively altered the scope of the legislation. The Bill as originally presented to the Assembly embraced the principle that a person should not be forced to endure the distress or pain or suffering that can sometimes accompany the dying process. The legislation finally passed by the Assembly embraces a narrower principle, which might be summarised as sparing a person unnecessary pain and suffering where there is no chance of recovery. Therefore, even though there has been an expansion of the types of patients to whom the Act might apply, there has been a narrowing of the circumstances in which euthanasia may be exercised. It is suggested that this makes a much clearer legal principle upon which the practice of euthanasia may operate. The legislation identifies a circumstance (a person who has unrelievable severe pain and suffering brought about by a condition and whose death will ultimately result from that condition) in which assistance to die may be given...

The addition of other requirements
Two other significant additions were made to the legislation when it was returned to the Assembly.

Cooling-off period
First, in accordance with a recommendation of the Select Committee (Recommendation 5.5), a cooling-off period has been added between the time of the initial request for assistance and the giving of assistance to the patient to terminate his or her life. That period, designed presumably to ensure that the decision to request assistance to terminate life is not made without due consideration, is two tiered. A period of seven days must elapse between the

initial request to the medical practitioner and the signing of the "certificate of request": s 7(1)(i). A further 48 hours must then elapse between the signing of the certificate and the giving of assistance to terminate life: s 7(n). This is a similar scheme to the legislation in place in Oregon in the United States (*Death with Dignity Act*), although there the initial period is 14 days. The difficulty in setting in place a cooling-off period is to balance the need to guard against decisions made in haste and perhaps at a low point in the patient's illness with the very purpose of the legislation, that is to relieve a patient from unnecessary pain and suffering. This legislation probably achieves that balance. The initial request can be made by a patient who is experiencing "pain, suffering and/or distress to an extent unacceptable" to them: s 4. The patient does not have to be at a point where the pain in unrelieved by palliative care. That requirement is one which operates at the time that the practitioner gives assistance. In practice then, the cooling-off period might work this way. The patient is experiencing pain, suffering and/or distress. He or she has been informed that there may be a point in the illness where the pain and suffering may no longer be relieved by medication. The patient can tell his or her practitioner that they would wish to be assisted to terminate their life when they reach that point. The patient must then wait at least seven days before he or she completes the required form requesting assistance. This could also be done at a time when the patient is still comfortable. No measures may be taken for at least another 48 hours and then *only* when palliative care has ceased to provide relief and there is no indication from the patient of a change of mind.

Interpreter

A further requirement which was added by amendment to the original Bill is that the assistance of an interpreter is now required where the patient and the medical practitioners do not share the same first language: s 7(4). Where an interpreter has been used, the interpreter is required to be present when the certificate of request is signed and must certify, inter alia, that the patient has understood the nature and the meaning of the certificate: s 7(1). This addition was particularly relevant for the Northern territory where there is a large Aboriginal population who do not speak English as a first language (in many cases English is spoken as a third or fourth language) and for whom the English words "kill" and "die" do not always carry the clear meaning that they do to those who have English as a first language. Tribal Aboriginal people will sometimes talk about a person being "killed a little bit" as opposed to being "proper dead". The difficulties for a medical practitioner are obvious.

The patient's request

The request from the patient for assistance to terminate his or her life is also the subject of conditions imposed by s 7.

A "certificate of request" (defined in s 3) in or in the effect of the form in the Schedule entitled "Request for assistance to end my life in a humane and dignified manner" must be completed, signed and witnessed in accordance with the Act. The certificate need only be witnessed by the first medical practitioner: s 7(1)(j). The second medical practitioner is only required to sign the certificate in the presence of the patient and the first medical practitioner (s 7(1)(k)) after consultation with the first medical practitioner and the patient to satisfy themselves as to the patient's soundness of mind and of the voluntary nature of the patient's decision, and that the other conditions required by s 7 have been met.

It is not always necessary for the patient to be the person signing the certificate. An adult (that is, a "person who has attained the age of 18 years": s 9(1)) other than the two medical practitioners specified in s 7, may sign the certificate on the patient's behalf if he or she is "physically unable to sign the certificate of request": s 9(1). Two safeguards have been added to the original provision. First, a person who "is likely to receive a financial benefit directly or indirectly as a result of the death of the patient" is precluded from signing on the patient's behalf: s 9(1). Secondly, if such a person does sign, he or she forfeits any financial or other benefit that they would have gained from the death of the patient: s 9(2).

The medical practitioner must also be satisfied that the patient has considered the implications of the decision on his or her family (s 7(1)(g)), although there is no requirement that the family be informed of the patient's decision prior to any action being taken.

Section 7(1)(o) imposes a requirement that, before assisted to end his or her life, the patient must at no time have given to the medical practitioner an indication that it was no longer the patient's wish to end his or her life. This requirement changes the emphasis from the previous s 6(m) which required the medical practitioner to have "no reasonable grounds for doubting that it continues to be the patient's wish to end his or her life". The original requirement was likely to cause difficulties in practice. Some practitioners may have interpreted the provision as allowing them to proceed as long as the patient had not given any indication of a change of mind, whereas others may have decided that, where a patient had subsequently become incompetent as a manifestation of the illness, they could not be satisfied that it continued to be the patient's wish to terminate his or her life. That situation would clearly frustrate the purpose of the legislation. The new provision therefore places the onus on the patient to communicate a change of mind. Where the patient becomes incompetent without expressing such a change, the medical practitioner may proceed on the basis that there is no indication that the patient has changed his or her wish to end their life.

Records and reporting procedures
Part 3 of the legislation deals with the keeping of certain medical records and the reporting of cases involving voluntary euthanasia. Again, the original provisions of the Bill have been amended to provide further safeguards. The original provisions did not specify who was to have the responsibility for preserving those records, nor was there any penalty attached for failure to keep records. It is now the responsibility of the medical practitioner who assists the patient to terminate his or her life to keep the prescribed medical records (s 12) and that section carries a penalty of $10,000 or imprisonment for two years.

Under s 14, a copy of the death certificate and "so much of the medical record of the patient (including that required by section 12 to be kept) as relates to the terminal illness and death of the patient" must be sent to the coroner. This section replaces the previous provision that required only the sending of the certificate of death and the "certificate of request". This amendment will allow the coroner to scrutinise requirements such as the independence of the relationship of the two medical practitioners and their professional experience and is partially in accordance with a recommendation of the Select Committee (Recommendation 5.11).

The coroner has the responsibility of notifying the Attorney-General of the number of patients who have died as a result of assistance given under the Act and the Attorney-General is then required to report the number to the Legislative Assembly: s 14(2).

Additionally, the coroner is now given the power to report to the Attorney-General on the operation of the Act and the Attorney-General is required to table such a report within three sitting days of the Assembly after the report has been received.

The Legislative Assembly did not take up the recommendation of the Select Committee that the Register of Death Certificate should record that the patient died as a result of euthanasia (Recommendation 5.10)....

One further matter needs to be noticed and it relates to one of the conditions for aid in dying set out in s 7(1)(c) of the Act concerned with the second medical opinion.

Margaret F A Otlowski 'Voluntary Euthanasia and the Common Law' (1997)

The original Bill had contained a requirement that the medical practitioner's opinion be confirmed by a second medical practitioner who has examined the patient. During the course of amendments made to the legislation prior to its passage, this requirement was tightened up to ensure the independence of the second medical practitioner. In addition, a requirement was added to section 7(1)(c) that the second medical practitioner must hold a diploma of psychological medicine or its equivalent. By requiring the second medical practitioner to have some background in psychiatry or psychology, the focus of this precondition was to verify the patient's mental state, in particular that the patient is not suffering from a treatable clinical depression in respect of the illness. However, as was pointed out in the course of the original legislative debate by parliamentarians opposed to the legislation, the decision to define the category of second medical practitioner principally in reference to their qualification to determine the patient's mental state was made at the expense of not providing for expert confirmation of diagnosis and prognosis by a doctor specializing in the field of the patient's terminal illness.

Since the passage of the legislation, it has come to light that the 'diploma of psychological medicine' referred to in this section is an obsolete qualification. An amendment Bill has recently been brought before the Northern Territory Parliament to address this difficulty. The Rights of the Terminally Ill Amendment Bill 1995 (NT) was introduced in November 1995 and passed with only minor amendment in February 1996 (Rights of the Terminally Ill Amendment Act 1996). The effect of this amendment is to replace the provision requiring the second medical practitioner to hold a diploma of psychological medicine or its equivalent with a twofold requirement: the patient must be examined by a second medical practitioner and by a qualified psychiatrist, both of whom must be independent from the first medical practitioner, (see s 7(1)(c) which specifies that neither the second medical practitioner nor the qualified psychiatrist can be a relative or employee of or a member of the same medical practice as the first medical practitioner or each other). The significance of this amendment is that the two distinct aspects of the role of second medical practitioner as originally provided for, namely confirming the opinion of the first medical practitioner regarding the patient's condition and prognosis and confirming that the patient is not suffering from a treatable clinical depression in respect of the illness, are now to be performed by specialists in each of these areas. As was noted, the principal impetus for this amendment was to rectify the difficulty regarding the 'diploma of psychological medicine' referred to under the original Act. This has been achieved by now setting down a more stringent requirement that the patient be examined by a qualified psychiatrist (section 7(1)(c)(ii)) who must confirm that the patient is not suffering from a treatable clinical depression in respect of the illness (section 7(1)(c)(iv)) before a doctor can proceed to assist a patient to die under the Act. Having removed the requirement that the second medical practitioner have qualifications in psychological medicine or its equivalent (this role of assessing the patient's mental state now falling within the responsibility of a psychiatrist) the opportunity has been taken to amend the legislation to ensure that the second medical practitioner has appropriate expertise in the area of the patient's terminal illness. The new section 7(1)(c)(i) stipulates that the second medical practitioner must hold prescribed professional qualifications, or have prescribed experience in the treatment of the terminal illness from which the patient is suffering. One of the key preconditions for the performance of active voluntary euthanasia or assisting the suicide of a patient under this Act is that the second medical practitioner examine the patient and confirm the findings of the first medical practitioner with regard to the existence and seriousness of the illness; that the patient is likely to die as a result of the illness; and the patient's prognosis. (This is now set out in s 7(1)(c)(iii).)

(For further discussion of the legislation, see Mullen (1995) 3 J Law & Med 121; Mendelson (1995) 3 J Law & Med 136; Gillett (1995) 3 J Law & Med 145; Ashby (1995) 3 J Law & Med 152; Buchan (1995) 3 J Law & Med 161 and Ranson (1995) 3 J Law & Med 169.)

Anticipatory decisions

So far, we have been concerned with decisions made by competent patients at the time they are being treated. Now we turn to consider the extent to which a patient while competent may make a decision about possible medical treatment in the future at a time when he is no longer competent by reason for example, of accident or supervening illness.

A. NATURE OF 'ADVANCE DIRECTIVES' OR 'LIVING WILLS'

1. Statements, wishes and decisions

Advance statements about future medical care take a number of forms. The statement may be oral or committed to writing. The statement may request treatment, express the patient's wishes, beliefs or values, state a clear refusal of all (or some) treatment in any circumstances or where the patient has a particular medical condition. Such statements are also variously referred to as 'advance directives' or 'living wills'.

The BMA in its 1995 Code of Practice (1995) illustrates the variations.

BMA *Advance Statements About Medical Treatment* (1995)

2.1 *Advance statements:* People who understand the implications of their choices can state in advance how they wish to be treated if they suffer loss of mental capacity. Just as adults must be consulted about treatment options, young people under the age of majority (age 18) are entitled to have their views taken into account. An advance statement (sometimes known as a living will) can be of various types (see also figure 1):

- a requesting statement reflecting an individual's aspirations and preferences. This can help health professionals identify how the person would like to be treated without binding them to that course of action, if it conflicts with professional judgement.
- a statement of the general beliefs and aspects of life which an individual values. This provides a summary of individual responses to a list of questions about a person's past and present wishes and future desires. It makes no specific request or refusal but attempts to give a biographical portrait of the individual as an aid to deciding what he or she would want.

- a statement which names another person who should be consulted at the time a decision has to be made. The views expressed by that named person should reflect what the patient would want. This can supplement and clarify the intended scope of a written statement but the named person's views are presently not legally binding in England & Wales. In Scotland, the powers of a tutor dative may cover such eventualities.
- a clear instruction refusing some or all medical procedures (advance directive). Made by a competent adult, this does, in certain circumstances, have legal force.
- a statement which, rather than refusing any particular treatment, specifies a degree of irreversible deterioration (such as a diagnosis of persistent vegetative state) after which no life sustaining treatment should be given. For adults, this again can have legal force.
- a combination of the above, including requests, refusals and the nomination of a representative. Those sections expressing clear refusal may have legal force in the case of adult patients.

The legal effect of these will vary. A patient's wishes or beliefs may be relevant in determining what treatment (or non-treatment) is in his best interests (see *supra*, ch 6). In the United States, 'values history forms' have been developed to provide greater opportunity for this. The leading health law text in the US explains these.

Barry R Furrow et al *Health Law* (vol 2) (1995)

§ 17–27. The Values History
Perhaps the best model for a source of information that can contribute to decision making concerning life sustaining treatment is the "values history," a kind of declaratory, non-mandatory advance directive (See, Ben A Rich, 'The Values History: A New Standard of Care', 40 Emory LJ, 1109, 1141–80 (1991)). Unlike other similar documents, the "values history" is not limited to specific questions about whether a person would want particular kinds of medical intervention; the answer to any such question depends on too great a variety of contingencies. Although many people would not want ventilator support if it were unlikely to return them to a cognitive state, most people would want to be placed on a ventilator under some conditions. Instead, the values history asks questions about those values, general interests, desires, fears, and expectations that are most likely to be significant when a surrogate must make a decision about life sustaining treatment. It provides the information necessary to make a reasonable and thoughtful decision; it does not purport to be the decision itself. The values history is likely to be extraordinarily valuable to thoughtful surrogate decision makers, and thus, it is likely to be well respected by most courts as a source of relevant information about the patient's likely decision.

(See further J Gibson 'Reflecting on Values' (1990) 51 Ohio St LJ 451 and Emmanuel and Emmanuel 'The Medical Directive – A New Comprehensive Advanced Care Document' (1989) 261 J Am Med Ass 3288.)

Requests for treatment may, likewise, be relevant to those who have the care of the patient in making decisions about his best interests. But, it is clear that in English law they are not of binding effect, since the law will not require a doctor to act contrary to his judgment of a patient's best interests (see eg *Re J (a minor) (child in care: medical treatment)* [1993] Fam 15 (CA) discussed *supra*, ch 6).

Likewise, requests to consult a relative or named individual or purported attempts to create another as a proxy have no legal effect in England. There is, at present, no mechanism for achieving this. At common law, any agency would terminate on the patient's incapacity and the Enduring Power of Attorney Act 1985 does not apply to decisions about medical treatment (see *infra*,).

2. Advance consents

What we are concerned with here, therefore, are advance *decisions* taken by patients in anticipation of their incapacity. Of course, decisions can be either to consent to treatment or to refuse it. We will concentrate on anticipatory *refusals*, although we point out here that every time a consent form for surgery is signed this is, of course, an example of an anticipatory *consent*. As such, it raises the issues of capacity; that it is based upon adequate information and voluntariness we saw earlier in Chapter 5. However, advance consents may be legally problematic. The patient may consent in advance to a procedure which is not in his 'best interests'. Is this legally effective? We have seen how the law may impose public policy limitations upon a competent patient's legal ability to consent to some procedures (see *supra*, ch 5). Clearly, an advance consent could be no more effective. However, the public policy limitation is not based upon the patient's 'best interests'. A competent patient can undoubtedly give consent to some procedures which are not in his best interests, eg organ or tissue donation. Can an advance consent likewise make legal what would otherwise be unlawful as not being in the incompetent patient's best interests? The Law Commission in its Report on *Mental Incapacity* (No 231 1995) took the view that it could not. At 5.13, the Law Commission states:

> We have now recommended that reasonable treatment which is in a person's best interests will be lawful. Advance consent to *other* sorts of treatment would not, however, have the effect of rendering them lawful. (Emphasis in original.)

A real illustration of this is the practice of 'elective ventilation', which we discussed in Chapter 15. This practice would allow for the maintenance of an incompetent patient on life-support in an intensive care unit in order to arrange for organ donation immediately following his inevitable death. As we saw, the practice is illegal as it cannot be said to be in the *patient's* best interests (*supra*, ch 15).

What, however, if the patient had anticipated this possibility and had given an advance consent to the life-support even though it would not be in his best interests? Assuming that the consent would otherwise be valid, could it make lawful the procedure by 'trumping' the application of the 'best interests' test? 'No', according to the Law Commission (*op cit*). It could be argued, however, that to the extent that advance *refusals* of treatment are given legal recognition, whatever underlies that ought to apply to advance *consents* subject always to the 'long-stop' of public policy. The better view, as we stated earlier (*supra*, ch 15) is that advance consents cannot override a doctor's obligation to act in the patient's 'best interests', though the patient's wishes may be relevant in making that determination.

B. RECOGNITION OF ADVANCE REFUSALS

1. Respect for autonomy

The principled basis for recognising the validity of advance refusals of medical treatment is respect for the patient's autonomy. To the extent that we respect a competent person's decision to refuse treatment, even life-sustaining treatment, likewise the patient's interests should be respected when they become incompetent. To respect the patient's decision furthers both the patient's current interests and also important interests of the patient – how they wish to live or die – which 'survive' incompetence (see R Dworkin *Life's Dominion* (1993), especially at 21–216). Allan Buchanan expresses it as follows in his paper 'Advance Directives and the Personal Identity Problem' (1988) 17 Philosophy & Public Affairs 277 at 278, n 1):

> ... a person who takes an interest in the well-being of others can use an advance directive to contribute to their well-being in two ways: (i) while still competent, the author's anxiety about the distress to which loved ones will be subjected in making difficult decisions without

guidance will be reduced; (ii) '... there is a sense in which our interests can survive us. I have an interest in how my family will fare after my death, and that interest survives me in the sense that whether or not it is satisfied will depend on events that occur after I am gone. An advance directive can help me ensure that my "surviving interests" are satisfied.'

Others disagree, and argue that a competent patient's advance wishes need not be followed, at least in some cases, because *their* interests will not be those of the person (now incompetent) about whose medical treatment a decision now has to be made. The best example of this is said to be the seriously demented patient who has made an advance refusal of treatment but seems content with his or her 'lot in life' (see eg Dresser and Robertson 'Quality-of-Life and Non-Treatment Decisions for Incompetent Patients: A Critique of the Orthodox Approach' (1989) 17 Law, Medicine and Health Care 234; and Dresser 'Missing Persons: Legal Perceptions of Incompetent Patients' (1994) 609 Rutgers Law Review 636).

The arguments are considered in an important paper by Derek Morgan.

Derek Morgan, 'Odysseus and the Binding Directive: Only a Cautionary Tale?' (1994) 14 Legal Studies 411

1 ODYSSEUS AND AUTONOMY

Before Odysseus navigates the rocks on which live Scylla and Charybdis he is lulled by the Sirens, promising advance disclosure of earthly adventures. Forewarned by Circe, he enjoins his crew first to contain him; later (on pain of death) to release him from the mast to which he is bound. Held to his originally expressed wishes, they refuse, and bind him more tightly. In this way, Odysseus creates what may have been one of the first advance directives. Its enforcement illustrates one of the concerns which have latterly been expressed about making binding health care choices, possibly many years before they might take effect.

'People do not always mean what they say; they do not always say what they want; and they do not always want what they say they want. That much is, if not exactly clear, at least uncontroversial. What is controversial is, recognizing this, how to proceed.' (Carl Elliott, 'Meaning What You Say' in Linda Emanuel (advisory editor), 'Advance Directives: Expectations, Experience and Future Practice' (1993) 4(1) Journal of Clinical Ethics 61 at 61.)

People change their minds. The lesson which the Odyssian directive affords is that we may wish to bring to the consideration of advance directives a certain caution. As it happens, holding him to his previous wishes may be thought to have benefited Odysseus in this case. Some would argue that his autonomy was respected (even enhanced), not only in that his welfare was protected, but also because a crucial dimension of autonomy might be thought to be the ability to enter into *binding* agreements. In trying to protect people from coming later to regret their previously expressed decisions we may be refusing to treat them 'as an autonomous and responsible person.' And, for some people, consideration of autonomy has come to occupy a central place, not just in the examination of the value and validity of advance directives, but in debates about medical law and jurisprudence more generally.

In an article generally cautious about the use of living wills, Joanne Lynn has suggested that there may be particular advantages to living wills in specific cases. These include where any form of legally sanctioned surrogate might be controversial (the mother or the long-term partner of an AIDS patient); where a patient expresses particularly specific priorities or unusual preferences (such as never to be treated again in a particular hospital, or not to have a particular treatment option) and for those whom laying anxiety to rest is a particularly important part of their care. But as Allen Buchanan has suggested, this limited catalogue of benefits would be a seriously incomplete weighting of the value of advance directives. This appreciation is one which some of the members of the courts which disposed of the *Bland* case in 1992 and 1993 perceived and sought to address ([1993] 1 All ER 821, [1993] 2 WLR 316). Importantly, Buchanan argues that advance directives might be seen to contribute to a new form of altruism; to ensuring that a person's 'surviving interests' are satisfied, thus that their interests in general are enhanced, and thus that their *present* interests are augmented or secured (Allen Buchanan 'Advance Directives and the Personal Identity Problem' (1988) 17 Philosophy & Public Affairs 277).

There are problems and difficulties with advance directives, some of which I want to allude to here, and there are seen to be particular advantages in their development. The most frequently cited are that they allow for greater self-determination and afford protection from unwarranted, or futile interventions at the end of life. It is in part, in the fear of such interventions, that the debate about other forms of intervention at the endings of life have been discussed...

5 A FRAIL REFLECTION

The assumption in the enthusiastic reception given by courts and commentators to advance directives is that if competent individuals have a virtually unlimited right to refuse immediate treatment then the same choice ought to be respected when the competent individual makes it concerning a future consideration (Joanne Lynn 'Why I Don't Have a Living Will' in Alexander Capron (ed), 'Medical Decision Making and the "Right to Die" after Cruzan' (1991) 19 Law Medicine and Health Care 101 at 102). I want to examine that assumption and test against it several arguments. The first examines the basis of the argument from competent choices and explores possible asymmetries between present and future directions. The second involves a cluster of issues around identity, and arises most clearly in the case of neurological degeneration which affects personality, and whether and to what extent the personal identity of the advance director changes over time, in such a way that *it cannot be said that we are now speaking of the same person*. In which case the direction given by P1 cannot bind P2, now described, even by those who knew them most intimately, as 'a different person'. A third troubling issue might be though to relate to the contested question of interpretation itself, and the difficulties inherent in 'a *genuine attempt* to identify the *true intentions* of the maker' of the advance direction (The Law Commission, Consultation Paper No 129, 'Mentally Incapacitated Adults and Decision Making: Medical Treatment and Research). Finally, there is a deep and contested question on the meaning of self-determination in respect of death, and the establishment of what has fashionably come to be called 'a right to die'. I cannot presently extensively treat each of these difficulties, but I can introduce the nature of the arguments involved.

(i) Competent choices

The first argument is that competent and incompetent people simply do not have the same rights, or for that matter, interests. In the case of Tony Bland, Lord Justice Butler-Sloss averred that the principle of sanctity of life 'was not an absolute one' ([1993] 1 All ER 821 at 861g). She rejected the approach which placed pain and suffering in a unique category and observed that the two exceptions which English law already admits (those of self-determination and where the pain and suffering outweighs any concomitant benefit) should be supplemented by other factors, particularly how one will be thought of by others after death. This entailed that incompetent individuals should and do have the same rights as competent ones to refuse and terminate medical treatment (see [1993] 1 All ER 821 at 847b). Lord Justice Hoffmann, Sir Thomas Bingham, Lord Goff, Lord Keith and the Ontario Court of Appeal all equate the conscious choice of a competent adult with one expressed to take effect at a future date contingent upon specified conditions.

One objection to this is that it looks to involve as much of a non-sequitur as that committed by Justice Brennan in his dissenting opinion in the Supreme Court decision in *Cruzan*. Recall that Brennan J argued that because competent people have the right to refuse medical treatment, and that because artificial feeding and hydration are medical treatments (all the Justices – even the concurring ones – seem to agree on this point), and since being incompetent does not deprive people of their fundamental rights, it follows that Nancy Cruzan had a 'right' to have her earlier choice respected and thus to have the feeding tube withdrawn. One commentator, Ron Stephens, has objected that this latter argument of Brennan J appears fallacious:

> ... in that the basis of his first condition is competency, and it seems quite clear ... that the right to "choose", or even "refuse", uphold possibilities that are uniquely absent in the incompetent individual such as Nancy Cruzan. And while one can agree with his second condition, and reasoning; that is, incompetent patients are not to be deprived of their "rights", it unhappily does not follow that competent and incompetent individuals have the same rights, particularly when the rights in question (by definition) inherently require competency (that is, the capacity to "choose" or to "refuse"). Consequently, Justice Brennan's concluding argument that Nancy has the right to "refuse" artificial feeding is simply erroneous.

This appears to be saying that even if a competent choice gives us, in virtue of its being such, some reason to respect it at the time, this reason only persists as long as the chooser remains competent. Stephens' argument is open to the strong objection that in observing her wishes, the doctors are not upholding her fundamental right to '... "refuse" artificial feeding' but rather a stronger claim not subject to the supposed fallacy. The 'fundamental rights' in question are not to have the feeding tube withdrawn, but rather to have one's (earlier) choices respected. The withdrawal of the feeding tubes is nothing more than an ancillary consequence of respecting that choice.

Of course, the demurer which Stephens enters may be stronger than this. It may be that he is really observing that if a competent choice gives us, in virtue of its being such, some reason to respect it at the time, *this* reason persists so long as the chooser *remains* incompetent. This then presents a more radical objection, which I consider below, that to respect an advance directive can only be justified if either (i) we are committed to respecting the wishes of the 'dead' (not in itself an insurmountable obstacle), or (ii) we hold that the person while competent can bind the person when incompetent. This gives rise to what may be thought to be difficult questions of personal identity and interpretation to which I shall come.

Second and subsequent objections to the 'equal rights assumption' are canvassed by Allen Buchanan who has challenged it because:

> ... it overlooks several morally significant asymmetries between the contemporaneous choice of a competent individual and the issuance of an advance directive to cover future decisions. (Allen Buchanan 'Advance Directives and the Personal Identity Problem' (supra) 278.)

These asymmetries, he suggests, are first, that therapeutic options and prognosis may change over time and that the director, as the House of Lords Committee following Donaldson in *Re T* were concerned, should make a decision on the proper basis of alternatives available. Secondly, the assumption that a competent person is the best judge of their own interests is weakened in the case of choice about future contingencies under conditions in which '... those interests have changed in radical and unforeseen ways.' (Ibid at 279.) Again, as I have commented, this weighed with the Select Committee's report. Finally, and perhaps of greatest force, is that:

> ... important informal safeguards that tend to restrain imprudent or unreasonable contemporaneous choices are not likely to be present, or if present, to be as effective, in the case of an advance directive. (Ibid at 280.)

A competent patient might be urged to reconsider their decision, and the protective effects of family or close friends are less likely to be operative when the anticipated refusal is a distant or theoretical possibility. Nonetheless, the law might take the view that the dangers of medical paternalism robbing patients of the value of their future choices outweigh any perceived difficulties which these asymmetries suggest.

Let me reflect briefly on these objections. Buchanan's first two points may look the same – circumstances and interests may change – and it would be wrong for the executors not to assess decisions in the light of such changes. Thus, a person's choices about death carry a lot of weight but are, of course, open to review. This is true of all decisions to be acted on later when the decider is inaccessible for *any* reason. Accordingly, it is misleading to suggest that my status as a judge of my future interests is weakened, as though the status of others as judges of those interests are not affected in just the same way. The mere fact that the future is uncertain, does not in principle weaken by status as a decider *in any way relevant to another deciding for me*, though obviously contingencies may make them or me the better informed. Buchanan's third point is puzzling. He suggests that we are less likely to take into account the views of others (as though we might be obliged to) when deciding for the distant future, and that we are therefore more likely to be imprudent and unreasonable. This may be the case, but it ignores the fact that the refusal (or choice) is not distant, it is taken now, when the advance directive is made.

(ii) *The identity question*

A far more troubling issue for Buchanan, however, is the question of personal identity, which represents a much more profound and potentially grave threat to the moral authority of advance directives. This gives rise to the objection that:

> ... the very process that renders the individual incompetent and brings the advance directive into play can – and indeed often does – destroy the conditions necessary for her personal identity and thereby undercut entirely the moral authority of the directive. (Ibid at 280.)

He seeks then to find a position which will enable the moral authority of advance directives to withstand such an assault, while not surrendering to what he calls dubious metaphysical theories of personal identity. In other words, he wants to rescue advance directives from the damage which a psychological continuity theory of personal identity might inflict if it were asked '*who* is dying?'

The most difficult, and perhaps common, case is not that of PVS, but is presented by Alzheimer's disease which results in such extensive, permanent neurological damage that the patient's memory is destroyed, cognitive processes are virtually obliterated and all that remains is basic perceptual awareness. One argument, by Rebecca Dresser ('Life, Death and Incompetent Patients: Conceptual Infirmities and Hidden Values in the Law' (1986) 28 Arizona Law Rev 379) suggests that because one person's advance directive has no moral authority to bind another, and because psychological continuity may be so severely disrupted that the person who issued the advance directive no longer exists therefore:

> in such cases the advance directive has no moral authority to determine what is to happen to the individual who remains after neurological damage has destroyed the person who issued the advance directive. (Ibid.)

Buchanan responds to this by suggesting that just as where the threshold is set for decision-making competence is a matter of *choice*, so too is the degree of psychological continuity regarded as necessary to speak about the destruction of a person (op cit 282). Challenging Parfitt who has suggested that the moral and social significance we attach to personal identity should reflect the fact that being the same person is not an either/or proposition, but a matter of more or less (op cit 294), Buchanan contends that there is:

> nothing incoherent about designating a certain degree of psychological continuity as necessary for the presence of personal identity *and* recognizing that psychological continuity is a matter of degree *and* admitting that psychological continuity is all there is to personal identity. (Ibid 300–01.)

It follows that there is nothing inconsistent in holding that the moral authority of an advance directive should diminish as the degree of psychological continuity decreases below the threshold, whether as a matter of judgment that is set at a high or at a meagre level. The importance of this conclusion is that it allows us to preserve the core of some of our most valuable practices and institutions, those which presuppose the use of all-or-nothing identity judgments, while acknowledging that:

> personal identity is simply a matter of psychological continuity and does not depend on some deeper, metaphysical fact. This compromise approach allows us to make a significant place for advance directives among our social institutions and practices without presupposing a dubious metaphysical theory of personal identity. (Ibid 301.)

These considerations do not appear to have disturbed the Select Committee's deliberations.

(iii) Identity and interpretation
I cannot here survey the literature to which the vexed question of interpretation has given rise in the past 30 years. I want only to recall that it has been argued that the relationship between author, text, reader and interpretation is a contested and controversial one. The point, in passing, is this; it cannot be assumed that the business of interpreting an advance directive, of discovering the director's true intent through genuine endeavour is straightforward, uncontested or without particular significance of meaning.

One of the difficulties with living wills of a standard format is claimed to be that it attends to priorities that are not one's own, addresses procedures rather than outcomes, and 'requires substantial interpretation without guaranteeing a reliable interpreter' (Joanne Lynn 'Why I Don't Have a Living Will' (1991) 19 Law Medicine & Health Care 101 at 101). Written documents cannot easily capture the subtle cues that might give one cause to doubt whether a person does, in fact, mean what he says. Unfortunately, there is evidence that:

> substitute decision makers, even those who have had a long, intimate familiarity with a patient, may not be accurate predictor's of patients' preferences. In the absence of better placed interpreters, we must make do with what the patient said, and perhaps more importantly, with how it says he behaved. (Carl Elliott 'Meaning What You Say' in Linda Emanuel (advisory editor), 'Advance Directives: Expectations, Experience and Future Practice' (1993) supra.)

The fact that a person took the time and the trouble to formulate and authenticate an advance directive and bring it to the physician's notice does imply something about that person's character and the seriousness with which he or she approaches these issues, 'but not much about the individual's preferences and priorities' (Lynn, supra at 102).

But this search of the 'meaning' of a provision in a living will is not necessarily the starting point of the endeavour. In a more critical understanding,

> … meaning is always to be argued for and never to be argued from. It is neither a sacred shard of archaeological excavation nor an ephemeral whim of narcissistic indulgence. (Allan Hutchinson 'Identity Crisis: the Politics of Interpretation' (1992) 26 New England Law Rev 1173.)

When this is allied with the question of identity which Buchanan has discussed, the layers of complexity become more profound. Thus, a more radical response to Buchanan is that the notion of a psychological continuity theory of identity (from which he seeks to rescue living wills) is itself seriously contestable and a limited rendition of what identity might consist of. As Hutchinson has suggested, 'the relation between persons and their contexts is like that between writers and texts – *nothing necessarily follows.*' (ibid.) Thus, identity '… is relative, not intrinsic; fluid not fixed; perspectival, not neutral; and protean, not perfected.' To speak, then, of devining the 'true intent' of an advance directive when the question of identity may be fulcral may be a journey of Odyssean duration, direction and difficulty.

(iv) Directing what; advancing where?

Leon Kass has written recently that 'to speak of rights in the very troubling matter of medically managed death is ill suited both to sound personal decision making and to sensible public policy.' (Leon Kass 'Is There a Right to Die?' (1993) 23(1). In arguing from this premise he concludes there is no firm philosophical or legal argument for a 'right to die'. 'My body and my life, while mine to use, are not mine to dispose of.' Hastings (Center Report 34 at 34).

In contrast with this view is that of Ronald Dworkin, in his recent book *Life's Dominion: An Argument about Abortion and Euthanasia* (ibid). Here, Dworkin has argued that there is no doubt that most people treat the manner of their deaths as of special, symbolic importance: they want their deaths, if possible, to express and in that way vividly to confirm the values they believe most important to their lives. The idea of a good (or less bad) death is not exhausted by how one dies – whether in battle or in bed – but includes timing, and I would add geography, as well. It helps to explain the premium people often put on living to 'see' some particular event, after which the idea of their own death seems less tragic to them (ibid 211).

It does not follow, however, that Dworkin would establish a right to die. While we almost all accept that human life in all its forms is sacred – that it has an intrinsic and objective value quite apart from any value it might have to the person whose life it is, we disagree about the source and character of that sacred value and therefore about which decisions respect and which dishonour it (ibid 25). From this he suggests that while many believe or concede that Lillian Boyes and Tony Bland were 'better off' dead, they nevertheless insist that killing her and letting him die was wrong, precisely because human life has this independent, sacred value. But this illustrates a fundamental distinction between morality and the state's responsibility for promoting, policing and enforcing law. Any legal regime which permits doctors and other health care workers to allow a patient to die – including those in which the person has made an advance declaration or stipulation of their wishes – must demand caution. It must be so structured as to protect the patient's 'real reflective wishes' and to avoid 'patients or relatives making an unwitting choice for death ...' (ibid 216).

The crucial question may be not whether to respect the sanctity of life, but which decision(s) best respect it. Those who believe that being 'kept alive' permanently unconscious, sedated beyond sense, or in some other way grossly compromised, may believe that this degrades rather than respects life. As Gray forcefully pleads,

> the absurdity and moral horror in which we currently warehouse for survival those who would, often enough, vastly prefer to exercise the ultimate form of exit option ... is not wisdom, conservative or otherwise, but rather a fetishisation of physical survival. (John Gray 'Beyond the New Right: Markets, Government and the Common Environment' (London, Routledge, 1993) 171.)

Others counter that the abandonment of care is at the centre of decisions to end a patient's life or for the patient to seek assistance to do so, or to refuse what would otherwise be life-sustaining treatment or care (John Finnis 'Bland: Crossing the Rubicon' (1992) 109 LQR 329–37). The resolution of these issues by the state in the form or absence of law will in part disclose the relationships between law and morality of that society, but will also disclose whether the state believes it has the authority to impose views on its citizens in areas which, whatever their individual moral convictions, may be none of the law's concern.

You will see in this extract reference to Ronald Dworkin's support for advance directives in *Life's Dominion* (*op cit*) and the work of Rebecca Dresser arguing against them when it is sought to implement them in the case of conscious, incompetent patients, specifically those with incurable dementia. The arguments against respecting a patient's past wishes – and thereby choosing instead to further his current and future interests – are subject to less challenge in the case of the unconscious (or barely conscious) incompetent patient (eg Tony Bland).

In an article debating Dworkin's position, Professor Rebecca Dresser returns to what she perceives as the problematic case.

Rebecca Dresser 'Dworkin on Dementia: Elegant Theory, Questionable Policy' (1995) 25 Hastings Center Report 32

In *Life's Dominion*, Dworkin considers Margo as a potential subject of his approach. In one variation, he asks us to suppose that

> years ago, when fully competent, Margo had executed a formal document directing that if she should develop Alzheimer's disease ... she should not receive treatment for any

other serious, life-threatening disease she might contract. Or even in that event she should be killed as soon and as painlessly as possible (p 226).

He presents an elegant and philosophically sophisticated argument for giving effect to her prior wishes, despite the value she appears to obtain from her life as an individual with dementia.

Dworkin's position emerges from his inquiry into the values of autonomy, beneficence, and sanctity of life. To understand their relevance to a case such as Margo's, he writes, we must first think about why we care about how we die. And to understand that phenomenon, we must understand why we care about how we live. Dworkin believes our lives are guided by the desire to advance two kinds of interests. *Experiential* interests are those we share to some degree with all sentient creatures. In Dworkin's words:

> We all do things because we like the experience of doing them: playing softball, perhaps, or cooking and eating well, or watching football, or seeing *Casablanca* for the twelfth time, or walking in the woods in October, or listening to *The Marriage of Figaro*, or sailing fast just off the wind, or just working hard at something. Pleasures like these are essential to a good life—a life within nothing that is marvellous only because of how it feels would be not pure but preposterous (p 201).

But Dworkin deems these interests less important than the second sort of interests we possess. Dworkin argues that we also seek to satisfy our *critical* interests, which are the hopes and aims that lend genuine meaning and coherence to our lives. We pursue projects such as establishing close friendships, achieving competence in our work, and raising children, not simply because we want the positive experiences they offer, but also because we believe we should want them, because our lives as a whole will be better if we take up these endeavors.

Dworkin admits that not everyone has a conscious sense of the interests they deem critical to their lives, but he thinks that "even people whose lives feel unplanned are nevertheless often guided by a sense of the general style of life they think appropriate, of what choices strike them as not only good at the moment but in character for them" (p 202). In this tendency, Dworkin sees us aiming for the ideal of integrity, seeking to create a coherent narrative structure for the lives we lead.

Our critical interests explain why many of us care about how the final chapter of our lives turns out. Although some of this concern originates in the desire to avoid experiential burdens, as well as burdens on our families, much of it reflects the desire to escape dying under circumstances that are out of character with the prior stages of our lives. For most people, Dworkin writes, death has a "special, symbolic importance: they want their deaths, if possible, to express and in that way vividly to confirm the values they believe most important to their lives" (p 211). And because critical interests are so personal and widely varied among individuals, each person must have the right to control the manner in which life reaches its conclusion. Accordingly, the state should refrain from imposing a "uniform, general view [of appropriate end-of-life-care] by way of sovereign law" (p 213).

Dworkin builds on this hierarchy of human interests to defend his ideas about how autonomy and beneficence should apply to someone else like Margo. First, he examines the generally accepted principle that we should in most circumstances honor the competent person's autonomous choice. One way to justify this principle is to claim that people generally know better than anyone else what best serves their interests; thus, their own choices are the best evidence we have of the decision that would most protect their welfare. Dworkin labels this the *evidentiary* view of autonomy. But Dworkin believes the better explanation for the respect we accord to individual choice lies in what he calls the *integrity* view of autonomy. In many instances, he contends, we grant freedom to people to act in ways that clearly conflict with their own best interests. We do this, he argues, because we want to let people "lead their lives out of a distinctive sense of their own character, a sense of what is important to them" (p 224). The model once again assigns the greatest moral significance to the individual's critical interests, as opposed to the less important experiential interests that also contribute to a person's having a good life.

The integrity view of autonomy partially accounts for Dworkin's claim that we should honor Margo's prior choice to end her life if she developed Alzheimer disease. In making this choice, she was exercising, in Dworkin's phrase, her "precedent autonomy" (p 226). The evidentiary view of autonomy fails to supply support for deferring to the earlier decision, Dworkin observes, because "[p]eople are not the best judges of what their own best interests would be under circumstances they have never encountered and in which their preferences and desires may drastically have changed" (p 226). He readily admits that Andrew Firlik and others evaluating Margo's life with dementia would perceive a conflict between her prior instructions and her current welfare. But the integrity view of autonomy furnishes compelling support for honoring Margo's advance directives. Margo's interest in living her life in character includes an interest in controlling the circumstances in which others should permit her life as an Alzheimer patient to continue. Limiting that control would in Dworkin's view be "an unacceptable form of moral paternalism" (p 231).

Dworkin finds additional support for assigning priority to Margo's former instructions in the moral principle of beneficence. People who are incompetent to exercise autonomy have a right to beneficence from those entrusted to decide on their behalf. The best interests standard typically has been understood to require the decision that would best protect the incompetent individual's current welfare. On this view, the standard would support some (though not necessarily all) life-extending decisions that depart from Margo's prior directives. But Dworkin invokes his concept of critical interests to construct a different best interests standard. Dworkin argues that Margo's critical interests persist, despite her current inability to appreciate them. Because critical interests have greater moral significance than the experiential interests Margo remains able to appreciate, and because "we must judge Margo's critical interest as she did when competent to do so" (p 231), beneficence requires us to honor Margo's prior preferences for death. In Dworkin's view, far from providing a reason to override Margo's directives, compassion counsels us to follow them, for it is compassion "toward the whole person" that underlies the duty of beneficence (p 232).

To honor the narrative that is Margo's life, then, we must honor her earlier choices. A decision to disregard them would constitute unjustified paternalism and would lack mercy as well. Dworkin concedes that such a decision might be made for other reasons —because we "find ourselves unable to deny medical help to anyone who is conscious and does not reject it" (p 232), or deem it "morally unforgiveable not to try to save the life of someone who plainly enjoys her life" (p 228), or find it "beyond imagining that we should actually kill her" (p 228), or "hate living in a community whose officials might make or license either of [Margo's] decisions" (pp 228–29). Dworkin does not explicitly address whether these or other aspects of the state's interest in protecting life should influence legal policy governing how people like Margo are treated....

Advance Directives and Precedent Autonomy

First, an observation. Dworkin makes an impressive case that the power to control one's future as an incompetent patient is a precious freedom that our society should go to great lengths to protect. But how strongly do people actually value this freedom? Surveys show that a relatively small percentage of the US population engages in end-of-life planning, and that many in that group simply designate a trusted relative or friend to make future treatment decisions, choosing not to issue specific instructions on future care. Though this widespread failure to take advantage of the freedom to exercise precedent autonomy may be attributed to a lack of publicity or inadequate policy support for advance planning, it could also indicate that issuing explicit instructions to govern the final chapter of one's life is not a major priority for most people. If it is not, then we may question whether precedent autonomy and the critical interests it protects should be the dominant model for our policies on euthanasia for incompetent people.

Dworkin constructs a moral argument for giving effect to Margo's directives, but does not indicate how his position could be translated into policy. Consider how we might approach this task. We would want to devise procedures to ensure that people issuing such directives were competent, their actions voluntary, and their decisions informed. In other medical settings, we believe that a person's adequate understanding of the information relevant to treatment decisionmaking is a prerequisite to the exercise of true self-determination. We should take the same view of Margo's advance planning.

What would we want the competent Margo to understand before she chose death over life in the event of dementia? At a minimum, we would want her to understand that the experience of dementia differs among individuals, that for some it appears to be a persistently frightening and unhappy existence, but that most people with dementia do not exhibit the distress and misery we competent people tend to associate with the condition. I make no claims to expertise in this area, but my reading and discussions with clinicians, caregivers, and patients themselves suggest that the subjective experience of dementia is more positive than most of us would expect. Some caregivers and other commentators also note that patients' quality of life is substantially dependent on their social and physical environments, as opposed to the neurological condition itself (See generally R Dresser, "Missing Persons: Legal Perceptions of Incompetent Patients" Rutgers Law Review 609 (1994)). Thus, the "tragedy" and "horror" of dementia is partially attributable to the ways in which others respond to people with this condition.

We also want Margo to understand that Alzheimer disease is a progressive condition, and that options for forgoing life-sustaining interventions will arise at different points in the process. Dworkin writes that his ideas apply only to the late stages of Alzheimer disease, but he makes implementation of Margo's former wishes contingent on the mere development of the condition (pp 219, 226). If we were designing policy, we would want to ensure that competent individuals making directives knew something about the general course of the illness and the points at which various capacities are lost. We would want them to be precise about the behavioral indications that should trigger the directive's implementation. We would want them to think about what their lives could be like at different stages of the disease, and about how invasive and effective various possible interventions might be. We would want to give them the opportunity to talk with physicians, caregivers, and individuals diagnosed with Alzheimer disease, and perhaps, to discuss their potential choices with a counselor.

The concern for education is one that applies to advance treatment directives generally, but one that is not widely recognized or addressed at the policy level. People complete advance directives in private, perhaps after discussion with relatives, physicians, or attorneys, but often with little understanding of the meaning or implications of their decisions. In one study of dialysis patients who had issued instructions on treatment in the event of advanced Alzheimer disease, a subsequent inquiry revealed that almost two-thirds of them wanted families and physicians to have some freedom to override the directives to protect their subsequent best interests (Ashwini Sehgal et al, "How Strictly Do Dialysis Patients Want Their Advance Directives Followed?" JAMA 267 (1992): 59–63). The patients' failure to include this statement in their directives indicates that the instructions they recorded did not reflect their actual preferences. A survey of twenty-nine people participating in an advance care planning workshop found ten agreeing with both of the following inconsistent statements: "I would never want to be on a respirator in an intensive care unit"; and "If a short period of extremely intensive medical care could return me to near-normal condition, I would want it." (Lachlan Forrow, Edward Gogel and Elizabeth Thomas, "Advance Directives for Medical Care" NEJM 325 (1991): 1255.) Meanwhile, some promoters of advance care planning have claimed that subjects can complete directives during interviews lasting fifteen minutes (Linda L Emanuel et al, "Advance Directives for Medical Care – A Case for Greater Use" NEJM 324 (1991): 889–95).

We do not advance people's autonomy by giving effect to choices that originate in insufficient or mistaken information. Indeed, interference in such choices is often considered a form of justified paternalism. Moreover, advance planning for future dementia treatment is more complex than planning for other conditions, such as permanent unconsciousness. Before implementing directives to hasten death in the event of dementia, we should require people to exhibit a reasonable understanding of the choices they are making.

Some shortcomings of advance planning are insurmountable, however. People exercising advance planning are denied knowledge of treatments and other relevant information that may emerge during the time between making a directive and giving it effect. Opportunities for clarifying misunderstandings are truncated, and decisionmakers are not asked to explain or defend their choices to the clinicians, relatives, and friends whose care and concern may lead depressed or imprudent individuals to alter their wishes. Moreover, the rigid adherence to advance planning Dworkin endorses leaves no room for the changes of heart that can lead us to deviate from our earlier choices. All of us are familiar with decisions we have later come to recognize as ill-suited to our subsequent situations. As Dworkin acknowledges, people may be mistaken about their future experiential interests as incompetent individuals. A policy of absolute adherence to advance directives means that we deny people like Margo the freedom we enjoy as competent people to change our decisions that conflict with our subsequent experiential interests.

Personal identity theory, which addresses criteria for the persistence of a particular person over time, provides another basis for questioning precedent autonomy's proper moral and legal authority. In *Life's Dominion*, Dworkin assumes that Margo the dementia patient is the same person who issued the earlier requests to die, despite the drastic psychological alteration that has occurred. Indeed, the legitimacy of the precedent autonomy model absolutely depends on this view of personal identity. Another approach to personal identity would challenge this judgment, however. On this view, substantial memory loss and other psychological changes may produce a new person, whose connection to the earlier one could be less strong, indeed, could be no stronger than that between you and me. Subscribers to this view of personal identity can argue that Margo's earlier choices lack moral authority to control what happens to Margo the dementia patient.

These shortcomings of the advance decisionmaking process are reasons to assign less moral authority to precedent autonomy than to contemporaneous autonomy. I note that Dworkin himself may believe in at least one limit on precedent autonomy in medical decisionmaking. He writes that people "who are repelled by the idea of living demented, totally dependent lives, speaking gibberish," ought to be permitted to issue advance directives "stipulating that if they become permanently and seriously demented, and then develop a serious illness, they should not be given medical treatment except to avoid pain" (p 231). Would he oppose honoring a request to avoid all medical treatment, including pain-relieving measures, that was motivated by religious or philosophical concerns? The above remark suggests that he might give priority to Margo's existing experiential interests in avoiding pain over her prior exercise of precedent autonomy. In my view, this would be a justified limit on precedent autonomy, but I would add others as well....

The State's Interest in Margo's Life

My final thoughts concern Dworkin's argument that the state has no legitimate reason to interfere with Margo's directives or her family's best interests judgment to end her life. A great deal of *Life's Dominion* addresses the intrinsic value of human life and the nature of the state's interest in protecting that value. Early in the book, Dworkin defends the familiar view that only conscious individuals can possess interests in not being destroyed or otherwise harmed. On this view, until the advent of sentience and other capacities, human fetuses lack interests of their own that would support a state policy restricting abortion. A policy that restricted abortion prior to this point would rest on what Dworkin calls a *detached* state interest in protecting human life. Conversely, a policy that restricts abortion after fetal sentience (which coincides roughly with viability) is supported by the state's *derivative* interest in valuing life, so called because it derives from the fetus's own interests (pp 10–24, 168–70). Dworkin believes that detached state interests in ensuring respect for the value of life justify state prohibitions on abortion only after pregnant women are given a reasonable opportunity to terminate an unwanted pregnancy. Prior to this point, the law should permit women to make decisions about pregnancy according to their own views on how best to respect the value of life. After viability, however, when fetal neurological development is sufficiently advanced to make sentience possible, the state may severely limit access to abortion, based on its legitimate role in protecting creatures capable of having interests of their own (pp 168–70).

Dworkin's analysis of abortion provides support, in my view, for a policy in which the state acts to protect the interests of conscious dementia patients like Margo. Although substantially impaired, Margo retains capacities for pleasure, enjoyment, interaction, relationships, and so forth. I believe her continued ability to participate in the life she is living furnishes a defensible basis for state limitations on the scope of her precedent autonomy, as well as on the choices her intimates make on her behalf. Contrary to Dworkin, I believe that such moral paternalism is justified when dementia patients have a quality of life comparable to Margo's. I am not arguing that all directives regarding dementia care should be overridden, nor that family choices should always be disregarded. I think directives and family choices should control in the vast majority of cases, for such decisions rarely are in clear conflict with the patient's contemporaneous interests. But I believe that state restriction is justified when a systematic evaluation by clinicians and others involved in patient care produces agreement that a minimally intrusive life-sustaining intervention is likely to preserve the life of someone as contented and active as Margo.

Many dementia patients do not fit Margo's profile. Some are barely conscious, others appear frightened, miserable, and unresponsive to efforts to mitigate their pain. Sometimes a proposed life-sustaining treatment will be invasive and immobilizing, inflicting extreme terror on patients unable to understand the reasons for their burdens. In such cases, it is entirely appropriate to question the justification for treatment, and often to withhold it, as long as the patient can be kept comfortable in its absence. This approach assumes that observors can accurately assess the experiential benefits and burdens of patients with neurological impairments and decreased ability to communicate. I believe that such assessments are often possible, and that there is room for a great deal of improvement in meeting this challenge…

We shall see later when we consider the Law Commission's proposals for reform that practical or pragmatic objections are often raised against giving binding effect to anticipatory refusals of treatment (see eg *Report of the Select Committee on Medical Ethics* (1994) HL Paper 21–I at paras 191–215).

2. The common law

In a series of cases, the English courts have recognised the legal effect at common law of advance or anticipated refusals of medical treatment, including life-sustaining treatment.

Re T (adult: refusal of medical treatment) [1992] 4 All ER 649, (1992) 9 BMLR 46 (CA)

T was injured in a car accident when she was 34 weeks pregnant. She was admitted to hospital and the possibility of her requiring a blood transfusion arose. T had been brought up by her mother, who was a Jehovah's Witness, but she was not herself a member of that religious sect. After a private conversation with her mother, T told the staff nurse that she used to belong to a religious sect which believed blood transfusion to be a sin and a bar to eternal salvation, that she still maintained some beliefs of the sect and that she did not want a blood transfusion. Shortly afterwards she went into labour and because of her distressed condition it was decided that delivery should be by Caesarian section. After being alone with her mother, T again told medical staff that she did not want a blood transfusion and was informed that other solutions to expand the blood could be used and that blood transfusions were not often necessary after a Caesarian section. T then blindly signed a form of refusal of consent to blood transfusions but it was not explained to her that it might be necessary to give a blood transfusion to save her life. After undergoing an emergency Caesarian operation her condition deteriorated and she was transferred to an intensive care unit where, given a free hand, the consultant anaesthetist would unhesitatingly have administered a blood transfusion but felt inhibited from doing so in the light of T's expressed wishes. T was instead put on a ventilator and paralysing drugs were administered. T's father and boyfriend applied to the court for assistance and following an emergency hearing the judge authorised the administration of a blood transfusion to T and declared that, in the circumstances then prevailing, it would not be unlawful for the hospital to do so, despite the absence of her consent, because a blood transfusion appeared manifestly to be in her best interests. At a second hearing the judge held that T had neither consented to nor refused a blood transfusion in the emergency which had arisen and accordingly that it was lawful for the doctors to treat her in whatever way they considered, in the exercise of their clinical judgment, to be in her best interests. T appealed.

In dismissing T's appeal, the Court of Appeal held that on the facts T's refusal of treatment was vitiated by her mother's undue influence [see *supra*, ch 5]. The judges, nevertheless, went on to consider the validity, in principle, of a patient's anticipatory refusal of treatment.

Lord Donaldson MR: There seems to be a view in the medical profession that in ... emergency circumstances the next of kin should be asked to consent on behalf of the patient and that, if possible, treatment should be postponed until that consent has been obtained. This is a misconception because the next of kin has no legal right either to consent or to refuse consent. This is not to say that it is an undesirable practice if the interests of the patient will not be adversely affected by any consequential delay. I say this because contact with the next of kin may reveal that the patient has made an anticipatory choice which, if clearly established and applicable in the circumstances – two major 'ifs' – would bind the practitioner...

The scope and basis of the patient's decision
If the doctors consider that the patient had the capacity to decide and has exercised his right to do so, they still have to consider what was the true scope and basis of that decision. If at the time the issue arises the patient still has capacity to decide, they can not only explore the scope of his decision with the patient, but can seek to persuade him to alter that decision. However this problem will usually arise at that time when this *cannot* be done. In such circumstances what the doctors cannot do is to conclude that if the patient still had had the necessary capacity in the changed situation he would have reversed his decision. This would be simply to deny his right of decision. What they *can* do is to consider whether at the time the decision was made it was intended by the patient to apply in the changed situation. It may well have been so intended, as it was in the Canadian Case of *Malette v Shulman* (1990) 72 OR (2d) 417 where the Jehovah's Witness carried a card stating in unequivocal terms that she did not wish blood to be administered to her in *any* circumstances. But it may not have so intended. It may have been of more limited scope, eg 'I refuse to have a blood transfusion, so long as there is an effective alternative'. Or again it may have been based upon an assumption, eg 'As there is an effective alternative, I refuse to have a blood transfusion'. If the factual situation falls outside the scope of the refusal or if the assumption upon which it is based is falsified, the refusal ceases to be effective. The doctors are then faced with a situation in which the patient has made no decision and, he by then being unable to decide for himself, they have both the right and the duty to treat him in accordance with what in the exercise of their clinical judgment they consider to be his best interests.

Refusal forms
I was surprised to find that hospitals appear to have standard forms of refusal to accept a blood transfusion and was dismayed at the layout of the form used in this case. It is clear that such forms are designed primarily to protect the hospital from legal action. They will be wholly ineffective for this purpose if the patient is incapable of understanding them, they are not explained to him and there is no good evidence (apart from the patient's signature) that he had that understanding and fully appreciated the significance of signing it. With this in mind it is for consideration whether such forms should not be redesigned to separate the disclaimer of liability on the part of the hospital from what really matters, namely the declaration by the patient of his decision with a full appreciation of the possible terms and emphasised by a different and larger type face, by underlining, the employment of coloured print or otherwise.

Informed refusal
As Ward J put it in his judgment, English law does not accept the transatlantic concept of 'informed consent' and it follows that it would reject any concept of 'informed refusal'. What is required is that the patient knew in broad terms the nature and effect of the procedure

to which consent (or refusal) was given. There is indeed a duty on the part of doctors to give the patient appropriately full information as to the nature of the treatment proposed, the likely risks (including any special risks attaching to the treatment being administered by particular persons), but a failure to perform this duty sounds in negligence and does not, as such, vitiate a consent or refusal. On the other hand, misinforming a patient, whether or not innocently, and the withholding of information which is expressly or impliedly sought by the patient may well vitiate either a consent or a refusal.

Butler-Sloss LJ: I agree with the reasoning of the Court of Appeal in Ontario in their decision in *Malette v Shulman* (1990) 72 OR (2d) 417 (a blood transfusion given to an unconscious card-carrying Jehovah's Witness). Robins JA said (at 432):

> At issue here is the freedom of the patient as an individual to exercise her right to refuse treatment and accept the consequences of her own decision. Competent adults, as I have sought to demonstrate, are generally at liberty to refuse medical treatment even at the risk of death. The right to determine what shall be done with one's own body is a fundamental right in our society. The concepts inherent in this right are the bedrock upon which the principles of self-determination and individual autonomy are based. Free individual choice in matters affecting this right should, in my opinion, be accorded very high priority....

The question may arise as to whether the decision to consent or to reject treatment is made by a patient who has the capacity to make the decision, in other words whether he is fit to make it, or whether he has genuinely made the decision....

The patient may make a decision which is limited in scope, and there may also be the situation where no decision is made and in those circumstances the principle of necessity will apply as set out in the speech of Lord Goff of Chieveley in *F v West Berkshire Health Authority (Mental Health Act Commission intervening)* [1989] 2 All ER 545 at 565–566, [1990] 2 AC 1 at 75–76....

There is ... the question whether she made a decision which was limited in duration and to which she would not have adhered if she had been alerted to dangers of a refusal to accept blood transfusions or similar blood-based treatment....

Limited refusal – the scope of her decision
The judge based his decision upon this point. In my view on the facts as found by the judge this issue does not arise since she was not able to make a genuine decision. But I can see circumstances in which a patient is unwilling to have certain procedures carried out and says so under the impression that in any even the emergency which would bring those procedures into play will not happen. If the patient has been misled or misinformed he may not have given a genuine consent or refusal. This is not to bring in the doctrine of informed consent which is not the law of this country. But on the present facts Miss T did not want a blood transfusion but she did ask whether there was a substitute treatment and was told, erroneously, I believe, that there was. She was also told in order to calm her down that a blood transfusion was most unlikely and she did not have to face, it appears, the possible serious or even fatal consequences of her decision. Had she been making a genuine decision to refuse the treatment, it would be necessary in a case such as this to find out of if the patient had received any advice as to the consequences of a refusal to accept treatment. In *Malette v Shulman* (1990) 72 OR (2d) 417 the answer was clear. It may be less clear in other situations.

Staughton LJ: The second reason why an apparent consent or refusal of consent may not be a true consent or refusal is that it may not have been made with reference to the particular circumstances in which it turns out to be relevant. A patient who consents, even in the widest terms, to a dental operation under anaesthetic does not give a true consent to the amputation of a leg. Nor does a patient who refuses consent in some circumstances necessarily give a true refusal of consent to treatment in any quite different circumstances which may arise: an example is to be found in *Werth v Taylor* (1991) 190 Mich App 141....

In *Malette v Shulman* (1990) 72 OR (2d) 417 a Canadian court upheld an award of $20,000 to a patient who had been given a blood transfusion in order to save her life but against her known wishes. I doubt if an English court would have awarded such a sum; but the liability would exist.

Subsequently, three of the judges in the *Bland* case specifically confirmed the legal effect of anticipatory decisions (per Lord Keith at 860 and Lord Goff at 866).

Lord Keith: The first point to make is that it is unlawful, so as to constitute both a tort and the crime of battery, to administer medical treatment to an adult, who is conscious and of sound mind, without his consent: see *F v West Berkshire Health Authority (Mental Health Act Commission intervening)* [1989] 2 All ER 545, [1990] 2 AC 1. Such a person is completely at liberty to decline to undergo treatment, even if the result of his doing so will be that he will die. This extends to the situation where the person, in anticipation of this, through one cause or another, entering into a condition such as PVS, gives clear instructions that in such event he is not to be given medical care, including artificial feeding, designed to keep him alive.

Lord Goff: Moreover the same principle [that respect must be given to the patient's wishes] applies where the patient's refusal to give his consent has been expressed at an earlier date, before he became unconscious or otherwise incapable of communicating it; though in such circumstances special care may be necessary to ensure that the prior refusal of consent is still properly to be regarded as applicable in the circumstances which have subsequently occurred.

(See also Lord Mustill at 892.)

Of course, in *Re T* the Court of Appeal avoided giving effect to the patient's wishes and in *Bland*, the patient had not expressed any view about the treatment he should receive if he became permanently unconscious. Any doubt that the law would not recognise the binding effect of a validly made anticipatory refusal was dispelled in the following case.

Re C (adult: refusal of medical treatment) [1994] 1 All ER 819 (Fam Div)

C, a 68-year-old patient suffering from paranoid schizophrenia, developed gangrene in a foot during his confinement in a secure hospital while serving a seven-year term of imprisonment. He was removed to a general hospital, where the consultant surgeon diagnosed that he was likely to die imminently if the leg was not amputated below the knee. The prognosis was that he had a 15% chance of survival without amputation. C refused to consider amputation. The hospital authorities considered whether the operation could be performed without C's consent and made arrangements for a solicitor to see him concerning his competence to give a reasoned decision. In the meantime, treatment with antibiotics and conservative surgery averted the immediate threat of imminent death but the hospital refused to give an undertaking to the solicitor that in recognition of his repeated refusals it would not amputate in any future circumstances. There was a possibility that C would develop gangrene again. An application was made on C's behalf to the court for an injunction restraining the hospital from carrying out an amputation without his express written consent. On behalf of the hospital it was contended that C's capacity to give a definitive decision had been impaired by his mental illness and that he had failed to appreciate the risk of death if the operation was not performed.

Thorpe J: Thanks to the recent decision in *Re T (adult: refusal of medical treatment)* [1992] 4 All ER 649, [1993] Fam 95 and *Airedale NHS Trust v Bland* [1993] 1 All ER 821, [1993] AC 789, the legal principles applicable to this case are readily ascertained. Lord Donaldson MR's judgment in *Re T* concludes with a helpful summary. The propositions contained in the first four numbered paragraphs govern this case. Those propositions are ([1992] 4 All ER 649 at 664, [1993] Fam 95 at 115):

(1) Prima facie every adult has the right and capacity to decide whether or not he will accept medical treatment, even if a refusal may risk permanent injury to his health or even lead to premature death. Furthermore, it matters not whether the reasons for the refusal were rational or irrational, unknown or even non-existent. This is so, notwithstanding the very strong public interest in preserving the life and health of all citizens. However, the presumption of capacity to decide, which stems from the fact that the patient is an adult, is rebuttable. (2) An adult patient may be deprived of his capacity to decide by long-term mental incapacity … (3) If an adult patient did not have the capacity to decide at the time of the purported refusal and still does not have that capacity, it is the duty of the doctors to treat him in whatever way they consider, in the exercise of clinical judgment, to be in his best interests. (4) Doctors faced with a refusal of consent have to give very careful and detailed consideration to what was the patient's capacity to decide at the time when the decision was made. It may not be a case of capacity or no capacity. It may be a case of reduced capacity. What matters is whether at that time the patient's capacity was reduced below the level needed in the case of a refusal of that importance, for refusals can vary in importance. Some may involve a risk to life or of irreparable damage to health. Others may not.

Those propositions are common ground. It is also common ground that a refusal can take the form of a declaration of intention never to consent in the future or never to consent in some future circumstances, to borrow the words of Lord Donaldson MR in *Re T*. That proposition has been confirmed by the judgments and speeches in *Bland*'s case.

However, submissions divide over the definition of the capacity which enables an individual to refuse treatment. Mr Gordon argues for what he calls the minimal competence test, which he defines as the capacity to understand in broad terms the nature and effect of the proposed treatment. It is common ground that C has the legal capacity to initiate these proceedings without a next friend, within the terms of RSC Ord 80. Mr Gordon contends that the capacity to refuse treatment is no higher and is equally no higher than the capacity to contract. I reject that submission. I think that the question to be decided is whether it has been established that C's capacity is so reduced by his chronic mental illness that he does not sufficiently understand the nature, purpose and effects of the proffered amputation.

I consider helpful Dr Eastman's analysis of the decision-making process into three stages: first, comprehending and retaining treatment information, second, believing it and, third, weighing it in the balance to arrive at choice. The Law Commission has proposed a similar approach in para 2.20 of its consultation paper 129, *Mentally Handicapped Adults and Decision-Making*. Applying that test to my findings on the evidence, I am completely satisfied that the presumption that C has the right of self-determination has not been displaced. Although his general capacity is impaired by schizophrenia, it has not been established that he does not sufficiently understand the nature, purpose and effects of the treatment he refuses. Indeed, I am satisfied that he has understood and retained the relevant treatment information, that in his own way he believes it, and that in the same fashion he has arrived at a clear choice.

I accept Mr Jackson's submission that C might have the capacity to make a present refusal but lack the capacity to make an anticipatory refusal, but I reject that conclusion because in weighing the consequences of facing a future acute phase without amputation he has the experience of a recent acute attack to guide him.

The relief sought by the originating summons is, in summary, an injunction preventing Heatherwood Hospital from amputation now or in the future without C's express written consent ... Order accordingly.

The cases show the clear acceptance by the courts of the validity of an anticipatory refusal. The constituent elements of a valid refusal are: (1) that the patient be competent at the time the decision was made; (2) that the patient be free from undue influence; (3) that the patient be sufficiently informed; and (4) that the patient intend his refusal to apply to the circumstances which subsequently arise.

The first two of these elements raise no special problems here. You will, however, notice the rather curious remark by Thorpe in *Re C* (*supra*) that 'C might have the capacity to make a present refusal but lack the capacity to make an anticipatory refusal'. If this suggests that a greater *ability* is required of a patient who wishes to make an advance refusal, it is unhelpful. If, by contrast, Thorpe J merely meant that a patient might require more information and thus contemplate more when the decision is to take effect in the future – and this is probably the sense of his remark – he is reflecting no more than a patient may have to understand or contemplate more complex information when he is anticipating the future and his (then) medical treatment (see also *Re T* (*supra*) per Lord Donaldson MR at 661: 'capacity commensurate in the gravity of the decision'). The other two do, however, require further consideration. As regards being 'sufficiently informed', it is important to recognise that the Court of Appeal in *Re T* did not create a doctrine of 'informed refusal'. Instead, the court held that a refusal may be valid provided a patient is aware of the 'nature and effect of the procedure' which he is refusing. There is no need, as Lord Donaldson MR makes clear, for the patient to be aware of other matters such as risks associated with the procedure. However, a patient who is not aware of the relevant risks and alternatives may not satisfy element 4, ie he may not be held to have intended his decision to apply in the circumstances which subsequently arise. Indeed, that was just the case in *Re T* itself where the patient's misunderstanding of the alternatives available to blood transfusion led the court to conclude that Miss T had not contemplated her refusal of treatment as applying if her life were threatened.

This fourth element as developed by Lord Donaldson MR in *Re T* may, therefore, be a Trojan horse. It may allow the courts (and therefore doctors) to undermine the law's apparent commitment to the patient's right of self-determination. If the court wishes, it can, on the basis of the fourth element in *Re T*, require that the patient specifically give his mind to the precise circumstances that have arisen and indicate that, should they arise, he refuses treatment. This may well be a hard criterion to satisfy. The following American case referred to in *Re T* highlights this danger.

Werth v Taylor (1991) 475 NW 2d 426 (Mich CA)

Neff PJ: Plaintiffs filed a civil battery claim against defendant Taylor based on his authorization of a blood transfusion for Cindy Werth despite plaintiff's refusals. Plaintiffs also filed a medical malpractice claim against Taylor and other defendants. The medical malpractice claim is not the subject of this appeal.

The facts are not in dispute. Cindy and her husband Donald are Jehovah's Witnesses. It is unquestioned that they are both devoted adherents to the tenets of their chosen faith. According to Cindy Werth's deposition testimony, one of the most deeply held of these tenets is the belief that it is a sin to receive blood transfusions.

In August 1985, Cindy, the mother of two children, became pregnant with twins. About two months before the expected date of delivery, Cindy went to Alpena General Hospital to preregister. She filled out several forms including a 'Refusal to Permit Blood Transfusion' form. Cindy went into labor on May 8, 1986, and entered Alpena General Hospital on that date. While she was being admitted, Donald signed another 'Refusal to Permit Blood Transfusion' form.

Cindy gave birth to her twins on the evening of May 8, 1986. Following delivery, Cindy was found to be bleeding from her uterus. Around 11:30 pm, Dr Cheryl Parsons was called. She performed a pelvic examination and discovered a great deal of clotting and a fair amount of bleeding. Dr Parsons then discussed performing a dilation of the cervix and curettage of the uterine lining (D& C). As a result, Dr Parsons began discussing with plaintiffs their refusals of blood transfusions.

Following this discussion, Cindy was taken to surgery. In the early hours of May 9, 1986, she was placed under general anesthesia, and Dr Parsons proceeded to perform a D & C. The bleeding, however, continued. Defendant Taylor, an anethesiologist, was then called to the hospital to examine Cindy. Cindy's blood pressure had risen significantly. At approximately 1:30 am, defendant Taylor observed mottling and cooling of the skin peripherally, premature ventricular activity, oozing of crystalloid material from her eyes, and a fairly rapid and significant fall in blood pressure. These observations prompted defendant Taylor to determine that a blood transfusion was medically necessary to preserve Cindy's life. He ordered the transfusion of packed red blood cells, but before the transfusion was given, Dr Parsons informed him that Cindy was a Jehovah's Witness. Dr Parsons testified that defendant responded by saying something like 'that may be, but she needs the blood'. A blood transfusion was then given.

Plaintiffs thereafter filed their medical malpractice action, alleging negligence by various defendants, including Taylor, and alleging battery against defendant Taylor…

Plaintiffs contend that the trial court erred in granting summary disposition where there refusal of a blood transfusion was made deliberately and voluntarily…

Defendant Taylor, on the other hand, contends that the trial court did not err in granting summary disposition, because plaintiffs did not unequivocally refuse the blood transfusion. He claims that, in the face of a life-threatening emergency, without a fully conscious and contemporaneous refusal, his decision to transfuse blood was appropriate and the court did not err in finding an implicit consent to the procedure authorized by him…

Here, the trial court determined that Cindy's refusals were made when she was contemplating merely routine elective surgery and not when life-threatening circumstances were present and concluded that it could not be said that she made the decision to refuse a blood transfusion while in a competent state and while fully aware that death would result from such refusal. The record reflects the unexpected development of a medical emergency requiring blood transfusion to prevent death or serious compromise of the patient's well-being.

The decision of the trial court is supported by one reached by the Supreme Court of Pennsylvania in *In Re Estate of Dorone*, 517 Pa 3, 543 A 2d 452 (1987). In *Dorone*, the patient was a twenty-two-year-old Jehovah's Witness who required a blood transfusion during a cranial operation to relieve an acute subdural hematoma. Without the operation or transfusion, death was imminent. The patient was unconscious, and his parents refused consent to the blood transfusion. The court overruled the parents' refusal, stating:

> Turning to the ultimate decisions the judge rendered, we feel that they were absolutely required under the facts he had before him. Those facts established that medical intervention, which necessarily included blood transfusions, could preserve Mr Dorone's life. When evidence of this nature is measured against third party speculation as to what an unconscious patient would want there can be no doubt that medical intervention is required. Indeed, in a situation like the present, where there is an emergency calling for an immediate decision, nothing less than a fully conscious contemporaneous decision *by the patient* will be sufficient to override evidence of medical necessity. [*Id*, p 9, 534 A 2d 452.]

Here, both plaintiffs signed 'Refusal to Permit Blood Transfusion' forms. Following Cindy's delivery of twins, Dr Parsons discussed these refusals with both plaintiffs. Cindy recalled their conversation as follows:

> She – okay. We told her – she said, 'I understand that you're one of Jehovah's Witnesses and that you won't take blood,' and Don and I both said, 'That's correct,' And she said, 'You mean to tell me if your wife's dying on the table that you're not going to give her blood?' And we said – Don said, 'That's – well, I don't want her to have blood, but I don't want her to die. We want the alternative treatment'...
>
> She said there would be no problem. It was a routine D & C, there was no problem with the blood...
>
> The idea of a blood transfusion, she made it sound that it wouldn't even be a problem. Blood wouldn't come into the picture. That's how I understood it.

Donald also testified regarding the conversation as follows:

> At the time of the consent form, she gave it to my wife and had her look it over and read it, and she said – she acknowledged us as being one of Jehovah's Witnesses, and then she said, 'Would you accept blood?' And we replied, 'No.' And then she made the remark. 'Even if she was to die, you'd let her die?'
>
> And at that point, I questioned, I said, 'Well, how serious of a, you know, condition was she?' And the reason why we asked that is because, like I say, in different situations like there are Witnesses who have gone to hospitals, you know, if there was some type of real emergency, a lot of times they're shipped out or flown out. Different ones have gone to Ann Arbor and other places.
>
> So at that time, I was just kind of questioning, well, how serious was it, you know. First of all, you say it's a routine D & C; then you mention that if she was to die, and so that's why I questioned it, and then she reassured us that there was no problem, nothing to it.

The following colloquy then occurred between defense counsel and Donald:

> Q. So you never answered the question.
> A. Oh, as far as the idea of dying?
> Q. Yes.
> A. I said no. The answer was no.
> Q. Even if she was to die, you said 'No blood.'
> A. Right.
> Q. What did your wife say to that?
> A. Well, she was right there and that was her feeling also.
> Q. But you didn't have the feeling that that was part of the problem or a possibility? It was kind of an academic discussion, that she might die?
> A. Well, she said it in a joking manner. It wasn't done as a serious matter. Being with a joking manner, that's why I asked her how serious it was and then she just – 'Oh, there's no problem.'
> Q. Okay. So you weren't really biting the bullet because it didn't seem to be part of the problem that she was going to die or there was a risk of her dying.
> A. At that point, no.

Dr Parsons testified to the conversation as follows:

> I recall discussing with her and her husband the fact that they were Jehovah's Witnesses and that she indicated that this was true. And I said, 'Is it true that you do not want any blood transfusions?' She said 'No.' He looked at me and said, 'Do you think it's that bad?' And I said, 'Not right now.' And I didn't get any further answer from him in terms of whether he felt that if it became that bad me might change his mind. And I left it at that.

She also described Donald's response as 'wishy-washy'.

Following this discussion, Cindy underwent surgery. She was placed under general anesthesia, and Dr Parsons performed a D & C. Cindy did not regain consciousness again until after the operation and transfusion of blood were performed. Defendant Taylor testified that he was aware, before deciding to infuse blood, that Cindy was a Jehovah's Witness. No attempt was made to bring Cindy to consciousness in order to obtain her approval, and defendant Taylor testified that this option was 'fool-hardy'. No attempt was made to discuss his decision with Donald because defendant saw nothing to be gained from it. He did not believe Donald could give or deny permission for a blood transfusion.

We agree with the principle in *Dorone* that it is the patient's fully informed, contemporaneous decision which alone is sufficient to override evidence of medical necessity…It is undisputed that Cindy was unconscious when the critical decision regarding the blood transfusion to avoid her death was being made. Her prior refusals had not been made when her life was hanging in the balance or when it appeared that death might be a possibility if a transfusion were not given. Clearly, her refusals were, therefore, not contemporaneous or informed. Thus, a record could not be developed regarding Cindy's refusal which would leave open an issue upon which reasonable minds could offer.

Our holding in this case is narrow. Without contemporaneous refusal of treatment by a fully informed competent adult patient, no action lies for battery and summary disposition was proper.
Shepherd and McDonald JJ agreed.

(See also *In the Matter of Alice Hughes* (1992) 611 A 2d 1148 (Sup NJ App Div).)

The situation is not saved by Lord Donaldson MR's assertion in *Re T* that if the patient was not informed of such matters as risks, he would have an action in negligence against his doctor (even though his refusal of treatment would be invalid by not being properly directed to what in fact arose). Any action in negligence against the doctor would, of course, fail even if the doctor were in breach of his duty because the patient would be unable to show that he had suffered any harm (see eg *Anderson v St Francis-St George Hospital* (1996) 671 NE 2d 225 (Ohio Sup Ct)). Alternatively, the action for 'wrongful living' or 'prolongation of life' may offend the court's moral sensibilities since the damages will flow from the patient being alive (*McKay v Essex AHA* [1982] QB 1166 (CA) – 'wrongful life'; *McFarlane v Tayside Health Board* [1999] 4 All ER 961 (HL) – 'wrongful conception'). Thus, Lord Donaldson MR takes away with one hand and does not give back with the other. In our view, a patient's right to refuse can only have any real substance if the fourth element we referred to above is not used in such a way so as to undermine the patient's right.

Re T and *Werth* seem to have gone to some lengths to construe the patients' refusals so as to narrow the scope of their application and thereby ignore them. By contrast, the Ontario Court of Appeal in the following case adopted a more sensitive approach.

Malette v Shulman (1990) 67 DLR (4th) 321, [1991] 2 Med LR 162 (Ont CA)

Robins JA: The question to be decided in this appeal is whether a doctor is liable in law for administering blood transfusions to an unconscious patient in a potentially life-threatening situation when the patient is carrying a card stating that she is a Jehovah's Witness and, as a matter of religious belief, rejects blood transfusions under any circumstances.

In the early afternoon of June 30, 1979, Mrs Georgette Malette, then aged 57, was rushed, unconscious, by ambulance to the Kirkland and District Hospital in Kirkland Lake, Ontario. She had been in an accident. The car in which she was a passenger, driven by her husband, had collided head-on with a truck. Her husband had been killed. She suffered serious injuries.

On arrival at the hospital, she was attended by Dr David L Shulman, a family physician practicing in Kirkland Lake who served two or three shifts a week in the emergency department of the hospital and who was on duty at the time. Dr Shulman's initial examination of Mrs Malette showed, among other things, that she had severe head and face injuries and was bleeding profusely. The doctor concluded that she was suffering from incipient shock by reason of blood loss, and ordered that she be given intravenous glucose followed immediately by Ringer's Lactate. The administration of a volume expander, such as Ringer's Lactate, is standard medical procedure in cases of this nature. If the patient does not respond with significantly increased blood pressure, transfusions of blood are then administered to carry essential oxygen to tissues and to remove waste products and prevent damage to vital organs.

At about this time, a nurse discovered a card in Mrs Malette's purse which identified her as a Jehovah's Witness and in which she requested, on the basis of her religious convictions, that she be given no blood transfusions under any circumstances. The card, which was not dated or witnessed was printed in French and signed by Mrs Malette. Translated into English, it read:

NO BLOOD TRANSFUSION!

As one of Jehovah's Witnesses with firm religious convictions, I request that no blood or blood products be administered to me under any circumstances. I fully realize the implications of this position, but I have resolutely decided to obey the Bible command: 'Keep abstaining…from blood.' (Acts 15:28, 29). However, I have no religious objection to use the nonblood alternatives, such as Dextran, Haemaccel, PVP, Ringer's Lactate or saline solution.

Dr Shulman was promptly advised of the existence of this card and its contents.

Mrs Malette was next examined by a surgeon on duty in the hospital. He concluded, as had Dr Shulman, that to avoid irreversible shock, it was vital to maintain her blood volume. He had Mrs Malette transferred to the X-ray department for X-rays on her skull, pelvis and chest. However, before the X-rays could be satisfactorily completed, Mrs Malette's condition deteriorated. Her blood pressure dropped markedly, her respiration became increasingly distressed, and her level of consciousness dropped. She continued to bleed profusely and could be said to be critically ill.

At this stage, Dr Shulman decided that Mrs Malette's condition had deteriorated to the point that transfusions were necessary to replace her lost blood and to preserve her life and health. Having made that decision, he personally administered transfusions to her, in spite of the Jehovah's Witness card, while she was in the X-ray department and after she was transferred to the intensive care unit. Dr Shulman was clearly aware of the religious objection to blood manifested in the card carried by Mrs Malette and the instruction that 'NO BLOOD TRANSFUSION!' be given under any circumstances. He accepted full responsibility then, as he does now, for the decision to administer the transfusion...

[H]e was not satisfied that the card signed by Mrs Malette expressed her current instructions because, on the information he then had, he did not know whether she might have changed her religious beliefs before the accident; whether the card may have been signed because of family or peer pressure; whether at the time she signed the card she was fully informed of the risks or refusal of blood transfusions; or whether, if conscious, she might have changed her mind in the face of medical advice as to her perhaps imminent but avoidable death.

As matters developed, by about midnight Mrs Malette's condition had stabilized sufficiently to permit her to be transferred early the next morning by air ambulance to Toronto General Hospital where she received no further blood transfusions. She was discharged on August 11, 1979. Happily, she made a very good recovery from her injuries...

What then is the legal effect, if any, of the Jehovah's Witness card carried by Mrs Malette? Was the doctor bound to honour the instructions of his unconscious patient or, given the emergency and his inability to obtain conscious instructions from his patient, was he entitled to disregard the card and act according to his best medical judgment?

To answer these questions and determine the effect to be given to the Jehovah's Witness card, it is first necessary to ascertain what rights a competent patient has to accept or reject medical treatment and to appreciate the nature and extent of those rights...

A competent adult is generally entitled to reject a specific treatment or all treatment, or to select an alternative form of treatment, even if the decision may entail risks as serious as death and may appear mistaken in the eyes of the medical profession or of the community. Regardless of the doctor's opinion, it is the patient who has the final say on whether to undergo the treatment. The patient is free to decide, for instance, not to be operated on or not to undergo therapy or, by the same token, not to have a blood transfusion. If a doctor were to proceed in the face of a decision to reject the treatment, he would be civilly liable for his unauthorized conduct notwithstanding his justifiable belief that what he did was necessary to preserve the patient's life or health...

On the facts of the present case, Dr Shulman was clearly faced with an emergency. He had an unconscious, critically ill patient on his hands who, in his opinion, needed blood transfusions to save her life or preserve her health. If there were no Jehovah's Witness card he undoubtedly would have been entitled to administer blood transfusions as part of the emergency treatment and could not have been held liable for so doing. In those circumstances he would have had no indication that the transfusions would have been refused had the patient then been able to make her wishes known and, accordingly, no reason to expect that, as a reasonable person, she would not consent to the transfusions.

However, to change the facts, if Mrs Malette, before passing into unconsciousness, had expressly instructed Dr Shulman, in terms comparable to those set forth on the card, that her religious convictions as a Jehovah's Witness were such that she was not to be given a blood transfusion under any circumstances and that she fully realized the implications of this position, the doctor would have been confronted with an obviously different situation. Here, the patient, anticipating an emergency in which she might be unable to make decisions about her health care contemporaneous with the emergency, has given explicit instructions that blood transfusions constitute an unacceptable medical intervention and are not to be administered to her. Once the emergency arises, is the doctor none the less entitled to administer transfusions on the basis of his honest belief that they are needed to save a patient's life?

The answer, in my opinion, is clearly no. A doctor is not free to disregard a patient's advance instructions any more than he would be free to disregard instructions given at the time of the emergency. The law does not prohibit a patient from withholding consent to emergency medical treatment, nor does the law prohibit a doctor from following his patient's instructions. While the law may disregard the absence of consent in limited emergency circumstances, it otherwise supports the right of competent adults to make decisions concerning their own health care by imposing civil liability on those who perform medical treatment without consent.

The patient's decision to refuse blood in the situation I have posed was made prior to and in anticipation of the emergency. While the doctor would have had the opportunity to dissuade her on the basis of his medical advice, her refusal to accept his advice or her unwillingness to discuss or consider the subject would not relieve him of his obligation to follow her instructions. The principles of self-determination and individual autonomy compel the conclusion that the patient may reject blood transfusions even if harmful consequences may result and even if the decision is generally regarded as foolhardy. Her decision in this instance would be operative after she lapsed into unconsciousness, and the doctor's conduct would be unauthorized. To transfuse a Jehovah's Witness in the face of her explicit instructions to the contrary would, in my opinion, violate her right to control her own body and show disrespect for the religious values by which she has chosen to live her life...

Accepting for the moment that there is no reason to doubt that the card validly expressed Mrs Malette's desire to withhold consent to blood transfusions, why should her wishes not be respected? Why should she be transfused against her will? The appellant's answer, in essence, is that the card cannot be effective when the doctor is unable to provide the patient with the information she would need before making a decision to withhold consent in this specific emergency situation...

In this case, the patient, in effect, issued standing orders that she was to be given 'NO BLOOD TRANSFUSION!' in any circumstances. She gave notice to the doctor and the hospital, in the only practical way open to her, of her firm religious convictions as a Jehovah's Witness and her resolve to abstain from blood. Her instructions plainly contemplated the situation in which she found herself as a result of her unfortunate accident. In light of those instructions, assuming the validity, she cannot be said to have consented to blood transfusions in this emergency. Nor can the doctor be said to have proceeded on the reasonable belief that the patient would have consented had she been in a condition to do so. Given his awareness of her instructions and his understanding that blood transfusions were anathema to her on religious grounds, by what authority could he administer the transfusions? Put another way, if the card evidences the patient's intent to withhold consent, can the doctor none the less ignore the card and subject the patient to a procedure that is manifestly contrary to her express wishes and unacceptable to her religious beliefs?...

In the particular doctor-patient relationship which arose in these emergency circumstances it is apparent that the doctor could not inform the patient of the risks involved in her prior decision to refuse consent to blood transfusions in any circumstances. It is apparent also that her decision did not emerge out of a doctor-patient relationship. Whatever the doctor's obligation to provide the information needed to make an informed choice may be in other doctor-patient relationships, he cannot be in breach of any such duty in the circumstances of this relationship. The patient manifestly made the decision on the basis of her religious convictions. It is not for the doctor to second-guess the reasonableness of the decision or to pass judgment on the religious principles which motivated it. The fact that he had no opportunity to offer medical advice cannot nullify instructions plainly intended to govern in circumstances where such advice is not possible. Unless the doctor had reason to believe that the instructions in the Jehovah's Witness card were not valid instructions in the sense that they did not truly represent the patient's wishes, in my opinion he was obliged to honor them. He has no authorization under the emergency doctrine to override the patient's wishes. In my opinion, she was entitled to reject in advance of an emergency a medical procedure inimical to her religious values...On my reading of the record, there was no reason not to regard this card as a valid advance directive. Its instructions were clear, precise and unequivocal, and manifested a calculated decision to reject a procedure offensive to the patient's religious convictions. The instructions excluded from potential emergency treatment a single medical procedure well known to the lay public and within its comprehension. The religious belief of Jehovah's Witnesses with respect to blood transfusions was known to the doctor and, indeed, is a matter of common knowledge to providers of health care. The card undoubtedly belonged to and was signed by Mrs Mallette; its authenticity was not questioned by anyone at the hospital and realistically, could not have been questioned. The trial judge found, '[t]here [was] no basis in evidence to indicate that the card [did] not represent the current intention and instruction of the card holder' [p 268 OR, p 43 DLR]. There was nothing to give credence to or provide support for the speculative inferences implicit in questions as to the current strength of Mrs Malette's religious beliefs or as to the circumstances under which the card was signed or her state of mind at the time. The fact that a card of this nature was carried by her can itself be taken as verification of her continuing and current resolve to reject blood 'fully realiz[ing] the implications of this position'.

In short, the card on its fact set forth unqualified instructions applicable to the circumstances presented by this emergency. In the absence of any evidence to the contrary, those instructions should be taken as validly representing the patient's wish not to be transfused. If, of course, there were evidence to the contrary – evidence which cast doubt on whether the card was a true expression of the patient's wishes – the doctor, in my opinion, would be entitled to proceed as he would in the usual emergency case. In this case, however, there was no such contradictory evidence. Accordingly, I am of the view that the card had the effect of validly restricting the treatment that could be provided to Mrs Malette and constituted the doctor's administration of the transfusions a battery.

Advance directives

A. DEVELOPMENTS IN OTHER COMMON LAW JURISDICTIONS

Legislation designed to give effect to patients' anticipatory decisions first emerged in the United States during the mid-1970s in the form of 'living will' statutes. Subsequent developments involved legislation permitting a patient to appoint an agent, or health care proxy, to make treatment decisions on his behalf after the onset of incompetence. A species of hybrid statute then began to appear combining the two forms, ie living will and durable powers of attorney. Together these developments have come known as 'advance directives'.

President's Commission *Deciding to Forgo Life-Sustaining Treatment* (1983)

Advance directives

An 'advance directive' lets people anticipate that they may be unable to participate in future decisions about their own health care – an 'instruction directive' specifies the types of care a person wants (or does not want) to receive; a 'proxy directive' specifies the surrogate a person wants to make such decisions if the person is ever unable to do so; and the two forms may be combined. Honoring such a directive shows respect for self-determination in that it fulfils two of the three values that underlie self-determination. First, following a directive, particularly one that gives specific instructions about types of acceptable and unacceptable interventions, fulfils the instrumental role of self-determination by promoting the patient's subjective, individual evaluation of well-being. Second, honoring the directive shows respect for the patient as a person.

An advance directive does not, however, provide self-determination in the sense of active moral agency by the patient on his or her own behalf. The discussion between patient and health care professional leading up to a directive would involve active participation and shared decisionmaking, but at the point of actual decision the patient is incapable of participating. Consequently, although self-determination is involved when a patient establishes a way to project his or her wishes into a time of anticipated incapacity, it is a sense of self-determination lacking in one important attribute: active, contemporaneous personal choice. Hence a decision not to follow an advance directive may sometimes be justified even when it would not be acceptable to disregard a competent patient's contemporaneous choice. Such a decision would most often rest on a finding that the patient did not adequately envision and consider the particular situation within which the actual medical decision must be made.

Advance directives are not confined to decisions to forego life-sustaining treatment but may be drafted for use in any health care situation in which people anticipate they will lack capacity to make decisions for themselves. However, the best-known type of directive – formulated pursuant to a 'natural death' act – does deal with decisions to forego life-sustaining treatment...

Despite a number of unresolved issues about how advance directives should be drafted, given legal effect, and used in clinical practice, the Commission recommends that advance directives should expressly be endowed with legal effect under state law. For such documents to assist decisionmaking, however, people must be encouraged to develop them for their individual use, and health care professionals should be encouraged to respect and abide by advance directives whenever reasonably possible, even without specific legislative authority.

Existing alternative documents. Several forms of advance directives are currently used. 'Living wills' were initially developed as documents without any binding legal effects; they are ordinarily instruction directives. The intent behind the original 'natural death' act was simply to give legal recognition to living wills drafted according to certain established requirements. They are primarily instruction directives, although their terms are poorly enough defined that the physician and surrogate who will carry them out will have to make substantial interpretations. 'Durable power of attorney' statutes are primarily proxy directives, although by limiting or describing the circumstances in which they are to operate they also contain elements of instruction directives. Furthermore, durable powers of attorney may incorporate extensive personal instructions...

Living wills. People's concerns about the loss of ability to direct care at the end of their lives have led a number of commentators as well as religious, educational, and professional groups to promulgate documents, usually referred to as living wills, by which individuals can indicate their preference not to be given 'heroic' or 'extraordinary' treatments. There have been many versions proposed, varying widely in their specificity. Some explicitly detailed directives have been drafted by physicians – outlining a litany of treatments to be forgone or disabilities they would not wish to suffer in their final days. The model living wills proposed by educational groups have somewhat more general language; they typically mention 'life-sustaining procedures which would serve only to artificially prolong the dying process'. One New York group has distributed millions of living wills. The columnist who writes 'Dear Abby' reports receiving tens of thousands of requests for copies each time she deals with the subject. Despite their popularity, their legal force and effect is uncertain. The absence of explicit statutory authorization in most jurisdictions raises a number of important issues that patients and their lawyers or other advisors should keep in mind when drafting living wills.

First, it is uncertain whether health care personnel are required to carry out the terms of a living will; conversely, those who, in good faith, act in accordance with living wills are not assured immunity from civil or criminal prosecution. No penalties re provided for the destruction, concealment, forgery or other misuse of living wills, which leaves them somewhat vulnerable to abuse. The question of whether a refusal of life-sustaining therapy constitutes suicide is unresolved, as are the insurance implications of a patient's having died as a result of a physician's withholding treatment pursuant to a living will.

Yet even in states that have not enacted legislation to recognize and implement advance directives, living wills may still have some legal effect. For example, should a practitioner be threatened with civil liability or criminal prosecution for having acted in accord with such a document, it should at least serve as evidence of a patient's wishes and assessment of benefit when he or she was competent. Indeed, no practitioner has been successfully subjected to civil liability or criminal prosecution for having followed the provisions in a living will, nor do there appear to be any cases brought for having acted against one...

Proxy directives allow patients to control decisionmaking in a far broader range of cases than the instruction directives authorized by most existing natural death acts...

A power of attorney – general or limited – may be employed in making decisions not only about property but about personal matters as well, and in this role powers of attorney might be used to delegate authority to others to make health care decisions. A power of attorney, therefore, can be an advance proxy directive. Using it, a person can nominate another to make health care decisions if he or she becomes unable to make those decisions.

One barrier to this use of a power of attorney, however, is that the usual power of attorney becomes inoperative at precisely the point it is needed; a common-law power of attorney automatically terminates when the principal becomes incapacitated. To circumvent this barrier, many states have enacted statutes creating a power of attorney that is 'durable' – which means that an agent's authority to act continues after his or her principal is incapacitated. As a result, durable power of attorney acts offer a simple, flexible, and powerful device for making health care decisions on behalf of incapacitated patients.

Although not expressly enacted for the problems of incompetent patients' health care decisionmaking, the language of these statutes can accommodate the appointment of a surrogate for that purpose and nothing in the statutes explicitly precludes such a use. The flexibility of the statutes allows directives to be drafted that are sensitive to both the different needs of patients in appointing proxy decisionmakers and to the range of situations in which decisions may have to be made.

The first living will statute was the National Death Act 1976 in California (currently, Cal Health and Safety Code, s 7185 to 7194.5: for details of the original (unamended) statute, see *First Edition* p 1123). The President's Commission in a 1983 report discussed (at 141–145) critically the California legislation and other early 'living will' statutes.

President's Commission *Deciding to Forgo Life-Sustaining Treatment* (1983)

Natural death acts. To overcome the uncertain legal status of living wills, 13 states and the District of Columbia have followed the lead set by California in 1976 and enacted statutes that formally establish the requirements for a 'directive to physicians'. The California statute was labeled a 'natural death' act and this term is now used generically to refer to other state statutes. Although well-intended, these acts raise a great many new problems without solving many of the old ones.

No natural death act yet deals with all the issues raised when living wills are used without specific statutory sanction. For instance, the acts differ considerably in their treatment of penalties for failing to act in accord with a properly executed directive or to transfer the patient to a physician who will follow the directive. In some jurisdictions, the statutes consider these failures to be unprofessional conduct and therefore grounds for professional discipline, including the suspension of a license to practice medicine. Other statutes fail to address the issue. Presumably, however, existing remedies such as injunctions or suits for breach of contract or for battery are available to patients or their heirs, although there do not appear to be any instances of such penalties being sought.

Some of the statutes attempt to provide patients with adequate opportunity to reconsider their decision by imposing a waiting period between the time when a patient decides that further treatment is unwanted and the time when the directive becomes effective. Under the California statute, for example, a directive is binding only if it is signed by a 'qualified patient', technically defined as someone who has been diagnosed as having a 'terminal condition'. This is defined as an incurable condition that means death is 'imminent' regardless of the 'life-sustaining procedures' used. A patient must wait 14 days after being told of the diagnosis before he or she can sign a directive, which would require a miraculous cure, a misdiagnosis, or a very loose interpretation of the word 'imminent' in order for the directive to be of any use to a patient. The statute requires that when a directive is signed, the patient must be fully competent and not overwhelmed by disease or by the effects of treatment, but a study of California physicians one year after the new law was enacted found that only about half the patients diagnosed as terminally ill even remain conscious for 14 days. There is an inherent tension between ensuring that dying patients have a means of expressing their wishes about treatment termination before they are overcome by incompetence and ensuring that people do not make binding choices about treatment on the basis of hypothetical rather than real facts about their illness and dying process. If a waiting period is deemed necessary to resolve this tension the time should be defined in a way that does not substantially undercut the objective of encouraging advance directives by people who are at risk of becoming incapacitated.

Although the California statute was inspired in part by the situation of Karen Quinlan, whose father had to pursue judicial relief for a year in order to authorize the removal of her respirator, it would not apply in a case like hers.

> The only patients covered by this statute are those who are on the edge of death *despite the doctor's efforts*. The very people for whom the greatest concern is expressed about a prolonged and undignified dying process are unaffected by the statute because their deaths are not imminent.

The class of person thus defined by many of the statutes, if it indeed contains any members, at most constitutes a small percentage of those incapacitated individuals for whom decisions about life-sustaining treatment must be made. Although some statutes have not explicitly adopted the requirement that treatments may be withheld or withdrawn only if death is imminent whether or not they are used, this requirement is still found in one of the most recently passed natural death acts. Such a limitation greatly reduces an act's potential.

Some of the patients for whom decisions to forgo life-sustaining treatment need to be made are residents of nursing homes rather than hospitals. Concerned that they might be under undue pressure to sign a directive, the California legislature provided additional safeguards for the voluntariness of their directives by requiring that a patient advocate or ombudsman serve as a witness. The Commission believes that health care providers should make reasonable efforts to involve disinterested parties, not only as witnesses to the signing of a directive under a natural death act, but also as counselors to patients who request such a directive to ensure that they are acting as voluntarily and competently as possible. Yet statutory requirements of this sort may have the effect of precluding use of advance directives by long-term care residents, even though some residents of these facilities might be as capable as any other person of using the procedure in a free and knowing fashion.

Paradoxically, natural death acts may restrict patients' ability to have their wishes about life-sustaining treatment respected. If health care providers view these as the exclusive means for making and implementing a decision to forego treatment and, worse, if they believe that such a decision cannot be made by a surrogate on behalf of another but only in accordance with an advance directive properly executed by a patient, some dying patients may be subject to treatment that is neither desired nor beneficial. In fact, although 6.5% of the physicians surveyed in California reported that during the first year after passage of the act there they withheld or withdrew procedures they previously would have administered, 10% of the physicians reported that they provided treatment they formerly would have withheld.

In addition there is the danger that people will infer that a patient who has not executed a directive in accordance with the natural death act does not desire life-sustaining treatment to be ended under any circumstances. Yet the person may fail to sign a directive because of ignorance of its existence, inattention to its significance, uncertainty about how to execute one, or failure to foresee the kind of medical circumstances that in fact develop. Unfortunately, even the explicit disclaimer contained in many of these laws – that the act is not intended to impair or supersede any preexisting common law legal rights or responsibilities that patients and practitioners may have with respect to the withholding or withdrawing of life-sustaining procedures – does not in itself correct this difficulty.

First, the declarations about the right of competent patients to refuse 'life-sustaining procedures' take on a rather pale appearance since such procedures are defined by the statutes as those that cannot stop an imminent death. (In other words, competent patients may refuse futile treatments.) second, it is hard to place great reliance on preexisting common law rights, since had the common law established such rights there would have been no real need for the statutes. Thus, if health care providers are to treat patients appropriately in states that have adopted natural death acts, they will need the encouragement of their attorneys – backed by sensible judicial interpretation of the statutes – to read the acts as authorizing a new, additional means for patients to exercise 'informed consent' regarding life-saving treatment, but not as a means that limits decisionmaking of patients who have not executed binding directives pursuant to the act.

The greatest value of the natural death acts is the impetus they provide for discussions between patients and practitioners about decisions to forgo life-sustaining treatment. This educational effect might be obtained, however, without making the documents binding by statute and without enforcement and punishment provisions.

One particular matter which bedevilled the early American legislation concerns what may be described as the 'triggering event', ie, that event which brings into operation the living will. The President's Commission took the view that living wills 'are not confined to decisions to forgo *life-sustaining* treatment' (our emphasis). This may imply that the onset of incompetence would be enough of itself to trigger the provisions of a living will whatever the directions in the living will might be and whether or not the patient was dying. In fact, however, in all the early statutes in the United States there was an insistence that the patient should be suffering from a terminal illness, or that death be imminent or some such expression. The limitations of the early statutes are discussed in the following extract.

G Gelfand 'Living Will Statutes: The First Decade' (1987) Wisconsin LR 737

Every existing living will act requires that the patient's physical condition or prognosis be 'terminal' or sufficiently poor in order to bring the provisions of a living will into effect. Subtle differences in the way the various statutes define this requirement are crucial because medical treatments may not be withheld unless the declarant's condition qualifies under the statute.

The most significant difference among the various statutory definitions concerns whether the patient's terminal status must be determined irrespective of the effect of the life-supporting treatments. Surprisingly, half of the current living will statutes require that the patient be in a condition where death will occur shortly *whether or not* life-supporting treatments are employed. If the patient will die shortly with or without life-supporting treatment, there is little reason to engage in euthanasia.

Further, if the intent of living will statutes was to permit the 'natural death' of persons who would otherwise linger for years maintained by modern machinery in a vegetative but 'alive' state, then the requirement that death be imminent whether or not treatment is withdrawn nullifies the purpose of such statutes. Even states that have repeatedly 'fine-tuned' their living will statutes through amendments, however, continue to define the necessary patient prognosis as requiring imminent death even with medical treatment. This contradiction between legislative intent and action almost certainly occurs by oversight, as many such statutes are internally inconsistent with regard to this point. In jurisdictions with such inconsistent statutes, a physician presented with a typical and seemingly proper case for the application of a living will – that is, a comatose, terminal individual who can be mechanically maintained with no change in prognosis for years – would have to seek judicial clarification of the statutory definition or risk a homicide prosecution for ending the life of such a patient.

A related question involves the timing of death generally for the purposes of defining a qualified terminally ill patient. A number of statutes require that the patient's condition be such that medical treatments serve only to postpone the moment of dying. This may be the best definition possible, for it conveys more of a sense of the futility of treatment than a time frame for death. Yet such a provision would be far too broad if taken literally. Most medical interventions serve only to postpone the moment of death, even in an otherwise healthy patient.

Other statutes require that death be 'imminent', or that it will occur within a 'short time'. These provisions seem to contain the most appropriate standard since the objective of living will statutes was to allow for the euthanatising of patients with little or no remaining life. However, this standard substitutes a time measure for what is really a more profound question about the futility of medical treatment. If a patient will linger, even for a considerable time, in a vegetative state which medical treatment cannot improve, the intent of living will statutes arguably should be to allow such a patient to die. Perhaps the most satisfactory codification of this intent is found in Alabama's living will statute which allows discontinuance of treatment where 'death is imminent or [the patient's] condition is hopeless'...

Perhaps the most important question, however, concerns the need for such a definition of any kind in the statutes. Political compromise has produced the present requirement that the patient's prognosis be terminal. Yet there may be many cases in which a patient could live for a substantial period, but only if he endures great pain, total physical incapacity, or drastic treatment such as amputation. Since living will statutes reflect a dramatic step toward the recognition of patient autonomy, it can be expected that future provisions will permit the decision to decline treatment in such non-terminal cases.

Given the various criticisms, not least the concern over the limited application of the legislation, a second wave of statutes permitting the creation of durable powers of attorney specifically concerned with health care decisions, emerged. The first and best-known example was again in California: the Durable Power of Attorney Health Carer Act 1983 (currently Cal Civil Code, s 2430 to 2445; for text, see *First Edition* pp 1145–1150).

A third generation of statutes emerged subsequently, combining provisions related to living wills with the option of appointing a proxy decision-maker (eg in Florida). Finally, a fourth generation of statutes of a somewhat different nature has emerged which vests decision-making power in the patient's family members in circumstances where the patient has not made an advance directive (eg in Indiana).

The decision of the Supreme Court of the United States in *Cruzan v Director, Missouri Dept of Health* (1990) 497 US 261 added significant impetus to state legislators in two respects (for a discussion of *Cruzan's* implications, see A Meisel, 'A Retrospective on *Cruzan*' (1992) 20 Law, Medicine and Health Care 340 and generally the special issue (1991) vol 19 (1–2) of Law, Medicine and Health Care entitled 'Medical Decision-Making and the 'Right to Die' after *Cruzan*'). First, the Supreme Court drew no distinction between the withdrawal of other medical treatment and artificial hydration and nutrition. Secondly, a number of the judges took the view that advance directives were beneficial to further patients' choices and, in the case of Justice O'Connor, that the Constitution may actually protect a patient's right to have his wishes respected as reflected in an advance directive. As a consequence, following the *Cruzan* decision, a flurry of legislative activity broke out in the United States, both to amend existing legislation to take account of the artificial hydration and nutrition point (eg in Ohio) and the enactment of new legislation to give effect to a patients' advance directives where previously there had been no such legislation (eg in New York and Massachusetts).

Also, the Federal Government passed the Patient Self-Determination Act 1990 (which came into force in December 1991) which, *inter alia*, requires health care institutions receiving federal funds to advise patients at the time of their admission of their rights under state law to make an advance directive. It also requires institutions to have in effect policies regarding advance directives and to document whether or not a patient has executed one (see discussion in Special Supplement, *Practising the PSDA* (1991) 21 Hastings Center Report). Legislation has not been limited to the United States. In Australia, the Northern Territory has enacted legislation giving effect to advance refusals (see Natural Death Act 1988 (NT) – for a discussion, see D Lanham and B Fehlberg, 'Living Wills and the Right to Die with Dignity' (1991) 18 Melbourne University Law Review 329). Victoria, the ACT and South Australia have adopted statutory frameworks for making anticipatory refusals of treatment *and* to allow a patient to appoint an agent or proxy (see Medical Treatment Act 1988 (as amended) (Vic) – discussed by D Lanham and S Woodford 'Refusal by Agents of Life-Sustaining Medical Treatment' (1992) 18 Melbourne University Law Review 659 and D Lanham 'The Right to Choose to Die with Dignity' (1990) 14 Criminal Law Journal 401; Consent to Medical Treatment and Palliative Care Act 1995 (SA); Medical Treatment Act 1994 (ACT)).

In Canada, a number of Provinces have enacted statutes giving effect to advance directives, whether as living wills or as durable powers of attorney (see, eg, Consent to Treatment Act 1992 and Substitute Decisions Act 1992 (Ontario); The Health Care Directives Act 1992 (Manitoba)).

B. ENGLAND

1. Existing law

As regards 'living wills', we have already seen that at common law they have legal effect providing they meet the elements necessary for validity set out in *Re T*. There is, of course, as yet no legislation covering 'living wills' in England.

As regards powers of attorney, the Enduring Powers of Attorney Act 1985 does provide that the grant of a power of attorney may survive the onset of the maker's incompetence. The Act, however, does not cover decisions about medical treatment since it is restricted to the 'property and affairs' of an individual (s 3).

The Living Will: Consent to Treatment at the End of Life (1988) (Working Party Report, Age Concern and Centre of Medical Law and Ethics, King's College) (pp 48–49)

Powers of attorney

As regards powers of attorney, under the Common Law it is arguable that an adult patient could nominate another as his agent so that the other may take decisions concerning the patient's health. There seems, however, to be no reported case in which this has occurred. In any event, any agency would (in the absence of any statutory provision) terminate on the incompetence of the patient.

As for statute law, the agency which a person may create for the management of his affairs under the Powers of Attorney Act 1971, terminates on the incompetence of that person. The Enduring Powers of Attorney Act 1985, however, permits the creation of a power of attorney which, providing certain statutory conditions are met, continues after the creator has become incompetent. Although the Act was designed to give power to deal specifically with the financial affairs of the individual, the question arises whether section 3(1) of the Act, which states that the scope of the general authority of an enduring power of attorney extends to an incompetent's 'property or affairs', thereby covers health care decisions, specifically about treatment. It is most unlikely that a court would so construe the statute in the light of the treatment of what is now Section 95 of the Mental Health Act, 1983 in *Re W (EEM)* [1971] Ch 123. When interpreting the Court of Protection's powers 'with respect to the property and affairs of a patient' in relation to this case Ungoed-Thomas J stated that the court did not have jurisdiction over 'the management of care of the patient's person'…

It seems, therefore, that without a specific statutory provision creating an enduring power of attorney in relation to health care decisions, this form of advance directive has no legal validity, unlike for example in California, since the Durable Power of Attorney Health Care Act, 1983.

(See also *Re F (mental patient: sterilisation)* [1990] 2 AC 1 (HL) per Lord Brandon at 59–60 and per Lord Goff at 71.)

2. Reforming the law

There are two issues which must be addressed:
(a) Is there a need for legislation to give effect to advance directives?
(b) If law is desirable, what provisions should it contain?

(a) The need for legislation

A study prepared for the Centre of Medical Law and Ethics, King's College London examined the attitudes towards advance directives of a group of patients with HIV infection or AIDS and of those caring for them (doctors and nurses).

C Schlyter *Advance Directives and AIDS* (1992)

The results of this study indicate that there is a substantial degree of dissatisfaction with current practice of medical decision-making about life-sustaining care in all three of the groups studied. Moreover, a great majority of the participants in the study believe that advance directives in some form would be helpful...

Problems in Current Practice

A number of concerns were put forward by participants which related to the ways in which decisions about life-sustaining treatment are currently managed in HIV care. It was feared by some that these shortcomings led to a large number of decisions being taken without any knowledge of, or reference to, the patient's wishes. Three areas of concern emerged.

First, *discussions with patients about life-sustaining treatment did not take place as often as the groups consulted would wish*. The view was put forward during interviews with doctors and under 'other comments' on the questionnaires in all groups that early discussions between a doctor and patient was the preferred way in which to ensure patient involvement. Such a discussion, held when the patient was not too ill, would give the patient an opportunity to let the doctor know about his or her personal attitude to life-sustaining treatment. At the same time, the doctor would be able to make sure that the patient was aware of the nature and possible effects of different treatments which were available.

However, in many cases discussions of this kind did not take place. The study showed that only a little less than a third of the people who had symptoms of HIV or AIDS had discussed life-sustaining care with a doctor. Of the remaining two-thirds (who had not done so), 93% said they would like to. During interviews, several doctors and nurses said that discussions were sometimes postponed to a stage when it was too late for communication.

A possible reason why life-sustaining treatment is not often discussed is the fact that the subject is not easy for either party to bring up. For example, a doctor may hesitate to initiate such a discussion for fear that it would make the patient anxious or even depressed. The patient, on the other hand, may be uncertain as to the doctor's reaction to questions about treatments for which there is not any present need.

Where a patient is developing new, serious symptoms, it is likely that many doctors would initiate a discussion with the patient about treatments which may have to be considered. Fifteen out of 35 doctors consulted in this study would initiate such a discussion with a patient who had AIDS at the time of significant deterioration of the patient's condition, or when a new problem developed. However, a doctor may be more reluctant to initiate, or even invite, a discussion where a patient had HIV, but is unlikely to experience any serious illness for a long time.

Therefore, a patient who would like to discuss life-sustaining treatment early on would do best to initiate this him- or herself. This, however, requires that patients are aware that they are entitled to have an input in the course of their care, and that their questions are not met with astonishment. It is possible that some people refrain from mentioning concerns regarding treatment to a doctor not because they do not wish to discuss it, but because they do not think they can influence decisions on what treatments are administered. A number of doctors consulted mentioned that they considered it normal practice to explain to patients what treatments were available, and let him or her make the choices. Despite this, some nurses claimed to have been asked by patients whether or not it was possible for the patient to influence treatment decisions. It can hardly be expected that patients will take the initiative to express their wishes about treatment, if they are not aware that they are entitled to.

Secondly, *concerns were expressed regarding the way in which participation of persons close to the patient was managed*. A large majority (89%) of the doctors surveyed said that they would 'normally' turn to someone who knows the patient for advice when the patient could not communicate. However, 71% of the doctors said it was not always obvious *who* should be consulted. According to some of the doctors consulted in interviews, it would emerge from the context who should be consulted. It would, for example, be the person who most frequently visited the patient. Others said it would often be the person the patient had put down as 'next-of-kin' or 'contact person' when admitted to the hospital.

A problem with relying on the person put down on the admission form by the patient is that the patient may not have realized that the person named could be consulted about treatment issues, and might otherwise have chosen someone else. If the term 'next-of-kin' has been used on such a form, there is also a risk of confusion about the meaning of this concept. A number of doctors interviewed thought that 'next-of-kin' in this context was specified by law. If this is also what patients believe, they may be likely to name their closest relative. However, many of the persons with HIV/AIDS surveyed did not wish their treatment decisions to be taken by a relative. Of the 91% of persons with HIV/AIDS who said they would like to name a proxy, only 13% would choose a family member, while 37% would name a friend, and 38% a spouse or partner.

Thirdly, *persons with HIV/AIDS may encounter several different doctors during the course of their treatment.* While free of any serious symptoms, their care may be managed by an out-patient doctor or a GP. Patients who get seriously ill will sometimes encounter one or several new doctors in hospital. If the patient is unable to communicate, decisions about treatment may be taken by doctors who have never previously met the patient. Even where life-sustaining care has been discussed with a doctor at an earlier stage, views expressed by the patient will then not be communicated unless the new doctor contacts the earlier one.

Would Advance Directives Help?

A large majority of participants in all three groups were in favour of a more wide-spread use of advance directives, both in the form of living wills, and by the naming of proxies. A variety of benefits with the use of advance directives were envisaged by participants, some of which might help avoid the problems described above.

It was expected by many that *advance directives, if they were to become more common, would encourage and help to initiate discussions about life-sustaining treatment.* If there were more information regarding advance directives, and possibly also forms available for making such directives, these could help reassure a person who had been concerned about treatment at the end of life that theirs was a valid concern shared by others. A discussion with a doctor could be more easily initiated if the patient presented the doctor with a draft living will and asked for comments or advice. Such a discussion would also give the patient an opportunity to establish whether or not his or her doctor was sympathetic to the idea of writing down wishes about treatment in a living will. Where this was not the case, the person might want to consider changing doctors.

A doctor who was told that his or her patient had made an advance directive might ask if the patient wanted to discuss it. A number of doctors put forward the view that once a discussion had been initiated, the patient and the doctor might – provided they had found they had been able to agree, and were able to continue a dialogue – decide that the living will was no longer necessary.

Further, *advance directives could be expected to lead to better practices regarding participation of persons close to the patient in decision making.* If a person has named someone, either in a living will or separately, to be his or her proxy, this will inform the doctor of whom the patient thinks is in the best position to advise the doctor about his or her views. This might be particularly helpful when the patient is visited regularly by a number of different people, for example a partner, parents, relatives, or friends who do not communicate between themselves, and who may also have different views about what the patient would have decided. It would, however, require that doctors be aware that there is no legal obligation on them to consult the next-of-kin unless named by the patient.

An advance directive could also give a doctor a helpful indication of the views of a patient whom he or she has not previously attended. This may, for example, be the case where the patient suddenly becomes very ill, and has to be brought to a hospital at which he or she has never previously been treated. However, advance directives may also be helpful where the patient encounters a new doctor at his or her regular hospital, or where the attending doctor has failed to discuss life-sustaining treatment with the patient while he or she was able to.

This requires that the attending doctor is aware of the existence of the advance directive. This can be achieved in different ways. If the directive is known to another doctor, it may have been attached to the patient's notes. If nobody knows about the directive, or if the patient is in a new hospital, the advance directive could be brought to the doctor's attention by an appointed proxy or another person close to the patient who holds a copy of it. Another, but probably less practical, possibility is that the patient carries a copy of the advance directive.

It can be argued that *the overall benefit of advance directives is that they would enable patients to have more control over what treatment is given.* This was the advantage put forward by the largest number of the nurses in the study (16 out of 28), and a comment made by a number of persons with HIV/AIDS on the questionnaires. Making an advance directive might give the sense to a patient who is able to communicate of being able to influence treatments which are being given at present, as well as care which might be given at a stage where he or she can no longer communicate.

Even where life-sustaining treatment has been discussed with a doctor, having one's wishes documented in a living will, or transmitted to an appointed proxy, might give the patient more hope of having his or her wishes respected. Sixty-three percent of persons with HIV/AIDS in the study, and 78% of those who had AIDS wanted a doctor to be legally bound to comply with a living will. These figures can be seen to indicate that the idea of having some control over what treatment is administered when one can no longer express one's wishes is important.

It is also possible that *advance directives might encourage patients to start a process of thinking about what they feel about life-sustaining treatment*. This aspect was emphasized by the two HIV/AIDS counsellors consulted in the study. It could also help the patient bring up the subject with those close to him or her and friends. Even if the patient did not state a wish until a very late stage, perhaps not until the need for a decision might seem imminent, the chance of the patient making a well-thought-through decision may be better if he or she is not confronted with the idea of influencing the choice of treatment for the first time at that stage.

Finally, *advance directives may be of benefit to persons close to the patient in that it could relieve such persons of the burden of making difficult decisions*. If the patient has written down his or her wishes about life-sustaining care such a person would no longer feel obliged to take a decision regarding matters which they may not have discussed with the patient. They would also be able to satisfy themselves that a decision, if taken according to a living will, is likely to be in accordance with the patient's wishes.

Potential Dangers

As we have seen, it is possible that a more widespread use of advance directives may lead to better practices in decision making about life-sustaining care. However, a number of potential problems or risks which may have to be taken into consideration were put forward by respondents.

For example, one doctor pointed out that although doctors could keep living will forms in their offices, they should be very careful about offering it to a patient without a direct enquiry from the patient about advance directives in order not to harm the relationship between the doctor and the patient. Otherwise, there would be a risk that a patient might feel obliged to make a living will when a form was brought out by an enthusiastic doctor.

In fact, one respondent was concerned that if the living will was initiated by doctors, it could become a weapon at the disposal of doctors who wished to withdraw treatment as early as possible. By pretending that all patients – especially those suffering from the same condition as the patient concerned – opted for making a living will, such a doctor might pressure the patient to reach a certain decision by inflicting feelings of guilt and fear in him or her.

Two doctors in the study were concerned that living wills, instead of stimulating discussions, might replace them. If a doctor was aware that a patient had a living will in which he or she expressed a wish only to receive care which was designed to keep him or her comfortable once terminally ill, the doctor might see it as a pretext for not communicating with the patient to confirm his or her wishes, even where the patient was able to.

The view was also put forward by a number of participants from all groups that a living will should not only enable a person to turn down life-sustaining treatment (which is normally understood to be the purpose of a living will), but also make it possible for a person to state that he or she would wish all treatments which are available and reasonable in the circumstances. The concept of advance directives would otherwise not appeal to those people who were concerned that their treatment would be withdrawn earlier than they would want. This group might also have fears and concerns, and could benefit from writing down their wishes and discussing them with a doctor.

A concern put forward by 13 out of 35 doctors, and eight out of 28 nurses, was that the patient might change his or her mind. This is related to the point made by some that a condition perceived as intolerable by the patient might seem tolerable once it occurs. In the light of these concerns, it may be concluded that a living will should not be made too early. However, a view put forward by, among others, a person with experience of counselling persons with HIV/AIDS at the Royal Free Hospital was that it might be very helpful for a person to make a living will at a stage where he or she is not very ill, but that it must be made clear that a living will was not a 'final' document, but could be changed by the person at a later stage, and should be reconsidered from time to time.

Some respondents pointed out that changes in the relationship between a patient and those close to him or her could be a problem where that person was named as a proxy. According to an HIV/AIDS counsellor at the Salvation Army who was consulted in the study, it was not uncommon for relationships with partners, friends or parents to change at a very late stage. Thus, a person named by the patient early on might not be among those who spend time with the patient at a stage when the proxy would be consulted. This would be a reason for not naming a proxy without also giving some written declarations, so that some indications of the patient's wishes remain even if the proxy cannot – or does not want to – be consulted.

A concern brought up by some was the difficulty of deciding when a patient is terminally ill, so as to trigger implementation of the wishes written down in a living will. This is related to the uncertainty of diagnosis mentioned by some. Others, however, described these as uncertainties which were present in the care of very ill and dying patients, whether or not advance directives were being used. Where no indication of the patient's wishes existed, it was regarded as good practice for a doctor to withhold or withdraw treatment he or she thinks would not benefit the patient, where recovery was very unlikely.

Finally, there was widespread concern in all groups regarding the legal status of a living will. A majority of persons with HIV/AIDS who were consulted would prefer advance directives to be legally binding on a doctor. All but seven doctors wanted living wills to be advisory only. In interviews with doctors, and during the discussion with a group of persons with HIV/AIDS at the organisation CARA, the question was also discussed as to what might happen if the effect of a living will, or a documented naming of a proxy, was ever to be tested in court. This legal uncertainty created worries among persons with HIV and AIDS that their advance directives would not be taken into account. Among doctors, there was concern regarding what might happen if a court found them to be guilty of failure to comply with an advance directive (should it be found to be legally binding). A reverse scenario would be that they might face criminal charges for withdrawing treatment in accordance with a living will.

SUMMARY OF CONCLUSIONS

The results of this study indicate that there is a great interest in advance directives in the groups surveyed. Fifty-five out of 64 persons with HIV/AIDS consulted would consider writing a living will, and another seven would 'maybe' do so. Among the doctors consulted, 33 out of 35 thought living wills would be helpful, and the remaining two thought they would be helpful in some circumstances. Twenty-seven out of 28 nurses thought it should be possible to make a living will (one expressed no opinion). The level of interest in and support for the nomination of someone whom the patient wanted to be consulted regarding life-sustaining care was similar.

A common expectation was that a more widespread use of advance directives would stimulate discussions about life-sustaining care between patient and doctor. The results from the study indicate that such discussions do not take place as often as participants would wish. For example, only ten out of 23 persons with AIDS had discussed life-sustaining treatment with a doctor, but of the 13 who had not, all said they would wish to. Also among the respondents who were infected with HIV, but did not have AIDS, a very large group would like to discuss life-sustaining care with a doctor if given the opportunity.

It was also thought that advance directives could change the way in which participation of persons close to the patient was managed. A large majority of the doctors who were consulted (89%) would turn to someone who knows the patient for advice when the patient could not communicate. However, 71% of the doctors said it was not always obvious *who* should be consulted. There appeared to be a widespread, albeit mistaken, belief in all the groups that the law defined who was next-of-kin and that this person had certain decision-making powers about life-sustaining care. This might make many doctors uncertain as to whether or not they could consult a partner or a friend where this seemed more appropriate. All 35 doctors said it would be helpful if the patient had decided in advance who should be consulted in matters relating to life-sustaining care.

Few of those with HIV/AIDS said they would like to name a relative to take decisions about medical care for them. Only eight would name a family member, while 23 would name a spouse or partner and 22 would name a friend. This suggests that those in this position should consider specifying through an advance directive (or otherwise) the person whom they want to act as decision-maker, in order to prevent conflicts among persons close to the patient at a later stage.

The concern most commonly expressed by doctors and nurses about advance directives was that the patient may change his or her mind. This suggests that it must be made clear that a living will is not a final document, but can be changed by the patient either orally or in writing. It should also be pointed out that a proxy appointment can be changed. The concern may be lessened if living wills are made the basis of continuing discussions between doctor and patient. The study indicates that many of the participants did view discussions as a part of the process of making an advance directive. Thus, 84% of respondents with HIV/AIDS said they would like to discuss their living will with their doctors, while more than half of the doctors (66%) would be less likely to take a living will into account if it had not been discussed with a doctor.

Persons with HIV/AIDS and doctors expressed diverging views as to whether or not advance directives should be legally binding. Among persons with HIV/AIDS, 55% wanted the proxy to be the sole decision-maker, and 63% wanted doctors to be legally obliged to comply with a living will. The latter figure was even higher (78%) among persons with AIDS than among those who had HIV but not AIDS. In contrast, only 20% of doctors wanted living wills to be legally binding.

Perhaps the most interesting conclusion is that when it came to the question whether advance directives should have the force of law, a large majority of patients were in favour of their having legal force. By contrast, the doctors in the study were largely opposed. This remains a recurrent theme in the medical press. As we have seen, if an advance directive in the form of an enduring power of attorney is to have legal force, legislation would be required. Experience in other countries certainly demonstrates the value of legislation which goes beyond merely recognising living wills. It would follow that if the expression of support for advance directives of patients (assuming the views of those patients in the study are typical) and health care workers are to be reflected in law, legislation would appear to be necessary. Before a final view can be reached, however, let us briefly examine some of the advantages an disadvantages of such legislation.

C Schlyter *Advance Directives and AIDS* (1992)

Benefits and disadvantages of legislation

There appear to be a number of advantages of regulating advance directives, were these to be more commonly used.

First, a doctor may be expected to take an advance directive more seriously if he or she were legally obliged to follow instructions given in a living will or through a proxy, not only because of fear of the legal consequences of non-compliance, but also because legislation may give advance directives a more 'accepted' status. This is the most likely reason why a majority of the people with HIV/AIDS consulted in the study wished advance directives to be legally binding.

Secondly, a possible advantage for doctors might be that legislation could (and does where it exists) give the doctor immunity from civil or criminal charges for withdrawing or withholding treatment in accordance with a living will or instructions from a proxy.

Third, legislation could contain specific instructions about what directions could be given, and provide definitions relevant to the writing and interpretation of a directive, all of which could lead to increased awareness both for doctors as well as those who make an advance directive.

Finally, legislation could contain safeguards for such things as witnessing and storing of a directive. This might, for example, increase the possibilities of verifying that the directive was actually written by the patient, and that he or she was not being pressured into doing so.

A disadvantage of introducing legislation in the field of medical decision-making is the rigidity it might bring. Legislation may be particularly unhelpful in the case of decision-making about life-sustaining treatment where decisions may have to be taken with a large degree of flexibility to suit each individual case. An example would be a situation where a doctor may feel compelled to comply with a living will because of fear of legal repercussions, despite having strong reasons to suspect that the patient had changed his or her mind since the writing of the will.

Another possible risk is that legislation creates an air of mutual distrust between patients an doctors, thereby possibly discouraging discussions about life-sustaining care.

Moreover, the binding force of a legally endorsed advance directive may in part be illusory, since it will in any event be the doctor who decides when a patient is in a *terminal condition* (which is a criterion common to all legislation on advance directives and widely recognized outside the legislative arena). This dilemma is illustrated in an American case, *Evans v Bellevue Hospital.*(Footnote.) In this case, doctors refused to act in accordance with a durable power of attorney's directive to terminate treatment since they did not find that a patient with toxoplasmosis was terminally ill as defined by the living will.

Is There a Case for Legislation in the UK?

The advantages of legislation in this field are likely to have contributed to the decision to legislate in respect of advance directives in the US, Canada and Australia. It is, however, not to be taken for granted that these same advantages can be used as reasons for enacting legislation on advance directives in the UK.

In the case of the US, legal decisions have had a greater effect on medical decision-making than in the UK, and there is also more reliance on legislation in the area of medical practice. Thus, not to legislate in the area of advance directives might in the US have been regarded as not giving enough support for a widespread use of these documents, and might also have been seen as leaving patients, relatives and doctors in doubt of what constitutes a valid advance directive.

Since this is less likely to be the case in the UK, and since there are, as we saw above, some substantial disadvantages to legislating on advance directives, it should be considered whether some of the above-mentioned benefits could be achieved without the enactment of legislation.

The benefits of having principles laid out as to the contents of advance directives and the circumstances in which they apply should not be ignored, nor should the importance of some mechanism for witnessing a living will in order to prevent abuse. However, certain principles which would apply, such as that which says that treatment which sustains life may be withheld or withdrawn but that no measures aimed solely to hasten death may be undertaken, are already accepted as good medical practice in UK hospitals and by professional bodies. Additional principles, such as that advance directives cannot be considered as long as the patient is able to communicate, and the witnessing requirements, could be set out in guidelines on advance directives.

Moreover, since medical practice in the UK accepts that decisions to end treatment for patients who are terminally ill may be taken in certain circumstances, no legal immunity from criminal charges need be created as long as this practice is respected.

There are, however, some foreseeable reasons why legislation regarding advance directives might have to be considered in the UK. One reason to consider legislation would be if, were advance directives to become more widely used, uncertainty prevented their use. For example, doctors might be reluctant to take into account a living will or a proxy's viewpoint simply because there is no statutory support or requirement to do so, and the legal consequences therefore would appear uncertain to the doctors. Legislation would overcome this problem.

Another reason to consider legislation is if a situation should arise where a court is asked to comment on the legal validity of an advance directive. This could occur if advance directives were to be more commonly used. Whether or not a court actually expressed support for the idea that written directives be legally binding, such a decision could well provoke a call for legislation to clarify matters.

Footnote: *Evans v Bellevue Hospital*, NYLJ (July 28, 1987) at 11 col 1 (NY County, July 27, 1987). The patient, a man with AIDS Related Complex, was suffering from toxoplasmosis and unable to communicate. The patient's power of attorney wanted treatment to be terminated following the patient's wishes in a living will. The hospital respondent refused to withhold treatment, claiming that the patient was not dying from his condition. The living will stated that life-sustaining treatment should be withheld 'when there is no reasonable expectation of recovery or regaining a meaningful quality of life'. The toxoplasmosis was, in fact, treatable. The court held that although there was no recovery from AIDS, there was hope of recovery from toxoplasmosis. The court asked the patient's power of attorney to present 'clear and convincing' evidence that there was no hope of recovery for the patient. In the absence of such evidence, the court dismissed the application to terminate treatment. Two weeks after the decision, the life-support system was removed under the pretext that the patient would not recover from the toxoplasmosis. He died shortly afterwards.

In its 1994 Report, the House of Lords Select Committee on Medical Ethics (HL Paper 21–I) (*supra*) rejected calls for legislation whilst generally approving of advance directives.

ADVANCE DIRECTIVES

263. We commend the development of advance directives. They enable patients to express in advance their individual preferences and priorities in respect of medical treatment should they subsequently become incompetent. Their preparation can (and indeed should) stimulate discussion of those preferences between doctors and patients. They can assist the health-care team and other carers in making decisions about appropriate treatment in respect of patients who are no longer able to take part in that debate. Advance directives may express refusal of any treatment or procedure which would require the consent of the patient if competent. We emphasise however that they should not contain requests for any unlawful intervention or omission; nor can they require treatment to be given which the health-care team judge is not clinically appropriate.

264. We have given careful consideration to the terms of Lord Allen of Abbeydale's private member's bill, and to the points which he set out in his two memoranda. We have also considered the arguments of other witnesses who advocated legislation on the subject of advance directives. But we conclude that legislation for advance directives generally is unnecessary. Doctors are increasingly recognising their ethical obligation to comply with advance directives. The development of case law is moving in the same direction. We agree with the assessment of the Crown Prosecution Service and confidently expect that a doctor who acted in accordance with an advance directive, where the clinical circumstances were such as the patient had considered, would not be guilty of negligence or any criminal offence. Adequate protection for doctors exists in terms of the current law and in trends in medical practice. We suggest that it could well be impossible to give advance directives in general greater legal force without depriving patients of the benefit of the doctor's professional expertise and of new treatments and procedures which may have become available since the advance directive was signed. We recognise that it would be possible to specify precisely particular categories of treatment which a patient would find unacceptable in **any** circumstances, such as a blood transfusion in the case of a Jehovah's Witness.

265. Instead of legislation for advance directives generally, we recommend that the colleges and faculties of all the health-care professions should jointly develop a code of practice to guide their members. The BMA's Statement on Advance Directives has to recommend it as a basis for such a code. The informing premise of the code should be that advance directives must be respected as an authoritative statement of the patient's wishes in respect of treatment. Those wishes should be overruled only where there are reasonable grounds to believe that

the clinical circumstances which actually prevail are significantly different from those which the patient had anticipated, or that the patient had changed his or her views since the directive was prepared. A directive may also be overruled if it requests treatment which the doctor judges is not clinically indicated, or if it requests any illegal action. There should be a presumption, in the absence of any explicit instruction to the contrary, in favour of all ordinary care and clinically-indicated treatment being given. A doctor who treats a patient in genuine ignorance of the provisions of a directive should not be considered culpable if the treatment proves to have been contrary to the wishes therein expressed, and there should be no expectation that treatment in an emergency should be delayed while enquiry is made about a possible advance directive. Doctors who anticipate having conscientious objections to complying with the directives of their patients should make this clear at an early stage in their preparation, so that patients may transfer to other doctors if they wish.

266. The code of practice should also encourage professionals to disseminate information about advance directives. It should establish procedures for a directive to be lodged by a patient with the general practitioner, who should be required to produce it to any other health-care professional who has care of the patient, for example on the patient's admission to hospital. The existence of an advance directive could be indicated by a card which the patient would carry, and the code should make provision for such a practice.

267. We also recommend that the proposed code of practice should encourage, though not require, regular review and re-endorsement by patients of the provisions of their advance directives. This would not only go some way towards eliminating the danger of a directive becoming out of line both with medical practice and with the patient's current wishes but would also demonstrate the patient's continuing commitment to the directive, which would reinforce its value as a statement of the patient's wishes.

Subsequently, the British Medical Association responded to the call for a Code of Practice producing a booklet entitled *Advance Statements About Medical Practice* (1995).

You may feel that the Select Committee under-emphasised the benefits of legislation in terms of clarity and certainty and, additionally, because of the educational advantages this would have for both the public and medical profession. As we shall see, the Law Commission took a different view from the Select Committee and recommended legislation (see *Mental Incapacity* (Report No 231) (1995) and *infra*). It would appear that this aspect of the Law Commission's Report 'aroused the greatest public concern' (see *Who Decides?* (Cm 3803) (LCD 1997) at para 4.2). The Lord Chancellor's Green Paper *Who Decides?* (*op cit*) sought to consult further on whether there should be legislation on advance directives – both in the form of anticipatory refusals (para 4.8) and continuing powers of attorney (para 6.9). In the result, the Government has decided to bring forward legislation only in relation to the latter: see *Making Decisions* (Cm 4465) (1999) at para 12.

(b) Framing the legislation

The North American experience would suggest that the optimal form of legislation would have two parts: the first dealing with anticipatory decisions by patients and the second dealing with decision-making through proxies.

(i) ANTICIPATORY DECISIONS

As regards this part of the legislation, the King's College Working Party Report argued as follows.

The Living Will: Consent to Treatment at the End of Life (Working Party Report, Age Concern and Centre of Medical Law and Ethics, King's College) (1988)

There are three principal prerequisites for making the living will perform its function as a prospective expression of autonomy. They are: (1) the phrasing of a declaration should reflect what the person considers to be the circumstances in which it might be used; (2) these circumstances should be identifiable; and (3) the recommendations contained in the declaration should be capable of being implemented within the accepted ethical and legal standards of medical practice.

In order to ensure that these prerequisites can be interpreted in a clinical setting the text of a living will should be precisely drafted. Particular attention needs to be directed to the event which will trigger the living will and to the procedures to be carried out when the time for implementation arrives.

In respect of the *triggering event* three alternatives are possible. The trigger can be incompetence alone, or incompetence with the addition of a particular condition or disability, or incompetence with the addition of terminal illness. Each of these definitions gives rise to particular difficulties. Incompetence alone may cause a living will to be implemented in circumstances which some people would consider inappropriate, for example, a moderate degree of dementia without other disability. Incompetence plus specified conditions or disabilities may lead to problems because of the impossibility of itemising every conceivable event triggering clinical circumstances, and the uncertainty in interpreting those which are specified. Incompetence plus terminal illness does not capture all the circumstances under which many people would wish a living will to be instituted. It may also cause problems if clinicians interpret terminal illness restrictively, as occurred in the operation of the California Natural Death Act 1976.

Whichever of these definitions is adopted it should be noted that they apply only to people who are permanently incompetent. It is not uncommon for those who are chronically ill, for example, with dementia, to demonstrate fluctuating competence, and it would be both inappropriate and unworkable to attempt to apply advance directives in such circumstances.

In respect of the *procedures to be adopted* once the living will has come into operation, the more vague the declaration, the less reassured might the patient be that his wishes would be met, and the less able might the doctor be to decide whether or when to implement those wishes. Furthermore, imprecise situations might be thought to oblige both patient and doctor to discuss and agree what they thought each other had in mind. This might require lengthy discussion, which could still be inconclusive. Also, if these discussions were not carefully recorded, they could well be ignored, given the high chance that the doctor who had to decide on the issue when the patient was incompetent would not be the same doctor.

These arguments favour detailed specific instructions, but some would take the view that the declared spirit in which the living will is used in the first place allows those responsible for the patient's care sufficient discretion to implement the living will even in those circumstances in which particular disease states are not specifically mentioned. There might also be a conflict for individuals who found it easy and comforting to sign a readily prepared declaration, whilst at the same time wishing to trust the doctor to attend to them as he saw fit, once it came to be implemented. 'The patient ordinarily trusts his physician not only to act in his best interest during his life but also to see that his death is as comfortable, decent and peaceful an event as possible. This is an implied trust that he may not want to verbalise or discuss.' So, equally, there is a counter-argument favouring more general instructions.

Another issue is whether a prescribed form should be used in drawing up a living will. The American Legal Advisors Committee of Concern for Dying proposed a 'Model Act for the Right to Refuse Treatment' in which the following recommendation was made: 'No specific form or document is included because we believe the individuals' wishes will be more likely to be set forth if their own words are used.' This recommendation assumes that people are capable of expressing their wishes unambiguously. The many versions of the living will in the USA are testimony, however, to the fact that even for those experienced in the field, it is not easy to find an appropriate form of words (although there is broad uniformity of sense). A further difficulty arising from allowing complete individual freedom to write a living will is that there may be a considerable gap between the patient's expectations and medical and legal reality. Patients might well make requests for that which would be medically unsound or legally untenable. In such a case, the doctor responsible for implementing the living will may be exposed to ethical and legal insecurity. Whether a prescribed form is advised or not it is recommended that all those preparing living wills are advised to consult with a professional experienced in the field, most probably their own general practitioner or solicitor, before drawing up the document.

There are therefore advantages and disadvantages to having a prescribed form of declaration. On balance, however, such a form is probably desirable...

Practical and procedural matters
Some of the practical and procedural matters which might arise in relation to living wills are discussed briefly below...

(b)   Capacity
The person making a living will should be a competent adult. Provided competence is defined, the question whether the test is satisfied is a matter for clinical judgment. In the event of a dispute as to whether the person was competent to execute the document, it is suggested that it should be presumed that he was, ie the onus of proving that he was not is upon the person

so claiming. Alternatively, it could be a requirement that the witness (see (c) below) sign a declaration that the person appears to be of sound mind when the instrument is executed.

(c) Signature and witnesses
A living will document, whether of a standard type or in the person's own words, would have to be signed and dated by the person making it. It is a uniform requirement of existing legislation on living wills that there should be witnesses, as a safeguard against coercion. It is suggested that there should be two competent adults, one of whom might be the person's family doctor or a hospital consultant in the case of a hospitalised patient.

A question arises as to whether certain persons, such as creditors or potential beneficiaries, should be excluded from witnessing. It is unlikely that creditors would be selected as witnesses. Perhaps the best solution is that at least one witness must be neither a relative nor a person who would take any part of the estate by will or otherwise on the death of the person involved.

(d) Notification and recording
The person making the living will would notify near relatives or friends (if any) of his action, and also his medical practitioner (if not a witness), and legal adviser. The medical practitioner would make a written note in the case records. There would also be a procedure for having the information recorded in any appropriate hospital records.

(e) Availability of blank forms
If prescribed living will declaration forms were to be used, consideration should be given to methods of making blank forms readily available, possibly from doctors' surgeries and hospital wards, and from professional legal advisers.

(f) Notice and implementation
The means whereby a living will might be brought into effect will vary. Provision should be made for ensuring the existence of a living will is brought to the attention of the doctor (see (d) above). The most common ways of implementing it would probably be as follows:
(i) *The patient.* A seriously ill patient, when still conscious and competent, might implement a previously signed living will as a means of substantiating and formalising a request for treatment to be withheld or withdrawn. At a particular juncture in an illness the patient might ask the attending doctors to refer to the living will and to consider implementing it forthwith.
   Alternatively, a patient when already gravely ill could request a copy of a living will for signature and subsequent implementation when the circumstances were deemed to be suitable.
(ii) *A relative or friend.* When a patient has become incompetent and a relative or close friend with knowledge of the patient's living will considered that the time was approaching or had arrived to consider implementing it, an approach could be made to a member of the medical staff.
(iii) *The legal adviser.* If the patient had notified his legal adviser that he had signed a living will form, the legal adviser, either from his own knowledge of the patient's serious condition or by information from others, could suggest to the medical staff that it might be appropriate to implement the living will.
(iv) *The doctor.* The patient's general practitioner or a hospital doctor knowing of a living will in the case records could suggest to the doctor in charge of the patient that the circumstances of implementing the living will might be considered.
(v) *A nurse, social worker, minister or other person involved in the care of the patient.* Any person with medical knowledge who was aware of the patient's state of health and of the living will could indicate to the medical attendants an opinion that the time might have come to implement the living will.

(g) Consultation procedure
When a doctor caring for a patient known to have completed a living will determines (spontaneously or at another's suggestion) that the circumstances might be appropriate to implement the living will, it may be appropriate to notify any next of kin, if possible. If the patient's wishes would be met by implementing the living will and the circumstances were deemed appropriate, it would be advisable to record the relevant facts and opinions in the medical record.

(h) Revocation
It is essential to an acceptance of the notion of living wills that it be clear that a person may revoke his living will at any time, by destroying or defacing it, or by asking someone else to do so on his behalf. The living will may be revoked at any time by verbal or written instructions from the signatory to his doctor, legal adviser, or other responsible person. Any legal or medical records must thereupon be amended to take note of the revocation, and any such alteration should be signed and dated. The execution of a living will should also revoke any earlier instrument.

More problematic is the question of revocation when incompetent. The logical expectation is that an incompetent person cannot revoke, as in the case of ordinary wills, for example. However, most of the American legislation permits revocation even after loss of competence. Although at first sight this seems to defeat the object of the exercise, the point is that it would be invidious to refuse treatment which the patient, although confused, is at present requesting. This is a strong argument for accepting revocation despite the person's incompetence. Even if it is thought that the person should only be able to revoke while competent, it should be presumed that he was competent at the time of revocation, so that the onus of proving the contrary is on the person so claiming.

(i)   Time limits
Should a living will lapse after a specified number of years? On the one hand it might be undesirable if the person's fate should be determined by means of an instrument executed decades ago and now forgotten, while on the other hand the person may fail to recognise the passing of a time limit and therefore fail to reconsider the matter. It would clearly be desirable that the provisions of a living will should be reviewed on a regular basis perhaps every five or ten years. People completing living wills should therefore be advised accordingly, but to make this mandatory would be administratively complex and costly and some people might prefer not to undertake such review at specified times. Therefore it is thought that, on balance, it is better that no obligatory review or time limit is imposed.

(j)   Liability
A doctor who reasonably and in good faith and after appropriate consultation, acted upon a living will would not be exposed to subsequent civil liability or criminal prosecution. Further, no question of professional misconduct would arise in such circumstances.

If the doctor deliberately disregards the instructions of a living will, consideration should be given as to what if any sanctions should apply and to whether these should go beyond professional censure.

Recourse to fraud, forgery, concealment or destruction in the preparation or implementation of a living will would clearly attract appropriate criminal liability.

(k)   Life assurance
It would be necessary to make it clear as a matter of law, whether by agreement with assurance companies or by legislation, that the completion or implementation of a living will was to have no effect upon the terms of an existing life assurance policy, particularly as regards any provision excluding cover in the case of suicide (ie execution of a living will and then compliance by others with its terms do not amount to suicide).

(l)   Pregnancy
If a living will comes into operation in relation to a woman who is pregnant, any instructions to forego life-sustaining treatment should be regarded as invalid during the course of the pregnancy.

In 1995 the Law Commission proposed a comprehensive scheme, *inter alia*, covering the medical treatment of incompetent adults: *Mental Incapacity* (Report No 231). We have made mention of this on a number of occasions already in this chapter. We saw earlier in Chapter 6 that the central feature of the Law Commission's scheme was the 'general authority' to act in an incompetent patient's best interests. By way of exception to that, the Law Commission proposed for anticipatory refusals which would be legally binding upon doctors.

Law Commission *Mental Incapacity* (Report No 231) (1995)

5.16 To maintain the effect of the present law is consistent with our policy aim of enabling people to make such decisions as they are able to make for themselves. In order to give full effect to this aim, special provision is now required for cases where a person makes an anticipatory refusal of treatment which is intended to remain in effect even when the maker no longer has capacity to review the decision made.

We recommend that an 'advance refusal of treatment' should be defined as a refusal made by a person aged eighteen or over with the necessary capacity of any medical, surgical or dental treatment or other procedure and intended to have effect at any subsequent time when he or she may be without capacity to give or refuse consent. (Draft Bill, clause 9(1).)

Capacity to make an advance refusal
5.17 'The right to decide one's own fate presupposes a capacity to do so.' (*Re T (Adult: Refusal of Treatment)* [1993] Fam 95, 112, per Lord Donaldson of Lymington MR.) It should therefore be an essential characteristic of an advance refusal that it was made at

a time when the maker had capacity to make it. (This is not necessarily coterminous with capacity to make a contemporaneous refusal, (*Re C (Adult: Refusal of Treatment)* [1994] 1 WLR 290, 295 obiter). The new statutory definition of incapacity will be applied in any case where a doubt about capacity needs to be resolved.

Age

5.18 There would be little point in our recommending that an anticipatory refusal of treatment can be made by persons under the age of eighteen since it is now settled if controversial law that the court in the exercise of its statutory and/or inherent jurisdiction (and possibly also any person who has parental responsibility) may overrule the refusal of a minor, competent or not, to accept medical treatment (*Re W (A Minor) (Medical Treatment: Courts Jurisdiction)* [1993] Fam 64).

Terminal conditions

5.19 None of our respondents disagreed with our preliminary view that it would be wrong to stipulate that advance decisions can only apply when a patient is in a 'terminal condition'. Such stipulations were common in early statutes in the United States which laid down strict formalities for the making of 'living wills', but they would be out of place in a scheme which seeks to build upon and clarify the fundamental legal principle that patients with capacity can refuse *any* treatment.

5.20 If an 'advance refusal' has been made then a treatment provider cannot rely on the authority which would otherwise be available to enable a patient without capacity to be treated reasonably and in his or her best interests. Obviously, the treatment provider will not be liable for proceeding with treatment unless he or she knows or has reasonable grounds for believing that there is an advance refusal.

We recommend that the general authority should not authorise any treatment or procedure if an advance refusal or treatment by the person concerned applies to that treatment or procedure in the circumstances of the case. (Draft Bill, clause 9(2).)

Validity and applicability

5.21 The recommendation made in paragraph 5.20 above will effectively take the place of the proposition in *Re T* that an advance refusal of treatment must be 'clearly established' and 'applicable in the circumstances' (see Consultation Paper No 129, paras 3.4–3.5 and *Re T (Adult: Refusal of Treatment)* [1993] Fam 95, 114). As was made clear in *Re T*, 'doctors will need to consider what is *the true scope and basis* of the decision' (ibid p 116 (emphasis added)). They must ask whether the patient has refused consent to the treatment or procedure which it is now desired to carry out, in the circumstances in which it would now be carried out. Inevitably, problems of evidence will sometimes arise. Equally, however, it can be seen from certain model forms that patients are already able to make the terms of their refusals absolutely clear. A Jehovah's Witness might have stated that 'my express refusal of blood is absolute and is not to be overridden in ANY circumstances'. Someone else might have provided that 'if I become permanently unconscious with no likelihood of regaining consciousness...I wish medical treatment to be limited to keeping me comfortable and free from pain, and I REFUSE all other medical treatment'.

5.22 Statutory provisions cannot resolve the problems and questions which may arise in relation to the validity and applicability of advance refusals. The development of a code of practice and of model forms which direct patients towards making the terms of any refusal clear will help to address the most likely problems. In the words of Lord Donaldson, 'what really matters' is 'the declaration by the patient of his decision with a full appreciation of the possible consequences, the latter being expressed in the simplest possible terms' (*Re T (Adult: Refusal of Treatment)* [1993] Fam 95, pp 114–115). It may be that the most effective format will be one which uses succinct and non-technical language, and avoids detailed provisions about particular ailments or conditions or particular treatments or procedures. As a matter of evidence, a document which refers to particular circumstances, but not to those which have arisen, may be found not to apply to the present circumstances. Similarly, a document which does not mention, expressly or impliedly, the particular treatment which is now proposed would not be an effective refusal of that treatment. The technique (adopted by the THT/King's College model form) of referring to treatment with particular purposes rather than any particular treatments may be one way of avoiding some of the difficulties. We do not believe that primary legislation can elucidate the many questions which can arise about the 'applicability' of a particular advance refusal. Our respondents consistently raised with us two matters in particular in relation to questions about applicability and we would expect to see these points addressed in any code of practice. First, many respondents were anxious to ensure that treatment which has become available since the time the refusal was made should not be withheld unless it was very clear that the patient intended to refuse this treatment as well. Secondly, it was said that a statement about health care matters which was made independently of any discussion with a health care professional might often be based on erroneous ideas and information. This is not to suggest that any refusal made without such a discussion would always be 'inapplicable'; a Jehovah's Witness would be unlikely to be swayed by any such discussion. These are, however, two of the many matters which will be relevant to the determination of whether any advance refusal 'applies to' the treatment or procedure now proposed 'in the circumstances of the case'.

Life-sustaining treatment

5.23 A number of north American cases indicate the great reluctance of both doctors and courts to approve the withholding of treatment which is imperative to prevent death, unless any refusal of such treatment expressly contemplates the possibility of such an avoidable death (*In re Estate of Dorone* (1987) 534 A 2d 452, *Werth v Taylor* (1991) 475 NW 2d 426, *In the Matter of Alice Hughes* (1992) 611 A 2d 1148). This was also an issue in the leading English case of *Re T*. The public interest in preserving the life and health of citizens does not prevent an adult patient from refusing life-sustaining treatment, although any doubt will be resolved in favour of the preservation of life (*Re T (Adult: Refusal of Treatment)* [1993] Fam 95, 112 per Lord Donaldson of Lymington MR). Patients should therefore be aware that they should address their minds to the possibility of dying if they wish any refusal of treatment to apply notwithstanding this possibility. Some model forms already make express reference to the danger of death.

Pregnant women

5.24 The case of *Re S* (*Re S (Adult: Refusal of Treatment)* [1993] Fam 123) involved a refusal by a pregnant woman to consent to a Caesarian section. The woman's refusal was effectively overruled by the High Court, which declared (after a brief hearing arranged at very short notice) that it would be lawful to perform the operation in the circumstances. Either this decision is in conflict with the later decision in *Re C* (*Re C (Adult: Refusal of Treatment)* [1994] 1 WLR 290) or its ratio is limited to cases where the life of an unborn viable foetus is in danger. It has been heavily criticised and a number of our respondents urged us to address the problem of principle it appears to pose, namely that a pregnant woman may lawfully be subjected to what would otherwise be an unlawful battery.

5.25 The majority of the US states with living will legislation set statutory limits to the effectiveness of any declarations during the maker's pregnancy. Similarly, it has been suggested here that '[i]f a living will comes into operation in relation to a woman who is pregnant, any instructions to forego life-sustaining treatment should be regarded as invalid during the course of the pregnancy'. We do not, however, accept that a woman's right to determine the sorts of bodily interference which she will tolerate somehow evaporates as soon as she becomes pregnant. There can, on the other hand, be no objection to acknowledging that many women do in fact alter their views as to the interventions they find acceptable as a direct result of the fact that they are carrying a child. By analogy with cases where life might be needlessly shortened or lost, it appears that a refusal which did not mention the possibility that the life of a foetus might be endangered would be likely to be found not to apply in circumstances where a treatment intended to save the life of the foetus was proposed. Women of child-bearing age should therefore be aware that they should address their minds to this possibility if they wish to make advance refusals of treatment.

A presumption of non-applicability

5.26 There are likely to be particular problems in relation to questions of applicability where life-sustaining treatment or treatment which would save the life of a foetus are at issue. The best way of balancing the continuing right of the patient to refuse such treatment with the public interest in preserving life is to create a statutory presumption in favour of the preservation of life.

We recommend that in the absence of any indication to the contrary it shall be presumed that an advance refusal of treatment does not apply in circumstances where those having the care of the person who made it consider that the refusal (a) endangers that person's life or (b) if that person is a woman who is pregnant, the life of the foetus. (Draft Bill, clause 9(3).)

Liability of health care providers

5.27 The maker of an advance refusal should be on notice that the treatment provider who withholds treatment as a result of the refusal will not be liable for the consequences. Equally, the treatment provider is entitled to reassurance that he or she will be relieved of liability (in the tort of negligence) for failing to provide treatment. This does not change the present law but it appears to us that the importance of the rule is such that it should be set out in the statute. Conversely, however, a doctor should not be liable for providing treatment which has in fact been refused if the doctor did not know or have any reason to believe that there was a relevant advance refusal. It is the responsibility of a patient making an advance refusal to ensure that the existence of the refusal comes to the notice of any treatment provider.

We recommend **that no person should incur liability (1) for the consequences of withholding any treatment or procedure if he or she has reasonable grounds for believing that an advance refusal of treatment applies; or (2) for carrying out any treatment or procedure to which an advance refusal applies unless he or she knows or has reasonable grounds for believing that an advance refusal applies.** (Draft Bill, clause 9(4).)

Conscientious objections

5.28 We have experienced some difficulty with the notion, put forward by a very small number of our respondents, that special provisions should cater for the fact that doctors may have a 'conscientious objection' to withholding treatment which a patient has refused. The law, clearly stated in *Re T*, is that treating a patient despite a refusal of consent 'will constitute the civil wrong of trespass to the person and may constitute a crime' (*Re T (Adult: Refusal of Treatment)* [1993] Fam 95, 102). The majority of our respondents were keen to see statutory force given to this clear principle and we ourselves fail to see the significance of the fact that some doctors may disagree with a patient's motives in making a refusal or advance refusal of treatment. If the principle of self-determination means anything, the patient's refusal must be respected. There is therefore no need for any specific statutory provision. We note the clear view of the BMA that it is unethical for a doctor to flout a competent refusal of treatment, including one made in advance; and that a doctor placed in difficulties by such an advance directive 'should relinquish the patient's management to colleagues' (BMA Statement on Advance Directives (revised January 1994) para 6).

Formalities

5.29 In the consultation paper we discussed the possible merits of a prescribed form for anticipatory decisions. We suggested that the importance of flexibility was such that there should simply be a presumption that written, signed and witnessed decisions was 'clearly established' (para 3.19). Our respondents generally favoured maximum flexibility, although a number of them told us that a model form would often be very helpful to patients. Some model forms are already widely available and more seem always to be being produced. Both the BMA and the Law Society expressed misgivings about any rules which would invalidate a patient's genuine choices simply because those choices were made in ways which fell short of formalities laid down in statute. To disregard valid decisions on that account would be contrary to our aims of policy. Matters of form and execution are essentially questions of evidence in any particular case. We have said that the present common law position is that the issue is the 'true scope and basis' of the decision, rather than the way it has been recorded. The existence of a formal document is no guarantee of either validity or applicability, nor is the absence of such a document any guarantee that a valid and applicable advance refusal has not been made. Although we gave careful consideration to the introduction of statutory requirements prescribing the form and contents of any advance refusal, we concluded that these would benefit no-one.

5.30 We do, however, see merit in at least encouraging patients to express any advance refusals of treatment in writing, to sign the document and to have their signature witnessed. Such a step would be likely to furnish some definite proof that the refusal was made by the patient and intended to have effect in the future. We take the view that a rebuttable presumption is the best way to balance the need for flexibility and the desirability of formal writing. It would not, of course, answer the questions the doctor must ask as to whether (1) the patient had capacity to make the refusal and whether (2) the refusal applies to the treatment now proposed and in the circumstances which now exist.

We recommend **that in the absence of any indication to the contrary it should be presumed that an advance refusal was validly made if it is in writing, signed and witnessed.** (Draft Bill, clause 9(5).)

We would certainly expect any code of practice to recommend the making of any refusal in writing.

Withdrawing or altering an advance refusal

5.31 The consultation paper suggested that it should be possible to revoke an anticipatory decision at any time when the maker has capacity to do so (paras 3.32–3.34). Consultees favoured a flexible approach to 'revocation', although some concern was expressed about the possibility of claims being made that a carefully considered refusal had been revoked in the privacy of a doctor's consulting room. This, again, is inevitably a question of fact and evidence in any particular case. It would seem entirely wrong to stipulate that an advance refusal must stand until, for example, paper and pencil and an independent witness can be found.

5.32 Some respondents pointed out that disputes could arise as to whether a 'revocation' was intended to be permanent, or only to apply to a particular proposed procedure. This led us to conclude that 'revocation' was an unhelpful term in the context of a policy favouring maximum flexibility. The essential point is that the maker should retain power, commensurate with his or her capacity, to depart from the terms of an advance refusal.

We recommend **that an advance refusal of treatment may at any time be withdrawn or altered by the person who made it, if he or she has capacity to do so.** (Draft Bill, clause 9(6).)

5.33 Respondents generally agreed with our provisional view that automatic revocation after a period of time would be unduly restrictive. We would expect any code of practice to give guidance to patients on updating any refusal on a regular basis, so as to reduce the risk of it being found not to apply to circumstances which arise many years later.

Exclusion of 'basic care'

5.34 In the consultation paper we proposed that an advance directive should never be effective in refusing either pain relief or basic care. On consultation, there was general agreement to the proposition that a patient's right to self-determination could properly be limited by considerations based on public policy. A number of respondents highlighted the effect on staff and other patients if patients were to have power to refuse in advance even the most basic steps to ensure comfort and cleanliness. One respondent argued that since a patient with capacity can refuse all types of treatment the same rule should apply to those making anticipatory refusals, but this minority view did not appeal to us. We were grateful for the assistance of the BMA on the details of the proposed exclusion clause. We accept that patients with capacity regularly refuse certain types or levels of pain relief because they prefer to maintain alertness, and we prefer now to refer only to the alleviation of severe pain. We have also replaced reference to 'spoon-feeding' with reference to direct oral feeding, to cater for the administration of nutrition and hydration by syringe or cup. Our proposed definition of 'basic care' reflects a level of care which it would be contrary to public policy to withhold from a patient without capacity.

We recommend **that an advance refusal of treatment should not preclude the provision of 'basic care', namely care to maintain bodily cleanliness and to alleviate severe pain, as well as the provision of direct oral nutrition and hydration.** (Draft Bill, clause 9(7)(a) and (8).)

Accident and emergency situations

5.35 One of our respondents suggested that any provision restricting the power or duty to treat should not be applicable in accident and emergency situations. The House of Lords Select Committee stated that 'there should be no expectation that treatment in an emergency should be delayed while enquiry is made about a possible advance directive' (Report of the Select Committee on Medical Ethics (1993) HL 21–1 para 265). The broad scheme of a general authority based on reasonable treatment in a patient's best interests appears to us quite flexible enough to cover any distinction there might be between emergency situations and others. There is no need for any special provision exempting accident and emergency personnel from the broad terms of that scheme.

The role of the court

5.36 Most respondents agreed with our provisional proposal that the court should not have power to override a valid and applicable anticipatory decision in the exercise of its 'best interests' jurisdiction. Although some respondents appeared to favour such a power, it was apparent on close reading that they were concerned about out-of-date refusals (where new treatment had become available), or those made in a state of depression or mental frailty. These issues go to applicability and validity respectively and do not necessitate any power to 'override'. Resort to the court will only be available and necessary where a decision is required about the validity of the refusal (including any issue as to whether it has been withdrawn or altered) or its applicability. Where there is any doubt about such matters and an application to the court is made, treatment providers should have authority to take minimum steps to prevent the patient's death or deterioration in the interim.

We recommend **that an advance refusal should not preclude the taking of any action necessary to prevent the death of the maker or a serious deterioration in his or her condition pending a decision of the court on the validity or applicability of an advance refusal or on the question whether it has been withdrawn or altered.** (Draft Bill, clause 9(7)(b).)

Independent supervision

5.37 Certain types of health-care decision should require independent sanction from a court or a second-opinion doctor. Where, however, the patient has already refused the procedure in a valid and applicable advance refusal then there can be no question of it being carried out. No reference to the court or a second-opinion doctor will change that.

An offence of concealing or destroying a document

5.38 In the consultation paper we proposed the creation of new offences of falsifying, forging, concealing, altering or destroying an 'advance directive' (para 3.36) and many respondents agreed that criminal sanctions were appropriate in such circumstances. Some expert respondents, however, believed that the existing law would cover such behaviour, and we accept that no new offence is required in relation to forging or falsifying. It is not, however, clear that the existing criminal law would cover the concealment or destruction of a document containing an advance refusal with intent to deceive the treatment provider.

We recommend that it should be an offence punishable with a maximum of two years imprisonment to conceal or destroy a written advance refusal of treatment with intent to deceive. (Draft Bill, clause 33.)

The main provision giving effect to these recommendations was clause 9 of the Draft Mental Health Incapacity Bill:

9. – (1) In this Act an 'advance refusal of treatment' means a refusal by a person who has attained the age of eighteen and has the necessary capacity of any medical, surgical or dental treatment or other procedure, being a refusal intended to have effect at any subsequent time when he may be without capacity to give or refuse his consent.

(2) Section 4 above does not authorise any such treatment or procedure as is mentioned in subsection (1) above if an advance refusal of treatment by the person concerned applies to that treatment or procedure in the circumstances of the case.

(3) In the absence of any indication to the contrary, it shall be presumed that an advance refusal of treatment does not apply in circumstances where those having the care of the person who made it consider that the refusal –

(a) endangers that person's life; or
(b) if that person is a woman who is pregnant, the life of the foetus.

(4) No person shall incur any liability –

(a) for the consequences of withholding any treatment or procedure if he has reasonable grounds for believing that an advance refusal of treatment by the person concerned applies to that treatment or procedure; or
(b) for carrying out any treatment or procedure to which an advance refusal of treatment by the person concerned applies unless he knows, or has reasonable grounds for believing, that an advance refusal of treatment by the person concerned applies to the treatment or procedure.

(5) Without prejudice to any other method of expressing an advance refusal of treatment, such a refusal may take the form of an instrument in writing; and, in the absence of any indication to the contrary, it shall be presumed that an advance refusal of treatment was validly made if it takes the form of an instrument in writing which is signed by the person by whom it is made and by at least one other person as a witness to his signature.

(6) An advance refusal of treatment may at any time be withdrawn or altered by the person who made it if he then has the capacity to do so.

(7) Notwithstanding the foregoing provisions, an advance refusal of treatment shall not preclude –

(a) the provision for the person who made it of basic care; or
(b) the taking of any action necessary to prevent his death or a serious deterioration in his condition pending a decision of the court on the validity or applicability of an advance refusal of treatment or on the question whether it has been withdrawn or altered.

(8) In subsection (7)(a) above 'basic care' means care to maintain bodily cleanliness and to alleviate severe pain and the provision of direct oral nutrition and hydration.

A number of the features of the proposed legislation are discussed in the following:

Petra Wilson 'The Law Commission's Report on Mental Incapacity: Medically Vulnerable Adults or Politically Vulnerable Law?' (1996) 4 Med L Rev 227

Where, however, a person with mental capacity wants to prohibit a given medical or surgical intervention affecting her when she no longer has the capacity to refuse consent, the Law

Commission agreed that she should be able to prepare (or have prepared) a written document which would have a legally binding status. It is argued that the evidential requirements for such documents should be as simple as possible. A person should simply be able to prepare a written statement, sign it and have it witnessed in order to complete a legally binding advance refusal. Any questions concerning the validity and scope of a given advance refusal could however be referred to the Court by treatment providers.

Bearing in mind the fears of the medical profession expressed in the British Medical Association (BMA) Report (BMA Statement on Advance Directives (1992)) and the opinions of the Government expressed in *Government Response to the Report of the Select Committee on Medical Ethics* (Cmnd 2553 (H.M.S.O. 1994)), the Law Commission has proposed certain limiting factors and presumptions concerning advance refusals. First, they should apply only when made by a person over 18 years of age. Although the draft legislation is generally applicable to people over 16 years of age, the Law Commission does not choose to recommend reform of the common law provisions that a court may overrule the refusal of a minor to accept medical treatment (*Re W (A Minor) (Medical Treatment: Courts Jurisdiction)* [1993] Fam 64 (CA)). Second, where a refusal endangers a person's life, there shall be a presumption of non-applicability. The court may be called upon to decide the validity of any advance refusal which if followed would result in the patient's death. It should be noted however, that the court may only allow the treatment provider to override an advance refusal of that kind, if it seems that the creator of the advance refusal had not foreseen her death as a result of her decision. It is accepted that an advance refusal is as good as any contemporaneous refusal by a mentally competent patient, in which a patient may of course refuse treatment even if doing so would result in her death (*Re T (Adult: Refusal of Treatment)* [1993] Fam 95).

A further presumption of non-applicability exists where the incapacitated party is pregnant. The Law Commission argues that unless a woman has expressly provided that her advance refusal should continue to operate notwithstanding her pregnancy, a treatment provider should assume that refusal does not apply if to follow it would endanger the life of the fetus. It should be noted, however, that the Commission does not leave a woman without the right to make an advance refusal which could compromise the fetus' life: 'We do not, however, accept that a woman's right to determine the sorts of bodily interference which she will tolerate somehow evaporates as soon as she becomes pregnant' (Law Commission No 231 at para 5.25).

One final point: it should be noted that the Law Commission's Scheme for anticipatory refusals would exist in parallel to the common law which would apply to oral refusals or written refusals that did not satisfy the requirements of clause 9 of the Bill. The Government has, as we noted earlier, now made it clear that it does not intend to enact the Law Commission's proposals on advance directives: *Making Decisions* (Cm 4465), (1999) at paras 12–20.

(ii) ENDURING POWERS OF ATTORNEY

The respective advantages and disadvantages of living wills and enduring powers of attorney were examined by the Working Party of King's College, London in 1988 with a view to establishing how the goal of patient autonomy could be best achieved.

The Living Will: Consent to Treatment at the End of Life (Working Party Report, Age Concern and Centre of Medical Law and Ethics, Kings College) (1988)

(a) Drafting problems
Existing examples of living will legislation seem to suffer from unsatisfactory drafting. The problem is to strike a balance between terms which are too general and those which are too specific. If the declaration is too general, it might fail to achieve the goal of patient autonomy because a large measure of discretion will inevitably be left with the doctor. If it is too specific, it may not deal with the particular problem which arises. While the drafting could be improved, it seems inevitable that the durable power of attorney must be more advantageous in this respect. Whatever criterion governs the agent's decision-making…the point is that he will make his decision in the light of the actual circumstances at the time the question arises. Hence a durable power of attorney, or a durable power combined with a living will declaration, must be preferable in this respect to a living will alone.

(b) Non-medical considerations
Of less importance, but not entirely without significance, is the question whether non-medical matters can play any part in the decision process. The timing of death can have financial consequences, for example, in the tax context. A living will is unlikely to permit such considerations to be taken into account. This raises the issue of whether the doctor can take such matters into consideration in a case involving no living will or durable power of attorney. For example, would the doctor be acting in the patient's interests if he kept him alive until a particular date for tax reasons, or until a relative gets married or arrives from Australia? To the extent that the doctor could take non-medical matters into account, then a person acting under a power of attorney should also be entitled to do so. In the absence of express provision, however, the point remains unclear. This is a matter which would affect only a small minority of patients, but some consideration should be given to the problem.

(c) Abuse
There is always a possibility that a person's free will may be overborne by the exercise of undue influence or pressure. This is so whatever the nature of the transaction, whether it is a living will, an ordinary will, a durable power of attorney or any other power of attorney. As far as contracts, gifts and other dispositions are concerned, the law deals with the problem by allowing the transaction to be set aside in certain circumstances. The requirements of writing, signature and witnesses are directed to minimising the possibility of undue pressure, and are a feature of wills, living wills and powers of attorney. It is not thought that a durable power of attorney is either more or less inherently liable to abuse in this respect.

However, one possible disadvantage of the durable power of attorney is that there is a possibility of abuse at the later stage, when the decision is made. It is not suggested that the agent is likely to act deliberately in bad faith. (If he did, some review procedure might be necessary, as discussed below.) The person in whose favour the power of attorney is executed is likely to be close to the patient. It is not impossible that he might be subconsciously influenced by improper considerations, for example, the prospect of release from the burden of caring for the patient at home. Persons who have an interest (financial or otherwise) in the patient's fate might be prevented from acting as witnesses, but it would be difficult to exclude them from the power of decision-making under a durable power of attorney, because an 'interested party' is the very person most patients would choose.

(d) Procedure
It is likely that the procedure for creating a durable power of attorney (see, for example, the Enduring Powers of Attorney Act 1985) will be more cumbersome than the procedure for executing a living will declaration. This is inevitable if the necessary safeguards are to be incorporated. A degree of formality will, however, be required in both cases.

(e) Lack of suitable agent
It may be that some people, for example, childless widows or widowers, would have difficulty in finding a trusted person to act. A living will would obviously be more advantageous in such a case, but this does not detract from the advantages of a durable power of attorney for those who do have a trusted friend or relative. One candidate could be a solicitor, but it may be doubted that such a person would have sufficiently intimate knowledge of the patient. For those with limited access to professional legal advice and with no suitable agent, the relative simplicity of a living will may have greater appeal.

(f) Resources
The question of resources…should not be regarded as a relevant consideration in deciding whether to choose living wills or durable powers of attorney. In any case it is thought that there is little distinction between them in the resources that are likely to be saved.
The above survey indicates that each option has its own advantages and disadvantages, so that it would not be desirable to recommend living will legislation to the exclusion of durable power of attorney legislation or vice versa. The remainder of this section deals with the question whether the two options should be separately available, or used in combination, or both.

The advantages of the combined document are twofold:
(i)   any uncertainty resulting from the drafting of the living will declaration (see (a) above) can be resolved by allowing the chosen agent, as opposed to the doctor, to make the decision;
(ii) the statement of wishes contained in the living will declaration provides guidance to the agent (assuming that he is to be guided by the patient's previously expressed wishes, as discussed below).

There is, however, a fundamental problem. If it is recommended that a living will declaration should not be mandatory, ie should take the form of a *request* only, then it is difficult to see what scope there could be for a durable power of attorney. The notion of an agent who has no legal power is unacceptable. It would therefore be impossible to have a combined instrument, part of which was not legally enforceable (the living will) and part of which was (the durable power). Even if the durable power were to be a separate instrument instead of part of the living will instrument, the position would still be unsatisfactory. If the preferred view is that there should be no legal force in a living will, then it should not be possible to achieve legal enforceability via a different route. The conclusion is that a durable power of attorney, either alone or in combination with a living will, can only be recommended, indeed, only makes sense, if the living will is to be legally binding. It is a matter of balancing, on the one hand, the reasons why a living will should be directory rather than mandatory with, on the other hand, the advantages which a durable power has over a living will, which would be lost if the living will is not to be legally binding.

If, in view of the above, it is concluded that the living will should be legally binding, further problems remain, in particular where a combined instrument is not used. It is possible to imagine a person crating more than one living will, or more than one durable power of attorney. The likely solution is, by analogy with the law of wills, that the later document would revoke the earlier either expressly or to the extent of any inconsistency. (See, for example, the Californian Durable Power of Attorney for Health Care Act 1983, which provides that a valid durable power of attorney for health care revokes any prior durable power of attorney for health care.) If a person executed a living will *and* a power of attorney in separate instruments, legislation should clarify whether the later document should revoke the earlier (assuming the order of execution is known), or whether the power of attorney should be construed as designed for the implementation of the living will.

Terms of a durable power of attorney

(a) Drafting

As with a living will, the problem is whether the instrument creating the power of attorney should attempt to be specific as to the types of treatment which the agent is empowered to sanction or refuse. Minimum requirements are that the instrument, or at any rate the legislation, should make clear what is the 'triggering event' and what are the criteria for decision-making. These two aspects are discussed below. Of course, the wording of the instrument will vary according to whether the durable power is created in isolation or in combination with a living will declaration…

The conclusion of the President's Commission Report was that 'by combining a proxy directive with specific instructions, an individual could control both the content and the process of decision-making about care in case of incapacity' (pp 155–160). Although no specific form of document is included, the Model Act attempts to put this into effect by 'permitting the declarant both to define what interventions are refused, and to name an authorised individual to make decisions consistent with the declarant's desires as expressed in the declaration'. Thus Section 1 defines 'competent person', 'medical procedure or treatment' and 'palliative care', and then Section 5 gives the declarant the right to appoint a person to order the administration, withholding or withdrawing of the defined treatments. The trigger is incompetence, and the criterion is 'substituted judgment' (explained below). It seems that these provisions meet the minimum standards of certainty…

Turning to the Californian statute, the Durable Power of Attorney for Health Care 1983, the Act defines 'health care', the 'trigger' is the principal's inability to give informed consent in respect of the particular decision, and the criterion is 'substituted judgment' unless the desires of the principal are unknown, in which case it is 'best interests' (explained below). No particular form of wording is prescribed, except that printed forms sold for use by a person who does not have legal advice must contain a warning notice specified in the Act, and the Act specifies a form of wording which must (in substance) be adopted in the declaration of the witnesses or the notary public, as the case may be.

(b) The 'triggering event'

The basic question is whether the durable power of attorney should come into operation merely upon the supervening incompetence of the principal, or whether some further event should be required, for example terminal illness or some other kind of illness…

For present purposes, suffice it to say that the definitions adopted for durable powers of attorney should be the same as those which apply in living wills and to any code of practice dealing with the treatment of competent and incompetent persons.

(c) The criterion for decision-making by the agent

This is a matter of choosing between 'substituted judgment' and 'best interests'. The 'substituted judgment' criterion is where the agent's decision is based on the known wishes of the principal, ie the agent makes the decision which the principal would have made but for his incompetence. The 'best interests' test is different, as that requires a decision which, objectively, is deemed to be in the best interests of the principal, even if it is not the decision he would have made.

As far as the treatment of incompetents generally is concerned, it may be that 'best interests' is the preferable test because if a person has never been competent, it is a matter of speculation as to what he or she would have decided if competent. [See, for example, discussion of this point in the Canadian case of *Re Eve* [1986] considered in Chapter 4.] However, in the present case we are dealing with people who have been competent, and who are likely to have made their wishes known. For this reason the 'substituted judgment' test is to be preferred. This was the view of the President's Commission Report.

> The Commission believes that, when possible, decision-making for incapacitated patients should be guided by the principle of substituted judgment, which promotes the underlying values of self-determination and well-being better than the best interests standard does. When a patient's likely decision is unknown, however, a surrogate decision-maker should use the best interests standard and choose a course that will promote the patient's well-being as it would probably be conceived by a reasonable person in the patient's circumstances. On certain points, of course, no consensus may exist about what most people would prefer, and surrogates retain discretion to choose among a range of acceptable choices (p 136).

Substituted judgment is the standard applied in the Concern for Dying Model Act and in the Californian Durable Power of Attorney for Health Care Act 1983 which provides that the attorney has a duty to act 'consistent with the desires of the principal as expressed in the durable power of attorney or otherwise made known to the attorney in fact at any time or, if the principal's desires are unknown, to act in the best interests of the principal'.

When the durable power is combined with a living will declaration, the arguments for applying the substituted judgment test are even stronger. However one consequence of adopting this criterion might be that there would be no scope for taking non-medical matters into account (see above). Even if the best interests standards were adopted, it is unclear whether such matters could be considered in the absence of express statutory provision.

Practical and procedural matters

The practical and procedural matters already discussed...in relation to living wills, apply equally or very similarly to durable powers of attorney. These will not be dealt with again. However, there are a number of additional matters which are relevant to durable powers of attorney alone.

(a) Capacity of agent

As with the principal, the agent should be a competent adult, the test for competence presumably being the same in each case. However in a recent judgment relating to the Enduring Powers of Attorney Act 1985 [*Re K: Re F* [1988] 1 All ER 358], the test of competence applied to the principal was a low one, and lower than that required of the agent. Another question is whether it should be possible to have joint agents in order to provide a further safeguard. In the Law Commission report on the Incapacitated Principal, the notion that joint attorneys should be *compulsory* was rejected. The Enduring Powers of Attorney Act 1985 does, however, *permit* joint agents. It is suggested that this is too cumbersome and that only one should be appointed.

(b) Witnesses

Clearly the person in whose favour the power of attorney is executed should not be a witness. Reference has already been made...to the difficulty that would arise if potential beneficiaries were to be excluded not merely from witnessing but from acting under a power of attorney.

(c) Forms

It has already been suggested that the durable power of attorney must be in writing, signed and witnessed...It does not seem necessary that the document should be in prescribed form. Nor does it seem necessary that there should be a requirement of prior discussion with an informed official, though this would usually be desirable. However, there may be a case for requiring the document to contain explanatory information, for the protection of the principal, in the case where printed power of attorney forms are available to the public at large (see the 1983 Californian Act). It should be noted that the Enduring Powers of Attorney Act 1985 requires both a prescribed form and the incorporation of explanatory information.

(d) Revocation

The main issues have already been discussed...and the following are additional points, relevant to durable powers of attorney.

The execution of a durable power should revoke any earlier power, and dissolution of marriage should revoke the appointment of the spouse as agent. This is analogous to the law of wills and is also found in the Californian Act of 1983.

In considering whether the principal should be entitled to revoke if he becomes incompetent, the President's Commission Report took the view that he should have power to override the agent as far as life-sustaining treatment is concerned. The Model Act (Section 6) permits revocation without specifying any requirements for continuing capacity.

The Californian Act of 1983 seems to achieve a compromise. On the one hand it provides the principal can only revoke if he still has capacity (although there is a rebuttable presumption that he does). On the other hand, it further provides that the agent has no authority to consent to or refuse health care necessary to keep the principal alive if the principal objects. In such a case, the matter is governed by the law that would apply if there were no durable power of attorney. This seems to be the most satisfactory solution.

(e)   Limits on the agent's power
The question arises whether certain matters should be excluded from the agent's sphere of authority. This could be done by limiting his role to 'life-sustaining procedures' (which must be defined)...or in some other way. There is much to be said for the provision in the Model Act that he cannot authorise the withholding of palliative care unless the instrument expressly so provides. It is unlikely, however, that there is any justification here for excluding such matters as are excluded in the Californian Act of 1983, for example psychosurgery. The agent should not have any power to make decisions, including consent to abortion, if the principal is pregnant.

There must also be provision for allowing the doctor to give emergency treatment without consulting the agent. (See the Californian Act 1983).

(f)   Delegation by the agent
If the agent is temporarily or permanently unable or unwilling to act (as to which, see also Disclaimer, below) the question arises as to whether he can delegate. The President's Commission Report (p 151) suggests such a possibility. It is thought, however, that this is undesirable. The principal should be able to choose a 'reserve'...but if he does not, the position will be as if no durable power existed if the agent cannot or will not act.

(g)   Disclaimer by the agent
It would seem impossible to provide that the agent is to be compelled to make a decision. When the time comes he may not wish to take the responsibility. The Californian Act 1983 does not seem to provide for this, but the Enduring Powers of Attorney Act 1985 allows disclaimer by permitting the agent to give notice to the principal while the latter is still competent, or, if he is not, by notice to the court. Disclaimer by notice to the competent principal seems unobjectionable, but a requirement of notice to the court in the present context seems too cumbersome. It is suggested that if the agent declines to act and no reserve has been designated by the principal, then the position will be as if no durable power existed.

(h)   Can the agent's decision be challenged?
What happens if there is a suspicion of bad faith, or an apparently unreasonable interpretation of the principal's wishes? The President's Commission Report (pp 152–3) suggests the possibility of an independent review, either 'intrainstitutional' or by way of court proceedings. Certainly the principal's interests must be safeguarded, but the notion of review by the court seems cumbersome. The statute could perhaps provide for review by a body such as the hospital ethics committee, on specified grounds, for example where the agent has not applied the correct criterion...to his decision.

(i)   Medical records
Should the agent be entitled to see the principal's records? He must have the necessary information in order to make a decision, but, on the other hand, the principal's privacy must be respected. Taking the latter point into account, the President's Commission Report suggests that it may be advisable to limit the agent's access to information needed for the particular decision in question. This may not work, since the agent may not know what is relevant until he has looked at everything. The Californian Act 1983 provides that the agent has the same right as the principal to receive information, unless the right is limited in the instrument creating the power. The Model Act is on similar lines. It is thought that this is preferable to the suggestion of the President's Commission.

(j)   Notice to relatives
The Enduring Powers of Attorney Act 1985 provides that the agent is obliged to notify various relatives when he applies to register the power (which he must do when he believes the principal is or is becoming incompetent). The relatives then have a chance to object on certain grounds, for example that the power is invalid, or the principal is not incompetent. This obviously provides an extra safeguard, but would probably be too cumbersome in the present context, especially if provision is made for a review procedure (see (h) above).

In its 1995 report, *Mental Incapacity* (No 231), the Law Commission proposed that legislation should provide for 'continuing powers of attorney' (CPA), which would replace enduring power of attorney under the Enduring Powers of Attorney 1985. The new CPA would extend to 'personal welfare' decisions, including those relating to medical treatment. Its proposed scheme is complex (see cls 12–22, Draft Mental Incapacity Bill).

Scope of a Continuing Power of Attorney

7.7 As the law now stands, the donor of an EPA can only delegate continuing decision-making authority over his or her 'property and affairs' (1985 Act, s 3(1) and *Re F (Mental Patient: Sterilisation)* [1990] 2 AC 1). In Consultation Paper No 128 we suggested that donors should be permitted to delegate authority over 'personal welfare' decisions, while in Consultation Paper No 129 we extended this proposal to health care decisions. Our consultees almost universally supported the proposal that a donor should be able to delegate non-financial decision-making in advance, in such a way that the authority would outlast any supervening incapacity of the donor. It was said that the great advantage of appointing an attorney to take health care decisions is the ability of the attorney to respond to new situations as they arise. For this reason, some respondents who expressed reservations about the advisability of 'advance directives' for health care were nonetheless enthusiastic about allowing people to appoint proxy decision-makers. In its report, the House of Lords Select Committee on Medical Ethics acknowledged 'the strong current of opinion in favour of proxy decision-making' about health care matters but concluded that it did not favour the more widespread development of such a system. The committee feared that a person's choice of proxy might become out of date, that the proxy might not make the same choice the patient would have made, and that the proxy might lack objectivity whether as a result of financial self-interest or psychological stress. Exactly the same arguments could be made against allowing people to delegate their financial powers. They appear to us to be arguments in favour of adequate safeguards rather than arguments against the extension of the popular EPA scheme to personal and medical matters. As the Lord Chancellor said in responding to the committee's report, 'some people might prefer to appoint a trusted family member rather than try to draw up a complicated living will or leave it all up to the doctors.' (Hansard (HL) 9 May 1994, vol 554, col 1353.) In our view, the appointment of an attorney with a range of powers should be one option available to those who wish to plan for the possibility of future incapacity. As under the present law, it should always be open to a donor to impose specific conditions or restrictions on the attorney.

We recommend that a CPA may extend to matters relating to a donor's personal welfare, health care and property and affairs (including the conduct of legal proceedings); and may be subject to conditions or restrictions. (Draft Bill, clause 16(1).)

7.8 In the consultation papers we suggested that a donor should always retain power to do any act in relation to which he or she has capacity at the time (Consultation Paper No L 128, paras 7.5–7.10; Consultation Paper No 129, para 5.6). Respondents all agreed with this principle. The general law in relation to powers of attorney has always catered for donor and attorney having simultaneous authority to act and we see no reason to depart from this principle. The issue only merits mention because the 1985 Act restricts the ability of the donor of a registered EPA to change the terms of the document (1985 Act, 7(1)(a) and (c) and s 7 (2)). It should be noted, however, that in 1983 this Commission clearly stated that 'if the donor after registration has sufficient capacity to do his shopping or run his bank account he should be able to do so independently of the attorney; and people with whom the donor deals should not be prevented from relying on his instructions just because they know that an EPA granted by him has been registered.' (Law Commission No 122, para 4.70.) Imposing any restriction on a donor, merely because authority to act has also been given to an attorney, would conflict with the policy aim of enabling people to act for themselves whenever they have capacity to do so. We do not, therefore, recommend any statutory provision to restrict the common law power of a donor of a power of attorney to act personally where he or she has capacity to do so.

7.9 The general law in relation to powers of attorney will continue to underlie our proposed scheme for Continuing Powers of Attorney. It would, however, be confusing and unhelpful if a document intended to take effect as a CPA, but which failed to meet some of the specific statutory requirements, could be taken to operate as an ordinary power of attorney. Nor does this possibility fit with the simplified procedures which we recommend, whereby registration of the CPA will act as a trigger to its effectiveness. We take the view that express provision to rule out any question of an unregistered (and therefore ineffective) CPA operating as an ordinary power would be helpful.

> ***We recommend*** **that where an instrument purports to create a CPA but does not comply with the statutory requirements it should confer no powers on the donee.** (Draft Bill, clause 12(4).)

Duties and powers of attorneys under CPAs

7.10 'An unpaid attorney need not do anything' (T Aldridge 'Powers of Attorney (8th ed 1991) p 72). Although a number of our respondents expressed dissatisfaction with this principle, the arguments against the imposition of a duty to act seem to us even stronger when the attorney may have authority over difficult and delicate personal and medical matters. An attorney with such powers may genuinely be unable to arrive at a firm decision. The new legislation we propose will of course identify others with lawful authority to act, including the court in the last resort. All our respondents, however, agreed with our provisional proposal that where the attorney does exercise his or her authority to act on behalf of the donor then this should be done in the best interests of the donor, with reference to the statutory check-list. This represents a slight shift in the nature of an attorney's duty, which currently depends on the law in relation to contractual and fiduciary relationships. While this may have been entirely adequate when an attorney could only be involved in financial matters, the concept of 'best interests' is better adapted to non-financial decisions and can equally well be applied to financial ones.

> ***We recommend*** **that an attorney acting under a Continuing Power of Attorney should act in the best interests of the donor, having regard to the statutory factors.** (Draft Bill, clause 3.)

7.11 The general law in relation to fiduciary obligations restricts an ordinary attorney from acting so as to benefit himself or herself. The 1985 Act, however, made specific provision relaxing the common law restriction so as to allow the attorney (1) to benefit persons other than the donor and (2) to make gifts in some circumstances. In view of our recommendation that an attorney under a CPA should be subject to the same duty to act in the donor's best interests as any other decision-maker, we see no need for comparable provisions in the new legislation. The power to act in the donor's best interests is a more flexible and slightly wider power than the power of an ordinary attorney at common law. Since it requires the attorney to consider the wishes and feelings of the donor and the factors he or she would have taken into account, the attorney would in appropriate cases be quite able to meet another person's needs (including the attorney's own needs) or make seasonal or charitable gifts, while still acting within the parameters of the best interests duty.

Statutory conditions and restrictions on CPAs

7.13 If an attorney under a CPA has powers in relation to personal and health care matters then that attorney should be bound by the general restriction against acts of confinement or coercion which we have recommended as a qualification upon the general authority of informal decision-makers. It is a well-established facet of the general law in relation to powers of attorney that the donor may revoke the power either expressly or impliedly, by doing acts inconsistent with the continued existence of the power. The active objection of a donor is highly likely to be an act amounting to implied revocation. It might therefore be argued that no express restriction on the authority of attorneys under CPAs to confine or coerce donors is needed. It appears to us, however, that the arguments in favour of express provision apply to attorneys as they apply to informal decision-makers.

> ***We recommend*** **that the restriction against coercion or confinement should apply equally to attorneys.** (Draft Bill, clauses 16(4) and (5).)

(2)   The donor has capacity to act personally

7.14 The origins of the EPA scheme in the 1985 Act lie in the general law relating to powers of attorney and it is no part of that act that a donor or principal must lack capacity before an attorney or agent may act. We suggested in the consultation papers, however, that while no such restriction need apply to personal welfare powers (Consultation Paper No 128, paras 7.8–7.9), an attorney should only have power to take a medical treatment decision if the donor lacks capacity to take that decision for himself or herself (Consultation Paper No 129, para 5.5). The difference in the health care context is that the health care provider is always under a personal obligation to assess the patient's capacity to consent to any treatment proposed. There is therefore nothing unduly burdensome in expecting both doctor and attorney to investigate whether the donor can give or refuse personal consent to any particular treatment. Respondents supported our provisional views.

We recommend that no attorney may consent to or refuse any treatment unless the donor is, or is reasonably believed by the attorney to be, without capacity to give or refuse personal consent to that treatment. (Draft Bill, clause 16(3)(a).)

(3)   Admission to hospital under the 1983 Act

7.15 The Mental Health Act 1983 provides that persons may be compulsorily admitted to hospital to be assessed or treated for mental disorder. In fact, the vast majority of people so assessed or treated are not detained under the compulsory powers but have agreed (or at least not objected) to the hospital admission. We see no objection to an attorney who holds health care powers assisting and arranging such an admission within the terms of his or her obligation to act in the donor's best interests. However, the situation is entirely different where the donor actively objects to the proposed hospital admission. We have already recommended a general restriction on attorneys where the donor actively objects to what is being done. However, for the avoidance of doubt,

We recommend that no attorney should have power to consent to the donor's admission to hospital for assessment or treatment for mental disorder, where such admission is against the will of the donor. (Draft Bill, clause 16(3)(b).)

This simply means that the safeguards and procedures of the 1983 Act cannot be avoided by reference to the consent of an attorney.

(4)   Basic care

7.16 We suggested in Consultation Paper No 129 (para 5.20 and paras 3.25 and 3.26) that no attorney with health care powers should be able to refuse, on a donor's behalf, the sort of basic care which maintains the patient in a hygienic pain-free state and provides spoon-feeding. All but one of our consultees agreed with this proposed restriction. We intend a similar restriction to apply to decisions by way of 'advance refusal' and have already explained that our thinking is based on considerations of public policy (para 5.34 above). We have referred to the BMA's submission to us that patients can wish to limit the amount of pain relief administered so as to retain a higher level of consciousness and interaction. The definition of 'basic care' adopted in our draft legislation acknowledges that not *all* forms of pain relief must be accepted, but that all 'direct oral' forms of nutrition and hydration should be covered.

We recommend that no attorney should be authorised to withhold basic care from the donor or refuse consent to its provision. (Draft Bill, clauses 16(3)(c) and 9(8).)

(5)   The donor has made an advance refusal

7.17 It may be that people will wish to give written directions about their future health care, as well as appointing another person under a CPA. It follows from our discussion of advance refusals of treatment in Part V above that an attorney can have no more power than any other person (or the court) to override a valid and applicable advance refusal. In Consultation Paper No 129 (para 5.20) we suggested that an attorney might override an advance refusal if the refusal itself provided for this eventuality. An example might be 'I refuse cardio-pulmonary resuscitation unless my attorney consents to it'. There is, however, no need for any special provision to cover the possibility of such wording; the refusal will simply not 'apply in the circumstances' of the attorney consenting. The situation may be less clear and easy to resolve where a donor has granted a general power over health care matters to an attorney, but *subsequently* makes an advance refusal. We think it would be helpful to specify that, in the absence of express provision to the contrary in the CPA, the attorney may not consent to procedures covered by an advance refusal. In relation to advance statements which are not 'advance refusals' the attorney, acting in the best interests of the donor, will still be obliged to consider the donor's expressed wishes and feelings. An attorney will also be able to take into account such factors as changes in medical technology and changes in the donor's outlook and attitudes. In this way the appointment of an attorney will, importantly, allow a flexible and adaptable approach to future health care issues to be constructed by a donor.

We recommend that, unless expressly authorised to do so, no attorney may consent to any treatment refused by the donor by an advance refusal of treatment. (Draft Bill, clause 16(3)(d)(i).)

(6)   Procedures requiring independent supervision

7.18 In Consultation Paper No 129 we provisionally proposed that an attorney should never be able to consent to procedures requiring independent supervision. In discussing such procedures in Part VI above, we recommend instead that if a donor clearly intends his or her attorney to displace the need for independent supervision then the law should respect that decision. We think this represents a sensible compromise, neither forbidding a donor to delegate a certain range of decisions nor allowing power over controversial decisions to be handed over without careful consideration. In each case, the donor must give the attorney express authority to consent to any of the 'independent supervision' procedures.

We recommend that, unless expressly authorised to do so, no attorney may consent on a donor's behalf to:

(1) a procedure requiring court approval,

(2) a procedure requiring a certificate from an independent medical practitioner,

(3) discontinuance of artificial nutrition or hydration,

(4) procedures for the benefit of others, or

(5) **participation in non-therapeutic research.** (Draft Bill, clauses 16(3)(d)(ii) and 16(5).)

(7) Life-sustaining treatment

7.19 Many respondents agreed with our preliminary view that power over certain sorts of serious medical decision (and not only those requiring independent supervision) should require express authorization by a donor. Such decisions would never be covered by a 'general power' and would require express 'opting-in' on the donor's part. In the consultation paper we suggested that a donor might be required to take a positive decision about granting power to refuse 'life-saving treatment'. It was clear on consultation that many people might want to appoint a health care attorney precisely so as to ensure that someone makes appropriate 'treatment-limiting' decisions for them. While there is therefore no question of preventing donors from giving attorneys such powers, it is entirely appropriate to require that the donor should have made express provision in the CPA.

We recommend **that, unless expressly authorised to do so, no attorney may refuse consent to any treatment necessary to sustain life.** (Draft Bill, clause 16(3)(d)(iii).)

Requirements affecting the donor and donee

(1) The donor

7.20 Under the current law, a donor of an EPA must be an individual with capacity to create the power. There are no other restrictions on donors, and it was stated in Law Com No 122 that minors and undischarged bankrupts would be able to create EPAs, albeit that this would be unusual and that any attorney's authority might be restricted by the general law. The general law as to the effect of a minor appointing an attorney remains complex, and it may be that the appointment itself is voidable by the minor if not for his or her benefit. Where CPAs are concerned, it would not be satisfactory to rely on the fact that a minor has power to 'avoid' transactions by an attorney. There may be physical, emotional or psychological consequences of a personal welfare or health care decision which cannot easily be reversed by the payment of a compensatory sum of money. Since a CPA may cover personal welfare matters and health care decisions, there would also be very significant complications with the law in relation to parental responsibility and the inherent jurisdiction of the High Court if a CPA could be created by a minor. We think it entirely appropriate that the right to create a document with such far-reaching legal consequences as a Continuing Power of Attorney should be restricted to adults.

We recommend **that a CPA may only be created by an individual who has attained the age of eighteen.** (Draft Bill, clause 14(1).)

(2) The donee

7.21 The 1985 Act specifically provided that the donee executing an EPA must be either an individual (over eighteen and not bankrupt) or a trust corporation. It would not be appropriate for a trust corporation to exercise personal or health care powers, but apart from that there is no need for any change in the law. In the consultation papers we provisionally proposed that it should never be possible for a public official *in his or her official capacity* to be appointed attorney. However, we were influenced by the views of the Public Trustee and the Association of Directors of Social Services (among others) that there might be occasions where a public official should be available to act as attorney of last resort. This would not require specific provision, since all the likely candidates will be either 'individuals' or trust corporations. For the avoidance of doubt, we think the legislation should specify that an individual can be identifiable by reference to an office or position (eg, the manager for the time being of the X branch of the Y Bank, or the Director of Social Services of Z Region). The person fulfilling the description at the time of execution would have to execute the CPA as donee of the power, even though a successor might subsequently act as attorney. Appointing an office-holder is probably possible under the existing law, but is uncommon. Where it is not intended to put the CPA into immediate effect, there will often be good reasons for avoiding the appointment of an office-holder. The result of local government or NHS re-organisation, or of business changes in a solicitors' firm or a financial institution, might be that there is no person fulfilling the description of the attorney when a time arrives when the CPA is needed. In cases where the CPA is to be registered and put into effect at once, however, the appointment of an office-holder might be a useful facility.

We recommend that an individual donee of a CPA may be described as the holder for the time being of a specified office or position. (Draft Bill, clause 14(3).)

(3) Multiple donees

7.22 The present law makes special provision for multiple attorneys, specifically allowing joint or 'joint and several' attorneys. (1985 Act, s 11(1).) We suggested in the consultation papers that, in contrast with the present law, donors should also be permitted to appoint an 'alternate' attorney to act if the original fails or ceases to act for some reason. Respondents agreed that there would be advantages in allowing for such a possibility. In order to ensure consistency with the registration system we describe below, replacement attorneys should only be available in circumstances where the original donee has ceased to act for a reason which can be established by objective evidence.

We recommend that a donor may, in a CPA, appoint a person to replace the donee in the event of the donee disclaiming, dying, becoming bankrupt or becoming divorced from the donor. (Draft Bill, clause 20(1)).

It should also be possible to appoint joint or joint and several attorneys under a CPA. (Draft Bill, clause 20(2)). Our draft Bill applies the rules in relation to CPAs to the case of multiple attorneys. (Draft Bill, clause 20(3) and (4).)

Formalities and safeguards

7.23 We will now deal with the formal and procedural aspects of our proposed scheme for Continuing Powers of Attorney. In the consultation papers we proposed some radical departures from the formalities and safeguards constructed by the 1985 Act. We have reconsidered our original suggestions in the light of helpful comments, and significant reservations, expressed by those whom we consulted. We believe that our recommendations now strike the right balance between protection for donors who may come to lack capacity and procedural simplicity, encouraging ever greater use of the provisions.

(1) A prescribed form

7.24 We see no need to depart from the principle that a power of attorney which is going to outlast the donor's incapacity must be in a form prescribed by the Lord Chancellor, and include prescribed explanatory information (1985 Act, s 2(1)(a) and (c). Draft Bill, clause 13(1)(a) and (c) and clause 13(2)). This should describe the general effect of creating and accepting the power (1985 Act, s 2(2)(a); draft Bill, clause 13(3)(a)). The form should include a statement by the donor that he or she intends the power to continue in spite of supervening mental incapacity and that he or she has read (or had read to him or her) the explanatory information (1985 Act, s 2(2)(b); draft Bill, clause 13(3)(b)(i)). The 1985 Act stipulates that the form must include a statement by the attorney in relation to the duty to register the EPA (1985 Act, s 2(2)(b)(iii)). No such duty will apply to donees of CPA but

We recommend that a CPA must contain a statement by the donee that he or she understands the duty to act in the best interests of the donor in relation to any decision which the donor is, or is reasonably believed by the donee to be, without capacity to make. (Draft Bill, clause 13(3)(b)(ii).)

7.25 In Consultation Paper No 128 we expressed reservations about a 'general power of attorney being used in relation to personal welfare matters (para 5.7). Numerous respondents, however, saw disadvantages in requiring donors to use a more complex prescribed form. Few agreed that a more complex form would offer any significant protection to vulnerable donors. Some recalled the days before the 1971 Act, when every power of attorney had to specify the powers being granted and many of them ran into copious pages of small print. Respondents to Consultation Paper No 129 (para 5.7) were in favour of a standard form which could be adapted as required by an individual donor. We are now persuaded that there is no objection in principle to donors granting wide 'general' powers so long as explanatory information makes clear the nature of the powers granted. As we have explained (para 7.7), donors can impose their own restrictions and there will be certain conditions and restrictions imposed by law.

We recommend **that a CPA may be expressed to confer general authority on a donee.**
(Draft Bill, clause 16(2).)

7.26 While the details of any prescribed form are for secondary legislation, we should report
that both the Law Society and the BMA submitted to us that a power of attorney for
health care decisions should always be a completely separate document from one dealing
with personal welfare or property and affairs. We are not ourselves persuaded, in the
context of the unified scheme we recommend throughout this report, that people need
be put to the trouble and expense of preparing and executing two separate documents.
We take it that a great many people would find it entirely appropriate to give power
over all three areas to a spouse, life-partner or other relative. A single form with separate
sections in relation to (1) personal welfare matters (2) health care matters and (3) property
and affairs might be a possible solution.

(2) Execution requirements

7.27 In the consultation papers, we proposed creating much more stringent formalities for
execution than those which have been imposed in relation to EPAs (Consultation paper
No 128, para 7.15; Consultation Paper 129 para 5.8). The 1985 Act stipulates that an
EPA must be executed in the prescribed manner (1985 Act, s 2(1)(b)). At present, the
relevant regulations require signature by both donor and donee, each in the presence of
a witness (Enduring Powers of Attorney (Prescribed Form) Regulations 1990 (SI 1990
No 1376), reg 3(1)). Our provisional proposal that the donor's capacity to execute should
be certified by a solicitor and a doctor at the time of execution did not commend itself
to the majority of our consultees. Numerous respondents said that any such requirement
would present practical difficulties and force donors to incur extra costs. Concern focused
on the idea that *both* a doctor *and* a lawyer need be involved in every case. It should in
any event be a matter of good practice for all health professionals not to witness a signature
without considering the question of the person's capacity to execute the document. Lawyers
involved in drawing up powers of attorney should also, as a matter of good practice, be
very clear that the client to whom the duty of care is owed is the donor of the power and
no-one else. In appropriate cases good practice already demands that an appropriate medical
certificate should be obtained and/or appropriate records kept on file. The provisional
proposal for a certification procedure was a corollary to the proposed abolition of any
form of registration, which, as we explain below, we are no longer pursuing. In those
circumstances, the draft Bill simply provides that a CPA (like an EPA) must be executed
in the prescribed manner by both donor and donee. (Clause 13(1)(b)).

(3) Registration of Continuing Powers of Attorney,

7.28 The 1985 Act requires an attorney under an EPA to notify a listed set of relatives and
then apply to register the EPA with the Court of Protection, once the donor 'is or is
becoming' mentally incapable (1985 Act, s 4). In the consultation papers we suggested
that the 1985 registration scheme was flawed, and should be abandoned and replaced with
a different set of safeguards for donors (Consultation Paper No 128, paras 7.20–7.23;
Consultation Paper No 129, para 5.11). Consultees who commented on this were evenly
divided between those who wanted some form of registration scheme retained and those
who did not. Although many of those with detailed knowledge of the workings of the
present scheme subscribed to our provisional view, others were convinced that registration
operated as a significant protection for donors. We have carefully reconsidered this
matter in the light of the many helpful comments made on consultation.

7.29 We have also been assisted in our deliberations by discussions with our colleagues in
the Scottish Law Commission. They, in a sense, approach the matter from the opposite
direction. As a temporary measure, pending a full review of the various options by the
Commission, Scots law simply provides that no power of attorney is revoked by the
donor's mental incapacity (Law Reform (Miscellaneous Provisions) (Scotland) Act 1990,
s 71. This section only has effect in relation to those powers of attorney 'granted on or
after the date on which this section comes into force'; s 71 came into force on 1 January
1991). There are no special formalities and no registration requirements. The Scottish
Law Commission originally proposed that adequate safeguards ensuring that a donor
had capacity to execute a CPA would be preferable to any form of registration. The
Commission's consultees, however, favoured a simple scheme of registration with an
administrative body, and we understand that some form of registration procedure is
likely to be recommended by our Scottish counterparts.

7.30 A straightforward administrative registration procedure can have the merit of bringing
a document into the public domain and establishing its formal validity. A mark of validity
can be of benefit to both donor and donee. A process of registration involving a public
body will undoubtedly discourage some people who might abuse powers which remain

in the private domain and will provide a point of reference for those who have queries or concerns about the status of a particular document. Registration can also serve to distinguish CPAs from ordinary powers of attorney. We therefore considered whether every CPA should be registered under such a scheme at the time of execution. Some donors, however, currently execute their EPAs well in advance of any loss of capacity. These are sometimes called 'insurance policy' EPAs; the need for the attorney to exercise any of the powers granted might never materialise. A requirement to register upon execution might needlessly burden a well-organised donor, as well as the registration authority.

7.31 Any registration scheme should direct its benefits towards those donors who are in need of them. Under the scheme in the 1985 Act, this leads to the requirement to register only when the donor 'is or is becoming' mentally incapable. In the consultation paper (Consultation Paper No 128, paras 7.7 and 7.20) we expressed particular concern about the fact that this requirement leads on to a statutory assumption that the donor of a registered EPA lacks capacity, and in particular capacity to revoke the EPA. We take the view that registration should no longer purport to identify those donors who are losing their capacity, but should instead apply to those donors of CPA's whose attorneys wish to *use* the powers granted in the instrument. A firm distinction should therefore be drawn between an 'ordinary power of attorney' and one which is in the prescribed form for a CPA, and in particular contains the essential statement by the donor that it is intended to last beyond incapacity. It should no longer be possible to operate an unregistered CPA as if it were an ordinary power of attorney. Every potential CPA must be a *registered* CPA before the donee can exercise any of the powers conferred in the document.

We recommend that no document should create a Continuing Power of Attorney until it has been registered in the prescribed manner. (Draft Bill, clause 15(1).)

7.32 The 1985 Act allocated numerous administrative and judicial functions in relation to EPAs to the Court of Protection. Many of the administrative functions, especially those concerned with registration, having in reality been carried out in the Public Trust Office rather than by the Court itself. New Rules which have been brought into force now that the Public Trust Office has acquired agency status provide for the division of functions between the Court of Protection and the Public Trustee (The Court of Protection (Enduring Powers of Attorney) Rules 1994 (SI 1994 No 3047)). The registration scheme we now recommend will be purely administrative in nature and we would expect it to be operated by the Public Trust Office, many of whose staff have been performing administrative functions in relation to EPAs for the past eight years. It will, however, be for the Lord Chancellor to determine which administrative body should discharge the functions described in our Bill.

We recommend that a registration authority appointed by the Lord Chancellor should register CPAs. (Draft Bill, clause 5(1).)

7.33 Any donee of a CPA who seeks to *use* the powers granted in the document will be obliged to apply for registration of the document. Questions about the donor's capacity will not concern the registration authority, which will register the power upon the donee making an application for registration in the prescribed form, subject only to the CPA complying with the prescribed formalities (Draft Bill, clause 15(2)). If the document is an 'insurance policy' CPA then the donee will probably not wish to go to the trouble of registration until the need arises.

(4) Notification to the donor

7.34 We favour the retention of a requirement that a donee must notify a donor of his or her intention to register a CPA. It may be some time since the document was executed and, in any event, the act of registration will significantly alter matters by triggering the attorney's power to act. The donor must be warned that this is in prospect and be given an opportunity to prevent registration. The registration authority will have no power to determine disputes and such matters will always have to go to the court. Thus, if the registration authority is informed by a donor that he or she objects to registration of a CPA then the registration authority will have no power to register it in the absence of a direction from the court. There is no need to specify any particular grounds on which a donor may object to registration.

We recommend that if a donor objects to registration of a CPA then the registration authority should inform the donee and should not register the document unless the court directs it to do so. (Draft Bill, clause 15(4).)

7.35 As at present, the court should have power to dispense with notification if it would serve no useful purpose (1985 Act, s 4(3) and Sched 1 paras 4(2) and 3(2)(b); draft Bill, clause 15(5)). Examples would be where the donor is in a coma or severely demented. We were told on consultation that at present an attorney is often embarrassed by having to spell out for the donor the attorney's belief that he or she is becoming mentally incapacitated. In future, there will be no necessary link between the intention to register and incipient incapacity. We therefore see no need to reproduce the extremely wide power in the 1985 Act for notification to the donor to be dispensed with because it would be 'undesirable' or 'impractical' (1985 Act, s 4(3) and Sched 1 paras 3(2)(a) and 4(2)).

7.36 The fact that a CPA has been registered will not necessarily signify any loss of capacity on the donor's part. It is therefore only right that notice should also be given to the donor once registration takes place.

We recommend that once a CPA has been registered the registration authority should give notice of that fact in the prescribed form to the donor. (Draft Bill, clause 15(6)(a).)

(5)   Notification to relatives or others

7.37 In Consultation Paper No 128 we suggested that requiring an attorney to notify listed relatives of the donor was hard to justify in the context of 'least restrictive intervention' (para 7.6). Many respondents endorsed this view. There was particular concern about the fact that the statutory list makes no acknowledgment that close and important relationships may exist outside of legal marriage and blood ties. It conflicts with the autonomy principle to require, regardless of the donor's wishes, that certain relatives must be notified of a private arrangement to govern future decision-making. Our respondents strongly supported the idea that a donor should be able to choose who might be notified about his or her power of attorney (see Consultation Paper No 128, paras 7.17–7.18 and Consultation Paper No 129, para 5.9).

7.38 We see a place for the notification of relatives or others as part of the 'publicity' facet of the new registration scheme. It should, however, differ in two marked respects from the present notification scheme. First, it should be a notification that a CPA *has been* registered rather than a notification of an intention to register. We see no reason for the law to assume that the donor's actions are such that his or her relatives should have a right to object. The assumption should be that the donor has made valid arrangements, although properly concerned relatives will be able to take positive steps to challenge those arrangements. Secondly, it is for the donor to say who should be notified and not for statute to lay down a list.

We recommend that once a CPA has been registered the registration authority should give notice of that fact in the prescribed form to a maximum of two people (not including the donee) as specified in the CPA. (Draft Bill, clause 15(6)(b).)

7.39 Although some respondents expressed concern about donors who had no friends or relatives to name for the purposes of notification, the same problem arises under the present statutory list arrangements. Notification can only ever be one small part of the protection afforded to donors. We note that more than one respondent to Consultation Paper No 129 suggested that a GP would be an appropriate person to be notified about a health care power of attorney.

Termination of Continuing Powers of Attorney

7.40 At common law a power of attorney comes to an end when (1) disclaimed by the attorney, (2) revoked (expressly or impliedly) by the donor or (3) terminated by operation of law (for example, upon the incapacity, death or bankruptcy of the parties). It can also terminate by expiry, having been granted for a fixed term or until the happening of a particular event. It seems most unlikely that a donor of a CPA, whose whole purpose is to provide for a future time when he or she will lack capacity, would wish to fix an expiry date for his or her CPA. We will now deal with the circumstances in which Continuing Powers of Attorney will terminate. As we will explain later (see para 7.58), the court will also have power to terminate a CPA in certain circumstances.

(1)   Disclaimer by the donee

7.41 The donee of a CPA is under no duty to act on behalf of the donor and, until the CPA is registered, has no power so to act. There is no scope for any special disclaimer rules in relation to unregistered (and therefore ineffective) CPAs. Once a CPA is registered, however, a disclaiming attorney should notify both the donor (since registration does not signify that the donor lacks capacity) and the registration authority.

We recommend that no disclaimer of a registered CPA should be valid unless notice is given to the donor and the registration authority. (Draft Bill, clause 15(7).)

(2) Revocation by the donor

7.42 There is a common law principle that a donor of a power can revoke all or any of it, either expressly (for example by saying so, or by tearing up the document) or impliedly, by doing an act which is inconsistent with the continuation of the power (for example, concealing the whereabouts of all assets from the attorney). The general rule as to capacity applies to revocation and a donor's revocation is only effective if he or she has capacity to revoke, in other words understands the nature and effect of the action being taken. The 1985 Act does not affect the common law position until the attorney makes an application for registration, whereupon it radically alters it. Our predecessors recommended that the ability of a donor of an EPA to deal in any way with *a registered power* should be curtailed, in order to preserve "the 'sanctity' of registration". The 1985 Act therefore provides that 'no revocation of …[a registered] power by the donor shall be valid unless and until the court confirms the revocation… .' (1985 Act, s 7(1)(a) Subsection (2) stresses that subsection (1) applies 'for so long as the instrument is registered …' whether or not the donor is for the time being mentally incapable.)

7.43 We suggested in the consultation papers that a donor with capacity to do so should always be able to revoke a power of attorney. Respondents unanimously agreed with this policy and some of them mentioned that it was particularly important not to restrict, and not even to impose any delay upon, a donor's ability to revoke a health care power. In relation to CPAs covering health care decisions, we have explained that no attorney's authority will ever coincide with that of a donor who is still able personally to consent to or refuse any treatment offered. Where a donor does, however, lack capacity to take the decision in question, he or she may still have capacity to revoke the CPA ('I don't want X deciding things for me any more'). It would be most unappealing to require that a treatment-provider must continue to honour the decision of an attorney when faced with a donor who is now revoking the authority granted. We therefore think it necessary to stress, by way of an explicit provision, that a donor should always retain the power to revoke his or her CPA.

We recommend an express provision that nothing in the legislation should preclude the donor of a CPA from revoking it at any time when he or she has the capacity to do so. (Draft Bill, clause 12(3).)

7.44 Some of our expert legal consultees, however, raised the matter of protection for attorneys and third parties. The clear effect of the 1985 Act is that an attorney or third party can confidently ignore any purported revocation by a donor if 'confirmation' has not been received from the court. This provision conflicts with the principles underlying our project. Can adequate protection for attorneys or third parties be provided by some other means? As we mentioned in Consultation Paper No 128 (para 7.10), the Powers of Attorney Act 1971 already provides protection for attorneys and third parties where revocation may be an issue. For attorneys, it states that:

> A donee of a power of attorney who acts in pursuance of the power at a time when it has been revoked shall not, by reason of the revocation, incur any liability (either to the donor or to any other person) if at that time he did not know that the power had been revoked (1971 Act, s 5(1)).

For third parties, it states that:

> Where a power of attorney has been revoked and a person, without knowledge of the revocation, deals with the donee of the power, the transaction between them shall, in favour of that person, be as valid as if the power had then been in existence (1971 Act, s 5(2)).

We take the view that these provisions, looking at the *knowledge* of the attorney or third party, provide clear and adequate protection for them in all the circumstances where it is appropriate. They should apply equally to Continuing Powers of Attorney.

We recommend that section 5 of the Powers of Attorney Act 1971 should apply to Continuing Powers of Attorney. (Draft Bill, clause 19(6).)

(3) Termination by operation of law

7.45 The rules about bankruptcy in relation to CPAs need to distinguish between the grant of powers over 'property and affairs' and the grant of powers over personal and health care matters. Although the existing rules whereby a bankrupt cannot act as an attorney should continue to apply to any powers over 'property and affairs', we see no reason for an absolute rule that a bankrupt may not act as an attorney in relation to personal and health care matters. Those parts of a CPA which relate to personal or health care matters need not, therefore, be revoked by the donee's bankruptcy.

7.46 A bankrupt may not be appointed as a donee of powers over property and financial affairs in a CPA. The supervening bankruptcy of a donee revokes an EPA and so should the supervening bankruptcy of a donee of powers over property and affairs in a CPA revoke his or her appointment as the donee of such powers. The 1985 Act provides that where two or more attorneys are appointed to act jointly then the bankruptcy of any one should revoke the powers of all; where they may act jointly and severally, however, the bankruptcy of any of them does not revoke the powers of the others (1985 Act, Sched 3 paras 2 and 7). Similar provision is made in the draft Bill (Draft Bill, clause 20(3)(d)).

7.47 The authority of an attorney is revoked by the later bankruptcy of the donor. (*Markwick v Hardingham* (1880) 15 Ch 339). This rule applies to transactions relating to property of which the donor is divested by the vesting of it in the trustee in bankruptcy and it would not therefore apply to personal or health care matters. The 1985 Act did not give the rule a statutory form. In view of the fact that CPAs can extend beyond financial matters, express provision in the new legislation would be helpful.

We recommend that any part of a CPA which relates to matters other than property and financial affairs should not be revoked by the donor's bankruptcy. (Draft Bill, clause 16(6).)

Our draft legislation provides for the consequences of the partial revocation of a CPA so far as the registration of the document is concerned (Draft Bill, clause 18(2)).

7.48 The 1985 Act makes no specific provision for cases where a donor and donee who were married at the time the donee was appointed have subsequently divorced. Since a CPA cannot take effect immediately, but must first be registered, we think it appropriate to provide for such circumstances. The law already makes provision for the situation where a testator appointed a divorced spouse executor or beneficiary under his or her will (Wills Act 1837, s 18A). A donor of a CPA may be equally unable to remedy the original, now inappropriate, appointment.

We recommend that, in the absence of a contrary intention, the appointment of the donee's spouse as an attorney under a CPA should be revoked by the subsequent dissolution or annulment of the parties' marriage. (Draft Bill, clause 14(5).)

A reminder might helpfully be placed on the standard form decree absolute of divorce. By analogy with the case where one attorney becomes bankrupt but multiple attorneys have been appointed to act jointly and severally, the divorce between the donor and one of multiple joint and several donees should not terminate the powers of other donees to act (Draft Bill, clause 20(3)(d)).

Powers of the registration authority

7.49 The role of the registration authority should simply be (1) to register CPAs and give notice of registration, (2) to cancel registrations and (3) to amend registrations in cases of partial revocation or the appointment of replacement attorneys. Since the registration authority will be an administrative rather than a judicial body, cancellation or amendment should only be effected on the receipt of specified types of objective evidence. If a change to the registration requires a determination of some disputed fact, or the exercise of discretion, then the court will make the necessary determination and then give instructions to the registration authority.

We recommend that the registration authority should cancel the registration of a CPA on receipt of a revocation by the donor, a disclaimer by the donee or evidence that the power has expired or been revoked by death, bankruptcy, winding up or the dissolution of the parties' marriage. (Draft Bill, clause 18(1).)

The registration authority should attach an appropriate note to any registered CPA which has been partially revoked, or in relation to which a replacement donee has gained power to act. (Draft Bill, clause 18(2) and (5).)

The draft Bill provides that the registration authority should give notice to the donee in appropriate cases (clause 18(3)), and that instruments should be delivered up to the registration authority for cancellation (clause 18(6)).

Powers of the court

7.50 Under the 1985 Act, the Court of Protection was given some judicial control over attorneys acting under registered EPAs (s 8), and over attorneys where the donor is or is becoming mentally incapable (s 5). Although our scheme for CPAs distinguishes very clearly between the administrative powers of the registration authority and the judicial powers of the court, many of the court's powers over CPAs will mirror the powers of the Court of Protection in relation to EPAs. We will simply mention such powers here for the sake of completeness.

7.51 The court should have power to determine any question as to the meaning or effect of a CPA, whether the donor had capacity to create or revoke it, and whether it has been effectively revoked (1985 Act, s 8(2)(a), s 4(5) and s 8(3); draft Bill, clause 17(3)(a) and (b)).

7.52 It will be remembered that the fact that a CPA has been registered will in future signify only that the attorney expects to seek to use it, rather than that the donor is losing capacity. The powers of the court to direct or control the attorney should only arise in relation to matters where the donor no longer has capacity, and the draft Bill therefore provides that he court should have power to give directions to the attorney and to give any consent or authorisation which the donor might have given had he or she had capacity (1985 Act, s 8(2)(b)(i) and (d); draft Bill, clause 17(3)(a) and (b)).

7.53 The court should also retain some supervisory powers where donors of CPAs lack capacity. Thus, the court should have power to give directions to an attorney in relation to reports, accounts and records (1985 Act, s 8(2)(b)(ii); draft Bill, clause 17(5)(a)); to require an attorney to produce information, documents or things (1985 Act, s 8(2)(i); draft Bill, clause 17(5)(b)); to give directions to an attorney in relation to remuneration or expenses (1985 Act, s 8(2)(b)(iii); draft Bill, clause 17(5)(i)); and to relieve an attorney from liability for breach of duty (1985 Act, s 8(2)(f); draft Bill, clause 17(5)(d)). Where the court finds that fraud or undue pressure was used to induce the donor to create a purported CPA, it should have power to direct that the document shall not be registered, or to revoke it if it has been registered (1985 Act, s 8(4)(f) and (5); draft Bill, cause 17(6)(a)). Where it follows from the decision of the court that the registration of the CPA should be cancelled, then the court should have power to direct the registration authority to cancel the registration (Draft Bill, clause 18(4)).

7.54 We suggested in the consultation papers (Consultation Paper No 128, paras 7.35–7.37; Consultation Paper No 129, para 5.21) that it might be appropriate to extend the powers which the Court of Protection has possessed in relation to EPAs. All those who responded supported our provisional proposals and we now recommend that the court should have certain new and additional powers in relation to CPAs.

(1) A dispensing power

7.55 A number of our respondents expressed concern about the rejection of EPAs on 'pettifogging' technical grounds, in some cases the donor will have suffered irreversible loss of capacity by the time the rejection of registration is made, with the result that a technically valid EPA can no longer be executed. The 1985 Act does provide that a document which 'differs in an immaterial respect' from the prescribed form shall be treated as sufficient (1985 Act, s 2(6)). This is a useful provision of general application and we have retained it in our draft Bill. (Draft Bill, clause 13(4)). Respondents did, however, give an enthusiastic welcome to our provisional proposal for a wider power whereby a judicial forum could 'cure' technical defects in a document (Consultation Paper No 128, para 7.37; Consultation Paper No 129, para 5.21). This would enable the court to look to the intention of the donor in executing any document which fails to conform to all the prescribed formalities.

We recommend that the court should have power to declare that a document not in the prescribed form shall be treated as if it were in that form if the court is satisfied that the persons executing it intended it to create a CPA. (Draft Bill, clause 17(1).)

(2) Power to appoint a new attorney

7.56 We suggested in the consultation papers that the court might appoint a replacement attorney for an attorney who is unable or unwilling to act (ibid). Although this may appear to be a radical departure from the pure concepts of agency law which underlie the law on powers of attorney, none of our consultees expressed opposition to the suggestion. This suggests a general acceptance of the fact that strict agency principles have already been fundamentally altered by the statutory provision that an agency granted in an EPA can survive the incapacity of the principal. In the context of special statutory rules for CPAs, a donor may be better served by changes being made to a CPA which contains clear and valuable guidance to the attorney, than by the CPA being disregarded and a court-appointed manager being given a new set of powers. We would note that a number of our respondents saw no objection to the court simply 'appointing' an 'attorney' even where no attempt to appoint one has been made by the person concerned. This, we think, offends too greatly against the personal and contractual elements of the donor-donee relationship. On balance, however, we believe that the creation of a power in the court to appoint a new attorney can be justified. The question will be whether it is in the best interests of the donor to build on the provisions of the CPA even though the basis on which it was made has altered or, alternatively, to put the CPA on one side and appoint a manager. This is an example of the flexibility which can be achieved when the same judicial forum has jurisdiction over both CPAs and court-based decision-making. The court should not be able to act in this way if the donor has stipulated that it should not have power to appoint a new attorney.

We recommend that, subject to any contrary intention expressed in the document, the court should have power to appoint a donee in substitution for or in addition to the donee mentioned in a CPA. The court may act where the donor is without capacity to act and the court thinks it desirable to do so. (Draft Bill, clause 17(3)(c)(i).)

(3) Power to modify or extend the scope of CPA

7.57 In the consultation papers we suggested that the court might be given power to modify or extend the scope of an attorney's powers, though only if the donor had specifically directed that the court could do so (Consultation Paper No 128, para 7.37; Consultation Paper No 129, para 5.21). Few respondents commented specifically on this suggestion. The arguments which have to be balanced are similar to those discussed above in relation to a power to appoint a new attorney. Again, we take the view that a power to modify or extend the scope of the powers would sometimes be a useful one for the court to deploy in the best interests of the donor. For example, a donor may have appointed her husband as attorney with comprehensive financial powers over substantial assets. Once the donor has lost capacity, it may then transpire that a series of decisions will have to be taken about her medical treatment or about where she should live. Another family member may seek authority to take those decisions as a court-appointed manager. If the court takes the view that the husband should in fact take the personal and medical decisions as well then there would seem little objection to the scope of the existing CPA being extended to cover them. Again, however, the donor should be able to exclude the possibility of the court exercising the power to modify or extend the scope of the power.

We recommend that, subject to any contrary intention expressed in the document, the court should have power to modify or extend the scope of the donee's power to act. The court may act where the donor is without capacity to act and the court thinks it desirable to do so. (Draft Bill, clause 17(3)(c)(ii).)

(4) Power to revoke based on the donee's behaviour

7.58 The 1985 Act provides that the court shall cancel the registration of, and revoke, an EPA if 'the attorney is unsuitable to be the donor's attorney' (1985 Act, s 8(4)(g) and (5)). In Consultation Paper No 129 (para 5.22) we suggested that this power to revoke should be linked to the question of whether the attorney was acting in the donor's best interests. Respondents supported this proposal, with some seeking reassurance that the court should not be able to override a patient's advance decisions about health care by revoking the appointment of an attorney. We have already recommended that an attorney under a CPA should be under a duty to act in the donor's best interests. It is therefore logical to use this terminology, rather than that of 'unsuitability', in relation to the court's power to displace an attorney. Express provision should also be made for revocation by the court where an attorney's acts contravene the terms of the authority granted by the donor.

We recommend that the court may, on behalf of a donor without capacity to do so, either direct that a purported CPA should not be registered or revoke a CPA where the donee or intended donee has behaved, is behaving or proposes to behave in a way that (1) contravenes or would contravene the authority granted in the CPA or (2) is not or would not be in the donor's best interests. (Draft Bill, clause 17(6)(b).)

The Government's Green Paper, *Who Decides?* (Cm 3803, 1997) by and large supported the Law Commission's proposals whilst raising some detailed concerns (see paras 6.11–6.75).

The scheme is considered in the following extract.

Petra Wilson 'The Law Commission's Report on Mental Incapacity: Medically Vulnerable Adults or Politically Vulnerable Law?' (1996) 4 Med L Rev 227

Formalities of creation and enforcement. The Law Commission proposes that a CPA may be created only by a person over the age of 18 years. Although this goes against the general applicability of the new legislation, it is argued that the law in relation to parental responsibility and the inherent jurisdiction of the High Court over minors would pose too many complications if a person of 16 or 17 were allowed to create a CPA.

The donee of a CPA must also be a person over the age of 18 years, although it should be noted that the Law Commission recommends that such a person could be described as the holder for the time being of an office (Law Commission No 231 at paras 7.20–7.22 and Draft Bill Clauses 14(1) and 14(3)). It would be possible for the donor therefore to give all decision-making powers to the manager of a care home if she should want to do so, thus relieving her relatives of such a burden but ensuring that her specific wishes are registered in an official manner.

Where the document relates to the donor's property and affairs only, the donee may be a trust corporation (as with the EPA). In appointing a donee who will have powers over property and affairs, the EPA restriction on bankrupts should continue to apply, although bankruptcy should have no impact upon welfare decision-making powers (Law Commission No 231 at paras 7.45–7.47 and Draft Bill clause 16(6)).

In order to allow the donor maximum capacity to control her later life, the donor should be able to appoint joint and several donees (as with the EPA) and should be able to appoint an alternate donee should the first disclaim, die, or (where she has powers over property) be declared bankrupt (Law Commission No 231 at para 7.22 and Draft Bill clause 20(1)). Where the donee of the CPA is the spouse of the donor, a presumption should exist that if the parties divorce the powers of the donee should cease (Law Commission No 231 at para 7.48 and Draft Bill clause 14(5)).

As to the form of the document, its registration and execution, the Law Commission have proposed a very comprehensive set of rules. Most significant among these are that the donee must sign a statement that she understands that she must act in the donor's best interests which are defined on the basis of the contents of the CPA as well as the general guidelines on 'best interests' contained in the proposed legislation. In keeping with the stated aim of the Law Commission to propose legislation that would empower an incapacitated person to make as many decisions as she can, it recommends that upon registration of a CPA only two people nominated by the donor should have to be notified. This marks a considerable change from the EPA legislation which provides for a list of relatives to be notified but does not allow the donor to nominate people not related by blood or marriage (Law Commission No 231 at paras 7.37–7.39 and Draft Bill Clause 15(6)(b)).

For the security and comfort of the donor it is envisaged the CPA will only be operable once registered (unlike an EPA which may operate as an ordinary power of attorney without registration), however, registration should signify simply that the donee wishes to use the powers, not that the donor is losing or has lost her capacity to decide. Where a donor continues to have the capacity to make decisions, a contemporaneous decision-making power shall exist. Therefore, if a bank manager knows a CPA has been registered, but believes that the donor has the capacity to control her bank account, she may still accept instructions from the donor.

As already noted, one of the central aims of the proposed legislation is that in deciding the best interests of an incapacitated person, reference should be made to any known wishes of that person. Accordingly, it is proposed that where a purported CPA has not been properly created, or where for some reason the current needs of a donor without capacity are not met by the stipulations of the CPA, the Court should have the power to declare that the document nevertheless constitutes a CPA and also (subject to any contrary intention of the donor) to modify or extend the CPA in order to meet the incapacitated donor's needs (Law Commission No 231 at para 7.57 and Draft Bill clause 17(3)(c)(i)).

The donee of a CPA will be able to exercise a wide range of powers delegated to her by the donor, or in some cases by the court. However, the donee will not be under a duty to act. One might argue that it is unfortunate that the Law Commission did not envisage that a donee should have to act when the donor has trusted her to do so, although it is of course difficult to envisage how one might force a person to act and then demand that she do so in another's best interest. Where a donee refuses to act and the donor no longer has the capacity to appoint a new attorney, the court will be able to appoint a new attorney to ensure that the donor's wishes will be met (Law Commission No 231 at para 7.10 and Draft Bill clause 17(3)(c)(i)).

Restrictions on use. As the proposed CPA will apply to matters of personal welfare and health, as well as to financial matters, the Law Commission proposes particular restrictions on powers relating to non-financial matters. Generally, therefore, where the donee has powers over the health care of a person, the donee should be bound by the same general restriction as those acting under the 'general authority'. Thus the attorney may not coerce the donor or seek her confinement against her will, or refuse basic care on her behalf (Law Commission No 231 at para 7.12–7.16 and Draft Bill clauses 16(4)and 16(3)(c)). The potential powers of the attorney in matters of health care are however very wide, since the donor may indicate that she would wish her attorney to make *all* necessary health-care decisions for her, including those procedures which would otherwise need court approval or a certificate from an independent medical practitioner (Law Commission No 231 at para 7.12–7.16 and Draft Bill clause 16(3)(d)(ii)). The attorney may, therefore, if empowered, on the one hand override any advance refusal of treatment and may, on the other, refuse life-sustaining treatment on behalf of the donor even where no such advance refusal has been made (Law Commission No 231 at para 7.12–7.16 and Draft Bill clause 16(3)(d)(i)and 16(3)(d)(iii)). Furthermore, in contrast to the possible contemporaneous powers to decide financial matters of the donor and donee, in matters of health care the donee should only have decision-making powers where a doctor has decided, in accordance with the capacity test described above, that the donor does not have the requisite capacity to consent to a proposed treatment or procedure (Law Commission No 231 at para 7.14 and Draft Bill clause 16(3)(a)).

The Government has stated that it will enact the Law Commission's proposals, with some changes, when legislative time allows: *Making Decisions* (Cm 4465) (1999) ch 2. The Government intends to put in place further safeguards including prescribing the form of a CPA and requiring notification by the attorney to others *prior* to registration rather than after it (*op cit*).

The Law Commission referred in its 1985 Report to the 'living will' prepared by the Terrence Higgins Trust and the Centre of Medical Law and Ethics at King's College, London. This advance directive is, in fact, a model based upon the hybrid approach which we have seen emerging in North America, ie it incorporates both a power of attorney provision (currently legally ineffective) and anticipatory refusals. Its terms are as follows.

Living Will
Declaration

This is an important document. Before you fill it in, please read the notes which are attached to this form. We recommend that you discuss your Living Will with a doctor, but you do not have to.

Your name and address

Your name:

Your address:

I make this Living Will to record my wishes in case I become unable to communicate, and cannot take part in decisions about my medical care.

If you discuss this Living Will with a doctor before or after you fill it in, please fill in this section.

I have discussed this Living Will with the following doctor.
Doctor's name:

Doctor's address:

Doctor's phone number:

Living Will
Advance Directives

1 – Medical treatment in general

Three possible health conditions are described below.

For each condition, choose 'A' or 'B' by ticking the appropriate box, or leave both boxes blank if you have no preference.

The choice between 'A' and 'B' is exactly the same in each case.

Treat each case separately. You do not have to make the same choice for each one.

I declare that my wishes concerning medical treatment are as follows.

Case 1 – Life-threatening condition

Here are my wishes if:
- I have a physical illness from which there is no likelihood of recovery; *and*
- the illness is so serious that my life is nearing its end.

A I want to be kept alive for as long as is reasonably possible using whatever forms of medical treatment are available. ☐

B I do not want to be kept alive by medical treatment. I want medical treatment to be limited to keeping me comfortable and free from pain. ☐

I refuse all other medical treatment.

Case 2 – Permanent mental impairment

Here are my wishes if:
- my mental functions have become permanently impaired:
- the impairment is so severe that I do not understand what is happening to me:
- there is no likelihood of improvement; and
- my physical condition then becomes so bad that I would need medical treatment to keep me alive.

A I want to be kept alive for as long as is reasonably possible using whatever forms of medical treatment are available. ☐

B I do not want to be kept alive by medical treatment. I want medical treatment to be limited to keeping me comfortable and free from pain. ☐

I refuse all other medical treatment

Case 3 – Permanent unconsciousness

Here are my wishes if:
- I become permanently unconscious and there is no likelihood I will regain consciousness.

A I want to be kept alive for as long as is reasonably possible using whatever forms of medical treatment are available. ☐

B I do not want to be kept alive by medical treatment. I want medical treatment to be limited to keeping me comfortable and free from pain. ☐

I refuse all other medical treatment

Living Will
Advance Directives

2 – Particular treatments or tests

If you have any wishes about particular medical treatments or tests, you can record them here. If you want to refuse a particular treatment or test, you should say so clearly. You should speak to a doctor before you write anything in this space.

I have the following wishes about particular medical treatments or tests.

3 – Having a friend or relative with you if your life is in danger

You can fill in this section if you would like a particular person to be with you if your life is in danger. It may not be possible to contact the person you name, or for him or her to arrive in time.

If my life is in danger, I want the following person to be contacted to give him or her a chance to be with me before I die.

Name:

Address:

Daytime phone number: Evening phone number:

Tick this box if you fill in a name in this section, and you want to be kept alive for as long as is reasonable to give the person you name a chance to reach you. ☐

If you tick this box, any wishes you have stated above in Section 1 – *Medical treatment in general* and Section 2 – *Particular treatments or tests* may be **temporarily disregarded**. This is explained in the notes with this form.

Living Will
Health Care Proxy

I appoint the following person to take part in decisions about my medical care on my behalf and to represent my views about the decisions if I am unable to do so. I want him or her to be consulted about and involved in those decisions and I want anyone who is caring for me to respect the views he or she expresses on my behalf.

Name:

Address:

Daytime phone number: Evening phone number:

This Living Will remains effective until I make clear that my wishes have changed.

Signatures

Sign and date the form here in the presence of a witness.

Date:

Your signature:

The witness must sign here after you have signed the form. The witness should then print his or her name and address in the spaces provided. Please read the notes to this form to see who should not be a witness.

Signature of witness:

Name of witness:

Address of witness:

Before we leave the problem of decision-making in the case of incompetent patients we should, perhaps, notice one development rejected by the Law Commission but which has found favour in North America. You will recall we referred earlier to the 'fourth generation' of statutes in North America empowering family members to make decisions on behalf of the incompetent patient. These statutes allow family members to make decisions when the patient has not made an anticipatory decision nor created an enduring power of attorney. In other words, family members are allowed to act as proxies in default of the patient's exercising any choice. The background to these statutes and their content is described in the following extract.

Barry R Furrow et al *Health Law* vol 2 (1995)

17–23 ...physicians (and the courts) have been relying on families to make such health care decisions for most of the last century, despite the absence of any legal basis for the practice. In 1983, the President's Commission assumed (without citation to any authority) that such a longstanding practice must have gained legal acceptance, and the Commission pointed out five reasons that deference to family members is appropriate:

(1) The family is generally most concerned about the good of the patient. (2) The family will usually be the most knowledgeable about the patient's goals, preferences, and values. (3) The family deserves recognition as an important social unit that ought to be treated, within limits, as a responsible decision-maker in matters that intimately affect its members. (4) Especially in a society in which many other traditional forms of community have eroded, participation in a family is often an important dimension of personal fulfillment. (5) Since a protected sphere of privacy and autonomy is required for the flourishing of this interpersonal union, institutions and the state should be reluctant to intrude, particularly regarding matters that are personal and on which there is a wide range of opinion in society...

Growing concern over the formal legal status of family decision making in the 1980s caused many state legislatures to recognize the practice and regulate it by statute. These 'family consent' statutes vary from state to state. Some have been added to state living will statutes to provide a back-up mechanism for making decisions regarding life-sustaining treatment on behalf of those who did not execute any advance directive; others are free-standing statutes that either apply to life-sustaining treatment or health care decisions generally. While most statutes discourage families and health care workers from seeking judicial review of the vast majority of health care decisions made under the statutes (W Va Code § 16–30B–7 (providing that court approval is not required)), some require judicial confirmation of decisions which result in the death of the patient (Ohio Rev Code Ann § 2123.08 (requiring probable court approval before withdrawing artificial nutrition and hydration)).

Despite their differences, family consent statutes have many common attributes. They become effective only when the patient is incompetent, and some require a certificate that the patient is incompetent before the family is authorized to make any health care decision. They authorize designated close family members to act on behalf of the patient, although the procedure for designation of the family member varies from state to state. All of the statutes prescribe a hierarchy of family members, with agreement by all of the members at the highest available class required to make a decision on behalf of the patient. No state prescribes precisely the same hierarchy as that recognized for purposes of intestate succession in the state's probate code because state legislatures have recognized that the purposes of the probate code are not reflected in the need for surrogate decision makers, and an alternative hierarchy is appropriate. Because some statutes recognize that family members may not be available for these decisions, close friends are included in the hierarchy, typically at the lowest level (see Ariz. Rev. Stat § 36–3231 (also providing for a domestic partner)). In addition, instead of a rigid hierarchy, Colorado simply grants authority to a person who has a close relationship and who is most likely to be currently informed of the patient's wishes regarding medical treatment (West Colo. Rev. Stat Ann § 15–18.5–101). Two states provide that the decision making power rests with the physician, not the family, although the physician must consult with the family before deciding to terminate life-sustaining treatment (Conn. Gen. Stat. Ann § 19A–571; Harv. Rev. Stat § 327D–21). All family consent statutes provide that a patient's specific designations of health care decisionmakers (through a durable power of attorney, for example) or of particular decisions (through a living will, for example) take priority over a family member exercising authority under the statute. Thus, there can be no conflict between a living will or durable power and a family member's decisions: the decisions made in the living will, or by the agent appointed by the durable power, prevail over the family member's decisions.

Like living will statutes, family consent laws usually are permissive, not mandatory, upon health care providers. Family members and health care providers who act in accordance with consent given under the terms of the acts are relieved of liability for depending on such consent. Some family consent statutes formally recognize the principle of substituted judgment, and they require authorized family members to attempt to discover what the patient would wish if competent. Finally, family consent laws generally provide some mechanism for resort to the judiciary to resolve disputes among family members at similar levels in the hierarchy, and many provide that no resort to the judiciary is necessary absent such disputes.

Because the common law status of family decision making remains unclear, it is difficult to know whether a family consent statute necessarily preempts all nonstatutory family decision making, or whether the family consent statute operates only within the sometimes very limited scope of the statute itself. These new statutes have been the subject of very little litigation, perhaps because they do no more than bring formal recognition to an arrangement which is so clearly based in common sense and which has been accepted by the medical profession (and by families) for so long.

Common sense they may be, but the Law Commission would not contemplate such legislation! Commenting on this approach, the Law Commission in its Consultation Paper No 129 *Mentally Incapacitated Adults and Decision-Making: Medical Treatment and Research* stated:

3.68 A few respondents supported the introduction of a duty to seek the consent of relatives or others caring for an incapacitated patient. Recent legislation in Ontario provides that consent may be given or refused by the first person from a list of relatives, who is at least 16 and is available, capable and willing to give or refuse consent. The list includes: the patient's spouse or partner; child; parent; brother or sister; and any other relative.

3.69 The difficulty with such schemes is that no statutory list will ever identify the most appropriate relative in every case. While many people might trust their spouses to make decisions for them, fewer will have the same confidence in their nephews. The fact that a person is the patient's next of kin may not be enough if there has been no contact with the patient for twenty years. In the proposals in Alberta, relatives would not have authority to make health care decisions on the incapacitated person's behalf unless they have had personal contact with the patient at some time during the preceding twelve months. Under legislation in New South Wales, except in an emergency the consent of the 'person responsible' is required for all medical treatment other than treatments such as sterilisation which require the consent of the Guardianship Board. The person responsible is the patient's spouse, or if there is no spouse, the person who has care of the patient, unless the patient lives in institutional care, in which case it is the person who cared for him immediately before the admission.

3.70 We are not at present persuaded that there is a need to introduce a scheme which gives relatives or carers an automatic authority to consent to, and also to refuse, medical treatment on behalf of an incapacitated person. Although one respondent argued that relatives might only be provided with sufficient information if a treatment provider was required to seek their consent, we believe that an appropriately formulated duty to consult relatives would be a better response to this problem. In New South Wales it has been suggested that incapacitated patients may sometimes not receive treatment because of the formalities required to obtain the consent of the person responsible. The President of the Victorian Guardianship and Administration Board has suggested that if someone automatically has the legal authority to consent it is too easy for doctors just to accept that person's consent without making a proper assessment of the risks involved in a proposed treatment. In Consultation Paper No 128 we rejected an automatic authority for relatives, and we also do so in the context of medical treatment. The limited authority which we proposed for those who have care of an incapacitated person was intended to be no more than was required to allow the incapacitated person to be appropriately cared for. We do not believe that the interests of the incapacitated person require this to include an authority to give or refuse consent to medical treatment.

The furthest that the Law Commission would go in its 1985 report, *Mental Incapacity* (*op cit*), was to require consultation with any person named by the patient or having the care of the patient in determining the patient's 'best interests', at least to the extent that such consultation was 'practicable and appropriate' (Draft Mental Incapacity Bill, cl 3(2)(c)). Vesting decision-making power in family members also failed to find favour with the House of Lords Select Committee (*op cit*) and in the Government's Green Paper, *Who Decides? (op cit).*

Chapter 17

The end(ing) of life: the incompetent patient

In any analysis of the law relating to medical treatment at the end of life it was natural to start with a consideration of the position of the competent patient who is able to make his own decisions about treatment before considering the position of the incompetent patient. We have already seen in the previous chapter and Chapter 6 concerned with decision-making and incompetent patients in general, many of the issues which we will address in this chapter. Unlike the situation of the competent patient, the law is largely not concerned with decisions made by the patient themselves. Since, however, the decision may result in the death of the patient, the law is more problematic and courts are more hesitant.

An illustrative case

Although it is an American case, *In the Matter of Conroy* raises the issues that any common law courts would face.

In the Matter of Claire Conroy (1985) 486 A 2d 1209 (NJ Sup Ct)

Schrieber J: At issue here are the circumstances under which life-sustaining treatment may be withheld or withdrawn from incompetent, institutionalised, elderly patients with severe and permanent mental and physical impairments and a limited life expectancy...

At the time of trial, Ms Conroy was no longer ambulatory and was confined to bed unable to move from a semi-fetal position. She suffered from arteriosclerotic heart disease, hypertension, and diabetes mellitus; her left leg was gangrenous to her knee; she had several necrotic decubitus ulcers (bed sores) on her left foot, leg, and hip; an eye problem required irrigation; she had a urinary catheter in place and could not control her bowels; she could not speak; and her ability to swallow was very limited. On the other hand, she interacted with her environment in some limited ways: she could move her head, neck, hands, and arms to a minor extent; she was able to scratch herself, and had pulled at her bandages, tube and catheter; she moaned occasionally when moved or fed through the tube, or when her bandages were changed; her eyes sometimes followed individuals in the room; her facial expressions were different when she was awake from when she was asleep; and she smiled on occasions when her hair was combed, or when she received a comforting rub.

Dr Kazemi and Dr Davidoff, a specialist in internal medicine who observed Ms Conroy before testifying as an expert on behalf of the guardian, testified that Ms Conroy was not brain dead, comatose, or in a chronic vegetative state. They stated, however, that her intellectual capacity was very limited, and that her mental condition probably would never improve. Dr Davidoff characterised her as awake, but said that she was severely demented, was unable to respond to verbal stimuli, and, as far as he could tell, had no higher functioning or consciousness. Dr Kazemi, in contrast, said that although she was confused and unaware, 'she responds somehow'...

The starting point in analysing whether life-sustaining treatment may be withheld or withdrawn from an incompetent patient is to determine what rights a competent patient has to accept or reject medical care. It is therefore necessary at the outset of this discussion to identify the nature and extent of a patient's rights that are implicated by such decisions.

The right of a person to control his own body is a basic societal concept, long recognised in the common law:

No right is held more sacred, or is more carefully guarded by the common law, than the right of every individual to the possession and control of his own person, free from all restraint or interference of others, unless by clear and unquestionable authority of law. As well said by Judge Cooley, 'The right to one's person may be said to be a right of complete immunity: to be let alone.' Cooley on Torts, 29. [*Union Pac Rly Co v Botsford* 141 US 250 at 251, 11 *S Ct* 1000 at 1001, 35 *L Ed* 734, 737 (1891) (refusing to compel personal injury plaintiff to undergo pretrial medical examination).]

Accord Perna v Pirozzi, 92 NJ 446 at 459–65, 457, A 2d 431 (1983). Judge Cardozo succinctly captured the essence of this theory as follows: 'Every human being of adult years and sound mind has a right to determine what shall be done with his own body; and a surgeon who performs an operation without his patient's consent commits an assault, for which he is liable in damages.' *Schloendorff v Society of New York Hosp* 211 NY 125 at 129–30, 105 NE 92 at 93 (1914).

The doctrine of informed consent is a primary means developed in the law to protect this personal interest in the integrity of one's body. 'Under this doctrine, no medical procedure may be performed without a patient's consent, obtained after explanation of the nature of the treatment, substantial risks, and alternative therapies.' Cantor, 'A Patient's Decision to Decline Life-Saving Medical Treatment: Bodily Integrity Versus the Preservation of Life', 26 *Rutgers L Rev* 288, 237 (1973) (footnote omitted); see also *Perna v Pirozzi, supra*, 92 NJ at 461, 457 A 2d 431 ('Absent an emergency, patients have the right to determine not only whether surgery is to be performed on them, but who shall perform it').

The doctrine of informed consent presupposes that the patient has the information necessary to evaluate the risks and benefits of all the available options and is competent to do so. Cf Wanzer, Adelstein, Cranford, Federman, Hook, Moertel, Saar, Stone, Taussig & Van Eys, 'The Physician's Responsibility Toward Hopelessly Ill Patients', 310 *New Eng J Med* 955, 957 (1984) ('There are three basic prerequisites for informed consent: the patient must have the capacity to reason and make judgments, the decision must be made voluntarily and without coercion, and the patient must have a clear understanding of the risks and benefits of the proposed treatment alternatives or nontreatment, along with a full understanding of the nature of the disease and the prognosis'). In general, it is the doctor's role to provide the necessary medical facts and the patient's role to make the subjective treatment decision based on his understanding of those facts. Cf Hilfiker, *supra* 308 *New Eng J Med* at 718 (acknowledging that 'our ability [as doctors] to phrase opinions, stress information, and present our own advice gives us tremendous power').

The patient's ability to control his bodily integrity through informed consent is significant only when one recognises that this right also encompasses a right to informed refusal. Note 'Informed Consent and the Dying Patient', 83 *Yale LJ* 1632, 1648 (1974). Thus, a competent adult person generally has the right to decline to have any medical treatment initiated or continued. See *Superintendent of Belchertown State School v Saikewicz* 373 *Mass* 728 at 738, 370 *NE 2d* 417 at 424 (1977); In *Re Quackenbush*, 156 *NJ Super* 282 at 290, 383 *A 2d* 785 (Cty Ct 1978); cf *Bennan v Parsonnet*, 83 *NJL* 20 at 22–23, 26–27, 83 *A* 948 (Sup Ct 1912) (acknowledging common-law rule that patient is 'the final arbiter as to whether he shall take his chances with the operation or take his chances of living without it', but holding that surgeon had implied consent while patient was unconscious to perform necessary surgical operation).

The right to make certain decisions concerning one's body is also protected by the federal constitutional right of privacy. The Supreme Court first articulated the right of privacy in *Griswold v Connecticut*, 381 *US* 479, 85 *S Ct* 1678, 14 *L Ed 2d* 510 (1965), which held that married couples have a constitutional right to use contraceptives. The Court in *Roe v Wade* 410 *US* 113, 93 S *Ct* 705, 35 *L Ed 2d* 147 (1973), further extended its recognition of the privacy right to protect a woman's decision to abort a pregnancy although the woman's right to choose abortion directly conflicted with the state's legitimate and important interest in preserving the potentiality of fetal life. Finally, in *Quinlan, supra* 70 *NJ* at 40, 355 *A 2d* 647, we indicated that the right of privacy enunciated by the Supreme Court 'is broad enough to encompass a patient's decision to decline medical treatment under certain circumstances', even if that decision might lead to the patient's death. *Accord Saikewicz, supra*, 373 *Mass* at 738, 370 *NE 2d* at 424; *Quackenbush, supra*, 156 *NJ Super* at 289–90, 383 *A 2d* 785. While this right of privacy might apply in a case such as this, we need not decide that issue since the right to decline medical treatment is, in any event, embraced within the common-law right to self-determination. *Accord In Re Storar* 52 *NY 2d* 363 at 376–77, 420 *NE 2d* 64 at 70, 438 *NYS 2d* 266 at 272–73; *cert* denied, 454 *US* 858, 102 *S Ct* 309, 70 *L Ed 2d* 153 (1981); Note, 'Live or Let Die; Who Decides an Incompetent's Fate? In *Re Storar and Eichner*', *1982 BYUL Rev* 387, 390–92.

...In view of the case law, we have no doubt that Ms Conroy, if competent to make the decision and if resolute in her determination, could have chosen to have her nasogastric tube withdrawn. Her interest in freedom from nonconsensual invasion of her bodily integrity would outweigh any state interest in preserving life or in safeguarding the integrity of the medical profession. In addition, rejecting her artificial means of feeding would not constitute attempted suicide, as the decision would probably be based on a wish to be free of medical intervention rather than a specific intent to die, and her death would result, if at all, from her underlying medical condition, which included her inability to swallow. Finally, removal of her feeding tube would not create a public health or safety hazard, nor would her death leave any minor dependents without care or support...

Whether based on common-law doctrines or on constitutional theory, the right to decline life-sustaining medical treatment is not absolute. In some cases, it may yield to countervailing societal interests in sustaining the person's life. Courts and commentators have commonly identified four state interests that may limit a person's right to refuse medical treatment: preserving life, preventing suicide, safeguarding the integrity of the medical profession, and protecting innocent third parties. *See, eg Satz v Perlmutter* 362 *So 2d* at 162; *Re Spring, 380 Mass* 629, 640, 405 *NE 2d* 115, 123 (1980); *Comr of Correction v Myers*, 379 *Mass* 255, 261, 399 *NE 2d* 452, 456 (1979); *Saikewicz, supra*, 373 *Mass* at 728, 370 *NE 2d* at 425; *Re Torres, 357 NW 2d* 332, 339 (Minn 1984); *Re Colyer*, 99 *Wash 2d* 114, 121, 660 *P 2d* 738, 743 (1983); *President's Commission Report, supra*, at 31–32; Note, '*Re Storar:* The Right to Die and Incompetent Patients', 43 *U Pitt L Rev* 1087, 1092 (1982).

The state's interest in preserving life is commonly considered the most significant of the four state interests. *See, eg, Spring, supra*, 380 *Mass* at 633, 405 *NE 2d* at 119; *Saikewicz, supra*, 373 *Mass* at 740, 370 *NE 2d* at 425; *President's Commission Report, supra*, at 32. It may be seen as embracing two separate but related concerns: an interest in preserving the life of the particular patient, and an interest in preserving the sanctity of all life. Cantor, '*Quinlan*, Privacy, and the Handling of Incompetent Dying Patients', 30 *Rutgers L Rev* 239, 249 (1977); *see* Annas, 'In re Quinlan: Legal Comfort for Doctors', *Hastings Center Rep*, June 1976, at 29.

While both of these state interests in life are certainly strong, in themselves they will usually not foreclose a competent person from declining life-sustaining medical treatment for himself. This is because the life that the state is seeking to protect in such a situation is the life of the same person who has competently decided to forego the medical intervention; it is not some other actual or potential life that cannot adequately protect itself. *Cf Roe v Wade, supra*, 410 *US* 113, 93 *S Ct* 705, 35 *L Ed 2d* 147 (authorising state restrictions or proscriptions of woman's right to abortion in final trimester of pregnancy to protect viable fetal life); *State v Perricone*, 37 *NJ* 463, 181 *A 2d* 751, *cert* denied, 371 *US* 890, 83 *S Ct* 189, 9 *L Ed 2d* 124 (1962) (affirming trial court's appointment of guardian with authority to consent to blood transfusion for infant over parents' religious objections); *Muhlenberg Hosp v Patterson*, 128 *NJ Super* 498, 320 *A 2d* 518 (Law Div 1974) (authorising blood transfusion to save infant's life over parents' religious objections).

In cases that do not involve the protection of the actual or potential life of someone other than the decision maker, the state's indirect and abstract interest in preserving the life of the competent patient generally gives way to the patient's much stronger personal interest in directing the course of his own life. *See, eg, Quackenbush, supra*, 156 *NJ Super* at 290, 383 *A 2d* 785; *Cantor, supra*, 30 *Rutgers L Rev* at 249–50. Indeed, insofar as the 'sanctity of individual free choice and self-determination [are] fundamental constituents of life,' the value of life may be lessened rather than increased 'by the failure to allow a competent human being the right of choice'. *Saikewicz, supra*, 373 *Mass* at 742, *NE 2d* at 426; *see also* Cantor, *supra*, 30 *Rutgers L Rev*n at 250 ('Government tolerance of the choice to resist treatment reflects concern for individual self-determination, bodily integrity, and avoidance of suffering, rather than a depreciation of life's value.').

It may be contended that in conjunction with its general interest in preserving life, this state has a particular legislative policy of preventing suicide. *See NJSA* 30: 4–26.3a (subjecting any person who attempts suicide to temporary hospitalisation when the person's behaviour suggests the existence of mental illness and constitutes a peril to life, person, or property); *see also* NJSA 2C:11–6 ('A person who purposely aids another to commit suicide is guilty of a crime of the second degree if his conduct causes such suicide or an attempted suicide, and otherwise of a crime of the fourth degree.'). This state interest in protecting people from direct and purposeful self-destruction is motivated by, if not encompassed within, the state's more basic interest in preserving life. Thus, it is questionable whether it is a distinct state interest worthy of independent consideration.

In any event, declining life-sustaining medical treatment may not properly be viewed as an attempt to commit suicide. Refusing medical intervention merely allows the disease to take its natural course; if death were eventually to occur, it would be the result, primarily, of the underlying disease, and not the result of a self-inflicted injury. See *Satz v Perlmutter, supra*, 362 *So 2d* at 162; *Saikewicz, supra*, 373 *Mass* at 743 n 11, 370 *NE 2d* at 426 n 11; *Colyer, supra* 99 *Wash* 2d at 121, 660 *P 2d* at 743; *see also President's Commission Report, supra*, at 38 (summarising case law on the subject). But cf *Caulk*, NH 480 *A 2d* 93, 96–97 (1984) (stating that attempt of an otherwise healthy prisoner to starve himself to death because he preferred death to life in prison was tantamount to attempted suicide, and that the state, to prevent such suicide, could force him to eat). In addition, people who refuse life-sustaining medical treatment may not harbour a specific intent to die, *Saikewicz, supra*, 373 *Mass* at 743, n 11, 370 *NE* 2d at 426 n 11; rather, they may fervently wish to live, but to do so free of unwanted medical technology, surgery, or drugs, and without protracted suffering, see *Satz v Perlmutter, supra* 362 *So* 2d at 162–63 ('The testimony of Mr Perlmutter... is that he really wants to live, but [to] do so God and Mother Nature willing, under his own power.').

Recognising the right of a terminally ill person to reject medical treatment respects that person's intent, not to die, but to suspend medical intervention at a point consonant with the individual's view respecting a personally preferred manner of concluding life. Note, 'The Tragic Choice: Termination of Care for Patients in a Permanent Vegetative State', *51 NYUL Rev* 285, 310 (1976). The difference is between self-infliction or self-destruction and self-determination. See Byrn, 'Compulsory Lifesaving Treatment for the Competent Adult', 44 *Fordham L Rev* 1, 16–23 (1975). To the extent that our decision in *John F Kennedy Memorial Hosp v Heston, 58 NJ* 576, 581–82, 279 *A* 2d 670 (1971), implies the contrary, we now overrule it.

The third state interest that is frequently asserted as a limitation on a competent patient's right to refuse medical treatment is the interest in safeguarding the integrity of the medical profession. This interest, like the interest in preventing suicide, is not particularly threatened by permitting competent patients to refuse life-sustaining medical treatment. Medical ethics do not require medical intervention in disease at all costs. As long ago as 1624, Francis Bacon wrote, 'I esteem it the office of a physician not only to restore health, but to mitigate pain and dolours; and not only when such mitigation may conduce to recovery, but when it may serve to make a fair and easy passage.' *F Bacon, New Atlantis, quoted in* Mannes, 'Euthanasia vs The Right to Life', 27 *Baylor L Rev* 68, 69 (1975). More recently, we wrote in *Quinlan, supra*, 70 *NJ* at 47, 355 *A* 2d 647, that modern-day 'physicians distinguish between curing the ill and comforting and easing the dying; that they refuse to treat the curable as if they were dying or ought to die, and that they have sometimes refused to treat the hopeless and dying as if they were curable'. Indeed, recent surveys have suggested that a majority of practising doctors now approve of passive euthanasia and believe that it is being practised by members of the profession. See sources cited in *Storar, supra NY* 2d at 385–386 n 3, 420 *NE* 2d at 75–76 n 3, 438 *NYS* 2d at 277–78 n 3 (Jones J, dissenting), and in Collester, 'Death, Dying and the Law: A Prosecutorial View of the *Quinlan* Case', 30 *Rutgers L Rev* 304, n 3, 312 & n 27.

Moreover, even if doctors were exhorted to attempt to cure or sustain their patients under all circumstances, that moral and professional imperative, at least in cases of patients who were clearly competent, presumably would not require doctors to go beyond advising the patient of the risks of foregoing treatment and urging the patient to accept the medical intervention. *Storar, supra*, 52 *NY* 2d at 377, 420 *NE* 2d at 71, 438 *NYS* 2d at 273; see *Colyer, supra*, 99 *Wash* 2d at 121–23, 660 *P* 2d at 743–44, citing *Saikewicz, supra*, 373 *Mass* at 743–44, 370 *NE* 2d at 417. If the patient rejected the doctor's advice, the onus of that decision would rest on the patient, not the doctor. Indeed, if the patient's right to informed consent is to have any meaning at all, it must be accorded respect even when it conflicts with the advice of the doctor or the values of the medical profession as a whole.

The fourth asserted state interest in overriding a patient's decision about his medical treatment is the interest in protecting innocent third parties who may be harmed by the patient's treatment decision. When the patient's exercise of his free choice could adversely and directly affect the health, safety, or security of others, the patient's right of self-determination must frequently give way. Thus, for example, courts have required competent adults to undergo medical procedures against their will if necessary to protect the public health. *Jacobson v Massachusetts, 197 US 11, 25 S Ct 358, 49 L Ed* 643 (1905) (recognising enforceability of compulsory smallpox vaccination law); to prevent a serious risk to prison security, *Myers, supra 379 Mass* at 263, 265, 399 *NE* 2d at 457, 458 (compelling prisoner with kidney disease to submit to dialysis over his protest rather than acquiescing in his demand to be transferred to a lower-security prison); *accord Caulk, supra*, 480 *A* 2d at 96; or to prevent the emotional and financial abandonment of the patient's minor children, *Application of President & Directors of Georgetown College, Inc, 331 F* 2d 1000, 1008 (DC Cir), *cert* denied, 377 *US* 978, 84 *S Ct* 1883, 12 *L Ed* 2d 746 (1964) (ordering mother of seven-month-old infant to submit to blood transfusion over her religious objections because of the mother's 'responsibility to the community care for her infant'); *Holmes v Silver Cross Hosp, 340 F Supp* 125, 130 (ND Ill 1972) (indicating that patient's status as father of minor child might justify authorising blood transfusion to save his life despite his religious objections).

On balance, the right to self-determination ordinarily outweighs any countervailing state interests, and competent persons generally are permitted to refuse medical treatment, even at the risk of death. Most of the cases that have held otherwise, unless they involved the interest in protecting innocent parties, have concerned the patient's competency to make a rational and considered choice of treatment. See Annot, 93 *ALR* 3D 67, AT 80–85 (1979) ('Patient's Right To Refuse Treatment Allegedly Necessary to Sustain Life'). For example, in *Heston, supra, 58 NJ* 576, 270 *A* 2d 670, this Court approved a blood transfusion to save the life of a twenty-two-year-old Jehovah's Witness who had been severely injured and was rushed to the hospital for treatment, despite the fact that a tenet of her faith forbade blood transfusions. The evidence indicated that she was in shock on admittance to the hospital and was then or soon became disoriented and incoherent. Part of the Court's rationale was that hospitals, upon which patients' care is thrust, 'exist to aid the sick and the injured', *id 58 NJ* at 582, 279 *A* 2d 670, and that it is difficult for them to assess a patient's intent in an emergency and to determine whether a desire to refuse treatment is firmly and competently held, *id 58 NJ* at 581, 582, 279 *A* 2d 670. Similarly, courts in other states have authorised blood transfusions over the objections of Jehovah's Witnesses when the patient's opposition to the treatment was expressed in equivocal terms. *Compare Georgetown College, supra,* 331 F 2d at 1006–07 (authorising transfusion to save life of patient who said that for religious reasons she would not consent to the transfusion, but who seemed to indicate that she would not oppose the transfusion if court ordered it since it would not then be her responsibility), *and United States v George,* 239 *F Supp* 752, 753 (D Conn 1965) (transfusion was authorised for patient who told court that he would not agree to the transfusion, but volunteered that if the court ordered it he would not resist in any way since it would be the court's will and not his), *with Re Osborne,* 294 *A* 2d 372, 374, 375 (DC 1972) (stating that guardian should not be appointed to consent to transfusion on behalf of man who told court that he would be deprived of 'everlasting life' if compelled by a court to submit to the transfusion, and who explained, 'it is between me and Jehovah; not the courts...I'm willing to take my chances. My faith is that strong.')...

...We are now faced with [the] situation:...of elderly, formerly competent nursing-home residents who...are awake and conscious and can interact with their environment to a limited extent, but whose mental and physical functioning is severely and permanently impaired and whose life expectancy, even with the treatment, is relatively short. The capacities of such people, while significantly diminished, are not as limited as those of irreversibly comatose persons, and their deaths, while no longer distant, may not be imminent. Large numbers of aged, chronically ill, institutionalised persons fall within this general category.

Such people (like newborns, mentally retarded persons, permanently comatose individuals, and members of other groups with which this case does not deal) are unable to speak for themselves on life-and-death issues concerning their medical care. This does not mean, however, that they lack a right to self-determination. The right of an adult who, like Claire Conroy, was once competent, to determine the course of her medical treatment remains intact even when she is no longer able to assert that right or to appreciate its effectuation. *John F Kennedy Memorial Hosp., Inc. v Bludworth,* 452 So.2d 921, 924 (Fla. 1984). As one commentator has noted:

> Even if the patient becomes too insensate to appreciate the honoring of his or her choice, self-determination is important. After all, law respects testamentary dispositions even if the testator never views his gift being bestowed. [Cantor, *supra, 30 Rutgers L. Rev.* at 259.]

...Any other view would permit obliteration of an incompetent's panoply of rights merely because the patient could no longer sense the violation of those rights. [*Id.* At 252.]

Since the condition of an incompetent patient makes it impossible to ascertain definitively his present desires, a third party acting on the patient's behalf often cannot say with confidence that his treatment decision for the patient will further rather than frustrate the patient's right to control his own body. Cf Smith, '*In Re Quinlan*: Defining the Basis for Terminating Life Support Under the Right of Privacy', 12 *Tulsa LJ* 150, 161 (1976) (arguing that permitting a guardian to make personal medical decisions for an incompetent patient actually interferes with the patient's right of privacy). Nevertheless, the goal of decision-making for incompetent patients should be to determine and effectuate, insofar as possible, the decision that the patient would have made if competent. Ideally, both aspects of the patient's right to bodily integrity – the right to consent to medical intervention and the right to refuse it – should be respected.

In light of these rights and concerns, we hold that life-sustaining treatment may be withheld or withdrawn from an incompetent patient when it is clear that the particular patient would have refused the treatment under the circumstances involved. The standard we are enunciating is a subjective one, consistent with the notion that the right that we are seeking to effectuate is a very personal right to control one's own life. The question is not what a reasonable or average person would have chosen to do under the circumstances but what the particular patient would have done if able to choose for himself.

The patient may have expressed, in one or more ways, an intent not to have life-sustaining medical intervention. Such an intent might be embodied in a written document, or 'living will', stating the person's desire not to have certain types of life-sustaining treatment administered under certain circumstances. It might also be evidenced in an oral directive that the patient gave to a family member or friend, or health care provider. It might consist of a durable power of attorney or appointment of a proxy authorising a particular person to make the decisions on the patient's behalf if he is no longer capable of making them for himself. See *NJSA* 46; 2b–8 (providing that principal may confer authority on agent that is to be exercisable 'notwithstanding later disability or incapacity of the principal at law or later uncertainty as to whether the principal is dead or alive'). It might take the form of reactions that the patient voiced regarding medical treatment administered to others. See, eg, *Storar, supra,* 52 *NY* 2d 363, 420 *NE* 2d 64, 438 *NYS* 2d 266 (withdrawal of respirator was justified as an effectuation of patient's stated wishes when patient, as member of Catholic religious order, had stated more than once in formal discussions concerning the moral implications of the *Quinlan* case, most recently two months before he suffered cardiac arrest that left him in an irreversible coma, that he would not want extraordinary means used to keep him alive under similar circumstances). It might also be deduced from a person's religious beliefs and the tenets of that religion, *id* at 378, 420 *NE* 2d at 72, 438 *NYS* 2d at 274, or from the patient's consistent pattern of conduct with respect to prior decisions about his own medical care. Of course, dealing with the matter in advance in some sort of thoughtful and explicit way is best for all concerned.

Any of the above types of evidence, and any other information bearing on the person's intent, may be appropriate aides in determining what course of treatment the patient would have wished to pursue. In this respect, we now believe that we were in error in *Quinlan, supra, 70 NJ* at 21, 41, 355 *A* 2d 647, to disregard evidence of statements that Ms Quinlan made to friends concerning artificial prolongation of the lives of others who were terminally ill. See criticism of this portion of *Quinlan* opinion in Collester, *supra, 30 Rutgers L Rev* at 318; Smith, *supra, 12 Tulsa LJ* at 163; and *D Meyers, supra,* at 282 n 65. Such evidence is certainly relevant to shed light on whether the patient would have consented to the treatment if competent to make the decision.

Although all evidence tending to demonstrate a person's intent with respect to medical treatment should properly be considered by surrogate decision-makers, or by a court in the event of any judicial proceedings, the probative value of such evidence may vary depending on the remoteness, consistency, and thoughtfulness of the prior statements or actions and the maturity of the person at the time of the statements or acts. *Colyer, supra, 99 Wash* 2d at 131, 660 *P* 2d at 748. Thus, for example, an offhand remark about not wanting to live under certain circumstances made by a person when young and in the peak of health would not in itself constitute clear proof twenty years later that he would want life-sustaining treatment withheld under those circumstances. In contrast, a carefully considered position, especially if written, that a person had maintained over a number of years or that he had acted upon in comparable circumstances might be clear evidence of his intent.

Another factor that would affect the probative value of a person's prior statements of intent would be their specificity. Of course, no one can predict with accuracy the precise circumstances with which he ultimately might be faced. Nevertheless, any details about the level of impaired functioning and the forms of medical treatment that one would find tolerable should be incorporated into advance directives to enhance their later usefulness as evidence.

Medical evidence bearing on the patient's condition, treatment and prognosis, like evidence of the patient's wishes, is an essential prerequisite to decision-making under the subjective test. The medical evidence must establish that the patient fits within the Claire Conroy pattern: an elderly, incompetent nursing-home resident with severe and permanent mental and physical impairments and a life expectancy of approximately one year or less. In addition, since the goal is to effectuate the patient's right of informed consent, the surrogate decision-maker must have at least as much medical information upon which to base his decision about what the patient would have chosen as one would expect a competent patient to have before consenting to or rejecting treatment. Such information might include evidence about the patient's present level of physical, sensory, emotional, and cognitive functioning; the degree of physical pain resulting from the medical condition, treatment, and termination of treatment, respectively; the degree of humiliation, dependence, and loss of dignity probably resulting from the condition and treatment; the life expectancy and prognosis for recovery with and without treatment' the various treatment options; and the risks, side effects, and benefits of each of those options. Particular care should be taken not to base a decision on a premature diagnosis or prognosis. See *Colyer, supra 99 Wash* 2d at 143–45, 660 *P* 2d at 754–55 (Dore J, dissenting).

We recognise that for some incompetent patients it might be impossible to be clearly satisfied as to the patient's intent either to accept or reject the life-sustaining treatment. Many people may have spoken of their desires in general or casual terms, or, indeed, never considered or resolved the issue at all. In such cases, a surrogate decision-maker cannot presume that treatment decisions made by a third party on the patient's behalf will further the patient's right to self-determination, since effectuating another person's right to self-determination presupposes that the substitute decision-maker knows what the person would have wanted. Thus, in the absence of adequate proof of the patient's wishes, it is naive to pretend that the right to self-determination serves as the basis for substituted decision-making. See *Storar, supra, 52 NY* 2d at 378–380, 420 *NE* 2d at 72–73, 438 *NYS* 2d at 274–75; Veatch,

'an Ethical Framework for Terminal Care Decisions: A New Classification of Patients',
32(9) *J Am Geriatrics Soc'y*, 666 (1984).

We hesitate, however, to foreclose the possibility of humane actions, which may involve
termination of life-sustaining treatment, for persons who never clearly expressed their desires
about life-sustaining treatment but who are now suffering a prolonged and painful death. An
incompetent, like a minor child, is a ward of the state, and the state's *parens patriae* power
supports the authority of its courts to allow decisions to be made for an incompetent that
serve the incompetent's best interests, even if the person's wishes cannot be clearly established.
This authority permits the state to authorise guardians to withhold or withdraw life-sustaining
treatment from an incompetent patient if it is manifest that such action would further the
patient's best interests in a narrow sense of the phrase, even though the subjective test that
we articulated above may not be satisfied. We therefore hold that life-sustaining treatment
may also be withheld or withdrawn from a patient in Claire Conroy's situation if either of
two 'best interests' tests – a limited-objective or a pure-objective test – is satisfied.

Under the limited-objective test, life-sustaining treatment may be withheld or withdrawn
from a patient in Claire Conroy's situation when there is some trustworthy evidence that the
patient would have refused the treatment, and the decision-maker is satisfied that it is clear that
the burdens of the patient's continued life with the treatment outweigh the benefits of that life
for him. By this we mean that the patient is suffering, and will continue to suffer throughout the
expected duration of his life, unavoidable pain, and that the net burdens of his prolonged life
(the pain and suffering of his life with the treatment less the amount and duration of pain that
the patient would likely experience if the treatment were withdrawn) markedly outweigh any
physical pleasure, emotional enjoyment, or intellectual satisfaction that the patient may still be
able to derive from life. This limited-objective standard permits the termination of treatment
for a patient who had not unequivocally expressed his desires before becoming incompetent,
when it is clear that the treatment in question would merely prolong the patient's suffering.

Medical evidence will be essential to establish that the burdens of the treatment to the
patient in terms of pain and suffering outweigh the benefits that the patient is experiencing.
The medical evidence should make it clear that the treatment would merely prolong the patient's
suffering and not provide him with any net benefit. Information is particularly important with
respect to the degree, expected duration, and constancy of pain with and without treatment, and
the possibility that the pain could be reduced by drugs or other means short of terminating the
life-sustaining treatment. The same types of medical evidence that are relevant to the subjective
analysis, such as the patient's life expectancy, prognosis, level of functioning, degree of
humiliation and dependency, and treatment options, should also be considered.

This limited-objective test also requires some trustworthy evidence that the patient would
have wanted the treatment terminated. This evidence could take any one or more of the
various forms appropriate to prove the patient's intent under the subjective test. Evidence
that, taken as a whole, would be too vague, casual, or remote to constitute the clear proof of
the patient's subjective intent that is necessary to satisfy the subjective test – for example,
informally expressed reactions to other people's medical conditions and treatment – might
be sufficient to satisfy this prong of the limited-objective test.

In the absence of trustworthy evidence, or indeed any evidence at all, that the patient
would have declined the treatment, life-sustaining treatment may still be withheld or
withdrawn from a formerly competent person like Claire Conroy if a third, pure-objective
test is satisfied. Under that test, as under the limited-objective test, the net burdens of the
patient's life with the treatment should clearly and markedly outweigh the benefits that the
patient derives from life. Further, the recurring, unavoidable and severe pain of the patient's
life with the treatment should be such that the effect of administering life-sustaining treatment
would be inhumane. Subjective evidence that the patient would not have wanted the treatment
is not necessary under this pure-objective standard. Nevertheless, even in the context of severe
pain, life-sustaining treatment should not be withdrawn from an incompetent patient who had
previously expressed a wish to be kept alive in spite of any pain that he might experience.

Although we are condoning a restricted evaluation of the nature of a patient's life in terms
of pain, suffering, and possible enjoyment under the limited-objective and pure-objective
tests, we expressly decline to authorise decision-making based on assessments of the personal
worth or social utility of another's life, or the value of that life to others. We do not believe
that it would be appropriate for a court to designate a person with the authority to determine
that someone else's life is not worth living simply because, to that person, the patient's
'quality of life' or value to society seems negligible. The mere fact that a patient's functioning
is limited or his prognosis dim does not mean that he is not enjoying what remains of his life
or that it is in his best interests to die. But cf *In Re Dinnerstein, 6 Mass App Ct* 466 at 473,
380 *NE* 2d 134 at 138 (1978) (indicating, in reference to possible resuscitation of half-
paralysed, elderly victim of Alzheimer's disease, that prolongation of life is not required if
there is no hope to return to a 'normal, integrated, functioning, cognitive existence'); see

also *President's Commission Report, supra*, at 135 (endorsing termination of treatment whenever surrogate decision-maker in his discretion believes it is in the patient's best interests, defined broadly to 'take into account such factors as the relief of suffering, the preservation or restoration of functioning, and the quality as well as the extent of life sustained'). More wide-ranging powers to make decisions about other people's lives, in our view, would create an intolerable risk for socially isolated and defenceless people suffering from physical or mental handicaps.

We are aware that it will frequently be difficult to conclude that the evidence is sufficient to justify termination of treatment under either of the 'best interests' tests that we have described. Often, it is unclear whether and to what extent a patient such as Claire Conroy is capable of, or is in fact, experiencing pain. Similarly, medical experts are often unable to determine with any degree of certainty the extent of a nonverbal person's intellectual functioning or the depth of his emotional life. When the evidence is insufficient to satisfy either the limited-objective or pure-objective standard, however, we cannot justify the termination of life-sustaining treatment as clearly furthering the best interests of a patient like Ms Conroy.

The surrogate decision-maker should exercise extreme caution in determining the patient's intent and in evaluating medical evidence of the patient's pain and possible enjoyment, and should not approve withholding or withdrawing life-sustaining treatment unless he is manifestly satisfied that one of the three tests that we have outlined has been met. Cf *In Re Grady*, 85 *NJ* 235, at 266, 426, *A* 2d 467 (1981) (requiring that evidence be clear and convincing before a court would approve sterilisation of an incompetent, mentally retarded adult). When evidence of a person's wishes or physical or mental condition is equivocal, it is best to err, if at all, in favour of preserving life. See *Osborne, supra*, 294 *A* 2d at 374 (stating in dictum that when a patient is 'suffering impairment of capacity for choice, it may be better to give weight to the known instinct for survival'); Dyck, 'Ethical Aspects of Care for the Dying Incompetent', 32(9) *J Am Geriatrics Soc'y* 661, 663 (1984). ('[S]ituations in which [decision-makers] are uncertain about what is best should be resolved in favor of extending life where possible.') Or, as one writer has said as a justification for requiring a high degree of safety and certainty of diagnosis in the determination of brain death; '[I]f there is a lot to lose by being wrong, it is generally better to stick to the safer, known way in the absence of the highest probability for proceeding otherwise.' D Walton, *Ethics of Withdrawal of Life-Support Systems: Case Studies on Decision Making in Intensive Care 82* (1983).

In the event, the court determined that the evidence did not satisfy any of the three tests laid down by the court. However, since Ms Conroy had subsequently died the case was not remanded to the trial court for further hearing. Examining the evidence Schrieber J concluded as follows:

The evidence that Claire Conroy would have refused the treatment, although sufficient to meet the lower showing of intent required under the limited-objective test, was certainly not the 'clear' showing of intent contemplated under the subjective test. More information should, if possible, have been obtained by the guardian with respect to Ms Conroy's intent. What were her ethical, moral, and religious beliefs? She did try to refuse initial hospitalisation, and indeed had 'scorned medicine'. 188 *NJ Super* at 525, 457 *A* 2d 1232. However, she allowed her nephew's wife, a registered nurse, to care for her during several illnesses. It was not clear whether Ms Conroy permitted the niece to administer any drugs or other forms of medical treatment to her during these illnesses. Although it may often prove difficult, and at times impossible, to ascertain a person's wishes, the Conroy case illustrates the sources to which the guardian might turn. For example, in more than eight decades of life in the same house, it is possible that she revealed to persons other than her nephew her feelings regarding medical treatments, other values, and her goals in life. Some promising avenues for such an inquiry about her personal values included her response to the illnesses and deaths of her sisters and others, and her statements with respect to not wanting to be in a nursing home.

Moreover, there was insufficient information concerning the benefits and burdens of Ms Conroy's life to satisfy either the limited-objective or pure-objective test. Although the treating doctor and the guardian's expert testified as to Claire Conroy's condition, neither testified conclusively as to whether she was in pain or was capable of experiencing pain or thirst. There was medical agreement that removal of the tube would have caused pain during the period of approximately one week that would have elapsed before her death, or at least until she were to lapse into a coma. On the other hand, there was little, if any, evidence of the discomfort, suffering, and pain she would endure if she continued to be fed and medicated through the tube during her remaining life – contemplated to be up to one year. Apparently her feedings sometimes occasioned moaning, but it remains unclear whether these were reflex responses or expressions of discomfort. Moreover, although she tried to remove the tube, it is not clear that this was intentional, and there was little evidence that she was in distress. Her treating physician also offered contradictory views as to whether the contractures of her legs caused pain or whether, indeed, they might be the result of pain, without offering any evidence on that issue. The trial court rejected as superfluous the offer to present as an expert witness a neurologist, who might have been able to explain what Ms Conroy's reaction to the environment indicated about her perception of pain.

The evidence was also unclear with respect to Ms Conroy's capacity to feel pleasure, another issue as to which the information supplied by a neurologist might have been helpful. What was known of her awareness of the world? Although Ms Conroy had some ability to smile and scratch, the relationship of these activities to external stimuli apparently was quite variable.

The trial transcript reveals no exploration of the discomfort and risks that attend nasogastric feedings. A casual mention by the nurse/administrator of the need to restrain the patient to prevent the removal of the tube was not followed by an assessment of the detrimental impact, if any, of those restraints. Alternative modalities, including gastrostomies, intravenous feeding, subcutaneous or intramuscular hydration, or some combination, were not investigated. Neither of the expert witnesses presented empirical evidence regarding the treatment options for such a patient.

It can be seen that the evidence at trial was inadequate to satisfy the subjective, the limited-objective, or the pure-objective standard that we have set forth.

You will see that the New Jersey Supreme Court established a procedural framework within which treatment decisions at the end of life should be made. We are not concerned with that framework here since it relates to the particular law of New Jersey and has little relevance in England. Subsequently, in a series of cases, the court expanded upon its framework and broadened its application: see *Re Peter* (1987) 529 A 2d 419; *Re Jobes* (1987) 529 A 2d 434; *Re Farrell* (1987) 529 A 2d 404 (a competent patient). (For a discussion by one of the Justices of the Court, see S Pollock 'Life and Death Decisions: Who Makes Them and by What Standards?' (1989) 41 Rutgers LR 505.)

However, a number of matters in *Conroy* are important for us here. First, there are the substantive principles identified by the court, in particular, its adoption of the three tests: '*the subjective*', the '*limited-objective*' and the '*pure-objective*' tests. We will see shortly how the English law resolves the same question and whether its approach is the same or similar to that adopted in *Conroy*.

Secondly, *Conroy* acknowledges that the law must strike a balance between its concern for a patient's right of self-determination and society's interests, which may conflict (see *supra*, ch 6).

Thirdly, the court exposes the fallacies in a number of arguments often marshalled in cases concerning treatment decisions at the end of life, for example, between ordinary and extraordinary treatment and withdrawing and withholding treatment.

The value of our setting out at some length the decision in *Conroy* is that it offers a *tour d'horizon* of this difficult area. This is not to say that *Conroy* is the last word on the subject. Indeed, later cases in New Jersey and elsewhere demonstrated the imperfections of *Conroy* and improved upon it. *Conroy* is nevertheless a significant decision because of the court's struggle to develop a comprehensive legal framework. As such it represented a considerable advance upon the earlier case law and, in particular, the much relied upon (yet much criticised) decision of the Massachusetts' Supreme Judicial Court in *Saikewicz*.

Superintendent of Belchertown v Saikewicz (1977) 370 NE 2d 417 (Mass Sup Jud Ct)

Liacos J:...Joseph Saikewicz, at the time the matter arose, was sixty-seven years old, with an IQ of ten and a mental age of approximately two years and eight months. He was profoundly mentally retarded. The record discloses that, apart from his leukemic condition, Saikewicz enjoyed generally good health. He was physically strong and well built, nutritionally nourished, and ambulatory. He was not, however, able to communicate verbally – resorting to gestures and grunts to make his wishes known to others and responding only to gestures or physical contacts. In the course of treatment for various medical conditions arising during Saikewicz's residency at the school, he had been unable to respond intelligibly to inquiries such as whether he was experiencing pain. It was the opinion of a consulting psychologist, not contested by the other experts relied on by the judge below, that Saikewicz was not aware of dangers and was disoriented outside his immediate environment. As a result of his condition Saikewicz had lived in State institutions since 1923 and had resided at the Belchertown State School since 1928. Two of his sisters, the only members of his family who could be located, were notified of his condition and of the hearing, but they preferred not to attend or otherwise become involved.

On April 19, 1976, Saikewicz was diagnosed as suffering from acute myeloblastic momocytic leukemia...

Chemotherapy, as was testified at the hearing in the Probate Court, involves the administration of drugs over several weeks, the purpose of which is to kill the leukemia cells. This treatment unfortunately affects normal cells as well...Estimates of the effectiveness of chemotherapy are complicated in cases, such as the one presented here, in which the patient's age becomes a factor. According to the medical testimony before the court below, persons over age sixty have more difficulty tolerating chemotherapy and the treatment is likely to be less successful than in younger patients. This prognosis may be compared with the doctor's estimates that, left untreated, a patient in Saikewicz's condition would live for a matter of weeks or, perhaps, several months. According to the testimony, a decision to allow the disease to run its natural course would not result in pain for the patient, and death would probably come without discomfort.

An important facet of the chemotherapy process, to which the judge below directed careful attention, is the problem of serious adverse side effects caused by the treating drugs. Among these side effects are severe nausea, bladder irritation, numbness and tingling of the extremities, and loss of hair. The bladder irritation can be avoided, however, if the patient drinks fluids, and the nausea can be treated by drugs. It was the opinion of the guardian *ad litem*, as well as the doctors who testified before the probate judge, that most people elect to suffer the side effects of chemotherapy rather than to allow their leukemia to run its natural course.

Drawing on the evidence before him, including the testimony of the medical experts, and the report of the guardian *ad litem*, the probate judge issued detailed findings, with regard to the costs and benefits of allowing Saikewicz to undergo chemotherapy. The judge's findings are reproduced in part here because of the importance of clearly delimiting the issues presented in this case. The judge below found:

5. That the majority of persons suffering from leukemia who are faced with a choice of receiving or foregoing such chemotherapy, and who are able to make an informed judgment thereon, choose to receive treatment in spite of its toxic side effects and risks of failure.
6. That such toxic side effects of chemotherapy include pain and discomfort, depressed bone marrow, pronounced anemia, increased chance of infection, possible bladder irritation, and possible loss of hair.
7. That administration of such chemotherapy requires cooperation from the patient over several weeks of time, which cooperation said Joseph Saikewicz is unable to give due to his profound retardation.
8. That, considering the age and general state of health of said Joseph Saikewicz, there is only a 30–40 percent chance that chemotherapy will produce a remission of said leukemia, which remission would probably be for a period of time of from 2 to 13 months, but that said chemotherapy will certainly not completely cure such leukemia.
9. That if such chemotherapy is to be administered at all it should be administered immediately, inasmuch as the risks involved will increase and the chances of successfully bringing about remission will decrease as time goes by.
10. That, at present, said Joseph Saikewicz's leukemia condition is stable and is not deteriorating.
11. That said Joseph Saikewicz is not now in pain and will probably die within a matter of weeks or months a relatively painless death due to the leukemia unless other factors should intervene to themselves cause death.
12. That it is impossible to predict how long said Joseph Saikewicz will probably live without chemotherapy or how long he will probably live with chemotherapy, but it is to a very high degree medically likely that he will die sooner, without treatment than with it.

Balancing these various factors, the judge concluded that the following considerations weighed *against* administering chemotherapy to Saikewicz: '(1) his age, (2) his inability to cooperate with the treatment, (3) probable adverse side effects of treatment, (4) low chance of producing remission, (5) the certainty that treatment will cause immediate suffering, and (6) the quality of life possible for him even if the treatment does bring about remission.'

The following considerations were determined to weigh in *favor* of chemotherapy: '(1) the chance that his life may be lengthened thereby; and (2) the fact that most people in his situation when given a chance to do so elect to take the gamble of treatment.'

Concluding that, in this case, the negative factors of treatment exceeded the benefits, the probate judge ordered on May 13, 1976, that no treatment be administered to Saikewicz for his condition of acute myeloblastic momocytic leukemia except by further order of the court. The judge further ordered that all reasonable and necessary supportive measures be taken, medical or otherwise, to safeguard the well-being of Saikewicz in all other respects and to reduce as far as possible any suffering or discomfort which he might experience.

...Saikewicz died on September 4, 1976, at the Belchertown State School hospital. Death was due to bronchial pneumonia, a complication of the leukemia. Saikewicz died without pain or discomfort.

...The question what legal standards govern the decision whether to administer potentially life-prolonging treatment to an incompetent person encompasses two distinct and important subissues. First, does a choice exist? That is, is it the unvarying responsibility of the State to order medical treatment in all circumstances involving the care of an incompetent person? Second, if a choice does exist under certain conditions, what considerations enter into the decision-making process?

We think that principles of equality and respect for all individuals require the conclusion that a choice exists...we recognize a general right in all persons to refuse medical treatment in appropriate circumstances. The recognition of that right must extend to the case of an incompetent, as well as a competent, patient because the value of human dignity extends to both.

This is not to deny that the State has a traditional power and responsibility, under the doctrine of *parens patriae*, to care for and protect the 'best interests' of the incompetent person. Indeed, the existence of this power and responsibility has impelled a number of courts to hold that the 'best interests' of such a person mandate an unvarying responsibility by the courts to order necessary medical treatment for an incompetent person facing an immediate and severe danger to life. *Application of the President & Directors of Georgetown College, Inc,* 118 US App DC 80, 331 F 2d 1000; cert denied 377 US 978, 84 S Ct 1883, 12 L Ed 2d 746 (1964). *Long Island Jewish-Hillside Medical Center v Levitt,* 73 Misc 2d 395, 342 NYS 2d 356 (NY Sup Ct 1973). Cf *In Re Weberlist,* 79 Misc 2d 753, 360 NYS 2d 783 (NY Sup Ct 1974). Whatever the merits of such a policy where life-saving treatment is available – a situation unfortunately not presented by this case – a more flexible view of the 'best interests' of the incompetent patient is not precluded under other conditions. For example, other courts have refused to take it on themselves to order certain forms of treatment or therapy which are not immediately required although concededly beneficial to the innocent person. *In Re CFB* 497 SW 2d 831 (Mo App 1973). *Green's Appeal,* 448 Pa 338, 292 A 2d 387 (1972). *In Re Frank,* 41 Wash 2d 294, 248 P 2d 553 (1952). Cf *In Re Rotkowitz,* 175 Misc 948, 25 NYS 2d 624 (NY Dom Rel Ct 1941); *Mitchell v Davis,* 205 SW 2d 812 (Tex App 1947). While some of these cases involved children who might eventually be competent to make the necessary decisions without judicial interference, it is also clear that the additional period of waiting might make the task of correction more difficult. See, eg, *In Re Frank, supra.* These cases stand for the proposition that, even in the exercise of the *parens patriae* power, there must be respect for the bodily integrity of the child or respect for the rational decision of those parties, usually the parents, who for one reason or another are seeking to protect the bodily integrity or other personal interest of the child. See *In Re Hudson,* 13 Wash 2d 673, 126 P 2d 765 (1942).

The 'best interests' of an incompetent person are not necessarily served by imposing on such persons results not mandated as to competent persons similarly situated. It does not advance the interest of the State or the ward to treat the ward as a person of lesser status or dignity than others. To protect the incompetent person within its power, the State must recognize the dignity and worth of such a person and afford to that person the same panoply of rights and choices it recognizes in competent persons. If a competent person faced with death may choose to decline treatment which not only will not cure the person but which substantially may increase suffering in exchange for a possible yet brief prolongation of life, then it cannot be said that it is always in the 'best interests' of the ward to require submission to such treatment. Nor do statistical factors indicating that a majority of competent persons similarly situated choose treatment resolve the issue. The significant decisions of life are more complex than statistical determinations. Individual choice is determined not by the vote of the majority but by the complexities of the singular situation viewed from the unique perspective of the person called on to make the decision. To presume that the incompetent person must always be subject to what many rational and intelligent persons may decline is to downgrade the status of the incompetent person by placing a lesser value on his intrinsic human worth and vitality.

The trend in the law has been to give incompetent persons the same rights as other individuals. *Boyd v Registrars of Voters of Belchertown,* 334 NE 2d 629 (1975). Recognition of this principle of equality requires understanding that in certain circumstances it may be appropriate for a court to consent to the withholding of treatment from an incompetent individual. This leads us to the question of how the right of an incompetent person to decline treatment might best be exercised so as to give the fullest possible expression to the character and circumstances of that individual.

The problem of decision-making presented in this case is one of first impression before this court, and we know of no decision in other jurisdictions squarely on point. The well publicized decision of the New Jersey Supreme Court in *Re Quinlan* 70 NJ 10, 355 A 2d 647 (1976), provides a helpful starting point for analysis, however. [Karen Quinlan was diagnosed as being in a persistent vegetative state sustained by a ventilator. The case concerned an application by her father as guardian under New Jersey law to discontinue her treatment on the ventilator.]

The exposition by the New Jersey court of the principle of substituted judgment, and of the legal standards that were to be applied by the guardian in making this decision, bears repetition here.

If a putative decision by Karen to permit this non-cognitive, vegetative existence to terminate by natural forces is regarded as a valuable incident of her right of privacy, as we believe to be, then it should not be discarded solely on the basis that her condition prevents her conscious exercise of the choice. The only practical way to prevent destruction of the right is to *permit the guardian and family of Karen to render their best judgment*, subject to the qualifications [regarding consultation with attending physicians and hospital 'Ethics Committee'] hereinafter stated, *as to whether she would exercise it in these circumstances*. If their conclusion is in the affirmative this decision should be accepted by a society the overwhelming majority of whose members would, we think, in similar circumstances, exercise such a choice in the same way for themselves or for those closest to them. It is for this reason that we determine that Karen's right of privacy may be asserted in her behalf, in this respect, by her guardian and family under the particular circumstances presented by this record (emphasis supplied). *Id* at 41–42, 355 A 2d 647.

The court's observation that most people in like circumstances would choose a natural death does not, we believe detract from or modify the central concern that the guardian's decision conforms, to the extent possible, to the decision that would have been made by Karen Quinlan herself. Evidence that most people would or would not act in a certain way is certainly an important consideration in attempting to ascertain the predilections of any individual, but care must be taken, as in any analogy, to ensure that operative factors are similar or at least take notice of the dissimilarities. With this in mind, it is profitable to compare the situations presented in the *Quinlan* case and the case presently before us. Karen Quinlan, subsequent to her accident, was totally incapable of knowing or appreciating life, was physically debilitated, and was pathetically reliant on sophisticated machinery to nourish and clean her body. Any other person suffering from similar massive brain damage would be in a similar state of total incapacity, and thus it is not unreasonable to give weight to a supposed general, and widespread, response to the situation.

Karen Quinlan's situation, however, must be distinguished from that of Joseph Saikewicz. Saikewicz was profoundly medically retarded. His mental state was a cognitive one but limited in his capacity to comprehend and communicate. Evidence that most people choose to accept the rigors of chemotherapy has no direct bearing on the likely choice that Joseph Saikewicz would have made. Unlike most people, Saikewicz had no capacity to understand his present situation or his prognosis. The guardian *ad litem* gave expression to this important distinction in coming to grips with this 'most troubling aspect' of withholding treatment from Saikewicz. 'If he is treated with toxic drugs he will be involuntarily immersed in a state of painful suffering, the reason for which he will never understand. Patients who request treatment know the risks involved and can appreciate the painful side-effects when they arrive. They know the reason for the pain and their hope makes it tolerable.' To make a worthwhile comparison, one would have to ask whether a majority of people would choose chemotherapy if they were told merely that something outside of their previous experience was going to be done to them, that this something would cause them pain and discomfort, that they would be removed to strange surroundings and possibly restrained for extended periods of time, and that the advantages of this course of action were measured by concepts of time and mortality beyond their ability to comprehend.

To put the above discussion in proper perspective, we realize that an inquiry into what a majority of people would do in circumstances that truly were similar assumes an objective viewpoint not far removed from a 'reasonable person' inquiry. While we recognise the value of this kind of indirect evidence, we should make it plain that the primary test is subjective in nature – that is, the goal is to determine with as much accuracy as possible the wants and needs of the individual involved. This may or may not conform to what is thought wise or prudent by most people. The problems of arriving at an accurate substituted judgment in matters of life and death vary greatly in degree, if not in kind, in different circumstances. For example, the responsibility of Karen Quinlan's father to act as she would have wanted could be discharged by drawing on many years of what was apparently an affectionate and close relationship. In contrast, Joseph Saikewicz was profoundly retarded and non communicative his entire life, which was spent largely in the highly restrictive atmosphere of an institution. While it may thus be necessary to rely to a greater degree on objective criteria, such as the supposed inability of profoundly retarded persons to conceptualize or fear death, the effort to bring the substituted judgment into step with the values and desires of the affected individual must not, and need not be abandoned.

The 'substituted judgment' standard which we have described commends itself simply because of its straightforward respect for the integrity and autonomy of the individual…[W]e now reiterate the substituted judgment doctrine as we apply it to the instant case. We believe that both the guardian *ad litem* in his recommendation and the judge in his decision should have attempted (as they did) to ascertain the incompetent person's actual interests and preferences. In short, the decision in cases such as this should be that which would be made by the incompetent person, if that person were competent, but taking into account the present and future competency of the individual as one of the factors which would necessarily enter into the decision-making process of the competent person. Having recognized the right of a competent person to make for himself the same decision as the court made in this case, the question is, do the facts on the record support the proposition that Saikewicz himself would have made the decision under the standard set forth. We believe they do.

The two factors considered by the probate judge to weigh in favor of administering chemotherapy were: (1) the fact that most people elect chemotherapy and (2) the chance of a longer life. Both are appropriate indicators of what Saikewicz himself would have wanted, provided that due allowance is taken for this individual's present and future incompetency. We have already discussed the perspective this brings to the fact that most people choose to undergo chemotherapy. With regard to the second factor, the chance of a longer life carries the same weight for Saikewicz as for any other person, the value of life under the law having no relation to intelligence or social position. Intertwined with this consideration is the hope that a cure, temporary or permanent, will be discovered during the period of extra weeks or months potentially made available by chemotherapy. The guardian *ad litem* investigated this possibility and found no reason to hope for a dramatic breakthrough in the time frame relevant to the decision.

The probate judge identified six factors weighing against administration of chemotherapy. Four of these – Saikewicz's age, the probable side effects of treatment, the low chance of producing remission, and the certainty that treatment will cause immediate suffering – were clearly established by the medical testimony to be considerations that any individual would weigh carefully. A fifth factor – Saikewicz's inability to cooperate with the treatment – introduces those considerations that are unique to this individual and which therefore are essential to the proper exercise of substituted judgment. The judge heard testimony that Saikewicz would have no comprehension of the reasons for the severe disruption of his formerly secure and stable environment occasioned by chemotherapy. He therefore would experience fear without the understanding from which other patients draw strength. The inability to anticipate and prepare for the severe side effects of the drugs leaves room only for confusion and disorientation. The possibility that such a naturally uncooperative patient would have to be physically restrained to allow the slow intravenous administration of drugs could only compound his pain and fear, as well as possibly jeopardize the ability of his body to withstand the toxic effects of the drugs.

The sixth factor identified by the judge as weighing against chemotherapy was 'the quality of life possible for him even if the treatment does bring about remission.' To the extent that this formulation equates the value of life with any measure of the quality of life, we firmly reject it. A reading of the entire record clearly reveals, however, the judge's concern that special care be taken to respect the dignity and worth of Saikewicz's life precisely because of his vulnerable position. The judge, as well as all the parties, were keenly aware that the supposed ability of Saikewicz, by virtue of his mental retardation, to appreciate or experience life had no place in the decision before them. Rather than reading the judge's formulation in a manner that demeans the value of the life of one who is mentally retarded, the vague, and perhaps ill-chosen, term 'quality of life' should be understood as a reference to the continuing state of pain and disorientation precipitated by the chemotherapy treatment. Viewing the term in this manner, together with the other factors properly considered by the judge, we are satisfied that the decision to withhold treatment from Saikewicz was based on a regard for his actual interests and preferences and that the facts supported this decision…

In this case, a ward of a State institution was discovered to have an invariably fatal illness, the only effective – in the sense of life-prolonging – treatment for which involved serious and painful intrusions on the patient's body. While an emergency existed with regard to taking action to begin treatment, it was not a case in which immediate action was required. Nor was this a case in which life-saving, as distinguished from life-prolonging, procedures were available. Because the individual involved was thought to be incompetent to make the necessary decisions, the officials of the State institutions properly initiated proceedings in the Probate Court.

...We note here that many health care institutions have developed medical ethics committees or panels to consider many of the issues touched on here. Consideration of the findings and advice of such groups as well as the testimony of the attending physicians and other medical experts ordinarily would be of great assistance to a probate judge faced with such a difficult decision. We believe it desirable for a judge to consider such views wherever available and useful to the court. We do not believe, however, that this option should be transformed by us into a required procedure. We take a dim view of any attempt to shift the ultimate decision-making responsibility away from the duly established courts of proper jurisdiction to any committee, panel or group, ad hoc or permanent. Thus, we reject the approach adopted by the New Jersey Supreme Court in the *Quinlan* case of entrusting the decision whether to continue artificial life support to the patient's guardian, family, attending doctors, and hospital 'ethics committee'. 70 NJ at 55, 355 A 2d 647, 671. One rationale for such a delegation was expressed by the lower court judge in the *Quinlan* case, and quoted by the New Jersey Supreme Court: 'The nature, extent and duration of care by societal standards is the responsibility of a physician. The morality and conscience of our society places this responsibility in the hands of the physician. What justification is there to remove it from the control of the medical profession and place it in the hands of the courts'? *Id* at 44, 355 A 2d at 655. For its part, the New Jersey Supreme Court concluded that 'a practice of applying to a court to confirm such decisions would generally be inappropriate, not only because that would be a gratuitous encroachment upon the medical profession's field of competence, but because it would be impossibly cumbersome. Such a requirement is distinguishable from the judicial overview traditionally required in other matters such as the adjudication and commitment of mental incompetents. This is not to say that in the case of an otherwise justiciable controversy access to the courts would be foreclosed; we speak rather of a general practice and procedure.' *Id* at 50, 355 A 2d at 669.

We do not view the judicial resolution of this most difficult and awesome question – whether potentially life-prolonging treatment should be withheld from a person incapable of making his own decision – as constituting a 'gratuitous encroachment' on the domain of medical expertise. Rather, such questions of life and death seem to us to require the process of detached but passionate investigation and decision that forms the ideal on which the judicial branch of government was created. Achieving this ideal is our responsibility and that of the lower court, and is not to be entrusted to any other group purporting to represent the 'morality and conscience of our society', no matter how highly motivated or impressively constituted.

Conroy enlarges on the test suggested by *Saikewicz* by making clear, as we saw, that there are *three* tests. The first test in *Conroy* – the 'subjective test' – demands that the decision-maker must follow the treatment choice which the incompetent person made prior to the onset of incompetence. Thus, the law requires that the patient's earlier decision be complied with (see *supra*, ch 16 'anticipatory decisions'). (See *Re Peter* (1987) 529 A 2d 419 (NJ Sup Ct) permitting discontinuation of artificial hydration and nutrition on the basis of the 'subjective test'.)

The second test in *Conroy* – the 'limited-objective' test – was intended by the court to reflect to some extent the decision that the patient *would* have made, while providing for some element of objective evaluation of the patient's interests. As Handler J explained in the subsequent case of *Re Jobes* (1987) 529 A 2d 434 at 458, this test seeks out a 'middle-ground which combined elements of both self-determination and objective physical factors'. This test calls for careful examination. On the one hand, it represents an improvement on the law as stated in *Saikewicz* but, on the other hand, it too has its drawbacks. In *Saikewicz* you will recall that Liacos J used the test of 'substituted judgment'. This, in truth, should be the second *Conroy* test. Liacos J misused it by applying it to a patient who never was competent to have views or express wishes on the treatment he would like to receive. Substituted judgment, properly understood, requires that the decision-maker should take account of the views and values of the now incompetent person as a guide in determining what the now incompetent person *would have chosen* for himself. The decision-maker acts as the substitute for the patient who can no longer speak for himself. He does *not* substitute his view for that of the patient. Clearly, if the patient has never had the capacity to have a view then the 'substituted judgment' test can have no application (see *supra*, ch 6). *Conroy* recognises this (and the error committed by Liacos J). But *Conroy* takes a wrong turning in that its second test is not pure substituted judgment (as it should be) but it is what the court calls 'limited objective'. The addition of an objective element undermines the commitment of the court to give effect wherever possible to the views and values of the patient. The flaw in the *Conroy* approach was subsequently exposed by the same court in the case of *Re Jobes* (1987) 529 A 2d 434. This case concerned a patient in a persistent vegetative state. There was no evidence that Mrs Jobes had made a prior decision concerning her treatment. The New Jersey Supreme Court permitted her family members to decide what treatment she should receive on the basis of the substituted judgment test.

Garibaldi J explained the test as follows:

> **Garibaldi J:** [Substituted judgment] is intended to ensure that the surrogate decision-maker effectuates as much as possible the decision that the incompetent patient would make if he or she were competent. Under the substituted judgment doctrine where an incompetent's wishes are not clearly expressed, a surrogate decisionmaker considers the patient's personal value system for guidance. The surrogate considers the patient's prior statements about and reactions to medical issues, and all the facets of the patient's personality that the surrogate is familiar with – with, of course, particular reference to his or her relevant philosophical, theological, and ethical values – in order to extrapolate what course of medical treatment the patient would choose.

She continued:

> Where an irreversibly vegetative patient like Mrs Jobes has not clearly expressed her intentions with respect to medical treatment, the *Quinlan* 'substituted judgment' approach best accomplishes the goal of having the patient make her own decision. In most cases in which the 'substituted judgment' doctrine is applied, the surrogate decisionmaker will be a family member or close friend of the patient. Generally it is the patient's family or other loved ones who support and care for the patient, and who best understand the patient's personal values and beliefs. Hence they will be best able to make a substituted medical judgment for the patient.

In a concurring judgment Handler J added:

> **Handler J:** Today this Court holds that though Mrs Jobes' intention to accept or refuse life-sustaining treatment has not been clearly established by clear and convincing evidence, the Court will uphold the decision of close family members who made the treatment determination based on what they believe Mrs Jobes would have decided. *Ante* at 446–447. The court is satisfied to effectuate the decision of the patient's family. It has in these circumstances adopted the individual right of self-determination reflected by the substituted judgment of a surrogate decisionmaker as the standard for resolving the fundamental issue of whether to terminate life-sustaining treatment.
>
> While this 'substituted judgment' standard fits well the facts of this case, the Court notes that in many cases this standard will not be workable, eg, in cases where the patient has always been incompetent or when there is no one sufficiently familiar with the patient to be able to know how the patient would have decided. *Ante* at 449–450. The Court does not suggest standards for how treatment decisions should be made in such cases. *Id.* I would add that there will be difficult cases in which the relationship of family members or putative friends of the patient may not be close enough for them to be an appropriate source for the awesome decision of whether to discontinue life-perpetuating treatment.
>
> In the cases now before the Court, the decision to discontinue or to refuse treatment was either made by the patient herself or made by the patient's guardian on the basis of trustworthy evidence of what the patient would have decided.

The third *Conroy* test – the 'pure objective test' – appears to be no different from the 'best interests' test familiar to English law. It can be argued, however, that *Conroy*, while developing the law, again muddied the waters. The majority of the court recognised that any decision about 'best interests' involves weighing burdens and benefits. Curiously, however, they restricted the relevant burdens to *pain and suffering*. This is clearly too narrow, not least because it either prejudges the answer which will be arrived at, or is of no assistance, where a patient can no longer feel pain – for example, when in a persistent vegetative state. This is because the absence of burden (ie no pain) suggests either that the benefit of treating mandates that treatment continue or, if it is recognised that treatment produces no benefit, in such a case there is neither burden nor benefit and so the test is meaningless. Any decision about treatment should, therefore, be based upon a test where burden is not limited to pain. Handler J in a concurring opinion in *Conroy* reflects the force of these arguments:

Handler J: In my opinion, the Court's objective tests too narrowly define the interests of people like Miss Conroy. While the basic standard purports to account for several concerns, it ultimately focuses on pain as the critical factor. The presence of significant pain in effect becomes the sole measure of such a person's best interests. 'Pain' thus eclipses a whole cluster of other human values that have a proper place in the subtle weighing that will ultimately determine how life should end.

The Court's concentration on pain as the exclusive criterion in reaching the life-or-death decision in reality transmutes the best-interests determination into an exercise of avoidance and nullification rather than confrontation and fulfilment. In most cases the pain criterion will dictate that the decision be one not to withdraw life-prolonging treatment and not to allow death to occur naturally. First, pain will not be an operative factor in a great many cases. '[P]resently available drugs and techniques allow pain to be reduced to a level acceptable to virtually every patient, usually without unacceptable sedation.' *President's Commission Report, supra*, at 50–51. See *id* at 19 n 19 *citing* Saunders, 'Current Views on Pain Relief and Terminal Care' in *The Therapy of Pain* 215 (Swerdlow, ed 1981) (a hospice reports complete control of pain in over 99% of its dying patients). See generally *id* at 277–94. See also generally *The Management of Terminal Disease* (Saunders, ed 1978); *The Experience of Dying* (Pattison, ed 1977); *Psychopharmacologic Agents for the Terminally Ill and Bereaved* (Goldberg *et al*, eds 1973). Further, as was true in Miss Conroy's case, health care providers frequently encounter difficulty in evaluating the degree of pain experienced by a patient. Finally, '[o]nly a minority of patients – fewer than half of those with malignancies, for example – have substantial problems with pain…' *President's Commission Report, supra*, at 278 *citing* Twycross, 'Relief of Pain' in *The Management of Terminal Disease, supra*, at 66. Thus, in a great many cases, the pain test will become an absolute bar to the withdrawal of life-support therapy.

The pain requirement, as applied by the Court in its objective tests, effectively negates other highly relevant considerations that should appropriately bear on the decision to maintain or to withdraw life-prolonging treatment. The pain standard may dictate the decision to prolong life despite the presence of other factors that reasonably militate in favour of the termination of such procedures to allow a natural death. The exclusive pain criterion denies relief to that class of people who, at the very end of life, might strongly disapprove of an artificially extended existence in spite of the absence of pain. See *Re Torres*, 357 NW 2d 332 at 340 (Minn 1984) (although a patient 'cannot feel pain', that patient may have a guardian petition to forego life-sustaining treatment). Thus, some people abhor dependence on others as much, or more, than they fear pain. Other individuals value personal privacy and dignity, and prize independence from others when their personal needs and bodily functions are involved. Finally, the ideal of bodily integrity may become more important than simply prolonging life at its most rudimentary level. Persons, like Miss Conroy, 'may well have wished to avoid …[t]he ultimate horror [not of] death but the possibility of being maintained in limbo, in a sterile room, by machines controlled by strangers.' In *Re Torres, supra*, 357 NW 2d at 340, quoting Steel, 'The Right to Die: New Options in California', 93 *Christian Century* [July–Dec 1976].

Clearly, a decision to focus exclusively on pain as the single criterion ignores and devalues other important ideals regarding life and death. Consequently, a pain standard cannot serve as an indirect proxy for additional and significant concerns that bear on the decision to forego life-prolonging treatments…

I would therefore have the Court adopt a test that does not rely exclusively on pain as the ultimately determinative criterion. Rather, the standard should consist of an array of factors to be medically established and then evaluated by the decisionmaker both singly and collectively to reach a balance that will justify the determination whether to withdraw or to continue life-prolonging treatment. The withdrawal of life-prolonging treatment from an unconscious or comatose, terminally ill individual near death, whose personal views concerning life-ending treatment cannot be ascertained, should be governed by such a standard.

Several important criteria bear on this critical determination. The person should be terminally ill and facing imminent death. There should also be present the permanent loss of conscious thought processes in the form of a comatose state or profound unconsciousness. Further, there should be the irreparable failure of at least one major and essential bodily organ or system. See, eg, *Re Quinlan*, 70 NJ 10, 355 A 2d 647 (1976) (respiratory system); *Barber, supra* (same); *Re Dinnerstein*, 6 *Mass App* 466, 380 NE 2d 134 (1978) (heart);

Saikewicz, supra (circulatory system); *Conroy, supra* (swallowing reflex); *Torres, supra* (cerebral cortex and brain-stem); *Re Hamlin, 102 Wash* 2d 810, 689 P 2d 1372 (1984) (cerebral cortex). Obviously the presence or absence of significant pain is highly relevant.

In addition, the person's general physical condition must be of great concern. The presence of progressive, irreversible, extensive and extreme physical deterioration, such as ulcers, lesions, gangrene, infection, incontinence and the like, which frequently afflict the bed-ridden, terminally ill, should be considered in the formulation of an appropriate standard. The medical and nursing treatment of individuals *in extremis* and suffering from these conditions entails the constant and extensive handling and manipulation of the body. At some point, such a course of treatment upon the insensate patient is bound to touch the sensibilities of even the most detached observer. Eventually, pervasive bodily intrusion, even for the best motives, will arouse feelings akin to humiliation and mortification for the helpless patient. When cherished values of human dignity and personal privacy, which belong to every person living or dying, are sufficiently transgressed by what is being done to the individual, we should be ready to say: enough.

Against this analytical background we now turn to the English law. The question is whether English law brings the same subtlety of analysis found in the judgments in New Jersey. The New Jersey cases reflect, of course, the very significant commitment of the courts in the United States to the patient's right to self-determination whenever this can safely be effected. English courts, by contrast, have historically been wary of the language of rights. Furthermore, as we have seen in Chapter 6, they are not slow, the moment there is the slightest doubt as to a patient's views, to fall back on the 'best interests' test with a dash of *Bolam* thrown in for good measure. This may reflect the tendency towards paternalism and 'doctor knows best' which is endemic in English medical law.

Decision-making in English law

A. WHO DECIDES?

It is as well to remember that although we have been considering cases concerning adult patients, the incompetent also include young children. We are concerned with both in this chapter. You will have noticed in the American cases that while the law relating to decision-making in the case of children is similar to English law, as regards adults there are significant differences. The differences lie not in the type of decision that may be made or the basis for making it, but in the decision-maker. Most American jurisdictions provide for family members to make decisions either as of right (under what are known as 'family consent statutes') or after application to a court to be appointed a guardian (see *supra*, ch 16). In England neither of these possibilities exists (contrast Scotland *Law Hospital NHS Trust v Lord Advocate* 1996 SLT 848). We have set out in detail in Chapter 6 the law which pertains in England as to who may be the decision-maker in the case of incompetent adults. In short, you will recall that in *Re F* the House of Lords vested decision-making in doctors, subject that is, in some instances, to cases where court involvement is desirable (but notice *Re R (adult: medical treatment)* (1996) 31 BMLR 127 requiring consent of a parent before withholding antibiotics from a severely disabled adult, discussed *infra*).

We also saw in Chapter 6 the legislative scheme for decision-making and incompetent adults proposed by the Law Commission in its Report, *Mental Incapacity* (No 231), 1995. The 'general authority' to act reasonably in the patient's best interests would encompass many of the decisions we are concerned with in this chapter. The Law Commission, however, would have removed one category of case – withdrawal of artificial hydration or nutrition from a patient in a persistent vegetative state (PVS) (see Report, paras 6.16–6.21 and cl 10 of the Mental Incapacity Bill). Only the court or an appropriately authorised attorney or court manager could make such a decision. The final scheme accepted by the Government in *Making Decisions* (Cm 4465), 1999 LCD, is somewhat different. Such decisions would seem to fall within the 'general authority' which it is proposed to enact (see its absence from the list of exclusions, *op cit*, para 1.23). also, if the court is involved only it, and not its appointed manager, could make such decisions (para 3.8).

B. BASIS FOR DECIDING

Whether the patient is a young child or an adult, the law which comes into play is the same. It is as well to remember the context: the possible end of a patient's life and the consequent responsibility of the doctor (and parent). In matters of life or death the criminal law, specifically the law of murder, comes to the fore and sets the agenda. Of course, as ever, the law of tort – specifically negligence and battery – and family law in the case of children remain central. Thus, an analysis of the criminal law will, for the most part, provide a means for resolving the issues which arise in tort and family law concerning the respective legal duties of doctors and parents. You will see that the crucial legal question is 'what is the legal duty of the doctor (or parent)? Here, as always now, we must also consider the impact of the Human Rights Act 1998.

1. Unhelpful arguments

Before we can begin to answer this question we must recognise that there are a number of unhelpful arguments which bedevil this area of law and need to be addressed at the outset.

(a) Sanctity of life

We discussed at some length the principle of the 'sanctity of life' in Chapter 16. We do not repeat that here.

Kenneth M Boyd (ed) *The New Dictionary of Medical Ethics* (1997)

> This essentially religious concept has its basis in the notion that life is a gift from God. An additional factor within Christianity is the belief that humans are created in the image of God. In non-religious circles the term is used to indicate the utmost respect with which human life should be treated.

For the law, the principle has become understood to entail an obligation to preserve life.

The courts in England have been anxious to assert the law's commitment to the sanctity of life. As Lord Donaldson MR put it in *Re J (A Minor) (Wardship: Medical Treatment)* [1990] 3 All ER 930 at 938: 'We know that the instinct and desire for survival is very strong. We all believe in and assert the sanctity of human life.' The courts have gone on, however, to demonstrate that they do not see this 'principle' in absolute terms. While recognising its importance, it has not been endorsed as a form of slogan designed to prevent the court from considering competing principles. In *Re J*, Taylor LJ stated (at 943) that, 'the court's high respect for the sanctity of human life imposes a strong presumption in favour of taking all steps capable of preserving it, save in exceptional circumstances'.

The principle of the 'sanctity of life' received its most careful examination by an English court in the case of *Airedale NHS Trust v Bland* [1993] 1 All ER 821 by Lords Keith (at 861) Goff (at 865–866) and Mustill (at 891).

> **Lord Keith:** The principle [of the sanctity of life] is not an absolute one. It does not compel a medical practitioner on pain of criminal sanctions to treat a patient, who will die if he does

not, contrary to the express wishes of the patient. It does not authorise forcible feeding of prisoners on hunger strike. It does not compel the temporary keeping alive of patients who are terminally ill where to do so would merely prolong their suffering.

Lord Goff: The fundamental principle…of the sanctity of human life [is]…a principle long recognised not only in our own society but also in most, if not all, civilised societies throughout the modern world, as is indeed evidenced by its recognition both in art 2 of the European Convention on Human Rights (Convention for the Protection of Human Rights and Fundamental Freedoms, Rome 4 November 1950; TS 71 (1953); (Cmd 8969)) and in at 6 of the International Covenant on Civil and Political Rights (New York, 19 December 1966; TS6 (1977); Cmd 6702).

But this principle, fundamental though it is, is not an absolute. Indeed there are circumstances in which it is lawful to take another man's life, for example by a lawful act of self-defence, or (in the days when capital punishment was acceptable in our society) by lawful execution.

Lord Mustill: The interest of the state in preserving the lives of its citizens is very strong, but it is not absolute. There are contrary interests, and sometimes these prevail; as witness the over-mastering effect of the patient's refusal of treatment, even where this makes death inevitable.

(For a trenchant criticism of the judges' understanding of 'sanctity of life', see J Keown 'Restoring Moral and Intellectual Shape to the Law After *Bland*' (1997) 113 LQR 481.)

You will notice Lord Goff's reference in *Bland* to art 2 of the European Convention. What, if any, impact does this have on treatment decisions that result in a patient's death? It is not 'an unhelpful argument' to consider art 2 but we will do so here for convenience (see also *supra*).

Article 2 provides as follows:

> *Right to life*
>
> 1. Everyone's right to life shall be protected by law. No one shall be deprived of his life intentionally save in the execution of a sentence of a court following his conviction of a crime for which this penalty is provided by law.
>
> 2. Deprivation of life shall not be regarded as inflicted in contravention of this Article when it results from the use of force which is no more than absolutely necessary:
> (a) in defence of any person from unlawful violence;
> (b) in order to effect a lawful arrest or to prevent the escape of a person lawfully detained;
> (c) in action lawfully taken for the purpose of quelling a riot or insurrection.

Certainly, these situations could not fall within the justifying circumstances specified in art 2(2). We saw earlier (*supra*, chs 6 and 16) how the courts could accommodate decision-making in a patient's 'best interests' with art 2 when that decision results in death even, as in cases such as *Bland*, where it is intentionally brought about (see eg *In re the Matter of a Ward of Court* [1995] 2 IRLM 401 (Ir Sup Ct), per Hamilton CJ at 426 interpreting a similar provision in the Irish Constitution). A court could conclude that if a doctor had no 'duty' to provide the treatment, his failure to do so did not 'deprive' the patient of his life (see *Shortlands v Northland Health Ltd* (1997) 50 BMLR 255 (NZ CA) at 266–267 interpreting art 8 of the NZ Bill of Rights). It is interesting and instructive that courts in other jurisdictions who have a constitutionally protected 'right to life' do not see decisions to withhold or withdraw treatment as infringing that right where the common law leads to the conclusion there is no duty to provide or continue the treatment (see eg *Cruzan v Director, Missouri Department of Health* (1990) 497 US 261 (US Sup Ct) and *Rodriquez v A-G of British Columbia* [1993] 3 SCR 519 (Can Sup Ct)). English courts would undoubtedly reach the same result (see *A NHS Trust v D* (2000) Times, 19 July (Fam Div) – not providing resuscitation to severely disabled child not contrary to arts 2 and 3 if treatment not in his best interests).

Furthermore, it is possible that *continued* intervention could in extreme circumstances amount to a breach of art 3 of the Convention prohibiting 'torture' or 'inhuman or degrading treatment', for example where it results in severe pain or distress for the patient.

(b) Ordinary/extraordinary treatment

The argument based on the distinction between ordinary and extraordinary treatment, accepting as it does the moral propriety of withholding treatment in some cases, can, of course, only be advanced once an absolutist view of the sanctity of life is rejected. An outstanding analysis, pinpointing the deficiencies of this argument, can be found in the President's Commission for the Study of Ethical Problems in Medical and Biomedical and Behavioural Research, Report of 1983 (1983) pp 82–88.

President's Commission *Deciding to Forego Life-Sustaining Treatment* (1983)

Ordinary versus extraordinary treatment. In many discussions and decisions about life-sustaining treatment, the distinction between ordinary and extraordinary (also termed 'heroic' or 'artificial') treatment plays an important role. In its origins within moral theology, the distinction was used to mark the difference between obligatory and nonobligatory care – ordinary care being obligatory for the patient to accept and others to provide, and extraordinary care being optional. It has also played a role in professional policy statements and recent judicial decisions about life-sustaining treatment for incompetent patients. As with the other terms discussed, defining and applying a distinction between ordinary and extraordinary treatment is both difficult and controversial and can lead to inconsistent results, which makes the terms of questionable value in the formulation of public policy in this area.

The meaning of the distinction. 'Extraordinary' treatment has an unfortunate array of alternative meanings, as became obvious in an exchange that took place at a Commission hearing concerning a Florida case [*Satz v Perlmutter* 379 So 2d 358 (1980)] involving the cessation of life-sustaining treatment at the request of a 76-year-old man dying of amyotrophic lateral sclerosis. The attending physician testified:

I deal with respirators every day of my life. To me, this is not heroic. This is standard procedure…I have other patients who have run large corporations who have been on portable respirators. Other people who have been on them and have done quite well for as long as possible.

By contrast, the trial judge who had decided that the respirator could be withdrawn told the Commission:

Certainly there is no question legally that putting a hole in a man's trachea and inserting a mechanical respirator is extraordinary life-preserving means. I do not think that the doctor would in candor allow that that is not an extraordinary means of preserving life. I understand that he deals with them every day, but in the sense of ordinary as against extraordinary, I believe it to be extraordinary.

There was no question in this case, nobody ever raised the question that this mechanical respirator was not an extraordinary means of preserving life.

The most natural understanding of the ordinary/extraordinary distinction is as the difference between common and unusual care, with those terms understood as applying to a patient in a particular condition. This interprets the distinction in a literal, statistical sense and, no doubt, is what some of its users intend. Related, though different, is the idea that ordinary care is simple and that extraordinary care is complex, elaborate, or artificial, or that it employs elaborate technology and/or great efforts or expense. With either of these interpretations, for example, the use of antibiotics to fight a life-threatening infection would be considered ordinary treatment. On the statistical interpretation, a complex of resuscitation measures (including physical, chemical and electrical means) might well be ordinary for a hospital patient, whereas on the technological interpretation, resuscitation would probably be considered extraordinary. Since both common/unusual and simple/complex exist on continuums with no precise dividing line, on either interpretation there will be borderline cases engendering disagreement about whether a particular treatment is ordinary or extraordinary.

A different understanding of the distinction, one that has its origins in moral theology, inquires into the usefulness and burdensomeness of a treatment. Here, too, disagreement persists about which outcomes are considered useful or burdensome. Without entering to the complexity of these debates, the Commission notes that any interpretation of the ordinary/extraordinary distinction in terms of usefulness and burdensomeness to an individual patient has an important advantage over the common/unusual or simple/complex interpretations in that judgments about usefulness and burdensomeness rest on morally important differences.

Despite the fact that the distinction between what is ordinary and what is extraordinary is hazy and variably defined, several courts have employed the terms in discussing cases involving the cessation of life-sustaining treatment of incompetent patients. In some cases, the courts used these terms because they were part of the patient's religious tradition. In other cases, the terms have been used to characterise treatments as being required or permissibly foregone. For example, the New Jersey Supreme Court in the *Quinlan* case [*Re Quinlan* (1976) 355 A 2d] recognised a distinction based on the possible benefit to the individual patient.

> One would have to think that the use of the same respirator or life support could be considered 'ordinary' in the context of the possibly curable patient but 'extraordinary' in the context of the forced sustaining by cardio-respiratory processes of an irreversibly doomed patient.

Likewise, the Massachusetts Supreme Judicial Court [*Superintendent of Belchertown State School v Saikewicz* (1977) 370 NE 2d 417] quoted an article in a medical journal concerning the proposition that ordinary treatment could become extraordinary when applied in the context of a patient for whom there is no hope:

> We should not use *extraordinary* means of prolonging life or its semblance when, after careful consideration, consultation and application of the most well conceived therapy it becomes apparent that there is no hope for the recovery of the patient. Recovery should not be defined simply as the ability to remain alive; it should mean life without intolerable suffering.

Even if the patient or a designated surrogate is held to be under no obligation to accept 'extraordinary' care, there still remains the perplexing issue about what constitutes the dividing line between the two. The courts have most often faced the question of what constitutes 'ordinary' care in cases when the respirator was the medical intervention at issue. Generally the courts have recognised, in the words of one judge, that 'the act of turning off the respirator is the termination of an optional, extraordinary medical procedure which will allow nature to take its course'.

For many, the harder questions lie in less dramatic interventions, including the use of artificial feeding and antibiotics. In one criminal case involving whether the defendant's robbery and assault killed his victim or whether she died because life-supporting treatments were later withdrawn after severe brain injury was confirmed, the court held that 'heroic' (and unnecessary) measures included 'infusion of drugs in order to reduce the pressure in the head when there was no obvious response to those measures of therapy'. In another case, in which a patient's refusal of an amputation to prevent death from gangrene was overridden, antibiotics were described by the physician 'as heroic measures meaning quantities in highly unusual amounts risking iatrogenic disease in treating gangrene'. Here the assessment, in addition to relying on 'benefits', also seems to rely to some degree upon the risk and invasiveness of the intervention. One court did begin to get at the scope of the questions underlying the ordinary/extraordinary distinction. Faced with the question of treatment withdrawal for a permanently unconscious automobile accident victim, the Delaware Supreme Court [*Severns v Wilmington Medical Center* (1980) 421 A 2d 1334] asked what might constitute life-sustaining measures for a person who has been comatose for many months:

> Are 'medicines' a part of such life-sustaining systems? If so, which medicines? Is food or nourishment a part of such life-sustaining systems? If so, to what extent? What extraordinary measures (or equipment) are a part of such systems? What measures (or equipment) are regarded by the medical profession as not extraordinary under the circumstances? What ordinary equipment is used? How is a respirator regarded in this context?

The moral significance of the distinction. Because of the varied meanings of the distinction, whether or not it has moral significance depends upon the specific meaning assigned to it. The Commission believes there is no basis for holding that whether a treatment is common or unusual, or whether it is simple or complex, is in itself significant to a moral analysis of whether the treatment is warranted or obligatory. An unusual treatment may have a lower success rate than a common one; if so, it is the lower success rate rather than the unusualness of the procedure that is relevant to evaluating the therapy. Likewise, a complex, technological treatment may be costlier than a simple one, and this difference may be relevant to the desirability of the therapy. A patient may choose a complex therapy and shun a simple one, and the patient's choice is always relevant to the moral obligation to provide the therapy.

If the ordinary/extraordinary distinction is understood in terms of the usefulness and burdensomeness of a particular therapy, however, the distinction does have moral significance.

When a treatment is deemed extraordinary because it is too burdensome for a particular patient, the individual (or surrogate) may appropriately decide not to undertake it. The reasonableness of this is evident – a patient should not have to undergo life-prolonging treatment without consideration of the burdens that the treatment would impose. Of course, whether a treatment is warranted depends on its usefulness or benefits as well. Whether serious burdens of treatment (for example, the side effects of chemotherapy treatments for cancer) are worth enduring obviously depends on the expected benefits – how long the treatment will extend life, and under what conditions. Usefulness might be understood as mere extension of life, no matter what the conditions of that life. But so long as mere biological existence is not considered the *only* value, patients may want to take the nature of that additional life into account as well.

This line of reasoning suggests that extraordinary treatment is that which, in the patient's view, entails significantly greater burdens than benefits and is therefore undesirable and not obligatory, while ordinary treatment is that which, in the patient's view, produces greater benefits than burdens and is therefore reasonably desirable and undertaken. The claim, then, that the treatment is extraordinary is more of an expression of the conclusion than a justification for it.

Professor Raanon Gillon supports the view of the President's Commission:

Raanon Gillon 'Editorial' (1981) 7 Journal of Medical Ethics 56

…[T]houghtful proponents of the use of the distinction between ordinary and extraordinary means agree with opponents that the moral assessment of any individual's case must properly come *before* it is decided whether any particular treatment is to be classified as ordinary and extraordinary; moreover not only the 'means' (ie the proposed means of treatment) but also the patient's particular circumstances and the anticipated harms and benefits to him in those circumstances of those means of treatment must be assessed before the means can be classified as being either ordinary and extraordinary. Thus there is no question of observing whether some proposed means of treatment X is, as a matter of non-evaluative fact, ordinary and extraordinary and then using this observation or 'fact' to decide whether or not patient Y in circumstances Z should be treated with X; rather it is a matter of first deciding whether or not it would be *right* to treat patient Y in context Z with treatment X and then, depending on that decision, classifying X as ordinary and extraordinary means of treatment.

Non-Catholics are often – perhaps always – surprised at this revelation when first they meet it, supposing reasonably enough that 'ordinary' means 'usual, common-place, not exceptional' (to quote the Oxford English Dictionary) and conversely that 'extraordinary' means 'unusual, uncommon, exceptional'. However, although these concepts may obliquely enter the analysis of specific cases it is clear that, as Strong explicitly states, the conflation of 'ordinary' with 'customary' and of 'extraordinary' with 'unusual' must be rejected; he indeed goes further and suggests that for the purpose of medical ethics 'perhaps we would avoid confusion if we used the terms 'ethically indicated,' and 'ethically non-indicated' in place of the terms 'ordinary' and 'extraordinary'. Of course once we accept such understanding of the distinction it remains open to ask what are the criteria upon which it should be made – what are the substantive moral principles upon which we can decide whether treatment X is or is not 'ethically indicated' (ie indicated by some process of ethical analysis) for patient Y in circumstances Z.

Roman Catholic authorities have proposed excessive expense, excessive pain, excessive difficulty or other inconvenience, and no reasonable or 'proportionate' hope of benefit as criteria for deciding that a treatment is 'extraordinary' in the context of a particular patient in particular circumstances. This approach is reflected by the Church of England. Thus the moral theologian Professor G R Dunstan in an article on this subject in the *Dictionary of Medical Ethics* suggests that the distinction has different connotations for moralists and for doctors but is used by both with the same intention, notably 'to insist that it is the patient's ultimate interest which should determine the treatment he receives, that interest being seen in relation to his unique being and his unique human and social environment'. Dunstan states that ordinary (and hence morally obligatory) procedures are for the moralist those which, when relativized to a particular patient in a particular context offer the patient 'a reasonable hope of benefit, without excessive expense, pain or other serious inconvenience'. Similarly in a medical usage 'ordinary' would indicate 'what is normal, established, well-tried; of known effectiveness, within the resources and skills available; of calculable and acceptable risk; of generally low morality; involving pain, disturbance, inconvenience, all within predictable limits of acceptability and control; and all proportionate to an expected and lasting benefit to the patient'.

Conversely 'extraordinary' (and hence morally optional) means are for the moralist those means which, when relativized to a particular patient in a particular context, do not satisfy the criteria for being 'ordinary' and which would impose on the patient 'undue suffering or expense, or, it may be, an undue distortion of his personality or a barrier in his relationships with his kin, a lessening of his human capacity, and all without a reasonable hope of benefit'. In the medical connotation extraordinary procedures would be those which in relation to a particular patient in a particular context would fail to meet the criteria for being ordinary – they would include for instance 'investigatory and experimental procedures of uncertain efficacy, or even carrying a high mortality rate; those involving a heavy disproportion between the pain, mutilation, disfigurement or psychological disruption of the patient and any immediate or long-term benefit reasonably predictable; or of disproportionate cost.'

There can be few people involved in making medical-ethical decisions, whether in practice or merely in theory, who would disagree with the general principles of assessment proposed in either the Roman Catholic or Church of England positions as outlined above. Both, however, knowingly leave many important moral questions unanswered. What is to count as 'excessive' expense, pain, difficulty or other inconvenience; what is a 'reasonable' or 'proportionate' hope of benefit; what indeed is to count as a 'benefit'; and who should decide these weighty matters? No attempt is made to answer such questions here. Rather, the crucial point for health workers not versed in Christian theology to appreciate is that an appeal to the ordinary/extraordinary means distinction cannot help them to answer these questions, for the distinction itself can only be made *after* the questions have been answered.

The distinction between ordinary means and extraordinary means has a dangerously deceptive appearance of simplicity. It appears to be a distinction made by assessing means of treatment, whereas in fact, as Dunstan puts it 'the criteria for decision relate primarily to the patient not to the remedy'. It appears to be a distinction made by determining whether particular means of treatment are usual or unusual, and again this is not the case. It appears to give a single *criterion* for making a moral decision whereas in fact it is only a label for a decision-making process which uses a cluster of different moral criteria; above all it appears to be a distinction based upon a simple, uncontroversial, morally non-evaluative assessment, whereas in fact it is based upon complex potentially controversial and essentially moral assessments.

Those who are motivated by their religious orientations to use the distinction between ordinary and extraordinary means in the context of medical ethics may be expected to be aware of all this; those who are not so motivated need to appreciate these complexities before using the distinction at all. However all health workers will risk less confusion, if not for themselves then at least for their patients and for the patients' relatives, if they specify the moral criteria which they believe should be used when deciding whether or not to undertake particular treatments for particular patients in particular circumstances. Specifying the criteria, which may well relate to risks, costs, pain, likelihood of success, anticipated results and side effects, both physical and psychological, of a proposed treatment, will not only reduce confusion but will also provide an opportunity for discussion of the complex issues, both among staff involved and also with patients and/or their relatives. Moreover once the actual criteria of decision are specified the misleading labels 'ordinary means' and 'extraordinary means' become superfluous and may be safely allowed to 'drop out of the picture' by those who have no special reason to retain them.

In short, the distinction is unhelpful in that the words represent a conclusion reached in the light of the consideration of a number of factors. It is the identification and relevance of these factors which any proper analysis of the doctor's (or parent's) duty should concentrate upon.

(c) Acts and omissions

Traditionally, the criminal law has drawn a distinction between acts and omissions. Criminal liability has ordinarily depended upon there being *an act* done by the defendant. Given the difficulties involved in determining precisely what conduct amounts to an act or omission, it will come as no surprise that this distinction has bedevilled medical law just as it has created problems elsewhere. Before trying to find a way out of the problem, not least the question of what is an act as distinct from an omission, it is important to take note of what the traditional approach consists of.

(i) ACTS

Although positive conduct in the form of an act is ordinarily required for there to be criminal liability, it does not follow that every positive act when death results by a doctor in caring for an incompetent patient will be unlawful. Some obviously are unlawful; some may not be. Professor Skegg (1984) analyses this issue:

P Skegg *Law, Ethics and Medicine* (1984)

The fact that a patient would be severely handicapped if he were to live, or would find life a burden, does not affect the general principle that it is murder to kill a person by doing some positive act, with the intention of hastening death. There were several statements to this effect in Farquharson J's direction to the jury in *R v Arthur*. He said that it was an important principle of law that 'However serious the case may be; however much the disadvantage of a mongol or, indeed, any other handicapped child, no doctor has the right to kill it.' There was, he said, no special power, facility, or licence to kill children who are handicapped or seriously disadvantaged in any irreversible way. *R v Arthur* resulted from the death of a newly-born child, but what was said on this matter is equally applicable to other patients.

As the consent of the patient or others, or the patient's medical condition, will not provide a doctor with a defence if he administers a drug for the purpose of ending the patient's life, it is as well to consider whether the doctor's exemplary motive, medical qualifications, or compliance with medical ethics, would provide him with a defence…[I]t is clear that the motive of alleviating suffering will not provide a legal justification for a doctor who intentionally administers what he knows to be a lethal dose of a drug. In *R v Arthur* Farquharson J said that it was accepted that the doctor had acted from the highest of motives, but directed the jury that 'however noble his motives were…that is irrelevant to the question of your deciding what his intent was'…If a doctor acts with the intention of bringing about the death of a patient, the fact that he was acting to alleviate suffering, or for some other exemplary motive, would not at present provide him with a defence to a charge of murder.

In some circumstances the fact that a person has particular medical qualifications will affect that person's liability for murder or manslaughter. If a patient died in the course of a heart transplant operation, performed by a doctor with appropriate qualifications and experience, the doctor would not normally be liable. But if the operation were performed by a layman it would be very difficult to resist the conclusion that he exposed the patient to an unjustified risk, and that he was grossly negligent in attempting the operation. However, the fact that someone was medically qualified would make no difference if he administered a drug – or took any other action – for the purpose of hastening the death of a patient. In the few cases in which doctors have been prosecuted for murder or attempted murder in consequence of things done in the course of medical practice, trial judges have stressed that the law does not place doctors in any special position. In *R v Adams* Devlin J said that the law was the same for all: there was not any special defence for medical men. And in *R v Arthur* Farquharson J said there 'is no special law…that places doctors in a separate category and gives them extra protection over the rest of us'. They are, he said, 'given no special power…to commit an act which causes death'.

Even if a doctor acted in compliance with statements on medical ethics propounded by the British Medical Association, or any other organisation, this would not of itself provide a doctor with a defence if he administered a drug – or did any other act – for the purpose of hastening the death of a patient. In *R v Arthur* Farquharson J commented that it was customary for a profession to agree on rules of conduct for its members but instructed the jury that 'that does not mean that any profession can set out a code of ethics and say that the law must accept it and take notice of it. It may be that in any particular feature the ethic is wrong'. He said that 'whatever a profession may evolve as a system of standards of ethics, it cannot stand on its own, and cannot survive if it is in conflict with the law'. It would therefore be open to a jury to find a doctor guilty of murder even though they believed that he acted in accordance with the ethical standards currently accepted by the medical profession.

The conclusion must be that neither the consent of the patient or anyone else, nor the condition of the patient, nor the doctor's exemplary motive, professional qualifications, or compliance with accepted standards of medical ethics, would provide any defence for a doctor who prescribed or administered a drug – or did any other act – for the purpose of hastening the death of the patient.

Some acts, however, are lawful even though they may hasten death:

R v Bodkin Adams [1957] CLR 365 (CCC)

Devlin J: But that does not mean that a doctor who is aiding the sick and the dying has to calculate in minutes, or even in hours, and perhaps not in days or weeks, the effect upon a patient's life of the medicines which he administers or else be in peril of a charge of murder. If the first purpose of medicine, the restoration of health, can no longer be achieved there is still much for a doctor to do, and he is entitled to do all that is proper and necessary to relieve pain and suffering, even if the measures he takes may incidentally shorten life. That is not because there is any special defence for medical men; it is not because doctors are put into any category different from other citizens for this purpose. The law is the same for all, and what I have said to you rests simply upon this: no act is murder which does not cause death. 'Cause' means nothing philosophical or technical or scientific. It means what you twelve men and women sitting as a jury in the jury box would regard in a common-sense way as the cause…If, for example, because a doctor has done something or has omitted to do something death occurs, it can be scientifically proved – if it could – at eleven o'clock instead of twelve o'clock, or even on Monday instead of Tuesday, no people of common sense would say, 'Oh, the doctor caused her death'. They would say the cause of her death was the illness or the injury, or whatever it was, which brought her into hospital, and the proper medical treatment that is administered and that has incidental effect of determining the exact moment of death, or may have, is not the cause of death in any sensible use of the term. But it remains the fact, and it remains the law, that no doctor, nor any man, no more in the case of the dying man than of the healthy, has the right deliberately to cut the thread of life.

We must be very clear what Devlin J means, because it must be clear that we are on the edge of a discussion about euthanasia, voluntary or otherwise. The mere mention of the word 'euthanasia' is instantly a recipe for confused (and emotive) thinking. Devlin J may be resting his conclusion that 'no act is murder which does not cause death' on either of two legal grounds.

I. No intention

Devlin J may have been saying that although the doctor did an act which 'played some part in' the death of the patient, the doctor should not be liable unless he intended to bring about the death. Devlin J must have meant that the doctor should not be held to have intended the death because of the theory of 'double effect', if the jury found that his primary intention was to relieve the pain of his patient. The theory of 'double effect' which Devlin J introduces into English criminal law purports to be a theory about intention. It seems to say that if an act may have two effects and the actor *desires* only one of them, which is considered a *good* effect, then he should be regarded as blameless even though his act also provides a bad effect providing that is justified (for a discussion see: O P T Price 'Euthanasia, Pain Relief and Double Effect' (1997) 17 Legal Studies 323). The words 'primary' and 'secondary' are used to describe the intention concerning the good and the bad effect (see *Re J (A Minor) (Wardship: Medical Treatment)* (1990) 6 BMLR 25 at 34 per Lord Donaldson MR).

For the lawyer, this theory is not without difficulties:

Glanville Williams *The Sanctity of Life and the Criminal Law* (1957)

…When you know that your conduct will have two consequences, one in itself good and one in itself evil, you are compelled as a moral agent to choose between acting and not acting by making a judgment of value, that is to say by deciding whether the good is more to be desired than the evil is to be avoided. If this is what the principle of double effect means, well and good; but if it means that the necessity of making a choice of values can be avoided merely by keeping your mind off one of the consequences, it can only encourage a hypocritical attitude towards moral problems.

What is true of morals is true of the law. There is no legal difference between desiring or intending a consequence as following from your conduct, and persisting in your conduct with a knowledge that the consequence as following from your conduct, and persisting in your conduct with a knowledge that the consequence will inevitably follow from it, though not desiring that consequence. When a result is foreseen as certain, it is the same as if it were desired or intended. It would be an undue refinement to distinguish between the two.

Professor Williams must be right on the law when he makes clear that the consequence that is undesired may nevertheless be intended in law. Despite the protestations of some philosophers and academic lawyers, it is clear that a defendant does, *in law*, intend a consequence of his actions if he knows it to be a virtually certain outcome of his actions (*R v Woollin* [1998] 4 All ER 103 (HL)). Thus for the lawyer, if not for the moral philosopher, the judgment that an act is blameless cannot analytically rest on a theory of intention as expressed in the 'double effect' theory. It must rest, if anywhere, on a judgment that some acts (though intended) ought as a matter of moral judgment and public policy to be regarded as attracting no blame because of their social worth. This, of course, raises its own problems; what is the principle which underlies any specific determination that a particular course of conduct is blameless?

II. Absence of causation

Devlin J in *Adams* may, in the alternative, have meant to rely on causation: that a doctor's act in such circumstances would not be regarded in law as the cause of the patient's death.

Again, Glanville Williams addresses the issue as follows in his book, *The Sanctity of Life and the Criminal Law* at pp 289–290:

> ...While I am reluctant to criticise a legal doctrine that gives a beneficial result, the use of the language of causation seems here to conceal rather than to reveal the valuation that is being made. To take an example, suppose that it were shown that the administration of morphine in regular medical practice caused a patient to die of respiratory failure or pneumonia. Medically speaking, this death would not be caused by the disease: it would be caused by the administration of morphine. There seems to be some difficulty in asserting that for legal purposes the causation is precisely the opposite.

Lord Devlin responded to this observation in a lecture in 1960 later published in his *Samples of Law Making* (1962). Having referred to his direction to the jury concerned with double effect, the judge went on, at p 95:

> This direction was not, however, given on the basis that the relief of pain justified an act that would otherwise be murder in law. Before a man can be convicted of murder, it must be proved that his act was the cause of the death. That does not invariably, or even frequently, mean the medical cause of death. Medicine is concerned with the immediate physical cause and the criminal law with the guilty cause. On a death certificate no one would put dangerous driving, for example, as a cause of death; but there is an offence known to the law as causing death by dangerous driving. If a man injured in a road crash by dangerous driving was taken to hospital and there died, the driver could not escape conviction unless he could show that there was improper treatment in the hospital of a man who would otherwise have lived. The law might regard negligent treatment as a new and supervening cause of death, but proper medical treatment consequent upon illness or injury plays no part in legal causation; and to relieve the pains of death is undoubtedly proper medical treatment.

Attractive as Lord Devlin's response may be, is it not somewhat question-begging to say that the criminal law is concerned with the 'guilty' cause? Surely our problem is to determine which cause *is* the guilty cause? Has not Lord Devlin in fact conceded Professor Williams' point and admitted that the doctor by his acts does cause the death of a patient but now seeks to rely on another ground? Is not this other ground the same as that which was hinted at in our discussion of intention?

It is suggested that the more appropriate analysis is as follows: the doctor by his act *intends* (on any proper understanding of the term) the death of his patient and by his act *causes* (on any proper understanding of the term) the death of his patient, but the intention is not culpable and the cause is not blameworthy because the law permits the doctor to do the act in question.

On what basis, as a matter of principle, does the law permit the doctor to *act* in this way? In the House of Lords decision in *Airedale NHS Trust v Bland* [1993] 1 All ER 821, Lord Goff (at 868) offered a way of resolving the question:

> **Lord Goff:** The established rule [is] that a doctor may, when caring for a patient who is, for example, dying of cancer, lawfully administer painkilling drugs despite the fact that he knows that an incidental effect of that application will be to abbreviate the patient's life. Such a decision may properly be made as part of the care of the living patient, in his best interests' and, on this basis, the treatment will be lawful. Moreover, where the doctor's treatment of his patient is lawful, the patient's death will be regarded in law as exclusively caused by the injury or disease to which his condition is attributable.

By contrast, Lord Mustill in *Bland* (at 892–893) was not prepared to follow the view of Lord Goff that lawful treatment could not be a cause of the patient's death.

Lord Mustill: One argument in support of the conclusion that if the proposed conduct is carried out and Anthony Bland then dies the doctors will nevertheless be guilty of no offence depends upon a very special application of the doctrine of causation. This has powerful academic support: Skegg *Law, Ethics and Medicine* (1985) ch 6, where it presents the author's chosen solution, and also Glanville Williams *Textbook of Criminal Law* (2nd edn, 1983) pp 282–283 and Professor Ian Kennedy's paper *Treat Me Right, Essays in Medical Law and Ethics* (1988) pp 360–361, where it is offered by way of alternative. Nevertheless I find it hard to grasp. At several stages of his discussion Professor Skegg frankly accepts that some manipulation of the law of causation will be needed to produce the desired result. I am bound to say that the argument seems to me to require not manipulation of the law so much as its application in an entirely new and illogical way. In one form the argument presented to the House asserts that for the purpose of both civil and criminal liability the cause of Anthony Bland's death, if and when it takes place, will be the Hillsborough disaster. As a matter of the criminal law of causation, this may well be right, once it is assumed that the conduct is lawful: see *R v Blaue* [1975] 3 All ER 446 [1975] 1 WLR 1411, *R v Malcherek* [1981] 2 All ER 422, [1981] 1 WLR 690 and *Finlayson v HM Advocate* 1979 JC 33. It does not perhaps follow that the conduct of the doctors is not also causative, but this is of no interest since if the conduct is lawful the doctors have nothing to worry about. If on the other hand the proposed conduct is unlawful, then it is in the same case as active euthanasia or any other unlawful act by doctors or laymen. In common sense they must all be causative or none; and it must be all, for otherwise euthanasia would never be murder.

A variant of the argument appears to put the ordinary law of causation into reverse. Normally, when faced with an act and a suggested consequence one begins by asserting the quality of the act and then, if it is found to be unlawful, one considers its connection to the consequence. This variant, by contrast, seems to begin the inquiry with the connection and then by applying a special rule of causation determine the character of the act. I confess that I cannot understand what mechanism enables this to be done. If the declarations are wrong and the proposed conduct is unlawful it is in my judgment perfectly obvious that the conduct will be, as it is intended to be, the cause of death, and nothing in the literature or the reported cases from other jurisdictions persuades me to any other conclusion.

III. A practical outcome

There is wide support for recognising the legality of pain-relieving treatment properly administered, even if it incidentally shortens life. The legality of the practice has been acknowledged by the US and Canadian Supreme Courts (see, respectively, *Washington v Glucksberg* (1997) 50 BMLR 65 (US Sup Ct) at 86 per O'Connor J (and Ginsburg J), at 92–94 per Stevens J, at 111 per Souter J and at 117–118 per Breyer, J; *Rodriquez v A-G of British Columbia* [1993] 3 SCR 519 at 560 per Lamer CJ (dissenting) and at 606 per Sopinka J). Some jurisdictions have put the legality of the practice beyond doubt through legislation (see eg Consent to Medical Treatment and Palliative Care Act 1995, s 17 (South Australia)).

Four aspects of the practice should be noted. First, the notion of 'pain relief' should not be narrowly construed and limited to *physical* pain. It could include demonstrable severe distress. This was accepted by all parties in the 1997 case involving Annie Linsell, who suffered from motor neurone disease. She sought to establish the legality of providing her palliative medication to avoid her *severe distress* from choking. Her action for a declaration was withdrawn when it became clear that the defendant and judge accepted that what was proposed was lawful (see *Hansard*, HL, cols 721–744 (November 20, 1997)).

Secondly, the 'pain relief' that is necessary in order to alleviate the patient's symptoms may result in the patient lapsing into a coma. The New York State Task Force on Life and the Law in its Report, *When Death is Sought: Assisted Suicide and Euthanasia in the Medical Context* (1994), described the practice:

Palliative care experts believe that the number of patients with unavoidable and intolerable pain is very small. For these patients, sedation to a sleeplike state, while far from an ideal option, would prevent the patient from experiencing severe pain and suffering. This option is considered in rare cases for terminally ill patients during the last days or weeks of their lives.

This practice, known as 'terminal sedation', may result in the subsequent withdrawal of artificial nutrition leading to the patient's death. To the extent that the latter is a necessary part of the doctor's treatment plan, the practice may be legally more problematic than the usual situation of administering 'pain relief'. It will be a necessary part of a course of conduct intended to cause death. One solution might be for the law to see the course of conduct as a whole as an omission to treat and, given the extreme circumstances of the patient, not a breach of duty (see analysis in *Bland, infra*, in relation to permanently unconscious patients in PVS).

Thirdly, the legality of administering 'pain-relieving' drugs is not limited to competent patients who request such medication. It may be lawful to administer such drugs to an incompetent patient also. The patient's consent may, of course, be relevant in that the patient's 'pain' may arise because they have refused another treatment unacceptable to them. That, of course, is their right. However, thereafter, the need for pain relief will arise as it would just as if no other treatment were available. The legal analysis is then the same.

Fourthly, although the issue will usually arise in relation to a 'terminally ill' patient, in principle it may be lawful to administer potentially life-shortening pain relief to other patients. Here, the legal issue will be whether what was done was *acceptable* practice and, in the case of a non-terminally ill patient, it may be more difficult to justify life-shortening treatment.

Finally, therefore, returning to the usual situation the legal difficulties only arise where there can be no doubt that the shortening of life *is known* by the doctor to be the effect of the drugs as in *R v Cox*. The reality, in practice, may however be otherwise. The House of Lords' Select Committee on Medical Ethics both identified and approved of the medical practice.

House of Lords Select Committee on Medical Ethics (1993–94) HL–21, vol 1

Double Effect

242. In the small and diminishing number of cases in which pain and distress cannot be satisfactorily controlled, we are satisfied that the professional judgment of the health-care team can be exercised to enable increasing doses of medication (whether of analgesics or sedatives) to be given in order to provide relief, even if this shortens life. The adequate relief of pain and suffering in terminally ill patients depends on doctors being able to do all that is necessary and possible. In many cases this will mean the use of opiates or sedative drugs in increasing doses. In some cases patients may in consequence die sooner than they would otherwise have done but this is not in our view a reason for withholding treatment that would give relief, as long as the doctor acts in accordance with responsible medical practice with the objective of relieving pain or distress, and with no intention to kill.

243. Some witnesses suggested that the double effect of some therapeutic drugs when given in large doses was being used as a cloak for what in effect amounted to widespread euthanasia, and suggested that this implied medical hypocrisy. We reject that charge while acknowledging that the doctor's intention, and evaluation of the pain and distress suffered by the patient, are of crucial significance in judging double effect. If this intention is the relief of severe pain or distress, and the treatment given is appropriate to that end, then the possible double effect should be no obstacle to such treatment being given. Some may suggest that intention is not readily ascertainable. But juries are asked every day to assess intention in all sorts of cases, and could do so in respect of double effect if in a particular instance there was any reason to suspect that the doctor's primary intention was to kill the patient rather than to relieve pain and suffering. They would no doubt consider the actions of the doctor, how they compared with usual medical practice directed towards the relief of pain and distress, and all the circumstances of the case. We have confidence in the ability of the medical profession to discern when the administration of drugs has been inappropriate or excessive. An additional safeguard is that increased emphasis on team working makes it improbable that doctors could deliberately and recklessly shorten the lives of their patients without their actions arousing suspicion.

244. We would add that the effects of opiates (the drugs most commonly involved in double effect) and of some other pain-relieving and sedative drugs are so uncertain that the outcome of a particular dose can never be predicted with total confidence. The body weight, metabolism, habituation and general condition of the individual patient all affect the response. There have been cases where an error in dispensing resulted in the administration of a dose which seemed likely to be lethal, yet the patient flourished. A doctor called to testify in the case of Dr Bodkin Adams asserted that a particular dose must certainly kill, only to be told that the patient had previously been given that dose and had survived. The primary effect (relief of pain and distress) can be predicted with reasonable confidence but there can be no certainty that the secondary effect (shortening of life) will result. Decisions about dosage are not easy, but the practice of medicine is all about the weighing of risks and benefits.

What we see here is the denial that the usual case will prove legally problematic. The doctor will simply not have, or *at least will not be proved to have*, beyond reasonable doubt, the intention to bring about the patient's death. The uncertainties of medicine come to his rescue. Any lesser intention could only expose the doctor to a charge of manslaughter (whether 'unlawful act' or 'gross negligence manslaughter'). But, if he has prescribed appropriate medication to relieve the pain, his conduct is unlikely to be judged negligent, let alone to be grossly negligent as would be necessary for a successful prosecution for manslaughter.

(ii) OMISSIONS

Let us now consider the other half of the traditional analysis – omissions. Professor Glanville Williams writes, in his *Textbook of Criminal Law* (2nd edn 1983), at pp 148–149:

A crime can be committed by omission, but there can be no omission in law in the absence of a duty to act. The reason is obvious. If there is an act, someone acts; but if there is an omission, everyone (in a sense) omits. We omit to do everything in the world that is not done. Only those of us omit in law who are under a duty to act.

Ordinarily, there is no liability under the criminal law if a person omits to act to save life. An exception to this proposition exists where the law imposes an obligation to act. The problem arises as to what amounts to an omission and how it can be distinguished from an act.

The difficulty in defining what is an omission does not lie in saying what it is, that much is clear; it is a non-action or failure to act. Rather, the difficulty lies in saying whether in any particular set of circumstances there is, in a person's behaviour (the propriety of which is under scrutiny), something that can be called an omission rather than an act since the former less readily attracts liability. If, for example, the facts are that 'X' has suffered harm and 'Y' appears responsible, a court may set out on a voyage of discovery to find some act by 'Y' on which to base liability. That the voyage may lead to the land of Humpty Dumpty can be seen in the following analysis by Professor Williams, of a doctor who turns off the respirator of a patient who is not dead. For Professor Williams, a traditionalist in his analysis here, the issue can be put as follows (*Textbook of Criminal Law* (1st edn 1978) p 237):

The question then arises whether stopping a respirator is an act of killing or a decision to let nature take its course. Common sense suggests it is the latter. Suppose that the respirator worked only as long as the doctor turned a handle. If he stopped turning, he would be regarded as merely commencing to omit to save the patient's life. Suppose, alternatively, that the respirator worked electrically but was made to shut itself off every 24 hours. Then the deliberate failure to restart it would be an omission. It can make no moral difference that the respirator is constructed to run continuously and has to be stopped. Stopping the respirator is not a positive act of killing the patient, but a decision not to strive any longer to save him.

Another commentator, Roger Leng, suggests the following:

Roger Leng 'Death and the Criminal Law' (1982) 45 MLR 206

It is submitted that it is correct to characterise termination [of life support] as an omission. This entails recognition that the act/omission distinction does not rest upon what is done, or upon a concept of willed muscular contraction, but upon the impact of what is done on the victim. The *provision* of life support is in fact a series of acts (albeit accomplished mechanically): termination of support is an omission to continue such acts which has no positive effect on the patient but merely fails to avert the natural cessation of vital functions.

If this characterisation and the general proposition that the doctor/patient relationship imports a duty recognised by the criminal law are accepted, a doctor deliberately discontinuing support to a patient who is not legally dead escapes liability only if it is further accepted that sometimes *it lies within a doctor's duty to allow a patient to die.*

This proposition may not be as problematic as first appears. Whereas the jurisprudence of duty relationships is well developed there has been relatively little consideration of the scope of a duty once found. Where duty and breach have been established the act required has not been onerous: eg alerting a doctor or social worker, provision of food at no personal expense or performing one's contract of employment. The law clearly allows some balancing of the interests of the person under the duty as against those of the person to whom it is owed. Stated briefly the doctor's duty is to preserve life and health. This is an unreal oversimplification. The doctor (with the policeman and judge) implements the state's broad duty to preserve the life and health of citizens. The state does not take every measure to preserve life but must balance competing calls upon its resources. The doctor gives practical effect to this balance. He must take decisions on allocation of skilled attention, drugs, blood and equipment, involving qualitative judgments of cost-effectiveness, likelihood of survival, and the value of the life involved. Some such decisions will adversely affect chances of survival. From this broad perspective, a responsible and procedurally correct decision to terminate life-support to a brain-dead patient may fall within a doctor's duty although it leads to immediate death as traditionally defined.

The distinction between acts and omissions, and its contribution to analysis, fell four-square to be addressed in the *Bland* case. The case involved a 21-year-old patient in a persistent vegetative state after being crushed in the infamous Hillsborough Football Stadium disaster in 1989. The question for the court was whether it would be lawful to discontinue artificial life-support in the form of hydration and nutrition given both the hopelessness of his condition and also that this would lead to his death. In determining that the doctors would behave lawfully the court was forced to indulge in the act/omission analysis.

Airedale NHS Trust v Bland [1993] 1 All ER 821, (1993) 12 BMLR 64 (HL)

Lord Browne-Wilkinson: Murder consists of causing the death of another with intent so to do. What is proposed in the present case is to adopt a course with the intention of bringing about Anthony Bland's death. As to the element of intention, or mens rea, in my judgment there can be no real doubt that it is present in this case: the whole purpose of stopping artificial feeding is to bring about the death of Anthony Bland.

As to the guilty act, or actus reus, the criminal law draws a distinction between the commission of a positive act which causes death and the omission to do an act which would have prevented death. In general an omission to prevent death is not an actus reus and cannot give rise to a conviction for murder. But where the accused was under a duty to the deceased to do the act which he omitted to do, such omission can constitute the actus reus of homicide, either murder (*R v Gibbins* (1918) 13 Cr App Rep 134) or manslaughter (*R v Stone* [1977] 2 All ER 341, [1977] QB 354) depending upon the mens rea of the accused. The Official Solicitor submits that the actus reus of murder is present on two alternative grounds, viz (1) the withdrawal of artificial feeding is a positive act of commission or (2) if what is proposed is only an omission, the hospital and the doctors have assumed a duty to care for Anthony Bland (including feeding him) and therefore the omission to feed him would constitute the actus reus of murder…

Mr Munby QC, in his powerful but balanced argument for the Official Solicitor, submits that the removal of the nasogastric tube necessary to provide artificial feeding and the discontinuance of the existing regime of artificial feeding constitute positive acts of commission. I do not accept this. Apart from the act of removing the nasogastric tube, the mere failure to continue to do what you have previously done is not, in any ordinary sense, to do anything positive: on the contrary it is by definition an omission to do what you have previously done.

The positive act of removing the nasogastric tube presents more difficulty. It is undoubtedly a positive act, similar to switching off a ventilator in the case of a patient whose life is being sustained by artificial ventilation. But in my judgment in neither case should the act be classified as positive, since to do so would be to introduce intolerably fine distinctions. If, instead of removing the nasogastric tube, it was left in place but no further nutrients were provided for the tube to convey to the patient's stomach, that would not be an act of commission. Again, as has been pointed out (Skegg, *Law, Ethics and Medicine* (1985) pp 169 ff), if the switching off of a ventilator were to be classified as a positive act, exactly the same result can be achieved by installing a time-close which requires to be reset every 12 hours: the failure to reset the machine could not be classified as a positive act. In my judgment, essentially what is being done is to omit to feed or to ventilate: the removal of the nasogastric tube or the switching off of a ventilator are merely incidents of that omission: see Glanville Williams, *Texbook of Criminal Law* (2nd edn, 1983) p 282 and Skegg p 169.

In my judgment, there is a further reason why the removal of the nasogastric tube in the present case could not be regarded as a positive act causing the death. The tube itself, without the food being supplied through it, does nothing. The removal of the tube by itself does not cause the death since by itself it did not sustain life. Therefore even if, contrary to my view, the removal of the tube is to be classified as a positive act, it would not constitute the actus reus of murder since such a positive act would not be the cause of death.

Lord Goff: At the heart of this distinction lies a theoretical question. Why is it that the doctor who gives his patient a lethal injection which kills him commits an unlawful act and indeed is guilty of murder, whereas a doctor who, by discontinuing life support, allows his patient to die may not act unlawfully and will not do so, if he commits no breach of duty to his patient? Professor Glanville Williams has suggested (see *Textbook of Criminal Law* (2nd edn, 1983) p 282) that the reason is that what the doctor does when he switches off a life support machine 'is in substance not an act but an omission to struggle' and that 'the omission is not a breach of duty by the doctor, because he is not obliged to continue in a hopeless case'.

I agree that the doctor's conduct in discontinuing life support can properly be categorised as an omission. It is true that it may be difficult to describe what the doctor actually does as an omission, for example where he takes some positive step to bring the life support to an end. But discontinuation of life support is, for present purposes, no different from not initiating life support in the first place. In each case, the doctor is simply allowing his patient to die in the sense that he is desisting from taking a step which might, in certain circumstances, prevent his patient from dying as a result of his pre-existing condition; and as a matter of general principle an omission such as this will not be unlawful unless it constitutes a breach of duty to the patient. I also agree that the doctor's conduct is to be differentiated from that of, for example, an interloper who may perform exactly the same act as the doctor, who discontinues life support, his doing so constitutes interference with the life-prolonging treatment then being administered by the doctor. Accordingly, whereas a doctor, in discontinuing life support, is simply allowing his patient to die of his pre-existing condition, the interloper is actively intervening to stop the doctor from prolonging the patient's life, and such conduct cannot possibly be categorised as an omission.

The distinction appears, therefore, to be useful in the present context in that it can be invoked to explain how discontinuance of life support can be differentiated from ending a patient's life by a lethal injection. But in the end the reason for that difference is that, whereas the law considers that discontinuance of life support may be consistent with the doctor's duty to care for his patient, it does not, for reasons of policy, consider that it forms any part of his duty to give his patient a lethal injection to put him out of his agony.

(See also Lord Mustill at 890–891 and 894–895.)

(iii) THE WAY OUT

You may well feel that reliance on the acts/omissions distinction is unhelpful. Indeed, you may wonder whether such a complicated question of responsibility can be resolved by being encapsulated in one word. It is even more unhelpful when it is recalled that the act/omission distinction, whatever it is, ceases to be of legal significance where there is a duty to act. Doctors caring for patients are under a *duty* to care for their patients; any liability for their conduct will turn on whether they have breached this duty, *whether by act or omission*. Lord Mustill in *Bland* accepted the unhelpfulness of the act/omission distinction (at 890–891):

Lord Mustill: The English criminal law, and also it would appear from the cases cited, the law of transatlantic state jurisdictions, draws a sharp distinction between acts and omissions. If an act resulting in death is done without lawful excuse and with intent to kill it is murder. But an omission to act with the same result and with the same intent is in general no offence at all. So also with lesser crimes. To this general principle there are limited statutory exceptions, irrelevant here. There is also one important general exception at common law, namely that a person may be criminally liable for the consequences of an omission if he stands in such a relation to the victim that he is under a duty to act. Where the result is death the offence will usually be manslaughter, but if the necessary intent is proved it will be murder: see *R v Gibbins* (1918) 13 Cr App Rep 134.

Precisely in what circumstances such a duty should be held to exist is at present quite unclear…For the time being all are agreed that the distinction between acts and omissions exists, and that we must give effect to it.

2.   The duty to the patient

If *duty* is the basis for analysing the legality of treatment decisions at the end of life, as it clearly is, the only issue is what is the content of the duty. We saw in Chapter 6 that, in principle, the law requires a doctor or parent to act in the 'best interests' of the incompetent patient. This is the test which the courts have embraced notwithstanding the limitations and imperfections of resort to this intrinsically imprecise formula. We also saw, when we considered the case of *In the Matter of Conroy* earlier, that two further tests could be relevant in this context. We discussed earlier the question of 'anticipatory decisions' by once competent patients (see *supra*, ch 16). However, in the case of adults (or indeed children) who *have been competent*, the court could adopt the 'substituted judgment' test which we discussed in Chapter 6. We also that the test to be applied by the doctor or parent is set by the law. In the case of children, the court may, under its inherent jurisdiction, review decisions made by others and act in the child's best interests. Such a jurisdiction does not exist in English law in the case of adults (but notice the proposals for reform in *Making Decisions* (Cm 4465), 1999, LCD *supra*, ch 6). Nevertheless, the court's function when deciding about treatment in the case of an incompetent adult should be no different in the sense that the court has to decide where the 'best interests' of the patient lie (for a not wholly convincing judicial attempt to distinguish the court's roles in the case of children and adults see, *Airedale NHS Trust v Bland* [1993] 1 All ER 821 at 882 per Lord Browne-Wilkinson). So the courts have decided that, in the case of incompetent patients, the test to be used by the decision-maker is that of the 'best interests' of the patient.

We now turn to consider how the courts have *applied* the test of 'best interests' in the case of an incompetent patient, whether child or adult, in making treatment decisions at the end of life. In doing so, it will be helpful to separate out a number of factual situations.

(a) The dying patient

We are concerned with the dying. We use this description conscious of its limitations, as expressed by the President's Commission:

President's Commission *Deciding to Forego Life-Sustaining Treatment* (1983)

Other phrases – though useful as general descriptions – are similarly unacceptable when an unambiguous definition is required. For example, attempts – such as those in several statutes – to make the obligations of patients and providers different when a patient is 'terminally ill' are dubious for several reasons. First, although a decision to undertake life-sustaining treatment will frequently depend on whether the patient believes the treatment is likely to extend life substantially enough to be worth its burdens, patients with similar prognoses evaluate relevant facts very differently. The closeness of death may be strongly felt by someone who has only a remote chance of dying soon, while for another person it may not seem imminent until his or her organs have nearly ceased to function. Moreover, prognostication near the end of life is notoriously uncertain. At best, confidence in predicting death is possible only in the final few hours. Patients with the same stage of a disease but with different family settings, personalities, and 'things to live for' actually do live for strikingly varied periods of time. It seems difficult to devise or to justify policies that restrict people's discretion to make appropriate decisions by allowing some choices only to 'terminally ill' patients or by denying them other choices.

Although the Commission has attempted to avoid rhetorical slogans so as to escape the ambiguities and misunderstandings that often accompany them, it uses 'dying' and 'terminally ill' as descriptive terms for certain patients, not as ironclad categories. There seem to be no other terms to use for a patient whose illness is likely to cause death within what is to that person a very short time. Of course, the word 'dying' is in some ways an unilluminating modifier for 'patient' – since life is always a 'terminal' condition – and further refinements, such as 'imminently', do little to clarify the situation. Therefore, words like 'dying' are used in the Report in the colloquial sense and with a caution against regarding them as a source of precision that is not theirs to bestow.

The dying patient is the patient for whom there is no prospect of cure nor of preventing the continued progress of the disease to imminent death. What is the scope and extent of the doctor's duty to care for his dying patient? A doctor faced with a dying patient should change his treatment from treatment for living to treatment for dying. The primary duty is to comfort the patient by symptomatic relief and other appropriate care (see M Somerville, 'Pain and Suffering at the Interfaces of Medicine and the Law' (1986) 36 U of Toronto LJ 186). The British Medical Association helpfully makes this point in its guidance, *Withholding and Withdrawing Life-Prolonging Medical Treatment* (1999) (at para 4.1):

> Developments in technology have led to a misperception in society that death can almost always be postponed. There needs to be a recognition that there comes a point in all lives where no more can reasonably or helpfully be done to benefit patients other than keeping them comfortable and free from pain.

We have seen that it may include the administration of drugs which may hasten death if the primary intention is the relief of pain. In his summing up to the jury in *R v Bodkin Adams* [1957] CLR 365 (discussed *supra*), Devlin J said:

> If the first purpose of medicine, the restoration of health, can no longer be achieved there is still much for a doctor to do, and he is entitled to do all that is proper and necessary to relieve pain and suffering, even if the measures he takes may incidentally shorten life.

The obligation of the doctor is discussed by the President's Commission:

President's Commission *Deciding to Forego Life-Sustaining Treatment* (1983)

The explanation lies in the importance of defining physicians' responsibilities regarding these choices and of developing an accepted and well-regulated social role that allows the choices to be made with due care. The search for medical treatment that will benefit a patient often involves risk, sometimes great risk, for the patient: for example, some surgery still carries a sizeable risk of mortality, as does much of cancer therapy. Furthermore, seeking to cure disease and to prolong life is only a part of the physician's traditional role in caring for patients; another important part is to comfort patients and relieve their suffering. Sometimes these goals conflict, and a physician and patient (or patient's surrogate) have the authority to decide which goal has priority. Medicine's role in relieving suffering is especially important when a patient is going to die soon, since the suffering of such a patient is not an unavoidable aspect of treatment that might restore health, as it might be for a patient with a curable condition. Consequently, the use of pain-relieving medications is distinguished from the use of poisons, though both may result in death, and society places the former into the category of acceptable treatment while continuing the traditional prohibition against the latter. Indeed, in the Commission's view it is not only possible but desirable to draw this distinction. If physicians (and other health professionals) became the dispensers of 'treatments' that could only be understood as deliberate killing of patients, patients' trust in them might be seriously undermined. And irreparable damage could be done to health care professionals' self-image and to their ability to devote themselves wholeheartedly to the often arduous task of treating gravely ill patients. Moreover, whether or not one believes there are some instances in which giving a poison might be morally permissible, the Commission considers that the obvious potential for abuse of a public, legal policy condoning such action argues strongly against it. For the use of morphine or other pain-relieving medication that can lead to death to be socially and legally acceptable, physicians must act within the socially defined bounds of their role. This means that they are not only proceeding with the necessary agreement of the patient (or surrogate) and in a professionally skilful fashion (for example, by not taking a step that is riskier than necessary), but that there are sufficiently weighty reasons to run the risk of the patient dying. For example, were a person experiencing great pain from a condition that will be cured in a few days, use of morphine at doses that would probably lead to death by inducing respiratory depression would usually be unacceptable. On the other hand, for a patient in great pain – especially from a condition that has proved to be untreatable and that is expected to be rapidly fatal – morphine can be both morally and legally acceptable if pain relief cannot be achieved by less risky means.

This analysis rests on the special role of physicians and on particular professional norms of acceptability that have gained social sanction (such as the difference between morphine, which can relieve pain, and strychnine, which can only cause death). Part of acceptable behaviour – from the medical as well as the ethical and legal standpoints – is for the physician to take into account all the foreseeable effects, not just the intended goals, in making recommendations and in administering treatment. The degree of care and judgment exercised by the physician should therefore be guided not only by the technical question of whether pain can be relieved but also by the broader question of whether care providers are certain enough of the facts in this case, including the patient's priorities and subjective experience, to risk death in order to relieve suffering. If this can be answered affirmatively, there is no moral or legal objection to using the kinds and amounts of drugs necessary to relieve the patient's pain.

An English case concerned with a dying patient, at least on the court's view of the facts, was *Re C* in 1989.

Re C (a minor) (wardship: medical treatment) [1989] 2 All ER 782 (CA)

Lord Donaldson MR: I have, most regretfully, to start with one fundamental and inescapable fact. Baby C is dying and nothing that the court can do, nothing that the doctors can do and nothing known to medical science can alter that fact.

The problem of how to treat the terminally ill is as old as life itself. Doctors and nurses have to confront it frequently, but it is never easy. Parents and relatives have to confront it less often and that makes it all the more difficult for them. Judges are occasionally faced with it when terminally ill children are wards of court. It is an awesome responsibility only made easier for them than for parents to the extent that judges are available to approach it with greater detachment and less emotional involvement.

The present case is one of the saddest which can be imagined. Not only are we concerned with a very young baby, but one who became terminally ill before she was ever born, a fact which only became apparent at a later date.

C was born prematurely on 23 December 1988. She is now 16 weeks old. At birth she was found to be afflicted with a much more serious condition than the usual type of hydrocephalus. There was not merely a blockage of cerebral spinal fluid within the brain, but as a result the brain structure itself was poorly formed. Her progress since then and further examinations have revealed how exceptionally she has been affected...

One of the first decisions which the court had to make was whether or not to agree to the child being operated on to relieve pressure on the brain. This is often done in cases of hydrocephalus with good results, but alas in the case of C all that could be hoped for was that it would prevent her head becoming so enlarged that nursing would become impossible. The damage to her brain had been done before birth and was irreparable.

Those who, understandably, have been moved by the story of C, but who have no personal involvement, have publicly commented that this operation should have been performed. I am bound to say that I think it might have been better if they had first made sure of the facts. In fact, the registrar of the court readily consented to its being undertaken and it was. The actual order was dated 11 January 1989 and it required that C 'who is suffering from congenital hydrocephalus, receive such treatment, including surgical treatment, as is considered medically appropriate' to her condition. It was pursuant to this order that the doctors operated on C and inserted a shunt to relieve pressure on her brain.

At all times since her birth C has received the finest and most caring medical and nursing attention which this country has to offer. However, the time came when a decision had to be made on what further treatment should be provided. In a critical situation such as this such decisions should not be, and are not, taken without wide consultation. And so it came about that the local authority's medical and social services departments became involved. The essential problem was what treatment should be given in the best interests of C if, as sooner or later was inevitable, she suffered some infection or illness over and above the handicaps from which she was already suffering. In the middle of last month a social worker expressed the view that in such a situation the court would expect the doctors to embark on 'treatment appropriate to a non handicapped child'. The legal department of the local authority, on the other hand, expressed the view that C should 'receive such treatment as is appropriate to her condition'.

For my part, I have no doubt that the legal department was right and the social worker was wrong. You do not treat a blind child as if she was sighted, or one with a diseased heart as if she was wholly fit. But this difference of opinion created a problem for Dr W, the physician in charge of C, for his paediatric colleague, Dr S, and for the nursing staff. Sooner or later he or the local authority would have been bound to seek instructions from the court because, as Heilbron J said in *Re D (a minor) (wardship: sterilisation)* [1976] 1 All ER 326 at 335, [1976] Fam 185 at 196:

> …once a child is a ward of court, no important step in the life of that child, can be taken without the consent of the court…

In the circumstances, and quite rightly, the local authority decided to consult the court sooner rather than later. In previous correspondence, which was of course made available to the judge, Dr W had raised the question of what he should do if the time came when it proved impossible to feed C through a syringe, in itself a procedure fraught with difficulty. In such circumstances should he resort to the use of a nasal-gastric tube? If C vomited, should he set up an intravenous drip? If C developed a terminal respiratory infection, should she be given antibiotics? All these were legitimate and difficult questions, given the sad but fundamental truth that C was dying and the only question was how soon this would happen.

Faced with these problems, the judge invited the intervention of the Official Solicitor, who asked one of the nation's foremost paediatricians to examine C and to make recommendations. I do not name him, simply because it might serve to identify where C is being treated; I refer simply to 'the professor'. The professor reported as follows and I read from his report:

> The records revealed that at birth she had a much more serious condition than the usual type of hydrocephalus. The detailed investigations which were done showed that there was not merely a blockage of cerebro-spinal fluid within the brain, but that the brain structure itself was poorly formed. Thus the operation that was done to relieve the pressure within the brain was no more than a palliative procedure to prevent her head from becoming so excessively large that nursing would be impossible. The operation could not be expected to restore brain function. [C's] appearance is of a tiny baby. Although she is 16 weeks old, she is the size of a 4 week baby apart from her head, which is unusually large by way of being tall and thin – squashed because of sleeping on her side. She lies quiet until handled and then she cries as if irritated. Her eyes move wildly in an uncoordinated way and she does not appear to see. (Her pupils do not respond to light so it is most unlikely that the mechanism for vision is present). She did not respond to very loud noises that I made, though the nurses said that she sometimes seems startled by their loud noises. However, my impression was that she did not hear, or had very poor hearing. She holds her limbs in a stiff flexed position. More detailed examination suggested that she had generalised spasticity of all her limbs as a result of the brain damage. The only social response she makes is the irritable crying when handled, though sometimes she can be pacified by stroking her face. She does not smile and does not respond in any other way. The only certain evidence of her feeling or appreciating events is the report of her quietening when her face is stroked. Thus she does not have the developmental skills and abilities of a normal new born baby. It is inconceivable that appreciable skills will develop, bearing in mind that there has been no progress during the past four months. She has severe brain damage. She is very thin and has not gained weight despite devoted nursing care at [the hospital]. She is receiving regular small doses of the sedative Chloral. If she does not receive that she cries 'as if in pain', though the carers are unsure where the pain originates. I do not believe that there is any treatment which will alter the ultimate prognosis, which appears to be hopeless. She has massive handicap as a result of a permanent brain lesion. Her handicap appears to be a mixture of severe mental handicap, blindness, probable deafness and spastic cerebral palsy of all four limbs. In addition, although given a normal amount of food, her body is not absorbing or using it in the normal way so that she is not growing. I do not believe

that she can be said to be enjoying her life and I find it hard to know if she is experiencing very much, though the reports of irritable crying suggest that certain things upset her. She is receiving outstandingly devoted care...which could not be replicated in many children's units, or in many homes. The high standard of care makes it difficult to forecast how long she will live...In the event of her acquiring a serious infection, or being unable to take feeds normally by mouth I do not think it would be correct to give antibiotics, to set up intravenous fusions or nasal-gastrict feeding regimes. Such action would be prolonging a life which has no future and which appears to be unhappy for her. However, the opinions of the local nurses and carers should be taken into account for they know her well, show great love to her, and have a feeling for her needs that an outsider cannot have. Thus if they believed she was in pain or would suffer less by a particular course of action, it would be correct to consider that course of action, always bearing in mind the balance between short-term gain and needless prolongation of suffering.

It will be seen that the professor took the view that the goal should be to ease the suffering of C rather than to achieve a short prolongation of her life. But he did not rule out the giving of antibiotics, intravenous fusions or nasal-gastric feeding if this would achieve this result. Above all, he felt that, in reaching decisions as events unfolded, the opinions of local nurses an carers should be given the greatest possible weight.

In giving the reasons for his decision Ward J said:

That poor baby has now been nursed and attended by the hospitals with a degree of devotion to duty which deserves the very highest commendation, and I pay tribute to those who have had part of the care of this ward, and I give my thanks to those for so looking after my ward on my behalf. I have had the advantage of a report by an eminent professor of paediatrics, instructed by the Official Solicitor, whom I caused to become involved in this matter to represent the interests of the baby. The professor observes in his report that the outstandingly devoted care she has received could not be replicated in many children's units or in many children's homes, and it is important that that should receive its proper tribute and its proper commendation. Sadly, notwithstanding that devotion this child has not prospered. I have had the benefit of reading the report and hearing the evidence of Dr W, who is the consultant physician at the hospital, a physician of 21 years' experience, and I gave him my thanks for the assistance he has given me. He reports to me that this baby has made virtually no progress since her birth.

I omit some matters and quote again from the judge's judgment, where he said: 'The damage which she has suffered is quite exceptionally severe.' Then he set out the evidence in support of that proposition and continued:

The medical evidence satisfies me that the damage to the cortex of the brain is gross and abnormally severe. The cortex of the brain is that part of the brain which serves the higher functions; those functions of intellect which make human life distinguishable, perhaps, from other forms of life. That damage, moreover, is irreparable, and about that all the medical witnesses are wholly agreed. There is, therefore, no prospect of a happy life for this child, sadly; no prospect whatever. The prognosis, in the conclusion of [the professor], is that it is inconceivable that appreciable skills will ever develop, and that is, of course, confirmed by the total failure of progress in those few short weeks of her life. There is, in the united opinion of the medical experts, no treatment which will alter that prognosis, and the prognosis is therefore one of hopelessness. I am therefore dealing with a child massively handicapped by a mixture of severe or permanent brain lesions, blindness, probable deafness and generalised spastic cerebral palsy of all four limbs...

[C] is, as I have already said, dying, and there is no medical or surgical treatment which can alter this fact. The judge continued in his judgment, saying:

But here I am quite satisfied that the damage is severe and irreparable. In so far as I can assess the quality of life, which as a test in itself raises as many questions as it can answer, I adjudge that any quality of life has already been denied to this child because it cannot flow from a brain incapable of even limited intellectual function. Inasmuch as one judges, as I do, intellectual function to be a hallmark of our humanity, her functioning on that level is negligible if it exists at all. Coupled with her total physical handicap, the quality of her life will be demonstrably awful and intolerable...Asking myself what capacity she has to interact mentally, socially, physically, I answer none. This is her permanent condition.

It was shortly after this that the judge, in a brief passage in his judgment, failed to express himself with his usual felicity. He said:

Putting the interests of this child first and putting them foremost so that they override all else, and in fulfilment of the awesome responsibility which Parliament has entrusted on me, I direct that leave be given to the hospital authorities to treat the ward to die, to die with the greatest dignity and the least of pain, suffering and distress.

No judge giving an extempore judgment has not, at one time or another, realised that he has not expressed himself as he intended. For this reason, and because the reasons for a decision in one case are published and are rightly taken into account in deciding others, it has long been the practice for judges in appropriate cases to make small revisions in the wording of their judgments when they receive a transcript from the shorthand writers. So it was in this case. The judge revised the first sentence of that passage to read:

I direct that leave be given to the hospital authorities to treat the ward in such a way that she may end her life and die peacefully with the greatest dignity and the least of pain, suffering and distress.

Unfortunately, the formal order also contained the misleading phrase 'treat the minor to die'. Such orders are not seen by the judge unless he specifically asks to approve its wording, and the judge was at first unaware of its phraseology. When it was drawn to his attention, he at once exercised his powers under the slip rule to amend that part of the order to read: 'the hospital authority be at liberty to allow her life to come to an end peacefully and with dignity'.

The Official Solicitor in appealing to this court does not take issue on this part of the judge's order. Nor do the local authority or the mother, both of whom have been represented. All concerned accept that the judge correctly directed himself that the first and paramount consideration was the well-being, welfare and interests of C as required by the decision of this court in *Re B (a minor) (wardship: medical treatment)* and by the House of Lords in a later and different case with the same name, *Re B (a minor) (wardship: sterilisation)* [1987] 2 All ER 206 at 211, [1988] AC 199 at 202 per Lord Hailsham LC.

Counsel for the local authority nevertheless felt it his duty to direct our attention to a decision of the British Columbia Supreme Court in *Re SD* [1983] 3 WWR 618, while submitting that the facts were very different. In so doing he was fulfilling the fundamental duty of members of the legal profession to assist the courts in the administration of justice, regardless of the views or interests of their client. He was wholly right so to do. In the event, I am fully satisfied that it does nothing to cast doubts on the correctness of his clients', and the judge's, view that the advice of the professor should be accepted. It was another case in which a child suffered from hydrocephalus, but the child concerned was very much older. The child had twice been operated on to implant a shunt and the question was whether he should now undergo a third operation.

He was undoubtedly severely handicapped, but not as severely as some in his class at the hospital school. If a third operation were to be performed he would probably continue to live as he had done before and would do so for some years. The parents thought that there should be no operation and that he should be allowed to die at once. The higher court authorised the operation, saying it was too simplistic to say, as did the parents, that the child would be allowed to die in peace. There was a real possibility that, without the operation, the child would endure in a state of progressive disability and pain. That is a wholly different case.

The Official Solicitor in bringing this appeal had three objectives. The first was to question the propriety of an order expressed to be 'liberty to treat the minor to die.' As I hope I have made clear, neither Ward J nor anyone else would uphold such phraseology and he himself amended it. Second, the Official Solicitor wished to question that part of the order of the judge which appeared to provide that in no circumstances should certain treatment be undertaken. To that I will return in a moment. Third, the Official Solicitor wished to allay anxieties in some quarters that the hospital staff were treating C in a way designed to bring about her death. These anxieties, while no doubt sincerely felt, were wholly without foundation and, when expressed, were deeply wounding to the dedicated staff caring for C who, as the professor said, were providing C with devoted care which could not be replicated in many children's units.

Balcombe and Nicholls LJJ agreed.

The conclusion arrived at by the Master of the Rolls seems eminently the right one and puts the law beyond doubt. Parenthetically it may be objected that a close examination of the facts suggests that C was not in fact dying. You will notice that Ward J, the trial judge, refers to C's prognosis as being one of 'hopelessness', namely, C was very severely disabled and would not get better. This is not the same as saying she was dying, ie that she would die regardless of any care or treatment which she received. This view of the facts of the case does not, of course, affect its status as the leading authority on the doctor's duty to a dying patient. On the other hand, it could be said that by regarding C as dying the Court of Appeal was able to duck the far more difficult problem of the patient who is disabled but who is not dying – but not for long (see *Re J* (*infra*)).

Before we leave the law relating to the doctor's duty to the dying, two final points must be made. First, it is all very well for the courts to say that the doctor's duty is to comfort and 'ease the suffering' of the patient. We have already seen from our consideration of the acts/omissions distinction that the courts talk easily of the doctor having a duty to care but not to kill. How does this square with the facts of modern medicine? Morphine to relieve suffering is legally permissible but poison to kill is not. But what of increasing doses of morphine which will comfort *and* kill and which is known to do this? All we say here is that the rhetoric of the courts in dealing with the care of the dying obscures the fact that what happens in practice is lawful or unlawful depending entirely on how it is described rather than on what is done.

Secondly, you will notice that *Re C* contemplated the withholding/withdrawal of medicines and life-support including artificial hydration and nutrition. We shall see later that the issue of whether the latter (and *a fortiori* manual feeding) may be withdrawn is problematic. In the context of the dying, however, the duty to comfort and 'ease the suffering' of the patient would in some instances countenance their withdrawal/withholding if that was in the patient's 'best interests', ie it served 'no purpose' other than to forestall an inevitable and imminent death subject always to the importance of avoiding, by whatever appropriate means if necessary, any suffering for the patient. Professional guidance recognises that this is ethical, at least to the extent that it is *artificial* feeding or nutrition. Hence, in its guidance, *Withholding and Withdrawing Life – Prolonging Medical Treatment* (1999), the British Medical Association states:

> 21.3 **Where the patient's imminent death is believed to be inevitable, artificial nutrition and hydration may be withheld or withdrawn if it is not considered to be a benefit to the patient.**
> Once an individual's condition has reached the stage where death is imminent, such as in the final stages of a terminal illness, the focus of care changes from attempting to prolong life to keeping the patient as comfortable as possible until death occurs. In these final stages, active treatment and the provision of artificial nutrition and hydration may become unnecessarily intrusive and merely prolong the dying process rather than offering a benefit to the patient. Basic care should, however, always be provided (including the offer of oral nutrition and hydration and any procedure necessary to keep the patient comfortable).

(See also, Royal College of Paediatrics and Child Health *Withholding or Withdrawing Life Saving Treatment in Children* (1997) para 3.1.4.)

It may be that the law would go further and in some circumstances permit the withholding of manual or oral provision of food or water (see *infra*).

(b) The patient who is not dying but who will do so if not given life-sustaining treatment

We can divide this category of patient into two broad groups. First, there is the patient who is in a state which we may call a 'living death' (group 1). Perhaps the best known manifestation of this is the persistent vegetative state (PVS). Secondly, there are those patients for whom medical intervention may offer some benefit but the question arises whether the benefit to be gained by the patient justifies the intervention (group 2).

In analysing the law in respect of these two groups of patients you will notice that we will be concerned with two questions in particular. First, what test must the decision-maker use when deciding on treatment in any particular case.

Secondly, are there circumstances in which a doctor or parent must refer the decision to the court and cannot make it himself? As we have suggested throughout this chapter, the crucial question for the law is to determine what is the *doctor's duty to his patient*. It is with this that we shall primarily be concerned in analysing the law as it applies to the two groups of patients described above.

(i) GROUP 1 PATIENTS

The persistent, or permanent, vegetative state is a rare phenomenon where the brain damage results in the patient remaining alive and 'awake but unaware'. As a medical condition, its diagnosis is not without controversy as is its management (see eg, A Grubb, P Walsh, N Lambe, T Murrells and S Robinson *Doctors' Views on the Management of Patients in Persistent Vegetative State (PVS): A UK Study* (1997), Centre of Medical Law & Ethics, King's College London, Occasional Papers Series 1). What decisions may be taken about the care and management of such patients, including withholding treatment and withdrawing nutrition and hydration continues to be a problematic issue in Britain and elsewhere giving rise to court cases and professional guidance (see P Walsh (ed) *The Vegetative State: Persisting Problems in Law and Regulation* (1999) Centre of Medical Law & Ethics, King's College London, Occasional Papers Series 3).

Until recently, the state of English law was uncertain although there had been numerous cases decided in the United States (see eg *In Re Quinlan* (1976) 355 A 2d 647 (NJ Sup Ct) and *Cruzan v Director, Missouri Department of Health* (1990) 110 S Ct 2841 (US Sup Ct). The case law is discussed in A Meisel *The Right to Die* (2nd edn, 1995) vols 1 and 2, especially para 9.53. For a discussion of legal and other developments in Europe and elsewhere, see A Grubb, P Walsh and N Lambe 'Reporting on the Persistent Vegetative State in Europe' (1998) 6 Med L Rev 161). The House of Lords in the *Bland* case established the law in England (and for similar reasoning and result by a Scottish court, see: *Law Hospital NHS Trust v Lord Advocate* 1996 SLT 848 (CS(IH)) and Commentary, (1996) 4 Med L Rev 300 (AG)). We will see, however, that the Law Lords differ in their approach and reasoning.

Airedale NHS Trust v Bland [1993] 1 All ER 821, (1993) 12 BMLR 64 (HL)

Lord Goff: My Lords, the facts of the present case are not in dispute…

They reveal a tragic state of affairs, which has evoked great sympathy, both for Anthony Bland himself and for his devoted family, and great respect for all those who have been responsible for his medical treatment and care since he was admitted to hospital following the terrible injuries which he suffered at Hillsborough in April 1989. For present purposes, I propose simply to adopt the sympathetic and economical summary of Sir Thomas Bingham MR…which, for convenience of reference, I will now incorporate into this opinion.

Mr Anthony David Bland, then aged 17½, went to the Hillsborough ground on 15 April 1989 to support the Liverpool Football Club. In the course of the disaster which occurred on that day his lungs were crushed and punctured and the supply of oxygen to his brain was interrupted. As a result, he suffered catastrophic and irreversible damage to the higher centres of the brain. The condition from which he suffers, and has suffered since April 1989, is known as a persistent vegetative state (PVS). PVS is a recognised medical condition quite distinct from other conditions sometimes known as 'irreversible coma', the 'Guillain-Barre syndrome', the 'locked-in syndrome' and 'brain death'. Its distinguishing characteristics are that the brain stem remains alive and functioning while the cortex of the brain loses its function and activity. Thus the PVS patient continues to breathe unaided and his digestion continues to function. But, although his eyes are open, he cannot see. He cannot hear. Although capable of reflex movement, particularly in respect to painful stimuli, the patient is incapable of voluntary movement and can feel no pain. He cannot taste or smell. He cannot speak or communicate in any way. He has no cognitive function and can thus feel no emotion, whether pleasure or distress. The absence of cerebral function is not a matter of surmise; it can be scientifically demonstrated. The space which the brain should occupy is full of watery fluid. The medical witnesses in this case include some of the outstanding authorities in the country on this condition. All are agreed on the diagnosis. All are agreed on the prognosis also: there is no hope of any improvement or recovery. One witness of great experience describes Mr Bland as the worst PVS case he had ever seen. Mr Bland lies in bed in the Airedale General Hospital, his eyes open, his mind vacant, his limbs crooked and taut. He cannot swallow, and so cannot be spoon-fed without a high risk that food will be inhaled into the lung. He is fed by means of a tube, threaded through the nose and down into the stomach, through which liquefied food is mechanically pumped. His bowels are evacuated by enema. His bladder is drained by catheter. He has been subject to repeated bouts of infection affecting his urinary tract and chest, which have been treated with antibiotics. Drugs have also been administered to reduce salivation, to reduce muscle tone and severe sweating and to encourage gastric emptying. A tracheostomy tube has been inserted and removed. Urino-genitary problems have required surgical intervention. A patient in this condition requires very skilled nursing and close medical attention if he is to survive. The Airedale National Health Service Trust have, it is agreed, provided both to Mr Bland. Introduction of the nasogastric tube is itself a task of some delicacy even in an insensate patient. Thereafter it must be monitored to ensure that it has not become dislodged and to control inflammation, irritation and infection to which it may give rise. The catheter must be monitored: it may cause infection (and has repeatedly done so); it has had to be resited, in an operation performed without anaesthetic. The mouth and other parts of the body must be constantly tended. The patient must be repeatedly moved to avoid pressure sores. Without skilled nursing and close medical attention a PVS patient will quickly succumb to infection. With such care, a young and otherwise healthy patient may live for many years. At no time before the disaster did Mr Bland give any indication of his wishes should he find himself in such a condition. It is not a topic most adolescents address. After careful thought his family agreed that the feeding tube should be removed and felt that this was what Mr Bland would have wanted. His father said of his son in evidence: 'He certainly wouldn't want to be left like that.' He could see no advantage at all in continuation of the current treatment. He was not cross-examined. It was accordingly with the concurrence of Mr Bland's family, as well as the consultant in charge of his case and the support of two independent doctors, that the Airedale NHS Trust as plaintiff in this action applied to the Family Division of the High Court for declarations that they might – (1)...lawfully discontinue all life-sustaining treatment and medical support measures designed to keep AB [Mr Bland] alive in his existing persistent vegetative state including the termination of ventilation nutrition and hydration by artificial means; and (2)...lawfully discontinue and thereafter need not furnish medical treatment to AB except for the sole purpose of enabling AB to end his life and die peacefully with the greatest dignity and the least of pain suffering and distress.' After a hearing in which he was assisted by an amicus curiae instructed by the Attorney General, Sir Stephen Brown P made these declarations (subject to a minor change of wording) on 19 November 1992. He declined to make further declarations which were also sought.

The Official Solicitor, acting on behalf of Anthony Bland, appealed against that decision to the Court of Appeal, which dismissed the appeal. Now, with the leave of the Court of Appeal, the Official Solicitor has appealed to your Lordships' House...

The central issue in the present case has been aptly stated by Sir Thomas Bingham MR to be whether artificial feeding and antibiotic drugs may lawfully be withheld from an insensate patient with no hope of recovery when it is known that if that is done the patient will shortly thereafter die. The Court of Appeal, like Sir Stephen Brown P, answered this question generally in the affirmative, and (in the declarations made or approved by them) specifically also in the affirmative in relation to Anthony Bland. I find myself to be in agreement with the conclusions so reached by all the judges below, substantially for the reasons given by them. But the matter is of such importance that I propose to express my reasons in my own words.

I start with the simple fact that, in law, Anthony is still alive...

[I]n many cases not only may the patient be in no condition to be able to say whether or not he consents to the relevant treatment or care, but also he may have given no prior indication of his wishes with regard to it. In the case of a child who is a ward of court, the court itself will decide whether medical treatment should be provided in the child's best interests, taking into account medical opinion. But the court cannot give its consent on behalf of an adult patient who is incapable of himself deciding whether or not to consent to treatment. I am of the opinion that there is nevertheless no absolute obligation upon the doctor who has the patient in his care to prolong his life, regardless of the circumstances. Indeed, it would be most startling, and could lead to the most adverse and cruel effects upon the patient, if any such absolute rule were held to exist. It is scarcely consistent with the primacy given to the principle of self-determination in those cases in which the patient of sound mind has declined to give his consent that the law should provide no means of enabling treatment to be withheld in appropriate circumstances where the patient is in no condition to indicate, if that was his wish, that he did not consent to it. The point was put forcibly in the judgment of the Supreme Judicial Court of Massachusetts in *Belchertown State School Superintendent v Saikewicz* (1977) 373 Mass 728 747 as follows:

> To presume that the incompetent person must always be subjected to what many rational and intelligent persons may decline is to downgrade the status of the incompetent person by placing a lesser value on his intrinsic human worth and vitality...

I return to the patient who, because for example he is of unsound mind or has been rendered unconscious by accident or illness, is incapable of stating whether or not he consents to treatment or care. In such circumstances, it is now established that a doctor may lawfully treat such a patient if he acts in his best interests, and indeed that, if the patient is already in his care, he is under a duty so to treat him: see *F v West Berkshire Health Authority* [1989] 2 All ER 545, [1990] 2 AC 1, in which the legal principles governing treatment in such circumstances were stated by this House. For my part I can see no reason why, as a matter of principle, a decision by a doctor whether or not to initiate, or to continue to provide, treatment or care which could or might have the effect of prolonging such a patient's life should not be governed by the same fundamental principle. Of course, in the great majority of cases, the best interests of the patient are likely to require that treatment of this kind, if available, should be given to a patient. But this may not always be so. To take a simple example given by Thomas J in the High Court of New Zealand in *Auckland Area Health Board v A-G* [1993] 1 NZLR 235 at 253, to whose judgment in that case I wish to pay tribute, it cannot be right that a doctor, who has under his care a patient suffering painfully from terminal cancer, should be under an absolute obligation to perform upon him major surgery to abate another condition which, if unabated, would or might shorten his life still further. The doctor who is caring for such a patient cannot, in my opinion, be under an absolute obligation to prolong his life by any means available to him, regardless of the quality of the patient's life. Common humanity requires otherwise, as do medical ethics and good medical practice accepted in this country and overseas. As I see it, the doctor's decision whether or not to take any such step must (subject to his patient's ability to give or withhold his consent) be made in the best interests of the patient...

It is of course the development of modern medical technology, and in particular the development of life support systems, which has rendered cases such as the present so much more relevant than in the past. Even so, where, for example, a patient is brought into hospital in such a condition that, without the benefit of a life support system, he will not continue to live, the decision has to be made whether or not to give him that benefit, if available. That decision can only be made in the best interests of the patient. No doubt, his best interests will ordinarily require that he should be placed on a life support system as soon as necessary, if only to make an accurate assessment of his condition and a prognosis for the future. But, if he neither recovers sufficiently to be taken off it nor dies, the question will ultimately arise whether he should be kept on it indefinitely. As I see it, that question (assuming the continued availability of the system) can only be answered by reference to the best interests of the patient himself, having regard to established medical practice. Indeed, if the justification for treating a patient who lacks the capacity to consent lies in the fact that the treatment is provided in his best interests, it must follow that the treatment may, and indeed ultimately should, be discontinued where it is no longer in his best interests to provide it. The question which lies at the heart of the present case is, as I see it, whether on that principle the doctors responsible for the treatment and care of Anthony Bland can justifiably discontinue the process of artificial feeding upon which the prolongation of his life depends.

It is crucial for the understanding of this question that the question itself should be correctly formulated. The question is not whether the doctor should take a course which will kill his patient, or even take a course which has the effect of accelerating his death. The question is whether the doctor should or should not continue to provide his patient with medical treatment or care which, if continued, will prolong his patient's life. The question is sometimes put in striking or emotional terms, which can be misleading. For example, in the case of a life support system, it is sometimes asked: should a doctor be entitled to switch it off, or to pull the plug? And then it is asked: can it be in the best interests of the patient that a doctor should be able to switch the life support system off, when this will inevitably result in the patient's death? Such an approach has rightly been criticised as misleading, for example by Professor Ian Kennedy (in his paper in *Treat Me Right, Essays in Medical Law and Ethics* (1988)), and by Thomas J in *Auckland Area Health Board v A-G* [1993] 1 NZLR 235 at 247. This is because the question is not whether it is in the best interests of the patient that he should die.

The question is whether it is in the best interests of the patient that his life should be prolonged by the continuance of this form of medical treatment or care.

The correct formulation of the question is of particular importance in a case such as the present, where the patient is totally unconscious and where there is no hope whatsoever of any amelioration of his condition. In circumstances such as these, it may be difficult to say that it is in his best interests that the treatment should be ended. But, if the question is asked, as in my opinion it should be, whether it is in his best interests that treatment which has the effect of artificially prolonging his life should be continued, that question can sensibly be answered to the effect that it is not in his best interests to do so...

[In PVS cases] there is in reality no weighing operation to be performed. Here the condition of the patient, who is totally unconscious and in whose condition there is no prospect of any improvement, is such that life-prolonging treatment is properly regarded as being, in medical terms, useless. As Sir Thomas Bingham MR pointed out in the present case, medical treatment or care may be provided for a number of different purposes. It may be provided, for example, as an aid to diagnosis, for the treatment of physical or mental injury or illness, to alleviate pain or distress, or to make the patient's condition more tolerable. Such purposes may include prolonging the patient's life, for example to enable him to survive during diagnosis and treatment. But for my part I cannot see that medical treatment is appropriate or requisite simply to prolong a patient's life when such treatment has no therapeutic purpose of any kind, as where it is futile because the patient is unconscious and there is no prospect of any improvement in his condition. It is reasonable also that account should be taken of the invasiveness of the treatment and of the indignity to which, as the present case shows, a person has to be subjected if his life is prolonged by artificial means, which must cause considerable distress to his family – a distress which reflects not only their own feelings but their perception of the situation of their relative who is being kept alive. But in the end, in a case such as the present, it is the futility of treatment which justifies its termination. I do not consider that, in circumstances such as these, a doctor is required to initiate or to continue life-prolonging treatment or care in the best interests of his patient. It follows that no such duty rests upon the respondents, or upon Dr Howe, in the case of Anthony Bland, whose condition is in reality no more than a living death, and for whom such treatment or care would, in medical terms, be futile.

In the present case it is proposed that the doctors should be entitled to discontinue both the artificial feeding of Anthony and the use of antibiotics. It is plain from the evidence that Anthony, in his present condition, is very prone to infection and that, over some necessarily uncertain but not very long period of time, he will succumb to infection which, if unchecked, will spread and cause his death. But the effect of discontinuing the artificial feeding will be that he will inevitably die within one or two weeks.

Objection can be made to the latter course of action on the ground that Anthony will thereby be starved to death, and that this would constitute a breach of the duty to feed him which must form an essential part of the duty which every person owes to another in his care. But here again it is necessary to analyse precisely what this means in the case of Anthony. Anthony is not merely incapable of feeding himself. He is incapable of swallowing, and therefore of eating or drinking in the normal sense of those words. There is overwhelming evidence that, in the medical profession, artificial feeding is regarded as a form of medical treatment; and, even if it is not strictly medical treatment, it must form part of the medical care of the patient. Indeed, the function of artificial feeding in the case of Anthony, by means of a nasogastric tube, is to provide a form of life support analogous to that provided by a ventilator which artificially breathes air in and out of the lungs of a patient incapable of breathing normally, thereby enabling oxygen to reach the bloodstream. The same principles must apply in either case when the question is asked whether the doctor in charge may lawfully discontinue the life-sustaining treatment or care; and, if in either case the treatment is futile in the sense I have described, it can properly be concluded that it is no longer in the best interests of the patient to continue it. It is true that, in the case of discontinuance of artificial feeding, it can be said that the patient will as a result starve to death; and this may bring before our eyes the vision of an ordinary person slowly dying of hunger and suffering all the pain and distress associated with such a death. But here it is clear from the evidence that no such pain or distress will be suffered by Anthony, who can feel nothing at all. Furthermore, we are told that the outward symptoms of dying in such a way, which might otherwise cause distress to the nurses who care for him or to members of his family who visit him, can be suppressed by means of sedatives. In these circumstances, I can see no ground in the present case for refusing the declarations applied for simply because the course of action proposed involves the discontinuance of artificial feeding.

In *F v West Berkshire Health Authority* [1989] 2 All ER 545, [1990] 2 AC 1 it was stated that, where a doctor provides treatment for a person who is incapacitated from saying whether or not he consents to it, the doctor must, when deciding on the form of treatment, act in accordance with a responsible and competent body of relevant professional opinion, on the principles set down in *Bolam v Friern Hospital Management Committee* [1957] 2 All ER 118, [1957] 1 WLR 582. In my opinion, this principle must equally be applicable to decisions to initiate, or to discontinue, life support, as it is to other forms of treatment. However, in a matter of such importance and sensitivity as discontinuance of life support, it is to be expected that guidance will be provided for the profession; and, on the evidence in the present case, such guidance is for a case such as the present to be found in a discussion paper on *Treatment of Patients in Persistent Vegetative State*, issued in September 1992 by the medical ethics committee of the British Medical Association. Anybody reading this substantial paper will discover for himself the great care with which this topic is being considered by the profession. Mr Francis for the respondents drew to the attention of the Appellate Committee four safeguards in particular which, in the committee's opinion, should be observed before discontinuing life support for such patients. They are: (1) every effort should be made at rehabilitation for at least six months after the injury; (2) the diagnosis of irreversible PVS should not be considered confirmed until at least 12 months after the injury, with the effect that any decision to withhold life-prolonging treatment will be delayed for that period; (3) the diagnosis should be agreed by two other independent doctors; and (4) generally, the wishes of the patient's immediate family will be given great weight.

In fact, the views expressed by the committee on the subject of consultation with the relatives of PVS patients are consistent with the opinion expressed by your Lordships' House in *F v West Berkshire Health Authority* that it is good practice for the doctor to consult relatives. Indeed the committee recognises that, in the case of PVS patients, the relatives themselves will require a high degree of support and attention. But the committee is firmly of the opinion that the relatives' views cannot be determinative of the treatment. Indeed, if that were not so, the relatives would be able to dictate to the doctors what is in the best interests of the patient, which cannot be right. Even so, a decision to withhold life-prolonging treatment, such as artificial feeding, must require close co-operation with those close to the patient; and it is recognised that, in practice, their views and the opinions of doctors will coincide in many cases.

Study of this document left me in no doubt that if a doctor treating a PVS patient acts in accordance with the medical practice now being evolved by the medical ethics committee of the British Medical Association he will be acting with the benefit of guidance from a responsible and competent body of relevant professional opinion, as required by the *Bolam* test. I also feel that those who are concerned that a matter of life and death, such as is involved in a decision to withhold life support in a case of this kind, should be left to the doctors would do well to study this paper. The truth is that, in the course of their work, doctors frequently have to make decisions which may affect the continued survival of their patients, and are in reality far more experienced in matters of this kind than are the judges. It is nevertheless the function of the judges to state the legal principles upon which the lawfulness of the actions of doctors depend; but in the end the decisions to be made in individual cases must rest with the doctors themselves. In these circumstances, what is required is a sensitive understanding by both the judges and the doctors of each other's respective functions, and in particular a determination by the judges not merely to understand the problems facing the medical profession in cases of this kind, but also to regard their professional standards with respect. Mutual understanding between the doctors and the judges is the best way to ensure the evolution of a sensitive and sensible legal framework for the treatment and care of patients, with a sound ethical base, in the interests of the patients themselves. This is a topic to which I will return at the end of this opinion, when I come to consider the extent to which the view of the court should be sought, as a matter of practice, in cases such as the present…

Certainly, in *F v West Berkshire Health Authority* your Lordships' House adopted a straightforward test based on the best interests of the patient; and I myself do not see why the same test should not be applied in the case of PVS patients, where the question is whether life-prolonging treatment should be withheld. This was also the opinion of Thomas J in *Auckland Area Health Board v A-G* [1993] 1 NZLR 235, a case concerned with the discontinuance of life support provided by ventilator to a patient suffering from the last stages of incurable Guillain-Barre syndrome. Of course, consistent with the best interests test, anything relevant to the application of the test may be taken into account; and, if the personality of the patient is relevant to the application of the test (as it may be in cases where the various relevant factors have to be weighed) it may be taken into account, as was done in *Re J (a minor) (wardship: medical treatment)* [1990] 3 All ER 930, [1991] Fam 33. But, where the question is whether life support should be withheld from a PVS patient, it is difficult to see how the personality of the patient can be relevant, though it may be of comfort to his relatives if they believe, as in the present case, and indeed may well be so in many other cases, that the patient would not have wished his life to be artificially prolonged if he was totally unconscious and there was no hope of improvement in his condition.

I wish to add however that, like the courts below, I have derived assistance and support from decisions in a number of American jurisdictions to the effect that it is lawful to discontinue life-prolonging treatment in the case of PVS patients where there is no prospect of improvement in their condition. Furthermore, I wish to refer to the section in Working Paper No 28 (1982) on *Euthanasia, Aiding Suicide and Cessation of Treatment* published by the Law Reform Commission of Canada concerned with cessation of treatment, to which I also wish to express my indebtedness. I believe the legal principles as I have stated them to be broadly consistent with the conclusions summarised in the Working Paper (at pp 65–66), which was substantially accepted in the Report of the Commission (1983) pp 32–35. Indeed, I entertain a strong sense that a community of view on the legal principles applicable in cases of discontinuing life support is in the course of development and acceptance throughout the common law world.

In setting out my understanding of the relevant principles, I have had very much in mind the submissions advanced by Mr Munby on behalf of the Official Solicitor, and I believe that I have answered, directly or indirectly, all his objections to the course now proposed. I do not, therefore, intend any disrespect to his argument if I do not answer each of his submissions seriatim. In summary, his two principal arguments were as follows. First, he submitted that the discontinuance of artificial feeding would constitute an act which would inevitably cause, and be intended to cause, Anthony's death; and as such, it would be unlawful, and indeed criminal. As will be plain from what I have already said, I cannot accept this proposition. In my opinion, for the reasons I have already given, there is no longer any duty upon the doctors to continue with this form of medical treatment or care in his case, and it follows that it cannot be unlawful to discontinue it. Second, he submitted that discontinuance of the artificial feeding of Anthony would be a breach of the doctor's duty to care for and feed him; and since it will (as it is intended to do) cause his death, it will necessarily be unlawful. I have considered this point earlier in this opinion, when I expressed my view that artificial feeding is, in a case such as the present, no different from life support by a ventilator, and as such can lawfully be discontinued when it no longer fulfils any therapeutic purpose. To me, the crucial point in which I found myself differing from Mr Munby was that I was unable to accept his treating the discontinuance of artificial feeding in the present case as equivalent to cutting a mountaineer's rope, or severing the air pipe of a deep sea diver. Once it is recognised, as I believe it must be, that the true question is not whether the doctor should take a course in which he will actively kill his patient, but rather whether he should continue to provide his patient with medical treatment or care which, if continued, will prolong his life, then, as I see it, the essential basis of Mr Munby's submission disappears. I wish to add that I was unable to accept his suggestion that recent decisions show that the law is proceeding down a 'slippery slope', in the sense that the courts are becoming more and more ready to allow doctors to take steps which will result in the ending of life. On the contrary, as I have attempted to demonstrate, the courts are acting within a structure of legal principle, under which in particular they continue to draw a clear distinction between the bounds of lawful treatment of a living patient and unlawful euthanasia.

I turn finally to the extent to which doctors should, as a matter of practice, seek the guidance of the court, by way of an application for declaratory relief, before withholding life-prolonging treatment from a PVS patient. Sir Stephen Brown P considered that the opinion of the court should be sought in all cases similar to the present. In the Court of Appeal Sir Thomas Bingham MR expressed his agreement with Sir Stephen Brown P in the following words (see p 842, ante):

> This was in my respectful view a wise ruling, directed to the protection of patients, the protection of doctors, the reassurance of patients' families and the reassurance of the public. The practice proposed seems to me desirable. It may well be that with the passage of time a body of experience and practice will build up which will obviate the need for application in every case but for the time being I am satisfied that the practice which Sir Stephen Brown P described should be followed.

Before the Appellate Committee this view was supported both by Mr Munby for the Official Solicitor and by Mr Lester as amicus curiae. For the respondents, Mr Francis suggested that an adequate safeguard would be provided if reference to the court was required in certain specific cases, ie (1) where there was known to be a medical disagreement as to the diagnosis or prognosis, and (2) problems had arisen with the patient's relatives – disagreement by the next of kin with the medical recommendation; actual or apparent conflict of interest between the next of kin and the patient; dispute between members of the patient's family; or absence of any next of kin to give their consent. There is, I consider, much to be said for the view that an application to the court will not be needed in every case, but only in particular circumstances, such as those suggested by Mr Francis. In this connection I was impressed not only by the care being taken by the medical ethics committee to provide guidance to the profession, but also by information given to the Appellate Committee about the substantial number of PVS patients in the country, and the very considerable cost of obtaining guidance from the court in cases such as the present. However, in my opinion this is a matter which would be better kept under review by the President of the Family Division than resolved now by your Lordships' House. I understand that a similar review is being undertaken in cases concerned with the sterilisation of adult women of unsound mind, with a consequent relaxation of the practice relating to applications to the court in such cases. For my part, I would therefore leave the matter as proposed by Sir Thomas Bingham MR; but I wish to express the hope that the President of the Family Division, who will no doubt be kept well informed about developments in this field, will soon feel able to relax the present requirement so as to limit applications for declarations to those cases in which there is a special need for the procedure to be invoked...

For these reasons, I would dismiss the appeal.

Lord Keith and Lord Lowry, while delivering short concurring speeches, agreed with the reasons given by Lord Goff.

Lord Keith: The first point to make is that it is unlawful, so as to constitute both a tort and the crime of battery, to administer medical treatment to an adult, who is conscious and of sound mind, without his consent: see *F v West Berkshire Health Authority (Mental Health Act Commission intervening)* [1989] 2 All ER 545, [1990] 2 AC 1. Such a person is completely at liberty to decline to undergo treatment, even if the result of his doing so will be that he will die. This extends to the situation where the person, in anticipation of this, through one cause or another, entering into a condition such as PVS, gives clear instructions that in such event he is not to be given medical care, including artificial feeding, designed to keep him alive...

The object of medical treatment and care is to benefit the patient. It may do so by taking steps to prevent the occurrence of illness, or, if an illness does occur, by taking steps towards curing it. Where an illness or the effects of an injury cannot be cured, then efforts are directed towards preventing deterioration of relieving pain and suffering. In Anthony Bland's case the first imperative was to prevent him from dying, as he would certainly have done in the absence of the steps that were taken. If he had died, there can be no doubt that the cause of this would have been the injuries which he had suffered. As it was, the steps taken prevented him from dying, and there was instituted the course of treatment and care which still continues. For a time, no doubt, there was some hope that he might recover sufficiently for him to be able to live a life that had some meaning. Some patients who have suffered damage to the cerebral cortex have, indeed, made a complete recovery. It all depends on the degree of damage. But sound medical opinion takes the view that if a PVS patient shows no signs of recovery after six months, or at most a year, then there is no prospect of any recovery. There are techniques available which make it possible to ascertain the state of the cerebral cortex, and in Anthony Bland's case these indicate that, as mentioned above, it has degenerated into a mass of watery fluid. The fundamental question then comes to be whether continuance of the present regime of treatment and care, more than three years after the injuries that resulted in the PVS, would confer any benefit on Anthony Bland...

In the case of a permanently insensate being, who if continuing to live would never experience the slightest actual discomfort, it is difficult, if not impossible, to make any relevant comparison between continued existence and the absence of it. It is, however, perhaps permissible to say that to an individual with no cognitive capacity whatever, and no prospect of ever recovering any such capacity in this world, it must be a matter of complete indifference whether he lives or dies.

Where one individual has assumed responsibility for the care of another who cannot look after himself or herself, whether as a medical practitioner or otherwise, that responsibility cannot lawfully be shed unless arrangements are made for the responsibility to be taken over by someone else. Thus a person having charge of a baby who fails to feed it, so that it dies, will be guilty at least of manslaughter. The same is true of one having charge of an adult who is frail and cannot look after herself: see *R v Stone* [1977] 2 All ER 341, [1977] QB 354. It was argued for the guardian ad litem, by analogy with that case, that here the doctors in charge of Anthony Bland had a continuing duty to feed him by means of the nasogastric tube and that if they failed to carry out that duty they were guilty of manslaughter, if not murder. This was coupled with the argument that feeding him by means of the nasogastric tube was not medical treatment at all, but simply feeding indistinguishable from feeding by normal means. As regards this latter argument, I am of opinion that regard should be had to the whole regime, including the artificial feeding, which at present keeps Anthony Bland alive. That regime amounts to medical treatment and care, and it is incorrect to direct attention exclusively to the fact that nourishment is being provided. In any event, the administration of nourishment by the means adopted involves the application of a medical technique. But it is, of course, true that in general it would not be lawful for a medical practitioner who assumed responsibility for the care of an unconscious patient simply to give up treatment in circumstances where continuance of it would confer some benefit on the patient. On the other hand a medical practitioner is under no duty to continue to treat such a patient where a large body of informed and responsible medical opinion is to the effect that no benefit at all would be conferred by continuance. Existence in a vegetative state with no prospect of recovery is by that opinion regarded as not being a benefit, and that, if not unarguably correct, at least forms a proper basis for the decision to discontinue treatment and care: see *Bolam v Friern Hospital Management Committee* [1957] 2 All ER 118, [1957] 1 WLR 582...

The decision whether or not the continued treatment and care of a PVS patient confers any benefit on him is essentially one for the practitioners in charge of his case. The question is whether any decision that it does not and that the treatment and care should therefore be discontinued should as a matter of routine be brought before the Family Division for indorsement or the reverse. The view taken by Sir Stephen Brown P and the Court of Appeal was that it should, at least for the time being and until a body of experience and practice has been built up which might obviate the need for application in every case. As Sir Thomas Bingham MR said (at p 842, ante), this would be in the interests of the protection of patients, the protection of doctors, the reassurance of patients' families and the reassurance of the public. I respectfully agree that these considerations render desirable the practice of application.

Lord Lowry: In answer to the respondents' reliance on accepted medical opinion that feeding (nutrition and hydration), particularly by sophisticated artificial methods, is part of the life-supporting medical treatment, [the Official Solicitor] says that the duty to feed a helpless person, such as a baby or an unconscious patient, is something different – an elementary duty to keep the patient alive which exists independently of all questions of treatment and which the person in charge cannot omit to perform: to omit deliberately to perform this duty in the knowledge that the omission will lead to the death of the helpless one, and indeed with the intention, as in the present case, of conducing that death, will render those in charge guilty of murder. One of the respondents' counter-arguments, albeit not conclusive, is based on the overwhelming verdict of informed medical opinion worldwide, with particular reference to the common law jurisdictions, where the relevant law generally corresponds closely with our own, that therapy and life-supporting care, including sophisticated methods of artificial feeding, are components of medical treatment and cannot be separated as the Official Solicitor contends. In this connection it may also be emphasised that an artificial feeding regime is inevitably associated with the continuous use of catheters and enemas and the sedulous avoidance and combating of potentially deadly infection. I consider that the court, when intent on reaching a decision according to law, ought to give weight to informed medical opinion both on the point now under discussion and also on the question of what is in the best interests of a patient...

The real answer to the Official Solicitor, as your Lordships are already agreed, is that his argument starts from the fallacious premise, which can be taken as correct in ordinary doctor-patient relationships, namely that feeding in order to sustain life is *necessarily* for the benefit of the patient. But in the prevailing circumstances the opposite view is overwhelmingly held by the doctors and the validity of that view has been accepted by the courts below. The doctors consider that in the patient's best interests they ought not to feed him and the law, as applied by your Lordships, has gone further by saying that they are not entitled to feed him without his consent, which cannot be obtained. So the theory of the 'duty to feed' is founded on a misapprehension and the Official Solicitor's argument leads to a legally erroneous conclusion. Even though the intention to bring about the patient's death is there, there is no proposed guilty act because, if it is not in the interests of an insentient patient to continue the life-supporting care and treatment, the doctor would be acting unlawfully if he continued the care and treatment and would perform no guilty act by discontinuing.

Lords Browne-Wilkinson and Mustill also delivered speeches agreeing that the appeal should be dismissed.

I. Understanding *Bland*

Nature of the duty The House of Lords confirmed that the relevant test to determine a doctor's duty was that of 'best interests'. The judges relied upon their earlier decision in *Re F*. The interesting question is how the judges explained the meaning of that test. All agreed that the correct question was whether it was in Anthony Bland's 'best interests' to continue to receive treatment and not whether it was in his 'best interests' to die. To some, this question involved the traditional concern whether there was any benefit accruing to the patient by the continuation of the treatment (per Lord Goff, Lord Lowry and Lord Browne-Wilkinson, *sed quaere* Lord Keith). They accepted that Tony Bland was permanently insensate. Thus, he could not possibly benefit, since his condition could not be improved. Lord Goff, you will recall, referred to the treatment as being in 'medical terms futile'. Further, it was burdensome to Tony Bland by reason of 'the invasiveness of the treatment and of [its] indignity…'

To others of their Lordships (Lord Mustill and, perhaps, Lord Keith), however, if 'best interests' means weighing the benefits of treatment against the burdens of treatment and non-treatment, this could have alarming implications when what is being weighed is, in effect, whether the patient lives or dies. Thus, for these judges, the task was to endorse 'best interests' as the test generally but then immediately to try to find a way to avoid what they saw as its implications in the case. The way they chose was to say that in a case of PVS the law need not proceed to weigh the various interests of the patient because the patient by being permanently insensate *has no interests*. In particular, the patient has no interest in treatment being continued:

> **Lord Keith:** In the case of a permanently insensate being, who if continuing to live would never experience the slightest actual discomfort, it is difficult, if not impossible, to make any relevant comparison between continued existence and the absence of it. It is, however, perhaps permissible to say that to an individual with no cognitive capacity whatever, and no prospect of ever recovering any such capacity in this world, it must be a matter of complete indifference whether he lives or dies.

The argument is more elaborately put by Lord Mustill.

> **Lord Mustill:** Just as in *F v West Berkshire Health Authority*, so the argument runs, the best interests of the patient demand a course of action which would normally be unlawful without the patient's consent. Just as in *F v West Berkshire Health Authority* the patient is unable to decide for himself. In practice, to make no decision is to decide that the care and treatment shall continue. So that the decision shall not thus be made by default it is necessary that someone other than Anthony Bland should consider whether in his own best interests his life should now be brought to an end, and if the answer is affirmative the proposed conduct can be put into effect without risk of criminal responsibility.
>
> I cannot accept this argument, which, if sound, would serve to legitimate a termination by much more direct means that are now contemplated. I can accept that a doctor in charge of a patient suffering the mental torture of Guillain-Barre syndrome, rational but trapped and mute in an unresponsive body, could well feel it imperative that a decision on whether to terminate life could wait no longer and that the only possible decision in the interests of the patient, even leaving out all the other interests involved, would be to end it here and now by a speedy and painless injection. Such a conclusion would attract much sympathy, but no doctrine of best interests could bring it within the law.
>
> Quite apart from this the case of Anthony Bland seems to me quite different. He feels no pain and suffers no mental anguish. Stress was laid in argument on the damage to his personal dignity by the continuation of the present medical regime, and on the progressive erosion of the family's happy recollections by month after month of distressing and hopeless care. Considerations of this kind will do doubt carry great weight when Parliament comes to consider the whole question in the round. But it seems to me to be stretching the concept of personal rights beyond breaking point to say that Anthony Bland has an interest in ending these sources of others' distress. Unlike the conscious patient he does not know what is happening to his body, and cannot be affronted by it; he does not know of his family's continuing sorrow. By ending his life the doctors will not relieve him of a burden become intolerable, for others carry the burden and he has none. What other considerations could make it better for him to die now rather than later? None that we can measure, for of death we know nothing. The distressing truth which must not be shirked is that the proposed conduct is not in the best interests of Anthony Bland, for he has no best interests of any kind…
>
> After much expression of negative opinions I turn to an argument which in my judgment is logically defensible and consistent with the existing law. In essence it turns the previous argument on its head by directing the inquiry to the interests of the patient, not in the termination of life but in the continuation of his treatment. It runs as follows. (i) The cessation of nourishment and hydration is an omission not an act. (ii) Accordingly, the cessation will not be a criminal act unless the doctors are under present duty to continue the regime. (iii) At the time when Anthony Bland came into the care of the doctors decisions had to be made

about his care which he was unable to make for himself. In accordance with *F v West Berkshire Health Authority* [1989] 2 All ER 545, [1990] 2 AC 1 these decisions were to be made in his best interests. Since the possibility that he might recover still existed his best interests required that he should be supported in the hope that this would happen. These best interests justified the application of the necessary regime without his consent. (iv) All hope of recovery has now been abandoned. Thus, although the termination of his life is not in the best interests of Anthony Bland, his best interests in being kept alive have also disappeared, taking with them the justification for the non-consensual regime and the correlative duty to keep it in being. (v) Since there is no longer a duty to provide nourishment and hydration a failure to do so cannot be a criminal offence…

I therefore consider the argument to be soundly based. Now that the time has come when Anthony Bland has no further interest in being kept alive, the necessity to do so, created by his inability to make a choice, has gone; and the justification for the invasive care and treatment together with the duty to provide it have also gone. Absent a duty, the omission to perform what had previously been a duty will no longer be a breach of the criminal law.

(For views arguing that the *Bland* decision allows intentional killing of a patient by the withdrawal of 'basic care' which is not 'futile' since it maintains his life, see J Finnis '*Bland*: Crossing the Rubicon?' (1993) 109 LQR 329 and J Keown 'Restoring Moral and Intellectual Shape to the Law after *Bland*' (1997) 113 LQR 481.)

Whose decision? Their Lordships make it clear that it is the doctor, following *Re F*, who applies the 'best interests' test in any particular case (or, in the case of a child, the parents in consultation with the doctor). Just as we saw, however, in the cases on sterilisation on intellectually disabled women (see Chapter 9), the Law Lords were anxious that, at least for a time, the court should have a supervisory role (per Lord Keith, Lord Goff, Lord Lowry and Lord Browne-Wilkinson). The Law Lords approved the view of Sir Thomas Bingham MR expressed in the Court of Appeal (at 842):

Sir Thomas Bingham MR: [In] cases of this kind application should be made to the court to obtain its sanction for the course proposed. This was in my respectful view a wise ruling, directed to the protection of patients, the protection of doctors, the reassurance of patients' families and the reassurance of the public. The practice proposed seems to me desirable. It may very well be that with the passage of time a body of experience and practice will build up which will obviate the need for application in every case, but for the time being I am satisfied that the practice…should be followed.

One of the most difficult issues in PVS cases is determining whether the patient is, in fact, in such a condition (see *Swindon and Marlborough NHS Trust v S* [1995] 3 Med LR 84; *Re D* (1997) 41 BMLR 81 and *Re H (Adult: Incompetent)* (1997) 38 BMLR 11). The court's involvement, together with the Official Solicitor, seeks a full factual investigation of the patient's circumstances and, in particular, evidence from two independent medical experts of his diagnosis and prognosis (*Practice Note* [1996] 2 FLR 375). (But contrast *Frenchay Healthcare NHS Trust v S* [1994] 2 All ER 403 (CA) and Commentary (1994) 2 Med L Rev 206 (AG) relaxing the latter requirement where an emergency arose when the patient's feeding tube became detached.)

In *Bland*, the House of Lords approved the BMA's interim guidance that a diagnosis that the VS is permanent should not be made (or at least acted upon by the court) until the patient has been insentient for 12 months (for the final guidance, see BMA *Guidelines on Treatment Decisions for Patients in Persistent Vegetative State* (1996)). Others consider that the diagnosis *can* be, but need not be, made earlier in some cases (see Royal College of Physician's Working Group on the Permanent Vegetative State' (1995) 29 J of Roy College of Physicians 381). There remains, however, documented evidence of the risk of misdiagnosis (see K Andrews, L Murphy, R Munday and C Littlewood 'Misdiagnosis of the Vegetative State: Retrospective Study in a Rehabilitation Unit' (1996) 313 BMJ 13).

The courts have, however, remained cautious maintaining the 12-month period before any treatment limiting decision can be made.

It remains unclear whether the court should be involved *only* where feeding or nutrition is to be withdrawn rather than any other form of treatment (see, Royal College of Physician's Working Group 'The Permanent Vegetative State' (1996) 30 J of Royal College of Physicians 119 at 120–121). The Law Commission likewise considered decisions to withdraw feeding or nutrition, but not other treatment, should be for the courts (see *Mental Incapacity*, Report No 231 at para 6.21). The ultimate view of the Lord Chancellor's department seems to be, however, that these decisions *could* be taken under the new statutory general authority (see *Making Decisions* (Cm 4465) (1999), para 12 (no legislation on independent supervision of medical procedures).

II. Questions which arise from *Bland*

The relevance of Bolam Four of the Law Lords regarded the *Bolam* test as a central factor in determining the doctor's duty ie, in determining whether to continue treatment is in the patient's 'best interests'. For example, Lord Browne-Wilkinson put it as follows (at 882):

[A] doctor's decision whether invasive care is in the best interests of the patient falls to be assessed by reference to the test laid down in *Bolam v Friern Hospital Management Committee* [1957] 2 All ER 118, [1957] 1 WLR 582, viz is the decision in accordance with a practice accepted at the time by a responsible body of medical opinion?

The difficulty of using *Bolam* to determine the *legality* of a doctor's conduct as opposed to its reasonableness, is made clear by Lord Mustill (at 895):

I venture to feel some reservations about the application of the principle of civil liability in negligence laid down in *Bolam v Friern Hospital Management Committee* [1957] 2 All ER 118, [1957] 1 WLR 582 to decisions on 'best interests' in a field dominated by the criminal law. I accept without difficulty that this principle applies to the ascertainment of the medical raw materials such as diagnosis, prognosis and appraisal of the patient's cognitive functions. Beyond this point, however, it may be said that the decision is ethical, not medical, and that there is no reason in logic why on such a decision the opinions of doctors should be decisive. If there had been a possibility that this question might make a difference to the outcome of the appeal I would have wished to consider it further, but since it does not I prefer for the moment to express no opinion on it.

As we saw in Chapter 6, the genesis of the approach in *Bland* is the House of Lords decision in *Re F*. In that case, the court (in our view, quite without justification) translated a test from an area in which it sits at best uncomfortably (medical negligence) to an area where it has no place at all, ie judgments as to the legality of future professional conduct. *Bolam* may have a place in facilitating the evaluation of conduct after a mishap has taken place. It is hard to argue that it has a place when the inquiry is not concerned with the responsibility for the mishap but how to respond to it. In our view, the latter question cannot be a matter of professional opinion and practice and in deciding that it is, the House of Lords has taken the law in the wrong direction (cf *Frenchay Healthcare NHS Trust v S* [1994] 2 All ER 403 (CA) – court's duty to determine patient's best interests).

In the Court of Appeal in *Bland*, Hoffmann LJ (at 858) would have taken the law in a different direction.

Hoffmann LJ: Sir Stephen Brown P laid some emphasis upon the fact that according to professional medical opinion and the BMA's statement on ethics, ending artificial feeding would be in accordance with good medical practice. Some have felt concern at the suggestion that questions of whether patients should live or die should be decided according to what was thought to be good practice by the medical profession. Once again, I sympathise with this concern.

I do not think that Sir Stephen Brown P was saying that the views of the medical profession should determine the legal and moral questions which I have discussed in this judgment. Nor do I think that the profession would be grateful to the court for leaving the full responsibility for such decisions in his hands. It seems to me that the medical profession can tell the court about the patient's condition and prognosis and about the probably consequences of giving or not giving certain kinds of treatment or care, including the provision of artificial feeding. But whether in those circumstances it would be lawful to provide or withhold the treatment or care is a matter for the law and must be decided with regard to the general moral considerations of which I have spoken. As to these matters, the medical profession will no doubt have views which are entitled to great respect, but I would expect medical ethics to be formed by the law rather than the reverse.

An irony of the approach adopted by the Law Lords is that it appears to have been unnecessary. If Lord Goff's speech is seen as representing the majority view, it is clear that by reference to the general principle of 'best interests' he had already reached the conclusion that Tony Bland need no longer be treated with artificial hydration and nutrition. The reliance on *Bolam* seems at best designed to bolster him in the conclusion he had already reached, rather than provide the critical legal justification for that conclusion (for a recent retrenchment by the courts, see *Re A (medical treatment: male sterilisation)* (1999) 53 BMLR 66 and *Re S* (2000) Times, 26 May (CA) discussed *supra*, ch 6).

Duty not to treat? When the doctor arrives at the conclusion that it is not in the patient's 'best interests' to continue treatment any longer, what must he do? On one view, he may have a discretion to withdraw treatment. On another view, however, once the doctor decides that continuation is not in the patient's 'best interests' his legal licence to treat (following *Re F*) no longer exists and he *must cease* treatment. Indeed, is it really possible to have two views about whether continuation is in the patient's best interests once the diagnosis/prognosis is confirmed? Arguably not (but see *infra* for an argument that there could be). In *Bland* Lord Browne-Wilkinson (at 882–883) clearly endorses this latter view.

> **Lord Browne-Wilkinson:** [I]f there comes a stage where the responsible doctor comes to the reasonable conclusion (which accords with the views of a responsible body of medical opinion) that further continuance of an intrusive life support system is not in the best interests of the patient, he can no longer lawfully continue that life support system: to do so would constitute the crime of battery and the tort of trespass to the person. Therefore he cannot be in breach of any duty to maintain the patient's life…perpetuation of life can only be achieved if it is lawful to continue to invade the bodily integrity of the patient by invasive medical care. Unless the doctor has reached the affirmative conclusion that it is in the patient's best interest to continue the invasive care, such care must cease.

(See also Lord Lowry at 876–877.)

Lord Browne-Wilkinson's categorical assertion that to continue to treat after a determination that it would not be in the best interests of the patient to do so, would be a tort and a crime, although entailed from his previous analysis, is not free from difficulty. Indeed, should we not go further and say that, given the approach of the Law Lords, continued intervention is not in the patient's best interests? This approach might, for example, create problems for the 'conscientious objector' who felt unable to withdraw feeding (see A Grubb 'The Persistent Vegetative State: A Duty (Not) to Treat and Conscious Objection' (1997) 4 European Journal of Health Law 157 at 163–168). Consider also the case of a patient from whom it is hoped to remove a kidney to transplant into another. A number of hospitals have adopted the practice of managing the dying of a patient in such a way that vital organs intended for transplantation will not be damaged in the process of dying (see *supra*, ch 15). If Lord Browne-Wilkinson's views were taken literally this practice, which is already of doubtful ethical and legal propriety, would most certainly be unlawful. In this context it is interesting to notice Lord Browne-Wilkinson's comment (at 879):

…it is not legitimate in reaching a view as to what is for the benefit of one individual whose life is in issue to take into account the impact on third parties of altering the time at which death occurs.

A corollary of Lord Browne-Wilkinson's approach is that just as the doctor is not entitled to continue treatment so the relatives may not insist on treatment being continued. Further, a doctor may not purport to justify a continuation of treatment simply by reference to requests by the relatives (see discussion of *Re J* [1992] 4 All ER 614, *supra*, ch 6). Subsequently, in *Re G (Persistent Vegetative State)* [1995] 2 FCR 46 the role of the patients relatives was examined.

Re G (Persistent Vegetative State) [1995] 2 FCR 46 (Fam Div)

In 1991, G, a married man, then aged 24, suffered a serious accident on his motorcycle. He never regained any awareness of those about him and was in profound and persistent vegetative state, diagnosed by a senior neurologist in December 1992 and since confirmed by a further four leading consultant neurologists. G's wife visited daily, G's mother was equally devoted to G. The family had felt that G was not in so severe a state of PVS as Tony Bland had been: see *Airedale NHS Trust v Bland* [1994] 1 FCR 485. The medical report presented to the Official Solicitor by an eminent medical specialist (who had also examined Mr Bland) concluded: "…it is my professional opinion that Mr G is, if anything, in a deeper state of the vegetative state than was Mr Bland in that he has fewer responses…".

The wife had, reluctantly come to accept that (a) having regard to views her husband had expressed to her in the past and (b) in the light of all the medical evidence as to his best interests, consideration be given to withdrawing the automatic feeding which had since July 1992 been provided by gastrotomy tube. G's mother, whose views also merited very serious consideration, accepted the overwhelming medical evidence, but felt that it could not be conclusive.

Sir Stephen Brown P: There is no dispute before me that the condition of Mr G is that of the persistent vegetative state. The Official Solicitor who appears for this insensate patient has taken extensive steps to seek the best advice in this case on behalf of Mr G. Other neurologists and neuro-surgeons have been consulted. The court has heard from Dr Cartledge who, like Dr Andrews, examined Mr Bland and gave evidence in the case of Mr Bland in 1992. Further at the instance of Mr G's mother, to whom I shall refer in due course, Professor Jennett, one of the leading authorities on the persistent vegetative state, has considered the position of Mr G and is of the opinion that this is clearly a classic example of this condition.

It is a very sad and tragic condition, particularly because those nearest and dearest find it difficult in certain instances to accept that the subject is in fact completely unaware of anything that takes place about him. In 1993, after the case of Mr Bland – *Airedale NHS Trust v Bland* [1993] AC 789; [1994] 1 FCR 485 – the British Medical Association issued guidelines on treatment decisions for patients in the persistent vegetative state. This document has been produced in the hearing before me and it includes what is termed a summary of advice. It is helpful to refer to para 5 which is headed, 'The views of people close to the patient'. I quote:

> It is good practice for the doctors to consult the wishes of people close to the patient but their views alone cannot determine the treatment of the PVS patient. People close to the patient may be able to throw light on the wishes of the PVS patient regarding the prolongation of treatment and this is likely to be helpful in decision-making. Treatment decisions however must be based upon the doctors' assessment of the patient's best interests.

As long ago as 1991 the wife of Mr G in consultation with Mr J, the orthopaedic consultant in charge of this case, decided that, if Mr G should suffer a cardiac arrest, there should be no attempt at resuscitation. However, he was in fact treated with antibiotics in August and October of 1991 when he developed a chest infection and subsequently a urinary tract infection. In July 1992 a gastrotomy was performed. In June 1993 his wife, who had been a constant daily visitor to the bedside of her of her husband, met Mr J, the consultant in charge of this patient, to discuss future treatment. At that time further examinations were still being made by independent neurologists but it appears that careful consideration was then given to the question of withdrawing the automatic feeding routine which had been set up.

The wife, if I may say so, is a shining example of devotion. She has been to the bedside of her husband every day except three for the last three-and-a-half years. She has taken part in the nursing routines and is constant in her continued devotion to her unfortunate husband. She indicated to Mr J that it would be, in her view, in the best interests of her husband, particularly having regard to views which he had expressed to her in his full life, that consideration should be given to withdrawing the automatic feeding which would result in death. She has found this a very difficult situation to come to terms with and to make a decision about. She has given evidence before me. She has made it clear that she finds it a very difficult decision, but she does not oppose the clinical decision of Mr J in the light of all the medical evidence that such a course would be in the best interests of her husband.

Another party to the originating summons which was issued on 16 February 1994 seeking declaratory relief in this matter is Mr G's mother. She is devoted to her son. She has been a regular visitor to his bedside. She is unable to agree to the course proposed by Mr J, which is of course the subject of this application. She believes, despite the overwhelming medical evidence, which she says that she accepts, that it cannot be conclusive. She has some undefined hope that the reality which is revealed in the medical reports and opinions, is not in fact the final position. Her views are very important because she is clearly a person who is very close to her son. The emotions involved are high indeed and this court can only pay tribute to the way in which these two ladies have borne their tragedy over these three-and-a-half years.

However, the difficulty is made plain when one has to consider where the responsibility lies for the treatment of Mr G. I have no doubt that the law requires, as the B.M.A. guidelines indicate, that treatment decisions must be based upon the doctor's assessment of the patient's best interests. The basic facts of this case follow almost precisely the position of the patient in the case of *Airedale NHS Trust v Bland*, to which I have referred. The condition of Mr G is, if anything, more severe than was that of Mr Bland. However, there is the difference in this case that in contradistinction to the situation in Mr Bland's case, a close relative is not in agreement with the course which the doctors propose. I have had to consider very carefully how the mother's opposition should be treated for, as the B.M.A. guidelines make clear, it is very important that all those who have to consider the future treatment of a PVS patient should take into account the views of close relatives.

In this case I have no doubt at all that Mr J has taken into account all those views. Nobody has any criticism of any kind to make of Mr J or indeed of the care which has been afforded by this excellent hospital and its outstanding nursing staff. I have read the affidavits sworn by the nursing staff. It is quite plain that everything that could possibly be done has been done, in this case and indeed is still being done. Nevertheless the situation has been arrived at when the considered view of all the distinguished medical advisers indicates that this is a case where there is no chance at all of recovery and where the patient has no awareness of any kind of anything which is going on around him in life. He suffers no pain. He is not aware of the presence of his loved ones, although they may find that difficult to accept having regard to the reflex actions to which Dr Andrews referred. There is therefore a situation where the doctor in charge has a duty to consider the best interests of this patient. Mr J has made it clear that albeit somewhat reluctantly he is of the view that the best interests of this patient lie in the withdrawal of the automatic feeding regime to which the patient is presently subject.

I need not say more in this case about the sad and tragic details of the condition of this patient. The facts, as I have said, in that regard are very similar to those which have been made very widely known in the case of Mr Bland and, as I have already said, there is no dispute of any kind between the medical advisers who have considered this case. I have no doubt that, although the mother's views must be taken into account, they cannot prevail so as to prevent the course being taken which is considered to be in the best interests of this patient.

Counsel for the mother submitted that her opposition should operate as a veto. That, I feel, cannot be a correct view of the law. It would indeed be an appalling burden to place upon any relative to transfer as it were the responsibility for making a decision in a case of this nature to that relative. In this case the responsibility must ultimately remain with the doctors in charge of the case, albeit taking fully into account views of the relatives.

Mr J has said in evidence that although a declaration may be granted permitting him to take the course which he seeks leave to take, if afterwards the wife were to withdraw her support in a positive way and in effect said, "No, do not do it", he would feel unable to proceed to pursue the withdrawal of the automatic feeding regime. It is abundantly plain that all those who bear responsibility in this case have been placed under enormous emotional pressure. It is a remarkable tribute to all of them that they are able calmly, coolly and clinically to review the situation. I have nothing but praise to offer to Mr J who has accepted the primary responsibility as the medical officer in charge of this case. He has of course sought expert opinion from independent sources in the widest sense and he has obtained it. I have no doubt at all that in this case there is no likelihood of recovery and there is no question of awareness on the part of this unfortunate patient. I have no doubt that Mr J's application is well-founded in seeking to give effect to the patient's best interests.

I accordingly propose to grant the declarations which are sought…

His wife has said that she wishes to be involved right up until the end and that wish is supported by the doctors. It is her wish that there should be sedative treatment in advance of the final result. That again is accepted and I have no doubt that all these matters will be carefully taken into account and that the wishes of the patient's wife in that regard will be fully respected and implemented.

(For a further case, see *Swindon & Marlborough NHS Trust v S* [1995] 3 Med LR 84 (Ward J).)

Sir Stephen Brown P followed the statement of the British Medical Association in its *Guidelines on Treatment Decisions for Patients in Persistent Vegetative State* (1992) that the relatives' views are relevant and should be taken into account by the patient's doctor but that ultimately it is the doctor's duty to act in the patient's 'best interests' even if this does not comport with the views of one or all the relatives. Hence, the judge held that G's mother could not have a veto on withdrawal of artificial hydration and nutrition from G if that would be in his best interests.

The judge's decision in *Re G* must be a correct extrapolation of the law from the *Bland* decision. On the face of it, once a diagnosis of PVS is made – which at present requires a 12-month gap since the injury – continuing intervention is not in the patient's best interests as it is medically futile. This is the legal precedent set by the *Bland* case. Under the current framework for making decisions for incapacitated adults in England, the decision must be the doctor's alone. What is interesting about Sir Stephen Brown P's view in *Re G* is that he seems to make *consultation* with the relatives a legal requirement. For many, this was previously thought only to be a matter of good medical practice. He, however, makes it a legal necessity by making consultation a procedural requirement as part of the process by which the doctor forms his view of the patient's best interests. As a *legal* requirement, this is novel and is by no means unproblematic. Of course, it makes good sense and practice but if it is a legal requirement the medical lawyer must ask what is the legal sanction for not consulting?

It may be that, in some cases, a failure to consult would lead a doctor to take a mistaken view of the patient's best interests. For example, if the doctor failed to consult the relatives of someone who turned out to be a Jehovah's Witness, and in ignorance of this he gave a blood transfusion when an alternative was available (see Lord Donaldson MR's remarked in *Re T (Adult: Refusal of Treatment)* [1992] 4 All ER 649 at 653 (CA)). However, providing the doctor forms a correct view of a patient's 'best interests' (or as the current law curiously stands *a* view defensible under *Bolam*), failure to consult cannot lead to any legal sanction. It is doubtful, therefore, whether in itself consultation can be said to be a *legal* requirement. The logic of *Re G*, which it is suggested is right, is that once a doctor forms the view that it is not in the patient's best interest to continue treatment or care the views of the relatives (even if unanimously opposed to withdrawal) are of no *legal* effect.

Hydration and nutrition: is it treatment? The House of Lords refused to draw a distinction between the provision of food and fluids by artificial means (eg by naso-gastric tube) and medical treatment. It was argued by the Official Solicitor that artificial hydration and nutrition were of a different order from medical treatment since they represented the basic necessities of life. Thus, while medical treatment might be withheld or discontinued, food and water could not be so, not least because the patient would then starve to death. As to this argument, as the speeches set out earlier make clear, Lord Keith (at 861) and Lord Lowry (at 877) describe hydration and nutrition as being included within the general term 'medical treatment and care'. Lord Goff also held that if not 'medical treatment' they are 'part of the medical care' of the patient (at 871) (see also Lord Mustill referring to 'care and treatment' at 895).

In deciding this issue in this way, the House of Lords avoids (at least as regards *artificial* hydration and nutrition), the controversy which dogged the American courts because of its emotive association with both euthanasia and suicide until the US Supreme Court's decision in *Cruzan v Director, Missouri Department of Heath* (1990) 110 S Ct 2841. While the plurality of the US Supreme Court did not specifically address the question, Justice O'Connor (in her concurrence) and Justice Brennan (in his dissent, with whom Marshall and Blackmun JJ agreed) both reached the same view as the House of Lords in *Bland*.

Cruzan v Director, Missouri Department of Health (1990) 110 S Ct 2841 (US Sup Ct)

O'Connor J: Artificial feeding cannot readily be distinguished from other forms of medical treatment. See, eg, Council on Ethical and Judicial Affairs, American Medical Association, AMA Ethical Opinion 2.20, Withholding or Withdrawing Life-Prolonging Medical Treatment, Current Opinions 13 (1989); The Hastings Center, Guidelines on the Termination of Life-Sustaining Treatment and the Care of the Dying 59 (1987). Whether or not the techniques used to pass food and water into the patient's alimentary tract are terms 'medical treatment' it is clear they all involve some degree of intrusion and restraint. Feeding a patient by means of a nasogastric tube requires a physician to pass a long flexible tube through the patient's nose, throat and esophagus and into the stomach. Because of the discomfort such a tube causes, '[m]any patients need to be restrained forcibly and their hands put into large mittens to prevent them from removing the tube.' Major, The Medical Procedures for Providing Food and Water: Indications and Side Effects, in By No Extraordinary Means: The Choice to Forgo Life-Sustaining Food and Water 25 (J Lynn ed 1986). A gastrostomy tube (as was used to provide food and water to Nancy Cruzan, see *ante*, at 2) or jejunostomy tube must be surgically implanted into the stomach or small intestine. Office of Technology Assessment Task Force, Life-Sustaining Technologies and the Elderly 282 (1988). Requiring a competent adult to endure such procedures against her will burdens the patient's liberty, dignity, and freedom to determine the course of her own treatment. Accordingly, the liberty guaranteed by the Due Process Clause must protect, if it protects anything, an individual's deeply personal decision to reject medical treatment, including the artificial delivery of food and water.

Brennan J: No material distinction can be drawn between the treatment to which Nancy Cruzan continues to be subject – artificial nutrition and hydration – and any other medical treatment. See *ante*, (O'Connor, J, concurring). The artificial delivery of nutrition and hydration is undoubtedly medical treatment. The technique to which Nancy Cruzan is subject – artificial feeding through a gastrostomy tube – involves a tube implanted surgically into her stomach and through incisions in her abdominal wall. It may obstruct the intestinal tract, erode and pierce the stomach wall or cause leakage of the stomach's contents into the abdominal cavity. See Page, Andrassy, & Sandler, Techniques in Delivery of Liquid Diets, in Nutrition in Clinical Surgery 66–67 (M Deitel 2nd edn 1985). The tube can cause pneumonia from redux of the stomach's contents into the lung. See Bernard & Forlaw, Complications and Their Prevention, in Enteral and Tube Feeding 553 (J Rombeau & M Caldwell eds 1984). Typically, and in this case (see Tr 377), commercially prepared formulas are used, rather than fresh food. See Matarese, Enteral Alimentation, in Surgical Nutrition 726 (J Fischer edn 1983). The type of formula and method of administration must be experimented with to avoid gastrointestinal problems. *Id*, at 748. The patient must be monitored daily by medical personnel as to weight, fluid intake and fluid output; blood tests must be done weekly. *Id*, at 749, 751.

Artificial delivery of food and water is regarded as medical treatment by the medical profession and the Federal Government. According to the American Academy of Neurology, '[t]he artificial provision of nutrition and hydration is a form of medical treatment...analogous to other forms of life-sustaining treatment, such as the use of the respirator. When a patient is unconscious, both a respirator and an artificial feeding device serve to support or replace normal bodily functions that are compromised as a result of the patient's illness'. Position of the American Academy of Neurology on Certain Aspects of the Care and Management of the Persistent Vegetative State Patient, 39 Neurology 125 (Jan 1989). See also Council on Ethical and Judicial Affairs of the American Medical Association, Current Opinions, Opinion 2.20 (1989) ('Life-prolonging medical treatment includes medication and artificially or technologically supplied respiration, nutrition or hydration'); President's Commission 88 (life-sustaining treatment includes respirators, kidney dialysis machines, special feeding procedures).

Not all commentators agree with the law's position.

John Keown 'Restoring Moral and Intellectual Shape to the Law after Bland' (1997) 113 LQR 481

Why was tube-feeding not basic care which the hospital and its medical and nursing staff were under a duty to provide? The Lords held that tube-feeding was part of a regime of "medical treatment and care" (see, *eg*, [1993] AC 789 at p 858 *per* Lord Keith of Kinkel). The insertion of a gastrostomy tube into the stomach requires a minor operation, which is clearly a medical procedure. But it is not at all clear that the insertion of a nasogastric tube is medical intervention. And, even if it were, the intervention had already been carried out in Tony Bland's case. The question in such a case is why the pouring of food down the tube constitutes medical treatment. What is it supposed to be treating? Nor does the difficulty evaporate by classifying it, as did the Law Lords, as medical treatment or medical care. As Professor Finnis observes:

> The judgments all seem to embrace a fallacious inference, that if tube-feeding *is* part of medical 'treatment or care', tube-feeding is therefore *not* part of the non-medical (home or nursing) care which decent families and communities provide or arrange for their utterly dependent members. The non-sequitur is compounded by failure to note that although naso-gastric tube-feeding will not normally be established without a doctor's decision, no distinctively medical skills are needed to insert a naso-gastric tube or to maintain the supply of nutrients through it. (J M Finnis *'Bland: Crossing the Rubicon?'* (1993) 109 LQR 329.)

> Their Lordships seemed to place great weight on the fact that tube-feeding is regarded by the medical profession as medical treatment. (See, *eg* [1993] AC 789 at p 870 *per* Lord Goff.) But whether an intervention is medical is not a matter to be determined by medical opinion, nor by the mere fact that it is an intervention typically performed by doctors. A doctor may do many things in the course of his practice, such as reassuring patients or fitting catheters, which are not distinctively medical in nature. And, if it is opinion which is crucial, the answer one gets may well depend on whom one asks. Tube-feeding may be regarded as medical treatment by many doctors, but many nurses regard it as ordinary care.
> Further, Lord Goff's analogy between tube-feeding and mechanical ventilation is (although accepted by Mr Munby QC ([1993] AC 789 at p 822)) unpersuasive. Ventilation is standardly part of a therapeutic endeavour to stabilise, treat and cure: tube-feeding is not. Moreover, ventilation replaces the patient's capacity to breathe whereas a tube does not replace the capacity to digest and merely delivers food to the stomach. Nor have all patients who are tube-fed (including, it appears, those in pvs) lost the capacity to swallow. Tube-feeding may be instituted solely to minimise the risk of the patient inhaling food and/or because spoon-feeding is thought to be too time-consuming. Even if the patient has lost the capacity to swallow, the tube would still not be treating anything. A feeding-tube by which liquid is delivered to the patient's stomach is surely no more medical treatment than a catheter by which it is drained from the patient's bladder.

(See further, Finnis (1993) 109 LQR 329 and Gormally (ed) *Euthanasia, Clinical Practice and the Law* (1994).)

In its 1994 Report, the Select Committee of the House of Lords on Medical Ethics (HL Paper 21–94) was divided on whether tube-feeding should be considered to be 'basic care' or not. Instead, the Committee chose to finesse the practical problem by agreeing that the withdrawal or withholding of antibiotics would be proper as they were undoubtedly medical treatment and avoided the need to consider withdrawing feeding (para 257).

But where does that leave hydration and nutrition which is not artificially administered, eg where the patient can swallow and is spoon-fed? Is this a form of medical treatment and thus may be discontinued or withheld? Or, is it a separate regime of care which the doctor is obliged to continue even though the patient's condition is hopeless and further medical treatment is agreed to be futile? One view is that there is a difference and oral provision of nutrition or hydration is 'basic care' which there is a duty to provide. Professional opinion is, perhaps, represented by the views of the British Medical Association.

BMA *Withholding and Withdrawing Life-prolonging Medical Treatment: Guidance for decision making* (1999)

> 3.5   *Oral nutrition and hydration*: Where nutrition and hydration are provided by ordinary means – such as by cup, spoon or any other method for delivering food or nutritional supplements into the patient's mouth – or the moistening of a patient's mouth for comfort, this forms part of basic care and should not be withdrawn.
>
>   Food or water to be given by these means should always be offered but should not be forced upon patients who resist or express a clear refusal. It should also not be forced upon patient's for whom the process of feeding produces an unacceptable level of burden, such as where it causes unavoidable choking or aspiration of the food or fluid. In the latter case, it would be appropriate to consider whether artificial nutrition and hydration would provide a benefit to the patient…

In our view, the solution to the problem does not lie in the process of labelling the intervention as 'treatment' or 'care' or indeed anything else. Instead, the solution lies in reminding ourselves that the doctor's obligation is to act in the 'best interests' of the patient which in the example we have given means that the patient be allowed to die. Continuing to spoon-feed the patient could frustrate this end and thus might not be in the patient's 'best interests'. Of course, the validity of this analysis must be set against the quite natural repugnance some might feel at the idea of denying a patient what look like the basic requirements of life. Indeed, this repugnance may persuade a court to accept that there is a difference between artificial feeding and spoon-feeding. In *Re Conroy* (*op cit*), the New Jersey Supreme Court did precisely this:

> **Schrieber J:** Once one enters the realms of complex, high-technology medical care, it is hard to shed the 'emotional symbolism' of food. *See Barber, 147 Cal App 3d* at 1016, 195 *Cal Rptr* at 490. However, artificial feedings such as nasogastric tubes, gastrostomies, and intravenous infusions are significantly different from bottle-feeding or spoon-feeding – they are medical procedures with inherent risks and possible side effects, instituted by skilled health-care providers to compensate for impaired physical functioning.

While understandable, we think this is wrong. This is not to say that we argue that the patient should suffer before he dies. Rather, we revert to the doctor's general duty to comfort which would entitle the doctor to administer whatever medicine necessary to alleviate any distress which may be caused to the patient but what that would be in the case of an insentient patient is unclear.

Substituted judgment? Tony Bland had never expressed any views on what should be done if he was ever rendered incompetent. As we saw in Chapter 6, in such a case the court (or indeed anyone else) cannot apply the 'substituted judgment' test, ie determine what the patient would have wished in the light of his previously expressed views and values. Therefore, any decision *must* be based upon the 'best interests' test. Nevertheless, both Lord Goff and Lord Mustill went out of their way to reject the 'substituted judgment' test as not being part of English law (see *op cit* at 872–873 and 892 respectively). It may be said that both judges' rejection of it was based upon a misunderstanding of the true nature of the test (*supra*, ch 6). (For a proper application of the 'substituted judgment' tests in a PVS case, see Garibaldi and Handler JJ in *Re Jobes* (1987) 529 A 2d 434 (NJ Sup Ct).) As Handler J put it in *Re Jobes*: 'the decision to discontinue or to refuse treatment was made by the patient's guardian on the basis of *trustworthy* evidence of what the patient would have decided' (our emphasis). (See also: *Brophy v New England Sinai Hospital* (1986) 497 NE 2d 626 (Mass Sup Jud Ct); *In Re Estate of Longeway* (1989) 549 NE 2d 292 (Ill Sup Ct) and see the cases discussed in *Cruzan, supra*.)

We have already examined the test of 'substituted judgment' in some detail (*supra*, ch 6). It is our view that properly understood and applied appropriately it could, and should, have a place in English law and the courts should adopt it.

Having said this, the Law Commission's Report, *Mental Incapacity* (No 231), (1995) specifically rejects it in favour of a modified version of the best interests test to include consideration of the 'ascertainable past and present wishes and feelings of the person concerned and the factors the person would consider if able to do so' (paras 3.28–3.31), discussed *supra*, ch 6.

The difficulty with this proposal – which the Government intends to enact: *Making Decisions* (Cm 4465) (1999) para 1.11 – is that it appears to look simultaneously in two different directions. It both looks to the objective 'best interests' of the patient and urges that account be taken, in effect, of what the patient himself considered to be in his 'best interests'. No solution is offered for the situation in which these two do not coincide. In so far as the English courts seem always to fall back on the 'best interests' test, any such conflict would most likely be decided by reference to what *others* consider to be in the patient's best interests, thereby weakening any purported concern to take account of the patient's views.

Having said this, there is, however, another possible view which the common law could adopt allowing the patient's views to shape the decision made such that, for example, his religious or other moral perspective could be taken into account, perhaps even be determinative, of whether the intervention continues.

Andrew Grubb 'The Persistent Vegetative State: A Duty (Not) To Treat and Conscientious Objection' (1997) 4 EJHL 157

I would like to suggest that the courts might have regard to an argument or approach advocated by Ronald Dworkin in his important book, *Life's Dominion* (Harper Collins, 1993). In his book, Professor Dworkin develops a dichotomy between a person's experiential and critical interest (*Ibid.* at 199–217). The former reflects those aspects of a person's life which he likes and consider to be for his 'good' or 'well-being'; to add to his enjoyment of the world, for example, listening to Mozart or viewing Picasso. But, significantly, these interests can only be enjoyed or defeated if a person is able to experience them and, of course, one person's joy may not be shared by others who may not like the same thing. The permanently insensate PVS patient, therefore, lacks these interests. By contrast, a person's 'critical' interests represent not just their view of how life should be enjoyed but rather how life coheres into a worthwhile whole: if you like the vision of what enriches a life beyond interstitial experiences. Having a family, being true to one's self and one's friends, contributing to understanding in a particular discipline: each of these could be an aspect of a person's 'critical' interests. What is crucial here is that 'critical' interests, as opposed to 'experiential' interests survive the loss of capacity to know whether the interest is being fulfilled. Thus, even patients in PVS possess these interests and, on this argument, Lord Mustill was wrong in *Bland* to state dismissively that such a patient had no interests.

So what is the relevance here? Dworkin argues, convincingly, that how, and in what circumstances, we die is capable of being one of a person's critical interests. We may even, I think, presume that people regard the manner of their death as 'of special, symbolic importance: they want their deaths, if possible, to express and in that way vividly confirm the values they believe most important to their lives' (*Ibid*, at 211). For some, perhaps most, this would encompass a 'good' or 'dignified' death: not a meaningless existence in a permanently unconscious state. Nor, I would suggest, given sufficient evidence of the patient's life, would it contemplate a death in which others, such as members of his family, are severely distressed and burdened by their relative's physical disintegration.

Thus, in an appropriate case, a patient's 'best interests' – his 'critical' ones – may include consideration of his view of his death ('I would like to be kept alive whatever.' 'I would like to die a dignified death.'); and of his family's plight – whether financial or emotional. Consequently, a court could determine that it was in a PVS patient's 'best interests' to remain alive – notwithstanding the medical and other opinion that treatment was medically futile – if there was clear and persuasive evidence that the patient valued being alive in whatever condition they would survive. Similarly, in an appropriate case, the court could have regard to the effects on the family of keeping the patient alive in making a decision whether or not to allow withdrawal of treatment. Of course, the evidence must be clear and great care should be taken to identify the patient's conception of a 'good life' and a 'good death'. What I do not think this approach deals with is the wider question of allocation of resources in society. Here, it remains the case, even on the view proposed, that the 'critical interests' of the patient are not implicated.

I offer this only as a tentative solution. Some philosophers would not accept the notion of 'critical' interests at all, or if they did, agree on their proper location or importance within a framework of moral obligations (J. Harris, *'Euthanasia and the Value of Life'* in J Keown (ed) (1995) *'Euthanasia Examined'*, Cambridge). Indeed, the approach comes close to a recognition of the 'substituted judgment' test beloved of American courts but so far rejected in England. It does, however, have some resonances in the Law Commission's proposed 'checklist' for determining an incompetent person's 'best interests' set out in its *Mental Incapacity Report* (*Mental Incapacity*, Law Commission Report No 231, at para 3.33). Further, one can see some judicial nodding in the direction of what is being suggested. Certainly, the Court of Appeal's decision in *Bland* contains a number of remarks reminiscent of this approach. Sir Thomas Bingham MR considered that the court should have regard to 'wider and less tangible considerations' in assessing the patient's 'best interests' (*supra*, at 813):

> …the constant invasions and humiliations to which his inert body is subject; to the desire he would naturally have to be remembered as a cheerful, carefree, gregarious teenager and not an object of pity; to the prolonged ordeal imposed on all the members of his family…, even, perhaps…to a belief that finite resources are better devoted to enhancing life than averting death.

Butler-Sloss LJ spoke of his 'right to be respected…[and]…to avoid unnecessary humiliation and degrading invasion of his body…' (*supra*, at 822). The third member of the Court of Appeal, Hoffmann LJ, having referred to Professor Dworkin's work, spoke in the language of critical interests without ever using the phrase and held that the patient had 'a recognisable interest in the manner of his life and death…' (*supra*, at 829). The House of Lords was, of course, a good deal less sympathetic to this approach although Lord Goff referred to the 'indignity' of Anthony Bland's treatment (*supra*, at 869). Its change of tack was, I think largely because the judges felt the notion of a 'medical futility' and absence of 'benefit' were safe refuges from the controversial issue of valuing life and presented a more solid evidential base for the decision.

3.4 Concluding Remark
It remains possible, therefore, for the courts to broaden the current conception of a PVS patient's interests so as to be more sensitive to that patient's pre-PVS view of himself and his family. What remains untouched is the court's inability to focus on anyone other than the patient and so contemplate a decision being based upon the limited resources available to sustain a patient in PVS. The courts are not likely to follow the view of Hoffmann LJ in *Bland* that '…in principle the allocation of resources between patients is a matter for the health authority and not for the courts' (*supra*, at 833). To do so might allow a decision whether to withdraw life-support to be made on the basis of available resources. This must be a matter for Parliament but to say that is to recognise that the issue will never be decided: it is simply too controversial.

Further support could be found in the European Convention on Human Rights. As we saw earlier (*supra*, ch 6) there is a strong argument that art 8 – the right to private and family life – could be interpreted so as to *require* the court (or other decision-maker) to apply a 'substituted judgment' test in an appropriate case. It was, after all, a PVS case where the US Supreme Court in *Cruzan v Director, Missouri Dept of Health* (1990) 110 S Ct 2841 held that a patient's 'liberty' interest under the 14th Amendment to the US Constitution required just such an approach. There are, however, two notes of caution which must be entered. First, it may be that an English court would not, any more than the common law has already, read the 'right' so broadly. Secondly, as the *Cruzan* case makes clear, the majority's view that requiring 'clear and convincing evidence' of the patient's wishes – which was the law in Missouri under challenge – was consistent with the patient's 'right' given the risks of abuse and error in surrogate decision-making, probably leaves little room for anything other than anticipated or advance refusals of treatment.

Rehnquist CJ put it as follows in *Cruzan v Director, Missouri Dept of Health* (1990) 110 S Ct 2841 (US Sup Ct):

Rehnquist CJ: In sum, we conclude that a State may apply a clear and convincing evidence standard in proceedings where a guardian seeks to discontinue nutrition and hydration of a person diagnosed to be in a persistent vegetative state.

The Supreme Court of Missouri held that in this case the testimony adduced at trial did not amount to clear and convincing proof of the patient's desire to have hydration and nutrition withdrawn. The testimony adduced at the trial consisted primarily of Nancy Cruzan's statements made to a housemate about a year before her accident that she would not want to live should she face life as a 'vegetable', and other observations to the same effect. The observations did not deal in terms with withdrawal of medical treatment or of hydration and nutrition. We cannot say that the Supreme Court of Missouri committed constitutional error in reaching the conclusion that it did.

Petitions alternatively contend that Missouri must accept the 'substituted judgment' of close family members even in the absence of substantial proof that their views reflect the views of the patient.

[W]e do not think the Due Process Clause requires the State to repose judgment on these matters with anyone but the patient herself. Close family members may have a strong feeling – a feeling not at all ignoble or unworthy, but not entirely disinterested either – that they do not wish the continuation of the life of a loved one which they regard as hopeless, meaningless, and even degrading. But there is no automatic assurance that the view of close family members will necessarily be the same as the patient's would have been had she been confronted with the prospect of her situation while competent. All of the reasons previously discussed for allowing Missouri to require clear and convincing evidence of the patient's wishes lead us to conclude that the State may choose to defer only to those wishes, rather than confide the decision to close family members.

(For a discussion of the relationship between anticipatory refusals, 'substituted judgment' and the 'clear and convincing' evidence requirement in a PVS case, see *De Grella v Elston* (1993) 858 SW 2d (Ky Sup Ct) and Commentary (1994) 2 Med L Rev 225 (AG).)

III.   Applying *Bland* Beyond PVS

On one view the law as expressed by the Law Lords in *Bland* is applicable only to decisions regarding the treatment of patients in PVS. The judges appeared prepared to accept the lawfulness of withholding or withdrawing treatment because Tony Bland was permanently insensate, which they took to mean that he no longer had any interests which counted in any calculation of his best interests (see especially per Lord Keith at 860–861 and Lord Mustill at 894). The much more difficult question concerning medical decisions when the patient is *not* insensate clearly troubled the court. It is to this question that we must turn. First, however, we must notice that the borderline between patients who are insensate and those who are not is by no means well defined. Two cases will help to illustrate the boundaries of the *Bland* decision. The crucial point in *Bland* was that the patient was permanently insensate. In one post-*Bland* decision (*Re H*) the court approved the withdrawal of food and water when the evidence was not so clear.

Re H (adult: incompetent) (1997) 38 BMLR 11 (Fam Div)

H, now aged 43, suffered very serious brain damage following a road traffic accident in May 1994. Since then she had been without all but a rudimentary awareness and had been kept alive by artificial feeding and by a tracheostomy operation. Expert evidence by several doctors was unanimous that H was in a permanent vegetative state. However, she did not fit fully within the criteria for the establishment of permanent vegetative state issued by the Royal College of Physicians in 1996. A consultant clinical psychologist had found, on occasions, that he had been able to obtain a visual tracking movement from H and believed that she could focus on an object and that she could be aroused by the sound of clapping, or by touch and movement of her arms. The National Health Service trust, in whose care H had been, applied for the declaration that it would be in her best interests for the administration of life-sustaining treatment, including the artificial administration of nutrition and hydration, to cease. The Official Solicitor supported the application.

Sir Stephen Brown P: A complication, or apparent complication, arose in this case because the Royal College of Physicians, in a report published in March 1996, issued criteria in order to assist in the diagnosis of the permanent vegetative state. Dr Wade, and indeed Professor McClellan, who gave evidence on behalf of the Official Solicitor, both agree that this patient does not fit four squarely within one particular guideline in the light of evidence of 'visual tracking', as it has been called. However, it is the opinion of Dr Wade and also of Professor

McClellan that she does fit within, and fully within, the assessment criteria published by an international working party in a report on the vegetative state issued in February 1996 which was prepared for the Royal Hospital for Neuro-Disability at Putney. The working party consisted of an international body of members headed by the very experienced Dr Keith Andrews as chairman, who has very great experience in this field. He is the director of medical and research services at the Royal Hospital for Neuro-Disability, and has in fact given evidence on a number of occasions to this court in cases of this nature.

The working party report includes, at p 56, a section headed: 'Vegetative Presentations'. It is the view of Professor McClellan and, indeed, of other witnesses in this case, that this patient fits within what is described there as the third category of vegetative presentations:

> The patient has sleep awake patterns, single limb response dissimulation, withdrawal or intermittent localisation to touch, sound or visual stimulation may occur, tracking eye movements may occur but the patient does not focus on objects or people. No turn to sound or touch.

In this instance it may be that a precise label is not of significant importance. This is, of course, a developing field for medical analysis and it is now, I think, 25 years since Professor Jennet and Professor Plumb coined the phrase 'persistent vegetative state' now known by the initials PVS. There is no doubt, in the view of all the witnesses who have given evidence, that, in Dr Wade's terms, the patient is wholly unaware of herself or of her environment and that there is no possibility of any change.

I have heard the evidence of two important nursing witnesses. The first of those senior nurses gave evidence that she sees this patient twice a week if not more frequently. She has never herself seen any sign of awareness. One gets the feeling, she said, sometimes that she is 'there', but her view is that that is not a reality. The entries in certain of the nursing records to which I have been referred, have not in fact been substantiated in any meaningful way by the repeated examinations of the numerous medical experts.

I am quite satisfied, having heard the consultant trauma and orthopaedic surgeon, who although not a neurologist is nevertheless experienced in acute trauma cases, together with the consultant neurologists, that this is a case of a vegetative state which, although it may not fall precisely within the Royal College guidelines, is, and can properly be described as being, permanent.

Because of the possibilities which might have appeared from the nursing records, the NHS trust also sought the assistance of a distinguished consultant clinical psychologist, Professor McMillen, who has some 15 years' experience of working with traumatic brain injury patients. He spent some 11 to 12 hours with this patient. He found that he was able on some occasions to obtain a tracking movement and he believed she would focus on an object; but he also concluded that she could be aroused by the sound of clapping or by touch and by movement of the arms. He said, although he was first encouraged by what he described as the movement of her thumb, he came to the conclusion that in fact she is not susceptible to any change and, although not a doctor but a clinical psychologist, he nevertheless stated quite explicitly that he agreed that, in this case, it would be wholly appropriate to cease the artificial feeding which would inevitably lead to physical death.

I heard, in addition to Dr Wade and Professor McMillen, the evidence of Dr Greenhall, a consultant neurologist who had seen H on three occasions. He said that he believed that she is in a vegetative state, which is permanent. He agreed that he did not in fact find that the Royal College guidelines were completely fulfilled. Nevertheless, he had no doubt that it would be correct to describe her as being in a vegetative state which is, in his view, permanent. He said that he would accept her condition as being consistent with that diagnosis.

Not content with Dr Greenhall and Dr Wade, the NHS trust also consulted a consultant neurologist from Southampton, Dr Philip Kennedy, who is also experienced in this class of case. He saw the patient twice in the autumn of 1995 and again in the autumn of 1996 when he carried out a joint examination with Professor McClellan. He noted the various features which have been referred to: the matter of the tracking and the response to visual threat which was apparent on occasions and which, without appropriate consideration, might suggest the possibility of some improvement, but, again, he came to the conclusion that it was, in his words, almost inconceivable that she had any awareness.

The term 'awareness' has received some analytical consideration in the course of this hearing. It has been used in different senses by certain of the witnesses. It certainly does not mean, in the case of this patient, according to any of the witnesses, that she knows what is going on, or is aware of herself in the way in which conscious persons are aware of themselves.

The degree of awareness has been described by the phrase 'rudimentary awareness', particularly by Professor McClellan, but he means it in the sense, as I understand his evidence, of some person, as it were, awaking from sleep; being still half asleep, not aware of their surroundings: they might appreciate that a light was coming through the curtains, or something of that kind. But these phrases really have little meaning in assessing this patient.

What the witnesses have described is, in effect, an insentient patient completely dependant upon artificial feeding by tube and tracheostomy for breathing; utterly dependent upon round the clock nursing for all physical needs; unable to communicate and unable to acknowledge anything which is taking place. Of course, patients in this situation require the most careful assessment. I am quite satisfied that this patient has had the most careful continuous assessment over the past three years.

Professor McClellan, who has given evidence for the Official Solicitor and therefore, in effect, on behalf of the patient herself, has applied his critical faculties in full to the condition of this patient. I found him to be a most convincing witness, if I may say so. He explained quietly, but with authority, the situation of this patient. It is a desperately tragic situation. It is one which must bear very heavily on the relatives and friends. It has continued now for over three years and there is no possibility of any improvement...

In this case, I have no doubt, having heard all the evidence, and in particular the evidence of the very distinguished medical witnesses who have exercised their analytical skills in this case now over a period of three years, that the application for the declarations which are sought in this case should be granted. These are very anxious cases. The sanctity of life is of vital importance. It is not, however, paramount, and, in this case, I am satisfied that it is in the best interests of this patient that the life sustaining treatment presently being artificially administered should be brought to a conclusion.

(For another case where the RCP guidelines were not satisfied, see *Re D* (1997) 41 BMLR 81.)

The New Zealand case of *Auckland AHB v A-G* [1993] 1 NZLR 235, cited with approval by Lords Goff and Mustill in *Bland*, offers another example.

Auckland AHB v A-G [1993] 1 NZLR 235 (NZ HCt)

Thomas J: At the present moment Mr L is lying in a hospital bed in the intensive care unit of the Auckland Hospital. He is suffering from an extreme case of Guillain-Barre syndrome. This terrible disease affects the nervous system. Although Mr L is not what is called 'brain dead', his brain is unable to communicate with his body or his body with his brain. The two are disconnected. In stark terms, Mr L has a living, but impaired, brain which is entirely disengaged from his body. So he cannot move a muscle or limb. He lies lifeless and motionless, unable to communicate by even elementary means. His condition is so severe that he has no prospect of recovery.

If nature were to have taken its course Mr L would long since be dead. None of his 'vital functions' would be active. But as part of his early treatment he was connected with a ventilatory-support system. By this mechanical means his breathing and heartbeat were maintained. Now, many months later, it is clear that his condition will never improve and that there is no therapeutic or medical benefit in continuing with the artificial ventilation. The unanimous view of eight specialists who have examined Mr L is that the support cannot be medically justified.

If and when the artificial ventilation is discontinued, Mr L will suffer an almost immediate cardiac arrest and quickly, but painlessly, die. Otherwise he will continue to exist in his current condition indefinitely.

In these tragic circumstances, the doctors who have been caring for Mr L decided to withdraw the ventilatory support. They have the full support of Mrs L, and they have adopted and meticulously followed a cautious procedure in reaching their decision...

The question in issue, therefore, is whether the doctors' action in withdrawing the artificial ventilatory-support system from Mr L would make them guilty of culpable homicide...

[T]he Auckland Area Health Board seek to establish...that the doctors would not, in withdrawing Mr L's ventilator in the circumstances of this case, be guilty of culpable homicide and that, for that purpose, ss 151(1) and 164 [of the Crimes Act 1961] have no application in this case...

Mr L was born on 13 April 1933. He is now 59 years old. He was a truck driver, and he and his wife lived in Eltham. On about 14 March 1990 Mr L was involved in a motor vehicle accident. He was admitted to Taranaki Base Hospital suffering from facial and rib fractures. A left femoral fracture was fixed internally with a pin. Mr L was discharged from the hospital and readmitted on 17 July 1991 to have the pin removed. At this stage, he was apparently well. He was discharged again on 22 July 1991 but returned to the hospital the following day suffering from numbness in his right hand.

On 26 July Mr L was readmitted to the Taranaki Base Hospital suffering from numbness in his other hand. He was unable to raise his arms. Upon his readmission, doctors noted that Mr L suffered profound weakness in both arms, weakness in his hips and a complete loss of deep tendon reflexes. Arrangements were made for him to be transferred to the neurology ward at Auckland Hospital on 29 July. He was brought into the hospital in a wheelchair in a weak state and a diagnosis of Guillain-Barre syndrome was confirmed.

Mr L's condition continued to deteriorate. The Guillain-Barre syndrome started to adversely affect his ability to breathe. On 4 August Mr L was transferred to the department of critical care medicine to guard against the possibility that he might require artificial ventilation. Initially, he did not require this assistance and was transferred back to the neurological ward but, later in the same day, he was brought back and connected to an artificial ventilator. Since 4 August a tracheostomy was performed to facilitate his care.

The deterioration continued. Mr L lost the ability to move his limbs altogether. He could not control any muscles governed by the brain stem, including the muscles in his face and eyes. For a while the doctors were able to establish limited communication with him, but by 11 August he could barely blink, either to communicate or to keep his corneas lubricated. By 15 August there was only a flicker of eyebrow movement and Mr L was totally paralysed. His eyeball muscles became inert and his pupils became fixed and dilated.

Extensive tests undertaken by the doctors revealed a complete absence of conduction along Mr L's nerves and the degeneration of the nerve axons. Beginning with marked demyelineation, the syndrome had progressed to secondary axonal degeneration. The nerves involving hearing do not function and, although the visual pathways are seemingly intact when tested neurophysiologically, it is not known whether Mr L receives visual impressions or not. (The visual function is not wholly dependent on the peripheral nervous system.) As best as can be ascertained, Mr L's brain is in a drowsy semi-working state, but this is probably due to sensory deprivation rather than brain damage. Mr L has no responses and displays no awareness to anything happening in his room or to himself. His muscles have now degenerated and are transforming into useless fibrous tissue.

Mr L is not brain dead. However, in effect, his brain is not connected to any part of his body apart, possibly, from his visual faculties. He is denervated and unable to interact in any way with his environment. He is properly described as being in a 'locked in' and 'locked out' state. For that reason, he is incapable of an independent existence and is completely dependent on artificial ventilatory support.

Mr L's prognosis is now hopeless. It must be concluded that his condition is irreversible. Overseas opinions which were obtained 10 months ago may have held out some remote hope of improvement, but no evidence emerged to justify even that guarded optimism. Dr Trubuhovich reiterated in cross-examination that a current examination had confirmed that the degeneration is continuing and that there is no sign of improvement. Nor is there any prospect of improvement…

[T]he proceeding is concerned with a [narrow] question; whether a doctor is obliged to continue treatment which has no therapeutic or medical benefit, notwithstanding that the discontinuance of the treatment may result in the clinical death of the patient.

The problem arises when life passes into death but obscurely. It is a problem made acute by the enormous advances made in technology and medical science in recent decades. With the use of sophisticated life-support systems, life may be perpetually well beyond the reach of the natural disease. The process of living can become the process of dying so that it is unclear whether life is being sustained or death being deferred.

This is the plight of the irreversibly doomed patient. Maintained by mechanical means they exist suspended in a state of moribund inanimation. Whether a body devoid of a mind or, as in the case of Mr L, a brain destitute of a body, does not matter in any sensible way. In their chronic and persistent vegetative condition they lack self-awareness or awareness of their surroundings in any cognitive sense. They are the 'living dead'. Whether, in such circumstances, or in this particular case, it is fairer to say that the life-support system is being used to sustain life or being used to defer death is at the heart of the question I must resolve…

Section 151(1) seeks to ensure that those who have the care of one who cannot care for him- or herself supply that person with the necessaries of life. The section reads:

151. Duty to provide the necessaries of life – (1) Every one who has charge of any other person unable, by reason of detention, age, sickness, insanity, or any other cause, to withdraw himself from such charge, and unable to provide himself with the necessaries of life, is (whether such charge is undertaken by him under any contract or is imposed upon him by law or by reason of his unlawful act or otherwise howsoever) under a legal duty to supply that person with the necessaries of life, and is criminally responsible for omitting without lawful excuse to perform such duty if the death of that person is caused, or if his life is endangered or his health permanently injured, by such omission.

In his carefully prepared submission, Mr Collins advanced four arguments in support of the claim that, in withdrawing the ventilatory support from Mr L, the doctors would not be in breach of this section. First, he submitted that in his case ventilatory support is not a necessity of life; secondly, he argued that the withdrawing of the ventilatory support would not be the cause of death; thirdly, he contended that there is no legal duty to continue to maintain Mr L on the ventilator; and, finally, he urged that the doctors concerned have a 'lawful excuse' to turn off the ventilator.

During the course of argument it was accepted by Mr Collins that the third point had no validity independently of his other submissions and it was abandoned.

(i) Cause of death?

For reasons which will become clear, I propose to first address the question of whether the withdrawal of the ventilator would be the cause of Mr L's death.

The contention advanced is that artificial ventilation cannot prevent, cure or alleviate Mr L's extreme Guillain-Barre syndrome so as to enable him to survive the illness. If the artificial ventilator is disconnected, argued Mr Collins, Mr L will not die because he no longer has the benefits of the machine. He will have died because of the effects of extreme Guillain-Barre syndrome. The point is expressed in this way by Dr Gillett: 'In my opinion it would be fair to conclude that in this case what caused his [Mr L's] death was the underlying disease process which prevented him from breathing on his own or sustaining his own vital functions.' This observation formed the basis of the acknowledgement proffered by Ms Goddard as part of the agreed facts. It reads: 'His [Mr L's] death will be caused by the underlying disease process of Guillain-Barre syndrome which prevents him from breathing on his own or sustaining his own vital functions.'

In the case of Mr L it is an argument which is easy to accept. But with due respect to counsel I am not certain that the point can be advanced in these relatively straightforward terms. There may be many circumstances in which a patient is kept alive by a life-support system where it would not be appropriate to discontinue that support. A polio victim unable to breathe or avoid cardiac arrest without mechanical assistance but who is nevertheless alive, and even perhaps desirous of remaining alive, is one example. No question of withdrawing the ventilator-support system would arise in such a case unless requested by the patient. But if the patient's doctor did in fact withdraw the support it is not acceptable that he or she should escape criminal responsibility on the ground that their action was not the cause of death. Yet, as a matter of logic, it is difficult to distinguish this example from a case such as Mr L's. The fact that in one case the application of ventilatory support is futile and has no real therapeutic or medical benefit is not a difference which could, at least on the face of it, go to the question of causation.

I suspect that the reason why this argument is pressed in a case such as Mr L's is that it accords with common sense. A doctor who withdraws a life-support system from a patient who is effectively lifeless should not be held responsible for the ensuing death when the support system is disconnected. Nor should he or she be obliged to regard their action as the cause of death. The difficulty is to perceive the rationale which would allow it to be said that the underlying disease was the cause of death when the doctors withdraw the life-support apparatus of one whose condition is irretrievably hopeless but not the cause of death when a doctor withdraws the support from one whose continued life is sustainable.

...The basic question must be whether the doctor was legally justified in doing what he did. Essentially, this is to ask whether the doctor was under a duty to continue the life-support system or had a 'lawful excuse' for withdrawing it. To my mind, these two questions are the critical questions. If the doctor is not under a legal duty to provide or continue with the life-support system, or he has a 'lawful excuse' for discontinuing it, it may then be said that he or she has not *legally* caused the death of the patient. This point may be re-examined later, but it is useful first to turn to these two critical questions.

(ii) The duty to provide the necessaries of life

There is no doubt that the section applies to a patient admitted to hospital care. Nor is there any doubt that the phrase 'necessaries of life' includes medical treatment. 'Medical aid', *R v Senior* [1899] 1 QB 283; *R v Burney* [1958] NZLR 745, 'medical care', *R v Books* (1902) 9 BCR 13, and 'medical attention', *R v Moore* [1954] NZLR 893, have been all held to be a necessary of life. I agree with Mr Collins that nothing hinges upon interchanging terminology. But in all these cases the medical intervention which was construed to be a necessary of life was medical intervention necessary to prevent, cure or alleviate a disease that threatened life or health; see also *R v Tutton* (1989) 48 CCC (3d) 129.

No cases are known – and I believe counsel's researches will have been exhaustive – in which the question of whether a ventilator is to be construed as a necessary of life has been in issue. So the question can be approached afresh. To my mind, however, there is no absolute answer; the answer in each case must depend on the facts. Thus, the provision of artificial respiration may be regarded as a necessary of life where it is required to prevent, cure or alleviate a disease that endangers the health or life of the patient. If, however, the patient is surviving only by virtue of the mechanical means which induces heartbeat and breathing and is beyond recovery, I do not consider that the provision of a ventilator can properly be construed as a necessary of life. It is repugnant that a doctor who has in good faith and with complete medical propriety undertaken treatment which has failed should be held responsible to continue that treatment on the basis that it is, or continues to be, a necessary of life. Nor is it possible to say at one and the same time that a life-support machine is serving no other purpose than deferring certain death and, on the other hand, regard the provision of the machine as a necessary of life in the sense that the term is used in the section. Such a patient has passed the point of 'life' and the obligation contemplated by the section is otiose.

However, as I have indicated, this would not be the case if a life-support system served the purpose of preventing, curing or alleviating a disease which threatened the life or health of the patient. Artificial ventilation may have this effect in many cases. In itself it does not prevent or cure the condition which threatens life or death. Rather, it has a therapeutic or medical advantage in that it may enable a patient to live long enough to recover from the illness. In such a case it alleviates the effects of the illness while nature or other medical intervention overcomes the condition. In that sense it has a therapeutic or medical function.

In Mr L's case there is no prospect of any improvement. Neither further medical treatment nor nature itself can intervene to repel the disease. Without the life-support system death is unavoidable. In these circumstances it serves no purpose and, for that reason, properly cannot be regarded as a necessary of life.

(iii) Lawful excuse

Even if it could be said, however, that the doctors are under a duty to provide the ventilator support to Mr L as a necessary of life, I am of the firm view that for the purpose of the section they are legally justified in withdrawing that support. They would not be acting without 'lawful excuse'.

The phrase 'lawful excuse' has no defined meaning. The Court of Appeal in *R v Burney* (at p 753) approved the dicta of the Privy Council in *Wong Pooh Yin v Public Prosecutor* [1955] AC 93 where it was said at p 100:

> Their Lordships doubt if it is possible to define the expression 'lawful excuse' in a comprehensive and satisfactory manner and they do not propose to make the attempt. They agree with the Court of Appeal that it would be undesirable to do so and that each case requires to be examined on its individual facts.

In my view, doctors have a lawful excuse to discontinue ventilation when there is no medical justification for continuing that form of medical assistance. To require the administration of a life-support system when such a system has no further medical function or purpose and serves only to defer the death of a patient is to confound the purpose of medicine. In such circumstances, the continuation of the artificial ventilation may be lawful, but that does not make it unlawful to discontinue it if the discontinuance accords with good medical practice.

A phrase such as 'good medical practice' may not have the precision of meaning that the medical profession or the public would desire. But that imprecision is inherent in the problem itself. There can be no single or fixed rule as to exactly when a doctor may withhold a life-support system which would cover the infinite variety of factual situations arising in practice. Consequently, the criterion can only be a general phrase such as 'good medical practice'.

Nor is it imperative that the phrase 'good medical practice' be accepted in any exclusive or dogmatic sense. It has been selected because it already enjoys some currency. But any description such as 'sound medical practice' or 'proper medical standards and procedures' would serve equally well. What is important is its perceived content. Clearly, it must begin with a bona fide decision on the part of the attending doctors as to what, in their judgment, is in the best interests of the patient. Equally, it must encompass the prevailing medical standards, practices, procedures and traditions which command general approval within the medical profession. All relevant tests would need to be carried out. In making vital decisions of the present kind specialist opinions and agreement will no doubt be required and extended consultation with other consultants is likely to be appropriate. Consultation with the medical profession's recognised ethical body is also critical. It must approve the doctor's decision. Finally, the patient's family or guardian must be fully informed and freely concur in what is proposed. It is knowledge of this practice, and the assurance that the procedures are conscientiously followed, which will provide the public with the confidence to accept the decisions which are then made.

I have already made the point that it is unacceptable to suggest that what constitutes good medical practice should not at the same time constitute a 'lawful excuse' for the purpose of s 151. Doctors who follow good medical practice should not, it is suggested, be liable to be held 'criminally responsible' in terms of s 151 or any related section. The strength of this contention was recognised by Ms Goddard for the Attorney-General. She acknowledged that:

> …if the Court were to comment that 'lawful excuse' in this medical context encompasses a collegiate decision made by doctors charged with the care of a patient, endorsed by the appropriate medical ethical committee and with the informed consent of family members concerned, then prima facie such a decision must be lawful. It could only be unlawful if, in a particular case, the decision itself had been made on a wrong exercise of principle, or, if account had not been taken of differing opinion or practice accepted as proper by a responsible body of medical opinion.

I agree. In the present case, the decision that Mr L's life-support system should be discontinued has been made by a number of medical specialists and supported by others. Extensive tests have been carried out and repeated. Overseas consultants have been approached. The decision has been endorsed by the appropriate medical ethical body, and the informed consent of the family members has been obtained. There is, in this process, the assurance of good medical practice...

[T]he determination of what is good medical practice in any particular situation can be best assisted by having regard to the essential nature of a doctor's duty in attending a patient whose life-support system has ceased to serve any therapeutic or medical function. Indeed, what is good practice probably cannot be determined without regard to the fundamental duty which arises from this doctor/patient relationship. This is because it needs to be recognised that a doctor is under no legal duty to prolong life – or to defer death – in circumstances such as exist in this case.

While they are not numerous, there are sufficient authorities which support this proposition for it to be accepted that it represents the law, certainly when combined with the dictates of common sense.

Questions of good medical practice, with some modification, form the basis of a number of decisions in the United Kingdom which enable doctors to perform sterilisation procedures upon adults unable to consent to such operations because of mental disability; see eg *T v T* [1988] 1 All ER 613; and *F v West Berkshire Health Authority* [1989] 2 All ER 545...

As I perceive it, what is involved is not just medical treatment, but medical treatment in accordance with the doctor's best judgment as to what is in the best interests of his or her patient. They remain responsible for the kind and extent of the treatment administered and, ultimately, for its duration. In exercising their best judgment in this regard it is crucial for the patient and in the overall interests of society that they should not be inhibited by considerations pertinent to their own self-interest in avoiding criminal sanctions. Their judgment must be a genuinely independent judgment as to what will best serve the well-being of their dying patients.

Conscientious doctors will undoubtedly continue to strive with dedication to preserve and promote the life and health of their patients. That is their primary mission. But with a patient such as Mr L, where 'life' is being prolonged for no therapeutic or medical purpose or, in other words, death is merely being deferred, the doctor is not under a duty to avert that death at all costs. If, in his judgment, the proper medical practice would be to discontinue the life-support system, and that would be in the best interests of his patient, he may do so subject to adhering to a procedure which provides a safeguard against the possibility of individual error.

A doctor acting responsibly and in accordance with good medical practice recognised and approved as such in the medical profession would not therefore be liable, in my opinion, to any criminal sanction based upon the application of s 151(1). He or she will have acted with lawful excuse.

(iv) The question of the cause of death re-examined
Before leaving this section I will briefly revert to the question of causation. From what I have said it will be plain, I think, that it is not enough to hold that, where the doctor discontinues the life-support system, the resulting brain-stem death is caused by the patient's illness. Apart from this test being equally appropriate in the case of the polio victim which I have previously given, it would, without further qualification, exonerate a doctor who did not adhere to good medical practice or follow the accepted procedure for terminating the operation of a life-support system. To my mind, therefore, it can only be said that the withdrawal of the ventilatory system is not the cause of death as a *matter of law* if and when one or other of the two primary conditions have been met, that is, the doctor is not under a duty to provide the ventilator as part of the necessaries of life or has a lawful excuse for declining to do so. Both questions then turn on whether or not the doctor has followed good medical practice and the guidelines or procedures which have been laid down.

To leave the matter there, however, would be unfair to doctors. Finding that, in such circumstances, they are not *legally* the cause of death may suggest that they are morally or otherwise the cause of death. This is not so. Indeed, the opposite is the case. Most objective observers would accept that where a life-support system which has ceased to serve any medical purpose or benefit to the patient is withdrawn, the certain death which it had for a time arrested would be the outcome of the original disease and not the withdrawal of the support. Nature has been permitted to take its course. To hold, therefore, that where a doctor is under no legal duty to provide that support and has a lawful excuse for withholding it, the discontinuance of the life support is not *legally* the cause of death is simply to make the law coincide with the perception dictated by good sense...

There will therefore be an order in the following terms:
If:
(i) the doctors responsible for the care of Mr L, taking into account a responsible body of medical opinion, conclude that there is no reasonable possibility of Mr L ever recovering from his present clinical condition;

(ii) there is no therapeutic or medical benefit to be gained by continuing to maintain Mr L on artificial ventilatory support, and to withdraw that support accords with good medical practice, as recognised and approved within the medical profession; and

(iii) Mrs L and the ethics committee of the Auckland Area Health Board concur with the decision to withdraw the artificial ventilatory support;

then, ss 151 and/or 164 of the Crimes Act 1961 will not apply, and the withdrawal of the artificial ventilatory support from Mr L will not constitute culpable homicide for the purposes of that Act.

If *Bland* is to be understood as limited to cases where the patient has no interests, how should we perceive Mr L in the above case? On one level he is *not* insensate in that his higher brain is functioning. On the other hand, given that he is 'locked in' and 'locked out', ie receiving no sensory input and incapable of responding to the environment around him, he could be described as insensate and, therefore, having no interests. In our view the idea of an individual having 'no interests', given that it is philosophically problematic, is best restricted (if indeed valid at all) to the patient in a persistent vegetative state.

The consequence is that even in the extreme case of Mr L, the court is required to engage in a different reasoning process from that which the judges in the House of Lords were able to avail themselves of in *Bland*. The court in using the 'best interests' test cannot avoid being drawn into weighing the burdens and benefits of continued medical intervention. This task which is crudely captured in the notion of making life or death decisions was thought at least by Lord Browne-Wilkinson (at 877–878 and 884) and Lord Mustill (at 888 and 889) to be possibly beyond the remit of the courts and, therefore, one for Parliament.

Lord Browne-Wilkinson: [B]ehind the questions of law lie moral, ethical, medical and practical issues of fundamental importance to society. As Hoffmann LJ in the Court of Appeal emphasised, the law regulating the termination of artificial life support being given to patients must, to be acceptable, reflect a moral attitude which society accepts. This has led judges into the consideration of the ethical and other non-legal problems raised by the ability to sustain life artificially which new medical technology has recently made possible. But in my judgment in giving the legal answer to these questions judges are faced with a dilemma. The ability to sustain life artificially is of relatively recent origin. Existing law may not provide an acceptable answer to the new legal questions which it raises. Should judges seek to develop new law to meet a wholly new situation? Or is this a matter which lies outside the area of legitimate development of the law by judges and requires society, through the democratic expression of its views in Parliament, to reach its decisions on the underlying moral and practical problems and then reflect those decisions in legislation?

I have no doubt that it is for Parliament, not the courts, to decide the broader issues which this case raises...

I am very conscious that I have reached my conclusions on narrow, legalistic, grounds which provide no satisfactory basis for the decision of cases which will arise in the future where the facts are not identical. I must again emphasise that this is an extreme case where it can be overwhelmingly proved that the patient is and will remain insensate: he neither feels pain from treatment nor will feel pain in dying and has no prospect of any medical care improving his condition. Unless, as I very much hope, Parliament reviews the law, the courts will be faced with cases where the chances of improvement are slight, or the patient has very slight sensate awareness. I express no view on what should be the answer in such circumstances, my decision does not cover such a case.

Lord Mustill: The formulation of the necessary broad social and moral policy is an enterprise which the courts have neither the means nor in my opinion the right to perform. This can only be achieved by democratic process through the medium of Parliament...

My Lords, I believe that I have said enough to explain why, from the outset, I have felt serious doubts about whether this question is justiciable, not in the technical sense, but in the sense of being a proper subject for legal adjudication. The whole matter cries out for exploration in depth by Parliament and then for the establishment by legislation not only of a new set of ethically and intellectually consistent rules, distinct from the general criminal law, but also of a sound procedural framework within which the rules can be applied to individual cases. The rapid advance of medical technology makes this an ever more urgent task, and I venture to hope that Parliament will soon take it in hand.

(ii) GROUP 2 PATIENTS

The patients in our group 2 may be babies, children or adults. They are ill and may be dying but are patients for whom there is some therapy available. The therapy offers either the possibility of benefit to the patient but is accompanied by very considerable risks of harm or does nothing to benefit the patient's *underlying* condition which is itself severely debilitating whether physically or mentally.

I. Best interests: 'quality of life'

We saw earlier an example of a case concerned with a patient in what we have called Group 2 – the important decision in *Saikewicz*. We saw there how the Massachusetts' Supreme Judicial Court sanctioned the withdrawal of treatment applying a 'substituted judgment' test. Of course, the case is problematic for English law because of the English courts' reluctance to embrace the 'substituted judgment' test (notwithstanding that it was inapplicable, if properly understood, to Joseph Saikewicz who had always been incompetent). However, a close reading of the case demonstrates that the court, in essence, balanced the burdens of treatment against any benefits that would accrue, ie the court applied a 'best interests' (in the sense of 'quality of life') test in reality though not in form.

The baby cases How would English law approach a case which necessitates the court's having to balance burdens and benefits? (For an analysis of the position in other European countries, see H McHaffie et al 'Withholding/Withdrawing Treatment from Neonates: Legislation and Official Guidelines Across Europe' (1999) 25 Journal of Medical Ethics 440.) The first case in which a court considered this question was in *Re B*.

Re B (a minor) (wardship: medical treatment) [1981] 1 WLR 1421 (CA)

Templeman LJ: This is a very poignantly sad case. Although we sit in public, for reasons which I think will be obvious to everybody in court, and if not will be obvious in the course of this judgment, it would be lamentable if the names of the parents of the child concerned were revealed in any way to the general public. The press and people who frequent these courts are usually very helpful in referring to names by initials, and this is a case where nothing ought to be leaked out to identify those concerned with the case.

It concerns a little girl who was born on July 28, 1981. She was born suffering from Down's syndrome, which means that she will be a mongol. She was also born with an intestinal blockage which will be fatal unless it is operated upon. When the parents were informed of the condition of the child they took the view that it would be unkind to this child to operate upon her, and that the best thing to do was for her not to have the operation, in which case she would die within a few days. During those few days she could be kept from pain and suffering by sedation. They took the view that would be the kindest thing in the interests of the child. They so informed the doctors at the hospital, and refused to consent to the operation taking place. It is agreed on all hands that the parents came to that decision with great sorrow. It was a firm decision: they genuinely believed that it was in the best interests of this child. At the same time, it is of course impossible for parents in the unfortunate position of these parents to be certain that their present view should prevail. The shock to caring parents finding that they have given birth to a child who is a mongol is very great indeed, and therefore while great weight ought to be given to the views of the parents they are not views which necessarily must prevail.

What happened then was that the doctors being informed that the parents would not consent to the operation contacted the local authority who very properly made the child a ward of court and asked the judge to give care and control to the local authority and to authorise them to direct that the operation be carried out. And the judge did so direct. But when the child was moved from the hospital where it was born to another hospital for the purposes of the operation a difference of medical opinion developed. The surgeon who was to perform the operation declined to do so when he was informed that the parents objected. In a statement he said that when the child was referred to him for the operation he decided he wished to speak to the parents of the child personally and he spoke to them on the telephone and they stated that in view of the fact that the child was mongoloid they did not wish to have the operation performed. He further stated:

I decided therefore to respect the wishes of the parents and not to perform the operation, a decision which would, I believe (after about 20 years in the medical profession), be taken by the great majority of surgeons faced with a similar situation.

Therefore the local authority came back to the judge. The parents were served in due course and appeared and made their submissions to the judge, and in addition inquiries were made and it was discovered that the surgeon in the hospital where the child was born and another surgeon in a neighbouring hospital were prepared and advised that the operation should be carried out. So there is a difference of medical opinion.

This morning the judge was asked to decide whether to continue his order that the operation should be performed or whether to revoke that order, and the position now is stark. The evidence, as I have said, is that if this little girl does not have this operation she will die within a matter of days. If she has the operation there is a possibility that she will suffer heart trouble as a result and that she may die within two to three months. But if she has the operation and it is successful, she has Down's syndrome, she is mongoloid, and the present evidence is that her life expectancy is short, about 20 to 30 years.

The parents say that no one can tell what will be the life of a mongoloid child who survives during that 20 or 30 years, but one thing is certain. She will be very handicapped mentally and physically and no one can expect that she will have anything like a normal existence. They make that point not because of the difficulties which will be occasioned to them but in the child's interests. This is not a case in which the court is concerned with whether arrangements could or could not be made for the care of this child, if she lives, during the next 20 or 30 years; the local authority is confident that the parents having for good reason decided that it is in the child's best interests that the operation should not be performed, nevertheless good adoption arrangements could be made and that in so far as any mongol child can be provided with a happy life then such a happy life can be provided.

The question which this court has to determine is whether it is in the interests of this child to be allowed to die within the next week or to have the operation in which case if she lives she will be a mongoloid child, but no one can say to what extent her mental or physical defects will be apparent. No one can say whether she will suffer or whether she will be happy in part. On the one hand the probability is that she will not be a cabbage as it is called when people's faculties are entirely destroyed. On the other hand it is certain that she will be very severely mentally and physically handicapped.

On behalf of the parents, Mr Gray has submitted very movingly, if I may say so, that this is a case where nature should not be interfered with. He has also submitted that in this kind of decision the views of responsible and caring parents, as these are, should be respected, and that their decision that it is better for the child to be allowed to die should be respected. Fortunately or unfortunately, in this particular case the decision no longer lies with the parents or with the doctors, but lies with the court. It is a decision which of course must be made in the light of the evidence and views expressed by the parents and the doctors, but at the end of the day it devolves on this court in this particular instance to decide whether the life of this child is demonstrably going to be so awful that in effect the child must be condemned to die, or whether the life of this child is still so imponderable that it would be wrong for her to be condemned to die. There may be cases, I know not, of severe proved damage where the future is so certain and where the life of the child is so bound to be full of pain and suffering that the court might be driven to a different conclusion, but in the present case the choice which lies before the court is this: whether to allow an operation to take place which may result in the child living for 20 to 30 years as a mongoloid or whether (and I think this must be brutally the result) to terminate the life of a mongoloid child because she also has an intestinal complaint. Faced with that choice I have no doubt that it is the duty of this court to decide that the child must live. The judge was much affected by the reasons given by the parents and came to the conclusion that their wishes ought to be respected. In my judgment he erred in that the duty of the court is to decide whether it is in the interests of the child that an operation should take place. The evidence in this case only goes to show that if the operation takes place and is successful then the child may live the normal span of a mongoloid child with the handicaps and defects and life of a mongol child, and it is not for this court to say that life of that description ought to be extinguished.

Accordingly the appeal must be allowed and the local authority must be authorised themselves to authorise and direct the operation to be carried out on the little girl.

Dunn LJ: I agree, and as we are differing from the view expressed by the judge I would say a few words of my own. I have great sympathy for the parents in the agonising decision to which they came. As they put it themselves, 'God or nature has given the child a way out.' But the child now being a ward of court, although due weight must be given to the decision of the parents which everybody accepts was an entirely responsible one, doing what they considered was the best, the fact of the matter is that this court now has to make the decision.

It cannot hide behind the decision of the parents or the decision of the doctors; and in making the decision this court's first and paramount consideration is the welfare of this unhappy little baby.

One of the difficulties in the case is that there is no prognosis as to the child's future, except that as a mongol her expectation of life is confined to 20 or 30 years. We were told that no reliable prognosis can be made until probably she is about two years old. That in itself leads me to the route by which the court should make its decision, because there is no evidence that this child's short life is likely to be an intolerable one. There is no evidence at all as the quality of life which the child may expect. As Mr Turcan on behalf of the Official Solicitor said, the child should be put into the same position as any other mongol child and must be given the chance to live an existence. I accept that way of putting it.

I agree with Templeman LJ that the court must step in to preserve this mongol baby's life.

The approach adopted by the Court of Appeal in *Re B* seems to mean that 'best interests', became for the court, 'quality of life', another general (and in itself, meaningless) test; but one which offers some hope for further analysis and articulation. Also, if 'quality of life' is the test this serves to highlight two further critical points. First, the test is not factual but *normative*. Secondly, being normative, it has to be *established* as a matter of principle by the courts (though it will ordinarily be *applied* in particular cases by those caring for the patient).

The vagueness and imprecision involved in recourse to the 'quality of life' test in the context of neonates is well put by Professor Gostin.

L Gostin 'A Moment in Human Development: Legal Protection, Ethical Standards and Social Policy on the Selective Non-Treatment of Handicapped Neonates' (1985) 11 American Journal of Law and Medicine 32

The term 'quality of life' has been introduced into Anglo-American jurisprudence[24] and by commentators [see eg, Goldstein, 'Medical Care for the Child at Risk: On State Supervention of Parental Autonomy' 86 Yale LJ 645 (1977) at 651–61; Williams, 'Down's Syndrome and the Duty to Preserve Life' 131 New LJ 1020 (1981) at 1020–21] to justify the withholding of medically indicated treatment for severely handicapped infants whose life would be so bereft of enjoyment as not to be worth living. As under social utilitarian thought, medically effective treatment, even if available and efficacious for an otherwise normal infant, could be withheld based upon broader consideration of the infant's handicaps. The relevant factors under a 'quality of life' assessment relate not to social worth or to economic cost, but to the infant's potential for human contentment.

It is difficult to argue with the premise underlying the 'quality of life' position, for there must come a point for most of us where life is so devoid of meaning and contentment that it is not worth living. As a philosophic position, its weakness is that the factors which would justify forsaking continued life are seldom, if ever, specified. If one accepts that continued life is not in the infant's interests, then those who make this decision must be clear about the criteria to be adopted. Yet the basis for identifying and measuring those interests under a 'quality of life' standard is unclear.

In practice, the term 'quality of life' often is not used as a coherent moral theory which defines with any certainty which handicapping conditions should or should not be treated. Rather, the term is employed as a signal by those who believe that selective non-treatment decisions are too delicate and complex to be governed by any coherent legal or ethical standard. Accordingly, most of those who advocate a 'quality of life' assessment seek to maintain the decision-making process within a confidential doctor/patient framework.

Footnote 24: Courts have been reluctant expressly to adopt a 'quality of life' criterion and have been careful not to demarcate a class of individuals, such as the mentally retarded or senile, as deserving a lower standard of legal protection. Yet several courts have made implicit assessments of personal quality of life and normalcy in coming to their decisions. It is helpful to distinguish between two groupings of cases to determine whether a court is actually employing a 'quality of life' standard. The first are cases which are decided principally by an assessment of medical benefits, risk and adverse effects of the treatment in question. (Is there a 'substantial chance for cure?' Are there 'medically effective alternative treatments?') Here, the court's decision follows directly from the medical assessment. The principal finding is factual, ie, whether a medical consensus exists that the treatment is indicated and that there are no medically recognised alternatives. Given this finding of fact courts will usually come to the same decision, irrespective of the legal standard applied. See, eg, *Custody of a*

Minor, 373 Mass 733, 379 NE 2d 1053 (1978), *affd*, 378 Mass 732, 393 NE 2d 836 (1979) (order permitting chemotherapy for minor patient suffering from acute lymphocytic leukemia over parental objection; court found chemotherapy offered a 'substantial chance for cure' and the alternative treatment of metabolic therapy was medically ineffective and poisonous); *Hofbauer Re*, 65 AD 2d 108, 411 NYS 2d 416 (1978), affd, 47 NY 2d 648, 393 NE 2d 1109, 419 NYS 2d 936 (1979) (a child suffering from Hodgkins Disease whose parents failed to follow attending physician's recommendation for treatment by radiation and chemotherapy, but rather placed child under care of licensed physician advocating nutritional or metabolic therapy, was not a neglected child; court found parents had justifiable concerns about deleterious effects of radiation and chemotherapy, that alternative treatments were controlling the child's condition, and that conventional treatments would be administered if child's condition so warranted); *Ex rel Cicero*, 101 Misc 2d 699, 421 NYS 2d 965 (Sup Ct 1979) (guardian appointed to consent to corrective surgery for infant born with meningomyelocele. The court found child unlikely to live beyond 24 months without surgery and that surgery would permit the child to walk with leg braces and to have 'normal intellectual development' with little future risk of mental retardation).

The cases cited about should be distinguished from those where the court is influenced not only by its findings of fact as to the choices of treatment, but also by the person's wider characteristics, including his or her potential for intellectual and social functioning. See, eg, *Re Phillip B*, 92 Cal App 3d 796, 156 Cal Rptr 48 (1979), cert denied sub nom 445 US 949 (1980) (court declined to order life-prolonging heart surgery for minor suffering from congenital ventricular septal heart defect. The trial court found corrective surgery to be medically indicated with 5 to 10 per cent mortality rate but noted that the child had Down's syndrome; the judge commented that he personally could not handle it, 'if it happened to me'); *Infant Doe*, [*in re the Treatment and Care of Infant Doe*, No GU 8204– 004A (Ind Cir Ct, April 12, 1982)] (court order barring doctors from providing nourishment or treatment for Down's Syndrome infant born with a deformity in the stomach wall which prevented food being digested; the condition could have been corrected by surgery which was serious but considered within the range of standard medical practice); *Re Spring*, 380 Mass 529, 405 NE 2d 115 (1980) (court approval for removal of 78 year old patient from kidney dialysis, probate court found patient to be senile and incapable of restoration to a 'normal, cognitive, integrated functioning existence'); *Superintendent of Belchertown State School v Saikewicz*, 373 Mass 728, 370 NE 2d 417 (1977) (authorisation for non-treatment of 67 year old mentally retarded ward suffering from acute myeloblastic monocytic leukemia; probate court found chemotherapy was life-prolonging and was treatment of choice, but patient's profound retardation was a significant issue in the case); *Re Conroy* 98 NJ 321, 486 A 2d 1209 (1985) (nursing home resident with severe and permanent mental and physical defects and limited life expectancy could have life-sustaining treatment withdrawn in certain circumstances).

If one were to remove the wider 'quality of life' element from the facts of these cases the results would appear anomalous and, in some instances, clearly erroneous. It is highly probable that the court in each of these cases would have opted to prolong a life it considered worth living. See Annas, *Quality of Life in the Courts: Early Spring in Fantasyland*, 10 Hast Cen Rpt 9 (Aug 1980). A further, albeit less apparent, instance of a quality of life assessment occurred in *Re Quinlan*, 70 NJ 10, 355 A 2d 647, cert denied, 429 US 922 (1976) and its progeny…See also, Annas, *Reconciling Quinlan and Saikewicz Decision-Making for the Terminally Ill Incompetent*, 4 Am JL & Med 367 (1979).

An analysis of 'best interests' in the context of neonates is helpfully set out in the President's Commission Report.

President's Commission *Deciding to Forego Life-Sustaining Treatment* (1983)

Best interests of the infant. In most circumstances, people agree on whether a proposed course of therapy is in a patient's best interests. Even with seriously ill newborns, quite often there is no issue – either a particular therapy plainly offers net benefits or no effective therapy is available. Sometimes, however, the right outcome will be unclear because the child's 'best interests' are difficult to assess.

The Commission believes that decision-making will be improved if an attempt is made to decide which of three situations applies in a particular case – (1) a treatment is available that would clearly benefit the infant, (2) all treatment is expected to be futile, or (3) the probable benefits to an infant from different choices are quite uncertain (see Table 1…). The three situations need to be considered separately, since they demand differing responses. *Clearly defined beneficial therapies.* The Commission's inquiries indicate that treatments are rarely withheld when there is a medical consensus that they would provide a net benefit to a child. Parents naturally want to provide necessary medical care in most circumstances, and parents who are hesitant at first about having treatment administered usually come to recognise the desirability of providing treatment after discussions with physicians, nurses and others. Parents should be able to choose among alternative treatments with similarly beneficial results and among providers, but not to reject treatment that is reliably expected to benefit a seriously ill newborn substantially, as is usually true if life can be saved.

Table 1:
Treatment options for seriously ill newborns – physician's assessment in relation to parents' preference

Physician's Assessment of Treatment Options*	Parents Prefer to Accept Treatment**	Parents Prefer to Forego Treatment**
Clearly beneficial	Provide treatment	Provide treatment during review process
Ambiguous or uncertain	Provide treatment	Forego treatment
Futile	Provide treatment unless provider declines to do so	Forego treatment

*The assessment of the value to the infant of the treatments available will initially be by the attending physician. Both when this assessment is unclear and when the joint decision between parents and physician is to forego treatment, this assessment would be reviewed by intra-institutional mechanisms and possibly thereafter by court.
**The choice made by the infant's parents or other duly authorised surrogate who has adequate decision-making capacity and has been adequately informed, based on their assessment of the infant's best interests.

Many therapies undertaken to save the lives of seriously ill newborns will leave the survivors with permanent handicaps, either from the underlying defect (such as heart surgery not affecting the retardation of a Down's Syndrome infant) or from the therapy itself (as when mechanical ventilation for a premature baby results in blindness or a scarred trachea). One of the most troubling and persistent issues in this entire area is whether, or to what extent, the expectation of such handicaps should be considered in deciding to treat or not to treat a seriously ill newborn. The Commission has concluded that a very restrictive standard is appropriate: such permanent handicaps justify a decision not to provide life-sustaining treatment only when they are so severe that continued existence would not be a net benefit to the infant. Though inevitably somewhat subjective and imprecise in actual application, the concept of 'benefit' excludes honoring idiosyncratic views that might be allowed if a person were deciding about his or her own treatment. Rather, net benefit is absent only if the burdens imposed on the patient by the disability or its treatment would lead a competent decision-maker to choose to forego the treatment. As in all surrogate decision-making, the surrogate is obligated to try to evaluate benefits and burdens from the infant's own perspective. The Commission believes that the handicaps of Down's Syndrome, for example, are not in themselves of this magnitude and do not justify failing to provide medically proven treatment, such as surgical correction of a blocked intestinal tract.

This is a very strict standard in that it excludes consideration of the negative effects of an impaired child's life on other persons, including parents, siblings, and society. Although abiding by this standard may be difficult in specific cases, it is all too easy to undervalue the lives of handicapped infants; the Commission finds it imperative to counteract this by treating them no less vigorously than their healthy peers or than older children with similar handicaps would be treated.

Clearly futile therapies. When there is no therapy that can benefit an infant, as in anencephaly or certain severe cardiac deformities, a decision by surrogates and providers not to try predictably futile endeavors is ethically and legally justifiable. Such therapies do not help the child, are sometimes painful for the infant (and probably distressing to the parents), and offer no reasonable probability of saving life for a substantial period. The moment of death for these infants might be delayed for a short time – perhaps as long as a few weeks – by vigorous therapy. Of course, the prolongation of life – and hope against hope – may be enough to lead some parents to want to try a therapy believed by physicians to be futile. As long as this choice does not cause substantial suffering for the child, providers should accept it, although individual health care professionals who find it personally offensive to engage in futile treatment may arrange to withdraw from the case.

Just as with older patients, even when cure or saving of life are out of reach, obligations to comfort and respect a dying person remain. Thus infants whose lives are destined to be brief are owed whatever relief from suffering and enhancement of life can be provided, including feeding, medication for pain, and sedation, as appropriate. Moreover, it may be possible for parents to hold and comfort the child once the elaborate means of life-support are withdrawn, which can be very important to all concerned in symbolic and existential as well as physical terms.

Ambiguous cases. Although for most seriously ill infants there will be either a clearly beneficial option or no beneficial therapeutic options at all, hard questions are raised by the smaller number for whom it is very difficult to assess whether the treatments available offer prospects of benefit – for example, a child with a debilitating and painful disease who might live with therapy, but only for a year or so, or a respirator-dependent premature infant whose long-term prognosis becomes bleaker with each passing day.

Much of the difficulty in these cases arises from factual uncertainty. For the many infants born prematurely, and sometimes for those with serious congenital defects, the only certainty is that without intensive care they are unlikely to survive; very little is known about how each individual will fare with treatment. Neonatology is too new a field to allow accurate predictions of which babies will survive and of the complications, handicaps and potentials that the survivors might have.

The longer some of these babies survive, the more reliable the prognosis for the infant becomes and the clearer parents and professionals can be on whether further treatment is warranted or futile. Frequently, however, the prospect of long-term survival and the quality of that survival remain unclear for days, weeks, and months, during which time the infants may have an unpredictable and fluctuating course of advances and setbacks.

One way to avoid confronting the difficulties involved in evaluating each case is to adopt objective criteria to distinguish newborns who will receive life-sustaining treatment from those who will not. Such criteria would be justified if there were evidence that their adoption would lead to decisions more often being made correctly.

Strict treatment criteria proposed in the 1970s by a British physician for deciding which newborns with spina bifida should receive treatment rested upon the location of the lesion (which influences degree of paralysis), the presence of hydrocephalus (fluid on the brain, which influences degree of retardation), and the likelihood of an infection. Some critics of this proposal argued with it on scientific grounds, such as objecting that long-term effects of spina bifida cannot be predicted with sufficient accuracy at birth. Other critics, however, claimed this whole approach to ambiguous cases exhibited the 'technical criteria fallacy'. They contended that an infant's future life – and hence the treatment decisions based on it – involves value considerations that are ignored when physicians focus solely on medical prognosis.

> The decision [to treat or not] must also include evaluation of the meaning of existence with varying impairments. Great variation exists about these essentially evaluative elements among parents, physicians, and policy makers. It must be an open question whether these variations in evaluation are among the relevant factors to consider in making a treatment decision. When Lorber uses the phrase 'contraindications to active therapy', he is medicalising what are really value choices.

The Commission agrees that such criteria necessarily include value considerations. Supposedly objective criteria such as birth weight limits or checklists for severity of spina bifida have not been shown to improve the quality of decision-making in ambiguous and complex cases. Instead, their use seems to remove the weight of responsibility too readily from those who should have to face the value questions – parents and health care providers.

Furthermore, any set of standards, when honestly applied, leaves some difficult or uncertain cases. When a child's best interests are ambiguous, a decision based upon them will require prudent and discerning judgment. Defining the category of cases in a way that appropriately protects and encourages the exercise of parental judgment will sometimes be difficult.

(See for further professional guidance in the UK, Royal College of Paediatrics and Child Health *Withholding or Withdrawing Life Saving Treatment in Children: A Framework for Practice* (1997) and BMA *Withholding and Withdrawing Life-prolonging Medical Treatment: Guidance for Decision making* (1999).)

A study written for the Law Reform Commission of Canada by Edward Keyserlinck takes the analysis further.

E Keyserlinck 'Sanctity of Life or Quality of Life' (1979)

The answer of course depends upon what is meant, or what meaning *we give* to 'quality of life'. What makes the question one of practical relevance and not just academic interest is that quality of life concerns are already and long have been influencing medical decisions.

But what makes the question an urgent and somewhat worrisome one for society, medicine and law is that quality of life can and does mean many different things, has no single, generally accepted meaning, and some of its connotations and the uses to which the concept is put are definitely opposed to and in conflict with the sanctity of life principle as outlined earlier.

It is probably its very elusiveness which makes the concept so attractive to media and public. It is so vague and glibly used in such quite different contexts (environmental and medical for instance) and in support of such quite different positions (for instance to improve the quality of air, or to cease medical treatment) that the concept seems to commit one to nothing specific, and is seldom given tangible content.

But its very elusiveness encourages as well the polarised, extreme and hostile views about its moral legitimacy and usefulness. There are those who think it answers all questions, and those who thing it answers none. There are those who would welcome the replacement of the 'traditional' ethic of the absolute value of human life by an ethic of its relative value. There are others who see any recognition of quality of life factors as a danger to be resisted at all costs.

But it is also possible, and in my view legitimate and preferable, to see no need to choose between an old ethic and a new one. Instead, to recognise an urgent need to on the one hand articulate and refine the 'old' ethic, and on the other hand to propose a carefully delineated and restricted meaning and purpose for quality of life. The purpose of such an exercise would be to encourage both medical decision-making and (perhaps) law-making to more formally recognise an interest in considering and protecting *both* the intrinsic value of each human life, *and* the quality of those lives, even when this involves a decision to cease or not initiate treatment or life support.

But to make this case successfully depends first of all of course on the meaning we intend for quality of life…

Quality is a comparative property, an evaluative property. And it is true that quality of life used in environmental/social contexts does essentially involve a comparison with other things – a ranking of the conditions which maximise optimal human life or general happiness requirements of a region. Implicit in the comparison is a readiness to discard or improve certain conditions because of where they rank on the scale.

But in the medical/health context, quality of life *need* not involve a comparison of *different human lives* as the basis for decisions to treat some and not others. Ideally, at the heart of quality of life concerns in this context should be only a comparison of the qualities *this patient* now has with the qualities deemed by *this patient* (or if incompetent or irreversibly comatose, by the patient's agents) to be normative and desirable, and either still or no longer present actually or potentially.

The real comparison in question is in a sense one between what the patient is and was, is and can or cannot be in the future. The quality of life comparison or evaluation in the medical context need not be a comparison *with others* or a relativising of persons' lives. And the quality of life norm and decision need not be arbitrary or based upon how treatment or non-treatment will relieve or burden others or society. The norm can and must include whatever the value sciences, medicine and public policy agree upon concerning the essential quality or qualities of a human person; and the decision can and must be in the first instance by, and for the benefit of the patient and no one else.

To include quality of life considerations in life saving or life support decision-making by no means must imply *harm* rather than improvement or benefit to the patients. If quality of life is limited only to what is intended here, then quite the contrary is the case and must be the case if the concept is to have any justifiably normative value.

In the first place, investigations, prognoses and conclusions arrived at concerning a patient's actual or potential level of function or degree of suffering, need not inevitably and exclusively lead to decisions *to cease* or *not to initiate* life supporting treatment. Given that the sanctity of life principle imposes the burden of proof on those who would cease to support life, the consideration of quality of life factors should more often lead to the opposite decision – to initiate or continue that treatment if there is any realistic hope of minimal human function and controllable pain and suffering.

Secondly, even when quality of life factors do contribute to a decision to cease or not initiate life saving or supporting treatment, there remains the continuing obligation to seek to improve the newborn's or the patient's *care and comfort*. Neither physician nor patient are usually faced with only two options – to continue or discontinue life support treatment. The third option and continuing responsibility of health care professionals and families, no matter how damaged the patient's condition, is to seek to improve the level of care and comfort of the dying, including being physically present to them. The sanctity of life surely calls for at least the same respect and consideration for dying life as for healthy life. And if greater needs call for greater care and concern, then the dying deserve more, not less of it, than the healthy.

Thirdly, even decisions to cease or not initiate life saving treatments, based partly on quality of life considerations, can and must offer a reasonable hope of *benefit* to the patient.

In other words, death should not always be resisted at any cost in terms of present and future suffering and damage, as if anything is an improvement over death. It is an integral part of my thesis that this is not so, that some conditions of human life are so damaged, and will likely remain so or become worse if treatment is continued or initiated, that death can reasonably be seen as beneficial, as an improvement for that patient.

The final weighing and balancing of reasons and criteria normally belongs to the patient, and within morally acceptable parameters different patients may and will weigh the criteria differently and come to different decisions. For the incompetent, the determination of benefit to patient or newborn must be made by proxies. While it remains enormously difficult to make such decisions in the interests and for the benefit of others, it is my contention that they must sometimes be made, and that reasonable and morally justifiable decisions for the benefit of others, based partially at least on quality of life matters, are possible. There will be occasion to come back to the 'who decides' question and the other points in more detail as the argument unfolds.

In the light of the above, quality of life in the medical context need not come out the loser when compared to quality of life in the environmental/social context. As noted, there are of course great differences in the contexts and the functions within them of quality of life criteria. But in both contexts the ultimate aim of these criteria is objective improvement and benefit, even if in the medical context that will often be limited to reducing rather than eliminating the patient's discomfort and indignity. In claiming this, the medical cases envisioned are primarily those in which the quality of life criteria are used in decisions made *by others* for the incompetent patient. In such cases the use of these criteria for the patient's objective improvement or reduction of discomfort or some other benefit is a realistic aim. Obviously it may be otherwise for patients able to *themselves* accept or refuse treatment. Since, as I shall argue below, competent patients have the right to refuse treatment on any grounds at all, whether they seem reasonable or foolish to others, there can be no guarantee at all of objective improvement and benefit in the decisions made and criteria used by competent patients for themselves.

Just before attempting to put flesh on the dry bones, to offer more argument for the claims made, the thesis of this quality of life section of the paper should be summarised.

Quality of life need not mean the 'relativising of lives'. Excluded here in this paper from that concept and its criteria are considerations such as social worth, social utility, social status or relative worth. The sanctity of life principle rightly insists on the intrinsic worth and equal value of every life. In excluding these elements from the meaning intended for quality of life, one need not of course deny that they can be ingredients of quality of life in wider contexts than our own. At least some of them are factors which a 'general' quality of life theory must consider and weigh in other contexts. I am only excluding these factors from this particular context of medical decision-making in life and death matters, and primarily when such decisions are made by proxies or patients' agents for patients or newborns unable to make these decisions themselves. Whatever the merits and realities of characteristics such as social status in other areas of concern, here I do not believe they should have determinative weight.

New circumstances such as increasingly sophisticated life support systems and treatment have challenged us to recognise in human life a distinction between mere existence and quality with more clarity than previously needed. But that does not mean that in our context the shifting sands of new medical technology, evolving social realities or subjective preferences comprise an adequate source for the meaning and criteria of a quality of life concept, or in themselves validly answer our questions. What is involved here, or should be, is a search for and a weighing of the *inherent features* of human life. That is an objective meaning of 'quality' light years away from mere considerations of relative and changing circumstances, facts and values. It does not make the task easier, or ensure an immediate consensus but at least the task is defensible.

In this sense, meaning and criteria for quality of life in life or death decision-making, should focus not on features or conditions which permit patients to act comfortably, well and without burdening others or society, but rather on features and conditions which allow them to at *all*, even to a minimal extent. The real question and issue raised by considerations of quality of life is not about the value of this patient's *life* – it is about the value of this patient's *treatment*.

The meaning and criteria of quality of life should focus on *benefit to the patient*, and in some circumstances to initiate treatment or prolong or postpone death can reasonably be seen as non-beneficial to the patient. One such circumstance is *excruciating, intractable and prolonged pain and suffering*. Another is the lack of capacity for what can be considered an inherent feature of human life, namely a *minimal capacity to experience, to relate with other human beings*. In such instances to preserve life could in some cases be a dishonouring of the sanctity of life itself, and allowing even death could be a demonstration of respect for the individual and for human life in general...

In particular there are two such quality of life criteria, relevant to decisions to treat, or to continue treatment or to stop treatment. The first considers the capacity to experience, to relate. The second considers the intensity and susceptibility to control of the patient's pain and suffering. If despite treatment there is not and cannot be even a minimal capacity to experience, and to relate, or if the level of pain and suffering will be prolonged, excruciating and intractable, then a decision to cease or not initiate treatment (of for instance a comatose patient) can be preferable to treatment.

The word 'life' can mean two things in this context. It can mean vital or metabolic processes alone, a life incapable of experiencing or communicating and one which therefore could be called 'human biological life'. Or it could mean a level or quality of life which includes *both* metabolic functions and at least a minimal capacity to experience or communicate, which together could be called 'human personal life'…

Given that the sanctity of life principle imposes the burden of proof on those who would cease to support the lives of others, the consideration of quality of life criteria should not inevitably and exclusively lead to decisions to cease or not initiate life supporting or saving treatment. Quite the opposite should just as often or more often be the case.

While a degree of 'indignity' is an inescapable element of death and dying, and while not every instance of a patient's life being externally supported is thereby undignified, there are cases in which the refusal to consider and weigh the patient's quality of life can result in a prolongation of treatment to the point that a real and further indignity is being done.

Both medical decision-making and law should continue to protect the intrinsic sanctity and value of each human life. But medicine (and perhaps law as well) should formally acknowledge that in some cases the quality or conditions of a patient's life can be so damaged and minimal that treatment or further treatment could be a violation precisely of that life's sanctity and value.

Even in those cases for which it is decided to cease or not initiate external life supporting *treatment*, there always remains a continuing obligation no matter how damaged the patient's condition, to provide whatever amount of *care and comfort* is needed and possible.

The elusiveness of the concept of 'quality of life' leading, perhaps, to confusion, is well illustrated by the judgment of Liacos J in *Superintendent of Belchertown v Saikewicz* (1976) 370 NE 2d 417. Liacos J appeared to want to take advantage of the concept and yet not be seen to be engaging in the calculation that the concept necessarily entails. When discussing whether a mentally retarded person suffering from acute myeloblastic monocytic leukaemia, who was adult but incompetent to consent, should have chemotherapy, he said:

Liacos J: The sixth factor identified by the judge as weighing against chemotherapy was 'the quality of life possible for him even if the treatment does bring about remission'. To the extent that this formulation equates the value of life with any measure of the quality of life, we firmly reject it. A reading of the entire record clearly reveals, however, the judge's concern that special care be taken to respect the dignity and worth of Saikewicz's life precisely because of his vulnerable position. The judge, as well as all the parties, were keenly aware that the supposed ability of Saikewicz, by virtue of his mental retardation, to appreciate or experience life had no place in the decision before them. Rather than reading the judge's formulation in a manner that demeans the value of the life of one who is mentally retarded, the vague, and perhaps ill-chosen term 'quality of life' should be understood as a reference to the continuing state of pain and disorientation precipitated by the chemotherapy treatment.

Clearly, the Court of Appeal in *Re B* was feeling its way towards what we can call a 'quality of life' approach. The court's judgment was, however, *ex tempore*, delivered within an hour of argument, given the urgency of the case. It is no surprise, therefore, that later cases would return to the issue. The landmark decision in English law which sought to do so was *Re J (a minor) (wardship: medical treatment)* [1990] 3 All ER 930 (CA). We must consider this case carefully. Before doing so, however, we need to notice what was at the time a case of considerable notoriety but which from the point of view of legal analysis must be regarded as aberrant.

In *R v Arthur* (1981) 12 BMLR 1, a baby was born with Down's syndrome. His mother told the consultant paediatrician, Dr Leonard Arthur, that 'she did not wish the baby to survive' as recorded in the medical notes. Thereafter, Dr Arthur prescribed dihydrocodeine, a powerful analgesic, and 'nursing care only'. Shortly afterwards, the baby died. Dr Arthur was charged with murder but after medical evidence showed that the prosecution could not prove the cause of death, the charge was reduced to one of attempted murder. In his summing up to the jury, Farquharson J set out the law as he saw it.

R v Arthur (1981) 12 BMLR 1 (Leicester Crown Ct)

Farquharson J: In this case the act, or acts, upon which the prosecution rely to say this was an attempt to kill on the part of Dr Arthur, is the preparation of those two documents: the case notes and the treatment chart. It was his endorsement on the case notes to the effect that the child should receiving nursing care only, coupled with the prescription he wrote into the treatment chart, that the child should have 5 mg of dihydrocodeine not less than every four hours and at the discretion of the nurse in charge of the child; that is to say, it was under the general heading 'as required'. The prosecution contend before you that those acts set in train the course of events which could only have resulted in the child's death and therefore, they say, that the preparation and endorsement of those treatment charges and case notes must have amounted to an attempt to kill. Whether it does or not is one of the important and vital questions that you have got to decide.

The defence, of course, contend that this does not amount to an act that could properly be described as an attempt. They point out the act was revocable; it could have been stopped, haltered and reversed because at any time the mother could have changed the opinion which, in the agony of giving birth, she had already expressed. The fact that the treatment prescribed by Dr Arthur can be recalled, or revoked, does not in itself mean that it could not be an attempt, but it is something that you should take very carefully into account.

…the defence do not rest their case there. They go further and say that Dr Arthur was not committing an act, a positive act, at all; he was simply prescribing a treatment which involved the creation of a set of circumstances whereby the child would peacefully die, and that there is all the difference in the world between the one and the other…The nurses were acting as the doctor's agents, in carrying out that task, contend the prosecution.

…However serious the case may be; however much the disadvantage of a mongol or, indeed, any other handicapped child, no doctor has the right to kill it.

There is no special law in this country that places doctors in a separate category and gives them extra protection over the rest of us. Neither, in law, is there any special power, facility or licence to kill children who are handicapped or seriously disadvantaged in an irreversible way.

But, perhaps the most agonising part of this case, is that it has become very clear that it is a very difficult area to decide precisely where a doctor is doing an act, a positive act, or allowing a course of events, or a set of circumstances to ensue. It is because no doctor has a special exemption, or a special right in this way, that this case comes before you.

We have heard a good deal about medical ethics and it is a fact that in virtually every profession, or any trade where there is a guild or association of any kind, rules of conduct are set out, and when those rules are broken, the professional body or guild would take action to punish the offender.

But that does not mean that any profession can set out a code of ethics and say that the law must accept it. In this case it has been suggested that what Dr Arthur did here, whatever may be the medical ethics of the matter, has gone beyond what any doctor is entitled to do and has committed a crime. If a child is born with a serious handicap – for example, where a mongol has an ill-formed intestine whereby that child will die of the ailment if he is not operated on – a surgeon may say: 'as this child is a mongol I do not propose to operate; I shall allow nature to take its course'. No one could say that that surgeon was committing an act or murder by declining to take a course which would save the child.

Equally, if a child not otherwise going to die, who is severely handicapped, is given a drug in such an excessive amount by the doctor that the drug itself will cause his death and the doctor does that intentionally it would be open to the jury to say: 'Yes, he was killing; he was murdering that child'. It is very easy to draw the line between those two examples. They are opposite ends of the spectrum. It is very much more difficult to say where the line should be drawn in relation to this case.

Where, perhaps, somebody is suffering from the agonies of terminal cancer and the doctor is obliged to give increasing dosages of an analgesic to relieve the pain, there comes a point where the amounts of those doses are such that in themselves they will kill off the patient, but he is driven to it on medical grounds. There again, you will, undoubtedly, say that that could never be murder. That would be a proper practice of medicine.

Where a child gets pneumonia and is a child with an irreversible handicap whose mother has rejected him, if the doctor said: 'I am not going to give it antibiotics', and by a merciful dispensation of providence he dies, once again it would be very unlikely, I would suggest, that you (or any other jury) would say that that doctor was committing murder. But what is the position here? Was what Dr Arthur did, in setting out that course of management, prescribing that drug in the way of a holding operation – in the nature of setting conditions where the child could, if it contracted pneumonia, die peacefully? Or, if it revealed any other organic defect, die peacefully? Or, was it a positive act on the part of Dr Arthur which was likely to kill the child and represented an attempt (within the definition I have given you), accompanied by an intent on his part that it should, as a result of the treatment that he prescribed, die?

If the prosecution have proved the latter, members of the jury, and you draw the line, so to speak, at that point, well then he would be guilty of attempted murder. If, on the other hand, they have not been able to do so and what Dr Arthur here prescribed and arranged comes into that first category – of a management that represents a holding operation, but not in the nature of a positive act – then he would not be guilty.

...[I]t appears there was a discussion as to whether the mother should or should not keep the child. The result of that discussion is shown in the middle of page 3 [of the notes], 'Parents do not wish the baby to survive. Nursing care only.'...[T]he houseman who was the specialist in gynaecology, although he had done his paediatric work previously, said that:

> Nursing care only involves dealing with the bodily functions; the child must be kept warm, fed and cherished. I mean fed with an ordinary feed. One has to consider all the options. If pneumonia developed, I would understand nursing care only to mean that the baby should not be treated but kept comfortable, warm and cherished.

...By the time the nurses were in fact looking after the child, it had plainly developed pneumonia. By that stage, whichever side is right about the legal effect of what happened, by that stage at all events, it was accepted that the child had reached a stage where, if infection overcame it, it was going to be left to die...[In his statement to the police Dr Arthur said 'If a non-treatment course of conduct with mongol children is adopted, it is in accordance with my own practice, which is accepted by modern paediatric thought. If non-treatment is elected it means it would be wrong to treat infection with antibiotics. The withholding of food is accepted by many doctors as part of non-treatment. Some lay people feel that this is distasteful. Sometimes we do feed babies, even if non-treatment is decided upon, if the parents or nurses wish it. But our major aim is to relieve distress in the child. The baby will take water or water and sugar. If it is fed milk it may be that it will inhale it and suffer a distressing condition. Paediatricians may use any of these foods or water. It really contributes little to the ultimate outcome. When non-treatment is decided upon the paediatrician may hope that parents will change their mind after the immediate shock of the birth. If they do not do so the course is continued in the hope that the baby will die peacefully from infection.']

The jury acquitted Dr Arthur.

The view taken by Farquharson J of the law relating to the doctor's duty is difficult, if not impossible, to reconcile with that in *Re B*. Recourse to language such as 'a holding operation' or 'allowing nature to take its course', is at best unhelpful and, at worst, fails to recognise that a doctor may have a duty to act so as, for example, not to 'allow nature to take its course'. In our view, Farquharson J was wrong to draw a clear line between the acts and omissions of Dr Arthur without properly relating it to the issue of duty. Furthermore, it is a matter of some surprise that the judge did not take advantage of the language used by Templeman LJ in *Re B*. This case has been decided shortly before and had itself attracted wide attention.

Before leaving *Arthur* we should remind ourselves that if the criminal law does ultimately set the agenda for the analysis of the scope of the doctor's duty, there is an aspect of the criminal law not mentioned in *Arthur* but worthy of brief comment. The Children and Young Persons Act 1933, s 1 creates the offence of 'wilful neglect' of a child. This provision does not, however, clinch any argument, since it begs the central question of whether to adopt a new regime of management which allows a baby to die is necessarily 'wilful neglect'. A doctor cannot be liable under the Act since he would not in law be regarded as 'ha[ving] responsibility [for the child]', since the section is limited to those with 'parental responsibility'. A parent, however *can* be guilty under s 1 for failing to provide adequate medical treatment (eg *R v Senior* [1899] 1 QB 283, *R v Lowe* [1973] QB 702, *Oakey v Jackson* [1914] 1 KB 216). The scope of s 1 was established by the House of Lords in *R v Sheppard* [1981] AC 394, [1980] 3 All ER 899. It should be noticed that the failure to provide 'adequate medical aid' must be 'wilful' and must 'cause [the child] unnecessary suffering or injury to health'.

R v Sheppard [1980] 3 All ER 899, [1981] AC 394 (HL)

The appellants were a young couple of low intelligence living in deprived conditions. Following the death of their 16-month-old son from hypothermia and malnutrition, they were charged under s 1(1) of the Children and Young Persons Act 1933 with wilfully neglecting the child in a manner likely to cause it unnecessary suffering or injury to its health. At the trial it was alleged that the appellants had failed to provide the child with adequate medical aid on several occasions, especially during the week immediately preceding his death. The appellants' defence was, in effect, that they had not realised that the child was ill enough to see a doctor, and that although they had observed his loss of appetite and failure to ingest food they had genuinely thought that that was due to some minor upset which would cure itself. The trial judge applying previous authority treated the offence as one of strict liability and directed the jury that the test of the appellants' guilt was to be judged objectively by whether a reasonable parent, with knowledge of the facts that were known to the appellants, would have appreciated that failure to have the child examined was likely to cause unnecessary suffering or injury to health. The appellants were convicted and appealed unsuccessfully against their convictions to the Court of Appeal. On appeal to the House of Lords, by a majority, the House of Lords allowed the appeal (Lords Fraser and Scarman dissenting).

Lord Diplock: [a] failure [to provide a child with such medical aid as is needed] as it seems to me could not be properly described as 'wilful' unless the parent *either* (1) had directed his mind to the question whether there was some risk (though it might fall far short of a probability) that the child's health might suffer unless he were examined by a doctor and provided with such curative treatment as the examination might reveal as necessary, and had made a conscious decision, for whatever reason, to refrain from arranging for such medical examination, *or* (2) had so refrained because he did not care whether the child might be in need of medical treatment or not.

...I have referred to the parents' knowledge of the existence of some risk of injury to health rather than of a probability. The section speaks of an act or omission that is 'likely' to cause unnecessary suffering or injury to health. This word is imprecise. It is capable of covering a whole range of possibilities from 'it's on the cards' to 'it's more probable than not', but, having regard to the ordinary parents' lack of skill in diagnosis and to the very serious consequences which may result from failure to provide a child with timely medical attention, it should in my view be understood as excluding only what would fairly be described as highly unlikely...

Lord Edmund-Davies: The justice (and, with respect, the common sense) of the matter is surely that, as Professor Glanville Williams has put in his *Textbook of Criminal Law* (1978, p 88):

> We do not run to a doctor whenever a child is a little unwell. We invoke medical aid only when we think that a doctor is reasonably necessary and may do some good. The requirement of wilfulness means, or should mean, that a parent who omits to call in the doctor to his child is not guilty of the offence if he does not know that the child needs this assistance.

But to that must be added that a parent reckless about the state of his child's health, not caring whether or not he is at risk, cannot be heard to say that he never gave the matter a thought and was therefore not wilful in not calling in a doctor. In such circumstances recklessness constitutes mens rea no less than positive awareness of the risk involved in failure to act...

Lord Keith: This appeal is concerned solely with a failure to provide adequate medical care. The word 'adequate', as applied to medical care, may mean no more than 'ordinarily competent'. If it is related to anything, I think it is related to the prevention of unnecessary suffering or injury to health, as mentioned in s 1(1), where in my view the adjective 'unnecessary' qualifies both 'suffering' and 'injury to health'. There could be no question of a finding of neglect against a parent who provided ordinarily competent medical care, but whose child nevertheless suffered further injury to its health, for example paralysis in a case of poliomyelitis, because the injury to health would not in the circumstances have been unnecessary, in the sense that it could have been prevented through the provision by the parent of adequate medical care. Failure to provide adequate medical care may be deliberate, as when the child's need for it is perceived yet nothing is done, negligent, as when the need ought reasonably to have been perceived but was not, or entirely blameless, as when the need was not perceived but was not such as ought to have been perceived by an ordinary reasonable parent. I would say that in all three cases the parent has neglected the child in the sense of the statute, since I am of opinion that in a proper construction of s 1(2)(a) it is to be ascertained objectively and in the light of events whether the parents failed to provide ordinarily competent medical care which as a matter of fact the child needed in order to prevent unnecessary suffering or injury to its health.

Lord Keith appears to regard 'adequate' to be a matter of fact. However, it is really a matter of judgment based on normative criteria. In other words, 'adequate' also connotes 'appropriate'. If this is so, arguably we are no further in determining the extent of parental duty and thus what regime of management is lawful after reading Lord Keith's speech. Likewise, the cases of *Senior*, *Lowe* and *Oakey v Jackson* (*supra*), though establishing potential parental liability, throw little light on the problem we are considering since they are all cases where medical treatment was called for on any reasonable view of the facts.

In any event, the *Arthur* case can be consigned to legal history for the oddity it is. The 1990 decision of the Court of Appeal in *Re J* is the leading case.

Re J (a minor) (wardship: medical treatment) [1990] 3 All ER 930, [1991] Fam 33 (CA)

Lord Donaldson MR: Baby J has suffered almost every conceivable misfortune. He was a very premature baby, born after 27 weeks' gestation on 28 May 1990. He weighed only 1.1 kg (2.5lb) at birth. He was not breathing. Almost immediately he was placed on a ventilator and given antibiotics to counteract an infection. He was put on a drip. His pulse rate frequently became very low and for ten days it was touch and go whether he survived.

One month later, on 28 June, the doctors were able to take him off the ventilator, but he was, and still is, a very sick and handicapped baby. There followed recurrent convulsions and episodes when he stopped breathing (apnoea). As a result he was oxygen-dependent until early August. At the end of August the doctors thought that he could be allowed to go home, although the prognosis was gloomy in the extreme. Four days later, on 1 September 1990, he had to be readmitted to hospital because he had choked and become cyanosed.

The subsequent history of J has been traumatic both for him, his parents and those professionally involved in caring for him. On 3 September it was noted that J had become cyanosed when he cried. On 5 September he collapsed suddenly and was again cyanosed. He was without a pulse, but was resuscitated. Two days later he again collapsed and had to be put on a ventilator. Between then and 23 September he was continuously on a ventilator. During that period four attempts were made to wean him from it. The first three failed because he suffered fits which interfered with the efficiency of the ventilator and on one occasion the doctors had to paralyse him in order to make his oxygen level safe. Since 23 September J has been breathing independently and in some ways his condition has slightly improved. However this improvement is from a base line which can only be described as abysmally low.

Needless to say the doctors have been concerned to discover what are likely to be J's long-term disabilities. As a result it is clear that he has suffered very severe brain damage due to shortage of oxygen and impaired blood supply around the time of his birth. This is no one's fault, but stems from his prematurity. Ultrasound scans of his brain were conducted on 22 August and 10 September. They showed a large area of fluid-filled cavities where there ought to have been brain tissue. The body is incapable of making this good. Of the three neo-natalogists who have been concerned with his care, the most optimistic is Dr W. His view is that J is likely to develop serious spastic quadriplegia, that is to say paralysis of both his arms and legs. It is debatable whether he will ever be able to sit up or to hold his head upright. J appears to be blind, although there is a possibility that some degree of sight may return. He is likely to be deaf. He may be able to make sounds which reflect his mood, but he is unlikely ever to be able to speak, even to the extent of saying 'Mum' or 'Dad'. It is highly unlikely that he will develop even limited intellectual abilities. Most unfortunately of all, there is a likelihood that he will be able to feel pain to the same extent as a normal baby, because pain is a very basic response. It is possible that he may achieve the ability to smile and to cry. Finally, as one might expect, his life expectancy has been considerably reduced at most into his late teens, but even Dr W would expect him to die long before then.

This assessment of J's present state and likely future development is not based only on the skills and experience of the doctors caring for him. It is supported by the ultrasound scans to which I have already referred and by other objective scientific testing.

The problem which now has to be faced by all concerned is what is to be done if J suffers another collapse. This may occur at any time, but is not inevitable. In most cases this would be a matter to be discussed and decided by the doctors in consultation with the parents. By this I do not mean that the parents could tell the doctors what to do, but they would have the right to withhold consent to treatment, subject to the right of the doctors to apply to make the child a ward of court and to seek the guidance of the court. In practice it might be expected that the parents would have confidence in the doctors and that the doctors, recognising the agonising dilemma facing the parents, would take all the time that was necessary to explain the very limited options which were available and, if at all possible, would agree with the parents on a course of action or inaction. In the present case there has been no real difference of opinion between the doctors and the parents, but for extraneous reasons into which it is unnecessary to go J has in fact been made a ward of court and, accordingly, the right and duty to give or refuse consent to treatment is vested in the court.

On 11 October Scott Baker J made an order authorising the hospital to treat J within the parameters of the opinion expressed by Dr W in his report of 4 October 1990, subject to amendments to paras 24, 25 and 26 made in the course of his oral evidence. This opinion, as amended and explained in the course of the hearing before this court, was as follows:

> 24 I am of the opinion that it would not be in [J's] best interests to re-ventilate him [using a ventilation machine] in the event of his stopping breathing, unless to do so seems appropriate to the doctors caring for him given the prevailing clinical situation. However, I think it would be reasonable to suck out his airway to remove any plug of mucous or milk and to give oxygen by his face mask.
>
> 25 If he developed a chest infection I would recommend treatment with antibiotics and maintenance of hydration, but not prolonged [manual] ventilation.
>
> 26 [Various recommendations to take effect on the assumption that baby J did not in the event have to face a critical condition as a result of his stopping breathing or otherwise].

The Official Solicitor has appealed against this decision. The parents do not formally appeal, but naturally and very reasonably feel that they are in a dilemma. Their solicitor took immense trouble to explain Scott Baker J's decision to them and at that time they were minded to accept it as being a decision taken in the best interests of their son. However, the fact that the Official Solicitor has appealed has caused them to wonder whether they were right.

The Official Solicitor submits that there are two justifications for an appeal. (i) *Re C (a minor) (wardship: medical treatment)* [1989] 2 All ER 782, [1990] Fam 26 gives guidance on the approach which it is appropriate to adopt in relation to the medical treatment of children who are dying and whose deaths can only be postponed for a short while. *Re B (a minor) (wardship: medical treatment)* (1981) [1990] 3 All ER 927, [1981] 1 WLR 1421 gives similar guidance in relation to severely, but not grossly, handicapped children with a shortened, but nevertheless substantial, expectation of life. In the Official Solicitor's view, the present case illustrates a different category falling between these two on which guidance should be given. (ii) Whilst Scott Baker J rightly directed himself that he must act in what he considered to be the best interests of the child, in the Official Solicitor's submission he erred in that a court is never justified in withholding consent to treatment which could enable a child to survive a life-threatening condition, whatever the quality of the life which it would experience thereafter. This is the absolutist approach. Alternatively, he submits that the judge erred in that a court is only justified in withholding consent to such treatment if it is certain that the quality of the child's subsequent life would be 'intolerable' to the child, 'bound to be full of pain and suffering' and 'demonstrably...so awful that in effect the child must be condemned to die' (see *Re B* (1981) [1990] 3 All ER 927, 930, [1981] 1 WLR 1421 at 1424 per Dunn and Templeman LJJ). In this case, in the Official Solicitor's submission, this has not been shown...

[Counsel for the Official Solicitor's] first, or absolutist, submission is that a court is never justified in withholding consent to treatment which could enable a child to survive a life-threatening condition, whatever the pain or other side effects inherent in the treatment and whatever the quality of the life which it would experience thereafter. In making this submission, he distinguishes a case such as that of *Re C (a minor) (wardship: medical treatment)* [1989] 2 All ER 782, [1990] Fam 26, where the child was dying and no amount of medical skill or care could do more than achieve a brief postponement of the moment of death. He submits, rightly, that in such a case neither the parents nor the court, in deciding whether to give or to withhold consent, nor the doctors in deciding what treatment they recommend or would be prepared to administer, are balancing life against death. In such a case death is inevitable, not in the sense that it is inevitable for all of us, but in the sense that the child is actually dying. What is being balanced is not life against death, but a marginally longer life of pain against a marginally shorter life free from pain and ending in death with dignity. He also distinguished and excepted from his proposition the case of the child whose faculties have been entirely destroyed, the so-called 'cabbage' case.

In support of his submission counsel for the Official Solicitor draws attention to the decision of this court in *McKay v Essex Area Health Authority* [1982] 2 All ER 771, [1982] QB 1166...

I do not regard this decision as providing us with either guidance or assistance in the context of the present problem. The child was claiming damages and the decision was that no monetary comparison could be made between the two states [of life and death]. True it is that it contains an assertion of the importance of the sanctity of human life, but that is not in issue.

Counsel for the Official Solicitor then turns to the decision of the Supreme Court of British Columbia in *Re Superintendent of Family and Child Service and Dawson* (1983) 145 DLR (3d) 610, which is also reported and referred to in *Re C* sub nom *Re SD* [1983] 3 WWR 618.

There the issue was whether a severely brain damaged child should be subjected to a relatively simple kind of surgical treatment which would assure the continuation of his life or whether, as the parents considered was in the child's best interests, consent to the operation should be refused with a view to the child being allowed to die in the near future with dignity rather than to continue a life of suffering. Counsel for the Official Solicitor relies on the first paragraph of the judgment of McKenzie J, but I think that that paragraph read in isolation is capable of being misleading. The full quotation is (145 DLR (3d) 610 at 620–621):

> I do not think that it lies within the prerogative of any parent or of this court to look down upon a disadvantaged person and judge the quality of that person's life to be so low as not to be deserving of continuance. The matter was well put in an American decision – *Re Weberlist* ((1974) 360 NYS 2d 783 at 787), where Justice Asch said: 'There is a strident cry in America to terminate the lives of *other* people – deemed physically or mentally defective…Assuredly, one test of a civilization is its concern with the survival of the 'unfittest', a reversal of Darwin's formulation…In this case, the court must decide what its ward would choose, if he were in a position to make a sound judgment.' This last sentence puts it right. It is not appropriate for an external decision maker to apply his standards of what constitutes a liveable life and exercise the right to impose death if that standard is not met in his estimation. The decision can only be made in the context of the disabled person viewing the worthwhileness or otherwise of his life in its own context as a disabled person – and in that context he would not compare his life with that of a person enjoying normal advantages. He would know nothing of a normal person's life having never experienced it.

I am in complete agreement with McKenzie J that the starting point is not what might have been, but what is. He was considering the best interests of a severely handicapped child, not of a normal child, and the latter's feelings and interests were irrelevant. I am also in complete agreement with his implied assertion of the vast importance of the sanctity of human life. I cavil mildly, although it is a very important point, with his use of the phrase 'the right to impose death'. No such right exists in the court or the parents. What is in issue in these cases is not a right to impose death, but a right to choose a course of action which will fail to avert death. The choice is that of the patient, if of full age and capacity, the choice is that of the parents or court if, by reason of his age, the child cannot make the choice and it is a choice which must be made solely *on behalf* of the child and in what the court or parents conscientiously believe to be his best interests.

In my view the last sentence of the passage which I have quoted from the judge's judgment shows that he was rejecting a particular comparison as a basis for decision rather than denying that there was a balancing exercise to be performed. I do not therefore think that this decision supports the absolutist approach which I would in any event unhesitatingly reject. In real life there are presumptions, strong presumptions and almost overwhelming presumptions, but there are few, if any, absolutes.

I turn, therefore, to the alternative submission of counsel for the Official Solicitor that a court is only justified in withholding consent to treatment which could enable a child to survive a life-threatening condition if it is certain that the quality of the child's subsequent life would be 'intolerable to the child', 'bound to be full of pain and suffering' and 'demonstrably so awful that in effect the child must be condemned to die'. As I have already mentioned, this submission owes much to the decision of this court in *Re B* (1981) [1990] 3 All ER 927, [1981] 1 WLR 1421.

It is I think, important to remember the facts of that case and what was in issue. B was born suffering from Down's syndrome and was a mongol. At birth she also had an intestinal blockage. Nothing could be done to reverse the effect of Down's syndrome, but the intestinal blockage could be cured without great difficulty and, if this was not done, the child would die. The parents with great sorrow came to the conclusion that it was not in the best interests of the child that the intestinal blockage should be relieved, as to do so would lead to their child experiencing 20 to 30 years of life with severe mental and physical handicaps.

From the point of view of the parents, this was an immensely difficult decision and in truth they were in no position to take it. They were suffering from the shock of finding that they had a mongoloid child and they may well have had little or no experience of the quality of life of such a child, viewed from its own point of view. The decision devolved on the court when the local authority made the child a ward.

There was no issue between the doctors that the operation could and, subject to the views of the parents, should be performed. The difference of medical opinion arose out of those views. One surgeon declined to operate saying that he would wish to respect the wishes of the parents and that in the light of 20 years' experience in the profession he thought that the great majority of surgeons would adopt the same attitude. Two other surgeons said that they would operate, subject to obtaining the consent of the court and notwithstanding the expressed wishes of the parents.

The judge originally decided to give the court's consent to the operation, but changed his mind in the light of the arguments adduced by the parents *and* the fact that the parents did not wish the operation to be performed. This court held that whilst the arguments adduced by the parents were of the utmost relevance in deciding where the best interests of the child lay, their wishes (perhaps their evaluation of the child's best interests is a better description) were irrelevant, since the duty of decision had passed from them to the court.

This court then gave consent. Templeman LJ said ([1990] 3 All ER 927, [1981] 1 WLR 1421 at 1424):

...at the end of the day it devolves on this court in this particular instance to decide whether the life of this child is demonstrably going to be so awful that in effect the child must be condemned to die, or whether the life of this child is still so imponderable that it would be wrong for her to be condemned to die. There may be cases, I know not, of severe proved damage where the future is so certain and where the life of the child is so bound to be full of pain and suffering that the court might be driven to a different conclusion, but in the present case the choice which lies before the court is this: whether to allow an operation to take place which may result in the child living for 20 or 30 years as a mongoloid or whether (and I think this must be brutally the result) to terminate the life of a mongoloid child because she also has an intestinal complaint. Faced with that choice I have no doubt that it is the duty of this court to decide that the child must live.

Dunn LJ said ([1990] 3 All ER 927 at 930, [1981] 1 WLR 1421 at 1424–1425):

One of the difficulties in the case is that there is no prognosis as to the child's future, except that as a mongol her expectation of life is confined to 20 to 30 years. We were told that no reliable prognosis can be made until probably she is about two years old. That in itself leads me to the route by which the court should make its decision, because there is no evidence that this child's short life is likely to be an intolerable one. There is no evidence at all as to the quality of life which the child may expect. As counsel for the Official Solicitor said, the child should be put into the same position as any other mongol child and must be given the chance to live an existence. I accept that way of putting it.

Again I have to cavil at the use of such an expression as 'condemn to die' and 'the child must live' in Templeman LJ's judgment, which, be it noted, was not a reserved judgment. 'Thou shalt not kill' is an absolute commandment in this context. But, to quote the well-known phrase of Arthur Hugh Clough in *The Latest Decalogue*, in this context it is permissible to add 'but need'st not strive officiously to keep alive'. The decision on life and death must and does remain in other hands. What doctors and the court have to decide is whether, in the best interests of the child patient, a particular decision as to medical treatment should be taken which *as a side effect* will render death more or less likely. This is not a matter of semantics. It is fundamental. At the other end of the age spectrum, the use of drugs to reduce pain will often be fully justified, notwithstanding this will hasten the moment of death. What can never be justified is the use of drugs or surgical procedures with the primary purpose of doing so.

Re B seems to me to come very near to being a binding authority for the proposition that there is a balancing exercise to be performed in assessing the course to be adopted in the best interests of the child. Even if it is not, I have no doubt that this should be and is the law.

This brings me face to face with the problem of formulating the critical equation. In truth it cannot be done with mathematical or any precision. There is without doubt a very strong presumption in favour of a course of action which will prolong life, but, even excepting the 'cabbage' case to which special considerations may well apply, it is not irrebuttable. As this court recognised in *Re B*, account has to be taken of the pain and suffering and quality of life which the child will experience if life is prolonged. Account must also to be taken of the pain and suffering involved in the proposed treatment itself. *Re B* was probably not a borderline case and I do not think that we are bound to, or should, treat Templeman LJ's use of the words 'demonstrably so awful' or Dunn LJ's use of the word 'intolerable' as providing a quasi-statutory yardstick.

For my part I prefer the formulation of Asch J in *Re Weberlist* (1974) 360 NYS 2d 783 at 787 as explained by McKenzie J in the passage from his judgment in *Dawson's* case (1983) 145 DLR (3d) 610 at 620–621 which I have quoted, although it is probably merely another way of expressing the same concept. We know that the instinct and desire for survival is very strong. We all believe in and assert the sanctity of human life. As explained, this formulation takes account of this and also underlines the need to avoid looking at the problem from the point of view of the decider, but instead requires him to look at it from the assumed point of view of the patient. This gives effect, as it should, to the fact that even very severely handicapped people find a quality of life rewarding which to the unhandicapped may seem manifestly intolerable. People have an amazing adaptability. But in the end there will be cases in which the answer must be that it is not in the interests of the child to subject it to treatment which will cause increased suffering and produce no commensurate benefit, giving the fullest possible weight to the child's, and mankind's, desire to survive.

I make no apology for having spent time on the generality of the problem which faces doctors and the courts in cases of this nature. The Official Solicitor invited us to do so and if we can succeed in achieving any degree of clarification, it will be worthwhile in terms of assisting those who have to make these very difficult decisions at short notice and in distressing circumstances. However, I now turn to the instant appeal.

The issue here is whether it would be in the best interests of the child to put him on a mechanical ventilator and subject him to all the associated processes of intensive care, if at some future time he could not continue breathing unaided. Let me say at once that I can understand the doctors wishing to ascertain the court's wishes at this stage, because it is an eventuality which could occur at any time and, if it did, an immediate decision might well have to be made. However, the situation is significantly different from being asked whether or not to consent on behalf of the child to particular treatment which is more or less immediately in prospect. The judge has found that the odds are about even whether the need for artificial ventilation, whether mechanical or manual, will ever arise. If it does arise, the very fact that it has arisen will mean that the more optimistic end of the range of prognoses, pessimistic though the whole range is, will have been falsified. On the other hand, the child's state of health might change at any time for the better as well as for the worse, even though there are distinct limits to what could be hoped for, let alone anticipated.

The doctors were unanimous in recommending that there should be no mechanical reventilation in the event of his stopping breathing, subject only to the qualifications injected by Dr W and accepted by the judge that in the event of a chest infection short term manual ventilation would be justified and that in the event of the child stopping breathing the provisional decision to abstain from mechanical ventilation could and should be revised, if this seemed appropriate to the doctors caring for him in the then prevailing clinical situation.

There can be no criticism of the judge for indorsing this approach on the footing that he was thereby abdicating his responsibility and leaving it to the doctors to decide. He had reviewed and considered the basis of the doctors' views and recommendations in the greatest detail and with the greatest care. Nothing could be more inimical to the interests of the child than the judge should make an order which restricted the doctors' freedom to revise their present view in favour of more active means to preserve the life of the child, if the situation changed and this then seemed to them to be appropriate.

The basis of the doctors' recommendations, approved by the judge, was that mechanical ventilation is itself an invasive procedure which, together with its essential accompaniments, such as the introduction of a naso-gastric tube, drips which have to be resited and constant blood sampling, would cause the child distress. Furthermore, the procedures involve taking active measures which carry their own hazards, not only to life but in terms of causing even greater brain damage. This had to be balanced against what could possibly be achieved by the adoption of such active treatment. The chances of preserving the child's life might be improved, although even this was not certain and account had to be taken of the extremely poor quality of life at present enjoyed by the child, the fact that he had already been ventilated for exceptionally long periods, the unfavourable prognosis with or without ventilation and a recognition that if the question of reventilation ever arose, his situation would have deteriorated still further.

I can detect no error in the judge's approach and in principle would affirm his decision. This is subject to two qualifications. (i) Although all concerned have, as they know, liberty to apply to the judge at any time and he had arranged to review his decision in December, I think that he should have asked for periodic reports meanwhile on J's condition, so that he could, if he thought it appropriate, review the matter before then of his own motion. (ii) I do not think that his order should have been in the form of 'The [local authority] shall direct the relevant health authority to continue to treat…'because neither the court in wardship proceedings, nor, I think, a local authority having care and control of the baby is able to require the authority to follow a particular course of treatment. What the court can do is to withhold consent to treatment of which it disapproves and it can express its approval of other treatment proposed by the authority and its doctors. There is ample precedent for the judge's formula, but I think that it is wrong and obscures the co-operative nature of the relationship between court and medical authorities. I would prefer 'Approval is given to the continuation of the treatment of…'

Taylor LJ: Three preliminary principles are not in dispute. First, it is settled law that the court's prime and paramount consideration must be the best interests of the child. That is easily said but not easily applied. What it does involve is that the views of the parents, although they should be heeded and weighed, cannot prevail over the court's view of the ward's best interests. In the present case the parents, finding themselves in hideous dilemma, have not taken a strong view so that no conflict arises.

Second, the court's high respect for the sanctity of human life imposes a strong presumption in favour of taking all steps capable of preserving it, save in exceptional circumstances. The problem is to define those circumstances.

Third, and as a corollary to the second principle, it cannot be too strongly emphasised that the court never sanctions steps to terminate life. That would be unlawful. There is no question of approving, even in a case of the most horrendous disability, a course aimed at terminating life or accelerating death. The court is concerned only with the circumstances in which steps should not be taken to prolong life.

Two decisions of this court have dealt with cases at the extremes of the spectrum of affliction. *Re C (a minor) (wardship: medical treatment)* [1989] 2 All ER 782, [1990] Fam 26 was a case in which a child had severe irreversible brain damage such that she was hopelessly and terminally ill. This court held that the best interests of the child required approval of recommendations designed to ease her suffering and permit her life to come to an end peacefully with dignity rather than seek to prolong her life.

By contrast, in the earlier case of *Re B (a minor) (wardship: medical treatment)* (1981) [1990] 3 All ER 927, [1981] 1 WLR 1421, the court was concerned with a child suffering from Down's syndrome, who quite separately was born with an intestinal obstruction. Without an operation this intestinal condition would quickly have been fatal. On the other hand, the operation had a good chance of successfully removing the obstruction, once and for all, thereby affording the child a life expectancy of some 20 to 30 years as a mongol. The parents genuinely believed it was in the child's interests to refrain from operating and allow her to die. The court took a different view...

Those two cases thus decide that where the child is terminally ill the court will not require treatment to prolong life; but where, at the other extreme, the child is severely handicapped although not intolerably so and treatment for a discrete condition can enable life to continue for an appreciable period, albeit subject to that severe handicap, the treatment should be given.

I should say that, in my view, the phrase 'condemned to die' which occurs twice in the passage cited from the judgment of Templeman LJ is more emotive than accurate. As already indicated, the court in these cases has to decide, not whether to end life, but whether to prolong it by treatment without which death would ensue from natural causes.

It is to be noted that Templeman LJ did not say, even obiter, that where the child's life would be bound to be full of pain and suffering there would come a point at which the court should rule against prolonged life by treatment. He went no further than to say there may be cases where the court might take that view.

This leads to the arguments presented by counsel for the Official Solicitor. His first submission propounded an absolute test, that, except where the ward is terminally ill, the court's approach should always be to prolong life by treatment if this is possible, regardless of the quality of life being preserved and regardless of any added suffering caused by the treatment itself. I cannot accept this test which in my view is so hard as to be inconsistent at its extreme with the best interests of the child. Counsel for the Official Solicitor submits that the court cannot play God and decide whether the quality of life which the treatment would give the child is better or worse than death...

Despite the court's inability to compare a life afflicted by the most severe disability with death, the unknown, I am of the view that there must be extreme cases in which the court is entitled to say: 'The life which this treatment would prolong would be so cruel as to be intolerable.' If, for example, a child was so damaged as to have negligible use of its faculties and the only way of preserving its life was by the continuous administration of extremely painful treatment such that the child either would be in continuous agony or would have to be so sedated continuously as to have no conscious life at all, I cannot think counsel's absolute test should apply to require the treatment to be given. In those circumstances, without there being any question of deliberately ending the life or shortening it, I consider the court is entitled in the treatment of the child to say that deliberate steps should not be taken artificially to prolong its miserable life span.

Once the absolute test is rejected, the proper criteria must be a matter of degree. At what point in the scale of disability and suffering ought the court to hold that the best interests of the child do not require further endurance to be imposed by positive treatment to prolong its life? Clearly, to justify withholding treatment, the circumstances would have to be extreme. Counsel for the Official Solicitor submitted that if the court rejected his absolute test, then at least it would have 'to be certain that the life of the child, were the treatment to be given, would be intolerably awful'.

I consider that the correct approach is for the court to judge the quality of life the child would have to endure if given the treatment and decide whether in all the circumstances such a life would be so afflicted as to be intolerable to that child. I say 'to that child' because the test should not be whether the life would be tolerable to the decider. The test must be whether the child in question, if capable of exercising sound judgment, would consider the life tolerable. This is the approach adopted by McKenzie J in *Re Superintendent of Family and Child Service and Dawson* (1983) 145 DLR (3d) 610 at 620–621 in the passage cited with approval by Lord Donaldson MR. It takes account of the strong instinct to preserve one's life even in circumstances which an outsider, not himself at risk of death, might consider unacceptable. The circumstances to be considered would, in appropriate cases, include the degree of existing disability and any additional suffering or aggravation of the disability which the treatment itself would superimpose. In an accident case, as opposed to one involving disablement from birth, the child's pre-accident quality of life and its perception of what has been lost may also be factors relevant to whether the residual life would be intolerable to that child.

Counsel for the Official Solicitor argued that, before deciding against treatment, the court would have to be *certain* that the circumstances of the child's future would comply with the extreme requirements to justify that decision. Certainty as to the future is beyond human judgment. The courts have not, even in the trial of capital offences, required certainty of proof. But, clearly the court must be satisfied to a high degree of probability.

In the present case, the doctors were unanimous that in his present condition, J should not be put back on to a mechanical ventilator. That condition is very grave indeed. I do not repeat the description of it given by Lord Donaldson MR. In reaching his conclusion, the judge no doubt had three factors in mind. First, the severe lack of capacity of the child in all his faculties which even without any further complication would make his existence barely sentient. Second, that, if further mechanical ventilation were to be required, that very fact would involve the risk of a deterioration in B's condition, because of further brain damage flowing from the interruption of breathing. Third, all the doctors drew attention to the invasive nature of mechanical ventilation and the intensive care required to accompany it. They stressed the unpleasant and distressing nature of that treatment. To add such distress and the risk of further deterioration to an already appalling catalogue of disabilities was clearly capable in my judgment of producing a quality of life which justified the stance of the doctors and the judge's conclusion. I therefore agree that, subject to the minor variations to the judge's order proposed by Lord Donaldson MR, this appeal should be dismissed.

Balcombe LJ agreed.

The language adopted by the court in *Re J* makes it clear that the court rejected any absolute notion of the sanctity of life in favour of an inquiry into the patient's quality of life as the means of determining his 'best interests'. That the judges did so cautiously, conscious of the implications of their decision, cannot be denied, but they did so none the less. Three points deserve attention.

First (a minor point), two of the judges curiously purport to apply the 'substituted judgment' test. As we have seen, this has no place where the patient has never been competent so as to express a view or hold values. Taylor LJ, however, talks of whether life would be 'intolerable to *that child*' (our emphasis). By this he clearly intended to direct the decision-maker's attention to what the child would consider intolerable: '[t]he test must be whether the child in question, *if capable of exercising sound judgment*, would consider the life tolerable' (our emphasis). (See also Lord Donaldson MR at 936.) This is an impossible test to apply given the circumstances of the child (see *supra*, ch 6).

Secondly, any reference to 'quality of life' still leaves unanswered the question which 'quality' or 'qualities' are relevant. For the Court of Appeal it would appear that the condition of the patient must be extreme before any consideration of withholding or withdrawing treatment may be contemplated. Arguably, the judges only permit the decision-maker to balance the benefits and burdens of treatment so as to let the patient die in such cases. The judges appear to erect a strong presumption in favour of treatment unless the patient's life will be intolerable or 'demonstrably' awful. It cannot be argued that these terms have any great ring of precision. Indeed, it is not clear whether the judges agree as to how extreme the patient's condition must be. Certainly, it seems that Taylor LJ, by adopting the language of Templeman LJ in *Re B*, would only contemplate letting the patient die in *the most* extreme circumstances. Lord Donaldson MR (and, perhaps Balcombe LJ also), however, as we saw, rejected the language in *Re B* and, as a consequence, may have 'left the door open' for less extreme cases (per Butler-Sloss LJ in *Airedale NHS Trust v Bland* [1993] 1 All ER 821 at 845). The Court of Appeal in *Bland* did little to make the matter any clearer. It is arguable, however, that both Sir Thomas Bingham MR and Hoffmann LJ (like Taylor LJ in *Re J*) opt for a more extreme test emphasising that 'full weight has to be given to the principle of the sanctity of life before deciding that a test of best interests justifies a decision to allow the patient to die' (per Hoffmann LJ at 857). Subsequently, in *Re C (A Minor) (Medical Treatment)* [1998] Lloyd's Rep Med 1, the court was not faced with the most extreme situation and yet authorised the withholding of ventilation. The case was primarily concerned with how the court should approach a decision where the parents wished treatment to continue (see *supra*, ch 6).

Re C (a minor) (medical treatment) [1998] Lloyd's Rep Med 1 (Fam Div)

Sir Stephen Brown P: Little C (as I shall call her) was born on July 3, 1996. She is now 16 months of age. She suffers from a dreadful fatal disease, spinal muscular atrophy, type 1. It is known in short as SMA 1. This is a tragic case. She came into hospital first in March of this year. She then weighed 7½ kilograms. She now weighs only 5½ kilograms. When she came into hospital in March she remained only for a few days and was then allowed to go home, but she came back in July and briefly stayed in hospital. She went with her parents to Israel in October 1997 and was there for two weeks. She has been in hospital in intensive care since that time and is on ventilation. This is known as intermittent positive pressure ventilation which is designed to support her own breathing.

She is seriously disabled. The disease means that she is seriously emaciated. She has little movement of her feet and no other movement in her legs. She does not have what is termed anti-gravity movement in her arms, and is in what the doctor responsible for her care termed as a 'no chance' situation. That is a phrase which appears in a publication of the Royal College of Paediatrics and Child Health issued in September of this year entitled 'Withholding or Withdrawing Lifesaving Treatment in Children, a Framework for Practice'. It defined the 'no chance' situation as

> ...where the child has such severe disease that life-sustaining treatment simply delays death without significant alleviation of suffering. Medical treatment in this situation may thus be deemed inappropriate.

The doctor, a consultant paediatric neurologist, having the responsibility for the care of C considers that this is a grave case within that bracket and is so grave that it is not in her best interests that she should be further ventilated, and if, when ventilation is withdrawn, it should not be reinstituted in the event of a further respiratory arrest. The doctor's view is that such treatment would be futile, it would not improve her quality of life and would subject her to further suffering without conferring any benefit. It is the inevitable and dreadfully sad feature of this disease that the life expectancy is very short indeed. Not many children survive one year of life in this condition. Nevertheless, she is conscious and is able to recognise her parents and is able to smile. She can move her hands laterally, that is, not in an anti-gravity way. But she has grave difficulties clearly and the future is very bleak indeed.

The doctors having her care – Dr H is responsible with other doctors who have also been concerned – have come to the conclusion that it is not in the best interests of this little child that she continue on indefinite ventilation which would produce increasing distress and would inevitably involve a tracheostomy operation under anaesthetic which might of itself give rise to epilepsy, but that she should be taken off ventilation at this stage and if she were then, as they believe is highly probable, to suffer a further respiratory relapse it would be against her interests to seek to place her back on ventilation or indeed to engage in resuscitative treatment.

This is a serious situation for doctors to contend with. It is a dreadful situation for the parents to have to face. The parents of C are highly responsible religious orthodox Jews. They love their child. They have other children. They cannot bring themselves to face what seems to be the inevitable future for this little child. They visit her and see a reaction which is a favourable reaction in her face towards them. They do not believe that it is within their religious tenets to contemplate the possibility of indirectly shortening life, even if that is not the purpose of the course which the doctors believe to be appropriate in order to spare her further suffering.

Accordingly, they have not been able to consent to the proposed course of treatment which the doctors have recommended. That is to say that whilst they believe that she should be taken off ventilation as a last attempt, as it were, to see whether she might survive for a time without the intermittent positive pressure ventilation presently being administered, they believe that they should be able to be assured that should she suffer further respiratory relapse or arrest she should be replaced on to ventilation. The doctors are unable to contemplate undertaking such a course of treatment in the best interests of the child...

The medical evidence is not in dispute. There is no issue in this case that this is a fatal disease and that in real terms this little child is approaching death. She has a desperately tragic existence. She is emaciated. Although she is conscious there is the prospect of increasing suffering as the days go by. The doctors are all of the view that it would be in her best interests that she be removed from ventilation and that in the event of what they believe to be an inevitable respiratory arrest it would follow that she should not be replaced on ventilation which would of itself give rise to increased suffering and distress...

In this case I have no doubt on the evidence before me, including the evidence of the parents themselves, that in this desperate situation it is in the best interests of C that she should now be taken off the ventilation presently being administered and that it should not be reimposed or restored if she should suffer a further respiratory arrest. It is a desperately sad situation for all concerned. The anxiety of the doctors as well as the parents can be well understood. Their objective in their profession is to save and to preserve life but, as has been said in earlier cases that whilst the sanctity of life is vitally important, it is not the paramount consideration. The paramount consideration here is the best interests of little C...what the court is being asked to do in this case is to exercise its inherent jurisdiction to approve the course of treatment which is now proposed by the doctors and for which they cannot gain the consent of the parents. In other words, to seek the court's consent in the absence of the consent of the parents. I am very conscious indeed of the grave responsibility which rests not only upon the doctors but in this situation upon the court. Dr H has made it very clear that she could not agree to the course which the parents propose, that is to say to restore ventilation in the event of a further respiratory arrest, and she would have to seek to replace her part in the supervision of the case by somebody else if they were willing to undertake it. It is, if I may say so, an extremely difficult situation but it is the reality of the present position.

I have been assisted greatly by Mr Michael Nicholls as *amicus curiae*. He has the advantage of having been a party to the preparation of the publication to which I have already briefly referred, that is the publication entitled 'Withholding or Withdrawing Lifesaving Treatment in Children, a Framework for Practice', published by the Royal College of Paediatrics and Child Health in September 1997. In that document at p 10 entitled 'Practice later in childhood', para 2.2.2 begins in these terms:

> Withdrawal of treatment in paediatric intensive care units accounts for up to 65% of deaths. Examples might be [and the second example is] the paediatric neurologist might reasonably withhold ventilator care in a child with progressive respiratory failure from anterior horn (cell) disease.

That is in fact this same disease, SMA 1. So it is clear that what is being proposed by the doctors has the support of the Royal College of Paediatrics and Child Health who considered the wide field of these matters in their meetings which led to the publication of that document.

I believe that in this case I should assent to the course which is proposed by the Hospital Trust. I do so with a feeling of grave solemnity because I realise that the parents themselves will be greatly disappointed. It is a sad feature of this matter that there is, in fact, no hope for C, and what has to be considered is her best interests to prevent her from suffering as would be inevitable if this course were not to be taken.

Accordingly I propose to grant relief in the following terms:

> That there be leave to treat the minor, C, as advised by Dr H, such treatment to include the withdrawal of artificial ventilation and non-resuscitation in the event of a respiratory arrest and palliative care to ease her suffering and permit her life to end peacefully and with dignity, such treatment being in C's best interests.

One view would be that baby C's condition, though undoubtedly extreme, was not such that she had little or no quality of life. She could, after all, smile and recognise her parents. Her outlook, though bleak and without long-term hope, was not one which was so 'demonstrably awful'. The judge, of course, did not agree and relied upon a publication of the Royal College of Paediatrics and Child Health.

It is becoming a feature of medicine that the profession as a whole (through, for example, the Medical Ethics Committee of the British Medical Association), or specialists, (through, for example, the Royal Colleges), have begun to develop and publish guidelines relating to clinical practice. Very often, these guidelines represent the views of non-doctors as well as doctors, since the relevant committees ordinarily do not have an exclusively medical membership. It is not surprising, indeed it is to be encouraged, that courts wrestling with a legal/moral issue arising from clinical practice, should be able to refer to a professional view, not only for an understanding of the facts but for what the proper response might be. Provided that they remember that the final decision always rests with the court, the judges can only benefit from this practice, not least because it is desirable to ensure that the law takes proper account of professional views.

A difficulty arises, however, if the guidelines which emerge have not received general approval within the profession and, indeed, are deemed somewhat unhelpful. The guidance relied upon, and indeed also the BMA's more recent guidelines, have proved controversial. The categorisation of a child as being in a 'no chance' situation could be said to be both insensitive if used in clinical practice and unhelpful. The latter is so because it merely identifies that patient as suffering from a condition that cannot be treated such as to delay death (see further Commentary (1998) 6 Med L Rev 99 (IK)).

Notwithstanding the above, what appears to emerge is a requirement that the patient must have little or no prospect of any meaningful interaction with others or his environment before a decision to withhold or withdraw treatment can be taken (see also *Re C (A Baby)* (1996) 32 BMLR 44 (Stephen Brown P) and Commentary (1997) 5 Med L Rev 102 (IK) – withdrawal of ventilation from a baby whose condition was extreme, with very low awareness and her prognosis was 'hopeless'). After all, the Court of Appeal cited with approval the decision of McKenzie J in the British Columbia case of *Dawson* and it is hard to imagine circumstances of more extreme disability than those suffered by Stephen Dawson (but see *Re: Representation Attorney-General* (1995) 3 Med L Rev 316 (Jersey Ry Ct)).

Re Superintendent of Family and Child Service and Dawson (1983) 145 DLR (3d) 610 (BC Sup Ct)

McKenzie J: [Stephen Dawson] is a severely retarded boy approaching seven years, who shortly after birth suffered profound brain damage through meningitis which inflamed the lining of his brain and left him with no control over his faculties, limbs or bodily functions. At the age of five months life-support surgery was performed by implanting a shunt which is a plastic tube which drains excess cerebrospinal fluid from the head to another body cavity from which it is expelled or absorbed.

[He] is legally blind, with atrophied optic nerves, partly deaf, incontinent, cannot hold a spoon to feed himself, cannot stand, walk, talk, or hold objects. [His parents] say that he has no method of communicating with his environment and think he is in pain. The sounds he makes are too soft to be heard from any distance. He is subject to seizures despite anticonvulsant medication. He is restrained by splints which are bandages on his arms to keep his elbows straight so that he cannot chew on his hands and roughly handle his face. Staff carry him from bed to wheelchair, which has a moulded 'insert' to ensure he is held securely and he is belted in with a hip belt.

This description applies to his condition as it existed when he was a patient in Sunnyhill Hospital before the shunt stopped operating. About six weeks ago a blockage in the shunt was detected and the parents gave their consent to remedial surgery but, after a day's reflection, withdrew their consent on the ground that the boy should be allowed to die with dignity rather than continue to endure a life of suffering. They continued to maintain that position…

I respect and have given anxious consideration to the views of the parents. In so doing I must give some weight to the fact that they were divorced in mid-1980 after extended matrimonial discord. Also I must give weight to my conclusion based on the evidence that they thought Stephen better dead long before the need for the critical decision arose about replacement of the shunt. Despite the evidence of highly qualified professionals, in whom I place great reliance, they are satisfied Stephen will promptly die if treatment is denied. My finding is that it is by no means a certainty that death will soon follow and a real possibility exists that his life will go no indefinitely but in pain and progressive deterioration. I must reject their assertion that they would consent to the operation if they could be assured that he would thereafter be comfortable and free of pain when at the same time they reject the opinions of competent professionals that such will probably be the case. I believe that their minds are firmly made up and closed shut.

I regret having to make such findings…

I cannot accept their view that Stephen would be better off dead. If it is to be decided that 'it is in the best interests of Stephen Dawson that his existence cease', then it must be decided that, for him, non-existence is the better alternative. This would mean regarding the life of a handicapped child as not only less valuable than the life of a normal child, but so much less valuable that it is not worth preserving. I tremble at contemplating the consequences if the lives of disabled persons are dependent upon such judgments.

To refer back to the words of Templeman LJ I cannot in conscience find that this is a case of severe proved damage 'where the future is so certain and where the life of the child is so bound to be full of pain and suffering that the court might be driven to a different conclusion'. I am not satisfied that 'the life of this child is demonstrably going to be so awful that in effect the child must be condemned to die'. Rather I believe that 'the life of this child is still so imponderable that it would be wrong for her to be condemned to die'.

There is not a simple choice here of allowing the child to live or die according to whether the shunt is implanted or not. There looms the awful possibility that without the shunt the child will endure in a state of progressing disability and pain. It is too simplistic to say that the child should be allowed to die in peace.

It is a matter which ultimately eludes rational analysis whether the condition of Baby J was more extreme, so as to warrant the withholding of treatment, than that of Stephen Dawson. There is, however, one pointer which suggests a difference between the condition of the patients in *Re J* and *Dawson* – that of pain, albeit the difference is not between its presence or absence, but between degrees of pain. You will recall that Stephen Dawson would suffer 'progressing pain' if he were *not* treated.

As for our third point, this relates to the emphasis placed upon the patient being in pain. The difficulty of identifying pain as the key to determining whether the quality of a patient's life is sufficiently intolerable to justify withdrawing or withholding care is that pain itself is an elusive concept and, more important, it is and should be only one of the factors in assessing 'quality of life'. If 'pain' were elevated to a special status, it would mean that the patient who is free of pain should always be treated if there is even the slightest benefit to be gained thereby (leaving aside what precisely 'benefit' means). You will recall Handler J's concurring opinion in the *Matter of Conroy* (1985) 486 A 2d 1209 (NJ Sup Ct):

Handler J: In my opinion, the Court's objective tests too narrowly define the interests of people like Miss Conroy. While the basic standard purports to account for several concerns, it ultimately focuses on pain as the critical factor. The presence of significant pain in effect becomes the sole measure of such a person's best interests. 'Pain' thus eclipses a whole cluster of other human values that have a proper place in the subtle weighing that will ultimately determine how life should end.

The Court's concentration on pain as the exclusive criterion in reaching the life-or-death decision in reality transmutes the best-interests determination into an exercise of avoidance and nullification rather than confrontation and fulfilment. In most cases the pain criterion will dictate that the decision to be one not to withdraw life-prolonging treatment and not to allow death to occur naturally. First, pain will not be an operative factor in a great many cases. '[P]resently available drugs and techniques allow pain to be reduced to a level acceptable to virtually every patient, usually without unacceptable sedation.' *President's Commission Report, supra,* at 50–51. *See id* at 19 n 19 *citing* Saunders, 'Current Views on Pain Relief and Terminal Care' in *The Therapy of Pain* 215 (Swerdlow, ed. 1981) (a hospice reports complete control of pain in over 99% of its dying patients). *See generally id* at 277–95. *See also generally The Management of Terminal Disease* (Saunders, ed 1978); *The Experience of Dying* (Pattison, ed 1977); *Psychopharmacologic Agents for the Terminally Ill and Bereaved* (Goldberg *et al*, eds 1973). Further, as was true in Miss Conroy's case, health care providers frequently encounter difficulty in evaluating the degree of pain experienced by a patient. Finally, '[o]nly a minority of patients – fewer than half of those with malignancies, for example – have substantial problems with pain…' *President's Commission Report, supra* at 278 *citing* Twycross, 'Relief of Pain' in *The Management of Terminal Disease, supra* at 66. Thus, in a great many cases, the pain test will become an absolute bar to the withdrawal of life-support therapy.

The pain requirement, as applied by the Court in its objective tests, effectively negates other highly relevant considerations that should appropriately bear on the decision to maintain or to withdraw life-prolonging treatment. The pain standard may dictate the decision to prolong life despite the presence of other factors that reasonably militate in favor of the termination of such procedures to allow a natural death. The exclusive pain criterion denies relief to that class of people who, at the very end of life, might strongly disapprove of an artificially extended existence in spite of the absence of pain. *See In Re Torres*, 357 NW 2d 332, 340 (Minn 1984) (although a patient 'cannot feel pain,' that patient may have a guardian petition to forego life-sustaining treatment). Thus, some people abhor dependence on others as much, or more, than they fear pain. Other individuals value personal privacy and dignity, and prize independence from others when their personal needs and bodily functions are involved. Finally, the ideal of bodily integrity may become more important than simply prolonging life at its most rudimentary level. Persons, like Miss Conroy, 'may well have wished to avoid…[t]he ultimate horror [not of] death but the possibility of being maintained in limbo, in a sterile room, by machines controlled by strangers.' *In Re Torres, supra* 357 NW 2d at 340, quoting Steel, 'The Right to Die: New Options in California,' 93 *Christian Century* [July–Dec 1976].

Clearly, a decision to focus exclusively on pain as the single criterion ignores and devalues other important ideals regarding life and death. Consequently, a pain standard cannot serve as an indirect proxy for additional and significant concerns that bear on the decision to forego life-prolonging treatments…

I share the Court's discomfiture with a standard that does not attempt to identify reasonably verifiable measures of a person's quality of life. However, there is no intrinsic reason why a quality-of-life standard must remain any more vague and undefined than a standard that includes pain…

I would therefore have the Court adopt a test that does not rely exclusively on pain as the ultimately determinative criterion. Rather, the standard should consist of an array of factors to be medically established and then evaluated by the decision-maker both singly and collectively to reach a balance that will justify the determination whether to withdraw or to continue life-prolonging treatment. The withdrawal of life-prolonging treatment from an unconscious or comatose, terminally ill individual near death, whose personal views concerning life-ending treatment cannot be ascertained, should be governed by such a standard.

Several important criteria bear on this critical determination. The person should be terminally ill and facing imminent death. There should also be present the permanent loss of conscious thought processes in the form of a comatose state or profound unconsciousness. Further, there should be the irreparable failure of at least one major and essential bodily organ or system. *See, eg, In Re Quinlan*, 70 NJ 10, 355, A 2d 647 (1976) (respiratory system); *Barber, supra* (same); *In Re Dinnerstein*, 6 Mass App 466, 380 NE 2d 134 (1978) (heart); *Saikewicz, supra* (circulatory system); *Conroy, supra* (swallowing reflex); *Torres, supra* (cerebral cortex and brain-stem); *In Re Hamlin*, 102 Wash 2d 810, 689 P 2d 1372 (1984) (cerebral cortex). Obviously the presence or absence of significant pain is highly relevant.

In addition, the person's general physical condition must be of great concern. The presence of progressive, irreversible, extensive, and extreme physical deterioration, such as ulcers, lesions, gangrene, infection, incontinence and the like, which frequently afflict the bed-ridden, terminally ill, should be considered in the formulation of an appropriate standard. The medical and nursing treatment of individuals *in extremis* and suffering from these conditions entails the constant and extensive handling and manipulation of the body. At some point, such a course of treatment upon the insensate patient is bound to touch the sensibilities of even the most detached observer. Eventually, pervasive bodily intrusions, even for the best motives, will arouse feelings akin to humiliation and mortification for the helpless patient. When cherished values of human dignity and personal privacy, which belong to every person living or dying, are sufficiently transgressed by what is being done to the individual, we should be ready to say: enough.

When the *Bland* case was before the Court of Appeal, all three judges accepted that pain was not the critical factor in the process of weighing so as to determine a patient's best interests.

Sir Thomas Bingham MR: I accept the argument…that account may be taken of wider and less tangible considerations. An objective assessment of Mr Bland's best interests…would in my opinion give weight to the constant invasions and humiliations to which his inert body is subject; to the desire he would naturally have to be remembered as a cheerful, carefree, gregarious teenager and not an object of pity; to the prolonged ordeal imposed on all members of his family, but particularly on his parents; even, perhaps, if altruism still lives, to a belief that finite resources are better devoted to enhancing life than simply averting death.

Butler-Sloss LJ: [Counsel for the Official Solicitor] argued in *Re J* the fundamentalist or absolutist approach, that the pain and suffering experienced and to be experienced by that child should not displace the sanctity of life, including the preservation of the life of that child, whatever it was to be. This court rejected that approach and placed on the other side of the critical equation the tragic situation of the child concerned and the quality of his life. Lord Donaldson MR did not feel bound to follow the views expressed (obiter) in *Re B (a minor)* *(wardship: medical treatment)* [1981] 1 WLR 1421 as to the degree of awfulness or intolerability of treatment which might be proposed as providing a quasi-statutory yardstick. He left the door open. Apart from preferring to use a word other than 'cabbage', I respectfully agree with him...

[Counsel for the Official Solicitor's] answer was that severe pain and suffering as experienced by the child in *Re J* is the only factor which can be put on the other side of the equation to the sanctity of life. He reserved his position to argue elsewhere that *Re J* was wrongly decided and there was nothing to place in the balance against the sanctity of life. In his argument to this court the interests of the PVS patient are limited to that sole consideration.

To place pain and suffering in a unique category, the existence of which may justify foregoing the preservation of the sanctity of life, does not appear to me to be justifiable. Two reasons come immediately to mind. First, on a practical level, according to [counsel for the Official Solicitor] the exception of extreme pain can be justified on the basis that it can be objectively verified. The degree of resistance to pain varies enormously from person to person and is intensively subjective however its existence as such may be objectively verified. It is not an absolute state and it will always be a matter of degree as to whether the state of pain of an incompetent patient is sufficiently severe to meet the necessary criterion. If it is to be the only criterion, excluding all other considerations, the lack of clarity in formulating when it comes into play, creates for me a logical problem in accepting it alone on the other side of the equation.

There is however a second and more fundamental objection. The case for the universal sanctity of life assumes a life in the abstract and allows nothing for the reality of Mr Bland's actual existence. There are clearly dangers in departing from the fundamental approach to the preservation of life, but in the American decisions it is not conclusive. Two exceptions are already recognised in English common law, the right of self-determination and the *Re J* situation of extreme pain and suffering. The quality of life has already been recognised as a factor and placed in the equation to allow a life not to be prolonged at all costs. Taylor LJ said in *Re J* [1990] 3 All ER 930 at 945, [1991] Fam 33 at 35: 'Once the absolute test is rejected, the proper criteria must be a matter of degree.' To limit the quality of life to extreme pain is to take a demeaning view of a human being. There must be something more for the humanity of the person of a PVS patient. He remains a person and not an object of concern. In *Re Conroy* (1985) 98 NJ 321 at 396, Handler J supports this approach:

> Clearly, a decision to focus exclusively on pain and the single criterion ignores and devalues other important ideals regarding life and death. Consequently, a pain standard cannot serve as an indirect proxy for additional and significant concerns that bear on the decision to forego life-prolonging treatments.

That concentration exclusively upon pain is to me an unacceptable approach to a patient in Anthony Bland's extreme situation. There are other factors to be placed in the critical equation.

Those other factors have not so far been explored in English decisions but they have been considered extensively in the United States and in a recent case in New Zealand. In *Cruzan v Director, Missouri Dept of Health* (1990) 110 S Ct 2841 at 2885–2886 (a PVS case) Stevens J (in a dissenting opinion) said:

> But Nancy Cruzan's interest in life, no less than any other person, includes an interest in how she will be thought of after her death by those whose opinions mattered to her. There can be no doubt that her life made her dear to her family, and to others. How she dies will affect how that life is remembered.

In *Guardianship of Jane Doe* (1992) 411 Mass 512 the Supreme Judicial Court of Massachusetts (in a PVS case where the patient had always been incompetent) held that incompetent individuals have the same rights as competent individuals to refuse and terminate medical treatment. Abrams J, giving the majority opinion, accepted the rights of the patient to bodily integrity and privacy and upheld the judge's decision to terminate nasoduodenal feeding and hydration. *Re Jobes* (1987) 108 NJ 394 (a PVS patient) following *Re Quinlan* (1976) 70 NJ 10 upheld the principle of self-determination for the incompetent. The views of the family were accepted in each of those cases. Handler J in a concurring opinion considered the best interests test and, after describing the extreme physical condition of Mrs Jobes (very similar to Mr Bland) quoted a passage in his opinion in *Re Conroy* (1985) 98 NJ 321 at 398–399:

> the medical and nursing treatment of individuals in extremis and suffering from these conditions entails the constant and extensive handling and manipulation of the body. At some point, such a course of treatment upon the insensate patient is bound to touch the sensibilities of even the most detached observer. Eventually, pervasive bodily intrusions, even for the best of motives, will arouse feelings akin to humiliation and mortification for the helpless patient. When cherished values of human dignity and personal privacy, which belong to every person living or dying, are sufficiently transgressed by what is

being done to the individual, we should be ready to say: enough'. Based upon such factors it should be possible to structure critical treatment decisions that are reliable, understandable and acceptable. (See 108 NJ 394 at 443–444.)

Auckland Area Health Board v A-G [1993] 1 NZLR 235 was an extreme example of a Guillain-Barre syndrome, causing a condition somewhat similar to a PVS patient, where the doctors sought a declaration that to withdraw artificial ventilation would not constitute culpable homicide. Thomas J granted the declaration and in doing so considered decisions from a number of common law jurisdictions including the American and our own. He referred (at 245) to

> values of human dignity and personal privacy…Human dignity and personal privacy belong to every person, whether living or dying. Yet, the sheer invasiveness of the treatment and the manipulation of the human body which it entails, the pitiful and humiliating helplessness of the patient's state and the degradation and dissolution of all bodily functions invoke these values…

The judge based his decision upon the best interests test. Mr Munby [counsel for the Official Solicitor] accepted that there was no difference in principle between the ventilator and the nasogastric tube.

Although the American decisions are often based upon the principle of achieving the right of an incompetent patient to make decisions as if competent through the device of a substituted judgment, in many cases the distinction from best interests is blurred as Handler J pointed out in *Re Jobes* (1987) 108 NJ 394 at 436, and in some cases it is clearly an objective assessment of best interests and the decisions are persuasive support for considerations far wider than the factor of pain to be taken into account in balancing the critical equation.

We all of course recognise that a patient unable to choose cannot himself exercise his right of self-determination and he cannot make the irrational decision he might notionally have made if in possession of his faculties. But not to be able to be irrational does not seem to me to be a good reason to be deprived of a rational decision which could be taken on his behalf in his best interests. Otherwise, if, as I believe they are, other factors as well as pain are relevant considerations, he is put at an unfair disadvantage.

A mentally incompetent patient has interests to be considered and protected, the basic one being the right to be properly cared for by others. He retains the right to have proceedings taken on his behalf, for instance to claim damages for negligence, or to have his estate or other property managed for him, or to respond to actions or proceedings taken against him, such as divorce proceedings. He retains in my view the right to be well regarded by others, and to be well remembered by his family. That right is separate from that of his family to remember him and to have the opportunity to grieve for him when he is dead. He has the right to be respected. Consequently he has a right to avoid unnecessary humiliation and degrading invasion of his body for no good purpose…

The considerations as to the quality of life of Mr Bland now and in the future in his extreme situation are in my opinion rightly to be placed on the other side of the critical equation from the general principle of the sanctity and inviolability of life.

Hoffmann LJ: The best interests of the patient in my judgment embrace not only recovery or the avoidance of pain (neither of which apply in this case) but also a dignified death. On this issue I respectfully agree with the dissenting judgments of Handler J in *Re Conroy* (1985) 98 NJ 321 and Brennan and Stevens JJ in *Cruzan v Director, Missouri Dept of Health* (1990) 497 US 261.

The adult cases We have already made it clear that the legal principles relevant to decisions concerning medical treatment at the end of life are of equal application to babies and to others who are incompetent, whether children or adults. Thus the analysis applied in the case of the severely disabled neonates applies to the senile elderly and disabled or terminally ill young adult.

Until recently, surprisingly, there had been no English cases concerned with adults other than the PVS cases. That the applicable principles are the same is illustrated by the decision in *Re R* (1996) 31 BMLR 127, where the judge relied upon the Court of Appeal's decision in *Re J* (1990), which we saw earlier was so central to the analysis for neonates. We set out the decision in full as we consider it to be an important case and one where it is essential to see the medical evidence presented to the court.

Re R (adult: medical treatment) (1996) 31 BMLR 127 (Fam Div)

Sir Stephen Brown P: R is 23 years of age. He was born on 7 December 1972, with a serious malformation of the brain and cerebral palsy. At eight months of age he developed severe epilepsy. He had and has profound learning disability and has not developed any formal means of communication or any consistent interactions with the social environment. He is spastic and is unable to walk or to sit upright unaided or, indeed, to reach for objects. It is believed that he is blind, although it is possible that he may perceive light. He is probably deaf, although it is possible that he showed some reaction to a buzzer when recently examined by a medical expert. He is incontinent and has no control over his motions. He suffers from serious constipation and his bowels have to be evacuated manually. He cannot chew, and food has to be syringed to the back of his mouth. He suffers from thrush and has ulcers 'all the way through his guts'. The only response to touch appears to be when he is cuddled, when he gives an indication of pleasure. According to Dr Keith Andrews, the Director of Medical and Research Service at the Royal Hospital for Neuro Disability at Putney he 'exists in a low awareness state'. He is not in the category of someone in a persistent vegetative state, but in the scale of gravity of the low awareness state he would rate between 1 and 2 on the scale of 10. He appears to respond to pain, and grimaces, but Dr Andrews is not sure whether he really feels it. He is totally dependent.

Until he was 17 years of age he lived at home. His devoted parents cared for him. Since 1989 he has resided at a NHS trust residential home, which is managed by a registered nurse for the mentally handicapped. The home has a staff of eight. R goes home to his parents for three weekends out of four. During the week he attends a day care centre operated by the authority social services between 9.00 am and 3.30 pm. There he is looked after by instructors who are not medically qualified but who are experienced in dealing with adults and disabilities. R's present condition and circumstances are summarised in the reports and evidence of two independent medical experts, whose advice has been sought by the Official Solicitor (who represents R in the proceedings now before this court): Dr Piachaud, a consultant psychiatrist in learning disability, and Dr Keith Andrews, to whom I have already referred. Dr Piachaud says:

> I feel R is operating cognitively and neurologically at the level of a newborn infant. He has a vague sensory input from his eyes, his ears, touch, taste and perhaps smell. He was liked by the people who are around him and who spoke gently and kindly to him.

He also said:

> R receives a very high quality of care. I was deeply impressed by all those people I met with regard to how they cared for R and were acting out of concern for him, even though they have formed different opinions as to what is right for him.

Dr Keith Andrews said:

> It is my opinion that he has very little, if any, real cognitive awareness at a level where he can interpret what is going on in his environment. He reacts at the most basic level by responding to comfort, warmth and a safe environment by being relaxed and producing the occasional smile. He responds to discomfort, pain and threatening situations by becoming distressed and crying. These are very basic level responses and do not imply any thought processes.

The medical care and treatment of R is the responsibility of his general practitioner, Dr V, and a consultant psychiatrist in learning disabilities, Dr S. There is unanimous praise for the quality of the medical care provided to R and the commitment of all those who have a part in looking after him. Dr S believes that R's condition is deteriorating neurologically and physically. He is frail and weighs only 5 stone. He suffers from recurrent chest infections, severe constipation, bleeding from ulceration of the oesophagus, epileptic fits, dehydration and under-nutrition. In 1995 he was admitted to hospital on five occasions. The manager of the residential home says: 'I have never worked with anybody as physically or mentally handicapped as R.' After the fifth distressing hospital admission, in September 1995, Dr S, the consultant responsible for his medical care, came to the conclusion which she expressed in her affidavit:

> To hospitalise R if he had another life-threatening crisis would, in my clinical judgment, be nothing more than striving officiously to keep him alive for no gain to him. In my opinion, this is tantamount to a failing against a basic duty of humanity. Indeed, at the last few admissions to hospital, I have had real concern as to whether it was ethical to treat him actively. That said, I would never withhold treatment against the wishes of his parents. In summary, taking R's best interests into account and whilst taking into account the basic premise of the sanctity of human life, it is in my judgment unquestionably in

R's best interests to allow nature to take its course next time he has a life-threatening crisis and to allow him to die with some comfort and dignity. That would relieve him of physical, mental and emotional suffering.

In March 1993 the British Medical Association and the Royal College of Nursing published a joint statement entitled 'Cardio-Pulmonary Resuscitation: A Statement from the R.C.N. and the B.M.A.'. The introduction reads:

Cardio-Pulmonary Resuscitation (C.P.R.) can be attempted on any individual in whom cardiac or respiratory function ceases. Such events are inevitable as part of dying and thus C.P.R. can theoretically be used on every individual prior to death. It is therefore essential to identify patients for whom Cardio-Pulmonary arrest represents a terminal event in their illness and in whom C.P.R. is inappropriate.

Under the heading 'Background' appears the following:

Do not resuscitate (D.N.R.) orders may be a potent source of misunderstanding and dissent amongst doctors, nurses and others involved in the care of patients. Many of the problems in this difficult area would be avoided if communication and explanation of the decision were improved.

A later paragraph in the statement says:

in a survey, the Royal College of Nursing found that most Health Authorities and Health Boards have taken steps to ensure that appropriate health workers are proficient in C.P.R. The problem of who should be resuscitated has not been addressed and several authorities stated they would welcome guidance. The factors surrounding a decision whether or not to initiate C.P.R. involve complex clinical considerations and emotional issues. The decision for the case of one patient may be inappropriate in a superficially similar case.

These guidelines, therefore, should be viewed as a framework, providing basic principles within which decisions regarding local policies on CPR may be formulated. Further assistance for doctors and nurses, where individual problems arise, can be obtained from their respective professional organisations.

Guidelines
The guidelines state:

It is appropriate to consider a do-not-resuscitate (D.N.R.) decision in the following circumstances: (a) where the patient's condition indicates that effective cardio-pulmonary resuscitation (C.P.R.) is unlikely to be successful. (b) where C.P.R. is not in accord with the recorded sustained wishes of the patient who is mentally competent. (c) where successful C.P.R. is likely to be followed by a lengthened quality of the life which would not be acceptable to the patient.
  2. Where a D.N.R. order has not been made and the express wishes of the patient are unknown, resuscitation should be initiated if cardiac or pulmonary arrest occurs. Anyone initiating C.P.R. in such circumstances, should be supported by their senior and medical nursing colleagues.
  3. The overall responsibility for a D.N.R. decision rests with the consultant in charge of the patient's care. This should be made after appropriate consultation and consideration of all aspects of the patients condition. The perspectives of other members of the medical and nursing team, the patient, and with due regard to patient confidentiality, the patient's relatives or close friends, may all be valuable in forming the consultant's decision.
  5. Although responsibility for C.P.R. policy rests with the consultant, he or she should be prepared always to discuss the decision for an individual patient with other health professionals involved in the patient's care.

Paragraph 9 states:

when the basis for a D.N.R. order is the absence of any likely medical benefit, discussion with the patient, or others close to the patient, should aim at securing an understanding and acceptance of the clinical decision which has been reached. If a D.N.R. decision is based on quality of life considerations, the views of the patient where these can be ascertained are particularly important. If the patient cannot express a view, the opinion of others close to the patient may be sought regarding the patient's best interests.

In December 1993 the NHS Trust in question published its own version of the statement issued jointly by the BMA and the RCN. Its wording was slightly different and, in particular, in para 2(c) used the phrase 'because of unacceptable quality of life'. That differed slightly from the wording of the joint BMA/RCN guidance, which referred to 'the length and quality of life which would not be acceptable to the patient'. However, the document issued by this NHS Trust made it clear in the first paragraph on p 2 that, 'the overall responsibility for such a D.N.R. decision rests with the consultant in charge of the patient's care. This should be made after appropriate consultation and consideration of all aspects of the patient's condition.'

Following the patient R's fifth discharge from hospital in September 1995, Dr S discussed the position with his parents. They agreed that if, in the future, R should suffer a life-threatening condition involving a cardiac arrest, he should not be subjected to cardio-pulmonary resuscitation. Dr S, and all the other medical witnesses who have given evidence to this court, have made it clear that it would be a dangerous operation, having regard to the physical frailty of R and the risk of enhanced brain damage in any event. Accordingly, on 22 September 1995, Dr S signed an NHS trust direction headed 'Do not resuscitate', giving the name of R and his date of birth, followed by these words: 'it is agreed that cardio-pulmonary resuscitation is not to be given to the above-named person.' Under the heading 'Next of kin', the mother's signature appears, then the consultant's signature and also the signature of the home manager. It should be made quite plain that that step was taken by Dr S with the full support of R's parents and that they have maintained their consistent support for the course which she took in issuing that notice.

However, certain members of the instructor staff at the day care centre which R attended became concerned when they learned of the existence of this notice. They made their concerns known to Dr S and there was a staff meeting on 4 October 1995 with Dr S, at which the concerns of the day care centre staff were made known. The day care centre staff did not agree that the quality of R's life was 'unacceptable'. It would appear from the document headed 'Minutes of the Meeting held on 4 October 1995' that there was a degree of confusion in the mind of the author of this document as to the effect of the DNR notice. The minute refers to 'a no treatment policy'. Dr S has made it quite plain that it is not her wish or the wish of the NHS trust that there should be a 'no treatment policy'. Indeed, R is receiving treatment and will continue to receive treatment. The DNR notice referred only to the question of cardio-pulmonary resuscitation (CPR). In fact, the accuracy of the contents of the document headed 'Minutes of the Meeting' is questioned both by Dr S and the manager of the residential home, who disagree with certain passages. As a result of the concern expressed by the care centre staff, one of their number, on their behalf, arranged for an application for leave to apply for judicial review to be issued on behalf of R by a 'next friend', who was an employee of the Disability Law Service, acting as a conduit for information provided by the social workers involved in the day care of the applicant. The notice of application for leave was issued on 7 February 1996, and it sought an order of certiorari to quash what was stated to be 'a decision of the NHS trust (the respondent) to apply 'its do not resuscitate policy' to the applicant, and a decision to apply 'a no treatment policy' in or around September 1995'. The basis of the application was stated to be that the respondent's DNR policy and its 'no treatment policy' are irrational and unlawful, in that they permit medical treatment to be withheld on the basis of an assessment of a patient's quality of life. On 8 February 1996 the NHS trust issued an originating summons in the Family Division of the High Court, seeking a declaration that, despite the inability of the first defendant (R) to give a valid consent, and in circumstances where he requires treatment by means of cardio-pulmonary resuscitation or develops a potentially life-threatening condition, it shall be lawful and in R's best interests for the plaintiff and or the responsible medical practitioners: (a) to withhold such life-sustaining treatment and medical support measures designed to keep the first defendant alive in his existing catastrophically brain damaged state, including: (i) resuscitation and ventilation; (ii) nutrition and hydration by artificial means; and (iii) the administration of antibiotics; and (b) to furnish such treatment and nursing care as may be appropriate to ensure that R suffers the least distress and retains the greatest dignity until such time as his life comes to an end.

On 9 February 1996 McCullough J in the Queen's Bench Division granted leave to apply for judicial review and referred the application to a judge of the Family Division to be heard together with the originating summons. On 19 February, at a directions hearing, it was ordered that the application for judicial review should be adjourned, with liberty to restore following the disposal of the originating summons, which specifically raised the lawfulness of the application of a 'do not resuscitate' policy to R. The Official Solicitor was appointed to act as the guardian ad litem of R in these proceedings. At this hearing the court has accordingly proceeded to hear the originating summons. The summons as originally issued has been amended and the relief now sought is more restricted than that originally sought. It has further been made clear that the NHS trust, the plaintiff in the present proceedings, has amended its own 'do not resuscitate' policy. It now relies strictly upon the policy as stated in the joint BMA/RCN statement. Moreover, it has been made abundantly clear during this hearing that there is not now, and never has been, a 'do not treat' policy. The trust seeks declarations that it shall be lawful and in the patient's best interests for the trust and/or the responsible medical practitioners having the responsibility at the time for the patient's treatment and care: (a) to perform a proposed gastrostomy; (b) to withhold cardio-pulmonary resuscitation of the patient; and (c) to withhold the administration of antibiotics in the event of the patient developing a potentially life-threatening infection which would otherwise call for the administration of antibiotics but only if, immediately prior to withholding the same: (i) the Trust is so advised both by the general medical practitioner and by the consultant psychiatrist having the responsibility at the time for the patient's treatment and care; and (ii) one or other or both of the parents first give their consent thereto; and (d) generally to furnish such treatment and nursing care as may from time to time be appropriate to ensure that the patient suffers the least distress and retains the greatest dignity.

The trust no longer seeks a declaration that it shall be lawful to withhold such life-sustaining treatment and medical support measures designed to keep the patient alive in his existing catastrophically brain damaged state *including nutrition and hydration by artificial means.* The medical evidence now adduced to the court makes it clear that the parties all agree that it is in R's interests that a gastrostomy should be performed and, accordingly, that it would be premature, in the light of that decision, for the question of withdrawing artificial nutrition/ hydration to be considered at this stage. This part of the originating summons is therefore the subject of an application that it should be adjourned generally, with liberty to restore. That course is proposed by the trust and is agreed to by the Official Solicitor on behalf of the patient and his parents and, accordingly, I proposed to adjourn that particular part of the application on the terms indicated. In the result, the court is now effectively considering only an application that it shall be lawful to withhold cardio-pulmonary resuscitation of the patient and, further, to withhold the administration of antibiotics in the event of the patient developing a potentially life-threatening infection which would otherwise call for the administration of antibiotics upon the conditions which I have already indicated.

It is apparent, therefore, that, as these proceedings have developed, the orders sought are somewhat more restricted than those originally envisaged. Furthermore, the court now has before it an extensive body of wholly independent expert opinion, which focuses on the needs and interests of the patient and which was not available when the judicial review proceedings were launched at the beginning of February 1996. The trust has now decided to perform a gastrostomy. A date at the beginning of May has been arranged for this to take place. As I have already indicated, in the light of this proposal it would be inappropriate for the court to consider at this stage the question of the possible withdrawal of artificial nutrition or hydration. That aspect of the originating application will therefore be adjourned generally. Accordingly, the hearing has been principally concerned with the withholding of cardio-pulmonary resuscitation in the event of the patient suffering a cardiac arrest. Dr Andrews points out that a 'do not resuscitate' policy is a well-recognised procedure in health care. He draws attention to the joint statement of the British Medical Association and the Royal College of Nurses to which I have already referred. I reiterate that the three guidelines under which such a policy would be appropriate are stated in that document to be: (a) where the patient's condition indicates that effective cardio-pulmonary resuscitation (CPR) is unlikely to be successful; (b) where CPR is not in accord with the recorded sustained wishes of the patient who is mentally competent; and (c) where successful CPR is likely to be followed by a length and quality of life which would not be acceptable to the patient.

He points out that (b) and (c) involve the views of the patient and therefore are not appropriate to this particular situation. It is (a), where the guideline deals with the effectiveness of CPR, which is particularly relevant in the present case. Dr Andrews said that, even in hospital settings, on average only about 13% of patients receiving CPR survive to discharge. In a residential home, without medical staff present, the chances of a successful resuscitation would be almost nil. There would also be a very real risk in the case of someone with deformities of the kind which the patient R has of his receiving injuries, such as broken ribs, from the procedure. Dr Andrews, gave it as his considered opinion that, in the light of the extremely small potential for success and the distress which injuries would cause, it would be wholly inappropriate to give this treatment to R. accordingly, a 'do not resuscitate' policy is, in his view, appropriate, based on the likely futility of attempts to resuscitate R successfully in a residential setting.

All the medical witnesses in this case support the view that CPR would not be appropriate in R's case. Dr S, the responsible consultant, has expressed that view very firmly. Dr Greenwood, a consultant neurologist, has also expressed that view. Dr John Morgan, a consultant psychiatrist for people with learning disability, stated in his report: 'There is a danger that if cardio-pulmonary resuscitation were attempted, he might suffer further brain damage, and his body is relatively fragile and excessive pressure or enthusiasm might lead to damage to his ribs or more serious complications.'

Dr Piachaud has also expressed the opinion that CPR would not be appropriate in this patient's case. The Official Solicitor, on behalf of R, has made a report, and counsel on his behalf has made it clear that the Official Solicitor, in the light of his own expert's opinions and all the other evidence before the court, supports the view that the procedure of CPR and ventilation would be inappropriate in this patient's case.

So far as the withholding of antibiotics is concerned, Dr Andrews stated that this is a matter which can only properly be decided at the time when a potentially life-threatening situation from infection arises. There should not be, as it were, a global 'do not treat' policy. The plaintiff trust has indicated that it is content to accept that position. The decision as to the withholding of the administration of antibiotics in a potentially life-threatening situation is a matter fully within the responsibility of the consultant having the responsibility for treating the patient. It is a matter which should be considered in conjunction with the general practitioner and, furthermore, in the case of R, with his parents. The Official Solicitor submits that it would be appropriate for the court at this stage to make a declaration that it would be lawful to withhold the administration of antibiotics in the event of the patient developing a potentially life-threatening infection, which would otherwise call for the administration of antibiotics, but only if immediately prior to withholding the same: (a) the trust is so advised both by the general medical practitioner and by the consultant psychiatrist having the responsibility at the time of the patient's treatment and care, and (b) one or other or both of the parents first give their consent thereto. Such a declaration would recognise the ultimate and effective clinical responsibility of the consultant having responsibility at the time for the patient's treatment and care. A declaration in these terms would be a modification of the declaration which was initially sought in the originating summons.

In this case there is no question of the court being asked to approve a course aimed at terminating life or accelerating death. The court is concerned with circumstances in which steps should not be taken to prolong life. The facts are very different from those in the case of *Airedale NHS Trust v Bland* (1993) 12 BMLR 64, [1993] AC 789. The principle of law to be applied in this case is that of the 'best interests of the patient', as made clear by the Court of Appeal in *Re J (a minor) (wardship: medical treatment)* (1990) 6 BMLR 25, [1991] Fam 33…

Although this present case concerns a handicapped adult and not a child who is a ward of court, the overriding principle, in my judgment, is the same. The operative words in this passage from the judgment of Lord Taylor to which I have referred are 'so afflicted as to be intolerable'. The extensive medical evidence in this case is unanimous in concluding that it would not be in the best interests of R to subject him to cardio-pulmonary resuscitation in the event of his suffering a cardiac arrest. The conclusions of the doctors are supported by R's parents. The Official Solicitor on behalf of R agrees that this is an appropriate course to be followed. He submits that, in the context of the facts of this case, it would be appropriate for the court to make a declaration that it shall be lawful as being in the patient's best interests for the trust and/or the responsible medical practitioners having the responsibility at the time for the patient's treatment and care to withhold cardio-pulmonary resuscitation of the patient. I agree that this declaration should be made.

The withholding in the future of the administration of antibiotics in the event of the patient developing a potentially life-threatening infection which would otherwise call for the administration of antibiotics is a decision which can only be taken at the time by the patient's responsible medical practitioners in the light of the prevailing circumstances. This requires a clinical judgment in the light of the prevailing circumstances…

Mr Munby…submits that, in the light of the medical evidence and all the factual material in this case, it would be appropriate for the court to make a declaration in terms which would not require a future further application to the court. He suggests a declaration in the following terms:

> To withhold the administration of antibiotics in the event of the patient developing a potentially life threatening infection which would otherwise call for the administration of antibiotics but only if immediately prior to withholding the same: (a) the trust is so advised both by the general medical practitioner and by the consultant psychiatrist having the responsibility at the time for the patient's treatment and care; and (b) one or other or both of the parents first give their consent thereto.

Counsel for the plaintiff trust agrees with that proposal. In my judgment, it would reflect the reality of the situation. The decision to withhold antibiotics in a given situation falls fairly and squarely within the clinical responsibility of the consultant treating the patient. I am quite satisfied on the evidence in this case that the consultant and the general practitioner having the responsibility for R's treatment do have R's best interests in mind. They are fully supported by the parents. I am accordingly satisfied that it would be in the best interests of R to make a declaration in these terms.

It is abundantly clear that the Official Solicitor has ensured that all relevant matters of fact and law have been fully and properly investigated and scrutinised in this tragic case. He has submitted a draft of proposed declarations to the court which has the approval of counsel for the plaintiffs and of the parents. I am satisfied that the court should order and declare that, notwithstanding (1) that the patient is unable to give a valid consent thereto; and (2) if such be the case, that no further order of the court shall have been obtained in the meantime, it shall be lawful as being in the patient's best interests for the trust and/or the responsible medical practitioners having the responsibility at the time for the patient's treatment and care: (a) to perform the said proposed gastrostomy; (b) to withhold cardio-pulmonary resuscitation of the patient; (c) to withhold the administration of antibiotics in the event of the patient developing a potentially life-threatening infection which would otherwise call for the administration of antibiotics but only if, immediately prior to withholding the same, (i) the trust is so advised both by the general medical practitioner and by the consultant psychiatrist having the responsibility at the time for the patient's treatment and care; and (ii) one or other or both of the parents first give their consent thereto; (d) generally to furnish such treatment and nursing care as may from time to time be appropriate to ensure that the patient suffers the least distress and retains the greatest dignity.

There are a number of important points raised by this case.

Importantly, the range of issues falling for decision by the court was much more narrow than when the case had first been launched. The initial approach of seeking a 'global' order stipulating 'do not treat' was accepted as inappropriate. Instead, specific treatment options were evaluated.

As you will have seen, initially it was proposed to withhold artificial nutrition and hydration, this was not pursued. The first question for the court concerned the lawfulness of the proposed DNR order. The court was told in evidence that such orders are a regular feature of medical care and are made in accordance with Guidelines jointly agreed in 1993 between the British Medical Association and the Royal College of Nursing (for the most recent guidance, see BMA/RCN *Decisions Relating to Cardiopulmonary Resuscitation* (1999)). The particular Hospital Trust modified these Guidelines in the instant case, before subsequently reverting to strict adherence to them. The Guidelines contemplate that '[i]t is appropriate to consider' a DNR order in three sets of circumstances. It was agreed that the two of the three did not apply, since they contemplated taking account of the patient's views. Thus, the court chose to consider the applicability of the other ground: 'that effective cardio-pulmonary resuscitation is unlikely to be successful.'

This is the first occasion on which a court has been asked to decide on the place of DNRs in medical law (see also, *R v Portsmouth Hospitals NHS Trust, ex p Glass* (1999) 50 BMLR 269 (CA)). It is important, therefore, to notice what the case did not, as well as what it did, decide. The court placed great reliance on the Guidelines. When such professional guidance relates to what are, primarily technical questions, this is both understandable and desirable. When professional guidance goes beyond this, the weight to be accorded to it is necessarily dependent on the extent to which it properly reflects the existing law. Of the three circumstances identified in the Guidelines, the first refers to the patient's quality of life. Clearly, this is not a technical matter. It is justified, however, and thus may lawfully be followed, in that it contemplates the involvement of the patient: a DNR order may be considered 'where successful CPR is likely to be followed by a lengthened quality of life *which would not be acceptable to the patient*', (emphasis added). A second circumstance set out in the Guidelines refers to following 'the recorded sustained wishes of the patient'. This again is not a technical matter. It does, however accord with current law and is not, therefore, objectionable nor does it require any further judicial scrutiny.

The third circumstance and, as has been said, the one relied on in the instant case, is when 'the patient's condition indicates that effective CPR is unlikely to be successful'. This *is* a technical matter. It does not address the futility of the treatment (CPR) in quality of life terms, but in the pragmatic sense of will it in fact work. The court was persuaded on the evidence that the chances of successful CPR were slight. This, coupled with the evidence that attempts at CPR could, in fact, exacerbate the patient's already parlous condition, persuaded the court to find that the proposed DNR was lawful.

DNR orders of the kind in *Re R* do not contemplate nor do they purport to validate decisions as to whether or not to continue treatment, in circumstances in which, with the treatment the patient would survive but without it he would die. Such decisions, now part of medical law and practice, are, of course taken. They may not, however be taken under the guise of a DNR order. They must be taken openly, after due attention to the principles laid down by law.

By contrast, the judge noticed that only one of the Guidelines was relevant: the one concerning the effectiveness of the treatment. This did not warrant any consideration of quality of life. But, he then chose to take account of and purport to apply the leading case on quality of life, *Re J (a minor) (wardship: medical treatment)* (1990) 6 BMLR 25. With respect, this quite unnecessarily muddies the water as to the status of DNR orders. It introduces a perspective which is not contemplated in the Guidelines, which is unnecessary for their successful operation and which involves a wholly undesirable element of controversy. He refers to Taylor LJ's criterion in *Re J* that the life in question should be 'so afflicted as to be intolerable'. But, there is no real analysis of what this might mean and its application to the facts. Certainly, R was very severely disabled. But, as was conceded in the judgment, some of those who cared for R on a day-to-day basis did not regard the quality of his life as 'hopeless'. What Sir Stephen Brown P chose was to endorse the prevailing medical view. Arguably, he should have avoided questions of quality of life. In failing to do so, he added to the fear that consideration of a patient's 'best interests', vague enough and insubstantial in itself, means no more than agreeing with and endorsing the views of the attending doctors. Moreover, by virtue of this approach, DNR orders were wrongly characterised as falling into the black hole of 'best interests'.

Where 'quality of life' was relevant was in relation to the second question which was whether it would be lawful to withhold antibiotics in the event of the patient's contracting an infection. Now, this, in contrast to the DNR order, is clearly not a technical matter. It is, and was recognised to be, a quality of life decision: whether, in short, R's quality of life was such that treatment, otherwise necessary to preserve his life, should be withheld. As has just been said, therefore, it is a decision which must be taken openly, with due regard for legal principle. Unhappily, whereas Sir Stephen Brown P considered and purported to apply *Re J* in the context of the DNR order, where it was unnecessary and inappropriate, it barely got a look in when it came to withholding treatment. Instead, rather remarkably, he held that this was 'a decision which can only be taken at the time by the patient's responsible medical practitioners in the light of the prevailing circumstances'. With the greatest respect, this is unhelpful. Certainly, it is true that the doctors will have to make the actual clinical decision. This is indisputable but tells us nothing. Medical law is concerned with the principles which the doctors are obliged by law to take account of. This is a 'decision' for the court. It is simply not good enough to say that it must be taken 'in the light of prevailing circumstances'.

As we have seen, it is arguable whether R's quality of life was of the extreme nature seen in the neonate cases such as *Re B* and *Re J* that we saw earlier. Certainly, it was not a case of a patient with extremely limited interaction with the world (contrast *In Re the Matter of a Ward of Court* [1995] 2 ILRM 401 (IR Sup Ct) – patient 'very nearly' in PVS with minimal cognitive abilities; discussed by D Feenan 'A "Terrible Beauty", the Irish Supreme Court, and Dying' (1996) 3 European Journal of Health Law 29). A more extreme case, perhaps, occurred in Massachusetts.

Re Dinnerstein (1978) 380 NE 2d 134 (App Ct Mass)

Armstrong J:...The patient is a sixty-seven year old woman who suffers from a condition known as Alzheimer's disease. It is a degenerative disease of the brain of unknown origin, described as presenile dementia, and results in destruction of brain tissue and, consequently, deterioration in brain function. The condition is progressive and unremitting, leading in stages to disorientation, loss of memory, personality disorganisation, loss of intellectual function, and ultimate loss of all motor function. The disease typically leads to a vegetative or comatose condition and then to death. The course of the disease may be gradual or precipitous, averaging five to seven years. At this time medical science knows of no cure for the disease and no treatment which can slow or arrest its course. No medical breakthrough is anticipated.

The patient's condition was diagnosed as Alzheimer's disease in July 1975, although the initial symptoms of the disease were observed as early as 1972. She entered a nursing home in November 1975, where her (by that time) complete disorientation, frequent psychotic outbursts, and deteriorating ability to control elementary bodily functions made her dependent on intensive nursing care. In February, 1978, she suffered a massive stroke, which left her totally paralysed on her left side. At the present time she is confined to a hospital bed, in an essentially vegetative state, immobile, speechless, unable to swallow without choking, and barely able to cough. Her eyes occasionally open and from time to time appear to fix on or follow an object briefly; otherwise she appears to be unaware of her environment. She is fed through a naso-gastric tube, intravenous feeding having been abandoned because it came to cause her pain. It is probable that she is experiencing some discomfort from the naso-gastric tube, which can cause irritation, ulceration, and infection in her throat and esophageal tract, and which must be removed from time to time, and that procedure itself causes discomfort. She is catheterised and also, of course, requires bowel care. Apart from her Alzheimer's disease and paralysis, she suffers from high blood pressure which is difficult to control; there is risk in lowering it due to a construction in an artery leading to a kidney. She has a serious, life-threatening coronary artery disease, due to arteriosclerosis. Her condition is hopeless, but it is difficult to predict exactly when she will die. Her life expectancy is no more than a year, but she could go into cardiac or respiratory arrest at any time. One of these, or another stroke, is most likely to be the immediate cause of her death.

In this situation her attending physician has recommended that, when (and if) cardiac or respiratory arrest occurs, resuscitation efforts should not be undertaken. Such efforts typically involve the use of cardiac massage or chest compression and delivery of oxygen under compression through an endotracheal tube into the lungs. An electrocardiogram is connected to guide the efforts of the resuscitation team and to monitor the patient's progress. Various plastic tubes are usually inserted intravenously to supply medications or stimulants directly to the heart. Such medications may also be supplied by direct injection into the heart by means of a long needle. The defibrillator may be used, applying electric shock to the heart to induce contractions. A pacemaker, in the form of an electrical conducting wire, may be fed through a large blood vessel directly to the heart's surface to stimulate contractions and to regulate beat. These procedures, to be effective, must be initiated with a minimum delay as cerebral anoxia, due to a cutoff of oxygen to the brain, will normally produce irreversible brain damage within three to five minutes and total brain death within fifteen minutes. Many of these procedures are obviously highly intrusive, and some are violent in nature. The defibrillator, for example, causes violent (and painful) muscle contractions which, in a patient suffering (as this patient is) from osteoporosis, may cause fracture of vertebrae or other bones. Such fractures, in turn, cause pain, which may be extreme.

The patient's family, consisting of a son, who is a physician practising in New York City, and a daughter, with whom the patient lived prior to her admission to the nursing home in 1975, concur in the doctor's recommendation that resuscitation should not be attempted in the event of cardiac or respiratory arrest. They have joined with the doctor and the hospital in bringing the instant action for declaratory relief, asking for a determination that the doctor may enter a 'no-code' order [ie an order not to resuscitate] on the patient's medical record without judicial authorisation or, alternatively, if such authorisation is a legal prerequisite to the validity of a 'no-code' order, that that authorisation be given. The probate judge appointed a guardian *ad litem*, who has taken a position in opposition to the prayers of the complaint.

…This case does not offer a life-saving or life-prolonging treatment alternative within the meaning of the *Saikewicz* case. It presents a question peculiarly within the competence of the medical profession of what measures are appropriate to ease the imminent passing of an irreversibly, terminally ill patient in light of the patient's history and condition and the wishes of her family. That question is not one for judicial decision, but one for the attending physician, in keeping with the highest traditions of his profession, and subject to court review only to the extent that it may be contended that he has failed to exercise 'the degree of care and skill of the average qualified practitioner, taking into account the advances in the profession'.

The case is remanded to the Probate Court, where a judgment is to enter in accordance with the prayers of the complaint for declaratory relief, declaring that on the findings made by the judge the law does not prohibit a course of medical treatment which excludes attempts at resuscitation in the event of cardiac or respiratory arrest and that the validity of an order to that effect does not depend on prior judicial approval.

It should be noted that the patient's condition in *Dinnerstein* was extreme. She was not in what is sometimes called 'a happily demented stated'. Her medical condition had deteriorated considerably. Even if an English court would reach the same result applying a 'best interests' test, this would not give any support for treatment-limiting decisions in a less serious state. The law remains very hazy in the context of incompetent adults even though, as we have already stated, the principles (such that they are) reflect those in the baby cases. In some ways, the baby cases often produce 'cleaner' factual situations where the patient is demonstrably unaware or only minimally aware of his surroundings. The very immaturity of the patient means that developmentally they will have limited interaction with their environment. In younger children, as we saw in *Dawson*, this is less clear or simply is not so. Adult cases, by contrast, will often involve patients who interact with the world even if severely disabled, as did the patient in *Re R*. The judgment to withhold or withdraw treatment is then that much more problematical both in practice and in reaching a conclusion that theirs is a life 'not worth living'. The happily demented Alzheimer's patient is not within this category and the courts would no doubt say so. There would have to be extreme circumstances such as occurred in *Dinnerstein* to tempt the court to approve a treatment-limiting decision that would lead to death.

The lack of precision demonstrated in the cases coupled with the knowledge that a patient's life or death is at stake would undoubtedly give the English courts cause to pause. Indeed, as we saw earlier, some members of the House of Lords in *Bland* found the exercise so fraught with difficulty as not to be a proper matter for the judges. It was, they said, a matter for Parliament.

Lord Browne-Wilkinson: Where a case raises wholly new moral and social issues, in my judgment it is not for the judges to seek to develop new, all-embracing, principles of law in a way which reflects the individual judges' moral stance when society as a whole is substantially divided on the relevant moral issues. Moreover, it is not legitimate for a judge in reaching a view as to what is for the benefit of the one individual whose life is in issue to take into account the wider practical issues as to allocation of limited financial resources or the impact on third parties of altering the time at which death occurs.

For these reasons, it seems to me imperative that the moral, social and legal issues raised by this case should be considered by Parliament. The judges' function in this area of the law should be to apply the principles which society, through the democratic process, adopts, not to impose their standards on society. If Parliament fails to act, then judge-made law will of necessity through a gradual and uncertain process provide a legal answer to each new question as it arises. But in my judgment that is not the best way to proceed.

(See also Lord Mustill at 888 and 889.)

Before moving on, we should finally note one other issue in *Re R*. The Official Solicitor proposed to the court that there be included in the court's declaration the following: '...it shall be lawful [to withhold CPR and the administration of antibiotics...but only if immediately prior to withholding the same...one or other or both of the parents first give their consent thereto'. Why did the court incorporate this proposal into the declaration which was granted? To insist on parental consent, as a matter of law, explicitly purports to recognise that the parents have a right in law to a say in the treatment of an adult, including a right of veto over future treatment options. This seems entirely inconsistent with the law as generally understood. It may be that, as a matter of good clinical practice and out of concern for the life of their adult child, it is crucial to involve the parents. But this is a matter of ethics, not law. The law vests no authority in them. By stipulating that they consent, Sir Stephen Brown P introduces unnecessary confusion into the law.

II. Challenging 'quality of life'

Lord Goff and Lord Browne-Wilkinson in *Bland* expressly reserved their positions on cases such as *Re J* where balancing factors which touch upon quality of life are required of the court (at 870 and 884). Lord Mustill went further (at 891):

> **Lord Mustill:** The interest of the state in preserving the lives of its citizens is very strong, but it is not absolute. There are contrary interests, and sometimes these prevail; as witness the over-mastering effect of the patient's refusal of treatment, even where this makes death inevitable. It has been suggested, for example in *Re Quinlan* (1976) 70 NJ 10, that the balance may also be tipped, not by the weight of an opposing policy but by the attenuation of the interest in preserving life, where the 'quality' of the life is diminished by disease or incapacity. My Lords, I would firmly reject this argument. If correct it would validate active as well as passive euthanasia, and thus require a change in the law of murder. In any event whilst the fact that a patient is in great pain may give him or her a powerful motive for wanting to end it, to which in certain circumstances it is proper to accede, that is not at all the same as the proposition that because of incapacity or infirmity one life is intrinsically worth less than another. This is the first step on a very dangerous road indeed, and one which I am not willing to take.

And later (at 896):

> I have no doubt that the best interests of Anthony Bland no longer demand the continuance of his present care and treatment. This is not at all to say that I would reach the same conclusion in less extreme cases, where the glimmerings of awareness may give the patient an interest which cannot be regarded as null. The issues, both legal and ethical, will then be altogether more difficult. As Mr Munby has pointed out, in this part of the law the court has moved a long way in a short time. Every step forward requires the greatest caution.

Where does this leave the law as regards patients who are other than permanently insensate, ie not in a persistent vegetative state? We have seen both how the Family Division and the Court of Appeal have gone beyond *Bland* in cases such as *Re B*, *Re J* and *Re R*. In our view, despite the understandable caution of the judges, the House of Lords would endorse the law as expressed at least by Taylor LJ in *Re J*. That is that, if the circumstances of the patient were extreme enough, withholding or withdrawing treatment would be lawful. The court would, however, be anxious to insist on a very high threshold of 'intolerability'. Of course, this is perhaps easier to identify, as we have argued, in the case of a very severely disabled new born baby than it is in the case of a senile patient who falls ill. As regards the latter it may be that the anxieties expressed by the judges in *Bland* would mean that they would not contemplate the withholding or withdrawing of treatment.

C. CONCLUDING REMARK

There can be little doubt that the law relating to the treatment of the incompetent at the end of life is less than satisfactory. This should come as no surprise given the pace of technological development. As Lord Mustill put it in *Bland* (at 888): 'the law has been left behind by the rapid advances of medical technology' opening up a 'gap between old law and new medicine'. In the wake of the *Bland* decision the House of Lords in its legislative capacity set up a Select Committee to investigate the legal, ethical and social issues surrounding treatment decisions at the end of life. In the result, its Report published in 1994 was a missed opportunity to engage in a rigorous debate of the issues (see *Report of the Select Committee on Medical Ethics* (1993–94), HL–21, 2 vols). For a critical analysis, see L Gormally 'Walton, Davies, Boyd and the Legalization of Euthanasia' in J Keown (ed) *Euthanasia Examined* (1995) ch 10.

Chapter 18

Death and dead bodies

Death

A. INTRODUCTION

C Pallis and DH Hartley *ABC of Brain Stem Death* (2nd edn, 1996)

The need to reappraise death

A dead brain in a body with a still beating heart is one of the more macabre products of modern technology. During the past 40 years techniques have developed that can artificially maintain ventilation (through resort to ever more sophisticated equipment), circulation (by the user of pressor amines), appropriate nutrition (by the intravenous route), and elimination of waste products of metabolism (by dialysis) in a body whose brain has irreversibly ceased to function. Such cases began to appear in all countries as their intensive care facilities reached a certain standard. What we do when confronted with such circumstances raises important questions. Brain death has compelled doctors (and society as a whole) to re-evaluate assumptions that go back for millennia.

Brain death was well described as early as 1959. Renal transplantation was then in its infancy, whole body irradiation being the only means of modifying the immune response. It is important to emphasise this because some critics seem to believe that brain death was invented by neurologists, neurosurgeons, anaesthetists, or intensive care specialists to satisfy the demands of transplant surgeons. If transplantation were superseded tomorrow by better methods of treating end stage organ failure, well run intensive care units would still ensure the production of many brain dead people in many parts of the world.

Over half a million people die in Great Britain each year. Whether at home or in the general wards of hospitals, they "die their own death." No machines or elaborate interventions are involved. Their heart stops, and that is the beginning and end of it. But there is another group of people who have sustained acute, irreparable, structural brain damage as a result of head injury, massive stroke, or very severe cerebral anoxia. The brain damage in question has plunged them into the deepest coma, with permanent loss of the capacity to breathe spontaneously. But prompt action by doctors ensures that ventilation is taken over by a machine before the resulting anoxia can stop the heart…

Concepts and criteria

All talk of the criteria of death – and thereby all arguments about better criteria – must be related to some overall concept of what death means. When we consider death, the tests we carry out and the decisions we make should be logically derived from explicitly stated conceptual and philosophical premises. There can be no free-floating criteria, unrelated to such premises. The box lists several concepts that have prevailed from time to time or that are currently being discussed.

> **Concepts**
>
> - Entering certain monastic orders in the Middle Ages
> - The soul leaving the body
> - "Ashes to ashes; dust to dust"
> - Irreversible loss of the capacity for consciousness and of the capacity to breathe
> - Loss of personal identity (the "higher brain" formulation)

Esoteric concepts
In the Middle Ages, if one entered certain monastic orders one ceased to enjoy the limited rights and heavy obligations of the outside world. One would be deemed "dead" by civil society. The appropriate criterion for such a concept of death would presumably be a certificate from the father superior of the monastery confirming that one had entered it. Esoteric concepts would be met by esoteric criteria.

The departure of the soul from the body
The identification of death with the departure of the soul from the body was central to ancient Egyptian culture. It then formed the basis of both Hellenic and Judeo-Christian concepts of death and eventually of the Islamic concept. It would, however, be impossible to derive criteria of death from this concept because of the impossibility of ascertaining the anatomical locus of the "soul." In 1957 Pope Pius XII, speaking to an international congress of anaesthetists, raised the question of whether one should "continue the resuscitation process despite the fact that the soul may already have left the body." The determination of when that had occurred was left for physicians to decide.

Death (irreversible loss of function) of the whole organism
Some people have held that the surest notion of death is the biblical one: "Ashes to ashes, dust to dust." The appropriate criterion for such a concept would be putrefaction, but no one today would argue that this is necessary before a person can be pronounced dead. We all readily grasp the difference between "is this woman dead?" and "has every enzyme stopped working, in every cell of her body?" The controversy is between those who think of death as "dissolution of the organism as a whole" and those who insist that it can mean only the "dissolution of the whole organism". This is no philological quibble. It is well established that different tissues die (that is, irreversibly cease to function) at different rates after asystole.

Asked what they mean by death, most people will probably talk about the heart "having stopped for good". This is by far the commonest mechanism of death (and, until relatively recently, it was also a universal attribute of a cadaver). But is it really a concept of death? When asked whether a person is dead whose cardiac function has, for a while, been taken over by a machine, many people begin to realise that a beating heart is not an end in itself but a means to another end: the perfusion of the brain with oxygenated blood. This centrality of the brain has been unconsciously perceived by people with little or no knowledge of physiology: we have been hanging and decapitating for centuries.

Irreversible loss of the capacity for consciousness plus irreversible loss of the capacity to breathe
We consider human death to be a state in which there is irreversible loss of the capacity for consciousness combined with irreversible loss of the capacity to breathe spontaneously (and hence to maintain a spontaneous heart beat). Alone, neither be sufficient. Both are essentially brainstem functions (predominantly represented, incidentally, at different ends of the brainstem). The concept is, admittedly, a hybrid one, expressing philosophical, cultural, and physiological concerns. The loss of the capacity for consciousness can be thought of as a reformulation (in terms of modern neurophysiology) of the older cultural concept of the departure of the "conscious soul" from the body. In the same perspective, irreversible apnoea can also be thought of as the permanent loss of "the breath of life". This approach corresponds perhaps to an intermediate stage of current concerns, seeking to maintain a footing on both types of ground. Although seldom explicitly formulated, this view of death is, we believe, widely shared in the West. It is the implicit basis for British practice in diagnosing "brainstem death."

"Cognitive death" and other "higher brain" formulations
Some people, particularly in the United States, have gone further and proposed a concept of death that would equate it with the loss of personal identity or with the "irreversible loss of that which is essentially significant to the nature of man." "Cognitive death" is already being evaluated as part of the "next generation of problems." We are opposed to "higher brain" formulations of death because we fear they are the first step along a slippery slope. If one starts equating the loss of higher functions with death, then which higher functions? Damage to one hemisphere or to both? If to one hemisphere, the "verbalising" dominant one or to the "attentive" non-dominant one? One soon starts arguing frontal versus parietal lobes.

Over the past 100 years people have sought to "secularise their philosophical understanding of their nature" and have sought to find "more biological formulations of what it meant to be dead." When we strike these existential chords, however, the responses are likely to be implicitly philosophical. If we understand this, we will be more tolerant of the diversity of answers people will give when asked, "What is it that is so central to your humanity that when you lose it you are dead?"

Death: an event or a process?
In 1968 the 22nd World Medical Assembly in Sydney stated: "Death is a gradual process at the cellular level, with tissues varying in their ability to withstand deprivation of oxygen. But clinical interest lies not in the state of preservation of isolated cells but in the fate of a person. Here the point of death of the different cells and organs is not so important as the certainty that the process has become irreversible, whatever techniques of resuscitation may be employed." In thus defining death the delegates in Sydney were endorsing – whether they knew it or not – one of the options offered by the *Concise Oxford Dictionary*, which describes death both as "dying" (a process) and "being dead" (a state).

It has, of course, been thought for centuries that growth of the hair and nails continues after the heart has stopped. Surgeons discovered years ago that they could harvest skin 24 hours after irreversible asystole and transplant it. A bone graft or an arterial graft would "take" even if the tissue had been collected 48 hours after death. In the light of such observations the classic signs of death (permanent cessation of breathing and of the heartbeat) will be perceived rather differently: they will be seen as major and easily detectable events, triggering a final, rapid sequence of biological changes. They are the usual points of no return in the dissolution of the organism as a whole and proof positive that the process leading to death of the whole organism has indeed become irreversible.

Legal constraints and dictionary definitions have probably delayed acceptance of the notion of death as a process. A quarter of a century ago an editorial in a leading American journal talked of the "end point" of existence "which ought to be as clear and sharp as in a chemical titration." In fact the simultaneous destruction of all tissues – death as an event – is rare indeed. The sudden carbonisation of the whole body by a nuclear explosion is the only example that readily comes to mind.

In the heat of the public controversy about brain death in 1981 a limerick was written which summed up the simple wisdom that death is a process:

> In our graveyards with winter winds blowing
> There's a great deal of to-ing and fro-ing
> But can it be said
> That the buried are dead
> When their nails and their hair are still growing?

We think all cultures capable of asking such a question would answer it with an unequivocal "yes" whether the premises were true or not.

There are other points of no return. One type of event epitomises the fact that death may precede cessation of the heart beat: decapitation. Once the head has been severed from the neck the heart continues to beat for up to an hour. Is that person alive or dead? If those who hold that a person can be truly dead only when the heart has stopped believe that a decapitated person is still alive simply because parts of the heart are still beating, they have a concept of life so different from ours that we doubt if bridges could be built. The example given is one of *anatomical* decapitation. Brain death is *physiological* decapitation and usually occurs when the intracranial pressure has lastingly exceeded the arterial pressure. Nevertheless, the implications of the two types of decapitation are similar. They are that the death of the brain is the necessary and sufficient condition for the death of the individual person.

The persistent vegetative state, whole brain death, and death of the brainstem
About 25 years ago a picture of an unsuccessfully decapitated chicken appeared in a leading magazine. The forebrain had been amputated and lay on the ground. The brainstem was still in situ. The animal, still breathing, was photographed some time after the decapitation. Was it alive or dead?

In our opinion the animal must be considered alive so long as its brainstem is functioning. Let us extrapolate the argument to a child with hydranencephaly. There is a spinal cord, a brainstem, and perhaps some diencephalic structures but certainly no cerebral hemispheres. The cranial cavity is full of cerebrospinal fluid, transilluminates when a light is applied to it, and there is no detectable electroencephalographic activity. The child can breathe spontaneously, swallow, and grimace in response to painful stimuli. Its eyes are open. The heart can beat normally for many weeks. No culture would declare that child dead. This emphasises the centrality we instinctively allocate to persisting brainstem function, even in the absence of anything we would describe as cerebration.

These examples may help one grasp the essence of a much more common and important condition: the persistent vegetative state. This is a chronic condition, the result of either cerebral anoxia (which may devastate the cortical mantle of the brain) or of impact injury to the head (which may massively shear the subcortical white matter, disconnecting the cortex from underlying structures). Other pathological processes may also on occasion be responsible. Affected people, if adequately nursed, may survive for years. They open their eyes so that by definition they cannot be described as comatose. But, although awake, they show no behavioural evidence of awareness. Conjugate roving movements of the eye are common, orientating movements rare. The patients do not speak or initiate purposeful movement of their limbs. Abnormal motor responses to stimulation may often be seen. Like the hydranencephalic child, the patients grimace, swallow, and breath spontaneously. Their pupillary and corneal reflexes are usually preserved. They have a working brainstem but show no evidence of meaningful function above the level of the tentorium. Excellent reviews of the pathological basis of the persistent vegetative state and of the difficulties in determining its limits have been recently published.

We have described the persistent vegetative state to contrast it with brainstem death. Patients whose brainstems are dead are in deep irreversible coma. They show no sleep-wake sequences. Their brainstem reflexes cannot be elicited. They have irreversibly lost the capacity to breathe. Brainstem death is the physiological kernel of brain death, the anatomical substratum of its cardinal signs (apnoeic coma with absent brainstem reflexes), and the main determinant of its invariable cardiac prognosis: inevitable asystole. [A controversy] has developed in the United States between the vast majority who have accepted death as synonymous with "death of all structures above the foramen magnum"(so called "whole brain death") and others, mainly philosophers, suggesting that death of large parts of both cerebral hemispheres ("neocortical death," "cognitive death," "persistent vegetative state") might itself be enough to consider a patient dead. It also shows the shift of emphasis that has occurred in the United Kingdom from a concept of brain death as a state in which "all functions of the brain have permanently and irreversibly ceased" to another in which the brainstem is perceived as "the critical system of the critical system" and in which "permanent functional loss of the brainstem constitutes brain death."

Another controversy centres on whether physicians can identify death of the brainstem by exclusively clinical (non-instrumental) methods and about what flows from such an identification. When people engaged in one discussion are suddenly parachuted into one of the others communication is bound, for a while, to be difficult.

B. UNDERSTANDING DEATH

Robert Veatch *Death, Dying and the Biological Revolution* (revised edn, 1989)

Four separate levels in [the definition of death] debate must be distinguished. First, there is the purely formal analysis of the term *death*, an analysis that gives the structure and specifies the framework that must be given content. Second, there is the concept of death which attempts to fill the content of the formal definition. At this level the question is: What is so essentially significant about life that its loss is termed death? Third, there is the question of the locus of death: Where in the organism ought one to look to determine whether death has occurred? Fourth, one must ask the question of the criteria of death: What technical tests must be applied at the locus to determine if an individual is living or dead?

Serious mistakes have been made in slipping from one level of the debate to another and in presuming that expertise on one level necessarily implies expertise on another. These problems began to emerge early in the debate. They can be seen in the historically important Report of the Ad Hoc Committee of the Harvard Medical School to Examine the Definition of Brain Death entitled 'A Definition of Irreversible Coma'. The title suggests that the committee members intend simply to report empirical measures that are criteria for predicting an irreversible coma. Yet the name of the committee seems to point more to the question of locus. The committee was established to examine the death of the brain. The implication is that the empirical indications of irreversible coma are also indications of 'brain death'. We now know that to be mistaken even at the empirical level, but the committee's confusion were even more serious. In the first sentence of the report the committee members claim that their 'primary purpose is to define irreversible coma as a new criterion for death'. They have now shifted so that they are interested in 'death'. They must be presuming a philosophical concept of death – that a person in irreversible coma should be considered dead – but they neither argue this nor state it as a presumption.

Even the composition of the Harvard committee signals some uncertainty of purpose. If empirical criteria were the principal concern, the inclusion of non-scientists on the panel was strange. If the philosophical concept of death was the main concern, medically trained people were overrepresented. As it happened, the committee did not deal at all with the conceptual matter of what it really means to be dead, yet that was the important policy issue raised in the shift to a brain-orientated definition of death. The committee and its interpreters have confused the questions at different levels.

As for the formal analysis of the term 'death', Veatch (*op cit*) offers the following (p 17):

> A strictly formal definition of death might be the following: Death means a complete change in the status of a living entity characterised by the irreversible loss of those characteristics that are essentially significant to it.

He points out, however, that (p 17):

> Such a definition would apply equally well to a human being, a nonhuman animal, a plant, an organ, a cell, or even metaphorically to a society or to any temporally limited entity like a research project, a sports event, or a language. To define the death of a human being, we must recognise its essential human characteristics. It is quite inadequate to limit the discussion to the death of the heart or the brain.

1. The concept

Veatch (*op cit*) pp 19–30 approaches the issue of the concept of death as follows:

> To ask what is essentially significant to a human being is a philosophical question – a question of ethical and other values. Many features have been suggested to be the one that makes human beings unique – their opposable thumbs, their possession of rational souls, their ability to form cultures and manipulate symbol systems, their upright posture, their being created in the image of God, and so on. Any concept of death will depend directly upon how one evaluates these qualities. Four choices seem to me to cover the most plausible approaches.
>
> *Irreversible loss of flow of vital fluids*
> At first it would appear that the irreversible cessation of heart and lung activity would represent a simple and straightforward statement of the traditional understanding of the concept of death in Western culture. Yet upon reflection this cannot be. If patients permanently lose control of their lungs and are supported by mechanical respirators, they are still living persons as long as they continue to get oxygen. If modern technology produced an efficient, compact heart-lung machine capable of being carried on the back or in a pocket, people using such devices would not be considered dead, even though both heart and lungs were permanently non-functioning. Some might consider such a technological person an affront to human dignity; some might argue that such a device should never be connected to a human; but even they would, in all likelihood, agree that such people were alive…
>
> *Irreversible loss of the soul from the body*
> There is a long-standing tradition, sometimes called vitalism, that holds the essence of humans to be independent of the chemical reactions and electrical forces that account for the flow of the bodily fluids…
>
> The departure of the soul might seem by believers as occurring at about the time that the fluids stop flowing. But it would be a mistake to equate these two concepts of death, as according to the first fluid stops from natural, if unexplained, causes, and death means nothing more than that stopping of the flow, which is essential to being treated as alive. According to the second view, the fluid stops flowing at the time the soul departs, and it stops because the soul is no longer present. Here the essential thing is the loss of the soul, not the loss of the fluid flow.
>
> *The irreversible loss of the capacity for bodily integration*
> In the debate between those who held a traditional religious notion of the animating force of the soul and those who had the more naturalistic concept of the irreversible loss of the flow of bodily fluids, the trend to secularism and empiricism made the loss of fluid flow more and more the operative concept of death in society. But human intervention in the dying process through cardiac pacemakers, respirators, intravenous medication and feeding, and extravenous purification of the blood has forced a sharper examination of the naturalistic concept of death. It is now possible to manipulate the dying process so that some parts of the body cease to function while other parts are maintained indefinitely…
>
> We now must consider whether concepts of death that focus on the flow of fluids or the departure of the soul are philosophically appropriate. The reason that the question arises as a practical matter is fear of a 'false positive' determination that human life is present. There are several ways of handling doubtful cases. Many would argue that when there is moral or philosophical doubt about whether someone is dead, it would be (morally) safer to act as if the individual were alive. An intermediate position is that we may follow a course of action

whose morality is in doubt if (and only if) it is more likely to be than not. Another position, called probabilism, offers the most leeway, holding that a 'probable opinion' may be followed even though the contrary opinion is also probable or even more probable. In the case under consideration, the probabilist could consider the individual dead even though moral doubt, even perhaps serious doubt, remained. Holders of the more rigorous positions would argue that we should take the morally safer course and consider the person alive even though the heart, lungs, and fluid flow had permanently stopped functioning.

Even the probabilist, however, traditionally has placed restrictions on legitimising actions supported by a probable opinion, for instance, when a life may be saved by taking one of the probable courses of action. This is clearly the sort of case involved in trying to decide whether to treat an individual as dead.

Thus, when modifying our traditional concept of death to pronounce dead some individual who would under older concepts be considered alive (that is, those with heart and lung but no brain function), the problem of moral doubt must be resolved … [T]he most plausible [solution is] to treat the situation as one of perplexed conscience. There are two relevant and important moral principles at stake: preservation of an individual life and preservation of the dignity of an individual by being able to distinguish a dead person from a living one. The introduction of a moral obligation to treat the dead as dead leaves one perplexed. It creates moral pressures in each direction. The defenders of the older concepts, which may lead to false pronouncements of living, must defend their action as well. It seems to me that only when such positive moral pressure is introduced on both sides of the argument can we plausibly overcome the claim that we must take the morally safer course. We must consider that it may be not only right to call persons dead, but also wrong to call them alive. This will still mean minimising the life-saving exception, but at least at this point there will be a positive moral argument for doing so. It is, thus, quite difficult to justify any divergence from the older, more traditional concepts of death, but the case for a neurologically centred concept can be made.

At first it would appear that the irreversible loss of brain activity is the concept of death held by those no longer satisfied with the vitalistic concept of the departure of the soul or the animalistic concept of the irreversible cessation of fluid flow. This is why the name *brain death* is frequently, if ambiguously, given to the new proposals, but the term is unfortunate for two reasons.

First, as we have seen, it is not the heart and lungs as such that are essentially significant but rather the vital function – the flow of liquids – that we believe according to the best empirical human physiology to be associated with these organs. An 'artificial brain' is not possible at present, but a walking, talking, thinking individual who had one would certainly be considered living. It is not the collection of physical tissues called the brain, but rather their functions – consciousness; motor control; sensory feeling; ability to reason; control over bodily functions including respiration and circulation; major integrating reflexes controlling blood pressure, ion levels and pupil size; and so forth – that are given essential significance by those who advocate adoption of a new concept of death or clarification of the old one. In short they see the body's capacity for integrating its functions as the essentially significant indication of life. Although there are occasional suggestions that it is the anatomical structure of the brain that is important, now almost any one arguing for a brain-orientated definition of death will accept that it is not technically the death of the brain that is critical, but the irreversible loss of the functions normally carried on by the brain.

Second, as I suggested earlier, we are not interested in the death of particular cells, organs, or organ systems, but in the death of the person as a whole – the point at which the person as a whole undergoes a quantum change through the loss of characteristics held to be essentially significant – and so terms such as brain death or heart death should be avoided. At the public policy level, this has practical consequences. A statute adopted in Kansas in 1970 specifically referred to 'alternative definitions of death' and said that they are 'to be used for all purposes in this state …' According to this language, which resulted from talking of brain and heart death, a person in Kansas could simultaneously be dead according to one definition and alive according to another. When a distinction must be made, it should be made directly on the basis of the philosophical significance of the functions mentioned above rather than on the importance of the tissue collection called the brain. For purposes of simplicity I shall use the phrase *the capacity for bodily integration* to refer to the total list of integrating mechanisms possessed by the body. A case for these mechanisms being the ones that are essential to humanness can indeed be made. Humans are more than the flowing of liquids. They are complex, integrated organisms with capacities for internal regulation. With and only with these integrating mechanisms is homo sapiens really human.

There appear to be two general aspects to this concept of what is essential significant: first, a capacity for integrating one's internal bodily environment (which is done for the most part unconsciously through highly complex homeostatic, feedback mechanisms) and, second, a capacity for integrating one's self, including one's body with the social environment through consciousness, which permits interaction with other persons. Together these offer a more profound understanding of the nature of the human than does the simple flow of bodily fluids. Whether it is a more profound concept than that which focuses simply on the presence or absence of the soul, it is clearly a very different one. The ultimate test between the two is that of meaningfulness and plausibility. For many in modern secular society, the concept of loss of capacity for bodily integration seems a more meaningful and accurate description of the essential significance of the human and of what is lost at the time of death. According to this view, when individuals lose all of these 'truly vital' capacities we should call them dead and behave accordingly …

The irreversible loss of the capacity for consciousness or social interaction
The fourth major alternative for a concept of death draws on the characteristics of the third concept and has often been confused with it. Henry Beecher offers a summary of what he considers to be essential to man's nature' … the individual's personality, his conscious life, his uniqueness, his capacity for remembering, judging, reasoning, acting, enjoying, worrying, and so on.'

Beecher goes on immediately to ask the anatomical question of locus. He concludes that these functions reside in the brain and that when the brain no longer functions, the individual is dead. What is remarkable is that Beecher's list, with the possible exception of 'uniqueness', is composed entirely of functions explicitly related to consciousness and the capacity to relate to one's social environment through interaction with others. All the functions that give the capacity to integrate one's internal bodily environment through unconscious, complex, homeostatic reflex mechanisms – respiration, circulation, and major integrating reflexes – are omitted. In fact, when asked what was essentially significant to man's living. Beecher replied simply, 'Consciousness.'

Thus a fourth possible concept of death is the irreversible loss of the capacity for mental or social functioning. If a group of hypothetical human beings had irreversibly lost the capacity for consciousness or social interaction, they would have lost the essential character of humanness and, according to this definition, they would be dead even if they had capacity for integration of bodily function.

Even if one moves to the so-called higher functions and away from the mere capacity to integrate bodily functions through reflex mechanisms, it is still not clear precisely what is ultimately valued as essential. We must have a more careful specification of mental or social function. Are these two capacities synonymous and, if not, what is the relationship between them? Before taking up that question, I must first make clear what is meant by capacity.

The meaning of capacity
Holders of this concept of death and related concepts of the human essence specifically do not say that individuals must be valued by others in order to be human. This would place life at the mercy of other human beings who may well be cruel or insensitive. Nor does this concept imply that the essence of humanness is the fact of social interaction with others, as this would also place a person at the mercy of others. The infant raised in complete isolation from other human contact would still be human, provided that the child retained the capacity for social interaction. This view of what is essentially significant to humanness makes no quantitative or qualitative judgments. It need not lead to the view that those who have more capacity for social integration are more human. The concepts of life and death are essentially bipolar, threshold concepts. People should either be treated as living or they should not …

The meaning of capacity
Holders of this concept of death and related concepts of the human essence specifically do not say that individuals must be valued by others in order to be human. This would place life at the mercy of other human beings who may well be cruel or insensitive. Nor does this concept imply that the essence of humanness is the factor of social interaction with others, as this would also place a person at the mercy of others. The infant raised in complete isolation from other human contact would still be human, provided that the child retained the capacity for social interaction. This view of what is essentially significant to humanness makes no quantitative or qualitative judgments. It need not lead to the view that those who have more capacity for social integration are more human. The concepts of life and death are essentially bipolar, threshold concepts. People should either be treated as living or they should not …

Specifying mental and social function
Precisely what are the functions considered to be ultimately significant to human life according to this concept? There are several possibilities.

Rationality. The capacity for rationality is one candidate. The human capacity for reasoning is so unique and important that some suggest it is the critical element in human nature. But certainly infants lack any such capacity, and they are considered living human beings.

Nor is possession of the potential for reasoning what is important. Including potential might resolve the problems of infants, but it does not explain why those who have no potential for rationality (such as the permanently backward psychotic or the senile individual) are considered to be humanly living in a real if not full sense and to be entitled to the protection of civil and moral law.

There is some confusion here because some philosophers are inclined to make a great deal out of labelling some human beings 'persons'. Their view seems to be that among those who are living beings some are persons. Persons are those who can reason, manipulate symbol systems, or otherwise partake in moral discourse. In this narrow, technical sense persons are seen by the proponents of this usage as morally in a different category from other living humans. For them a person apparently is a rights bearing human being by definition while some other humans are not.

I have consistently avoided this usage. Whenever I use the term *person*, it is synonymous with living human beings, and I leave open the question of whether all living humans are equally bearers of rights. In pressing the meaningfulness of the definition of death debate, however, I imply that it is plausible to think of all living human beings as standing in a moral position different from that of those who are dead. To wit, living human beings deserve to be treated differently from those who are dead, as subject to the moral and legal protections of the society such as those granted by the Constitution. They are individuals for whom death behaviours are not yet appropriate. That leaves entirely open the questions of whether there is some subgroup of living humans who have additional moral status and why they would be given that status, whether it be because they have the capacity to reason, to manipulate symbol systems, or to generate claims. It strikes me that it is hard to defend the position that some such subgroup exists, but that is not a problem for a discussion of the definitions of life and death.

Consciousness. Consciousness is a second candidate for that critical function that qualifies one to be treated as living. If the rationalist tradition is reflected in the previous notion, then the empiricist philosophical tradition seems to be represented in the emphasis on consciousness. What may be of central significance is the capacity for experience. This would include the infant and the individual who lacks the capacity for nationality, and it focuses attention on the capacity for sensory awareness, summarised as consciousness. Yet, this is a very individualistic understanding of the human's nature. It describes what is essentially significant to the human life without any reference to other human beings.

Personal identity. A third possibility has been proposed by philosophers Michael B Green and Daniel Wikler [(1980) 9(2) *Philosophy and Public Affairs* 105] and has been considered by the President's Commission. They argue that it is personal identity that is critical in deciding when a person is dead. Their position is that 'a given person ceases to exist with the destruction of whatever processes there are which normally underlie that person's psychological continuity and connectedness'.

They go on to argue against my position. They suggest that I am making an essentially moral argument for a so-called higher-brain conception of death. In this they are certainly correct. I have repeatedly claimed that all that is at stake in the public policy debate over the definition of death in determining when death behaviours are appropriate.

They claim that this is 'ontological gerrymandering', or arranging a concept of death to fit moral judgments. They argue against doing this by apparently reducing moral judgments to judgments about subjective value. Instead they want what they refer to as an ontological argument for the concept of death, which simply clarifies the concept without going on to reach moral conclusions. They cite as an example the possibility that some society valuing sports might find it congenial to classify the lame as dead. Since it is clearly absurd to do so, they apparently believe that they have demonstrated that the definition of death is not a matter of moral judgment.

Perhaps Green and Wikler have too modest a notion of the ontological status of moral judgments. I would analyse the problem of the lame as follows. The question being debated is a moral one: should lame persons be treated like the dead? The answer is clearly negative, and it is a moral answer. That however, does not make it less ontological. If one believes that moral judgments should be viewed as if they had ontological grounding in reality rather than being merely subjective expressions of a society's values, then one could say of the society that wanted to treat the lame as dead that they have made a mistake. Although they do not value the lame, they are wrong to the extent that they treat them as though they were dead. I would claim they are morally wrong just as Green and Wikler would claim they are conceptually wrong. This has nothing whatsoever to do with the empirical question of whether a society, in fact, values certain of its members. The concept of being dead, for me, can be reduced to being in a state in which one is appropriately treated the way dead people are treated.

Green and Wikler go on to argue that an individual is appropriately considered dead when personal identity (that is, psychological continuity and connectedness) is destroyed. In so far as being dead precipitates what I have called death behaviour, I am sure Green and Wikler are wrong in equating irreversible loss of personal identity and death. The test case is that of a (possibly hypothetical) individual – call him Jones – who suffers a severe head trauma that leaves him with permanent amnesia. These are, in fact, the kinds of cases Green and Wikler address in their article.

Suppose that Jones eventually recovers consciousness, but it is established that there is a total and irreversible break in psychological continuity and connectedness. He does recover, however, to the point where he can leave the hospital and, after substantial education in language and the skills of living, return to society. The question that Green and Wikler should have difficulty answering in a way that squares with intuitions is whether Jones has died and a new person (say, Smith) has been created. They must say that Jones has died and that a new and different person comes out of the hospital.

I have no problem if they want to claim that according to their theory of personal identity a new person with a new identity emerges, but that question is not really the same as debating whether an individual has died. I am only interested in whether any of the behaviours that society appropriately initiates upon death and would be appropriate for Jones. Would, we, for example, read his will and transfer his assets to his beneficiaries, leaving Smith destitute? Smith, a new and different person who is a stranger? I am convinced that Jones's relatives would have no problem remaining identified with him and that no traditional death behaviours would be appropriate. If Green and Wikler want to say that there is a destruction of personal identity, fine, but they surely cannot say that Jones has died. Anyone who did so would be confusing irreversible loss of personal identity with death.

Social interaction. Social interaction is a fourth candidate. The Western tradition in both its Judeo-Christian and Greek manifestations has long held that the human is essentially a social or political animal. Perhaps the human's capacity or potential for social interaction has such ultimate significance that its loss is considered death. The claim here is a radical one. It is not merely that human life would be boring or miserable lived in total isolation. It is rather that the essence of being human would be lost. I believe that anyone who stands in this tradition must ultimately maintain that it is the capacity for social interaction that is essential for being treated as living.

Is this in any sense different from the capacity for consciousness? Certainly it is conceptually different and places a very different emphasis on the human's essential role. Yet it may well be that the two functions, experience and social interaction, are completely coterminous. For all practical purposes it may make no difference whether we speak of the critical characteristic as capacity for consciousness, or social interaction. Thus even though it is crucial for a philosophical understanding of the human's nature to distinguish between these two functions, it may not be necessary for deciding when an individual has died. Thus, for our purposes we can say that the fourth concept of death is one in which the essential element that is lost is the capacity for consciousness or social interaction or both.

The concept presents one further problem. The Western tradition, which emphasises social interaction, also emphasises, as we have seen, the importance of the body. Consider the admittedly remote possibility that the electrical impulses of the brain could be transferred by recording devices onto magnetic computer tape. Would that tape together with some kind of minimum sensory device be a living human being and would erasure of the tape be considered murder. If the body is really essential, then we might well decide that such a creature would not be a living human being.

This may help explain why Jones, the victim of permanent amnesia, did not die but is still Jones. He still has the same body, to which his family would relate. As long as he did not have another person's identity (the sort of case envisioned in the brain transplant scenarios), I think no one would have difficulty treating the conscious individual with bodily continuity as the same individual. (Whether he is the same person or not is irrelevant). It also helps explain why we are so repulsed at the thought of a brain transplant. Assuming the consciousness of one person is merged with the body of another, a moral monster would be created, one having all of the components of living people, but containing the bodily trace of one person and the mental trace of another. If continuity of bodily and mental functions is critical then the merging of two produces a chimera. It is not merely the continuation of one person (the one who supplied the mental component) in a new body as some modern day gnostics would have us believe.

Where does this leave us? The earlier concepts of death – the irreversible loss of the soul and the irreversible stopping of the flow of vital body fluids – strike me as quite implausible. The soul as an independent nonphysical entity that is necessary and sufficient for a person to be considered alive is a relic from the era of dichotomised anthropologies. Animalistic fluid flow is simply too base a function to be the human essence. The capacity for bodily integration is more plausible, but I suspect it is attractive primarily because it includes those higher functions that we normally take to be central – consciousness, the ability to think and feel and relate to others. When the reflex networks that regulate such things as blood pressure and respiration are separated from the higher functions, I am led to conclude that it is the higher functions that are so essential that their loss ought to be taken as the death of the individual. While consciousness is certainly important, the human's social nature and embodiment seem to me to be the truly essential characteristics. I therefore believe that death is most appropriately thought of as the irreversible loss of the embodied capacity for social interaction.

As you have just seen Robert Veatch favours the 'irreversible loss of the embodied capacity for social interaction' as the most appropriate concept of death. David Lamb's analysis in his book *Death, Brain Death and Ethics* leads to a somewhat different conclusion.

D Lamb *Death, Brain Death and Ethics* (1985)

[W]hilst it is important to separate the sphere of the philosophical from the medical, it is equally important to stress that in any discussion of death neither party can afford to ignore the contributions of the other. Medical judgments are informed by philosophical presuppositions, whether or not the latter are explicitly formulated. The diagnosis of any illness may be clinical and empirical, but it would be lacking in significance if there were no underlying concepts of health and disease. Whether a patient is classified as dead or alive depends on our understanding of the relevant concept of death. According to Capron and Kass [(1972) 121 Univ Penn LR 87] ... the departure from the traditional concept of death manifest in the employment of brain-related criteria has brought these extra-medical concepts to the forefront of concern. Whilst traditional criteria, based on the cessation of cardio-respiratory functions, remained congruent with public conceptions of death, the phenomenon of death remained exclusively a matter of medical concern. But once medicine appeared to depart from traditional criteria for determining death, clarification of these extra-medical concepts of death became a matter of urgent concern for those responsible for the management of death. In view of the importance attached to a diagnosis of death in terms of the social, religious, political and ethical consequences, it is essential that this challenge be met and that the concept of death be made explicit. Furthermore, it is essential that criteria and tests for death should be logically derived from the appropriate concept of death.

The concept of death involves a philosophical judgment that a significant change has taken place, which presupposes an idea of the necessary conditions of life. These may range from the faculties involved in social interaction to the capacity to maintain bodily integration. Concepts of death may vary according to cultural patterns, religious traditions and scientific practice ...They may include such distinct formulations as 'the separation of soul and body', 'destruction of all physical structures', 'loss of the capacity for social interaction', 'irreversible loss of consciousness', 'loss of bodily integration', and many others. Related to these concepts are appropriate criteria, and tests to ascertain that the criteria have been met. It follows that any shift in the concept of death will necessitate corresponding changes in the criteria and tests for death. However, it does not follow that new criteria and tests mean that a change of concept has taken place. They may indicate nothing more than refinements of previous criteria and tests. For example, the employment of stethoscopes and cardiograms constituted technically better tests for death which did not entail any departure from the traditional cardio-respiratory-based concept of death.

Criteria for death only have meaning if they can be shown to be logically derived from the appropriate concept of death. It is therefore meaningless to use 'free-floating criteria' which are not derived from a clearly-determined concept of death ... Clarity concerning the concept of death provides a point of reference when deciding upon criteria, but some definitions of death are philosophically inadequate despite the fact that criteria can be logically derived from them ... Concepts of death, such as 'entering a monastery' or exclusion from the family, tribe or clan, are widely used and yield appropriate criteria. But they can refer to death only in a metaphorical sense.

The essential point here is that some concepts are more relevant than others. The requirement for a definition of death is a demand for the selection of a concept that is superior to others. For this reason vaguely formulated and indeterminate concepts should be eschewed. Thus a concept of death as 'the loss of that which is essentially significant to the nature of man' is unsatisfactory, since we can say that a patient has lost what is essentially significant but is still alive. This is because concepts like 'essentially significant' are by their very nature undetermined. For if by 'the loss of what is essentially significant' is meant 'the loss of the capacity for social interaction' then various interpretations are possible, from loss of libido to blindness, from senility to dementia, which will provide appropriate criteria. But the question of which, if any, of these states might best fulfil the requirements of the definition cannot be answered without further conceptual guidelines. On what grounds can it be inferred that 'massive brain damage' or 'loss of reproductive function' and so on amount to the 'loss of what is essentially significant'? Furthermore, all of the fore-mentioned criteria may be fulfilled when it is patently obvious that the patient is alive and, in some cases, that his situation is even reversible. If the 'loss of that which is essentially significant' is to have any meaning as a concept of death, then it must be framed so that it involves an irreversible state where the organism as a whole cannot function.

Only a concept which specifies the irreversible loss of specified functions (due to the destruction of their anatomical substratum) can avoid the anomalous situation where a patient is said to be alive according to one concept but dead according to another. The only wholly satisfactory concept of death is that which trumps other concepts of death in so far as it yields a diagnosis of death which is beyond dispute. It follows that any criterion which, when fulfilled, leaves it possible for the organism as a whole to continue to function is inadequate. It should not be possible to say that the person is still alive although the criterion has been met, nor to say that the person is dead although the criterion has not been met....

The concept of death that will be proposed and defended in this chapter is the '*irreversible loss of function of the organism as a whole*'. There is confusion between this and 'death of the whole organism'. This is often present – although unformulated – in arguments which maintain that the concept of death should be left undetermined, or that death is a process with no special point at which a non-arbitrary diagnosis can be factually ascertained.... Criteria for the 'death of the whole organism' could only be met by tests for putrefaction, since cellular life in certain tissues can continue long after it has ceased in others, and long past the point where the organism as a whole has ceased to function. However, putrefaction has never been seriously advanced as a definition of death by either physicians or philosophers. Consequently, the argument that the concept of death should remain undetermined has no place in a world where practical decisions regarding the criteria of death necessitate an acceptable concept. In contrast criteria for 'irreversible loss of function of the organism as a whole' is a biological concept which yields clinical criteria and tests. It presupposes the irreversible loss of the capacity for consciousness and the irreversible loss of the capacity to breathe, and hence sustain a spontaneous heartbeat. It supersedes ethical and religious-based concepts and its appropriate criterion is the death of the critical system as measured by tests for the irreversible cessation of brainstem function.

Failure to understand the relationship between the concept and criteria for death may lead to serious errors of judgment in practical matter. A patient in a vegetative state, it is argued, may meet a concept of death as 'a worthless existence' but, unless the individual's critical system is dead, it will not satisfy the concept of death formulated above as the 'irreversible loss of function of the organism as a whole'. The latter concept is currently employed in medical practice, if not explicitly formulated. It explains why an anencephalic infant would not be regarded as dead as long as its brainstem remained intact....

For the above reasons it has become commonplace in the literature on brain death to describe the concept of death as a philosophical matter and the development of diagnostic criteria as a task for medical expertise and to warn against conflating definitions of what death is with the problem of when death occurs. The philosophical analysis of death is held to identify what it is that the diagnostic criteria are supposed to determine....

Whilst this distinction is important, it is nevertheless equally important that it should not be drawn too rigidly. Philosophical issues do not exist in complete isolation from technical and scientific issues; they interact and interpenetrate. For this reason a more flexible distinction has been formulated by Bernat, Culver and Gert [(1981) 94(3) Annals of Int Med 389]...

> Providing a definition is primarily a philosophical task: the choice of the criteria is primarily medical: and the selection of tests to prove that the criterion is satisfied is solely a medical matter.
>
> This formulation can be illustrated as follows: suppose the concept of death were 'absence of fluid flow', then the criteria would be based on cessation of pulse, heartbeat and respiration, and could be determined by relatively straightforward empirical tests. If, however, the concept were the 'integrated functioning of the organism as a whole', one would have to decide which organ has decisive responsibility for this. If it is a matter of general agreement that the brain has this responsibility, then tests for measuring brain functions will be important. The formulation proposed by Bernat *et al* has the merit of maintaining the distinction between philosophical discourse regarding the concept of death and medical discourse. Yet it recognised that, whilst philosophical and practical issues can be distinguished at one level, they interact at another level. It is therefore important to be wary of attempts to settle – at the outset of any discussion – which kinds of problems belong exclusively to philosophy and which belong exclusively to medicine. Whilst Veatch's and Korein's [(1978) 315 Annals of NY Acad Sci 19] formulations correctly identify the concept of death as a philosophical issue and the criteria for death as a practical matter, the three-level distinction between concept, criteria and practical tests, which is proposed by Bernat *et al*, is preferable because it acknowledges the interaction between conceptual issues and the application of criteria in a practical context.

Whether we subscribe to the view of Veatch or Lamb, it is clear that we must look to the brain as the appropriate 'locus' (as Veatch puts it) and not to the heart and lungs. Further we must remind ourselves of Lamb's observation (at p 13) that: 'Only a concept which specifies the irreversible loss of specified functions (due to the destruction of their anatomical substratum) can avoid the anomalous situation where a patient is said to be alive according to one concept but dead according to another.' This entails that the relevant locus chosen must be that which is physiologically responsible for the functions deemed critical to the relevant concept of brain death.

2. The criteria

What we are concerned with here is the means of identifying the presence or absence of the relevant functions of the locus (ie the whole brain or a part thereof). If the appropriate concept of death is *loss of the capacity for social interaction* then the correct locus of death is the brain. The criterion will then be the permanent and irreversible loss of function of the *higher brain*.

The President's Commission for the Study of Ethical Problems in Medicine and Biomedical and Behavioral Research: 'Medical, Legal and Ethical Issues in the Determination of Death: *Defining Death*' (1981), criticises the criterion (pp 38 and 40):

The 'higher brain' formulations
When all brain processes cease, the patient loses two important sets of functions. One set encompasses the integrating and coordinating functions, carried out principally but not exclusively by the cerebellum and brainstem. The other set includes the psychological functions which make consciousness, thought, and feeling possible. These latter functions are located primarily but not exclusively in the cerebrum, especially the neocortex. The two 'higher brain' formulations of brain-orientated definitions of death discussed here are premised on the fact that loss of cerebral functions strips the patient of his psychological capacities and properties.

A patient whose brain has permanently stopped functioning will, by definition, have lost those brain functions which sponsor consciousness, feeling and thought. Thus the higher brain rationales support classifying as dead bodies which meet 'whole brain' standards ... The converse is not true, however. If there are parts of the brain which have no role in sponsoring consciousness, the higher brain formulation would regard their continued functioning as compatible with death.

The concepts: Philosophers and theologians have attempted to derive the attributes a living being must have to be a person. 'Personhood' consists of the complex of activities (or of capacities to engage in them) such as thinking, reasoning, feeling, human intercourse which make the human different from, or superior to, animals or things. One higher brain formulation would define death as the loss of what is essential to a person. Those advocating the personhood definition often relate these characteristics to brain functioning. Without brain activity, people are incapable of these essential activities. A breathing body, the argument goes, is not in itself a person; and, without functioning brains, patients are merely breathing bodies. Hence personhood ends when the brain suffers irreversible loss of function.

For other philosophers, a certain concept of 'personal identity' supports a brain-orientated definition of death. According to this argument, a patient literally ceases to exist as an individual when his or her brain ceases functioning, even if the patient's body is biologically alive. Actual decapitation creates a similar situation: the body might continue to function for a short time, but it would no longer be the 'same' person. The persistent identity of a person as an individual from one moment to the next is taken to be dependent on the continuation of certain mental processes which arise from brain functioning. When the brain processes cease (whether due to decapitation or to 'brain death') the person's identity also lapses. The mere continuation of biological activity in the body is irrelevant to the determination of death, it is argued, because after the brain has ceased functioning the body is no longer identical with the person.

Critique: Theoretical and practical objections to these arguments led the Commission to rely on them only as confirmatory of other views in formulating a definition of death. First, crucial to the personhood argument is acceptance of one particular concept of those things that are essential to being a person, while there is no general agreement on this very fundamental point among philosophers, much less physicians or the general public. Opinions about what is essential to personhood vary greatly from person to person in our society – to say nothing of intercultural variations.

The argument from personal identity does not rely on any particular conception of personhood, but it does require assent to a single solution to the philosophical problem of identity. Again, this problem has persisted for centuries despite the best attempts by philosophers to solve it. Regardless of the scholarly merits of the various philosophical solutions, their abstract technicality makes them less useful to public policy.

Further, applying either of these arguments in practice would give rise to additional important problems. Severely senile patients, for example, might not clearly be persons, let alone ones with continuing personal identities; the same might be true of the severely retarded. Any argument that classified these individuals as dead would not meet with public acceptance.

Equally problematic for the 'higher brain' formulations, patients in whom only the neocortex or subcortical areas have been damaged may return or regain spontaneous respiration and circulation. Karen Quinlan is a well-known example of a person who apparently suffered permanent damage to the higher centres of the brain but whose lower brain continues to function. Five years after being removed from the respirator that supported her breathing for nearly a year, she remains in a persistent vegetative state but with heart and lungs that function without mechanical assistance. Yet the implication of the personhood and personal identity arguments is that Karen Quinlan, who retains brainstem function and breathing spontaneously, is just as dead as a corpse in the traditional sense. The Commission rejects this conclusion and the further implication that such patients could be buried or otherwise treated as dead persons.

If, however, the preferred concept of death is *loss of bodily integration*, then the correct locus is again the brain. However, here the criterion will be the permanent and irreversible loss of functions of the brain.

For some, particularly in the United States, this 'permanent and irreversible loss of function of the *brain*' means: of the *usable brain*. The President's Commission (*op cit*) writes (pp 32 and 35–36):

> One characteristic of living things which is absent in the dead is the body's capacity to organize and regulate itself. In animals, the neural apparatus is the dominant locus of these functions. In higher animals and man, regulation of both maintenance of the internal environment (homeostasis) and interaction with the external environment occurs primarily within the cranium.
>
> External threats, such as heat or infection, or internal ones, such as liver failure or endogenous lung disease, can stress the body enough to overwhelm its ability to maintain organization and regulation. If the stress passes a certain level, the organism as a whole is defeated and death occurs.
>
> This process and its denouement are understood in two major ways. Although they are sometimes stated as alternative formulations of a 'whole brain definition' of death, they are actually mirror images of each other. The Commission has found them to be complementary; together they enrich one's understanding of the 'definition'. The first focuses on the integrated functioning of the body's major organ systems, while recognizing the centrality of the whole brain, since it is neither revivable nor replaceable. The other identifies the functioning of the whole brain as the hallmark of life because the brain is the regulator of the body's integration....
>
> A (more) significant criticism shares the view that life consists of the coordinated functioning of the various bodily systems, in which process the whole brain plays a crucial role. At the same time, it notes that in some adult patients lacking all brain functions it is possible through intensive support to achieve constant temperature, metabolism, waste disposal, blood pressure, and other conditions typical of living organisms and not found in dead ones. Even with extraordinary medical care, these functions cannot be sustained indefinitely – typically, no longer than seven days – but it is argued that this shows only that patients with nonfunctional brains are dying, not that they are dead. In this view, the respirator, drugs and other resources of the modern intensive-care unit collectively substitute for the lower brain, just as a pump used in cardiac surgery takes over the heart's function.
>
> This criticism rests, however, on a premise about the role of artificial support vis-a-vis brainstem which the Commission believes is mistaken or at best incomplete. While the respirator and its associated medical techniques do substitute for the functions of the intercostal muscles and the diaphragm, which without neuronal stimulation from the brain cannot function spontaneously, they cannot replace the myriad functions of the brainstem or of the rest of the brain. The startling contrast between bodies lacking *all* brain functions and patients with intact brainstems (despite severe neocortical damage) manifests this. The former lie with fixed pupils, motionless except for the chest movements produced by their respirators. The latter can not only breathe, metabolize, maintain temperature and blood pressure, and so forth, *on their own* but also sigh, yawn, track light with their eyes, and react to pain or reflex stimulation.
>
> It is not easy to discern precisely what it is about patients in this latter group that makes them alive while those in the other category are not. It is in part that in the case of the first category (ie, absence of all brain functions) when the mask created by the artificial medical support is stripped away what remains is not an integrated organism but 'merely a group of artificially maintained sub-systems'. Sometimes, of course, an artificial substitute can forge

the link that restores the organism as a whole to unified functioning. Heart or kidney transplants, kidney dialysis, or the iron lung used to replace physically-impaired breathing ability in a polio victim, for example, restore the integrated functioning of the organism as they replace the failed function of a part. Contrast such situations, however, with the hypothetical one of a decapitated body treated so as to prevent the outpouring of blood and to generate respiration: continuation of bodily functions in that case would not have restored the requisites of human life.

However in the United Kingdom a different view is taken. Pallis and Harley explain the English approach (pp 5–9, 17):

C Pallis and DH Harley *ABC of Brainstem Death* (2nd edn, 1996)

FROM BRAIN DEATH TO BRAINSTEM DEATH

The earliest references in the neurological literature to states resembling what would today be called "brain death" go back to the end of the nineteenth century, when Victor Horsley reported that patients suffering from depressed fractures of the skull, cerebral haemorrhage, and brain tumours "die from respiratory and not from cardiac failure, as is often supposed." Clinical observations had led him to conclude that in such cases "the respiration suddenly ceased, the heart continuing to beat." "Such" he wrote, "was the common end of practically all cases of pathological intracranial tension."

Four years later, in 1898, Sir Dyce Duckworth, honorary physician to HRH the Prince of Wales, read a paper (in French) to an international congress in Moscow in which he described "some cases of cerebral disease in which the function of respiration entirely ceases for some hours before that of the circulation." Two of his patients had temporosphenoidal abscesses, one had a cerebellar abscess, and one had a cerebral haemorrhage that had ruptured into the ventricles. All were comatose, and artificial respiration was resorted to in each case. Duckworth commented that "with respiratory cessation death had practically already begun." Harvey Cushing (1902) had finally emphasised the importance of such cases when he wrote "in death from a fatal increase in intracranial tension the arrest of respiration precedes that of the heart ... prompt surgical relief, with a wide opening of the calvarium, may save life even in desperate cases with pronounced medullary involvement." This early emphasis on the centrality of brainstem function (and in particular of apnoea) and on the importance of excluding reversible causes of such disturbances has a very modern resonance.

Despite these early references to what was probably brain death the condition was only to be described in some detail in 1959 when two French physicians identified a condition they called "coma dépassé" – literally, a state beyond coma. Twenty of their 23 patients were suffering from primary intracranial disorders and the three others from the cerebral effects of cardiorespiratory arrest. All the classic features of brain death are found in this early report. As well as obvious signs indicating death of both brain and spinal cord the authors mentioned poikilothermia, diabetes insipidus, a sustained hypotension which proved increasingly difficult to control with pressor amines, and a progressive acidosis, initially respiratory and later metabolic. Awed by the potential of resuscitatory techniques the authors described the condition created as both "une révélation et une rançon." The revelation related to the capacities of the contemporaneous intensive care technology and the ransom to what the maintenance of patients in this state imposed on others. Those affected were said to have the appearance of "corpses with a good volume pulse."

Articles published in the early 1960s already hinted that the cerebral circulation was "blocked" by raised intracranial pressure in most of these cases. These early publications also suggested the presence of cerebral oedema and intracranial hypertension. Within a few years "blocked" cerebral circulation was to be recognised as a very common concomitant of the condition.

Although major French contributions can be said to have heralded all modern discussions about brain death, it was the 1968 report of the ad hoc committee of Harvard Medical School which brought awareness of brain death to a much wider audience. Possibly influenced by the French, the committee initially used the term "irreversible coma" to describe the brain death syndrome; this has led to untold confusion as the words "irreversible coma" were later to be used to describe a very different clinical entity. A major multicentre project on brain death ... used the words "irreversible coma" to refer to "a vegetating state in which all functions attributed to the cerebrum are lost but certain vital functions such as respiration, temperature, and blood pressure regulation may be retained." This could have been a classic pre-emptive description of the persistent vegetative state. In view of these ambiguities the words "irreversible coma" are best avoided altogether.

The Harvard criteria demanded that the patient should be unreceptive and unresponsive, the most intensely painful stimuli evoking "no vocal or other response, not even a groan, withdrawal of a limb or quickening of respiration" *(sic)*. No movements were to occur during observation for one hour. Apnoea was to be confirmed by three minutes off the respirator (the centrality of apnoea, properly defined and tested for, had already been appreciated). The quantification in terms of Paco$_2$ levels reached during disconnection tests came only much later as a result of British experience. The Harvard criteria also required that there should be "no reflexes," the emphasis being on brainstem reflexes. A flat or isoelectric electroencephalogram at high gain was of "great confirmatory value." All the tests were to be repeated at least 24 hours later with no changes in the findings.

Harvard criteria (1968)

- Unreceptive and unresponsive
- No movements (observe for one hour)
- Apnoea (3 minutes off respirator)
- Absence of elicitable reflexes
- Isoelectric electroencephalogram "of great confirmatory value" (at 5 μv/mm)

All the above tests should be repeated at least 24 hours later, and there should be no change.

The report unambiguously proposed that this clinical state should be accepted as death, recognised the moral, ethical, religious, and legal implications, and boldly saw itself as preparing the way "for better insight into all these matters as well as for better law than is currently applicable." A year later Beecher, the chairman of the Harvard committee, stated that this body was "unanimous in its belief that an electroencephalogram was not essential to a diagnosis of irreversible coma," although it could provide "valuable supporting data."

Within three years of this radical yet human proposal two neurosurgeons from Minneapolis made the challenging suggestion that "in patients with known but irreparable intracranial lesions" irreversible damage to the brainstem was the "point of no return." The diagnosis "could be based on clinical judgment."

The Minnesota neurosurgeons had introduced the notion of aetiological preconditions. (Twenty of their 25 patients had sustained massive craniocerebral trauma, and the remaining five were suffering from other primary intracranial disorders.) They emphasised the importance of apnoea in the determination of brain death; in fact they insisted on four minutes of disconnection from the respirator.

(Alarmingly to us today, they did not mention pre-oxygenation *before* disconnection or diffusion oxygenation *during* the procedure.) They demanded absent brainstem reflexes, stated that the finding should not change for at least 12 hours, and emphasised that the electroencephalogram was not mandatory for the diagnosis. Their recommendations later became known as the Minnesota criteria and were to influence thinking and practice in the United Kingdom considerably. We are emphasising this because it has been suggested that doctors in the United Kingdom have been overcritical of much American work on this subject.

Minnesota criteria (1971)

- Known and irreparable intracranial lesion
- No spontaneous movement
- Apnoea (4 minutes)
- Absent brainstem reflexes
- All findings unchanged for at least 12 hours

Electroencephalography **not** mandatory

Since 1971 doctors have sought to identify the necessary and sufficient component (or physiological kernel) of brain death. It was soon realised that absent tendon reflexes (deemed essential in both the French and Harvard criteria) really implied loss of function of the spinal cord and that this was irrelevant in a diagnosis of brain death. The original insistence of the French on areflexia is strange for the works of Babinski contain accounts of knee jerks persisting for up to eight minutes after decapitation on the guillotine. Death of the brain and death of the whole nervous system are not the same thing. If the heart beat continues for long enough many patients with dead brains will recover tendon reflexes in their limbs or show pathological limb reflexes. The presence or absence of such reflexes, while providing useful clues as to whether the spinal cord is alive or dead, tell us nothing about whether the brainstem is functioning or not. Spinal areflexia is in fact the exception in brain death (established by the angiographic demonstration of a non-perfused brain).

The limb reflexes in brainstem death

- The tendon (stretch) reflexes of the limbs are segmental spinal reflexes
- Brainstem death may be complicated by spinal shock causing areflexia
- After an interval if the spinal cord is viable abnormal reflexes will appear below the level of a dead brainstem
- The reflex pattern in the limbs is of no prognostic value in cases of brainstem death

---

In retrospect it is interesting that insight into the importance of the brainstem had been achieved as early as 1964, seven years before the publication of the Minnesota criteria when Professor Keith Simpson, asked by the Medical Protection Society for words to use in a test case, suggested that "there is life so long as a circulation of oxygenated blood is maintained to live brainstem centres."

Irreversible loss of brainstem function

The box highlights the implications of the memoranda on brain death issued by the Conference of Medical Royal Colleges and their Faculties in the United Kingdom in 1976 and 1979. The first memorandum (which we will call the United Kingdom code) emphasises that "permanent functional death of the brainstem constitutes brain death" and that this should be diagnosed in a defined context (irremediable structural brain damage) and after certain specified conditions have been excluded. It showed how the permanent loss of brainstem function can be determined clinically and describes simple tests for recognising the condition. The second memorandum identified brain death with death itself but did not explain the basis of the identification. These documents mark a milestone in thinking about brain death and have already influenced practice in most English speaking countries and in many others. A more recent report published in 1995 reinforced the previous views and stipulated yet again that instrumental diagnosis was not essential. It defined death as "the irreversible loss of the capacity for consciousness combined with the irreversible loss of the capacity to breathe" and recommended that when death is diagnosed on neurological grounds the condition should be referred to as "brainstem death."

The basic propositions

- Irreversible loss of brainstem function is as valid a yardstick of death as cessation of the heart beat
- The loss of brainstem function can be determined operationally in clinical terms
- The irreversibility of the loss is determined by:
- A context of irremediable structural brain damage
- The exclusion of reversible causes of loss of brainstem function (hypothermia, drugs, severe metabolic disturbances)

What the proposals imply

Two major conceptual strides are necessary before one can accept the propositions implicit in the Conference memoranda or reports.

The first is the step from classic death to whole brain death. In most countries medical opinion accepted the basic concept of brain death, although there are still a few influenced by religious or other considerations who oppose it. Leading spokespeople of all the main Western religions have endorsed it, and publications on the subject are numerous.

Doctors were still taking this first step when they were faced with another challenge: that the brainstem was "the critical system of the critical system" and that death of the brainstem was the necessary and sufficient component of whole brain death. It has already been explained how death of the brainstem relates to a given philosophical concept of death (the irreversible loss of the capacity for consciousness combined with the irreversible loss of the capacity to breathe). The task is now to convince people that this condition can be identified clinically and that it is not in conflict with more traditional notions of brain death or of death itself.

Two important conceptual steps

- From classic death ⇨ whole brain death
- From whole brain death ⇨ brainstem death

Some neurologists – and many experts in electroencephalography – have been caught off balance by these essentially conceptual developments. Some of the early and influential proponents of the idea of whole brain death (their first battle won, the role of their electroencephalographs well defined, their skill widely accepted) have proved reluctant to take the second step.

It has long been known that small, strategically situated lesions of the brainstem of acute onset and affecting the paramedian tegmental area bilaterally cause prolonged coma because they damage critical parts of the ascending reticular activating system.

The reticular formation constitutes the central core of the brainstem and projects to wide areas of the limbic system and neocortex. Projections from the upper part of the brainstem are responsible for alerting mechanisms. These can be thought of as generating the *capacity* for consciousness. The *content* of consciousness (what a person knows, thinks, or feels) is a function of activated cerebral hemispheres. But unless there is a functioning brainstem "switching on" the hemispheres one cannot envisage such a content. There is evidence that brainstem injury in humans may massively reduce cerebral oxidative metabolism, cerebral blood flow, or both. Apart from mechanisms essential for respiration the brainstem contains others which contribute to maintaining blood pressure. All the motor outputs from the hemispheres have to travel through the brainstem, as do all the sensory inputs to the brain (other than sight and smell).

Because the brainstem nuclei are so near one another brainstem function can be clinically evaluated in a unique way. Testing the various cranial nerve reflexes probes the brainstem slice by slice as if it were salami. Respiratory function can also be assessed accurately. An acute, massive, and irreversible brainstem lesion (primary or secondary) prevents meaningful functioning of the "brain as a whole," even if groups of nerve cells may for a short while still emit signals of biological activity. The relevance (or irrelevance) of any residual activity above (or below) a dead brainstem should always be related to an overall philosophical concept of death. Those who think such activity important should always be asked to what concept of death they believe it to be relevant.

The difference between functional death (death of the organism as a whole) and total cellular death (death of the whole organism) has already been emphasised. The box summarises the parallel argument in relation to the brain as a whole and the whole brain.

The irreversible cessation of respiration and heart beat implies death *of the patient as a whole*. It does not necessarily imply the immediate death *of every cell in the body*

The irreversible cessation of brainstem function implies death *of the brain as a whole*. It does not necessarily imply the immediate death *of every cell in the brain*.

Mechanisms of brainstem death

A severe head injury may be associated with cerebral oedema and a pronounced rise in intracranial pressure, even in the absence of a subdural or extradural haemorrhage. Similar rises (based on a different mechanism) may be seen after subarachnoid haemorrhage. Intracranial hypertension is also a feature of the cerebral oedema that almost invariably complicates acute anoxic insults to the brain. The initial effects, in such cases, are often complicated by the development of various intracranial "shifts." There may be downward spreading oedema and caudal displacement of the diencephalon and brainstem with stretching of the perforating pontine branches of the basilar artery and secondary haemorrhages in their territory, or the brainstem may be compressed from uncal herniation into the tentorial opening. Several factors may operate in any given case.

A pressure cone at the level of the foramen magnum may further damage the brainstem. Venous drainage may be compromised. Ischaemic changes may be striking. If ventilation is continued at room temperature in the presence of a dead brain, autolysis will occur. The whole brain may liquefy. Fragments of the destroyed cerebellar tonsils may become detached and be found even as far away as the roots of the cauda equina. The severity of the pathological changes may vary widely. Among the factors responsible for such variations are the duration of ventilation after arrest of the cerebral circulation and the proportion of cases, in some American series, which were not due to primary structural brain damage.

About half the patients in whom brainstem death is diagnosed in the United Kingdom have sustained a recent head injury. Another 30% have had a very recent intracranial haemorrhage (either intracerebral or subarachnoid). Other primary intracranial conditions are meningitis or encephalitis. Not all such cases will be suitable as organ donors. In cases of cerebral tumour brainstem death may occur after operation or, rarely, when a prior decision has been taken, with the relatives' consent, to put the patient on a ventilator when in terminal coma (with the aim of making organs available for transplantation). Cardiac and respiratory arrest (and hypoperfusion of the brain complicating profound shock) are less common causes of brainstem death. They result more often in a persistent vegetative state.

Primary lesions of the brainstem (haemorrhages or infarcts) seldom cause total loss of brainstem function. Restricted lesions (causing restricted deficits) are more common. Massive lesions may occur, however, and result in brainstem death.

Judicial hanging is another cause of lethal, primary brainstem injury. Death in such cases is widely believed to be due to a fracture-dislocation of the odontoid with compression of the upper two segments of the spinal cord. Although such a lesion may be found in some cases, the late Professor Simpson, Home Office pathologist when capital punishment was still resorted to in the United Kingdom, informed one of us (CP) that a rupture of the brainstem (between pons and medulla) was more common.

In judicial hanging respiration stops immediately because of the effect of the rupture of the brainstem on the respiratory centre. Consciousness is also lost immediately as a result of the abrupt damage to the ascending reticular formation. The carotid or vertebral arteries may remain patent. The heart may go on beating for 20 minutes. Circulation continues, and parts of the brain are probably irrigated with blood (of diminishing oxygen saturation) for several minutes. We surmise that an electroencephalogram might, for a short while, continue to show some activity, despite the lethal injury to the brainstem. Is such a person alive or dead? The very posing of such a question forces one to focus attention on the reversibility or irreversibility of the inflicted brainstem lesion.

Aware of the different views held in the United States, Pallis and Harley go on (pp 29–30):

One of the main criticisms of codes based on the clinical identification of a dead brainstem is that they could result in diagnoses of death in some patients who might still show some electroencephalographic activity at maximum amplification. It has been emphasised that "the prediction of a fatal outcome is not a valid criterion for the accuracy of standards designed to determine that death has already occurred." We take this to mean that predicting someone is going to die is not the same as saying he or she is already dead. Superficially, this sounds unexceptionable. But it has meaning only if the words "fatal outcome," "dead," and "death" are unquestionably (and perhaps even reflexly) used in a doubly traditional sense – that is, either as synonyms for "asystole" or as shorthand for the eventual development of an "isoelectric" electroencephalographic pattern characterised (in 1969) as "no activity over 2 μV when recording from scalp electrode pairs 10 or more centimetres apart, with interelectrode resistances of under 10,000 ohms (or impedance under 6000 ohms)."

If one rejects these premises and believes that a person is dead when he or she has irreversibly and as a result of a single event lost both the capacity for consciousness and the capacity to breathe spontaneously, this kind of "critique" assumes a different dimension. It is reduced to the trite conclusion that if a dead brainstem heralds asystole (or the imminent extinction of the electroencephalogram) the differing notions of death are doomed to converge. The words doctors use are indeed important.

How long in fact may cardiac action persist after a diagnosis of brainstem death? Published evidence suggests that in most cases asystole develops within days. Of the 63 patients diagnosed as brain dead (and maintained on the ventilator) in a large Danish series, 29 developed asystole within 12 hours, 10 after 12–24 hours, 16 after 24–72 hours, and eight after 72–211 hours. Experience from Great Britain and elsewhere is in line with these observations. A case in the United States achieved wide publicity because asystole failed to develop during the two months that followed a diagnosis of brain death. The brainstem would not have been declared dead in this case as early as it was had United Kingdom type criteria been used.

The Department of Health's *Code of Practice For the Diagnosis of Brain Stem Death* (March 1998) adopts the 'brain-stem death' approach.

1. The Definition of Death
Death entails the irreversible loss of those essential characteristics which are necessary to the existence of a living human person. Thus, it is recommended that the definition of death should be regarded as 'irreversible loss of the capacity for consciousness, combined with irreversible loss of the capacity to breathe'. The irreversible cessation of brain stem function (brain stem death) whether induced by intra-cranial events or the result of extra-cranial phenomena, such as hypoxia, will produce this clinical state and therefore brain stem death equates with the death of the individual.

The current position in law is that there is no statutory definition of death in the United Kingdom. Subsequent to the proposal of the 'brain death criteria' by the Conference of Royal Colleges in 1976 and 1979, the courts in England and Northern Ireland have adopted these criteria, as part of the law, for the diagnosis of death. There is no reason to believe that courts in other parts of the United Kingdom would not follow this approach.

(see also 'Criteria for the Diagnosis of Brain Stem Death' (1995) 29 Journal of Royal College of Physicians 381 (Working Party of RCP).)

Having seen the medical background and philosophical analysis, how then does the law respond?

C. THE LAW

1. The background

It is no surprise that the definition of death did not historically trouble the courts. It was only with the development of medical technology, as we have seen, that the issue became problematic. The following case reflects the time when everything seemed relatively straightforward.

Smith v Smith (1958) 317 SW 2d 275 (Sup Ct Ark)

This case raised the question of whose estate inherited Mr Smith's property. In turn the court had to determine whether Mr and Mrs Smith died simultaneously in the accident.

Harris CJ: Hugh Smith and Lucy Coleman Smith, his wife, lived at Siloam Springs, Arkansas. They had no children. On April 22, 1947, Mrs Smith executed a will leaving all property to her husband. On November 3, 1952, Mr Smith executed a will leaving all property to his wife. On April 19, 1957, while riding together in an automobile, the Smiths had an accident. Hugh Smith was dead when assistance arrived at the scene, and Lucy Coleman Smith was unconscious, and remained so until her death seventeen days later on May 6th.... Let it first be observed that in reading appellant's petition, as a whole, the assertion of the death of Lucy Coleman Smith appears to be predicated on the theory that such demise occurred 'as a matter of medical science', and of course, appellant could not have meant otherwise, for he had already filed the petitions, heretofore mentioned, in the probate court, together with the physician's letter, stating that Mrs Smith was a patient in the hospital, and would be incapacitated for several months. Black's Law Dictionary, 4th Edition, page 488, defines death as follows;

The cessation of life, the ceasing to exist; defined by physicians as a total stoppage of the circulation of the blood, and a cessation of the animal and vital functions consequent thereon, such as respiration, pulsation, etc.

Admittedly, this condition did not exist, and as a matter of fact, it would be too much of a strain on credulity for us to believe any evidence offered to the effect that Mrs Smith was dead, scientifically or otherwise, unless the conditions set out in the definition existed....

To summarise and conclude, this litigation is determined by two facts. First, Hugh Smith and Lucy Coleman Smith did not die simultaneously ...

It may be that, judged against the background of philosophical argument and the realities generated by technological advance, the definition adopted by the court is not entirely satisfactory.

2. England

In England, there is no statute defining death. Also, there is little English case law concerning the definition of death. The English law, as one might expect, did not historically need to resolve the question of when someone was dead.

In *R v Malcherek; R v Steel* [1981] 2 All ER 422 (CA), the Court of Appeal was concerned with the criminal liability of two defendants who attacked and severely injured their victims. In both instances, the victims' ventilators were switched off by their doctors who had decided their prognoses' were hopeless. It was argued that each victim was already dead, as they were brain stem dead, when the ventilators were switched off. Hence, the switching off did not break the chain of causation to the defendants' violent assaults. Not all the tests for diagnosing brain stem death were, however, carried out. The Court of Appeal sidestepped the issue of whether the victims were already dead, preferring to decide the case on the basis that, whether or not they were dead, the switching off of the ventilators did not break the chain of causation because the defendants' actions 'continued to be an operating cause of death'. As Peter Skegg points out in his book *Law, Ethics and Medicine* (1984), the trial judge in *Malcherek* seems to have adopted 'brain stem' death (p 196):

> The judge at Malcherek's original trial was reported to have said: 'To have kept her on the respirator would have been, in effect, to ventilate a corpse.' This statement, and his ruling that there was no evidence to show that the victim was still alive when the doctors switched off the machine, indicated the trial judge's acceptance of the view that once brain death [semble brain stem death] is established a person is dead for the purpose of the law of homicide, even though the heart continues to beat.

It should be noted that courts in a number of jurisdictions have in similar circumstances to *Malcherek and Steel* confirmed that court's view on causation without finding it necessary to determine whether the victim was already dead when the ventilator was turned off (*Finlayson v HM Advocate* 1978 SLT (Notes) 60 (Scotland); *R v Kitching and Adams* [1976] 6 WWR 697 (Manitoba); *R v Kinash* [1982] Qld R 648 (Qd)).

The issue was subsequently raised, curiously enough, in a case in which an issue of copyright turned on whether one of the alleged copyright holders was dead.

Mail Newspapers plc v Express Newspapers plc [1987] FSR 90 (Ch D)

Millet J: Mrs B had suffered a brain haemorrhage while 24 weeks pregnant. She was being kept on a life-support system in the hope that the baby could be born alive. The evidence suggested that Mrs B was probably clinically dead, but tests had not been undertaken.

Seven national newspapers obtained and published, without any authority from Mr B, photographs of the couple's wedding. Thereafter Mr B entered into an agreement with the plaintiffs granting them exclusive rights to all his archive photographs and undertaking to pose exclusively for the plaintiffs for photographs with his baby within 24 hours of its birth, all rights to those photographs to be owned by the plaintiffs. The plaintiffs wrote to many national newspapers informing them that they held the exclusive rights to Mr B's photographs and warning them not to publish these. The defendants replied that they intended to use the photographs. The plaintiffs therefore obtained *ex parte* injunctions restraining the defendants from publishing the photographs.

On the *inter partes* hearing of the motion, the defendants argued that the copyright in the photographs vested either in Mrs B alone or in Mr and Mrs B together, and that Mr B was unable to grant an exclusive licence since Mrs B was still alive and had not consented. The evidence was that before the wedding Mr B had asked his fiancée to arrange for the photographs to be taken, but that afterwards Mr B paid the bill....

The evidence, such as it is, suggests that Mrs Bell is probably clinically dead, that is to say, that her brain had ceased to function altogether, although she is breathing and her bodily functions are being kept going. Medical tests to determine whether or not Mrs Bell is clinically dead have not been undertaken, and understandably no one has thought it appropriate to obtain a death certificate.

...[I]n submitting to me that the plaintiffs have no real prospect of succeeding at the trial Mr Shaw was really submitting that Mrs B is unarguably still alive. The evidence before me does not go nearly far enough to warrant any such conclusion. I have no doubt at all that there is at the very least a serious question to be tried whether Mrs Bell is alive or dead. Indeed, so far as the evidence before me goes, it supports the conclusion that she is probably already legally dead.

Millet J does not seem to advance the cause of clarity, so necessary in this area, when he uses expressions such as Mrs Bell was 'clinically dead' and, a little later, that she was 'legally dead' implying as a consequence that there are different types of death. Subsequently, however, the English law seems to have settled the question.

Re A [1992] 3 Med LR 303 (Fam Div)

Johnson J: These proceedings concern a boy, A, who was born on April 24, 1990. He and his family come from overseas and there are three other children in the family. A was taken to the Accident & Emergency Department of a hospital near where his family live on January 17 of this year. It was not the first time that he had been taken to a hospital as an emergency because in December he had been taken to hospital suffering from facial bruising and greenstick fractures of both his left femur and tibia and he had been kept in hospital until the beginning of January.

When he arrived at hospital again on January 17 the doctors who examined him could detect no heartbeat. It was said by his mother that he had fallen from a table on to a carpeted floor and had struck his head against a toy of some kind. She also said that some minutes later he had begun to breathe heavily and seemed to be having a convulsion which seemed to last about ten minutes.

On the same day he was transferred to another hospital where extensive attempts at resuscitation were made, but on the following day he was transferred to Guy's Hospital for intensive care and assessment. There the records show that he was found to have bruising on the inside of his right upper ear as well as what is described as a 'probable bruise' behind his left ear. He still had a plaster on his left leg from his earlier admission to hospital. A brain scan showed blood, the presence and distribution of which are said to be typical of non-accidental injury. A was in intensive care. Vigorous attempts were made to improve his situation, but there were no signs of recovery. However, it is plain from the evidence which I have heard that he was not then 'brain-stem dead'.

I have had the advantage of evidence from a consultant paediatric neurologist at Guy's Hospital. She gave her evidence with great clarity and precision. I judged her to be an extremely impressive member of her profession and I have no hesitation in accepting her evidence. A has been under her care ever since he arrived at Guy's Hospital. He has been on a ventilator. Put briefly in lay terms, the brain-stem controls the vital functions of the body. The ventilator enables the body to breathe by introducing oxygen and extracting carbon dioxide and that mechanism enables the heart to keep beating.

On January 20 – that is last Monday – the consultant removed A briefly from the ventilator to see whether he was capable of supporting himself without the ventilator. When she did so she heard slight gasping noises which led her to believe that A was not brain-stem dead according to criteria now generally accepted in medical circles.

The precise definition of death has been the subject of recommendations by both the Royal College of Surgeons and the Royal College of Physicians and a working party of the British Paediatric Association. Applying the criteria laid down by her profession the consultant concluded on January 20 that A was not then brain-stem dead. On the following day she again carried out the tests which are necessary to determine whether the necessary criteria are satisfied. The consultant described those tests to me and she explained to me that each one was satisfied. The tests lasted overall about half an hour.

Describing the criteria and her observations of A, and expressing myself in lay terms, her evidence was to the following effect. A's pupils were fixed and dilated. On movement of the head his eyes moved with his head. What is called the 'doll's eye response' was absent. On his eye being touched with a piece of cotton wool there was no response. On cold water being passed into his ear there was no eye movement in response. On steps being taken, in effect, to cause him to 'gag' there was no reflex reaction, neither was there reaction to pain being applied to his central nervous system. Finally, on his temporary removal from the ventilator to enable the carbon dioxide content of his body to increase there was no respiratory response. All in all, the consultant was satisfied that A was brain-stem dead....

On the same day the consultant had arranged for a colleague consultant paediatric neurologist to carry out the same tests that she had, herself, carried out the previous day with a view to confirming or otherwise the validity of her own professional conclusion. Under professional guidelines it was not necessary for her to seek a second opinion in that way, but she decided that in the particular circumstances of the case it would be a wise thing for her to do. Accordingly, the tests were carried out again on Wednesday of last week, January 22, by this colleague who reached the same conclusion as had been reached by the first consultant.

Both doctors were at pains to exclude other possibilities for A's state, including the possibility of his suffering from extreme hypothermia or some abnormality of his biochemistry. Moreover, they tested for drugs, lest his brain-stem function should have been suppressed by the administration of some drug of which they had not been aware, although he had, in fact, been under the consultant's supervision for three days in Guy's Hospital and they would have been aware had drugs been administered to him. Nonetheless they carried out the necessary checks and satisfied themselves that no such drug was present.

Both doctors concluded that A was brain-stem dead....

It is now Monday, January 27. I have no hesitation at all in holding that A has been dead since Tuesday of last week, January 21.

(For commentary see, (1993) 1 Med L Rev 98 (IK).)

Even more emphatic was the view expressed by a majority of the Law Lords in *Airedale NHS Trust v Bland* [1993] 1 All ER 821. You will recall that this was the case concerning the legality of the withdrawal of hydration and nutrition from a patient in a persistent vegetative state. Three of the Law Lords reasoned as follows:

Lord Keith: Anthony Bland has for over three years been in the condition known as persistent vegetative state ("PVS"). It is unnecessary to go into all the details about the manifestations of this state which are fully set out in the judgments of the courts below. It is sufficient to say that it arises from the destruction, through prolonged deprivation of oxygen, of the cerebral cortex, which has resolved into a watery mass. The cortex is that part of the brain which is the seat of cognitive function and sensory capacity. Anthony Bland cannot see, hear or feel anything. He cannot communicate in any way. The consciousness which is the essential feature of individual personality has departed for ever. On the other hand the brain stem, which controls the reflexive functions of the body, in particular heartbeat, breathing and digestion, continues to operate. In the eyes of the medical world and of the law a person is not clinically dead so long as the brain stem retains its function.

Lord Goff: I start with the simple fact that, in law, Anthony is still alive. It is true that his condition is such that it can be described as a living death; but he is nevertheless still alive. This is because, as a result of developments in modern medical technology, doctors no longer associate death exclusively with breathing and heartbeat, and it has come to be accepted that death occurs when the brain, and in particular the brain stem, has been destroyed.... The evidence is that Anthony's brain stem is still alive and functioning and it follows that, in the present state of medical science, he is still alive and should be so regarded as a matter of law.

Lord Browne-Wilkinson: Until recently there was no doubt what was life and what was death. A man was dead if he stopped breathing and his heart stopped beating. There was no artificial means of sustaining these indications of life for more than a short while. Death in the traditional sense was beyond human control. Apart from cases of unlawful homicide, death occurred automatically in the course of nature when the natural functions of the body failed to sustain the lungs and the heart.

Recent developments in medical science have fundamentally affected these previous certainties. In medicine, the cessation of breathing or of heartbeat is no longer death. By the use of a ventilator, lungs which in the unaided course of nature would have stopped breathing can be made to breathe, thereby sustaining the heartbeat. Those, like Anthony Bland, who would previously have died through inability to swallow food can be kept alive by artificial feeding. This has led the medical profession to redefine death in terms of brain stem death, ie, the death of that part of the brain without which the body cannot function at all without assistance. In some cases it is now apparently possible, with the use of the ventilator, to sustain a beating heart even though the brain stem, and therefore in medical terms the patient, is dead; 'the ventilated corpse'.

I do not refer to these factors because Anthony Bland is already dead, either medically or legally. His brain stem is alive and so is he....

Undoubtedly, these views form part of the *ratio decidendi* of the case. It was a necessary step in the reasoning of the Law Lords that Anthony Bland was alive otherwise no question of the doctor's duty as regards treatment would have arisen. Brain-stem death was also applied by the High Court in Northern Ireland in *Re TC (a minor)* (1994) 2 Med L Rev 376 (declaration that child on ventilator was dead).

The fascination with 'brain-stem death' has the potential to confuse. Is it the only *legal* definition of death or does the (irreversible) cessation of the heart still equate to death? Putting it another way, are there two ways to die legally or only one? Professor Skegg analyses the relationship between the 'old' definition of death and the 'new' brain-stem death definition and the difficulties of the 'old' definition itself.

P D G Skegg *Law, Ethics and Medicine* (1984)

There are undoubtedly some circumstances in which a patient must be regarded as alive, even though his heart has stopped beating for a time. Quite apart from elective cardiac arrest in the course of open-heart surgery, spontaneous cardiac arrest is often followed by successful resuscitation. Although such patients are sometimes said to have 'died', but to have been 'brought back to life' (see eg *Lim v Camden and Islington AHA* [1979] QB 196, 214; *Croke v Wiseman* [1982] 1 WLR 71, 74), for legal purposes death must be a once-and-for-all occurrence. If respiration and circulation are restored in a patient who is not brain dead, he is obviously alive. He must also be regarded as having been alive during the time his heart ceased beating.

But what of the patient whose respiration and circulation cease, and who is not successfully resuscitated? Is the patient to be considered dead from the time respiration and circulation ceased, or from some later time? Professor Glanville Williams has twice discussed an imaginary situation in which a potential legatee plunges a dagger into a patient after his heart has stopped beating, thereby ensuring that the patient is not resuscitated. Would this be an offence against the person, or would he be merely interfering with a corpse? A quarter of a century ago Professor Williams suggested that (Williams, Glanville '*Sanctity of Life and the Criminal Law*' 18):

perhaps death is only when the heart stops beating beyond the known limit of medical recall. On this view, we cannot tell whether a man is dead or merely in a state of suspended animation, until such time has elapsed as puts revivification out of the question. But such a definition would introduce some indeterminacy into the time of death.

More recently he wrote that it seems 'that the legal moment of death is not to be postponed by reference to a possible resuscitation that does not take place, because the contrary view would create formidable difficulties' (Williams, Glanville '*Textbook of Criminal Law*' 236). On this approach the potential legatee would simply have interfered with a corpse, even if but for that interference the patient would have been resuscitated.

Professor Williams's approach would not avoid all uncertainty. Immediately after respiration and circulation ceased it would sometimes be impossible to determine whether the body was that of a living human being or whether it was a corpse. It would all depend upon whether the patient was subsequently resuscitated. Nevertheless, in many circumstances Professor Williams's approach would make it easier to specify a precise 'moment of death' than would an approach involving a test of irreversibility. But this advantage has not been sufficient to lead legislatures or law reform bodies to prefer a test of permanency to one of irreversibility in this context. If adopted, Professor Williams's approach would have remarkable consequences. If a patient's respiration and circulation ceased, in circumstances where he could easily be resuscitated, a doctor would always be free to 'let the patient die'. The patient would then be accounted dead from the time of the cessation, and the doctor could hardly be said to be under a duty to resuscitate what was, in retrospect, already a corpse. And, as Professor Williams recognizes (Williams, '*Textbook*' 236), a surgeon would not commit any offence against the person if he removed that patient's heart for transplantation, even if the patient could still have been resuscitated.

Until there has been an irreversible cessation of the function or functions which are accepted as being of crucial significance, a patient should not be regarded as dead. But it would now be wrong to assume that, in cases where respiration and circulation have ceased, the only alternatives to tests focusing on the 'permanent' cessation of respiration and circulation are ones focusing on their 'irreversible' cessation.

For, now that it is accepted that a patient will not be regarded as alive if he is brain dead, even though his heart continues to beat, the question arises whether a patient should ever be regarded as dead before there is an irreversible cessation of brain function. In other words, should brain death be the sole, or simply an alternative, test of death? Leading Commonwealth law reform bodies have expressed different views on this matter.

In Australia the Law Reform Commission has recommended enactment of a provision stating: (*Human Tissue Transplants'* (Law Reform Commission, Report No 7, 1977) 63)

A person has died when there has occurred:

(a) irreversible cessation of all function of the brain of the person; or
(b) irreversible cessation of circulation of blood in the body of the person.

On this approach, if the irreversible cessation of the circulation of blood occurs before brain death, the patient is already dead for legal purposes.

By contrast, the Law Reform Commission of Canada has recommended the enactment of a provision stating that for all purposes within the jurisdiction of the Parliament of Canada (*Criteria for the Determination of Death* (Law Reform Commission of Canada, Report 15, 1981) p 25):

(1) a person is dead when an irreversible cessation of all that person's brain functions has occurred.
(2) the irreversible cessation of brain functions can be determined by the prolonged absence of spontaneous circulatory and respiratory functions.
(3) when the determination of the prolonged absence of spontaneous circulatory and respiratory functions is made impossible by the use of artificial means of support, the irreversible cessation of brain functions can be determined by any means recognized by the ordinary standards of current medical practice.

On this approach, brain death is the crucial factor in all cases, even though it will often be determined by the prolonged absence of the conventional signs of life, rather than by the more complicated tests which are necessary when the body is being maintained on a ventilator.

The Canadian proposal avoids giving the impression that there are two definitions of death, and shows how the traditional tests can be linked to the new approach. In the United Kingdom the Conference of Medical Royal Colleges' report on *Diagnosis of Death* lends support to an approach in which the occurrence of brain death is always the event of crucial importance. Having stated that to most people the one aspect of death that is beyond doubt is its irreversibility, the report explained that although brain death sometimes occurs before the failure of heartbeat and respiration, in the majority of cases 'successive organic failures eventually reach a point at which brain death occurs and this is the point of no return' ([1979] 1 Br Med J 332, para 5; [1979] 1 Lancet 261, 262, para 5). It went on to state that whatever the mode of its production 'brain death represents the stage at which a patient becomes truly dead, because by then all functions of the brain have permanently and irreversibly ceased' (ibid para 7). This statement may well encourage the English courts to adopt the view that, just as a patient is not be regarded as alive after brain death has occurred, nor is a patient to be regarded as dead before brain death occurs.

We endorse Skegg's views. There can only be one *legal* definition of death and it is 'brain-stem death'. The Australian proposal, which has been widely adopted by the states, and the US approach of having two definitions is simply wrong (see also, I Kennedy 'The Kansas Statute of Death – An Appraisal' (1971) 285 New England Journal of Medicine 946). Irreversible – and we emphasise that – cessation of the heart is evidence of this, given that shortly after it has occurred 'brain-stem death' will usually follow.

3. Brain death in the world

Pallis and Harley (*op cit*) helpfully survey the recognition of brain death in other countries.

C Pallis and D H Harley *ABC of Brainstem Death* (2nd edn, 1996)

Other countries

Different developments were meanwhile taking place elsewhere. At the end of 1979 the renal transplant organisations in 40 countries were questioned by the departments of surgery of the University of Chicago and of the Albert Einstein College of Medicine, New York, and by the department of neurology at the Hennepin County Medical Center, Minneapolis. Neurosurgical societies were also questioned. We have tabulated updated information concerning the legal status of brain death (and about the tests currently required to establish the diagnosis) in various parts of the world.

All the countries responding to the 1979 questionnaire demanded apnoeic coma and absent brainstem reflexes as integral components of the definition of brain death. Most countries which specified preconditions of structural brain disease did not require additional instrumental tests. Countries which did not specify preconditions – that is, where brain death could be diagnosed in patients suffering from severe drug intoxication, metabolic coma, and so on – required either one or two electroencephalograms, separated by variable periods of time, or one or more angiograms (to show a blocked cerebral circulation), or both electroencephalograms and angiograms.

The situation today varies widely. It has least changed in France, where the concept of *coma dépassé* triggered all subsequent discussion. The *Circulaire Jeanneney* (a document issued by the Ministry of Social Affairs on 24 April 1968) became incorporated in a law (the *loi Caillavet*) in December 1976. The 1968 circular had stipulated that what was needed to diagnose death on neurological grounds were "concordant proofs" (clinical and electroencephalographic) concerning the "irreversibility of lesions incompatible with life." Among the clinical requirements were "dilated pupils, complete hypotonia, and the abolition of all reflexes." A 1986 review suggested that aging precept and current practice were beginning to diverge. This is probably inevitable when the law seeks to "freeze" medical concepts, confining them to what prevailed at earlier points in time.

In Germany, criteria of brain death published in 1982 had already made the useful distinction between primarily intracranial and primarily extracranial causes of the condition. The publication of "third generation criteria" in 1987 was to make further distinctions between primary supratentorial and primary infratentorial lesions. Under certain conditions "the extinction of evoked potentials" could establish the loss of brainstem function and "might offer an alternative" to an isoelectric electroencephalogram or the demonstration of a blocked cerebral circulation. Overall, however, the medical regulatory body (Bundesärzteskammer) currently insists on the use of electroencephalography or flow detection methods to determine brain death after brainstem reflexes have been shown to be absent.

In Italy, there is a requirement for "instrumental techniques" to confirm clinical findings. A new law (No 582) was promulgated in 1994. Clinical findings indicating a non-functioning brainstem are required, but an electroencephalogram is still mandatory. Assessment of cerebral blood flow is still required in children under the age of 1 year, in the presence of pharmacological or metabolic factors which might affect clinical evaluation, and in cases where the clinical evaluation, for whatever reason, cannot properly be carried out. In Scandinavia, criteria for brainstem death were first accepted in Finland in 1971, Sweden in 1988 and Denmark in 1990. The Swedish road to consensus proved difficult but informative, the Danish particularly bumpy (eg Rix, BA '*Danish Ethics Council rejects brain death as the criterion of death*' J Med Ethics 1990:16:5–7).

In both Spain and Portugal, brain death has legal status, but the diagnosis requires EEG "confirmation." The Greek code, published in March 1985, closely mirrors that in the United Kingdom. No electroencephalography is required. The Swiss code is uniquely detailed. In May 1983 the country's Senate approved new directives for the definition and diagnosis of death. These insisted that in testing for brain death firm pressure be applied over the emergence point of the second division of the trigeminal. They also specified not only a target of $Paco_2$ for the disconnection test (6.65 kPa – 59 mm Hg) but an arterial pH of "less than 7.4." Two isoelectric electroencephalograms at 24 hours' interval were said to be diagnostically useful "in some cases of metabolic coma." An excellent review, in German, evaluates the guidelines currently prevailing in Germany, Austria, and Switzerland. Hungary passed a law in 1988 explicitly recognising that brainstem death was legally death. No electroencephalography was required. Surprisingly, in Holland, traditionally a forward-looking and liberal country, electroencephalography or angiography is required in all brainstem dead patients who are to become organ donors, even those who fulfil the preconditions and brainstem death criteria . . . Poland was unusual. Although brain death was accepted, its logical extension (the concept of what we have called a "beating heart cadaver") was not. Brain death was not unequivocally equated with death. Brain death warranted withdrawal of ventilatory support, but organs could not be removed while the heart was still beating.

Brain death is legally recognised in Argentina, Brazil, Chile, Colombia, Peru, Uruguay, and Venezuela. It is also legally recognised in Cuba, and the first International Symposium on Brain Death was held in Havana in September 1992. There were representatives from many South American countries, as well as from Europe and the United States. The most useful outcome of the symposium was the very positive response evoked by the recommendation to refer to the condition being discussed as *muerte encefálica* (whole brain death) rather than *muerte cerebral* (with its implication of pathology confined to the cerebral hemispheres.) This first major linguistic hurdle overcome, it became possible to focus more sharply on the different components of *muerte encefálica*. Advocacy of brainstem death got a good hearing, merging with important local work being done on brainstem auditory evoked potentials. In Argentina the recent editorial of a widely read neurological journal bore the title "*Muerte Encefálica, Muerte Cerebral o Muerte Troncal?*" and concluded that 'in the future we will be speaking of death of the brain stem (*muerte troncal*) when referring to what we currently think of as "whole-brain death."' This statement marks a major step forward in Latin American opinion.

In 1982 both brain death and organ transplantation were declared *hallal* (permissible) by the Ulema Commission, the highest religious authority on such matters in Saudi Arabia, and hence throughout the Islamic world.

Turkey (where electroencephalography or angiography must be performed) has now legally accepted brain death.

In Israel, a 1987 regulation issued by the Ministry of Health stated explicitly that brain death was death. It also stressed that irreversible loss of brainstem function was the factual equivalent of brain death. Political and cultural considerations have precluded the regulation becoming law, but as rules issued by the ministry carry legal authority as far as medical matters are concerned, the arrangement has successfully legitimised brain death and the transplantation procedures that it permits, while avoiding a formal Knesset vote on a very sensitive issue. The emphasis on properly documented apnoea secured the endorsement of a body known as the "Council for the Adaptation of Talmudic Doctrine to Recent Advances in Science and Technology."

Little information could be obtained about practice in the former Soviet Union. A law was passed in 1987 permitting the recognition of the brain dead state and the harvesting of organs, but the concept was not widely accepted. The present situation among the various republics is confused. In China, details are scanty. It is known that organ donation takes place from executed prisoners with, allegedly, their consent. These are not, as far is known, beating heart donors. Evidence has been collected to indicate that ethical standards are low in the methods used to obtain these donations.

The Taiwanese code closely mirrors the United Kingdom code. Neither electroencephalograms or angiograms are required. Taiwanese neurologists have conduced the first ever large prospective study to assess the prognosis of deeply comatose patients on ventilators, when given maximum circulatory support. They concluded that "if strict attention is paid to preconditions and exclusions brainstem death can be reliably diagnosed on clinical grounds alone."

In Japan, organ transplantation from brain dead donors is currently forbidden, although cadaveric donation is legally acceptable. Although the majority of the Japanese medical profession agrees with the concept of "whole brain death" and are very ready to "confirm" it with the use of electroencephalography, there is no social consensus on the use of organ donation from such patients. Very interesting papers have been published discussing the cultural roots of Japanese attitudes (the "polluting" effect of receiving organs from the dead; the blurring of distinctions between "self" and "non-self", the practice of leaving the problem of whether to recognise brain death as death to the individual choice of relatives, in the name of self determination, etc.)

The reasoning underpinning current practice in Australia and New Zealand is, for us, difficult to understand. Their 1993 Guidelines on the Certification of Brain Death ('Statement and Guidelines on brain death and Organ Donation' Australian and New Zealand Intensive Care Society, 1993) state that "the legal definition of brain death is irreversible cessation of all functions of the brain" and that "the medical means by which this is diagnosed is to demonstrate irreversible loss of consciousness and irreversible loss of brainstem function." The two are, of course, largely synonymous, both because the ascending reticular activating system of the brainstem generates the capacity for consciousness, and because the death of the brainstem is, in the overwhelming majority of cases, the terminal infratentorial repercussion of catastrophic supratentorial events. The guidelines however, object to the use of such terms as "whole brain death" and "brainstem death", objections to the latter centring on the fact that "it cannot be reconciled with the legal definition of death." This seems to be a Catch 22 situation: the desire to remain within the legal framework leads to the pursuit of an unattainable objective. No currently available technique or combination of techniques can ever hope to assess "all functions of the entire brain." In the clinical context of suspected brain death there is a great deal more than isolate cellular activity that simply cannot be evaluated. There is no way of adequately testing, for instance, such important brain functions as those of the thalamus, basal ganglia, or cerebellum. If the irreversible loss of all brain function is the diagnostic target aimed at, we cannot understand the deafening silence concerning the role of electroencephalography, which might have helped a little in the pursuit of this unachievable objective.

The 1987 Canadian Guidelines for the Diagnosis of Brain Death drawn up by the Canadian Congress of Neurological Sciences and endorsed by the Canadian Medical Association, very closely resemble the United Kingdom code (Canadian Medical Association '*Guidelines for the diagnosis of brain death*' Can Med Assoc J 1987; 136: 200A–200B). Brain death, it is stated, "can be established by clinical criteria alone." Special tests "can be used to support and in some instances supplement the clinical diagnosis." An updated code was drafted by the congress in 1988, which it was hoped would prove "helpful and sufficient for many years."

The Irish Working Party on brain death, whose members were from the medical and surgical Colleges in Ireland, published a memorandum in 1988 ('*Memorandum on brain death*' Ir Med J 1988; 42–5). The case for brainstem death was put quite explicitly. The memorandum said "the essential element in brain death is brainstem death. If brainstem function is irreversibly lost, what goes on elsewhere in the brain is immaterial; life cannot return." All signatories to the memorandum were "agreed that the EEG was not necessary for the diagnosis of brainstem death."

The report of the President's Commission

In July 1981 the President's Commission for the Study of Ethical Problems in Medicine and Biomedical and Behavioural Research submitted a report (*Defining Death*) to the president, congress, and the relevant departments of government. The report accurately described the British criteria and contained the statement that "if the brainstem completely lacks function, the brain as a whole cannot function."

Among the appendices to the report were "*Guidelines for the Determination of Death*" drawn up by a large panel of medical consultants to the Commission (JAMA 1981; 246: 2185–6). The guidelines emphasised the importance of accurate testing for apnoea. They specifically mention the preoxygenation of the patient, the use of an oxygen and carbon dioxide mixture, disconnection from the ventilator for 10 minutes, and diffusion oxygenation during the period of disconnection. The United Kingdom technique has clearly been taken as a model.

The Commission worked closely with three organisations which had proposed model legislation on the subject: the American Medical Association, the American Bar Association, and the National Conference of Commissioners on Uniform State Laws. These groups endorsed a statute, and the report recommended its adoption by congress for all areas under federal jurisdiction. The proposed statute was to be called the Uniform Determination of Death Act. It states:

"An individual who has sustained either (1) irreversible cessation of circulatory and respiratory functions, or (2) irreversible cessation of all functions of the entire brain, including the brainstem, is dead. A determination of death must be made in accordance with accepted medical standards."

The statute is already law in nearly all states. When all states have endorsed it the unsettling situation where differing statutes have been drawn up by various legislatures will finally come to an end. In 1981 there were seven different patterns of legal statute concerning brain death in 33 states, though many states had no statutes. One could have been declared dead in one state and not in another. A wit once claimed that "the shortest road to resurrection was crossing a state boundary." The taxonomy of these statutes had almost become a study in its own right.

The content of the statute is not entirely satisfactory. The "cessation of all functions of the entire brain" is, quite simply, something that is impossible to determine. No available technique or combination of techniques can ever hope to assess "all functions of the entire brain." The Commission's report correctly states that all functions cannot be taken to include "electrical and metabolic activity at the level of individual cells or even groups of cells," but in the clinical context of suspected brain death there is a great deal more than this (cerebellar and thalamic activity for instance, and the functions of the basal ganglia) that simply cannot be directly evaluated.

The statute will give the impression, at least to a lay public, of seeking to identify "death of the whole brain" rather than "death of the brain as a whole." The medical guidelines accompanying the report make the disingenuous disclaimer that "all functions of the entire brain" means only "those functions that are clinically ascertainable," but the introduction to the report states wisely that "in language as well as content, any legislation ought to make personal sense to lay people." The average lay person does not know that many if not most cerebral functions cannot be clinically tested in the context under discussion. And, if someone in a glass house may be allowed to throw a pebble, our own code has also erred in much the same way when it stated that in brain death "*all* functions of the brain have permanently and irreversibly ceased" (our emphasis). All functions are undoubtedly on the verge of ceasing. And all relevant – that is, brainstem – functions have certainly ceased. But neither of these statements is quite the same as asserting that all brain functions have actually ceased. This seems to be as untestable a proposition in London as it is in Washington. But this very untestability is less relevant to those who equate death with permanent loss of brainstem function (for which there are tests) than for those who insist that the neurological deficit should include all the other intracranial systems (some of which cannot be clinically assessed).

The Uniform Determination of Death Act encountered another type of criticism within the United States itself – namely, that "it contains the most serious flaw that the Commission finds in previous statutes: it provides two independent standards of death without explaining the relationship between them." The same point had been raised over a decade earlier in a detailed critique of the Kansas Statute (the first in the common law world seeking to define death.) Kennedy had then shrewdly emphasised that it was "in no way inspiring of confidence in one's doctor to learn that there are two types of death." The new critics point out that "irreversible cessation of circulatory and respiratory functions" works as a test of death (in the absence of cardiopulmonary support) only because it produces the true standard of death: the irreversible cessation of whole brain function. This approach incorporates the useful distinction between a standard or concept of death and a test for death. Their proposed alternative statute would define death in terms of "irreversible cessation of all functions of the entire brain" and then show how such a state could be ascertained in one of two ways: either by establishing an absence of spontaneous circulation and respiration of adequate duration, or (in the presence of artificial cardiovascular support) by tests specifically directed at brain function. This alternative statute would clearly reconcile the claims of conceptual clarity and of practical relevance. All that would then remain would be to amend this so that it read "irreversible cessation of brainstem functions" instead of "all functions of the entire brain." This would be more relevant because of the ease and thoroughness with which these functions can be tested, because of the prognostic implications of their loss, and because of the relation of this loss to an acceptable philosophical concept of death. Although the debate continues there are signs that logic and clinical expertise are getting the upper hand. A very recent (1995) document from the American Academy of Neurology seeks to provide guidelines in the form of "practice parameters" for "determining brain death in adults." Brain death is no longer unrealistically perceived as the "irreversible cessation of all functions of the entire brain including the brainstem" but as "the absence of clinical brain function when the proximate cause is known and demonstrably irreversible." An accompanying "special article" states: "the clinical diagnosis of brain death is equivalent to irreversible loss of all brainstem function." The practice parameters point out this is a clinical diagnosis and that "confirmatory" tests are "not mandatory" but just "desirable in patients in whom specific components of clinical testing cannot reliably be evaluated." Bedside experience seems to have reasserted its primacy and led to a belated convergence of British and American practice over a very wide field.

4. Applying the brain-stem death criterion in English law

(a) The Code of Practice

You will recall that Johnson J in *Re A* and other sources we have set out referred to the Report of the Conference of Medical Royal Colleges and their Faculties in 1976. As part of the Report there was included a memorandum by way of a Code of Practice.

'Diagnosis of Brain Death' (1976) 2 British Medical Journal 1187

Conditions under which the diagnosis of brain death should be considered

1. The patient is deeply comatose.
(a) There should be no suspicion that this state is due to depressant drugs. *Note 1*
(b) Primary hypothermia as a cause of coma should have been excluded.
(c) Metabolic and endocrine disturbances which can be responsible for or can contribute to coma should have been excluded. *Note 2*
2. The patient is being maintained on a ventilator because spontaneous respiration had previously become inadequate or had ceased altogether.
(a) Relaxants (neuromuscular blocking agents) and other drugs should have been excluded as a cause of respiratory inadequacy or failure. *Note 3*
3. There should be no doubt that the patient's condition is due to irremediable structural brain damage. The diagnosis of a disorder which can lead to brain death should have been fully established. Note 4

Notes

Note 1
Narcotics, hypnotics, and tranquillisers may have prolonged duration of action particularly when some hypothermia exists. The benzodiazepines are markedly cumulative and persistent

in their actions and are commonly used as anticonvulsants or to assist synchronisation with mechanical ventilators. It is therefore recommended that the drug history should be carefully reviewed and adequate intervals allowed for the persistence of drug effects to be excluded. This is of particular importance in patients where the primary cause of coma lies in the toxic effects of drugs followed by anoxic cerebral damage.

Note 2
Metabolic and endocrine factors contributing to the persistence of coma must be subject to careful assessment. There should be no profound abnormality of the serum-electrolytes, acid-balance, or blood-glucose.

Note 3
Immobility, unresponsiveness, and lack of spontaneous respiration may be due to the use of neuromuscular blocking drugs and the persistence of their effects should be excluded by elicitation of spinal reflexes (flexion or stretch) or by the demonstration of adequate neuromuscular conduction with a conventional nerve stimulator. Equally, persistent effects of hypnotics and narcotics should be excluded as the cause of respiratory failure.

Note 4
It may be obvious within hours of a primary intra-cranial event such as severe head injury, spontaneous intra-cranial haemorrhage or following neurosurgery that the condition is irremediable. However, when a patient has suffered primarily from cardiac arrest, hypoxia or severe circulatory insufficiency with an indefinite period of cerebral anoxia, or is suspected of having cerebral air or fat embolism then it may take much longer to establish the diagnosis and to be confident of the prognosis. In some patients the primary pathology may be a matter of doubt and a confident diagnosis may only be reached by continuity of clinical observation and investigation.

Diagnostic tests for the confirmation of brain death

All brainstem reflexes are absent:
(i) The pupils are fixed in diameter and do not respond to sharp changes in the intensity of incident light.
(ii) There is no corneal reflex.
(iii) The vestibulo-ocular reflexes are absent. *Note (a)*
(iv) No motor responses within the cranial nerve distribution can be elicited by adequate stimulation of any somatic area.
(v) There is no gag reflex response to bronchial stimulation by a suction catheter passed down the trachea.
(vi) No respiratory movements occur when the patient is disconnected from the mechanical ventilator for long enough to ensure that the arterial carbon dioxide tension rises above the threshold for stimulation of respiration. *Note (b)*

Note (a)
Vestibulo-ocular reflexes – These are absent when no eye movement occurs during or following the slow injection of 20 ml of ice-cold water into each external auditory meatus in turn, clear access to the tympanic membrane having been established by direct inspection. This test may be contra-indicated on one or other side by local trauma.

Note (b)
Disconnection from the ventilator. – During this test it is necessary for the arterial carbon-dioxide tension to exceed the threshold for respiratory stimulation – that is the $PaCO_2$ should normally reach 50 mm Hg (6.65 kPa). This is best achieved by measurement of the blood gases; if this facility is available it is recommended that the patient should be disconnected when the $PaCO_2$ reaches 40–45 mm Hg following administration of 5% CO_2 in oxygen through the ventilator. This starting level has been chosen because patients may be moderately hypothermic (35°C–37°C), flaccid, and with a depressed metabolic rate, so that arterial carbon-dioxide tension rises only slowly in apnoea (about 2mm Hg/min). (Hypoxia during disconnection should be prevented by delivering oxygen at 6 litres/min through a catheter into the trachea.) If blood-gas analysis is not available to measure the $PaCO_2$ and PaO_2 the alternative procedure is to supply the ventilator with pure oxygen for 10 minutes (pre-oxygenation), then with 5% CO_2 in oxygen for five minutes and to disconnect the ventilator for 10 minutes, while delivering oxygen at 6 litres/minute by catheter into the trachea. This establishes diffusion oxygenation and ensures that during apnoea hypoxia will not occur even in ten or more minutes of respiratory arrest. Those patients with preexisting chronic respiratory insufficiency, who may be unresponsive to raised levels of carbon dioxide and who normally exist on an hypoxic drive, are special cases and should be expertly investigated with careful blood-gas monitoring.

Other considerations

1. Repetition of testing

It is customary to repeat the tests to ensure that there has been no observer error. The interval between tests must depend upon the primary pathology and the clinical course of the disease. Note 4 indicates some conditions where it would be unnecessary to repeat them since a prognosis of imminent brain death can be accepted as being obvious.

In some conditions the outcome is not so clear cut and in these it is recommended that the tests should be repeated. The interval between tests depends upon the progress of the patient and might be as long as 24 hours. This is a matter for medical judgement and repetition time must be related to the signs of improvement, stability, or deterioration which present themselves.

2. Integrity of spinal reflexes

It is well established that spinal-cord function can persist after insults which irretrievably destroy brainstem function. Reflexes of spinal origin may persist or return after an initial absence in brain dead patients.

3. Confirmatory investigations

It is now widely accepted that electro-encephalography is not necessary for the diagnosis of brain death. Indeed this view was expressed from Harvard in 1969 [(1969) 281 N Eng J Med 1070] only a year after the publication of their original criteria.

Electroencephalography has its principal value at earlier stages in the care of patients, in whom the original diagnosis is in doubt. When electroencephalography is used, the strict criteria recommended by the Federation of EEG Societies must be followed.

Other investigations such as cerebral angiography or cerebral blood-flow measurements are not required for the diagnosis of brain death.

4. Body temperature

The body temperature of these patients may be low because of depression of central temperature regulation by drugs or by brainstem damage and it is recommended that it should be not less than 35°C before the diagnostic tests are carried out. A low-reading thermometer should be used.

5. Specialist opinion and the status of the doctors concerned

Experienced clinicians in intensive-care units, acute medical wards, and accident and emergency departments should not normally require specialist advice. Only when the primary diagnosis is in doubt is it necessary to consult with a neurologist or neurosurgeon.

Decision to withdraw artificial support should be made after all the criteria presented above have been fulfilled and can be made by any one of the following combination of doctors:

(a)   A consultant who is in charge of the case and one other doctor.
(b)   In the absence of a consultant, his deputy, who should have been registered for 5 years or more *and* who should have had adequate previous experience in the care of such cases, and one other doctor.

An addendum was produced in 1979.

'Memorandum on the diagnosis of death' (1979) 1 British Medical Journal 332

1. In October 1976 the Conference of Royal Colleges and their Faculties (UK) published a report unanimously expressing the opinion that 'Brain Death', when it had occurred, could be diagnosed with certainty. The report has been widely accepted.

The Conference was not at that time asked whether or not it believed that death itself should be presumed to occur when brain death takes place or whether it would come to some other conclusion. The present report examines this point and should be considered as an addendum to the original report.

2. Exceptionally, as a result of massive trauma, death occurs instantaneously or near-instantaneously. Far more commonly, death is not an event, it is a process, the various organs and systems supporting the continuation of life failing and eventually ceasing altogether to function, successively and at different times.

3. Cessation of respiration and cessation of the heart beat are examples of organic failure occurring during the process of dying and since the moment that the heart beat ceases is usually detectable with simplicity by no more than clinical means, it has for many centuries been accepted as the moment of death itself, without any serious attempt being made to assess the validity of this assumption.

4. It is now universally accepted, by the lay public as well as by the medical profession, that it is not possible to equate death itself with cessation of the heart beat. Quite apart from the elective cardiac arrest of open-heart surgery, spontaneous cardiac arrest followed by successful resuscitation is today a commonplace and although the more sensational accounts of occurrences of this kind still refer to the patient being 'dead' until restoration of the heartbeat, the use of the quote marks usually demonstrates that this word is not taken literally, for to most people the one aspect of death that is beyond debate is its irreversibility.

5. In the majority of cases, in which a dying patient passes through the processes leading to the irreversible state we call death, successive organic failures eventually reach a point at which brain death occurs and this is the point of no return.

6. In a minority of cases, brain death does not occur as a result of the failure of other organs or systems but as a direct result of severe damage to the brain itself from, perhaps, a head injury or a spontaneous intracranial haemorrhage. Here the order of events is reversed; instead of the failure of such vital functions as heart beat and respiration eventually resulting in brain death, brain death results in the cessation of spontaneous respiration; this is normally followed within minutes of cardiac arrest due to hypoxia. If, however, oxygenation is maintained by artificial ventilation the heartbeat can continue for some days, and haemoperfusion will for a time be adequate to maintain function in other organs, such as the liver and kidneys.

7. Whatever the mode of its production, brain death represents the state at which a patient becomes truly dead, because by then all functions of the brain have permanently and irreversibly ceased. It is not difficult or illogical in any way to equate this with the concept in many religions of the departure of the spirit from the body.

8. In the majority of cases, since brain death is part or the culmination of a failure of all vital functions, there is no necessity for a doctor specifically to identify brain death individually before concluding that the patient is dead. In a minority of cases in which it is brain death that causes failure of other organs and systems, the fact that these systems can be artificially maintained even after brain death has made it important to establish a diagnostic routine which will identify with certainty the existence of brain death.

Conclusion

9. It is the conclusion of the Conference that the identification of brain death means that the patient is dead, whether or not the function of some organs, such as a heartbeat, is still maintained by artificial means.

(For two further additions see Robson (1981) 295 BMJ 505 and [1981] ii Lancet 365.)

Given the near universal acceptance of the approach adopted in this Code, it is no surprise that the court in *Re A* adopted the concept of death that is reflected, at least implicitly, in the Code; adopted the locus (ie brain); and adopted the criteria for determining the presence or absence of the relevant functions and the means of determining clinically these criteria. (There remain, however, adherents to the more traditional definition, see eg RD Truog 'Is it Time to Abandon Brain Death?' (1997) 27 CD Hastings Center Report 29.)

Subsequently, the Department of Health has issued *A Code of Practice for the Diagnosis of Brain Stem Death* (March 1998). In replacing the 1983 Code, *Cadaveric Organs for Transplantation including the Diagnosis of Brain Death*, it provides comprehensive and up-to-date guidance on the diagnosis of 'brain-stem death'. Importantly, it replaces the term 'brain death' used in the 1983 Code with the more precise one of 'brain-stem death'. It repeats the criteria in the 1976/79 Conference of Colleges documents. Since it is not entirely clear whether it has totally superseded the latter, we set out for completeness the relevant parts of the 1998 Code.

DoH *A Code of Practice for the Diagnosis of Brain Stem Death* (1998)

2. Conditions Under Which the Diagnosis of Brain Stem Death Should be Considered

2.1 There should be no doubt that the patient's condition is due to irremediable brain damage or known aetiology. It may be obvious within hours of a primary intracranial event such as a severe head injury, or spontaneous intracranial haemorrhage that the condition is irremediable. However, when a patient has suffered primarily from cardiac arrest, hypoxia or severe circulatory insufficiency with an indefinite period of cerebral hypoxia, or is suspected of having cerebral air or fat embolism it may take longer to establish the diagnosis and to be confident of the prognosis. In some patients the primary pathology may be a matter of doubt and a confident diagnosis may only be reached by continuing clinical observation and investigation.

2.2 The patient is deeply unconscious.

2.2.1 There should be no evidence that this state is due to depressant drugs. Narcotics, hypnotics and tranquillisers may have prolonged action, particularly when hypothermia coexists or in the context of renal or hepatic failure. The benzodiazepines are markedly cumulative and persistent in their actions and are commonly used as anticonvulsants or to assist synchronisation with mechanical ventilators. It is therefore essential that the drug history should be carefully reviewed and any possibility of intoxication being the cause of, or contributing to, the patient's comatose state should preclude a diagnosis of brain stem death. It is important to recognise that, in some patients, hypoxia may have followed the ingestion of a drug but in this situation the criteria for brain stem death will not be applicable until such a time as the drug effects have been excluded as a continuing cause of the unresponsiveness.

2.2.2 Primary hypothermia as the cause of unconsciousness must have been excluded.

2.2.3 Potentially reversible circulatory, metabolic and endocrine disturbances must have been excluded as the cause of the continuation of unconsciousness. It is recognised that circulatory, metabolic and endocrine disturbances are a likely accompaniment of brain stem death (eg hypernatraemia, diabetes insipidus) but these are the effect rather than the cause of that condition and do not preclude the diagnosis of brain stem death.

2.3 The patient is being maintained on the ventilator because spontaneous respiration has been inadequate or ceased altogether. Relaxants (neuromuscular blocking agents) and other drugs must have been excluded as the cause of respiratory inadequacy or failure. Immobility, unresponsiveness, and lack of spontaneous respiration may be due to the use of neuromuscular blocking drugs and the persistence of their effects should be excluded by elicitation of deep tendon reflexes or by the demonstration of adequate neuromuscular conduction with a conventional nerve stimulator. Persistent effects of hypnotics or narcotics must be excluded as the cause of respiratory failure . . .

3.1 All brain stem reflecxes are absent.

3.1.1 The pupils are fixed and do not respond to sharp changes in the intensity of incident light.

3.1.2 There is no corneal reflex – care should be taken to avoid damage to the cornea.

3.1.3 The vestibulo-ocular reflexes are absent. No eye movements are seen during or following the slow injection of at least 50mls of ice cold water over one minute into each external auditory meatus in turn. Clear access to the tympanic membrane must be established by direct inspection and the head should be flexed at 30°. The performance of this manoeuvre may be prevented on one or other side by local injury or disease but this does not invalidate the diagnosis of brain stem death.

3.1.4 No motor responses within the cranial nerve distribution can be elicited by adequate stimulation of any somatic area. There is no limb response to supraorbital pressure.

3.1.5 There is no gag reflex or reflex response to bronchial stimulation by suction catheter placed down the trachea.

3.1.6 No respirator movements occur when the patient is disconnected from the mechanical ventilator. During this test it is necessary for the arterial carbon dioxide to exceed the threshold for respiratory stimulation, that is, the $PaCO_2$ shoudl reach 6.65kPa. This should be ensured by measurement of the blood gases.

The patient may be moderately hypothermic, flaccid and with a depressed metabolic rate such that the arterial carbon dioxide tension rises slowly during apnoea. Hypoxia during disconnection should be prevented by delivering oxygen at 6 litres per minute through a catheter in the trachea. If the facility for administering 5% CO_2 in oxygen exists, this is the preferred method for performing this test. The patient should first be venilated with 100% oxygen for 10 minutes, then with 5% CO_2 in oxygen for 5 minutes. The ventilator should then be disconnected for 10 minutes. During this period, oxygen should be delivered through a catheter as above.

Those patients with pre-existing chronic respiratory disease who may be responsive only to supra-normal levels of carbon dioxide and who depend upon hypoxic drive are special cases who should be managed in consultation with an expert in respiratory disease.

3.4 The beating heart in brain stem death. Even if ventilation is continued both adults and children will suffer cessation of heart beat within a few days, very occasionally a few weeks, of the diagnosis of brain stem death.

3.5 Endocrine, metabolic and circulatory abnormalities. Abnormalities, such as diabetes insipidus, hypo or hypernatraemia, hypothermia and disturbance of cardiac rhythm or blood pressure may occur in patients following anoxic, haemorrhagic or traumatic cerebral injury. These abnormalities may be consequences of brain stem failure and must be differentiated from abnormalities of endocrinological, biochemical or autonomic function contributing to failure of brain stem function.

3.6 Limb and trunk movements. Reflex movements of the limbs and torso may occur after brain stem death has been identified. The doctor should be able to explain clearly the significance of these movements to relatives, nurses and other staff who should be given sufficient information to enable them to understand that they are of spinal reflex origin and do not involve the brain at all.

3.7 Investigations. The safety of the clinical criteria for the diagnosis of brain stem death during the past 17 years provides justification for not including the results of neurophysiological or imaging investigations as part of those criteria. At present there is no evidence that imaging, electroencephalography or evoked potentials assist in the determination of brain stem death and, though such techniques will be kept under review, they should not presently form part of the diagnostic requirements.

3.8 Peripheral neurological syndromes of intensive care. There is a range of overlapping neuropathic, neuromuscular and myopathic syndromes which may occur in the context of intensive therapy and may cause problems in weaning a patient from a ventilator. This is not true apnoea (respiratory centre paralysis) and should not be taken as evidence for brain stem death.

3.9 The permanent vegetative state. Problems relating to the diagnosis and management of the permanent vegetative state must not be confused with those relating to brain stem death and the guidelines endorsed by the Conference of the Royal Colleges emphasise the important differences.

(b) Non-compliance with codes

Questions concerning compliance or non-compliance with the Codes only arise, of course, in those circumstances in which the patient's vital functions are being artificially maintained. Clearly, if the patient dies in other circumstances the death will be recognised by the prolonged irreversible absence of vital functions. If the patient is receiving artificial life-support, will non-compliance with the Codes have any legal consequences? There are two sets of problems:

(a) the determination of death;
(b) the legality of the doctor's conduct.

It may be useful to divide non-compliance with the Codes by looking at the three stages contemplated in the Codes. We concentrate here on the Conference of the Royal Colleges' Code.

Stage 1 requires that the doctor exclude patients with certain conditions; see Code (1)(a), (b) and (c) and (2) and (3), *supra*.

Stage 2 requires that the doctor perform the specific clinical 'tests for confirming brain death', *supra*.

Stage 3 requires that the doctor repeat the testing.

(i) THE DETERMINATION OF DEATH

The question we are concerned with here is, would a court when presented with evidence of non-compliance with the Code, hold that a patient was not dead when the doctor stated that he was? Undoubtedly, whether a person is dead will always ultimately be a question for the court. A court in making a determination will make a finding that death occurred on a basis of medical evidence (save in the most obvious circumstances). The medical evidence must *prima facie* include a demonstration that the doctor has complied with the Code. If the doctor's non-compliance occurs at *stage 1* it would be open to the court, on appropriate facts, to find that the patient was not dead at the time certified.

If the non-compliance occurs at *stage 2*, what has to be tested is whether a court would decide that a patient was not dead because, for example, the doctor failed to carry out one or more of the stipulated tests. At first blush, this would seem to be a somewhat recondite point, but we are assuming here, so as to test the analysis, that the precise moment of death is important legally. We take the view that a court, in the absence of evidence of irresponsible behaviour by the doctor, would be reluctant to find that the patient was not dead at the time asserted. But, how can this conclusion be justified in the face of the fact that a person must be presumed to be living until shown to be dead? The justification may be that, although the determination of death is a matter for the court, medical evidence is the only material upon which the court can act. We have no doubt that if responsible medical evidence was that the omission of the test(s) was irrelevant on the particular facts the court would not question this. (See *R v Malcherek*, where two tests were not carried out by the doctors and Lord Lane CJ stated: '[r]easons were given for neither of these tests having been carried out'. The court did not cast doubt on the doctors' determination of death.) This would obviously be the case where the test could not physically be carried out but may also be the case in other circumstances where good medical reasons exist for omitting it. It would, of course, be more difficult to sustain this view if none of the prescribed tests have been carried out.

If the non-compliance occurs at *stage 3*, again the only relevant legal question is whether the patient was dead at the time the first set of tests was carried out. If the purpose of the repetition of the tests is *confirmatory*, in view of what has been said before, it must follow that a court would hold that death had occurred no later than the completion of the first set of tests. Of course, if the repeat tests were more than confirmatory, major problems arise not merely concerning repetition of the tests but concerning the validity of the tests themselves. Obviously if a second set of tests are called for why not a third and so on? Pallis and Harley addressed this point:

C Pallis and D H Harley *ABC of Brain Stem Death* (2nd edn, 1996)

Virtually all codes urge that testing be carried out twice. The recommended intervals between the relevant tests have progressively shortened. There are several reasons why this has happened. Firstly, the objections to ventilating corpses have become more widely accepted. Secondly, when the first and second examinations for brain death were separated by as long as 24 hours several patients would develop asystole before the second examination. Finally, it became widely recognised that provided scrupulous attention was given to the preconditions and exclusions the second examination always confirmed the first. In other words, the more time spent in ascertaining the irremediable nature of the structural brain damage causing the coma the less important does the interval between tests become.

What is the purpose of retesting in a patient with a non-functioning brain stem due to well established, irremediable, structural brain damage? The United Kingdom code claims that it is to ensure that there has been no observer error. This is entirely praiseworthy, although no properly documented case has been published where the diagnosis of brain stem death has been revised after repeat testing. In our opinion retesting usually has a different purpose. It ensures that the non-functioning of the brain stem is not just a single observation at one point in time but that it has persisted. For how long? For a period several hundredfold that during which brain stem neurons could survive the total ischaemia of a non-perfused brain. At Hammersmith Hospital we like to separate our tests by two or three hours, which is more than enough to ensure that the findings are irreversible.

The 1998 Code of Practice issued by the Department of Health confirms the purpose of the two sets of tests is 'to remove the risk of observer error'. It also accepts that, while death is pronounced after the second set of tests, death occurred no later than the first set. Reliance is placed upon Johnson J's approach in *Re A, supra*.

DoH *A Code of Practice for the Diagnosis of Brain Stem Death* (1998)

3.3 Repetition of testing. The diagnosis of brain stem death should be made by at least two medical practitioners who have been registered for more than five years, are competent in this field and are not members of the transplant team, at least one of the doctors should be a consultant. Two sets of tests should always be performed, these may be carried out by the two practitioners separately or together. The tests are repeated to remove the risk of observer error. The timing of the interval between the tests is a matter for clinical judgement but the time should be adequate for the reassurance of all those directly concerned. The interval between the tests will depend upon the primary pathology, the clinical course of the disease and the progress of the patient. Although death is not pronounced until the second test has been completed the legal time of death is when the first test indicates brain stem death.

One further point which may be noted arises from the final paragraph of the 1976 Code. Although not entirely clearly drafted, the paragraph seems to contemplate that the determination should be made (or confirmed) by medical practitioners of appropriate standing and experience. (In 1981 it was clarified that one should be a consultant and the other a consultant or senior registrar: Robson [1981] ii Lancet 364. The 1998 DoH Code speaks of two doctors of more than 5 years registration with the GMC who are competent to make the diagnosis.) If this procedure was not complied with, again would a court hold that the patient certified as dead was not dead? Provided the tests were carried out with appropriate skill and the results were not doubted by informed medical opinion, we have no doubt that a court would find the patient was dead as certified despite the imprecise compliance.

(ii) THE LEGALITY OF THE DOCTOR'S CONDUCT

The concern here is with the possible criminal liability of the doctor for homicide and civil liability in negligence for failing to comply with the Code. Apart from the issue of the doctor's *mens rea* for the purpose of homicide (to which we shall return shortly), there seems to be two common features necessary to establish either civil or criminal liability. *First*, was the doctor's conduct in breach of his duty to his patient? *Secondly*, if it was, did the breach cause the patient's death?

The doctor's conduct will only be unlawful if the court has found that the patient is not dead either because there has been a failure to comply with the pre-conditions (at stage 1) or an irresponsible performance or failure to perform the tests (at stage 2). To make this issue abundantly clear, we are not here concerned with the doctor's decision in good faith to 'treat for dying' even to the point of withdrawing a patient from a ventilator (see *supra*, ch 17). Here, instead we are concerned with the doctor who by reason of non-compliance with the Code wrongly believes that the patient is dead, and then through his conduct brings about the patient's death, ie, by removing the patient's life-support system.

In these circumstances, we have no doubt that a court would decide that the doctor was both in breach of his legal duty to his patient and that his conduct was a legal cause of death. It follows, therefore, that a doctor could be guilty of gross negligence manslaughter (see *R v Adomako* [1995] 1 AC 171 (HL)) and could be civilly liable in negligence for the patient's death. Establishing the crime of murder would be more problematic since that requires proof that the defendant intended to kill (ie bringing about the death of), or cause serious bodily harm to, another human being. The doctor's belief that the patient was dead would be inconsistent with this state of mind.

5. A special case – the anencephalic

The anencephalic is a baby born with a fatal neurological condition – anencephaly – involving the absence of all, or most of, the cerebral hemispheres, ie the higher brain. The question is, how should the law respond to the anencephalic baby? The question is of general importance but arises specifically from proposals to harvest the organs of such babies for others while the anencephalic is still breathing.

G Annas 'From Canada with Love: Anencephalic Newborns as Organ Donors' (1987) 17 Hastings Center Report 36

Determining death

The central issue in the debate about using anencephalic infants as organ sources is whether they must be dead, and if so, how death can be determined. Some have argued that since they lack higher brain function anencephalics should not be considered living human beings and thus their organs should be available for immediate use. Although almost all agree that anencephalic infants – unlike nearly every other handicapped newborn – need not be treated to prolong their lives, the majority believe that they are living human beings and that killing them would be murder.

In January 1987, transplant surgeon Calvin Stiller convened an international group, among them Leonard Bailey, in London, Ontario, to discuss this issue. Diverse views were expressed, including that anencephalic infants could be used as organ donors, but only upon pronouncement of death using classical brain death criteria. To utilise such criteria, it would be necessary to put the child on a mechanical ventilator, because simply permitting him or her to stop breathing naturally would normally result in organs that deteriorate as the child's breathing becomes more compromised. This intervention would likely prolong the child's life; in the most extreme (but unlikely) scenario, the child's brain-stem might become strong enough to sustain independent breathing for weeks, or even months or years.

Arthur Caplan represented the position to the London meeting that anencephalic infants should be considered a separate category of human ('living but brain absent') and that parents should be able to donate their newborns' organs prior to their death. He justifies this position on the basis that the anencephalic child can never develop even a 'semblance of personhood', that the 'need for these organs is real', and that (most convincing for Caplan), 'many parents are eager to have their dead or anencephalic child used as a donor in the hope that something good might come of a tragic situation'. He does not believe that existing brain death criteria can be applied, and so is content with less exacting criteria to determine if anencephalic newborns are eligible for organ donation.

Declaring brain death in children

Since the country's first human heart transplant – in which the donor was, in fact, an anencephalic infant – great strides have been made in the mechanics of determining death. There is now general medical, legal and ethical agreement that an individual is dead either when he or she has irreversible cessation of circulation and respiration, or irreversible cessation 'of all functions of the entire brain, including the brain stem'. However, the medical consultants to the President's Commission concluded in 1981 that because of the 'increased resistance to damage' of their brains, 'physicians should be particularly cautious in applying neurologic criteria to determine death in children younger than five years'.

Responding to that challenge, a Task Force for the Determination of Brain Death in Children was established to develop guidelines for children under five. After years of study and deliberation, the group's report, which has been widely endorsed, was published in June, 1987. The guidelines provide accepted clinical criteria for determining brain death in three categories of children: those over one year of age; those aged two months to one year; and those aged seven days to two months. The criteria are inapplicable to infants under seven days of age; for infants less than two months, in addition to meeting strict clinical criteria, two electroencephalograms separated by at least forty-eight hours are recommended. The guidelines are recommendations only and are not meant as universal requirements. The group did not specifically deal with anencephalic infants, but the basic determination to be made is that the insult to the brain is 'irreversible'. Since anencephalic newborns have no higher brain function, different clinical criteria could be used to determine brain death for them.

New clinical criteria for anencephalics?

This leaves essentially two policy choices: we can abandon attempts to justify use of anencephalic infants as organ donors because there is currently no clinically accepted means to declare brain death in these infants; or we can carry out the research necessary to establish a clinically valid procedure for doing so. The Canadian group has decided to take the second route and experiment on methods to use as organ donors anencephalic newborns who can be validly declared brain-dead on classic criteria. The group has developed a basic protocol that calls for the parent to agree, prior to birth, that: (1) the infant will be resuscitated; (2) periodic testing will be done to determine brain death (removal from the ventilator at six-to-twelve hour intervals for a ten-minute period to determine ability to breathe spontaneously); (3) organ donation is acceptable; and (4) a definite time limit (to be determined by the parents but not more than fourteen days) after which the infant will be removed from the ventilator and permitted to die. Low dose morphine is administered to prevent potential suffering on the part of the infant, although whether anencephalic newborns can suffer is unknown.

This is a true experiment in the sense that there has never been a clinical trial to determine how anencephalic infants do with full ventilator support. They have almost never been so supported, primarily because the condition is quickly and universally fatal. As one paediatric intensive care specialist put it, it would be 'futile and inhumane' to support respiration in these infants artificially. How can we determine if this research is legally and ethically proper?

First, we must determine if it is proper to use dying newborns to help others rather than as ends in themselves. Anencephalic infants differ from all other organ donors in that they are not placed on life-support systems initially for their own sake, but solely for the sake of others. Specifically, since anencephalic newborns are not routinely resuscitated, intubated, or placed on ventilators and given other support, we cannot justify these interventions as 'treatment' for these infants. Rather, these interventions can only be seen as treatment for the benefit of the ultimate organ recipient, and perhaps as treatment for parents. If we determine that it is never ethically appropriate to prolong an unconsenting person's dying process for the sake of another, then our inquiry is at an end. If we conclude that it may be appropriate to do so (for example, if the harm to the dying child is trivial and the benefit to others is enormous), we can go on to the second step.

This second step would entail research, like that underway in Canada, to determine how long anencephalic infants can survive with the support available in an intensive care unit; whether they feel pain or have other sensations; the state of their kidneys, liver, and heart, which will determine their general usefulness for transplantation; and whether it is true that the condition of anencephaly can be easily and accurately distinguished from all other abnormalities of infants.

Professor Capron puts the argument against considering anencephalics as dead.

Alexander Morgan Capron 'Anencephalic Donors: Separate the Dead from the Dying' (1987) 17 Hastings Center Report 5

Adding anencephalics to the category of dead persons would be a radical change, both in the social and medical understanding of what it means to be dead and in the social practices surrounding death. Anencephalic infants may be dying, but they are still alive and breathing. Calling them 'dead' will not change physiologic reality or otherwise cause them to resemble those (cold and nonrespiring) bodies that are considered appropriate for post-mortem examinations and burial ... Physicians do not consider anencephalic infants as dead, but as dying. Their perception is borne out of statistics. One study of liveborn infants with anencephaly, conducted over a thirty-year period, found an equal distribution among males and females. Significantly more males survived the first day of life, but none lived longer than seven days, while female survival was comparable to male after the first day. One female (1.1 percent) survived 14 days:

> The results of this study show that over 40 percent of anencephalic infants can be expected to survive longer than 24 hours (51% males, 34% females), and of these, 35 percent will still be alive on the third day and 5 percent on the seventh day.

For most of the infants in this study, anencephaly was the only neural tube defect, and most of these had no anomalies in other organ systems. Among those infants who also had spina bifida or encephalocele (a protrusion of the brain substance through an opening in the skull), one third had defects in another major organ system.

... Although the diagnosis is usually made accurately by neurologists, authors of the thirty-year study just mentioned found that in 'conducting this study, it became obvious that it is important to verify the diagnosis of anencephaly'. They describe several cases of long survival:

> One infant initially coded as anencephaly, who survived over 4 months, had hydranencephaly rather than anencephaly, and another who lived for 12 days actually had amniotic band syndrome mimicking anencephaly.

Misdiagnosis by itself would not appear to be a great enough risk to preclude the use of anencephaly as a category to trigger further action (such as declaration of 'death'). But the observed relationship to – or even overlapping with – other congenital neurological defects underlines the problems that the proposal would create. For example, hydranencephalics have normal brain development early in gestation; as a result of some event (such as an in utero infection) their cerebral hemispheres are destroyed and replaced with fluid. Like anencephalics, hydranencephalics survive depending upon the extent to which their brain stems are able to regulate vegetative functioning, but they usually survive somewhat longer because their skulls are intact and thus their brains are not open to infection.

To further complicate the picture, other neurological conditions, such as certain types of microcephaly, are also inconsistent with long-term survival. Microcephaly, – literally, a small head – covers a spectrum of problems, including cases in which the hemispheres fail to form. Whatever their clinical differences from anencephalic babies, hydranencephalic and some microcephalic infants are *conceptually* indistinguishable if the characteristic separating anencephalics from normal children is their lethal neurological condition.

Because of the existence of these other diagnostic categories, decision makers will be pressured to expand the 'definition' to sweep in other similarly situated 'dead' neonates. Indeed, Dr Alan Shewmon, a pediatric neurologist at UCLA, has pointed out that babies – such as hydranencephalics – who typically live a little longer than anencephalics are actually likely to be *more* attractive sources of organs because of the extra time for development. At present, the regional organ procurement association for California does not accept organs from infants younger than two months of age because of physiologic difficulties (such as the tendency of vessels to clot).

More important, these other diagnostic categories serve as a reminder that the proposals involve a variety of infants who are going to die in a relatively short time. Distinguishing those who will die within a day or two from those (including *some* microcephalics and hydranencephalics as well as the remaining anencephalics) who will die over the following two weeks is inevitably imprecise. The distinctions rest on clinical judgment, not moral principle....

'Defining' anencephalics as dead would place these patients into the same category as patients who lack the capacity to breathe on their own, which has always been taken as a basic sign of life. Perhaps the proponents of this change do not see this as a major alteration because they think the law already lumps together some people who are 'more dead' (those whose hearts have stopped) with others who are merely 'brain dead'. But all persons found to meet the standards of the UDDA [the Uniform Determination of Death Act] are equally dead; it is merely the means of measuring the absence of the integrated functioning of heart, lungs and brain that differs between those who are and those who are not being tested by methods that can induce breathing and heartbeat.

Defining anencephalics as dead so that they may be used as organ donors could, ironically, actually decrease organ donation. Imagine the effect of the law on the process of seeking organ donations from the relatives of a deceased person. At present, when that situation arises, the person seeking permission can explain that the patient is dead; despite the heaving chest and other appearances of life, if the physicians were to cease the mechanical interventions, it would immediately be apparent that the body is in the same state that we have always recognised as dead. The next-of-kin are told that they do not face a difficult decision over whether to let the patient die; instead they face the reality that their loved one is now a corpse – albeit a corpse with artificially generated heartbeat and breathing – whose organs are still being maintained in a way that would make them useful for transplants. (Remember that only a fraction of persons declared dead on the basis of absence of brain functions are candidates for organ donation.)

If anencephalic babies were also regarded as dead bodies suitable for organ donation, this certainty would be lost. For in these cases, decisions about the extent of treatment remain – indeed, some parents may even wish to try heroic or experimental means to lengthen their child's life. The message to those involved in organ transplantation – both as relatives of potential donors and as physicians, nurses, and others seeking permission for donation – is thus likely to introduce new elements of uncertainty. Is *any* particular patient – and not just an anencephalic baby – *really* dead? Or do the physicians mean only that the outlook for the patient's survival is poor, so why not allow the organs to be taken and bring about death in this (useful) fashion?

Alternatively, perhaps some who favor the anencephalic standard for death *do* mean to change the law radically. A few commentators have argued for many years that the statutes on death should move beyond new means for measuring the traditional state of death and should instead declare that persons who have lost only the higher (neocortical) functions of their brains are also dead. These suggestions have been uniformly rejected by legislators across the country – as well as by most medical, ethical, and legal writers. Yet the inclusion of anencephalics in the 'definition' of death would amount to the first recognition of a 'higher brain' standard – and a first step toward a broader use of this standard – because these babies, despite the massive deficit in their brains, still have some functions (principally at the brain stem level).

To state that such patients are dead would be equivalent to saying that the late Karen Quinlan was 'dead' for the more than ten years that she lived after her respirator was removed. Like the anencephalic babies, Ms Quinlan and other patients in a persistent vegetative state lack the ability to think, to communicate, and probably even to process any sensations of pain and pleasure (at least in the way that we think of these phenomena). Some people may consider such a life as unrewarding, but that does not justify loose use of language about who is 'dead'. Emotionally, one may be tempted to say that a person in a permanent coma is 'as good as dead' because he or she cannot participate in any of the activities that give life meaning. But such a breathing, metabolising patient does not embody what we mean by dead and is not ready for burial – or organ donation.

A statute that labels anencephalics 'dead' is a bad idea because either it will treat differently another group that is identical on the relevant criteria (the permanently comatose, who are dying and lacking consciousness) or it will lead to a further revision in medical and legal standards under which the permanently comatose would also be regarded as 'dead' although many of them can survive for years with nothing more than ordinary nursing care.

For many people, the prospect of being in a permanent coma is unacceptable; if that occurred, they would want to be allowed to die without further treatment. But that is a separate problem to which society is already responding in other ways. It would be highly controversial – and, indeed, would be rejected by most people – to call people who are in a coma but who still breathe on their own 'dead', especially when the purpose is to allow removal of their vital organs, which *would* then cause their death as that term is now used. That was the nightmarish scenario that took place in the Jefferson Institute in Robin Cook's novel *Coma*.

In 1988, the Working Party of the Medical Royal Colleges on 'Organ Transplantation in Neonates', chaired by Sir Raymond Hoffenberg, considered, *inter alia*, the question of the status of the anencephalic baby. It concluded that:

5.1 It is understood that, providing there was professional confidence that brain stem death criteria could be applied to the neonate of a certain gestational age, then there could be no legal or ethical objection to the parents agreeing to, and a surgeon undertaking, organ retrieval. 5.2 There is little firm evidence that the well-established criteria used for diagnosing brain stem death in older children and adults can be applied to neonates with beating hearts in the first seven days of life for the purpose of organ removal. The ethics committee of the Child Neurology Society in the United States has concluded that there is insufficient information to diagnose brain death at this age and in that country a joint task force is investigating the matter further and will report soon. 5.3 Until acceptable criteria for brain stem death in the first seven days of life are agreed it is the view of the Working Party that the brain stem death criteria used in older children and adults cannot be used to justify the removal or organs from such neonates with beating hearts for transplantation.

In the light of this, the Working Party recommended the following:

4.7.3 … Tests of brain stem functions are applied in adults because the absence of such function establishes that the brain is dead; they are clearly inapplicable when the forebrain itself is missing. Such infants clearly have a major neurological deficiency incompatible with life for longer than a few hours. A view which commended itself to the Working Party was that organs could be removed from an anencephalic infant when two doctors (who are not members of the transplant team) agreed that spontaneous respiration had ceased. In the adult the diagnosis of brain death plus apnoea is recognised as death. The Working Party felt by analogy that the absence of the forebrain in these infants plus apnoea would similarly be recognised as death.

What we see here is, as has been said, a general problem in adopting the 'brainstem death' criteria for children under two months of age. The recent Department of Health Code of Practice (*op cit*) (March 1998) at para 3.2 confirms this:

3.2 Children. A report of a working party of the British Paediatric Association of 1991 supported by the Council of the Royal College of Physicians suggested that, in children over the age of 2 months, the brain stem death criteria should be the same as those in adults. Between 37 weeks of gestation and 2 months of age, it is rarely possible confidently to diagnose brain stem death and below 37 weeks of gestation, the criteria for brain stem death cannot be applied. A Working Party of the Conference of Colleges on Organ Transplantation in Neonates recommended that organs for transplantation may be removed from anencephalic infants when two doctors, who are not members of the transplant team, agree that spontaneous respiration has ceased. The conclusions of these reports are endorsed by the current Working Party.

In the following case, the Florida Supreme Court examined both Florida's statutory definition of death and the common law.

Re TACP (1992) 609 So 2d 588 (Fla Sup Ct)

Kogan J:

I. Facts

At or about the eighth month of pregnancy, the parents of the child TACP were informed that she would be born with anencephaly. This is a birth defect invariably fatal, in which the child typically is born with only a "brain stem" but otherwise lacks a human brain. In TACP's case, the back of the skull was entirely missing and the brain stem was exposed to the air, except for medical bandaging. The risk of infection to the brain stem was considered very high. Anencephalic infants sometimes can survive several days after birth because the brain stem has a limited capacity to maintain autonomic bodily functions such as breathing and heartbeat. This ability soon ceases, however, in the absence of regulation from the missing brain.

In this case, TACP actually survived only a few days after birth. The medical evidence in the record shows that the child TACP was incapable of developing any sort of cognitive process, may have been unable to feel pain or experience sensation due to the absence of the upper brain, and at least for part of the time was placed on a mechanical ventilator to assist her breathing. At the time of the hearing below, however, the child was breathing unaided, although she died soon thereafter.

On the advice of physicians, the parents continued the pregnancy to term and agreed that the mother would undergo caesarean section during birth. The parents agreed to the caesarean procedure with the express hope that the infant's organs would be less damaged and could be used for transplant in other sick children. Although TACP had no hope of life herself, the parents both testified in court that they wanted to use this opportunity to give life to others. However, when the parents requested that TACP be declared legally dead for this purpose, her health care providers refused out of concern that they thereby might incur civil or criminal liability....

III. Legal Definitions of "Death" & "Life"

As the parties and amici have argued, the common law in some American jurisdictions recognized a cardiopulmonary definition of "death": A human being was not considered dead until breathing and heartbeat had stopped entirely, without possibility of resuscitation. Eg, *Thomas v Anderson* 96 Cal App 2d 371, 215 P 2d 478, 482 (Cal App 1950); see Jay A. Friedman, Taking the Camel by the Nose: The Anencephalic as a Source for Pediatric Organ Transplants, 90 Colum L Rev 917, 925–26 (1990).

However, there is some doubt about the exact method by which this definition was imported into the law of some states. Apparently the definition was taken from earlier editions of *Black's Law Dictionary*, which itself did not cite to an original source. C Anthony Friloux, Jr, Death, When Does It Occur?, 27 Baylor L Rev 10, 12–13 (1975). The definition thus may only have been the opinion of Black's earlier editors.

We have found no authority showing that Florida ever recognized the original *Black's Law Dictionary* definition or any other definition of "death" as a matter of our own common law. Even if we had adopted such a standard, however, it is equally clear that modern medical technology has rendered the earlier Black's definition of "death" seriously inadequate. With the invention of life-support devices and procedures, human bodies can be made to breathe and blood to circulate even in the utter absence of brain function.

As a result, the ability to withhold or discontinue such life support created distinct legal problems in light of the "cardiopulmonary" definition of death originally used by *Black's Dictionary*. For example, health care providers might be civilly or criminally liable for removing transplantable organs from a person sustained by life support, or defendants charged with homicide might argue that their victim's death actually was caused when life support was discontinued. Andrea K. Scott, Death Unto Life: Anencephalic Infants as Organ Donors 74 Va L Rev 1527, 1538–41 (1988) (citing actual cases).

In light of the inadequacies of a cardiopulmonary definition of "death," a number of jurisdictions began altering their laws in an attempt to address the medical community's changing conceptions of the point in time at which life ceases. An effort was made to synthesize many of the new concerns into a Uniform Determination of Death Act issued by the National Conference of Commissioners on Uniform State Laws. The uniform statute states:

> An individual who has sustained either (1) irreversible cessation of circulatory and respiratory functions, or (2) irreversible cessation of all functions of the entire brain, including the brain stem, is dead. A determination of death must be made in accordance with accepted medical standards.

Uniform Determination of Death Act @ 1, 12 ULA 340 (Supp 1991). Thus the uniform act both codified the earlier common law standard and extended it to deal with the specific problem of "whole brain death." While some American jurisdictions appear to have adopted substantially the same language, Florida is not among these . . .

Indeed, Florida appears to have struck out on its own. The statute cited as controlling by the trial court does not actually address itself to the problem of anencephalic infants, nor indeed to any situation other than patients actually being sustained by artificial life support. The statute provides:

> For legal and medical purposes, where respiratory and circulatory functions are maintained by artificial means of support so as to preclude a determination that these functions have ceased, the occurrence of death may be determined where there is the irreversible cessation of the functioning of the entire brain, including the brain stem, determined in accordance with this section.

@ 382.009(1), Fla Stat (1991) (emphasis added). A later subsection goes on to declare:

> Except for a diagnosis of brain death, the standard set forth in this section is not the exclusive standard for determining death or for the withdrawal of life-support systems.

@382.009(4), Fla Stat (1991). This language is highly significant for two reasons.

First, the statute does not purport to codify the common law standard applied in some other jurisdictions, as does the uniform act. The use of the permissive word "may" in the statute in tandem with the savings clause of section 382.009(4) buttresses the conclusion that the legislature envisioned other ways of defining "death." Second, the statutory framers clearly did not intend to apply the statutes language to the anencephalic infant not being kept alive by life support. To the contrary, the framers expressly limited the statute to that situation in which "respiratory and circulatory functions are maintained by artificial means of support."

There are a few Florida authorities that have addressed the definitions of "life" and "death" in somewhat analogous though factually distinguishable contexts. Florida's Vital Statistics Act, for example, defines "live birth" as:

> the complete expulsion or extraction of a product of human conception from its mother, irrespective of the duration of pregnancy, which, after such expulsion, breathes or shows any other evidence of life such as beating of the heart, pulsation of the umbilical cord, and definite movement of the voluntary muscles, whether or not the umbilical cord has been cut or the placenta is attached.

@382.002(10), Fla Stat (1991). Conversely, "fetal death" is defined as:

> death prior to the complete expulsion or extraction of a product of human conception from its mother if the 20th week of gestation has been reached and the death is indicated by the fact that after such expulsion or extraction the fetus does not breathe or show any other evidence of life such as beating of the heart, pulsation of the umbilical cord, or definite movement of voluntary muscles.

@382.002(7) Fla Stat (1991). From these definitions, it is clear that TACP was a "live birth" and not a "fetal death," at least for purposes of the collection of vital statistics in Florida. These definitions obviously are inapplicable to the issues at hand today, but they do shed some light on the Florida legislature's thoughts regarding a definition of "life" and "death."

Similarly, an analogous (if distinguishable) problem has arisen in Florida tort law. In cases alleging wrongful death, our courts have held that fetuses are not "persons" and are not "born alive" until they acquire an existence separate and independent from the mother. Eg *Duncan v Flynn* 358 So 2d 178, 178–179 (Fla 1978). We believe the weight of the evidence supports the conclusion that TACP was "alive" in this sense because she was separated from the womb, and was capable of breathing and maintaining a heartbeat independently of her mother's body for some duration of time thereafter. Once again, however, this conclusion arises from law that is only analogous and is not dispositive of the issue at hand.

We also note that the 1988 Florida Legislature considered a bill that would have defined "death" to include anencephaly. Fla HB 1089 (1988). The bill died in committee. While the failure of legislation in committee does not establish legislative intent, it nevertheless supports the conclusion that as recently as 1988 no consensus existed among Florida's lawmakers regarding the issue we confront today.

The parties have cited to no authorities directly dealing with the question of whether anencephalics are "alive" or "dead." Our own research has disclosed no other federal or Florida law or precedent arguably on this point or applicable by analogy. We thus are led to the conclusion that no legal authority binding upon this Court has decided whether an anencephalic child is alive for purposes of organ donation. In the absence of applicable legal authority, this Court must weigh and consider the public policy considerations at stake here . . .

IV Common Law & Policy

Initially, we must start by recognizing that section 382.009, Florida Statutes (1991), provides a method for determining death in those cases in which a person's respiratory and circulatory functions are maintained artificially. @ 382.009(4), Fla Stat (1991). Likewise, we agree that a cardiopulmonary definition of death must be accepted in Florida as a matter of our common law, applicable whenever section 382.009 does not govern. Thus, if cardiopulmonary function is not being maintained artificially as stated in section 382.009, a person is dead who has sustained irreversible cessation of circulatory and respiratory functions as determined in accordance with accepted medical standards. We have found no credible authority arguing that this definition is inconsistent with the existence of death, and we therefore need not labor the point further.

The question remaining is whether there is good reason in public policy for this Court to create an additional common law standard applicable to anencephalics. Alterations of the common law, while rarely entertained or allowed, are within this Court's prerogative. Eg *Hoffman v Jones*, 280 So 2d 431 (Fla 1973). However, the rule we follow is that the common law will not be altered or expanded unless demanded by public necessity, *Coastal Petroleum Co v Mobil Oil Corp* 583 So 2d 1022, 1025 (Fla 1991), or where required to vindicate fundamental rights. *Haag v State*, 591 So 2d 614, 618 (Fla 1992). We believe, for example, that our adoption of the cardiopulmonary definition of death today is required by public necessity and, in any event, merely formalizes what has been the common practice in this state for well over a century.

Such is not the case with petitioners' request. Our review of the medical, ethical, and legal literature on anencephaly discloses absolutely no consensus that public necessity or fundamental rights will be better served by granting this request.

We are not persuaded that a public necessity exists to justify this action, in light of the other factors in this case – although we acknowledge much ambivalence about this particular question. We have been deeply touched by the altruism and unquestioned motives of the parents of TACP. The parents have shown great humanity, compassion, and concern for others. The problem we as a Court must face, however, is that the medical literature shows unresolved controversy over the extent to which anencephalic organs can or should be used in transplants.

There is an unquestioned need for transplantable infant organs. See Kathleen L Paliokas, Anencephalic Newborns as Organ Donors: An Assessment of "Death" and Legislative Policy, 31 Wm & Mary L Rev 197, 238–39 (1989); Andrea K Scott, Death Unto Life: Anencephalic Infants as Organ Donors, 74 Va L Rev 1527, 1565–56 (1988). Yet some medical commentators suggest that the organs of anencephalics are seldom usable, for a variety of reasons, and that so few organ transplants will be possible from anencephalics as to render the enterprise questionable in light of the ethical problems at stake – even if legal restrictions were lifted. D Alan Shewmon et al, The Use of Anencephalic Infants as Organ Sources, 261 JAM 1773, 1774–75, (1989).

Others note that prenatal screening now is substantially reducing the number of anencephalics born each year in the United States and that, consequently, anencephalics are unlikely to be a significant source of organs as time passes. Shlomo Shinnar et al, Ethical Issues in the Use of Anencephalic Infants as Organ Donors, 7 Ethical Issues in Neurologic Practice 729, 741 (1989). And still others have frankly acknowledged that there is no consensus and that redefinition of death in this content should await the emergence of a consensus. Norman Frost, Removing Organs from Anencephalic Infants: Ethical and Legal Considerations, 16 Neonatal Neurology 331, 336 (1989). But see Charles N Rock, The Living Dead: Anencephaly and Organ Donation, 7 J Hum Rts, 243, 276–77 (1989) (arguing a consensus may be developing).

A presidential commission in 1981 urged strict adherence to the Uniform Determination of Death Act's definition, which would preclude equating anencephaly with death. President's Commission for the Study of Ethical Problems, Biomedical, and Behavioral Research, Defining Death: Medical, Legal and Ethical Issues in the Determination of Death 2 (1981). Several sections of the American Bar Association have reached much the same conclusion. National Conference on Birth, Death, and Law, Report on Conference, 29 Jurimetrics J 403, 421 (Lori B Andrews et al eds 1989).

Some legal commentators have urged that treating anencephalics as dead equates them with "nonpersons," presenting a "slippery slope" problem with regard to all other persons who lack cognition for whatever reason. Debra H Berger, The Infant with Anencephaly: Moral and Legal Dilemmas, 5 Issues in L & Med 67, 84–85 (1989). Others have quoted physicians involved in infant-organ transplants as stating, "The slippery slope is real," because some physicians have proposed transplants from infants with defects less severe than anencephaly. Beth Brandon, Anencephalic Infants as Organ Donors: A Question of Life or Death, 40 Case Western L Rev 781, 802 (1989–90).

We express no opinion today about who is right and who is wrong on these issues – if any "right" or "wrong" can be found here. The salient point is that no consensus exists as to: (a) the utility of organ transplants of the type at issue here; (b) the ethical issues involved; or (c) the legal and constitutional problems implicated.

V. Conclusions

Accordingly, we find no basis to expand the common law to equate anencephaly with death. We acknowledge the possibility that some infants' lives might be saved by using organs from anencephalics who do not meet the traditional definition of "death" we reaffirm today. But weighed against this is the utter lack of consensus, and the questions about the overall utility of such organ donations. The scales clearly tip in favour of not extending the common law in this instance.

To summarize: We hold that Florida common law recognizes the cardiopulmonary definition of death as stated above; and Florida statutes create a "whole-brain death" exception applicable whenever cardiopulmonary function is being maintained artificially. There are no other legal standards for determining death under present Florida law.

Because no Florida statute applies to the present case, the determination of death in this instance must be judged against the common law cardiopulmonary standard. The evidence shows that TACP's heart was beating and she was breathing at the times in question. Accordingly, she was not dead under Florida law, and no donation of her organs would have been legal.

Barkett, CJ and Overton, McDonald, Shaw, Grimes and Harding, JJ agreed.

The court concluded that the common law definition of death was limited to irreversible cardiopulmonary failure. The Florida Legislation created an exception of 'whole brain death' for those on artificial life support. Of course, in England the common law recognises 'brain-stem death', as we have seen. Like the Florida court, an English court (as opposed to Parliament) is most unlikely to take the further step that is required to bring anencephalic babies within the category of 'dead' person. It may be worth noting, perhaps, that such a baby would, of course, if a change occurred, be dead at birth. Having never been 'born alive' and hence a legal person, the Human Tissue Act 1961 would not apply.

6. Cognitive or higher brain death

Can it be argued that the law should recognise death as having occurred even when the individual has not irreversibly lost the capacity for consciousness *and* to breathe? We have already seen mention of this possibility. Some have argued for the recognition of 'cognitive' or 'higher brain death' where the person has only irreversibly lost the capacity for consciousness (eg R M Veatch 'The Impending Collapse of the Whole-Brain Definition of Death' (1993) 23(4) Hastings Center Report 18 and R J Devettere, 'Neocortical Death and Human Death' (1990) 18, Law Medicine and Health Care 96). The obvious example of such a 'person' would be the patient in a permanent vegetative state (PVS) but there may be others, such as anencephalics we have just been considering. Clearly, the law in England (or indeed elsewhere) has not gone this far. Should it?

P D G Skegg *Law, Ethics and Medicine* **(1984)**

Many of the arguments for regarding as dead those patients whose hearts continue to beat, but who are brain dead apply also to those who are in an irreversible non-cognitive condition. But the fundamental argument is that, once cognitive death has occurred, the person may be said to have ceased to exist, even if the body continues to breathe spontaneously. Doctors, as well as philosophers and theologians, have supported this approach. For example, one doctor (who uses 'cerebral death' to refer to what is here described as 'cognitive death') has written (S D Clinger, '*Medical Death*' (1975) 27 Baylor Law Review 22, 22–4):

The personal, identifiable life of an individual human can be equated with the living function of that part of the brain called the cerebrum.

Central function is manifested in consciousness, awareness, memory, anticipation, recognition and emotions. ... There is no human life in the [irreversible] absence of these....

I would emphasize ... that 'cerebral death' and 'brain death' are different things, and that the term 'cerebral death' expresses the medical concept which is equated with the death of the individual person.

If a doctor acted upon this view in practice, and removed a heart from a patient who had sustained cognitive death, but whose brain-stem was still functioning, the courts might be forced to consider the issue. It could come before the courts in other ways also. For example, the defendant in a personal injury claim could argue that as the plaintiff had sustained cognitive death he was no longer a living person, and hence not entitled to damages on the basis that he was still alive. Were such a case to come before the courts, it would be particularly important that the courts make a clear distinction between the medical facts about the patient's condition and the separate issue of whether, given those facts, the patient was to be regarded as alive or dead. Whether the patient is in an irreversible non-cognitive condition is undoubtedly a medical question. But whether a patient in this condition is alive or dead, for the purpose of English law, is not a matter on which the courts should feel obliged to follow the views of the doctors who gave evidence, or even the views of the medical profession generally…

For the foreseeable future, conventional usage will be so clear that patients in an irreversible non-cognitive state must be regarded as alive for the purpose of English law. But the currently accepted view is likely to come under increasing attack, and it is possible that opinion will become so divided that the courts will have to take account of other considerations. It is therefore as well to consider some of the arguments and considerations which might, in that event, influence the courts.

Many of the reasons which have been put forward for regarding as dead those patients who have sustained brain death apply also to those patients who have sustained cognitive death. For example, the first of the two reasons offered in the Harvard Report, in support of the 'new criterion for death', was that (H K Beecher et al, '*A Definition of Irreversible Coma*' (1968) 205 JAMA 337–340):

> Improvements in resuscitative and supportive measures have led to increased efforts to save those who are desperately injured. Sometimes these efforts have only partial success so that the result is an individual whose heart continues to beat but whose brain is irreversibly damaged. The burden is great on patients who suffer permanent loss of intellect, on their families, on the hospitals, and on those in need of hospital beds already occupied by these comatose patients.

Although this consideration can hardly stand on its own as a sufficient reason for regarding anyone as dead, it has much greater application to those who have sustained cognitive death than to those who have sustained brain death. Even if doctors were not free to withdraw artificial ventilation when brain death was established, those bodies can rarely be kept functioning for more than a few days. By contrast, patients who have sustained cognitive death may continue in that state for months, and sometimes even years.

The other reason often given for regarding brain-dead patients as dead is the desirability of doctors being free to remove organs from such bodies for transplantation. Patients who have sustained cognitive death would be a particularly suitable source of organs for transplantation, as their hearts, livers, and kidneys will often be in excellent condition. But such patients would provide a very small proportion of the organs required for transplantation, so the possible benefit to transplantation if those patients were regarded as dead would not be comparable with the benefit which would accrue in the saving of medical resources.

The debate about cognitive death has been unlike much of that about brain death, for most of those who favour patients in an irreversibly non-cognitive condition being regarded as dead have not relied on the incidental advantages of such an approach. They have focused on more fundamental issues. Death being the cessation of life, many of them have sought to determine what is distinctive about the life of a human person, as opposed to other members of the animal kingdom. They argue that if a person's brain is damaged to such an extent that he can never return to consciousness, can never perform any cognitive function, then that person has died. The Co-ordinator of the Protection of Life Project of the Law Reform Commission of Canada, E W Keyserlingk has taken this view. In a study written for the Commission, (Protection of Life Series, Study Paper, (1979), 62) he stated:

> In my view, if the medical tests have in fact determined that there is no potential for spontaneous cerebral brain function, even if spontaneous respiration continues, then the human person is dead. Obviously this view is based on the conviction that man is essentially more than a biological 'respiratory' being, and is essentially a rational, experiencing, communicating being. It is based as well on the strong medical evidence that the specific loci in the brain in which these latter functions reside are cerebral or higher brain centres…

If the courts were to hold that someone who was once a living person, but who had sustained cognitive death, was dead for legal purposes, it is difficult to see that there could be any legal objection to these spontaneously breathing bodies being cremated or buried.

Even if a judge did have freedom of decision in this matter he might consider that, although there are very significant differences between patients who have sustained cognitive death and patients who have not lost their cognitive faculties, there are also significant differences between patients who have sustained cognitive death but continue to breathe spontaneously and almost all corpses. He would be likely to recognize that a move to regard as dead all patients who have sustained cognitive death would be very controversial, and that a trial was a particularly unsuitable occasion to determine such an issue (*R v Kitching and Adams* [1976]

6 WWR 697, 714 (Man CA)). Even if a judge was personally in favour of a statute providing that a person is dead once cognitive death occurs, considerations such as these could be expected to lead him to persist with the view that – in the absence of statutory intervention – a patient who is breathing spontaneously is not be regarded as dead. He would not consider that it was for him to introduce a fundamental distinction between personal and bodily life.

Of course, it could be argued that acceptance of the view that a patient who has sustained brain death is dead, even though his heart continues to beat, has already involved acceptance of a distinction between human personal life, and human biological life, in relation to some bodies which would not in the past have been regarded as corpses. A patient who has sustained brain death may be maintained on a ventilator for some days before systemic death occurs. But the fact that there has been a relatively small departure from the traditional approach, whereby a person was not regarded as dead before his heart stopped pumping blood around his body, is not necessarily an argument for a much more striking departure. The argument may lead to doubt as to the wisdom of having taken the first step, rather than encourage the taking of the second or third.

As dying is invariably a process, it is not surprising that wherever the line between life and death is drawn there will be cases on either side of it which do not appear all that different. The problem would be shifted, rather than avoided, if patients in an irreversibly non-cognitive condition were regarded as dead. It would then be possible to point to those patients whose brains were damaged to such an extent that they could never have more than a minimal degree of cognition. Why, it could be asked, should the possibility of such an extremely limited function be considered so significant as to warrant making such a fundamental distinction between this patient and one in whom this very limited capacity was absent?

The 'slippery slope' argument may be seen as a reason for drawing the line short of cognitive death. One writer who supports the view that patients in an irreversible non-cognitive state are no longer living persons has proposed a list of 'possible human criteria'. One of these is minimal intelligence, and concerning this he writes that 'An individual of the species *Homo sapiens* who falls below the IQ grade of 40-mark in a standard Stanford-Binet test, amplified if you like by other tests, is questionably a person; below the 20-mark, not a person. Others who favour the view that patients who have sustained cognitive death should be regarded as dead also use arguments which, if logically applied, would deny the status of a living human person to others who are not in an irreversible non-cognitive condition. Indeed, the approach of most of those who believe that patients who have sustained cognitive death should be regarded as dead, could lead to the conclusion that some patients who have not reached this stage are also dead. They identify certain functions, capacities, or qualities as essential to 'personal' or truly 'human' life, and go on to say that where these have been irreversibly lost, 'personal' or 'human' life has ceased, so the individual is by definition dead. There is unlikely to be agreement as to what are these 'indicators of humanhood' or personhood. The irreversible loss of cognitive functions is at present the lowest common denominator, but there is no reason why this approach should be restricted to these cases alone.

Thus far, this discussion of cognitive death has proceeded on the assumption that it is possible to determine with certainty that some patients who are not brain dead are nevertheless in an irreversible non-cognitive condition. Many doctors believe that this is so, but there is less agreement about the identification of this state than there is now about the identification of brain death. Hence it could be argued that it is, at the very least, premature to accept that a person whom doctors believe to be in an irreversibly non-cognitive condition is dead for legal purposes.

Even once it is generally accepted that in some cases it can be established with certainty that a patient is in an irreversibly non-cognitive condition, there are likely to be many other cases in which it is not clear whether or not patients have sustained cognitive death. Doctors would doubtless treat them as alive until death was conclusively established, as they do patients who may be brain dead. But the problem would occur over a longer time-scale than it does with brain death, and it would be unsatisfactory if a great number of long-term patients were suspected of being dead, but were being treated as alive simply because death had not been established conclusively. There could also be undesirable consequences if the law failed to provide a presumption that such patients were alive until it was clearly established that they were dead.

Conclusion

The conclusion, then, is that while patients who have sustained brain death can now be regarded as dead for the purpose of English law, those who have merely sustained cognitive death will not now, or in the near future, be regarded as dead for the purpose of English law. Even if conventional usage becomes much less clear, and doctors come to favour reclassification, judges should be wary of giving effect to the new view in advance of its very widespread acceptance, or its adoption by statute.

(For a sustained philosophical argument, see K Gervais *Redefining Death* (1986).)

Use of and dealing with dead bodies

A. LEGAL STATUS

What is the legal status of the corpse or parts removed from it? This is a general jurisprudential question raising the issue of the place of human remains in the law's catalogue. Is a corpse a person? Clearly not. Some might describe it as an 'ex-person', because of what it was. But, after death, the body (or its parts) is not in law treated as a person. Could a body (or its parts) fall within the law's realm of property? As such, it could be amenable to legal control and allow others to exercise proprietary rights over it. It could be stolen, damage to it could amount to criminal damage and individuals who acquire parts of the body could have rights over those parts protected as their property (see, for a recent discussion, R Atherton 'Claims on the Deceased: The Corpse as Property' (2000) 7 JLM 361). As we saw in Chapter 15, the same question calls for a solution where parts of a living person's body are excised or separated from him .We saw there, that the law may be influenced by its attitude to dead bodies and the so-called 'no property' rule which has it that a corpse is not in law property and cannot be 'owned' or otherwise subject to property rights. The law can be usefully illustrated by the important decision of the Australian High Court in *Doodeward v Spence* (1908) 6 CLR 406.

Doodeward v Spence (1908) 6 CLR 406 (HC of A)

Griffith CJ: The subject matter of the action was the preserved body of what has been spoken of in the case as "a two-headed baby." It appears from the evidence that the mother of the baby gave birth to it in New Zealand forty years ago, that it was still-born (by which I understand that it never had an independent existence), that the mother's medical attendant, a Dr Donahoe, who arrived after the birth, took the body away with him preserved it with spirits in a bottle, and kept it in his surgery as a curiosity, that at his death in 1870 it was sold by auction with his other personal effects and realized between £30 and £40, and that it afterwards came into the possession of the appellant. It must be assumed that Dr Donahoe's possession of the body was lawful, so far as the possession of such an object can be lawful.

The Supreme Court were of opinion that there can be no right of property in the dead body of a human being, and consequently that such a body cannot be the subject of an action for detinue or trover. Pring J further expressed the opinion that there can be no right of property in a portion of a human body which has been severed from it.

The authorities referred to in support of the decision of the Supreme Court, with one exception, relate (as was pointed out by Cohen J) to human bodies awaiting burial, and they appear to assert a general rule that when a human being dies property in his body does not vest in anyone, although certain persons have duties, and perhaps rights, with respect to it. Thus, a mandamus will lie to compel delivery of a corpse to the person charged with the duty of burying it: *R v Fox* ((1841) 2 QB 246). But it cannot at that moment, while awaiting burial, be the subject of larceny, since the ownership could not be laid in any one. The circumstance, however, that a thing was not the subject of larceny at common law did not determine the question whether an action of detinue could be brought in respect of it. For instance, deeds relating to land were not at common law the subject of larceny, but detinue would lie in respect of them (see *Fitz-Herbert de Naturá Brevium*, p 138 a). An unburied corpse awaiting burial is *nullius in rebus*. All that is said by the authorities to which we were referred, except *Dr Handyside's Case* . . . appears to have been said from this point of view. It does not appear who was the plaintiff in that case, which might apparently have been decided on the ground that the plaintiff had not established any right of possession in himself. But it does not follow from the fact that an object is at one time *nullius in rebus* that it is incapable of becoming the subject of ownership. For instance, the dead body of an animal *ferae naturae* is not at death the property of any one, but it may be appropriated by the finder. So, it does not follow from the mere fact that a human body at death is not the subject of ownership that it is for ever incapable of having an owner. If that is the law, it must have some other foundation. After burial a corpse forms part of the land in which it is buried, and the right of possession goes with the land. Even, however, if the asserted rule was intended to be of general application – which, I doubt – it does not follow that there can be no exception to it. Many doctrines have been asserted on the supposed authority of learned persons, who, addressing themselves to one aspect of a question, have used language which has been generalized in a manner at which no one would have been more surprised than the supposed authors of the doctrines. I do not, myself, accept the dogma of the verbal inerrancy of ancient text writers. Indeed, equally respectable authority, and of equal antiquity, may be cited for establishing as a matter of law the reality of witchcraft. But in my opinion none of the authorities cited afford any assistance in the present case. We are, therefore, free to regard it as a case of first instance arising in the 20th century, and to decide it in accordance with general principles of law, which are usually in accord with reason and common sense.

The foundation of the argument for the respondent must be that the continued possession of an unburied human body after death by any one except for the purpose of burial is necessarily unlawful. If it is, it follows that no action can be founded upon a disturbance of that possession.

But, if it is not necessarily unlawful, then in my opinion it equally follows that, in any case in which the possession is lawful, the law will by appropriate remedies redress any such disturbance. The very term "lawful possession" connotes a right to invoke the law for its protection. A lawful possession which does not involve any right cognizable by law is a contradiction in terms...

The question to be determined, then, is whether the continued possession of a human corpse unburied is *in re ipsá* unlawful. If it is, the reason must be that such possession is injurious to the public welfare, and the notion that it is so injurious must be founded upon considerations of religion or public health or public decency. The question whether a particular act is injurious to the public on any such grounds is a mixed question of law and fact, so that what may be injurious at one time or under one set of circumstances may not be so at another time and under different circumstances. For instance, a discussion which would, not so very long ago, have been held to be rank blasphemy might not now be considered to be even irreverent. What would have been regarded a century ago as gross negligence in the treatment of a disease might now be thought the adoption of necessary and obvious precautions, and *via versá.* I am not sure that notions of public decency are not equally liable to change.

On what ground, then, can it be asserted that the continued possession of a corpse unburied is in all cases and at all events injurious to the public welfare? So far as any argument is based upon the ecclesiastical law as part of the common law it is sufficient to say that that part (if it be a part) of the common law was never in force in Australia. The question whether the possession of a corpse is injurious to the public health is manifestly not an abstract question of law, but a concrete question of fact, depending upon the circumstances of the particular case. As to public decency, some dealings with a corpse no doubt constitute a misdemeanour, but I know of no authority for saying that the retention of a human body unburied is *ipso facto* a misdemeanour.

It is idle to contend in these days that the possession of a mummy, or of a prepared skeleton, or of a skull, or other parts of a human body, is necessarily unlawful; if it is, the many valuable collections of anatomical and pathological specimens or preparations formed and maintained by scientific bodies, were formed and are maintained in violation of the law.

In my opinion there is no law forbidding the mere possession of a human body, whether born alive or dead, for purposes other than immediate burial. *A fortiori* such possession is not unlawful if the body possesses attributes of such a nature that its preservation may afford valuable or interesting information or instruction. If the requirements of public health or public decency are infringed, quite different considerations arise.

To apply these principles to the present case. Neither public health nor public decency is endangered by the mere preservation of a perhaps unique specimen of malformation. Public decency may, perhaps, be offended by the public exhibition of such an object. But the fact that an object may not be publicly exhibited affords no criterion for determining the lawfulness of the possession of that object. In my opinion it is not *contra bonos mores* to retain such a specimen unburied. If one medical or scientific student may lawfully possess it, he may transfer the possession to another. The manner of use may be controlled, but the possession is not of itself unlawful.

If, then, there can, under some circumstances, be a continued rightful possession of a human body unburied, I think, as I have already said, that the law will protect that rightful possession by appropriate remedies. I do not know of any definition of property which is not wide enough to include such a right of permanent possession. By whatever name the right is called, I think it exists, and that, so far as it constitutes property, a human body, or a portion of a human body, is capable by law of becoming the subject of property. It is not necessary to give an exhaustive enumeration of the circumstances under which such a right may be acquired, but I entertain no doubt that, when a person has by the lawful exercise of work or skill so dealt with a human body or part of a human body in his lawful possession that it has acquired some attributes differentiating it from a mere corpse awaiting burial, he acquires a right to retain possession of it, at least as against any person not entitled to have it delivered to him for the purpose of burial, but subject, of course, to any positive law which forbids its retention under the particular circumstances.

In the present case the evidence showed that the body came, not unlawfully, into Dr Donahoe's possession, that some – perhaps not much – work and skill had been bestowed by him upon it, and that it had acquired an actual pecuniary value. Under these circumstances, and in the absence of any positive law to the contrary, I think that an action will lie for an interference with the right of possession. I do not think that the Anatomy Act has any bearing on the case. I express no opinion on the question whether a still-born child falls within the authorities relating to human corpses.

Griffith CJ stated the 'no property' in a corpse rule, recognised an exception based upon the 'exercise of work or skill' on it and held that the body of the 'still-born' child was property lawfully in the possession of the plaintiff. As a result, he could maintain an action in detinue (in England it would today be for conversion) based upon his right to possession of it.

Barton J agreed in the result but his reasoning differed somewhat.

Barton J: [The corpse] has never existed independently of the physical attachment to the mother. It was never alive in the ordinary sense of human life. It has never drawn the breath of life so as to have expired, for it was still-born. It has been preserved in a jar or bottle with spirits since the day of its birth, now forty years ago. Add to these facts that it is an aberration of nature, having two heads. Can such a thing be, without shock to the mind, associated with the notion of the process that we know as Christian burial? Does it not almost seem indecent to associate that notion with such facts? Do not all these considerations lead us to doubt whether such a thing as a dead-born foetal monster, preserved in spirits as a curiosity during four decades, can now be regarded as a corpse awaiting burial, the thing which Judges have discussed in decisions and lawyers in textbooks? It would have been difficult to admit that this dead foetus answered that description at the time, almost immediately after its birth, when Dr Donahoe was allowed to take it away and when he preserved it in spirits. The difficulty has increased since. If it were ever a corpse awaiting burial, was that a correct description of it when the plaintiff's possession of it was interfered with? It had then been in a state of preservation for thirty-nine years. It had acquired, as the evidence shows, a considerable monetary value, not as a corpse, but as something so unlike an ordinary corpse as to be a curiosity, a well-preserved specimen of nature's freaks. To take the simplest test, is it possible to affirm that the meaning conveyed by the term "unburied corpse" to one who had never seen such an object as this would include it? There can only be one answer to that question.

On the facts, which are not disputed, I think we are really not discussing the thing which has been the subject of decision in the cases cited. Their authority I do not doubt, but they do not, I think, apply so as to deprive the appellant of redress.

That conclusion clears the case of the difficulties which authority would otherwise place in the way of a determination on ordinary grounds of legal principle, applying sense and reason to the exceptional facts of this case.

Now, I have given the matter close and repeated consideration in that aspect, and I must say that the impression I formed during the argument has been confirmed. I have read the judgement of the Chief Justice, and I entirely agree with the reasons it embodies, which I hold it unnecessary to amplify. I would add that I do not wish it to be supposed that I cast the slightest doubt upon the general rule that an unburied corpse is not the subject of property, or upon the legal authorities which require the proper and decent disposal of the dead. Further, the gross indecency of publicly exhibiting this object must not be thought to be endorsed as lawful by anything I have said.

Barton J, as you will observe, also accepted the 'no property' rule but did not consider it applicable to a still-born child which was not a 'corpse' (of a dead person) awaiting burial. He did not expressly rely upon the exception referred to by Griffith CJ although he expressed his completed agreement with the latter's reasons.

Higgins J dissented. He did so on the basis that the 'no property rule' applied. He also accepted Griffith CJ's exception but considered it inapplicable as 'no skill or labour has been exercised and there has been no change in its character' (at 417).

1. The 'no property rule'

The 'no property rule' has a long historical lineage though its provenance is doubtful. Professor Skegg analyses the case law such that it is.

P D G Skegg 'Human Corpses, Medical Specimens and the Law of Property' (1976) Anglo-Am LR 412

The view that the corpse cannot be the subject of property appears to have originated from a passage in the Third Part of Coke's *Institutes* first published in 1644. He wrote:

> It is to be observed, that in every Sepulcher, that hath a monument, two things are to be considered, *viz* the monument, and the sepultre or buriall of the dead.
>
> The buriall of the *Cadaver* (that is, *caro data vermibus*) is *nullius in bonis*, and belongs to Ecclesiastical cognizance, but as to the monument, action is given (as hath been said) at the Common Law for defacing thereof.

In a marginal note, Coke referred to a passage in the late thirteenth century legal work, Britton. However, neither that passage, nor anything else in Britton, establishes Coke's proposition that the 'buriall of the *Cadaver* ... is *nullius in bonis*'.

It should be noted that Coke did not assert that a corpse could never be the subject of property. He was concerned only with the 'burial of the corpse', with 'flesh given to worms'. At that time, corpses were normally buried in consecrated ground. Once there, they were protected by ecclesiastical law. Unburied corpses, and corpses buried in unconsecrated ground, were not then, or subsequently, protected by ecclesiastical law. But the fact that corpses buried in consecrated ground were the subject of ecclesiastical cognizance, was hardly a good reason for regarding them as *nullius in bonis* at common law. Monuments in consecrated ground were also subject to ecclesiastical jurisdiction but, as Coke himself indicated, an action would lie at common law if someone defaced them.

The no property rule appears to have been first mentioned in a court of law in the eighteenth century, in *Dr Handyside*'s. Trover was there brought against the doctor, for the body of a pair of 'Siamese twins'. The case was not reported, nor was it mentioned in the legal works published later in the eighteenth century, where reference to it might have been expected. It was first noted early in the nineteenth century, by East, who could not have had any personal knowledge of the case. He simply recorded that in 'the case of Dr Handyside, where trover was brought against him for two children that grew together; Lord CJ Willes held the action would not lie, as no person had any property in corpses'. Unfortunately, there is no indication whether the corpse had ever been buried, how it came to be in the doctor's possession, who the plaintiff was, or on what ground he brought the action. Nor was there any indication whether there were any submissions on the no property point, and what, if any, authority was cited in connection with it. Although it is the only English case in which the no property rule appears to have been the sole ground of the decision, it has not been cited in subsequent English cases.

More than a century passed before the courts returned to the question of property in corpses. But in the intervening years, there were two important developments whereby the common law courts established a considerable measure of control over corpses.

The leading case in the first development was *R v Lynn* ((1788) 2 TR 733) which came before the Court of King's Bench in 1788. Lynn had been convicted on indictment for entering a burial ground and disinterring a corpse, which he took away for dissection. Counsel moved in arrest of judgment that the offence, if such it were, was one of solely ecclesiastical cognizance, and sought to invoke Coke's dictum that 'The burial of the *Cadaver* ... is *nullius in bonis*, and belongs to Ecclesiastical cognizance'. However, the Court of King's Bench did not accept this submission, insisting that Lynn's conduct was cognizable on a criminal court 'as being highly indecent, and contra bonus mores'. The form of indictment in *R v Lynn* is indicative of the acceptance of the view, expressed by Blackstone, that 'stealing the corpse itself, which has no owner ... is no felony, unless some of the grave-clothes be stolen with it'.

However, the decision itself showed an unwillingness to be hindered by Coke's assertion that a buried corpse belonged – by implication, exclusively – to ecclesiastical jurisdiction.

Just over half a century later, in *R v Fox* ((1841) 2 QB 246) the Court of Queen's Bench delivered a judgment which further established its control over corpses. A debtor had died while in prison and, after an inquest, the coroner issued an order for burial. The executors requested that the body be delivered up to them. However, the gaoler refused to comply with this request, and said he would do so only when the executors paid him the sum he claimed to be due from the deceased. They refused to do this. The Solicitor General then moved for mandamus, peremptory in the first instance, commanding those responsible to give up for interment the body of the deceased. The court awarded the mandamus applied for. The implication of this decision was that the executors had a right to possession of the corpse prior to burial, and that in appropriate circumstances the court would act to protect that right. Once again, they did not treat the corpse as solely a matter of ecclesiastical cognizance.

By the middle of the nineteenth century, the common law courts had a well-established jurisdiction over corpses. At the same time, more corpses were being buried in unconsecrated ground. These corpses were not protected in any way be ecclesiastical law, which was itself of steadily decreasing importance. However, it was in the latter half of the century that there were decided the only properly reported cases in which English Judges have lent support to the no property rule.

In three of the four cases, all references to the absence of property in, or ownership of, a corpse, was clearly obiter. In these three cases, there does not appear to have been any reference to the no property rule in any of the counsels' submissions. Nor did the judges cite any authorities in support of their dicta. It is proposed to deal first with these three cases.

In *R v Sharpe* ((1856–57) Dears & Bell 160) the court was in effect applying and extending the principle in *R v Lynn*. Sharpe's mother had been interred in the burial ground of a congregation of dissenters. By a misrepresentation, Sharpe obtained access to the grave. He removed the corpse, with the intention of burying it with that of his recently deceased father, in a nearby churchyard. He was subsequently convicted of a common law misdemeanor for removing the corpse from the grave without lawful authority. The judges confirmed that his conduct constituted such a crime. Erle J delivered their judgment, and in the course of it said:

> Our law recognises no property in a corpse, and the protection of the grave at common law, as contradistinguished from the ecclesiastical protection to consecrated ground, depends upon this form of indictment.

However, this was simply to explain the form of indictment, which was not in this particular court's control in any event. Even if it had been accepted that the corpse was the subject of property, this would not have justified an owner disinterring it. Things buried with the deceased are said to remain the property of the owner, but it is scarcely arguable that the owner is justified in disinterring a corpse simply because he wishes to recover them.

Foster v Dodd ((1866) LR 1 QB 475, (1867) LR 3 QB 67) concerned the validity of an Order in Council and an order of the Secretary of State. The Court of Queen's Bench, and then the Court of Exchequer Chamber, held that the relevant provisions of the Burial Acts did not apply to the land in respect of which the orders were made. The orders were therefore invalid. The sole reference to the status of the corpse came in the final judgment on appeal. Byles J said he desired to add one observation, 'That the effect of our judgment may not be misunderstood'. He stressed that the court was simply concerned with whether the action taken had been in pursuance of a valid order, and said

> A dead body belongs to no one, and is, therefore, under the protection of the public. If it lies in consecrated ground, the ecclesiastical law will interpose for its protection; but, whether in ground consecrated or unconsecrated, indignities offered to human remains in improperly and indecently disinterring them, are the grounds of an indictment.

It is not clear that it is because a corpse 'belongs to no one' that it is 'under the protection of the public'. After all, tombstones are the subject of property, but they are nonetheless protected by the criminal law. *R v Price* ([1884] 12 QBD 247) arose out of the attempt of the 84-year-old Price to burn the corpse of a baby, whose father he was said to be. Price had put the corpse into a ten gallon cask of petroleum, and set fire to the cask, petroleum and corpse. The case is famous for Stephen, J's decision that the burning of the corpse of a human being did not amount to a crime at common law, unless it were done in a way which amounted to a common law nuisance. In his charge to the Grand Jury at Assizes, Stephen J reviewed a number of earlier cases, including *R v Lynn*. He said

> It is to be observed in reference to this case that the act done would have been a peculiarly indecent theft if it had not been for the technical reason that a dead body is not the subject of property.

This is undoubtedly the probable explanation of the form of indictment in that case. However, this observation of Stephen J, was wholly incidental to the question before him.

The one properly reported case in which an English judge has used the no property doctrine to support his decision is *Williams v Williams* ((1882) 20 Ch D 659). In a codicil to his will, a testator directed that 'within three days after my death, or as soon as conveniently may be, my body shall be given to my friend Miss Eliza Williams, to be dealt with by her in such manner as I have directed to be done in a private letter to her'. He also directed that the executors were to reimburse her for any expenses she incurred in carrying out his instructions. The letter expressed his wish that his body be burnt, and the remains placed in a vase, to be disposed of as Miss Williams wished. On the testator's death his executors and family had his body buried, despite some protest from Miss Williams. On the pretext that she was going to have the body reburied in consecrated ground, Miss Williams obtained from the Home Secretary a license permitting the removal of the body. Two years later, she had the remains disinterred, taken to Italy, and burnt. The ashes were then placed in a vase, and buried in consecrated ground. Miss Williams then demanded payment of the £321 she had spent in carrying out the testator's instructions. When payment was refused, she brought an action against the executors and the residuary legatees.

The case was heard in Chancery before Kay J. At an early stage of counsel's submissions, the Judge asked how, given that there was no property in a corpse, the gift was good. However, counsel had not, and did not, suggest that there had been a bequest of the body. Furthermore, he conceded the no property point. What he did submit was that a man could give directions as to what was to be done with his body, in a way not contrary to law, and that he could devote part of his estate to the carrying out of his directions. In delivering his judgment, Kay J said that in English law there can be no property in the dead body of a human being. He quoted Erle J's dictum in *R v Sharpe* to support the view. He then went on to discuss the executor's right to possession of the body prior to burial, and said that it followed from this that a man could not dispose of his body by will. Having reached this conclusion, he said that it also followed from there being no property in a corpse, that a man could not dispose of it by will.

It is extremely doubtful that the testator had been seeking to bequeath his body. In directing that 'within three days after my death or as soon as conveniently may be, my body shall be given to my friend Miss Eliza Williams', to be dealt with in the manner in which he had directed here, it is likely that he simply intended to provide for the body to be delivered up to her, so that she could arrange its cremation. But quite apart from Kay J's interpretation of the direction as an attempted bequest, his reasoning is open to question. The common law rule that the executors have the right to possession of the corpse, and can themselves determine what is to be done with it, is not necessarily dependent on their being no property in a corpse. A legal system could refuse to recognize property in a corpse, but recognizes a power to give binding directions as to what is to be done with it. Conversely, a legal system could recognize property in a corpse (so that, for example, the law of theft and the possessory actions applied to it), but have a rule that property vests in, say, the executors, who would have a discretion as to what they did with it.

Whatever may be thought of Kay J's reasoning, it does seem that he used the rule that a corpse is not the subject of property as an additional ground for his conclusions that it was impossible to dispose of a corpse by will. This conclusion was one of the four grounds given by Kay J for any one of which the action would have failed.

Since these four cases were decided – the most recent of them, now more than 90 years ago – the question whether there can be property in a corpse does not appear to have been mentioned in the ordinary English courts.

It is remarkable how slight is the authority in favour of the no property rule. *Dr Handyside's* case and *Williams v Williams* are the only cases in which the no property rule appears to have constituted at least part of the *ratio decidendi*. Neither of these cases is binding on the higher English courts. But, granted that these courts are free to take a different view, are there cogent reasons for their doing so?

A change in the traditional view need not bring about very far-reaching changes in the law relating to corpses. It has already been suggested that treating the corpse as the subject of property need not of itself enable a person to bequeath his body, or to give binding directions as to what is done with it after his death. Ownership could vest in the executors, or whoever else is now under the duty to dispose of it and has a right to possession for that purpose. Then, as now, that person could have a considerable discretion as to the mode of disposal.

Treating the corpse as the subject of property would not necessarily affect the sale of bodies, or parts of bodies. The property interest in the corpse could be treated as one which could not be divested. In any case, the fact that corpses have not been regarded as the subject of property has not prevented payments for whole corpses in the past, and does not prevent payments for parts of corpses at present. If the traditional view caused practical difficulties in this context, it would be simple to formulate the contracts as being for the service of providing the corpse, or part thereof, rather than for the sale of goods. In this context, the important issue is not whether a corpse, or part thereof, is the subject of property. It is whether there is a common law offence which prohibits any or all such transactions – and, if there is not, whether the contracts are in any case void on grounds of public policy. These questions arise whether the contract is viewed as one for the sale of goods, or for services.

If corpses were treated as the subject of property, this would have some effect on liability for unauthorized interferences with them, and the control which the law could exercise over them. But even here the difference is much less than it would have been two hundred years ago. This is the result of the development of the common law crime prohibiting the unauthorized disinterment of a corpse, and the development of a legally enforceable right to possession of a corpse, for the purpose of disposal. The crime prevents the removal of corpses from graves as effectively as the law of theft would. The right to possession could be used by the person who has that right, as the basis of an action to recover possession of the corpse, or to recover damages for an interference with that right.

However, there are a number of *lacunae* which the recognition of a property interest in a corpse would help to fill. For example, interferences with unburied corpses, or parts of corpses, will only sometimes come within the range of any established crime. If they were the subject of property, the law of theft and criminal damage would apply. Where a corpse, or part of a corpse, is removed from the custody of someone who is lawfully in possession of it, but who cannot show that he is under the duty to dispose of it, he will normally be without legal remedies. If the corpse were the subject of property, he could recover possession or damages, except where the person who removed it had a right to do so.

It is undesirable that, for example, many anatomical specimens on the shelves of medical schools, and cadaveric organs and tissues awaiting transplantation, should be to a greater or lesser extent outside the range of the law. Quaint anomaly that the no property rule may be, there is little to be said for retaining it if it has this effect and could be jettisoned without undesirable consequences...

Scots institutional writers, and *dicta* in the Court of Justiciary in *Dewar v HM Advocate* (1945 JC 5) support the view that in Scots law a corpse is the subject of property (and can therefore be stolen), until such time as it is buried or otherwise disposed of. This view appears to have resulted from a misunderstanding of an earlier case. However, it is more in keeping with the raison d'etre of the traditional English view than any of the other approaches, including the one hitherto adopted in the English courts. It was only after the corpse had been buried in consecrated ground that ecclesiastical law prevented interferences with it. Buried corpses are now perfectly adequately protected by the common law crime exemplified in *R v Sharpe*, which is the English equivalent of the Scots crime of violation of sepulchres. Where English law is inadequate is in the rather limited protection it extends to corpses or parts of corpses prior to burial or cremation. This inadequacy could be overcome by the courts taking the view that, until such time as a corpse or part thereof is buried, cremated, or otherwise disposed of, it is the subject of property. Unburied corpses, and anatomical specimens and transplant material removed from corpses, would then be protected by, amongst other things, the crime of theft and the tort of trespass to goods.

It would be desirable for the English courts to go further than Scots authority yet does, and take the view that it is only while corpses or the remains of corpses are buried, or dispersed following cremation, that they are not the subject of property. This would enable the courts to extend more effective legal control, not only over corpses awaiting burial and cremation, but also over ashes which had not been buried or dispersed, and human remains which had been disinterred.

You will notice Skegg's reference to parts of dead bodies which have been removed, for example, during post-mortems or as anatomical specimens. We will return to the legal status of 'parts' shortly. We will also see the regulatory regime of such practices which, certainly in relation to anatomy, strongly suggest that excised parts are seen, albeit implicitly by Parliament, as the 'property' of the authorised retainer under the Anatomy Act 1984. For now we should return the legal status of whole corpses. The 'no-property' rule has been doubted by academic writers as of questionable provenance being based upon little or no authority (see P Matthews 'Whose Body? People as Property? [1983] CLP 193). In particular, Professor Matthews identifies the confusion caused by reliance upon *Haynes'* case (1614) 12 Co Rep 113 which is not authority for the proposition that there is 'no property in a dead corpse' but rather than a corpse cannot *own* property (see at 197–198). The misreading is 'a complete perversion of the case' (at 197). Likewise, Professor Matthews convincingly demonstrates that the case of *Dr Handyside*, referred to in Skegg's article, was probably never a case where a decision was reached to support the proposition that 'no person had any property in corpses' (see at 208–210).

Nevertheless, despite all these doubts the Court of Appeal in *R v Kelly* [1998] 3 All ER 741 at 749 has accepted that a corpse (or part thereof) is not property under the common law. Rose LJ stated as follows:

We return to the first question, that is to say whether or not a corpse or part of a corpse is property. We accept that, however questionable the historical origins of the principle, it has now been the common law for 150 years at least that neither a corpse, nor parts of a corpse, are in themselves and without more capable of being property protected by rights (see eg Erle J, delivering the judgment of a powerful Court of Crown Cases Reserved in *R v Sharpe* (1857) Dears & B 160 at 163, 169 ER 959 at 960, where he said:

Our law recognises no property in a corpse, and the protection of the grave at common law, as contradistinguished from ecclesiastical protection to consecrated ground, depends upon this form of indictment ...

He was there referring to an indictment which charged not theft of a corpse but removal of a corpse from a grave.

If that principle is now to be changed, in our view, it must be by Parliament, because it has been express or implicit in all the subsequent authorities and writing to which we have been referred that a corpse or part of it cannot be stolen....

2. Exceptions

There are, however, exceptions to the general 'no property' rule. The first concerns the right of relatives of the deceased to possession of the corpse for the purposes of burial or cremation. The second recognises that those who expend work and exercise skill on a corpse or an excised part may acquire property rights over it.

(a) Right to possession for the purposes of burial or cremation

While maintaining the 'no-property-in-a-corpse' rule, English law recognises that certain individuals have a duty to arrange for the disposal of a dead body (by burial or cremation) which should not to be confused with the distinct duty to pay the funeral expenses (see eg *Rees v Hughes* [1946] 2 All ER 47 (CA)–deceased wife's estate, and not the husband, liable to pay). The common law accepts as a concomitant to the former duty that the person has a legal *right to possess* the dead body for the purpose of disposal (see P D G Skegg *Law, Ethics and Medicine* (1984) pp 232–235). These certainly include the deceased's executor where a will has been made (*Williams v Williams* (1882) 20 Ch D 659) or an administrator where the deceased has died intestate and one has been appointed (see *Holtham v Arnold* (1986) 2 BMLR 123 (Hoffmann J)).

In *Dobson v North Tyneside HA* [1996] 4 All ER 474 (CA) Peter Gibson LJ, however, doubted whether a deceased's next of kin had a duty to dispose of the body and hence a right of possession. It is unclear the extent to which others, in particular, the relatives of the deceased have a duty to arrange the disposal of and right to possess the body. There is nineteenth century and modern authority that a parent of an unmarried child certainly does (*R v Vann* (1851) 2 Den 325 and *R v Gwynedd CC, ex p B* (1991) 7 BMLR 120 (CA)). Likewise, it has long been accepted that close relatives of a deceased have a right to possess the body for this purpose (see P D G Skegg, *op cit* at pp 234–235). It may be, however, that the *independent* duty (and concomitant right) of the relatives does not exist (see recent doubts expressed in *Dobson v North Tyneside HA* [1996] 4 All ER 474 at 478 (CA)). It is more likely that the obligation is based upon one or two other bases: first, their having actual possession of the body due to the body being on their premises and there is nobody such as an executor or administrator with a prior duty of disposal (see, by analogy, *R v Stewart* (1840) 12 Ad & El 773 and *R v Feist* (1858) Dears & B 590) or, secondly (and it is suggested this is more likely), as the person(s) next entitled to be appointed the administrator of the deceased's estate under the Non-Contentious Probate Rules 1987 (SI 1987 No 2024), r 22, *ie* the surviving spouse, children, parents, siblings etc (see P Matthews and J Freeman (eds) *Jervis on Coroners* (11th edn, 1993) at para 7–05).

Recognising the obligation of the next of kin is a workable and sensible solution. In cases of dispute between relatives the courts should adopt a rigid lexical ordering (*Burnes v Richards* (1993) NSW Lexis 1339 (6 October) (NSWSC) (daughter and sister versus common law husband); and *Warner v Levitt* (1994) NSW Lexis 2115 (23 August) (NSWSC) (foster parents versus natural parents)) rather than any vague notion of what is equitable unless more than one person stands on an equal footing (but see *Calma v Sesar* [1992] 2 NTLR 37 (father versus mother) and *Buchanan v Milton* (1999) 53 BMLR 176 (Hale J)). (For Australian developments, see L Griggs and K Mackie (2000) 7 JLM 404.)

It is important to notice that the right to possession is for the specific purpose of lawfully disposing of the dead body. There is no right to possession for other purposes, for example, to obtain evidence for a potential negligence action arising out of the medical treatment of the deceased (see *Dobson v North Tyneside HA* [1996] 4 All ER 474 (CA)).

(b) Work/skill exception

We have already seen the exception stated by Griffith CJ in *Doodeward v Spence* (1908) 6 CLR 406 (HC of A). We should remind ourselves of what he said:

> **Griffith CJ:** ... I entertain no doubt that, when a person has by the lawful exercise of work or skill so dealt with a human body or part of a human body in his lawful possession that it has acquired some attributes differentiating it from a mere corpse awaiting burial, he acquires a right to retain possession of it, at least as against any person not entitled to have it delivered to him for the purpose of burial, but subject, of course, to any positive law which forbids its retention under the particular circumstances.

Doodeward, of course, concerned a whole corpse, albeit of a still-born child. The exception would also apply to excised parts upon which work and/or skill has been exercised. This would, therefore, cover anatomical or other specimens but not all.

P D G Skegg 'Human Corpses, Medical Specimens and the Law of Property' (1976) Anglo-Am LR 412

> One drawback of Griffith, CJ's principle is the difficulty of its application. If the principle were adopted in England, it would no doubt apply to Egyptian mummies in museum collections and probably also to shrunken heads, or head which had been tattooed after death. But much more difficult would be the question of whether it would apply to anatomical specimens, and tissues and organs awaiting transplantation. If the English courts were prepared to apply the principle in the same way as the majority of the High Court of Australia in *Doodeward v Spence*, these objects might very often be considered the subject of property. However, when dealing with an object on which no more labour or skill had been expended than was on the corpse in *Doodeward v Spence*, which had simply been placed in spirits, an English court might favour the approach of the dissenting Judge in *Doodeward v Spence*. He said that 'No skill or labour has been exercised on it; and there has been no change in its character'.

Does the exception represent English law? In *Dobson v North Tyneside HA* [1996] 4 All ER 474, the Court of Appeal was content to accept that it was 'properly arguable' (see per Peter Gibson LJ at 479). The exception was, however, inapplicable where the deceased's brain had been fixed in [sic] paraffin.

More importantly, and decisively, the Court of Appeal applied the exception in *R v Kelly* [1998] 3 All ER 741.

R v Kelly [1998] 3 All ER 741 (CA)

> K, an artist, had privileged access to the Royal College of Surgeons where he was permitted to draw anatomical specimens which were used by doctors training to be surgeons. L was employed at the college as a junior technician, and K asked L to remove a number of body parts. Approximately 35 to 40 body parts were removed, and K made casts of them. Most of the body parts were buried in a field; part of a leg was found in K's attic and the remaining parts were found in the basement of a flat belonging to friends. K and L were charged with theft, contrary to s 1 of the Theft Act 1968. At the trial, the defence submitted at the close of the prosecution case (i) that parts of bodies were not in law capable of being property and therefore could not be stolen, and (ii) that the specimens were not in the lawful possession of

the college at the time they were taken because they had been retained beyond the period of two years before burial stipulated in the Anatomy Act 1832, and so did not belong to it. The trial judge rejected those submissions, ruling that there was an exception to the traditional common law rule that there was no property in a corpse, namely that once a human body or body part had undergone a process of skill by a person authorised to perform it, with the object of preserving it for the purpose of medical or scientific examination, or for the benefit of medical science, it became something quite different from an interred corpse and it thereby acquired a usefulness or value and it was capable of becoming property in the usual way, and could be stolen. K and L were convicted, and they appealed against their conviction.

Rose LJ: On behalf of the appellant, Lindsay, in submissions adopted by counsel on behalf of Kelly, Mr Thornton QC submits, as we have indicated, that the jury's verdict was unsafe, first, because the body parts were not property and therefore could not be stolen, secondly, because they did not belong to the Royal College of Surgeons because they were not lawfully in their possession, and thirdly, because the judge's direction that the college was in lawful possession was a prejudicial misdirection of the jury.

In support of those submissions, Mr Thornton advanced eight propositions. First, that the common law rule applies to corpses to be buried but not yet buried. Such, he submits, are not property. Secondly there has been, until this case, no prosecution for theft of a body or body parts, although there do exist in other Acts, in particular the Anatomy Act 1832, certain statutory offences, in relation to corpses and parts of corpses, which are – it is perhaps worth noting in passing– susceptible to a maximum sentence of imprisonment of three months. Thirdly, the common law rule extends to parts of bodies as well as to the entire corpse. Fourthly, the body parts in the present case were not property, they were intended by their donors for burial, and the resolution of that matter, clearly one of fact, was one which could only be favourable to the defence. Fifthly, there is no exception to the general common law rule.

For this part of his submission, it was pertinent for him to take the court, as he did, to *Doodeward v Spence* ...

Mr Thornton draws attention to the fact that that authority, which related to a two headed still born foetus preserved as a curio, arose from a claim in detinue and he relies, as we have said, on the dissenting judgment of Higgins J. The facts of that case, he says, are plainly distinguishable from the present, because the nature of the object there in dispute rendered it something wholly different from a corpse or part of a corpse.

He submitted that there cannot be property for the purposes of the 1968 Act, unless there is a permanent right to possession vested in the person from whom the property is taken. He submitted that the decision of the English Court of Appeal in *Dobson v North Tyneside Health Authority* [1996] 4 All ER 474, [1997] 1 WLR 596 does not lend succour to the *Doodeward v Spence* exception. He submitted that no amount of skill expended on a body part can affect its ownership; at the highest, it might affect possessory rights....

We return to the first question, that is to say whether or not a corpse or part of a corpse is property. We accept that, however questionable the historical origins of the principle, it has now been the common law for 150 years at least that neither a corpse, nor parts of a corpse, are in themselves and without more capable of being property protected by rights (see eg Erle J, delivering the judgment of a powerful Court of Crown Cases Reserved in *R v Sharpe* (1857) Dears & B 160 at 163, 169 ER 959 at 960, where he said:

Our law recognised no property in a corpse, and the protection of the grave at common law, as contradistinguished from ecclesiastical protection to consecrated ground, depends upon this form of indictment ...

He was there referring to an indictment which charged not theft of a corpse but removal of a corpse from a grave.

If that principle is now to be changed, in our view, it must be by Parliament, because it has been express or implicit in all the subsequent authorities and writings to which we have been referred that a corpse or part of it cannot be stolen.

To address the point as it was addressed before the trial judge and to which his certificate relates, in our judgment, parts of a corpse are capable of being property within s 4 of the Theft Act, if they have acquired different attributes by virtue of the application of skill, such as dissection or preservation techniques, for exhibition or teaching purposes: see *Doodeward v Spence*, in the judgment of Griffith CJ to which we have already referred and *Dobson v North Tyneside Health Authority* [1996] 4 All ER 474 at 479, [1997] 1 WLR 596 at 601, where this proposition is not dissented from and appears, in the judgment of this court, to have been accepted by Peter Gibson LJ; otherwise, his analysis of the facts of *Dobson*'s case, which appears at that page in the judgment, would have been, as it seems to us, otiose. Accordingly the trial judge was correct to rule as he did.

Furthermore, the common law does not stand still. It may be that if, on some future occasion, the question arises, the courts will hold that human body parts are capable of being property for the purposes of s 4, even without the acquisition of different attributes, if they have a use or significance beyond their mere existence. This may be so if, for example, they are intended for use in an organ transplant operation, for the extraction of DNA or, for that matter, as an exhibit in a trial. It is to be noted that in *Dobson*'s case, there was no legal or other requirement for the brain, which was then the subject of litigation, to be preserved (see the judgment of Peter Gibson LJ [1996] 4 All ER 474 at 479, [1997] 1 WLR 596 at 601).

(For a discussion of other aspects of *Kelly*, see Commentary (1998) 6 Med L Rev 247 (AG)).

How, then, are we to understand the decision in *Kelly*? One of us offers the following:

Andrew Grubb 'I, Me, Mine: Bodies, Parts & Property' (1998) Medical Law International 299

Four observations about *Kelly*.

First, on one reading it could be said that the Court of Appeal was concerned with "property" in the limited sense of a description of the "thing". Well, of course it was, but that would be too narrow a reading of the decision. The court determined that the body parts were "property" in that sense but further, were property over which the Royal College had rights – to possess – which entitled them to exclude others from the parts. This is "property" in the other sense I described earlier, looking to the relationship between the "thing" and an individual.

Secondly, the exception in *Doodeward* and *Kelly* may be seen as a reflection of the related philosophical arguments that an individual is entitled to property rights where he performs useful work or, what has been described as the 'creation-without-wrong argument' (JW Harris 'Who Owns My Body? (1996) 16 OJLS 55, 67–68) based upon the views of Locke and Mill. In *Kelly*, this might work in the way it was intended: to give the artificer of the Royal College rights over the parts just as it did the original "worker" and his successors in *Doodeward*. But, arguably it only did so because until that time in both instances there was no "property" in either sense I have used it. Until then it was part of the woman who gave birth to the stillborn child or of the corpses that were to be subject to anatomical examination. Otherwise, in English law if another had "rights" over the thing, the artificer would not extinguish those rights (*Falcke v Scottish Imperial Insurance Co* (1886) 34 CH D 234), unless he created a 'new thing' the *nova species* of specification. But even that, as we have seen, may not be correct and the source may retain his proprietary interests subject to a claim in full for conversion extinguishing them (Torts (Interference with Goods) Act 1977, s 5). Both *Doodeward* and *Kelly* may be better explained as cases of "first possession" conferring property rights. The analogy would, in law, be with wild animals that are killed or wild flowers that are cut, the "first possessor" acquires the rights over them when previously there had been none.

Thirdly, there is considerable uncertainty about how the exception should be applied. Will mere preservation do? 'Yes', according to Griffith CJ in *Doodeward* – nothing else had been done to the stillborn baby. 'No', according to Higgins J in that case and the Court of Appeal in *Dobson* – where preservation ("fixing") was all that had occurred to the body part (brain) there in question. In *Dobson*, Peter Gibson LJ considered that the exception did not apply since the preservation of the brain was not on a par with "stuffing or embalming a corpse or preserving an anatomical or pathological specimen for a scientific collection or with preserving a freak such as a double-headed foetus that had some value for exhibition purposes" as had occurred in *Doodeward* (at 479). Leaving aside whether *Doodeward* is actually different, what should be the crucial indicia of the exception? It is not just a matter of what is done but also the purpose for which the work or skill is deployed. There must be an intention to create a novel item with a use of its own. It is the deliberate creation of a novel item which justifies the common law in conferring proprietary status on the "item" in order to give legal protection to the artificer as reward for his expended effort; an argument which looks to notions of justice, sometimes encapsulated in the so-called 'sweat/equity' argument.

But should the exception go further? Griffith CJ in *Doodeward* specifically stated that his exception was not an "exhaustive enumeration of the circumstances under which [a property] right may be acquired" (at 414). There are pragmatic reasons why the law should protect the "possession" of a body part in some circumstances even where the possessor cannot rely upon on "sweat/equity" argument to justify his proprietary interest. Of course, the possession should not offend what Griffith CJ in *Doodeward* called "any positive law which forbids … retention under the particular circumstances", such as public health or public decency laws. However, where the "possessor" holds the part for a legitimate purpose recognised by society as appropriate why should not the common law protect that individual's possession such that he may prevent its taking by others and obtain its return if taken unlawfully. In *Kelly*, the Court of Appeal hypothesised that the common law might well develop in this way. Rose LJ stated that body parts that "have a use of significance beyond their mere existence" might be property for the purposes of theft even if they did not fall within Griffith CJ's formulation in *Doodeward*, ie, they had not acquired different attributes through skill or work (at 750). The judge gave a number of helpful examples, which, it is suggested, would fully justify an expansion of the current exception: parts intended for use in an organ transplantation operation, for the extraction or DNA or as an exhibit in a trial.

This would, however, in effect re-write the 'no property' rule itself such that it became: there is 'no property' in corpses (excluding excised body parts). In the vast majority of instances, perhaps even all, there would be little purpose in removing a body part from a dead body unless the part was "of use" or was "significant" for some purpose. The exception would now prove a new, and more limited, rule but there would be nothing wrong with that since it would be entirely consistent with modern demands on the common law and concerns about public decency and public health.

B. MEDICAL EDUCATION AND RESEARCH

We have already seen in Chapter 15 the law relating to the use of cadavers (corpses) for transplantation purposes contained in the Human Tissue Act 1961. As we saw, the 1961 Act sets out the requirements for the removal and *therapeutic use of parts* as a dead body. It is important to notice three matters. First, the 1961 Act is not restricted to therapeutic use. It also covers removal and use for the purposes of 'medical education or research' (s 1(1)). It follows that *parts* of a dead body may also be removed and used for these purposes provided the requirements of the 1961 Act, which we saw in Chapter 15, are satisfied. By contrast, whole bodies may be used for anatomy in accordance with the Anatomy Act 1984. This would also cover the removal and use of parts. Whilst the provisions of the 1984 Act are similar to those of the 1961 Act, the regulation of anatomy is different. To avoid an overlap between the 1961 and 1984 Acts, the Anatomy Act 1984 provides that the removal and use is not covered by the Anatomy Act 1984 where it has been authorised under the 1961 Act.

Section 1(5) of the Anatomy Act 1984 provides as follows:

> 1(5) If part of a body is authorised under section 1 of the Human Tissues Act 1961 to be removed for purposes of medical education or research, that section (and not this Act) applies to the removal and use of the part, even if the education or research consists of or involves anatomical examination; but the preceding provisions of this subsection do not prevent this Act applying as regards the body after such removal or where no such removal is made.

Secondly, what is meant by 'medical education or research'?

P D G Skegg 'The Use of Corpses for Medical Education and Research: the Legal Requirements' (1991) 31 Med Sci Law 345

The Human Tissue Act does not provide a definition of 'medical education or research'. 'Medical education' would here be taken to include the education, both formal and informal, of medical students and of medical practitioners. In this context, it should also be taken to include the education of nurses, physiotherapists, and other 'paramedicals'. Specimens removed from dead bodies are sometimes used in the course of the education of such persons and it would be unfortunate if the Act were interpreted in a way that provided an obstacle to parts being removed and used for this purpose.

'Medical education' could be interpreted in a still wider sense, to include the education of the general public in medical matters. If this were accepted, whole mount sections of normal lung, emphysema and lung cancer could be used, by virtue of the Act, by education officers of a Cancer Society or by psychologists leading 'stop smoking' sessions. The problem with this interpretation is that it gives the qualifying word 'medical' very little effect. In practice, such specimens will have been removed and prepared for use in the education of doctors and paramedicals as well, and problems are most unlikely to arise if the specimens are used, without personal identification, for other educational purposes.

> Section 1 of the Human Tissue Act does not provide for the use of whole bodies for
> medical education or research, even in those cases where the deceased had 'expressed a
> request that his body ... be used after his death' for one or both of these purposes. ... It
> provides only for authorization of the removal for use of 'any part', or 'the specified part'.
> But there is no limit on the parts that can be removed if appropriate authorization is given: a
> complete skeleton could be removed, part by part, for use in medical education.

Thirdly, as you will have noticed, Professor Skegg points out that the 1961 Act
does not authorise the use of *whole bodies* for medical education or research,
only parts of bodies. Does this mean that whole bodies cannot be used for
medical research or education? Clearly, this is highly desirable in order to train
and educate doctors (and others) for their professional practice and to conduct
proper research and study for the benefit of the health of the living. The practice
of anatomy involving dissection is permitted and regulated by the Anatomy
Act 1984 and will be considered below. Not all teaching, study or research
involving dead bodies is, however, covered by the Anatomy Act because it will
not involve 'dissection' or be for the purposes of 'morphology', ie the study of
the form and structure of the body (see definition of 'anatomical examination'
in s 1(1) of the Anatomy Act 1984 *infra*. An example of such an educational
use might be the use of cadavers to train medical students or others in
resuscitation techniques (see discussion of the practice in M Ardagh 'May We
Practise Endotracheal Intubation on the Newly Dead?' (1997) 23 Journal of
Medical Ethics 289).

The legality of these latter types of procedure turns upon the question of whether
they are *otherwise* legal. Compliance with legislation such as the Human Tissue
Act 1961 means that the procedure is lawful (see 1(3) of the 1961 Act). The converse
that non-compliance renders the procedure unlawful, – is not, however, true. We
discussed the issue of non-compliance with the 1961 Act in Chapter 15 (*supra*).
As we saw then, the use of cadavers for transplantation purposes would, in
most instances, be legal even if the 1961 Act were not complied with. In relation
to the unauthorised use of corpses for medical education or research, Professor
Skegg reaches the same conclusion in the following extract.

P D G Skegg 'Criminal Liability for the Unauthorised Use of Corpses for Medical Education and Research' (1992) 37 Med Sci Law 51

If those responsible for an unauthorized post-mortem examination knew that their conduct
would obstruct coronial or police inquiries, they might commit a common law offence of
obstruction of a coroner (see generally *R v Purcy* (1933) 24 Cr App R 70), or possible even
the equivalent statutory offence of obstruction of a constable (Police Act 1964, s 51(3)). A
common law crime of perverting the course of justice might also be held to apply . However,
many unauthorized uses of a corpse for medical education or research would not amount to
any of these offences.

Except for the unauthorized and long-term detention of a body for anatomical examination,
few uses of a body for medical education and research would be likely to amount to the
common law offence of preventing the lawful and decent disposal of a corpse (as to which
see *R v Hunter* [1974] QB 95, and see also *R v Le Grand* [1983] Crim LR 626). For example,
an unauthorized post-mortem examination of the body need not prevent the entire body
being buried or cremated within the customary time. Furthermore, the retention of some
parts of the body for medical education and research need not prevent the burial or cremation
of the body as a whole. (Bodies are often buried or cremated following post-mortem
examinations carried out at the coroner's request, even though some parts have been retained
for further investigation, or the inquest.) The common law crime of preventing the lawful
and decent disposal of a corpse would therefore rarely apply.

In some circumstances, the public display of part of a dead body would amount to a
common law offence of outraging public decency (see *R v Gibson and Sylveire* [1990] 2 QB
619 which resulted from the conviction of an artist and an art curator for exhibiting ear-rings
made from two human foetuses). However, the display of parts of a body in a medical school
museum, for the purpose of medical education, would not amount to such an offence.

There is surprisingly little authority in support of the existence of a common law offence which prohibits unauthorized interferences with corpses prior to burial and cremation. However, in some circumstances (such as prosecution following interference with a corpse for a sexual purpose) a court might well hold that there is a common law offence which prohibits at least some interferences with corpses awaiting burial or cremation. The question would then arise whether the unauthorized use of a corpse for medical education or research would amount to such a crime. Prior to the enactment of the Anatomy Act 1832, the means by which bodies were acquired for the practice of anatomy were sometimes unlawful … . However, it appears that the practice of anatomy was itself lawful at common law (see eg *R v Price* (1884) 12 QBD 247, 251, 252, 253). Furthermore, before the Human Tissue Act 1961 provided for the authorization of post-mortem examinations (in addition to those directed or requested by a coroner or other lawful authority), such post-mortem examinations had long been performed. Judges would therefore have no difficulty in holding that the unauthorized use of a corpse for medical education and research did not amount to any common law offence which prohibits certain unauthorized interferences with a corpse prior to burial or cremation. Such an approach cannot, however, be guaranteed.

The conclusion must be that there are no well-established common law offences that will apply to most unauthorized uses of corpses for medical education or research, although there are some offences which could sometimes be applicable. There is also a possibility that some judges would adopt the view that the unauthorized use of corpses for medical education or research amounts to a common law offence of unlawful interference with a corpse.

Skegg also considers the possibility of theft and criminal damage, only to dismiss them on the basis that the corpse is not in English law 'property', which is a requirement for either offence (for a recent affirmation of this historical rule, see *R v Kelly* [1998] 3 All ER 741 (CA) at 749 per Rose LJ). We discussed this issue earlier (see *supra*).

One final issue which we should consider is whether the removal and use contrary to, or outside, the legislative scheme of the 1961 Act, could give rise to an action in damages (see, generally, P D G Skegg (1974) 14 Medicine, Science and the Law 53 and (1977) 17 Medicine Science and the Law 123; I Kennedy (1976) 16 Medicine, Science and the Law 49). There are two possibilities: reliance upon *Wilkinson v Downton* [1897] 2 QB 57 and an action in negligence for any psychiatric injury caused. We discussed these in Chapter 15 in relation to use of *parts* of a dead body. The issues here are similar.

If the defendant interfered with the body intending to cause harm to the plaintiff, then the rule in *Wilkinson v Downton* ([1897] 2 QB 57 (Wright J)) would apply and an action would lie for any recognised psychiatric injury. But what if the interference and the harm were only negligently caused? Clearly, the plaintiff would have to suffer more than 'mere distress' or 'grief' amounting to a recognised psychiatric injury. Even so, there are considerable difficulties in the way of recovering damages in these circumstances.

Could it be argued that a relative's right to possession of the body for the purposes of disposal has been infringed giving rise to a claim for damages? It is unlikely that an English court would allow an action in damages for deliberate or negligent infringement of this right when, and if, it exists (contrast, *Mackey v US* (1993) 8 F 3d 826 (DC Cir) and Commentary (1995) 3 Med L Rev 222 (IK), the latter arguing an action could be brought only for intentional infringement of the right). First, the right is a limited one: there would, in any event, only be an argument in cases where the interference prevented the relatives burying or cremating the body. Thus, not every mishandling of a body would be covered, for example, dropping the body or coffin (*Owens v Liverpool Corpn* [1938] 4 All ER 727 (CA)) or the wrongful removal of an organ or tissue (cf *Edmond v Armstrong Funeral Home Ltd* [1931] 1 DLR 676 (Alt CA)). The right would seem only to be infringed where the defendants did not comply with the plaintiff's request to bury the body. By contrast, merely holding onto the body, not refusing to hand it over when requested, would not have been an infringement of the right.

Secondly, in any event, English judges are reluctant to create new actions for infringement of rights. Given the absence of authority on a damages' action, the courts are likely to confine the remedy for an infringement of right at most to an order for the return of the body. Thirdly, the judges are most likely to want to develop, if at all, these claims incrementally through the familiar territory of the law of negligence analogising with the existing cases on recovery for psychiatric injury.

Even here in the familiar territory of negligence, there are considerable difficulties in the way of a successful action. Could the relatives bring themselves within the *McLoughlin/Alcock* rules as 'secondary victims'? The law requires: (i) a close relationship between the victim and the plaintiff such that psychiatric injury is foreseeable to the plaintiff; (ii) propinquity in time and space between the victim's 'accident' and the plaintiff's discovery of the victim's injury, ie at the scene or its 'immediate aftermath'; (iii) that the plaintiff discovers that injury by sight and sound; and (iv) that as a result the plaintiff suffers psychiatric illness through an affront to her senses. As a preliminary point, there is, of course, a major difficulty here. There is no primary victim who is injured or killed. Would this be an insuperable obstacle to a relative who, otherwise, satisfied the *McLoughlin/Alcock* rules? It is suggested that it should not be and that the courts should see the deceased as the 'primary victim' and apply by analogy the same approach. The rationale behind the 'relationship' requirement is twofold: first, it positively identifies those plaintiffs who really are likely to suffer psychiatric injury as a result of the negligence; and secondly, it negatively acts as a gatekeeper to keep out speculative claims and excluding those who are expected to 'endure the calamities of modern life' (*Alcock v Chief Constable of South Yorkshire Police* [1991] 4 All ER 907 per Lord Ackner at 919). That the 'victim' has already died should not make a difference.

Indeed, in *Owens v Liverpool Corpn* [1938] 4 All ER 727, the Court of Appeal allowed a claim for psychiatric injury by relatives of a deceased who witnessed an accident involving the hearse carrying the dead body. The court rejected the argument that a claim could only be brought if there was injury or threat of injury to another. The merits of mourners who feared that the coffin would spill out onto the road were accepted even if others might put forward unfounded claims (see per MackKinnon LJ at 729–731). Subsequently, however, the House of Lords doubted *Owens* (*Bourhill v Young* [1942] 2 All ER 396, per Lord Thankerton at 400; per Lord Wright at 406; per Lord Porter at 408–409). These dicta could be put to one side as the product of the still developing (and then narrow) law of the time, were it not for the fact that in *Alcock* Lord Oliver refers to them approvingly (at 927). It is not clear, however whether Lord Oliver really disapproves of *Owens*, since he treats the case as one involving claims not by close relatives but by 'mere spectators' (as did *Bourhill v Young*). Of course, this was not so and their claims would fall foul of the 'relationship' requirement in the *McLoughlin/Alcock* rules in any event.

Thus, the limitations explicit in the *McLoughlin/Alcock* rules would act as a control on outrageous or unmeritorious claims. In addition to the need to be a close relative, the claimant would have had to witness the mishandling of the dead body, as in *Owens*. Invisible mishandling would not give rise to a claim. So, where the body is detained against the relatives' wishes, there would be no liability. For the same reason, there would be no action where an organ or tissue was wrongly removed. In other words, the extension of the law would be constrained by the existing policy of the law embodied in the *McLoughlin/Alcock* rules. The arguments which have compelled the courts not to allow damages to be recovered where the 'primary victim' is alive apply with equal force where he is already dead.

C. POST-MORTEMS

Post-mortems or autopsies usually involve the dissection of dead bodies in order to determine the cause of death. First, they may be directed or requested by the Coroner under the Coroners Act 1988 (ss 19–21). Usually, this will be where he has reasonable cause to suspect that the person had died a sudden death of which the cause is unknown, or a violent or unnatural death, and it is his opinion that a post-mortem may prove an inquest to be necessary (Coroners Act 1988, s 19(1)). Alternatively, he may do so after he has decided to hold an inquest (s 20). Secondly, post-mortems may be carried out with the authority of the person 'lawfully in possession of the body' under s 2(2) of the Human Tissue Act 1961. The law is discussed by Professor Skegg in the following extract.

P D G Skegg 'The Use of Corpses for Medical Education and Research: the Legal Requirements' (1991) 31 Med Sci Law 345

The Human Tissue Act 1961 and the Coroners Act 1988 both contain provisions relating to post-mortem examinations, but neither Act contains a definition of post-mortem examination. There can, however, be no doubt that 'post-mortem examination' is synonymous with 'autopsy', and that it usually involves the dissection of parts of the body (see the 'Post-Mortem Examination Report' form, provided in schedule 2 to the Coroners Rules 1984, SI 1984/552).

Post-mortem examinations can be carried out for various purposes, but they are usually performed either to ascertain the cause of death or to investigate the deceased patient's disease and its response to treatment. The scope of the post-mortem examination will sometimes vary according to the purpose for which it is carried out.

For legal purposes, post-mortem examinations may be divided into two categories, depending upon whether or not they are performed in pursuance of the authorization of 'the coroner or any other competent legal authority' (Human Tissue Act 1961, s 2(2)). Post-mortem examinations which are performed in pursuance of the authorization of a coroner or other official will here be discussed under the heading 'official post-mortem examinations'; the others under the heading 'unofficial post-mortem examinations'.

Official post-mortem examinations

Coroners are not the only officials who sometimes authorize post-mortem examinations, other than in exercise of the power conferred by section 2(2) of the Human Tissue Act 1961. For example, the Cremation Regulations specify the circumstances in which the Medical Referee 'shall require a post-mortem examination to be held' (Cremation Regulations 1930, SR & O 1930/1016, reg 12(5); see also ibid regs 8(b), 10, 11, 14, sch Form D). However, by far the most important category of official post-mortem examinations are those requested or directed by a coroner.

Post-mortem examinations performed at the request or direction of a coroner are not conducted primarily for the purpose of medical education and research. However, they sometimes contribute to the medical education of those who perform or attend them, and also of the doctors who have been responsible for the patients. They also provide information about causes of death which is sometimes of assistance to research. It is therefore appropriate to take account of these post-mortem examinations in this article.

Coroners may request or direct a registered medical practitioner to carry out a post-mortem examination when they are under a duty to hold an inquest and also in some cases where they are of the opinion that a post-mortem examination may prove an inquest to be unnecessary. The cases in which coroners may request or direct a post-mortem examination therefore include those where they have reasonable cause to suspect that people have died violent or unnatural deaths, or sudden deaths of which the cause is unknown (see Coroners Act 1988, ss 8, 19(1), 21). Coroners may request or direct post-mortem examinations in these cases, whether or not they have reason to believe that a post-mortem examination would be contrary to the previously expressed wishes of the deceased, or the wishes of the surviving spouse and relatives. (As to which medical practitioners may be directed, rather than simply requested, to perform post-mortem examinations, see Coroners Act 1988, ss 19(1), 21, but note also Coroners Rules 1984, SI 1984/552, r 6, esp r 6(1)(a).)

In addition to the power to request or direct that a post-mortem examination to be carried out, a coroner may also request a special examination of the body (Coroners Act 1988, s 20). 'Special examination' in relation to a body here means (ibid, s 20(4)):

a special examination by way of analysis, test or otherwise of such parts or contents of the body or such other substances or things as ought in the opinion of the coroner to be submitted to analyses, tests or other examination with a view to ascertaining how the deceased came by his death.

The power to request a special examination of the body implies that certain 'parts ... of the body' may be retained after the post-mortem examination itself, for the special examination. The Coroners Rules 1984 also provide that a person making a post-mortem examination shall make provision, so far as possible, 'for the preservation of material which in his opinion bears upon the cause of death', for such period 'as the coroner thinks fit' (r 9).

A coroner's request or direction that a post-mortem examination be made does not by implication authorize the removal and retention of parts for therapeutic purposes, or for purposes of medical education or research. If this is to be done, authorization should be obtained from the person lawfully in possession of the body, and the removal effected in compliance with the requirements of section 1 of the Human Tissue Act.

Unofficial post-mortem examinations

Post-mortem examinations 'not directed or requested by the coroner or any other competent legal authority' (Human Tissue Act 1961, s 2(2)) are sometimes referred to as academic, clinical, hospital or unofficial post-mortem examinations. Such post-mortem examinations have long been performed, but it is only since 1961 that an English statute has provided for their authorization.

Section 2(2) of the Human Tissue Act 1961 enables the person lawfully in possession of the body (or, in some cases, someone designated by that person) to authorize a post-mortem examination if certain conditions are fulfilled. The first part of section 2(2) is expressed to apply to all post-mortem examinations for it states:

No post-mortem examination shall be carried out otherwise than by or in accordance with the instructions of a fully registered medical practitioner ...

But section 2(2) continues:

... and no post-mortem examination which is not directed or requested by the coroner or any other competent legal authority shall be carried out without the authority of the person lawfully in possession of the body; and subsections (2), (5) (6) and (7) of section one of this Act shall, with the necessary modifications, apply with respect to the giving of that authority.

Section 1(2) is the most important of the provisions which apply, 'with the necessary modifications', to the authorization of clinical post-mortem examinations. Because of the reference to it in section 2(2), the person lawfully in possession of the body may authorize a post-mortem examination if, having made such reasonable enquiry as may be practicable, he or she has no reason to believe that the deceased had expressed (and not withdrawn) an objection to a post-mortem examination being carried out, or that the surviving spouse or any surviving relative of the deceased objects to a post-mortem examination being performed.

In consequence of the adoption of some of the other provisions of section 1, a person may not give or act upon authority if that person has reason to believe that an inquest or a coroner's post-mortem examination may be required (s 1(5)); authorization cannot be given by a person who has been entrusted with the body for the purpose only of its interment or cremation (s 1(6)); and, in the case of a body lying in a hospital or other institution, any authority under section 2(2) may be given on behalf of the person who has management or control of the institution, by anyone whom that person has designated for that purpose (s 1(7)). But other provisions were not adopted, including section 1(8) which provides that nothing in section 1 shall be construed as rendering unlawful any dealing with, or with any part of, the body of a deceased person which is lawful apart from the Act. This omission, together with the statement in section 2(2) that no post-mortem examination which is not directed or requested by the coroner or other competent legal authority 'shall be carried out without the authority of the person lawfully in possession of the body', excludes the possibility of unofficial post-mortem examinations being authorized by others.

Although section 2(2) adopts section 1(2), it does not adopt section 1(1). Hence a post-mortem examination cannot be authorized under section 2 if the person lawfully in possession of the body has reason to believe that the surviving spouse or any surviving relative objects to a post-mortem examination being performed, even if the deceased had requested that a post-mortem examination be carried out. Sometimes objections could be circumvented by reporting the death to the coroner as one of which the cause is unknown, for this almost always leads to a post-mortem examination being requested or directed, whatever the previously expressed wishes of the deceased or the objections of the spouse or relatives. Alternatively, if the deceased had requested, in the required manner, that his or her body be used after death for medical education or research, the person lawfully in possession of the body could authorize the removal of parts under section 1(1) of the Human Tissue Act, for their further examination for medical education or research.

There is nothing in the Human Tissue Act which indicates whether a person performing a post-mortem examination may remove tissue for further examination at a different place, or later time. However, the removal and processing of samples for histological study is now regarded as a proper part of a post-mortem examination. Where one of the aims of the post-mortem examination is the demonstration of an abnormal condition to the practitioner who was involved in the care of the patient, this will often necessitate the retention of tissue. Authorization of a post-mortem examination can therefore be taken to include authorization for the removal and retention of some tissue. But the tissue must be retained for purposes implicit in the authorization of the post-mortem examination itself, such as the confirmation of the cause of death or the investigation of an abnormal condition.

Post-mortem examinations also offer a convenient opportunity to remove tissue for therapeutic purposes, or for other purposes of medical education and research. For example, heart valves, corneas and long bones have sometimes been removed for therapeutic purposes during post-mortem examinations. Similarly, portions of brain, inner ear, coronary artery, trachea, gut and bladder, have been removed during post-mortem examinations, for research purposes. Such research is often highly desirable, even when (as is usually the case) it has no direct diagnostic application in relation to the post-mortem examination in question. Even in relation to pathology itself, it is desirable to collect samples of apparently normal tissue so pathologists may appreciate the range of appearances resulting from intrinsic biological variability, and thus identify correctly the abnormal. It is also desirable to collect and store tissues showing unusual or poorly understood abnormalities in the hope of establishing a pattern or process of disease when several cases can be compared. Post-mortem examinations also provide an excellent opportunity to remove specimens of diseased tissue for the teaching of pathology (Dr M D Sage, personal communication).

The authorisation of a post-mortem examination, in exercise of the power conferred by section 2(2) of the Human Tissue Act 1961, does not of itself provide authorization for the removal and use of parts for purposes unrelated to the post-mortem examination, such as those mentioned in the preceding paragraph. It is, however, open to the person lawfully in possession of the body to authorize the removal and use of parts for therapeutic purposes, or for purposes of medical education and research, at the same time as he or she authorizes the performance of a post-mortem examination under section 2(2).

To overcome difficulties that might otherwise arise when tissue is removed and retained following a post-mortem examination, the Department of Health and Social Security prepared a 'Post-Mortem Declaration Form' to ensure that enquiries were made not only as to any relevant objection to the post-mortem examination itself, but also to the removal and retention of tissue (HC (77) 28, Appendix 2). The Department suggested that in appropriate cases a relative should be invited to sign the declaration form (ibid para 4), to read as follows:

> I do not object to a post mortem examination being carried out on the body of … and I am not aware that he/she had expressed objection or that another relative objects.
>
> I understand that this examination is carried out:
>
> (a) to verify the cause of death and to study the effects of treatment, which may involve the retention of tissue for laboratory study.
>
> (b) to remove amounts of tissue for the treatment of other patients and for medical education and research.

If the person lawfully in possession of the body establishes that this form has been signed, or that equivalent enquiries have been made, it could usually be said that he or she has made 'such reasonable enquiry as may be practicable' for the purpose of section 1(2) as well as section 2(2). It would then be open to the person who is lawfully in possession of the body to authorize both a post-mortem examination and the removal and use of tissues for therapeutic purposes, or for the purposes of medical education and research.

There is, however, one minor complication. An unofficial post-mortem examination may be carried out either by a fully registered medical practitioner or by someone acting in accordance with the instructions of such a practitioner. In practice, technicians often remove parts in the course of post-mortem examinations. But if tissue (other than an eye or part of an eye) is to be removed under section 1 for therapeutic purposes or for the purposes of medical education and research, the removal must be effected by a registered medical practitioner (Human Tissue Act 1961, s 1(4), discussed above).

You will notice the discussion of control over tissue and parts removed during a post-mortem (for an analysis, see Bristol Royal Infirmary Interim Report *Removal and Retention of Human Material* (2000)). As Skegg points out, where this is performed for the coroner, the Coroners Rules 1984 (SI 1984 No 552) r 9 requires that the material be preserved for such period 'as the coroner thinks fit'. The rules do not, however, state what should happen after the coroner no longer requires their preservation either expressly or impliedly because his inquiries, or inquest, are complete. It may be that what is done to the tissue or whatever becomes the 'property' of the pathologist (or more likely his employing institution) under the *Doodeward v Spence* exception applied in *R v Kelly* [1998] 3 All ER 741 (CA) discussed *supra*. Alternatively, and more persuasively, the pathologist may 'receive' the property merely as the agent of the coroner who, if anyone, has the ultimate entitlement to the samples until such time as the coroner's inquiry is over when the executor (or whoever) may be entitled to possession for the purposes of disposal. The work/skill exception may not, however, apply where all that is done is that the tissue (or part) is preserved. The point arose in *Dobson v North Tyneside HA* [1996] 4 All ER 474 (CA), where the plaintiffs argued, *inter alia*, that the deceased's brain, when removed and preserved during a post-mortem, became their 'property'. The Court of Appeal rejected the argument.

> **Peter Gibson LJ:** Does this mean that it is arguable that when Dr Perry fixed the brain in paraffin, he thereby transformed it into an item the right to possession of which or the property in which belonged to the plaintiffs? For my part, I do not think so. The removal of the brain was lawfully performed in the course of the post mortem which at the coroner's request Dr Perry had undertaken to determine the cause of the deceased's death. Dr Perry was under an obligation imposed by r 9 of the Coroners Rules 1984, SI 1984/552, to make provision for the preservation of material which in his opinion bore upon the cause of death, but only for such period as the coroner thought fit. It is not alleged that Dr Perry was in breach of that obligation, and once the cause of death had been determined by the coroner with Dr Perry's help and the time for challenge to that determination had passed, there could be no continuing obligation under the rule to preserve that material. There is nothing in the pleading or evidence before us to suggest that the actual preservation of the brain after the post mortem was on a par with stuffing or embalming a corpse or preserving an anatomical or pathological specimen for a scientific collection or with preserving a human freak such as a double-headed foetus that had some value for exhibition purposes. There was no practical possibility of, nor any sensible purpose in, the brain being reunited with the body for burial purposes. Mr Hone accepted that organs would not usually be preserved by the pathologist who caries out a post mortem and that if Dr Perry had disposed of the brain without fixing it in paraffin, the plaintiffs would have no cause for complaint. I do not see how the fact that the brain was so fixed rendered it an item to possession of which the plaintiffs ever became entitled for the purpose of interment or any other purpose, still less that the plaintiffs ever acquired the property in it.

Two points should be made. Surely the plaintiff's claim was misplaced, even if the exception applied? The 'property' would have vested in the person exercising the skill or carrying out the work (or his employer) rather than the plaintiffs (see *supra* for the argument based upon 'first possessor'). Secondly, arguably the brain (or other excised part or tissue) fell within the extended exception to the 'no property rule' tentatively proposed by the Court of Appeal in *Kelly*. There may be reason to confer property rights upon those who remove the tissue during a post-mortem (or indeed anatomical examination) and retain lawful *de facto* possession for research, educational or other such purposes (see P D G Skegg 'Medical Uses of Corpses and the "No Property" Rule' (1992) 32 Medicine, Science and the Law 311 at 317; but contrast, Bristol Royal Infirmary Interim Report, *op cit*, Annex B).

D. ANATOMY

The practice of anatomy has long been part of medical education and research. Dissecting the bodies of paupers or executed felons was common practice for English surgeons and notorious instances of grave robbing or body snatching such as by Burke and Hare are well documented. The history of anatomy, leading to its regularisation in the Anatomy Act 1832, is told elsewhere (see R Richardson *Death, Dissection and the Destitute* (1988)). It may well be that the practice of anatomy was lawful at common law (see *R v Price* (1884) 12 QBD 247, at 251–252 per Stephen J). Nevertheless, it remained unregulated until the 1832 Act. The 1832 Act created for the first time a licensing system for the carrying out of anatomical examinations, an inspectorate of premises, the conditions under which bodies could be donated, and placed a duty on the licensee to inter the body after examination and, in any event, within (ultimately) two years of the body being first received.

1. The Anatomy Act 1984

The 1832 Act (together with the Anatomy Act 1871) were repealed by the Anatomy Act 1984 when it came into force on 14 February 1988 (see Anatomy Act 1984 (Commencement) Order 1988 (SI 1988 No 81)). The 1984 Act created a new regulatory requirement for the practice of anatomy. As we shall see below, it provides for the licensing of premises where anatomy may be performed, of practitioners of anatomy and for the possession of anatomical specimens (s 3). It provides for an inspectorate of anatomy with extensive powers of entry and inspection (ss 9 and 10). The Act sets out the conditions under which a body may be used for anatomical examination (ss 4 and 6). Unlike the 1832 Act, the new legislation deals with the retention of parts of a body following anatomical examination (s 5). In creating the regulatory regime, the Act makes it a criminal offence where there is a failure to comply with the Act's requirements, for example, for carrying out the examination or possessing an anatomical specimen or body or part following an examination, as well as to act in contravention of a condition to the practitioner's licence to practice (s 11).

The Act applies only to persons who died after it came into force. Hence, s 13(4) states that: 'Nothing in this Act affects anything done in relation to the body or part of the body of a person who died before the coming into force of section 4.' Thus, anatomical examinations of such persons are, on the face of it, outside the 1984 Act and, curiously, not governed by the 1832 Act since it was repealed at the same time. However, regulations provide transitional provisions which seem to assume the opposite. Regulation 3(4) of the Anatomy Act 1984 (Commencement) Order 1988 (SI 1988 No 81) states that:

> Any direction or permission given under the 1832 Act to permit or cause the body of a deceased person to undergo anatomical examination shall be deemed for the purposes of the Act to be an authority given in pursuance of the Act.

The Act referred to is, of course, the Anatomy Act 1984. Arguably, this part of the regulations is *ultra vires*, since it purports to cover bodies of persons who died before the 1984 Act came into force and thus is contrary to s 13(4) of the 1984 Act. The point is, of course, largely academic given the time gap that now exists since the 1984 Act came into force (but for a case where it might have had relevance see *R v Kelly* [1998] 3 All ER 741 (CA)). If this argument is correct, the effect is that anatomical examination of the bodies of those who died before the 1984 Act but which was carried out after that Act came into force, was not governed by either piece of legislation. The applicable law would be the common law, both as regards the legality of carrying out the examination itself and in relation to the permissibility of retaining parts of the body as medical specimens for educational, teaching or other purposes (on which see *supra*).

2. Scope of the 1984 Act

The Act applies to 'anatomical examinations' and to 'anatomical specimens'. These are defined in s 1 as follows:

Definitions, and scope of Act

1. – (1) In this Act "anatomical examination" means the examination by dissection of a body for purposes of teaching or studying, or researching into, morphology; and where parts of a body are separated in the course of its anatomical examination, such examination includes the examination by dissection of the parts for those purposes.

(2) In this Act "anatomical specimen" means –

(a) a body to be used for anatomical examination, or

(b) a body in course of being used for anatomical examination (including separated parts of such a body).

(3) In this Act "body" means the body of a deceased person.

You will notice a number of points. First, there is a very specific definition of 'anatomical examination' in the Act. It requires 'dissection' of a dead body or its parts and also that must be for one of the specific purposes set out, ie teaching, studying or researching into morphology (the form of the body). Thus, the use of dead bodies (or their parts) for artistic purposes or as exhibits would not be covered (see eg *R v Kelly* [1998] 3 All ER 741 (CA)). Secondly, a body (or its parts) is only an anatomical specimen before or during its anatomical examination. Once the latter has ceased, the body or its part also ceases to be an 'anatomical specimen'. As we shall see, this has implications for the regulation of possession of bodies or their parts.

Finally, there is the potential for overlapping legislative schemes. We have already seen the potential overlap between the Human Tissue Act 1961 and the Anatomy Act 1984 (see *supra*, discussing s 1(5) of the 1984 Act). The 1984 Act does not apply to the removal or use of any part of a dead body for the purposes of 'medical education or research' authorised under the Human Tissue Act even if that consists of or involves 'anatomical examination' which would otherwise fall within the scheme of the 1984 Act (s 1(5)).

Likewise, there can be an overlap with post-mortem examinations (on which see *supra*). Section 1(4) of the Anatomy Act 1984 seeks to resolve any such overlap and is discussed by Professor Skegg in the following extract.

P D G Skegg 'Use of Corpses for Medical, Education and Research' (1991) 31 Med Sci Law 345

The Anatomy Act 1984 contains an express provision which determines the relationship of its provisions to post-mortem examinations. This is in section 1(4) of the Act, which states:

Nothing in this Act applies to anything done for the purposes of a post-mortem examination requested or required or directed to be made by a competent legal authority or carried out for the purpose of establishing or confirming the causes of death or of investigating the existence or nature of abnormal conditions.

This exclusionary provision clearly applies to all official post-mortem examinations, for they are 'requested or required or directed to be made by a competent legal authority'. It also applies to unofficial post-mortem examinations 'carried out for the purpose of establishing or confirming the causes of death or of investigating the existence or nature of abnormal conditions', whether or not they are authorized and performed in compliance with section 2(2) of the Human Tissue Act 1961.

It is possible that an unofficial post-mortem examination could be authorized and performed in accordance with section 2(2) of the Human Tissue Act, yet not be carried out for a purpose specified in section 1(4) of the Anatomy Act 1984. But even if section 1(4) does not apply to some post-mortem examinations, it would not follow that these post-mortem examinations were subject to general provisions relating to anatomical examinations. Section 1(1) of the Anatomy Act defines 'anatomical examination' as the examination by dissection of a body 'for purposes of teaching or studying, or researching into, morphology'. In view of this definition, the examination by dissection of a body for any other purpose is not subject to the provisions relating to anatomical examinations, whether or not it comes within the ambit of section 1(4).

3. Legal requirements for anatomical examinations and possession of anatomical specimens

(a) Who and where?

Who may carry out 'anatomical examinations', where they may be performed and who may have possession of an 'anatomical specimen' is governed by ss 2 and 3 of the 1984 Act.

Control of examinations and possession

2. – (1) No person shall carry out an anatomical examination unless –

(a) he carries it out on premises which at the time of the examination are licensed under section 3(1).

(b) he is authorised to carry it out under section 3(3).

(c) at the time the examination is carried out it is lawful by virtue of section 4, and

(d) death has been registered in the case of the body concerned, under section 15 of the 1953 Act or section 22 of the 1965 Act.

(2) Subject to subsection (3), no person shall have an anatomical specimen in his possession unless –

(a) he is authorised to have possession under section 3(4).

(b) anatomical examination of the specimen is at the time concerned lawful by virtue of section 4 and,

(c) a certificate of cause of death has been signed, in the case of the body concerned, in accordance with section 22(1) of the 1953 Act or section 24 of the 1965 Act.

(3) Subsection (2) does not apply where a person came into lawful possession of a body immediately after death and retained possession prior to its removal to the place where anatomical examination is to take place.

(4) In this section "the 1953 Act" means the Births and Deaths Registration Act 1953 and "the 1965 Act" means the Registration of Births, Deaths and Marriages (Scotland) Act 1965.

Licences

3. – (1) The Secretary of State may grant a licence of the use of premises for carrying out anatomical examinations.

(2) The Secretary of State may grant a licence to a person to do one or both of the following:–

(a) carry out anatomical examinations;

(b) have possession of anatomical specimens.

(3) A person is authorised under this subsection to carry out an anatomical examination if –

(a) at the time of the examination he is licensed to carry it out under subsection (2)(a), or

(b) he carries out the examination in the course of teaching or studying, or researching into, morphology and has permission (general or particular) to carry out the examination from a person who is so licensed at the time of the examination.

(4) A person is authorised under this subsection to have possession of an anatomical specimen if –

(a) at the time he has possession he is licensed to do so under subsection (2)(b), or

(b) he has, from a person who is so licensed at that time, permission (general or particular) to have such possession.

(5) A person to whom a licence has been granted under subsection (2) shall –

(a) compile such records in relation to anatomical examinations and anatomical specimens as may be specified by regulations made by the Secretary of State, and

(b) retain for such period as may be so specified in records compiled in accordance with paragraph (a).

(6) The power to make regulations under subsection (5) shall be exercisable by statutory instrument subject to annulment in pursuance of a resolution of either House of Parliament.

In essence, a licensing scheme for persons and premises is created. Section 11(1) creates offences for breaches of s 2(1) (carrying out anatomical examinations) and s 2(2) (possession of anatomical specimens) with a penalty of a fine or imprisonment not exceeding three months. These are exclusive offences such that no other offence at common law or otherwise will be committed if there is no offence under s 11(1) (see s 11(10)).

You will notice that not only the licensed individual may carry out an anatomical examination or possess an anatomical specimen but so may someone who acts with his general or particular authority (ss 3(3)(b) and 4(6)). Thus, non-licensed demonstrators of anatomy and students may do so.

Regulation 4 of the Anatomy Regulations 1988 (SI 1988 No 44 (as amended by SI 1988, No 198)) imposes a duty upon a licence holder in relation to a body subject to anatomical examination as follows:

4. (1) Except in relation to a body to which paragraph (3) of this regulation applies, a person to whom a licence has been granted under section 3(2) of the Act shall ensure that –

(a)   as soon as practicable after a body is received at the place where anatomical examination is to take place the body is subjected to a suitable process for its preservation;

(b)   a body is held in possession only for such period as an adequate state of preservation of the body is maintained;

(c)   all bodies in his possession are stored in an orderly and hygienic manner in suitably designed rooms equipped with adequate facilities for regulating temperatures;

(d)   where an anatomical examination is carried out by a person who is authorised to carry out the examination by virtue of section 3(3)(b) of the Act, (in this paragraph referred to as "the authorised person") the authorised person is adequately supervised by a person who is licensed under section 3(2)(a) of the Act unless the authorised person is sufficiently qualified and trained to carry out anatomical examinations in an orderly and efficient manner without such supervision; …

(3) This regulation shall not apply in relation to the body of a person who died before the coming into force of these Regulations.

Finally, you will notice the provisions in s 3(5) which impose a duty on the licence holder to compile and retain records in relation to anatomical examinations and specimens. The detailed provisions are contained in the Anatomy Regulations 1988. Regulation 2 provides as follows:

2. (1) A person to whom a licence has been granted under section 3(2) of the Act shall compile records in a permanent form in relation to each anatomical specimen which is in his possession or in the possession of another person to whom he has given permission to have possession of the anatomical specimen which records shall contain the particulars specified in paragraph (2) of this regulation.

(2) The particulars referred to in paragraph (1) of this regulation are as follows:–

(a)   the full names and sex of the deceased person whose body is used for anatomical examination, his date of death, his age at the time of death and the cause of death;

(b)   the date and time at which the body is received by him at the premises where the anatomical examination is to be carried out;

(c)   whether authority for the anatomical examination of the body was given in pursuance of subsection (2) or (3) of section 4 of the Act and the name and address of the person lawfully in possession of the body who authorised the use of the body in accordance with subsection (2) or (3) of that section, as the case may be;

(d)   the name and address of any person to whom he has given permission under section 3(4)(b) of the Act to have possession of the body or any separated part of the body who retains possession of the body or such separated part for a period exceeding one month;

(e)   particulars of any wishes expressed by the deceased person or the surviving spouse or any surviving relative of that person in relation to the disposal of the body after the anatomical examination has been concluded;

(f)   the date and method of disposal of the body after the anatomical examination has been concluded.

(3) Subject to paragraph (4) of this regulation, a person to whom a licence has been granted under section 3(2) of the Act shall retain records compiled in accordance with paragraph (1) above for a period of 5 years beginning with the date of disposal of the body.

(4) Where a person to whom a licence has been granted under section 3(2)(a) of the Act is licensed under section 5(5) of the Act to have possession of parts of the body and retains parts after the body has been disposed of he shall retain such records compiled in accordance with paragraph (1) of this regulation as are required for the purposes of regulation 3(1) of these Regulations for the period specified in regulation 3(3) of these Regulations.

Failure to comply with s 3(5) and the regulations is a summary criminal offence punishable with a fine (s 11(5), (7), (8) and reg 5).

(b) On whose authority?

Section 4 of the Anatomy Act 1984 sets out the circumstances in which an 'anatomical examination' will be lawful.

Lawful examinations

4. – (1) Subsection (2) applies if a person, either in writing at any time or orally in the presence of two or more witnesses during his last illness, has expressed a request that his body be used after his death for anatomical examination.

(2) If the person lawfully in possession of the body after death has no reason to believe that the request was withdrawn, he may authorise the use of the body in accordance with the request.

(3) Without prejudice to subsection (2), the person lawfully in the possession of a body may authorise it to be used for anatomical examination if, having made such reasonable inquiry as may be practicable, he has no reason to believe –

(a) that the deceased, either in writing at any time or orally in the presence of two or more witnesses during his last illness, had expressed an objection to his body being so used after his death, and had not withdrawn it, or

(b) that the surviving spouse or any surviving relative of the deceased objects to the body being so used.

(4) Subject to subsections (5) to (8), the anatomical examination of a body in accordance with an authority given in pursuance of this section is lawful by virtue of this section.

(5) Where a person has reason to believe that an inquest may be required to be held on any body or that a post-mortem examination of any body may be required by the coroner, he shall not, except with the coroner's consent –

(a) give an authority under this section in respect of the body, or

(b) act on such an authority given by any other person.

This subsection does not apply in Scotland ...

(7) No authority shall be given under this section in respect of a body by a person entrusted with the body for the purpose only of its interment or cremation.

(8) Authority under this section expires at the end of the statutory period (even if the person lawfully in possession of the body concerned authorises its use under subsection (2) or (3) for a longer or a shorter period or for no particular period).

(9) In the case of a body lying in a hospital, nursing home or other institution, any authority under this section may be given on behalf of the person having the control and management of the institution by any officer or person designated for that purpose by the first mentioned person.

(10) In subsection (8) "the statutory period" means the period of 3 years (or such other period as the Secretary of State may from time to time by order specify for the purposes of this subsection) beginning with the date of the deceased's death.

You will notice the similarity between this provision and the Human Tissue Act 1961. There are, however, important differences. Professor Skegg discusses them:

P D G Skegg 'Use of Corpses for Medical Education and Research' (1991) 31 Med Sci Law 345

An anatomical examination may not be performed without the authorization of the person lawfully in possession of the body. The circumstances in which that person may authorize this use of the body vary according to whether or not the deceased had requested that the body be used for anatomical examination.

If the deceased had requested, in the appropriate way, that his or her body be used after death for anatomical examination, the person lawfully in possession of the body is usually free to authorize the use of the body for that purpose. Where there is a relevant request, there is no obligation on the person lawfully in possession of the body to enquire into, or take account of, the views of the surviving spouse or relatives. This is by virtue of section 4(1) and (2) of the Anatomy Act 1984, which are the equivalent of section 1(1) of the Human Tissue Act 1961. Section 4(1) states:

> Subsection (2) applies if a person, either in writing at any time or orally in the presence of two or more witnesses during his last illness, has expressed a request that his body be used after his death for anatomical examination.

Section 4(2) then provides:

> If the person lawfully in possession of the body after death has no reason to believe that the request was withdrawn, he may authorise the use of the body in accordance with the request.

The person lawfully in possession of a body is sometimes free to authorize the use of the body even though the deceased did not request that this be done. Section 4(3) enables authorization to be given if, after making the required enquiry, the person lawfully in possession of the body has no reason to believe that there is a relevant objection. Section 4(3) provides:

Without prejudice to subsection (2), the person lawfully in possession of a body may authorise it to be used for anatomical examination if, having made such reasonable inquiry as may be practicable, he has no reason to believe –

(a) that the deceased, either in writing at any time or orally in the presence of two or more witnesses during his last illness, had expressed an objection to his body being so used after his death, and had not withdrawn it, or

(b) that the surviving spouse or any surviving relative of the deceased objects to the body being so used.

Section 4(3) is the equivalent of section 1(2) of the Human Tissue Act 1961. There is, however, a significant difference in the wording of the paragraph (a) in these two provisions. In consequence of the wording of paragraph (a) in section 4(3) of the Anatomy Act 1984, the person lawfully in possession of the body may disregard a known objection of the deceased if it was not expressed 'in writing at any time or orally in the presence of two or more witnesses during his last illness'.

Section 4(8) of the Anatomy Act 1984 provides:

Authority under this section expires at the end of the statutory period (even if the person lawfully in possession of the body concerned authorises its use under subsection (2) or (3) for a longer or a shorter period or for no particular period).

The 'statutory period' is currently three years, beginning with the day of the deceased's death (Anatomy Act 1984 s 4(10)), but the Secretary of State has the power to specify, by order, a longer or a shorter period (Anatomy Act 1984, s 4(10); see also s 4(11)). Section 1 of the Human Tissue Act does not contain any equivalent provision.

As with the 1961 Act, authority must be given by the person 'lawfully in possession of the body' (on which see *supra*). One further difference we have already noted before. Unlike the 1961 Act, the Anatomy Act makes it crystal clear that failure to comply with its provisions will be a criminal offence. As we saw, the 1961 Act is silent upon the consequences of its being breached (*supra*, ch 15).

4. Completion of anatomical examination

Two issues arise: first, when must an 'anatomical examination' be completed? and, secondly, what are the legal consequences for the body and its parts thereafter?

(a) Completion

The 'anatomical examination' of a body must be concluded by the expiry of the statutory period. Section 11(1) states that this is three years from the date of the deceased's death (it was two years prior to the 1984 Act), although the period may be altered by the Home Secretary by statutory instrument. Of course, the examination may end sooner in practice. Importantly, s 4(7) of the Act makes it clear that the 'authority' under s 4 (necessary for the examination and possession of the body) is the statutory period *even if* the person lawfully in possession of the body specified a longer or even *shorter* period. Thus, whilst the body must be used in accordance with the 'authority' given by the person lawfully in possession, this cannot be subject to a time constraint.

(b) The body and its parts thereafter

Once an 'anatomical examination' is completed, or in fact must cease because the statutory period expires, possession of the body and its parts is governed by ss 5 and 6 of the Act.

Control of possession after examination
5. –(1) This section applies where –
(a) authority under section 4 to use a body for anatomical examination has expired, or
(b) the anatomical examination of a body has been concluded before the expiry of such authority.

(2) Subject to subsections (3) and (4), no person shall have the body or part of the body in his possession.

(3) Subsection (2) does not apply where a person has possession of the body or part for the purpose only of its decent disposal.

(4) Subsection (2) does not apply where –

(a) a person has possession of part of a body whose anatomical examination has been concluded before the expiry of authority under section 4,

(b) the part is such that the person from whose body it came cannot be recognised simply by examination of the part,

(c) the person with possession is authorised to have possession under subsection (5), and

(d) possession of the part is lawful by virtue of section 6.

(5) If the Secretary of State thinks it desirable to do so in the interests of education or research, he may grant a licence to a person to have possession of parts of bodies, and a person is authorised under this subsection to have possession of a part of a body if –

(a) at the time he has possession he is licensed to do so under this subsection, or

(b) he has, from a person who is so licensed at that time, permission (general or particular) to have such possession.

(6) A person to whom a licence has been granted under subsection (5) shall –

(a) compile such records in relation to parts of bodies as may be specified by regulations made by the Secretary of State, and

(b) retain for such period as may be so specified any records compiled in accordance with paragraph *(a)*.

(7) The power to make regulations under subsection (6) shall be exercisable by statutory instrument subject to annulment in pursuance of a resolution of either House of Parliament.

Lawful possession

6. – (1) Subsection (2) applies if a person, in expressing a request as mentioned in section 4(1), has given permission for possession of parts (or any specified parts) of his body to be held after its anatomical examination is concluded.

(2) If the person lawfully in possession of the body after death has no reason to believe that the permission was withdrawn, he may, in giving authority under section 4(2), give authority for possession to be held in accordance with the permission.

(3) Without prejudice to subsection (2), the person lawfully in possession of a body may, in giving authority under section 4(3), give authority for possession of parts (or any specified parts) of the body to be held after an anatomical examination is concluded if, having made such reasonable inquiry as may be practicable, he has no reason to believe –

(a) that the deceased, either in writing at any time or orally in the presence of two or more witnesses during his last illness, had expressed an objection to such possession being held, and had not withdrawn it, or

(b) that the surviving spouse or any surviving relative of the deceased objects to such possession being held.

(4) It is lawful by virtue of this section to have possession of part of a body if possession is held in accordance with an authority given in pursuance of this section.

As regards the body, it may only be lawfully possessed for the purposes of 'decent disposal' (s 5(2) and (3)). Nothing further is stated in the Act. However, the Anatomy Regulations 1988 (*supra*) state:

4.(1) Except in relation to a body to which paragraph (3) of this regulation applies, a person to whom a licence has been granted under section 3(2) of the Act shall ensure that – ...

(e) after anatomical examination of a body has been concluded its disposal shall, so far as practicable, be in accordance with any wishes expressed by the deceased or any surviving spouse or surviving relative of his and that separated parts of the body, other than those parts which are held in possession by virtue of section 6 of the Act, are, so far as practicable, disposed of with the body from which they were removed ...

(3) This regulation shall not apply in relation to the body of a person who died before the coming into force of these Regulations.

On its face, this does not explicitly impose upon the licence-holder a duty to dispose of the body. It could be said that the duty remains, as it would otherwise be, on the executor or administrator of the deceased's estate etc (see *supra*). The better view is, however, that reg 4(1)(e) implicitly imposes a duty upon the licence-holder which is inconsistent, in the usual case, with any other having such a duty since the wishes of the surviving spouse or relatives–one of whom would normally have the duty–are for him to act in accordance with if practicable.

As regards parts of the body that have been removed during the anatomical examination, ss 5 and 6 make particular provision for their retention. This contrasts markedly with the Anatomy Act 1832, where no provision was made although specimens were frequently retained. The practice, whilst widespread, was not beyond question. Section 13 of that Act imposed a duty to 'make provision that such bodies, after undergoing anatomical examination, be decently interred in consecrated ground, or in some public burial ground in use for persons of that religious persuasion to which the person belonged'. Failure to do so was a criminal offence (s 18). It was said in *Doodeward v Spence* (1908) 6 CLR 406 (HC of A)– a case we saw earlier–that failure to bury the whole body infringed the Act (or its Australian equivalent) (see per Higgins J at 423). It depends, of course, on whether the 'body' minus the parts can still constitute the body under s 13. Perhaps different conclusions would be reached where only internal organs were retained, as opposed to the head or torso of the body (see Commentary (1998) 6 Med L Rev 247 at 252 (AG)). In any event, the 1984 Act clarifies the law and makes possession lawful in certain circumstances. Professor Skegg explains the provisions we have already set out:

P D G Skegg 'Use of Corpses for Medical Education and Research' (1991) 31 Med Sci Law 345

The Anatomy Act 1984 specifies the circumstances in which people may have in their possession bodies that are to be used for anatomical examination, or bodies in the course of being used for anatomical examination, including separated parts of such bodies (Anatomy Act 1984, ss 1(2), 2(2), (3), 3(2), (4)). Once the anatomical examination of the body has been concluded, or the 'statutory period' for anatomical examination has expired, it is usually unlawful for people to have these bodies or parts of bodies in their possession, except for the purpose of disposing of them (Anatomy Act 1984, s 5 (1)–(3)).

The Anatomy Act does, however, permit the retention of parts of bodies if certain conditions are fulfilled (Anatomy Act 1984, s 5(4)–(7); see also Anatomy Regulations 1988, reg 4(2)). One is that the person lawfully in possession of the body must have given authority for possession of the part or parts in question, at the time of authorizing the anatomical examination itself (Anatomy Act 1983, s 6(2), (3)). If the deceased gave permission for parts of the body to be held after the anatomical examination was concluded, and the person lawfully in possession of the body had no reason to believe that the permission was withdrawn, he or she may give authority for possession to be held in accordance with the permission (Anatomy Act 1984, s 6(1), (2)). Alternatively, the person lawfully in possession of the body may give authority for parts to be held after the anatomical examination is concluded if, having made 'such reasonable enquiry as may be practicable', he or she has no reason to believe that there is any relevant objection (Anatomy Act 1984, s 6(3)). The objections which are relevant in relation to the giving of this authority are the same as those which are relevant in relation to the authorization of the anatomical examination itself.

Possession of parts after the conclusion of the anatomical examination is not lawful simply because it has been authorized by the person lawfully in possession of the body, at the time of authorization of the anatomical examination itself. The person with possession must either have been granted a licence by the Secretary of State to have possession of parts of bodies, after the conclusion of anatomical examinations, or else have been granted permission by a licensed person (Anatomy Act 1984 s 5(5); see also ibid, s 5(6), (7)). The anatomical examination must also have been concluded before the expiration of the statutory period, and the part must be such that the person from whose body it came could not be recognized simply by examination of the part (Anatomy Act 1984, s 5(4)(a),(b)).

The last two points made by Professor Skegg merit emphasis. It is often assumed, wrongly, that the Act permits the retention of parts regardless of when the anatomical examination concluded. Section 5 (4)(a) makes it clear that the examination must have been concluded before the expiry of the statutory period, ie three years after death. For s 5 to apply, the examination must have been concluded before this. Also, not all parts may be retained. The authority given by the person lawfully in possession may be specific to some parts under s 6. In any event, s 5 (4)(b) states that the deceased person must not be recognisable by examination of the part. Retention of heads would, therefore, be unlawful. But, equally, although unlikely, any other distinctive part could not be retained, for example, an arm with an identifiable tattoo.

Index